SCOTT

2001 Standard Postage Stamp Catalogue

ONE HUNDRED AND FIFTY-SEVENTH EDITION IN SIX VOLUMES

VOLUME 1

UNITED STATES
and Affiliated Territories
UNITED NATIONS
COUNTRIES OF THE WORLD
A-B

VICE PRESIDENT/PUBLISHER	Stuart J. Morrissey
EDITOR	James E. Kloetzel
ASSOCIATE EDITOR	William W. Cummings
NEW ISSUES MANAGING EDITOR	David C. Akin
ASSISTANT EDITOR FOR NEW ISSUES	Martin J. Frankevicz
VALUING ANALYST	Leonard J. Gellman
ELECTRONIC PRODUCT DEVELOPMENT COORDINATOR	Denise Oder
EDITORIAL ASSISTANTS	Judith E. Bertrand, Beth Brown
ART/PRODUCTION DIRECTOR	Janine C. S. Apple
PRODUCTION COORDINATOR	Nancy S. Martin
MARKETING/SALES DIRECTOR	William Fay
ADVERTISING	Angela M. Nolte
CIRCULATION/PRODUCT PROMOTION MANAGER	Tim Wagner

Released April 2000

Includes New Stamp Listings through the March, 2000 *Scott Stamp Monthly* Catalogue Update

Scott Publishing Co.

911 Vandemark Road, Sidney, OH 45365-0828

A division of AMOS PRESS, INC., publishers of *Linn's Stamp News, Coin World, Cars & Parts* magazine and *The Sidney Daily News.*

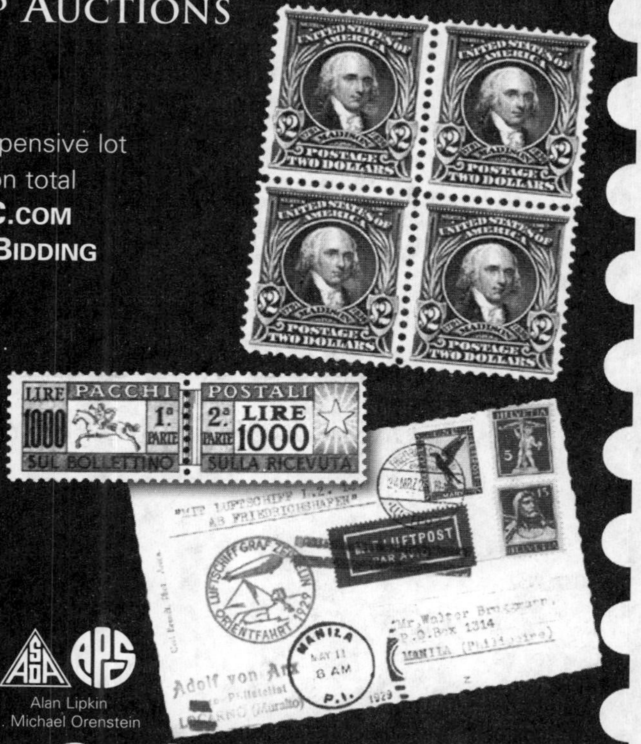

UNITED STATES OF AMERICA
POSTAGE TWO DOLLARS
LIRE PACCHI POSTALI
1000
LIRE 1000
SUL BOLLETTINO
SULLA RICEVUTA
LUFTPOST

Table of Contents

Scott Publishing Mission Statement

The Scott Publishing Team exists to serve the recreational, educational and commercial hobby needs of stamp collectors and dealers.

We strive to set the industry standard for philatelic information and products by developing and providing goods that help collectors identify, value, organize and present their collections.

Quality customer service is, and will continue to be, our highest priority. We aspire toward achieving total customer satisfaction.

ISBN 0-89487-260-5

Library of Congress Card No. 2-3301

Scott Publishing Co.

SCOTT 911 VANDEMARK ROAD, SIDNEY, OHIO 45365 937-498-0802

Dear Scott Catalogue User:

With constantly spiraling prices for better stamps and the well-established presence of stamp sales online, we are faced with a philatelic world that grows ever more complex and fractionalized.

Ebay.com dominates its niche as the virtual stamp bourse of choice online. The consequences have been huge: declining advertising sales for the philatelic weeklies, lower stamp show attendance and more sales of stamp supplies and accessories.

The average stamp that sells on eBay is about $15. This is not much when one considers all of the more expensive stamps out there. The next question: who will be the first to populate a website with premium stamps to match the volume of eBay? Will it be an auctioneer, a stamp dealer or another unknown, such as eBay, coming out of nowhere?

The Scott editorial staff does not pay much attention to stamp sales data from eBay, because it doesn't fit our criteria. I suspect this may change in the future.

Almost 15,000 values have changed in Volume 1 and this does not include stamps that have been raised as the result of the new minimum value of 20 cents. Access to current market information is more important than ever for the active collector. And now for the self-imposed interview.

What's up with U.S. stamp values?

There is a trend among the philatelic elite to focus on the *U.S. Specialized Catalogue* and not to pay much attention to the additional changes in Volume 1. With more than 1500 value changes in the stamps of U.S. and related areas since the publication of the *U.S. Specialized* such a narrow outlook could cost you money.

There is much upward movement in the 1857-61 perforated issues. The 1858 5 cent brick red, type I, Scott 27, which jumped to $19,000 unused from $15,000 in last year's *U.S. Specialized*, jumps slightly again, now to $20,000.

Many other classic values show increases, including the 1867 grills where values rise for almost all major Scott numbers. The 1869 Pictorials, which have seen many value increases in recent Scott editions, see further increases for 2001. Classic special printings show a 5%-10% movement upward for all sets, from the reprints of the 1857-61 issue, Scott 40-47, through the special printings of the 1879 issue, Scott 192-204.

Beginning with the small Banknote issues, Scott 219-229, the continuing trend of a widening gap between unused hinged and mint never hinged is once again evident in the new Scott values. The 1890 issue unused moves upward about 10% across the board, but the movement for mint never hinged values is far greater.

Starting with the 1893 Columbians, unused values tend to remain static while values for mint never-hinged examples rise. The $5 Columbian, a harbinger of U.S. stamp values, rises to $8,000 mint never-hinged from $7,500 in last year's *U.S. Specialized*. In last year's Volume 1, the same $5 Columbian had a catalogue value of $6,750. Keep in mind that stamps such as the $5 Columbian, with very fine centering and mint never-hinged gum, are "condition rarities" and represent the upper neck in the wine bottle of condition.

The 1894-95 First Bureau issue, Scott 246-278, and the 1902-03 Second Bureau issue, Scott 300-313, each move upward both unused and mint never hinged, again with the values for mint never-hinged condition leading the way.

In the back-of-the-book category, Newspaper stamps continue their recent rise in value. Large value increases are evident in the Carrier section, based on the recent auction sale of the now legendary David Golden collection.

What's the scoop for A-B Countries?

In Australia, the 1915 2sh brown Kangaroo, watermarked Wide Crown and Narrow A, perf. 11 1/2, Scott 43, pushes to $400 unused and $90 used, from $375 unused and $87.50 used. The popular 1928 Kookaburra pane of 4, Scott 95a, moves to $125 unused, $190 mint never hinged and $150 used, from $110 unused, $175 mint never hinged and $135 used. The 1932 5sh Sydney Harbor Bridge, Scott 132, remains steady at $350 unused, $575 mint never hinged and $200 used.

Important Bermuda collection auction sales in 1999 have resulted in new, higher values for several rarities. The 1p red on bluish Perot Postmaster stamp, Scott X5, rises one notch to $130,000 from $125,000. The 1865 6p brown lilac, Scott 4, moves to $1,200 unused from $900.

Is there any truth to the rumor that Scott is raising its minimum value?

Yes. For the first time since the 1992 edition, the minimum value for stamps in the Scott catalogues has been raised, this time to 20 cents. The previous minimum value was 15 cents. Given the cost to a dealer of selling an individual stamp to a collector, it is Scott's belief that 20 cents is the minimum that one should expect to pay for a single stamp purchased separately. Collectors should keep in mind that almost all of this 20 cents represents handling costs and does not represent the inherent value of the stamp itself. A reminder is given that a group of stamps with minimum values, whether it be a packet, a long run of catalogue numbers or even a single set, invariably will cost less or much less than the total of the minimum catalogue values. What can you buy for 20 cents anymore? Think about it.

What about other editorial changes?

Two additions to the foreign section of Volume 1 stand out as especially important. The first is the addition of 143 new major number Postal Fiscal stamps from four different Australian states: Queensland, Tasmania, Victoria and Western Australia. These stamps from the 1880s and 1890s did both postal and revenue duty, and all were authorized for postal use. Values range from $8 to $3500.

The other major addition to the 2001 Volume 1 is a multi-page Bosnia and Herzegovina listing comprising the stamps issued from 1993 to the present. Included are the stamps issued by the government in Sarajevo and the Bosnian Croat administration located in Mostar, as well as the Bosnian Serb administration located in Banja Luca.

New listings for individual stamps or sets in never-hinged condition have been added to Allenstein (entire country), Spanish Andorra, Antigua, Australia (entire country) and Bechuanaland Protectorate.

What else is new?

You probably noticed that we have a new typeface. New systems software has swept our office and working environment allowing this change to be possible. Hopefully you will find the new type easier to read. We had been using a software system custom designed for the Scott operation that performed a multitude of tasks including the creation of type and layout, adding up set values, ad placement and more, but in the rapid world of computer development it was starting to get clunky. We have invested considerable dollars in new state-of-the-art systems to make sure that we can store, process and deliver the stamp information you need in a variety of media.

Happy collecting,

Stuart Morrissey

Stuart Morrissey/Publisher

Acknowledgments

Our appreciation and gratitude go to the following individuals who have assisted us in preparing information included in the 2001 Scott Catalogues. Some helpers prefer anonymity. These individuals have generously shared their stamp knowledge with others through the medium of the Scott Catalogue.

Those who follow provided information that is in addition to the hundreds of dealer price lists and advertisements and scores of auction catalogues and realizations which were used in producing the catalogue values. It is from those noted here that we have been able to obtain information on items not normally seen in published lists and advertisements. Support from these people goes beyond data leading to catalogue values, for they also are key to editorial changes.

B.J. Ammel (The Nile Post)
Robert Ausubel
Jack Hagop Barsoumian
Jules K. Beck
John Birkinbine II
Torbjorn Bjork (Paradise Valley Stamp Company, Inc.)
Jeff Brasor (Honduras Coll. Club, Associated Coll. of El Salvador)
Roger S. Brody
Joseph Bush
Lawrence A. Bustillo (Suburban Stamp Inc.)
A. Bryan Camarda
Alan C. Campbell
Nathan Carlin
Henry Chlanda
Laurie Conrad
Frank D. Correl
Steven D. Crippe
Andrew Cronin (Canadian Society of Russian Philately)
Charles E. Cwiakala
Norman S. Davis
Kenneth E. Diehl
Bob Dumaine (Sam Houston Duck Company)
William S. Dunn
Paul G. Eckman
Stephen G. Esrati
J.A. Farrington
Peter R. Feltus
Leon Finik (Loral Stamps)
Henry Fisher
Geoffrey Flack
Joseph E. Foley (Eire Philatelic Association)
Huguette Gagnon (Ethiopian Philatelic Society)
Gary Griffith
Henry Hahn (Society for Czechoslovak Philately, Inc.)
Rudolf Hamar (Estonian Philatelic Society)
Erich E. Hamm (Philactica)
Robert R. Hegland
Clifford O. Herrick (Fidelity Trading Company)
Lee H. Hill, Jr.
Steven Hines
Dr. Eugene H. Holmok (Tatra Stamps, Reg'd.)
Wilson Hulme
Kalman V. Illyefalvi (Society for Hungarian Philately)
John I. Jamieson (Saskatoon Stamp Centre)
Peter C. Jeannopoulos
A.E. Buzz Jehle
Clyde Jennings
Allan Katz
Stanford M. Katz
Lewis Kaufman
Dr. James W. Kerr
Charles F. Kezbers
William V. Kriebel
Dr. Stanley Kronenberg
William Langs
Steve Levine
Gary B. Little
William A. Litle
Pedro Llach (Filatelia Llach S.L.)
William Thomas Lockard
F. Brian Marshall (Sarawak Specialists' Society)
Marilyn R. Mattke
Dr. Hector R. Mena (Society for Costa Rica Collectors)
Robert Meyersburg
Giorgio Migliavacca
Jack E. Molesworth (Jack E. Molesworth, Inc.)
Chuck Q. Moo
William E. Mooz
Gary M. Morris (Pacific Midwest Co.)
Peter Mosiondz, Jr.
Bruce M. Moyer (Moyer Stamps & Collectibles)
Richard H. Muller (Richard's Stamps)
James Natale
Gregg Nelson
Robert Odenweller
Victor Ostolaza
Souren V. Panirian
John E. Pearson (Pittwater Philatelic Service)
Donald J. Peterson
Vernon W. Pickering
Stanley M. Piller (Stanley M. Piller & Associates)
Louis E. Repeta
Peter A. Robertson
Michael Rogers (Michael Rogers, Inc.)
Jon W. Rose
Frans H.A. Rummens (American Society for Netherlands Philately)
Richard H. Salz
Jacques C. Schiff, Jr. (Jacques C. Schiff, Jr., Inc.)
F. Burton Sellers
Michael Shamilzadeh
Jeff Siddiqui (Pakistan Study Circle)
Sergio & Liane Sismondo (The Classic Collector)
Dr. Russell V. Skavaril (St. Helena, Ascension & Tristan da Cunha Philatelic Society)
Dr. Hubert C. Skinner
Roger D. Skinner (Nepal & Tibet Philatelic Study Group)
Jay Smith
Jack Solens (Armstrong Philatelics)
Ekrem Spahich (Croatian Philatelic Society)
Richard Stambaugh
Richard Stark
Jay Tell (Americana Stamp & Coin Galleries, Inc.)
Scott R. Trepel (Siegel Auction Galleries, Inc.)
Ming W. Tsang (Hong Kong Stamp Society)
A. John Ultee
James O. Vadeboncoeur (Mexico-Elmhurst Philatelic Society Intl.)
Xavier Verbeck
Hal Vogel
George P. Wagner
Jerome S. Wagshal
Philip T. Wall
William R. Wallace (Rhodesian Study Circle)
Daniel C. Warren
Richard A. Washburn
Giana Wayman
Dr. Gary B. Weiss
William R. Weiss, Jr. (Weiss Philatelics)
Hans A. Westphal
Ralph Yorio
Val Zabijaka
Alfonso G. Zulueta

A special acknowledgment to Liane and Sergio Sismondo of The Classic Collector for their extraordinary assistance and knowledge sharing that has aided in the preparation of this year's Standard and Classic Specialized Catalogues.

Addresses, Telephone Numbers, Web Sites, E-Mail Addresses of General & Specialized Philatelic Societies

Collectors can contact the following groups for information about the philately of the areas within the scope of these societies, or inquire about membership in these groups. Aside from the general societies, we limit this list to groups that specialize in particular fields of philately, particular areas covered by the Scott Standard Postage Stamp Catalogue, and topical groups. Many more specialized philatelic societies exist than those listed below. These addresses were compiled in January 2000, and are, to the best of our knowledge, correct and current. Groups should inform the editors of address changes whenever they occur. The editors also want to hear from other such specialized groups not listed.

Unless otherwise noted all website addresses begin with http://

General "Umbrella" Societies

American Philatelic Society
PO Box 8000
State College PA 16803
Ph: (814) 237-3803
www.stamps.org
E-mail: relamb@stamps.org

American Stamp Dealers' Association
Joseph Savarese
3 School St.
Glen Cove NY 11542
Ph: (516) 759-7000
www.asdaonline.com
E-mail: asda@erols.com

International Society of Worldwide Stamp Collectors
Anthony Zollo
PO Box 150407
Lufkin TX 75915-0407
www.iswsc.homepage.com/
E-mail: stamptmf@frontiernet.net

Junior Philatelists of America
Ellie Chapman
PO Box 850
Boalsburg PA 16827-0850
www.jpastamps.org
E-mail: jpaellie@aol.com

Royal Philatelic Society
41 Devonshire Place
London, United Kingdom W1N 1PE

Royal Philatelic Society of Canada
PO Box 929, Station Q
Toronto, ON, Canada M4T 2P1
www.interlog.com/~rspc
E-mail: rpsc@interlog.com

Groups focusing on fields or aspects found in world-wide philately (some may cover U.S. area only)

American Air Mail Society
Stephen Reinhard
PO Box 110
Mineola NY 11501
ourworld.compuserve.com/homepages/aams/
E-mail: sr1501@aol.com

American First Day Cover Society
Douglas Kelsey
PO Box 65960
Tucson AZ 85728-5960
Ph: (520) 321-0880
E-mail: afdcs@aol.com

American Revenue Association
Eric Jackson
PO Box 728
Leesport PA 19533-0728
Ph: (610) 926-6200
www.revenuer.org
E-mail: eric@revenuer.com

American Topical Association
Paul E. Tyler
PO Box 50820
Albuquerque NM 87181-0820
Ph: (505) 323-8595
prcn.org/~pauld/ata/
E-mail: ATAStamps@aol.com

Errors, Freaks and Oddities Collectors Club
Jim McDevitt
138 East Lakemont Dr.
Kingsland GA 31548
Ph: (912) 729-1573
E-mail: cwouscg@aol.com

Fakes and Forgeries Study Group
Anthony Torres
107 Hoover Rd.
Rochester NY 14617-3611

First Issues Collectors Club
Peter F. Kaminski
1347 Prosser Drive
Sycamore IL 60178
Ph: (815) 895-2819
E-mail: pkaminsk@niu.edu

International Philatelic Society of Joint Stamp Issues Collectors
Richard Zimmermann
124, Avenue Guy de Coubertin
Saint Remy Les Chevreuse,
France F-78470
perso.clubinternet.fr/rzimmerm/index.htm
E-mail: rzimmerm@club-internet.fr

National Duck Stamp Collectors Society
Anthony J. Monico
PO Box 43
Harleysville PA 19438-0043

No Value Identified Club
Albert Sauvanet
Le Clos Royal B, Boulevard des Pas Enchantes
St. Sebastien-sur Loire, France 44230
E-mail: alain.vailly@irin.univ_nantes.fr

The Perfins Club
Kurt Ottenheimer
462 West Walnut St.
Long Beach NY 11561
Ph: (516) 431-3412
E-mail: oak462@juno.com

Post Mark Collectors Club
David Proulx
7629 Homestead Drive
Baldwinsville NY 13027
E-mail: stampdance@baldcom.net

Postal History Society
Kalman V. Illyefalvi
8207 Daren Court
Pikesville MD 21208-2211
Ph: (410) 653-0665

Precancel Stamp Society
176 Bent Pine Hill
North Wales PA 19454
Ph: (215) 368-6082
E-mail: abentpine1@aol.com

United Postal Stationery Society
Joann Thomas
PO Box 48
Redlands CA 92373
www.upss.org

Groups focusing on U.S. area philately as covered in the Standard Catalogue

Bureau Issues Association
David G. Lee
PO Box 2641
Reston VA 20195-0641
www.usstamps.org

Canal Zone Study Group
Richard H. Salz
60 27th Ave.
San Francisco CA 94121

Carriers and Locals Society
Steven M. Roth
PO Box 57160
Washington DC 20036
Ph: (202) 293-6813
E-mail: smroth@wizard.net

Confederate Stamp Alliance
Richard L. Calhoun
PO Box 581
Mt. Prospect IL 60056-0581

Hawaiian Philatelic Society
Kay H. Hoke
PO Box 10115
Honolulu HI 96816-0115
Ph: (808) 521-5721
E-mail: bannan@pixi.com

Plate Number Coil Collectors Club
Gene C. Trinks
3603 Bellows Court
Troy MI 48083
www.geocities.com/Heartland/Hills/6283
E-mail: gctrinks@sprynet.com

United Nations Philatelists
Blanton Clement, Jr.
292 Springdale Terrace
Yardley PA 19067-3421
www.unpi.com
E-mail: bclement@prodigy.net

U.S. Cancellation Club
Roger Rhoads
3 Ruthana Way
Hockessin DE 19707
www.geocities.com/athens/2088/uscchome.htm
E-mail:rrrhoads@aol.com

U.S. Philatelic Classics Society
Mark D. Rogers
PO Box 80708
Austin TX 78708-0708
www.scruz.net/~eho/uspcs
E-mail: mdr@texas.net

U.S. Possessions Philatelic Society
David S. Durbin
1608 S. 22nd St.
Blue Springs MO 64015
Ph: (816) 224-3666

Groups focusing on philately of foreign countries or regions

Albania Study Circle
Paul Eckman
620 North Hoover St.
Los Angeles CA 90004-2311

Andorran Philatelic Study Circle
D. Hope
17 Hawthorn Dr.
Stalybridge, Cheshire, United Kingdom SK15 1UE
www.chy-an-piran.demon.co.uk/
E-mail: apsc@chy-an-piran.demon.co.uk

American Society of Polar Philatelists (Antarctic areas)
Richard Julian
1153 Fairview Dr.
York PA 17403
E-mail: rajulian@netrax.net

Australian States Study Circle
Ben Palmer
GPO 1751
Sydney, N.S.W., Australia 1043

American Belgian Philatelic Society
Kenneth L. Costilow
621 Virginius Dr.
Virginia Beach VA 23452-4417
Ph: (757) 463-6081
E-mail: klc32@erols.com

Bermuda Collectors Society
Thomas J. McMahon
PO Box 1949
Stuart FL 34995

Brazil Philatelic Association
Kurt Ottenheimer
462 West Walnut St.
Long Beach NY 11561
Ph: (516) 431-3412
E-mail: oak462@juno.com

British Caribbean Philatelic Study Group
Gale J. Raymond
Bali-Hai, PO Box 228
Sugar Land TX 77478-0228

British North America Philatelic Society (Canada & Provinces)
Alexander Unwin
PO Box 1686
Bellevue WA 98009-1686
www.wep.ab.ca/bnaps
E-mail: alecunwin@msn.com

British West Indies Study Circle
W. Clary Holt
PO Drawer 59
Burlington NC 27216
Ph: (336) 227-7461

Burma Philatelic Study Circle
A. Meech
7208 91st Ave.
Edmonton, AB, Canada T6B 0R8
E-mail: ameech@telusplanet.net

Ceylon Study Group
R. W. P. Frost
42 Lonsdale Road, Cannington
Bridgewater, Somerset, United Kingdom TA5 2JS

China Stamp Society
Paul H. Gault
PO Box 20711
Columbus OH 43220
www.chinastampsociety.org
E-mail: gault.1@osu.edu

Colombia / Panama Philatelic Study Group
PO Box 2245
El Cajon CA 92021
E-mail: jimacross@juno.com

Society for Costa Rica Collectors
Dr. Hector R. Mena
PO Box 14831
Baton Rouge LA 70808
E-mail: hrmena1@home.com

Croatian Philatelic Society (Croatia & other Balkan areas)
Ekrem Spahich
502 Romero, PO Box 696
Fritch TX 79036-0696
Ph: (806) 857-0129
www.dalmatia.net/cps/index.htm
E-mail: ou812@arn.net

Cuban Philatelic Society of America
Ernesto Cuesta
PO Box 8309
Silver Spring MD 20907-8309

Cyprus Study Circle
A. R. Everett
29 Diomed Drive
Great Barton
Bury St. Edmunds, Suffolk, United Kingdom IP31 2TN

Society for Czechoslovak Philately
Robert T. Cossaboom
PO Box 25332
Scott AFB IL 62225-0332
ww.erols.com/sibpost
E-mail: klfck1@aol.com

Danish West Indies Study Unit of the Scandinavian Collectors Club
John L. Dubois
Thermalogic Corp.
22 Kane Industrial Drive
Hudson MA 01749
Ph: (800) 343-4492
dwi.thlogic.com
E-mail: jld@thlogic.com

East Africa Study Circle
Ken Hewitt
16 Ashleigh Road
Solihull, United Kingdom B91 1AE
E-mail: 106602.2410@compuserve.com

Egypt Study Circle
G. A. Jeyes
4 Ravine Court
Meriden Close, Canford Cliffs, Poole, Dorset, United Kingdom BH13 7JU

Estonian Philatelic Society
Rudolf Hamar
1912 Nugget Drive
Felton CA 95018

Ethiopian Philatelic Society
Huguette Gagnon
110-10662 151A Street
Surrey, BC, Canada V3R 8T3
Ph: (604) 584-1701

Falkland Islands Philatelic Study Group
Carl J. Faulkner
Williams Inn, On-the-Green
Williamstown MA 01267-2620
Ph: (413) 458-9371

Faroe Islands Study Circle
Norman Hudson
28 Enfield Road
Ellesmere Port, Cheshire, United Kingdom CH65 8BY
www.on-trac.com/faroes/fisc.shtml
E-mail: jntropics@mcmail.com

Former French Colonies Specialist Society
BP 628
75367 Paris Cedex 08, France
www.ifrance.com/colfra
E-mail: clubcolfra@aol.com

France & Colonies Philatelic Society
Walter Parshall
103 Spruce St.
Bloomfield NJ 07003-3514

Germany Philatelic Society
PO Box 779
Arnold MD 21012-4779
www.gps.nu
E-mail: germanyphilatelic@juno.com

German Democratic Republic Study Group of the German Philatelic Society
Ken Lawrence
PO Box 8040
State College PA 16803-8040
Ph: (814) 237-3803
E-mail: apsken@aol.com

Gibraltar Study Circle
D. Brook
80 Farm Road
Weston Super Mare, Avon, United Kingdom BS22 8BD
www.abel.co.uk/~stirrups/GSC.HTM
E-mail: drstirrups@dundee.ac.uk

Great Britain Collectors Club
Janet Gordon
PO Box 42324
Cincinnati OH 45242-0324
www.gbstamps.com/gbcc
E-mail: jangnp@aol.com

Hellenic Philatelic Society of America (Greece & related areas)
Dr. Nicholas Asimakopulos
541 Cedar Hill Ave.
Wyckoff NJ 07481
Ph: (201) 447-6262

International Society of Guatemala Collectors
Mrs. Mae Vignola
105 22nd Ave.
San Francisco CA 94121

Haiti Philatelic Society
Ubaldo Del Toro
5709 Marble Archway
Alexandria VA 22315
E-mail: u007ubi@aol.com

Honduras Collectors Club
Jeff Brasor
PO Box 173
Coconut Creek FL 33097

Hong Kong Stamp Society
Dr. An-Min Chung
120 Deerfield Rd.
Broomall PA 19008
Ph: (215) 576-6850

Hungary Philatelic Society
Thomas Phillips
PO Box 1162
Fairfield CT 06432-1162
home.sprintmail.com/~aahoover/shp/shphome.htm
E-mail: h.alanhoover@lycosemail.com

India Study Circle
John Warren
PO Box 7326
Washington DC 20044
Ph: (202) 564-6876
E-mail: warren.john@epamail.epa.gov

Indian Ocean Study Circle
K. B. Fitton
50 Firlands
Weybridge, Surrey, United Kingdom KT13 0HR
E-mail: keithfitton@intonet.co.uk

Society of Indochina Philatelists
Paul Blake
1466 Hamilton Way
San Jose CA 95125

Iran Philatelic Study Circle
Darrell R. Hill
1410 Broadway
Bethlehem PA 18015-4025
www.iranphilatelic.org
E-mail: hillstamps@email.msn.com

Eire Philatelic Association (Ireland)
Myron G. Hill III
PO Box 1210
College Park MD 20741-1210
ourworld.compuserve.com/homepages/aranman/epa.htm
E-mail: mhill@radix.net

Society of Israel Philatelists
Paul S. Aufrichtig
300 East 42nd St.
New York NY 10017

Italy and Colonies Study Circle
Andrew D'Anneo
1085 Dunweal Lane
Calistoga CA 94515

International Society for Japanese Philately
Kenneth Kamholz
PO Box 1283
Haddonfield NJ 08033
www.west.net/~lmevans/isjp.html
E-mail: kamholz@uscom.com

Korea Stamp Society
John E. Talmage
PO Box 6889
Oak Ridge TN 37831
E-mail: jtalmage@usit.net

Latin American Philatelic Society
Piet Steen
197 Pembina Ave.
Hinton, AB, Canada T7V 2B2

Latvian Philatelic Society
J. Ronis
7 Lowes Ave.
Brampton, ON, Canada L6X 1R8

Liberian Philatelic Society
William Thomas Lockard
PO Box 106
Wellston OH 45692
Ph: (740) 384-2020
E-mail: tlockard@zoomnet.net

Liechtenstudy USA (Liechtenstein)
Ralph Schneider
PO Box 23049
Belleville IL 62223
Ph: (618) 277-8543
www.rschneiderstamps.com/info.html
E-mail: rsstamps@aol.com

Lithuania Philatelic Society
John Variakojis
3715 W. 68th St.
Chicago IL 60629
Ph: (773) 585-8649
www.public.osf.lt/~vasaris/e_bend_0.htm
E-mail: variakojis@earthlink.net

Luxembourg Collectors Club
Gary B. Little
3304 Plateau Dr.
Belmont CA 94002-1312
www.luxcentral.com/stamps/LCC
E-mail: lcc@luxcentral.com

Malaya Study Group
Joe Robertson
12 Lisa Court
Downsland Road
Basingstoke, Hampshire, United Kingdom RG21 8TU
home.freeuk.net/johnmorgan/msg.htm

Malta Study Circle
A. Webster
50 Worcester Road
Sutton, Surrey, United Kingdom SM2 6QB
E-mail: lander.jgc@btinternet.com

Mexico-Elmhurst Philatelic Society International
David Pietsch
PO Box 50997
Irvine CA 92619-0997
E-mail: mepsi@msn.com

Society for Moroccan and Tunisian Philately
206, bld. Pereire
75017 Paris, France
members.aol.com/Jhaik5811/p1E.html
E-mail: jhaik5814@aol.com

Nepal & Tibet Philatelic Study Group
Roger D. Skinner
1020 Covington Road
Los Altos CA 94024-5003
Ph: (650) 968-4163

American Society of Netherlands Philately
Jan Enthoven
W6428 Riverview Drive
Onalaska WI 54650
Ph: (608) 781-8612
www.cs.cornell.edu/Info/People/aswin/NL/neth
E-mail: jenthoven@centuryinter.net

Nicaragua Study Group
Erick Rodriguez
11817 S.W. 11th St.
Miami FL 33184-2501
clubs.yahoo.com/clubs/nicaraguastudygroup
E-mail: nsgsec@yahoo.com

Society of Australasian Specialists / Oceania
Henry Bateman
PO Box 4862
Monroe LA 71211-
Ph: (800) 571-0293
members.aol.com/stampsho/saso.html
E-mail: ck100@iamerica.net

Orange Free State Study Circle
J. R. Stroud
28 Oxford St.
Burnham-on-sea, Somerset,
United Kingdom TA8 1LQ
www.ofssc.org
E-mail: jrstroud@classicfm.net

Pacific Islands Study Group
John Ray
24 Woodvale Avenue
London, United Kingdom SE25 4AE
dspace.dial.pipex.com/jray/pisc.html
E-mail: jray@dial.pipex.com

Pakistan Study Circle
Jeff Siddiqui
PO Box 7002
Lynnwood WA 98046
E-mail: jeffsiddiqui@msn.com

Papuan Philatelic Society
Steven Zirinsky
PO Box 49, Ansonia Station
New York NY 10023
Ph: (212) 665-0765
E-mail: szirinsky@compuserve.com

International Philippine Philatelic Society
Robert F. Yacano
PO Box 100
Toast NC 27049
Ph: (336) 783-0768
E-mail: yacano@advi.net

Pitcairn Islands Study Group
Nelson A. L. Weller
2940 Wesleyan Lane
Winston-Salem NC 27106
Ph: (336) 724-6398
E-mail: nalweller@aol.com

Plebiscite-Memel-Saar Study Group of the German Philatelic Society
Clay Wallace
100 Lark Court
Alamo CA 94507
E-mail: wallace@earthlink.net

Polonus Philatelic Society (Poland)
Roman H. Strzelecki
PO Box 458
Berwyn IL 60402
Ph: (708) 749-9345

International Society for Portuguese Philately
Clyde Homen
1491 Bonnie View Rd.
Hollister CA 95023-5117
E-mail: cjh@hollinet.com

Rhodesian Study Circle
William R. Wallace
PO Box 16381
San Francisco CA 94116
www.rsc.stamps.org.uk/
E-mail: bwall8rscr@earthlink.net

Romanian Chapter of Croatian Philatelic Society
Dan Demetriade
PO Box 09700
Detroit MI 48209

Canadian Society of Russian Philately
Andrew Cronin
PO Box 5722, Station A
Toronto, ON, Canada M5W 1P2
Ph: (905) 764-8968
www3.sympatico.ca/postrider/postrider/index.html
E-mail: postrider@sympatico.ca

Rossica Society of Russian Philately
George G. Werbizky
409 Jones Rd.
Vestal NY 13850-3246

Ryukyu Philatelic Specialist Society
Carmine J. DiVincenzo
PO Box 381
Clayton CA 94517-0381

St. Helena, Ascension & Tristan Da Cunha Philatelic Society
Dr. Russell V. Skavaril
222 East Torrance Road
Columbus OH 43214-3834
Ph: (614) 262-3046
ourworld.compuserve.com/homepages/st_helena_ascen_tdc

St. Pierre & Miquelon Philatelic Society
David Salovey
PO Box 464
New York NY 10014-0464

Associated Collectors of El Salvador
Jeff Brasor
PO Box 173
Coconut Creek FL 33097

Fellowship of Samoa Specialists
Jack R. Hughes
1541 Wellington St.
Oakland CA 94602-1751
members.aol.com/tongaJan/foss.html

Sarawak Specialists' Society
Stu Leven
4031 Samson Way
San Jose CA 95124-3733
Ph: (408) 978-0193
E-mail: stulev@ix.netcom.com

Scandinavian Collectors Club
Donald B. Brent
PO Box 13196
El Cajon CA 92020
www.scc-online.org
E-mail: dbrent47@sprynet.com

Slovakia Stamp Society
Jack Benchik
PO Box 555
Notre Dame IN 46556

Philatelic Society for Greater Southern Africa
William C. Brooks VI
PO Box 4158
Cucamonga CA 91729-4158
Ph: (909) 484-2806
www.homestead.com/psgsa/index.html
E-mail: bbrooks@dpss.co.san-bernardino.ca.us

Spanish Philatelic Society
Robert H. Penn
1108 Walnut Drive
Danielsville PA 18038
Ph: (610) 767-6793

Sudan Study Group
Charles Hass
PO Box 3435
Nashua NH 03061-3435
Ph: (603) 888-4160
E-mail: hassstamps@aol.com

American Helvetia Philatelic Society (Switzerland, Liechtenstein)
Richard T. Hall
PO Box 666
Manhattan Beach CA 90267-0666
E-mail: rtravish@pacbell.net

Tannu Tuva Collectors Society
Ken Simon
513 Sixth Ave. So.
Lake Worth FL 33460-4507
Ph: (561) 588-5954
www.seflin.org/tuva
E-mail: p003115b@pb.seflin.org

Society for Thai Philately
H. R. Blakeney
PO Box 25644
Oklahoma City OK 73125
E-mail:HRBlakeney@aol.com

Turkish and Ottoman Philatelic Society
Robert Stuchell
173 Valley Stream Lane
Wayne PA 19087

Ukrainian Philatelic & Numismatic Society
Bohdan O. Pauk
PO Box 11184
Chicago IL 60611-0184
Ph: (773) 276-0355
E-mail: bpauk@excite.com

Vatican Philatelic Society
Sal Quinonez
2 Aldersgate, Apt. 119
Riverhead NY 11901
Ph: (516) 727-6426

British Virgin Islands Philatelic Society
Roger Downing
PO Box 11156
St. Thomas VI 00801-4156
Ph: (284) 494-3510
www.islandsun.com/FEATURES/bviphil9198.html
E-mail: issun@caribsurf.com

West Africa Study Circle
Jack Ince
PO Box 858
Stirling, ON, Canada K0K 3E0
Ph: (613) 395-1926
ourworld.compuserve.com/homepages/FrankWalton
E-mail: pamjack@bel.auracom.com

Western Australia Study Group
Brian Pope
PO Box 423
Claremont, Western Australia,
Australia 6910

Yugoslavia Study Group of the Croatian Philatelic Society
Michael Lenard
1514 North 3rd Ave.
Wausau WI 54401

Topical Groups

Americana Unit
Dennis Dengel
17 Peckham Rd.
Poughkeepsie NY 12603-2018
www.americanaunit.org
E-mail: info@americanaunit.org

Astronomy Study Unit
George Young
PO Box 632
Tewksbury MA 01876-0632
Ph: (978) 851-8283
www.fandm.edu/departments/astronomy/miscell/astunit.html
E-mail: george-young@msn.com

Bicycle Stamp Club
Norman Batho
358 Iverson Place
East Windsor NJ 08520
Ph: (609) 448-9547
members.tripod.com/~bicyclestamps
E-mail: normbatho@worldnet.att.net

Bird Stamp Society
G. P. Horsman
9 Cowley Drive, Worthy Down
Winchester, Hants., United Kingdom
SO21 2OW

Biology Unit
Alan Hanks
34 Seaton Dr.
Aurora, ON, Canada L4G 2K1
Ph: (905) 727-6993

Canadiana Study Unit
John Peebles
PO Box 3262, Station "A"
London, ON, Canada N6A 4K3
E-mail: john.peebles@odyssey.on.ca

Captain Cook Study Unit
Brian P. Sandford
173 Minuteman Dr.
Concord MA 01742-1923
freespace.virgin.net/chris.jones/ccsu.htm
E-mail: ian.boreham@virgin.net

Casey Jones Railroad Unit
Oliver Atchison
PO Box 31631
San Francisco CA 94131-0631
Ph: (415) 648-8057
E-mail: cjrrunit@aol.com

Cats on Stamps Study Unit
Mary Ann Brown
3006 Wade Rd.
Durham NC 27705
E-mail: ma.brown@duke.edu

Chemistry & Physics Study Unit
Dr. Roland Hirsch
20458 Water Point Lane
Germantown MD 20874
E-mail: rfhirsch@erols.com

Chess on Stamps Study Unit
Anne Kasonic
7625 County Road #153
Interlaken NY 14847
www.iglobal.net/home/reott/stamps1.htm#cossu
E-mail: akasonic@epix.net

Christmas Philatelic Club
Linda Lawrence
312 Northwood Drive
Lexington KY 40505
Ph: (606) 293-0151
www.hwcn.org/link/cpc
E-mail: stamplinda@aol.com

Christopher Columbus Philatelic Society
Donald R. Ager
PO Box 71
Hillsboro NH 03244
Ph: (603) 464-5379
E-mail: don_ager@conknet.com

Collectors of Religion on Stamps
Verna Shackleton
425 North Linwood Avenue #110
Appleton WI 54914
Ph: (920) 734-2417
www.powernetonline.com/corosec/coros1.htm
E-mail: corosec@powernetonline.com

Dogs on Stamps Study Unit
Morris Raskin
202A Newport Rd.
Monroe Township NJ 08831
Ph: (609) 655-7411
www.dossu.org
E-mail: mraskin@worldnet.att.net

Earth's Physical Features Study Group
Fred Klein
515 Magdalena Ave.
Los Altos CA 94024
www.philately.com/society_news/earths_physical.htm

Ebony Society of Philatelic Events and Reflections (African-American topicals)
Sanford L. Byrd
PO Box 1864
Midland MI 48641-1864
Ph: (212) 928-5165
www.slsabyrd.com/esper.htm
E-mail: esper@ibm.net

Embroidery, Stitchery, Textile Unit
Helen N. Cushman
1001 Genter St., Apt. 9H
La Jolla CA 92037
Ph: (619) 459-1194

Europa Study Unit
Hank Klos
PO Box 611
Bensenville IL 60106
E-mail: eunity@aol.com

Fine & Performing Arts
Ruth Richards
10393 Derby Dr.
Laurel MD 20723
www.philately.com/society_news/fap.htm
E-mail: bersec@aol.com

Gay & Lesbian History on Stamps Club
Joe Petronie
PO Box 515981
Dallas TX 75251-5981
home.earthlink.net/~glhsc/index.html
E-mail: glhsc@aol.com

Gems, Minerals & Jewelry Study Group
George Young
PO Box 632
Tewksbury MA 01876-0632
Ph: (978) 851-8283
www.rockhounds.com/rockshop/gmjsuapp.txt
E-mail: george-young@msn.com

Graphics Philately Association
Mark Winnegrad
1450 Parkchester Road
Bronx NY 10462

Journalists, Authors & Poets on Stamps
Louis Forster
7561 East 24th Court
Wichita KS 67226

Lighthouse Stamp Society
Dalene Thomas
8612 West Warren Lane
Lakewood CO 80227-2352
Ph: (303) 986-6620
www.lighthousestampsociety.homepage.com
E-mail: dalene1@uswest.net

Lions International Stamp Club
John Bargus
RR #1
Mill Bay, BC, Canada V0R 2P0
Ph: (250) 743-5782

Mahatma Gandhi On Stamps Study Circle
Pramod Shivagunde
Pratik Clinic, Akluj
Solapur, Maharashtra, India 413101

Mask Study Unit
Carolyn Weber
1220 Johnson Drive #104
Ventura CA 93003-0540
www.philately.com/philately/masks.htm

Mathematical Study Unit
Estelle Buccino
5615 Glenwood Rd.
Bethesda MD 20817-6727
Ph: (301) 718-8898

Medical Subjects Unit
Dr. Frederick C. Skvara
PO Box 6228
Bridgewater NJ 08807
E-mail: fcskvara@bellatlantic.net

Mesoamerican Archeology Study Unit
Chris Moser
PO Box 1442
Riverside CA 92502
www.arrive.at/codexfilatelica
E-mail:cmoser@ci.riverside.ca.us

Napoleonic Age Philatelists
Ken Berry
7513 Clayton Dr.
Oklahoma City OK 73132-5636
Ph: (405) 721-0044

Parachute Study Group
Bill Wickert
3348 Clubhouse Road
Virginia Beach VA 23452-5339
Ph: (757) 486-3614
E-mail: bw47psg@worldnet.att.net

Petroleum Philatelic Society International
Linda W. Corwin
5427 Pine Springs Court
Conroe TX 77304

Philatelic Computing Study Group
Robert de Violini
PO Box 5025
Oxnard CA 93031
www.west.net/~stamps1/pcsg/pcsg.html
E-mail: dviolini@west.net

Philatelic Music Circle
Cathleen Osborne
PO Box 1781
Sequim WA 98382
Ph: (360) 683-6373
www.stampshows.com/pmc.html

Rainbow Study Unit
Shirley Sutton
PO Box 37
Lone Pine, AB, Canada T0G 1M0
Ph: (780) 584-2268
E-mail: george-young@msn.com

Rotary on Stamps Unit
Donald Fiery
PO Box 333
Hanover PA 17331
Ph: (717) 632-8921

Scouts on Stamps Society International
Carl Schauer
PO Box 526
Belen NM 87002
Ph: (505) 864-0098
www.sossi.org
E-mail: rfrank@sossi.org

Ships on Stamps Unit
Robert Stuckert
2750 Highway 21 East
Paint Lick KY 40461
Ph: (606) 925-4901

Space Unit
Carmine Torrisi
PO Box 780241
Maspeth NY 11378
Ph: (718) 386-7882
stargate.1usa.com/stamps/

Sports Philatelists International
Margaret Jones
5310 Lindenwood Ave.
St. Louis MO 63109-1758
www.concentric.net/~laimins/spi.html

Stamps on Stamps Collectors Club
William Critzer
1360 Trinity Drive
Menlo Park CA 94025
Ph: (650) 234-1136
ourworld.compuserve.com/homepages/soscu
E-mail: willcrit@aol.com

Windmill Study Unit
Walter J. Hollien
PO Box 346
Long Valley NJ 07853-0346

Wine on Stamps Study Unit
James D. Crum
5132 Sepulveda
San Bernardino CA 92404-1134
Ph: (909) 886-3186
E-mail: jdakcrum@aol.com

Women on Stamps Study Unit
Phebe Quattrucci
259 Middle Road
Falmouth ME 04105

Zeppelin Collectors Club
Cheryl Ganz
PO Box A3843
Chicago IL 60690-3843

Expertizing Services

The following organizations will, for a fee, provide expert opinions about stamps submitted to them. Collectors should contact these organizations to find out about their fees and requirements before submitting philatelic material to them. The listing of these groups here is not intended as an endorsement by Scott Publishing Co.

General Expertizing Services

American Philatelic Expertizing Service (a service of the American Philatelic Society)
PO Box 8000
State College PA 16803
Ph: (814) 237-3808
Fax: (814) 237-6128
www.stamps.org
E-mail: ambristo@stamps.org
Areas of Expertise: Worldwide

B. P. A. Expertising, Ltd.
PO Box 137
Leatherhead, Surrey, United Kingdom KT22 0RG
E-mail: sec.bpa@tcom.co.uk
Areas of Expertise: British Commonwealth, Great Britain, Classics of Europe, South America and the Far East

Philatelic Foundation
501 Fifth Ave., Rm. 1901
New York NY 10017
Areas of Expertise: U.S. & Worldwide

Professional Stamp Experts
PO Box 43-0055
Miami FL 33243-0055
Ph: (305) 971-9010
Fax: (305) 259-4701
www.stampexpert.com
E-mail: randyshoemaker@netscape.net
Areas of Expertise: Stamps and covers of U.S., U.S. Possessions, British Commonwealth

Royal Philatelic Society Expert Committee
41 Devonshire Place
London, United Kingdom W1N 1PE
Areas of Expertise: All

Expertizing Services Covering Specific Fields Or Countries

Canadian Society of Russian Philately Expertizing Service
PO Box 5722, Station A
Toronto, ON, Canada M5W 1P2
Fax: (416)932-0853
Areas of Expertise: Russian areas

Confederate Stamp Alliance Authentication Service
522 Old State Road
Lincoln DE 19960-9797
Ph: (302) 422-2656
Fax: (302) 424-1990
www.webuystamps.com/csaauth.htm
E-mail: trish@ce.net
Areas of Expertise: Confederate stamps and postal history

Croatian Philatelic Society Expertizing Service
PO Box 696
Fritch TX 79036-0696
Ph: (806) 857-0129
E-mail: ou812@arn.net
Areas of Expertise: Croatia and other Balkan areas

Errors, Freaks and Oddities Collectors Club Expertizing Service
138 East Lakemont Dr.
Kingsland GA 31548
Ph: (912) 729-1573
Areas of Expertise: U.S. errors, freaks and oddities

Estonian Philatelic Society Expertizing Service
39 Clafford Lane
Melville NY 11747
Ph: (516) 421-2078
E-mail: esto4@aol.com
Areas of Expertise: Estonia

Hawaiian Philatelic Society Expertizing Service
PO Box 10115
Honolulu HI 96816-0115
Areas of Expertise: Hawaii

Hong Kong Stamp Society Expertizing Service
PO Box 206
Glenside PA 19038
Fax: (215) 576-6850
Areas of Expertise: Hong Kong

International Society for Japanese Philately Expertizing Committee
32 King James Court
Staten Island NY 10308-2910
Ph: (718) 227-5229
Areas of Expertise: Japan and related areas, except WWII Japanese Occupation issues

International Society for Portuguese Philately Exertizing Service
PO Box 43146
Philadelphia PA 19129-3146
Ph: (215) 843-2106
Fax: (215) 843-2106
E-mail: s.s.washburne@worldnet.att.net
Areas of Expertise: Portugal and colonies

Mexico-Elmhurst Philatelic Society International Expert Committee
PO Box 1133
West Covina CA 91793
Areas of Expertise: Mexico

Philatelic Society for Greater Southern Africa Expert Panel
13955 W. 30th Ave.
Golden CO 80401
Areas of expertise: Entire South and South West Africa area, Bechuanalands, Basutoland, Swaziland

Ryukyu Philatelic Specialist Society Expertizing Service
1710 Buena Vista Ave.
Spring Valley CA 91977-4458
Ph: (619) 697-3205
Areas of Expertise: Ryukyu Islands

Ukrainian Philatelic & Numismatic Society Expertizing Service
30552 Dell Lane
Warren MI 48092-1862
Ph: (810) 751-5754
Areas of Expertise: Ukraine, Western Ukraine

V. G. Greene Philatelic Research Foundation
Box 100, First Canadian Place
Toronto, ON, Canada M5X 1B2
Ph: (416) 863-4593
Fax: (416) 863-4592
Areas of Expertise: British North America

Information on Catalogue Values, Grade and Condition

Catalogue Value

The Scott Catalogue value is a retail value; that is, an amount you could expect to pay for a stamp in the grade of Very Fine with no faults. Any exceptions to the grade valued will be noted in the text. The general introduction on the following pages and the individual section introductions further explain the type of material that is valued. The value listed for any given stamp is a reference that reflects recent actual dealer selling prices for that item.

Dealer retail price lists, public auction results, published prices in advertising and individual solicitation of retail prices from dealers, collectors and specialty organizations have been used in establishing the values found in this catalogue. Scott Publishing Co. values stamps, but Scott is not a company engaged in the business of buying and selling stamps as a dealer.

Use this catalogue as a guide for buying and selling. The actual price you pay for a stamp may be higher or lower than the catalogue value because of many different factors, including the amount of personal service a dealer offers, or increased or decreased interest in the country or topic represented by a stamp or set. An item may occasionally be offered at a lower price as a "loss leader," or as part of a special sale. You also may obtain an item inexpensively at public auction because of little interest at that time or as part of a large lot.

Stamps that are of a lesser grade than Very Fine, or those with condition problems, generally trade at lower prices than those given in this catalogue. Stamps of exceptional quality in both grade and condition often command higher prices than those listed.

Values for pre-1900 unused issues are for stamps with approximately half or more of their original gum. Stamps with most or all of their original gum may be expected to sell for more, and stamps with less than half of their original gum may be expected to sell for somewhat less than the values listed. On rarer stamps, it may be expected that the original gum will be somewhat more disturbed than it will be on more common issues. Post-1900 unused issues are assumed to have full original gum. From breakpoints in most countries' listings, stamps are valued as never hinged, due to the wide availability of stamps in that condition. These notations are prominently placed in the listings and in the country information preceding the listings. Some countries also feature listings with dual values for hinged and never-hinged stamps.

Grade

A stamp's grade and condition are crucial to its value. The accompanying illustrations show examples of Very Fine stamps from different time periods, along with examples of stamps in Fine to Very Fine and Extremely Fine grades as points of reference.

FINE stamps (illustrations not shown) have designs that are noticeably off center on two sides. Imperforate stamps may have small margins, and earlier issues may show the design touching one edge of the stamp design. For perforated stamps, perfs may barely clear the design on one side, and very early issues normally will have the perforations slightly cutting into the design. Used stamps may have heavier than usual cancellations.

FINE-VERY FINE stamps may be somewhat off center on one side, or slightly off center on two sides. Imperforate stamps will have two margins of at least normal size, and the design will not touch any edge. For perforated stamps, the perfs are well clear of the design, but are still noticeably off center. *However, early issues of a country may be printed in such a way that the design naturally is very close to the edges. In these cases, the perforations may cut into the design very slightly.* Used stamps will not have a cancellation that detracts from the design.

VERY FINE stamps may be slightly off center on one side, but the design will be well clear of the edge. The stamp will present a nice, balanced appearance. Imperforate stamps will have three normal-sized margins. *However, early issues of many countries may be printed in such a way that the perforations may touch the design on one or more sides. Where this is the case, a boxed note will be found defining the centering and margins of the stamps being valued.* Used stamps will have light or otherwise neat cancellations. This is the grade used to establish Scott Catalogue values.

EXTREMELY FINE stamps are close to being perfectly centered. Imperforate stamps will have even margins that are larger than normal. Even the earliest perforated issues will have perforations clear of the design on all sides.

Scott Publishing Co. recognizes that there is no formally enforced grading scheme for postage stamps, and that the final price you pay or obtain for a stamp will be determined by individual agreement at the time of transaction.

Condition

Grade addresses only centering and (for used stamps) cancellation. *Condition* refers to factors other than grade that affect a stamp's desirability.

Factors that can increase the value of a stamp include exceptionally wide margins, particularly fresh color, the presence of selvage, and plate or die varieties. Unusual cancels on used stamps (particularly those of the 19th century) can greatly enhance their value as well.

Factors other than faults that decrease the value of a stamp include loss of original gum, regumming, a hinge remnant or foreign object adhering to the gum, natural inclusions, straight edges, and markings or notations applied by collectors or dealers.

Faults include missing pieces, tears, pin or other holes, surface scuffs, thin spots, creases, toning, short or pulled perforations, clipped perforations, oxidation or other forms of color changelings, soiling, stains, and such man-made changes as reperforations or the chemical removal or lightening of a cancellation.

Grading Illustrations

On the following two pages are illustrations of various stamps from countries appearing in this volume. These stamps are arranged by country, and they represent early or important issues that are often found in widely different grades in the marketplace. The editors believe the illustrations will prove useful in showing the margin size and centering that will be seen on the various issues.

In addition to the matters of margin size and centering, collectors are reminded that the very fine stamps valued in the Scott catalogues also will possess fresh color and intact perforations, and they will be free from defects.

Most examples shown are computer – manipulated images made from single digitized master illustrations.

Fine-Very Fine →

SCOTT CATALOGUES VALUE STAMPS IN THIS GRADE

Very Fine →

Extremely Fine →

Fine-Very Fine →

SCOTT CATALOGUES VALUE STAMPS IN THIS GRADE

Very Fine →

Extremely Fine →

Fine-Very Fine

SCOTT CATALOGUES VALUE STAMPS IN THIS GRADE

Very Fine

Extremely Fine

Fine-Very Fine

SCOTT CATALOGUES VALUE STAMPS IN THIS GRADE

Very Fine

Extremely Fine

For purposes of helping to determine the gum condition and value of an unused stamp, Scott Publishing Co. presents the following chart which details different gum conditions and indicates how the conditions correlate with the Scott values for unused stamps. Used together, the Illustrated Grading Chart on the previous pages and this Illustrated Gum Chart should allow catalogue users to better understand the grade and gum condition of stamps valued in the Scott catalogues.

Gum Categories:	MINT N.H.	ORIGINAL GUM (O.G.)				NO GUM
	Mint Never Hinged *Free from any disturbance*	**Lightly Hinged** *Faint impression of a removed hinge over a small area*	**Hinge Mark or Remnant** *Prominent hinged spot with part or all of the hinge remaining*	**Large part o.g.** *Approximately half or more of the gum intact*	**Small part o.g.** *Approximately less than half of the gum intact*	**No gum** *Only if issued with gum*
Commonly Used Symbol:	★★	★	★	★	★	(★)
Pre-1900 Issues (Pre-1890 for U.S.)	*Very fine pre-1900 stamps in these categories trade at a premium over Scott value*			Scott Value for "Unused"		Scott "No Gum" listings for selected unused classic stamps
From 1900 to break-points for listings of never-hinged stamps	Scott "Never Hinged" listings for selected unused stamps	Scott Value for "Unused" (Actual value will be affected by the degree of hinging of the full o.g.)				
From breakpoints noted for many countries	Scott Value for "Unused"					

Never Hinged (NH; ★★): A never-hinged stamp will have full original gum that will have no hinge mark or disturbance. The presence of an expertizer's mark does not disqualify a stamp from this designation.

Original Gum (OG; ★): Pre-1900 stamps should have approximately half or more of their original gum. On rarer stamps, it may be expected that the original gum will be somewhat more disturbed that it will be on more common issues. Post-1900 stamps should have full original gum. Original gum will show some disturbance caused by a previous hinge(s) which may be present or entirely removed. The actual value of a post-1900 stamp will be affected by the degree of hinging of the full original gum.

Disturbed Original Gum: Gum showing noticeable effects of humidity, climate or hinging over more than half of the gum. The significance of gum disturbance in valuing a stamp in any of the Original Gum categories depends on the degree of disturbance, the rarity and normal gum condition of the issue and other variables affecting quality.

Regummed (RG; (★)): A regummed stamp is a stamp without gum that has had some type of gum privately applied at a time after it was issued. This normally is done to deceive collectors and/or dealers into thinking that the stamp has original gum and therefore has a higher value. A regummed stamp is considered the same as a stamp with none of its original gum for purposes of grading.

CATALOGUE TABS

Looking up listings in the Scott Catalogue has never been easier!

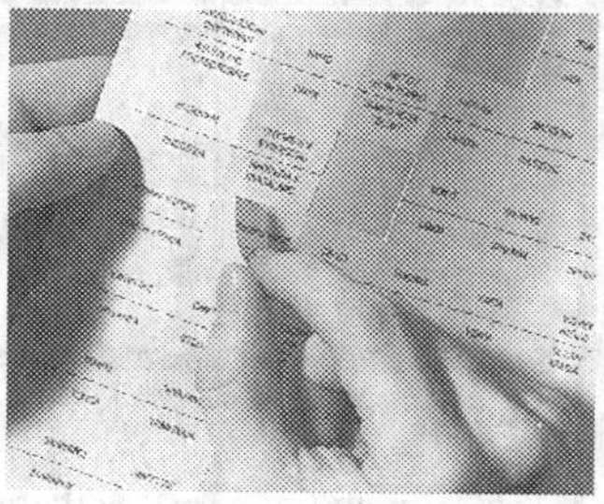

1. Scott Catalogue Tabs make referencing listings quick and easy.Simply select the country name or specialty area from the sheet.

2. Affix a portion of the tab to the appropriate page. Fold tab in half at the dotted line.

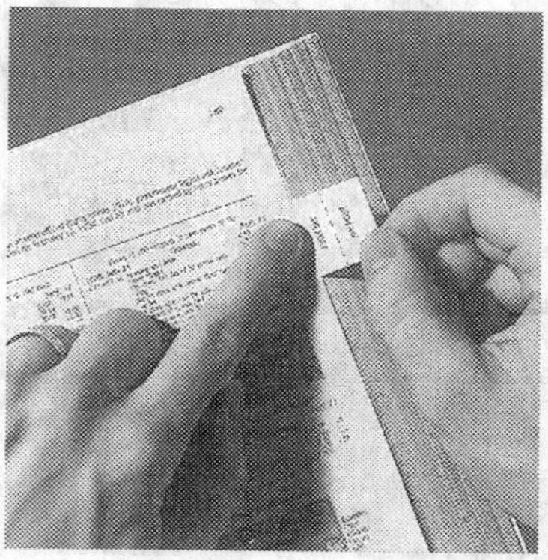

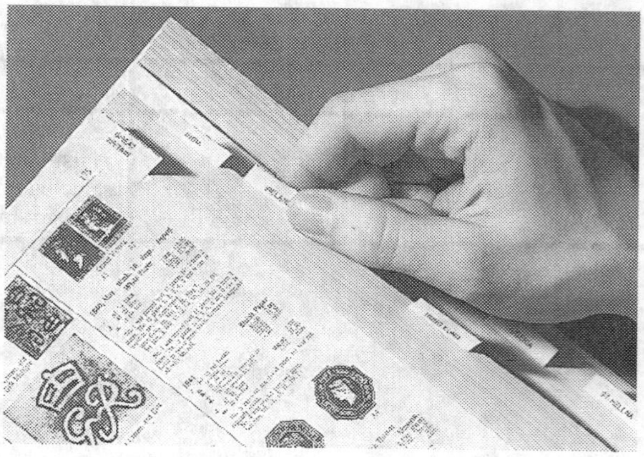

3. Use the tabs to reference catalogue listings. Blank tabs also included.

Tabs available for each Volume of the Scott Catalogue

CT1	Catalogue Tabs Volume 1 U.S. and Countries A - B	$2.95
CT2	Catalogue Tabs Volume 2 Countries C - F	$2.95
CT3	Catalogue Tabs Volume 3 Countries G - I	$2.95
CT4	Catalogue Tabs Volume 4 Countries J - O	$2.95
CT5	Catalogue Tabs Volume 5 Countries P - Slovenia	$2.95
CT6	Catalogue Tabs Volume 6 Countries Solomon Islands - Z	$2.95
CLGT6	Catalogue Tabs U.S. Specialized	$2.95
CLGTC	Catalogue Tabs Classic Specialized	$2.95

Scott Catalogue Tabs are available from your favorite stamp dealer or direct from:

SCOTT®

1-800-572-6885

P.O. Box 828 Sidney OH 45365-0828

www.scottonline.com

Catalogue Listing Policy

It is the intent of Scott Publishing Co. to list all postage stamps of the world in the *Scott Standard Postage Stamp Catalogue*. The only strict criteria for listing is that stamps be decreed legal for postage by the issuing country. Whether the primary intent of issuing a given stamp or set was for sale to postal patrons or to stamp collectors is not part of our listing criteria. Scott's role is to provide basic comprehensive postage stamp information. It is up to each stamp collector to choose which items to include in a collection.

It is Scott's objective to seek reasons why a stamp should be listed, rather than why it should not. Nevertheless, there are certain types of items that will not be listed. These include the following:

1. Unissued items that are not officially distributed or released by the issuing postal authority. Even if such a stamp is "accidentally" distributed to the philatelic or even postal market, it remains unissued. If such items are officially issued at a later date by the country, they will be listed. Unissued items consist of those that have been printed and then held from sale for reasons such as change in government, errors found on stamps or something deemed objectionable about a stamp subject or design.
2. Stamps "issued" by non-existent postal entities or fantasy countries, such as Nagaland, Occusi-Ambeno, Staffa, Sedang, Torres Straits and others.
3. Semi-official or unofficial items not required for postage. Examples include items issued by private agencies for their own express services. When such items are required for delivery, or are valid as prepayment of postage, they are listed.
4. Local stamps issued for local use only. Postage stamps issued by governments specifically for "domestic" use, such as Haiti Scott 219-228, or the United States non-denominated stamps, are not considered to be locals, since they are valid for postage throughout the country of origin.
5. Items not valid for postal use. For example, a few countries have issued souvenir sheets that are not valid for postage. This area also includes a number of worldwide charity labels (some denominated) that do not pay postage.
6. Intentional varieties, such as imperforate stamps that look like their perforated counterparts and are issued in very small quantities. These are often controlled issues intended for speculation.
7. Items distributed by the issuing government only to a limited group, such as a stamp club, philatelic exhibition or a single stamp dealer, and later brought to market at inflated prices. These items normally will be included in a footnote.

The fact that a stamp has been used successfully as postage, even on international mail, is not in itself sufficient proof that it was legitimately issued. Numerous examples of so-called stamps from non-existent countries are known to have been used to post letters that have successfully passed through the international mail system.

There are certain items that are subject to interpretation. When a stamp falls outside our specifications, it may be listed along with a cautionary footnote.

A number of factors are considered in our approach to analyzing how a stamp is listed. The following list of factors is presented to share with you, the catalogue user, the complexity of the listing process.

Additional printings — "Additional printings" of a previously issued stamp may range from an item that is totally different to cases where it is impossible to differentiate from the original. At least a minor number (a small-letter suffix) is assigned if there is a distinct change in stamp shade, noticeably redrawn design, or a significantly different perforation measurement. A major number (numeral or numeral and capital-letter combination) is assigned if the editors feel the "additional printing" is sufficiently different from the original that it constitutes a different issue.

Commemoratives — Where practical, commemoratives with the same theme are placed in a set. For example, the U.S. Civil War Centenniel set of 1961-65 and the Constitution Bicentennial series of 1989-90 appear as sets. Countries such as Japan and Korea issue such material on a regular basis, with an announced, or at least predictable, number of stamps known in advance. Occasionally, however, stamp sets that were released over a period of years have been separated. Appropriately placed footnotes will guide you to each set's continuation.

Definitive sets — Blocks of numbers generally have been reserved for definitive sets, based on previous experience with any given country. If a few more stamps were issued in a set than originally expected, they often have been inserted into the original set with a capital-letter suffix, such as U.S. Scott 1059A. If it appears that many more stamps than the originally allotted block will be released before the set is completed, a new block of numbers will be reserved, with the original one being closed off. In some cases, such as the British Machin Head series or the U.S. Transportation and Great Americans series, several blocks of numbers exist. Appropriately placed footnotes will guide you to each set's continuation.

New country — Membership in the Universal Postal Union is not a consideration for listing status or order of placement within the catalogue. The index will tell you in what volume or page number the listings begin.

"No release date" items — The amount of information available for any given stamp issue varies greatly from country to country and even from time to time. Extremely comprehensive information about new stamps is available from some countries well before the stamps are released. By contrast some countries do not provide information about stamps or release dates. Most countries, however, fall between these extremes. A country may provide denominations or subjects of stamps from upcoming issues that are not issued as planned. Sometimes, philatelic agencies, those private firms hired to represent countries, add these later-issued items to sets well after the formal release date. This time period can range from weeks to years. If these items were officially released by the country, they will be added to the appropriate spot in the set. In many cases, the specific release date of a stamp or set of stamps may never be known.

Overprints — The color of an overprint is always noted if it is other than black. Where more than one color of ink has been used on overprints of a single set, the color used is noted. Early overprint and surcharge illustrations were altered to prevent their use by forgers.

Se-tenants — Connected stamps of differing features (se-tenants) will be listed in the format most commonly collected. This includes pairs, blocks or larger multiples. Se-tenant units are not always symmetrical. An example is Australia Scott 508, which is a block of seven stamps. If the stamps are primarily collected as a unit, the major number may be assigned to the multiple, with minors going to each component stamp. In cases where continuous-design or other unit se-tenants will receive significant postal use, each stamp is given a major Scott number listing. This includes issues from the United States, Canada, Germany and Great Britain, for example.

Understanding the Listings

On the opposite page is an enlarged "typical" listing from this catalogue. Below are detailed explanations of each of the highlighted parts of the listing.

1 Scott number — Scott catalogue numbers are used to identify specific items when buying, selling or trading stamps. Each listed postage stamp from every country has a unique Scott catalogue number. Therefore, Germany Scott 99, for example, can only refer to a single stamp. Although the Scott catalogue usually lists stamps in chronological order by date of issue, there are exceptions. When a country has issued a set of stamps over a period of time, those stamps within the set are kept together without regard to date of issue. This follows the normal collecting approach of keeping stamps in their natural sets.

When a country issues a set of stamps over a period of time, a group of consecutive catalogue numbers is reserved for the stamps in that set, as issued. If that group of numbers proves to be too few, capital-letter suffixes, such as "A" or "B," may be added to existing numbers to create enough catalogue numbers to cover all items in the set. A capital-letter suffix indicates a major Scott catalogue number listing. Scott uses a suffix letter only once. Therefore, a catalogue number listing with a capital-letter prefix will not also be found with the same letter (lower case) used as a minor-letter listing. If there is a Scott 16A in a set, for example, there will not also be a Scott 16a.

Suffix letters are cumulative. A minor variety of Scott 16A would be Scott 16Ab, not Scott 16b.

There are times when a reserved block of Scott catalogue numbers is too large for a set, leaving some numbers unused. Such gaps in the numbering sequence also occur when the catalogue editors move an item's listing elsewhere or have removed it entirely from the catalogue. Scott does not attempt to account for every possible number, but rather attempts to assure that each stamp is assigned its own number.

Scott numbers designating regular postage normally are only numerals. Scott numbers for other types of stamps, such as air post, semi-postal, postal tax, postage due, occupation and others have a prefix consisting of one or more capital letters or a combination of numerals and capital letters.

2 Illustration number — Illustration or design-type numbers are used to identify each catalogue illustration. For most sets, the lowest face-value stamp is shown. It then serves as an example of the basic design approach for other stamps not illustrated. Where more than one stamp use the same illustration number, but have differences in design, the design paragraph or the description line clearly indicates the design on each stamp not illustrated. Where there are both vertical and horizontal designs in a set, a single illustration may be used, with the exceptions noted in the design paragraph or description line.

When an illustration is followed by a lower-case letter in parentheses, such as "A2(b)," the trailing letter indicates which overprint or surcharge illustration applies.

Illustrations normally are 75 percent of the original size of the stamp. An effort has been made to note all illustrations not illustrated at that percentage. Virtually all souvenir sheet illustrations are reduced even more. Overprints and surcharges are shown at 100 percent of their original size, unless otherwise noted. In some cases, the illustration will be placed above the set, between listings or omitted completely. Overprint and surcharge illustrations are not placed in this catalogue for purposes of expertizing stamps.

3 Paper color — The color of a stamp's paper is noted in italic type when the paper used is not white.

4 Listing styles — There are two principal types of catalogue listings: major and minor.

Major listings are in a larger type style than minor listings. The catalogue number is a numeral that can be found with or without a capital-letter suffix, and with or without a prefix.

Minor listings are in a smaller type style and have a small-letter suffix or (if the listing immediately follows that of the major number) may show only the letter. These listings identify a variety of the major item. Examples include perforation, color, watermark or printing method differences, multiples (some souvenir sheets, booklet panes and se-tenant combinations), and singles of multiples.

Examples of major number listings include 16, 28A, B97, C13A, 10N5, and 10N6A. Examples of minor numbers are 16a and C13Ab.

5 Basic information about a stamp or set — Introducing each stamp issue is a small section (usually a line listing) of basic information about a stamp or set. This section normally includes the date of issue, method of printing, perforation, watermark and, sometimes, some additional information of note. *Printing method, perforation and watermark apply to the following sets until a change is noted.* Stamps created by overprinting or surcharging previous issues are assumed to have the same perforation, watermark and printing method as the original. Dates of issue are as precise as Scott is able to confirm and often reflect the dates on first-day covers, rather than the actual date of release.

6 Denomination — This normally refers to the face value of the stamp; that is, the cost of the unused stamp at the post office at the time of issue. When a denomination is shown in parentheses, it does not appear on the stamp. This includes the non-denominated stamps of the United States, Brazil and Great Britain, for example.

7 Color or other description — This area provides information to solidify identification of a stamp. In many recent cases, a description of the stamp design appears in this space, rather than a listing of colors.

8 Year of issue — In stamp sets that have been released in a period that spans more than a year, the number shown in parentheses is the year that stamp first appeared. Stamps without a date appeared during the first year of the issue. Dates are not always given for minor varieties.

9 Value unused and Value used — The Scott catalogue values are based on stamps that are in a grade of Very Fine unless stated otherwise. Unused values refer to items that have not seen postal, revenue or any other duty for which they were intended. Pre-1900 unused stamps that were issued with gum must have at least most of their original gum. Later issues are assumed to have full original gum. From breakpoints specified in most countries' listings, stamps are valued as never hinged. Stamps issued without gum are noted. Modern issues with PVA or other synthetic adhesives may appear ungummed. Self-adhesive stamps are valued as appearing undisturbed on their original backing paper. For a more detailed explanation of these values, please see the "Catalogue Value," "Condition" and "Understanding Valuing Notations" elsewhere in this introduction.

In some cases, where used stamps are more valuable than unused stamps, the value is for an example with a contemporaneous cancel, rather than a modern cancel or a smudge or other unclear marking. For those stamps that were released for postal and fiscal purposes, the used value represents a postally used stamp. Stamps with revenue cancels generally sell for less.

10 Changes in basic set information — Bold type is used to show any changes in the basic data given for a set of stamps. This includes perforation differences from one stamp to the next or a different paper, printing method or watermark.

11 Total value of a set — The total value of sets of three or more stamps issued after 1900 are shown. The set line also notes the range of Scott numbers and total number of stamps included in the grouping. The actual value of a set consisting predominantly of stamps having the minimum value of twenty cents may be less than the total value shown.

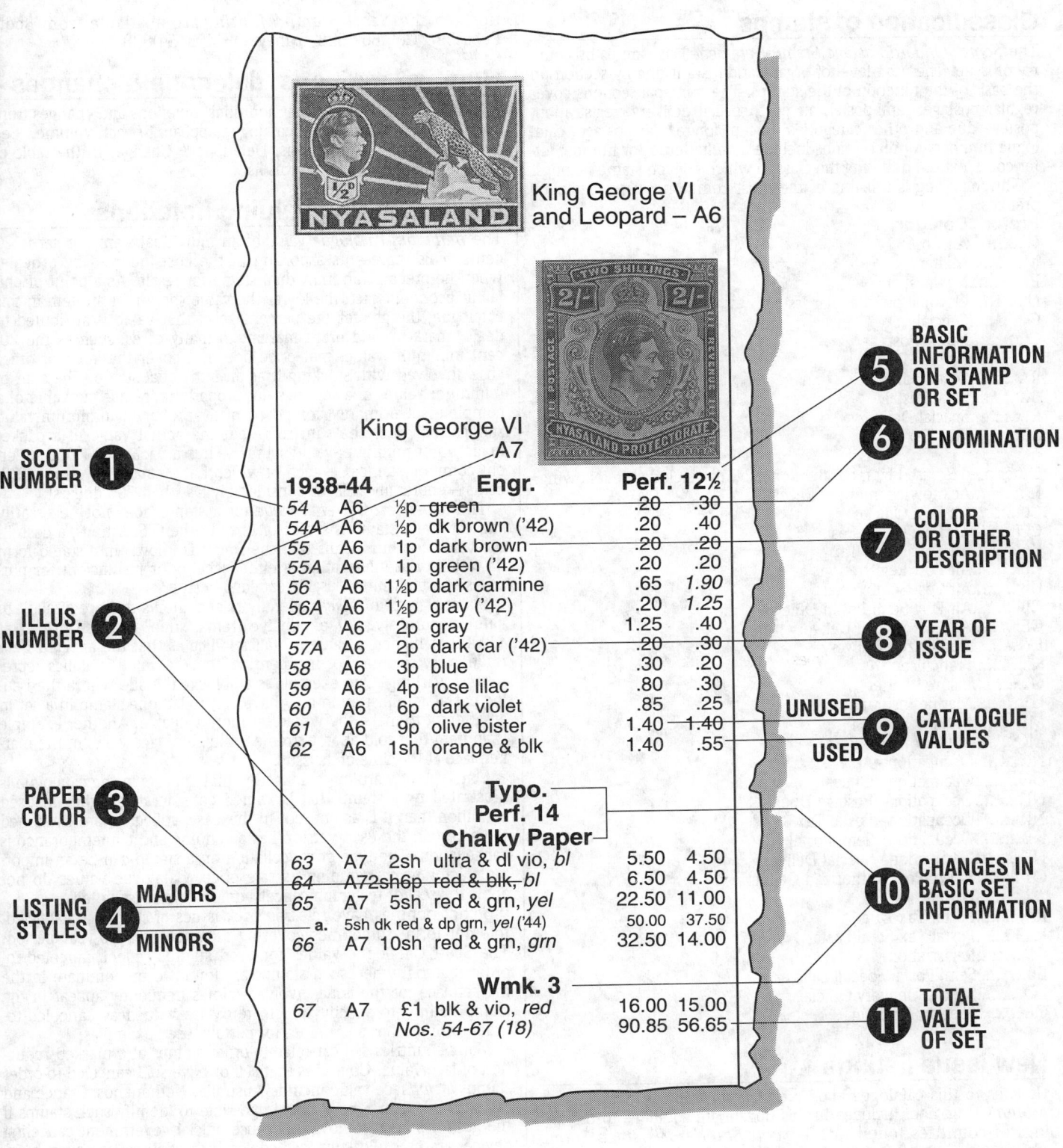

King George VI and Leopard – A6

King George VI
A7

1938-44 Engr. Perf. 12½

54	A6	½p	green	.20	.30
54A	A6	½p	dk brown ('42)	.20	.40
55	A6	1p	dark brown	.20	.20
55A	A6	1p	green ('42)	.20	.20
56	A6	1½p	dark carmine	.65	*1.90*
56A	A6	1½p	gray ('42)	.20	*1.25*
57	A6	2p	gray	1.25	.40
57A	A6	2p	dark car ('42)	.20	.30
58	A6	3p	blue	.30	.20
59	A6	4p	rose lilac	.80	.30
60	A6	6p	dark violet	.85	.25
61	A6	9p	olive bister	1.40	1.40
62	A6	1sh	orange & blk	1.40	.55

Typo.
Perf. 14
Chalky Paper

63	A7	2sh	ultra & dl vio, *bl*	5.50	4.50
64	A7	2sh6p	red & blk, *bl*	6.50	4.50
65	A7	5sh	red & grn, *yel*	22.50	11.00
a.			5sh dk red & dp grn, *yel* ('44)	50.00	37.50
66	A7	10sh	red & grn, *grn*	32.50	14.00

Wmk. 3

67	A7	£1	blk & vio, *red*	16.00	15.00
			Nos. 54-67 (18)	90.85	56.65

1 SCOTT NUMBER
2 ILLUS. NUMBER
3 PAPER COLOR
4 LISTING STYLES — MAJORS, MINORS
5 BASIC INFORMATION ON STAMP OR SET
6 DENOMINATION
7 COLOR OR OTHER DESCRIPTION
8 YEAR OF ISSUE
9 CATALOGUE VALUES — UNUSED, USED
10 CHANGES IN BASIC SET INFORMATION
11 TOTAL VALUE OF SET

Special Notices

Classification of stamps

The *Scott Standard Postage Stamp Catalogue* lists stamps by country of issue. The next level of organization is a listing by section on the basis of the function of the stamps. The principal sections cover regular postage, semi-postal, air post, special delivery, registration, postage due and other categories. Except for regular postage, catalogue numbers for all sections include a prefix letter (or number-letter combination) denoting the class to which a given stamp belongs.

The following is a listing of the most commonly used catalogue prefixes.

Prefix ...Category
C ....Air Post
M...........Military
P............Newspaper
N ....Occupation - Regular Issues
O ....Official
Q ....Parcel Post
J.............Postage Due
RA ....Postal Tax
B............Semi-Postal
E............Special Delivery
MR ....War Tax

Other prefixes used by more than one country include the following:
H ....Acknowledgment of Receipt
CO.........Air Post Official
CQ.........Air Post Parcel Post
RAC ....Air Post Postal Tax
CF..........Air Post Registration
CB ....Air Post Semi-Postal
CBO.......Air Post Semi-Postal Official
CE ....Air Post Special Delivery
EY..........Authorized Delivery
S ....Franchise
G ....Insured Letter
GY ....Marine Insurance
MC ....Military Air Post
MQ.........Military Parcel Post
NC..........Occupation - Air Post
NO..........Occupation - Official
NJ ....Occupation - Postage Due
NRA.......Occupation - Postal Tax
NB ....Occupation - Semi-Postal
NE ....Occupation - Special Delivery
QY ....Parcel Post Authorized Delivery
AR ....Postal-fiscal
RAJ ....Postal Tax Due
RAB ....Postal Tax Semi-Postal
F ....Registration
EB..........Semi-Postal Special Delivery
EO ....Special Delivery Official
QE ....Special Handling

New issue listings

Updates to this catalogue appear each month in the *Scott Stamp Monthly* magazine. Included in this update are additions to the listings of countries found in the *Scott Standard Postage Stamp Catalogue* and the *Specialized Catalogue of United States Stamps*, as well as corrections and updates to current editions of this catalogue.

From time to time there will be changes in the final listings of stamps from the *Scott Stamp Monthly* to the next edition of the catalogue. This occurs as more information about certain stamps or sets becomes available.

The catalogue update section of the *Scott Stamp Monthly* is the most timely presentation of this material available. Annual subscriptions to the *Scott Stamp Monthly* are available from Scott Publishing Co., Box 828, Sidney, OH 45365-0828.

Number additions, deletions & changes

A listing of catalogue number additions, deletions and changes from the previous edition of the catalogue appears in each volume. See Catalogue Number Additions, Deletions & Changes in the table of contents for the location of this list.

Understanding valuing notations

The *minimum catalogue value* of an individual stamp or set is 20 cents. This represents a portion of the cost incurred by a dealer when he prepares an individual stamp for resale. As a point of philatelic-economic fact, the lower the value shown for an item in this catalogue, the greater the percentage of that value is attributed to dealer mark up and profit margin. In many cases, such as the 20-cent minimum value, that price does not cover the labor or other costs involved with stocking it as an individual stamp. The sum of minimum values in a set does not properly represent the value of a complete set primarily composed of a number of minimum-value stamps, nor does the sum represent the actual value of a packet made up of minimum-value stamps. Thus a packet of 1,000 different common stamps — each of which has a catalogue value of 20-cents — normally sells for considerably less than 200 dollars!

The *absence of a retail value* for a stamp does not necessarily suggest that a stamp is scarce or rare. In the U.S. listings, a dash in the value column means that the stamp is known in a stated form or variety, but information is either lacking or insufficient for purposes of establishing a usable catalogue value.

Stamp values in *italics* generally refer to items that are difficult to value accurately. For expensive items, such as those priced at $1,000 or higher, a value in italics indicates that the affected item trades very seldom. For inexpensive items, a value in italics represents a warning. One example is a "blocked" issue where the issuing postal administration may have controlled one stamp in a set in an attempt to make the whole set more valuable. Another example is an item that sold at an extreme multiple of face value in the marketplace at the time of its issue.

One type of warning to collectors that appears in the catalogue is illustrated by a stamp that is valued considerably higher in used condition than it is as unused. In this case, collectors are cautioned to be certain the used version has a genuine and contemporaneous cancellation. The type of cancellation on a stamp can be an important factor in determining its sale price. Catalogue values do not apply to fiscal or telegraph cancels, unless otherwise noted.

Some countries have released back issues of stamps in canceled-to-order form, sometimes covering as much as a 10-year period. The Scott Catalogue values for used stamps reflect canceled-to-order material when such stamps are found to predominate in the marketplace for the issue involved. Notes frequently appear in the stamp listings to specify which items are valued as canceled-to-order, or if there is a premium for postally used examples.

Many countries sell canceled-to-order stamps at a marked reduction of face value. Countries that sell or have sold canceled-to-order stamps at *full* face value include Australia, Netherlands, France and Switzerland. It may be almost impossible to identify such stamps if the gum has been removed, because official government canceling devices are used. Postally used copies of these items on cover, however, are usually worth more than the canceled-to-order stamps with original gum.

Abbreviations

Scott Publishing Co. uses a consistent set of abbreviations throughout this catalogue to conserve space, while still providing necessary information.

COLOR ABBREVIATIONS

amb.....amber	crim.....crimson	ol.........olive
anil......aniline	cr.........cream	olvn.....olivine
ap.........apple	dk.........dark	org.......orange
aqua.....aquamarine	dl.........dull	pck.......peacock
az.........azure	dp.........deep	pnksh...pinkish
bis........bister	db.........drab	Prus.....Prussian
bl.........blue	emer....emerald	pur.......purple
bld.......blood	gldn.....golden	redsh....reddish
blk.......black	grysh....grayish	res.......reseda
bril.......brilliant	grn.......green	ros.......rosine
brn.......brown	grnsh....greenish	ryl........royal
brnsh...brownish	hel.......heliotrope	sal........salmon
brnz.....bronze	hn.........henna	saph.....sapphire
brt.......bright	ind........indigo	scar......scarlet
brnt.....burnt	int........intense	sep.......sepia
car.......carmine	lav.......lavender	sien......sienna
cer.......cerise	lem......lemon	sil.........silver
chlky....chalky	lil.........lilac	sl..........slate
cham....chamois	lt..........light	stl.........steel
chnt.....chestnut	mag.....magenta	turq.....turquoise
choc.....chocolate	man.....manila	ultra.....ultramarine
chr.......chrome	mar......maroon	Ven......Venetian
cit........citron	mv.......mauve	ver.......vermilion
cl.........claret	multi....multicolored	vio.......violet
cob......cobalt	mlky....milky	yel.......yellow
cop......copper	myr......myrtle	yelsh....yellowish

When no color is given for an overprint or surcharge, black is the color used. Abbreviations for colors used for overprints and surcharges include: "(B)" or "(Blk)," black; "(Bl)," blue; "(R)," red; and "(G)," green.

Additional abbreviations in this catalogue are shown below:

Adm. ....Administration
AFL ....American Federation of Labor
Anniv. ....Anniversary
APS ....American Philatelic Society
Assoc...............Association
ASSR. ....Autonomous Soviet Socialist Republic
b.......................Born
BEP ....Bureau of Engraving and Printing
Bicent. ....Bicentennial
Bklt...................Booklet
Brit. ....British
btwn.................Between
Bur....................Bureau
c. or ca..............Circa
Cat. ....Catalogue
Cent..................Centennial, century, centenary
CIO ....Congress of Industrial Organizations
Conf. ....Conference
Cong.................Congress
Cpl. ....Corporal
CTO ....Canceled to order
d........................Died
Dbl....................Double
EKU..................Earliest known use
Engr..................Engraved
Exhib................Exhibition
Expo.................Exposition
Fed....................Federation
GB.....................Great Britain
Gen. ....General
GPO ....General post office
Horiz................Horizontal
Imperf..............Imperforate
Impt. ....Imprint
Intl. ....International
Invtd.................Inverted
L........................Left
Lieut., lt............Lieutenant
Litho.................Lithographed
LL......................Lower left
LR ....Lower right
mm....................Millimeter
Ms.....................Manuscript
Natl. ....National
No.....................Number
NY.....................New York
NYC ....New York City
Ovpt. ....Overprint
Ovptd. ....Overprinted
P........................Plate number
Perf....................Perforated, perforation
Phil....................Philatelic
Photo.................Photogravure
PO ....Post office
Pr. ....Pair
P.R.....................Puerto Rico
Prec...................Precancel, precanceled
Pres. ....President
PTT ....Post, Telephone and Telegraph
Rio.....................Rio de Janeiro
Sgt. ....Sergeant
Soc. ....Society
Souv...................Souvenir
SSR....................Soviet Socialist Republic, see ASSR
St.......................Saint, street
Surch..................Surcharge
Typo. ....Typographed
UL ....Upper left
Unwmkd. ....Unwatermarked
UPU ....Universal Postal Union
UR.....................Upper Right
US ....United States
USPOD..............United States Post Office Department
USSR ....Union of Soviet Socialist Republics
Vert. ....Vertical
VP ....Vice president
Wmk. ....Watermark
Wmkd. ....Watermarked
WWI ....World War I
WWII ....World War II

Examination

Scott Publishing Co. will not comment upon the genuineness, grade or condition of stamps, because of the time and responsibility involved. Rather, there are several expertizing groups that undertake this work for both collectors and dealers. Neither will Scott Publishing Co. appraise or identify philatelic material. The company cannot take responsibility for unsolicited stamps or covers sent by individuals.

How to order from your dealer

When ordering stamps from a dealer, it is not necessary to write the full description of a stamp as listed in this catalogue. All you need is the name of the country, the Scott catalogue number and whether the desired item is unused or used. For example, "Japan Scott 422 unused" is sufficient to identify the unused stamp of Japan listed as "422 A206 5y brown."

Basic Stamp Information

A stamp collector's knowledge of the combined elements that make a given stamp issue unique determines his or her ability to identify stamps. These elements include paper, watermark, method of separation, printing, design and gum. On the following pages each of these important areas is briefly described.

Paper

Paper is an organic material composed of a compacted weave of cellulose fibers and generally formed into sheets. Paper used to print stamps may be manufactured in sheets, or it may have been part of a large roll (called a web) before being cut to size. The fibers most often used to create paper on which stamps are printed include bark, wood, straw and certain grasses. In many cases, linen or cotton rags have been added for greater strength and durability. Grinding, bleaching, cooking and rinsing these raw fibers reduces them to a slushy pulp, referred to by paper makers as "stuff." Sizing and, sometimes, coloring matter is added to the pulp to make different types of finished paper.

After the stuff is prepared, it is poured onto sieve-like frames that allow the water to run off, while retaining the matted pulp. As fibers fall onto the screen and are held by gravity, they form a natural weave that will later hold the paper together. If the screen has metal bits that are formed into letters or images attached, it leaves slightly thinned areas on the paper. These are called watermarks.

When the stuff is almost dry, it is passed under pressure through smooth or engraved rollers - dandy rolls - or placed between cloth in a press to be flattened and dried.

Stamp paper falls broadly into two types: wove and laid. The nature of the surface of the frame onto which the pulp is first deposited causes the differences in appearance between the two. If the surface is smooth and even, the paper will be of fairly uniform texture throughout. This is known as *wove paper.* Early papermaking machines poured the pulp onto a continuously circulating web of felt, but modern machines feed the pulp onto a cloth-like screen made of closely interwoven fine wires. This paper, when held to a light, will show little dots or points very close together. The proper name for this is "wire wove," but the type is still considered wove. Any U.S. or British stamp printed after 1880 will serve as an example of wire wove paper.

Closely spaced parallel wires, with cross wires at wider intervals, make up the frames used for what is known as *laid paper.* A greater thickness of the pulp will settle between the wires. The paper, when held to a light, will show alternate light and dark lines. The spacing and the thickness of the lines may vary, but on any one sheet of paper they are all alike. See Russia Scott 31-38 for examples of laid paper.

Batonne, from the French word meaning "a staff," is a term used if the lines in the paper are spaced quite far apart, like the printed ruling on a writing tablet. Batonne paper may be either wove or laid. If laid, fine laid lines can be seen between the batons. The laid lines, which are a form of watermark, may be geometrical figures such as squares, diamonds, rectangles or wavy lines.

Quadrille is the term used when the lines in the paper form little squares. *Oblong quadrille* is the term used when rectangles, rather than squares, are formed. See Mexico-Guadalajara Scott 35-37 for examples of oblong quadrille paper.

Paper also is classified as thick or thin, hard or soft, and by color if dye is added during manufacture. Such colors may include yellowish, greenish, bluish and reddish.

Brief explanations of other types of paper used for printing stamps, as well as examples, follow.

Pelure — Pelure paper is a very thin, hard and often brittle paper that is sometimes bluish or grayish in appearance. See Serbia Scott 169-170.

Native — This is a term applied to handmade papers used to produce some of the early stamps of the Indian states. Stamps printed on native paper may be expected to display various natural inclusions that are normal and do not negatively affect value. Japanese paper, originally made of mulberry fibers and rice flour, is part of this group. See Japan Scott 1-18.

Manila — This type of paper is often used to make stamped envelopes and wrappers. It is a coarse-textured stock, usually smooth on one side and rough on the other. A variety of colors of manila paper exist, but the most common range is yellowish-brown.

Silk — Introduced by the British in 1847 as a safeguard against counterfeiting, silk paper contains bits of colored silk thread scattered throughout. The density of these fibers varies greatly and can include as few as one fiber per stamp or hundreds. U.S. revenue Scott R152 is a good example of an easy-to-identify silk paper stamp.

Silk-thread paper has uninterrupted threads of colored silk arranged so that one or more threads run through the stamp or postal stationery. See Great Britain Scott 5-6 and Switzerland Scott 14-19.

Granite — Filled with minute cloth or colored paper fibers of various colors and lengths, granite paper should not be confused with either type of silk paper. Austria Scott 172-175 and a number of Swiss stamps are examples of granite paper.

Chalky — A chalk-like substance coats the surface of chalky paper to discourage the cleaning and reuse of canceled stamps, as well as to provide a smoother, more acceptable printing surface. Because the designs of stamps printed on chalky paper are imprinted on what is often a water-soluble coating, any attempt to remove a cancellation will destroy the stamp. *Do not soak these stamps in any fluid.* To remove a stamp printed on chalky paper from an envelope, wet the paper from underneath the stamp until the gum dissolves enough to release the stamp from the paper. See St. Kitts-Nevis Scott 89-90 for examples of stamps printed on this type of chalky paper.

India — Another name for this paper, originally introduced from China about 1750, is "China Paper." It is a thin, opaque paper often used for plate and die proofs by many countries.

Double — In philately, the term double paper has two distinct meanings. The first is a two-ply paper, usually a combination of a thick and a thin sheet, joined during manufacture. This type was used experimentally as a means to discourage the reuse of stamps.

The design is printed on the thin paper. Any attempt to remove a cancellation would destroy the design. U.S. Scott 158 and other Banknote-era stamps exist on this form of double paper.

The second type of double paper occurs on a rotary press, when the end of one paper roll, or web, is affixed to the next roll to save time feeding the paper through the press. Stamp designs are printed over the joined paper and, if overlooked by inspectors, may get into post office stocks.

Goldbeater's Skin — This type of paper was used for the 1866 issue of Prussia, and was a tough, translucent paper. The design was printed in reverse on the back of the stamp, and the gum applied over the printing. It is impossible to remove stamps printed on this type of paper from the paper to which they are affixed without destroying the design.

Ribbed — Ribbed paper has an uneven, corrugated surface made by passing the paper through ridged rollers. This type exists on some copies of U.S. Scott 156-165.

Various other substances, or substrates, have been used for stamp manufacture, including wood, aluminum, copper, silver and gold foil, plastic, and silk and cotton fabrics.

Wove Laid Granite

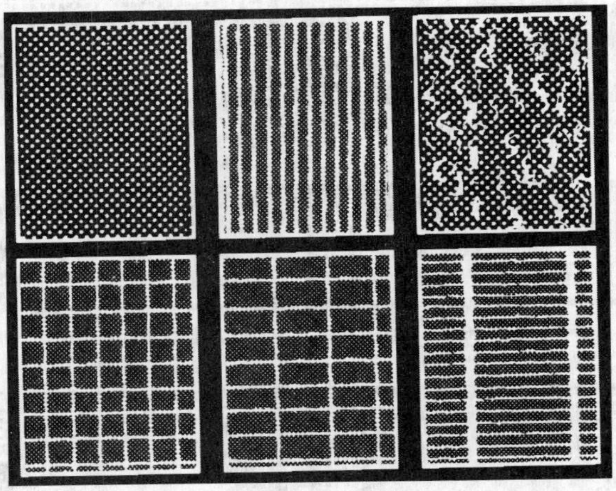

Quadrille Oblong Quadrille Batonne

Watermarks

Watermarks are an integral part of some papers. They are formed in the process of paper manufacture. Watermarks consist of small designs, formed of wire or cut from metal and soldered to the surface of the mold or, sometimes, on the dandy roll. The designs may be in the form of crowns, stars, anchors, letters or other characters or symbols. These pieces of metal - known in the paper-making industry as "bits" - impress a design into the paper. The design sometimes may be seen by holding the stamp to the light. Some are more easily seen with a watermark detector. This important tool is a small black tray into which a stamp is placed face down and dampened with a fast-evaporating watermark detection fluid that brings up the watermark image in the form of dark lines against a lighter background. These dark lines are the thinner areas of the paper known as the watermark. Some watermarks are extremely difficult to locate, due to either a faint impression, watermark location or the color of the stamp. There also are electric watermark detectors that come with plastic filter disks of various colors. The disks neutralize the color of the stamp, permitting the watermark to be seen more easily.

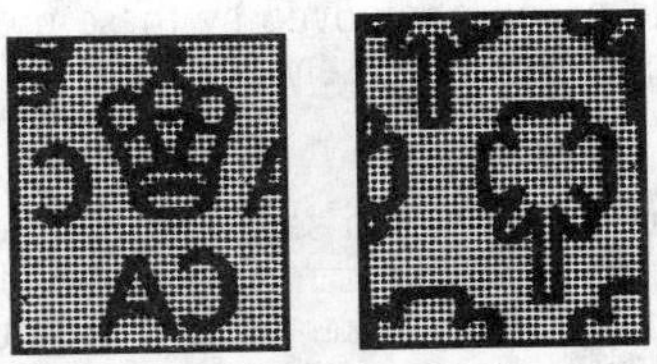

Multiple watermarks of Crown Agents and Burma

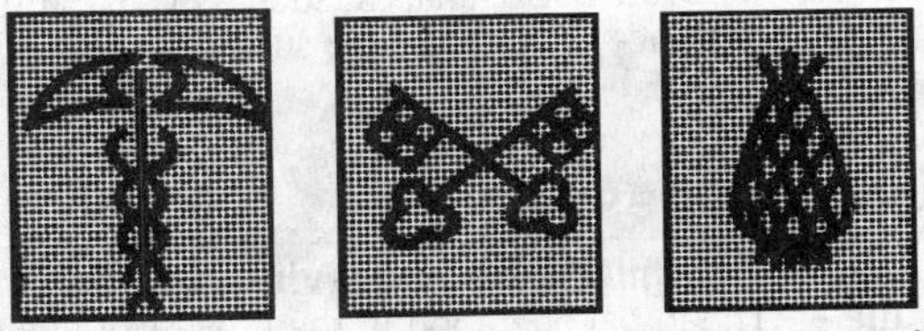

Watermarks of Uruguay, Vatican City and Jamaica

WARNING: Some inks used in the photogravure process dissolve in watermark fluids (Please see the section on Soluble Printing Inks). Also, see "chalky paper."

Watermarks may be found normal, reversed, inverted, reversed and inverted, sideways or diagonal, as seen from the back of the stamp. The relationship of watermark to stamp design depends on the position of the printing plates or how paper is fed through the press. On machine-made paper, watermarks normally are read from right to left. The design is repeated closely throughout the sheet in a "multiple-watermark design." In a "sheet watermark," the design appears only once on the sheet, but extends over many stamps. Individual stamps may carry only a small fraction or none of the watermark.

"Marginal watermarks" occur in the margins of sheets or panes of stamps. They occur on the outside border of paper (ostensibly outside the area where stamps are to be printed). A large row of letters may spell the name of the country or the manufacturer of the paper, or a border of lines may appear. Careless press feeding may cause parts of these letters and/or lines to show on stamps of the outer row of a pane.

Soluble Printing Inks

WARNING: Most stamp colors are permanent; that is, they are not seriously affected by short-term exposure to light or water. Many colors, especially of modern inks, fade from excessive exposure to light. There are stamps printed with inks that dissolve easily in water or in fluids used to detect watermarks. Use of these inks was intentional to prevent the removal of cancellations. Water affects all aniline inks, those on so-called safety paper and some photogravure printings - all such inks are known as *fugitive colors. Removal from paper of such stamps requires care and alternatives to traditional soaking.*

Separation

"Separation" is the general term used to describe methods used to separate stamps. The three standard forms currently in use are perforating, rouletting and die-cutting. These methods are done during the stamp production process, after printing. Sometimes these methods are done on-press or sometimes as a separate step. The earliest issues, such as the 1840 Penny Black of Great Britain (Scott 1), did not have any means provided for separation. It was expected the stamps would be cut apart with scissors or folded and torn. These are examples of imperforate stamps. Many stamps were first issued in imperforate formats and were later issued with perforations. Therefore, care must be observed in buying single imperforate stamps to be certain they were issued imperforate and are not perforated copies that have been altered by having the perforations trimmed away. Stamps issued imperforate usually are valued as singles. However, imperforate varieties of normally perforated stamps should be collected in pairs or larger pieces as indisputable evidence of their imperforate character.

PERFORATION

The chief style of separation of stamps, and the one that is in almost universal use today, is perforating. By this process, paper between the stamps is cut away in a line of holes, usually round, leaving little bridges of paper between the stamps to hold them together. Some types of perforation, such as hyphen-hole perfs, can be confused with roulettes, but a close visual inspection reveals that paper has been removed. The little perforation bridges, which project from the stamp when it is torn from the pane, are called the teeth of the perforation.

As the size of the perforation is sometimes the only way to differentiate between two otherwise identical stamps, it is necessary to be able to accurately measure and describe them. This is done with a perforation gauge, usually a ruler-like device that has dots or graduated lines to show how many perforations may be counted in the space of two centimeters. Two centimeters is the space universally adopted in which to measure perforations.

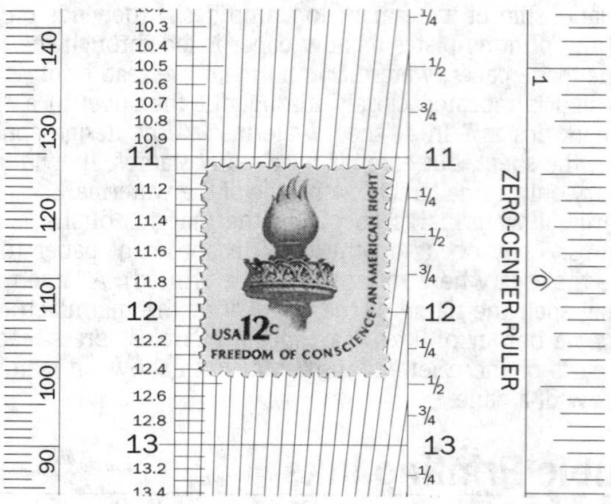

Perforation gauge

To measure a stamp, run it along the gauge until the dots on it fit exactly into the perforations of the stamp. If you are using a graduated-line perforation gauge, simply slide the stamp along the surface until the lines on the gauge perfectly project from the center of the bridges or holes. The number to the side of the line of dots or lines that fit the stamp's perforation is the measurement. For example, an "11" means that 11 perforations fit between two centimeters. The description of the stamp therefore is "perf. 11." If the gauge of the perforations on the top and bottom of a stamp differs from that on the sides, the result is what is known as *compound perforations.* In measuring compound perforations, the gauge at top and bottom is always given first, then the sides. Thus, a stamp that measures 11 at top and bottom and 10 1/2 at the sides is "perf. 11 x 10 1/2." See U.S. Scott 632-642 for examples of compound perforations.

Stamps also are known with perforations different on three or all four sides. Descriptions of such items are clockwise, beginning with the top of the stamp.

A perforation with small holes and teeth close together is a "fine perforation." One with large holes and teeth far apart is a "coarse perforation." Holes that are jagged, rather than clean-cut, are "rough perforations." *Blind perforations* are the slight impressions left by the perforating pins if they fail to puncture the paper. Multiples of stamps showing blind perforations may command a slight premium over normally perforated stamps.

The term *syncopated perfs* describes intentional irregularities in the perforations. The earliest form was used by the Netherlands from 1925-33, where holes were omitted to create distinctive patterns. Beginning in 1992, Great Britain has used an oval perforation to help prevent counterfeiting. Several other countries have started using the oval perfs.

A new type of perforation, still primarily used for postal stationery, is known as microperfs. Microperfs are tiny perforations (in some cases hundreds of holes per two centimeters) that allows items to be intentionally separated very easily, while not accidentally breaking apart as easily as standard perforations. These are not currently measured or differentiated by size, as are standard perforations.

perce en arc

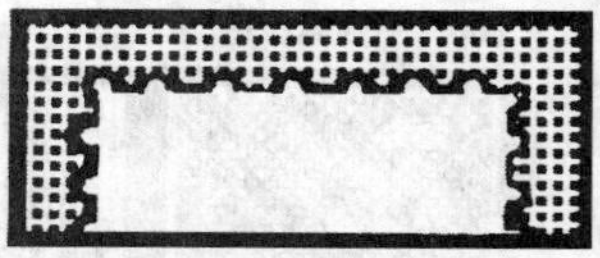

perce en lignes

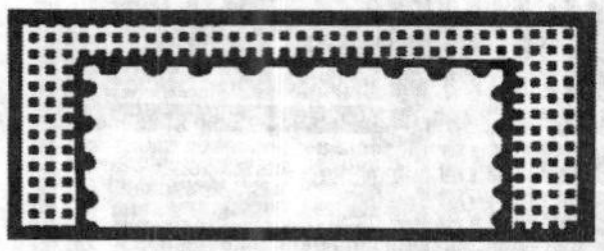

perce en points

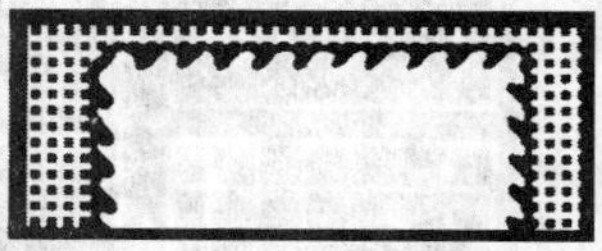

oblique roulette

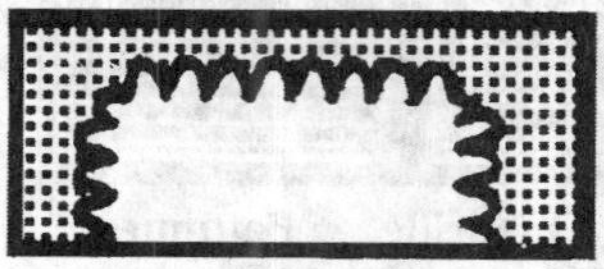

perce en scie

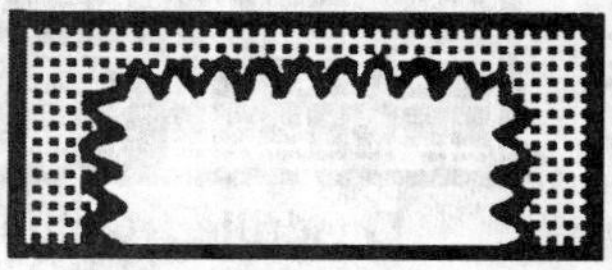

perce serpentin

ROULETTING

In rouletting, the stamp paper is cut partly or wholly through, with no paper removed. In perforating, some paper is removed. Rouletting derives its name from the French roulette, a spur-like wheel. As the wheel is rolled over the paper, each point makes a small cut. The number of cuts made in a two-centimeter space determines the gauge of the roulette, just as the number of perforations in two centimeters determines the gauge of the perforation.

The shape and arrangement of the teeth on the wheels varies. Various roulette types generally carry French names:

Perce en lignes - rouletted in lines. The paper receives short, straight cuts in lines. This is the most common type of rouletting. See Mexico Scott 500.

Perce en points - pin-rouletted. This differs from a small perforation because no paper is removed, although round, equidistant holes are pricked through the paper. See Mexico Scott 242-256.

Perce en arc and *perce en scie* - pierced in an arc or saw-toothed designs, forming half circles or small triangles. See Hanover (German States) Scott 25-29.

Perce en serpentin - serpentine roulettes. The cuts form a serpentine or wavy line. See Brunswick (German States) Scott 13-18.

Once again, no paper is removed by these processes, leaving the stamps easily separated, but closely attached.

DIE-CUTTING

The third major form of stamp separation is die-cutting. This is a method where a die in the pattern of separation is created that later cuts the stamp paper in a stroke motion. Although some standard stamps bear die-cut perforations, this process is primarily used for self-adhesive postage stamps. Die-cutting can appear in straight lines, such as U.S. Scott 2522, shapes, such as U.S. Scott 1551, or imitating the appearance of perforations, such as New Zealand Scott 935A and 935B.

Printing Processes

ENGRAVING (Intaglio, Line-engraving, Etching)

Master die — The initial operation in the process of line engraving is making the master die. The die is a small, flat block of softened steel upon which the stamp design is recess engraved in reverse.

Master die

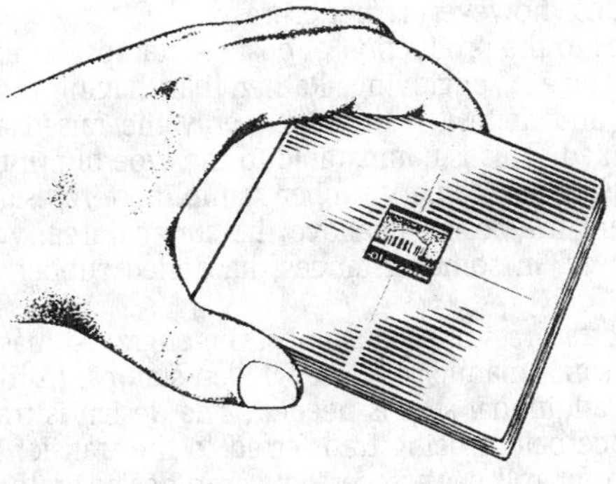

Photographic reduction of the original art is made to the appropriate size. It then serves as a tracing guide for the initial outline of the design. The engraver lightly traces the design on the steel with his graver, then slowly works the design until it is completed. At various points during the engraving process, the engraver hand-inks the die and makes an impression to check his progress. These are known as progressive die proofs. After completion of the engraving, the die is hardened to withstand the stress and pressures of later transfer operations.

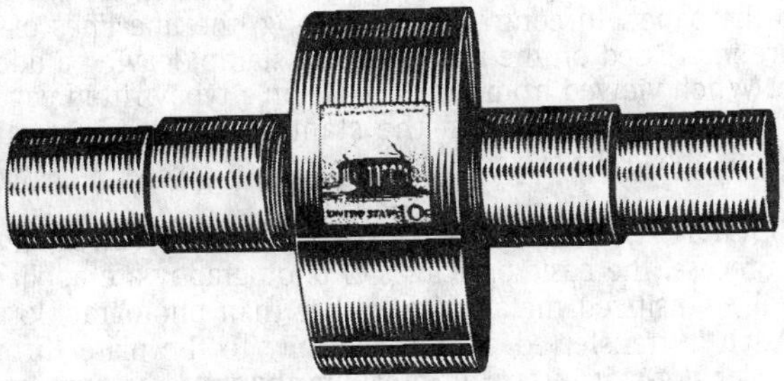

Transfer roll

Transfer roll — Next is production of the transfer roll that, as the name implies, is the medium used to transfer the subject from the master die to the printing plate. A blank roll of soft steel, mounted on a mandrel, is placed under the bearers of the transfer press to allow it to roll freely on its axis. The hardened die is placed on the bed of the press and the face of the transfer roll is applied to the die, under pressure. The bed or the roll is then rocked back and forth under increasing pressure, until the soft steel of the roll is forced into every engraved line of the die. The resulting impression on the roll is known as a "relief" or a "relief transfer." The engraved image is now positive in appearance and stands out from the steel. After the required number of reliefs are "rocked in," the soft steel transfer roll is hardened.

Different flaws may occur during the relief process. A defective relief may occur during the rocking in process because of a minute piece of foreign material lodging on the die, or some other cause. Imperfections in the steel of the transfer roll may result in a breaking away of parts of the design. This is known as a relief break, which will show up on finished stamps as small, unprinted areas. If a damaged relief remains in use, it will transfer a repeating defect to the plate. Deliberate alterations of reliefs sometimes occur. "Altered reliefs" designate these changed conditions.

Plate — The final step in pre-printing production is the making of the printing plate. A flat piece of soft steel replaces the die on the bed of the transfer press. One of the reliefs on the transfer roll is positioned over this soft steel. Position, or layout, dots determine the correct position on the plate. The dots have been lightly marked on the plate in advance. After the correct position of the relief is determined, the design is rocked in by following the same method used in making the transfer roll. The difference is that this time the image is being transferred from the transfer roll, rather than to it. Once the design is entered on the plate, it appears in reverse and is recessed. There are as many transfers entered on the plate as there are subjects printed on the sheet of stamps. It is during this process that double and shifted transfers occur, as well as re-entries. These are the result of improperly entered images that have not been properly burnished out prior to rocking in a new image.

Modern siderography processes, such as those used by the U.S. Bureau of Engraving and Printing, involve an automated form of rocking designs in on preformed cylindrical printing sleeves. The same process also allows for easier removal and re-entry of worn images right on the sleeve.

Transferring the design to the plate

Following the entering of the required transfers on the plate, the position dots, layout dots and lines, scratches and other markings generally are burnished out. Added at this time by the siderographer are any required *guide lines, plate numbers* or other *marginal markings.* The plate is then hand-inked and a proof impression is taken. This is known as a plate proof. If the impression is approved, the plate is machined for fitting onto the press, is hardened and sent to the plate vault ready for use.

On press, the plate is inked and the surface is automatically wiped clean, leaving ink only in the recessed lines. Paper is then forced under pressure into the engraved recessed lines, thereby receiving the ink. Thus, the ink lines on engraved stamps are slightly raised, and slight depressions (debossing) occur on the back of the stamp. Prior to the advent of modern high-speed presses and more advanced ink formulations, paper had to be dampened before receiving the ink. This sometimes led to uneven shrinkage by the time the stamps were perforated, resulting in improperly perforated stamps, or misperfs. Newer presses use drier paper, thus both *wet* and *dry printings* exist on some stamps.

Rotary Press — Until 1914, only flat plates were used to print engraved stamps. Rotary press printing was introduced in 1914, and slowly spread. Some countries still use flat-plate printing.

After approval of the plate proof, older *rotary press plates* require additional machining. They are curved to fit the press cylinder. "Gripper slots" are cut into the back of each plate to receive the "grippers," which hold the plate securely on the press. The plate is then hardened. Stamps printed from these bent rotary press plates are longer or wider than the same stamps printed from flat-plate presses. The stretching of the plate during the curving process is what causes this distortion.

Re-entry — To execute a re-entry on a flat plate, the transfer roll is re-applied to the plate, often at some time after its first use on the press. Worn-out designs can be resharpened by carefully burnishing out the original image and re-entering it from the transfer roll. If the original impression has not been sufficiently removed and the transfer roll is not precisely in line with the remaining impression, the resulting double transfer will make the re-entry obvious. If the registration is true, a re-entry may be difficult or impossible to distinguish. Sometimes a stamp printed from a successful re-entry is identified by having a much sharper and clearer impression than its neighbors. With the advent of rotary presses, post-press re-entries were not possible. After a plate was curved for the rotary press, it was impossible to make a re-entry. This is because the plate had already been bent once (with the design distorted).

However, with the introduction of the previously mentioned modern-style siderography machines, entries are made to the preformed cylindrical printing sleeve. Such sleeves are dechromed and softened. This allows individual images to be burnished out and re-entered on the curved sleeve. The sleeve is then rechromed, resulting in longer press life.

Double Transfer — This is a description of the condition of a transfer on a plate that shows evidence of a duplication of all, or a portion of the design. It usually is the result of the changing of the registration between the transfer roll and the plate during the rocking in of the original entry. Double transfers also occur when only a portion of the design has been rocked in and improper positioning is noted. If the worker elected not to burnish out the partial or completed design, a strong double transfer will occur for part or all of the design.

It sometimes is necessary to remove the original transfer from a plate and repeat the process a second time. If the finished reworked image shows traces of the original impression, attributable to incomplete burnishing, the result is a partial double transfer.

With the modern automatic machines mentioned previously, double transfers are all but impossible to create. Those partially doubled images on stamps printed from such sleeves are more than likely re-entries, rather than true double transfers.

Re-engraved — Alterations to a stamp design are sometimes necessary after some stamps have been printed. In some cases, either the original die or the actual printing plate may have its "temper" drawn (softened), and the design will be re-cut. The resulting impressions from such a re-engraved die or plate may differ slightly from the original issue, and are known as "re-engraved." If the alteration was made to the master die, all future printings will be consistently different from the original. If alterations were made to the printing plate, each altered stamp on the plate will be slightly different from each other, allowing specialists to reconstruct a complete printing plate.

Dropped Transfers — If an impression from the transfer roll has not been properly placed, a dropped transfer may occur. The final stamp image will appear obviously out of line with its neighbors.

Short Transfer — Sometimes a transfer roll is not rocked its entire length when entering a transfer onto a plate. As a result, the finished transfer on the plate fails to show the complete design, and the finished stamp will have an incomplete design printed. This is known as a "short transfer." U.S. Scott No. 8 is a good example of a short transfer.

TYPOGRAPHY (Letterpress, Surface Printing, Flexography, Dry Offset, High Etch)

Although the word "Typography" is obsolete as a term describing a printing method, it was the accepted term throughout the first century of postage stamps. Therefore, appropriate Scott listings in this catalogue refer to typographed stamps. The current term for this form of printing, however, is "letterpress."

As it relates to the production of postage stamps, letterpress printing is the reverse of engraving. Rather than having recessed areas trap the ink and deposit it on paper, only the raised areas of the design are inked. This is comparable to the type of printing seen by inking and using an ordinary rubber stamp. Letterpress includes all printing where the design is above the surface area, whether it is wood, metal or, in some instances, hardened rubber or polymer plastic.

For most letterpress-printed stamps, the engraved master is made in much the same manner as for engraved stamps. In this instance, however, an additional step is needed. The design is transferred to another surface before being transferred to the transfer roll. In this way, the transfer roll has a recessed stamp design, rather than one done in relief. This makes the printing areas on the final plate raised, or relief areas.

For less-detailed stamps of the 19th century, the area on the die not used as a printing surface was cut away, leaving the surface area raised. The original die was then reproduced by stereotyping or electrotyping. The resulting electrotypes were assembled in the required number and format of the desired sheet of stamps. The plate used in printing the stamps was an electroplate of these assembled electrotypes.

Once the final letterpress plates are created, ink is applied to the raised surface and the pressure of the press transfers the ink impression to the paper. In contrast to engraving, the fine lines of letterpress are impressed on the surface of the stamp, leaving a debossed surface. When viewed from the back (as on a typewritten page), the corresponding line work on the stamp will be raised slightly (embossed) above the surface.

PHOTOGRAVURE (Gravure, Rotogravure, Heliogravure)

In this process, the basic principles of photography are applied to a chemically sensitized metal plate, rather than photographic paper. The design is transferred photographically to the plate through a halftone, or dot-matrix screen, breaking the reproduction into tiny dots. The plate is treated chemically and the dots form depressions, called cells, of varying depths and diameters, depending on the degrees of shade in the design. Then, like engraving, ink is applied to the plate and the surface is wiped clean. This leaves ink in the tiny cells that is lifted out and deposited on the paper when it is pressed against the plate.

Gravure is most often used for multicolored stamps, generally using the three primary colors (red, yellow and blue) and black. By varying the dot matrix pattern and density of these colors, virtually any color can be reproduced. A typical full-color gravure stamp will be created from four printing cylinders (one for each color). The original multicolored image will have been photographically separated into its component colors.

Modern gravure printing may use computer-generated dot-matrix screens, and modern plates may be of various types including metal-coated plastic. The catalogue designation of Photogravure (or "Photo") covers any of these older and more modern gravure methods of printing.

For examples of the first photogravure stamps printed (1914), see Bavaria Scott 94-114.

LITHOGRAPHY (Offset Lithography, Stone Lithography, Dilitho, Planography, Collotype)

The principle that oil and water do not mix is the basis for lithography. The stamp design is drawn by hand or transferred from engraving to the surface of a lithographic stone or metal plate in a greasy (oily) substance. This oily substance holds the ink, which will later be transferred to the paper. The stone (or plate) is wet with an acid fluid, causing it to repel the printing ink in all areas not covered by the greasy substance.

Transfer paper is used to transfer the design from the original stone or plate. A series of duplicate transfers are grouped and, in turn, transferred to the final printing plate.

Photolithography — The application of photographic processes to lithography. This process allows greater flexibility of design, related to use of halftone screens combined with line work. Unlike photogravure or engraving, this process can allow large, solid areas to be printed.

Offset — A refinement of the lithographic process. A rubber-covered blanket cylinder takes the impression from the inked lithographic plate. From the "blanket" the impression is *offset* or transferred to the paper. Greater flexibility and speed are the principal reasons offset printing has largely displaced lithography. The term "lithography" covers both processes, and results are almost identical.

EMBOSSED (Relief) Printing

Embossing, not considered one of the four main printing types, is a method in which the design first is sunk into the metal of the die. Printing is done against a yielding platen, such as leather or linoleum. The platen is forced into the depression of the die, thus forming the design on the paper in relief. This process is often used for metallic inks.

Embossing may be done without color (see Sardinia Scott 4-6); with color printed around the embossed area (see Great Britain Scott 5 and most U.S. envelopes); and with color in exact registration with the embossed subject (see Canada Scott 656-657).

HOLOGRAMS

For objects to appear as holograms on stamps, a model exactly the same size as it is to appear on the hologram must be created. Rather than using photographic film to capture the image, holography records an image on a photoresist material. In processing, chemicals eat away at certain exposed areas, leaving a pattern of constructive and destructive interference. When the phororesist is developed, the result is a pattern of uneven ridges that acts as a mold. This mold is then coated with metal, and the resulting form is used to press copies in much the same way phonograph records are produced.

A typical reflective hologram used for stamps consists of a reproduction of the uneven patterns on a plastic film that is applied to a reflective background, usually a silver of gold foil. Light is reflected off the background through the film, making the pattern present on the film visible. Because of the uneven pattern of the film, the viewer will perceive the objects in their proper three-dimensional relationships with appropriate brightness.

The first hologram on a stamp was produced by Austria in 1988 (Scott 1441).

FOIL APPLICATION

A modern tecnique of applying color to stamps involves the application of metallic foil to the stamp paper. A pattern of foil is applied to the stamp paper by use of a stamping die. The foil usually is flat, but it may be textured. Canada Scott 1735 has three different foil applications in pearl, bronze and gold. The gold foil was textured using a chemical-etch copper embossing die. The printing of this stamp also involved two-color offset lithography plus embossing.

COMBINATION PRINTINGS

Sometimes two or even three printing methods are combined in producing stamps. In these cases, such as Austria Scott 933 or Canada 1735 (described in the preceding paragraph), the multiple-printing technique can be determined by studing the individual characteristics of each printing type. A few stamps, such as Singapore Scott 684-684A, combine as many as three of the four major printing types (lithography, engraving and typography). When this is done it often indicates the incorporation of security devices against counterfeiting.

INK COLORS

Inks or colored papers used in stamp printing often are of mineral origin, although there are numerous examples of organic-based pigments. As a general rule, organic-based pigments are far more subject to varieties and change than those of mineral-based origin.

The appearance of any given color on a stamp may be affected by many aspects, including printing variations, light, color of paper, aging and chemical alterations.

Numerous printing variations may be observed. Heavier pressure or inking will cause a more intense color, while slight interruptions in the ink feed or lighter impressions will cause a lighter appearance. Stamps printed in the same color by water-based and solvent-based inks can differ significantly in appearance. This affects several stamps in the U.S. Prominent Americans series. Hand-mixed ink formulas (primarily from the 19th century) produced under different conditions (humidity and temperature) account for notable color variations in early printings of the same stamp (see U.S. Scott 248-250, 279B, for example). Different sources of pigment can also result in significant differences in color.

Light exposure and aging are closely related in the way they affect stamp color. Both eventually break down the ink and fade colors, so that a carefully kept stamp may differ significantly in color from an identical copy that has been exposed to light. If stamps are exposed to light either intentionally or accidentally, their colors can be faded or completely changed in some cases.

Papers of different quality and consistency used for the same stamp printing may affect color appearance. Most pelure papers, for example, show a richer color when compared with wove or laid papers. See Russia Scott 181a, for an example of this effect.

The very nature of the printing processes can cause a variety of differences in shades or hues of the same stamp. Some of these shades are scarcer than others, and are of particular interest to the advanced collector.

Luminescence

All forms of tagged stamps fall under the general category of luminescence. Within this broad category is fluorescence, dealing with forms of tagging visible under longwave ultraviolet light, and phosphorescence, which deals with tagging visible only under shortwave light. Phosphorescence leaves an afterglow and fluorescence does not. These treated stamps show up in a range of different colors when exposed to UV light. The differing wavelengths of the light activates the tagging material, making it glow in various colors that usually serve different mail processing purposes.

Intentional tagging is a post-World War II phenomenon, brought about by the increased literacy rate and rapidly growing mail volume. It was one of several answers to the problem of the need for more automated mail processes. Early tagged stamps served the purpose of triggering machines to separate different types of mail. A natural outgrowth was to also use the signal to trigger machines that faced all envelopes the same way and canceled them.

Tagged stamps come in many different forms. Some tagged stamps have luminescent shapes or images imprinted on them as a form of security device. Others have blocks (United States), stripes, frames (South Africa and Canada), overall coatings (United States), bars (Great Britain and Canada) and many other types. Some types of tagging are even mixed in with the pigmented printing ink (Australia Scott 366, Netherlands Scott 478 and U.S. Scott 1359 and 2443).

The means of applying taggant to stamps differs as much as the intended purposes for the stamps. The most common form of tagging is a coating applied to the surface of the printed stamp. Since the taggant ink is frequently invisible except under UV light, it does not interfere with the appearance of the stamp. Another common application is the use of phosphored papers. In this case the paper itself either has a coating of taggant applied before the stamp is printed, has taggant applied during the papermaking process (incorporating it into the fibers), or has the taggant mixed into the coating of the paper. The latter method, among others, is currently in use in the United States.

Many countries now use tagging in various forms to either expedite mail handling or to serve as a printing security device against counterfeiting. Following the introduction of tagged stamps for public use in 1959 by Great Britain, other countries have steadily joined the parade. Among those are Germany (1961); Canada and Denmark (1962); United States, Australia, France and Switzerland (1963); Belgium and Japan (1966); Sweden and Norway (1967); Italy (1968); and Russia (1969). Since then, many other countries have begun using forms of tagging, including Brazil, China, Czechoslovakia, Hong Kong, Guatemala, Indonesia, Israel, Lithuania, Luxembourg, Netherlands, Penrhyn Islands, Portugal, St. Vincent, Singapore, South Africa, Spain and Sweden to name a few.

In some cases, including United States, Canada, Great Britain and Switzerland, stamps were released both with and without tagging. Many of these were released during each country's experimental period. Tagged and untagged versions are listed for the aforementioned countries and are noted in some other countries' listings. For at least a few stamps, the experimentally tagged version is worth far more than its untagged counterpart, such as the 1963 experimental tagged version of France Scott 1024.

In some cases, luminescent varieties of stamps were inadvertently created. Several Russian stamps, for example, sport highly fluorescent ink that was not intended as a form of tagging. Older stamps, such as early U.S. postage dues, can be positively identified by the use of UV light, since the organic ink used has become slightly fluorescent over time. Other stamps, such as Austria Scott 70a-82a (varnish bars) and Obock Scott 46-64 (printed quadrille lines), have become fluorescent over time.

Various fluorescent substances have been added to paper to make it appear brighter. These optical brighteners, as they are known, greatly affect the appearance of the stamp under UV light. The brightest of these is known as Hi-Brite paper. These paper varieties are beyond the scope of the Scott Catalogue.

Shortwave UV light also is used extensively in expertizing, since each form of paper has its own fluorescent characteristics that are impossible to perfectly match. It is therefore a simple matter to detect filled thins, added perforation teeth and other alterations that involve the addition of paper. UV light also is used to examine stamps that have had cancels chemically removed and for other purposes as well.

Gum

The Illustrated Gum Chart in the first part of this introduction shows and defines various types of gum condition. Because gum condition has an important impact on the value of unused stamps, we recommend studying this chart and the accompanying text carefully.

The gum on the back of a stamp may be shiny, dull, smooth, rough, dark, white, colored or tinted. Most stamp gumming adhesives use gum arabic or dextrine as a base. Certain polymers such as polyvinyl alcohol (PVA) have been used extensively since World War II.

The *Scott Standard Postage Stamp Catalogue* does not list items by types of gum. The *Scott Specialized Catalogue of United States Stamps* does differentiate among some types of gum for certain issues.

Reprints of stamps may have gum differing from the original issues. In addition, some countries have used different gum formulas for different seasons. These adhesives have different properties that may become more apparent over time.

Many stamps have been issued without gum, and the catalogue will note this fact. See, for example, United States Scott 40-47. Sometimes, gum may have been removed to preserve the stamp. Germany Scott B68, for example, has a highly acidic gum that eventually destroys the stamps. This item is valued in the catalogue with gum removed.

Reprints and Reissues

These are impressions of stamps (usually obsolete) made from the original plates or stones. If they are valid for postage and reproduce obsolete issues (such as U.S. Scott 102-111), the stamps are *reissues.* If they are from current issues, they are designated as *second, third,* etc., *printing.* If designated for a particular purpose, they are called *special printings.*

When special printings are not valid for postage, but are made from original dies and plates by authorized persons, they are *official reprints. Private reprints* are made from the original plates and dies by private hands. An example of a private reprint is that of the 1871-1932 reprints made from the original die of the 1845 New Haven, Conn., postmaster's provisional. *Official reproductions* or imitations are made from new dies and plates by government authorization. Scott will list those reissues that are valid for postage if they differ significantly from the original printing.

The U.S. government made special printings of its first postage stamps in 1875. Produced were official imitations of the first two stamps (listed as Scott 3-4), reprints of the demonetized pre-1861 issues (Scott 40-47) and reissues of the 1861 stamps, the 1869 stamps and the then-current 1875 denominations. Even though the official imitations and the reprints were not valid for postage, Scott lists all of these U.S. special printings.

Most reprints or reissues differ slightly from the original stamp in some characteristic, such as gum, paper, perforation, color or watermark. Sometimes the details are followed so meticulously that only a student of that specific stamp is able to distinguish the reprint or reissue from the original.

Remainders and Canceled to Order

Some countries sell their stock of old stamps when a new issue replaces them. To avoid postal use, the *remainders* usually are canceled with a punch hole, a heavy line or bar, or a more-or-less regular-looking cancellation. The most famous merchant of remainders was Nicholas F. Seebeck. In the 1880s and 1890s, he arranged printing contracts between the Hamilton Bank Note Co., of which he was a director, and several Central and South American countries. The contracts provided that the plates and all remainders of the yearly issues became the property of Hamilton. Seebeck saw to it that ample stock remained. The "Seebecks," both remainders and reprints, were standard packet fillers for decades.

Some countries also issue stamps *canceled-to-order (CTO),* either in sheets with original gum or stuck onto pieces of paper or envelopes and canceled. Such CTO items generally are worth less than postally used stamps. In cases where the CTO material is far more prevalent in the marketplace than postally used examples, the catalogue value relates to the CTO examples, with postally used examples noted as premium items. Most CTOs can be detected by the presence of gum. However, as the CTO practice goes back at least to 1885, the gum inevitably has been soaked off some stamps so they could pass as postally used. The normally applied postmarks usually differ slightly from standard postmarks, and specialists are able to tell the difference. When applied individually to envelopes by philatelically minded persons, CTO material is known as *favor canceled* and generally sells at large discounts.

Cinderellas and Facsimiles

Cinderella is a catch-all term used by stamp collectors to describe phantoms, fantasies, bogus items, municipal issues, exhibition seals, local revenues, transportation stamps, labels, poster stamps and many other types of items. Some cinderella collectors include in their collections local postage issues, telegraph stamps, essays and proofs, forgeries and counterfeits.

A *fantasy* is an adhesive created for a nonexistent stamp-issuing authority. Fantasy items range from imaginary countries (Occusi-Ambeno, Kingdom of Sedang, Principality of Trinidad or Torres Straits), to non-existent locals (Winans City Post), or nonexistent transportation lines (McRobish & Co.'s Acapulco-San Francisco Line).

On the other hand, if the entity exists and could have issued stamps (but did not) or was known to have issued other stamps, the items are considered *bogus* stamps. These would include the Mormon postage stamps of Utah, S. Allan Taylor's Guatemala and Paraguay inventions, the propaganda issues for the South Moluccas and the adhesives of the Page & Keyes local post of Boston.

Phantoms is another term for both fantasy and bogus issues.

Facsimiles are copies or imitations made to represent original stamps, but which do not pretend to be originals. A catalogue illustration is such a facsimile. Illustrations from the Moens catalogue of the last century were occasionally colored and passed off as stamps. Since the beginning of stamp collecting, facsimiles have been made for collectors as space fillers or for reference. They often carry the word "facsimile," "falsch" (German), "sanko" or "mozo" (Japanese), or "faux" (French) overprinted on the face or stamped on the back. Unfortunately, over the years a number of these items have had fake cancels applied over the facsimile notation and have been passed off as genuine.

Forgeries and Counterfeits

Forgeries and counterfeits have been with philately virtually from the beginning of stamp production. Over time, the terminology for the two has been used interchangeably. Although both forgeries and counterfeits are reproductions of stamps, the purposes behind their creation differ considerably.

Among specialists there is an increasing movement to more specifically define such items. Although there is no universally accepted terminology, we feel the following definitions most closely mirror the items and their purposes as they are currently defined.

Forgeries (also often referred to as *Counterfeits*) are reproductions of genuine stamps that have been created to defraud collectors. Such spurious items first appeared on the market around 1860, and most old-time collections contain one or more. Many are crude and easily spotted, but some can deceive experts.

An important supplier of these early philatelic forgeries was the Hamburg printer Gebruder Spiro. Many others with reputations in this craft included S. Allan Taylor, George Hussey, James Chute, George Forune, Benjamin & Sarpy, Julius Goldner, E. Oneglia and L.H. Mercier. Among the noted 20th-century forgers were Francois Fournier, Jean Sperati and the prolific Raoul DeThuin.

Forgeries may be complete replications, or they may be genuine stamps altered to resemble a scarcer (and more valuable) type. Most forgeries, particularly those of rare stamps, are worth only a small fraction of the value of a genuine example, but a few types, created by some of the most notable forgers, such as Sperati, can be worth as much or more than the genuine. Fraudulently produced copies are known of most classic rarities and many medium-priced stamps.

In addition to rare stamps, large numbers of common 19th- and early 20th-century stamps were forged to supply stamps to the early packet trade. Many can still be easily found. Few new philatelic forgeries have appeared in recent decades. Successful imitation of well-engraved work is virtually impossible. It has proven far easier to produce a fake by altering a genuine stamp than to duplicate a stamp completely.

Counterfeit (also often referred to as *Postal Counterfeit* or *Postal Forgery*) is the term generally applied to reproductions of stamps that have been created to defraud the government of revenue. Such items usually are created at the time a stamp is current and, in some cases, are hard to detect. Because most counterfeits are seized when the perpetrator is captured, postal counterfeits, particularly used on cover, are usually worth much more than a genuine example to specialists. The first postal counterfeit was of Spain's 4-cuarto carmine of 1854 (the real one is Scott 25). Apparently, the counterfeiters were not satisfied with their first version, which is now very scarce, and they soon created an engraved counterfeit, which is common. Postal counterfeits quickly followed in Austria, Naples, Sardinia and the Roman States. They have since been created in many other countries as well, including the United States.

An infamous counterfeit to defraud the government is the 1-shilling Great Britain "Stock Exchange" forgery of 1872, used on telegraph forms at the exchange that year. The stamp escaped detection until a stamp dealer noticed it in 1898.

Fakes

Fakes are genuine stamps altered in some way to make them more desirable. One student of this part of stamp collecting has estimated that by the 1950s more than 30,000 varieties of fakes were known. That number has grown greatly since then. The widespread existence of fakes makes it important for stamp collectors to study their philatelic holdings and use relevant literature. Likewise, collectors should buy from reputable dealers who guarantee their stamps and make full and prompt refunds should a purchased item be declared faked or altered by some mutually agreed-upon authority. Because fakes always have some genuine characteristics, it is not always possible to obtain unanimous agreement among experts regarding specific items. These students may change their opinions as philatelic knowledge increases. More than 80 percent of all fakes on the philatelic market today are regummed, reperforated (or perforated for the first time), or bear forged overprints, surcharges or cancellations.

Stamps can be chemically treated to alter or eliminate colors. For example, a pale rose stamp can be re-colored to resemble a blue shade of high market value. In other cases, treated stamps can be made to resemble missing color varieties. Designs may be changed by painting, or a stroke or a dot added or bleached out to turn an ordinary variety into a seemingly scarcer stamp. Part of a stamp can be bleached and reprinted in a different version, achieving an inverted center or frame. Margins can be added or repairs done so deceptively that the stamps move from the "repaired" into the "fake" category.

Fakers have not left the backs of the stamps untouched either. They may create false watermarks, add fake grills or press out genuine grills. A thin India paper proof may be glued onto a thicker backing to create the appearance an issued stamp, or a proof printed on cardboard may be shaved down and perforated to resemble a stamp. Silk threads are impressed into paper and stamps have been split so that a rare paper variety is added to an otherwise inexpensive stamp. The most common treatment to the back of a stamp, however, is regumming.

Some in the business of faking stamps have openly advertised fool-proof application of "original gum" to stamps that lack it, although most publications now ban such ads from their pages. It is believed that very few early stamps have survived without being hinged. The large number of never-hinged examples of such earlier material offered for sale thus suggests the widespread extent of regumming activity. Regumming also may be used to hide repairs or thin spots. Dipping the stamp into watermark fluid, or examining it under longwave ultraviolet light often will reveal these flaws.

Fakers also tamper with separations. Ingenious ways to add margins are known. Perforated wide-margin stamps may be falsely represented as imperforate when trimmed. Reperforating is commonly done to create scarce coil or perforation varieties, and to eliminate the naturally occurring straight-edge stamps found in sheet margin positions of many earlier issues. Custom has made straight-edged stamps less desirable. Fakers have obliged by perforating straight-edged stamps so that many are now uncommon, if not rare.

Another fertile field for the faker is that of overprints, surcharges and cancellations. The forging of rare surcharges or overprints began in the 1880s or 1890s. These forgeries are sometimes difficult to detect, but experts have identified almost all. Occasionally, overprints or cancellations are removed to create non-overprinted stamps or seemingly unused items. This is most commonly done by removing a manuscript cancel to make a stamp resemble an unused example. "SPECIMEN" overprints may be removed by scraping and repainting to create non-overprinted varieties. Fakers use inexpensive revenues or pen-canceled stamps to generate unused stamps for further faking by adding other markings. The quartz lamp or UV lamp and a high-powered magnifying glass help to easily detect removed cancellations.

The bigger problem, however, is the addition of overprints, surcharges or cancellations - many with such precision that they are very difficult to ascertain. Plating of the stamps or the overprint can be an important method of detection.

Fake postmarks may range from many spurious fancy cancellations to a host of markings applied to transatlantic covers, to adding normally appearing postmarks to definitives of some countries with stamps that are valued far higher used than unused. With the increased popularity of cover collecting, and the widespread interest in postal history, a fertile new field for fakers has come about. Some have tried to create entire covers. Others specialize in adding stamps, tied by fake cancellations, to genuine stampless covers, or replacing less expensive or damaged stamps with more valuable ones. Detailed study of postal rates in effect at the time a cover in question was mailed, including the analysis of each handstamp used during the period, ink analysis and similar techniques, usually will unmask the fraud.

Restoration and Repairs

Scott Publishing Co. bases its catalogue values on stamps that are free of defects and otherwise meet the standards set forth earlier in this introduction. Most stamp collectors desire to have the finest copy of an item possible. Even within given grading categories there are variances. This leads to a controversial practice that is not defined in any universal manner: stamp *restoration.*

There are broad differences of opinion about what is permissible when it comes to restoration. Carefully applying a soft eraser to a stamp or cover to remove light soiling is one form of restoration, as is washing a stamp in mild soap and water to clean it. These are fairly accepted forms of restoration. More severe forms of restoration include pressing out creases or removing stains caused by tape. To what degree each of these is acceptable is dependent upon the individual situation. Further along the spectrum is the freshening of a stamp's color by removing oxide build-up or the effects of wax paper left next to stamps shipped to the tropics.

At some point in this spectrum the concept of *repair* replaces that of restoration. Repairs include filling thin spots, mending tears by reweaving or adding a missing perforation tooth. Regumming stamps may have been acceptable as a restoration or repair technique many decades ago, but today it is considered a form of fakery.

Restored stamps may or may not sell at a discount, and it is possible that the value of individual restored items may be enhanced over that of their pre-restoration state. Specific situations dictate the resultant value of such an item. Repaired stamps sell at substantial discounts from the value of sound stamps.

Terminology

Booklets — Many countries have issued stamps in small booklets for the convenience of users. This idea continues to become increasingly popular in many countries. Booklets have been issued in many sizes and forms, often with advertising on the covers, the panes of stamps or on the interleaving.

The panes used in booklets may be printed from special plates or made from regular sheets. All panes from booklets issued by the United States and many from those of other countries contain stamps that are straight edged on the sides, but perforated between. Others are distinguished by orientation of watermark or other identifying features. Any stamp-like unit in the pane, either printed or blank, that is not a postage stamp, is considered to be a *label* in the catalogue listings.

Scott lists and values booklet panes only. Complete booklets are listed and valued in only a few cases, such as Grenada Scott 1055 and some forms of British prestige booklets. Individual booklet panes are listed only when they are not fashioned from existing sheet stamps and, therefore, are identifiable from their sheet stamp counterparts.

Panes usually do not have a used value assigned to them because there is little market activity for used booklet panes, even though many exist used and there is some demand for them.

Cancellations — The marks or obliterations put on stamps by postal authorities to show that they have performed service and to prevent their reuse are known as cancellations. If the marking is made with a pen, it is considered a "pen cancel." When the location of the post office appears in the marking, it is a "town cancellation." A "postmark" is technically any postal marking, but in practice the term generally is applied to a town cancellation with a date. When calling attention to a cause or celebration, the marking is known as a "slogan cancellation." Many other types and styles of cancellations exist, such as duplex, numerals, targêts, fancy and others. See also "precancels," below.

Coil Stamps — These are stamps that are issued in rolls for use in dispensers, affixing and vending machines. Those coils of the United States, Canada, Sweden and some other countries are perforated horizontally or vertically only, with the outer edges imperforate. Coil stamps of some countries, such as Great Britain and Germany, are perforated on all four sides and may in some cases be distinguished from their sheet stamp counterparts by watermarks, counting numbers on the reverse or other means.

Covers — Entire envelopes, with or without adhesive postage stamps, that have passed through the mail and bear postal or other markings of philatelic interest are known as covers. Before the introduction of envelopes in about 1840, people folded letters and wrote the address on the outside. Some people covered their letters with an extra sheet of paper on the outside for the address, producing the term "cover." Used airletter sheets, stamped envelopes and other items of postal stationery also are considered covers.

Errors — Stamps that have some major, consistent, unintentional deviation from the normal are considered errors. Errors include, but are not limited to, missing or wrong colors, wrong paper, wrong watermarks, inverted centers or frames on multicolor printing, inverted or missing surcharges or overprints, double impressions, missing perforations and others. Factually wrong or misspelled information, if it appears on all examples of a stamp, are not considered errors in the true sense of the word. They are errors of design. Inconsistent or randomly appearing items, such as misperfs or color shifts, are classified as freaks.

Overprints and Surcharges — Overprinting involves applying wording or design elements over an already existing stamp. Overprints can be used to alter the place of use (such as "Canal Zone" on U.S. stamps), to adapt them for a special purpose ("Porto" on Denmark's 1913-20 regular issues for use as postage due stamps, Scott J1-J7) or to commemorate a special occasion (United States Scott 647-648).

A *surcharge* is a form of overprint that changes or restates the face value of a stamp or piece of postal stationery.

Surcharges and overprints may be handstamped, typeset or, occasionally, lithographed or engraved. A few hand-written overprints and surcharges are known.

Precancels — Stamps that are canceled before they are placed in the mail are known as precancels. Precanceling usually is done to expedite the handling of large mailings and generally allow the affected mail pieces to skip certain phases of mail handling.

In the United States, precancellations generally identified the point of origin; that is, the city and state. This information appeared across the face of the stamp, usually centered between parallel lines. More recently, bureau precancels retained the parallel lines, but the city and state designations were dropped. Recent coils have a service inscription that is present on the original printing plate. These show the mail service paid for by the stamp. Since these stamps are not intended to receive further cancellations when used as intended, they are considered precancels. Such items often do not have parallel lines as part of the precancellation.

In France, the abbreviation *Affranchts* in a semicircle together with the word *Postes* is the general form of precancel in use. Belgian precancellations usually appear in a box in which the name of the city appears. Netherlands precancels have the name of the city enclosed between concentric circles, sometimes called a "lifesaver." Precancellations of other countries usually follow these patterns, but may be any arrangement of bars, boxes and city names.

Precancels are listed in the Scott catalogues only if the precancel changes the denomination (Belgium Scott 477-478); if the precanceled stamp is different from the non-precanceled version (such as untagged U.S. precancels); or if the stamp exists only precanceled (France Scott 1096-1099, U.S. Scott 2265).

Proofs and Essays — Proofs are impressions taken from an approved die, plate or stone in which the design and color are the same as the stamp issued to the public. Trial color proofs are impressions taken from approved dies, plates or stones in colors that vary from the final version. An essay is the impression of a design that differs in some way from the issued stamp. "Progressive die proofs" generally are considered to be essays.

Provisionals — These are stamps that are issued on short notice and intended for temporary use pending the arrival of regular issues. They usually are issued to meet such contingencies as changes in government or currency, shortage of necessary postage values or military occupation.

During the 1840s, postmasters in certain American cities issued stamps that were valid only at specific post offices. In 1861, postmasters of the Confederate States also issued stamps with limited validity. Both of these examples are known as "postmaster's provisionals."

Se-tenant — This term refers to an unsevered pair, strip or block of stamps that differ in design, denomination or overprint.

Unless the se-tenant item has a continuous design (see U.S. Scott 1451a, 1694a) the stamps do not have to be in the same order as shown in the catalogue (see U.S. Scott 2158a).

Specimens — The Universal Postal Union required member nations to send samples of all stamps they released into service to the International Bureau in Switzerland. Member nations of the UPU received these specimens as samples of what stamps were valid for postage. Many are overprinted, handstamped or initial-perforated "Specimen," "Canceled" or "Muestra." Some are marked with bars across the denominations (China-Taiwan), punched holes (Czechoslovakia) or back inscriptions (Mongolia).

Stamps distributed to government officials or for publicity purposes, and stamps submitted by private security printers for official approval, also may receive such defacements.

The previously described defacement markings prevent postal use, and all such items generally are known as "specimens."

Tete Beche — This term describes a pair of stamps in which one is upside down in relation to the other. Some of these are the result of intentional sheet arrangements, such as Morocco Scott B10-B11. Others occurred when one or more electrotypes accidentally were placed upside down on the plate, such as Colombia Scott 57a. Separation of the tete-beche stamps, of course, destroys the tete beche variety.

Currency Conversion

Country	Dollar	Pound	S Franc	Guilder	Yen	Lira	HK Dollar	D-Mark	Fr Franc	Cdn Dollar	Aust Dollar
Australia	1.5544	2.5110	0.9895	0.7201	0.0151	0.0008	0.2000	0.8113	0.2419	1.0531	....
Canada	1.4760	2.3843	0.9396	0.6837	0.0143	0.0008	0.1899	0.7704	0.2297	....	.09496
France	6.4256	10.3799	4.0904	2.9766	0.0623	0.0034	0.8267	3.3538	....	4.3534	4.1338
Germany	1.9159	3.0949	1.2196	0.8875	0.0186	0.0010	0.2465	....	0.2982	1.2980	1.2326
Hong Kong	7.7726	12.556	4.9479	3.6006	0.0754	0.0041	....	4.0569	1.2096	5.2660	5.0004
Italy	1896.72	3063.97	1207.41	878.64	18.394	....	244.03	989.99	295.18	1285.04	1220.23
Japan	103.11	166.57	65.641	47.767	....	0.0544	13.266	53.821	16.048	69.861	66.337
Netherlands	2.1587	3.4872	1.3742	....	0.0209	0.0011	0.2777	1.1267	0.3360	1.4625	1.3888
Switzerland	1.5709	2.5376	....	0.7277	0.0152	0.0008	0.2021	0.8199	0.2445	1.0643	1.0106
U.K.	0.6190	....	0.3941	0.2868	0.0060	0.0003	0.0796	0.3231	0.0963	0.4194	0.3983
U.S.	....	1.6154	0.6366	0.4632	0.0097	0.0005	0.1287	0.5219	0.1556	0.6775	0.6433

Country	Currency	U.S. $ Equiv.
Afghanistan	afghani	.0002
Aitutaki	New Zealand dollar	.5082
Albania	lek	.0074
Algeria	dinar	.0145
Andorra (French)	franc	.1556
Andorra (Spanish)	peseta	.0061
Angola	kwanza	.1831
Anguilla	East Caribbean dollar	.3703
Antigua	East Caribbean dollar	.3703
Argentina	peso	1.00
Aruba	guilder	.5586
Ascension	British pound	1.6154
Australia	dollar	.6433
Australian Antarctic Territory	dollar	.6433
Austria	schilling	.0741
Azerbaijan	manat	.00023
Bahamas	dollar	1.00
Bahrain	dinar	2.63
Bangladesh	taka	.0196
Barbados	dollar	.5000
Barbuda	East Caribbean dollar	.3703
Belgium	franc	.0253
Belize	dollar	.5000
Benin	Community of French Africa (CFA) franc	.00155
Bermuda	dollar	1.00
Bhutan	ngultrum	.0229
Bolivia	boliviano	.1675
Botswana	pula	.2164
Brazil	real	.5434
British Antarctic Territory	British pound	1.6154
British Indian Ocean Territory	British pound	1.6154
Brunei	dollar	.5970
Bulgaria	lev	.5235
Burkina Faso	CFA franc	.00155
Burma	kyat	.1591
Burundi	franc	.0016
United Nations-New York	U.S. dollar	1.00
United Nations-Geneva	Swiss franc	.6366
United Nations-Vienna	Austria shilling	.0741
United States	dollar	1.00

Source: ***Wall Street Journal*** *Dec. 20, 1999. Figures reflect values as of Dec. 17, 1999.*

Common Design Types

Pictured in this section are issues where one illustration has been used for a number of countries in the Catalogue. Not included in this section are overprinted stamps or those issues which are illustrated in each country.

EUROPA

Europa, 1956

The design symbolizing the cooperation among the six countries comprising the Coal and Steel Community is illustrated in each country.

Belgium	496-497
France	805-806
Germany	748-749
Italy	715-716
Luxembourg	318-320
Netherlands	368-369

Europa, 1958

"E" and Dove
CD1

European Postal Union at the service of European integration.

1958, Sept. 13

Belgium	527-528
France	889-890
Germany	790-791
Italy	750-751
Luxembourg	341-343
Netherlands	375-376
Saar	317-318

Europa, 1959

6-Link Endless Chain – CD2

1959, Sept. 19

Belgium	536-537
France	929-930
Germany	805-806
Italy	791-792
Luxembourg	354-355
Netherlands	379-380

Europa, 1960

19-Spoke Wheel – CD3

First anniverary of the establishment of C.E.P.T. (Conference Europeenne des Administrations des Postes et des Telecommunications.)

The spokes symbolize the 19 founding members of the Conference.

1960, Sept.

Belgium	553-554
Denmark	379
Finland	376-377
France	970-971
Germany	818-820
Great Britain	377-378
Greece	688
Iceland	327-328
Ireland	175-176
Italy	809-810
Luxembourg	374-375
Netherlands	385-386
Norway	387
Portugal	866-867
Spain	941-942
Sweden	562-563
Switzerland	400-401
Turkey	1493-1494

Europa, 1961

19 Doves Flying as One – CD4

The 19 doves represent the 19 members of the Conference of European Postal and Telecommunications Administrations C.E.P.T.

1961-62

Belgium	572-573
Cyprus	201-203
France	1005-1006
Germany	844-845
Great Britain	383-384
Greece	718-719
Iceland	340-341
Italy	845-846
Luxembourg	382-383
Netherlands	387-388
Spain	1010-1011
Switzerland	410-411
Turkey	1518-1520

Europa, 1962

Young Tree with 19 Leaves
CD5

The 19 leaves represent the 19 original members of C.E.P.T.

1962-63

Belgium	582-583
Cyprus	219-221
France	1045-1046
Germany	852-853
Greece	739-740
Iceland	348-349
Ireland	184-185
Italy	860-861
Luxembourg	386-387
Netherlands	394-395
Norway	414-415
Switzerland	416-417
Turkey	1553-1555

Europa, 1963

Stylized Links, Symbolizing Unity – CD6

1963, Sept.

Belgium	598-599
Cyprus	229-231
Finland	419
France	1074-1075
Germany	867-868
Greece	768-769
Iceland	357-358
Ireland	188-189
Italy	880-881
Luxembourg	403-404
Netherlands	416-417
Norway	441-442
Switzerland	429
Turkey	1602-1603

Europa, 1964

Symbolic Daisy
CD7

5th anniversary of the establishment of C.E.P.T. The 22 petals of the flower symbolize the 22 members of the Conference.

1964, Sept.

Austria	738
Belgium	614-615
Cyprus	244-246
France	1109-1110
Germany	897-898
Greece	801-802
Iceland	367-368
Ireland	196-197
Italy	894-895
Luxembourg	411-412
Monaco	590-591
Netherlands	428-429
Norway	458
Portugal	931-933
Spain	1262-1263
Switzerland	438-439
Turkey	1628-1629

Europa, 1965

Leaves and "Fruit"
CD8

1965

Belgium	636-637
Cyprus	262-264
Finland	437
France	1131-1132
Germany	934-935
Greece	833-834
Iceland	375-376
Ireland	204-205
Italy	915-916
Luxembourg	432-433
Monaco	616-617
Netherlands	438-439
Norway	475-476
Portugal	958-960
Switzerland	469
Turkey	1665-1666

Europa, 1966

Symbolic Sailboat
CD9

1966, Sept.

Andorra, French	172
Belgium	675-676
Cyprus	275-277
France	1163-1164
Germany	963-964
Greece	862-863
Iceland	384-385
Ireland	216-217
Italy	942-943
Liechtenstein	415
Luxembourg	440-441
Monaco	639-640
Netherlands	441-442
Norway	496-497
Portugal	980-982
Switzerland	477-478
Turkey	1718-1719

Europa, 1967

Cogwheels
CD10

1967

Andorra, French	174-175
Belgium	688-689
Cyprus	297-299
France	1178-1179
Germany	969-970
Greece	891-892
Iceland	389-390
Ireland	232-233
Italy	951-952
Liechtenstein	420
Luxembourg	449-450
Monaco	669-670
Netherlands	444-447
Norway	504-505
Portugal	994-996
Spain	1465-1466
Switzerland	482
Turkey	B120-B121

Europa, 1968

Golden Key with C.E.P.T. Emblem
CD11

1968

Andorra, French	182-183
Belgium	705-706
Cyprus	314-316
France	1209-1210
Germany	983-984
Greece	916-917
Iceland	395-396
Ireland	242-243
Italy	979-980
Liechtenstein	442
Luxembourg	466-467
Monaco	689-691
Netherlands	452-453
Portugal	1019-1021
San Marino	687
Spain	1526
Turkey	1775-1776

Europa, 1969

"EUROPA" and "CEPT" – CD12

Tenth anniversary of C.E.P.T.

1969

Andorra, French	188-189
Austria	837
Belgium	718-719
Cyprus	326-328
Denmark	458
Finland	483
France	1245-1246
Germany	996-997
Great Britain	585
Greece	947-948
Iceland	406-407
Ireland	270-271
Italy	1000-1001
Liechtenstein	453
Luxembourg	474-475
Monaco	722-724
Netherlands	475-476
Norway	533-534
Portugal	1038-1040
San Marino	701-702
Spain	1567

Sweden 814-816
Switzerland 500-501
Turkey 1799-1800
Vatican 470-472
Yugoslavia 1003-1004

Europa, 1970

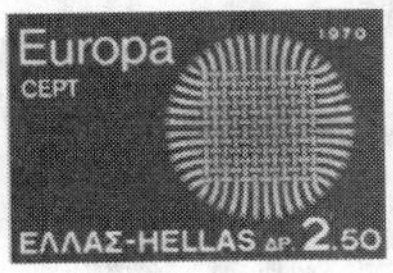

Interwoven Threads CD13

1970
Andorra, French 196-197
Belgium 741-742
Cyprus 340-342
France 1271-1272
Germany 1018-1019
Greece 985, 987
Iceland 420-421
Ireland 279-281
Italy 1013-1014
Liechtenstein 470
Luxembourg 489-490
Monaco 768-770
Netherlands 483-484
Portugal 1060-1062
San Marino 729-730
Spain 1607
Switzerland 515-516
Turkey 1848-1849
Yugoslavia 1024-1025

Europa, 1971

"Fraternity, Cooperation, Common Effort" – CD14

1971
Andorra, French 205-206
Belgium 803-804
Cyprus 365-367
Finland 504
France 1304
Germany 1064-1065
Greece 1029-1030
Iceland 429-430
Ireland 305-306
Italy 1038-1039
Liechtenstein 485
Luxembourg 500-501
Malta 425-427
Monaco 797-799
Netherlands 488-489
Portugal 1094-1096
San Marino 749-750
Spain 1675-1676
Switzerland 531-532
Turkey 1876-1877
Yugoslavia 1052-1053

Europa, 1972

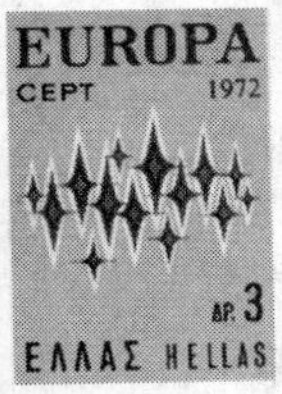

Sparkles, Symbolic of Communications CD15

1972
Andorra, French 210-211
Andorra, Spanish 62
Belgium 825-826
Cyprus 380-382
Finland 512-513
France 1341
Germany 1089-1090
Greece 1049-1050
Iceland 439-440
Ireland 316-317
Italy 1065-1066
Liechtenstein 504
Luxembourg 512-513
Malta 450-453
Monaco 831-832
Netherlands 494-495
Portugal 1141-1143
San Marino 771-772
Spain 1718
Switzerland 544-545
Turkey 1907-1908
Yugoslavia 1100-1101

Europa, 1973

Post Horn and Arrows CD16

1973
Andorra, French 319-320
Andorra, Spanish 76
Belgium 839-840
Cyprus 396-398
Finland 526
France 1367
Germany 1114-1115
Greece 1090-1092
Iceland 447-448
Ireland 329-330
Italy 1108-1109
Liechtenstein 528-529
Luxembourg 523-524
Malta 469-471
Monaco 866-867
Netherlands 504-505
Norway 604-605
Portugal 1170-1172
San Marino 802-803
Spain 1753
Switzerland 580-581
Turkey 1935-1936
Yugoslavia 1138-1139

PORTUGAL & COLONIES

Vasco da Gama

Fleet Departing CD20

Fleet Arriving at Calicut CD21

Embarking at Rastello CD22

Muse of History – CD23 San Gabriel, da Gama and Camoens – CD24

Archangel Gabriel, the Patron Saint CD25

Flagship San Gabriel CD26

Vasco da Gama CD27

Fourth centenary of Vasco da Gama's discovery of the route to India.

1898
Azores 93-100
Macao 67-74
Madeira 37-44
Portugal 147-154
Port. Africa 1-8
Port. Congo 75-98
Port. India 189-196
St. Thomas & Prince Islands 170-193
Timor 45-52

Pombal

POSTAL TAX

POSTAL TAX DUES

Marquis de Pombal CD28

Planning Reconstruction of Lisbon, 1755 CD29

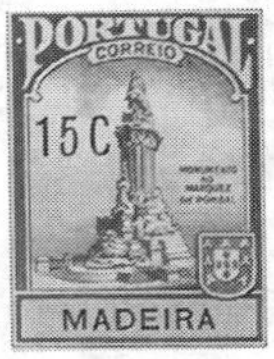

Pombal Monument, Lisbon CD30

Sebastiao Jose de Carvalho e Mello, Marquis de Pombal (1699-1782), statesman, rebuilt Lisbon after earthquake of 1755. Tax was for the erection of Pombal monument. Obligatory on all mail on certain days throughout the year.

Postal Tax Dues are inscribed "Multa."

1925
Angola RA1-RA3, RAJ1-RAJ3
Azores RA9-RA11, RAJ2-RAJ4
Cape Verde RA1-RA3, RAJ1-RAJ3
Macao RA1-RA3, RAJ1-RAJ3
Madeira RA1-RA3, RAJ1-RAJ3
Mozambique RA1-RA3, RAJ1-RAJ3
Nyassa RA1-RA3, RAJ1-RAJ3
Portugal RA11-RA13, RAJ2-RAJ4
Port. Guinea RA1-RA3, RAJ1-RAJ3
Port. India RA1-RA3, RAJ1-RAJ3
St. Thomas & Prince Islands RA1-RA3, RAJ1-RAJ3
Timor RA1-RA3, RAJ1-RAJ3

Vasco da Gama CD34

Mousinho de Albuquerque CD35

Dam CD36

Prince Henry the Navigator – CD37

Affonso de Albuquerque CD38

Plane over Globe CD39

1938-39
Angola 274-291, C1-C9
Cape Verde 234-251, C1-C9
Macao 289-305, C7-C15
Mozambique 270-287, C1-C9
Port. Guinea 233-250. C1-C9
Port. India 439-453, C1-C8
St. Thomas & Prince Islands 302-319, 323-340, C1-C18
Timor 223-239, C1-C9

Lady of Fatima

Our Lady of the Rosary, Fatima, Portugal CD40

1948-49
Angola 315-318
Cape Verde 266
Macao 336
Mozambique 325-328
Port. Guinea 271
Port. India 480
St. Thomas & Prince Islands 351
Timor 254

A souvenir sheet of 9 stamps was issued in 1951 to mark the extension of the 1950 Holy Year. The sheet contains: Angola No. 316, Cape Verde No. 266, Macao No. 336, Mozambique No. 325, Portuguese Guinea No. 271, Portugese India Nos. 480, 485, St. Thomas & Prince Islands No. 351, Timor No. 254.

The sheet also contains a portrait of Pope Pius XII and is inscribed "Encerramento do Ano Santo, Fatima 1951." It was sold for 11 escudos.

Holy Year

Church Bells and Dove CD41

Angel Holding Candelabra CD42

Holy Year, 1950.

1950-51
Angola 331-332
Cape Verde 268-269
Macao 339-340
Mozambique 330-331
Port. Guinea 273-274
Port. India 490-491, 496-503
St. Thomas & Prince Islands 353-354
Timor 258-259

A souvenir sheet of 8 stamps was issued in 1951 to mark the extension of the Holy Year. The sheet contains: Angola No. 331, Cape Verde No. 269, Macao No. 340, Mozambique No. 331, Portuguese Guinea No. 275, Portuguese India No. 490, St. Thomas & Prince Islands No. 354, Timor No. 258, some with colors changed. The sheet contains doves and is inscribed "Encerramento do Ano Santo, Fatima 1951." It was sold for 17 escudos.

Holy Year Conclusion

Our Lady of Fatima CD43

Conclusion of Holy Year. Sheets contain alternate vertical rows of stamps and labels bearing quotation from Pope Pius XII, different for each colony.

1951

Angola	357
Cape Verde	270
Macao	352
Mozambique	356
Port. Guinea	275
Port. India	506
St. Thomas & Prince Islands	355
Timor	270

Medical Congress

CD44

First National Congress of Tropical Medicine, Lisbon, 1952.

Each stamp has a different design.

1952

Angola	358
Cape Verde	287
Macao	364
Mozambique	359
Port. Guinea	276
Port. India	516
St. Thomas & Prince Islands	356
Timor	271

POSTAGE DUE STAMPS

CD45

1952

Angola	J37-J42
Cape Verde	J31-J36
Macao	J53-J58
Mozambique	J51-J56
Port. Guinea	J40-J45
Port. India	J47-J52
St. Thomas & Prince Islands	J52-J57
Timor	J31-J36

Sao Paulo

Father Manuel de Nobrega and View of Sao Paulo CD46

Founding of Sao Paulo, Brazil, 400th anniv.

1954

Angola	385
Cape Verde	297
Macao	382
Mozambique	395
Port. Guinea	291
Port. India	530
St. Thomas & Prince Islands	369
Timor	279

Tropical Medicine Congress

CD47

Sixth International Congress for Tropical Medicine and Malaria, Lisbon, Sept. 1958.

Each stamp shows a different plant.

1958

Angola	409
Cape Verde	303
Macao	392
Mozambique	404
Port. Guinea	295
Port. India	569
St. Thomas & Prince Islands	371
Timor	289

Sports

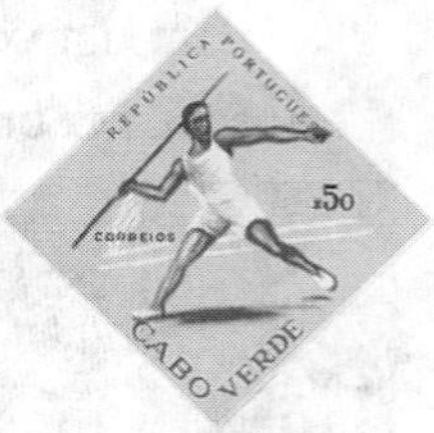

CD48

Each stamp shows a different sport.

1962

Angola	433-438
Cape Verde	320-325
Macao	394-399
Mozambique	424-429
Port. Guinea	299-304
St. Thomas & Prince Islands	374-379
Timor	313-318

Anti-Malaria

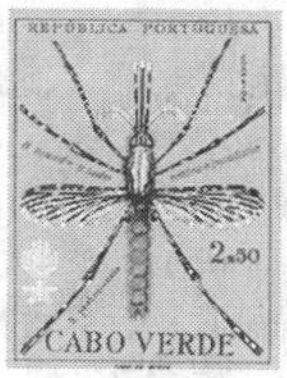

Anopheles Funestus and Malaria Eradication Symbol CD49

World Health Organization drive to eradicate malaria.

1962

Angola	439
Cape Verde	326
Macao	400
Mozambique	430
Port. Guinea	305
St. Thomas & Prince Islands	380
Timor	319

Airline Anniversary

Map of Africa, Super Constellation and Jet Liner CD50

Tenth anniversary of Transportes Aereos Portugueses (TAP).

1963

Angola	490
Cape Verde	327
Mozambique	434
Port. Guinea	318
St. Thomas & Prince Islands	381

National Overseas Bank

Antonio Teixeira de Sousa CD51

Centenary of the National Overseas Bank of Portugal.

1964, May 16

Angola	509
Cape Verde	328
Port. Guinea	319
St. Thomas & Prince Islands	382
Timor	320

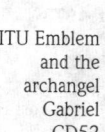

ITU

ITU Emblem and the archangel Gabriel CD52

International Communications Union, Cent.

1965, May 17

Angola	511
Cape Verde	329
Macao	402
Mozambique	464
Port. Guinea	320
St. Thomas & Prince Islands	383
Timor	321

National Revolution

CD53

40th anniv. of the National Revolution.

Different buildings on each stamp.

1966, May 28

Angola	525
Cape Verde	338
Macao	403
Mozambique	465
Port. Guinea	329
St. Thomas & Prince Islands	392
Timor	322

Navy Club

CD54

Centenary of Portugal's Navy Club.

Each stamp has a different design.

1967, Jan. 31

Angola	527-528
Cape Verde	339-340
Macao	412-413
Mozambique	478-479
Port. Guinea	330-331
St. Thomas & Prince Islands	393-394
Timor	323-324

Admiral Coutinho

CD55

Centenary of the birth of Admiral Carlos Viegas Gago Coutinho (1869-1959), explorer and aviation pioneer.

Each stamp has a different design.

1969, Feb. 17

Angola	547
Cape Verde	355
Macao	417
Mozambique	484
Port. Guinea	335
St. Thomas & Prince Islands	397
Timor	335

Administration Reform

Luiz Augusto Rebello da Silva CD 56

Centenary of the administration reforms of the overseas territories.

1969, Sept. 25

Angola	549
Cape Verde	357
Macao	419
Mozambique	491
Port. Guinea	337
St. Thomas & Prince Islands	399
Timor	338

Marshal Carmona

CD57

Birth centenary of Marshal Antonio Oscar Carmona de Fragoso (1869-1951), President of Portugal.

Each stamp has a different design.

1970, Nov. 15

Angola	563
Cape Verde	359
Macao	422
Mozambique	493
Port. Guinea	340
St. Thomas & Prince Islands	403
Timor	341

Olympic Games

CD59

20th Olympic Games, Munich, Aug. 26-Sept. 11.

Each stamp shows a different sport.

1972, June 20

Angola	569
Cape Verde	361
Macao	426
Mozambique	504
Port. Guinea	342
St. Thomas & Prince Islands	408
Timor	343

Lisbon-Rio de Janeiro Flight

CD60

50th anniversary of the Lisbon to Rio de Janeiro flight by Arturo de Sacadura and Coutinho, March 30-June 5, 1922.

Each stamp shows a different stage of the flight.

1972, Sept. 20

Angola	570
Cape Verde	362
Macao	427
Mozambique	505
Port. Guinea	343
St. Thomas & Prince Islands	409
Timor	344

WMO Centenary

WMO Emblem CD61

Centenary of international meterological cooperation.

1973, Dec. 15

Angola	571
Cape Verde	363
Macao	429
Mozambique	509
Port. Guinea	344
St. Thomas & Prince Islands	410
Timor	345

FRENCH COMMUNITY

Upper Volta can be found under Burkina Faso in Vol. 1

Madagascar can be found under Malagasy in Vol. 3

Colonial Exposition

People of French Empire CD70

Women's Heads CD71

France Showing Way to Civilization CD72

"Colonial Commerce" CD73

International Colonial Exposition, Paris.

1931

Cameroun 213-216
Chad 60-63
Dahomey 97-100
Fr. Guiana 152-155
Fr. Guinea 116-119
Fr. India 100-103
Fr. Polynesia 76-79
Fr. Sudan 102-105
Gabon 120-123
Guadeloupe 138-141
Indo-China 140-142
Ivory Coast 92-95
Madagascar 169-172
Martinique 129-132
Mauritania 65-68
Middle Congo 61-64
New Caledonia 176-179
Niger 73-76
Reunion 122-125
St. Pierre & Miquelon 132-135
Senegal 138-141
Somali Coast 135-138
Togo 254-257
Ubangi-Shari 82-85
Upper Volta 66-69
Wallis & Futuna Isls. 85-88

Paris International Exposition
Colonial Arts Exposition

"Colonial Resources"
CD74 CD77

Overseas Commerce – CD75

Exposition Building and Women CD76

"France and the Empire" CD78

Cultural Treasures of the Colonies CD79

Souvenir sheets contain one imperf. stamp.

1937

Cameroun 217-222A
Dahomey 101-107
Fr. Equatorial Africa 27-32, 73
Fr. Guiana 162-168
Fr. Guinea 120-126
Fr. India 104-110
Fr. Polynesia 117-123
Fr. Sudan 106-112
Guadeloupe 148-154
Indo-China 193-199
Inini 41
Ivory Coast 152-158
Kwangchowan 132
Madagascar 191-197
Martinique 179-185
Mauritania 69-75
New Caledonia 208-214
Niger 72-83
Reunion 167-173
St. Pierre & Miquelon 165-171
Senegal 172-178
Somali Coast 139-145
Togo 258-264
Wallis & Futuna Isls. 89

Curie

Pierre and Marie Curie CD80

40th anniversary of the discovery of radium. The surtax was for the benefit of the Intl. Union for the Control of Cancer.

1938

Cameroun B1
Cuba B1-B2
Dahomey B2
France B76
Fr. Equatorial Africa B1
Fr. Guiana B3
Fr. Guinea B2
Fr. India B6
Fr. Polynesia B5
Fr. Sudan B1
Guadeloupe B3
Indo-China B14
Ivory Coast B2
Madagascar B2
Martinique B2
Mauritania B3
New Caledonia B4
Niger B1
Reunion B4
St. Pierre & Miquelon B3
Senegal B3
Somali Coast B2
Togo B1

Caillie

Rene Caille and Map of Northwestern Africa - CD81

Death centenary of Rene Caillie (1799-1838), French explorer.

All three denominations exist with colony name omitted.

1939

Dahomey 108-110
Fr. Guinea 161-163
Fr. Sudan 113-115
Ivory Coast 160-162
Mauritania 109-111
Niger 84-86
Senegal 188-190
Togo 265-267

New York World's Fair

Natives and New York Skyline CD82

1939

Cameroun 223-224
Dahomey 111-112
Fr. Equatorial Africa 78-79
Fr. Guiana 169-170
Fr. Guinea 164-165
Fr. India 111-112
Fr. Polynesia 124-125
Fr. Sudan 116-117
Guadeloupe 155-156
Indo-China 203-204
Inini 42-43
Ivory Coast 163-164
Kwangchowan 121-122
Madagascar 209-210
Martinique 186-187
Mauritania 112-113
New Caledonia 215-216
Niger 87-88
Reunion 174-175
St. Pierre & Miquelon 205-206
Senegal 191-192
Somali Coast 179-180
Togo 268-269
Wallis & Futuna Isls. 90-91

French Revolution

Storming of the Bastille – CD83

French Revolution, 150th anniv. The surtax was for the defense of the colonies.

1939

Cameroun B2-B6
Dahomey B3-B7
Fr. Equatorial Africa B4-B8, CB1
Fr. Guiana B4-B8, CB1
Fr. Guinea B3-B7
Fr. India B7-B11
Fr. Polynesia B6-B10, CB1
Fr. Sudan B2-B6
Guadeloupe B4-B8
Indo-China B15-B19, CB1
Inini B1-B5
Ivory Coast B3-B7
Kwangchowan B1-B5
Madagascar B3-B7, CB1
Martinique B3-B7
Mauritania B4-B8
New Caledonia B5-B9, CB1
Niger B2-B6
Reunion B5-B9, CB1
St. Pierre & Miquelon B4-B8
Senegal B4-B8, CB1
Somali Coast B3-B7
Togo B2-B6
Wallis & Futuna Isls. B1-B5

Plane over Coastal Area CD85

All five denominations exist with colony name omitted.

1940

Dahomey C1-C5
Fr. Guinea C1-C5
Fr. Sudan C1-C5
Ivory Coast C1-C5
Mauritania C1-C5
Niger C1-C5
Senegal C12-C16
Togo C1-C5

Colonial Infantryman CD86

1941

Cameroun B13B
Dahomey B13
Fr. Equatorial Africa B8B
Fr. Guiana B10
Fr. Guinea B13
Fr. India B13
Fr. Polynesia B12
Fr. Sudan B12
Guadeloupe B10
Indo-China B19B
Inini B7
Ivory Coast B13
Kwangchowan B7
Madagascar B9
Martinique B9
Mauritania B14
New Caledonia B11
Niger B12
Reunion B11
St. Pierre & Miquelon B8B
Senegal B14
Somali Coast B9
Togo B10B
Wallis & Futuna Isls. B7

Cross of Lorraine & Four-motor Plane CD87

1941-5

Cameroun C1-C7
Fr. Equatorial Africa C17-C23
Fr. Guiana C9-C10
Fr. India C1-C6
Fr. Polynesia C3-C9
Fr. West Africa C1-C3
Guadeloupe C1-C2
Madagascar C37-C43
Martinique C1-C2
New Caledonia C7-C13
Reunion C18-C24
St. Pierre & Miquelon C1-C7
Somali Coast C1-C7

Transport Plane CD88

Caravan and Plane CD89

1942

Dahomey C6-C13
Fr. Guinea C6-C13
Fr. Sudan C6-C13
Ivory Coast C6-C13
Mauritania C6-C13
Niger C6-C13
Senegal C17-C25
Togo C6-C13

Red Cross

Marianne CD90

The surtax was for the French Red Cross and national relief.

1944

Cameroun B28
Fr. Equatorial Africa B38
Fr. Guiana B12
Fr. India B14
Fr. Polynesia B13
Fr. West Africa B1
Guadeloupe B12

Madagascar B15
Martinique B11
New Caledonia.....................................B13
Reunion B15
St. Pierre & Miquelon B13
Somali Coast B13
Wallis & Futuna Isls. B9

Eboue

CD91

Felix Eboue, first French colonial administrator to proclaim resistance to Germany after French surrender in World War II.

1945
Cameroun 296-297
Fr. Equatorial Africa 156-157
Fr. Guiana 171-172
Fr. India 210-211
Fr. Polynesia 150-151
Fr. West Africa....................................15-16
Guadeloupe 187-188
Madagascar 259-260
Martinique 196-197
New Caledonia...............................274-275
Reunion...238-239
St. Pierre & Miquelon......................322-323
Somali Coast..................................238-239

Victory

Victory – CD92

European victory of the Allied Nations in World War II.

1946, May 8
Cameroun...C8
Fr. Equatorial Africa C24
Fr. Guiana C11
Fr. India...C7
Fr. Polynesia C10
Fr. West Africa C4
Guadeloupe C3
Indo-China...C19
Madagascar..C44
Martinique...C3
New Caledonia C14
Reunion C25
St. Pierre & Miquelon C8
Somali Coast..C8
Wallis & Futuna Isls................................C1

Chad to Rhine

Leclerc's Departure from Chad – CD93

Battle at Cufra Oasis – CD94

Tanks in Action, Mareth – CD95

Normandy Invasion – CD96

Entering Paris – CD97

Liberation of Strasbourg – CD98

"Chad to the Rhine" march, 1942-44, by Gen. Jacques Leclerc's column, later French 2nd Armored Division.

1946, June 6
Cameroun C9-C14
Fr. Equatorial Africa C25-C30
Fr. Guiana C12-C17
Fr. India C8-C13
Fr. Polynesia C11-C16
Fr. West Africa C5-C10
Guadeloupe......................................C4-C9
Indo-China C20-C25
Madagascar C45-C50
Martinique C4-C9
New Caledonia C15-C20
Reunion...C26-C31
St. Pierre & Miquelon......................C9-C14
Somali Coast..................................C9-C14
Wallis & Futuna Isls. C2-C7

UPU

French Colonials, Globe and Plane CD99

Universal Postal Union, 75th anniv.

1949, July 4
Cameroun...C29
Fr. Equatorial Africa C34
Fr. India...C17
Fr. Polynesia...C20
Fr. West Africa C15
Indo-China...C26
Madagascar..C55
New Caledonia C24
St. Pierre & Miquelon C18
Somali Coast..C18
Togo..C18
Wallis & Futuna Isls..............................C10

Tropical Medicine

Doctor Treating Infant CD100

The surtax was for charitable work.

1950
Cameroun B29
Fr. Equatorial Africa.............................B39
Fr. India...B15
Fr. Polynesia...B14
Fr. West Africa B3
Madagascar..B17
New Caledonia......................................B14
St. Pierre & Miquelon B14
Somali Coast B14
Togo B11

Military Medal

Medal, Early Marine and Colonial Soldier CD101

Centenary of the creation of the French Military Medal.

1952
Cameroun 332
Comoro Isls. 39
Fr. Equatorial Africa..............................186
Fr. India 233
Fr. Polynesia..179
Fr. West Africa 57
Madagascar 286
New Caledonia.......................................295
St. Pierre & Miquelon.............................345
Somali Coast..267
Togo..327
Wallis & Futuna Isls. 149

Liberation

Allied Landing, Victory Sign and Cross of Lorraine – CD102

Lberation of France, 10th anniv.

1954, June 6
Cameroun..C32
Comoro Isls...C4
Fr. Equatorial Africa C38
Fr. India..C18
Fr. Polynesia C22
Fr. West Africa C17
Madagascar...C57
New Caledonia C25
St. Pierre & Miquelon C19
Somali Coast...C19
Togo C19
Wallis & Futuna Isls...............................C11

FIDES

Plowmen CD103

Efforts of FIDES, the Economic and Social Development Fund for Overseas Possessions (Fonds d' Investissement pour le Developpement Economique et Social).

Each stamp has a different design.

1956
Cameroun 326-329
Comoro Isls. 43
Fr. Polynesia 181
Fr. West Africa.....................................65-72
Madagascar 292-295
New Caledonia.......................................303
Somali Coast..268
Togo...331

Flower

CD104

Each stamp shows a different flower.

1958-9
Cameroun 333
Comoro Isls. 45
Fr. Equatorial Africa.........................200-201
Fr. Polynesia 192
Fr. So. & Antarctic Terr. 11
Fr. West Africa.....................................79-83
Madagascar 301-302
New Caledonia..................................304-305
St. Pierre & Miquelon................................357
Somali Coast...270
Togo...348-349
Wallis & Futuna Isls. 152

Human Rights

Sun, Dove and U.N. Emblem – CD105

10th anniversary of the signing of the Universal Declaration of Human Rights.

1958
Comoro Isls. 44
Fr. Equatorial Africa..................................202
Fr. Polynesia..191
Fr. West Africa 85
Madagascar 300
New Caledonia...306
St. Pierre & Miquelon.................................356
Somali Coast..274
Wallis & Futuna Isls. 153

C.C.T.A.

CD106

Commission for Technical Cooperation in Africa south of the Sahara, 10th anniv.

1960
Cameroun 335
Cent. Africa 3
Chad 66
Congo, P.R. 90
Dahomey..138
Gabon 150
Ivory Coast 180
Madagascar 317
Mali 9
Mauritania..117
Niger..104
Upper Volta 89

Air Afrique, 1961

Modern and Ancient Africa, Map and Planes – CD107

Founding of Air Afrique (African Airlines).

1961-62
Cameroun...C37
Cent. Africa C5
Chad...C7
Congo, P.R..C5
Dahomey C17
Gabon...C5
Ivory Coast C18
Mauritania C17
Niger C22
Senegal C31
Upper Volta...C4

Anti-Malaria

CD108

World Health Organization drive to eradicate malaria.

1962, Apr. 7

Cameroun	B36
Cent. Africa	B1
Chad	B1
Comoro Isls.	B1
Congo, P.R.	B3
Dahomey	B15
Gabon	B4
Ivory Coast	B15
Madagascar	B19
Mali	B1
Mauritania	B16
Niger	B14
Senegal	B16
Somali Coast	B15
Upper Volta	B1

Abidjan Games

CD109

Abidjan Games, Ivory Coast, Dec. 24-31, 1961. Each stamp shows a different sport.

1962

Chad	83-84
Cent. Africa	19-20
Congo, P.R.	103-104
Gabon	163-164, C6
Niger	109-111
Upper Volta	103-105

African and Malagasy Union

Flag of Union CD110

First anniversary of the Union.

1962, Sept. 8

Cameroun	373
Cent. Africa	21
Chad	85
Congo, P.R.	105
Dahomey	155
Gabon	165
Ivory Coast	198
Madagascar	332
Mauritania	170
Niger	112
Senegal	211
Upper Volta	106

Telstar

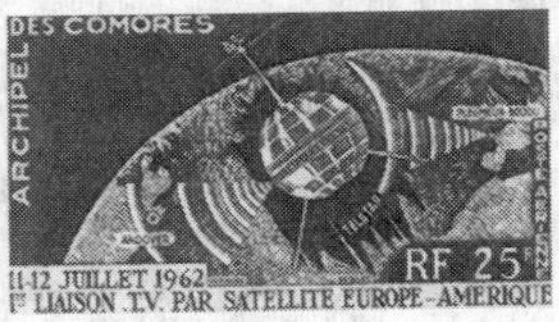

Telstar and Globe Showing Andover and Pleumeur-Bodou – CD111

First television connection of the United States and Europe through the Telstar satellite, July 11-12, 1962.

1962-63

Andorra, French	154
Comoro Isls.	C7
Fr. Polynesia	C29
Fr. So. & Antarctic Terr.	C5
New Caledonia	C33
Somali Coast	C31
St. Pierre & Miquelon	C26
Wallis & Futuna Isls.	C17

Freedom From Hunger

World Map and Wheat Emblem CD112

U.N. Food and Agriculture Organization's "Freedom from Hunger" campaign.

1963, Mar. 21

Cameroun	B37-B38
Cent. Africa	B2
Chad	B2
Congo, P.R.	B4
Dahomey	B16
Gabon	B5
Ivory Coast	B16
Madagascar	B21
Mauritania	B17
Niger	B15
Senegal	B17
Upper Volta	B2

Red Cross Centenary

CD113

Centenary of the International Red Cross.

1963, Sept. 2

Comoro Isls.	55
Fr. Polynesia	205
New Caledonia	328
St. Pierre & Miquelon	367
Somali Coast	297
Wallis & Futuna Isls.	165

African Postal Union, 1963

UAMPT Emblem, Radio Masts, Plane and Mail CD114

Establishment of the African and Malagasy Posts and Telecommunications Union.

1963, Sept. 8

Cameroun	C47
Cent. Africa	C10
Chad	C9
Congo, P.R.	C13
Dahomey	C19
Gabon	C13
Ivory Coast	C25
Madagascar	C75
Mauritania	C22
Niger	C27
Rwanda	36
Senegal	C32
Upper Volta	C9

Air Afrique, 1963

Symbols of Flight – CD115

First anniversary of Air Afrique and inauguration of DC-8 service.

1963, Nov. 19

Cameroun	C48
Chad	C10
Congo, P.R.	C14
Gabon	C18
Ivory Coast	C26
Mauritania	C26
Niger	C35
Senegal	C33

Europafrica

Europe and Africa Linked CD116

Signing of an economic agreement between the European Economic Community and the African and Malagasy Union, Yaounde, Cameroun, July 20, 1963.

1963-64

Cameroun	402
Chad	C11
Cent. Africa	C12
Congo, P.R.	C16
Gabon	C19
Ivory Coast	217
Niger	C43
Upper Volta	C11

Human Rights

Scales of Justice and Globe CD117

15th anniversary of the Universal Declaration of Human Rights.

1963, Dec. 10

Comoro Isls.	58
Fr. Polynesia	206
New Caledonia	329
St. Pierre & Miquelon	368
Somali Coast	300
Wallis & Futuna Isls.	166

PHILATEC

Stamp Album, Champs Elysees Palace and Horses of Marly – CD118

Intl. Philatelic and Postal Techniques Exhibition, Paris, June 5-21, 1964.

1963-64

Comoro Isls.	60
France	1078
Fr. Polynesia	207
New Caledonia	341
St. Pierre & Miquelon	369
Somali Coast	301
Wallis & Futuna Isls.	167

Cooperation

CD119

Cooperation between France and the French-speaking countries of Africa and Madagascar.

1964

Cameroun	409-410
Cent. Africa	39
Chad	103
Congo, P.R.	121
Dahomey	193
France	1111
Gabon	175
Ivory Coast	221
Madagascar	360
Mauritania	181
Niger	143
Senegal	236
Togo	495

ITU

Telegraph, Syncom Satellite and ITU Emblem CD120

Intl. Telecommunication Union, Cent.

1965, May 17

Comoro Isls.	C14
Fr. Polynesia	C33
Fr. So. & Antarctic Terr.	C8
New Caledonia	C40
New Hebrides	124-125
St. Pierre & Miquelon	C29
Somali Coast	C36
Wallis & Futuna Isls.	C20

French Satellite A-1

Diamant Rocket and Launching Installation – CD121

Launching of France's first satellite, Nov. 26, 1965.

1965-66

Comoro Isls.	C15-C16
France	1137-1138
Fr. Polynesia	C40-C41
Fr. So. & Antarctic Terr.	C9-C10
New Caledonia	C44-C45
St. Pierre & Miquelon	C30-C31
Somali Coast	C39-C40
Wallis & Futuna Isls.	C22-C23

French Satellite D-1

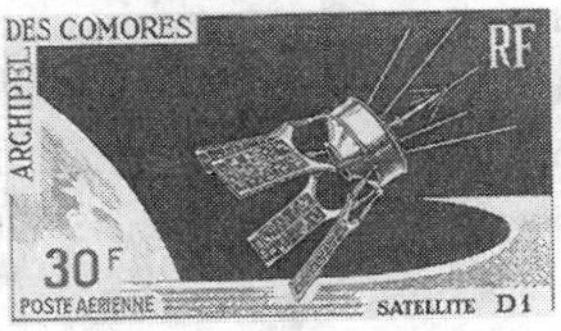

D-1 Satellite in Orbit – CD122

Launching of the D-1 satellite at Hammaguir, Algeria, Feb. 17, 1966.

1966

Comoro Isls.	C17
France	1148
Fr. Polynesia	C42
Fr. So. & Antarctic Terr.	C11
New Caledonia	C46
St. Pierre & Miquelon	C32
Somali Coast	C49
Wallis & Futuna Isls.	C24

Air Afrique, 1966

Planes and Air Afrique Emblem – CD123

Introduction of DC-8F planes by Air Afrique.

1966

Cameroun	C79
Cent. Africa	C35
Chad	C26
Congo, P.R.	C42
Dahomey	C42

Gabon	C47
Ivory Coast	C32
Mauritania	C57
Niger	C63
Senegal	C47
Togo	C54
Upper Volta	C31

African Postal Union, 1967

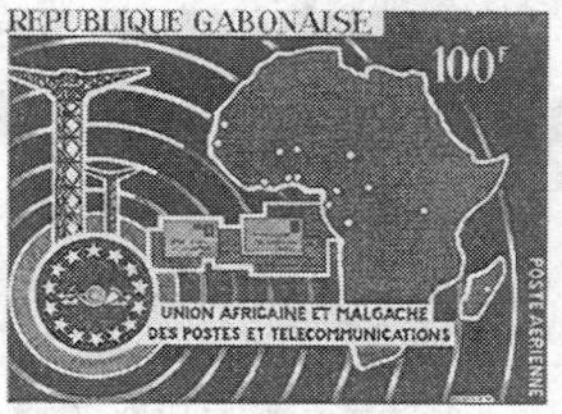

Telecommunications Symbols and Map of Africa – CD124

Fifth anniversary of the establishment of the African and Malagasy Union of Posts and Telecommunications, UAMPT.

1967

Cameroun	C90
Cent. Africa	C46
Chad	C37
Congo, P.R.	C57
Dahomey	C61
Gabon	C58
Ivory Coast	C34
Madagascar	C85
Mauritania	C65
Niger	C75
Rwanda	C1-C3
Senegal	C60
Togo	C81
Upper Volta	C50

Monetary Union

Gold Token of the Ashantis, 17-18th Centuries CD125

West African Monetary Union, 5th anniv.

1967, Nov. 4

Dahomey	244
Ivory Coast	259
Mauritania	238
Niger	204
Senegal	294
Togo	623
Upper Volta	181

WHO Anniversary

Sun, Flowers and WHO Emblem CD126

World Health Organization, 20th anniv.

1968, May 4

Afars & Issas	317
Comoro Isls.	73
Fr. Polynesia	241-242
Fr. So. & Antarctic Terr.	31
New Caledonia	367
St. Pierre & Miquelon	377
Wallis & Futuna Isls.	169

Human Rights Year

Human Rights Flame CD127

1968, Aug. 10

Afars & Issas	322-323
Comoro Isls.	76
Fr. Polynesia	243-244
Fr. So. & Antarctic Terr.	32
New Caledonia	369
St. Pierre & Miquelon	382
Wallis & Futuna Isls.	170

2nd PHILEXAFRIQUE

CD128

Opening of PHILEXAFRIQUE, Abidjan, Feb. 14. Each stamp shows a local scene and stamp.

1969, Feb. 14

Cameroun	C118
Cent. Africa	C65
Chad	C48
Congo, P.R.	C77
Dahomey	C94
Gabon	C82
Ivory Coast	C38-C40
Madagascar	C92
Mali	C65
Mauritania	C80
Niger	C104
Senegal	C68
Togo	C104
Upper Volta	C62

Concorde

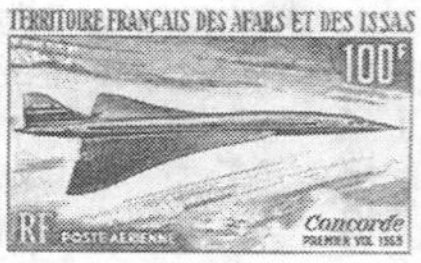

Concorde in Flight CD129

First flight of the prototpye Concorde super-sonic plane at Toulouse, Mar. 1, 1969.

1969

Afars & Issas	C56
Comoro Isls.	C29
France	C42
Fr. Polynesia	C50
Fr. So. & Antarctic Terr.	C18
New Caledonia	C63
St. Pierre & Miquelon	C40
Wallis & Futuna Isls.	C30

Development Bank

Bank Emblem CD130

African Development Bank, fifth anniv.

1969

Cameroun	499
Chad	217
Congo, P.R.	181-182
Ivory Coast	281
Mali	127-128
Mauritania	267
Niger	220
Senegal	317-318
Upper Volta	201

ILO

ILO Headquarters, Geneva, and Emblem – CD131

Intl. Labor Organization, 50th anniv.

1969-70

Afars & Issas	337
Comoro Isls.	83
Fr. Polynesia	251-252
Fr. So. & Antarctic Terr.	35
New Caledonia	379
St. Pierre & Miquelon	396
Wallis & Futuna Isls.	172

ASECNA

Map of Africa, Plane and Airport – CD132

10th anniversary of the Agency for the Security of Aerial Navigation in Africa and Madagascar (ASECNA, Agence pour la Securite de la Navigation Aerienne en Afrique et a Madagascar).

1969-70

Cameroun	500
Cent. Africa	119
Chad	222
Congo, P.R.	197
Dahomey	269
Gabon	260
Ivory Coast	287
Mali	130
Niger	221
Senegal	321
Upper Volta	204

U.P.U. Headquarters

CD133

New Universal Postal Union headquarters, Bern, Switzerland.

1970

Afars & Issas	342
Algeria	443
Cameroun	503-504
Cent. Africa	125
Chad	225
Comoro Isls.	84
Congo, P.R.	216
Fr. Polynesia	261-262
Fr. So. & Antarctic Terr.	36
Gabon	258
Ivory Coast	295
Madagascar	444
Mali	134-135
Mauritania	283
New Caledonia	382
Niger	231-232
St. Pierre & Miquelon	397-398
Senegal	328-329
Tunisia	535
Wallis & Futuna Isls.	173

De Gaulle

CD134

First anniversay of the death of Charles de Gaulle, (1890-1970), President of France.

1971-72

Afars & Issas	356-357
Comoro Isls.	104-105
France	1322-1325
Fr. Polynesia	270-271
Fr. So. & Antarctic Terr.	52-53
New Caledonia	393-394
Reunion	377, 380
St. Pierre & Miquelon	417-418
Wallis & Futuna Isls.	177-178

African Postal Union, 1971

UAMPT Building, Brazzaville, Congo – CD135

10th anniversary of the establishment of the African and Malagasy Posts and Telecommunications Union, UAMPT.

Each stamp has a different native design.

1971, Nov. 13

Cameroun	C177
Cent. Africa	C89
Chad	C94
Congo, P.R.	C136
Dahomey	C146
Gabon	C120
Ivory Coast	C47
Mauritania	C113
Niger	C164
Rwanda	C8
Senegal	C105
Togo	C166
Upper Volta	C97

West African Monetary Union

African Couple, City, Village and Commemorative Coin – CD136

West African Monetary Union, 10th anniv.

1972, Nov. 2

Dahomey	300
Ivory Coast	331
Mauritania	299
Niger	258
Senegal	374
Togo	825
Upper Volta	280

African Postal Union, 1973

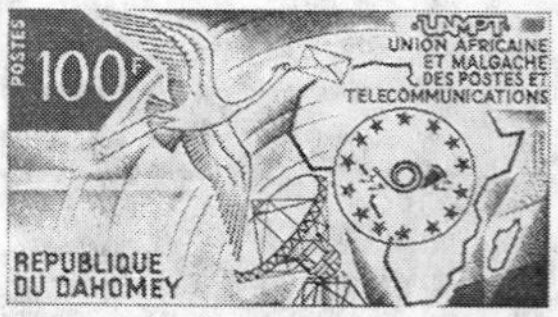

Telecommunications Symbols and Map of Africa – CD137

11th anniversary of the African and Malagasy Posts and Telecommunications Union (UAMPT).

1973, Sept. 12

Cameroun	574
Cent. Africa	194
Chad	294
Congo, P.R.	289
Dahomey	311
Gabon	320
Ivory Coast	361
Madagascar	500
Mauritania	304
Niger	287
Rwanda	540
Senegal	393
Togo	849
Upper Volta	297

Philexafrique II — Essen

CD138

CD139

Designs: Indigenous fauna, local and German stamps.

Types CD138-CD139 printed horizontally and vertically se-tenant in sheets of 10 (2x5). Label between horizontal pairs alternately commemoratives Philexafrique II, Libreville, Gabon, June 1978, and 2nd International Stamp Fair, Essen, Germany, Nov. 1-5.

1978-1979

Benin ... C285-C286
Central Africa ... C200-C201
Chad ... C238-C239
Congo Republic ... C245-C246
Djibouti ... C121-C122
Gabon ... C215-C216
Ivory Coast ... C64-C65
Mali ... C356-C357
Mauritania ... C185-C186
Niger ... C291-C292
Rwanda ... C12-C13
Senegal ... C146-C147
Togo ... C363-C364
Upper Volta ... C253-C254

BRITISH COMMONWEALTH OF NATIONS

The listings follow established trade practices when these issues are offered as units by dealers. The Peace issue, for example, includes only one stamp from the Indian state of Hyderabad. The U.P.U. issue includes the Egypt set. Pairs are included for those varieties issues with bilingual designs se-tenant.

Silver Jubilee

Windsor Castle and King George V
CD301

Reign of King George V, 25th anniv.

1935

Antigua ... 77-80
Ascension ... 33-36
Bahamas ... 92-95
Barbados ... 186-189
Basutoland ... 11-14
Bechuanaland Protectorate ... 117-120
Bermuda ... 100-103
British Guiana ... 223-226
British Honduras ... 108-111
Cayman Islands ... 81-84
Ceylon ... 260-263
Cyprus ... 136-139
Dominica ... 90-93
Falkland Islands ... 77-80
Fiji ... 110-113
Gambia ... 125-128
Gibraltar ... 100-103
Gilbert & Ellice Islands ... 33-36
Gold Coast ... 108-111
Grenada ... 124-127
Hong Kong ... 147-150
Jamaica ... 109-112
Kenya, Uganda, Tanganyika ... 42-45
Leeward Islands ... 96-99
Malta ... 184-187
Mauritius ... 204-207
Montserrat ... 85-88
Newfoundland ... 226-229
Nigeria ... 34-37
Northern Rhodesia ... 18-21
Nyasaland Protectorate ... 47-50
St. Helena ... 111-114
St. Kitts-Nevis ... 72-75
St. Lucia ... 91-94
St. Vincent ... 134-137
Seychelles ... 118-121
Sierra Leone ... 166-169
Solomon Islands ... 60-63
Somaliland Protectorate ... 77-80
Straits Settlements ... 213-216
Swaziland ... 20-23
Trinidad & Tobago ... 43-46
Turks & Caicos Islands ... 71-74
Virgin Islands ... 69-72

The following have different designs but are included in the omnibus set:

Great Britain ... 226-229
  Offices in Morocco ... 67-70, 226-229, 422-425, 508-510
Australia ... 152-154
Canada ... 211-216
Cook Islands ... 98-100
India ... 142-148
Nauru ... 31-34
New Guinea ... 46-47
New Zealand ... 199-201
Niue ... 67-69
Papua ... 114-117
Samoa ... 163-165
South Africa ... 68-71
Southern Rhodesia ... 33-36
South-West Africa ... 121-124
249 stamps

Coronation

Queen Elizabeth and King George VI
CD302

1937

Aden ... 13-15
Antigua ... 81-83
Ascension ... 37-39
Bahamas ... 97-99
Barbados ... 190-192
Basutoland ... 15-17
Bechuanaland Protectorate ... 121-123
Bermuda ... 115-117
British Guiana ... 227-229
British Honduras ... 112-114
Cayman Islands ... 97-99
Ceylon ... 275-277
Cyprus ... 140-142
Dominica ... 94-96
Falkland Islands ... 81-83
Fiji ... 114-116
Gambia ... 129-131
Gibraltar ... 104-106
Gilbert & Ellice Islands ... 37-39
Gold Coast ... 112-114
Grenada ... 128-130
Hong Kong ... 151-153
Jamaica ... 113-115
Kenya, Uganda, Tanganyika ... 60-62
Leeward Islands ... 100-102
Malta ... 188-190
Mauritius ... 208-210
Montserrat ... 89-91
Newfoundland ... 230-232
Nigeria ... 50-52
Northern Rhodesia ... 22-24
Nyasaland Protectorate ... 51-53
St. Helena ... 115-117
St. Kitts-Nevis ... 76-78
St. Lucia ... 107-109
St. Vincent ... 138-140
Seychelles ... 122-124
Sierra Leone ... 170-172
Solomon Islands ... 64-66
Somaliland Protectorate ... 81-83
Straits Settlements ... 235-237
Swaziland ... 24-26
Trinidad & Tobago ... 47-49
Turks & Caicos Islands ... 75-77
Virgin Islands ... 73-75

The following have different designs but are included in the omnibus set:

Great Britain ... 234
  Offices in Morocco ... 82, 439, 514
Canada ... 237
Cook Islands ... 109-111
Nauru ... 35-38
Newfoundland ... 233-243
New Guinea ... 48-51
New Zealand ... 223-225
Niue ... 70-72
Papua ... 118-121
South Africa ... 74-78
Southern Rhodesia ... 38-41
South-West Africa ... 125-132
202 stamps

Peace

King George VI and
Parliament Buildings, London – CD303

Return to peace at the close of World War II.

1945-46

Aden ... 28-29
Antigua ... 96-97
Ascension ... 50-51
Bahamas ... 130-131
Barbados ... 207-208
Bermuda ... 131-132
British Guiana ... 242-243
British Honduras ... 127-128
Cayman Islands ... 112-113
Ceylon ... 293-294
Cyprus ... 156-157
Dominica ... 112-113
Falkland Islands ... 97-98
Falkland Islands Dep. ... 1L9-1L10
Fiji ... 137-138
Gambia ... 144-145
Gibraltar ... 119-120
Gilbert & Ellice Islands ... 52-53
Gold Coast ... 128-129
Grenada ... 143-144
Jamaica ... 136-137
Kenya, Uganda, Tanganyika ... 90-91
Leeward Islands ... 116-117
Malta ... 206-207
Mauritius ... 223-224
Montserrat ... 104-105
Nigeria ... 71-72
Northern Rhodesia ... 46-47
Nyasaland Protectorate ... 82-83
Pitcairn Island ... 9-10
St. Helena ... 128-129
St. Kitts-Nevis ... 91-92
St. Lucia ... 127-128
St. Vincent ... 152-153
Seychelles ... 149-150
Sierra Leone ... 186-187
Solomon Islands ... 80-81
Somaliland Protectorate ... 108-109
Trinidad & Tobago ... 62-63
Turks & Caicos Islands ... 90-91
Virgin Islands ... 88-89

The following have different designs but are included in the omnibus set:

Great Britain ... 264-265
  Offices in Morocco ... 523-524
Aden
  Kathiri State of Seiyun ... 12-13
  Qu'aiti State of Shihr and
    Mukalla ... 12-13
Australia ... 200-202
Basutoland ... 29-31
Bechuanaland Protectorate ... 137-139
Burma ... 66-69
Cook Islands ... 127-130
Hong Kong ... 174-175
India ... 195-198
  Hyderabad ... 51
New Zealand ... 247-257
Niue ... 90-93
Pakistan-Bahawalpur ... O16
Samoa ... 191-194
South Africa ... 100-102
Southern Rhodesia ... 67-70
South-West Africa ... 153-155
Swaziland ... 38-40
Zanzibar ... 222-223
164 stamps

Silver Wedding

King George VI and Queen Elizabeth
CD304 CD305

1948-49

Aden ... 30-31
  Kathiri State of Seiyun ... 14-15
  Qu'aiti State of Shihr and
    Mukalla ... 14-15
Antigua ... 98-99
Ascension ... 52-53
Bahamas ... 148-149
Barbados ... 210-211
Basutoland ... 39-40
Bechuanaland Protectorate ... 147-148
Bermuda ... 133-134
British Guiana ... 244-245
British Honduras ... 129-130
Cayman Islands ... 116-117
Cyprus ... 158-159
Dominica ... 114-115
Falkland Islands ... 99-100
Falkland Islands Dep. ... 1L11-1L12
Fiji ... 139-140
Gambia ... 146-147
Gibraltar ... 121-122
Gilbert & Ellice Islands ... 54-55
Gold Coast ... 142-143
Grenada ... 145-146
Hong Kong ... 178-179
Jamaica ... 138-139
Kenya, Uganda, Tanganyika ... 92-93
Leeward Islands ... 118-119
Malaya
  Johore ... 128-129
  Kedah ... 55-56
  Kelantan ... 44-45
  Malacca ... 1-2
  Negri Sembilan ... 36-37
  Pahang ... 44-45
  Penang ... 1-2
  Perak ... 99-100
  Perlis ... 1-2
  Selangor ... 74-75
  Trengganu ... 47-48
Malta ... 223-224
Mauritius ... 229-230
Montserrat ... 106-107
Nigeria ... 73-74
North Borneo ... 238-239
Northern Rhodesia ... 48-49
Nyasaland Protectorate ... 85-86
Pitcairn Island ... 11-12
St. Helena ... 130-131
St. Kitts-Nevis ... 93-94
St. Lucia ... 129-130
St. Vincent ... 154-155
Sarawak ... 174-175
Seychelles ... 151-152
Sierra Leone ... 188-189
Singapore ... 21-22
Solomon Islands ... 82-83
Somaliland Protectorate ... 110-111
Swaziland ... 48-49
Trinidad & Tobago ... 64-65
Turks & Caicos Islands ... 92-93
Virgin Islands ... 90-91
Zanzibar ... 224-225

The following have different designs but are included in the omnibus set:

Great Britain ... 267-268
  Offices in Morocco ... 93-94, 525-526
Bahrain ... 62-63
Kuwait ... 82-83
Oman ... 25-26
South Africa ... 106
South-West Africa ... 159
138 stamps

U.P.U.

Mercury and Symbols of
Communications – CD306

Plane, Ship and Hemispheres
CD307

Mercury Scattering Letters over Globe
CD308

U.P.U. Monument, Bern
CD309

Universal Postal Union, 75th anniversary.

1949

Aden 32-35
  Kathiri State of Seiyun 16-19
  Qu'aiti State of Shihr and Mukalla 16-19
Antigua 100-103
Ascension 57-60
Bahamas 150-153
Barbados 212-215
Basutoland 41-44
Bechuanaland Protectorate 149-152
Bermuda 138-141
British Guiana 246-249
British Honduras 137-140
Brunei 79-82
Cayman Islands 118-121
Cyprus 160-163
Dominica 116-119
Falkland Islands 103-106
Falkland Islands Dep. 1L14-1L17
Fiji 141-144
Gambia 148-151
Gibraltar 123-126
Gilbert & Ellice Islands 56-59
Gold Coast 144-147
Grenada 147-150
Hong Kong 180-183
Jamaica 142-145
Kenya, Uganda, Tanganyika 94-97
Leeward Islands 126-129
Malaya
  Johore 151-154
  Kedah 57-60
  Kelantan 46-49
  Malacca 18-21
  Negri Sembilan 59-62
  Pahang 46-49
  Penang 23-26
  Perak 101-104
  Perlis 3-6
  Selangor 76-79
  Trengganu 49-52
Malta 225-228
Mauritius 231-234
Montserrat 108-111
New Hebrides, British 62-65
New Hebrides, French 79-82
Nigeria 75-78
North Borneo 240-243
Northern Rhodesia 50-53
Nyasaland Protectorate 87-90
Pitcairn Islands 13-16
St. Helena 132-135
St. Kitts-Nevis 95-98
St. Lucia 131-134
St. Vincent 170-173
Sarawak 176-179
Seychelles 153-156
Sierra Leone 190-193
Singapore 23-26
Solomon Islands 84-87
Somaliland Protectorate 112-115
Southern Rhodesia 71-72
Swaziland 50-53
Tonga 87-90
Trinidad & Tobago 66-69
Turks & Caicos Islands 101-104
Virgin Islands 92-95
Zanzibar 226-229

The following have different designs but are included in the omnibus set:

Great Britain 276-279
  Offices in Morocco 546-549
Australia 223
Bahrain 68-71
Burma 116-121
Ceylon 304-306
Egypt 281-283
India 223-226
Kuwait 89-92
Oman 31-34
Pakistan-Bahawalpur 26-29, O25-O28
South Africa 109-111
South-West Africa 160-162
  319 stamps

University

Arms of University College
CD310

Alice, Princess of Athlone
CD311

1948 opening of University College of the West Indies at Jamaica.

1951

Antigua 104-105
Barbados 228-229
British Guiana 250-251
British Honduras 141-142
Dominica 120-121
Grenada 164-165
Jamaica 146-147
Leeward Islands 130-131
Montserrat 112-113
St. Kitts-Nevis 105-106
St. Lucia 149-150
St. Vincent 174-175
Trinidad & Tobago 70-71
Virgin Islands 96-97
  28 stamps

Coronation

Queen Elizabeth II
CD312

1953

Aden 47
  Kathiri State of Seiyun 28
  Qu'aiti State of Shihr and Mukalla 28
Antigua 106
Ascension 61
Bahamas 157
Barbados 234
Basutoland 45
Bechuanaland Protectorate 153
Bermuda 142
British Guiana 252
British Honduras 143
Cayman Islands 150
Cyprus 167
Dominica 141
Falkland Islands 121
Falkland Islands Dependencies 1L18
Fiji 145
Gambia 152
Gibraltar 131
Gilbert & Ellice Islands 60
Gold Coast 160
Grenada 170
Hong Kong 184
Jamaica 153
Kenya, Uganda, Tanganyika 101
Leeward Islands 132
Malaya
  Johore 155
  Kedah 82
  Kelantan 71
  Malacca 27
  Negri Sembilan 63
  Pahang 71
  Penang 27
  Perak 126
  Perlis 28
  Selangor 101
  Trengganu 74
Malta 241
Mauritius 250
Montserrat 127
New Hebrides, British 77
Nigeria 79
North Borneo 260
Northern Rhodesia 60
Nyasaland Protectorate 96
Pitcairn 19
St. Helena 139
St. Kitts-Nevis 119
St. Lucia 156
St. Vincent 185
Sarawak 196
Seychelles 172
Sierra Leone 194
Singapore 27
Solomon Islands 88
Somaliland Protectorate 127
Swaziland 54
Trinidad & Tobago 84
Tristan da Cunha 13
Turks & Caicos Islands 118
Virgin Islands 114

The following have different designs but are included in the omnibus set:

Great Britain 313-316
  Offices in Morocco 579-582
Australia 259-261
Bahrain 92-95
Canada 330
Ceylon 317
Cook Islands 145-146
Kuwait 113-116
New Zealand 280-284
Niue 104-105
Oman 52-55
Samoa 214-215
South Africa 192
Southern Rhodesia 80
South-West Africa 244-248
Tokelau Islands 4
  106 stamps

Royal Visit 1953

Separate designs for each country for the visit of Queen Elizabeth II and the Duke of Edinburgh.

1953

Aden 62
Australia 267-269
Bermuda 163
Ceylon 318
Fiji 146
Gibraltar 146
Jamaica 154
Kenya, Uganda, Tanganyika 102
Malta 242
New Zealand 286-287
  13 stamps

West Indies Federation

Map of the Caribbean
CD313

Federation of the West Indies, April 22, 1958.

1958

Antigua 122-124
Barbados 248-250
Dominica 161-163
Grenada 184-186
Jamaica 175-177
Montserrat 143-145
St. Kitts-Nevis 136-138
St. Lucia 170-172
St. Vincent 198-200
Trinidad & Tobago 86-88
  30 stamps

Freedom from Hunger

Protein Food
CD314

U.N. Food and Agricultural Organization's "Freedom from Hunger" campaign.

1963

Aden 65
Antigua 133
Ascension 89
Bahamas 180
Basutoland 83
Bechuanaland Protectorate 194
Bermuda 192
British Guiana 271
British Honduras 179
Brunei 100
Cayman Islands 168
Dominica 181
Falkland Islands 146
Fiji 198
Gambia 172
Gibraltar 161
Gilbert & Ellice Islands 76
Grenada 190
Hong Kong 218
Malta 291
Mauritius 270
Montserrat 150
New Hebrides, British 93
North Borneo 296
Pitcairn 35
St. Helena 173
St. Lucia 179
St. Vincent 201
Sarawak 212
Seychelles 213
Solomon Islands 109
Swaziland 108
Tonga 127
Tristan da Cunha 68
Turks & Caicos Islands 138
Virgin Islands 140
Zanzibar 280
  37 stamps

Red Cross Centenary

Red Cross and Elizabeth II – CD315

1963

Antigua 134-135
Ascension 90-91
Bahamas 183-184
Basutoland 84-85
Bechuanaland Protectorate 195-196
Bermuda 193-194
British Guiana 272-273
British Honduras 180-181
Cayman Islands 169-170
Dominica 182-183
Falkland Islands 147-148
Fiji 203-204
Gambia 173-174
Gibraltar 162-163
Gilbert & Ellice Islands 77-78
Grenada 191-192
Hong Kong 219-220
Jamaica 203-204
Malta 292-293
Mauritius 271-272
Montserrat 151-152
New Hebrides, British 94-95
Pitcairn Islands 36-37
St. Helena 174-175
St. Kitts-Nevis 143-144
St. Lucia 180-181
St. Vincent 202-203
Seychelles 214-215
Solomon Islands 110-111
South Arabia 1-2
Swaziland 109-110
Tonga 134-135
Tristan da Cunha 69-70
Turks & Caicos Islands 139-140
Virgin Islands 141-142
  70 stamps

Shakespeare

Shakespeare Memorial Theatre, Stratford-on-Avon – CD316

400th anniversary of the birth of William Shakespeare.

1964

Antigua 151
Bahamas 201
Bechuanaland Protectorate 197
Cayman Islands 171
Dominica 184
Falkland Islands 149
Gambia 192
Gibraltar 164
Montserrat 153
St. Lucia 196
Turks & Caicos Islands 141
Virgin Islands 143
  12 stamps

ITU

ITU Emblem CD317

Intl. Telecommunication Union, cent.

1965

Antigua	153-154
Ascension	92-93
Bahamas	219-220
Barbados	265-266
Basutoland	101-102
Bechuanaland Protectorate	202-203
Bermuda	196-197
British Guiana	293-294
British Honduras	187-188
Brunei	116-117
Cayman Islands	172-173
Dominica	185-186
Falkland Islands	154-155
Fiji	211-212
Gibraltar	167-168
Gilbert & Ellice Islands	87-88
Grenada	205-206
Hong Kong	221-222
Mauritius	291-292
Montserrat	157-158
New Hebrides, British	108-109
Pitcairn Islands	52-53
St. Helena	180-181
St. Kitts-Nevis	163-164
St. Lucia	197-198
St. Vincent	224-225
Seychelles	218-219
Solomon Islands	126-127
Swaziland	115-116
Tristan da Cunha	85-86
Turks & Caicos Islands	142-143
Virgin Islands	159-160

64 stamps

Intl. Cooperation Year

ICY Emblem – CD318

1965

Antigua	155-156
Ascension	94-95
Bahamas	222-223
Basutoland	103-104
Bechuanaland Protectorate	204-205
Bermuda	199-200
British Guiana	295-296
British Honduras	189-190
Brunei	118-119
Cayman Islands	174-175
Dominica	187-188
Falkland Islands	156-157
Fiji	213-214
Gibraltar	169-170
Gilbert & Ellice Islands	104-105
Grenada	207-208
Hong Kong	223-224
Mauritius	293-294
Montserrat	176-177
New Hebrides, British	110-111
New Hebrides, French	126-127
Pitcairn Islands	54-55
St. Helena	182-183
St. Kitts-Nevis	165-166
St. Lucia	199-200
Seychelles	220-221
Solomon Islands	143-144
South Arabia	17-18
Swaziland	117-118
Tristan da Cunha	87-88
Turks & Caicos Islands	144-145
Virgin Islands	161-162

64 stamps

Churchill Memorial

Winston Churchill and St. Paul's, London, During Air Attack – CD319

1966

Antigua	157-160
Ascension	96-99
Bahamas	224-227
Barbados	281-284
Basutoland	105-108
Bechuanaland Protectorate	206-209
Bermuda	201-204
British Antarctic Territory	16-19
British Honduras	191-194
Brunei	120-123
Cayman Islands	176-179
Dominica	189-192
Falkland Islands	158-161
Fiji	215-218
Gibraltar	171-174
Gilbert & Ellice Islands	106-109
Grenada	209-212
Hong Kong	225-228
Mauritius	295-298
Montserrat	178-181
New Hebrides, British	112-115
New Hebrides, French	128-131
Pitcairn Islands	56-59
St. Helena	184-187
St. Kitts-Nevis	167-170
St. Lucia	201-204
St. Vincent	241-244
Seychelles	222-225
Solomon Islands	145-148
South Arabia	19-22
Swaziland	119-122
Tristan da Cunha	89-92
Turks & Caicos Islands	146-149
Virgin Islands	163-166

136 stamps

Royal Visit, 1966

Queen Elizabeth II and Prince Philip CD320

Caribbean visit, Feb. 4 - Mar. 6, 1966.

1966

Antigua	161-162
Bahamas	228-229
Barbados	285-286
British Guiana	299-300
Cayman Islands	180-181
Dominica	193-194
Grenada	213-214
Montserrat	182-183
St. Kitts-Nevis	171-172
St. Lucia	205-206
St. Vincent	245-246
Turks & Caicos Islands	150-151
Virgin Islands	167-168

26 stamps

World Cup Soccer

Soccer Player and Jules Rimet Cup CD321

World Cup Soccer Championship, Wembley, England, July 11-30.

1966

Antigua	163-164
Ascension	100-101
Bahamas	245-246
Bermuda	205-206
Brunei	124-125
Cayman Islands	182-183
Dominica	195-196
Fiji	219-220
Gibraltar	175-176
Gilbert & Ellice Islands	125-126
Grenada	230-231
New Hebrides, British	116-117
New Hebrides, French	132-133
Pitcairn Islands	60-61
St. Helena	188-189
St. Kitts-Nevis	173-174
St. Lucia	207-208
Seychelles	226-227
Solomon Islands	167-168
South Arabia	23-24
Tristan da Cunha	93-94

42 stamps

WHO Headquarters

World Health Organization Headquarters, Geneva – CD322

1966

Antigua	165-166
Ascension	102-103
Bahamas	247-248
Brunei	126-127
Cayman Islands	184-185
Dominica	197-198
Fiji	224-225
Gibraltar	180-181
Gilbert & Ellice Islands	127-128
Grenada	232-233
Hong Kong	229-230
Montserrat	184-185
New Hebrides, British	118-119
New Hebrides, French	134-135
Pitcairn Islands	62-63
St. Helena	190-191
St. Kitts-Nevis	177-178
St. Lucia	209-210
St. Vincent	247-248
Seychelles	228-229
Solomon Islands	169-170
South Arabia	25-26
Tristan da Cunha	99-100

46 stamps

UNESCO Anniversary

"Education" – CD323

"Science" (Wheat ears & flask enclosing globe). "Culture" (lyre & columns).
20th anniversary of the UNESCO.

1966-67

Antigua	183-185
Ascension	108-110
Bahamas	249-251
Barbados	287-289
Bermuda	207-209
Brunei	128-130
Cayman Islands	186-188
Dominica	199-201
Gibraltar	183-185
Gilbert & Ellice Islands	129-131
Grenada	234-236
Hong Kong	231-233
Mauritius	299-301
Montserrat	186-188
New Hebrides, British	120-122
New Hebrides, French	136-138
Pitcairn Islands	64-66
St. Helena	192-194
St. Kitts-Nevis	179-181
St. Lucia	211-213
St. Vincent	249-251
Seychelles	230-232
Solomon Islands	171-173
South Arabia	27-29
Swaziland	123-125
Tristan da Cunha	101-103
Turks & Caicos Islands	155-157
Virgin Islands	176-178

84 stamps

Silver Wedding, 1972

Queen Elizabeth II and Prince Philip CD324

Designs: borders differ for each country.

1972

Anguilla	161-162
Antigua	295-296
Ascension	164-165
Bahamas	344-345
Bermuda	296-297
British Antarctic Territory	43-44
British Honduras	306-307
British Indian Ocean Territory	48-49
Brunei	186-187
Cayman Islands	304-305
Dominica	352-353
Falkland Islands	223-224
Fiji	328-329
Gibraltar	292-293
Gilbert & Ellice Islands	206-207
Grenada	466-467
Hong Kong	271-272
Montserrat	286-287
New Hebrides, British	169-170
Pitcairn Islands	127-128
St. Helena	271-272
St. Kitts-Nevis	257-258
St. Lucia	328-329
St.Vincent	344-345
Seychelles	309-310
Solomon Islands	248-249
South Georgia	35-36
Tristan da Cunha	178-179
Turks & Caicos Islands	257-258
Virgin Islands	241-242

60 stamps

Princess Anne's Wedding

Princess Anne and Mark Phillips CD325

Wedding of Princess Anne and Mark Phillips, Nov. 14, 1973.

1973

Anguilla	179-180
Ascension	177-178
Belize	325-326
Bermuda	302-303
British Antarctic Territory	60-61
Cayman Islands	320-321
Falkland Islands	225-226
Gibraltar	305-306
Gilbert & Ellice Islands	216-217
Hong Kong	289-290
Montserrat	300-301
Pitcairn Island	135-136
St. Helena	277-278
St. Kitts-Nevis	274-275
St. Lucia	349-350
St. Vincent	358-359
St. Vincent Grenadines	1-2
Seychelles	311-312
Solomon Islands	259-260
South Georgia	37-38
Tristan da Cunha	189-190
Turks & Caicos Islands	286-287
Virgin Islands	260-261

44 stamps

Elizabeth II Coronation Anniv.

CD326

CD327

CD328

Designs: Royal and local beasts in heraldic form and simulated stonework. Portrait of Elizabeth II by Peter Grugeon.
25th anniversary of coronation of Queen Elizabeth II.

1978

Ascension	229
Barbados	474
Belize	397
British Antarctic Territory	71
Cayman Islands	404
Christmas Island	87
Falkland Islands	275
Fiji	384
Gambia	380
Gilbert Islands	312
Mauritius	464
New Hebrides, British	258
St. Helena	317
St. Kitts-Nevis	354
Samoa	472
Solomon Islands	368
South Georgia	51
Swaziland	302
Tristan da Cunha	238
Virgin Islands	337

20 sheets

Queen Mother Elizabeth's 80th Birthday

CD330

Designs: Photographs of Queen Mother Elizabeth. Falkland Islands issued in sheets of 50; others in sheets of 9.

1980

Ascension	261
Bermuda	401
Cayman Islands	443
Falkland Islands	305
Gambia	412
Gibraltar	393
Hong Kong	364
Pitcairn Islands	193
St. Helena	341
Samoa	532
Solomon Islands	426
Tristan da Cunha	277

12 stamps

Royal Wedding, 1981

Prince Charles and Lady Diana
CD331

Wedding of Charles, Prince of Wales, and Lady Diana Spencer, St. Paul's Cathedral, London, July 29, 1981.

1981

Antigua	623-625
Ascension	294-296
Barbados	547-549
Barbuda	497-499
Bermuda	412-414
Brunei	268-270
Cayman Islands	471-473
Dominica	701-703
Falkland Islands	324-326
Falkland Islands Dep.	1L59-1L61
Fiji	442-444
Gambia	426-428
Ghana	759-761
Grenada	1051-1053
Grenada Grenadines	440-443
Hong Kong	373-375
Jamaica	500-503
Lesotho	335-337
Maldive Islands	906-908
Mauritius	520-522
Norfolk Island	280-282
Pitcairn Islands	206-208
St. Helena	353-355
St. Lucia	543-545
Samoa	558-560
Sierra Leone	509-517
Solomon Islands	450-452
Swaziland	382-384
Tristan da Cunha	294-296
Turks & Caicos Islands	486-488
Caicos Island	8-10
Uganda	314-316
Vanuatu	308-310
Virgin Islands	406-408

Princess Diana

CD332 CD333

Designs: Photographs and portrait of Princess Diana, wedding or honeymoon photographs, royal residences, arms of issuing country. Portrait photograph by Clive Friend. Souvenir sheet margins show family tree, various people related to the princess. 21st birthday of Princess Diana of Wales, July 1.

1982

Antigua	663-666
Ascension	313-316
Bahamas	510-513
Barbados	585-588
Barbuda	544-546
British Antarctic Territory	92-95
Cayman Islands	486-489
Dominica	773-776
Falkland Islands	348-351
Falkland Islands Dep.	1L72-1L75
Fiji	470-473
Gambia	447-450
Grenada	1101A-1105
Grenada Grenadines	485-491
Lesotho	372-375
Maldive Islands	952-955
Mauritius	548-551
Pitcairn Islands	213-216
St. Helena	372-375
St. Lucia	591-594
Sierra Leone	531-534
Solomon Islands	471-474
Swaziland	406-409
Tristan da Cunha	310-313
Turks and Caicos Islands	530A-534
Virgin Islands	430-433

250th anniv. of first edition of Lloyd's List (shipping news publication) & of Lloyd's marine insurance.

CD335

Designs: First page of early edition of the list; historical ships, modern transportation or harbor scenes.

1984

Ascension	351-354
Bahamas	555-558
Barbados	627-630
Cayes of Belize	10-13
Cayman Islands	522-525
Falkland Islands	404-407
Fiji	509-512
Gambia	519-522
Mauritius	587-590
Nauru	280-283
St. Helena	412-415
Samoa	624-627
Seychelles	538-541
Solomon Islands	521-524
Vanuatu	368-371
Virgin Islands	466-469

Queen Mother 85th Birthday

CD336

Designs: Photographs tracing the life of the Queen Mother, Elizabeth. The high value in each set pictures the same photograph taken of the Queen Mother holding the infant Prince Henry.

1985

Ascension	372-376
Bahamas	580-584
Barbados	660-664
Bermuda	469-473
Falkland Islands	420-424
Falkland Islands Dep.	1L92-1L96
Fiji	531-535
Hong Kong	447-450
Jamaica	599-603
Mauritius	604-608
Norfolk Island	364-368
Pitcairn Islands	253-257
St. Helena	428-432
Samoa	649-653
Seychelles	567-571
Solomon Islands	543-547
Swaziland	476-480
Tristan da Cunha	372-376
Vanuatu	392-396
Zil Elwannyen Sesel	101-105

Queen Elizabeth II, 60th Birthday

CD337

1986, April 21

Ascension	389-393
Bahamas	592-596
Barbados	675-679
Bermuda	499-503
Cayman Islands	555-559
Falkland Islands	441-445
Fiji	544-548
Hong Kong	465-469
Jamaica	620-624
Kiribati	470-474
Mauritius	629-633
Papua New Guinea	640-644
Pitcairn Islands	270-274
St. Helena	451-455
Samoa	670-674
Seychelles	592-596
Solomon Islands	562-566
South Georgia	101-105
Swaziland	490-494
Tristan da Cunha	388-392
Vanuatu	414-418
Zambia	343-347
Zil Elwannyen Sesel	114-118

Royal Wedding

Marriage of Prince Andrew and Sarah Ferguson
CD338

1986, July 23

Ascension	399-400
Bahamas	602-603
Barbados	687-688
Cayman Islands	560-561
Jamaica	629-630
Pitcairn Islands	275-276
St. Helena	460-461
St. Kitts	181-182
Seychelles	602-603
Solomon Islands	567-568
Tristan da Cunha	397-398
Zambia	348-349
Zil Elwannyen Sesel	119-120

Queen Elizabeth II, 60th Birthday

Queen Elizabeth II Inspecting Guard, 1946
CD339

Designs: Photographs tracing the life of Queen Elizabeth II.

1986

Anguilla	674-677
Antigua	925-928
Barbuda	783-786
Dominica	950-953
Gambia	611-614
Grenada	1371-1374
Grenada Grenadines	749-752
Lesotho	531-534
Maldive Islands	1172-1175
Sierra Leone	760-763
Uganda	495-498

Royal Wedding, 1986

CD340

Designs: Photographs of Prince Andrew and Sarah Ferguson during courtship, engagement and marriage.

1986

Antigua	939-942
Barbuda	809-812
Dominica	970-973
Gambia	635-638
Grenada	1385-1388
Grenada Grenadines	758-761
Lesotho	545-548
Maldive Islands	1181-1184
Sierra Leone	769-772
Uganda	510-513

Lloyds of London, 300th Anniv.

CD341

Designs: 17th century aspects of Lloyds, representations of each country's individual connections with Lloyds and publicized disasters insured by the organization.

1986

Ascension	454-457
Bahamas	655-658
Barbados	731-734
Bermuda	541-544
Falkland Islands	481-484
Liberia	1101-1104
Malawi	534-537
Nevis	571-574
St. Helena	501-504
St. Lucia	923-926
Seychelles	649-652
Solomon Islands	627-630
South Georgia	131-134
Trinidad & Tobago	484-487
Tristan da Cunha	439-442
Vanuatu	485-488
Zil Elwannyen Sesel	146-149

Moon Landing, 20th Anniv.

CD342

Designs: Equipment, crew photographs, spacecraft, official emblems and report profiles created for the Apollo Missions. Two stamps in each set are square in format rather than like the stamp shown; see individual country listings for more information.

1989

Ascension Is.	468-472
Bahamas	674-678
Belize	916-920
Kiribati	517-521
Liberia	1125-1129
Nevis	586-590
St. Kitts	248-252
Samoa	760-764
Seychelles	676-680
Solomon Islands	643-647
Vanuatu	507-511
Zil Elwannyen Sesel	154-158

Queen Mother, 90th Birthday

CD343 CD344

Designs: Portraits of Queen Elizabeth, the Queen Mother. See individual country listings for more information.

1990

Ascension Is.	491-492
Bahamas	698-699
Barbados	782-783
British Antarctic Territory	170-171
British Indian Ocean Territory	106-107
Cayman Islands	622-623
Falkland Islands	524-525
Kenya	527-528
Kiribati	555-556
Liberia	1145-1146
Pitcairn Islands	336-337
St. Helena	532-533
St. Lucia	969-970
Seychelles	710-711
Solomon Islands	671-672
South Georgia	143-144
Swaziland	565-566
Tristan da Cunha	480-481
Zil Elwannyen Sesel	171-172

Queen Elizabeth II, 65th Birthday, and Prince Philip, 70th Birthday

CD345 CD346

Designs: Portraits of Queen Elizabeth II and Prince Philip differ for each country. Printed in sheets of 10 + 5 labels (3 different) between. Stamps alternate, producing 5 different triptychs.

1991

Ascension Is.	505-506
Bahamas	730-731
Belize	969-970
Bermuda	617-618
Kiribati	571-572
Mauritius	733-734
Pitcairn Islands	348-349
St. Helena	554-555
St. Kitts	318-319
Samoa	790-791
Seychelles	723-724
Solomon Islands	688-689
South Georgia	149-150
Swaziland	586-587
Vanuatu	540-541
Zil Elwannyen Sesel	177-178

Royal Family Birthday, Anniversary

CD347

Queen Elizabeth II, 65th birthday, Charles and Diana, 10th wedding anniversary: Various photographs of Queen Elizabeth II, Prince Philip, Prince Charles, Princess Diana and their sons William and Henry.

1991

Antigua	1446-1455
Barbuda	1229-1238
Dominica	1328-1337
Gambia	1080-1089
Grenada	2006-2015
Grenada Grenadines	1331-1340
Guyana	2440-2451
Lesotho	871-875
Maldive Islands	1533-1542
Nevis	666-675
St. Vincent	1485-1494
St. Vincent Grenadines	769-778
Sierra Leone	1387-1396
Turks & Caicos Islands	913-922
Uganda	918-927

Queen Elizabeth II's Accession to the Throne, 40th Anniv.

CD348

CD349

Various photographs of Queen Elizabeth II with local Scenes.

1992 - CD348

Antigua	1513-1518
Barbuda	1306-1309
Dominica	1414-1419
Gambia	1172-1177
Grenada	2047-2052
Grenada Grenadines	1368-1373
Lesotho	881-885
Maldive Islands	1637-1642
Nevis	702-707
St. Vincent	1582-1587
St. Vincent Grenadines	829-834
Sierra Leone	1482-1487
Turks and Caicos Islands	978-987
Uganda	990-995
Virgin Islands	742-746

1992 - CD349

Ascension Islands	531-535
Bahamas	744-748
Bermuda	623-627
British Indian Ocean Territory	119-123
Cayman Islands	648-652
Falkland Islands	549-553
Gibraltar	605-609
Hong Kong	619-623
Kenya	563-567
Kiribati	582-586
Pitcairn Islands	362-366
St. Helena	570-574
St. Kitts	332-336
Samoa	805-809
Seychelles	734-738
Soloman Islands	708-712
South Georgia	157-161
Tristan da Cunha	508-512
Vanuatu	555-559
Zambia	561-565
Zil Elwannyen Sesel	183-187

Royal Air Force, 75th Anniversary

CD350

1993

Ascension	557-561
Bahamas	771-775
Barbados	842-846
Belize	1003-1008
Bermuda	648-651
British Indian Ocean Territory	136-140
Falkland Is.	573-577
Fiji	687-691
Montserrat	830-834
St. Kitts	351-355
Samoa	957-961

Royal Air Force, 80th Anniv.

Design CD350 Re-inscribed

1998

Ascension	697-701
Bahamas	907-911
British Indian Ocean Terr	198-202
Cayman Islands	754-758
Fiji	814-818
Gibraltar	755-759
Samoa	957-961
Turks & Caicos Islands	1258-1265
Tuvalu	763-767
Virgin Islands	879-883

End of World War II, 50th Anniv.

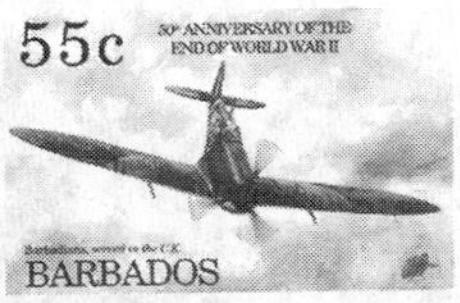

CD351

CD352

1995

Ascension	613-617
Bahamas	824-828
Barbados	891-895
Belize	1047-1050
British Indian Ocean Territory	163-167
Cayman Islands	704-708
Falkland Islands	634-638
Fiji	720-724
Kiribati	662-668
Liberia	1175-1179
Mauritius	803-805
St. Helena	646-654
St. Kitts	389-393
St. Lucia	1018-1022
Samoa	890-894
Solomon Islands	799-803
South Georgia & S. Sandwich Is.	198-200
Tristan da Cunha	562-566

UN, 50th Anniv.

CD353

1995

Bahamas	839-842
Barbados	901-904
Belize	1055-1058
Jamaica	847-851
Liberia	1187-1190
Mauritius	813-816
Pitcairn Islands	436-439
St. Kitts	398-401
St. Lucia	1023-1026
Samoa	900-903
Tristan da Cunha	568-571
Virgin Islands	807-810

Queen Elizabeth, 70th Birthday

CD354

1996

Ascension	632-635
British Antarctic Territory	240-243
British Indian Ocean Territory	176-180
Falkland Islands	653-657
Pitcairn Islands	446-449
St. Helena	672-676
Samoa	912-916
Tokelau	223-227
Tristan da Cunha	576-579
Virgin Islands	824-828

Diana, Princess of Wales (1961-97)

CD355

1998

Ascension	696
Bahamas	901A-902
Barbados	950
Belize	1091
Bermuda	753
Botswana	659-663
British Antarctic Territory	258
British Indian Ocean Terr.	197
Cayman Islands	752A-753
Falkland Islands	694
Fiji	819-820
Gibraltar	754
Kiribati	719A-720
Namibia	909
Niue	706
Norfolk Island	644-645
Papua New Guinea	937
Pitcairn Islands	487
St. Helena	711
St. Kitts	437A-438
Samoa	955A-956
Seycelles	802
Solomon Islands	866-867
South Georgia & S. Sandwich Islands	220
Tokelau	253
Tonga	980
Niuafo'ou	201
Tristan da Cunha	618
Tuvalu	762
Vanuatu	719

Wedding of Prince Edward and Sophie Rhys-Jones

CD356

1999

Ascension	729-730
Cayman Islands	775-776
Falkland Islands	729-730
Pitcairn Islands	505-506
St. Helena	733-734
Samoa	971-972
Tristan da Cunha	636-637
Virgin Islands	908-909

1st Manned Moon Landing,

30th Anniv.

CD357

1999

Ascension 731-735
Bahamas 942-946
Barbados 967-971
Bermuda 778
Cayman Islands 777-781
Fiji 853-857
Jamaica 889-893
Kirbati 746-750
Nauru 465-469
St. Kitts 460-464
Samoa 973-977
Solomon Islands 875-879
Tuvalu 800-804
Virgin Islands 910-914

Queen Mother's Century

CD358

1999

Ascension 736-740
Bahamas 951-955
Cayman Islands 782-786
Fiji 858-862
Norfolk Island 688-692
St. Helena 740-744
Samoa 978-982
Solomon Islands 880-884
South Georgia & South
  Sandwich Islands 231-235
Tristan da Cunha 638-642
Tuvalu 805-809

UNITED STATES

yu-ˌnī-təd 'stāts

GOVT. — Republic
AREA — 3,615,211 sq. mi.
POP. — 226,545,805 (1980)
CAPITAL — Washington, DC

In addition to the 50 States and the District of Columbia, the Republic includes Guam, the Commonwealth of Puerto Rico, the Virgin Islands, American Samoa, Wake, Midway, and a number of small islands in the Pacific Ocean, all of which use stamps of the United States.

100 Cents = 1 Dollar

Catalogue values for unused stamps in this country are for Never Hinged items, beginning with Scott 772 in the regular postage section, Scott C19 in the air post section, Scott E17 in the special delivery section, Scott FA1 in the certified mail section, Scott O127 in officials section, Scott J88 in the postage due section, Scott R733 in the revenues section, Scott RW1 in the hunting permit stamps section.

Watermarks

Wmk. 190- "USPS" in Single-lined Capitals

Wmk. 191- Double-lined "USPS" in Capitals

Wmk. 190PI - PIPS, used in the Philippines
Wmk. 191PI - PIPS, used in the Philippines
Wmk. 191C - US-C, used for Cuba
Wmk. 191R - USIR

PROVISIONAL ISSUES BY POSTMASTERS

Values for Envelopes are for entires.

ALEXANDRIA, VA

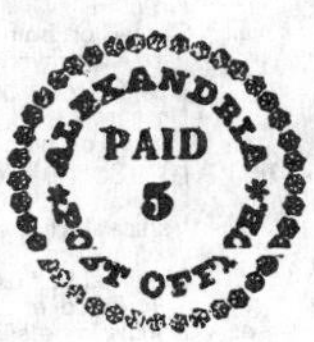

A1

Type I - 40 asterisks in circle.
Type II - 39 asterisks in circle.

1846 **Typeset** ***Imperf.***

1X1 A1 5c black, *buff*, Type I —
a. 5c black, *buff*, Type II 75,000.
1X2 A1 5c black, *blue*, Type I, on cover —

All known copies of Nos. 1X1-1X2 are cut to shape.

ANNAPOLIS, MD

ENVELOPE

E1

1846

2XU1 E1 5c carmine red 210,000.

Handstamped impressions of the circular design with "2" in blue or red exist on envelopes and letter sheets. Values: blue $2,500, red $3,500.

A letter sheet exists with circular design and "5" handstamped in red. Values: blue $3,500, red $5,000.

A similar circular design in blue was used as a postmark.

BALTIMORE, MD

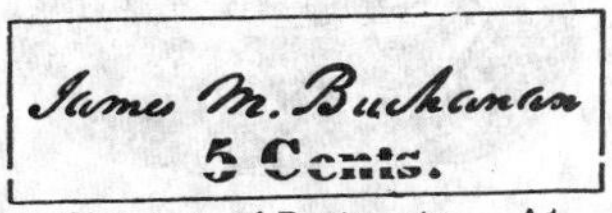

Signature of Postmaster — A1

1845 **Engr.** ***Imperf.***

3X1 A1 5c black 5,000.
3X2 A1 10c black, on cover 50,000.
3X3 A1 5c black, *bluish* 65,000. 5,000.
3X4 A1 10c black, *bluish* 60,000.

Nos. 3X1-3X4 were printed from a plate of 12 (2x6) containing nine 5c and three 10c.

Envelopes

E1

The color given is that of the "PAID 5" and oval. "James M. Buchanan" is handstamped in black, blue or red. The paper is manila, buff, white, salmon or grayish.

1845 **Handstamped**

Various Papers

3XU1 E1 5c blue 6,000.
3XU2 E1 5c red 10,000.
3XU3 E1 10c blue 20,000.
3XU4 E1 10c red 20,000.

On the formerly listed "5+5" envelopes, the second "5" in oval is believed not to be part of the basic prepaid marking.

BOSCAWEN, NH

A1

1846(?) **Typeset** ***Imperf.***

4X1 A1 5c dull blue, *yellowish*, on cover 175,000.

BRATTLEBORO, VT

Initials of Postmaster (FNP) — A1

Plate of 10 (5x2).

1846 **Engr.** ***Imperf.***

5X1 A1 5c black, *buff* 9,000.

LOCKPORT, NY

A1

Handstamped, "5" in Black Ms

1846

6X1 A1 5c red, *buff*, on cover 150,000.

MILLBURY, MA

George Washington — A1

Printed from a Woodcut

1846 ***Imperf.***

7X1 A1 5c blue, *bluish* 130,000. 20,000.

NEW HAVEN, CT

Envelopes

E1

1845 **Handstamped**

Signed in Blue, Black, Magenta or Red

8XU1 E1 5c red (Bl or M) 75,000.
8XU2 E1 5c red, *light bluish* (Bk) 100,000.
8XU3 E1 5c dull blue, *buff* (Bl) 100,000.
8XU4 E1 5c dull blue (Bl) 100,000.

Values of Nos. 8XU1-8XU4 are a guide to value. They are based on auction realizations and retail sales and take condition into consideration. All New Haven envelopes are of almost equal rarity. An entire of No. 8XU2 is the finest example known. The other envelopes are valued according to condition as much as rarity.

Reprints were made at various times between 1871 and 1932. They can be distinguished from the originals, primarily due to differences in paper.

NEW YORK, NY

George Washington — A1

Plate of 40 (5x8). Nos. 9X1-9X3 and varieties unused are valued without gum. Examples with original gum are extremely scarce and will command higher prices.

1845-46 **Engr.** ***Imperf.***

Bluish Wove Paper

9X1 A1 5c blk, signed ACM, connected ('46) 1,300. 500.
a. Signed ACM, AC connected 1,600. 550.
b. Signed A.C.M. 3,750. 700.
c. Signed MMJr 9,000.
d. Signed RHM 13,000. 3,250.
e. Without signature 3,250. 750.

These stamps were usually initialed "ACM" in magenta ink, as a control, before being sold or passed through the mails.

A plate of 9 (3x3) was made from which proofs were printed in black on white and deep blue papers; also in blue, green, brown and red on white bond paper.

1847 **Engr.** ***Imperf.***

Blue Wove Paper

9X2 A1 5c blk, signed ACM, connected 6,500. 3,500.
a. Signed RHM 11,000. 7,250.
d. Without signature

On the listing example of No. 9X2a the "R" is illegible and does not match those of the other "RHM" signatures.

1847 **Engr.** ***Imperf.***

Gray Wove Paper

9X3 A1 5c blk, signed ACM, connected 5,250. 2,100.
a. Signed RHM 7,000.
b. Without signature 7,000.

PROVIDENCE, RI

A1

A2

1846 **Engr.** ***Imperf.***

10X1 A1 5c gray black 400. 1,750.
10X2 A2 10c gray black 1,250. 15,000.
a. Pair, #10X1-10X2 2,150.

Plate of 12 (3x4) contains 11-5c and 1-10c.

Reprints were made in 1898. Each stamp bears one of the following letters on the back: B. O. G. E. R. T. D. U. R. B. I. N. Value of 5c, $50; 10c, $125; sheet, $725.

Reprint singles or sheets without back print sell for more.

ST. LOUIS, MO

Missouri Coat of Arms

A1 A2 A3

Unused are valued without gum.

1845-46 **Engr.** ***Imperf.***

Greenish Wove Paper

11X1 A1 5c black 5,000. 2,750.
11X2 A2 10c black 4,500. 2,500.
11X3 A3 20c black 20,000.

Three varieties of 5c, 3 of 10c, 2 of 20c.

1846

Gray Lilac Paper

11X4 A1 5c black — 4,250.
11X5 A2 10c black 4,500. 2,200.
11X6 A3 20c black 13,500.

One variety of 5c, 3 of 10c, 2 of 20c.

1847

Pelure Paper

11X7 A1 5c black *bluish* — 6,250.
11X8 A2 10c blk, *bluish* 6,250.
a. Impression of 5c on back —

Three varieties of 5c, 3 of 10c.
Used values are for pencanceled copies.

For Tuscumbia, Alabama, formerly listed as United States postmasters' provisional No. 12XU1, see the "3c 1861 Postmasters' Provisionals" section before the Confederate States of America Postmasters' Provisionals.

GENERAL ISSUES

All Issues from 1847 to 1894 are Unwatermarked.

Benjamin Franklin
A1

George Washington
A2

1847, July 1 Engr. *Imperf.*

1	A1	5c red brown, *bluish*	5,250.	600.
		No gum	2,500.	
	a.	5c dark brown, *bluish*	5,500.	625.
		No gum	2,600.	
	b.	5c orange brown, *bluish*	6,500.	850.
		No gum	3,100.	
	c.	5c red orange, *bluish*	*12,500.*	*5,000.*
		No gum	7,500.	
	d.	Double impression		—
		Pen cancel		300.

The only known double impression shows part of the design doubled.

2	A2	10c black, *bluish*	*26,000.*	1,400.
		No gum	*14,000.*	
	a.	Diagonal half used as 5c on cover		*13,000.*
	b.	Vertical half used as 5c on cover		*35,000.*
	c.	Horizontal half used as 5c on cover		—
		Pen cancel		750.

REPRODUCTIONS

Actually, official imitations made from new plates by order of the Post Office Department.

A3

A4

1875 *Imperf.*

Bluish Paper Without Gum

3	A3	5c red brown	850.
4	A4	10c black	1,100.

Reproductions. The letters R. W. H. & E. at the bottom of each stamp are less distinct on the reproductions than on the originals.

5c. On the originals the left side of the white shirt frill touches the oval on a level with the top of the "F" of "Five." On the reproductions it touches the oval about on a level with the top of the figure "5."

10c. On the reproductions, line of coat at left points to right tip of "X" and line of coat at right points to center of "S" of CENTS. On the originals, line of coat points to "T" of TEN and between "T" and "S" of CENTS. On the reproductions the eyes have a sleepy look, the line of the mouth is straighter, and in the curl of hair near the left cheek is a strong black dot, while the originals have only a faint one.

VALUES FOR VERY FINE STAMPS

Stamps are valued in the grade of very fine unless otherwise indicated.

Values for unused stamps with no gum are for examples with certificates of authenticity or examples sold with the buyer having the right of certification. Beware of unused, no gum stamps that are offered "as is." Expertization by competent authorities is recommended.

Franklin — A5

ONE CENT

Type I. Has complete curved lines outside the labels with "U.S. Postage" and "One Cent." The scrolls below the lower label are turned under, forming little balls. The ornaments at top are substantially complete.

Values for type I are for stamps showing the marked characteristics plainly. Copies of type I showing the balls indistinctly sell for much lower prices.

Type Ib. Same as I but balls below the bottom label are not so clear. The plumelike scrolls at bottom are not complete.

A6

Type Ia. Same as I at bottom but top ornaments and outer line at top are partly cut away.

Type Ic. Same as Ia, but bottom right plume and ball ornament incomplete. Bottom left plume complete or nearly complete.

A7

Type II. The little balls of the bottom scrolls and the bottoms of the lower plume ornaments are missing. The side ornaments are complete.

A8

Type III. The top and bottom curved lines outside the labels are broken in the middle. The side ornaments are complete.

Type IIIa. Similar to type III with the outer line broken at top or bottom but not both.

A9

Type IV. Similar to type II, but with the curved lines outside the labels recut at top or bottom or both.

Washington — A10

THREE CENTS

Type I. There is an outer frame line on all four sides.

Thomas Jefferson — A11

FIVE CENTS

Type I. There are projections on all four sides.

Washington — A12

TEN CENTS

Type I. The "shells" at the lower corners are practically complete. The outer line below the label is very nearly complete. The outer lines are broken above the middle of the top label and the "X" in each upper corner.

A13

Type II. The design is complete at the top. The outer line at the bottom is broken in the middle. The shells are partly cut away.

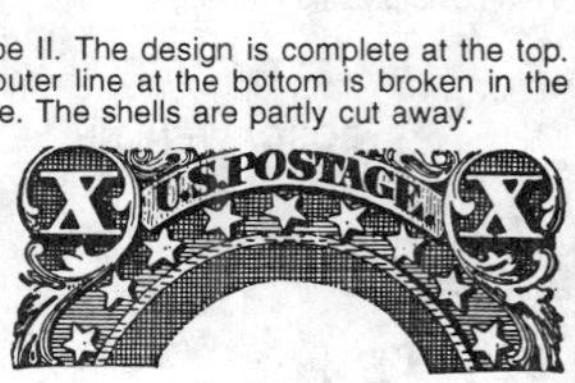
A14

Type III. The outer lines are broken above the top label and the "X" numerals. The outer line at the bottom and the shells are partly cut away, similar to Type II.

A15

Type IV. The outer lines have been recut at top or bottom or both.

Types I, II, III and IV have complete ornaments at the sides of the stamps and three pearls at each outer edge of the bottom panel.

Washington — A16

In Nos. 5-17, the 1c, 3c, and 12c have very small margins between the stamps. The 5c and 10c have moderate size margins. The values of these stamps take the margin size into consideration.

Values for No. 5A, 6b and 19b are for the less distinct positions. Best examples sell for more.

Values for No. 16 are for outer line recut at top. Other recuts sell for more.

1851-57 *Imperf.*

5	A5	1c blue, I	*175,000.*	*37,500.*

Values for No. 5 are for copies with margins touching or slightly cutting into the design. Value unused is for an example with no gum.

5A	A5	1c blue, Ib	*13,000.*	*5,000.*
		No gum	*6,750.*	
6	A6	1c blue, Ia ('57)	*32,500.*	*9,000.*
		No gum	*19,000.*	
	b.	Type Ic	*6,000.*	*1,400.*
		No gum	*3,500.*	
7	A7	1c blue, II	1,000.	160.
		No gum	500.	
8	A8	1c blue, III	*10,000.*	2,500.
		No gum	*5,750.*	

Values for type III are for at least a 2mm break in each outer line. Examples of type III with wider breaks in outer lines command higher prices; those with smaller breaks sell for less.

8A	A8	1c blue, IIIa	*4,000.*	975.
		No gum	2,250.	

Stamps of type IIIa with bottom line broken command higher prices than those with top line broken. See note after No. 8 on width of break of outer lines.

9	A9	1c blue, IV ('52)	675.	125.
		No gum	375.	
	a.	Printed on both sides, reverse inverted		—
10	A10	3c org brown, I	2,750.	100.
		No gum	1,500.	
	a.	Printed on both sides		—
11	A10	3c dull red, I	240.	10.
		No gum	100.	
	c.	Vertical half used as 1c on cover		*5,000.*
	d.	Diagonal half used as 1c on cover		*5,000.*
	e.	Double impression		*5,000.*
12	A11	5c red brown, I ('56)	*16,000.*	1,250.
		No gum	*9,500.*	
13	A12	10c green, I ('55)	*13,000.*	800.
		No gum	*7,500.*	
14	A13	10c green, II ('55)	3,250.	225.
		No gum	1,600.	
15	A14	10c green, III ('55)	3,250.	225.
		No gum	1,600.	
16	A15	10c green, IV ('55)	*22,500.*	1,600.
		No gum	*13,500.*	
17	A16	12c black	4,000.	325.
		No gum	2,250.	
	a.	Diagonal half used as 6c on cover		*2,500.*
	b.	Vertical half used as 6c on cover		*8,500.*
	c.	Printed on both sides		*10,000.*

Same Designs as 1851-56 Issues

Franklin — A20

ONE CENT

Type V. Similar to type III of 1851-57 but with side ornaments partly cut away.

Washington — A21

THREE CENTS

Type II. The outer frame line has been removed at top and bottom. The side frame lines were recut so as to be continuous from the top to the bottom of the plate. Stamps from the top or bottom rows show the ends of the side frame lines and may be mistaken for type IIa.

Type IIa. The side frame lines extend only to the top and bottom of the stamp design.

Jefferson — A22

FIVE CENTS

Type II. The projections at top and bottom are partly cut away.

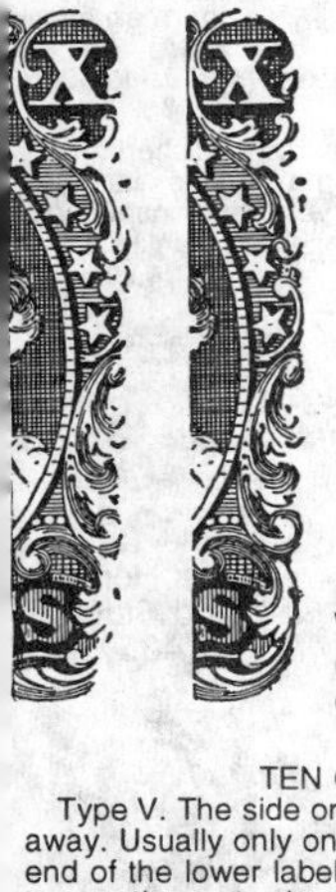

Washington (Two typical examples) — A23

TEN CENTS

Type V. The side ornaments are slightly cut away. Usually only one pearl remains at each end of the lower label but some copies show two or three pearls at the right side. At the bottom the outer line is complete and the shells nearly so. The outer lines at top are complete except over the right "X."

Washington A17

Franklin A18

Washington — A19

TWELVE CENTS

Plate I. Outer frame lines complete.

Plate III. Outer frame lines noticeably uneven or broken, sometimes partly missing.

Nos. 18-39 have small or very small margins. The values take into account the margin size.

1857-61 *Perf. 15½*

18	A5	1c blue, type I ('61)	1,600.	550.
		No gum	850.	
19	A6	1c blue, type Ia	17,000.	5,000.
		No gum	10,000.	
b.		Type Ic	2,600.	1,100.
		No gum	1,500.	
20	A7	1c blue, type II	900.	250.
		No gum	475.	
21	A8	1c blue, type III	11,000.	1,800.
		No gum	5,750.	
a.		Horiz. pair, imperf. btwn.		16,000.
22	A8	1c blue, type IIIa	1,750.	425.
		No gum	950.	
b.		Horiz. pair, imperf. btwn.		5,000.

One pair of No. 22b has been reported. Beware of pairs with blind perforations.

23	A9	1c blue, type IV	6,500.	575.
		No gum	3,750.	
24	A20	1c blue, type V	175.	40.
		No gum	85.	
b.		Laid paper		—
25	A10	3c rose, type I	2,000.	75.
		No gum	1,100.	
b.		Vert. pair, imperf. horiz.		10,000.
26	A21	3c dull red, type II	75.	5.
		No gum	30.	
a.		3c dull red, type IIa	200.	45.
		No gum	105.	
b.		Horiz. pair, imperf. vert., type II	4,000.	—
c.		Vert. pair, imperf. horiz., type II		—
d.		Horizontal pair, imperf. between, type II		—
e.		Dbl. impression, type II		2,500.
f.		Horiz. strip of 3, imperf. vert., type IIa, on cover		8,250.
27	A11	5c brick red, type I ('58)	20,000.	1,200.
		No gum	10,500.	
28	A11	5c red brown, type I	3,500.	600.
		No gum	1,900.	
b.		5c bright red brown	3,750.	800.
		No gum	2,100.	
28A	A11	5c Indian red, type I ('58)	25,000.	3,000.
		No gum	16,000.	
29	A11	5c brown, type I ('59)	2,000.	325.
		No gum	1,100.	
30	A22	5c org brown, type II ('61)	1,100.	1,100.
		No gum	600.	
30A	A22	5c brown, type II ('60)	1,750.	260.
		No gum	850.	
b.		Printed on both sides	4,250.	4,500.
31	A12	10c green, type I	15,000.	750.
		No gum	8,000.	
32	A13	10c green, type II	4,500.	275.
		No gum	2,500.	
33	A14	10c green, type III	4,500.	275.
		No gum	2,500.	
34	A15	10c green, type IV	29,000.	2,100.
		No gum	16,000.	
35	A23	10c green, type V ('59)	275.	65.
		No gum	140.	
36	A16	12c black, plate I	1,200.	200.
		No gum	650.	
a.		Diagonal half used as 6c on cover (I)		17,500.
b.		12c black, plate III ('59)	725.	170.
		No gum	375.	
c.		Horizontal pair, imperf. between (I)		12,500.
37	A17	24c gray lilac ('60)	1,250.	350.
a.		24c gray	1,250.	350.
		No gum	625.	
38	A18	30c orange ('60)	1,750.	450.
		No gum	900.	
39	A19	90c blue ('60)	2,500.	5,500.
		No gum	1,400.	
		Pen cancel		1,250.

See Die and Plate proofs in the Scott United States Specialized Catalogue for imperfs. of the 12c, 24c, 30c, 90c.

Genuine cancellations on the 90c are rare.

REPRINTS OF 1857-60 ISSUE

White Paper

Without Gum

1875 *Perf. 12*

40	A5	1c bright blue	625.
41	A10	3c scarlet	2,500.
42	A22	5c orange brown	1,050.
43	A12	10c blue green	2,100.
44	A16	12c greenish blk	2,750.
45	A17	24c black violet	2,750.
46	A18	30c yellow orange	2,750.
47	A19	90c deep blue	4,250.
		Nos. 40-47 (8)	18,775.

Nos. 41-46 are valued in the grade of fine.
Nos. 40-47 exist imperf., value, set $25,000.

Essays - Trial Color Proofs

The paper of former Nos. 55-62 (Nos. 63E11e, 65-E15h, 67-E9e, 69-E6e, 72-E7h, Essay section, Nos. 70eTC, 71bTC, Trial Color Proof section, Scott U.S. Specialized) is thin and semitransparent. That of the postage issues is thicker and more opaque, except Nos. 62B, 70c and 70d.

Franklin — A24

1c - There is a dash under the tip of the ornament at right of the numeral in upper left corner. There is no dash on the essay.

Washington — A25

3c - Ornaments at corners are large and end in a small ball. The ornaments are smaller and there is no ball on the essay.

Jefferson — A26

5c - Leaflets appear at each corner. These do not appear on the essay.

Washington — A27

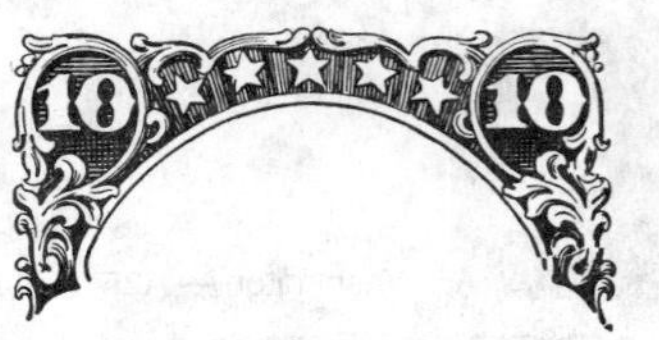

A27a

A27

10c - On A27 a heavy curved line appears below the stars and an outer line above them which does not appear on A27a.

Washington — A28

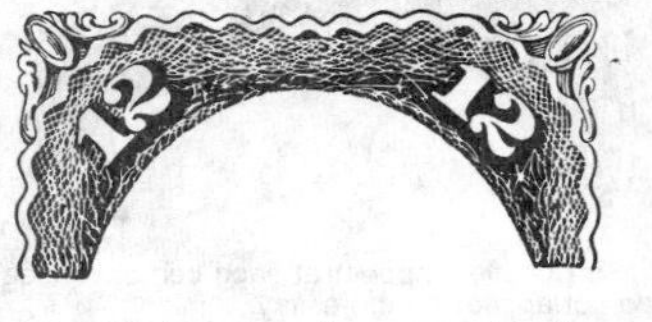

12c - Ovals and scrolls appear at each corners. These do not appear on the essay.

Washington
A29

Franklin
A30

Washington — A31

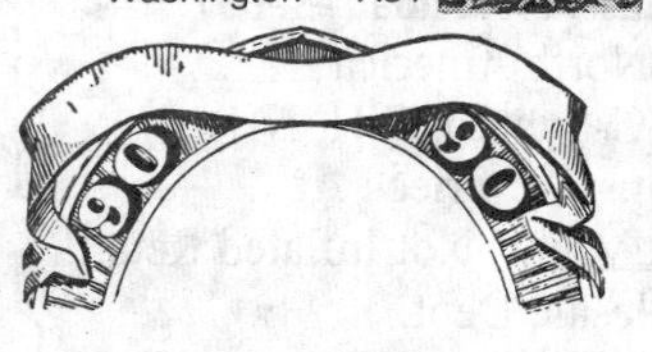

90c. Two pairs of parallel lines form an angle above the ribbon with "U. S. Postage"; between these lines is a row of dashes, and there is a point of color to the apex of the lower pair. These do not appear on the essay.

1861 ***Perf. 12***

62B A27a 10c dark green *6,250.* 800.
No gum *3,500.*

1861-62 ***Perf. 12***

63 A24 1c blue 300.00 30.00
No gum 140.00
a. 1c ultramarine 675.00 240.00
No gum 350.00
b. 1c dark blue 500.00 70.00
No gum 260.00
c. Laid paper — —
d. Vert. pair, imperf. horiz. —
e. Printed on both sides — *2,500.*
64 A25 3c pink 6,000. 675.00
No gum *3,500.*
a. 3c pigeon blood pink *15,000.* *3,250.*
No gum *8,500.*
b. 3c rose pink 450.00 125.00
No gum 210.00
65 A25 3c rose 125.00 2.50
No gum 55.00
b. Laid paper — —
d. Vert. pair, imperf. horiz. *3,500.* *750.00*
e. Printed on both sides *2,400.* *2,000.*
f. Double impression *6,000.*

The 3c lake can be found under No. 66 in the Trial Color Proofs section of the Scott U.S. Specialized Catalogue. The imperf 3c lake under No. 66P in the same section. The imperf 3c rose can be found in the Die and Plate Proofs section of the Specialized.

67 A26 5c buff *15,000.* 750.00
a. 5c brown yellow *15,000.* 750.00
No gum *8,500.*
b. 5c olive yellow — 825.00

Values for Nos. 67, 67a, 67b reflect the normal small margins.

68 A27 10c yellow green 550.00 50.00
No gum 260.00
a. 10c dark green 575.00 52.50
No gum 275.00
b. Vert. pair, imperf. horiz. *3,500.*
69 A28 12c black 900.00 85.00
No gum 500.00
70 A29 24c red lilac ('62) 1,500. 150.00
No gum 800.00
a. 24c brown lilac 1,400. 130.00
No gum 725.00
b. 24c steel blue *6,500.* 550.00
No gum *4,000.*
c. 24c violet, thin paper *9,000.* 1,100.
No gum *5,250.*
d. 24c pale gray violet, thin paper 2,750. 800.00
No gum 1,500.
71 A30 30c orange 1,250. 140.00
No gum 675.00
a. Printed on both sides —

Values for No. 71 are for copies with small margins, especially at sides. Large margined examples sell for much more.

72 A31 90c blue 2,400. 400.00
a. 90c pale blue 2,400. 400.00
No gum 1,350.
b. 90c dark blue 2,600. 450.00
No gum 1,500.

Nos. 70c, 70d are on a thinner, harder and more transparent paper than Nos. 70, 70a, 70b, or the later Nos. 78, 78a, 78b and 78c.

VALUES FOR VERY FINE STAMPS

Stamps are valued in the grade of very fine unless otherwise indicated.

Values for unused stamps with no gum are for examples with certificates of authenticity or examples sold with the buyer having the right of certification. Beware of unused, no gum stamps that are offered "as is." Expertization by competent authorities is recommended.

Designs as 1861 Issue

Andrew
Jackson
A32

Abraham
Lincoln
A33

1861-66 ***Perf. 12***

73 A32 2c black ('63) 325.00 50.00
No gum 140.00
a. Diag. half used as 1c as part of 3c rate on cover 1,250.
b. Diagonal half used alone as 1c on cover *3,000.*
c. Horiz. half used as 1c as part of 3c rate on cover *3,500.*
d. Vert. half used as 1c as part of 3c rate on cover 1,250.
e. Printed on both sides *5,000.*
f. Laid paper — —

The 3c scarlet can be found under No. 74 in the Scott U.S. Specialized Catalogue Trial Color Proofs section.

75 A26 5c red brown ('62) 4,000. 450.00
No gum 2,200.
76 A26 5c brown ('63) 900.00 100.00
No gum 475.00
a. 5c black brown 1,000. 125.00
No gum 550.00
b. Laid paper —
77 A33 15c black ('66) 1,200. 150.00
No gum 650.00
78 A29 24c lilac ('63) 900.00 95.00
a. 24c grayish lilac 900.00 95.00
b. 24c gray 900.00 95.00
No gum 475.00
c. 24c blackish violet *30,000.* *1,750.*
No gum *20,000.*
d. Printed on both sides *3,500.*

Values for Nos. 75, 76, 76a reflect the normal small margins.

Grill

Same as 1861-66 Issues
Embossed with grills of various sizes

Grill with Points Up

Grills A and C were made by a roller covered with ridges shaped like an inverted V. Pressing the ridges into the stamp paper forced the paper into the pyramidal pits between the ridges, causing irregular breaks in the paper.

Grill B was made by a roller with raised bosses.

A. Grill covering the entire stamp

1867 ***Perf. 12***

79 A25 3c rose 4,000. 950.
No gum 2,250.
b. Printed on both sides —
80 A26 5c brown — *80,000.*
a. 5c dark brown *80,000.*
81 A30 30c orange *50,000.*

Nos. 79, 79b, are valued for fine - very fine centering but with minor perforation faults.

An essay which is often mistaken for No. 79 (#79-E15) shows the points of the grill as small squares faintly impressed in the paper, but not cutting through it. On No. 79 the grill breaks through the paper. Copies free from defects are rare.

Eight copies of Nos. 80 and 80a (four unused, four used), and eight copies of No. 81 (one institutionalized and not available to collectors) are known. All are more or less faulty and/or off-center. Values are for off-center examples with small perforation faults.

The imperf. of the 3c rose can be found in the Scott U.S. Specialized Catalogue Die and Plate Proofs section.

B. Grill about 18x15mm (22 by 18 points)

82 A25 3c rose *160,000.*

The four known copies of No. 82 are fine.

C. Grill about 13x16mm (16 to 17 by 18 to 21 points)

83 A25 3c rose 4,500. 850.
No gum 2,500.

The grilled area on each of four C grills in the sheet may total about 18x15mm when a normal C grill adjoins a fainter grill extending to the right or left edge of the stamp. This is caused by a partial erasure on the grill roller when it was changed to produce C grills instead of the all-over A grill.

The imperf. can be found in the Scott U.S. Specialized Catalogue Die and Plate Proofs section.

Grill with Points Down

The grills were produced by rollers with the surface covered by pyramidal bosses. On the Z grill the tips of the pyramids are very short horizontal ridges. On the D, E and F grills the ridges are vertical.

D. Grill about 12x14mm (15 by 17 to 18 points)

84 A32 2c black *13,000.* 2,500.
No gum 7,750.

No. 84 is valued in the grade of fine.

85 A25 3c rose 5,500. 900.
No gum 2,750.

Z. Grill about 11x14mm (13 to 14 by 17 to 18 points)

85A A24 1c blue *935,000.*
85B A32 2c black 6,000. 900.
No gum 3,250.
85C A25 3c rose 9,000. 2,500.
No gum 4,750.
85D A27 10c green *90,000.*
85E A28 12c black 8,000. 1,100.
No gum 4,500.
85F A33 15c black *220,000.*

Two copies of No. 85A are known. One is contained in the New York Public Library collection. Value represents 1998 auction sale price of the single example available to collectors.

Six copies of No. 85D are known. One is in the New York Public Library collection. Value is for a well-centered example with small faults.

Two copies of No. 85F are known. Value represents 1998 auction sale price of the much finer example.

E. Grill about 11x13mm (14 by 15 to 17 points)

86 A24 1c blue 2,500. 450.
No gum 1,350.
a. 1c dull blue 2,500. 425.
No gum 1,350.
87 A32 2c black 1,250. 125.
No gum 700.
a. Half used as 1c on cover, diagonal or vert. *2,000.*
88 A25 3c rose 700. 20.
No gum 350.
a. 3c lake red 750. 19.
No gum 375.
89 A27 10c green 4,000. 300.
No gum 2,250.
90 A28 12c black 3,950. 325.
No gum 2,000.
91 A33 15c black 8,000. 625.
No gum 4,250.

F. Grill about 9x13mm (11 to 12 by 15 to 17 points)

92 A24 1c blue 950. 175.
a. 1c pale blue 950. 175.
No gum 500.
93 A32 2c black 450. 45.00
No gum 225.
a. Vert. or diag. half used as 1c as part of 3c rate on cover *1,250.*
c. Horiz. or diagonal half used alone as 1c on cover *2,500.*
94 A25 3c red 325. 6.00
a. 3c rose 325. 6.00
No gum 160.
c. Vert. pair, imperf. horiz. *1,100.*
d. Printed on both sides *1,200.*

The imperf. 3c can be found in the Scott U.S. Specialized Catalogue Die and Plate Proofs section.

95 A26 5c brown 2,500. 650.
No gum 1,350.
a. 5c black brown 2,750. 775.
No gum 1,500.

Values for Nos. 95, 95a reflect the normal small margins.

96 A27 10c yellow green 2,100. 200.
a. 10c dark green 2,100. 200.
No gum 1,200.
97 A28 12c black 2,500. 225.
No gum 1,300.
98 A33 15c black 2,750. 300.
No gum 1,450.
99 A29 24c gray lilac 5,000. 700.
No gum 2,750.
100 A30 30c orange 4,750. 650.
No gum 2,600.

Values for No. 100 are for copies with small margins, especially at sides. Large-margined examples sell for much more.

101 A31 90c blue 8,500. 1,300.
No gum 4,500.

Some authorities believe that more than one size of grill probably existed on one of the grill rolls.

Re-issue of 1861-66 Issues
Without Grill
Hard White Paper
White Crackly Gum

1875 ***Perf. 12***

102 A24 1c blue *750.* *1,000.*
No gum *400.*
103 A32 2c black *2,750.* *4,500.*
No gum *1,750.*
104 A25 3c brown red *3,000.* *5,000.*
No gum *2,000.*
105 A26 5c brown *2,250.* *2,750.*
No gum *1,450.*
106 A27 10c green *2,400.* *4,500.*
No gum *1,550.*
107 A28 12c black *3,250.* *5,250.*
No gum *2,100.*
108 A33 15c black *3,250.* *5,500.*
No gum *2,100.*
109 A29 24c deep violet *4,000.* *7,000.*
No gum *2,600.*
110 A30 30c brownish org *4,250.* *8,000.*
No gum *2,750.*
111 A31 90c blue *5,250.* *40,000.*
No gum *3,500.*

These stamps can be distinguished from the 1861-66 issues by the shades and the paper which is hard and very white instead of yellowish. The gum is white and crackly.

Franklin
A34

Post Horse
and Rider
A35

Locomotive
A36

Washington
A37

Shield and
Eagle
A38

S. S.
Adriatic
A39

Landing of Columbus — A40

FIFTEEN CENTS

Type I. Picture unframed.

A40a

Type II. Picture framed.

Type III. Same as type I but without fringe of brown shading lines around central vignette.

"The Declaration of Independence" A41

Shield, Eagle and Flags A42

Lincoln — A43

G. Grill measuring 9½x9mm (12 by 11 to 11½ points)

1869 ***Perf. 12***

112	A34	1c buff	650.00	150.00
		No gum	325.00	
b.		Without grill	*4,000.*	
113	A35	2c brown	600.00	60.00
		No gum	300.00	
b.		Without grill	*2,250.*	
c.		Half used as 1c on cover, diagonal, vert. or horiz.		*3,000.*
d.		Printed on both sides		*9,000.*
114	A36	3c ultramarine	300.00	20.00
		No gum	150.00	
a.		Without grill	*950.00*	
b.		Vertical one third used as 1c on cover		—
c.		Vertical two thirds used as 2c on cover		*4,000.*
d.		Double impression		*3,500.*
e.		Printed on both sides		—
115	A37	6c ultramarine	2,250.	200.00
		No gum	1,150.	
b.		Vertical half used as 3c on cover		—
116	A38	10c yellow	1,750.	140.
		No gum	900.	
117	A39	12c green	1,900.	150.
		No gum	1,000.	
118	A40	15c brn & blue, Type I	6,250.	600.
		No gum	3,500.	
a.		Without grill	*7,000.*	
119	A40a	15c brn & blue, Type II	2,750.	250.
		No gum	1,400.	
b.		Center inverted	*275,000.*	*18,500.*
c.		Center dbl., one invtd.		*35,000.*
120	A41	24c green & vio	5,500.	750.
		No gum	3,250.	
a.		Without grill	*8,000.*	
b.		Center inverted	*275,000.*	*20,000.*
121	A42	30c ultra & car	6,000.	550.
		No gum	3,500.	
a.		Without grill	*6,250.*	
b.		Flags inverted	*210,000.*	*65,000.*
122	A43	90c car & black	8,500.	2,200.
		No gum	4,500.	
a.		Without grill	*15,000.*	

Values of varieties of Nos. 112-122 without grill are for copies with original gum.

Most copies of Nos. 119b, 120b are faulty. Values are for fine centered copies with only minimal faults.

Re-issues of the 1869 Issue
Without Grill
Hard White Paper
White Crackly Gum

1875 ***Perf. 12***

123	A34	1c buff	500.	325.
		No gum	275.	
124	A35	2c brown	600.	450.
		No gum	350.	
125	A36	3c blue	*4,500.*	*14,000.*
		No gum	2,900.	

Used value for No. 125 is for an attractive copy with minimal faults.

126	A37	6c blue	1,250.	1,400.
		No gum	750.	
127	A38	10c yellow	1,900.	1,600.
		No gum	1,200.	
128	A39	12c green	2,250.	*2,500.*
		No gum	1,400.	
129	A40	15c brown & blue, type III	1,800.	1,000.
		No gum	1,100.	
a.		Imperf. horiz., single	2,500.	—

Type III is same as type I but without fringe of brown shading lines around central vignette.

130	A41	24c green & violet	1,800.	1,200.
		No gum	1,100.	
131	A42	30c ultra & carmine	2,500.	2,250.
		No gum	1,600.	
132	A43	90c carmine & black	4,750.	*5,250.*
		No gum	3,000.	

1880-81

Soft Porous Paper

133	A34	1c buff	300.	200.
		No gum	150.	
a.		1c brown orange ('81)	225.	175.

No. 133 was issued with gum, No. 133a without gum.

Printed by the National Bank Note Company

Franklin — A44

A44

Jackson — A45

A45

Washington — A46

A46

Lincoln — A47

A47

Edwin M. Stanton — A48

A48

Jefferson — A49

A49

Henry Clay — A50

A50

Daniel Webster — A51

A51

Gen. Winfield Scott A52

Alexander Hamilton A53

Commodore O. H. Perry — A54

Two varieties of grill are known on this issue.

H. Grill about 10x12mm
(11 to 13 by 14 to 16 points)
On all values, 1c to 90c
I. Grill about 8½x10mm
(10 to 11 by 10 to 13 points)
On 1, 2, 3, 6, 7 and 15c

On the 1870-71 stamps the grill impressions are usually faint or incomplete. This is especially true of the H grill, which often shows only a few points.

Values for 1c - 7c are for stamps showing well-defined grills.

White Wove Paper

1870-71 *Perf. 12*

134 A44 1c ultramarine 1,750. 125.00
No gum 900.00

135 A45 2c red brown 1,000. 65.00
No gum 500.00
a. Diagonal half used as 1c on cover —
b. Vertical half used as 1c on cover —

136 A46 3c green 675.00 17.50
No gum 325.00

The imperf. 3c can be found in the Scott U.S. Specialized Catalogue Die and Plate Proofs section.

137 A47 6c carmine 3,600. 500.
No gum 1,850.

138 A48 7c vermilion ('71) 2,500. 400.
No gum 1,300.

139 A49 10c brown 4,000. 650.
No gum 2,100.

140 A50 12c dull violet *19,000.* 2,750.
No gum *10,000.*

141 A51 15c orange 4,750. 1,100.
No gum 2,500.

142 A52 24c purple — *6,500.*

No. 142 is valued in the grade of fine.

143 A53 30c black 10,000. 2,100.
No gum 6,000.

144 A54 90c carmine 11,500. 1,400.
No gum 6,250.

Without Grill
White Wove Paper

1870-71 *Perf. 12*

145 A44 1c ultramarine 390.00 14.00
No gum 190.00

146 A45 2c red brown 300.00 9.00
No gum 140.00
a. Half used as 1c on cover, diagonal or vert. —
c. Double impression —

147 A46 3c green 275.00 1.50
No gum 130.00
a. Printed on both sides *1,750.*
b. Double impression *1,250.*

The imperf. 3c can be found in the Scott U.S. Specialized Catalogue Die and Plate Proofs section.

148 A47 6c carmine 575.00 22.50
No gum 280.00
a. Vert. half used as 3c on cover —
b. Double impression *1,500.*

149 A48 7c vermilion ('71) 700.00 90.00
No gum 350.00

150 A49 10c brown 575.00 20.00
No gum 280.00

151 A50 12c dull violet 1,425. 140.00
No gum 750.00

152 A51 15c bright orange 1,550. 140.00
No gum 800.00
a. Double impression *1,600.*

153 A52 24c purple 1,425. 130.00
No gum 750.00

154 A53 30c black 3,750. 150.00
No gum 2,000.

155 A54 90c carmine 3,400. 275.00
No gum 1,800.

Printed by the Continental Bank Note Co.

Designs of the 1870-71 Issue with secret marks on the values from 1c to 15c as described and illustrated below.

Franklin — A44a

1c. In pearl at left of numeral "1" is a small crescent.

Jackson — A45a

2c. Under the scroll at the left of "U. S." there is a small diagonal line. This mark seldom shows clearly. The stamp, No. 157, can be distinguished by its color.

Washington — A46a

3c. The under part of the upper tail of the left ribbon is heavily shaded.

Lincoln — A47a

6c. The first four vertical lines of the shading in the lower part of the left ribbon have been strengthened.

Stanton — A48a

7c. Two small semi-circles are drawn around the ends of the lines that outline the ball in the lower right hand corner.

Jefferson — A49a

10c. There is a small semi-circle in the scroll at the right end of the upper label.

Clay — A50a

12c. The balls of the figure "2" are crescent shaped.

Webster — A51a

15c. In the lower part of the triangle in the upper left corner two lines have been made heavier forming a "V." This mark can be found on some of the Continental and American (1879) printings, but not all stamps show it.

Secret marks were added to the dies of the 24c, 30c and 90c but new plates were not made from them. The various printings of these stamps can be distinguished only by the shades and paper.

White Wove Paper, thin to thick
Without Grill*

1873 *Perf. 12*

156 A44a 1c ultramarine 200.00 3.00
No gum 95.00
e. With grill *2,000.*
f. Imperf., pair — *550.00*

157 A45a 2c brown 360.00 17.50
No gum 175.00
c. With grill *1,800.* *700.00*
d. Double impression — —
e. Vertical half used as 1c on cover —

158 A46a 3c green 125.00 .40
No gum 50.00
e. With grill *325.00*
h. Horiz. pair, imperf. vert. —
i. Horiz. pair, imperf. btwn. *1,300.*
j. Double impression *1,250.*
k. Printed on both sides —

The imperf. 3c, with and without grill, can be found in the Scott U.S. Specialized Catalogue Die and Plate Proofs section.

159 A47a 6c dull pink 425.00 17.50
No gum 210.00
b. With grill *1,800.*

160 A48a 7c orange ver 875.00 75.00
No gum 450.00
a. With grill *2,650.*

161 A49a 10c brown 600.00 17.50
No gum 290.00
c. With grill *3,000.*
d. Horiz. pair, imperf. btwn. *2,500.*

162 A50a 12c black violet 1,500. 90.00
No gum 775.00
a. With grill *4,500.*

163 A51a 15c yellow orange 1,650. 100.00
No gum 850.00
a. With grill *4,500.*

164 A52 24c purple —

165 A53 30c gray black 1,750. 100.00
No gum 900.00
c. With grill *4,250.*

166 A54 90c rose carmine 2,750. 250.00
No gum 1,550.

The Philtelic Foundation has certified as genuine a 24c on vertically ribbed paper, and that is the unique stamp listed as No. 164. Specialists believe that only Continental used ribbed paper. It is not known for sure whether or not Continental also printed the 24c value on regular paper; if it did, specialists currently are not able to distinguish these from No. 153.

* All values except 24c, 90c exist with experimental (J) grill, about 7x9½mm.

Special Printing of the 1873 Issue

Hard, White Wove Paper
Without Gum

1875 *Perf. 12*

167 A44a 1c ultramarine *9,500.*
168 A45a 2c dark brown *4,250.*
169 A46a 3c blue green *11,000.* —
170 A47a 6c dull rose *10,000.*
171 A48a 7c redsh vermilion *2,500.*
172 A49a 10c pale brown *10,000.*
173 A50a 12c dark violet *3,750.*
174 A51a 15c bright orange *10,000.*
175 A52 24c dull purple *2,400.* *5,000.*
176 A53 30c greenish black *7,500.*
177 A54 90c violet carmine *9,000.*

Although perforated, these stamps were usually cut apart with scissors. As a result, the perforations are often much mutilated and the design is frequently damaged.

These can be distinguished from the 1873 issue by the shades, also by the paper, which is very white instead of yellowish.

These and the subsequent issues listed under this heading are special printings of stamps then in current use which, together with the reprints and reissues, were made for sale to collectors. They were available for postage except for the Officials and demonetized issues.

Zachary Taylor — A55

Yellowish Wove Paper

1875, June 21 *Perf. 12*

178 A45a 2c vermilion 350.00 8.50
No gum 160.00
b. Half used as 1c on cover —
c. With grill 500.00

The imperf. 2c can be found in the Scott U.S. Specialized Catalogue Die and Plate Proofs section.

179 A55 5c blue 475.00 17.50
No gum 225.00
c. With grill 1,500.

Almost all of the stamps of the Continental Bank Note Co. printing including the Department stamps and some of the Newspaper stamps may be found upon a paper that shows more or less of the characteristics of a ribbed paper.

Special Printing of the 1875 Issue

Hard, White Wove Paper
Without Gum

1875

180 A45a 2c carmine ver *26,000.*
181 A55 5c bright blue *42,500.*

VALUES FOR VERY FINE STAMPS

Stamps are valued in the grade of very fine unless otherwise indicated.

Values for unused stamps with no gum are for examples with certificates of authenticity or examples sold with the buyer having the right of certification. Beware of unused, no gum stamps that are offered "as is." Expertization by competent authorities is recommended.

Printed by the American Bank Note Company

Same as 1870-75 Issues
Soft Porous Paper
Varying from Thin to Thick

1879 *Perf. 12*

182 A44a 1c dark ultra 275.00 2.50
No gum 120.00

183 A45a 2c vermilion 120.00 2.50
No gum 55.00
a. Double impression — *500.00*

184 A46a 3c green 95.00 .40
No gum 37.50
b. Double impression —

The imperf. 3c can be found in the Scott U.S. Specialized Catalogue Die and Plate Proofs section.

185 A55 5c blue 475.00 12.00
No gum 210.00

186 A47a 6c pink 850.00 19.00
No gum 400.00

187 A49 10c brown (without secret mark) 1,750. 25.00
No gum 875.00

188 A49a 10c brown (with secret mark) 1,300. 25.00
No gum 625.00

189 A51a 15c red orange 325.00 22.50
No gum 150.00

190 A53 30c full black 1,000. 55.00
No gum 500.00

191 A54 90c carmine 2,100. 250.00
No gum 1,150.

The ABN Co. used many Continental plates to print the postage, Departmental and Newspaper stamps. Therefore, stamps bearing the Continental imprint were not always its product.

The ABN Co. also used the National 90c plate and possibly the 30c plate.

Early printings of No. 188 were from Continental plates 302 and 303 which contained the normal secret mark of 1873. After those plates were re-entered by the ABN Co. in 1880, pairs or multiple pieces contained combinations of normal, hairline or missing marks. The pairs or other multiples usually found contain at least one hairline mark which tended to disappear as the plate wore.

ABN Co. plates 377 and 378 were made in 1881 from the National transfer roll of 1870. No. 187 from those plates has no secret mark.

Perf 12 Trial Color Proofs on gummed stamp paper exist, as does a 15c without the blue "SAMPLE" overprint.

The ABN Co. used many Continental plates to print the postage, Departmental and Newspaper stamps. Therefore, stamps bearing the Continental imprint were not always its product. The imperf. 90c can be found in the Scott U.S. Specialized Catalogue Die and Plate Proofs section.

Special Printing of the 1879 Issue

Soft Porous Paper
Without Gum

1880 *Perf. 12*

192 A44a 1c dark ultra *16,000.*
193 A45a 2c black brown *8,000.*
194 A46a 3c blue green *22,500.*
195 A47a 6c dull rose *16,000.*
196 A48a 7c scar vermilion *3,000.*
197 A49a 10c deep brown *16,000.*
198 A50a 12c black purple *4,750.*
199 A51a 15c orange *16,000.*
200 A52 24c dark violet *4,750.*
201 A53 30c grnsh black *11,000.*
202 A54 90c dull carmine *12,000.*
203 A45a 2c scar vermilion *24,000.*
204 A55 5c deep blue *40,000.*

No. 197 was printed from Continental plate 302 (or 303) after plate was re-entered, therefore stamp may show normal, hairline or missing secret mark.

James A. Garfield — A56

1882, Apr. 10 *Perf. 12*

205 A56 5c yellow brown 225.00 8.00
No gum 100.00

Special Printing

Soft Porous Paper
Without Gum

1882

205C A56 5c gray brown *25,000.*

Designs of 1873 Re-engraved

Franklin — A44b

1c. The vertical lines in the upper part of the stamp have been so deepened that the background often appears to be solid. Lines of shading have been added to the upper arabesques.

Washington — A46b

3c. The shading at the sides of the central oval appears only about one-half the previous width. A short horizontal dash has been cut about 1mm below the "TS" of "CENTS."

Lincoln — A47b

6c. On the original stamps four vertical lines can be counted from the edge of the panel to the outside of the stamp. On the re-engraved stamps there are but three lines in the same place.

Jefferson — A49b

10c. On the original stamps there are five vertical lines between the left side of the oval and the edge of the shield. There are only four lines on the re-engraved stamps. In the lower part of the latter, also, the horizontal lines of the background have been strengthened.

1881-82 — *Perf. 12*

206	A44b 1c gray blue	70.00	.90
	No gum	30.00	
207	A46b 3c blue green	70.00	.55
	No gum	30.00	
c.	Double impression		—
208	A47b 6c rose ('82)	475.00	70.00
	No gum	225.00	
a.	6c deep brown red	425.00	100.00
	No gum	190.00	
209	A49b 10c brown ('82)	140.00	4.25
	No gum	60.00	
b.	10c black brown	500.00	40.00
	No gum	260.00	
c.	Double impression		—
	Nos. 206-209 (4)	755.00	75.70

Specimen stamps without overprint exist in a brown shade that differs from No. 209 and in green. The unoverprinted brown specimen is cheaper than No. 209.

Washington A57

Jackson A58

1883, Oct. 1 — *Perf. 12*

210	A57 2c red brown	47.50	.40
	No gum	20.00	
211	A58 4c blue green	220.00	12.50
	No gum	95.00	

Imperfs. can be found in the Scott U.S. Specialized Catalogue Die and Plate Proofs section.

Special Printings of 1883 follow.

Special Printing

Soft Porous Paper

1883-85

211B	A57 2c pale red brown	550.	—
	No gum	250.	
c.	Horiz. pair, imperf. btwn.	*2,000.*	
211D	A58 4c deep blue green	*22,500.*	

No. 211D is without gum.

Franklin — A59

1887 — *Perf. 12*

212	A59 1c ultramarine	100.00	1.40
	No gum	40.00	
213	A57 2c green	42.50	.35
	No gum	15.00	
b.	Printed on both sides		—
214	A46b 3c vermilion	75.00	55.00
	No gum	32.50	
	Nos. 212-214 (3)	217.50	56.75

Imperf. 1c, 2c can be found in the Scott U.S. Specialized Catalogue Die and Plate Proofs section.

1888 — *Perf. 12*

215	A58 4c carmine	200.00	17.50
	No gum	85.00	
216	A56 5c indigo	210.00	10.00
	No gum	90.00	
217	A53 30c orange brown	425.00	95.00
	No gum	200.00	
218	A54 90c purple	1,200.	225.00
	No gum	650.00	
	Nos. 215-218 (4)	2,035.	347.50

Imperfs. can be found in the Scott U.S. Specialized Catalogue Die and Plate Proofs section.

IMPORTANT INFORMATION REGARDING VALUES FOR NEVER-HINGED STAMPS

Collectors should be aware that the values given for never-hinged stamps from No. 219 on are for stamps in the grade of very fine. The never-hinged premium as a percentage of value will be larger for stamps in extremely fine or superb grades, and the premium will be smaller for fine-very fine, fine or poor examples. This is particularly true of the issues of the late-19th and early-20th centuries. For example, in the grade of very fine, an unused stamp from this time period may be valued at $100 hinged and $160 never hinged. The never-hinged premium is thus 60%. But in a grade of extremely fine, this same stamp will not only sell for more hinged, but the never-hinged premium will increase, perhaps to 100%-300% or more over the higher extremely fine value. In a grade of superb, a hinged copy will sell for much more than a very fine copy, and additionally the never-hinged premium will be much larger, perhaps as large as 300%-400% or more. On the other hand, the same stamp in a grade of fine or fine-very fine not only will sell for less than a very fine stamp in hinged condition, but additionally the never-hinged premium will be smaller than the never-hinged premium on a very fine stamp, perhaps as small as 15%-30%.

Please note that the above statements and percentages are NOT a formula for arriving at the values of stamps in hinged or never-hinged condition in the grades of fine, fine to very fine, extremely fine or superb. The percentages given apply only to the size of the premium for never-hinged condition that might be added to the stamp value for hinged condition. The marketplace will determine what this value will be for grades other than very fine. Further, the percentages given are only generalized estimates. Some stamps or grades may have percentages for never-hinged condition that are higher or lower than the ranges given.

Franklin A60

Washington A61

Jackson — A62

Lincoln — A63

Ulysses S. Grant — A64

Garfield — A65

William T. Sherman — A66

Daniel Webster — A67

Henry Clay — A68

Jefferson — A69

Perry — A70

1890-93 — *Perf. 12*

219	A60 1c dull blue	27.50	.30
	Never hinged	50.00	
219D	A61 2c lake	210.00	.80
	Never hinged	375.00	
220	A61 2c carmine	22.50	.30
	Never hinged	40.00	
a.	Cap on left "2"	75.00	2.25
	Never hinged	135.00	
c.	Cap on both "2's"	275.00	17.50
	Never hinged	500.00	
221	A62 3c purple	72.50	7.00
	Never hinged	130.00	
222	A63 4c dark brown	75.00	2.50
	Never hinged	135.00	
223	A64 5c chocolate	72.50	2.50
	Never hinged	130.00	
224	A65 6c brown red	75.00	19.00
	Never hinged	135.00	
225	A66 8c lilac ('93)	57.50	12.00
	Never hinged	105.00	
226	A67 10c green	155.00	3.00
	Never hinged	275.00	
227	A68 15c indigo	200.00	19.00
	Never hinged	360.00	
228	A69 30c black	325.00	27.50
	Never hinged	575.00	
229	A70 90c orange	500.00	120.00
	Never hinged	900.00	
	Nos. 219-229 (12)	1,792.	213.90

The "cap on right 2" variety is due to imperfect inking, not a plate defect.

Imperfs. can be found in the Scott U.S. Specialized Catalogue Die and Plate Proofs section.

Columbian Exposition Issue

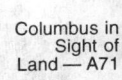

Columbus in Sight of Land — A71

Landing of Columbus A72

Flagship of Columbus A73

Fleet of Columbus A74

Columbus Soliciting Aid from Isabella — A75

Columbus Welcomed at Barcelona A76

Columbus Restored to Favor — A77

Columbus Presenting Natives — A78

Columbus Announcing his Discovery A79

Columbus at La Rábida — A80

Recall of Columbus A81

Isabella Pledging her Jewels — A82

Columbus in Chains — A83

Columbus Describing his Third Voyage — A84

Isabella and Columbus A85

Columbus A86

1893 ***Perf. 12***

230	A71	1c deep blue	25.00	.40
		Never hinged	42.50	
231	A72	2c brown violet	22.50	.20
		Never hinged	40.00	
232	A73	3c green	62.50	15.00
		Never hinged	115.00	
233	A74	4c ultra	87.50	7.50
		Never hinged	160.00	
a.		4c blue (error)	*19,000.*	*5,500.*
		Never hinged	27,500.	
234	A75	5c chocolate	95.00	8.00
		Never hinged	175.00	
235	A76	6c purple	90.00	22.50
		Never hinged	170.00	
a.		6c red violet	90.00	22.50
		Never hinged	170.00	
236	A77	8c magenta	80.00	11.00
		Never hinged	145.00	
237	A78	10c black brown	135.00	8.00
		Never hinged	240.00	
238	A79	15c dark green	240.00	65.00
		Never hinged	425.00	
239	A80	30c orange brown	300.00	85.00
		Never hinged	550.00	
240	A81	50c slate blue	600.00	160.00
		Never hinged	1,150.	
241	A82	$1 salmon	1,500.	650.00
		Never hinged	2,900.	
		No gum	725.00	
242	A83	$2 brown red	1,550.	600.00
		Never hinged	3,000.	
		No gum	725.00	
243	A84	$3 yellow green	2,400.	1,000.
		Never hinged	4,750.	
		No gum	1,100.	
a.		$3 olive green	2,400.	1,000.
		Never hinged	4,750.	
		No gum	1,100.	
244	A85	$4 crimson lake	3,250.	1,350.
		Never hinged	6,500.	
		No gum	1,500.	
a.		$4 rose carmine	3,250.	1,350.
		Never hinged	6,500.	
		No gum	1,500.	
245	A86	$5 black	3,750.	1,600.
		Never hinged	8,000.	
		No gum	1,750.	

World's Columbian Expo., Chicago, May 1-Oct. 30, 1893.

Nos. 230-245 are known imperf., but were not regularly issued. (See Scott U. S. Specialized Catalogue Die and Plate Proofs for the 2c.)

Never-Hinged Stamps

See note after No. 218 regarding premiums for never-hinged stamps.

Bureau Issues

Starting in 1894, the Bureau of Engraving and Printing at Washington has produced most U.S. postage stamps. Until 1965 Bureau-printed stamps were engraved except Nos. 525-536, which are offset. The combination of lithography and engraving (see No. 1253) was first used in 1964, and photogravure (see No. 1426) in 1971.

Franklin A87

Washington A88

Jackson A89

Lincoln A90

Grant A91

Garfield A92

Sherman A93

Webster A94

Clay A95

Jefferson A96

Perry A97

James Madison A98

John Marshall — A99

TWO CENTS

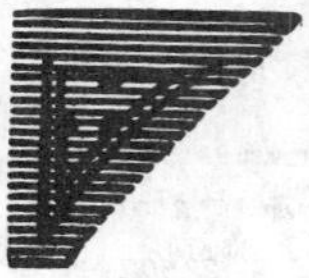

Triangle A (Type I)

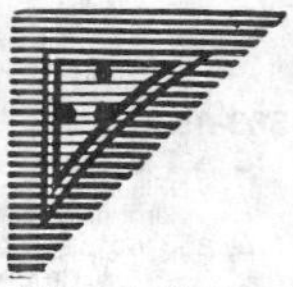

Triangle B (Type II)

Type I. The horizontal lines of the ground work run across the triangle and are of the same thickness within it as without.

Type II. The horizontal lines cross the triangle but are thinner within it than without.

Triangle C (Types III and IV)

Type III. The horizontal lines do not cross the double frame lines of the triangle. The lines within the triangle are thin, as in type II. Otherwise, design as type II.

Type IV

Type IV. Same triangle C as type III, but other design differences including, (1) re-cutting and lengthening of hairline, (2) shaded toga button, (3) strengthening of lines on sleeve, (4) additional dots on ear, (5) "T" of "TWO" straight at right, (6) background lines extend into white oval opposite "U" of "UNITED." Many other differences exist.

ONE DOLLAR

Type I

Type I. The circles enclosing "$1" are broken where they meet the curved line below "One Dollar." The 15 left vert. rows of impressions from plate 76 are Type I, the balance Type II.

Type II

Type II. The circles are complete.

1894 **Unwmk.** ***Perf. 12***

246	A87	1c ultramarine	32.50	4.00
		Never hinged	55.00	
247	A87	1c blue	67.50	2.00
		Never hinged	115.00	
248	A88	2c pink, Type I	27.50	3.00
		Never hinged	47.50	
249	A88	2c carmine lake, Type I	145.00	2.50
		Never hinged	250.00	
250	A88	2c car, Type I	30.00	.75
		Never hinged	52.50	
a.		2c rose, type I	30.00	1.50
		Never hinged	52.50	
b.		2c scarlet, type I ('95)	30.00	.40
		Never hinged	52.50	
c.		Vert. pair, imperf. horiz.	*1,500.*	
d.		Horiz. pair, imperf. btwn.	*1,500.*	
251	A88	2c car, Type II	250.00	4.50
		Never hinged	450.00	
a.		2c scarlet, type II	250.00	3.50
		Never hinged	450.00	
252	A88	2c car, Type III	120.00	4.50
		Never hinged	210.00	
a.		2c scarlet, type III	120.00	4.50
		Never hinged	210.00	
b.		Horiz. pair, imperf. vert.	*1,500.*	
c.		Horiz. pair, imperf. btwn.	*1,750.*	
253	A89	3c purple	105.00	8.00
		Never hinged	180.00	
254	A90	4c dark brown	135.00	3.75
		Never hinged	240.00	
255	A91	5c chocolate	100.00	4.75
		Never hinged	175.00	
c.		Vert. pair, imperf. horiz.	*1,750.*	
256	A92	6c dull brown	150.00	21.00
		Never hinged	260.00	
a.		Vert. pair, imperf. horiz.	*900.00*	
257	A93	8c vio brn ('95)	140.00	14.00
		Never hinged	250.00	
258	A94	10c dark green	250.00	10.00
		Never hinged	440.00	
259	A95	15c dark blue	300.00	45.00
		Never hinged	525.00	
260	A96	50c orange	450.00	95.00
		Never hinged	775.00	
261	A97	$1 black, Type I	900.00	275.00
		Never hinged	1,600.	
		No gum	325.	
261A	A97	$1 black, Type II	2,200.	600.00
		Never hinged	3,900.	
		No gum	750.	
262	A98	$2 bright blue	3,000.	875.00
		Never hinged	5,250.	
		No gum	1,050.	
263	A99	$5 dark green	4,500.	1,900.
		Never hinged	8,000.	
		No gum	2,000.	

For imperfs. and the 2c pink, vert. pair, imperf. horiz., see Scott U. S. Specialized Catalogue Die and Plate Proofs.

Same as 1894 Issue

1895 **Wmk. 191** ***Perf. 12***

264	A87	1c blue	6.50	.25
		Never hinged	11.50	
265	A88	2c car, Type I	30.00	.80
		Never hinged	52.50	
266	A88	2c car, Type II	30.00	3.00
		Never hinged	52.50	
267	A88	2c car, Type III	5.50	.25
		Never hinged	9.50	
a.		2c pink, type III ('97	6.00	.30
		Never hinged	10.50	
b.		2c vermilion, type III ('99)	*27.50*	
c.		2c rose carmine, type III ('99)		—

The three left vertical rows from plate 170 are Type II, the balance being Type III.

268	A89	3c purple	37.50	1.10
		Never hinged	65.00	
269	A90	4c dark brown	40.00	1.60
		Never hinged	67.50	
270	A91	5c chocolate	37.50	1.90
		Never hinged	65.00	
271	A92	6c dull brown	95.00	4.25
		Never hinged	165.00	
a.		Wmkd. USIR	*2,750.*	800.00
272	A93	8c violet brown	65.00	1.25
		Never hinged	115.00	
a.		Wmkd. USIR	2,250.	175.00
273	A94	10c dark green	95.00	1.50
		Never hinged	165.00	
274	A95	15c dark blue	225.00	9.00
		Never hinged	400.00	
275	A96	50c orange	300.00	20.00
		Never hinged	525.00	
a.		50c red orange	325.00	24.00
		Never hinged	575.00	
276	A97	$1 blk, Type I	650.00	70.00
		Never hinged	1,150.	
		No gum	190.00	
276A	A97	$1 blk, Type II	1,300.	160.00
		Never hinged	2,350.	
		No gum	425.00	
277	A98	$2 bright blue	1,100.	325.00
		Never hinged	2,000.	
		No gum	375.00	
a.		$2 dark blue	1,100.	325.00
		Never hinged	2,000.	
		No gum	375.00	
278	A99	$5 dark green	2,500.	450.00
		Never hinged	4,500.	
		No gum	950.	

For imperfs. and the 1c horiz. pair, imperf. vert., see Scott U. S. Specialized Catalogue Die and Plate Proofs.

For "I.R." overprints see Nos. R155-R158.

TEN CENTS

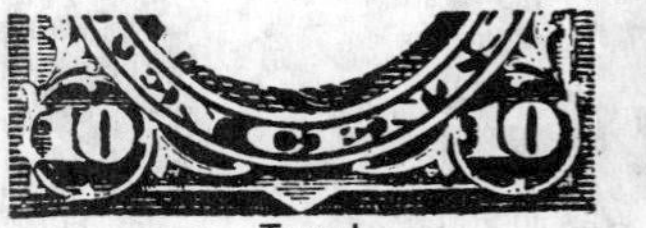

Type I

Type I. Tips of foliate ornaments do not impinge on white curved line below "TEN CENTS."

Type II

Type II. Tips of ornaments break curved line below "E" of "TEN" and "T" of "CENTS."

1897-1903 **Wmk. 191** ***Perf. 12***

279	A87	1c deep grn ('98)	9.00	.25
		Never hinged	16.00	

279B A88 2c red, type IV ('99) 9.00 .25
Never hinged 16.00
c. 2c rose carmine, type IV ('99) 240.00 65.00
Never hinged 425.00
d. 2c orange red, type IV ('00) 10.00 .30
Never hinged 17.50
e. Booklet pane of 6 ('00) 425.00 *425.00*
Never hinged 725.00
f. 2c carmine, type IV 10.00 .25
Never hinged 17.50
g. 2c pink, type IV 11.00 .40
Never hinged 19.00
h. 2c vermilion, type IV ('99) 10.00 .25
Never hinged 17.50
i. 2c brown orange, type IV ('99) *100.00* *5.00*
Never hinged *175.00*
280 A90 4c rose brn ('98) 30.00 .90
Never hinged 52.50
a. 4c lilac brown 30.00 .90
Never hinged 52.50
b. 4c orange brown 30.00 .90
Never hinged 52.50
281 A91 5c dark blue ('98) 35.00 .75
Never hinged 60.00
282 A92 6c lake ('98) 45.00 2.50
Never hinged 77.50
a. 6c purple lake 60.00 3.50
Never hinged 105.00
282C A94 10c brn, Type I ('98) 180.00 2.50
Never hinged 325.00
283 A94 10c org brn, Type II 110.00 2.00
Never hinged 190.00
284 A95 15c olive grn ('98) 150.00 7.50
Never hinged 260.00
Nos. 279-284 (8) 568.00 16.65

For "I.R." overprints see Nos. R153-R154.

VALUES FOR VERY FINE STAMPS
Please note: Stamps are valued in the grade of Very Fine unless otherwise indicated.

Trans-Mississippi Exposition Issue

Marquette on the Mississippi A100

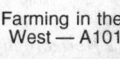

Farming in the West — A101

Indian Hunting Buffalo — A102

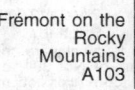

Frémont on the Rocky Mountains A103

Troops Guarding Wagon Train — A104

Hardships of Emigration A105

Western Mining Prospector A106

Western Cattle in Storm — A107

Mississippi River Bridge — A108

1898, June 17 Wmk. 191 *Perf. 12*
285 A100 1c dk yel green 30.00 6.00
Never hinged 52.50
286 A101 2c copper red 25.00 1.50
Never hinged 45.00
287 A102 4c orange 140.00 22.50
Never hinged 250.00
288 A103 5c dull blue 130.00 20.00
Never hinged 230.00
289 A104 8c violet brown 175.00 40.00
Never hinged 310.00
a. Vert. pair, imperf. horiz. *19,000.*
290 A105 10c gray violet 170.00 25.00
Never hinged 300.00
291 A106 50c sage green 625.00 180.00
Never hinged 1,100.
292 A107 $1 black 1,250. 525.00
Never hinged 2,250.
No gum 600.
293 A108 $2 orange brown 2,100. 900.00
Never hinged 3,750.
No gum 1,000.
Nos. 285-293 (9) 4,645. 1,720.

Trans-Mississippi Exposition, Omaha, Neb., June 1 to Nov. 1, 1898.
For "I.R." overprints see #R158A-R158B.

Never-Hinged Stamps
See note after No. 218 regarding premiums for never-hinged stamps.

Pan-American Exposition Issue

Fast Lake Navigation A109

"Empire State" Express A110

Electric Automobile A111

Bridge at Niagara Falls A112

Canal Locks at Sault Ste. Marie A113

Fast Ocean Navigation A114

1901, May 1 Wmk. 191 *Perf. 12*
294 A109 1c green & black 18.00 3.00
Never hinged 32.50
a. Center inverted *10,000.* *7,000.*
Never hinged *15,000.*
295 A110 2c car & black 17.50 1.00
Never hinged 31.00
a. Center inverted *37,500.* *15,000.*
296 A111 4c dp red brn & black 82.50 15.00
Never hinged 150.00
a. Center inverted *21,000.*
297 A112 5c ultra & black 95.00 14.00
Never hinged 170.00
298 A113 8c brn vio & black 120.00 50.00
Never hinged 210.00
299 A114 10c yel brn & black 170.00 25.00
Never hinged 300.00
Nos. 294-299 (6) 503.00 108.00
Nos. 294-299, never hinged 893.50

Buffalo, NY, May 1-Nov. 1, 1901.
No. 296a was a special printing.
Almost all unused copies of Nos. 295a and 296a have partial or disturbed gum. Values are for examples with full original gum that is slightly disturbed.

Franklin A115

Washington A116

Jackson A117

Grant A118

Lincoln A119

Garfield A120

Martha Washington A121

Webster A122

Benjamin Harrison A123

Clay A124

Jefferson A125

David G. Farragut A126

Madison A127

Marshall A128

1902-03 Wmk. 191 *Perf. 12*
300 A115 1c blue grn ('03) 11.00 .20
Never hinged 19.00
b. Booklet pane of 6 525.00 —
Never hinged 875.00
301 A116 2c carmine ('03) 15.00 .20
Never hinged 26.00
c. Booklet pane of 6 450.00 —
Never hinged 750.00
302 A117 3c brt violet ('03) 52.50 2.75
Never hinged 95.00
303 A118 4c brown ('03) 57.50 1.25
Never hinged 105.00
304 A119 5c blue ('03) 57.50 1.50
Never hinged 105.00
305 A120 6c claret ('03) 70.00 2.50
Never hinged 125.00
306 A121 8c violet black 42.50 2.00
Never hinged 75.00
307 A122 10c pale red brn ('03) 65.00 1.40
Never hinged 115.00
308 A123 13c purple black 47.50 7.50
Never hinged 85.00
309 A124 15c olive green ('03) 160.00 4.75
Never hinged 290.00
310 A125 50c orange ('03) 450.00 22.50
Never hinged 800.00
311 A126 $1 black ('03) 750.00 55.00
Never hinged 1,350.
No gum 175.00
312 A127 $2 dark blue ('03) 1,200. 170.00
Never hinged 2,150.
No gum 300.
313 A128 $5 dark green ('03) 2,900. 675.00
Never hinged *5,250.*
No gum 825.
Nos. 300-313 (14) 5,878. 946.55

For listings of designs A127 and A128 with Perf. 10, see Nos. 479 and 480.

1906-08 *Imperf.*
314 A115 1c blue green 20.00 15.00
Never hinged 32.50
314A A118 4c brown ('08) *27,500.* *22,500.*
Never hinged —
315 A119 5c blue ('08) 275.00 *475.00*
Never hinged 450.00

No. 314A was issued imperforate but all copies were privately perforated with large oblong perforations at the sides (Schermack type III).
Beware of copies of No. 303 with trimmed perforations and fake private perfs added.
Used copies of Nos. 314 & 315 must have contemporaneous cancels.

Coil Stamps

Imperforate stamps are known fraudulently perforated to resemble coil stamps and part perforate varieties.

1908 *Perf. 12 Horizontally*
316 A115 1c blue green, pair *100,000.* —
317 A119 5c blue, pair *12,500.* —
Never hinged *20,000.*

Perf. 12 Vertically
318 A115 1c blue green, pair *10,000.* —

Coil stamps for use in vending and affixing machines are perforated on two sides only, either horizontally or vertically. They were first issued in 1908, using perf. 12. This was changed to 8½ in 1910, and to 10 in 1914.
Imperforate sheets of certain denominations were sold to the vending machine companies which applied a variety of private perforations and separations.
Several values of the 1902 and later issues are found on an apparently coarse ribbed paper. This is caused by worn blankets on the printing press and is not a true paper variety.

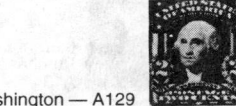

Washington — A129

Type I

Type II

Type I. Leaf next to left "2" penetrates the border.
Type II. Strong line forming border left of leaf.

1903, Nov. 12 Wmk. 191 *Perf. 12*
319 A129 2c carmine (I) 5.75 .20
Never hinged 9.50
a. 2c lake (I) —
b. 2c carmine rose (I) 7.75 .35
Never hinged 13.00
c. 2c scarlet (I) 5.75 .25
Never hinged 9.50
d. Vert. pair, imperf. horiz. *3,500.*
e. Vert. pair, imperf. btwn. *1,250.*
f. 2c lake (II) 7.50 .25
Never hinged 12.50
g. Booklet pane of 6, car (I) 110.00 *150.00*
Never hinged 180.00
h. As "g" (II) 240.00
Never hinged 400.00
i. 2c carmine (II) 27.50 *50.00*
Never hinged 45.00
j. 2c carmine rose (II) 20.00 .75
Never hinged 32.50
k. 2c scarlet (II) 17.50 .45
Never hinged 29.00
m. As "g," lake (I) *2,500.*
n. As "g," car rose (I) 160.00 *200.00*
Never hinged 260.00
p. As "g," scarlet (I) 150.00 *150.00*
Never hinged 250.00
q. As "g," lake (II) 190.00 *300.00*
Never hinged 310.00

1906, Oct. 2 *Imperf.*
320 A129 2c carmine (I) 19.00 12.00
Never hinged 30.00
a. 2c lake (II) 50.00 40.00
Never hinged 77.50
b. 2c scarlet (I) 19.00 12.50
Never hinged 30.00
c. 2c carmine rose (I) 60.00 40.00
Never hinged 95.00
d. 2c carmine (II) —

Coil Stamps

1908 *Perf. 12 Horizontally*
321 A129 2c car, pair (I) *125,000.* *170,000.*

Four or five authenticated unused pairs are known. The used value is for a single on cover, of which 2 authenticated examples are known, both used from Indianapolis in 1908. Numerous counterfeits exist.

Perf. 12 Vertically

322 A129 2c carmine, pair (II) *9,000.* *5,500.*

Louisiana Purchase Exposition

St. Louis, Mo., Apr. 30 - Dec. 1, 1904

Robert R. Livingston
A130

Thomas Jefferson
A131

James Monroe
A132

William McKinley
A133

Map of Louisiana Purchase
A134

1904, Apr. 30 Wmk. 191 *Perf. 12*

323 A130 1c green	30.00	4.00
Never hinged	52.50	
324 A131 2c carmine	27.50	1.75
Never hinged	50.00	
a. Vert. pair, imperf. horiz.	*10,000.*	
325 A132 3c violet	90.00	30.00
Never hinged	160.00	
326 A133 5c dark blue	95.00	20.00
Never hinged	165.00	
327 A134 10c red brown	180.00	27.50
Never hinged	325.00	
Nos. 323-327 (5)	422.50	83.25
Nos. 323-327, never hinged	752.50	

Jamestown Exposition Issue

Captain John Smith
A135

Founding of Jamestown
A136

Pocahontas
A137

1907 Wmk. 191 *Perf. 12*

328 A135 1c green	30.00	4.00
Never hinged	52.50	
329 A136 2c carmine	35.00	3.50
Never hinged	62.50	
330 A137 5c blue	135.00	27.50
Never hinged	240.00	
Nos. 328-330 (3)	200.00	35.00
Nos. 328-330, never hinged	355.00	

Jamestown Expo., Hampton Roads, Va., Apr. 26 to Dec. 1.

Franklin
A138

Washington
A139

Washington — A140

There are several types of some of the 2c and 3c stamps of this and succeeding issues. These types are described under the dates when they first appeared.

Illustrations of Types I-VII of the 2c (A140) and Types I-IV of the 3c (A140) are reproduced by permission of H. L. Lindquist.

TYPE I

THREE CENTS

Type I. The top line of the toga rope is weak and the rope shading lines are thin. The fifth line from the left is missing.

The line between the lips is thin.

Used on both flat plate and rotary press printings.

1908-09 Wmk. 191 *Perf. 12*

331 A138 1c green	7.00	.20
Never hinged	12.00	
a. Booklet pane of 6	160.00	*140.00*
Never hinged	240.00	
332 A139 2c carmine	6.50	.20
Never hinged	11.00	
a. Booklet pane of 6	135.00	*125.00*
Never hinged	200.00	
333 A140 3c deep violet, Type I	32.50	2.50
Never hinged	55.00	
334 A140 4c orange brown	40.00	1.00
Never hinged	67.50	
335 A140 5c blue	50.00	2.00
Never hinged	85.00	
336 A140 6c red orange	62.50	5.00
Never hinged	105.00	
337 A140 8c olive green	47.50	2.50
Never hinged	80.00	
338 A140 10c yellow ('09)	67.50	1.40
Never hinged	115.00	
339 A140 13c blue green ('09)	40.00	19.00
Never hinged	67.50	
340 A140 15c pale ultra ('09)	65.00	5.50
Never hinged	110.00	
341 A140 50c violet ('09)	325.00	20.00
Never hinged	550.00	
342 A140 $1 vio brown ('09)	500.00	75.00
Never hinged	850.00	
Nos. 331-342 (12)	1,243.	134.30

For listings of China Clay papers see the Scott U.S. Specialized Catalogue.

For listing of other perforated stamps of designs A138, A139 and A140 see

#357-366	Bluish Paper	
#374-382, 405-407	Single line wmk.	Perf. 12
#424-430	Single line wmk.	Perf. 10
#461	Single line wmk.	Perf. 11
#462-469	Unwmkd.	Perf. 10
#498-507	Unwmkd.	Perf. 11
#519	Double line wmk.	Perf. 11
#525-530, 536	Offset printing	
#538-546	Rotary press printing	

Imperf

343 A138 1c green	5.75	4.50
Never hinged	9.00	
344 A139 2c carmine	7.00	3.00
Never hinged	11.00	
345 A140 3c dp violet, Type I	13.00	20.00
Never hinged	20.00	
346 A140 4c org brown ('09)	22.50	22.50
Never hinged	35.00	
347 A140 5c blue ('09)	40.00	35.00
Never hinged	62.50	
Nos. 343-347 (5)	88.25	85.00

For listings of other imperforate stamps of designs A138, A139 and A140 see

#383 & 384, 408 & 409, 459	Single line wmk.
#481-485	Unwmkd.
#531-535	Offset printing

Coil Stamps

1908-10 *Perf. 12 Horizontally*

348 A138 1c green	35.00	19.00
Never hinged	60.00	
349 A139 2c carmine ('09)	65.00	11.00
Never hinged	110.00	
350 A140 4c orange brown ('10)	150.00	100.00
Never hinged	250.00	
351 A140 5c blue ('09)	165.00	140.00
Never hinged	280.00	
Nos. 348-351 (4)	415.00	270.00

1909 *Perf. 12 Vertically*

352 A138 1c green	75.00	40.00
Never hinged	130.00	
353 A139 2c carmine	82.50	11.00
Never hinged	140.00	
354 A140 4c orange brown	180.00	75.00
Never hinged	310.00	
355 A140 5c blue	190.00	100.00
Never hinged	325.00	
356 A140 10c yellow	2,250.	1,050.
Never hinged	3,500.	

Beware of stamps offered as No. 356 which may be examples of No. 338 with perforations trimmed at top and/or bottom. Beware also of plentiful fakes in the marketplace of Nos. 348-355. Authentication of all these coil stamps is advised.

For listings of other coil stamps of designs A138, A139 and A140 see

#385-396, 410-413, 441-458	Single line wmk.
#486-496	Unwmkd.

Bluish Paper

This was made with 35 per cent rag stock instead of all wood pulp. The grayish blue color goes through the paper showing clearly on the back as well as on the face.

1909 *Perf. 12*

357 A138 1c green	95.00	100.00
Never hinged	150.00	
358 A139 2c carmine	90.00	100.00
Never hinged	145.00	
359 A140 3c dp violet, Type I	1,800.	*2,250.*
Never hinged	2,800.	
360 A140 4c orange brown	*20,000.*	
Never hinged	*27,000.*	
361 A140 5c blue	4,500.	*6,500.*
Never hinged	*6,500.*	
362 A140 6c red orange	1,350.	*1,900.*
Never hinged	2,100.	
363 A140 8c olive green	*21,500.*	
Never hinged	*28,500.*	
364 A140 10c yellow	1,600.	*2,100.*
Never hinged	2,500.	
365 A140 13c blue green	2,800.	*2,250.*
Never hinged	4,250.	
366 A140 15c pale ultra	1,350.	*1,600.*
Never hinged	2,100.	

Nos. 360, 363 not regularly issued.

Lincoln Centenary of Birth Issue

Lincoln — A141

1909, Feb. 12 Wmk. 191 *Perf. 12*

367 A141 2c carmine	5.50	1.75
Never hinged	8.50	

Imperf

368 A141 2c carmine	22.50	20.00
Never hinged	37.50	

Bluish Paper

1909 *Perf. 12*

369 A141 2c carmine	225.00	*260.00*
Never hinged	350.00	

Alaska-Yukon-Pacific Exposition Issue

William H. Seward — A142

1909, June 1 Wmk. 191 *Perf. 12*

370 A142 2c carmine	9.00	2.00
Never hinged	13.50	

1909 *Imperf.*

371 A142 2c carmine	28.00	25.00
Never hinged	42.50	

Seattle, Wash., June 1 to Oct. 16.

Hudson-Fulton Celebration Issue

"Half Moon" and Steamship
A143

1909, Sept. 25 Wmk. 191 *Perf. 12*

372 A143 2c carmine	13.00	4.50
Never hinged	19.00	

Imperf

373 A143 2c carmine	32.50	25.00
Never hinged	47.50	

Tercentenary of the discovery of the Hudson River and Centenary of Robert Fulton's steamship.

Designs of 1908-09 Issue

1910-11 Wmk. 190 *Perf. 12*

374 A138 1c green	6.50	.20
Never hinged	10.50	
a. Booklet pane of 6	140.00	*100.00*
Never hinged	210.00	
375 A139 2c carmine	6.50	.20
Never hinged	10.50	
a. Booklet pane of 6	95.00	*85.00*
Never hinged	145.00	
b. 2c lake	*250.00*	
Never hinged	375.00	
376 A140 3c dp vio, Type I ('11)	19.00	1.40
Never hinged	30.00	
377 A140 4c brown ('11)	30.00	.50
Never hinged	50.00	
378 A140 5c blue ('11)	30.00	.50
Never hinged	50.00	
379 A140 6c red orange ('11)	35.00	.70
Never hinged	57.50	
380 A140 8c olive green ('11)	110.00	12.50
Never hinged	180.00	
381 A140 10c yellow ('11)	100.00	3.75
Never hinged	165.00	
382 A140 15c pale ultra ('11)	260.00	15.00
Never hinged	430.00	
Nos. 374-382 (9)	597.00	34.75

1910 *Imperf.*

383 A138 1c green	2.60	2.00
Never hinged	4.00	
384 A139 2c carmine	4.25	2.50
Never hinged	6.75	

Coil Stamps

1910 *Perf. 12 Horizontally*

385 A138 1c green	30.00	15.00
Never hinged	50.00	
386 A139 2c carmine	55.00	20.00
Never hinged	90.00	

1910-11 *Perf. 12 Vertically*

387 A138 1c green	125.00	50.00
Never hinged	210.00	
388 A139 2c carmine	800.00	350.00
Never hinged	1,300.	
389 A140 3c dp vio, Type I ('11)	*52,500.*	*10,000.*
Never hinged	*80,000.*	

Stamps sold as No. 388 frequently are privately perforated examples of No. 384, or examples of No. 375 with top and/or bottom perfs trimmed.

Stamps offered as No. 389 sometimes are examples of No. 376 with top and/or bottom perfs trimmed.

Expertization by competent authorities is recommended.

1910 *Perf. 8½ Horizontally*

390 A138 1c green	4.50	*6.00*
Never hinged	7.50	
391 A139 2c carmine	35.00	12.50
Never hinged	57.50	

1910-13 *Perf. 8½ Vertically*

392 A138 1c green	20.00	19.00
Never hinged	32.50	
393 A139 2c carmine	40.00	7.75
Never hinged	65.00	
394 A140 3c dp vio, Type I ('11)	50.00	47.50
Never hinged	82.50	
395 A140 4c brown ('12)	50.00	42.50
Never hinged	80.00	
396 A140 5c blue ('13)	50.00	42.50
Never hinged	80.00	
Nos. 392-396 (5)	210.00	159.25

Panama-Pacific Exposition Issue

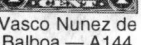

Vasco Nunez de Balboa — A144

Pedro Miguel Locks, Panama Canal — A145

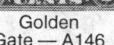

Golden Gate — A146

Discovery of San Francisco Bay — A147

1913 Wmk. 190 *Perf. 12*

397 A144 1c green 17.50 1.50
Never hinged 29.00
398 A145 2c carmine 21.00 .50
Never hinged 35.00
a. 2c carmine lake *575.00*
Never hinged *875.00*
399 A146 5c blue 75.00 9.50
Never hinged 125.00
400 A147 10c orange yellow 125.00 20.00
Never hinged 210.00
400A A147 10c orange 210.00 16.00
Never hinged 350.00
Nos. 397-400A (5) 448.50 47.50
Nos. 397-400A, never hinged 720.00

1914-15 *Perf. 10*

401 A144 1c green 25.00 5.50
Never hinged 42.50
402 A145 2c carmine ('15) 75.00 1.50
Never hinged 125.00
403 A146 5c blue ('15) 175.00 15.00
Never hinged 290.00
404 A147 10c orange ('15) 925.00 62.50
Never hinged 1,500.
Nos. 401-404 (4) 1,200. 84.50
Nos. 401-404, never hinged 1,957.

San Francisco, Cal., Feb. 20 to Dec. 4.

TYPE I

TWO CENTS

Type I. There is one shading line in the first curve of the ribbon above the left "2" and one in the second curve of the ribbon above the right "2."

The button of the toga has a faint outline.

The top line of the toga rope, from the button to the front of the throat, is also very faint.

The shading lines at the face terminate in front of the ear with little or no joining, to form a lock of hair.

Used on both flat and rotary press printings.

1912-14 Wmk. 190 *Perf. 12*

405 A140 1c green 5.50 .20
Never hinged 9.00
a. Vert. pair, imperf. horiz. *650.00* —
b. Booklet pane of 6 60.00 *45.00*
Never hinged 95.00
406 A140 2c carmine, Type I 5.50 .20
Never hinged 9.00
a. Booklet pane of 6 60.00 *60.00*
Never hinged 95.00
b. Double impression —
c. 2c lake, type II *350.00* —
407 A140 7c black ('14) 80.00 11.00
Never hinged 130.00
Nos. 405-407 (3) 91.00 11.40

1912 *Imperf.*

408 A140 1c green 1.15 .55
Never hinged 1.75
409 A140 2c carmine, Type I 1.40 .60
Never hinged 2.10

Coil Stamps

1912 *Perf. 8½ Horizontally*

410 A140 1c green 6.00 4.00
Never hinged 10.00
411 A140 2c carmine, Type I 10.00 3.75
Never hinged 16.50

Perf. 8½ Vertically

412 A140 1c green 25.00 5.50
Never hinged 42.50
413 A140 2c carmine, Type I 42.50 1.10
Never hinged 70.00
Nos. 410-413 (4) 83.50 14.35

Franklin — A148

1912-14 Wmk. 190 *Perf. 12*

414 A148 8c pale olive green 45.00 1.25
Never hinged 75.00
415 A148 9c salmon red ('14) 55.00 12.50
Never hinged 90.00
416 A148 10c orange yellow 45.00 .40
Never hinged 75.00
a. 10c brown yellow *500.00* —
Never hinged *750.00*
417 A148 12c claret brown ('14) 50.00 4.25
Never hinged 82.50
418 A148 15c gray 85.00 3.50
Never hinged 140.00
419 A148 20c ultra ('14) 200.00 15.00
Never hinged 350.00
420 A148 30c orange red ('14) 125.00 15.00
Never hinged 210.00
421 A148 50c violet ('14) 425.00 17.50
Never hinged 725.00
Nos. 414-421 (8) 1,030. 69.40

No. 421 almost always has an offset of the frame lines on the back under the gum. No. 422 does not have this offset.

VALUES FOR VERY FINE STAMPS
Please note: Stamps are valued in the grade of Very Fine unless otherwise indicated.

1912, Feb. 12 Wmk. 191 *Perf. 12*

422 A148 50c violet 250.00 15.00
Never hinged 425.00
423 A148 $1 violet brown 525.00 60.00
Never hinged 875.00

Other stamps of type A148:

#431-440	Single line wmk.	Perf. 10
#460	Double line wmk.	Perf. 10
#470-478	Unwmkd.	Perf. 10
#508-518	Unwmkd.	Perf. 11

1914-15 Wmk. 190 *Perf. 10*

424 A140 1c green 2.30 .20
Never hinged 3.75
a. Perf. 12x10 *2,750.* *2,500.*
b. Perf. 10x12 *950.00*
c. Vert. pair, imperf. horiz. *425.00* *250.00*
d. Booklet pane of 6 4.75 *3.00*
Never hinged 7.25
e. As "d," imperf. *1,600.*

Most copies of No. 424b are precanceled Dayton, Ohio, to which the value applies.

All known examples of No. 424e are without gum.

425 A140 2c rose red, Type I 2.20 .20
Never hinged 3.60
c. Perf. 10x12 —
d. Perf. 12x10 *6,500.* *3,500.*
e. Booklet pane of 6 16.00 *12.50*
Never hinged 25.00
426 A140 3c deep vio, Type I 14.00 1.25
Never hinged 23.00
427 A140 4c brown 35.00 .50
Never hinged 57.50
428 A140 5c blue 32.50 .50
Never hinged 55.00
a. Perf. 12x10 *5,500.*
429 A140 6c red orange 47.50 1.40
Never hinged 77.50
430 A140 7c black 85.00 4.00
Never hinged 140.00
431 A148 8c pale olive green 35.00 1.50
Never hinged 57.50
432 A148 9c salmon red 50.00 7.50
Never hinged 82.50
433 A148 10c orange yellow 47.50 .40
Never hinged 77.50
434 A148 11c dark green ('15) 22.50 7.50
Never hinged 37.50
435 A148 12c claret brown 26.00 4.00
Never hinged 42.50
a. 12c copper red 29.00 4.00
Never hinged 47.50
437 A148 15c gray 125.00 7.25
Never hinged 210.00
438 A148 20c ultra 210.00 4.00
Never hinged 350.00
439 A148 30c orange red 250.00 16.00
Never hinged 410.00
440 A148 50c violet ('15) 550.00 16.00
Never hinged 900.00
Nos. 424-440 (16) 1,534. 72.20

Coil Stamps

1914 *Perf. 10 Horizontally*

441 A140 1c green 1.00 1.00
Never hinged 1.60
442 A140 2c carmine, Type I 8.00 6.00
Never hinged 13.00

1914 *Perf. 10 Vertically*

443 A140 1c green 22.50 5.00
Never hinged 37.50
444 A140 2c carmine, Type I 35.00 1.50
Never hinged 55.00
445 A140 3c violet, Type I 220.00 125.00
Never hinged 350.00
446 A140 4c brown 120.00 42.50
Never hinged 190.00
447 A140 5c blue 42.50 27.50
Never hinged 67.50
Nos. 443-447 (5) 440.00 201.50

TYPE II

TWO CENTS

Type II. Shading lines in ribbons as on type I.

The toga button, rope, and shading lines are heavy.

The shading lines of the face at the lock of hair end in a strong vertical curved line.

Used on rotary press printings only.

TYPE III

TWO CENTS

Type III. Two lines of shading in the curves of the ribbons.

Other characteristics similar to type II.

Used on rotary press printings only.

Fraudulently altered copies of Type III (Nos. 455, 488, 492 and 540) have had one line of shading scraped off to make them resemble Type II (Nos. 454, 487, 491 and 539).

ROTARY PRESS STAMPS

The Rotary Press stamps are printed from plates that are curved to fit around a cylinder. This curvature produces stamps that are slightly larger, either horizontally or vertically, than those printed from flat plates. Stamps from flat plates measure about 18½-19mm wide by 22mm high. When the impressions are placed sideways on the curved plates the stamps are 19½-20mm wide; when they are placed vertically the stamps are 23mm high.

Coil Stamps

Rotary Press Printing

1915-16 *Perf. 10 Horizontally*

448 A140 1c green 6.00 3.25
Never hinged 9.50
449 A140 2c red, Type I 2,600. 450.00
Never hinged 3,800.
450 A140 2c car, Type III ('16) 9.50 3.00
Never hinged 15.00

1914-16 *Perf. 10 Vertically*

452 A140 1c green 10.00 2.00
Never hinged 16.00
453 A140 2c carmine rose, Type I 130.00 4.25
Never hinged 210.00
454 A140 2c red, Type II 82.50 10.00
Never hinged 130.00
455 A140 2c carmine, Type III 8.50 1.00
Never hinged 13.50
456 A140 3c violet, Type I ('16) 240.00 90.00
Never hinged 375.00
457 A140 4c brown ('16) 25.00 17.50
Never hinged 40.00
458 A140 5c blue ('16) 30.00 17.50
Never hinged 47.50
Nos. 452-458 (7) 526.00 142.25

1914, June 30 *Imperf.*

459 A140 2c car, Type I 250.00 *950.00*
Never hinged 350.00

No. 459 is a horizontal coil.

The used value is for a copy with a contemporaneous cancel.

Flat Plate Printings

1915, Feb. 8 Wmk. 191 *Perf. 10*

460 A148 $1 violet black 825.00 85.00
Never hinged 1,350.

1915, June 17 Wmk. 190 *Perf. 11*

461 A140 2c pale carmine red, Type I 140.00 *250.00*
Never hinged 225.00

Fraudulently perforated copies of No. 409 are offered as No. 461.

The used value is for a copy with a contemporaneous cancel.

Unwatermarked

From 1916 onward all postage stamps except Nos. 519 and 832b are on unwatermarked paper.

1916-17 Unwmk. *Perf. 10*

462 A140 1c green 6.50 .35
Never hinged 10.50
a. Booklet pane of 6 9.00 *2.50*
Never hinged 13.50
463 A140 2c carmine, Type I 4.25 .25
Never hinged 6.75
a. Booklet pane of 6 90.00 *45.00*
Never hinged 135.00
464 A140 3c violet, Type I 75.00 12.50
Never hinged 120.00
465 A140 4c orange brown 45.00 1.70
Never hinged 72.50
466 A140 5c blue 75.00 1.70
Never hinged 120.00
467 A140 5c car (error in plate of 2c, '17) 550.00 675.00
Never hinged 875.00
468 A140 6c red orange 95.00 7.00
Never hinged 150.00
469 A140 7c black 120.00 11.00
Never hinged 190.00
470 A148 8c olive green 57.50 5.50
Never hinged 92.50
471 A148 9c salmon red 57.50 14.00
Never hinged 97.50
472 A148 10c orange yel 105.00 1.25
Never hinged 170.00
473 A148 11c dark green 37.50 16.00
Never hinged 60.00
474 A148 12c claret brown 50.00 5.00
Never hinged 80.00
475 A148 15c gray 190.00 10.50
Never hinged 300.00
476 A148 20c lt ultra 240.00 12.00
Never hinged 390.00
476A A148 30c orange red *4,000.* —
Never hinged *5,250.*
477 A148 50c lt violet ('17) 1,050. 60.00
Never hinged 1,750.
478 A148 $1 violet black 775.00 16.00
Never hinged 1,250.
Nos. 462-466,468-476,477-478 (16) 2,983. 174.75

No. 476A is valued in the grade of fine.

Types of 1903 Issue

1917, Mar. 22 *Perf. 10*

479 A127 $2 dark blue 300.00 40.00
Never hinged 500.00
480 A128 $5 light green 240.00 42.50
Never hinged 400.00

TYPE Ia

TWO CENTS

Type Ia. Design characteristics similar to type I except that all lines of design are stronger.

The toga button, toga rope and rope shading lines are heavy. The latter characteristics are those of type II, which, however, occur only on impressions from rotary plates.

Used only on flat plates 10208 and 10209.

TYPE II

THREE CENTS

Type II. The top line of the toga rope is strong and the rope shading lines are heavy and complete.

The line between the lips is heavy.

Used on both flat plate and rotary press printings.

1916-17 ***Imperf.***

481	A140	1c green	1.00	.55
		Never hinged	1.50	
482	A140	2c carmine, Type I	1.50	1.25
		Never hinged	2.25	
482A	A140	2c dp rose, Type Ia		*12,000.*

No. 482A was issued imperforate but all copies were privately perforated with large oblong perforations at the sides (Schermack type III).

No. 500 exists with imperforate top sheet margin. Copies have been altered by trimming perforations. Some also have faked Schermack perfs.

483	A140	3c violet, Type I ('17)	14.00	7.50
		Never hinged	21.00	
484	A140	3c violet, Type II	11.00	5.00
		Never hinged	16.50	
485	A140	5c car (error in plate of 2c) ('17)	*10,000.*	
		Never hinged	*13,000.*	

Although #485 is valued as a single stamp, such examples are not seen in the marketplace. #485 usually is seen as the center stamp in a block of 9 with 8 #482 (value with #485 never hinged, $17,000) or as two center stamps in a block of 12 (value with both #485 never hinged, $25,000).

Coil Stamps

Rotary Press Printing

1916-19 ***Perf. 10 Horizontally***

486	A140	1c green ('18)	.90	.25
		Never hinged	1.40	
487	A140	2c car, Type II	14.00	3.00
		Never hinged	22.50	
488	A140	2c car, Type III ('19)	2.50	1.75
		Never hinged	3.75	
489	A140	3c violet, Type I ('17)	5.00	1.50
		Never hinged	7.50	
		Nos. 486-489 (4)	22.40	6.50

1916-22 ***Perf. 10 Vertically***

490	A140	1c green	.55	.25
		Never hinged	.90	
491	A140	2c car, Type II	2,100.	550.00
		Never hinged	3,000.	
492	A140	2c car, Type III	9.00	.25
		Never hinged	14.50	
493	A140	3c vio, Type I ('17)	16.00	3.00
		Never hinged	25.00	
494	A140	3c vio, Type II ('18)	10.00	1.00
		Never hinged	16.00	
495	A140	4c org brown ('17)	10.00	4.00
		Never hinged	16.00	
496	A140	5c blue ('19)	3.50	1.00
		Never hinged	5.50	
497	A148	10c orange yel ('22)	20.00	10.50
		Never hinged	32.50	
		Nos. 490,492-497 (7)	69.05	20.00

See note above #448 regarding #487, 491.

Blind Perfs.

Listings of imperforate-between varieties are for examples which show no trace of "blind perfs.," traces of impressions from the perforating pins which do not cut into the paper.

Types of 1912-14 Issue

Flat Plate Printings

1917-19 ***Perf. 11***

498	A140	1c green	.35	.25
		Never hinged	.60	
	a.	Vert. pair, imperf. horiz.	175.00	
	b.	Horiz. pair, imperf. btwn.	100.00	
	c.	Vert. pair, imperf. btwn.	*450.00*	—
	d.	Double impression	175.00	
	e.	Booklet pane of 6	2.50	*.75*
		Never hinged	4.00	
	f.	Booklet pane of 30	*1,000.*	
		Never hinged	*1,350.*	
499	A140	2c rose, Type I	.35	.25
		Never hinged	.60	
	a.	Vert. pair, imperf. horiz.	150.00	
	b.	Horiz. pair, imperf. vert.	275.00	*150.00*
	c.	Vert. pair, imperf. btwn.	*650.00*	*225.00*
	e.	Booklet pane of 6	4.00	*1.00*
		Never hinged	6.25	
	f.	Booklet pane of 30	*27,500.*	
		Never hinged	*33,000.*	
	g.	Double impression	160.00	—
500	A140	2c deep rose, Type Ia	275.00	180.00
		Never hinged	450.00	
501	A140	3c lt violet, Type I	11.00	.25
		Never hinged	17.50	
	b.	Booklet pane of 6	70.00	*30.00*
		Never hinged	110.00	
	c.	Vert. pair, imperf. horiz.	350.00	
	d.	Double impression	275.00	
502	A140	3c dk violet, Type II	14.00	.40
		Never hinged	22.50	
	b.	Booklet pane of 6	60.00	*30.00*
		Never hinged	92.50	
	c.	Vert. pair, imperf. horiz.	250.00	125.00
	d.	Double impression	200.00	
503	A140	4c brown	10.00	.25
		Never hinged	16.00	
	b.	Double impression	—	
504	A140	5c blue	9.00	.25
		Never hinged	14.50	
	a.	Horiz. pair, imperf. btwn.	*2,500.*	—
505	A140	5c rose (error in plate of 2c)	375.00	*500.00*
		Never hinged	575.00	
506	A140	6c red orange	12.50	.25
		Never hinged	20.00	
507	A140	7c black	27.50	1.10
		Never hinged	45.00	
508	A148	8c olive bister	12.00	.50
		Never hinged	19.00	
	b.	Vert. pair, imperf. btwn.	—	—
509	A148	9c salmon red	14.00	1.75
		Never hinged	22.50	
510	A148	10c orange yellow	17.00	.20
		Never hinged	27.50	
	a.	10c brown yellow	*350.00*	—
		Never hinged	*525.00*	
511	A148	11c lt green	9.00	2.50
		Never hinged	14.50	
512	A148	12c claret brown	9.00	.35
		Never hinged	14.50	
	a.	12c brown carmine	9.50	.40
		Never hinged	15.00	
513	A148	13c apple green ('19)	11.00	6.00
		Never hinged	17.50	
514	A148	15c gray	37.50	1.00
		Never hinged	60.00	
515	A148	20c light ultra	47.50	.25
		Never hinged	75.00	
	b.	Vert. pair, imperf. btwn.	*325.00*	
	c.	Double impression	*1,250.*	

Beware of pairs with blind perforations inside the design of the top stamp that are offered as No. 515b.

516	A148	30c orange red	37.50	1.00
		Never hinged	60.00	
	b.	Double impression	—	
517	A148	50c red violet	67.50	.50
		Never hinged	110.00	
	b.	Vert. pair, imperf. btwn. & at bottom	*1,750.*	*1,000.*
518	A148	$1 violet brown	52.50	1.50
		Never hinged	85.00	
	b.	$1 deep brown	*1,600.*	*1,000.*
		Never hinged	*2,550.*	
		Nos. 498-504,506-518 (20)	674.20	198.55

No. 518b is valued in the grade of fine to very fine.

Type of 1908-09 Issue

1917, Oct. 10 Wmk. 191 ***Perf. 11***

519	A139	2c carmine	400.00	*750.00*
		Never hinged	650.00	

Fraudulently perforated copies of No. 344 are offered as No. 519.

The used value is for a stamp with a contemporaneous cancel.

Franklin — A149

1918, Aug. 19 Unwmk. ***Perf. 11***

523	A149	$2 orange red & blk	625.00	230.00
		Never hinged	1,000.	
524	A149	$5 dp grn & black	220.00	35.00
		Never hinged	350.00	

See No. 547 for $2 carmine & black.

Types of 1912-14 Issue

TYPE IV

TWO CENTS

Type IV. Top line of toga rope is broken. Shading lines in toga button are so arranged that the curving of the first and last form a "D (reversed) ID."

Line of color in left "2" is very thin and usually broken.

Used on offset printings only.

TYPE V

TWO CENTS

Type V. Top line of toga is complete.

Five vertical shading lines in toga button.

Line of color in left "2" is very thin and usually broken.

Shading dots on the nose and lip are as indicated on the diagram.

Used on offset printings only.

TYPE Va

TWO CENTS

Type Va. Characteristics same as type V, except in shading dots of nose. Third row from bottom has 4 dots instead of 6. Overall height of type Va is ⅓mm less than type V.

Used on offset printings only.

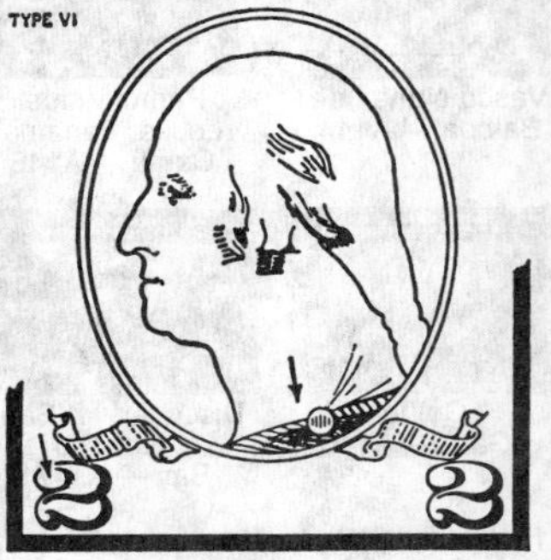

TYPE VI

TWO CENTS

Type VI. General characteristics same as type V, except that line of color in left "2" is very heavy.

Used on offset printings only.

TYPE VII

TWO CENTS

Type VII. Line of color in left "2" is invariably continuous, clearly defined, and heavier than in type V or Va, but not as heavy as in type VI.

Additional vertical row of dots has been added to the upper lip.

Numerous additional dots have been added to hair on top of head.

Used on offset printings only.

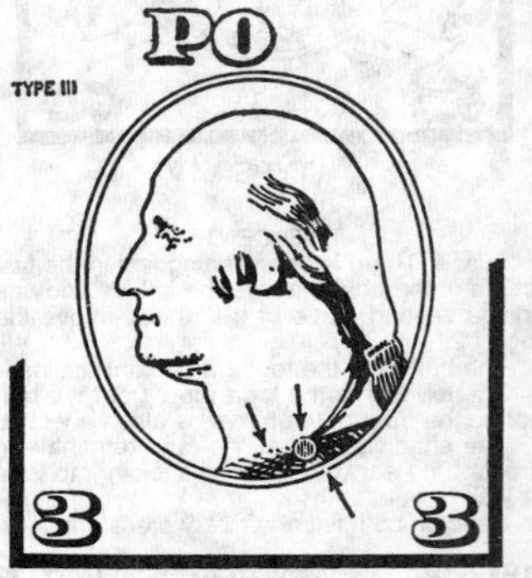

TYPE III

THREE CENTS

Type III. The top line of the toga rope is strong but the fifth shading line is missing as in type I.

Center shading line of the toga button consists of two dashes with a central dot.

The "P" and "O" of "POSTAGE" are separated by a line of color.

The frame line at the bottom of the vignette is complete.

Used on offset printings only.

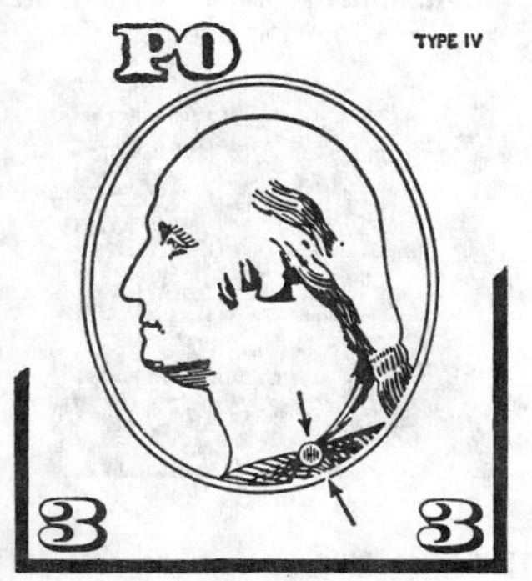

TYPE IV

THREE CENTS

Type IV. Shading lines of toga rope are complete.

Second and fourth shading lines in toga button are broken in the middle and the third line is continuous with a dot in the center.

"P" and "O" of "POSTAGE" are joined.

Frame line at bottom of vignette is broken.

Used on offset printings only.

1918-20 Offset Printing *Perf. 11*

525	A140 1c gray green	2.50	.50
	Never hinged	4.00	
a.	1c dark green	2.75	.95
	Never hinged	4.40	
c.	Horiz. pair, imperf. btwn.	100.00	
d.	Double impression	27.50	25.00
526	A140 2c car, Type IV ('20)	27.50	3.50
	Never hinged	45.00	
527	A140 2c car, Type V ('20)	20.00	1.00
	Never hinged	32.50	
a.	Double impression	60.00	10.00
b.	Vert. pair, imperf. horiz.	*600.00*	
c.	Horiz. pair, imperf. vert.	*1,000.*	—
528	A140 2c car, Type Va ('20)	9.00	.25
	Never hinged	14.50	
c.	Double impression	27.50	
g.	Vert. pair, imperf. btwn.	*2,000.*	
528A	A140 2c car, Type VI ('20)	52.50	1.50
	Never hinged	85.00	
d.	Double impression	160.00	—
f.	Vert. pair, imperf. horiz.	—	
h.	Vert. pair, imperf. btwn.	*1,000.*	
528B	A140 2c car, Type VII ('20)	22.50	.35
	Never hinged	35.00	
e.	Double impression	70.00	
529	A140 3c vio, Type III	3.25	.25
	Never hinged	5.25	
a.	Double impression	32.50	—
b.	Printed on both sides	*450.00*	
530	A140 3c pur, Type IV	1.60	.20
	Never hinged	2.50	
a.	Double impression	20.00	6.00
b.	Printed on both sides	*250.00*	
	Nos. 525-530 (8)	138.85	7.55

1918-20 *Imperf.*

531	A140 1c green ('19)	9.00	8.00
	Never hinged	14.50	
532	A140 2c car rose, Type IV ('20)	40.00	27.50
	Never hinged	65.00	
533	A140 2c car, Type V ('20)	140.00	80.00
	Never hinged	225.00	
534	A140 2c car, Type Va ('20)	11.00	6.50
	Never hinged	17.50	
534A	A140 2c car, Type VI ('20)	40.00	22.50
	Never hinged	65.00	
534B	A140 2c car, Type VII ('20)	1,900.	950.00
	Never hinged	3,000.	
535	A140 3c vio, Type IV	9.00	5.00
	Never hinged	14.50	
a.	Double impression	100.00	—
	Nos. 531-534A,535 (6)	249.00	149.50

1919, Aug. 15 *Perf. 12½*

536	A140 1c gray green	20.00	20.00
	Never hinged	32.50	
a.	Horiz. pair, imperf. vert.	*700.00*	

Victory Issue

"Victory" and Flags of the Allies — A150

Flat Plate Printing

1919, Mar. 3 Engr. *Perf. 11*

537	A150 3c violet	9.50	3.25
	Never hinged	15.00	
a.	3c deep red violet	*600.00*	*150.00*
	Never hinged	*850.00*	
b.	3c light reddish violet	9.50	3.00
	Never hinged	15.00	
c.	3c red violet	40.00	12.00
	Never hinged	65.00	

Victory of Allies in World War I.

No. 537a is valued in the grade of fine.

Rotary Press Printings

1919 *Perf. 11x10*

Size: 19½ to 20mm wide by 22 to 22¼mm high

538	A140 1c green	12.00	8.50
	Never hinged	18.00	
a.	Vert. pair, imperf. horiz.	50.00	*100.00*
	Never hinged	75.00	
539	A140 2c carmine rose, Type II	2,800.	*4,250.*
	Never hinged	4,000.	
540	A140 2c carmine rose, Type III	14.00	8.50
	Never hinged	21.00	
a.	Vert. pair, imperf. horiz.	50.00	*100.00*
	Never hinged	75.00	
b.	Horiz. pair, imperf. vert.	*750.00*	
541	A140 3c vio, Type II	45.00	30.00
	Never hinged	70.00	

The part perforate varieties of Nos. 538a and 540a were issued in sheets and may be had in blocks; similar part perforate varieties, Nos. 490 and 492, are from coils and are found only in strips.

See note over No. 448 regarding No. 539.

No. 539 is valued in the grade of fine.

Size: 19x22½-22¾mm

1920, May 26 *Perf. 10x11*

542	A140 1c green	13.50	1.10
	Never hinged	20.00	

Size: 19x22½mm

1921 *Perf. 10*

543	A140 1c green	.50	.25
	Never hinged	.75	
a.	Horiz. pair, imperf. btwn.	*1,100.*	

Size: 19x22½mm

1922 *Perf. 11*

544	A140 1c green	*14,500.*	*3,250.*
	Never hinged	*22,500.*	

No. 544 is valued in the grade of fine.

Size: 19½-20x22mm

1921 *Perf. 11*

545	A140 1c green	190.00	160.00
	Never hinged	300.00	
546	A140 2c car rose, Type III	125.00	*150.00*
	Never hinged	200.00	

Flat Plate Printing

1920, Nov. 1 *Perf. 11*

547	A149 $2 carmine & black	200.00	40.00
	Never hinged	325.00	

Pilgrim Tercentenary Issue

"Mayflower" A151

Landing of the Pilgrims A152

Signing of the Compact — A153

1920, Dec. 21 *Perf. 11*

548	A151 1c green	4.50	2.25
	Never hinged	6.75	
549	A152 2c carmine rose	6.50	1.60
	Never hinged	10.00	
550	A153 5c deep blue	42.50	12.50
	Never hinged	65.00	
	Nos. 548-550 (3)	53.50	16.35
	Nos. 548-550, never hinged	81.75	

Tercentenary of the landing of the Pilgrims at Plymouth, Mass.

Nathan Hale A154

Franklin A155

Harding A156

Washington A157

Lincoln A158

Martha Washington A159

Theodore Roosevelt A160

Garfield A161

McKinley A162

Grant A163

Jefferson A164

Monroe A165

Rutherford B. Hayes A166

Grover Cleveland A167

American Indian A168

Statue of Liberty A169

Golden Gate — A170

Niagara Falls — A171

American Buffalo A172

Arlington Amphitheater A173

Lincoln Memorial A174

US Capitol A175

Head of Freedom Statue, Capitol Dome — A176

1922-25 *Perf. 11*

551	A154 ½c olive brn ('25)	.20	.20
	Never hinged	.25	
552	A155 1c dp green ('23)	1.40	.20
	Never hinged	2.50	
a.	Booket pane of 6	6.00	*1.50*
	Never hinged	9.50	
553	A156 1½c yel brn ('25)	2.60	.15
	Never hinged	3.90	
554	A157 2c carmine ('23)	1.40	.20
	Never hinged	2.20	
a.	Horiz. pair, imperf. vert.	200.00	
b.	Vert. pair, imperf. horiz.	*750.00*	
c.	Booklet pane of 6	6.50	*2.00*
	Never hinged	10.50	
555	A158 3c violet ('23)	18.00	1.00
	Never hinged	29.00	
556	A159 4c yel brn ('23)	19.00	.25
	Never hinged	30.00	
a.	Vert. pair, imperf. horiz.	—	
557	A160 5c dark blue	19.00	.20
	Never hinged	30.00	
a.	Imperf., pair	*1,500.*	
b.	Horiz. pair, imperf. vert.	—	
558	A161 6c red orange	35.00	.85
	Never hinged	55.00	
559	A162 7c black ('23)	9.00	.55
	Never hinged	13.50	
560	A163 8c olive grn ('23)	47.50	.60
	Never hinged	75.00	
561	A164 9c rose ('23)	13.50	1.10
	Never hinged	22.50	
562	A165 10c orange ('23)	18.00	.20
	Never hinged	29.00	
a.	Vert. pair, imperf. horiz.	*1,250.*	
b.	Imperf., pair	*1,250.*	
563	A166 11c light blue	1.30	.40
	Never hinged	2.20	
d.	Imperf., pair		—
564	A167 12c brn vio ('23)	6.00	.20
	Never hinged	9.50	
a.	Horiz. pair, imperf. vert.	*1,000.*	
565	A168 14c blue ('23)	4.00	.75
	Never hinged	6.50	
566	A169 15c gray	22.50	.20
	Never hinged	37.50	
567	A170 20c car rose ('23)	21.00	.20
	Never hinged	35.00	
a.	Horiz. pair, imperf. vert.	*1,500.*	
568	A171 25c yellow green	18.00	.45
	Never hinged	29.00	
b.	Vert. pair, imperf. horiz.	*850.00*	
569	A172 30c olive brn ('23)	32.50	.35
	Never hinged	52.50	
570	A173 50c lilac	55.00	.20
	Never hinged	87.50	
571	A174 $1 vio black ('23)	45.00	.45
	Never hinged	72.50	
572	A175 $2 dp blue ('23)	90.00	9.00
	Never hinged	145.00	
573	A176 $5 car & bl ('23)	150.00	15.00
	Never hinged	250.00	
a.	$5 carmine lake & dark blue	175.00	16.00
	Never hinged	280.00	
	Nos. 551-573 (23)	629.90	32.70
	Nos. 551-573, never hinged	1,021.	

For listings of other perforated stamps of designs A154 to A176 see

#578-579	Perf. 11x10
#581-591	Perf. 10
#594-595	Perf. 11
#632-642, 653, 692-696	Perf. 11x10½
#697-701	Perf. 10½x11

This series includes Nos. 622-623 (perf. 11).

1923-25 *Imperf.*

575	A155 1c green	7.50	5.00
	Never hinged	11.50	
576	A156 1½c yel brn ('25)	1.60	1.50
	Never hinged	2.40	
577	A157 2c carmine	1.75	1.25
	Never hinged	2.60	
	Nos. 575-577 (3)	10.85	7.75
	Nos. 555-577, never hinged	16.50	

The 1½c A156 rotary press imperforate is listed as No. 631.

Rotary Press Printings

Perf. 11x10

578	A155 1c green	95.00	*140.00*
	Never hinged	150.00	
579	A157 2c carmine	85.00	*125.00*
	Never hinged	135.00	

Nos. 578-579 were made from coil waste of Nos. 597, 599 and measure approximately 19¾x22¼mm.

1923-26 *Perf. 10*

581	A155 1c green	10.00	.65
	Never hinged	16.00	
582	A156 1½c brown ('25)	5.00	.60
	Never hinged	8.00	
583	A157 2c carmine ('24)	2.75	.25
	Never hinged	4.50	
a.	Booklet pane of 6	90.00	*27.50*
	Never hinged	135.00	
584	A158 3c violet ('25)	30.00	2.25
	Never hinged	48.00	
585	A159 4c yel brn ('25)	17.50	.45
	Never hinged	28.00	

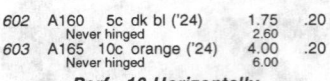

586 A160 5c blue ('25) 17.50 .25
Never hinged 28.00
a. Horiz. pair, imperf. btwn. —
587 A161 6c red org ('25) 8.25 .35
Never hinged 13.25
588 A162 7c black ('26) 12.00 5.50
Never hinged 19.00
589 A163 8c ol grn ('26) 27.50 3.50
Never hinged 44.00
590 A164 9c rose ('26) 5.50 2.25
Never hinged 8.75
591 A165 10c orange ('25) 65.00 .25
Never hinged 105.00
Nos. 581-591 (11) 201.00 16.30
Nos. 581-591, never hinged 322.50

Perf. 11

594 A155 1c green *18,000.* 5,500.
595 A157 2c carmine 300. 300.
Never hinged 475.

Nos. 594-595 were made from coil waste of Nos. 597 and 599, and measure approximately 19¾x22¼mm.

No. 594 unused is valued without gum; both unused and used are valued with perforations just touching frameline on one side.

Perf. 11

596 A155 1c green *60,000.*
Precanceled *45,000.*

No. 596 was made from rotary press sheet waste and measures approximately 19¼x22½mm. A majority of the copies carry the Bureau precancel "Kansas City, Mo." No. 596 is valued in the grade of fine.

ROTARY PRESS DOUBLE PAPER

The web of paper used on rotary presses must be continuous, therefore any break in the paper must be lapped and pasted, causing the "double paper" varieties. These are no longer listed since they may occur on any rotary press stamp.

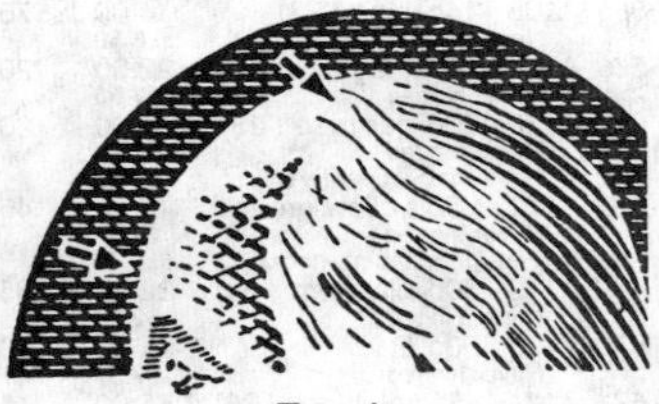

Type I

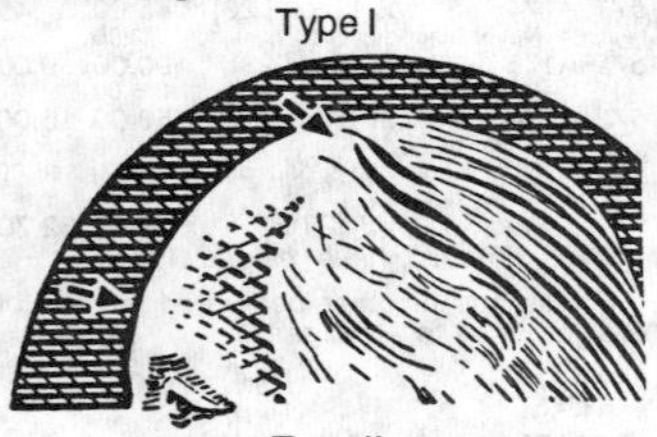

Type II

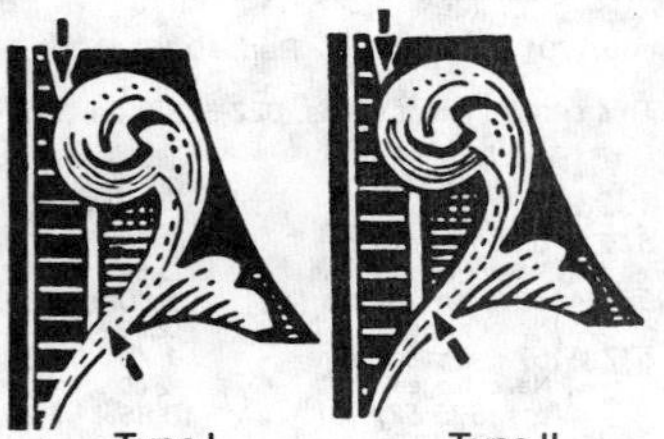

Type I Type II

Type I. No heavy hair lines at top center of head. Outline of left acanthus scroll generally faint at top and toward base at left side.

Type II. The heavy hair lines at top center of head; two being outstanding in the white area. Outline of left acanthus scroll very strong and clearly defined at top (under left edge of lettered panel) and at lower curve (above and to left of numeral oval). Type II is found only on Nos. 599A and 634A.

Coil Stamps

Rotary Press Printing

1923-29 ***Perf. 10 Vertically***

597 A155 1c green .30 .20
Never hinged .45
598 A156 1½c brown ('25) 1.00 .20
Never hinged 1.50
599 A157 2c car, Type I ('23) .40 .20
Never hinged .60
599A A157 2c car, Type II ('29) 125.00 11.00
Never hinged 200.00
600 A158 3c violet ('24) 7.25 .20
Never hinged 11.00
601 A159 4c yellow brown 4.50 .35
Never hinged 6.75
602 A160 5c dk bl ('24) 1.75 .20
Never hinged 2.60
603 A165 10c orange ('24) 4.00 .20
Never hinged 6.00

Perf. 10 Horizontally

604 A155 1c green ('24) .35 .20
Never hinged .50
605 A156 1½c yel brn ('25) .35 .20
Never hinged .50
606 A157 2c carmine .35 .20
Never hinged .50
Nos. 597-599,600-606 (10) 20.25 2.15
Nos. 597-599, 600-606, never hinged 30.40

Harding Memorial Issue

Warren G. Harding — A177

Flat Plate Printing
(19¼x22¼mm)

1923, Sept. 1 ***Perf. 11***

610 A177 2c black .65 .20
Never hinged 1.00
a. Horiz. pair, imperf. vert. *1,750.*

1923, Nov. 15 ***Imperf.***

611 A177 2c black 6.50 4.00
Never hinged 10.00

Rotary Press Printing
(19¼x22½mm)

1923, Sept. 12 ***Perf. 10***

612 A177 2c black 17.50 1.75
Never hinged 26.00

1923 ***Perf. 11***

613 A177 2c black *25,000.*

Tribute to President Warren G. Harding, who died August 2, 1923.

Nos. 610a, 613 valued in the grade of fine.

Huguenot-Walloon Tercentenary Issue

"New Netherland" A178

Landing at Fort Orange A179

Monument to Jan Ribault at Duvall County, Fla. — A180

Flat Plate Printings

1924, May 1 ***Perf. 11***

614 A178 1c dark green 3.00 3.25
Never hinged 4.25
615 A179 2c carmine rose 6.00 2.10
Never hinged 8.50
616 A180 5c dark blue 25.00 12.50
Never hinged 35.00
Nos. 614-616 (3) 34.00 17.85
Nos. 614-616, never hinged 47.75

Tercentenary of the settling of the Walloons and in honor of the Huguenots.

Lexington-Concord Issue

Washington at Cambridge A181

"Birth of Liberty," by Henry Sandham A182

The Minute Man, by Daniel Chester French A183

1925, Apr. 4 ***Perf. 11***

617 A181 1c deep green 2.80 2.40
Never hinged 4.00
618 A182 2c carmine rose 5.50 3.90
Never hinged 7.75
619 A183 5c dark blue 22.50 12.50
Never hinged 32.50
Nos. 617-619 (3) 30.80 18.80
Nos. 617-619, never hinged 44.25

150th anniv. of the Battle of Lexington-Concord.

Norse-American Issue

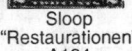

Sloop "Restaurationen" A184

Viking Ship A185

1925, May 18 ***Perf. 11***

620 A184 2c carmine & black 4.00 3.00
Never hinged 6.00
621 A185 5c dk blue & black 15.00 10.50
Never hinged 22.50

100th anniv. of the arrival in NY on Oct. 9, 1825, of the sloop "Restaurationen" with the first group of immigrants from Norway to the US.

Benjamin Harrison A186

Woodrow Wilson A187

1925-26 ***Perf. 11***

622 A186 13c green ('26) 13.50 .45
Never hinged 21.00
623 A187 17c black 15.00 .25
Never hinged 24.00

Sesquicentennial Exposition Issue

Liberty Bell — A188

1926, May 10 ***Perf. 11***

627 A188 2c carmine rose 3.25 .50
Never hinged 4.50

150th anniv. of the Declaration of Independence, Philadelphia, June 1-Dec. 1.

Statue of John Ericsson A189

Alexander Hamilton's Battery A190

Ericsson Memorial Issue

1926, May 29 ***Perf. 11***

628 A189 5c gray lilac 6.50 3.25
Never hinged 9.50

John Ericsson, builder of the "Monitor."

Battle of White Plains Issue

1926, Oct. 18 ***Perf. 11***

629 A190 2c carmine rose 2.25 1.70
Never hinged 3.25
a. Vertical pair, imperf. btwn. —

Battle of White Plains, NY, 150th anniv.

International Philatelic Exhibition

Souvenir Sheet

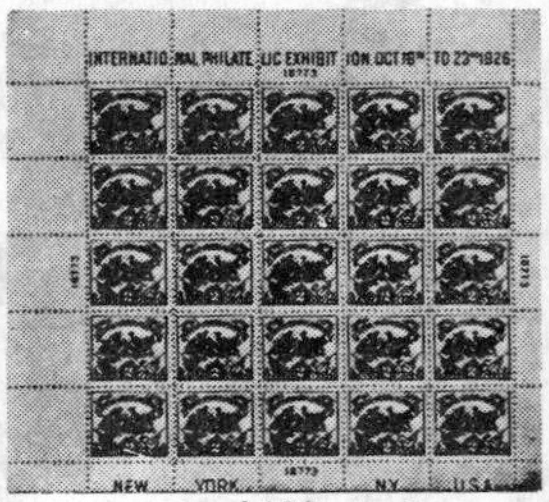

A190a

1926, Oct. 18 ***Perf. 11***

630 A190a 2c carmine rose, sheet of 25 400.00 450.00
Never hinged 550.00

Intl. Phil. Exhib. in NYC, Oct. 16-23. Size: 158-160¼x136-146½mm.

Condition Valued:

Centering: Overall centering will average very fine, but individual stamps may be better or worse.

Perforations: No folds along rows of perforations.

Gum: There may be some light gum bends but no gum creases.

Hinging: There may be hinge marks in the selvage and on up to two or three stamps, but no heavy hingling or hinge remnants (except in the ungummed portion of the wide selvage).

Margins: Top panes should have about ½ inch bottom margin and 1 inch top margin.

Bottom panes should have about ½ inch top margin and just under ¾ inch bottom margin. Both will have one wide side (usually 1½ inches plus) and one narrow (½ inch) side margin. The wide margin corner will have a small diagonal notch on top panes.

Types of 1922-26

Rotary Press Printings

1926, Aug. 27 ***Imperf.***

631 A156 1½c yellow brown 2.00 1.70
Never hinged 2.75

1926-34 ***Perf. 11x10½***

632 A155 1c green ('27) .20 .20
Never hinged .20
a. Booklet pane of 6 5.50 *1.50*
Never hinged 7.00
b. Vert. pair, imperf. btwn. 1,600. *125.00*
Never hinged 2,500.
c. Horiz. pair, imperf. btwn. —
633 A156 1½c yel brown ('27) 2.00 .20
Never hinged 2.60
634 A157 2c car, Type I .20 .20
Never hinged .20
b. 2c carmine lake — —
c. Horiz. pair, imperf. btwn. *2,000.*
d. Booklet pane of 6 1.75 *.90*
Never hinged 2.50
634A A157 2c car, Type II ('28) 350.00 13.50
Never hinged 475.00
635 A158 3c violet ('27) .45 .20
Never hinged .55
a. 3c bright violet ('34) .25 .20
Never hinged .30
636 A159 4c yel brown ('27) 2.25 .20
Never hinged 3.00
637 A160 5c dk blue ('27) 2.25 .20
Never hinged 3.00
638 A161 6c red orange ('27) 2.25 .20
Never hinged 3.00
639 A162 7c black ('27) 2.25 .20
Never hinged 3.00
a. Vert. pair, imperf. btwn. 275.00 85.00
640 A163 8c ol grn ('27) 2.25 .20
Never hinged 3.00
641 A164 9c rose ('27) 2.25 .20
Never hinged 3.00
642 A165 10c orange ('27) 3.75 .20
Never hinged 5.00
Nos. 632-634,635-642 (11) 20.10 2.20
Nos. 632-634, 635-642 never hinged 26.45

The 1½c, 2c, 4c, 5c, 6c, 8c imperf. (dry print) are printer's waste.

For ½c, 11c-50c see Nos. 653, 692-701.

Vermont Sesquicentennial Issue

Green Mountain Boy — A191

Flat Plate Printing

1927, Aug. 3 ***Perf. 11***

643 A191 2c carmine rose 1.40 .80
Never hinged 2.00

Battle of Bennington, Vt., and independence of the State of Vermont, 150th anniv.

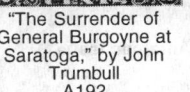

"The Surrender of General Burgoyne at Saratoga," by John Trumbull
A192

Washington at Prayer
A193

Burgoyne Campaign Issue

1927, Aug. 3 ***Perf. 11***

644 A192 2c carmine rose 3.50 2.10
Never hinged 5.00

Battles of Bennington, Oriskany, Fort Stanwix and Saratoga.

Valley Forge Issue

1928, May 26 ***Perf. 11***

645 A193 2c carmine rose 1.05 .40
Never hinged 1.40
a. 2c lake —
Never hinged —

150th anniv. of Washington's encampment at Valley Forge, Pa.

Battle of Monmouth Issue

No. 634 Overprinted **MOLLY PITCHER**

Rotary Press Printing

1928, Oct. 20 ***Perf. 11x10½***

646 A157 2c carmine 1.10 1.10
Never hinged 1.45
a. "Pitcher" only —

The normal space between a vertical pair of the overprints is 18mm, but pairs are known with the space measuring 28mm.

150th anniv. of the Battle of Monmouth, NJ, and as a memorial to "Molly Pitcher" (Mary Ludwig Hays), the heroine of the battle.

Hawaii Sesquicentennial Issue

Nos. 634 and 637 Overprinted **HAWAII 1778 - 1928**

Rotary Press Printing

1928, Aug. 13 ***Perf. 11x10½***

647 A157 2c carmine 5.00 4.50
Never hinged 6.75
648 A160 5c dark blue 14.50 13.50
Never hinged 20.00

150th anniv. of the discovery of the Hawaiian Islands by Captain Cook.

These stamps were on sale at post offices in the Hawaiian Islands and at the Postal Agency in Washington, DC They were not on sale at post offices in the Continental US, though they were valid for postage there.

Normally the overprints were placed 18mm apart vertically, but pairs exist with a space of 28mm between the overprints.

Aeronautics Conference Issue

Wright Airplane
A194

Globe and Airplane
A195

Flat Plate Printing

1928, Dec. 12 ***Perf. 11***

649 A194 2c carmine rose 1.25 .80
Never hinged 1.75
650 A195 5c blue 5.25 3.25
Never hinged 7.00

Intl. Civil Aeronautics Conf. at Washington, DC, Dec. 12-14, 1928, and of the 25th anniv. of the 1st airplane flight by the Wright brothers, Dec. 17, 1903.

George Rogers Clark Issue

Surrender of Fort Sackville
A196

1929, Feb. 25 ***Perf. 11***

651 A196 2c carmine & black .65 .50
Never hinged .90

150th anniv. of the surrender of Fort Sackville, the present site of Vincennes, Ind., to George Rogers Clark.

Type of 1925

Rotary Press Printing

1929, May 25 ***Perf. 11x10½***

653 A154 ½c olive brown .20 .20
Never hinged .20

Edison's First Lamp
A197

Maj. Gen. John Sullivan
A198

Electric Light Jubilee Issue

1929 **Flat Plate Printing** ***Perf. 11***

654 A197 2c carmine rose .70 .70
Never hinged 1.00

Rotary Press Printing

Perf. 11x10½

655 A197 2c carmine rose .65 .20
Never hinged .90

Coil Stamp (Rotary Press)

Perf. 10 Vertically

656 A197 2c carmine rose 14.00 1.75
Never hinged 20.00
Nos. 654-656 (3) 15.35 2.65

50th anniv. of invention of the incandescent lamp by Thomas Alva Edison, Oct. 21, 1879. Issued: No. 654, June 5; Nos. 655-656, June 11.

Sullivan Expedition Issue

Flat Plate Printing

1929, June 17 ***Perf. 11***

657 A198 2c carmine rose .70 .60
Never hinged 1.00
a. 2c lake 500.00 —
Never hinged 750.00

150th anniv. of the Sullivan Expedition in NY State during the Revolutionary War.

Nos. 632-634, 635-642 Overprinted **Kans.**

Rotary Press Printing

1929 ***Perf. 11x10½***

658 A155 1c green 2.50 2.00
Never hinged 3.60
a. Vert. pair, one without ovpt. 325.00
659 A156 1½c brown 4.00 2.90
Never hinged 5.75
a. Vert. pair, one without ovpt. 350.00
660 A157 2c carmine 4.50 1.10
Never hinged 6.50
661 A158 3c violet 22.50 15.00
Never hinged 32.50
a. Vert. pair, one without ovpt. 425.00
662 A159 4c yellow brown 22.50 9.00
Never hinged 32.50
a. Vert. pair, one without ovpt. 425.00
663 A160 5c deep blue 14.00 9.75
Never hinged 20.00
664 A161 6c red orange 32.50 18.00
Never hinged 47.50
665 A162 7c black 30.00 27.50
Never hinged 44.00
a. Vert. pair, one without ovpt. —
666 A163 8c olive green 110.00 75.00
Never hinged 160.00
667 A164 9c light rose 16.00 11.25
Never hinged 24.00
668 A165 10c orange yel 25.00 12.00
Never hinged 35.00
Nos. 658-668 (11) 283.50 183.50
Nos. 658-668, never hinged 411.35

The existence of No. 665a has been questioned by specialists. The editors would like to see authenticated evidence of such a pair.

See note following No. 679.

Overprinted **Nebr.**

669 A155 1c green 4.00 2.25
Never hinged 5.75
a. Vert. pair, one without ovpt. —
b. No period after "Nebr." (19338, 19339 UR 26, 36) 50.00
670 A156 1½c brown 3.75 2.50
Never hinged 5.50
671 A157 2c carmine 3.75 1.30
Never hinged 5.50
672 A158 3c violet 15.00 12.00
Never hinged 22.00
a. Vert. pair, one without ovpt. 425.00
673 A159 4c yellow brown 22.50 15.00
Never hinged 32.50
674 A160 5c deep blue 20.00 15.00
Never hinged 29.00
675 A161 6c red orange 47.50 24.00
Never hinged 67.50
676 A162 7c black 27.50 18.00
Never hinged 40.00
677 A163 8c olive green 37.50 25.00
Never hinged 55.00
678 A164 9c light rose 42.50 27.50
Never hinged 62.50
a. Vert. pair, one without ovpt. 650.00
679 A165 10c orange yel 135.00 22.50
Never hinged 195.00
Nos. 669-679 (11) 359.00 165.05
Nos. 669-679, never hinged 520.25

Nos. 658-660, 669-673, 677 and 678 are known with the overprints on vertical pairs spaced 32mm apart instead of the normal 22mm.

The existence of No. 669a has been questioned by specialists. The editors would like to see authenticated evidence of such a pair.

Important: Nos. 658-679 with original gum have either one horizontal gum breaker ridge per stamp or portions of two at the extreme top and bottom of the stamps, 21mm apart. Multiple complete gum breaker ridges indicate a fake overprint. Absence of the gum breaker ridges indicates either regumming or regumming and a fake overprint.

Gen. Anthony Wayne Memorial — A199

Lock No. 5, Monongahela River — A200

Battle of Fallen Timbers Issue

Flat Plate Printing

1929, Sept. 14 ***Perf. 11***

680 A199 2c carmine rose .80 .80
Never hinged 1.10

General Anthony Wayne memorial and the 135th anniv. of the Battle of Fallen Timbers, Ohio.

Ohio River Canalization Issue

1929, Oct. 19 ***Perf. 11***

681 A200 2c carmine rose .70 .65
Never hinged .90

Completion of the Ohio River Canalization Project between Cairo, Ill. and Pittsburgh.

Massachusetts Bay Colony Issue

Mass. Bay Colony Seal — A201

1930, Apr. 8 ***Perf. 11***

682 A201 2c carmine rose .60 .50
Never hinged .80

300th anniv. of the founding of the Massachusetts Bay Colony.

Carolina-Charleston Issue

Gov. Joseph West and Chief Shadoo, a Kiowa — A202

1930, Apr. 10 ***Perf. 11***

683 A202 2c carmine rose 1.20 1.20
Never hinged 1.60

260th anniv. of the founding of the Province of Carolina, and the 250th anniv. of the City of Charleston, SC.

Warren G. Harding — A203

William H. Taft — A204

Type of 1922-26 Issue

Rotary Press Printing

1930 ***Perf. 11x10½***

684 A203 1½c brown .35 .20
Never hinged .45
685 A204 4c brown .90 .20
Never hinged 1.25

Coil Stamps

Perf. 10 Vertically

686 A203 1½c brown 1.80 .20
Never hinged 2.50
687 A204 4c brown 3.25 .45
Never hinged 4.50

Braddock's Field Issue

Statue of Col. George Washington — A205

Flat Plate Printing

1930, July 9 ***Perf. 11***

688 A205 2c carmine rose 1.00 .85
Never hinged 1.30

175th anniv. of the Battle of Braddock's Field, otherwise the Battle of Monongahela.

General von Steuben
A206

General Casimir Pulaski
A207

Von Steuben Issue

1930, Sept. 17 ***Perf. 11***

689 A206 2c carmine rose .55 .55
Never hinged .70
a. Imperf., pair 2,500.
Never hinged 3,250.

Gen. Baron Friedrich Wilhelm von Steuben (1730-1794), German soldier who served with distinction in American Revolution.

Pulaski Issue

1931, Jan. 16 ***Perf. 11***

690 A207 2c carmine rose .30 .20
Never hinged .40

150th anniv. (in 1929) of the death of Gen. Count Casimir Pulaski (1748-1779), Polish patriot and hero of American Revolution.

Types of 1922-26

Rotary Press Printing

1931 ***Perf. 11x10½***

692 A166 11c light blue 2.60 .20
Never hinged 3.70
693 A167 12c brown violet 5.50 .20
Never hinged 7.75
694 A186 13c yellow green 2.00 .20
Never hinged 2.80
695 A168 14c dark blue 3.75 .25
Never hinged 5.25
696 A169 15c gray 8.00 .20
Never hinged 11.25

Perf. 10½x11

697 A187 17c black 4.50 .20
Never hinged 6.25
698 A170 20c carmine rose 8.75 .20
Never hinged 12.50
699 A171 25c blue green 9.00 .20
Never hinged 12.50
700 A172 30c brown 17.50 .20
Never hinged 25.00
701 A173 50c lilac 40.00 .20
Never hinged 55.00
Nos. 692-701 (10) 101.60 2.05
Nos. 692-701, never hinged 142.00

"The Greatest Mother" A208

Count de Rochambeau, Washington, Count de Grasse A209

Red Cross Issue
Flat Plate Printing

1931, May 21 ***Perf. 11***

702 A208 2c black & red .25 .20
Never hinged .30
a. Red cross omitted *40,000.*

50th anniv. of the founding of the American Red Cross Society.

Yorktown Issue

1931, Oct. 19 ***Perf. 11***

703 A209 2c carmine rose & black .40 .25
Never hinged .50
a. 2c lake & black 4.50 .75
Never hinged 6.25
b. 2c dark lake & black *375.00*
Never hinged *525.00*
c. Horiz. pair, imperf. vert. *5,000.*
Never hinged *6,250.*

Surrender of Yorktown, sesquicentennial.

Washington Bicentennial Issue
Various Portraits of George Washington

A210

A211

A212

A213

A214

A215

A216

A217

A218

A219

A220

A221

Rotary Press Printings

1932, Jan. 1 ***Perf. 11x10½***

704 A210 ½c olive brown .20 .20
Never hinged .20
705 A211 1c green .20 .20
Never hinged .20
706 A212 1½c brown .40 .20
Never hinged .55
707 A213 2c carmine rose .20 .20
Never hinged .20
708 A214 3c deep violet .55 .20
Never hinged .80
709 A215 4c light brown .25 .20
Never hinged .35
710 A216 5c blue 1.60 .20
Never hinged 2.25
711 A217 6c red orange 3.25 .20
Never hinged 4.50
712 A218 7c black .25 .20
Never hinged .35
713 A219 8c olive bister 2.75 .50
Never hinged 3.75
714 A220 9c pale red 2.40 .20
Never hinged 3.25
715 A221 10c orange yellow 10.00 .20
Never hinged 14.00
Nos. 704-715 (12) 22.05 2.70
Nos. 704-715, never hinged 30.25

200th anniv. of the birth of Washington.

Skier — A222

Boy and Girl Planting Tree — A223

Olympic Winter Games Issue
Flat Plate Printing

1932, Jan. 25 ***Perf. 11***

716 A222 2c carmine rose .40 .20
Never hinged .50

Olympic Winter Games, Lake Placid, NY, Feb. 4-13.

Arbor Day Issue
Rotary Press Printing

1932, Apr. 22 ***Perf. 11x10½***

717 A223 2c carmine rose .20 .20
Never hinged .20

60th anniv. of the 1st observance of Arbor Day in Nebr., April, 1872, and the birth centenary of Julius Sterling Morton, who conceived the plan and the name "Arbor Day," while a member of the Nebr. State Board of Agriculture.

10th Olympic Games Issue

Runner at Starting Mark A224

Myron's Discobolus A225

1932, June 15 ***Perf. 11x10½***

718 A224 3c violet 1.40 .20
Never hinged 1.75
719 A225 5c blue 2.20 .20
Never hinged 2.75

Los Angeles, Cal., July 30-Aug. 14.

Washington — A226

1932, June 16 ***Perf. 11x10½***

720 A226 3c deep violet .20 .20
Never hinged .20
b. Booklet pane of 6 37.50 *7.50*
Never hinged 50.00
c. Vert. pair, imperf. btwn. 325.00 *250.00*
Never hinged 425.00

Coil Stamps
Rotary Press Printing

1932, June 24 ***Perf. 10 Vertically***

721 A226 3c deep violet 2.75 .20
Never hinged 3.50

1932, Oct. 12 ***Perf. 10 Horizontally***

722 A226 3c deep violet 1.50 .35
Never hinged 2.00

Garfield Type of 1922-26 Issue

1932, Aug. 18 ***Perf. 10 Vertically***

723 A161 6c deep orange 11.00 .30
Never hinged 14.50

William Penn A227

Daniel Webster A228

William Penn Issue
Flat Plate Printing

1932, Oct. 24 ***Perf. 11***

724 A227 3c violet .25 .20
Never hinged .35
a. Vert. pair, imperf. horiz. —

250th anniv. of the arrival in America of William Penn (1644-1718), English Quaker and founder of Pennsylvania.

Daniel Webster Issue

1932, Oct. 24 ***Perf. 11***

725 A228 3c violet .30 .25
Never hinged .40

Daniel Webster (1782-1852), statesman.

Georgia Bicentennial Issue

Gen. James Edward Oglethorpe — A229

1933, Feb. 12 ***Perf. 11***

726 A229 3c violet .25 .20
Never hinged .35

200th anniv. of the founding of the Colony of Georgia and James Edward Oglethorpe, who landed from England, Feb. 12th, 1733, and personally supervised the establishing of the colony.

Peace of 1783 Issue

Washington's Headquarters, Newburgh, NY — A230

Rotary Press Printing

1933, Apr. 19 ***Perf. 10½x11***

727 A230 3c violet .20 .20
Never hinged .20

150th anniv. of the Proclamation of Peace between the US and Great Britain at the end of the Revolutionary War.
See No. 752.

Century of Progress Issue

Restoration of Fort Dearborn A231

Federal Building at Chicago, 1933 A232

1933, May 25 ***Perf. 10½x11***

728 A231 1c yellow green .20 .20
Never hinged .20
729 A232 3c violet .20 .20
Never hinged .20

"Century of Progress" Intl. Phil. Exhib., Chicago, 1933 and 100th anniv. of the incorporation of Chicago as a city.

American Philatelic Society Issue
Souvenir Sheets
Without Gum
Flat Plate Printing

1933, Aug. 25 ***Imperf.***

730 Sheet of 25 27.50 27.50
a. A231 1c deep yellow green .75 .45
731 Sheet of 25 25.00 25.00
a. A232 3c deep violet .65 .45

Sheet measures 134x120mm.
See Nos. 766-767.

National Recovery Act Issue

Group of Workers — A233

Rotary Press Printing

1933, Aug. 15 ***Perf. 10½x11***

732 A233 3c violet .20 .20
Never hinged .20

Issued to direct attention to and arouse support of the Nation for the NRA.

Byrd Antarctic Issue

World Map on van der Grinten's Projection — A234

Flat Plate Printing

1933, Oct. 9 ***Perf. 11***

733 A234 3c dark blue .50 .50
Never hinged .60

Second Antarctic expedition of Rear Admiral Richard E. Byrd.
In addition to the 3 cents postage, letters sent by the ships of the expedition to be canceled in Little America were subject to a service charge of 50 cents each.
See Nos. 735, 753.

Kosciuszko Issue

Statue of Gen. Tadeusz Kosciuszko — A235

1933, Oct. 13 ***Perf. 11***

734 A235 5c blue .55 .25
Never hinged .65
a. Horiz. pair, imperf. vert. *2,250.*
Never hinged *2,800.*

Gen. Tadeusz Kosciuszko (1746-1807), Polish soldier and statesman who served in American Revolution. 150th anniv. of grant of American citizenship.

National Stamp Exhibition Issue
Souvenir Sheet
Without Gum

1934, Feb. 10 ***Imperf.***

735 Sheet of 6 12.50 10.00
a. A234 3c dark blue 2.00 1.65

Sheet measures 87x93mm. See #768.

Maryland Tercentenary Issue

"The Ark" and "The Dove" — A236

1934, Mar. 23 ***Perf. 11***

736 A236 3c carmine rose .20 .20
Never hinged .20

300th anniv. of the founding of Maryland.

Mothers of America Issue

Adaptation of Whistler's Portrait of his Mother A237

Rotary Press Printing

1934, May 2 ***Perf. 11x10½***

737 A237 3c deep violet .20 .20
Never hinged .20

Flat Plate Printing
Perf. 11

738 A237 3c deep violet .20 .20
Never hinged .20

Mother's Day. See No. 754.

Wisconsin Tercentenary Issue

Nicolet's Landing A238

1934, July 7 *Perf. 11*

739 A238 3c deep violet .20 .20
Never hinged .20
a. Vert. pair, imperf. horiz. *350.00*
Never hinged *450.00*
b. Horiz. pair, imperf. vert. *450.00*
Never hinged *575.00*

Tercentenary of the arrival of French explorer Jean Nicolet at Green Bay, Wis.
See No. 755.

National Parks Issue

El Capitan, Yosemite (California) A239

Old Faithful, Yellowstone (Wyoming) A243

Grand Canyon (Arizona) A240

Mt. Rainier and Mirror Lake (Washington) A241

Mesa Verde (Colorado) A242

Crater Lake (Oregon) A244

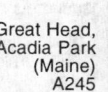

Great Head, Acadia Park (Maine) A245

Great White Throne, Zion Park (Utah) A246

Great Smoky Mts. (North Carolina) A248

Mt. Rockwell (Mt. Sinopah) and Two Medicine Lake, Glacier Natl. Park (Montana) A247

1934 Flat Plate Printing *Perf. 11*

740 A239 1c green .20 .20
Never hinged .20
a. Vert. pair, imperf. horiz., with gum *450.00*
Never hinged *575.00*
741 A240 2c red .20 .20
Never hinged .20
a. Vert. pair, imperf. horiz., with gum *450.00*
Never hinged *575.00*
b. Horiz. pair, imperf. vert., with gum *425.00*
Never hinged *550.00*
742 A241 3c deep violet .20 .20
Never hinged .20
a. Vert. pair, imperf. horiz., with gum *425.00*
Never hinged *550.00*
743 A242 4c brown .35 .40
Never hinged .45
a. Vert. pair, imperf. horiz., with gum *700.00*
Never hinged *1,000.*
744 A243 5c blue .70 .65
Never hinged .95
a. Horiz. pair, imperf. vert., with gum *500.00*
Never hinged *725.00*
745 A244 6c dark blue 1.10 .85
Never hinged 1.50
746 A245 7c black .60 .75
Never hinged .85
a. Horiz. pair, imperf. vert., with gum *700.00*
Never hinged *1,000.*
747 A246 8c sage green 1.60 1.50
Never hinged 2.20
748 A247 9c red orange 1.50 .65
Never hinged 2.10
749 A248 10c gray black 3.00 1.25
Never hinged 4.25
Nos. 740-749 (10) 9.45 6.65
Nos. 740-749, never hinged 12.75

National Parks Year.
See Nos. 750-751, 756-765, 769-770, 797.

American Philatelic Society Issue

Souvenir Sheet

1934, Aug. 28 *Imperf.*

750 Sheet of 6 30.00 27.50
Never hinged 37.50
a. A241 3c deep violet 3.50 3.25
Never hinged 4.50

Sheet measures approximately 98x93mm.
See #770.

Trans-Mississippi Philatelic Exposition Issue

Souvenir Sheet

1934, Oct. 10 *Imperf.*

751 Sheet of 6 12.50 12.50
Never hinged 16.00
a. A239 1c green 1.40 1.60
Never hinged 1.85

Sheet measures approximately 92x99mm.
See #769.

Special Printing (Nos. 752-771)

"Issued for a limited time in full sheets as printed, and in blocks thereof, to meet the requirements of collectors and others who may be interested."—From Postal Bulletin, No. 16614.

Issuance of the following 20 stamps in complete sheets resulted from the protest of collectors and others at the practice of presenting, to certain government officials, complete sheets of unsevered panes, imperforate (except Nos. 752 and 753) and generally ungummed.

Without Gum.

Note. In 1940 the P.O. Department offered to and did gum full sheets of Nos. 754 to 771 sent in by owners.

Type of Peace Issue
Issued in sheets of 400

Rotary Press Printing

1935, Mar. 15 *Perf. 10½x11*

752 A230 3c violet .20 .20

Type of Byrd Issue

Issued in sheets of 200

Flat Plate Printing

Perf. 11

753 A234 3c dark blue .50 .45

No. 753 is similar to No. 733. Positive identification is by pairs or blocks showing a guide line between stamps. These lines are found only on No. 753.

Type of Mothers of America Issue
Issued in sheets of 200
Imperf

754 A237 3c deep violet .55 .55

Type of Wisconsin Issue
Issued in sheets of 200
Imperf

755 A238 3c deep violet .55 .55

Types of National Parks Issue
Issued in sheets of 200
Imperf

756	A239	1c green	.20	.20
757	A240	2c red	.25	.25
758	A241	3c deep violet	.50	.45
759	A242	4c brown	.95	.95
760	A243	5c blue	1.50	1.30
761	A244	6c dark blue	2.40	2.10
762	A245	7c black	1.50	1.40
763	A246	8c sage green	1.60	1.50
764	A247	9c red orange	1.90	1.65
765	A248	10c gray black	3.75	3.25
		Nos. 756-765 (10)	14.55	13.05

Souvenir Sheets
Type of Century of Progress Issue
Issued in sheets of 9 panes of 25 stamps each

Note: Single items from these sheets are identical with other varieties, 766 & 730, 766a & 730a, 767 & 731, 767a & 731a, 768 & 735, 768a & 735a, 769 & 756, 770 & 758. Positive identification is by blocks or pairs showing wide gutters between stamps. These wide gutters occur only on Nos. 766 to 770 and measure, horizontally, 13mm on Nos. 766-767; 16mm on No. 768, and 23mm on Nos. 769-770.

Imperf

766	Pane of 25	25.00	25.00
a.	A231 1c yellow green	.70	.40
767	Pane of 25	23.50	23.50
a.	A232 3c violet	.60	.40

National Exhibition Issue
Type of Byrd Issue
Issued in sheets of 25 panes of 6 stamps each
Imperf

768	Pane of 6	20.00	15.00
a.	A234 3c dark blue	2.80	2.40

Types of National Parks Issue
Issued in sheets of 20 panes of 6 stamps each
Imperf

769	Pane of 6	12.50	11.00
a.	A239 1c green	1.85	1.80
770	Pane of 6	30.00	24.00
a.	A241 3c deep violet	3.25	3.10

Type of Air Post Special Delivery
Issued in sheets of 200
Imperf

771 APSD1 16c dark blue 2.25 2.25

Catalogue values for unused stamps in this section, from this point to the end of the section, are for Never Hinged items.

Connecticut Tercentenary Issue

Charter Oak — A249

Rotary Press Printing

1935, Apr. 26 ***Perf. 11x10½***

772 A249 3c violet .20 .20

300th anniv. of the settlement of Conn.
See No. 778a.

California-Pacific Exposition Issue

View of San Diego Exposition A250

1935, May 29 ***Perf. 11x10½***

773 A250 3c purple .20 .20

California-Pacific Expo., San Diego.
See No. 778b.

Boulder Dam Issue

Boulder Dam — A251

Flat Plate Printing

1935, Sept. 30 ***Perf. 11***

774 A251 3c purple .20 .20

Dedication of Boulder Dam.

Michigan Centenary Issue

Michigan State Seal — A252

Rotary Press Printing

1935, Nov. 1 ***Perf. 11x10½***

775 A252 3c purple .20 .20

Advance celebration of Michigan statehood centenary. Michigan was admitted to Union Jan. 26, 1837.
See No. 778c.

Texas Centennial Issue

Sam Houston, Stephen F. Austin and the Alamo A253

1936, Mar. 2 ***Perf. 11x10½***

776 A253 3c purple .20 .20

Centennial of Texas independence.
See No. 778d.

Rhode Island Tercentenary Issue

Statue of Roger Williams — A254

1936, May 4 ***Perf. 10½x11***

777 A254 3c purple .20 .20

Settlement of Rhode Island, 1636.

Third International Philatelic Exhibition Issue
Souvenir Sheet

A254a

Flat Plate Printing

1936, May 9 ***Imperf.***

778	A254a Sheet of 4	1.75	1.75
a.	A249 3c violet	.40	.30
b.	A250 3c violet	.40	.30
c.	A252 3c violet	.40	.30
d.	A253 3c violet	.40	.30

Sheet measures 98x66mm.

Arkansas Centennial Issue

Arkansas Post, Old and New State Houses A255

Rotary Press Printing

1936, June 15 ***Perf. 11x10½***

782 A255 3c purple .20 .20

Centennial of Arkansas statehood.

Map of Oregon Territory A256

Susan B. Anthony A257

Oregon Territory Issue

1936, July 14 ***Perf. 11x10½***

783 A256 3c purple .20 .20

Centenary of Oregon Territory opening.

Susan B. Anthony Issue

1936, Aug. 26 ***Perf. 11x10½***

784 A257 3c dark violet .20 .20

Susan Brownell Anthony (1820-1906), woman suffrage advocate, honored on 16th anniv. of ratification of 19th Amendment granting American women the right to vote.

Army Issue

George Washington, Nathanael Greene and Mount Vernon A258

Andrew Jackson, Winfield Scott and the Hermitage A259

Generals Sherman, Grant and Sheridan A260

Generals Robert E. Lee, "Stonewall" Jackson and Stratford Hall — A261

US Military Academy, West Point — A262

1936-37 ***Perf. 11x10½***

785	A258	1c green	.20	.20
786	A259	2c carmine ('37)	.20	.20
787	A260	3c purple ('37)	.20	.20
788	A261	4c gray ('37)	.30	.20
789	A262	5c ultra ('37)	.60	.20
		Nos. 785-789 (5)	1.50	1.00

Issued in honor of the United States Army.

Navy Issue

John Paul Jones and John Barry — A263

Stephen Decatur and Thomas MacDonough A264

Admirals David G. Farragut and David D. Porter A265

Admirals William T. Sampson, George Dewey and Winfield S. Schley A266

Seal of US Naval Academy and Naval Cadets A267

1936-37 ***Perf. 11x10½***

790	A263	1c green	.20	.20
791	A264	2c carmine ('37)	.20	.20
792	A265	3c purple ('37)	.20	.20
793	A266	4c gray ('37)	.30	.20
794	A267	5c ultra ('37)	.60	.20
		Nos. 790-794 (5)	1.50	1.00

Issued in honor of the United States Navy.

Northwest Ordinance Sesquicentennial Issue

Manasseh Cutler, Rufus Putnam and Map of Northwest Territory A268

1937, July 13 ***Perf. 11x10½***

795 A268 3c red violet .20 .20

150th anniv. of the adoption of the Ordinance of 1787 and the creation of the Northwest Territory.

Virginia Dare Issue

Virginia Dare and Parents — A269

Flat Plate Printing

1937, Aug. 18 ***Perf. 11***

796 A269 5c gray blue .20 .20

350th anniv. of the birth of Virginia Dare and the settlement at Roanoke Island. Virginia was the first child born in America of English parents (Aug. 18, 1587).

Society of Philatelic Americans
Souvenir Sheet

A269a

1937, Aug. 26 ***Imperf.***

797 A269a 10c blue green .60 .40

Sheet measures 67x78mm.

Constitution Sesquicentennial Issue

Signing of the Constitution A270

Rotary Press Printing

1937, Sept. 17 ***Perf. 11x10½***

798 A270 3c bright red violet .20 .20

Sesquicentennial of the Signing of the Constitution, Sept. 17, 1787.

Territorial Issues
Hawaii

Statue of Kamehameha I, Honolulu — A271

1937, Oct. 18 ***Perf. 10½x11***

799 A271 3c violet .20 .20

Alaska

Landscape with Mt. McKinley A272

1937, Nov. 12 ***Perf. 11x10½***

800 A272 3c violet .20 .20

Puerto Rico

La Fortaleza, San Juan — A273

1937, Nov. 25 ***Perf. 11x10½***

801 A273 3c bright violet .20 .20

Virgin Islands

Charlotte Amalie A274

1937, Dec. 15 ***Perf. 11x10½***

802 A274 3c light violet .20 .20

Presidential Issue

Benjamin Franklin A275 — George Washington A276

Martha Washington A277 — John Adams A278

Thomas Jefferson A279 — James Madison A280

White House A281

James Monroe A282

John Q. Adams A283

Andrew Jackson A284

Martin Van Buren A285

William H. Harrison A286

John Tyler A287

James K. Polk A288

Zachary Taylor A289

Millard Fillmore A290

Franklin Pierce A291

James Buchanan A292

Abraham Lincoln A293

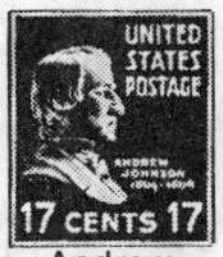

Andrew Johnson A294

Ulysses S. Grant A295

Rutherford B. Hayes A296

James A. Garfield A297

Chester A. Arthur A298

Grover Cleveland A299

Benjamin Harrison A300

William McKinley A301

Theodore Roosevelt A302

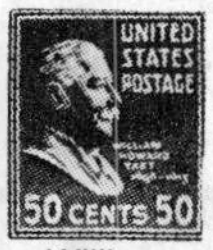

William Howard Taft A303

Woodrow Wilson A304

Warren G. Harding A305

Calvin Coolidge A306

1938-54 ***Perf. 11x10½***

803	A275	½c deep orange	.20	.20
804	A276	1c green	.20	.20
b.		Booklet pane of 6	2.00	.35
805	A277	1½c bister brown	.20	.20
b.		Horiz. pair, imperf. btwn.	175.00	30.00
806	A278	2c rose carmine	.20	.20
b.		Booklet pane of 6	4.75	.85
807	A279	3c deep violet	.20	.20
a.		Booklet pane of 6	8.50	1.25
b.		Horiz. pair, imperf. btwn.	900.00	—
c.		Imperf., pair	2,500.	
808	A280	4c red violet	.75	.20
809	A281	4½c dark gray	.20	.20
810	A282	5c bright blue	.20	.20
811	A283	6c red orange	.20	.20
812	A284	7c sepia	.25	.20
813	A285	8c olive green	.30	.20
814	A286	9c rose pink	.30	.20
815	A287	10c brown red	.25	.20
816	A288	11c ultra	.65	.20
817	A289	12c bright violet	.90	.20
818	A290	13c blue green	1.25	.20
819	A291	14c blue	.90	.20
820	A292	15c blue gray	.40	.20
821	A293	16c black	.90	.25
822	A294	17c rose red	.85	.20
823	A295	18c brown car	1.75	.20
824	A296	19c bright violet	1.25	.35
825	A297	20c brt blue green	.70	.20
826	A298	21c dull blue	1.25	.20
827	A299	22c vermilion	1.00	.40
828	A300	24c gray black	3.50	.20
829	A301	25c deep red lilac	.60	.20
830	A302	30c deep ultra	3.75	.20
831	A303	50c lt red violet	5.75	.20

Flat Plate Printing
Perf. 11

832	A304	$1 pur & black	7.00	.20
a.		Vert. pair, imperf. horiz.	1,600.	
b.		Wmkd. USIR ('51)	250.00	65.00
c.		$1 red violet & black ('54)	6.00	.20
d.		As "c," vert. pair, imperf. horiz.	1,250.	
e.		Vert. pair, imperf. btwn.	2,750.	
f.		As "c," vert. pair, imperf. btwn.	7,000.	
833	A305	$2 yel grn & blk	20.00	3.75
834	A306	$5 car & black	95.00	3.00
a.		$5 red brown & black	3,250.	1,500.
		Hinged	2,500.	
		Nos. 803-834 (32)	150.85	13.15

No. 805b used is always Bureau precanceled St. Louis Mo., and are generally with gum. Value is for gummed pair.

No. 832c is printed on thick white paper with smooth, colorless gum.

No. 834 can be chemically altered to resemble No. 834a. No. 834a should be purchased only with competent expert certification.

See Nos. 839-851.

Constitution Ratification Issue

Old Court House, Williamsburg, Va. — A307

Rotary Press Printing

1938, June 21 ***Perf. 11x10½***

835 A307 3c deep violet .25 .20

150th anniv. of the ratification of the US Constitution.

Landing of the Swedes and Finns — A308

Statue Symbolizing Colonization of the West — A309

Swedish-Finnish Tercentenary Issue
Flat Plate Printing

1938, June 27 ***Perf. 11***

836 A308 3c red violet .20 .20

Tercentenary of the founding of the Swedish and Finnish settlement at Wilmington, Del.

Northwest Territory Issue
Rotary Press Printing

1938, July 15 ***Perf. 11x10½***

837 A309 3c bright violet .20 .20

Sesquicentennial of the settlement of the Northwest Territory.

Iowa Territory Centennial Issue

Old Capitol, Iowa City — A310

1938, Aug. 24 ***Perf. 11x10½***

838 A310 3c violet .20 .20

Centenary of Iowa Territory.

Presidential Types of 1938
Coil Stamps

Rotary Press Printing

1939 ***Perf. 10 Vertically***

839	A276	1c green	.30	.20
840	A277	1½c bister brown	.30	.20
841	A278	2c rose carmine	.40	.20
842	A279	3c deep violet	.50	.20
843	A280	4c red violet	8.00	.40
844	A281	4½c dark gray	.70	.40
845	A282	5c bright blue	5.00	.35
846	A283	6c red orange	1.10	.20
847	A287	10c brown red	11.00	.50

Perf. 10 Horizontally

848	A276	1c green	.85	.20
849	A277	1½c bister brown	1.25	.30
850	A278	2c rose carmine	2.50	.40
851	A279	3c deep violet	2.25	.35
		Nos. 839-851 (13)	34.15	3.90

"Tower of the Sun" A311

Trylon and Perisphere A312

Golden Gate International Exposition Issue
Rotary Press Printing

1939, Feb. 18 ***Perf. 10½x11***

852 A311 3c bright purple .20 .20

Golden Gate Intl. Expo., San Francisco.

New York World's Fair Issue

1939, Apr. 1 ***Perf. 10½x11***

853	A312	3c deep purple	.20	.20

Washington Inauguration Issue

George Washington Taking Oath of Office — A313

Flat Plate Printing

1939, Apr. 30 ***Perf. 11***

854	A313	3c bright red violet	.40	.20

Sesquicentennial of the inauguration of George Washington as 1st president.

Baseball Centennial Issue

Sand-lot Baseball Game — A314

Rotary Press Printing

1939, June 12 ***Perf. 11x10½***

855	A314	3c violet	1.75	.20

Centennial of baseball.

Panama Canal Issue

Theodore Roosevelt, Gen. George W. Goethals and Gaillard Cut — A315

Flat Plate Printing

1939, Aug. 15 ***Perf. 11***

856	A315	3c deep red violet	.25	.20

25th anniv. of the Panama Canal opening.

Printing Tercentenary Issue

Stephen Daye Press — A316

Rotary Press Printing

1939, Sept. 25 ***Perf. 10½x11***

857	A316	3c violet	.20	.20

300th anniv. of printing in Colonial America.

50th Anniversary of Statehood Issue.

Map of North and South Dakota, Montana and Washington A317

1939, Nov. 2 ***Perf. 11x10½***

858	A317	3c rose violet	.20	.20

50th anniv. of admission to Statehood of North Dakota, South Dakota, Montana and Washington.

United States stamps can be mounted in the Scott National and Minuteman albums.

Famous Americans Issues
Authors

Washington Irving A318

James Fenimore Cooper A319

Ralph Waldo Emerson A320

Louisa May Alcott A321

Samuel L. Clemens (Mark Twain) — A322

1940 ***Perf. 10½x11***

859	A318	1c bright blue green	.20	.20
860	A319	2c rose carmine	.20	.20
861	A320	3c bright red violet	.20	.20
862	A321	5c ultra	.30	.20
863	A322	10c dark brown	1.65	1.20
		Nos. 859-863 (5)	2.55	2.00

Poets

Henry W. Longfellow A323

John Greenleaf Whittier A324

James Russell Lowell A325

Walt Whitman A326

James Whitcomb Riley — A327

1940 ***Perf. 10½x11***

864	A323	1c bright blue green	.20	.20
865	A324	2c rose carmine	.20	.20
866	A325	3c bright red violet	.20	.20
867	A326	5c ultra	.35	.20
868	A327	10c dark brown	1.75	1.25
		Nos. 864-868 (5)	2.70	2.05

Educators

Horace Mann A328

Mark Hopkins A329

Charles W. Eliot A330

Frances E. Willard A331

Booker T. Washington — A332

1940 ***Perf. 10½x11***

869	A328	1c bright blue green	.20	.20
870	A329	2c rose carmine	.20	.20
871	A330	3c bright red violet	.20	.20
872	A331	5c ultra	.40	.20
873	A332	10c dark brown	1.25	1.10
		Nos. 869-873 (5)	2.25	1.90

Scientists

John James Audubon A333

Dr. Crawford W. Long A334

Luther Burbank A335

Dr. Walter Reed A336

Jane Addams — A337

1940 ***Perf. 10½x11***

874	A333	1c bright blue green	.20	.20
875	A334	2c rose carmine	.20	.20
876	A335	3c bright red violet	.20	.20
877	A336	5c ultra	.25	.20
878	A337	10c dark brown	1.10	.85
		Nos. 874-878 (5)	1.95	1.65

Composers

Stephen Collins Foster A338

John Philip Sousa A339

Victor Herbert A340

Edward MacDowell A341

Ethelbert Nevin — A342

1940 ***Perf. 10½x11***

879	A338	1c bright blue green	.20	.20
880	A339	2c rose carmine	.20	.20
881	A340	3c bright red violet	.20	.20
882	A341	5c ultra	.40	.20
883	A342	10c dark brown	3.75	1.20
		Nos. 879-883 (5)	4.75	2.00

Artists

Gilbert Charles Stuart A343

James A. McNeill Whistler A344

Augustus Saint-Gaudens A345

Daniel Chester French A346

Frederic Remington — A347

1940 ***Perf. 10½x11***

884	A343	1c bright blue green	.20	.20
885	A344	2c rose carmine	.20	.20
886	A345	3c bright red violet	.20	.20
887	A346	5c ultra	.50	.20
888	A347	10c dark brown	1.75	1.25
		Nos. 884-888 (5)	2.85	2.05

Inventors

Eli Whitney A348

Samuel F. B. Morse A349

Cyrus Hall McCormick A350

Elias Howe A351

Alexander Graham Bell — A352

1940 ***Perf. 10½x11***

889	A348	1c brt blue green	.20	.20
890	A349	2c rose carmine	.20	.20
891	A350	3c bright red violet	.25	.20
892	A351	5c ultra	1.10	.30
893	A352	10c dark brown	11.00	2.00
		Nos. 889-893 (5)	12.75	2.90
		Nos. 859-893 (35)	29.80	14.55

Pony Express Issue

Pony Express Rider — A353

1940, Apr. 3 ***Perf. 11x10½***

894	A353	3c henna brown	.25	.20

80th anniv. of the Pony Express.

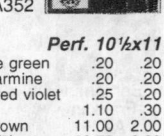

Pan American Union Issue

The Three Graces from Botticelli's "Spring" — A354

1940, Apr. 14 ***Perf. 10½x11***

895 A354 3c light violet .20 .20

Pan American Union founding, 50th anniv.

Idaho Statehood Issue

Idaho Capitol, Boise — A355

1940, July 3 ***Perf. 11x10½***

896 A355 3c bright violet .20 .20

Idaho statehood, 50th anniv.

Wyoming Statehood Issue

Wyoming State Seal — A356

1940, July 10 ***Perf. 10½x11***

897 A356 3c brown violet .20 .20

Wyoming statehood, 50th anniv.

Coronado Expedition Issue

"Coronado and His Captains" Painted by Gerald Cassidy A357

1940, Sept. 7 ***Perf. 11x10½***

898 A357 3c violet .20 .20

400th anniv. of the Coronado Expedition.

National Defense Issue

Statue of Liberty — A358

90-millimeter Anti-aircraft Gun — A359

Torch of Enlightenment — A360

1940, Oct. 16 ***Perf. 11x10½***

899 A358 1c bright blue green .20 .20
- *a.* Vert. pair, imperf. btwn. *650.00* —
- *b.* Horiz. pair, imperf. btwn. 35.00 —

900 A359 2c rose carmine .20 .20
- *a.* Horiz. pair, imperf. btwn. 40.00 —

901 A360 3c bright violet .20 .20
- *a.* Horiz. pair, imperf. btwn. 27.50 —

Nos. 899-901 (3) .60 .60

Thirteenth Amendment Issue

"Emancipation," Statue of Lincoln and Slave, by Thomas Ball — A361

1940, Oct. 20 ***Perf. 10½x11***

902 A361 3c deep violet .20 .20

75th anniv. of the 13th Amendment to the Constitution.

Vermont Statehood Issue

Vermont Capitol, Montpelier A362

1941, Mar. 4 ***Perf. 11x10½***

903 A362 3c light violet .20 .20

Vermont statehood, 150th anniv.

Kentucky Statehood Issue

Daniel Boone and Three Frontiersmen, from Mural by Gilbert White — A363

1942, June 1 ***Perf. 11x10½***

904 A363 3c violet .20 .20

Kentucky statehood, 150th anniv.

American Eagle A364

Lincoln, Sun Yat-sen and Map A365

Win the War Issue

1942, July 4 ***Perf. 11x10½***

905 A364 3c violet .20 .20
- *b.* 3c purple — —

Chinese Resistance Issue

1942, July 7 ***Perf. 11x10½***

906 A365 5c bright blue .30 .20

Five years' resistance of the Chinese people to Japanese aggression.

Allegory of Victory A366

Liberty Holding Torch of Freedom and Enlightenment A367

Allied Nations Issue

1943, Jan. 14 ***Perf. 11x10½***

907 A366 2c rose carmine .20 .20

Four Freedoms Issue

1943, Feb. 12 ***Perf. 11x10½***

908 A367 1c bright blue green .20 .20

Overrun Countries Issue

Flag of Poland A368

Frames Engraved, Centers Offset Letterpress

Rotary Press Printing

1943-44 **Unwmk.** ***Perf. 12***

909	A368	5c	Poland	.20	.20
910	A368	5c	Czechoslovakia	.20	.20
911	A368	5c	Norway	.20	.20
912	A368	5c	Luxembourg	.20	.20
913	A368	5c	Netherlands	.20	.20
914	A368	5c	Belgium	.20	.20
915	A368	5c	France	.20	.20
916	A368	5c	Greece	.35	.25
917	A368	5c	Yugoslavia	.25	.20
918	A368	5c	Albania	.20	.20
919	A368	5c	Austria	.20	.20
920	A368	5c	Denmark	.20	.20
921	A368	5c	Korea ('44)	.20	.20
			Nos. 909-921 (13)	2.80	2.65

Transcontinental Railroad Issue

"Golden Spike Ceremony" Painting by John McQuarrie A369

Engraved; Rotary Press Printing

1944, May 10 ***Perf. 11x10½***

922 A369 3c violet .20 .20

75th anniv. of the completion of the first transcontinental railroad.

Steamship Issue

"Savannah" A370

1944, May 22 ***Perf. 11x10½***

923 A370 3c violet .20 .20

125th anniv. of the first steamship to cross the Atlantic Ocean.

Telegraph Issue

Telegraph Wires and the First Transmitted Words "What Hath God Wrought" A371

1944, May 24 ***Perf. 11x10½***

924 A371 3c bright red violet .20 .20

100th anniv. of the 1st message transmitted by telegraph.

Philippines Issue

View of Corregidor A372

1944, Sept. 27 ***Perf. 11x10½***

925 A372 3c deep violet .20 .20

Final resistance of the US and Philippine defenders on Corregidor.

Motion Pictures, 50th Anniv.

Motion Picture Showing for the Armed Forces in South Pacific A373

1944, Oct. 31 ***Perf. 11x10½***

926 A373 3c deep violet .20 .20

Florida Statehood Centenary

Old Florida Seal, St. Augustine Gates and State Capitol A374

1945, Mar. 3 ***Perf. 11x10½***

927 A374 3c bright red violet .20 .20

United Nations Conference Issue

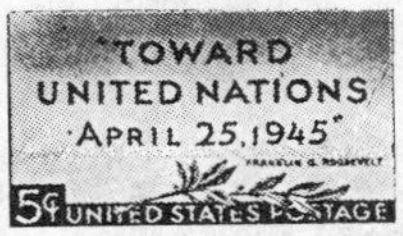

A375

1945, Apr. 25 ***Perf. 11x10½***

928 A375 5c ultramarine .20 .20

United Nations conference, San Francisco.

Iwo Jima (Marines) Issue

Marines Raising the Flag on Mt. Suribachi, Iwo Jima — A376

1945, July 11 ***Perf. 10½x11***

929 A376 3c yellow green .20 .20

Achievements of the US Marines in WWII.

Franklin D. Roosevelt Issue

Roosevelt and Hyde Park Home — A377

Roosevelt and "Little White House," Warm Springs, Georgia A378

Roosevelt and White House A379

Roosevelt, Globe and Four Freedoms A380

1945-46 ***Perf. 11x10½***

930	A377	1c	blue green	.20	.20
931	A378	2c	carmine rose	.20	.20
932	A379	3c	purple	.20	.20
933	A380	5c	bright blue ('46)	.20	.20
			Nos. 930-933 (4)	.80	.80

Franklin Delano Roosevelt (1882-1945).

Army Issue

US Troops Passing Arch of Triumph, Paris — A381

1945, Sept. 28 ***Perf. 11x10½***

934 A381 3c olive .20 .20

Achievements of the US Army in WWII.

Navy Issue

US Sailors
A382

1945, Oct. 27 ***Perf. 11x10½***
935 A382 3c blue .20 .20

Achievements of the US Navy in WWII.

Coast Guard Issue

Coast Guard Landing Craft and Supply Ship — A383

1945, Nov. 10 ***Perf. 11x10½***
936 A383 3c bright blue green .20 .20

Achievements of the US Coast Guard in WWII.

Alfred E. Smith
A384

US and Texas State Flags
A385

Alfred E. Smith Issue

1945, Nov. 26 ***Perf. 11x10½***
937 A384 3c purple .20 .20

Smith (1873-1944), governor of NY.

Texas Statehood Centenary

1945, Dec. 29 ***Perf. 11x10½***
938 A385 3c dark blue .20 .20

Liberty Ship Unloading Cargo
A386

Honorable Discharge Emblem
A387

Merchant Marine Issue

1946, Feb. 26 ***Perf. 11x10½***
939 A386 3c blue green .20 .20

Achievements of the US Merchant Marine in WWII.

Veterans of World War II Issue

1946, May 9 ***Perf. 11x10½***
940 A387 3c dark violet .20 .20

Issued to honor all veterans of WWII.

Tennessee Statehood, 150th Anniv.

Andrew Jackson, John Sevier and Tennessee Capitol
A388

1946, June 1 ***Perf. 11x10½***
941 A388 3c dark violet .20 .20

Iowa Statehood Centenary

Iowa State Flag and Map — A389

1946, Aug. 3 ***Perf. 11x10½***
942 A389 3c deep blue .20 .20

Smithsonian Institution Issue

Smithsonian Institution
A390

1946, Aug. 10 ***Perf. 11x10½***
943 A390 3c violet brown .20 .20

Centenary of the establishment of the Smithsonian Institution, Washington, DC.

Kearny Expedition Issue

"Capture of Santa Fe" by Kenneth M. Chapman
A391

1946, Oct. 16 ***Perf. 11x10½***
944 A391 3c brown violet .20 .20

Centenary of the entry of General Stephen Watts Kearny into Santa Fe.

Thomas Alva Edison Issue

Thomas A. Edison, Birth Centenary — A392

1947, Feb. 11 ***Perf. 10½x11***
945 A392 3c bright red violet .20 .20

Joseph Pulitzer Birth Centenary

Joseph Pulitzer and Statue of Liberty
A393

1947, Apr. 10 ***Perf. 11x10½***
946 A393 3c purple .20 .20

US Postage Stamp Centenary

Washington and Franklin, Early and Modern Mail-carrying Vehicles
A394

1947, May 17 ***Perf. 11x10½***
947 A394 3c deep blue .20 .20

Centenary International Philatelic Exhibition (CIPEX)

Souvenir Sheet

A395

Flat Plate Printing

1947, May 19 ***Imperf.***

948	A395 Sheet of 2	.55	.45
a.	A1 5c blue	.20	.20
b.	A2 10c brown orange	.25	.25

Sheet size varies: 96-98x66-68mm

Doctors Issue

"The Doctor," by Sir Luke Fildes — A396

Rotary Press Printing

1947, June 9 ***Perf. 11x10½***
949 A396 3c brown violet .20 .20

Issued to honor the physicians of America.

Utah Settlement Centenary

Pioneers Entering the Valley of Great Salt Lake — A397

1947, July 24 ***Perf. 11x10½***
950 A397 3c dark violet .20 .20

US Frigate Constitution Issue

Naval Architect's Drawing of Frigate Constitution
A398

1947, Oct. 21 ***Perf. 11x10½***
951 A398 3c blue green .20 .20

150th anniv. of the launching of the US Frigate Constitution ("Old Ironsides").

Everglades National Park Issue

Great White Heron and Map of Florida — A399

1947, Dec. 5 ***Perf. 10½x11***
952 A399 3c bright green .20 .20

Dedication of Everglades Natl. Park, Florida, Dec. 6, 1947.

Dr. George Washington Carver Issue

Dr. George Washington Carver — A400

1948, Jan. 5 ***Perf. 10½x11***
953 A400 3c bright red violet .20 .20

5th anniv. of the death of Dr. George Washington Carver, scientist.

California Gold Centennial Issue

Sutter's Mill, Coloma, California
A401

1948, Jan. 24 ***Perf. 11x10½***
954 A401 3c dark violet .20 .20

Discovery of gold in California, centenary.

Mississippi Territory, 150th Anniv.

Map, Seal and Gov. Winthrop Sargent
A402

1948, Apr. 7 ***Perf. 11x10½***
955 A402 3c brown violet .20 .20

Four Chaplains Issue

Four Chaplains and Sinking S. S. Dorchester
A403

1948, May 28 ***Perf. 11x10½***
956 A403 3c gray black .20 .20

Honoring George L. Fox, Clark V. Poling, John P. Washington and Alexander D. Goode, the four chaplains who sacrificed their lives in the sinking of the SS Dorchester, Feb. 3, 1943.

Wisconsin Statehood Centenary

Map on Scroll and State Capitol
A404

1948, May 29 ***Perf. 11x10½***
957 A404 3c dark violet .20 .20

Swedish Pioneer Issue

Swedish Pioneer with Covered Wagon Moving Westward
A405

1948, June 4 ***Perf. 11x10½***
958 A405 5c deep blue .20 .20

Centenary of the coming of the Swedish pioneers to the Middle West.

Progress of Women Issue

Elizabeth Stanton, Carrie C. Catt and Lucretia Mott — A406

1948, July 19 ***Perf. 11x10½***
959 A406 3c dark violet .20 .20

Century of progress of American women.

William Allen White Issue

William Allen White, Editor and Author — A407

1948, July 31 ***Perf. 10½x11***
960 A407 3c bright red violet .20 .20

US-Canada Friendship Centenary

Niagara Railway Suspension Bridge
A408

1948, Aug. 2 ***Perf. 11x10½***
961 A408 3c blue .20 .20

Francis Scott Key Issue

Key and American Flags of 1814 and 1948 — A409

1948, Aug. 9 ***Perf. 11x10½***
962 A409 3c rose pink .20 .20

Francis Scott Key (1779-1843), Maryland lawyer and author of "The Star-Spangled Banner" (1813).

Salute to Youth Issue

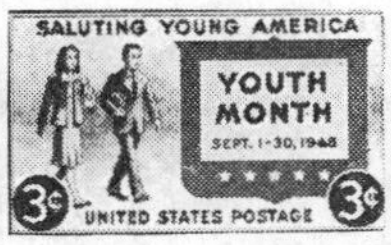

Girl and Boy Carrying Books — A410

1948, Aug. 11 ***Perf. 11x10½***
963 A410 3c deep blue .20 .20

Youth of America and "Youth Month," Sept. 1948.

Oregon Territory Issue

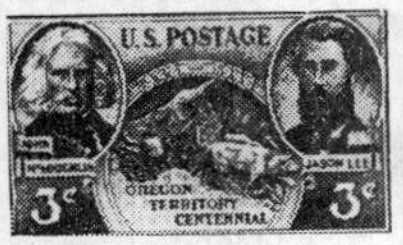

John McLoughlin, Jason Lee and Wagon on Oregon Trail — A411

1948, Aug. 14 ***Perf. 11x10½***
964 A411 3c brown red .20 .20

Centenary of the establishment of Ore. Terr.

Chief Justice Harlan Fiske Stone — A412

Observatory, Palomar Mt., Cal. — A413

Harlan Fiske Stone Issue

1948, Aug. 25 ***Perf. 10½x11***
965 A412 3c bright red violet .20 .20

Palomar Mountain Observatory Issue

1948, Aug. 30 ***Perf. 10½x11***
966 A413 3c blue .20 .20
a. Vert. pair, imperf btwn. *550.00*

Clara Barton, 1821-1912

Founder of the American Red Cross (1882) A414

1948, Sept. 7 ***Perf. 11x10½***
967 A414 3c rose pink .20 .20

Poultry Industry Issue

Light Brahma Rooster A415

1948, Sept. 9 ***Perf. 11x10½***
968 A415 3c sepia .20 .20

Centenary of the establishment of the American poultry industry.

Gold Star Mothers Issue

Star and Palm Frond — A416

1948, Sept. 21 ***Perf. 10½x11***
969 A416 3c orange yellow .20 .20

Honoring mothers of deceased members of the US armed forces.

Fort Kearny Issue

Fort Kearny and Pioneer Group — A417

1948, Sept. 22 ***Perf. 11x10½***
970 A417 3c violet .20 .20

Cent. of the establishment of Fort Kearny, Nebr.

Volunteer Firemen Issue

Peter Stuyvesant; Early and Modern Fire Engines A418

1948, Oct. 4 ***Perf. 11x10½***
971 A418 3c bright rose carmine .20 .20

300th anniv. of the organization of the 1st volunteer firemen in America by Peter Stuyvesant (1592-1672), Dutch colonial gov. of New Netherland.

Indian Centennial Issue

Map of Indian Territory and Seals of Five Tribes A419

1948, Oct. 15 ***Perf. 11x10½***
972 A419 3c dark brown .20 .20

Cent. of the arrival in Indian Territory, later Okla., of the Five Civilized Indian Tribes.

Rough Riders Issue

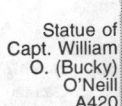

Statue of Capt. William O. (Bucky) O'Neill A420

1948, Oct. 27 ***Perf. 11x10½***
973 A420 3c violet brown .20 .20

50th anniv. of the organization of the Rough Riders of the Spanish-American War.

Low and Girl Scout Emblem A421

Will Rogers A422

Juliette Low Issue

1948, Oct. 29 ***Perf. 11x10½***
974 A421 3c blue green .20 .20

Juliette Gordon Low (1860-1927), organizer of the Girl Scouts of America.

Will Rogers Issue

1948, Nov. 4 ***Perf. 10½x11***
975 A422 3c bright red violet .20 .20

Will Rogers, 1879-1935, humorist and political commentator.

Fort Bliss and Rocket A423

Moina Michael and Poppy Plant A424

Fort Bliss Centennial Issue

1948, Nov. 5 ***Perf. 10½x11***
976 A423 3c henna brown .20 .20

Centenary of Fort Bliss, Texas.

Moina Michael Issue

1948, Nov. 9 ***Perf. 11x10½***
977 A424 3c rose pink .20 .20

Michael (1870-1944), educator who originated (1918) Flanders Field Poppy Day idea as memorial to war dead.

Gettysburg Address Issue

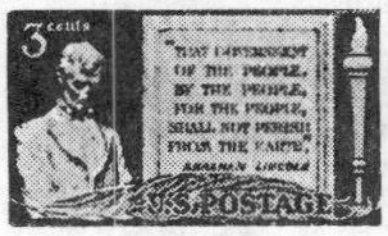

Lincoln and Quotation from Gettysburg Address A425

1948, Nov. 19 ***Perf. 11x10½***
978 A425 3c bright blue .20 .20

85th anniv. of Abraham Lincoln's address at Gettysburg, Pa.

Torch and American Turners' Emblem A426

Joel Chandler Harris A427

American Turners Issue

1948, Nov. 20 ***Perf. 10½x11***
979 A426 3c carmine .20 .20

Centenary of the formation of the American Turners Society.

Joel Chandler Harris Issue

1948, Dec. 9 ***Perf. 10½x11***
980 A427 3c bright red violet .20 .20

Harris (1848-1908), editor and author.

Minnesota Territory Issue

Pioneer and Red River Oxcart A428

1949, Mar. 3 ***Perf. 11x10½***
981 A428 3c blue green .20 .20

Cent. of the establishment of Minn. Terr.

Washington and Lee University Issue

George Washington, Robert E. Lee and University Building A429

1949, Apr. 12 ***Perf. 11x10½***
982 A429 3c ultramarine .20 .20

200th anniv. of the founding of Washington and Lee Univ.

Puerto Rico Election Issue

Puerto Rican Farmer Holding Cogwheel and Ballot Box — A430

1949, Apr. 27 ***Perf. 11x10½***
983 A430 3c green .20 .20

1st gubernatorial election in the Territory of P.R., Nov. 2, 1948.

Annapolis Tercentenary Issue

Stoddert's 1718 Map of Regions about Annapolis, Redrawn A431

1949, May 23 ***Perf. 11x10½***
984 A431 3c aquamarine .20 .20

300th anniv. of the founding of Annapolis, Md.

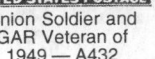

Union Soldier and GAR Veteran of 1949 — A432

Edgar Allan Poe — A433

GAR Issue

1949, Aug. 29 ***Perf. 11x10½***
985 A432 3c bright rose carmine .20 .20

Final encampment of the Grand Army of the Republic, Indianapolis, Aug. 28 to Sept. 1.

Edgar Allan Poe Issue

1949, Oct. 7 ***Perf. 10½x11***
986 A433 3c bright red violet .20 .20

Poe (1809-1849), writer and poet.

Coin, Symbolizing Fields of Banking Service A434

Samuel Gompers A435

Bankers Issue

1950, Jan. 3 ***Perf. 11x10½***
987 A434 3c yellow green .20 .20

75th anniv. of the formation of the American Bankers Assoc.

Samuel Gompers Issue

1950, Jan. 27 ***Perf. 10½x11***
988 A435 3c bright red violet .20 .20

Gompers (1850-1924), labor leader.

National Capital Sesquicentennial Issue

Statue of Freedom on Capitol Dome A436

Executive Mansion A437

Supreme Court Building A438

United States Capitol — A439

1950 ***Perf. 10½x11, 11x10½***

989 A436 3c bright blue .20 .20
990 A437 3c deep green .20 .20
991 A438 3c light violet .20 .20
992 A439 3c bright red violet .20 .20
Nos. 989-992 (4) .80 .80

150th anniv. of the establishment of the National Capital, Washington, DC.

Issued: Apr. 20, June 12, Aug. 2 and Nov. 22.

Railroad Engineers Issue

"Casey" Jones and Locomotives of 1900 and 1950 — A440

1950, Apr. 29 ***Perf. 11x10½***

993 A440 3c violet brown .20 .20

Kansas City, Missouri, Issue

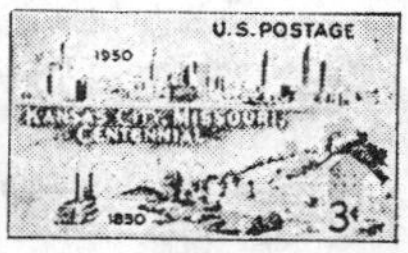

Kansas City Skyline, 1950 and Westport Landing, 1850 — A441

1950, June 3 ***Perf. 11x10½***

994 A441 3c violet .20 .20

Cent. of the incorporation of Kansas City, Mo.

Boy Scouts Issue

Three Boys, Statue of Liberty and Scout Badge A442

1950, June 30 ***Perf. 11x10½***

995 A442 3c sepia .20 .20

Honoring the BSA on the occasion of the 2nd Natl. Jamboree, held at Valley Forge, Pa.

Indiana Territory Issue

Gov. William Henry Harrison and First Indiana Capitol, Vincennes A443

1950, July 4 ***Perf. 11x10½***

996 A443 3c bright blue .20 .20

150th anniv. of the establishment of Ind. Terr.

California Statehood Centenary

Gold Miner, Pioneers and S.S. *Oregon* A444

1950, Sept. 9 ***Perf. 11x10½***

997 A444 3c yellow orange .20 .20

United Confederate Veterans Final Reunion Issue

Confederate Soldier and United Confederate Veteran A445

1951, May 30 ***Perf. 11x10½***

998 A445 3c gray .20 .20

Final reunion of the United Confederate Veterans, Norfolk, Va, May 30, 1951.

Nevada Settlement Centennial

Carson Valley, c. 1851 A446

1951, July 14 ***Perf. 11x10½***

999 A446 3c light olive green .20 .20

Landing of Cadillac Issue

Detroit Skyline and Cadillac Landing A447

1951, July 24 ***Perf. 11x10½***

1000 A447 3c blue .20 .20

250th anniv. of the landing of Antoine de la Mothe Cadillac at Detroit.

Colorado Statehood Issue

Colorado Capitol and Mount of the Holy Cross A448

1951, Aug. 1 ***Perf. 11x10½***

1001 A448 3c blue violet .20 .20

Colorado statehood, 75th anniv. Design includes columbine and statue, "The Bronco Buster," by A. Phimister Proctor.

American Chemical Society Issue

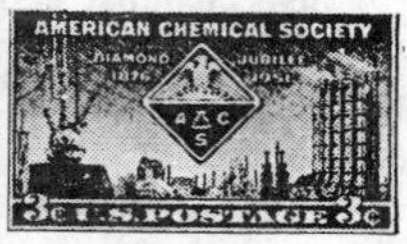

A. C. S. Emblem and Symbols of Chemistry A449

1951, Sept. 4 ***Perf. 11x10½***

1002 A449 3c violet brown .20 .20

American Chemical Soc., 75th anniv.

Battle of Brooklyn Issue

Gen. George Washington Evacuating Army — A450

1951, Dec. 10 ***Perf. 11x10½***

1003 A450 3c violet .20 .20

175th anniv. of the Battle of Brooklyn. Design includes Fulton Ferry House.

Betsy Ross Issue

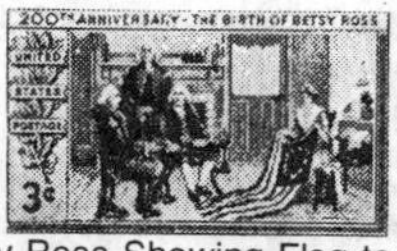

Betsy Ross Showing Flag to Gen. George Washington, Robert Morris and George Ross — A451

1952, Jan. 2 ***Perf. 11x10½***

1004 A451 3c carmine rose .20 .20

200th anniv. of the birth of Betsy Ross, maker of the 1st American flag.

4-H Club Issue

Farm, Club Emblem, Boy and Girl — A452

1952, Jan. 15 ***Perf. 11x10½***

1005 A452 3c blue green .20 .20

B. & O. Railroad Issue

Charter and Three Stages of Rail Transportation A453

1952, Feb. 28 ***Perf. 11x10½***

1006 A453 3c bright blue .20 .20

125th anniv. of the granting of a charter to the Baltimore and Ohio Railroad Company by the Maryland Legislature.

A. A. A., 50th Anniv.

School Girls and Safety Patrolman, Automobiles of 1902 and 1952 A454

1952, Mar. 4 ***Perf. 11x10½***

1007 A454 3c deep blue .20 .20

Torch of Liberty and Globe A455

Spillway, Grand Coulee Dam A456

NATO Issue

1952, Apr. 4 ***Perf. 11x10½***

1008 A455 3c deep violet .20 .20

3rd anniv. of the signing of the North Atlantic Treaty.

Grand Coulee Dam Issue

1952, May 15 ***Perf. 11x10½***

1009 A456 3c blue green .20 .20

50 years of Federal cooperation in developing the resources of rivers and streams in the West.

Lafayette Issue

Marquis de Lafayette, Flags, Cannon and Landing Party — A457

1952, June 13 ***Perf. 11x10½***

1010 A457 3c bright blue .20 .20

175th anniv. of the arrival of Lafayette in America.

Mt. Rushmore Memorial Issue

Sculptured Heads on Mt. Rushmore — A458

1952, Aug. 11 ***Perf. 10½x11***

1011 A458 3c blue green .20 .20

25th anniv. of the dedication of the Mt. Rushmore Natl. Memorial.

Engineering Centennial Issue

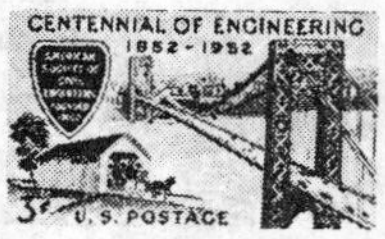

George Washington Bridge and Covered Bridge of 1850's A459

1952, Sept. 6 ***Perf. 11x10½***

1012 A459 3c violet blue .20 .20

Centenary of the founding of the American Soc. of Civil Engineers.

Service Women Issue

Women of the Marine Corps, Army, Navy and Air Force — A460

1952, Sept. 11 ***Perf. 11x10½***

1013 A460 3c deep blue .20 .20

Honoring the women in the US Armed Services.

Gutenberg Bible Issue

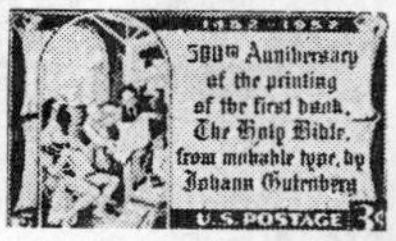

Gutenberg Showing Proof to the Elector of Mainz — A461

1952, Sept. 30 ***Perf. 11x10½***

1014 A461 3c violet .20 .20

500th anniv. of the printing of the 1st book, the Holy Bible, from movable type, by Johann Gutenberg.

Newspaper Boys Issue

Newspaper Boy, Torch and Group of Homes A462

1952, Oct. 4 ***Perf. 11x10½***

1015 A462 3c violet .20 .20

Red Cross Issue

Globe, Sun and Cross — A463

Perf. 11x10½

1952, Nov. 21 **Cross Typo.**

1016 A463 3c deep blue & carmine .20 .20

National Guard Issue

National Guardsman and Amphibious Landing A464

1953, Feb. 23 ***Perf. 11x10½***

1017 A464 3c bright blue .20 .20

Ohio Statehood Sesquicentennial

Map and Ohio State Seal — A465

1953, Mar. 2 ***Perf. 11x10½***

1018 A465 3c chocolate .20 .20

Washington Territory Issue

Medallion, Pioneers and Washington Scene — A466

1953, Mar. 2 ***Perf. 11x10½***

1019 A466 3c green .20 .20

Centenary of the organization of Washington Territory.

Louisiana Purchase, 150th Anniv.

Monroe, Livingston and Barbé-Marbois A467

1953, Apr. 30 ***Perf. 11x10½***

1020 A467 3c violet brown .20 .20

Opening of Japan Centennial Issue

Commodore Perry and 1st Anchorage off Tokyo Bay — A468

1953, July 14 ***Perf. 11x10½***

1021 A468 5c green .20 .20

Cent. of Commodore Matthew Calbraith Perry's negotiations with Japan, which opened her doors to foreign trade.

American Bar Association, 75th Anniv.

Section of Frieze, Supreme Court Room A469

1953, Aug. 24 ***Perf. 11x10½***

1022 A469 3c rose violet .20 .20

Sagamore Hill Issue

Home of Theodore Roosevelt A470

1953, Sept. 14 ***Perf. 11x10½***

1023 A470 3c yellow green .20 .20

Opening of Sagamore Hill, Theodore Roosevelt's home, as a national shrine.

Future Farmers Issue

Agricultural Scene and Future Farmer A471

1953, Oct. 13 ***Perf. 11x10½***

1024 A471 3c deep blue .20 .20

25th anniv. of the organization of Future Farmers of America.

Trucking Industry Issue

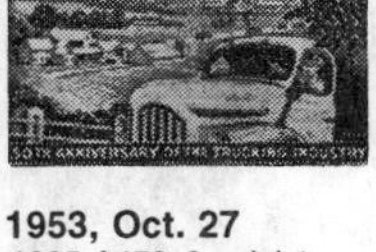

Truck, Farm and Distant City — A472

1953, Oct. 27 ***Perf. 11x10½***

1025 A472 3c violet .20 .20

Trucking Industry in the US, 50th anniv.

General Patton Issue

Gen. George S. Patton, Jr., and Tank in Action — A473

1953, Nov. 11 ***Perf. 11x10½***

1026 A473 3c blue violet .20 .20

Honoring Patton and the armored forces of the US army.

New York City, 300th Anniv.

Dutch Ship in New Amsterdam Harbor A474

1953, Nov. 20 ***Perf. 11x10½***

1027 A474 3c bright red violet .20 .20

Gadsden Purchase Issue

Map and Pioneer Group — A475

1953, Dec. 30 ***Perf. 11x10½***

1028 A475 3c copper brown .20 .20

Centenary of James Gadsden's purchase of territory from Mexico, to adjust US-Mexico boundary.

Columbia University, 200th Anniv.

Low Memorial Library A476

1954, Jan. 4 ***Perf. 11x10½***

1029 A476 3c blue .20 .20

Wet and Dry Printings

In 1953 the Bureau of Engraving and Printing began experiments in printing on "dry" paper (moisture content 5-10 per cent). In previous "wet" printings the paper had a moisture content of 13-35 per cent.

The new process required a thicker, stiffer paper, special types of inks and greater pressure to force the paper into the recessed plates. The "dry" printings show whiter paper, a higher sheen on the surface, feel thicker and stiffer, and the designs stand out more clearly than on the "wet" printings.

Nos. 832c and 1041 (flat plate) were the first "dry" printings to be issued of flat-plate, regular-issue stamps. No. 1063 was the first rotary-press stamp to be produced entirely by "dry" printing.

All postage stamps have been printed by the "dry" process since the late 1950's.

See the Scott Specialized Catalogue of United States Stamps for listings of the wet and dry printings and for No. 1033 on Silkote paper.

Liberty Issue

Franklin A477

Washington A478

Palace of the Governors, Santa Fe A478a

Mount Vernon A479

Thomas Jefferson A480

Bunker Hill Monument, Mass. Flag, 1776 A481

Statue of Liberty A482

Abraham Lincoln A483

The Hermitage A484

James Monroe A485

Theodore Roosevelt A486

Woodrow Wilson A487

Statue of Liberty

A488 A489

John J. Pershing A489a

The Alamo A490

Independence Hall — A491

Statue of Liberty A491a

Benjamin Harrison A492

John Jay A493

Monticello A494

Paul Revere A495

Robert E. Lee A496

John Marshall A497

Susan B. Anthony A498

Patrick Henry A499

Alexander Hamilton A500

Perf. 11x10½, 10½x11

1954-68 **Rotary Press Printing**

1030 A477 ½c red orange ('55) .20 .20
1031 A478 1c dark green .20 .20
1031A A478a 1¼c turq ('60) .20 .20
1032 A479 1½c brown carmine ('56) .20 .20
1033 A480 2c car rose .20 .20
1034 A481 2½c gray blue ('59) .20 .20
1035 A482 3c deep violet .20 .20
  a. Booklet pane of 6 4.00 *.90*
  b. Tagged ('66) .25 .25
  c. Imperf., pair *2,000.*
  d. Horiz. pair, imperf. btwn. —
  g. As "a," vert. imperf. btwn. *5,000.*

No. 1057a measures about 19½x22mm; No. 1035c, about 18¾x22½mm.

1036 A483 4c red violet .20 .20
  a. Booklet pane of 6 ('58) 2.75 *.80*
  b. Tagged ('63) .50 .40
  d. As "a," imperf. horiz. —
1037 A484 4½c blue green ('59) .20 .20
1038 A485 5c deep blue .20 .20
1039 A486 6c car ('55) .25 .20
  a. Imperf., pair —
1040 A487 7c rose carmine ('56) .20 .20
  a. 7c dark rose carmine .20 .20

Flat Plate Printing

Perf. 11

Size: 22.7mm high

1041 A488 8c dk vio blue & car .25 .20
  a. Double impression of carmine *650.00*

Rotary Press Printing

Size: 22.9mm high

1041B A488 8c dk vio blue & car .25 .20

Giori Press Printing

Redrawn Design

1042 A489 8c dk vio bl & car rose ('58) .20 .20

Rotary Press Printing

Perf. 11x10½, 10½x11

1042A A489a 8c brown ('61) .20 .20
1043 A490 9c rose lilac ('56) .30 .20
  a. 9c dark rose lilac .30 .20
1044 A491 10c rose lake ('56) .25 .20
  b. 10c dark rose lake .25 .20
  d. Tagged ('66) 2.00 1.00

Giori Press Printing
Perf. 11

1044A A491a 11c car & dk vio blue ('61) .30 .20
c. Tagged ('67) 2.00 1.60

Rotary Press Printing
Perf. 11x10½, 10½x11

1045 A492 12c red ('59) .35 .20
a. Tagged ('68) .35 .20
1046 A493 15c rose lake ('58) .60 .20
a. Tagged ('66) 1.10 .35
1047 A494 20c ultra ('56) .40 .20
a. 20c deep bright ultra .40 .20
1048 A495 25c green ('58) 1.10 .20
1049 A496 30c black ('55) .70 .20
b. 30c intense black .70 .20
1050 A497 40c brown red ('55) 1.50 .20
1051 A498 50c brt purple ('55) 1.50 .20
1052 A499 $1 purple ('55) 5.00 .20

Flat Plate Printing
Perf. 11

1053 A500 $5 black ('56) 75.00 6.75
Nos. 1030-1053 (28) 90.35 12.15

Luminescence

During 1963 quantities of certain issues (Nos. C64a, 1213b, 1213c and 1229a) were overprinted with phosphorescent coating, "tagged," for use in testing automated facing and canceling machines. Listings for tagged varieties of stamps previously issued without tagging start with Nos. 1035b and C59a.

The entire printings of Nos. 1238, 1278, 1280-1281, 1283B, 1286-1288, 1298-1305, 1323-1340, 1342-1362, 1364, and C69-C75 and all following listings, unless otherwise noted, were tagged.

Stamps tagged with zinc orthosilicate glow yellow green. Airmail stamps with calcium silicate overprint glow orange red. Both tagging overprints are activated only by shortwave ultraviolet light.

Coil Stamps
Perf. 10 Vert., Horiz. (1¼c, 4½c)

1954-73

1054 A478 1c dark green .20 .20
b. Imperf., pair 2,500. —
1054A A478a 1¼c turq ('60) .20 .20
1055 A480 2c rose car .20 .20
a. Tagged ('68) .20 .20
b. Imperf., pair (Bureau precanceled) 550.00
c. As "a," imperf. pair 575.00
1056 A481 2½c gray blue ('59) .25 .25
1057 A482 3c dp violet .20 .20
a. Imperf., pair 1,750. —
b. Tagged ('66) 1.00 .50

No. 1057a measures about 19½x22mm; No. 1035c, about 18¾x22½mm.

1058 A483 4c red vio ('58) .20 .20
a. Imperf., pair 120.00 70.00
1059 A484 4½c blue grn ('59) 1.50 1.20
1059A A495 25c grn ('65) .50 .30
b. Tagged ('73) .65 .20
c. Imperf., pair 50.00
Nos. 1054-1059A (8) 3.25 2.75

Value for No. 1059c is for fine centering.

Nebraska Territory Issue

Mitchell Pass, Scotts Bluff and "The Sower," by Lee Lawrie A507

1954, May 7 ***Perf. 11x10½***
1060 A507 3c violet .20 .20

Centenary of the establishment of the Nebraska Territory.

> ***Buying Sets***
> *It is often less expensive to purchase complete sets than individual stamps that make up the set.*

Kansas Territory Issue

Wheat Field and Pioneer Wagon Train A508

1954, May 31 ***Perf. 11x10½***
1061 A508 3c brown orange .20 .20

Centenary of the establishment of the Kansas Territory.

George Eastman Issue

George Eastman (1854-1932), Inventor and Philanthropist — A509

1954, July 12 ***Perf. 10½x11***
1062 A509 3c violet brown .20 .20

Lewis and Clark Expedition Sesquicentennial

Landing of Lewis and Clark — A510

1954, July 28 ***Perf. 11x10½***
1063 A510 3c violet brown .20 .20

Pennsylvania Acad. of the Fine Arts

Charles Willson Peale in his Museum, Self-portrait — A511

1955, Jan. 15 ***Perf. 10½x11***
1064 A511 3c violet brown .20 .20

150th anniv. of the founding of the Pa. Acad. of the Fine Arts, Philadelphia.

Land Grant Colleges Issue

Open Book and Symbols of Subjects Taught A512

1955, Feb. 12 ***Perf. 11x10½***
1065 A512 3c green .20 .20

Cent. of the founding of Mich. State College and Penn. State Univ., 1st of the land-grant institutions.

Rotary International, 50th Anniv.

Torch, Globe and Rotary Emblem A513

1955, Feb. 23 ***Perf. 11x10½***
1066 A513 8c deep blue .20 .20

Armed Forces Reserve Issue

Marine, Coast Guard, Army, Navy, and Air Force Personnel A514

1955, May 21 ***Perf. 11x10½***
1067 A514 3c purple .20 .20

New Hampshire Issue

Great Stone Face — A515

1955, June 21 ***Perf. 10½x11***
1068 A515 3c green .20 .20

Honor NH on the occasion of the sesquicentennial of the discovery of the "Old Man of the Mountains."

Soo Locks Opening, Centenary

Map of Great Lakes and Two Steamers A516

1955, June 28 ***Perf. 11x10½***
1069 A516 3c blue .20 .20

Atoms for Peace Policy

Atomic Energy Encircling the Hemispheres A517

1955, July 28 ***Perf. 11x10½***
1070 A517 3c deep blue .20 .20

Fort Ticonderoga Bicentenary

Map of the Fort, Ethan Allen and Artillery A518

1955, Sept. 18 ***Perf. 11x10½***
1071 A518 3c light brown .20 .20

Andrew W. Mellon Issue

Andrew W. Mellon — A519

1955, Dec. 20 ***Perf. 10½x11***
1072 A519 3c rose carmine .20 .20

Mellon, US Sec. of the Treasury (1921-32), financier and art collector.

Benjamin Franklin Issue

"Franklin Taking Electricity from the Sky," by Benjamin West — A520

1956, Jan. 17 ***Perf. 10½x11***
1073 A520 3c bright carmine .20 .20

250th anniv. of the birth of Franklin.

Booker T. Washington Issue

Log Cabin — A521

1956, Apr. 5 ***Perf. 11x10½***
1074 A521 3c deep blue .20 .20

Washington (1856-1915), black educator.

Fifth Intl. Phil. Exhib. Issues
Souvenir Sheet

A522

Flat Plate Printing

1956, Apr. 28 ***Imperf.***
1075 A522 Sheet of 2 2.00 2.00
a. A482 3c deep violet .80 .80
b. A488 8c dk vio bl & carmine 1.00 1.00

No. 1075 measures 108x73mm; Nos. 1075a and 1075b measure 24x28mm.

New York Coliseum and Columbus Monument A523

Rotary Press Printing

1956, Apr. 30 ***Perf. 11x10½***
1076 A523 3c deep violet .20 .20

FIPEX, New York City, Apr. 28-May 6.

Wildlife Conservation Issue

Wild Turkey A524

Pronghorn Antelope A525

King Salmon A526

1956 ***Perf. 11x10½***
1077 A524 3c rose lake .20 .20
1078 A525 3c brown .20 .20
1079 A526 3c blue green .20 .20
Nos. 1077-1079 (3) .60 .60

Emphasizing the importance of Wildlife conservation in America.
Issued: May 5, June 22, Nov. 9.
See Nos. 1098, 1392.

Pure Food and Drug Laws, 50th Anniv.

Harvey W. Wiley — A527

1956, June 27 ***Perf. 10½x11***
1080 A527 3c dark blue green .20 .20

Wheatland Issue

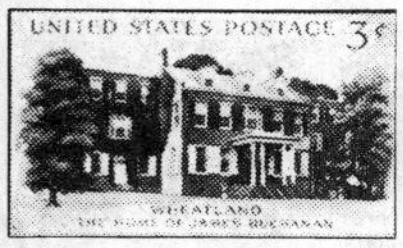

President Buchanan's Home, "Wheatland," Lancaster, PA — A528

1956, Aug. 5 ***Perf. 11x10½***
1081 A528 3c black brown .20 .20

Labor Day Issue

Mosaic, AFL-CIO Headquarters — A529

1956, Sept. 3 ***Perf. 10½x11***
1082 A529 3c deep blue .20 .20

Nassau Hall Issue

Nassau Hall, Princeton, NJ — A530

1956, Sept. 22 ***Perf. 11x10½***
1083 A530 3c black, *orange* .20 .20

200th anniv. of Nassau Hall, Princeton University.

Devils Tower Issue

Devils Tower — A531

1956, Sept. 24 ***Perf. 10½x11***
1084 A531 3c violet .20 .20

50th anniv. of the Federal law providing for protection of American natural antiquities. Devils Tower Natl. Monument, Wyoming, is an outstanding example.

Children's Issue

Children of the World A532

1956, Dec. 15 ***Perf. 11x10½***
1085 A532 3c dark blue .20 .20

Promoting friendship among the world's children.

Alexander Hamilton Issue

Alexander Hamilton (1757-1804) and Federal Hall — A533

1957, Jan. 11 ***Perf. 11x10½***
1086 A533 3c rose red .20 .20

Polio Issue

Allegory — A534

1957, Jan. 15 ***Perf. 10½x11***
1087 A534 3c red lilac .20 .20

Honoring "those who helped fight polio," and 20th anniv. of the Natl. Foundation for Infantile Paralysis and the March of Dimes.

Coast and Geodetic Survey Issue

Flag of Coast and Geodetic Survey and Ships at Sea — A535

1957, Feb. 11 ***Perf. 11x10½***
1088 A535 3c dark blue .20 .20

150th anniv. of the establishment of the Coast and Geodetic Survey.

Architects Issue

Corinthian Capital and Mushroom Type Head and Shaft — A536

1957, Feb. 23 ***Perf. 11x10½***
1089 A536 3c red lilac .20 .20

Centenary of the American Institute of Architects.

Steel Industry Centenary

American Eagle and Pouring Ladle — A537

1957, May 22 ***Perf. 10½x11***
1090 A537 3c bright ultra .20 .20

International Naval Review Issue

Aircraft Carrier and Jamestown Festival Emblem A538

1957, June 10 ***Perf. 11x10½***
1091 A538 3c blue green .20 .20

Intl. Naval Review and Jamestown Festival.

Oklahoma Statehood, 50th Anniv.

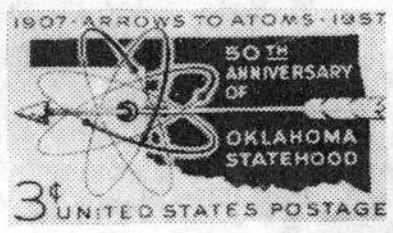

Map of Oklahoma, Arrow and Atom Diagram A539

1957, June 14 ***Perf. 11x10½***
1092 A539 3c dark blue .20 .20

School Teachers Issue

Teacher and Pupils — A540

1957, July 1 ***Perf. 11x10½***
1093 A540 3c rose lake .20 .20

Honoring the school teachers of America.

Flag Issue

"Old Glory" (48 Stars) — A541

Giori Press Printing

1957, July 4 ***Perf. 11***
1094 A541 4c dk blue & dp carmine .20 .20

Shipbuilding Issue

"Virginia of Sagadahock" and Seal of Maine — A542

Rotary Press Printing

1957, Aug. 15 ***Perf. 10½x11***
1095 A542 3c deep violet .20 .20

350th anniv. of shipbuilding in America.

Champion of Liberty Issue

Ramon Magsaysay, (1907-1957), Philippines President — A543

Giori Press Printing

1957, Aug. 31 ***Perf. 11***
1096 A543 8c carmine, ultra & ocher .20 .20

For other Champion of Liberty issues, see Nos. 1110-1111, 1117-1118, 1125-1126, 1136-1137, 1147-1148, 1159-1160, 1165-1166, 1168-1169, 1174-1175.

Marquis de Lafayette A544

Whooping Cranes A545

Lafayette Bicentenary Issue

Rotary Press Printing

1957, Sept. 6 ***Perf. 10½x11***
1097 A544 3c rose lake .20 .20

Bicentenary of the birth of Lafayette.

Wildlife Conservation Issue

Giori Press Printing

1957, Nov. 22 ***Perf. 11***
1098 A545 3c blue, ocher & green .20 .20

Emphasizing the importance of Wildlife Conservation in America.

Bible, Hat and Quill Pen A546

"Bountiful Earth" A547

Religious Freedom Issue

Rotary Press Printing

1957, Dec. 27 ***Perf. 10½x11***
1099 A546 3c black .20 .20

Flushing Remonstrance, 300th anniv.

Gardening-Horticulture Issue

1958, Mar. 15
1100 A547 3c green .20 .20

Garden clubs of America and cent. of the birth of Liberty Hyde Bailey, horticulturist.

Brussels Fair Issue

US Pavilion at Brussels A551

Rotary Press Printing

1958, Apr. 17 ***Perf. 11x10½***
1104 A551 3c deep claret .20 .20

Opening of the Universal and Intl. Exhib., Brussels, Apr. 17.

James Monroe Issue

James Monroe, by Gilbert Stuart — A552

1958, Apr. 28 ***Perf. 11x10½***
1105 A552 3c purple .20 .20

Monroe (1758-1831), 5th pres. of the US.

Minnesota Statehood Centenary

Minnesota Lakes and Pines — A553

Rotary Press Printing

1958, May 11
1106 A553 3c green .20 .20

Geophysical Year (IGY, 1957-58)

Solar Disc and Hands from Michelangelo's "Creation of Adam" A554

Giori Press Printing

1958, May 31 ***Perf. 11***
1107 A554 3c black & red orange .20 .20

Gunston Hall Issue

Gunston Hall, Virginia A555

Rotary Press Printing

1958, June 12 ***Perf. 11x10½***
1108 A555 3c light green .20 .20

Bicent. of Gunston Hall and honoring George Mason, author of the Constitution of Va. and the Va. Bill of Rights.

Mackinac Bridge A556

Simon Bolivar A557

Mackinac Bridge Issue

1958, June 25 *Perf. 10½x11*

1109 A556 3c bright greenish blue .20 .20

Dedication of Mackinac Bridge, Mich.

Champion of Liberty Issue
Rotary Press Printing

1958, July 24 *Perf. 10½x11*

1110 A557 4c olive bister .20 .20

Giori Press Printing
Perf. 11

1111 A557 8c carmine, ultra & ocher .20 .20

Simon Bolivar, So. American freedom fighter.

Atlantic Cable Centennial Issue

Neptune, Globe and Mermaid A558

Rotary Press Printing

1958, Aug. 15 *Perf. 11x10½*

1112 A558 4c reddish purple .20 .20

Centenary of the Atlantic Cable, linking the Eastern and Western hemispheres.

Lincoln Sesquicentennial Issue

Lincoln, by George Healy A559

Lincoln, by Gutzon Borglum A560

Abraham Lincoln and Stephen A. Douglas Debating A561

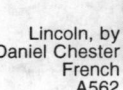

Lincoln, by Daniel Chester French A562

1958-59 *Perf. 10½x11, 11x10½*

1113 A559 1c green ('59) .20 .20
1114 A560 3c purple ('59) .20 .20
1115 A561 4c sepia .20 .20
1116 A562 4c dark blue ('59) .20 .20
Nos. 1113-1116 (4) .80 .80

No. 1114 also for the founding of Cooper Union cent., NYC. No. 1115 also for the Lincoln-Douglas debates, cent.

Issue dates: Nos. 1113, 1114, 1116, Feb. 12, Feb. 27 and May 30. No. 1115, Aug. 27.

Lajos Kossuth, (1802-1892) A563

Early Press and Hand Holding Quill A564

Champion of Liberty Issue
Rotary Press Printing

1958, Sept. 19 *Perf. 10½x11*

1117 A563 4c green .20 .20

Giori Press Printing
Perf. 11

1118 A563 8c carmine, ultra & ocher .20 .20

Kossuth, Hungarian freedom fighter.

Freedom of Press Issue
Rotary Press Printing

1958, Sept. 22 *Perf. 10½x11*

1119 A564 4c black .20 .20

Honoring journalism and freedom of the press in connection with the 50th anniv. of the 1st School of Journalism at the Univ. of Mo.

Overland Mail Centenary

Mail Coach and Map of Southwest US — A565

1958, Oct. 10 *Perf. 11x10½*

1120 A565 4c crimson rose .20 .20

Noah Webster A566

Forest Scene A567

Noah Webster Issue

1958, Oct. 16 *Perf. 10½x11*

1121 A566 4c dark carmine rose .20 .20

Webster (1758-1843), lexicographer.

Forest Conservation Issue
Giori Press Printing

1958, Oct. 27 *Perf. 11*

1122 A567 4c green, yel & brown .20 .20

Publicizing forest conservation and the protection of natural resources and honoring Theodore Roosevelt, a leading forest conservationist, on the cent. of his birth.

Fort Duquesne Issue

Occupation of Fort Duquesne A568

Rotary Press Printing

1958, Nov. 25 *Perf. 11x10½*

1123 A568 4c blue .20 .20

Bicentennial of Fort Duquesne (Fort Pitt).

Oregon Statehood Centenary

Covered Wagon and Mt. Hood — A569

1959, Feb. 14 *Perf. 11x10½*

1124 A569 4c blue green .20 .20

José de San Martin — A570

NATO Emblem — A571

Champion of Liberty Issue
Rotary Press Printing

1959, Feb. 25 *Perf. 10½x11*

1125 A570 4c blue .20 .20
a. Horiz. pair, imperf. btwn. *1,500.*

Giori Press Printing
Perf. 11

1126 A570 8c car, ultra & ocher .20 .20

San Martin, South American soldier and statesman.

NATO Issue
Rotary Press Printing

1959, Apr. 1 *Perf. 10½x11*

1127 A571 4c blue .20 .20

North Atlantic Treaty Organ., 10th anniv.

Arctic Explorations Issue

North Pole, Dog Sled and "Nautilus" A572

1959, Apr. 6 *Perf. 11x10½*

1128 A572 4c brt greenish blue .20 .20

Conquest of the Arctic by land by Rear Admiral Robert Edwin Peary in 1909 and by sea by the submarine "Nautilus" in 1958.

World Peace Through World Trade Issue

Globe and Laurel — A573

1959, Apr. 20 *Perf. 11x10½*

1129 A573 8c rose lake .20 .20

Issued in conjunction with the 17th Cong. of the Intl. Chamber of Commerce, Washington, DC, Apr. 19-25.

Silver Centennial Issue

Henry Comstock at Mount Davidson Site — A574

1959, June 8 *Perf. 11x10½*

1130 A574 4c black .20 .20

Cent. of the discovery of silver at the Comstock Lode, Nev.

St. Lawrence Seaway Issue

Great Lakes, Maple Leaf and Eagle Emblems A575

Giori Press Printing

1959, June 26 *Perf. 11*

1131 A575 4c red & dark blue .20 .20

Opening of the St. Lawrence Seaway, June 26, 1959. See Canada No. 387.

49-Star Flag Issue

US Flag, 1959 — A576

1959, July 4 *Perf. 11*

1132 A576 4c ocher, dk blue & dp car .20 .20

Soil Conservation Issue

Modern Farm — A577

1959, Aug. 26

1133 A577 4c blue, green & ocher .20 .20

Tribute to farmers and ranchers who use soil and water conservation measures.

Petroleum Industry Issue

Oil Derrick — A578

Rotary Press Printing

1959, Aug. 27 *Perf. 10½x11*

1134 A578 4c brown .20 .20

Cent. of the completion of the nation's 1st oil well at Titusville, Pa.

Dental Health Issue

Children A579

1959, Sept. 14 *Perf. 11x10½*

1135 A579 4c green .20 .20

Publicizing dental health and cent. of the American Dental Assoc.

Ernst Reuter A580

Dr. Ephraim McDowell A581

Champion of Liberty Issue
Rotary Press Printing

1959, Sept. 29 *Perf. 10½x11*

1136 A580 4c gray .20 .20

Giori Press Printing
Perf. 11

1137 A580 8c carmine, ultra & ocher .20 .20
a. Ocher omitted *3,750.*
b. Ultramarine omitted *3,750.*
c. Ocher & ultramarine omitted *4,000.*
d. All colors omitted —

Ernst Reuter, mayor of Berlin 1948-53.

Dr. Ephraim McDowell Issue
Rotary Press Printing

1959, Dec. 3 *Perf. 10½x11*

1138 A581 4c rose lake .20 .20
a. Vert. pair, imperf. btwn. *450.00*
b. Vert. pair, imperf. horiz. *350.00*

Honoring McDowell on the 150th anniv. of the 1st successful ovarian operation performed in the US.

American Credo Issue

Quotation from Washington's Farewell Address, 1796 — A582

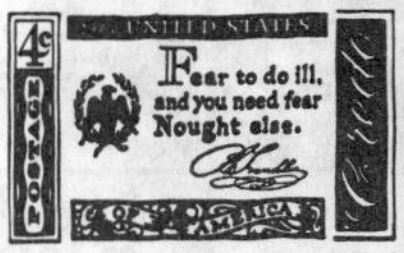

Benjamin Franklin Quotation A583

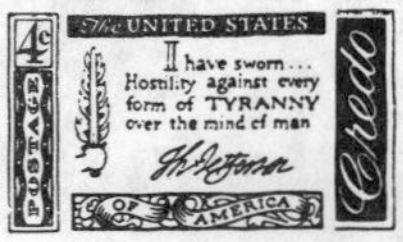

Thomas Jefferson Quotation A584

Francis Scott Key Quotation A585

Abraham Lincoln Quotation A586

Patrick Henry Quotation A587

Giori Press Printing

1960-61 *Perf. 11*

1139 A582 4c dk violet blue & car .20 .20
1140 A583 4c olive bister & green .20 .20
1141 A584 4c gray & vermilion .20 .20
1142 A585 4c carmine & dark blue .20 .20
1143 A586 4c magenta & green .20 .20
1144 A587 4c green & brown ('61) .20 .20
Nos. 1139-1144 (6) 1.20 1.20

Re-emphasizing the ideals upon which America was founded and honoring those great Americans who wrote or uttered the credos.

Issue dates: Jan. 20, Mar. 31, May 18, Sept. 14, Nov. 19, and Jan. 11.

Boy Scout Jubilee Issue

Boy Scout Giving Scout Sign — A588

Giori Press Printing

1960, Feb. 8 *Perf. 11*

1145 A588 4c red, dk blue & dk bis .20 .20

Boy Scouts of America, 50th anniv.

Olympic Rings and Snowflake A589

Thomas G. Masaryk A590

Olympic Winter Games Issue

Rotary Press Printing

1960, Feb. 18 *Perf. 10½x11*

1146 A589 4c dull blue .20 .20

Opening of the 8th Olympic Winter Games, Squaw Valley, Feb. 18-29.

Champion of Liberty Issue

Rotary Press Printing

1960, Mar. 7 *Perf. 10½x11*

1147 A590 4c blue .20 .20
a. Vert. pair, imperf. btwn. *3,250.*

Giori Press Printing

Perf. 11

1148 A590 8c carmine, ultra & ocher .20 .20
a. Horiz. pair, imperf. btwn.

Masaryk, founder and pres. of Czechoslovakia (1918-35), on the 110th anniv. of his birth.

World Refugee Year Issue

Refugee Family Walking Toward New Life — A591

Rotary Press Printing

1960, Apr. 7 *Perf. 11x10½*

1149 A591 4c gray black .20 .20

WRY, July 1, 1959-June 30, 1960.

Water Conservation Issue

Water, from Watershed to Consumer A592

Giori Press Printing

1960, Apr. 18 *Perf. 11*

1150 A592 4c dk blue, brn org & green .20 .20
a. Brown orange omitted

Stressing the importance of water conservation, and 7th Watershed Cong., Washington, DC.

SEATO Issue

SEATO Emblem — A593

Rotary Press Printing

1960, May 31 *Perf. 10½x11*

1151 A593 4c blue .20 .20
a. Vert. pair, imperf. btwn. *175.00*

South-East Asia Treaty Org. and the SEATO Conf., Washington, DC, May 31-June 3.

American Woman Issue

Mother and Daughter A594

1960, June 2 *Perf. 11x10½*

1152 A594 4c deep violet .20 .20

A tribute to American women and their accomplishments in civic affairs, education, arts and industry.

50-Star Flag Issue

US Flag, 1960 — A595

Giori Press Printing

1960, July 4 *Perf. 11*

1153 A595 4c dark blue & red .20 .20

Pony Express Centennial Issue

Pony Express Rider — A596

Rotary Press Printing

1960, July 19 *Perf. 11x10½*

1154 A596 4c sepia .20 .20

Man in Wheelchair Operating Drill Press — A597

5th World Forestry Congress Seal — A598

Employ the Handicapped Issue

1960, Aug. 28 *Perf. 10½x11*

1155 A597 4c dark blue .20 .20

Promoting employment of the physically handicapped and publicizing the 8th World Cong. of the Intl. Soc. for the Welfare of Cripples, NYC.

World Forestry Congress Issue

1960, Aug. 29

1156 A598 4c green .20 .20

5th World Forestry Cong., Seattle, Wash., Aug. 29-Sept. 10.

A599

A600

Mexican Independence Issue

Giori Press Printing

1960, Sept. 16 *Perf. 11*

1157 A599 4c Independence Bell .20 .20

150th anniv. of Mexican independence. See Mexico No. 910.

US-Japan Treaty Issue

1960, Sept. 28 *Perf. 11*

Washington Monument and Cherry Blossoms

1158 A600 4c blue & pink .20 .20

Cent. of the US-Japan Treaty of Amity and Commerce.

Ignacy Jan Paderewski A601

Robert A. Taft A602

Champion of Liberty Issue

Rotary Press Printing

1960, Oct. 8 *Perf. 10½x11*

1159 A601 4c blue .20 .20

Giori Press Printing

Perf. 11

1160 A601 8c carmine, ultra & ocher .20 .20

Paderewski (1866-1941), Polish statesman and musician.

Senator Taft Memorial Issue

Rotary Press Printing

1960, Oct. 10 *Perf. 10½x11*

1161 A602 4c dull violet .20 .20

Senator Taft (1889-1953), of Ohio.

Wheels of Freedom Issue

Globe and Steering Wheel with Tractor, Car and Truck — A603

1960, Oct. 15 *Perf. 11x10½*

1162 A603 4c dark blue .20 .20

Honoring the automotive industry and in connection with the National Automobile Show, Detroit, Oct. 15-23.

Boys' Clubs of America Issue

Profile of a Boy — A604

Giori Press Printing

1960, Oct. 18 *Perf. 11*

1163 A604 4c indigo, slate & rose red .20 .20

Cent. of the Boys' Clubs of America movement.

Automated Post Office Issue

Architect's Sketch of New Post Office, Providence, RI — A605

1960, Oct. 20 *Perf. 11*

1164 A605 4c dk blue & carmine .20 .20

Opening of the 1st automated PO in the US.

Baron Gustaf Emil Mannerheim A606

Camp Fire Girls Emblem A607

Champion of Liberty Issue

Rotary Press Printing

1960, Oct. 26 *Perf. 10½x11*

1165 A606 4c blue .20 .20

Giori Press Printing

Perf. 11

1166 A606 8c car, ultra & ocher .20 .20

Mannerheim (1867-1951), marshal and pres. of Finland.

Camp Fire Girls Issue

Giori Press Printing

1960, Nov. 1 *Perf. 11*

1167 A607 4c dk blue & brt red .20 .20

50th anniv. of the Camp Fire Girls' movement and with their Golden Jubilee Convention celebration.

Giuseppe Garibaldi (1807-1882) A608

Walter F. George (1878-1957) A609

Champion of Liberty Issue
Rotary Press Printing

1960, Nov. 2 ***Perf. 10½x11***
1168 A608 4c green .20 .20

Giori Press Printing
Perf. 11

1169 A608 8c carmine, ultra & ocher .20 .20

Garibaldi, Italian patriot and freedom fighter.

Senator George Memorial Issue
Rotary Press Printing

1960, Nov. 5 ***Perf. 10½x11***
1170 A609 4c dull violet .20 .20

Senator Walter F. George of Georgia.

Andrew Carnegie A610

John Foster Dulles A611

Andrew Carnegie Issue

1960, Nov. 25
1171 A610 4c deep claret .20 .20

Carnegie (1835-1919), industrialist and philanthropist.

John Foster Dulles Memorial Issue

1960, Dec. 6 ***Perf. 10½x11***
1172 A611 4c dull violet .20 .20

John Foster Dulles (1888-1959), Sec. of State (1953-1959).

Echo I — Communications for Peace Issue

Radio Waves Connecting Echo I and Earth — A612

1960, Dec. 15 ***Perf. 11x10½***
1173 A612 4c deep violet .20 .20

World's 1st communications satellite, Echo I, placed in orbit by NASA, Aug. 12, 1960.

Champion of Liberty Issue

Mahatma Gandhi — A613

Rotary Press Printing

1961, Jan. 26 ***Perf. 10½x11***
1174 A613 4c red orange .20 .20

Giori Press Printing
Perf. 11

1175 A613 8c carmine, ultra & ocher .20 .20

Mohandas K. Gandhi, leader in India's struggle for independence.

Range Conservation Issue

The Trail Boss and Modern Range A614

Giori Press Printing

1961, Feb. 2 ***Perf. 11***
1176 A614 4c blue, slate & brown orange .20 .20

Importance of range conservation and meeting of the American Soc. of Range Management, Washington, DC. "The Trail Boss" from a drawing by Charles M. Russell is the Society's emblem.

Horace Greeley Issue

Horace Greeley (1811-1872), Publisher and Editor — A615

Rotary Press Printing

1961, Feb. 3 ***Perf. 10½x11***
1177 A615 4c dull violet .20 .20

Civil War Centennial Issue

Sea Coast Gun of 1861 — A616

Rifleman at Shiloh, 1862 — A617

Blue and Gray at Gettysburg, 1863 — A618

Battle of the Wilderness, 1864 A619

Appomattox, 1865 A620

1961-65 ***Perf. 11x10½***
1178 A616 4c light green .20 .20
1179 A617 4c blk, *peach blossom* .20 .20

Giori Press Printing
Perf. 11

1180 A618 5c gray & blue .20 .20
1181 A619 5c dark red & black .20 .20
1182 A620 5c Prus blue & black .25 .20
a. Horiz. pair, imperf. vert. *4,500.*
Nos. 1178-1182 (5) 1.05 1.00

Cent. of the firing on Fort Sumter, No. 1178; cent. of the Battle of Shiloh, No. 1179; cent. of the Battle of Gettysburg, No. 1180; cent. of the Battle of the Wilderness, No. 1181; cent. of the surrender of Gen. Robert E. Lee to Lt. Gen. Ulysses S. Grant at Appomattox Court House, No. 1182.

Issued: #1178-1182, 4/12; 4/7/62; 7/1/63; 5/5/64; 4/9/65.

Kansas Statehood Centenary

Sunflower, Pioneer Couple and Stockade A621

Giori Press Printing

1961, May 10 ***Perf. 11***
1183 A621 4c brn, dk red & grn, *yellow* .20 .20

Senator George W. Norris Issue

Norris and Norris Dam, Tenn. — A622

Rotary Press Printing

1961, July 11 ***Perf. 11x10½***
1184 A622 4c blue green .20 .20

Norris (1861-1944) of Nebraska.

Naval Aviation, 50th Anniv.

Navy's First Plane (Curtiss A-1 of 1911) and Naval Air Wings A623

1961, Aug. 20
1185 A623 4c blue .20 .20

Scales of Justice, Factory, Worker and Family A624

Remington's "Smoke Signal" A625

Workmen's Compensation Issue

1961, Sept. 4 ***Perf. 10½x11***
1186 A624 4c ultra, *grayish* .20 .20

50th anniv. of the 1st successful Workmen's Compensation Law, enacted by the Wis. legislature.

Frederic Remington Issue

Giori Press Printing

1961, Oct. 4 ***Perf. 11***
1187 A625 4c multicolored .20 .20

Frederic Remington (1861-1909), artist of the West. The design is from an oil painting, Amon Carter Museum of Western Art, Fort Worth, Texas.

Sun Yat-sen A626

Basketball A627

Republic of China, 50th Anniv.

Rotary Press Printing

1961, Oct. 10 ***Perf. 10½x11***
1188 A626 4c blue .20 .20

Naismith-Basketball Issue

1961, Nov. 6 ***Perf. 10½x11***
1189 A627 4c brown .20 .20

Honoring basketball and James A. Naismith (1861-1939), who invented the game in 1891.

Nursing Issue

Student Nurse Lighting Candle — A628

Giori Press Printing

1961, Dec. 28 ***Perf. 11***
1190 A628 4c blue, green, org & blk .20 .20

New Mexico Statehood, 50th Anniv.

Shiprock A629

1962, Jan. 6 ***Perf. 11***
1191 A629 4c lt blue, maroon & bis .20 .20

Arizona Statehood, 50th Anniv.

Giant Saguaro Cactus — A630

1962 Feb. 14 ***Perf. 11***
1192 A630 4c car, vio blue & green .20 .20

Project Mercury Issue

"Friendship 7" Capsule and Globe A631

1962, Feb. 20 ***Perf. 11***
1193 A631 4c dark blue & yellow .20 .20

First orbital flight of a US astronaut, Lt. Col. John H. Glenn, Jr., Feb. 20, 1962. Imperfs. are printers waste.

Malaria Eradication Issue

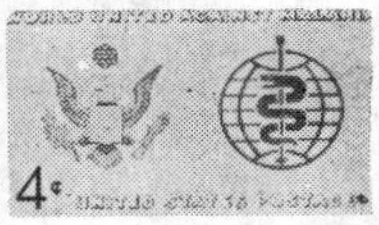

Great Seal of US and WHO Symbol A632

1962, Mar. 30 ***Perf. 11***
1194 A632 4c blue & bister .20 .20

WHO drive to eradicate malaria.

Charles Evans Hughes A633

Space Needle and Monorail A634

Charles Evans Hughes Issue

Rotary Press Printing

1962, Apr. 11 ***Perf. 10½x11***
1195 A633 4c black, *buff* .20 .20

Hughes (1862-1948), Gov. of NY, Chief Justice of the US.

Seattle World's Fair Issue

Giori Press Printing

1962, Apr. 25 ***Perf. 11***
1196 A634 4c red & dark blue .20 .20

"Century 21" Intl. Expo., Seattle, Wash., Apr. 21-Oct. 21.

Louisiana Statehood Sesquicentennial

Riverboat on the Mississippi A635

1962, Apr. 30 ***Perf. 11***
1197 A635 4c blue, dk sl grn & red .20 .20

Homestead Act Centenary

Sod Hut and Settlers A636

Rotary Press Printing

1962, May 20 ***Perf. 11x10½***
1198 A636 4c slate .20 .20

Girl Scout of America, 50th Anniv.

Senior Girl Scout and Flag — A637

1962, July 24 ***Perf. 11x10½***
1199 A637 4c rose red .20 .20

Senator Brien McMahon Issue

Brien McMahon and Atomic Diagram A638

1962, July 28 ***Perf. 11x10½***
1200 A638 4c violet .20 .20

Honoring Sen. McMahon, Conn., for his role in opening the way to peaceful uses of atomic energy.

Apprenticeship Issue

Machinist Handing Micrometer to Apprentice A639

1962, Aug. 31 ***Perf. 11x10½***
1201 A639 4c black, *yellow bister* .20 .20

Natl. Apprenticeship Program and 25th anniv. of the Natl. Apprenticeship Act.

Sam Rayburn Issue

Sam Rayburn and Capitol — A640

Giori Press Printing

1962, Sept. 16 ***Perf. 11***
1202 A640 4c dk blue & red brown .20 .20

Sam Rayburn (1882-1961), Speaker of the House of Representatives.

Dag Hammarskjold Issue

UN Headquarters and Dag Hammarskjold A641

Giori Press Printing

1962, Oct. 23 ***Perf. 11***
1203 A641 4c black, brown & yellow .20 .20

Hammarskjold, Sec. Gen. of the UN, 1953-61.

Hammarskjold Special Printing

1962, Nov. 16
1204 A641 4c blk, brn & yel (yel inverted) .20 .20

No. 1204 was issued following discovery of No. 1203 with yellow background inverted.

Wreath and Candles A642

Map of US and Lamp A643

Christmas Issue

Giori Press Printing

1962, Nov. 1 ***Perf. 11***
1205 A642 4c green & red .20 .20

Higher Education Issue

1962, Nov. 14 ***Perf. 11***
1206 A643 4c blue green & black .20 .20

Higher education's role in American cultural and industrial development in connection with the centenary celebrations of the signing of the law creating land-grant colleges and universities.

Winslow Homer Issue

"Breezing Up" — A644

1962, Dec. 15 ***Perf. 11***
1207 A644 4c multicolored .20 .20
a. Horiz. pair, imperf. btwn. & at right *6,750.*

Winslow Homer (1836-1910), painter (showing his oil which hangs in the Natl. Gallery, Washington, DC).

Flag Issue

Flag over White House — A645

1963-66 ***Perf. 11***
1208 A645 5c blue & red .20 .20
a. Tagged ('66) .20 .20
b. Horiz. pair, imperf. btwn. *1,500.*

Issue dates: #1208, Jan. 9. #1208a, Aug. 25.

Beware of pairs with faint blind perforations between offered as No. 1208b.

Regular Issue

Andrew Jackson A646

George Washington A650

Rotary Press Printing

1962-66 ***Perf. 11x10½***
1209 A646 1c green ('63) .20 .20
a. Tagged ('66) .20 .20
1213 A650 5c dark blue gray .20 .20
a. Booklet pane 5 + label 3.00 *1.75*
b. Tagged ('63) .50 .20
c. As "a," tagged ('63) 2.00 *1.50*

See Luminescence note after No. 1053.

Three different messages are found on the label in No. 1213a, and two messages on that of No. 1213c.

Unused catalogue numbers (1210-1212, 1214-1224, 1226-1228) were left vacant for additional denominations in this regular series which were not produced.

Coil Stamps; Rotary Press

1962-66 ***Perf. 10 Vertically***

1225 A646 1c green ('63) .20 .20
- **a.** Tagged ('66) .20 .20

1229 A650 5c dark blue gray 1.25 .20
- **a.** Tagged ('63) 1.25 .20
- **b.** Imperf., pair *450.00*

Carolina Charter Issue

First Page of Carolina Charter A662

Giori Press Printing

1963, Apr. 6 ***Perf. 11***

1230 A662 5c dk carmine & brown .20 .20

Carolina Charter, 1663, granting to 8 Englishmen lands, extending coast-to-coast roughly along the present border of Va. to the north and Fla. to the south. Original charter on display at Raleigh.

Food for Peace-Freedom from Hunger

Wheat — A663

1963, June 4 ***Perf. 11***

1231 A663 5c green, buff & red .20 .20

American "Food for Peace" program and FAO "Freedom from Hunger" campaign.

West Virginia Statehood Centenary

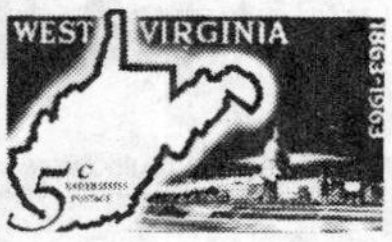

Map of West Virginia and State Capitol A664

1963, June 20

1232 A664 5c green, red & blk .20 .20

Emancipation Proclamation Issue

Severed Chain — A665

1963, Aug. 16 ***Perf. 11***

1233 A665 5c dk blue, black & red .20 .20

Cent. of Lincoln's Emancipation Proclamation, freeing about 3,000,000 slaves in 10 southern states.

Alliance for Progress Issue

Alliance Emblem A666

1963, Aug. 17

1234 A666 5c ultra & green .20 .20

2nd anniv. of the Alliance for Progress, which aims to stimulate economic growth and raise living standards in Latin America.

Cordell Hull Issue

Cordell Hull (1871-1955), Sec. of State (1933-44) — A667

Rotary Press Printing

1963, Oct. 5 ***Perf. 10½x11***

1235 A667 5c blue green .20 .20

Eleanor Roosevelt Issue

Mrs. Franklin D. Roosevelt (1884-1962) A668

1963, Oct. 11 ***Perf. 11x10½***

1236 A668 5c bright purple .20 .20

Science Issue

"The Universe" A669

Giori Press Printing

1963, Oct. 14 ***Perf. 11***

1237 A669 5c Prus blue & black .20 .20

Honoring the sciences and cent. of the Natl. Academy of Science.

Free City Mail Delivery Centenary

Letter Carrier, 1863 — A670

1963, Oct. 26 **Tagged** ***Perf. 11***

1238 A670 5c gray, dark blue & red .20 .20

International Red Cross Centenary

Cuban Refugees on S.S. *Morning Light* and Red Cross Flag — A671

1963, Oct. 29 ***Perf. 11***

1239 A671 5c bluish black & red .20 .20

Christmas Issue

National Christmas Tree and White House — A672

1963, Nov. 1 ***Perf. 11***

1240 A672 5c dk blue, bluish black & red .20 .20
- **a.** Tagged .65 .40

See Luminescence note after No. 1053.

"Columbia Jays" A673

Sam Houston A674

John James Audubon Issue

1963, Dec. 7 ***Perf. 11***

1241 A673 5c dark blue & multi .20 .20

John James Audubon (1785-1851), ornithologist and artist. The birds pictured are actually Collie's magpie jays.

Sam Houston Issue

Rotary Press Printing

1964, Jan. 10 ***Perf. 10½x11***

1242 A674 5c black .20 .20

Sam Houston (1793-1863), soldier, pres. of Texas, US senator.

Charles M. Russell Issue

"Jerked Down" — A675

Giori Press Printing

1964, Mar. 19 ***Perf. 11***

1243 A675 5c indigo, red brn & olive .20 .20

Russell (1864-1926), painter. The design is from a painting, Thomas Gilcrease Inst. of American History and Art, Tulsa, Okla.

New York World's Fair (1964-65)

Mall with Unisphere and "Rocket Thrower," by Donald De Lue — A676

Rotary Press Printing

1964, Apr. 22 ***Perf. 11x10½***

1244 A676 5c blue green .20 .20

John Muir Issue

John Muir (1838-1914), naturalist and conservationist and Redwood Forest — A677

Giori Press Printing

1964, Apr. 29 ***Perf. 11***

1245 A677 5c brn, grn, yel grn & ol .20 .20

Kennedy Memorial Issue

Pres. John F. Kennedy (1917-63) and Eternal Flame A678

Rotary Press Printing

1964, May 29 ***Perf. 11x10½***

1246 A678 5c blue gray .20 .20

New Jersey Tercentenary Issue

Philip Carteret Landing at Elizabethtown, and Map of New Jersey — A679

1964, June 15 ***Perf. 10½x11***

1247 A679 5c bright ultra .20 .20

300th anniv. of English colonization of NJ. The design is from a mural by Howard Pyle in the Essex County Courthouse, Newark.

Nevada Statehood Centenary

Virginia City and Map of Nevada A680

Giori Press Printing

1964, July 22 ***Perf. 11***

1248 A680 5c red, yellow & blue .20 .20

Flag A681

William Shakespeare A682

Register and Vote Issue

Giori Press Printing

1964, Aug. 1 ***Perf. 11***

1249 A681 5c dark blue & red .20 .20

Campaign to draw more voters to the polls.

Shakespeare Issue

Rotary Press Printing

1964, Aug. 14 ***Perf. 10½x11***

1250 A682 5c black brown, *tan* .20 .20

400th anniv. of the birth of Shakespeare (1564-1616).

Doctors Mayo Issue

Drs. William and Charles Mayo — A683

1964, Sept. 11 ***Perf. 10½x11***

1251 A683 5c green .20 .20

William (1861-1939) and his brother, Charles (1865-1939), surgeons who founded the Mayo Foundation for Medical Education and Research in affiliation with the Univ. of Minn. at Rochester. From a sculpture by James Earle Fraser.

American Music Issue

Lute, Horn, Laurel, Oak and Music Score — A684

Giori Press Printing

1964, Oct. 15 ***Perf. 11***

Gray Paper with Blue Threads

1252 A684 5c red, black & blue .20 .20
- **a.** Blue omitted *1,000.*

50th anniv. of the founding of ASCAP (American Soc. of Composers, Authors and Publishers).

Beware of copies offered as No. 1252a which have traces of blue.

Homemakers Issue

Farm Scene Sampler A685

Lithographed, Engraved (Giori)

1964, Oct. 26 ***Perf. 11***

1253 A685 5c multicolored .20 .20

Honoring American women as homemakers and 50th anniv. of the passage of the Smith-Lever Act. By providing consumer experts under an extension service of the US Dept. of Agriculture, this legislation helped to improve homelife.

Christmas Issue

Holly A686 / Mistletoe A687

Poinsettia A688 / Sprig of Conifer A689

Giori Press Printing

1964, Nov. 9 ***Perf. 11***

1254	A686 5c green, car & black	.25	.20
a.	Tagged	.60	.50
1255	A687 5c car, green & black	.25	.20
a.	Tagged	.60	.50
1256	A688 5c car, green & black	.25	.20
a.	Tagged	.60	.50
1257	A689 5c black, green & car	.25	.20
a.	Tagged	.60	.50
b.	Block of 4, #1254-1257	1.10	1.00
c.	Block of 4, #1254a-1257a	2.50	2.00

Tagged stamps issued Nov. 10.

Verrazano-Narrows Bridge Issue

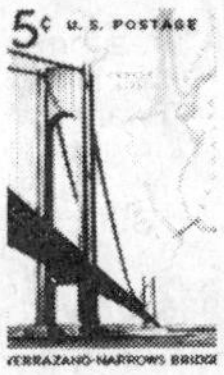

Verrazano-Narrows Bridge and Map of NY Bay — A690

Rotary Press Printing

1964, Nov. 21 ***Perf. 10½x11***

1258 A690 5c blue green .20 .20

Opening of the Verrazano-Narrows Bridge connecting Staten Island and Brooklyn, NY.

Fine Arts Issue

Abstract Design by Stuart Davis — A691

Giori Press Printing

1964, Dec. 2 ***Perf. 11***

1259 A691 5c ultra, blk & dull red .20 .20

Amateur Radio Issue

Radio Waves and Dial — A692

Rotary Press Printing

1964, Dec. 15 ***Perf. 10½x11***

1260 A692 5c red lilac .20 .20

Honoring radio amateurs on the 50th anniv. of the American Radio Relay League.

Battle of New Orleans Issue

General Andrew Jackson and Sesquicentennial Medal — A693

Giori Press Printing

1965, Jan. 8 ***Perf. 11***

1261 A693 5c dp car, violet blue & gray .20 .20

Battle of New Orleans, Chalmette Plantation, Jan. 8-18, 1815, which established 150 years of peace and friendship between the US and Great Britain.

Discus Thrower A694

Microscope and Stethoscope A695

Physical Fitness-Sokol Issue

1965, Feb. 15 ***Perf. 11***

1262 A694 5c maroon & black .20 .20

Importance of physical fitness and cent. of the founding of the Sokol (athletic) org. in America.

Crusade Against Cancer Issue

1965, Apr. 1 ***Perf. 11***

1263 A695 5c blk, pur & red org .20 .20

"Crusade Against Cancer" and stressing the importance of early diagnosis.

Churchill Memorial Issue

Winston Churchill — A696

Rotary Press Printing

1965, May 13 ***Perf. 10½x11***

1264 A696 5c black .20 .20

Sir Winston Spencer Churchill (1874-1965), British statesman and WWII leader.

Magna Carta Issue

Procession of Barons and King John's Crown A697

Giori Press Printing

1965, June 15 ***Perf. 11***

1265 A697 5c blk, yel ocher & red lilac .20 .20

750th anniv. of the Magna Carta, the basis of English and American common law.

International Cooperation Year Issue

ICY Emblem A698

1965, June 26 ***Perf. 11***

1266 A698 5c dull blue & black .20 .20

ICY, 1965, and 20th anniv. of the UN.

A699

Dante — A700

Salvation Army Issue

1965, July 2 ***Perf. 11***

1267 A699 5c red, black & dark blue .20 .20

Cent. of the founding of the Salvation Army in London by William Booth.

Dante Alighieri Issue

Rotary Press Printing

1965, July 17 ***Perf. 10½x11***

1268 A700 5c maroon, *tan* .20 .20

Dante Alighieri (1265-1321), Italian poet. Design after a 16th cent. painting.

Herbert Hoover Issue

Pres. Herbert Clark Hoover (1874-1964) — A701

1965, Aug. 10 ***Perf. 10½x11***

1269 A701 5c rose red .20 .20

Robert Fulton Issue

Robert Fulton and Clermont A702

Giori Press Printing

1965, Aug. 19 ***Perf. 11***

1270 A702 5c black & blue .20 .20

Fulton (1765-1815), inventor of the 1st commercial steamship.

Settlement of Florida Issue

Spanish Explorer, Royal Flag of Spain and Ships — A703

Giori Press Printing

1965, Aug. 28

1271	A703 5c red, yel & blk	.20	.20
a.	Yellow omitted	*400.00*	

400th anniv. of the settlement of Fla., and the 1st permanent European settlement in the continental US, St. Augustine, Fla. See Spain #1312.

Traffic Safety Issue

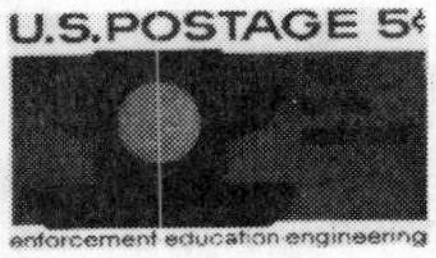

Traffic Signal A704

1965, Sept. 3 ***Perf. 11***

1272 A704 5c emerald, black & red .20 .20

Traffic safety and the prevention of traffic accidents.

John Singleton Copley Issue

Elizabeth Clarke Copley — A705

1965, Sept. 17

1273 A705 5c black, brown & olive .20 .20

Copley (1738-1815), painter. The portrait of the artist's daughter is from the oil painting "The Copley Family," which hangs in the Natl. Gallery of Art, Washington, DC.

International Telecommunication Union Centenary

Gall Projection World Map and Radio Sine Wave — A706

1965, Oct. 6 ***Perf. 11***

1274 A706 11c black, car & bister .35 .20

Adlai E. Stevenson A707

Angel with Trumpet, 1840 Weather Vane A708

Adlai E. Stevenson Issue

1965, Oct. 23 **Litho., Engr. (Giori)**

1275 A707 5c pale blue, blk, car & vio blue .20 .20

Stevenson (1900-65), gov. of Ill., US ambassador to the UN.

Christmas Issue

Giori Press Printing

1965, Nov. 2 ***Perf. 11***

1276	A708 5c car, dk ol grn & bis	.20	.20
a.	Tagged	.75	.25

Prominent Americans Issue

Thomas Jefferson A710

Albert Gallatin A711

Frank Lloyd Wright and Guggenheim Museum, New York A712

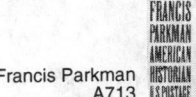

Francis Parkman A713

Lincoln
A714

Washington
A715

Washington
(Redrawn)
A715a

Franklin D.
Roosevelt
A716

Albert
Einstein
A717

Andrew
Jackson
A718

Henry Ford, 1909
Model T
A718a

John F.
Kennedy
A719

Oliver
Wendell
Holmes
A720

George
Catlett
Marshall
A721

Frederick
Douglass
A722

John Dewey
A723

Thomas
Paine
A724

Lucy Stone
A725

Eugene
O'Neill
A726

John
Bassett
Moore
A727

Perf. 11x10½, 10½x11

1965-78 Rotary Press Printing

1278 A710 1c green, tagged .20 .20
- *a.* Booklet pane of 8 1.00 *.50*
- *b.* Bklt. pane of 4 + 2 labels .80 *.30*
- *c.* Untagged (Bureau precanceled) .20

1279 A711 1¼c lt green .20 .20
1280 A712 2c dk blue gray, tagged .20 .20
- *a.* Booklet pane of 5 + label 1.25 *.60*
- *b.* Untagged (Bureau precanceled) .20
- *c.* Booklet pane of 6 1.00 *.50*

1281 A713 3c vio, tagged .20 .20
- *a.* Untagged (Bureau precanceled) .20

1282 A714 4c black .20 .20
- *a.* Tagged .20 .20

1283 A715 5c blue .20 .20
- *a.* Tagged .20 .20

1283B A715a 5c blue, tagged .20 .20
- *d.* Untagged (Bureau precanceled) .20

1284 A716 6c gray brown .20 .20
- *a.* Tagged .20 .20
- *b.* Booklet pane of 8 1.50 *.75*
- *c.* Booklet pane of 5 + label 1.50 *.75*
- *d.* Horiz. pair, imperf. between —

1285 A717 8c violet .20 .20
- *a.* Tagged .20 .20

1286 A718 10c lilac, tagged .20 .20
- *b.* Untagged (Bureau precanceled) .20

1286A A718a 12c black, tagged .25 .20
- *c.* Untagged (Bureau precanceled) .25

1287 A719 13c brn, tagged .30 .20
- *a.* Untagged (Bureau precanceled) .35

1288 A720 15c magenta, tagged .30 .20
- *a.* Untagged (Bureau precanceled) .30
- *d.* Type II .55 .20

Type II: necktie does not touch coat at bottom.

Perf. 10

1288B A720 15c magenta (from bklt. pane) .30 .20
- *c.* Booklet pane of 8 2.50 *1.75*
- *e.* As "c," vert. imperf. btwn. —

Perf. 11x10½, 10½x11

1289 A721 20c deep olive .40 .20
- *a.* Tagged .40 .20

1290 A722 25c rose lake .55 .20
- *a.* Tagged .45 .20
- *b.* 25c magenta 25.00 —

1291 A723 30c red lilac .60 .20
- *a.* Tagged .50 .20

1292 A724 40c blue black .85 .20
- *a.* Tagged .65 .20

1293 A725 50c rose magenta 1.00 .20
- *a.* Tagged .80 .20

1294 A726 $1 dull purple 2.25 .20
- *a.* Tagged 1.65 .20

1295 A727 $5 gray black 9.50 2.25
- *a.* Tagged 8.00 2.00

Nos. 1278-1295 (21) 18.30 6.25

On No. 1283B the highlights and shadows have been softened.

No. 1288B issued in booklets only. All stamps have one or two straight edges.

Issue dates (without tagging)—1965: 4c, Nov. 19.

1966: 5c, Feb. 22; 6c, Jan. 29; 8c, Mar. 14; $5, Dec. 3.

1967: 1¼c, Jan. 30; 20c, Oct. 24; 25c, Feb. 14; $1, Oct. 16.

1968: 30c, Oct. 21; 40c, Jan. 29; 50c, Aug. 13.

Dates for tagged: 1965: 4c, Dec. 1.

1966: 2c, June 8; 5c, Feb. 23; 6c, Dec. 29; 8c, July 6.

1967: 3c, Sept. 16; No. 1283B, Nov. 17; No. 1284b, Dec. 28; 10c, Mar. 15; 13c, May 29.

1968: 1c & No. 1284c, Jan. 12; No. 1280a, Jan. 8; 12c, July 30; 15c, Mar. 8.

1973: 20c, 25c, 30c, 40c, 50c, $1, $5, Apr. 3.

1978: No. 1288B, June 14.

Franklin D.
Roosevelt — A727a

Coil Stamps

Rotary Press Printing

1966-81 Tagged *Perf. 10 Horiz.*

1297 A713 3c violet .20 .20
- *a.* Imperf., pair 30.00
- *b.* Untagged (Bureau precanceled) .20
- *c.* As "b," imperf. pair 6.00

1298 A716 6c gray brn .20 .20
- *a.* Imperf., pair 2,250.

Perf. 10 Vertically

1299 A710 1c green .20 .20
- *a.* Untagged (Bureau precanceled) .20
- *b.* Imperf., pair 30.00 —

1303 A714 4c black .20 .20
- *a.* Untagged (Bureau precanceled) .20
- *b.* Imperf., pair 900.00

1304 A715 5c blue .20 .20
- *a.* Untagged (Bureau precanceled) .20
- *b.* Imperf., pair 175.00
- *e.* As "a," imperf. pair 400.00

No. 1304b is valued in the grade of fine.

1304C A715a 5c blue .20 .20
- *d.* Imperf., pair 800.

1305 A727a 6c gray brn .20 .20
- *a.* Imperf., pair 75.00
- *b.* Untagged (Bureau precanceled) .20

1305E A720 15c magenta .25 .20
- *f.* Untagged (Bureau precanceled) .30
- *g.* Imperf., pair 30.00
- *h.* Pair, imperf. between 200.00
- *i.* Type II .35 .20
- *j.* Imperf., pair, type II 90.00

1305C A726 $1 dull pur 1.75 .20
- *d.* Imperf., pair 2,250.

Nos. 1297-1305C (9) 3.40 1.80

Issued: 1c, 1/12/68; 3c, 11/4/75; 4c, 5/28/66; #1304, 9/8/66; 6c, #1298, 12/28/67; #1305, 2/ 28/68; $1, 1/12/73; 15c, 6/14/78.

See Nos. 1393-1395, 1397-1402 for more Prominent Americans.

Migratory Bird Treaty Issue

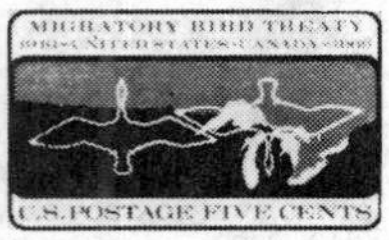

Migratory
Birds over
Canada-US
Border
A728

Giori Press Printing

1966, Mar. 16 *Perf. 11*

1306 A728 5c blk, crim & dk blue .20 .20

50th anniv. of the Migratory Bird Treaty between the US and Canada.

Humane Treatment of Animals Issue

Mongrel
A729

Lithographed, Engraved (Giori)

1966, Apr. 9 *Perf. 11*

1307 A729 5c org brown & black .20 .20

Humane treatment of all animals and cent. of the ASPCA.

Indiana Statehood Sesquicentennial

Sesquicentennial Seal;
Map of Indiana with 19
Stars and Old Capitol at
Corydon — A730

Giori Press Printing

1966, Apr. 16

1308 A730 5c yel, ocher & vio blue .20 .20

American Circus Issue

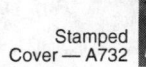

Clown — A731

1966, May 2 *Perf. 11*

1309 A731 5c multicolored .20 .20

Honoring the American circus on the cent. of the birth of John Ringling.

Sixth Intl. Phil. Exhib. Issues

Stamped
Cover — A732

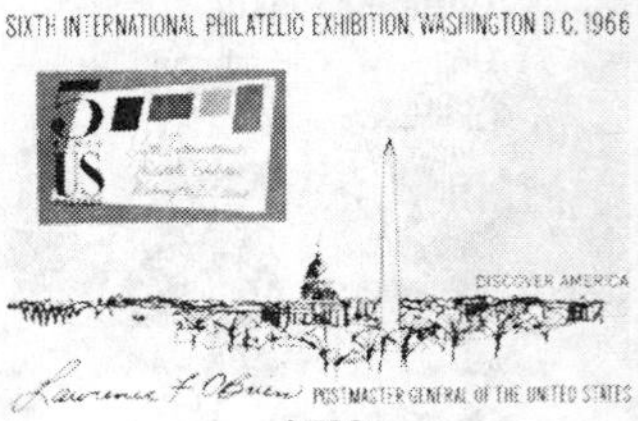

A733

Lithographed, Engraved (Giori)

1966, May *Perf. 11*

1310 A732 5c multicolored .20 .20

Souvenir Sheet

Imperf

1311 A733 5c multicolored .20 .20

SIPEX, Washington, DC, May 21-30.
No. 1311 measures 108x74mm.
Issue dates: #1310, 21st; #1311, 23rd.

"Freedom"
Checking
"Tyranny"
A734

Polish Eagle
and Cross
A735

Bill of Rights, 175th Anniv.

Giori Press Printing

1966, July 1 *Perf. 11*

1312 A734 5c carmine, dk & lt blue .20 .20

Polish Millennium Issue

Rotary Press Printing

1966, July 30 *Perf. 10½x11*

1313 A735 5c red .20 .20

1000th anniv. of the adoption of Christianity in Poland.

Tagging Extended

During 1966 experimental use of tagged stamps was extended to the Cincinnati Postal Region covering offices in Indiana, Kentucky and Ohio. To supply these offices about 12 percent of the following nine issues (Nos. 1314-1322) were tagged.

National Park Service Issue

National Park
Service
Emblem
A736

Lithographed, Engraved (Giori)

1966, Aug. 25 *Perf. 11*

1314 A736 5c yel, black & green .20 .20
- *a.* Tagged .30 .25

50th anniv. of the Natl. Park Service of the Interior Dept. The design "Parkscape U.S.A." identifies Natl. Park Service facilities. No. 1314a was issued Aug. 26.

Marine Corps Reserve Issue

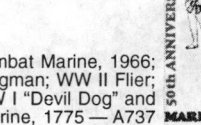

Combat Marine, 1966;
Frogman; WW II Flier;
WW I "Devil Dog" and
Marine, 1775 — A737

Lithographed, Engraved (Giori)

1966, Aug. 29 *Perf. 11*

1315 A737 5c black, bister, red & ultra .20 .20
- *a.* Tagged .30 .20
- *b.* Black & bister (engr.) omitted *16,000.*

50th anniv. of the founding of the US Marine Corps Reserve.

General Federation of Women's Clubs

Women of 1890 and 1966 — A738

Giori Press Printing

1966, Sept. 12 *Perf. 11*

1316 A738 5c black, pink & blue .20 .20
- *a.* Tagged .30 .20

75 years of service by the Gen. Fed. of Women's Clubs. No. 1316a was issued Sept. 13.

American Folklore Issue

Johnny Appleseed — A739

1966, Sept. 24 *Perf. 11*

1317 A739 5c green, red & black .20 .20
- *a.* Tagged .30 .20

Johnny Appleseed, (John Chapman, 1774-1845), who wandered over 100,000 square miles planting apple trees, and who gave away and sold seedlings to Midwest pioneers. No. 1317a issued Sept. 26.

Beautification of America Issue

Jefferson Memorial, Tidal Basin and Cherry Blossoms A740

1966, Oct. 5 *Perf. 11*

1318 A740 5c emerald, pink & black .20 .20
- *a.* Tagged .30 .20

Pres. Johnson's "Plant for a more beautiful America" campaign.

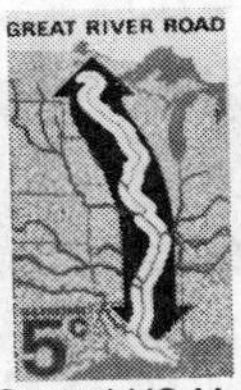

Central US Map With Great River Road — A741

Statue of Liberty and "Old Glory" — A742

Great River Road Issue

Lithographed, Engraved (Giori)

1966, Oct. 21 *Perf. 11*

1319 A741 5c ver, yellow, blue & green .20 .20
- *a.* Tagged .30 .20

5,600-mile Great River Road connecting New Orleans with Kenora, Ontario, following the Mississippi most of the way. No. 1319a issued Oct. 22.

Savings Bond-Servicemen Issue

1966, Oct. 26

1320 A742 5c red, dk & lt blue, black .20 .20
- *a.* Tagged .30 .20
- *b.* Red, dark blue & black omitted *5,000.*
- *c.* Dark blue (engr.) omitted *9,000.*

25th anniv. of US Savings Bonds, and to honor American servicemen. No. 1320a issued Oct. 27.

Christmas Issue

Madonna and Child, by Hans Memling — A743

Lithographed, Engraved (Giori)

1966, Nov. 1 *Perf. 11*

1321 A743 5c multicolored .20 .20
- *a.* Tagged .30 .20

The design is from "Madonna and Child with Angels," by the Flemish artist Hans Memling (c. 1430-1494), National Gallery of Art, Washington, DC. No. 1321a was issued Nov. 2. See No. 1336.

Mary Cassatt Issue

"The Boating Party" — A744

Giori Press Printing

1966, Nov. 17 *Perf. 11*

1322 A744 5c multicolored .20 .20
- *a.* Tagged .30 .25

Cassatt (1844-1926), painter. The original painting is in the Natl. Gallery of Art, Washington, DC.

National Grange Issue

Grange Poster, 1870 — A745

1967, Apr. 17 **Tagged** *Perf. 11*

1323 A745 5c multicolored .20 .20

Cent. of the founding of the National Grange, American farmers' organization.

Phosphor Tagging

From No. 1323 onward, all postage issues are tagged, unless otherwise noted.

Tagging Omitted

Inadvertent omissions of tagging occurred on Nos. 1238, 1278, 1281, 1298 and 1305. In addition most tagged issues from 1967 on exist with tagging unintentionally omitted.

Canada Centenary Issue

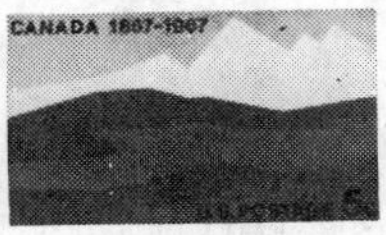

Canadian Landscape A746

Giori Press Printing

1967, May 25 *Perf. 11*

1324 A746 5c multicolored .20 .20

Cent. of Canada's emergence as a nation.

Erie Canal Issue

Stern of Early Canal Boat — A747

Lithographed, Engraved (Giori)

1967, July 4 *Perf. 11*

1325 A747 5c multicolored .20 .20

150th anniv. of the Erie Canal groundbreaking ceremony. The canal links Lake Erie and NYC.

"Peace"—Lions Issue

Peace Dove — A748

Giori Press Printing

1967, July 5 *Perf. 11*

Gray Paper with Blue Threads

1326 A748 5c blue, red & black .20 .20

Publicizing the Search for Peace. This was the theme of an essay contest for young men and women sponsored by Lions Intl. on its 50th anniv.

Henry David Thoreau Issue

Henry David Thoreau (1817-1862), Writer — A749

1967, July 12

1327 A749 5c red, black & green .20 .20

Nebraska Statehood Centenary

Hereford Steer and Corn — A750

Lithographed, Engraved (Giori)

1967, July 29 *Perf. 11*

1328 A750 5c dk red brn, lem & yel .20 .20

Voice of America Issue

Radio Transmission Tower and Waves — A751

1967, Aug. 1 **Giori Press Printing**

1329 A751 5c red, blue, black & car .20 .20

25th anniv. of the radio branch of the US Information Agency (USIA).

American Folklore Issue

Davy Crockett (1786-1836) and Scrub Pines — A752

Lithographed, Engraved (Giori)

1967, Aug. 17 *Perf. 11*

1330 A752 5c green, black & yellow .20 .20
- *a.* Vert. pair, imperf. btwn. *6,000.*
- *b.* Green (engr.) omitted —
- *c.* Black & green (engr.) omitted —

Crockett, frontiersman and congressman, died in defense of the Alamo.

A foldover on a pane of No. 1330 resulted in one example each of Nos. 1330b-1330c. Part of the colors appear on the back of the selvage and one freak stamp. An engraved black-and-green-only impression appears on the gummed side of one almost-complete "stamp."

Space Accomplishments Issue

Space-Walking Astronaut — A753

Gemini 4 Capsule and Earth A754

Lithographed, Engraved (Giori)

1967, Sept. 29 *Perf. 11*

1331 A753 5c multicolored .55 .20

1332 A754 5c multicolored .55 .20
- *b.* Pair, #1331-1332 1.25 1.25

US accomplishments in space.

View of Model City — A755

Finnish Coat of Arms — A756

Urban Planning Issue

Lithographed, Engraved (Giori)

1967, Oct. 2 *Perf. 11*

1333 A755 5c dk & lt blue, black .20 .20

Importance of Urban Planning and the Intl. Conf. of the American Inst. of Planners, Washington, DC, Oct. 1-6.

Finnish Independence, 50th Anniv.

Engraved (Giori)

1967, Oct. 6 *Perf. 11*

1334 A756 5c blue .20 .20

Thomas Eakins Issue

"The Biglin Brothers Racing" (Sculling on Schuylkill River, Philadelphia) A757

1967, Nov. 2 **Photo.** *Perf. 12*

1335 A757 5c gold & multi .20 .20

Eakins (1844-1916), painter and sculptor. The painting is in the Natl. Gallery of Art, Washington, DC.

Christmas Issue

Madonna and Child, by Hans Memling — A758

Lithographed, Engraved (Giori)

1967, Nov. 6 *Perf. 11*

1336 A758 5c multicolored .20 .20

See note after No. 1321.

Footnotes near stamp listings often refer to other stamps of the same design.

Magnolia
A759

Flag and White House
A760

Mississippi Statehood, 150th Anniv.

Giori Press Printing

1967, Dec. 11 ***Perf. 11***

1337 A759 5c brt grnsh blue, green & red brown .20 .20

Flag Issue

Giori Press Printing

1968-71 ***Perf. 11***

Size: 19x22mm

1338 A760 6c dk blue, red & green .20 .20
- *k.* Vert. pair, imperf. btwn. *550.00*
- *s.* Red omitted —

Vert. pairs have been offered as imperf. horiz. Some have had the gum washed off to make it difficult to detect blind perfs.

Coil Stamp

Multicolor Huck Press

Perf. 10 Vert.

Size: 18¼x21mm

1338A A760 6c dk blue, red & green ('69) .20 .20
- *b.* Imperf., pair *500.00*

Multicolor Huck Press

Perf. 11x10½

Size: 18¼x21mm

1338D A760 6c dk blue, red & green ('70) .20 .20
- *e.* Horiz. pair, imperf. btwn. *175.00*

1338F A760 8c multi ('71) .20 .20
- *i.* Vert. pair, imperf. 45.00
- *j.* Horiz. pair, imperf. btwn. 55.00
- *p.* Slate green omitted *425.00*
- *t.* Horiz. pair, imperf. vert. —

Issued: #1338, Jan. 24, 1968; #1338A, May 30, 1969; #1338D, Aug. 7, 1970; 8c, May 10, 1971.

Coil Stamp

1971, May 10 ***Perf. 10 Vert.***

Size: 18¼x21mm

1338G A760 8c multi ('71) .20 .20
- *h.* Imperf., pair *55.00*

Farm House and Fields of Ripening Grain
A761

Map of North and South America
A762

Illinois Statehood, 150th Anniv.

Lithographed, Engraved (Giori)

1968, Feb. 12 ***Perf. 11***

1339 A761 6c multicolored .20 .20

HemisFair '68 Issue

1968, Mar. 30 ***Perf. 11***

1340 A762 6c blue, rose red & white .20 .20
- *a.* White omitted *1,400.*

HemisFair '68 exhib. at San Antonio, Tex., Apr. 6-Oct. 6, for the 250th anniv. of San Antonio.

Airlift Issue

Eagle Holding Pennant
A763

Lithographed, Engraved (Giori)

1968, Apr. 4 Untagged ***Perf. 11***

1341 A763 $1 sep, dk blue, ocher & brn red 2.25 1.25

Issued to pay for airlift of parcels from and to US ports to servicemen overseas and in Alaska, Hawaii and P.R. Valid for all regular postage.

On Apr. 26, 1969, the POD ruled that henceforth No. 1341 "may be used toward paying the postage or fees for special services on airmail articles."

"Youth"—Elks Issue

Girls and Boys — A764

Lithographed, Engraved (Giori)

1968, May 1 ***Perf. 11***

1342 A764 6c ultra & orange red .20 .20

Support Our Youth program, and honoring the Benevolent and Protective Order of Elks, which extended its youth service program in observance of its centennial year.

Policeman and Small Boy
A765

Eagle Weather Vane
A766

Law and Order Issue

Giori Press Printing

1968, May 17 ***Perf. 11***

1343 A765 6c chlky blue, blk & red .20 .20

The police as protector and friend and respect for law and order.

Register and Vote Issue

Lithographed, Engraved (Giori)

1968, June 27 ***Perf. 11***

1344 A766 6c blk, yel & org .20 .20

Campaign to draw more voters to the polls. The weather vane is from an old house in the Russian Hill section of San Francisco.

Historic Flag Series

Ft. Moultrie, 1776
A767

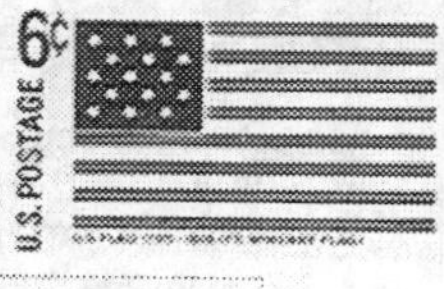

Ft. McHenry, 1795-1818
A768

Washington's Cruisers, 1775 — A769

Bennington, 1777
A770

Rhode Island, 1775
A771

First Stars and Stripes, 1777
A772

Bunker Hill, 1775
A773

Grand Union, 1776
A774

Philadelphia Light Horse, 1775
A775

First Navy Jack, 1775
A776

Engraved (Giori) (#1345-1348, 1350): Engr. & Litho. (#1349, 1351-1354)

1968, July 4 ***Perf. 11***

1345 A767 6c dark blue .40 .25
1346 A768 6c dk blue & red .30 .25
1347 A769 6c dk blue & ol green .25 .25
1348 A770 6c dk blue & red .25 .25
1349 A771 6c dk blue, yel & red .25 .25
1350 A772 6c dk blue & red .25 .25
1351 A773 6c dk bl, ol grn & red .25 .25
1352 A774 6c dk blue & red .25 .25
1353 A775 6c dk blue, yel & red .25 .25
1354 A776 6c dk blue, red & yel .25 .25
- *a.* Strip of 10, Nos. 1345-1354 2.75 2.75

Flags carried by American colonists and by citizens of the new United States. The flag sequence on the upper panes is as listed. On the lower panes the sequence is reversed with the Navy Jack in the 1st row and the Fort Moultrie flag in the 10th.

Walt Disney Issue

Disney and Children of the World — A777

1968, Sept. 11 Photo. ***Perf. 12***

1355 A777 6c multicolored .20 .20
- *a.* Ocher (Walt Disney, 6c, etc.) omitted *800.* —
- *b.* Vert. pair, imperf. horiz. *750.*
- *c.* Imperf., pair *675.*
- *d.* Black omitted *2,000.*
- *e.* Horiz. pair, imperf. btwn. *4,750.*
- *f.* Blue omitted *2,250.*

Disney (1901-1966), cartoonist, film producer, creator of Mickey Mouse.

Father Marquette Issue

Father Marquette and Louis Jolliet Exploring the Mississippi
A778

Giori Press Printing

1968, Sept. 20 ***Perf. 11***

1356 A778 6c black, apple green & org brn .20 .20

Father Jacques Marquette (1637-1675). French Jesuit missionary, who with Louis Jolliet explored the Mississippi and its tributaries.

American Folklore Issue

Daniel Boone (1734-1820)

Pennsylvania Rifle, Powder Horn, Tomahawk Pipe and Knife — A779

Lithographed, Engraved (Giori)

1968, Sept. 26 ***Perf. 11***

1357 A779 6c yel, dp yel, mar & blk .20 .20

Daniel Boone, frontiersman and trapper.

Arkansas River Navigation Issue

Ship's Wheel, Power Transmission Tower and Barge — A780

1968, Oct. 1 ***Perf. 11***

1358 A780 6c brt bl, dk bl & blk .20 .20

Opening of the Arkansas River to commercial navigation.

Leif Erikson Issue

Leif Erikson, by Stirling Calder — A781

1968, Oct. 9 Litho., Engr. ***Perf. 11***

1359 A781 6c lt gray brn & blk brn .20 .20

Erikson, 11th cent. Norse explorer, was the 1st European to set foot on the American continent, at a place he called Vinland. The statue by an American sculptor is in Reykjavik, Iceland.

The light gray brown ink carries the tagging element.

Cherokee Strip Issue

Homesteaders Racing to Cherokee Strip — A782

Rotary Press Printing

1968, Oct. 15 ***Perf. 11x10½***

1360 A782 6c brown .20 .20

75th anniv. of the opening of the Cherokee Strip to settlers, Sept. 16, 1893.

John Trumbull Issue

Detail from "The Battle of Bunker's Hill" — A783

Lithographed, Engraved

1968, Oct. 18 ***Perf. 11***

1361 A783 6c multicolored .20 .20

Trumbull (1756-1843), painter. The stamp shows Lt. Thomas Grosvenor and his attendant, Peter Salem. The painting is at Yale Univ., New Haven, CT.

Waterfowl Conservation Issue

Wood Ducks — A784

Lithographed, Engraved (Giori)

1968, Oct. 24 *Perf. 11*

1362 A784 6c black & multi .20 .20
- *a.* Vert. pair, imperf. btwn. 550.
- *b.* Red & dark blue omitted 1,050.
- *c.* Red omitted —

Gabriel, from van Eyck's Annunciation A785

Chief Joseph, by Cyrenius Hall A786

Christmas Issue

Engraved (Multicolor Huck)

1968, Nov. 1 Tagged *Perf. 11*

1363 A785 6c multicolored .20 .20
- *a.* Untagged .20 .20
- *b.* Imperf., pair, tagged 250.00
- *c.* Light yellow omitted 75.00
- *d.* Imperf., pair, untagged 300.00

"The Annunciation" by the 15th cent. Flemish artist Jan van Eyck is in the Natl. Gallery of Art, Washington, DC. No. 1363a was issued Nov. 2.

Luminescence

No. 1364 and all following postage stamps are tagged, unless otherwise noted.

American Indian Issue

Lithographed, Engraved (Giori)

1968, Nov. 4 *Perf. 11*

1364 A786 6c black & multi .20 .20

Honoring American Indians and the opening of the Natl. Portrait Gallery, Oct. 5, 1968. Chief Joseph (Indian name Thunder Traveling over the Mountains) a leader of the Nez Percé tribe, was born c. 1840 in eastern Oregon and died at the Colesville Reservation in Washington in 1904.

Beautification of America Issue

Capitol, Azaleas and Tulips A787

Washington Monument, Potomac River and Daffodils A788

Poppies and Lupines along Highway A789

Blooming Crabapples along Street A790

Lithographed, Engraved (Giori)

1969, Jan. 16 *Perf. 11*

1365 A787 6c multicolored .35 .20
1366 A788 6c multicolored .35 .20
1367 A789 6c multicolored .35 .20
1368 A790 6c multicolored .35 .20
- *a.* Block of 4, #1365-1368 1.65 1.75

Natural Beauty Campaign for more beautiful cities, parks, highways and streets.

Eagle from Great Seal of US A791

July Fourth, by Grandma Moses A792

American Legion, 50th Anniv.

Lithographed, Engraved (Giori)

1969, Mar. 15 *Perf. 11*

1369 A791 6c red, blue & black .20 .20

American Folklore Issue

Grandma Moses

Lithographed, Engraved (Giori)

1969, May 1 *Perf. 11*

1370 A792 6c multicolored .20 .20
- *a.* Horiz. pair, imperf. btwn. 225.00
- *b.* Black and Prus blue omitted 900.00

Grandma Moses (Anna Mary Robertson Moses, 1860-1961), primitive painter of American life.

Beware of pairs with blind perfs. being offered as No. 1370a. No. 1370b often comes with mottled or disturbed gum. Such stamps sell for about two-thirds as much as copies with perfect gum.

Apollo 8 Issue

Moon Surface and Earth — A793

Giori Press Printing

1969, May 5 *Perf. 11*

1371 A793 6c black, blue & ocher .20 .20

Apollo 8 mission, which put the 1st men into orbit around the moon, Dec. 21-27, 1968. Imperfs. exist from printer's waste.

William Christopher Handy Issue

W. C. Handy (1873-1958), Jazz Musician and Composer A794

Lithographed, Engraved (Giori)

1969, May 17 *Perf. 11*

1372 A794 6c multicolored .20 .20

California Settlement, 200th Anniv.

Carmel Mission Belfry — A795

1969, July 16 *Perf. 11*

1373 A795 6c multicolored .20 .20

John Wesley Powell Issue

Powell Exploring Colorado River — A796

1969, Aug. 1 *Perf. 11*

1374 A796 6c multicolored .20 .20

Powell (1834-1902), geologist and explorer of the Green and Colorado Rivers, 1869-1875.

Alabama Statehood, 150th Anniv.

Camellia and Yellow-shafted Flicker A797

1969, Aug. 2 *Perf. 11*

1375 A797 6c multicolored .20 .20

Botanical Congress Issue

Douglas Fir (Northwest) A798

Lady's-slipper (Northeast) A799

Ocotillo (Southwest) A800

Franklinia (Southeast) A801

Lithographed, Engraved (Giori)

1969, Aug. 23 *Perf. 11*

1376 A798 6c multicolored .45 .20
1377 A799 6c multicolored .45 .20
1378 A800 6c multicolored .45 .20
1379 A801 6c multicolored .45 .20
- *a.* Block of 4, #1376-1379 2.00 2.25

11th Intl. Botanical Cong., Seattle, Wash., Aug. 24-Sept. 2.

Dartmouth College Case Issue

Daniel Webster and Dartmouth Hall — A802

Rotary Press Printing

1969, Sept. 22 *Perf. 10½x11*

1380 A802 6c green .20 .20

Sesquicentennial of the Dartmouth College case, argued by Daniel Webster before the Supreme Court, which reasserted the sanctity of contracts.

Professional Baseball Centenary

Batter — A803

Lithographed, Engraved (Giori)

1969, Sept. 24 *Perf. 11*

1381 A803 6c yel, red, black & green .65 .20
- *a.* Black (1869-1969, United States, 6c, Professional Baseball) omitted 1,100.

Intercollegiate Football Centenary

Football Player and Coach A804

1969, Sept. 26 *Perf. 11*

1382 A804 6c red & green .20 .20

Dwight D. Eisenhower Issue

Dwight D. Eisenhower — A805

Giori Press Printing

1969, Oct. 14 *Perf. 11*

1383 A805 6c blue, black & red .20 .20

Gen. Eisenhower, 34th Pres. (1890-1969).

Christmas Issue

Winter Sunday in Norway, Maine A806

Engraved (Multicolor Huck)

1969, Nov. 3 *Perf. 11x10½*

1384 A806 6c dk green & multi .20 .20
- Precanceled .50 .20
- *b.* Imperf., pair 1,000.
- *c.* Light green omitted 25.00
- *d.* Lt grn, red & yel omitted 1,000. —
- *e.* Yellow omitted 2,250.
- *g.* Red & yellow omitted —

The precancel value applies to the experimental precancel printed in four cities with the names between lines 4½mm apart: in black or green "ATLANTA, GA" and in green only "BALTIMORE, MD," "MEMPHIS, TN" and "NEW HAVEN, CT." They were sold freely to the public and could be used on any class of mail at all post offices during the experimental program and thereafter.

Most examples of No. 1384c show orange where the offset green was. Value is for this variety. Copies without orange sell for a premium.

Cured Child A807

"Old Models" A808

Hope for Crippled Issue

Lithographed, Engraved (Giori)

1969, Nov. 20 *Perf. 11*

1385 A807 6c multicolored .20 .20

Issued to encourage the rehabilitation of crippled children and adults, and to honor the Natl. Soc. for Crippled Children and Adults (Easter Seal Soc.) on its 50th anniv.

William M. Harnett Issue

1969, Dec. 3 *Perf. 11*

1386 A808 6c multicolored .20 .20

Harnett (1848-1892), painter. The painting is in the Museum of Fine Arts, Boston.

Natural History Issue

American Bald Eagle — A809

African Elephant Herd — A810

Tlingit Chief in Haida Ceremonial Canoe — A811

Brontosaurus, Stegosaurus and Allosaurus from Jurassic Period — A812

Lithographed, Engraved (Giori)

1970, May 6 ***Perf. 11***

1387 A809 6c multicolored .20 .20
1388 A810 6c multicolored .20 .20
1389 A811 6c multicolored .20 .20
1390 A812 6c multicolored .20 .20
a. Block of 4, #1387-1390 .50 .60

1969-1970 celebration of the cent. of the American Museum of Natural History in NYC. The design of No. 1390 is a detail from a mural by Rudolph Zallinger in Yale's Peabody Museum.

Maine Statehood Issue

Lighthouse at Two Lights, Maine — A813

Lithographed, Engraved (Giori)

1970, July 9 ***Perf. 11***

1391 A813 6c black & multi .20 .20

Sesquicentennial of Maine statehood. The painting by Edward Hopper (1882-1967) hangs in the Metropolitan Museum of Art, NYC.

Wildlife Conservation Issue

American Buffalo A814

Rotary Press Printing

1970, July 20 ***Perf. 10½x11***

1392 A814 6c black, *light brown* .20 .20

Regular Issue

Dwight David Eisenhower

A815
Dot between "R" and "U"

A815a
No dot between "R" and "U"

Benjamin Franklin A816

USPS Emblem A817

Fiorello H. LaGuardia A817a

Ernest Taylor Pyle A818

Dr. Elizabeth Blackwell A818a

Amadeo P. Giannini A818b

Rotary (6c, 7c, 14c, 16c, 18c, 21c, #1395); Giori (#1394); Photo. (#1396)

Perf. 11x10½, 10½x11; 11 (#1394)

1970-74

1393 A815 6c dark blue gray .20 .20
a. Booklet pane of 8 1.50 *.65*
b. Booklet pane of 5 + label 1.50 *.65*
c. Untagged (Bureau precanceled) .20
1393D A816 7c brt blue ('72) .20 .20
e. Untagged (Bureau precanceled) .20
1394 A815a 8c blk, red & bl gray ('71) .20 .20
1395 A815 8c dp claret ('71) .20 .20
a. Booklet pane of 8 1.80 *1.25*
b. Booklet pane of 6 1.25 *.90*
c. Booklet pane of 4 + 2 labels ('72) 1.65 *.80*
d. Booklet pane of 7 + label ('72) 1.90 *1.00*
1396 A817 8c multi ('71) .20 .20
1397 A817a 14c gray brn ('72) .25 .20
a. Untagged (Bureau precanceled) .25
1398 A818 16c brown ('71) .30 .20
a. Untagged (Bureau precanceled) .35
1399 A818a 18c violet ('74) .35 .20
1400 A818b 21c green ('73) .40 .20
Nos. 1393-1400 (9) 2.30 1.80

No. 1395 was issued in booklets only. All stamps have one or two straight edges.

Issued: 6c, 8/6/70; 7c, 10/20/72; #1394-1395, 5/10/71; #1396, 7/1/71; 14c, 4/24/72; 16c, 5/7/71; 18c, 1/23/74; 21c, 6/27/73.

Coil Stamps

Rotary Press

1970-71 ***Perf. 10 Vert.***

1401 A815 6c dark blue gray .20 .20
a. Untagged (Bureau precanceled) .20
b. Imperf., pair *2,000.*
1402 A815 8c deep claret .20 .20
a. Imperf., pair 45.00
b. Untagged (Bureau precanceled) .20
c. Pair, imperf. btwn. *6,250.*

Issue dates: 6c, Aug. 6; 8c, May 10, 1971.

Edgar Lee Masters Issue

Edgar Lee Masters (1869-1950), Poet — A819

Lithographed, Engraved (Giori)

1970, Aug. 22 ***Perf. 11***

1405 A819 6c black & olive bister .20 .20

Woman Suffrage Issue

Suffragettes, 1920, and Woman Voter, 1970 A820

Giori Press Printing

1970, Aug. 26 ***Perf. 11***

1406 A820 6c blue .20 .20

50th anniv. of the 19th Amendment, which gave women the vote.

South Carolina Issue

Symbols of South Carolina A821

Lithographed, Engraved (Giori)

1970, Sept. 12 ***Perf. 11***

1407 A821 6c bister, black & red .20 .20

300th anniv. of the founding of Charles Town (Charleston), the 1st permanent settlement of SC. Against a background of pine wood the line drawings of the design represent the economic and historic development of SC: the spire of St. Phillip's Church, Capitol, state flag, a ship, 17th cent. man and woman, a Fort Sumter cannon, barrels, cotton, tobacco and yellow jessamine.

Stone Mountain Memorial Issue

Robert E. Lee, Jefferson Davis and "Stonewall" Jackson A822

Giori Press Printing

1970, Sept. 19 ***Perf. 11***

1408 A822 6c gray .20 .20

Dedication of the Stone Mountain Confederate Memorial, GA, May 9, 1970.

Fort Snelling Issue

Fort Snelling, Keelboat and Tepees A823

Lithographed, Engraved (Giori)

1970, Oct. 17 ***Perf. 11***

1409 A823 6c yellow & multi .20 .20

150th anniv. of Fort Snelling, MN, which was an important outpost for the opening of the Northwest.

Anti-Pollution Issue

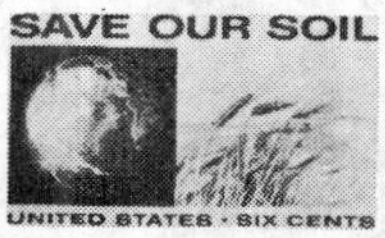

Globe and Wheat — A824

Globe and City — A825

Globe and Bluegill A826

Globe and Seagull A827

1970, Oct. 28 Photo. ***Perf. 11x10½***

1410 A824 6c multicolored .20 .20
1411 A825 6c multicolored .20 .20
1412 A826 6c multicolored .20 .20
1413 A827 6c multicolored .20 .20
a. Block of 4, #1410-1413 1.00 1.25

Issued to focus attention on the mounting problems of pollution.

Christmas Issue

Nativity, by Lorenzo Lotto (1480-1556) A828

Tin and Cast-iron Locomotive A829

Toy Horse on Wheels A830

Mechanical Tricycle A831

Doll Carriage A832

1970, Nov. 5 Photo. ***Perf. 10½x11***

1414 A828 6c multicolored .20 .20
a. Precanceled .20 .20
b. Black omitted *600.00*
c. As "a," blue omitted *1,500.*

Perf. 11x10½

1415 A829 6c multicolored .30 .20
a. Precanceled .75 .20
b. Black omitted *2,500.*
1416 A830 6c multicolored .30 .20
a. Precanceled .75 .20
b. Black omitted *2,500.*
c. Imperf., pair (#1416, 1418) *4,000.*
1417 A831 6c multicolored .30 .20
a. Precanceled .75 .20
b. Black omitted *2,500.*
1418 A832 6c multicolored .30 .20
a. Precanceled .75 .20
b. Block of 4, #1415-1418 1.25 1.50
c. As "b," precanceled 3.25 3.25
d. Black omitted *2,500.*
Nos. 1414-1418 (5) 1.40 1.00

Nos. 1415-1418 are antique Christmas toys.

The precanceled stamps, Nos. 1414a-1418a, were furnished to 68 cities. The plates include two straight (No. 1414a) or two wavy (Nos. 1415a-1418a) black lines that make up the precancellation. Unused values are for copies with gum and used values are for copies with an additional cancellation or without gum.

United Nations, 25th Anniv.

"UN" and UN Emblem A833

Lithographed, Engraved (Giori)

1970, Nov. 20 ***Perf. 11***

1419 A833 6c black, ver & ultra .20 .20

Landing of the Pilgrims Issue

Mayflower and Pilgrims — A834

Lithographed, Engraved (Giori)

1970, Nov. 21 ***Perf. 11***

1420 A834 6c black, org, yel, brn, mag & blue .20 .20
- *a.* Orange & yellow omitted *900.00*
- *b.* Magenta omitted —

Mayflower landing, 350th anniv.

Disabled Veterans and Servicemen Issue

A835 A836

Lithographed, Engraved (Giori)

1970, Nov. 24 ***Perf. 11***

1421 A835 6c multicolored .20 .20

Engr.

1422 A836 6c dk blue, black & red .20 .20
- *a.* Pair, #1421-1422 .25 .30

50th anniv. of the Disabled Veterans of America Organization (No. 1421); honoring the contribution of servicemen, particularly those who were prisoners of war or missing in action (No. 1422).

Ewe and Lamb A837

Douglas MacArthur A838

American Wool Industry Issue

Lithographed, Engraved (Giori)

1971, Jan. 19 ***Perf. 11***

1423 A837 6c multicolored .20 .20
- *b.* Teal blue ("United States") omitted —

450th anniv. of the introduction of sheep to the No. American continent and the beginning of the American wool industry.

No. 1423b was caused by the misregistration of the intaglio printing.

Gen. Douglas MacArthur Issue

Giori Press Printing

1971, Jan. 26

1424 A838 6c black, red & dk blue .20 .20

MacArthur (1880-1964), Chief of Staff, Supreme Commander for the Allied Powers in the Pacific Area during WW II and Supreme Commander in Japan after the war.

Blood Donor Issue

"Giving Blood Saves Lives" — A839

1971, Mar. 12 ***Perf. 11***

1425 A839 6c lt blue, scar & indigo .20 .20

Salute to blood donors and spur to participation in the blood donor program.

Missouri Sesquicentennial Issue

"Independence and the Opening of the West," Detail, by Thomas Hart Benton A840

1971, May 8 Photo. ***Perf. 11x10½***

1426 A840 8c multicolored .20 .20

The stamp design shows a Pawnee facing a hunter-trapper and a group of settlers.

Wildlife Conservation Issue

Trout A841

Alligator — A842

Polar Bear and Cubs A843

California Condor — A844

Lithographed, Engraved (Giori)

1971, June 12 ***Perf. 11***

1427 A841 8c multicolored .20 .20
- *a.* Red omitted *1,250.*

1428 A842 8c multicolored .20 .20

1429 A843 8c multicolored .20 .20

1430 A844 8c multicolored .20 .20
- *a.* Block of 4, #1427-1430 .80 .90
- *b.* As "a," lt grn & dk grn omitted from #1427-1428 *4,500.*
- *c.* As "a," red omitted from #1427, 1429-1430 *9,000.*

Antarctic Treaty Issue

Map of Antarctica A845

Giori Press Printing

1971, June 23

1431 A845 8c red & dark blue .20 .20
- *b.* Both colors omitted —

10th anniv. of the Antarctic Treaty pledging peaceful uses of and scientific cooperation in Antarctica.

No. 1431b was caused by an extraneous piece of paper blocking the impression. It should be collected se-tenant with a normal stamp and/or a partially printed stamp.

American Revolution Bicentennial

Bicentennial Commission Emblem — A846

Lithographed, Engraved (Giori)

1971, July 4 ***Perf. 11***

1432 A846 8c red, blue, gray & black .20 .20
- *a.* Gray & black omitted *700.00*
- *b.* Gray ("U.S. Postage 8c") omitted *1,250.*

John Sloan Issue

The Wake of the Ferry A847

1971, Aug. 2 ***Perf. 11***

1433 A847 8c multicolored .20 .20

Sloan (1871-1951), painter.

Space Achievement Decade Issue

Earth, Sun, Landing Craft on Moon A848

Lunar Rover and Astronauts A849

Lithographed, Engraved (Giori)

1971, Aug. 2 ***Perf. 11***

1434 A848 8c blk, bl, yel & red .20 .20

1435 A849 8c blk, bl, yel & red .20 .20
- *b.* Pair, #1434-1435 .40 .45
- *d.* As "b," bl & red (litho.) omitted *1,500.*

A decade of space achievements. Apollo 15 moon exploration mission July 26-Aug. 7.

Emily Elizabeth Dickinson A850

Sentry Box, Morro Castle, San Juan A851

Emily Dickinson Issue

Lithographed, Engraved (Giori)

1971, Aug. 28 ***Perf. 11***

1436 A850 8c multi, *greenish* .20 .20
- *a.* Black & olive (engr.) omitted *800.*
- *b.* Pale rose omitted *7,500.*
- *c.* Red omitted —

Dickinson (1830-1886), poet.

San Juan, PR, 450th Anniv.

1971, Sept. 12

1437 A851 8c multicolored .20 .20

Young Woman Drug Addict A852

Hands Reaching for CARE A853

Prevent Drug Abuse Issue

1971, Oct. 5 Photo. ***Perf. 10½x11***

1438 A852 8c bl, dp bl & blk .20 .20

Drug Abuse Prevention Week, Oct. 3-9.

CARE Issue

1971, Oct. 27

1439 A853 8c multicolored .20 .20
- *a.* Black omitted *4,750.*

25th anniv. of CARE, a US-Canadian Cooperative for American Relief Everywhere.

Historic Preservation Issue

Decatur House, Washington, DC — A854

Whaling Ship Charles W. Morgan, Mystic, Conn. — A855

Cable Car, San Francisco — A856

San Xavier del Bac Mission, Tucson, Ariz. — A857

Lithographed, Engraved (Giori)

1971, Oct. 29 Buff Paper ***Perf. 11***

1440 A854 8c blk brn & ocher .20 .20

1441 A855 8c blk brn & ocher .20 .20

1442 A856 8c blk brn & ocher .20 .20

1443 A857 8c blk brn & ocher .20 .20
- *a.* Block of 4, #1440-1443 .75 .85
- *b.* As "a," black brown omitted *2,500.*
- *c.* As "a," ocher omitted —

Christmas Issue

Adoration of the Shepherds, by Giorgione A858

Partridge in a Pear Tree, by Jamie Wyeth A859

1971, Nov. 10 Photo. *Perf. 10½x11*

1444 A858 8c gold & multi .20 .20
a. Gold omitted 550.00
1445 A859 8c multicolored .20 .20

Sidney Lanier (1842-1881) A860

Peace Corps Poster, by David Battle A861

Sidney Lanier Issue
Giori Press Printing

1972, Feb. 3 *Perf. 11*

1446 A860 8c black, brown & lt blue .20 .20

Lanier, poet, musician, lawyer, educator.

Peace Corps Issue

1972, Feb. 11 Photo. *Perf. 10½x11*

1447 A861 8c dk blue, light blue & red .20 .20

National Parks Centennial Issue

Hulk of Ship A862 — Cape Hatteras Lighthouse A863

Laughing Gulls on Driftwood A864 — Laughing Gulls and Dune A865

Wolf Trap Farm, Vienna, Va. — A866

Old Faithful, Yellowstone A867

Mt. McKinley, Alaska A868

Lithographed, Engraved (Giori)

1972 *Perf. 11*

1448 A862 2c black & multi .20 .20
1449 A863 2c black & multi .20 .20
1450 A864 2c black & multi .20 .20
1451 A865 2c black & multi .20 .20
a. Block of 4, #1448-1451 .25 .25
b. As "a," black (litho.) omitted 2,750.
1452 A866 6c black & multi .20 .20
1453 A867 8c blk, blue, brn & multi .20 .20
1454 A868 15c black & multi .30 .20

Cent. of Yellowstone Natl. Park, the 1st Natl. Park, and of the Natl. Park System. The four 2c stamps were issued for Cape Hatteras, NC, Natl. Seashore.

Issued: 2c, 4/5; 6c, 6/26; 8c, 3/1; 15c, 7/28.

See No. C84.

Family Planning Issue

Family — A869

1972, Mar. 18

1455 A869 8c black & multi .20 .20
a. Yellow omitted 1,250.
b. Dark brown & olive omitted —
c. Dark brown omitted 9,500

American Bicentennial
Colonial American Craftsmen

Glassmaker A870

Silversmith A871

Wigmaker A872

Hatter A873

1972, July 4 Engr. *Perf. 11x10½*
Dull Yellow Paper

1456 A870 8c deep brown .20 .20
1457 A871 8c deep brown .20 .20
1458 A872 8c deep brown .20 .20
1459 A873 8c deep brown .20 .20
a. Block of 4, #1456-1459 .65 .75

Olympic Games Issue

Bicycling and Olympic Rings — A874

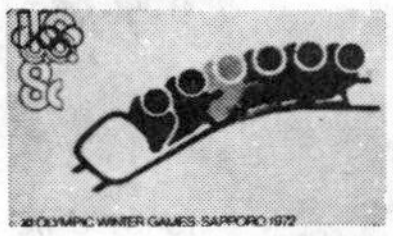

Bobsledding A875

Running A876

1972, Aug. 17 Photo. *Perf. 11x10½*

1460 A874 6c multicolored .20 .20
1461 A875 8c multicolored .20 .20
1462 A876 15c multicolored .30 .20
Nos. 1460-1462 (3) .70 .60

11th Winter Olympic Games, Sapporo, Japan, Feb. 3-13, and 20th Summer Olympic Games, Munich, Germany, Aug. 26-Sept. 11.

See No. C85.

Parent Teacher Association, 75th Anniv.

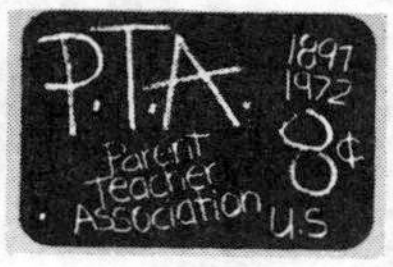

Blackboard A877

Perf. 11x10½

1972, Sept. 15 Photo.

1463 A877 8c yellow & black .20 .20

Wildlife Conservation Issue

Fur Seals A878

Cardinal — A879

Brown Pelican A880

Bighorn Sheep — A881

Lithographed, Engraved

1972, Sept. 20 *Perf. 11*

1464 A878 8c multicolored .20 .20
1465 A879 8c multicolored .20 .20
1466 A880 8c multicolored .20 .20
1467 A881 8c multicolored .20 .20
a. Block of 4, #1464-1467 .65 .75
b. As "a," brown omitted 4,000.
c. As "a," green & blue omitted 4,750.
d. As "a," red & brown omitted 4,500.

Mail Order Issue

Rural Post Office Store A882

Perf. 11x10½

1972, Sept. 27 Photo.

1468 A882 8c multicolored .20 .20

Cent. of mail order business, originated by Aaron Montgomery Ward, Chicago.

Osteopathic Medicine Issue

Man's Quest for Health — A883

1972, Oct. 9 Photo. *Perf. 10½x11*

1469 A883 8c yel, org & dk brn .20 .20

75th anniv. of the American Osteopathic Assoc., founded by Dr. Andrew T. Still.

American Folklore Issue

Tom Sawyer, by Norman Rockwell — A884

Lithographed, Engraved (Giori)

1972, Oct. 13 *Perf. 11*

1470 A884 8c black & multi .20 .20
a. Horiz. pair, imperf. btwn. 4,500.
b. Red & black (engr.) omitted 2,000.
c. Yellow & tan (litho.) omitted 2,400.

Tom Sawyer, hero of "The Adventures of Tom Sawyer," by Mark Twain.

Angel from "Mary, Queen of Heaven" A885

Santa Claus A886

1972, Nov. 9 Photo. *Perf. 10½x11*

1471 A885 8c multicolored .20 .20
a. Pink omitted 190.00
b. Black omitted 4,000.
1472 A886 8c multicolored .20 .20

Design of No. 1471 shows detail from a painting by the Master of the St. Lucy Legend.

Pharmacy Issue

Mortar and Pestle, Bowl of Hygeia, 19th Century Medicine Bottles A887

Lithographed, Engraved (Giori)

1972, Nov. 10 *Perf. 11*

1473 A887 8c black & multi .20 .20
a. Blue & orange omitted 900.00
b. Blue omitted 2,250.
c. Orange omitted 2,250.

Honoring American druggists, and 120th anniv. of the American Pharmaceutical Assoc.

Stamp Collecting Issue

US No. 1 Under Magnifying Glass A888

1972, Nov. 17 *Perf. 11*

1474 A888 8c dark blue green, black & brown .20 .20
a. Black (litho.) omitted 800.00

Love Issue

"Love," by Robert Indiana A889

1973, Jan. 26 Photo. *Perf. 11x10½*

1475 A889 8c red, emer & vio blue .20 .20

American Bicentennial
Communications in Colonial Times

Printer and Patriots Examining Pamphlet A890

Posting a Broadside A891

Postrider A892

Drummer A893

1973 Giori Press Printing ***Perf. 11***

1476 A890 8c ultra, grnsh blk & red .20 .20
1477 A891 8c black, ver & ultra .20 .20

Lithographed, Engraved (Giori)

1478 A892 8c multicolored .20 .20
1479 A893 8c multicolored .20 .20
Nos. 1476-1479 (4) .80 .80

Issue dates: No. 1476, Feb. 16; No. 1477, Apr. 13; No. 1478, June 22; No. 1479, Sept. 28.

Boston Tea Party

British Merchantman A894

British Three-master A895

Boats and Ship's Hull — A896

Boat and Dock — A897

Lithographed, Engraved (Giori)

1973, July 4 ***Perf. 11***

1480 A894 8c black & multi .20 .20
1481 A895 8c black & multi .20 .20
1482 A896 8c black & multi .20 .20
1483 A897 8c black & multi .20 .20
a. Block of 4, #1480-1483 .65 .75
b. As "a," black (engr.) omitted 1,500.
c. As "a," black (litho.) omitted 1,500.

American Arts Issue

Gershwin, Sportin' Life, Porgy and Bess A898

Robinson Jeffers, Man and Children of Carmel with Burro A899

Henry Ossawa Tanner, Palette and Rainbow A900

Willa Cather, Pioneer Family and Covered Wagon A901

1973 Photo. ***Perf. 11***

1484 A898 8c dp green & multi .20 .20
a. Vert. pair, imperf. horiz. 250.00
1485 A899 8c Prus blue & multi .20 .20
a. Vert. pair, imperf. horiz. 250.00
1486 A900 8c yel brown & multi .20 .20
1487 A901 8c dp brown & multi .20 .20
a. Vert. pair, imperf. horiz. 275.00
Nos. 1484-1487 (4) .80 .80

Honoring: No. 1484, George Gershwin (1898-1937), composer. No. 1485, Robinson Jeffers (1887-1962), poet. No. 1486, Henry Ossawa Tanner (1859-1937), black painter (portrait by Thomas Eakins). No. 1487, Willa Sibert Cather (1873-1947), novelist.

Issue dates: No. 1484, Feb. 28; No. 1485, Aug. 13; No. 1486, Sept. 10; No. 1487, Sept. 20.

Copernicus Issue

Nicolaus Copernicus (1473-1543), Polish Astronomer — A902

Lithographed, Engraved (Giori)

1973, Apr. 23 ***Perf. 11***

1488 A902 8c black & orange .20 .20
a. Orange omitted 1,000.
b. Black (engraved) omitted 1,200.

The orange color can be chemically removed.

Postal Service Employees' Issue

Stamp Counter — A903

Mail Collection — A904

Letter Facing on Conveyor Belt — A905

Parcel Post Sorting — A906

Mail Canceling — A907

Manual Letter Routing — A908

Electronic Letter Routing — A909

Loading Mail on Truck — A910

Mailman — A911

Rural Mail Delivery — A912

1973, Apr. 30 Photo. ***Perf. 10½x11***

1489 A903 8c multicolored .20 .20
1490 A904 8c multicolored .20 .20
1491 A905 8c multicolored .20 .20
1492 A906 8c multicolored .20 .20
1493 A907 8c multicolored .20 .20
1494 A908 8c multicolored .20 .20
1495 A909 8c multicolored .20 .20
1496 A910 8c multicolored .20 .20
1497 A911 8c multicolored .20 .20
1498 A912 8c multicolored .20 .20
a. Strip of 10, Nos. 1489-1498 1.50 1.75

A tribute to USPS employees. Emerald inscription on back, printed beneath gum in water-soluble ink, includes the USPS emblem, "People Serving You" and a statement, differing for each of the 10 stamps, about some aspect of postal service.

Each stamp in top or bottom row has a tab with blue inscription enumerating various jobs in postal service.

Harry S Truman Issue

Harry S Truman, 33rd President (1884-1972) A913

Giori Press Printing

1973, May 8 ***Perf. 11***

1499 A913 8c car rose, black & blue .20 .20

Electronics Progress Issue

Marconi's Spark Coil and Gap — A914

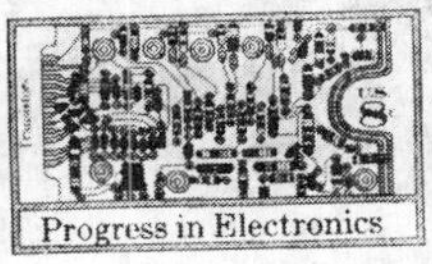

Transistors and Printed Circuit Board A915

Microphone, Speaker, Vacuum Tube, TV Camera Tube A916

Lithographed, Engraved (Giori)

1973, July 10 ***Perf. 11***

1500 A914 6c lilac & multi .20 .20
1501 A915 8c tan & multi .20 .20
a. Black (inscriptions & "U.S. 8c") omitted 600.
b. Tan (background) & lilac omitted 1,250.
1502 A916 15c gray green & multi .30 .20
a. Black (inscriptions & "U.S. 15c") omitted 1,500.
Nos. 1500-1502 (3) .70 .60

No. 1501b hinged is ½ unhinged value.
See No. C86.

Lyndon B. Johnson Issue

Lyndon B. Johnson (1908-1973), 36th President — A917

1973, Aug. 27 Photo. ***Perf. 11***

1503 A917 8c black & multi .20 .20
a. Horiz. pair, imperf. vert. 350.00

Rural America Issue

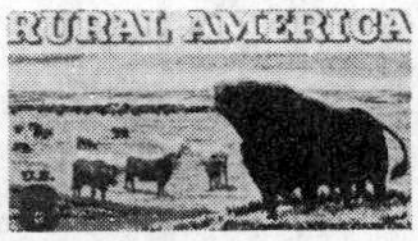

Angus and Longhorn Cattle A918

Chautauqua Tent and Buggies A919

Wheat Fields and Train A920

Lithographed, Engraved (Giori)

1973-74 ***Perf. 11***

1504 A918 8c multicolored .20 .20
a. Green & red brown omitted 1,000.
b. Vert. pair, imperf. between —
1505 A919 10c multicolored .20 .20
a. Black (litho.) omitted
1506 A920 10c multicolored .20 .20
a. Black & blue (engr.) omitted 900.
Nos. 1504-1506 (3) .60 .60

Cent. of introduction of Aberdeen Angus cattle to US (No. 1504); of Chautauqua Institution (No. 1505); of introduction of hard winter wheat into Kansas by Mennonite immigrants (No. 1506).

Issue dates: No. 1504, Oct. 5, 1973. No. 1505, Aug. 6, 1974. No. 1506, Aug. 16, 1974.

Christmas Issue

Small Cowper Madonna, by Raphael A921

Christmas Tree in Needlepoint A922

1973, Nov. 7 Photo. ***Perf. 10½x11***

1507 A921 8c tan & multi .20 .20
1508 A922 8c green & multi .20 .20
a. Vert. pair, imperf. btwn. 300.00

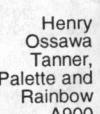

50-Star and 13-Star Flags — A923

Jefferson Memorial and Signature — A924

Mail Transport — A925

Liberty Bell — A926

Multicolor Huck Press

1973-74 Tagged *Perf. 11x10½*

1509 A923 10c red & blue .20 .20
- *a.* Horiz. pair, imperf. btwn. *50.* —
- *b.* Blue omitted *175.*
- *c.* Vert. pair, imperf. *1,100.*
- *d.* Horiz. pair, imperf. vert. *1,000.*

Rotary Press Printing

1510 A924 10c blue .20 .20
- *a.* Untagged (Bureau precanceled) .20
- *b.* Booklet pane of 5 + label 1.65 .55
- *c.* Booklet pane of 8 1.65 .70
- *d.* Booklet pane of 6 ('74) 5.25 1.00
- *e.* Vert. pair, imperf. horiz. *525.00*
- *f.* Vert. pair, imperf. btwn. —

1511 A925 10c multi, photo .20 .20
- *a.* Yellow omitted *65.00*

The yellow can be chemically removed.

Coil Stamps

Perf. 10 Vert.

Rotary Press Printing

1518 A926 6.3c brick red .20 .20
- *a.* Untagged (Bureau precanceled) .20
- *b.* Imperf., pair *200.00*
- *c.* As "a," imperf. pair *100.00*

Multicolor Huck Press

1519 A923 10c red & blue .20 .20
- *a.* Imperf., pair 37.50

Rotary Press Printing

1520 A924 10c blue .25 .20
- *a.* Untagged (Bureau precanceled) .25
- *b.* Imperf., pair 40.00

Issued: #1509, 1519, 12/8/73; #1510, 1520, 12/14/73; #1511, 1/4/74; #1518, 10/1/74.

Veterans of Foreign Wars Issue

V.F.W. Emblem A928

Giori Press Printing

1974, Mar. 11 *Perf. 11*

1525 A928 10c red & dark blue .20 .20

75th anniv. of Veterans of Spanish American and other Foreign Wars.

Robert Frost Issue

Robert Frost (1874-1963), Poet — A929

Rotary Press Printing

1974, Mar. 26 *Perf. 10½x11*

1526 A929 10c black .20 .20

EXPO '74 Issue

"Cosmic Jumper" A930

1974, Apr. 18 Photo. *Perf. 11*

1527 A930 10c multicolored .20 .20

EXPO '74, Spokane, Wash., May 4-Nov. 4. Theme, "Preserve the Environment."

Horse Racing Issue

Horses Rounding Turn — A931

1974, May 4 Photo. *Perf. 11x10½*

1528 A931 10c yellow & multi .20 .20
- *a.* Blue ("Horse Racing") omitted *1,000.*
- *b.* Red ("U.S. postage 10 cents") omitted —

Beware of stamps offered as No. 1528b that have traces of red.

Skylab Issue

Skylab A932

Lithographed, Engraved (Giori)

1974, May 14 *Perf. 11*

1529 A932 10c multicolored .20 .20
- *a.* Vert. pair, imperf. btwn.

1st anniv. of the launching of Skylab and to honor all who participated in the Skylab projects.

Centenary of UPU Issue

Michelangelo, from "School of Athens," by Raphael — A933

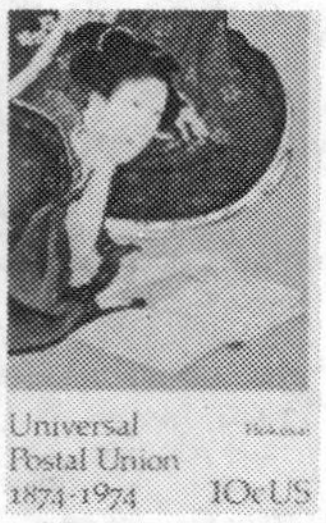

"Five Feminine Virtues," by Hokusai — A934

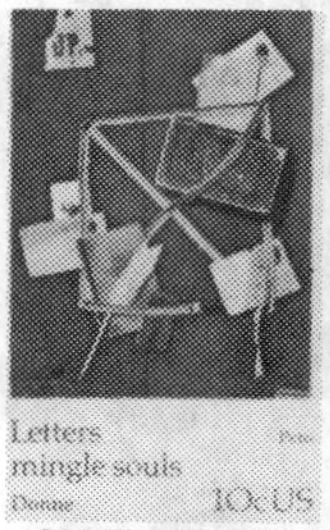

Old Time Letter Rack, by Peto — A935

Mlle. La Vergne, by Jean Liotard — A936

Lady Writing Letter, by Gerard Terborch — A937

Inkwell and Quill, by Jean Chardin — A938

Mrs. John Douglas, by Thomas Gainsborough A939

Don Antonio Noreiga, by Francisco de Goya A940

1974, June 6 Photo. *Perf. 11*

1530 A933 10c multicolored .20 .20
1531 A934 10c multicolored .20 .20
1532 A935 10c multicolored .20 .20
1533 A936 10c multicolored .20 .20
1534 A937 10c multicolored .20 .20
1535 A938 10c multicolored .20 .20
1536 A939 10c multicolored .20 .20
1537 A940 10c multicolored .20 .20
- *a.* Block or strip of 8, #1530-1537 1.60 1.60
- *b.* As "a" (block), imperf. vert. *7,500.*

Mineral Heritage Issue

Petrified Wood A941

Tourmaline — A942

Amethyst A943

Rhodochrosite — A944

Lithographed, Engraved (Giori)

1974, June 13 *Perf. 11*

1538 A941 10c lt blue & multi .20 .20
- *a.* Light blue & yellow omitted —

1539 A942 10c lt blue & multi .20 .20
- *a.* Light blue omitted —
- *b.* Black & purple omitted —

1540 A943 10c lt blue & multi .20 .20
- *a.* Light blue & yellow omitted —

1541 A944 10c lt blue & multi .20 .20
- *a.* Block or strip of 4, #1538-1541 .80 .90
- *b.* As "a," lt bl & yel omitted *2,000.*
- *c.* Light blue omitted —
- *d.* Black & red omitted —

Kentucky Settlement Issue

Fort Harrod — A945

Lithographed, Engraved (Giori)

1974, June 15 *Perf. 11*

1542 A945 10c green & multi .20 .20
- *a.* Dull black (litho.) omitted *900.*
- *b.* Green (engr. & litho.), black (engr. & litho.), blue omitted *3,750.*
- *c.* Green (engr.) omitted —
- *d.* Grn (engr.), blk (litho.) omitted —

American Bicentennial

First Continental Congress

Carpenters' Hall A946

A947

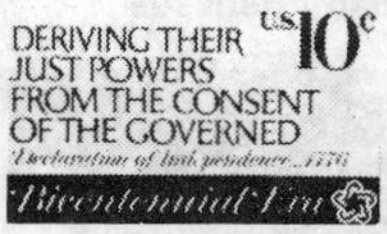

A948

Independence Hall — A949

Giori Press Printing

1974, July 4 *Perf. 11*

1543 A946 10c dark blue & red .20 .20
1544 A947 10c gray, dk blue & red .20 .20
1545 A948 10c gray, dk blue & red .20 .20
1546 A949 10c red & dark blue .20 .20
- *a.* Block of 4, #1543-1546 .80 .90

Energy Conservation Issue

Molecules and Drops of Gasoline and Oil — A950

Lithographed, Engraved (Giori)

1974, Sept. 23 *Perf. 11*

1547	A950 10c multicolored	.20	.20
a.	Blue & orange omitted	*900.*	
b.	Orange & green omitted	*750.*	
c.	Green omitted	*800.*	

To publicize the importance of conserving all forms of energy.

American Folklore Issue
Legend of Sleepy Hollow

Headless Horseman Pursuing Ichabod Crane A951

Lithographed, Engraved (Giori)

1974, Oct. 10 *Perf. 11*

1548	A951 10c dk blue, black, org & yel	.20	.20

Legend of Sleepy Hollow, by Washington Irving.

Retarded Children Issue

Retarded Child — A952

Giori Press Printing

1974, Oct. 12 *Perf. 11*

1549	A952 10c brn red & dk brn	.20	.20

Natl. Assoc. of Retarded Citizens.

Christmas Issue

Angel, from Perussis Altarpiece, 1480 — A953

"The Road-Winter," by Currier and Ives — A954

Dove Weather Vane, Mount Vernon A955

1974 **Photo.** *Perf. 10½x11*

1550	A953 10c multicolored	.20	.20

Perf. 11x10½

1551	A954 10c multicolored	.20	.20
a.	Buff omitted	35.00	

No. 1551a is difficult to identify. Competent expertization is necessary.

Die Cut, Paper Backing Rouletted
Self-adhesive
Inscribed "Precanceled"
Untagged

1552	A955 10c multicolored	.20	.20

Issued: #1550-1551, Oct. 23; #1552, Nov. 15.

Unused value of No. 1552 is for copy on rouletted paper backing as issued. Used value is for copy on piece, with or without postmark. Most copies are becoming discolored, probably from the adhesive. Unused and used values are for discolored copies.

Die cutting includes crossed slashes through dove, applied to prevent removal and re-use of stamp. The stamp will separate into layers if soaked.

American Arts Issue

Benjamin West, Self-portrait A956

Paul Laurence Dunbar A957

D. W. Griffith and Projector A958

1975 **Photo.** *Perf. 10½x11*

1553	A956 10c multicolored	.20	.20

Perf. 11

1554	A957 10c multicolored	.20	.20
a.	Imperf., pair	*1,300.*	

Litho., Engr. (Giori)

1555	A958 10c multicolored	.20	.20
a.	Brown (engr.) omitted	*600.*	
	Nos. 1553-1555 (3)	.60	.60

Honoring: West (1738-1820), painter (#1553). Dunbar (1872-1906), poet (#1554). David Lewelyn Wark Griffith (1875-1948), motion picture producer (#1555).

Issued: #1553, 2/10; #1554, 5/1; #1555, 5/27.

Space Issue

Pioneer 10 Passing Jupiter A959

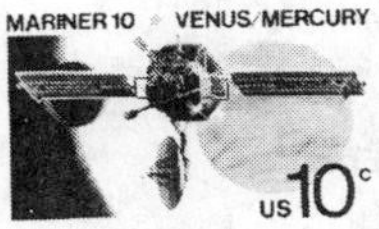

Mariner 10, Venus and Mercury A960

Lithographed, Engraved (Giori)

1975 *Perf. 11*

1556	A959 10c lt yel, dk yel, red, blue, & 2 dk blues	.20	.20
a.	Red & dk yel omitted	*1,400.*	
b.	Dk blues (engr.) omitted	*950.*	
d.	Dark yellow omitted	—	

Imperfs. exist from printer's waste.

1557	A960 10c blk, red, ultra & bis	.20	.20
a.	Red omitted	*550.*	
b.	Ultra & bister omitted	*2,000.*	

US unmanned accomplishments in space. Pioneer 10 passed within 81,000 miles of Jupiter, Dec. 3, 1973. Mariner 10 explored Venus and Mercury in 1974, and Mercury again in Mar. 1975.

Issue dates: #1556, Feb. 28; #1557, Apr. 4.

Collective Bargaining Issue

"Labor and Management" A961

1975, Mar. 13 **Photo.** *Perf. 11*

1558	A961 10c multicolored	.20	.20

Collective Bargaining Law, enacted 1935 with Wagner Act. Imperfs. are printers waste.

American Bicentennial
Contributors to the Cause

Sybil Ludington A962

Salem Poor — A963

Haym Salomon A964

Peter Francisco A965

1975, Mar. 25 **Photo.** *Perf. 11x10½*

1559	A962 8c multicolored	.20	.20
a.	Back inscription omitted	*225.00*	
1560	A963 10c multicolored	.20	.20
a.	Back inscription omitted	*225.00*	
1561	A964 10c multicolored	.20	.20
a.	Back inscription omitted	*225.00*	
b.	Red omitted	*250.00*	
1562	A965 18c multicolored	.35	.20
	Nos. 1559-1562 (4)	.95	.80

Ludington, age 16, rallied militia Apr. 26, 1777. Poor, black freeman, fought in Battle of Bunker Hill. Salomon, Jewish immigrant, raised money to finance Revolutionary War. Francisco, Portuguese-French immigrant, joined Continental Army at 15.

Emerald inscription on back, printed beneath gum in water-soluble ink, gives thumbnail sketch of portrayed contributor.

Lexington-Concord Battle, 200th Anniv.

"Birth of Liberty," by Henry Sandham A966

1975, Apr. 19 **Photo.** *Perf. 11*

1563	A966 10c multicolored	.20	.20
a.	Vert. pair, imperf. horiz.	*425.00*	

Battle of Bunker Hill, 200th Anniv.

Battle of Bunker Hill, by John Trumbull — A967

1975, June 17 *Perf. 11*

1564	A967 10c multicolored	.20	.20

Military Uniforms

Soldier with Flintlock Musket, Uniform Button — A968

Sailor with Grappling Hook, First Navy Jack, 1775 — A969

Marine with Musket, Full-rigged Ship — A970

Militiaman with Musket, Powder Horn — A971

1975, July 4 *Perf. 11*

1565	A968 10c multicolored	.20	.20
1566	A969 10c multicolored	.20	.20
1567	A970 10c multicolored	.20	.20
1568	A971 10c multicolored	.20	.20
a.	Block of 4, #1565-1568	.85	.90

Bicentenary of US Military Services.

Apollo Soyuz Space Issue

Apollo and Soyuz After Docking and Earth — A972

Spacecraft Before Docking, Earth and Project Emblem — A973

1975, July 15 **Photo.** *Perf. 11*

1569	A972 10c multicolored	.20	.20
1570	A973 10c multicolored	.20	.20
a.	Pair, #1569-1570	.45	.40
c.	As "a," vert. pair, imperf. horiz.	*2,000.*	

Apollo Soyuz space test project (Russo-American cooperation); launching, July 15; link-up, July 17.

Completely imperf varieties of No. 1570 are from printer's waste.

See Russia Nos. 4339-4340.

International Women's Year Issue

Worldwide Equality for Women A974

1975, Aug. 26 **Photo.** *Perf. 11x10½*

1571	A974 10c blue, org & dk blue	.20	.20

Postal Service Bicentennial Issue

Stagecoach and Trailer Truck A975

Old and New Locomotives — A976

Early Mail Plane and Jet — A977

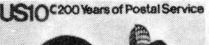

Satellite for Transmission of Mailgrams — A978

1975, Sept. 3 Photo. *Perf. 11x10½*

1572 A975 10c multicolored .20 .20
1573 A976 10c multicolored .20 .20
1574 A977 10c multicolored .20 .20
1575 A978 10c multicolored .20 .20
a. Block of 4, #1572-1575 .85 .90
b. As "a," red ("10c") omitted *9,500.*

World Peace Through Law Issue

Law Book, Olive Branch and Globe A979

Giori Press Printing

1975, Sept. 29 *Perf. 11*

1576 A979 10c green, Prus blue & rose brown .20 .20
b. Horiz. pair, imperf. vert. —

A prelude to 7th World Conf. of the World Peace Through Law Center at Washington, DC, Oct. 12-17.

Banking and Commerce Issue

Engine Turning, Indian Head Penny and Morgan Silver Dollar A980

Seated Liberty Quarter, $20 Gold (Double Eagle), Engine Turning A981

Lithographed, Engraved (Giori)

1975, Oct. 6 *Perf. 11*

1577 A980 10c multicolored .20 .20
1578 A981 10c multicolored .20 .20
a. Pair, #1577-1578 .40 .40
b. As "a," brown & blue (litho.) omitted *2,250.*
c. As "a," brown, blue & yellow (litho.) omitted *2,750.*

Banking and commerce in the US and for the Centennial Convention of the American Bankers Association.

Christmas Issue

Madonna, by Domenico Ghirlandaio A982

Christmas Card, by Louis Prang, 1878 A983

1975, Oct. 14 Photo. *Perf. 11*

1579 A982 (10c) multicolored .20 .20
a. Imperf., pair *90.00*
1580 A983 (10c) multicolored .20 .20
a. Imperf., pair *90.00*
b. Perf. 10½x11 .60 .20

Americana Issue

Inkwell and Quill — A984

Speaker's Stand — A985

Early Ballot Box A987

Books, Bookmark, Eyeglasses A988

Dome of Capitol — A994

Contemplation of Justice — A995

Early American Printing Press — A996

Torch — A997

Liberty Bell — A998

Eagle and Shield — A999

Fort McHenry Flag — A1001

Head, Statue of Liberty — A1002

Old North Church, Boston A1003

Fort Nisqually A1004

Sandy Hook Lighthouse, NJ — A1005

Morris Township School No. 2, Devils Lake, ND — A1006

Iron "Betty" Lamp, 17th-18th Cent. — A1007

Rush Lamp and Candle Holder — A1008

Kerosene Table Lamp — A1009

Railroad Conductor's Lantern, c. 1850 — A1010

1975-81 Engr. *Perf. 11x10½*

1581 A984 1c dk blue, *grnsh* .20 .20
a. Untagged (Bureau pre-canceled) .20
1582 A985 2c red brown, *grnsh* .20 .20
a. Untagged (Bureau pre-canceled) .20
b. Cream paper ('81) .20 .20
1584 A987 3c olive, *grnsh* .20 .20
a. Untagged (Bureau pre-canceled) .20
1585 A988 4c rose mag, *cr* .20 .20
a. Untagged (Bureau pre-canceled) 1.25

Size: 17½x20½mm

1590 A994 9c slate green .45 .20
a. Perf. 10 20.00 12.50

Size: 18½x22½mm

1591 A994 9c slate green, *gray* .20 .20
a. Untagged (Bureau pre-canceled) .20
1592 A995 10c violet, *gray* .20 .20
a. Untagged (Bureau pre-canceled) .25
1593 A996 11c orange, *gray* .20 .20
1594 A997 12c brown red, *beige* .25 .20
1595 A998 13c brown .25 .20
a. Booklet pane of 6 1.90 *.75*
b. Booklet pane of 7 + label 1.75 *.75*
c. Booklet pane of 8 2.00 *1.00*
d. Booklet pane of 5 + label ('76) 1.50 *.75*
e. Vert. pair, imperf btwn. *1,200.*

Photo.
Perf. 11

1596 A999 13c multicolored .25 .20
a. Imperf., pair *50.00* —
b. Yellow omitted *180.00*

Engr.

1597 A1001 15c gray, dk blue & red .30 .20
a. Vert. pair, imperf. *20.00*
b. Gray omitted *700.00*
c. Vert. strip of 3, imperf. btwn. & at top or bottom —

Perf. 11x10½

1598 A1001 15c gray, dk blue & red .35 .20
a. Booklet pane of 8 3.50 *.80*
1599 A1002 16c blue .35 .20
1603 A1003 24c red, *blue* .45 .20
1604 A1004 28c brown, *blue* .55 .20
1605 A1005 29c blue, *blue* .55 .20
1606 A1006 30c green, *blue* .55 .20

Engr. & Litho.
Perf. 11

1608 A1007 50c tan, black & org .85 .20
a. Black omitted *300.00*
b. Vert. pair, imperf. horiz. *1,750.*

Beware of copies offered as No. 1608b that have blind perfs.

1610 A1008 $1 tan, brn, org & yel 1.75 .20
a. Brown (engraved) omitted *275.*
b. Tan, orange & yel omitted *350.*
c. Brown inverted *14,500.*
1611 A1009 $2 tan, dk grn, org & yel 3.25 .75
1612 A1010 $5 tan, red brn, yel & org 7.50 1.75
Nos. 1581-1612 (22) 19.05 6.50

Nos. 1590, 1590a, 1595, 1598 issued in booklets only. All stamps have one or two straight edges.

Years of issue: #1591, 1595-1596, 11c, 24c, 1975. #1590, 1c-4c, 10c, 1977. #1597-1598, 16c, 28c, 29c, $2, 1978. 30c-$1, $5, 1979. 12c, 1981.

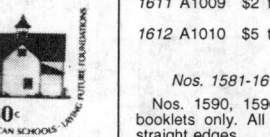

Guitar A1011

Saxhorns A1012

Drum A1013

Piano A1014

Coil Stamps
Engr.
Perf. 10 Vertically

1613 A1011 3.1c brown, *yel* .20 .20
a. Untagged (Bureau precanceled) .50
b. Imperf., pair *1,400.*
1614 A1012 7.7c brown, *brt yel* .20 .20
a. Untagged (Bureau precanceled) .35
b. As "a," imperf., pair *1,600.*
1615 A1013 7.9c carmine, *yel* .20 .20
a. Untagged (Bureau precanceled) .20
b. Imperf., pair *600.00*
1615C A1014 8.4c dk blue, *yel* .20 .20
d. Untagged (Bureau precanceled) .30
e. As "d," pair, imperf. btwn. 60.00
f. As "d," imperf., pair 17.50
1616 A994 9c sl green, *gray* .20 .20
a. Imperf., pair *160.00*
b. Untagged (Bureau precanceled) .35
c. As "b," imperf., pair *700.00*
1617 A995 10c violet, *gray* .20 .20
a. Untagged (Bureau precanceled) .25
b. Imperf., pair *60.00*
1618 A998 13c brown .25 .20
a. Untagged (Bureau precanceled) .45
b. Imperf., pair 25.00
g. Pair, imperf. between —
h. As "a," imperf., pair —
1618C A1001 15c gray, dk blue & red .40 .20
d. Imperf., pair 25.00
e. Pair, imperf. between *150.00*
f. Gray omitted *40.00*
1619 A1002 16c blue .35 .20
a. Huck press printing .50 .20
Nos. 1613-1619 (9) 2.20 1.80

The 15c was printed on two different presses. Huck press printings have white background without bluish tinge, are a fraction of a millimeter smaller and have block instead of overall tagging. Cottrell press printings show a joint line.

Years of issue: 9c, 13c, 1975. 7.7c, 7.9c, 1976. 10c, 1977. 8.4c, 15c, 16c, 1978. 3.1c, 1979.

See Nos. 1811, 1813, 1816.

13-Star Flag, Independence Hall — A1015

Flag over Capitol — A1016

Multicolor Huck Press

1975-77 *Perf. 11x10½*

No.	Design	Description	Unused	Used
1622	A1015	13c dark blue & red	.25	.20
a.		Horiz. pair, imperf. btwn.	50.	
b.		Vert. pair, imperf.	1,100.	
c.		Perf. 11 ('81)	.65	.20
d.		As "c," vert. pair, imperf.	150.	
e.		Horiz. pair, imperf. vert.	—	

No. 1622 has large block tagging and nearly vertical multiple gum ridges. No. 1622c has small block tagging and flat gum.

No.	Design	Description	Unused	Used
1623	A1016	13c blue & red ('77)	.25	.20
a.		Booklet pane of 8 (1 #1590 and 7 #1623)	2.25	1.10
b.		Perf. 10	1.00	1.00
c.		Booklet pane of 8 (1 #1590a + 7 #1623b)	26.00	—
d.		Se-tenant pair, #1590 & 1623	.70	.70
e.		Se-tenant pair, #1590a & 1623b	22.50	20.00

Coil Stamp

Perf. 10 Vertically

No.	Design	Description	Unused	Used
1625	A1015	13c dark blue & red	.25	.20
a.		Imperf., pair	25.00	

Nos. 1623 and 1623b issued in booklets only. All stamps have one or two straight edges.

American Bicentennial — Spirit of '76

Drummer Boy
A1019

Old Drummer
A1020

Fifer — A1021

Designed after painting "The Spirit of '76," by Archibald M. Willard.

1976, Jan. 1 **Photo.** *Perf. 11*

No.	Design	Description	Unused	Used
1629	A1019	13c multicolored	.20	.20
a.		Imperf., vert. pair	—	
1630	A1020	13c multicolored	.20	.20
1631	A1021	13c multicolored	.20	.20
a.		Strip of 3, #1629-1631	.60	.65
b.		As "a," imperf.	1,100.	
c.		Imperf., vert. pair #1631	800.	

Interphil Issue

"Interphil 76"
A1022

Lithographed, Engraved (Giori)

1976, Jan. 17 *Perf. 11*

No.	Design	Description	Unused	Used
1632	A1022	13c dk blue, red & ultra	.20	.20

Interphil 76 Intl. Phil. Exhib., Philadelphia, Pa., May 29-June 6.

State Flags

A1023-A1072

1976, Feb. 23 **Photo.** *Perf. 11*

No.	Design	Description	Unused	Used
1633	A1023	13c Delaware	.25	.20
1634	A1024	13c Pennsylvania	.25	.20
1635	A1025	13c New Jersey	.25	.20
1636	A1026	13c Georgia	.25	.20
1637	A1027	13c Connecticut	.25	.20
1638	A1028	13c Massachusetts	.25	.20
1639	A1029	13c Maryland	.25	.20
1640	A1030	13c South Carolina	.25	.20
1641	A1031	13c New Hampshire	.25	.20
1642	A1032	13c Virginia	.25	.20
1643	A1033	13c New York	.25	.20
1644	A1034	13c North Carolina	.25	.20
1645	A1035	13c Rhode Island	.25	.20
1646	A1036	13c Vermont	.25	.20
1647	A1037	13c Kentucky	.25	.20
1648	A1038	13c Tennessee	.25	.20
1649	A1039	13c Ohio	.25	.20
1650	A1040	13c Louisiana	.25	.20
1651	A1041	13c Indiana	.25	.20
1652	A1042	13c Mississippi	.25	.20
1653	A1043	13c Illinois	.25	.20
1654	A1044	13c Alabama	.25	.20
1655	A1045	13c Maine	.25	.20
1656	A1046	13c Missouri	.25	.20
1657	A1047	13c Arkansas	.25	.20
1658	A1048	13c Michigan	.25	.20
1659	A1049	13c Florida	.25	.20
1660	A1050	13c Texas	.25	.20
1661	A1051	13c Iowa	.25	.20
1662	A1052	13c Wisconsin	.25	.20
1663	A1053	13c California	.25	.20
1664	A1054	13c Minnesota	.25	.20
1665	A1055	13c Oregon	.25	.20
1666	A1056	13c Kansas	.25	.20
1667	A1057	13c West Virginia	.25	.20
1668	A1058	13c Nevada	.25	.20
1669	A1059	13c Nebraska	.25	.20
1670	A1060	13c Colorado	.25	.20
1671	A1061	13c North Dakota	.25	.20
1672	A1062	13c South Dakota	.25	.20
1673	A1063	13c Montana	.25	.20
1674	A1064	13c Washington	.25	.20
1675	A1065	13c Idaho	.25	.20
1676	A1066	13c Wyoming	.25	.20
1677	A1067	13c Utah	.25	.20
1678	A1068	13c Oklahoma	.25	.20
1679	A1069	13c New Mexico	.25	.20
1680	A1070	13c Arizona	.25	.20
1681	A1071	13c Alaska	.25	.20
1682	A1072	13c Hawaii	.25	.20
a.		Pane of 50	13.00	—

Telephone Centenary Issue

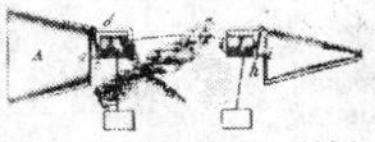

Bell's Telephone Patent Application
A1073

Engraved (Giori)

1976, Mar. 10 *Perf. 11*

No.	Design	Description	Unused	Used
1683	A1073	13c blk, pur & red, *tan*	.25	.20
a.		Black & purple omitted	—	

1st telephone call by Alexander Graham Bell, Mar. 10, 1876.

No. 1683a comes from a partially printed pane. The errors have only tiny traces of red present so are best collected as a horiz. strip of 5 with 2 or 3 error stamps.

Commercial Aviation Issue

Ford-Pullman Monoplane and Laird Swallow Biplane
A1074

1976, Mar. 19 **Photo.** *Perf. 11*

No.	Design	Description	Unused	Used
1684	A1074	13c blue & multi	.25	.20

50th anniv. of 1st contract airmail flights: Dearborn, MI to Cleveland, OH, Feb. 15, 1926; and Pasco, WA to Elko, NV, Apr. 6, 1926.

Chemistry Issue

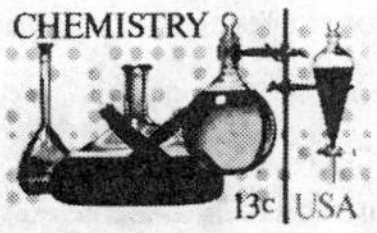

Various Flasks, Separatory Funnel, Computer Tape
A1075

1976, Apr. 6 **Photo.** *Perf. 11*

No.	Design	Description	Unused	Used
1685	A1075	13c multicolored	.25	.20

Honoring American chemists, cent. of the American Chemical Society.

American Bicentennial Issues

Designs, from Left to Right, No. 1686: a, Two British officers. b, Gen. Benjamin Lincoln. c, George Washington. d, John Trumbull, Col. Cobb, von Steuben, Lafayette, Thomas Nelson. Alexander Hamilton, John Laurens, Walter Stewart, all vert.

No. 1687: a, John Adams, Roger Sherman, Robert R. Livingston. b, Jefferson, Franklin. c, Thomas Nelson, Jr., Francis Lewis, John Witherspoon, Samuel Huntington. d, John Hancock, Charles Thomson. e, George Read, John Dickinson, Edward Rutledge (a, d, vert., b, c, e, horiz.).

No. 1688: a, Boatsman. b, Washington. c, Flag bearer. d, Men in boat. e, Men on shore (a, d, horiz., b, c, e, vert.).

No. 1689: a, Two officers. b, Washington. c, Officer, black horse. d, Officer, white horse. e, Three soldiers (a, c, e, horiz., b, d, vert.).

1976, May 29 Litho. *Perf. 11*

Souvenir Sheets

1686	A1076	Sheet of 5	3.25	—
a.-e.		13c multi, any single	.45	.40
f.		USA 13c omitted on "b," "c" & "d," imperf., untagged	—	*2,250.*
g.		USA 13c omitted on "a" & "e"	*450.*	—
h.		Imperf., untagged		*2,250.*
i.		USA 13c omitted on "b," "c" & "d"	*450.*	
j.		USA 13c double on "b"	—	
k.		USA 13c omitted on "c" & "d"	*800.*	
l.		USA 13c omitted on "e"	*500.*	
m.		USA 13c omitted, imperf., untagged	—	—
n.		As "g," imperf., untagged		—
1687	A1077	Sheet of 5	4.25	—
a.-e.		18c multi, any single	.55	.55
f.		Design & marginal inscriptions omitted	*3,000.*	
g.		USA 18c omitted on "a" & "c"	*800.*	
h.		USA 18c omitted on "b," "d" & "e"	*500.*	
i.		USA 18c omitted on "d"	*550.*	*500.*
j.		Black omitted in design	*2,000.*	
k.		USA 18c omitted, imperf., untagged	*3,000.*	
m.		USA 18c omitted on "b" & "e"	*500.*	
n.		USA 18c omitted on "b" & "d"	—	
p.		Imperf., tagged	—	
q.		USA 18c omitted on "c"	—	
1688	A1078	Sheet of 5	5.25	—
a.-e.		24c multi, any single	.70	.70
f.		USA 24c omitted, imperf., untagged	*3,500.*	
g.		USA 24c omitted on "d" & "e"	*450.*	*450.*
h.		Design & marginal inscriptions omitted	*3,250.*	
i.		USA 24c omitted on "a," "b" & "c"	*500.*	—
j.		Imperf., untagged	*3,000.*	
k.		USA 24c of "d" & "e" inverted	—	
1689	A1079	Sheet of 5	6.25	—
a.-e.		31c multi, any single	.85	.85
f.		USA 31c omitted, imperf.	*2,750.*	
g.		USA 31c omitted on "a" & "c"	*425.*	
h.		USA 31c omitted on "b," "d" & "e"	*450.*	—
i.		USA 31c omitted on "e"	*475.*	
j.		Black omitted in design	*2,000.*	
k.		Imperf., untagged		*2,250.*
l.		USA 31c omitted on "b" & "d"	—	
m.		USA 31c omitted on "a" "c" & "e"	—	
n.		As "m," imperf., untagged	—	
p.		As "h," imperf., untagged		*2,500.*
q.		As "g," imperf., untagged	*2,750.*	
r.		USA 31c omitted on "d" & "e"	—	
s.		As "f," untagged	2,250.	
		Nos. 1686-1689 (4)	19.00	

Nos. 1688-1689 exist with inverted perforations.

Issued in connection with Interphil 76 Intl. Phil. Exhib., Philadelphia, Pa., May 29-June 6. Size of sheets: 203x152mm; stamps: 25x39½mm, 39½x25mm.

Benjamin Franklin Issue

Franklin and Map of North America, 1776 — A1080

Lithographed, Engraved (Giori)

1976, June 1 *Perf. 11*

1690	A1080	13c ultra & multi	.25	.20
a.		Light blue omitted	*250.00*	

American Bicentennial; Franklin (1706-1790), deputy postmaster general for the colonies (1753-1774) and statesman.

See Canada No. 691.

American Bicentennial Issue

Declaration of Independence, by John Trumbull

A1081 A1082 A1083 A1084

1976, July 4 Photo. *Perf. 11*

1691	A1081	13c multicolored	.25	.20
1692	A1082	13c multicolored	.25	.20
1693	A1083	13c multicolored	.25	.20
1694	A1084	13c multicolored	.25	.20
a.		Strip of 4, #1691-1694	1.00	1.10

Olympic Games Issue

Diving A1085 Skiing A1086

Running A1087 Skating A1088

1976, July 16 Photo. *Perf. 11*

1695	A1085	13c multicolored	.25	.20
1696	A1086	13c multicolored	.25	.20
1697	A1087	13c multicolored	.25	.20
1698	A1088	13c multicolored	.25	.20
a.		Block of 4, #1695-1698	1.10	1.10
b.		As "a," imperf.	*700.00*	

12th Winter Olympic Games, Innsbruck, Austria, Feb. 4-15, and 21st Summer Olympic Games, Montreal, Canada, July 17-Aug. 1.

Clara Maass Issue

Clara Maass, Newark German Hospital Pin — A1089

1976, Aug. 18 Photo. *Perf. 11*

1699	A1089	13c multicolored	.25	.20
a.		Horiz. pair, imperf. vert.	*450.00*	

Clara Maass (1876-1901), volunteer in fight against yellow fever, birth centenary.

Adolph S. Ochs Issue

Adolph S. Ochs (1858-1935), Publisher of the NY Times, 1896-1935 A1090

Giori Press Printing

1976, Sept. 18 *Perf. 11*

1700	A1090	13c black & gray	.25	.20

Christmas Issue

Nativity, by John Singleton Copley A1091

"Winter Pastime," by Nathaniel Currier A1092

1976, Oct. 27 Photo. *Perf. 11*

1701	A1091	13c multicolored	.25	.20
a.		Imperf., pair	*100.00*	
1702	A1092	13c multicolored	.25	.20
a.		Imperf., pair	*100.00*	
1703	A1092	13c multicolored	.25	.20
a.		Imperf., pair	*110.00*	
b.		Vert. pair, imperf. btwn.	—	
d.		Red omitted	—	
e.		Yellow omitted	—	
		Nos. 1701-1703 (3)	.75	.60

No. 1702 has overall tagging. Lettering at base is black and usually ½mm below design. As a rule, no "snowflaking" in sky or pond. Pane of 50 has margins on 4 sides with slogans.

No. 1703 has block tagging the size of printed area. Lettering at base is gray black and usually ¾mm below design. "Snowflaking" generally in sky and pond. Pane has margin only at right or left, and no slogans. Copies are known with various amounts of red or yellow missing. Nos. 1703d and 1703e have the color totally omitted. Expertization is recommended.

American Bicentennial Issue

Washington at Princeton

Washington, Nassau Hall, Hessians, 13-Star Flag, by Charles Willson Peale — A1093

1977, Jan. 3 Photo. *Perf. 11*

1704	A1093	13c multicolored	.25	.20
a.		Horiz. pair, imperf. vert.	*550.00*	

Washington's victory at Princeton over Lord Cornwallis, bicentennial.

Sound Recording Issue

Tin Foil Phonograph A1094

Lithographed, Engraved (Giori)

1977, Mar. 23 *Perf. 11*

1705	A1094	13c black & multi	.25	.20

Centenary of invention of the phonograph by Thomas Alva Edison, and development of sophisticated recording industry.

American Folk Art Issue

Pueblo Pottery

Zia Pot — A1095

San Ildefonso Pot — A1096

Hopi Pot — A1097

Acoma Pot — A1098

1977, Apr. 13 Photo. *Perf. 11*

1706	A1095	13c multicolored	.25	.20
1707	A1096	13c multicolored	.25	.20
1708	A1097	13c multicolored	.25	.20
1709	A1098	13c multicolored	.25	.20
a.		Block or strip of 4	1.00	1.00
b.		As "a," imperf. vert.	*2,500.*	

Pueblo art, 1880-1920, from museums in NM, AZ and CO.

Lindbergh Flight Issue

Spirit of St. Louis A1099

1977, May 20 Photo. *Perf. 11*

1710	A1099	13c multicolored	.25	.20
a.		Imperf., pair	*1,100.*	

Charles A. Lindbergh's solo transatlantic flight from NY to Paris, 50th anniv.

Colorado Statehood Issue

Columbine and Rocky Mountains — A1100

1977, May 21 Photo. *Perf. 11*

1711	A1100	13c multicolored	.25	.20
a.		Horiz. pair, imperf. btwn.	*600.00*	
b.		Horiz. pair, imperf. vert.	*900.00*	

Colorado became a state in 1876.

Butterfly Issue

Swallowtail A1101

Checkerspot A1102

Dogface A1103

Orange Tip — A1104

1977, June 6 Photo. *Perf. 11*

1712	A1101	13c tan & multi	.25	.20
1713	A1102	13c tan & multi	.25	.20
1714	A1103	13c tan & multi	.25	.20
1715	A1104	13c tan & multi	.25	.20
a.		Block of 4, #1712-1715	1.00	1.00
b.		As "a," imperf. horiz.	*15,000.*	

American Bicentennial Issues

Lafayette

Marquis de Lafayette — A1105

1977, June 13 Engr. *Perf. 11*

1716	A1105	13c blue, black & red	.25	.20

200th anniv. of Lafayette's landing on the coast of SC, north of Charleston.

Skilled Hands for Independence

Seamstress A1106

Blacksmith A1107

Wheelwright A1108

Leatherworker A1109

1977, July 4 Photo. *Perf. 11*

1717	A1106	13c multicolored	.25	.20
1718	A1107	13c multicolored	.25	.20
1719	A1108	13c multicolored	.25	.20
1720	A1109	13c multicolored	.25	.20
a.		Block of 4, #1717-1720	1.00	1.00

Peace Bridge Issue

Peace Bridge and Dove — A1110

1977, Aug. 4 Engr. *Perf. 11x10½*

1721	A1110	13c blue	.25	.20

50th anniv. of the Peace Bridge, connecting Buffalo, NY with Fort Erie, Ontario.

American Bicentennial Issue

Battle of Oriskany

Herkimer at Oriskany, by Frederick Yohn A1111

1977, Aug. 6 Photo. *Perf. 11*

1722	A1111	13c multicolored	.25	.20

200th anniv. of Battle of Oriskany, American Militia led by Brig. Gen. Nicholas Herkimer (1728-1777).

Energy Issue

Energy Conservation A1112

Energy Development A1113

1977, Oct. 20 Photo. *Perf. 11*

1723	A1112	13c multicolored	.25	.20
1724	A1113	13c multicolored	.25	.20
a.		Pair, #1723-1724	.50	.50

Conservation and development of nation's energy resources.

Alta California Issue

Farm Houses A1114

Litho. & Engraved (Giori)

1977, Sept. 9 *Perf. 11*

1725	A1114	13c black & multi	.25	.20

El Pueblo de San José de Guadalupe, 1st civil settlement in Alta California, 200th anniv.

American Bicentennial Issue

Articles of Confederation

Members of Continental Congress in Conference A1115

Engraved (Giori)

1977, Sept. 30 *Perf. 11*

1726	A1115	13c red & brn, *cream*	.25	.20
b.		Red omitted	—	
c.		Red & brown omitted	—	

200th anniv. of drafting the Articles of Confederation, York Town, Pa.

No. 1726b also has most of the brown color omitted. No. 1726c must be collected as a

American Bicentennial Issues
Souvenir Sheets

Surrender of Cornwallis at Yorktown, by John Trumbull A1076

Declaration of Independence, by John Trumbull A1077

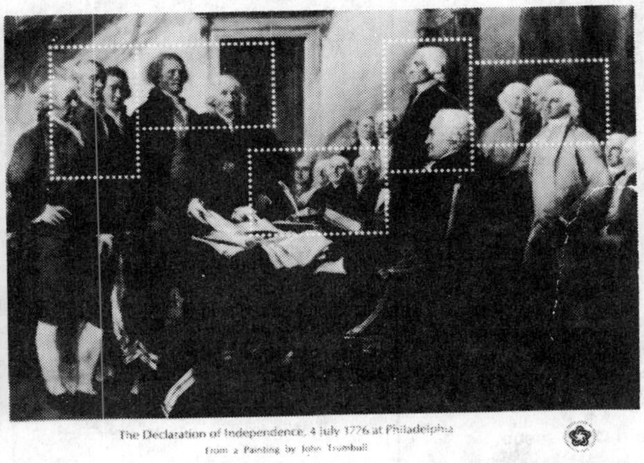

Washington Crossing the Delaware, by Emanuel Leutze/Eastman Johnson A1078

Washington Reviewing Army at Valley Forge, by William T. Trego A1079

transition multiple, certainly with No. 1726b and preferably also with No. 1726.

Talking Picture, 50th Anniv. Issue

Movie Projector and Phonograph A1116

Litho. & Engraved (Giori)

1977, Oct. 6 *Perf. 11*

1727 A1116 13c multicolored	.25	.20

American Bicentennial Issue

Surrender at Saratoga

Surrender of Burgoyne, by John Trumbull A1117

1977, Oct. 7 **Photo.** *Perf. 11*

1728 A1117 13c multicolored	.25	.20

200th anniv. of Gen. John Burgoyne's surrender at Saratoga.

Christmas Issue

Washington at Valley Forge A1118

Rural Mailbox A1119

1977, Oct. 21 **Photo.** *Perf. 11*

1729 A1118 13c multicolored	.25	.20
a. Imperf., pair	*75.00*	
1730 A1119 13c multicolored	.25	.20
a. Imperf., pair	*300.00*	

Carl Sandburg Issue

Carl Sandburg, by William A. Smith, 1952 — A1120

Engraved (Giori)

1978, Jan. 6 *Perf. 11*

1731 A1120 13c black & brown	.25	.20
a. Brown omitted	—	

Sandburg (1878-1967), poet, biographer and collector of American folk songs.

Captain Cook Issue

Capt. Cook, by Nathaniel Dance, 1776 A1121

"Resolution" and "Discovery," by John Webber A1122

Giori Press Printing

1978, Jan. 20 *Perf. 11*

1732 A1121 13c dark blue	.25	.20
1733 A1122 13c green	.25	.20
a. Vert. pair, imperf. horiz.	—	
b. Pair, #1732-1733	.50	.50
c. As "b," imperf. between	*4,500.*	

Capt. James Cook, 200th anniv. of his arrival in Hawaii, at Waimea, Kauai, Jan. 20, 1778, and of his anchorage in Cook Inlet, near Anchorage, Alaska, June 1, 1778. Nos. 1732-1733 issued in panes of 50, containing 25 each of Nos. 1732-1733 including 5 No. 1732a. Design of No. 1733 is after etching "A View of Karakekooa in Owyhee."

Indian Head Penny, 1877 A1123

Eagle A1124

Roses — A1126

Engraved (Giori)

1978, Jan. 11 *Perf. 11*

1734 A1123 13c brown & blue green, *bister*	.25	.20
a. Horiz. pair, imperf. vert.	*300.00*	

1978, May 22 **Photo.** *Perf. 11*

1735 A1124 (15c) orange	.25	.20
a. Imperf., pair	*100.00*	
b. Vert. pair, imperf. horiz.	*700.00*	

Engr. *Perf. 11x10½*

1736 A1124 (15c) orange	.25	.20
a. Booklet pane of 8	2.25	*.90*

See No. 1743

1978, July 11 **Engr.** *Perf. 10*

1737 A1126 15c multicolored	.25	.20
a. Booklet pane of 8	2.25	*.90*
b. As "a," imperf.	—	

Nos. 1736, 1737 issued in booklets only. All stamps have 1 or 2 straight edges.

Robertson Windmill, Williamsburg A1127

Old Windmill, Portsmouth A1128

Cape Cod Windmill, Eastham A1129

Dutch Mill, Batavia A1130

Southwestern Windmill — A1131

1980, Feb. 7 **Engr.** *Perf. 11*

Booklet Stamps

1738 A1127 15c sepia, *yellow*	.30	.20
1739 A1128 15c sepia, *yellow*	.30	.20
1740 A1129 15c sepia, *yellow*	.30	.20
1741 A1130 15c sepia, *yellow*	.30	.20
1742 A1131 15c sepia, *yellow*	.30	.20
a. Bklt. pane, 2 each #1738-1742	3.50	*3.00*
b. Strip of 5, #1738-1742	1.50	1.40

Coil Stamp

1978, May 22 **Engr.** *Perf. 10 Vert.*

1743 A1124 (15c) orange	.25	.20
a. Imperf., pair	90.00	

No. 1743a is valued in the grade of fine.

Black Heritage Issue

Harriet Tubman (1820-1913), Cart Carrying Slaves — A1133

1978, Feb. 1 **Photo.** *Perf. 10½x11*

1744 A1133 13c multicolored	.25	.20

Tubman, born a slave, helped more than 300 slaves escape to freedom.

American Folk Art Issue

American Quilts, Basket Design

A1134 A1135

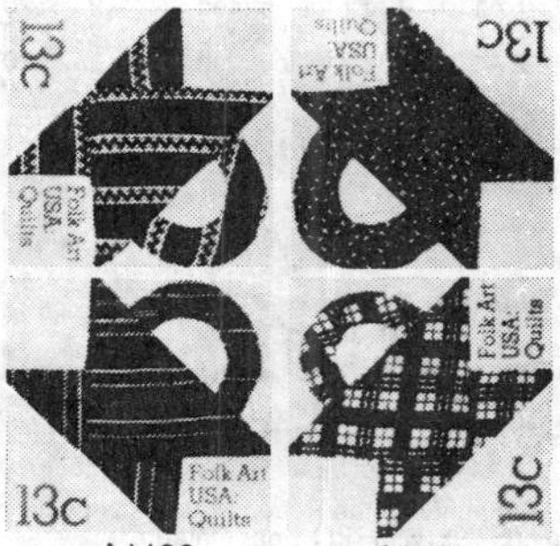

A1136 A1137

1978, Mar. 8 **Photo.** *Perf. 11*

1745 A1134 13c multicolored	.25	.20
1746 A1135 13c multicolored	.25	.20
1747 A1136 13c multicolored	.25	.20
1748 A1137 13c multicolored	.25	.20
a. Block of 4, #1745-1748	1.00	1.00

American Dance Issue

Ballet A1138

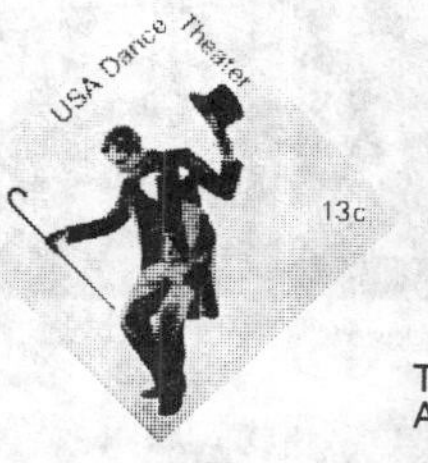

Theater A1139

Folk Dance A1140

20-Cent Minimum Value

The minimum value for a single stamp is 20 cents. This value reflects the costs of handling inexpensive stamps.

Modern Dance A1141

1978, Apr. 26 **Photo.** *Perf. 11*

1749 A1138 13c multicolored	.25	.20
1750 A1139 13c multicolored	.25	.20
1751 A1140 13c multicolored	.25	.20
1752 A1141 13c multicolored	.25	.20
a. Block of 4, #1749-1752	1.00	1.00

American Bicentennial Issue

French Alliance

Louis XVI and Franklin, Porcelain Sculpture by C. G. Sauvage — A1142

Giori Press Printing

1978, May 4 *Perf. 11*

1753 A1142 13c blue, black & red	.25	.20

Bicent. of French Alliance, signed in Paris, Feb. 6, 1778, and ratified by Continental Cong., May 4.

Early Cancer Detection Issue

Dr. George Papanicolaou (1883-1962), his Signature and Microscope — A1143

1978, May 18 **Engr.** *Perf. 10½x11*

1754 A1143 13c brown	.25	.20

Papanicolaou, developer of Pap Test, early cancer detection in women.

Performing Arts Issues

Jimmie Rodgers and Locomotive A1144

George M. Cohan, "Yankee Doodle Dandy" and Stars A1145

1978 **Photo.** *Perf. 11*

1755 A1144 13c multicolored	.25	.20
1756 A1145 15c multicolored	.25	.20

Rodgers (1897-1933), the "Singing Brakeman, Father of Country Music," and Cohan (1878-1942), actor and playwright.

Issue dates: #1755, May 24; #1756, July 3.

CAPEX Issue

Wildlife from Canadian-US Border — A1146

Litho. & Engr. (Giori)

1978, June 10 *Perf. 11*

1757	A1146 Block of 8	2.00	2.00
a.	13c Cardinal	.25	.20
b.	13c Mallard	.25	.20
c.	13c Canada goose	.25	.20
d.	13c Blue jay	.25	.20
e.	13c Moose	.25	.20
f.	13c Chipmunk	.25	.20
g.	13c Red fox	.25	.20
h.	13c Raccoon	.25	.20
i.	Yellow, green, red, brown, blue, black (litho.) omitted	*6,500.*	
j.	Strip of 4 (a-d), imperf. vert.	—	
k.	Strip of 4 (e-h), imperf. vert.	—	

CAPEX, Canadian Intl. Phil. Exhib., Toronto, Ont., June 9-18.

Photography Issue

Photographic Equipment A1147

1978, June 26 **Photo.** *Perf. 11*

1758	A1147 15c multicolored	.30	.20

Viking Missions to Mars Issue

Viking 1 Lander Scooping Up Soil on Mars A1148

1978, July 20 **Litho. & Engr.**

1759	A1148 15c multicolored	.30	.20

2nd anniv. of landing of Viking 1 on Mars.

American Owls Issue

Great Gray Owl A1149

Saw-whet Owl A1150

Barred Owl A1151

Great Horned Owl A1152

1978, Aug. 26 **Engr.** *Perf. 11*

1760	A1149 15c multicolored	.30	.20
1761	A1150 15c multicolored	.30	.20
1762	A1151 15c multicolored	.30	.20
1763	A1152 15c multicolored	.30	.20
a.	Block of 4, #1760-1763	1.25	1.25

American Trees Issue

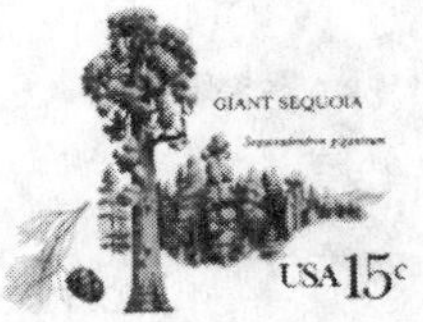

Giant Sequoia A1153

White Pine A1154

White Oak A1155

Gray Birch A1156

1978, Oct. 9 **Photo.** *Perf. 11*

1764	A1153 15c multicolored	.30	.20
1765	A1154 15c multicolored	.30	.20
1766	A1155 15c multicolored	.30	.20
1767	A1156 15c multicolored	.30	.20
a.	Block of 4, #1764-1767	1.25	1.25
b.	As "a," imperf. horiz.	*15,000.*	

Christmas Issue

Madonna and Child with Cherubim, by Andrea della Robbia — A1157

Child on Hobby-horse and Christmas Trees — A1158

1978, Oct. 18 **Photo.** *Perf. 11*

1768	A1157 15c blue & multi	.30	.20
a.	Imperf., pair	*90.00*	
1769	A1158 15c red & multi	.30	.20
a.	Imperf., pair	*100.00*	
b.	Vert. pair, imperf. horiz.	*2,000.*	

Value for #1768a is for an uncreased pair.

Robert F. Kennedy Issue

Robert F. Kennedy (1925-68), US Attorney General — A1159

1979, Jan. 12 **Engr.** *Perf. 11*

1770	A1159 15c blue	.30	.20

Black Heritage Issue

Dr. Martin Luther King, Jr. (1929-68), and Civil Rights Marchers — A1160

1979, Jan. 13 **Photo.** *Perf. 11*

1771	A1160 15c multicolored	.30	.20
a.	Imperf., pair		

Civil rights leader.

Year of the Child Issue

Children A1161

1979, Feb. 15 **Engr.** *Perf. 11*

1772	A1161 15c orange red	.30	.20

International Year of the Child.

John Steinbeck A1162

Albert Einstein A1163

John Steinbeck Issue

1979, Feb. 27 **Engr.** *Perf. 10½x11*

1773	A1162 15c dark blue	.30	.20

John Ernst Steinbeck (1902-68), novelist.

Albert Einstein Issue

1979, Mar. 4 **Engr.** *Perf. 10½x11*

1774	A1163 15c chocolate	.30	.20

Einstein (1879-1955), theoretical physicist.

American Folk Art Issue
Pennsylvania Toleware

Coffeepot A1164

Tea Caddy A1165

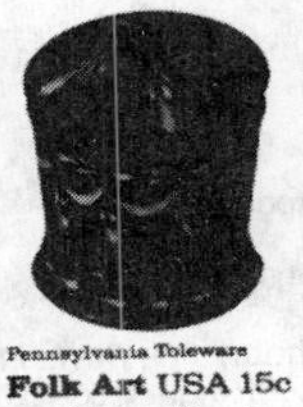

Sugar Bowl A1166

Coffeepot A1167

1979, Apr. 19 **Photo.** *Perf. 11*

1775	A1164 15c multicolored	.30	.20
1776	A1165 15c multicolored	.30	.20
1777	A1166 15c multicolored	.30	.20
1778	A1167 15c multicolored	.30	.20
a.	Block of 4, #1775-1778	1.25	1.25
b.	As "a," imperf. horiz.	*4,250.*	

American Architecture Issue

Virginia Rotunda, by Thomas Jefferson A1168

Baltimore Cathedral, by Benjamin Latrobe A1169

Boston State House, by Charles Bulfinch A1170

Philadelphia Exchange, by William Strickland A1171

1979, June 4 **Engr.** *Perf. 11*

1779	A1168 15c black & brick red	.30	.20
1780	A1169 15c black & brick red	.30	.20
1781	A1170 15c black & brick red	.30	.20
1782	A1171 15c black & brick red	.30	.20
a.	Block of 4, #1779-1782	1.25	1.25

Endangered Flora Issue

Persistent Trillium A1172

Hawaiian Wild Broadbean A1173

Contra Costa Wallflower A1174

Antioch Dunes Evening Primrose A1175

1979, June 7 **Photo.** *Perf. 11*

1783	A1172 15c multicolored	.30	.20
1784	A1173 15c multicolored	.30	.20
1785	A1174 15c multicolored	.30	.20
1786	A1175 15c multicolored	.30	.20
a.	Block of 4, #1783-1786	1.25	1.25
b.	As "a," imperf.	*600.00*	

Seeing Eye Dogs Issue

German Shepherd Leading Man — A1176

1979, June 15

1787	A1176 15c multicolored	.30	.20
a.	Imperf., pair	*425.00*	

Special Olympics Issue

Child Holding Winner's Medal — A1177

1979, Aug. 9 ***Perf. 11***

1788 A1177 15c multicolored .30 .20

Special Olympics for special children, Brockport, NY, Aug. 8-13.

John Paul Jones Issue

John Paul Jones, by Charles Willson Peale — A1178

1979, Sept. 23 Photo. ***Perf. 11x12***

1789 A1178 15c multicolored .30 .20
- *a.* Perf. 11 .30 .20
- *b.* Perf. 12 *1,900. 1,000.*
- *c.* Vert. pair, imperf. horiz. *175.*
- *d.* As "a," vert. pair, imperf horiz. *150.*

John Paul Jones (1747-1792), Naval Commander, American Revolution.

Imperfs., perf. or imperf. gutter pairs and blocks exist from printer's waste.

Olympic Games Issue

Javelin A1179

Running A1180

Swimming A1181

Rowing A1182

Equestrian A1183

1979 Photo. ***Perf. 11***

1790 A1179 10c multicolored .20 .20
1791 A1180 15c multicolored .30 .20
1792 A1181 15c multicolored .30 .20
1793 A1182 15c multicolored .30 .20
1794 A1183 15c multicolored .30 .20
- *a.* Block of 4, #1791-1794 1.25 1.25
- *b.* As "a," imperf. *1,600.*

22nd Summer Olympic Games, Moscow, July 19-Aug. 3, 1980.

Issue dates: 10c, Sept. 5; 15c, Sept. 28.

Winter Olympic Games Issue

Speed Skating A1184

Downhill Skiing A1185

Ski Jump A1186

Ice Hockey A1187

1980, Feb. 1 Photo. ***Perf. 11x10½***

1795 A1184 15c multicolored .35 .20
- *a.* Perf. 11 1.05 —

1796 A1185 15c multicolored .35 .20
- *a.* Perf. 11 1.05 —

1797 A1186 15c multicolored .35 .20
- *a.* Perf. 11 1.05 —

1798 A1187 15c multicolored .35 .20
- *a.* Perf. 11 1.05 —
- *b.* Block of 4, #1795-1798 1.50 1.40
- *c.* Block of 4, #1795a-1798a 4.25 —

13th Winter Olympic Games, Lake Placid, NY, Feb. 12-24.

Christmas Issue

Virgin and Child, by Gerard David A1188

Santa Claus, Christmas Tree Ornament A1189

1979, Oct. 18 Photo. ***Perf. 11***

1799 A1188 15c multicolored .30 .20
- *a.* Imperf., pair *90.*
- *b.* Vert. pair, imperf. horiz. *700.*
- *c.* Vert. pair, imperf. btwn. *2,250.*

1800 A1189 15c multicolored .30 .20
- *a.* Green & yellow omitted *700.*
- *b.* Green, yellow & tan omitted *750.*

Nos. 1800a, 1800b always have the remaining colors misaligned,

No. 1800b is valued in the grade of fine.

Performing Arts Issue

Will Rogers (1879-1935), Actor and Humorist — A1190

1979, Nov. 4 Photo. ***Perf. 11***

1801 A1190 15c multicolored .30 .20
- *a.* Imperf., pair *225.00*

Viet Nam Veterans Issue

Ribbon for Viet Nam Service Medal A1191

1979, Nov. 11 Photo. ***Perf. 11***

1802 A1191 15c multicolored .30 .20

A tribute to veterans of the Viet Nam War.

Performing Arts Issue

W.C. Fields (1880-1946), actor and comedian — A1192

1980, Jan. 29 Photo. ***Perf. 11***

1803 A1192 15c multicolored .30 .20
- *a.* Imperf., pair —

Black Heritage

Benjamin Banneker (1731-1806), Astronomer and Mathematician, Transverse — A1193

1980, Feb. 15 Photo. ***Perf. 11***

1804 A1193 15c multicolored .30 .20
- *a.* Horiz. pair, imperf. vert. *800.00*

Imperf. printer's waste has been fraudulently perforated to simulate No. 1804a. Legitimate examples of No. 1804a do not have colors misregistered.

Letter Writing

Letters Preserve Memories A1194

P.S. Write Soon A1195

Letters Lift Spirits A1196

Letters Shape Opinions A1197

1980, Feb. 25

1805 A1194 15c multicolored .30 .20
1806 A1195 15c purple & multi .30 .20
1807 A1196 15c multicolored .30 .20
1808 A1195 15c green & multi .30 .20
1809 A1197 15c multicolored .30 .20
1810 A1195 15c red & multi .30 .20
- *a.* Vert. strip of 6 #1805-1810 1.85 2.00

Nos. 1805-1810 (6) 1.80 1.20

Natl. Letter Writing Week, Feb. 24-Mar. 1.

Americana Type

Weaver Violins — A1199

Coil Stamps

1980-81 Engr. ***Perf. 10 Vert.***

1811 A984 1c dk blue, *grnsh* .20 .20
- *a.* Imperf., pair *175.00*

1813 A1199 3.5c purple, *yel* .20 .20
- *a.* Untagged (Bureau precanceled, lines only) .20
- *b.* Imperf., pair *225.00*

1816 A997 12c brown red, *beige* ('81) .25 .20
- *a.* Untagged (Bureau precanceled) .25
- *b.* Imperf., pair *200.00*

A1207

1981, Mar. 15 Photo. ***Perf. 11x10½***

1818 A1207 (18c) violet .35 .20

Engr. ***Perf. 10***

Booklet Stamp

1819 A1207 (18c) violet .40 .20
- *a.* Booklet pane of 8 3.50 *1.75*

Coil Stamp

Perf. 10 Vert.

1820 A1207 (18c) violet .40 .20
- *a.* Imperf., pair *100.00*

Nos. 1818-1820 (3) 1.15 .60

Frances Perkins

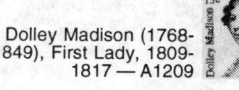

Frances Perkins (1882-1965), Sec. of Labor, 1933-45 (1st Woman Cabinet Member) — A1208

1980, Apr. 10 ***Perf. 10½x11***

1821 A1208 15c Prus blue .30 .20

Dolley Madison

Dolley Madison (1768-1849), First Lady, 1809-1817 — A1209

1980, May 20 ***Perf. 11***

1822 A1209 15c red brown & sepia .30 .20

Emily Bissell

Emily Bissell (1861-1948), Social Worker; Introduced Christmas seals in US — A1210

1980, May 31

1823 A1210 15c black & red .30 .20
- *a.* Vert. pair, imperf. horiz. *400.00*

Helen Keller

Helen Keller and Anne Sullivan — A1211

Litho. & Engr.

1980, June 27 ***Perf. 11***

1824 A1211 15c multicolored .30 .20

Keller (1880-1968), blind and deaf writer and lecturer taught by Sullivan (1867-1936).

Veterans Admin-istration Emblem A1212

Gen. Bernardo de Galvez A1213

Veterans Administration

1980, July 21 **Photo.**
1825 A1212 15c car & vio bl .30 .20
a. Horiz. pair, imperf. vert. *475.00*

General Bernardo de Galvez

1980, July 23 **Engr.** ***Perf. 11***
1826 A1213 15c multicolored .30 .20
a. Red, brn & bl (engr.) omitted *800.*
b. Red, brn, bl (engr.), bl & yel (litho.) omitted *1,400.*

Galvez (1746-1786), helped defeat British in Battle of Mobile, 1780.

Coral Reefs

Brain Coral, Beaugregory Fish A1214

Elkhorn Coral, Porkfish A1215

Chalice Coral, Moorish Idol Fish A1216

Finger Coral, Sabertooth Blenny Fish A1217

1980, Aug. 26 **Photo.** ***Perf. 11***
1827 A1214 15c multicolored .30 .20
1828 A1215 15c multicolored .30 .20
1829 A1216 15c multicolored .30 .20
1830 A1217 15c multicolored .30 .20
a. Block of 4, #1827-1830 1.25 1.10
b. As "a," imperf. *1,000.*
c. As "a," vert. imperf. btwn. —
d. As "a," imperf. vert. *3,000.*

American Bald Eagle A1218

Edith Wharton A1219

Organized Labor

1980, Sept. 1 **Photo.** ***Perf. 11***
1831 A1218 15c multicolored .30 .20
a. Imperf., pair *375.00*

Edith Wharton

1980, Sept. 5 **Engr.** ***Perf. 10½x11***
1832 A1219 15c purple .30 .20

Edith Wharton (1862-1937), writer.

American Education

"Homage to the Square: Glow," by Josef Albers — A1220

1980, Sept. 12 **Photo.** ***Perf. 11***
1833 A1220 15c multicolored .30 .20
a. Horiz. pair, imperf. btwn. *250.00*

American Folk Art

Pacific Northwest Indian Masks

Heiltsuk, Bella Bella Tribe A1221

Chilkat Tlingit Tribe A1222

Tlingit Tribe A1223

Bella Coola Tribe A1224

1980, Sept. 25
1834 A1221 15c multicolored .30 .20
1835 A1222 15c multicolored .30 .20
1836 A1223 15c multicolored .30 .20
1837 A1224 15c multicolored .30 .20
a. Block of 4, #1834-1837 1.25 1.25

American Architecture

Smithsonian Institution, by James Renwick A1225

Trinity Church, Boston, by Henry Hobson Richardson A1226

Pennsylvania Academy of Fine Arts, by Frank Furness — A1227

Lyndhurst, Tarrytown, NY, by Alexander Jackson Davis A1228

1980, Oct. 9 **Engr.** ***Perf. 11***
1838 A1225 15c black & brick red .30 .20
1839 A1226 15c black & brick red .30 .20
1840 A1227 15c black & brick red .30 .20
1841 A1228 15c black & brick red .30 .20
a. Block of 4, #1838-1841 1.25 1.25
b. As "a," red omitted on Nos. 1838, 1839 *350.00*

No. 1841b was caused by a misregistration of the perforations.

Christmas

Madonna and Child A1229

Wreath, Toys on Windowsill A1230

1980, Oct. 31 **Photo.** ***Perf. 11***
1842 A1229 15c multicolored .30 .20
a. Imperf., pair *75.00*
1843 A1230 15c multicolored .30 .20
a. Imperf., pair *75.00*
b. Buff omitted *25.00*
c. Vert. pair, imperf. horiz. —
d. Horiz. pair, imperf. between *4,000.*

No. 1843b is difficult to identify and should have a competent certificate.

Great Americans

A1231

A1232

A1233

A1234

A1235

A1236

A1237

A1238

A1239

A1240

A1241

A1242

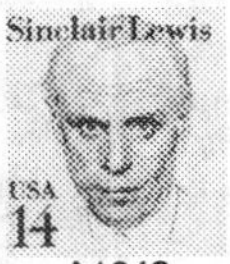

A1243

A1244

A1245

A1246

A1247

A1248

A1249

A1250

A1251

A1252

A1253

A1254

A1255

A1256

Perf. 11x10½, 11 (1, 6-11, 14, #1862, 22, 30, 39, 40, 50c)

1980-85 **Engr.**
1844 A1231 1c black .20 .20
a. Imperf. pair *400.*
b. Vert. pair, imperf. btwn. and at bottom *3,000.*
e. Vert. pair, imperf. horiz. —
1845 A1232 2c brown black .20 .20
1846 A1233 3c olive green .20 .20
1847 A1234 4c violet .20 .20
1848 A1235 5c henna brown .20 .20
1849 A1236 6c orange ver .20 .20
a. Vert. pair, imperf. btwn. and at bottom *2,250.*
1850 A1237 7c brt carmine .20 .20
1851 A1238 8c olive black .20 .20
1852 A1239 9c dark green .20 .20
1853 A1240 10c Prus blue .20 .20
b. Vert. pair, imperf. btwn. & at bottom *1,000.*
c. Horiz. pair, imperf. btwn. *2,250.*

Completely imperforate tagged or untagged stamps are from printer's waste.

1854 A1241 11c dark blue .25 .20
1855 A1242 13c lt maroon .25 .20
1856 A1243 14c slate green .30 .20
b. Vert. pair, imperf. horiz. *125.*
c. Horiz. pair, imperf. btwn. *9.00*
d. Vert. pair, imperf. btwn. *1,900.*
e. All color omitted —

No. 1856e comes from a partially printed pane and should be collected as a vertical strip of 10, one stamp normal, one stamp transitional and 8 stamps with color omitted.

1857 A1244 17c green .35 .20
1858 A1245 18c dark blue .35 .20
1859 A1246 19c brown .40 .20
1860 A1247 20c claret .40 .20
1861 A1248 20c green .45 .20
1862 A1249 20c black .40 .20
1863 A1250 22c dk chalky blue .55 .20
d. Vert. pair, imperf. horiz. *2,500.*
e. Vert. pair, imperf. btwn. —
f. Horiz. pair, imperf. btwn. *2,500.*
1864 A1251 30c olive gray .55 .20
1865 A1252 35c gray .70 .20
1866 A1253 37c blue .75 .20
1867 A1254 39c rose lilac .80 .20
a. Vert. pair, imperf. horiz. *600.*
b. Vert. pair, imperf. btwn. *2,000.*

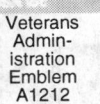

1868 A1255 40c dark green .80 .20
1869 A1256 50c brown .95 .20
Nos. 1844-1869 (26) 10.25 5.20

Years of issue: 19c, 1980. 17c, 18c, 35c, 1981. No. 1860, 2c, 13c, 37c, 1982. No. 1861, 1c, 3c-5c, 1983. No. 1862, 10c, 30c, 40c, 1984. 6c-9c, 11c, 14c, 22c, 39c, 50c, 1985.

A1261

A1262

Everett Dirksen

1981, Jan. 4 ***Perf. 11***
1874 A1261 15c gray .30 .20
a. All color omitted —

Everett Dirksen (1896-1969), Senate Minority Leader, 1960-69.

No. 1874a comes from a parially printed pane and may be collected as either a vertical strip of 3 or 5 (1 or 3 stamps normal, one stamp transitional and one stamp with color omitted) or as a pair with one partially printed stamp.

Black Heritage

1981, Jan. 30 **Photo.** ***Perf. 11***
1875 A1262 15c multicolored .30 .20

Whitney Moore Young (1921-71), civil rights leader.

Flowers

A1263 A1264

A1265 A1266

1981, Apr. 23 ***Perf. 11***
1876 A1263 18c multicolored .35 .20
1877 A1264 18c multicolored .35 .20
1878 A1265 18c multicolored .35 .20
1879 A1266 18c multicolored .35 .20
a. Block of 4, #1876-1879 1.40 1.25

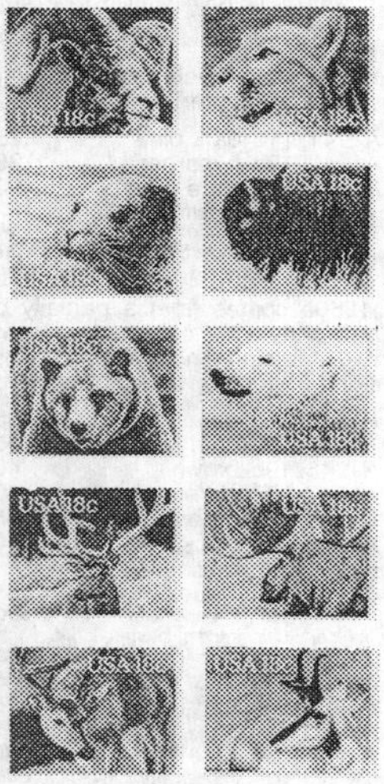
A1267-A1276

1981, May 14 **Engr.** ***Perf. 11***
Booklet Stamps

1880 A1267 18c Bighorn .55 .20
1881 A1268 18c Puma .55 .20
1882 A1269 18c Harbor seal .55 .20
1883 A1270 18c American Buffalo .55 .20
1884 A1271 18c Brown bear .55 .20
1885 A1272 18c Polar bear .55 .20
1886 A1273 18c Elk (wapiti) .55 .20
1887 A1274 18c Moose .55 .20
1888 A1275 18c White-tailed deer .55 .20
1889 A1276 18c Pronghorn .55 .20
a. Bklt. pane of 10, #1880-1889 8.00 7.00
Nos. 1880-1889 (10) 5.50 2.00

See No. 1949.

A1277

A1278

A1279

A1280

Multicolor Huck Press

1981, Apr. 24 ***Perf. 11***
1890 A1277 18c multicolored .35 .20
a. Imperf., pair 110.00
b. Vert. pair, imperf. horiz. 900.00

Coil Stamp
Perf. 10 Vert.

1891 A1278 18c multicolored .35 .20
a. Imperf., pair 25.00
b. Pair, imperf. btwn. —

Beware of pairs offered as imperf. between that have faint blind perfs.

Booklet Stamps
Perf. 11

1892 A1279 6c multicolored .50 .20
1893 A1280 18c multicolored .30 .20
a. Booklet pane, 2 #1892, 6 #1893 3.00 2.25
b. As "a," vert. imperf. btwn. 75.00
c. Pair, #1892, 1893 .90 1.00

Bureau Precanceled Coils

Starting with No. 1895e, Bureau precanceled coil stamps are valued unused as well as used. The coils issued with dull finish gum may be difficult to distinguish. When used normally these stamps do not receive any postal markings so that used stamps with an additional post-cancellation of any kind are worth considerably less than the values shown here.

A1281

1981, Dec. 17 ***Perf. 11***
1894 A1281 20c blk, dk blue & red .40 .20
a. Vert. pair, imperf. 35.00
b. Vert. pair, imperf. horiz. 600.00
c. Dark blue omitted 90.00
d. Black omitted 325.00

Coil Stamp
Perf. 10 Vertical

1895 A1281 20c blk, dk blue & red .35 .20
b. Untagged (Bureau precanceled) .50 .50
d. Imperf., pair 10.00
e. Pair, imperf. btwn. 1,250.
f. Black omitted 55.00
g. Dark blue omitted 1,500.

Booklet Stamp
Perf. 11x10½

1896 A1281 20c blk, dk blue & red .35 .20
a. Booklet pane of 6 2.50 2.00
b. Booklet pane of 10 4.25 3.25

Transportation Coils

A1282

A1283

A1284

A1285

A1286

A1287

A1288

A1289

A1290

A1291

A1292

A1293

A1294

A1295

1981-84 **Engr.** ***Perf. 10 Vert.***
1897 A1282 1c violet .20 .20
b. Imperf., pair 675.00
1897A A1283 2c black .20 .20
e. Imperf., pair 55.00

For similar designs to the 1c and 2c, see Nos. 2225-2226.

1898 A1284 3c dk green .20 .20
1898A A1285 4c redsh brown .20 .20
b. Untagged (Bureau precanceled) .20 .20
c. As "b," imperf., pair 750.00
d. No. 1898A, imperf., pair 900.00 —
1899 A1286 5c gray green .20 .20
a. Imperf., pair 2,750.
1900 A1287 5.2c carmine .20 .20
a. Untagged (Bureau precanceled) .20 .20
1901 A1288 5.9c blue .20 .20
a. Untagged (Bureau precanceled, lines only) .20 .20
b. As "a," imperf., pair 200.00
1902 A1289 7.4c brown .20 .20
a. Untagged (Bureau precanceled) .20 .20
1903 A1290 9.3c car rose .30 .20
a. Untagged (Bureau precanceled, lines only) .25 .25
b. As "a," imperf., pair 125.00
1904 A1291 10.9c purple .25 .20
a. Untagged (Bureau precanceled, lines only) .25 .25
b. As "a," imperf., pair 150.00
1905 A1292 11c red .25 .20
a. Untagged .25 .20
1906 A1293 17c ultra .35 .20
a. Untagged (Bureau precanceled, Presorted First Class) .35 .35
b. Imperf., pair 165.00
c. As "a," imperf., pair 650.00
1907 A1294 18c dark brown .35 .20
a. Imperf., pair 150.00
1908 A1295 20c vermilion .35 .20
a. Imperf., pair 110.00
Nos. 1897-1908 (14) 3.45 2.80

Years of issue: 9.3c, 17c-20c, 1981. 2c, 4c, 5.9c, 10.9c, 1982. 1c, 3c, 5c, 5.2c, 1983. 7.4, 11c, 1984.

See Nos. 2123-2136, 2225-2231, 2252-2266, 2451-2468.

A1296

Perf. 10 Vert. on 1 or 2 Sides
1983, Aug. 12 **Photo.**
1909 A1296 $9.35 multi 21.00 14.00
a. Booklet pane of 3 65.00 —

A1297

A1298

American Red Cross Centennial

1981, May 1 ***Perf. 10½x11***
1910 A1297 18c multicolored .35 .20

Savings & Loan Sesquicentennial

1981, May 8 ***Perf. 11***
1911 A1298 18c multicolored .35 .20

Space Achievement

A1299 A1300

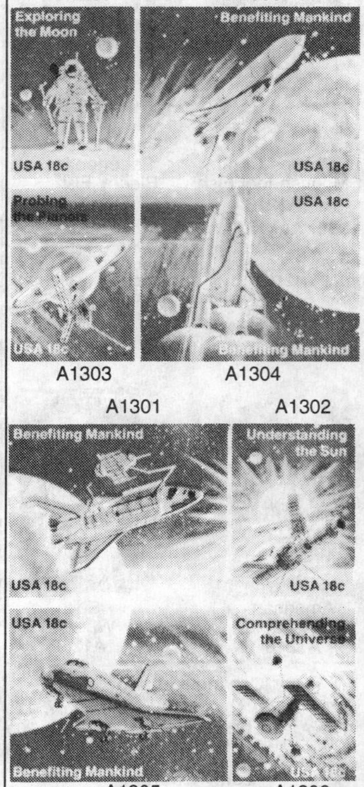

A1303 A1304
A1301 A1302
A1305 A1306

1981, May 21 ***Perf. 11***
1912 A1299 18c multicolored .35 .20
1913 A1300 18c multicolored .35 .20
1914 A1301 18c multicolored .35 .20
1915 A1302 18c multicolored .35 .20
1916 A1303 18c multicolored .35 .20
1917 A1304 18c multicolored .35 .20

1918 A1305 18c multicolored		.35	.20
1919 A1306 18c multicolored		.35	.20
a.	Block of 8, #1912-1919	3.00	3.00
b.	As "a," imperf.	9,000.	

Professional Management

Joseph Wharton
A1307

1981, June 18

1920 A1307 18c blue & black	.35	.20

Preservation of Wildlife Habitats

A1308 A1309

A1310 A1311

1981, June 26

1921 A1308 18c multicolored		.35	.20
1922 A1309 18c multicolored		.35	.20
1923 A1310 18c multicolored		.35	.20
1924 A1311 18c multicolored		.35	.20
a.	Block of 4, #1921-1924	1.50	1.25

International Year of the Disabled

Man Looking through Microscope
A1312

1981, June 29 Photo. *Perf. 11*

1925 A1312 18c multicolored		.35	.20
a.	Vert. pair, imperf. horiz.	2,750.	

Edna St. Vincent Millay, 1892-1950

A1313

Litho. & Engr.

1981, July 10 *Perf. 11*

1926 A1313 18c multicolored		.35	.20
a.	Black (engr., inscriptions) omitted	400.00	—

Alcoholism

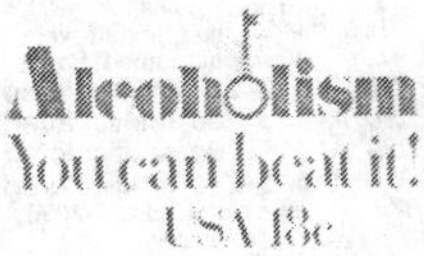

A1314

1981, Aug. 19 Engr. *Perf. 11*

1927 A1314 18c blue & black		.40	.20
a.	Imperf., pair	400.	
b.	Vert. pair, imperf. horiz.	2,500.	

American Architecture

New York University Library by Sanford White
A1315

Biltmore House by Richard Morris Hunt
A1316

Palace of the Arts by Bernard Maybeck
A1317

National Farmer's Bank by Louis Sullivan
A1318

1981, Aug. 28 Engr. *Perf. 11*

1928 A1315 18c black & red		.40	.20
1929 A1316 18c black & red		.40	.20
1930 A1317 18c black & red		.40	.20
1931 A1318 18c black & red		.40	.20
a.	Block of 4, #1928-1931	1.65	1.50

Athletes

Mildred Didrikson Zaharias
A1319

Robert Tyre Jones
A1320

1981, Sept. 22 Engr. *Perf. 10½x11*

1932 A1319 18c purple	.35	.20
1933 A1320 18c green	.35	.20

Frederic Remington, 1861-1909

Coming Through the Rye — A1321

1981, Oct. 9 *Perf. 11*

1934 A1321 18c gray, green & brown		.35	.20
a.	Vert. pair, imperf. btwn.	275.00	
b.	Brown omitted	500.00	

James Hoban, 1762?-1831

Irish-American Architect of White House — A1322

1981, Oct. 13 Photo. *Perf. 11*

1935 A1322 18c multicolored	.35	.20
1936 A1322 20c multicolored	.35	.20

See Ireland No. 504.

American Bicentennial

Battle of Yorktown
A1323

Battle of Virginia Capes
A1324

Litho. & Engr.

1981, Oct. 16 *Perf. 11*

1937 A1323 18c multicolored		.35	.20
1938 A1324 18c multicolored		.35	.20
a.	Pair, #1937-1938	.90	.75
b.	As "a," black (engr., inscriptions) omitted	400.00	

Christmas

Madonna and Child, Botticelli
A1325

Felt Bear on Sled
A1326

1981, Oct. 28 Photo. *Perf. 11*

1939 A1325 (20c) multicolored		.40	.20
a.	Imperf., pair	125.	
b.	Vert. pair, imperf. horiz.	1,650.	
1940 A1326 (20c) multicolored		.40	.20
a.	Imperf., pair	325.	
b.	Vert. pair, imperf. horiz.	2,500.	

John Hanson, 1721-1783

First President of Continental Congress — A1327

1981, Nov. 5 Photo. *Perf. 11*

1941 A1327 20c multicolored	.40	.20

Desert Plants

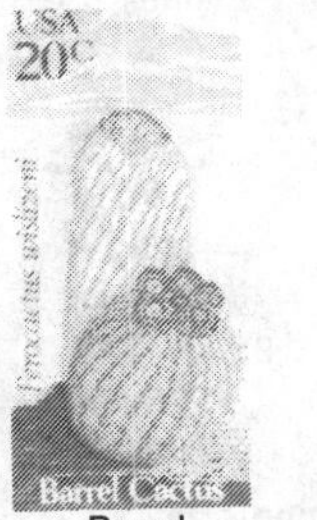

Barrel Cactus — A1328

Saguaro — A1331

Agave — A1329

Beavertail Cactus — A1330

1981, Dec. 11 Litho. & Engr.

1942 A1328 20c multicolored	.35	.20
1943 A1329 20c multicolored	.35	.20
1944 A1330 20c multicolored	.35	.20

1945 A1331 20c multicolored		.35	.20
a.	Block of 4, #1942-1945	1.50	1.25
b.	As "a," deep brown omitted	7,500.	
c.	No. 1945 imperf., vert. pair	5,250.	

A1332 A1333 A1334

1981, Oct. 11 Photo. *Perf. 11x10½*

1946 A1332 (20c) brown	.40	.20

Coil Stamp

Perf. 10 Vert.

1947 A1332 (20c) brown		.60	.20
a.	Imperf., pair	1,500.	

Booklet Stamp

Perf. 11x10½

1948 A1333 (20c) brown		.40	.20
a.	Booklet pane of 10	4.50	3.00

1982, Jan. 8 Engr. *Perf. 11*

1949 A1334 20c dk blue (from bklt. pane)		.50	.20
a.	Booklet pane of 10	5.00	2.50
b.	As "a," vert. imperf. btwn.	110.00	
c.	Type II	.50	.20
d.	As "c," booklet pane of 10	10.00	—

No. 1949 is 18¾mm wide and has overall tagging. No. 1949c is 18½mm wide and has block tagging.

See No. 1880.

Franklin Delano Roosevelt

A1335

1982, Jan. 30 Engr. *Perf. 11*

1950 A1335 20c blue	.40	.20

A1336

1982, Feb. 1 Photo. *Perf. 11x10½*

1951 A1336 20c multicolored		.65	.20
a.	Perf. 11	.40	.20
b.	Imperf., pair	300.00	
c.	Blue omitted	225.00	
d.	Yellow omitted	—	
e.	Purple omitted	—	

No. 1951c is valued in the grade of fine.

A1337 A1338-A1387

George Washington

1982, Feb. 22 Photo. *Perf. 11*

1952 A1337 20c multicolored	.40	.20

State Birds & Flowers

1982, Apr. 14 Photo. *Perf. 10½x11*

1953 A1338 20c Alabama	.50	.25
1954 A1339 20c Alaska	.50	.25
1955 A1340 20c Arizona	.50	.25
1956 A1341 20c Arkansas	.50	.25
1957 A1342 20c California	.50	.25
1958 A1343 20c Colorado	.50	.25
1959 A1344 20c Connecticut	.50	.25
1960 A1345 20c Delaware	.50	.25
1961 A1346 20c Florida	.50	.25
1962 A1347 20c Georgia	.50	.25
1963 A1348 20c Hawaii	.50	.25
1964 A1349 20c Idaho	.50	.25
1965 A1350 20c Illinois	.50	.25
1966 A1351 20c Indiana	.50	.25
1967 A1352 20c Iowa	.50	.25
1968 A1353 20c Kansas	.50	.25
1969 A1354 20c Kentucky	.50	.25
1970 A1355 20c Louisiana	.50	.25

1971	A1356	20c	Maine	.50	.25
1972	A1357	20c	Maryland	.50	.25
1973	A1358	20c	Massachusetts	.50	.25
1974	A1359	20c	Michigan	.50	.25
1975	A1360	20c	Minnesota	.50	.25
1976	A1361	20c	Mississippi	.50	.25
1977	A1362	20c	Missouri	.50	.25
1978	A1363	20c	Montana	.50	.25
1979	A1364	20c	Nebraska	.50	.25
1980	A1365	20c	Nevada	.50	.25
1981	A1366	20c	New Hampshire	.50	.25
1982	A1367	20c	New Jersey	.50	.25
1983	A1368	20c	New Mexico	.50	.25
1984	A1369	20c	New York	.50	.25
1985	A1370	20c	North Carolina	.50	.25
1986	A1371	20c	North Dakota	.50	.25
1987	A1372	20c	Ohio	.50	.25
1988	A1373	20c	Oklahoma	.50	.25
1989	A1374	20c	Oregon	.50	.25
1990	A1375	20c	Pennsylvania	.50	.25
1991	A1376	20c	Rhode Island	.50	.25
1992	A1377	20c	South Carolina	.50	.25
1993	A1378	20c	South Dakota	.50	.25
1994	A1379	20c	Tennessee	.50	.25
1995	A1380	20c	Texas	.50	.25
1996	A1381	20c	Utah	.50	.25
1997	A1382	20c	Vermont	.50	.25
1998	A1383	20c	Virginia	.50	.25
1999	A1384	20c	Washington	.50	.25
2000	A1385	20c	West Virginia	.50	.25
2001	A1386	20c	Wisconsin	.50	.25
2002	A1387	20c	Wyoming	.50	.25
a.			#1953a-2002a, any single, perf. 11	.55	.30
b.			Pane of 50, perf. 10½x11	25.00	—
c.			Pane of 50, perf. 11	27.50	—
d.			Pane of 50, imperf.	*27,500.*	

US-Netherlands

200th Anniv. of Diplomatic Recognition by the Netherlands
A1388

1982, Apr. 20 Photo. *Perf. 11*

2003 A1388 20c ver, brt blue & gray black .40 .20
a. Imperf., pair *325.00*

See Netherlands Nos. 640-641.

Library of Congress

A1389

1982, Apr. 21 Engr. *Perf. 11*

2004 A1389 20c red & black .40 .20

Consumer Education

A1390

Coil Stamp

1982, Apr. 27 Engr. *Perf. 10 Vert.*

2005 A1390 20c sky blue .55 .20
a. Imperf., pair *100.00*

Knoxville World's Fair

A1391

A1392

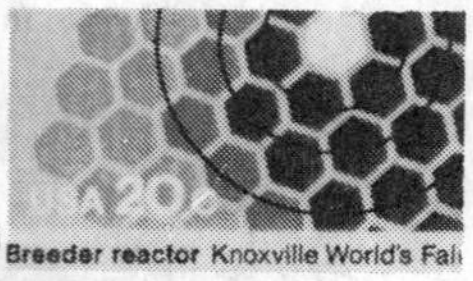

A1393

A1394

1982, Apr. 29 Photo. *Perf. 11*

2006 A1391 20c multicolored .40 .20
2007 A1392 20c multicolored .40 .20
2008 A1393 20c multicolored .40 .20
2009 A1394 20c multicolored .40 .20
a. Block of 4, #2006-2009 1.65 1.50

American Author, 1832-1899

Frontispiece from "Ragged Dick" — A1395

1982, Apr. 30 Engr. *Perf. 11*

2010 A1395 20c red & black, *tan* .40 .20
a. Red & Black omitted —

The Philatelic Foundation has issued a certificate for a pane of 50 with red and black colors omitted. Recognition of this error is by the paper and by a tiny residue of red ink from the tagging roller. The engraved plates did not strike the paper.

Aging Together

A1396

1982, May 21 *Perf. 11*

2011 A1396 20c brown .40 .20

A1397

A1398

Performing Arts

Design: Actors John, Ethel & Lionel Barrymore.

1982, June 8 Photo. *Perf. 11*

2012 A1397 20c multicolored .40 .20

Dr. Mary E. Walker, 1832-1919

1982, June 10 Photo. *Perf. 11*

2013 A1398 20c multicolored .40 .20

International Peace Garden

A1399

1982, June 30 Photo. *Perf. 11*

2014 A1399 20c multicolored .40 .20
a. Black & green (engr.) omitted *275.00*

A1400

A1401

America's Libraries

1982, July 13 Engr. *Perf. 11*

2015 A1400 20c red & black .40 .20
a. Vert. pair, imperf. horiz. *300.00*

Jackie Robinson, 1919-1972

1982, Aug. 2 Photo. *Perf. 10½x11*

2016 A1401 20c multicolored 1.10 .20

Touro Synagogue

A1402

Photogravure, Engraved

1982, Aug. 22 *Perf. 11*

2017 A1402 20c multicolored .40 .20
a. Imperf., pair *2,500.*

Wolf Trap Farm Park

A1403

1982, Sept. 1 Photo. *Perf. 11*

2018 A1403 20c multicolored .40 .20

American Architecture

Fallingwater, Mill Run, Pa., by Frank Lloyd Wright — A1404

Illinois Institute of Technology by Ludwig Mies van der Rohe A1405

Gropius House, Lincoln, Mass., by Walter Gropius A1406

Dulles Airport, by Eero Saarinen A1407

1982, Sept. 30 Engr. *Perf. 11*

2019 A1404 20c black & brown .40 .20
2020 A1405 20c black & brown .40 .20
2021 A1406 20c black & brown .40 .20
2022 A1407 20c black & brown .40 .20
a. Block of 4, #2019-2022 1.75 1.60

St. Francis of Assisi, 1182-1226

A1408

1982, Oct. 7 Photo. *Perf. 11*

2023 A1408 20c multicolored .40 .20

Ponce de Leon, 1527-1591

A1409

1982, Oct. 12 Photo. *Perf. 11*

2024 A1409 20c multicolored .40 .20
a. Imperf., pair *500.00*
b. Vert. pair, Imperf. btwn. and at top —

Christmas

A1410

A1411

A1412

A1413

A1414

A1415

1982, Nov. 3 Photo. *Perf. 11*

2025 A1410 13c multicolored .25 .20
a. Imperf., pair *650.00*

1982, Oct. 28

2026 A1411 20c multicolored .40 .20
a. Imperf., pair *150.00*
b. Horiz. pair, imperf. vert. —
c. Vert. pair, imperf. horiz. —
2027 A1412 20c multicolored .45 .20
2028 A1413 20c multicolored .45 .20
2029 A1414 20c multicolored .45 .20
2030 A1415 20c multicolored .45 .20
a. Block of 4, #2027-2030 2.00 1.50
b. As "a," imperf. *2,750.*
c. As "a," imperf. horiz. *3,250.*
Nos. 2025-2030 (6) 2.45 1.20

Science & Industry

A1416

Litho. & Engr.

1983, Jan. 19 ***Perf. 11***
2031 A1416 20c multicolored .40 .20
a. Black (engr.) omitted *1,400.*

Balloons

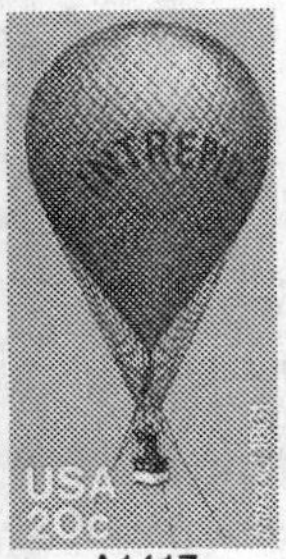

A1417

A1420

A1418

A1419

1983, Mar. 31 **Photo.** ***Perf. 11***
2032 A1417 20c multicolored .40 .20
2033 A1418 20c multicolored .40 .20
2034 A1419 20c multicolored .40 .20
2035 A1420 20c multicolored .40 .20
a. Block of 4, #2032-2035 1.65 1.50
b. As "a," imperf. *4,250.*
c. As "a," right stamp perf., otherwise imperf. *4,500.*

US-Sweden

A1421

1983, Mar. 24 **Engr.** ***Perf. 11***
2036 A1421 20c multicolored .40 .20

See Sweden No. 1453.

Civilian Conservation Corps

A1422

1983, Apr. 5 **Photo.** ***Perf. 11***
2037 A1422 20c multicolored .40 .20
a. Imperf., pair *2,750.*
b. Vert. pair, imperf. horiz. —

Joseph Priestley, 1733-1804

A1423

1983, Apr. 13 **Photo.** ***Perf. 11***
2038 A1423 20c multicolored .40 .20

Voluntarism

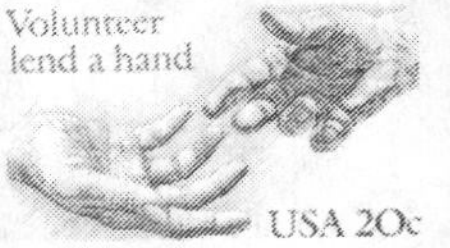

A1424

1983, Apr. 20 **Engr.** ***Perf. 11***
2039 A1424 20c red & black .40 .20
a. Imperf., pair *800.00*

US-Germany

Concord, 1683
A1425

1983, Apr. 29 ***Perf. 11***
2040 A1425 20c brown .40 .20

See Germany No. 1397.

Brooklyn Bridge

A1426

1983, May 17 **Engr.** ***Perf. 11***
2041 A1426 20c blue .40 .20

T.V.A.

A1427

Photo. & Engr.

1983, May 18 ***Perf. 11***
2042 A1427 20c multicolored .40 .20

Physical Fitness

A1428

1983, May 14 **Photo.** ***Perf. 11***
2043 A1428 20c multicolored .40 .20

Scott Joplin, 1868-1917

A1429

1983, June 9 **Photo.**
2044 A1429 20c multicolored .40 .20
a. Imperf., pair *475.00*

Medal of Honor

A1430

Litho. & Engr.

1983, June 7 ***Perf. 11***
2045 A1430 20c multicolored .40 .20
a. Red omitted *300.00*

A1431

A1432

George Herman Ruth, 1895-1948

1983, July 6 **Engr.** ***Perf. 10½x11***
2046 A1431 20c blue 1.10 .20

Nathaniel Hawthorne, 1804-1864

1983, July 8 **Photo.** ***Perf. 11***
2047 A1432 20c multicolored .40 .20

1984 Summer Olympics

Discus
A1433

High Jump
A1434

Archery
A1435

Boxing
A1436

1983, July 28 **Photo.** ***Perf. 11***
2048 A1433 13c multicolored .35 .20
2049 A1434 13c multicolored .35 .20
2050 A1435 13c multicolored .35 .20
2051 A1436 13c multicolored .35 .20
a. Block of 4, #2048-2051 1.50 1.25

Signing of Treaty of Paris

John Adams, Franklin, John Jay, David Hartley
A1437

1983, Sept. 2 **Photo.** ***Perf. 11***
2052 A1437 20c multicolored .40 .20

Civil Service

A1438

1983, Sept. 9 **Photo. & Engr.**
2053 A1438 20c buff, blue & red .40 .20

Metropolitan Opera

A1439

1983, Sept. 14 **Litho. & Engr.**
2054 A1439 20c yellow & maroon .40 .20

American Inventors

A1440

A1441

A1442

A1443

1983, Sept. 21 **Litho. & Engr**
2055 A1440 20c multicolored .40 .20
2056 A1441 20c multicolored .40 .20
2057 A1442 20c multicolored .40 .20
2058 A1443 20c multicolored .40 .20
a. Block of 4, #2055-2058 1.60 1.25
b. As "a," black omitted *400.00*

Streetcars

A1444

A1445

A1446

A1447

1983, Oct. 8 — Photo. & Engr.

2059 A1444 20c multicolored	.40	.20
2060 A1445 20c multicolored	.40	.20
2061 A1446 20c multicolored	.40	.20
2062 A1447 20c multicolored	.40	.20
a. Block of 4, #2059-2062	1.70	1.40
b. As "a," black omitted	*425.00*	
c. As "a," black omitted on #2059, 2061	—	

Christmas

A1448

A1449

1983, Oct. 28 — Photo. — *Perf. 11*

2063 A1448 20c multicolored	.40	.20
2064 A1449 20c multicolored	.40	.20
a. Imperf., pair	*175.00*	

A1450

Caribou and Alaska Pipeline — A1451

Martin Luther, 1483-1546

1983, Nov. 11 — Photo. — *Perf. 11*

2065 A1450 20c multicolored .40 .20

25th Anniv. of Alaska Statehood

1984, Jan. 3 — Photo. — *Perf. 11*

2066 A1451 20c multicolored .40 .20

Winter Olympic Games

Ice Dancing A1452 — Downhill Skiing A1453

Cross-country Skiing A1454 — Hockey A1455

1984, Jan. 6 — *Perf. 10½x11*

2067 A1452 20c multicolored	.45	.20
2068 A1453 20c multicolored	.45	.20
2069 A1454 20c multicolored	.45	.20
2070 A1455 20c multicolored	.45	.20
a. Block of 4, #2067-2070	1.85	1.50

14th Winter Olympic Games, Sarajevo, Yugoslavia, Feb. 8-19.

A1456 — A1457

Federal Deposit Insurance Corp., 50th Anniv.

1984, Jan. 12 — *Perf. 11*

2071 A1456 20c multicolored .40 .20

Love

1984, Jan. 31 — Photo. & Engr.

2072 A1457 20c multicolored	.40	.20
a. Horiz. pair, imperf. vert.	*175.00*	

Carter G. Woodson (1875-1950), Writer — A1458 — A1459

Black Heritage Issue

1984, Feb. 1 — Photo.

2073 A1458 20c multicolored	.40	.20
a. Horiz. pair, imperf. vert.	*1,600.*	

Soil and Water Conservation

1984, Feb. 6

2074 A1459 20c multicolored .40 .20

50th Anniv. of Credit Union Act

Dollar Sign, Coin — A1460

1984, Feb. 10 — Photo. — *Perf. 11*

2075 A1460 20c multicolored .40 .20

Orchids

A1461 — A1462

A1463 — A1464

1984, Mar. 5

2076 A1461 20c Wild pink	.45	.20
2077 A1462 20c Yellow lady's-slipper	.45	.20
2078 A1463 20c Spreading pogonia	.45	.20
2079 A1464 20c Pacific calypso	.45	.20
a. Block of 4, #2076-2079	1.85	1.50

25th Anniv. of Hawaii Statehood

Eastern Polynesian Canoe, Golden Plover, Mauna Loa Volcano A1465

1984, Mar. 12 — Photo. — *Perf. 11*

2080 A1465 20c multicolored .40 .20

National Archives

Abraham Lincoln, George Washington — A1466

1984, Apr. 16 — Photo. — *Perf. 11*

2081 A1466 20c multicolored .40 .20

1984 Los Angeles Olympics

Diving A1467 — Long Jump A1468

Wrestling A1469 — Kayak A1470

1984, May 4 — *Perf. 11*

2082 A1467 20c multicolored	.50	.20
2083 A1468 20c multicolored	.50	.20
2084 A1469 20c multicolored	.50	.20
2085 A1470 20c multicolored	.50	.20
a. Block of 4, #2082-2085	2.25	1.90
b. As "a," imperf. btwn. vert.	—	

New Orleans World Exposition

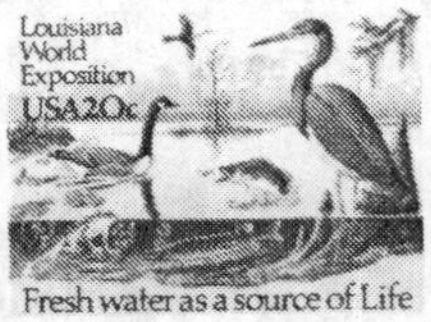

River Wildlife A1471

1984, May 11 — *Perf. 11*

2086 A1471 20c multicolored .40 .20

Health Research

Lab Equipment A1472

1984, May 17 — *Perf. 11*

2087 A1472 20c multicolored .40 .20

Actor Douglas Fairbanks (1883-1939) A1473

A1474

Performing Arts

1984, May 23 — Photo. & Engr.

2088 A1473 20c multicolored	.40	.20
b. Horiz. pair, imperf btwn.	—	

Jim Thorpe, 1888-1953

1984, May 24 — Engr. — *Perf. 11*

2089 A1474 20c dark brown .40 .20

Performing Arts

Tenor John McCormack (1884-1945) — A1475

1984, June 6 — Photo. — *Perf. 11*

2090 A1475 20c multicolored .40 .20

See Ireland No. 594.

25th Anniv. of St. Lawrence Seaway

Aerial View of Seaway, Freighters A1476

1984, June 26 — Photo. — *Perf. 11*

2091 A1476 20c multicolored .40 .20

50th Anniv. of Waterfowl Preservation Act

"Mallards Dropping In," by Jay N. Darling A1477

1984, July 2 — Engr. — *Perf. 11*

2092 A1477 20c blue	.50	.20
a. Horiz. pair, imperf. vert.	*400.00*	

See No. RW1.

A1478 — Author — A1479

Roanoke Voyages

1984, July 13 — Photo. — *Perf. 11*

2093 A1478 20c multicolored .40 .20

Herman Melville (1819-1891)

1984, Aug. 1 Engr. *Perf. 11*
2094 A1479 20c sage green .40 .20

Horace Moses (1862-1947)

Junior Achievement Founder — A1480

1984, Aug. 6 Engr.
2095 A1480 20c orange & dk brown .45 .20

Smokey Bear — A1481

Clemente, Puerto Rican Flag — A1482

1984, Aug. 13 Litho. & Engr.
2096 A1481 20c multicolored .40 .20
- *a.* Horiz. pair, imperf. btwn. *300.*
- *b.* Vert. pair, imperf. btwn. *250.*
- *c.* Block of 4, imperf. btwn, vert. and horiz. *5,500.*
- *d.* Horiz. pair, imperf. vert. *1,750.*

Roberto Clemente (1934-1972)

1984, Aug. 17 Photo. *Perf. 11*
2097 A1482 20c multicolored 1.40 .20
- *a.* Horiz. pair, imperf. vert. *2,000.*

Dogs

Beagle, Boston Terrier A1483

Chesapeake Bay Retriever, Cocker Spaniel — A1484

Alaskan Malamute, Collie A1485

Black & Tan Coonhound, American Foxhound — A1486

1984, Sept. 7 Photo. *Perf. 11*
2098 A1483 20c multicolored .40 .20
2099 A1484 20c multicolored .40 .20
2100 A1485 20c multicolored .40 .20
2101 A1486 20c multicolored .40 .20
- *a.* Block of 4, #2098-2101 1.75 1.75

Crime Prevention

McGruff, The Crime Dog — A1487

1984, Sept. 26 Photo. *Perf. 11*
2102 A1487 20c multicolored .40 .20

Hispanic Americans

A1488

1984, Oct. 31 Photo. *Perf. 11*
2103 A1488 20c multicolored .40 .20
- *a.* Vert. pair, imperf. horiz. *2,000.*

A1489

A1490

Family Unity

1984, Oct. 1 Photo. & Engr.
2104 A1489 20c multicolored .40 .20
- *a.* Horiz. pair, imperf. vert. *550.00*
- *c.* Vert. pair, imperf. btwn. and at bottom —
- *d.* Horiz. pair, imperf. between —

Eleanor Roosevelt

1984, Oct. 11 Engr. *Perf. 11*
2105 A1490 20c deep blue .40 .20

Nation of Readers

Lincoln, Son Tad — A1491

1984, Oct. 16 Engr. *Perf. 11*
2106 A1491 20c brown & maroon .40 .20

Christmas

Madonna and Child by Fra Filippo Lippi — A1492

Santa Claus — A1493

1984, Oct. 30 Photo. *Perf. 11*
2107 A1492 20c multicolored .40 .20
2108 A1493 20c multicolored .40 .20
- *a.* Horiz. pair, imperf. vert. *950.00*

No. 2108a is valued in the grade of fine.

Vietnam Veterans Memorial

Memorial Wall — A1494

1984, Nov. 10 Engr. *Perf. 10½*
2109 A1494 20c multicolored .40 .20

Performing Arts

Composer Jerome Kern (1885-1945) — A1495

1985, Jan. 23 Photo. *Perf. 11*
2110 A1495 22c multicolored .40 .20

A1496

A1497

1985, Feb. 1 Photo. *Perf. 11*
2111 A1496 (22c) green .55 .20
- *a.* Vert. pair, imperf. *40.*
- *b.* Vert. pair, imperf. horiz. *1,350.*

Coil Stamp
Perf. 10 Vert.

2112 A1496 (22c) green .60 .20
- *a.* Imperf., pair 47.50

Booklet Stamp
Perf. 11

2113 A1497 (22c) green .80 .20
- *a.* Booklet pane of 10 8.50 *3.00*
- *b.* As "a," imperf. btwn. horiz. —

A1498

Flag over Capitol Dome A1499

1985, Mar. 29 Engr. *Perf. 11*
2114 A1498 22c blue, red & black .40 .20

Coil Stamp
Perf. 10 Vert.

2115 A1498 22c blue, red & black .40 .20
- *a.* Imperf., pair 15.00
- *b.* Inscribed "T" at bottom ('87) .50 .20
- *c.* Black field of stars

Booklet Stamp
Perf. 10 Horiz. on 1 or 2 Sides

2116 A1499 22c blue, red & black .50 .20
- *a.* Booklet pane of 5 2.50 *1.25*

Seashells

Frilled Dogwinkle A1500

Reticulated Helmet A1501

New England Neptune A1502

Calico Scallop A1503

Lightning Whelk — A1504

1985, Apr. 4 Engr. *Perf. 10*
Booklet Stamps

2117 A1500 22c black & brown .40 .20
2118 A1501 22c multicolored .40 .20
2119 A1502 22c black & brown .40 .20
2120 A1503 22c black & violet .40 .20
2121 A1504 22c multicolored .40 .20
- *a.* Booklet pane of 10, 2 ea #2117-2121 4.00 *2.50*
- *b.* As "a," violet omitted *850.00*
- *c.* As "a," vert. imperf. btwn. *600.00*
- *d.* As "a," imperf. —
- *e.* Strip of 5, #2117-2121 2.00 —

Eagle and Half Moon A1505

Type I. Washed out, dull appearance most evident in the black of the body of the eagle, and the red in the background between the eagle's shoulder and the moon. "$10.75" appears splotchy or grainy (P# 11111).

Type II. Brighter, more intense colors most evident in the black on the eagle's body, and red in the background. "$10.75" appears smoother, brighter, and less grainy (P# 22222).

Perf. 10 Vert. on 1 or 2 Sides
1985, Apr. 29 Photo. Untagged

2122 A1505 $10.75 multi, type I 17.00 7.00
- *a.* Booklet pane of 3 52.50 —
- *b.* Type II 17.00 —
- *c.* As "b," booklet pane of 3 52.50 —

Issued in booklets only.

Transportation Coils

A1506

A1507

A1508

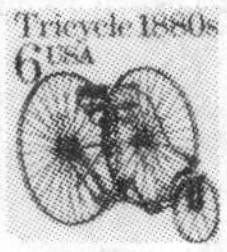

A1509

A1510

A1511

A1512

A1513

A1514

A1515

A1516

A1517

A1518

A1519

1985-87 Engr. *Perf. 10 Vert.*

2123 A1506 3.4c dk bluish green .20 .20
- *a.* Untagged (Bureau precanceled) .20 .20

2124 A1507 4.9c brn blk .20 .20
- *a.* Untagged (Bureau precanceled) .20 .20

2125 A1508 5.5c deep mag .20 .20
- *a.* Untagged (Bureau precanceled) .20 .20

2126 A1509 6c red brown .20 .20
- *a.* Untagged (Bureau precanceled) .20 .20
- *b.* As "a," imperf., pair 200.00

2127 A1510 7.1c lake .20 .20
- *a.* Untagged (Bureau precanceled) .20 .20

2128 A1511 8.3c green .20 .20
- *a.* Untagged (Bureau precanceled) .20 .20

For similar stamp see No. 2231.

2129 A1512 8.5c dk Prus green .20 .20
- *a.* Untagged (Bureau precanceled) .20 .20

2130 A1513 10.1c slate blue .25 .20
- *a.* Untagged (Bureau precanceled) .25 .25
- *b.* As "a," imperf., pair (red precancel) 15.00
- As "b," black precancel *100.00*

2131 A1514 11c dk green .25 .20

2132 A1515 12c dk bl, type I .25 .20
- *a.* Untagged (Bureau precanceled) .25 .25
- *b.* Type II, untagged (Bureau precanceled) .25 .25

Type II has "Stanley Steamer 1909" ½mm shorter (17½mm) than No. 2132 (18mm).

2133 A1516 12.5c olive green .25 .20
- *a.* Untagged (Bureau precanceled) .25 .25
- *b.* As "a," imperf., pair 55.00

2134 A1517 14c sky bl, type I .30 .20
- *a.* Imperf., pair 100.00
- *b.* Type II .30 .20

Type II design is ¼mm narrower (17¼mm) than No. 2134 (17½mm) and has block tagging. No. 2134 has overall tagging.

2135 A1518 17c sky blue .30 .20
- *a.* Imperf., pair *500.00*

2136 A1519 25c org brown .45 .20
- *a.* Imperf., pair 10.00
- *b.* Pair, imperf. between —

Nos. 2123-2136 (14) 3.45 2.80

Years of issue: 3.4c, 4.9c, 6c, 8.3c, 10.1c-14c, 1985. 5.5c, 17c, 25c, 1986. 7.1c, 8.5c, 1987.

See Nos. 1897-1908, 2225-2231, 2252-2266, 2451-2468.

Black Heritage Issue

Mary McLeod Bethune (1875-1955), Educator — A1520

1985, Mar. 5 Photo. *Perf. 11*

2137 A1520 22c multicolored .40 .20

Duck Decoys

Broadbill A1521

Mallard A1522

Canvasback A1523

Redhead A1524

1985, Mar. 22 Photo. *Perf. 11*

2138 A1521 22c multicolored .60 .20
2139 A1522 22c multicolored .60 .20
2140 A1523 22c multicolored .60 .20
2141 A1524 22c multicolored .60 .20
- *a.* Block of 4, #2138-2141 3.75 2.25

Winter Special Olympics

Ice Skater, Emblem, Skier A1525

1985, Mar. 25 Photo. *Perf. 11*

2142 A1525 22c multicolored .40 .20
- *a.* Vert. pair, imperf. horiz. *600.00*

Love

A1526

1985, Apr. 17 Photo.

2143 A1526 22c multicolored .40 .20
- *a.* Imperf., pair *1,500.*

Rural Electrification Administration

Electrified Farm A1527

1985, May 11 Photo. & Engr.

2144 A1527 22c multicolored .45 .20
- *a.* Vert. pair, imperf. btwn. —

AMERIPEX '86

US No. 134 — A1528

1985, May 25 Litho. & Engr.

2145 A1528 22c multicolored .40 .20
- *a.* Red, black & blue omitted *200.*
- *b.* Red & black omitted *1,250.*
- *c.* Red omitted —

US First Lady

Abigail Adams (1744-1818) — A1529

1985, June 14 Litho. *Perf. 11*

2146 A1529 22c multicolored .40 .20
- *a.* Imperf., pair *275.00*

Architect, Sculptor

Frederic Auguste Bartholdi (1834-1904), Statue of Liberty A1530

1985, July 18 Litho. & Engr.

2147 A1530 22c multicolored .40 .20
- *a.* Black (engr.) omitted —

Examples exist with most, but not all, of the engraved black omitted. Expertization of No. 2147a is recommended.

George Washington, Washington Monument A1532

Envelopes A1533

COIL STAMPS

1985 Photo. *Perf. 10 Vert.*

2149 A1532 18c multicolored .35 .20
- *a.* Untagged (Bureau precanceled) .35 .35
- *b.* Imperf., pair *950.00*
- *c.* As "a," imperf., pair *800.00*

2150 A1533 21.1c multicolored .40 .20
- *a.* Untagged (Bureau precanceled) .40 .40

Issue dates: 18c, Nov. 6; 21.1c, Oct. 22.

Precancellations on Nos. 2149a ("PRESORTED FIRST CLASS"), 2150a ("ZIP+4") do not have lines.

Korean War Veterans

American Troops in Korea A1535

1985, July 26 Engr. *Perf. 11*

2152 A1535 22c gray grn & rose red .40 .20

Social Security Act, 50th Anniv.

Men, Women, Children, Corinthian Columns A1536

1985, Aug. 14 Photo. *Perf. 11*

2153 A1536 22c deep blue & lt blue .40 .20

World War I Veterans

The Battle of Marne, France, by Harvey Dunn A1537

1985, Aug. 26 Engr. *Perf. 11*

2154 A1537 22c gray grn & rose red .40 .20

Horses

Quarter Horse A1538

Morgan A1539

Saddlebred A1540

Appaloosa A1541

1985, Sept. 25 Photo. *Perf. 11*

2155 A1538 22c multicolored .90 .20
2156 A1539 22c multicolored .90 .20
2157 A1540 22c multicolored .90 .20
2158 A1541 22c multicolored .90 .20
- *a.* Block of 4, #2155-2158 5.50 4.50

Public Education in America

Quill Pen, Apple, Spectacles, Penmanship Quiz — A1542

1985, Oct. 1 Photo. *Perf. 11*

2159 A1542 22c multicolored .45 .20

International Youth Year

YMCA Youth Camping, Cent. A1543

Boy Scouts, 75th Anniv. A1544

Big Brothers/Big Sisters Fed., 40th Anniv. A1545

Camp Fire, Inc., 75th Anniv. A1546

1985, Oct. 7 Photo. *Perf. 11*

2160 A1543 22c multicolored	.60	.20
2161 A1544 22c multicolored	.60	.20
2162 A1545 22c multicolored	.60	.20
2163 A1546 22c multicolored	.60	.20
a. Block of 4, #2160-2163	2.75	2.25

Help End Hunger

Youths and the Elderly Suffering from Malnutrition
A1547

1985, Oct. 15 Photo.

2164 A1547 22c multicolored	.45	.20

Christmas

Genoa Madonna, Enameled Terra-Cotta by Luca Della Robbia (1400-1482) — A1548

Poinsettia Plants
A1549

1985, Oct. 30 Photo.

2165 A1548 22c multicolored	.40	.20
a. Imperf., pair	*100.00*	
2166 A1549 22c multicolored	.40	.20
a. Imperf., pair	*130.00*	

Arkansas Statehood, 150th Anniv.

Old State House, Little Rock
A1550

1986, Jan. 3 Photo. *Perf. 11*

2167 A1550 22c multicolored	.40	.20
a. Vert. pair, imperf. horiz.	—	

Great Americans

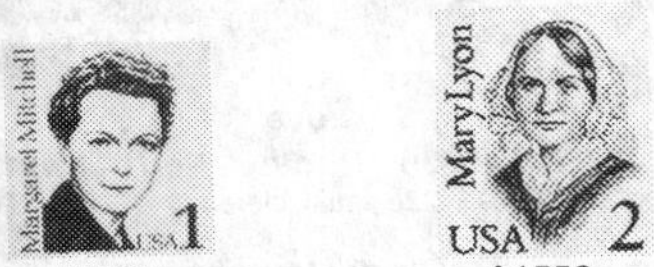

A1551 A1552

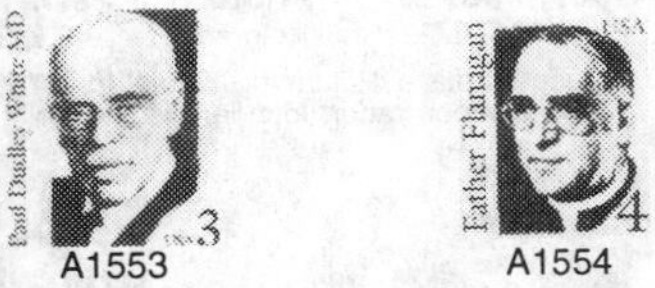

A1553 A1554

A1555 A1556

A1557 A1558

A1559 A1560

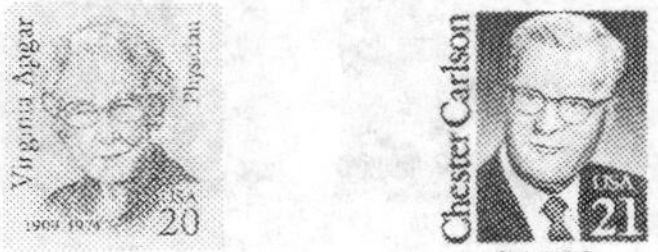

A1561 A1562

A1563 A1564

A1565 A1566

A1567 A1568

A1569 A1570

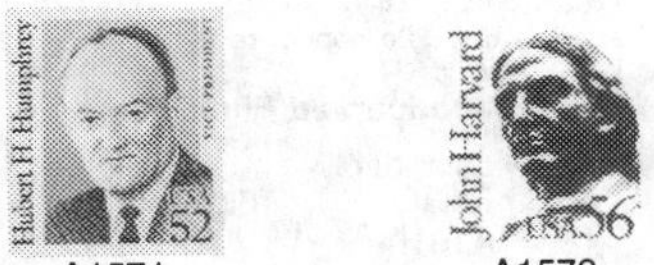

A1571 A1572

A1573 A1574

A1575 A1576

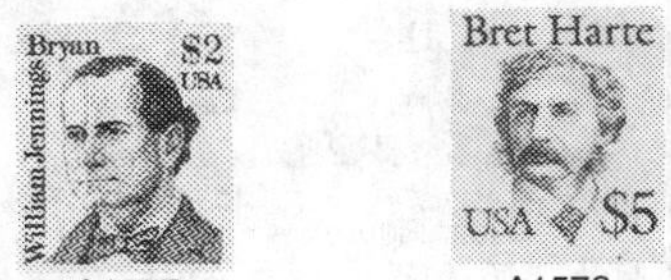

A1577 A1578

Perf. 11, 11½x11 (#2185), 11.1x11 (#2179)

1986-94 Engr.

2168 A1551 1c brnsh ver	.20	.20
2169 A1552 2c bright blue	.20	.20
a. Untagged	.20	.20
2170 A1553 3c bright blue	.20	.20
a. Untagged	.20	.20
2171 A1554 4c blue violet	.20	.20
a. 4c grayish violet, untagged	.20	.20
b. 4c deep grayish blue, untagged	.20	.20
2172 A1555 5c dk ol grn	.20	.20
2173 A1556 5c carmine	.20	.20
a. Untagged	.20	.20
2175 A1557 10c lake	.20	.20
e. 10c carmine	.25	.20
2176 A1558 14c crimson	.25	.20
2177 A1559 15c claret	.30	.20
2178 A1560 17c dull bl grn	.35	.20
2179 A1561 20c red brown	.40	.20
a. 20c orange brown	.40	.20
2180 A1562 21c blue vio	.40	.20
2181 A1563 23c purple	.45	.20
2182 A1564 25c blue	.45	.20
a. Booklet pane of 10 ('88)	4.50	*3.75*
2183 A1565 28c myrtle grn	.50	.20
2184 A1566 29c blue	.55	.20
2185 A1567 29c indigo	.50	.20
2186 A1568 35c black	.65	.20
2187 A1569 40c dark blue	.70	.20
2188 A1570 45c bright blue	.85	.20
a. 45c blue	1.65	—
2189 A1571 52c purple	1.10	.20
2190 A1572 56c scarlet	1.10	.20
2191 A1573 65c dark blue	1.20	.20
2192 A1574 75c dp magenta	1.30	.20
2193 A1575 $1 dk Prus grn	2.25	.50
2194 A1576 $1 intense deep blue	1.75	.50
b. $1 deep blue	1.75	—
d. $1 dark blue	1.75	—
e. $1 blue	1.75	—
2195 A1577 $2 brt violet	3.50	.50
2196 A1578 $5 copper red	8.00	1.00
Nos. 2168-2196 (28)	27.95	7.30

Booklet Stamp

Perf. 10 on 2 or 3 sides

2197 A1564 25c blue	.45	.20
a. Booklet pane of 6	3.00	2.25

The intense deep blue of No. 2194 is much deeper than the deep blue and dark blue of the other $1 varieties.

Issued: #2182, 1/11/86; #2172, 2/27/86; $2, 3/19/86; 17c, 6/18/86; 1c, 6/30/86; 4c, 7/14/86; 56c, 9/3/86; 3c, 9/15/86; #2193, 9/23/86; 14c, 2/12/87; 2c, 2/28/87; 10c, 8/15/87; $5, 8/25/87; #2183a, 2197, 5/3/88; 15c, 6/6/88; 45c, 6/17/88; 21c, 10/21/88; 23c, 11/4/88; 65c, 11/5/88; # 2197, 1988; #2194, 6/7/89; 28c, 9/14/89; #2173, 2/18/90; 40c, 9/6/90; #2188a, 2194b, 1990; 35c, 4/3/91; 52c, 6/3/91; 75c, 2/16/92; #2184, 3/9/92; #2194d, 1992; #2185, 4/13/93; #2171b, 2194e, 1993; 20c, 10/24/94; #2170a, 1994.

Stamp Collecting

Handstamped Cover, No. 213, Philatelic Memorabilia
A1581

Boy Examining Stamp Collection
A1582

No. 836 Under Magnifying Glass, Sweden Nos. 268, 271 — A1583

1986 Presidents Miniature Sheet — A1584

Perf. 10 Vert. on 1 or 2 Sides

1986, Jan. 23 Litho. & Engr.

Booklet Stamps

2198 A1581 22c multicolored	.45	.20
2199 A1582 22c multicolored	.45	.20
2200 A1583 22c multicolored	.45	.20
2201 A1584 22c multicolored	.45	.20
a. Bklt. pane of 4, #2198-2201	2.00	1.75
b. As "a," black omitted on #2198, 2201	55.00	
c. As "a," blue (litho.) omitted on #2198-2200	*2,500.*	
d. As "a," buff (litho.) omitted	—	

See Sweden Nos. 1585-1588.

A1585

A1586

Love

1986, Jan. 30 Photo. *Perf. 11*

2202 A1585 22c Puppy	.40	.20

Black Heritage Issue

1986, Feb. 4 Photo. *Perf. 11*

2203 A1586 22c multicolored	.40	.20

Sojourner Truth (c. 1797-1883), abolitionist.

Republic of Texas, 150th Anniv.

Texas State Flag and Silver Spur — A1587

1986, Mar. 2 Photo.

2204 A1587 22c dk bl, dk red & grysh blk	.40	.20
a. Horiz. pair, imperf. vert.	*1,100.*	
b. Dark red omitted	*2,750.*	
c. Dark blue omitted	*8,500.*	

Fish

Muskellunge — A1588

Atlantic Cod
A1589

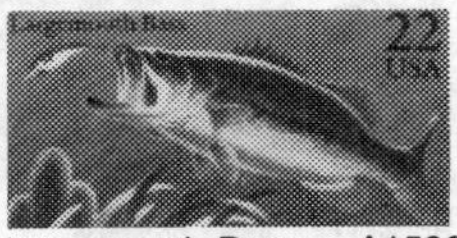

Largemouth Bass — A1590

Bluefin Tuna
A1591

Catfish
A1592

Perf. 10 Horiz. on 1 or 2 Sides

1986, Mar. 21 Photo.

Booklet Stamps

2205 A1588 22c multicolored .50 .20
2206 A1589 22c multicolored .50 .20
2207 A1590 22c multicolored .50 .20
2208 A1591 22c multicolored .50 .20
2209 A1592 22c multicolored .50 .20
a. Bklt. pane of 5, #2205-2209 4.50 *2.75*
b. As "a," red omitted —

Public Hospitals

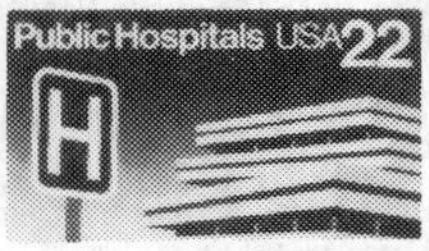

A1593

1986, Apr. 11 Photo. *Perf. 11*

2210 A1593 22c multicolored .40 .20
a. Vert. pair, imperf. horiz. *325.*
b. Horiz. pair, imperf. vert. *1,350.*

Performing Arts

Edward Kennedy "Duke" Ellington (1899-1974), Jazz Composer — A1594

1986, Apr. 29 Photo. *Perf. 11*

2211 A1594 22c multicolored .40 .20
a. Vert. pair, imperf. horiz. *1,000.* —

Miniature Sheets

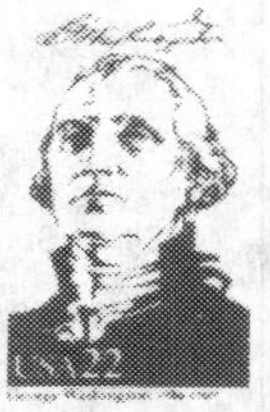

35 Presidents — A1599

No. 2216: a, Washington. b, John Adams. c, Jefferson. d, Madison. e, Monroe. f, John Quincy Adams. g, Jackson. h, Van Buren. i, Harrison.

No. 2217; a, Tyler. b, Polk. c, Taylor. d, Fillmore. e, Pierce. f, Buchanan. g, Lincoln. h, Andrew Johnson. i, Grant.

No. 2218: a, Hayes. b, Garfield. c, Arthur. d, Cleveland. e, Harrison. f, McKinley. g, Theodore Roosevelt. h, Taft. i, Wilson.

No. 2219: a, Harding. b, Coolidge. c, Hoover. d, Franklin Delano Roosevelt. e, White House. f, Truman. g, Eisenhower. h, Kennedy. i, Lyndon B. Johnson.

1986, May 22 Litho. & Engr.

2216 Sheet of 9 3.75 —
a.-i. A1599 22c any single .40 .25
j. Blue omitted *3,500.*
k. Black inscription omitted *2,000.*
l. Imperf. *10,500.*
2217 Sheet of 9 3.75 —
a.-i. A1599 22c any single .40 .25
j. Black inscription omitted *3,750.*
2218 Sheet of 9 3.75 —
a.-i. A1599 22c any single .40 .25
j. Brown omitted —
k. Black inscription omitted *3,000.*
2219 Sheet of 9 3.75 —
a.-i. A1599 22c any single .40 .25
j. Blackish blue (engr.) inscription omitted on a.-b., d.-e., g.-h. —
Nos. 2216-2219 (4) 15.00

Issued at AMERIPEX '86 Intl. Phil. Exhib., Chicago, IL, May 22-June 1.

Arctic Explorers

Elisha Kent Kane A1600

Adolphus W. Greely A1601

Vilhjalmur Stefansson — A1602

Robert E. Peary and Matthew Alexander Henson A1603

1986, May 28 Photo. *Perf. 11*

2220 A1600 22c multicolored .65 .20
2221 A1601 22c multicolored .65 .20
2222 A1602 22c multicolored .65 .20
2223 A1603 22c multicolored .65 .20
a. Block of 4, #2220-2223 2.75 2.25
b. As "a," black (engr.) omitted *9,500.*
c. As "a," #2220 & 2221 black (engr.) omitted —

Statue of Liberty, Cent. — A1604

1986, July 4 Engr. *Perf. 11*

2224 A1604 22c scarlet & dark blue .40 .20

See France No. 2014.

Transportation Coils

Types of 1982-85 and

A1604a

A1604b

1986-87 Engr. *Perf. 10 Vert.*

2225 A1604a 1c violet .20 .20
b. Untagged .20 .20
c. Imperf., pair *2,250.*
2226 A1604b 2c black ('87) .20 .20
a. Untagged .20 .20
2228 A1285 4c reddish brown .20 .20
b. Imperf., pair *300.00*
2231 A1511 8.3c grn (Bureau precancel) .20 .20
Nos. 2225-2231 (4) .80 .80

Issue dates: 1c, Nov. 26. 2c, Mar. 6. Earliest known usage of 4c, Aug. 15, 1986. 8.3c, Aug. 29.

On No. 2228 "Stagecoach 1890s" is 17½mm long, on No. 1898A 19½mm long. On No. 2231 "Ambulance 1860s" is 18mm long, on No. 2128 18½mm long.

No. 2226 inscribed "2 USA;" No. 1897A inscribed "USA 2c."

Navajo Art

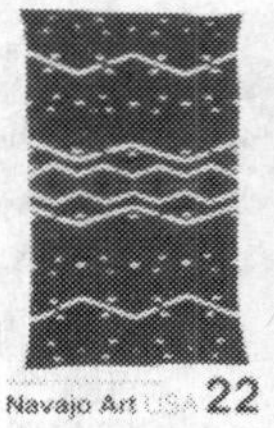

A1605

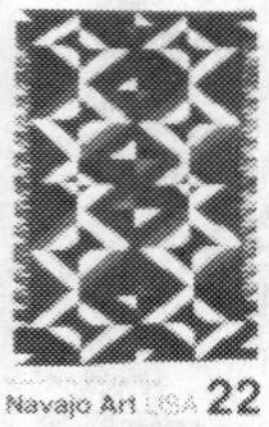

A1606

A1607

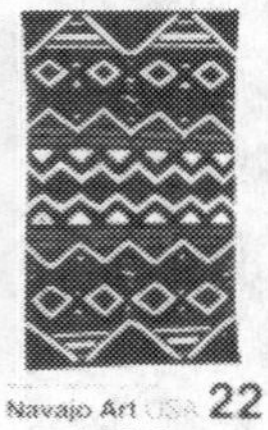

A1608

Blankets in the Museum of the American Indian and Lowe Art Museum.

Litho. & Engr.

1986, Sept. 4 *Perf. 11*

2235 A1605 22c multicolored .45 .20
2236 A1606 22c multicolored .45 .20
2237 A1607 22c multicolored .45 .20
2238 A1608 22c multicolored .45 .20
a. Block of 4, #2235-2238 2.25 2.00
b. As "a," blk (engr.) omitted *400.00*

Literary Arts

T. S. Eliot (1888-1965), Poet — A1609

1986, Sept. 26 Engr. *Perf. 11*

2239 A1609 22c copper red .40 .20

Woodcarved Figurines

Highlander Figure A1610

Ship Figurehead A1611

Nautical Figure A1612

Cigar Store Figure A1613

1986, Oct. 1 Photo. *Perf. 11*

2240 A1610 22c multicolored .40 .20
2241 A1611 22c multicolored .40 .20
2242 A1612 22c multicolored .40 .20
2243 A1613 22c multicolored .40 .20
a. Block of 4, #2240-2243 1.75 1.75
b. As "a," imperf. vert. *1,500.*

Christmas

Madonna, by Perugino (c. 1450-1523) A1614

Village Scene A1615

1986, Oct. 24 *Perf. 11*

2244 A1614 22c multicolored .40 .20
a. Imperf., pair —
2245 A1615 22c multicolored .40 .20

Michigan Statehood Sesquicent.

White Pine — A1616

1987, Jan. 26 Photo. *Perf. 11*

2246 A1616 22c multicolored .40 .20

Pan American Games, Indianapolis, August 7-25

Runner in Full Stride A1617

1987, Jan. 29 *Perf. 11*

2247 A1617 22c multicolored .40 .20
a. Silver omitted *1,500.*

No. 2247a is valued in the grade of fine.

A1618

A1619

Love

1987, Jan. 30 Photo. *Perf. 11½x11*

2248 A1618 22c multicolored .40 .20

Black Heritage

1987, Feb. 20 Photo. *Perf. 11*

2249 A1619 22c multicolored .40 .20

Jean Baptiste Pointe du Sable (c. 1750-1818), pioneer trader, founder of Chicago

A1620

A1621

Performing Arts

Enrico Caruso (1873-1921), Opera Tenor

Photo. & Engr.

1987, Feb. 27 *Perf. 11*

2250 A1620 22c multicolored .40 .20
a. Black (engr.) omitted *5,000.*

Girl Scouts, 75th Anniv.
Litho. & Engr.

1987, Mar. 12 *Perf. 11*

2251 A1621 22c 14 Achievement Badges .40 .20
- *a.* All litho. colors omitted 2,400

All known examples of No. 2251a have been expertized, and certificate must accompany purchase.

Transportation Coils

A1622

A1623

A1624

A1625

A1626

A1627

A1628

A1629

A1630

A1631

A1632

A1633

A1634

A1635

A1636

1987-88 **Engr.** *Perf. 10 Vert.*

2252 A1622 3c claret .20 .20
- *a.* Untagged .20 .20

2253 A1623 5c black .20 .20
2254 A1624 5.3c blk (Bureau precancel in scarlet) .20 .20
2255 A1625 7.6c brn (Bureau precancel in scarlet) .20 .20
2256 A1626 8.4c dp clar (Bureau precancel in red) .20 .20
- *a.* Imperf., pair 700.00

2257 A1627 10c sky blue .20 .20
2258 A1628 13c blk (Bureau precancel in red) .25 .25
2259 A1629 13.2c slate grn (Bureau precancel in red) .25 .25
- *a.* Imperf., pair 100.00

2260 A1630 15c violet .25 .20
- *c.* Imperf., pair 800.00

2261 A1631 16.7c rose (Bureau precancel in black) .30 .30
- *a.* Imperf., pair 225.00

All known copies of No. 2261a are miscut top to bottom.

2262 A1632 17.5c dark violet .30 .20
- *a.* Untagged (Bureau precancel) .30 .30
- *b.* Imperf., pair 2,250.

2263 A1633 20c blue vio .35 .20
- *a.* Imperf., pair 75.00

2264 A1634 20.5c rose (Bureau precancel in black) .40 .40
2265 A1635 21c olive grn (Bureau precancel in red) .40 .40
- *a.* Imperf., pair 65.00

2266 A1636 24.1c deep ultra (Bureau precancel) .45 .45
Nos. 2252-2266 (15) 4.15 3.85

The 5.3c, 7.6c, 8.4c, 13c, 13.2c, 16.7c, 20.5c, 21c and 24.1c are only available precanceled and are untagged.

Years of issue: 5c, 10c, 17.5c, 1987; others, 1988.

See Nos. 1897-1908, 2123-2136, 2225-2231, 2451-2468.

Special Occasions

A1637

A1638

A1639

A1640

A1641

A1642

A1643

A1644

Perf. 10 on 1, 2, or 3 sides

1987, Apr. 20 **Photo.**

Booklet Stamps

2267 A1637 22c multicolored .55 .20
2268 A1638 22c multicolored .55 .20
2269 A1639 22c multicolored .55 .20
2270 A1640 22c multicolored .55 .20
2271 A1641 22c multicolored .55 .20
2272 A1642 22c multicolored .55 .20
2273 A1643 22c multicolored .55 .20
2274 A1644 22c multicolored .55 .20
- *a.* Bklt. pane of 10, #2268-2271, 2273-2274, 2 each #2267, 2272 8.00 5.00

Nos. 2267-2274 (8) 4.40 1.60

United Way Centenary

Six Profiles A1645

Litho. & Engr.

1987, Apr. 28 *Perf. 11*

2275 A1645 22c multicolored .40 .20

A1646

A1647

A1648

A1649

Pheasant A1649a

Grosbeak A1649b

Owl A1649c

Honeybee A1649d

Photo., Engr. (No. 2280), Litho. & Engr. (No. 2281)

1987-88 *Perf. 11*

2276 A1646 22c multicolored .40 .20
- *a.* Booklet pane of 20 8.50 —
- *b.* As "a." vert. pair, imperf. btwn. —

2277 A1647 (25c) multi ('88) .45 .20
2278 A1648 25c multi ('88) .40 .20
Nos. 2276-2278 (3) 1.25 .60

Coil Stamps
Perf. 10 Vertical

2279 A1647 (25c) multi ('88) .45 .20
- *a.* Imperf., pair 90.00 —

2280 A1649 25c Green trees ('88) .45 .20
- *c.* Imperf., pair 15.00
- *e.* Black trees 100.00 —
- *f.* Pair, imperf. btwn. 800.00

2281 A1649d 25c multi ('88) .45 .20
- *a.* Imperf., pair 45.00
- *b.* Black (engr.) omitted 65.00
- *c.* Black (litho.) omitted 550.00
- *d.* Pair, imperf. between 1,000.
- *e.* Yellow (litho.) omitted 1,250.

Nos. 2279-2281 (3) 1.35 .60

Beware of copies with traces of the litho. black that are offered as No. 2281c. Vertical pairs or blocks of No. 2281 and imperfs. with the engr. black missing are from printer's waste.

No. 2280c is on prephosphored paper (mottled tagging). Imperfs are also known with large block tagging, value, unused, $35.

Booklet Stamps
Perf. 10 on 2 or 3 Sides, 11 on 2 or 3 sides (#2283)

2282 A1647 (25c) multi ('88) .50 .20
- *a.* Booklet pane of 10 6.50 3.50

Vert. pairs, imperf between, are printer's waste. Other "varieties" probably exist.

2283 A1649a 25c multi ('88) .50 .20
- *a.* Booklet pane of 10 6.00 3.50
- *b.* 25c multi, red removed from sky 6.00 .20
- *c.* As "b," booklet pane of 10 65.00 —
- *d.* As "a," horiz. imperf. between 2,250.

Imperfs. are printer's waste.

2284 A1649b 25c multi ('88) .45 .20
2285 A1649c 25c multi ('88) .45 .20
- *b.* Bklt. pane of 10, 5 each Nos. 2284-2285 4.50 3.50
- *d.* Pair, Nos. 2284-2285 1.00 .25

2285A A1648 25c multi ('88) .45 .20
- *c.* Booklet pane of 6 2.75 2.00

Nos. 2282-2285A (5) 2.35 1.00

Issued: #2276, 5/9; #2277, 2279, 2282, 3/22; #2278, 5/6; #2280, 5/20; #2281, 9/2; #2283, 4/29; #2284-2285, 5/28; #2285A, 7/5.

North American Wildlife A1650-A1699

1987, June 13 **Photo.** *Perf. 11*

2286 A1650 22c Barn swallow .85 .20
2287 A1651 22c Monarch butterfly .85 .20
2288 A1652 22c Bighorn sheep .85 .20
2289 A1653 22c Broad-tailed hummingbird .85 .20
2290 A1654 22c Cottontail .85 .20
2291 A1655 22c Osprey .85 .20
2292 A1656 22c Mountain lion .85 .20
2293 A1657 22c Luna moth .85 .20
2294 A1658 22c Mule deer .85 .20
2295 A1659 22c Gray squirrel .85 .20
2296 A1660 22c Armadillo .85 .20
2297 A1661 22c Eastern chipmunk .85 .20
2298 A1662 22c Moose .85 .20
2299 A1663 22c Black bear .85 .20
2300 A1664 22c Tiger swallowtail .85 .20
2301 A1665 22c Bobwhite .85 .20
2302 A1666 22c Ringtail .85 .20
2303 A1667 22c Red-winged blackbird .85 .20
2304 A1668 22c American lobster .85 .20
2305 A1669 22c Black-tailed jack rabbit .85 .20
2306 A1670 22c Scarlet tanager .85 .20
2307 A1671 22c Woodchuck .85 .20
2308 A1672 22c Roseate spoonbill .85 .20
2309 A1673 22c Bald eagle .85 .20
2310 A1674 22c Alaskan brown bear .85 .20
2311 A1675 22c Iiwi .85 .20
2312 A1676 22c Badger .85 .20
2313 A1677 22c Pronghorn .85 .20
2314 A1678 22c River otter .85 .20
2315 A1679 22c Ladybug .85 .20
2316 A1680 22c Beaver .85 .20
2317 A1681 22c White-tailed deer .85 .20
2318 A1682 22c Blue jay .85 .20
2319 A1683 22c Pika .85 .20
2320 A1684 22c American Buffalo .85 .20
2321 A1685 22c Snowy egret .85 .20
2322 A1686 22c Gray wolf .85 .20
2323 A1687 22c Mountain goat .85 .20
2324 A1688 22c Deer mouse .85 .20
2325 A1689 22c Black-tailed prairie dog .85 .20
2326 A1690 22c Box turtle .85 .20
2327 A1691 22c Wolverine .85 .20
2328 A1692 22c American elk .85 .20
2329 A1693 22c California sea lion .85 .20
2330 A1694 22c Mockingbird .85 .20
2331 A1695 22c Raccoon .85 .20
2332 A1696 22c Bobcat .85 .20
2333 A1697 22c Black-footed ferret .85 .20
2334 A1698 22c Canada goose .85 .20
2335 A1699 22c Red fox .85 .20
- *a.* Pane of 50, #2286-2335 47.50
- *b.* 2286b-2335b, any single, red omitted —

Ratification of the Constitution

A1700

A1701

A1702

A1703

A1704

A1705

A1706

A1707

A1708

A1709

A1710

A1711

A1712

Litho. & Engr., Photo. (#2337, 2343-2344, 2347)

1987-90 *Perf. 11*

2336 A1700 22c multi .40 .20
2337 A1701 22c multi .40 .20
2338 A1702 22c multi .40 .20
 a. Black (engr.) omitted *6,000.*
2339 A1703 22c multi ('88) .40 .20
2340 A1704 22c multi ('88) .40 .20
2341 A1705 22c dk blue & dk red ('88) .40 .20
2342 A1706 22c multi ('88) .40 .20
2343 A1707 25c multi ('88) .45 .20
 a. Strip of 3, vert. imperf. btwn. —
2344 A1708 25c multi ('88) .45 .20
2345 A1709 25c multi ('88) .45 .20
2346 A1710 25c multi ('88) .45 .20
2347 A1711 25c multi ('89) .45 .20
2348 A1712 25c multi ('90) .45 .20
 Nos. 2336-2348 (13) 5.50 2.60

Issued: #2336, 7/4; #2337, 8/26; #2238, 9/11; #2339, 1/6; #2340, 1/9; #2341, 2/6; 32342, 2/15; #2343, 5/23; #2344, 6/21; #2345, 6/25; #2346, 7/26; # 2347, 8/22; #2348, 5/29.

US-Morocco Diplomatic Relations Bicentennial

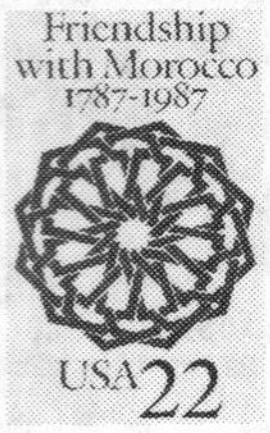

Arabesque, Dar Batha Palace, Fez — A1713

Litho. & Engr.

1987, July 18 ***Perf. 11***

2349 A1713 22c scar & blk .40 .20
 a. Black (engr.) omitted *325.00*

See Morocco No. 642.

Literary Arts

William Cuthbert Faulkner (1897-1962), Novelist — A1714

1987, Aug. 3 **Engr.** ***Perf. 11***

2350 A1714 22c bright green .40 .20

Imperfs. are from printer's waste.

Folk Art Issue

A1715

A1716

A1717

A1718

Litho. & Engr.

1987, Aug. 14 ***Perf. 11***

2351 A1715 22c ultra & white .45 .20
2352 A1716 22c ultra & white .45 .20
2353 A1717 22c ultra & white .45 .20
2354 A1718 22c ultra & white .45 .20
 a. Block of 4, #2351-2354 1.90 1.90
 b. As "a," white omitted *1,000.*

Drafting of the Constitution Bicentennial

A1719
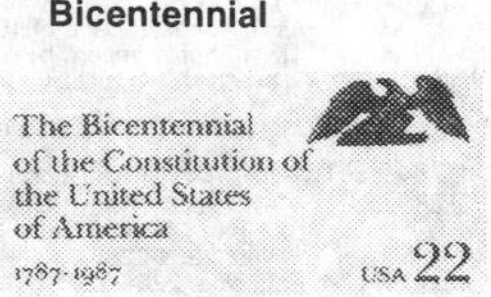

A1720

A1721

A1722

A1723

Perf. 10 Horiz. on 1 or 2 Sides

1987, Aug. 28 **Photo.**

Booklet Stamps

2355 A1719 22c multicolored .50 .20
 a. Grayish grn (background) omitted —
2356 A1720 22c multicolored .50 .20
 a. Grayish grn (background) omitted —
2357 A1721 22c multicolored .50 .20
 a. Grayish grn (background) omitted —
2358 A1722 22c multicolored .50 .20
 a. Grayish grn (background) omitted —
2359 A1723 22c multicolored .50 .20
 a. Bklt. pane of 5, #2355-2359 2.50 *2.25*
 b. Grayish grn (background) omitted —

A1724

A1725

Signing of the Constitution

Litho. & Engr.

1987, Sept. 17 ***Perf. 11***

2360 A1724 22c multicolored .40 .20

Certified Public Accounting

1987, Sept. 21 **Litho. & Engr.**

2361 A1725 22c multicolored 1.90 .20
 a. Black (engr.) omitted *900.00*

Locomotives

Stourbridge Lion, 1829 A1726

Best Friend of Charleston, 1830 A1727

John Bull, 1831 A1728

Brother Jonathan, 1832 A1729

Gowan & Marx, 1839 A1730

Perf. 10 Horiz. on 1 or 2 Sides

1987, Oct. 1

Booklet Stamps

2362 A1726 22c multicolored .55 .20
2363 A1727 22c multicolored .55 .20
2364 A1728 22c multicolored .55 .20
2365 A1729 22c multicolored .55 .20
 a. Red omitted —
2366 A1730 22c multicolored .55 .20
 a. Bklt. pane of 5, #2362-2366 2.75 *2.50*
 b. As No. 2366, black (engr.) omitted (single) —
 c. As No. 2366, blue omitted (single) —

Christmas

Moroni Madonna A1731

Christmas Ornaments A1732

1987, Oct. 23 **Photo.** ***Perf. 11***

2367 A1731 22c multicolored .40 .20
2368 A1732 22c multicolored .40 .20

1988 Winter Olympics, Calgary

Skiing — A1733

1988, Jan. 10 **Photo.** ***Perf. 11***

2369 A1733 22c multicolored .40 .20

Australia Bicentennial

Caricature of Australian Koala and American Bald Eagle — A1734

1988, Jan. 10 **Photo.** ***Perf. 11***

2370 A1734 22c multicolored .40 .20

See Australia No. 1052.

Black Heritage

James Weldon Johnson, 1871-1938, Author, Lyricist — A1735

1988, Feb. 2 **Photo.** ***Perf. 11***

2371 A1735 22c multicolored .40 .20

Siamese, Exotic Shorthair A1736

Abyssinian, Himalayan A1737

Maine Coon, Burmese A1738

American Shorthair, Persian A1739

1988, Feb. 5			*Perf. 11*	
2372	A1736 22c	multicolored	.45	.20
2373	A1737 22c	multicolored	.45	.20
2374	A1738 22c	multicolored	.45	.20
2375	A1739 22c	multicolored	.45	.20
a.	Block of 4, #2372-2375		1.90	1.90

American Sports Issues

A1740

A1741

1988, Mar. 9		**Litho. & Engr.**		
2376	A1740 22c	multicolored	.40	.20

Knute Kenneth Rockne (1888-1931), Notre Dame football coach.

1988, June 13	**Photo.**		*Perf. 11*	
2377	A1741 25c	multicolored	.45	.20

Francis Ouimet (1893-1967), 1st amateur golfer to win the US Open Championship.

Love Issue

Rose — A1742

A1743

1988	**Photo.**		*Perf. 11*	
2378	A1742 25c	multicolored	.45	.20
a.	Imperf., pair		*3,000.*	
2379	A1743 45c	multicolored	.65	.20

Issue dates: 25c, July 4; 45c, Aug. 8.

1988 Summer Olympics, Seoul

Gymnastic Rings A1744

1988, Aug. 19	**Photo.**		*Perf. 11*	
2380	A1744 25c	multicolored	.45	.20

Classic Automobiles

1928 Locomobile — A1745

1929 Pierce-Arrow A1746

1931 Cord A1747

1932 Packard A1748

1935 Duesenberg — A1749

Perf. 10 Horiz. on 1 or 2 Sides

1988, Aug. 25		**Litho. & Engr.**		
		Booklet Stamps		
2381	A1745 25c	multicolored	.50	.20
2382	A1746 25c	multicolored	.50	.20
2383	A1747 25c	multicolored	.50	.20
2384	A1748 25c	multicolored	.50	.20
2385	A1749 25c	multicolored	.50	.20
a.	Bklt. pane of 5, #2381-2385		5.00	*2.25*
	Nos. 2381-2385 (5)		2.50	1.00

Antarctic Explorers

Nathaniel Palmer (1799-1877) A1750

Lt. Charles Wilkes (1798-1877) A1751

Richard E. Byrd (1888-1957) A1752

Lincoln Ellsworth (1880-1951) A1753

1988, Sept. 14	**Photo.**		*Perf. 11*	
2386	A1750 25c	multicolored	.65	.20
2387	A1751 25c	multicolored	.65	.20
2388	A1752 25c	multicolored	.65	.20
2389	A1753 25c	multicolored	.65	.20
a.	Block of 4, #2386-2389		2.75	2.00
b.	Black (engr.) omitted		*1,500.*	
c.	As "a," imperf. horiz.		*3,000.*	

Folk Art Issue

Carousel Animals

Deer A1754

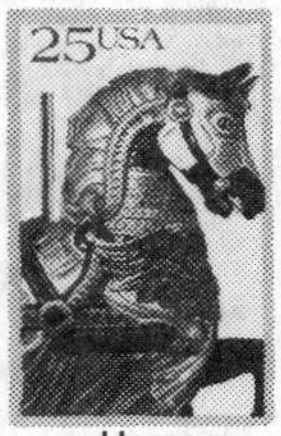

Horse A1755

Camel A1756

Goat A1757

Litho. & Engr.

1988, Oct. 1			*Perf. 11*	
2390	A1754 25c	multicolored	.65	.20
2391	A1755 25c	multicolored	.65	.20
2392	A1756 25c	multicolored	.65	.20
2393	A1757 25c	multicolored	.65	.20
a.	Block of 4, #2390-2393		3.00	2.00

Express Mail Rate

Eagle in Flight — A1758

Litho. & Engr.

1988, Oct. 4			*Perf. 11*	
2394	A1758 $8.75	multi	13.50	8.00

Special Occasions

Happy Birthday — A1759

Best Wishes — A1760

Thinking of You — A1761

Love You — A1762

Perf. 11 on 2 or 3 sides

1988, Oct. 22			**Photo.**	
		Booklet Stamps		
2395	A1759 25c	multicolored	.50	.20
2396	A1760 25c	multicolored	.50	.20
a.	Bklt. pane of 6, 3 #2395 + 3 #2396 with gutter btwn.		3.50	*3.25*
2397	A1761 25c	multicolored	.50	.20
2398	A1762 25c	multicolored	.50	.20
a.	Bklt. pane of 6, 3 #2397 + 3 #2398 with gutter btwn.		3.50	*3.25*
b.	As "a," imperf. horiz.		—	
	Nos. 2395-2398 (4)		2.00	.80

Madonna and Child, by Botticelli A1763

One-horse Open Sleigh and Village Scene A1764

Litho. & Engr., Photo. (No. 2400)

1988, Oct. 20			*Perf. 11½*	
2399	A1763 25c	multicolored	.45	.20
a.	Gold omitted		30.00	
2400	A1764 25c	multicolored	.45	.20

Montana Statehood Centennial

C.M. Russell and Friends, by Charles M. Russell (1865-1926) A1765

Litho. & Engr.

1989, Jan. 15			*Perf. 11*	
2401	A1765 25c	multicolored	.45	.20

Imperfs without gum exist from printer's waste.

Black Heritage Issues

Asa Philip Randolph (1889-1979), Labor and Civil Rights Leader — A1766

1989, Feb. 3	**Photo.**		*Perf. 11*	
2402	A1766 25c	multicolored	.45	.20

North Dakota Statehood Centennial

A1767

1989, Feb. 21			*Perf. 11*	
2403	A1767 25c	multicolored	.45	.20

Washington Statehood Centennial

A1768

1989, Feb. 22			*Perf. 11*	
2404	A1768 25c	multicolored	.45	.20

Steamboats

Experiment, 1788-1790 — A1769

Phoenix, 1809 — A1770

New Orleans, 1812 — A1771

Washington, 1816 — A1772

Walk in the Water, 1818 — A1773

Perf. 10 Horiz. on 1 or 2 sides
1989, Mar. 3 Litho. & Engr.
Booklet Stamps

2405	A1769	25c multicolored	.45	.20
2406	A1770	25c multicolored	.45	.20
2407	A1771	25c multicolored	.45	.20
2408	A1772	25c multicolored	.45	.20
2409	A1773	25c multicolored	.45	.20
a.		Bklt. pane of 5, #2405-2409	2.25	1.75

A1774

A1775

World Stamp Expo '89

Nov. 17-Dec. 3, Washington, DC

Litho. & Engr.

1989, Mar. 16 *Perf. 11*

2410	A1774	25c No. 122	.45	.20

Performing Arts

Arturo Toscanini (1867-1975), Italian Conductor

1989, Mar. 25 Photo. *Perf. 11*

2411	A1775	25c multicolored	.45	.20

Constitution Bicentennial

House of Representatives A1776

Senate A1777

Executive Branch A1778

Supreme Court A1779

1989-90 Litho. & Engr. *Perf. 11*

2412	A1776	25c multicolored	.45	.20
2413	A1777	25c multicolored	.45	.20
2414	A1778	25c multicolored	.45	.20
2415	A1779	25c multicolored	.45	.20
		Nos. 2412-2415 (4)	1.80	.80

Issue dates: #2412, Apr. 4; #2413, Apr. 6; #2414, Apr. 16. #2415, Feb. 2, 1990.

South Dakota State Centenary

State Flower, Pioneer Woman and Sod House on Grasslands A1780

1989, May 3 Photo. *Perf. 11*

2416	A1780	25c multicolored	.45	.20

American Sports

Henry Louis "Lou" Gehrig (1903-1941), Baseball Player for the New York Yankees — A1781

1989, June 10 Photo. *Perf. 11*

2417	A1781	25c multicolored	.50	.20

Literary Arts

Ernest Hemingway (1899-1961), Nobel Prize-winner for Literature, 1954 — A1782

1989, July 17 Photo. *Perf. 11*

2418	A1782	25c multicolored	.45	.20
a.		Vert. pair, imperf. horiz.	—	

Moon Landing, 20th Anniv.

Raising the Flag on Lunar Surface, July 20, 1969 — A1783

Litho. & Engr.

1989, July 20 *Perf. 11x11½*

2419	A1783	$2.40 multicolored	4.00	2.00
a.		Black (engr.) omitted	*2,500.*	
b.		Imperf., pair	*750.00*	
c.		Black (litho.) omitted	*4,500.*	

Natl. Assoc. of Letter Carriers, Cent.

Letter Carriers A1784

1989, Aug. 30 Photo. *Perf. 11*

2420	A1784	25c multicolored	.45	.20

Constitution Bicentennial

Bill of Rights — A1785

Litho. & Engr.

1989, Sept. 25 *Perf. 11*

2421	A1785	25c multicolored	.45	.20
a.		Black (engr.) omitted	*375.00*	

Prehistoric Animals

Tyrannosaurus Rex — A1786

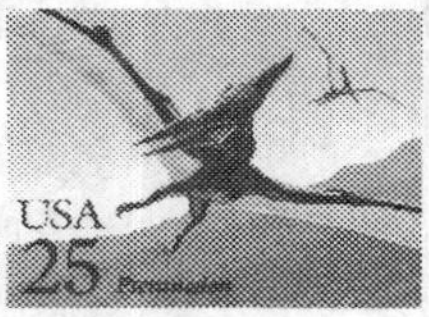

Pteranodon A1787

Stegosaurus A1788

Brontosaurus A1789

Litho. & Engr.

1989, Oct. 1 *Perf. 11*

2422	A1786	25c multicolored	.65	.20
2423	A1787	25c multicolored	.65	.20
2424	A1788	25c multicolored	.65	.20
2425	A1789	25c multicolored	.65	.20
a.		Block of 4, #2422-2425	3.00	2.00
b.		As "a," black (engr.) omitted	*1,000.*	

The correct name for "Brontosaurus" is "Apatosaurus."

No. 2425b is valued in the grade of fine.

Pre-Columbian America Issue

Southwest Carved Figure, A. D. 1150-1350 — A1790

Emblem of the Postal Union of the Americas and Spain (UPAE) and Southwestern Wood-carved Ritual Figure, Mogollon Culture, Mimbres Period, a Forerunner of the Hopi Indian Kachina Doll, A.D. 1150-1350.

1989, Oct. 12 Photo. *Perf. 11*

2426	A1790	25c multicolored	.45	.20

Discovery of America, 500th anniv. (in 1992). See No. C121.

Christmas

Madonna and Child, by Caracci A1791

Sleigh Full of Presents A1792

Litho. & Engr.

1989, Oct. 19 *Perf. 11½*

2427	A1791	25c multicolored	.45	.20
a.		Booklet pane of 10	4.75	*3.50*
b.		Red (litho.) omitted	*900.00*	
c.		As "a," imperf.	—	

Photo.

Perf. 11

2428	A1792	25c multicolored	.45	.20
a.		Vert. pair, imperf. horiz.	*2,000.*	

Booklet Stamp

Perf. 11½ on 2 or 3 sides

2429	A1792	25c multicolored	.45	.20
a.		Booklet pane of 10	4.75	*3.50*
b.		As "a," imperf. horiz.	—	
c.		Vert. pair, imperf. horiz.	—	
d.		As "a," red omitted	—	
e.		Imperf., pair	—	

Marked differences exist between Nos. 2428 and 2429: The runners on the sleigh in No. 2429 are twice as thick as those in No. 2428; in No. 2429 the package at upper left in the sleigh has a red bow, whereas the same package in No. 2428 has a red and black bow; and the ribbon on the upper right package in No. 2429 is green, whereas the same ribbon in No. 2428 is black.

Eagle and Shield — A1793

1989, Nov. 10 Photo. *Die Cut*

Self-Adhesive

2431	A1793	25c multicolored	.50	.20
a.		Booklet pane of 18	11.00	
b.		Vert. pair, no die cutting between	*850.00*	
c.		Pair, no die cutting	—	

Issued unfolded in panes of 18; peelable paper backing is booklet cover. Sold for $5.

Also available in strips of 18 with stamps spaced for use in affixing machines to service first day covers. Sold for $5.

Sold in 15 test cities and through the philatelic agency only.

Souvenir Sheet

World Stamp Expo, Washington, DC, Nov. 17-Dec. 3 — A1794

Litho. & Engr.

1989, Nov. 17 *Imperf.*

2433	A1794	Sheet of 4	14.00	9.00
a.		90c like No. 122	2.00	1.75
b.		90c like No. 132TC (blue frame, brown center)	2.00	1.75
c.		90c like No. 132TC (green frame, blue center)	2.00	1.75
d.		90c like No. 132TC (scarlet frame, blue center)	2.00	1.75

Traditional Mail Delivery

Stagecoach, c. 1850 — A1795

Paddlewheel Steamer — A1796

Biplane A1797

Depot-hack Type Automobile A1798

Litho. & Engr.

1989, Nov. 19 ***Perf. 11***

2434	A1795 25c multicolored	.45	.20
2435	A1796 25c multicolored	.45	.20
2436	A1797 25c multicolored	.45	.20
2437	A1798 25c multicolored	.45	.20
a.	Block of 4, #2434-2437	2.00	2.00
b.	As "a," dk blue (engr.) omitted	*1,000.*	

No. 2437b is valued in the grade of fine. Very fine blocks exist and sell for somewhat more.

1989, Nov. 28 ***Imperf.***

2438	Sheet of 4	4.00	1.75
a.	A1795 25c multicolored	.65	.25
b.	A1796 25c multicolored	.65	.25
c.	A1797 25c multicolored	.65	.25
d.	A1798 25c multicolored	.65	.25
e.	Dark blue & gray (engr.) omitted	*7,000.*	

20th Universal Postal Union Congress.

Idaho State Centenary

Mountain Bluebird, Sawtooth Mountains — A1799

1990, Jan. 6 **Photo.** ***Perf. 11***

2439 A1799 25c multicolored .45 .20

Love Issue

A1800

1990, Jan. 18 **Photo.** ***Perf. 12½x13***

2440	A1800 25c brt bl, dk pink & emer grn	.45	.20
a.	Imperf., pair	*850.00*	

Booklet Stamp

Perf. 11½ on 2 or 3 sides

2441	A1800 25c ultra, brt pink & dk grn	.45	.20
a.	Booklet pane of 10	4.75	*3.50*
b.	As "a," bright pink omitted	*2,100.*	
c.	As "b," single stamp	*200.*	

No. 2441c may be obtained from booklet panes containing both normal and color-omitted stamps.

Black Heritage

Ida B. Wells (1862-1931), Journalist — A1801

1990, Feb. 1 **Photo.** ***Perf. 11***

2442 A1801 25c multicolored .45 .20

Beach Umbrella — A1802

1990, Feb. 3 **Photo.** ***Perf. 11***

Booklet Stamp

2443	A1802 15c multicolored	.30	.20
a.	Booklet pane of 10	3.00	2.00
b.	As "a," blue omitted	*2,000.*	
c.	As No. 2443, blue omitted	*180.*	

Wyoming State Centenary

High Mountain Meadows, by Conrad Schwiering A1803

Litho. & Engr.

1990, Feb. 23 ***Perf. 11***

2444	A1803 25c multicolored	.45	.20
a.	Black (engr.) omitted	*2,500.*	—

Classic Films

The Wizard of Oz — A1804

Gone With the Wind — A1805

Beau Geste A1806

Stagecoach A1807

1990, Mar. 23 **Photo.** ***Perf. 11***

2445	A1804 25c multicolored	1.00	.20
2446	A1805 25c multicolored	1.00	.20
2447	A1806 25c multicolored	1.00	.20
2448	A1807 25c multicolored	1.00	.20
a.	Block of 4, #2445-2448	4.50	3.50

Literary Arts Series

Marianne Craig Moore (1887-1972), Poet — A1808

1990, Apr. 18 **Photo.** ***Perf. 11***

2449 A1808 25c multicolored .45 .20

TRANSPORTATION ISSUE

A1810

A1811

A1811a

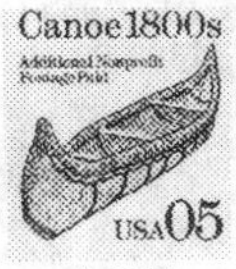

A1812

A1816

A1822

A1823

A1825

A1827

Engr., Photo. (#2452B, 2452D, 2454, 2458)

Perf. 9.8 Vert.

1990-95 **Coil Stamps**

Untagged: #2452B, 2452D, 2453, 2454, & 10c

2451	A1810	4c claret	.20	.20
a.		Imperf., pair	*700.00*	
b.		Untagged	.20	.20
2452	A1811	5c carmine	.20	.20
a.		Untagged	.20	.20
c.		Imperf., pair	*900.00*	
2452B	A1811	5c carmine	.20	.20
2452D	A1811a	5c carmine	.20	.20
e.		Imperf., pair	—	
2453	A1812	5c brn (Bureau precancel in gray)	.20	.20
a.		Imperf., pair	*350.00*	
b.		Gray omitted	—	
2454	A1812	5c red (Bureau precancel in gray)	.20	.20
2457	A1816	10c grn (Bureau precancel in gray)	.20	.20
a.		Imperf., pair	*350.00*	
2458	A1816	10c grn (Bureau precancel in black)	.20	.20
2463	A1822	20c green	.40	.20
a.		Imperf., pair	*150.00*	
2464	A1823	23c dark blue	.45	.20
b.		Imperf., pair	*175.00*	
2466	A1825	32c blue	.60	.20
a.		Imperf., pair	—	
b.		32c bright blue	6.00	—
2468	A1827	$1 blue & scar	1.75	.50
a.		Imperf., pair	*2,500.*	
		Nos. 2451-2468 (12)	4.80	2.70

Issued: $1, 4/20; #2452, 8/31; 4c, 1/25/91; #2453, 2457, 5/25/91; #2454, 10/22/91; 23c, 4/12/91; #2452B, 12/8/92; #2458, 5/25/94; #2452D, 3/20/95; 32c, 6/2/95; #2463, 6/9/95

This is an expanding set. Numbers will change if necessary.

Some pairs of No. 2468 appear to be imperf but have some blind perfs on the gum. Beware of copies with the gum removed.

Lighthouses

Admiralty Head, WA — A1829

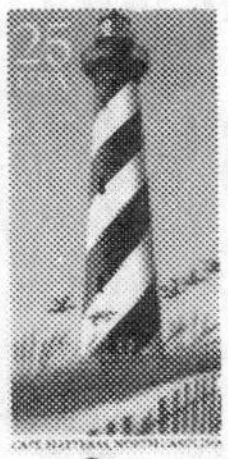

Cape Hatteras, NC — A1830

West Quoddy Head, ME — A1831

American Shoals, FL — A1832

Sandy Hook, NJ — A1833

Perf. 10 Vert. on 1 or 2 Sides

1990, Apr. 26 **Litho. & Engr.**

Booklet Stamps

2470	A1829 25c multicolored	.45	.20
2471	A1830 25c multicolored	.45	.20
2472	A1831 25c multicolored	.45	.20
2473	A1832 25c multicolored	.45	.20
2474	A1833 25c multicolored	.45	.20
a.	Bklt. pane of 5, #2470-2474	2.50	*2.00*
b.	As "a," white (USA 25) omitted	*75.00*	

Flag

A1834

1990, May 18 **Photo.** ***Die Cut***

Self-adhesive

2475	A1834 25c dk red & dk bl	.50	.25
a.	Pane of 12	6.00	

Sold only in panes of 12; peelable plastic backing inscribed in light ultramarine. Available for a test period of six months at 22 First National Bank automatic teller machines in Seattle.

Flora and Fauna Series

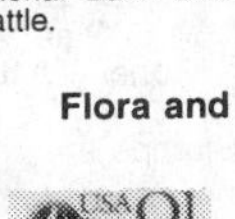

American Kestrel

A1840 A1841

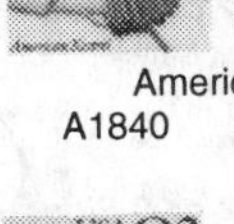

Eastern Bluebird — A1842

Fawn — A1843

Cardinal
A1844

Pumpkinseed Sunfish
A1845

Bobcat
A1846

Perf. 11, 11.2 (#2477)

1990-95 Litho. Untagged

2476 A1840 1c multicolored .20 .20
2477 A1841 1c multicolored .20 .20
2478 A1842 3c multicolored .20 .20

Photo.

Perf. 11½x11

2479 A1843 19c multicolored .35 .20
b. Red omitted *850.00*

On No. 2479b other colors are shifted.

2480 A1844 30c multicolored .50 .20

Litho. & Engr.

Perf. 11

2481 A1845 45c multicolored .80 .20
a. Black (engr.) omitted *600.00* —
2482 A1846 $2 multicolored 3.00 1.25
a. Black (engr.) omitted *325.00*
Nos. 2476-2482 (7) 5.25 2.45

Issued: $2, 6/1/90; 19c, 3/11/91; 3c, 30c, #2476, 6/22/91; 45c, 12/2/92; #2477, 5/10/95.

See Nos. 3031, 3044. Compare design A1842 with A2336.

Blue Jay — A1847

Wood Duck — A1848

African Violets — A1849

Peach — A1850

Pear — A1851

Red Squirrel — A1852

Rose — A1853

Pine Cone — A1854

Booklet Stamps

1991-95 ***Perf. 10.9x9.8***

2483 A1847 20c multicolored .40 .20
a. Booklet pane of 10 4.00 *2.25*

See No. 3053.

Perf. 10 on 2 or 3 Sides

2484 A1848 29c black & multi .50 .20
a. Booklet pane of 10 5.50 *3.75*
b. As "a," horiz. imperf. between —

Perf. 11 on 2 or 3 Sides

2485 A1848 29c red & multi .50 .20
a. Booklet pane of 10 5.50 *4.00*
b. Vert. pair, imperf. between *275.00*
c. As "b," booklet pane of 10 *1,500.*

Perf. 10x11 on 2 or 3 Sides

2486 A1849 29c multicolored .50 .20
a. Booklet pane of 10 5.50 *4.00*
2487 A1850 32c multicolored .60 .20
2488 A1851 32c multicolored .60 .20
a. Bklt. pane, 5 each #2487-2488 6.00 *4.25*
b. Pair, #2487-2488 1.25 .30

Issued: #2484-2485, 4/12/91; #2486, 10/8/93; 20c, 6/15/95; 32c 7/8/95.

Booklet Stamps

Die Cut 11¼x11¾ on 2, 3 or 4 sides

1993-95 Photo.

Self-Adhesive

2489 A1852 29c multicolored .50 .20
a. Booklet pane of 18 10.00
2490 A1853 29c red, green & black .50 .20
a. Booklet pane of 18 10.00
2491 A1854 29c multicolored .50 .20
a. Booklet pane of 18 11.00
b. Horiz. pair, no die cutting between —
c. Coil with plate #B1 — 4.25

Serpentine Die Cut

2492 A1853 32c pk, grn & blk ('95) .60 .20
a. Booklet pane of 20+label 12.00
b. Booklet pane of 15+label ('96) 8.75
c. Horiz. pair, no die cutting between —
d. As "a," 2 stamps and parts of 7 others printed on backing liner —
e. Booklet pane of 14 21.00
f. Booklet pane of 16 21.00
g. Coil with plate #S111 — 3.50
2493 A1850 32c multi ('95) .60 .20
2494 A1851 32c multi ('95) .60 .20
a. Booklet pane, 10 each #2493-2494+label 12.50

Coil Stamps

Serpentine Die Cut Vert.

2495 A1850 32c multi ('95) .60 .20
2495A A1851 32c multi ('95) .60 .20
b. Pair, #2495-2495A 1.25

Except for #2491c and 2492g with plate numbers, coil stamps of these issues are indistinguishable from booklet stamps once they are removed from the backing paper.

Issued: #2489, June 25; #2490, Aug. 19; #2491, Nov. 5.

See Nos. 3048-3049, 3053-3054.

Olympians

Jesse Owens, 1936
A1855

Ray Ewry, 1900-08
A1856

Hazel Wightman, 1924
A1857

Eddie Eagan, 1920, 1932
A1858

Helene Madison, 1932
A1859

1990, July 6 Photo. ***Perf. 11***

2496 A1855 25c multicolored .60 .20
2497 A1856 25c multicolored .60 .20
2498 A1857 25c multicolored .60 .20
2499 A1858 25c multicolored .60 .20
2500 A1859 25c multicolored .60 .20
a. Strip of 5, #2496-2500 3.25 2.50

Indian Headdresses

Assiniboin
A1860

Cheyenne
A1861

Comanche
A1862

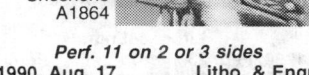

Flathead
A1863

Shoshone
A1864

Perf. 11 on 2 or 3 sides

1990, Aug. 17 Litho. & Engr.

Booklet Stamps

2501 A1860 25c multicolored .55 .20
2502 A1861 25c multicolored .55 .20
2503 A1862 25c multicolored .55 .20
2504 A1863 25c multicolored .55 .20
2505 A1864 25c multicolored .55 .20
a. Bklt. pane, 2 each #2501-2505 5.50 *3.50*
b. As "a," black (engr.) omitted *3,250.*
c. Strip of 5, #2501-2505 2.75 1.00
d. As "a," horiz. imperf. btwn. —

Micronesia, Marshall Islands

Canoe and Flag of the Federated States of Micronesia — A1865

Stick Chart, Canoe and Flag of the Republic of the Marshall Islands
A1866

1990, Sept. 28 ***Perf. 11***

2506 A1865 25c multicolored .45 .20
2507 A1866 25c multicolored .45 .20
a. Pair, #2506-2507 .90 .60
b. As "a," black (engr.) omitted *4,000.*

See Micronesia Nos. 124-126 and Marshall Islands No. 381.

Sea Creatures

Killer Whales
A1867

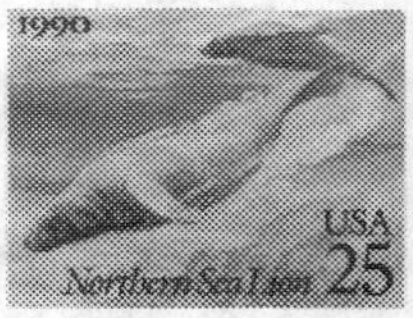
Northern Sea Lions
A1868

Sea Otter
A1869

Common Dolphin
A1870

Litho. & Engr.

1990, Oct. 3 ***Perf. 11***

2508 A1867 25c multicolored .45 .20
2509 A1868 25c multicolored .45 .20
2510 A1869 25c multicolored .45 .20
2511 A1870 25c multicolored .45 .20
a. Block of 4, #2508-2511 1.90 1.75
b. As "a," blk (engr.) omitted *900.00*

See Russia Nos. 5933-5936.

Pre-Columbian America Issue

Grand Canyon
A1871

1990, Oct. 12 Photo. ***Perf. 11***

2512 A1871 25c multicolored .45 .20

Dwight David Eisenhower

A1872

1990, Oct. 13 Photo. ***Perf. 11***

2513 A1872 25c multicolored .45 .20
a. Imperf., pair *2,250.*

Christmas

Madonna and Child by Antonello da Messina
A1873

Christmas Tree
A1874

Litho. & Engr.

1990, Oct. 18 ***Perf. 11½***

2514 A1873 25c multicolored .45 .20
a. Booklet pane of 10 5.00 *3.25*

Photo.

Perf. 11

2515 A1874 25c multicolored .45 .20
a. Vert. pair, imperf horiz. *1,100.*

Perf. 11½x11 on 2 or 3 Sides

2516 A1874 25c multicolored .45 .20
a. Booklet pane of 10 5.00 *3.25*
Nos. 2514-2516 (3) 1.35 .60

Marked differences exist between Nos. 2515 and 2516. The background red on No. 2515 is even while that on No. 2516 is splotchy. The bands across the tree and "GREETINGS" are blue green on No. 2515 and yellow green on No. 2516.

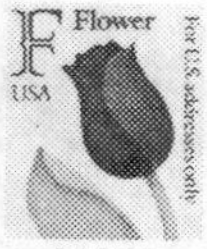

A1875

A1876

A1877

1991, Jan. 22 Photo. *Perf. 13*

2517 A1875 (29c) yel, blk, red & yel grn .50 .20
- *a.* Imperf., pair 750.00
- *b.* Horiz. pair, imperf. vert. 1,250.

Do not confuse No. 2517a with No. 2518a. See note after No. 2518.

Coil Stamp

Perf. 10 Vert.

2518 A1875 (29c) yel, blk, dull red & dk yel grn .50 .20
- *a.* Imperf., pair 37.50

"For U.S. addresses only" is 17½mm long on No. 2517, 16½mm long on No. 2518. Design of No. 2517 measures 21½x17½mm, No. 2518, 21x18mm.

Booklet Stamps

Perf. 11 on 2 or 3 Sides

2519 A1875 (29c) yel, blk, dull red & dk grn .50 .20
- *a.* Booklet pane of 10 6.50 *4.50*

2520 A1875 (29c) pale yel, blk, red & brt grn .50 .20
- *a.* Booklet pane of 10 18.00 *4.50*
- *b.* As "a," imperf horiz. —

No. 2519 has bullseye perforations that measure approximately 11.2. No. 2520 has less pronounced black lines in the leaf, which is a much brighter green than on No. 2519.

Litho.

Perf. 11

2521 A1876 (4c) bister & car .20 .20
- *a.* Vert. pair, imperf. horiz. 110.00
- *b.* Imperf., pair —

Photo.

Imperf., Die Cut

Self-Adhesive

2522 A1877 (29c) blk, dk blue & red .50 .25
- *a.* Pane of 12 7.00

No. 2522 sold only in panes of 12; peelable plastic backing inscribed in light ultramarine. Available during a test period at 22 First National Bank automatic teller machines in Seattle.

Flag Over Mt. Rushmore A1878

Flower A1879

1991, Mar. 29 Engr. *Perf. 10 Vert.*

Coil Stamps

2523 A1878 29c bl, red & claret .50 .20
- *b.* Imperf., pair 22.50
- *c.* Blue, red & brown 5.00 —

Photo.

2523A A1878 29c blue, red & brown .50 .20

On No. 2523A, USA and 29 are not outlined in white and appear farther from edge of design.

Issue dates: #2523, Mar. 29. #2523A, July 4.

1991-92 Photo. *Perf. 11*

2524 A1879 29c dull yel, blk, red & pale yel grn .50 .20
- *a.* Perf. 13x12½ .60 .20

Coil Stamps

Roulette 10 Vert.

2525 A1879 29c pale yel, blk, red & yel grn .50 .20

Perf. 10 Vert.

2526 A1879 29c pale yel, blk, red & yel grn .50 .20

Perf. 11 on 2 or 3 Sides

Booklet Stamp

2527 A1879 29c pale yel, blk, red & brt grn .50 .20
- *a.* Booklet pane of 10 5.50 *3.50*
- *b.* As "a," imperf. vert. 1,500.
- *c.* Horiz. pair, imperf. vert. *300.*
- *d.* As "a," imperf horiz. *2,750.*

Flower on No. 2524 has grainy appearance, inscriptions look rougher.

Issue dates: #2524, 2527, Apr. 5. #2525, Aug. 16. #2526, Mar. 3, 1992.

Flag, Olympic Rings — A1880

Perf. 11 on 2 or 3 Sides

1991, Apr. 21 Photo.

Booklet Stamp

2528 A1880 29c multicolored .50 .20
- *a.* Booklet pane of 10 5.25 *3.50*
- *b.* As "a," horiz. imperf. between —
- *c.* Vert. pair, imperf between —
- *d.* Vert. strip of 3, top pair imperf between —

No. 2528c comes from the misperfed booklet pane of No. 2528b. No. 2528d resulted from a paper foldover after normal perforating and before cutting into panes. Two No. 2528d are known.

Fishing Boat A1881

Balloon A1882

1991-94 Photo. *Perf. 9.8 Vert.*

Coil Stamps

2529 A1881 19c multicolored .35 .20
- *a.* Type II ('93) .35 .20
- *b.* As "a," untagged ('93) 1.00 .40

2529C A1881 19c multicolored .50 .20

Design of Type II stamps is created by a finer dot pattern. The vertical sides of "1" are smooth on Type II and jagged on Type I stamps.

No. 2529C has one loop of rope tying boat to piling, numerals and USA are taller and thinner.

Issued: No. 2529, 8/8/91; No. 2529C, 6/25/94.

Perf. 10 on 2 or 3 Sides

1991, May 17 Photo.

Booklet Stamp

2530 A1882 19c multicolored .35 .20
- *a.* Booklet pane of 10 3.50 *2.75*

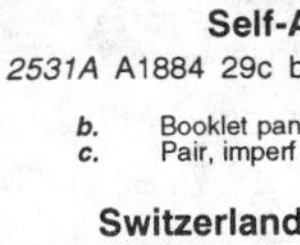

Flags on Parade — A1883

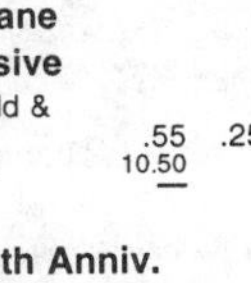

Liberty Torch — A1884

1991, May 30 Photo. *Perf. 11*

2531 A1883 29c multicolored .50 .20

1991, June 25 Photo. *Die Cut*

Booklet Pane

Self-Adhesive

2531A A1884 29c blk, gold & grn .55 .25
- *b.* Booklet pane of 18 10.50
- *c.* Pair, imperf —

Switzerland, 700th Anniv.

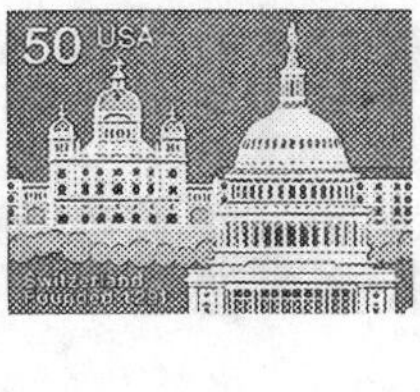

A1887

1991, Feb. 22 Photo. *Perf. 11*

2532 A1887 50c multicolored 1.00 .25
- *a.* Vert. pair, imperf horiz. *1,750.*

Imperfs exist from printers' waste.

See Switzerland No. 888.

A1888

A1889

Vermont Statehood Bicentennial

1991, Mar. 1 *Perf. 11*

2533 A1888 29c multicolored .50 .20

Savings Bonds, 50th Anniv.

1991, Apr. 30 Photo. *Perf. 11*

2534 A1889 29c multicolored .50 .20

Love

A1890

A1891

1991, May 9 Photo. *Perf. 12½x13*

2535 A1890 29c multicolored .50 .20
- *a.* Perf. 11 .60 .20
- *b.* Imperf., pair —

Perf. 11 on 2 or 3 Sides

Booklet Stamp

2536 A1890 29c multicolored .50 .20
- *a.* Booklet pane of 10 5.25 *3.50*

"29" is closer to edge of design on No. 2536 than on No. 2535.

Perf. 11

2537 A1891 52c multicolored .90 .20

Literary Arts Series

William Saroyan A1892

1991, May 22 Photo. *Perf. 11*

2538 A1892 29c multicolored .50 .20

See Russia No. 6002.

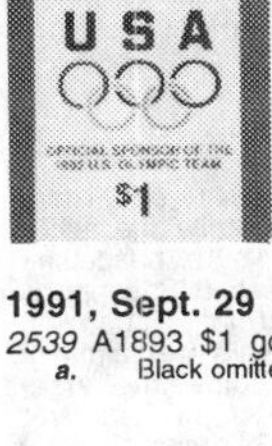

Eagle, Olympic Rings — A1893

1991, Sept. 29 Photo. *Perf. 11*

2539 A1893 $1 gold & multi 1.75 .50
- *a.* Black omitted —

A1894

A1895

A1896

1991 Litho. & Engr. *Perf. 11*

Untagged (#2541-2542)

2540 A1894 $2.90 Priority 5.00 2.50
- *a.* Vert. pair, imperf horiz. —

2541 A1895 $9.95 Domestic express 15.00 7.50
- *a.* Imperf., pair —

2542 A1896 $14 Intl. express 22.50 10.00
- *a.* Red (engr. inscriptions) omitted *1,500.*

Nos. 2540-2542 (3) 42.50 20.00

Issued: $2.90, 7/7; $9.95, 6/16; $14, 8/31.

Priority Mail Rate

Futuristic Space Shuttle A1897

Space Shuttle Challenger A1898

Litho. & Engr.

1993, June 3 *Perf. 11x10½*

2543 A1897 $2.90 multicolored 5.00 2.25

Litho. & Engr.

1995, June 22 *Perf. 11.2*

2544 A1898 $3 multi, dated "1995" 5.25 2.25
- *b.* Dated "1996" 5.25 2.25

Express Mail Rate

Space Shuttle Endeavour A1898a

Litho. & Engr.

1995, Aug. 4 *Perf. 11*

2544A A1898a $10.75 multi 17.50 7.50

Fishing Flies

Royal Wulff
A1899

Jock Scott
A1900

Apte Tarpon Fly — A1901

Lefty's Deceiver
A1902

Muddler Minnow
A1903

Perf. 11 Horiz. on 1 or 2 Sides

1991, May 31 Photo.

Booklet Stamps

2545	A1899	29c multicolored	.55	.20
a.		Black omitted	—	
2546	A1900	29c multicolored	.55	.20
a.		Black omitted	—	
2547	A1901	29c multicolored	.55	.20
a.		Black omitted	—	
2548	A1902	29c multicolored	.55	.20
2549	A1903	29c multicolored	.55	.20
a.		Bklt. pane of 5, #2545-2549	3.00	*2.50*

Horiz. pairs, imperf. vert., exist from printers' waste.

A1904

A1905

Performing Arts

Cole Porter (1891-1964), Composer

1991, June 8 Photo. *Perf. 11*

2550	A1904	29c multicolored	.50	.20
a.		Vert. pair, imperf. horiz.	*650.00*	

Operations Desert Shield & Desert Storm

1991, July 2 Photo. *Perf. 11*

2551	A1905	29c Southwest Asia service medal	.50	.20
a.		Vert. pair, imperf horiz.	*2,000.*	

No. 2551 is 21mm wide.

Perf. 11 Vert. on 1 or 2 Sides

Booklet Stamp

2552	A1905	29c multicolored	.50	.20
a.		Booklet pane of 5	2.75	*2.25*

No. 2552 is 20½mm wide. Inscriptions are shorter than on No. 2551.

Summer Olympics

Pole Vault
A1907

Discus
A1908

Women's Sprints
A1909

Javelin
A1910

Women's Hurdles
A1911

1991, July 12 Photo. *Perf. 11*

2553	A1907	29c multicolored	.50	.20
2554	A1908	29c multicolored	.50	.20
2555	A1909	29c multicolored	.50	.20
2556	A1910	29c multicolored	.50	.20
2557	A1911	29c multicolored	.50	.20
a.		Strip of #2553-2557	2.75	2.25

Numismatics

1858 Flying Eagle Cent, 1907 Standing Liberty Double Eagle, Series 1875 $1 Note, Series 1902 $10 National Currency Note — A1912

Litho. & Engr.

1991, Aug. 13 *Perf. 11*

2558	A1912	29c multicolored	.50	.20

World War II

A1913

Designs and events of 1941: a, Military vehicles (Burma Road, 717-mile lifeline to China). b, Recruits (America's 1st peacetime draft). c, Shipments for allies (US supports allies with Lend-Lease Act). d, Roosevelt, Churchill (Atlantic Charter sets war aims of allies). e, Tank (America becomes the "arsenal of democracy"). f, Sinking of Destroyer Reuben James, Oct. 31. g, Gas mask, helmet (Civil defense mobilizes Americans at home). h, Liberty Ship, sea gull (1st Liberty ship delivered Dec. 30). i, Sinking ships (Japanese bomb Pearl Harbor, Dec. 7). j, Congress in session (US declares war on Japan, Dec. 8). Central label is the size of 15 stamps and shows world map, extent of Axis control.

Illustration reduced.

Litho. & Engr.

1991, Sept. 3 *Perf. 11*

2559	A1913	Block of 10	5.25	4.50
a.-j.		29c any single	.50	.30
k.		Black (engr.) omitted	*10,000.*	

Basketball, 100th Anniversary

Basketball, Hoop, Players' Arms — A1914

1991, Aug. 28 Photo. *Perf. 11*

2560	A1914	29c multicolored	.55	.20

District of Columbia Bicentennial

Capitol Building from Pennsylvania Avenue, Circa 1903 — A1915

Litho. & Engr.

1991, Sept. 7 *Perf. 11*

2561	A1915	29c multicolored	.50	.20
a.		Black (engr.) omitted	*150.00*	

Comedians

Stan Laurel and Oliver Hardy
A1916

Edgar Bergen and Charlie McCarthy
A1917

Jack Benny
A1918

Fanny Brice
A1919

Bud Abbott and Lou Costello
A1920

Perf. 11 on 2 or 3 Sides

1991, Aug. 29 Litho. & Engr.

Booklet Stamps

2562	A1916	29c multicolored	.50	.20
2563	A1917	29c multicolored	.50	.20
2564	A1918	29c multicolored	.50	.20
2565	A1919	29c multicolored	.50	.20
2566	A1920	29c multicolored	.50	.20
a.		Bklt. pane, 2 each #2562-2566	5.50	*3.50*
b.		As "a," scarlet & bright violet (engr.) omitted	*900.00*	
c.		Strip of 5, #2562-2566	2.50	—

Black Heritage

Jan E. Matzeliger (1852-1889), Inventor — A1921

1991, Sept. 15 Photo. *Perf. 11*

2567	A1921	29c multicolored	.50	.20
a.		Horiz. pair, imperf. vert.	*1,750.*	
b.		Vert. pair, imperf. horiz.	*1,500.*	
c.		Imperf, pair	*2,750.*	

Space Exploration

Mercury, Mariner 10
A1922

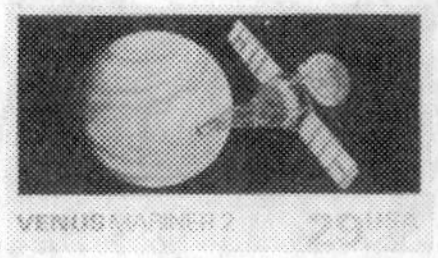

Venus, Mariner 2
A1923

Earth, Landsat
A1924

Moon, Lunar Orbiter
A1925

Mars, Viking Orbiter
A1926

Jupiter, Pioneer 11
A1927

Saturn, Voyager 2
A1928

Uranus, Voyager 2
A1929

Neptune, Voyager 2
A1930

Pluto
A1931

Perf. 11 on 2 or 3 Sides

1991, Oct. 1 Photo.

Booklet Stamps

2568	A1922	29c multicolored	.50	.20
2569	A1923	29c multicolored	.50	.20
2570	A1924	29c multicolored	.50	.20
2571	A1925	29c multicolored	.50	.20
2572	A1926	29c multicolored	.50	.20
2573	A1927	29c multicolored	.50	.20
2574	A1928	29c multicolored	.50	.20
2575	A1929	29c multicolored	.50	.20
2576	A1930	29c multicolored	.50	.20
2577	A1931	29c multicolored	.50	.20
a.		Bklt. pane of 10, #2568-2577	5.50	*3.50*

Christmas

Madonna and Child by Antoniazzo Romano
A1933

Santa Claus in Chimney
A1934

Santa Checking List — A1935

Santa with Present — A1936

Santa at Fireplace
A1937

Santa and Sleigh
A1938

Litho. & Engr.

1991, Oct. 17 *Perf. 11*

2578 A1933 (29c) multicolored .50 .20
a. Booklet pane of 10 5.75 *3.25*
b. As "a," single, red & black (engr.) omitted *3,500.*

Photo.

2579 A1934 (29c) multicolored .50 .20
a. Horiz. pair, imperf. vert. *325.00*
b. Vert. pair, imperf. horiz. *525.00*

Booklet Stamps
Size: 25x18½mm
Perf. 11 on 2 or 3 Sides

2580 A1934 (29c) Type I 1.75 .20
2581 A1934 (29c) Type II 1.75 .20
a. Pair, #2580, 2581 3.50 .25
b. Bklt. pane, 2 each #2580, 2581 7.50 1.25
2582 A1935 (29c) multicolored .50 .20
a. Booklet pane of 4 2.00 *1.25*
2583 A1936 (29c) multicolored .50 .20
a. Booklet pane of 4 2.00 *1.25*
2584 A1937 (29c) multicolored .50 .20
a. Booklet pane of 4 2.00 *1.25*
2585 A1938 (29c) multicolored .50 .20
a. Booklet pane of 4 2.00 *1.25*
Nos. 2578-2585 (8) 6.50 1.60

The extreme left brick in top row of chimney is missing from Type II, No. 2581.

A1939

A1942

A1944

James K. Polk (1795-1849)

1995, Nov. 2 Engr. *Perf. 11.2*

2587 A1939 32c red brown .60 .20

Surrender of Gen. John Burgoyne

1994, May 5 Engr. *Perf. 11.5*

2590 A1942 $1 blue 1.90 .50

Washington and Jackson

1994, Aug. 19 Engr. *Perf. 11.5*

2592 A1944 $5 slate green 8.00 2.50

Pledge of Allegiance
A1946

Eagle and Shield
A1947

A1950

Statue of Liberty — A1951

Perf. 10 on 2 or 3 sides

1992-93 Photo.

Booklet Stamps

2593 A1946 29c black & multi .50 .20
a. Booklet pane of 10 5.25 *4.25*
b. Perf. 11x10 on 2 or 3 sides .50 .20
c. As "b," booklet pane of 10 5.50 *4.25*

Perf. 11x10 on 2 or 3 Sides

2594 A1946 29c red & multi .50 .20
a. Booklet pane of 10 5.25 *4.25*
b. Imperf., pair *900.00*

Denomination is red on #2594 and black on #2593.
Issue dates: #2593, Sept. 8. #2594, 1993.

1992-94 Litho. & Engr. ***Die Cut***
Self-Adhesive

2595 A1947 29c brown & multi .50 .25
a. Bklt. pane of 17 + label 13.00
b. Pair, no die cutting *225.00*
c. Brown (engr.) omitted *500.00*
d. As "a," no die cutting *1,800.*

Photo.

2596 A1947 29c green & multi .50 .25
a. Bklt. pane of 17 + label 12.00
2597 A1947 29c red & multi .50 .25
a. Bklt. pane of 17 + label 10.00
2598 A1950 29c red, cream & blue .50 .20
a. Booklet pane of 18 10.00
b. Coil with plate #111 — 3.50
2599 A1951 29c multicolored .50 .20
a. Booklet pane of 18 10.00
b. Coil with plate #D111 — 3.50

Plate No. and inscription reads down on No. 2595a and up on Nos. 2596a-2597a. Design is sharper and more finely detailed on Nos. 2595, 2597.

Except for #2598b and 2599b with plate numbers, coil stamps of these issues are indistinguishable from booklet stamps once they are removed from the backing paper.

Issued unfolded in panes of 17 + label; peelable paper backing is booklet cover. Sold for $5.

Issue dates: No. 2598, Feb. 4, 1994; No. 2599, June 24, 1994; others, Sept. 25, 1992.

See Nos. 3122, 3122E.

A1956

A1957

A1959

A1960

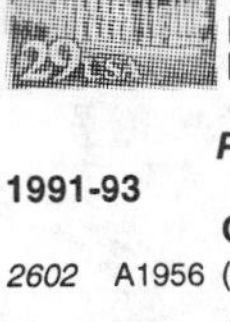

Flag Over White House — A1961

Perf. 10 Vert.

1991-93 Photo. Untagged
Coil Stamps

2602 A1956 (10c) multicolored .20 .20
a. Imperf., pair
2603 A1957 (10c) orange yel & multi .20 .20
a. Imperf., pair *30.00*
b. Tagged 2.00
2604 A1957 (10c) gold & multi .20 .20
2605 A1959 23c multi (Bureau precancel in blue) .40 .40
2606 A1960 23c multi (Bureau Precanceled) .40 .40
2607 A1960 23c multi (Bureau precanceled) .40 .40
c. Imperf., pair *100.00*
2608 A1960 23c vio blue, red & blk (Bureau Precanceled) .40 .40
a. Imperf., pair —

"23" is 7mm long on No. 2607. "First Class" is 8½mm long on No. 2608.

Engr.

2609 A1961 29c blue & red .50 .20
a. Imperf., pair *20.00*
b. Pair, imperf between *100.00*
Nos. 2602-2609 (8) 2.70 2.40

Issued: #2602, 12/13/91; #2603-2604, 5/29/93; #2605, 9/27/91; #2606, 7/21/92; #2607, 10/9/92; #2608, 5/14/93; 29c, 4/23/92.

See Nos. 2907, 3270-3271.

Winter Olympics

Hockey
A1963

Figure Skating
A1964

Speed Skating
A1965

Skiing
A1966

Bobsledding
A1967

1992, Jan. 11 Photo. *Perf. 11*

2611 A1963 29c multicolored .50 .20
2612 A1964 29c multicolored .50 .20
2613 A1965 29c multicolored .50 .20
2614 A1966 29c multicolored .50 .20
2615 A1967 29c multicolored .50 .20
a. Strip of 5, #2611-2615 2.75 2.25

A1968

A1969

World Columbian Stamp Expo

1992, Jan. 24 Litho. & Engr.

2616 A1968 29c Detail from #129 .50 .20

Black Heritage

Litho. & Engr.

1992, Jan. 31 *Perf. 11*

2617 A1969 29c multicolored .50 .20

W.E.B. Du Bois (1868-1963), writer and civil rights leader.

Love

A1970

1992, Feb. 6 Photo. *Perf. 11*

2618 A1970 29c multicolored .50 .20
a. Horiz. pair, imperf vert. *800.00*

Olympic Baseball

A1971

1992, Apr. 3 Photo. *Perf. 11*

2619 A1971 29c multicolored .50 .20

Voyages of Columbus

Seeking Queen Isabella's Support
A1972

Crossing the Atlantic
A1973

Approaching Land
A1974

Coming Ashore
A1975

Litho. & Engr.

1992, Apr. 24 *Perf. 11*

2620 A1972 29c multicolored .50 .20
2621 A1973 29c multicolored .50 .20
2622 A1974 29c multicolored .50 .20
2623 A1975 29c multicolored .50 .20
a. Block of 4, #2620-2623 2.00 1.90

See Italy Nos. 1877-1880.

Voyages of Columbus
Souvenir Sheets

A1976

A1977

A1978

A1979

A1980

A1981

Illustrations reduced.
Margins on Nos. 2624-2628 are lithographed. Nos. 2624a-2628c, 2629 are similar in design to Nos. 230-245 but are dated 1492-1992.

Litho. & Engr.

1992, May 22 *Perf. 10½*

2624	A1976	Sheet of 3	1.75	—
a.	A71	1c deep blue	.20	.20
b.	A74	4c ultramarine	.20	.20
c.	A82	$1 salmon	1.65	1.00
2625	A1977	Sheet of 3	6.75	—
a.	A72	2c brown violet	.20	.20
b.	A73	3c green	.20	.20
c.	A85	$4 crimson lake	6.50	4.00
2626	A1978	Sheet of 3	1.40	—
a.	A75	5c chocolate	.20	.20
b.	A80	30c orange brown	.50	.30
c.	A81	50c slate blue	.80	.50
2627	A1979	Sheet of 3	5.25	—
a.	A76	6c purple	.20	.20
b.	A77	8c magenta	.20	.20
c.	A84	$3 yellow green	4.75	3.00
2628	A1980	Sheet of 3	3.75	—
a.	A78	10c black brown	.20	.20
b.	A79	15c dark green	.25	.20
c.	A83	$2 brown red	3.25	2.00
2629	A1981	$5 Sheet of 1	8.50	—
a.	A86	$5 black	8.50	5.00
		Nos. 2624-2629 (6)	27.40	

Imperforate examples are known of all the Columbus souvenir sheets, but these are not listed in this catalogue. Their appearance several years after the issue date, in substantial quantities of all six sheets at the same time and, evidently, from a single source, with many small faults such as wrinkles and light creases that are not normally seen on these sheets, raises serious concerns about the legitimacy of these imperforate sheets as issued errors.

These circumstances have led the Scott editors to adopt the position that these imperforate sheets are indeed almost certainly printer's waste rather than issued errors. While it is possible that actual imperforate errors of one or more of the sheets may exist that were legitimately sold by the USPS, it is not possible to separate these (should they exist) from the many more numerous examples that apparently are printer's waste.

See Italy Nos. 1883-1888, Portugal Nos. 1918-1923 and Spain Nos. 2677-2682.

New York Stock Exchange Bicentennial

A1982

Litho. & Engr.

1992, May 17 *Perf. 11*

2630 A1982 29c green, red & black .50 .20

Space Accomplishments

Cosmonaut, US Space Shuttle — A1983

Astronaut, Russian Space Station — A1984

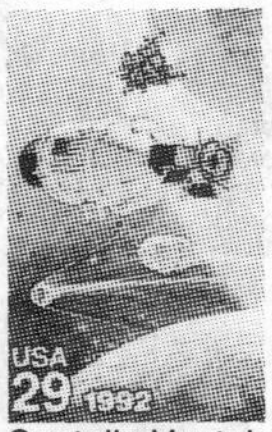

Sputnik, Vostok, Apollo Command & Lunar Modules
A1985

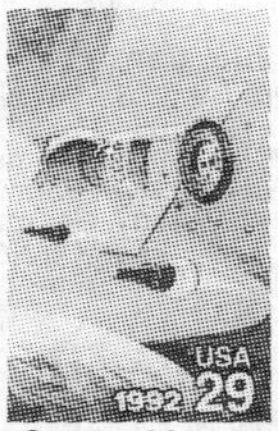

Soyuz, Mercury and Gemini Spacecraft
A1986

1992, May 29 **Photo.** *Perf. 11*

2631	A1983	29c multicolored	.50	.20
2632	A1984	29c multicolored	.50	.20
2633	A1985	29c multicolored	.50	.20
2634	A1986	29c multicolored	.50	.20
a.		Block of 4, #2631-2634	2.00	1.75

See Russia Nos. 6080-6083.

Alaska Highway, 50th Anniversary

A1987

Litho. & Engr.

1992, May 30 *Perf. 11*

2635	A1987	29c multicolored	.50	.20
a.		Black (engr.) omitted	500.00	

Most known examples of No. 2635a have poor to fine centering. It is valued in the grade of fine. Very fine examples sell for much more.

Kentucky Statehood Bicentennial

A1988

1992, June 1 **Photo.** *Perf. 11*

2636 A1988 29c multicolored .50 .20

Summer Olympics

Soccer
A1989

Gymnastics
A1990

Volleyball
A1991

Boxing
A1992

Swimming
A1993

1992, June 11 **Photo.** *Perf. 11*

2637	A1989	29c multicolored	.50	.20
2638	A1990	29c multicolored	.50	.20
2639	A1991	29c multicolored	.50	.20
2640	A1992	29c multicolored	.50	.20
2641	A1993	29c multicolored	.50	.20
a.		Strip of 5, #2637-2641	2.50	2.25

Hummingbirds

Ruby-throated
A1994

Broad-billed
A1995

Costa's
A1996

Rufous
A1997

Calliope — A1998

Perf. 11 Vert. on 1 or 2 sides

1992, June 15 **Photo.**

Booklet Stamps

2642	A1994	29c multicolored	.50	.20
2643	A1995	29c multicolored	.50	.20
2644	A1996	29c multicolored	.50	.20
2645	A1997	29c multicolored	.50	.20
2646	A1998	29c multicolored	.50	.20
a.		Bklt. pane of 5, #2642-2646	2.75	*2.25*

Wildflowers

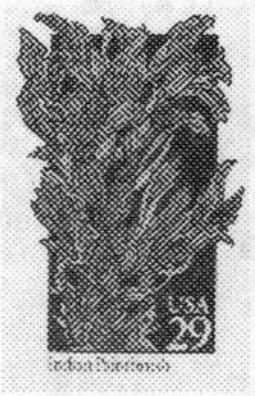

A1999-A2048

1992, July 24 **Litho.** *Perf. 11*

2647	A1999	29c Indian paintbrush	.50	.20
2648	A2000	29c Fragrant water lily	.50	.20
2649	A2001	29c Meadow beauty	.50	.20
2650	A2002	29c Jack-in-the-pulpit	.50	.20
2651	A2003	29c California poppy	.50	.20
2652	A2004	29c Large-flowered trillium	.50	.20
2653	A2005	29c Tickseed	.50	.20
2654	A2006	29c Shooting star	.50	.20
2655	A2007	29c Stream violet	.50	.20
2656	A2008	29c Bluets	.50	.20
2657	A2009	29c Herb Robert	.50	.20
2658	A2010	29c Marsh marigold	.50	.20
2659	A2011	29c Sweet white violet	.50	.20
2660	A2012	29c Claret cup cactus	.50	.20
2661	A2013	29c White mountain avens	.50	.20
2662	A2014	29c Sessile bellwort	.50	.20
2663	A2015	29c Blue flag	.50	.20
2664	A2016	29c Harlequin lupine	.50	.20
2665	A2017	29c Twinflower	.50	.20
2666	A2018	29c Common sunflower	.50	.20
2667	A2019	29c Sego lily	.50	.20
2668	A2020	29c Virginia bluebells	.50	.20
2669	A2021	29c Ohi'a lehua	.50	.20
2670	A2022	29c Rosebud orchid	.50	.20
2671	A2023	29c Showy evening primrose	.50	.20

2672 A2024 29c Fringed gentian .50 .20
2673 A2025 29c Yellow lady's slipper .50 .20
2674 A2026 29c Passionflower .50 .20
2675 A2027 29c Bunchberry .50 .20
2676 A2028 29c Pasqueflower .50 .20
2677 A2029 29c Round-lobed hepatica .50 .20
2678 A2030 29c Wild columbine .50 .20
2679 A2031 29c Fireweed .50 .20
2680 A2032 29c Indian pond lily .50 .20
2681 A2033 29c Turk's cap lily .50 .20
2682 A2034 29c Dutchman's breeches .50 .20
2683 A2035 29c Trumpet honeysuckle .50 .20
2684 A2036 29c Jacob's ladder .50 .20
2685 A2037 29c Plains prickly pear .50 .20
2686 A2038 29c Moss campion .50 .20
2687 A2039 29c Bearberry .50 .20
2688 A2040 29c Mexican hat .50 .20
2689 A2041 29c Harebell .50 .20
2690 A2042 29c Desert five spot .50 .20
2691 A2043 29c Smooth Solomon's seal .50 .20
2692 A2044 29c Red maids .50 .20
2693 A2045 29c Yellow skunk cabbage .50 .20
2694 A2046 29c Rue anemone .50 .20
2695 A2047 29c Standing cypress .50 .20
2696 A2048 29c Wild flax .50 .20
a. Pane of 50, #2647-2696 25.00 —

World War II

A2049

Designs and events of 1942: a, B-25's take off to raid Tokyo, Apr. 18. b, Ration coupons (food and other commodities rationed). c, Divebomber and deck crewman (US wins Battle of the Coral Sea, May). d, Prisoners of war (Corregidor falls to Japanese, May 6). e, Dutch Harbor buildings on fire (Japan invades Aleutian Islands, June). f, Headphones, coded message (Allies decipher secret enemy codes). g, Yorktown lost, US wins at Midway. h, Woman with drill (millions of women join war effort). i, Marines land on Guadalcanal, Aug. 7. j, Tank in desert (Allies land in North Africa, Nov.).

Central label is the size of 15 stamps and shows world map, extent of axis control.

Illustration reduced.

Litho. & Engr.

1992, Aug. 17 ***Perf. 11***
2697 A2049 Block of 10 5.25 4.50
a.-j. 29c any single .50 .30
k. Red (litho.) omitted 10,000.

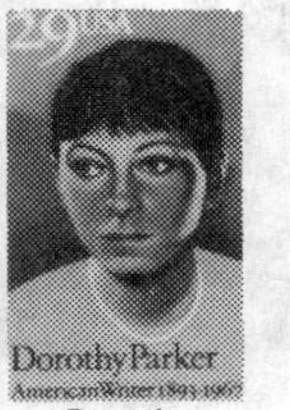

Dorothy Parker — A2050

A2051

Literary Arts Series

1992, Aug. 22 Photo. *Perf. 11*
2698 A2050 29c multicolored .50 .20

1992, Aug. 31 Photo. *Perf. 11*
2699 A2051 29c multicolored .50 .20

Dr. Theodore von Karman (1881-1963), rocket scientist.

Minerals

Azurite — A2052

Copper — A2053

Variscite A2054

Wulfenite A2055

Litho. & Engr.

1992, Sept. 17 ***Perf. 11***
2700 A2052 29c multicolored .50 .20
2701 A2053 29c multicolored .50 .20
2702 A2054 29c multicolored .50 .20
2703 A2055 29c multicolored .50 .20
a. Block or strip of 4, #2700-2703 2.00 1.75
b. As "a," silver (litho.) omitted 8,500.
c. As "a," red (litho.) omitted —

Juan Rodriguez Cabrillo

Cabrillo (d. 1543), Ship, Map of San Diego Bay Area — A2056

Litho. & Engr.

1992, Sept. 28 ***Perf. 11***
2704 A2056 29c multicolored .50 .20
a. Black (engr.) omitted

Wild Animals

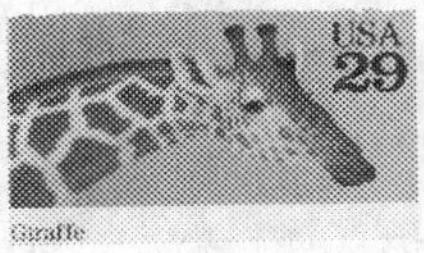

Giraffe A2057

Giant Panda A2058

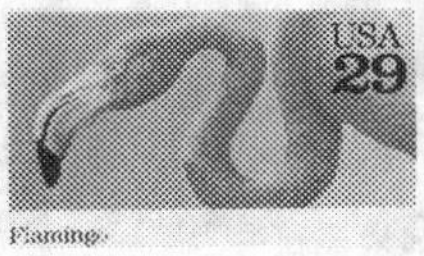

Flamingo A2059

King Penguins A2060

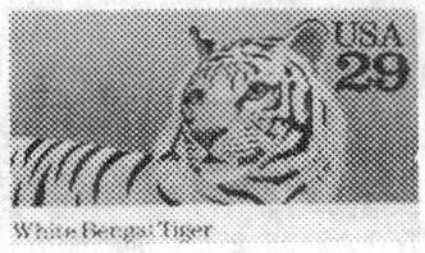

White Bengal Tiger A2061

Perf. 11 Horiz. on 1 or 2 sides

1992, Oct. 1 Photo.

Booklet Stamps

2705 A2057 29c multicolored .50 .20
2706 A2058 29c multicolored .50 .20
2707 A2059 29c multicolored .50 .20
2708 A2060 29c multicolored .50 .20
2709 A2061 29c multicolored .50 .20
a. Booklet pane of 5, #2705-2709 2.50 *2.00*
b. As "a," imperforate 3,000.

Christmas

Madonna and Child, by Giovanni Bellini — A2062

A2063 A2064

A2065 A2066

1992 Litho. & Engr. *Perf. 11.2*
2710 A2062 29c multicolored .50 .20
a. Booklet pane of 10 5.25 *3.50*

Litho.

Perf. 11½x11
2711 A2063 29c multicolored .50 .20
2712 A2064 29c multicolored .50 .20
2713 A2065 29c multicolored .50 .20
2714 A2066 29c multicolored .50 .20
a. Block of 4, #2711-2714 2.00 1.10

Booklet Stamps

Photo.

Perf. 11 on 2 or 3 Sides
2715 A2063 29c multicolored .50 .20
2716 A2064 29c multicolored .50 .20
2717 A2065 29c multicolored .50 .20
2718 A2066 29c multicolored .50 .20
a. Bklt. pane of 4, #2715-2718 2.25 *1.25*
b. As "a," imperf horiz. —
c. As "a," imperf —

Self-Adhesive

Die Cut
2719 A2064 29c multicolored .60 .20
a. Booklet pane of 18 11.00

Issued: #2710-2718, Oct. 22; #2719, Oct. 28.

"Greetings" is 27mm long on Nos. 2711-2714, 25mm long on Nos. 2715-2718 and 21½mm long on No. 2719. Nos. 2715-2719 differ in color from Nos. 2711-2714.

Chinese New Year

Year of the Rooster A2067

Litho. & Engr.

1992, Dec. 30 ***Perf. 11***
2720 A2067 29c multicolored .50 .20

American Music Series

Elvis Presley A2068

Oklahoma! A2069

Hank Williams A2070

Elvis Presley A2071

Bill Haley A2072

Clyde McPhatter A2073

Ritchie Valens A2074

Otis Redding A2075

Buddy Holly A2076

Dinah Washington A2077

1993, Jan. 8 Photo. *Perf. 11*
2721 A2068 29c multicolored .50 .20

1993, Mar. 30 Photo. *Perf. 10*
2722 A2069 29c multicolored .50 .20

1993
2723 A2070 29c multicolored .50 .20
a. Perf. 11.2x11.4 20.00 *3.00*
2724 A2071 29c multicolored .50 .20
2725 A2072 29c multicolored .50 .20
2726 A2073 29c multicolored .50 .20
2727 A2074 29c multicolored .50 .20
2728 A2075 29c multicolored .50 .20
2729 A2076 29c multicolored .50 .20
2730 A2077 29c multicolored .50 .20
a. Vertical strip of 7, #2724-2730 3.50 —

Booklet Stamps

Perf. 11 Horiz.

2731 A2071 29c multicolored	.50	.20
2732 A2072 29c multicolored	.50	.20
2733 A2073 29c multicolored	.50	.20
2734 A2074 29c multicolored	.50	.20
2735 A2075 29c multicolored	.50	.20
2736 A2076 29c multicolored	.50	.20
2737 A2077 29c multicolored	.50	.20
a. Booklet pane, 2 #2731, 1 each #2732-2737	4.25	*2.25*
b. Booklet pane of 4, #2731, 2735-2737 + tab	2.25	*1.50*

Issued: No. 2723, June 9; others, June 16.

See Nos. 2769, 2771, 2775 and designs A2112-A2117.

Space Fantasy

A2086 A2087

A2088 A2089

A2090

Perf. 11 Vert. on 1 or 2 Sides

1993, Jan. 25 Photo.

Booklet Stamps

2741 A2086 29c multicolored	.50	.20
2742 A2087 29c multicolored	.50	.20
2743 A2088 29c multicolored	.50	.20
2744 A2089 29c multicolored	.50	.20
2745 A2090 29c multicolored	.50	.20
a. Bklt. pane of 5, #2741-2745	2.50	*2.00*

Black Heritage

Percy Lavon Julian (1899-1975), Chemist — A2091

Litho. & Engr.

1993, Jan. 29 ***Perf. 11***

2746 A2091 29c multicolored	.50	.20

Oregon Trail

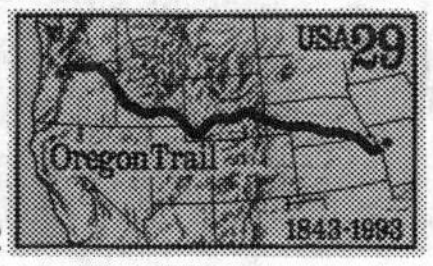

A2092

Litho. & Engr.

1993, Feb. 12 ***Perf. 11***

2747 A2092 29c multicolored	.50	.20

World University Games

A2093

1993, Feb. 25 Photo. ***Perf. 11***

2748 A2093 29c multicolored	.50	.20

Grace Kelly (1929-1982)

Actress, Princess of Monaco — A2094

1993, Mar. 24 Engr. ***Perf. 11***

2749 A2094 29c blue	.50	.20

See Monaco No. 1851.

Circus

Clown A2095 Ringmaster A2096

Trapeze Artist A2097 Elephant A2098

Illustrations reduced.

1993, Apr. 6 Litho. ***Perf. 11***

2750 A2095 29c multicolored	.50	.20
2751 A2096 29c multicolored	.50	.20
2752 A2097 29c multicolored	.50	.20
2753 A2098 29c multicolored	.50	.20
a. Block of 4, #2750-2753	2.00	1.75

Cherokee Strip Land Run, Centennial

A2099

Litho. & Engr.

1993, Apr. 17 ***Perf. 11***

2754 A2099 29c multicolored	.50	.20

Dean Acheson (1893-1971)

Secretary of State — A2100

1993, Apr. 21 Engr. ***Perf. 11***

2755 A2100 29c greenish gray	.50	.20

Sporting Horses

Steeplechase — A2101

Thoroughbred Racing — A2102

Harness Racing A2103

Polo A2104

Litho. & Engr.

1993, May 1 ***Perf. 11x11½***

2756 A2101 29c multicolored	.50	.20
2757 A2102 29c multicolored	.50	.20
2758 A2103 29c multicolored	.50	.20
2759 A2104 29c multicolored	.50	.20
a. Block of 4, #2756-2759	2.00	1.75
b. As "a," black (engr.) omitted	*1,600.*	

Garden Flowers

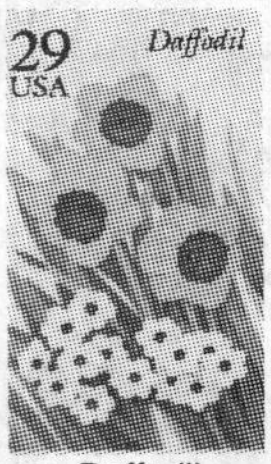

Hyacinth A2105 Daffodil A2106

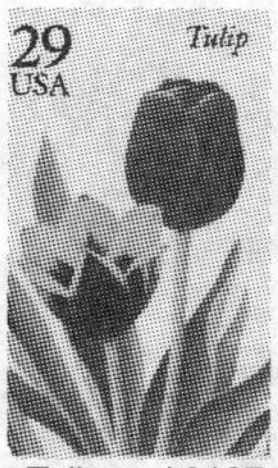

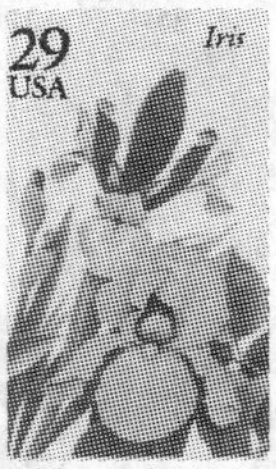

Tulip — A2107 Iris — A2108

Lilac — A2109

Litho. & Engr.

1993, May 15 ***Perf. 11 Vert.***

2760 A2105 29c multicolored	.50	.20
2761 A2106 29c multicolored	.50	.20
2762 A2107 29c multicolored	.50	.20
2763 A2108 29c multicolored	.50	.20
2764 A2109 29c multicolored	.50	.20
a. Booklet pane of 5, #2760-2764	2.50	*2.00*
b. As "a," black (engr.) omitted	*375.00*	
c. As "a," imperf	*2,500.*	

World War II

A2110

Designs and events of 1943: a, Destroyers (Allied forces battle German U-boats). b, Military medics treat the wounded. c, Amphibious landing craft on beach (Sicily attacked by Allied forces, July). d, B-24s hit Ploesti refineries, August. e, V-mail delivers letters from home. f, PT boat (Italy invaded by Allies, Sept.). g, Nos. WS7, WS8, savings bonds (Bonds and stamps help war effort). h, "Willie and Joe" keep spirits high. i, Banner in window (Gold Stars mark World War II losses). j, Marines assault Tarawa, Nov.

Central label is the size of 15 stamps and shows world map with extent of Axis control and Allied operations.

Illustration reduced.

Litho. & Engr.

1993, May 31 ***Perf. 11***

2765 A2110 Block of 10 + label	5.25	4.50
a.-j. 29c any single	.50	.30

Joe Louis (1914-1981)

A2111

Litho. & Engr.

1993, June 22 ***Perf. 11***

2766 A2111 29c multicolored	.50	.20

American Music Series

Oklahoma! Type and

Show Boat A2112

Porgy & Bess A2113

My Fair Lady A2114

Perf. 11 Horiz. on 1 or 2 Sides

1993, July 14 Photo.

Booklet Stamps

2767 A2112 29c multicolored	.50	.20
2768 A2113 29c multicolored	.50	.20
2769 A2069 29c multicolored	.50	.20
2770 A2114 29c multicolored	.50	.20
a. Booklet pane of 4, #2767-2770	2.50	*2.00*

No. 2769 has smaller design size, brighter colors and shorter inscription than No. 2722, as well as a frameline around the design and other subtle design differences.

Hank Williams Type and

Patsy Cline
A2115

The Carter Family
A2116

Bob Wills
A2117

1993, Sept. 25 Photo. *Perf. 10*

2771 A2070 29c multicolored	.50	.20
2772 A2115 29c multicolored	.50	.20
2773 A2116 29c multicolored	.50	.20
2774 A2117 29c multicolored	.50	.20
a. Block or horiz. strip of 4, #2771-2774	2.00	1.75

Booklet Stamps

Perf. 11 Horiz.

With Black Frameline

2775 A2070 29c multicolored	.50	.20
2776 A2116 29c multicolored	.50	.20
2777 A2115 29c multicolored	.50	.20
2778 A2117 29c multicolored	.50	.20
a. Booklet pane of 4, #2775-2778	2.50	*2.00*
b. As "a," imperf	—	

Inscription at left measures 27mm on No. 2771, 27 ½mm on No. 2723 and 22mm on No. 2775. No. 2723 shows only two tuning keys on guitar, while No. 2771 shows those two and parts of two others.

National Postal Museum

Independence Hall, Benjamin Franklin, Printing Press, Colonial Post Rider — A2118

Pony Express Rider, Civil War Soldier, Concord Stagecoach
A2119

JN-4H Biplane, Charles Lindbergh, Railway Mail Car, 1931 Model A Ford Mail Truck
A2120

California Gold Rush Miner's Letter, Nos. 39, 295, C3a, C13, Barcode and Circular Date Stamp
A2121

Litho. & Engr.

1993, July 30 *Perf. 11*

2779 A2118 29c multicolored	.50	.20
2780 A2119 29c multicolored	.50	.20
2781 A2120 29c multicolored	.50	.20
2782 A2121 29c multicolored	.50	.20
a. Block or strip of 4, #2779-2782	2.00	1.75
b. As "a," engr. maroon (USA/29) & black ("My Dear...") omitted	—	
c. As "a," imperf	*3,500.*	

American Sign Language

A2122

A2123

Designs:

1993, Sept. 20 Photo. *Perf. 11½*

2783 A2122 29c multicolored	.50	.20
2784 A2123 29c multicolored	.50	.20
a. Pair, #2783-2784	1.00	.65

Classic Books

A2124

A2125

A2126

A2127

Designs: No. 2785, Rebecca of Sunnybrook Farm, by Kate Douglas Wiggin. No. 2786, Little House on the Prairie, by Laura Ingalls Wilder. No. 2787, The Adventures of Huckleberry Finn, by Mark Twain. No. 2788, Little Women, by Louisa May Alcott.

Litho. & Engr.

1993, Oct. 23 *Perf. 11*

2785 A2124 29c multicolored	.50	.20
2786 A2125 29c multicolored	.50	.20
2787 A2126 29c multicolored	.50	.20
2788 A2127 29c multicolored	.50	.20
a. Block or horiz. strip of 4, #2785-2788	2.00	1.75
b. As "a," imperf	*3,000.*	

Christmas

Madonna and Child in a Landscape, by Giovanni Battista Cima — A2128

Jack-in-the-Box
A2129

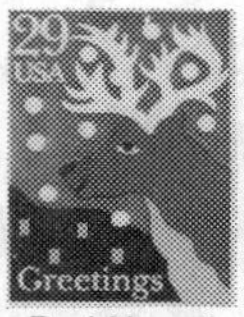

Red-Nosed Reindeer
A2130

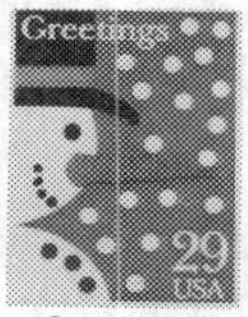

Snowman
A2131

Toy Soldier Blowing Horn
A2132

Litho. & Engr.

1993, Oct. 21 *Perf. 11*

2789 A2128 29c multicolored	.50	.20

Booklet Stamp

Size: 18x25mm

Perf. 11½x11 on 2 or 3 Sides

2790 A2128 29c multicolored	.50	.20
a. Booklet pane of 4	2.25	*1.75*
b. Imperf pair	—	
c. As "a," imperf	—	

No. 2790 has darker colors and smaller inscriptions than No. 2789.

1993 Photo. *Perf. 11½*

2791 A2129 29c multicolored	.50	.20
2792 A2130 29c multicolored	.50	.20
2793 A2131 29c multicolored	.50	.20
2794 A2132 29c multicolored	.50	.20
a. Block or strip of 4, #2791-2794	2.00	1.75

Booklet Stamps

Size: 18x21mm

Perf. 11x10 on 2 or 3 Sides

2795 A2132 29c multicolored	.50	.20
2796 A2131 29c multicolored	.50	.20
2797 A2130 29c multicolored	.50	.20
2798 A2129 29c multicolored	.50	.20
a. Booklet pane, 3 each #2795-2796, 2 each #2797-2798	5.00	*4.00*
b. Booklet pane, 3 each #2797-2798, 2 each #2795-2796	5.00	*4.00*

Self-Adhesive

Size: 19½x26½mm

Die Cut

2799 A2131 29c multicolored	.50	.20
a. Coil with plate #V1111111	—	3.50
2800 A2132 29c multicolored	.50	.20
2801 A2129 29c multicolored	.50	.20
2802 A2130 29c multicolored	.50	.20
a. Bklt. pane, 3 each #2799-2802	7.00	

Size: 17x20mm

2803 A2131 29c multicolored	.50	.20
a. Booklet pane of 18	10.00	

Except for #2799a with plate number, coil stamps are indistinguishable from booklet stamps once they are removed from the backing paper.

Issue dates: Nos. 2791-2798, Oct. 21; Nos. 2799-2803, Oct. 28.

Snowman on Nos. 2793, 2799 has three buttons and seven snowflakes beneath nose (placement differs on both stamps). No. 2796 has two buttons and five snowflakes beneath nose. No. 2803 has two orange buttons and four snowflakes beneath nose.

Mariana Islands

A2133

Litho. & Engr.

1993, Nov. 4 *Perf. 11*

2804 A2133 29c multicolored	.50	.20

Columbus' Landing in Puerto Rico, 500th Anniv.

A2134

1993, Nov. 19 Photo. *Perf. 11.2*

2805 A2134 29c multicolored	.50	.20

AIDS Awareness

A2135

1993, Dec. 1 Photo. *Perf. 11.2*

2806 A2135 29c black & red	.50	.20
a. Perf. 11 vert. on 1 or 2 sides, from bklt. pane	.50	.20
b. As "a," booklet pane of 5	2.50	*2.00*

Winter Olympics

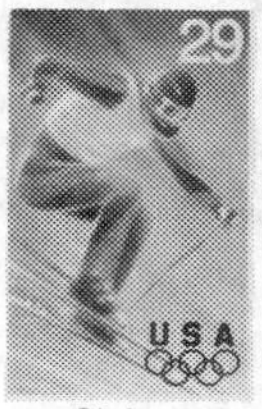

Slalom
A2136

Luge
A2137

Ice Dancing
A2138

Cross-Country Skiing
A2139

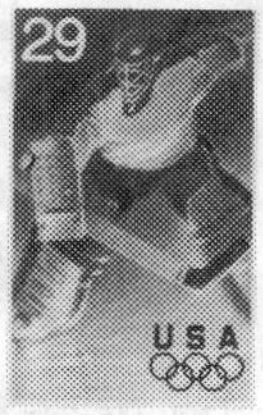

Ice Hockey — A2140

1994, Jan. 6 Litho. *Perf. 11.2*

2807 A2136 29c multicolored	.50	.20
2808 A2137 29c multicolored	.50	.20
2809 A2138 29c multicolored	.50	.20
2810 A2139 29c multicolored	.50	.20
2811 A2140 29c multicolored	.50	.20
a. Strip of 5, #2807-2811	2.50	2.25

Edward R. Murrow, Journalist (1908-65)

A2141

1994, Jan. 21 Engr. *Perf. 11.2*

2812 A2141 29c brown	.50	.20

Love

A2142

A2143

A2144

1994 Litho. & Engr. *Die Cut*

Self-Adhesive (No. 2813)

2813 A2142 29c multicolored .50 .20
- *a.* Booklet pane of 18 11.00
- *b.* Coil with plate #B1 — 3.50

Photo.

Perf. 10.9x11.1

2814 A2143 29c multicolored .50 .20
- *a.* Booklet pane of 10 5.50 *3.50*
- *b.* As "a," imperf —
- *e.* Horiz. pair, imperf. between —

Litho. & Engr.

Perf. 11.1

2814C A2143 29c multicolored .50 .20

Photo. & Engr.

Perf. 11.2

2815 A2144 52c multicolored 1.00 .20

Size of No. 2814C is 20x28mm. No. 2814 is 18x24½mm.

Except for #2813b with plate number, coil stamps are indistinguishable from booklet stamps once they are removed from the backing paper.

Issued: No. 2813, Jan. 27. Nos. 2814-2815, Feb. 14. No. 2814C, June 24.

No. 2814 was issued in booklets only.

Black Heritage

Dr. Allison Davis (1902-83), Social Anthropologist, Educator — A2145

1994, Feb. 1 Engr. *Perf. 11.2*

2816 A2145 29c red brown & brown .50 .20

Chinese New Year

Year of the Dog A2146

1994, Feb. 5 Photo. *Perf. 11.2*

2817 A2146 29c multicolored .50 .20

Buffalo Soldiers

A2147

Perf. 11.5x11.2

1994, Apr. 22 Litho. & Engr.

2818 A2147 29c multicolored .50 .20

Silent Screen Stars

Rudolph Valentino (1895-1926) A2148

Clara Bow (1905-65) A2149

Charlie Chaplin (1889-1977) A2150

Lon Chaney (1883-1930) A2151

John Gilbert (1895-1936) A2152

Zasu Pitts (1898-1963) A2153

Harold Lloyd (1894-1971) A2154

Keystone Cops A2155

Theda Bara (1885-1955) A2156

Buster Keaton (1895-1966) A2157

Litho. & Engr.

1994, Apr. 27 *Perf. 11.2*

2819 A2148 29c red, blk & brt vio .50 .20
2820 A2149 29c red, blk & brt vio .50 .20
2821 A2150 29c red, blk & brt vio .50 .20
2822 A2151 29c red, blk & brt vio .50 .20
2823 A2152 29c red, blk & brt vio .50 .20
2824 A2153 29c red, blk & brt vio .50 .20
2825 A2154 29c red, blk & brt vio .50 .20
2826 A2155 29c red, blk & brt vio .50 .20
2827 A2156 29c red, blk & brt vio .50 .20
2828 A2157 29c red, blk & brt vio .50 .20
- *a.* Block of 10, #2819-2828 5.00 4.00
- *b.* As "a," black (litho.) omitted —
- *c.* As "a," black, red & brt vio (litho.) omitted —

Garden Flowers

Lily A2158

Zinnia A2159

Gladiola A2160

Marigold A2161

Rose — A2162

Perf. 10.9 Vert.

1994, Apr. 28 Litho. & Engr.

Booklet Stamps

2829 A2158 29c multicolored .50 .20
2830 A2159 29c multicolored .50 .20
2831 A2160 29c multicolored .50 .20
2832 A2161 29c multicolored .50 .20
2833 A2162 29c multicolored .50 .20
- *a.* Booklet pane of 5, #2829-2833 2.50 —
- *b.* As "a," imperf *2,500.*
- *c.* As "a," black (engr.) omitted *425.00*

1994 World Cup Soccer Championships

A2163

A2164

A2165

Design: 40c, Soccer player, diff.

1994, May 26 Photo. *Perf. 11.1*

2834 A2163 29c multicolored .50 .20
2835 A2163 40c multicolored .80 .20
2836 A2164 50c multicolored 1.00 .20
Nos. 2834-2836 (3) 2.30 .60

Souvenir Sheet

2837 A2165 Sheet of 3, #a.-c. 2.50 2.00

Nos. 2834-2836 are printed on phosphor-coated paper, while Nos. 2837a (29c), 2837b (40c), 2837c (50c) are block tagged. No. 2837c has a portion of the yellow map in the LR corner.

World War II

A2166

Designs and events of 1944: a, Allied forces retake New Guinea. b, P-51s escort B-17s on bombing raids. c, Troops running from landing craft (Allies in Normandy, D-Day, June 6). d, Airborne units spearhead attacks. e, Officer at periscope (Submarines shorten war in Pacific). f, Parade (Allies free Rome, June 4; Paris, Aug. 25). g, Soldier firing flamethrower (US troops clear Saipan bunkers). h, Red Ball Express speeds vital supplies. i, Battleship firing main battery (Battle for Leyte Gulf, Oct. 23-26). j, Soldiers in snow (Bastogne and Battle of the Bulge, Dec.).

Central label is size of 15 stamps and shows world map with extent of Axis control and Allied operations.

Illustration reduced.

Litho. & Engr.

1994, June 6 *Perf. 10.9*

2838 A2166 Block of 10 + label 5.25 4.50
- *a.-j.* 29c any single .50 .30

Norman Rockwell

A2167

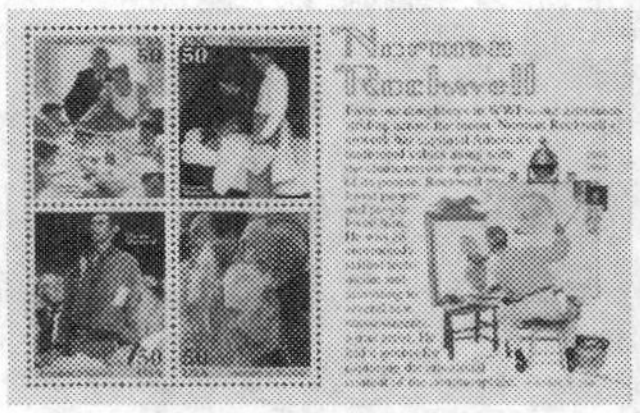

A2168

Perf. 10.9x11.1

1994, July 1 Litho. & Engr.

2839 A2167 29c multicolored .50 .20

Souvenir Sheet

Litho.

2840 A2168 Sheet of 4 4.00 2.75
- *a.* 50c Freedom from Want 1.00 .65
- *b.* 50c Freedom from Fear 1.00 .65
- *c.* 50c Freedom of Speech 1.00 .65
- *d.* 50c Freedom of Worship 1.00 .65

Moon Landing, 25th Anniv.

A2169

A2170

Perf. 11.2x11.1

1994, July 20 **Litho.**

Miniature Sheet

2841	A2169	Sheet of 12		7.50	—
a.		29c Single stamp		.60	.60

Litho. & Engr.

Perf. 10.7x11.1

2842	A2170	$9.95	multicolored	17.50	7.50

Locomotives

Hudson's General A2171

McQueen's Jupiter A2172

Eddy's No. 242 A2173

Ely's No. 10 A2174

Buchanan's No. 999 A2175

Perf. 11 Horiz.

1994, July 28 **Photo.**

Booklet Stamps

2843	A2171	29c	multicolored	.50	.20
2844	A2172	29c	multicolored	.50	.20
2845	A2173	29c	multicolored	.50	.20
2846	A2174	29c	multicolored	.50	.20
2847	A2175	29c	multicolored	.50	.20
a.		Booklet pane of 5, #2843-2847		2.50	*2.00*
b.		As "a," imperf		—	

George Meany, Labor Leader (1894-1980)

A2176

1994, Aug. 16 **Engr.** ***Perf. 11.1x11***

2848	A2176	29c	blue	.50	.20

American Music Series

Al Jolson (1886-1950) A2177

Bing Crosby (1904-77) A2178

Ethel Waters (1896-1977) A2179

Nat "King" Cole (1919-65) A2180

Ethel Merman (1908-84) A2181

Bessie Smith (1894-1937) A2182

Muddy Waters (1915-83) A2183

Billie Holiday (1915-59) A2184

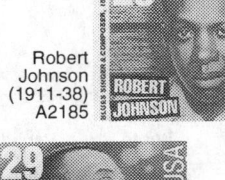

Robert Johnson (1911-38) A2185

Jimmy Rushing (1902-72) A2186

"Ma" Rainey (1886-1939) A2187

Mildred Bailey (1907-51) A2188

Howlin' Wolf (1910-76) A2189

1994 **Photo.** ***Perf. 10.1x10.2***

2849	A2177	29c	multicolored	.50	.20
2850	A2178	29c	multicolored	.50	.20
2851	A2179	29c	multicolored	.50	.20
2852	A2180	29c	multicolored	.50	.20
2853	A2181	29c	multicolored	.50	.20
a.		Vert. strip of 5, #2849-2853		2.50	2.00

Perf. 11x10.8

Litho.

2854	A2182	29c	multicolored	.50	.20
2855	A2183	29c	multicolored	.50	.20
2856	A2184	29c	multicolored	.50	.20
2857	A2185	29c	multicolored	.50	.20
2858	A2186	29c	multicolored	.50	.20
2859	A2187	29c	multicolored	.50	.20
2860	A2188	29c	multicolored	.50	.20
2861	A2189	29c	multicolored	.50	.20
a.		Block of 9, #2854-2861 +1 additional stamp		4.50	3.50

Issued: Nos. 2849-2853, 9/1/94; Nos. 2854-2861, 9/17/94.

Literary Arts Series

James Thurber (1894-1961) A2190

Litho. & Engr.

1994, Sept. 10 ***Perf. 11***

2862	A2190	29c	multicolored	.50	.20

Wonders Of The Sea

Diver, Motorboat A2191

Diver, Ship A2192

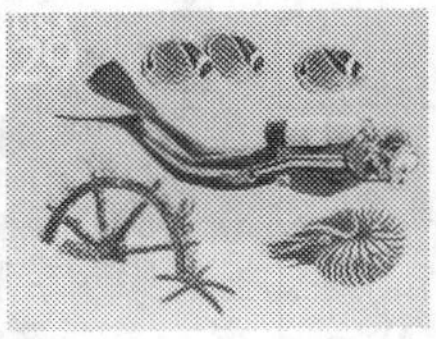

Diver, Ship's Wheel A2193

Diver, Coral A2194

1994, Oct. 3 **Litho.** ***Perf. 11x10.9***

2863	A2191	29c	multicolored	.50	.20
2864	A2192	29c	multicolored	.50	.20
2865	A2193	29c	multicolored	.50	.20
2866	A2194	29c	multicolored	.50	.20
a.		Block of 4, #2863-2866		2.00	1.50
b.		As "a," imperf		*2,000.*	

Cranes

Black-Necked A2195

Whooping A2196

Litho. & Engr.

1994, Oct. 9 ***Perf. 10.8x11***

2867	A2195	29c	multicolored	.50	.20
2868	A2196	29c	multicolored	.50	.20
a.		Pair, #2867-2868		1.00	.65
b.		Black & magenta (engr.) omitted		—	
c.		As "a," dble. impression of engr. blk (Birds' names, "USA") & mag ("29")		—	
d.		As "a," dble. impression of engr. blk ("USA") & mag ("29")		—	

See People's Republic of China Nos. 2528-2529.

Legends Of The West

Miniature Pane

A2197

g. Bill Pickett (1870-1932) (Revised)

Designs: a, Home on the Range. b, Buffalo Bill Cody (1846-1917). c, Jim Bridger (1804-81). d, Annie Oakley (1860-1926). e, Native American Culture. f, Chief Joseph (c. 1840-1904). h, Bat Masterson (1853-1921). i, John C. Fremont (1813-90). j, Wyatt Earp (1848-1929). k, Nellie Cashman (c. 1849-1925). l, Charles Goodnight (1826-1929). m, Geronimo (1823-1909). n, Kit Carson (1809-68). o, Wild Bill Hickok (1837-76). p, Western Wildlife. q, Jim Beckwourth (c. 1798-1866). r, Bill Tilghman (1854-1924). s, Sacagawea (c. 1787-1812). t, Overland Mail.

1994, Oct. 18 **Photo.** ***Perf. 10.1x10***

2869	A2197	Pane of 20		12.00	—
a.-t.		29c any single		.60	.20
u.		As No. 2869, a.-e. imperf, f.-j. part perf.		—	

Legends Of The West (Recalled)

Miniature Pane

g. Bill Pickett (Recalled)

Nos. 2870b-2870d, 2870f-2870o, 2870q-2870s have a frameline around the vignette that is half the width of the frameline on similar stamps in No. 2869. Other design differences may exist.

1994 Photo. *Perf. 10.1x10*

2870 A2197 29c Pane of 20 190.00 —

150,000 panes were made available through a drawing. Panes were delivered in an envelope. Value is for pane without envelope.

Christmas

Madonna and Child, by Elisabetta Sirani A2200

Stocking A2201

Santa Claus A2202

Cardinal in Snow A2203

Litho. & Engr.

1994, Oct. 20 *Perf. 11.1*

2871 A2200 29c multicolored .50 .20
a. Perf. 9.8x10.8, from bklt. pane .50 .20
b. As "a," booklet pane of 10 5.25 *3.50*
c. As "a," imperf —

Litho.

2872 A2201 29c multicolored .50 .20
a. Booklet pane of 20 10.50 *3.00*
b. Imperf., pair —
c. As "a," imperf. horiz. —

Booklet Stamps
Photo.
Die Cut
Self-Adhesive

2873 A2202 29c multicolored .50 .20
a. Booklet pane of 12 6.25
b. Coil with plate #V1111 — 3.50
2874 A2203 29c multicolored .50 .20
a. Booklet pane of 18 9.50

Except for #2873b with plate number, coil stamps are indistinguishable from booklet stamps once they are removed from the backing paper.

Bureau Of Engraving & Printing
Souvenir Sheet

A2204

Litho. & Engr.

1994, Nov. 3 *Perf. 11*

2875 A2204 Sheet of 4 15.00 —
a. $2 Single stamp 3.00 1.25

Chinese New Year

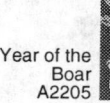

Year of the Boar A2205

Perf. 11.2x11.1

1994, Dec. 30 Photo.

2876 A2205 29c multicolored .50 .20

A2206

A2207

A2208

A2208a

A2209

A2210

1994, Dec. 13 Litho. *Perf. 11x10.8*
Untagged

2877 A2206 (3c) tan, bright blue & red .20 .20
a. Imperf, pair 200.00

Perf. 10.8x10.9

2878 A2206 (3c) tan, dark blue & red .20 .20

Inscriptions on #2877 are in a thin typeface. Those on #2878 are in heavy, bold type.

Photo.
Perf. 11.2x11.1
Tagged

2879 A2207 (20c) black "G," yellow & multi .40 .20
a. Imperf, pair —

Perf. 11x10.9

2880 A2207 (20c) red "G," yellow & multi .45 .20

Perf. 11.2x11.1

2881 A2208 (32c) black "G" & multi .70 .20
a. Booklet pane of 10 6.00 *3.75*

Perf. 11x10.9

2882 A2208 (32c) red "G" & multi .60 .20

Distance on #2882 from bottom of red G to top of flag immediately above is 13¾mm. Illustration A2208a shows #2885 superimposed over #2882.

Booklet Stamps
Perf. 10x9.9 on 2 or 3 Sides

2883 A2208 (32c) black "G" & multi .60 .20
a. Booklet pane of 10 6.25 *3.75*

Perf. 10.9 on 2 or 3 Sides

2884 A2208 (32c) blue "G" & multi .60 .20
a. Booklet pane of 10 6.00 *3.75*
b. As "a," imperf —

Perf. 11x10.9 on 2 or 3 Sides

2885 A2208a (32c) red "G" & multi .60 .20
a. Booklet pane of 10 6.00 *3.75*
b. Pair, imperf vert. —

Distance on #2885 from bottom of red G to top of flag immediately above is 13½mm. See note below #2882.

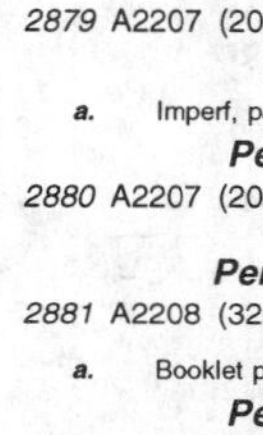

A2208b

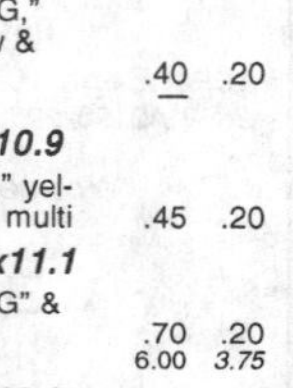

A2208c

Die Cut
Self-Adhesive

2886 A2208b (32c) gray, blue, lt blue, red & blk .60 .20
a. Booklet pane of 18 11.00
b. Coil with plate #V11111 — 3.25

No. 2886 is printed on pre-phosphored paper and has only a small number of blue shading dots in the white stripes immediately below the flag's blue field.

Except for #2886b with plate number, coil stamps are indistinguishable from booklet stamps once they are removed from the backing paper.

2887 A2208c (32c) black, blue & red .60 .20
a. Booklet pane of 18 11.00

No. 2887 has noticeable blue shading in the white stripes immediately below the blue field and has overall tagging.

COIL STAMPS

1994-95 *Perf. 9.8 Vert.*

2888 A2209 (25c) black "G" .50 .20
2889 A2208 (32c) black "G" .60 .20
a. Imperf., pair *300.00*
2890 A2208 (32c) blue "G" .60 .20
2891 A2208 (32c) red "G" .60 .20

Rouletted 9.8 Vert.

2892 A2208 (32c) red "G" .60 .20

Perf. 9.8 Vert.

2893 A2210 (5c) green & multi .20 .20

Nos. 2888-2892 issued 12/13/94. No. 2893 was only available through the Philatelic Fullfillment Center after its announcement 1/12/95.

Eagle and Shield Type of 1993 and:

Flag Over Porch A2212

Butte A2217

Mountain A2218

Auto A2220

Auto Tail Fin A2223

Juke Box A2225

Flag Over Field — A2230

1995-97 Photo. *Perf. 10.4*

2897 A2212 32c multicolored .60 .20
a. Imperf., vert. pair *175.00*

COIL STAMPS
Self-Adhesive (#2902B, 2904A-2904B, 2906-2907, 2910, 2912A-2912B, 2915-2915D, 2919-2921)
Photo.
Perf. 9.8 Vert.

2902 A2217 (5c) yel, red & bl .20 .20
a. Imperf., pair 750.00

Serpentine Die Cut 11.5 Vert.

2902B A2217 (5c) yellow, red & blue .20 .20

Perf. 9.8 Vert.

2903 A2218 (5c) purple & multi .20 .20

Letters of inscription "USA NONPROFIT ORG." outlined in purple on #2903.

2904 A2218 (5c) blue & multi .20 .20
c. Imperf., pair 500.00

Letters of inscription have no outline on #2904.

Serpentine Die Cut 11.2 Vert.

2904A A2218 (5c) pur & multi .20 .20

Serpentine Die Cut 9.8 Vert.

2904B A2218 (5c) pur & multi .20 .20

Letters of inscription outlined in purple on #2904B, not outlined on No. 2904A.

Perf. Perf. 9.8 Vert.

2905 A2220 (10c) blk, red brn & brn .20 .20

Serpentine Die Cut 11.5 Vert.

2906 A2220 (10c) blk, brn & red brn .20 .20
2907 A1957 (10c) gold & multi .20 .20

Perf. 9.8 Vert.

2908 A2223 (15c) dk org yel & multi .30 .30

No. 2908 has dark, bold colors, heavy shading lines and heavily shaded chrome.

2909 A2223 (15c) buff & multi .30 .30

No. 2909 has shinier chrome, more subdued colors and finer details than No. 2908.

Serpentine Die Cut 11.5 Vert.

2910 A2223 (15c) buff & multi .30 .30

Perf. 9.8 Vert.

2911 A2225 (25c) dk red, dk yel grn & multi .50 .50

No. 2911 has dark, saturated colors and dark blue lines in the music selection board.

2912 A2225 (25c) brt org red, brt yel grn & multi .50 .50

No. 2912 has bright colors, less shading and light blue lines in the music selection board.

Serpentine Die Cut 11.5 Vert.

2912A A2225 (25c) brt org red, brt yel grn & multi .50 .50

Serpentine Die Cut 9.8 Vert.

2912B A2225 (25c) dark red, dark yellow green & multi .50 .50

See No. 3132.

Perf. 9.8 Vert.

2913 A2212 32c bl, tan, brn, red & lt bl .60 .20
a. Imperf., pair *60.00*

No. 2913 has pronounced light blue shading in the flag and red "1995" at left bottom. See No. 3133.

2914 A2212 32c bl, yel brn, red & gray .60 .20

No. 2914 has pale gray shading in the flag and blue "1995" at left bottom.

Serpentine Die Cut 8.7 Vert.

2915 A2212 32c multicolored .60 .30

Serpentine Die Cut 9.8 Vert.

2915A A2212 32c dk bl, tan, brn, red & lt bl .60 .20
h. Imperf., pair —
i. Tan omitted —

On No. 2915Ai all other colors except brown are severly shifted.

Serpentine Die Cut 11.5 Vert.

2915B A2212 32c As #2915A .60 .20

Serpentine Die Cut 10.9 Vert.

2915C A2212 32c As #2915A .60 .20

Serpentine Die Cut 9.8 Vert.

2915D A2212 32c dk bl, tan, brn, red & lt bl .60 .20

Die cutting on #2915D starts and ends with straight cuts and has 9 teeth between. Die cutting on #2915A has a straight cut at bottom and 11 teeth above. Stamps on multiples of No. 2915A touch, and are on a peelable backing the same size as the stamps, while those of No. 2915D are separated on the peelable backing, which is larger than the stamps.

No. 2915D has red "1997" at left bottom; No. 2915A has red "1996" at left bottom.

Sky on No. 3133 shows color gradation at lower right not on No. 2915D, and it has blue "1996" at left bottom.

Booklet Stamps
Perf. 10.8x9.8 on 2 or 3 Adjacent Sides

2916 A2212 32c bl, tan, brn, red & lt bl .60 .20
a. Booklet pane of 10 6.00

b. As "a," imperf —

Die Cut

2919 A2230 32c multicolored .60 .20
- *a.* Booklet pane of 18 11.00
- *b.* Vert. pair, no die cutting btwn. —

Serpentine Die Cut 8.7 on 2, 3 or 4 Adjacent Sides

2920 A2212 32c multi, large blue "1995" date .60 .20
- *a.* Booklet pane of 20+label 12.00
- *b.* Small blue "1995" date 1.75 .20
- *c.* As "b," booklet pane of 20+label 50.00
- *d.* Serpentine die cut 11.3, blue "1996" date, from bklt. pane .60 .20
- *e.* As "d," booklet pane of 10 6.00
- *f.* As #2920, pane of 15+label *9.00* —
- *g.* As "a," partial pane of 10, 3 stamps and parts of 7 stamps printed on backing liner —
- *h.* As #2920, booklet pane of 15 *9.00*

No. 2920d is dated "1996." Date on No. 2920 is nearly twice as large as date on No. 2920b. No. 2920f comes in various configurations.

No. 2920h is a pane of 16 with one stamp removed. The missing stamp is the lower right stamp in the pane. No. 2920h cannot be made from No. 2920f, a pane of 15 + label. The label is located in the second or third row of the pane and is die cut. If the label is removed, an impression of the die cutting appears on the backing paper.

Serpentine Die Cut 9.8 on 2 or 3 Adjacent Sides

2921 A2212 32c dk bl, tan, brn, red & lt bl, red "1996" date .60 .20
- *a.* Booklet pane of 10, red "1996" date 6.00
- *b.* As #2921, red "1997" date .60 .20
- *c.* As "a," red "1997" date 6.00
- *d.* Booklet pane of 5 + label, red "1997" date 3.25
- *e.* As "a," imperf —

Issued: #2902, 2905, 3/10/95; #2908-2909, 2911-2912, 2919, 3/17/95; #2915, 2920, 4/18/95; #2897, 2913-2914, 2916, 5/19/95; #2920d, 1/20/96; #2904B, 2912B, 2915D 1/24/96; #2903-2904, 3/16/96; #2915A, 5/21/96; #2907, 2921, 5/21/96; #2902B, 2904A, 2906, 2910, 2912A, 2915B, 6/15/96; #2915C, 5/21/96; #2921d, 1/24/97.

See Nos. 3132-3133.

Great Americans Issue

A2248

A2249

A2250

A2251

A2253

A2255

A2256

A2257

A2258

Perf. 11, Serpentine Die Cut 11½ (#2941), 11¾x11½ (#2942)

1995-99 Engr.

Self-Adhesive (#2941-2942)

2933 A2248 32c brown .60 .20
2934 A2249 32c green .60 .20
2935 A2250 32c lake .60 .20
2936 A2251 32c blue .60 .20
2938 A2253 46c carmine .90 .20
2940 A2255 55c green 1.10 .20
- *a.* Imperf., pair —

2941 A2256 55c black 1.10 .20
2942 A2257 77c blue 1.50 .20
2943 A2258 78c bright violet 1.60 .20
- *a.* 78c Dull violet 1.60 .20
- *b.* 78c Pale violet 1.75 .30

Nos. 2933-2943 (9) 8.60 1.80

Issued: #2933, 9/13; 46c, 10/20; 55c, 7/11; 78c, 8/18; #2934, 5/26/96; #2935, 4/3/98; #2936, 7/16/98; #2942, 11/9/98; #2941, 7/17/99.

This is an expanding set. Nos. will change.

Love

Cherub from Sistine Madonna, by Raphael
A2263 A2264

Litho. & Engr.

1995, Feb. 1 ***Perf. 11.2***

2948 A2263 (32c) multicolored .60 .20

Self-Adhesive

Die Cut

2949 A2264 (32c) multicolored .60 .20
- *a.* Booklet pane of 20 + label 12.00
- *b.* As No. 2949, red (engr.) omitted —
- *c.* As "a," red (engr.) omitted —

Florida Statehood, 150th Anniv.
A2265

1995, Mar. 3 Litho. ***Perf. 11.1***

2950 A2265 32c multicolored .60 .20

Earth Day

Earth Clean-Up
A2266

Solar Energy
A2267

Tree Planting
A2268

Beach Clean-Up
A2269

1995, Apr. 20 Litho. ***Perf. 11.1x11***

2951 A2266 32c multicolored .60 .20
2952 A2267 32c multicolored .60 .20
2953 A2268 32c multicolored .60 .20
2954 A2269 32c multicolored .60 .20
- *a.* Block of 4, #2951-2954 2.40 1.75

Richard M. Nixon

Richard M. Nixon, 37th President (1913-94) — A2270

Litho. & Engr.

1995, Apr. 26 ***Perf. 11.2***

2955 A2270 32c multicolored .60 .20
- *a.* Red (engr.) omitted *1,400.*

No. 2955 is known with red (engr. "Richard Nixon") inverted, and with red (engr.) omitted but only half of Nixon portrait present, both from printer's waste.

No. 2955a shows a complete Nixon portrait.

Black Heritage

Bessie Coleman (d. 1926), Aviator — A2271

1995, Apr. 27 Engr. ***Perf. 11.2***

2956 A2271 32c red & black .60 .20

Love

A2272

A2273

Cherubs from Sistine Madonna, by Raphael — A2274

Litho. & Engr.

1995, May 12 ***Perf. 11.2***

2957 A2272 32c multicolored .60 .20
2958 A2273 55c multicolored 1.10 .20

BOOKLET STAMPS

Perf. 9.8x10.8

2959 A2272 32c multicolored .60 .20
- *a.* Booklet pane of 10 6.00 *3.25*
- *b.* As "a," imperf —

Self-Adhesive

Die Cut

2960 A2274 55c multicolored 1.10 .20
- *a.* Booklet pane of 20 + label 22.50

Recreational Sports

Volleyball
A2275

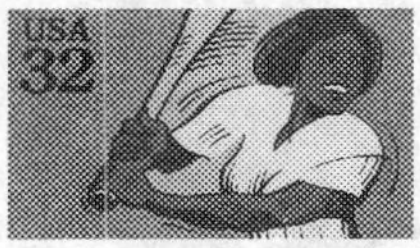

Softball
A2276

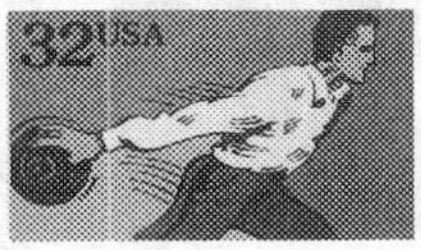

Bowling
A2277

Tennis
A2278

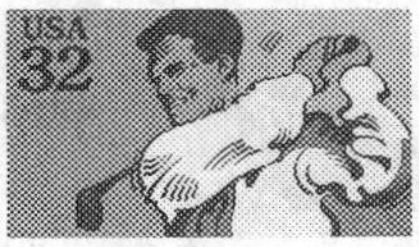

Golf
A2279

1995, May 20 Litho. ***Perf. 11.2***

2961 A2275 32c multicolored .60 .20
2962 A2276 32c multicolored .60 .20
2963 A2277 32c multicolored .60 .20
2964 A2278 32c multicolored .60 .20
2965 A2279 32c multicolored .60 .20
- *a.* Vert. strip of 5, #2961-2965 3.00 2.00
- *b.* As "a," imperf *2,500.*
- *c.* As "a," yellow omitted *2,500.*
- *d.* As "a," yel, bl & mag omitted *2,500.*

Prisoners of War & Missing in Action

A2280

1995, May 29 ***Perf. 11.2***

2966 A2280 32c multicolored .60 .20

Legends of Hollywood

Marilyn Monroe (1926-62) — A2281

1995, June 1 Photo. ***Perf. 11.1***

2967 A2281 32c multicolored .60 .20
- *a.* Imperf., pair *600.00*

Texas Statehood

A2282

1995, June 16 Litho. ***Perf. 11.2***

2968 A2282 32c multicolored .60 .20

Great Lakes Lighthouses

Split Rock, Lake Superior
A2283

St. Joseph, Lake Michigan
A2284

Spectacle Reef, Lake Huron
A2285

Marblehead, Lake Erie
A2286

Thirty Mile Point, Lake Ontario — A2287

Perf. 11.2 Vert.

1995, June 17 **Photo.**

Booklet Stamps

2969	A2283	32c multicolored	.60	.20
2970	A2284	32c multicolored	.60	.20
2971	A2285	32c multicolored	.60	.20
2972	A2286	32c multicolored	.60	.20
2973	A2287	32c multicolored	.60	.20
a.		Booklet pane of 5, #2969-2973	3.00	*2.25*

U.N., 50th Anniv.

A2288

1995, June 26 **Engr.** ***Perf. 11.2***

2974	A2288	32c blue	.60	.20

Civil War

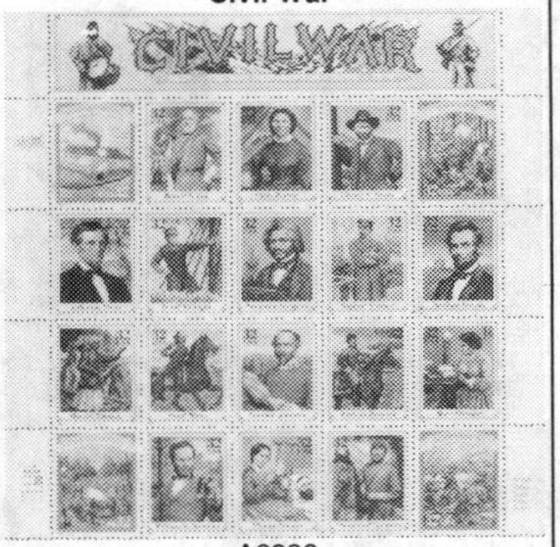

A2289

Designs: a, Monitor and Virginia. b, Robert E. Lee. c, Clara Barton. d, Ulysses S. Grant. e, Battle of Shiloh. f, Jefferson Davis. g, David Farragut. h, Frederick Douglass. i, Raphael Semmes. j, Abraham Lincoln. k, Harriet Tubman. l, Stand Watie. m, Joseph E. Johnston. n, Winfield Hancock. o, Mary Chesnut. p, Battle of Chancellorsville. q, William T. Sherman. r, Phoebe Pember. s, "Stonewall" Jackson. t, Battle of Gettysburg.

1995, June 29 **Photo.** ***Perf. 10.1***

2975	A2289 Pane of 20		12.00	—
a.-t.	32c any single		.60	.20
u.	As "No. 2975," a.-e. imperf, f.-j. part perf			—
v.	As "No. 2975," k.-t. imperf, f.-j. part perf			—
w.	As "No. 2975," imperf		*1,500.*	
x.	Block of 9 (f.-h., k.-m., p.-r.), k.-l., p.-q. imperf vert.			—

Carousel Horses

A2290

A2291

A2292

A2293

1995, July 21 **Litho.** ***Perf. 11***

2976	A2290	32c multicolored	.60	.20
2977	A2291	32c multicolored	.60	.20
2978	A2292	32c multicolored	.60	.20
2979	A2293	32c multicolored	.60	.20
a.		Block of 4, #2976-2979	2.40	1.75

Woman Suffrage

A2294

Litho. & Engr.

1995, Aug. 26 ***Perf. 11.1x11***

2980	A2294	32c multicolored	.60	.20
a.		Black (engr.) omitted	425.00	
b.		Imperf, pair	*1,500.*	

No. 2980a is valued in the grade of fine. Very fine examples sell for much more.

World War II

A2295

Designs and events of 1945: a, Marines raise flag on Iwo Jima. b, Fierce fighting frees Manila by March 3, 1945. c, Soldiers advancing (Okinawa, the last big battle). d, Destroyed bridge (US and Soviets link up at Elbe River). e, Allies liberate Holocaust survivors. f, Germany surrenders at Reims. g, Refugees (by 1945, World War II has uprooted millions). h, Truman announces Japan's surrender. i, Sailor kissing nurse (news of victory hits home). j, Hometowns honor their returning veterans.

Central label is size of 15 stamps and shows world map with extent of Axis control and Allied operations.

Illustration reduced.

Litho. & Engr.

1995, Sept. 2 ***Perf. 11.1***

2981	A2295	Block of 10	6.00	4.50
a.-j.		32c any single	.60	.30

American Music Series

Louis Armstrong (1901-71) A2296

Coleman Hawkins (1904-69) A2297

James P. Johnson (1894-1955) A2298

Jelly Roll Morton (1890-1941) A2299

Charlie Parker (1920-55) A2300

Eubie Blake (1883-1983) A2301

Charles Mingus (1922-79) A2302

Thelonious Monk (1917-82) A2303

John Coltrane (1926-67) A2304

Erroll Garner (1921-77) A2305

1995 **Litho.** ***Perf. 11.1x11***

2982	A2296	32c white "32c"	.60	.20
2983	A2297	32c multicolored	.60	.20
2984	A2296	32c black "32c"	.60	.20
2985	A2298	32c multicolored	.60	.20
2986	A2299	32c multicolored	.60	.20
2987	A2300	32c multicolored	.60	.20
2988	A2301	32c multicolored	.60	.20
2989	A2302	32c multicolored	.60	.20
2990	A2303	32c multicolored	.60	.20
2991	A2304	32c multicolored	.60	.20
2992	A2305	32c multicolored	.60	.20
a.		Vert. block of 10, #2983-2992, top selvage	6.00	—
b.		Pane of 20, dark blue (inscriptions) omitted	—	

Issued: No. 2982, 9/1/95; others, 9/16/95.

Garden Flowers

Aster A2306

Chrysanthemum A2307

Dahlia A2308

Hydrangea A2309

Rudbeckia — A2310

Perf. 10.9 Vert.

1995, Sept. 19 **Litho. & Engr.**

Booklet Stamps

2993	A2306	32c multicolored	.60	.20
2994	A2307	32c multicolored	.60	.20
2995	A2308	32c multicolored	.60	.20
2996	A2309	32c multicolored	.60	.20
2997	A2310	32c multicolored	.60	.20
a.		Booklet pane of 5, #2993-2997	3.00	*2.25*

Eddie Rickenbacker (1890-1973), Aviator

A2311

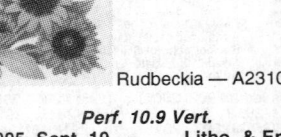

1995, Sept. 25 **Photo.** ***Perf. 11.1***

2998	A2311	60c multicolored	1.25	.25

Republic of Palau

A2312

1995, Sept. 29 **Litho.** ***Perf. 11.1***

2999	A2312	32c multicolored	.60	.20

Comic Strips

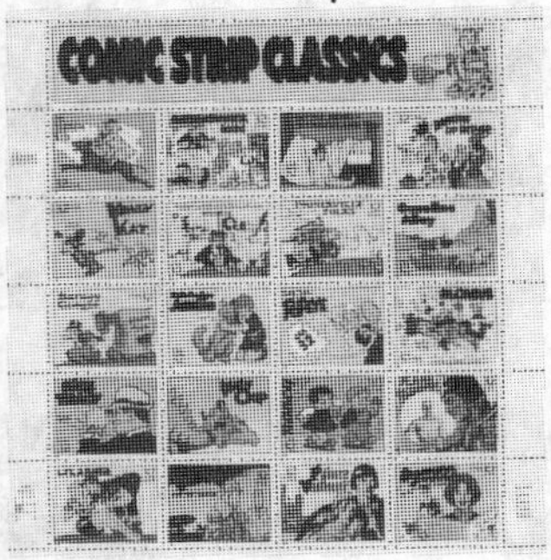

A2313

Designs: a, The Yellow Kid. b, Katzenjammer Kids. c, Little Nemo in Slumberland. d, Bringing Up Father. e, Krazy Kat. f, Rube Goldberg's Inventions. g, Toonerville Folks. h, Gasoline Alley. i, Barney Google. j, Little Orphan Annie. k, Popeye. l, Blondie. m, Dick Tracy. n, Alley Oop. o, Nancy. p, Flash Gordon. q, Li'l Abner. r, Terry and the Pirates. s, Prince Valiant. t, Brenda Starr, Reporter.

1995, Oct. 1 Photo. *Perf. 10.1*

3000 A2313	Pane of 20	12.00	—
a.-t.	32c any single	.60	.20
u.	As No. 3000, a.-h. imperf., i.-l. part perf	—	
v.	As No. 3000, m.-t. imperf., i.-l. part perf	—	
w.	As No. 3000, a.-l. imperf., m.-t. imperf vert.	—	

Inscriptions on back of each stamp describe the comic strip.

U.S. Naval Academy, 150th Anniversary

A2314

1995, Oct. 10 Litho. *Perf. 10.9*

3001 A2314 32c multicolored .60 .20

Literary Arts Series

Tennessee Williams (1911-83) A2315

1995, Oct. 13 Litho. *Perf. 11.1*

3002 A2315 32c multicolored .60 .20

Christmas

Madonna and Child, by Giotto di Bondone — A2316

Santa Claus Entering Chimney A2317

Child Holding Jumping Jack A2318

Child Holding Tree A2319

Santa Claus Working on Sled A2320

Midnight Angel A2321

Children Sledding A2322

1995 Litho. & Engr. *Perf. 11.2*

3003 A2316	32c multicolored	.60	.20
a.	Perf. 9.8x10.8, from bklt. pane	.60	.20
b.	As "a," booklet pane of 10	6.00	*4.00*
c.	As #3003, black (engr. denomination) omitted	*250.00*	

Lithographed

3004 A2317	32c multicolored	.60	.20
3005 A2318	32c multicolored	.60	.20
3006 A2319	32c multicolored	.60	.20
3007 A2320	32c multicolored	.60	.20
a.	Block or strip of 4, #3004-3007	2.40	1.25
b.	Booklet pane of 10, 3 each #3004-3005, 2 each #3006-3007	6.00	*4.00*
c.	Booklet pane of 10, 2 each #3004-3005, 3 each #3006-3007	6.00	*4.00*
d.	As "a," imperf.	*750.00*	

Self-Adhesive Stamps

Photogravure

Serpentine Die Cut

3008 A2320	32c multicolored	.60	.20
3009 A2318	32c multicolored	.60	.20
3010 A2317	32c multicolored	.60	.20
3011 A2319	32c multicolored	.60	.20
a.	Booklet pane of 20, 5 each #3008-3011 + label	12.00	

Lithographed

3012 A2321	32c multicolored	.60	.20
a.	Booklet pane of 20 + label	12.00	
c.	Booklet pane of 15 + label	9.00	
d.	Booklet pane of 15	—	

Colors of No. 3012c are deeper than those on #3012a. Label on #3012c has die-cutting, not found on label of #3012a.

No. 3012d is a pane of 16 with one stamp removed. The missing stamp is from the second row, either from the top or bottom, of the pane. No. 3012d cannot be made from No. 3012c, a pane of 15 + label. The label is die cut. If the label is removed, an impression of the die cutting appears on the backing paper.

Photogravure

Die Cut

3013 A2322	32c multicolored	.60	.20
a.	Booklet pane of 18	11.00	

Self-Adhesive Coil Stamps

Serpentine Die Cut Vert.

3014 A2320	32c multicolored	.60	.30
3015 A2318	32c multicolored	.60	.30
3016 A2317	32c multicolored	.60	.30
3017 A2319	32c multicolored	.60	.30
a.	Strip of 4, #3014-3017	2.40	

Lithographed

3018 A2321 32c multicolored .60 .30

Nos. 3014-3018 were only available through the Philatelic Fullfillment Center in Kansas City.

Issued: #3003, 3012-3013, 3018, 10/19; #3004-3011, 3014-3017, 9/30.

Antique Automobiles

1893 Duryea A2323

1894 Haynes A2324

1898 Columbia A2325

1899 Winton A2326

1901 White A2327

1995, Nov. 3 Photo. *Perf. 11.1*

3019 A2323	32c multicolored	.60	.20
3020 A2324	32c multicolored	.60	.20
3021 A2325	32c multicolored	.60	.20
3022 A2326	32c multicolored	.60	.20
3023 A2327	32c multicolored	.60	.20
a.	Vert. or horiz. strip of 5, #3019-3023	3.00	2.00

Vert. and horiz. strips are all in different order.

Utah Statehood Centenary

Delicate Arch, Arches Natl. Park — A2328

1996, Jan. 4 Litho. *Perf. 11.1*

3024 A2328 32c multicolored .60 .20

Garden Flowers

Crocus A2329

Winter Aconite A2330

Pansy A2331

Snowdrop A2332

Anemone — A2333

Perf. 10.9 Vert.

1996, Jan. 19 Litho. & Engr.

Booklet Stamps

3025 A2329	32c multicolored	.60	.20
3026 A2330	32c multicolored	.60	.20
3027 A2331	32c multicolored	.60	.20
3028 A2332	32c multicolored	.60	.20
3029 A2333	32c multicolored	.60	.20
a.	Booklet pane of 5, #3025-3029	3.00	*2.25*
b.	As "a," imperf	—	

Love

Cherub from Sistine Madonna, by Raphael — A2334

Serpentine Die Cut 11¼x11¾

1996, Jan. 20

Self-Adhesive

Booklet Stamp

3030 A2334	32c multicolored	.60	.20
a.	Booklet pane of 20 + label	12.00	
b.	Booklet pane of 15 + label	9.00	
c.	Red omitted	—	

Flora and Fauna Series

Kestrel Type of 1995 and

Red-headed Woodpecker A2335

Eastern Bluebird A2336

Red Fox A2339

Ring-necked Pheasant A2350

Coral Pink Rose — A2351

Self-Adhesive Serpentine Die Cut 10¾

1996-99 Litho.

3031 A1841 1c multicolored .20 .20

Perf. 11.1

3032 A2335	2c multicolored	.20	.20
3033 A2336	3c multicolored	.20	.20

Serpentine Die Cut 11.5x11.3

Self-Adhesive

3036 A2339 $1 multicolored 2.00 .50

COIL STAMPS

Perf. 9¾ Vert.

3044 A1841	1c multicolored	.20	.20
a.	Large date	.20	.20
3045 A2335	2c multicolored	.20	.20

Date on #3044 is 1mm long, on #3044a 1.5mm.

Issued: #3032, 2/2/96; #3033, 4/3/96; #3044, 1/20/96; #3036, 8/14/98; #3045, 6/22/99; #3031, 11/19/99.

Blue Jay & Rose Types of 1993-95

Serpentine Die Cut 10.4x10.8 on 3 Sides

1996-98 Photo.

Self-Adhesive

Booklet Stamps

3048 A1847	20c multicolored	.40	.20
a.	Booklet pane of 10	4.00	

Serpentine Die Cut 11.3x11.7

3049 A1853	32c yellow, orange, green & black	.60	.20
a.	Booklet pane of 20 + label	12.00	
b.	Booklet pane of 4	2.75	
c.	Booklet pane of 5 + label	3.00	
d.	Booklet pane of 6	3.60	

Serpentine Die Cut 11.2 on 3 Sides

3050 A2350	20c multicolored	.40	.20
a.	Booklet pane of 10	4.00	

Serpentine Die Cut 10½x11 on 3 Sides

3051 A2350 20c multicolored .40 .20
- *a.* Serpentine die cut 10½ on 3 sides .40 .20
- *b.* Booklet pane of 5, 4 #3051, 1 #3051a 4.00

No. 3051a is turned sideways at the top or bottom of No. 3051b.

Serpentine Die Cut 11½x11¼ on 2, 3 or 4 Sides

3052 A2351 33c multicolored .65 .20
- *a.* Booklet pane of 4 2.60
- *b.* Booklet pane of 5 + label 3.25
- *c.* Booklet pane of 6 3.90
- *d.* Booklet pane of 20 + label 13.00

COIL STAMPS

Serpentine Die Cut 11.6 Vert.

3053 A1847 20c multicolored .40 .20

Serpentine Die Cut 9.8 Vert.

Litho.

Self-Adhesive

3054 A1853 32c yel, org, blk & grn .60 .20
- *a.* Imperf, pair 90.00
- *b.* Blk, yel & grn omitted —
- *c.* Blk, yel & grn omitted, imperf pair —
- *d.* Black omitted —
- *e.* Black omitted, imperf pair —

Nos. 3054b and 3054d also are miscut and with shifted die cuttings.

3055 A2350 20c multicolored .40 .20
- *a.* Imperf, pair —

Issued: #3048, 3053, 8/2/96; #3049, 10/24/96; #3054, 8/1/97; #3050, 3055, 7/31/98; #3051, 7/99; #3052, 8/13/99.

Black Heritage

Ernest E. Just (1883-1941), Marine Biologist — A2358

1996, Feb. 1 Litho. *Perf. 11.1*

3058 A2358 32c gray & black .60 .20

Smithsonian Institution, 150th Anniversary

A2359

1996, Feb. 7 *Perf. 11.1*

3059 A2359 32c multicolored .60 .20

Chinese New Year

Year of the Rat A2360

1996, Feb. 8 Photo. *Perf. 11.1*

3060 A2360 32c multicolored .60 .20
- *a.* Imperf, pair —

Pioneers of Communication

Eadweard Muybridge (1830-1904), Photographer — A2361

Ottmar Mergenthaler (1854-99), Inventor of Linotype — A2362

Frederic E. Ives (1856-1937), Developer of Halftone Process A2363

William Dickson (1860-1935), Co-developer of Kinetoscope — A2364

1996, Feb. 22 Litho. *Perf. 11.1x11*

3061 A2361 32c multicolored .60 .20
3062 A2362 32c multicolored .60 .20
3063 A2363 32c multicolored .60 .20
3064 A2364 32c multicolored .60 .20
- *a.* Block or strip of 4, #3061-3064 2.40 1.75

Fulbright Scholarships, 50th Anniversary

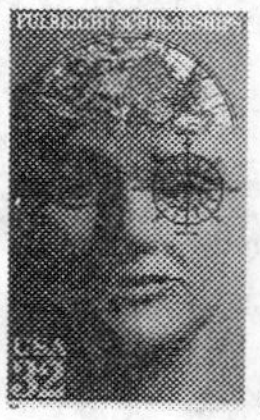

A2365

Litho. & Engr.

1996, Feb. 28 *Perf. 11.1*

3065 A2365 32c multicolored .60 .20

Jacqueline Cochran (1910-80), Pilot

A2366

Litho. & Engr.

1996, Mar. 9 *Perf. 11.1*

3066 A2366 50c multicolored 1.00 .20
- *a.* Black (eng.) omitted 70.00

Marathon

A2367

1996, Apr. 11 Litho. *Perf. 11.1*

3067 A2367 32c multicolored .60 .20

1996 Summer Olympic Games

A2368

Designs: a, Decathlon (javelin). b, Canoeing. c, Women's running. d, Women's diving. e, Cycling. f, Freestyle wrestling. g, Women's gymnastics. h, Women's sailboarding. i, Shot put. j, Women's soccer. k, Beach volleyball. l, Rowing. m, Sprints. n, Women's swimming. o, Women's softball. p, Hurdles. q, Swimming. r, Gymnastics (pommel horse). s, Equestrian. t, Basketball.

1996, May 2 Photo. *Perf. 10.1*

3068 A2368 Pane of 20 12.00 —
- *a.-t.* 32c any single .60 .20
- *u.* As No. 3068, imperf 1,500.
- *v.* As No. 3068, back inscriptions omitted on a, f, k, p, incorrect back inscriptions on others —

Inscription on back of each stamp describes the sport shown.

Georgia O'Keeffe (1887-1986)

A2369

Perf. 11.6x11.4

1996, May 23 Photo.

3069 A2369 32c multicolored .60 .20
- *a.* Imperf, pair 200.00

Tennessee Statehood Bicentennial

A2370

1996, May 31 Photo. *Perf. 11.1*

3070 A2370 32c multicolored .60 .20

Booklet Stamp

Self-Adhesive

Serpentine Die Cut 9.9x10.8

3071 A2370 32c multicolored .60 .30
- *a.* Booklet pane of 20 12.00
- *b.* Horiz. pair, no die cutting btwn. —

American Indian Dances

Fancy A2371

Butterfly A2372

Traditional A2373

Raven A2374

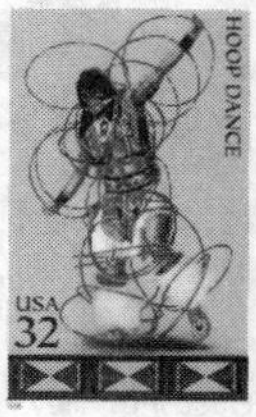

Hoop — A2375

1996, June 7 Litho. *Perf. 11.1*

3072 A2371 32c multicolored .60 .20
3073 A2372 32c multicolored .60 .20
3074 A2373 32c multicolored .60 .20
3075 A2374 32c multicolored .60 .20
3076 A2375 32c multicolored .60 .20
- *a.* Strip of 5, #3072-3076 3.00 1.75

Prehistoric Animals

Eohippus A2376

Woolly Mammoth A2377

Mastodon A2378

Saber-tooth Cat A2379

1996, June 8 Litho. *Perf. 11.1x11*

3077 A2376 32c multicolored .60 .20
3078 A2377 32c multicolored .60 .20
3079 A2378 32c multicolored .60 .20
3080 A2379 32c multicolored .60 .20
- *a.* Block or strip of 4, #3077-3080 2.40 1.50

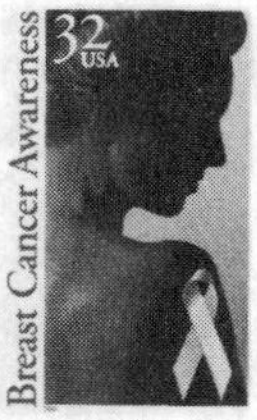

A2380

A2381

Breast Cancer Awareness

1996, June 15 Litho. *Perf. 11.1*

3081 A2380 32c multicolored .60 .20

Legends of Hollywood
James Dean (1931-55)

1996, June 24 Photo. ***Perf. 11.1***
3082 A2381 32c multicolored .60 .20
a. Imperf. pair 425.00
b. As "a," red (USA 32c) omitted —

Folk Heroes

A2382

A2383

A2384

A2385

1996, July 11 Litho. ***Perf. 11.1x11***
3083 A2382 32c multicolored .60 .20
3084 A2383 32c multicolored .60 .20
3085 A2384 32c multicolored .60 .20
3086 A2385 32c multicolored .60 .20
a. Block or strip of 4, #3083-3086 2.40 1.50

Myron's Discobolus
A2386

Young Corn, by Grant Wood
A2387

Centennial Olympic Games

1996, July 19 Engr. ***Perf. 11.1***
3087 A2386 32c brown .60 .20

Sheet margin of the pane of 20 is lithographed.

Iowa Statehood, 150th Anniversary

1996, Aug. 1 Litho. ***Perf. 11.1***
3088 A2387 32c multicolored .60 .20

Booklet Stamp
Self-Adhesive
Serpentine Die Cut 11.6x11.4

3089 A2387 32c multicolored .60 .30
a. Booklet pane of 20 12.00

Rural Free Delivery, Cent.

A2388

Litho. & Engr.

1996, Aug. 7 ***Perf. 11.2x11***
3090 A2388 32c multicolored .60 .20

Riverboats

Robt. E. Lee
A2389

Sylvan Dell
A2390

Far West
A2391

Rebecca Everingham
A2392

Bailey Gatzert
A2393

Self-Adhesive
Serpentine Die Cut 11x11.1

1996, Aug. 22 Photo.
3091 A2389 32c multicolored .60 .20
3092 A2390 32c multicolored .60 .20
3093 A2391 32c multicolored .60 .20
3094 A2392 32c multicolored .60 .20
3095 A2393 32c multicolored .60 .20
a. Vertical strip of 5, #3091-3095 3.00
b. As "a," with special die cutting 75.00 50.00

The serpentine die cutting runs through the peelable backing to which Nos. 3091-3095 are affixed. No. 3095a exists with stamps in different sequences.

On the long side of each stamp in No. 3095b, the die cutting is missing 3 "perforations" between the stamps, one near each end and one in the middle. This allows a complete strip to be removed from the backing paper for use on a first day cover.

American Music Series
Big Band Leaders

Count Basie
A2394

Tommy & Jimmy Dorsey
A2395

Glenn Miller
A2396

Benny Goodman
A2397

Songwriters

Harold Arlen
A2398

Johnny Mercer
A2399

Dorothy Fields
A2400

Hoagy Carmichael
A2401

1996, Sept. 11 Litho. ***Perf. 11.1x11***
3096 A2394 32c multicolored .60 .20
3097 A2395 32c multicolored .60 .20
3098 A2396 32c multicolored .60 .20
3099 A2397 32c multicolored .60 .20
a. Block or strip of 4, #3096-3099 2.40 1.50
3100 A2398 32c multicolored .60 .20
3101 A2399 32c multicolored .60 .20
3102 A2400 32c multicolored .60 .20
3103 A2401 32c multicolored .60 .20
a. Block or strip of 4, #3100-3103 2.40 1.50

Literary Arts

F. Scott Fitzgerald (1896-1940)
A2402

1996, Sept. 27 Photo. ***Perf. 11.1***
3104 A2402 23c multicolored .45 .20

Endangered Species

A2403

Designs: a, Black-footed ferret. b, Thick-billed parrot. c, Hawaiian monk seal. d, American crocodile. e, Ocelot. f, Schaus swallowtail butterfly. g, Wyoming toad. h, Brown pelican. i, California condor. j, Gila trout. k, San Francisco garter snake. l, Woodland caribou. m, Florida panther. n, Piping plover. o, Florida manatee.

1996, Oct. 2 Litho. ***Perf. 11.1x11***
3105 A2403 Pane of 15 9.00 —
a.-o. 32c any single .60 .20

See Mexico No. 1995.

Computer Technology

A2404

Perf. 10.9x11.1

1996, Oct. 8 Litho. & Engr.
3106 A2404 32c multicolored .60 .20

Christmas

Madonna and Child from Adoration of the Shepherds, by Paolo de Matteis — A2405

Family at Fireplace
A2406

Decorating Tree
A2407

Dreaming of Santa Claus
A2408

Holiday Shopping
A2409

Skaters — A2410

1996 Litho. & Engr. ***Perf. 11.1x11.2***
3107 A2405 32c multicolored .60 .20

Litho.
Perf. 11.3

3108 A2406 32c multicolored .60 .20
3109 A2407 32c multicolored .60 .20
3110 A2408 32c multicolored .60 .20
3111 A2409 32c multicolored .60 .20
a. Block or strip of 4, #3108-3111 2.40 1.50
b. Strip of 4, #3110-3111, 3108-3109, with #3109 imperf, #3108 imperf at right —

Self-Adhesive Booklet Stamps
Litho. & Engr.
Serpentine Die Cut 10 on 2, 3 or 4 Sides

3112 A2405 32c multicolored .60 .20
a. Booklet pane of 20 + label 12.00
b. No die cutting, pair 75.00
c. As "a," no die cutting

Litho.
Serpentine Die Cut 11.8x11.5 on 2, 3 or 4 Sides

3113 A2406 32c multicolored .60 .20
3114 A2407 32c multicolored .60 .20
3115 A2408 32c multicolored .60 .20
3116 A2409 32c multicolored .60 .20
a. Booklet pane, 5 ea #3113-3116 12.00
b. As "a," no die cutting —

Photo.
Die Cut

3117 A2410 32c multicolored .60 .20
a. Booklet pane of 18 11.00

Issued: #3108-3111, 3113-3117, 10/8; #3107, 3112, 11/1.

Hanukkah

A2411

Serpentine Die Cut 11.1

1996, Oct. 22 Photo.

Self-Adhesive

3118 A2411 32c multicolored .60 .20

See No. 3352. See Israel No. 1289.

Cycling
Souvenir Sheet

A2412

1996, Nov. 1 Photo. *Perf. 11x11.1*

3119 A2412 Sheet of 2 2.00 2.00
- *a.* 50c orange & multi 1.00 1.00
- *b.* 50c blue green & multi 1.00 1.00

Chinese New Year

Year of the Ox — A2413

1997, Jan. 5 Photo. *Perf. 11.2*

3120 A2413 32c multicolored .60 .20

Black Heritage

Brig. Gen. Benjamin O. Davis, Sr. (1880-1970) — A2414

Self-Adhesive

Serpentine Die Cut 11.4

1997, Jan. 28 Litho.

3121 A2414 32c multicolored .60 .20

Statue of Liberty Type of 1994

Serpentine Die Cut 11 on 2, 3 or 4 Sides

1997, Feb. 1 Photo.

Self-Adhesive

3122 A1951 32c red, lt bl, dk bl & yel .60 .20
- *a.* Booklet pane of 20 + label 12.00
- *b.* Booklet pane of 4 3.20
- *c.* Booklet pane of 5 + label 3.00
- *d.* Booklet pane of 6 3.60
- *h.* As "a," no die cutting —

Serpentine Die Cut 11.5x11.8 on 2, 3 or 4 Sides

1997 Photo.

Self-Adhesive

3122E A1951 32c red, lt bl, dk bl & yel .60 .20
- *f.* Booklet pane of 20 + label 12.00
- *g.* Booklet pane of 6 3.60

Love

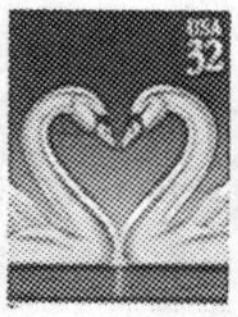

Swans

A2415 A2416

Serpentine Die Cut 11.8x11.6 on 2, 3 or 4 Sides

1997, Feb. 7 Litho.

Self-Adhesive

3123 A2415 32c multicolored .60 .20
- *a.* Booklet pane of 20 + label 12.00
- *b.* No die cutting, pair 250.00
- *c.* As "a," no die cutting —
- *d.* As "a," black omitted —

Serpentine Die Cut 11.6x11.8 on 2, 3 or 4 Sides

3124 A2416 55c multicolored 1.00 .20
- *a.* Booklet pane of 20 + label 21.00

Helping Children Learn

A2417

Serpentine Die Cut 11.6x11.7

1997, Feb. 18 Photo.

Self-Adhesive

3125 A2417 32c multicolored .60 .20

Merian Botanical Prints

Citron, Moth, Larvae, Pupa, Beetle A2418

Flowering Pineapple, Cockroaches A2419

No. 3128 (r), No. 3129 (l), No. 3128a below

Serpentine Die Cut 10.9x10.2 on 2, 3 or 4 Sides

1997, Mar. 3 Photo.

Self-Adhesive

3126 A2418 32c multicolored .60 .20

3127 A2419 32c multicolored .60 .20
- *a.* Booklet pane of 20, 10 ea #3126-3127 + label 12.00

Size: 18.5x24mm

Serpentine Die Cut 11.2x10.8 on 2 or 3 Sides

3128 A2418 32c multicolored .60 .20
- *a.* See footnote .60 .20
- *b.* Booklet pane of 5, 2 ea #3128-3129, 1 #3128a 3.00

3129 A2419 32c multicolored .60 .20
- *a.* See footnote .60 .20
- *b.* Booklet pane of 5, 2 ea #3128-3129, 1 #3129a 3.00

Nos. 3128a-3129a are placed sideways on the pane and are serpentine die cut 11.2 on top and bottom, 10.8 on left side. The right side is 11.2 broken by a large perf where the stamp meets the vertical perforations of the two stamps above it. See illustration above.

Pacific '97

Sailing Ship — A2420

Stagecoach — A2421

1997, Mar. 13 Engr. *Perf. 11.2*

3130 A2420 32c blue .60 .20

3131 A2421 32c red .60 .20
- *a.* Pair, #3130-3131 1.25 .30

Juke Box and Flag Over Porch Types of 1995

COIL STAMPS

1997, Mar. 14 Photo. *Imperf.*

Self-Adhesive

3132 A2225 (25c) brt org red, brt yel grn & multi .50 .50

Tagged

Serpentine Die Cut 9.9 Vert.

3133 A2212 32c dk bl, tan, brn, red & lt bl .60 .20

Nos. 3132-3133 were issued without backing paper. No. 3132 has simulated perforations ending in black bars at the top and bottom edges of the stamp.

Sky on No. 3133 shows color gradation at lower right that is not on Nos. 2915A or 2915D, and it has blue "1996" at left bottom.

Literary Arts

Thornton Wilder (1897-1975) A2422

1997, Apr. 17 Litho. *Perf. 11.1*

3134 A2422 32c multicolored .60 .20

Raoul Wallenberg (1912-47)

Wallenberg and Jewish Refugees A2423

1997, Apr. 24 Litho. *Perf. 11.1*

3135 A2423 32c multicolored .60 .20

Dinosaurs

A2424

Designs: a, Ceratosaurus. b, Camptosaurus. c, Camarasaurus. d, Brachiosaurus. e, Goniopholis. f, Stegosaurus. g, Allosaurus. h, Opisthias. i, Edmontonia. j, Einiosaurus. k, Daspletosaurus. l, Palaeosaniwa. m, Corythosaurus. n, Ornithominus. o, Parasaurolophus.

Illustration reduced.

1997, May 1 Litho. *Perf. 11x11.1*

3136 A2424 Sheet of 15 9.00 —
- *a.-o.* 32c any single .60 .20
- *p.* As #3136, bottom seven stamps imperf —

Bugs Bunny

A2425

Serpentine Die Cut 11

1997, May 22 Photo.

3137 Pane of 10 6.00
- *a.* A2425 32c single .60 .20
- *b.* Booklet pane of 9 5.40
- *c.* Booklet pane of 1 .60

Die cutting on #3137b does not extend through the backing paper.

3138 Pane of 10 *125.00*
- *a.* A2425 32c single *2.00*
- *b.* Booklet pane of 9 —
- *c.* Booklet pane of 1, imperf —

Die cutting on #3138b extends through the backing paper. Used examples of #3138a are identical to those of #3137a.

An untagged promotional piece similar to No. 3137c exists on the same backing paper as the booklet pane, with the same design image, but without Bugs' signature and the single stamp. Replacing the stamp is an enlarged "32 / USA" in the same style as used on the stamp.

Pacific 97

Franklin A2426

Washington A2427

1997 Litho. & Engr. *Perf. 10.5x10.4*

3139 Pane of 12 12.00 —
- *a.* A2426 50c single 1.00 .50

3140 Pane of 12 14.50 —
- *a.* A2427 60c single 1.20 .60

Margins on Nos. 3139-3140 are lithographed.

Issued: No. 3139, 5/29; No. 3140, 5/30.

Marshall Plan, 50th Anniv.

Gen. George C. Marshall, Map of Europe A2428

1997, June 4 *Perf. 11.1*

3141 A2428 32c multicolored .60 .20

Classic American Aircraft

A2429

Designs: a, Mustang. b, Model B. c, Cub. d, Vega. e, Alpha. f, B-10. g, Corsair. h, Stratojet. i, GeeBee. j, Staggerwing. k, Flying Fortress. l, Stearman. m, Constellation. n, Lightning. o, Peashooter. p, Tri-Motor. q, DC-3. r, 314 Clipper. s, Jenny. t, Wildcat.

Illustration reduced.

1997, July 19 Photo. *Perf. 10.1*

3142 A2429 Pane of 20 12.00 —
- *a.-t.* 32c any single .60 .20

Inscriptions on back of each stamp describe the airplane.

Football Coaches

Bear Bryant A2430

Pop Warner A2431

Vince Lombardi A2432

George Halas A2433

1997	Litho.	Perf. 11.2	
3143 A2430	32c multicolored	.60	.20
3144 A2431	32c multicolored	.60	.20
3145 A2432	32c multicolored	.60	.20
3146 A2433	32c multicolored	.60	.20
a.	Block or strip of 4, #3143-3146	2.40	—

With Red Bar Above Coach's Name

Perf. 11

3147 A2432	32c multicolored	.60	.30
3148 A2430	32c multicolored	.60	.30
3149 A2431	32c multicolored	.60	.30
3150 A2433	32c multicolored	.60	.30

Issued: #3143-3146, 7/25; #3147, 8/5; #3148, 8/7; #3149, 8/8; #3150, 8/16.

A2434

Designs: a, "Alabama Baby," and doll by Martha Chase. b, "Columbian Doll." c, Johnny Gruelle's "Raggedy Ann." d, Doll by Martha Chase. e, "American Child." f, "Baby Coos." g, Plains Indian. h, Doll by Izannah Walker. i, "Babyland Rag." j, "Scootles." k, Doll by Ludwig Greiner. l, "Betsy McCall." m, Percy Crosby's "Skippy." n, "Maggie Mix-up." o, Dolls by Albert Schoenhut.

Illustration reduced.

1997, July 28		Perf. 10.9x11.1	
3151 A2434	Pane of 15	9.00	—
a.-o.	32c any single	.60	.20

A2435

A2436

Legends Of Hollywood

Humphrey Bogart (1899-1957)

1997, July 31	Photo.	Perf. 11.1	
3152 A2435	32c multicolored	.60	.20

Perforations in corner of each stamp are star-shaped.

"The Start and Stripes Forever!"

1997, Aug. 21		Perf. 11.1	
3153 A2436	32c multicolored	.60	.20

American Music Series Opera Singers

Lily Pons A2437

Richard Tucker A2438

Lawrence Tibbett A2439

Rosa Ponselle A2440

Classical Composers & Conductors

Leopold Stokowski A2441

Arthur Fiedler A2442

George Szell A2443

Eugene Ormandy A2444

Samuel Barber A2445

Ferde Grofé A2446

Charles Ives A2447

Louis Moreau Gottschalk A2448

1997	Litho.	Perf. 11	
3154 A2437	32c multicolored	.60	.20
3155 A2438	32c multicolored	.60	.20
3156 A2439	32c multicolored	.60	.20
3157 A2440	32c multicolored	.60	.20
a.	Block or strip of 4, #3154-3157	2.40	—
3158 A2441	32c multicolored	.60	.20
3159 A2442	32c multicolored	.60	.20
3160 A2443	32c multicolored	.60	.20
3161 A2444	32c multicolored	.60	.20
3162 A2445	32c multicolored	.60	.20
3163 A2446	32c multicolored	.60	.20
3164 A2447	32c multicolored	.60	.20
3165 A2448	32c multicolored	.60	.20
a.	Block of 8, #3158-3165	4.80	—

Issued: #3154-3157, 9/10; #3158-3165, 9/12.

Padre Félix Varela (1788-1853)

A2449

1997, Sept. 15	Litho.	Perf. 11.2	
3166 A2449	32c purple	.60	.20

Department of the Air Force, 50th Anniv.

Thunderbirds Aerial Demonstration Squadron — A2450

Perf. 11.2x11.1

1997, Sept. 18		Litho.	
3167 A2450	32c multicolored	.60	.20

Beginning with #3167, a hidden 3-D design can be seen on some stamps when they are viewed with a special viewer sold by the post office.

Classic Movie Monsters

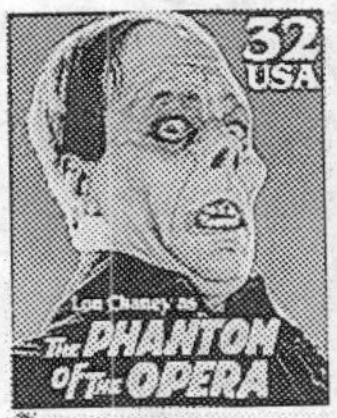

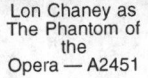

Lon Chaney as The Phantom of the Opera — A2451

Bela Lugosi as Dracula — A2452

Boris Karloff as Frankenstein's Monster — A2453

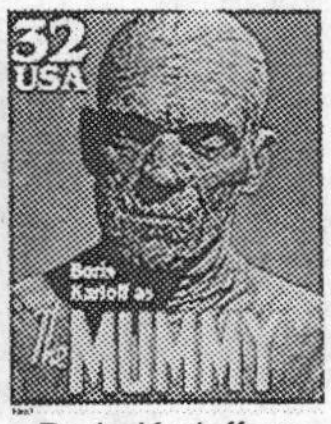

Boris Karloff as The Mummy — A2454

Lon Chaney, Jr. as The Wolf Man — A2455

1997, Sept. 30	Photo.	Perf. 10.2	
3168 A2451	32c multicolored	.60	.20
3169 A2452	32c multicolored	.60	.20
3170 A2453	32c multicolored	.60	.20
3171 A2454	32c multicolored	.60	.20
3172 A2455	32c multicolored	.60	.20
a.	Strip of 5, #3168-3172	3.00	—

First Supersonic Flight, 50th Anniv.

A2456

Serpentine Die Cut 11.4

1997, Oct. 14 Litho.

Self-Adhesive

3173 A2456	32c multicolored	.60	.20

Women In Military Service

A2457

1997, Oct. 18	Litho.	Perf. 11.1	
3174 A2457	32c multicolored	.60	.20

Kwanzaa

A2458

Serpentine Die Cut 11

1996, Oct. 22 Photo.

Self-Adhesive

3175 A2458	32c multicolored	.60	.20

See No. 3368.

Christmas

Madonna and Child, by Sano di Pietro A2459

Holly A2460

Serpentine Die Cut 9.9 on 2, 3 or 4 Sides

1997 Litho.

Booklet Stamps

Self-Adhesive

3176 A2459	32c multicolored	.60	.20
a.	Booklet pane of 20 + label	12.00	

Serpentine Die Cut 11.2x11.8 on 2, 3 or 4 Sides

3177 A2460 32c multicolored		.60	.20
a.	Booklet pane of 20 + label	12.00	
b.	Booklet pane of 4	2.50	
c.	Booklet pane of 5 + label	3.00	
d.	Booklet pane of 6	3.75	

Issued: No. 3176, 10/27; No. 3177, 10/30.

Mars Pathfinder
Souvenir Sheet

Mars Rover Sojourner — A2461

Illustration reduced.

1997, Dec. 10 Photo. *Perf. 11x11.1*
3178 A2461 $3 multicolored 6.00 —

The perforations at the bottom of the stamp include the letters "USA." Vertical rouletting extends from the vertical perforations of the stamp to the bottom of the souvenir sheet.

Chinese New Year

Year of the Tiger
A2462

1998, Jan. 5 Photo. *Perf. 11.2*
3179 A2462 32c multicolored .60 .20

A2463

A2464

Alpine Skiing
1998, Jan. 22 Litho. *Perf. 11.2*
3180 A2463 32c multicolored .60 .20

Black Heritage
Serpentine Die Cut 11.6x11.3
1998, Jan. 28
Self-Adhesive
3181 A2464 32c sepia & black .60 .20

Madam C.J. Walker (1867-1919), entrepreneur.

Celebrate the Century

1900s — A2465

No. 3182: a, Model T Ford. b, Theodore Roosevelt. c, Motion picture "The Great Train Robbery," 1903. d, Crayola Crayons introduced, 1903. e, St. Louis World's Fair, 1904. f, Design used on Hunt's Remedy stamp (#RS56), Pure Food & Drug Act, 1906. g, Wright Brothers first flight, Kitty Hawk, 1903. h, Boxing match shown in painting "Stag at Sharkey's," by George Bellows of the Ash Can School. i, Immigrants arrive. j, John Muir, preservationist. k, "Teddy" Bear created. l, W.E.B. Du Bois, social activist. m, Gibson Girl. n, First baseball World Series, 1903. o, Robie House, Chicago, designed by Frank Lloyd Wright.

1910s — A2466

No. 3183: a, Charlie Chaplin as the Little Tramp. b, Federal Reserve System created, 1913. c, George Washington Carver. d, Avant-garde art introduced at Armory Show, 1913. e, First transcontinental telephone line, 1914. f, Panama Canal opens, 1914. g, Jim Thorpe wins decathlon at Stockholm Olympics, 1912. h, Grand Canyon National Park, 1919. i, U.S. enters World War I. j, Boy Scouts started in 1910, Girl Scouts formed in 1912. k, Woodrow Wilson. l, First crossword puzzle published, 1913. m, Jack Dempsey wins heavyweight title, 1919. n, Construction toys. o, Child labor reform.

1920s — A2467

No. 3184: a, Babe Ruth. b, The Gatsby style. c, Prohibition enforced. d, Electric toy trains. e, 19th Amendment (woman voting). f, Emily Post's Etiquette. g, Margaret Mead, anthropologist. h, Flappers do the Charleston. i, Radio entertains America. j, Art Deco style (Chrysler Building). k, Jazz flourishes. l, Four Horsemen of Notre Dame. m, Lindbergh flies the Atlantic. n, American realism (The Automat, by Edward Hopper). o, Stock Market crash, 1929.

1930s — A2468

No. 3185: a, Franklin D. Roosevelt. b, The Empire State Building. c, 1st Issue of Life Magazine, 1936. d, Eleanor Roosevelt. e, FDR's New Deal. f, Superman arrives, 1938. g, Household conveniences. h, "Snow White and the Seven Dwarfs," 1937. i, "Gone with the Wind," 1936. j, Jesse Owens. k, Streamline design. l, Golden Gate Bridge. m, America survives the Depression. n, Bobby Jones wins Grand Slam, 1938. o, The Monopoly Game.

1940s — A2469

No. 3186: a, World War II. b, Antibiotics save lives. c, Jackie Robinson. d, Harry S Truman. e, Women support war effort. f, TV entertains America. g, Jitterbug sweeps nation. h, Jackson Pollock, Abstract Expressionism. i, GI Bill, 1944. j, Big Band Sound. k, Intl. style of architecture (UN Headquarters). l, Postwar baby boom. m, Slinky, 1945. n, "A Streecar Named Desire," 1947. o, Orson Welles' "Citizen Kane."

1950s — A2470

No. 3187: a, Polio vaccine developed. b, Teen fashions. c, The "Shot Heard 'Round the World." d, US launches satellites. e, Korean War. f, Desegregating public schools. g, Tail fins, chrome. h, Dr. Seuss' "The Cat in the Hat." i, Drive-in movies. j, World Series rivals. k, Rocky Marciano, undefeated. l, "I Love Lucy." m, Rock 'n Roll. n, Stock car racing. o, Movies go 3-D.

1960s — A2471

No. 3188: a, Martin Luther King, Jr., "I Have a Dream." b, Woodstock. c, Man walks on the moon. d, Green Bay Packers. e, Star Trek. f, The Peace Corps. g, Viet Nam War. h, Ford Mustang. i, Barbie Doll. j, Integrated circuit. k, Lasers. l, Super Bowl I. m, Peace symbol. n, Roger Maris, 61 in '61. o, The Beatles "Yellow Submarine."

1970s — A2472

No. 3189: a, Earth Day celebrated. b, "All in the Family" television series. c, "Sesame Street" television series character, Big Bird. d, Disco music. e, Pittsburgh Steelers win four Super Bowls. f, US Celebrates 200th birthday. g, Secretariat wins Triple Crown. h, VCRs transform entertainment. i, Pioneer 10. j, Women's rights movement. k, 1970s fashions. l, "Monday Night Football." m, Smiley face buttons. n, Jumbo jets. o, Medical imaging.

1980s — A2473

No. 3190: a, Space shuttle program. b, "Cats" Broadway show. c, San Francisco 49ers. d, Hostages in Iran come home. e, Figure skating. f, Cable TV. g, Vietnam Veterans Memorial. h, Compact discs. i, Cabbage Patch Kids. j, "The Cosby Show" television series. k, Fall of the Berlin Wall. l, Video games. m, "E. T. The Extra-Terrestrial" movie. n, Personal computers. o, Hip-hop culture.

Litho. & Engr. (#3182m, 3183f, 3184m, 3185b, 3186k, 3187a, 3188c, 3189h), Litho.

1998-2000 ***Perf. 11½***

3182	A2465	Pane of 15	9.00	—
a.-o.		32c any single	.60	.30
3183	A2466	Pane of 15	9.00	—
a.-o.		32c any single	.60	.30
3184	A2467	Pane of 15	9.00	—
a.-o.		32c any single	.60	.30
3185	A2468	Pane of 15	9.00	—
a.-o.		32c any single	.60	.30
3186	A2469	Pane of 15	9.75	—
a.-o.		33c any single	.65	.30
3187	A2470	Pane of 15	9.75	—
a.-o.		33c any single	.65	.30
3188	A2471	Pane of 15	9.75	—
a.-o.		33c any single	.65	.30
3189	A2472	Pane of 15	9.75	—
a.-o.		33c any single	.65	.30
3190	A2473	Pane of 15	9.75	—
a.-o.		33c any single	.65	.30
	Nos. 3182-3190 (9)		84.75	

Issued: #3182-3183, 2/3; #3184, 5/28; #3185, 9/10; #3186, 2/18/99; #3187, 5/26/99; #3188, 9/17/99; #3189, 11/18/99; #3190, 1/12/00.

Numbers have been reserved for one additional sheet in this set.

"Remember The Maine"

A2475

Litho. & Engr.

1998, Feb. 15 *Perf. 11.2x11*

3192	A2475	32c red & black	.60	.20

Flowering Trees

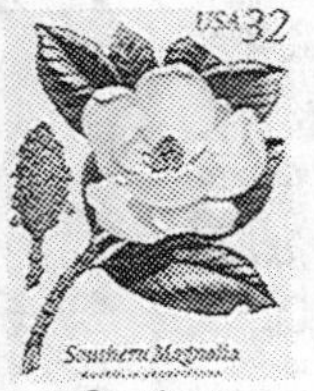
Southern Magnolia A2476

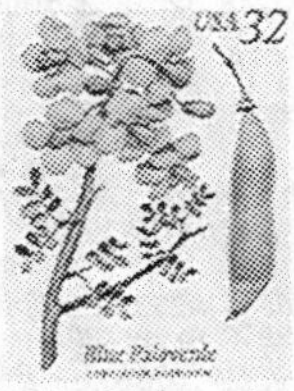
Blue Paloverde A2477

Yellow Poplar — A2478

Prairie Crab Apple — A2479

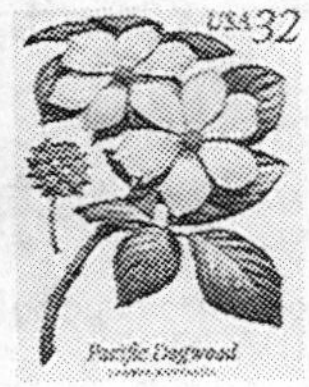
Pacific Dogwood — A2480

Die Cut Perf 11.3

1998, Mar. 19 **Litho.**

Self-Adhesive

3193	A2476	32c multicolored	.60	.20
3194	A2477	32c multicolored	.60	.20
3195	A2478	32c multicolored	.60	.20
3196	A2479	32c multicolored	.60	.20
3197	A2480	32c multicolored	.60	.20
a.		Strip of 5, #3193-3197	3.00	

Alexander Calder (1898-1976), Sculptor

Black Cascade, 13 Verticals, 1959 — A2481

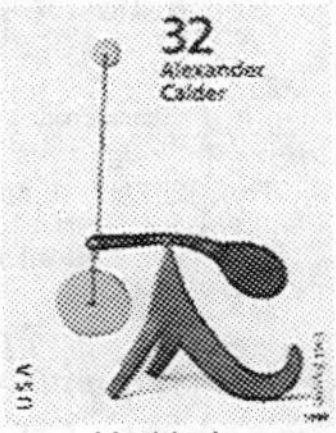
Untitled, 1965 — A2482

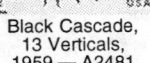

Rearing Stallion, 1928 — A2483

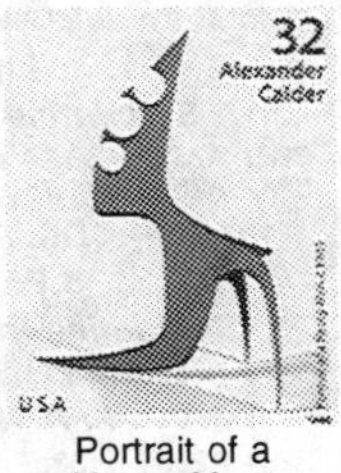
Portrait of a Young Man, c. 1945 — A2484

Un Effet du Japonais, 1945 — A2485

1998, Mar. 25 **Photo.** *Perf. 10.2*

3198	A2481	32c multicolored	.60	.20
3199	A2482	32c multicolored	.60	.20
3200	A2483	32c multicolored	.60	.20
3201	A2484	32c multicolored	.60	.20
3202	A2485	32c multicolored	.60	.20
a.		Strip of 5, #3198-3202	3.00	—

Cinco De Mayo

A2486

Serpentine Die Cut 11.7x10.9

1998, Apr. 16 **Photo.**

Self-Adhesive

3203	A2486	32c multicolored	.60	.20

See No. 3309. See Mexico No. 2066.

A2487

A2488

Sylvester & Tweety

Serpentine Die Cut 11.1

1998, Apr. 27

Self-Adhesive

3204	Pane of 10	6.00	
a.	A2487 32c single	.60	.20
b.	Booklet pane of 9 #3204a	5.40	
c.	Booklet pane of 1 #3204a	.60	

Die cutting on #3204b does not extend through the backing paper.

3205	Pane of 10	*10.00*	
a.	A2487 32c single	*.60*	
b.	Booklet pane of 9 #3205a	—	
c.	Booklet pane of 1, imperf.	—	

Die cutting on #3205a extends through the backing paper. Used examples of No. 3205a are identical to those of No. 3204a.

Wisconsin Statehood

Serpentine Die Cut 10.8x10.9

1998, May 29 **Photo.**

Self-Adhesive

3206	A2488	32c multicolored	.60	.30

See note after No. 3167.

Wetlands A2489

Diner A2490

COIL STAMPS

1998 **Photo.** *Perf. 10 Vert.*

Self-Adhesive (#3207A, 3208A)

3207	A2489	(5c) multicolored	.20	.20

Serpentine Die Cut 9.7 Vert.

3207A	A2489	(5c) multicolored	.20	.20

Perf. 10 Vert.

3208	A2490	(25c) multicolored	.50	.50

Serpentine Die Cut 9.7 Vert.

3208A	A2490	(25c) multicolored	.50	.50

Issued: #3207-3208, 6/5; #3208A, 9/30; #3207A, 12/14.

1898 Trans-Mississippi Stamps, Cent.

A2491

Litho. & Engr.

1998, June 18 *Perf. 12x12.4*

3209	A2491	Pane of 9	7.75	5.00
a.	A100	1c green & black	.20	.20
b.	A108	2c red brown & black	.20	.20
c.	A102	4c orange & black	.20	.20
d.	A103	5c blue & black	.20	.20
e.	A104	8c dark lilac & black	.20	.20
f.	A105	10c purple & black	.20	.20
g.	A106	50c green & black	1.00	.60
h.	A107	$1 red & black	2.00	1.25
i.	A101	$2 red brown & black	4.00	2.50

Vignettes on Nos. 3209b and 3209i are reversed in comparison to the original issue.

3210	A107	$1 Pane of 9 #3209h	18.00	—

Berlin Airlift, 50th Anniv.

A2492

1998, June 26 **Photo.** *Perf. 11.2*

3211	A2492	32c multicolored	.60	.20

American Music Series Folk Singers

Huddie "Leadbelly" Ledbetter (1888-1949) A2493

Woody Guthrie (1912-67) A2494

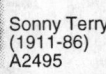

Sonny Terry (1911-86) A2495

Josh White (1908-69) A2496

Gospel Singers

Mahalia Jackson (1911-72) A2497

Roberta Martin (1917-69) A2498

Clara Ward (1924-73) A2499

Sister Rosetta Tharpe (1921-73) A2500

1998, June 26 *Perf. 10.1x10.2*

3212	A2493	32c multicolored	.60	.20
3213	A2494	32c multicolored	.60	.20
3214	A2495	32c multicolored	.60	.20
3215	A2496	32c multicolored	.60	.20
a.		Block or strip of 4, #3212-3215	2.40	—

Perf. 10.1x10.3

1998, July 15 **Photo.**

3216	A2497	32c multicolored	.60	.20
3217	A2498	32c multicolored	.60	.20
3218	A2499	32c multicolored	.60	.20
3219	A2500	32c multicolored	.60	.20
a.		Block or strip of 4, #3216-3219	2.40	—

Spanish Settlement of the Southwest

La Mision de San Miguel de San Gabriel, Española, NM A2501

1998, July 11 **Litho.** *Perf. 11.2*

3220	A2501	32c multicolored	.60	.20

Literary Arts

Stephen Vincent Benét (1898-43) A2502

1998, July 22 **Litho.** *Perf. 11.2*

3221	A2502	32c multicolored	.60	.20

Tropical Birds

Antillean Euphonia A2503

Green-throated Carib — A2504

Crested Honeycreeper — A2505

Cardinal Honeyeater
A2506

1998, July 29 Litho. *Perf. 11.2*

3222	A2503	32c multicolored	.60	.20
3223	A2504	32c multicolored	.60	.20
3224	A2505	32c multicolored	.60	.20
3225	A2506	32c multicolored	.60	.20
a.		Block of 4, #3222-3225	2.40	—

A2507

A2508

Legends of Hollywood

1998, Aug. 3 Photo. *Perf. 11.1*

3226 A2507 32c multicolored .60 .20

Alfred Hitchcock (1899-1980). Perforations in corner of each stamp are star-shaped. Hitchcock's profile in the UL corner of each stamp is laser cut.

Organ & Tissue Donation

Serpentine Die Cut 11.7

1998, Aug. 5 Photo.

Self-Adhesive

3227 A2508 32c multicolored .60 .20

MODERN BICYCLE

A2509

COIL STAMPS

Serpentine Die Cut 9.8 Vert.

1998, Aug. 14 Photo. Untagged

Self-Adhesive

3228 A2509 (10c) multicolored .20 .20

Perf. 9.9 Vert.

3229 A2509 (10c) multicolored .20 .20

Bright Eyes

Dog
A2510

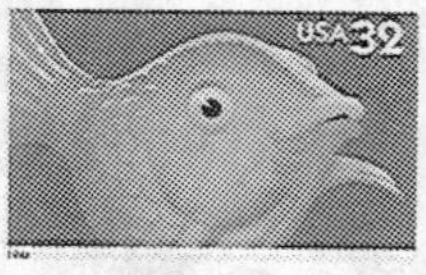

Fish
A2511

Cat
A2512

Parakeet
A2513

Hamster
A2514

Serpentine Die Cut 9.9

1998, Aug. 20 Photo.

Self-Adhesive

3230	A2510	32c multicolored	.60	.20
3231	A2511	32c multicolored	.60	.20
3232	A2512	32c multicolored	.60	.20
3233	A2513	32c multicolored	.60	.20
3234	A2514	32c multicolored	.60	.20
a.		Strip of 5, #3230-3234	3.00	

See note after No. 3167.

Klondike Gold Rush, Centennial

A2515

1998, Aug. 21 Litho. *Perf. 11.1*

3235 A2515 32c multicolored .60 .20

American Art

A2516

Paintings: a, "Portrait of Richard Mather," by John Foster. b, "Mrs. Elizabeth Freake and Baby Mary," by The Freake Limner. c, "Girl in Red Dress with Cat and Dog," by Ammi Phillips. d, "Rubens Peale with a Geranium," by Rembrandt Peale. e, "Long-billed Curlew, Numenius Longrostris," by John James Audubon. f, "Boatmen on the Missouri," by George Caleb Bingham. g, "Kindred Sprits," by Asher B. Durand. h, "The Westwood Children," by Joshua Johnson. i, "Music and Literature," by William Harnett. j, "The Fog Warning," by Winslow Homer. k, "The White Cloud, Head Chief of the Iowas," by George Catlin. l, "Cliffs of Green River," by Thomas Moran. m, "The Last of the Buffalo," by Alfred Bierstadt. n, "Niagara," by Frederic Edwin Church. o, "Breakfast in Bed," by Mary Cassatt. p, "Nighthawks," by Edward Hopper. q, "American Gothic," by Grant Wood. r, "Two Against the White," by Charles Sheeler. s, "Mahoning," by Franz Kline. t, "No. 12," by Mark Rothko.

1998, Aug. 27 Photo. *Perf. 10.2*

3236	A2516	Pane of 20	12.00	—
a.-t.		32c any single	.60	.20

Inscriptions on the back of each stamp describe the painting and the artist.

American Ballet

A2517

Perf. 10.9x11.1

1998, Sept. 16 Litho.

3237 A2517 32c multicolored .60 .20

SPACE DISCOVERY

A2518

A2519

A2520

A2521

A2522

1998, Oct. 1 Photo. *Perf. 11.1*

3238	A2518	32c multicolored	.60	.20
3239	A2519	32c multicolored	.60	.20
3240	A2520	32c multicolored	.60	.20
3241	A2521	32c multicolored	.60	.20
3242	A2522	32c multicolored	.60	.20
a.		Strip of 5, #3238-3242	3.00	—

See note after No. 3167.

Giving and Sharing

A2523

Serpentine Die Cut 11.1

1998, Oct. 7 Photo.

Self-Adhesive

3243 A2523 32c multicolored .60 .20

Christmas

Madonna and Child, Florence, 15th Cent. — A2524

Evergreen Wreath — A2525

Victorian Wreath — A2526

Chili Pepper Wreath — A2527

Tropical Wreath — A2528

Serpentine Die Cut 10.1x9.9 on 2, 3 or 4 Sides

1998, Oct. 15 Litho.

Booklet Stamps

3244	A2524	32c multicolored	.60	.20
a.		Booklet pane of 20 + label	12.00	

Serpentine Die Cut 11.3x11.6 on 2 or 3 Sides

3245	A2525	32c multicolored	.60	.20
3246	A2526	32c multicolored	.60	.20
3247	A2527	32c multicolored	.60	.20
3248	A2528	32c multicolored	.60	.20
a.		Bklt. pane of 4, #3245-3248	2.50	
b.		Bklt. pane of 5, #3245-3246, 3248, 2 #3247 + label	3.00	
c.		Booklet pane of 6, #3247-3248, 2 each #3245-3246	3.60	

Size: 23x30mm

Serpentine Die Cut 11.4x11.6 on 2, 3 or 4 Sides

3249	A2525	32c multicolored	.60	.20
3250	A2526	32c multicolored	.60	.20
3251	A2527	32c multicolored	.60	.20
3252	A2528	32c multicolored	.60	.20
a.		Block of 4, #3249-3252	2.40	
b.		Bklt. pane, 5 each #3249-3252	12.00	
c.		As "a," red ("Greetings 32 USA" and "1998") omitted on #3249, 3252)		—

Weather Vane
A2529

Uncle Sam
A2530

Uncle Sam's Hat
A2531

Space Shuttle Landing
A2532

Piggyback Space Shuttle
A2533

1998 Litho. *Perf. 11.2*

Self-Adhesive (#3259, 3261-3263, 3265-3269)

3257	A2529	(1c) multi	.20	.20
a.		Black omitted		
3258	A2529	(1c) multi	.20	.20

No. 3257 is 18mm high, has thin letters, white USA, and black 1998. No. 3258 is 17mm high, has thick letters, pale blue USA and blue 1998.

Photo.

Serpentine Die Cut 10.8

3259 A2530 22c multi .45 .20

See No. 3353.

Perf. 11.2

3260 A2531 (33c) multi .65 .20

Litho.

Serpentine Die Cut 11.5

3261	A2532	$3.20 multi	6.00	3.00
3262	A2533	$11.75 multi	22.50	11.50

COIL STAMPS

Photo.

Serpentine Die Cut 9.9 Vert.

3263 A2530 22c multi .45 .20

Perf. 9.8 Vert.

3264 A2531 (33c) multi .65 .20

Serpentine Die Cut 9.9 Vert.

3265	A2531	(33c) multi	.65	.20
a.		Imperf., pair	—	
b.		Red omitted	—	
c.		Black omitted	—	
d.		Black omitted, imperf., pair	—	

Unused examples of No. 3265 are on backing paper the same size as the stamps.

On No. 3265b, the blue and gray colors are shifted down and to the right.

Serpentine Die Cut 9.7 Vert.

3266 A2531 (33c) multi .65 .20

Unused examples of No. 3266 are on backing paper larger than the stamps. Corners of stamps are rounded.

BOOKLET STAMPS

Serpentine Die Cut 9.9 on 2 or 3 Sides

3267 A2531 (33c) multi .65 .20
a. Booklet pane of 10 6.50

Serpentine Die Cut 11.2x11.1 on 2, 3 or 4 Sides

3268 A2531 (33c) multi .65 .20
a. Booklet pane of 10 6.50
b. Booklet pane of 20 + label 13.00

Die Cut 8 on 2, 3 or 4 Sides

3269 A2531 (33c) multi .65 .20
a. Booklet pane of 18 12.00

Issued: No. 3262, 11/19; others, 11/9.

A2534

COIL STAMPS

1998, Dec. 14 Photo. *Perf. 10 Vert.*

3270 A2534 (10c) multicolored .20 .20

Serpentine Die Cut 10 Vert.

Self-Adhesive

3271 A2534 (10c) multicolored .20 .20

Compare to Nos. 2602-2604, 2907.

Chinese New Year

Year of the Rabbit A2535

1999, Jan. 5 Photo. *Perf. 11.2*

3272 A2535 33c multicolored .65 .20

Black Heritage

Malcolm X (1925-65), Civil Rights Activist — A2536

Serpentine Die Cut 11.4

1999, Jan. 20 Litho.

Self-Adhesive

3273 A2536 33c multicolored .65 .20

Love

A2537 A2538

1999, Jan. 28 Photo. *Die Cut*

Booklet Stamp

Self-Adhesive

3274 A2537 33c multicolored .65 .20
a. Booklet pane of 20 13.00
3275 A2538 55c multicolored 1.10 .20

Hospice Care

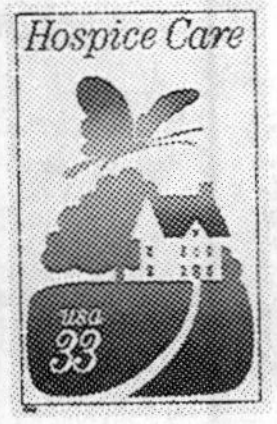

A2539

Serpentine Die Cut 11.4

1998, Feb. 9 Litho.

3276 A2539 33c multicolored .65 .20

Flag and City — A2540

1999 Photo. *Perf. 11.2*

Self-Adhesive (#3278-3279, 3281-3282)

3277 A2540 33c multicolored .65 .20

Serpentine Die Cut 11.1 on 2, 3 or 4 Sides

3278 A2540 33c multicolored .65 .20
a. Booklet pane of 4 2.60
b. Booklet pane of 5 + label 3.25
c. Booklet pane of 6 3.90
d. Booklet pane of 10 6.50
e. Booklet pane of 20 + label 13.00

BOOKLET STAMPS

Serpentine Die Cut 11½x11¾ on 2, 3 or 4 Sides

3278F A2540 33c multicolored .65 .20
g. Booklet pane of 20 + label 13.00

Serpentine Die Cut 9.8 on 2 or 3 Sides

3279 A2540 33c multicolored .65 .20
a. Booklet pane of 10 6.50

COIL STAMPS

Perf. 9.9 Vert.

3280 A2540 33c multicolored .65 .20

Serpentine Die Cut 9.8 Vert.

3281 A2540 33c multicolored .65 .20
a. Imperf., pair —

Corners are square on #3281. Unused examples are on backing paper the same size as the stamps.

3282 A2540 33c multicolored .65 .20

Corners are rounded on #3282. Unused examples are on backing paper larger than the stamps.

Flag and Chalkboard — A2541

Booklet Stamp

Serpentine Die Cut 7.9 on 2, 3 or 4 Sides

1999, Mar. 13 Photo.

Self-Adhesive

3283 A2541 33c multicolored .65 .20
a. Booklet pane of 18 12.00

Irish Immigration

A2542

1999, Feb. 26 Litho. *Perf. 11.2*

3286 A2542 33c multicolored .65 .20

Alfred Lunt (1892-1977), Lynn Fontanne (1887-1983), Actors

A2543

1999, Mar. 2 Litho. *Perf. 11.2*

3287 A2543 33c multicolored .65 .20

Arctic Animals

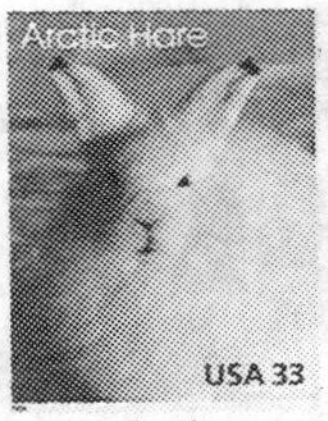

Arctic Hare — A2544 Arctic Fox — A2545

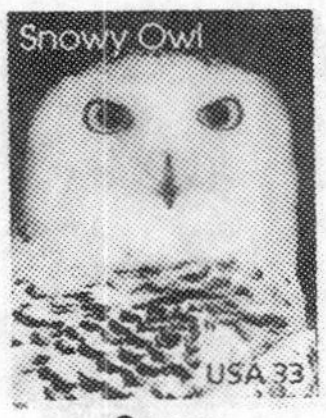

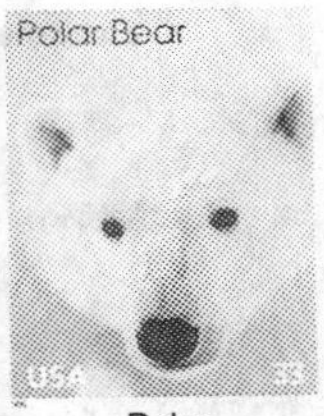

Snowy Owl — A2546 Polar Bear — A2547

Gray Wolf — A2548

1999, Mar. 12 Litho. *Perf. 11*

3288 A2544 33c multicolored .65 .20
3289 A2545 33c multicolored .65 .20
3290 A2546 33c multicolored .65 .20
3291 A2547 33c multicolored .65 .20
3292 A2548 33c multicolored .65 .20
a. Strip of 5, #3288-3292 3.25 —

Sonoran Desert

A2549

Designs: a, Cactus wren, brittlebush, teddy bear cholla. b, Desert tortoise. c, White-winged dove, prickly pear. d, Gambel quail. e, Saguaro cactus. f, Desert mule deer. g, Desert cottontail, hedgehog cactus. h, Gila monster. i, Western diamondback rattlesnake, cactus mouse. i, Gila woodpecker.

Serpentine Die Cut Perf 11.2

1999, Apr. 6 Litho.

Self-Adhesive

3293 A2549 Pane of 10 6.50
a.-j. 33c any single .65 .20

Berries

Blueberries A2550 Raspberries A2551

Strawberries A2552 Blackberries A2553

Serpentine Die Cut 11.2x11.7 on 2, 3 or 4 Sides

1999, Apr. 10 Photo.

Self-Adhesive

3294 A2550 33c multicolored .65 .20
3295 A2551 33c multicolored .65 .20
3296 A2552 33c multicolored .65 .20
3297 A2553 33c multicolored .65 .20
a. Booklet pane of 5 each, #3294-3297 + label 13.00

Serpentine Die Cut 9.5x10 on 2 or 3 Sides

3298 A2550 33c multicolored .65 .20
3299 A2552 33c multicolored .65 .20
3300 A2551 33c multicolored .65 .20
3301 A2553 33c multicolored .65 .20
a. Booklet pane of 15, 4 each #3298-3300, 3 #3301 9.75

COIL STAMPS

Serpentine Die Cut 8.5 Vert.

3302 A2550 33c multicolored .65 .20
3303 A2551 33c multicolored .65 .20
3304 A2553 33c multicolored .65 .20
3305 A2552 33c multicolored .65 .20

A2554 A2555

Daffy Duck

Serpentine Die Cut 11.1

1999, Apr. 16 Photo.

Self-Adhesive

3306 Pane of 10 6.50
a. A2554 33c single .65 .20
b. Booklet pane, 9 #3306a 5.85
c. Booklet pane, 1 #3306a .65

Die cutting on #3306b does not extend through the backing paper.

3307 Pane of 10 *6.50*
a. A2554 33c single *.65*
b. Booklet pane, 9 #3307a *5.85*
c. Booklet pane, 1 #3307a imperf. *.65*

Die cutting on #3307a extends through the backing paper. Used examples of No. 3307a are identical to those of No. 3206a.

Nos. 3306b-3306c and 3307b-3307c are separated by a vertical line of microperforations.

Literary Arts

Ayn Rand (1905-82)

1999, Apr. 22 Litho. *Perf. 11.2*

3308 A2555 33c multicolored .65 .20

Cinco De Mayo Type of 1998

Serpentine Die Cut 11.6x11.3

1999, Apr. 27 Photo.

Self-Adhesive

3309 A2486 33c multicolored .65 .20

Tropical Flowers

Bird of Paradise A2556

Royal Poinciana A2557

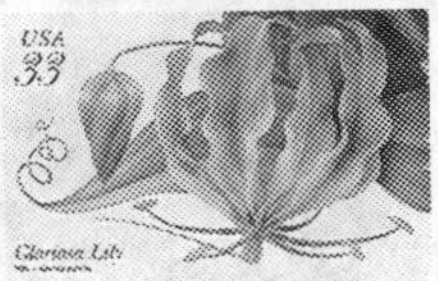

Gloriosa Lily A2558

Chinese Hibiscus A2559

BOOKLET STAMPS

Serpentine Die Cut 10.9 on 2 or 3 Sides

1999, May 1 Photo.

Self-Adhesive

3310 A2556 33c multicolored .65 .20
3311 A2557 33c multicolored .65 .20
3312 A2558 33c multicolored .65 .20
3313 A2559 33c multicolored .65 .20
a. Block of 4, #3310-3313 2.60
b. Booklet pane, 5 #3313a 13.00

John (1699-1777) & William (1739-1823) Bartram, Botanists

Franklinia Alatamaha, by William Bartram — A2560

1999, May 18 Litho. *Perf. 11½*
Self-Adhesive

3314	A2560	33c	multicolored	.65	.20

Prostate Cancer Awareness

A2561

1999, May 28 Photo. *Perf. 11*
Self-Adhesive

3315	A2561	33c	multicolored	.65	.20

California Gold Rush, 150th Anniv.

A2562

1999, June 18 Litho. *Perf. 11¼*

3316	A2562	33c	multicolored	.65	.20

Aquarium Fish
Reef Fish

A2563

A2564

A2565

A2566

#3317, Yellow fish, red fish, cleaner shrimp. #3318, Fish, thermometer. #3319, Red fish, blue & yellow fish. #3320, Fish, heater/airator.

Serpentine Die Cut 11½
1999, June 24Z Litho.
Self-Adhesive

3317	A2563	33c	multicolored	.65	.20
3318	A2564	33c	multicolored	.65	.20
3319	A2565	33c	multicolored	.65	.20
3320	A2566	33c	multicolored	.65	.20
b.	Strip of 4, #3317-3320			2.60	

Extreme Sports

Skateboarding A2567

BMX Biking A2568

Snowboarding A2569

Inline Skating A2570

Serpentine Die Cut 11
1999, June 25 Photo.
Self-Adhesive

3321	A2567	33c	multicolored	.65	.20
3322	A2568	33c	multicolored	.65	.20
3323	A2569	33c	multicolored	.65	.20
3324	A2570	33c	multicolored	.65	.20
a.	Block of 4, #3321-3324			2.60	

American Glass

Free-Blown Glass A2571

Mold-Blown Glass A2572

Pressed Glass A2573

Art Glass A2574

1999, June 29 Litho. *Perf. 11*

3325	A2571	33c	multicolored	.65	.20
3326	A2572	33c	multicolored	.65	.20
3327	A2573	33c	multicolored	.65	.20
3328	A2574	33c	multicolored	.65	.20
a.	Strip or block of 4, #3325-3328			2.60	—

A2575

A2576

Legends of Hollywood
James Cagney (1899-1986)

Perf. 11
1999, July 22 Photo. Tagged

3329	A2575	33c	multicolored	.65	.20

Perforations in corner of each stamp are star-shaped.

Gen. William "Billy" L. Mitchell (1879-1936), Aviation Pioneer

Serpentine Die Cut 9¾x10
1999, July 30 Photo.

3330	A2576	55c	multicolored	1.10	.20

Honoring Those Who Served

A2577

Serpentine Die Cut 11
1999, Aug. 16 Photo.
Self-Adhesive

3331	A2577	33c	black, blue & red	.65	.20

Universal Postal Union

A2578

1999, Aug. 25 Litho. *Perf. 11*

3332	A2578	45c	multicolored	.90	.20

Famous Trains

Daylight A2579

Congressional — A2580

20th Century Limited A2581

Hiawatha A2582

Super Chief A2583

1999, Aug. 26 Litho. *Perf. 11*

3333	A2579	33c	multicolored	.65	.20
3334	A2580	33c	multicolored	.65	.20
3335	A2581	33c	multicolored	.65	.20
3336	A2582	33c	multicolored	.65	.20
3337	A2583	33c	multicolored	.65	.20
a.	Strip of 5, #3333-3337			3.25	—

Stamps in No. 3337a are arranged in four different orders.

Frederick Law Olmstead (1822-1903), Landscape Architect

A2584

1999, Sept. 12 Litho. *Perf. 11*

3338	A2584	33c	multicolored	.65	.20

American Music Series
Hollywood Composers

Max Steiner (1888-1971) A2585

Dimitri Tiomkin (1894-1975) A2586

Bernard Herrmann (1911-75) A2587

Franz Waxman (1906-67) A2588

Alfred Newman (1907-70) A2589

Erich Wolfgang Korngold (1897-1957) A2590

1999, Sept. 16 Litho. *Perf. 11*

3339	A2585	33c	multicolored	.65	.20
3340	A2586	33c	multicolored	.65	.20
3341	A2587	33c	multicolored	.65	.20
3342	A2588	33c	multicolored	.65	.20
3343	A2589	33c	multicolored	.65	.20
3344	A2590	33c	multicolored	.65	.20
a.	Block of 6, #3339-3344			3.90	—

Broadway Songwriters

Ira (1896-1983) & George (1898-1937) Gershwin A2591

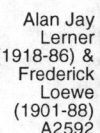

Alan Jay Lerner (1918-86) & Frederick Loewe (1901-88) A2592

Lorenz Hart (1895-1943) A2593

Richard Rodgers (1902-79) & Oscar Hammerstein II (1895-1960) — A2594

Meredith Willson (1902-84) A2595

Frank Loesser (1910-69) A2596

1999, Sept. 21 Litho. *Perf. 11*

3345 A2591 33c multicolored .65 .65
3346 A2592 33c multicolored .65 .65
3347 A2593 33c multicolored .65 .65
3348 A2594 33c multicolored .65 .65
3349 A2595 33c multicolored .65 .65
3350 A2596 33c multicolored .65 .65
a. Block of 6, #3345-3350 3.90 —

Insects & Spiders

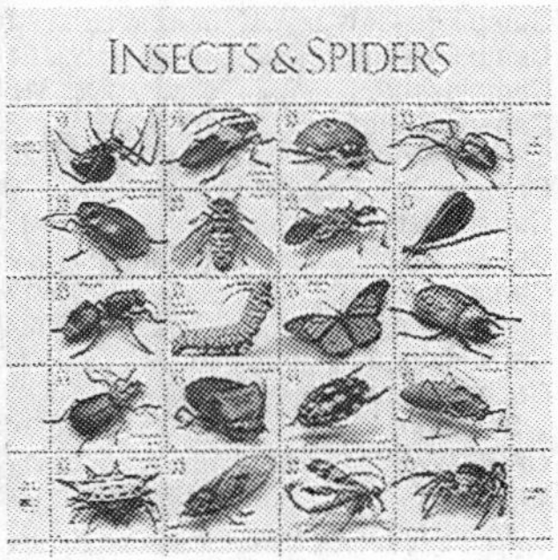

A2597

a, Black widow. b, Elderberry longhorn. c, Lady beetle. d, Yellow garden spider. e, Dogbane beetle. f, Flower fly. g, Assassin bug. h, Ebony jewelwing. i, Velvet ant. j, Monarch caterpillar. k, Monarch butterfly. l, Eastern Hercules beetle. m, Bombardier beetle. n, Dung beetle. o, Spotted water beetle. p, True katydid. q, Spinybacked spider. r, Periodical cicada. s, Scorpionfly. t, Jumping spider.

1999, Oct. 1 Litho. *Perf. 11*

3351 A2597 Pane of 20 13.00 —
a.-t. 33c any single .65 .20

Hanukkah Type of 1996
Serpentine Die Cut 11
1999, Oct. 8 Photo.
Self-adhesive

3352 A2411 33c multicolored .65 .20

Uncle Sam Type of 1998
COIL STAMP
1999, Oct. 8 Photo. *Perf. 9¾*

3353 A2530 22c multicolored .45 .20

NATO, 50th Anniv.

A2598

1999, Oct. 13 Litho. *Perf. 11¼*

3354 A2598 33c multicolored .65 .20

Christmas

Madonna and Child, by Bartolomeo Vivarini A2599

Deer A2600

Serpentine Die Cut 11¼ on 2 or 3 sides
1999, Oct. 20 Litho.
Booklet Stamp
Self-Adhesive

3355 A2599 33c multicolored .65 .20
a. Booklet pane of 20 13.00

Serpentine Die Cut 11¼

3356 A2600 33c gold & red .65 .20
3357 A2600 33c gold & blue .65 .20
3358 A2600 33c gold & purple .65 .20
3359 A2600 33c gold & green .65 .20
a. Block or strip, #3356-3359 2.60

Booklet Stamps
Serpentine Die Cut 11¼ on 2, 3 or 4 sides

3360 A2600 33c gold & red .65 .20
3361 A2600 33c gold & blue .65 .20
3362 A2600 33c gold & purple .65 .20
3363 A2600 33c gold & green .65 .20
a. Booklet pane of 20, 5 each #3360-3363 13.00

Size: 21x19mm
Serpentine Die Cut 11½x11¼ on 2 or 3 sides

3364 A2600 33c gold & red .65 .20
3365 A2600 33c gold & blue .65 .20
3366 A2600 33c gold & purple .65 .20
3367 A2600 33c gold & green .65 .20
a. Booklet pane of 15, 4 each #3364-3366, 3 #3367 +label 9.75

The frame on Nos. 3356-3359 is narrow and the space between it and the hoof is a hairline. The frame on Nos. 3360-3363 is much thicker, and the space between it and the hoof is wider.

Kwanzaa Type of 1997
Serpentine Die Cut 11
1999, Oct. 29 Photo.
Self-Adhesive

3368 A2458 33c multicolored .65 .20

Year 2000

Baby New Year — A2601

Serpentine Die Cut 11¼
1999, Dec. 27 Litho.
Self-Adhesive

3369 A2601 33c multicolored .65 .20

Chinese New Year

Year of the Dragon A2602

2000, Jan. 6 Litho. *Perf. 11¼*

3370 A2602 33c multicolored .65 .20

Black Heritage

Patricia Roberts Harris (1924-85), First Black Woman Cabinet Secretary — A2603

Serpentine Die Cut 11½x11¼
2000, Jan. 27 Litho.
Self-Adhesive

3371 A2603 33c indigo .65 .20

Subject Index of Regular & Air Post Issues

SEMI-POSTAL STAMP

Breast Cancer Awareness

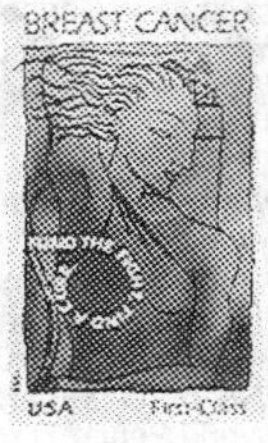

SP1

Serpentine Die Cut 11

1998, July 29 **Photo.**

Self-Adhesive

B1 SP1 (32c+8c) multicolored .80 .60

After the Jan. 10, 1999 1st class postage rate change, #B1 became a 33c stamp with 7c additional for cancer research.

AIR POST STAMPS

For prepayment of postage on all mailable matter sent by airmail.

Curtiss Jenny — AP1

Engraved (Flat Plate Printing)

1918 **Unwmk.** ***Perf. 11***

C1 AP1 6c orange 75.00 30.00
Never hinged 110.00
C2 AP1 16c green 105.00 35.00
Never hinged 155.00
C3 AP1 24c car rose & blue 105.00 35.00
Never hinged 155.00
a. Center inverted *150,000.*
Never hinged *180,000.*
Nos. C1-C3 (3) 285.00 100.00
Nos. C1-C3, never hinged 420.00

Wooden Propeller and Radiator AP2

Emblem of Air Service AP3

De Havilland Biplane — AP4

1923

C4 AP2 8c dark green 27.50 14.00
Never hinged 40.00
C5 AP3 16c dark blue 105.00 30.00
Never hinged 155.00
C6 AP4 24c carmine 120.00 30.00
Never hinged 180.00
Nos. C4-C6 (3) 252.50 74.00
Nos. C4-C6, never hinged 375.00

Map of US and Two Mail Planes AP5

1926-27

C7 AP5 10c dark blue 3.00 .35
Never hinged 4.50
C8 AP5 15c olive brown 3.50 2.50
Never hinged 5.25
C9 AP5 20c yellow green ('27) 9.00 2.00
Never hinged 13.50
Nos. C7-C9 (3) 15.50 4.85
Nos. C7-C9, never hinged 23.25

Lindbergh's Airplane "Spirit of St. Louis" — AP6

1927, June 18

C10 AP6 10c dark blue 8.50 2.50
Never hinged 12.50
a. Booklet pane of 3 85.00 *65.00*
Never hinged 120.00

Singles from No. C10a are imperf. at sides or imperf. at sides and bottom.

Nos. C1-C10 were available for ordinary postage.

Beacon on Rocky Mountains AP7

1928, July 25 ***Perf. 11***

C11 AP7 5c carmine & blue 5.25 .75
Never hinged 8.00
a. Vertical pair, imperf. btwn. *5,500.*

Winged Globe AP8

1930, Feb. 10 ***Perf. 11***

Size: 46½x19mm

C12 AP8 5c violet 11.00 .50
Never hinged 16.50
a. Horiz. pair, imperf. btwn. *4,500.*

See Nos. C16-C17, C19.

Graf Zeppelin Issue

Zeppelin over Atlantic Ocean AP9

Zeppelin between Continents — AP10

Zeppelin Passing Globe — AP11

1930, Apr. 19 ***Perf. 11***

C13 AP9 65c green 250.00 160.00
Never hinged 360.00
C14 AP10 $1.30 brown 500.00 375.00
Never hinged 725.00
C15 AP11 $2.60 blue 800.00 575.00
Never hinged 1,150.
Nos. C13-C15 (3) 1,550. 1,110.
Nos. C13-C15, never hinged 2,235.

Issued for use on mail carried on first Europe-Pan-America round-trip flight of Graf Zeppelin, May, 1930.

Type of 1930 Issue

Rotary Press Printing

1931-32 ***Perf. 10½x11***

Size: 47½x19mm

C16 AP8 5c violet 5.50 .60
Never hinged 8.25
C17 AP8 8c olive bister ('32) 2.50 .40
Never hinged 3.75

Century of Progress Issue

Airship "Graf Zeppelin" — AP12

Flat Plate Printing

1933, Oct. 2 ***Perf. 11***

C18 AP12 50c green 75.00 70.00
Never hinged 110.00

Flight of the "Graf Zeppelin" in Oct. 1933, to Miami, Akron and Chicago, and from the last city to Europe.

Catalogue values for unused stamps in this section, from this point to the end of the section, are for Never Hinged items.

Type of 1930 Issue

Rotary Press Printing

1934, June 30 ***Perf. 10½x11***

C19 AP8 6c dull orange 3.50 .25

Transpacific Issues

The "China Clipper" over the Pacific AP13

Flat Plate Printing

1935, Nov. 22 ***Perf. 11***

C20 AP13 25c blue 1.40 1.00

Issued to pay postage on mail carried on the Transpacific air post service inaugurated Nov. 22, 1935.

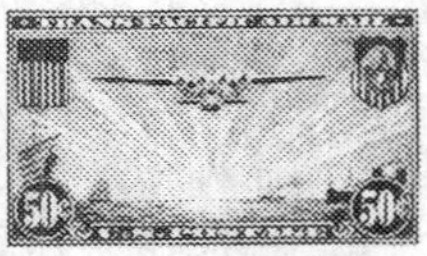

The "China Clipper" over the Pacific AP14

1937, Feb. 15 ***Perf. 11***

C21 AP14 20c green 11.00 1.75
C22 AP14 50c carmine 10.00 5.00

Eagle Holding Shield, Olive Branch and Arrows AP15

1938, May 14 ***Perf. 11***

C23 AP15 6c dk blue & carmine .50 .20
a. Vert. pair, imperf. horiz. 350.00
b. Horiz. pair, imperf. vert. *12,500.*

Transatlantic Issue

Winged Globe AP16

1939, May 16 ***Perf. 11***

C24 AP16 30c dull blue 10.50 1.50

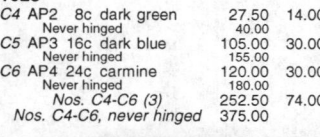

Twin-Motored Transport Plane — AP17

Rotary Press Printing

1941-44 ***Perf. 11x10½***

C25 AP17 6c carmine .20 .20
a. Booklet pane of 3 ('43) 5.00 *1.50*
b. Horiz. pair, imperf. between *2,250.*
C26 AP17 8c olive green ('44) .20 .20
C27 AP17 10c violet 1.25 .20
C28 AP17 15c brown carmine 2.75 .35
C29 AP17 20c bright green 2.25 .30
C30 AP17 30c blue 2.50 .35
C31 AP17 50c orange 11.00 3.00
Nos. C25-C31 (7) 20.15 4.60

Singles from No. C25a are imperf. at sides or imperf. at sides and bottom.

DC-4 Skymaster AP18

1946, Sept. 25 ***Perf. 11x10½***

C32 AP18 5c carmine .20 .20

DC-4 Skymaster — AP19

1947, Mar. 26 ***Perf. 10½x11***

C33 AP19 5c carmine .20 .20

See Nos. C37, C39, C41.

Pan American Union Building, Washington, DC — AP20

Statue of Liberty and New York Skyline AP21

Plane over San Francisco-Oakland Bay Bridge — AP22

1947 ***Perf. 11x10½***

C34 AP20 10c black .25 .20
C35 AP21 15c brt blue green .35 .20
a. Horiz. pair, imperf. between *2,000.*
C36 AP22 25c blue .85 .20
Nos. C34-C36 (3) 1.45 .60

No. C35a is valued in the grade of fine.

Coil Stamp

1948, Jan. 15 ***Perf. 10 Horiz.***

C37 AP19 5c carmine 1.00 .80

New York City Issue

Map of Five Boroughs, Circular Band and Planes — AP23

1948, July 31 ***Perf. 11x10½***

C38 AP23 5c bright carmine .20 .20

50th anniv. of the consolidation of the 5 boroughs of NYC.

Type of 1947

1949, Jan. 18 ***Perf. 10½x11***

C39 AP19 6c carmine .20 .20
a. Booklet pane of 6 10.00 *5.00*

Alexandria Bicentennial Issue

Home of John Carlyle, Alexandria Seal and Gadsby's Tavern AP24

Rotary Press Printing

1949, May 11 ***Perf. 11x10½***

C40 AP24 6c carmine .20 .20

Founding of Alexandria, Va, 200th anniv.

Type of 1947

Coil Stamp

1949, Aug. 25 ***Perf. 10 Horiz.***

C41 AP19 6c carmine 3.25 .20

Universal Postal Union Issue

Post Office Department Building AP25

Globe and Doves Carrying Messages AP26

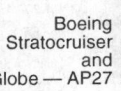

Boeing Stratocruiser and Globe — AP27

1949	Unwmk.	*Perf. 11x10½*	
C42 AP25	10c violet	.20	.20
C43 AP26	15c ultramarine	.30	.25
C44 AP27	25c rose carmine	.50	.40
	Nos. C42-C44 (3)	1.00	.85

75th anniv. of the UPU.

Wright Brothers Issue

Wilbur and Orville Wright and their Plane — AP28

1949, Dec. 17		*Perf. 11x10½*	
C45 AP28	6c magenta	.20	.20

46th anniv. of the Wright Brothers' 1st flight, Dec. 17, 1903.

Diamond Head, Honolulu, Hawaii AP29

1952, Mar. 26		*Perf. 11x10½*	
C46 AP29	80c brt red violet	5.00	1.25

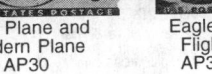

First Plane and Modern Plane AP30

Eagle in Flight AP31

Powered Flight Issue

1953, May 29		*Perf. 11x10½*	
C47 AP30	6c carmine	.20	.20

50th anniversary of powered flight.

For Domestic Post Cards

1954, Sept. 3		*Perf. 11x10½*	
C48 AP31	4c bright blue	.20	.20

See No. C50.

Air Force Issue

B-52 Stratofortress and F-104 Starfighters AP32

Rotary Press Printing

1957, Aug. 1		*Perf. 11x10½*	
C49 AP32	6c blue	.20	.20

50th anniv. of US Air Force.

Flying Eagle Type of 1954
For Domestic Post Cards

1958, July 31		*Perf. 11x10½*	
C50 AP31	5c rose red	.20	.20

Silhouette of Jet Airliner — AP33

1958, July 31		*Perf. 10½x11*	
C51 AP33	7c blue	.20	.20
a.	Booklet pane of 6	14.00	*7.00*
b.	Vert. pair, imperf btwn. (from bklt. pane)	—	

Coil Stamp

Perf. 10 Horizontally

C52 AP33	7c blue	2.25	.20

No. C51b resulted from a paper foldover after perforating and before cutting into panes. Two pairs are known.

See Nos. C60-C61.

Alaska Statehood Issue

Big Dipper, North Star and Map of Alaska AP34

Rotary Press Printing

1959, Jan. 3		*Perf. 11x10½*	
C53 AP34	7c dark blue	.20	.20

Alaska's admission to statehood.

Balloon Jupiter Issue

Balloon and Crowd — AP35

Giori Press Printing

1959, Aug. 17		*Perf. 11*	
C54 AP35	7c dark blue & red	.20	.20

Cent. of the carrying of mail by the balloon Jupiter from Lafayette to Crawfordsville, Ind.

Hawaii Statehood Issue

Alii Warrior, Map of Hawaii and Star of Statehood AP36

Rotary Press Printing

1959, Aug. 21		*Perf. 11x10½*	
C55 AP36	7c rose red	.20	.20

Hawaii's admission to statehood.

Pan American Games Issue

Runner Holding Torch — AP37

Giori Press Printing

1959, Aug. 27		*Perf. 11*	
C56 AP37	10c violet blue & brt red	.25	.25

3rd Pan American Games, Chicago, Aug. 27-Sept. 7.

Liberty Bell — AP38

Statue of Liberty AP39

Abraham Lincoln AP40

Giori Press Printing

1959-66		*Perf. 11*	
C57 AP38	10c blk & grn ('60)	1.25	.70
C58 AP39	15c black & orange	.35	.20
C59 AP40	25c blk & mar ('60)	.50	.20
a.	Tagged ('66)	.60	.30
	Nos. C57-C59 (3)	2.10	1.10

Luminescence

See note following No. 1053. "Tagged" varieties of untagged airmail stamps start with No. C59a and end with No. C67a.

Airmail stamps starting with No. C69 are tagged unless otherwise noted.

Type of 1958

Rotary Press Printing

1960, Aug. 12		*Perf. 10½x11*	
C60 AP33	7c carmine	.20	.20
a.	Booklet pane of 6	17.50	*8.00*
b.	Vert. pair, imperf between	*5,500.*	

No. C60b resulted from a paper foldover after perforating and before cutting into panes. Twp pairs are known.

Type of 1958
Coil Stamp

1960, Oct. 22		*Perf. 10 Horiz.*	
C61 AP33	7c carmine	4.25	.25

Type of 1959-60 and

Statue of Liberty AP41

Giori Press Printing

1961-67		*Perf. 11*	
C62 AP38	13c black & red	.40	.20
a.	Tagged ('67)	.75	.50
C63 AP41	15c black & orange	.30	.20
a.	Tagged ('67)	.35	.20
b.	As "a," horiz. pair, imperf. vert.	*15,000.*	

No. C63 has a gutter between the two parts of the design; No. C58 has none.

Jet Airliner Over Capitol — AP42

Rotary Press Printing

1962, Dec. 5		*Perf. 10½x11*	
C64 AP42	8c carmine	.20	.20
a.	Tagged ('63)	.20	.20
b.	Booklet pane 5 + label	7.00	*3.00*
c.	As "b," tagged ('64)	2.00	*.75*

Three different messages are found on the label in No. C64b, and one on No. C64c.

Coil Stamp

Perf. 10 Horizontally

C65 AP42	8c carmine	.40	.20
a.	Tagged ('65)	.35	.20

The 1st luminescent tagged US issue was No. C64a issued Aug. 1, 1963, at Dayton, OH. Initial experiments there used tagged stamps and an automated facer-canceler to extract airmail as an aid to dispatch.

Montgomery Blair AP43

Bald Eagle AP44

Montgomery Blair Issue

Giori Press Printing

1963, May 3	Unwmk.	*Perf. 11*	
C66 AP43	15c car, dp claret & blue	.60	.55

Blair (1813-1883), Postmaster Gen. (1861-64), who called the 1st Intl. Postal Conf., Paris, 1863, forerunner of the UPU.

For Domestic Post Cards

Rotary Press Printing

1963, July 12		*Perf. 11x10½*	
C67 AP44	6c red	.20	.20
a.	Tagged ('67)	4.00	3.00

Amelia Earhart Issue

Amelia Earhart and Lockheed Electra — AP45

Giori Press Printing

1963, July 24		*Perf. 11*	
C68 AP45	8c carmine & maroon	.20	.20

Earhart (1898-1937), 1st woman to fly across the Atlantic.

Dr. Robert H. Goddard Issue

Robert H. Goddard, Atlas Rocket and Launching Tower, Cape Kennedy
AP46

1964, Oct. 5 Unwmk. Tagged
C69 AP46 8c blue, red & bister .40 .20

Goddard (1882-1945), physicist and pioneer rocket researcher.

Tlingit Totem, Southern Alaska
AP47

"Columbia Jays," by Audubon
AP48

Alaska Purchase Issue
Giori Press Printing

1967, Mar. 30 ***Perf. 11***
C70 AP47 8c brown .25 .20

Cent. of the Alaska Purchase. The Tlingit totem is from the Alaska State Museum, Juneau.

1967, Apr. 26 ***Perf. 11***
C71 AP48 20c multicolored .80 .20

See note after No. 1241.

50-Star Runway — AP49

Rotary Press Printing

1968, Jan. 5 Unwmk. ***Perf. 11x10½***
C72 AP49 10c carmine .20 .20
- ***b.*** Booklet pane of 8 2.00 .75
- ***c.*** Booklet pane of 5 + label 3.75 .75
- ***d.*** Vert. pair, imperf btwn. (from bklt. pane) *8,000.*

Coil Stamp
Perf. 10 Vertically

C73 AP49 10c carmine .30 .20
- ***a.*** Imperf., pair *600.00*

No. C72d resulted from a paper foldover after perforating and before cutting into panes. Only one pair is known.

The $1 Air Lift stamp is listed as No. 1341.

Air Mail Service Issue

Curtiss Jenny
AP50

Lithographed, Engraved (Giori)

1968, May 15 ***Perf. 11***
C74 AP50 10c blue, black & red .25 .20
- ***a.*** Red (tail stripe) omitted —

50th anniv. of regularly scheduled US air mail service.

USA and Jet — AP51

1968, Nov. 22 ***Perf. 11***
C75 AP51 20c red, blue & black .35 .20

See No. C81.

Moon Landing Issue

First Man on the Moon — AP52

Litho. & Engr. (Giori)

1969, Sept. 9 ***Perf. 11***
C76 AP52 10c multicolored .25 .20
- ***a.*** Rose red (litho.) omitted *500.00* —

Man's 1st landing on the moon, July 20, 1969. US astronauts Neil A. Armstrong and Col. Edwin E. Aldrin, Jr., with Lieut. Col. Michael Collins piloting Apollo 11.

On No. C76a, the litho. rose red is missing from the entire vignette—the dots on top of the yellow areas as well as the flag shoulder patch.

Type of 1968 and:

Silhouette of Delta Wing Plane — AP53

Silhouette of Jet Airliner — AP54

Winged Airmail Envelope — AP55

Statue of Liberty
AP56

Design: 21c, "USA" and jet (as C75).

Rotary Press Printing

1971-73 ***Perf. 10½x11***
C77 AP53 9c red .20 .20

Perf. 11x10½

C78 AP54 11c carmine .20 .20
- ***a.*** Booklet pane of 4 + 2 labels 1.25 *.75*
- ***b.*** Untagged (Bureau precanceled) .30

C79 AP55 13c carmine ('73) .25 .20
- ***a.*** Booklet pane of 5 + label ('73) 1.50 *.75*
- ***b.*** Untagged (Bureau precanceled) .30

Giori Press Printing
Perf. 11

C80 AP56 17c bluish black, red & dark green .30 .20

Litho. & Engr. (Giori)
Perf. 11

C81 AP51 21c red, blue & black .35 .20
Nos. C77-C81 (5) 1.30 1.00

Issue dates: 9c, May 15; 11c, May 7; 17c, July 13; 21c, May 21, 1971; 13c, Nov. 16, 1973.

The 9c was for use on domestic post cards. No. C78b is precanceled "WASHINGTON D.C." (or "DC") and No. C79b "WASHINGTON DC" for the use of Congressmen and the public.

Coil Stamps
Rotary Press Printing

1971-73 ***Perf. 10 Vertically***
C82 AP54 11c carmine .25 .20
- ***a.*** Imperf., pair *250.00*

C83 AP55 13c carmine ('73) .30 .20
- ***a.*** Imperf., pair 75.00

Issue dates: 11c, May 7; 13c, Dec. 27.

National Parks Centennial Issue

Kii Statue and Temple, City of Refuge, Hawaii — AP57

Litho. & Engr. (Giori)

1972, May 3 ***Perf. 11***
C84 AP57 11c orange & multi .20 .20
- ***a.*** Blue & green (litho) omitted *1,000.*

Cent. of the Natl. Parks system. No. C84 shows view of the City of Refuge Natl. Historical Park at Honaunau.

Olympic Games Issue

Skiing and Olympic Rings — AP58

Photogravure (Andreotti)

1972, Aug. 17 ***Perf. 11x10½***
C85 AP58 11c multicolored .20 .20

11th Winter Olympic Games, Sapporo, Japan, Feb. 3-13, and 20th Summer Olympic Games, Munich, Germany, Aug. 26-Sept. 11.

Electronics Progress Issue

De Forest Audions
AP59

Litho. & Engr. (Giori)

1973, July 10 ***Perf. 11***
C86 AP59 11c multicolored .20 .20
- ***a.*** Vermilion & olive (litho.) omitted *1,400.*

Statue of Liberty
AP60

Mt. Rushmore National Memorial
AP61

1974 Giori Press Printing ***Perf. 11***
C87 AP60 18c car, black & ultra .35 .25
C88 AP61 26c ultra, black & car .50 .20

Issue dates: 18c, Jan. 11; 26c, Jan. 2.

Plane and Globes
AP62

Plane, Globes and Flag — AP63

Giori Press Printing

1976, Jan. 2 ***Perf. 11***
C89 AP62 25c ultra, red & black .45 .20
C90 AP63 31c ultra, red & black .50 .20

Wright Brothers Issue

Orville and Wilbur Wright, Flyer A — AP64

Wright Brothers, Flyer A and Shed — AP65

Litho. & Engr.

1978, Sept. 23 ***Perf. 11***
C91 AP64 31c ultra & multi .60 .30
C92 AP65 31c ultra & multi .60 .30
- ***a.*** Vert. pair, #C91-C92 1.20 1.10
- ***b.*** As "a," ultramarine & black (engr.) omitted *800.00*
- ***c.*** As "a," black (engr.) omitted —
- ***d.*** As "a," black, yellow, magenta, blue & brown (litho.) omitted *2,250.*

75th anniv. of 1st powered flight, Kill Devil Hill, NC, Dec. 17, 1903.

Octave Chanute Issue

Chanute and Biplane Hangglider
AP66

Biplane Hanggliders and Chanute
AP67

Litho. & Engr.

1979, Mar. 29 ***Perf. 11***
C93 AP66 21c ultra & multi .70 .30
C94 AP67 21c ultra & multi .70 .30
- ***a.*** Vert. pair, #C93-C94 1.40 1.10
- ***b.*** As "a," ultramarine & black (engr.) omitted *4,500.*

Octave Chanute (1832-1910), civil engineer and aviation pioneer.

Wiley Post Issue

Wiley Post and "Winnie Mae" — AP68

NR-105 W, Post in Pressurized Suit, Portrait — AP69

Litho. & Engr.

1979, Nov. 20 ***Perf. 11***
C95 AP68 25c ultra & multi 1.10 .35
C96 AP69 25c ultra & multi 1.10 .35
- ***a.*** Vert. pair, #C95-C96 2.25 1.25

Post (1899-1935), 1st man to fly around the world alone and high-altitude flying pioneer.

Olympic Games Issue

High Jump
AP70

1979, Nov. 1 Photo. ***Perf. 11***
C97 AP70 31c multicolored .65 .30

22nd Olympic Games, Moscow, July 19-Aug. 3, 1980.

Philip Mazzei (1730-1816), Italian-born Political Writer — AP71

1980, Oct. 13 Photo. *Perf. 11*

C98 AP71 40c multicolored .75 .20
- *a.* Perf. 10½x11 5.00 —
- *b.* Imperf., pair 3,250.
- *c.* Horiz. pair, imperf. vert.

Blanche Stuart Scott (1886-1970) AP72

Glenn Curtiss (1878-1930) AP73

1980, Dec. 30

C99 AP72 28c multicolored .55 .20
- *a.* Imperf., pair —

C100 AP73 35c multicolored .60 .20

Scott, 1st woman pilot, and Curtiss, aviation pioneer and aircraft designer.

1984 Olympic Games

AP81

1983, June 17 *Perf. 11*

C101 AP81 28c Gymnast 1.00 .30
C102 AP81 28c Hurdler 1.00 .30
C103 AP81 28c Basketball 1.00 .30
C104 AP81 28c Soccer 1.00 .30
- *a.* Block of 4, #C101-C104 4.50 2.00
- *b.* As "a," imperf. vert. —

Nos. C101-C104 are vertical.

1983, Apr. 8

C105 AP81 40c Shot put .90 .40
C106 AP81 40c Gymnast .90 .40
C107 AP81 40c Swimmer .90 .40
C108 AP81 40c Weightlifting .90 .40
- *b.* Block of 4, #C105-C108 4.25 2.50
- *d.* As "b," imperf. 1,250.

1983, Nov. 4

C109 AP81 35c Women's fencing .90 .50
C110 AP81 35c Cycling .90 .50
C111 AP81 35c Women's volleyball .90 .50
C112 AP81 35c Pole vaulting .90 .50
- *a.* Block of 4, #C109-C112 4.00 3.00

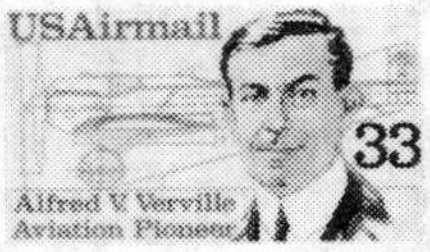

Alfred V. Verville AP86

Lawrence and Elmer Sperry AP87

1985, Feb. 13 Photo.

C113 AP86 33c multicolored .65 .20
- *a.* Imperf., pair 900.00

C114 AP87 39c multicolored .75 .25
- *a.* Imperf., pair 1,400.

Alfred V. Verville (1890-1970), aircraft designer, Lawrence Sperry (1892-1931), designer and pilot, and Elmer Sperry (1860-1930), inventor.

Transpacific Airmail AP88

1985, Feb. 15 Photo.

C115 AP88 44c multicolored .85 .25
- *a.* Imperf., pair 900.00

Fr. Junipero Serra (1713-84)
California Missionary

Outline Map of Southern California, Portrait, San Gabriel Mission AP89

1985, Aug. 22 Photo. *Perf. 11*

C116 AP89 44c multicolored 1.00 .30
- *a.* Imperf., pair 1,500.

Settling of New Sweden, 350th Anniv. AP90

Design: 17th Cent. European settler negotiating with two American Indians, map of New Sweden, the Swedish ships *Kalmar Nyckel* and *Fogel Grip*, based on an 18th cent. illustration from a Swedish book about the Colonies.

1988, Mar. 29 Litho. & Engr.

C117 AP90 44c multicolored 1.00 .25

See Finland No. 768 and Sweden No. 1672.

Samuel Pierpont Langley (1834-1906)
Astronomer, Aviation Pioneer and Inventor

Langley and Unmanned Aerodrome No. 5 — AP91

Litho. & Engr.

1988, May 14 *Perf. 11*

C118 AP91 45c multicolored .90 .20

Igor Sikorsky (1889-1972)
Aeronautic Engineer

Sikorsky and VS300 Helicopter, 1939 AP92

1988, June 23 Photo. *Perf. 11*

C119 AP92 36c multicolored .70 .20

French Revolution, Bicent.

Liberty, Equality and Fraternity — AP93

Litho. & Engr.

1989, July 14 *Perf. 11½x11*

C120 AP93 45c multicolored .95 .20

See France Nos. 2143-2145a.

Pre-Columbian America Issue

UPAE Emblem and Southeastern Figure, *Key Marco Cat,* Calusa Culture, Pre-Columbian Mississippian Period, A.D. 700-1450 — AP94

1989, Oct. 12 Photo. *Perf. 11*

C121 AP94 45c multicolored .90 .20

Discovery of America, 500th anniv. (in 1992).

Futuristic Mail Delivery

Spacecraft AP95 — Air-suspended Hover Car AP96

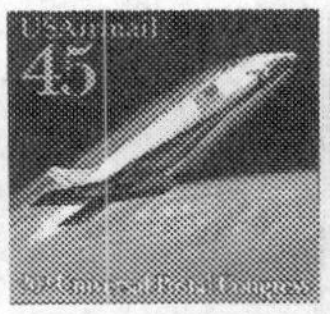

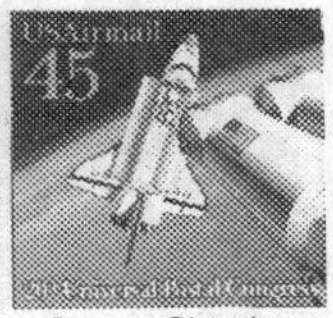

Moon Rover AP97 — Space Shuttle AP98

1989, Nov. 27 *Perf. 11*

C122 AP95 45c multicolored 1.00 .40
C123 AP96 45c multicolored 1.00 .40
C124 AP97 45c multicolored 1.00 .40
C125 AP98 45c multicolored 1.00 .40
- *a.* Block of 4, Nos. C122-C125 4.00 3.00
- *b.* As "a," light blue (engr.) omitted 1,000.

Litho. & Engr.

1989, Nov. 24 *Imperf.*

C126 Sheet of 4 4.50 3.25
- *a.* AP95 45c multicolored 1.00 .50
- *b.* AP96 45c multicolored 1.00 .50
- *c.* AP97 45c multicolored 1.00 .50
- *d.* AP98 45c multicolored 1.00 .50

World Stamp Expo '89, 20th UPU Congress. See Russia No. 5837.

Pre-Columbian America Issue

Tropical Coast AP99

1990, Oct. 12 Photo. *Perf. 11*

C127 AP99 45c multicolored .90 .20

Harriet Quimby, Bleriot Aircraft AP100

1991, Apr. 27 Photo. *Perf. 11*

C128 AP100 50c multicolored 1.00 .25
- *a.* Vert. pair, imperf. horiz. 2,000.
- *b.* Perf. 11.2 ('93) 1.00 .25

William T. Piper, Piper Cub AP101

1991, May 17

C129 AP101 40c multicolored .80 .20

See No. C132.

Antarctic Treaty, 30th Anniv. AP102

1991, June 21 Photo. *Perf. 11*

C130 AP102 50c multicolored 1.00 .25

Pre-Columbian America Issue

First Americans Crossed Over From Asia AP103

1991, Oct. 12 Photo. *Perf. 11*

C131 AP103 50c multicolored 1.00 .25

Piper Type of 1991

1993 Photo. *Perf. 11*

C132 AP101 40c multicolored 1.00 .20

Piper's hair touches top edge of design. Bullseye perf. 11.2.

"All LC (Letters and Cards) mail receives First-Class Mail service in the United States, is dispatched by the fastest transportation available, and travels by airmail or priority service in the destination country. All LC mail should be marked 'AIRMAIL' or 'PAR AVION.'" (U.S. Postal Service, Pub. 51).

No. C133 listed below was issued to meet the LC rate to Canada and Mexico and is inscribed with the silhouette of a jet plane next to the denomination indicating the need for airmail service. This is unlike No. 2998, which met the LC rate to other countries, but contained no indication that it was intended for that use.

Future issues that meet a specific international airmail rate and contain the airplane silhouette will be treated by Scott as Air Post stamps. Stamps similar to No. 2998 will be listed in the Postage section.

Niagara Falls

AP104

1999, May 12 Photo. *Perf. 11*

Self-Adhesive

C133 AP104 48c multicolored .95 .20

Rio Grande

AP105

Serpentine Die Cut 11

1999, July 30 Photo.

Self-Adhesive

C134 AP105 40c multicolored .80 .60

Grand Canyon

AP106

Serpentine Die Cut 11¼x11½

2000, Jan. 20 Litho.

Self-Adhesive

C135 AP106 60c multicolored 1.25 .25

AIR POST SPECIAL DELIVERY STAMPS

To provide for the payment of both the postage and the special delivery fee in one stamp.

Great Seal of United States APSD1

Flat Plate Printing

1934 Unwmk. *Perf. 11*

CE1 APSD1 16c dark blue .60 .65
Never hinged .80

For imperforate variety see No. 771.

1936

CE2 APSD1 16c red & blue .40 .25
Never hinged .50
a. Horiz. pair, imperf. vert. *4,000.*

SPECIAL DELIVERY STAMPS

When affixed to any letter or article of mailable matter, secure immediate delivery, between 7 A. M. and midnight, at any post office.

Messenger Running SD1

Flat Plate Printing

1885 Unwmk. *Perf. 12*

E1 SD1 10c blue 300.00 45.00
Never hinged 525.00

Messenger Running SD2

1888

E2 SD2 10c blue 275.00 17.50
Never hinged 475.00

1893

E3 SD2 10c orange 180.00 22.50
Never hinged 310.00

Messenger Running SD3

Line under "Ten Cents"

1894

E4 SD3 10c blue 650.00 30.00
Never hinged 1,150.

1895 Wmk. 191

E5 SD3 10c blue 160.00 3.50
Never hinged 275.00
b. Printed on both sides —

Messenger on Bicycle SD4

1902

E6 SD4 10c ultramarine 105.00 3.25
Never hinged 180.00
a. 10c blue 105.00 3.25
Never hinged 180.00

Helmet of Mercury and Olive Branch — SD5

1908

E7 SD5 10c green 60.00 40.00
Never hinged 105.00

1911 Wmk. 190 *Perf. 12*

E8 SD4 10c ultramarine 100.00 5.25
Never hinged 175.00
b. 10c violet blue 100.00 5.25
Never hinged 175.00

1914 *Perf. 10*

E9 SD4 10c ultramarine 175.00 6.50
Never hinged 300.00
a. 10c blue 210.00 6.50
Never hinged 360.00

1916 Unwmk. *Perf. 10*

E10 SD4 10c pale ultra 275.00 27.50
Never hinged 475.00
a. 10c blue 310.00 27.50
Never hinged 525.00

1917 *Perf. 11*

E11 SD4 10c ultramarine 19.00 .50
Never hinged 32.50
b. 10c gray violet 19.00 .50
Never hinged 32.50
c. 10c blue 50.00 2.50
Never hinged 85.00

Postman and Motorcycle SD6

Post Office Truck — SD7

1922-25

E12 SD6 10c gray violet 32.50 .50
Never hinged 55.00
a. 10c deep ultramarine 37.50 .60
Never hinged 65.00
E13 SD6 15c deep orange ('25) 27.50 1.00
Never hinged 47.50
E14 SD7 20c black ('25) 2.00 .85
Never hinged 3.00
Nos. E12-E14 (3) 62.00 2.35

No. E12 measures 36x21½mm
No. E15 measures 36½x21¾mm
No. E13 measures 36½x21½mm
No. E16 measures 36¾x22¼mm
No. E14 measures 35½x21½mm
No. E19 measures 36¼x22mm

Rotary Press Printing

1927-31 *Perf. 11x10½*

E15 SD6 10c gray violet .60 .20
Never hinged .80
a. 10c red lilac .60 .20
Never hinged .80
b. 10c gray lilac .60 .20
Never hinged .80
c. Horiz. pair, imperf. btwn. 300.00
E16 SD6 15c orange ('31) .70 .20
Never hinged .90

Catalogue values for unused stamps in this section, from this point to the end of the section, are for Never Hinged items.

1944-51

E17 SD6 13c blue .60 .20
E18 SD6 17c orange yellow 2.75 1.75
E19 SD7 20c black ('51) 1.25 .20
Nos. E17-E19 (3) 4.60 2.15

Special Delivery Letter, Hand to Hand — SD8

1954-57 *Perf. 11x10½*

E20 SD8 20c deep blue .40 .20
E21 SD8 30c lake ('57) .50 .20

Arrows — SD9

Giori Press Printing

1969-71 *Perf. 11*

E22 SD9 45c car & vio blue 1.25 .25
E23 SD9 60c vio blue & car ('71) 1.25 .20

Issue dates: 45c, Nov. 21; 60c, May 10.

REGISTRATION STAMP

Issued for the prepayment of registry fees; not usable for postage.

Eagle — RS1

Wmk. 190

1911, Dec. 1 Engr. *Perf. 12*

F1 RS1 10c ultramarine 75.00 7.50
Never hinged 120.00

CERTIFIED MAIL STAMP

For use on first-class mail for which no indemnity value is claimed, but for which proof of mailing and proof of delivery are available at less cost than registered mail.

Catalogue values for unused stamps in this section are for Never Hinged items.

Letter Carrier — CM1

Rotary Press Printing

Perf. 10½x11

1955, June 6 Unwmk.

FA1 CM1 15c red .45 .30

POSTAGE DUE STAMPS

For affixing, by a postal clerk to any piece of mailable matter, to denote the amount to be collected from the addressee because of insufficient prepayment of postage.

Unused Values for Nos. J1-J14 are for stamps with full original gum.

D1

D2

Printed by the American Bank Note Company

1879 Unwmk. Engraved *Perf. 12*

J1 D1 1c brown 50.00 8.50
J2 D1 2c brown 325.00 7.50
J3 D1 3c brown 45.00 4.50
J4 D1 5c brown 525.00 45.00
J5 D1 10c brown 550.00 25.00
a. Imperf., pair *1,750.*
J6 D1 30c brown 275.00 50.00
J7 D1 50c brown 425.00 60.00
Nos. J1-J7 (7) 2,195. 200.50

Special Printing

1879

J8 D1 1c deep brown *9,000.*
J9 D1 2c deep brown *7,000.*
J10 D1 3c deep brown *10,000.*
J11 D1 5c deep brown *6,000.*
J12 D1 10c deep brown *3,250.*
J13 D1 30c deep brown *3,250.*
J14 D1 50c deep brown *3,250.*

1884

J15 D1 1c red brown 50.00 4.50
J16 D1 2c red brown 60.00 4.50
J17 D1 3c red brown 900.00 175.00
J18 D1 5c red brown 450.00 25.00
J19 D1 10c red brown 425.00 17.50
J20 D1 30c red brown 150.00 50.00
J21 D1 50c red brown 1,500. 175.00
Nos. J15-J21 (7) 3,535. 451.50

1891

J22 D1 1c bright claret 22.50 1.00
J23 D1 2c bright claret 27.50 1.00
J24 D1 3c bright claret 55.00 8.00
J25 D1 5c bright claret 67.50 8.00
J26 D1 10c bright claret 110.00 17.50
J27 D1 30c bright claret 425.00 150.00
J28 D1 50c bright claret 450.00 150.00
Nos. J22-J28 (7) 1,157. 335.50

See Die and Plate Proofs in the Scott U.S. Specialized for imperfs. on stamp paper.

Printed by the Bureau of Engraving and Printing

1894

J29 D2 1c vermilion 1,400. 400.
Never hinged 2,250.
J30 D2 2c vermilion 600. 125.
Never hinged 950.

1894

J31 D2 1c deep claret 45.00 6.00
Never hinged 75.00
b. Vert. pair, imperf. horiz. —
J32 D2 2c deep claret 37.50 4.00
Never hinged 62.50
J33 D2 3c deep claret 150.00 30.00
Never hinged 250.00
J34 D2 5c deep claret 225.00 35.00
Never hinged 375.00
J35 D2 10c deep claret 225.00 25.00
Never hinged 375.00
J36 D2 30c deep claret 375.00 90.00
a. 30c carmine 375.00 100.00
Never hinged 625.00
b. 30c pale rose 310.00 85.00
Never hinged 500.00
J37 D2 50c deep claret 1,100. 250.00
Never hinged 1,800.
a. 50c pale rose 1,050. 250.00
Never hinged 1,750.
Nos. J31-J37 (7) 2,157. 440.00

Shades are numerous in the 1894 and later issues.

See Die and Plate Proofs in the Scott U.S. Specialized for 1c imperf. on stamp paper.

1895 Wmk. 191

J38 D2 1c deep claret 8.00 .75
Never hinged 13.00
J39 D2 2c deep claret 8.00 .70
Never hinged 13.00
J40 D2 3c deep claret 55.00 1.75
Never hinged 90.00
J41 D2 5c deep claret 60.00 1.75
Never hinged 100.00
J42 D2 10c deep claret 62.50 3.50
Never hinged 105.00
J43 D2 30c deep claret 500.00 50.00
Never hinged 825.00
J44 D2 50c deep claret 325.00 37.50
Never hinged 525.00
Nos. J38-J44 (7) 1,018. 95.95

1910-12 Wmk. 190

J45 D2 1c deep claret 30.00 3.00
Never hinged 47.50
a. 1c rose carmine 27.50 3.00
Never hinged 45.00
J46 D2 2c deep claret 30.00 1.00
Never hinged 47.50
a. 2c rose carmine 27.50 1.00
Never hinged 45.00
J47 D2 3c deep claret 550.00 30.00
Never hinged 875.00
J48 D2 5c deep claret 85.00 6.50
Never hinged 135.00
a. 5c rose carmine 80.00 6.50
Never hinged 130.00
J49 D2 10c deep claret 110.00 12.50
Never hinged 175.00
a. 10c rose carmine 105.00 12.50
Never hinged 170.00
J50 D2 50c deep claret ('12) 850.00 120.00
Never hinged 1,350.
Nos. J45-J50 (6) 1,655. 173.00

1914 *Perf. 10*

J52 D2 1c carmine lake 55.00 11.00
Never hinged 90.00
a. 1c dull rose 65.00 11.00
Never hinged 105.00
J53 D2 2c carmine lake 45.00 .40
Never hinged 72.50
a. 2c dull rose 50.00 .40
Never hinged 80.00
b. 2c vermilion 50.00 .40
Never hinged 80.00
J54 D2 3c carmine lake 825.00 37.50
Never hinged 1,350.
a. 3c dull rose 825.00 37.50
Never hinged 1,350.
J55 D2 5c carmine lake 36.00 2.50
Never hinged 57.50
a. 5c dull rose 36.00 2.50
Never hinged 57.50
J56 D2 10c carmine lake 55.00 2.00
Never hinged 90.00
a. 10c dull rose 65.00 2.00
Never hinged 105.00
J57 D2 30c carmine lake 225.00 17.50
Never hinged 360.00
J58 D2 50c carmine lake *9,500.* 800.00
Never hinged *15,000.*
Nos. J52-J58 (7) 10,741. 870.90

1916 Unwmk. *Perf. 10*

J59 D2 1c rose 2,400. 325.00
Never hinged 3,900.
J60 D2 2c rose 150.00 20.00
Never hinged 240.00

1917 *Perf. 11*

J61 D2 1c carmine rose 2.75 .25
Never hinged 4.50
a. 1c rose red 2.75 .25
Never hinged 4.50
b. 1c deep claret 2.75 .25
Never hinged 4.50
J62 D2 2c carmine rose 2.50 .25
Never hinged 4.00
a. 2c rose red 2.50 .25
Never hinged 4.00
b. 2c deep claret 2.50 .25
Never hinged 4.00
J63 D2 3c carmine rose 11.00 .25
Never hinged 17.50
a. 3c rose red 11.00 .25
Never hinged 17.50
b. 3c deep claret 11.00 .35
Never hinged 17.50
J64 D2 5c carmine 11.00 .25
Never hinged 17.50
a. 5c rose red 11.00 .25
Never hinged 17.50
b. 5c deep claret 11.00 .25
Never hinged 17.50
J65 D2 10c carmine rose 17.00 .30
Never hinged 27.50
a. 10c rose red 17.00 .25
Never hinged 27.50
b. 10c deep claret 17.00 .25
Never hinged 27.50
J66 D2 30c carmine rose 87.50 .75
Never hinged 140.00
a. 30c deep claret 87.50 .75
Never hinged 140.00
J67 D2 50c carmine rose 110.00 .30
Never hinged 175.00
a. 50c rose red 110.00 .30
Never hinged 175.00
b. 50c deep claret 110.00 .30
Never hinged 175.00
Nos. J61-J67 (7) 241.75 2.35

1925

J68 D2 ½c dull red 1.00 .25
Never hinged 1.50

D3

D4

1930 *Perf. 11*

J69 D3 ½c carmine 4.50 1.40
Never hinged 6.00
J70 D3 1c carmine 3.00 .25
Never hinged 4.25
J71 D3 2c carmine 4.00 .25
Never hinged 5.75
J72 D3 3c carmine 21.00 1.75
Never hinged 32.50
J73 D3 5c carmine 19.00 2.50
Never hinged 30.00
J74 D3 10c carmine 40.00 1.00
Never hinged 65.00
J75 D3 30c carmine 110.00 2.00
Never hinged 160.00
J76 D3 50c carmine 140.00 .75
Never hinged 250.00
J77 D4 $1 carmine 30.00 .25
Never hinged 40.00
a. $1 scarlet 25.00 .25
Never hinged 35.00
J78 D4 $5 carmine 37.50 .25
Never hinged 57.50
a. $5 scarlet 32.50 .25
Never hinged 47.50
Nos. J69-J78 (10) 409.00 10.40

Rotary Press Printing

1931-56 *Perf. 11x10½*

J79 D3 ½c dull carmine .90 .20
Never hinged 1.30
J80 D3 1c dull carmine .20 .20
Never hinged .30
J81 D3 2c dull carmine .20 .20
Never hinged .30
J82 D3 3c dull carmine .25 .20
Never hinged .40
J83 D3 5c dull carmine .40 .20
Never hinged .60
J84 D3 10c dull carmine 1.10 .20
Never hinged 1.60
J85 D3 30c dull carmine 7.50 .25
Never hinged 10.00
J86 D3 50c dull carmine 10.00 .25
Never hinged 15.00

J79a D3 ½c scarlet .90 .20
Never hinged 1.30
J80a D3 1c scarlet .20 .20
Never hinged .30
J81a D3 2c scarlet .20 .20
Never hinged .30
J82a D3 3c scarlet .25 .20
Never hinged .40
J83a D3 5c scarlet .40 .20
Never hinged .60
J84a D3 10c scarlet 1.10 .20
Never hinged 1.60
J85a D3 30c scarlet 7.50 .25
Never hinged 10.00
J86a D3 50c scarlet 10.00 .25
Never hinged 15.00

Perf. 10½x11

J87 D4 $1 scarlet ('56) 32.50 .25
Never hinged 47.50
Nos. J79-J87 (17) 73.60 3.65
Nos. J79a-J86a (8) 20.55 1.70

Catalogue values for unused stamps in this section, from this point to the end of the section, are for Never Hinged items.

D5

Denominations added by rubber plates in an operation similar to precanceling.

Rotary Press Printing
Perf. 11x10½

1959, June 19 **Unwmk.**

Denomination in Black

J88 D5 ½c carmine rose 1.50 1.10
J89 D5 1c carmine rose .20 .20
a. Denomination omitted 350.00
b. Pair, one without "1 CENT" 600.00
J90 D5 2c carmine rose .20 .20
J91 D5 3c carmine rose .20 .20
a. Pair, one without "3 CENTS" 750.00
J92 D5 4c carmine rose .20 .20
J93 D5 5c carmine rose .20 .20
a. Pair, one without "5 CENTS" 1,250.
J94 D5 6c carmine rose .20 .20
a. Pair, one without "6 CENTS" 850.00
J95 D5 7c carmine rose .20 .20
J96 D5 8c carmine rose .20 .20
a. Pair, one without "8 CENTS" 850.00
J97 D5 10c carmine rose .20 .20
J98 D5 30c carmine rose .75 .20
J99 D5 50c carmine rose 1.10 .20

Straight Numeral Outlined in Black

J100 D5 $1 carmine rose 2.00 .20
J101 D5 $5 carmine rose 9.00 .20
Nos. J88-J101 (14) 16.15 3.70

All single copies with value omitted are catalogued as No. J89a.

1978-85

Denomination in Black

J102 D5 11c carmine rose .25 .20
J103 D5 13c carmine rose .25 .20
J104 D5 17c carmine rose ('85) .40 .35
Nos. J102-J104 (3) .90 .75
Nos. J88-J104 (17) 17.05 4.45

Issue dates: Jan. 2, 1978, June 10, 1985.

UNITED STATES OFFICES IN CHINA

Issued for sale by the postal agency at Shanghai, at their surcharged value in local currency. Valid to the amount of their original values for the prepayment of postage on mail dispatched from the US postal agency at Shanghai to addresses in the US.

SHANGHAI
2¢
CHINA

Nos. 498-499, 502-504, 506-510, 512, 514-518 Surcharged

1919 **Unwmk.** *Perf. 11*

K1 A140 2c on 1c green 25.00 *27.50*
Never hinged 40.00
K2 A140 4c on 2c rose, type I 25.00 *27.50*
Never hinged 40.00
K3 A140 6c on 3c vio, type II 50.00 *65.00*
Never hinged 82.50
K4 A140 8c on 4c brown 55.00 *65.00*
Never hinged 90.00
K5 A140 10c on 5c blue 60.00 *65.00*
Never hinged 100.00
K6 A140 12c on 6c red org 77.50 *95.00*
Never hinged 130.00
K7 A140 14c on 7c black 82.50 *110.00*
Never hinged 135.00
K8 A148 16c on 8c ol bis 60.00 *70.00*
Never hinged 100.00
a. 16c on 8c olive green 55.00 *60.00*
Never hinged 90.00
K9 A148 18c on 9c sal red 60.00 *75.00*
Never hinged 100.00
K10 A148 20c on 10c org yel 55.00 *60.00*
Never hinged 90.00
K11 A148 24c on 12c brn car 65.00 *70.00*
Never hinged 110.00
a. 24c on 12c claret brown 87.50 *110.00*
Never hinged 145.00
K12 A148 30c on 15c gray 82.50 *125.00*
Never hinged 135.00
K13 A148 40c on 20c dp ultra 125.00 *190.00*
Never hinged 210.00
K14 A148 60c on 30c org red 110.00 *160.00*
Never hinged 180.00
K15 A148 $1 on 50c lt vio 475.00 *550.00*
Never hinged 800.00
K16 A148 $2 on $1 vio brown 400.00 *500.00*
Never hinged 675.00
a. Double surcharge *4,500.* *4,750.*
Never hinged *6,750.*
Nos. K1-K16 (16) 1,807. 2,255.

SHANGHAI
2 Cts.
CHINA

Nos. 498 and 528B Surcharged

1922, July 3

K17 A140 2c on 1c green 120.00 110.00
Never hinged 190.00
K18 A140 4c on 2c carmine, type VII 105.00 95.00
Never hinged 170.00

OFFICIAL STAMPS

The franking privilege having been abolished, as of July 1, 1873, these stamps were provided for each of the departments of Government for the prepayment of postage on official matter.

These stamps were supplanted on May 1, 1879, by penalty envelopes and on July 5, 1884, were declared obsolete.

Designs, except Post Office, resemble those illustrated but are not identical. Each bears the name of Department. Portraits are as follows: 1c, Franklin; 2c, Jackson; 3c, Washington; 6c, Lincoln; 7c, Stanton; 10c, Jefferson; 12c, Clay; 15c, Webster; 24c, Scott; 30c, Hamilton; 90c, Perry.

Grade, condition and original gum are very important in valuing #O1-O120 unused.

Printed by the Continental Bank Note Co.
Thin Hard Paper

O1

1873 **Unwmk.** **Engr.** ***Perf. 12***

Dept. of Agriculture

O1 O1 1c yellow 160.00 125.00
O2 O1 2c yellow 130.00 50.00
O3 O1 3c yellow 115.00 9.50
O4 O1 6c yellow 125.00 40.00
O5 O1 10c yellow 260.00 160.00
O6 O1 12c yellow 350.00 200.00
O7 O1 15c yellow 290.00 170.00
O8 O1 24c yellow 290.00 160.00
O9 O1 30c yellow 375.00 225.00
Nos. O1-O9 (9) 2,095. 1,139.

Special printings overprinted "SPECIMEN" follow No. O120.

Executive Dept.

O10 O1 1c carmine 575.00 350.00
O11 O1 2c carmine 375.00 160.00
O12 O1 3c carmine 450.00 160.00
a. 3c violet rose 450.00 160.00
O13 O1 6c carmine 675.00 425.00
O14 O1 10c carmine 625.00 500.00
Nos. O10-O14 (5) 2,700. 1,595.

Special printings overprinted "SPECIMEN" follow No. O120.

Dept. of the Interior

O15 O1 1c vermilion 35.00 8.00
O16 O1 2c vermilion 30.00 9.00
O17 O1 3c vermilion 47.50 5.00
O18 O1 6c vermilion 35.00 5.00
O19 O1 10c vermilion 35.00 15.00
O20 O1 12c vermilion 50.00 7.75
O21 O1 15c vermilion 85.00 17.00
O22 O1 24c vermilion 62.50 14.00
a. Double impression —
O23 O1 30c vermilion 85.00 14.00
O24 O1 90c vermilion 190.00 37.50
Nos. O15-O24 (10) 655.00 132.25

Special printings overprinted "SPECIMEN" follow No. O120.

Dept. of Justice

O25 O1 1c purple 105.00 77.50
O26 O1 2c purple 175.00 82.50
O27 O1 3c purple 175.00 17.00
O28 O1 6c purple 160.00 25.00
O29 O1 10c purple 180.00 55.00
O30 O1 12c purple 140.00 37.50
O31 O1 15c purple 275.00 125.00
O32 O1 24c purple 700.00 275.00
O33 O1 30c purple 600.00 160.00
O34 O1 90c purple 900.00 425.00
Nos. O25-O34 (10) 3,410. 1,279.

Special printings overprinted "SPECIMEN" follow No. O120.

Navy Dept.

O35 O1 1c ultramarine 75.00 37.50
a. 1c dull blue 85.00 40.00
O36 O1 2c ultramarine 60.00 17.00
a. 2c dull blue 70.00 15.00
O37 O1 3c ultramarine 60.00 8.00
a. 3c dull blue 70.00 11.00
O38 O1 6c ultramarine 60.00 14.00
a. 6c dull blue 70.00 14.50
O39 O1 7c ultramarine 375.00 140.00
a. 7c dull blue 425.00 150.00
O40 O1 10c ultramarine 80.00 27.50
a. 10c dull blue 85.00 27.50
O41 O1 12c ultramarine 95.00 25.00
O42 O1 15c ultramarine 175.00 50.00
O43 O1 24c ultramarine 175.00 55.00
a. 24c dull blue 200.00 —
O44 O1 30c ultramarine 140.00 27.50
O45 O1 90c ultramarine 700.00 175.00
a. Double impression *3,750.*
Nos. O35-O45 (11) 1,995. 576.50

Special printings overprinted "SPECIMEN" follow No. O120.

O6

Post Office Dept.

O47 O6 1c black 12.50 7.50
O48 O6 2c black 16.00 7.00
a. Double impression 325.00 300.00
O49 O6 3c black 5.25 1.00
a. Printed on both sides *3,000.*
O50 O6 6c black 16.00 6.00
a. Diagonal half used as 3c on cover *3,000.*
O51 O6 10c black 70.00 40.00
O52 O6 12c black 35.00 8.25
O53 O6 15c black 47.50 14.00
O54 O6 24c black 60.00 17.00
O55 O6 30c black 60.00 17.00
O56 O6 90c black 90.00 14.00
Nos. O47-O56 (10) 412.25 131.75

Stamps of the POD are often on paper with a gray surface. This is due to insufficient wiping of the plates during printing.

Special printings overprinted "SPECIMEN" follow No. O120.

Seward — O8

Dept. of State

O57 O1 1c dark green 110.00 40.00
O58 O1 2c dark green 210.00 60.00
O59 O1 3c bright green 85.00 17.00
O60 O1 6c bright green 80.00 19.00
O61 O1 7c dark green 160.00 40.00
O62 O1 10c dark green 125.00 27.50
O63 O1 12c dark green 200.00 82.50
O64 O1 15c dark green 210.00 55.00
O65 O1 24c dark green 425.00 140.00
O66 O1 30c dark green 400.00 110.00
O67 O1 90c dark green 750.00 250.00
O68 O8 $2 green & black 850.00 650.00
O69 O8 $5 green & black 6,000. 3,250.
O70 O8 $10 green & black 4,000. 2,250.
O71 O8 $20 green & black 3,250. 1,700.

Nos. O68-O71 with pen cancels sell for approximately 25-40% of the values shown.

Special printings overprinted "SPECIMEN" follow No. O120.

Treasury Dept.

O72 O1 1c brown 37.50 4.50
O73 O1 2c brown 47.50 4.50
O74 O1 3c brown 32.50 1.25
a. Double impression —
O75 O1 6c brown 42.50 2.25
O76 O1 7c brown 90.00 22.50
O77 O1 10c brown 90.00 7.75
O78 O1 12c brown 90.00 6.00
O79 O1 15c brown 85.00 7.75
O80 O1 24c brown 425.00 65.00
O81 O1 30c brown 145.00 9.00
O82 O1 90c brown 150.00 10.00
Nos. O72-O82 (11) 1,235. 140.50

Special printings overprinted "SPECIMEN" follow No. O120.

War Dept.

O83 O1 1c rose 140.00 7.25
O84 O1 2c rose 125.00 9.50
O85 O1 3c rose 130.00 2.75
O86 O1 6c rose 425.00 6.00
O87 O1 7c rose 125.00 72.50
O88 O1 10c rose 42.50 15.00
O89 O1 12c rose 145.00 9.00
O90 O1 15c rose 37.50 11.00
O91 O1 24c rose 37.50 6.75
O92 O1 30c rose 40.00 6.75
O93 O1 90c rose 90.00 40.00
Nos. O83-O93 (11) 1,337. 186.50

Special printings overprinted "SPECIMEN" follow No. O120.

Printed by the American Bank Note Co.

1879 **Soft Porous Paper**

Dept. of Agriculture

O94 O1 1c yel, no gum 3,000.
O95 O1 3c yellow 290.00 55.00

Dept. of the Interior

O96 O1 1c vermilion 210.00 190.00
O97 O1 2c vermilion 4.00 1.25
O98 O1 3c vermilion 3.50 1.00
O99 O1 6c vermilion 5.25 5.50
O100 O1 10c vermilion 65.00 60.00
O101 O1 12c vermilion 125.00 90.00
O102 O1 15c vermilion 300.00 225.00
O103 O1 24c vermilion *3,000.* —

Dept. of Justice

O106 O1 3c bluish purple 85.00 55.00
O107 O1 6c bluish purple 190.00 160.00

Post Office Dept.

O108 O6 3c black 15.00 5.00

Treasury Dept.

O109 O1 3c brown 45.00 6.75
O110 O1 6c brown 85.00 35.00
O111 O1 10c brown 125.00 40.00
O112 O1 30c brown 1,250. 275.00
O113 O1 90c brown 2,000. 275.00
Nos. O109-O113 (5) 3,505. 631.75

War Dept.

O114 O1 1c rose red 3.50 2.75
O115 O1 2c rose red 5.00 3.25
O116 O1 3c rose red 5.00 1.20
a. Imperf., pair *900.00*
b. Double impression *750.00*
O117 O1 6c rose red 4.50 1.00
O118 O1 10c rose red 37.50 37.50
O119 O1 12c rose red 30.00 10.00
O120 O1 30c rose red 80.00 67.50
Nos. O114-O120 (7) 165.50 123.20

SPECIAL PRINTINGS

Special printings of Official stamps were made in 1875 at the time the other Reprints, Re-issues and Special Printings were printed. They are ungummed.

Although perforated, these stamps were sometimes (but not always) cut apart with scissors. As a result the perforations may be mutilated and the design damaged.

All values exist imperforate.

Printed by the Continental Bank Note Co.

Overprinted in Block Letters **SPECIMEN**

1875 ***Perf. 12***

Thin, hard white paper

Type D

AGRICULTURE

Carmine Overprint

O1S D 1c yellow 14.00
a. "Sepcimen" error 700.00
b. Small dotted "i" in "Specimen" 425.00
c. Horiz. ribbed paper 20.00
O2S D 2c yellow 27.50
a. "Sepcimen" error 750.00
O3S D 3c yellow 75.00
a. "Sepcimen" error *3,000.*
O4S D 6c yellow 130.00
a. "Sepcimen" error *5,500.*
O5S D 10c yellow 130.00
a. "Sepcimen" error *3,250.*
O6S D 12c yellow 125.00
a. "Sepcimen" error *3,750.*
O7S D 15c yellow 125.00
a. "Sepcimen" error *3,250.*
O8S D 24c yellow 125.00
a. "Sepcimen" error *3,250.*
O9S D 30c yellow 125.00
a. "Sepcimen" error *3,250.*
Nos. O1S-O9S (9) 876.50

EXECUTIVE

Blue Overprint

O10S D 1c carmine 14.00
a. Small dotted "i" in "Specimen" 325.00
b. Ribbed paper 20.00
O11S D 2c carmine 27.50
O12S D 3c carmine 27.50
O13S D 6c carmine 27.50
O14S D 10c carmine 27.50
Nos. O10S-O14S (5) 124.00

INTERIOR

Blue Overprint

O15S D 1c vermilion 27.50
O16S D 2c vermilion 35.00
a. "Sepcimen" error *3,750.*
O17S D 3c vermilion 475.00
O18S D 6c vermilion 450.00
O19S D 10c vermilion 450.00
O20S D 12c vermilion 475.00
O21S D 15c vermilion 475.00
O22S D 24c vermilion 475.00
O23S D 30c vermilion 475.00
O24S D 90c vermilion 475.00
Nos. O15S-O24S (10) 3,812.

JUSTICE

Blue Overprint

O25S D 1c purple 15.00
a. "Sepcimen" error 675.00
b. Small dotted "i" in "Specimen" 275.00
c. Horiz. ribbed paper 20.00
O26S D 2c purple 30.00
a. "Sepcimen" error 1,100.
O27S D 3c purple 250.00
a. "Sepcimen" error *3,750.*
O28S D 6c purple 250.00
O29S D 10c purple 250.00
O30S D 12c purple 250.00
a. "Sepcimen" error *4,000.*
O31S D 15c purple 275.00
a. "Sepcimen" error *4,000.*
O32S D 24c purple 300.00
a. "Sepcimen" error *4,000.*
O33S D 30c purple 300.00
a. "Sepcimen" error *4,000.*
O34S D 90c purple 325.00
Nos. O25S-O34S (10) 2,245.

NAVY

Carmine Overprint

O35S D 1c ultramarine 17.50
a. "Sepcimen" error 550.00
O36S D 2c ultramarine 35.00
a. "Sepcimen" error 675.00
O37S D 3c ultramarine 300.00
O38S D 6c ultramarine 350.00
O39S D 7c ultramarine 150.00
a. "Sepcimen" error 3,000.
O40S D 10c ultramarine 350.00
a. "Sepcimen" error *4,250.*
O41S D 12c ultramarine 300.00
a. "Sepcimen" error *4,000.*
O42S D 15c ultramarine 300.00
a. "Sepcimen" error *7,500.*
O43S D 24c ultramarine 300.00
a. "Sepcimen" error *4,000.*
O44S D 30c ultramarine 300.00
a. "Sepcimen" error *4,500.*
O45S D 90c ultramarine 300.00
Nos. O35S-O45S (11) 2,702.

POST OFFICE

Carmine Overprint

O47S D 1c black 25.00
a. "Sepcimen" error 650.00
b. Inverted overprint *1,000.*
O48S D 2c black 65.00
a. "Sepcimen" error 1,750.
O49S D 3c black 450.00
a. "Sepcimen" error —
O50S D 6c black 425.00
O51S D 10c black 275.00
a. "Sepcimen" error *4,250.*
O52S D 12c black 400.00
O53S D 15c black 475.00
a. "Sepcimen" error *4,250.*
O54S D 24c black 425.00
a. "Sepcimen" error *4,250.*
O55S D 30c black 425.00
O56S D 90c black 425.00
a. "Sepcimen" error *8,000.*
Nos. O47S-O56S (10) 3,390.

STATE

Carmine Overprint

O57S D 1c bluish green 15.00
a. "Sepcimen" error 400.00
b. Small dotted "i" in "Specimen" 400.00
c. Horiz. ribbed paper 20.00
d. Double overprint —
O58S D 2c bluish green 30.00
a. "Sepcimen" error 550.00
O59S D 3c bluish green 45.00
a. "Sepcimen" error 2,000.
O60S D 6c bluish green 95.00
a. "Sepcimen" error 2,250.
O61S D 7c bluish green 47.50
a. "Sepcimen" error 1,750.
O62S D 10c bluish green 180.00
a. "Sepcimen" error *7,500.*
O63S D 12c bluish green 190.00
a. "Sepcimen" error *3,500.*
O64S D 15c bluish green 180.00
O65S D 24c bluish green 180.00
a. "Sepcimen" error *3,500.*
O66S D 30c bluish green 180.00
a. "Sepcimen" error *3,750.*
O67S D 90c bluish green 180.00
a. "Sepcimen" error *3,750.*
O68S D $2 green & black *7,250.*
O69S D $5 green & black *12,000.*
O70S D $10 green & black *16,000.*
O71S D $20 green & black *19,000.*
Nos. O57S-O67S (11) 1,322.

TREASURY

Blue Overprint

O72S D 1c dark brown 27.50
O73S D 2c dark brown 130.00
O74S D 3c dark brown 475.00
O75S D 6c dark brown 425.00
O76S D 7c dark brown 250.00
O77S D 10c dark brown 450.00
O78S D 12c dark brown 475.00
O79S D 15c dark brown 475.00
O80S D 24c dark brown 375.00
O81S D 30c dark brown 500.00
O82S D 90c dark brown 500.00
Nos. O72S-O82S (11) 4,082.

WAR

Blue Overprint

O83S D 1c deep rose 17.50
a. "Sepcimen" error 550.00
O84S D 2c deep rose 35.00
a. "Sepcimen" error 1,000.
O85S D 3c deep rose 350.00
a. "Sepcimen" error *4,000.*
O86S D 6c deep rose 350.00
a. "Sepcimen" error *4,250.*
O87S D 7c deep rose 72.50
a. "Sepcimen" error 1,900.
O88S D 10c deep rose 325.00
a. "Sepcimen" error *4,250.*
O89S D 12c deep rose 375.00
a. "Sepcimen" error *4,250.*
O90S D 15c deep rose 375.00
a. "Sepcimen" error *4,250.*
O91S D 24c deep rose 375.00
a. "Sepcimen" error *4,250.*
O92S D 30c deep rose 375.00
a. "Sepcimen" error *4,250.*
O93S D 90c deep rose 375.00
a. "Sepcimen" error *4,750.*
Nos. O83S-O93S (11) 3,025.

SOFT POROUS PAPER

1881 **EXECUTIVE**

Blue Overprint

O10xS D 1c violet rose 45.00

NAVY

Carmine Overprint

O35xS D 1c gray blue 50.00
a. Double overprint 850.00

STATE

O57xS D 1c yellow green 200.00

Official Postal Savings Mail

These stamps were used to prepay postage on official correspondence of the Postal Savings Division of the POD. Discontinued Sept. 23, 1914.

O11

1911 **Wmk. 191**

O121 O11 2c black 14.00 1.50
Never hinged 22.50
O122 O11 50c dark green 140.00 40.00
Never hinged 225.00
O123 O11 $1 ultra 130.00 11.00
Never hinged 210.00

Wmk. 190

O124 O11 1c dark violet 7.50 1.50
Never hinged 12.00
O125 O11 2c black 45.00 5.50
Never hinged 72.50
O126 O11 10c carmine 17.00 1.60
Never hinged 27.50
Nos. O121-O126 (6) 353.50 61.10

Catalogue values for unused stamps in this section, from this point to the end of the section, are for Never Hinged items.

Catalogue values for used stamps are for regularly used copies, not copies removed from first day covers.

Official Mail

O12

O13

Type O13 has frame line completely around blue design.

1983-85 **Unwmk.** ***Perf. 11***

O127 O12 1c red, bl & blk .20 .20
O128 O12 4c red, bl & blk .20 .25
O129 O12 13c red, bl & blk .45 .75
O129A O12 14c red, bl & blk ('85) .45 .50
O130 O12 17c red, bl & blk .55 .40
O132 O12 $1 red, bl & blk 2.00 1.00
O133 O12 $5 red, bl & blk 9.00 9.00
Nos. O127-O133 (7) 12.85 12.10

Coil Stamps

Perf. 10 Vert.

O135 O12 20c red, bl & blk 1.75 *2.00*
a. Imperf., pair *2,000.*
O136 O12 22c red, bl & blk ('85) .70 *2.00*

No. O129A does not have a "c" after the "14."

Inscribed: Postal Card Rate D

1985, Feb. 4 ***Perf. 11***

O138 O12 (14c) red, bl & blk 5.25 *5.00*

Coil Stamps

Inscribed: No. O139, Domestic Letter Rate D. No. O140, Domestic Mail E.

1985-88 ***Perf. 10 Vert.***

O138A O13 15c red, bl & blk .45 .50
O138B O13 20c red, bl & blk .45 .30
O139 O12 (22c) red, bl & blk 5.25 *3.00*
O140 O13 (25c) red, bl & blk .75 *2.00*
O141 O13 25c red, bl & blk .65 .50
a. Imperf., pair *1,750.* —
Nos. O138A-O141 (5) 7.55 6.30

Issue dates: 1985; E, Mar. 22, 1988; 15c, June 11; 20c, May 19; 25c, June 11.

See Nos. O143, O145-O151, O153-O156.

1989, July 5 **Litho.** ***Perf. 11***

O143 O13 1c red, blue & black .20 .20

O14

1991, Jan. 22 **Litho.** ***Perf. 10 Vert.***

Coil Stamp

O144 O14 (29c) red, blue & black .75 .50

See No. O152.

Official Type of 1985

1991, May 24 **Litho.** ***Perf. 10 Vert.***

Coil Stamp

O145 O13 29c red, blue & black .65 .30

1991-93 ***Perf. 11***

O146 O13 4c red, blue & black .20 .30
O146A O13 10c red, blue & black .25 .30
O147 O13 19c red, blue & black .40 .50

O148	O13	23c red, blue & black		.45	.30
	a.	Imperf., pair		*200.00*	
O151	O13	$1 red, blue & black		2.00	.75

Nos. O146A, O151 have a line of microscopic printing below eagle. Nos. O147 and O148 have blue background made up of crosshatched lines, thicker lettering and thinner numerals.

Issued: #O146, 4/6; #O147, O148, 5/24; 10c, 10/19/93; #O151, 9/1993.

COIL STAMP

1994, Dec. 13 Litho. *Perf. 9.8 Vert.*

Inscribed: No. O152, For U.S. addresses only G.

O152	O14	(32c) red, blue & black	.65	—

Type of 1985

1995, May 9 Litho. *Perf. 9¾ Vert.*

COIL STAMP

O153	O13	32c red, blue & black	.65	.30

1995, May 9 ***Perf. 11.2***

O154	O13	1c red, blue & black	.20	.20
O155	O13	20c red, blue & black	.45	.30
O156	O13	23c red, blue & black	.50	.30

COIL STAMP

1999, Oct. 8 Litho. *Perf. 9¾ Vert.*

O157	O13	33c red, blue & black	.65	—

Nos. O153-O157 have a line of microscopic text below the eagle.

NEWSPAPER STAMPS

For the prepayment of postage on bulk shipments of newspapers and periodicals. From 1875 on, the stamps were affixed to pages of receipt books, sometimes canceled and retained by the post office. Discontinued on July 1, 1898.

Most used stamps of Nos. PR1-PR4, PR9-PR32, PR57-PR79 and PR81-PR89 are pen canceled (or uncanceled). Handstamp cancellations on any of these issues are rare and sell for much more than catalogue values which are for pen-canceled examples. Used values for Nos. PR102-PR125 are for stamps with handstamp cancellations.

Washington N1

Franklin N2

Lincoln — N3

Printed by the National Bank Note Co.

Thin Hard Paper, No Gum

1865 Unwmk. Typo. *Perf. 12*

Size: 51x95mm

Colored Border

PR1	N1	5c dark blue	350.00	—
	a.	5c light blue	375.00	—
PR2	N2	10c blue green	140.00	—
	a.	10c green	140.00	—
	b.	Pelure paper	165.00	—
PR3	N3	25c orange red	190.00	—
	a.	25c carmine red	220.00	—
	b.	Pelure paper	190.00	

White Border

Yellowish Paper

PR4	N1	5c light blue	87.50	—
	a.	5c dark blue	87.50	—
	b.	Pelure paper	87.50	—
		Nos. PR1-PR4 (4)	767.50	

Reprints of 1865 Issue

Printed by the National Bank Note Co.

Hard White Paper, Without Gum

1875

PR5	N1	5c dull blue	100.00	
	a.	Printed on both sides		—
PR6	N2	10c dk bluish green	110.00	
	a.	Printed on both sides	*2,000.*	
PR7	N3	25c dark carmine	135.00	
		Nos. PR5-PR7 (3)	345.00	

The 5c has white border, 10c and 25c have colored borders.

Printed by the American Bank Note Co.

Soft Porous Paper

1880

White Border

PR8	N1	5c dark blue	250.

Statue of Freedom — N4

"Justice" — N5

Ceres — N6

"Victory" — N7

Clio — N8

Minerva — N9

Vesta — N10

"Peace" — N11

"Commerce" N12

Hebe N13

Indian Maiden — N14

Printed by the Continental Bank Note Co.

Engraved Thin Hard Paper

1875 Size: 24x35mm

PR9	N4	2c black	37.50	22.50
PR10	N4	3c black	45.00	25.00
PR11	N4	4c black	45.00	22.50
PR12	N4	6c black	55.00	25.00
PR13	N4	8c black	65.00	35.00
PR14	N4	9c black	140.00	80.00
PR15	N4	10c black	70.00	30.00
PR16	N5	12c rose	160.00	70.00
PR17	N5	24c rose	200.00	80.00
PR18	N5	36c rose	250.00	90.00
PR19	N5	48c rose	425.00	150.00
PR20	N5	60c rose	225.00	80.00
PR21	N5	72c rose	500.00	190.00
PR22	N5	84c rose	750.00	275.00
PR23	N5	96c rose	450.00	160.00
PR24	N6	$1.92 dark brn	550.00	225.00
PR25	N7	$3 vermilion	800.00	240.00
PR26	N8	$6 ultra	1,250.	400.00
PR27	N9	$9 yellow	1,600.	450.00
PR28	N10	$12 blue grn	1,750.	575.00
PR29	N11	$24 dk gray vio	1,750.	575.00
PR30	N12	$36 brn rose	2,000.	700.00
PR31	N13	$48 red brn	2,500.	850.00
PR32	N14	$60 violet	2,500.	850.00

Special Printing of the 1875 Issue

Printed by the Continental Bank Note Co.

Hard White Paper

Without Gum

PR33	N4	2c gray black	275.
	a.	Horizontally ribbed paper	275.
PR34	N4	3c gray black	290.
	a.	Horizontally ribbed paper	300.
PR35	N4	4c gray black	325.
PR36	N4	6c gray black	400.
PR37	N4	8c gray black	475.
PR38	N4	9c gray black	550.
PR39	N4	10c gray black	700.
	a.	Horizontally ribbed paper	750.
PR40	N5	12c pale rose	850.
PR41	N5	24c pale rose	1,250.
PR42	N5	36c pale rose	1,500.
PR43	N5	48c pale rose	1,750.
PR44	N5	60c pale rose	2,000.
PR45	N5	72c pale rose	2,400.
PR46	N5	84c pale rose	*3,000.*
PR47	N5	96c pale rose	*4,500.*
PR48	N6	$1.92 dk brown	*10,000.*
PR49	N7	$3 vermilion	*19,000.*
PR50	N8	$6 ultra	*25,000.*
PR51	N9	$9 yellow	*40,000.*
PR52	N10	$12 blue green	*35,000.*
PR53	N11	$24 dk gray vio	—
PR54	N12	$36 brown rose	—
PR55	N13	$48 red brown	—
PR56	N14	$60 violet	—

Nos. PR33 to PR56 exist imperf. but were not regularly issued. (See the Scott U.S. Specialized Catalogue.)

Printed by the American Bank Note Co.

1879

Soft Porous Paper

PR57	N4	2c black	17.50	5.50
PR58	N4	3c black	22.50	7.00
PR59	N4	4c black	20.00	7.00
PR60	N4	6c black	40.00	15.00
PR61	N4	8c black	40.00	15.00
PR62	N4	10c black	40.00	15.00
PR63	N5	12c red	200.00	60.00
PR64	N5	24c red	200.00	60.00
PR65	N5	36c red	500.00	175.00
PR66	N5	48c red	450.00	130.00
PR67	N5	60c red	375.00	110.00
	a.	Imperf., pair	*1,000.*	
PR68	N5	72c red	675.00	210.00
PR69	N5	84c red	575.00	160.00
PR70	N5	96c red	375.00	110.00
PR71	N6	$1.92 pale brown	275.00	105.00
PR72	N7	$3 red ver	275.00	105.00
PR73	N8	$6 blue	450.00	160.00
PR74	N9	$9 orange	325.00	110.00
PR75	N10	$12 yellow grn	475.00	150.00
PR76	N11	$24 dk violet	550.00	180.00
PR77	N12	$36 Indian red	675.00	200.00
PR78	N13	$48 yellow brown	800.00	275.00
PR79	N14	$60 purple	725.00	275.00
		Nos. PR57-PR70 (14)	3,530.	1,079.

See the Scott U.S. Specialized Catalogue Die and Plate Proof section for other imperforates.

Special Printing of the 1879 Issue

Printed by the American Bank Note Co.

1881

PR80	N4	2c intense black	550.00

1885

PR81	N4	1c black	17.50	7.50
PR82	N5	12c carmine	55.00	17.50
PR83	N5	24c carmine	57.50	20.00
PR84	N5	36c carmine	82.50	30.00
PR85	N5	48c carmine	120.00	45.00
PR86	N5	60c carmine	165.00	65.00
PR87	N5	72c carmine	175.00	70.00
PR88	N5	84c carmine	360.00	160.00
PR89	N5	96c carmine	275.00	120.00
		Nos. PR81-PR89 (9)	1,307.	535.00

See the Scott U.S. Specialized Catalogue Die and Plate Proof section for imperforates.

Printed by the Bureau of Engraving and Printing

1894 Soft Wove Paper

PR90	N4	1c intense black	150.00	—
PR91	N4	2c intense black	150.00	
PR92	N4	4c intense black	160.00	
PR93	N4	6c intense black	2,250.	
PR94	N4	10c intense black	350.00	
PR95	N5	12c pink	1,000.	—
PR96	N5	24c pink	1,000.	
PR97	N5	36c pink	*11,000.*	
PR98	N5	60c pink	*11,000.*	—
PR99	N5	96c pink	*12,500.*	
PR100	N7	$3 scarlet	*15,000.*	
PR101	N8	$6 pale blue	*22,500.*	—

Statue of Freedom N15

"Justice" N16

"Victory" — N17

Clio — N18

Vesta — N19

"Peace" — N20

"Commerce" N21

Indian Maiden N22

1895 **Unwmk.**

Sizes: 1c-50c, 21x34mm, $2-$100, 24x35mm

PR102	N15	1c black	60.00	12.50
		Never hinged	95.00	
PR103	N15	2c black	60.00	12.50
		Never hinged	95.00	
PR104	N15	5c black	80.00	20.00
		Never hinged	130.00	
PR105	N15	10c black	175.00	52.50
		Never hinged	275.00	
PR106	N16	25c carmine	250.00	55.00
		Never hinged	375.00	
PR107	N16	50c carmine	600.00	150.00
		Never hinged	925.00	
PR108	N17	$2 scarlet	700.00	110.00
		Never hinged	1,100.	
PR109	N18	$5 ultra	950.00	225.00
		Never hinged	1,450.	
PR110	N19	$10 green	1,100.	250.00
		Never hinged	1,700.	
PR111	N20	$20 slate	1,500.	450.00
		Never hinged	2,300.	
PR112	N21	$50 dull rose	1,600.	450.00
		Never hinged	2,500.	
PR113	N22	$100 purple	1,600.	525.00
		Never hinged	2,500.	
		Nos. PR102-PR113 (12)	8,675.	2,312.

1895-97 **Wmk. 191**

PR114	N15	1c black ('96)	6.00	4.00
		Never hinged	9.50	
PR115	N15	2c black	6.50	4.00
		Never hinged	10.00	
PR116	N15	5c black ('96)	10.00	6.50
		Never hinged	16.00	
PR117	N15	10c black	6.50	4.25
		Never hinged	10.00	
PR118	N16	25c carmine	12.50	10.00
		Never hinged	19.50	
PR119	N16	50c carmine	15.00	15.00
		Never hinged	24.00	
PR120	N17	$2 scar ('97)	20.00	22.50
		Never hinged	32.50	
PR121	N18	$5 dk blue ('96)	35.00	35.00
		Never hinged	55.00	
a.		$5 light blue	175.00	70.00
		Never hinged	280.00	
PR122	N19	$10 green ('96)	35.00	35.00
		Never hinged	55.00	
PR123	N20	$20 slate ('96)	37.50	37.50
		Never hinged	60.00	
PR124	N21	$50 dl rose ('97)	50.00	42.50
		Never hinged	80.00	
PR125	N22	$100 purple ('96)	55.00	47.50
		Never hinged	87.50	
		Nos. PR114-PR125 (12)	289.00	263.75

In 1899 the Government sold 26,989 sets of these stamps, but, as the stock of the high values was not sufficient to make up the required number, the $5, $10, $20, $50 and $100 were reprinted. These are virtually indistinguishable from earlier printings.

For overprints see Nos. R159-R160.

PARCEL POST STAMPS

Issued for the prepayment of postage on parcel post packages only.

Post Office Clerk — PP1

City Carrier PP2

Railway Postal Clerk — PP3

Rural Carrier PP4

Mail Train — PP5

Steamship and Mail Tender PP6

Automobile Service PP7

Airplane Carrying Mail — PP8

Manufacturing PP9

Dairying PP10

Harvesting PP11

Fruit Growing PP12

1913 **Engr.** **Wmk. 190** ***Perf. 12***

Q1	PP1	1c carmine rose	5.25	1.50
		Never hinged	8.75	
Q2	PP2	2c carmine rose	6.75	1.25
		Never hinged	11.25	
Q3	PP3	3c carmine	13.50	5.75
		Never hinged	22.50	
Q4	PP4	4c carmine rose	37.50	3.00
		Never hinged	62.50	
Q5	PP5	5c carmine rose	32.50	2.25
		Never hinged	52.50	
Q6	PP6	10c carmine rose	52.50	3.00
		Never hinged	87.50	
Q7	PP7	15c carmine rose	67.50	12.00
		Never hinged	110.00	
Q8	PP8	20c carmine rose	140.00	25.00
		Never hinged	230.00	
Q9	PP9	25c carmine rose	67.50	6.75
		Never hinged	110.00	
Q10	PP10	50c carmine rose	275.00	40.00
		Never hinged	450.00	
Q11	PP11	75c carmine rose	95.00	35.00
		Never hinged	160.00	
Q12	PP12	$1 carmine rose	350.00	30.00
		Never hinged	575.00	
		Nos. Q1-Q12 (12)	1,143.	165.50
		Nos. Q1-Q12, never hinged	1,880.	

PARCEL POST POSTAGE DUE STAMPS

For affixing by a postal clerk, to any parcel post package, to denote the amount to be collected from the addressee because of insufficient prepayment of postage.

PPD1

1913 **Engr.** **Wmk. 190** ***Perf. 12***

JQ1	PPD1	1c dark green	11.00	4.50
		Never hinged	18.00	
JQ2	PPD1	2c dark green	85.00	17.50
		Never hinged	140.00	
JQ3	PPD1	5c dark green	15.00	5.50
		Never hinged	25.00	
JQ4	PPD1	10c dark green	175.00	45.00
		Never hinged	290.00	
JQ5	PPD1	25c dark green	105.00	5.00
		Never hinged	175.00	
		Nos. JQ1-JQ5 (5)	391.00	77.50
		Nos. JQ1-JQ5, never hinged	648.00	

SPECIAL HANDLING STAMPS

For use on fourth-class mail to secure the same expeditious handling accorded to first-class mail matter.

PP13

1925-29 **Unwmk.** **Engr.** ***Perf. 11***

QE1	PP13	10c yellow grn ('28)	1.50	1.00
		Never hinged	2.25	
QE2	PP13	15c yellow grn ('28)	1.75	.90
		Never hinged	2.60	
QE3	PP13	20c yellow grn ('28)	2.75	1.50
		Never hinged	4.10	
QE4	PP13	25c yellow grn ('29)	20.00	7.50
		Never hinged	30.00	
a.		25c deep green ('25)	30.00	5.50
		Never hinged	45.00	
		Nos. QE1-QE4 (4)	26.00	10.90
		Nos. QE1-QE4, never hinged	38.95	

COMPUTER VENDED POSTAGE

CVP1

CVP2

1989, Aug. 23 **Tagged** ***Guillotined***

Self-Adhesive

Washington, DC, Machine 82

Any Date Other Than 1st Day

1	CVP1	25c **1st Class**	6.00	—
a.		1st day dated, serial #12501-15500	4.50	—
b.		1st day dated, serial #00001-12500	4.50	—
c.		1st day dated, serial over #27500	—	—
2	CVP1	$1 **3rd Class**	—	—
a.		1st day dated, serial #24501-27500	—	—
b.		1st day dated, serial over #27500	—	—
3	CVP2	$1.69 **Parcel Post**	—	—
a.		1st day dated, serial #21501-24500	—	—
b.		1st day dated, serial over #27500	—	—
4	CVP1	$2.40 **Priority Mail**	—	—
a.		1st day dated, serial #18501-21500	—	—
b.		Priority Mail ($2.74), with bar code (CVP2)	*100.00*	
c.		1st day dated, serial over #27500	—	—
5	CVP1	$8.75 **Express Mail**	—	—
a.		1st day dated, serial #15501-18500	—	—
b.		1st day dated, serial over #27500	—	—
		Nos. 1a-5a (5)	82.50	—

Washington, DC, Machine 83

Any Date Other Than 1st Day

6	CVP1	25c **1st Class**	6.00	—
a.		1st day dated, serial #12501-15500	4.50	—
b.		1st day dated, serial #00001-12500	4.50	—
c.		1st day dated, serial over #27500	—	—
7	CVP1	$1 **3rd Class**	—	—
a.		1st day dated, serial #24501-27500	—	—
b.		1st day dated, serial over #27500	—	—
8	CVP2	$1.69 **Parcel Post**	—	—
a.		1st day dated, serial #21501-24500	—	—
b.		1st day dated, serial over #27500	—	—
9	CVP1	$2.40 **Priority Mail**	—	—
a.		1st day dated, serial #18501-21500	—	—
b.		1st day dated, serial over #27500	—	—
c.		Priority Mail ($2.74), with bar code (CVP2)	*100.00*	
10	CVP1	$8.75 **Express Mail**	—	—
a.		1st day dated, serial #15501-18500	—	—
b.		1st day dated, serial over #27500	—	—
		Nos. 6a-10a (5)	57.50	—

1989, Sept. 1

Kensington, MD, Machine 82

Any Date Other Than 1st Day

11	CVP1	25c **1st Class**	6.00	—
a.		1st day dated, serial #12501-15500	4.50	—
b.		1st day dated, serial #00001-12500	4.50	—
c.		1st day dated, serial over #27500	—	—
12	CVP1	$1 **3rd Class**	—	—
a.		1st day dated, serial #24501-27500	—	—
b.		1st day dated, serial over #27500	—	—
13	CVP2	$1.69 **Parcel Post**	—	—
a.		1st day dated, serial #21501-24500	—	—
b.		1st day dated, serial over #27500	—	—
14	CVP1	$2.40 **Priority Mail**	—	—
a.		1st day dated, serial #18501-21500	—	—
b.		1st day dated, serial over #27500	—	—
c.		Priority Mail ($2.74), with bar code (CVP2)	*100.00*	
15	CVP1	$8.75 **Express Mail**	—	—
a.		1st day dated, serial #15501-18500	—	—
b.		1st day dated, serial over #27500	—	—
		Nos. 11a-15a (5)	57.50	—
		Nos. 1b, 11b (2)	9.00	—

Kensington, MD, Machine 83

Any Date Other Than 1st Day

16	CVP1	25c **1st Class**	6.00	—
a.		1st day dated, serial #12501-15500	4.50	—
b.		1st day dated, serial #00001-12500	4.50	—
c.		1st day dated, serial over #27500	—	—
17	CVP1	$1 **3rd Class**	—	—
a.		1st day dated, serial #24501-27500	—	—
b.		1st day dated, serial over #27500	—	—

18 CVP2 $1.69 **Parcel Post** — —
a. 1st day dated, serial #21501-24500 — —
b. 1st day dated, serial over #27500 — —
19 CVP1 $2.40 **Priority Mail** — —
a. 1st day dated, serial #18501-21500 — —
b. 1st day dated, serial over #27500 — —
c. Priority Mail ($2.74), with bar code (CVP2) 100.00
20 CVP1 $8.75 **Express Mail** — —
a. 1st day dated, serial #15501-18500 — —
b. 1st day dated, serial over #27500 — —
Nos. 16a-20a (5) 57.50 —
Nos. 6b, 16b (2) 9.00 —

1989, Nov.

Washington, DC, Machine 11

21 CVP1 25c **1st Class** *150.00*
a. 1st Class, with bar code (CVP2) —

Stamps in CVP1 design, probably certified 1st class, with $1.10 denominations exist.

22 CVP1 $1 **3rd Class** *500.00*
23 CVP2 $1.69 **Parcel Post** *500.00*
24 CVP1 $2.40 **Priority Mail** *500.00*
a. Priority Mail ($2.74), with bar code (CVP2) —
25 CVP1 $8.75 **Express Mail** *500.00*

Washington, DC, Machine 12

26 CVP1 25c **1st Class** *150.00*

A $1.10 certified 1st Class stamp, dated Nov. 20, exists on cover.

27 CVP1 $1 **3rd Class** —

A $1.40 Third Class stamp of type CVP2, dated Dec. 1 is known on a Dec. 2 cover.

28 CVP2 $1.69 **Parcel Post** —
29 CVP1 $2.40 **Priority Mail** —
a. Priority Mail ($2.74), with bar code (CVP2) —
30 CVP1 $8.75 **Express Mail** —

An $8.50 Express Mail stamp, dated Dec. 2, exists on cover.

Type I — CVP3

Type II — CVP3

1992, Aug. 20 Engr. *Perf. 10 Horiz.*

Coil Stamp

31 CVP3 29c red & blue, type I .60 .25
c. 32c, type II ('94) .80 .25

No. 31 was available in all denominations from 1c to $99.99. The listing is for the first class rate. Other denominations, se-tenant combinations, or "errors" will not be listed.

Type II denomination has large sans-serif numerals preceded by an asterisk measuring 2mm across. No. 31 has small numerals with serifs preceded by an asterisk 1½mm across.

CVP4

1994, Feb. 19 Photo. *Perf. 9.9 Vert.*

Coil Stamp

32 CVP4 29c dark red & dark blue .60 .25

No. 32 was available in all denominations from 19c to $99.99. The listing is for the first class rate at time of issue. Other denominations, se-tenant combinations, or "errors" will not be listed.

1996, Jan. 26 Photo. *Perf. 9.9 Vert.*

33 CVP4 32c bright red & blue .60 .25

Letters in "USA" on No. 33 are thicker than on No. 32. Numerous other design differences exist in the moire pattern and in the bunting. No. 33 has "1996" in the lower left corner; No. 32 has no date.

For No. 33, the 32c value has been listed because it was the first class rate at time of issue.

CARRIERS' STAMPS

OFFICIAL ISSUES

Issued by the US Government to facilitate payment of fees for delivering and collecting letters.

Franklin OC1

Eagle OC2

1851 Unwmk. Engr. *Imperf.*

LO1 OC1 (1c) dull blue, *rose* *4,500.* *5,500.*
LO2 OC2 1c blue 25.00 *50.00*

1875

REPRINTS OF 1851 ISSUE

Without Gum

LO3 OC1 (1c) blue, *rose*, imperf. 50.00
LO4 OC1 (1c) blue, perf. 12 *15,500.*
LO5 OC2 1c blue, imperf. 25.00
LO6 OC2 1c blue, perf. 12 200.00

Reprints of the Franklin Carrier are printed in dark blue, instead of the dull blue or deep blue of the originals. The reprints of the Eagle carrier are on hard white paper, ungummed and sometimes perforated, and also on a coarse wove paper. Originals are on yellowish paper with brown gum.

SEMI-OFFICIAL ISSUES

Issued by officials or employees of the US Government for the purpose of securing or indicating payment of carriers' fees.

BALTIMORE, MD.

C1

1850-55 Typo. *Imperf.*

1LB1 C1 1c red, *bluish* 180. 160.
1LB2 C1 1c blue, *bluish* 200. 150.
a. Bluish laid paper — —
1LB3 C1 1c blue 160. 100.
a. Laid paper 190. 130.
1LB4 C1 1c green — 850.
1LB5 C1 1c red 2,250. 1,750.

Ten varieties.

C2

C3

1856 Typo.

1LB6 C2 1c blue 130. 90.
1LB7 C2 1c red 130. 90.

Shades exist of Nos. 1LB6-1LB7.

1857

1LB8 C3 1c black 65. 50.
a. "SENT" 100. 75.
b. Short rays 100. 75.
1LB9 C3 1c red 100. 90.
a. "SENT" 140. 110.
b. Short rays 140. 110.

Ten varieties of C3.

BOSTON, MASS.

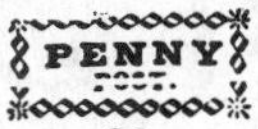

C6

C7

1849-50 Typeset

3LB1 C6 1c blue 375. 180.
3LB2 C7 1c blue (shades), *slate* 190. 100.

CHARLESTON, S. C.

C8

C10

1849 Typo.

4LB1 C8 2c black, *brn rose* *10,000.*
Cut to shape *3,000.*
4LB2 C8 2c black, *yellow*, cut to shape —

No. 4LB1 unused is a unique uncanceled stamp on piece. The used cut-to-shape stamp is also unique. In addition two covers exist bearing No. 4LB1.

No. 4LB2 unused (uncanceled) off cover is unique; four known on cover. See the *Scott U.S. Specialized Catalogue.*

1854 Typeset

4LB3 C10 2c black *1,500.*

C11

1849-50 Typeset

4LB5 C11 2c black, *bluish*, pelure *750.* *500.*
4LB7 C11 2c black, *yellow* *750.* *1,000.*

Several varieties of C11.

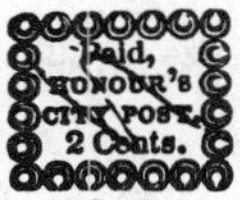

C13

C14

C15

1851-58 Typeset

4LB8 C13 2c blk, *bluish* 300. 150.
a. Period after "Paid" 500. 250.
b. "Cens" 600. *800.*
c. "Conours" and "Bents" —
4LB9 C13 2c blk, *bluish*, pelure *850.* *950.*
4LB11 C14 (2c) blk, *bluish* — *375.*
4LB12 C14 (2c) blk, *bluish*, pelure — —
4LB13 C15 (2c) blk, *bluish* ('58) 500. 250.
a. Comma after "PAID" *1,000.*
b. No period after "Post" *1,300.*

Several varieties of C13.

C16

C17

1851-58 Typeset

4LB14 C16 2c black, *bluish* *550.* *625.*
4LB15 C17 2c black, *bluish* *700.* *700.*

Several varieties of each.

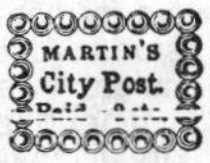

C18

1858 Typeset

4LB16 C18 2c black, *bluish* *8,000.*

Several varieties.

Same as C19, but Inscribed "Beckmann's City Post"

1860

4LB17 C19 2c black —

One copy exists, on cover.

C19

C20

1859 Typeset

4LB18 C19 2c black, *bluish* —
4LB19 C20 2c black, *bluish* *5,000.* —
4LB20 C20 2c black, *pink* *200.* —
4LB21 C20 2c black, *yellow* 175.

CINCINNATI, OHIO

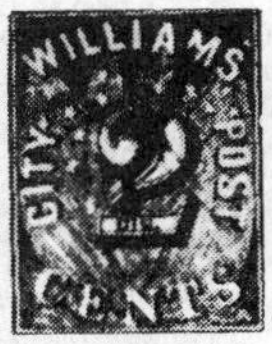

C20a

1854 Litho. Wove Paper

9LB1 C20a 2c brown *3,000.* *3,000.*

CLEVELAND, OHIO

C20b

C20c

1854 Wove Paper Litho.

10LB1 C20b blue *2,000.* *2,000.*

Vertically Laid Paper

10LB2 C20c 2c black, *bluish* — *3,750.*

LOUISVILLE, KY.

C21

C22

1857-58 Litho.

5LB1 C21 (2c) bluish green 100.
5LB2 C22 (2c) blue ('58) 175. *425.*
5LB3 C22 (2c) black ('58) *3,000.* *15,000.*

NEW YORK, N.Y.

C23

1842 Engr.

6LB1 C23 3c black, *grayish* *1,500.*

Used copies are Carriers' stamps only when canceled with the regular government cancellation "U.S." in octagonal frame (see illustration), "U.S.CITY DESPATCH POST," or New York circular postmark. When canceled "FREE" in frame they were used as local stamps (see No. 40L1 in the Scott Specialized Catalogue of United States Stamps).

C24

1842-45 **Engr.**

Unsurfaced Paper, Colored Through

6LB2	C24	3c black, *rosy buff*	1,500.		
6LB3	C24	3c blk, *light blue*	500.	500.
6LB4	C24	3c black, *green*	—	

Some authorities consider No. 6LB2 to be an essay, and No. 6LB4 to be a color changeling.

Glazed Paper, Surface Colored

6LB5	C24	3c black, *blue green (shades)*	175.	140.
a.		Double impression		500.
b.		3c, black, *blue*	650.	200.
c.		As "b," double impression		750.
d.		3c, black, *green*	1,000.	900.
e.		As "d," double impression		—

No. 6LB5 Surcharged in Red — C25

1846

6LB7	C25	2c on 3c, on cover	55,000.

The City Despatch 2c red is listed in the *Scott U.S. Specialized Catalogue* as a Local stamp.

C27

1849-50 **Typo.**

6LB9	C27	1c black, *rose*	90.	75.
6LB10	C27	1c black, *yellow*	90.	90.
6LB11	C27	1c black, *buff*	90.	75.
a.		Pair, one stamp sideways	2,250.	

PHILADELPHIA, PA.

C28

C29

1849-50 **Typeset**

7LB1	C28	1c blk, *rose* (with letters L.P.)	300.	
7LB2	C28	1c black, *rose* (with letter S)	3,000.	
7LB3	C28	1c blk, *rose* (with letter H)	275.	
7LB4	C28	1c blk, *rose* (with letters L.S.)	275.	500.
7LB5	C28	1c black, *rose* (with letters J.J.)		7,500.
7LB6	C29	1c black, *rose*	300.	250.
7LB7	C29	1c blk, *blue, glazed*	1,000.	
7LB8	C29	1c blk, *ver, glazed*	700.	
7LB9	C29	1c blk, *yel*, glazed	3,000.	2,250.

Several varieties of each.

Nos. 7LB1-7LB9 normally received no cancellation.

Two examples reported of No. 7LB5, one uncanceled on a cover front, the other uncanceled on full cover with U.S. 5c (No. 1). Value here is for stamp on cover front; for full cover see the *Scott U.S. Specialized Catalogue.*

The 1c black on buff (unglazed), type C29, is believed to be a color changeling.

C30

C31

C32

1850-52 **Litho.**

7LB11	C30	1c gold, *black, glazed*	140.	110.
7LB12	C30	1c blue	350.	275.
7LB13	C30	1c black	—	550.

25 varieties of C30.

Handstamped

7LB14	C31	1c blue, *buff*	3,000.	
7LB16	C31	1c black		5,000.

1856(?)

7LB18	C32	1c black	1,250.	2,000.

Labels in these designs are not believed to be Carrier stamps.

ST. LOUIS, MO.

C36

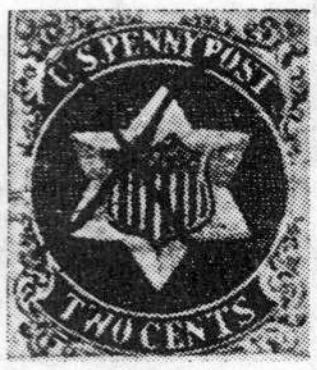

(Actual size) — C37

Several varieties.

1849 **Litho.**

8LB1	C36	2c black	6,000.	10,000.

1857 **Litho.**

8LB2	C37	2c blue	22,500.

Carrier stamps Nos. 9LB1, 10LB1-10LB2 are listed following No. 4LB21.

STAMPED ENVELOPES AND WRAPPERS

VALUES

Values are for cut squares in a grade of very fine. Very fine cut squares will have the design well centered within moderately large margins. Precanceled cut squares must include the entire precancellation. Values for unused entires are for those without printed or manuscript address. Values for letter sheets are for folded entires. Unfolded copies sell for more. A "full corner" includes back and side flaps and commands a premium. (Entire envelopes and wrappers are listed in the Scott U.S. Specialized Catalogue.)

Wrappers are listed with envelopes of corresponding designs, and indicated by prefix letter "W" instead of "U."

Envelopes with the stamp printed by error in colorless embossing from an uninked die, are "albinos." They are worth more than normal, inked impressions. Albinos of earlier issues, canceled while current, are scarce.

The papers of these issues vary greatly in texture, and in color from yellowish to bluish white and from amber to dark buff.

"+" Some authorities claim that Nos. U37, U48, U49, U110, U124, U125, U130, U133A, U137A, U137B, U137C, W138, U145, U162, U178A, U185, U220, U285, U286, U298, U299, UO3, UO32, UO38, UO45 and UO45A (each with "+" before number) were not regularly issued and are not known to have been used.

Washington

U1 U2

U1 — "THREE" in short label with curved ends; 13mm wide at top.

U2 — "THREE" in short label with straight ends; 15½mm wide at top.

U3

U4

U3 — "THREE" in short label with octagon ends.

U4 — "THREE" in wide label with straight ends; 20mm wide at top.

U5

U6

U5 — "THREE" in medium wide label with curved ends; 14½mm wide at top.

U7

U8

U7 — "TEN" in short label; 15½mm wide at top.

U8 — "TEN" in wide label 20mm wide at top.

On Diagonally Laid Paper

1853-55

U1	U1	3c red	250.00	20.00
U2	U1	3c red, *buff*	80.00	11.00
U3	U2	3c red	900.00	35.00
U4	U2	3c red, *buff*	275.00	20.00
U5	U3	3c red ('54)	4,500.	375.00
U6	U3	3c red, *buff* ('54)	250.00	42.50
U7	U4	3c red	750.00	85.00
U8	U4	3c red, *buff*	1,500.	100.00
U9	U5	3c red ('54)	35.00	3.00
U10	U5	3c red, *buff* ('54)	17.50	3.00
U11	U6	6c red	180.00	65.00
U12	U6	6c red, *buff*	130.00	55.00
U13	U6	6c green	250.00	100.00
U14	U6	6c green, *buff*	200.00	80.00
U15	U7	10c green ('55)	225.00	70.00
U16	U7	10c green, *buff* ('55)	80.00	50.00
a.		10c pale green, *buff*	70.00	45.00
U17	U8	10c green ('55)	275.00	100.00
a.		10c pale green	225.00	100.00
U18	U8	10c green, *buff* ('55)	125.00	60.00
a.		10c pale green, *buff*	125.00	60.00

Nos. U9, U10, U11, U12, U13, U14, U17 and U18 have been reprinted on white and buff papers, wove or vertically laid, and are not known entire. The originals are on diagonally laid paper. Value of 8 reprints on laid, $225. Reprints on wove sell for more.

Franklin, Period after "POSTAGE."

U9 U10

U10 — Bust touches inner frame-line at front and back.

No period after "POSTAGE" U11

Washington U12

Envelopes are on diagonally laid paper. Wrappers on vertically or horizontally laid paper.

1860-61

U19	U9	1c blue, *buff*	32.50	15.00
W20	U9	1c blue, *buff* ('61)	65.00	50.00
W21	U9	1c blue, *man* ('61)	45.00	45.00
W22	U9	1c blue, *org* ('61)	2,750.	
U23	U10	1c blue, *org*	450.00	350.00
U24	U11	1c blue, *buff*	225.00	90.00
W25	U11	1c blue, *man* ('61)	3,250.	2,750.
U26	U12	3c red	30.00	15.00
U27	U12	3c red, *buff*	22.50	12.50
U28	U12+9	3c + 1c red & blue	350.00	240.00
U29	U12+9	3c + 1c red & blue, *buff*	300.00	225.00
U30	U12	6c red	2,400.	1,250.
U31	U12	6c red, *buff*	2,250.	900.00
U32	U12	10c green	1,200.	350.00
U33	U12	10c green, *buff*	1,100.	250.00

Nos. U26, U27, U30 to U33 have been reprinted on the same vertically laid paper as the reprints of the 1853-55 issue, and are not known entire. Value, Nos. U26-U27, $160; Nos. U30-U33, $100.

U13

U14

Washington

U15 U16

Envelopes are on diagonally laid paper.

1861

U34	U13	3c pink	22.50	5.50
U35	U13	3c pink, *buff*	21.00	5.00
U36	U13	3c pink, *bl* (letter sheet)	80.00	50.00
+U37	U13	3c pink, *org*	3,500.	
U38	U14	6c pink	110.00	80.00
U39	U14	6c pink, *buff*	70.00	60.00
U40	U15	10c yellow green	35.00	30.00
a.		10c blue green	32.50	27.50
U41	U15	10c yel green, *buff*	30.00	27.50
a.		10c blue green, *buff*	30.00	27.50
U42	U16	12c red & brown, *buff*	190.00	160.00
a.		12c lake & brown, *buff*	800.00	
U43	U16	20c red & bl, *buff*	200.00	175.00
U44	U16	24c red & green, *buff*	200.00	175.00
a.		24c lake & green, *sal*	275.00	200.00
U45	U16	40c black & red, *buff*	300.00	300.00

Nos. U38 and U39 have been reprinted on the same papers as the reprints of the 1853-55 issue and are not known entire. Value of two reprints, $60.

Jackson — U17

Jackson — U18

"U.S. POSTAGE" above

U17 — The downstroke and tail of the "2" unite near the point.

U18 — The downstroke and tail of the "2" touch but do not merge.

Jackson — U19

Jackson — U20

"U.S. POST" above

U19 — Stamp measures 24 to 25mm in width.

U20 — Stamp measures 25½ to 26¼mm in width.

Envelopes are on diagonally laid paper. Wrappers on vertically or horizontally laid paper.

1863-64

U46	U17	2c	black, *buff*	35.00	17.50
W47	U17	2c	black, *dk man*	47.50	35.00
+U48	U18	2c	black, *buff*	2,250.	
+U49	U18	2c	black, *orange*	1,200.	
U50	U19	2c	blk, *buff* ('64)	14.00	9.00
W51	U19	2c	blk, *buff* ('64)	175.00	150.00
U52	U19	2c	blk, *org* ('64)	12.50	9.00
W53	U19	2c	black, *dk man* ('64)	40.00	25.00
U54	U20	2c	blk, *buff* ('64)	14.00	9.00
W55	U20	2c	blk, *buff* ('64)	75.00	55.00
U56	U20	2c	blk, *org* ('64)	12.00	8.00
W57	U20	2c	blk, *lt man* ('64)	14.00	11.50

Washington U21

Washington U22

1864-65

U58	U21	3c	pink	8.00	1.50
U59	U21	3c	pink, *buff*	5.75	1.00
U60	U21	3c	brown ('65)	45.00	27.50
U61	U21	3c	brn, *buff* ('65)	45.00	25.00
U62	U21	6c	pink	70.00	27.50
U63	U21	6c	pink, *buff*	35.00	27.50
U64	U21	6c	purple ('65)	50.00	27.50
U65	U21	6c	pur, *buff* ('65)	42.50	19.00
U66	U22	9c	lem, *buff* ('65)	425.00	250.00
U67	U22	9c	org, *buff* ('65)	100.00	80.00
a.			9c orange yellow, *buff*	90.00	85.00
U68	U22	12c	brn, *buff* ('65)	350.00	250.00
U69	U22	12c	red brn, *buff* ('65)	90.00	55.00
U70	U22	18c	red, *buff* ('65)	90.00	90.00
U71	U22	24c	bl, *buff* ('65)	95.00	80.00
U72	U22	30c	grn, *buff* ('65)	75.00	75.00
a.			30c yellow green, *buff*	70.00	*80.00*
U73	U22	40c	rose, *buff* ('65)	92.50	*300.00*

Reay Issue

The engravings in this issue are finely executed.

Franklin — U23

Jackson — U24

U23 — Bust points to the end of the "N" of "ONE".

U24 — Bust narrow at back. Small, thick figures of value.

Washington U25

Lincoln U26

U25 — Queue projects below bust.

U26 — Neck very long at the back.

Stanton — U27

Jefferson — U28

U27 — Bust pointed at the back, figures "7" are normal.

U28 — Queue forms straight line with the bust.

Clay — U29

Webster — U30

U29 — Ear partly concealed by hair, mouth large, chin prominent.

U30 — Has side whiskers.

Scott — U31

Hamilton — U32

U31 — Straggling locks of hair at top of head; ornaments around the inner oval end in squares.

U32 — Back of bust very narrow, chin almost straight; labels containing figures of value are exactly parallel.

Perry — U33

U33 — Front of bust very narrow and pointed; inner lines of shields project very slightly beyond the oval.

1870-71

U74	U23	1c	blue	35.00	27.50
a.			1c ultramarine	60.00	32.50
U75	U23	1c	blue, *amber*	32.50	27.50
a.			1c ultramarine, *amb*	50.00	30.00
U76	U23	1c	blue, *org*	17.50	15.00
W77	U23	1c	blue, *man*	40.00	35.00
U78	U24	2c	brown	37.50	15.00
U79	U24	2c	brown, *amb*	17.50	8.50
U80	U24	2c	brown, *org*	10.00	6.00
W81	U24	2c	brown, *man*	25.00	20.00
U82	U25	3c	green	7.50	.85
U83	U25	3c	green, *amb*	6.25	1.90
U84	U25	3c	green, *cream*	9.50	4.00
U85	U26	6c	dark red	22.50	16.00
a.			6c vermilion	17.50	16.00
U86	U26	6c	dk red, *amb*	22.50	15.00
a.			6c vermilion, *amber*	21.00	15.00
U87	U26	6c	dk red, *cr*	27.50	15.00
a.			6c vermilion, *cream*	22.50	15.00
U88	U27	7c	ver, *amb* ('71)	47.50	*180.00*
U89	U28	10c	olive black	550.00	425.00
U90	U28	10c	ol blk, *amb*	550.00	425.00
U91	U28	10c	brown	50.00	70.00
U92	U28	10c	brn, *amb*	72.50	50.00
a.			10c dark brown, *amb*	60.00	60.00
U93	U29	12c	plum	110.00	82.50
U94	U29	12c	plum, *amb*	110.00	110.00
U95	U29	12c	plum, *cr*	225.00	225.00
U96	U30	15c	red orange	67.50	70.00
a.			15c orange	67.50	
U97	U30	15c	red org, *amb*	140.00	180.00
a.			15c orange, *amber*	140.00	
U98	U30	15c	red org, *cr*	250.00	225.00
a.			15c orange, *cream*	240.00	
U99	U31	24c	purple	130.00	120.00
U100	U31	24c	pur, *amb*	185.00	300.00
U101	U31	24c	pur, *cream*	185.00	300.00
U102	U32	30c	black	80.00	100.00
U103	U32	30c	blk, *amb*	200.00	250.00
U104	U32	30c	blk, *cream*	220.00	400.00
U105	U33	90c	carmine	140.00	225.00
U106	U33	90c	car, *amb*	350.00	400.00
U107	U33	90c	car, *cream*	450.00	650.00

Plimpton Issue

The profiles in this issue are inferior to the fine engraving of the Reay issue.

U34

U35

U34 — Bust forms an angle at the back near the frame. Lettering poorly executed. Distinct circle in "O" of "POSTAGE."

U35 — Lower part of bust points to the end of the "E" in "ONE." Head inclined downward.

U36

U37

U36 — Bust narrow at back. Thin figures of value. The head of the "P" in "POSTAGE" is very narrow. The bust at front is broad and ends in sharp corners.

U37 — Bust broad. Figures of value in long ovals.

U38

U39

U38 — Similar to die 2 but the figure "2" at the left touches the oval.

U39 — Similar to die 2 but the "O" of "TWO" has the center netted instead of plain. The "G" of "POSTAGE" and the "C" of "CENTS" have diagonal crossline.

U40

U41

U40 — Bust broad; numerals in ovals short and thick.

U41 — Similar to die 5 but the ovals containing the numerals are much heavier. A diagonal line runs from the upper part of the "U" to the white frame-line.

U42

U43

U42 — Similar to die 5 but the middle stroke of "N" in "CENTS" is as thin as the vertical strokes.

U43 — Bottom of bust cut almost semi-circularly.

U44

U45

U44 — Thin lettering, long thin figures of value.

U45 — Thick lettering, well-formed figures of value, queue does not project below bust.

U46

U46 — Top of head egg-shaped; knot of queue well marked and projects triangularly.

Taylor — U47

Die 1

Die 2

Die 1 — Figures of value with thick curved tops.

Die 2 — Figures of value with long, thin tops.

U48

U49

U48 — Neck very short at the back.

U49 — Figures of value turned up at the ends.

U50

U51

U50 — Very large head.

U51 — Knot of queue stands out prominently.

U52

U53

U52 — Ear prominent, chin receding.

U53 — No side whiskers, forelock projects above head.

U54

U55

U54 — Hair does not project; ornaments around the inner oval end in points.

U55 — Back of bust rather broad, chin slopes considerably; labels containing figures of value are not exactly parallel.

U56

U56 — Front of bust sloping; inner lines of shields project considerably into the inner oval.

1874-86

U34

U108	1c dark blue	100.00	70.00
a.	1c light blue	110.00	75.00
U109	1c dk blue, *amb*	120.00	75.00
+U110	1c dk blue, *cr*	1,050.	
U111	1c dk blue, *org*	20.00	16.00
a.	1c light blue, *org*	22.50	15.00
W112	1c dk blue, *man*	50.00	40.00

U35

U113	1c light blue	1.60	.75
a.	1c dark blue	7.50	7.50
U114	1c lt blue, *amb*	4.25	4.00
a.	1c dark blue, *amb*	15.00	10.00
U115	1c blue, *cr*	4.50	4.50
a.	1c dark blue, *cr*	17.50	8.00
U116	1c lt blue, *org*	.75	.40
a.	1c dark blue, *org*	3.50	3.50
U117	1c lt bl, *bl* ('80)	6.50	5.25
U118	1c light blue, *fawn* ('79)	6.25	5.50
U119	1c lt blue, *man* ('86)	6.00	3.25
W120	1c lt blue, *man*	1.50	1.00
a.	1c dark blue, *man*	7.00	8.00
U121	1c lt blue, *amb man* ('86)	11.00	10.00

U36

U122	2c brown	90.00	37.50
U123	2c brown, *amb*	55.00	40.00
+U124	2c brown, *cr*	*775.00*	
+U125	2c brown, *org*	*12,500.*	
W126	2c brown, *man*	110.00	65.00
W127	2c ver, *man*	1,250.	250.00

U37

U128	2c brown	45.00	32.50
U129	2c brown, *amb*	65.00	37.50
+U130	2c brown, *cr*	*40,000.*	
W131	2c brown, *man*	17.50	15.00

U38

U132	2c brown	60.00	27.50
U133	2c brown, *amb*	190.00	55.00
+U133A	2c brown, *cr*	—	

U39

U134	2c brown	575.00	135.00
U135	2c brown, *amb*	400.00	110.00
U136	2c brown, *org*	47.50	27.50
W137	2c brown, *man*	60.00	35.00
+U137A	2c vermilion	*18,500.*	
+U137B	2c ver, *amb*	*18,500.*	
+U137C	2c ver, *org*	*18,500.*	
+W138	2c ver, *man*	*17,500.*	

U40

U139	2c brown ('75)	40.00	32.50
U140	2c brown, *amb* ('75)	75.00	62.50
U140A	2c brown, *org* ('75)	*17,500.*	
W141	2c brown, *man* ('75)	35.00	25.00
U142	2c ver ('75)	6.00	2.75
a.	2c pink	8.50	6.50
U143	2c ver, *amber* ('75)	6.00	2.75
U144	2c ver, *cr* ('75)	12.50	6.00
+U145	2c ver, *org* ('75)	*12,500.*	
U146	2c ver, *bl* ('80)	125.00	30.00
U147	2c ver, *fawn* ('75)	6.00	4.50
W148	2c ver, *man* ('75)	3.75	3.50

U41

U149	2c ver ('78)	45.00	30.00
a.	2c pink	45.00	30.00
U150	2c ver, *amber* ('78)	22.50	17.50
U151	2c ver, *bl* ('80)	12.50	9.00
a.	2c pink, *blue*	10.00	9.00
U152	2c ver, *fawn* ('78)	11.00	4.50

U42

U153	2c ver ('76)	55.00	25.00
U154	2c ver, *amb* ('76)	275.00	85.00
W155	2c ver, *man* ('76)	21.00	9.50

U43

U156	2c ver ('81)	600.00	130.00
U157	2c ver, *amb* ('81)	*35,000.*	*15,000.*
W158	2c ver, *man* ('81)	80.00	62.50

U44

U159	3c green	22.50	6.50
U160	3c green, *amb*	27.50	10.00
U161	3c green, *cr*	35.00	12.50
+U162	3c green, *blue*	—	

U45

U163	3c green	1.40	.25
U164	3c green, *amb*	1.40	.65
U165	3c green, *cr*	8.00	6.75
U166	3c green, *blue*	8.00	6.00
U167	3c green, *fawn* ('75)	5.00	3.50

U46

U168	3c green ('81)	500.00	55.00
U169	3c green, *amb* ('81)	225.00	100.00
U170	3c grn, *bl* ('81)	*8,000.*	*2,250.*
U171	3c green, *fawn* ('81)	*40,000.*	*2,500.*

U47

U172	5c blue, die 1 ('75)	11.00	8.00
U173	5c blue, die 1, *amb* ('75)	11.00	9.00
U174	5c blue, die 1, *cr* ('75)	95.00	40.00
U175	5c blue, die 1, *bl* ('75)	25.00	15.00
U176	5c blue, die 1, *fawn* ('75)	110.00	55.00
U177	5c blue, die 2 ('75)	8.00	6.50
U178	5c blue, die 2, *amb* ('75)	8.00	7.50
+U178A	5c blue, die 2, *cr* ('76)	*4,250.*	
U179	5c blue, die 2, *blue* ('75)	15.00	9.00
U180	5c blue, die 2, *fawn* ('75)	100.00	45.00

U48

U181	6c red	7.00	6.00
a.	6c vermilion	5.75	5.50
U182	6c red, *amber*	12.50	6.00
a.	6c vermilion, *amber*	10.00	6.00
U183	6c red, *cream*	20.00	12.50
a.	6c vermilion, *cream*	20.00	12.50
U184	6c red, *fawn* ('75)	20.00	12.50

U49

+U185	7c vermilion	*1,500.*	
U186	7c ver, *amber*	95.00	60.00

U50

U187	10c brown	35.00	20.00
U188	10c brown, *amb*	60.00	32.50

U51

U189	10c choc ('75)	8.00	4.25
a.	10c bister brown	8.50	5.00
b.	10c yellow ocher	1,250.	
U190	10c choc, *amb* ('75)	8.50	7.50
a.	10c bister brown, *amb*	8.50	7.50
b.	10c yellow ocher, *amb*	1,050.	
U191	10c brn, *oriental buff* ('86)	10.00	8.50
U192	10c brn, *bl* ('86)	12.50	8.50
a.	10c gray black, *blue*	11.00	7.50
b.	10c red brown, *blue*	11.00	7.50
U193	10c brown, *man* ('86)	14.00	10.00
a.	10c red brown, *man*	12.50	9.50
U194	10c brown, *amb man* ('86)	15.00	9.00
a.	10c red brown, *amber manila*	17.50	9.00

U52

U195	12c plum	180.00	85.00
U196	12c plum, *amb*	170.00	150.00
U197	12c plum, *cream*	225.00	175.00

U53

U198	15c orange	45.00	37.50
U199	15c orange, *amb*	135.00	100.00
U200	15c org, *cream*	350.00	350.00

U54

U201	24c purple	150.00	125.00
U202	24c purple, *amb*	160.00	125.00
U203	24c pur, *cream*	160.00	125.00

U55

U204	30c black	60.00	27.50
U205	30c black, *amb*	70.00	60.00
U206	30c black, *cream*	375.00	375.00
U207	30c blk, *oriental buff* ('86)	100.00	80.00
U208	30c blk, *bl* ('86)	105.00	80.00
U209	30c black, *man* ('86)	90.00	80.00
U210	30c black, *amb man* ('86)	125.00	80.00

U56

U211	90c carmine ('75)	125.00	80.00
U212	90c car, *amb* ('75)	160.00	225.00
U213	90c car, *cr* ('75)	1,300.	
U214	90c car, *oriental buff* ('86)	210.00	275.00
U215	90c car, *bl* ('86)	190.00	250.00
U216	90c car, *man* ('86)	130.00	250.00
U217	90c car, *amb man* ('86)	125.00	200.00

See Nos. U336-U347.

United States Centennial Issue

Single line under "POSTAGE" U57

Double line under "POSTAGE" U58

1876

U218	U57	3c red	50.00	25.00
U219	U57	3c green	45.00	17.50
+U220	U58	3c red	*25,000.*	
U221	U58	3c green	52.50	22.50

Cent. of the US, and the World's Fair at Philadelphia.

See No. U582.

Garfield U59

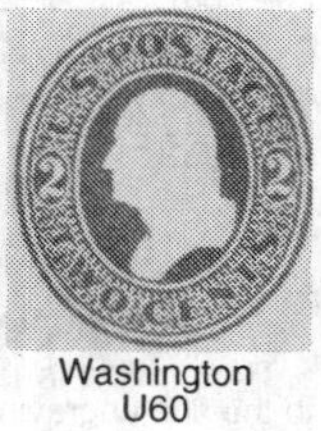
Washington U60

1882-86

U222	U59	5c brown	4.00	2.75
U223	U59	5c brown, *amb*	4.75	3.25
U224	U59	5c brn, *oriental buff* ('86)	110.00	70.00
U225	U59	5c brown, *blue*	60.00	35.00
U226	U59	5c brown, *fawn*	240.00	

1883, Oct.

U227	U60	2c red	3.75	2.25
a.		2c brown (error), entire	*3,000.*	
U228	U60	2c red, *amber*	4.75	2.75
U229	U60	2c red, *blue*	7.00	5.00
U230	U60	2c red, *fawn*	8.00	5.25

Wavy lines fine and clear — U61

Wavy lines thick and blurred — U62

Four Wavy Lines in Oval

1883, Nov.

U231	U61	2c red	3.75	2.25
U232	U61	2c red, *amber*	5.00	3.75
U233	U61	2c red, *blue*	8.00	7.00
U234	U61	2c red, *fawn*	6.00	4.50
W235	U61	2c red, *manila*	17.50	6.00

1884, June

U236	U62	2c red	7.50	4.00
U237	U62	2c red, *amber*	11.00	10.00
U238	U62	2c red, *blue*	17.50	10.00
U239	U62	2c red, *fawn*	12.00	9.50

See Nos. U260-W269.

3½ links over left "2" — U63

2 links below right "2" — U64

Round "O" in "TWO" — U65

U240	U63	2c red	70.00	40.00
U241	U63	2c red, *amber*	750.00	325.00
U242	U63	2c red, *fawn*		*6,500.*
U243	U64	2c red	90.00	55.00
U244	U64	2c red, *amber*	160.00	75.00
U245	U64	2c red, *blue*	375.00	140.00
U246	U64	2c red, *fawn*	375.00	140.00
U247	U65	2c red	1,500.	350.00
U248	U65	2c red, *amber*	2,500.	850.00
U249	U65	2c red, *fawn*	600.00	375.00

See Nos. U270-U276.

Jackson — U66

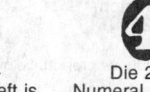

Die 1 — Numeral at left is 2¾mm wide

Die 2 — Numeral at left is 3¼mm wide

1883-86

U250	U66	4c grn, die 1	3.75	3.50
U251	U66	4c grn, die 1, *amb*	4.75	3.50
U252	U66	4c grn, die 1, *oriental buff* ('86)	8.00	9.00
U253	U66	4c grn, die 1, *bl* ('86)	8.00	6.50

U254	U66	4c grn, die 1, *man* ('86)	10.00	7.50
U255	U66	4c grn, die 1, *amb man* ('86)	17.50	10.00
U256	U66	4c grn, die 2	5.50	5.00
U257	U66	4c grn, die 2, *amb*	11.00	7.00
U258	U66	4c grn, die 2, *man* ('86)	10.00	7.50
U259	U66	4c grn, die 2, *amb man* ('86)	11.00	7.50

1884, May

U260	U61	2c brown	13.00	5.75
U261	U61	2c brn, *amber*	12.00	6.75
U262	U61	2c brn, *blue*	13.00	9.50
U263	U61	2c brn, *fawn*	12.00	9.00
W264	U61	2c brn, *manila*	14.00	10.00

1884, June **Retouched Die**

U265	U62	2c brown	15.00	6.00
U266	U62	2c brn, *amber*	65.00	40.00
U267	U62	2c brn, *blue*	13.00	6.00
U268	U62	2c brn, *fawn*	15.00	11.00
W269	U62	2c brn, *manila*	22.50	15.00

2 Links Below Right "2"

U270	U64	2c brown	95.00	37.50
U271	U64	2c brn, *amber*	200.00	90.00
U272	U64	2c brn, *fawn*	*3,500.*	*1,250.*

Round "O" in "Two"

U273	U65	2c brown	160.00	80.00
U274	U65	2c brn, *amber*	200.00	80.00
U275	U65	2c brn, *blue*		*15,000.*
U276	U65	2c brn, *fawn*	825.00	650.00

Washington

U67 U68

U67 — Extremity of bust below the queue forms a point.

U68 — Extremity of bust is rounded.

Similar to U61

Two wavy lines in oval

1884-86

U277	U67	2c brown	.50	.20
a.		2c brown lake	20.00	22.50
U278	U67	2c brn, *amber*	.65	.45
a.		2c brown lake, *amber*	30.00	12.50
U279	U67	2c brn, *oriental buff* ('86)	2.90	2.00
U280	U67	2c brn, *blue*	2.50	2.00
U281	U67	2c brn, *fawn*	3.00	2.25
U282	U67	2c brn, *man* ('86)	10.00	4.00
W283	U67	2c brn, *man*	6.00	5.00
U284	U67	2c brn, *amb man* ('86)	5.50	5.75
+U285	U67	2c red	575.00	
+U286	U67	2c red, *blue*	250.00	
W287	U67	2c red, *man*	110.00	
U288	U68	2c brown	150.00	35.00
U289	U68	2c brn, *amb*	14.00	12.50
U290	U68	2c brn, *blue*	950.00	140.00
U291	U68	2c brn, *fawn*	20.00	19.00
W292	U68	2c brn, *man*	20.00	17.50

Grant — US1

1886 **Letter Sheet**

U293	US1	2c green, entire	25.00	16.00

See the Scott U.S. Specialized Catalogue for perforation and inscription varieties..

Franklin U69 Washington U70

U70 — Bust points between 3rd and 4th notches of inner oval; "G" of "POSTAGE" has no bar.

U71 U72

U71 — Bust points between second and third notches of inner oval; "G" of "POSTAGE" has a bar; ear is indicated by one heavy line; one vertical line at corner of mouth.

U72 — Frame same as die 2; upper part of head more rounded; ear indicated by two curved lines with two locks of hair in front; two vertical lines at corner of mouth.

Jackson — U73

Grant — U74 U75

U74 — There is a space between the beard and the collar of the coat. A button is on the collar.

U75 — The collar touches the beard and there is no button.

1887-94

U294	U69	1c blue	.55	.20
U295	U69	1c dk bl ('94)	7.50	2.50
U296	U69	1c bl, *amb* ('94)	3.50	1.25
U297	U69	1c dk blue, *amb* ('94)	47.50	22.50
+U298	U69	1c bl, *oriental buff* ('94)	*3,750.*	
+U299	U69	1c bl, *bl* ('94)	*8,000.*	
U300	U69	1c bl, *man* ('94)	.65	.35
W301	U69	1c bl, *man* ('94)	.45	.30
U302	U69	1c dk blue, *man* ('94)	25.00	10.00
W303	U69	1c dk blue, *man* ('94)	12.00	9.50
U304	U69	1c bl, *amb man*	5.50	4.25
U305	U70	2c green	11.00	9.00
U306	U70	2c grn, *amb*	22.50	14.00
U307	U70	2c grn, *oriental buff*	75.00	30.00
U308	U70	2c grn, *blue*	*8,000.*	1,000.
U309	U70	2c grn, *man*	*4,500.*	500.00
U310	U70	2c grn, *amb man*	1,800.	1,250.
U311	U71	2c green	.35	.20
U312	U71	2c grn, *amb*	.45	.20
U313	U71	2c grn, *oriental buff*	.60	.25
U314	U71	2c grn, *blue*	.60	.30
U315	U71	2c grn, *man*	1.80	.50
W316	U71	2c grn, *man*	3.25	2.50
U317	U71	2c grn, *amb man*	2.75	1.90
U318	U72	2c green	110.00	12.50
U319	U72	2c grn, *amb*	175.00	25.00
U320	U72	2c grn, *oriental buff*	170.00	40.00
U321	U72	2c grn, *blue*	190.00	65.00
U322	U72	2c grn, *man*	175.00	65.00
U323	U72	2c grn, *amb man*	375.00	72.50
U324	U73	4c carmine	2.50	1.75
a.		4c lake	2.75	2.00
b.		4c scarlet ('94)	2.75	2.00
U325	U73	4c car, *amb*	3.00	2.25
a.		4c lake, *amber*	3.25	2.50
b.		4c scarlet, *amber* ('94)	3.25	3.25
U326	U73	4c car, *oriental buff*	5.50	3.00
a.		4c lake, *oriental buff*	6.50	3.50
U327	U73	4c car, *blue*	5.00	4.00
a.		4c lake, *blue*	5.00	4.00
U328	U73	4c car, *man*	6.25	5.50
a.		4c lake, *manila*	7.25	6.00
b.		4c pink, *manila*	7.50	4.50
U329	U73	4c car, *amb man*	4.50	2.75
a.		4c lake, *amb manila*	4.25	3.25
b.		4c pink, *amb manila*	5.50	3.75
U330	U74	5c blue	3.50	4.00
U331	U74	5c bl, *amber*	4.50	2.25
U332	U74	5c bl, *oriental buff*	4.50	3.75
U333	U74	5c bl, *blue*	10.00	5.50
U334	U75	5c blue ('94)	12.50	5.50
U335	U75	5c bl, *amb* ('94)	11.00	5.50
U336	U55	30c red brown	45.00	37.50
a.		30c yellow brown	50.00	45.00
b.		30c chocolate	50.00	47.50
U337	U55	30c red brn, *amb*	47.50	50.00
a.		30c yel brown, *amber*	45.00	42.50
b.		30c choc, *amber*	45.00	42.50
U338	U55	30c red brn, *oriental buff*	42.50	42.50
a.		30c yel brn, *oriental buff*	37.50	42.50
U339	U55	30c red brn, *bl*	42.50	42.50
a.		30c yellow brown, *blue*	37.50	42.50
U340	U55	30c red brn, *manila*	45.00	42.50
a.		30c brown, *manila*	42.50	37.50
U341	U55	30c red brown, *amb man*	50.00	27.50
a.		30c yel brn, *amb man*	47.50	27.50
U342	U56	90c purple	62.50	70.00
U343	U56	90c pur, *amb*	77.50	75.00
U344	U56	90c pur, *oriental buff*	77.50	80.00
U345	U56	90c pur, *blue*	82.50	85.00
U346	U56	90c pur, *man*	85.00	85.00
U347	U56	90c pur, *amb manila*	87.50	85.00

Columbian Exposition Issue

Columbus and Liberty U76

1893

U348	U76	1c deep blue	2.00	1.10
U349	U76	2c violet	1.75	.50
a.		2c dark slate (error)	*1,750.*	
U350	U76	5c chocolate	8.50	7.50
a.		5c slate brown (error)	775.00	750.00
U351	U76	10c slate brown	30.00	25.00
		Nos. U348-U351 (4)	42.25	34.10

Franklin U77 Washington U78

U78 — Bust points to first notch of inner oval and is only slightly concave below.

U79 U80

U79 — Bust points to middle of second notch of inner oval and is quite hollow below. Queue has ribbon around it.

U80 — Same as die 2 but hair flowing and no ribbon around queue.

Lincoln — U81

Pointed but not draped.

U82 U83

U82 — Bust broad and draped.

U83 — Head larger, inner oval has no notches.

Grant — U84

Similar to designs of 1887-95 but smaller

1899

U352	U77	1c green	.60	.20
U353	U77	1c grn, *amb*	4.75	1.50
U354	U77	1c grn, *oriental buff*	11.00	2.75
U355	U77	1c grn, *bl*	11.00	7.50
U356	U77	1c grn, *man*	2.25	.95
W357	U77	1c grn, *man*	2.50	1.10
U358	U78	2c carmine	3.00	1.75
U359	U78	2c car, *amb*	20.00	14.00
U360	U78	2c car, *oriental buff*	19.00	8.00
U361	U78	2c car, *blue*	57.50	27.50
U362	U79	2c carmine	.35	.20
a.		2c dark lake	27.50	32.50
U363	U79	2c car, *amb*	1.40	.20
U364	U79	2c car, *oriental buff*	1.20	.20
U365	U79	2c car, *blue*	1.50	.55
W366	U79	2c car, *man*	8.00	3.25
U367	U80	2c carmine	4.50	2.75
U368	U80	2c car, *amber*	9.00	6.75
U369	U80	2c car, *oriental buff*	25.00	12.50
U370	U80	2c car, *blue*	12.50	10.00
U371	U81	4c brown	17.50	11.00
U372	U81	4c brn, *amb*	17.50	12.50
U373	U82	4c brown	*6,250.*	375.00
U374	U83	4c brown	12.50	8.00
U375	U83	4c brn, *amb*	40.00	17.50
W376	U83	4c brn, *man*	17.50	8.25
U377	U84	5c blue	10.00	9.50
U378	U84	5c blue, *amb*	14.00	10.00

Franklin U85 Washington U86

U86 — One short and two long vertical lines at right of "CENTS."

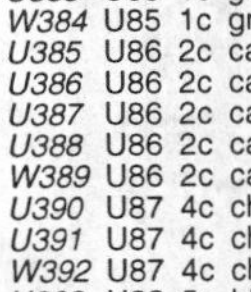
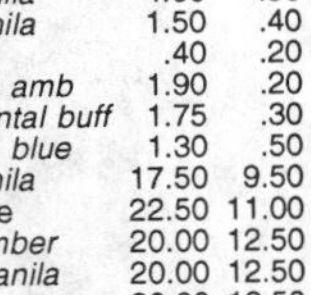

Grant — U87 Lincoln — U88

1903

U379	U85	1c green	.70	.20
U380	U85	1c green, *amb*	13.50	2.00
U381	U85	1c grn, *oriental buff*	15.00	2.50
U382	U85	1c green, *blue*	20.00	2.50
U383	U85	1c grn, *manila*	4.00	.90
W384	U85	1c grn, *manila*	1.50	.40
U385	U86	2c carmine	.40	.20
U386	U86	2c carmine, *amb*	1.90	.20
U387	U86	2c car, *oriental buff*	1.75	.30
U388	U86	2c carmine, *blue*	1.30	.50
W389	U86	2c car, *manila*	17.50	9.50
U390	U87	4c chocolate	22.50	11.00
U391	U87	4c choc, *amber*	20.00	12.50
W392	U87	4c choc, *manila*	20.00	12.50
U393	U88	5c blue	20.00	12.50
U394	U88	5c blue, *amber*	20.00	12.50

U89

The three lines at the right of "CENTS" and at the left of "TWO" are usually all short; the lettering is heavier and the ends of the ribbons slightly changed.

1904 **Re-cut Die**

U395	U89 2c carmine	.50	.20
U396	U89 2c car, *amber*	8.00	1.00
U397	U89 2c car, *oriental buff*	5.50	1.10
U398	U89 2c carmine, *blue*	3.50	.90
W399	U89 2c car, *manila*	12.00	9.50

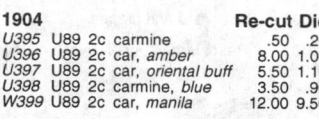

Franklin — U90

Die 1

Die 2

Die 3

Die 4

Die 1. Wide "D" in "UNITED."
Die 2. Narrow "D" in "UNITED."
Die 3. Wide "S-S" in "STATES" (1910).
Die 4. Sharp angle at back of bust, "N" and "E" of "ONE" are parallel (1912).

1907-16 **Die 1**

U400	U90 1c green	.30	.20
a.	Die 2	.80	.25
b.	Die 3	.80	.35
c.	Die 4	.75	.30
U401	U90 1c green, *amber*	.85	.40
a.	Die 2	.95	.70
b.	Die 3	1.05	.75
c.	Die 4	.95	.65
U402	U90 1c grn, *oriental buff*	4.50	1.00
a.	Die 2	5.75	1.50
b.	Die 3	6.50	1.50
c.	Die 4	5.00	1.50
U403	U90 1c green, *blue*	5.00	1.50
a.	Die 2	5.00	1.50
b.	Die 3	5.00	3.00
c.	Die 4	4.25	1.25
U404	U90 1c grn, *manila*	3.00	1.90
a.	Die 3	3.75	3.00
W405	U90 1c grn, *manila*	.50	.25
a.	Die 2	40.00	25.00
b.	Die 3	7.50	4.00
c.	Die 4	40.00	

Die 1, Washington — U91

Die 2

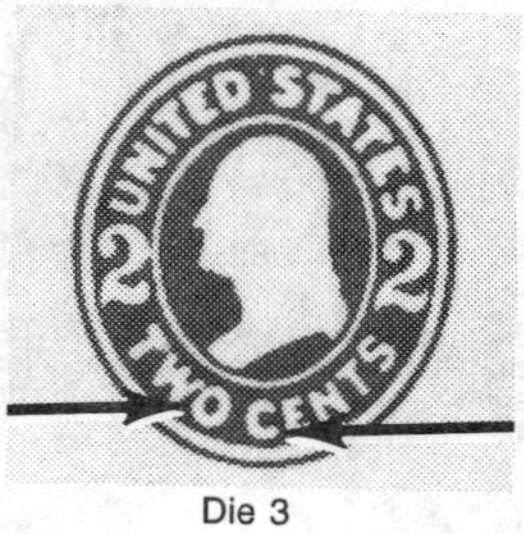

Die 3

Die 4

Die 5

Die 6

Die 7

Die 8

Die 1. Oval "O" in "TWO" and "C" in "CENTS," front of bust broad.

Die 2. Similar to 1 but hair in two distinct locks at top of head.

Die 3. Round "O" in "TWO" and "C" in "CENTS," coarse lettering.

Die 4. Similar to 3 but lettering fine and clear, hair lines clearly embossed. Inner oval thin and clear.

Die 5. All "S's" wide (1910).

Die 6. Similar to 1 but front of bust narrow (1913).

Die 7. Similar to 6 but upper corner of front of bust cut away (1916).

Die 8. Similar to 7 but lower stroke of "S" in "CENTS" is a straight line. Hair as in Die 2 (1916).

Die I

U406	U91 2c brown red	.80	.20
a.	Die 2	27.50	6.25
b.	Die 3	.55	.20
U407	U91 2c brn red, *amb*	5.50	2.00
a.	Die 2	100.00	45.00
b.	Die 3	3.50	1.00
U408	U91 2c brown red, *oriental buff*	7.00	1.50
a.	Die 2	125.00	55.00
b.	Die 3	6.50	2.50
U409	U91 2c brn red, *blue*	4.50	1.75
a.	Die 2	125.00	100.00
b.	Die 3	4.50	1.50
W410	U91 2c brn red, *man*	40.00	32.50
U411	U91 2c carmine	.25	.20
a.	Die 2	.45	.20
b.	Die 3	.75	.35
c.	Die 4	.40	.20
d.	Die 5	.55	.30
e.	Die 6	.40	.20
f.	Die 7	12.50	10.00
g.	Die 8	13.00	10.00
h.	Die 1, with added impression of 1c grn (#U400), entire	325.00	
i.	Die 1, with added impression of 4c blk (#U416a), entire	300.00	
U412	U91 2c carmine, *amb*	.25	.20
a.	Die 2	.45	.25
b.	Die 3	1.30	.45
c.	Die 4	.40	.25
d.	Die 5	.60	.35
e.	Die 6	.55	.35
f.	Die 7	11.00	8.00
U413	U91 2c car, *oriental buff*	.45	.20
a.	Die 2	.55	.45
b.	Die 3	6.00	3.00
c.	Die 4	.40	.20
d.	Die 5	2.75	1.25
e.	Die 6	.55	.35
f.	Die 7	35.00	17.50
g.	Die 8	11.00	8.50
U414	U91 2c carmine, *blue*	.50	.20
a.	Die 2	.50	.35
b.	Die 3	.80	.60
c.	Die 4	.50	.25
d.	Die 5	.65	.30
e.	Die 6	.55	.30
f.	Die 7	12.50	7.50
g.	Die 8	12.50	7.50
W415	U91 2c car, *manila*	4.50	2.00
a.	Die 2	4.50	1.10
b.	Die 5	4.50	2.25
c.	Die 7	40.00	35.00

"F" 1mm from left "4" — Die 1

"F" 1¾mm from left "4" — Die 2

U416	U90 4c black, die 2	4.00	2.25
a.	Die 1	4.50	3.00
U417	U90 4c black, *amb,* die 2	5.50	2.50
a.	Die 1	5.50	2.50

Die 1-Tall "F" in "FIVE"

Die 2-Short "F" in "FIVE"

U418	U91 5c blue, die 2	6.50	2.25
a.	Die 1	6.50	2.25
b.	5c blue, *buff,* die 2 (error)	*1,000.*	
c.	5c blue, *blue,* die 2 (error)	*1,000.*	
d.	5c blue, *blue,* die 1 (error)	*1,100.*	
U419	U91 5c blue, *amber,* die 2	14.00	11.00
a.	Die 1	12.50	11.00

Franklin — U92

Die 1

Die 2

Die 3

Die 4

Die 5

(The 1c and 4c dies are the same except for figures of value.)

Die 1. UNITED nearer inner circle than outer circle.

Die 2. Large U; large NT closely spaced.

Die 3. Knob of hair at back of neck. Large NT widely spaced.

Die 4. UNITED nearer outer circle than inner circle.

Die 5. Narrow oval C, (also O and G).

1915-32 **Die 1**

U420	U92 1c green ('16)	.20	.20
a.	Die 2	90.00	55.00
b.	Die 3	.30	.20
c.	Die 4	.40	.40
d.	Die 5	.40	.35
U421	U92 1c grn, *amber* ('16)	.60	.30
a.	Die 2	300.00	175.00
b.	Die 3	1.10	.65
c.	Die 4	1.25	.85
d.	Die 5	1.00	.55
U422	U92 1c grn, *oriental buff* ('16)	2.00	.90
a.	Die 4	4.25	1.25
U423	U92 1c green, *blue* ('16)	.45	.35
a.	Die 3	.75	.45
b.	Die 4	1.25	.65
c.	Die 5	.80	.35
U424	U92 1c grn, (unglazed), *manila* ('16)	6.50	4.00
W425	U92 1c grn, (unglazed), *manila* ('16)	.20	.20
a.	Die 3	140.00	125.00
U426	U92 1c grn, (glazed) *brown* ('20)	30.00	15.00
W427	U92 1c grn, (glazed) *brown* ('20)	65.00	
U428	U92 1c grn, (unglazed) *brown* ('20)	8.00	7.50

Die 1, Washington — U93

Die 2

Die 3

Die 4

Die 5

Die 6

Die 7

Die 8

Die 9

(The 1½c, 2c, 3c, 5c, and 6c are the same except for figures of value.)

Die 1. Letters broad. Numerals vertical. Large head (9¼mm) from tip of nose to back of neck. E closer to inner circle than N of cents.

Die 2. Similar to 1; but U far from left circle.

Die 3. Similar to 2; but all inner circles very thin (Rejected Die).

Die 4. Similar to 1; but C very close to left circle.

Die 5. Small head (8¾mm) from tip of nose to back of neck. T and S of CENTS close at bottom.

Die 6. Similar to 5; but T and S of CENTS far apart at bottom. Left numeral slopes to right.

Die 7. Large head. Both numerals slope to right. Clean cut lettering. All letters T have short top strokes.

Die 8. Similar to 7; but all letters T have long top strokes.

Die 9. Narrow oval C (also O and G).

Die 1

U429 U93 2c carmine, *Dec. 20, 1915* .20 .20
- *a.* Die 2 9.00 6.00
- *b.* Die 3 30.00 25.00
- *c.* Die 4 9.00 7.50
- *d.* Die 5 .50 .35
- *e.* Die 6 .60 .30
- *f.* Die 7 .65 .25
- *g.* Die 8 .45 .20
- *h.* Die 9 .40 .20
- *i.* 2c grn, error, die 1, entire 8,000.
- *j.* 2c car, die 1 with added impression of 1c grn (#U420), die 1 450.00
- *k.* Die 1, with added impression of 4c blk (#U416a), entire 700.00
- *l.* Die 1, with added impression of 1c grn (#U400), die 1, entire 500.00

U430 U93 2c car, *amber* ('16) .25 .20
- *a.* Die 2 9.25 7.50
- *b.* Die 4 20.00 10.00
- *c.* Die 5 1.10 .35
- *d.* Die 6 .95 .40
- *e.* Die 7 .70 .35
- *f.* Die 8 .65 .30
- *g.* Die 9 .60 .20

U431 U93 2c car, *oriental buff* ('16) 2.25 .65
- *a.* Die 2 100.00 40.00
- *b.* Die 4 30.00 30.00
- *c.* Die 5 2.75 1.75
- *d.* Die 6 3.00 2.00
- *e.* Die 7 2.75 1.75

U432 U93 2c carmine, *blue* ('16) .25 .20
- *b.* Die 2 25.00 20.00
- *c.* Die 3 100.00 90.00
- *d.* Die 4 25.00 25.00
- *e.* Die 5 .80 .30
- *f.* Die 6 .85 .40
- *g.* Die 7 .75 .35
- *h.* Die 8 .60 .25
- *i.* Die 9 .90 .30

U432A U93 2c car, *manila*, die 7, entire *25,000.*

W433 U93 2c car, *manila* ('16) .25 .20

W434 U93 2c car, (glazed) *brn* ('20) 90.00 50.00

W435 U93 2c car, (unglazed) *brn* ('20) 95.00 50.00

U436 U93 3c dk violet ('17) .55 .20
- *a.* 3c purple, die 1 ('32) .30 .20
- *b.* 3c dark violet, die 5 1.65 .75
- *c.* 3c dark violet, die 6 2.00 1.40
- *d.* 3c dark violet, die 7 1.40 .95
- *e.* 3c purple, die 7 ('32) .65 .30
- *f.* 3c purple, die 9 ('32) .40 .20
- *g.* 3c carmine (error), die 1 30.00 27.50
- *h.* 3c carmine (error), die 5 32.50 30.00
- *i.* 3c dk vio, die 1, with added impression of 1c grn (#U420), die 1, entire 600.00
- *j.* 3c dk vio, die 1, with added impression of 2c car (#U429), die 1, entire 700.00 —

U437 U93 3c dk violet, *amb* 3.25 1.25
- *a.* 3c purple, die 1 ('32) .35 .20
- *b.* 3c dark vio, die 5 4.50 2.50
- *c.* 3c dark vio, die 6 4.50 2.50
- *d.* 3c dark vio, die 7 3.75 2.25
- *e.* 3c purple, die 7 ('32) .75 .20
- *f.* 3c purple, die 9 ('32) .50 .20
- *g.* 3c carmine (error), die 5 450.00 275.00
- *h.* 3c black (error), die 1 165.00 —

U438 U93 3c dk vio, *oriental buff* 22.50 1.50
- *a.* Die 5 22.50 1.00
- *b.* Die 6 32.50 1.65
- *c.* Die 7 32.50 3.50

U439 U93 3c dk violet, *bl* 6.50 2.00
- *a.* 3c purple, die 1 ('32) .30 .20
- *b.* 3c dark violet, die 5 6.50 4.00
- *c.* 3c dark violet, die 6 6.00 4.25
- *d.* 3c dark violet, die 7 9.00 5.50
- *e.* 3c purple, die 7 ('32) .75 .25
- *f.* 3c purple, die 9 ('32) .50 .20
- *g.* 3c carmine (error), die 5 300.00 300.00

U440 U92 4c black ('16) 1.50 .60
- *a.* 4c black with added impression of 2c car (#U429), die 1, entire 250.00

U441 U92 4c black, *amb* ('16) 3.00 .85

U442 U92 4c black, *bl* ('21) 3.25 .85

U443 U93 5c blue ('16) 3.25 2.75

U444 U93 5c blue, *amber* ('16) 3.75 1.60

U445 U93 5c bl, *blue* ('21) 4.00 3.25

See Nos. U481-U485, U529-U531.

Listings of double or triple surcharges of 1920-25 are for specimens with the surcharges directly or partly upon the stamp.

Surcharged Type 1

1920-21

U446 U93 2c on 3c dk vio (U436, die 1) 12.00 10.00
- *a.* Die 5 (U436b) 12.00 10.00

Surcharged Type 2

Rose Surcharge

U447 U93 2c on 3c dk vio (U436, die 1) 7.75 6.50
- *b.* Die 6 (U436c) 10.00 8.50

Black Surcharge

U447A U93 2c on 2c car (U429, die 1) —

U447C U93 2c on 2c car, *amb* (U430, die 1) —

U448 U93 2c on 3c dk vio (U436, die 1) 2.50 2.00
- *a.* Die 5 (U436b) 2.50 2.00
- *b.* Die 6 (U436c) 3.25 2.00
- *c.* Die 7 (U436d) 2.50 2.00

U449 U93 2c on 3c dk vio, *amb* (U437, die 1) 6.50 6.00
- *a.* Die 5 (U437b) 10.00 7.50
- *b.* Die 6 (U437c) 7.50 6.00
- *c.* Die 7 (U437d) 7.00 6.50

U450 U93 2c on 3c dk vio, *oriental buff* (U438, die 1) 17.50 14.00
- *a.* Die 5 (U438a) 17.50 14.00
- *b.* Die 6 (U438b) 17.50 14.00
- *c.* Die 7 (U438c) 100.00 90.00

U451 U93 2c on 3c dk vio, *blue* (U439, die 1) 12.50 10.00
- *b.* Die 5 (U439b) 12.50 10.00
- *c.* Die 6 (U439c) 12.50 10.00
- *d.* Die 7 (U439d) 25.00 20.00

Surcharged Type 3

Bars 2mm apart

U451A U90 2c on 1c grn (U400, die 1) 2,250.

U452 U92 2c on 1c grn (U420, die 1) 1,750.
- *a.* Die 3 (U420b) 1,750.
- *b.* As No. U452, dbl. surch. 1,500.

U453 U91 2c on 2c car (U411b, die 3) 1,500.
- *a.* Die 1 (U411) 1,750.

U453B U91 2c on 2c car, *bl* (U414e, die 6) 1,250.

U453C U91 2c on 2c car, *oriental buff* (U413e, die 6) 1,100. 700.00
- *d.* Die 1 (U413) 1,250.

U454 U93 2c on 2c car (U429e, die 6) 82.50
- *a.* Die 1 (U429) 150.00
- *b.* Die 5 (U429d) 300.00
- *c.* Die 7 (U429f) 82.50

U455 U93 2c on 2c car, *amb* (U430, die 1) 1,250.
- *a.* Die 6 (U430d) 1,250.
- *b.* Die 7 (U430e) 1,250.

U456 U93 2c on 2c car, *oriental buff* (U431a, die 2) 200.00
- *a.* Die 5 (U431c) 200.00
- *b.* Die 7 (U431e) 200.00
- *c.* As #U456, double surcharge 250.00

U457 U93 2c on 2c car, *bl* (U432f, die 6) 225.00
- *a.* Die 5 (U432e) 250.00
- *b.* Die 7 (U432g) 225.00

U458 U93 2c on 3c dk vio (U436, die 1) .50 .35
- *a.* Die 5 (U436b) .50 .40
- *b.* Die 6 (U436c) .50 .35
- *c.* Die 7 (U436d) .50 .35
- *d.* As #U458, double surcharge 14.00 7.50
- *e.* As #U458, triple surcharge 35.00
- *f.* As #U458, dbl. surch., one in magenta 65.00
- *g.* As #U458, double surcharge, types 2 & 3 100.00
- *h.* As "a," double surcharge 27.50 15.00
- *i.* As "a," triple surcharge 50.00
- *j.* As "a," double surcharge, both magenta 65.00
- *k.* As "b," double surcharge 16.00 8.00
- *l.* As "c," double surcharge 16.00 8.00
- *m.* As "c," triple surcharge 35.00

U459 U93 2c on 3c dk vio, *amb* (U437c, die 6) 3.00 1.00
- *a.* Die 1 (U437) 4.00 1.00
- *b.* Die 5 (U437b) 4.00 1.00
- *c.* Die 7 (U437d) 3.00 1.00
- *d.* As No. U459, dbl. surch. 24.00
- *e.* As "a," double surcharge 24.00
- *f.* As "b," double surcharge 24.00
- *g.* As "b," double surcharge, types 2 & 3 80.00
- *h.* As "c," double surcharge 18.00

U460 U93 2c on 3c dk vio, *oriental buff* (U438a, die 5) 2.75 1.00
- *a.* Die 1 (U438) 3.00 1.50
- *b.* Die 6 (U438b) 3.00 2.00
- *c.* As No. U460, dbl. surch. 12.50
- *d.* As "a," double surcharge 12.50
- *e.* As "b," double surcharge 12.50
- *f.* As "b," triple surcharge 27.50

U461 U93 2c on 3c dk vio, *bl* (U439, die 1) 4.25 1.00
- *a.* Die 5 (U439b) 4.25 1.00
- *b.* Die 6 (U439c) 4.25 1.00
- *c.* Die 7 (U439d) 10.00 2.00
- *d.* As No. U461, dbl. surch. 12.50
- *e.* As "a," double surcharge 12.50
- *f.* As "b," double surcharge 12.50
- *g.* As "c," double surcharge 12.50

U462 U87 2c on 4c choc (U390) 350.00 160.00

U463 U87 2c on 4c choc, *amb* (U391) 350.00 100.00

U463A U90 2c on 4c blk (U416, die 2) 1,100. 375.00

U464 U93 2c on 5c bl (U443) 1,000.

Surcharged Type 4

Similar to Type 3, but bars 1½mm apart.

U465 U92 2c on 1c grn (U420, die 1) 1,100.
- *a.* Die 3 (U420b) 1,150.

U466 U91 2c on 2c car (U411e, die 6) *7,500.*

U466A U93 2c on 2c car (U429, die 1) 240.00
- *c.* Die 5 (U429d) 375.00
- *d.* Die 6 (U429e) 450.00
- *e.* Die 7 (U429f) 325.00

U466B U93 2c on 2c car, *amb* (U430) *5,000.*

U467 U45 2c on 3c grn (U163) 225.00

U468 U93 2c on 3c dk vio (U436, die 1) .70 .45
- *a.* Die 5 (U436b) .70 .50
- *b.* Die 6 (U436c) .70 .50
- *c.* Die 7 (U436d) .70 .50
- *d.* As No. U468, double surcharge 15.00
- *e.* As No. U468, triple surcharge 20.00
- *f.* As No. U468, dbl. surch., types 2 & 4 75.00
- *g.* As "a," double surcharge 15.00
- *h.* As "b," double surcharge 15.00
- *i.* As "c," double surcharge 15.00
- *j.* As "c," triple surcharge 20.00
- *k.* As "c," inverted surcharge 75.00
- *l.* 2c on 3c car (error) (U436h) 450.00

U469 U93 2c on 3c dk vio, *amber* (U437, die 1) 3.50 2.25
- *a.* Die 5 (U437b) 3.50 2.25
- *b.* Die 6 (U437c) 3.50 2.25
- *c.* Die 7 (U437d) 3.50 2.25
- *d.* As No. U469, dbl. surch. 20.00
- *e.* As "a," double surcharge 20.00
- *f.* As "a," double surcharge, types 2 & 4 60.00
- *g.* As "b," double surcharge 20.00
- *h.* As "c," double surcharge 20.00

U470 U93 2c on 3c dk vio, *oriental buff* (U438, die 1) 4.50 2.50
- *a.* Die 5 (U438a) 4.50 2.50
- *b.* Die 6 (U438b) 4.50 2.50
- *c.* Die 7 (U438c) 35.00 32.50
- *d.* As No. U470, dbl. surch. 18.50
- *e.* As No. U470, double surcharge, types 2 & 4 60.00
- *f.* As "a," double surcharge 18.50
- *g.* As "b," double surcharge 22.50

U471 U93 2c on 3c dk vio, *bl* (U439, die 1) 4.50 1.75
- *a.* Die 5 (U439b) 4.50 1.75
- *b.* Die 6 (U439c) 4.50 1.75
- *c.* Die 7 (U439d) 10.00 6.00
- *d.* As No. U471, dbl. surch. 22.50
- *e.* As No. U471, double surcharge, types 2 & 4 150.00
- *f.* As "a," double surcharge 22.50
- *g.* As "b," double surcharge 22.50

U472 U87 2c on 4c choc (U390) 12.00 8.00
- *a.* Double surcharge 37.50

U473 U87 2c on 4c choc, *amb* (U391) 16.00 10.00

Dbl. Surch., Type 4 and as above

U474 U93 2c on 1c on 3c dk vio (U436, die 1) 250.00
- *a.* Die 5 (U436b) 325.00
- *b.* Die 7 (U436d) 475.00

U475 U93 2c on 1c on 3c dk vio, *amb* (U437, die 1) 250.00

Surcharged Type 5

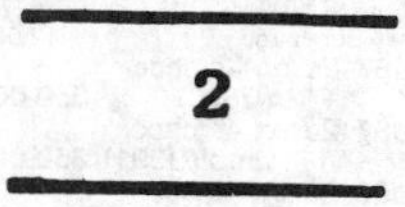

U476 U93 2c on 3c dk vio, *amb* (U437, die 1) 135.00
- *a.* Die 6 (U437c) 600.00
- *b.* As No. U476, double surcharge —

Surcharged Type 6

U477 U93 2c on 3c dk vio (U436, die 1) 120.00
- *a.* Die 5 (U436b) 150.00
- *b.* Die 6 (U436c) 175.00
- *c.* Die 7 (U437d) 175.00

U478 U93 2c on 3c dk vio, *amb* (U437, die 1) 240.00

Handstamped Surcharge in Black or Violet—Type 7

U479 U93 2c on 3c dk vio (Bk) (U436b, die 5) 325.00
- *a.* Die 1 (U436) 375.00
- *b.* Die 7 (U436d) 325.00

U480 U93 2c on 3c dk vio (V) (U436d, die 7) 2,500.

Expertization by competent authorities is recommened for Nos. U479-U480.

Type of 1916-32 Issue

1925-34

Die 1

U481 U93 1½c brown .20 .20
- *a.* Die 8 .60 .25
- *b.* 1½c purple (error) ('34) 90.00

U482 U93 1½c brown, *amber* .90 .40
- *a.* Die 8 1.40 .75

U483 U93 1½c brn, *bl* 1.50 .95
- *a.* Die 8 1.75 1.25

U484 U93 1½c brown, *manila* 6.00 3.00

W485 U93 1½c brown, *manila* .80 .20
- *a.* With added impression of No. W433 120.00 —

Surcharged Type 8

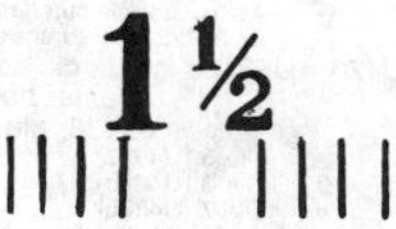

1925

U486 U71 1½c on 2c grn (U311) 675.00

U487 U71 1½c on 2c grn, *amb* (U312) 850.00

U488 U77 1½c on 1c grn (U352) 575.00

U489 U77 1½c on 1c grn, *amb* (U353) 90.00 60.00

U490 U90 1½c on 1c grn (U400, die 1) 4.00 3.50
- *a.* Die 2 (U400a) 12.00 9.00
- *b.* Die 3 (U400b) 25.00 17.50
- *c.* Die 4 (U400c) 6.00 2.50

U491 U90 1½c on 1c grn, *amb* (U401c, die 4) 4.50 2.25
- *a.* Die 1 (U401) 8.00 2.50
- *b.* Die 2 (U401a) 80.00 65.00
- *c.* Die 3 (U401b) 35.00 30.00

U492 U90 1½c on 1c grn, *oriental buff* (U402a, die 2) 210.00 80.00
- *a.* Die 4 (U402c) 600.00 80.00

U493 U90 1½c on 1c grn, *bl* (U403c, die 4) 85.00 52.50
- *a.* Die 2 (U403a) 85.00 52.50

U494 U90 1½c on 1c grn, *man* (U404, die 1) 240.00 72.50
- *a.* Die 3 (U404a) 300.00

U495 U92 1½c on 1c grn (U420, die 1) .50 .25
- *a.* Die 2 (U420a) 50.00 50.00
- *b.* Die 3 (U420b) 1.60 .60
- *c.* Die 4 (U420c) 1.75 .75
- *d.* As No. U495, dbl. surch. 4.00 1.90
- *e.* As "b," double surcharge 7.00 3.00
- *f.* As "c," double surcharge 6.00 3.00

U496 U92 1½c on 1c grn, *amb* (U421, die 1) 17.50 12.50
- *a.* Die 3 (U421b) 500.00
- *b.* Die 4 (U421c) 17.50 12.50

U497 U92 1½c on 1c grn, *oriental buff* (U422, die 1) 3.25 1.90
- *a.* Die 4 (U422b) 50.00

U498 U92 1½c on 1c grn, *bl* (U423c, die 4) 1.25 .75
- *a.* Die 1 (U423) 2.25 1.50
- *b.* Die 3 (U423b) 1.75 1.50

U499 U92 1½c on 1c grn, *man* (U424) 12.50 6.00

U500 U92 1½c on 1c grn, *brn* (unglazed) (U428) 60.00 30.00

U501 U93 1½c on 1c grn, *brn* (glazed) (U426) 60.00 25.00

U502 U93 1½c on 2c car (U429, die 1) 225.00 —
- *a.* Die 5 (U429d) 300.00
- *b.* Die 7 (U429f) 300.00

U503 U93 1½c on 2c car, *oriental buff* (U431c, die 5) 275.00 —
- *a.* Double surcharge —
- *b.* Dbl. surch., one inverted *525.00*

U504 U93 1½c on 2c car, *bl* (U432, die 1) 275.00 —
- *a.* Die 7 (U432g) 275.00

On Envelopes of 1925

U505 U93 1½c on 1½c brn (U481, die 1) 425.00
- *a.* Die 8 (U481a) 425.00

U506 U93 1½c on 1½c brn, *bl* (U483a, die 8) 350.00

The paper of No. U500 is not glazed and appears to be the same as that used for wrappers of 1920.

Surcharged Type 9

Black Surcharge

U507 U69 1½c on 1c bl (U294) 1,400.

U508 U77 1½c on 1c grn, *amb* (U353) 55.00

U508A U85 1½c on 1c grn (U379) 2,250.

U509 U85 1½c on 1c grn, *amb* (U380) 14.00 10.00
- *a.* Double surcharge 30.00

U509B U85 1½c on 1c grn, *oriental buff* (U381) 50.00 40.00

U510 U90 1½c on 1c grn (U400, die 1) 2.40 1.25
- *b.* Die 2 (U400a) 6.50 4.00
- *c.* Die 3 (U400b) 17.50 8.00
- *d.* Die 4 (U400c) 3.25 1.25
- *e.* As No. U510, double surcharge 8.00

U511 U90 1½c on 1c grn, *amb* (U401, die 1) 150.00 72.50

U512 U90 1½c on 1c grn, *oriental buff* (U402, die 1) 7.00 4.00
- *a.* Die 4 (U402c) 17.50 14.00

U513 U90 1½c on 1c grn, *bl* (U403, die 1) 5.25 2.50
- *a.* Die 4 (U403c) 5.25 4.00

U514 U90 1½c on 1c grn, *man* (U404, die 1) 25.00 9.00
- *a.* Die 3 (U404a) 55.00 37.50

U515 U92 1½c on 1c grn (U420, die 1) .35 .20
- *a.* Die 2 (U420a) 20.00 15.00
- *b.* Die 3 (U420b) .35 .20
- *c.* Die 4 (U420c) .35 .20
- *d.* As No. U515, double surcharge 6.00
- *e.* As No. U515, inverted surch. 9.00
- *f.* As No. U515, triple surcharge 11.00
- *g.* As No. U515, dbl. surch., one invtd., entire —
- *h.* As "b," double surcharge 6.00
- *i.* As "b," inverted surcharge 9.00
- *j.* As "b," triple surcharge 11.00
- *k.* As "c," double surcharge 6.00
- *l.* As "c," inverted surcharge 9.00

U516 U92 1½c on 1c grn, *amb* (U421c, die 4) 40.00 25.00
- *a.* Die 1 (U421) 45.00 30.00

U517 U92 1½c on 1c grn, *oriental buff* (U422, die 1) 4.25 1.25
- *a.* Die 4 (U422a) 5.50 1.50

U518 U92 1½c on 1c grn, *bl* (U423b, die 4) 4.50 1.25
- *a.* Die 1 (U423) 6.50 2.50
- *b.* Die 3 (U423a) 20.00 7.50
- *c.* As "a," double surcharge 9.00

U519 U92 1½c on 1c grn, *man* (U424) 22.50 10.00
- *a.* Double surcharge 27.50

U520 U93 1½c on 2c car (U429, die 1) 275.00 —
- *a.* Die 5 (U429d) 275.00
- *b.* Die 6 (U429e) 275.00
- *c.* Die 7 (U429f) 275.00

Magenta Surcharge

U521 U92 1½c on 1c grn (U420b, die 3) 4.50 3.50
- *a.* Double surcharge 25.00

Sesquicentennial Exposition Issue

Liberty Bell — U94

Die 1. The center bar of "E" of "POSTAGE" is shorter than top bar.
Die 2. The center bar of "E" of "POSTAGE" is of same length as top bar.

1926

U522 U94 2c carmine, die 1 1.10 .50
- *a.* Die 2 7.00 3.75

See note below No. 627.

Washington Bicentennial Issue

Mount Vernon — U95

2 cent:
Die 1. "S" of "POSTAGE" normal.
Die 2. "S" of "POSTAGE" raised.

1932

U523	U95	1c olive green	1.00	.80
U524	U95	1½c chocolate	2.00	1.50
U525	U95	2c car, die 1	.40	.20
a.		Die 2	70.00	16.00
b.		Die 1, *blue*, entire (error)	*27,500.*	
U526	U95	3c violet	2.00	.35
U527	U95	4c black	18.00	16.00
U528	U95	5c dark blue	4.00	3.50
		Nos. U523-U528 (6)	27.40	22.35

Bicen. of the birth of Washington.

1932 **Die 7**

U529	U93	6c orange	5.50	4.00
U530	U93	6c orange, *amber*	11.00	8.00
U531	U93	6c orange, *blue*	11.00	10.00

Franklin U96

Washington U97

Die 1

Die 2

Die 3

Die 1. Short (3½mm) and thick "1" in thick circle.

Die 2. Tall (4½mm) and thin "1" in thin circle; upper and lower bars of E in ONE long and 1mm from circle.

Die 3. As in Die 2, but E normal and 1½mm from circle.

1950

U532	U96	1c green, die 1	5.00	1.75
a.		Die 2	6.50	3.00
b.		Die 3	6.00	3.00
		Die 3, precanceled		.50

Die 1

Die 2

Die 3

Die 4

Die 1. Thick "2" in circle; toe of "2" is an acute angle.

Die 2. Thin "2" in thin circle; toe of "2" is almost right angle; line through stand of "E" in POSTAGE goes considerably below tip of chin; "N" of UNITED is tall; "O" of TWO is high.

Die 3. Thin "2" in thin circle; toe of "2" is almost right angle; short UN in UNITED: thin crossbar in A of STATES.

Die 4. Tall UN in UNITED; thick crossbar in A of STATES; otherwise like Die 3.

U533	U97	2c carmine, die 3	.75	.25
a.		Die 1	.85	.30
b.		Die 2	1.50	.85
c.		Die 4	1.40	.60

Die 1

Die 2

Die 3

Die 4 Die 5

Die 1. Thick and tall (4½mm) "3" in thick circle; long top bars and short stems in T's of STATES.
Die 2. Thin and tall (4½mm) "3" in medium circle; short top bars and long stems in T's of STATES.
Die 3. Thin and short (4mm) "3" in thin circle; lettering wider than Dies 1 and 2; line from left stand of N to stand of E is distinctly below tip of chin.
Die 4. Figure and letters as in Die 3. Line hits tip of chin; short N in UNITED and thin crossbar in A of STATES.
Die 5. Figure, letter and chin line as in Die 4; but tall N in UNITED and thick crossbar in A of STATES.

U534 U97 3c dk violet, die 4		.40	.20
a.	Die 1	2.00	.70
b.	Die 2	.80	.50
c.	Die 3	.60	.25
d.	Die 5	.80	.45

Washington — U98

1952

U535 U98 1½c brown	5.00	3.50
Precanceled		.50

Die 1 Die 2

Die 3

Die 1. Head high in oval (2mm below T of STATES). Circle near (1mm) bottom of colored oval.
Die 2. Head low in oval (3mm). Circle 1 ½mm from edge of oval. Right leg of A of POSTAGE shorter than left. Short leg on P.
Die 3. Head centered in oval (2½mm). Circle as in Die 2. Legs of A of POSTAGE about equal. Long leg on P.

1958

U536 U96 4c red violet, die 1		.80	.20
a.	Die 2	1.05	.20
b.	Die 3	1.05	.20

Nos. U429, U429f, U429h, U533, U533a-U533c Surcharged in Red at Left of Stamp - b

1958

U537 U93 2c + 2c car, die 1		3.25	1.50
a.	2c + 2c carmine, die 7	10.00	7.00
b.	2c + 2c carmine, die 9	5.00	5.00
U538 U97 2c + 2c car, die 1		.75	.20
a.	2c + 2c carmine, die 2	1.00	—
b.	2c + 2c carmine, die 3	.80	.25
c.	2c + 2c carmine, die 4	.80	—

Nos. U436a, U436e-U436f, U534a-U534d Surcharged in Green at Left of Stamp - a

U539 U93 3c + 1c pur, die 1		15.00	11.00
a.	3c + 1c purple, die 7	12.00	9.00
b.	3c + 1c purple, die 9	30.00	15.00
U540 U97 3c + 1c dk violet, die 3		.50	.20
a.	3c + 1c dk violet, die 2, entire	*1,000.*	—
b.	3c + 1c dark violet, die 4	.75	.20
c.	3c + 1c dark violet, die 5	.75	.20

See No. U545.

Franklin U99 Washington U100

Die 1 Die 2

Dies of 1¼c
Die 1. The "4" is 3mm high. Upper leaf in left cluster 2mm from "U."
Die 2. The "4" is 3½mm high. Leaf clusters are larger. Upper leaf at left is 1mm from "U."

1960

U541 U99 1¼c turquoise, die 1		.75	.50
	Die 1, precanceled		.20
a.	Die 2, precanceled		1.50
U542 U100 2½c dull blue		.85	.50
	Precanceled		.25

Precanceled Cut Squares

Precanceled envelopes do not normally receive another cancellation. Since the lack of a cancellation makes it impossible to distinguish between cut squares from used and unused envelopes, they are valued here as used only.

Pony Express Centennial Issue

Pony Express Rider U101

Envelope White Outside, Blue Inside

1960, July 19

U543 U101 4c brown	.60	.30

Abraham Lincoln — U102

Die 1 Die 2

Die 3

Die 1. Center bar of E of POSTAGE is above the middle. Center bar of E of STATES slants slightly upward. Nose sharper, more pointed. No offset ink specks inside envelope on back of die impression.
Die 2. Center bar of E in POSTAGE in middle. P of POSTAGE has short stem. Ink specks on back of die impression.
Die 3. FI of FIVE closer than Die 1 or 2. Second T of STATES seems taller than ES. Ink specks on back of die impression.

1962, Nov. 19

U544 U102 5c dark blue, die 2		.85	.20
a.	Die 1	.85	.25
b.	Die 3	.90	.35
c.	Die 2 with albino impression of 4c (#U536)	50.00	—
d.	Die 3 with albino impression of 4c (#U536)	70.00	—
e.	Die 3 with complete impression of 4c (#U536)		—

No. U536 Surcharged Type "a" in Green at Left of Stamp

Two types of surcharge "a":
Type I. "U.S. POSTAGE" 18½mm high. Serifs on cross of T both diagonal. Two lines of shading in C of CENT.
Type II. "U.S. POSTAGE" 17½mm high. Right serif on cross of T is vertical. Three shading lines in C.

1962, Nov.

U545 U96 4c + 1c red vio, Type I		1.40	.50
a.	Type II	1.10	.50

New York World's Fair (1964-65)

Globe with Satellite Orbit U103

1964, Apr. 22

U546 U103 5c carmine rose	.60	.40

Liberty Bell U104 Old Ironsides U105

Eagle — U106 Head of Statue of Liberty — U107

1965-69 **Tagged (6c)**

U547 U104 1¼c brown			.20
U548 U104 1⁴⁄₁₀c brown ('68)			.20
U548A U104 1⁶⁄₁₀c orange ('69)			.20
U549 U105 4c bright blue		.75	.20
U550 U106 5c bright purple		.75	.20
a.	Tagged ('67)	1.25	.20
U551 U107 6c lt green ('68)		.70	.20

Issue dates: 5c, Jan. 5; 1¼c, Jan. 6; 6c, Jan. 4; 1⁴⁄₁₀c, Mar. 26; 1⁶⁄₁₀c, June 16.

No. U550a has a luminescent panel 9x29mm at left of stamp. It glows yellow green under ultraviolet light.

Nos. U549-U550 Surcharged Types "b" and "a" in Red or Green at Left of Stamp

1968, Feb. 5

U552 U105 4c + 2c brt blue (R)		3.75	2.00
U553 U106 5c + 1c brt purple (G)		3.50	2.50
a.	Tagged	3.50	2.75

Tagging

Envelopes from No. U554 onward are tagged, with the tagging element in the ink unless otherwise noted.

Herman Melville Issue

Moby Dick — U108

1970, Mar. 7

U554 U108 6c light blue	.50	.20

Herman Melville (1819-91), writer, and the whaling industry.

Youth Conference Issue

Youth Conference Emblem U109

1971, Feb. 24

U555 U109 6c light blue	.75	.20

White House Conference on Youth, Estes Park, Colo., Apr. 18-22.

Bell Type of 1965-69 and

Eagle — U110

1971 **Untagged (1⁷⁄₁₀c)**

U556 U104 1⁷⁄₁₀c deep lilac		.20
U557 U110 8c bright ultra	.40	.20

Issue dates: 1⁷⁄₁₀c, May 10; 8c, May 6.

Nos. U551 and U555 Surcharged in Green at Left of Stamp

1971, May 16

U561 U107 6c + (2c) light green	1.00	.30
U562 U109 6c + (2c) light blue	2.00	1.60

Bowling Issue

Bowling Ball and Pin — U111

1971, Aug. 21

U563 U111 8c rose red	.50	.20

Salute to bowling and 7th World Tournament of the Intl. Bowling Fed., Milwaukee, WI.

Aging Conference Issue

Conference Symbol — U112

1971, Nov. 5

U564 U112 8c light blue	.50	.20

White House Conference on Aging, Washington, DC, Nov. 28-Dec. 2, 1971.

International Transportation Exhibition Issue

Transportation Exhibition Emblem U113

Illustration ⅔ actual size.

1972, May 2

U565 U113 8c ultra & rose red .50 .20

US Intl. Transportation Exhib., Dulles Intl. Airport, Washington, May 27-June 4.

No. U557 Surcharged Type "b" in Ultramarine at Left of Stamp

1973, Dec. 1

U566 U110 8c + 2c bright ultra .40 .20

Liberty Bell — U114

1973, Dec. 5

U567 U114 10c emerald .40 .20

"Volunteer Yourself" — U115

1974, Aug. 23 **Untagged**

U568 U115 1⁸⁄₁₀c blue green .20

US Tennis Centenary Issue

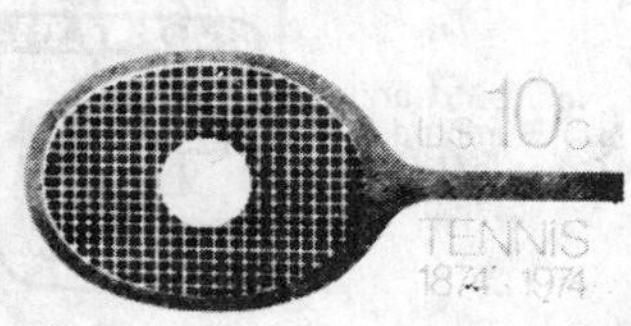

Tennis Racquet — U116

1974, Aug. 31

U569 U116 10c yel, brt blue & lt grn .30 .20

Bicentennial Era Issue

The Seafaring Tradition--Compass Rose — U118

The American Homemaker--Quilt Pattern — U119

The American Farmer--Sheaf of Wheat — U120

The American Doctor — U121

The American Craftsman--Tools, c. 1750 — U122

Designs (in brown on left side of envelope): 10c, Norwegian sloop Restaurationen. No. U572, Spinning wheel. No. U573, Plow. No. U574, Colonial era medical instruments and bottle. No. U575, Shaker rocking chair.

Light Brown Diagonally Laid Paper

1975-76

U571 U118 10c brown & blue .30 .20
- *a.* Brown ("10c/USA," etc.) omitted, entire 125.00

U572 U119 13c brn & bl grn .35 .20
- *a.* Brown ("13c/USA," etc.) omitted, entire 125.00

U573 U120 13c brn & brt grn .35 .20
- *a.* Brown ("13c/USA," etc.) omitted, entire 125.00

U574 U121 13c brown & orange .35 .20
- *a.* Brown ("13c/USA," etc.) omitted, entire —

U575 U122 13c brown & car .35 .20
- *a.* Brown ("13c/USA," etc.) omitted, entire 125.00

Issue dates: 10c, Oct. 13, 1975. No. U572, Feb. 2, 1976. No. U573, Mar. 15, 1976. No. 574, June 30, 1976. No. U575, Aug. 6, 1976.

Liberty Tree, Boston, 1646 — U123

1975, Nov. 8

U576 U123 13c orange brown .30 .20

Precanceled Cut Squares
See note following No. U542.

Star and Pinweel — U124

U125

U126

Eagle — U127

"Uncle Sam" — U128

1976-78

U577 U124 2c red, untagged ('76) .20

U578 U125 2.1c yel grn, untagged ('77) .20

U579 U126 2.7c grn, untagged ('78) .20

U580 U127 (15c) orange ('78) .40 .20

U581 U128 15c red ('78) .40 .20

Issued: 2c, 9/10; 2.1c 6/3; 2.7c, 7/5; A, 5/22; 15c, 6/3.

Bicentennial Issue

Centennial Envelope, 1876 — U129

1976, Oct. 15

U582 U129 13c emerald .35 .20

See Nos. U218-U221.

Golf Issue

Golf Club in Motion and Golf Ball — U130

1977, Apr. 7

U583 U130 13c blk, bl & yel green .45 .20
- *a.* Black omitted, entire 650.00
- *b.* Black & blue omitted, entire 550.00

Energy Issue

Energy Conservation U131

Energy Development U132

1977, Oct. 20

U584 U131 13c blk, red & yel .40 .20
- *a.* Red & yel omitted, entire 250.00
- *b.* Yellow omitted, entire 175.00
- *c.* Black omitted, entire 175.00
- *d.* Black & red omitted, entire 425.00

U585 U132 13c blk, red & yel .40 .20

Nos. U584-U585 have a luminescent panel at left of stamp.

Olive Branch and Star — U133

1978, July 28

U586 U133 15c on 16c blue .35 .20
- *a.* Surcharge omitted, entire 225.00 —
- *b.* Surcharge on #U581, entire — —

Auto Racing Issue

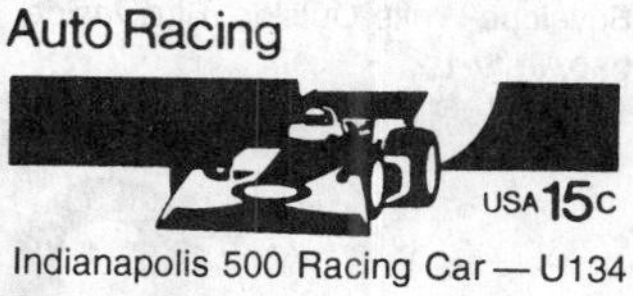

Indianapolis 500 Racing Car — U134

1978, Sept. 2

U587 U134 15c red, blue & black .35 .20
- *a.* Black omitted, entire 120.00
- *b.* Black & blue omitted, entire —
- *c.* Red omitted, entire 120.00
- *d.* Red & blue omitted, entire —

No. U576 Surcharged at left of Stamp Like No. U586

1978, Nov. 28 **Embossed**

U588 U123 15c on 13c org brown .35 .20

Precanceled Cut Squares
See note following No. U542.

U135

Weaver Violins — U136

U137

Eagle U138

Star — U139

Eagle U140

1979-82

Untagged (3.1c, 3.5c, 5.9c)

U589 U135 3.1c ultramarine .20

U590 U136 3.5c purple .20

U591 U137 5.9c brown .20

U592 U138 (18c) violet .45 .20

U593 U139 18c dark blue .45 .20

U594 U140 (20c) brown .45 .20

Issued: 3.1c, 5/18; 3.5c, 6/23; 5.9c, 2/17/82; #U592, 3/15/81; #U593, 4/2/81; #U594, 10/11/81.

Veterinary Medicine Issue

Seal of Veterinarians U141

Design on left side of envelope shows 5 animals and a bird in brown and "Veterinary Medicine" in gray.

1979, July 24

U595 U141 15c brown & gray .35 .20
- *a.* Gray omitted, untagged, entire 650.00
- *b.* Brown omitted, entire 950.00

Olympic Games Issue

U142

Design (multicolored on left side of envelope) shows two soccer players with ball.

1979, Dec. 10

U596 U142 15c red, green & black .60 .20
- *a.* Red & green omitted, untagged, entire *225.00*
- *b.* Blk omitted, untagged, entire *225.00*
- *c.* Black & green omitted, entire *225.00*
- *d.* Red omitted, untagged, entire 400.00

22nd Olympic Games, Moscow, July 19-Aug. 3, 1980.

Bicycling Issue

Highwheeler Bicycle — U143

Design (on left side of envelope) shows racing bicycle.

1980, May 16

U597 U143 15c bl & rose claret .40 .20
- *a.* Blue ("15c USA") omitted *100.00*

America's Cup Yacht Races Issue

Racing Yacht — U144

1980, Sept. 15

U598 U144 15c light blue .40 .20

Italian Honeybee and Orange Blossoms U145

Bee & Petals Colorless Embossed

1980, Oct. 10

U599 U145 15c multicolored .35 .20
- *a.* Brown ("USA 15c") omitted, entire *125.00*

U146

Design: Hand and braille colorless embossed

1981, Oct. 11

U600 U146 18c blue & red .45 .20
- *a.* Blue omitted, untagged, entire —
- *b.* Red omitted, entire

Capitol Dome U147

1981, Nov. 13

U601 U147 20c deep magenta .45 .20

U148

Illustration reduced.

1982, June 15

U602 U148 20c dk blue, blk & mag .45 .20
- *a.* Dark blue omitted, entire *150.00*
- *b.* Dark blue & magenta omitted, entire —

U149

1982, Aug. 6

U603 U149 20c purple & black .45 .20
- *a.* Black omitted, entire —

U150

1983, Mar. 21 **Untagged**

U604 U150 5.2c orange .20

U151

1983, Aug. 3

U605 U151 20c red, blue & black .45 .20
- *a.* Red omitted, entire —
- *b.* Blue omitted, entire
- *c.* Red & black omitted, entire *140.00*
- *d.* Blue & black omitted, entire *140.00*
- *e.* Black omitted, entire *225.00*

U152

Design shows storefronts at lower left.

Stamp and design continue on back of envelope.

1984, May 7 **Photo.**

U606 U152 20c multicolored .50 .20

U153

1985, Feb. 1 **Embossed**

U607 U153 (22c) deep green .55 .20

American Buffalo U154

1985, Feb. 25 **Embossed**

U608 U154 22c violet brown .55 .20
- *a.* Untagged, precanceled with 3 blue lines .20

Frigate U.S.S. Constitution, "Old Ironsides" — U155

Embossed

1985, May 3 **Untagged**

U609 U155 6c green blue .20

Mayflower — U156

Embossed

1986, Dec. 4 **Untagged**

Precanceled

U610 U156 8.5c black & gray .20

Stars — U157

1988, Mar. 26 **Embossed & Typo.**

U611 U157 25c dk bl & dk red .60 .20
- *a.* Dark red ("25") omitted, entire *75.00* —

Sea Gulls, Frigate USS Constellation — U158

Embossed & Typo.

1988, Apr. 12 **Untagged**

Precanceled

U612 U158 8.4c black & brt blue .20
- *a.* Black omitted, entire *600.00*

Snowflake — U159

"Holiday Greetings!" inscribed at lower left.

1988, Sept. 8 **Typo.**

U613 U159 25c dark red & green .60 .25

Stars and "*Philatelic Mail*" Continuous in Dark Red Below Vignette — U160

1989, Mar. 10 **Typo.**

U614 U160 25c dk red & dp bl .50 .25

"USA" and Stars — U161

1989, July 10 **Typo.** **Unwmk.**

U615 U161 25c dk red & dp bl .50 .25
- *a.* Dark red omitted, entire —

Love — U162

Litho. & Typo.

1989, Sept. 25 **Unwmk.**

U616 U162 25c dark red & blue .50 .25

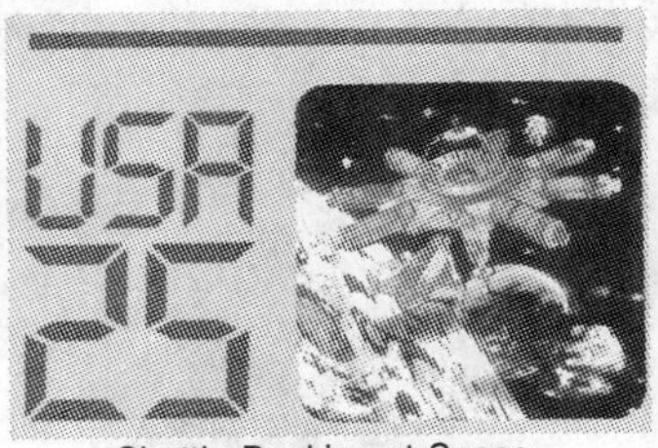

Shuttle Docking at Space Station — U163

1989, Dec. 3 **Typo.** **Unwmk.**

U617 U163 25c ultramarine .60 .30
- *a.* Ultramarine omitted, entire *600.00*

A hologram, visible through the die cut window to the right of "USA 25," is affixed to the inside of the envelope. Available only in No. 9 size. No. 9 envelopes are 225mm by 100mm.

See Nos. U625, U639.

Vince Lombardi Trophy, Football Players — U164

1990, Sept. 9 **Litho.** **Unwmk.**

U618 U164 25c vermilion .50 .25

A hologram, visible through the die cut window to the right of "USA 25," is affixed to the inside of the envelope.

Star
U165

Has embossed bars above and below the design.

1991, Jan. 24 Embossed & Typo.

U619 U165 29c ultra & rose .60 .30
- *a.* Ultramarine omitted, entire —
- *b.* Rose omitted, entire —

Precanceled Cut Squares
See note following No. U542.

Birds — U166

Stamp and design continue on back of envelope.

1991, May 3 Typo. Wmk.
Untagged
Precanceled

U620 U166 11.1c blue & red .20

Love — U167

1991, May 9 Litho.

U621 U167 29c lt blue, maroon & brt rose .60 .30
- *a.* Bright rose omitted, entire *500.00*

Magazine Industry, 250th Anniv. — U168

Photo. & Typo.

1991, Oct. 7 Unwmk.

U622 U168 29c multicolored .60 .30

The photogravure vignette, visible through the die cut window to the right of "USA 29," is affixed to the inside of the envelope. Available only in No. 10 size.

Star
U169

Stamp and design continue on back of envelope.

1991, July 20 Typo.

U623 U169 29c ultra & rose .60 .30
- *a.* Ultra omitted, entire —
- *b.* Rose omitted, entire —

Lined with a blue design to provide security for enclosures. Available only in No. 9 size.

Country Geese — U170

Litho. & Typo.

1991, Nov. 8 Wmk.

U624 U170 29c blue gray & yellow .60 .60

Space Shuttle Type of 1989

1992, Jan. 21 Typo. Unwmk.

U625 U163 29c yellow green .60 .25

A hologram, visible through the die cut window to the right of "USA 29," is affixed to the inside of the envelope. Available only in No. 10 size.

See No. U617a for envelopes with hologram only.

U171

Typo. & Litho.

1992, Apr. 10 Unwmk. *Die Cut*

U626 U171 29c multicolored .60 .30

The lithographed vignette, visible through the die cut window to the right of "USA 29," is affixed to the inside of the envelope.

Hillebrandia — U172

Illustration reduced.

1992, Apr. 22

U627 U172 29c multicolored .60 .30

The lithographed vignette, visible through the die cut window to the right of "29 USA," is affixed to the inside of the envelope.

U173

Typo. & Embossed

1992, May 19 Untagged
Precanceled

U628 U173 19.8c red & blue .40

Disabled Americans

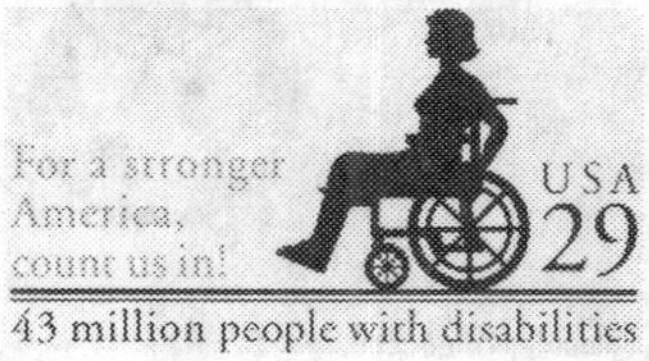

U174

1992, July 22 Typo. Unwmk.

U629 U174 29c red & blue .60 .30

U175

Illustration reduced.

Typo. & Litho.

1993, Oct. 2 Unwmk. *Die Cut*

U630 U175 29c multicolored .60 .30

The lithographed vignette, visible through the die cut window to the right of "USA 29," is affixed to the inside of the envelope.

U176

Typo. & Embossed

1994, Sept. 17 Unwmk.

U631 U176 29c brown & black .60 .30
- *a.* Black ("29/USA") omitted, entire —

See No. U638.

Liberty Bell — U177

Typo. & Embossed

1995, Jan. 3 Unwmk.

U632 U177 32c greenish blue & blue .65 .30
- *a.* Greenish blue omitted, entire —
- *b.* Blue ("USA 32") omitted, entire *150.00*

U178

Design size: 49x38mm (#U633), 53x44mm (#U634). Stamp and design continue on back of envelope.

1995 Typo. Unwmk.

U633 U178 (32c) blue & red .65 .30
U634 U178 (32c) blue & red .65 .30
- *a.* Red color and tagging omitted, entire —
- *b.* Blue omitted, entire —

Originally, Nos. U633-U634 were only available through the Philatelic Fullfillment Center after their announcement 1/12/95.

U179

Design size: 58x25mm. Stamp and design continue on back of envelope.

1995, Mar. 10 Typo. Unwmk.
Precanceled

U635 U179 (5c) green & red brown .20

Graphic Eagle — U180

1995, Mar. 10 Typo. Unwmk.
Precanceled

U636 U180 (10c) dark carmine & blue .20

Spiral Heart — U181

1995, May 12 Typo. Unwmk.

U637 U181 32c red, *light blue* .65 .30

Liberty Bell Type of 1995

1995, May 16 Typo. Unwmk.

U638 U177 32c greenish blue & blue .65 .30

Space Shuttle Type of 1989

Unwmk.

1995, Sept. 22 Typo. *Die Cut*

U639 U163 32c carmine rose .65 .35

A hologram, visible through the die cut window to the right of "USA 32," is affixed to the inside of the envelope.

U182

Typo. & Litho.

1996, Apr. 20 Unwmk. *Die Cut*

U640 U182 32c multicolored .60 .30

The lithographed vignette, visible through the die cut window to the right of "USA 32c," is affixed to the inside of the envelope.

U183

1996, May 2

U641 U183 32c multicolored .60 .30
- *a.* Black & red omitted, entire —
- *b.* Blue & gold omitted, entire —
- *c.* Red omitted, entire —

U184

Type & Embossed

1999, Jan. 11 **Unwmk.**

U642 U184 33c yellow, blue & red .65 .30

1999, Jan. 11 **Typo.** **Unwmk.**

U643 U184 33c blue & red .65 .30

U185

1999, Jan. 28 **Litho.**

U644 U185 33c violet .65 .30

Lincoln — U186

Typo. & Litho.

1999, June 5 **Unwmk.**

U645 U186 33c blue & black .65 .30

AIR POST STAMPED ENVELOPES AND AIR LETTER SHEETS

UC1

UC2

UC1 — Vertical rudder is not semi-circular but slopes down to the left. The tail of the plane projects into the G of POSTAGE.

UC2 — Vertical rudder is semi-circular. The tail of the plane touches but does not project into the G of POSTAGE.

6c: Same as UC2 except 3 types of numeral.

Die 2a- Numeral "6" 6½mm wide.
Die 2b- Numeral "6" 6mm wide.
Die 2c- Numeral "6" 5½mm wide.
Die 3- Vertical rudder leans forward. S closer to O than to T of POSTAGE. E of POSTAGE has short center bar.

1929-44 **Embossed**

UC1 UC1 5c blue 3.50 2.00
UC2 UC2 5c blue 11.00 5.00
UC3 UC2 6c org, die 2a ('34) 1.45 .40
 a. No. UC3 with added impression of 3c pur (#U436a), entire without border 3,000.
UC4 UC2 6c org, die 2b ('42) 2.75 2.00
UC5 UC2 6c org, die 2c ('44) .75 .30
UC6 UC2 6c org, die 3 ('42) 1.00 .35
 a. 6c org, *blue* (error), entire 3,500. 2,400.
UC7 UC2 8c olive green ('32) 13.00 3.50

Surcharged in black on envelopes indicated by numbers in brackets.

1945

UC8 U93 6c on 2c (U429) 1.25 .65
 a. 6c on 1c grn, error, (U420) 1,750.
 b. 6c on 3c purple, error, (U436a) 2,000.
 c. 6c on 3c purple, error, *amb* (U437a) 3,000.
 d. 6c on 3c vio, error, (U526) 3,000.
UC9 U95 6c on 2c (U525) 75.00 40.00

Nos. UC8a-UC8d are known only entire.

Surcharged in Black on 6c Orange Air Post Envelopes without borders

1946

UC10 UC2 5c on 6c, die 2a 2.75 1.50
 a. Double surcharge 60.00
UC11 UC2 5c on 6c, die 2b 9.00 5.50
UC12 UC2 5c on 6c, die 2c .75 .50
 a. Double surcharge 60.00 60.00
UC13 UC2 5c on 6c, die 3 .80 .60
 a. Double surcharge 60.00

The 6c borderless envelopes and the revalued envelopes were issued primarily for use to and from members of the armed forces.

The 5c rate came into effect Oct. 1, 1946.

DC-4 Skymaster UC3

Die 1. The end of the wing at the right is a smooth curve. The juncture of the front end of the plane and the engine forms an acute angle. The first T of STATES and the E's of UNITED STATES lean to the left.

Die 2. The end of the wing at the right is a straight line. The juncture of the front end of the plane and the engine is wide open. The first T of STATES and the E's of UNITED STATES lean to the right.

1946 **Embossed**

UC14 UC3 5c carmine, die 1 .75 .20
UC15 UC3 5c carmine, die 2 .85 .25

See Nos. UC18, UC26.

DC-4 Skymaster — UC4

Letter Sheet for Foreign Postage

"Air Letter" on face, 2-line inscription on back.

1947, Apr. 29 **Typo.**

UC16 UC4 10c brt red, *pale bl*, entire 7.50 6.00
 a. "Air Letter" on face, 4-line inscription on back ('51), entire 16.00 14.00
 b. As "a," 10c chocolate, *pale bl*, entire 400.00
 c. "Air Letter" and "Aerogramme" on face, 4-line inscription on back ('53), entire 45.00 12.50
 d. As "c," 3-line inscription on back ('55), entire 8.00 8.00

Washington and Franklin, Early and Modern Mail-carrying Vehicles — UC5

Embossed, Rotary Press Printing

1947, May 21

UC17 UC5 5c car, (22¼mm high) .40 .25
 a. Flat plate (21¾mm high) .50 .30

Cent. of the 1st postage stamps issued by the US Government.

Type of 1946

Type I- 6's lean to right.
Type II- 6's upright.

1950, Sept. 22

UC18 UC3 6c carmine, Type I .35 .20
 a. Type II .75 .25

Several other types differ slightly from the two listed.

Nos. UC14, UC15, UC18 Surcharged in Red at Left of Stamp

1951

UC19 UC3 6c on 5c car, die 1 .85 .50
UC20 UC3 6c on 5c car, die 2 .80 .50
 a. 6c on 6c car, error, entire 1,500.
 b. 6c on 5c, double surcharge 250.00 —

Nos. UC14, UC15 and UC17 Surcharged in Red at Left of Stamp

1952

UC21 UC3 6c on 5c, die 1 27.50 17.50
UC22 UC3 6c on 5c, die 2 3.50 2.50
 a. Double surcharge 75.00
UC23 UC5 6c on 5c, entire 1,850.

The 6c on 4c black (No. U440) is believed to be a favor printing.

Eagle in Flight — UC6

1956, May 2 **Embossed**

UC25 UC6 6c red .75 .50

FIPEX, NYC, Apr. 28-May 6. Two types exist, differing mainly in the clouds at top.

Skymaster Type of 1946

1958, July 31

UC26 UC3 7c blue .65 .50

Nos. UC3-UC5, UC18 and UC25 Surcharged in Green at Left of Stamp

1958

UC27 UC2 6c + 1c, die 2a 250.00 225.00
UC28 UC2 6c + 1c, die 2b 65.00 75.00
UC29 UC2 6c + 1c, die 2c 37.50 50.00
UC30 UC3 6c + 1c, type I 1.00 .50
 a. Type II 1.00 .50
UC31 UC6 6c + 1c 1.00 .50

Jet Airliner — UC7

Letter Sheet for Foreign Postage.

Two types:
Type I - Back inscription in 3 lines.
Type II - Back inscription in 2 lines.

1958-59 **Typo.**

UC32 UC7 10c bl & red, *bl*, II ('59), entire 6.00 5.00
 a. Type I ('58), entire 10.00 5.00
 b. Red omitted, II, entire —
 c. Blue omitted, II, entire —

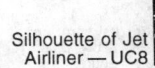

Silhouette of Jet Airliner — UC8

1958, Nov. 21 **Embossed**

UC33 UC8 7c blue .60 .25

1960, Aug. 18

UC34 UC8 7c carmine .60 .25

Jet Plane and Globe — UC9

Letter Sheet for Foreign Postage

1961, Nov. 16 **Typo.**

UC35 UC9 11c red & bl, *bl*, entire 2.75 1.50
 a. Red omitted, entire 875.00
 b. Blue omitted, entire 875.00

UC10

UC11

1962, Nov. 17 **Embossed**

UC36 UC10 8c red .55 .20

1965, Jan. 7

UC37 UC11 8c red .35 .20
 a. Tagged ('67) 1.25 .30

No. UC37a has a luminescent panel ⅜x1 inches at left of stamp. It glows orange red under ultraviolet light.

Pres. John F. Kennedy and Jet Plane UC12

Letter Sheets for Foreign Postage

1965-67 **Typo.**

UC38 UC12 11c red & dk bl, *blue*, entire 3.25 1.50
UC39 UC12 13c red & dk bl, *blue*, entire 3.00 1.50
 a. Red omitted 500.00
 b. Dark blue omitted 500.00

Issued: 11c, May 29, 1965; 13c, May 29, 1967.

UC13

1968, Jan. 8 **Tagged** **Embossed**

UC40 UC13 10c red .50 .20

No. UC37 Surcharged in Red at Left of Stamp

1968, Feb. 5

UC41 UC11 8c + 2c red .65 .20

Tagging

Envelopes and Letter Sheets from No. UC42 onward are tagged unless otherwise noted.

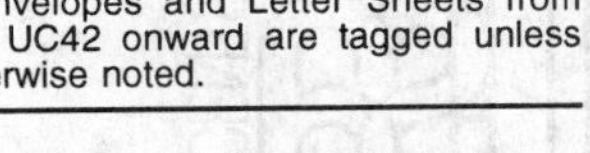

Globes and Flock of Birds — UC14

Letter Sheet for Foreign Postage

1968, Dec. 3 **Photo.**

UC42 UC14 13c gray, brn, org & blk, *blue*, entire 8.00 4.00

a. Orange omitted, entire —

b. Brown omitted, entire 400.00

c. Black omitted, entire —

Intl. Human Rights Year, and 20th anniv. of the UN Declaration of Human Rights.

UC15

1971, May 6 **Embossed**

UC43 UC15 11c red & blue .50 .20

Birds in Flight and "usa" — UC16

Letter Sheet for Foreign Postage
"postage 15c" in Gray

1971, May 28 **Photo.**

UC44 UC16 15c gray, red, white & blue, *blue*, entire 1.50 1.10

a. "AEROGRAMME" added, entire 1.50 1.10

Folding instructions (2 steps) in capitals on No. UC44; (4 steps) in upper and lower case on No. UC44a. No. UC44a issued Dec. 13. See No. UC46.

No. UC40 Surcharged in Green at Left of Stamp

1971, June 28 **Embossed**

UC45 UC13 10c + (1c) red 1.50 .20

Letter Sheet for Foreign Postage
"usa" Type of 1971

Design: Three balloons and cloud at left in address section; no birds beside stamp.

"postage 15c" in Blue

1973, Feb. 10 **Photo.**

UC46 UC16 15c red, white & bl, *blue*, entire .75 .40

Hot Air Ballooning World Championships, Albuquerque, NM, Feb. 10-17. Folding instructions as on No. UC44a, with "INTERNATIONAL HOT AIR BALLOONING" added to inscription.

Bird in Flight — UC17

1973, Dec. 1 **Embossed**

UC47 UC17 13c rose red .30 .20

Beginning with No. UC48 all letter sheets are for Foreign Postage unless noted otherwise.

UC18

1974, Jan. 4 **Photo.**

UC48 UC18 18c red & blue, *blue*, entire .90 .30

a. Red omitted, entire —

UC19

Design: "NATO" and NATO emblem in multicolor at left in address section.

1974, Apr. 4 **Photo.**

UC49 UC19 18c red & blue, *blue*, entire .90 .40

25th anniv. of NATO.

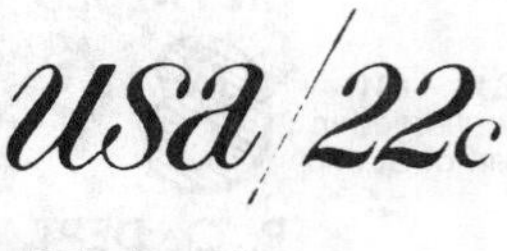

UC20

1976, Jan. 16 **Photo.**

UC50 UC20 22c red & blue, *blue*, entire .90 .40

UC21

1978, Nov. 3 **Photo.**

UC51 UC21 22c bl, *bl*, entire .70 .25

UC22

Design (multicolored in bottom left corner) shows discus thrower.

1979, Dec. 5 **Photo.**

UC52 UC22 22c red, blk & grn, *bluish*, entire 1.50 .25

22nd Olympic Games, Moscow, July 19-Aug. 3, 1980.

UC23

Design shows Statue of Liberty at lower left. Inscribed "Tour the United States," folding area shows tourist attractions.

1980-81 **Photo.**

UC53 UC23 30c bl, red & brn, *bl*, entire .65 .30

a. Red ("30c") omitted, entire 70.00

UC54 UC23 30c yel, magenta, bl & blk, *bl*, entire ('81) .65 .30

Issued: Dec. 29, 1980; Sept. 21, 1981.

UC24

"Made in USA . . . world's best buys."

1982, Sept. 16 **Photo.**

UC55 UC24 30c multi, *bl*, entire .65 .30

World Communications Year Issue

World Map Showing Locations of Satellite Tracking Stations — UC25

1983, Jan. 7 **Photo.**

UC56 UC25 30c multi, *bl*, entire .65 .30

1984 Olympics

UC26

1983, Oct. 14 **Photo.**

UC57 UC26 30c multi, *bl*, entire .65 .30

UC27

Design: Satellite over Earth at lower left, with Landsat photographs on folding area. Inscribed: Landsat views the Earth.

1985, Feb. 14 **Photo.**

UC58 UC27 36c multi, *bl*, entire .70 .35

National Tourism Week

Urban Skyline UC28

1985, May 21 **Photo.**

UC59 UC28 36c multi, *bl*, entire .70 .35

a. Black omitted, entire —

Mark Twain (1835-1910) and Halley's Comet

Comet Tail Viewed from Space — UC29

1985, Dec. 4 **Photo.**

UC60 UC29 36c multi, entire .70 .35

UC30

1988, May 9 **Litho.**

UC61 UC30 39c multi, entire .80 .40

Montgomery Blair and Pres. Lincoln — UC31

Design: Mail bags and text at lower left. Globe, locomotive, bust of Blair, UPU emblem and text contained on reverse folding area.

1989, Nov. 20 **Litho.**

UC62 UC31 39c multi, entire .80 .40

UC32

1991, May 17 **Litho.**

UC63 UC32 45c gray, red & blue, *blue*, entire .90 .45

a. White paper, entire .90 .45

Thaddeus Lowe (1832-1913), Balloonist — UC33

Letter Sheet for Foreign Postage

1995, Sept. 23 **Litho.**

UC64 UC33 50c multicolored, *blue*, entire 1.00 .50

Voyageurs Natl. Park, Minnesota UC34

Letter Sheet of Foreign Postage

1999, May 15 **Litho.** **Tagged**

UC65 UC34 60c multicolored, *blue*, entire 1.25 .65

POSTAL CARDS
"R.F." CONTROL OVERPRINT
STAMPED ENVELOPES
are listed in the Scott Specialized Catalogue of United States Stamps.
NEWSPAPER WRAPPERS
Included in listings of Stamped Envelopes with prefix "W" instead of "U"
LETTER SHEETS Included with Stamped Envelopes

OFFICIAL STAMPED ENVELOPES

Post Office Department

"2" 9mm high — UO1

"3" 9mm high — UO2

"6" 9½mm high — UO3

1873

UO1	UO1	2c black, *lemon*	15.00	8.00
UO2	UO2	3c black, *lemon*	9.00	6.00
+UO3	UO2	3c black	*20,000.*	
UO4	UO3	6c black, *lemon*	17.50	14.00

"2" 9¼mm high — UO4

"3" 9¼mm high — UO5

"6" 10½mm high — UO6

1874-79

UO5	UO4	2c black, *lemon*	6.00	4.00
UO6	UO4	2c black	70.00	32.50
UO7	UO5	3c black, *lemon*	3.00	.75
UO8	UO5	3c black	1,500.	850.00
UO9	UO5	3c black, *amber*	45.00	35.00
UO10	UO5	3c black, *blue*	*17,500.*	
UO11	UO5	3c blue, *blue*	*15,000.*	
UO12	UO6	6c black, *lemon*	8.00	6.00
UO13	UO6	6c black	1,150.	

Postal Service

UO7

1877

UO14	UO7	black	7.00	3.75
UO15	UO7	black, *amber*	55.00	27.50
UO16	UO7	blue, *amber*	50.00	30.00
UO17	UO7	blue, *blue*	8.00	6.00
	Nos. UO14-UO17 (4)		120.00	67.25

War Department

Franklin — UO8

Jackson — UO9

UO8 — Bust points to the end of "N" of "ONE."

UO9 — Bust narrow at the back.

Washington UO10

Lincoln UO11

UO10 — Queue projects below the bust.

UO11 — Neck very long at the back.

Jefferson UO12

Clay UO13

UO12 — Queue forms straight line with bust.

UO13 — Ear partly concealed by hair, mouth large, chin prominent.

Webster — UO14

Scott — UO15

UO14 — Has side whiskers.

Hamilton — UO16

Back of bust very narrow, chin almost straight; the labels containing the letters "U S" are exactly parallel.

1873

Reay Issue

UO18	UO8	1c dark red	525.00	300.00
UO19	UO9	2c dark red	850.00	425.00
UO20	UO10	3c dark red	60.00	40.00
UO21	UO10	3c dark red, *amb*	*17,500.*	
UO22	UO10	3c dark red, *cr*	450.00	225.00
UO23	UO11	6c dark red	210.00	90.00
UO24	UO11	6c dark red, *cr*	2,250.	425.00
UO25	UO12	10c dark red	6,000.	350.00
UO26	UO13	12c dark red	110.00	50.00
UO27	UO14	15c dark red	110.00	55.00
UO28	UO15	24c dark red	110.00	50.00
UO29	UO16	30c dark red	450.00	150.00
UO30	UO8	1c vermilion	135.00	
WO31	UO8	1c ver, *man*	12.50	12.50
+UO32	UO9	2c vermilion	275.00	
WO33	UO9	2c ver, *man*	200.00	
UO34	UO10	3c vermilion	70.00	40.00
UO35	UO10	3c ver, *amb*	80.00	
UO36	UO10	3c ver, *cr*	16.00	12.50
UO37	UO11	6c vermilion	70.00	
+UO38	UO11	6c ver, *cr*	325.00	
UO39	UO12	10c vermilion	200.00	
UO40	UO13	12c vermilion	135.00	
UO41	UO14	15c vermilion	210.00	
UO42	UO15	24c vermilion	375.00	
UO43	UO16	30c vermilion	375.00	

UO17

UO18

UO17--Bottom serif on "S" is thick and short, bust at bottom below hair forms sharp point.

UO18--Bottom serif on "S" is thick and short front part of bust is rounded.

UO19

UO20

UO19--Bottom serif on "S" is short, queue does not project below bust.

UO20--Neck very short at the back.

UO21

UO22

UO21--Knot of queue stands out prominently.

UO22--Ear prominent, chin receding.

UO23

UO24

UO23--Has no side whiskers, forelock projects above head.

UO24--Back of bust rather broad; chin slopes considerably; the labels containing letters "U S" are not exactly parallel.

1875

Plimpton Issue

UO44	UO17	1c red	120.00	80.00
+UO45	UO17	1c red, *amb*	750.00	
+UO45A	UO17	1c red, *org*	*35,000.*	
WO46	UO17	1c red, *man*	4.00	2.75
UO47	UO18	2c red	90.00	
UO48	UO18	2c red, *amb*	25.00	14.00
UO49	UO18	2c red, *org*	45.00	12.50
WO50	UO18	2c red, *man*	75.00	40.00
UO51	UO19	3c red	12.50	9.00
UO52	UO19	3c red, *amb*	14.00	9.00
UO53	UO19	3c red, *cr*	6.50	3.75
UO54	UO19	3c red, *bl*	3.50	2.75
UO55	UO19	3c red, *fawn*	4.50	2.75
UO56	UO20	6c red	40.00	30.00
UO57	UO20	6c red, *amb*	70.00	40.00
UO58	UO20	6c red, *cr*	175.00	87.50
UO59	UO21	10c red	150.00	82.50
UO60	UO21	10c red, *amb*	1,100.	
UO61	UO22	12c red	42.50	40.00
UO62	UO22	12c red, *amb*	625.00	
UO63	UO22	12c red, *cr*	600.00	
UO64	UO23	15c red	160.00	140.00
UO65	UO23	15c red, *amb*	700.00	
UO66	UO23	15c red, *cr*	675.00	
UO67	UO24	30c red	160.00	140.00
UO68	UO24	30c red, *amb*	900.00	
UO69	UO24	30c red, *cr*	900.00	

POSTAL SAVINGS STAMPED ENVELOPES

UO25

1911

UO70	UO25	1c green	60.00	20.00
UO71	UO25	1c grn, *oriental buff*	175.00	65.00
UO72	UO25	2c carmine	11.00	3.75
a.		2c carmine, *manila* (error)	*1,900.*	

Used Values

Catalogue values for regularly used entires. Those with first day cancels generally sell for much less.

OFFICIAL MAIL

UO26

1983, Jan. 12

UO73	UO26	20c blue, entire	1.25	*30.00*

UO27

1985, Feb. 26

UO74	UO27	22c blue, entire	.90	*5.00*

UO28

1987, Mar. 2 **Typo.**

UO75	UO28	22c blue, entire	1.00	*20.00*

Used exclusively to mail US Savings Bonds.

UO29

1988, Mar. 22 **Typo.**

UO76	UO29	(25c) blk & bl, entire	1.20	*20.00*

Used exclusively to mail US Saving Bonds.

UO30

1988, Apr. 11 **Embossed & Typo.**

UO77	UO30	25c blk & blue, entire	.80	*15.00*
a.		Denomination & lettering as No. UO78	—	—

UO31

1988, Apr. 11 **Typo.**

UO78	UO31	25c black & blue, entire	1.00	*25.00*
a.		Denomination & lettering as No. UO77	—	—

Used exclusively to mail US Saving Bonds.

Used Values

The appearance in the marketplace of postally used examples of the entires used to mail passports (Nos. UO79-UO82, UO86-UO87) is so infrequent that it currently is not possible to establish accurate values.

1990, Mar. 17 **Typo.**
UO79 UO31 45c blk & bl, entire 1.25 —
UO80 UO31 65c blk & bl, entire 1.75 —

Used exclusively to mail US passports.

UO32

Type UO32: sharp impression, stars and "E Pluribus Unum" are clear and distinct. Official is 14½mm long, USA is 17mm long.

1990, Aug. 10 **Typo.**
UO81 UO32 45c blk & bl, entire 1.25 —
UO82 UO32 65c blk & bl, entire 1.60 —

Used exclusively to mail US passports.

UO33

1991, Jan. 22 **Typo.** **Wmk.**
UO83 UO33 (29c) blk & bl, entire 1.10 *20.00*

Used exclusively to mail US Saving Bonds.

UO34

1991, Apr. 6 **Typo. & Embossed**
UO84 UO34 29c black & blue, entire .75 *2.00*

UO35

1991, Apr. 17 **Typo.** **Wmk.**
UO85 UO35 29c blk & bl, entire .70 *20.00*

Used exclusively to mail US Saving Bonds.

Consular Service, Bicent. UO36

1992, July 10 **Litho.** **Unwmk.**
UO86 UO36 52c blue & red, entire 1.25 —
UO87 UO36 75c blue & red, entire 1.75 —

Used exclusively to mail US passports.

UO37

Typo. & Embossed

1995, May 9 **Unwmk.**
UO88 UO37 32c blue & red, entire .75 *10.00*

OFFICIAL WRAPPERS

Included in listings of Official Stamped Envelopes with prefix letters "WO" instead of "UO"

REVENUE STAMPS

Nos. R1-R102 were used to pay taxes on documents and proprietary articles including playing cards. Until Dec. 25, 1862, the law stated that a revenue stamp could be used only for payment of the tax upon the particular instrument or article specified on its face. After that date stamps, except the Proprietary, could be used indiscriminately.

Values quoted are for pen-canceled copies. Stamps with handstamped cancellations sell at higher prices. Stamps canceled with cuts, punches or holes sell for less. See the Scott U.S. Specialized Catalogue.

General Issue

First Issue. Head of Washington in Oval. Various Frames as Illustrated.

Old Paper

Perf. 12

Nos. R1b to R42b, part perforate, occur perforated sometimes at sides only and sometimes at top and bottom only. The higher values, part perforate, are perforated at sides only. Imperforate and part perforate revenues often bring much more in pairs or blocks than as single copies.

The experimental silk paper is a variety of the old paper and has only a very few minute fragments of fiber.

Some of the stamps were in use eight years and were printed several times. Many color variations occurred, particularly when unstable pigments were used and the color was intended to be purple or violet, such as the 4c Proprietary, 30c and $2.50 stamps. Before 1868 dull colors predominate on these and the early red stamps. In later printings of the 4c Proprietary, 30c and $2.50 stamps, red predominates in the mixture, and on the dollar values the red is brighter. The early $1.90 stamp is dull purple, imperf. or perforated. In a later printing, perforated only, the purple is darker.

R1

R2

R3

R4

R5

1862-71 **Engr.**

R1 R1 1c Express, red 1.25
a. Imperf. 55.00
b. Part perf. 35.00
d. Silk paper 85.00
R2 R1 1c Playing Cards, red 130.00
a. Imperf. 1,050.
b. Part perf. 750.00
R3 R1 1c Proprietary, red .50
a. Imperf. 725.00
b. Part perf. 120.00
d. Silk paper 22.50
R4 R1 1c Telegraph, red 11.00
a. Imperf. 375.00
R5 R2 2c Bank Check, blue .25
a. Imperf. 1.00
b. Part perf. 1.75
e. Vertical pair, imperf. between, old paper *400.00*
R6 R2 2c Bank Check, orange .25
b. Part perf. 55.00
d. Silk paper 250.00
e. Old paper, *green* 400.00
R7 R2 2c Certificate, blue 25.00
a. Imperf. 12.50
R8 R2 2c Certificate, orange 27.50
R9 R2 2c Express, blue .40
a. Imperf. 12.50
b. Part perf. 20.00
R10 R2 2c Express, orange 7.50
b. Part perf. —
d. Silk paper 65.00
R11 R2 2c Playing Cards, blue 4.00
b. Part perf. 175.00
R12 R2 2c Playing Cards, orange 35.00
R13 R2 2c Proprietary, blue .40
a. Imperf. *350.00*
b. Part perf. 120.00
d. Silk paper 55.00
e. Ultramarine 180.00
R14 R2 2c Proprietary, orange 37.50
R15 R2 2c U.S. Int. Rev., orange ('64) .20
d. Silk paper .25
e. Old paper, *green* 525.00
R16 R3 3c For. Exch., green 3.50
b. Part perf. 260.00
d. Silk paper 50.00
R17 R3 3c Playing Cards, green ('63) 120.00
a. Imperf. *8,500.*
R18 R3 3c Proprietary, green 3.25
b. Part perf. 300.00
d. Silk paper 30.00
e. Printed on both sides, old paper *1,600.*
R19 R3 3c Telegraph, green 2.75
a. Imperf. 60.00
b. Part perf. 22.50
R20 R3 4c Inland Exch., brown ('63) 1.75
d. Silk paper 50.00
R21 R3 4c Playing Cards, slate ('63) 500.00
R22 R3 4c Proprietary, purple 6.50
a. Imperf. —
b. Part perf. 210.00
d. Silk paper 65.00

Many shade and color variations of Nos. R21-R22. See foreword, "Revenue Stamps."

R23 R3 5c Agreement, red .30
d. Silk paper 1.50
R24 R3 5c Certificate, red .30
a. Imperf. 2.50
b. Part perf. 11.00
d. Silk paper .35
R25 R3 5c Express, red .30
a. Imperf. 5.00
b. Part perf. 6.00
R26 R3 5c Foreign Exchange, red .30
b. Part perf. —
d. Silk paper 200.00
R27 R3 5c Inland Exch., red .25
a. Imperf. 5.00
b. Part perf. 3.75
d. Silk paper 15.00
R28 R3 5c Playing Cards, red ('63) 20.00
R29 R3 5c Proprietary, red ('64) 25.00
d. Silk paper 110.00
R30 R3 6c Inland Exch., org ('63) 1.75
d. Silk paper 70.00
R31 R3 6c Proprietary, orange ('71) *1,600.*

Nearly all copies of No. R31 are faulty or repaired and poorly centered.

The Catalogue value is for a fine centered copy with minor faults which do not detract from its appearance.

R32 R3 10c Bill of Lading, blue 1.00
a. Imperf. 45.00
b. Part perf. 200.00
R33 R3 10c Certificate, blue .25
a. Imperf. 130.00
b. Part perf. 225.00
d. Silk paper 5.00
R34 R3 10c Contract, blue .35
b. Part perf. 160.00
d. Silk paper 2.25
e. Ultramarine, part perf. 425.00
f. Ultramarine, old paper 1.00
R35 R3 10c For. Exch., blue 7.00
d. Silk paper —
e. ultra, old paper 9.75
R36 R3 10c Inland Exch., blue .20
a. Imperf. 175.00
b. Part perf. 3.50
d. Silk paper 30.00
R37 R3 10c Power of Attorney, blue .50
a. Imperf. 450.00
b. Part perf. 22.50
R38 R3 10c Proprietary, blue ('64) 15.00
R39 R3 15c For. Exch., brown ('63) 15.00
R40 R3 15c Inland Exch., brown 1.25
a. Imperf. 30.00
b. Part perf. 12.50
R41 R3 20c For. Exch., red 32.50
a. Imperf. 40.00
R42 R3 20c Inland Exch., red .35
a. Imperf. 15.00
b. Part perf. 17.50
d. Silk paper —
R43 R4 25c Bond, red 2.50
a. Imperf. 150.00
b. Part perf. 6.00
R44 R4 25c Certificate, red .25
a. Imperf. 10.00
b. Part perf. 6.00
d. Silk paper 2.75
e. Printed on both sides, old paper *1,750.*
f. Impression of No. R48 on back, old paper —
R45 R4 25c Entry of Goods, red .75
a. Imperf. 17.50
b. Part perf. 65.00
d. Silk paper 22.50
R46 R4 25c Insurance, red .25
a. Imperf. 10.00
b. Part perf. 10.00
d. Silk paper 4.50
R47 R4 25c Life Insurance, red 6.50
a. Imperf. 35.00
b. Part perf. 225.00
R48 R4 25c Power of Attorney, red .30
a. Imperf. 6.00
b. Part perf. 27.50
R49 R4 25c Protest, red 6.75
a. Imperf. 30.00
b. Part perf. 260.00
R50 R4 25c Warehouse Receipt, red 22.50
a. Imperf. 42.50
b. Part perf. 235.00
R51 R4 30c For. Exch., lilac 52.50
a. Imperf. 72.50
b. Part perf. 950.00
d. Silk paper —
R52 R4 30c Inland Exch., lilac 3.50
a. Imperf. 50.00
b. Part perf. 65.00
d. Silk paper —

Many shade and color variations of Nos. R51-R52. See foreword, "Revenue Stamps."

R53 R4 40c Inland Exch., brown 3.50
a. Imperf. 575.00
b. Part perf. 7.00
R54 R5 50c Conveyance, blue .20
a. Imperf. 14.00
b. Part perf. 1.60
d. Silk paper 3.00
e. Ultramarine, old paper .25
f. Ultramarine, silk paper —
R55 R5 50c Entry of Goods, blue .40
b. Part perf. 12.00
d. Silk paper 40.00
R56 R5 50c For. Exch., blue 5.00
a. Imperf. 45.00
b. Part perf. 47.50
R57 R5 50c Lease, blue 8.50
a. Imperf. 24.00
b. Part perf. 60.00
R58 R5 50c Life Insurance, blue 1.00
a. Imperf. 30.00
b. Part perf. 45.00
R59 R5 50c Mortgage, blue .50
a. Imperf. 14.00
b. Part perf. 2.50
d. Silk paper —
R60 R5 50c Original Process, blue .60
a. Imperf. 3.00
b. Part perf. *550.00*
d. Silk paper 1.60
R61 R5 50c Passage Ticket, blue 1.25
a. Imperf. 75.00
b. Part perf. 150.00
R62 R5 50c Probate of Will, blue 19.00
a. Imperf. 35.00
b. Part perf. 60.00
R63 R5 50c Surety Bond, blue .30
a. Imperf. 150.00
b. Part perf. 2.50
e. Ultramarine, old paper .75
R64 R5 60c Inland Exch., org 6.00
a. Imperf. 85.00
b. Part perf. 47.50
d. Silk paper 32.50
R65 R5 70c For. Exch., green 8.00
a. Imperf. 325.00
b. Part perf. 95.00
d. Silk paper 47.50

R6

R7

R8

R9

R10

(Illustration sideways) — R11

Old Paper

R66 R6	$1	Conveyance, red	15.00
a.		Imperf.	12.00
b.		Part perf.	425.00
d.		Silk paper	90.00
R67 R6	$1	Entry of Goods, red	1.90
a.		Imperf.	32.50
d.		Silk paper	50.00
R68 R6	$1	For. Exch., red	.60
a.		Imperf.	70.00
d.		Silk paper	45.00
R69 R6	$1	Inland Exch., red	.45
a.		Imperf.	12.50
b.		Part perf.	325.00
d.		Silk paper	2.75
R70 R6	$1	Lease, red	2.25
a.		Imperf.	35.00
R71 R6	$1	Life Insurance, red	6.50
a.		Imperf.	150.00
R72 R6	$1	Manifest, red	27.50
a.		Imperf.	42.50
R73 R6	$1	Mortgage, red	175.00
a.		Imperf.	20.00
R74 R6	$1	Passage Ticket, red	200.00
a.		Imperf.	250.00
R75 R6	$1	Power of Attorney, red	2.10
a.		Imperf.	75.00
R76 R6	$1	Probate of Will, red	35.00
a.		Imperf.	70.00
R77 R7	$1.30	For. Exch., orange ('63)	55.00
a.		Imperf.	*3,000.*
R78 R7	$1.50	Inland Exch., blue	3.25
a.		Imperf.	22.50
R79 R7	$1.60	For. Exch., green ('63)	105.00
a.		Imperf.	900.00
R80 R7	$1.90	For. Exch., purple ('63)	90.00
a.		Imperf.	*3,750.*
d.		Silk paper	—

Many shade and color variations of No. R80. See foreword, "Revenue Stamps."

R81 R8	$2	Conveyance, red	2.75
a.		Imperf.	100.00
b.		Part perf.	1,300.
d.		Silk paper	25.00
R82 R8	$2	Mortgage, red	3.00
a.		Imperf.	100.00
d.		Silk paper	55.00
R83 R8	$2	Probate of Will, red ('63)	50.00
a.		Imperf.	*3,250.*
R84 R8	$2.50	Inland Exch., pur ('63)	6.50
a.		Imperf.	2,500.
d.		Silk paper	22.50
R85 R8	$3	Charter Party, green	5.00
a.		Imperf.	110.00
d.		Silk paper	85.00
e.		Printed on both sides	*2,000.*
g.		Impression of #RS208 on back	*4,000.*
R86 R8	$3	Manifest, green	25.00
a.		Imperf.	110.00
R87 R8	$3.50	Inland Exch., blue ('63)	50.00
a.		Imperf.	*2,750.*
e.		Printed on both sides	—

Many shade and color variations of the $2.50. See foreword, "Revenue Stamps." The $3.50 has stars in upper corners.

R88 R9	$5	Charter Party, red	6.00
a.		Imperf.	240.00
d.		Silk paper	65.00
R89 R9	$5	Conveyance, red	6.00
a.		Imperf.	35.00
d.		Silk paper	65.00
R90 R9	$5	Manifest, red	77.50
a.		Imperf.	110.00
R91 R9	$5	Mortgage, red	17.00
a.		Imperf.	110.00
R92 R9	$5	Probate of Will, red	17.50
a.		Imperf.	475.00
R93 R9	$10	Charter Party, green	25.00
a.		Imperf.	550.00
R94 R9	$10	Conveyance, green	60.00
a.		Imperf.	90.00
R95 R9	$10	Mortgage, green	25.00
a.		Imperf.	350.00
R96 R9	$10	Probate of Will, green	27.50
a.		Imperf.	1,150.
R97 R10	$15	Mortgage, blue	120.00
a.		Imperf.	1,100.
e.		Ultramarine, old paper	190.00
R98 R10	$20	Conveyance, org	65.00
a.		Imperf.	125.00
d.		Silk paper	110.00
R99 R10	$20	Probate of Will, orange	1,050.
a.		Imperf.	1,200.
R100 R10	$25	Mortgage, red ('63)	115.00
a.		Imperf.	950.00
d.		Silk paper	175.00
e.		Horiz. pair, imperf. btwn., old paper	*1,100.*
R101 R10	$50	U.S. Int. Rev., green ('63)	90.00
a.		Imperf.	190.00
R102 R11	$200	U.S. Int. Rev., green & red ('64)	625.00
a.		Imperf.	1,400.

DOCUMENTARY STAMPS

Second Issue

After release of the First Issue revenue stamps, the Bureau of Internal Revenue received many reports of fraudulent cleaning and re-use. The Bureau ordered a Second Issue with new designs and colors, using a patented "chameleon" paper which is usually slightly violet or pinkish, with silk fibers.

R12

R12a

R13a

R13

R13b

Head of Washington in Black within Octagon. Various Frames and Numeral Arrangements.

1871 ***Perf. 12***

R103 R12	1c	blue & black	40.00
		Cut cancel	19.00
a.		Inverted center	*950.00*
R104 R12	2c	blue & black	1.10
		Cut cancel	.20
a.		Inverted center	*3,750.*
R105 R12a	3c	blue & black	17.50
		Cut cancel	9.00
R106 R12a	4c	blue & black	60.00
		Cut cancel	30.00
R107 R12a	5c	blue & black	1.50
		Cut cancel	.50
a.		Inverted center	*1,650.*
R108 R12a	6c	blue & black	90.00
		Cut cancel	50.00
R109 R12a	10c	blue & black	1.00
		Cut cancel	.20
a.		Inverted center	*1,650.*
R110 R12a	15c	blue & black	25.00
		Cut cancel	14.00
R111 R12a	20c	blue & black	6.00
		Cut cancel	2.75
a.		Inverted center	*8,000.*

Head of Washington in Black within Circle

Various Frames

R112 R13	25c	blue & black	.60
		Cut cancel	.20
a.		Inverted center	*8,000.*
b.		Sewing machine perf.	95.00
c.		Perf. 8	275.00
R113 R13	30c	blue & black	65.00
		Cut cancel	35.00
R114 R13	40c	blue & black	40.00
		Cut cancel	20.00
R115 R13a	50c	blue & black	.60
		Cut cancel	.20
a.		Sewing machine perf.	75.00
b.		Inverted center	800.00
		Inverted center, punch cancellation	250.00
R116 R13a	60c	blue & black	90.00
		Cut cancel	45.00
R117 R13a	70c	blue & black	35.00
		Cut cancel	17.50
a.		Inverted center	*2,750.*
R118 R13b	$1	blue & black	3.00
		Cut cancel	1.25
a.		Inverted center	*4,250.*
		Invtd. center, punch cancel	*750.*
R119 R13b	$1.30	blue & black	275.00
		Cut cancel	150.00
R120 R13b	$1.50	blue & black	12.50
		Cut cancel	7.00
a.		Sewing machine perf.	450.00
R121 R13b	$1.60	blue & black	350.00
		Cut cancel	225.00
R122 R13b	$1.90	blue & black	175.00
		Cut cancel	100.00
R123 R13b	$2	blue & black	15.00
		Cut cancel	7.50
R124 R13b	$2.50	blue & black	27.50
		Cut cancel	15.00
R125 R13b	$3	blue & black	30.00
		Cut cancel	17.50
R126 R13b	$3.50	blue & black	150.00
		Cut cancel	75.00
R127 R13b	$5	blue & black	17.50
		Cut cancel	9.00
a.		Inverted center	*2,400.*
		Invtd. center, punch cancel	*725.*
R128 R13b	$10	blue & black	100.00
		Cut cancel	60.00
R129 R13b	$20	blue & black	350.00
		Cut cancel	225.00
R130 R13b	$25	blue & black	350.00
		Cut cancel	225.00
R131 R13b	$50	blue & black	350.00
		Cut cancel	225.00
R132 R13b	$200	red, blue & blk	*5,000.*
		Cut cancel	*2,800.*
R133 R13b	$500	red org, grn & blk	*12,500.*

Fraudulently produced inverted centers exist, some excellently made.

Value for No. R133 is for a very fine appearing example with a light cut cancel or with minor flaws.

Third Issue

Violet "Chameleon" Paper with Silk Fibers. Various Frames and Numeral Arrangements.

1871-72 ***Perf. 12***

R134 R12	1c	claret & blk ('72)	30.00
		Cut cancel	17.50
R135 R12	2c	orange & blk	.20
		Cut cancel	.20
a.		2c vermilion & black (error)	*550.00*
b.		Inverted center	300.00
c.		Imperf., pair	—
R136 R12a	4c	brown & blk ('72)	35.00
		Cut cancel	17.50
R137 R12a	5c	orange & black	.25
		Cut cancel	.20
a.		Inverted center	*3,250.*
R138 R12a	6c	orange & blk ('72)	40.00
		Cut cancel	20.00
R139 R12a	15c	brown & blk ('72)	8.50
		Cut cancel	4.00
a.		Inverted center	*8,000.*
R140 R13	30c	orange & blk ('72)	15.00
		Cut cancel	7.50
a.		Inverted center	*2,250.*
R141 R13	40c	brown & blk ('72)	35.00
		Cut cancel	17.50
R142 R13	60c	orange & blk ('72)	65.00
		Cut cancel	32.50
R143 R13	70c	green & blk ('72)	45.00
		Cut cancel	22.50
R144 R13b	$1	green & blk ('72)	1.35
		Cut cancel	.55
a.		Inverted center	*5,500.*
R145 R13b	$2	ver & black ('72)	22.50
		Cut cancel	14.00
R146 R13b	$2.50	claret & blk ('72)	37.50
		Cut cancel	21.00
a.		Inverted center	*13,500.*
R147 R13b	$3	green & blk ('72)	37.50
		Cut cancel	21.00
R148 R13b	$5	ver & black ('72)	22.50
		Cut cancel	11.00
R149 R13b	$10	green & blk ('72)	85.00
		Cut cancel	45.00
R150 R13b	$20	orange & blk ('72)	475.00
		Cut cancel	250.00
a.		$20 vermilion & black (error)	600.00

1874 ***Perf. 12***

R151 R12	2c	orange & black, *green*	.20
		Cut cancel	.20
a.		Inverted center	350.00

Liberty — R14

1875-78 ***Perf. 12***

R152 R14 2c blue, *blue*, silk paper	.20	
b. Wmk. 191R ('78)	.20	
c. Wmk. 191R, rouletted	32.50	
d. Vert. pair, imperf. horiz.	175.00	
e. As "b," imperf., pair	*250.00*	

The rouletted stamps probably were introduced in 1881.

Nos. 279, 267a, 267, 279Bg, 279B, 272-274 Overprinted in Red or Blue

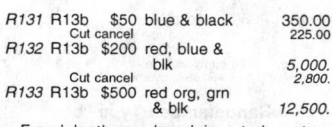

I. R.   **I.R.**

a   b

1898 **Wmk. 191** ***Perf. 12***

R153 A87(a)	1c green (R)	3.00	2.50
R154 A87(b)	1c green (R)	.20	.20
a.	Overprint inverted	20.00	*17.50*
b.	Overprint on back instead of face, inverted	—	
c.	Pair, one without ovpt.	—	
R155 A88(b)	2c pink, type III (Bl)	.20	.20
b.	2c carmine, type III	.25	*.20*
c.	As #R155, overprint inverted	4.50	*2.75*
d.	Vert. pair, one without ovpt.	*750.00*	
e.	Horiz. pair, one without ovpt.	—	
f.	As #R155, overprinted on back instead of face, inverted	—	

R155A A88(b) 2c pink, type IV (Bl) .20 .20
g. 2c carmine, type IV .20 .20
h. As #R155A, overprint inverted 2.50 1.75

Handstamped Type "b"

R156 A93 8c vio brn 4,000.
R157 A94 10c dark green 4,000.
R158 A95 15c dark blue 4,750.

Nos. R156-R158 were emergency provisionals, privately prepared, not officially issued.

Privately Prepared Provisionals

No. 285 Overprinted in Red

I. R.
L. H. C.

1898	Wmk. 191	Perf. 12	
R158A A100 1c dk yel grn		8,500.	7,750.

Same Overprinted "I.R./P.I.D. & Son" in Red

R158B A100 1c dk yel grn — 10,000.

Nos. R158A-R158B were overprinted with federal government permission by the Purvis Printing Co. upon order of Capt. L.H. Chapman of the Chapman Steamboat Line. Both the Chapman line and P.I. Daprix & Son operated freight-carrying steamboats on the Erie Canal. The Chapman Line touched at Syracuse, Utica, Little Falls and Fort Plain; the Daprix boat ran between Utica and Rome. 250 of each stamp were overprinted.

Dr. Kilmer & Co. provisional overprints are listed in the Scott Specialized Catalogue of United States Stamps under Private Die Medicine Stamps, Nos. RS307-RS315.

Newspaper Stamp No. PR121 Surcharged Vertically in Red

INT. REV.
$5.
DOCUMENTARY.

1898 Wmk. 191 Perf. 12

Reading Down

R159 N18 $5 on $5 dk blue 250.00 160.00

Reading Up

R160 N18 $5 on $5 dk blue 110.00 70.00

Battleship R15

Inscribed: "Series of 1898" and "Documentary."

There are 2 styles of rouletting for the 1898 proprietary and documentary stamps, an ordinary roulette 5½ and one where small rectangles of the paper are cut out, called hyphen hole perf. 7.

1898 Wmk. 191R Rouletted 5½

R161 R15 ½c orange 2.50 7.50
R162 R15 ½c dark gray .25 .20
a. Vert. pair, imperf. horiz. 75.00
R163 R15 1c pale blue .20 .20
a. Vert. pair, imperf. horiz. 7.50
b. Imperf., pair 350.00
R164 R15 2c carmine rose .25 .25
a. Vert. pair, imperf. horiz. 65.00
b. Imperf., pair 200.00
c. Horiz. pair, imperf. vert. —
R165 R15 3c dark blue 1.50 .20
R166 R15 4c pale rose 1.00 .20
a. Vert. pair, imperf. horiz. 125.00
R167 R15 5c lilac .20 .20
a. Pair, imperf. horiz. or vert. 200.00 150.00
b. Horiz. pair, imperf. btwn. 450.00
R168 R15 10c dark brown 1.50 .20
a. Vert. pair, imperf. horiz. 35.00 30.00
b. Horiz. pair, imperf. vert. —
R169 R15 25c purple brown 2.00 .20
R170 R15 40c blue lilac 125.00 1.00
Cut cancellation .30
R171 R15 50c slate violet 15.00 .20
a. Imperf., pair 300.00
R172 R15 80c bister 80.00 .25
Cut cancellation .20

No. R167b may not be genuine.

Hyphen Hole Perf. 7

R163p 1c .25 .20
R164p 2c .30 .20
R165p 3c 15.00 1.00
R166p 4c 5.00 1.50
R167p 5c 5.00 .20
R168p 10c 4.00 .20
R169p 25c 6.50 .25
R170p 40c 175.00 30.00
R171p 50c 25.00 .75
b. Horiz. pair, imperf. btwn. — 250.00
R172p 80c 200.00 40.00

Commerce — R16

1898 Rouletted 5½

R173 R16 $1 dark green 8.00 .20
a. Vert. pair, imperf. horiz. —
b. Horiz. pair, imperf. vert. — 300.00
p. Hyphen hole perf. 7 15.00 .65
R174 R16 $3 dark brown 20.00 .85
Cut cancellation .20
a. Horiz. pair, imperf. vert. 450.00
p. Hyphen hole perf. 7 25.00 2.25
Cut cancellation .25

Hyphen Hole Perf. 7

R175 R16 $5 orange red 25.00 1.40
Cut cancellation .20
R176 R16 $10 black 70.00 2.75
Cut cancellation .50
a. Horiz. pair, imperf. vert. —
R177 R16 $30 red 210.00 110.00
Cut cancellation 45.00
R178 R16 $50 gray brown 110.00 5.50
Cut cancellation 2.00

See Nos. R182-R183.

John Marshall — R17

Alexander Hamilton R18

James Madison R19

Inscribed "Series of 1898"

1899 Without Gum Imperf.

R179 R17 $100 yel brn & black 130.00 30.00
Cut cancellation 20.00
R180 R18 $500 car lake & black 750.00 500.00
Cut cancellation 225.00
R181 R19 $1000 grn & blk 750.00 300.00
Cut cancellation 110.00

See Nos. R224-R227, R246-R252, R282-R286.

Type of 1898

1900 Hyphen-Hole Perf. 7

R182 R16 $1 carmine 16.00 .50
Cut cancellation .20
R183 R16 $3 lake 120.00 45.00
Cut cancellation 7.00

Surcharged in Black

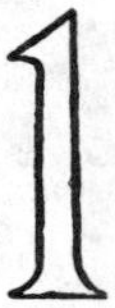

a

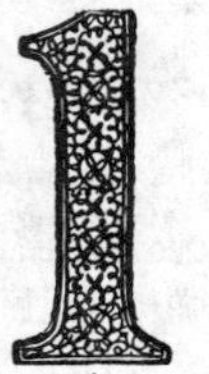

b

Surcharged type "a"

1900

R184 R16 $1 gray 11.00 .20
Cut cancellation .20
a. Horiz. pair, imperf. vert. —
b. Surcharge omitted 125.00
As "b", cut cancellation 80.00
R185 R16 $2 gray 11.00 .20
Cut cancellation .20
R186 R16 $3 gray 55.00 11.00
Cut cancellation 3.00
R187 R16 $5 gray 37.50 6.50
Cut cancellation 1.00
R188 R16 $10 gray 65.00 17.50
Cut cancellation 3.00
R189 R16 $50 gray 650.00 400.00
Cut cancellation 85.00

Surcharged type "b"

1902

R190 R16 $1 green 17.50 3.75
Cut cancellation .20
a. Inverted surcharge 175.00
R191 R16 $2 green 15.00 1.30
Cut cancellation .25
a. Surcharged as #R185 75.00 75.00
b. Surch. as #R185, in vio 1,300. —
c. Double surcharge 100.00
d. Triple surcharge —
R192 R16 $5 green 125.00 25.00
Cut cancellation 4.00
a. Surcharge omitted 140.00
b. Pair, one without surch. 325.00
R193 R16 $10 green 325.00 125.00
Cut cancellation 45.00
R194 R16 $50 green 950.00 800.00
Cut cancellation 225.00

Warning: If Nos. R190-R194 are soaked, the center part of the surcharged numeral may wash off. Before surcharging, a square of soluble varnish was applied to the middle of some stamps.

R20

Liberty — R21

Inscribed "Series of 1914"

Offset Printing

1914 Wmk. 190 Perf. 10

R195 R20 ½c rose 7.50 3.50
R196 R20 1c rose 1.40 .20
R197 R20 2c rose 2.00 .20
R198 R20 3c rose 47.50 30.00
R199 R20 4c rose 14.00 2.00
R200 R20 5c rose 4.00 .20
R201 R20 10c rose 3.25 .20
R202 R20 25c rose 27.50 .55
R203 R20 40c rose 17.50 1.00
R204 R20 50c rose 6.00 .20
R205 R20 80c rose 85.00 10.00
Nos. R195-R205 (11) 215.65 48.05

Wmk. 191R

R206 R20 ½c rose 1.50 .50
R207 R20 1c rose .20 .20
R208 R20 2c rose .20 .20
R209 R20 3c rose 1.40 .20
R210 R20 4c rose 3.50 .45
R211 R20 5c rose 1.75 .25
R212 R20 10c rose .60 .20
R213 R20 25c rose 5.00 1.25
R214 R20 40c rose 65.00 12.50
Cut cancellation .45
R215 R20 50c rose 15.00 .25
R216 R20 80c rose 95.00 17.50
Cut cancellation 1.00
Nos. R206-R216 (11) 189.15 33.50

Engr.

R217 R21 $1 green 30.00 .30
Cut cancellation .20
a. $1 yellow green — .20
R218 R21 $2 carmine 45.00 .50
Cut cancellation .20
R219 R21 $3 purple 55.00 2.50
Cut cancellation .45
R220 R21 $5 blue 47.50 2.75
Cut cancellation .50
R221 R21 $10 orange 110.00 5.00
Cut cancellation .75
R222 R21 $30 vermilion 225.00 11.00
Cut cancellation 2.00
R223 R21 $50 violet 1,250. 800.00
Cut cancellation 350.00

See #R240-R245, R257-R259, R276-R281.

Portrait Types of 1899 Inscribed "Series of 1915" (#R224), or "Series of 1914"

1914-15 Without Gum Perf. 12

R224 R19 $60 brn (Lincoln) — 100.00
Cut cancellation 45.00
R225 R17 $100 grn (Washington) 60.00 40.00
Cut cancellation 15.00
R226 R18 $500 blue — 450.00
Cut cancellation 200.00
R227 R19 $1000 orange — 375.00
Cut cancellation 175.00

The stamps of types R17, R18 and R19 in this and subsequent issues are issued in vert. strips of 4 which are imperf. at the top, bottom and right side; therefore, single copies are always imperf. on 1 or 2 sides.

R22

Offset Printing

1917 Wmk. 191R Perf. 11

R228 R22 1c carmine rose .20 .20
R229 R22 2c carmine rose .20 .20
R230 R22 3c carmine rose 1.25 .35
R231 R22 4c carmine rose .50 .20
R232 R22 5c carmine rose .20 .20
R233 R22 8c carmine rose 1.75 .30
R234 R22 10c carmine rose .35 .20
R235 R22 20c carmine rose .60 .20
R236 R22 25c carmine rose 1.10 .20
R237 R22 40c carmine rose 1.50 .40
R238 R22 50c carmine rose 2.00 .20
R239 R22 80c carmine rose 5.00 .20
Nos. R228-R239 (12) 14.65 2.85

Type of 1914 without "Series 1914"

1917-33 Engr.

R240 R21 $1 yellow green 6.50 .20
a. $1 green 6.50 .20
R241 R21 $2 rose 11.00 .20
R242 R21 $3 violet 35.00 .75
Cut cancellation .20
R243 R21 $4 yellow brown ('33) 25.00 1.75
Cut cancellation .20
R244 R21 $5 dark blue 17.50 .25
Cut cancellation .20
R245 R21 $10 orange 30.00 .90
Cut cancellation .20

Portrait Types of 1899-1915 without "Series of" and Date

Portraits: $30, Grant. $100, Washington.

1917 Without Gum Perf. 12

R246 R17 $30 dp org, grn numerals 45.00 10.00
Cut cancellation 1.00
a. Imperf., pair 750.00
b. Numerals in blue 70.00 1.90
As "b," cut cancellation 1.00
R247 R19 $60 brown 55.00 7.00
Cut cancellation .80
R248 R17 $100 green 32.50 1.00
Cut cancellation .35
R249 R18 $500 blue, red numerals 230.00 35.00
Cut cancellation 10.00
a. Numerals in orange 275.00 50.00
R250 R19 $1000 orange 130.00 12.50
Cut cancellation 4.00
a. Imperf., pair 900.00

See note after No. R227.

1928-29 Offset Printing Perf. 10

R251 R22 1c carmine rose 2.00 1.50
R252 R22 2c carmine rose .60 .20
R253 R22 4c carmine rose 5.50 3.75
R254 R22 5c carmine rose 1.25 .50
R255 R22 10c carmine rose 1.75 1.25
R256 R22 20c carmine rose 5.50 4.50
Nos. R251-R256 (6) 16.60 11.70

Engr.

R257 R21 $1 green 90.00 30.00
Cut cancellation 5.00
R258 R21 $2 rose 35.00 2.50
R259 R21 $10 orange 120.00 40.00
Cut cancellation 25.00

1929 Offset Printing *Perf. 11x10*

R260	R22	2c	carmine rose	2.75	2.50
R261	R22	5c	carmine rose	2.00	1.75
R262	R22	10c	carmine rose	7.50	6.50
R263	R22	20c	carmine rose	15.00	8.00

Used values for Nos. R264-R734 are for copies which are neither cut nor perforated with initials. Copies with cut cancellations or perforated initials are valued in the Scott U. S. Specialized Catalogue.

Types of 1917-33 Overprinted in Black SERIES 1940

1940 Offset Printing *Perf. 11*

R264	R22	1c	rose pink	2.75	2.25
R265	R22	2c	rose pink	2.75	1.75
R266	R22	3c	rose pink	8.25	4.00
R267	R22	4c	rose pink	3.50	.55
R268	R22	5c	rose pink	3.75	.90
R269	R22	8c	rose pink	16.00	12.50
R270	R22	10c	rose pink	1.75	.45
R271	R22	20c	rose pink	2.25	.60
R272	R22	25c	rose pink	5.50	1.00
R273	R22	40c	rose pink	5.50	.65
R274	R22	50c	rose pink	6.00	.50
R275	R22	80c	rose pink	11.00	.90
			Nos. R264-R275 (12)	69.00	26.05

Engr.

R276	R21	$1	green	35.00	.80
R277	R21	$2	rose	35.00	1.00
R278	R21	$3	violet	50.00	25.00
R279	R21	$4	yellow brown	87.50	30.00
R280	R21	$5	dark blue	50.00	11.00
R281	R21	$10	orange	125.00	27.50

Types of 1917 Handstamped in Green Like Nos. R264-R281

Perf. 12

Without Gum

R282	R17	$30	vermilion		500.
a.			With black 2-line handstamp in larger type		—
R283	R19	$60	brown		700.
a.			As #R282a, cut cancel		—
R284	R17	$100	green		1,100.
R285	R18	$500	blue		1,400.
a.			As #R282a	*2,250.*	*2,000.*
b.			Blue handstamp, double transfer		—
R286	R19	$1000	orange		650.

Alexander Hamilton — R23

Levi Woodbury — R24

Thomas Corwin — R25

Portraits: 2c, Oliver Wolcott, Jr. 3c, Samuel Dexter. 4c, Albert Gallatin. 5c, George Washington Campbell. 8c, Alexander Dallas. 10c, William H. Crawford. 20c, Richard Rush. 25c, Samuel D. Ingham. 40c, Louis McLane. 50c, William J. Duane. 80c, Roger B. Taney. $2, Thomas Ewing. $3, Walter Forward. $4, John Canfield Spencer. $5, George M. Bibb. $10, Robert J. Walker. $20, William M. Meredith. $50, James Guthrie. $60, Howell Cobb. $100, P. F. Thomas. $500, John Adams Dix. $1,000, Salmon P. Chase.

Overprinted in Black Like Nos. R264-R281

1940 *Perf. 11*

Various Portraits

R288	R23	1c	carmine	4.00	3.00
R289	R23	2c	carmine	4.50	2.75
R290	R23	3c	carmine	17.50	9.00
R291	R23	4c	carmine	40.00	20.00
R292	R23	5c	carmine	3.00	.60
R293	R23	8c	carmine	60.00	45.00
R294	R23	10c	carmine	2.50	.45
R295	R23	20c	carmine	3.75	2.50
R296	R23	25c	carmine	2.75	.50
R297	R23	40c	carmine	40.00	20.00
R298	R23	50c	carmine	4.50	.40
R299	R23	80c	carmine	90.00	60.00
R300	R24	$1	carmine	35.00	.55
R301	R24	$2	carmine	42.50	.75
R302	R24	$3	carmine	125.00	75.00
R303	R24	$4	carmine	70.00	30.00
R304	R24	$5	carmine	42.50	2.00
R305	R24	$10	carmine	75.00	6.00
R305A	R24	$20	carmine	*1,500.*	550.00
b.			Imperf., pair	600.00	

Various Frame Designs

Perf. 12

Without Gum

R306	R25	$30	carmine	120.00	40.00
R306A	R25	$50	carmine	—	1,500.
R307	R25	$60	carmine	240.00	55.00
a.			Vert. pair, imperf. between		*1,450.*
R308	R25	$100	carmine	175.00	60.00
R309	R25	$500	carmine	—	1,250.
R310	R25	$1000	carmine	—	425.00

The $30 to $1,000 denominations in this and following similar issues, and the $2,500, $5,000 and $10,000 stamps of 1952-58 have straight edges on one or two sides. They were issued without gum through No. R723.

Overprinted in Black "SERIES 1941"

1941 Size: 19x22mm *Perf. 11*

R311	R23	1c	carmine	3.00	2.25
R312	R23	2c	carmine	3.00	.90
R313	R23	3c	carmine	7.50	3.50
R314	R23	4c	carmine	5.00	1.25
R315	R23	5c	carmine	1.00	.25
R316	R23	8c	carmine	14.00	7.50
R317	R23	10c	carmine	1.25	.20
R318	R23	20c	carmine	3.00	.45
R319	R23	25c	carmine	1.75	.20
R320	R23	40c	carmine	11.00	2.50
R321	R23	50c	carmine	2.50	.20
R322	R23	80c	carmine	47.50	10.00
			Nos. R311-R322 (12)	100.50	29.20

Size: 21½x36¼mm

R323	R24	$1	carmine	9.00	.25
R324	R24	$2	carmine	11.00	.35
R325	R24	$3	carmine	19.00	2.75
R326	R24	$4	carmine	30.00	17.50
R327	R24	$5	carmine	35.00	.60
R328	R24	$10	carmine	55.00	3.50
R329	R24	$20	carmine	500.00	175.00

Size: 28½x42mm

Perf. 12

Without Gum

R330	R25	$30	carmine	55.00	25.00
R331	R25	$50	carmine	190.00	160.00
R332	R25	$60	carmine	75.00	45.00
R333	R25	$100	carmine	50.00	19.00
R334	R25	$500	carmine	—	220.00
R335	R25	$1000	carmine	—	125.00

Overprinted in Black "SERIES 1942"

1942 Size: 19x22mm *Perf. 11*

R336	R23	1c	carmine	.50	.45
R337	R23	2c	carmine	.45	.45
R338	R23	3c	carmine	.70	.60
R339	R23	4c	carmine	1.20	.90
R340	R23	5c	carmine	.45	.20
R341	R23	8c	carmine	5.50	4.25
R342	R23	10c	carmine	1.20	.25
R343	R23	20c	carmine	1.20	.45
R344	R23	25c	carmine	2.10	.45
R345	R23	40c	carmine	4.75	1.20
R346	R23	50c	carmine	3.00	.20
R347	R23	80c	carmine	16.00	10.00
			Nos. R336-R347 (12)	37.05	19.40

Size: 21½x36¼mm

R348	R24	$1	carmine	7.50	.25
R349	R24	$2	carmine	9.00	.25
R350	R24	$3	carmine	15.00	2.00
R351	R24	$4	carmine	22.50	3.75
R352	R24	$5	carmine	25.00	.90
R353	R24	$10	carmine	57.50	2.50
R354	R24	$20	carmine	110.00	35.00

Size: 28½x42mm

Perf. 12

Without Gum

R355	R25	$30	carmine	45.00	20.00
R356	R25	$50	carmine	350.00	250.00
R357	R25	$60	carmine	700.00	625.00
R358	R25	$100	carmine	160.00	120.00
R359	R25	$500	carmine	—	200.00
R360	R25	$1000	carmine	—	100.00

Overprinted in Black "SERIES 1943"

1943 Size: 19x22mm *Perf. 11*

R361	R23	1c	carmine	.60	.50
R362	R23	2c	carmine	.45	.35
R363	R23	3c	carmine	2.50	2.50
R364	R23	4c	carmine	1.00	1.00
R365	R23	5c	carmine	.50	.30
R366	R23	8c	carmine	4.25	3.00
R367	R23	10c	carmine	.60	.25
R368	R23	20c	carmine	1.90	.65
R369	R23	25c	carmine	1.50	.25
R370	R23	40c	carmine	5.00	2.25
R371	R23	50c	carmine	1.25	.20
R372	R23	80c	carmine	12.50	5.50
			Nos. R361-R372 (12)	32.05	16.75

Size: 21½x36¼mm

R373	R24	$1	carmine	5.00	.35
R374	R24	$2	carmine	10.00	.25
R375	R24	$3	carmine	19.00	2.25
R376	R24	$4	carmine	25.00	3.25
R377	R24	$5	carmine	30.00	.60
R378	R24	$10	carmine	47.50	4.00
R379	R24	$20	carmine	100.00	22.50

Size: 28½x42mm

Perf. 12

Without Gum

R380	R25	$30	carmine	37.50	18.00
R381	R25	$50	carmine	70.00	30.00
R382	R25	$60	carmine	175.00	75.00
R383	R25	$100	carmine	25.00	10.00
R384	R25	$500	carmine	—	175.00
R385	R25	$1000	carmine	—	150.00

Overprinted in Black "Series 1944"

1944 Size: 19x22mm *Perf. 11*

R386	R23	1c	carmine	.40	.35
R387	R23	2c	carmine	.40	.35
R388	R23	3c	carmine	.40	.35
R389	R23	4c	carmine	.55	.50
R390	R23	5c	carmine	.30	.20
R391	R23	8c	carmine	1.75	1.25
R392	R23	10c	carmine	.40	.20
R393	R23	20c	carmine	.75	.20
R394	R23	25c	carmine	1.40	.20
R395	R23	40c	carmine	2.75	.60
R396	R23	50c	carmine	3.00	.20
R397	R23	80c	carmine	14.00	4.00
			Nos. R386-R397 (12)	26.10	8.40

Size: 21½x36¼mm

R398	R24	$1	carmine	6.00	.20
R399	R24	$2	carmine	8.75	.25
R400	R24	$3	carmine	14.00	2.00
R401	R24	$4	carmine	20.00	10.00
R402	R24	$5	carmine	22.50	.25
R403	R24	$10	carmine	42.50	1.40
R404	R24	$20	carmine	90.00	15.00

Size: 28½x42mm

Perf. 12

Without Gum

R405	R25	$30	carmine	55.00	22.50
R406	R25	$50	carmine	22.50	15.00
R407	R25	$60	carmine	110.00	45.00
R408	R25	$100	carmine	40.00	9.00
R409	R25	$500	carmine	—	1,200.
R410	R25	$1000	carmine	—	175.00

Overprinted in Black "Series 1945"

1945 Size: 19x22mm *Perf. 11*

R411	R23	1c	carmine	.20	.20
R412	R23	2c	carmine	.25	.20
R413	R23	3c	carmine	.50	.45
R414	R23	4c	carmine	.30	.30
R415	R23	5c	carmine	.25	.20
R416	R23	8c	carmine	4.25	2.00
R417	R23	10c	carmine	.80	.20
R418	R23	20c	carmine	4.50	1.00
R419	R23	25c	carmine	1.10	.30
R420	R23	40c	carmine	4.75	1.00
R421	R23	50c	carmine	2.75	.20
R422	R23	80c	carmine	19.00	8.00
			Nos. R411-R422 (12)	38.65	14.05

Size: 21½x36¼mm

R423	R24	$1	carmine	7.50	.20
R424	R24	$2	carmine	8.00	.25
R425	R24	$3	carmine	16.00	2.25
R426	R24	$4	carmine	22.50	3.00
R427	R24	$5	carmine	22.50	.40
R428	R24	$10	carmine	45.00	1.40
R429	R24	$20	carmine	90.00	11.00

Size: 28½x42mm

Without Gum

Perf. 12

R430	R25	$30	carmine	65.00	25.00
R431	R25	$50	carmine	70.00	25.00
R432	R25	$60	carmine	125.00	42.50
R433	R25	$100	carmine	35.00	14.00
R434	R25	$500	carmine	200.00	160.00
R435	R25	$1000	carmine	100.00	82.50

Overprinted in Black "Series 1946"

1946 Wmk. 191R *Perf. 11*

Size: 19x22mm

R436	R23	1c	carmine	.20	.25
R437	R23	2c	carmine	.35	.30
R438	R23	3c	carmine	.35	.30
R439	R23	4c	carmine	.60	.50
R440	R23	5c	carmine	.30	.20
R441	R23	8c	carmine	1.25	1.10
R442	R23	10c	carmine	.70	.20
R443	R23	20c	carmine	1.25	.40
R444	R23	25c	carmine	4.00	.20
R445	R23	40c	carmine	2.50	.75
R446	R23	50c	carmine	3.00	.20
R447	R23	80c	carmine	11.00	4.25
			Nos. R436-R447 (12)	25.50	8.65

Size: 21½x36¼mm

R448	R24	$1	carmine	7.50	.20
R449	R24	$2	carmine	11.00	.20
R450	R24	$3	carmine	16.50	5.00
R451	R24	$4	carmine	22.50	10.00
R452	R24	$5	carmine	22.50	.45
R453	R24	$10	carmine	45.00	1.50
R454	R24	$20	carmine	90.00	11.00

Size: 28½x42mm

Without Gum

Perf. 12

R455	R25	$30	carmine	45.00	12.00
R456	R25	$50	carmine	22.50	9.00
R457	R25	$60	carmine	45.00	16.00
R458	R25	$100	carmine	50.00	10.00
R459	R25	$500	carmine	—	105.00
R460	R25	$1000	carmine	—	100.00

Overprinted in Black "Series 1947"

1947 Wmk. 191R *Perf. 11*

Size: 19x22mm

R461	R23	1c	carmine	.65	.50
R462	R23	2c	carmine	.55	.50
R463	R23	3c	carmine	.55	.50
R464	R23	4c	carmine	.70	.60
R465	R23	5c	carmine	.35	.30
R466	R23	8c	carmine	1.20	.70
R467	R23	10c	carmine	1.10	.25
R468	R23	20c	carmine	1.80	.50
R469	R23	25c	carmine	2.40	.60
R470	R23	40c	carmine	3.75	.90
R471	R23	50c	carmine	3.00	.25
R472	R23	80c	carmine	8.25	6.00
			Nos. R461-R472 (12)	24.30	11.60

Size: 21½x36¼mm

R473	R24	$1	carmine	6.00	.25
R474	R24	$2	carmine	9.50	.50
R475	R24	$3	carmine	11.00	5.00
R476	R24	$4	carmine	12.00	4.50
R477	R24	$5	carmine	19.00	.50
R478	R24	$10	carmine	42.50	2.00
R479	R24	$20	carmine	65.00	10.00

Size: 28½x42mm

Perf. 12

Without Gum

R480	R25	$30	carmine	65.00	17.50
R481	R25	$50	carmine	32.50	12.00
R482	R25	$60	carmine	80.00	35.00
R483	R25	$100	carmine	32.50	10.00
R484	R25	$500	carmine	—	150.00
R485	R25	$1000	carmine	—	80.00

Overprinted in Black "Series 1948"

1948 Wmk. 191R *Perf. 11*

Size: 19x22mm

R486	R23	1c carmine	.25	.25
R487	R23	2c carmine	.35	.30
R488	R23	3c carmine	.45	.35
R489	R23	4c carmine	.40	.30
R490	R23	5c carmine	.35	.20
R491	R23	8c carmine	.75	.35
R492	R23	10c carmine	.60	.20
R493	R23	20c carmine	1.75	.30
R494	R23	25c carmine	1.50	.20
R495	R23	40c carmine	4.50	1.50
R496	R23	50c carmine	2.25	.20
R497	R23	80c carmine	7.50	4.50
		Nos. R486-R497 (12)	20.65	8.65

Size: 21½x36¼mm

R498	R24	$1 carmine	7.50	.20
R499	R24	$2 carmine	11.00	.20
R500	R24	$3 carmine	15.00	2.50
R501	R24	$4 carmine	22.50	2.75
R502	R24	$5 carmine	19.00	.50
R503	R24	$10 carmine	42.50	1.00
a.		Pair, one dated "1946"		—
R504	R24	$20 carmine	85.00	10.00

Size: 28½x42mm

Perf. 12

Without Gum

R505	R25	$30 carmine	42.50	20.00
R506	R25	$50 carmine	42.50	17.50
a.		Vert. pair, imperf. btwn.	—	
R507	R25	$60 carmine	65.00	27.50
a.		Vert. pair, imperf. btwn.	*1,100*	
R508	R25	$100 carmine	55.00	10.00
a.		Vert. pair, imperf. btwn.	*850.00*	
R509	R25	$500 carmine	125.00	100.00
R510	R25	$1000 carmine	87.50	60.00

Overprinted in Black "Series 1949"

1949 Wmk. 191R *Perf. 11*

Size: 19x22mm

R511	R23	1c carmine	.25	.25
R512	R23	2c carmine	.55	.35
R513	R23	3c carmine	.40	.35
R514	R23	4c carmine	.60	.50
R515	R23	5c carmine	.35	.20
R516	R23	8c carmine	.70	.60
R517	R23	10c carmine	.40	.25
R518	R23	20c carmine	1.30	.60
R519	R23	25c carmine	1.80	.70
R520	R23	40c carmine	4.25	2.10
R521	R23	50c carmine	3.50	.30
R522	R23	80c carmine	9.00	4.75
		Nos. R511-R522 (12)	23.10	10.95

Size: 21½x36¼mm

R523	R24	$1 carmine	7.50	.40
R524	R24	$2 carmine	9.50	2.00
R525	R24	$3 carmine	15.00	6.00
R526	R24	$4 carmine	19.00	6.00
R527	R24	$5 carmine	19.00	2.25
R528	R24	$10 carmine	42.50	2.50
R529	R24	$20 carmine	85.00	9.00

Size: 28½x42mm

Perf. 12

Without Gum

R530	R25	$30 carmine	55.00	22.50
R531	R25	$50 carmine	65.00	35.00
R532	R25	$60 carmine	90.00	40.00
R533	R25	$100 carmine	50.00	15.00
R534	R25	$500 carmine	—	180.00
R535	R25	$1000 carmine	—	110.00

Overprinted in Black "Series 1950"

1950 Wmk. 191R *Perf. 11*

Size: 19x22mm

R536	R23	1c carmine	.20	.20
R537	R23	2c carmine	.30	.25
R538	R23	3c carmine	.35	.30
R539	R23	4c carmine	.50	.40
R540	R23	5c carmine	.30	.20
R541	R23	8c carmine	1.25	.65
R542	R23	10c carmine	.60	.20
R543	R23	20c carmine	1.00	.35
R544	R23	25c carmine	1.50	.35
R545	R23	40c carmine	3.25	1.75
R546	R23	50c carmine	4.00	.20
R547	R23	80c carmine	7.50	4.00
		Nos. R536-R547 (12)	20.75	8.85

Size: 21½x36¼mm

R548	R24	$1 carmine	7.50	.25
R549	R24	$2 carmine	9.50	2.00
R550	R24	$3 carmine	11.00	4.00
R551	R24	$4 carmine	15.00	5.00
R552	R24	$5 carmine	19.00	.80
R553	R24	$10 carmine	42.50	8.50
R554	R24	$20 carmine	85.00	9.00

Size: 28½x42mm

Perf. 12

Without Gum

R555	R25	$30 carmine	70.00	40.00
R556	R25	$50 carmine	42.50	14.00
a.		Vert. pair, imperf. horiz.		—
R557	R25	$60 carmine	100.00	50.00
R558	R25	$100 carmine	55.00	17.50
R559	R25	$500 carmine	—	100.00
R560	R25	$1000 carmine	—	75.00

Overprinted in Black "Series 1951"

1951 Wmk. 191R *Perf. 11*

Size: 19x22mm

R561	R23	1c carmine	.20	.20
R562	R23	2c carmine	.30	.25
R563	R23	3c carmine	.25	.25
R564	R23	4c carmine	.30	.25
R565	R23	5c carmine	.30	.20
R566	R23	8c carmine	1.00	.35
R567	R23	10c carmine	.55	.20
R568	R23	20c carmine	1.25	.45
R569	R23	25c carmine	1.25	.40
R570	R23	40c carmine	3.00	1.25
R571	R23	50c carmine	2.50	.35
R572	R23	80c carmine	6.50	2.50
		Nos. R561-R572 (12)	17.40	6.65

Size: 21½x36¼mm

R573	R24	$1 carmine	7.50	.20
R574	R24	$2 carmine	9.50	.50
R575	R24	$3 carmine	14.00	3.50
R576	R24	$4 carmine	19.00	5.00
R577	R24	$5 carmine	15.00	.60
R578	R24	$10 carmine	37.50	2.25
R579	R24	$20 carmine	80.00	8.50

Size: 28½x42mm

Perf. 12

Without Gum

R580	R25	$30 carmine	70.00	10.00
a.		Imperf., pair		*750.00*
R581	R25	$50 carmine	55.00	16.00
R582	R25	$60 carmine	90.00	40.00
R583	R25	$100 carmine	45.00	12.50
R584	R25	$500 carmine	125.00	82.50
R585	R25	$1000 carmine	—	95.00

Overprinted in Black "Series 1952"

Designs: 55c, $1.10, $1.65, $2.20, $2.75, $3.30, L. J. Gage; $2500, William Windom; $5000, C. J. Folger; $10,000, W. Q. Gresham.

1952 Wmk. 191R *Perf. 11*

Size: 19x22mm

R586	R23	1c carmine	.20	.20
R587	R23	2c carmine	.35	.25
R588	R23	3c carmine	.30	.25
R589	R23	4c carmine	.30	.25
R590	R23	5c carmine	.25	.20
R591	R23	8c carmine	.65	.45
R592	R23	10c carmine	.40	.20
R593	R23	20c carmine	1.00	.35
R594	R23	25c carmine	1.50	.40
R595	R23	40c carmine	3.00	1.00
R596	R23	50c carmine	2.75	.20
R597	R23	55c carmine	19.00	10.00
R598	R23	80c carmine	11.00	3.00
		Nos. R586-R598 (13)	40.70	16.75

Size: 21½x36¼mm

R599	R24	$1 carmine	5.00	1.50
R600	R24	$1.10 carmine	37.50	25.00
R601	R24	$1.65 carmine	130.00	45.00
R602	R24	$2 carmine	9.50	.65
R603	R24	$2.20 carmine	105.00	60.00
R604	R24	$2.75 carmine	115.00	60.00
R605	R24	$3 carmine	22.50	4.00
a.		Horiz. pair, imperf. btwn.	*600.00*	
R606	R24	$3.30 carmine	105.00	60.00
R607	R24	$4 carmine	19.00	4.00
R608	R24	$5 carmine	19.00	1.25
R609	R24	$10 carmine	37.50	1.25
R610	R24	$20 carmine	60.00	9.00

Size: 28½x42mm

Perf. 12

Without Gum

R611	R25	$30 carmine	47.50	18.00
R612	R25	$50 carmine	42.50	12.00
R613	R25	$60 carmine	150.00	50.00
R614	R25	$100 carmine	37.50	8.00
R615	R25	$500 carmine	—	100.00
R616	R25	$1000 carmine	—	30.00
R617	R25	$2500 carmine	—	165.00
R618	R25	$5000 carmine	—	1,400.
R619	R25	$10,000 carmine	—	*1,250.*

Overprinted in Black "Series 1953"

1953 Wmk. 191R *Perf. 11*

Size: 19x22mm

R620	R23	1c carmine	.20	.20
R621	R23	2c carmine	.20	.20
R622	R23	3c carmine	.25	.20
R623	R23	4c carmine	.35	.25
R624	R23	5c carmine	.20	.20
a.		Vert. pair, imperf. horiz.		*650.00*
R625	R23	8c carmine	.75	.35
R626	R23	10c carmine	.40	.20
R627	R23	20c carmine	.75	.40
R628	R23	25c carmine	1.00	.50
R629	R23	40c carmine	1.75	1.00
R630	R23	50c carmine	2.50	.20
R631	R23	55c carmine	3.50	2.00
a.		Horiz. pair, imperf. vert.	*350.00*	
R632	R23	80c carmine	6.00	2.00
		Nos. R620-R632 (13)	17.85	7.70

Size: 21½x36¼mm

R633	R24	$1 carmine	4.00	.25
R634	R24	$1.10 carmine	7.00	2.25
a.		Horiz. pair, imperf. vert.	500.00	
b.		Imperf., pair	550.00	
R635	R24	$1.65 carmine	8.00	4.00
R636	R24	$2 carmine	6.00	.65
R637	R24	$2.20 carmine	11.00	6.00
R638	R24	$2.75 carmine	15.00	7.00
R639	R24	$3 carmine	8.50	3.00
R640	R24	$3.30 carmine	24.00	8.00
R641	R24	$4 carmine	17.50	7.50
R642	R24	$5 carmine	17.50	1.00
R643	R24	$10 carmine	37.50	1.75
R644	R24	$20 carmine	75.00	18.00

Size: 28½x42mm

Perf. 12

Without Gum

R645	R25	$30 carmine	42.50	13.50
R646	R25	$50 carmine	80.00	27.50
R647	R25	$60 carmine	300.00	175.00
R648	R25	$100 carmine	37.50	12.00
R649	R25	$500 carmine	250.00	115.00
R650	R25	$1000 carmine	125.00	57.50
R651	R25	$2500 carmine	550.00	500.00
R652	R25	$5000 carmine	—	*1,500.*
R653	R25	$10,000 carmine	—	*1,500.*

Types of 1940 without Overprint

1954 Wmk. 191R *Perf. 11*

Size: 19x22mm

R654	R23	1c carmine	.20	.20
a.		Horiz. pair, imperf. vert.	—	
R655	R23	2c carmine	.20	.20
R656	R23	3c carmine	.20	.20
R657	R23	4c carmine	.20	.20
R658	R23	5c carmine	.20	.20
R659	R23	8c carmine	.25	.20
R660	R23	10c carmine	.25	.20
R661	R23	20c carmine	.50	.30
R662	R23	25c carmine	.60	.35
R663	R23	40c carmine	1.25	.60
R664	R23	50c carmine	1.65	.20
a.		Horiz. pair, imperf. vert	275.00	
R665	R23	55c carmine	1.50	1.25
R666	R23	80c carmine	2.25	1.75
		Nos. R654-R666 (13)	9.25	5.85

Size: 21½x36¼mm

R667	R24	$1 carmine	1.50	.30
R668	R24	$1.10 carmine	3.25	2.50
R669	R24	$1.65 carmine	95.00	65.00
R670	R24	$2 carmine	1.75	.35
R671	R24	$2.20 carmine	4.50	3.75
R672	R24	$2.75 carmine	100.00	60.00
R673	R24	$3 carmine	3.00	2.00
R674	R24	$3.30 carmine	6.50	5.00
R675	R24	$4 carmine	4.00	3.50
R676	R24	$5 carmine	6.00	.45
R677	R24	$10 carmine	12.50	1.25
R678	R24	$20 carmine	32.50	5.75

Overprinted in Black "Series 1954"

Perf. 12

Size: 28½x42mm

Without Gum

R679	R25	$30 carmine	32.50	12.00
R680	R25	$50 carmine	42.50	17.50
R681	R25	$60 carmine	70.00	20.00
R682	R25	$100 carmine	32.50	7.00
R683	R25	$500 carmine	—	75.00
R684	R25	$1000 carmine	150.00	55.00
R685	R25	$2500 carmine	—	175.00
R686	R25	$5000 carmine	—	850.00
R687	R25	$10,000 carmine	—	500.00

Overprinted in Black "Series 1955"
Without Gum

1955 Wmk. 191R *Perf. 12*

Size: 28½x42mm

R688	R25	$30 carmine	42.50	11.50
R689	R25	$50 carmine	42.50	13.50
R690	R25	$60 carmine	75.00	25.00
R691	R25	$100 carmine	37.50	7.00
R692	R25	$500 carmine	—	125.00
R693	R25	$1000 carmine	—	35.00
R694	R25	$2500 carmine	—	140.00
R695	R25	$5000 carmine	*1,000.*	900.00
R696	R25	$10,000 carmine	—	600.00

Overprinted in Black
"Series 1956"
Without Gum

1956 Size: 28½x42mm

R697	R25	$30 carmine	55.00	13.50
R698	R25	$50 carmine	60.00	17.00
R699	R25	$60 carmine	75.00	35.00
R700	R25	$100 carmine	55.00	12.50
R701	R25	$500 carmine	—	85.00
R702	R25	$1000 carmine	—	60.00
R703	R25	$2500 carmine	—	275.00
R704	R25	$5000 carmine	—	1,400.
R705	R25	$10,000 carmine	—	500.00

Overprinted in Black "Series 1957"
Without Gum

1957 Size: 28½x42mm

R706	R25	$30 carmine	70.00	27.50
R707	R25	$50 carmine	55.00	24.00
R708	R25	$60 carmine	—	150.00
R709	R25	$100 carmine	50.00	12.50
R710	R25	$500 carmine	175.00	90.00
R711	R25	$1000 carmine	—	80.00
R712	R25	$2500 carmine	—	525.00
R713	R25	$5000 carmine	—	600.00
R714	R25	$10,000 carmine	—	450.00

Overprinted in Black "Series 1958"
Without Gum

1958 Size: 28½x42mm

R715	R25	$30 carmine	80.00	20.00
R716	R25	$50 carmine	65.00	20.00
R717	R25	$60 carmine	75.00	25.00
R718	R25	$100 carmine	55.00	10.00
R719	R25	$500 carmine	125.00	57.50
R720	R25	$1000 carmine	—	67.50
R721	R25	$2500 carmine	—	750.00
R722	R25	$5000 carmine	—	1,750.
R723	R25	$10,000 carmine	—	900.00

Documentary Stamps and Type of 1940 Without Overprint
With Gum

1958 Size: 28½x42mm

R724	R25	$30 carmine	37.50	7.00
a.		Vert. pair, imperf. horiz.		
R725	R25	$50 carmine	42.50	7.00
a.		Vert. pair, imperf. horiz.		
R726	R25	$60 carmine	80.00	20.00
R727	R25	$100 carmine	19.00	4.75
R728	R25	$500 carmine	85.00	25.00
R729	R25	$1000 carmine	55.00	20.00
a.		Vert. pair, imperf. horiz.		*750.00*
R730	R25	$2500 carmine	—	140.00
R731	R25	$5000 carmine	—	150.00
R732	R25	$10,000 carmine	—	125.00

Internal Revenue Building, Washington, DC — R26

Giori Press Printing

1962, July 1 Unwmk. *Perf. 11*

R733	R26	10c vio bl & brt grn	.80	.35
		Never hinged	1.10	

Centenary of Internal Revenue Service.

"Established 1862" Removed

1963

R734	R26	10c vio blue & brt green	2.50	.35
		Never hinged	3.50	

Documentary revenue stamps were no longer required after Dec. 31, 1967.

PROPRIETARY STAMPS

Stamps for use on proprietary articles were included in the first general issue of 1862-71. They are Nos. R3, R13, R14, R18, R22, R29, R31 and R38.

Washington — RB1

Various Frames and Sizes
Violet or Green Paper with Silk Threads

1871-74 Engr. *Perf. 12*

a. left column = Violet Paper (1871)

b. right column = Green Paper (1874)

RB1	RB1	1c green & blk	5.00	9.00
c.		Imperf.	80.00	
d.		Inverted center	*2,500.*	
RB2	RB1	2c green & blk	6.00	20.00
c.		Invtd. center, *violet*	*40,000.*	
d.		Invtd. center, *green*		8,500.
RB3	RB1	3c green & blk	17.50	50.00
c.		Sewing machine perf.	225.00	
d.		Inverted center	*16,000.*	
RB4	RB1	4c green & blk	10.00	17.50
c.		Inverted center	*22,500.*	
RB5	RB1	5c green & blk	130.00	150.00
c.		Inverted center	*80,000.*	
RB6	RB1	6c green & blk	35.00	100.00
RB7	RB1	10c green & blk ('73)	175.00	50.00
RB8	RB1	50c green & blk ('73)	500.00	900.00
RB9	RB1	$1 green & blk ('73)	*1,100.*	*4,250.*
RB10	RB1	$5 green & blk ('73)	*3,250.*	*27,500.*

Washington — RB2

Various Frames and Sizes
Green Paper

Wmk. 191R, Unwmkd. (Silk Paper)
1875-81
b. left column = Perf.
c. right column = Rouletted 6

RB11 RB2 1c green .40 70.00
a. Silk paper 1.90
d. Vert. pair, imperf btwn. 250.00
RB12 RB2 2c brown 1.40 90.00
a. Silk paper 2.50
RB13 RB2 3c orange 3.00 90.00
a. Silk paper 12.50
d. Horiz. pair, imperf. btwn. —
RB14 RB2 4c red brown 5.50
a. Silk paper 6.00
RB15 RB2 4c red 4.50 140.00
RB16 RB2 5c black 90.00 1,250.
a. Silk paper 110.00
RB17 RB2 6c violet blue 20.00 240.00
a. Silk paper 25.00
RB18 RB2 6c violet 30.00 —
RB19 RB2 10c blue ('81) 300.00

Many fraudulent roulettes exist.
The existence of No. RB18c has been questioned by specialists. The editors would like to see authenticated evidence proving its existence.

Battleship — RB3

Rouletted 5½
1898 Wmk. 191R Engr.

RB20 RB3 1/8c yellow green .20 .20
a. Vert. pair, imperf. horiz. —
RB21 RB3 1/4c brown .20 .20
a. 1/4c red brown .20 .20
b. 1/4c yellow brown .20 .20
c. 1/4c orange brown .20 .20
d. 1/4c bister .20 .20
e. Vert. pair, imperf. horiz. —
f. Printed on both sides —
RB22 RB3 3/8c deep orange .20 .20
a. Horiz. pair, imperf. vert. 10.00
b. Vert. pair, imperf. horiz. —
RB23 RB3 5/8c deep ultra .20 .20
a. Vert. pair, imperf. horiz. 75.00
b. Horiz. pair, imperf. btwn. 300.00
RB24 RB3 1c dark green 1.50 .20
a. Vert. pair, imperf. horiz. 300.00
RB25 RB3 1 1/4c violet .20 .20
a. 1 1/4c brown violet .20 .20
b. Vert. pair, imperf. btwn. —
RB26 RB3 1 7/8c dull blue 10.00 1.50
RB27 RB3 2c vio brown 1.00 .20
a. Horiz. pair, imperf. vert. 50.00
RB28 RB3 2 1/2c lake 3.00 .20
a. Vert. pair, imperf. horiz. 175.00
RB29 RB3 3 3/4c olive gray 35.00 10.00
RB30 RB3 4c purple 10.00 1.00
RB31 RB3 5c brown org 10.00 1.00
a. Vert. pair, imperf. horiz. — 300.00
b. Horiz. pair, imperf. vert. — 400.00
Nos. RB20-RB31 (12) 71.50 15.10

Hyphen Hole Perf. 7

RB20p 1/8c .20 .20
RB21p 1/4c .20 .20
g. 1/4c yellow brown .20 .20
h. 1/4c orange brown .20 .20
RB22p 3/8c .25 .20
RB23p 5/8c .25 .20
RB24p 1c 20.00 12.50
RB25p 1 1/4c .20 .20
c. 1 1/4c brown violet .20 .20
RB26p 1 7/8c 27.50 7.50
RB27p 2c 6.00 .75
RB28p 2 1/2c 4.00 .25
RB29p 3 3/4c 65.00 20.00
RB30p 4c 60.00 17.50
RB31p 5c 65.00 20.00

See note before No. R161.

RB4

RB5

Offset Printing
1914 Wmk. 190 *Perf. 10*

RB32 RB4 1/8c black .20 .20
RB33 RB4 1/4c black 1.75 1.00
RB34 RB4 3/8c black .20 .20
RB35 RB4 5/8c black 3.50 1.75
RB36 RB4 1 1/4c black 2.50 .80
RB37 RB4 1 7/8c black 35.00 15.00
RB38 RB4 2 1/2c black 7.50 2.50
RB39 RB4 3 1/8c black 80.00 50.00
RB40 RB4 3 3/4c black 35.00 20.00
RB41 RB4 4c black 50.00 27.50
RB42 RB4 4 3/8c black 1,100. —
RB43 RB4 5c black 110.00 70.00
Nos. RB32-RB41,RB43 (11) 325.65 188.95

Wmk. 191R

RB44 RB4 1/8c black .20 .20
RB45 RB4 1/4c black .20 .20
RB46 RB4 3/8c black .60 .30
RB47 RB4 1/2c black 3.00 2.75
RB48 RB4 5/8c black .20 .20
RB49 RB4 1c black 4.25 4.00
RB50 RB4 1 1/4c black .35 .25
RB51 RB4 1 1/2c black 3.00 2.25
RB52 RB4 1 7/8c black 1.00 .60
RB53 RB4 2c black 5.00 4.00
RB54 RB4 2 1/2c black 1.25 1.00
RB55 RB4 3c black 4.00 2.75
RB56 RB4 3 1/8c black 5.00 3.00
RB57 RB4 3 3/4c black 11.00 7.50
RB58 RB4 4c black .30 .20
RB59 RB4 4 3/8c black 14.00 8.00
RB60 RB4 5c black 3.00 2.50
RB61 RB4 6c black 55.00 40.00
RB62 RB4 8c black 17.50 11.00
RB63 RB4 10c black 11.00 7.00
RB64 RB4 20c black 22.50 17.50
Nos. RB44-RB64 (21) 162.35 115.20

1919 *Perf. 11*

RB65 RB5 1c dark blue .20 .20
RB66 RB5 2c dark blue .20 .20
RB67 RB5 3c dark blue 1.00 .60
RB68 RB5 4c dark blue 1.00 .50
RB69 RB5 5c dark blue 1.25 .60
RB70 RB5 8c dark blue 14.00 9.00
RB71 RB5 10c dark blue 5.00 2.00
RB72 RB5 20c dark blue 7.50 3.00
RB73 RB5 40c dark blue 45.00 10.00
Nos. RB65-RB73 (9) 75.15 26.10

FUTURE DELIVERY STAMPS

Issued to facilitate the collection of a tax upon each sale, agreement of sale or agreement to sell any products or merchandise at any exchange or board of trade, or other similar place for future delivery.

Documentary Stamps Nos. R228 to R250 Overprinted in Black or Red

FUTURE
DELIVERY

Offset Printing
1918-34 Wmk. 191R *Perf. 11*
Overprint Horizontal
(Lines 8mm apart)

RC1 R22 2c car rose 3.50 .20
RC2 R22 3c car rose ('34) 30.00 22.50
Cut cancellation 12.50
RC3 R22 4c car rose 6.00 .20
RC3A R22 5c car rose ('33) 75.00 5.00
RC4 R22 10c car rose 11.00 .20
a. Double overprint — 5.00
b. "FUTURE" omitted — 200.00
c. "DELIVERY FUTURE" 35.00
RC5 R22 20c car rose 15.00 .20
a. Double overprint 20.00
RC6 R22 25c car rose 35.00 .40
Cut cancellation .20
RC7 R22 40c car rose 40.00 .75
Cut cancellation .20
RC8 R22 50c car rose 8.50 .20
a. "DELIVERY" omitted — 100.00
RC9 R22 80c car rose 75.00 10.00
Cut cancellation 1.00
a. Double overprint 35.00
Cut cancellation 6.00
Nos. RC1-RC9 (10) 299.00 39.65

Overprint Vertical, Reading Up
(Lines 2mm apart)
Engr.

RC10 R21 $1 green (R) 30.00 .25
Cut cancellation .20
a. Overprint reading down 275.00
b. Black overprint —
Cut cancellation 125.00
RC11 R21 $2 rose 35.00 .25
Cut cancellation .20
RC12 R21 $3 violet (R) 80.00 2.50
Cut cancellation .20
a. Overprint reading down — 50.00
RC13 R21 $5 dark blue (R) 60.00 .35
Cut cancellation .20
RC14 R21 $10 orange 80.00 .75
Cut cancellation .20
a. "DELIVERY FUTURE" 100.00
RC15 R21 $20 olive bis 150.00 4.00
Cut cancellation .50
Nos. RC10-RC15 (6) 435.00 8.10

Perf. 12
Overprint Horizontal
(Lines 11½mm apart)
Without Gum

RC16 R17 $30 ver, green numerals 70.00 3.50
Cut cancellation 1.25
a. Numerals in blue 60.00 3.50
Cut cancellation 1.50
b. As "a," imperf. 100.00
RC17 R19 $50 olive green 47.50 1.25
Cut cancellation .40
a. $50 olive bister 47.50 1.00
Cut cancellation .40
RC18 R19 $60 brown 70.00 2.25
Cut cancellation .75
a. Vert. pair, imperf. horiz. 400.00
RC19 R17 $100 yel green ('34) 110.00 27.50
Cut cancellation 7.00
RC20 R18 $500 blue, red numerals (R) 80.00 11.00
Cut cancellation 4.50
a. Numerals in orange — 50.00
Cut cancellation 11.00
RC21 R19 $1000 orange 95.00 5.50
Cut cancellation 1.50
a. Vert. pair, imperf. horiz. 900.00
Nos. RC16-RC21 (6) 472.50 51.00

See note after No. R227.

1923-24 Offset Printing *Perf. 11*
Overprint Horiz.
(Lines 2mm apart)

RC22 R22 1c carmine rose 1.00 .20
RC23 R22 80c carmine rose 65.00 1.75
Cut cancellation .35

Documentary Stamps of 1917 Overprinted in Red or Black

FUTURE
DELIVERY

1925-34 Engr.

RC25 R21 $1 green (R) 27.50 .75
Cut cancellation .20
RC26 R21 $10 orange (Bk) ('34) 90.00 15.00
Cut cancellation 10.00

Overprinted like Nos. RC1-RC9

1928-29 Offset Printing *Perf. 10*

RC27 R22 10c carmine rose 1,500.
RC28 R22 20c carmine rose 1,500.

STOCK TRANSFER STAMPS

Issued to facilitate the collection of a tax on all sales or agreements to sell, or memoranda of sales or delivery of, or transfers of legal title to shares or certificates of stock.

Documentary Stamps Nos. R228 to R259 Overprinted in Black or Red

STOCK
TRANSFER

Offset Printing
1918-29 Wmk. 191R *Perf. 11*
Overprint Horiz. (Lines 8mm apart)

RD1 R22 1c car rose .85 .20
a. Double overprint — —
RD2 R22 2c car rose .20 .20
a. Double overprint — 5.00
Cut cancellation 2.50
RD3 R22 4c car rose .20 .20
a. Double overprint — 4.00
Cut cancellation 2.00
b. "STOCK" omitted 10.00
d. Overprint lines 10mm apart —
RD4 R22 5c car rose .25 .20
RD5 R22 10c car rose .25 .20
a. Double overprint — 5.00
Cut cancellation 2.50
b. "STOCK" omitted
RD6 R22 20c car rose .50 .20
a. Double overprint 6.00
b. "STOCK" double —
RD7 R22 25c car rose 1.50 .20
Cut cancellation .20
RD8 R22 40c car rose ('22) 1.25 .20
RD9 R22 50c car rose .65 .20
a. Double overprint — —
RD10 R22 80c car rose 3.00 .30
Cut cancellation .20
Nos. RD1-RD10 (10) 8.65 2.10

Overprint Vertical, Reading Up
(Lines 2mm apart)
Engr.

RD11 R21 $1 green (R) 85.00 20.00
Cut cancellation 3.00
a. Ovpt. reading down 125.00 20.00
Cut cancellation 7.50
RD12 R21 $1 green (Bk) 2.50 .25
a. Pair, one without ovpt. — 150.00
b. Ovptd. on back instead of face, inverted — 100.00
c. Ovpt. reading down — 6.00
d. $1 yellow green 2.75 .20
RD13 R21 $2 rose 2.50 .20
a. Ovpt. reading down 10.00
Cut cancellation 1.50
b. Vert. pair, imperf. horiz. 500.00
RD14 R21 $3 violet (R) 17.50 4.25
Cut cancellation .20
RD15 R21 $4 yellow brn 9.00 .20
Cut cancellation .20
RD16 R21 $5 dk blue (R) 6.00 .20
Cut cancellation .20
a. Ovpt. reading down 20.00 1.00
Cut cancellation .20
RD17 R21 $10 orange 16.00 .30
Cut cancellation .20
RD18 R21 $20 ol bis ('21) 75.00 20.00
Cut cancellation 3.00
Nos. RD11-RD18 (8) 213.50 45.40

1918 Without Gum *Perf. 12*
Overprint Horizontal (Lines 11½mm apart)

RD19 R17 $30 ver, green numerals 17.50 4.50
Cut cancellation 1.00
a. Numerals in blue 55.00
RD20 R19 $50 olive green, (Cleveland) 110.00 55.00
Cut cancellation 20.00
RD21 R19 $60 brown 110.00 20.00
Cut cancellation 9.00
RD22 R17 $100 green 22.50 5.50
Cut cancellation 2.25
RD23 R18 $500 blue (R) 300.00 110.00
Cut cancellation 65.00
a. Numerals in orange 140.00
RD24 R19 $1000 orange 165.00 72.50
Cut cancellation 25.00

See note after No. R227.

1928-32 Offset Printing *Perf. 10*
Overprint Horiz. (Lines 8mm apart)

RD25 R22 2c carmine rose 2.50 .25
RD26 R22 4c carmine rose 2.50 .25
RD27 R22 10c carmine rose 2.00 .25
a. Inverted overprint 1,000.
RD28 R22 20c carmine rose 3.00 .25
RD29 R22 50c carmine rose 3.50 .25

Overprint Vertical, Reading Up
(Lines 2mm apart)
Engr.

RD30 R21 $1 green 30.00 .20
a. $1 yellow green — —
RD31 R21 $2 car rose 30.00 .20
a. Pair, one without overprint 200.00 175.00
RD32 R21 $10 orange 32.50 .35
Cut cancellation .20
Nos. RD25-RD32 (8) 106.00 2.00

Overprinted Horiz. in Black

STOCK
TRANSFER

1920-28 Offset Printing *Perf. 11*

RD33 R22 2c carmine rose 7.50 .70
RD34 R22 10c carmine rose 1.25 .30
b. Inverted overprint 1,500.
RD35 R22 20c carmine rose 1.00 .20
a. Horiz. pair, one without overprint 175.00
d. Inverted overprint (perf. initials) —
RD36 R22 50c carmine rose 3.00 .20

Engr.

RD37 R21 $1 green 40.00 8.00
Cut cancellation .25
RD38 R21 $2 rose 35.00 8.00
Cut cancellation .25
Nos. RD33-RD38 (6) 87.75 17.40

Shifted overprints on the 10c, 20c and 50c result in "TRANSFER STOCK," "TRANSFER" omitted, "STOCK" omitted, pairs, one without overprint and other varieties.

Perf. 10
Offset Printing

RD39 R22 2c carmine rose 6.50 .50
RD40 R22 10c carmine rose 1.50 .50
RD41 R22 20c carmine rose 2.50 .25
Nos. RD39-RD41 (3) 10.50 1.25

Used values for Nos. RD42-RD372 are for copies which are neither cut nor perforated with initials. Copies with cut cancellations or perforated initials are valued in the Scott U.S. Specialized Catalogue.

SERIES 1940

Documentary Stamps of 1917-33 Overprinted in Black

STOCK TRANSFER

1940 *Perf. 11*

RD42 R22 1c rose pink 3.00 .45
a. "Series 1940" inverted — 225.00
RD43 R22 2c rose pink 3.00 .50
RD45 R22 4c rose pink 3.00 .20
RD46 R22 5c rose pink 3.50 .20
RD48 R22 10c rose pink 3.50 .20
RD49 R22 20c rose pink 7.50 .20
RD50 R22 25c rose pink 7.50 .60
RD51 R22 40c rose pink 5.00 .75
RD52 R22 50c rose pink 6.00 .25
RD53 R22 80c rose pink 95.00 50.00
Nos. RD42-RD53 (10) 137.00 53.35

Engr.

RD54 R21 $1 green 22.50 .35
RD55 R21 $2 rose 22.50 .60
RD56 R21 $3 violet 140.00 9.00
RD57 R21 $4 yel brown 47.50 1.00
RD58 R21 $5 dark blue 47.50 1.00
RD59 R21 $10 orange 110.00 6.00
RD60 R21 $20 olive bister 240.00 75.00
Nos. RD54-RD60 (7) 630.00 92.95

Stock Transfer Stamps of 1918 Handstamped in Blue "Series 1940"

1940 **Without Gum** *Perf. 12*

RD61 R17 $30 vermilion *900.* 550.
RD62 R19 $50 olive green *900.* 750.
a. Dbl. ovpt. (perf. initials canc.) *350.*
RD63 R19 $60 brown 1,150.
RD64 R17 $100 green 750. 550.
RD65 R18 $500 blue *2,200.*
RD66 R19 $1000 orange *2,400.*

Alexander Hamilton — ST1

Levi Woodbury — ST2 Thomas Corwin — ST3

Portraits (see R23-R25): 2c, Wolcott. 4c, Gallatin. 5c, Campbell. 10c, Crawford. 20c, Rush. 25c, Ingham. 40c, McLane. 50c, Duane. 80c, Taney. $2, Ewing. $3, Forward. $4, Spencer. $5, Bibb. $10, Walker. $20, Meredith. $50, Guthrie. $60, Cobb. $100, Thomas. $500, Dix. $1,000, Chase.

Overprinted in Black SERIES 1940

1940 **Wmk. 191R** *Perf. 11*

Various Portraits

Size: 19x22mm

RD67 ST1 1c brt green 9.50 2.75
RD68 ST1 2c brt green 5.75 1.40
RD70 ST1 4c brt green 11.00 3.75
RD71 ST1 5c brt green 6.50 1.40
a. Without overprint (cut canc.) *250.00*
RD73 ST1 10c brt green 9.00 1.75
RD74 ST1 20c brt green 11.00 2.00
RD75 ST1 25c brt green 30.00 8.00
RD76 ST1 40c brt green 57.50 30.00
RD77 ST1 50c brt green 9.00 1.75
RD78 ST1 80c brt green 75.00 50.00
Nos. RD67-RD78 (10) 224.25 102.80

Size: 21½x36¼mm

RD79 ST2 $1 brt green 32.50 3.50
a. Without overprint (perf. initials canc.) *225.00*
RD80 ST2 $2 brt green 37.50 8.50
RD81 ST2 $3 brt green 57.50 10.00
RD82 ST2 $4 brt green 260.00 200.00
RD83 ST2 $5 brt green 52.50 12.50
RD84 ST2 $10 brt green 130.00 35.00
RD85 ST2 $20 brt green 475.00 70.00

Perf. 12

Without Gum

Size: 28½x42mm

Various Frame Designs

RD86 ST3 $30 brt green — 140.00
RD87 ST3 $50 brt green 325.00 250.00
RD88 ST3 $60 brt green — 425.00
RD89 ST3 $100 brt green — 190.00
RD90 ST3 $500 brt green — 1,100.
RD91 ST3 $1000 brt green — 1,100.

Overprinted in Black "Series 1941" SERIES 1941

1941 **Size: 19x22mm** *Perf. 11*

RD92 ST1 1c brt green .65 .50
RD93 ST1 2c brt green .45 .25
RD95 ST1 4c brt green .40 .20
RD96 ST1 5c brt green .35 .20
RD98 ST1 10c brt green .75 .20
RD99 ST1 20c brt green 1.75 .25
RD100 ST1 25c brt green 1.75 .40
RD101 ST1 40c brt green 2.50 .75
RD102 ST1 50c brt green 3.75 .35
RD103 ST1 80c brt green 20.00 7.50
Nos. RD92-RD103 (10) 32.35 10.60

Size: 21½x36¼mm

RD104 ST2 $1 brt green 12.50 .20
RD105 ST2 $2 brt green 14.00 .25
RD106 ST2 $3 brt green 21.00 1.50
RD107 ST2 $4 brt green 37.50 6.50
RD108 ST2 $5 brt green 37.50 .60
RD109 ST2 $10 brt green 80.00 4.00
RD110 ST2 $20 brt green 150.00 55.00
Nos. RD104-RD110 (7) 352.50 68.05

Perf. 12

Without Gum

Size: 28½x42mm

RD111 ST3 $30 brt green 150.00 125.00
RD112 ST3 $50 brt green 240.00 175.00
RD113 ST3 $60 brt green 450.00 200.00
RD114 ST3 $100 brt green — 75.00
RD115 ST3 $500 brt green 875.00 *1,000.*
RD116 ST3 $1000 brt green — *1,100.*

Overprinted in Black "Series 1942"

1942 **Size: 19x22mm** *Perf. 11*

RD117 ST1 1c brt green .50 .30
RD118 ST1 2c brt green .40 .35
RD119 ST1 4c brt green 3.00 1.00
RD120 ST1 5c brt green .40 .20
a. Ovpt. inverted (cut cancel) *225.00*
RD121 ST1 10c brt green 1.75 .20
RD122 ST1 20c brt green 2.00 .20
RD123 ST1 25c brt green 2.00 .35
RD124 ST1 40c brt green 4.25 .35
RD125 ST1 50c brt green 5.25 .20
RD126 ST1 80c brt green 19.00 5.25
Nos. RD117-RD126 (10) 38.55 8.25

Size: 21½x36¼mm

RD127 ST2 $1 brt green 11.50 .35
RD128 ST2 $2 brt green 17.00 .35
RD129 ST2 $3 brt green 24.00 1.00
RD130 ST2 $4 brt green 37.50 17.50
RD131 ST2 $5 brt green 32.50 .35
a. Double overprint (perf. initials cancel) —
RD132 ST2 $10 brt green 62.50 7.50
RD133 ST2 $20 brt green 140.00 32.50
Nos. RD127-RD133 (7) 325.00 59.55

Perf. 12

Without Gum

Size: 28½x42mm

RD134 ST3 $30 brt green 100.00 45.00
RD135 ST3 $50 brt green 170.00 90.00
RD136 ST3 $60 brt green 200.00 150.00
RD137 ST3 $100 brt green 125.00 77.50
RD138 ST3 $500 brt green — *8,000.*
RD139 ST3 $1000 brt green — 500.00

Overprinted in Black "Series 1943"

1943 **Size: 19x22mm** *Perf. 11*

RD140 ST1 1c brt green .40 .25
RD141 ST1 2c brt green .50 .40
RD142 ST1 4c brt green 1.75 .20
RD143 ST1 5c brt green .50 .20
RD144 ST1 10c brt green 1.00 .20
RD145 ST1 20c brt green 1.75 .20
RD146 ST1 25c brt green 3.75 .25
RD147 ST1 40c brt green 3.75 .25
RD148 ST1 50c brt green 3.75 .20
RD149 ST1 80c brt green 14.00 4.50
Nos. RD140-RD149 (10) 31.15 6.65

Size: 21½x36¼mm

RD150 ST2 $1 brt green 14.00 .20
RD151 ST2 $2 brt green 16.00 .35
RD152 ST2 $3 brt green 19.00 1.00
RD153 ST2 $4 brt green 37.50 15.00
RD154 ST2 $5 brt green 52.50 .35
RD155 ST2 $10 brt green 75.00 4.50
RD156 ST2 $20 brt green 135.00 37.50
Nos. RD150-RD156 (7) 349.00 58.90

Perf. 12

Without Gum

Size: 28½x42mm

RD157 ST3 $30 brt green 220.00 100.00
RD158 ST3 $50 brt green 300.00 125.00
RD159 ST3 $60 brt green — 325.00
RD160 ST3 $100 brt green 75.00 50.00
RD161 ST3 $500 brt green — 425.00
RD162 ST3 $1000 brt green — 250.00

Overprinted in Black "Series 1944"

Portraits: $2,500, William Windom. $5,000, C. J. Folger. $10,000, Walter Q. Gresham.

1944 **Wmk. 191R** *Perf. 11*

Size: 19x22mm

RD163 ST1 1c brt green .65 .60
RD164 ST1 2c brt green .45 .20
RD165 ST1 4c brt green .60 .25
RD166 ST1 5c brt green .50 .20
RD167 ST1 10c brt green .75 .20
RD168 ST1 20c brt green 1.25 .20
RD169 ST1 25c brt green 2.00 .30
RD170 ST1 40c brt green 8.00 5.00
RD171 ST1 50c brt green 4.50 .20
RD172 ST1 80c brt green 7.50 4.50
Nos. RD163-RD172 (10) 26.20 11.65

Size: 21½x36¼mm

RD173 ST2 $1 brt green 8.00 .40
RD174 ST2 $2 brt green 32.50 .60
RD175 ST2 $3 brt green 30.00 1.25
RD176 ST2 $4 brt green 35.00 5.00
RD177 ST2 $5 brt green 32.50 .90
RD178 ST2 $10 brt green 65.00 4.50
RD179 ST2 $20 brt green 110.00 9.00
Nos. RD173-RD179 (7) 313.00 21.65

Perf. 12

Without Gum

Size: 28½x42mm

Bright Green

RD180 ST3 $30 135.00 60.00
RD181 ST3 $50 90.00 50.00
RD182 ST3 $60 160.00 110.00
RD183 ST3 $100 135.00 50.00
RD184 ST3 $500 — 425.00
RD185 ST3 $1000 (cut cancel) — 225.00
RD185A ST3 $2500 — —
RD185B ST3 $5000 — —
RD185C ST3 $10,000 (cut cancel) — *1,500.*

Overprinted in Black "Series 1945"

1945 **Wmk. 191R** *Perf. 11*

Size: 19x22mm

RD186 ST1 1c brt green .20 .20
RD187 ST1 2c brt green .25 .20
RD188 ST1 4c brt green .25 .20
RD189 ST1 5c brt green .25 .20
RD190 ST1 10c brt green .75 .35
RD191 ST1 20c brt green 1.25 .30
RD192 ST1 25c brt green 2.00 .35
RD193 ST1 40c brt green 3.00 .20
RD194 ST1 50c brt green 3.50 .25
RD195 ST1 80c brt green 6.50 2.50
Nos. RD186-RD195 (10) 17.95 4.75

Size: 21½x36¼mm

RD196 ST2 $1 brt green 14.00 .25
RD197 ST2 $2 brt green 19.00 .45
RD198 ST2 $3 brt green 32.50 .80
RD199 ST2 $4 brt green 32.50 2.50
RD200 ST2 $5 brt green 21.00 .50
RD201 ST2 $10 brt green 47.50 6.50
RD202 ST2 $20 brt green 75.00 10.00

Perf. 12

Without Gum

Size: 28½x42mm

Bright green

RD203 ST3 $30 95.00 60.00
RD204 ST3 $50 65.00 21.00
RD205 ST3 $60 160.00 125.00
RD206 ST3 $100 55.00 32.50
RD207 ST3 $500 — 500.00
RD208 ST3 $1000 — 550.00
RD208A ST3 $2500 — —
RD208B ST3 $5000 — —
RD208C ST3 $10,000 cut canc. — *1,500.*

Overprinted in Black "Series 1946"

1946 **Wmk. 191R** *Perf. 11*

Size: 19x22mm

RD209 ST1 1c brt green .20 .20
a. Pair, one dated "1945" *475.00*
RD210 ST1 2c brt green .35 .20
RD211 ST1 4c brt green .30 .20
RD212 ST1 5c brt green .35 .20
RD213 ST1 10c brt green .75 .20
RD214 ST1 20c brt green 1.50 .20
RD215 ST1 25c brt green 1.50 .25
RD216 ST1 40c brt green 3.50 .60
RD217 ST1 50c brt green 4.50 .20
RD218 ST1 80c brt green 9.50 6.00
Nos. RD209-RD218 (10) 22.45 8.25

Size: 21½x36¼mm

RD219 ST2 $1 brt green 8.50 .50
RD220 ST2 $2 brt green 9.50 .50
RD221 ST2 $3 brt green 19.00 1.25
RD222 ST2 $4 brt green 19.00 6.25
RD223 ST2 $5 brt green 27.50 1.10
RD224 ST2 $10 brt green 55.00 2.60
RD225 ST2 $20 brt green 87.50 42.50
Nos. RD219-RD225 (7) 226.00 54.70

Perf. 12

Without Gum

Size: 28½x42mm

RD226 ST3 $30 brt grn 77.50 35.00
RD227 ST3 $50 brt grn 60.00 40.00
RD228 ST3 $60 brt grn 140.00 82.50
RD229 ST3 $100 brt grn 85.00 42.50
RD230 ST3 $500 brt grn — 165.00
RD231 ST3 $1000 brt grn — 150.00
RD232 ST3 $2500 brt grn (cut cancel) — *5,750.*
RD233 ST3 $5000 brt grn — *5,500.*
RD234 ST3 $10,000 brt grn (cut cancel) — *2,000.*

Overprinted in Black "Series 1947"

1947 **Wmk. 191R** *Perf. 11*

Size: 19x22mm

RD235 ST1 1c brt green .65 .55
RD236 ST1 2c brt green .60 .50
RD237 ST1 4c brt green .50 .40
RD238 ST1 5c brt green .45 .35
RD239 ST1 10c brt green .60 .50
RD240 ST1 20c brt green 1.10 .50
RD241 ST1 25c brt green 1.75 .50
RD242 ST1 40c brt green 3.00 .75
RD243 ST1 50c brt green 4.00 .30
RD244 ST1 80c brt green 15.00 10.00
Nos. RD235-RD244 (10) 27.65 14.35

Size: 21½x36¼mm

RD245 ST2 $1 brt green 8.00 .50
RD246 ST2 $2 brt green 14.00 .75
RD247 ST2 $3 brt green 22.50 1.50
RD248 ST2 $4 brt green 35.00 6.00
RD249 ST2 $5 brt green 30.00 1.50
RD250 ST2 $10 brt green 47.50 5.00
RD251 ST2 $20 brt green 90.00 30.00
Nos. RD245-RD251 (7) 247.00 45.25

Perf. 12

Without Gum

Size: 28½x42mm

RD252 ST3 $30 brt grn 65.00 40.00
RD253 ST3 $50 brt grn 135.00 82.50
RD254 ST3 $60 brt grn 165.00 125.00
RD255 ST3 $100 brt grn 75.00 35.00
RD256 ST3 $500 brt grn — 250.00
RD257 ST3 $1000 brt grn — 85.00
RD258 ST3 $2500 brt grn (cut canc.) — *350.00*
RD259 ST3 $5000 brt grn (cut canc.) — *300.00*
RD260 ST3 $10,000 brt grn (cut canc.) — 55.00
a. Horiz. pair, imperf. vert. (cut canc.) —

Overprinted in Black "Series 1948"

1948 **Wmk. 191R** *Perf. 11*

Size: 19x22mm

RD261 ST1 1c brt green .25 .25
RD262 ST1 2c brt green .25 .25
RD263 ST1 4c brt green .30 .30
RD264 ST1 5c brt green .25 .24
RD265 ST1 10c brt green .30 .25
RD266 ST1 20c brt green 1.40 .35
RD267 ST1 25c brt green 1.40 .40
RD268 ST1 40c brt green 1.75 .35
RD269 ST1 50c brt green 4.25 .30
RD270 ST1 80c brt green 12.50 6.00
Nos. RD261-RD270 (10) 22.65 9.09

Size: 21½x36¼mm

RD271 ST2 $1 brt green 9.00 .40
RD272 ST2 $2 brt green 14.50 .60
RD273 ST2 $3 brt green 16.00 3.75
RD274 ST2 $4 brt green 19.00 11.00
RD275 ST2 $5 brt green 27.50 2.50
RD276 ST2 $10 brt green 47.50 4.50
RD277 ST2 $20 brt green 80.00 18.00
Nos. RD271-RD277 (7) 213.50 40.75

Perf. 12

Without Gum

Size: 28½x42mm

RD278 ST3 $30 brt grn 100.00 42.50
RD279 ST3 $50 brt grn 65.00 42.50
RD280 ST3 $60 brt grn 165.00 110.00
RD281 ST3 $100 brt grn 55.00 17.50
RD282 ST3 $500 brt grn — 210.00
RD283 ST3 $1000 brt grn — 100.00
RD284 ST3 $2500 brt grn 300.00 275.00
RD285 ST3 $5000 brt grn — 250.00
RD286 ST3 $10,000 brt grn (cut canc.) — 55.00

Overprinted in Black "Series 1949"

1949 Wmk. 191R *Perf. 11*

Size: 19x22mm

RD287	ST1	1c	brt green	.50	.45
RD288	ST1	2c	brt green	.50	.45
RD289	ST1	4c	brt green	.60	.50
RD290	ST1	5c	brt green	.60	.50
RD291	ST1	10c	brt green	1.30	.60
RD292	ST1	20c	brt green	2.10	.50
RD293	ST1	25c	brt green	3.00	.85
RD294	ST1	40c	brt green	5.50	1.50
RD295	ST1	50c	brt green	5.00	.25
RD296	ST1	80c	brt green	12.50	6.50
	Nos. RD287-RD296 (10)			31.60	12.10

Size: 21½x36¼mm

RD297	ST2	$1	brt green	11.00	.75
RD298	ST2	$2	brt green	16.50	.90
RD299	ST2	$3	brt green	35.00	4.50
RD300	ST2	$4	brt green	32.50	7.50
RD301	ST2	$5	brt green	42.50	2.00
RD302	ST2	$10	brt green	55.00	4.00
RD303	ST2	$20	brt green	125.00	15.00
	Nos. RD297-RD303 (7)			317.50	34.65

Perf. 12

Without Gum

Size: 28½x42mm

RD304	ST3	$30	brt grn	110.00	65.00
RD305	ST3	$50	brt grn	150.00	75.00
RD306	ST3	$60	brt grn	175.00	160.00
RD307	ST3	$100	brt grn	90.00	57.50
RD308	ST3	$500	brt grn	—	210.00
RD309	ST3	$1000	brt grn	—	85.00
RD310	ST3	$2500	brt grn (cut canc.)	—	*450.00*
RD311	ST3	$5000	brt grn (cut canc.)	—	*400.00*
RD312	ST3	$10,000	brt grn	—	300.00
a.			Pair, one without ovpt. (cut cancel)		—

Overprinted in Black "Series 1950"

1950 Wmk. 191R *Perf. 11*

Size: 19x22mm

RD313	ST1	1c	brt green	.40	.35
RD314	ST1	2c	brt green	.40	.30
RD315	ST1	4c	brt green	.40	.35
RD316	ST1	5c	brt green	.40	.20
RD317	ST1	10c	brt green	2.00	.30
RD318	ST1	20c	brt green	3.00	.50
RD319	ST1	25c	brt green	4.25	.60
RD320	ST1	40c	brt green	5.00	.90
RD321	ST1	50c	brt green	8.25	.35
RD322	ST1	80c	brt green	11.00	5.00
	Nos. RD313-RD322 (10)			35.10	8.85

Size: 21½x36¼mm

RD323	ST2	$1	brt green	11.00	.40
RD324	ST2	$2	brt green	19.00	.75
RD325	ST2	$3	brt green	30.00	4.00
RD326	ST2	$4	brt green	32.50	9.00
RD327	ST2	$5	brt green	37.50	1.75
RD328	ST2	$10	brt green	87.50	5.00
RD329	ST2	$20	brt green	125.00	25.00
	Nos. RD323-RD329 (7)			342.50	45.90

Perf. 12

Without Gum

Size: 28½x42mm

RD330	ST3	$30	brt grn	90.00	60.00
RD331	ST3	$50	brt grn	80.00	70.00
RD332	ST3	$60	brt grn	175.00	110.00
RD333	ST3	$100	brt grn	65.00	35.00
a.			Vert. pair, Imperf betwn.		—
RD334	ST3	$500	brt grn	—	175.00
RD335	ST3	$1000	brt grn	—	75.00
RD336	ST3	$2500	brt grn	—	*1,100.*
RD337	ST3	$5000	brt grn	—	650.00
RD338	ST3	$10,000	brt grn	—	450.00

Overprinted in Black "Series 1951"

1951 Wmk. 191R *Perf. 11*

Size: 19x22mm

RD339	ST1	1c	brt green	1.10	.35
RD340	ST1	2c	brt green	1.10	.30
RD341	ST1	4c	brt green	1.50	.50
RD342	ST1	5c	brt green	1.10	.35
RD343	ST1	10c	brt green	1.50	.30
RD344	ST1	20c	brt green	3.75	.90
RD345	ST1	25c	brt green	5.00	.90
RD346	ST1	40c	brt green	14.00	9.00
RD347	ST1	50c	brt green	9.00	.90
RD348	ST1	80c	brt green	16.50	10.00
	Nos. RD339-RD348 (10)			54.55	23.50

Size: 21½x36¼mm

RD349	ST2	$1	brt green	19.00	.80
RD350	ST2	$2	brt green	27.50	1.25
RD351	ST2	$3	brt green	37.50	10.00
RD352	ST2	$4	brt green	42.50	12.00
RD353	ST2	$5	brt green	52.50	2.50
RD354	ST2	$10	brt green	85.00	8.50
RD355	ST2	$20	brt green	140.00	17.50
	Nos. RD349-RD355 (7)			404.00	52.55

Perf. 12

Without Gum

Size: 28½x42mm

RD356	ST3	$30	brt grn	110.00	60.00
RD357	ST3	$50	brt grn	100.00	50.00
RD358	ST3	$60	brt grn	—	*600.00*
RD359	ST3	$100	brt grn	100.00	55.00
RD360	ST3	$500	brt grn	—	175.00
RD361	ST3	$1000	brt grn	—	82.50
RD362	ST3	$2500	brt grn	—	*1,100.*
RD363	ST3	$5000	brt grn	—	*1,250.*
RD364	ST3	$10,000	brt grn	—	120.00

Overprinted in Black "Series 1952"

1952 Wmk. 191R *Perf. 11*

Size: 19x22mm

RD365	ST1	1c	brt green	30.00	15.00
RD366	ST1	10c	brt green	30.00	15.00
RD367	ST1	20c	brt green	350.00	—
RD368	ST1	25c	brt green	450.00	—
RD369	ST1	40c	brt green	90.00	35.00

Size: 21½x36¼mm

RD370	ST2	$4	brt green	1,100.	550.
RD371	ST2	$10	brt green	*2,000.*	—
RD372	ST2	$20	brt green	*3,250.*	—

Stock Transfer stamps were discontinued in 1952.

See the Scott United States Specialized Catalogue for other categories of Revenue stamps.

HUNTING PERMIT STAMPS

The receipts of the sales of these "Migratory Bird Hunting" stamps help to maintain waterfowl life in the United States.

See the Scott United States Specialized Catalogue for other categories of Revenue stamps. Catalogue values for unused stamps in this section are for Never Hinged items.

Department of Agriculture

Used Values

Used value for No. RW1 is for stamp with handstamp or manuscript cancel, though technically it was illegal to deface the stamp. Beginning with No. RW2, the used value is for stamps with manuscript signature.

HP1

Various Designs
Inscribed "U. S. Department of Agriculture"

Engraved; Flat Plate Printing

1934 Unwmk. *Perf. 11*

"Void after June 30, 1935"

RW1	HP1 $1 blue		700.00	125.00
	Hinged		350.00	
	No gum		160.00	
a.	Imperf., pair		—	
b.	Vert. pair, imperf. horiz.		—	

1935 "Void after June 30, 1936"

RW2	$1 *Canvasback Ducks Taking to Flight*	650.00	130.00
	Hinged	375.00	
	No gum	175.00	

1936 "Void after June 30, 1937"

RW3	$1 *Canada Geese in Flight*	325.00	72.50
	Hinged	190.00	
	No gum	95.00	

1937 "Void after June 30, 1938"

RW4	$1 *Scaup Ducks Taking to Flight*	275.00	57.50
	Hinged	150.00	
	No gum	75.00	

1938 "Void after June 30, 1939"

RW5	$1 *Pintail Drake and Duck Alighting*	350.00	57.50
	Hinged	190.00	
	No gum	75.00	

Department of the Interior

Green-Winged Teal — HP2

Various Designs
Inscribed: "U. S. Department of the Interior"

1939 "Void after June 30, 1940"

RW6	HP2 $1 chocolate	200.00	45.00
	Hinged	110.00	
	No gum	50.00	

1940 "Void after June 30, 1941"

RW7	$1 *Black Mallards*	200.00	45.00
	Hinged	110.00	
	No gum	50.00	

1941 "Void after June 30, 1942"

RW8	$1 *Family of Ruddy Ducks*	200.00	45.00
	Hinged	110.00	
	No gum	50.00	

1942 "Void after June 30, 1943"

RW9	$1 *Baldpates*	200.00	45.00
	Hinged	110.00	
	No gum	50.00	

1943 "Void after June 30, 1944"

RW10	$1 *Wood Ducks*	75.00	40.00
	Hinged	50.00	
	No gum	42.50	

1944 "Void after June 30, 1945"

RW11	$1 *White-fronted Geese*	87.50	27.50
	Hinged	50.00	
	No gum	32.50	

1945 "Void after June 30, 1946"

RW12	$1 *Shoveller Ducks in Flight*	60.00	25.00
	Hinged	35.00	
	No gum	27.50	

1946 "Void after June 30, 1947"

RW13	$1 *Redhead Ducks*	45.00	14.00
	No gum	18.00	
a.	$1 bright rose pink		—

1947 "Void after June 30, 1948"

RW14	$1 *Snow Geese*	45.00	14.00
	No gum	18.00	

1948 "Void after June 30, 1949"

RW15	$1 *Bufflehead Ducks in Flight*	50.00	14.00
	No gum	21.00	

Goldeneye Ducks
HP3

1949 "Void after June 30, 1950"

RW16	HP3 $2 bright green	60.00	14.00
	No gum	22.50	

1950 "Void after June 30, 1951"

RW17	$2 *Trumpeter Swans in Flight*	72.50	11.00
	No gum	25.00	

1951 "Void after June 30, 1952"

RW18	$2 *Gadwall Ducks*	72.50	11.00
	No gum	25.00	

1952 "Void after June 30, 1953"

RW19	$2 *Harlequin Ducks*	72.50	11.00
	No gum	25.00	

1953 "Void after June 30, 1954"

RW20	$2 *Blue-winged Teal*	75.00	10.00
	No gum	25.00	

1954 "Void after June 30, 1955"
RW21 $2 *Ring-necked Ducks* 75.00 9.50
No gum 25.00

1955 "Void after June 30, 1956"
RW22 $2 *Blue Geese* 75.00 9.50
No gum 25.00

1956 "Void after June 30, 1957"
RW23 $2 *American Merganser* 75.00 9.50
No gum 25.00

1957 "Void after June 30, 1958"
RW24 $2 *American Eiders* 75.00 9.50
No gum 25.00
a. Back inscription inverted —

1958 "Void after June 30, 1959"
RW25 $2 *Canada Geese* 72.50 9.00
No gum 25.00

Labrador Retriever Carrying Mallard Drake HP4

1959 Giori Press Printing
"Void after June 30, 1960"
RW26 HP4 $3 blue, ocher & blk 92.50 9.50
No gum 35.00
a. Back inscription inverted —

Redhead Ducks HP5

1960 "Void after June 30, 1961"
RW27 HP5 $3 red brn, dk bl & bister 80.00 9.50
No gum 35.00

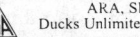

1961 "Void after June 30, 1962"
RW28 $3 *Mallard Hen and Ducklings* 82.50 9.50
No gum 37.50

Pintail Drakes Coming in for Landing HP6

1962 "Void after June 30, 1963"
RW29 HP6 $3 dk bl, dk red brn & black 95.00 10.50
No gum 55.00

1963 "Void after June 30, 1964"
RW30 $3 *Pair of Brant landing* 95.00 10.50
No gum 55.00

1964 "Void after June 30, 1965"
RW31 $3 *Hawaiian Nene Geese* 95.00 10.50
No gum 55.00

1965 "Void after June 30, 1966"
RW32 $3 *3 Canvasback Drakes* 92.50 10.00
No gum 55.00

Whistling Swans HP7

1966 "Void after June 30, 1967"
RW33 HP7 $3 ultra, sl grn & blk 92.50 10.50
No gum 50.00

1967 "Void after June 30, 1968"
RW34 $3 *Old Squaw Ducks* 100.00 10.00
No gum 50.00

1968 "Void after June 30, 1969"
RW35 $3 *Hooded Mergansers* 57.50 9.00
No gum 25.00

MIGRATORY BIRD HUNTING STAMP
White-winged Scoters — HP8

1969 "Void after June 30, 1970"
RW36 HP8 $3 gray, brn, indigo & brn red 57.50 7.00
No gum 25.00

1970 Litho. & Engr.
"Void after June 30, 1971"
RW37 $3 *Ross' Geese* 57.50 7.00
No gum 22.50

1971 "Void after June 30, 1972"
RW38 $3 *3 Cinnamon Teal* 40.00 7.00
No gum 21.00

1972 "Void after June 30, 1973"
RW39 $5 *Emperor Geese* 25.00 7.00
No gum 12.50

1973 "Void after June 30, 1974"
RW40 $5 *Steller's Eiders* 21.00 7.00
No gum 12.00

1974 "Void after June 30, 1975"
RW41 $5 *Wood Ducks* 20.00 6.00
No gum 9.50

1975 "Void after June 30, 1976"
RW42 $5 *Weathered canvasback duck decoy and flying ducks* 15.00 6.00
No gum 8.00

1976 Engr.
"Void after June 30, 1977"
RW43 $5 *Family of Canada Geese* 14.00 6.00
No gum 7.50

1977 Engr. & Litho.
"Void after June 30, 1978"
RW44 $5 *Ross' Geese, pair* 15.00 6.00
No gum 7.50

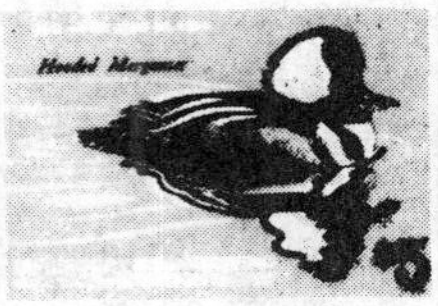

Hooded Merganser HP9

1978 "Void after June 30, 1979"
RW45 HP9 $5 multicolored 12.50 6.00
No gum 7.50

1979 "Void after June 30, 1980"
RW46 $7.50 *Green-winged teal* 14.00 6.00
No gum 8.00

1980 "Void after June 30, 1981"
RW47 $7.50 *Mallards* 14.00 6.00
No gum 8.00

1981 "Void after June 30, 1982"
RW48 $7.50 *Ruddy Ducks* 14.00 6.00
No gum 8.00

1982 "Void after June 30, 1983"
RW49 $7.50 *Canvasbacks* 15.00 6.00
No gum 8.00
a. Orange & violet omitted —

1983 "Void after June 30, 1984"
RW50 $7.50 *Pintails* 15.00 6.00
No gum 8.00

1984 "Void after June 30, 1985"
RW51 $7.50 *Widgeons* 15.00 6.00
No gum 8.00

1985 "Void after June 30, 1986"
RW52 $7.50 *Cinnamon Teal* 14.00 6.00
No gum 8.00

1986 "Void after June 30, 1987"
RW53 $7.50 *Fulvous Whistling Duck* 15.00 6.00
No gum 8.00
a. Black omitted *3,750.*

1987 *Perf. 11½x11*
"Void after June 30, 1988"
RW54 $10 *Redheads* 15.00 9.00
No gum 10.00

1988 "Void after June 30, 1989"
RW55 $10 *Snow Goose* 16.00 9.00
No gum 10.00

1989 "Void after June 30, 1990"
RW56 $12.50 *Lesser Scaups* 19.00 10.00
No gum 12.00

1990 "Void after June 30, 1991"
RW57 $12.50 *Black Bellied Whistling Duck* 19.00 10.00
No gum 12.00
a. Back inscription omitted *425.00*

The back inscription is on top of the gum so beware of copies with gum removed. Used examples of No. RW57a cannot exist.

King Eiders — HP10

1991 "Void after June 30, 1992"
RW58 HP10 $15 multicolored 22.50 11.00
No gum 15.00
a. Black (engr.) omitted 8,500.

1992 "Void after June 30, 1993"
RW59 $15 *Spectacled Eider* 22.50 11.00
No gum 15.00

1993 "Void after June 30, 1994"
RW60 $15 *Canvasbacks* 22.50 11.00
No gum 15.00
a. Black (engr.) omitted 3,250.

1994 "Void after June 30, 1995"
RW61 $15 *Red-breasted mergansers* 22.50 11.00
No gum 15.00

1995 "Void after June 30, 1996"
RW62 $15 *Mallards* 22.50 11.00
No gum 15.00

1996 "Void after June 30, 1997"
RW63 $15 *Surf Scoters* 22.50 11.00
No gum 15.00

1997 "Void after June 30, 1998"
RW64 $15 *Canada Goose* 22.50 11.00
No gum 15.00

1998 "Void after June 30, 1999"
RW65 $15 *Barrow's Goldeneye* 22.50 11.00
No gum 15.00

Self-Adhesive
Serpentine Die Cut
RW65A $15 *Barrow's Goldeneye* 22.50 11.00

#RW65 was sold in panes of 30, #RW65A in panes of 1.

1999 "Void after June 30, 2000"
RW66 $15 *Greater Scaup* 22.50 11.00
No gum 15.00

Self-Adhesive
Die Cut 10
RW66A $15 *Greater Scaup* 22.50 11.00

See footnote following No. RW65A.

CONFEDERATE STATES

3c 1861 POSTMASTERS' PROVISIONALS

With the secession of South Carolina from the Union on Dec. 20, 1860, a new era began in U.S. history as well as its postal history. Other Southern states quickly followed South Carolina's lead, which in turn led to the formation of the provisional government of the Confederate States of America on Feb. 4, 1861.

President Jefferson Davis' cabinet was completed Mar. 6, 1861, with the acceptance of the position of Postmaster General by John H. Reagan of Texas. The provisional government had already passed regulations that required payment for postage in cash and that effectively carried over the U.S. 3c rate until the new Confederate Post Office Department took over control of the system.

Soon after entering on his duties, Reagan directed the postmasters in the Confederate States and in the newly seceded states to "continue the performance of their duties as such, and render all accounts and pay all moneys (sic) to the order of the Government of the U.S. as they have heretofore done, until the Government of the Confederate States shall be prepared to assume control of its postal affairs."

As coinage was becoming scarce, postal patrons began having problems buying individual stamps or paying for letters individually, especially as stamp stocks started to run short in certain areas. Even though the U.S. Post Office Department was technically in control of the postal system and southern postmasters were operating under Federal authority, the U.S.P.O. was hesitant in re-supplying seceded states with additional stamps and stamped envelopes.

The U.S. government had made the issuance of postmasters' provisionals illegal many years before, but the southern postmasters had to do what they felt was necessary to allow patrons to pay for postage and make the system work. Therefore, a few postmasters took it upon themselves to issue provisional stamps in the 3c rate then in effect. Interestingly, these were stamps and envelopes that the U.S. government did not recognize as legal, but they did do postal duty unchallenged in the Confederate States. Yet the proceeds were to be remitted to the U.S. government in Washington! Six authenticated postmasters' provisionals in the 3c rate have been recorded.

On May 13, 1861, Postmaster General Reagan issued his proclamation "assuming control and direction of postal service within the limits of the Confederate States of America on and after the first day of June," with new postage rates and regulations. The Federal government suspended operations in the Confederate States (except for western Virginia and the seceding state of Tennessee) by a proclamation issued by Postmaster General Montgomery Blair on May 27, 1861, effective from May 31, 1861, and June 10 for western and middle Tennessee. As Tennessee did not join the Confederacy until July 2, 1861, the unissued 3c Nashville provisional was produced in a state that was in the process of seceding, while the other provisionals were used in the Confederacy before the June 1 assumption of control of postal service by the Confederate States of America.

Illustrations in this section are reduced in size.

XU numbers are envelope entires.

HILLSBORO, N.C.

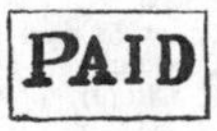

A1

Handstamped Adhesive

1AX1	A1	3c bluish black, on cover	—

This is the same handstamp as used for No. 39X1. 3c usage is determined from the May 27, 1861 circular date stamp.

See Nos. 39X1, 39XU1.

JACKSON, MISS.

E1

Handstamped Envelope

2AXU1	E1	3c black	—

See Nos. 43XU1-43XU4.

MADISON COURT HOUSE, FLA.

A1

"CNETS"

Typeset Adhesive

3AX1	A1	3c bronze	—	—
a.		"CNETS"		—

See No. 137XU1.

NASHVILLE, TENN.

A1

Typeset Adhesive (5 varieties)

4AX1	A1	3c carmine	150.

No. 4AX1 was prepared by Postmaster McNish with the U.S. rate, but the stamp was never issued.

See Nos. 61X2-61XU2.

SELMA, ALA.

E1

Handstamped Envelope

5AXU1	E1	3c black	—

See Nos. 77XU1-77XU3.

TUSCUMBIA, ALA.

E1

Handstamped Envelope

Impression at upper right

6AXU1	E1	3c dull red, *buff*	*17,500.*

See Nos. 84XU1-84XU3.

PROVISIONAL ISSUES

These stamps and envelopes were issued by individual postmasters generally during the interim between June 1, 1861, when the use of U.S. stamps stopped in the Confederacy, and Oct. 16, 1861, when the 1st Confederate Government stamps were issued. They were occasionally issued at later periods, especially in Texas, when regular issues of Government stamps were unavailable.

Canceling stamps of the post offices were often used to produce envelopes, some of which were supplied in advance by private citizens. These envelopes and other stationery therefore may be found in a wide variety of papers, colors, sizes and shapes, including patriotic and semi-official types. It is often difficult to determine whether the impression made by the canceling stamp indicates provisional usage or merely postage paid at the time the letter was deposited in the post office. Occasionally the same mark was used for both purposes.

The *press-printed* provisional envelopes are in a different category. They were produced in quantity, using envelopes procured in advance by the postmaster, such as those of Charleston, Lynchburg, Memphis, etc. *The press-printed envelopes are listed and valued on all known papers.*

The handstamped provisional envelopes are listed and valued according to type and variety of handstamp, but not according to paper. Many exist on such a variety of papers that they defy accurate, complete listing. The value of a handstamped provisional envelope is determined *primarily* by the clarity of the markings and its overall condition and attractiveness, rather than the type of paper. *All handstamped provisional envelopes, when used, should also show the postmark of the town of issue.*

Most handstamps are impressed at top right, although they exist from some towns in other positions.

Illustrations in this section are reduced in size.

XU numbers are envelope entires.

E1

E1a

ABERDEEN, MISS.

Handstamped Envelopes

1XU1	E1	5c black	2,500.	
1XU2	E1	10c (ms.) on 5c black		—

ABINGDON, VA.

Handstamped Envelopes

2XU1	E1a	2c black		*11,000.*
2XU2	E1a	5c black		1,000.
2XU3	E1a	10c black	*2,200.*	*3,500.*

No. 2XU1 is unique. The unused No. 2XU3 is a unique mint example.

ALBANY, GA.

E1

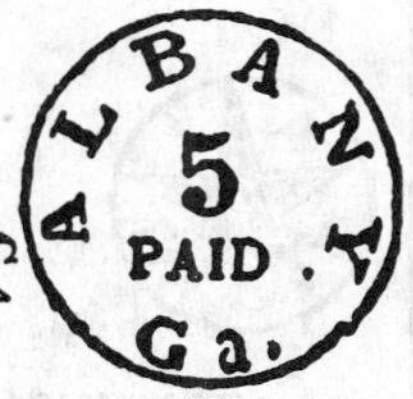

E2

Handstamped Envelopes

3XU1	E1	5c greenish blue		700.
3XU2	E1	10c greenish blue		*2,000.*
3XU3	E1	10c on 5c grnsh blue		*2,500.*
3XU5	E2	5c greenish blue		—
3XU6	E2	10c greenish blue		*2,250.*

E1

Two varieties — A1

ANDERSON COURT HOUSE, S.C.

Handstamped Envelopes

4XU1	E1	5c black	1,500.
4XU2	E1	10c (ms.) black	*2,500.*

ATHENS, GA.

Typographed Adhesives

5X1	A1	5c purple (shades)	900.	1,100.
a.		Vertical tete beche pair		*4,000.*
5X2	A1	5c red	—	3,000.

ATLANTA, GA.

E1

E2

E3

Handstamped Adhesives

6XU1	E1	5c red		3,500.
6XU2	E1	5c black	175.	600.
6XU3	E1	10c on 5c black		1,500.
6XU4	E2	2c black		*5,000.*
6XU5	E2	5c black		1,500.
6XU6	E2	10c black		850.
6XU7	E2	10c on 5c black		2,500.
6XU8	E3	5c black		3,500.
6XU9	E3	10c blk ("10" upright)		2,750.

AUGUSTA, GA.

E1

Handstamped Envelope

7XU1	E1	5c black	

Provisional status questioned.

E1

E1a

AUSTIN, MISS.

Typeset Envelope

8XU1	E1	5c red, *amber*	*75,000.*

No. 8XU1 is unique.

AUSTIN, TEX.

Handstamped Adhesive

9X1	E1a	10c black	—

Handstamped Envelope

9XU1	E1a	10c black	1,500.

AUTAUGAVILLE, ALA.

E1

E2

Handstamped Envelopes

10XU1	E1	5c black	*8,000.*
10XU2	E2	5c black	*12,000.*

BALCONY FALLS, VA.

E1

Handstamped Envelope

122XU1 E1 5c black —

BARNWELL COURT HOUSE, S.C.

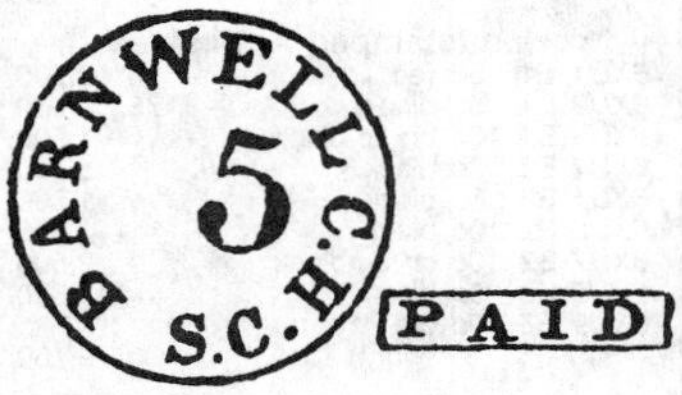

E1

Handstamped Envelope

123XU1 E1 5c black —

These are two separate handstamps.

BATON ROUGE, LA.

A1

A2

A3

A4

Ten varieties each of A1, A2 and A3

Typeset Adhesives

11X1	A1 2c green		*5,000.*	*3,750.*
a.	"McCcrmick"		*10,000.*	*8,500.*
11X2	A2 5c green & car		1,250.	1,100.
a.	"McCcrmick"		—	*2,000.*
11X3	A3 5c green & car		*4,500.*	*1,750.*
a.	"McCcrmick"			*3,250.*
11X4	A4 10c blue			*6,000.*

BEAUMONT, TEX.

A1

A2

Several varieties of A1

Typeset Adhesives

12X1	A1 10c black, *yellow*	*4,500.*
12X2	A1 10c black, *pink*	*12,500.*
12X3	A2 10c blk, *yel*, on cover	*90,000.*

E1

A1

BLUFFTON, S.C.

Handstamped Envelope

124XU1 E1 5c black —

BRIDGEVILLE, ALA.

Handstamped Adhesive

13X1 A1 5c black & red *20,000.*

CAMDEN, S.C.

E1

E2

Handstamped Envelopes

125XU1 E1 5c black —
125XU2 E2 10c black —

No. 125XU2 unused was privately carried and is addressed but has no postal markings. No. 125XU2 is indistinguishable from a handstamp paid cover when used.

CANTON, MISS.

E1

Handstamped Envelopes

14XU1	E1 5c black	2,250.
14XU2	E1 10c (ms.) on 5c black	5,000.

CAROLINA CITY, N.C.

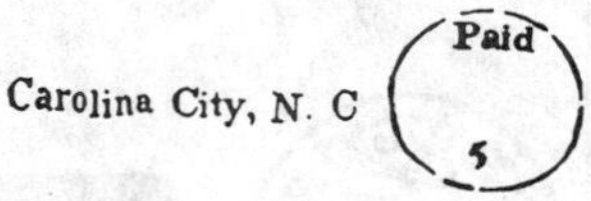

E1

Handstamped Envelope

118XU1 E1 5c black *3,500.*

CARTERSVILLE, GA.

E1

Handstamped Envelope

126XU1 E1 (5c) red —

CHAPEL HILL, N.C.

E1

Handstamped Envelope

15XU1 E1 5c black 2,500.

CHARLESTON, S.C.

A1

E1

E2

Lithographed Adhesive

16X1 A1 5c blue 900. 750.

Typographed from Woodcut Envelopes

16XU1	E1 5c blue	1,100.	*3,500.*
16XU2	E1 5c blue, *amber*	1,100.	*3,500.*
16XU3	E1 5c blue, *orange*	1,100.	*3,500.*
16XU4	E1 5c blue, *buff*	1,100.	*3,500.*
16XU5	E1 5c blue, *blue*	1,100.	*3,500.*
16XU6	E2 10c blue, *orange*		*77,500.*

Handstamped Envelope

16XU7 E2 10c black *3,000.*

The No. 16XU6 entire is unique. There is also only one copy known of No. 16XU7. It is a cut-out, not an entire. It may not have been mailed from Charleston and may not have paid postage.

CHARLOTTESVILLE, VA.

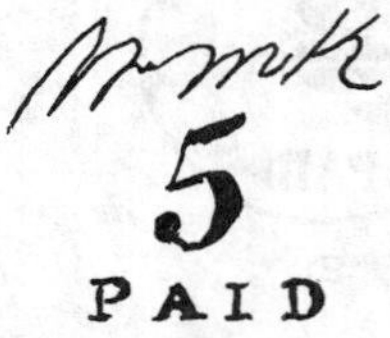

E1

Handstamped Envelopes Manuscript Initials

127XU1 E1 5c blue —
127XU2 E1 10c blue —

CHATTANOOGA, TENN.

E1

Handstamped Envelopes

17XU2	E1 5c black		1,600.
17XU3	E1 5c on 2c black	*3,250.*	

CHRISTIANSBURG, VA.

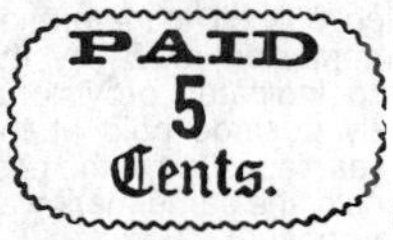

E1

Typeset Envelopes

Impressed at top right

99XU1	E1 5c black, *blue*	*2,000.*
99XU2	E1 5c blue	*1,400.*
99XU3	E1 5c black, *orange*	*2,000.*
99XU4	E1 5c green, on US envelope #U27	*4,500.*
99XU5	E1 10c blue	*3,500.*

COLAPARCHEE, GA.

E1

Control

Handstamped Envelope

119XU1 E1 5c black *3,500.*

COLUMBIA, S.C.

E1

E2

Handstamped Envelopes

18XU1	E1 5c blue	500.	*900.*
18XU2	E1 5c black	600.	*900.*
18XU3	E1 10c on 5c blue		*3,500.*
18XU4	E2 5c blue (seal on front)		*2,500.*
a.	Seal on back		*1,000.*
18XU5	E2 10c blue (seal on back)		*2,750.*

Circular Seal similar to E2, 27mm diameter

18XU6 E2 5c blue (seal on back) *4,000.*

E1

E1a

COLUMBIA, TENN.

Handstamped Envelope

113XU1 E1 5c red *3,500.*

COLUMBUS, GA.

Handstamped Envelopes

19XU1	E1a 5c blue	700.
19XU2	E1a 10c red	*2,250.*

E1

E1a

COURTLAND, ALA.

Handstamped Envelopes from Woodcut

103XU1 E1 5c black —
103XU2 E1 5c red *10,000.*

Provisional status of No. 103XU1 questioned.

DALTON, GA.

Handstamped Envelopes

20XU1 E1a 5c black 500.
  a. Denomination omitted (5c rate) 650.
20XU2 E1a 10c black 700.
20XU3 E1a 10c (ms.) on 5c black 1,500.

DANVILLE, VA.

A1

Design measures 60x37mm — E1

E2

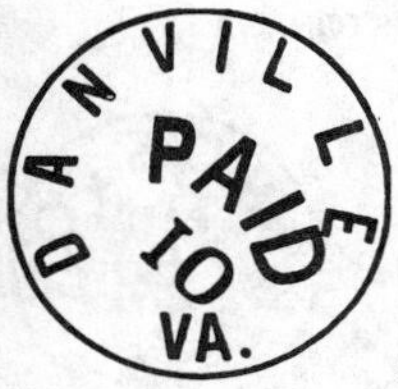

E3

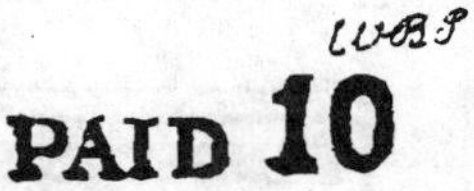

E4

Typeset Adhesives

21X1 A1 5c red, wove paper 5,500.
21X2 A1 5c red, laid paper 6,500.

Typographed Envelopes

Two types: "SOUTHERN" in straight or curved line.

21XU1 E1 5c black 5,500.
21XU2 E1 5c black, *amber* 5,500.
21XU3 E1 5c black, *dark buff* 5,250.

An unissued 10c envelope (type E1, in red) is known. All recorded examples are envelopes on which added stamps paid the postage.

Handstamped Envelopes

21XU3A E4 5c black (ms "WBP") —
21XU4 E2 10c black 2,000.
21XU5 E2 10c blue
21XU6 E3 10c black 2,750.
21XU7 E4 10c black (ms "WBP") —

The existence of No. 21XU5 has been questioned.

DEMOPOLIS, ALA.

E1

Handstamped Envelopes
Ms Signature

22XU1 E1 5c black ("Jno. Y. Hall") 2,000.
22XU2 E1 5c black ("J. Y. Hall") 2,000.
22XU3 E1 5c (ms.) blk ("J. Y. Hall") 2,500.

EATONTON, GA.

E1

Handstamped Envelopes

23XU1 E1 5c black 3,000.
23XU2 E1 5c + 5c black 1,250.

EMORY, VA.

A1

E1

E2

Handstamped Adhesive

On sheet selvage of US 1857 1c stamps

Perf. 15 on Three Sides

24X1 A1 5c blue 3,500.

No. 24X1 exists with "5" above or below "PAID."

Handstamped Envelopes

24XU1 E1 5c blue 2,000.
24XU2 E2 10c blue 4,400.

E1

E1a

FINCASTLE, VA.

Typeset Envelope

104XU1 E1 10c black 20,000.

No. 104XU1 is unique.

FORSYTH, GA.

Handstamped Envelope

120XU1 E1a 10c black 1,350.

FRANKLIN, N.C.

E1

E1a

Typeset Envelope

25XU1 E1 5c blue, *buff* 30,000.

No. 25XU1 is unique.

FRAZIERSVILLE, S.C.

Handstamped Envelope
Manuscript "5"

128XU1 E1a 5c black —

FREDERICKSBURG, VA.

A1

Typeset Adhesives

Ten varieties

Thin Bluish Paper

26X1 A1 5c blue, *bluish* 250. 750.
26X2 A1 10c red (shades), *bluish* 900.

GAINESVILLE, ALA.

E1

E2

Handstamped Envelopes

27XU1 E1 5c black 5,000.
27XU2 E2 10c black 6,000.

GALVESTON, TEX.

E1

E2

Handstamped Envelopes

98XU1 E1 5c black 500. 1,500.
98XU2 E1 10c black 1,750.
98XU3 E2 10c black 550. 2,400.
98XU4 E2 20c black 3,500.

GASTON, N.C.

E1

Handstamped Envelope

129XU1 E1 5c black —

GEORGETOWN, S.C.

E1

Control

Handstamped Envelope

28XU1 E1 5c black 800.

GOLIAD, TEX.

A1

A2

Typeset Adhesives

Several varieties of A1 and A2

29X1 A1 5c black 5,000.
29X2 A1 5c black, *gray* 4,500.
29X3 A1 5c black, *rose* 5,000.
29X4 A1 10c black — 5,000.
29X5 A1 10c black, *rose* 5,000.

Type A1 stamps bear ms. control: "Clarke P.M."

29X6 A2 5c black, *gray* 7,000.
  a. "Goilad" 8,000.
29X7 A2 10c black, *gray* 5,000.
  a. "Goilad" 5,500.
29X8 A2 5c black, *dark blue* —
29X9 A2 10c black, *dark blue* —

GONZALES, TEX.

A1

Typographed Adhesives

30X1 A1 (5c) gold, *dark blue* 7,500.
30X2 A1 (10c) gold, *garnet*, on cover, *1864* —
30X3 A1 (10c) gold, *black*, on cover, *1865* —

No. 30X1 must bear double-circle town cancel as validating control. The control was applied to the labels in the sheet before their sale as stamps. When used, the stamps bear an additional Gonzales double-circle postmark.

GREENSBORO, ALA.

E1

E2

Handstamped Envelopes

31XU1 E1 5c black 1,500.
31XU2 E1 10c black 2,750.
31XU3 E2 10c black 4,250.

GREENSBORO, N.C.

E1

Handstamped Envelope

32XU1 E1 10c red 1,250.

GREENVILLE, ALA.

A1

A2

Typeset Adhesives

33X1 A1 5c blue & red	22,500.	
33X2 A2 10c red & blue	—	

Nos. 33X1-33X2 exist used on cover.

GREENVILLE COURT HOUSE, S.C.

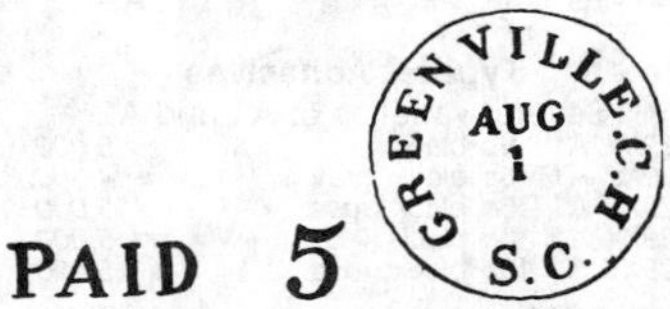

E1 Control

Handstamped Envelopes
Several types

34XU1 E1 5c black	1,800.	
34XU2 E1 10c black	2,000.	
34XU3 E1 20c (ms.) on 10c black	3,000.	

Envelopes must bear the black circle control on the back.

GREENWOOD DEPOT, VA.

A1

Handstamped "PAID" Adhesive
Ms Value and Signature

35X1 A1 10c black, *gray blue*, laid paper, on cover	16,000.	

Six examples are known of No. 35X1, all on covers. On only one cover is the stamp tied, and the catalogue value refers to this cover. Examples on cover but uncanceled are valued at $4,500.

GRIFFIN, GA.

E1

Handstamped Envelope

102XU1 E1 5c black		1,750.

A1

A1a

GROVE HILL, ALA.
Typographed Adhesive

36X1 A1 5c black		—

Two examples are recorded. One is on cover tied by the postmark. The other is canceled by magenta pen on a cover front.

HALLETTSVILLE, TEX.

Handstamped Adhesive
Ruled Letter Paper

37X1 A1a 10c black, *gray blue*, on cover	15,000.	

HAMBURGH, S.C.

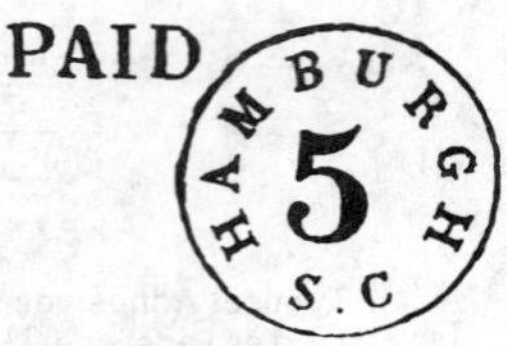

E1

Handstamped Envelope

112XU1 E1 5c black	2,000.	

HARRISBURGH (Harrisburg), TEX.

E1

Handstamped Envelope

130XU1 E1 5c black	—	

No. 130XU1 is indistinguishable from a handstamp paid cover when used.

A1

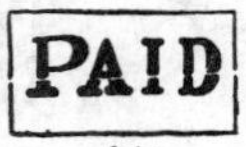

A1a

HELENA, TEX.
Typeset Adhesives
Several varieties

38X1 A1 5c black, *buff*	7,500.	6,000.
38X2 A1 10c black, *gray*		5,000.

On 10c "Helena" is in upper and lower case italics.

Used examples are valued with small faults or repairs, as all recorded have faults.

HILLSBORO, N.C.

Handstamped Adhesive

39X1 A1a 5c black, on cover	15,000.	

Manuscript Envelope

39XU1 10c "paid 10"	—	

No. 39XU1 has undated town cancel as control on face.

See 3c 1861 Postmaster Provisional No. 1AX1.

E1

E1a

HOLLANDALE, TEX.
Handstamped Envelope

132XU1 E1 5c black		—

HOUSTON, TEX.

Handstamped Envelopes

40XU1 E1a 5c red	—	700.
40XU2 E1a 10c red	—	1,250.
40XU3 E1a 10c black		2,000.
40XU4 E1a 5c + 10c red		2,500.
40XU5 E1a 10c + 10c red		2,500.
40XU6 E1a 10c (ms.) on 5c red		3,000.

HUNTSVILLE, TEX.

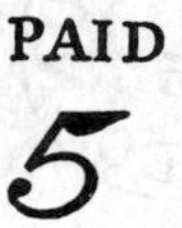

E1 Control

Handstamped Envelope

92XU1 E1 5c black		2,500.

No. 92XU1 exists with "5" outside or within control circle.

A1

E1

INDEPENDENCE, TEX.
Handstamped Adhesives

41X1 A1 10c black, *buff*, on cover		8,000.
41X2 A1 10c blk, *dull rose*, on cover		8,500.
41X3 A1 10c blk, *buff*, small "10," Ms "Pd," on cover		10,000.

All known examples of Nos. 41X1-41X3 are uncanceled on covers with black "INDEPENDANCE TEX." (sic) postmark.

No. 41X3 is known only cut to shape.

ISABELLA, GA.

Handstamped Envelope
Manuscript "5"

133XU1 E1 5c black		—

E1

E1a

IUKA, MISS.
Handstamped Envelope

42XU1 E1 5c black		1,600.

JACKSON, MISS.

Handstamped Envelopes

43XU1 E1a 5c black		500.
43XU2 E1a 10c black		2,000.
43XU3 E1a 10c on 5c black		2,750.
43XU4 E1a 10c on 5c blue		2,750.

The 5c also exists on a lettersheet.

See 3c 1861 Postmaster Provisional No. 2AXU1.

E1

E1a

JACKSONVILLE, ALA.
Handstamped Envelope

110XU1 E1 5c black	—	1,500.

JACKSONVILLE, FLA.

Handstamped Envelope

134XU1 E1a 5c black		—

Undated double circle postmark control on reverse.

A1

E1

JETERSVILLE, VA.
Handstamped "5"; Ms "AHA."
Adhesive
Laid Paper

44X1 A1 5c black, vert. pair on cover, uncanceled		16,000.

JONESBORO, TENN.

Handstamped Envelopes

45XU1 E1 5c black		3,750.
45XU2 E1 5c dark blue		6,500.

KINGSTON, GA.

E1

E2

E4

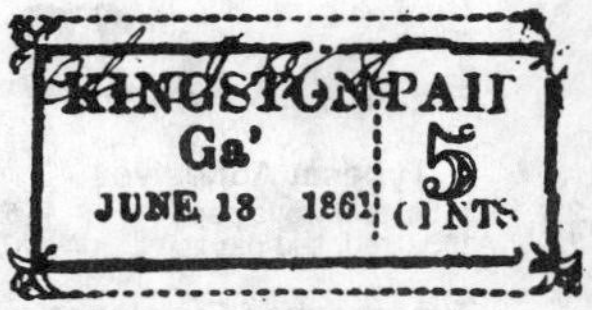

E3

Typo. (E1-E3); Handstamped (E4)
Envelopes

46XU1 E1 5c black		2,000.
46XU2 E2 5c black	—	3,250.
a. No "C" or "S" at sides of numeral		—
46XU3 E2 5c black, *amber*		2,750.
46XU4 E3 5c black		—
46XU5 E4 5c black		2,000.

Only one example of No. 46XU3 is recorded.

KNOXVILLE, TENN.

A1

Woodcut Adhesives
Grayish White Laid Paper

47X1 A1 5c brick red	1,250.	900.
47X2 A1 5c carmine	1,750.	1,500.
47X3 A1 10c green, on cover		57,750.

The 5c has been reprinted in red, brown and chocolate on white and bluish wove and laid paper.

E1

E2

Typographed Envelopes

47XU1 E1 5c blue 750. *1,500.*
47XU2 E1 5c blue, *orange* 750. *2,000.*
47XU3 E1 10c red (cut to shape) *1,800.*
47XU4 E1 10c red, *orange* (cut to shape) *1,800.*

Handstamped Envelopes

47XU5 E2 5c black 750. *1,500.*
47XU6 E2 10c on 5c black *3,500.*

Type E2 exists with "5" above or below "PAID."

LA GRANGE, TEX.

E1

Handstamped Envelopes

48XU1 E1 5c black — 2,000.
48XU2 E1 10c black 2,500.

LAKE CITY, FLA.

E1

Control

Handstamped Envelope

96XU1 E1 10c black *2,000.*

Envelopes have black circle control mark, or printed name of E.R. Ives, postmaster, on face or back.

LAURENS COURT HOUSE, S.C.

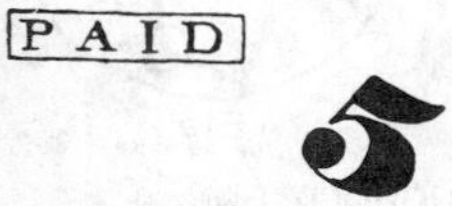

E1

Handstamped Envelope

116XU1 E1 5c black —

LENOIR, N.C.

A1

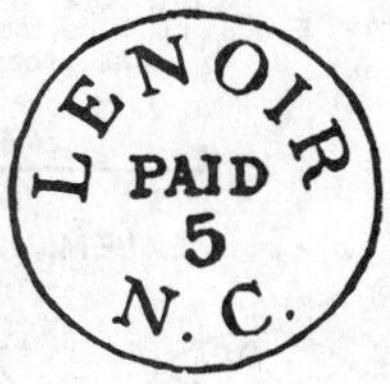

E1

Handstamped Adhesive from Woodcut

Paper has ruled lines in orange

49X1 A1 5c blue *3,250.* *2,750.*

Handstamped Envelopes

49XU1 A1 5c black *3,500.*
49XU2 A1 10c (5c + 5c) blue *25,000.*
49XU3 E1 5c blue *2,500.*
49XU4 E1 5c black

The existence of No. 49XU4 has been questioned.
No. 49XU2 is unique.

LEXINGTON, MISS.

E1

Handstamped Envelopes

50XU1 E1 5c black *5,000.*
50XU2 E1 10c black *5,000.*

LEXINGTON, VA.

E1

Handstamped Envelopes

135XU1 E1 5c black —
135XU2 E1 10c black —

Nos. 135XU1-135XU2 by themselves are indistinguishable from a handstamp paid cover when used.

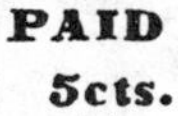

A1

A1a

LIBERTY, VA. (and SALEM, VA.)

Typeset Adhesive

Laid Paper

74X1 A1 5c blk, on cover, uncanceled *8,000.*

Three known on covers: two on covers with Liberty, Va. postmark, one on cover with Salem, Va., postmark.

LIMESTONE SPRINGS, S.C.

Handstamped Adhesive

121X1 A1a 5c black, on cover 4,000.

Stamps are cut round, square or rectangular. Covers are not postmarked.

LIVINGSTON, ALA.

A1

Lithographed Adhesive

51X1 A1 5c blue *7,000.*

LYNCHBURG, VA.

A1

E1

Stereotyped Adhesive from Woodcut

52X1 A1 5c blue (shades) 600. *1,000.*

Typographed Envelopes

52XU1 E1 5c black *2,500.*
52XU2 E1 5c black, *amber* 650. *2,500.*
52XU3 E1 5c black, *buff* *2,500.*
52XU4 E1 5c black, *brown* 900. *2,500.*

MACON, GA.

A1

A2

A3

A4

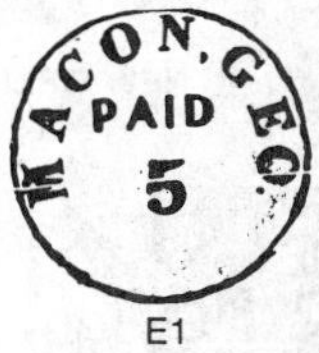

E1

Typeset Adhesives

Several varieties of each. Ten of A2.

Wove Paper

53X1 A1 5c blk, *lt blue green* (shades) 850. 600.
53X3 A2 5c black, *yellow* 2,500. 800.
53X4 A3 5c blk, *yel* (shades) 2,750. 1,250.
a. Vertical tete beche pair —
53X5 A4 2c black, *gray green* *6,500.*

No. 53X4a is unique.

Laid Paper

53X6 A2 5c black, *yellow* *3,000.* *3,500.*
53X7 A3 5c black, *yellow* *6,000.*
53X8 A1 5c blk, *lt blue green* 1,750. *2,000.*

Handstamped Envelope

Two types of "PAID" and "5"

53XU1 E1 5c black 250. *500.*

MADISON, GA.

E1

E1a

Handstamped Envelope

136XU1 E1 5c black —

No. 136XU1 is indistinguishable from a handstamp paid cover when used.

MADISON COURT HOUSE, FLA.

Typeset Envelope

137XU1 E1 5c black —

See 3c 1861 Postmaster Provisional No. 3AX1.

MARIETTA, GA.

E1

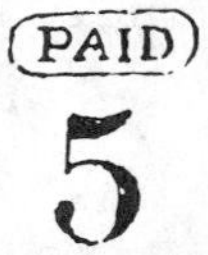

E2

Handstamped Envelopes

Two types of "PAID" and numerals

54XU1 E1 5c black 300.
54XU2 E1 10c on 5c black *1,750.*
54XU3 E1 10c black
54XU4 E2 5c black *2,000.*

The existence of No. 54XU3 is questioned.

MARION, VA.

A1

Handstamped Numeral, Typeset Frame Adhesives

Wove Paper

55X1 A1 5c black *5,000.*
55X2 A1 10c black *16,500.* *10,000.*

Bluish Laid Paper

55X3 A1 5c black —

The 2c, 3c, 15c and 20c are believed to be bogus.

MEMPHIS, TENN.

A1

A2

Stereotyped Adhesives from Woodcut

56X1 A1 2c blue (shades) 90. *1,250.*
56X2 A2 5c red (shades) 140. *175.*
a. Tete beche pair 1,500.
b. Pair, one sideways 750.
c. Pelure paper — —

Typographed Envelopes

56XU1 A2 5c red 2,500.
56XU2 A2 5c red, *amber* 4,000.
56XU3 A2 5c red, *orange* 2,500.

MICANOPY, FLA.

E1

Handstamped Envelope

105XU1 E1 5c black *11,500.*

No. 105X1 is unique.

MILLEDGEVILLE, GA.

E1

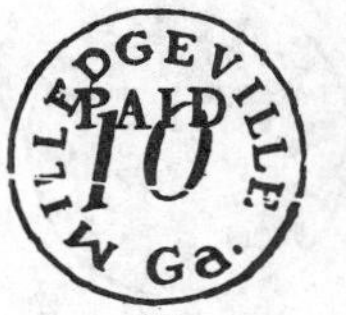

E2

E3

Handstamped Envelopes

57XU1 E1	5c black		250.
57XU2 E1	5c blue		800.
57XU3 E1	10c on 5c black		1,000.
57XU4 E2	10c black	225.	*1,000.*
57XU5 E3	10c black		700.

E1

A1

MILTON, N.C.

Handstamped Envelope
Manuscript "5"

138XU1 E1 5c black *2,000.*

Two examples of No. 138XU1 are recorded.

MOBILE, ALA.

Lithographed Adhesives

58X1 A1	2c black	2,000.	1,000.
58X2 A1	5c blue	275.	225.

MONTGOMERY, ALA.

E1

E2

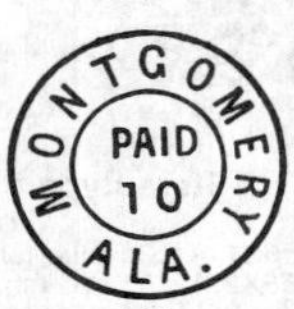

E3

Handstamped Envelopes

59XU1 E1	5c red		1,200.
59XU2 E1	5c blue	400.	*900.*
59XU3 E1	10c red		800.
59XU4 E1	10c blue		*1,500.*
59XU5 E1	10c black		800.
59XU6 E1	10c on 5c red		*2,750.*

The 10c design is larger than the 5c.

59XU7 E2	2c red	*2,500.*
59XU7A E2	2c blue	*3,500.*
59XU8 E2	5c black	*2,250.*
59XU9 E3	10c black	*2,750.*
59XU10 E3	10c red	*1,500.*

MT. LEBANON, LA.

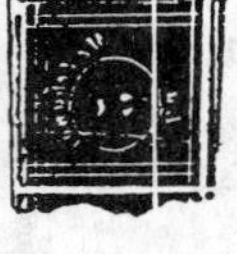

A1

Woodcut Adhesive, Design Reversed

60X1 A1 5c red brown, on cover *385,000.*

No. 60X1 is unique. Value represents sale price at 1999 auction.

NASHVILLE, TENN.

Stereotyped Adhesives from Woodcut

Gray Blue Ribbed Paper

61X2 A2	5c carmine (shades)	850.	500.
a.	Vertical tete beche pair		*3,000.*
61X3 A2	5c brick red	850.	450.
61X4 A2	5c gray (shades)	850.	625.
61X5 A2	5c violet brown	750.	475.
a.	Vertical tete beche pair	*3,500.*	*2,500.*
61X6 A2	10c green	*3,000.*	*3,000.*

Handstamped Envelopes

61XU1 E1	5c blue	750.
61XU2 E1	5c + 10c blue	*2,400.*

See 3c Postmaster Provisional No. 4AX1.

A2

E1

NEW ORLEANS, LA.

A1

A2

E1

Stereotyped Adhesives from Woodcut

62X1 A1	2c blue	150.	*500.*
a.	Printed on both sides	1,750.	
62X2 A1	2c red (shades)	125.	*1,000.*
62X3 A2	5c brown, *white*	250.	150.
a.	Printed on both sides		*1,750.*
b.	5c ocher	650.	600.
62X4 A2	5c red brown, *bluish*	280.	175.
a.	Printed on both sides		*2,750.*
62X5 A2	5c yel brn, *off-white*	125.	*225.*
62X6 A2	5c red	—	*7,500.*
62X7 A2	5c red, *bluish*		*10,000.*

Handstamped Envelopes

62XU1 E1	5c black	4,500.
62XU2 E1	10c black	*12,500.*

"J L. RIDDELL, P.M." omitted

62XU3 E1 2c black *9,500.*

NEW SMYRNA, FLA.

A1

E1

Handstamped Adhesive

63X1 A1 10c ("01") on 5c black *45,000.*

No. 63X1 is unique.

NORFOLK, VA.

Handstamped Envelopes
Ms Initials on Front or Back

139XU1 E1	5c black	—
139XU2 E1	10c black	—

A1

E1

OAKWAY, S.C.

Handstamped Adhesive

115X1 A1 5c black, on cover *66,000.*

Two used examples of No. 115X1 are recorded, both on cover. Value represents 1997 auction realization for the cover on which the stamp is tied by manuscript "Paid."

PENSACOLA, FLA.

Handstamped Envelopes

106XU1 E1	5c black	*3,750.*
106XU2 E1	10c (ms.) on 5c black	*4,250.*

PETERSBURG, VA.

A1

A1a

Typeset Adhesive (10 varieties)

65X1 A1 5c red (shades) *1,500.* 450.

PITTSYLVANIA COURT HOUSE, VA.

Typeset Adhesives

66X1 A1a	5c red, wove paper	*6,000.*	*5,000.*
66X2 A1a	5c red, laid paper		*6,500.*

PLAINS OF DURA, GA.

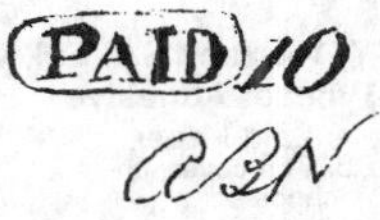

E1

Handstamped, Ms initials Envelopes

140XU1 E1	5c black	—
140XU2 E1	10c black	—

PLEASANT SHADE, VA.

A1

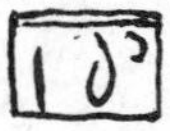

E1

Typeset Adhesive (5 varieties)

67X1 A1 5c blue *2,500.* *15,000.*

PLUM CREEK, TEX.

Manuscript Adhesive

141X1 E1 10c black, *blue*, on cover —

The ruled lines and "10" are done by hand. Size and shape of the stamp varies.

PORT GIBSON, MISS.

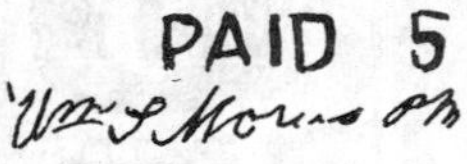

E1

Handstamped Envelope
Ms Signature

142XU1 E1 5c black —

A1

E1

PORT LAVACA, TEX.

Typeset Adhesive

107X1 A1 10c black, on cover *25,000.*

No. 107X1 is unique.

RALEIGH, N.C.

Handstamped Envelopes

68XU1 E1	5c red	500.
68XU2 E1	5c blue	*2,500.*

A1

E1

RHEATOWN, TENN.

Typeset Adhesive

Three varieties

69X1 A1 5c red *2,000.* *2,750.*

RICHMOND, TEX.

Handstamped Envelopes

70XU1 E1	5c red	1,500.
70XU2 E1	10c red	1,000.
70XU3 E1	10c on 5c red	*5,000.*
70XU4 E1	15c (ms.) on 10c red	*5,000.*

E1

E1a

RINGGOLD, GA.

Handstamped Envelope

71XU1 E1 5c blue black *3,000.*

RUTHERFORDTON, N.C.

Handstamped Adhesive
"Paid 5cts" in ms.

72X1 E1a 5c black, cut round, on cover (uncanceled) *25,000.*

No. 72X1 is unique.

SALEM, N.C.

"Paid 5" in Ms.
E1

"Paid 5" Handstamped
E2

Handstamped Envelopes

73XU1 E1 5c black 1,150.
73XU2 E1 10c black *1,500.*
73XU3 E2 5c black 1,500.
73XU4 E2 10c on 5c black *2,800.*

Reprints exist on various papers. They either lack the "Paid" and value or have them counterfeited.

Salem, Va.
See No. 74X1 under Liberty, Va.

SALISBURY, N.C.

E1

Typeset Envelope
Impressed at top left

75XU1 E1 5c black, *greenish* *5,000.*

One example known with part of envelope torn away, leaving part of design missing. Illustration E1 partly suppositional.

SAN ANTONIO, TEX.

E1

E2

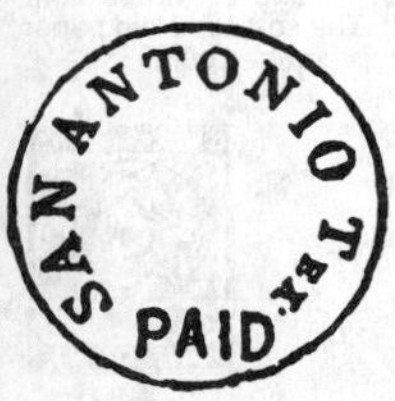

Control

Handstamped Envelopes

76XU1 E1 10c black 275. *2,000.*
76XU1A E2 5c black —
76XU2 E2 10c black *2,500.*

Black circle control mark is on front or back.

SAVANNAH, GA.

E1

Control

E2

Handstamped Envelopes

101XU1 E1 5c black 400.
101XU2 E2 5c black 600.
101XU3 E1 10c black 750.
101XU4 E2 10c black 750.
101XU5 E1 10c on 5c black 1,500.
101XU6 E2 20c on 5c black 2,000.

Envelope must bear octagonal control mark. One example is known of No. 101XU6.

E1

E1a

SELMA, ALA.

Handstamped Envelopes
Ms Signature

77XU1 E1 5c black *1,250.*
77XU2 E1 10c black *2,500.*
77XU3 E1 10c on 5c black *3,000.*

See 3c Postmaster Provisional No. 5AXU1.

SPARTA, GA.

Handstamped Envelopes

93XU1 E1a 5c red — 1,000.
93XU2 E1a 10c red *2,250.*

SPARTANBURG, S.C.

A1

A2

Handstamped Adhesives on Ruled or Plain Wove Paper

78X1 A1 5c black *3,500.*
a. "5" omitted —
78X2 A2 5c black, *bluish* *4,000.*
78X3 A2 5c black, *brown* *4,000.*

Most examples of Nos. 78X1-78X3 are cut round. Cut square examples in sound condition are worth much more.

STATESVILLE, N.C.

E1

Handstamped Envelopes

79XU1 E1 5c black 175. 450.
79XU2 E1 10c on 5c black *2,000.*

SUMTER, S.C.

E1

Handstamped Envelopes

80XU1 E1 5c black 300.
80XU2 E1 10c black 300.
80XU3 E1 10c on 5c black *800.*
80XU4 E1 2c (ms.) on 10c black *1,100.*

Used examples of Nos. 80XU1-80XU2 are indistinguishable from handstamped "Paid" covers.

TALBOTTOM, GA.

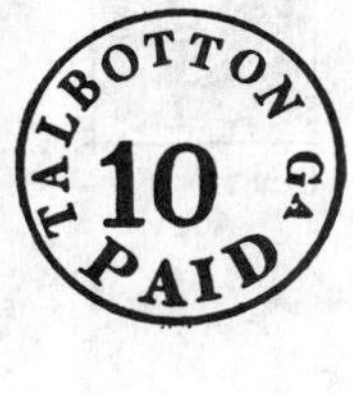

E1

Handstamped Envelopes

94XU1 E1 5c black 1,000.
94XU2 E1 10c black 1,000.
94XU3 E1 10c on 5c black *2,000.*

E1

A1

TALLADEGA, ALA.

Handstamped Envelopes

143XU1 E1 5c black —
143XU2 E1 10c black —

TELLICO PLAINS, TENN.

Typeset Adhesives
Laid Paper

81X1 A1 5c red 1,250. —
81X2 A1 10c red 2,500.

THOMASVILLE, GA.

E1

Control

E2

Handstamped Envelopes

82XU1 E1 5c black 500.
82XU2 E2 5c black 900.

TULLAHOMA, TENN.

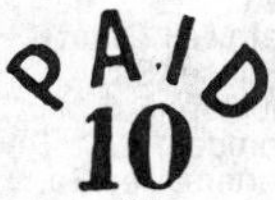

E1

Control

Handstamped Envelope

111XU1 E1 10c black *3,000.*

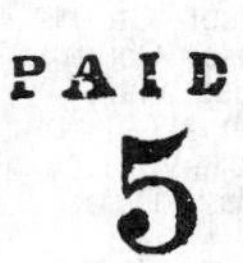

E1

E1a

TUSCALOOSA, ALA.

Handstamped Envelopes

83XU1 E1 5c black 250.
83XU2 E1 10c black 250.

Used examples of Nos. 83XU1-83XU2 are indistinguishable from handstamped "Paid" covers.

TUSCUMBIA, ALA.

Handstamped Envelopes

84XU1 E1a 5c black 2,250.
84XU2 E1a 5c red 3,000.
84XU3 E1a 10c black 3,500.

See 3c 1861 Postmasters Provisional No. 6AXU1.

E1

Union City, Tenn.
The use of E1 to produce provisional envelopes is doubtful.

A1

A1a

UNIONTOWN, ALA.

Typeset Adhesives in settings of 4 (2x2)
Four varieties of each value
Laid Paper

86X1 A1 2c dark blue, *gray blue*, on cover —
86X2 A1 2c dark blue *15,000.*
86X3 A1 5c green, *gray blue* 2,750. 2,000.
86X4 A1 5c green 2,750. 2,000.
86X5 A1 10c red, *gray blue*, on cover *32,500.*

Although No. 86X2 is valued as a single stamp, it exists only in a unique sheet of 4.

UNIONVILLE, S.C.

Handstamped Adhesive
Wove Paper with Blue Ruled Lines

87X1 A1a 5c black, *grayish* —

VALDOSTA, GA.

E1

Control

Handstamped Envelopes

100XU1 E1 10c black *2,000.*
100XU2 E1 5c + 5c black —

The black circle control must appear on front or back of envelope.
There is one recorded cover each of Nos. 100XU1-100XU2.

A1

E1

VICTORIA, TEX.

Typeset Adhesives

88X1 A1 5c red brown, *green* 8,000.
88X2 A1 10c red brown, *green* 9,000. 5,500.

Pelure Paper

88X3 A1 10c red brn, *grn,* "10" in bold face type 6,250. 6,250.

WALTERBOROUGH, S.C.

Handstamped Envelopes

108XU1 E1 10c black, *buff* 4,000.
108XU2 E1 10c carmine 3,750.

WARRENTON, GA.

E1

Handstamped Envelopes

89XU1 E1 5c black 1,250.
89XU2 E1 10c (ms.) on 5c black 850.

E1

E1a

WASHINGTON, GA.

Handstamped Envelope

117XU1 E1 10c black 2,000.

WEATHERFORD, TEX.

Handstamped Envelopes

Woodcut with "PAID" inserted in type

109XU1 E1a 5c black 2,000.
109XU2 E1a 5c + 5c black 11,000.

One example is known of No. 109XU2.

WINNSBOROUGH, S.C.

E1

Control

Handstamped Envelopes

97XU1 E1 5c black 1,500.
97XU2 E1 10c black 2,000.

Envelopes must bear black circle control on front or back.

WYTHEVILLE, VA.

E1

Control

Handstamped Envelope

114XU1 E1 5c black 900.

For later additions, listed out of numerical sequence, see:

No. 74X1,	Liberty, Va. (and Salem, Va.)
No. 92XU1,	Huntsville, Tex.
No. 93XU1,	Sparta, Ga.
No. 94XU1,	Talbotton, Ga.
No. 96XU1,	Lake City, Fla.
No. 97XU1,	Winnsborough, S.C.
No. 98XU1,	Galveston, Tex.
No. 99XU1,	Christiansburg, Va.
No. 100XU1,	Valdosta, Ga.
No. 101XU1,	Savannah, Ga.
No. 102XU1,	Griffin, Ga.
No. 103XU1,	Courtland, Ala.
No. 104XU1,	Fincastle, Va.
No. 105XU1,	Micanopy, Fla.
No. 106XU1,	Pensacola, Fla.
No. 107X1,	Port Lavaca, Tex.
No. 108XU1,	Walterborough, S.C.
No. 109XU1,	Weatherford, Tex.
No. 110XU1,	Jacksonville, Ala.
No. 111XU1,	Tullahoma, Tenn.
No. 112XU1,	Hamburgh, S.C.
No. 113XU1,	Columbia, Tenn.
No. 114XU1,	Wytheville, Va.
No. 115X1,	Oakway, S.C.
No. 116XU1,	Laurens Court House, S.C.
No. 117XU1,	Washington, Ga.
No. 118XU1,	Carolina City, N.C.
No. 119XU1,	Colaparchee, Ga.
No. 120XU1,	Forsyth, Ga.
No. 121XU1,	Limestone Springs, S.C.
No. 122XU1,	Balcony Falls, Va.
No. 123XU1,	Barnwell Court House, S.C.
No. 124XU1,	Bluffton, S.C.
No. 125XU1,	Camden, S.C.
No. 126XU1,	Cartersville, Ga.
No. 127XU1,	Charlottesville, Va.
No. 128XU1,	Fraziersville, S.C.
No. 129XU1,	Gaston, N.C.
No. 130XU1,	Harrisburgh, Tex.
No. 132XU1,	Hollandale, Tex.
No. 133XU1,	Isabella, Ga.
No. 134XU1,	Jacksonville, Fla.
No. 135XU1,	Lexington, Va.
No. 136XU1,	Madison, Ga.
No. 137XU1,	Madison Court House, Fla.
No. 138XU1,	Milton, N.C.
No. 139XU1,	Norfolk, Va.
No. 140XU1,	Plains of Dura, Ga.
No. 141X1,	Plum Creek, Tex.
No. 142XU1,	Port Gibson, Miss.
No. 143XU1,	Talladega, Ala.

GENERAL ISSUES

Jefferson Davis
A1

Thomas Jefferson
A2

1861 Unwmk. Litho. *Imperf.*

1	A1	5c green	250.00	150.00
		No gum	185.00	
a.		5c light green	250.00	150.00
		No gum	185.00	
b.		5c dark green	275.00	175.00
		No gum	200.00	
c.		5c olive green	275.00	175.00
		No gum	200.00	
2	A2	10c blue	280.00	190.00
		No gum	220.00	
a.		10c light blue	280.00	190.00
		No gum	220.00	
b.		10c dark blue	550.00	240.00
		No gum	425.00	
c.		10c indigo	*2,750.*	*2,250.*
		No gum	*2,000.*	
d.		Printed on both sides	—	—
e.		10c greenish blue	475.00	300.00
		No gum	350.00	

The earliest printings of No. 2 were made by Hoyer & Ludwig, the later ones by J. T. Paterson & Co. Stamps of the later printings usually have a small colored dash below the lowest point of the upper left spandrel.

See Nos. 4-5.

Andrew Jackson
A3

Jefferson Davis
A4

1862

3	A3	2c green	700.00	650.00
		No gum	550.00	
a.		2c bright yellow green	*1,750.*	—
		No gum	*1,400.*	
4	A1	5c blue	180.00	110.00
		No gum	135.00	
a.		5c dark blue	240.00	160.00
		No gum	170.00	
b.		5c light milky blue	270.00	200.00
		No gum	190.00	
5	A2	10c rose	1,250.	500.00
		No gum	950.00	
a.		10c carmine	*2,800.*	*1,750.*
		No gum	*2,100.*	

Typo.

6	A4	5c lt blue (London print)	10.00	*27.50*
		No gum	7.00	
7	A4	5c blue (local print)	13.00	*20.00*
		No gum	9.00	
a.		5c deep blue	16.00	*35.00*
		No gum	11.00	
b.		Printed on both sides	*2,500.*	950.00

No. 6 has fine, clear impression. No. 7 has coarser impression and the color is duller and often blurred.

Both 2c and 10c stamps, types A4 and A10, were privately printed in various colors.

Andrew Jackson — A5

1863 Engr.

8	A5	2c brown red	70.00	*350.00*
		No gum	55.00	
a.		2c pale red	90.00	*450.00*
		No gum	70.00	

Jefferson Davis
A6 A6a

Thick or Thin Paper

9	A6	10c blue	850.	525.
		No gum	650.	
a.		10c milky blue	850.	525.
		No gum	650.	
b.		10c gray blue	900.	625.
		No gum	700.	
10	A6a	10c blue (with frame line)	3,750.	1,250.
		No gum	3,000.	
a.		10c milky blue	3,750.	1,250.
		No gum	3,000.	
b.		10c greenish blue	4,250.	1,350.
		No gum	3,400.	
c.		10c dark blue	4,250.	1,350.
		No gum	3,400.	

Values of Nos. 10, 10a, 10b and 10c are for copies showing parts of lines on at least three sides. Stamps showing 4 complete lines sell for 300%-400% of the values given.

A7

A8

There are many slight differences between A7 and A8, the most noticeable being the additional line outside the ornaments at the corners of A8.

11	A7	10c blue	9.00	*15.00*
		No gum	7.50	
a.		10c milky blue	22.50	*37.50*
		No gum	19.00	
b.		10c dark blue	18.50	*25.00*
		No gum	15.00	
c.		10c greenish blue	17.50	17.50
		No gum	12.50	
d.		10c green	70.00	*75.00*
		No gum	60.00	
e.		Officially perforated 12½	300.00	275.00
12	A8	10c blue	11.00	*17.50*
		No gum	9.00	
a.		10c milky blue	25.00	*35.00*
		No gum	20.00	
b.		10c light blue	11.00	*17.50*
		No gum	9.00	
c.		10c greenish blue	20.00	*45.00*
		No gum	16.50	
d.		10c dark blue	11.00	*20.00*
		No gum	9.00	
e.		10c green	90.00	*110.00*
		No gum	75.00	
f.		Officially perforated 12½	325.00	300.00

The paper of Nos. 11 and 12 varies from thin hard to thick soft. The so-called laid paper is probably due to thick streaky gum.

George Washington
A9

John C. Calhoun
A10

13	A9	20c green	37.50	*400.00*
		No gum	27.50	
a.		20c yellow green	70.00	*450.00*
		No gum	47.50	
b.		20c dark green	65.00	*500.00*
		No gum	45.00	
c.		Diag. half used as 10c on cover		*2,000.*
d.		Horiz. half used as 10c on cover		*3,500.*

1862 Typo.

14	A10	1c orange	90.00	
		No gum	70.00	
a.		1c deep orange	115.00	
		No gum	90.00	

The 1c was never put in use.

CANAL ZONE

kə-ˈnal ˈzōn

LOCATION — A strip of land 10 miles wide, extending through the Republic of Panama, between the Atlantic and Pacific Oceans.

GOVT. — From 1904-79 a US Government Reservation; from 1979-99 under joint control of the Republic of Panama and the U.S..

AREA — 552.8 sq. mi.

POP. — 41,800 (est. 1976)

The Canal Zone, site of the Panama Canal, was leased in perpetuity to the US for a cash payment of $10,000,000 and a yearly rental. Treaties between the two countries provided for joint jurisdiction by the U.S. and Panama, 1979-1999, with Panama handling postal service. At the end of 1999, the canal, in its entirety, reverted to Panama.

100 Centavos = 1 Peso
100 Centesimos = 1 Balboa
100 Cents = 1 Dollar

Catalogue values for unused stamps in this country are for Never Hinged items, beginning with Scott 118 in the regular postage section and Scott C6 in the air post section.

Watermarks

Wmk. 190- "USPS" in Single-lined Capitals

Wmk. 191- Double-lined "USPS" in Capitals

Map of Panama — A1

Violet to Violet-blue Handstamp, "CANAL ZONE," on Panama Nos. 72-72c, 78 and 79

1904 Unwmk. *Perf. 12*

1	A1	2c rose, both "PANAMA" up or down	550.00	425.00
a.		"CANAL ZONE" inverted	850.00	850.00
b.		"CANAL ZONE" double	2,000.	2,000.
c.		"CANAL ZONE" double, both inverted	*15,000.*	
d.		"PANAMA" reading down and up	700.00	650.00
e.		As "d," "CANAL ZONE" inverted	6,500.	6,500.
f.		Vert. pair, "PANAMA" reading up on top 2c, down on other	2,000.	2,000.
2	A1	5c blue	225.00	175.00
a.		"CANAL ZONE" inverted	600.00	600.00
b.		"CANAL ZONE" double	2,250.	1,500.
c.		Pair, one without "CANAL ZONE"	5,000.	5,000.
d.		"CANAL ZONE" diagonal, running down to right	700.00	700.00
3	A1	10c yellow	375.00	225.00
a.		"CANAL ZONE" inverted	625.00	600.00
b.		"CANAL ZONE" double		*12,500.*
c.		Pair, one without "CANAL ZONE"	*6,000.*	*5,000.*
		Nos. 1-3 (3)	1,150.	825.00

On the 2c stamp "PANAMA" is normally about 13mm; on the 5c and 10c about 15mm.

Varieties of "PANAMA" overprint exist on the 2c with inverted "V" for "A," accent on "A," inverted "N," etc.

Counterfeit "CANAL ZONE" overprints exist.

US Nos. 300, 319, 304, 306 and 307 Overprinted in Black

CANAL ZONE
PANAMA

1904 Wmk. 191

4	A115	1c blue green	32.50	22.50
5	A129	2c carmine	30.00	25.00
a.		2c scarlet	35.00	30.00
6	A119	5c blue	100.00	65.00
7	A121	8c violet black	175.00	85.00
8	A122	10c pale red brown	150.00	90.00
		Nos. 4-8 (5)	487.50	287.50

Beware of fake overprints.

A2

A3

CANAL ZONE
Regular Type

CANAL ZONE
Antique Type

Black Overprint on Stamps of Panama

1904-06 Unwmk.

9	A2	1c green	2.75	2.25
a.		"CANAL" in antique type	100.00	100.00
b.		"ZONE" in antique type	70.00	70.00
c.		Inverted overprint	*5,000.*	*2,250.*
d.		Double overprint	*2,000.*	*1,500.*
10	A2	2c rose	4.50	2.50
a.		Inverted overprint	225.00	275.00
b.		"L" of "CANAL" sideways	2,500.	2,500.

Overprinted "CANAL ZONE" Black, "PANAMA" and Bar in Red on Panama Nos. 77-79 "PANAMA" 15mm long

11	A3	2c rose	7.50	5.00
a.		"ZONE" in antique type	200.00	200.00
b.		"PANAMA" inverted, bar at bottom	350.00	350.00
12	A3	5c blue	8.00	3.75
a.		"CANAL" in antique type	75.00	65.00
b.		"ZONE" in antique type	75.00	65.00
c.		"CANAL ZONE" double	600.00	600.00
d.		"PANAMA" ovpt. dbl.	1,050.	850.00
e.		"PANAMA" inverted, bar at bottom		1,250.
13	A3	10c yellow	22.50	12.50
a.		"CANAL" in antique type	200.00	200.00
b.		"ZONE" in antique type	175.00	160.00
c.		"PANAMA" ovpt. dbl.	650.00	650.00
d.		"PANAMA" overprint in red brown	27.50	27.50
		Nos. 11-13 (3)	38.00	21.25

With Added Surcharge in Red on Panama No. 81

8 cts

14	A3	8c on 50c bis brn	32.50	22.50
a.		"ZONE" in antique type	1,100.	1,100.
b.		"CANAL ZONE" invtd.	425.00	400.00
c.		Rose brown overprint	40.00	40.00
d.		As "c," "CANAL" in antique type	2,250.	
e.		As "c," "ZONE" in antique type	2,250.	
f.		As "c," "8 cts" double	*850.00*	
g.		As "c," "8" omitted	*4,250.*	

Panama No. 74 Overprinted "CANAL ZONE" in Regular Type in Black and Surch. Like No. 14 in Red. Both "PANAMA" Reading Up. "PANAMA" 13mm long.

1905

15	A3	8c on 50c bis brn	2,750.	*4,500.*
a.		"PANAMA" reading down & up	6,500.	—

On No. 15 with original gum the gum is almost always disturbed.

Panama Nos. 19 and 21 Surcharged in Black:

a
PANAMA CANAL ZONE 1 ct. PANAMA

b
PANAMA CANAL ZONE 1 ct. PANAMA

c
PANAMA CANAL ZONE 1 ct. PANAMA

d
PANAMA CANAL ZONE 2 cts. PANAMA

e
PANAMA CANAL ZONE 2 cts. PANAMA

f
PANAMA CANAL ZONE 2 cts. PANAMA

There were 3 printings of each denomination differing mainly in the relative position of the various parts of the surcharges. Varieties occur with invtd. "V" for the 3rd "A" in "PANAMA," "CA" spaced, "ZO" spaced, "2c" spaced, accents in various positions, and with bars shifted so that 2 bars appear on top or bottom of the stamp (either with or without the corresponding bar on top or bottom) and sometimes with only 1 bar at top or bottom.

1906

16	A4	1c on 20c vio, type a	2.00	1.60
a.		Surcharge type b	2.00	1.60
b.		Surcharge type c	2.00	1.60
c.		As #16, double surcharge		*2,000.*
17	A4	2c on 1p lake, type d	2.75	2.75
a.		Surcharge type e	2.75	2.75
b.		Surcharge type f	20.00	20.00

Panama No. 74 Overprinted "CANAL ZONE" in Regular Type in Black and Surcharged in Red

8 cts.
b

8 cts
c

Both "PANAMA" reading up

1905-06

18	A3 (b)	8c on 50c bis brn	55.00	50.00
a.		"ZONE" in antique type	200.00	180.00
b.		"PANAMA" down & up	175.00	160.00
19	A3 (c)	8c on 50c bis brn ('06)	55.00	45.00
a.		"CANAL" in antique type	210.00	180.00
b.		"ZONE" in antique type	210.00	180.00
c.		"8 cts." double	*1,100.*	*1,100.*
d.		"PANAMA" down & up	110.00	90.00

On Nos. 18-19 with original gum the gum is usually disturbed.

Panama No. 81 Overprinted "CANAL ZONE" in Regular Type in Black and Surcharged in Red Type "c" plus Period.

"PANAMA" reading up and down

20	A3	8c on 50c bis brn	45.00	40.00
a.		"CANAL" in antique type	200.00	180.00
b.		"ZONE" in antique type	200.00	180.00
c.		"8 cts" omitted	750.00	750.00
d.		"8 cts" double	*1,500.*	

Numerous minor varieties of all these surcharges exist. Nos. 14, 18, 19 and 20 exist without CANAL ZONE overprint but were not regularly issued.

Vasco Nunez de Balboa
A5

Francisco Hernandez de Cordoba
A6

Justo Arosemena
A7

Manuel J. Hurtado
A8

Jose de Obaldia — A9

Stamps of Panama Ovptd. in Black

1906-07

Overprint Reading Up

21	A6	2c red & black	25.00	25.00
a.		"CANAL" only	*4,000.*	

Overprint Reading Down

22	A5	1c green & black	2.25	1.25
a.		Horiz. pair, imperf. btwn.	1,250.	1,250.
b.		Vert. pair, imperf. btwn.	*1,750.*	*1,750.*
c.		Vert. pair, imperf. horiz.	*2,250.*	*1,750.*
d.		Invtd. ovpt., reading up	550.00	550.00
e.		Double overprint	275.00	275.00
f.		Dbl. ovpt., one reading up	1,350.	1,350.
g.		Inverted center and ovpt. reading up	*4,000.*	*2,750.*
23	A6	2c red & black	3.25	1.40
a.		Horiz. pair, imperf. btwn.	2,000.	1,750.
b.		Vertical pair, one without overprint	1,750.	1,750.
c.		Double overprint	500.00	500.00
d.		Dbl. ovpt., one diagonal	750.00	750.00
e.		Pair, Nos. 23, 23d	1,750.	
f.		2c carmine red & black	5.00	2.75
g.		As "f," inverted center and overprint reading up		*5,000.*
h.		As "d," one "ZONE CANAL"	*4,000.*	
i.		"CANAL" double	*3,250.*	
24	A7	5c ultra & black	6.50	2.25
c.		Double overprint	450.00	350.00
d.		"CANAL" only	*3,500.*	
e.		"ZONE CANAL"	*4,500.*	
25	A8	8c purple & black	22.50	8.00
a.		Horizontal pair, imperf. between and at left margin	2,000.	—
26	A9	10c violet & black	20.00	8.00
a.		Dbl. ovpt., one reading up	*3,250.*	
b.		Overprint reading up	*3,500.*	
		Nos. 22-26 (5)	54.50	20.90

Nos. 22 to 25 occur with "CA" spaced.

Cordoba
A11

Arosemena
A12

Hurtado
A13

Jose de Obaldia
A14

Overprint Reading Down

1909

27	A11	2c vermilion & black	12.50	6.50
a.		Horiz. pair, one without ovpt.	*2,600.*	
b.		Vert. pair, one without ovpt.	*2,750.*	
28	A12	5c deep blue & black	45.00	12.50
29	A13	8c violet & black	37.50	14.00

30 A14 10c violet & black 40.00 15.00
a. Horiz. pair, one without ovpt. *2,400.*
b. Vert. pair, one without ovpt. *2,600.*
Nos. 27-30 (4) 135.00 48.00

Nos. 27-30 occur with "CA" spaced.

Do not confuse No. 27 with Nos. 39d or 53a.

For designs A11-A14 with overprints reading up, see Nos. 32-35, 39-41, 47-48, 53-54, 56-57.

Vasco Nunez de Balboa — A15

CANAL ZONE
Type I

Black Overprint, Reading Up

Type I Overprint: "C" with serifs both top and bottom. "L" "Z" and "E" with slanting serif.

Compare Type I overprint with Types II to V illustrated before Nos. 38, 46, 52 and 55. Illustrations of Types I to V are considerably enlarged and do not show actual spacing between lines of overprint.

1909-10

31 A15 1c dk green & blk 4.00 1.60
a. Inverted center and overprint reading down *15,000.*
c. Bklt. pane of 6 handmade, perf. margins 575.00
32 A11 2c vermilion & blk 4.50 1.60
a. Vert. pair, imperf. horiz 1,000. 1,000.
c. Bklt. pane of 6, handmade, perf. margins 750.00
d. Double overprint —
33 A12 5c dp blue & blk 15.00 4.00
a. Double overprint 375.00 375.00
34 A13 8c violet & blk ('10) 11.00 5.25
a. Vert. pair, one without ovpt. *1,500.*
35 A14 10c violet & black 50.00 20.00
Nos. 31-35 (5) 84.50 32.45

See Nos. 38, 46, 52, 55.

A16

A17

Black Surcharge

1911

36 A16 10c on 13c gray 6.00 2.25
a. "10 cts." inverted 275.00 275.00
b. "10 cts." omitted 275.00

1914

37 A17 10c gray 55.00 12.50

Type II: "C" with serif at top only. "L" and "E" with vertical serifs. "O" tilts to left

CANAL ZONE

Black Overprint, Reading Up

1912-16

38 A15 1c green & blk ('13) 11.00 3.00
a. Vert. pair, one without ovpt. 1,500. 1,500.
b. Booklet pane of 6 600.00
c. As "b," handmade, perf. margins 1,000.
39 A11 2c vermilion & blk 8.50 1.40
a. Horiz. pair, right stamp without ovpt. 1,250.
b. Horiz. pair, left stamp without ovpt. 1,750.
c. Booklet pane of 6 500.00
d. Overprint reading down 175.00
e. As "d," inverted center 700.00 750.00
f. As "e," booklet pane of 6 handmade, perf. margins *8,000.*
g. As "c," handmade, perf. margins 1,000.
h. As #39, "CANAL" only 1,100.
40 A12 5c dp blue & blk 22.50 3.25
a. With portrait of 2c *8,750.*
41 A14 10c violet & blk ('16) 47.50 8.50
Nos. 38-41 (4) 89.50 16.15

Map of Panama Canal — A18

Balboa Takes Possession of the Pacific Ocean — A19

Gatun Locks — A20

Culebra Cut — A21

Blue Overprint, Type II

1915

42 A18 1c dark green & black 8.50 6.50
43 A19 2c carmine & black 10.00 4.25
44 A20 5c blue & black 11.00 5.75
45 A21 10c orange & black 22.50 11.00
Nos. 42-45 (4) 52.00 27.50

Type III: Similar to Type I but letters appear thinner, particularly the lower bar of "L," "Z" and "E." Impressions are often light, rough and irregular

CANAL ZONE

Black Overprint, Reading Up

1915-20

46 A15 1c green & black 160.00 95.00
a. Overprint reading down 375.00
b. Double overprint 300.00
c. "ZONE" double *4,250.*
d. Dbl. ovpt., one "ZONE CANAL" 1,750.
47 A11 2c orange ver & blk 3,000. 100.00
48 A12 5c dp blue & black 550.00 175.00
Nos. 46-48 (3) 3,710. 370.00

S.S. "Panama" in Culebra Cut — A22

S.S. "Panama" in Culebra Cut — A23

S.S. "Cristobal" in Gatun Locks — A24

Blue Overprint, Type II

1917

49 A22 12c purple & black 17.50 5.50
50 A23 15c brt blue & black 55.00 25.00
51 A24 24c yel brown & black 45.00 15.00
Nos. 49-51 (3) 117.50 45.50

Type IV: "C" thick at bottom, "E" with center bar same length as top and bottom bars

CANAL ZONE

Black Overprint, Reading Up

1918-20

52 A15 1c green & black 32.50 11.00
a. Overprint reading down 175.00
b. Booklet pane of 6 650.00
c. Bklt. pane of 6, left vert. row of 3 without ovpt. *7,500.*
d. Bklt. pane of 6, right vert. row of 3 with dbl. ovpt. *7,500.*
e. Horiz. bklt. pair, left stamp without overprint *3,000.*
f. Horiz. bklt. pair, right stamp with dbl. overprint *3,000.*
53 A11 2c vermilion & blk 115.00 7.00
a. Overprint reading down 150.00 150.00
b. Horizontal pair, right stamp without overprint 2,000.
c. Booklet pane of 6 1,000.
d. Bklt. pane of 6, left vert. row of 3 without ovpt. *8,000.*
e. Horiz. bklt. pair, left stamp without overprint *3,000.* *4,500.*
54 A12 5c dp blue & black ('20) 200.00 35.00
Nos. 52-54 (3) 347.50 53.00

Normal spacing between words of overprint on Nos. 52 and 53 is 9¼mm. On No. 54 and the booklet printings of Nos. 52 and 53, the normal spacing is 9mm. Minor spacing varieties are known.

No. 53e used is unique and is on cover.

Type V: Smaller block type 1¾mm high. "A" with flat top

CANAL ZONE

Black Overprint, Reading Up

1920-21

55 A15 1c lt green & black 22.50 3.50
a. Overprint reading down 250.00 225.00
b. Horiz. pair, right stamp without ovpt. 1,750.
c. Horiz. pair, left stamp without ovpt. 1,000.
d. "ZONE" only *2,750.*
e. Booklet pane of 6 *1,750.*
f. "CANAL" double *1,250.*
56 A11 2c orange ver & blk 8.50 2.25
a. Double overprint 600.00
b. Double overprint, one reading down 650.00
c. Horiz. pair, right stamp without ovpt. 1,500.
d. Horiz. pair, left stamp without ovpt. 1,000.
e. Vert. pair, one without overprint 1,500.
f. "ZONE" double 1,000.
g. Booklet pane of 6 850.00
h. "CANAL" double 1,000.
57 A12 5c dp blue & black 325.00 55.00
a. Horiz. pair, right stamp without ovpt. *2,500.*
b. Horiz. pair, left stamp without ovpt. *2,500.*
Nos. 55-57 (3) 356.00 60.75

Drydock at Balboa — A25

Ship in Pedro Miguel Locks — A26

Black Overprint, Type V

1920

58 A25 50c orange & black 275.00 160.00
59 A26 1b dk violet & black 160.00 65.00

Jose Vallarino A27

The "Land Gate" A28

Bolivar's Tribute — A29

Municipal Building in 1821 and 1921 — A30

Statue of Balboa A31

Tomas Herrera A32

Jose de Fabrega — A33

Black or Red Overprint, Type V

1921

60 A27 1c green 3.75 1.40
a. "CANAL" double *2,500.*
b. Booklet pane of 6 *900.00*
61 A28 2c carmine 3.00 1.50
a. Overprint reading down 225.00 225.00
b. Double overprint 900.00
c. Vert. pair, one without overprint *3,500.*
d. "CANAL" double *1,900.*
f. Booklet pane of 6 *2,100.*
62 A29 5c blue (R) 11.00 4.50
a. Overprint reading down (R) 60.00
63 A30 10c violet 18.00 7.50
a. Overprint reading down 100.00
64 A31 15c light blue 47.50 17.50
65 A32 24c black brown 70.00 22.50
66 A33 50c black 150.00 100.00
Nos. 60-66 (7) 303.25 154.90

Experts question the status of the 5c blue with a small type V overprint in red or black.

Black Overprint, Type III

1924

67 A27 1c green 500. 200.
a. "ZONE CANAL" reading down 850.
b. "ZONE" reading down *1,900.*

Coat of Arms — A34

Black Overprint

1924

68 A34 1c dark green 11.00 4.50
69 A34 2c carmine 8.25 2.75

The 5c to lb values were prepared but never issued. See listing in the Scott U.S. Specialized Catalogue.

US Nos. 551-554, 557, 562, 564-566, and 569-571 Overprinted in Red or Black

CANAL
ZONE
Type A

Letters "A" with Flat Tops

Flat Plate Printing

1924-25 *Perf. 11*

70 A154 ½c olive brown (R) 1.25 .75
71 A155 1c deep green 1.40 .90
a. Inverted overprint 500.00 500.00
b. "ZONE" inverted 350.00 325.00
c. "CANAL" only 1,750.
d. "ZONE CANAL" 450.00
e. Booklet pane of 6 100.00
72 A156 1½c yellow brown 1.90 1.70
73 A157 2c carmine 7.50 1.70
a. Booklet pane of 6 175.00
74 A160 5c dark blue 19.00 8.50
75 A165 10c orange 45.00 25.00
76 A167 12c brown violet 35.00 32.50
a. "ZONE" inverted *3,750.* *3,000.*
77 A168 14c dark blue 30.00 22.50
78 A169 15c gray 50.00 37.50
79 A172 30c olive brown 35.00 22.50
80 A173 50c lilac 77.50 45.00
81 A174 $1 violet brown 225.00 95.00
Nos. 70-81 (12) 528.55 293.55

The space between the two lines of the overprint, on both type A and B, varies on some settings.

US Nos. 554, 555, 557, 562, 564-567, 569-571 and 623 Overprinted in Black or Red

Type B

CANAL

ZONE

Letters "A" with Sharp Pointed Tops

1925-26				
84	A157	2c carmine	30.00	8.00
a.		"CANAL" ONLY	*1,600.*	
b.		"ZONE CANAL"	375.00	
c.		Horiz. pair, one without overprint	*3,500.*	
d.		Booklet pane of 6	175.00	
85	A158	3c violet	4.00	3.25
a.		"ZONE ZONE"	600.00	550.00
86	A160	5c dark blue	4.00	2.25
a.		"ZONE ZONE"	*1,250.*	
b.		"CANAL" inverted	950.00	
c.		Inverted overprint	500.00	
d.		Pair, one without overprint	*3,250.*	
e.		"ZONE CANAL"	325.00	
f.		"ZONE" only	*2,000.*	
g.		Pair, one without ovpt., other ovpt. invtd.	*2,250.*	
h.		"CANAL" only	*2,250.*	
87	A165	10c orange	35.00	12.00
a.		"ZONE ZONE"	*3,000.*	
88	A167	12c brown violet	22.50	14.00
a.		"ZONE ZONE"	*5,250.*	
89	A168	14c dark blue	20.00	16.00
90	A169	15c gray	7.00	4.50
a.		"ZONE ZONE"	*5,500.*	
91	A187	17c black (R)	4.00	3.00
a.		"ZONE" only	900.00	
b.		"CANAL" only	*1,700.*	
c.		"ZONE CANAL"	175.00	
92	A170	20c carmine rose	7.25	3.25
a.		"CANAL" inverted	*3,600.*	
b.		"ZONE" inverted	*3,850.*	
c.		"ZONE CANAL"	*3,600.*	
93	A172	30c olive brown	5.00	4.00
94	A173	50c lilac	225.00	165.00
95	A174	$1 violet brown	125.00	60.00
		Nos. 84-95 (12)	488.75	295.25

Overprint Type B on US Sesquicentennial Stamp No. 627

1926				
96	A188	2c carmine rose	4.50	3.75

On this stamp there is a space of 5mm between the two words of the overprint.

Overprint Type B on US Nos. 583, 584 and 591

Rotary Press Printings

1927			***Perf. 10***	
97	A157	2c carmine	42.50	11.00
a.		Pair, one without overprint	*3,250.*	
b.		Booklet pane of 6	650.00	
c.		"CANAL" only	*2,000.*	
d.		"ZONE" only	*2,750.*	
98	A158	3c violet	8.00	4.25
99	A165	10c orange	17.50	7.50
		Nos. 97-99 (3)	68.00	22.75

Overprint Type B on US Nos. 632, 634, 635, 637 and 642

Rotary Press Printings

1927-31			***Perf. 11x10½***	
100	A155	1c green	2.25	1.40
a.		Pair, one without overprint	*3,000.*	
101	A157	2c carmine	2.50	1.00
a.		Booklet pane of 6	175.00	
102	A158	3c violet	4.25	2.75
a.		Booklet pane of 6, handmade, perf. margins	*6,500.*	
103	A160	5c dark blue	30.00	10.00
104	A165	10c orange	17.50	10.00
		Nos. 100-104 (5)	56.50	25.15

Wet and Dry Printings

Canal Zone stamps printed by both the "wet" and "dry" process are Nos. 105, 108-109, 111-114, 117, 138-140, C21-C24, C26, J25, J27. Starting with Nos. 147 and C27, the Bureau of Engraving and Printing used the "dry" method exclusively. See note following US Scott 1029.

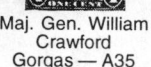

Maj. Gen. William Crawford Gorgas — A35

Maj. Gen. George Washington Goethals — A36

Gaillard Cut A37

Maj. Gen. Harry Foote Hodges A38

Lt. Col. David D. Gaillard — A39

Maj. Gen. William L. Sibert — A40

Jackson Smith — A41

Rear Adm. Harry H. Rousseau — A42

Col. Sydney B. Williamson — A43

J.C.S. Blackburn — A44

Flat Plate Printing

1928-40			***Perf. 11***	
105	A35	1c green	.20	.20
106	A36	2c carmine	.20	.20
a.		Booklet pane of 6	15.00	*20.00*
107	A37	5c blue ('29)	1.00	.40
108	A38	10c orange ('32)	.20	.20
109	A39	12c violet brown ('29)	.75	.60
110	A40	14c blue ('37)	.85	.85
111	A41	15c gray ('32)	.40	.35
112	A42	20c olive brown ('32)	.60	.20
113	A43	30c brown black ('40)	.80	.70
114	A44	50c lilac ('29)	1.50	.65
		Nos. 105-114 (10)	6.50	4.35

For surcharges & overprints see #J21-J24, O1-O8.

United States Nos. 720 and 695 Overprinted type B

Rotary Press Printing

1933			***Perf. 11x10½***	
115	A226	3c deep violet	2.75	.25
b.		"CANAL" only	*2,600.*	
c.		Bklt. pane of 6, handmade, perf. margins	225.00	
116	A168	14c dark blue	4.50	3.50
a.		"ZONE CANAL"	*1,500.*	

Gen. George Washington Goethals — A45

Flat Plate Printing

1934, Aug. 15			***Perf. 11***	
117	A45	3c deep violet	.20	.20
a.		Booklet pane of 6	45.00	*32.50*
b.		As "a," handmade, perf. margins	225.00	—

20th anniv. of the Panama Canal opening. See No. 153.

Catalogue values for unused stamps in this section, from this point to the end of the section, are for Never Hinged items.

US Nos. 803 and 805 Overprinted in Black **CANAL ZONE**

Rotary Press Printing

1939			***Perf. 11x10½***	
118	A275	½c deep orange	.20	.20
119	A277	1½c bister brown	.20	.20

Panama Canal Anniversary Issue

Balboa-Before A46

Balboa-After A47

Gaillard Cut-Before A48

Gaillard Cut-After A49

Bas Obispo-Before A50

Bas Obispo-After A51

Gatun Locks-Before A52

Gatun Locks-After A53

Canal Channel-Before — A54

Canal Channel-After A55

Gamboa-Before — A56

Gamboa-After A57

Pedro Miguel Locks-Before A58

Pedro Miguel Locks-After A59

Gatun Spillway-Before — A60

Gatun Spillway-After A61

Flat Plate Printing

1939, Aug. 15			***Perf. 11***	
120	A46	1c yellow green	.65	.30
121	A47	2c rose carmine	.65	.35
122	A48	3c purple	.65	.20
123	A49	5c dark blue	1.60	1.25
124	A50	6c red orange	3.00	3.00
125	A51	7c black	3.25	3.00
126	A52	8c green	4.75	3.50
127	A53	10c ultramarine	3.50	3.00
128	A54	11c blue green	8.00	8.50
129	A55	12c brown carmine	7.50	8.00
130	A56	14c dark violet	7.50	8.00
131	A57	15c olive green	10.00	6.00
132	A58	18c rose pink	10.00	8.50
133	A59	20c brown	12.50	7.50
134	A60	25c orange	17.50	17.50
135	A61	50c violet brown	22.50	6.00
		Nos. 120-135 (16)	113.55	84.60

25th anniv. of the Panama Canal.

Maj. Gen. George W. Davis — A62

Gov. Charles E. Magoon — A63

Theodore Roosevelt — A64

John F. Stevens — A65

John F. Wallace — A66

1946-49		**Size: 19x22mm**	***Perf. 11***	
136	A62	½c bright red ('48)	.40	.25
137	A63	1½c chocolate ('48)	.40	.25
138	A64	2c rose carmine ('49)	.20	.20
139	A65	5c deep blue	.35	.20
140	A66	25c yellow green ('48)	.85	.55
		Nos. 136-140 (5)	2.20	1.45

See #155, 162, 164. For overprint see #O9.

Map of Biological Area and Coati-Mundi A67

1948, Apr. 17			***Perf. 11***	
141	A67	10c black	1.25	.80

25th anniv. of the establishment of the Canal Zone Biological Area on Barro Colorado Is.

"Forty-niners" Arriving at Chagres — A68

Journey by "Bungo" to Las Cruces — A69

Canal Zone stamps can be mounted in the Scott U.S. Possessions album.

Las Cruces Trail to Panama — A70

Departure for San Francisco — A71

1949, June 1 *Perf. 11*
142 A68 3c blue .50 .25
143 A69 6c violet .65 .30
144 A70 12c bright green 1.10 .90
145 A71 18c deep red lilac 2.00 1.50
Nos. 142-145 (4) 4.25 2.95

Centenary of the California Gold Rush.

Workers in Culebra Cut — A72

Early Railroad Scene — A73

1951, Aug. 15
146 A72 10c carmine 2.25 1.50

Contribution of West Indian laborers in the construction of the Canal.

1955, Jan. 28 *Perf. 11*
147 A73 3c violet .60 .50

Cent. of the completion of the Panama Railroad and the 1st transcontinental railroad trip in Americas.

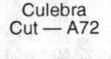

Gorgas Hospital and Ancon Hill — A74

1957, Nov. 17
148 A74 3c black, *blue green* .45 .35

75th anniv. of Gorgas Hospital. Printed on two shades of blue green paper.

S.S. Ancon A75

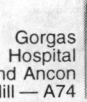

1958, Aug. 30 **Unwmk.**
149 A75 4c greenish blue .40 .30

Roosevelt Medal and Map — A76

1958, Nov. 15 *Perf. 11*
150 A76 4c brown .40 .30

Theodore Roosevelt (1858-1919).

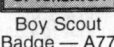

Boy Scout Badge — A77

Administration Building — A78

Giori Press Printing

1960, Feb. 8 *Perf. 11*
151 A77 4c dk blue, red & bister .50 .40

Boy Scouts of America, 50th anniv.

1960, Nov. 1 **Engr.** *Perf. 11*
152 A78 4c rose lilac .20 .20

Types of 1934, 1960 and 1946
Coil Stamps

1960-62 *Perf. 10 Vert.*
153 A45 3c deep violet .20 .20

Perf. 10 Horizontally
154 A78 4c deep rose lilac .20 .20

Perf. 10 Vertically
155 A65 5c deep blue .25 .20
Nos. 153-155 (3) .65 .60

Issue dates: 3c, 4c, 1960. 5c, Feb. 10, 1962.

Girl Scout Badge and Camp at Gatun Lake — A79

Giori Press Printing

1962, Mar. 12 *Perf. 11*
156 A79 4c blue, dk green & bister .50 .30

50th anniv. of Girl Scouts.

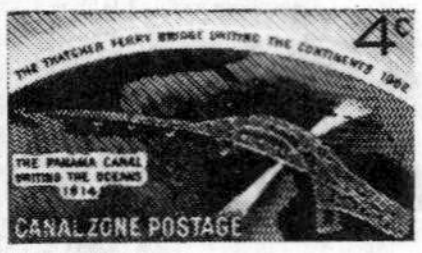

Thatcher Ferry Bridge and Map of Western Hemisphere A80

1962, Oct. 12
157 A80 4c black & silver .35 .25
a. Silver (bridge) omitted 7,500.

Opening of the Thatcher Ferry Bridge, spanning the Panama Canal.

Goethals Memorial, Balboa — A81

Fort San Lorenzo — A82

Giori Press Printing

1968-71 *Perf. 11*
158 A81 6c green & ultra .30 .30
159 A82 8c multicolored .35 .20

Issued: 6c, Mar. 15, 1968; 8c, July 14, 1971.

Portrait Type of 1928-48
Coil Stamps

1975, Feb. 14 **Engr.** *Perf. 10 Vert.*
160 A35 1c green .20 .20
161 A38 10c orange .70 .40
162 A66 25c yellow green 2.75 2.75
Nos. 160-162 (3) 3.65 3.35

Dredge Cascadas A83

Giori Press Printing

1976, Feb. 23 *Perf. 11*
163 A83 13c multicolored .35 .20
a. Booklet pane of 4 3.00 —

Stevens Type of 1946
Rotary Press Printing

1977 *Perf. 11x10½*
Size: 19x22½mm
164 A65 5c deep blue .60 .85
a. Tagged 9.50 —

Towing Locomotive, Ship in Lock — A84

1978, Oct. 25 **Engr.** *Perf. 11*
165 A84 15c dp green & blue green .35 .20

AIR POST STAMPS

AIR MAIL

Nos. 105-106 Surcharged in Dark Blue

25 CENTS 25

Type I- Flag of "5" pointing up **15**

Type II- Flag of "5" curved **15**

Flat Plate Printing

1929 **Unwmk.** *Perf. 11*
C1 A35 15c on 1c green, I 8.00 5.50
C2 A35 15c on 1c green, II 85.00 75.00
C3 A36 25c on 2c carmine 3.50 2.00
Nos. C1-C3 (3) 96.50 82.50

AIR MAIL

Nos. 114 and 106 Surcharged

≡10c

1929, Dec. 31
C4 A44 10c on 50c lilac 7.50 6.50
C5 A36 20c on 2c carmine 5.00 1.75
a. Dropped "2" in surcharge 80.00 60.00

Catalogue values for unused stamps in this section, from this point to the end of the section, are for Never Hinged items.

Gaillard Cut — AP1

1931-49 **Engr.**
C6 AP1 4c red violet ('49) .75 .70
C7 AP1 5c yellow green .60 .45
C8 AP1 6c yellow brown ('46) .75 .35
C9 AP1 10c orange 1.00 .35
C10 AP1 15c blue 1.25 .30
C11 AP1 20c red violet 2.00 .30
C12 AP1 30c rose lake ('41) 3.50 1.00
C13 AP1 40c yellow 3.50 1.10
C14 AP1 $1 black 8.50 1.90
Nos. C6-C14 (9) 21.85 6.45

For overprints see Nos. CO1-CO14.

Panama Canal Anniversary Issue

Douglas Plane over Sosa Hill — AP2

Planes and Map of Central America AP3

Pan American Clipper and Scene near Fort Amador AP4

Pan American Clipper at Cristobal Harbor — AP5

Pan American Clipper over Gaillard Cut — AP6

Pan American Clipper Landing AP7

1939, July 15
C15 AP2 5c greenish black 3.75 2.25
C16 AP3 10c dull violet 3.00 2.25
C17 AP4 15c light brown 4.25 1.25
C18 AP5 25c blue 13.00 8.00
C19 AP6 30c rose carmine 12.00 6.75
C20 AP7 $1 green 35.00 22.50
Nos. C15-C20 (6) 71.00 43.00

10th anniv. of Air Mail service and the 25th anniv. of the opening of the Panama Canal.

Globe and Wing — AP8

1951, July 16 **Unwmk.** *Perf. 11*
C21 AP8 4c red violet .75 .35
C22 AP8 6c brown .50 .25
C23 AP8 10c red orange .90 .35
C24 AP8 21c blue 7.50 4.00
C25 AP8 31c cerise 7.50 3.75
a. Horiz. pair, imperf. vert. 1,000. —
C26 AP8 80c gray black 4.50 1.50
Nos. C21-C26 (6) 21.65 10.20

1958, Aug. 16
C27 AP8 5c yellow green 1.00 .60
C28 AP8 7c olive 1.00 .45
C29 AP8 15c brown violet 3.75 2.75
C30 AP8 25c orange yellow 10.00 2.75
C31 AP8 35c dark blue 6.25 2.75
Nos. C27-C31 (5) 22.00 9.30
Nos. C21-C31 (11) 43.65 19.50

See No. C34.

Emblem of US Army Caribbean School — AP9

Giori Press Printing

1961, Nov. 21 *Perf. 11*
C32 AP9 15c red & dk blue 1.25 .75

Malaria Eradication Emblem and Mosquito AP10

1962, Sept. 24 **Unwmk.** *Perf. 11*
C33 AP10 7c yellow & black .45 .40

WHO drive to eradicate malaria.

Type of 1951
Rotary Press Printing

1963, Jan. 7 *Perf. 10½x11*
C34 AP8 8c carmine .40 .30

Alliance Emblem AP11

Giori Press Printing

1963, Aug. 17 Unwmk. *Perf. 11*

C35	AP11	15c gray, green & dk ultra	1.10	.85

2nd anniv. of the Alliance for Progress, which aims to stimulate economic growth and raise living standards in Latin America.

Jet over Cristobal AP12

Designs: 8c, Gatun Locks. 15c, Madden Dam. 20c, Gaillard Cut. 30c, Miraflores Locks. 80c, Balboa.

1964, Aug. 15 *Perf. 11*

C36	AP12	6c green & black	.45	.35
C37	AP12	8c rose red & black	.45	.35
C38	AP12	15c blue & black	1.00	.75
C39	AP12	20c rose lilac & blk	1.50	1.00
C40	AP12	30c redsh brown & blk	2.25	2.25
C41	AP12	80c ol bister & black	3.75	3.00
		Nos. C36-C41 (6)	9.40	7.70

50th anniv. of the Panama Canal.

Seal and Jet Plane — AP13

1965, July 15 Unwmk. *Perf. 11*

C42	AP13	6c green & black	.35	.30
C43	AP13	8c rose red & black	.30	.20
C44	AP13	15c blue & black	.50	.20
C45	AP13	20c lilac & black	.55	.30
C46	AP13	30c redsh brn & blk	.80	.30
C47	AP13	80c bister & black	2.00	.75
		Nos. C42-C47 (6)	4.50	2.05

1968-76

C48	AP13	10c dull orange & blk	.25	.20
a.		Booklet pane of 4 ('70)	4.25	—
C49	AP13	11c gray olive & blk	.25	.20
a.		Booklet pane of 4	3.50	—
C50	AP13	13c emerald & black	.80	.25
a.		Booklet pane of 4	6.00	—
C51	AP13	22c violet & black	.75	*2.00*
C52	AP13	25c pale yel green & blk	.60	.70
C53	AP13	35c salmon & black	.90	*2.00*
		Nos. C48-C53 (6)	3.55	*5.35*

Issued: 10c, 25c, 3/15/68; 11c, 9/24/71; 13c, 2/11/74; 22c, 35c, 5/10/76.

AIR POST OFFICIAL STAMPS

Officials and Air Post Officials were sold to the public only with a Balboa Heights, Canal Zone wavy line parcel post cancel while current. After being withdrawn from use, unused copies (except for Nos. CO8-CO12, O3 and O8) were sold at face value for three months beginning Jan. 2, 1952.

Used values are for the CTO copies, postally used copies being worth more.

Nos. C7, C9-C14 Overprinted in Black

OFFICIAL
PANAMA CANAL

Two Types of Overprint

1941-42 Unwmk. *Perf. 11*

"PANAMA CANAL" 19-20mm

CO1	AP1	5c yellow green	5.50	1.50
CO2	AP1	10c orange	8.50	2.00
CO3	AP1	15c blue	11.00	2.00
CO4	AP1	20c red violet	12.50	4.00
CO5	AP1	30c rose lake ('42)	17.50	5.00
CO6	AP1	40c yellow	17.50	7.50
CO7	AP1	$1 black	20.00	10.00
		Nos. CO1-CO7 (7)	92.50	32.00

Overprint varieties occur on Nos. CO1-CO7 and CO14: "O" over "N" of "PANAMA" (entire 3rd row). "O" broken at top (pos. 31). "O" over 2nd "A" of "PANAMA" (pos. 45). 1st "F" of "OFFICIAL" over 2nd "A" of "PANAMA" (pos. 50).

1941

"PANAMA CANAL" 17mm long

CO8	AP1	5c light green	—	160.00
CO9	AP1	10c orange	—	275.00
CO10	AP1	20c red violet	—	175.00
CO11	AP1	30c rose lake	—	65.00
CO12	AP1	40c yellow	—	180.00
		Nos. CO8-CO12 (5)		855.00

Same Overprint on No. C8

1947, Nov.

"PANAMA CANAL" 19-20mm long

CO14	AP1	6c yellow brown	12.50	5.00
a.		Inverted overprint		*2,500.*

POSTAGE DUE STAMPS

Postage Due Stamps of the US Nos. J45a, J46a and J49a Overprinted in Black

CANAL ZONE

1914, Mar. Wmk. 190 *Perf. 12*

J1	D2	1c rose carmine	85.00	15.00
J2	D2	2c rose carmine	250.00	45.00
J3	D2	10c rose carmine	850.00	40.00
		Nos. J1-J3 (3)	1,185.	100.00

Castle Gate (See footnote) — D1

Statue of Columbus D2

Pedro J. Sosa D3

Blue Overprint, Type II, on Postage Due Stamps of Panama

1915 Unwmk.

J4	D1	1c olive brown	12.50	5.00
J5	D2	2c olive brown	200.00	17.50
J6	D3	10c olive brown	50.00	10.00
		Nos. J4-J6 (3)	262.50	32.50

The 1c was intended to show a gate of San Lorenzo Castle, Chagres. By error the stamp actually shows the main gate of San Geronimo Castle, Portobelo.

Surcharged in Red

CANAL 2 ZONE

J7	D1	1c on 1c olive brn	105.00	15.00
J8	D2	2c on 2c olive brn	25.00	7.00
J9	D3	10c on 10c olive brn	22.50	5.00
		Nos. J7-J9 (3)	152.50	27.00

Columbus Statue — D4

Capitol, Panama City — D5

Carmine Surcharge

1919

J10	D4	2c on 2c olive brown	30.00	12.50
J11	D5	4c on 4c olive brown	35.00	15.00
a.		"ZONE" omitted	*7,500.*	
b.		"4" omitted	*7,500.*	

US Postage Due Stamps Nos. J61, J62b and J65b Overprinted in Black

CANAL

Type A

ZONE

Letters "A" with Flat Tops

1924 *Perf. 11*

J12	D2	1c carmine rose	110.00	27.50
J13	D2	2c deep claret	60.00	10.00
J14	D2	10c deep claret	250.00	50.00
		Nos. J12-J14 (3)	420.00	87.50

US Postage Stamps Nos. 552, 554 and 562 Overprinted Type A and additional Overprint in Red or Blue

POSTAGE
DUE

1925

J15	A155	1c deep green	90.00	13.00
J16	A157	2c carmine (Bl)	22.50	7.00
J17	A165	10c orange	50.00	11.00
a.		"POSTAGE DUE" double	450.00	
b.		"E" of "POSTAGE" missing	450.00	
c.		As "a" and "b"	*3,250.*	
		Nos. J15-J17 (3)	162.50	31.00

"CANAL ZONE" Type B Overprinted on US Nos. J61, J62, J65, J65a

Letters "A" with Sharp Pointed Tops

1925

J18	D2	1c carmine rose	8.00	3.00
a.		"ZONE ZONE"	1,250.	
J19	D2	2c carmine rose	15.00	4.00
a.		"ZONE ZONE"	1,500.	
J20	D2	10c carmine rose	150.00	20.00
a.		Pair, one without overprint	*1,750.*	
b.		10c rose red	*250.00*	150.00
c.		As "b," double overprint	*450.00*	—
		Nos. J18-J20 (3)	173.00	27.00

No. 107 Surcharged in Black

POSTAGE DUE
≡ 10 ≡

1929-30

J21	A37	1c on 5c blue	4.50	1.75
a.		"POSTAGE DUE" omitted	*5,500.*	
J22	A37	2c on 5c blue	7.50	2.50
J23	A37	5c on 5c blue	7.50	2.75
J24	A37	10c on 5c blue	7.50	2.75
		Nos. J21-J24 (4)	27.00	9.75

On No. J23 the horizontal bars in the lower corners of the surcharge are omitted.

Canal Zone Seal — D6

1932-41

J25	D6	1c claret	.20	.20
J26	D6	2c claret	.20	.20
J27	D6	5c claret	.35	.20
J28	D6	10c claret	1.40	1.50
J29	D6	15c claret ('41)	1.10	1.00
		Nos. J25-J29 (5)	3.25	3.10

The 1c and 5c are found in both "wet" and "dry" printings. (See note after US No. 1029.) The dry printings are in red violet.

OFFICIAL STAMPS

See note at beginning of Air Post Official Stamps.

Regular Issues of 1928-34 Overprinted in Black:

OFFICIAL
PANAMA
CANAL
Type 1

OFFICIAL
PANAMA CANAL
Type 2

Type 1 - "PANAMA" 10mm long.
Type 1A - "PANAMA" 9mm long.

1941 Unwmk. *Perf. 11*

O1	A35	1c yellow green (1)	2.25	.40
O2	A45	3c deep violet (1)	4.00	.75
O3	A37	5c blue (2)	*1,000.*	32.50
O4	A38	10c orange (1)	7.00	1.90
O5	A41	15c gray (1)	12.50	2.25
O6	A42	20c olive brown (1)	15.00	2.75
O7	A44	50c lilac (1)	37.50	5.50
O8	A44	50c rose lilac (1A)		625.00

Same Overprint on No. 139

1947

O9	A65	5c deep blue (1)	9.00	3.50

CUBA

'kyü-bə

LOCATION — The largest island of the West Indies; south of Florida.

GOVT. — socialist; under US military governor 1899-1902 and US provisional governor 1906-1909.

AREA — 44,206 sq. mi.

POP. — 9,710,000 (1981)

CAPITAL — Havana

Formerly a Spanish possession, Cuba's attempts to gain freedom led to US intervention in 1898. Under Treaty of Paris of that year, Spain relinquished the island to US trust. In 1902, a republic was established and Cuban Congress took over government from US military authorities.

100 Cents = 1 Dollar

Watermark

Wmk. 191- Double-lined "USPS" in Capitals

Values for Nos. 176-220 are for stamps in the grade of fine and in sound condition where such exist. Values for Nos. 221-J4 are for very fine examples.

King Alfonso XIII
A19 N2

United States Administration

Puerto Principe Issue

Issues of Cuba of 1898 and 1896 Surcharged:

HABILITADO
1
cent.
a

HABILITADO
1
cents.
b

HABILITADO
2
cents.
c

HABILITADO
2
cents.
d

HABILITADO 3 cents. (e)

HABILITADO 3 cents. (f)

HABILITADO 5 cents. (g)

HABILITADO 5 cents. (h)

HABILITADO 5 cents. (i)

HABILITADO 5 cents. (j)

HABILITADO 3 cents. (k)

HABILITADO 3 cents. (l)

HABILITADO 10 cents. (m)

Types a, c, d, e, f, g and h are 17½mm high, the others are 19½mm high.

Black Surcharge on #156-158, 160

1898-99

176 (a) 1c on 1m org brn 50. 30.
177 (b) 1c on 1m org brn 45. 35.
- *a.* Broken figure "1" 75. 65.
- *b.* Inverted surcharge 200.
- *d.* As "a," inverted 250.

178 (c) 2c on 2m org brn 22.50 18.
- *a.* Inverted surcharge 250. 50.

179 (d) 2c on 2m org brn 40. 35.
- *a.* Inverted surcharge 350. 100.

179B (k) 3c on 1m org brn 300. 175.
- *c.* Double surcharge 1,500. 750.

179D (l) 3c on 1m org brn *1,500.* *675.*
- *e.* Double surcharge — —

179F (e) 3c on 2m org brn *1,500.*

Value for No. 179F is for copies with minor faults.

179G (f) 3c on 2m org brn — *2,000.*

Value for No. 179G is for copies with minor faults.

180 (e) 3c on 3m org brown 27.50 30.
- *a.* Inverted surcharge 110.

181 (f) 3c on 3m org brown 75. 75.
- *a.* Inverted surcharge *200.*

182 (g) 5c on 1m org brown 700. 200.
- *a.* Inverted surcharge *500.*

183 (h) 5c on 1m org brown *1,300.* 500.
- *a.* Inverted surcharge *700.*

184 (g) 5c on 2m org brown 750. 250.
185 (h) 5c on 2m org brown 1,500. 500.
186 (g) 5c on 3m org brown 175.
- *a.* Inverted surcharge 700.

187 (h) 5c on 3m org brown 400.
- *a.* Inverted surcharge 1,000.

188 (g) 5c on 5m org brown 80. 60.
- *a.* Inverted surcharge 400. 200.
- *b.* Double surcharge — —

189 (h) 5c on 5m org brown 350. 250.
- *a.* Inverted surcharge 400.
- *b.* Double surcharge — —

Values for Nos. 188, 189 are for the 1st printing. The 2nd printing was surcharged using a shiny ink.

189C (i) 5c on 5m org brown *7,500.*

Black Surcharge on No. P25

190 (g) 5c on ½m blue grn 250. 75.
- *a.* Inverted surcharge 500. 150.
- *b.* Pair, one without surch. 500.

Value for No. 190b is for pair with unsurcharged copy at right. Exists with unsurcharged stamp at left.

191 (h) 5c on ½m blue grn 300. 90.
- *a.* Inverted surcharge 200.

192 (i) 5c on ½m blue grn 550. 200.
- *a.* Dbl. surch., one diagonal *11,500.*

193 (j) 5c on ½m blue grn 800. 300.

Red Surcharge on No. 161

196 (k) 3c on 1c black violet 65. 35.
- *a.* Inverted surcharge 300.

197 (l) 3c on 1c black violet 125. 55.
- *a.* Inverted surcharge 300.

198 (i) 5c on 1c black violet 25. 30.
- *a.* Inverted surcharge 125.
- *b.* Vert. surch., reading up *3,500.*
- *c.* Double surcharge 400. *600.*
- *d.* Double invtd. surcharge —

No. 198b exists reading down.

199 (j) 5c on 1c black vio 55. 55.
- *a.* Inverted surcharge 250.
- *b.* Vertical surcharge *2,000.*
- *c.* Double surcharge 1,000. 600.

200 (m) 10c on 1c black vio 20. *50.*
- *a.* Broken figure "1" 40. *100.*

Black Surcharge on Nos. P26-P30

201 (k) 3c on 1m blue green 350. 350.
- *a.* Inverted surcharge 450.
- *b.* "EENTS" 550. 450.
- *c.* As "b," inverted 850.

202 (l) 3c on 1m blue green 550. 400.
- *a.* Inverted surcharge 850.

203 (k) 3c on 2m blue green 850. 350.
- *a.* "EENTS" 1,250. 500.
- *b.* Inverted surcharge 850.
- *c.* As "a," inverted 950.

204 (l) 3c on 2m blue green 1,250. 600.
- *a.* Inverted surcharge 750.

205 (k) 3c on 3m blue green 900. 350.
- *a.* Inverted surcharge 500.
- *b.* "EENTS" 1,250. 450.
- *c.* As "b," inverted 700.

206 (l) 3c on 3m blue green 1,200. 550.
- *a.* Inverted surcharge 700.

211 (i) 5c on 1m blue green 1,800.
- *a.* "EENTS" — 2,500.

212 (j) 5c on 1m blue green 2,250.
213 (i) 5c on 2m blue green 1,800.
- *a.* "EENTS" — 1,900.

214 (j) 5c on 2m blue green 1,750.
215 (i) 5c on 3m blue green 550.
- *a.* "EENTS" 1,000.

216 (j) 5c on 3m blue green — 1,000.
217 (i) 5c on 4m blue green *2,500.* 900.
- *a.* "EENTS" *3,000.* 1,500.
- *b.* Inverted surcharge *2,000.*
- *c.* As "a," inverted 2,000.

218 (j) 5c on 4m blue green *1,250.*
- *a.* Inverted surcharge *2,000.*

219 (i) 5c on 8m blue green *2,500.* 1,250.
- *a.* Inverted surcharge 1,500.
- *b.* "EENTS" — 1,800.
- *c.* As "b," inverted 2,500.

220 (j) 5c on 8m blue green 2,000.
- *a.* Inverted surcharge 2,500.

US Nos. 279, 267, 267b, 279Bf, 279Bh, 268, 281, 282C and 283 Surcharged in Black

CUBA 1 c. de PESO.

1899 **Wmk. 191** ***Perf. 12***

221 A87 1c on 1c yellow green 5.25 .35
222 A88 2c on 2c reddish car, type III 10.00 .75
- *b.* 2c on 2c vermilion, type III 10.00 .75

222A A88 2c on 2c reddish car, type IV 5.75 .40
- *c.* 2c on 2c vermilion, type IV 5.75 .40
- *d.* As #222A, inverted surcharge *3,500.* *3,500.*

223 A88 2½c on 2c reddish car, type III 5.00 .80
- *b.* 2½c on 2c vermilion, type III 5.00 .80

223A A88 2½c on 2c reddish car, type IV 3.50 .50
- *c.* 2½c on 2c vermilion 3.50 .50

224 A89 3c on 3c purple 12.50 1.75
- *a.* "CUB.A" 35.00 35.00

225 A91 5c on 5c blue 12.50 2.00
226 A94 10c on 10c brn, type I 22.50 6.50
- *b.* "CUBA" omitted *4,000.* *4,000.*

226A A94 10c on 10c brn, type II *6,250.*

Nos. 221-226 (8) 77.00 13.05

The 2½c was sold and used as a 2 centavo stamp.

Excellent counterfeits of this and the preceding issue exist, especially inverted and double surcharges.

Issues of the Republic under US Military Rule

Statue of Columbus A20

Royal Palms A21

"Cuba" A22

Ocean Liner A23

Cane Field — A24

Wmk. U S-C (191C)

1899 **Engr.** ***Perf. 12***

227 A20 1c yellow green 3.50 .20
228 A21 2c carmine 3.50 .20
- *a.* 2c scarlet 3.50 .20
- *b.* Booklet pane of 6 *2,000.*

229 A22 3c purple 3.50 .20
230 A23 5c blue 4.50 .20
231 A24 10c brown 11.00 .50

Nos. 227-231 (5) 26.00 1.30

Unwatermarked stamps of designs A20-A24 were re-engraved and issued by the Cuban Republic. See Volume 2 for details of the re-engraving.

SPECIAL DELIVERY STAMPS

United States Administration

US No. E5 Surcharged in Red

CUBA. 10c. de PESO

1899 **Wmk. 191** ***Perf. 12***

E1 SD3 10c on 10c blue 130.00 100.00
- *a.* No period after "CUBA" 450.00 400.00

Issues of the Republic under US Military Rule

Special Delivery Messenger SD2

Inscribed: "Immediata"

1899 **Wmk. 191C** **Engr.**

E2 SD2 10c orange 45.00 15.00

POSTAGE DUE STAMPS

United States Administration

Postage Due Stamps of the US Nos. J38, J39, J41 and J42 Surcharged in Black Like Nos. 221-226A

1899 **Wmk. 191** ***Perf. 12***

J1 D2 1c on 1c deep claret 45.00 5.25
J2 D2 2c on 2c deep claret 45.00 5.25
- *a.* Inverted surcharge *2,750.*

J3 5c on 5c deep claret 45.00 5.25
J4 D2 10c on 10c deep claret 27.50 2.50

Nos. J1-J4 (4) 162.50 18.25

DANISH WEST INDIES

'dā-nish 'west 'in-dēs

LOCATION — Group of islands in the West Indies, lying east of Puerto Rico
GOVT. — Danish colony
AREA — 132 sq. mi.
POP. — 27,086 (1911)
CAPITAL — Charlotte Amalie

The US bought these islands in 1917 and they became the US Virgin Islands, using US stamps and currency.

100 Cents = 1 Dollar
100 Bit = 1 Franc (1905)

Watermarks

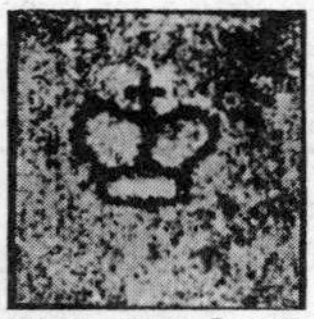

Wmk. 111- Small Crown

Wmk. 112- Crown

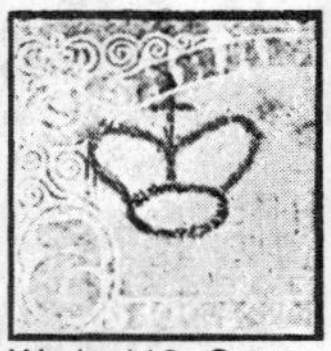
Wmk. 113- Crown

Wmk. 114- Multiple Crosses

Coat of Arms — A1

Yellowish Paper
Yellow Wavy-line Burelage, UL to LR

1856 Wmk. 111 Typo. *Imperf.*
1 A1 3c dk car, brown gum 175. 175.
a. 3c dark carmine, yellow gum 200. 200.
b. 3c carmine, white gum 4,500. —

Reprint: 1981, carmine, back-printed across two stamps ("Reprint by Dansk Post og Telegrafmuseum 1978"), value, pair, $10.

White Paper
Yellow Wavy-line Burelage, UR to LL

1866
2 A1 3c rose 45.00 60.00

No. 2 reprints unwatermarked: 1930 carmine, value $100. 1942 rose carmine, backprinted across each row ("Nytryk 1942 G. A. Hagemann Danmark og Dansk Vestindiens Friemaerker Bind 2"), value $50.

1872 *Perf. 12½*
3 A1 3c rose 85.00 150.00

1873
Without Burelage
4 A1 4c dull blue 175.00 325.00
a. Imperf., pair 750.00
b. Horiz. pair, imperf. vert. 550.00

#4 reprints, unwatermarked, imperf.: 1930, ultramarine, value $100. 1942, blue backprinted like 1942 reprint of #2, value $50.

A2

Normal Frame

Inverted Frame

The arabesques in the corners have a main stem and a branch. When the frame is in normal position, in the upper left corner the branch leaves the main stem half way between two little leaflets. In the lower right corner the branch starts at the foot of the second leaflet. When the frame is inverted the corner designs are, of course, transposed.

White Wove Paper, Varying from Thin to Thick

1874-79 Wmk. 112 *Perf. 14x13½*
5 A2 1c green & brn red 20.00 27.50
a. 1c grn & rose lilac, thin paper 85.00 140.00
b. 1c grn & red violet, medium paper 50.00 75.00
c. 1c green & violet, thick paper 20.00 27.50
e. Inverted frame 20.00 27.50
6 A2 3c blue & carmine 20.00 27.50
a. 3c light blue & rose carmine, thin paper 70.00 55.00
b. 3c deep blue & dark carmine, medium paper 40.00 20.00
c. 3c greenish blue & lake, thick paper 22.50 15.00
d. Imperf., pair 350.00
e. Inverted frame 22.50 15.00
7 A2 4c brn & dull blue 20.00 15.00
b. 4c brown & ultramarine 250.00 250.00
c. Diagonal half used as 2c on cover 125.00
d. As "b," inverted frame 1,250. 1,500.
8 A2 5c green & gray ('76) 20.00 15.00
a. 5c yellow green & dark gray, thin paper 50.00 35.00
b. Inverted frame 20.00 15.00
9 A2 7c lilac & orange 25.00 75.00
a. 7c lilac & yellow 55.00 55.00
b. Inverted frame 45.00 125.00
10 A2 10c blue & brn ('76) 20.00 17.50
a. 10c dark blue & black brown, thin paper 50.00 35.00
b. "cent.s" 22.50 17.50
c. Inverted frame 22.50 25.00
11 A2 12c red lilac & yel green ('77) 40.00 125.00
a. 12c lilac & deep green 125.00 175.00
12 A2 14c lilac & green 500.00 900.00
a. Inverted frame 2,250. 3,250.
13 A2 50c violet, thin paper ('79) 80.00 175.00
a. 50c gray violet, thick porous paper 150.00 300.00
Nos. 5-13 (9) 745.00 1,377.

The central element in the fan-shaped scrollwork at the outside of the lower left corner of Nos. 5a and 7b looks like an elongated diamond.

See Nos. 16-20. For surcharges see Nos. 14-15, 23-28, 40.

Nos. 9 and 13 Surcharged in Black

1 CENT

10 CENTS 1895

1887-95
14 A2 1c on 7c lilac & org 65.00 175.00
a. 1c on 7c lilac & yellow 90.00 200.00
b. Double surcharge 200.00 300.00
c. Inverted frame 90.00 300.00
15 A2 10c on 50c violet, thin paper ('95) 27.50 55.00

Type of 1874-79

1896-1901 *Perf. 13*
16 A2 1c green & red vio ('98) 11.00 17.50
a. Normal frame 250.00 375.00
17 A2 3c blue & lake ('98) 11.00 12.50
a. Normal frame 275.00 325.00
18 A2 4c bister & dull blue ('01) 12.50 12.50
a. Diagonal half used as 2c on cover 40.00
b. Inverted frame 45.00 75.00
c. As "b," diagonal half used as 2c on cover 250.00
19 A2 5c green & gray 45.00 32.50
a. Normal frame 600.00 1,150.
20 A2 10c blue & brown ('01) 65.00 110.00
a. Inverted frame 900.00 1,300.
b. "cent.s" 85.00 130.00
Nos. 16-20 (5) 144.50 185.00

Arms — A5

1900
21 A5 1c light green 2.50 2.50
22 A5 5c light blue 12.50 22.50

See Nos. 29-30. For surcharges see Nos. 41-42.

Nos. 6, 17, 20 Surcharged:

2 CENTS 1902
c

8 Cents 1902
d

Surcharge "c" in Black

1902 *Perf. 14x13½*
23 A2 2c on 3c blue & car 400.00 400.00
a. "2" in date with straight tail 425.00 450.00
b. Normal frame 3,500.

Perf. 13
24 A2 2c on 3c blue & lake 8.00 17.50
a. "2" in date with straight tail 15.00 20.00
b. Dated "1901" 325.00 400.00
c. Normal frame 150.00 200.00
d. Dark green surcharge 1,750.
e. As "d" & "a" —
f. As "d" & "c" —
25 A2 8c on 10c blue & brn 20.00 32.50
a. "2" with straight tail 20.00 35.00
b. On No. 20b 20.00 37.50
c. Inverted frame 250.00 350.00

Only one copy of No. 24f can exist.

Surcharge "d" in Black
27 A2 2c on 3c blue & lake 11.00 22.50
a. Normal frame 225.00 375.00
28 A2 8c on 10c blue & brn 11.00 11.00
a. On No. 20b 17.50 20.00
b. Inverted frame 175.00 350.00
Nos. 23-28 (5) 450.00 483.50

One example reported of No. 24f.

1903 Wmk. 113
29 A5 2c carmine 8.00 15.00
30 A5 8c brown 22.50 35.00

King Christian IX — A8

St. Thomas Harbor — A9

1905 Typo. *Perf. 13*
31 A8 5b green 3.50 3.00
32 A8 10b red 4.50 3.00
33 A8 20b green & blue 11.00 8.00
34 A8 25b ultramarine 8.00 8.00
35 A8 40b red & gray 9.00 8.00
36 A8 50b yellow & gray 9.00 11.00

Frame Typo., Center Engr.
Wmk. Two Crowns (113)
Perf. 12
37 A9 1fr green & blue 17.50 37.50
38 A9 2fr org red & brown 35.00 60.00
39 A9 5fr yellow & brown 85.00 225.00
Nos. 31-39 (9) 182.50

Favor cancels exist on #37-39. Value 25% less.

Nos. 18, 22, 30 Surcharged in Black

5 BIT 1905

1905 Wmk. 112 *Perf. 13*
40 A2 5b on 4c bis & dull blue 12.50 35.00
a. Inverted frame 40.00 75.00
41 A5 5b on 5c light blue 12.50 32.50

Wmk. 113
42 A5 5b on 8c brown 12.50 32.50
Nos. 40-42 (3) 37.50 100.00

Favor cancels exist on #40-42. Value 25% less.

Frederik VIII A10

Christian X A11

Frame Typo., Center Engr.
1907-08 Wmk. 113 *Perf. 13*
43 A10 5b green 1.75 1.25
44 A10 10b red 1.75 1.25
45 A10 15b violet & brown 4.00 4.00
46 A10 20b green & blue 35.00 27.50
47 A10 25b blue & dk blue 1.75 1.75
48 A10 30b claret & slate 45.00 45.00
49 A10 40b ver & gray 4.50 4.75
50 A10 50b yellow & brown 4.50 7.50
Nos. 43-50 (8) 98.25 93.00

1915 Wmk. 114 *Perf. 14x14½*
51 A11 5b yellow green 3.00 5.00
52 A11 10b red 3.00 35.00
53 A11 15b lilac & red brown 3.00 40.00
54 A11 20b green & blue 3.00 40.00
55 A11 25b blue & dark blue 3.00 10.00
56 A11 30b claret & black 3.00 50.00
57 A11 40b orange & black 3.00 50.00
58 A11 50b yellow & brown 3.00 50.00
Nos. 51-58 (8) 24.00

Forged and favor cancellations exist.

Danish West Indies stamps can be mounted in the Scott U.S. Possessions album.

POSTAGE DUE STAMPS

Royal Cipher, "Christian 9 Rex" — D1

1902 Unwmk. Litho. *Perf. 11½*
J1 D1 1c dark blue 5.00 10.00
J2 D1 4c dark blue 10.00 20.00
J3 D1 6c dark blue 20.00 50.00
J4 D1 10c dark blue 15.00 45.00
Nos. J1-J4 (4) 50.00 125.00

There are five types of each value. On the 4c they may be distinguished by differences in the figures "4"; on the other values the differences are minute.

Used values of Nos. J1-J4 are for canceled copies. Uncanceled examples without gum have probably been used. Value 60% of unused.

Counterfeits of Nos. J1-J4 exist.

D2

1905-13 *Perf. 13*
J5 D2 5b red & gray 4.00 5.00
J6 D2 20b red & gray 10.00 12.50
J7 D2 30b red & gray 7.00 12.50
J8 D2 50b red & gray 9.00 32.50
a. Perf. 14x14½ ('13) 35.00 125.00
b. Perf. 11½ 400.00
Nos. J5-J8 (4) 30.00 62.50

All values of this issue are known imperforate, but were not regularly issued.

Used values of Nos. J5-J8 are for canceled copies. Uncanceled examples without gum have probably been used. Value 60% of unused.

Counterfeits of Nos. J5-J8 exist.

Danish West Indies stamps were replaced by those of the US in 1917, after the US bought the islands.

GUAM

'gwäm

LOCATION — One of the Mariana Islands in the Pacific Ocean, about 1450 miles east of the Philippines
GOVT. — United States Possession
AREA — 206 sq. mi.
POP. — 9,000 (est. 1899)
CAPITAL — Agaña

Formerly a Spanish possession, Guam was ceded to the United States in 1898 following the Spanish-American War. Stamps overprinted "Guam" were superseded by the regular postage stamps of the United States in 1901.

100 Cents = 1 Dollar

US Nos. 279, 279B, 279Bc, 268, 280a, 281, 282, 272, 282C, 283, 284, 275, 275a, 276 and 276A Overprinted in Black (1c-50c) or Red ($1)

GUAM

1899 Wmk. 191 *Perf. 12*
1 A87 1c deep green 20.00 25.00
2 A88 2c red, type IV 17.50 25.00
a. 2c rose carmine, type IV 22.50 30.00
3 A89 3c purple 125.00 175.00
4 A90 4c lilac brown 135.00 175.00
5 A91 5c blue 30.00 45.00
6 A92 6c lake 125.00 200.00
7 A93 8c violet brown 125.00 200.00
8 A94 10c brown, type I 45.00 55.00
9 A94 10c brown, type II 3,500. —
10 A95 15c olive green 150.00 175.00
11 A96 50c orange 300.00 375.00
a. 50c red orange 500.00 —
12 A97 $1 black, type I 350.00 400.00
13 A97 $1 black, type II 3,750.
Nos. 1-8,10-12 (11) 1,422. 1,850.

SPECIAL DELIVERY STAMP

United States No. E5 Overprinted in Red **GUAM**

1899 Wmk. 191 ***Perf. 12***
E1 SD3 10c blue 150.00 *200.00*

Guam Guard Mail stamps of 1930 are listed in the Scott Specialized United States Catalogue.

HAWAII

hə-ˈwä-yē

LOCATION — Group of 20 islands in the Pacific Ocean, about 2,000 miles southwest of San Francisco.
GOVT. — Former Kingdom and Republic
AREA — 6,435 sq. mi.
POP. — 150,000 (est. 1899)
CAPITAL — Honolulu

Until 1893 an independent kingdom, from 1893 to 1898 a republic, the Hawaiian Islands were annexed to the US in 1898. The Territory of Hawaii achieved statehood in 1959.

100 Cents = 1 Dollar

Values for Nos. 1-4 are for examples with minor damage that has been skillfully repaired.

A1

A2

A3

Pelure Paper

1851-52 Unwmk. Typeset ***Imperf.***
1 A1 2c blue *660,000. 200,000.*
2 A1 5c blue *45,000. 25,000.*
3 A2 13c blue *22,500. 17,500.*
4 A3 13c blue *40,000. 27,500.*

Two varieties of each.
No. 1 unused is unique.

King Kamehameha III
A4 A5

Thick White Wove Paper

1853 **Engr.**
5 A4 5c blue 1,250. 950.
a. Line through "Honolulu" (Pos. 2) *2,250. 1,250.*
6 A5 13c dark red 600. *1,000.*

See #8-9. See Special Printings section, #10-11.

Hawaii stamps can be mounted in the Scott U.S. Possessions album.

A6

1857
7 A6 5c on 13c dark red *6,750. 9,000.*

1857

Thin White Wove Paper
8 A4 5c blue 600. 575.
a. Line through "Honolulu" (Pos. 2) *1,050. 1,000.*
b. Double impression *2,500. 3,500.*

1861

Thin Bluish Wove Paper
9 A4 5c blue 350. 250.
a. Line through "Honolulu" (Pos. 2) *750. 1,000.*

For Re-issues and Reprints of Types A4-A5 see Special Printings section.

Unused values for the Numeral stamps, Nos. 12-26, are for examples without gum.

A7

A8

A9

1859-62 **Typeset**
12 A7 1c lt blue, *bluish white* *7,500. 5,500.*
a. "1 Ce" omitted — *15,000.*
b. "nt" omitted —
13 A7 2c lt blue, *bluish white* *6,000. 3,500.*
a. 2c dark blue, *grayish white* *6,500. 3,750.*
b. Comma after "Cents" — *6,000.*
c. No period after "Leta" —
14 A7 2c blk, *grnsh blue* ('62) *6,000. 3,500.*
a. "2-Cents." — —

1863
15 A7 1c black, *grayish* 450. *1,000.*
a. Tete beche pair *3,500.*
b. "NTER" —
c. Period omitted after "Postage" 700.
16 A7 2c black, *grayish* 800. 600.
a. "2" at top of rectangle *3,500. 2,500.*
b. Printed on both sides — *20,000.*
c. "NTER" *3,000. 3,000.*
d. 2c black, *grayish white* 675. 575.
e. Period omitted after "Cents" —
f. Overlapping impressions — —
g. "TAGE." — —
17 A7 2c dk blue, *bluish* *7,500. 6,500.*
a. "ISL" — —
18 A7 2c black, *blue gray* *2,750. 4,500.*

1864-65
19 A7 1c black 450. *1,000.*
20 A7 2c black 600. *1,150.*
21 A8 5c blue, *blue* ('65) 750. 550.
a. Tete beche pair *7,500.*
b. 5c bluish black, *grayish white* *12,000.*
22 A9 5c blue, *blue* ('65) 500. *750.*
a. Tete beche pair *5,000.*
b. 5c blue, *grayish white* —
c. Overlapping impressions —

1864 **Laid Paper**
23 A7 1c black 250. *2,000.*
a. HA instead of HAWAIIAN *2,750.*
b. Tete beche pair *6,000.*
c. Tete beche pair, #23, 23a *17,500.*
24 A7 2c black 250. *1,000.*
a. "NTER" *2,250.*
b. "S" of "POSTAGE" omitted *1,000.*
c. Tete beche pair *5,250.*

A10

1865 **Wove Paper**
25 A10 1c dark blue 250. —
a. Double impression —
b. With inverted impression of #21 *6,500.*
26 A10 2c dark blue 250.

Nos. 12 to 26 were typeset and were printed in settings of ten, each stamp differing from the others.

King Kamehameha IV — A11

1861-63 **Litho.**

Horizontally Laid Paper
27 A11 2c pale rose 275. 250.
a. 2c carmine rose ('63) 1,750. *2,100.*

Vertically Laid Paper
28 A11 2c pale rose 275. 150.
a. 2c carmine rose ('63) 275. *325.*

For Re-issues and Reprints of Type A11 see Special Printings section.

Princess Victoria Kamamalu — A12

King Kamehameha IV — A13

King Kamehameha V
A14 A15

Mataio Kekuanaoa — A16

1864-86 Engr. ***Perf. 12***

Wove Paper
30 A12 1c purple ('86) 9.00 7.50
a. 1c mauve ('71) 35.00 15.00
b. 1c violet ('78) 15.00 10.00
31 A13 2c vermilion ('86) 15.00 9.00
a. 2c rose vermilion 35.00 12.50
b. Half used as 1c on cover *8,500.*
32 A14 5c blue ('66) 150.00 30.00
33 A15 6c yellow green ('71) 25.00 9.00
a. 6c bluish green ('78) 25.00 9.00
34 A16 18c dull rose ('71) 85.00 35.00
Nos. 30-34 (5) 284.00 90.50

No. 32 has traces of rectangular frame lines surrounding the design. Nos. 39 and 52C have no such frame lines.

For overprints see #53, 58-60, 65, 66C, 71.

King David Kalakaua
A17

Prince William Pitt Leleiohoku
A18

1875
35 A17 2c brown 7.50 3.00
36 A18 12c black 55.00 27.50

See Nos. 38, 43, 46. For overprints see Nos. 56, 62-63, 66, 69.

Princess Likelike — A19

King David Kalakaua — A20

Queen Kapiolani — A21

Statue of King Kamehameha I — A22

King William Lunalilo
A23

Queen Emma Kaleleonalani
A24

1882
37 A19 1c blue 6.00 *10.00*
38 A17 2c lilac rose 125.00 45.00
39 A14 5c ultramarine 15.00 3.25
a. Vert. pair, imperf. horiz. *4,250. 4,250.*
40 A20 10c black 35.00 20.00
41 A21 15c red brown 55.00 25.00
Nos. 37-41 (5) 236.00 103.25

1883-86
42 A19 1c green 2.75 1.90
43 A17 2c rose ('86) 4.00 1.00
a. 2c dull red 60.00 20.00
44 A20 10c red brown ('84) 30.00 10.00
45 A20 10c vermilion 32.50 12.50
46 A18 12c red lilac 75.00 32.50
47 A22 25c dark violet 125.00 55.00
48 A23 50c red 150.00 82.50
49 A24 $1 rose red 225.00 135.00
Maltese cross cancellation 75.00
Nos. 42-49 (8) 644.25 330.40

Other fiscal cancellations exist on No. 49. For overprints see Nos. 54-55, 57, 61-61B, 64, 67-68, 70, 72-73.

For Reproduction and Reprint of the 2c see Special Printings section.

Queen Liliuokalani — A25

1890-91 ***Perf. 12***
52 A25 2c dull violet ('91) 4.50 1.50
a. Vert. pair, imperf. horiz. *3,750.*
52C A14 5c deep indigo 105.00 135.00

Stamps of 1864-91 Overprinted in Red **Provisional GOVT. 1893**

1893
53 A12 1c purple 7.50 12.50
a. "189" instead of "1893" 400.00 —
b. No period after "GOVT" *200.00 200.00*
54 A19 1c blue 6.00 *12.50*
b. No period after "GOVT" *135.00 135.00*
55 A19 1c green 1.50 *3.00*
a. Pair, one without ovpt. *10,000.*
b. Double overprint 600.00 450.00
56 A17 2c brown 10.00 *20.00*
a. No period after "GOVT" *300.00* —
57 A25 2c dull violet 1.50 1.25
a. Inverted overprint *4,000. 3,500.*
b. Double overprint 850.00 650.00
c. "18 3" instead of "1893" *600.00 500.00*
58 A14 5c deep indigo 10.00 *25.00*
a. No period after "GOVT" *225.00 250.00*
59 A14 5c ultra 6.00 2.50
a. Inverted overprint *1,250. 1,250.*
b. Double overprint *5,000.*
60 A15 6c green 15.00 *25.00*
a. Double overprint *1,250.*

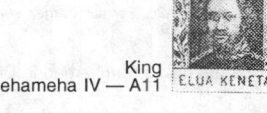

61	A20	10c black	9.00	15.00
a.		Double overprint	700.00	300.00
61B	A20	10c red brown	14,000.	29,000.
62	A18	12c black	9.00	17.50
b.		Double overprint	2,000.	
63	A18	12c red lilac	150.00	250.00
64	A22	25c dark violet	25.00	40.00
a.		No period after "GOVT"	325.00	300.00
		Nos. 53-61,62-64 (12)	250.50	424.25

Overprinted in Black

65	A13	2c vermilion	65.00	75.00
a.		No period after "GOVT"	250.00	250.00
66	A17	2c rose	1.25	2.25
a.		Double overprint	2,500.	
b.		No period after "GOVT"	50.00	60.00
66C	A15	6c green	14,000.	29,000.
67	A20	10c vermilion	15.00	30.00
68	A20	10c red brown	7.50	12.50
69	A18	12c red lilac	275.00	500.00
70	A21	15c red brown	20.00	30.00
a.		Double overprint	2,000.	
71	A16	18c dull rose	25.00	35.00
a.		Double overprint	350.00	
b.		Pair, one without ovpt.	2,500.	
c.		No period after "GOVT"	300.00	300.00
d.		"18 3" instead of "1893"	400.00	375.00
72	A23	50c red	60.00	90.00
b.		No period after "GOVT"	400.00	400.00
73	A24	$1 rose red	110.00	175.00
a.		No period after "GOVT"	450.00	400.00
		Nos. 65-66,67-73 (9)	578.75	949.75

Coat of Arms — A26

View of Honolulu — A27

Statue of Kamehameha I — A28

Stars and Palms — A29

S. S. "Arawa" — A30

Pres. Sanford Ballard Dole — A31

"CENTS" Added — A32

1894

74	A26	1c yellow	2.00	1.25
75	A27	2c brown	2.25	.60
76	A28	5c rose lake	4.00	1.50
77	A29	10c yellow green	6.00	4.50
78	A30	12c blue	12.50	17.50
79	A31	25c deep blue	12.50	17.50
		Nos. 74-79 (6)	39.25	42.85

1899

80	A26	1c dark green	1.50	1.25
81	A27	2c rose	1.35	1.00
a.		2c salmon	1.50	1.25
b.		Vert. pair, imperf. horiz.	4,500.	
82	A32	5c blue	5.50	3.00
		Nos. 80-82 (3)	8.35	5.25

OFFICIAL STAMPS

Lorrin Andrews Thurston — O1

1896 Unwmk. Engr. *Perf. 12*

O1	O1	2c green	35.00	17.50
O2	O1	5c black brown	35.00	17.50
O3	O1	6c deep ultra	35.00	17.50
O4	O1	10c bright rose	35.00	17.50
O5	O1	12c orange	35.00	17.50
O6	O1	25c gray violet	35.00	17.50
		Nos. O1-O6 (6)	210.00	105.00

Used values for Nos. O1-O6 are for copies canceled to order "FOREIGN OFFICE/HONOLULU H.I." in double circle without date.

The stamps of Hawaii were replaced by those of the United States.

SPECIAL PRINTINGS

Re-issues

1868

Ordinary White Wove Paper

10	A4	5c blue	25.00	
a.		Line through "Honolulu" (Pos. 2)	50.00	
11	A5	13c dull rose	250.00	

Reprints:

5c. Originals have two small dots near the left side of the square in the upper right corner. These dots are missing in the reprints.

13c. The bottom of the 3 of 13 in the upper left corner is flattened in the originals and rounded in the reprints. The "t" of "Cts" on the left side is as tall as the "C" in the reprints, but shorter in the originals.

On August 19, 1892, the remaining supply of reprints was overprinted in black "REPRINT." The reprints (both with and without overprint) were sold at face value. See the Scott U.S. Specialized Catalogue.

1869 Engr. Thin Wove Paper

29	A11	2c red	45.00	—

No. 29 was sold only at the Honolulu post office, at first without overprint and later with overprint "CANCELLED."

See note following No. 51.

Reproduction and Reprint

Yellowish Wove Paper

1886-89 *Imperf.*

50	A11	2c orange vermilion	150.00
51	A11	2c carmine ('89)	25.00

In 1885 the Postmaster General wished to have on sale complete sets of Hawaii's stamps as far back as type A11, but was unable to find either the stone from which Nos. 27 and 28, or the plate from which No. 29 was printed. He therefore sent a copy of No. 29 to the American Bank Note Co., with an order to engrave a new plate and print 10,000 stamps, of which 5000 were overprinted "Specimen" in blue.

The original No. 29 was printed in sheet of 15 (5x3), but the plate of these "Official Imitations" was made up of 50 stamps (10x5). Later, in 1887, the original die for No. 29 was discovered, and after retouching, a new plate was made and 37,500 stamps were printed. These, like the originals, were printed in sheets of 15. They were delivered during 1889 and 1890. In 1892 all remaining unsold in the Post Office were overprinted "Reprint."

No. 29 is red in color, and printed on very thin white wove paper. No. 50 is orange vermilion in color, on medium, white to buff paper. In No. 50 the vertical line on the left side of the portrait touches the horizontal line over the label "Elua Keneta", while in the other two varieties, Nos. 29 and 51, it does not touch the horizontal line by half a millimeter. In No. 51 there are three parallel lines on the left side of the King's nose, while in No. 29 and No. 50 there are no such lines. No. 51 is carmine in color and printed on thick, yellowish to buff wove paper.

It is claimed that both Nos. 50 and 51 were available for postage, although not made to fill a postal requirement.

PHILIPPINES

ˌfi-lə-ˈpēnz

LOCATION — Group of 7,100 islands and islets in the Malay Archipelago, north of Borneo, in the North Pacific Ocean

GOVT. — US Admin., 1898-1946

AREA — 115,748 sq. mi.

POP. — 16,971,100 (est. 1941)

CAPITAL — Quezon City

The islands were ceded to the US by Spain in 1898. On Nov. 15, 1935, they were given their independence, subject to a transition period which ended July 4, 1946. On that date the Commonwealth became the "Republic of the Philippines."

100 Cents = 1 Dollar (1899)
100 Centavos = 1 Peso (1906)

Watermarks

Wmk. 191PI- Double-lined PIPS

Wmk. 190PI- Single-lined PIPS

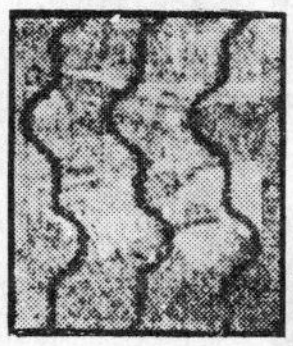

Wmk. 257- Curved Wavy Lines

Issued under US Administration

Issues of the US Overprinted in Black

On No. 260

1899-1901 Unwmk. *Perf. 12*

212	A96	50c orange	400.00	250.00

On Nos. 279, 279B, 279Bd, 279Be, 279Bf, 279Bc, 268, 281, 282C, 283, 284, 275 and 275a

Wmk. 191

213	A87	1c yellow green	3.00	.60
a.		Inverted overprint	13,500.	
214	A88	2c red, type IV	1.25	.60
a.		2c orange red, type IV ('01)	1.25	.60
b.		Booklet pane of 6, red, type IV ('00)	300.00	150.00
c.		2c reddish car, type IV	1.90	.90
d.		2c rose car, type IV	2.25	1.10
215	A89	3c purple	5.75	1.25
216	A91	5c blue	5.50	.90
a.		Inverted overprint		3,750.
217	A94	10c brown, type I	17.50	4.00
217A	A94	10c org brn, type II	200.00	32.50
218	A95	15c olive green	32.50	8.00
219	A96	50c orange	130.00	37.50
a.		50c red orange	260.00	
		Nos. 213-219 (8)	395.50	85.35

No. 216a is valued in the grade of fine.

On Nos. 280b, 282 and 272

1901

220	A90	4c orange brown	22.50	4.50
221	A92	6c lake	27.50	7.00
222	A93	8c violet brown	27.50	7.50
		Nos. 220-222 (3)	77.50	19.00

On Nos. 276, 276A, 277a and 278

Red Overprint

223	A97	$1 black, type I	425.	240.
223A	A97	$1 black, type II	2,250.	675.
224	A98	$2 dark blue	450.	250.
225	A99	$5 dark green	825.	700.

On Nos. 300-313 and shades

1903-04

Black Overprint

226	A115	1c blue green	4.00	.30
227	A116	2c carmine	7.50	1.10
228	A117	3c bright violet	67.50	12.50
229	A118	4c brown ('04)	75.00	22.50
a.		4c orange brown	75.00	20.00
230	A119	5c blue	11.00	1.00
231	A120	6c brnsh lake ('04)	80.00	22.50
232	A121	8c vio blk ('04)	40.00	12.50
233	A122	10c pale red brn ('04)	20.00	2.25
a.		10c red brown	25.00	3.00
b.		Pair, one without ovpt.		1,500.
234	A123	13c purple black	32.50	17.50
a.		13c brown violet	32.50	17.50
235	A124	15c olive green	60.00	15.00
236	A125	50c orange	130.00	35.00
		Nos. 226-236 (11)	527.50	142.15

Red Overprint

237	A126	$1 black	450.	250.
238	A127	$2 dk blue ('04)	725.	750.
239	A128	$5 dk green ('04)	950.	900.

On Nos. 319, 319c in Black

1904

240	A129	2c carmine	5.50	2.25
a.		Booklet pane of 6	1,100.	
b.		2c scarlet	6.25	2.75

Jose Rizal — A40

Arms of Manila — A41

Designs: 4c, McKinley. 6c, Magellan. 8c, Miguel Lopez de Legaspi. 10c, Gen. Henry W. Lawton. 12c, Lincoln. 16c, Adm. William T. Sampson. 20c, Washington. 26c, Francisco Carriedo. 30c, Franklin.

Each Inscribed "Philippine Islands/United States of America"

1906, Sept. 8 Engr. Wmk. 191PI

241	A40	2c deep green	.25	.20
a.		2c yellow green ('10)	.40	.20
b.		Booklet pane of 6	425.00	
242	A40	4c carmine	.30	.20
a.		4c carmine lake ('10)	.60	.20
b.		Booklet pane of 6	600.00	
243	A40	6c violet	1.25	.20
244	A40	8c brown	2.50	.65
245	A40	10c blue	1.75	.20
246	A40	12c brown lake	5.00	2.00
247	A40	16c violet black	3.75	.20
248	A40	20c orange brown	4.00	.30
249	A40	26c violet brown	6.00	2.25
250	A40	30c olive green	4.75	1.50
251	A41	1p orange	27.50	7.00
252	A41	2p black	35.00	1.25
253	A41	4p dark blue	100.00	15.00
254	A41	10p dark green	225.00	70.00
		Nos. 241-254 (14)	417.05	100.95

Change of Colors

1909-13 *Perf. 12*

255	A40	12c red orange	8.50	2.50
256	A40	16c olive green	3.50	.75
257	A40	20c yellow	7.50	1.25
258	A40	26c blue green	1.75	.75
259	A40	30c ultramarine	10.00	3.25
260	A41	1p pale violet	30.00	5.00
260A	A41	2p vio brown ('13)	85.00	2.75
		Nos. 255-260A (7)	146.25	16.25

1911 Wmk. 190PI *Perf. 12*

261	A40	2c green	.65	.20
a.		Booklet pane of 6	475.00	
262	A40	4c carmine lake	2.50	.20
a.		4c carmine	—	—
b.		Booklet pane of 6	525.00	
263	A40	6c deep violet	2.00	.20
264	A40	8c brown	8.50	.45
265	A40	10c blue	3.25	.20
266	A40	12c orange	2.50	.45
267	A40	16c olive green	2.50	.20
268	A40	20c yellow	2.00	.20
a.		20c orange	2.00	.20
269	A40	26c blue green	3.00	.20
270	A40	30c ultramarine	3.50	.45
271	A41	1p pale violet	22.50	.55
272	A41	2p violet brown	27.50	.75
273	A41	4p deep blue	625.00	80.00
274	A41	10p deep green	225.00	25.00
		Nos. 261-274 (14)	930.40	109.05

1914

275	A40	30c gray	10.00	.40

1914-23 *Perf. 10*

276	A40	2c green	1.75	.20
a.		Booklet pane of 6	400.00	
277	A40	4c carmine	1.75	.20
a.		Booklet pane of 6	400.00	
278	A40	6c light violet	37.50	9.00
a.		6c deep violet	42.50	6.00
279	A40	8c brown	40.00	10.00
280	A40	10c dark blue	25.00	.20
281	A40	16c olive green	75.00	4.50
282	A40	20c orange	22.50	.85
283	A40	30c gray	55.00	2.75
284	A41	1p pale violet	110.00	3.00
		Nos. 276-284 (9)	368.50	30.70

1918-26 *Perf. 11*

285	A40	2c green	20.00	4.25
a.		Booklet pane of 6	650.00	
286	A40	4c carmine	25.00	2.50
a.		Booklet pane of 6	1,250.	
287	A40	6c deep violet	35.00	1.75
287A	A40	8c light brown	200.00	25.00
288	A40	10c dark blue	52.50	1.50
289	A40	16c olive green	90.00	6.75
289A	A40	20c orange	60.00	7.50
289C	A40	30c gray	55.00	12.50
289D	A41	1p pale violet	70.00	14.00
		Nos. 285-289D (9)	607.50	75.75

1917-25 Unwmk. *Perf. 11*

290	A40	2c yellow green	.20	.20
a.		2c dark green	.20	.20
b.		Vert. pair, imperf. horiz.	1,500.	
c.		Horiz. pair, imperf. btwn.	1,500.	—

d. Vert. pair, imperf. btwn. *1,750.*
e. Booklet pane of 6 27.50
291 A40 4c carmine .20 .20
a. 4c light rose .20 .20
b. Booklet pane of 6 17.50 —
292 A40 6c deep violet .30 .20
a. 6c lilac .35 .20
b. 6c red violet .35 .20
c. Booklet pane of 6 *550.00* —
293 A40 8c yellow brown .20 .20
a. 8c orange brown .20 .20
294 A40 10c deep blue .20 .20
295 A40 12c red orange .30 .20
296 A40 16c light olive green 55.00 .25
a. 16c olive bister 55.00 .40
297 A40 20c orange yellow .30 .20
298 A40 26c green .45 .45
a. 26c blue green .55 .25
299 A40 30c gray .55 .20
300 A41 1p pale violet 27.50 1.00
a. 1p red lilac 27.50 1.00
b. 1p pale rose lilac 27.50 1.10
301 A41 2p violet brown 25.00 .75
302 A41 4p blue 22.50 .45
a. 4p dark blue 22.50 .45
Nos. 290-302 (13) 132.70 4.50

1923-26

Design: 16c, Adm. George Dewey.

303 A40 16c olive bister .90 .20
a. 16c olive green 1.30 .20
304 A41 10p deep green ('26) 45.00 5.00

See Nos. 326-353. For surcharges see Nos. 368-369, 450. For overprints see Nos. C1-C28, C36-C46, C54-C57, O5-O14.

Legislative Palace — A42

1926, Dec. 20 Unwmk. *Perf. 12*
319 A42 2c green & black .40 .25
a. Horiz. pair, imperf. btwn. *275.00*
b. Vert. pair, imperf. between *500.00*
320 A42 4c car & black .40 .35
a. Horiz. pair, imperf. btwn. *275.00*
b. Vert. pair, imperf. between *500.00*
321 A42 16c ol grn & black .75 .65
a. Horiz. pair, imperf. btwn. *350.00*
b. Vert. pair, imperf. between *550.00*
c. Double impression of center *575.00*
322 A42 18c lt brn & black .85 .50
a. Double impression of center *575.00*
b. Vert. pair, imperf. between *550.00*
323 A42 20c orange & black 1.20 .80
a. 20c orange & brown *500.00* —
b. Imperf., pair *450.00* *450.00*
c. As "a," imperf., pair *850.00*
d. Vert. pair, imperf. between *550.00*
324 A42 24c gray & black .85 .55
a. Vert. pair, imperf. between *550.00*
325 A42 1p rose lilac & blk 45.00 30.00
a. Vert. pair, imperf. between *625.00*
Nos. 319-325 (7) 49.45 33.10

Opening of the Legislative Palace.
For overprints see Nos. O1-O4.

Coil Stamp
Rizal Type of 1906

1928 *Perf. 11 Vertically*
326 A40 2c green 7.50 15.00

Types of 1906-23

1925-31 Unwmk. *Imperf.*
340 A40 2c yel grn ('31) .20 .20
a. green ('25) .25 .20
341 A40 4c car rose ('31) .20 .20
a. carmine ('25) .40 .20
342 A40 6c violet ('31) 1.00 1.00
a. deep violet ('25) 8.00 4.00
343 A40 8c brown ('31) .90 .90
a. yellow brown ('25) 6.00 3.00
344 A40 10c blue ('31) 1.00 1.00
a. deep blue ('25) 15.00 5.00
345 A40 12c dp orange ('31) 1.50 1.50
a. red orange ('25) 15.00 5.00
346 A40 16c olive green *(Dewey)* ('31) 1.10 1.10
a. bister green ('25) 12.50 4.00
347 A40 20c orange yel ('31) 1.10 1.10
a. yellow ('25) 12.50 4.00
348 A40 26c green ('31) 1.10 1.10
a. blue green ('25) 15.00 5.00
349 A40 30c light gray ('31) 1.25 1.25
a. gray ('25) 15.00 5.00
350 A41 1p lt violet ('31) 4.00 4.00
a. violet ('25) 70.00 30.00
351 A41 2p brn vio ('31) 10.00 10.00
a. violet brown ('25) 150.00 50.00
352 A41 4p blue ('31) 30.00 30.00
a. deep blue ('25) 700.00 300.00
353 A41 10p green ('31) 90.00 90.00
a. deep green ('25) 1,000. 500.00
Nos. 340-353 (14) 143.35 143.35
Nos. 340a-353a (14) 2,019. 915.40

Mount Mayon, Luzon — A43

Post Office, Manila — A44

Pier No. 7, Manila Bay A45

(See footnote) A46

Rice Planting A47

Rice Terraces A48

Baguio Zigzag — A49

1932, May 3 *Perf. 11*
354 A43 2c yellow green .40 .20
355 A44 4c rose carmine .35 .25
356 A45 12c orange .50 .50
357 A46 18c red orange 17.50 9.00
358 A47 20c yellow .65 .55
359 A48 24c deep violet 1.00 .65
360 A49 32c olive brown 1.00 .70
Nos. 354-360 (7) 21.40 11.85

The 18c vignette was intended to show Pagsanjan Falls in Laguna, central Luzon, and is so labeled. Through error, the stamp pictures Vernal Falls in Yosemite Natl. Park, CA.
For overprints see #C29-C35, C47-C51, C63.

Nos. 302, 302a Surcharged in Orange or Red

1932
368 A41 1p on 4p blue (O) 2.00 .45
a. 1p on 4p dark blue (O) 2.75 1.30
369 A41 2p on 4p dark blue (R) 3.50 .75
a. 2p on 4p blue (R) 3.50 .75

Baseball — A50

Tennis — A51

Basketball — A52

1934, Apr. 14 Typo. *Perf. 11½*
380 A50 2c yellow brown *1.50* *.80*
381 A51 6c ultramarine .25 .20
a. Vert. pair, imperf. between *1,250.*
382 A52 16c violet brown .50 .50
a. Vert. pair, imperf. horiz. *1,250.*

Tenth Far Eastern Championship Games.

Jose Rizal A53

Woman and Carabao A54

La Filipina — A55

Pearl Fishing — A56

Fort Santiago — A57

Salt Spring — A58

Magellan's Landing, 1521 A59

"Juan de la Cruz" A60

Rice Terraces — A61

"Blood Compact," 1565 — A62

Barasoain Church, Malolos A63

Battle of Manila Bay, 1898 — A64

Montalban Gorge A65

George Washington — A66

1935, Feb. 15 Engr. *Perf. 11*
383 A53 2c rose .20 .20
384 A54 4c yellow green .20 .20
385 A55 6c dark brown .20 .20
386 A56 8c violet .20 .20
387 A57 10c rose carmine .20 .20
388 A58 12c black .20 .20
389 A59 16c dark blue .20 .20
390 A60 20c light olive green .20 .20
391 A61 26c indigo .25 .25
392 A62 30c orange red .25 .25
393 A63 1p red orange & black 1.65 1.25
394 A64 2p bister brn & black 4.00 1.25
395 A65 4p blue & black 4.00 2.75
396 A66 5p green & black 8.00 2.00
Nos. 383-396 (14) 19.75 9.35

For overprints see Nos. 411-424, 433-446, 463-466, 468, 472-474, 478-484, 485-494, C52-C53, O15-O36, O38, O40-O43, N2-N3, NO6. For surcharges see Nos. 449, N4-N9, N28, NO2-NO5.

Commonwealth Issues

The Temples of Human Progress — A67

1935, Nov. 15
397 A67 2c carmine rose .20 .20
398 A67 6c deep violet .20 .20
399 A67 16c blue .20 .20
400 A67 36c yellow green .35 .30
401 A67 50c brown .55 .55
Nos. 397-401 (5) 1.50 1.45

Inauguration of the Philippine Commonwealth, Nov. 15th, 1935.

Jose Rizal — A68

President Manuel L. Quezon — A69

1936, June 19 *Perf. 12*
402 A68 2c yellow brown .20 .20
403 A68 6c slate blue .20 .20
a. Horiz. pair, imperf. vert. *1,350.*
404 A68 36c red brown .50 .45
Nos. 402-404 (3) .90 .85

75th anniv. of the birth of Jose Rizal.

1936, Nov. 15 *Perf. 11*
408 A69 2c orange brown .20 .20
409 A69 6c yellow green .20 .20
410 A69 12c ultramarine .20 .20
Nos. 408-410 (3) .60 .60

1st anniv. of the Commonwealth.
For overprints see Nos. 467, 475.

Nos. 383-396 Overprinted in Black

COMMON-
WEALTH
a

COMMONWEALTH
b

1936-37 *Perf. 11*
411 A53 (a) 2c rose .20 .20
a. Booklet pane of 6 2.50 *.65*
412 A54 (b) 4c yel grn ('37) .50 .40
413 A55 (a) 6c dark brown .20 .20
414 A56 (b) 8c violet ('37) .25 .20
415 A57 (b) 10c rose carmine .20 .20
a. "COMMONWEALT" — —
416 A58 (b) 12c black ('37) .20 .20
417 A59 (b) 16c dark blue .20 .20
418 A60 (a) 20c lt ol grn ('37) .65 .40
419 A61 (b) 26c indigo ('37) .45 .35
420 A62 (b) 30c orange red .35 .20
421 A63 (b) 1p red org & black .65 .20

422 A64 (b) 2p bister brn & black ('37) 5.00 2.75
423 A65 (b) 4p blue & blk ('37) 17.50 3.00
424 A66 (b) 5p green & black ('37) 1.75 1.25
Nos. 411-424 (14) 28.10
Nos. 411,413-424 (13) 9.35

Map of Philippines
A70

Arms of Manila
A71

1937, Feb. 3
425 A70 2c yellow green .20 .20
426 A70 6c light brown .20 .20
427 A70 12c sapphire .20 .20
428 A70 20c deep orange .25 .20
429 A70 36c deep violet .55 .40
430 A70 50c carmine .65 .35
Nos. 425-430 (6) 2.05 1.55

33rd Eucharistic Congress.

1937, Aug. 27 ***Perf. 11***
431 A71 10p gray 4.25 2.00
432 A71 20p henna brown 2.25 1.40

For overprints see Nos. 495-496. For surcharges see Nos. 451, C58.

Nos. 383-396 Overprinted in Black

COMMON-
WEALTH
a

COMMONWEALTH
b

1938-40 ***Perf. 11***
433 A53 (a) 2c rose ('39) .20 .20
a. Booklet pane of 6 3.50 .65
b. "WEALTH COMMON-" 4,000. —
c. Hyphen omitted — —
434 A54 (b) 4c yel grn ('40) 1.25 —
435 A55 (a) 6c dk brn ('39) .20 .20
a. 6c golden brown .20 .20
436 A56 (b) 8c violet ('39) .20 .20
a. "COMMONWEALT" (LR 31) 65.00
437 A57 (b) 10c rose car ('39) .20 .20
a. "COMMONWEALT" (LR 31) —
438 A58 (b) 12c black ('40) .20 .20
439 A59 (b) 16c dark blue .20 .20
440 A60 (a) 20c lt ol grn ('39) .20 .20
441 A61 (b) 26c indigo ('40) .20 .20
442 A62 (b) 30c org red ('39) 1.40 .70
443 A63 (b) 1p red org & blk .40 .20
444 A64 (b) 2p bis brn & blk 2.75 .75
445 A65 (b) 4p bl & blk ('40) 100.00 75.00
446 A66 (b) 5p grn & blk ('40) 4.50 2.75
Nos. 433-446 (14) 111.90
Nos. 433,435-446 (13) 81.00

Overprint "b" measures 18½x1¾mm. No. 433b occurs in booklet pane, No. 433a, position 5; all copies are straight-edged, left and bottom.

Stamps of 1917-37 Surcharged in Red, Violet or Black

FIRST
FOREIGN

TRADE
WEEK

2
CENTAVOS

MAY 21-27,1939

FIRST FOREIGN
TRADE WEEK

50CENTAVOS50

FIRST FOREIGN
TRADE WEEK

MAY 21-27, 1939
6CENTAVOS6

MAY 21-27,1939

1939, July 5
449 A54 2c on 4c yel green (R) .20 .20
450 A40 6c on 26c blue grn (V) .20 .20
a. 6c on 26c blue green .65 .30
451 A71 50c on 20p henna brn (Bk) 1.00 1.00
Nos. 449-451 (3) 1.40 1.40

Foreign Trade Week.

Triumphal Arch — A72

Malacanan Palace — A73

1939, Nov. 15 ***Perf. 11***
452 A72 2c yellow green .20 .20
453 A72 6c carmine .20 .20
454 A72 12c bright blue .20 .20
Nos. 452-454 (3) .60 .60

For overprints see Nos. 469, 476.

1939, Nov. 15
455 A73 2c green .20 .20
456 A73 6c orange .20 .20
457 A73 12c carmine .20 .20
Nos. 455-457 (3) .60 .60

#452-457 for 4th anniv. of the Commonwealth.
For overprint see No. 470.

Quezon Taking Oath of Office
A74

Jose Rizal
A75

1940, Feb. 8
458 A74 2c dark orange .20 .20
459 A74 6c dark green .20 .20
460 A74 12c purple .25 .20
Nos. 458-460 (3) .65 .60

4th anniversary of Commonwealth.
For overprints see Nos. 471, 477.

Rotary Press Printing

1941, Apr. 14 ***Perf. 11x10½***

Size: 19x22½mm

461 A75 2c apple green .20 .20

Flat Plate Printing

1941-43 ***Perf. 11***

Size: 18¾x22mm

462 A75 2c apple green ('43) .20 .20
a. 2c pale apple green .20 .20
b. Bklt. pane of 6 (apple green, '43) 1.25 1.25
c. Bklt. pane of 6 (pale apple green) 2.50 2.75

No. 462 was issued only in booklet panes and all copies have straight edges.
Further printings were made in 1942 and 1943 in different shades from the first supply of stamps sent to the islands.
For type A75 overprinted see Nos. 464, O37, O39, N1, NO1.

Philippine Stamps of 1935-41, Handstamped in Violet

VICTORY

1944 ***Perf. 11, 11x10½***
463 A53 2c (#411) *275.00 95.00*
a. Booklet pane of 6 *2,000.*
463B A53 2c (#433) *1,250. 1,200.*
464 A75 2c (#461) 2.50 2.25
465 A54 4c (#384) *25.00 25.00*
466 A55 6c (#385) *1,450. 1,350.*
467 A69 6c (#409) *115.00 85.00*
468 A55 6c (#413) *675.00 600.00*
469 A72 6c (#453) *140.00 110.00*
470 A73 6c (#456) *625.00 550.00*
471 A74 6c (#459) *170.00 150.00*
472 A56 8c (#436) 15.00 20.00
473 A57 10c (#415) *115.00 75.00*
474 A57 10c (#437) *140.00 110.00*
475 A69 12c (#410) *425.00 175.00*
476 A72 12c (#454) *3,750. 2,000.*
477 A74 12c (#460) *200.00 135.00*
478 A59 16c (#389) *725.00*
479 A59 16c (#417) *475.00 325.00*
480 A59 16c (#439) *170.00 100.00*
481 A60 20c (#440) 27.50 27.50
482 A62 30c (#420) *250.00 160.00*
483 A62 30c (#442) *350.00 250.00*
484 A63 1p (#443) *5,750. 4,000.*

Nos. 463-484 are valued in the grade of fine to very fine.

Types of 1935-37 Overprinted

VICTORY

COMMON-
WEALTH
a

VICTORY

COMMONWEALTH
b

1945 ***Perf. 11***
485 A53 (a) 2c rose .20 .20
486 A54 (b) 4c yellow green .20 .20
487 A55 (a) 6c golden brown .20 .20
488 A56 (b) 8c violet .20 .20
489 A57 (b) 10c rose carmine .20 .20
490 A58 (b) 12c black .20 .20
491 A59 (b) 16c dark blue .25 .20
492 A60 (a) 20c lt olive green .30 .20
493 A62 (b) 30c orange red .40 .35
494 A63 (b) 1p red org & black 1.10 .25

Nos. 431-432 Overprinted in Black VICTORY

495 A71 10p gray 40.00 13.50
496 A71 20p henna brown 35.00 15.00
Nos. 485-496 (12) 78.25 30.70

Jose Rizal — A76

Rotary Press Printing

1946, May 28 ***Perf. 11x10½***
497 A76 2c sepia .20 .20

For overprints see No. 503 (Philippines, Vol. 5) and No. O44.

Succeeding issues, released by the Philippine Republic on and after July 4, 1946, are listed in Vol. 5.

AIR POST STAMPS

Madrid-Manila Flight Issue

Regular Issue of 1917-26 Overprinted in Red or Violet

1926, May 13 **Unwmk.** ***Perf. 11***
C1 A40 2c green (R) 7.50 3.50
C2 A40 4c carmine 10.00 4.25
a. Inverted overprint *2,000.* —
C3 A40 6c lilac (R) 47.50 14.00
C4 A40 8c org brown 47.50 14.00
C5 A40 10c deep blue (R) 47.50 14.00
C6 A40 12c red orange 47.50 25.00
C7 A40 16c lt olive green (Sampson) *1,850. 1,550.*
C8 A40 16c ol bister (Sampson) (R) *3,250. 2,600.*
C9 A40 16c olive green (Dewey) 55.00 25.00
C10 A40 20c orange yellow 55.00 25.00
C11 A40 26c blue green 55.00 27.50
C12 A40 30c gray 55.00 27.50
C13 A41 2p vio brown (R) 475.00 260.00
C14 A41 4p dark blue (R) 675.00 450.00
C15 A41 10p deep green 1,050. 625.00

Same Overprint on No. 269

Wmk. 190PI

Perf. 12

C16 A40 26c blue green *2,400.*

Same Overprint on No. 284

Perf. 10

C17 A41 1p pale violet 175.00 100.00

Flight of Spanish aviators Gallarza and Loriga from Madrid to Manila.

London-Orient Flight Issue

Regular Issue of 1917-25 Overprinted in Red

L.O.F.

1928

1928, Nov. 9 **Unwmk.** ***Perf. 11***
C18 A40 2c green .40 .25
C19 A40 4c carmine .50 .40
C20 A40 6c violet 1.75 1.40
C21 A40 8c orange brown 1.90 1.60
C22 A40 10c deep blue 1.90 1.60
C23 A40 12c red orange 2.75 2.25
C24 A40 16c ol green *(Dewey)* 2.00 1.50
C25 A40 20c orange yellow 2.75 2.25
C26 A40 26c blue green 8.00 5.50
C27 A40 30c gray 8.00 5.50

Same Overprint on No. 271

Wmk. 190PI

Perf. 12

C28 A41 1p pale violet 45.00 25.00
Nos. C18-C28 (11) 74.95 47.25

Flight from London to Manila.

Nos. 354-360 Overprinted

1932, Sept. 27 **Unwmk.** ***Perf. 11***
C29 A43 2c yellow green .40 .30
C30 A44 4c rose carmine .40 .30
C31 A45 12c orange .60 .50
C32 A46 18c red orange 3.50 3.25
C33 A47 20c yellow 1.75 1.50
C34 A48 24c deep violet 1.75 1.50
C35 A49 32c olive brown 1.75 1.50
Nos. C29-C35 (7) 10.15 8.85

Visit of Capt. Wolfgang von Gronau on his round-the-world flight.

Regular Issue of 1917-25 Overprinted

F.REIN
MADRID-MANILA
FLIGHT-1933

1933, Apr. 11
C36 A40 2c green .40 .35
C37 A40 4c carmine .45 .35
C38 A40 6c deep violet .80 .75
C39 A40 8c orange brown 2.50 1.50
C40 A40 10c dark blue 2.25 1.00
C41 A40 12c orange 2.00 1.00
C42 A40 16c ol green *(Dewey)* 2.00 1.00
C43 A40 20c yellow 2.00 1.00
C44 A40 26c green 2.25 1.50
a. 26c blue green 3.00 1.80
C45 A40 30c gray 3.00 1.75
Nos. C36-C45 (10) 17.65 10.20

Flight from Madrid to Manila of aviator Fernando Rein y Loring.

Stamp of 1917 Overprinted

1933, May 26 **Unwmk.** ***Perf. 11***
C46 A40 2c green .50 .40

Regular Issue of 1932 Overprinted

C47 A44 4c rose carmine .20 .20
C48 A45 12c orange .30 .20
C49 A47 20c yellow .30 .20
C50 A48 24c deep violet .40 .25
C51 A49 32c olive brown .50 .35
Nos. C46-C51 (6) 2.20 1.60

Nos. 387 and 392 Overprinted in Gold

P.I.-U.S.
INITIAL FLIGHT

December-1935

1935, Dec. 2
C52 A57 10c rose carmine .30 .20
C53 A62 30c orange red .50 .35

China Clipper flight from Manila to San Francisco, Dec. 2-5, 1935.

Regular Issue of 1917-25 Surcharged in Various Colors

MANILA-MADRID ARNACAL FLIGHT-1936 2CENTAVOS2

1936, Sept. 6 *Perf. 11*
C54 A40 2c on 4c carmine (Bl) .20 .20
C55 A40 6c on 12c red org (V) .20 .20
C56 A40 16c on 26c blue green (Bk) .25 .20
a. 16c on 26c green (Bk) 1.25 .70
Nos. C54-C56 (3) .65 .60

Manila-Madrid flight by aviators Antonio Arnaiz and Juan Calvo.

Regular Issue of 1917-37 Surcharged in Black or Red

FIRST AIR MAIL EXHIBITION Feb 17 to 19, 1939 8 CENTAVOS 8

1939, Feb. 17
C57 A40 8c on 26c blue green .75 .40
a. 8c on 26c green 1.60 .55
C58 A71 1p on 10p gray (R) 3.00 2.25

1st Air Mail Exhib., Feb. 17-19, 1939.

Moro Vinta and Clipper — AP1

1941, June 30
C59 AP1 8c carmine 1.00 .60
C60 AP1 20c ultramarine 1.20 .45
C61 AP1 60c blue green 1.75 1.00
C62 AP1 1p sepia .70 .50
Nos. C59-C62 (4) 4.65 2.55

For overprint see No. NO7. For surcharges see Nos. N10-N11, N35-N36.

No. C47 Handstamped in Violet — VICTORY

1944, Dec. 3 **Unwmk.** *Perf. 11*
C63 A44 4c rose carmine *1,600. 1,600.*

SPECIAL DELIVERY STAMPS

US No. E5 Overprinted in Red — PHILIPPINES

1901, Oct. 15 **Wmk. 191** *Perf. 12*
E1 SD3 10c dark blue 120.00 100.00

Special Delivery Messenger SD2

1906 **Engr.** **Wmk. 191PI**
E2 SD2 20c ultramarine 30.00 7.50
b. 20c pale ultramarine 30.00 7.50

See Nos. E3-E6. For overprints see Nos. E7-E10, EO1.

Special Printing

Ovptd. in Red as #E1 on US #E6

1907
E2A SD4 10c ultramarine *2,250.*

1911 **Wmk. 190PI**
E3 SD2 20c deep ultramarine 20.00 1.75

1916 *Perf. 10*
E4 SD2 20c deep ultra 175.00 50.00

1919 **Unwmk.** *Perf. 11*
E5 SD2 20c ultramarine .60 .20
a. 20c pale blue .75 .20
b. 20c dull violet .60 .20

Type of 1906 Issue

1925-31 *Imperf.*
E6 SD2 20c dull violet ('31) 20.00 *17.50*

Type of 1919 Overprinted in Black — COMMONWEALTH

1939 *Perf. 11*
E7 SD2 20c blue violet .25 .20

Nos. E5b and E7, Handstamped in Violet — VICTORY

1944 *Perf. 11*
E8 SD2 20c (On #E5b) *700.00 500.00*
E9 SD2 20c (On #E7) *190.00 150.00*

Type SD2 Overprinted "VICTORY" As No. 486

1945
E10 SD2 20c blue violet .70 .55
a. "IC" close together 3.25 2.75

SPECIAL DELIVERY OFFICIAL STAMP

Type of 1906 Issue Overprinted — O. B.

1931 **Unwmk.** *Perf. 11*
EO1 SD2 20c dull violet .65 .40
a. No period after "B" 20.00 15.00
b. Double overprint —

POSTAGE DUE STAMPS

Postage Due Stamps of the US Nos. J38-J44 Overprinted in Black — PHILIPPINES

1899, Aug. 16 **Wmk. 191** *Perf. 12*
J1 D2 1c deep claret 5.75 1.25
J2 D2 2c deep claret 6.00 1.10
J3 D2 5c deep claret 15.00 2.25
J4 D2 10c deep claret 19.00 4.75
J5 D2 50c deep claret 200.00 90.00

No. J1 was used to pay regular postage Sept. 5-19, 1902.

1901, Aug. 31
J6 D2 3c deep claret 17.50 6.00
J7 D2 30c deep claret 225.00 95.00
Nos. J1-J7 (7) 488.25 200.35

Post Office Clerk — D3

Unwmk.

1928, Aug. 21 **Engr.** *Perf. 11*
J8 D3 4c brown red .20 .20
J9 D3 6c brown red .20 .20
J10 D3 8c brown red .20 .20
J11 D3 10c brown red .20 .20
J12 D3 12c brown red .20 .20
J13 D3 16c brown red .20 .20
J14 D3 20c brown red .20 .20
Nos. J8-J14 (7) 1.40 1.40

For overprints see Nos. O16-O22, NJ1. For surcharge see No. J15.

No. J8 Surcharged in Blue — 3 CVOS. 3

1937
J15 D3 3c on 4c brown red .20 .20

Nos. J8-J14 Handstamped in Violet — VICTORY

1944
J16 D3 4c brown red *125.00* —
J17 D3 6c brown red *80.00* —
J18 D3 8c brown red *85.00* —
J19 D3 10c brown red *80.00* —
J20 D3 12c brown red *80.00* —
J21 D3 16c brown red *85.00* —
J22 D3 20c brown red *85.00* —
Nos. J16-J22 (7) *620.00*

OFFICIAL STAMPS

Official Handstamped Overprints

"Officers purchasing stamps for government business may, if they so desire, overprint them with the letters "O.B." either in writing with black ink or by rubber stamps but in such a manner as not to obliterate the stamp that postmasters will be unable to determine whether the stamps have been previously used." C. M. Cotterman, Director of Posts, Dec. 26, 1905.

Beginning Jan. 1, 1906, all branches of the Insular Government used postage stamps to prepay postage instead of franking them as before. Some officials used manuscript, some utilized typewriting machines, some made press-printed overprints, but by far the larger number provided themselves with rubber stamps.

The majority of these read "O.B." but other forms were: "OFFICIAL BUSINESS" or "OFFICIAL MAIL" in 2 lines, with variations on many of these.

These "O.B." overprints are known on US 1899-1901 stamps; on 1903-06 stamps in red and blue; on 1906 stamps in red, blue, black, yellow and green.

"O.B." overprints were also made on the centavo and peso stamps of the Philippines, per order of May 25, 1907.

Beginning in 1926, the Bureau of Posts issued press-printed official stamps, but many government offices continued to handstamp ordinary postage stamps "O.B."

Regular Issue of 1926 Overprinted in Red — OFFICIAL

1926, Dec. 20 **Unwmk.** *Perf. 12*
O1 A42 2c green & black 2.25 1.00
O2 A42 4c carmine & black 2.25 1.20
a. Vertical pair, imperf. between 750.00
O3 A42 18c lt brown & black 7.00 4.00
O4 A42 20c orange & black 6.75 1.75
Nos. O1-O4 (4) 18.25 7.95

Opening of the Legislative Palace.

Regular Issue of 1917-26 Overprinted — O. B.

1931 *Perf. 11*
O5 A40 2c green .20 .20
a. No period after "B" 15.00 5.00
b. No period after "O" —
O6 A40 4c carmine .20 .20
a. No period after "B" 15.00 5.00
O7 A40 6c deep violet .20 .20
O8 A40 8c yellow brn .20 .20
O9 A40 10c deep blue .30 .20
O10 A40 12c red orange .25 .20
a. No period after "B" 32.50
O11 A40 16c lt ol green (Dewey) .25 .20
a. 16c olive bister 1.25 .20
O12 A40 20c orange yellow .25 .20
a. No period after "B" 22.50 15.00
O13 A40 26c green .40 .30
a. 26c blue green 1.00 .65
O14 A40 30c gray .30 .25
Nos. O5-O14 (10) 2.55 2.15

Same Overprint on Nos. 383-392

1935
O15 A53 2c rose .20 .20
a. No period after "B" 15.00 5.00
O16 A54 4c yellow green .20 .20
a. No period after "B" 15.00 8.50
O17 A55 6c dark brown .20 .20
a. No period after "B" 20.00 17.50
O18 A56 8c violet .20 .20
O19 A57 10c rose carmine .20 .20
O20 A58 12c black .20 .20
O21 A59 16c dark blue .20 .20
O22 A60 20c lt olive green .20 .20
O23 A61 26c indigo .25 .20
O24 A62 30c orange red .30 .25
Nos. O15-O24 (10) 2.15 2.05

Same Overprint on Nos. 411 and 418

1937-38 *Perf. 11*
O25 A53 2c rose .20 .20
a. No period after "B" 4.25 2.25
b. Period after "B" raised (UL 4) —
O26 A60 20c lt olive green ('38) .65 .50

Nos. 383-392 Overprinted in Black:

O. B.
COMMON-WEALTH
a

O. B.
b

1938-40
O27 A53(a) 2c rose .20 .20
a. Hyphen omitted 20.00 20.00
b. No period after "B" 25.00 25.00
O28 A54(b) 4c yellow green .20 .20
O29 A55(a) 6c dark brown .20 .20
O30 A56(b) 8c violet .20 .20
O31 A57(b) 10c rose carmine .20 .20
a. No period after "O" 30.00 30.00
O32 A58(b) 12c black .20 .20
O33 A59(b) 16c dark blue .20 .20
O34 A60(a) 20c lt ol green ('40) .25 .25
O35 A61(b) 26c indigo .30 .30
O36 A62(b) 30c orange red .25 .25
Nos. O27-O36 (10) 2.20 2.20

No. 461 Overprinted in Black — O. B.

Perf. 11x10½

1941, Apr. 14 **Unwmk.**
O37 A75 2c apple green .20 .20

Official Stamps Handstamped in Violet — VICTORY

1944 *Perf. 11, 11x10½*
O38 A53 2c #O27 *200.00 110.00*
O39 A75 2c #O37 6.50 3.00
O40 A54 4c #O16 *37.50 25.00*
O40A A55 6c #O29 *4,250.* —
O41 A57 10c #O31 *135.00*
a. No period after "O" —
O42 A60 20c #O22 *6,000.*
O43 A60 20c #O26 *1,550.*

No. 497 Overprinted Like No. O37 in Black

Perf. 11x10½

1946, June 19 **Unwmk.**
O44 A76 2c sepia .20 .20

OCCUPATIONSTAMPS

Issued under Japanese Occupation

Nos. 461, 438 and 439 Overprinted with Bars in Black

1942-43 **Unwmk.** *Perf. 11x10½, 11*
N1 A75 2c apple green .20 .20
a. Pair, one without overprint —
N2 A58 12c black ('43) .20 .20
N3 A59 16c dark blue 5.00 3.75
Nos. N1-N3 (3) 5.40 4.15

Nos. 435, 442, 443 and 423 Surcharged in Black

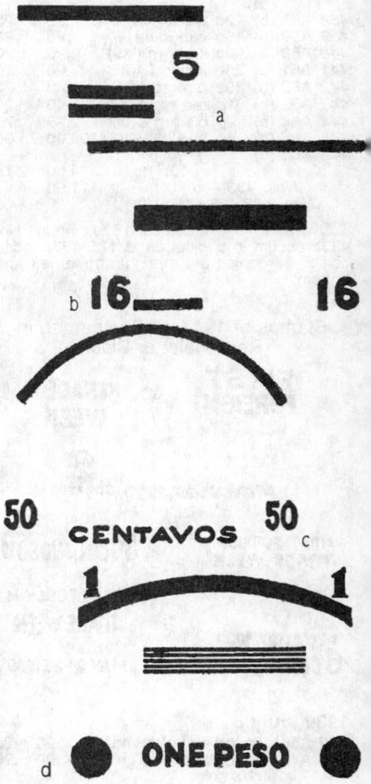

Perf. 11
N4 A55 5c on 6c golden brn .20 .20
a. Top bar shorter, thinner .20 .20
b. 5c on 6c dark brown .20 .20
c. As "b" and "a" .20 .20
N5 A62 16c on 30c orange red ('43) .25 .25
N6 A63 50c on 1p red org & black ('43) .60 .60
a. Double surcharge *300.00*

N7 A65 1p on 4p blue & black ('43) 110.00 120.00
Nos. N4-N7 (4) 111.05 121.05

On Nos. N4 and N4b, the top bar measures 1½x22½mm. On Nos. N4a and N4c, the top bar measures 1x21mm and the "5" is smaller and thinner.

No. 384 Surcharged in Black

CONGRATULATIONS
FALL OF
BATAAN AND
CORREGIDOR
1942
2

1942, May 18
N8 A54 2c on 4c yellow green 6.00 6.00

Japan's capture of Bataan and Corregidor. The American-Filipino forces finally surrendered May 7, 1942.

No. 384 Surcharged in Black

ダイトーアセンソー
イッシューネンキネン
12-8-1942 5

1942, Dec. 8
N9 A54 5c on 4c yellow green .50 .50

1st anniv. of the "Greater East Asia War."

Nos. C59 and C62 Surcharged in Black

ヒトー ギヨーセイフ
イッシューオン キネン
1-23-43
2

1943, Jan. 23
N10 AP1 2(c) on 8c carmine .25 .25
N11 AP1 5c on 1p sepia .50 .50

1st anniv. of the Philippine Executive Commission.

Nipa Hut — OS1

Rice Planting — OS2

Mt. Mayon and Mt. Fuji OS3

Moro Vinta OS4

Engr., Typo. (2, 6, 25c)

1943-44 Wmk. 257 *Perf. 13*

N12	OS1	1c deep orange	.20	.20
N13	OS2	2c bright green	.20	.20
N14	OS1	4c slate green	.20	.20
N15	OS3	5c orange brown	.20	.20
N16	OS2	6c red	.20	.20
N17	OS3	10c blue green	.20	.20
N18	OS4	12c steel blue	1.00	1.00
N19	OS4	16c dark brown	.20	.20
N20	OS1	20c rose violet	1.25	1.25
N21	OS3	21c violet	.20	.20
N22	OS2	25c pale brown	.20	.20
N23	OS3	1p deep carmine	.75	.75
N24	OS4	2p dull violet	5.00	5.00
N25	OS4	5p dark olive	8.50	8.50
		Nos. N12-N25 (14)	18.30	18.30

For surcharges see Nos. NB5-NB7.

Map of Manila Bay Showing Bataan and Corregidor OS5

1943, May 7 Photo. Unwmk.
N26 OS5 2c carmine red .20 .20
N27 OS5 5c bright green .25 .25

Fall of Bataan and Corregidor, 1st anniv.

No. 440 Surcharged in Black

Limbagan
1593 - 1943
12 12

1943, June 20 Engr. *Perf. 11*
N28 A60 12c on 20c lt olive green .20 .20
a. Double surcharge

350th anniv. of the printing press in the Philippines. "Limbagan" is Tagalog for "printing press."

Rizal Monument, Filipina and Philippine Flag — OS6

1943, Oct. 14 Photo. *Perf. 12*

N29	OS6	5c light blue	.20	.20
a.		Imperf.	.20	.20
N30	OS6	12c orange	.20	.20
a.		Imperf.	.20	.20
N31	OS6	17c rose pink	.20	.20
a.		Imperf.	.20	.20
		Nos. N29-N31 (3)	.60	.60

"Independence of the Philippines." Japan granted "independence" Oct. 14, 1943, when the puppet republic was founded.

The imperforate stamps were issued without gum.

Jose Rizal OS7

Rev. Jose Burgos OS8

Apolinario Mabini — OS9

1944, Feb. 17 Litho. *Perf. 12*

N32	OS7	5c blue	.20	.20
a.		Imperf.	.20	.20
N33	OS8	12c carmine	.20	.20
a.		Imperf.	.20	.20
N34	OS9	17c deep orange	.20	.20
a.		Imperf.	.20	.20
		Nos. N32-N34 (3)	.60	.60

Nos. C60 and C61 Surcharged in Black

REPÚBLIKÁ
NG PILIPINAS
5-7-44
5

1944, May 7 *Perf. 11*
N35 AP1 5c on 20c ultra .50 .35
N36 AP1 12c on 60c blue green 1.25 .85

Fall of Bataan and Corregidor, 2nd anniv.

Jose P. Laurel — OS10

Without Gum

1945, Jan. 12 Litho. *Imperf.*

N37	OS10	5c dull violet brown	.20	.20
N38	OS10	7c blue green	.20	.20
N39	OS10	20c chalky blue	.20	.20
		Nos. N37-N39 (3)	.60	.60

1st anniv. of the puppet Philippine Republic (Oct. 14, 1944). "S" stands for "sentimos."

OCCUPATION SEMI-POSTAL STAMPS

Woman, Farming and Cannery — OSP1

Unwmk.

1942, Nov. 12 Litho. *Perf. 12*

NB1	OSP1	2c + 1c pale violet	.20	.20
NB2	OSP1	5c + 1c brt green	.25	.20
NB3	OSP1	16c + 2c orange	25.00	25.00
		Nos. NB1-NB3 (3)	25.45	25.40

Campaign to produce and conserve food. The surtax aided the Red Cross.

Souvenir Sheet

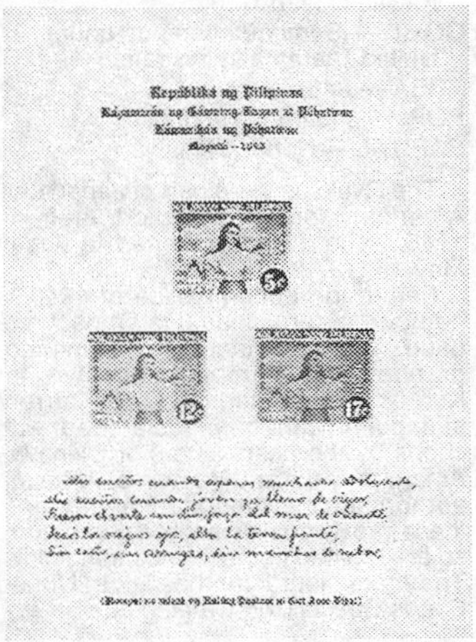

OSP2

Without Gum

1943, Oct. 14 *Imperf.*
NB4 OSP2 Sheet of 3 45.00 6.00

"Independence of the Philippines."

No. NB4 contains Nos. N29a-N31a. Lower inscription from Rizal's "Last Farewell." Sold for 2.50p.

Nos. N18, N20 and N21 Surcharged in Black

BAHA
1943
+21

1943, Dec. 8 Wmk. 257 *Perf. 13*

NB5	OS4	12c + 21c steel blue	.20	.20
NB6	OS1	20c + 36c rose violet	.20	.20
NB7	OS3	21c + 40c violet	.20	.20
		Nos. NB5-NB7 (3)	.60	.60

The surtax was for the benefit of victims of a Luzon flood.

"Baha" is Tagalog for "flood."

Souvenir Sheet

OSP3

Without Gum

Unwmk.

1944, Feb. 9 Litho. *Imperf.*
NB8 OSP3 Sheet of 3 5.00 *3.00*

No. NB8 contains Nos. N32a-N34a.

Sheet sold for 1p, surtax going to a fund for the care of heroes' monuments.

OCCUPATION POSTAGE DUE STAMP

No. J15 Ovptd. with Bar in Blue

1942, Oct. 14 Unwmk. *Perf. 11*
NJ1 D3 3c on 4c brown red 35.00 20.00

On copies of No. J15, two lines were drawn in India ink with a ruling pen across "United States of America" by employees of the Short Paid Section of the Manila Post Office.

This was to make a provisional 3c postage due stamp which was used from Sept. 1, 1942, (when the letter rate was raised from 2c to 5c) until Oct. 14 when No. NJ1 went on sale.

OCCUPATION OFFICIAL STAMPS

Nos. 461, 413, 435, 435a and 442 Overprinted or Surcharged in Black with Bars and

公用
(K. P.)

1943-44 Unwmk. *Perf. 11x10½, 11*

NO1	A75	2c apple green	.20	.20
a.		Double overprint	*500.00*	
NO2	A55	5c on 6c dk brown (#413, '44)	35.00	35.00
NO3	A55	5c on 6c gldn brn (No. 435a)	.20	.20
a.		Narrower spacing btwn. bars	.20	.20
b.		5c on 6c dark brown (#435)	.20	.20
c.		As "b," narrower spacing between bars	.20	.20
d.		Double surcharge	—	
NO4	A62	16c on 30c orange red	.30	.30
a.		Wider spacing between bars	.30	.30
		Nos. NO1-NO4 (4)	35.70	35.70

On Nos. NO3 and NO3b, the bar deleting "United States of America" is 9¾-10mm above the bar deleting "Common-." On Nos. NO3a and NO3c, the spacing is 8-8½mm.

On No. NO4 the center bar is 19mm long, 3½mm below the top bar and 6mm above the Japanese characters. On No. NO4a, the center bar is 20½mm long, 9mm below the top bar and 1mm above the Japanese characters.

"K. P." (Kagamitang Pampamahalaan) is Tagalog for "Official Business."

Nos. 435 and 435a Surcharged in Black

5
REPUBLIKA NG
PILIPINAS
(K. P.)

1944 *Perf. 11*
NO5 A55 5c on 6c golden brown .20 .20
a. 5c on 6c dark brown .20 .20

Nos. 034 and C62 Overprinted in Black

Pilipinas
REPUBLIKA

a

K.P.
REPUBLIKA NG PILIPINAS

(K. P.)

b

NO6 A60(a) 20c lt olive green .25 .25
NO7 AP1(b) 1p sepia .65 .65

PUERTO RICO

ˌpwer-tə-ˈrē-ˌkō

(Porto Rico)

LOCATION — Large island in the West Indies, east of Hispaniola
GOVT. — Former Spanish possession
AREA — 3,435 sq. mi.
POP. — 953,243 (1899)
CAPITAL — San Juan

The island was ceded to the US by the Treaty of 1898.

Spanish issues of 1855-73 used in both Puerto Rico and Cuba are listed as Cuba Nos. 1-4, 9-14, 18-21, 32-34, 35A-37, 39-41, 43-45, 47-49, 51-53, 55-57.

Spanish issues of 1873-1898 for Puerto Rico only are listed in Vol. 4 of this Catalogue.

100 Cents = 1 Dollar (1898)

Issued under US Administration
Ponce Issue

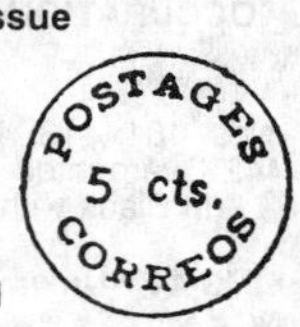

A11

1898 Unwmk. *Imperf.*

200	A11	5c violet, *yellowish*	*7,000.*

The only way No. 200 is known used is handstamped on envelopes. Both unused stamps and used envelopes have a violet control mark.

Counterfeits exist of Nos. 200-201.

Coamo Issue

A12

1898 Unwmk. *Imperf.*

201	A12	5c black	650.	*1,050.*

There are ten varieties in the setting (see the Scott United States Specialized Catalogue). The stamps bear the control mark "F. Santiago" in violet.

US Nos. 279, 279Bf, 281, 272 and 282C Overprinted in Black at 36 degree angle

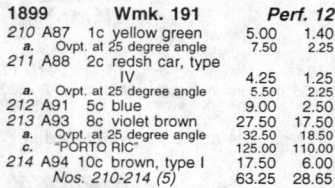

1899 Wmk. 191 *Perf. 12*

210	A87	1c yellow green	5.00	1.40
a.		Ovpt. at 25 degree angle	7.50	2.25
211	A88	2c redsh car, type IV	4.25	1.25
a.		Ovpt. at 25 degree angle	5.50	2.25
212	A91	5c blue	9.00	2.50
213	A93	8c violet brown	27.50	17.50
a.		Ovpt. at 25 degree angle	32.50	18.50
c.		"PORTO RIC"	125.00	110.00
214	A94	10c brown, type I	17.50	6.00
		Nos. 210-214 (5)	63.25	28.65

Misspellings of the overprint, actually broken letters (PORTO RICU, PORTU RICO, FORTO RICO), are found on 1c, 2c, 8c and 10c.

US Nos. 279 and 279B Overprinted Diagonally in Black

1900

215	A87	1c yellow green	6.00	1.40
216	A88	2c red, type IV	4.75	1.25
b.		Inverted overprint		*8,250.*

POSTAGE DUE STAMPS

US Nos. J38, J39, J42 Overprinted like Nos. 210-214

1899 Wmk. 191 *Perf. 12*

J1	D2	1c deep claret	22.50	5.50
a.		Overprint at 25 degree angle	22.50	7.50
J2	D2	2c deep claret	11.00	6.00
a.		Overprint at 25 degree angle	15.00	7.00
J3	D2	10c deep claret	160.00	60.00
a.		Overprint at 25 degree angle	180.00	85.00
		Nos. J1-J3 (3)	193.50	71.50

Stamps of Puerto Rico were replaced by those of the US.

RYUKYU ISLANDS

LOCATION — Chain of 63 islands between Japan and Formosa, separating the East China Sea from the Pacific Ocean
GOVT. — Semi-autonomous under United States administration
AREA — 848 sq. mi.
POP. — 945,465 (1970)
CAPITAL — Naha, Okinawa

The Ryukyus were part of Japan until American forces occupied them in 1945. The islands reverted to Japan May 15, 1972.

Before the general issue of 1948, a number of provisional stamps were used. These included a mimeographed-handstamped adhesive for Kume Island, and various current stamps of Japan handstamped with chops by the postmasters of Okinawa, Amami, Miyako and Yaeyama. Although authorized by American authorities, these provisionals were local in nature, so are omitted in the listings that follow. They are listed in the Scott United States Specialized Catalogue.

100 Sen = 1 Yen
100 Cents = 1 Dollar (1958)

Catalogue values for all unused stamps in this country are for Never Hinged items.

Watermark

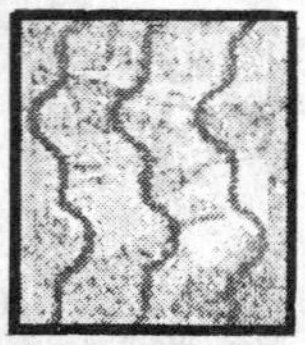

Wmk. 257

Cycad — A1

Lily — A2

Sailing Ship A3

Farmer A4

Wmk. 257

1949, July 18 Typo. *Perf. 13*

Second Printing

1	A1	5s magenta	1.50	1.50
2	A2	10s yellow green	6.00	5.50
3	A1	20s yellow green	2.50	2.50
4	A3	30s vermilion	1.50	1.50
5	A2	40s magenta	1.50	1.50
6	A3	50s ultramarine	3.00	3.25
7	A4	1y ultramarine	6.00	5.50
		Nos. 1-7 (7)	22.00	21.25

First Printing

1948, July 1

1a	A1	5s magenta	2.50	3.50
2a	A2	10s yellow green	1.40	2.00
3a	A1	20s yellow green	1.40	2.00
4a	A3	30s vermilion	2.50	3.25
5a	A2	40s magenta	50.00	50.00
6a	A3	50s ultramarine	2.50	3.50
7a	A4	1y ultramarine	450.00	290.00
		Nos. 1a-7a (7)	510.30	354.25

First printing: thick yellow gum, dull colors, rough perforations, grayish paper.

Second printing: white gum, sharp colors, cleancut perforations, white paper.

Roof Tiles — A5

Ryukyu University — A6

Designs: 1y, Ryukyu girl. 2y, Shuri Castle. 3y, Guardian dragon. 4y, Two women. 5y, Sea shells.

Perf. 13x13½

1950, Jan. 21 Unwmk. Photo.

8	A5	50s dark carmine rose	.20	.20
a.		White paper	.50	.50
9	A5	1y deep blue	2.50	2.00
10	A5	2y rose violet	11.00	6.00
11	A5	3y carmine rose	25.00	11.00
12	A5	4y grnsh gray	15.00	11.00
13	A5	5y blue green	7.50	5.00
		Nos. 8-13 (6)	61.20	35.20

No. 8a is on whiter paper with colorless gum. Issued Sept. 6, 1958.

No. 8 is on toned paper with yellowish gum.

For surcharges see Nos. 16-17.

1951, Feb. 12 *Perf. 13½x13*

14	A6	3y red brown	55.00	20.00

Opening of Ryukyu University, Feb. 12.

Pine Tree — A7

1951, Feb. 19 *Perf. 13*

15	A7	3y dark green	50.00	20.00

Reforestation Week, Feb. 18-24.

Nos. 8 and 10 Surcharged in Black

Three types of 10y surcharge:
I - Narrow-spaced rules, "10" normal spacing.
II - Wide-spaced rules, "10" normal spacing.
III - Rules and "10" both wide-spaced.

1952 *Perf. 13x13½*

16	A5	10y on 50s, type II	9.00	9.00
a.		Type I	35.00	35.00
b.		Type III	40.00	40.00
17	A5	100y on 2y rose vio	1,900.	1,200.

Surcharge forgeries are known of No. 17. Authentication by competent experts is recommended.

Dove, Bean Sprout and Map — A8

Madanbashi Bridge — A9

1952, Apr. 1 *Perf. 13½x13*

18	A8	3y deep plum	120.00	35.00

Establishment of the Government of the Ryukyu Islands (GRI), Apr. 1, 1952.

1952-53

Designs: 2y, Main Hall, Shuri Castle. 3y, Shurei Gate. 6y, Stone Gate, Sogenji temple, Naha. 10y, Benzaiten-do temple. 30y, Sonohan Utaki (altar) at Shuri Castle. 50y, Tamaudum (royal mausoleum), Shuri. 100y, Stone Bridge, Hosho Pond.

19	A9	1y red	.20	.20
20	A9	2y green	.25	.25
21	A9	3y aqua	.35	.35
22	A9	6y blue	1.75	1.75
23	A9	10y crimson rose	2.50	.90
24	A9	30y olive green	11.00	6.50
a.		30y light olive green ('58)	30.00	
25	A9	50y rose violet	15.00	8.25
26	A9	100y claret	20.00	6.25
		Nos. 19-26 (8)	51.05	24.45

Issued: 1y, 2y, 3y, 11/20/52; others, 1/20/53.

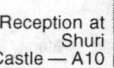

Reception at Shuri Castle — A10

Perry and American Fleet A11

1953, May 26 *Perf. 13½x13, 13x13½*

27	A10	3y deep magenta	12.50	6.50
28	A11	6y dull blue	1.25	1.25

Centenary of the arrival of Commodore Matthew Calbraith Perry at Naha, Okinawa.

Chofu Ota and Pencil-shaped Matrix — A12

Shigo Toma and Pen — A13

1953, Oct. 1 *Perf. 13½x13*

29	A12	4y yellow brown	10.00	5.00

3rd Newspaper Week.

1954, Oct. 1

30	A13	4y blue	13.00	7.50

4th Newspaper Week.

Ryukyu Pottery A14

Noguni Shrine and Sweet Potato Plant A15

Designs: 15y, Lacquerware. 20y, Textile design.

1954-55 Photo. *Perf. 13*

31	A14	4y brown	1.00	.60
32	A14	15y vermilion	4.00	2.00
33	A14	20y yellow orange	2.25	2.00
		Nos. 31-33 (3)	7.25	4.60

Issue dates: June 25, 1954, June 20, 1955.

For surcharges see Nos. C19, C21, C23.

1955, Nov. 26

34	A15	4y blue	11.00	7.00

350th anniv. of the introduction of the sweet potato to the Ryukyu Islands.

Stylized Trees
A16

Willow
Dance
A17

1956, Feb. 18 **Unwmk.**
35 A16 4y bluish green 10.00 5.00

Arbor Week, Feb. 18-24.

1956, May 1 ***Perf. 13***

Design: 8y, Straw hat dance. 14y, Dancer in warrior costume with fan.

36 A17 5y rose lilac .90 .60
37 A17 8y violet blue 2.00 1.65
38 A17 14y reddish brown 3.00 2.00
Nos. 36-38 (3) 5.90 4.25

For surcharges see Nos. C20, C22.

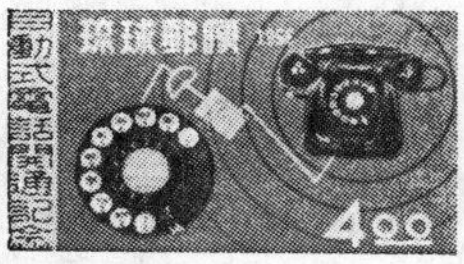
Telephone
A18

1956, June 8
39 A18 4y violet blue 15.00 8.00

Establishment of dial telephone system.

Garland of
Pine, Bamboo
and
Plum — A19

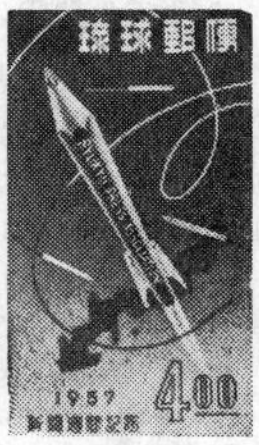
Map of
Okinawa and
Pencil
Rocket — A20

1956, Dec. 1 ***Perf. 13½x13***
40 A19 2y multicolored 2.00 2.00

New Year, 1957.

1957, Oct. 1 **Photo.** ***Perf. 13½x13***
41 A20 4y deep violet blue .75 .75

7th annual Newspaper Week, Oct. 1-7.

Phoenix — A21

1957, Dec. 1 **Unwmk.** ***Perf. 13***
42 A21 2y multicolored .25 .25

New Year, 1958.

Ryukyu Stamps — A22

1958, July 1 ***Perf. 13½***
43 A22 4y multicolored .80 .80

10th anniversary of first Ryukyu stamps.

Yen Symbol and
Dollar Sign — A23

1958, Sept. 16 **Typo.** ***Perf. 11***
Without Gum

44 A23 ½c orange .90 .90
a. Imperf., pair *1,000.*
b. Horiz. pair, imperf. btwn. 100.00
c. Vert. pair, imperf. btwn. 150.00
d. Vert. strip of 4, imperf. btwn. 500.00
45 A23 1c yellow green 1.40 1.40
a. Horiz. pair, imperf. btwn. 150.00
b. Vert. pair, imperf. btwn. 110.00
c. Vert. strip of 3, imperf. btwn. 450.00
d. Vert. strip of 4, imperf. btwn. 500.00
e. Block of 4, imperf. btwn. vert & horiz. —
46 A23 2c dark blue 2.25 2.25
a. Horiz. pair, imperf. btwn. 150.00
b. Vert. pair, imperf. btwn. *1,500.*
c. Horiz. strip of 3, imperf. btwn. 300.00
d. Horiz. strip of 4, imperf. btwn. 500.00
47 A23 3c deep carmine 1.75 1.50
a. Horiz. pair, imperf. btwn. 150.00
b. Vert. pair, imperf. btwn. 110.00
c. Vert. strip of 3, imperf. btwn. 300.00
d. Vert. strip of 4, imperf. btwn. 550.00
e. Block of 4, imperf. btwn. vert & horiz. —
48 A23 4c bright green 2.25 2.25
a. Horiz. pair, imperf. btwn. *500.00*
b. Vert. pair, imperf. btwn. 150.00
49 A23 5c orange 4.25 3.75
a. Horiz. pair, imperf. btwn. 150.00
b. Vert. pair, imperf. btwn. *750.00*
50 A23 10c aqua 5.75 4.75
a. Horiz. pair, imperf. btwn. 200.00
b. Vert. pair, imperf. btwn. 150.00
c. Vert. strip of 3, imperf. btwn. 550.00
51 A23 25c brt vio blue 8.00 6.00
a. Gummed paper ('61) 9.50 8.50
b. Horiz. pair, imperf. btwn. *1,400.*
c. Vert. pair, imperf. btwn. —
d. Vert. strip of 3, imperf. btwn. 600.00
52 A23 50c gray *17.50* 10.00
a. Gummed paper ('61) 10.50 10.00
b. Horiz. pair, imperf. btwn. *1,200.*
53 A23 $1 rose lilac 12.50 5.50
a. Horiz. pair, imperf. btwn. 400.00
b. Vert. pair, imperf. btwn. *1,750.*
Nos. 44-53 (10) 56.55 38.30

Printed locally. Perforation, paper and shade varieties exist.

Nos. 51a, 52a are on off-white paper and perf 10.3.

Gate of Courtesy — A24

1958, Oct. 15 **Photo.** ***Perf. 13½***
54 A24 3c multicolored 1.25 1.25

Restoration of Shureimon, Gate of Courtesy, on road leading to Shuri City.

Counterfeits exist.

Lion Dance
A25

Trees and
Mountains
A26

1958, Dec. 10 **Unwmk.** ***Perf. 13½***
55 A25 1½c multicolored .25 .25

New Year, 1959.

1959, Apr. 30 **Litho.** ***Perf. 13½x13***
56 A26 3c bl, yel grn, grn & red .70 .60

"Make the Ryukyus Green" movement.

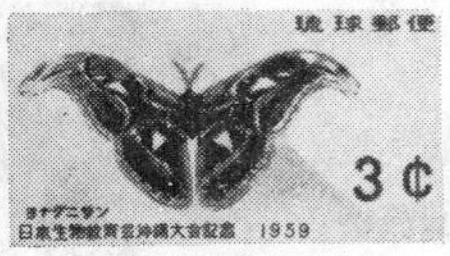
Yonaguni
Moth
A27

1959, July 23 **Photo.** ***Perf. 13***
57 A27 3c multicolored 1.10 1.00

Meeting of the Japanese Biological Education Society in Okinawa.

Hibiscus
A28

Toy(Yakaji)
A29

3c, Fish (Moorish idol). 8c, Sea shell (Phalium bandatum). 13c, Butterfly (Kallima Inachus Eucerca), denomination at left, butterfly going up. 17c, Jellyfish (Dactylometra pacifera Goette).

Inscribed 琉球郵便

1959, Aug. 10 ***Perf. 13x13½***
58 A28 ½c multicolored .20 .20
59 A28 3c multicolored .75 .40
60 A28 8c lt ultra, blk & ocher 10.00 5.50
61 A28 13c lt bl, gray & org 2.50 1.75
62 A28 17c vio bl, red & yel 20.00 9.00
Nos. 58-62 (5) 33.45 16.85

Four-character inscription measures 10x2mm on ½c; 12x3mm on 3c, 8c; 8½x2mm on 13c, 17c. See Nos. 76-80.

1959, Dec. 1 **Litho.**
63 A29 1½c gold & multi .55 .45

New Year, 1960.

University
Badge
A30

1960, May 22 **Photo.** ***Perf. 13***
64 A30 3c multicolored .95 .75

Opening of Ryukyu University, 10th anniv.

Dancer — A31

Designs: Various Ryukyu Dances.

1960, Nov. 1 **Photo.** ***Perf. 13***
Dark Gray Background

65 A31 1c yellow, red & vio 1.25 .80
66 A31 2½c crimson, bl & yel 3.00 1.00
67 A31 5c dk blue, yel & red .65 .50
68 A31 10c dk blue, yel & car .80 .65
Nos. 65-68 (4) 5.70 2.95

See Nos. 81-87, 220.

Torch and
Nago
Bay — A32

Runners at
Starting
Line
A33

1960, Nov. 8
72 A32 3c lt bl, grn & red 5.50 3.00
73 A33 8c orange & slate grn .75 .75

8th Kyushu Inter-Prefectural Athletic Meet, Nago, Northern Okinawa, Nov. 6-7.

Little Egret
and Rising
Sun
A34

1960, Dec. 1 **Unwmk.** ***Perf. 13***
74 A34 3c reddish brown 5.50 3.50

National census.

Okinawa Bull
Fight — A35

1960, Dec. 10 ***Perf. 13½***
75 A35 1½c bis, dk bl & red brn 1.75 1.50

New Year, 1961.

Type of 1959 With Japanese Inscription Redrawn:

琉球郵便

1960-61 **Photo.** ***Perf. 13x13½***
76 A28 ½c multicolored ('61) .45 .45
77 A28 3c multicolored ('61) .90 .35
78 A28 8c lt ultra, blk & ocher .90 .80
79 A28 13c blue, brn & red 1.10 .90
80 A28 17c violet bl, red & yel 15.00 6.00
Nos. 76-80 (5) 18.35 8.50

Size of Japanese inscription on Nos. 78-80 is 10½x11½mm. On No. 79 the denomination is at right, butterfly going down.

Issued: 8c-17c, July 1; 3c, Aug. 23; ½c, Oct.

Dancer Type of 1960 with "RYUKYUS" Added in English

1961-64 *Perf. 13*

81	A31	1c multicolored	.20	.20
82	A31	2½c multicolored ('62)	.20	.20
83	A31	5c multicolored ('62)	.25	.25
84	A31	10c multicolored ('62)	.45	.40
84A	A31	20c multicolored ('64)	3.00	1.40
85	A31	25c multicolored ('62)	1.00	.90
86	A31	50c multicolored	2.50	1.40
87	A31	$1 multicolored	6.00	.25
		Nos. 81-87 (8)	13.60	5.00

Issue dates: 50c, $1, Sept. 1. 1c, Dec. 5. 25c, Feb. 1. 2½c, 5c, 10c, June 20. 20c, Jan. 20.

Pine Tree — A36

1961, May 1 Photo. *Perf. 13*
88 A36 3c yellow green & red 1.50 1.25

"Make the Ryukyus Green" movement.

Naha, Steamer and Sailboat A37

1961, May 20
89 A37 3c aqua 2.10 1.50

40th anniversary of Naha.

White Silver Temple — A38

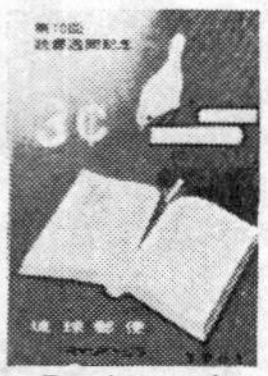

Books and Bird — A39

1961, Oct. 1 Typo. *Perf. 11*
90 A38 3c red brown 2.00 1.50
a. Horiz. pair, imperf. between 500.00
b. Vert. pair, imperf. between 600.00

Merger of townships Takamine, Kanegushiku and Miwa with Itoman.

1961, Nov. 12 Litho. *Perf. 13*
91 A39 3c multicolored 1.10 .90

Issued for Book Week.

Rising Sun and Eagles — A40

Symbolic Steps, Trees and Government Building — A41

1961, Dec. 10 Photo. *Perf. 13½*
92 A40 1½c gold, ver & blk 2.00 2.00

New Year, 1962.

1962, Apr. 1 Unwmk. *Perf. 13½*

Design: 3c, Government Building.

93 A41 1½c multicolored .60 .60
94 A41 3c brt green, red & gray .80 .80

10th anniv. of the Government of the Ryukyu Islands (GRI).

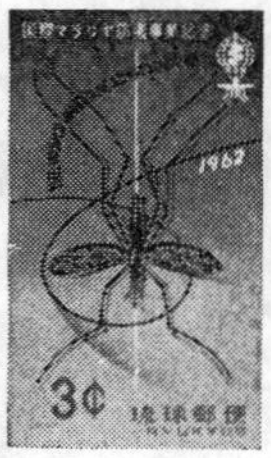

Anopheles Hyrcanus Sinensis — A42

8c, Malaria eradication emblem & Shurei gate.

1962, Apr. 7 *Perf. 13½x13*
95 A42 3c multicolored .60 .60
96 A42 8c multicolored .90 .75

WHO drive to eradicate malaria.

Dolls and Toys A43

Linden or Sea Hibiscus A44

1962, May 5 Litho. *Perf. 13½*
97 A43 3c red, blk, bl & buff 1.10 1.00

Issued for Children's Day.

1962, June 1 Photo.

Flowers: 3c, Indian coral tree. 8c, Iju (Schima liukiuensis Nakai). 13c, Touch-me-not (garden balsam). 17c, Shell flower (Alpinia speciosa).

98	A44	½c multicolored	.20	.20
99	A44	3c multicolored	.35	.20
100	A44	8c multicolored	.40	.40
101	A44	13c multicolored	.60	.55
102	A44	17c multicolored	1.00	.80
		Nos. 98-102 (5)	2.55	2.15

See #107, 114 for 1½c and 15c flower stamps.
For surcharge see No. 190.

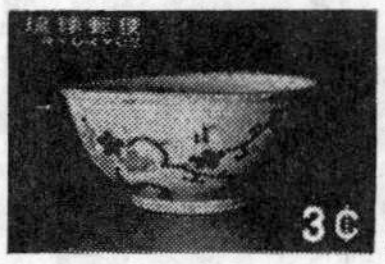

Earthenware A45

1962, July 5 *Perf. 13½x13*
103 A45 3c multicolored 3.50 2.50

Issued for Philatelic Week.

Japanese Fencing (Kendo) A46

1962, July 25 *Perf. 13*
104 A46 3c multicolored 4.00 3.00

All-Japan Kendo Meeting, Okinawa, July 25.

Rabbit Playing near Water, Bingata Cloth Design — A47

Young Man and Woman, Stone Relief — A48

1962, Dec. 10 *Perf. 13x13½*
105 A47 1½c gold & multi 1.00 .80

New Year, 1963.

1963, Jan. 15 Photo. *Perf. 13½*
106 A48 3c gold, black & blue .90 .80

Issued for Adult Day.

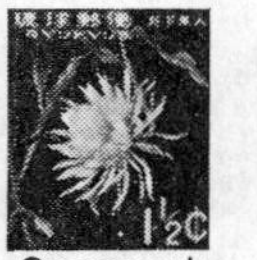

Gooseneck Cactus A49

Trees and Wooded Hills A50

1963, Apr. 5 *Perf. 13x13½*
107 A49 1½c dk bl, grn, yel & pink .20 .20

1963, Mar. 25 *Perf. 13½x13*
108 A50 3c ultra, green & red brn 1.00 .80

"Make the Ryukyus Green" movement.

Map of Okinawa A51

Hawks over Islands A52

1963, Apr. 30 Unwmk. *Perf. 13½*
109 A51 3c multicolored 1.25 1.00

Opening of the Round Road on Okinawa.

1963, May 10 Photo.
110 A52 3c multicolored 1.10 .95

Issued for Bird Day, May 10.

Shioya Bridge — A53

1963, June 5
111 A53 3c multicolored 1.10 .95

Opening of Shioya Bridge over Shioya Bay.

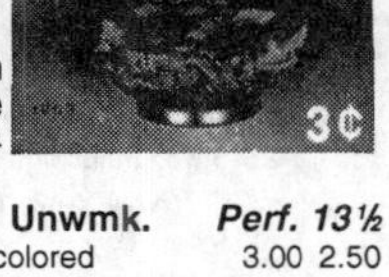

Tsuikin-wan Lacquerware Bowl — A54

1963, July 1 Unwmk. *Perf. 13½*
112 A54 3c multicolored 3.00 2.50

Issued for Philatelic Week.

Map of Far East and JCI Emblem — A55

1963, Sept. 16 Photo. *Perf. 13½*
113 A55 3c multicolored .70 .70

Meeting of the Intl. Junior Chamber of Commerce (JCI), Naha, Okinawa, Sept. 16-19.

Mamaomoto A56

Site of Nakagusuku Castle A57

1963, Oct. 15 *Perf. 13x13½*
114 A56 15c multicolored 2.00 .80

1963, Nov. 1 *Perf. 13½x13*
115 A57 3c multicolored .70 .60

Protection of national cultural treasures.

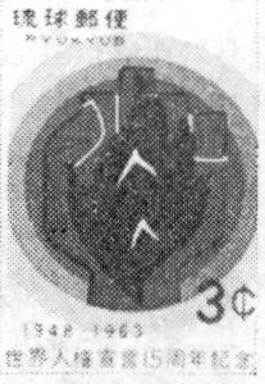

Flame — A58

Dragon (Bingata Pattern) — A59

1963, Dec. 10 *Perf. 13½*
116 A58 3c red, dk bl & yel .70 .60

15th anniversary of the Universal Declaration of Human Rights.

1963, Dec. 10 Photo.
117 A59 1½c multicolored .60 .50

New Year, 1964.

Carnation A60

Pineapples and Sugar Cane A61

1964, May 10 *Perf. 13½*
118 A60 3c blue, yel, blk & car .40 .35

Issued for Mother's Day.

1964, June 1
119 A61 3c multicolored .40 .35

Agricultural census.

Minsah Obi (Sash Woven of Kapok) — A62

1964, July 1 Unwmk. *Perf. 13½*
120 A62 3c dp bl, rose pink & ocher .55 .50
a. 3c dp bl, dp car & ocher .70 .65

Issued for Philatelic Week.

Girl Scout and Emblem — A63

1964, Aug. 31 **Photo.**
121 A63 3c multicolored .40 .35

10th anniversary of Ryukyuan Girl Scouts.

Shuri Relay Station — A64

Parabolic Antenna and Map — A65

1964, Sept. 1 **Unwmk.** ***Perf. 13½***
Black Overprint

122 A64 3c deep green	.65	.65
a. Figure "1" inverted	27.50	27.50
123 A65 8c ultra	1.25	1.25

Opening of the Ryukyu Islands-Japan microwave system carrying telephone and telegraph messages between the Ryukyus and Japan. Nos. 122-123 not issued without overprint.

Gate of Courtesy, Olympic Torch and Emblem — A66

1964, Sept. 7 **Photo.** ***Perf. 13½x13***
124 A66 3c ultra, yellow & red .20 .20

Relaying of the Olympic torch on Okinawa en route to Tokyo.

"Naihanchi," Karate Stance — A67

"Makiwara," Strengthening Hands and Feet — A68

"Kumite," Simulated Combat — A69

1964-65 **Photo.** ***Perf. 13½***

125 A67 3c dull claret, yel & blk	.50	.45
126 A68 3c yellow & multi ('65)	.40	.40
127 A69 3c gray, red & blk ('65)	.40	.40
Nos. 125-127 (3)	1.30	1.25

Karate, Ryukyuan self-defense sport.
Issued: #125, 10/5; #126, 2/5; #127, 6/5.

Miyara Dunchí A70

Snake and Iris (Bingata) A71

1964, Nov. 1 ***Perf. 13½***
128 A70 3c multicolored .25 .25

Protection of national cultural treasures. Miyara Dunchi was built as a residence by Miyara-pechin Toen in 1819.

1964, Dec. 10 **Photo.**
129 A71 1½c multicolored .30 .25

New Year, 1965.

Boy Scouts — A72

1965, Feb. 6 ***Perf. 13½***
130 A72 3c lt blue & multi .45 .40

10th anniversary of Ryukyuan Boy Scouts.

Main Stadium, Onoyama A73

1965, July 1 ***Perf. 13x13½***
131 A73 3c multicolored .25 .25

Inauguration of the main stadium of the Onoyama athletic facilities.

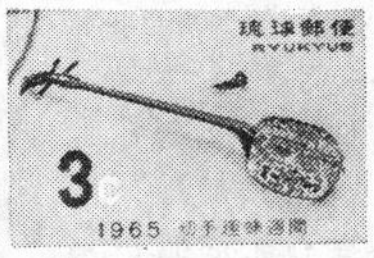

Samisen of King Shoko — A74

1965, July 1 **Photo.** ***Perf. 13½***
132 A74 3c buff & multi .45 .40

Issued for Philatelic Week.

Kin Power Plant — A75

ICY Emblem, Ryukyu Map — A76

1965, July 1
133 A75 3c green & multi .25 .25

Completion of Kin power plant.

1965, Aug. 24 **Photo.** ***Perf. 13½***
134 A76 3c multicolored .20 .20

UN, 20th anniv.; Intl. Cooperation Year, 1964-65.

Naha City Hall — A77

1965, Sept. 18 **Unwmk.** ***Perf. 13½***
135 A77 3c blue & multi .20 .20

Completion of Naha City Hall.

Chinese Box Turtle A78

Horse (Bingata) A79

Turtles: No. 137, Hawksbill turtle (denomination at top, country name at bottom). No. 138, Asian terrapin (denomination and country name on top).

1965-66 **Photo.** ***Perf. 13½***

136 A78 3c gldn brn & multi	.30	.30
137 A78 3c black, yel & brn	.30	.30
138 A78 3c gray & multi	.30	.30
Nos. 136-138 (3)	.90	.90

Issue dates: No. 136, Oct. 20, 1965. No. 137, Jan. 20, 1966. No. 138, Apr. 20, 1966.

1965, Dec. 10 **Photo.** ***Perf. 13½***

139 A79 1½c multicolored	.20	.20
a. Gold omitted	*1,200.*	—

New Year, 1966.
There are 92 unused and 2 used examples of No. 139a known.

Noguchi's Okinawa Woodpecker A80

Sika Deer A81

Ryukyu Bungalow Swallow — A82

1966, May 10 **Photo.** ***Perf. 13½***
143 A82 3c sky blue, blk & brn .20 .20

4th Bird Week, May 10-16.

Lilies and Ruins A83

1966, June 23 ***Perf. 13x13½***
144 A83 3c multicolored .20 .20

Memorial Day, commemorating the end of the Battle of Okinawa, June 23, 1945.

University of the Ryukyus A84

1966, July 1
145 A84 3c multicolored .20 .20

Transfer of the University of the Ryukyus from US authority to the Ryukyu Government.

1966 **Photo.** ***Perf. 13½***

140 A80 3c shown	.20	.20
141 A81 3c shown	.25	.25
142 A81 3c Dugong	.25	.25
Nos. 140-142 (3)	.70	.70

Nature conservation.
Issued: #140, 2/15; #141, 3/15; #142, 4/20.

Lacquerware, 18th Century A85

Tile-Roofed House and UNESCO Emblem A86

1966, Aug. 1 ***Perf. 13½***
146 A85 3c gray & multi .20 .20

Issued for Philatelic Week.

1966, Sept. 20 **Photo.** ***Perf. 13½***
147 A86 3c multicolored .20 .20

UNESCO, 20th anniv.

Government Museum and Dragon Statue — A87

1966, Oct. 6
148 A87 3c multicolored .20 .20

Completion of the GRI (Government of the Ryukyu Islands) Museum, Shuri.

Tomb of Nakasone-Tuimya Genga, Ruler of Miyako — A88

1966, Nov. 1 **Photo.** ***Perf. 13½***
149 A88 3c multicolored .20 .20

Protection of national cultural treasures.

Ram in Iris Wreath (Bingata) A89

Clown Fish A90

1966, Dec. 10 **Photo.** ***Perf. 13½***
150 A89 1½c dk blue & multi .20 .20

New Year, 1967.

1966-67

Fish: No. 152, Young boxfish (white numeral at lower left). No. 153, Forceps fish (pale buff numeral at lower right). No. 154, Spotted triggerfish (orange numeral). No. 155, Saddleback butterflyfish (carmine numeral, lower left).

151 A90 3c org red & multi	.20	.20
152 A90 3c org yel & multi ('67)	.20	.20
153 A90 3c multi ('67)	.30	.25
154 A90 3c multi ('67)	.30	.25
155 A90 3c multi ('67)	.30	.25
Nos. 151-155 (5)	1.30	1.15

Issue dates: #151, Dec. 20. #152, Jan. 10. #153, Apr. 10. #154, May 25. #155, June 10.

Tsuboya Urn — A91

Episcopal Miter — A92

1967, Apr. 20
156 A91 3c yellow & multi .20 .20

Issued for Philatelic Week.

1967-68 Photo. *Perf. 13½*

Seashells: No. 158, Venus comb murex. No. 159, Chiragra spider. No. 160, Green turban. No. 161, Euprotomus bulla.

157 A92 3c lt green & multi .20 .20
158 A92 3c grnsh bl & multi .20 .20
159 A92 3c emerald & multi .25 .20
160 A92 3c lt blue & multi .30 .25
161 A92 3c brt blue & multi .60 .50
Nos. 157-161 (5) 1.55 1.35

Issued: 1967, #157, July 20; #158, Aug. 30. 1968; #159, Jan. 18; #160, Feb. 20; #161, June 5.

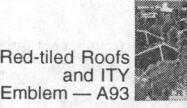

Red-tiled Roofs and ITY Emblem — A93

1967, Sept. 11 Photo. *Perf. 13½*
162 A93 3c multicolored .20 .20

International Tourist Year.

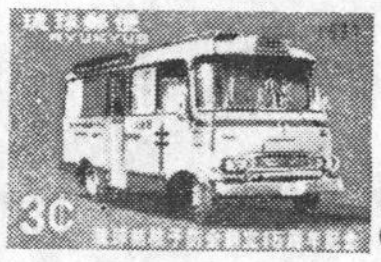
Mobile TB Clinic — A94

1967, Oct. 13 Photo. *Perf. 13½*
163 A94 3c lilac & multi .20 .20

Anti-Tuberculosis Society, 15th anniv.

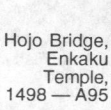

Hojo Bridge, Enkaku Temple, 1498 — A95

1967, Nov. 1
164 A95 3c blue grn & multi .20 .20

Protection of national cultural treasures.

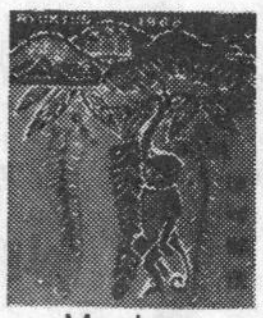
Monkey (Bingata) A96

TV Tower and Map A97

1967, Dec. 11 Photo. *Perf. 13½*
165 A96 1½c silver & multi .25 .20

New Year 1968.

1967, Dec. 22
166 A97 3c multicolored .25 .25

Opening of Miyako and Yaeyama television stations.

Dr. Kijin Nakachi and Helper — A98

Pill Box (Inro) — A99

1968, Mar. 15 Photo. *Perf. 13½*
167 A98 3c multicolored .25 .25

120th anniv. of the first vaccination in the Ryukyu Islands, performed by Dr. Kijin Nakachi.

1968, Apr. 18
168 A99 3c gray & multi .45 .45

Philatelic Week.

Young Man, Library, Book and Map of Ryukyu Islands A100

1968, May 13
169 A100 3c multicolored .30 .25

10th International Library Week.

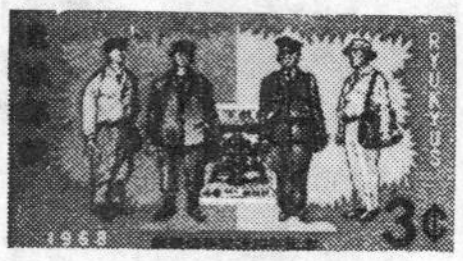
Mailmen's Uniforms and Stamp of 1948 A101

1968, July 1 Photo. *Perf. 13x13½*
170 A101 3c multicolored .30 .25

1st Ryukyuan postage stamps, 20th anniv.

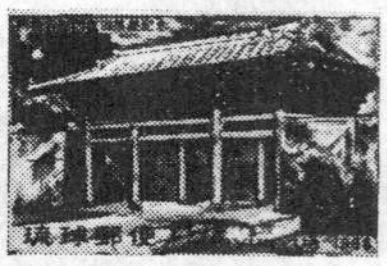
Main Gate, Enkaku Temple A102

Photo. & Engr.

1968, July 15 *Perf. 13½*
171 A102 3c multicolored .30 .25

Restoration of the main gate of the Enkaku Temple, built 1492-1495, and destroyed during WWII.

Old Man's Dance — A103

1968, Sept. 15 Photo. *Perf. 13½*
172 A103 3c gold & multi .30 .25

Issued for Old People's Day.

Mictyris Longicarpus A104

Crabs: No. 174, Uca dubia stimpson. No. 175, Baptozius vinosus. No. 176, Cardisoma carnifex. No. 177, Ocypode ceratophthalma pallas.

1968-69 Photo. *Perf. 13½*
173 A104 3c blue, ocher & blk .30 .25
174 A104 3c lt bl grn & multi .35 .30
175 A104 3c lt green & multi .35 .30
176 A104 3c lt ultra & multi .45 .40
177 A104 3c lt ultra & multi .45 .40
Nos. 173-177 (5) 1.90 1.65

Issued: #173, 10/10; #174, 2/5/69; #175, 3/5/69; #176, 5/15/69; #177, 6/2/69.

Saraswati Pavilion A105

1968, Nov. 1 Photo. *Perf. 13½*
178 A105 3c multicolored .30 .25

Restoration of the Saraswati Pavilion (in front of Enkaku Temple), destroyed during WWII.

Tennis Player A106

Cock and Iris (Bingata) A107

1968, Nov. 3 Photo. *Perf. 13½*
179 A106 3c green & multi .40 .35

35th All-Japan East-West Men's Soft-ball Tennis Tournament, Naha City, Nov. 23-24.

1968, Dec. 10
180 A107 1½c orange & multi .25 .20

New Year, 1969.

Boxer A108

Ink Slab Screen A109

1969, Jan. 3
181 A108 3c gray & multi .40 .30

20th All-Japan Amateur Boxing Championships, University of the Ryukyus, Jan. 3-5.

1969, Apr. 17 Photo. *Perf. 13½*
182 A109 3c salmon, indigo & red .40 .35

Philatelic Week.

Box Antennas and Map of Radio Link A110

Gate of Courtesy and Emblems A111

1969, July 1 Photo. *Perf. 13½*
183 A110 3c multicolored .25 .20

Opening of the UHF (radio) circuit system between Okinawa and the outlying Miyako-Yaeyama Islands.

1969, Aug. 1 Photo. *Perf. 13½*
184 A111 3c Prus bl, gold & ver .25 .20

22nd All-Japan Formative Education Study Conference, Naha, Aug. 1-3.

Tug of War Festival A112

Hari Boat Race A113

Izaiho Ceremony, Kudaka Island A114

Mortardrum Dance — A115

Sea God Dance A116

1969-70 Photo. *Perf. 13*
185 A112 3c multicolored .30 .25
186 A113 3c multicolored .35 .30
187 A114 3c multicolored .35 .30
188 A115 3c multicolored ('70) .50 .45
189 A116 3c multicolored ('70) .50 .45
Nos. 185-189 (5) 2.00 1.75

Folklore. Issue dates: #185, Aug. 1; #186, Sept. 5; #187, Oct. 3; #188, Jan. 20; #189, Feb. 27.

No. 99 Surcharged 改訂 ½¢

1969, Oct. 15 Photo. *Perf. 13½*
190 A44 ½c on 3c multi .90 .90

Nakamura-ke Farm House, Built 1713-51 A117

1969, Nov. 1 Photo. *Perf. 13½*
191 A117 3c multicolored .20 .20

Protection of national cultural treasures.

Statue of Kyuzo Toyama, Maps of Hawaiian and Ryukyu Islands A118

1969, Dec. 5 Photo. *Perf. 13½*
192 A118 3c lt ultra & multi .40 .40
a. Without overprint *2,500.*
b. Wide-spaced bars *725.00*

Ryukyu-Hawaii emigration led by Kyuzo Toyama, 70th anniversary.

The overprint - "1969" at lower left and bars across "1970" at upper right - was applied before No. 192 was issued.

Dog and Flowers (Bingata) A119

Sake Flask Made from Coconut A120

1969, Dec. 10

193 A119 1½c pink & multi .20 .20

New Year, 1970.

1970, Apr. 15 Photo. *Perf. 13½*

194 A120 3c multicolored .25 .25

Philatelic Week.

Classic Opera Issue

"The Bell" (Shushin Kaneiri) A121

Child and Kidnapper (Chu-nusudu) A122

Robe of Feathers (Mekarushi) A123

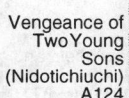

Vengeance of Two Young Sons (Nidotichiuchi) A124

The Virgin and the Dragon (Kokonomaki) A125

1970 Photo. *Perf. 13½*

195	A121	3c dull bl & multi	.40	.40
196	A122	3c lt blue & multi	.40	.40
197	A123	3c bluish grn & multi	.40	.40
198	A124	3c dull bl grn & multi	.40	.40
199	A125	3c multicolored	.40	.40
		Nos. 195-199 (5)	2.00	2.00
		195a-199a, 5 sheets of 4	22.50	25.00

Issue dates: #195, Apr. 28. #196, May 29. #197, June 30. #198, July 30. #199, Aug. 25.

Underwater Observatory and Tropical Fish — A126

1970, May 22

200 A126 3c blue grn & multi .30 .25

Completion of the underwater observatory at Busena-Misaki, Nago.

Noboru Jahana (1865-1908), Politician A127

Map of Okinawa and People A128

Portraits: No. 202, Saion Gushichan Bunjaku (1682-1761), statesman. No. 203, Choho Giwan (1823-1876), regent and poet.

1970-71 Engr. *Perf. 13½*

201	A127	3c rose claret	.50	.45
202	A127	3c dull blue green	.75	.65
203	A127	3c black	.50	.45
		Nos. 201-203 (3)	1.75	1.55

Issued: #201, 9/25; #202, 12/22; #203, 1/2271.

1970, Oct. 1 Photo.

204 A128 3c red & multi .25 .25

Oct. 1, 1970 census.

Great Cycad of Une — A129

1970, Nov. 2 Photo. *Perf. 13½*

205 A129 3c gold & multi .25 .25

Protection of national treasures.

Japanese Flag, Diet and Map of Ryukyus A130

Wild Boar and Cherry Blossoms (Bingata) A131

1970, Nov. 15 Photo. *Perf. 13½*

206 A130 3c ultra & multi .80 .75

Citizens' participation in national administration according to Japanese law of Apr. 24, 1970.

1970, Dec. 10

207 A131 1½c multicolored .20 .20

New Year, 1971.

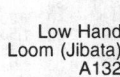

Low Hand Loom (Jibata) A132

Farmer Wearing Palm Bark Raincoat and Kuba Leaf Hat — A133

Fisherman's Wooden Box and Scoop — A134

Designs: No. 209, Woman running a filature (reel). No. 211, Woman hulling rice with cylindrical "Shiri-ushi."

1971 Photo. *Perf. 13½*

208	A132	3c lt blue & multi	.30	.25
209	A132	3c pale grn & multi	.30	.25
210	A133	3c lt blue & multi	.35	.30
211	A132	3c yellow & multi	.40	.35
212	A134	3c gray & multi	.35	.30
		Nos. 208-212 (5)	1.70	1.45

Issue dates: #208, Feb. 16; #209, Mar. 16; #210, Apr. 30; #211, May 20; #212, June 15.

Water Carrier (Taku) — A135

1971, Apr. 15 Photo. *Perf. 13½*

213 A135 3c blue grn & multi .35 .30

Philatelic Week.

Old and New Naha, and City Emblem A136

1971, May 20 *Perf. 13*

214 A136 3c ultra & multi .25 .20

50th anniversary of Naha as a municipality.

Caesalpinia Pulcherrima — A137

Design: 2c, Madder (Sandanka).

1971 Photo. *Perf. 13*

215	A137	2c gray & multi	.20	.20
216	A137	3c gray & multi	.20	.20

Issue dates: 2c, Sept. 30; 3c, May 10.

View from Mabuni Hill — A138

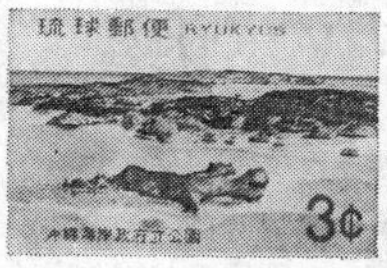

Mt. Arashi from Haneji Sea — A139

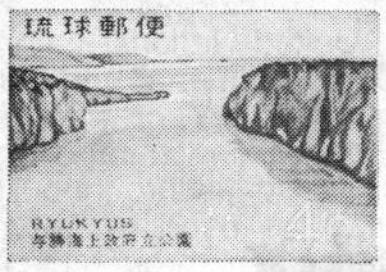

Yabuchi Island from Yakena Port — A140

1971-72

217	A138	3c green & multi	.20	.20
218	A139	3c blue & multi	.20	.20
219	A140	4c multi ('72)	.25	.20
		Nos. 217-219 (3)	.65	.60

Government parks. Issue dates: No. 217, July 30; No. 218, Aug. 30, 1971; No. 219, Jan. 20, 1972.

Dancer A141

Deva King, Torinji Temple A142

1971, Nov. 1 Photo. *Perf. 13*

220 A141 4c Prus blue & multi .20 .20

1971, Dec. 1

221 A142 4c dp blue & multi .20 .20

Protection of national cultural treasures.

Rat and Chrysanthemums A143

Student Nurse A144

1971, Dec. 10

222 A143 2c brown org & multi .20 .20

New Year 1972.

1971, Dec. 24

223 A144 4c lilac & multi .20 .20

Nurses' training, 25th anniversary.

Birds on Seashore A145

Sun over Islands A147

Coral Reef — A146

1972 Photo. *Perf. 13*

224	A145	5c brt blue & multi	.40	.35
225	A146	5c gray & multi	.40	.35
226	A147	5c ocher & multi	.40	.35
		Nos. 224-226 (3)	1.20	1.05

Issued: #224, 4/14; #225, 3/30; #226, 3/21.

Dove, US and Japanese Flags — A148

1972, Apr. 17 Photo. *Perf. 13*

227 A148 5c brt blue & multi .60 .60

Ratification of the Reversion Agreement with US under which the Ryukyu Islands were returned to Japan.

20-Cent Minimum Value

The minimum catalogue value is 20 cents. Separating se-tenant pieces into individual stamps does not increase the value of the stamps since demand for the separated stamps may be small.

Antique Sake Pot (Yushibin) — A149

1972, Apr. 20
228 A149 5c ultra & multi .50 .50

Philatelic Week.

Ryukyu stamps were replaced by those of Japan after May 15, 1972.

AIR POST STAMPS

Dove and Map of Ryukyus — AP1

Perf. 13x13½

1950, Feb. 15	Unwmk.	Photo.	
C1	AP1 8y bright blue	120.00	60.00
C2	AP1 12y green	35.00	30.00
C3	AP1 16y rose carmine	15.00	15.00
	Nos. C1-C3 (3)	170.00	105.00

Heavenly Maiden AP2

1951-54			
C4	AP2 13y blue	2.50	1.50
C5	AP2 18y green	3.50	2.25
C6	AP2 30y cerise	6.00	1.75
C7	AP2 40y red violet	7.00	5.50
C8	AP2 50y yellow orange	9.00	6.50
	Nos. C4-C8 (5)	28.00	17.50

Issue dates: Oct. 1, 1951, Aug. 16, 1954.

Heavenly Maiden Playing Flute — AP3

1957, Aug. 1	Engr.	*Perf. 13½*	
C9	AP3 15y blue green	9.00	3.50
C10	AP3 20y rose carmine	15.00	5.50
C11	AP3 35y yellow green	15.00	6.50
a.	35y light yellow green ('58)	150.00	
C12	AP3 45y reddish brown	16.00	8.00
C13	AP3 60y gray	18.00	10.00
	Nos. C9-C13 (5)	73.00	33.50

Same Surcharged in Brown Red or Light Ultramarine

改訂 9¢

1959, Dec. 20			
C14	AP3 9c on 15y (BrR)	2.50	1.50
a.	Inverted surcharge	950.00	
C15	AP3 14c on 20y (LU)	3.00	3.00
C16	AP3 19c on 35y (BrR)	8.00	5.00
C17	AP3 27c on 45y (LU)	17.50	6.00
C18	AP3 35c on 60y (BrR)	15.00	9.00
	Nos. C14-C18 (5)	46.00	24.50

Nos. 31-33, 36 and 38 Surcharged in Black, Brown, Red, Blue or Green

改訂 9¢

1960, Aug. 3	Photo.	*Perf. 13*	
C19	A14 9c on 4y	3.50	1.00
a.	Surch. invtd. and transposed	15,000.	15,000.
b.	Invtd. surch. (legend only)	12,000.	
c.	Surcharge transposed	1,500.	
d.	Legend of surcharge only	4,000.	
e.	Horiz. pair, one without surch.	—	
C20	A17 14c on 5y (Br)	4.00	2.25
C21	A14 19c on 15y (R)	2.50	2.00
C22	A17 27c on 14y (Bl)	9.00	2.75
C23	A14 35c on 20y (G)	6.00	4.50
	Nos. C19-C23 (5)	25.00	12.50

Nos. C19c and C19d are from a single sheet of 100 with surcharge shifted downward. Ten examples of No. C19c exist with "9c" also in bottom selvage. No. C19d is from the top row of the sheet.

No. C19e is unique, pos. 100, caused by paper foldover.

Wind God — AP4

Designs: 9c, Heavenly Maiden (as on AP2). 14c, Heavenly Maiden (as on AP3). 27c, Wind God at right. 35c, Heavenly Maiden over treetops.

1961, Sept. 21	Photo.	*Perf. 13½*	
C24	AP4 9c multicolored	.30	.20
C25	AP4 14c multicolored	.70	.60
C26	AP4 19c multicolored	.70	.70
C27	AP4 27c multicolored	3.00	.60
C28	AP4 35c multicolored	1.50	1.25
	Nos. C24-C28 (5)	6.20	3.35

Jet over Gate of Courtesy — AP5

Jet Plane — AP6

1963, Aug. 28		*Perf. 13x13½*	
C29	AP5 5½c multicolored	.25	.25
C30	AP6 7c multicolored	.25	.25

SPECIAL DELIVERY STAMP

Dragon and Map of Ryukyus — SD1

Perf. 13x13½

1950, Feb. 15	Unwmk.	Photo.	
E1	SD1 5y bright blue	30.00	16.00

UNITED NATIONS

yu-ˌnī-təd ˈnā-shənz

LOCATION — Headquarters in New York City

United Nations stamps are used on UN official mail sent from UN Headquarters, NY, or from the UN Offices in Geneva, Switzerland, and Vienna, Austria to points throughout the world. They may be used on private correspondence sent through the UN post offices, and are valid only at the individual UN post offices.

UN mail is carried by the US, Swiss and Austrian postal systems.

The UN stamps issued for use in Geneva and Vienna are listed in separate sections at the end of the NY issues. They are denominated in centimes and francs, and are valid only in Geneva or Vienna. The UN stamps issued for use in New York, denominated in cents and dollars, are valid only in New York.

Letters bearing Nos. 170-174 provide an exception as they were carried by the Canadian postal system.

See Switzerland Nos. 7O1-7O39 in Volume 6 for stamps issued by the Swiss Government for official use of the UN European Office in Geneva.

The 1962 UN Temporary Executive Authority (UNTEA) overprints on stamps of Netherlands New Guinea are listed under West Irian in Volume 6.

Catalogue values for all unused stamps in this country are for Never Hinged items.

Stamps are inscribed in English, French or Spanish or are multilingual.

Watermark

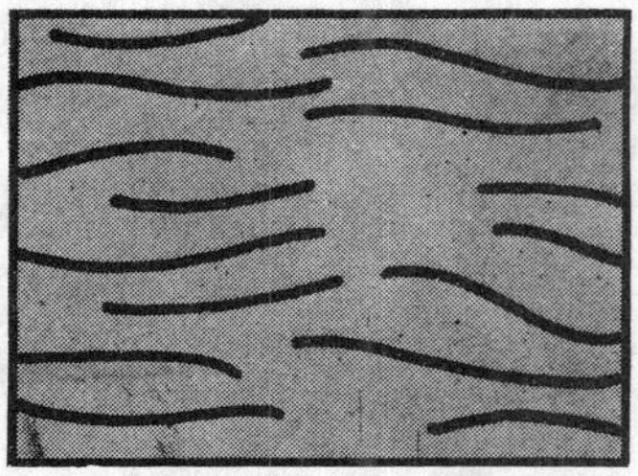
Wmk. 309- Wavy Lines

Peoples of the World — A1

UN Headquarters Building — A2

"Peace, Justice, Security" — A3

UN Flag — A4

UN Children's Fund — A5

World Unity — A6

Perf. 13x12½, 12½x13, 12½x13½ (2c, 5c)

1951	Unwmk.	Engr. & Photo.	
1	A1 1c magenta	.20	.20
2	A2 1½c blue green	.20	.20
3	A3 2c purple	.20	.20
4	A4 3c magenta & blue	.20	.20
5	A5 5c blue	.20	.20
6	A1 10c chocolate	.25	.20
7	A4 15c violet & blue	.25	.20
8	A6 20c dark brown	.35	.20
9	A4 25c ol gray & blue	.40	.20
10	A2 50c indigo	2.25	1.50
11	A3 $1 red	1.50	.65
	Nos. 1-11 (11)	6.00	3.95

See Offices in Geneva Nos. 4, 14.

Veteran's War Memorial Building, San Francisco A7

1952, Oct. 24	Engr.	*Perf. 12*	
12	A7 5c blue	.20	.20

7th anniv. of the signing of the UN charter.

Globe and Encircled Flame — A8

1952, Dec. 10		*Perf. 13½x14*	
13	A8 3c deep green	.20	.20
14	A8 5c blue	.20	.20

Fourth anniv. of the adoption of the Universal Declaration of Human Rights.

Refugee Family — A9

1953, Apr. 24		*Perf. 12½x13*	
15	A9 3c dk red brn & rose brn	.20	.20
16	A9 5c indigo & blue	.25	.25

"Protection for Refugees."

Envelope, UN Emblem and Map — A10

1953, June 12	Unwmk.	*Perf. 13*	
17	A10 3c black brown	.20	.20
18	A10 5c dark blue	.50	.45

Issued to honor the UPU.

Gearwheels and UN Emblem — A11

1953, Oct. 24		*Perf. 13x12½*	
19	A11 3c dark gray	.20	.20
20	A11 5c dark green	.35	.35

UN activities in the field of technical assistance.

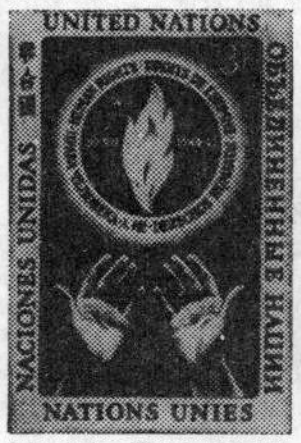

Hands Reaching Toward Flame — A12

Ear of Wheat — A13

1953, Dec. 10		*Perf. 12½x13*	
21	A12 3c bright blue	.20	.20
22	A12 5c rose red	1.10	.50

Human Rights Day.

1954, Feb. 11			
23	A13 3c dark green & yellow	.40	.20
24	A13 8c indigo & yellow	.85	.50

Issued to honor the FAO.

UN Emblem and Anvil — A14

1954, May 10 ***Perf. 12½x13***

25	A14 3c brown		.20	.20
26	A14 8c magenta		1.25	.75

Honoring the ILO.

UN European Office, Geneva A15

1954, Oct. 25 ***Perf. 14***

27	A15 3c dark blue violet		2.00	1.10
28	A15 8c red		.25	.25

UN Day.

Mother and Child — A16

1954, Dec. 10 ***Perf. 14***

29	A16 3c red orange		7.00	2.00
30	A16 8c olive green		.25	.25

Human Rights Day.

Symbol of Flight A17

1955, Feb. 9 ***Perf. 13½x14***

31	A17 3c blue		1.75	.65
32	A17 8c rose carmine		.75	.75

International Civil Aviation Organization.

UNESCO Emblem A18

1955, May 11 ***Perf. 13½x14***

33	A18 3c lilac rose		.20	.20
34	A18 8c light blue		.20	.20

Honoring the UN Educational, Scientific and Cultural Organization.

UN Charter A19

1955, Oct. 24 ***Perf. 13½x14***

35	A19 3c deep plum		.90	.50
36	A19 4c dull green		.35	.20
37	A19 8c bluish black		.20	.20
	Nos. 35-37 (3)		1.45	.90

10th anniv. of the UN.

Souvenir Sheet

Wmk. 309 ***Imperf.***

38	Sheet of 3		110.00	40.00
	a. A19 3c deep plum		10.00	1.50
	b. A19 4c dull green		10.00	1.50
	c. A19 8c bluish black		10.00	1.50

Two printings were made of No. 38. The first may be distinguished by the broken line of background shading on the 8c. It leaves a small white spot below the left leg of the "n" of "Unies." For the 2nd printing, the broken line was retouched, eliminating the white spot.

Hand Holding Torch — A20

1955, Dec. 9 Unwmk. ***Perf. 14x13½***

39	A20 3c ultra		.20	.20
40	A20 8c green		.20	.20

Human Rights Day, Dec. 10.

Symbols of Telecommunication — A21

1956, Feb. 17 ***Perf. 14***

41	A21 3c turquoise blue		.20	.20
42	A21 8c deep carmine		.30	.30

Honoring the ITU.

Globe and Caduceus — A22

1956, Apr. 6 ***Perf. 14***

43	A22 3c bright greenish blue		.20	.20
44	A22 8c golden brown		.20	.20

Honoring the World Health Organization.

General Assembly A23

1956, Oct. 24 ***Perf. 14***

45	A23 3c dark blue		.20	.20
46	A23 8c gray olive		.20	.20

UN Day, Oct. 24.

Flame and Globe — A24

1956, Dec. 10 ***Perf. 14***

47	A24 3c plum		.20	.20
48	A24 8c dark blue		.20	.20

Human Rights Day.

Weather Balloon — A25

1957, Jan. 28 ***Perf. 14***

49	A25 3c violet blue		.20	.20
50	A25 8c dark carmine rose		.20	.20

Honoring the World Meteorological Organization.

Badge of UN Emergency Force — A26

UN Emblem and Globe — A27

1957, Apr. 8 ***Perf. 14x12½***

51	A26 3c light blue		.20	.20
52	A26 8c rose carmine		.20	.20

UN Emergency Force.

Re-engraved

1957, Apr.-May

53	A26 3c blue		.20	.20
54	A26 8c rose carmine		.35	.20

On Nos. 53-54 the background within and around the circles is shaded lightly, giving a halo effect. The letters are more distinct with a line around each letter.

1957, Oct. 24 Engr. ***Perf. 12½x13***

55	A27 3c orange brown		.20	.20
56	A27 8c dark blue green		.20	.20

Honoring the Security Council.

Flaming Torch — A28

1957, Dec. 10 ***Perf. 14***

57	A28 3c red brown		.20	.20
58	A28 8c black		.20	.20

Human Rights Day.

Atom and UN Emblem A29

Central Hall, Westminster A30

1958, Feb. 10 ***Perf. 12***

59	A29 3c olive		.20	.20
60	A29 8c blue		.20	.20

Honoring the International Atomic Energy Agency.

1958, Apr. 14 ***Perf. 12***

61	A30 3c violet blue		.20	.20
62	A30 8c rose claret		.20	.20

Central Hall, Westminster, London, was the site of the first session of the UN General Assembly 1946.

UN Seal A31

Gearwheels A32

1958 ***Perf. 13½x14***

63	A31 4c red orange		.20	.20

Perf. 13x14

64	A31 8c bright blue		.20	.20

Issue dates: 4c, Oct. 24; 8c, June 2.

1958, Oct. 24 Engr. ***Perf. 12***

65	A32 4c dark blue green		.20	.20
66	A32 8c vermilion		.20	.20

Honoring the Economic and Social Council.

Hands Upholding Globe — A33

1958, Dec. 10 **Unwmk.**

67	A33 4c yellow green		.20	.20
68	A33 8c red brown		.20	.20

Human Rights Day and the 10th anniv. of the signing of the Universal Declaration of Human Rights.

New York City Building, Flushing Meadows A34

1959, Mar. 30 ***Perf. 12***

69	A34 4c light lilac rose		.20	.20
70	A34 8c aqua		.20	.20

Site of many General Assembly meetings, 1946-50.

UN Emblems and Symbols of Agriculture, Industry and Trade — A35

Figure Adapted from Rodin's "Age of Bronze" — A36

1959, May 18 ***Perf. 12***

71	A35 4c blue		.20	.20
72	A35 8c red orange		.20	.20

Honoring the UN Economic Commission for Europe.

1959, Oct. 23 Engr. ***Perf. 12***

73	A36 4c bright red		.20	.20
74	A36 8c dark olive green		.20	.20

Honor the Trusteeship Council.

World Refugee Year Emblem — A37

1959, Dec. 10 **Unwmk.**

75	A37 4c olive & red		.20	.20
76	A37 8c olive & brt greenish blue		.20	.20

World Refugee Year, July 1, 1959-June 30, 1960.

Chaillot Palace, Paris — A38

1960, Feb. 29 ***Perf. 14***

77	A38 4c rose lilac & blue		.20	.20
78	A38 8c dull green & brown		.20	.20

Chaillot Palace in Paris was the site of General Assembly meetings in 1948 and 1951.

Map of Far East and Steel Beam A39

1960, Apr. 11 Photo. *Perf. 13x13½*

79 A39 4c dp cl, bl grn & dl yel .20 .20
80 A39 8c ol green, blue & rose .20 .20

Honoring the Economic Commission for Asia and the Far East (ECAFE).

Tree, FAO and UN Emblems — A40

1960, Aug. 29 *Perf. 13½*

81 A40 4c green, dk blue & org .20 .20
  a. Imperf., pair —
82 A40 8c yel green, black & org .20 .20

5th World Forestry Congress, Seattle, Wash., Aug. 29-Sept. 10.

UN Headquarters and Preamble to UN Charter — A41

1960, Oct. 24 Engr. *Perf. 11*

83 A41 4c blue .20 .20
84 A41 8c gray .20 .20

Souvenir Sheet

Imperf

85 Sheet of 2 .50 .50
  a. A41 4c blue .25 .20
  b. A41 8c gray .25 .20

15th anniv. of the UN.

Block and Tackle — A42

Scales of Justice — A43

1960, Dec. 9 Photo. *Perf. 13½x13*

86 A42 4c multicolored .20 .20
87 A42 8c multicolored .20 .20
  a. Imperf., pair —

Honoring the International Bank for Reconstruction and Development.
No. 86 exists imperf.

1961, Feb. 13 Unwmk.

88 A43 4c yel, org brn & blk .20 .20
89 A43 8c yellow, green & black .20 .20

Honoring the International Court of Justice. The design was taken from Raphael's "Stanze."
Nos. 88-89 exist imperf.

Seal of International Monetary Fund A44

1961, Apr. 17 *Perf. 13x13½*

90 A44 4c bright bluish green .20 .20
91 A44 7c fawn & yellow .20 .20

Honoring the International Monetary Fund.
No. 90 exists imperf.

Abstract Group of Flags — A45

1961, June 5 *Perf. 11½*

92 A45 30c multicolored .40 .20

See Offices in Geneva No. 10.

Cogwheel and Map of Latin America — A46

1961, Sept. 18 *Perf. 13½*

93 A46 4c blue, red & citron .20 .20
94 A46 11c green, lilac & org ver .25 .20

Honoring the Economic Commission for Latin America.

Africa House, Addis Ababa, and Map — A47

1961, Oct. 24 Photo. *Perf. 11½*

95 A47 4c ultra, org, yel & brown .20 .20
96 A47 11c emer, org, yel & brown .25 .20

Honoring the Economic Commission for Africa.

Mother Bird Feeding Young and UNICEF Seal — A48

1961, Dec. 4 Unwmk. *Perf. 11½*

97 A48 3c brown, gold, org & yel .20 .20
98 A48 4c brown, gold, bl & emer .20 .20
99 A48 13c deep green, gold, purple & pink .20 .20
  Nos. 97-99 (3) .60 .60

15th anniv. of the UN Children's Fund.

Family and Symbolic Buildings A49

1962, Feb. 28 Photo. *Perf. 14½x14*

Central design multicolored

100 A49 4c bright blue .20 .20
  a. Black omitted 200.00
  b. Yellow omitted —
  c. Brown omitted —
101 A49 7c orange brown .20 .20
  a. Red omitted —
  b. Black omitted —

UN program for housing and urban development.

"The World Against Malaria" — A50

1962, Mar. 30 *Perf. 14x14½*

Word frame in gray

102 A50 4c org, yel, green & black .20 .20
103 A50 11c green, yel, brn & indigo .25 .20

Honoring the WHO and to call attention to the international campaign to eradicate malaria from the world.

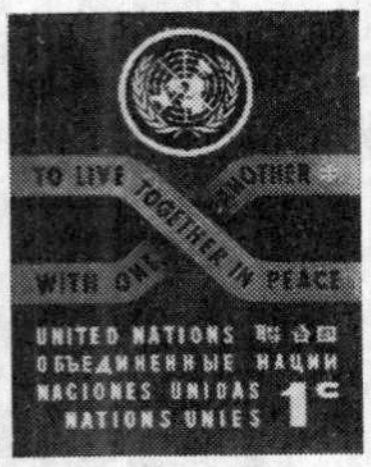

"Peace" — A51

UN Flag — A52

Hands Combining "UN" and Globe A53

UN Emblem over Globe — A54

Photogravure; Engraved (5c)

1962, May 25 *Perf. 14x14½*

104 A51 1c ver, blue, black & gray .20 .20
105 A52 3c lt green, Prus blue, yel & gray .20 .20

Perf. 12

Size: 36½x23½mm

106 A53 5c dark carmine rose .20 .20

Perf. 12½

107 A54 11c dk & lt blue & gold .25 .20
  Nos. 104-107 (4) .85 .80

See #167 and UN Offices in Geneva #2, 6.

Flag at Half-mast and UN Headquarters A55

World Map Showing Congo A56

1962, Sept. 17 Unwmk. *Perf. 11½*

108 A55 5c black, lt blue & blue .20 .20
109 A55 15c black, gray ol & blue .20 .20

1st anniv. of the death of Dag Hammarskjold, Secretary General of the UN 1953-61, in memory of those who died in the service of the UN.

1962, Oct. 24

110 A56 4c olive, org, black & yel .20 .20
111 A56 11c bl grn, org, blk & yel .20 .20

UN Operation in the Congo.

Globe in Universe and Palm Frond — A57

1962, Dec. 3 Engr. *Perf. 14x13½*

112 A57 4c violet blue .20 .20
113 A57 11c rose claret .25 .20

Honoring the Committee on Peaceful Uses of Outer Space.

Development Decade Emblem — A58

Perf. 11½

1963, Feb. 4 Unwmk. Photo.

114 A58 5c pale grn, mar, dk blue & Prus blue .20 .20
115 A58 11c yel, mar, dk blue & Prus blue .20 .20

UN Development Decade and the UN Conference on the Application of Science and Technology for the Benefit of the Less Developed Areas, Geneva, Feb. 4-20.

Stalks of Wheat — A59

1963, Mar. 22 *Perf. 11½*

116 A59 5c ver, green & yellow .20 .20
117 A59 11c ver, dp claret & yel .25 .20

"Freedom from Hunger" campaign of the FAO.

Bridge over Map of New Guinea — A60

1963, Oct. 1 Unwmk. *Perf. 11½*

118 A60 25c blue, green & gray .45 .30

1st anniv. of the UN Temporary Executive Authority (UNTEA) in West New Guinea (West Irian).

General Assembly Building, New York — A61

1963, Nov. 4 Photo. *Perf. 13*

119 A61 5c violet blue & multi .20 .20
120 A61 11c green & multi .20 .20

Since Oct. 1955 all sessions of the General Assembly have been held in the General Assembly Hall, UN Headquarters, N.Y.

Flame — A62

1963, Dec. 10 *Perf. 13*

121 A62 5c green, gold, red & yel .20 .20
122 A62 11c car, gold, blue & yel .20 .20

15th anniv. of the signing of the Universal Declaration of Human Rights.

Ships at Sea and IMCO Emblem — A63

1964, Jan. 13 ***Perf. 11½***

123 A63 5c blue, ol, ocher & yel .20 .20
124 A63 11c bl, dk grn, emer & yel .20 .20

Honoring the Intergovernmental Maritime Consultative Organization.

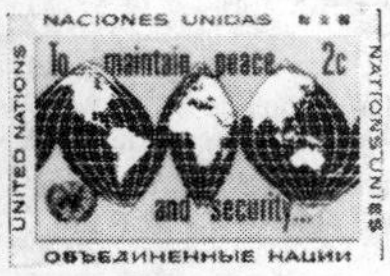

Map of the World — A64

UN Emblem — A65

Three Men United Before Globe — A66

Stylized Globe and Weather Vane — A67

1964-71 Unwmk. Photo. *Perf. 14*

125 A64 2c lt bl, dk blue, org & yel green .20 .20
a. Perf. 13x13½ ('71) .20 .20

Perf. 11½

126 A65 7c dk bl, org brn & blk .20 .20
127 A66 10c blue grn, ol grn & blk .20 .20
128 A67 50c multicolored .75 .45
Nos. 125-128 (4) 1.35 1.05

Dates of issue: 2c, 7c, 10c, May 29; 50c, Mar. 6, 1964. See UN Offices in Geneva Nos. 3, 12.

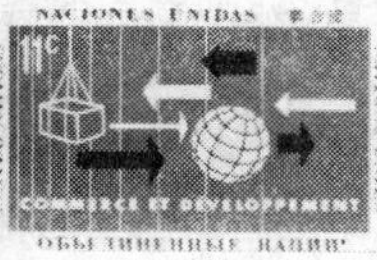

Arrows Showing Global Flow of Trade — A68

1964, June 15 ***Perf. 13***

129 A68 5c black, red & yellow .20 .20
130 A68 11c black, olive & yellow .20 .20

UN Conference on Trade and Development, Geneva, Mar. 23-June 15.

Poppy Capsule and Hands A69

1964, Sept. 21 Engr. *Perf. 12*

131 A69 5c rose red & black .20 .20
132 A69 11c emerald & black .20 .20

International efforts and achievements in the control of narcotics.

Padlocked Atomic Blast — A70

"Education for Progress" — A71

Photogravure and Engraved

1964, Oct. 23 ***Perf. 11x11½***

133 A70 5c dark red & dk brown .20 .20

Signing of the nuclear test ban treaty pledging an end to nuclear explosions in the atmosphere, outer space and under water.

1964, Dec. 7 Photo. *Perf. 12½*

134 A71 4c multicolored .20 .20
135 A71 5c multicolored .20 .20
136 A71 11c multicolored .20 .20
Nos. 134-136 (3) .60 .60

UNESCO world campaign for universal literacy and for free compulsory primary education.

Progress Chart of Special Fund, Key and Globe A72

Leaves and View of Cyprus A73

Perf. 13½x13

1965, Jan. 25 **Unwmk.**

137 A72 5c multicolored .20 .20
138 A72 11c multicolored .20 .20
a. Black omitted (UN emblem on key) —

Special Fund Program, which aims to speed economic growth and social advancement in low-income countries.

1965, Mar. 4 Photo. *Perf. 11½*

139 A73 5c org, olive & black .20 .20
140 A73 11c yel grn, blue grn & blk .20 .20

UN Peace-keeping Force on Cyprus.

"From Semaphore to Satellite" A74

1965, May 17 Unwmk. *Perf. 11½*

141 A74 5c multicolored .20 .20
142 A74 11c multicolored .20 .20

Cent. of the ITU.

ICY Emblem — A75

1965, June 26 Engr. *Perf. 14x13½*

143 A75 5c dark blue .20 .20
144 A75 15c lilac rose .20 .20

Souvenir Sheet

145 A75 Sheet of 2, #143-144 .35 .30

20th anniv. of the UN and Intl. Cooperation Year.

"Peace" — A76

Opening Words, UN Charter — A77

UN Headquarters and Emblem — A78

UN Emblem — A79

UN Emblem — A80

1965-66 Photo. *Perf. 13½*

146 A76 1c ver, bl, blk & gray .20 .20

Perf. 14

147 A77 15c ol bis, dull yel, blk & dp claret .25 .20

Perf. 12

148 A78 20c dk bl, bl, red & yel .30 .20
a. Yellow omitted —

Lithographed and Embossed

Perf. 14

149 A79 25c lt bl & dk blue .35 .20

Photo.

Perf. 11½

150 A80 $1 aqua & sapphire 1.75 1.50
Nos. 146-150 (5) 2.85 2.30

Issue dates: 1c, 25c, Sept. 20, 1965. 15c, 20c, Oct. 25, 1965. $1, Mar. 25, 1966.
See UN Offices in Geneva Nos. 5, 9 and 11.

Fields and People A81

Globe and Flags of UN Members A82

1965, Nov. 29 Photo. *Perf. 12*

151 A81 4c multicolored .20 .20
152 A81 5c multicolored .20 .20
153 A81 11c multicolored .20 .20
Nos. 151-153 (3) .60 .60

Emphasize the importance of the world's population growth and its problems and to call attention to population trends and developments.

1966, Jan. 31 Photo. *Perf. 11½*

154 A82 5c multicolored .20 .20
155 A82 15c multicolored .20 .20

World Federation of UN Associations.

WHO Headquarters, Geneva — A83

1966, May 26 Photo. *Perf. 12½x12*

Granite Paper

156 A83 5c multicolored .20 .20
157 A83 11c multicolored .20 .20

WHO Headquarters, Geneva.

Coffee — A84

1966, Sept. 19 ***Perf. 13½x13***

158 A84 5c multicolored .20 .20
159 A84 11c multicolored .20 .20

International Coffee Agreement of 1962.

UN Observer A85

Children of Various Races A86

1966, Oct. 24 Photo. *Perf. 11½*

Granite Paper

160 A85 15c multicolored .25 .20

Peace Keeping UN Observers.

1966, Nov. 28 Litho. *Perf. 13x13½*

Designs: 5c, Children riding locomotive and tender. 11c, Children in open railroad car playing medical team.

161 A86 4c pink & multi .20 .20
162 A86 5c pale green & multi .20 .20
a. Yellow omitted — —
163 A86 11c ultra & multi .20 .20
a. Imperf., pair —
b. Dark blue omitted —
Nos. 161-163 (3) .60 .60

20th anniv. of UNICEF.

Hand Rolling up Sleeve and Chart Showing Progress — A87

1967, Jan. 23 Photo. *Perf. 12½*

164 A87 5c multicolored .20 .20
165 A87 11c multicolored .20 .20

UN Development Program.

Type of 1962 and

UN Headquarters, New York and World Map — A88

1967 Photo. *Perf. 11½*

166 A88 1½c ultra, blk, org & ocher .20 .20

Size: 33x23mm

167 A53 5c red brn, brn & org yel .20 .20

Issue dates: 1½c, Mar. 17; 5c, Jan. 23.
See UN Offices in Geneva No. 1.

Fireworks — A89

1967, Mar. 17 ***Perf. 14x14½***

168 A89 5c dark blue & multi .20 .20
169 A89 11c brown lake & multi .20 .20

Honoring all nations which gained independence since 1945.

United Nations Headquarters in New York stamps can be mounted in the Scott U.N. Singles and Postal Stationery album.

"Peace"
A90

UN Pavilion, EXPO '67
A91

Litho. & Engr.; Litho. (8c)

1967, Apr. 28 *Perf. 11*

170	A90	4c shown	.20	.20
171	A90	5c Justice	.20	.20
172	A91	8c shown	.20	.20
173	A90	10c Fraternity	.20	.20
174	A90	15c Truth	.20	.20
		Nos. 170-174 (5)	1.00	1.00

Montreal World's Fair, EXPO '67, Apr. 28-Oct. 27. Under special agreement with the Canadian Government Nos. 170-174 were valid for postage only on mail posted at the UN pavilion during the fair. The denominations are expressed in Canadian currency.

Luggage Tags and UN Emblem
A92

Unwmk.

1967, June 19 **Litho.** *Perf. 14*

175	A92	5c multicolored	.20	.20
176	A92	15c multicolored	.25	.20

International Tourist Year, 1967.

Quotation from Isaiah 2:4 — A93

1967, Oct. 24 **Photo.**

177	A93	6c multicolored	.20	.20
178	A93	13c multicolored	.20	.20

UN General Assembly's resolutions on general and complete disarmament and for suspension of nuclear and thermonuclear tests.

Art at UN Issue
Miniature Sheet

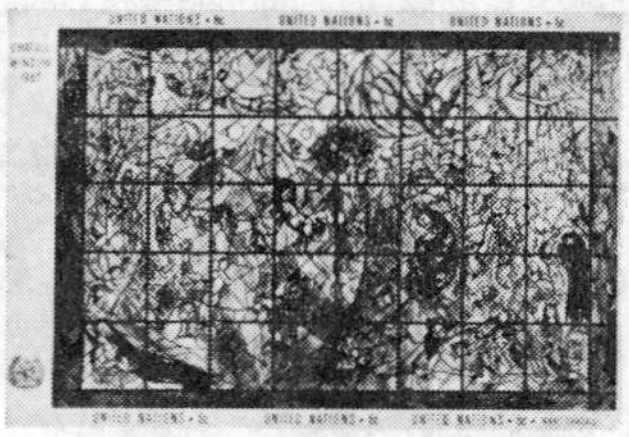

Memorial Window, by Marc Chagall — A94

"The Kiss of Peace" by Marc Chagall — A95

Sizes: a, 41x46nn. b, 24x46mm. c, 41x33½mm. d, 36x33½mm. e, 29x33½mm. f, 41½x47mm.

1967, Nov. 17 **Litho.** *Rouletted 9*

179	A94	Sheet of 6, a.-f.	.40	.30

Perf. 12½x13½

180	A95	6c multicolored	.20	.20

No. 179 contains six 6c stamps, each rouletted on 3 sides, imperf. on fourth side. On Nos. 179a-179c, "United Nations. 6c" appears at top; on Nos. 179d-179f, at bottom. No. 179f includes name "Marc Chagall."

Globe and Major UN Organs — A96

1968, Jan. 16 **Photo.** *Perf. 11½*

181	A96	6c multicolored	.20	.20
182	A96	13c multicolored	.20	.20

Honoring the UN Secretariat.

Statue by Henrik Starcke
A97

Factories and Chart
A98

Art at UN Issue

1968, Mar. 1 **Photo.** *Perf. 11½*

183	A97	6c blue & multi	.20	.20
184	A97	75c rose lake & multi	1.10	.85

The 6c is part of the "Art at UN" series. The 75c belongs to the definitive series. The 6c exists imperforate.

The Starcke statue represents mankind's search for freedom and happiness.

See UN Offices in Geneva No. 13.

1968, Apr. 18 **Litho.** *Perf. 12*

185	A98	6c multicolored	.20	.20
186	A98	13c multicolored	.20	.20

UN Industrial Development Organization.

UN Headquarters — A99

1968, May 31 **Litho.** *Perf. 13½*

187	A99	6c multicolored	.20	.20

Radarscope and Globes
A100

Perf. 13x13½

1968, Sept. 19 **Photo.**

188	A100	6c green & multi	.20	.20
189	A100	20c lilac & multi	.30	.20

World Weather Watch, a new weather system directed by the World Meterological Organization.

Human Rights Flame
A101

Books and UN Emblem
A102

Photogravure; Foil Embossed

1968, Nov. 22 *Perf. 12½*

190	A101	6c brt bl, dp ultra & gold	.20	.20
191	A101	13c rose red, dk red & gold	.20	.20

International Human Rights Year.

1969, Feb. 10 **Litho.** *Perf. 13½*

192	A102	6c yel green & multi	.20	.20
193	A102	13c bluish lilac & multi	.25	.20

UN Institute for Training and Research (UNITAR).

UN Building, Santiago, Chile
A103

1969, Mar. 14 **Litho.** *Perf. 14*

194	A103	6c lt blue, vio bl & lt grn	.20	.20
195	A103	15c pink, cr & red brown	.25	.20

The UN Building in Santiago, Chile is the seat of the UN Economic Commission for Latin America and of the Latin American Institute for Economic and Social Planning.

"UN" and UN Emblem
A104

UN Emblem and Scales of Justice
A105

1969, Mar. 14 **Photo.** *Perf. 13½*

196	A104	13c brt blue, black & gold	.20	.20

See UN Offices in Geneva No. 7.

1969, Apr. 21 **Photo.** *Perf. 11½*
Granite Paper

197	A105	6c brt green, ultra & gold	.20	.20
198	A105	13c crim, lilac & gold	.20	.20

20th anniv. session of the UN Intl. Law Commission.

Allegory of Labor, Emblems of UN and ILO — A106

1969, June 5 **Photo.** *Perf. 13*

199	A106	6c blue, dp bl, yel & gold	.20	.20
200	A106	20c org ver, mag, yel & gold	.25	.20

"Labor and Development" and the 50th anniv. of the ILO.

Art at UN Issue

Ostrich, Tunisian Mosaic, 3rd Century — A107

Design: 13c, Pheasant.

1969, Nov. 21 **Photo.** *Perf. 14*

201	A107	6c blue & multi	.20	.20
202	A107	13c red & multi	.20	.20

Art at UN Issue

Peace Bell, Gift of Japanese
A108

1970, Mar. 13 **Photo.** *Perf. 13½x13*

203	A108	6c vio blue & multi	.20	.20
204	A108	25c claret & multi	.35	.25

Mekong River, Power Lines and Map of Delta — A109

1970, Mar. 13 *Perf. 14*

205	A109	6c dk blue & multi	.20	.20
206	A109	13c dp plum & multi	.20	.20

Lower Mekong Basin, Viet Nam, Development project under UN auspices.

"Fight Cancer" — A110

1970, May 22 **Litho.** *Perf. 14*

207	A110	6c blue & black	.20	.20
208	A110	13c olive & black	.20	.20

Fight against cancer in connection with the 10th Intl. Cancer Congress of the International Union Against Cancer, Houston, Texas, May 22-29.

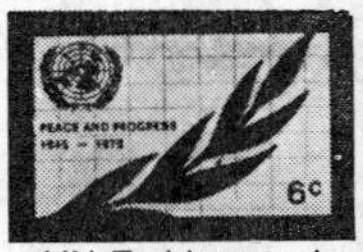

UN Emblem and Olive Branch
A111

UN Emblem
A112

1970, June 26 **Photo.** *Perf. 11½*

209	A111	6c red, gold, dk & lt blue	.20	.20
210	A111	13c dk bl, gold, grn & red	.20	.20

Perf. 12½

211	A112	25c dk blue, gold & lt blue	.35	.25
		Nos. 209-211 (3)	.75	.65

Souvenir Sheet
Imperf

212		Sheet of 3	.60	.60
a.	A111	6c multicolored	.20	.20
b.	A111	13c multicolored	.20	.20
c.	A112	25c multicolored	.30	.20

25th anniv. of the UN.

Scales, Olive Branch, Progress Symbol
A113

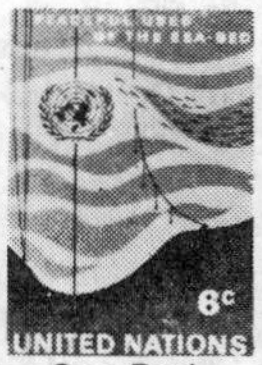

Sea Bed, Fish, Underwater Research
A114

1970, Nov. 20 **Photo.** *Perf. 13½*

213	A113	6c gold & multi	.20	.20
214	A113	13c silver & multi	.20	.20

Issued to publicize "Peace, Justice and Progress" in connection with the 25th anniv. of the UN.

Photogravure and Engraved

1971, Jan. 25 *Perf. 13*

215	A114	6c blue & multi	.20	.20

Peaceful uses of the sea bed. See Offices in Geneva No. 15.

Refugees, Sculpture by Kaare K. Nygaard — A115

Wheat and Globe — A116

1971, Mar. 12 Litho. *Perf. 13x12½*
216 A115 6c brown, ocher & black .20 .20
217 A115 13c ultra, grnsh blue & blk .20 .20

International support for refugees. See Offices in Geneva No. 16.

1971, Apr. 13 Photo. *Perf. 14*
218 A116 13c brn red, gold & green .20 .20

Publicizing the UN World Food Program. See Offices in Geneva No. 17.

UPU Headquarters, Bern — A117

1971, May 28 Photo. *Perf. 11½*
219 A117 20c brown org & multi .35 .20

Opening of new UPU Headquarters, Bern. See Offices in Geneva No. 18.

"Eliminate Racial Discrimination" A118

A119

1971, Sept. 21 Photo. *Perf. 13½*
220 A118 8c yel green & multi .20 .20
221 A119 13c blue & multi .20 .20

International Year Against Racial Discrimination. See Offices in Geneva Nos. 19-20.

UN Headquarters, New York — A120

UN Emblem and Symbolic Flags A121

1971, Oct. 22 *Perf. 13½; 13 (60c)*
222 A120 8c vio blue & multi .20 .20
223 A121 60c ultra & multi .75 .60

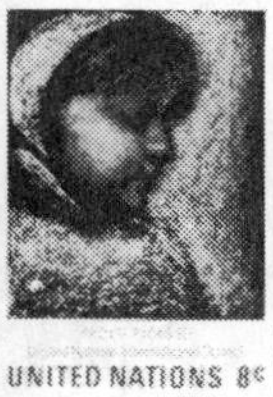
Maia by Pablo Picasso — A122

1971, Nov. 19 Photo. *Perf. 11½*
224 A122 8c olive & multi .20 .20
225 A122 21c ultra & multi .30 .20

UN Intl. School. See Offices in Geneva No. 21.

Letter Changing Hands A123

1972, Jan. 5 Litho. *Perf. 14*
226 A123 95c blue & multi 1.25 .95

"No More Nuclear Weapons" A124

1972, Feb. 14 Photo. *Perf. 13½x14*
227 A124 8c dull rose, blk, bl & gray .20 .20

To promote non-proliferation of nuclear weapons. See Offices in Geneva No. 23.

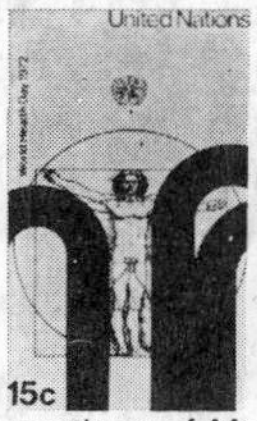
Proportions of Man (c. 1509), by Leonardo da Vinci A125

"Human Environment" A126

Lithographed and Engraved

1972, Apr. 7 *Perf. 13x13½*
228 A125 15c black & multi .25 .20

World Health Day, Apr. 7. See Offices in Geneva No. 24.

Lithographed and Embossed

1972, June 5 *Perf. 12½x14*
229 A126 8c multicolored .20 .20
230 A126 15c multicolored .25 .20

UN Conference on Human Environment, Stockholm, June 5-16, 1972.
See Offices in Geneva Nos. 25-26.

"Europe" and UN Emblem A127

The Five Continents, by José Maria Sert A128

1972, Sept. 11 Litho. *Perf. 13x13½*
231 A127 21c yel brown & multi .35 .20

Economic Commission for Europe, 25th anniv.
See Offices in Geneva No. 27.

Art at UN Issue

1972, Nov. 17 Photo. *Perf. 12x12½*
232 A128 8c gold, brn & gldn brn .20 .20
233 A128 15c gold, brn & blue grn .30 .20

See Offices in Geneva Nos. 28-29.

Olive Branch and Broken Sword — A129

1973, Mar. 9 Litho. *Perf. 13½x13*
234 A129 8c blue & multi .20 .20
235 A129 15c lilac rose & multi .35 .20

Disarmament Decade, 1970-79.
Nos. 234-235 exist imperf. See Offices in Geneva Nos. 30-31.

Poppy Capsule and Skull — A130

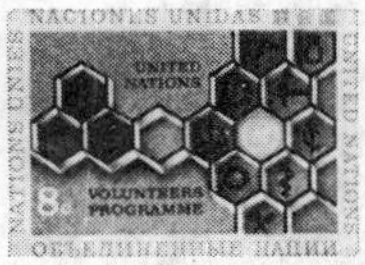
Honeycomb — A131

1973, Apr. 13 Photo. *Perf. 13½*
236 A130 8c multicolored .20 .20
237 A130 15c multicolored .35 .25

Fight against drug abuse. See Offices in Geneva No. 32.

1973, May 25 Photo. *Perf. 14*
238 A131 8c olive bister & multi .20 .20
239 A131 21c gray blue & multi .35 .20

5th anniv. of the UN Volunteer Program. See UN Offices in Geneva No. 33.

Map of Africa with Namibia — A132

1973, Oct. 1 Photo. *Perf. 13½*
240 A132 8c emerald & multi .20 .20
241 A132 15c brt rose & multi .35 .20

To publicize Namibia (South-West Africa), for which the UN General Assembly ended the mandate of South Africa and established the UN Council for Namibia to administer the territory until independence. See Offices in Geneva No. 34.

UN Emblem, Human Rights Flame — A133

1973, Nov. 16 Photo. *Perf. 13½*
242 A133 8c dp carmine & multi .20 .20
243 A133 21c blue green & multi .35 .20

25th anniv. of the adoption and proclamation of the Universal Declaration of Human Rights. See Offices in Geneva Nos. 35-36.

ILO Headquarters, Geneva A134

1974, Jan. 11 Photo. *Perf. 14*
244 A134 10c ultra & multi .20 .20
245 A134 21c blue green & multi .35 .20

New Headquarters of Intl. Labor Organization. See Offices in Geneva Nos. 37-38.

Post Horn Encircling Globe A135

1974, Mar. 22 Photo. *Perf. 14*
246 A135 10c multicolored .25 .20

Centenary of UPU. See Offices in Geneva Nos. 39-40.

Art at UN Issue

Peace Mural, by Candido Portinari — A136

1974, May 6 Photo. *Perf. 14*
247 A136 10c gold & multi .20 .20
248 A136 18c ultra & multi .40 .30

See Offices in Geneva Nos. 41-42.

Dove and UN Emblem A137

UN Headquarters A138

Globe, UN Emblem, Flags — A139

1974, June 10 Photo. *Perf. 14*
249 A137 2c dk bl & lt blue .20 .20
250 A138 10c multicolored .20 .20
251 A139 18c multicolored .30 .20
Nos. 249-251 (3) .70 .60

Children of the World — A140

Law of the Sea — A141

1974, Oct. 18 Photo. *Perf. 14*
252 A140 10c lt blue & multi .20 .20
253 A140 18c lilac & multi .40 .20

World Population Year. See Offices in Geneva Nos. 43-44.

1974, Nov. 22 Photo. *Perf. 14*
254 A141 10c green & multi .20 .20
255 A141 26c multicolored .40 .25

UN General Assembly declared the sea bed common heritage of mankind, exempt from arms race. See Offices in Geneva No. 45.

Satellite and Globe A142

1975, Mar. 14 Litho. *Perf. 13*
256 A142 10c multicolored .20 .20
257 A142 26c multicolored .40 .25

Peaceful uses of outer space (meteorology, industry, fishing, communications).
See Offices in Geneva Nos. 46-47.

Equality Between Men and Women — A143

1975, May 9 Litho. *Perf. 15*

258 A143 10c multicolored .20 .20
259 A143 18c multicolored .40 .20

International Women's Year 1975. See Offices in Geneva Nos. 48-49.

UN Flag and "XXX" — A144

1975, June 26 Litho. *Perf. 13*

260 A144 10c multicolored .20 .20
261 A144 26c purple & multi .50 .25

Souvenir Sheet

Imperf

262 Sheet of 2 .65 .20
a. A144 10c olive bister & multi .20 .20
b. A144 26c purple & multi .40 .20

30th anniv. of the UN. See Offices in Geneva Nos. 50-52.

Hand Reaching up over Map of Africa and Namibia A145

Wild Rose Growing from Barbed Wire A146

1975, Sept. 22 Photo. *Perf. 13½*

263 A145 10c multicolored .20 .20
264 A145 18c multicolored .35 .20

"Namibia—United Nations direct responsibility." See note after No. 241. See Offices in Geneva Nos. 53-54.

1975, Nov. 21 Engr. *Perf. 12½*

265 A146 13c ultramarine .25 .20
266 A146 26c rose carmine .50 .45

UN Peace-keeping Operations. See Offices in Geneva Nos. 55-56.

Symbolic Flags Forming Dove A147

UN Emblem A149

People of All Races A148

UN Flag — A150

Dove and Rainbow — A151

Perf. 13x13½, 13½x13, 14 (9c)

1976 Litho.; Photo. (9c)

267 A147 3c multicolored .20 .20
268 A148 4c multicolored .20 .20
269 A149 9c multicolored .20 .20
270 A150 30c blue, emer & black .40 .35
271 A151 50c multicolored .70 .65
Nos. 267-271 (5) 1.70 1.60

Issue dates: 9c, Nov. 19; others, Jan. 9. See Offices in Vienna No. 8.

Interlocking Bands — A152

1976, Mar. 12 Photo. *Perf. 14*

272 A152 13c blue, green & black .20 .20
273 A152 26c green & multi .35 .30

World Federation of UN Association. See Offices in Geneva No. 57.

Cargo, Globe and Graph — A153

Houses Around Globe — A154

1976, Apr. 23 Photo. *Perf. 11½*

274 A153 13c multicolored .20 .20
275 A153 31c multicolored .40 .30

UN Conference on Trade and Development (UNCTAD), Nairobi, Kenya, May 1976. See Offices in Geneva No. 58.

1976, May 28 Photo. *Perf. 14*

276 A154 13c multicolored .20 .20
277 A154 25c green & multi .40 .30

Habitat, UN Conference on Human Settlements, Vancouver, Canada, May 31-June 11. See Offices in Geneva Nos. 59-60.

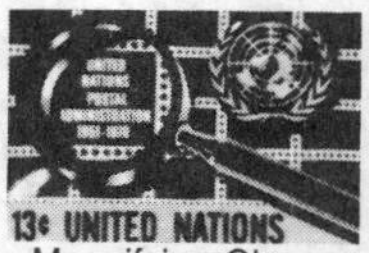

Magnifying Glass, Sheet of Stamps, UN Emblem — A155

Grain — A156

1976, Oct. 8 Photo. *Perf. 11½*

278 A155 13c blue & multi .20 .20
279 A155 31c green & multi 1.40 1.40

UN Postal Administration, 25th anniv. Sheets of 20. See Offices in Geneva #61-62.

1976, Nov. 19 Litho. *Perf. 14½*

280 A156 13c multicolored .25 .20

World Food Council. See Offices in Geneva No. 63.

WIPO Headquarters, Geneva — A157

1977, Mar. 11 Photo. *Perf. 14*

281 A157 13c citron & multi .20 .20
282 A157 31c brt green & multi .45 .30

World Intellectual Property Organization. See Geneva No. 64.

Drops of Water Falling into Funnel — A158

1977, Apr. 22 Photo. *Perf. 13½x13*

283 A158 13c yellow & multi .20 .20
284 A158 25c salmon & multi .45 .25

UN Water Conf., Mar del Plata, Argentina, Mar. 14-25. See Offices in Geneva #65-66.

Burning Fuse Severed A159

1977, May 27 Photo. *Perf. 14*

285 A159 13c purple & multi .20 .20
286 A159 31c dk blue & multi .45 .30

UN Security Council. See Geneva #67-68.

"Combat Racism" A160

1977, Sept. 19 Litho. *Perf. 13½x13*

287 A160 13c black & yellow .20 .20
288 A160 25c black & vermilion .40 .25

Fight against racial discrimination. See Geneva Nos. 69-70.

Atom, Grain, Fruit and Factory — A161

1977, Nov. 18 Photo.

289 A161 13c yellow bister & multi .20 .20
290 A161 18c dull green & multi .35 .20

Peaceful uses of atomic energy. See Geneva Nos. 71-72.

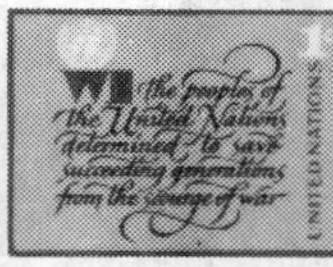

Opening Words of UN Charter A162

"Live Together in Peace" A163

People of the World — A164

1978, Jan. 27 Litho. *Perf. 14½*

291 A162 1c gold, brown & red .20 .20
292 A163 25c multicolored .35 .30
293 A164 $1 multicolored 1.20 1.25
Nos. 291-293 (3) 1.75 1.75

See Offices in Geneva No. 73.

Smallpox Virus — A165

1978, Mar. 31 Photo. *Perf. 12x11½*

294 A165 13c rose & black .20 .20
295 A165 31c blue & black .45 .40

Global eradication of smallpox. See Offices in Geneva Nos. 74-75.

Open Handcuff A166

Multicolored Bands and Clouds A167

1978, May 5 Photo. *Perf. 12*

296 A166 13c multicolored .20 .20
297 A166 18c multicolored .30 .20

Liberation, justice and cooperation for Namibia. See Offices in Geneva No. 76.

1978, June 12 Photo. *Perf. 14*

298 A167 13c multicolored .20 .20
299 A167 25c multicolored .40 .40

International Civil Aviation Organization for "Safety in the Air." See Offices in Geneva #77-78.

General Assembly A168

1978, Sept. 15 Photo. *Perf. 13½*

300 A168 13c multicolored .20 .20
301 A168 18c multicolored .35 .25

See Offices in Geneva Nos. 79-80.

Hemispheres as Cogwheels A169

1978, Nov. 17 Photo. *Perf. 14*

302 A169 13c multicolored .25 .20
303 A169 31c multicolored .60 .45

Technical Cooperation Among Developing Countries Conf., Buenos Aires, Argentina, Sept. 1978. See Offices in Geneva No. 81.

Hand Holding Olive Branch — A170

Tree of Various Races — A171

Globe, Dove with Olive Branch — A172

Birds and Globe — A173

1979, Jan. 19 Photo. Perf. 14

304 A170 5c multicolored .20 .20
305 A171 14c multicolored .20 .20
306 A172 15c multicolored .30 .25
307 A173 20c multicolored .30 .25
Nos. 304-307 (4) 1.00 .90

UNDRO Against Fire and Water — A174

1979, Mar. 9 Photo. Perf. 14

308 A174 15c multicolored .25 .20
309 A174 20c multicolored .35 .30

Office of the UN Disaster Relief Coordinator. See Offices in Geneva Nos. 82-83.

Child and ICY Emblem A175

1979, May 4 Photo. Perf. 14

310 A175 15c multicolored .20 .20
311 A175 31c multicolored .40 .40

International Year of the Child. See Offices in Geneva Nos. 84-85.

Map of Namibia, Olive Branch — A176

Scales and Sword of Justice — A177

1979, Oct. 5 Litho. Perf. 13½

312 A176 15c multicolored .20 .20
313 A176 31c multicolored .40 .40

For a free and independent Namibia. See Offices in Geneva No. 86.

1979, Nov. 9 Litho. Perf. 13x13½

314 A177 15c multicolored .20 .20
315 A177 20c multicolored .40 .35

Intl. Court of Justice, The Hague, Netherlands. See Offices in Geneva Nos. 87-88.

Graph of Economic Trends — A178

Key — A179

1980, Jan. 11 Perf. 15x14½

316 A178 15c multicolored .20 .20
317 A179 31c multicolored .50 .35

New International Economic Order. See Offices in Geneva No. 89; Vienna No. 7.

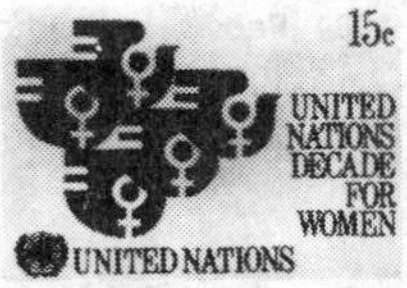

Women's Year Emblems A180

1980, Mar. 7 Litho. Perf. 14½x15

318 A180 15c multicolored .20 .20
319 A180 20c multicolored .30 .25

UN Decade for Women. See Offices in Geneva Nos. 90-91; Vienna Nos. 9-10.

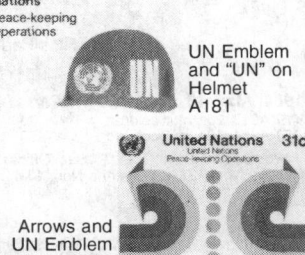

UN Emblem and "UN" on Helmet A181

Arrows and UN Emblem A182

1980, May 16 Litho. Perf. 14x13

320 A181 15c black & brt blue .25 .20
321 A182 31c multicolored .45 .40

UN Peace-keeping Operations. See Offices in Geneva No. 92; Vienna No. 11.

"35" and Flags — A183

Globe and Laurel — A184

1980, June 26 Litho. Perf. 13

322 A183 15c multicolored .20 .20
323 A184 31c multicolored .40 .30

Souvenir Sheet

Imperf

324 Sheet of 2 .60 .45
a. A183 15c multicolored .20
b. A184 31c multicolored .40

35th anniv. of the UN. See Offices in Geneva Nos. 93-95; Vienna Nos. 12-14.

Flag of Turkey A185

1980, Sept. 26 Litho. Perf. 12

Granite Paper

325 A185 15c shown .20 .20
326 A185 15c Luxembourg .20 .20
327 A185 15c Fiji .20 .20
328 A185 15c Viet Nam .20 .20
a. Se-tenant block of 4 .75 —
329 A185 15c Guinea .20 .20
330 A185 15c Surinam .20 .20
331 A185 15c Bangladesh .20 .20
332 A185 15c Mali .20 .20
a. Se-tenant block of 4 .75 —
333 A185 15c Yugoslavia .20 .20
334 A185 15c France .20 .20
335 A185 15c Venezuela .20 .20
336 A185 15c El Salvador .20 .20
a. Se-tenant block of 4 .75 —
337 A185 15c Madagascar .20 .20
338 A185 15c Cameroon .20 .20
339 A185 15c Rwanda .20 .20
340 A185 15c Hungary .20 .20
a. Se-tenant block of 4 .75 —
Nos. 325-340 (16) 3.20 3.20

Issued in 4 sheets of 16. Each sheet contains 4 blocks of 4 (Nos. 325-328, 329-332, 333-336, 337-340). A se-tenant block of 4 designs centers each sheet.

See #350-365, 374-389, 399-414, 425-440, 450-465, 477-492, 499-514, 528-543, 554-569, 690-697; 719-726, 744-751.

Symbolic Flowers A186

Symbols of Progress A187

1980, Nov. 21 Litho. Perf. 13½x13

341 A186 15c multicolored .30 .25
342 A187 20c multicolored .40 .35

Economic and Social Council (ECOSOC). See Offices in Geneva Nos. 96-97; Vienna Nos. 15-16.

Inalienable Rights of the Palestinian People A188

1981, Jan. 30 Photo.

343 A188 15c multicolored .25 .25

See Offices in Geneva #98; Vienna #17.

Interlocking Puzzle Pieces — A189

Stylized Person — A190

1981, Mar. 6 Photo.

344 A189 20c multicolored .35 .20
345 A190 35c multicolored .60 .40

Intl. Year of the Disabled. See Offices in Geneva Nos. 99-100; Vienna Nos. 18-19.

Divislava and Sebastocrator Kaloyan, Bulgarian Mural, 1259, Boyana Church, Sofia — A191

1981, Apr. 15 Photo. Perf. 11½

Granite Paper

346 A191 20c multicolored .30 .30
347 A191 31c multicolored .45 .40

See Offices in Geneva #101; Vienna #20.

Solar Energy A192

Conference Emblem — A193

1981, May 29 Litho. Perf. 13

348 A192 20c multicolored .30 .30
349 A193 40c multicolored .55 .50

Conference on New and Renewable Sources of Energy, Nairobi, Aug. 10-21. See Offices in Geneva No. 102; Vienna No. 21.

Flag Type of 1980

1981, Sept. 25 Litho.

Granite Paper

350 A185 20c Djibouti .25 .20
351 A185 20c Sri Lanka .25 .20
352 A185 20c Bolivia .25 .20
353 A185 20c Equatorial Guinea .25 .20
a. Se-tenant block of 4 1.25 —
354 A185 20c Malta .25 .20
355 A185 20c Czechoslovakia .25 .20
356 A185 20c Thailand .25 .20
357 A185 20c Trinidad & Tobago .25 .20
a. Se-tenant block of 4 1.25 —
358 A185 20c Ukrainian SSR .25 .20
359 A185 20c Kuwait .25 .20
360 A185 20c Sudan .25 .20
361 A185 20c Egypt .25 .20
a. Se-tenant block of 4 1.25 —
362 A185 20c US .25 .20
363 A185 20c Singapore .25 .20
364 A185 20c Panama .25 .20
365 A185 20c Costa Rica .25 .20
a. Se-tenant block of 4 1.25 —
Nos. 350-365 (16) 4.00 3.20

See note after No. 340.

Seedling and Tree Cross Section A194

"10" and Symbols of Progress A195

1981, Nov. 13 Litho.

366 A194 18c multicolored .30 .25
367 A195 28c multicolored .55 .45

UN Volunteers Program, 10th anniv. See Offices in Geneva #103-104; Vienna #22-23.

Respect for Human Rights — A196

Independence of Colonial Countries and People — A197

Second Disarmament Decade — A198

1982, Jan. 22 Perf. 11½x12

368 A196 17c multicolored .30 .20
369 A197 28c multicolored .50 .25
370 A198 40c multicolored .80 .40
Nos. 368-370 (3) 1.60 .85

10th Anniv. of UN Environment Program

A199 A200

1982, Mar. 19 Litho. ***Perf. 13½x13***

371 A199 20c multicolored .30 .25
372 A200 40c multicolored .75 .65

See Offices in Geneva #107-108; Vienna #25-26.

UN Emblem and Olive Branch in Outer Space — A201

Perf. 13 x 13½

1982, June 11 Litho.

373 A201 20c multicolored .35 .20

Exploration and Peaceful Uses of Outer Space. See Offices in Geneva Nos. 109-110; Vienna No. 27.

Flag Type of 1980

1982, Sept. 24 Litho. ***Perf. 12***

Granite Paper

374	A185 20c	Austria	.25	.20
375	A185 20c	Malaysia	.25	.20
376	A185 20c	Seychelles	.25	.20
377	A185 20c	Ireland	.25	.20
a.		Se-tenant block of 4	1.40	—
378	A185 20c	Mozambique	.25	.20
379	A185 20c	Albania	.25	.20
380	A185 20c	Dominica	.25	.20
381	A185 20c	Solomon Islands	.25	.20
a.		Se-tenant block of 4	1.40	—
382	A185 20c	Philippines	.25	.20
383	A185 20c	Swaziland	.25	.20
384	A185 20c	Nicaragua	.25	.20
385	A185 20c	Burma	.25	.20
a.		Se-tenant block of 4	1.40	—
386	A185 20c	Cape Verde	.25	.20
387	A185 20c	Guyana	.25	.20
388	A185 20c	Belgium	.25	.20
389	A185 20c	Nigeria	.25	.20
a.		Se-tenant block of 4	1.40	—
		Nos. 374-369 (16)	4.00	3.20

See note after No. 340.

Conservation and Protection of Nature — A202

1982, Nov. 19 Photo. ***Perf. 14***

390 A202 20c Leaf .40 .35
391 A202 28c Butterfly .55 .50

See Offices in Geneva Nos. 111-112; Vienna Nos. 28-29.

A203

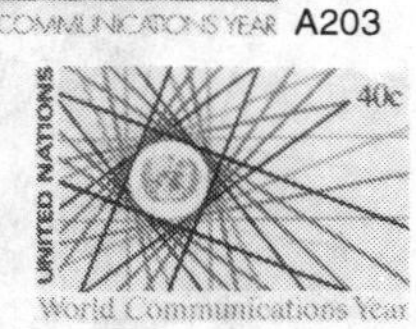

World Communications Year — A204

1983, Jan. 28 Litho. ***Perf. 13***

392 A203 20c multicolored .25 .25
393 A204 40c multicolored .70 .65

See Offices in Geneva #113; Vienna #30.

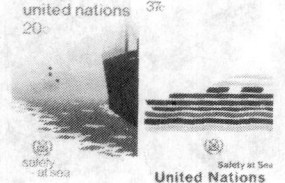

Safety at Sea

A205 A206

1983, Mar. 18 Litho. ***Perf. 14½***

394 A205 20c multicolored .30 .25
395 A206 37c multicolored .65 .65

See Offices in Geneva #114-115; Vienna #31-32.

World Food Program A207

1983, Apr. 22 Engr. ***Perf. 13½***

396 A207 20c rose lake .35 .30

See Offices in Geneva #116; Vienna #33-34.

Trade and Development

A208 A209

1983, June 6 Litho. ***Perf. 14***

397 A208 20c multicolored .30 .25
398 A209 28c multicolored .65 .60

See Offices in Geneva Nos. 117-118; Vienna Nos. 35-36.

Flag Type of 1980

1983, Sept. 23 Photo. ***Perf. 12***

Granite Paper

399	A185 20c	Great Britain	.25	.20
400	A185 20c	Barbados	.25	.20
401	A185 20c	Nepal	.25	.20
402	A185 20c	Israel	.25	.20
a.		Se-tenant block of 4	1.50	—
403	A185 20c	Malawi	.25	.20
404	A185 20c	Byelorussian SSR	.25	.20
405	A185 20c	Jamaica	.25	.20
406	A185 20c	Kenya	.25	.20
a.		Se-tenant block of 4	1.50	—
407	A185 20c	People's Republic of China	.25	.20
408	A185 20c	Peru	.25	.20
409	A185 20c	Bulgaria	.25	.20
410	A185 20c	Canada	.25	.20
a.		Se-tenant block of 4	1.50	—
411	A185 20c	Somalia	.25	.20
412	A185 20c	Senegal	.25	.20
413	A185 20c	Brazil	.25	.20
414	A185 20c	Sweden	.25	.20
a.		Se-tenant block of 4	1.50	—
		Nos. 399-414 (16)	4.00	3.20

See note after No. 340.

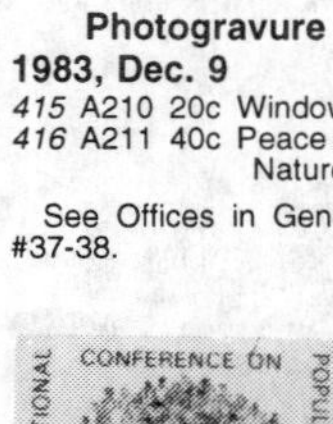

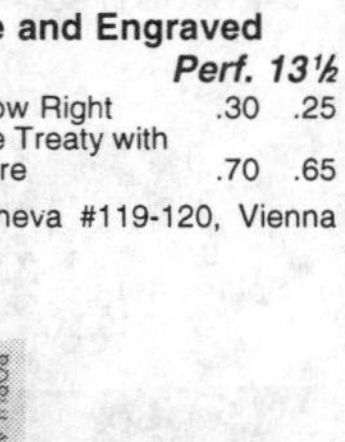

35th Anniv. of the Universal Declaration of Human Rights

A210 A211

Photogravure and Engraved

1983, Dec. 9 ***Perf. 13½***

415 A210 20c Window Right .30 .25
416 A211 40c Peace Treaty with Nature .70 .65

See Offices in Geneva #119-120, Vienna #37-38.

Intl. Population Conference A212

1984, Feb. 3 Litho. ***Perf. 14***

417 A212 20c multicolored .30 .25
418 A212 40c multicolored .60 .60

See Offices in Geneva #121; Vienna #39.

Tractor Plowing A213

Rice Paddy A214

1984, Mar. 15 Litho. ***Perf. 14½***

419 A213 20c multicolored .30 .25
420 A214 40c multicolored .60 .60

World Food Day, Oct. 16. See Offices in Geneva Nos. 122-123; Vienna Nos. 40-41.

Grand Canyon A215

Ancient City of Polonnaruwa, Sri Lanka A216

1984, Apr. 18 Litho. ***Perf. 14***

421 A215 20c multicolored .25 .20
422 A216 50c multicolored .70 .70

World Heritage (protection of world cultural and natural sites). See #601-602; Offices in Geneva #124-125, 211-212; Vienna #42-43, 125-126.

A217 A218

1984, May 29 Photo. ***Perf. 11½***

423 A217 20c multicolored .40 .35
424 A218 50c multicolored 1.00 .85

Future for Refugees. See Offices in Geneva Nos. 126-127; Vienna Nos. 44-45.

Flag Type of 1980

1984, Sept. 21 Photo. ***Perf. 12***

Granite Paper

425	A185 20c	Burundi	.55	.20
426	A185 20c	Pakistan	.55	.20
427	A185 20c	Benin	.55	.20
428	A185 20c	Italy	.55	.20
a.		Se-tenant block of 4	2.75	—
429	A185 20c	Tanzania	.55	.20
430	A185 20c	United Arab Emirates	.55	.20
431	A185 20c	Ecuador	.55	.20
432	A185 20c	Bahamas	.55	.20
a.		Se-tenant block of 4	2.75	—
433	A185 20c	Poland	.55	.20
434	A185 20c	Papua New Guinea	.55	.20
435	A185 20c	Uruguay	.55	.20
436	A185 20c	Chile	.55	.20
a.		Se-tenant block of 4	2.75	—
437	A185 20c	Paraguay	.55	.20
438	A185 20c	Bhutan	.55	.20
439	A185 20c	Central African Republic	.55	.20
440	A185 20c	Australia	.55	.20
a.		Se-tenant block of 4	2.75	—
		Nos. 425-440 (16)	8.80	3.20

See note after No. 340.

Intl. Youth Year — A219

ILO Turin Center — A220

1984, Nov. 15 Litho. ***Perf. 13½***

441 A219 20c multicolored .50 .30
442 A219 35c multicolored 1.50 .65

See Offices in Geneva #128; Vienna #46-47.

1985, Feb. 1 Engr.

443 A220 23c Turin Center emblem .60 .45

See Offices in Geneva #129-130; Vienna #48.

UN University A221

1985, Mar. 15 Photo. ***Perf. 13½***

444 A221 50c multicolored 1.25 .85

See Offices in Geneva #131-132; Vienna #49.

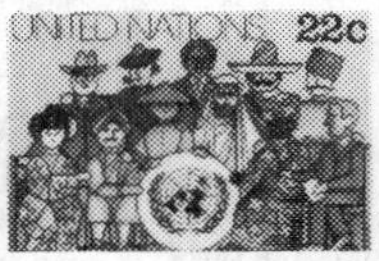

Peoples of the World — A222

Painting UN Emblem A223

1985, May 10 Litho. ***Perf. 14***

445 A222 22c multicolored .35 .30
446 A223 $3 multicolored 4.00 3.50

See Offices in Geneva #133-134; Vienna #50-51.

The Corner A224

Alvaro Raking Hay A225

Oil paintings (details) by American artist Andrew Wyeth.

1985, June 26 Photo. ***Perf. 12x11½***

447 A224 22c multicolored .50 .35
448 A225 45c multicolored 1.00 .85

Souvenir Sheet

Imperf

449 Sheet of 2 1.60 1.10
a. A224 22c multicolored .50 —
b. A225 45c multicolored 1.00 —

40th anniv. of the UN. No. 449 has multicolored margin with inscription and UN emblem. Size: 75x83mm. See Offices in Geneva Nos. 135-137; Vienna Nos. 52-54.

Flag Type of 1980

1985, Sept. 20 Photo. ***Perf. 12***

Granite Paper

450	A185 22c	Grenada	.60	.50
451	A185 22c	Federal Republic of Germany	.60	.50
452	A185 22c	Saudi Arabia	.60	.50

453 A185 22c Mexico	.60	.50
a. Se-tenant block of 4	3.25	—
454 A185 22c Uganda	.60	.50
455 A185 22c St. Thomas & Prince	.60	.50
456 A185 22c USSR	.60	.50
457 A185 22c India	.60	.50
a. Se-tenant block of 4	3.25	—
458 A185 22c Liberia	.60	.50
459 A185 22c Mauritius	.60	.50
460 A185 22c Chad	.60	.50
461 A185 22c Dominican Republic	.60	.50
a. Se-tenant block of 4	3.25	—
462 A185 22c Sultanate of Oman	.60	.50
463 A185 22c Ghana	.60	.50
464 A185 22c Sierra Leone	.60	.50
465 A185 22c Finland	.60	.50
a. Se-tenant block of 4	3.25	—
Nos. 450-465 (16)	9.60	8.00

See note after No. 340.

A226

A227

Photoravure and Engraved

1985, Nov. 22 ***Perf. 13½***

466 A226 22c Asian child	.35	.30
467 A226 33c Breastfeeding	.65	.60

UNICEF Child Survival Campaign. See Offices in Geneva #138-139; Vienna #55-56.

1986, Jan. 31 Photo. ***Perf. 11½***

468 A227 22c Abstract Painting by Wosene Kosrof	.60	.45

Africa in Crisis, campaign against hunger. See Offices in Geneva #140; Vienna #57.

Water Resources A228

1986, Mar. 14 Photo. ***Perf. 13½***

469 A228 22c Dam	1.25	1.10
470 A228 22c Irrigation	1.25	1.10
471 A228 22c Hygiene	1.25	1.10
472 A228 22c Well	1.25	1.10
a. Block of 4, #469-472	5.25	5.25

UN Development program. No. 472a has continuous design. See Offices in Geneva #141-144; Vienna #58-61.

Human Rights Stamp of 1954 — A229

Stamp collecting: 44c, Engraver.

1986, May 22 Engr. ***Perf. 12½***

473 A229 22c dk violet & brt blue	.30	.30
474 A229 44c brown & emer green	.85	.80

See Offices in Geneva #146-147; Vienna #62-63.

Birds Nest in Tree — A230

Peace in Seven Languages A231

Photo. & Embossed

1986, June 20 ***Perf. 13½***

475 A230 22c multicolored	.60	.45
476 A231 33c multicolored	1.50	1.25

Intl. Peace Year. See Offices in Geneva Nos. 148-149; Vienna Nos. 64-65.

Flag Type of 1980

1986, Sept. 19 Photo. ***Perf. 12***

Granite Paper

477 A185 22c New Zealand	.60	.45
478 A185 22c Lao PDR	.60	.45
479 A185 22c Burkina Faso	.60	.45
480 A185 22c Gambia	.60	.45
a. Se-tenant block of 4	3.25	—
481 A185 22c Maldives	.60	.45
482 A185 22c Ethiopia	.60	.45
483 A185 22c Jordan	.60	.45
484 A185 22c Zambia	.60	.45
a. Se-tenant block of 4	3.25	—
485 A185 22c Iceland	.60	.45
486 A185 22c Antigua & Barbuda	.60	.45
487 A185 22c Angola	.60	.45
488 A185 22c Botswana	.60	.45
a. Se-tenant block of 4	3.25	—
489 A185 22c Romania	.60	.45
490 A185 22c Togo	.60	.45
491 A185 22c Mauritania	.60	.45
492 A185 22c Colombia	.60	.45
a. Se-tenant block of 4	3.25	—
Nos. 477-492 (16)	9.60	7.20

See note after No. 340.

Souvenir Sheet

World Federation of UN Associations, 40th Anniv. — A232

Designs: 22c, Mother Earth, by Edna Hibel, US. 33c, Watercolor by Salvador Dali (b. 1904), Spain. 39c, New Dawn, by Dong Kingman, US. 44c, Watercolor by Chaim Gross, US.

1986, Nov. 14 Litho. ***Perf. 13x13½***

493 Sheet of 4	4.25	1.60
a. A232 22c multicolored	.50	—
b. A232 33c multicolored	.80	—
c. A232 39c multicolored	.95	—
d. A232 44c multicolored	1.10	—

See Offices in Geneva #150; Vienna #66.

Trygve Halvdan Lie (1896-1968), 1st Secretary-General A233

Photogravure and Engraved

1987, Jan. 30 ***Perf. 13½***

494 A233 22c multicolored	.90	.20

See Offices in Geneva #151; Vienna #67.

Intl. Year of Shelter for the Homeless A234

Perf. 13½x12½

1987, Mar. 13 Litho.

495 A234 22c Surveying, blueprint	.45	.20
496 A234 44c Cutting lumber	1.40	.45

See Offices in Geneva #154-155; Vienna #68-69.

Fight Drug Abuse A235

1987, June 12 Litho. ***Perf. 14½x15***

497 A235 22c Construction	.65	.20
498 A235 33c Education	1.25	.35

See Offices in Geneva #156-157; Vienna #70-71.

Flag Type of 1980

1987, Sept. 18 Photo. ***Perf. 12***

Granite Paper

499 A185 22c Comoros	.60	.50
500 A185 22c Yemen PDR	.60	.50
501 A185 22c Mongolia	.60	.50
502 A185 22c Vanuatu	.60	.50
a. Se-tenant block of 4	3.25	—
503 A185 22c Japan	.60	.50
504 A185 22c Gabon	.60	.50
505 A185 22c Zimbabwe	.60	.50
506 A185 22c Iraq	.60	.50
a. Se-tenant block of 4	3.25	—
507 A185 22c Argentina	.60	.50
508 A185 22c Congo	.60	.50
509 A185 22c Niger	.60	.50
510 A185 22c St. Lucia	.60	.50
a. Se-tenant block of 4	3.25	—
511 A185 22c Bahrain	.60	.50
512 A185 22c Haiti	.60	.50
513 A185 22c Afghanistan	.60	.50
514 A185 22c Greece	.60	.50
a. Se-tenant block of 4	3.25	—
Nos. 499-514 (16)	9.60	8.00

See note after No. 340.

UN Day — A236

Multinational people in various occupations.

1987, Oct. 23 Litho. ***Perf. 14½x15***

515 A236 22c multicolored	.40	.35
516 A236 39c multicolored	.60	.65

See Offices in Geneva #158-159; Vienna #74-75.

Immunize Every Child — A237

1987, Nov. 20 Litho. ***Perf. 15x14½***

517 A237 22c Measles	1.00	.60
518 A237 44c Tetanus	2.00	1.50

See Offices in Geneva #160-161; Vienna #76-77.

Intl. Fund for Agricultural Development (IFAD) — A238

1988, Jan. 29 Litho. ***Perf. 13½***

519 A238 22c Fishing	.55	.40
520 A238 33c Farming	1.10	.85

See Offices in Geneva #162-163; Vienna #78-79.

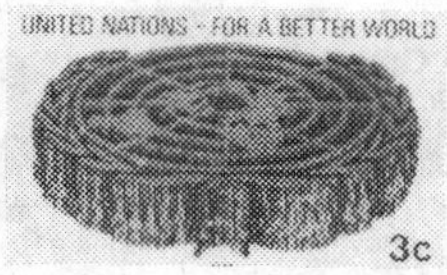

A239

1988, Jan. 29 Photo. ***Perf. 13½x14***

521 A239 3c multicolored ('88)	.20	.20

Survival of the Forests A240

1988, Mar. 18 Litho. ***Perf. 14x15***

522 A240 25c multicolored	1.00	1.00
523 A240 44c multicolored	1.75	1.75
a. Pair, #522-523	3.25	3.25

No. 523a has continuous design. See Offices in Geneva Nos. 165-166; Vienna Nos. 80-81.

Intl. Volunteer Day — A241

1988, May 6 ***Perf. 13x14, 14x13***

524 A241 25c Education, vert.	.45	.40
525 A241 50c Vocational training	1.10	1.00

See Offices in Geneva #167-168; Vienna #82-83.

Health in Sports A242

Perf. 13½x13, 13x13½

1988, June 17 Litho.

526 A242 25c Cycling, vert.	.55	.45
527 A242 38c Marathon	1.40	1.10

See Offices in Geneva #169-170; Vienna #84-85.

Flag Type of 1980

1988, Sept. 16 Photo. ***Perf. 12***

Granite Paper

528 A185 25c Spain	.60	.45
529 A185 25c St. Vincent & Grenadines	.60	.45
530 A185 25c Ivory Coast	.60	.45
531 A185 25c Lebanon	.60	.45
a. Se-tenant block of 4	3.25	—
532 A185 25c Yemen (Arab Republic)	.60	.45
533 A185 25c Cuba	.60	.45
534 A185 25c Denmark	.60	.45
535 A185 25c Libya	.60	.45
a. Se-tenant block of 4	3.25	—
536 A185 25c Qatar	.60	.45
537 A185 25c Zaire	.60	.45
538 A185 25c Norway	.60	.45
539 A185 25c German Democratic Republic	.60	.45
a. Se-tenant block of 4	3.25	—
540 A185 25c Iran	.60	.45
541 A185 25c Tunisia	.60	.45
542 A185 25c Samoa	.60	.45
543 A185 25c Belize	.60	.45
a. Se-tenant block of 4	3.25	—
Nos. 528-543 (16)	9.60	7.20

See note after No. 340.

A243

A244

1988, Dec. 9 **Photo. & Engr.**
544 A243 25c multicolored .60 .40

Souvenir Sheet

545 A243 $1 multicolored 1.25 1.25

Universal Declaration of Human Rights, 40th anniv.

See Offices in Geneva #171-172; Vienna #86-87.

1989, Jan. 27 **Litho.** ***Perf. 13x14***
546 A244 25c Energy and nature .75 .45
547 A244 45c Agriculture 1.50 1.00

World Bank. See Offices in Geneva Nos. 173-174; Vienna Nos. 88-89.

UN Peace-Keeping Force, 1988 Nobel Peace Prize Winner — A245

1989, Mar. 17 **Litho.** ***Perf. 14x13½***
548 A245 25c multicolored .55 .40

See Offices in Geneva #175, Vienna #90.

Aerial Photograph of New York Headquarters — A246

1989, Mar. 17 ***Perf. 14½x14***
549 A246 45c multicolored .75 .60

World Weather Watch, 25th Anniv. (in 1988) — A247

Satellite photographs: 25c, Storm system off the East Coast, US. 36c, Typhoon Abby in the North-West Pacific.

1989, Apr. 21 **Litho.** ***Perf. 13x14***
550 A247 25c multicolored .80 .50
551 A247 36c multicolored 1.75 1.25

See Offices in Geneva #176-177; Vienna #91-92.

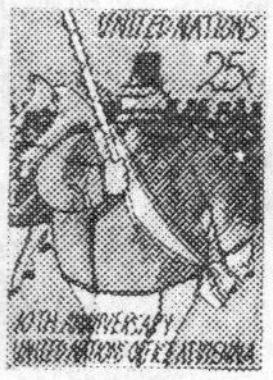

A248

A249

Photo. & Engr., Photo.

1989, Aug. 23 ***Perf. 14***
552 A248 25c multicolored 2.75 .50
553 A249 90c multicolored 2.25 1.75

Offices in Vienna, 10th anniv. See Offices in Geneva Nos. 178-179; Vienna Nos. 93-94.

Flag Type of 1980

1989, Sept. 22 **Photo.** ***Perf. 12***

Granite Paper

554 A185 25c Indonesia .65 .55
555 A185 25c Lesotho .65 .55
556 A185 25c Guatemala .65 .55
557 A185 25c Netherlands .65 .55
a. Se-tenant block of 4 3.50 —
558 A185 25c South Africa .65 .55
559 A185 25c Portugal .65 .55
560 A185 25c Morocco .65 .55
561 A185 25c Syrian Arab Republic .65 .55
a. Se-tenant block of 4 3.50 —
562 A185 25c Honduras .65 .55
563 A185 25c Kampuchea .65 .55
564 A185 25c Guinea-Bissau .65 .55
565 A185 25c Cyprus .65 .55
a. Se-tenant block of 4 3.50 —
566 A185 25c Algeria .65 .55
567 A185 25c Brunei .65 .55
568 A185 25c St. Kitts and Nevis .65 .55
569 A185 25c United Nations .65 .55
a. Se-tenant block of 4 3.50 —
Nos. 554-569 (16) 10.40 8.80

See note after No. 340.

Declaration of Human Rights, 40th Anniv. (in 1988) — A250

Paintings: 25c, *The Table of Universal Brotherhood*, by Jose Clemente Orozco. 45c, *Study for Composition II*, by Vassily Kandinsky.

1989, Nov. 17 **Litho.** ***Perf. 13½***
570 A250 25c multicolored .45 .45
571 A250 45c multicolored .95 .85

Printed in sheets of 12+12 se-tenant labels containing Articles 1 (25c) or 2 (45c) inscribed in English, French or German.

See Nos. 582-583, 599-600, 616-617, 627-628; Offices in Geneva Nos. 180-181, 193-194, 209-210, 224-225, 234-235; Vienna Nos. 95-96, 108-109, 123-124, 139-140, 150-151.

Intl. Trade Center A251

1990, Feb. 2 **Litho.** ***Perf. 14½x15***
572 A251 25c multicolored 1.60 1.10

See Offices in Geneva #182; Vienna #97.

Fight AIDS Worldwide A252

Perf. 13½x12½

1990, Mar. 16 **Litho.**
573 A252 25c shown .60 .55
574 A252 40c Shadow over crowd 1.50 1.25

See Offices in Geneva #184-185; Vienna #99-100.

Medicinal Plants — A253

1990, May 4 **Photo.** ***Perf. 11½***

Granite Paper

575 A253 25c *Catharanthus roseus* .50 .45
576 A253 90c *Panax quinquefolium* 2.00 1.50

See Off. in Geneva #186-187; Vienna #101-102.

United Nations, 45th Anniv. A254

1990, June 26 **Litho.** ***Perf. 14½x13***
577 A254 25c shown .90 .70
578 A254 45c "45," emblem 2.75 .85

Souvenir Sheet

579 Sheet of 2, #577-578 7.50 2.00

See Off. in Geneva #188-189; Vienna #103-104.

Crime Prevention — A255

1990, Sept. 13 **Photo.** ***Perf. 14***
580 A255 25c Crimes of youth 1.10 .70
581 A255 36c Organized crime 2.50 1.25

See Off. in Geneva #191-192; Vienna #106-107.

Human Rights Type of 1989

Artwork: 25c, Fragment from the sarcophagus of Plotinus, c. 270 A.D. 45c, Combined Chambers of the High Court of Appeal by Charles Paul Renouard.

1990, Nov. 16 **Litho.** ***Perf. 13½***
582 A250 25c black, gray & tan .45 .35
583 A250 45c black & brown .90 .75

See Off. in Geneva #193-194; Vienna #108-109.

Printed in sheets of 12+12 se-tenant labels containing Articles 7 (25c) or 8 (45c) inscribed in English, French or German.

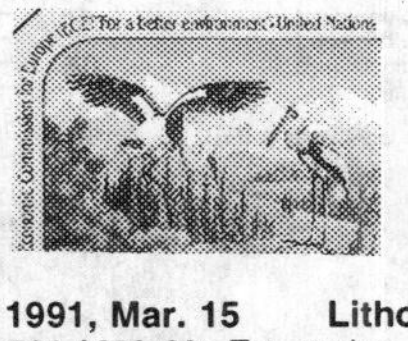

Economic Commission for Europe A256

1991, Mar. 15 **Litho.** ***Perf. 14***
584 A256 30c Two storks 1.10 .90
585 A256 30c Woodpecker, ibex 1.10 .90
586 A256 30c Capercaille, plover 1.10 .90
587 A256 30c Falcon, marmot 1.10 .90
a. Block of 4, #584-587 4.50 3.75

Namibian Independence A257

1991, May 10 **Litho.** ***Perf. 14***
588 A257 30c Dunes, Namib Desert 1.00 .65
589 A257 50c Savanna 2.00 1.50

See Off. in Geneva #199-200; Vienna #114-115.

A258

The Golden Rule by Norman Rockwell — A259

1991, Sept. 11 **Litho.** ***Perf. 13½***
590 A258 30c multicolored .65 .55

Photo.

Perf. 12x11½

591 A259 50c multicolored 1.10 1.00

UN Headquarters, New York — A260

1991, May 10 **Engr.** ***Perf. 13½***
592 A260 $2 dark blue 3.00 2.50

Rights of the Child A261

1991, June 14 **Litho.** ***Perf. 14½***
593 A261 30c Children, globe 1.25 .60
594 A261 70c Houses, rainbow 2.75 1.75

See Off. in Geneva #203-204; Vienna #117-118.

Banning of Chemical Weapons A262

Design: 90c, Hand holding back chemical drums.

1991, Sept. 11 **Litho.** ***Perf. 13½***
595 A262 30c multicolored 1.75 .75
596 A262 90c multicolored 4.00 2.75

See Off. in Geneva #205-206; Vienna #119-120.

UN Postal Administration, 40th Anniv. — A263

1991, Oct. 24 **Litho.** ***Perf. 14x15***
597 A263 30c No. 1 1.10 .60
598 A263 40c No. 3 1.50 1.10

See Off. in Geneva #207-208; Vienna #121-122.

Human Rights Type of 1989

Artwork: 30c, The Last of England, by Ford Madox Brown. 50c, The Emigration to the East, by Tito Salas.

1991, Nov. 20 **Litho.** ***Perf. 13½***
599 A250 30c multicolored .60 .30
600 A250 50c multicolored 1.00 .50

See Off. in Geneva #209-210; Vienna #123-124.

Printed in sheets of 12+12 se-tenant labels containing Articles 13 (30c) or 14 (50c) inscribed in English, French or German.

World Heritage Type of 1984

Designs: 30c, Uluru Natl. Park, Australia. 50c, The Great Wall of China.

1992, Jan. 24 Litho. *Perf. 13*
Size: 35x28mm

601 A215 30c multicolored .70 .60
602 A215 50c multicolored 1.25 1.00

See Off. in Geneva #211-212; Vienna #125-126.

Clean Oceans A264

1992, Mar. 13 Litho. *Perf. 14*

603 A264 29c Ocean surface .55 .55
604 A264 29c Ocean bottom .55 .55
a. Pair, #603-604 1.10 1.10

See Off. in Geneva #214-215; Vienna #127-128.
Printed in sheets of 12 containing 6 #604a.

Earth Summit A265

Designs: No. 605, Globe at LR. No. 606, Globe at LL. No. 607, Globe at UR. No. 608, Globe at UL.

1992, May 22 Photo. *Perf. 11½*

605 A265 29c multicolored .60 .50
606 A265 29c multicolored .60 .50
607 A265 29c multicolored .60 .50
608 A265 29c multicolored .60 .50
a. Block of 4, #605-608 2.50 2.00

See Off. in Geneva #216-219, Vienna #129-132.

Mission to Planet Earth — A266

Designs: No. 609, Satellites over city, sailboats, fishing boat. No. 610, Satellite over coast, passenger liner, dolphins, whale, volcano.

1992, Sept. 4 Photo. *Rouletted 8*
Granite Paper

609 A266 29c multicolored 3.25 .60
610 A266 29c multicolored 3.25 .60
a. Pair, #609-610 6.50 1.25

See Off. in Geneva #220-221, Vienna #133-134.

Science and Technology for Development — A267

Design: 50c, Animal, man drinking.

1992, Oct. 2 Litho. *Perf. 14*

611 A267 29c multicolored .50 .45
612 A267 50c multicolored .85 .70

See Off. in Geneva #222-223, Vienna #135-136.

UN University Building, Tokyo A268

UN Headquarters A269

Design: 40c, UN University Building, Tokyo, diff.

Perf. 14, 13½x13 (29c)
1992, Oct. 2 Litho.

613 A268 4c multicolored .20 .20
614 A269 29c multicolored .60 .55
615 A268 40c multicolored .80 .75
Nos. 613-615 (3) 1.60 1.50

Human Rights Type of 1989

Artwork: 29c, Lady Writing a Letter With her Maid, by Vermeer. 50c, The Meeting, by Ester Almqvist.

1992, Nov. 20 Litho. *Perf. 13½*

616 A250 29c multicolored .90 .55
617 A250 50c multicolored 1.10 1.00

See Off. in Geneva #224-225; Vienna #139-140.
Printed in sheets of 12+12 se-tenant labels containing Articles 19 (29c) and 20 (50c) inscribed in English, French or German.

Aging With Dignity — A270

Designs: 29c, Elderly couple, family. 52c, Old man, physician, woman holding fruit basket.

1993, Feb. 5 Litho. *Perf. 13*

618 A270 29c multicolored 1.00 .55
619 A270 52c multicolored 1.75 1.00

See Off. in Geneva #226-227; Vienna #141-142.

Endangered Species — A271

Designs: No. 620, Hairy-nosed wombat. No. 621, Whooping crane. No. 622, Giant clam. No. 623, Giant sable antelope.

1993, Mar. 3 Litho. *Perf. 13x12½*

620 A271 29c multicolored .55 .50
621 A271 29c multicolored .55 .50
622 A271 29c multicolored .55 .50
623 A271 29c multicolored .55 .50
a. Block of 4, #620-623 2.25 2.25

See #639-642, 657-660, 674-677, 700-703, 730-733, 757-760; Offices in Geneva #228-231, 246-249, 264-267, 280-283, 298-301, 318-321, 336-339; Vienna #143-146, 162-165, 180-183, 196-199, 214-217, 235-238, 253-256.

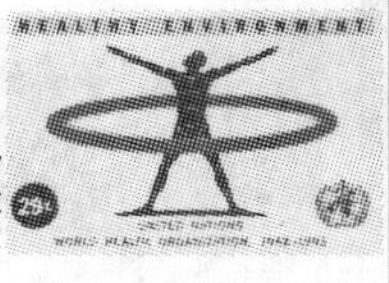

Healthy Environment A272

Designs: 29c, Personal. 50c, Family.

1993, May 7 Litho. *Perf. 15x14½*

624 A272 29c Man .75 .45
625 A272 50c Family 1.25 .75

WHO, 45th anniv.
See Off. in Geneva #232-233; Vienna #147-148.

A273

1993, May 7 Litho. *Perf. 15x14*

626 A273 5c multicolored .20 .20

Human Rights Type of 1989

Artwork: 29c, Shocking Corn, by Thomas Hart Benton. 35c, The Library, by Jacob Lawrence.

1993, June 11 Litho. *Perf. 13½*

627 A250 29c multicolored .90 .65
628 A250 35c multicolored 1.25 .80

See Off. in Geneva #234-235; Vienna #150-151.
Printed in sheets of 12 + 12 se-tenant labels containing Articles 25 (29c) and 26 (35c) inscribed in English, French or German.

Intl. Peace Day — A274

Denomination at: No. 629, UL. No. 630, UR. No. 631, LL. No. 632, LR.

Rouletted 12½
1993, Sept. 21 Litho. & Engr.

629 A274 29c blue & multi 2.00 .75
630 A274 29c blue & multi 2.00 .75
631 A274 29c blue & multi 2.00 .75
632 A274 29c blue & multi 2.00 .75
a. Block of 4, #629-632 9.00 7.00

See Off. in Geneva #236-239; Vienna #152-155.

Environment-Climate — A275

Designs: No. 633, Chameleon. No. 634, Palm trees, top of funnel cloud. No. 635, Bottom of funnel cloud, deer, antelope. No. 636, Bird of paradise.

1993, Oct. 29 Litho. *Perf. 14½*

633 A275 29c multicolored .70 .55
634 A275 29c multicolored .70 .55
635 A275 29c multicolored .70 .55
636 A275 29c multicolored .70 .55
a. Strip of 4, #633-636 3.00 2.25

See Off. in Geneva #240-243; Vienna #156-159.

Intl. Year of the Family — A276

Designs: 29c, Mother holding child, two children, woman. 45c, People tending crops.

1994, Feb. 4 Litho. *Perf. 13.1*

637 A276 29c green & multi 1.25 .75
638 A276 45c blue & multi 2.00 1.10

See Off. in Geneva #244-245; Vienna #160-161.

Endangered Species Type of 1993

Designs: No. 639, Chimpanzee. No. 640, St. Lucia Amazon. No. 641, American crocodile. No. 642, Dama gazelle.

1994, Mar. 18 Litho. *Perf. 12.7*

639 A271 29c multicolored .60 .50
640 A271 29c multicolored .60 .50
641 A271 29c multicolored .60 .50
642 A271 29c multicolored .60 .50
a. Block of 4, #639-642 2.50 2.25

See Off. in Geneva #246-249; Vienna #162-165.

Protection for Refugees — A277

Perf. 14.3x14.8
1994, Apr. 29 Litho.

643 A277 50c multicolored 1.25 .70

See Offices in Geneva #250; Vienna #166.

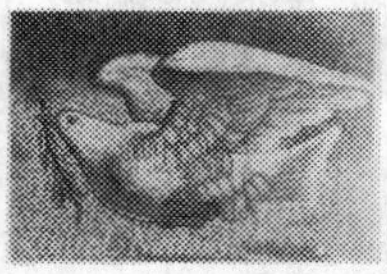

Dove of Peace — A278

Sleeping Child, by Stanislaw Wyspianski A279

Mourning Owl, by Vanessa Isitt A280

1994, Apr. 29 Litho. *Perf. 12.9*

644 A278 10c multicolored .20 .20
645 A279 19c multicolored .65 .40

Engr.
Perf. 13.1

646 A280 $1 red brown 2.50 2.00

Intl. Decade for Natural Disaster Reduction A281

Earth viewed from space, outline map of: No. 647, North America. No. 648, Eurasia. No. 649, South America, No. 650, Australia and South Asia.

1994, May 27 Litho. *Perf. 13.9x14.2*

647 A281 29c multicolored 1.75 .60
648 A281 29c multicolored 1.75 .60
649 A281 29c multicolored 1.75 .60
650 A281 29c multicolored 1.75 .60
a. Block of 4, #647-650 8.00 3.00

See Off. in Geneva #251-254; Vienna #170-173.

Population and Development — A282

Designs: 29c, Children playing. 52c, Family with house, car, other possessions.

1994, Sept. 1 Litho. ***Perf. 13.2x13.6***
651 A282 29c multicolored .75 .60
652 A282 52c multicolored 1.25 1.00

See Off. in Geneva #258-259; Vienna #174-175.

UNCTAD, 30th Anniv. — A283

1994, Oct. 28
653 A283 29c multicolored .55 .50
654 A283 50c multi, diff. .95 .70

See Off. in Geneva #260-261; Vienna #176-177.

UN, 50th Anniv. A284

Social Summit, Copenhagen A285

Litho. & Engr.

1995, Jan. 1 ***Perf. 13.4***
655 A284 32c multicolored 1.25 .90

See Offices in Geneva #262; Vienna #178.

Photo. & Engr.

1995, Feb. 3 ***Perf. 13.6x13.9***
656 A285 50c multicolored 1.10 1.00

See Offices in Geneva #263; Vienna #179.

Endangered Species Type of 1993

Designs: No. 657, Giant armadillo. No. 658, American bald eagle. No. 659, Fijian/Tongan banded iguana. No. 660, Giant panda.

1995, Mar. 24 Litho. ***Perf. 13x12½***
657 A271 32c multicolored .65 .55
658 A271 32c multicolored .65 .55
659 A271 32c multicolored .65 .55
660 A271 32c multicolored .65 .55
a. Block of 4, 657-660 2.75 2.25

See Off. in Geneva #264-267; Vienna #180-183.

Intl. Youth Year, 10th Anniv. — A286

32c, Seated child. 55c, Children cycling.

1995, May 26 Litho. ***Perf. 14.4x14.7***
661 A286 32c multicolored .75 .45
662 A286 55c multicolored 1.25 .85

See Off. in Geneva #268-269; Vienna #184-185.

UN, 50th Anniv. — A287

Designs: 32c, Hand with pen signing UN Charter, flags. 50c, Veterans' War Memorial, Opera House, San Francisco.

Perf. 13.3x13.6

1995, June 26 **Engr.**
663 A287 32c black .65 .45
664 A287 50c maroon 1.00 .70

Souvenir Sheet

Litho. & Engr.

Imperf

665 Sheet of 2, #663-664 2.25 2.00
a. A287 32c black .90 .75
b. A287 50c maroon 1.25 1.10

See Off. in Geneva #270-271; Vienna #186-187.

4th World Conference on Women, Beijing A288

Designs: 32c, Mother and child. 40c, Seated woman, cranes flying above.

1995, Sept. 5 Photo. ***Perf. 12***
666 A288 32c multicolored .80 .40

Size: 28x50mm

667 A288 40c multicolored 1.10 .50

See Off. in Geneva #273-274; Vienna #189-190.

UN Headquarters — A289

1995, Sept. 5 Litho. ***Perf. 15***
668 A289 20c multicolored .35 .20

Miniature Sheet

United Nations, 50th Anniv. — A290

Designs: #669a-669 l, Various people in continuous design (2 blocks of six stamps with gutter between).

1995, Oct. 24 Litho. ***Perf. 14***
669 Sheet of 12 9.00 5.00
a.-l. A290 32c any single .70 .40
670 Souvenir booklet 15.00
a. A290 32c Booklet pane of 3, vert. strip of 3 from UL of sheet 3.50 3.50
b. A290 32c Booklet pane of 3, vert. strip of 3 from UR of sheet 3.50 3.50
c. A290 32c Booklet pane of 3, vert. strip of 3 from LL of sheet 3.50 3.50
d. A290 32c Booklet pane of 3, vert. strip of 3 from LR of sheet 3.50 3.50

See Off. in Geneva #275-276; Vienna #191-192.

WFUNA, 50th Anniv. — A291

1996, Feb. 2 Litho. ***Perf. 13x13½***
671 A291 32c multicolored .50 .30

See Offices in Geneva #277; Vienna #193.

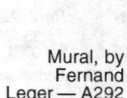

Mural, by Fernand Leger — A292

1996, Feb. 2 Litho. ***Perf. 14½x15***
672 A292 32c multicolored .50 .30
673 A292 60c multi, diff. 1.00 .60

Endangered Species Type of 1993

Designs: No. 674, Masdevallia veitchiana. No. 675, Saguaro cactus. No. 676, West Australian pitcher plant. No. 677, Encephalartos horridus.

1996, Mar. 14 Litho. ***Perf. 12½***
674 A271 32c multicolored .60 .30
675 A271 32c multicolored .60 .30
676 A271 32c multicolored .60 .30
677 A271 32c multicolored .60 .30
a. Block of 4, #674-677 2.50 —

See Off. in Geneva #280-283; Vienna #196-199.

City Summit (Habitat II) — A293

Designs: No. 678, Deer. No. 679, Man, child, dog sitting on hill, overlooking town. No. 680, People walking in park, city skyline. No. 681, Tropical park, Polynesian woman, boy. No. 682, Polynesian village, orchids, bird.

1996, June 3 Litho. ***Perf. 14x13½***
678 A293 32c multicolored .70 .30
679 A293 32c multicolored .70 .30
680 A293 32c multicolored .70 .30
681 A293 32c multicolored .70 .30
682 A293 32c multicolored .70 .30
a. Strip of 5, #678-682 3.50 —

See Off. in Geneva #284-288; Vienna #200-204.

Sport and the Environment — A294

1996 Summer Olympic Games, Atlanta, GA: 32c, Men's basketball, vert. 50c, Women's volleyball.

Perf. 14x14½, 14½x14

1996, July 19 **Litho.**
683 A294 32c multicolored 1.00 .40
684 A294 50c multicolored 2.00 .75

Souvenir Sheet

685 A294 Sheet of 2, #683-684 2.00 1.65

See Off. in Geneva #289-291; Vienna #205-207.

Plea for Peace — A295

Designs: 32c, Doves. 60c, Stylized dove.

1996, Sept. 17 Litho. ***Perf. 14½x15***
686 A295 32c multicolored .65 .30
687 A295 60c multicolored 1.25 .60

See Off. in Geneva #292-293; Vienna #208-209.

UNICEF, 50th Anniv. — A296

Fairy Tales: 32c, Yeh-Shen, China. 60c, The Ugly Duckling, by Hans Christian Andersen.

1996, Nov. 20 Litho. ***Perf. 14½x15***
688 A296 32c multicolored .65 .30
689 A296 60c multicolored 1.25 .60

Panes of 8 + label.

See Off. in Geneva #294-295; Vienna #210-211.

Flag Type of 1980

1997, Feb. 12 Photo. ***Perf. 12***

Granite Paper

690 A185 32c Tadjikistan .65 .30
691 A185 32c Georgia .65 .30
692 A185 32c Armenia .65 .30
693 A185 32c Namibia .65 .30
a. Block of 4, #690-693 2.60 1.20
694 A185 32c Liechtenstein .65 .30
695 A185 32c Republic of Korea .65 .30
696 A185 32c Kazakhstan .65 .30
697 A185 32c Latvia .65 .30
a. Block of 4, #694-697 2.60 1.20

See note after No. 340.

Cherry Blossoms, UN Headquarters A297

Peace Rose A298

1997, Feb. 12 Litho. ***Perf. 14½***
698 A297 8c multicolored .20 .20
699 A297 55c multicolored 1.10 .55

Endangered Species Type of 1993

Designs: No. 700, African elephant. No. 701, Major Mitchell's cockatoo. No. 702, Black-footed ferret. No. 703, Cougar.

1997, Mar. 13 Litho. ***Perf. 12½***
700 A271 32c multicolored .65 .30
701 A271 32c multicolored .65 .30
702 A271 32c multicolored .65 .30
703 A271 32c multicolored .65 .30
a. Block of 4, #700-703 2.60 1.20

See Off. in Geneva #298-301; Vienna #214-217.

Earth Summit, 5th Anniv. A299

Designs: No. 704, Sailboat. No. 705, Three sailboats. No. 706, Two people watching sailboat, sun. No. 707, Person, sailboat.

$1, Combined design similar to Nos. 704-707.

1997, May 30 Photo. ***Perf. 11.5***

Granite Paper

704 A299 32c multicolored .90 .40
705 A299 32c multicolored .90 .40
706 A299 32c multicolored .90 .40
707 A299 32c multicolored .90 .40
a. Block of 4, #704-707 3.75 1.75

Souvenir Sheet

708 A299 $1 multicolored 4.00 4.00
a. Ovptd. in sheet margin *20.00 20.00*

See Off. in Geneva #302-306; Vienna #218-222.

No. 708 contains one 60x43mm stamp. Overprint in sheet margin of No. 708a reads "PACIFIC 97 / World Philatelic Exhibition / San Francisco, California / 29 May - 8 June 1997."

Transportation A300

Ships: No. 709, Clipper ship. No. 710, Paddle steamer. No. 711, Ocean liner. No. 712, Hovercraft. No. 713, Hydrofoil.

1997, Aug. 29 Litho. *Perf. 14x14½*

709 A300 32c multicolored	.65	.30
710 A300 32c multicolored	.65	.30
711 A300 32c multicolored	.65	.30
712 A300 32c multicolored	.65	.30
713 A300 32c multicolored	.65	.30
a. Strip of 5, #709-713	3.25	1.50

See Off. in Geneva #307-311; Vienna #223-227.

No. 713a has continuous design.

Philately — A301

1997, Oct. 14 Litho. *Perf. 13½x14*

714 A301 32c No. 473	.90	.40
715 A301 50c No. 474	1.75	.75

See Off. in Geneva #312-313; Vienna #228-229.

World Heritage Convention, 25th Anniv. — A302

Terracotta warriors of Xian: 32c, Single warrior. 60c, Massed warriors.

No. 718: a, like #716. b, like #717. c, like Geneva #314. d, like Geneva #315. e, like Vienna #230. f, like Vienna #231.

1997, Nov. 19 Litho. *Perf. 13½*

716 A302 32c multicolored	.90	.40
717 A302 60c multicolored	1.75	.75
718 Souvenir booklet	8.00	
a.-f. A302 8c any single	.30	.30
g. Booklet pane of 4 #718a	1.25	1.25
h. Booklet pane of 4 #718b	1.25	1.25
i. Booklet pane of 4 #718c	1.25	1.25
j. Booklet pane of 4 #718d	1.25	1.25
k. Booklet pane of 4 #718e	1.25	1.25
l. Booklet pane of 4 #718f	1.25	1.25

See Off. in Geneva #314-316; Vienna #230-232.

Flag Type of 1980

1998, Feb. 13 Photo. *Perf. 12*

Granite Paper

719 A185 32c Micronesia	.65	.30
720 A185 32c Slovakia	.65	.30
721 A185 32c Democratic People's Republic of Korea	.65	.30
722 A185 32c Azerbaijan	.65	.30
a. Block of 4, #719-722	2.60	—
723 A185 32c Uzbekistan	.65	.30
724 A185 32c Monaco	.65	.30
725 A185 32c Czech Republic	.65	.30
726 A185 32c Estonia	.65	.30
a. Block of 4, #723-726	2.60	—

See note after No. 340.

A303

A304

A305

1998, Feb. 13 Litho. *Perf. 14½x15*

727 A303 1c multicolored	.20	.20
728 A304 2c multicolored	.20	.20

Perf. 15x14½

729 A305 21c multicolored	.45	.20

Endangered Species Type of 1993

Designs: No. 730, Lesser galago. No. 731, Hawaiian goose. No. 732, Golden birdwing. No. 733, Sun bear.

1998, Mar. 13 Litho. *Perf. 12½*

730 A271 32c multicolored	.65	.30
731 A271 32c multicolored	.65	.30
732 A271 32c multicolored	.65	.30
733 A271 32c multicolored	.65	.30
a. Block of 4, #730-733	2.75	1.40

See Off. in Geneva #318-321; Vienna #235-238.

Intl. Year of the Ocean — A306

1998, May 20 Litho. *Perf. 13x13½*

734 A306 Sheet of 12	6.25	4.00
a.-l. 32c any single	.50	.30

See Offices in Geneva #322; Vienna #239.

Rain Forests A307

1998, June 19 Litho. *Perf. 13x13½*

735 A307 32c Jaguar	.65	.30

Souvenir Sheet

736 A307 $2 like #735	4.00	2.00

See Off. in Geneva #323-324; Vienna #240-241.

U.N. Peacekeeping Forces, 50th Anniv. — A308

Designs: 33c, Commander with binoculars. 40c, Two soldiers on vehicle.

1998, Sept. 15 Photo. *Perf. 12*

737 A308 33c multicolored	.65	.30
738 A308 40c multicolored	.80	.40

See Off. in Geneva #325-326; Vienna #242-243.

Universal Declaration of Human Rights, 50th Anniv. — A309

Stylized people: 32c, Carrying flag. 55c, Carrying pens.

Litho. & Photo.

1998, Oct. 27 *Perf. 13*

739 A309 32c multicolored	.65	.30
740 A309 55c multicolored	1.10	.55

See Off. in Geneva #327-328; Vienna #244-245.

Schönnbrun Palace, Vienna — A310

>Designs: 33c, #743f, The Gloriette. 60c, #743b, Wall painting on fabric (detail), by Johann Wenzl Bergl, vert. No. 743a, Blue porcelain vase, vert. No. 743c, Porcelain stove, vert. No. 743d, Palace. No. 743e, Great Palm House (conservatory).

1998, Dec. 4 Litho. *Perf. 14*

741 A310 33c multicolored	.65	.30
742 A310 60c multicolored	1.25	.65
743 Souvenir booklet	6.00	
a.-c. A310 11c any single	.25	.25
d.-f. A310 15c any single	.30	.30
g. Booklet pane, 4 #743d	1.25	
h. Booklet pane, 3 #743a	.75	
i. Booklet pane, 3 #743b	.75	
j. Booklet pane, 3 #743c	.75	
k. Booklet pane, 4 #743e	1.25	
l. Booklet pane, 4 #743f	1.25	

See Off. in Geneva #329-331; Vienna #246-248.

Flag Type of 1980

Each pane contains 4 blocks of 4 (Nos. 744-747, 748-751). A se-tenant block of 4 designs centers each pane.

1999, Feb. 5 Photo. *Perf. 12*

744 A185 33c Lithuania	.65	.30
745 A185 33c San Marino	.65	.30
746 A185 33c Turkmenistan	.65	.30
747 A185 33c Marshall Islands	.65	.30
a. Block of 4, #744-747	2.60	—
748 A185 33c Moldova	.65	.30
749 A185 33c Kyrgyzstan	.65	.30
750 A185 33c Bosnia & Herzegovina	.65	.30
751 A185 33c Eritrea	.65	.30
a. Block of 4, #748-751	2.60	—

Flags and Globe — A311

Roses — A312

1999, Feb. 5 Litho. *Perf. 14x13½*

752 A311 33c multicolored	.65	.30

Photo.

Granite Paper

Perf. 11½x12

753 A312 $5 multicolored	10.00	5.00

World Heritage Sites, Australia A313

Designs: 33c, #756f, Willandra Lakes region. 60c, #756b, Wet tropics of Queensland. No. 756a, Tasmanian wilderness. No. 756c, Great Barrier Reef. No. 756d, Uluru-Kata Tjuta Natl. Park. No. 756e, Kakadu Natl. Park.

1999, Mar. 19 Litho. *Perf. 13*

754 A313 33c multicolored	.65	.30
755 A313 60c multicolored	1.25	.65
756 Souvenir booklet	5.00	
a.-c. A313 5c any single	.20	.20
d.-f. A313 15c any single	.30	.30
g. Booklet pane of 4, #756a	.40	
h. Booklet pane of 4, #756d	1.25	
i. Booklet pane of 4, #756b	.40	
j. Booklet pane of 4, #756e	1.25	
k. Booklet pane of 4, #756c	.40	
l. Booklet pane of 4, #756f	1.25	

See Offices in Geneva Nos. 333-335; Vienna Nos. 250-252.

Endangered Specied Type of 1993

#757, Tiger. #758, Secretary bird. #759, Green tree python. #760, Long-tailed chinchilla.

1999, Apr. 22 Litho. *Perf. 12½*

757	A271	33c multicolored	.65	.20
758	A271	33c multicolored	.65	.20
759	A271	33c multicolored	.65	.20
760	A271	33c multicolored	.65	.20
a.		Block of 4, #757-760	2.60	

See Offices in Geneva Nos. 336-339; Vienna Nos. 253-256.

UNISPACE III, Vienna — A314

#761, Probe on planet's surface. #762, Planetary rover. #763, Composite of #761-762.

1999, July 7 Photo. *Rouletted 8*

761	A314	33c multicolored	.65	.30
762	A314	33c multicolored	.65	.30
a.		Pair, #761-762	1.30	.60

Souvenir Sheet

Perf. 14½

763	A314	$2 multicolored	4.00	2.00

See Offices in Geneva #340-342; Vienna #257-259.

UPU, 125th Anniv. A315

Various people, 19th century methods of mail transportation, denomination at: No. 764, UL. No. 765, UR. No. 766, LL. No. 767, LR.

1999, Aug. 23 Photo. *Perf. 11¾*

764	A315	33c multicolored	.65	.30
765	A315	33c multicolored	.65	.30
766	A315	33c multicolored	.65	.30
767	A315	33c multicolored	.65	.30
a.		Block of 4, #764-767	2.60	—

See Offices in Geneva Nos. 343-346; Vienna Nos. 260-263.

In Memoriam A316

UN Headquarters. Size of $1 stamp: 34x63mm.

1999, Sept. 21 Litho. *Perf. 14½x14*

768	A316	33c multicolored	.65	.30

Souvenir Sheet

Perf. 14

769	A316	$1 multicolored	2.00	1.00

See Off. in Geneva #347-348, Vienna #264-265.

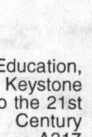

Education, Keystone to the 21st Century A317

Perf. 13½x13¾

1999, Nov. 18 Litho.

770	A317	33c Two readers	.65	.30
771	A317	60c Heart	1.25	.60

See Offices in Geneva Nos. 349-350, Vienna Nos. 266-267.

AIR POST STAMPS

Plane and Gull — AP1

Swallows and UN Emblem AP2

Unwmk.

1951, Dec. 14 Engr. *Perf. 14*

C1	AP1	6c henna brown	.20	.20
C2	AP1	10c bright blue green	.20	.20
C3	AP2	15c deep ultra	.20	.25
a.		15c Prussian blue	100.00	
C4	AP2	25c gray black	.80	.35
		Nos. C1-C4 (4)	1.40	1.00

The 6c, 15c and 25c exist imperforate.

Airplane Wing and Globe — AP3

1957, May 27 *Perf. 12½x14*

C5	AP3	4c maroon	.20	.20

1959, Feb. 9 *Perf. 12½x13½*

C6	AP3	5c rose red	.20	.20

UN Flag and Plane AP4

1959, Feb. 9 *Perf. 13½x14*

C7	AP4	7c ultramarine	.20	.20

Outer Space — AP5

UN Emblem — AP6

"Flight Across Globe" — AP8

Bird of Laurel Leaves — AP7

Jet Plane and Envelope — AP9

1963-64 Photo. *Perf. 11½*

C8	AP5	6c blk, blue & yel grn	.20	.20
C9	AP6	8c yel, ol green & red	.20	.20

Perf. 12½x12

C10	AP7	13c ultra, aqua, gray & car	.20	.20

Perf. 11½x12, 12x11½

C11	AP8	15c violet, buff, gray & pale grn ('64)	.25	.20
a.		Gray omitted	—	
C12	AP9	25c yel, org, gray, blue & red ('64)	.50	.30
		Nos. C8-C12 (5)	1.35	1.10

Dates of issue: 6c, 8c, 13c, June 17, 1963; 15c, 25c, May 1. See Offices in Geneva No. 8.

Jet Plane and UN Emblem AP10

1968, Apr. 18 Litho. *Perf. 13*

C13	AP10	20c multicolored	.30	.25

Wings, Envelopes and UN Emblem — AP11

1969, Apr. 21 Litho.

C14	AP11	10c org ver, org, yel & black	.20	.20

UN Emblem and Stylized Wing — AP12

Birds in Flight — AP13

Clouds AP14

"UN" and Plane — AP15

Lithogravd and Engraved

1972, May 1 *Perf. 13x13½*

C15	AP12	9c lt blue, dark red & vio blue	.20	.20

Photo. *Perf. 14x13½*

C16	AP13	11c blue & multi	.20	.20

Perf. 13½x14

C17	AP14	17c yel, red & orange	.25	.20

Perf. 13

C18	AP15	21c silver & multi	.30	.25

Globe and Jet — AP16

Pathways Radiating from UN Emblem AP17

Bird in Flight, UN Headquarters AP18

Perf. 13, 12½x13 (18c)

1974, Sept. 16 Litho.

C19	AP16	13c multicolored	.20	.20
C20	AP17	18c multicolored	.25	.20
C21	AP18	26c blue & multi	.35	.30
		Nos. C19-C21 (3)	.80	.70

Winged Airmail Letter — AP19

Symbolic Globe and Plane — AP20

1977, June 27 Photo. *Perf. 14*

C22	AP19	25c grnsh blue & multi	.35	.25
C23	AP20	31c magenta	.40	.30

OFFICES IN GENEVA, SWITZERLAND

For use only on mail posted at the Palais des Nations (UN European Office), Geneva. Inscribed in French unless otherwise stated.

100 Centimes = 1 Franc

Types of UN Issues 1961-69 and

UN European Office, Geneva — G1

Designs: 5c, UN Headquarters, New York, and world map. 10c, UN flag. 20c, Three men united before globe. 50c, Opening words of UN Charter. 60c, UN emblem over globe. 70c, "UN" and UN emblem. 75c, "Flight Across Globe." 80c, UN Headquarters and emblem. 90c, Abstract group of flags. 1fr, UN Emblem. 2fr, Stylized globe and weather vane. 3fr, Statue by Henrik Starcke. 10fr, "Peace, Justice, Security."

Perf. 13 (5c, 70c, 90c); Perf. 12½x12 (10c); Perf. 11½ (20c-60c, 3fr); Perf. 11½x12 (75c); Perf. 13½x14 (80c); Perf. 14 (1fr); Perf. 12x11½ (2fr); Perf. 12 (10fr)

Photogravure; Lithographed & Embossed (1fr); Engraved (10fr)

1969-70 Unwmk.

1	A88	5c purple & multi	.20	.20
a.		Green omitted	—	
2	A52	10c salmon & multi	.20	.20
3	A66	20c black & multi	.20	.20
4	G1	30c dk blue & multi	.20	.20
5	A77	50c ultra & multi	.20	.20
6	A54	60c dk brown, sal & gold	.20	.20
7	A104	70c red, black & gold	.20	.20
8	AP8	75c car rose & multi	.25	.25
9	A78	80c blue grn, red & yel	.25	.25
10	A45	90c blue & multi	.25	.25
11	A79	1fr lt & dk green	.30	.30
12	A67	2fr blue & multi	.60	.60

13 A97 3fr olive & multi .95 .95
14 A3 10fr deep blue 2.75 2.75
Nos. 1-14 (14) 6.75 6.75

The 20c, 80c and 90c are inscribed in French. The 75c and 10fr carry French inscription at top, English at bottom.

Issued: 60c, 10fr, 4/17/70; 70c, 80c, 90c, 2fr, 9/22/70; others, 10/4/69.

Sea Bed Type

Photogravure and Engraved

1971, Jan. 25 ***Perf. 13***
15 A114 30c green & multi .20 .20

Refugee Type

1971, Mar. 12 Litho. ***Perf. 13x12½***
16 A115 50c dp car, dp org & black .20 .20

Food Program Type

1971, Apr. 13 Photo. ***Perf. 14***
17 A116 50c dk purple, gold & grn .20 .20

UPU Headquarters Type

1971, May 28 Photo. ***Perf. 11½***
18 A117 75c green & multi .30 .30

Eliminate Discrimination Types

1971, Sept. 21 Photo. ***Perf. 13½***
19 A118 30c blue & multi .20 .20
20 A119 50c multicolored .25 .25

Picasso Type

1971, Nov. 19 Photo. ***Perf. 11½***
21 A122 1.10fr carmine & multi .75 .65

Palais des Nations, Geneva G2

1972, Jan. 5 Photo. ***Perf. 11½***
22 G2 40c olive & multi .20 .20

Nuclear Weapons Type

1972, Feb. 14 Photo. ***Perf. 13½x14***
23 A124 40c yel green, blk, rose & gray .25 .25

World Health Day Type

Lithographed and Engraved

1972, Apr. 7 ***Perf. 13x13½***
24 A125 80c black & multi .40 .40

Environment Type

Lithographed and Embossed

1972, June 5 ***Perf. 12½x14***
25 A126 40c multicolored .20 .20
26 A126 80c multicolored .40 .40

ECE Type

1972, Sept. 11 Litho. ***Perf. 13x13½***
27 A127 1.10fr red & multi 1.00 .90

Art at UN Type

1972, Nov. 17 Photo. ***Perf. 12x12½***
28 A128 40c gold, brown & red .30 .30
29 A128 80c gold, brown & olive .60 .60

Disarmament Type

1973, Mar. 9 Litho. ***Perf. 13½x13***
30 A129 60c violet & multi .40 .35
31 A129 1.10fr olive & multi .85 .75

Nos. 30-31 exist imperf.

Drug Abuse Type

1973, Apr. 13 Photo. ***Perf. 13½***
32 A130 60c blue & multi .45 .40

Volunteers Type

1973, May 25 Photo. ***Perf. 14***
33 A131 80c multicolored .35 .35

Namibia Type

1973, Oct. 1 Photo. ***Perf. 13½***
34 A132 60c red & multi .35 .35

Human Rights Type

1973, Nov. 16 Photo. ***Perf. 13½***
35 A133 40c ultra & multi .30 .30
36 A133 80c olive & multi .50 .50

ILO Headquarters Type

1974, Jan. 11 Photo. ***Perf. 14***
37 A134 60c violet & multi .45 .45
38 A134 80c brown & multi .65 .60

UPU Type

1974, Mar. 22 Photo. ***Perf. 14***
39 A135 30c multicolored .25 .20
40 A135 60c multicolored .60 .40

Art at UN Type

1974, May 6 Photo. ***Perf. 14***
41 A136 60c dark red & multi .40 .40
42 A136 1fr green & multi .70 .70

WPY Type

1974, Oct. 18 Photo. ***Perf. 14***
43 A140 60c brt green & multi .55 .45
44 A140 80c brown & multi .70 .55

Law of the Sea Type

1974, Nov. 22 Photo. ***Perf. 14***
45 A141 1.30fr blue & multi .95 .95

Outer Space Type

1975, Mar. 14 Litho. ***Perf. 13***
46 A142 60c multicolored .50 .35
47 A142 90c multicolored .75 .55

IWY Type

1975, May 9 Litho. ***Perf. 15***
48 A143 60c multicolored .45 .40
49 A143 90c multicolored .65 .55

30th Anniv. Type

1975, June 26 Litho. ***Perf. 13***
50 A144 60c green & multi .45 .40
51 A144 90c violet & multi .65 .60

Souvenir Sheet

Imperf

52 Sheet of 2 .75 .75
a. A144 60c green & multi .25 .25
b. A144 90c violet & multi .50 .50

Namibia Type

1975, Sept. 22 Photo. ***Perf. 13½***
53 A145 50c multicolored .30 .30
54 A145 1.30fr multicolored .95 .70

Peace-keeping Operations Type

1975, Nov. 21 Engr. ***Perf. 12½***
55 A146 60c greenish blue .35 .35
56 A146 70c bright violet .65 .50

WFUNA Type

1976, Mar. 12 Photo. ***Perf. 14***
57 A152 90c multicolored 1.00 .65

UNCTAD Type

1976, Apr. 23 Photo. ***Perf. 11½***
58 A153 1.10fr multicolored 1.00 .80

Habitat Type

1976, May 28 Photo. ***Perf. 14***
59 A154 40c multicolored .20 .20
60 A154 1.50fr violet & multi .80 .80

UN Emblem, Post Horn and Rainbow — G3

1976, Oct. 8 Photo. ***Perf. 11½***
61 G3 80c tan & multi .50 .50
62 G3 1.10fr lt green & multi 1.60 1.60

Sheets of 20.

Food Council Type

1976, Nov. 19 Litho. ***Perf. 14½***
63 A156 70c multicolored .60 .55

WIPO Type

1977, Mar. 11 Photo. ***Perf. 14***
64 A157 80c red & multi .60 .55

Drop of Water and Globe — G4

1977, Apr. 22 Photo. ***Perf. 13½x13***
65 G4 80c ultra & multi .60 .50
66 G4 1.10fr dark car & multi .85 .75

UN Water Conference, Mar del Plata, Argentina, Mar. 14-25.

Hands Protecting UN Emblem — G5

1977, May 24 Photo. ***Perf. 14***
67 G5 80c blue & multi .60 .50
68 G5 1.10fr emerald & multi .85 .75

UN Security Council.

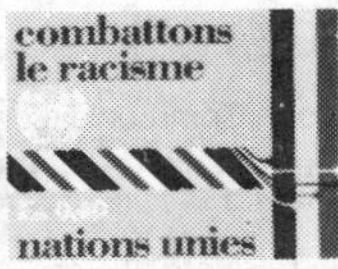

Colors of Five Races Spun into One Firm Rope — G6

1977, Sept. 19 Litho. ***Perf. 13***
69 G6 40c multicolored .25 .25
70 G6 1.10fr multicolored .65 .65

Fight against racial discrimination.

Atomic Energy Turning Partly into Olive Branch — G7

1977, Nov. 18 Photo.
71 G7 80c dark car & multi .50 .50
72 G7 1.10fr Prus blue & multi .75 .75

Peaceful uses of atomic energy.

"Tree" of Doves — G8

1978, Jan. 27 Litho. ***Perf. 14½***
73 G8 35c multicolored .20 .20

Globes with Smallpox Distribution G9

1978, Mar. 31 Photo. ***Perf. 12x11½***
74 G9 80c yellow & multi .50 .50
75 G9 1.10fr lt green & multi .75 .75

Global eradication of smallpox.

Namibia Type

1978, May 5 Photo. ***Perf. 12***
76 A166 80c multicolored .75 .60

United Nations Offices in Geneva stamps can be mounted in the Scott U.N. Singles and Postal Stationery album.

Jets and Flight Patterns — G10

1978, June 12 Photo. ***Perf. 14***
77 G10 70c multicolored .40 .30
78 G10 80c multicolored .70 .50

International Civil Aviation Organization for "Safety in the Air."

General Assembly, Flags and Globe G11

1978, Sept. 15 Photo. ***Perf. 13½***
79 G11 70c multicolored .55 .55
80 G11 1.10fr multicolored .90 .60

Technical Cooperation Type

1978, Nov. 17 Photo. ***Perf. 14***
81 A169 80c multicolored .70 .55

Seismograph Recording Earthquake G12

1979, Mar. 9 Photo. ***Perf. 14***
82 G12 80c multicolored .50 .40
83 G12 1.50fr multicolored .85 .85

Office of the UN Disaster Relief Coordinator (UNDRO).

Children and Rainbow G13

1979, May 4 Photo. ***Perf. 14***
84 G13 80c multicolored .35 .35
85 G13 1.10fr multicolored .65 .65

International Year of the Child.

Namibia Type

1979, Oct. 5 Litho. ***Perf. 13½***
86 A176 1.10fr multicolored .50 .50

International Court of Justice, Scales — G14

1979, Nov. 9 Litho. ***Perf. 13x13½***
87 G14 80c multicolored .40 .40
88 G14 1.10fr multicolored .60 .60

International Court of Justice, The Hague, Netherlands.

Economic Order Type

1980, Jan. 11 ***Perf. 15x14½***
89 A179 80c multicolored .75 .60

Women's Year Emblem G15

1980, Mar. 7 Litho. *Perf. 14½x15*
90 G15 40c multicolored .30 .30
91 G15 70c multicolored .75 .55

UN Decade for Women.

Peace-keeping Operations Type

1980, May 16 Litho. *Perf. 14x13*
92 A181 1.10fr blue & green .80 .70

35th Anniv. Type and

Dove and "35" — G16

1980, June 26 Litho. *Perf. 13*
93 G16 40c multicolored .35 .30
94 A183 70c multicolored .55 .50

Souvenir Sheet

Imperf

95 Sheet of 2 .75 .60
a. G16 40c multicolored .25 —
b. A183 70c multicolored .50 —

35th anniv. of the UN.

ECOSOC Type and

Family Climbing Line Graph — G17

1980, Nov. 21 Litho. *Perf. 13½x13*
96 A186 40c multicolored .30 .25
97 G17 70c multicolored .60 .50

Palestinian Rights Type

1981, Jan. 30 Photo.
98 A188 80c multicolored .60 .60

Disabled Type of UN, Vienna

1981, Mar. 6 Photo.
99 A190 40c multicolored .25 .25
100 V4 1.50fr multicolored 1.00 1.00

Art Type

1981, Apr. 15 Photo. *Perf. 11½*
101 A191 80c multicolored .75 .60

Energy Type

1981, May 29 Litho. *Perf. 13*
102 A192 1.10fr multicolored .75 .75

Volunteers Program Type and Symbols of Science, Agriculture and Industry — G18

1981, Nov. 13 Litho. *Perf. 13½x13*
103 A194 40c multicolored .45 .30
104 G18 70c multicolored .90 .65

Fight Against Apartheid G19

Flower of Flags G20

1982, Jan. 22 Photo. *Perf. 11½x12*
105 G19 30c multicolored .25 .20
106 G20 1fr multicolored .80 .65

Human Environment — G21

1982, Mar. 19 Litho. *Perf. 13½x13*
107 G21 40c multicolored .30 .20
108 A199 1.20fr multicolored 1.25 1.00

Outer Space Type and

Satellite Applications of Space Technology G22

1982, June 11 Litho. *Perf. 13x13½*
109 A201 80c multicolored .60 .45
110 G22 1fr multicolored .75 .60

Conservation and Protection of Nature

1982, Nov. 19 Photo. *Perf. 14*
111 A202 40c Bird .45 .35
112 A202 1.50fr Reptile 1.10 .75

World Communications Year Type

1983, Jan. 28 Litho. *Perf. 13*
113 A204 1.20fr multicolored 1.25 1.00

Safety at Sea Type and

Life Preserver and Radar — G23

1983, Mar. 18 Litho. *Perf. 14½*
114 A205 40c multicolored .35 .35
115 G23 80c multicolored .75 .75

World Food Program Type

1983, Apr. 22 Engr. *Perf. 13½*
116 A207 1.50fr blue 1.25 1.00

Type of UN and

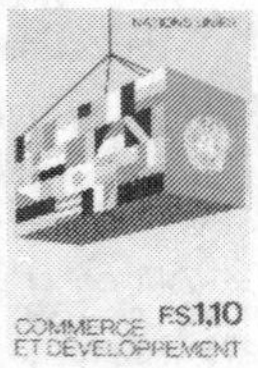

G24

1983, June 6 Litho. *Perf. 14*
117 A208 80c multicolored .50 .50
118 G24 1.10fr multicolored .90 .85

35th Anniv. of the Universal Declaration of Human Rights
G25 G26

Perf. 13½

1983, Dec. 9 Photo. Engr.
119 G25 40c Homo Humus Humanitas .45 .45
120 G26 1.20fr Right to Create .95 .90

Intl. Population Conference Type

1984, Feb. 3 Litho. *Perf. 14*
121 A212 1.20fr multicolored 1.00 .85

Fishing G27

Women Farm Workers, Africa G28

1984, Mar. 15 Litho. *Perf. 14½*
122 G27 50c multicolored .35 .30
123 G28 80c multicolored .65 .55

World Food Day.

Valletta, Malta — G29

Los Glaciares Natl. Park, Argentina G30

1984, Apr. 18 Litho. *Perf. 14*
124 G29 50c multicolored .55 .50
125 G30 70c multicolored .75 .70

World Heritage. See Nos. 211-212.

G31

G32

1984, May 29 Photo. *Perf. 11½*
126 G31 35c multicolored .35 .20
127 G32 1.50fr multicolored 1.25 .75

Refugees.

International Youth Year — G33

1984, Nov. 15 Litho. *Perf. 13½*
128 G33 1.20fr multicolored 1.25 1.00

ILO Type of UN and

Turin Center — G34

1985, Feb. 1 Engr.
129 A220 80c Turin Center emblem .60 .45
130 G34 1.20fr U Thant Pavilion .90 .70

UN University Type

1985, Mar. 15 Photo. *Perf. 13½*
131 A221 50c Farmer, discussion group .60 .45
132 A221 80c As above 1.00 .75

Postman G35

Doves — G36

1985, May 10 Litho. *Perf. 14*
133 G35 20c multicolored .25 .20
134 G36 1.20fr multicolored 1.40 1.00

40th Anniv. Type

1985, June 26 Photo. *Perf. 12x11½*
135 A224 50c multicolored .55 .35
136 A225 70c multicolored .80 .50

Souvenir Sheet

Imperf

137 Sheet of 2 2.25 1.10
a. A224 50c multicolored .75 —
b. A225 70c multicolored 1.00 —

UNICEF Child Survival Campaign

Photo. & Engr.

1985, Nov. 22 *Perf. 13½*
138 A226 50c Three girls *.40* .20
139 A226 1.20fr Infant drinking *1.00* .90

Africa in Crisis Type

Abstract painting by Alemayehou Gabremedhin.

1986, Jan. 31 Photo. *Perf. 11½*
140 A227 1.40fr Mother, hungry children 1.40 1.00

UN Development Program Type

1986, Mar. 14 Photo. *Perf. 13½*
141 A228 35c Erosion control 1.90 1.50
142 A228 35c Logging 1.90 1.50
143 A228 35c Lumber transport 1.90 1.50
144 A228 35c Nursery 1.90 1.50
a. Block of 4, #141-144 8.00 6.00

No. 144a has a continuous design.

Doves and Sun — G37

1986, Mar. 14 Litho. *Perf. 15x14½*
145 G37 5c multicolored .20 .20

UN Stamp Collecting Type

Designs: 50c, UN Human Rights stamp. 80c, UN stamps.

1986, May 22 Engr. *Perf. 12½*
146 A229 50c dk green & hn brn .60 .45
147 A229 80c dk green & yel org 1.00 .75

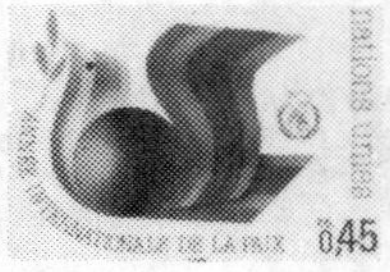

Flags and Globe as Dove — G38

Peace in French — G39

Photo. & Embossed

1986, June 20 *Perf. 13½*
148 G38 45c multicolored .60 .45
149 G39 1.40fr multicolored 1.65 1.25

Intl. Peace Year.

WFUNA Anniv. Type
Souvenir Sheet

Designs: 35c, Abstract by Benigno Gomez, Honduras. 45c, Abstract by Alexander Calder (1898-1976), US. 50c, Abstract by Joan Miro (b. 1893), Spain. 70c, Sextet with Dove, by Ole Hamann, Denmark.

1986, Nov. 14 Litho. *Perf. 13x13½*
150 Sheet of 4 4.25 2.00
a. A232 35c multicolored .55 —
b. A232 45c multicolored .75 —
c. A232 50c multicolored .95 —
d. A232 70c multicolored 1.25 —

Trygve Lie Type
Photo. & Engr.

1987, Jan. 30 *Perf. 13½*
151 A233 1.40fr multicolored 1.25 1.00

Sheaf of Colored Bands, by Georges Mathieu — G40

Armillary Sphere, Palais des Nations — G41

Photo., Photo. & Engr. (No. 153)
Perf. 11½x12, 13½ (No. 153)

1987, Jan. 30
152 G40 90c multicolored .75 .60
153 G41 1.40fr multicolored 1.25 .90

Perf. 13½x12½

1987, Mar. 13 Litho.
154 A234 50c Construction .60 .55
155 A234 90c Finishing interior 1.00 .90

Fight Drug Abuse Type

1987, June 12 Litho. *Perf. 14½*
156 A235 80c Mother and child .55 .55
157 A235 1.20fr Workers in rice paddy .95 .95

UN Day Type

Designs: Multinational people in various occupations.

1987, Oct. 23 Litho. *Perf. 14½x15*
158 A236 35c multicolored .45 .45
159 A236 50c multicolored .75 .75

Immunize Every Child Type

1987, Nov. 20 Litho. *Perf. 15x14½*
160 A237 90c Whooping cough 1.40 1.00
161 A237 1.70fr Tuberculosis 2.50 1.15

IFAD Type

1988, Jan. 29 Litho. *Perf. 13½*
162 A238 35c Flocks .40 .35
163 A238 1.40fr Fruit 1.65 1.40

G42

1988, Jan. 29 Photo. *Perf. 14*
164 G42 50c multicolored .80 .70

Survival of the Forests Type

1988, Mar. 18 Litho. *Perf. 14x15*
165 A240 50c Pine forest *1.50* 1.25
166 A240 1.10fr as 50c *4.00* 3.50
a. Pair, #165-166 *5.50* 5.00

No. 166a has a continuous design.

Intl. Volunteer Day Type
Perf. 13x14, 14x13

1988, May 6 Litho.
167 A241 80c Agriculture, vert. .95 .60
168 A241 90c Veterinary medicine 1.00 .70

Health in Sports Type
Perf. 13½x13, 13x13½

1988, June 17 Litho.
169 A242 50c Soccer, vert. .50 .40
170 A242 1.40fr Swimming 1.50 1.25

Human Rights Declaration Anniv. Type
Photo. & Engr.

1988, Dec. 9 *Perf. 12*
171 A243 90c multicolored .75 .60

Souvenir Sheet
172 A243 2fr multicolored 3.00 2.50

World Bank Type

1989, Jan. 27 Litho. *Perf. 13x14*
173 A244 80c Telecommunications 1.00 .75
174 A244 1.40fr Industry 2.25 1.75

Peace-Keeping Force Type

1989, Mar. 17 Litho. *Perf. 14x13½*
175 A245 90c multicolored 1.00 1.00

World Weather Watch Anniv. Type

Satellite photographs: 90c, Europe under the influence of Arctic air. 1.10fr, Surface temperatures of sea, ice and land surrounding the Kattegat between Denmark and Sweden.

1989, Apr. 21 Litho. *Perf. 13x14*
176 A247 90c multicolored 1.25 1.00
177 A247 1.10fr multicolored 2.00 1.50

G43

G44

Photo. & Engr., Photo.

1989, Aug. 23 *Perf. 14*
178 G43 50c multicolored 1.10 .70
179 G44 2fr multicolored 3.50 2.50

Offices in Vienna, 10th anniv.

Human Rights Type of 1989

Paintings and sculpture: 35c, *Young Mother Sewing,* by Mary Cassatt. 80c, *The Unknown Slave,* sculpture by Albert Mangones.

1989, Nov. 17 Litho. *Perf. 13½*
180 A250 35c multicolored .40 .40
181 A250 80c multicolored 1.10 1.10

Printed in sheets of 12+12 se-tenant labels containing Articles 3 (35c) or 4 (80c) inscribed in French, German or English.

Intl. Trade Center Type

1990, Feb. 2 Litho. *Perf. 14½x15*
182 A251 1.50fr multicolored 2.50 2.00

G45

1990, Feb. 2 Photo. *Perf. 14x13½*
183 G45 5fr multicolored 4.50 4.00

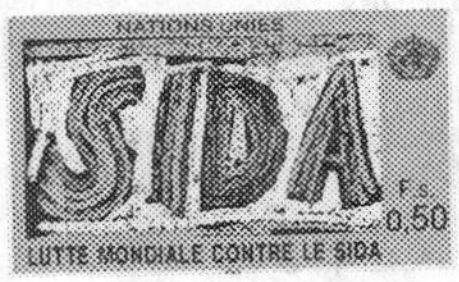

G46

Fight AIDS Worldwide G46a

Perf. 13½x12½

1990, Mar. 16 Litho.
184 G46 50c multicolored 1.10 1.00
185 G46a 80c multicolored 1.75 .50

Medicinal Plants Type

1990, May 4 Photo. *Perf. 11½*
Granite Paper
186 A253 90c *Plumeria rubra* 1.25 .70
187 A253 1.40fr *Cinchona officinalis* 2.25 1.50

UN 45th Anniv. Type

"45," emblem and: 90c, Symbols of clean environment, transportation and industry. 1.10fr, Dove in silhouette.

1990, June 26 Litho. *Perf. 14½x13*
188 A254 90c multicolored 1.25 .45
189 A254 1.10fr multicolored 2.25 1.50

Souvenir Sheet
190 A254 Sheet of 2, #188-189 5.75 2.75

Crime Prevention Type

1990, Sept. 13 Photo. *Perf. 14*
191 A255 50c Official corruption 1.25 .80
192 A255 2fr Environmental crime 3.50 2.75

Human Rights Type of 1989

Paintings: 35c, The Prison Courtyard by Vincent Van Gogh. 90c, Katho's Son Redeems the Evil Doer From Execution by Albrecht Durer.

1990, Nov. 16 Litho. *Perf. 13½*
193 A250 35c multicolored .55 .25
194 A250 90c black & brown 1.50 .65

Printed in sheets of 12+12 se-tenant labels containing Articles 9 (35c) or 10 (90c) inscribed in French, German or English.

Economic Commission for Europe Type

1991, Mar. 15 Litho. *Perf. 14*
195 A256 90c Owl, gull 1.40 .75
196 A256 90c Bittern, otter 1.40 .75
197 A256 90c Swan, lizard 1.40 .75
198 A256 90c Great crested grebe 1.40 .75
a. Block of 4, #195-198 5.75 3.50

Namibian Independence Type

1991, May 10 Litho. *Perf. 14*
199 A257 70c Mountains 1.25 1.00
200 A257 90c Baobab tree 2.25 1.75

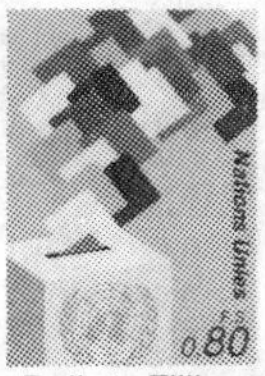

Ballots Filling Ballot Box — G47

UN Emblem — G48

1991, May 10 Litho. *Perf. 15x14½*
201 G47 80c multicolored 1.50 1.10
202 G48 1.50fr multicolored 3.00 2.25

G49

Rights of the Child G50

1991, June 14 Litho. *Perf. 14½*
203 G49 80c Hands holding infant 1.50 1.00
204 G50 1.10fr Children, flowers 2.00 1.50

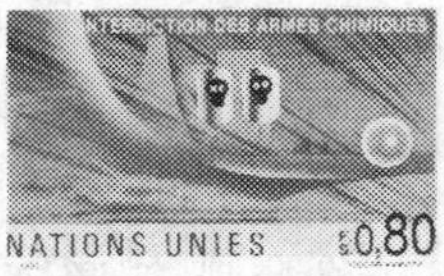

G51

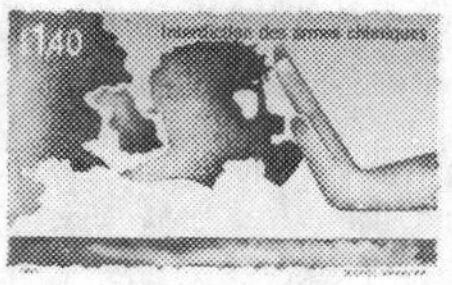

Banning of Chemical Weapons G52

1991, Sept. 11 Litho. *Perf. 13½*
205 G51 80c multicolored 1.75 1.25
206 G52 1.40fr multicolored 3.25 2.00

UN Postal Administration, 40th Anniv. Type

1991, Oct. 24 Litho. *Perf. 14x15*
207 A263 50c UN NY #7 .90 .70
208 A263 1.60fr UN NY #10 2.50 2.00

Human Rights Type of 1989

Artwork: 50c, Early Morning in Ro...1925, by Paul Klee. 90c, The Marriage of Giovanni Arnolfini and Fiovanna Cenami, by Jan Van Eyck.

1991, Nov. 20 Litho. *Perf. 13½*
209 A250 50c multicolored .85 .70
210 A250 90c multicolored 1.50 1.25

Printed in sheets of 12+12 se-tenant labels containing Articles 15 (50c) and 16 (90c) inscribed in French, German or English.

World Heritage Type of 1984

Designs: 50c, Sagarmatha Natl. Park, Nepal. 1.10fr, Stonehenge, United Kingdom.

1992, Jan. 24 Litho. *Perf. 13*
Size: 35x28mm
211 G29 50c multicolored 1.25 1.00
212 G29 1.10fr multicolored 2.50 1.65

G53

1992, Jan. 24 *Perf. 15x14½*
213 G53 3fr multicolored 3.50 3.00

Clean Oceans Type

1992, Mar. 13 Litho. *Perf. 14*
214 A264 80c Ocean surface, diff. 1.00 .75
215 A264 80c Ocean bottom, diff. 1.00 .75
a. Pair, #214-215 2.00 1.75

Printed in sheets of 12 containing 6 #215a.

Earth Summit Type

Designs: No. 216, Rainbow. No. 217, Faces shaped as clouds. No. 218, Two sailboats. No. 219, Woman with parasol, sailboat, flowers.

1992, May 22 Photo. *Perf. 11½*
216 A265 75c multicolored 1.10 .75
217 A265 75c multicolored 1.10 .75
218 A265 75c multicolored 1.10 .75
219 A265 75c multicolored 1.10 .75
a. Block of 4, #216-219 4.50 3.00

Mission to Planet Earth Type

Designs: No. 220, Space station. No. 221, Probes near Jupiter.

1992, Sept. 4 Photo. *Rouletted 8*
Granite Paper
220 A266 1.10fr multicolored 2.50 2.00
221 A266 1.10fr multicolored 2.50 2.00
a. Pair, #220-221 5.00 4.00

Science and Technology Type

Designs: 90c, Doctor, nurse. 1.60fr, Graduate seated before computer.

1992, Oct. 2 Litho. *Perf. 14*
222 A267 90c multicolored 1.50 .90
223 A267 1.60fr multicolored 2.50 1.75

Human Rights Type of 1989

Artwork: 50c, The Oath of the Tennis Court, by Jacques Louis David. 90c, Rocking Chair I, by Henry Moore.

1992, Nov. 20 Litho. *Perf. 13½*
224 A250 50c multicolored 1.00 .90
225 A250 90c multicolored 1.75 1.50

Printed in sheets of 12+12 se-tenant labels containing Articles 21 (50c) and 22 (90c) inscribed in French, German or English.

Aging With Dignity Type

Designs: 50c, Older man coaching soccer. 1.50fr, Older man working at computer terminal.

1993, Feb. 5 Litho. *Perf. 13*
226 A270 50c multicolored .80 .60
227 A270 1.50fr multicolored 2.50 1.75

Endangered Species Type

Designs: No. 228, Pongidae (gorilla). No. 229, Falco peregrinus (peregrine falcon). No. 230, Trichechus inunguis (Amazonian manatee). No. 231, Panthera uncia (snow leopard).

1993, Mar. 3 Litho. *Perf. 13x12½*
228 A271 80c multicolored 1.10 .90
229 A271 80c multicolored 1.10 .90
230 A271 80c multicolored 1.10 .90
231 A271 80c multicolored 1.10 .90
a. Block of 4, #228-231 4.50 4.00

Healthy Environment Type

1993, May 7 Litho. *Perf. 15x14½*
232 A272 60c Neighborhood 1.10 .70
233 A272 1fr Urban skyscrapers 2.50 1.50

Human Rights Type of 1989

Artwork: 50c, Three Musicians, by Pablo Picasso. 90c, Voice of Space, by Rene Magritte.

1993, June 11 Litho. *Perf. 13½*
234 A250 50c multicolored .75 .75
235 A250 90c multicolored 1.75 1.75

Printed in sheets of 12 + 12 se-tenant labels containing Article 27 (50c) and 28 (90c) inscribed in French, German or English.

Intl. Peace Day Type

Denomination at: No. 236, UL. No. 237, UR. No. 238, LL. No. 239, LR.

Rouletted 12½
1993, Sept. 21 Litho. & Engr.
236 A274 60c purple & multi 2.00 .90
237 A274 60c purple & multi 2.00 .90
238 A274 60c purple & multi 2.00 .90
239 A274 60c purple & multi 2.00 .90
a. Block of 4, #236-239 8.25 3.75

Environment-Climate Type

Designs: No. 240, Polar bears. No. 241, Whale sounding. No. 242, Elephant seal. No. 243, Penguins.

1993, Oct. 29 Litho. *Perf. 14½*
240 A275 1.10fr multicolored 1.50 1.25
241 A275 1.10fr multicolored 1.50 1.25
242 A275 1.10fr multicolored 1.50 1.25
243 A275 1.10fr multicolored 1.50 1.25
a. Strip of 4, #240-243 6.00 5.00

Intl. Year of the Family Type of 1993

Designs: 80c, Parents teaching child to walk. 1fr, Two women and child picking plants.

1994, Feb. 4 Litho. *Perf. 13.1*
244 A276 80c rose violet & multi 1.40 1.00
245 A276 1fr brown & multi 1.75 1.25

Endangered Species Type of 1993

Designs: No. 246, Mexican prairie dog. No. 247, Jabiru. No. 248, Blue whale. No. 249, Golden lion tamarin.

1994, Mar. 18 Litho. *Perf. 12.7*
246 A271 80c multicolored 1.10 .85
247 A271 80c multicolored 1.10 .85
248 A271 80c multicolored 1.10 .85
249 A271 80c multicolored 1.10 .85
a. Block of 4, #246-249 4.50 3.50

Protection for Refugees Type of 1994

Design: 1.20fr, Hand lifting figure over chasm.

Perf. 14.3x14.8
1994, Apr. 29 Litho.
250 A277 1.20fr multicolored 2.75 2.25

Intl. Decade for Natural Disaster Reduction Type of 1994

Earth seen from space, outline map of: No. 251, North America. No. 252, Eurasia. No. 253, South America. No. 254, Australia and South Pacific region.

1994, May 27 Litho. *Perf. 13.9x14.2*
251 A281 60c multicolored 1.50 .50
252 A281 60c multicolored 1.50 .50
253 A281 60c multicolored 1.50 .50
254 A281 60c multicolored 1.50 .50
a. Block of 4, #251-254 6.50 2.00

Palais des Nations, Geneva G54

Creation of the World, by Oili Maki — G55

1994, Sept. 1 Litho. *Perf. 14.3x14.6*
255 G54 60c multicolored .75 .55
256 G55 80c multicolored 1.00 .70
257 G54 1.80fr multi, diff. 2.25 1.75

Population and Development Type of 1994

Designs: 60c, People shopping at open-air market. 80c, People on vacation crossing bridge.

1994, Sept. 1 Litho. *Perf. 13.2x13.6*
258 A282 60c multicolored 1.25 .70
259 A282 80c multicolored 1.75 1.00

UNCTAD Type of 1994

1994, Oct. 28
260 A283 80c multi, diff. 1.25 1.00
261 A283 1fr multi, diff. 1.65 1.40
a. Grayish green omitted —

UN 50th Anniv. Type of 1995

Litho. & Engr.
1995, Jan. 1 *Perf. 13.4*
262 A284 80c multicolored 1.40 1.25

Social Summit Type of 1995

Photo. & Engr.
1995, Feb. 3 *Perf. 13.6x13.9*
263 A285 1fr multi, diff. 1.50 1.25

Endangered Species Type of 1993

Designs: No. 264, Crowned lemur, Lemur coronatus. No. 265, Giant Scops owl, Otus gurneyi. No. 266, Zetek's frog, Atelopus varius zeteki. No. 267, Wood bison, Bison bison athabascae.

1995, Mar. 24 Litho. *Perf. 13x12½*
264 A271 80c multicolored 1.40 1.10
265 A271 80c multicolored 1.40 1.10
266 A271 80c multicolored 1.40 1.10
267 A271 80c multicolored 1.40 1.10
a. Block of 4, 264-267 5.75 4.50

Intl. Youth Year Type of 1995

Designs: 80c, Farmer on tractor, fields at harvest time. 1fr, Couple standing by fields at night.

1995, May 26 Litho. *Perf. 14.4x14.7*
268 A286 80c multicolored 1.40 1.10
269 A286 1fr multicolored 1.75 1.40

UN, 50th Anniv. Type of 1995

Designs: 60c, Like No. 663. 1.80fr, Like No. 664.

Perf. 13.3x13.6
1995, June 26 Engr.
270 A287 60c maroon 1.00 .60
271 A287 1.80fr green 3.25 1.75

Souvenir Sheet
Litho. & Engr.
Imperf
272 Sheet of 2, #270-271 4.25 4.25
a. A287 60c maroon 1.00 1.00
b. A287 1.80fr green 3.25 3.25

Conference on Women Type of 1995

Designs: 60c, Black woman, cranes flying above. 1fr, Women, dove.

1995, Sept. 5 Photo. *Perf. 12*
273 A288 60c multicolored 1.50 .50

Size: 28x50mm
274 A288 1fr multicolored 2.50 .85

UN People, 50th Anniv. Type of 1995

1995, Oct. 24 Litho. *Perf. 14*
275 Sheet of 12 14.00 9.00
a.-l. A290 30c any single 1.10 .70
276 Souvenir booklet 15.00
a. A290 30c Booklet pane of 3, vert. strip of 3 from UL of sheet 3.50 3.50
b. A290 30c Booklet pane of 3, vert. strip of 3 from UR of sheet 3.50 3.50
c. A290 30c Booklet pane of 3, vert. strip of 3 from LL of sheet 3.50 3.50
d. A290 30c Booklet pane of 3, vert. strip of 3 from LR of sheet 3.50 3.50

WFUNA, 50th Anniv. Type of 1996

1996, Feb. 2 Litho. *Perf. 13x13½*
277 A291 80c multicolored 1.50 .65

The Galloping Horse Treading on a Flying Swallow, Chinese Bronzework, Eastern Han Dynasty (25-220 A.D.) — G56

Palais des Nations, Geneva G57

1996, Feb. 2 Litho. *Perf. 14½x15*
278 G56 40c multicolored .65 .30
279 G57 70c multicolored 1.10 .55

Endangered Species Type of 1993

Designs: No. 280, Paphiopedilum delenatii. No. 281, Pachypodium baronii. No. 282, Sternbergia lutea. No. 283, Darlingtonia californica.

1996, Mar. 14 Litho. *Perf. 12½*
280 A271 80c multicolored 1.10 .65
281 A271 80c multicolored 1.10 .65
282 A271 80c multicolored 1.10 .65
283 A271 80c multicolored 1.10 .65
a. Block of 4, #280-283 4.50 —

City Summit Type of 1996

Designs: No. 284, Asian family. No. 285, Oriental garden. No. 286, Fruit, vegetable vendor, mosque. No. 287, Boys playing ball. No. 288, Couple reading newspaper.

1996, June 3 Litho. *Perf. 14x13½*
284 A293 70c multicolored .90 .30
285 A293 70c multicolored .90 .30
286 A293 70c multicolored .90 .30
287 A293 70c multicolored .90 .30
288 A293 70c multicolored .90 .30
a. Strip of 5, #284-288 4.50 —

Sport and the Environment Type of 1996

Designs: 70c, Cycling, vert. 1.10fr, Sprinters.

Perf. 14x14½, 14½x14
1996, July 19 Litho.
289 A294 70c multicolored 1.25 .55
290 A294 1.10fr multicolored 1.75 .85

Souvenir Sheet
291 A294 Sheet of 2, #289-290 3.00 2.85

Plea for Peace Type of 1996

Designs: 90c, Tree filled with birds, vert. 1.10fr, Bouquet of flowers in rocket tail vase, vert.

1996, Sept. 17 Litho. *Perf. 15x14½*
292 A295 90c multicolored 1.40 .70
293 A295 1.10fr multicolored 1.75 .85

UNICEF Type of 1996

Fairy Tales: 70c, The Sun and the Moon, South America. 1.80fr, Ananse, Africa.

1996, Nov. 20 Litho. *Perf. 14½x15*
294 A296 70c multicolored 1.00 .55
295 A296 1.80fr multicolored 2.50 1.40

Panes of 8 + label.

UN Flag — G58

Palais des Nations Under Construction, by Massimo Campigli G59

1997, Feb. 12 Litho. *Perf. 14½*
296 G58 10c multicolored .20 .20
297 G59 1.10fr multicolored 1.50 .75

Endangered Species Type of 1993

Designs: No. 298, Ursus maritimus (polar bear). No. 299, Goura cristata (blue-crowned pigeon). No. 300, Amblyrhynchus cristatus (marine iguana). No. 703, Lama guanicoe (guanaco).

1997, Mar. 13 Litho. *Perf. 12½*
298 A271 80c multicolored 1.10 .55
299 A271 80c multicolored 1.10 .55
300 A271 80c multicolored 1.10 .55
301 A271 80c multicolored 1.10 .55
a. Block of 4, #298-301 4.50 2.25

Earth Summit Anniv. Type of 1997

Designs: No. 302, Person flying over mountain. No. 303, Mountain, person's face. No. 304, Person standing on mountain, sailboats. No. 305, Person, mountain, trees.

1.10fr, Combined design similar to Nos. 302-305.

1997, May 30 Photo. *Perf. 11.5*
Granite Paper
302 A299 45c multicolored .75 .30
303 A299 45c multicolored .75 .30
304 A299 45c multicolored .75 .30
305 A299 45c multicolored .75 .30
a. Block of 4, #302-305 3.00 1.20

Souvenir Sheet
306 A299 1.10fr multicolored 1.50 1.50

Transportation Type of 1997

Air transportation: No. 307, Zeppelin, Fokker tri-motor. No. 308, Boeing 314 Clipper, Lockheed Constellation. No. 309, DeHavilland Comet. No. 310, Boeing 747, Illyushin jet. No. 311, Concorde.

1997, Aug. 29 Litho. *Perf. 14x14½*
307 A300 70c multicolored 1.00 .50
308 A300 70c multicolored 1.00 .50
309 A300 70c multicolored 1.00 .50
310 A300 70c multicolored 1.00 .50
311 A300 70c multicolored 1.00 .50
a. Strip of 5, #307-311 5.00 2.50

No. 311a has continuous design.

Philately Type of 1997

Designs: 70c, No. 146. 1.10fr, No. 147.

1997, Oct. 14 Litho. *Perf. 13½x14*
312 A301 70c multicolored 1.00 .50
313 A301 1.10fr multicolored 1.50 .75

World Heritage Convention Type of 1997

Terracotta warriors of Xian: 45c, Single warrior. 70c, Massed warriors. No. 316a, like #716. No. 316b, like #717. No. 316c, like Geneva #314. No. 316d, like Geneva #315. No. 316e, like Vienna #230. No. 316f, like Vienna #231.

1997, Nov. 19 Litho. *Perf. 13½*
314 A302 45c multicolored .60 .30
315 A302 70c multicolored 1.00 .50
316 Souvenir booklet 3.75
a.-f. A302 10c any single .20 .20
g. Booklet pane of 4 #316a .60 .60
h. Booklet pane of 4 #316b .60 .60
i. Booklet pane of 4 #316c .60 .60
j. Booklet pane of 4 #316d .60 .60
k. Booklet pane of 4 #316e .60 .60
l. Booklet pane of 4 #316f .60 .60

Palais des Nations, Geneva G60

1998, Feb. 13 Litho. *Perf. 14½x15*
317 G60 2fr multicolored 2.75 1.40

Endangered Species Type of 1993

Designs: No. 318, Macaca thibetana (short-tailed Tibetan macaque). No. 319, Phoenicopterus ruber (Caribbean flamingo). No. 320, Ornithoptera alexandrae (Queen Alexandra's birdwing). No. 321, Dama mesopotamica (Persian fallow deer).

1998, Mar. 13 Litho. *Perf. 12½*
318 A271 80c multicolored 1.10 .55
319 A271 80c multicolored 1.10 .55
320 A271 80c multicolored 1.10 .55
321 A271 80c multicolored 1.10 .55
a. Block of 4, #318-321 4.50 2.25

Intl. Year of the Ocean — G61

1998, May 20 Litho. *Perf. 13x13½*
322 G61 Sheet of 12 8.00 4.50
a.-l. 45c any single .65 .35

Rain Forests Type of 1998

1998, June 19 *Perf. 13x13½*
323 A307 70c Orangutans 1.00 .50

Souvenir Sheet

324 A307 3fr like #323 4.00 2.00

Peacekeeping Type of 1998

Designs: 70c, Soldier with two children. 90c, Two soldiers, children.

1998, Sept. 15 Photo. *Perf. 12*
325 A308 70c multicolored 1.00 .50
326 A308 90c multicolored 1.40 .70

Declaration of Human Rights Type of 1998

Designs: 90c, Stylized birds. 1.80fr, Stylized birds flying from hand.

Litho. & Photo.

1998, Oct. 27 *Perf. 13*
327 A309 90c multicolored 1.40 .70
328 A309 1.80fr multicolored 2.75 1.40

Schönnbrun Palace Type of 1998

Designs: 70c, #331b, Great Palm House. 1.10fr, #331d, Blue porcelain vase, vert. No. 331a, Palace. No. 331c, The Gloriette (archway). No. 331e, Wall painting on fabric (detail), by Johann Wenzl Bergl, vert. No. 331f, Porcelain stove, vert.

1998, Dec. 4 Litho. *Perf. 14*
329 A310 70c multicolored 1.00 .50
330 A310 1.10fr multicolored 1.50 .75
331 Souvenir booklet 6.00
a.-c. A310 10c any single .20 .20
d.-f. A310 30c any single .45 .45
g. Booklet pane, 4 #331a .60
h. Booklet pane, 3 #331d 1.40
i. Booklet pane, 3 #331e 1.40
j. Booklet pane, 3 #331f 1.40
k. Booklet pane, 4 #331b .60
l. Booklet pane, 4 #331c .60

Palais Wilson, Geneva G62

1999, Feb. 5 Photo. *Perf. 11½*

Granite Paper

332 G62 1.70fr brown red 2.50 1.25

World Heritage, Australia Type of 1999

90c, #335e, Kakadu Natl. Park. 1.10fr, #335c, Great Barrier Reef. #335a, Tasmanian Wilderness. #335b, Wet tropics of Queensland. #335d, Uluru-Kata Tjuta Natl. Park. #335f, Willandra Lakes region.

1999, Mar. 19 Litho. *Perf. 13*
333 A313 90c multicolored 1.40 .70
334 A313 1.10fr multicolored 1.50 .75
335 Souvenir booklet 5.50
a.-c. A313 10c any single .20 .20
d.-f. A313 20c any single .35 .35
g. Booklet pane of 4, #335a .40
h. Booklet pane of 4, #335d 1.40
i. Booklet pane of 4, #335b .40
j. Booklet pane of 4, #335e 1.40
k. Booklet pane of 4, #335c .40
l. Booklet pane of 4, #335f 1.40

Endangered Specied Type of 1993

Designs: No. 336, Equus hemionus (Asiatic wild ass). No. 337, Anodorhynchus hyacinthinus (hyacinth macaw). No. 338, Epicrates subflavus (Jamaican boa). No. 339, Dendrolagus bennettianus (Bennetts' tree kangaroo).

1999, Apr. 22 Litho. *Perf. 12½*
336 A271 90c multicolored 1.40 .70
337 A271 90c multicolored 1.40 .70
338 A271 90c multicolored 1.40 .70
339 A271 90c multicolored 1.40 .70
a. Block of 4, #336-339 5.75

UNISPACE III Type

No. 340, Farm, satellite dish. No. 341, City, satellite in orbit. No. 342, Composite of #340-341.

1999, July 7 Photo. *Rouletted 8*
340 A314 45c multicolored .60 .30
341 A314 45c multicolored .60 .30
a. Pair, #340-341 1.25 .60

Souvenir Sheet

Perf. 14½

342 A314 2fr multicolored 2.75 1.40
a. Ovptd. in sheet margin 2.75 1.40

No. 342a is overprinted in violet blue "PHILEXFRANCE 99 / LE MONDIAL DU TIMBRE / PARIS / 2 AU 11 JUILLET 1999."

UPU Type

Various people, early 20th century methods of mail transportation, denomination at: No. 343, UL. No. 344, UR. No. 345, LL. No. 346, LR.

1999, Aug. 23 Photo. *Perf. 11¾*
343 A315 70c multicolored 1.00 .50
344 A315 70c multicolored 1.00 .50
345 A315 70c multicolored 1.00 .50
346 A315 70c multicolored 1.00 .50
a. Block of 4, #343-346 4.00 —

In Memoriam Type

Armillary sphere, Palais de Nations. Size of 2fr stamp: 34x63mm.

1999, Sept. 21 Litho. *Perf. 14½x14*
347 A316 1.10fr multicolored 1.60 .80

Souvenir Sheet

Perf. 14

348 A316 2fr multicolored 3.00 1.50

Education Type

Perf. 13½x13¾

1999, Nov. 18 Litho.
349 A317 90c Rainbow over globe 1.40 .70
350 A317 1.80fr Fish, tree, globe, book 2.60 1.25

OFFICES IN VIENNA, AUSTRIA

For use only on mail posted at the Vienna International Center for the UN and the International Atomic Energy Agency.

100 Groschen = 1 Schilling

Type of Geneva 1978, UN Types of 1961-72 and

Donaupark, Vienna — V1

Aerial View — V2

Perf. 11½

1979, Aug. 24 Photo. Unwmk.

Granite Paper

1 G8 50g multicolored .20 .20
2 A52 1s multicolored .20 .20
3 V1 4s multicolored .20 .20
4 AP13 5s multicolored .25 .25
5 V2 6s multicolored .35 .30
6 A45 10s multicolored .50 .45
Nos. 1-6 (6) 1.70 1.60

No. 6 has no frame.

Economic Order Type

1980, Jan. 11 Litho. *Perf. 15x14½*
7 A178 4s multicolored .70 .50

Dove Type

1980, Jan. 11 Litho. *Perf. 13x13½*
8 A147 2.50s multicolored .30 .20

Women's Year Emblem on World Map — V3

1980, Mar. 7 Litho. *Perf. 14½x15*
9 V3 4s lt green & dk green .40 .25
10 V3 6s bister brown .65 .45

UN Decade for Women.

Peace-keeping Operations Type

1980, May 16 Litho. *Perf. 14x13*
11 A182 6s multicolored .50 .50

35th Anniv. Types of Geneva and UN

1980, June 26 Litho. *Perf. 13*
12 G16 4s multicolored .40 .25
13 A184 6s multicolored .70 .45

Souvenir Sheet

Imperf

14 Sheet of 2 .55 .55
a. G16 4s multicolored .20 —
b. A184 6s multicolored .35 —

35th anniv. of the UN.

ECOSOC Types of UN and Geneva

1980, Nov. 21 Litho. *Perf. 13½x13*
15 A187 4s multicolored .30 .20
16 G17 6s multicolored .60 .20

Palestinian Rights Type

1981, Jan. 30 Photo.
17 A188 4s multicolored .45 .45

Disabled Type of UN and

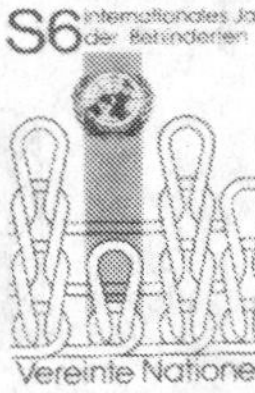

Interlocking Stitches — V4

1981, Mar. 6 Photo.
18 A189 4s multicolored .40 .35
19 V4 6s multicolored .60 .50

Art Type

1981, Apr. 15 Photo. *Perf. 11½*
20 A191 6s multicolored .75 .50

Energy Type

1981, May 29 Litho. *Perf. 13*
21 A193 7.50s multicolored .70 .50

Volunteers Program Types of UN and Geneva

1981, Nov. 13 Litho. *Perf. 13½x13*
22 A195 5s multicolored .55 .35
23 G18 7s multicolored 1.10 .65

"For a Better World" — V5

1982, Jan. 22 Photo. *Perf. 11½x12*
24 V5 3s multicolored .35 .20

Human Environment Types of UN and Geneva

1982, Mar. 19 Litho. *Perf. 13½x13*
25 A200 5s multicolored .45 .40
26 G21 7s multicolored .90 .55

Outer Space Type of Geneva

1982, June 11 Litho. *Perf. 13x13½*
27 G22 5s multicolored .70 .60

Conservation and Protection of Nature Type

1982, Nov. 19 Photo. *Perf. 14*
28 A202 5s Fish .50 .40
29 A202 7s Animal .70 .60

World Communications Year Type

1983, Jan. 28 Litho. *Perf. 13*
30 A203 4s multicolored .40 .40

Safety at Sea Types of Geneva and UN

1983, Mar. 18 Litho. *Perf. 14½*
31 G23 4s multicolored .45 .30
32 A206 6s multicolored .65 .55

World Food Program Type

1983, Apr. 22 Engr. *Perf. 13½*
33 A207 5s green .50 .35
34 A207 7s brown .70 .55

Trade and Development Types of Geneva and UN

1983, June 6 Litho. *Perf. 14*
35 G24 4s multicolored .45 .25
36 A209 8.50s multicolored .75 .65

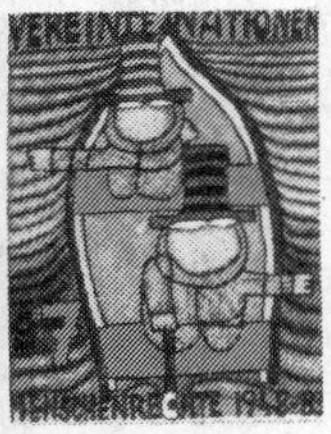

35th Anniv. of the Universal Declaration of Human Rights
V6 V7

Photogravure and Engraved

1983, Dec. 9 *Perf. 13½*
37 V6 5s The Second Skin .50 .40
38 V7 7s Right to Think .75 .70

Intl. Population Conference Type

1984, Feb. 3 Litho. *Perf. 14*
39 A212 7s multicolored .65 .50

Field Irrigation V8

Pest Control V9

1984, Mar. 15 Litho. *Perf. 14½*
40 V8 4.50s multicolored .50 .40
41 V9 6s multicolored .70 .60

World Food Day.

Serengeti Park, Tanzania V10

Ancient City of Shiban, People's Democratic Rep. of Yemen — V11

1984, Apr. 18 Litho. *Perf. 14*
42 V10 3.50s multicolored .30 .25
43 V11 15s multicolored 1.40 1.00

World Heritage. See Nos. 125-126.

V12

V13

1984, May 29 Photo. *Perf. 11½*
44 V12 4.50s multicolored .55 .45
45 V13 8.50s multicolored 1.40 .85

Refugees.

International Youth Year — V14

1984, Nov. 15 Litho. *Perf. 13½*
46 V14 3.50s multicolored .50 .40
47 V14 6.50s multicolored .80 .65

ILO Type of Geneva

1985, Feb. 1 Engr. *Perf. 13½*
48 G34 7.50s U Thant Pavilion .85 .65

UN University Type

1985, Mar. 15 Photo. *Perf. 13½*
49 A221 8.50s Rural scene, scientist 1.00 .80

Ship of Peace V15

Sharing Umbrella V16

1985, May 10 Litho. *Perf. 14*
50 V15 4.50s multicolored .35 .30
51 V16 15s multicolored 2.50 2.25

40th Anniv. Type

1985, June 26 Photo. *Perf. 12x11½*
52 A224 6.50s multicolored 1.00 .55
53 A225 8.50s multicolored 1.50 1.00

Souvenir Sheet

Imperf

54 Sheet of 2 3.00 2.00
a. A224 6.50s multicolored .70 .60
b. A225 8.50s multicolored .90 .75

UNICEF Child Survival Campaign

Photogravure and Engraved

1985, Nov. 22 *Perf. 13½*
55 A226 4s Spoonfeeding children .90 .65
56 A226 6s Mother hugging infant 1.50 1.25

Africa in Crisis Type

Abstract painting by Tesfaye Tessema.

1986, Jan. 31 Photo. *Perf. 11½*
57 A227 8s multicolored .85 .70

UN Development Program Type

1986, Mar. 14 Photo. *Perf. 13½*
58 A228 4.50s Developing crop strains 1.65 .25
59 A228 4.50s Animal husbandry 1.65 .25
60 A228 4.50s Technical instruction 1.65 .25
61 A228 4.50s Nutrition education 1.65 .25
a. Block of 4, #58-61 6.75 1.00

No. 61a has a continuous design.

UN Stamp Collecting Type

Designs: 3.50s, UN stamps. 6.50s, Engraver.

1986, May 22 Engr. *Perf. 12½*
62 A229 3.50s dk ultra & dk brown .45 .35
63 A229 6.50s int blue & brt rose .90 .85

Olive Branch, Rainbow, Earth — V17

Photogravure and Embossed

1986, June 20 *Perf. 13½*
64 V17 5s shown .90 .60
65 V17 6s Doves, UN emblem 1.10 .70

Intl. Peace Year.

WFUNA Anniv. Type

Souvenir Sheet

Designs: 4c, White Stallion, by Elisabeth von Janota-Bzowski, Germany. 5s, Surrealistic landscape by Ernst Fuchs, Austria. 6s, Geometric abstract by Victor Vasarely (b. 1908), France. 7s, Mythological abstract by Wolfgang Hutter (b. 1928), Austria.

1986, Nov. 14 Litho. *Perf. 13x13½*
66 Sheet of 4 4.25 4.00
a. A232 4s multicolored .75 .60
b. A232 5s multicolored .85 .70
c. A232 6s multicolored 1.00 .80
d. A232 7s multicolored 1.25 1.00

Trygve Lie Type

Photogravure and Engraved

1987, Jan. 30 *Perf. 13½*
67 A233 8s multicolored .90 .75

Shelter for the Homeless Type

Perf. 13½x12½

1987, Mar. 13 Litho.
68 A234 4s Family, homes .55 .40
69 A234 9.50s Entering home 1.25 1.10

Fight Drug Abuse Type

1987, June 12 Litho. *Perf. 14½x15*
70 A235 5s Soccer players .65 .50
71 A235 8s Family 1.00 .85

Donaupark, Vienna V18

Peace Embracing the Earth — V19

1987, June 12 *Perf. 14½x15*
72 V18 2s multicolored .30 .25
73 V19 17s multicolored 1.75 1.50

UN Day Type

1987, Oct. 23 Litho. *Perf. 14½x15*
74 A236 5s multicolored .85 .65
75 A236 6s multicolored 1.00 1.00

Immunize Every Child Type

1987, Nov. 20 *Perf. 15x14½*
76 A237 4s Polio .90 .35
77 A237 9.50s Diphtheria 2.00 .75

IFAD Type

1988, Jan. 29 Litho. *Perf. 13½*
78 A238 4s Grains .75 .55
79 A238 6s Vegetables 1.10 .90

Survival of the Forests Type

Deciduous forest in fall.

1988, Mar. 18 Litho. *Perf. 14x15*
80 A240 4s multicolored *2.50* 2.25
81 A240 5s multicolored *3.50* 3.25
a. Pair, #80-81 *6.00* 6.00

No. 81a has a continuous design.

Intl. Volunteer Day Type

Perf. 13x14, 14x13

1988, May 6 Litho.
82 A241 6s Medical care, vert. .85 .70
83 A241 7.50s Construction 1.25 1.10

Health in Sports Type

Perf. 13½x13, 13x13½

1988, June 17 Litho.
84 A242 6s Skiing, vert. .85 .70
85 A242 8s Tennis 1.40 1.25

Human Rights Declaration Anniv. Type

Photo. & Engr.

1988, Dec. 9 *Perf. 12*
86 A243 5s multicolored .75 .65

Souvenir Sheet

87 A243 11s multicolored 1.25 .50

World Bank Type

1989, Jan. 27 Litho. *Perf. 13x14*
88 A244 5.50s Transportation 1.25 .75
89 A244 8s Health care, education 1.90 1.75

Peace-Keeping Force Type

1989, Mar. 17 Litho. *Perf. 14x13½*
90 A245 6s multicolored .90 .80

World Weather Watch Anniv. Type

Designs: 4s, Helical cloud formation over Italy, the eastern Alps and parts of Yugoslavia. 9.50s, Rainfall in Tokyo, Japan.

1989, Apr. 21 Litho. *Perf. 13x14*
91 A247 4s multicolored 1.10 .75
92 A247 9.50s multicolored 2.50 2.25

V20

V21

Photo. & Engr., Photo.

1989, Aug. 23 *Perf. 14*
93 V20 5s multicolored 4.50 .50
94 V21 7.50s multicolored 1.00 .70

Offices in Vienna, 10th anniv.

Human Rights Type

Paintings: 4s, *The Prisoners,* by Kathe Kollwitz. 6s, *Justice,* by Raphael.

1989, Nov. 17 Litho. *Perf. 13½*
95 A250 4s multicolored .65 .60
96 A250 6s multicolored .90 .90

Printed in sheets of 12+12 se-tenant labels containing Articles 5 (4s) or 6 (6s) inscribed in German, English or French.

Intl. Trade Center Type

1990, Feb. 2 Litho. *Perf. 14½x15*
97 A251 12s multicolored 1.50 1.25

Painting by Kurt Regschek V22

1990, Feb. 2 Litho. *Perf. 13x13½*
98 V22 1.50s multicolored .30 .20

Fight AIDS Worldwide V23

Perf. 13½x12½

1990, Mar. 16 Litho.
99 V23 5s "AIDS" 1.00 .75
100 V23 11s Stylized figures, ink blot 2.50 2.00

Medicinal Plants Type

1990, May 4 Photo. *Perf. 11½*

Granite Paper

101 A253 4.50s *Bixa orellana* 1.00 .75
102 A253 9.50s *Momordica charantia* 2.50 2.00

UN 45th Anniv. Type

"45" and emblem.

1990, June 26 Litho. *Perf. 14½x13*
103 A254 7s multicolored 1.25 1.00
104 A254 9s multi, diff. 2.25 1.75

Souvenir Sheet

105 A254 Sheet of 2, #103-104 5.00 3.00

Crime Prevention Type

1990, Sept. 13 Photo. *Perf. 14*
106 A255 6s Domestic violence 1.25 1.00
107 A255 8s Crime against cultural heritage 2.25 1.75

Human Rights Type of 1989

Paintings: 4.50s, Before the Judge by Sandor Bihari. 7s, Young Man Greeted by a Woman Writing a Poem by Suzuki Harunobu.

1990, Nov. 16 Litho. *Perf. 13½*
108 A250 4.50s multicolored .45 .40
109 A250 7s multicolored 1.40 1.00

Printed in sheets of 12+12 se-tenant labels containing Articles 11 (4.50s) or 12 (7s) inscribed in German, English or French.

Economic Commission for Europe Type

1991, Mar. 15 Litho. *Perf. 14*
110 A256 5s Weasel, hoopoe 1.00 .75
111 A256 5s Warbler, swans 1.00 .75
112 A256 5s Badgers, squirrel 1.00 .75
113 A256 5s Fish 1.00 .75
a. Block of 4, #110-113 4.25 3.00

Namibian Independence Type

1991, May 10 Litho. *Perf. 14*
114 A257 6s Mountain, clouds 1.10 .75
115 A257 9.50s Dune, Namib Desert 2.50 2.00

United Nations Offices in Vienna stamps can be mounted in the Scott U.N. Singles and Postal Stationery album.

V24

1991, May 10 Litho. *Perf. 15x14½*
116 V24 20s multicolored 3.25 2.50

V25

Rights of the Child V26

1991, June 14 Litho. *Perf. 14½*
117 V25 7s Stick drawings 1.50 1.25
118 V26 9s Child, clock, fruit 2.00 1.65

V27

Banning of Chemical Weapons V28

1991, Sept. 11 Litho. *Perf. 13½*
119 V27 5s multicolored 1.25 .75
120 V28 10s multicolored 2.25 1.50

UN Postal Administration, 40th Anniv. Type

1991, Oct. 24 Litho. *Perf. 14x15*
121 A263 5s UN NY No. 8 .85 .75
122 A263 8s UN NY No. 5 2.00 1.90

Human Rights Type of 1989

Artwork: 4.50s, Pre-columbian Mexican pottery, c. 600 A.D. 7s, Windows, 1912, by Robert Delaunay.

1991, Nov. 20 Litho. *Perf. 13½*
123 A250 4.50s black & brown .80 .75
124 A250 7s multicolored 1.40 1.25

Printed in sheets of 12+12 se-tenant labels containing Articles 17 (4.50s) and 18 (7s) inscribed in German, English or French.

World Heritage Type of 1984

Designs: 5s, Iguacu Natl. Park, Brazil. 9s, Abu Simbel, Egypt.

1992, Jan. 24 Litho. *Perf. 13*
Size: 35x28mm
125 V10 5s multicolored 1.25 1.00
126 V10 9s multicolored 2.25 1.75

Clean Oceans Type

1992, Mar. 13 Litho. *Perf. 14*
127 A264 7s Ocean surface, diff. 1.10 .60
128 A264 7s Ocean bottom, diff. 1.10 .60
a. Pair, #127-128 2.25 1.20

Printed in sheets of 12 containing 6 #128a.

Earth Summit Type

1992, May 22 Photo. *Perf. 11½*
129 A265 5.50s Man in space 1.25 1.00
130 A265 5.50s Sun 1.25 1.00
131 A265 5.50s Man fishing 1.25 1.00
132 A265 5.50s Sailboat 1.25 1.00
a. Block of 4, #129-132 5.00 4.25

Mission to Planet Earth Type

Designs: No. 133, Satellite, person's mouth. No. 134, Satellite, person's ear.

1992, Sept. 4 Photo. *Rouletted 8*
Granite Paper
133 A266 10s multicolored 2.75 1.00
134 A266 10s multicolored 2.75 1.00
a. Pair, #133-134 5.50 2.00

Science and Technology Type

Designs: 5.50s, Woman emerging from computer screen. 7s, Green thumb growing flowers.

1992, Oct. 2 Litho. *Perf. 14*
135 A267 5.50s multicolored .80 .75
136 A267 7s multicolored 1.50 1.50

V29

Intl. Center, Vienna — V30

1992, Oct. 2 Litho. *Perf. 13x13½*
137 V29 5.50s multicolored 1.00 .75

Perf. 13½x13
138 V30 7s multicolored 1.50 1.50

Human Rights Type of 1989

Artwork: 6s, Les Constructeurs, by Fernand Leger. 10s, Sunday Afternoon on the Island of La Grande Jatte, by Georges Seurat.

1992, Nov. 20 Litho. *Perf. 13½*
139 A250 6s multicolored 1.10 .85
140 A250 10s multicolored 1.90 1.50

Printed in sheets of 12+12 se-tenant labels containing Articles 23 (6s) and 24 (10s) inscribed in German, English or French.

Aging With Dignity Type

Designs: 5.50s, Elderly couple, family working in garden. 7s, Older woman teaching.

1993, Feb. 5 Litho. *Perf. 13*
141 A270 5.50s multicolored 1.00 1.00
142 A270 7s multicolored 1.65 1.50

Endangered Species Type

Designs: No. 143, Equus grevyi (Grevy's zebra). No. 144, Spheniscus humboldti (Humboldt's penguins). No. 145, Varanus griseus (desert monitor). No. 146, Canis lupus (gray wolf).

1993, Mar. 3 Litho. *Perf. 13x12½*
143 A271 7s multicolored 1.25 1.00
144 A271 7s multicolored 1.25 1.00
145 A271 7s multicolored 1.25 1.00
146 A271 7s multicolored 1.25 1.00
a. Block of 4, #143-146 5.00 4.00

Healthy Environment Type

1993, May 7 Litho. *Perf. 15x14½*
147 A272 6s Wave in ocean 1.40 .75
148 A272 10s Globe 2.25 1.50

V31

1993, May 7 Photo. *Perf. 11½*
Granite Paper
149 V31 13s multicolored 2.50 2.25

Human Rights Type of 1989

Artwork: 5s, Lower Austrian Peasants' Wedding, by Ferdinand G. Waldmuller. 6s, Outback, by Sally Morgan.

1993, June 11 Litho. *Perf. 13½*
150 A250 5s multicolored 1.25 .75
151 A250 6s multicolored 1.50 .50

Printed in sheets of 12 + 12 se-tenant labels containing Article 29 (5s) and 30 (6s) inscribed in German, English or French.

Intl. Peace Day Type

Denomination at: No. 152, UL. No. 153, UR. No. 154, LL. No. 155, LR.

Rouletted 12½
1993, Sept. 21 Litho. & Engr.
152 A274 5.50s green & multi 2.00 .90
153 A274 5.50s green & multi 2.00 .90
154 A274 5.50s green & multi 2.00 .90
155 A274 5.50s green & multi 2.00 .90
a. Block of 4, #152-155 8.50 3.75

Environment-Climate Type

Designs: No. 156, Monkeys. No. 157, Bluebird, industrial pollution, volcano. No. 158, Volcano, nuclear power plant, tree stumps. No. 159, Cactus, tree stumps, owl.

1993, Oct. 29 Litho. *Perf. 14½*
156 A275 7s multicolored 1.50 1.25
157 A275 7s multicolored 1.50 1.25
158 A275 7s multicolored 1.50 1.25
159 A275 7s multicolored 1.50 1.25
a. Strip of 4, #156-159 6.00 5.00

Intl. Year of the Family Type of 1993

Designs: 5.50s, Adults, children holding hands. 8s, Two adults, child planting crops.

1994, Feb. 4 Litho. *Perf. 13.1*
160 A276 5.50s blue green & multi 1.25 1.25
161 A276 8s red & multi 2.00 1.50

Endangered Species Type of 1993

Designs: No. 162, Ocelot. No. 163, White-breasted silver-eye. No. 164, Mediterranean monk seal. No. 165, Asian elephant.

1994, Mar. 18 Litho. *Perf. 12.7*
162 A271 7s multicolored 1.40 1.25
163 A271 7s multicolored 1.40 1.25
164 A271 7s multicolored 1.40 1.25
165 A271 7s multicolored 1.40 1.25
a. Block of 4, #162-165 5.75 5.00

Protection for Refugees Type of 1994

Design: 12s, Protective hands surround group of refugees.

Perf. 14.3x14.8
1994, Apr. 29 Litho.
166 A277 12s multicolored 2.00 1.50

V32

V33

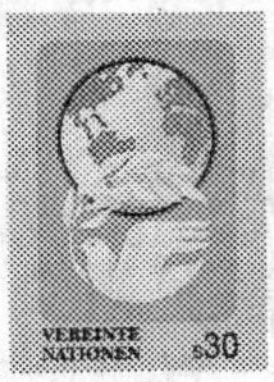

V34

1994, Apr. 29 Litho. *Perf. 12.9*
167 V32 50g multicolored .20 .20
168 V33 4s multicolored .70 .50
169 V34 30s multicolored 5.00 4.00
Nos. 167-169 (3) 5.90 4.70

Intl. Decade for Natural Disaster Reduction Type of 1994

Earth seen from space, outline map of: No. 170, North America. No. 171, Eurasia. No. 172, South America. No. 173, Australia and South Asia.

1994, May 27 Litho. *Perf. 13.9x14.2*
170 A281 6s multicolored 1.75 .80
171 A281 6s multicolored 1.75 .80
172 A281 6s multicolored 1.75 .80
173 A281 6s multicolored 1.75 .80
a. Block of 4, #170-173 7.00 3.50

Population and Development Type of 1994

Designs: 5.50s, Women teaching, running machine tool, coming home to family. 7s, Family on tropical island.

1994, Sept. 1 Litho. *Perf. 13.2x13.6*
174 A282 5.50s multicolored 1.25 .75
175 A282 7s multicolored 1.50 1.25

UNCTAD Type of 1994

1994, Oct. 28
176 A283 6s multi, diff. 1.10 .55
177 A283 7s multi, diff. 1.50 .65

UN 50th Anniv. Type of 1995

Litho. & Engr.
1995, Jan. 1 *Perf. 13.4*
178 A284 7s multicolored 1.65 .75

Social Summit Type of 1995

Photo. & Engr.
1995, Feb. 3 *Perf. 13.6x13.9*
179 A285 14s multi, diff. 2.50 1.50

Endangered Species Type of 1993

Designs: No. 180, Black rhinoceros, Diceros bicornis. No. 181, Golden conure, Aratinga guarouba. No. 182, Douc langur, Pygathrix nemaeus. No. 183, Arabian oryx, Oryx leucoryx.

1995, Mar. 24 Litho. *Perf. 13x12½*
180 A271 7s multicolored 1.25 1.25
181 A271 7s multicolored 1.25 1.25
182 A271 7s multicolored 1.25 1.25
183 A271 7s multicolored 1.25 1.25
a. Block of 4, 180-183 5.00 5.00

Intl. Youth Year Type of 1995

Designs: 6s, Village in winter. 7s, Teepees.

1995, May 26 Litho. *Perf. 14.4x14.7*
184 A286 6s multicolored 1.40 1.00
185 A286 7s multicolored 1.65 1.25

UN, 50th Anniv. Type of 1995

Designs: 7s, Like No. 663. 10s, Like No. 664.

Perf. 13.3x13.6
1995, June 26 Engr.
186 A287 7s green 1.40 1.25
187 A287 10s black 2.00 1.50

Souvenir Sheet
Litho. & Engr.
Imperf
188 Sheet of 2, #186-187 3.50 3.50
a. A287 7s green 1.40 1.40
b. A287 10s black 1.75 1.75

Conference on Women Type of 1995

Designs: 5.50s, Women amid tropical plants. 6s, Woman reading, swans on lake.

1995, Sept. 5 Photo. *Perf. 12*
189 A288 5.50s multicolored 1.25 .55

Size: 28x50mm
190 A288 6s multicolored 1.75 .65

UN People, 50th Anniv. Type of 1995

1995, Oct. 24 Litho. *Perf. 14*
191 Sheet of 12 16.00 11.00
a.-l. A290 3s any single 1.25 .85
192 Souvenir booklet 16.00
a. A290 3s Booklet pane of 3, vert. strip of 3 from UL of sheet 3.75 3.75
b. A290 3s Booklet pane of 3, vert. strip of 3 from UR of sheet 3.75 3.75
c. A290 3s Booklet pane of 3, vert. strip of 3 from LL of sheet 3.75 3.75
d. A290 3s Booklet pane of 3, vert. strip of 3 from LR of sheet 3.75 3.75

WFUNA, 50th Anniv. Type of 1996

Design: 7s, Harlequin holding dove.

1996, Feb. 2 Litho. *Perf. 13x13½*
193 A291 7s multicolored 1.35 .65

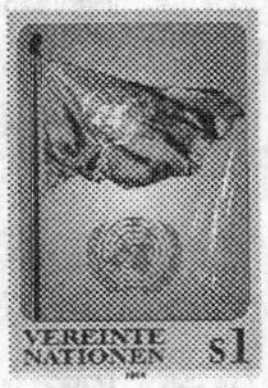

UN Flag — V35

Abstract, by Karl Korab — V36

1996, Feb. 2 Litho. *Perf. 15x14½*
194 V35 1s multicolored .20 .20
195 V36 10s multicolored 2.00 1.00

Endangered Species Type of 1993

Designs: No. 196, Cypripedium calceolus. No. 197, Aztekium ritteri. No. 198, Euphorbia cremersii. No. 199, Dracula bella.

1996, Mar. 14 Litho. *Perf. 12½*
196 A271 7s multicolored 1.30 .65
197 A271 7s multicolored 1.30 .65
198 A271 7s multicolored 1.30 .65
199 A271 7s multicolored 1.30 .65
a. Block of 4, #196-199 5.25 —

City Summit Type of 1996

Designs: No. 200, Arab family selling fruits, vegetables. No. 201, Woman beside stream, camels. No. 202, Woman carrying bundle on head, city skyline. No. 203, Woman threshing grain, yoke of oxen in field. No. 204, Native village, elephant.

1996, June 3 Litho. *Perf. 14x13½*
200 A293 6s multicolored 1.10 .30
201 A293 6s multicolored 1.10 .30
202 A293 6s multicolored 1.10 .30
203 A293 6s multicolored 1.10 .30
204 A293 6s multicolored 1.10 .30
a. Strip of 5, #200-204 5.50 —

Sport and the Environment Type of 1996

Designs: 6s, Men's parallel bars (gymnastics), vert. 7s, Hurdles.

Perf. 14x14½, 14½x14
1996, July 19 Litho.
205 A294 6s multicolored 1.10 .55
206 A294 7s multicolored 1.40 .65

Souvenir Sheet

207 A294 Sheet of 2, #205-206 2.50 2.40

Plea for Peace Type of 1996

7s, Dove & butterflies. 10s, Stylized dove, diff.

1996, Sept. 17 Litho. *Perf. 14½x15*
208 A295 7s multicolored 1.25 .65
209 A295 10s multicolored 1.90 .95

UNICEF Type of 1996

Fairy Tales: 5.50s, Hansel and Gretel, by the Brothers Grimm. 8s, How Maui Stole Fire from the Gods, South Pacific.

1996, Nov. 20 Litho. *Perf. 14½x15*
210 A296 5.50s multicolored 1.00 .50
211 A296 8s multicolored 1.50 .75

Panes of 8 + label.

V37

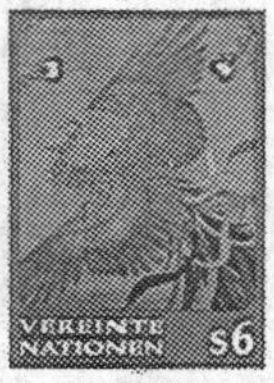

Phoenixes Flying Down (Detail), by Sagenji Yoshida — V38

1997, Feb. 12 Litho. *Perf. 14½*
212 V37 5s multicolored .85 .40
213 V38 6s multicolored 1.00 .50

Endangered Species Type of 1993

No. 214, Macaca sylvanus (Barbary macaque). No. 215, Anthropoides paradisea (blue crane). No. 216, Equus przewalskii (Przewalski horse). No. 217, Myrmecophaga tridactyla (giant anteater).

1997, Mar. 13 Litho. *Perf. 12½*
214 A271 7s multicolored 1.10 .55
215 A271 7s multicolored 1.10 .55
216 A271 7s multicolored 1.10 .55
217 A271 7s multicolored 1.10 .55
a. Block of 4, #214-217 4.50 2.25

Earth Summit Anniv. Type of 1997

Designs: No. 218, Person running. No. 219, Hills, stream, trees. No. 220, Tree with orange leaves. No. 221, Tree with pink leaves.

11s, Combined design similar to Nos. 218-221.

1997, May 30 Photo. *Perf. 11.5*
Granite Paper
218 A299 3.50s multicolored .60 .30
219 A299 3.50s multicolored .60 .30
220 A299 3.50s multicolored .60 .30
221 A299 3.50s multicolored .60 .30
a. Block of 4, #218-221 2.50 1.25

Souvenir Sheet

222 A299 11s multicolored 1.75 1.75

Transportation Type of 1997

Ground transportation: No. 223, 1829 Rocket, 1901 Darraque. No. 224, Steam engine from Vladikawska Railway, trolley. No. 225, Double-decker bus. No. 226, 1950s diesel locomotive, semi-trailer. No. 227, High-speed train, electric car.

1997, Aug. 29 Litho. *Perf. 14x14½*
223 A300 7s multicolored 1.10 .55
224 A300 7s multicolored 1.10 .55
225 A300 7s multicolored 1.10 .55
226 A300 7s multicolored 1.10 .55
227 A300 7s multicolored 1.10 .55
a. Strip of 5, #223-227 5.50 2.75

No. 227a has continuous design.

Philately Type of 1997

Designs: 6.50s, No. 62. 7s, No. 63.

1997, Oct. 14 Litho. *Perf. 13½x14*
228 A301 6.50s multicolored 1.25 .50
229 A301 7s multicolored 1.40 .55

World Heritage Convention Type of 1997

Terracotta warriors of Xian: 3s, Single warrior. 6s, Massed warriors. No. 232a, like #716. No. 232b, like #717. No. 232c, like Geneva #314. No. 232d, like Geneva #315. No. 232e, like Vienna #230. No. 232f, like Vienna #231.

1997, Nov. 19 Litho. *Perf. 13½*
230 A302 3s multicolored .50 .25
231 A302 6s multicolored 1.00 .50
232 Souvenir booklet 4.00
a.-f. A302 1s any single .20 .20
g. Booklet pane of 4 #232a .65 .65
h. Booklet pane of 4 #232b .65 .65
i. Booklet pane of 4 #232c .65 .65
j. Booklet pane of 4 #232d .65 .65
k. Booklet pane of 4 #232e .65 .65
l. Booklet pane of 4 #232f .65 .65

Japanese Peace Bell, Vienna — V39

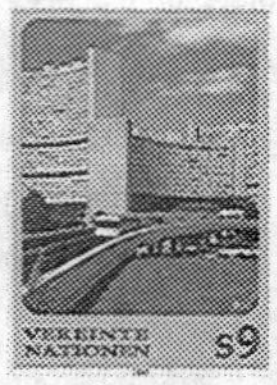

Vienna Subway, Vienna Intl. Center — V40

1998, Feb. 13 Litho. *Perf. 15x14½*
233 V39 6.50s multicolored 1.00 .50
234 V40 9s multicolored 1.40 .70

Endangered Species Type of 1993

Designs: No. 235, Chelonia mydas (green turtle). No. 236, Speotyto cunicularia (burrowing owl). No. 237, Trogonoptera brookiana (Rajah Brooke's birdwing). No. 238, Ailurus fulgens (lesser panda).

1998, Mar. 13 Litho. *Perf. 12½*
235 A271 7s multicolored 1.10 .55
236 A271 7s multicolored 1.10 .55
237 A271 7s multicolored 1.10 .55
238 A271 7s multicolored 1.10 .55
a. Block of 4, #235-238 4.50 2.25

Intl. Year of the Ocean — V41

1998, May 20 Litho. *Perf. 13x13½*
239 V41 Sheet of 12 7.50 4.00
a.-l. 3.50s any single .60 .35

Rain Forests Type of 1998

1998, June 19 *Perf. 13x13½*
240 A307 6.50s Ocelot 1.00 .50

Souvenir Sheet

241 A307 22s like #240 3.50 1.75

Peacekeeping Type of 1998

Designs: 4s, Soldier passing out relief supplies. 7.50s, UN supervised voting.

1998, Sept. 15 Photo. *Perf. 12*
242 A308 4s multicolored .70 .35
243 A308 7.50s multicolored 1.30 .65

Declaration of Human Rights Type of 1998

Designs: 4.50s, Stylized person. 7s, Gears.

Litho. & Photo.
1998, Oct. 27 *Perf. 13*
244 A309 4.50s multicolored .80 .40
245 A309 7s multicolored 1.25 .60

Schönnbrun Palace Type of 1998

Designs: 3.50s, #248d, Palace. 7s, #248c, Porcelain stove, vert. No. 248a, Blue porcelain vase, vert. No. 248b, Wall painting on fabric (detail), by Johann Wenzl Bergl, vert. No. 248e, Great Palm House (conservatory). No. 248f, The Gloriette (archway).

1998, Dec. 4 Litho. *Perf. 14*
246 A310 3.50s multicolored .60 .30
247 A310 7s multicolored 1.10 .55
248 Souvenir booklet 5.75
a.-c. A310 1s any single .20 .20
d.-f. A310 2s any single .30 .30
g. Booklet pane, 4 #248d 1.25
h. Booklet pane, 3 #248a .60
i. Booklet pane, 3 #248b .60
j. Booklet pane, 3 #248c .60
k. Booklet pane, 4 #248e 1.25
l. Booklet pane, 4 #248f 1.25

Volcanic Landscape — V42

1999, Feb. 5 Litho. *Perf. 13x13½*
249 V42 8s multicolored 1.40 .70

World Heritage, Australia Type of 1999

Designs: 4.50s, #252d, Uluru-Kata Tjuta Natl. Park. 6.50s, #252a, Tasmanian Wilderness. No. 252b, Wet tropics of Queensland. No. 252c, Great Barrier Reef. No. 252e, Kakadu Natl. Park. No. 252f, Willandra Lakes region.

1999, Mar. 19 Litho. *Perf. 13*
250 A313 4.50s multicolored .75 .35
251 A313 6.50s multicolored 1.10 .55
252 Souvenir booklet 6.75
a.-c. A313 1s any single .20 .20
d.-f. A313 2s any single .35 .35
g. Booklet pane of 4, #252a .80
h. Booklet pane of 4, #252d 1.40
i. Booklet pane of 4, #252b .80
j. Booklet pane of 4, #252e 1.40
k. Booklet pane of 4, #252c .80
l. Booklet pane of 4, #252f 1.40

Endangered Specied Type of 1993

No. 253, Pongo pygmaeus (oran-utan). No. 254, Pelecanus crispus (Dalmatian pelican). No. 255, Eunectes notaeus (yellow anaconda). No. 256, Caracal.

1999, Apr. 22 Litho. *Perf. 12½*
253 A271 7s multicolored 1.10 .55
254 A271 7s multicolored 1.10 .55
255 A271 7s multicolored 1.10 .55
256 A271 7s multicolored 1.10 .55
a. Block of 4, #253-256 4.50 —

UNISPACE III Type

#257, Satellite over ships. #258, Satellite up close. #259, Composite of #257-258.

1999, July 7 Photo. *Rouletted 8*
257 A314 3.50s multicolored .55 .30
258 A314 3.50s multicolored .55 .30
a. Pair, #257-258 1.10 .60

Souvenir Sheet
Perf. 14½

259 A314 13s multicolored 2.00 1.00

UPU Type

Various people, late 20th century methods of mail transportation, denomination at: No. 260, UL. No. 261, UR. No. 262, LL. No. 263, LR.

1999, Aug. 23 Photo. *Perf. 11¾*
260 A315 6.50s multicolored 1.10 .55
261 A315 6.50s multicolored 1.10 .55
262 A315 6.50s multicolored 1.10 .55
263 A315 6.50s multicolored 1.10 .55
a. Block of 4, #260-263 4.50 —

In Memoriam Type

Donaupark. Size of 14s stamp: 34x63mm.

1999, Sept. 21 Litho. *Perf. 14½x14*
264 A316 6.50s multicolored 1.10 .55

Souvenir Sheet
Perf. 14

265 A316 14s multicolored 2.40 1.25

Education Type

Perf. 13½x13¾
1999, Nov. 18 Litho.
266 A317 7s Boy, girl, book 1.25 .60
267 A317 13s Group reading 2.25 1.10

ABU DHABI

ˌä-bü-ˈthä-bē

LOCATION — Arabia, on Persian Gulf
GOVT. — Sheikdom under British protection
POP. — 25,000 (estimated)
CAPITAL — Abu Dhabi

Abu Dhabi is one of six Persian Gulf sheikdoms to join the United Arab Emirates, which proclaimed its independence Dec. 2, 1971. See United Arab Emirates.

100 Naye Paise = 1 Rupee
1000 Fils = 1 Dinar (1966)

Catalogue values for all unused stamps in this country are for Never Hinged items.

Sheik Shakbut bin Sultan — A1

Palace — A2

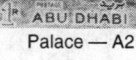

Designs: 40np, 50np, 75np, Gazelle. 5r, 10r, Oil rig and camels.

Perf. 14½
1964, Mar. 30 Photo. Unwmk.
1 A1 5np brt yellow green .20 .20
2 A1 15np brown .30 .20
3 A1 20np brt ultra .40 .20
4 A1 30np red orange .50 .25
5 A1 40np brt violet .65 .30
6 A1 50np brown olive .75 .35
7 A1 75np gray 1.25 .50

Engr. *Perf. 13x13½*
8 A2 1r light green 2.00 .75
9 A2 2r black 4.50 1.50
10 A2 5r carmine rose 12.50 4.75
11 A2 10r dark blue 25.00 12.00
Nos. 1-11 (11) 48.05 21.00

For surcharges see Nos. 15-25.

Falcon Perched on Wrist — A3

40np, Falcon facing left. 2r, Falcon facing right.

1965, Mar. 30 Photo. *Perf. 14½*

12	A3	20np chlky blue & brn	2.75	.50
13	A3	40np ultra & brown	6.75	2.00
14	A3	2r brt blue grn & gray brn	30.00	15.00
		Nos. 12-14 (3)	39.50	17.50

Nos. 1-11 Surcharged

5Fils ٥ فلس
a

Fils فلس
b

100 Fils ١٠٠ فلس
c

1966, Oct. 1 Photo. *Perf. 14½*

15	A1 (a)	5f on 5np	.20	.20
16	A1 (a)	15f on 15np	.60	.40
17	A1 (a)	20f on 20np	.80	.55
18	A1 (a)	30f on 30np	.90	.70
19	A1 (b)	40f on 40np	1.50	.90
20	A1 (b)	50f on 50np	6.50	8.00
21	A1 (b)	75f on 75np	8.00	8.00

Engr.
Perf. 13x13½

22	A2 (c)	100f on 1r	9.00	5.75
23	A2 (c)	200f on 2r	17.50	11.00
24	A2 (c)	500f on 5r	42.50	40.00
25	A2 (c)	1d on 10r	82.50	87.50
		Nos. 15-25 (11)	170.00	163.00

Overprint on No. 25 has "1 Dinar" on 1 line and 3 bars through old denomination.

Sheik Zaid bin Sultan al Nahayan

A4 A6

Dorcas Gazelle — A5

Designs: 5f, 15f, 20f, 35f, Crossed flags of Abu Dhabi. 200f, Falcon. 500f, 1d, Palace.

Engr.; Flags Litho.

1967, Apr. 1 *Perf. 13x13½*

26	A4	5f dull grn & red	.20	.20
27	A4	15f dk brown & red	.30	.20
28	A4	20f dk blue & red	.35	.25
29	A4	35f purple & red	.60	.40

Engr.

30	A4	40f green	.75	.55
31	A4	50f brown	1.00	.70
32	A4	60f blue	1.30	.80
33	A4	100f car rose	2.25	1.50

Litho.

34	A5	125f green & brn ol	2.75	1.90
35	A5	200f sky blue & brn	4.50	3.00
36	A5	500f org & brt pur	11.00	7.50
37	A5	1d green & vio bl	25.00	15.00
		Nos. 26-37 (12)	50.00	32.00

In 1969, the 15f was surcharged "25" in Arabic in black with a numbering machine.

1967, Aug. 6 Photo. *Perf. 14½x14*

38	A6	40f Prussian green	1.40	1.10
39	A6	50f brown	1.40	.75
40	A6	60f blue	2.25	1.00
41	A6	100f carmine rose	4.00	1.90
		Nos. 38-41 (4)	9.05	4.75

Human Rights Flame and Sheik Zaid A6a

Perf. 14½x14
1968, Apr. 1 Photo. Unwmk.
Emblem in Red and Green

42	A6a	35f peacock bl & gold	1.25	.50
43	A6a	60f dk blue & gold	2.00	.75
44	A6a	150f dk brown & gold	4.75	1.75
		Nos. 42-44 (3)	8.00	3.00

International Human Rights Year.

Sheik Zaid and Coat of Arms A7

Perf. 14x14½
1968, Aug. 6 Photo. Unwmk.

45	A7	5f green, sil, red & blk	.45	.20
46	A7	10f brn org, sil, red & blk	.70	.20
47	A7	100f lilac, gold, red & blk	4.25	1.50
48	A7	125f lt blue, gold, red & blk	6.00	2.25
		Nos. 45-48 (4)	11.40	4.15

Accession of Sheik Zaid, 2nd anniversary.

Abu Dhabi Airport — A8

5f, Buildings under construction and earth-moving equipment. 35f, New bridge and falcon. Each stamp shows different portrait of Sheik Zaid.

Perf. 12, 12½x13 (10f)
1969, Mar. 28 Litho.
Size: 5f, 35f, 59x34mm

49	A8	5f multicolored	1.00	.25
50	A8	10f multicolored	2.00	.60
51	A8	35f multicolored	7.00	2.50
		Nos. 49-51 (3)	10.00	3.35

Issued to publicize progress made in Abu Dhabi during preceding 2 years.

Sheik Zaid and Abu Dhabi Petroleum Co. — A9

Designs: 60f, Abu Dhabi Marine Areas drilling platform and helicopter. 125f, Zakum Field separator at night. 200f, Tank farm.

1969, Aug. 6 Litho. *Perf. 14x13½*

52	A9	35f olive grn & multi	.75	.25
53	A9	60f yel brown & multi	1.25	.65
54	A9	125f multicolored	3.00	1.10
55	A9	200f red brown & multi	5.00	2.00
		Nos. 52-55 (4)	10.00	4.00

Accession of Sheik Zaid, 3rd anniversary.

Sheik Zaid — A10

Sheik Zaid and Stallion A11

Designs: 5f, 25f, 60f, 90f, Oval frame around portrait. 150f, Gazelle and Sheik. 500f, Fort Jahili and Sheik. 1d, Grand Mosque and Sheik.

1970-71 Litho. *Perf. 14*

56	A10	5f lt green & multi	.20	.20
57	A10	10f bister & multi	.30	.20
58	A10	25f lilac & multi	.60	.20
59	A10	35f violet & multi	.90	.30
60	A10	50f sepia & multi	1.50	.40
61	A10	60f violet & multi	1.75	.45
62	A10	70f rose red & multi	2.25	.65
63	A10	90f car rose & multi	2.50	.70
64	A11	125f multi ('71)	4.00	.90
65	A11	150f multi ('71)	5.00	1.00
66	A11	500f multi ('71)	13.00	3.50
67	A11	1d multi ('71)	26.00	6.50
		Nos. 56-67 (12)	58.00	15.00

For surcharge see No. 80.

Sheik Zaid and Mt. Fuji — A12

1970, Aug. Litho. *Perf. 13½x13*

68	A12	25f multicolored	1.75	1.00
69	A12	35f multicolored	2.75	1.25
70	A12	60f multicolored	5.00	1.75
		Nos. 68-70 (3)	9.50	4.00

Issued to publicize EXPO '70 International Exhibition, Osaka, Japan, Mar. 15-Sept. 13.

Abu Dhabi Airport A13

Designs: 60f, Airport entrance. 150f, Aerial view of Abu Dhabi Town, vert.

Perf. 14x13½, 13½x14
1970, Sept. 22 Litho.

71	A13	25f multicolored	1.25	.50
72	A13	60f multicolored	4.00	1.25
73	A13	150f multicolored	7.25	3.00
		Nos. 71-73 (3)	12.50	4.75

Accession of Sheik Zaid, 4th anniversary.

Gamal Abdel Nasser — A14

1971, May 3 Litho. *Perf. 14*

74	A14	25f deep rose & blk	2.75	2.00
75	A14	35f rose violet & blk	4.00	3.00

In memory of Gamal Abdel Nasser (1918-1970), President of UAR.

Scout Cars A15

Designs: 60f, Patrol boat. 125f, Armored car in desert. 150f, Meteor jet fighters.

1971, Aug. 6 Litho. *Perf. 13*

76	A15	35f multicolored	2.25	1.00
77	A15	60f multicolored	3.25	1.50
78	A15	125f multicolored	4.50	2.25
79	A15	150f multicolored	5.00	3.00
		Nos. 76-79 (4)	15.00	7.75

Accession of Sheik Zaid, 5th anniversary.

٥ فلوس

No. 60 Surcharged in Green

5 Fils

1971, Dec. 8 *Perf. 14*

80	A10	5f on 50f multi	*65.00*	*45.00*

Dome of the Rock, Jerusalem — A16

Designs: Different views of Dome of the Rock.

1972, June 3 *Perf. 13*

81	A16	35f lt violet & multi	8.50	2.00
82	A16	60f lt violet & multi	12.50	2.50
83	A16	125f lilac & multi	24.00	5.50
		Nos. 81-83 (3)	45.00	10.00

Nos. 80-83 were issued after Abu Dhabi joined the United Arab Emirates Dec. 2, 1971. Stamps of UAE replaced those of Abu Dhabi. UAE Nos. 1-12 were used only in Abu Dhabi except the 10f and 25f which were issued later in Dubai and Sharjah.

ADEN

'ä-dən

LOCATION — Southern Arabia
GOVT. — British colony and protectorate
AREA — 112,075 sq. mi.
POP. — 220,000 (est. 1964)
CAPITAL — Aden

Aden used India stamps before 1937. In January, 1963, the colony of Aden (the port) and the sheikdoms and emirates of the Western Aden Protectorate formed the Federation of South Arabia. This did not include the Eastern Aden Protectorate with Kathiri and Qu'aiti States. Stamps of Aden, except those of Kathiri and Qu'aiti States, were replaced Apr. 1, 1965, by those of the Federation of South Arabia. See South Arabia and People's Democratic Republic of Yemen, Vol. 6.

12 Pies = 1 Anna
16 Annas = 1 Rupee
100 Cents = 1 Shilling (1951)

Catalogue values for unused stamps in this country are for Never Hinged items, beginning with Scott 28 in the regular postage section and for all of the items in the states' sections.

Dhow — A1

Perf. 13x11½

1937, Apr. 1 Engr. Wmk. 4

1 A1 ½a lt green 1.60 1.25
2 A1 9p dark green 1.60 1.50
3 A1 1a black brown 1.60 .65
4 A1 2a red 1.60 *1.75*
5 A1 2½a blue 1.50 .75
6 A1 3a carmine rose 4.25 *5.75*
7 A1 3½a gray blue 3.50 1.75
8 A1 8a rose lilac 9.00 5.00
9 A1 1r brown 13.50 5.50
10 A1 2r orange yellow 22.50 14.50
11 A1 5r rose violet 50.00 *57.50*
12 A1 10r olive green 140.00 *240.00*
Nos. 1-12 (12) 250.65 *335.90*
Set, never hinged 375.00

Common Design Types pictured following the introduction.

Coronation Issue
Common Design Type

1937, May 12 ***Perf. 13½x14***

13 CD302 1a black brown .45 *.75*
14 CD302 2½a blue .65 *1.35*
15 CD302 3½a gray blue 1.10 *2.40*
Nos. 13-15 (3) 2.20 *4.50*
Set, never hinged 3.00

Aidrus Mosque — A2

Designs: ¾a, 5r, Camel Corpsman. 1a, 2r, Aden Harbor. 1½a, 1r, Adenese dhow. 2½a, 8a, Mukalla. 3a, 14a, 10r, Capture of Aden, 1839.

1939-45 Engr. Wmk. 4 ***Perf. 12½***

16 A2 ½a green .25 *.45*
17 A2 ¾a red brown ('46) .65 *1.25*
18 A2 1a brt lt blue .25 .25
19 A2 1½a red .50 *.55*
20 A2 2a dark brown ('46) .25 .25
21 A2 2½a brt ultra .45 .30
22 A2 3a rose car & dk brn .55 .25
23 A2 8a orange .90 .40
23A A2 14a lt bl & brn blk ('45) 1.10 1.00
24 A2 1r bright green 1.25 *1.40*
25 A2 2r dp mag & bl blk ('44) 4.00 1.90
26 A2 5r dp ol & lake brn ('44) 10.00 7.25
27 A2 10r brt vio & brt sepia 16.00 11.00
Nos. 16-27 (13) 36.15 26.25
Set, never hinged 55.00

Catalogue values for unused stamps in this section, from this point to the end of the section, are for Never Hinged items.

Peace Issue
Common Design Type
Perf. 13½x14

1946, Oct. 15 Engr. Wmk. 4

28 CD303 1½a carmine .20 *.75*
29 CD303 2½a deep blue .30 .30

Return to peace at end of World War II.

Silver Wedding Issue
Common Design Types

1949, Jan. 17 Photo. ***Perf. 14x14½***

30 CD304 1½a scarlet .40 *.75*

Engraved; Name Typographed
Perf. 11½x11

31 CD305 10r purple 25.00 *28.00*

25th anniv. of the marriage of King George VI and Queen Elizabeth.

UPU Issue
Common Design Types
Surcharged with New Values in Annas and Rupees

Engr.; Name typo. on Nos. 33-34

1949, Oct. 10 ***Perf. 13½, 11x11½***

32 CD306 2½a on 20c dp ultra .75 *1.40*
33 CD307 3a on 30c dp car 1.60 1.40
34 CD308 8a on 50c org 1.75 1.50
35 CD309 1r on 1sh blue 2.50 2.75
Nos. 32-35 (4) 6.60 7.05

75th anniv. of the formation of the UPU.

Nos. 18 and 20-27 Surcharged with New Values in Black or Carmine

1951, Oct. 1 Wmk. 4 ***Perf. 12½***

36 A2 5c on 1a .25 *.40*
37 A2 10c on 2a .35 *.45*
38 A2 15c on 2½a .85 *1.20*
a. Double surcharge *650.00*
39 A2 20c on 3a 1.00 1.00
40 A2 30c on 8a (C) 1.00 1.00
41 A2 50c on 8a 1.00 .75
42 A2 70c on 14a 1.75 1.50
43 A2 1sh on 1r .65 *.70*
44 A2 2sh on 2r 6.00 5.00
45 A2 5sh on 5r 15.00 11.00
46 A2 10sh on 10r 22.50 20.00
Nos. 36-46 (11) 50.35 43.05

Surcharge on No. 40 includes 2 bars.

Coronation Issue
Common Design Type

1953, June 2 Engr. ***Perf. 13½x13***

47 CD312 15c dark green & black .45 .35

Minaret — A10

Camel Transport — A11

15c, Crater. 25c, Mosque. 35c, Dhow. 50c, Map. 70c, Salt works. 1sh, Dhow building. 1sh, 25c, Colony Badge. 2sh, Aden Protectorate levy. 5sh, Crater Pass. 10sh, Tribesman. 20sh, Aden in 1572.

Perf. 12, 12x13½ ('56)

1953-58 Engr. Wmk. 4

Size: 29x23, 23x29mm

48 A10 5c grn, perf. 12x13½ ('56) .20 .20
a. Perf. 12 .20 .20
49 A11 10c orange .20 .20
50 A11 15c blue green .90 .50
51 A11 25c carmine .60 .35
52 A10 35c ultra, perf. 12 1.75 1.75
a. 35c dp bl, perf. 12x13½ ('58) 3.00 2.00
53 A10 50c blue, perf. 12 .20 .20
a. Perf. 12x13½ ('56) .55 .20
54 A10 70c gray, perf. 12 .20 .20
a. Perf. 12x13½ ('56) .60 .20
55 A11 1sh pur & sepia .20 .20
55A A11 1sh vio & black ('55) 1.10 .20
56 A10 1sh25c blk & lt blue ('56) 1.65 .50
57 A10 2sh car rose & sep .90 .40
57A A10 2sh car & black ('56) 4.25 .40
58 A10 5sh blue & sepia .90 .40
58A A10 5sh dk blue & blk ('56) 3.75 .50
59 A10 10sh olive & sepia 1.25 *6.75*
60 A10 10sh ol gray & blk ('54) 9.50 1.10

Size: 36½x27mm
Perf. 13½x13

61 A11 20sh rose vio & dk brn 4.75 *8.50*
61A A11 20sh lt vio & blk ('57) 30.00 12.00
Nos. 48-61A (18) 62.30 34.35

Various shades from two or more printings exist. No. 60 has heavier shading on tribesman's lower garment than No. 59.

See #66-75. For overprints see #63-64.

Type of 1953
Inscribed: "Royal Visit 1954"

1954, Apr. 27 ***Perf. 12***

62 A11 1sh purple & sepia .40 .40

Nos. 50 and 56 Overprinted in Red

تعديل
الدستور
١٩٥٩
No. 63

REVISED
CONSTITUTION
1959
No. 64

1959, Jan. 26 ***Perf. 12, 12x13½***

63 A11 15c dark blue green .30 .30
64 A10 1sh25c black & light blue .80 .80

Introduction of a revised constitution.

Freedom from Hunger Issue
Common Design Type
Perf. 14x14½

1963, June 4 Photo. Wmk. 314

65 CD314 1sh25c green 1.50 .65

Types of 1953-57
Perf. 12x13½, 12 (#67-69, 73)

1964-65 Engr. Wmk. 314

66 A10 5c green ('65) .20 *.25*
67 A11 10c orange .25 .20
68 A11 15c Prus green .30 .25
69 A11 25c carmine .50 .25
70 A10 35c dk blue 2.50 .75
71 A10 50c dull blue 2.50 .75
72 A10 70c gray 2.75 1.25
73 A11 1sh vio & black 2.75 1.25
74 A10 1sh25c blk & lt blue 5.50 *7.25*
75 A10 2sh car & blk ('65) 10.00 *14.00*
Nos. 66-75 (10) 27.25 *26.20*

KATHIRI STATE OF SEIYUN

LOCATION — In Eastern Aden Protectorate
GOVT. — Sultanate
CAPITAL — Seiyun

Catalogue values for unused stamps in this section are for Never Hinged items.

Sultan Ja'far bin Mansur al Kathiri — A1

Seiyun — A2

Minaret at Tarim — A3

Designs: 2½a, Mosque at Seiyun. 3a, Palace at Tarim. 8a, Mosque at Seiyun, horiz. 1r, South Gate, Tarim. 2r, Kathiri House. 5r, Mosque at Tarim.

1942 Engr. Wmk. 4 ***Perf. 13⅞x14***

1 A1 ½a dark green .20 *.35*
2 A1 ¾a copper brown .30 *.55*
3 A1 1a deep blue .40 *.35*

Perf. 13x11½, 11½x13

4 A2 1½a carmine .40 *.40*
5 A3 2a sepia brown .30 *.65*
6 A3 2½a deep blue .70 *1.00*
7 A2 3a dk car rose & dull brn 1.20 *1.60*
8 A2 8a orange red .55 *.90*
9 A3 1r green 1.90 *1.50*
10 A2 2r rose vio & dk blue 6.50 *9.50*
11 A3 5r gray green & fawn 17.00 *12.50*
Nos. 1-11 (11) 29.45 *29.30*

For surcharges see Nos. 20-27.

Nos. 4, 6 Ovptd. in Black or Red:

VICTORY
ISSUE
8TH JUNE 1946
a

VICTORY
ISSUE
8TH JUNE
1946
b

Perf. 13x11½, 11½x13

1946, Oct. 15 Wmk. 4

12 A2 (a) 1½a dark car rose .20 *.25*
13 A3 (b) 2½a deep blue (R) .25 .25
a. Inverted overprint *425.00*
b. Double overprint —

Victory of the Allied Nations in WWII.

All examples of No. 13b have the 2nd overprint almost directly over the 1st.

Silver Wedding Issue
Common Design Types

1949, Jan. 17 Photo. ***Perf. 14x14½***

14 CD304 1½a scarlet .35 *2.00*

Engraved; Name Typo.
Perf. 11½x11

15 CD305 5r green 12.50 10.00

25th anniv. of the marriage of King George VI and Queen Elizabeth.

UPU Issue
Common Design Types
Surcharged with New Values in Annas and Rupees

Engr.; Name Typo. on Nos. 17-18

1949, Oct. 10 ***Perf. 13½, 11x11½***

16 CD306 2½a on 20c dp ultra .25 *.50*
17 CD307 3a on 30c dp car 1.00 .65
18 CD308 8a on 50c orange .55 *.75*
19 CD309 1r on 1sh blue 1.00 *1.10*
Nos. 16-19 (4) 2.80 *3.00*

75th anniv. of the formation of the UPU.

Nos. 3 and 5-11 Surcharged with New Values in Carmine or Black

Perf. 14, 13x11½, 11½x13

1951, Oct. 1 Engr. Wmk. 4

20 A1 5c on 1a (C) .20 .20
21 A3 10c on 2a .30 .20
22 A3 15c on 2½a .50 .50
23 A2 20c on 3a .25 *.60*
24 A2 50c on 8a .30 .25
25 A3 1sh on 1r 1.90 .75
26 A2 2sh on 2r 3.50 *13.00*
27 A3 5sh on 5r 14.50 *27.50*
Nos. 20-27 (8) 21.45 *43.00*

Coronation Issue
Common Design Type

1953, June 2 ***Perf. 13½x13***

28 CD312 15c dk green & blk .30 .25

Sultan Hussein A10

Qarn Adh Dhabi A11

Designs: 15c, Seiyun scene, horiz. 25c, Minaret at Tarim. 35c, Mosque at Seiyun. 50c, Palace at Tarim, horiz. 1sh, Mosque at Seiyun, horiz. 2sh, South Gate, Tarim. 5sh, Kathiri house, horiz. 10sh, Mosque entrance, Tarim.

1954, Jan. 15 Engr. ***Perf. 12½***

29 A10 5c dark brown .20 .20
30 A10 10c deep blue .20 .20

Perf. 13x11½, 11½x13

31 A11 15c dk blue green .20 .20
32 A11 25c dk car rose .20 .20
33 A11 35c deep blue .20 .20
34 A11 50c dk car rose & dk brn .20 .20
35 A11 1sh deep orange .35 .30
36 A11 2sh gray green 1.00 .85
37 A11 5sh vio & dk blue 2.25 *3.25*
38 A11 10sh vio & yel brn 5.25 *6.50*
Nos. 29-38 (10) 10.05 *12.10*

Perf. 11½x13, 13x11½

1964, July 1 Wmk. 314

Designs: 1sh25c, Seiyun, horiz. 1sh50c, View of Gheil Omer, horiz.

39 A11 70c black .50 .35
40 A11 1sh25c bright green .85 .60
41 A11 1sh50c purple 1.10 .80
Nos. 39-41 (3) 2.45 1.75

QUAITI STATE OF SHIHR AND MUKALLA

LOCATION — In Eastern Aden Protectorate
GOVT. — Sultanate
CAPITAL — Mukalla

Catalogue values for unused stamps in this section are for Never Hinged items.

Sultan Sir Saleh bin Ghalib al Qu'aiti — A1

Mukalla Harbor — A2

Buildings at Shibam — A3

Designs: 2a, Gateway of Shihr. 3a, Outpost of Mukalla. 8a, View of 'Einat. 1r, Governor's Castle, Du'an. 3r, Mosque in Hureidha. 5r, Meshhed.

1942 Engr. Wmk. 4 *Perf. 13¾x14*

1 A1 ½a blue green .50 .40
2 A1 ¾a copper brown .50 .30
3 A1 1a deep blue .60 .55

Perf. 13x11½, 11½x13

4 A2 1½a deep carmine .70 .40
5 A2 2a black brown .75 .55
6 A3 2½a deep blue .40 .30
7 A2 3a dk car rose & dl brn .75 .40
8 A3 8a orange red .50 .40
9 A2 1r green 2.25 1.75
10 A3 2r rose vio & dk blue 9.50 7.50
11 A3 5r gray green & fawn 13.50 10.00
Nos. 1-11 (11) 29.95 22.55

For surcharges see Nos. 20-27.

Nos. 4, 6 Ovptd. in Black or Carmine like Kathiri Nos. 12-13

1946, Oct. 15 *Perf. 11½x13, 13x11½*

12 A2 (b) 1½a dk car rose .20 *.30*
13 A3 (a) 2½a deep blue (C) .25 .20

Victory of the Allied Nations in WWII.

Silver Wedding Issue
Common Design Types

1949, Jan. 17 Photo. *Perf. 14x14½*

14 CD304 1½a scarlet .45 *1.75*

Engraved; Name Typo.
Perf. 11½x11

15 CD305 5r green 12.50 *10.50*

25th anniv. of the marriage of King George VI and Queen Elizabeth.

UPU Issue
Common Design Types
Surcharged with New Values in Annas and Rupees

Engr.; Name Typo. on Nos. 17 and 18

1949, Oct. 10 *Perf. 13½, 11x11½*

16 CD306 2½a on 20c dp ultra .20 .20
17 CD307 3a on 30c dp car .50 .50
18 CD308 8a on 50c org .65 .65
19 CD309 1r on 1sh blue 1.75 1.75
a. Surcharge omitted *1,300.*
Nos. 16-19 (4) 3.10 3.10

Nos. 3 and 5-11 Surcharged with New Values in Carmine or Black

Perf. 14, 13x11½, 11½x13

1951, Oct. 1 Engr. Wmk. 4

20 A1 5c on 1a (C) .20 .20
21 A2 10c on 2a .20 .20
22 A3 15c on 2½a .20 .20
23 A2 20c on 3a .30 .20
24 A3 50c on 8a .20 *.40*
25 A2 1sh on 1r .75 *.30*
26 A3 2sh on 2r 6.00 *8.75*
27 A3 5sh on 5r 9.00 *13.50*
Nos. 20-27 (8) 16.85 *23.75*

Coronation Issue
Common Design Type

1953, June 2 Engr. *Perf. 13½x13*

28 CD312 15c dk blue & black .45 .45

Qu'aiti State in Hadhramaut

Metal Work — A10

Fisheries A11

Designs: 10c, Mat making. 15c, Weaving. 25c, Pottery. 35c, Building. 50c, Date cultivation. 90c, Agriculture. 1sh25c, 10sh, Lime burning. 2sh, Dhow building. 5sh, Agriculture.

Perf. 11½x13, 13½x14

1955, Sept. 1 Engr. Wmk. 4

29 A10 5c greenish blue .20 .20
30 A10 10c black .20 .20
31 A10 15c dk green .20 .20
32 A10 25c carmine .20 .20
33 A10 35c ultra .20 .20
34 A10 50c red orange .40 .40
35 A10 90c brown .55 .55
36 A11 1sh purple & blk .65 .65
37 A11 1sh25c red org & blk .75 .75
38 A11 2sh dk blue & blk 2.50 .80
39 A11 5sh green & blk 3.50 2.50
40 A11 10sh car & black 5.00 *5.50*
Nos. 29-40 (12) 14.35 12.15

Types of 1955 with Portrait of Sultan Awadh Bin Saleh El-Qu'aiti

Design: 70c, Agriculture. Others as before.

1963, Oct. 20 Wmk. 314

41 A10 5c greenish blue .20 .20
42 A10 10c black .20 .20
43 A10 15c dark green .20 .20
44 A10 25c carmine .20 .20
45 A10 35c ultra .30 .25
46 A10 50c red orange .40 .35
47 A10 70c brown .65 .60
48 A11 1sh purple & blk .90 .85
49 A11 1sh25c red org & blk 1.00 *1.50*
50 A11 2sh dk blue & blk 2.50 1.25
51 A11 5sh green & backk 7.50 *9.00*
52 A11 10sh carmine & backk 10.50 *12.00*
Nos. 41-52 (12) 24.55 *26.60*

AFARS AND ISSAS

French Territory of the

'ä-‚fär(z) and ē-'sä(z)

LOCATION — East Africa
GOVT. — French Overseas Territory
AREA — 8,880 sq. mi.
POP. — 150,000 (est. 1974)
CAPITAL — Djibouti (Jibuti)

The French overseas territory of Somali Coast was renamed the French Territory of the Afars and Issas in 1967. It became the Djibouti Republic (which see) on June 27, 1977.

100 Centimes = 1 Franc

Catalogue values for all unused stamps in this country are for Never Hinged items.

Imperforates

Most stamps of Afars and Issas exist imperforate in issued and trial colors, and also in small presentation sheets in issued colors.

Grayheaded Kingfisher A48

1967 Engr. Unwmk. *Perf. 13*

310 A48 10fr Halcyon leucocephala 1.50 1.25
311 A48 15fr Haematopus ostralegus 2.00 1.50
312 A48 50fr Tringa nebularia 7.75 4.50
313 A48 55fr Coracias abyssinicus 9.50 5.25
314 A48 60fr Xerus rutilus, vert. 13.00 10.00
Nos. 310-314 (5) 33.75 22.50
Nos. 310-314,C50 (6) 48.75 30.00

Issued: 10fr, 55fr, Aug. 21; 15fr, 50fr, 60fr, Sept. 25. See No. C50.

Soccer A49

1967, Dec. 18 Engr. *Perf. 13*

315 A49 25fr shown 1.90 1.50
316 A49 30fr Basketball 2.50 2.00

Common Design Types
Pictured in section at front of book.

WHO Anniversary Issue
Common Design Type

1968, May 4 Engr. *Perf. 13*

317 CD126 15fr multicolored 1.25 1.00

20th anniv. of WHO.

Damerdjog Fortress A50

Administration Buildings: 25fr, Ali Adde. 30fr, Dorra. 40fr, Assamo.

1968, May 17 Engr. *Perf. 13*

318 A50 20fr slate, brn & emer .90 .50
319 A50 25fr brt grn, bl & brn .95 .50
320 A50 30fr brn ol, brn org & sl 1.10 .75
321 A50 40fr brn ol, sl & brt grn 2.00 1.50
Nos. 318-321 (4) 4.95 3.25

Human Rights Year Issue
Common Design Type

1968, Aug. 10 Engr. *Perf. 13*

322 CD127 10fr purple, ver & org .75 .60
323 CD127 70fr green, pur & org 1.50 1.10

International Human Rights Year.

Radio-television Station, Djibouti — A52

High Commission Palace, Djibouti — A53

Designs: 2fr, Justice Building. 5fr, Chamber of Deputies. 8fr, Great Mosque. 15fr, Monument of Free French Forces, vert. 40fr, Djibouti Post Office. 70fr, Residence of Gov. Léonce Lagarde at Obock. No. 332, Djibouti Harbormaster's Building. No. 333, Control tower, Djibouti Airport.

1968-70 Engr. *Perf. 13*

324 A52 1fr dk red, sky bl & ind .25 .20
325 A52 2fr green, bl & indigo .25 .20
326 A52 5fr brn, sky bl & grn .35 .20
327 A52 8fr choc, emer & gray .40 .20
328 A52 15fr grn, sky bl & yel brn 3.00 2.00
329 A52 40fr green, brn & slate 2.00 1.00
330 A53 60fr multicolored 2.25 1.50
331 A53 70fr dl grn, gray & ol bis 3.00 1.50
332 A53 85fr multicolored 4.00 2.00
333 A52 85fr dk grn, bl & gray 4.50 2.50
Nos. 324-333 (10) 20.00 11.30

Issue years: 1968 - 60fr; 1969 - 1fr-15fr, 70fr, 85fr; 1970 - 40fr, 85fr.

Locust A54

Designs: 50fr, Pest control by helicopter. 55fr, Pest control by plane.

1969, Oct. 6 Engr. *Perf. 13*

334 A54 15fr brn, grn & slate 2.50 1.00
335 A54 50fr dk grn, bl & ol brn 1.50 1.00
336 A54 55fr red brn, bl & brn 2.00 1.50
Nos. 334-336 (3) 6.00 3.50

Campaign against locusts.

ILO Issue
Common Design Type

1969, Nov. 24 Engr. *Perf. 13*

337 CD131 30fr orange, gray & lilac 1.25 .80

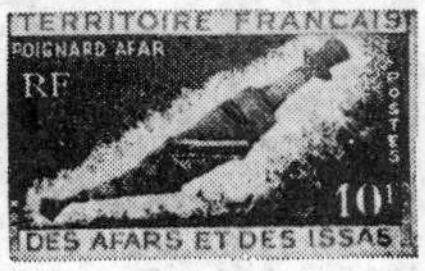

Afar Dagger in Ornamental Scabbard A56

1970, Apr. 3 Engr. *Perf. 13*

338 A56 10fr yel grn, dk grn & org brn .50 .35
339 A56 15fr yel grn, bl & org brn .60 .35
340 A56 20fr yel grn, red & org brn .80 .55
341 A56 25fr yel grn, plum & org brn 1.10 .55
Nos. 338-341 (4) 3.00 1.80

See No. 364.

UPU Headquarters Issue
Common Design Type

1970, May 20 Engr. *Perf. 13*

342 CD133 25fr brn, brt grn & choc 1.00 .60

Trapshooting A57

Motorboats A58

Designs: 50fr, Steeplechase. 55fr, Sailboat, vert. 60fr, Equestrians.

1970 Engr. *Perf. 13*

343 A57 30fr dp brn, yel grn & brt bl 1.60 .90
344 A58 48fr blue & multi 1.75 .90
345 A58 50fr cop red, bl & pur 2.25 1.25

346 A58 55fr red brn, bl & ol 1.75 1.25
347 A58 60fr ol, blk & red brn 2.75 1.75
Nos. 343-347 (5) 10.10 6.05

Issued: 30fr, June 5; 48fr, Oct. 9; 50fr, 60fr, Nov. 6.

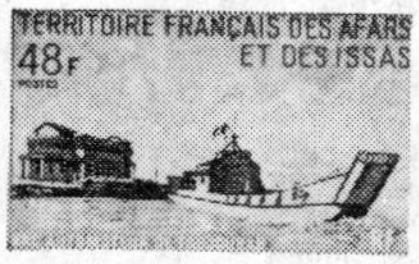

Automatic Ferry, Tadjourah
A59

1970, Nov. 25
348 A59 48fr blue, brn & grn 2.25 1.40

Volcanic Geode
A60

Diabase and Chrysolite
A61

10fr, Doleritic basalt. 15fr, Olivine basalt.

1971 Photo. *Perf. 13*
349 A61 10fr black & multi 1.25 .50
350 A61 15fr black & multi 1.75 .50
351 A60 25fr black, crim & brn 3.50 1.50
352 A61 40fr black & multi 6.50 2.00
Nos. 349-352 (4) 13.00 4.50

Issued: 10fr, 11/22; 15fr, 10/8; 25fr, 4/26; 40fr, 1/25.

A62

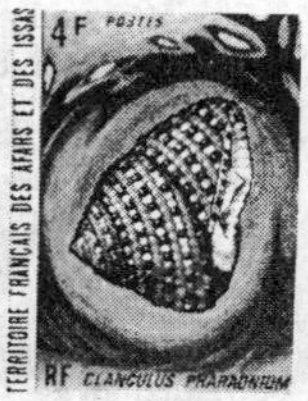

A63

1971, July 1 Photo. *Perf. 12x12½*
353 A62 4fr Manta birostris 1.25 .50
354 A62 5fr Coryphaena hippurus 1.25 .50
355 A62 9fr Pristis pectinatus 2.50 1.50
Nos. 353-355 (3) 5.00 2.50

See No. C60.

De Gaulle Issue
Common Design Type

Designs: 60fr, Gen. Charles de Gaulle, 1940. 85fr, Pres. de Gaulle, 1970.

1971, Nov. 9 Engr. *Perf. 13*
356 CD134 60fr dk vio bl & blk 2.00 1.50
357 CD134 85fr dk vio bl & blk 2.50 1.50

1972, Mar. 8 Photo. *Perf. 12½x13*

Shells: 4fr, Strawberry Top. 9fr, Cypraea pantherina. 20fr, Bull-mouth helmet. 50fr, Ethiopian volute.

358 A63 4fr olive & multi 1.25 .40
359 A63 9fr dk blue & multi 1.50 .60
360 A63 20fr dp green & multi 3.75 1.00
361 A63 50fr dp claret & multi 7.50 1.50
Nos. 358-361 (4) 14.00 3.50

Shepherd — A64

Design: 10fr, Dromedary breeding.

1973, Apr. 11 Photo. *Perf. 13*
362 A64 9fr blue & multi 1.00 .30
363 A64 10fr blue & multi 1.00 .30

Afar Dagger — A65

1974, Jan. 29 Engr. *Perf. 13*
364 A65 30fr slate grn & dk brn 1.10 .65

For surcharge see No. 379.

Flamingos, Lake Abbe — A66

Flamingos and different views of Lake Abbe.

1974, Feb. 22 Photo. *Perf. 13*
370 A66 5fr multicolored 1.25 .30
371 A66 15fr multicolored .60 .50
372 A66 50fr multicolored 1.90 1.25
Nos. 370-372 (3) 3.75 2.05

Soccer Ball — A67

1974, May 24 Engr. *Perf. 13*
373 A67 25fr black & emerald 1.25 .80

World Cup Soccer Championship, Munich, June 13-July 7.

Letters Around UPU Emblem
A68

Oleo Chrysophylla
A69

1974, Oct. 9 Engr. *Perf. 13*
374 A68 20fr multicolored 1.00 .50
375 A68 100fr multicolored 2.50 2.00

Centenary of Universal Postal Union.

1974, Nov. 22 Photo.
376 A69 10fr shown .75 .40
377 A69 15fr *Ficus species* 1.10 .60
378 A69 20fr *Solanum adoense* 2.25 1.00
Nos. 376-378 (3) 4.10 2.00

Day Primary Forest.

No. 364 Surcharged with New Value and Two Bars in Red

1975, Jan. 1 Engr. *Perf. 13*
379 A65 40fr on 30fr multi 1.50 .90

Treasury — A70

Design: 25fr, Government buildings.

1975, Jan. 7 Engr. *Perf. 13*
380 A70 8fr blue, gray & red .40 .30
381 A70 25fr red, blue & indigo .75 .60

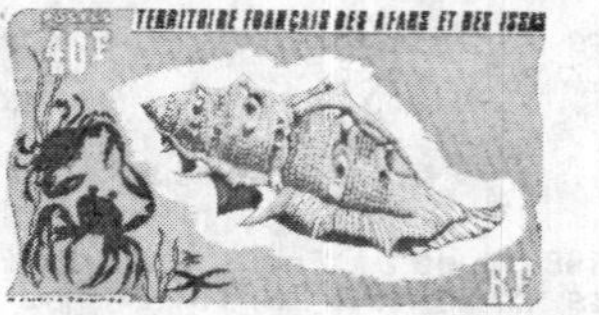

Ranella Spinosa — A71

Sea Shells: No. 382, Darioconus textile. No. 383, Murex palmarosa. 10fr, Conus sumatrensis. 15fr, Cypraea pulchra. No. 386, 45fr, Murex scolopax. No. 387, Cypraea exhusta. 55fr, Cypraea erythraensis. 60fr, Conus taeniatus.

1975-76 Engr. *Perf. 13*
382 A71 5fr blue grn & brn 1.25 .40
383 A71 5fr blue & multi ('76) .90 .20
384 A71 10fr lilac, blk & brn 1.25 .40
385 A71 15fr blue, indigo & brn 2.25 .60
386 A71 20fr purple & lt brn 3.00 1.60
387 A71 20fr brt grn & multi ('76) 1.10 .40
388 A71 40fr green & brown 6.00 1.00
389 A71 45fr green, bl & bister 5.00 1.00
390 A71 55fr turq & multi ('76) 3.00 1.25
391 A71 60fr buff & sepia ('76) 6.00 1.75
Nos. 382-391 (10) 29.75 8.60

Hypolimnas Misippus
A72

Butterflies: 40fr, Papilio nireus. 50fr, Acraea anemosa. 65fr, Holocerina smilax menieri. 70fr, Papilio demodocus. No. 397, Papilio dardanus. No. 398, Balachowsky gonimbrasca. 150fr, Vanessa cardui.

1975-76 Photo. *Perf. 13*
392 A72 25fr emerald & multi 1.90 1.00
393 A72 40fr yellow & multi 2.00 1.00
394 A72 50fr ultra & multi ('76) 2.25 1.50
395 A72 65fr olive & multi ('76) 3.25 1.50
396 A72 70fr violet & multi 4.25 2.00
397 A72 100fr blue & multi 5.50 2.00
398 A72 100fr Prus bl & multi ('76) 4.25 2.00
399 A72 150fr green & multi ('76) 6.00 2.00
Nos. 392-399 (8) 29.40 13.00

A73

Perf. 13x12½, 12½x13

1975-76 Photo.
400 A73 10fr Hyaena hyaena .55 .30
401 A73 15fr Cercopithecus aethiops 1.10 .50
402 A73 15fr Equus asinus somalicus .90 .50
403 A73 30fr Dorcatragus megalotis 1.60 .90
404 A73 50fr Ichneumia albicauda 2.25 1.00
405 A73 60fr Hystrix galasta 2.75 1.25
406 A73 70fr Ictonyx striatus 4.00 1.75
407 A73 200fr Orycteropus afar 6.75 4.00
Nos. 400-407 (8) 19.90 10.20

Nos. 401-402, 405 are vert.
Issued: 50fr, 60fr, 70fr, 2/21; No. 401, 200fr, 10/24; 10fr, No. 402, 30fr, 2/4/76.

A74

A75

1975-76 Photo. *Perf. 12½x13*
413 A74 20fr Vidua macroura 1.25 .80
414 A74 25fr Psittacula krameri 1.25 .40
415 A74 50fr Cinnyris venustus 2.50 1.50
416 A74 60fr Ardea goliath 3.50 1.75
417 A74 100fr Scopus umbretta 4.50 2.50
418 A74 100fr Oena capensis 3.50 1.75
419 A74 300fr Platalea alba 9.00 4.00
Nos. 413-419 (7) 25.50 12.70

Issued: 300fr, 6/15/76; 25fr, No. 418, 10/13/76; others 11/21 and 12/19/75.

1975, Dec. 19 Engr. *Perf. 13*
421 A75 20fr Palms 1.00 .40

Satellite and Alexander Graham Bell — A76

1976, Mar. 10 Engr. *Perf. 13*
422 A76 200fr dp bl, org & sl grn 4.00 2.25

Centenary of the first telephone call by Alexander Graham Bell, Mar. 10, 1876.

Basketball
A77

1976, July 7 Litho. *Perf. 12½*
423 A77 10fr shown .45 .20
424 A77 15fr Bicycling .60 .30
425 A77 40fr Soccer 1.10 .50
426 A77 60fr Running 1.40 .80
Nos. 423-426 (4) 3.55 1.80

21st Olympic Games, Montreal, Canada, July 17-Aug. 1.

Pterois Radiata — A78

1976, Aug. 10 Photo. *Perf. 13x13½*
428 A78 45fr blue & multi 2.50 1.00

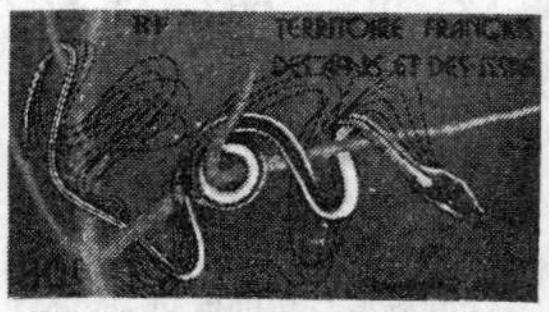

Psammophis Elegans — A79

Design: 70fr, Naja nigricollis, vert.

Perf. 13x13½, 13½x13

1976, Sept. 27 Photo.
430 A79 70fr ocher & multi 2.75 1.50
431 A79 80fr emerald & multi 3.25 1.75

Motorcyclist — A80

1977, Jan. 27 Litho. *Perf. 12x12½*
432 A80 200fr multicolored 5.25 2.75

Moto-Cross motorcycle race.

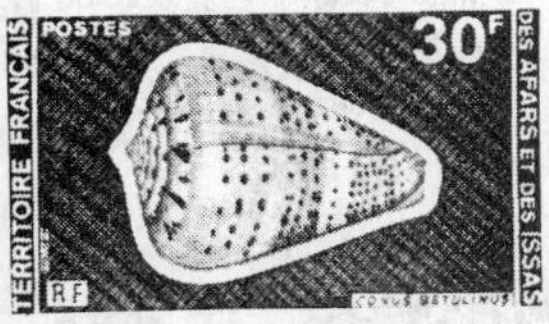

Conus Betulinus — A81

Sea Shells: 5fr, Cyprea tigris. 70fr, Conus striatus. 85fr, Cyprea mauritiana.

1977 Engr. *Perf. 13*
433 A81 5fr multicolored .90 .50
434 A81 30fr multicolored 1.40 .60
435 A81 70fr multicolored 4.75 1.75
436 A81 85fr multicolored 5.00 2.00
Nos. 433-436 (4) 12.05 4.85

Gaterin Gaterinus A82

1977, Apr. 15 Photo. *Perf. 13x12½*
437 A82 15fr shown 1.10 .40
438 A82 65fr Barracudas 3.25 1.10

AIR POST STAMPS

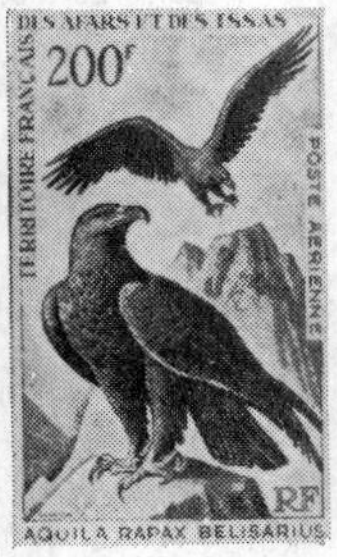

AP16 AP17

Unwmk.

1967, Aug. 21 Engr. *Perf. 13*
C50 AP16 200fr Aquila rapax belisarius 15.00 7.50

1968 Engr. *Perf. 13*
C51 AP17 48fr Parachutists 2.75 1.50
C52 AP17 85fr Water skier & skin diver 3.75 2.50

Issue dates: 48fr, Jan. 5; 85fr, Mar. 15.

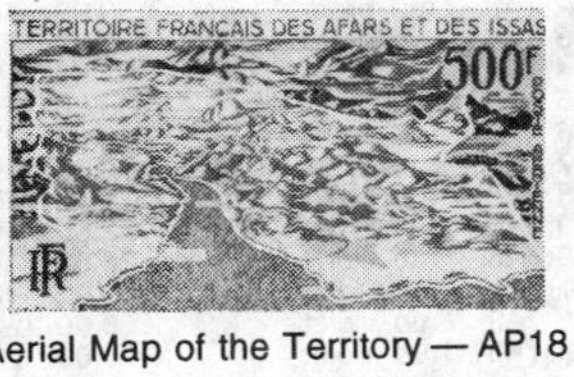

Aerial Map of the Territory — AP18

1968, Nov. 15 Engr. *Perf. 13*
C53 AP18 500fr bl, dk brn & ocher 26.00 8.00

Buildings Type of Regular Issue

100fr, Cathedral. 200fr, Sayed Hassan Mosque.

1969 Engr. *Perf. 13*
C54 A53 100fr multi, vert. 2.25 1.50
C55 A53 200fr multi, vert. 5.25 3.00

Issue dates: 100fr, Apr. 4; 200fr, May 8.

Concorde Issue
Common Design Type

1969, Apr. 17
C56 CD129 100fr org red & olive 17.50 10.00

Arta Ionospheric Station — AP19

Japanese Sword Guard, Fish Design — AP20

1970, May 8 Engr. *Perf. 13*
C57 AP19 70fr multicolored 3.00 2.00

Gold embossed

1970, Oct. 26 *Perf. 12½*

200fr, Japanese sword guard, horse design.

C58 AP20 100fr multicolored 7.50 5.00
C59 AP20 200fr multicolored 9.50 5.50

EXPO '70 International Exposition, Osaka, Japan, Mar. 15-Sept. 13.

Scarus vetula AP21

1971, July 1 Photo. *Perf. 12½*
C60 AP21 30fr black & multi 4.00 2.50

Djibouti Harbor — AP22

1972, Feb. 3
C61 AP22 100fr blue & multi 4.00 2.25

New Djibouti harbor.

AP23 AP24

1972 Photo. *Perf. 12½x13*
C62 AP23 30fr Pterocles lichtensteini 1.90 1.40
C63 AP23 49fr Uppupa epops 4.50 2.50
C64 AP23 66fr Capella media 5.75 3.25
C65 AP23 500fr Francolinus ochropectus 24.00 9.00
Nos. C62-C65 (4) 36.15 16.15

Issue dates: #C65, Nov. 3; others Apr. 21.

1972, June 8 Engr. *Perf. 13*

Olympic Rings and: 5fr, Running. 10fr, Basketball. 55fr, Swimming, horiz. 60fr, Olympic torch and Greek frieze, horiz.

C66 AP24 5fr multicolored .45 .25
C67 AP24 10fr multicolored .55 .40
C68 AP24 55fr multicolored 1.75 1.10
C69 AP24 60fr multicolored 2.25 1.25
Nos. C66-C69 (4) 5.00 3.00

20th Olympic Games, Munich, Aug. 26-Sept. 11.

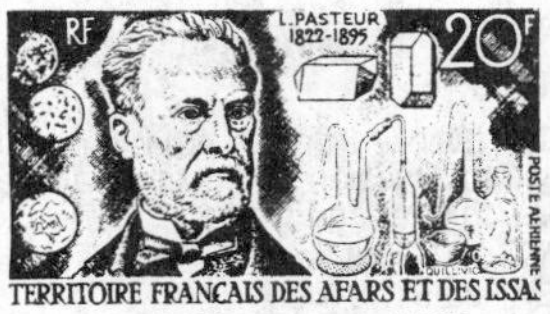

Louis Pasteur — AP25

Design: 100fr, Albert Calmette and C. Guérin.

1972, Oct. 5 Engr. *Perf. 13*
C70 AP25 20fr multicolored 1.25 .50
C71 AP25 100fr multicolored 4.00 2.50

Pasteur, Calmette, Guerin, chemists and bacteriologists, benefactors of mankind.

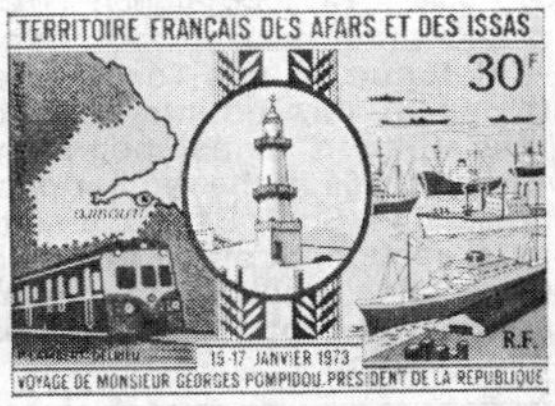

Map and Views of Territory — AP26

200fr, Woman and Mosque of Djibouti, vert.

1973, Jan. 15 Photo. *Perf. 13*
C72 AP26 30fr brown & multi 4.50 3.50
C73 AP26 200fr multicolored 8.00 6.00

Visit of Pres. Georges Pompidou of France, Jan. 15-17.

AP27

1973, Feb. 26 Photo. *Perf. 13x12½*
C74 AP27 30fr Oryx beisa 2.00 1.00
C75 AP27 50fr Madogua saltiana 2.75 1.50
C76 AP27 66fr Felis caracal 3.75 2.00
Nos. C74-C76 (3) 8.50 4.50

See Nos. C94-C96.

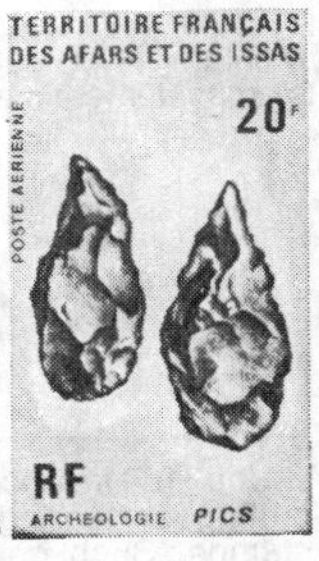

Celts — AP28

Various pre-historic flint tools. 40fr, 60fr, horiz.

1973 *Perf. 13*
C77 AP28 20fr yel grn, blk & brn 2.25 1.50
C78 AP28 40fr yellow & multi 2.75 2.00
C79 AP28 49fr lilac & multi 5.00 3.00
C80 AP28 60fr blue & multi 3.75 2.50
Nos. C77-C80 (4) 13.75 9.00

Issued: 20fr, 49fr, Mar. 16; 40fr, 60fr, Sept. 7.

Octopus macropus — AP29

1973, Mar. 16
C81 AP29 40fr shown 3.00 1.00
C82 AP29 60fr Halicore dugong 5.00 2.50

AP30 AP31

Copernicus: 8fr, Nicolaus Copernicus, Polish astronomer. 9fr, William C. Roentgen, physicist, X-ray discoverer. No. C85, Edward Jenner, physician, discoverer of vaccination. No. C86, Marie Curie, discoverer of radium and polonium. 49fr, Robert Koch, physician and bacteriologist. 50fr, Clement Ader (1841-1925), French aviation pioneer. 55fr, Guglielmo Marconi, Italian electrical engineer, inventor. 85fr, Moliere, French playwright. 100fr, Henri Farman (1874-1937), French aviation pioneer. 150fr, Andre-Marie Ampere (1775-1836), French physicist. 250fr, Michelangelo Buonarroti (1475-1564), Italian sculptor, painter and architect.

1973-75 Engr. *Perf. 13*
C83 AP30 8fr multicolored .65 .30
C84 AP30 9fr multicolored 1.00 .40
C85 AP30 10fr multicolored .90 .50
C86 AP30 10fr multicolored .75 .40
C87 AP30 49fr multicolored 3.25 1.60
C88 AP30 50fr multicolored 2.50 1.25
C89 AP30 55fr multicolored 1.90 1.00
C90 AP30 85fr multicolored 3.75 1.75
C91 AP30 100fr multicolored 3.75 2.00
C92 AP30 150fr multicolored 3.75 2.00
C93 AP30 250fr multicolored 6.50 3.50
Nos. C83-C93 (11) 28.70 14.70

Issued: 8fr, 85fr, 5/9/73; 9fr, #C85, 49fr, 10/12/73; 100fr, 1/29/74; 55fr, 3/22/74; #C86, 8/23/74; 150fr, 7/24/75; 250fr, 6/26/75; 50fr, 9/25/75.

Perf. 12½x13, 13x12½

1973, Dec. 12 Photo.
C94 AP31 20fr Papio anubis 1.25 .60
C95 AP31 50fr Genetta tigrina, horiz. 2.50 .90
C96 AP31 66fr Lapus habessinicus 4.00 1.50
Nos. C94-C96 (3) 7.75 3.00

Spearfishing — AP32

1974, Apr. 14 Engr. *Perf. 13*
C97 AP32 200fr multicolored 7.50 4.50

No. C97 was prepared for release in Nov. 1972, for the 3rd Underwater Spearfishing Contest in the Red Sea. Dates were obliterated with a rectangle and the stamp was not issued without this obliteration.

The Scott Catalogue value is a retail value; that is, what you could expect to pay for the stamp in a grade of Very Fine. The value listed reflects recent actual dealer selling prices.

Rock Carvings, Balho — AP33

1974, Apr. 26
C98 AP33 200fr carmine & slate 7.00 5.00

Lake Assal — AP34

Designs (Lake Assal): 50fr, Rock formations on shore. 85fr, Crystallized wood.

1974, Oct. 25 Photo. *Perf. 13*
C99 AP34 49fr multicolored 1.25 .75
C100 AP34 50fr multicolored 1.75 1.00
C101 AP34 85fr multicolored 3.50 2.25
Nos. C99-C101 (3) 6.50 4.00

Columba guinea — AP35

1975, May 23 Photo. *Perf. 13*
C102 AP35 500fr multicolored 18.00 6.50

Djibouti Airport — AP36

1977, Mar. 1 Litho. *Perf. 12*
C103 AP36 500fr multicolored 10.00 7.50

Opening of new Djibouti Airport.

Thomas A. Edison and Phonograph — AP37

Design: 75fr, Alexander Volta, electric train, lines and light bulb.

1977, May 5 Engr. *Perf. 13*
C104 AP37 55fr multicolored 3.00 1.50
C105 AP37 75fr multicolored 4.50 2.50

Famous inventors: Thomas Alva Edison and Alexander Volta (1745-1827).

POSTAGE DUE STAMPS

Nomad's Milk Jug — D3

Perf. 14x13

1969, Dec. 15 Engr. Unwmk.
J49 D3 1fr red brn, red lil & slate .20 .20
J50 D3 2fr red brn, emer & slate .20 .20
J51 D3 5fr red brn, bl & slate .30 .30
J52 D3 10fr red brn, brn & slate .80 .80
Nos. J49-J52 (4) 1.50 1.50

AFGHANISTAN

af-'ga-nə-,stan

LOCATION — Central Asia, bounded by Iran, Russian Turkestan, Pakistan, Baluchistan and China
GOVT. — Republic
AREA — 251,773 sq. mi.
POP. — 23,500,000 (1995 est.)
CAPITAL — Kabul

Afghanistan changed from a constitutional monarchy to a republic in July 1973.

12 Shahi = 6 Sanar = 3 Abasi =
2 Krans = 1 Rupee Kabuli
60 Paisas = 1 Rupee (1921)
100 Pouls = 1 Rupee Afghani (1927)

Catalogue values for unused stamps in this country are for Never Hinged items, beginning with Scott 364 in the regular postage section, Scott B1 in the semi-postal section, Scott C7 in the air-post section, Scott O8 in officials section, and Scott RA6 in the postal tax section.

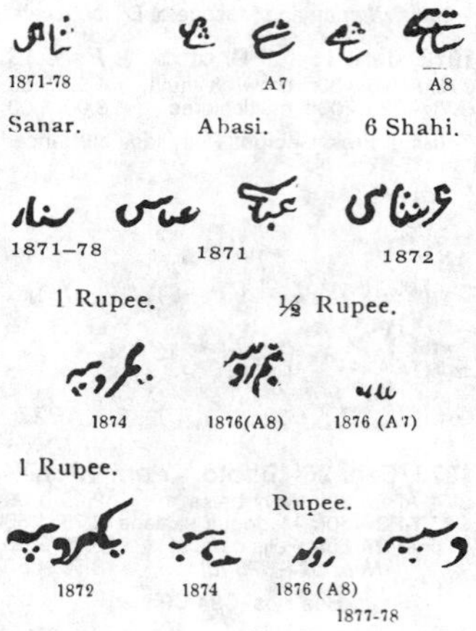

From 1871 to 1892 and 1898 the Moslem year date appears on the stamp. Numerals as follows:

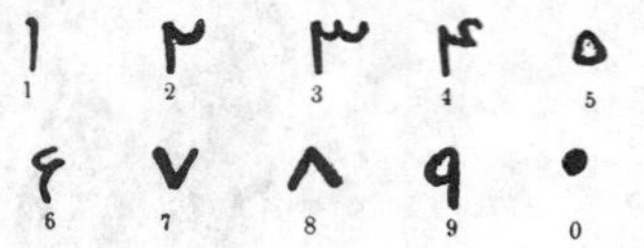

Until 1891 cancellation consisted of cutting or tearing a piece from the stamps. Such copies should not be considered as damaged.

Values are for cut square examples of good color. Cut to shape or faded copies sell for much less, particularly Nos. 2-10.

Nos. 2-108 are on laid paper of varying thickness except where wove is noted.

Until 1907 all stamps were issued ungummed.

The tiger's head on types A2 to A11 symbolizes the name of the contemporary amir, Sher (Tiger) Ali.

Kingdom of Kabul

Tiger's Head — A2

(Both circles dotted)

1871 Unwmk. Litho. *Imperf.*
Dated "1288"

2 A2 1sh black 110.00 22.50
3 A2 1sa black 75.00 20.00
4 A2 1ab black 37.50 20.00
Nos. 2-4 (3) 222.50 62.50

Thirty varieties of the shahi, 10 of the sanar and 5 of the abasi.

Similar designs without the tiger's head in the center are revenues.

A3

(Outer circle dotted)

Dated "1288"

5 A3 1sh black 175.00 35.00
6 A3 1sa black 75.00 22.50
7 A3 1ab black 37.50 22.50
Nos. 5-7 (3) 287.50 80.00

Five varieties of each.

A4

1872

Toned Wove Paper
Dated "1289"

8 A4 6sh violet *850. 750.*
9 A4 1rup violet *1,300. 1,100.*

Two varieties of each. Date varies in location. Printed in sheets of 4 (2x2) containing two of each denomination.

Most used copies are smeared with a greasy ink cancel.

A4a

1873

White Laid Paper
Dated "1290"

10 A4a 1sh black 10.00 4.50
a. Corner ornament missing *450.00 375.00*
b. Corner ornament retouched *60.00 25.00*

15 varieties. Nos. 10a, 10b are the sixth stamp on the sheet.

A5

1873

11 A5 1sh black 2.25 2.00
11A A5 1sh violet *500.00*

Sixty varieties of each.

1874

Dated "1291"

12 A5 1ab black 40.00 25.00
13 A5 ½rup black 20.00 17.50
14 A5 1rup black 22.50 20.00
Nos. 12-14 (3) 82.50 62.50

Five varieties of each.

Nos. 12-14 were printed on the same sheet. Se-tenant varieties exist.

A6

A7

1875

Dated "1292"

15 A6 1sa black *300.00 250.00*
a. Wide outer circle *600.00*
16 A6 1ab black 350.00 300.00
17 A6 1sa brown violet 22.50 22.50
a. Wide outer circle 110.00
18 A6 1ab brown violet 40.00 25.00

Ten varieties of the sanar, five of the abasi.

Nos. 15-16 and 17-18 were printed in the same sheets. Se-tenant pairs exist.

1876

Dated "1293"

19 A7 1sh black 300.00 150.00
20 A7 1sa black 375.00 200.00
21 A7 1ab black 600.00 325.00
22 A7 ½rup black 375.00 200.00
23 A7 1rup black 550.00 200.00
24 A7 1sh violet 375.00 200.00
25 A7 1sa violet 350.00 200.00
26 A7 1ab violet 425.00 200.00
27 A7 ½rup violet 90.00 55.00
28 A7 1rup violet 90.00 75.00

12 varieties of the shahi and 3 each of the other values.

A8

1876

Dated "1293"

29 A8 1sh gray 5.00 4.00
30 A8 1sa gray 7.50 4.00
31 A8 1ab gray 15.00 7.50
32 A8 ½rup gray 17.50 10.00
33 A8 1rup gray 22.50 10.00
34 A8 1sh olive blk 125.00
35 A8 1sa olive blk 175.00
36 A8 1ab olive blk 350.00
37 A8 ½rup olive blk 250.00
38 A8 1rup olive blk 275.00
39 A8 1sh green 22.50 3.75
40 A8 1sa green 35.00 15.00
41 A8 1ab green 50.00 37.50
42 A8 ½rup green 100.00 40.00
43 A8 1rup green 100.00 80.00
44 A8 1sh ocher 22.50 7.50
45 A8 1sa ocher 35.00 15.00
46 A8 1ab ocher 60.00 27.50
47 A8 ½rup ocher 75.00 60.00
48 A8 1rup ocher 125.00 110.00
49 A8 1sh violet 22.50 5.50
50 A8 1sa violet 22.50 7.50
51 A8 1ab violet 35.00 10.00
52 A8 ½rup violet 60.00 22.50
53 A8 1rup violet 75.00 35.00

12 varieties of the sanar, 6 of the abasi and 3 each of the ½ rupee and rupee.

24 varieties of the shahi, 4 of which show denomination written:

A9

1877

Dated "1294"

54	A9	1sh gray	3.50	2.25
55	A9	1sa gray	6.00	3.00
56	A9	1ab gray	9.00	6.00
57	A9	½rup gray	12.00	12.00
58	A9	1rup gray	12.00	12.00
59	A9	1sh black	10.00	
60	A9	1sa black	17.50	
61	A9	1ab black	42.50	
62	A9	½rup black	45.00	
63	A9	1rup black	45.00	
64	A9	1sh green	4.50	3.50
a.		Wove paper	12.00	
65	A9	1sa green	7.50	3.50
a.		Wove paper	16.00	12.00
66	A9	1ab green	10.00	10.00
a.		Wove paper	27.50	
67	A9	½rup green	14.00	14.00
a.		Wove paper	30.00	30.00
68	A9	1rup green	14.00	14.00
a.		Wove paper	30.00	30.00
69	A9	1sh ocher	3.50	2.00
70	A9	1sa ocher	10.00	3.50
71	A9	1ab ocher	17.50	16.00
72	A9	½rup ocher	30.00	30.00
73	A9	1rup ocher	30.00	30.00
74	A9	1sh violet	3.75	2.00
75	A9	1sa violet	7.50	2.75
76	A9	1ab violet	11.00	7.50
77	A9	½rup violet	17.50	14.00
78	A9	1rup violet	17.50	14.00

25 varieties of the shahi, 8 of the sanar, 3 of the abasi and 2 each of the ½ rupee and rupee.

A10

A11

1878

Dated "1295"

79	A10	1sh gray	1.50	1.50
80	A10	1sa gray	1.75	1.75
81	A10	1ab gray	3.75	3.75
82	A10	½rup gray	10.00	7.50
83	A10	1rup gray	10.00	7.50
84	A10	1sh black	3.00	
85	A10	1sa black	3.00	
86	A10	1ab black	10.00	
87	A10	½rup black	20.00	
88	A10	1rup black	20.00	
89	A10	1sh green	21.00	20.00
90	A10	1sa green	3.00	3.00
91	A10	1ab green	11.00	10.00
92	A10	½rup green	21.00	17.50
93	A10	1rup green	21.00	17.50
94	A10	1sh ocher	10.00	3.00
95	A10	1sa ocher	3.00	2.25
96	A10	1ab ocher	11.00	10.00
97	A10	½rup ocher	21.00	21.00
98	A10	1rup ocher	16.00	16.00
99	A10	1sh violet	1.75	1.75
100	A10	1sa violet	1.75	1.75
101	A10	1ab violet	5.50	5.50
102	A10	½rup violet	21.00	17.50
103	A10	1rup violet	21.00	17.50
104	A11	1sh gray	2.00	1.75
105	A11	1sh black	90.00	
106	A11	1sh green	1.75	1.75
107	A11	1sh ocher	1.40	1.40
108	A11	1sh violet	2.00	1.75

40 varieties of the shahi, 30 of the sanar, 6 of the abasi and 2 each of the ½ rupee and 1 rupee.

The 1876, 1877 and 1878 issues were printed in separate colors for each main post office on the Peshawar-Kabul-Khulm (Tashkurghan) postal route. Some specialists consider the black printings to be proofs or trial colors.

There are many shades of these colors.

1ab, Type I (26mm) — A12

1ab, Type II (28mm) — A13

A14

A15

Dated "1298", numerals scattered through design

Handstamped, in watercolor

1881-90

Thin White Laid Batonne Paper

109	A12	1ab violet	1.75	1.10
109A	A13	1ab violet	3.50	2.50
110	A12	1ab black brn	3.50	1.75
111	A12	1ab rose	2.00	2.00
b.		Se-tenant with No. 111A	16.00	
111A	A13	1ab rose	2.50	2.00
112	A14	2ab violet	1.75	1.50
113	A14	2ab black brn	5.00	4.00
114	A14	2ab rose	3.00	3.00
115	A15	1rup violet	2.50	1.50
116	A15	1rup black brn	6.50	6.50
117	A15	1rup rose	3.00	3.00

Thin White Wove Batonne Paper

118	A12	1ab violet	6.50	4.00
119	A12	1ab vermilion	4.25	
120	A12	1ab rose		
121	A14	2ab violet		
122	A14	2ab vermilion	5.00	
122A	A14	2ab black brn		
123	A15	1rup violet	8.25	
124	A15	1rup vermilion	6.50	
125	A15	1rup black brn	8.25	

Thin White Laid Batonne Paper

126	A12	1ab brown org	2.50	2.50
126A	A13	1ab brn org (II)	3.50	3.50
127	A12	1ab carmine lake	2.50	2.50
a.		Laid paper		
128	A14	2ab brown org	2.50	2.50
129	A14	2ab carmine lake	3.00	3.00
130	A15	1rup brown org	10.00	10.00
131	A15	1rup car lake	4.25	4.25

Yellowish Laid Batonne Paper

132	A12	1ab purple		3.50
133	A12	1ab red	6.50	3.50

1884

Colored Wove Paper

133A	A13	1ab purple, *yel* (II)	17.50	17.50
134	A12	1ab purple, *grn*	20.00	
135	A12	1ab purple, *blue*	32.50	21.00
136	A12	1ab red, *grn*	37.50	
137	A12	1ab red, *yel*	1.75	
139	A12	1ab red, *rose*	6.00	
140	A14	2ab red, *yel*	6.00	
142	A14	2ab red, *rose*	5.50	
143	A15	1rup red, *yel*	6.50	6.50
145	A15	1rup red, *rose*	7.00	7.00

Thin Colored Ribbed Paper

146	A14	2ab red, *yellow*	3.00	
147	A15	1rup red, *yellow*	8.25	
148	A12	1ab lake, *lilac*	4.00	
149	A14	2ab lake, *lilac*	5.00	
150	A15	1rup lake, *lilac*	4.00	
151	A12	1ab lake, *green*	2.00	
152	A14	2ab lake, *green*	4.00	
153	A15	1rup lake, *green*	4.00	

1886-88

Colored Wove Paper

155	A12	1ab black, *magenta*	27.50
156	A12	1ab claret brn, *org*	20.00
156A	A12	2ab red, *org*	2.00
156B	A14	2ab red, *org*	4.75
156C	A15	1rup red, *org*	3.50

Laid Batonné Paper

157	A12	1ab black, *lavender*	2.75
158	A12	1ab cl brn, *grn*	6.50
159	A12	1ab black, *pink*	17.50
160	A14	2ab black, *pink*	35.00
161	A15	1rup black, *pink*	20.00

Laid Paper

162	A12	1ab black, *pink*	6.50
163	A14	2ab black, *pink*	6.50
164	A15	1rup black, *pink*	6.50
165	A12	1ab brown, *yel*	6.50
166	A14	2ab brown, *yel*	6.50
167	A15	1rup brown, *yel*	6.50
168	A12	1ab blue, *grn*	6.50
169	A14	2ab blue, *grn*	6.50
170	A15	1rup blue, *grn*	6.50

1891

Colored Wove Paper

175	A12	1ab green, *rose*	22.50
176	A15	1rup pur, *grn batonne*	22.50

Nos. 109-176 fall into three categories:

1. Those regularly issued and in normal postal use from 1881 on, handstamped on thin white laid or wove paper in strip sheets containing 12 or more impressions of the same denomination arranged in two irregular rows, with the impressions often touching or overlappng.
2. The 1884 postal issues provisionally printed on smooth or ribbed colored wove paper as needed to supplement low stocks of the normal white paper stamps.
3. The "special" printings made in a range of colors on several types of laid or wove colored papers, most of which were never used for normal printings. These were produced periodically from 1886 to 1891 to meet philatelic demands. Although nominally valid for postage, most of the special printings were exported directly to fill dealers' orders, and few were ever postally used. Many of the sheets contained all three denominations with impressions separated by ruled lines. Sometimes different colors were used, so se-tenant multiples of denomination or color exist. Many combinations of stamp and paper colors exist besides those listed.

Various shades of each color exist.

Type A12 is known dated "1297."

Counterfeits, lithographed or typographed, are plentiful.

Kingdom of Afghanistan

A16

A17

A18

Dated "1309"

1891 **Pelure Paper** **Litho.**

177	A16	1ab slate blue	.85	.85
a.		Tete beche pair	14.00	
178	A17	2ab slate blue	6.00	5.00
179	A18	1rup slate blue	12.50	10.00
		Nos. 177-179 (3)	19.35	15.85

Revenue stamps of similar design exist in various colors.

Nos. 177-179 were printed in panes on the same sheet, so se-tenant gutter pairs exist. Examples in black or red are proofs.

A Mosque Gate and Crossed Cannons (National Seal) — A19

Dated "1310" in Upper Right Corner

1892

Flimsy Wove Paper

180	A19	1ab black, *green*	2.00	1.60
181	A19	1ab black, *orange*	2.50	2.50
182	A19	1ab black, *yellow*	2.00	1.60
183	A19	1ab black, *pink*	2.50	1.60
184	A19	1ab black, *lil rose*	2.50	2.50
185	A19	1ab black, *blue*	4.25	3.50
186	A19	1ab black, *salmon*	2.50	2.00
187	A19	1ab black, *magenta*	2.50	2.50
188	A19	1ab black, *violet*	2.50	2.50
188A	A19	1ab black, *scarlet*	2.50	1.75

Many shades exist.

A20

A21

Undated

1894

Flimsy Wove Paper

189	A20	2ab black, *green*	6.50	6.50
190	A21	1rup black, *green*	10.00	10.00

24 varieties of the 2 abasi and 12 varieties of the rupee.

Nos. 189-190 and F3 were printed se-tenant in the same sheet. Pairs exist.

A21a

Dated "1316"

1898

Flimsy Wove Paper

191	A21a	2ab black, *pink*	2.50
192	A21a	2ab black, *magenta*	2.50
193	A21a	2ab black, *yellow*	1.10
193A	A21a	2ab black, *salmon*	3.00
194	A21a	2ab black, *green*	1.40
195	A21a	2ab black, *purple*	1.75
195A	A21a	2ab black, *blue*	17.50
		Nos. 191-195A (7)	29.75

Nos. 191-195A were not regularly issued. Genuinely used copies are scarce. No. 195A was found in remainder stocks and probably was never released.

A22

A23

A24

1907 **Engr.** ***Imperf.***

Medium Wove Paper

196	A22	1ab blue green	10.00	2.50
a.		1ab emerald	17.00	5.00
197	A22	1ab brt blue	15.00	10.00
198	A23	2ab deep blue	5.00	5.00
199	A24	1rup green	9.00	*10.00*
a.		1rup blue green	10.00	*12.50*

Zigzag Roulette 10

200	A22	1ab green	55.00
201	A23	2ab blue	90.00
201A	A24	1rup blue green	*110.00*

1908 ***Perf. 12***

202	A22	1ab green	14.00	*20.00*
203	A23	2ab deep blue	5.00	5.00
204	A24	1rup blue green	17.50	17.50
		Nos. 202-204 (3)	36.50	42.50

Twelve varieties of the 1 abasi, 6 of the 2 abasi, 4 of the 1 rupee.

Nos. 196-204 were issued in small sheets containing 3 or 4 panes. Gutter pairs, normal and tête bêche, exist.

A25

A26

A27

1909-19 Typo. *Perf. 12*

205	A25	1ab ultra	3.00	1.00
a.		Imperf., pair	20.00	
206	A25	1ab red ('16)	.60	.60
a.		Imperf.	22.50	
207	A25	1ab rose ('18)	.80	.70
208	A26	2ab green	.50	.25
a.		Imperf., pair	20.00	
b.		Horiz. pair, imperf. btwn.		
208C	A26	2ab yellow ('16)	2.00	2.00
209	A26	2ab bis ('18-'19)	.90	*1.25*
210	A27	1rup lilac brn	4.00	4.00
a.		1rup red brown	4.00	4.00
211	A27	1rup ol bis ('16)	6.00	6.00
		Nos. 205-211 (8)	17.80	15.80

A28

1913

212	A28	2pa drab brown	1.25	1.25
a.		2pa red brown	1.25	1.25

No. 212 is inscribed "Tiket waraq dak" (Postal card stamps). It was usable only on postcards and not accepted for postage on letters.

Nos. 196-212 sometimes show letters of a papermaker's watermark, "Howard & Jones, London."

Royal Star — A29

1920, Aug. 24 *Perf. 12*

Size: 39x47mm

214	A29	10pa rose	30.00	20.00
215	A29	20pa red brown	50.00	40.00
216	A29	30pa green	100.00	100.00
		Nos. 214-216 (3)	180.00	160.00

Issued in sheets of two.

1921, Mar.

Size: 22½x28¼mm

217	A29	10pa rose	1.00	1.00
a.		Perf. 11 ('27)	12.00	10.00
218	A29	20pa red brown	2.00	2.00
219	A29	30pa yel green	3.00	2.50
a.		Tete beche pair	20.00	20.00
b.		30pa green	3.00	2.75
c.		As "b," Tete beche pair	20.00	20.00
		Nos. 217-219 (3)	6.00	5.50

Two types of the 10pa, three of the 20pa.

Crest of King Amanullah
A30 A32

1924, Feb. 26 *Perf. 12*

220	A30	10pa chocolate	27.50	27.50
a.		Tete beche pair	90.00	70.00

6th Independence Day.

Printed in sheets of four consisting of two tete beche pairs, and in sheets of two. Two types exist.

Some authorities believe that Nos. Q15-Q16 were issued as regular postage stamps.

1925, Feb. 26 *Perf. 12*

Size: 29x37mm

222	A32	10pa light brown	35.00	30.00

7th Independence Day.

Printed in sheets of 8 (two panes of 4).

1926, Feb. 28

Wove Paper

Size: 26x33mm

224	A32	10pa dark blue	5.00	5.00
a.		Imperf., pair	25.00	
b.		Horiz. pair, imperf. btwn.	50.00	
c.		Vert. pair, imperf. btwn.		
d.		Laid paper	10.00	10.00

7th anniv. of Independence. Printed in sheets of 4, and in sheets of 8 (two panes of 4). Tete beche gutter pairs exist.

Tughra and Crest of Amanullah — A33

1927, Feb.

225	A33	10pa magenta	10.00	9.00
a.		Vertical pair, imperf. between	47.50	

Dotted Background

226	A33	10pa magenta	12.00	10.00
a.		Horiz. pair, imperf. between	50.00	

The surface of No. 226 is covered by a net of fine dots.

8th anniv. of Independence. Printed in sheets of 8 (two panes of 4). Tete beche gutter pairs exist.

National Seal — A34

A35

A35a

A36

1927, Oct. *Imperf.*

227	A34	15p pink	1.00	1.00
228	A35	30p Prus green	2.00	.90
229	A36	60p light blue	3.00	2.50
a.		Tete beche pair	7.50	
		Nos. 227-229 (3)	6.00	4.40

1927-30 *Perf. 11, 12*

230	A34	15p pink	1.00	1.00
231	A34	15p ultra ('29)	1.00	1.00
232	A35	30p Prus green	2.00	1.00
233	A35a	30p dp green ('30)	1.00	.90
234	A36	60p bright blue	2.00	1.00
a.		Tete beche pair	9.00	9.00
235	A36	60p black ('29)	2.50	1.75
		Nos. 230-235 (6)	9.50	6.65

Nos. 230, 232 and 234 are usually imperforate on one or two sides.

No. 233 has been redrawn. A narrow border of pearls has been added and "30," in European and Arabic numerals, inserted in the upper spandrels.

Tughra and Crest of Amanullah A37

1928, Feb. 27

236	A37	15p pink	4.00	4.00
a.		Tete beche pair	9.00	7.50
b.		Horiz. pair, imperf. vert.	17.50	15.00
c.		As "a," imperf. vert., block of 4	25.00	

9th anniv. of Independence. This stamp is always imperforate on one or two sides.

A 15p blue of somewhat similar design was prepared for the 10th anniv., but was not issued due to Amanullah's dethronement. Value, $15.

A38

A39

A40

A41

A42

1928-30 *Perf. 11, 12*

237	A38	2p dull blue	2.50	1.60
a.		Vertical pair, imperf. between	17.50	
238	A38	2p lt rose ('30)	.25	.25
239	A39	10p gray green	1.00	.20
a.		Tete beche pair	12.00	5.00
b.		Vert. pair, imperf. horiz.	10.00	10.00
c.		Vertical pair, imperf. between		
240		10p choc ('30)	1.25	1.00
a.		10p brown purple ('29)	8.00	4.00
241	A40	25p car rose	1.00	.25
242	A40	25p Prus green ('29)	1.50	1.00
243	A41	40p ultra	1.25	.35
a.		Tete beche pair	13.00	*15.00*
244	A41	40p rose ('29)	1.50	1.25
a.		Tete beche pair	12.50	
b.		Vert. pair, imperf. horiz.	10.00	
245	A42	50p red	.60	.50
246	A42	50p dk blue ('29)	1.75	1.25
		Nos. 237-246 (10)	12.60	7.65

The sheets of these stamps are often imperforate at the outer margins.

Nos. 237-238 are newspaper stamps.

This handstamp was used for ten months by the Revolutionary Gov't in Kabul as a control mark on outgoing mail. It occasionally fell on the stamps but there is no evidence that it was officially used as an overprint. Unused copies were privately made.

Independence Monument — A46

Wmk. Large Seal in the Sheet

1931, Aug. Litho. *Perf. 12*

Laid Paper

Without Gum

262	A46	20p red	1.00	.60

13th Independence Day.

National Assembly Chamber — A47

A48

A50

National Assembly Building A49

National Assembly Chamber A51

National Assembly Building A52

1932 Unwmk. Typo. *Perf. 12*

Wove Paper

263	A47	40p olive	1.00	.40
264	A48	60p violet	.65	.50
265	A49	80p dark red	1.00	.80
266	A50	1af black	10.00	4.25
267	A51	2af ultra	3.50	2.75
268	A52	3af gray green	4.25	3.50
		Nos. 263-268 (6)	20.40	12.20

Formation of the Natl. Council. Imperforate or perforated examples on ungummed chalky paper are proofs.

See Nos. 304-305.

Mosque at Balkh — A53

Kabul Fortress — A54

Parliament House, Darul Funun — A55

Parliament House, Darul Funun — A56

Arch of Qalai Bist — A57

Memorial Pillar of Knowledge and Ignorance A58

Independence Monument A59

Minaret at Herat A60

Arch of Paghman — A61

Ruins at Balkh — A62

Minarets of Herat A63

Great Buddha at Bamian A64

1932 Typo. *Perf. 12*

269	A53	10p brown	.50	.20
270	A54	15p dk brown	.60	.20
271	A55	20p red	.30	.20
272	A56	25p dk green	.75	.20
273	A57	30p red	.40	.30
274	A58	40p orange	.65	.35
275	A59	50p blue	.80	.35
a.		Tete beche pair	5.50	
276	A60	60p blue	1.50	.50
277	A61	80p violet	1.75	1.00
278	A62	1af dark blue	2.75	.60
279	A63	2af dk red violet	3.75	2.00
280	A64	3af claret	4.25	2.50
		Nos. 269-280 (12)	18.00	8.40

Counterfeits of types A53-A65 exist.

See Nos. 290-295, 298-299, 302-303.

Entwined 2's — A65

Two types:

Type I - Numerals shaded. Size about 21x29mm.

Type II - Numerals unshaded. Size about 21¾x30mm.

1931-38 *Perf. 12, 11x12*

281	A65	2p red brn (I)	.25	.20
282	A65	2p olive blk (I) ('34)	.25	.20
283	A65	2p grnsh gray (I) ('34)	.35	.20
283A	A65	2p black (II) ('36)	.35	.20
284	A65	2p salmon (II) ('38)	.25	.20
284A	A65	2p rose (I) ('38)	.25	.20
b.		Imperf., pair	3.00	

Imperf

285	A65	2p black (II) ('37)	.75	.20
286	A65	2p salmon (II) ('38)	.25	.20
		Nos. 281-286 (8)	2.70	1.60

The newspaper rate was 2 pouls.

A66

A67

1932, Aug. *Perf. 12*

287 A66 1af Independence Monument 2.75 1.50

14th Independence Day.

1932, Oct. Typo.

1929 Liberation Monument, Kabul.

288 A67 80p red brown .85 .50

Arch of Paghman A68

1933, Aug.

289 A68 50p light ultra 1.25 1.25

15th Independence Day.

Types of 1932 and

Royal Palace, Kabul — A69

Darrah-Shikari Pass, Hindu Kush — A70

1934-38 Typo. *Perf. 12*

290	A53	10p deep violet	.20	.20
291	A54	15p turq green	.20	.20
292	A55	20p magenta	.25	.20
293	A56	25p deep rose	.30	.20
294	A57	30p orange	.40	.20
295	A58	40p blue black	.75	.30
296	A69	45p dark blue	1.50	1.00
297	A69	45p red ('38)	.50	.20
298	A59	50p orange	.30	.20
299	A60	60p purple	.85	.20
300	A70	75p red	1.00	.35
301	A70	75p dk blue ('38)	.60	.40
302	A61	80p brown vio	1.00	.50
303	A62	1af red violet	1.60	1.00
304	A51	2af gray black	3.00	2.00
305	A52	3af ultra	5.00	3.00
		Nos. 290-305 (16)	17.45	10.15

Nos. 290, 292, 300, 304, 305 exist imperf.

Independence Monument — A71

1934, Aug. Litho.

Without Gum

306	A71	50p pale green	2.50	1.25
a.		Tete beche pair	10.00	3.50

16th year of Independence. Each sheet of 40 (4x10) included 4 tete beche pairs as lower half of sheet was inverted.

Independence Monument A74

Fireworks Display A75

1935, Aug. 15

Laid Paper

309 A74 50p dark blue 1.25 1.25

17th year of Independence.

1936, Aug. 15 *Perf. 12*

Wove Paper

310 A75 50p red violet 1.25 1.00

18th year of Independence.

Independence Monument and Nadir Shah — A76

1937

311	A76	50p vio & bis brn	1.00	.60
a.		Imperf., pair	2.25	

19th year of Independence.

Mohammed Nadir Shah
A77 A78

1938 *Perf. 11x12*

Without Gum

315	A77	50p brt blue & sepia	5.00	2.50
a.		Imperf. pair	20.00	

20th year of Independence.

1939 *Perf. 11, 12x11*

317 A78 50p deep salmon 1.75 1.00

21st year of Independence.

National Arms A79

Parliament House, Darul Funun A80

Royal Palace, Kabul A81

Independence Monument A82

Independence Monument and Nadir Shah — A83

Mohammed Zahir Shah — A84

Mohammed Zahir Shah — A85

Perf. 11, 11x12, 12x11, 12

1939-61 Typo.

318	A79	2p intense blk	.20	.20
318A	A79	2p brt pink ('61)	1.50	.50
319	A80	10p brt purple	.20	.20
320	A80	15p brt green	.20	.20
321	A80	20p red lilac	.20	.20
322	A81	25p rose red	1.00	.25
322A	A81	25p green ('41)	.50	.20
323	A81	30p orange	.20	.20
324	A81	40p dk gray	.20	.20
325	A82	45p brt carmine	.20	.20
326	A82	50p dp orange	.30	.20
327	A82	60p violet	.60	.20
328	A83	75p ultra	3.00	.75
328A	A83	75p red vio ('41)	.75	.30
328C	A83	75p brt red ('44)	3.00	3.00
328D	A83	75p chnt brn ('49)	4.00	3.00
329	A83	80p chocolate	.50	.50
a.		80p dull red violet (error)		
330	A84	1af brt red violet	1.50	.75
330A	A85	1af brt red vio ('44)	3.00	1.50
331	A85	2af copper red	1.75	.50
a.		2af dp rose red	2.50	1.40
332	A84	3af deep blue	3.75	1.60
		Nos. 318-332 (21)	26.55	14.65

Many shades exist in this issue.

On No. 332 the King faces slightly left.

No. 318A issued with and without gum.

See #795A-795B. For similar design see #907A.

Mohammed Nadir Shah — A86

1940, Aug. 23 *Perf. 11*

333 A86 50p gray green .75 .60

22nd year of Independence.

Independence Monument A87

Arch of Paghman A88

1941, Aug. 23 *Perf. 12*

334	A87	15p gray green	8.00	2.75
335	A88	50p red brown	1.25	.85

23rd year of Independence.

Sugar Factory, Baghlan — A89

1942, Apr. *Perf. 12*

336	A89	1.25af blue (shades)	2.00	1.00
a.		1.25af ultra	2.00	1.00

In 1949, a 1.50af brown, type A89, was sold for 3af by the Philatelic Office, Kabul. It was not valid for postage. Value $3.50.

Independence Monument A90

Mohammed Nadir Shah and Arch of Paghman A91

1942, Aug. 23 *Perf. 12*

337	A90	35p bright green	2.75	2.00
338	A91	125p chalky blue	1.40	1.10

24th year of Independence.

Independence Monument and Nadir Shah — A92

Mohammed Nadir Shah — A93

Perf. 11x12, 12x11

1943, Aug. 25 Typo. Unwmk.

339 A92 35p carmine 18.00 6.00
340 A93 1.25af dark blue 3.00 1.75

25th year of Independence.

Tomb of Gohar Shad, Herat — A94

Ruins of Qalai Bist — A95

1944, May 1 ***Perf. 12, 11x12***

341 A94 35p orange .50 .30
342 A95 70p violet 1.00 .60
a. 70p rose lilac 3.50 .75

A96 A97

1944, Aug. ***Perf. 12***

343 A96 35p crimson .80 .60
344 A97 1.25af ultra 1.40 1.10

26th year of Independence.

A98 A99

1945, July

345 A98 35p dp red lil .75 .65
346 A99 1.25af blue 1.75 1.50

27th year of Independence.

Mohammed Zahir Shah A100

Independence Monument A101

Mohammed Nadir Shah — A102

1946, July

347 A100 15p emerald .45 .35
348 A101 20p dp red lilac .70 .55
349 A102 125p blue 1.75 1.75
Nos. 347-349 (3) 2.90 2.65

28th year of Independence.

Zahir Shah and Ruins of Qalai Bist — A103

A104 A105

1947, Aug.

350 A103 15p yellow green .30 .20
351 A104 35p plum .40 .20
352 A105 125p deep blue 1.40 1.40
Nos. 350-352 (3) 2.10 1.80

29th year of Independence.

Begging Child — A106

A107

1948, May Unwmk. Typo. ***Perf. 12***

353 A106 35p yel green 3.00 2.00
354 A107 125p gray blue 3.00 2.25

Children's Day, May 29, 1948, and valid only on that day. Proceeds were used for Child Welfare.

A108 A109

A110

1948, Aug.

355 A108 15p green .20 .20
356 A109 20p magenta .40 .20
357 A110 125p dark blue .75 .70
Nos. 355-357 (3) 1.35 1.10

30th year of Independence.

United Nations Emblem — A111

1948, Oct. 24

358 A111 125p dk violet blue 7.00 7.00

UN, 3rd anniv. Valid one day only. Sheets of 9.

Maiwand Victory Column, Kandahar — A112

Zahir Shah and Ruins of Qalai Bist — A113

Independence Monument and Nadir Shah — A114

1949, Aug. Typo. ***Perf. 12***

359 A112 25p green .25 .20
360 A113 35p magenta .35 .25
361 A114 1.25af blue .90 .75
Nos. 359-361 (3) 1.50 1.20

31st year of Independence.

Catalogue values for unused stamps in this section, from this point to the end of the section, are for Never Hinged items.

Nadir Shah — A117

1950, Aug.

364 A117 35p red brown .30 .30
365 A117 125p blue .65 .65

32nd year of Independence.

Medical School and Nadir Shah A119

1950, Dec. 22 Typo. ***Perf. 12***

Size: 38x25mm

367 A119 35p emerald .60 .60

Size: 46x30mm

368 A119 1.25af deep blue 1.90 1.90
a. 1.25af black (error) 6.00

19th anniv. of the founding of Afghanistan's Faculty of Medicine. On sale and valid for use on Dec. 22-28, 1950.

Minaret, Herat — A120

Zahir Shah — A121

Mosque of Khodja Abu Parsar, Balkh — A122

A123 A124

20p, Buddha at Bamian. 40p, Ruined arch. 45p, Maiwand Victory onument. 50p, View of Kandahar. 60p, Ancient tower. 70p, Afghanistan flag. 80p, 1af, Profile of Zahir Shah in uniform.

Photogravure, Engraved, Engraved and Lithographed

Perf. 12, 12½, 13x12½, 13½

1951, Mar. 21 Unwmk.

Imprint: "Waterlow & Sons Limited, London"

369 A120 10p yellow & brn .20 .20
370 A120 15p blue & brn .20 .20
371 A120 20p black 5.00 2.75
372 A121 25p green .20 .20
373 A122 30p cerise .20 .20
374 A121 35p violet .20 .20
375 A122 40p chestnut brn .25 .20
376 A120 45p deep blue .20 .20
377 A122 50p olive black .45 .20
378 A120 60p black 1.50 .75
379 A122 70p dk grn, blk, red & grn .25 .20
380 A123 75p cerise .75 .35
381 A123 80p carmine & blk .65 .35
382 A123 1af dp grn & vio .45 .35
383 A124 1.25af rose lil & blk 5.00 .35
384 A124 2af ultra 1.10 .35
385 A124 3af ultra & blk 2.50 .90
Nos. 369-385 (17) 19.10 7.95

Nos. 372, 374 and 381 to 385 are engraved, No. 379 is engraved and lithographed.

Imperfs. exist of the photogravure stamps.

See Nos. 445-451, 453, 552A-552D. For surcharges see Nos. B1-B2.

Arch of Paghman A125

Nadir Shah and Independence Monument A126

Overprint in Violet

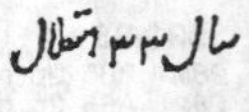

Perf. 13½x13, 13

1951, Aug. 25 Engr.

386 A125 35p dk green & blk .60 .35
387 A126 1.25af deep blue 1.40 .85

Overprint reads "Sol 33 Istiqlal" or "33rd Year of Independence." Overprint measures about 11mm wide.

See Nos. 398-399B, 441-442.

Proposed Flag of Pashtunistan — A127

Design: 125p, Flag and Pashtunistan warrior.

1951, Sept. 2 Litho. *Perf. 11½*

388 A127 35p dull chocolate .80 .65
389 A127 125p blue 2.00 1.75

Issued to publicize "Free Pashtunistan" Day.

Imperforates

From 1951 to 1958, quantities of nearly all locally-printed stamps were left imperforate and sold by the government at double face. From 1959 until March, 1964, many of the imperforates were sold for more than face value.

Avicenna — A128

1951, Nov. 4 Typo. *Perf. 11½*

390 A128 35p deep claret .50 .35
391 A128 125p blue 1.40 1.10

20th anniv. of the founding of the natl. Graduate School of Medicine.

A129

Dove and UN Symbols — A130

1951, Oct. 24

392 A129 35p magenta 1.40 1.00
393 A130 125p blue 3.50 2.75

7th anniv. of the UN.

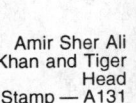

Amir Sher Ali Khan and Tiger Head Stamp — A131

Nos. 395, 397, Zahir Shah and stamp.

1951, Dec. 23 Litho.

394 A131 35p chocolate .35 .35
395 A131 35p rose lilac .35 .35
396 A131 125p ultra .65 .60
a. Cliche of 35p in plate of 125p 80.00 80.00
397 A131 125p aqua .65 .60
Nos. 394-397 (4) 2.00 1.90

76th anniv. of the UPU.

Stamps of 1951 Without Overprint

Perf. 13½x13, 13

1952, Aug. 24 Engr.

398 A125 35p dk green & blk 1.25 1.25
399 A126 1.25af deep blue 1.25 1.25

For overprints see #399A-399B, 441-442.

Same Overprinted in Violet

399A A125 35p dk grn & blk .60 .40
399B A126 1.25af deep blue 1.60 1.00

#398-399B issued for 34th Independence Day.

Globe — A132

Perf. 11½

1952, Oct. 25 Unwmk. Litho.

400 A132 35p rose .55 .45
401 A132 125p aqua 1.10 1.00

Issued to honor the United Nations.

Symbol of Medicine A134

Tribal Warrior, Natl. Flag A135

1952, Nov. *Perf. 11½*

403 A134 35p chocolate .40 .35
404 A134 125p violet blue 1.10 1.10

21st anniv. of the natl. Graduate School of Medicine.

No. 404 is inscribed in French with white letters on a colored background.

1952, Sept. 1 *Perf. 11*

405 A135 35p red .30 .30
406 A135 125p dark blue .60 .60

No. 406 is inscribed in French "Pashtunistan Day, 1952."

Flags of Afghanistan & Pashtunistan A139

Badge of Pashtunistan A140

Perf. 10½x11, 11

1953, Sept. 1 Unwmk.

411 A139 35p vermilion .20 .20
412 A140 125p blue .60 .45

Issued to publicize "Free Pashtunistan" Day.

Nadir Shah and Flag Bearer — A141

A142

1953, Aug. 24 *Perf. 11*

413 A141 35p green .20 .20
414 A142 125p violet .75 .60

35th anniv. of Independence.

United Nations Emblem — A143

1953, Oct. 24

415 A143 35p lilac .60 .60
416 A143 125p violet blue 1.50 1.25

United Nations Day, 1953.

Nadir Shah

A144 A145

1953, Nov. 29

417 A144 35p orange .65 .65
418 A145 125p chalky blue 1.50 1.50

22nd anniv. of the founding of the natl. Graduate School of Medicine.

Redrawn

35p. Original- Right character in second line of Persian inscription: ٣

Redrawn- Persian character: ٢

125p: Original- Inscribed "XXIII," "MADECINE" and "ANNIVERAIRE"
Redrawn- Inscribed "XXII," "MEDECINE" and "ANNIVERSAIRE"

1953

419 A144 35p deep orange 3.50
420 A145 125p chalky blue 4.25

Nadir Shah and Symbols of Independence A146

1954, Aug. Typo. *Perf. 11*

421 A146 35p carmine rose .35 .30
422 A146 125p violet blue 1.00 .80

36th year of Independence.

Raising Flag of Pashtunistan A147

1954, Sept. *Perf. 11½*

423 A147 35p chocolate .35 .30
424 A147 125p blue 1.00 .80

Issued to publicize "Free Pashtunistan" Day.

UN Flag and Map — A148

1954, Oct. 24 *Perf. 11*

425 A148 35p carmine rose .65 .65
426 A148 125p dk violet blue 2.00 2.00

9th anniv. of the United Nations.

UN Symbols — A149

Design: 125p, UN emblem & flags.

1955, June 26 Litho. *Perf. 11*

Size: 26½x36mm

427 A149 35p dark green .45 .40

Size: 28½x36mm

428 A149 125p aqua 1.10 .90

10th anniv. of the UN charter.

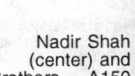

Nadir Shah (center) and Brothers — A150

1929 Civil War Scene and Zahir Shah — A151

Tribal Elders' Council and Pashtun Flag — A152

1955, Aug. Unwmk. *Perf. 11*

429 A150 35p brt pink .30 .30
430 A150 35p violet blue .30 .30
431 A151 125p rose lilac .90 .75
432 A151 125p light violet .90 .75
Nos. 429-432 (4) 2.40 2.10

37th anniv. of Independence.

1955, Sept. 5

433 A152 35p orange brown .20 .20
434 A152 125p yellow green .90 .65

Issued for "Free Pashtunistan" Day.

UN Flag — A153

A154

1955, Oct. 24 Unwmk. *Perf. 11*

435 A153 35p orange brown .75 .60
436 A153 125p brt ultra 1.40 1.10

10th anniv. of the United Nations.

1956, Aug. Litho.

437 A154 35p lt green .25 .20
438 A154 140p lt violet blue .90 .75

38th year of Independence.

Jesh'n Exhibition Hall — A155

1956, Aug. 25

439 A155 50p chocolate .25 .20
440 A155 50p lt violet blue .25 .20

International Exposition at Kabul.

Of the 50p face value, only 35p paid postage. The remaining 15p went to the Exposition.

Nos. 398-399 Handstamped in Violet

39 em Anv

a b

1957, Aug. Engr. *Perf. 13½x13, 13*

441 A125 (a) 35p dk green & blk .40 .20
442 A126 (b) 1.25af deep blue .60 .50

Arabic overprint measures 19mm.
39th year of independence.

Pashtunistan Flag — A156

1957, Sept. 1 Litho. *Perf. 11*

443	A156	50p	pale lilac rose	.60	.40
444	A156	155p	light violet	.90	.75

Issued for "Free Pashtunistan" Day. French inscription on No. 444. 15p of each stamp went to the Pashtunistan Fund.

Types of 1951 and

Game of Buzkashi A157

Perf. 12, 12½, 12½x13, 13, 13x12, 13x12½, 13½x14

Photo., Engr., Engr.& Litho.

1957, Nov. 23 Unwmk.

Imprint: "Waterlow & Sons Limited, London"

445	A122	30p	brown	.20	.20
446	A122	40p	rose red	.20	.20
447	A122	50p	yellow	.35	.20
448	A120	60p	ultra	.40	.20
449	A123	75p	brt violet	.50	.20
450	A123	80p	violet & brn	.50	.20
451	A123	1af	carmine & ultra	1.00	.20
452	A157	140p	olive & dp claret	2.00	.50
453	A124	3af	orange & blk	2.50	.50
			Nos. 445-453 (9)	7.65	2.40

No. 452 lacks imprint.

Nadir Shah and Flag-bearer A158

1958, Aug. 25 *Perf. 13½x14*

454	A158	35p	dp yellow green	.20	.20
455	A158	140p	brown	.55	.35

40th year of Independence.

Exposition Buildings A159

1958, Aug. 23 Litho. *Perf. 11*

456	A159	35p	brt blue green	.20	.20
457	A159	140p	vermilion	.50	.40

International Exposition at Kabul.

Pres. Celal Bayar of Turkey A160

Flags of UN and Afghanistan A161

1958, Sept. 13 Unwmk.

458	A160	50p	lt blue	.20	.20
459	A160	100p	brown	.35	.30

Visit of President Celal Bayar of Turkey.

1958, Oct. 24 Photo. *Perf. 14x13½*

Flags in Original Colors

460	A161	50p	dark gray	.60	.60
461	A161	100p	green	1.10	.90

United Nations Day, Oct. 24.

Atomic Energy Encircling the Hemispheres A162

1958, Oct. 20 *Perf. 13½x14*

462	A162	50p	blue	.60	.35
463	A162	100p	dp red lilac	.90	.55

Issued to promote Atoms for Peace.

UNESCO Building, Paris — A163

1958, Nov. 3

464	A163	50p	dp yellow grn	.50	.40
465	A163	100p	brown olive	.75	.60

UNESCO Headquarters in Paris opening, Nov. 3.

Globe and Torch — A164

Perf. 13½x14

1958, Dec. 10 Unwmk.

466	A164	50p	lilac rose	.35	.35
467	A164	100p	maroon	.65	.65

10th anniv. of the signing of the Universal Declaration of Human Rights.

Nadir Shah and Flags — A165

1959, Aug. Litho. *Perf. 11 Rough*

468	A165	35p	light vermilion	.20	.20
469	A165	165p	light violet	.65	.40

41st year of Independence.

Uprooted Oak Emblem — A166

1960, Apr. 7 *Perf. 11*

470	A166	50p	deep orange	.20	.20
471	A166	165p	blue	.35	.30

Issued to publicize World Refugee Year, July 1, 1959-June 30, 1960.

Two imperf. souvenir sheets exist. Both contain a 50p and a 165p, type A166, with marginal inscriptions and WRY emblem in maroon. On one sheet the stamps are in the colors of Nos. 470-471 (size 108x81mm). On the other, the 50p is blue and the 165p is deep orange (size 107x80mm). Value $4 each.

For surcharges see Nos. B35-B36.

Buzkashi A167

1960, May 4 *Perf. 11, Imperf.*

472	A167	25p	rose red	.25	.20
473	A167	50p	bluish green	.50	.35
a.			Cliche of 25p in plate of 50p	20.00	20.00

See Nos. 549-550A.

Independence Monument — A168

1960, Aug. *Perf. 11, 12*

474	A168	50p	light blue	.20	.20
475	A168	175p	bright pink	.40	.40

42nd Independence Day.

Globe and Flags — A169

1960, Oct. 24 Litho. *Perf. 11, 12*

476	A169	50p	rose lilac	.25	.20
477	A169	175p	ultra	.75	.65

UN Day.

An imperf. souvenir sheet contains one each of Nos. 476-477 with marginal inscriptions ("La Journée des Nations Unies 1960" in French and Persian) and UN emblem in light blue. Size: 127x85½mm. Value $4.

This sheet was surcharged "+20ps" in 1962. Value $8.50.

Teacher Pointing to Globe A170

1960, Oct. 23 *Perf. 11*

478	A170	50p	brt pink	.20	.20
479	A170	100p	brt green	.70	.45

Issued to publicize Teacher's Day.

Mohammed Zahir Shah — A171

1960, Oct. 15

480	A171	50p	red brown	.30	.20
481	A171	150p	dk car rose	.90	.30

Honoring the King on his 46th birthday.

Buzkashi A172

1960, Nov. 9 *Perf. 11*

482	A172	175p	lt red brown	1.00	.40

See Nos. 551-552.

No. 482 Overprinted "1960" and Olympic Rings in Bright Green.

1960, Dec. 24

483	A172	175p	red brown	2.00	1.75
a.			Souv. sheet of 1, imperf.	8.50	

17th Olympic Games, Rome, Aug. 25-Sept. 11.

Mir Wais — A173

1961, Jan. 5 Unwmk. *Perf. 10½*

484	A173	50p	brt rose lilac	.20	.20
485	A173	175p	ultra	.60	.40
a.			Souv. sheet of 2, #484-485, imperf.	2.00	2.00

Mir Wais (1665-1708), national leader.

No Postal Need

existed for the 1p-15p denominations issued with sets of 1961-63 (between Nos. 486 and 649, B37 and B65).

The lowest denomination actually used for non-philatelic postage in that period was 25p (except for the 2p newspaper rate for which separate stamps were provided).

Horse, Sheep and Camel A174

#487, 175p, Rock partridge. 10p, 100p, Afghan hound. 15p, 150p, Grain & grasshopper, vert.

1961, Mar. 29 Photo. *Perf. 13½x14*

486	A174	2p	maroon & buff		
487	A174	2p	ultra & org		
488	A174	5p	brown & yel		
489	A174	10p	black & salmon		
490	A174	15p	blue grn & yel		
491	A174	25p	black & pink		
492	A174	50p	black & citron		
493	A174	100p	black & pink		
494	A174	150p	green & yel		
495	A174	175p	ultra & pink		
			Nos. 486-495 (10)	2.00	

Two souvenir sheets, perf. and imperf., contain 2 stamps, 1 each of #492-493. Value $2 each.

Afghan Fencing A175

Designs: No. 497, 5p, 25p, 50p, Wrestlers. 10p, 100p, Man with Indian clubs. 15p, 150p, Afghan fencing. 175p, Children skating.

1961, July 6 *Perf. 13½x14*

496	A175	2p	green & rose lil		
497	A175	2p	brown & citron		
498	A175	5p	gray & rose		
499	A175	10p	blue & bister		
500	A175	15p	sl bl & dl lil		
501	A175	25p	black & dl bl		
502	A175	50p	sl grn & bis brn		
503	A175	100p	brown & bl grn		
504	A175	150p	brown & org yel		
505	A175	175p	black & blue		
			Nos. 496-505 (10)	3.00	

Issued for Children's Day.

A souvenir sheet exists, perf. and imperf., containing one each of Nos. 502-503. Value $4.50 each.

For surcharges see Nos. B37-B41.

Bande Amir Lakes A176

1961, Aug. 7 Photo. *Perf. 13½x14*

506	A176	3af	brt blue	.35	.30
507	A176	10af	rose claret	1.10	1.00

Nadir Shah — A177

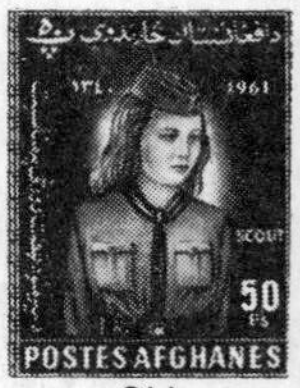

Girl Scout — A178

1961, Aug. 23 ***Perf. 14x13½***
508 A177 50p rose red & blk .50 .40
509 A177 175p brt grn & org brn 1.00 .80

43rd Independence Day.
Two souvenir sheets, perf. and imperf., contain one each of Nos. 508-509. Value, each $2.50.

Perf. 14x13½
1961, July 23 **Unwmk.**
510 A178 50p dp car & dk gray .40 .20
511 A178 175p dp grn & rose brn .90 .40

Issued for Women's Day.
Two souvenir sheets exist, perf. and imperf., containing one each of Nos. 510-511. Value $3 each.

Exhibition Hall, Kabul — A179

1961, Aug. 23 ***Perf. 13½x14***
512 A179 50p yel brn & yel grn .20 .20
513 A179 175p blue & brn .40 .30

International Exhibition at Kabul.

Pathan with Pashtunistan Flag — A180

1961, Aug. 31 **Photo.** ***Perf. 14x13½***
514 A180 50p blk, lil & red .20 .20
515 A180 175p brn, grnsh bl & red .35 .30

Issued for "Free Pashtunistan Day."
Souvenir sheets exist perf. and imperf. containing one each of Nos. 514-515. Value $2 each.

Assembly Building A181

1961, Sept. 10 ***Perf. 12***
516 A181 50p dk gray & brt grn .20 .20
517 A181 175p ultra & brn .45 .30

Anniv. of the founding of the Natl. Assembly.
Souvenir sheets exist, perf. and imperf., containing one each of Nos. 516-517. Value $1 each.

Exterminating Anopheles Mosquito A182

1961, Oct. 5 ***Perf. 13½x14***
518 A182 50p blk & brn lil .50 .30
519 A182 175p maroon & brt grn 1.10 .50

Anti-Malaria campaign. Souvenir sheets exist, perf. and imperf., containing one each of Nos. 518-519. Value $4 each.

Zahir Shah — A183

1961, Oct. 15 ***Perf. 13½***
520 A183 50p lilac & blue .20 .20
521 A183 175p emerald & red brn .40 .35

Issued to honor King Mohammed Zahir Shah on his 47th birthday.
See Nos. 609-612.

Pomegranates A184

Fruit: No. 523, 5p, 25p, 50p, Grapes. 10p, 150p, Apples. 15p, 175p, Pomegranates. 100p, Melons.

1961, Oct. 16 ***Perf. 13½x14***
Fruit in Natural Colors
522 A184 2p black
523 A184 2p green
524 A184 5p lilac rose
525 A184 10p lilac
526 A184 15p dk blue
527 A184 25p dull red
528 A184 50p purple
529 A184 100p brt blue
530 A184 150p brown
531 A184 175p olive gray
Nos. 522-531 (10) 1.75

For Afghan Red Crescent Society.
Souvenir sheets exist, perf. and imperf., containing one each of Nos. 528-529. Value $1.50 each.
For surcharges see Nos. B42-B46.

UN Headquarters, NY — A185

1961, Oct. 24 ***Perf. 13½x14***
Vertical Borders in Emerald, Red and Black
532 A185 1p rose lilac
533 A185 2p slate
534 A185 3p brown
535 A185 4p ultra
536 A185 50p rose red
537 A185 75p gray
538 A185 175p brt green
Nos. 532-538 (7) 1.50

16th anniv. of the UN. Souvenir sheets exist, perf. and imperf., containing one each of Nos. 536-538. Value $2 each.

Children Giving Flowers to Teacher — A186

People Raising UNESCO Symbol — A187

#540, 5p, 25p, 50p, Tulips. 10p, 100p, Narcissus. 15p, 150p, Children giving flowers to teacher. 175p, Teacher with children in front of school.

1961, Oct. 26 **Photo.** ***Perf. 12***
539 A186 2p multicolored
540 A186 2p multicolored
541 A186 5p multicolored
542 A186 10p multicolored
543 A186 15p multicolored
544 A186 25p multicolored
545 A186 50p multicolored
546 A186 100p multicolored
547 A186 150p multicolored
548 A186 175p multicolored
Nos. 539-548 (10) 1.75

Issued for Teacher's Day.
Souvenir sheets exist, perf. and imperf. containing one each of Nos. 545-546. Value, 2 sheets, $4.
For surcharges see Nos. B47-B51.

Buzkashi Types of 1960

1961-72 **Litho.** ***Perf. 10½, 11***
549 A167 25p violet .20 .20
b. 25p brt vio, typo. ('72) .20 .20
549A A167 25p citron ('63) .20 .20
550 A167 50p blue .30 .20
550A A167 50p yel org ('69) .20 .20
551 A172 100p citron .45 .20
551A A172 150p orange ('64) .30 .20
552 A172 2af lt green 1.10 .45
Nos. 549-552 (7) 2.75 1.65

Zahir Shah Types of 1951

Photo., Engr., Engr. & Litho.
1962 ***Perf. 13x12, 13***
Imprint: "Thomas De La Rue & Co. Ltd."
552A A123 75p brt purple 1.10 .25
552B A123 1af car & ultra 1.40 .35
552C A124 2af blue 1.75 .75
552D A124 3af orange & blk 4.00 1.10
Nos. 552A-552D (4) 8.25 2.45

1962, July 2 **Photo.** ***Perf. 14x13½***
553 A187 2p rose lil & brn
554 A187 2p ol bis & brn
555 A187 5p dp org & dk grn
556 A187 10p gray & mag
557 A187 15p blue & brn
558 A187 25p org yel & pur
559 A187 50p lt grn & pur
560 A187 75p brt cit & brn
561 A187 100p dp org & brn
Nos. 553-561 (9) 1.60

15th anniv. of UNESCO. Souvenir sheets exist, perf. and imperf. One contains Nos. 558-559; the other contains Nos. 560-561. Value, $3 each.
For surcharges see Nos. B52-B60.

Ahmad Shah — A188

Afghan Hound — A189

1962, Feb. 24 **Photo.** ***Perf. 13½***
562 A188 50p red brn & gray .20 .20
563 A188 75p green & salmon .25 .20
564 A188 100p claret & bister .40 .30
Nos. 562-564 (3) .85 .70

Ahmad Shah (1724-73), founded the Afghan kingdom in 1747 and ruled until 1773.

1962, Apr. 21 ***Perf. 14x13½***

Designs: 5p, 75p, Afghan cock. 10p, 100p, Kondjid plant. 15p, 125p, Astrakhan skins.

565 A189 2p rose & brn
566 A189 2p lt green & brn
567 A189 5p dp rose & claret
568 A189 10p lt grn & sl grn
569 A189 15p blue grn & blk
570 A189 25p blue & brn
571 A189 50p gray & brn
572 A189 75p rose lil & lil
573 A189 100p gray & dl grn
574 A189 125p rose brn & blk
Nos. 565-574 (10) 2.00

Agriculture Day. Perf. and imperf. souvenir sheets exist. Set of 4 sheets, value $4.

Athletes with Flag and Nadir Shah A190

Woman in National Costume A191

1962, Aug. 23 ***Perf. 12***
575 A190 25p multicolored .20 .20
576 A190 50p multicolored .20 .20
577 A190 150p multicolored .25 .20
Nos. 575-577 (3) .65 .60

44th Independence Day.

1962, Aug. 30 ***Perf. 11½x12***
578 A191 25p lilac & brn .20 .20
579 A191 50p green & brn .25 .20
Nos. 578-579,C15-C16 (4) 1.90 1.85

Issued for Women's Day. A souvenir sheet exists containing one each of #578-579, C15-C16. Value $3.

Man and Woman with Flag — A192

Malaria Eradication Emblem and Swamp — A193

1962, Aug. 31 **Photo.**
580 A192 25p black, pale bl & red .20 .20
581 A192 50p black, grn & red .20 .20
582 A192 150p black, pink & red .45 .20
Nos. 580-582 (3) .85 .60

Issued for "Free Pashtunistan Day."

1962, Sept. 5 ***Perf. 14x13½***
583 A193 2p dk grn & ol gray
584 A193 2p dk green & sal
585 A193 5p red brn & ol
586 A193 10p red brn & brt grn
587 A193 15p red brn & gray
588 A193 25p brt bl & bluish grn
589 A193 50p brt bl & rose lil
590 A193 75p black & blue
591 A193 100p black & brt pink
592 A193 150p black & bis brn
593 A193 175p black & orange
Nos. 583-593 (11) 2.50

WHO drive to eradicate malaria. Perf. and imperf. souvenir sheets exist. Set of 4 sheets, value $6.50.
For surcharges see Nos. B61-B71.

National Assembly Building A194

Perf. 10½, 11 (100p)
1962, Sept. 10 **Unwmk.** **Litho.**
594 A194 25p lt green .35 .25
595 A194 50p blue .55 .35
596 A194 75p rose .75 .55
597 A194 100p violet 1.10 .90
598 A194 125p ultra 1.25 1.10
Nos. 594-598 (5) 4.00 3.15

Establishment of the National Assembly.

Horse Racing — A195

Designs: 2p, Pole vaulting. 3p, Wrestling. 4p, Weight lifting. 5p, Soccer.

1962, Sept. 22 **Photo.** ***Perf. 12***
Black Inscriptions
599 A195 1p lt ol & red brn
600 A195 2p lt grn & red brn
601 A195 3p yellow & dk pur
602 A195 4p pale bl & grn
603 A195 5p bluish grn & dk brn
Nos. 599-603, C17-C22 (11) 2.50

4th Asian Games, Djakarta, Indonesia. Two souvenir sheets exist. A perforated one contains a 125p blue, dark blue and brown stamp in horse racing design. An imperf. one contains a 2af buff, purple and black stamp in soccer design. Value, $3.50 each.

Runners
A196

1p, 2p, Diver, vert. 4p, Peaches. 5p, Iris, vert.

Perf. 11½x12, 12x11½

1962, Oct. 2 **Unwmk.**

604	A196	1p rose lil & brn		
605	A196	2p blue & brn		
606	A196	3p brt blue & lil		
607	A196	4p ol gray & multi		
608	A196	5p gray & multi		
		Nos. 604-608, C23-C25 (8)	2.00	

Issued for Children's Day.

King Type of 1961, Dated "1962"

1962, Oct. 15 ***Perf. 13½***

Various Frames

609	A183	25p lilac rose & brn	.20	.20
610	A183	50p orange brn & grn	.20	.20
611	A183	75p blue & lake	.20	.20
612	A183	100p green & red brn	.30	.20
		Nos. 609-612 (4)	.90	.80

Issued to honor King Mohammed Zahir Shah on his 48th birthday.

Grapes
A197

1962, Oct. 16 ***Perf. 12***

613	A197	1p shown		
614	A197	2p Grapes		
615	A197	3p Pears		
616	A197	4p Wistaria		
617	A197	5p Blossoms		
		Nos. 613-617, C26-C28 (8)	1.00	

For the Afghan Red Crescent Society.

UN Headquarters, NY and Flags of UN and Afghanistan — A198

1962, Oct. 24 **Unwmk.**

618	A198	1p multicolored		
619	A198	2p multicolored		
620	A198	3p multicolored		
621	A198	4p multicolored		
622	A198	5p multicolored		
		Nos. 618-622, C29-C31 (8)	2.00	

UN Day. Souvenir sheets exist. One contains a single 4af ultramarine stamp, perforated; the other, a 4af ocher stamp, imperf. Value, 2 sheets, $5.

Boy Scout — A199 Pole Vault — A200

1962, Oct. 18 **Photo.** ***Perf. 12***

623	A199	1p yel, dk grn & sal		
624	A199	2p dl yel, slate & sal		
625	A199	3p rose, blk & sal		
626	A199	4p multicolored		
		Nos. 623-626, C32-C35 (8)	2.25	

Issued to honor the Boy Scouts.

1962, Oct. 25 **Unwmk.** ***Perf. 12***

3p, High jump. 4p, 5p, Different blossoms.

627	A200	1p lilac & dk grn		
628	A200	2p yellow grn & brn		
629	A200	3p bister & vio		
630	A200	4p sal pink, grn & ultra		
631	A200	5p yellow, grn & bl		
		Nos. 627-631, C36-C37 (7)	1.25	

Issued for Teacher's Day.

Rockets
A201

1962, Nov. 29

632	A201	50p pale lil & dk bl	.45	
633	A201	100p lt blue & red brn	.85	

UN World Meteorological Day. A souvenir sheet contains one 5af pink and green stamp. Value $6.

Ansari Mausoleum, Herat — A202

Perf. 13½

1963, Jan. 3 **Unwmk.** **Photo.**

634	A202	50p purple & green	.20	.20
635	A202	75p gray & magenta	.20	.20
636	A202	100p orange brn & brn	.30	.30
		Nos. 634-636 (3)	.70	.70

Khwaja Abdullah Ansari, Sufi, religious leader and poet, on the 900th anniv. of his death.

Sheep
A203

Silkworm, Cocoons, Moth and Mulberry Branch
A204

1963, Mar. 1 ***Perf. 12***

637	A203	1p grnsh blue & blk		
638	A203	2p yellow grn & blk		
639	A203	3p lilac rose & blk		
640	A204	4p gray, grn & brn		
641	A204	5p red lil, grn & brn		
		Nos. 637-641, C42-C44 (8)	2.25	

Issued for the Day of Agriculture.

Rice — A205

Designs: 3p, Corn. 300p, Wheat emblem.

1963, Mar. 27 **Unwmk.** ***Perf. 14***

642	A205	2p gray, claret & grn	.20	.20
643	A205	3p green, yel & ocher	.20	.20
644	A205	300p dk blue & yel	.30	.30
		Nos. 642-644 (3)	.70	.70

FAO "Freedom from Hunger" campaign.

Meteorological Measuring Instrument
A206

Designs: 3p, 10p, Weather station. 4p, 5p, Rockets in space.

1963, May 23 **Photo.** ***Perf. 13½x14***

645	A206	1p dp magenta & brn		
646	A206	2p brt blue & brn		
647	A206	3p red & brown		
648	A206	4p orange & lilac		
649	A206	5p green & dl vio		

Imperf

650	A206	10p red brn & grn		
		Nos. 645-650, C46-C50 (11)	7.50	

3rd UN World Meteorological Day, Mar. 23.

Independence Monument — A207

1963, Aug. 23 **Litho.** ***Perf. 10½***

651	A207	25p lt green	.20	.20
652	A207	50p orange	.20	.20
653	A207	150p rose carmine	.35	.20
		Nos. 651-653 (3)	.75	.60

45th Independence Day.

Pathans in Forest
A208

1963, Aug. 31 **Unwmk.** ***Perf. 10½***

654	A208	25p pale violet	.20	.20
655	A208	50p sky blue	.20	.20
655A	A208	150p dull red brn	.45	.35
		Nos. 654-655A (3)	.85	.75

Issued for "Free Pashtunistan Day."

4th Asian Games, Djakarta
A208a

Designs: 2p, 250p, 300p, Wrestling. 3p, 10p, Tennis. 4p, 500p, Javelin. 5p, 9af, Shot put.

1963, Sept. 3 **Litho.** ***Perf. 12***

656	A208a	2p rose vio & brn		
656A	A208a	3p olive grn & brn		
656B	A208a	4p blue & brn		
656C	A208a	5p yel grn & brn		
656D	A208a	10p lt bl grn & brn		
656E	A208a	300p yellow & vio		
656F	A208a	500p lt yel bis & brn		
656G	A208a	9af pale grn & vio		
		Nos. 656-656G (8)	1.75	

Souvenir Sheets

656H	A208a	250p lilac & vio		
656I	A208a	300p blue & blk		

Nos. 656-656F are airmail. Nos. 656-656I exist imperf.

National Assembly Building
A209

1963, Sept. 10 ***Perf. 11***

657	A209	25p gray	.20	.20
658	A209	50p dull red	.20	.20
659	A209	75p brown	.20	.20
660	A209	100p olive	.30	.20
661	A209	125p lilac	.40	.20
		Nos. 657-661 (5)	1.30	1.00

Issued to honor the National Assembly.

Balkh Gate
A210

1963, Oct. 8

662	A210	3af choc (screened margins)	.40	.30
a.		White margins	1.00	.35

In the original printing a halftone screen extended across the plate, covering the space between the stamps. A retouch removed the screen between the stamps (No. 662a).

Intl. Red Cross, Cent.
A210a

4p, 5p, 200p, 3af, Nurse holding patient, vert. 10p, 4af, 6af, Crown Prince Ahmed Shah.

1963, Oct. 9 ***Perf. 13½***

662B	A210a	2p olive, blk & red		
662C	A210a	3p blue, blk & red		
662D	A210a	4p lt grn, blk & red		
662E	A210a	5p lt vio, blk & red		
662F	A210a	10p gray grn, red & blk		
662G	A210a	100p dull bl grn, red & blk		
662H	A210a	200p lt brn, blk & red		
662I	A210a	4af brt bl grn, red & blk		
m.		Souvenir sheet of 1		
662J	A210a	6af lt brn, red & blk		

Souvenir Sheet

662K	A210a	3af dl blue, blk & red		

Nos. 662G-662K are airmail. Nos. 662B-662K exist imperf.

Zahir Shah — A211 Kemal Ataturk — A212

1963, Oct. 15 ***Perf. 10½***

663	A211	25p green	.20	.20
663A	A211	50p gray	.20	.20
663B	A211	75p carmine rose	.20	.20
663C	A211	100p dull redsh brn	.30	.20
		Nos. 663-663C (4)	.90	.80

King Mohammed Zahir Shah, 49th birthday.

1963, Oct. 10 ***Perf. 10½***

664	A212	1af blue	.20	.20
665	A212	3af rose lilac	.40	.35

25th anniv. of the death of Kemal Ataturk, president of Turkey.

Protection of Nubian Monuments
A213

Designs: 5af, 7.50af, 10af, Ruins, vert.

Perf. 12, Imperf. (150p, 250p, 10af)

1963, Nov. 16 **Photo.**

666	A213	100p	lil rose & blk
666A	A213	150p	rose lil & blk
666B	A213	200p	brown & blk
666C	A213	250p	ultra & blk
666D	A213	500p	green & blk
666E	A213	5af	greenish blue & gray bl
666F	A213	7.50af	red brn & gray bl
666G	A213	10af	ver & gray bl

#666E-666G are airmail. #666D exists imperf.

Women's Day — A213a

Boy and Girl Scouts — A213c

A213b

1964, Jan. 5 ***Perf. 14x13½***

667	A213a	2p	multicolored
667A	A213a	3p	multicolored
667B	A213a	4p	multicolored
667C	A213a	5p	multicolored
667D	A213a	10p	multicolored

Exist imperf.

1964, Jan. 5 ***Perf. 13½x14, 14x13½***

#668F-668G, 668K-668M, Girl with flag.

668	A213b	2p	multi
668A	A213b	3p	multi
668B	A213b	4p	multi
668C	A213b	5p	multi
668D	A213b	10p	multi
668E	A213c	2af	multi
668F	A213c	2af	multi
668G	A213c	2.50af	multi
668H	A213c	3af	multi
668I	A213c	4af	multi
668J	A213c	5af	multi
668K	A213c	12af	multi

Souvenir Sheets

668L	A213c	5af	multi
668M	A213c	6af	multi
668N	A213c	6af	multi
668O	A213c	10af	multi

Nos. 668E-668O are airmail. Nos 668-668K, 668N-668O exist imperf.

Children — A213d

1964, Jan. 22 ***Perf. 12***

669	A213d	2p	Playing ball
669A	A213d	3p	like #669
669B	A213d	4p	Swinging, jumping rope, vert.
669C	A213d	5p	Skiing, vert.
669D	A213d	10p	like #669
669E	A213d	200p	like #669C
669F	A213d	300p	like #669B

Nos. 669E-669F are airmail. All exist imperf.

Red Crescent Society — A213e

Designs: 100p, 200p, Pierre and Marie Curie, physicists. 2.50af, 7.50af Nurse examining child. 3.50af, 5af, Nurse and patients.

Perf. 14, Imperf. (#670A, 670C-670D)

1964, Feb. 8

670	A213e	100p	multi
670A	A213e	100p	multi
670B	A213e	200p	multi
670C	A213e	2.50af	multi
670D	A213e	3.50af	multi
670E	A213e	5af	multi
670F	A213e	7.50af	multi

Nos. 670B-670D are airmail.

Teachers' Day — A213f

Flowers: 2p, 3p, 3af, 4af, Tulips. 4p, 5p, 3.50af, 6af, Flax. 10p, 1.50af, 2af, Iris.

Perf. 12, Imperf. (1.50af, 2af)

1964, Mar. 3

671	A213f	2p	multicolored
671A	A213f	3p	multicolored
671B	A213f	4p	multicolored
671C	A213f	5p	multicolored
671D	A213f	10p	multicolored
671E	A213f	1.50af	multicolored
671F	A213f	2af	multicolored
671G	A213f	3af	multicolored
671H	A213f	3.50af	multicolored

Souvenir Sheets

671I	A213f	4af	multicolored
671J	A213f	6af	multi, imperf

#671E-671J are airmail. #671-671D exist imperf.

A213g

UN Day: 5p, 10p, 2af, 3af, 4af, Doctor and nurse, vert.

1964, Mar. 9 ***Perf. 14***

672	A213g	2p	multicolored
672A	A213g	3p	multicolored
672B	A213g	4p	multicolored
672C	A213g	5p	multicolored
672D	A213g	10p	multicolored
672E	A213g	100p	multicolored
672F	A213g	2af	multicolored
672G	A213g	3af	multicolored

Souvenir Sheets

672H	A213g	4af	multi, imperf.
672I	A213g	5af	multicolored

Nos. 672E-672G are airmail. Nos. 672-672G exist imperf.

For surcharges see Nos. B71A-B71J.

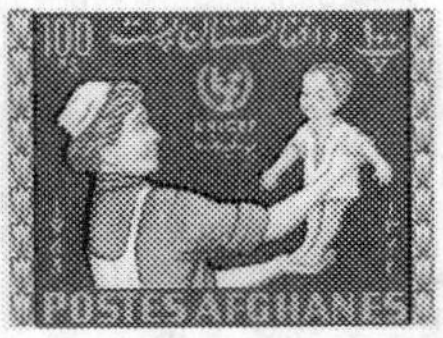

UNICEF A213h

Design: 5af, 7.50af, 10af, Children eating.

Perf. 14x13½, Imperf. (150p, 250p, 10af)

1964, Mar. 15

673	A213h	100p	multicolored	
673A	A213h	150p	multicolored	
673B	A213h	200p	multicolored	
673C	A213h	250p	multicolored	
673D	A213h	5af	multicolored	
673E	A213h	7.50af	multicolored	
673F	A213h	10af	multicolored	
	Nos. 673-673F (7)			10.00

Nos. 673D-673F are airmail.

Eradication of Malaria — A213i

Designs: 4p, 5p, 5af, 10af Spraying mosquitoes.

1964, Mar. 15 ***Perf. 13½***

674	A213i	2p	lt red brn & yel grn
674A	A213i	3p	olive grn & buff
674B	A213i	4p	dk vio & bl grn
674C	A213i	5p	brn & grn
674D	A213i	2af	Prus bl & ver
h.			Souvenir sheet of 1
674E	A213i	5af	dk grn & lt red brn, imperf.
i.			Souv. sheet of 1, imperf.
674F	A213i	10af	red brn & grnsh bl

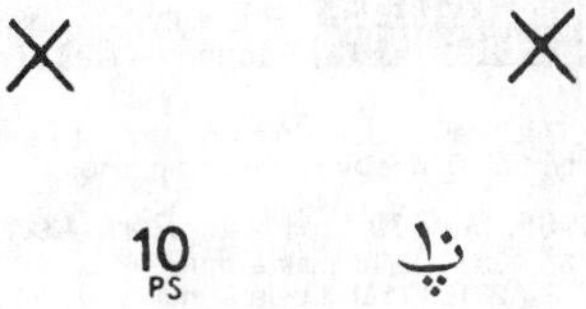

674G	A213i	10p on 4p	Prus bl & rose

No. 674G not issued without surcharge. Nos. 674-674C, 674G exist imperf. Nos. 674D-674F are airmail.

Exists imperf.

"Tiger's Head" of 1878 — A214

1964, Mar. 22 **Photo.** ***Perf. 12***

675	A214	1.25af	gold, grn & blk	.25	.20
676	A214	5af	gold, rose car & blk	.55	.35

Issued to honor philately.

Unisphere and Flags — A215

1964, May 3 ***Perf. 13½x14***

677	A215	6af	crimson, gray & grn	.30	.20

New York World's Fair, 1964-65.

Hand Holding Torch — A216

1964, May 12 **Photo.** ***Perf. 14x13½***

678	A216	3.75af	multicolored	.20	.20

1st UN Seminar on Human Rights in Kabul, May 1964. The denomination in Persian at right erroneously reads "3.25" but the stamp was sold and used as 3.75af.

Kandahar Airport A217

1964, Apr. **Litho.** ***Perf. 10½, 11***

679	A217	7.75af	dk red brown	.40	.20
680	A217	9.25af	lt green	.50	.20
681	A217	10.50af	lt green	.50	.30
682	A217	13.75af	carmine rose	.70	.40
	Nos. 679-682 (4)			2.10	1.10

Inauguration of Kandahar Airport.

Snow Leopard A218

50p, Ibex, vert. 75p, Head of argali. 5af, Yak.

1964, June 25 **Photo.** ***Perf. 12***

683	A218	25p	yellow & blue	.20	.20
684	A218	50p	dl red & grn	.20	.20
685	A218	75p	Prus bl & lil	.20	.20
686	A218	5af	brt grn & dk brn	.30	.30
	Nos. 683-686 (4)			.90	.90

View of Herat — A219

Flag and Map of Afghanistan A220

Tourist publicity: 75p, Tomb of Queen Gowhar Shad, vert.

1964, July 12 ***Perf. 13½x14, 14x13½***

687	A219	25p	sepia & bl	.20	.20
688	A219	75p	dp blue & buff	.20	.20
689	A220	3af	red, blk & grn	.30	.20
	Nos. 687-689 (3)			.70	.60

Wrestling A221

25p, Hurdling, vert. 1af, Diving, vert. 5af, Soccer.

1964, July 26 ***Perf. 12***

690	A221	25p	ol bis, blk & car	.20	.20
691	A221	1af	bl grn, blk & car	.20	.20
692	A221	3.75af	yel grn, blk & car	.20	.20
693	A221	5af	brn, blk & car	.30	.30
a.			Souv. sheet of 4, #690-693, imperf.	.90	.90
	Nos. 690-693 (4)			.90	.90

18th Olympic Games, Tokyo, Oct. 10-25, 1964. No. 693a sold for 15af. The additional 5af went to the Afghanistan Olympic Committee.

Flag and Outline of Nadir Shah's Tomb — A222

1964, Aug. 24 **Photo.**

695	A222	25p	multicolored	.20	.20
696	A222	75p	multicolored	.20	.20

Independence Day. The stamps were printed with an erroneous inscription in upper left corner: "33rd year of independence." This was locally obliterated with a typographed gold bar.

Pashtunistan Flag — A223

Zahir Shah — A225

1964, Sept. 1 **Unwmk.**
697 A223 100p gold, blk, red, bl & grn .20 .20

Issued for "Free Pashtunistan Day."

1964, Oct. 17 ***Perf. 14x13½***
699 A225 1.25af gold & yel grn .20 .20
700 A225 3.75af gold & rose .20 .20
701 A225 50af gold & gray 2.00 1.75
Nos. 699-701 (3) 2.40 2.15

King Mohammed Zahir Shah, 50th birthday.

Coat of Arms of Afghanistan and UN Emblem A226

1964, Oct. 24 ***Perf. 13½x14***
702 A226 5af gold, blk & dl bl .20 .20

Issued for United Nations Day.

Emblem of Afghanistan Women's Association A227

1964, Nov. 9 **Photo.** **Unwmk.**
703 A227 25p pink, dk bl & emer .50 .25
704 A227 75p aqua, dk bl & emer .75 .35
705 A227 1af sil, dk bl & emer 1.00 .50
Nos. 703-705 (3) 2.25 1.10

Issued for Women's Day.

Poet Mowlana Nooruddin Abdul Rahman Jami (1414-1492) A228

Perf. 11 Rough

1964, Nov. 23 **Litho.**
706 A228 1.50af blk, emer & yel .85 .85

Woodpecker A229

Birds: 3.75af, Black-throated jay, vert. 5af, Impeyan pheasant, vert.

Perf. 13½x14, 14x13½

1965, Apr. 20 **Photo.** **Unwmk.**
707 A229 1.25af multi 1.00 .50
708 A229 3.75af multi 1.75 .75
709 A229 5af multi 2.50 1.00
Nos. 707-709 (3) 5.25 2.25

ITU Emblem, Old and New Communication Equipment — A230

1965, May 17 ***Perf. 13½x14***
710 A230 5af lt bl, blk & red .35 .35

Cent. of the ITU.

"Red City," Bamian — A231

Designs: 3.75af, Ruins of ancient Bamian city. 5af, Bande Amir, mountain lakes.

1965, May 30 ***Perf. 13x13½***
711 A231 1.25af pink & multi .20 .20
712 A231 3.75af lt blue & multi .20 .20
713 A231 5af yellow & multi .30 .30
Nos. 711-713 (3) .70 .70

Issued for tourist publicity.

ICY Emblem A232

1965, June 25 ***Perf. 13½x13***
714 A232 5af multicolored .25 .25

International Cooperation Year, 1965.

ARIANA Air Lines Emblem and DC-3 — A233

Designs: 5af, DC-6 at right. 10af, DC-3 on top.

Perf. 13½x14

1965, July 15 **Photo.** **Unwmk.**
715 A233 1.25af brt bl, gray & blk .20 .20
716 A233 5af red lil, blk & bl .30 .30
717 A233 10af bis, blk, bl gray & grn .75 .75
a. Souv. sheet of 3, #715-717, imperf. 1.00 1.00
Nos. 715-717 (3) 1.25 1.25

10th anniv. of Afghan Air Lines, ARIANA.

Nadir Shah — A234

1965, Aug. 23 ***Perf. 14x13½***
718 A234 1af dl grn, blk & red brn .25 .20

For the 47th Independence Day.

Flag of Pashtunistan A235

Perf. 13½x14

1965, Aug. 31 **Photo.** **Unwmk.**
719 A235 1af multicolored .25 .20

Issued for "Free Pashtunistan Day."

Zahir Shah Signing Constitution — A236

1965, Sept. 11 ***Perf. 13x13½***
720 A236 1.50af brt grn & blk .25 .25

Promulgation of the new Constitution.

Zahir Shah and Oak Leaves — A237

1965, Oct. 14 ***Perf. 14x13½***
721 A237 1.25af blk, ultra & salmon .20 .20
722 A237 6af blk, lt bl & rose lil .40 .35

King Mohammed Zahir Shah, 51st birthday.

Flags of UN and Afghanistan A238

1965, Oct. 24 ***Perf. 13½x14***
723 A238 5af multicolored .20 .20

Issued for United Nations Day.

Dappled Ground Gecko — A239

Designs: 4af, Caucasian agamid (lizard). 8af, Horsfield's tortoise.

Perf. 13½x14

1966, May 10 **Photo.** **Unwmk.**
724 A239 3af tan & multi .75 .35
725 A239 4af brt grn & multi .85 .40
726 A239 8af violet & multi 1.50 .75
Nos. 724-726 (3) 3.10 1.50

Soccer Player and Globe — A240

1966, July 31 **Litho.** ***Perf. 14x13½***
727 A240 2af rose red & blk .65 .20
728 A240 6af violet bl & blk 1.10 .25
729 A240 12af bister brn & blk 2.25 .55
Nos. 727-729 (3) 4.00 1.00

World Cup Soccer Championship, Wembley, England, July 11-30.

Cotton Flower and Boll — A241

5af, Silkworm. 7af, Farmer plowing with oxen.

1966, July 31 ***Perf. 13½x14***
730 A241 1af multicolored .50 .20
731 A241 5af multicolored 1.00 .30
732 A241 7af multicolored 1.40 .40
Nos. 730-732 (3) 2.90 .90

Issued for the Day of Agriculture.

Independence Monument A242

1966, Aug. 23 **Photo.** ***Perf. 13½x14***
733 A242 1af multicolored .25 .20
734 A242 3af multicolored .75 .25

Issued to commemorate Independence Day.

Flag of Pashtunistan — A243

Perf. 11 Rough

1966, Aug. 31 **Litho.**
735 A243 1af bright blue .50 .20

"Free Pashtunistan Day."

Bagh-i-Bala Park Casino A244

Tourist publicity: 2af, Map of Afghanistan. 8af, Tomb of Abd-er-Rahman. The casino on 4af is the former summer palace of Abd-er-Rahman near Kabul.

1966, Oct. 3 **Photo.** ***Perf. 13½x14***
736 A244 2af red & multi .20 .20
737 A244 4af multicolored .40 .30
738 A244 8af multicolored .65 .60
a. Souvenir sheet of 3, #736-738, imperf. 3.50 3.50
Nos. 736-738 (3) 1.25 1.10

Zahir Shah — A245

UNESCO Emblem — A246

1966, Oct. 14 ***Perf. 14x13½***
739 A245 1af dk slate grn .20 .20
740 A245 5af red brown .50 .25

King Mohammed Zahir Shah, 52nd birthday. See Nos. 760-761.

1967, Mar. 6 **Litho.** ***Perf. 12***
741 A246 2af multicolored .60 .20
742 A246 6af multicolored .75 .20
743 A246 12af multicolored 1.50 .30
Nos. 741-743 (3) 2.85 .70

20th anniv. of UNESCO.

Zahir Shah and UN Emblem
A247

1967 **Photo.**
744 A247 5af multicolored .40 .20
745 A247 10af multicolored .75 .30

UN Intl. Org. for Refugees, 20th anniv.

New Power Station
A248

Designs: 5af, Carpet, vert. 8af, Cement factory.

1967, Jan. 7 **Photo.** ***Perf. 13½x14***
746 A248 2af red lil & ol grn .20 .20
747 A248 5af multicolored .20 .20
748 A248 8af blk, dk bl & tan .40 .25
Nos. 746-748 (3) .80 .65

Issued to publicize industrial development.

International Tourist Year Emblem — A249

Designs: 6af, International Tourist Year emblem and map of Afghanistan.

1967, May 11 **Photo.** ***Perf. 12***
749 A249 2af yel, blk & lt bl .20 .20
750 A249 6af bis brn, blk & lt bl .40 .20
a. Souvenir sheet of 2, #749-750, imperf. 1.00 1.00

Intl. Tourist Year, 1967. No. 750a sold for 10af.

Power Dam, Dorunta
A250

Macaque
A251

6af, Sirobi Dam, vert. 8af, Reservoir at Jalalabad.

1967, July 2 **Photo.** ***Perf. 12***
751 A250 1af dk green & lil .20 .20
752 A250 6af red brn & grnsh bl .35 .35
753 A250 8af plum & dk bl .50 .50
Nos. 751-753 (3) 1.05 1.05

Progress in agriculture through electricity.

1967, July 28 **Photo.** ***Perf. 12***

Designs: 6af, Striped hyena, horiz. 12af, Persian gazelles, horiz.

754 A251 2af dull yel & indigo .25 .20
755 A251 6af lt green & sepia .70 .35
756 A251 12af lt bl & red brn 1.50 .75
Nos. 754-756 (3) 2.45 1.30

Pashtun Dancers
A252

1967, Sept. 1 **Photo.** ***Perf. 12***
757 A252 2af magenta & violet .50 .20

Issued for "Free Pashtunistan Day."

Retreat of British at Maiwand
A253

Fireworks and UN Emblem
A254

1967, Aug. 24
758 A253 1af dk brn & org ver .25 .20
759 A253 2af dk brn & brt pink .50 .20

Issued to commemorate Independence Day.

King Type of 1966

1967, Oct. 15 **Photo.** ***Perf. 14x13½***
760 A245 2af brown red .20 .20
761 A245 8af dark blue .50 .25

Issued to honor King Mohammed Zahir Shah on his 53rd birthday.

1967, Oct. 24 **Litho.** ***Perf. 12***
762 A254 10af violet bl & multi .65 .35

Issued for United Nations Day.

Greco-Roman Wrestlers
A255

Said Jamalluddin Afghan
A256

Design: 6af, Free style wrestlers.

1967, Nov. 20 **Photo.**
763 A255 4af ol grn & rose lil .50 .20
764 A255 6af dp carmine & brn .80 .20
a. Souvenir sheet of 2, #763-764, imperf. 5.00 5.00

1968 Olympic Games.

1967, Nov. 27
765 A256 1af magenta .20 .20
766 A256 5af brown .35 .20

Said Jamalluddin Afghan, politician (1839-97).

Bronze Vase, 11th-12th Centuries
A257

WHO Emblem
A258

Design: 7af, Bronze vase, Ghasnavide era, 11th-12th centuries.

1967, Dec. 23 **Photo.** ***Perf. 12***
767 A257 3af lt green & brn .20 .20
768 A257 7af yel & slate grn .40 .30
a. Souvenir sheet of 2, #767-768, imperf. 2.50 2.50

1968, Apr. 7 **Photo.** ***Perf. 12***
769 A258 2af citron & brt bl .20 .20
770 A258 7af rose & brt bl .30 .20

20th anniv. of the WHO.

Karakul
A259

1968, May 20 **Photo.** ***Perf. 12***
771 A259 1af yellow & blk .25 .20
772 A259 6af lt blue & blk .70 .20
773 A259 12af ultra & dk brn 1.25 .40
Nos. 771-773 (3) 2.20 .80

Issued for the Day of Agriculture.

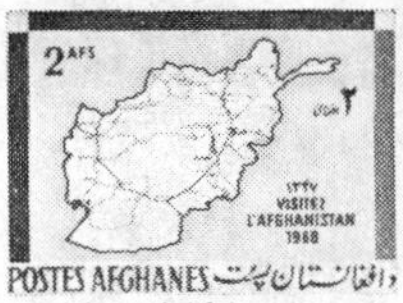

Map of Afghanistan
A260

Victory Tower, Ghazni
A261

Design: 16af, Mausoleum, Ghazni.

1968, June 3 ***Perf. 13½x14, 12***
774 A260 2af red, blk, lt bl & grn .20 .20
775 A261 3af yel, dk brn & lt bl .20 .20
776 A261 16af pink & multi .95 .50
Nos. 774-776 (3) 1.35 .90

Issued for tourist publicity.

Cinereous Vulture — A262

Birds: 6af, Eagle owl. 7af, Greater flamingoes.

1968, July 3 ***Perf. 12***
777 A262 1af sky blue & multi .75 .20
778 A262 6af yellow & multi 1.50 .20
779 A262 7af multicolored 1.75 .30
Nos. 777-779 (3) 4.00 .70

Game of "Pegsticking"
A263

2af, Olympic flame & rings, vert. 12af, Buzkashi.

1968, July 20 **Photo.** ***Perf. 12***
780 A263 2af multicolored .20 .20
781 A263 8af orange & multi .65 .30
782 A263 12af multicolored 1.00 .45
Nos. 780-782 (3) 1.85 .95

19th Olympic Games, Mexico City, Oct. 12-27.

Flower-decked Armored Car — A264

1968, Aug. 23
783 A264 6af multicolored .40 .20

Issued to commemorate Independence Day.

Flag of Pashtunistan
A265

1968 Aug. 31 **Photo.** ***Perf. 12***
784 A265 3af multicolored .25 .20

Issued for "Free Pashtunistan Day."

Zahir Shah
A266

Human Rights Flame
A267

1968, Oct. 14 **Photo.** ***Perf. 12***
785 A266 2af ultra .20 .20
786 A266 8af brown .45 .30

King Mohammed Zahir Shah, 54th birthday.

1968, Oct. 24
787 A267 1af multicolored .20 .20
788 A267 2af violet, bis & blk .20 .20
789 A267 6af vio blk, bis & vio .40 .20
Nos. 787-789 (3) .80 .60

Souvenir Sheet

Imperf

790 A267 10af plum, bis & red org 1.50 1.50

International Human Rights Year.

Maolana Djalalodine Balkhi
A268

Kushan Mural
A269

1968, Nov. 26 **Photo.** ***Perf. 12***
791 A268 4af dk green & mag .25 .20

Balkhi (1207-73), historian.

1969, Jan. 2 ***Perf. 12***

Design: 3af, Jug shaped like female torso.

792 A269 1af dk grn, mar & yel .25 .20
793 A269 3af violet, gray & mar .75 .20
a. Souv. sheet of 2, #792-793, imperf. 1.50 1.50

Archaeological finds at Bagram, 1st cent. B.C. to 2nd cent. A.D.

ILO Emblem
A270

1969, Mar. 23 **Photo.** ***Perf. 12***
794 A270 5af lt yel, lemon & blk .30 .20
795 A270 8af lt bl, grnsh bl & blk .50 .30

50th anniv. of the ILO.

Arms Type of 1939

1969, May (?) **Typo.**
795A A79 100p dark green .20 .20
795B A79 150p deep brown .25 .20

Nos. 795A-795B were normally used as newspaper stamps.

Badakhshan Scene
A271

Tourist Publicity: 2af, Map of Afghanistan. 7af, Three men on mules ascending the Pamir Mountains.

1969, July 6 Photo. *Perf. 13½x14*

796 A271 2af ocher & multi .20 .20
797 A271 4af multicolored .30 .20
798 A271 7af multicolored .75 .20
a. Souvenir sheet of 3, #796-798, imperf. 1.75 1.75
Nos. 796-798 (3) 1.25 .60

No. 798a sold for 15af.

Bust, from Hadda Treasure, 3rd-5th Centuries A272

Zahir Shah and Queen Humeira A273

Designs: 5af, Vase and jug. 10af, Statue of crowned woman. 5af and 10af from Bagram treasure, 1st-2nd centuries.

1969, Aug. 3 Photo. *Perf. 14x13½*

799 A272 1af olive grn & gold .20 .20
800 A272 5af purple & gold .20 .20
801 A272 10af dp blue & gold .40 .30
Nos. 799-801 (3) .80 .70

1969, Aug. 23 *Perf. 12*

802 A273 5af gold, dk bl & red brn .35 .20
803 A273 10af gold, dp lil & bl grn .65 .35

Issued to commemorate Independence Day.

Map of Pashtunistan and Rising Sun — A274

1969, Aug. 31 Typo. *Perf. 10½*

804 A274 2af lt blue & red .20 .20

Issued for "Free Pashtunistan Day."

Zahir Shah — A275

1969, Oct. 14 Photo. *Perf. 12*

Portrait in Natural Colors

805 A275 2af dk brown & gold .20 .20
806 A275 6af brown & gold .45 .20

King Mohammed Zahir Shah, 55th birthday.

UN Emblem and Flag of Afghanistan — A276

1969, Oct. 24 Litho. *Perf. 13½*

807 A276 5af blue & multi .25 .20

Issued for United Nations Day.

ITU Emblem — A277

Wild Boar — A278

1969, Nov. 12

808 A277 6af ultra & multi .30 .20
809 A277 12af rose & multi .60 .35

Issued for World Telecommunications Day.

1969, Dec. 7 Photo. *Perf. 12*

1af, Long-tailed porcupine. 8af, Red deer.

810 A278 1af yellow & multi .25 .20
811 A278 3af blue & multi .75 .50
812 A278 8af pink & multi 2.00 1.00
Nos. 810-812 (3) 3.00 1.70

Man's First Footprints on Moon, and Earth — A279

1969, Dec. 28 *Perf. 13½x14*

813 A279 1af yel grn & multi .20 .20
814 A279 3af yellow & multi .25 .20
815 A279 6af blue & multi .40 .20
816 A279 10af rose & multi .65 .30
Nos. 813-816 (4) 1.50 .90

Moon landing. See note after Algeria #427.

Anti-cancer Symbol — A280

Mirza Abdul Quader Bedel — A281

1970, Apr. 7 Photo. *Perf. 14*

817 A280 2af dk grn & rose car .20 .20
818 A280 6af dk bl & rose claret .40 .20

Issued to publicize the fight against cancer.

1970, May 6 *Perf. 14x13½*

819 A281 5af multicolored .25 .20

Mirza Abdul Quader Bedel (1643-1720), poet.

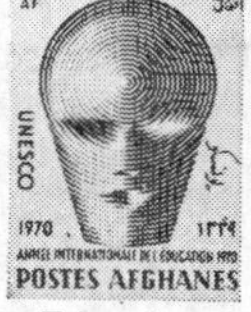

Education Year Emblem A282

Mother and Child A283

1970, June 7 Photo. *Perf. 12*

820 A282 1af black .20 .20
821 A282 6af deep rose .35 .20
822 A282 12af green .75 .35
Nos. 820-822 (3) 1.30 .75

International Education Year 1970.

1970, June 15 *Perf. 13½*

823 A283 6af yellow & multi .25 .20

Issued for Mother's Day.

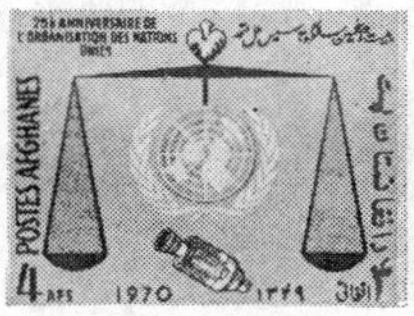

UN Emblem, Scales of Justice, Spacecraft A284

1970, June 26

824 A284 4af yel, dk bl & dp bl .20 .20
825 A284 6af pink, dk bl & brt bl .35 .20

25th anniversary of United Nations.

Mosque of the Amir of the two Swords, Kabul A285

2af, Map of Afghanistan. 7af, Arch of Paghman.

1970, July 6 *Perf. 12*

Size: 30½x30½mm

826 A285 2af lt bl, blk & citron .20 .20

Size: 36x26mm

827 A285 3af pink & multi .20 .20
828 A285 7af yellow & multi .40 .20
Nos. 826-828 (3) .80 .60

Issued for tourist publicity.

Zahir Shah Reviewing Troops A286

1970, Aug. 23 Photo. *Perf. 13½*

829 A286 8af multicolored .60 .25

Issued to commemorate Independence Day.

Pathans — A287

1970, Aug. 31 Typo. *Perf. 10½*

830 A287 2af ultra & red .20 .20

Issued for "Free Pashtunistan Day."

Quail — A288

4af, Golden eagle. 6af, Ringnecked pheasant.

1970, Sept. Photo. *Perf. 12*

831 A288 2af multicolored .50 .25
832 A288 4af multicolored 1.00 .50
833 A288 6af multicolored 1.50 .75
Nos. 831-833 (3) 3.00 1.50

Zahir Shah A289

Red Crescents A290

1970, Oct. 14 Photo. *Perf. 14x13½*

834 A289 3af green & vio .20 .20
835 A289 7af dk bl & vio brn .60 .25

King Mohammed Zahir Shah, 56th birthday.

1970, Oct. 16 Typo. *Perf. 10½*

836 A290 2af black, gold & red .20 .20

Issued for the Red Crescent Society.

UN Emblem and Charter A291

1970, Oct. 24 Photo. *Perf. 14*

837 A291 1af gold & multi .20 .20
838 A291 5af gold & multi .20 .20

United Nations Day.

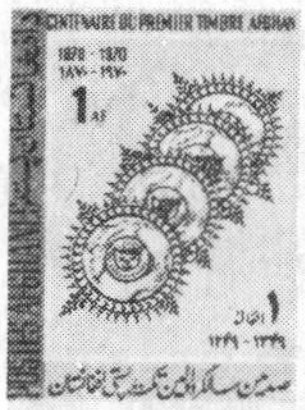

Tiger Heads of 1871 — A292

1970, Nov. 10 *Perf. 12*

839 A292 1af sal, lt grnsh bl & blk .25 .20
840 A292 4af lt ultra, yel & blk .50 .20
841 A292 12af lilac, lt bl & blk .85 .35
Nos. 839-841 (3) 1.60 .75

Cent. of the 1st Afghan postage stamps. The postal service was established in 1870, but the 1st stamps were issued in May, 1871.

Globe and Waves A293

1971, May 17 Photo. *Perf. 13½*

842 A293 12af green, blk & bl .60 .35

3rd World Telecommunications Day.

Callimorpha Principalis A294

Designs: 3af, Epizygaenella species. 5af, Parnassius autocrator.

1971, May 30 *Perf. 13½x14*

843 A294 1af vermilion & multi 1.00 .50
844 A294 3af yellow & multi 2.25 1.00
845 A294 5af ultra & multi 3.00 1.50
Nos. 843-845 (3) 6.25 3.00

"UNESCO" and Half of Ancient Kushan Statue — A295

1971, June 26 **Photo.** ***Perf. 13½***

846 A295 6af ocher & vio .40 .20
847 A295 10af lt blue & mar .65 .30

UNESCO-sponsored Intl. Kushani Seminar.

Tughra and Independence Monument — A296

1971, Aug. 23

848 A296 7af rose red & multi .40 .20
849 A296 9af red orange & multi .65 .30

Independence Day.

Pashtunistan Square, Kabul — A297

1971, Aug. 31 **Typo.** ***Perf. 10½***

850 A297 5af deep rose lilac .25 .20

"Free Pashtunistan Day."

Zahir Shah — A298

A299

1971, Oct. 14 **Photo.** ***Perf. 12½x12***

851 A298 9af lt green & multi .40 .30
852 A298 17af yellow & multi .75 .55

King Mohammed Zahir Shah, 57th birthday.

1971, Oct. 16 ***Perf. 14x13½***

Design: Map of Afghanistan, red crescent, various activities.

853 A299 8af lt bl, red, grn & blk .45 .25

For Afghan Red Crescent Society.

Equality Year Emblem A300

1971, Oct. 24 ***Perf. 12***

854 A300 24af brt blue 1.25 .70

International Year Against Racial Discrimination and United Nations Day.

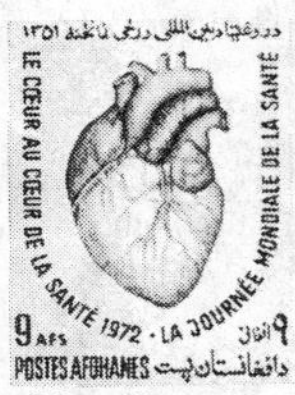

"Your Heart is your Health" — A301

Tulip — A302

1972, Apr. 7 **Photo.** ***Perf. 14***

855 A301 9af pale yellow & multi .75 .30
856 A301 12af gray & multi 1.50 .35

World Health Day.

1972, June 5 **Photo.** ***Perf. 14***

Designs: 10af, Rock partridge, horiz. 12af, Lynx, horiz. 18af, Allium stipitatum (flower).

857 A302 7af green & multi .50 .25
858 A302 10af blue & multi .75 .35
859 A302 12af lt green & multi 1.00 .35
860 A302 18af blue grn & multi 1.25 .60
Nos. 857-860 (4) 3.50 1.55

Buddhist Shrine, Hadda A302a

Designs: 7af, Greco-Bactrian animal seal, 250 B.C. 9af, Greco-Oriental temple, Ai-Khanoum, 3rd-2nd centuries B.C.

1972, July 16 **Photo.** ***Perf. 12***

861 A302a 3af brown & dl bl .50 .20
862 A302a 7af rose claret & dl grn .80 .20
863 A302a 9af green & lilac 1.10 .30
Nos. 861-863 (3) 2.40 .70

Tourist publicity.

King and Queen Reviewing Parade — A303

1972, Aug. 23 **Photo.** ***Perf. 13½***

864 A303 25af gold & multi 4.00 1.00

Independence Day.

Used as a provisional in 1978 with king and queen portion removed.

Wrestling A304

10af, 19af, 21af, Wrestling, different hold.

1972, Aug. 26

865 A304 4af ol bis & multi .25 .20
866 A304 8af lt blue & multi .50 .25
867 A304 10af yel grn & multi .60 .30
868 A304 19af multicolored 1.25 .40
869 A304 21af lilac & multi 1.40 .45
a. Souv. sheet of 5, #865-869, imperf. 3.00 3.00
Nos. 865-869 (5) 4.00 1.60

20th Olympic Games, Munich, Aug. 26-Sept. 11. No. 869a sold for 60af.

Pathan and View of Tribal Territory — A305

Zahir Shah — A306

1972, Aug. 31 ***Perf. 12½x12***

870 A305 5af ultra & multi .25 .20

Pashtunistan day.

1972, Oct. 14 **Photo.** ***Perf. 14x13½***

871 A306 7af gold, blk & Prus bl 1.50 .30
872 A306 14af gold, blk & lt brn 2.50 .50

58th birthday of King Mohammed Zahir Shah.

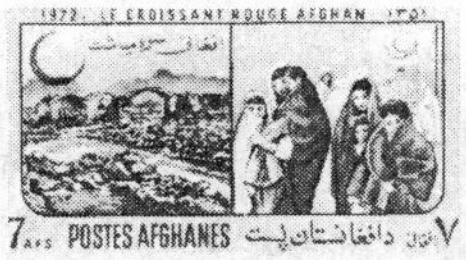

City Destroyed by Earthquake, Refugees — A307

1972, Oct. 16 ***Perf. 13½***

873 A307 7af lt bl, red & blk .40 .20

For Afghan Red Crescent Society.

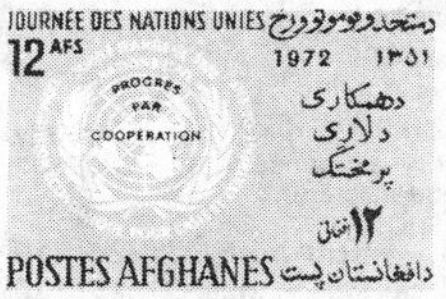

UN Emblem A308

1972, Oct. 24

874 A308 12af lt ultra & blk .65 .35

UN Economic Commission for Asia and the Far East (ECAFE), 25th anniv.

Ceramics A309

Designs: 9af, Leather coat, vert. 12af, Metal ware, vert. 16af, Inlaid artifacts.

1972, Dec. 10 **Photo.** ***Perf. 12***

875 A309 7af gold & multi .40 .20
876 A309 9af gold & multi .55 .30
877 A309 12af gold & multi .70 .35
878 A309 16af gold & multi 1.00 .50
a. Souv. sheet of 4, #875-878, imperf. 2.25 2.25
Nos. 875-878 (4) 2.65 1.35

Handicraft industries. No. 878a sold for 45af.

WMO and National Emblems — A310

1973, Apr. 3 **Photo.** ***Perf. 14***

879 A310 7af lt lil & dk grn .40 .20
880 A310 14af lt bl & dp claret .85 .45

Cent. of intl. meteorological cooperation.

Abu Rayhan al-Biruni — A311

Family — A312

1973, June 16 **Photo.** ***Perf. 13½***

881 A311 10af multicolored .55 .30

Millennium of birth (973-1048), philosopher and mathematician.

1973, June 30 **Photo.** ***Perf. 13½***

882 A312 9af orange & red lil .50 .30

Intl. Family Planning Fed., 21st anniv.

Republic

Impeyan Pheasant A313

Birds: 9af, Great crested grebe. 12af, Himalayan snow cock.

1973, July 29 **Photo.** ***Perf. 12x12½***

883 A313 8af yellow & multi 1.25 .25
884 A313 9af blue & multi 1.75 .30
885 A313 12af multicolored 2.00 .35
Nos. 883-885 (3) 5.00 .90

Stylized Buzkashi Horseman A314

1973, Aug. ***Perf. 13½***

886 A314 8af black .30 .25

Tourist publicity.

Fireworks A315

1973, Aug. 23 **Photo.** ***Perf. 12***

887 A315 12af multicolored .45 .35

55th Independence Day.

Lake Abassine, Pashtunistan Flag — A316

1973, Aug. 31 ***Perf. 14x13½***

888 A316 9af multicolored .50 .30

Pashtunistan Day.

Red Crescent — A317

1973, Oct. 16 **Perf. 13½**
889 A317 10af red, blk & gold .60 .30

Red Crescent Society.

Kemal Ataturk — A318

1973, Oct. 28 Litho. **Perf. 10½**
890 A318 1af blue .20 .20
891 A318 7af reddish brown .40 .20

50th anniversary of the Turkish Republic.

Human Rights Flame, Arms of Afghanistan A319

1973, Dec. 10 Photo. **Perf. 12**
892 A319 12af sil, blk & lt bl .45 .35

25th anniversary of the Universal Declaration of Human Rights.

Asiatic Black Bears A320

1974, Mar. 26 Litho. **Perf. 12**
893 A320 5af shown .35 .20
894 A320 7af Afghan hound .50 .20
895 A320 10af Persian goat .70 .30
896 A320 12af Leopard .90 .35
a. Souv. sheet of 4, #893-896, imperf. 5.00 5.00
Nos. 893-896 (4) 2.45 1.05

Worker and Farmer A321

1974, May 1 Photo. **Perf. 13½x12½**
897 A321 9af rose red & multi .40 .25

International Labor Day, May 1.

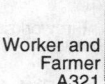

Independence Monument and Arch — A322

1974, May 27 Photo. **Perf. 12**
898 A322 4af blue & multi .20 .20
899 A322 11af gold & multi .35 .30

56th Independence Day.

Arms of Afghanistan and Symbol of Cooperation A323

Pres. Mohammad Daoud Khan — A324

Designs: 5af, Flag of Republic of Afghanistan. 15af, Soldiers and coat of arms of the Republic.

1974, July 25 **Perf. 13½x12½, 14**
Sizes: 4af, 15af, 36x22mm; 5af, 7af, 36x26, 26x36mm
900 A323 4af multicolored .20 .20
901 A323 5af multicolored .25 .20
902 A324 7af green, brn & blk .30 .20
a. Souv. sheet of 2, #901-902, imperf. .70 .70
903 A323 15af multicolored .65 .40
a. Souv. sheet of 2, #900, 903, imperf. 1.00 1.00
Nos. 900-903 (4) 1.40 1.00

1st anniv. of the Republic of Afghanistan.

Lesser Spotted Eagle A325

Birds: 6af, White-fronted goose, ruddy shelduck and gray-lag goose. 11af, European coots and European crane.

1974, Aug. 6 Photo. **Perf. 13½x13**
904 A325 1af car rose & multi .25 .20
905 A325 6af blue & multi .75 .20
906 A325 11af yellow & multi 1.50 .40
a. Strip of 3, #904-906 1.00 1.00
Nos. 904-906 (3) 2.50 .80

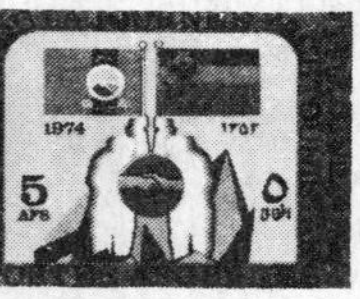

Flags of Pashtunistan and Afghanistan A326

1974, Aug. 31 Photo. **Perf. 14**
907 A326 5af multicolored .25 .20

Pashtunistan Day.

Natl. Arms A326a

1974, Aug. Typo. **Rough Perf. 11**
907A A326a 100p green

Coat of Arms A327

1974, Oct. 9
908 A327 7af gold, grn & blk .25 .20

Centenary of Universal Postal Union.

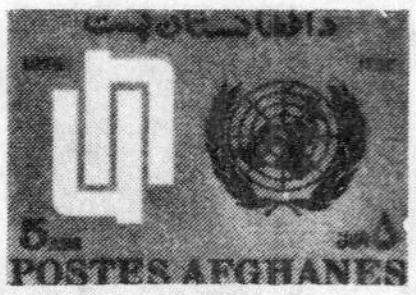

"un" and UN Emblem A328

1974, Oct. 24 Photo. **Perf. 14**
909 A328 5af lt ultra & dk bl .25 .20

United Nations Day.

Minaret of Jam — A329

Buddha, Hadda — A330

14af, Lady riding griffin, 2nd century, Bagram.

1975, May 5 Photo. **Perf. 13½**
910 A329 7af multicolored .25 .20
911 A330 14af multicolored .60 .30
912 A330 15af multicolored .65 .30
a. Souvenir sheet of 3, #910-912, imperf. 3.50 3.50
Nos. 910-912 (3) 1.50 .80

South Asia Tourism Year 1975.

New Flag of Afghanistan A331

1975, May 27 Photo. **Perf. 12**
913 A331 16af multicolored .75 .35

57th Independence Day.

Celebrating Crowd A332

1975, July 17 Photo. **Perf. 13½**
914 A332 9af blue & multi .45 .20
915 A332 12af carmine & multi .55 .30

Second anniversary of the Republic.

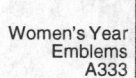

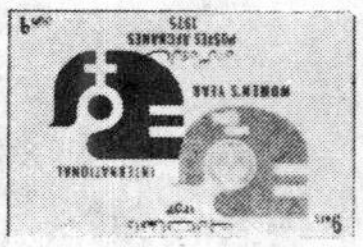

Women's Year Emblems A333

1975, Aug. 24 Photo. **Perf. 12**
916 A333 9af car, lt bl & blk .30 .20

International Women's Year 1975.

Pashtunistan Flag, Sun Rising Over Mountains A334

Mohammed Akbar Khan A335

1975, Aug. 31 **Perf. 13½**
917 A334 10af multicolored .30 .25

Pashtunistan Day.

1976, Feb. 4 Photo. **Perf. 14**
918 A335 15af lt brown & multi .45 .35

Mohammed Akbar Khan (1816-1846), warrior son of Amir Dost Mohammed Khan.

Pres. Mohammad Daoud Khan
A336 A337

1974-78 Photo. **Perf. 14**
919 A336 10af multi .55 .20
920 A336 16af multi ('78) 2.00 *.75*
921 A336 19af multi .75 .40
922 A336 21af multi 1.10 .45
923 A336 22af multi ('78) 3.00 *1.60*
924 A336 30af multi ('78) 4.00 *2.25*
925 A337 50af multi ('75) 2.25 1.10
926 A337 100af multi ('75) 4.50 2.00
Nos. 919-926 (8) 18.15 8.75

Arms of Republic, Independence Monument — A338

1976, June 1 Photo. **Perf. 14**
927 A338 22af blue & multi .65 .45

58th Independence Day.

Flag Raising — A339

1976, July 17 Photo. **Perf. 14**
928 A339 30af multicolored .90 .75

Republic Day.

Mountain Peaks and Flag of Pashtunistan
A340

1976, Aug. 31 Photo. ***Perf. 14***

929 A340 16af multicolored .50 .40

Pashtunistan Day.

Coat of Arms
A340a

1976, Sept. Litho. ***Perf. 11 Rough***

930 A340a 25p salmon .25 .20
931 A340a 50p lt green .25 .20
932 A340a 1af ultra .25 .20
Nos. 930-932 (3) .75 .60

Flag and Views on Open Book — A341

1977, May 27 Photo. ***Perf. 14***

937 A341 20af green & multi .60 .50

59th Independence Day.

Pres. Daoud and National Assembly — A342

President Taking Oath of Office
A343

Designs: 10af, Inaugural address. 18af, Promulgation of Constitution.

1977, June 22

938 A342 7af multicolored .65 .45
939 A343 8af multicolored .70 .60
940 A343 10af multicolored .90 .75
941 A342 18af multicolored 1.60 1.25
  a. Souvenir sheet of 4 3.00 3.00
Nos. 938-941 (4) 3.85 3.05

Election of 1st Pres. and promulgation of Constitution. No. 941a contains 4 imperf. stamps similar to Nos. 938-941.

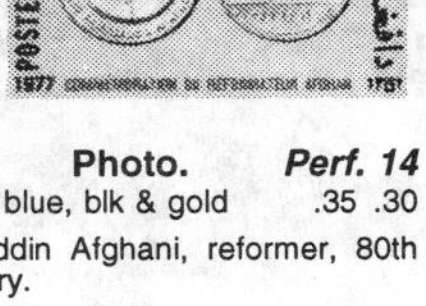

Jamalluddin Medal
A344

1977, July 6 Photo. ***Perf. 14***

942 A344 12af blue, blk & gold .35 .30

Sajo Jamalluddin Afghani, reformer, 80th death anniversary.

Afghanistan Flag over Crowd — A345

1977, July 17

943 A345 22af multicolored .65 .55

Dancers, Fountain, Pashtunistan Flag — A346

1977, Aug. 31

944 A346 30af multicolored .90 .75

Pashtunistan Day.

Arms and Carrier Pigeon
A346a

1977, Oct. 30 Litho. ***Perf. 11***

944A A346a 1af black & blue .20 .20

Members of Parliament Congratulating Pres. Daoud — A347

1978, Feb. 5 Litho. ***Perf. 14***

945 A347 20af multicolored 1.75

Election of first president, first anniversary.

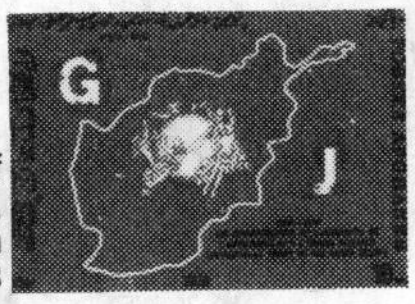

Map of Afghanistan, UPU Emblem
A348

1978, Apr. 1 Photo. ***Perf. 14***

946 A348 10af green, blk & gold .30 .25

Afghanistan's UPU membership, 50th anniv.

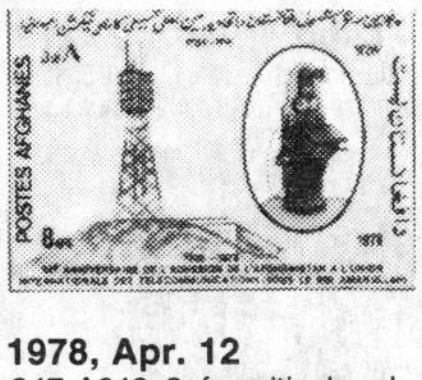

Wall Telephone and Satellite Station
A349

1978, Apr. 12

947 A349 8af multicolored .25 .20

Afghanistan's ITU membership, 50th anniv.

Democratic Republic

Arrows Pointing to Crescent, Cross and Lion — A350

1978, July 6 Litho. ***Perf. 11 Rough***

948 A350 3af black 1.00 .50

50th anniv. of Afghani Red Crescent Soc.

Khalq Party Emblem
A350a

1978, Aug. Litho. ***Perf. 11***

948A A350a 1af rose red & gold 1.25 .50
948B A350a 4af rose red & gold 1.75 .75

Qalai Bist Arch
A351

1978, Aug. 19 ***Perf. 14***

949 A351 16af Bamian Buddha 1.00 .40
949A A351 22af shown 1.25 .55
949B A351 30af Hazara Women 1.75 .90
Nos. 949-949B (3) 4.00 1.85

Men with Pashtunistan Flag — A352

Coat of Arms and Emblems — A353

1978, Aug. 31 ***Perf. 11 Rough***

950 A352 7af ultra & red .20 .20

Pashtunistan Day.

1978, Sept. 8 ***Perf. 11***

951 A353 20af rose red .60 .50

World Literacy Day.

A354

Perf. 11½ Rough

1978, Oct. 25 Litho.

952 A354 18af light green .55 .45

Hero of Afghanistan.

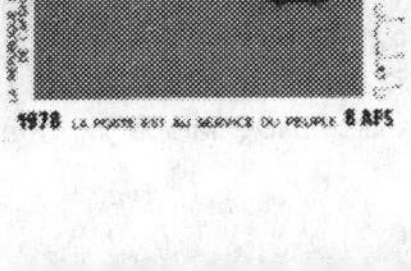

Khalq Party Flag — A355

1978, Oct. 19 Photo. ***Perf. 11½***

953 A355 8af black, red & gold .25 .20
954 A355 9af black, red & gold .30 .20

"The mail serving the people."

Nour Mohammad Taraki — A356

1979, Jan. 1 Litho. ***Perf. 12***

955 A356 12af multicolored .35 .20

Nour Mohammad Taraki, founder of People's Democratic Party of Afghanistan, installation as president.

Woman Breaking Chain — A357

1979, Mar. 8 Litho. ***Perf. 11***

956 A357 14af red & ultra 1.50 .50

Women's Day. Inscribed "POSSTES."

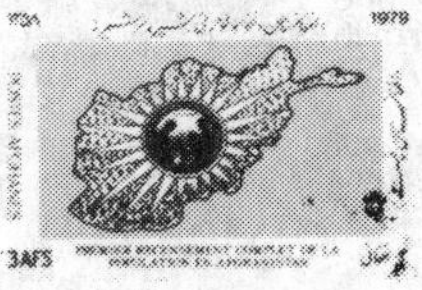

Map of Afghanistan, Census Emblem — A358

1979, Mar. 25 Litho. ***Perf. 12***

957 A358 3af multicolored .75 .50

First comprehensive population census.

Farmers
A359

1979, Mar. 21

958 A359 1af multicolored .50 .25

Agricultural advances.

Pres. Taraki Reading First Issue of Khalq — A360

1979, Apr. 11 ***Perf. 12½x12***

959 A360 2af multicolored .25 .20

Khalq, newspaper of People's Democratic Republic of Afghanistan.

Pres. Noor Mohammad Taraki
A361

Plaza with Tank Monument and Fountain — A362

House where Revolution Started — A363

Designs: 50p, Taraki, tank. 12af, House where 1st Khalq Party Congress was held.

Perf. 12, 12½x12 (A362)

1979, Apr. 27 Litho.

959A	A363	50p multicolored	.20	.20
960	A361	4af multicolored	.20	.20
961	A362	5af multicolored	.25	.20
962	A363	6af multicolored	.30	.25
963	A363	12af multicolored	.50	.45
		Nos. 959A-963 (5)	1.45	1.30

1st anniversary of revolution.

Carpenter and Blacksmith A364

1979, May 1 ***Perf. 12***
964 A364 10af multicolored .30 .25

Int'l Labor Day.

Children, Flag and Map of Afghanistan — A366

1979, June 1 Litho. ***Perf. 12½x12***
966 A366 16af multicolored 1.50 .75

International Year of the Child.

Doves Circling Asia in Globe A366a

1979 Litho. ***Perf. 11x10½***
966A A366a 2af red & blue 1.00 .20

Values quoted in this catalogue are for stamps graded Very Fine and with no faults. An illustrated guide to grade is provided in the "Catalogue Information" section of the Introduction.

Armed Afghans, Kabul Memorial and Arch — A367

Pashtunistan Citizens, Flag — A368

1979, Aug. 19 Litho. ***Perf. 12***
967 A367 30af multicolored 1.25 .75

60th independence day.

1979, Aug. 31
968 A368 9af multicolored .30 .20

Pashtunistan Day.

UPU Day — A369

1979, Oct. 9 Litho. ***Perf. 12***
969 A369 15af multicolored .45 .40

Tombstone — A369a

1979, Oct. 25 Litho. ***Perf. 12½x12***
969A A369a 22af multicolored 2.00 1.00

International Women's Day — A370

1980, Mar. 8 Litho. ***Perf. 12***
970 A370 8af multicolored *3.00 3.00*

Farmers' Day — A371

1980, Mar. 21 Litho. ***Perf. 11½x12***
971 A371 2af multicolored .50 .25

Non-smoker and Smoker — A372

1980, Apr. 7 ***Perf. 11½***
972 A372 5af multicolored .25 .20

Anti-smoking campaign; World Health Day.

Lenin, 110th Birth Anniversary A373

1980, Apr. 22 ***Perf. 12x12½***
973 A373 12af multicolored .35 .30

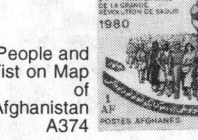

People and Fist on Map of Afghanistan A374

1980, Apr. 27 Litho. ***Perf. 12½x12***
974 A374 1af multicolored .25 .25

Saur Revolution, 2nd anniversary.

International Workers' Solidarity Day — A375

1980, May 1
975 A375 9af multicolored .30 .20

Wrestling, Moscow '80 Emblem A376

1980, July 19 ***Perf. 12x12½, 12½x12***

976	A376	3af Soccer, vert.	.60	.25
977	A376	6af shown	1.00	.45
978	A376	9af Buzkashi	1.60	.60
979	A376	10af Pegsticking	1.75	.75
		Nos. 976-979 (4)	4.95	2.05

22nd Summer Olympic Games, Moscow, July 19-Aug. 3.

61st Anniversary of Independence — A377

1980, Aug. 19 Litho. ***Perf. 12½x12***
980 A377 3af multicolored .25 .20

Pashtunistan Day — A378

1980, Aug. 30
981 A378 25af multicolored .80 .65

Intl. UPU Day A379

1980, Oct. 9 Litho. ***Perf. 12½x12***
982 A379 20af multicolored .60 .50

The resistance group headed by Amin Wardak released some stamps in 1980. Some of these are inscribed "WARDAK AFGHANISTAN," others "Solidarite Internationale Avec la Resistance Afghane." The status of these labels is questionable.

International Women's Day A381

1981, Mar. 9 Litho. ***Perf. 12½x12***
984 A381 15af multicolored .45 .40

Farmers' Day — A382

1981, Mar. 20 Litho. ***Perf. 12½x12***
985 A382 1af multicolored .25 .25

Bighorn Mountain Sheep (Protected Species) A383

1981, Apr. 4 ***Perf. 12x12½***
986 A383 12af multicolored 1.00 .75

Saur Revolution, 3rd Anniversary A384

Intl. Workers' Solidarity Day A385

1981, Apr. 27 ***Perf. 11***
987 A384 50p brown .20 .20

1981, May 1 ***Perf. 12½x12***
988 A385 10af multicolored .30 .25

13th World Telecommunications Day — A387

1981, May 17 Litho. *Perf. 12½x12*
990 A387 9af multicolored .30 .20

Intl. Children's Day — A388

1981, June 1 *Perf. 12x12½*
991 A388 15af multicolored .45 .40

People's Independence Monument 62nd Anniv. of Independence — A389

1981, Aug. 19
992 A389 4af multicolored .20 .20

Pashtunistan Day — A390

1981, Aug. 31 Litho. *Perf. 12*
992A A390 2af multicolored .25 .20

Intl. Tourism Day — A391

1981, Sept. 27 *Perf. 12½x12*
993 A391 5af multicolored .25 .20

World Food Day — A392

1981, Oct. 16
995 A392 7af multicolored .35 .20

Asia-Africa Solidarity Meeting A393

1981, Nov. 18 Litho. *Perf. 11*
996 A393 8af blue .25 .20

Struggle Against Apartheid A394

1300th Anniv. of Bulgaria A395

1981, Dec. 1 *Perf. 12½x12*
997 A394 4af multicolored .30 .20

1981, Dec. 9 *Perf. 12x12½*
998 A395 20af multicolored 1.25 1.00

Buzkashi Game A395a

1980 Photo. *Perf. 14*
998A A395a 50af multicolored 3.00 1.00
998B A395a 100af multicolored 6.00 2.00

Intl. Women's Day — A396

1982, Mar. 8 Litho. *Perf. 12*
999 A396 6af multicolored .50 .25

Farmers' Day — A397

1982, Mar. 21
1000 A397 4af multicolored .25 .20

Rhubarb Plant — A398

Saur Revolution, 4th Anniv. — A399

Designs: Various local plants.

1982, Apr. 9 Litho. *Perf. 12*
1001 A398 3af Judas trees .25 .20
1002 A398 4af Rose of Sharon .35 .20
1003 A398 16af shown 1.00 .40
Nos. 1001-1003 (3) 1.60 .80

1982, Apr. 27
1004 A399 1af multicolored .25 .20

George Dimitrov (1882-1947), First Prime Minister of Bulgaria — A400

1982, Apr. 30
1005 A400 30af multicolored .90 .75

Intl. Workers' Solidarity Day — A401

1982, May 1
1006 A401 10af multicolored .30 .25

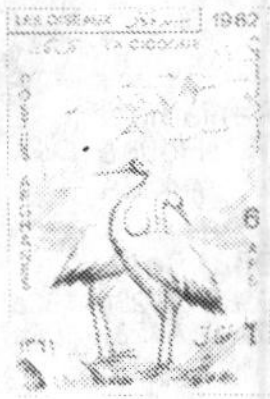

Storks — A402

1982, May 31
1007 A402 6af shown .50 .25
1008 A402 11af Nightingales 1.00 .45

Hedgehogs A403

1982, July 6 Litho. *Perf. 12*
1009 A403 3af shown .25 .20
1010 A403 14af Cobra .75 .50

See Nos. 1020-1022.

63rd Anniv. of Independence — A404

1982, Aug. 19
1011 A404 20af multicolored .60 .50

Pashtunistan Day — A405

1982, Aug. 31
1012 A405 32af multicolored 1.00 .80

World Tourism Day — A406

1982, Sept. 27 Litho. *Perf. 12*
1013 A406 9af multicolored .75 .50

UPU Day — A407

1982, Oct. 9
1014 A407 4af multicolored .50 .25

World Food Day — A408

1982, Oct. 16
1015 A408 9af multicolored .30 .20

37th Anniv. of UN — A409

1982, Oct. 24
1016 A409 15af multicolored .45 .40

ITU Plenipotentiaries Conference, Nairobi, Sept. — A410

1982, Oct. 26
1017 A410 8af multicolored .25 .20

TB Bacillus Centenary A411

Human Rights Declaration, 34th Anniv. A412

1982, Nov. 24 Litho. *Perf. 12*
1018 A411 7af multicolored .25 .20

1982, Dec. 10
1019 A412 5af multicolored .25 .20

Animal Type of 1982

1982, Dec. 16
1020 A403 2af Lions .25 .20
1021 A403 7af Donkeys .75 .20
1022 A403 12af Marmots, vert. 1.00 .25
Nos. 1020-1022 (3) 2.00 .65

Intl. Women's Day — A413

Mir Alicher Nawai Research Decade — A414

1983, Mar. 8
1023 A413 3af multicolored .25 .20

1983, Mar. 19
1024 A414 22af multicolored .70 .50

Farmers' Day — A415

1983, Mar. 21 Litho. *Perf. 12*
1025 A415 10af multicolored .30 .25

5th Anniv. of Saur Revolution A416

1983, Apr. 27 Litho. *Perf. 12*
1026 A416 15af multicolored 1.00 .50

Intl. Workers' Solidarity Day — A417

1983, May 1
1027 A417 2af multicolored .60 .50

World Communications Year — A418

1983, May 17
1028 A418 4af Modes of communication .25 .20
1029 A418 11af Building .75 .30

Intl. Children's Day — A419

1983, June 1 Litho. *Perf. 12*
1030 A419 25af multicolored 1.50 1.50

2nd Anniv. of National Front — A420

1983, June 15
1031 A420 1af multicolored .20 .20

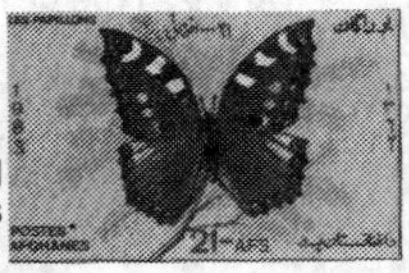
Local Butterflies A421

Various butterflies. 9af, 13af vert.

1983, July 6
1032 A421 9af multicolored .55 .55
1033 A421 13af multicolored .80 .80
1034 A421 21af multicolored 1.25 1.25
Nos. 1032-1034 (3) 2.60 2.60

Struggle Against Apartheid — A422

1983, Aug. 1 Litho. *Perf. 12*
1035 A422 10af multicolored .60 .60

64th Anniv of Independence — A423

1983, Aug. 19
1036 A423 6af multicolored .35 .35

Parliament House A423a

1983, Sept. Litho. *Perf. 12*
1036A A423a 50af shown 3.00 3.00
1036B A423a 100af Afghan Woman, Camel 6.00 6.00

A424

World Tourism Day — A425

1983, Sept. 27 Litho. *Perf. 12*
1037 A424 5af shown .30 .30
1038 A425 7af shown .45 .45
1039 A424 12af Golden statues .75 .75
1040 A425 16af Stone carving 1.00 1.00
Nos. 1037-1040 (4) 2.50 2.50

World Communications Year — A426

1983, Oct. 9 Litho. *Perf. 12*
1041 A426 14af Dish antenna, dove .85 .85
1042 A426 15af shown .90 .90

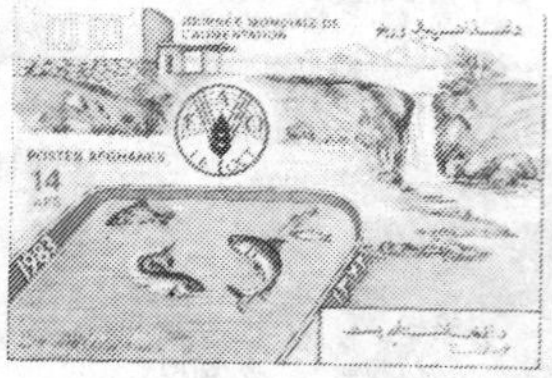
World Food Day A427

1983, Oct. 16 Litho. *Perf. 12*
1043 A427 14af multicolored .85 .85

Boxing A428

1983, Nov. 1 Litho. *Perf. 12*
1044 A428 1af Running .20 .20
1045 A428 18af shown 1.10 1.10
1046 A428 21af Wrestling 1.25 1.25
Nos. 1044-1046 (3) 2.55 2.55

Pashtunistan Day — A428a

1983,Nov. Litho. *Perf. 12*
1046A A428a 3af Pathans Waving Flag .20 .20

Handicrafts A429

1983, Nov. 22
1047 A429 2af Jewelry .20 .20
1048 A429 8af Stone ashtrays, dishes .50 .50
1049 A429 19af Furniture 1.10 1.10
1050 A429 30af Leather goods 1.90 1.90
Nos. 1047-1050 (4) 3.70 3.70

UN Declaration of Human Rights, 35th Anniv. A430

1983, Dec. 10 Litho. *Perf. 12*
1051 A430 20af multicolored 1.25 1.25

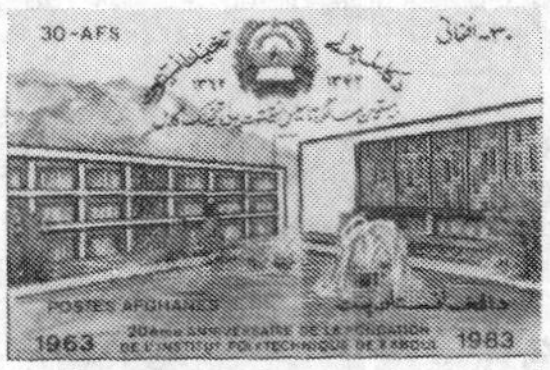
Kabul Polytechnical Institute, 20th Anniv. — A431

1983, Dec. 28 *Perf. 12½x12*
1052 A431 30af multicolored 1.90 1.90

1984 Winter Olympics A432

1984, Jan. *Perf. 12*
1053 A432 5af Figure skating .30 .30
1054 A432 9af Skiing .55 .55
1055 A432 11af Speed skating .65 .65
1056 A432 15af Hockey .90 .90
1057 A432 18af Biathlon 1.10 1.10
1058 A432 20af Ski jumping 1.25 1.25
1059 A432 22af Bobsledding 1.40 1.40
Nos. 1053-1059 (7) 6.15 6.15

Intl. Women's Day — A433

1984, Mar. 8
1060 A433 4af multicolored .25 .25

Farmers' Day A434

Various agricultural scenes.

1984, Mar. 21 Litho. *Perf. 12*
1061 A434 2af multicolored .20 .20
1062 A434 4af multicolored .25 .25
1063 A434 7af multicolored .40 .40
1064 A434 9af multicolored .55 .55
1065 A434 15af multicolored .95 .95
1066 A434 18af multicolored 1.10 1.10
1067 A434 20af multicolored 1.25 1.25
Nos. 1061-1067 (7) 4.70 4.70

World Aviation Day A435

1984, Apr. 12
1068 A435 5af Luna 1 .30 .30
1069 A435 8af Luna 2 .50 .50
1070 A435 11af Luna 3 .70 .70
1071 A435 17af Apollo 11 1.00 1.00
1072 A435 22af Soyuz 6 1.40 1.40
1073 A435 28af Soyuz 7 1.75 1.75
1074 A435 34af Soyuz 6, 7, 8 2.00 2.00
Nos. 1068-1074 (7) 7.65 7.65

Souvenir Sheet

Perf. 12x12½
1075 A435 25af S. Koroliov 1.50 1.50

No. 1075 contains one 30x41mm stamp.

Saur Revolution, 6th Anniv. A436

1984, Apr. 27 *Perf. 12*
1076 A436 3af multicolored .25 .25

65th Anniv. of Independence — A437

1984, Aug. 19 Litho. *Perf. 12*
1077 A437 6af multicolored .40 .40

Pashto's and Balutchi's Day A438

1984, Aug. 31
1078 A438 3af Symbolic sun, tribal terr. .25 .25

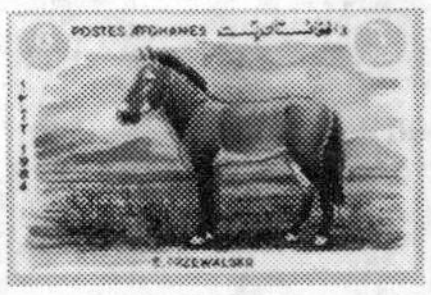
Wildlife A439

Perf. 12½x12, 12x12½

1984, May 5 Litho.
1079 A439 1af Cape hunting dog, vert. .20 .20
1080 A439 2af Argali sheep, vert. .20 .20
1081 A439 6af Przewalski's horse .40 .40
1082 A439 8af Wild boar, vert. .50 .50
1083 A439 17af Snow leopard 1.00 1.00
1084 A439 19af Tiger 1.25 1.25

1085 A439 22af Indian elephant, vert. 1.40 1.40
Nos. 1079-1085 (7) 4.95 4.95

19th UPU Congress, Hamburg A440

1984, June 18 ***Perf. 12x12½***

1086 A440 25af German postman, 17th cent. 1.50 1.50
1087 A440 35af Postrider, 16th cent. 2.00 2.00
1088 A440 40af Carrier pigeon, letter 2.50 2.50
Nos. 1086-1088 (3) 6.00 6.00

Souvenir Sheet

1089 A440 50af Hamburg No. 3 in black 4.00 4.00

No. 1089 contains one 30x40mm stamp.

Natl. Aviation, 40th Anniv. A441

Soviet civil aircraft.

1984, June 29

1090 A441 1af Antonov AN-2 .20 .20
1091 A441 4af Ilyushin IL-12 .25 .25
1092 A441 9af Tupolev TU-104 .55 .55
1093 A441 10af Ilyushin IL-18 .60 .60
1094 A441 13af Tupolev TU-134 .80 .80
1095 A441 17af Ilyushin IL-62 1.00 1.00
1096 A441 21af Ilyushin IL-28 1.25 1.25
Nos. 1090-1096 (7) 4.65 4.65

Ettore Bugatti (1881-1947), Type 43, Italy — A442

Classic automobiles and their designers: 5af, Henry Ford, 1903 Model A, US. 8af, Rene Panhard (1841-1908), 1899 Landau, France. 11af, Gottlieb Daimler (1834-1900), 1935 Daimler-Benz, Germany. 12af, Carl Benz (1844-1929), 1893 Victoris, Germany. 15af, Armand Peugeot (1848-1915), 1892 Vis-a-Vis, France. 22af, Louis Chevrolet (1879-1941), 1925 Sedan, US.

1984, June 30

1097 A442 2af multicolored .20 .20
1098 A442 5af multicolored .30 .30
1099 A442 8af multicolored .50 .50
1100 A442 11af multicolored .70 .70
1101 A442 12af multicolored .75 .75
1102 A442 15af multicolored .90 .90
1103 A442 22af multicolored 1.40 1.40
Nos. 1097-1103 (7) 4.75 4.75

Qalai Bist Arch — A443

World Tourism Day: 2af, Ornamental buckled harness. 5af, Victory Monument and Memorial Arch, Kabul. 9af, Standing sculpture of Afghani ruler and attendants. 15af, Buffalo riders in snow. 19af, Camel driver, tent, camel in caparison. 21af, Horsemen playing buzkashi.

1984, Sept. 27

1104 A443 1af multicolored .20 .20
1105 A443 2af multicolored .20 .20
1106 A443 5af multicolored .30 .30
1107 A443 9af multicolored .55 .55
1108 A443 15af multicolored .60 .60
1109 A443 19af multicolored 1.10 1.10
1110 A443 21af multicolored 1.25 1.25
Nos. 1104-1110 (7) 4.20 4.20

UN World Food Day — A444

Fruit-bearing trees.

1984, Oct. 16

1111 A444 2af multicolored .20 .20
1112 A444 4af multicolored .25 .25
1113 A444 6af multicolored .40 .40
1114 A444 9af multicolored .55 .55
1115 A444 13af multicolored .80 .80
1116 A444 15af multicolored .90 .90
1117 A444 26af multicolored 1.60 1.60
Nos. 1111-1117 (7) 4.70 4.70

People's Democratic Party, 20th Anniv. A445

1985, Jan. 1

1118 A445 25af multicolored 1.50 1.50

Farmer's Day A446

1985, Mar. 2

1119 A446 1af Oxen .20 .20
1120 A446 3af Mare, foal .20 .20
1121 A446 7af Brown horse .40 .40
1122 A446 8af White horse, vert. .50 .50
1123 A446 15af Sheep, sheepskins .90 .90
1124 A446 16af Shepherd, cattle, sheep 1.00 1.00
1125 A446 25af Family, camels 1.50 1.50
Nos. 1119-1125 (7) 4.70 4.70

Geologist's Day — A447

1985, Apr. 5

1126 A447 4af multicolored .25 .25

Lenin Leading Red Army, 1917 — A448

Lenin and: 10af, Soviet Workers' Party deputies, Smolny. 15af, Revolutionaries, 1917, Leningrad. 50af, Portrait.

1985, Apr. 21 ***Perf. 12x12½***

1127 A448 10af multicolored .60 .60
1128 A448 15af multicolored .90 .90
1129 A448 25af multicolored 1.50 1.50
Nos. 1127-1129 (3) 3.00 3.00

Souvenir Sheet

1130 A448 50af multicolored 4.00 4.00

Saur Revolution, 7th Anniv. — A449

1985, Apr. 27

1131 A449 21af multicolored 1.25 1.25

Berlin-Treptow Soviet War Memorial, Red Army at Siege of Berlin, 1945 — A450

9af, Victorious Motherland monument, fireworks over Kremlin. 10af, Caecilienhof, site of Potsdam Treaty signing, Great Britain, USSR & US flags.

1985, May 9 ***Perf. 12½x12***

1132 A450 6af multicolored .40 .40
1133 A450 9af multicolored .55 .55
1134 A450 10af multicolored .65 .65
Nos. 1132-1134 (3) 1.60 1.60

End of World War II, defeat of Nazi Germany, 40th anniv.

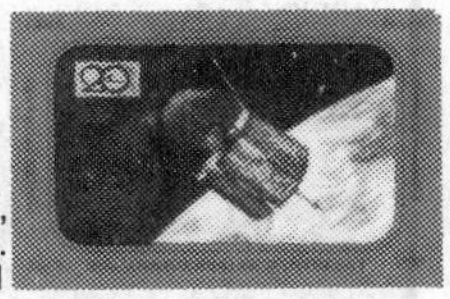
INTELSAT, 20th Anniv. A451

Designs: 6af, INTELSAT satellite orbiting Earth. 9af, INTELSAT III. 10af, Rocket launch, Baikanur Space Center, vert.

Perf. 12x12½, 12½x12

1985, Apr. 6 **Litho.**

1135 A451 6af multicolored .40 .40
1136 A451 9af multicolored .55 .55
1137 A451 10af multicolored .60 .60
Nos. 1135-1137 (3) 1.55 1.55

12th World Youth Festival, Moscow — A452

1985, May 5

1138 A452 7af Olympic stadium, Moscow .50 .50
1139 A452 12af Festival emblem .75 .75
1140 A452 13af Kremlin .80 .80
1141 A452 18af Folk doll, emblem 1.10 1.10
Nos. 1138-1141 (4) 3.15 3.15

Intl. Child Survival Campaign A453

1985, June 1

1142 A453 1af Weighing child .20 .20
1143 A453 2af Immunization .20 .20
1144 A453 4af Breastfeeding .25 .25
1145 A453 5af Mother, child .30 .30
Nos. 1142-1145 (4) .95 .95

Flowers A454

1985, July 5

1146 A454 2af Oenothera affinis .20 .20
1147 A454 4af Erythrina crista-galli .25 .25
1148 A454 8af Tillandsia aeranthos .50 .50
1149 A454 13af Vinca major .80 .80
1150 A454 18af Mirabilis jalapa 1.10 1.10
1151 A454 25af Cypella herbertii 1.50 1.50
1152 A454 30af Clytostoma callistegioides 1.90 1.90
Nos. 1146-1152 (7) 6.25 6.25

Souvenir Sheet

Perf. 12½x11½

1153 A454 75af Sesbania punicea, horiz. 6.00 6.00

ARGENTINA '85.

Independence, 66th Anniv. — A455

1985, Aug. 19 ***Perf. 12x12½***

1154 A455 33af Mosque 2.00 2.00

Pashto's and Balutchi's Day — A456

1985, Aug. 30

1155 A456 25af multicolored 1.50 1.50

UN Decade for Women A457

1985, Sept. 22

1156 A457 10af Emblems .60 .60

World Tourism Day, 10th Anniv. A457a

1985, Sept. 27 **Litho.** ***Perf. 12***

1156A A457a 1af Guldara Stupa .20 .20
1156B A457a 2af Mirwais Tomb, vert. .20 .20
1156C A457a 10af Statue of Bamyan, vert. .60 .60
1156D A457a 13af No Gumbad Mosque, vert. .80 .80
1156E A457a 14af Pule Kheshti Mosque .85 .85
1156F A457a 15af Bost Citadel .90 .90
1156G A457a 20af Ghazni Minaret, vert. 1.25 1.25
Nos. 1156A-1156G (7) 4.80 4.80

Sports
A457b

Perf. 12x12½, 12½x12

1985, Oct. 3 **Litho.**

1156H	A457b	1af Boxing	.20	.20
1156I	A457b	2af Volleyball	.20	.20
1156J	A457b	3af Soccer, vert.	.20	.20
1156K	A457b	12af Buzkashi	.90	.90
1156L	A457b	14af Weight lifting	1.00	1.00
1156M	A457b	18af Wrestling	1.25	1.25
1156N	A457b	25af Peg sticking	1.90	1.90
		Nos. 1156H-1156N (7)	5.65	5.65

World Food Day
A457c

1985, Oct. 16

1156O	A457c	25af multicolored	1.50	1.50

UN 40th Anniv. — A458

Birds — A459

1985, Oct. 24 ***Perf. 12½x12***

1157	A458	22af multicolored	1.40	1.40

1985, Oct. 25 ***Perf. 12½x12, 12x12½***

1158	A459	2af Jay	.20	.20
1159	A459	4af Plover, hummingbird	.25	.25
1160	A459	8af Pheasant	.50	.50
1161	A459	13af Hoopoe	.80	.80
1162	A459	18af Falcon	1.10	1.10
1163	A459	25af Partridge	1.50	1.50
1164	A459	30af Pelicans, horiz.	1.90	1.90
		Nos. 1158-1164 (7)	6.25	6.25

Souvenir Sheet

Perf. 12x12½

1165	A459	75af Parakeets	6.00	6.00

Mushrooms — A460

1985, June 10 **Litho.** ***Perf. 12½x12***

1165A	A460	3af Tricholomopsis rutilans	.20	.20
1166	A460	4af Boletus miniatoporus	.25	.25
1167	A460	7af Amanita rubescens	.45	.45
1168	A460	11af Boletus scaber	.65	.65
1169	A460	12af Coprinus atramentarius	.75	.75
1170	A460	18af Hypholoma	1.10	1.10
1171	A460	20af Boletus aurantiacus	1.25	1.25
		Nos. 1165A-1171 (7)	4.65	4.65

World Wildlife Fund — A461

1985, Nov. 25

1172	A461	2af Leopard, cubs	.20	.20
1173	A461	9af Adult's head	.55	.55
1174	A461	11af Adult	.70	.70
1175	A461	15af Cub	.90	.90
		Nos. 1172-1175 (4)	2.35	2.35

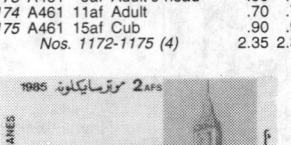

Motorcycle, Cent. — A462

Designs: Different makes and landmarks.

1985, Dec. 16

1176	A462	2af multicolored	.20	.20
1177	A462	4af multicolored	.25	.25
1178	A462	8af multicolored	.50	.50
1179	A462	13af multicolored	.75	.75
1180	A462	18af multicolored	1.00	1.00
1181	A462	25af multicolored	1.50	1.50
1182	A462	30af multicolored	1.75	1.75
		Nos. 1176-1182 (7)	5.95	5.95

Souvenir Sheet

Perf. 11½x12½

1183	A462	75af multicolored	6.00	6.00

People's Democratic Party, 21st Anniv. — A463

1986, Jan. 1 ***Perf. 12½x12***

1184	A463	2af multicolored	.25	.25

27th Soviet Communist Party Congress — A464

1986, Mar. 31

1185	A464	25af Lenin	1.50	1.50

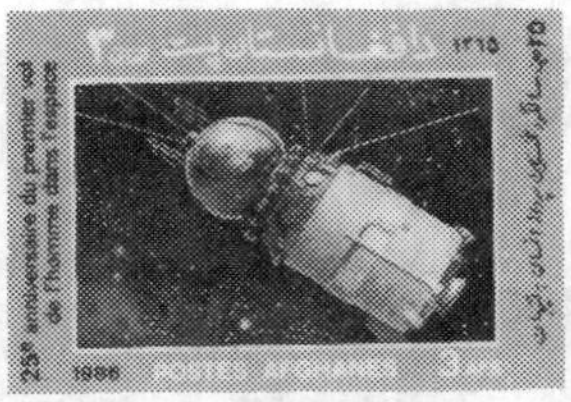

First Man in Space, 25th Anniv. — A465

Designs: 3af, Spacecraft. 7af, Soviet space achievement medal, vert. 9af, Rocket lift-off, vert. 11af, Yuri Gagarin, military decorations, vert. 13af, Gagarin, cosmonaut. 15af, Gagarin, politician. 17af, Gagarin wearing flight suit, vert.

Perf. 12½x12, 12x12½

1986, Apr. 12 **Litho.**

1186	A465	3af multicolored		
1187	A465	7af multicolored		
1188	A465	9af multicolored		
1189	A465	11af multicolored		
1190	A465	13af multicolored		
1191	A465	15af multicolored		
1192	A465	17af multicolored		
		Nos. 1186-1192 (7)	4.50	4.50

Loya Jirgah (Grand Assembly) of the People's Democratic Republic, 1st Anniv.
A465a

1986, Apr. 23 **Litho.** ***Perf. 12x12½***

1192A	A465a	3af multicolored	.25	.25

Intl. Day of Labor Solidarity — A465b

1986, May 1 ***Perf. 12½x12***

1192B	A465b	5af multicolored	.30	.30

Intl. Red Crescent Day
A465c

1986, May 8 ***Perf. 12x12½***

1192C	A465c	7af multicolored	.45	.45

Intl. Children's Day — A466

1986, June 1 ***Perf. 12***

1193	A466	1af Mother, children, vert.	.20	.20
1194	A466	3af Mother, child, vert.	.25	.25
1195	A466	9af Children, map	.40	.40
		Nos. 1193-1195 (3)	.85	.85

World Youth Day
A466a

1986, July 31 ***Perf. 12x12½***

1195A	A466a	15af multicolored	.90	.90

Pashtos' and Baluchis' Day — A467

1986, Aug. 31 ***Perf. 12x12½***

1196	A467	4af multicolored	.25	.25

Intl. Peace Year — A468

Perf. 12½x12

1986, Sept. 30 **Photo.**

1197	A468	12af black & Prus blue	.75	.75

A469

1986 World Cup Soccer Championships, Mexico — A470

Various soccer plays.

1986, Apr. 15 **Litho.** ***Perf. 12***

1198	A469	3af multi, vert.		
1199	A469	4af multicolored		
1200	A469	7af multicolored		
1201	A469	11af multi, vert.		
1202	A469	12af multicolored		
1203	A469	18af multi, vert.		
1204	A469	20af multi, vert.		
		Nos. 1198-1204 (7)	4.50	4.50

Souvenir Sheet

Perf. 12½x12

1205	A470	75af multicolored	6.00	6.00

A471

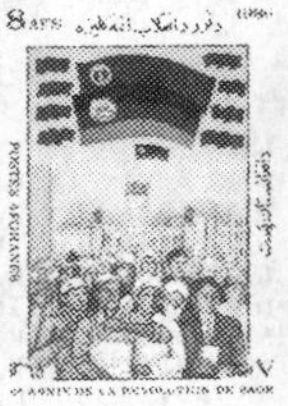

A472

1986, Apr. 21 ***Perf. 12½x12***

1206	A471	16af Lenin	1.00	1.00

1986, Apr. 27 **Litho.** ***Perf. 12½x12***

1207	A472	8af multicolored	.50	.50

Saur revolution, 8th anniv.

Natl. Independence, 67th Anniv. — A473

1986, Aug. 19 **Litho.** ***Perf. 12½x12***

1208	A473	10af multicolored	.65	.65

Literacy Day — A474

1986, Sept. 18 ***Perf. 12x12½***

1209	A474	2af multicolored	.25	.25

Dogs
A475

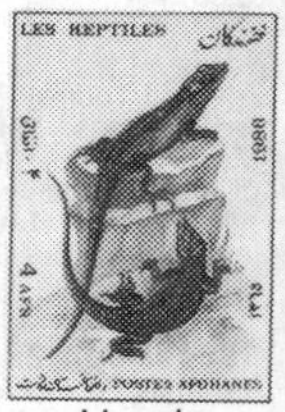

Lizards
A476

1986, May 19 Litho. *Perf. 12x12½*
1210 A475 5af St. Bernard
1211 A475 7af Collie
1212 A475 8af Pointer
1213 A475 9af Golden retriever
1214 A475 11af German shepherd
1215 A475 15af Bulldog
1216 A475 20af Afghan hound
Nos. 1210-1216 (7) 4.50 4.50

1986, July 7 *Perf. 12x12½, 12½x12*
1217 A476 3af Cobra
1218 A476 4af shown
1219 A476 5af Praying mantis
1220 A476 8af Beetle
1221 A476 9af Tarantula
1222 A476 10af Python
1223 A476 11af Scorpions
Nos. 1217-1223 (7) 3.00 3.00

Nos. 1217, 1219, 1221-1223 horiz.

STOCKHOLMIA '86 — A477

Ships.

1986, Aug. 28 *Perf. 12½x12*
1224 A477 4af multicolored
1225 A477 5af multicolored
1226 A477 6af multicolored
1227 A477 7af multicolored
1228 A477 8af multicolored
1229 A477 9af multicolored
1230 A477 11af multicolored
Nos. 1224-1230 (7) 3.00 3.00

Souvenir Sheet
1231 A477 50af Galley 4.00 4.00

A479

A480

1986, Sept. 14 *Perf. 12*
1232 A479 3af lt blue, blk & olive gray .25 .25

Reunion of Afghan tribes under the Supreme Girgah.

1986, Oct. 25 *Perf. 12½x12*
1233 A480 3af black & brt ver .25 .25

Natl. youth solidarity.

Locomotives — A481

1986, June 21 *Perf. 12½x12*
1234 A481 4af multicolored
1235 A481 5af multicolored
1236 A481 6af multicolored
1237 A481 7af multicolored
1238 A481 8af multicolored
1239 A481 9af multicolored
1240 A481 11af multicolored
Nos. 1234-1240 (7) 3.00 3.00

Fish
A482

Various fish.

1986, May 25
1241 A482 5af multicolored
1242 A482 7af multicolored
1243 A482 8af multicolored
1244 A482 9af multicolored
1245 A482 11af multicolored
1246 A482 15af multicolored
1247 A482 20af multicolored
Nos. 1241-1247 (7) 4.50 4.50

Saur Revolution, 9th Anniv.
A483

1987, Apr. 27 *Perf. 12*
1248 A483 3af multicolored .25 .25

Natl. Reconciliation — A484

1987, May 27 *Perf. 12x12½*
1249 A484 3af multicolored .25 .25

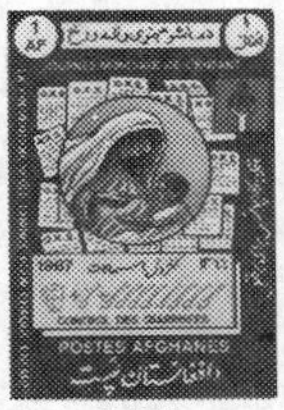

A485

A486

UN Child Survival Campaign — A487

1987, June 1 *Perf. 12*
1250 A485 1af multicolored .20 .20
1251 A486 5af multicolored .30 .30
1252 A487 9af multicolored .55 .55
Nos. 1250-1252 (3) 1.05 1.05

Conference of Clergymen and Ulema, 1st Anniv.
A488

1987, June 30
1253 A488 5af multicolored .30 .30

Butterflies — A489

A490

1987, July 3
1254 A489 7af multicolored
1255 A489 9af multi, diff.
1256 A489 10af multi, diff.
1257 A489 12af multi, diff.
1258 A489 15af multi, diff.
1259 A489 22af multi, diff.
1260 A489 25af multi, diff.
Nos. 1254-1260 (7) 6.00 6.00

10af, 15af and 22af horiz.

1987, Aug. 11
1261 A490 1af multicolored .25 .25

1st election of local representatives for State Power and Administration.

Natl. Independence, 68th Anniv. — A490a

1987, Aug. 19
1261A A490a 3af multicolored .25 .25

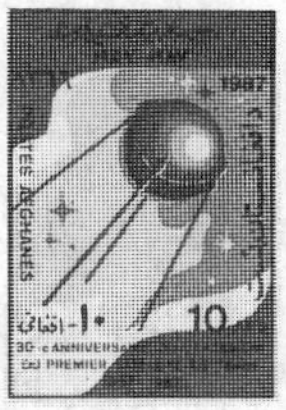

1st Artificial Satellite (Sputnik), 30th Anniv. — A491

1987, Oct. 4 Litho. *Perf. 12½x12*
1262 A491 10af Sputnik
1263 A491 15af Rocket launch
1264 A491 25af Soyuz
Nos. 1262-1264 (3) 3.00 3.00

World Post Day
A492

1987, Oct. 9 *Perf. 12x12½*
1265 A492 22af multicolored 1.40 1.40

Intl. Communications and Transport Day — A493

1987, Oct. 24 *Perf. 12½x12*
1266 A493 42af multicolored 2.50 2.50

October Revolution in Russia, 70th Anniv. — A494

Mice — A495

1987, Nov. 7
1267 A494 25af Lenin 1.50 1.50

1987, Dec. 6 *Perf. 12½x12, 12x12½*

Various mice. Nos. 1269-1272 horiz.

1268 A495 2af multicolored
1269 A495 4af multi, diff.
1270 A495 8af multi, diff.
1271 A495 16af multi, diff.
1272 A495 20af multi, diff.
Nos. 1268-1272 (5) 3.00 3.00

Medicinal Plants — A496

Pashto's and Baluchis' Day — A497

1987, Nov. 11 Litho. *Perf. 12*
1273 A496 3af Castor bean .20 .20
1274 A496 6af Licorice .35 .35
1275 A496 9af Chamomile .55 .55
1276 A496 14af Datura .80 .80
1277 A496 18af Dandelion 1.00 1.00
Nos. 1273-1277 (5) 2.90 2.90

1987, Aug. 30
1278 A497 4af multicolored .25 .25

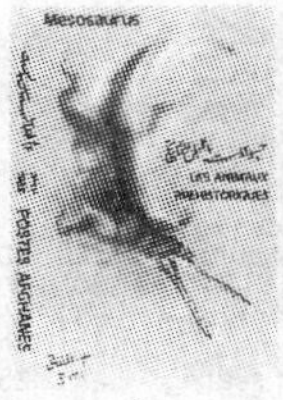

Dinosaurs
A498

Pashtos' and Baluchis' Day
A499

Perf. 12½x12, 12x12½
1988, June 6 Litho.
1279 A498 3af Mesosaurus .20 .20
1280 A498 5af Styracosaurus .30 .30
1281 A498 10af Uinatherium .60 .60
1282 A498 15af Protoceratops .90 .90
1283 A498 20af Stegosaurus 1.25 1.25
1284 A498 25af Ceratosaurus 1.50 1.50
1285 A498 30af Dinornis maximus 1.90 1.90
Nos. 1279-1285 (7) 6.65 6.65

Nos. 1280-1283 horiz.

1988, Aug. 30 *Perf. 12½x12*
1286 A499 23af multicolored 1.40 1.40

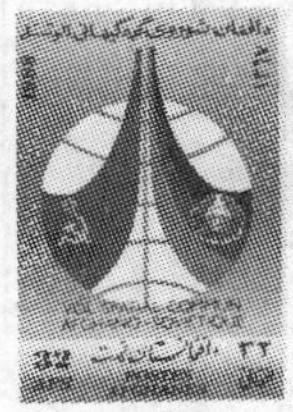

Afghan-Soviet Joint Space Flight — A500

Valentina Tereshkova, 1st Woman in Space, 25th Anniv. — A501

1988, Aug. 30
1287 A500 32af multicolored 2.00 2.00

1988, Oct. 16 *Perf. 12x12½, 12½x12*
1288 A501 10af Portrait, rocket, horiz. .60 .60
1289 A501 15af Lift-off, dove .90 .90
1290 A501 25af Spacecraft, Earth, horiz. 1.50 1.50
Nos. 1288-1290 (3) 3.00 3.00

Traditional Crafts — A502

Precious and Semiprecious Gems — A503

Perf. 12x12½, 12½x12

1988, Nov. 9 **Litho.**

1291 A502 2af Pitcher, bowls .20 .20
1292 A502 4af Vases .25 .25
1293 A502 5af Dress .30 .30
1294 A502 9af Mats, napkins .55 .55
1295 A502 15af Pocketbooks .90 .90
1296 A502 23af Jewelry 1.40 1.40
1297 A502 50af Furniture 3.00 3.00
Nos. 1291-1297 (7) 6.60 6.60

Nos. 1291-1292, 1294-1297 horiz.

1988, Dec. 5 ***Perf. 12½x12***

1298 A503 13af Emeralds .80 .80
1299 A503 37af Lapiz lazuli 2.25 2.25
1300 A503 40af Rubies 2.50 2.50
Nos. 1298-1300 (3) 5.55 5.55

1988 Winter Olympics, Calgary — A504

1988, Dec. 25

1301 A504 2af Women's figure skating .20 .20
1301A A504 5af Skiing .30 .30
1301B A504 9af Bobsledding .55 .55
1301C A504 22af Biathlon 1.40 1.40
1301D A504 37af Speed skating 2.25 2.25

Size: 80x60mm

1302 A504 75af Ice hockey 4.50 4.50
Nos. 1301-1302 (6) 9.20 9.20

A510

A511

A512

A513

A513a

Flowers — A514

Various flowering plants.

Perf. 12x12½, 12½x12

1988, Jan. 27 **Litho.**

1303 A510 3af multicolored .20 .20
1304 A511 5af multicolored .30 .30
1305 A511 7af multi, vert. .40 .40
1306 A512 9af multicolored .50 .50
1307 A513 12af multicolored .75 .75
1308 A513a 15af multicolored .90 .90
1309 A514 24af multicolored 1.50 1.50
Nos. 1303-1309 (7) 4.55 4.55

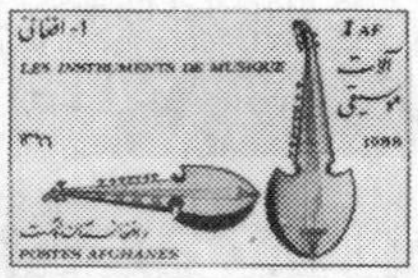

Traditional Musical Instruments A515

String and percussion instruments.

1988, Jan. 15 **Litho.** ***Perf. 12***

1310 A515 1af shown .20 .20
1311 A515 3af drums .20 .20
1312 A515 5af multi, diff. .30 .30
1313 A515 15af multi, diff. .90 .90
1314 A515 18af multi, diff. 1.10 1.10
1315 A515 25af multi, diff. 1.50 1.50
1316 A515 33af multi, diff. 2.00 2.00
Nos. 1310-1316 (7) 6.20 6.20

Admission of Afghanistan to the ITU and UPU, 60th Anniv. — A516

1988, Apr. 13 **Litho.** ***Perf. 12***

1317 A516 20af multicolored 1.25 1.25

Saur Revolution, 10th Anniv. A517

1988, Apr. 23

1318 A517 10af multicolored .65 .65

Fruit — A518

1988, July 18 **Litho.** ***Perf. 12***

1319 A518 2af Baskets, compote .20 .20
1320 A518 4af Four baskets .25 .25
1321 A518 7af Basket .45 .45
1322 A518 8af Grapes, vert. .50 .50
1323 A518 16af Market 1.00 1.00
1324 A518 22af Market, diff. 1.40 1.40
1325 A518 25af Vendor, vert. 1.50 1.50
Nos. 1319-1325 (7) 5.30 5.30

Jawaharlal Nehru (1889-1964), 1st Prime Minister of Independent India — A519

1988, Nov. 14

1326 A519 40af multicolored 2.50 2.50

Natl. Independence, 69th Anniv. — A520

1988, Aug. 1

1327 A520 24af multicolored 1.50 1.50

Intl. Red Cross and Red Crescent Organizations, 125th Annivs. — A521

1988, Sept. 26

1328 A521 10af multicolored .60 .60

Natl. Reconciliation Institute, 2nd Anniv. — A522

1989, Jan. 4

1329 A522 4af multicolored .25 .25

Chess A523

Boards, early matches and hand-made chessmen.

1989, Feb. 2 **Litho.** ***Perf. 12x12½***

1330 A523 2af Bishop .20 .20
1331 A523 3af Queen .20 .20
1332 A523 4af King (bust) .25 .25
1333 A523 7af King, diff. .40 .40
1334 A523 16af Knight 1.00 1.00
1335 A523 24af Pawn 1.50 1.50
1336 A523 45af Bishop, diff. 2.75 2.75
Nos. 1330-1336 (7) 6.30 6.30

Paintings by Picasso — A524

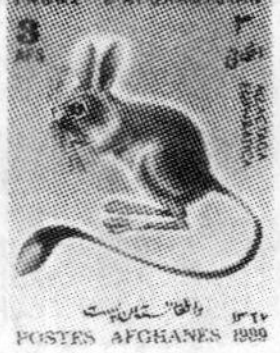

Fauna — A525

Designs: 4af, *The Old Jew.* 6af, *The Two Mountebanks.* 8af, *Portrait of Ambrouse Vollar.* 22af, *Woman of Majorca.* 35af, *Acrobat on the Ball.* 75af, *Usine a Horta de Ebro.*

1989, Feb. 13 **Litho.** ***Perf. 12½x12***

1341 A524 4af multicolored .25 .25
1342 A524 6af multicolored .35 .35
1343 A524 8af multicolored .50 .50
1344 A524 22af multicolored 1.40 1.40
1345 A524 35af multicolored 2.25 2.25

Size: 71x90mm

Imperf

1346 A524 75af multicolored 4.50 4.50
Nos. 1341-1346 (6) 9.25 9.25

1989, Feb. 20 **Litho.** ***Perf. 12½x12***

1347 A525 3af *Allactaga euphratica* .20 .20
1348 A525 4af *Equus hemionus* .25 .25
1349 A525 14af *Felis lynx* .85 .85
1350 A525 35af *Gypaetus barbatus* 2.25 2.25
1351 A525 44af *Capra falconeri* 2.75 2.75

Size: 71x91mm

Imperf

1352 A525 100af *Naja oxiana* 6.00 6.00
Nos. 1347-1352 (6) 12.30 12.30

Intl. Women's Day — A526

1989, Mar. 8 ***Perf. 12½x12***

1353 A526 8af multicolored .50 .50

Restoration and Development of San'a, Yemen A527

1988, Dec. 27 **Litho.** ***Perf. 12***

1354 A527 32af multicolored 2.00 2.00

Agriculture Day — A528

1989, Mar. 21

1355 A528 1af Cattle .20 .20
1356 A528 2af Old and new plows .20 .20
1357 A528 3af Field workers .20 .20
Nos. 1355-1357 (3) .60 .60

World Meteorology Day — A529

1989, Mar. 23

1358 A529 27af shown 1.60 1.60
1359 A529 32af Emblems 2.00 2.00
1360 A529 40af Weather station, balloon, vert. 2.50 2.50
Nos. 1358-1360 (3) 6.10 6.10

Saur Revolution, 11th Anniv. A530

1989, Apr. 27

1361 A530 20af multicolored 1.25 1.25

Classic Automobiles — A531

1989, Dec. 30 Litho. *Perf. 12½x12*

1362 A531 5af 1910 Duchs, Germany
1363 A531 10af 1911 Ford, US
1364 A531 20af 1911 Renault, France
1365 A531 25af 1911, Russo-Balte, Russia
1366 A531 30af 1926 Fiat, Italy

Asia-Pacific Telecommunity, 10th Anniv. — A532

1989, Aug. 3 *Perf. 12*

1367 A532 3af shown
1368 A532 27af Emblem, satellite dish

Teacher's Day — A533

1989, May 30 Litho. *Perf. 12*

1369 A533 42af multicolored 1.25

French Revolution, Bicent. — A534

1989, July Litho. *Perf. 12*

1370 A534 25af multicolored .80

Natl. Independence, 70th Anniv. — A535

1989, Aug. 18 Litho. *Perf. 12*

1371 A535 25af multicolored .80

A536

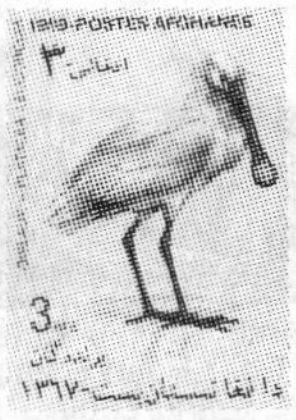

Birds — A537

1989, Aug. 30

1372 A536 3af multicolored .20

Pashtos' and Baluchis' Day.

1989, Dec. 5 Litho. *Perf. 12*

1373 A537 3af Platalea leucorodia .20
1374 A537 5af Porphyrio porhyrio .20
1375 A537 10af Botaurus stellaris, horiz. .30
1376 A537 15af Pelecanus onocrotalus .45
1377 A537 20af Netta rufina .60
1378 A537 25af Cygnus olor .75
1379 A537 30af Phalacrocorax carbo, horiz. .90
Nos. 1373-1379 (7) 3.40

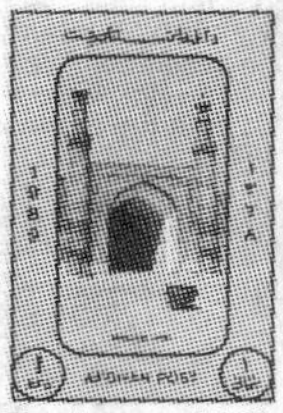

Tourism — A538

Mushrooms — A539

1989, Dec.

1380 A538 1af Mosque .20
1381 A538 2af Minaret .20
1382 A538 3af Buzkashi, horiz. .20
1383 A538 4af Jet over Hendo Kush, horiz. .20
Nos. 1380-1383 (4) .80

1996, July 20 Litho. *Perf. 12½x13*

Designs: 100af, Suillus luteus. 300af, Russula virescens. 400af, Clitocybe inversa. 500af, Volvariella bombycina. 600af, Macrolepiota procera. 800af, Cystoderma cinnabarinum.
4000af, Lycoperdon umbrinum.

1384 A539 100af multicolored .25
1385 A539 300af multicolored .70
1386 A539 400af multicolored .95
1387 A539 500af multicolored 1.10
1388 A539 600af multicolored 1.40
1389 A539 800af multicolored 1.75
Nos. 1384-1389 (6) 6.15

Souvenir Sheet

1390 A539 4000af multicolored 5.25

No. 1390 contains one 32x40mm stamp.

Bears A540

Designs: 500af, Ursus americanus, vert. 600af, Ursus maritimus. 800af, Helarctos malayanus. 900af, Ursus arctos horribilis. 1000af, Ursus arctos pyreneicus, vert.
4000af, Ursus arctos syriacus, vert.

Perf. 12½x13, 13x12½

1996, Aug. 15 Litho.

1391 A540 500af multicolored *.75*
1392 A540 600af multicolored *.90*
1393 A540 800af multicolored *1.25*
1394 A540 900af multicolored *1.40*
1395 A540 1000af multicolored *1.50*
Nos. 1391-1395 (5) *5.80*

Souvenir Sheet

Perf. 13

1396 A540 4000af multicolored *6.25*

No. 1396 contains one 32x40mm stamp.

1998 World Cup Soccer Championships, France — A541

Various soccer players.

1996, Sept. 18 Litho. *Perf. 13*

Background Color

1397 A541 500af green .75
1398 A541 600af purple .90
1399 A541 700af brown 1.00

Size: 28x42mm

1400 A541 800af yellow 1.25
1401 A541 900af blue 1.40
1402 A541 1000af vermilion 1.50
Nos. 1397-1402 (6) 6.80

Souvenir Sheet

Perf. 12½

1403 A541 4000d multicolored 6.00

No. 1403 contains one 32x40mm stamp.

Silkworms A542

Designs: 300af, Arctia caja. 400af, Sphinx ligustri. 500af, Zerynthia polyxema. 600af, Papilio machaon. 700af, Cerura vinula. 800af, Celerio euphorbiae.
3000af, Abraxes grossulariata.

1996, Oct. 7 *Perf. 12½*

1404 A542 300af multicolored .45
1405 A542 400af multicolored .60
1406 A542 500af multicolored .75
1407 A542 600af multicolored .90
1408 A542 700af multicolored 1.00
1409 A542 800af multicolored 1.25
Nos. 1404-1409 (6) 4.95

Souvenir Sheet

Perf. 13

1410 A542 3000af multicolored 4.50

No. 1410 contains one 40x32mm stamp.

Domestic Cats — A543

Designs: 200af, American shorthair. 500af, Japanese bobtail. 600af, British shorthair. 800af, Devon rex. 1000af, Colorpoint shorthair. 1200af, Somali.
4000af, Sphinx.

1996 Litho. *Perf. 12½*

1411 A543 200af multicolored .30
1412 A543 500af multicolored .75
1413 A543 600af multicolored .90
1414 A543 800af multicolored 1.25
1415 A543 1000af multicolored 1.50
1416 A543 1200af multicolored 1.75
Nos. 1411-1416 (6) 6.45

Souvenir Sheet

1417 A543 4000af multicolored 6.00

No. 1417 contains one 40x32mm stamp.

Horses A544

1996, Nov. 5

1418 A544 200af Eohippus .45
1419 A544 300af Miohippus .65
1420 A544 400af Merychippus .90
1421 A544 500af Pliohippus 1.10
1422 A544 600af Equus 1.25
Nos. 1418-1422 (5) 4.35

Souvenir Sheet

Perf. 13

1423 A544 3000af Trotter, sulky 6.00

No. 1423 contains one 40x32mm stamp. Inscription on No. 1418 reads "Echippus."

Tulips — A545

Designs: 300af, Jewel of Spring. 400af, Mrs. John Scheepers. 500af, Absalon. 600af, Queen of Sheba. 800af, Marlette. 1000af, Mary Housley,
3000af, Fosteriana Purissima.

1997 Litho. *Perf. 12½*

1424 A545 300af multicolored .45
1425 A545 400af multicolored .60
1426 A545 500af multicolored .70
1427 A545 600af multicolored .90
1428 A545 800af multicolored 1.10
1429 A545 1000af multicolored 1.50
Nos. 1424-1429 (6) 5.25

Souvenir Sheet

1430 A545 3000af multicolored 4.25

No. 1430 contains one 32x40mm stamp.

Llamas and Camels A546

Designs: 400af, Lama vicugna, vert. 600af, Lama guanicoe. 800af, Camelus dromedarius. 1000af, Lama guanicoe pacos, vert. 1200af, Lama guanicoe glama. 1500af, Camelus ferus bactrianus.
4000af, Camelus dromedarius, vert.

1997

1431 A546 400af multicolored .60
1432 A546 600af multicolored .85
1433 A546 800af multicolored 1.10
1434 A546 1000af multicolored 1.50
1435 A546 1200af multicolored 1.75
1436 A546 1500af multicolored 2.25
Nos. 1431-1436 (6) 8.05

Souvenir Sheet

1437 A546 4000af multicolored 5.75

No. 1437 contains one 32x40mm stamp.

Islamic Revolution, 4th Anniv. — A547

Design: 1500af, Farmer plowing beside stream.

1996 Litho. *Perf. 13*

1438 A547 800af multicolored 1.50
1439 A547 1500af multicolored 3.00

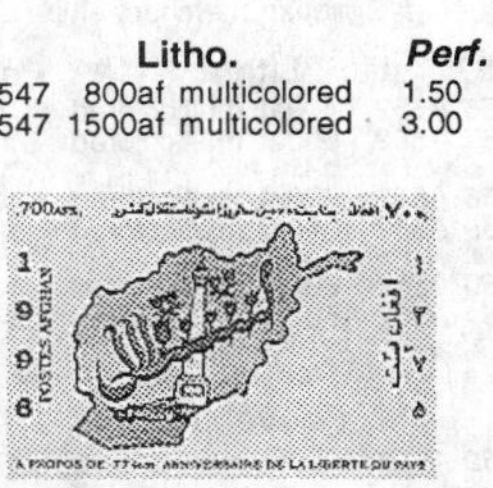

Independence, 77th Anniv. — A548

In Honor of Prophet Mohammed A549

1996

1440 A548 700af multicolored 1.40
1441 A549 1500af multicolored 3.00

Domestic Cats A550

Designs: 30af, Norwegian forest. 50af, Ragdoll. 100af, Longhair Scottish fold. 200af, Oriental longhair. 300af, Manx. 500af, Sphinx. 1200af, Manx, diff.

1997 *Perf. 12½*

1442	A550	30af	multicolored	.20
1443	A550	50af	multicolored	.20
1444	A550	100af	multicolored	.40
1445	A550	200af	multicolored	.80
1446	A550	300af	multicolored	1.25
1447	A550	500af	multicolored	2.00
			Nos. 1442-1447 (6)	4.85

Souvenir Sheet

Perf. 13

1448	A550	1200af	multicolored	4.50

No. 1448 contains one 40x32mm stamp.

Wildflowers A551

Designs: 50af, Nymphaea odorata. 100af, Nymphaea lotus. 200af, Aponogeton distachyus. 500af, Nymphaea capensis. 800af, Numphaea rubra. 1000af, Pontederia cordata. 3000af, Nymphaea daubenyana, horiz.

1997 **Litho.** *Perf. 12½*

1449	A551	50af	multicolored	.20
1450	A551	100af	multicolored	.20
1451	A551	200af	multicolored	.25
1452	A551	500af	multicolored	.65
1453	A551	800af	multicolored	1.00
1454	A551	1000af	multicolored	1.25
			Nos. 1449-1454 (6)	3.55

Souvenir Sheet

1455	A551	3000af	multicolored	3.75

No. 1455 contains one 40x32mm stamp.

Early Sailing Ships — A552

Designs: 400af, Hanseatic cog. 600af, Northern Europe dromond. 800af, Venetian cargo ship. 1000af, Northern Europe merchant ship. 1200af, Ladia Russian war ship. 1500af, Genoa merchant ship. 4000af, Egyptian merchant ship.

1997 **Litho.** *Perf. 12½*

1456	A552	400af	multicolored	.45
1457	A552	600af	multicolored	.70
a.			Pair, #1456-1457	1.15
1458	A552	800af	multicolored	.95
1459	A552	1000af	multicolored	1.25
a.			Pair, #1458-1459	2.25
1460	A552	1200af	multicolored	1.40
1461	A552	1500af	multicolored	1.75
a.			Pair, #1460-1461	3.15
			Nos. 1456-1461 (6)	6.50

Souvenir Sheet

1462	A552	4000af	multicolored	4.50

1998 World Cup Soccer Championships, France — A553

French flag, various soccer plays.

1997 **Litho.** *Perf. 12½*

1463	A553	400af	multicolored	.50
1464	A553	600af	multicolored	.70
1465	A553	800af	multicolored	.95
1466	A553	1000af	multicolored	1.25
1467	A553	1200af	multicolored	1.40
1468	A553	1500af	multicolored	1.75
			Nos. 1463-1468 (6)	6.55

Souvenir Sheet

1469	A553	4000af	multicolored	4.75

No. 1469 contains one 32x40mm stamp.

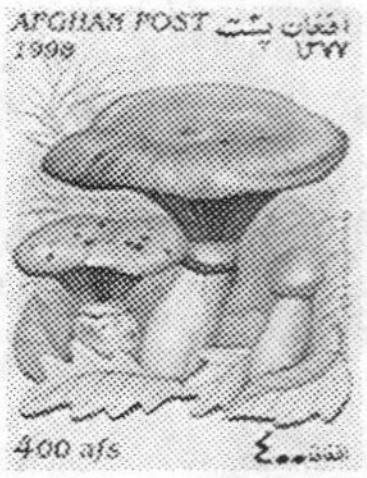

Mushrooms A554

Designs: 400af, Gomphidius glutinosus. 600af, Collybia fusipes. 800af, Stropharia aeruginosa. 1000af, Craterellus cornucopioides. 1200af, Guepinia helvelloides. 1500af, Ixocomus elegans. 4000af, Cantharellus cibarius.

1998 **Litho.** *Perf. 12½*

1470	A554	400af	multicolored	.45
1471	A554	600af	multicolored	.70
1472	A554	800sh	multicolored	.95
1473	A554	1000af	multicolored	1.60
1474	A554	1200af	multicolored	1.40
1475	A554	1500af	multicolored	1.75
			Nos. 1470-1475 (6)	6.85

Souvenir Sheet

Perf. 13

1476	A554	4000af	multicolored	4.50

No. 1476 contains one 40x32mm stamp.

Butterflies, Moths — A556

Designs: 400af, Fabriciana adippe, vert. 600af, Nymphalis antiopa. 800af, Polygonia c-album. 1000af, Nymphalis polychloros. 1200af, Pararge aegeria. 1500af, Melitaea phoebe, vert. 4000af, Aglais urticae.

1998, July 3 **Litho.** *Perf. 12½*

1478	A556	400af	multicolored	.50	.50
1479	A556	600af	multicolored	.75	.75
1480	A556	800af	multicolored	1.00	1.00
1481	A556	1000af	multicolored	1.25	1.25
1482	A556	1200af	multicolored	1.50	1.50
1483	A556	1500af	multicolored	1.90	1.90
			Nos. 1478-1483 (6)	6.90	6.90

Souvenir Sheet

Perf. 13

1484	A556	4000af	multicolored	4.75	4.75

No. 1484 contains one 40x32mm stamp.

A sheet of 9 stamps memorializing Princess Diana has been sold in the philatelic market. The editors do not believe that these stamps were sold in Afghanistan.

Ovis Vignei A557

World Wildlife Fund: a, 800af, Male. b, 1000af, Female nursing young. c, 1200af, Two males walking. d, 10,000af, Two males butting heads.

1998 **Litho.** *Perf. 12½*

1485	A557	Strip of 4, #a.-d.	7.00	7.00

Wildlife — A558

#1486, Panthera tigris, vert. #1487, Cepreolus capreolus, vert. #1488, Lutra lutra, vert. #1489, Cervus elaphus, vert. #1490, Dama dama, vert. #1491, Acinonyx jubatus, vert. #1492, Panthera leo. #1493, Sus scrofa. #1494, Martes foina. #1495, Martes martes. #1496, Vulpes vulpes. #1497, Capra ibex.

1998 **Litho.** *Perf. 12½*

1486	A558	400af	lilac	.45	.45
1487	A558	400af	orange	.45	.45
1488	A558	600af	blue	.70	.70
1489	A558	600af	brown	.70	.70
1490	A558	800af	blue green	.95	.95
1491	A558	800af	red	.95	.95
1492	A558	1000af	violet	1.10	1.10
1493	A558	1000af	green	1.10	1.10
1494	A558	1200af	brown	1.40	1.40
1495	A558	1200af	blue	1.40	1.40
1496	A558	1500af	black	1.75	1.75
1497	A558	1500af	green blue	1.75	1.75
			Nos. 1486-1497 (12)	12.70	12.70

Dogs A559

1998, Mar. 25 **Litho.** *Perf. 12¾*

1498	A559	400af	Bloodhound, vert.	.45	.45
1499	A559	600af	St. Bernard, vert.	.65	.65
1500	A559	800af	Rottweiler, vert.	.90	.90
1501	A559	1000af	Borzoi, vert.	1.10	1.10
1502	A559	1200af	Basset hound	1.25	1.25
1503	A559	1500af	Chow chow	1.75	1.75
			Nos. 1498-1503 (6)	6.10	6.10

Souvenir Sheet

Perf. 13

1504	A559	4000af	Vizsla, vert.	4.50	4.50

No. 1504 contains one 32x40mm stamp.

Trains A560

Designs: 400af, Large Bloomer, Great Britain. 600af, Mogul 2-6-0, US. 800af, Saddle Tank 0-4-0, US. 1000af, A4-4498, Great Britain. 1200af, 020201, Germany. 1500af, 3801, Australia. 4000af, Royal Hudson 2860, Canada.

1998, May **Litho.** *Perf. 12¾*

1505	A560	400af	multi	.45	.45
1506	A560	600af	multi	.65	.65
1507	A560	800af	multi	.90	.90
1508	A560	1000af	multi	1.10	1.10
1509	A560	1200af	multi	1.25	1.25
1510	A560	1500af	multi	1.75	1.75
			Nos. 1505-1510 (6)	6.10	6.10

Souvenir Sheet

Perf. 12½

1511	A560	4000af	multi	4.50	4.50

No. 1511 contains one 36x28mm stamp.

Prehistoric Animals — A561

400af, Mammuthu primigenius. 600af, Megaloceros. 800af, Ursus spelaeus. 1000af, Synthetoceras. 1200af, Coelodonta. 1500af, Hipparion. 4000af, Smilodon.

1998, May **Litho.** *Perf. 12¾*

1512	A561	400af	multi	.45	.45
1513	A561	600af	multi	.65	.65
1514	A561	800af	multi	.90	.90
1515	A561	1000af	multi	1.10	1.10
1516	A561	1200af	multi	1.25	1.25
1517	A561	1500af	multi	1.75	1.75
			Nos. 1512-1517 (6)	6.10	6.10

Souvenir Sheet

Perf. 12½

1518	A561	4000af	multi	4.50	4.50

No. 1518 contains one 32x40mm stamp.

SEMI-POSTAL STAMPS

Catalogue values for unused stamps in this section are for Never Hinged items.

No. 373 Surcharged in Violet

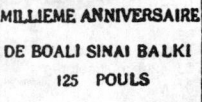

MILLIEME ANNIVERSAIRE
DE BOALI SINAI BALKI
125 POULS

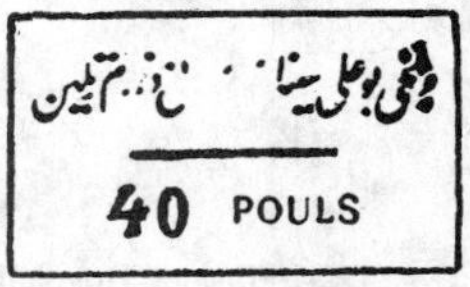

1952, July 12 **Unwmk.** *Perf. 12½*

B1	A122	40p + 30p	cerise	10.00	1.50
B2	A122	125p + 30p	cerise	12.50	2.00

1000th anniv. of the birth of Avicenna.

Children at Play — SP1

1955, July 3 **Typo.** *Perf. 11*

B3	SP1	35p + 15p	dk green	.50	.35
B4	SP1	125p + 25p	purple	1.00	.85

The surtax was for child welfare.

Amir Sher Ali Khan, Tiger Head Stamp and Zahir Shah — SP2

Children at Play — SP3

1955, July 2 **Litho.**

B5	SP2	35p + 15p	carmine	.40	.30
B6	SP2	125p + 25p	pale vio bl	.85	.55

85th anniv. of the Afghan post.

1956, June 20 **Typo.**

B7 SP3 35p + 15p brt vio bl .75 .25
B8 SP3 140p + 15p dk org brn 1.25 .75

Issued for Children's Day. The surtax was for child welfare. No. B8 inscribed in French.

Pashtunistan Monument, Kabul — SP4

1956, Sept. 1 **Litho.**

B9 SP4 35p + 15p dp violet .20 .20
B10 SP4 140p + 15p dk brown .60 .60

"Free Pashtunistan" Day. The surtax aided the "Free Pashtunistan" movement.

No. B9 measures 30½x19½mm; No. B10, 29x19mm. On sale and valid for use only on Sept. 1-2.

Globe and Sun — SP5

Children on Seesaw — SP6

1956, Oct. 24 ***Perf. 11***

B11 SP5 35p + 15p ultra .65 .60
B12 SP5 140p + 15p red brown 1.25 1.00

Afghanistan's UN admission, 10th anniv.

1957, June 20 **Unwmk.**

B13 SP6 35p + 15p brt rose .75 .25
B14 SP6 140p + 15p ultra 1.50 .90

Children's Day. Surtax for child welfare.

UN Headquarters and Emblems — SP7

1957, Oct. 24 ***Perf. 11 Rough***

B15 SP7 35p + 15p red brown .35 .20
B16 SP7 140p + 15p lt ultra .65 .55

United Nations Day.

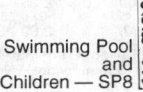

Swimming Pool and Children — SP8

1958, June 22 ***Perf. 11***

B17 SP8 35p + 15p rose .25 .20
B18 SP8 140p + 15p dl red brn .75 .60

Children's Day. Surtax for child welfare.

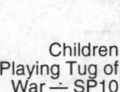

Pashtunistan Flag — SP9

1958, Aug. 31

B19 SP9 35p + 15p lt blue .20 .20
B20 SP9 140p + 15p red brown .60 .60

Issued for "Free Pashtunistan Day."

Children Playing Tug of War — SP10

1959, June 23 **Litho.** ***Perf. 11***

B21 SP10 35p + 15p brown vio .50 .20
B22 SP10 165p + 15p brt pink 1.00 .60

Children's Day. Surtax for child welfare.

Pathans in Tribal Dance — SP11

Perf. 11 Rough

1959, Sept. **Unwmk.**

B23 SP11 35p + 15p green .50 .20
B24 SP11 165p + 15p orange 1.00 .60

Issued for "Free Pashtunistan Day."

Afghan Cavalryman with UN Flag — SP12

1959, Oct. 24 ***Perf. 11 Rough***

B25 SP12 35p + 15p orange .20 .20
B26 SP12 165p + 15p lt bl grn .45 .40

Issued for United Nations Day.

Children SP13

1960, Oct. 23 **Litho.**

B27 SP13 75p + 25p lt ultra .75 .20
B28 SP13 175p + 25p lt green 1.50 .35

Children's Day. Surtax for child welfare.

Man with Spray Gun — SP14

1960, Sept. 6 ***Perf. 11 Rough***

B29 SP14 50p + 50p orange .80 1.00
B30 SP14 175p + 50p red brown 2.25 2.25

11th anniversary of the WHO malaria control program in Afghanistan.

SP15

1960, Sept. 1 **Unwmk.**

B31 SP15 50p + 50p rose .25 .20
B32 SP15 175p + 50p dk blue .55 .45

Issued for "Free Pashtunistan Day."

Ambulance — SP16

1960, Oct. 16 ***Perf. 11***

Crescent in Red

B33 SP16 50p + 50p violet .40 .30
B34 SP16 175p + 50p blue .90 .75

Issued for the Red Crescent Society.

Nos. 470-471 Surcharged in Blue or Orange

1960, Dec. 31 **Litho.** ***Perf. 11***

B35 A166 50p + 25p dp org (Bl) 1.50 1.50
B36 A166 165p + 25p blue (O) 1.50 1.50

The souvenir sheets described after No. 471 were surcharged in carmine "+25 Ps" on each stamp. Value $5 each.

See general note after No. 485.

Nos. 496-500 Surcharged

UNICEF
يونيسف
+25PS

Perf. 13½x14

1961 **Unwmk.** **Photo.**

B37 A175 2p + 25p green & rose lil
B38 A175 2p + 25p brown & cit
B39 A175 5p + 25p gray & rose
B40 A175 10p + 25p blue & bis
B41 A175 15p + 25p sl bl & dl lil
Nos. B37-B41 (5) 1.50

UNICEF. The same surcharge was applied to an imperf. souvenir sheet like that noted after No. 505. Value $4.50.

Nos. 522-526 Surcharged "+25PS" and Crescent in Red

1961, Oct. 16 ***Perf. 13½x14***

B42 A184 2p + 25p black
B43 A184 2p + 25p green
B44 A184 5p + 25p lilac rose
B45 A184 10p + 25p lilac
B46 A184 15p + 25p dk blue
Nos. B42-B46 (5) 2.00

Issued for the Red Crescent Society.

Nos. 539-543 Surcharged in Red: "UNESCO + 25PS"

1962 ***Perf. 12***

B47 A186 2p + 25p multi
B48 A186 2p + 25p multi
B49 A186 5p + 25p multi
B50 A186 10p + 25p multi
B51 A186 15p + 25p multi
Nos. B47-B51 (5) 1.50

UNESCO. The same surcharge was applied to the souvenir sheets mentioned after No. 548. Value, 2 sheets, $3.50.

Nos. 553-561 Surcharged: "Dag Hammarskjöld +20PS"

1962, Sept. 17 ***Perf. 14x13½***

B52 A187 2p + 20p
B53 A187 2p + 20p
B54 A187 5p + 20p
B55 A187 10p + 20p
B56 A187 15p + 20p
B57 A187 25p + 20p
B58 A187 50p + 20p
B59 A187 75p + 20p
B60 A187 100p + 20p
Nos. B52-B60 (9) 2.00

In memory of Dag Hammarskjold, Sec. Gen. of the UN, 1953-61. Perf. and imperf. souvenir sheets exist. Value, 2 sheets, $3.

Nos. 583-593 Surcharged "+15PS"

1963, Mar. 15 ***Perf. 14x13½***

B61 A193 2p + 15p
B62 A193 2p + 15p
B63 A193 5p + 15p
B64 A193 10p + 15p
B65 A193 15p + 15p
B66 A193 25p + 15p
B67 A193 50p + 15p
B68 A193 75p + 15p
B69 A193 100p + 15p
B70 A193 150p + 15p
B71 A193 175p + 15p
Nos. B61-B71 (11) 7.50

WHO drive to eradicate malaria.

Postally used copies of Nos. B37-B71 are uncommon and command a considerable premium over the values for unused copies.

Nos. 672-672G, 672I Surcharged in Various Positions

15ᵉ ANNIVERSAIRE DES DROITS HUMAINS

+
50
POULS

1964, Mar. 9

B71A A213g 2p + 50p
B71B A213g 3p + 50p
B71C A213g 4p + 50p
B71D A213g 5p + 50p
B71E A213g 10p + 50p
B71F A213g 100p + 50p
B71G A213g 2af + 50p
B71H A213g 3af + 50p

Souvenir Sheet

B71J A213g 5af + 50p

Nos. B71E-B71G are airmail semi-postals.

Blood Transfusion Kit — SP17

1964, Oct. 18 **Litho.** ***Perf. 10½***

B72 SP17 1af + 50p black & rose .50 .20

Issued for the Red Crescent Society and Red Crescent Week, Oct. 18-24.

First Aid Station SP18

1965, Oct. **Photo.** ***Perf. 13½x14***

B73 SP18 1.50af + 50p multi 1.00 .50

Issued for the Red Crescent Society.

Children Playing SP19

1966, Nov. 28 **Photo.** ***Perf. 13½x14***

B74 SP19 1af + 1af yel grn & cl .35 .20
B75 SP19 3af + 2af yel & brn .75 .20
B76 SP19 7af + 3af rose lil & grn 1.25 .40
Nos. B74-B76 (3) 2.35 .80

Children's Day.

Nadir Shah Presenting Society Charter SP20

1967 **Photo.** ***Perf. 13x14***

B77 SP20 2af + 1af red & dk grn .25 .20
B78 SP20 5af + 1af lil rose & brn .50 .25

Issued for the Red Crescent Society.

Vaccination SP21

Red Crescent SP22

1967, June 6 **Photo.** ***Perf. 12***

B79 SP21 2af + 1af yellow & blk .75 .20
B80 SP21 5af + 2af pink & brn 1.00 .25

The surtax was for anti-tuberculosis work.

1967, Oct. 18 **Photo.** ***Perf. 12***

Crescent in Red

B81 SP22 3af + 1af gray ol & blk .50 .20
B82 SP22 5af + 1af dl bl & blk .75 .20

Issued for the Red Crescent Society.

Queen Humeira SP23

Red Crescent SP24

1968, June 14 Photo. *Perf. 12*
B83 SP23 2af + 2af red brown .25 .20
B84 SP23 7af + 2af dull green .75 .50

Issued for Mother's Day.

1968, Oct. 16 Photo. *Perf. 12*
B85 SP24 4af + 1af yel, blk & red .45 .25

Issued for the Red Crescent Society.

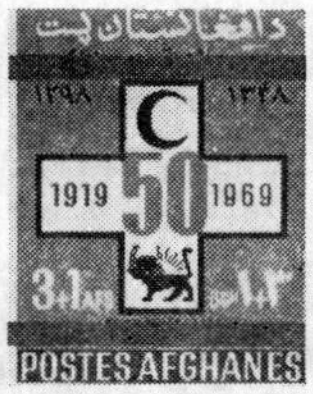

Red Cross, Crescent, Lion and Sun Emblems — SP25

Mother and Child — SP26

1969, May 5 Litho. *Perf. 14x13½*
B86 SP25 3af + 1af multicolored .75 .20
B87 SP25 5af + 1af multicolored 1.25 .30

League of Red Cross Societies, 50th anniv.

1969, June 14 Photo. *Perf. 12*
B88 SP26 1af + 1af yel org & brn .25 .20
B89 SP26 4af + 1af rose lil & pur .40 .25
a. Souvenir sheet of 2 1.00 1.00

Mother's Day. No. B89a contains 2 imperf. stamps similar to Nos. B88-B89. Sold for 10af.

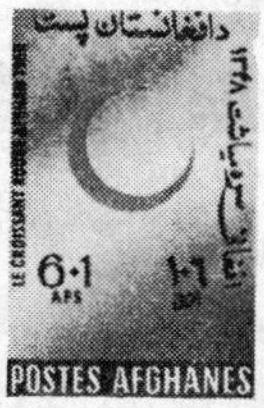

Red Crescent — SP27

1969, Oct. 16 Photo. *Perf. 12*
B90 SP27 6af + 1af multi .75 .30

Issued for the Red Crescent Society.

UN and FAO Emblems, Farmer SP28

1973, May 24 Photo. *Perf. 13½*
B91 SP28 14af + 7af grnsh bl & lil 1.10 .75

World Food Program, 10th anniversary.

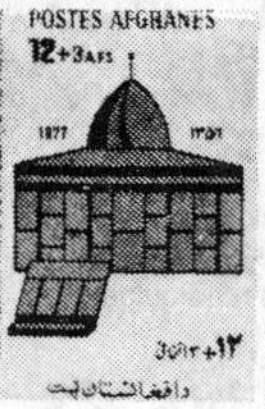

Dome of the Rock, Jerusalem — SP29

1977, Sept. 11 Photo. *Perf. 14*
B92 SP29 12af + 3af multi 1.50 .35

Surtax for Palestinian families and soldiers.

15 Cent. (lunar) of Islamic Pilgrimage (Hegira) — SP30

1981, Jan. 17 Litho. *Perf. 12½x12*
B93 SP30 13af + 2af multi .45 .40

Red Crescent Aid Programs SP31

1981, May 8 *Perf. 12x12½*
B94 SP31 1af + 4af multi 1.00 1.00

Intl. Year of the Disabled SP32

1981, Oct. 12 *Perf. 12x12½*
B95 SP32 6af + 1af multi .35 .25

AIR POST STAMPS

Plane over Kabul — AP1

Perf. 12, 12x11, 11
1939, Oct. 1 Typo. Unwmk.
C1 AP1 5af orange 3.75 2.25
a. Imperf., pair ('47) 22.50 22.50
b. Horiz. pair, imperf. vert. 20.00
C2 AP1 10af blue 3.75 1.75
a. 10af lt bl 5.00 5.00
b. Imperf., pair ('47) 22.50
c. Horiz. pair, imperf. vert. 20.00
C3 AP1 20af emerald 7.50 5.00
a. Imperf., pair ('47) 22.50
b. Horiz. pair, imperf. vert. 20.00
c. Vert. pair, imperf. horiz. 22.50
Nos. C1-C3 (3) 15.00 9.00

These stamps come with clean-cut or rough perforations. Counterfeits exist.

1948, June 14 *Perf. 12x11½*
C4 AP1 5af emerald 15.00 15.00
C5 AP1 10af red orange 15.00 15.00
C6 AP1 20af blue 15.00 15.00
Nos. C4-C6 (3) 45.00 45.00

Imperforates exist.

Catalogue values for unused stamps in this section, from this point to the end of the section, are for Never Hinged items.

Plane over Palace Grounds, Kabul AP2

1951-54 Engr. *Perf. 13½*
Imprint: "Waterlow & Sons, Limited, London"
C7 AP2 5af henna brn 2.50 .55
C8 AP2 5af dp grn ('54) 3.50 .50
C9 AP2 10af gray 4.00 1.40
C10 AP2 20af dark blue 6.50 2.25

1957
C11 AP2 5af ultra .90 .35
C12 AP2 10af dark vio 1.75 .75
Nos. C7-C12 (6) 19.15 5.80

See No. C38.

Ariana Plane over Hindu Kush — AP3

Perf. 11, Imperf.
1960-63 Litho. Unwmk.
C13 AP3 75p light vio .30 .30
C14 AP3 125p blue .40 .40

Perf. 10½, 11
C14A AP3 5af citron ('63) 1.10 1.10
Nos. C13-C14A (3) 1.80 1.80

Girl Scout — AP4

1962, Aug. 30 Photo. *Perf. 11½x12*
C15 AP4 100p ocher & brn .60 .60
C16 AP4 175p brt yel grn & brn .85 .85

Women's Day. See #578-579 and note on souvenir sheet.

Sports Type of Regular Issue, 1962

Designs: 25p, 50p, Horse racing. 75p, 100p, Wrestling. 150p, Weight lifting. 175p, Soccer.

1962, Sept. 25 Unwmk. *Perf. 12*
Black Inscriptions
C17 A195 25p rose & red brn
C18 A195 50p gray & red brn
C19 A195 75p pale vio & dk grn
C20 A195 100p gray ol & dk pur
C21 A195 150p rose lil & grn
C22 A195 175p sal & brn
Nos. C17-C22 2.25

Children's Day Type of Regular Issue
Perf. 11½x12, 12x11½
1962, Oct. 14 Unwmk.
C23 A196 75p Runners
C24 A196 150p Peaches
C25 A196 200p Iris, vert.

A souvenir sheet contains one each of Nos. C23-C25. Value $2.50.

Red Crescent Type of Regular Issue
1962, Oct. 16 *Perf. 12*
Fruit and Flowers in Natural Colors; Carmine Crescent
C26 A197 25p Grapes
C27 A197 50p Pears
C28 A197 100p Wistaria

Two souvenir sheets exist. One contains a 150p gray brown stamp in blossom design, the other a 200p gray stamp in wistaria design, imperf. Value, each $5.

UN Type of Regular Issue
1962, Oct. 24 Photo.
Flags in Original Colors, Black Inscriptions
C29 A198 75p blue
C30 A198 100p lt brn
C31 A198 125p brt grn

Boy Scout Type of Regular Issue
1962, Oct. 25 Unwmk. *Perf. 12*
C32 A199 25p gray, blk, dl grn & sal
C33 A199 50p grn, brn & sal
C34 A199 75p bl grn, red brn & sal
C35 A199 100p bl, slate & sal

Teacher's Day Type of Regular Issue
1962, Oct. 25
C36 A200 100p Pole vault
C37 A200 150p High jump

A souvenir sheet contains one 250p pink and slate green stamp in design of 150p. Value $2.50.

Type of 1951-54
1962 Engr. *Perf. 13½*
Imprint: "Thomas De La Rue & Co. Ltd."
C38 AP2 5af ultra 6.00 1.00

Agriculture Types of Regular Issue
Unwmk.
1963, Mar. 1 Photo. *Perf. 12*
C42 A204 100p dk car, grn & brn
C43 A203 150p ocher & blk
C44 A204 200p ultra, grn & brn

Hands Holding Wheat Emblem AP5

1963, Mar. 27 Photo. *Perf. 14*
C45 AP5 500p lil, lt brn & brn 1.75 .60

FAO "Freedom from Hunger" campaign.
Two souvenir sheets exist. One contains a 1000p blue green, light brown and brown, type AP5, imperf. The other contains a 200p brown and green and 300p ultramarine, yellow and ocher in rice and corn designs, type A205. Values $6 and $2.50.

Meteorological Day Type of Regular Issue

Designs: 100p, 500p, Meteorological measuring instrument. 200p, 400p, Weather station. 300p, Rockets in space.

1963, May 23 *Imperf.*
C46 A206 100p brn & bl

Perf. 13½x14
C47 A206 200p brt grn & lil
C48 A206 300p dk bl & rose
C49 A206 400p bl & dl red brn
C50 A206 500p car rose & gray grn

Nos. C47 and C50 printed se-tenant.
Two souvenir sheets exist. One contains a 125p red and brown stamp in rocket design. The other contains a 100p blue and dull red brown in "rockets in space" design. Values $5 and $7.50.

Kabul International Airport AP8

Perf. 12x11½
1964, Apr. Unwmk. Photo.
C57 AP8 10af red lil & grn .55 .20
C58 AP8 20af dk grn & red lil .80 .40
a. Perf. 12 ('68) 5.00 3.00
C59 AP8 50af dk bl & grnsh bl 2.25 1.00
a. Perf. 12 ('68) 8.00 5.00
Nos. C57-C59 (3) 3.60 1.60

Inauguration of Kabul Airport Terminal.
Nos. C58a-C59a are 36mm wide. Nos. C58-C59 are 35½mm wide.

Zahir Shah and Kabul Airport — AP9

Design: 100af, Zahir Shah and Ariana Plane.

1971 Photo. *Perf. 12½x13½*
C60 AP9 50af multi 10.00 8.00
C61 AP9 100af blk, red & grn 5.00 3.00

Remainders of No C60 were used, starting in 1978, with king's portrait removed.

REGISTRATION STAMPS

R1

Dated "1309"

1891 Unwmk. Litho. *Imperf.*

Pelure Paper

F1	R1 1r slate blue	2.00	
a.	Tete beche pair	12.50	

Genuinely used copies of No. F1 are rare. Counterfeit cancellations exist.

R2

Dated "1311"

1893 Thin Wove Paper

F2	R2 1r black, *green*	1.60	

Genuinely used copies of No. F2 are rare. Counterfeit cancellations exist.

R3

Undated

1894

F3	R3 2ab black, *green*	8.00	*10.00*

12 varieties. See note below Nos. 189-190.

R4

Undated

1898-1900

F4	R4 2ab black, *deep rose*	4.00	4.00
F5	R4 2ab black, *lilac rose*	4.00	4.00
F6	R4 2ab black, *magenta*	6.00	4.00
F7	R4 2ab black, *salmon*	2.50	*4.00*
F8	R4 2ab black, *orange*	6.00	4.00
F9	R4 2ab black, *yellow*	2.50	*4.00*
F10	R4 2ab black, *green*	6.00	4.00
	Nos. F4-F10 (7)	31.00	28.00

Many shades of paper.

Nos. F4-F10 come in two sizes, measured between outer frame lines: 52x36mm, 1st printing; 46x33mm, 2nd printing. The outer frame line (not pictured) is 3-6mm from inner frame line.

Used on P.O. receipts.

OFFICIAL STAMPS

(Used only on interior mail.)

Coat of Arms O1

1909 Unwmk. Typo. *Perf. 12*

Wove Paper

O1	O1 red	1.00	1.00
a.	Carmine ('19?)	2.25	*6.00*

Later printings of No. O1 in scarlet, vermilion, claret, etc., on various types of paper, were issued until 1927.

Coat of Arms — O2

1939-68? Typo. *Perf. 11, 12*

O3	O2 15p emerald	.35	.20
O4	O2 30p ocher ('40)	.50	.50
O5	O2 45p dark carmine	.40	.35
O6	O2 50p brt car ('68)	.30	.30
a.	50p carmine rose ('55)	.50	.40
O7	O2 1af brt red violet	.80	.80
	Nos. O3-O7 (5)	2.35	2.15

Size of 50p, 24x31mm, others 22½x28mm.

Catalogue values for unused stamps in this section, from this point to the end of the section, are for Never Hinged items.

1964-65 Litho. *Perf. 11*

O8	O2 50p rose	.75	.75
a.	50p salmon ('65)	1.50	1.50

Stamps of this type are revenues.

PARCEL POST STAMPS

Coat of Arms — PP1

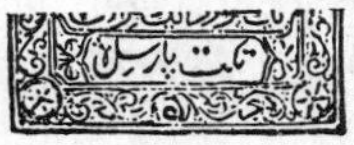

PP2

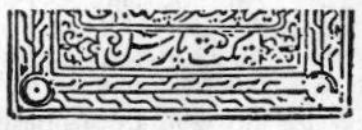

PP3

PP4

1909 Unwmk. Typo. *Perf. 12*

Q1	PP1 3sh bister	1.00	*2.00*
a.	Imperf., pair	*1.00*	
Q2	PP2 1kr olive gray	1.60	*3.00*
a.	Imperf., pair		
Q3	PP3 1r orange	3.00	3.00
Q4	PP3 1r olive green	18.00	4.00
Q5	PP4 2r red	3.50	3.50
	Nos. Q1-Q5 (5)	27.10	15.50

1916-18

Q6	PP1 3sh green	1.60	*3.00*
Q7	PP2 1kr pale red	2.50	1.25
a.	1kr rose red ('18)	3.25	3.25
Q8	PP3 1r brown org	1.25	1.25
a.	1r deep brown ('18)	10.00	2.50
Q9	PP4 2r blue	4.50	*5.00*
	Nos. Q6-Q9 (4)	9.85	*10.50*

Nos. Q1-Q9 sometimes show letters of the papermaker's watermark "HOWARD & JONES LONDON."

Ungummed copies are remainders. They sell for one-third the price of mint examples.

Old Habibia College, Near Kabul PP5

1921

Wove Paper

Q10	PP5 10pa chocolate	3.00	3.00
a.	Tete beche pair	15.00	15.00
Q11	PP5 15pa light brn	6.00	5.00
a.	Tete beche pair	20.00	
Q12	PP5 30pa red violet	9.00	7.00
a.	Tete beche pair	30.00	
b.	Laid paper	*15.00*	*10.00*
Q13	PP5 1r brt blue	10.00	9.00
a.	Tete beche pair	50.00	
	Nos. Q10-Q13 (4)	28.00	24.00

Stamps of this issue are usually perforated on one or two sides only.

The laid paper of No. Q12b has a papermaker's watermark in the sheet.

PP6

1924-26

Wove Paper

Q15	PP6 5kr ultra ('26)	35.00	35.00
Q16	PP6 5r lilac	15.00	15.00

A 15r rose exists, but is not known to have been placed in use.

PP7

PP8

1928-29 *Perf. 11, 11xImperf.*

Q17	PP7 2r yellow orange	10.00	3.00
Q18	PP7 2r green ('29)	3.00	3.00
Q19	PP8 3r deep green	7.50	4.00
Q20	PP8 3r brown ('29)	5.00	5.00
	Nos. Q17-Q20 (4)	25.50	15.00

POSTAL TAX STAMPS

Aliabad Hospital near Kabul PT1

Pierre and Marie Curie — PT2

Perf. 12x11½, 12

1938, Dec. 22 Typo. Unwmk.

RA1	PT1 10p peacock grn	1.50	*2.75*
RA2	PT2 15p dull blue	1.50	*2.75*

Obligatory on all mail Dec. 22-28, 1938. The money was used for the Aliabad Hospital. See note with CD80.

Begging Child

PT3 PT4

1949, May 28 Typo. *Perf. 12*

RA3	PT3 35p red orange	1.60	1.60
RA4	PT4 125p ultra	2.50	2.00

United Nations Children's Day, May 28. Obligatory on all foreign mail on that date. Proceeds were used for child welfare.

Paghman Arch and UN Emblem PT5

1949, Oct. 24

RA5	PT5 125p dk blue green	10.00	6.00

4th anniv. of the UN. Valid one day only. Issued in sheets of 9 (3x3).

Catalogue values for unused stamps in this section, from this point to the end of the section, are for Never Hinged items.

Zahir Shah and Map of Afghanistan — PT6

1950, Mar. 30 Typo.

RA6	PT6 125p blue green	2.00	1.25

Return of Zahir Shah from a trip to Europe for his health. Valid for two weeks. The tax was used for public health purposes.

Hazara Youth — PT7

1950, May 28 Typo. *Perf. 11½*

RA7	PT7 125p dk blue green	2.00	1.50

Tax for Child Welfare. Obligatory and valid only on May 28, 1950, on foreign mail.

Ruins of Qalai Bist and Globe PT8

1950, Oct. 24

RA8 PT8 1.25af ultramarine 7.50 4.00

5th anniv. of the UN. Proceeds went to Afghanistan's UN Projects Committee.

Zahir Shah and Medical Center PT9

1950, Dec. 22 Typo. *Perf. 11½*

Size: 38x25mm

RA9	PT9	35p carmine	1.00	1.00
RA10	PT9	1.25af black	4.50	2.25

The tax was for the national Graduate School of Medicine.

Koochi Girl with Lamb — PT10

Kohistani Boy and Sheep PT11

1951, May 28

RA11	PT10	35p emerald	.75	.65
RA12	PT11	1.25af ultramarine	.75	.65

The tax was for Child Welfare.

Distributing Gifts to Children — PT12

Qandahari Boys Dancing the "Attan" — PT13

1952, May 28 Litho.

RA13	PT12	35p chocolate	.25	.25
RA14	PT13	125p violet	.75	.75

The tax was for Child Welfare.

Soldier Receiving First Aid — PT14

1952, Oct.

RA15 PT14 10p light green .50 .35

Stretcher-bearers and Wounded — PT15

Soldier Assisting Wounded — PT16

1953, Oct.

RA16	PT15	10p yel grn & org red	.50	.40
RA17	PT16	10p vio brn & org red	.50	.40

Prince Mohammed Nadir — PT17

Map and Young Musicians — PT18

1953, May 28

RA18	PT17	35p orange yellow	.20	.20
RA19	PT17	125p chalky blue	.55	.55

No. RA19 is inscribed in French "Children's Day." The tax was for child welfare.

1954, May 28 Unwmk. *Perf. 11*

RA20	PT18	35p purple	.30	.20
RA21	PT18	125p ultra	1.10	1.10

No. RA21 is inscribed in French. The tax was for child welfare.

Red Crescent

PT19 PT20

1954, Oct. 17 *Perf. 11½*

RA22 PT19 20p blue & red .25 .20

1955, Oct. 18 *Perf. 11*

RA23 PT20 20p dull grn & car .50 .25

Zahir Shah and Red Crescent — PT21

1956, Oct. 18

RA24 PT21 20p lt grn & rose car .25 .20

Red Crescent Headquarters, Kabul — PT22

1957, Oct. 17

RA25 PT22 20p lt ultra & car .75 .50

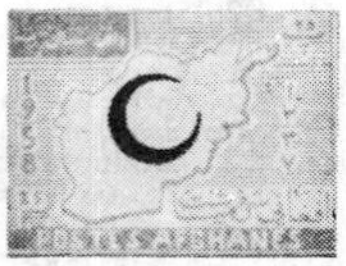

Map and Crescent PT23

1958, Oct. Unwmk. *Perf. 11*

RA26 PT23 25p yel grn & red .30 .30

PT24

1959, Oct. 17 Litho. *Perf. 11*

RA27 PT24 25p lt violet & red .20 .20

The tax on Nos. RA15-RA17, RA22-RA27 was for the Red Crescent Society. Use of these stamps was required for one week.

AGUERA, LA

LOCATION — An administrative district in southern Rio de Oro on the north-west coast of Africa.

GOVT. — Spanish possession

AREA — Because of indefinite political boundaries, figures for area and population are not available.

100 Centimos = 1 Peseta

Type of 1920 Issue of Rio de Oro Overprinted **LA AGÜERA**

1920, June Unwmk. *Perf. 13*

1	A8	1c	blue green	1.75	1.75
2	A8	2c	olive brown	1.75	1.75
3	A8	5c	deep green	1.75	1.75
4	A8	10c	light red	1.75	1.75
5	A8	15c	yellow	1.75	1.75
6	A8	20c	lilac	1.75	1.75
7	A8	25c	deep blue	1.75	1.75
8	A8	30c	dark brown	1.75	1.75
9	A8	40c	pink	1.75	1.75
10	A8	50c	bright blue	4.50	4.50
11	A8	1p	red brown	8.00	8.00
12	A8	4p	dark violet	25.00	25.00
13	A8	10p	orange	50.00	50.00
			Nos. 1-13 (13)	103.25	103.25
			Set, never hinged	155.00	

Very fine examples of Nos. 1-13 will be somewhat off center. Well centered examples are uncommon and will sell for more.

King Alfonso XIII — A2

1922, June Typo.

14	A2	1c	turquoise blue	.75	.75
15	A2	2c	dark green	.75	.75
16	A2	5c	blue green	.75	.75
17	A2	10c	red	.75	.75
18	A2	15c	red brown	.75	.75
19	A2	20c	yellow	.75	.75
20	A2	25c	deep blue	.75	.75
21	A2	30c	dark brown	.75	.75
22	A2	40c	rose red	1.00	1.00
23	A2	50c	red violet	3.50	3.50
24	A2	1p	rose	7.00	7.00
25	A2	4p	violet	15.00	15.00
26	A2	10p	orange	22.50	22.50
			Nos. 14-26 (13)	55.00	55.00
			Set, never hinged	80.00	

For later issues see Spanish Sahara.

AITUTAKI

,īt-ə-'täk-ē

LOCATION — One of the larger Cook Islands, in the South Pacific Ocean northeast of New Zealand

GOVT. — A dependency of New Zealand

AREA — 7 sq. mi.

POP. — 2,335 (1981)

The Cook Islands were attached to New Zealand in 1901. Stamps of Cook Islands were used in 1892-1903 and 1932-72.

Aitutaki acquired its own postal service in August 1972, though remaining part of Cook Islands.

12 Pence = 1 Shilling

100 Cents = 1 Dollar (1972)

Catalogue values for unused stamps in this country are for Never Hinged items, beginning with Scott 37.

Watermark

Wmk. 61- Single-lined NZ and Star Close Together

Stamps of New Zealand Surcharged in Red or Blue:

AITUTAKI. Ava Pene. — a

AITUTAKI. Tai Pene. — b

1903 Engr. Wmk. 61 *Perf. 14*

1	A18(a)	½p green (R)	4.00	*6.00*
2	A35(b)	1p rose (Bl)	4.50	*6.25*

AITUTAKI. Rua Pene Ma Te Ava. — c

AITUTAKI. Toru Pene. — d

AITUTAKI. Ono Pene. — e

AITUTAKI. Tai Tiringi. — f

Perf. 11

3	A22(c)	2½p blue (R)	10.50	*11.00*
4	A23(d)	3p yellow brn (Bl)	14.00	14.00
5	A26(e)	6p red (Bl)	27.50	27.50
6	A29(f)	1sh scarlet (Bl)	55.00	*80.00*
a.		1sh orange red (Bl)	60.00	*87.50*

1911 Typo. *Perf. 14x15*

7 A41(a) ½p yellow grn (R) 1.00 *2.75*

Engr.

Perf. 14

9 A22(c) 2½p deep blue (R) 7.50 *17.00*

AITUTAKI. Ono Pene. — g

AITUTAKI. Tai Tiringi. — h

1913-16 Typo.

10 A42(b) 1p rose (Bl) 2.75 *9.00*

Engr.

12 A41(g) 6p car rose (Bl) ('16) 37.50 *85.00*
13 A41(h) 1sh ver (Bl) ('14) 55.00 *130.00*

1916-17 ***Perf. 14x13½, 14x14½***

17 A45(g) 6p car rose (Bl) 10.00 *24.00*
18 A45(h) 1sh ver (Bl) ('17) 32.50 *85.00*
Nos. 1-18 (13) 261.75 *497.50*

New Zealand Stamps of 1909-19 Overprinted in Red or Dark Blue **AITUTAKI.**

1917-20 **Typo.** ***Perf. 14x15***

19 A43 ½p yellow grn ('20) .95 *5.50*
20 A42 1p car (Bl) ('20) 3.00 *19.00*
21 A47 1½p gray black 3.50 *27.50*
22 A47 1½p brown org ('19) .80 *6.50*
23 A43 3p choc (Bl) ('19) 3.25 *14.00*

Perf. 14x13½, 14x14½
Engr.

24 A44 2½p dull blue ('18) 1.65 *14.00*
25 A45 3p vio brn (Bl) ('18) 1.75 *16.00*
26 A45 6p car rose (Bl) 4.50 *19.00*
27 A45 1sh vermilion (Bl) 11.50 *26.00*
Nos. 19-27 (9) 30.90 *147.50*

Landing of Capt. Cook A15

Avarua Waterfront A16

Capt. James Cook — A17

Palm — A18

Houses at Arorangi — A19

Avarua Harbor — A20

1920 **Engr.** **Unwmk.** ***Perf. 14***

28 A15 ½p green & black 3.25 *22.50*
29 A16 1p carmine & black 3.25 *16.00*
30 A17 1½p brown & blk 5.50 *11.00*
31 A18 3p dp blue & blk 2.00 *14.00*
32 A19 6p slate & red brn 6.25 *15.00*
33 A20 1sh claret & blk 9.00 *24.00*
Nos. 28-33 (6) 29.25 *102.50*

Inverted centers, double frames, etc. are from printers waste.

Rarotongan Chief (Te Po) — A21

1926-27 **Wmk. 61** ***Perf. 14***

34 A15 ½p green & blk ('27) 2.00 *9.00*
35 A16 1p carmine & blk 5.75 *6.00*
36 A21 2½p blue & blk ('27) 7.50 *47.50*
Nos. 34-36 (3) 15.25 *62.50*

Catalogue values for unused stamps in this section, from this point to the end of the section, are for Never Hinged items.

Cook Islands Nos. 199-200, 202, 205-206, 210, 212-213, 215-217 Overprinted **Aitutaki**

Perf. 14x13½
1972 **Photo.** **Unwmk.**

37 A34 ½c gold & multi .60 *1.00*
38 A34 1c gold & multi 1.00 *1.50*
39 A34 2½c gold & multi 6.50 *7.50*
40 A34 4c gold & multi 1.00 *1.10*
41 A34 5c gold & multi 7.50 *8.75*
42 A34 10c gold & multi 6.50 6.50
43 A34 20c gold & multi 3.25 *3.50*
44 A34 25c gold & multi 1.00 *1.10*
45 A34 50c gold & multi 5.00 *3.50*
46 A35 $1 gold & multi 7.50 *7.50*
47 A35 $2 gold & multi 1.50 *1.10*
Nos. 37-47 (11) 41.35 *43.05*

Overprint horizontal on Nos. 46-47. On $2, overprint is in capitals of different font; size: 21x3mm.

Issued: Nos. 37-46, Aug. 9; No. 47, Nov. 24.

Same Overprint Horizontal in Silver On Cook Islands Nos. 330-332

1972, Oct. 27 ***Perf. 13½***

48 A53 1c gold & multi .20 .20
49 A53 5c gold & multi .25 .25
50 A53 10c gold & multi .40 .40
Nos. 48-50 (3) .85 .85

Fluorescence

Starting in 1972, stamps carry a "fluorescent security underprinting" in a multiple pattern of New Zealand's coat of arms with "Aitutaki" above, "Cook Islands" below and two stars at each side.

Silver Wedding Type of Cook Islands

1972, Nov. 20 **Photo.** ***Perf. 13½***
Size: 29x40mm

51 A54 5c silver & multi 3.25 2.50

Size: 66x40mm

52 A54 15c silver & multi 1.50 1.10

25th anniversary of the marriage of Queen Elizabeth II and Prince Philip. Nos. 51-52 printed in sheets of 5 stamps and one label.

Flower Issue of Cook Islands Overprinted AITUTAKI

1972, Dec. 11 **Photo.** ***Perf. 14x13½***

53 A34 ½c on #199 .20 .20
54 A34 1c on #200 .20 .20
55 A34 2½c on #202 .20 .20
56 A34 4c on #205 .20 .20
57 A34 5c on #206 .20 .20
58 A34 10c on #210 .30 .30
59 A34 20c on #212 .70 .70
60 A34 25c on #213 .90 .90
61 A34 50c on #215 1.75 1.75
62 A35 $1 on #216 3.75 3.75
Nos. 53-62 (10) 8.40 8.40

See Nos. 73-76.

The Passion of Christ, by Mathias Grunewald — A22

Paintings: No. 63b, St. Veronica, by Rogier van der Weyden. No. 63c, Crucifixion, by Raphael. No. 63d, Resurrection, by della Francesca. No. 64a, Last Supper, by Master of Amiens. No. 64b, Condemnation of Christ, by Hans Holbein, the Elder. No. 64c, Crucifixion, by Rubens. No. 64d, Resurrection, by El Greco. No. 65a, Passion of Christ, by El Greco. No. 65b, St. Veronica, by Jakob Cornelisz. No. 65c, Crucifixion, by Rubens. No. 65d, Resurrection, by Dierik Bouts.

Perf. 13½
1973, Apr. 6 **Photo.** **Unwmk.**

63 Block of 4 .25 .25
a.-d. A22 1c any single .20 .20
64 Block of 4 .80 .80
a.-d. A22 5c any single .20 .20
65 Block of 4 1.90 1.90
a.-d. A22 10c any single .45 .45
Nos. 63-65 (3) 2.95 2.95

Easter. Printed in blocks of 4 in sheets of 40. Design descriptions in top and bottom margins.

Coin Type of Cook Islands

Queen Elizabeth II Coins: 1c, Taro leaf. 2c, Pineapples. 5c, Hibiscus. 10c, Oranges. 20c, Fairy terns. 50c, Bonito. $1, Tangaroa, Polynesian god of creation, vert.

1973, May 14 ***Perf. 13x13½***
Size: 37x24mm

66 A55 1c dp car & multi .20 .20
67 A55 2c blue & multi .20 .20
68 A55 5c green & multi .20 .20

Size: 46x30mm

69 A55 10c vio blue & multi .20 .20
70 A55 20c green & multi .30 .30
71 A55 50c dp car & multi .70 .70

Size: 32x54½mm

72 A55 $1 blue, blk & sil 1.40 1.40
Nos. 66-72 (7) 3.20 3.20

Cook Islands coinage commemorating silver wedding anniv. of Queen Elizabeth II.

Printed in sheets of 20 stamps and label showing Westminster Abbey.

Cook Islands Nos. 208, 210, 212 and 215 Overprinted Like Nos. 53-62 and: "TENTH ANNIVERSARY/ CESSATION/ OF/ NUCLEAR TESTING/ TREATY"

1973, July **Photo.** ***Perf. 14x13½***

73 A34 8c gold & multi .20 .20
74 A34 10c gold & multi .20 .20
75 A34 20c gold & multi .50 .50
76 A34 50c gold & multi 1.10 1.10
Nos. 73-76 (4) 2.00 2.00

Nuclear Test Ban Treaty, 10th anniv., protest against French nuclear testing on Mururoa Atoll.

Princess Anne, Hibiscus A23

Design: 30c, Mark Phillips and hibiscus.

1973, Nov. 14 **Photo.** ***Perf. 13½x14***

77 A23 25c gold & multi .30 .30
78 A23 30c gold & multi .40 .40
a. Souvenir sheet of 2, #77-78 .80 .80

Wedding of Princess Anne and Capt. Mark Phillips.

Virgin and Child, by Il Perugino — A24

Paintings of the Virgin and Child by various masters - #79: a, Van Dyck. b, Bartolommeo Montagna. c, Carlo Crivelli. d, Il Perugino. #80: a, Cima da Conegliano. b, Memling. c, Verones. d, Verones. #81: a, Raphael. b, Lorenzo Lotto. c, Del Colle. d, Memling.

1973, Dec. **Photo.** ***Perf. 13***

79 A24 1c Block of 4, #a.-d. .25 .25
80 A24 5c Block of 4, #a.-d. .75 .75
81 A24 10c Block of 4, #a.-d. 1.90 1.90
Nos. 79-81 (3) 2.90 2.90

Christmas. Printed in blocks of 4 in sheets of 48. Design descriptions in margins.

Murex Ramosus A25

Terebra Maculata — A26

Pacific Shells: 1c, Nautilus macromphalus. 2c, Harpa major. 3c, Phalium strigatum. 4c, Cypraea talpa. 5c, Mitra stictica. 8c, Charonia tritonis. 10c, Murex triremis. 20c, Oliva sericea. 25c, Tritonalia rubeta. 60c, Strombus latissimus. $1, Biplex perca. $5, Cypraea hesitata.

1974-75 **Photo.** ***Perf. 13***

82 A25 ½c silver & multi .50 .40
83 A25 1c silver & multi .50 .40
84 A25 2c silver & multi .50 .40
85 A25 3c silver & multi .50 .40
86 A25 4c silver & multi .50 .40
87 A25 5c silver & multi .50 .40
88 A25 8c silver & multi 1.10 .50
89 A25 10c silver & multi 1.10 .50
90 A25 20c silver & multi 1.50 1.00
91 A25 25c silver & multi 1.75 1.00
92 A25 60c silver & multi 6.00 1.75
93 A25 $1 silver & multi 4.75 3.00

Perf. 14

94 A26 $2 silver & multi 7.50 4.25
95 A26 $5 silver & multi 27.50 16.00
Nos. 82-95 (14) 54.20 30.40

Issued: #82-93, 1/31/74; $2, 1/20/75; $5, 2/28/75.

For overprints see Nos. O1-O16.

William Bligh and "Bounty" A27

1974, Apr. 11 **Photo.** ***Perf. 13***
Size: 38x22mm

96 A27 1c shown .20 .20
97 A27 1c "Bounty" at sea .20 .20
98 A27 5c Bligh and "Bounty" off Aitutaki .45 .45
99 A27 5c Chart of Aitutaki, 1856 .45 .45
100 A27 8c James Cook and "Resolution" .95 .95
101 A27 8c Maps of Aitutaki and Pacific Ocean .95 .95
Nos. 96-101,C1-C6 (12) 10.00 10.00

Capt. William Bligh (1754-1817), European discoverer of Aitutaki, Apr. 11, 1789. Stamps of same denomination printed se-tenant in sheets of 32.

Aitutaki Nos. 1 & 2 Map and UPU Emblem A28

Design: 50c, Aitutaki Nos. 4 and 28, map of Aitutaki and UPU emblem.

1974, July 15 **Photo.** ***Perf. 13½***

102 A28 25c blue & multi .55 .55
103 A28 50c blue & multi 1.10 1.10
a. Souvenir sheet of 2, #102-103 1.90 1.90

UPU, cent. Printed in sheets of 5 plus label showing UPU emblem.

A29

A30

Designs: Paintings of the Virgin and Child.

1974, Oct. 11 Photo. *Perf. 13½*

104 A29 1c Van der Goes .20 .20
105 A29 5c Giovanni Bellini .20 .20
106 A29 8c Gerard David .20 .20
107 A29 10c Antonello da Messina .20 .20
108 A29 25c Joos van Cleve .50 .50
109 A29 30c Maitre de St. Catherine .55 .55
  a. Souvenir sheet of 6, #104-109 2.00 2.00
  Nos. 104-109 (6) 1.85 1.85

Christmas. #104-109 printed in sheets of 15 stamps and corner label. See #B1-B6.

1974, Nov. 29 Photo. *Perf. 14*

Designs: Churchill portraits.

110 A30 10c Dublin, Age 5 .20 .20
111 A30 25c As young man .25 .20
112 A30 30c Inspecting troops, WWII .35 .20
113 A30 50c Painting .70 .40
114 A30 $1 Giving V sign 1.40 .80
  a. Souvenir sheet of 5, #110-114 + label, perf. 13½ 4.50 3.75
  Nos. 110-114 (5) 2.90 1.80

Sir Winston Churchill (1874-1965). Nos. 110-114 printed in sheets of 5 stamps and corner label.

Emblem US & USSR Flags A31

Design: 50c, Icarus and Apollo Soyuz spacecraft.

1975, July 24 Photo. *Perf. 13x14½*

115 A31 25c multicolored .35 .35
116 A31 50c multicolored .90 .90
  a. Souvenir sheet of 2 1.75 1.75

Apollo Soyuz space test project (Russo-American cooperation), launching July 15; link-up July 17. Nos. 115 and 116 each printed in sheets of 5 stamps and one label showing area of Apollo splash-downs. No. 116a contains one each of Nos. 115-116 with gold and black border and inscription.

Madonna and Child, by Pietro Lorenzetti — A32

Paintings: 7c, Adoration of the Kings, by Rogier van der Weyden. 15c, Madonna and Child, by Bartolommeo Montagna. 20c, Adoration of the Shepherds.

1975, Nov. 24 Photo. *Perf. 14x13½*

117 A32 Strip of 3 .30 .30
  a. 6c St. Francis .20 .20
  b. 6c Madonna and Child .20 .20
  c. 6c St. John the Evangelist .20 .20
118 A32 Strip of 3 .30 .30
  a. 7c One King .20 .20
  b. 7c Madonna and Child .20 .20
  c. 7c Two Kings .20 .20
119 A32 Strip of 3 .75 .75
  a. 15c St. Joseph .25 .25
  b. 15c Madonna and Child .25 .25
  c. 15c St. John the Baptist .25 .25
120 A32 Strip of 3 1.25 1.25
  a. 20c One Shepherd .40 .40
  b. 20c Madonna and Child .40 .40
  c. 20c Two Shepherds .40 .40
  d. Souv. sheet of 12, #117-120, perf. 13½ 3.50 3.50
  Nos. 117-120 (4) 2.60 2.60

Christmas. Nos. 117-120 printed in sheets of 30 (10 strips of 3).

For surcharges see Nos. B7-B10.

Aitutaki stamps can be mounted in the Scott annual New Zealand Dependencies supplement.

Descent from the Cross, detail — A33

Designs (Painting, Flemish School, 16th Century): 30c, Virgin Mary, disciple and body of Jesus. 35c, Mary Magdalene and disciple.

1976, Apr. 5 Photo. *Perf. 13½*

121 A33 15c gold & multi .20 .20
122 A33 30c gold & multi .30 .30
123 A33 35c gold & multi .70 .70
  a. Souvenir sheet of 3 1.60 1.60
  Nos. 121-123 (3) 1.20 1.20

Easter. No. 123a contains 3 stamps similar to Nos. 121-123, perf. 13, in continuous design without gold frames and white margins.

Declaration of Independence — A34

Paintings by John Trumbull: 35c, Surrender of Cornwallis at Yorktown. 50c, Washington's Farewell Address. a, "1976 BICENTENARY." b, "UNITED STATES." c, "INDEPENDENCE 1776."

1976, June 1 Photo. *Perf. 13½*

124 A34 Strip of 3 1.50 1.50
  a.-c. 30c any single .50 .50
125 A34 Strip of 3 2.00 2.00
  a.-c. 35c any single .65 .65
126 A34 Strip of 3 2.75 2.75
  a.-c. 50c any single .90 .90
  d. Souvenir sheet of 9 (3x3) 6.25 6.25
  Nos. 124-126 (3) 6.25 6.25

American Bicentennial. Nos. 124-126 printed in sheets of 5 strips of 3 and 3-part corner label showing portrait of John Trumbull, commemorative inscription and portraits of Washington (30c), John Adams (35c) and Jefferson (50c). No. 126d contains 3 strips similar to Nos. 124-126.

Bicycling A35

Montreal Olympic Games Emblem and: 35c, Sailing. 60c, Field hockey. 70c, Running.

1976, July 15 Photo. *Perf. 13x14*

127 A35 15c multicolored .25 .20
128 A35 35c multicolored .55 .45
129 A35 60c multicolored .90 .75
130 A35 70c multicolored 1.10 .85
  a. Souvenir sheet of 4 3.00 2.25
  Nos. 127-130 (4) 2.80 2.25

21st Olympic Games, Montreal, Canada, July 17-Aug. 1. Nos. 127-130 printed in sheets of 5 stamps and label showing coat of Arms and Montreal Olympic Games emblem. No. 130a contains 4 stamps similar to Nos. 127-130 with gold margin around each stamp.

Nos. 127-130a Overprinted Diagonally: "ROYAL VISIT JULY 1976"

1976, July 30

131 A35 15c multicolored .20 .20
132 A35 35c multicolored .55 .55
133 A35 60c multicolored .75 .75
134 A35 70c multicolored 1.00 1.00
  a. Souvenir sheet of 4 3.00 3.00
  Nos. 131-134 (4) 2.50 2.50

Visit of Queen Elizabeth II to Montreal and official opening of the Games. Each stamp of No. 134a has diagonal overprint. Sheet margin has additional overprint: "ROYAL VISIT OF H.M. QUEEN ELIZABETH II/OFFICIALLY OPENED 17 JULY 1976."

Annunciation
A36 A37

Designs: Nos. 137-138, Angel appearing to the shepherds. Nos. 139-140, Nativity. Nos. 141-142, Three Kings.

1976, Oct. 18 *Perf. 13½x13*

135 A36 6c dk green & gold .20 .20
136 A37 6c dk green & gold .20 .20
137 A36 7c dk brown & gold .20 .20
138 A37 7c dk brown & gold .20 .20
139 A36 15c dk blue & gold .20 .20
140 A37 15c dk blue & gold .20 .20
141 A36 20c purple & gold .25 .25
142 A37 20c purple & gold .25 .25
  a. Souvenir sheet of 8 1.90 1.90
  Nos. 135-142 (8) 1.70 1.70

Christmas. Stamps of same denomination printed se-tenant in sheets of 50. No. 142a contains 8 stamps similar to Nos. 135-142 with white margin around each pair of stamps.

A. G. Bell and 1876 Telephone — A38

Design: 70c, Satellite and radar.

1977, Mar. 3 Photo. *Perf. 13½x13*

143 A38 25c rose & multi .25 .25
144 A38 70c violet & multi .85 .85
  a. Souvenir sheet of 2 1.65 1.65

Centenary of first telephone call by Alexander Graham Bell, Mar. 10, 1876. No. 144a contains a 25c in colors of 70c and 70c in colors of 25c.

Calvary (detail), by Rubens A39

Paintings by Rubens: 20c, Lamentation. 35c, Descent from the Cross.

1977, Mar. 31 Photo. *Perf. 13½x14*

145 A39 15c gold & multi .55 .55
146 A39 20c gold & multi .70 .70
147 A39 35c gold & multi 1.00 1.00
  a. Souv. sheet of 3, #145-147, perf. 13 2.75 2.75
  Nos. 145-147 (3) 2.25 2.25

Easter, and 400th birth anniv. of Peter Paul Rubens (1577-1640), Flemish painter.

Capt. Bligh, "Bounty" and George III — A40

Designs: 35c, Rev. John Williams, George IV, First Christian Church. 50c, British flag, map of Aitutaki, Queen Victoria. $1, Elizabeth II and family on balcony after coronation.

1977, Apr. 21 *Perf. 13½*

148 A40 25c gold & multi .20 .20
149 A40 35c gold & multi .35 .35
150 A40 50c gold & multi .50 .50
151 A40 $1 gold & multi 3.00 3.00
  a. Souvenir sheet of 4, #148-151 2.75 2.75
  Nos. 148-151 (4) 4.05 4.05

Reign of Queen Elizabeth II, 25th anniv.

For overprint and surcharge see Nos. O11, O15.

Annunciation
A41 A42

Designs: No. 154, Virgin, Child and ox. No. 155, Joseph and donkey (Nativity). No. 156, Three Kings. No. 157, Virgin and Child. No. 158, Joseph. No. 159, Virgin, Child and donkey (Flight into Egypt).

1977, Oct. 14 Photo. *Perf. 13½x14*

152 A41 6c multicolored .20 .20
153 A42 6c multicolored .20 .20
154 A41 7c multicolored .20 .20
155 A42 7c multicolored .20 .20
156 A41 15c multicolored .25 .25
157 A42 15c multicolored .25 .25
158 A41 20c multicolored .30 .30
159 A42 20c multicolored .30 .30
  a. Souvenir sheet of 8, #152-159 1.65 1.65
  Nos. 152-159 (8) 1.90 1.90

Christmas. Stamps of same denomination printed se-tenant in sheets of 32.

For surcharges see Nos. B19-B26a.

Hawaiian Wood Figurine — A43

Designs: 50c, Talbot hunting dog, figurehead of "Resoiution", horiz. $1, Temple figure.

1978, Jan. 19 Litho. *Perf. 13½*

160 A43 35c multicolored .55 .55
161 A43 50c multicolored .75 .75
162 A43 $1 multicolored 1.40 1.40
  a. Souvenir sheet of 3, #160-162 3.00 3.00
  Nos. 160-162 (3) 2.70 2.70

Bicentenary of Capt. Cook's arrival in Hawaii. Nos. 160-162 issued in sheets of 6.

Avignon Pietà, 15th Century A44

Paintings: 15c, Jesus Carrying Cross, by Simone di Martini. 35c, Christ at Emmaus, by Rembrandt.

1978, Mar. 17 Photo. *Perf. 13½x14*

163 A44 15c gold & multi .20 .20
164 A44 20c gold & multi .30 .30
165 A44 35c gold & multi .45 .45
  a. Souvenir sheet of 3 1.40 1.40
  Nos. 163-165 (3) .95 .95

Easter. No. 165a contains one each of Nos. 163-165, perf. 13½, and label showing Louvre, Paris. See Nos. B27-B29.

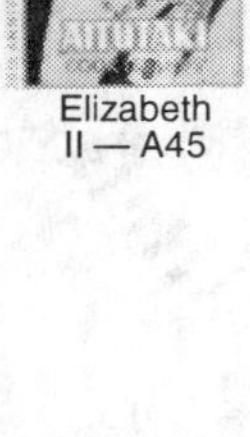

Elizabeth II — A45

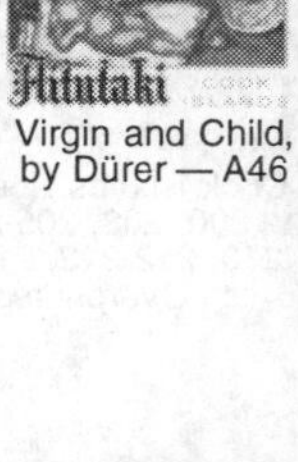

Virgin and Child, by Dürer — A46

Souvenir Sheets

1978, June 15 Photo. ***Perf. 13½x13***

166	Sheet of 6	2.75	2.75
a.	A45 $1 Yale of Beaufort	.25	.25
b.	A45 $1 shown	.25	.25
c.	A45 $1 Ancestral statue	.25	.25
d.	Souvenir sheet of 6	3.00	3.00

25th anniv. of coronation of Queen Elizabeth II. No. 166 contains 2 each of Nos. 166a-166c, silver marginal inscription and coats of arms. No. 166d contains 2 strips of Nos. 166a-166c separated by horizontal slate green gutter showing Royal family on balcony, silver marginal inscription.

1978, Dec. 4 Photo. ***Perf. 14½x13***

Designs: Various paintings of the Virgin and Child by Albrecht Dürer.

167	A46 15c multicolored	.30	.30
168	A46 17c multicolored	.35	.35
169	A46 30c multicolored	.70	.70
170	A46 35c multicolored	.90	.90
	Nos. 167-170 (4)	2.25	2.25

Christmas; 450th death anniv. of Albrecht Dürer (1471-1528), German painter. Nos. 167-170 issued in sheets of 5 stamps and corner label. See No. B30.

Capt. Cook, by Nathaniel Dance — A47

Boy Holding Hibiscus, IYC Emblem — A48

Design: 75c, "Resolution" and "Adventure," by William Hodges.

1979, July 20 Photo. ***Perf. 14x13½***

171	A47 50c multicolored	1.25	1.25
172	A47 75c multicolored	1.75	1.75
a.	Souvenir sheet of 2, #171-172	2.50	2.50

Capt. James Cook (1728-1779), explorer, death bicentenary.

1979, Oct. 1 Photo. ***Perf. 14x13½***

IYC Emblem and: 35c, Boy playing guitar. 65c, Boys in outrigger canoe.

173	A48 30c multicolored	.30	.30
174	A48 35c multicolored	.35	.35
175	A48 65c multicolored	.70	.70
	Nos. 173-175 (3)	1.35	1.35

See No. B31.

Aitutaki No. 102, Hill, Penny Black A49

Designs: Nos. 176, 178-179, 181, paintings of letter writers, Flemish School, 17th century.

1979, Nov. 14 Photo. ***Perf. 13***

176	A49 50c Gabriel Metsu	.55	.55
177	A49 50c shown	.55	.55
178	A49 50c Jan Vermeer	.55	.55
179	A49 65c Gerard Terborch	.65	.65
180	A49 65c No. 103 (like No. 177)	.65	.65
181	A49 65c Jan Vermeer	.65	.65
	Nos. 176-181 (6)	3.60	3.60

Souvenir Sheet

182	Sheet of 6	2.50	2.50
a.	A49 30c like No. 176	.40	.40
b.	A49 30c like No. 177	.40	.40
c.	A49 30c like No. 178	.40	.40
d.	A49 30c like No. 179	.40	.40
e.	A49 30c like No. 180	.40	.40
f.	A49 30c like No. 181	.40	.40

Sir Rowland Hill (1795-1879), originator of penny postage. Nos. 176-178 and 179-181 printed se-tenant in sheets of 9 (3x3).

Descent from the Cross, Detail — A50

Albert Einstein — A51

Easter: 30c, 35c, Descent from the Cross, by Quentin Metsys (details).

1980, Apr. 3 Photo. ***Perf. 13x13½***

183	A50 20c multicolored	.45	.45
184	A50 30c multicolored	.65	.65
185	A50 35c multicolored	.80	.80
	Nos. 183-185 (3)	1.90	1.90

See No. B32.

1980, July 21 Photo. ***Perf. 14***

186	A51 12c shown	.55	.55
187	A51 12c Formula, atom structure	.55	.55
188	A51 15c Portrait, diff.	.65	.65
189	A51 15c Atomic blast	.65	.65
190	A51 20c Portrait, diff.	.90	.90
191	A51 20c Atomic blast, trees	.90	.90
a.	Souv. sheet of 6, #186-191, perf. 13	4.25	4.25
	Nos. 186-191 (6)	4.20	4.20

Albert Einstein (1879-1955), theoretical physicist. Stamps of same denomination se-tenant.

A52

A53

1980, Sept. 26 Photo. ***Perf. 14***

192	A52 6c Ancestral Figure, Aitutaki	.20	.20
193	A52 6c God image staff, Rarotonga	.20	.20
194	A52 6c Trade adze, Mangaia	.20	.20
195	A52 6c Tangaroa carving, Rarotonga	.20	.20
196	A52 12c Wooden image, Aitutaki	.20	.20
197	A52 12c Hand club, Rarotonga	.20	.20
198	A52 12c Carved mace, Mangaia	.20	.20
199	A52 12c Fisherman's god, Rarotonga	.20	.20
200	A52 15c Ti'i image, Aitutaki	.20	.20
201	A52 15c Fisherman's god, diff.	.20	.20
202	A52 15c Carved mace, Cook Islands	.20	.20
203	A52 15c Tangaroa, diff.	.20	.20
204	A52 20c Chief's headdress, Aitutaki	.30	.30
205	A52 20c Carved mace, diff.	.30	.30
206	A52 20c God image staff, diff.	.30	.30
207	A52 20c like #195	.30	.30
a.	Souvenir sheet of 16, #192-207	3.50	
	Nos. 192-207 (16)	3.60	3.60

Third South Pacific Arts Festival, Port Moresby, Papua New Guinea. Stamps of same denomination se-tenant.

1980, Nov. 21 Photo. ***Perf. 13x13½***

Virgin and Child, Sculptures.

208	A53 15c 13th cent.	.20	.20
209	A53 20c 14th cent.	.30	.30
210	A53 25c 15th cent.	.35	.35
211	A53 35c 15th cent., diff.	.50	.50
	Nos. 208-211 (4)	1.35	1.35

Christmas. See No. B33.

Mourning Virgin, by Pedro Roldan — A54

Sturnus Vulgaris — A55

Easter (Roldan Sculptures): 40c, Christ. 50c, Mourning St. John.

1981, Mar. 31 Photo. ***Perf. 14***

212	A54 30c green & gold	.40	.40
213	A54 40c brt purple & gold	.50	.50
214	A54 50c dk blue & gold	.65	.65
	Nos. 212-214 (3)	1.55	1.55

See No. B34.

1981-82 ***Perf. 14x13½, 13½x14***

215	A55 1c shown	.25	.20
216	A55 1c Poephila gouldiae	.25	.20
217	A55 2c Petroica multicolor	.35	.20
218	A55 2c Pachycephala pectoralis	.35	.20
219	A55 3c Falco peregrinus	.40	.20
220	A55 3c Rhipidura rufifrous	.40	.20
221	A55 4c Tyto alba	.45	.20
222	A55 4c Padda oryzivora	.45	.20
223	A55 5c Artamus leucorhynchus	.50	.20
224	A55 5c Vini peruviana	.50	.20
225	A55 6c Columba livia	.60	.20
226	A55 6c Porphyrio porphyria	.60	.20
227	A55 10c Geopelia striata	.80	.35
228	A55 10c Lonchura castaneothorax	.80	.35
229	A55 12c Acridotheres tristis	.80	.40
230	A55 12c Egretta sacra	.80	.40
231	A55 15c Diomeda melanophris	.90	.45
232	A55 15c Numenius phaeopus	.90	.45
233	A55 20c Gygis alba	1.00	.65
234	A55 20c Pluvialis dominica	1.00	.65
235	A55 25c Sula leucogaster	1.10	.80
236	A55 25c Anas superciliosa	1.10	.80
237	A55 30c Anas acuta	1.90	.90
238	A55 30c Fregata minor	1.90	.90
239	A55 35c Stercorarius pomarinus	2.00	1.10
240	A55 35c Conopoderas caffra	2.00	1.10
241	A55 40c Lalage maculosa	2.25	1.10
242	A55 40c Gallirallus philippensis	2.25	1.10
243	A55 50c Vini stepheni	2.50	1.50
244	A55 50c Diomedea epomophora	2.50	1.50
245	A55 70c Ptilinopus victor	5.00	2.00
246	A55 70c Erythrura cyaneovirens	5.00	2.00

Photo. ***Perf. 13½***
Size: 35x47mm

246A	A55 $1 Myiagra azureocapilla	6.00	4.00
246B	A55 $2 Myiagra vanikorensis	10.00	8.00
246C	A55 $4 Amandava amandava	17.00	13.00
246D	A55 $5 Halcyon recurvirostris	18.00	16.00
	Nos. 215-246D (36)	92.60	61.90

Issued: #215-230, 4/6; #231-238, 5/8; #239-246, 1/14/82; #246A-246B, 2/15/82.

Stamps of same denomination se-tenant. Nos. 231-246 horiz.

For surcharges and overprint see Nos. 293-306, 452-454, O40-O41.

Prince Charles and Lady Diana — A56

Perf. 13x13½, 13½x13

1981, June 10 **Photo.**

247	A56 60c Charles, vert.	.65	.65
248	A56 80c Lady Diana, vert.	.85	.85
249	A56 $1.40 Shown	1.50	1.50
	Nos. 247-249 (3)	3.00	3.00

Royal Wedding. Issued in sheets of 4.

For overprints and surcharges see Nos. 265-267, 307, 309, 355, 405-407, B35-B37.

1982 World Cup Soccer — A57

Designs: Various soccer players.

1981, Nov. 30 Photo. ***Perf. 14***

250	A57 12c Pair, #250a-250b	.40	.40
251	A57 15c Pair, #251a-251b	.50	.50
252	A57 20c Pair, #252a-252b	.65	.65
253	A57 25c Pair, #253a-253b	.80	.80
	Nos. 250-253 (4)	2.35	2.35

See No. B38.

Christmas A58

Rembrandt Etchings: 15c, Holy Family, 1632, vert. 30c, Virgin with Child, 1634, vert. 40c, Adoration of the Shepherds, 1654. 50c, Holy Family with Cat, 1644.

1981, Dec. 10 ***Perf. 14***

254	A58 15c gold & dk brown	.20	.20
255	A58 30c gold & dk brown	.45	.45
256	A58 40c gold & dk brown	.60	.60
257	A58 50c gold & dk brown	.75	.75
	Nos. 254-257 (4)	2.00	2.00

Souvenir Sheets

258	A58 80c + 5c like #254	.95	.95
259	A58 80c + 5c like #255	.95	.95
260	A58 80c + 5c like #256	.95	.95
261	A58 80c + 5c like #257	.95	.95

Nos. 258-261 have multicolored margins showing entire etching. Surtax on Nos. 258-261 was for local charities.

21st Birthday of Princess Diana — A59

1982, June 24 Photo. ***Perf. 14***

262	A59 70c shown	.75	.75
263	A59 $1 Wedding portrait	1.00	1.00
264	A59 $2 Diana, diff.	2.25	2.25
a.	Souvenir sheet of 3, #262-264	4.50	4.50
	Nos. 262-264 (3)	4.00	4.00

See #268-270a. For surcharges see #308, 310.

Nos. 247-249 Overprinted: "21 June 1982 PRINCE WILLIAM OF WALES" or "COMMEMORATING THE ROYAL BIRTH"

1982, July 13 ***Perf. 13x13½,13½x13***

265	A56 60c multicolored	1.00	1.00
266	A56 80c multicolored	1.50	1.50
267	A56 $1.40 multicolored	2.50	2.50
	Nos. 265-267 (3)	5.00	5.00

Nos. 262-264a Inscribed: "ROYAL BIRTH 21 JUNE 1982 PRINCE WILLIAM OF WALES"

1982, Aug. 5 ***Perf. 14***

268	A59 70c multicolored	1.10	1.10
269	A59 $1 multicolored	1.50	1.50
270	A59 $2 multicolored	3.00	3.00
a.	Souvenir sheet of 3	5.25	5.25
	Nos. 268-270 (3)	5.60	5.60

Christmas — A60

Madonna and Child Sculptures, 12th-15th Cent.

1982, Dec. 10 Photo. *Perf. 13*
271 A60 18c multicolored .25 .25
272 A60 36c multicolored .55 .55
273 A60 48c multicolored .75 .75
274 A60 60c multicolored .90 .90
Nos. 271-274 (4) 2.45 2.45

Souvenir Sheet

275 Sheet of 4 2.75 2.75
a. A60 18c + 2c like 18c .30 .30
b. A60 36c + 2c like 36c .55 .55
c. A60 48c + 2c like 48c .75 .75
d. A60 60c + 2c like 60c .90 .90

Surtax was for children's charities.

Commonwealth Day — A61

1983, Mar. 14 Photo. *Perf. 13x13½*
276 A61 48c Bananas 1.25 1.25
277 A61 48c Ti'i statuette 1.25 1.25
278 A61 48c Boys canoeing 1.25 1.25
279 A61 48c Capt. Bligh, Bounty 1.25 1.25
a. Block of 4, #276-279 5.00 5.00

Scouting Year — A62

1983, Apr. 18 Photo. *Perf. 14*
280 A62 36c Campfire .55 .55
281 A62 48c Salute .75 .75
282 A62 60c Hiking .90 .90
Nos. 280-282 (3) 2.20 2.20

Souvenir Sheet

Perf. 13½

283 Sheet of 3 3.00 3.00
a. A62 36c + 3c like #280 .75 .75
b. A62 48c + 3c like #281 .90 .90
c. A62 60c + 3c like #282 1.25 1.25

Surtax was for benefit of Scouting.

Nos. 280-283 Overprinted: "15th WORLD SCOUT JAMBOREE"

1983, July 11 Photo. *Perf. 14*
284 A62 36c multicolored .55 .55
285 A62 48c multicolored .75 .75
286 A62 60c multicolored .90 .90
Nos. 284-286 (3) 2.20 2.20

Souvenir Sheet

287 Sheet of 3 3.00 3.00
a. A62 36c + 3c like #284 .75 .75
b. A62 48c + 3c like #285 .90 .90
c. A62 60c + 3c like #286 1.25 1.25

A63

A64

Manned Flight Bicentenary: Modern sport balloons.

1983, July 22 Photo. *Perf. 14x13*
288 A63 18c multicolored .25 .25
289 A63 36c multicolored .55 .55
290 A63 48c multicolored .75 .75
291 A63 60c multicolored .90 .90
Nos. 288-291 (4) 2.45 2.45

Souvenir Sheet

292 A63 $2.50 multicolored 3.00 3.00

Nos. 233-246, 246D, 248-249, 263-264 Surcharged

1983, Sept. 22
293 A55 18c on 20c, #233 .90 .35
294 A55 18c on 20c, #234 .90 .35
295 A55 36c on 25c, #235 1.25 .70
296 A55 36c on 25c, #236 1.25 .70
297 A55 36c on 30c, #237 1.25 .70
298 A55 36c on 30c, #238 1.25 .70
299 A55 36c on 35c, #239 1.25 .70
300 A55 36c on 35c, #240 1.25 .70
301 A55 48c on 40c, #241 2.00 .95
302 A55 48c on 40c, #242 2.00 .95
303 A55 48c on 50c, #243 2.00 .95
304 A55 48c on 50c, #244 2.00 .95
305 A55 72c on 70c, #245 3.00 1.50
306 A55 72c on 70c, #246 3.00 1.50
307 A56 96c on 80c, #248 5.50 1.90
308 A59 96c on $1, #263 5.50 1.90
309 A56 $1.20 on $1.40, #249 6.50 2.50
310 A59 $1.20 on $2, #264 6.50 2.50

Size: 35x47mm

311 A55 $5.60 on $5, #246D 16.00 11.00
Nos. 293-311 (19) 63.30 31.50

Nos. 293-306 printed in se-tenant pairs. Nos. 307-308, 310-311 vert.

1983, Sept. 29 Photo. *Perf. 14*
312 A64 48c shown .65 .65
313 A64 60c Communications satellite .85 .85
314 A64 96c Global coverage 1.50 1.50
a. Souvenir sheet of 3, #312-314 3.00 3.00
Nos. 312-314 (3) 3.00 3.00

World Communications Year.

Christmas A65

Raphael Paintings.

1983, Nov. 21 Photo. *Perf. 13½x14*
315 A65 36c Madonna of the Chair .50 .50
316 A65 48c Alba Madonna .65 .65
317 A65 60c Connestabile Madonna .80 .80
Nos. 315-317 (3) 1.95 1.95

Souvenir Sheet

318 Sheet of 3 2.50 2.50
a. A65 36c + 3c like #315 .60 .60
b. A65 48c + 3c like #316 .75 .75
c. A65 60c + 3c like #317 .90 .90

1983, Dec. 15 *Imperf.*

Size: 46x46mm

319 A65 85c + 5c like #315 1.25 1.25
320 A65 85c + 5c like #316 1.25 1.25
321 A65 85c + 5c like #317 1.25 1.25
Nos. 319-321 (3) 3.75 3.75

Surtax was for children's charities.

Local Birds — A66

1984 Photo. *Perf. 14*
322 A66 2c as No. 216 .25 .25
323 A66 3c as No. 215 .25 .25
324 A66 5c as No. 217 .25 .25
325 A66 10c as No. 218 .25 .25
326 A66 12c as No. 220 .35 .35
327 A66 18c as No. 219 .45 .45
328 A66 24c as No. 221 .65 .65
329 A66 30c as No. 222 .75 .75
330 A66 36c as No. 223 .90 .90
331 A66 48c as No. 224 1.25 1.25
332 A66 50c as No. 225 .90 .90
333 A66 60c as No. 226 1.25 1.25
334 A66 72c as No. 227 1.50 1.50
335 A66 96c as No. 228 2.00 2.00
336 A66 $1.20 as No. 229 2.25 2.25
337 A66 $2.10 as No. 230 4.00 4.00
338 A66 $3 as No. 246A 5.75 5.75
339 A66 $4.20 as No. 246B 7.00 7.00
340 A66 $5.60 as No. 246C 7.50 7.50
341 A66 $9.60 as No. 246D 12.50 12.50
Nos. 322-341 (20) 50.00 50.00

For overprints and surcharges see Nos. O17-O39.

1984 Summer Olympics — A67

1984, July 24 Photo. *Perf. 13x13½*
342 A67 36c Javelin .35 .35
343 A67 48c Shot put .45 .45
344 A67 60c Hurdles .55 .55
345 A67 $2 Handball 1.75 1.75
Nos. 342-345 (4) 3.10 3.10

Souvenir Sheet

346 Sheet of 4 3.50 3.50
a. A67 36c + 5c like #342 .40 .40
b. A67 48c + 5c like #343 .50 .50
c. A67 60c + 5c like #344 .60 .60
d. A67 $2 + 5c like #345 1.75 1.75

Surtax was for benefit of local sports.

Nos. 342-345 Overprinted in Gold on Black with Winners' Names, Event, Nationality

1984, Aug. 21 Photo. *Perf. 13x13½*
347 A67 36c multicolored .35 .35
348 A67 48c multicolored .45 .45
349 A67 60c multicolored .55 .55
350 A67 $2 multicolored 1.75 1.75
Nos. 347-350 (4) 3.10 3.10

Ausipex '84 — A68

1984, Sept. 14 Photo. *Perf. 14*
351 A68 60c William Bligh, map 1.10 1.10
352 A68 96c Bounty, map 1.75 1.75
353 A68 $1.40 Stamps, map 2.50 2.50
Nos. 351-353 (3) 5.35 5.35

Souvenir Sheet

354 Sheet of 3 5.50 5.50
a. A68 60c + 5c like #351 1.10 1.10
b. A68 96c + 5c like #352 1.60 1.60
c. A68 $1.40 + 5c like #353 2.25 2.25

For overprint see No. 399.

No. 247 Surcharged with Black Bar and New Value in Gold and: "15.9.84 Birth/Prince Henry"

1984, Oct. 10 Photo. *Perf. 13x13½*
355 A56 $3 multicolored 4.50 4.50

Issued in sheets of 4.

A69

A70

1984, Nov. 16 Photo. *Perf. 13*
356 A69 36c Annunciation .35 .35
357 A69 48c Nativity .45 .45
358 A69 60c Epiphany .55 .55
359 A69 96c Flight into Egypt .90 .90
Nos. 356-359 (4) 2.25 2.25

Souvenir Sheets

Size: 45x53mm

Imperf

360 A69 90c + 7c like #356 .90 .90
361 A69 90c + 7c like #357 .90 .90
362 A69 90c + 7c like #358 .90 .90
363 A69 90c + 7c like #359 .90 .90

Christmas.

1984, Dec. 10 Photo. *Perf. 13½x14*
364 A70 48c Diana, Henry .75 .75
365 A70 60c William, Henry .90 .90
366 A70 $2.10 Family 2.75 2.75
Nos. 364-366 (3) 4.40 4.40

Souvenir Sheet

367 Sheet of 3 4.50 4.50
a. A70 96c + 7c like #364 1.40 1.40
b. A70 96c + 7c like #365 1.40 1.40
c. A70 96c + 7c like #366 1.40 1.40

Christmas, Birth of Prince Henry, Sept. 15. Surtax was for benefit of local children's charities.

Audubon Birth Bicentenary A71

Illustrations of bird species by John J. Audubon.

1985, Mar. 22 Litho. *Perf. 13*
368 A71 55c Gray kingbird .80 .80
369 A71 65c Bohemian waxwing .95 .95
370 A71 75c Summer tanager 1.25 1.25
371 A71 95c Cardinal 1.50 1.50
372 A71 $1.15 White-winged crossbill 1.75 1.75
Nos. 368-372 (5) 6.25 6.25

Queen Mother, 85th Birthday — A72

Photographs: 55c, Lady Elizabeth Bowes-Lyon, age 7. 65c, Engaged to the Duke of York. 75c, Duchess of York with daughter, Elizabeth. $1.30, Holding the infant Prince Charles. $3, Portrait taken on 63rd birthday.

1985-86 *Perf. 13½x13*
373 A72 55c multicolored .50 .50
374 A72 65c multicolored .60 .60
375 A72 75c multicolored .65 .65
376 A72 $1.30 multicolored 1.25 1.25
a. Souvenir sheet of 4, #373-376 3.25 3.25
Nos. 373-376 (4) 3.00 3.00

Souvenir Sheet

377 A72 $3 multicolored 2.25 2.25

Nos. 373-376 printed in sheets of 4.
Issued: #376a, 8/4/86; others, 6/14/85.

Intl. Youth Year A73

Designs: 75c, The Calmady Children, by Thomas Lawrence (1769-1830). 90c, Madame Charpentier's Children, by Renoir (1841-1919). $1.40, Young Girls at Piano, by Renoir.

1985, Sept. 16 Photo. *Perf. 13*
378 A73 75c multicolored 1.40 1.40
379 A73 90c multicolored 1.65 1.65
380 A73 $1.40 multicolored 2.75 2.75
Nos. 378-380 (3) 5.80 5.80

Souvenir Sheet

381 Sheet of 3 3.75 3.75
a. A73 75c + 10c like #378 .90 .90
b. A73 90c + 10c like #379 1.10 1.10
c. A73 $1.40 + 10c like #380 1.75 1.75

Surcharged for children's activities.

Adoration of the Magi, by Giotto di Bondone (1276-1337) — A74

1985, Nov. 15 Photo. *Perf. 13½x13*

382 A74 95c multicolored 1.10 1.10
383 A74 95c multicolored 1.10 1.10
384 A74 $1.15 multicolored 1.40 1.40
385 A74 $1.15 multicolored 1.40 1.40
Nos. 382-385 (4) 5.00 5.00

Souvenir Sheet

Imperf

386 A74 $6.40 multicolored 7.50 7.50

Christmas, return of Halley's Comet, 1985-86. Stamps of the same denomination se-tenant.

Halley's Comet A75

Designs: 90c, Halley's Comet, A.D. 684, wood engraving, Nuremberg Chronicles. $1.25, Sighting of 1066, Bayeux Tapestry, detail, c. 1092, France. $1.75, The Comet Inflicting Untold Disasters, 1456, Lucerne Chronicles, by Diebolt Schilling. $4.20, Melancolia I, engraving by Durer.

1986, Feb. 25 Photo. *Perf. 13½x13*

387 A75 90c multicolored 1.00 1.00
388 A75 $1.25 multicolored 1.40 1.40
389 A75 $1.75 multicolored 2.00 2.00
Nos. 387-389 (3) 4.40 4.40

Souvenir Sheets

390 Sheet of 3 + label 3.00 3.00
a. A75 95c, like #387 1.00 1.00
b. A75 95c, like #388 1.00 1.00
c. A75 95c, like #389 1.00 1.00

Imperf

391 A75 $4.20 multicolored 4.75 4.75

Elizabeth II, 60th Birthday — A76

1986, Apr. 21 *Perf. 14*

392 A76 95c Coronation portrait 1.10 1.10

Souvenir Sheet

Perf. 13½

393 A76 $4.20 Portrait, diff. 5.00 5.00

No. 392 printed in sheets of 5 with label picturing U.K. flag and Queen's flag for New Zealand.

Statue of Liberty, Cent. A77

1986, June 27 Photo. *Perf. 14*

394 A77 $1 Liberty head 1.10 1.10
395 A77 $2.75 Statue 3.00 3.00

Souvenir Sheet

Perf. 13½

396 Sheet of 2 2.75 2.75
a. A77 $1.25 like $1 1.25 1.25
b. A77 $1.25 like $2.75 1.25 1.25

For surcharges see Nos B44, B49.

Wedding of Prince Andrew and Sarah Ferguson — A78

1986, July 23 *Perf. 14*

397 A78 $2 multicolored 2.25 2.25

Souvenir Sheet

Perf. 13½

398 A78 $5 multicolored 5.75 5.75

No. 397 printed in sheets of 5 plus label picturing Westminster Abbey.
For surcharge see No. B48.

No. 354 Ovptd. with Gold Circle over AUSIPEX Emblem, Black and Gold STAMPEX '86 Emblem

1986, Aug. 4 Photo. *Perf. 14*

399 Sheet of 3 6.00 6.00
a. A68 60c + 5c like #351 1.25 1.25
b. A68 96c + 5c like #352 2.00 2.00
c. A68 $1.40 + 5c like #353 2.75 2.75

STAMPEX '86, Adelaide, Aug. 4-10.

Christmas A79

Paintings by Albrecht Durer: 75c, No. 404a, St. Anne with Virgin and Child. $1.35, No. 404b, Virgin and Child. $1.95, No. 404c, Adoration of the Magi. $2.75, No. 404d, Rosary Festivity.

1986, Nov. 21 Litho. *Perf. 13½*

400 A79 75c multicolored .80 .80
401 A79 $1.35 multicolored 1.50 1.50
402 A79 $1.95 multicolored 2.00 2.00
403 A79 $2.75 multicolored 3.00 3.00
Nos. 400-403 (4) 7.30 7.30

Souvenir Sheet

404 Sheet of 4 7.00 7.00
a.-d. A79 $1.65 any single 1.75 1.75

For surcharges see Nos. B39-B44, B46-B47, B50-B54.

Nos. 247-249 Surcharged in Gold and Black

1987, Nov. 20 Photo. *Perf. 13x12½*

405 A56 $2.50 on 60c No. 247 3.00 3.00
406 A56 $2.50 on 80c No. 248 3.00 3.00
407 A56 $2.50 on $1.40 No. 249 3.00 3.00
Nos. 405-407 (3) 9.00 9.00

Issued in sheets of 4 with margin inscriptions overprinted with gold bar and "40th Anniversary of the Royal Wedding / 1947-1987" in black; "OVERPRINTED BY NEW ZEALAND GOVERNMENT PRINTER, / WELLINGTON, NOVEMBER 1987" at left.

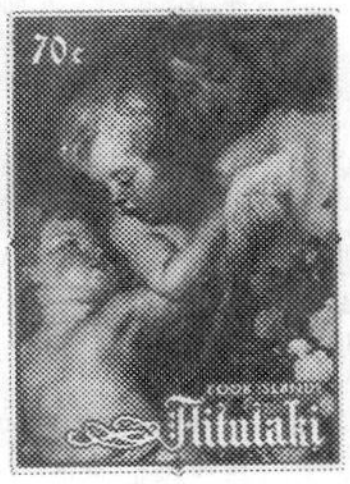

A80

The Virgin with Garland, by Rubens — A81

Painting details.

1987, Dec. 10 Photo. *Perf. 13x13½*

408 A80 70c UL .90 .90
409 A80 85c UR 1.10 1.10
410 A80 $1.50 LL 2.00 2.00
411 A80 $1.85 LR 2.50 2.50
Nos. 408-411 (4) 6.50 6.50

Souvenir Sheets

412 Sheet of 4 6.00 6.00
a. A80 95c like No. 408 1.50 1.50
b. A80 95c like No. 409 1.50 1.50
c. A80 95c like No. 410 1.50 1.50
d. A80 95c like No. 411 1.50 1.50

Perf. 13

413 A81 $6 multicolored 7.75 7.75

Christmas.

1988 Summer Olympics, Seoul — A82

Flags of Korea, Aitutaki, ancient and modern events, and Seoul Games emblem or $50 silver coin issued to commemorate the participation of Aitutaki athletes in the Olympics for the 1st time: 70c, No. 418a, Obverse of silver coin, chariot race, running. 85c, Emblem, running, soccer. 95c, Emblem, boxing, handball. $1.40, No. 418b, Reverse of coin, spearmen, women's tennis.

1988, Aug. 22 Photo. *Perf. 14½x15*

414 A82 70c multicolored .95 .95
415 A82 85c multicolored 1.10 1.10
416 A82 95c multicolored 1.25 1.25
417 A82 $1.40 multicolored 1.90 1.90
Nos. 414-417 (4) 5.20 5.20

Souvenir Sheet

418 Sheet of 2 5.50 5.50
a.-b. A82 $2 any single 2.75 2.75

Nos. 414-417 Ovptd. with Names of 1988 Olympic Gold Medalists

a. "FLORENCE GRIFFTH JOYNER / UNITED STATES / 100 M AND 200 M"
b. "GELINDO BORDIN / ITALY / MARATHON"
c. "HITOSHI SAITO / JAPAN / JUDO"
d. "STEFFI GRAF / WEST GERMANY / WOMEN'S TENNIS"

1988, Oct. 10 Litho. *Perf. 14½x15*

419 A82 (a) 70c on No. 414 .95 .95
420 A82 (b) 85c on No. 415 1.10 1.10
421 A82 (c) 95c on No. 416 1.25 1.25
422 A82 (d) $1.40 on No. 417 1.90 1.90
Nos. 419-422 (4) 5.20 5.20

Griffith is spelled incorrectly on No. 419.

Christmas A83

Paintings by Rembrandt: 55c, Adoration of the Shepherds (detail), National Gallery, London. 70c, Holy Family, Alte Pinakothek, Munich. 85c, Presentation in the Temple, Kunsthalle, Hamburg. 95c, The Holy Family, Louvre, Paris. $1.15, Presentation in the Temple, diff., Mauritshuis, The Hague. $4.50, Adoration of the Shepherds (entire painting).

1988, Nov. 2 Photo. *Perf. 13½*

423 A83 55c multicolored .70 .70
424 A83 70c multicolored .90 .90
425 A83 85c multicolored 1.10 1.10
426 A83 95c multicolored 1.25 1.25
427 A83 $1.15 multicolored 1.50 1.50
Nos. 423-427 (5) 5.45 5.45

Souvenir Sheet

Perf. 14

428 A83 $4.50 multicolored 5.75 5.75

No. 428 contains one 52x34mm stamp.

A84

Mutiny on the *Bounty,* 200th Anniv. — A85

1989, July 3 Photo. *Perf. 13½*

429 A84 55c Ship, Capt. Bligh 1.25 1.25
430 A84 65c Breadfruit 1.40 1.40
431 A84 75c Bligh, chart 1.60 1.60
432 A84 95c *Bounty* off Aitutaki 2.00 2.00
433 A84 $1.65 Christian, Bligh 3.75 3.75
Nos. 429-433 (5) 10.00 10.00

Souvenir Sheet

434 A85 $4.20 Castaways 9.00 9.00

Discovery of Aitutaki by William Bligh, bicent.

1st Moon Landing, 20th Anniv. — A86

Apollo 11 mission emblem, American flag, eagle, "The Eagle has landed" and: 75c, Astronaut standing on the lunar surface. $1.15, Conducting an experiment in front of the lunar module. $1.80, Carrying equipment. $6.40, Raising the flag.

1989, July 28 Photo. *Perf. 13½x13*

435 A86 75c multicolored .90 .90
436 A86 $1.15 multicolored 1.40 1.40
437 A86 $1.80 multicolored 2.25 2.25
Nos. 435-437 (3) 4.55 4.55

Souvenir Sheet

Perf. 13½

438 A86 $6.40 multicolored 7.50 7.50

No. 438 contains one 42x31mm stamp.

Christmas — A87

Details from *Virgin in Glory*, by Titian: 70c, Virgin. 85c, Christ child. 95c, Angel. $1.25, Cherubs. $6, Entire painting.

1989, Nov. 20 Photo. *Perf. 13½x13*

439	A87	70c multicolored	.90	.90
440	A87	85c multicolored	1.10	1.10
441	A87	95c multicolored	1.25	1.25
442	A87	$1.25 multicolored	1.60	1.60
		Nos. 439-442 (4)	4.85	4.85

Souvenir Sheet

Perf. 13½

443	A87	$6 multicolored	7.75	7.75

No. 443 contains one 45x60mm stamp.

World Environmental Protection — A88

Designs: a, Human comet, World Philatelic Programs emblem. b, Comet tail and "Protect The Endangered Earth!" $3, Human comet, emblem and inscription. (Illustration reduced.)

1990, Feb. 16 Photo. *Perf. 13½x13*

444	A88	Pair	4.50	4.50
a.-b.		$1.75 any single	2.25	2.25

Souvenir Sheet

445	A88	$3 multicolored	4.00	4.00

No. 376a Ovptd. "Ninetieth / Birthday" in Black on Gold

Designs: 55c, Lady Elizabeth Bowes-Lyon, 1907. 65c, Lady Elizabeth engaged to Duke of York. 75c, As Duchess of York with daughter Elizabeth. $1.30, As Queen Mother with grandson.

1990, July 16 Litho. *Perf. 13½x13*

446	Sheet of 4	4.00	4.00
a.	A72 55c multicolored	.65	.65
b.	A72 65c multicolored	.75	.75
c.	A72 75c multicolored	.90	.90
d.	A72 $1.30 multicolored	1.50	1.50

Christmas — A89

Paintings: 70c, Madonna of the Basket by Correggio. 85c, Virgin and Child by Morando. 95c, Adoration of the Child by Tiepolo. $1.75, Mystic Marriage of St. Catherine by Memling. $6, Donne Triptych by Memling.

1990, Nov. 28 Litho. *Perf. 14*

447	A89	70c multicolored	.85	.85
448	A89	85c multicolored	1.00	1.00
449	A89	95c multicolored	1.10	1.10
450	A89	$1.75 multicolored	2.25	2.25
		Nos. 447-450 (4)	5.20	5.20

Souvenir Sheet

451	A89	$6 multicolored	7.50	7.50

Nos. 246A-246B Overprinted

1990, Dec. 5 Photo. *Perf. 13½*

452	A55	$1 multicolored	1.90	1.90
453	A55	$2 multicolored	3.75	3.75

Birdpex '90, 20 Intl. Ornithological Congress, New Zealand.

No. 246D Overprinted "COMMEMORATING 65TH BIRTHDAY OF H.M. QUEEN ELIZABETH II"

1991, Apr. 22 Photo. *Perf. 13*

454	A55	$5 multicolored	6.25	6.25

Christmas — A90

Paintings: 80c, The Holy Family, by Mengs. 90c, Virgin and Child, by Fra Filippo Lippi. $1.05, Virgin and Child, by Durer. $1.75, Adoration of the Shepherds, by De La Tour. $6, The Holy Family, by Michelangelo.

1991, Nov. 13 Litho. *Perf. 14*

455	A90	80c multicolored	.90	.90
456	A90	90c multicolored	1.10	1.10
457	A90	$1.05 multicolored	1.25	1.25
458	A90	$1.75 multicolored	2.00	2.00
		Nos. 455-458 (4)	5.25	5.25

Souvenir Sheet

459	A90	$6 multicolored	7.00	7.00

1992 Summer Olympics, Barcelona — A91

1992, July 29 Litho. *Perf. 14*

460	A91	95c Hurdles	1.00	1.00
461	A91	$1.25 Weight lifting	1.40	1.40
462	A91	$1.50 Judo	1.75	1.75
463	A91	$1.95 Soccer	2.25	2.25
		Nos. 460-463 (4)	6.40	6.40

6th Festival of Pacific Arts, Rarotonga — A92

Canoes: 30c, Vaka Motu. 50c, Hamatafua. 95c, Alia Kalia Ndrua. $1.75, Hokule'a Hawaiian. $1.95, Tuamotu Pahi.

1992, Oct. 16 Litho. *Perf. 14x15*

464	A92	30c multicolored	.35	.35
465	A92	50c multicolored	.55	.55
466	A92	95c multicolored	1.10	1.10
467	A92	$1.75 multicolored	2.00	2.00
468	A92	$1.95 multicolored	2.25	2.25
		Nos. 464-468 (5)	6.25	6.25

Overprinted "ROYAL VISIT"

1992, Oct. 16

469	A92	30c on #464	.35	.35
470	A92	50c on #465	.55	.55
471	A92	95c on #466	1.10	1.10
472	A92	$1.75 on #467	2.00	2.00
473	A92	$1.95 on #468	2.25	2.25
		Nos. 469-473 (5)	6.25	6.25

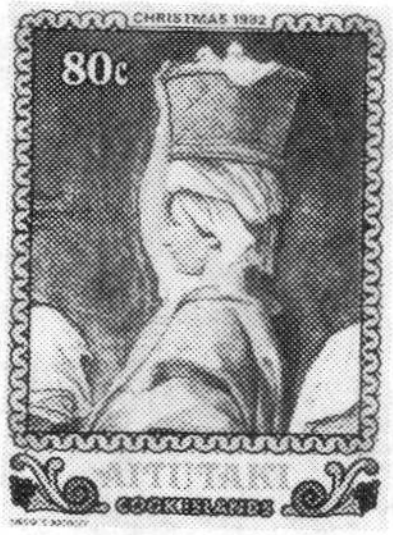

Christmas A93

Designs: Different details from Virgin's Nativity, by Guido Reni.

1992, Nov. 19 Litho. *Perf. 13½*

474	A93	80c multicolored	.90	.90
475	A93	90c multicolored	1.10	1.10
476	A93	$1.05 multicolored	1.25	1.25
477	A93	$1.75 multicolored	1.90	1.90
		Nos. 474-477 (4)	5.15	5.15

Souvenir Sheet

478	A93	$6 like #476	6.50	6.50

No. 478 contains one 39x50mm stamp.

Discovery of America, 500th Anniv. — A94

Designs: $1.25, Columbus being blessed as he departs from Spain. $1.75, Map of Columbus' four voyages. $1.95, Columbus landing in New World.

1992, Dec. 11 *Perf. 14x15*

479	A94	$1.25 multicolored	1.40	1.40
480	A94	$1.75 multicolored	1.90	1.90
481	A94	$1.95 multicolored	2.25	2.25
		Nos. 479-481 (3)	5.55	5.55

Coronation of Queen Elizabeth II, 40th Anniv. — A95

Designs: a, Victoria, Edward VII. b, George V, George VI. c, Elizabeth II.

1993, June 4 Litho. *Perf. 14*

482	A95	$1.75 Strip of 3, #a.-c.	6.00	6.00

Christmas — A96

Religious sculpture: 80c, Madonna and Child, by Nino Pisano. 90c, Virgin on Rosebush, by Luca Della Robbia. $1.15, Virgin with Child and St. John, by Juan Francisco Rustici. $1.95, Virgin with Child, by Michelangelo. $3, Madonna and Child, by Jacopo Della Quercia.

1993, Oct. 29 Litho. *Perf. 14*

483	A96	80c multicolored	.90	.90
484	A96	90c multicolored	1.00	1.00
485	A96	$1.15 multicolored	1.25	1.25
486	A96	$1.95 multicolored	2.25	2.25

Size: 32x47mm

Perf. 13½

487	A96	$3 multicolored	3.50	3.50
		Nos. 483-487 (5)	8.90	8.90

1994 Winter Olympics, Lillehammer — A97

Designs: a, Ice hockey. b, Ski jumping. c, Cross-country skiing.

1994, Feb. 11 Litho. *Perf. 14*

488	A97	$1.15 Strip of 3, #a.-c.	4.00	4.00

Flowers — A98

Hibiscus A98a

1994-97 Litho. *Perf. 13½*

489	A98	5c Prostrate morning glory	.20	.20
490	A98	10c White frangipani	.20	.20
491	A98	15c Red hibiscus	.20	.20
492	A98	20c Yellow allamanda	.20	.20
493	A98	25c Royal poinciana	.25	.25
494	A98	30c White gardenia	.35	.35
495	A98	50c Pink frangipani	.55	.55
496	A98	80c Morning glory	.90	.90
497	A98	85c Yellow mallow	.95	.95
498	A98	90c Red coral tree	1.00	1.00
499	A98	$1 Cup of gold	1.10	1.10
500	A98	$2 Red cordia	2.25	2.25
501	A98a	$3 multicolored	3.75	3.75
502	A98a	$5 multicolored	6.25	6.25
503	A98a	$8 multicolored	10.00	10.00
		Nos. 489-503 (15)	28.15	28.15

Issued: 5c-90c, 2/17; $1, $2, 4/29; $3, $5, 11/18; $8, 11/21/97. This is an expanding set. Numbers may change.

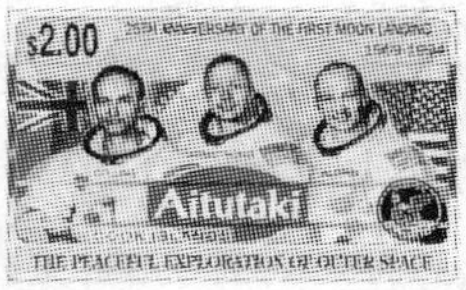

First Manned Moon Landing, 25th Anniv. A99

Designs: No. 506, Astronauts Collins, Armstrong, Aldrin. No. 507, Splash down in South Pacific.

1994, July 20 Litho. *Perf. 14*

506	A99	$2 multicolored	2.25	2.25
507	A99	$2 multicolored	2.25	2.25

Christmas — A100

Paintings: No. 508a, The Madonna of the Basket, by Corregio. b, Virgin & Child with Saints, by Hans Memling. c, The Virgin & Child with Flowers, by Dolci. d, Virgin & Child with Angels, by Bergognone.

No. 509a, The Adoration of the Kings, by Dosso. b, The Virgin & Child, by Bellini. c, The Virgin & Child, by Schiavone. d, Adoration of the Kings, by Dolci.

1994, Nov. 30 Litho. *Perf. 14*

508	A100	85c Block of 4, #a.-d.	3.75	3.75
509	A100	90c Block of 4, #a.-d.	4.00	4.00

End of World War II, 50th Anniv. — A101

Designs: a, Battle of Britain, 1940. b, Battle of Midway, June 1942.

1995, Sept. 4 Litho. ***Perf. 13½x13***

510 A101 $4 Pair, #a.-b. 10.50 10.50

No. 510 issued in sheets of 4 stamps.

Queen Mother, 95th Birthday A102

1995, Sept. 14 Litho. ***Perf. 13x13½***

511 A102 $4 multicolored 5.25 5.25

UN, 50th Anniv. — A103

1995, Oct. 18 Litho. ***Perf. 13½***

512 A103 $4.25 multicolored 5.50 5.50

Year of the Sea Turtle A104

1995, Dec. 1 Litho. ***Perf. 14x13½***

513 A104 95c Green turtle 1.25 1.25
514 A104 $1.15 Leatherback turtle 1.50 1.50
515 A104 $1.50 Olive Ridley turtle 2.00 2.00
516 A104 $1.75 Loggerhead turtle 2.25 2.25
Nos. 513-516 (4) 7.00 7.00

Queen Elizabeth II, 70th Birthday A105

1996, June 24 Litho. ***Perf. 14***

517 A105 $4.50 multicolored 6.00 6.00

No. 517 was issued in sheets of 4.

Modern Olympic Games, Cent. A106

Designs: No. 518, Pierre de Coubertin, Olympic torch, parading athletes, 1896. No. 519, Modern sprinters, US flag, Atlanta, 1996.

1996, July 11 Litho. ***Perf. 14***

518 A106 $2 multicolored 2.75 2.75
519 A106 $2 multicolored 2.75 2.75
a. Pair, #518-519 5.50 5.50

Queen Elizabeth II and Prince Philip, 50th Wedding Anniv. A107

$2.50, Queen Elizabeth II, Prince Philip, Queen Mother, and King George VI. $6, like #520, close-up.

1997, Nov. 20 Litho. ***Perf. 14***

520 A107 $2.50 multicolored 3.25 3.25

Souvenir Sheet

521 A107 $6 multicolored 7.75 7.75

No. 520 was issued in sheets of 4.

Diana, Princess of Wales (1961-97) — A108

1998, Apr. 15 Litho. ***Perf. 14***

522 A108 $1 multicolored 1.25 1.25

Souvenir Sheet

523 A108 $4 like #522 4.75 4.75

No. 522 was issued in sheets of 5 + label. No. 523 is a continuous design.
For surcharge see No. B55.

SEMI-POSTAL STAMPS

Christmas Type of 1974

Designs: 1c+1c, like #104. 5c+1c, like #105. 8c+1c, like #106. 10c+1c, like #107. 25c+1c, like #108. 30c+1c, like #109.

1974, Dec. 2 Photo. ***Perf. 13½***

B1 A29 1c + 1c multicolored .20 .20
B2 A29 5c + 1c multicolored .20 .20
B3 A29 8c + 1c multicolored .20 .20
B4 A29 10c + 1c multicolored .20 .20
B5 A29 25c + 1c multicolored .30 .30
B6 A29 30c + 1c multicolored .30 .30
Nos. B1-B6 (6) 1.40 1.40

Surtax was for child welfare.

Nos. 117-120 Surcharged in Silver

1975, Dec. 19 Photo. ***Perf. 14x13½***

B7 A32 Strip of 3 .30 .30
a.-c. 6c+1c any single .20 .20
B8 A32 Strip of 3 .35 .35
a.-c. 7c+1c any single .20 .20
B9 A32 Strip of 3 .90 .90
a.-c. 15c+1c any single .30 .30
B10 A32 Strip of 3 1.25 1.25
a.-c. 20c+1c any single .40 .40
Nos. B7-B10 (4) 2.80 2.80

Christmas. The surtax was for children's activities during holiday season.

Nos. 135-142a Surcharged in Silver

1976, Nov. 19 Photo. ***Perf. 13½x13***

B11 A36 6c + 1c multicolored .20 .20
B12 A37 6c + 1c multicolored .20 .20
B13 A36 7c + 1c multicolored .20 .20
B14 A37 7c + 1c multicolored .20 .20
B15 A36 15c + 1c multicolored .20 .20
B16 A37 15c + 1c multicolored .20 .20
B17 A36 20c + 1c multicolored .30 .30
B18 A37 20c + 1c multicolored .30 .30
a. Souvenir sheet of 8 1.60 1.60
Nos. B11-B18 (8) 1.80 1.80

Surtax was for child welfare. Stamps of No. B18a each surcharged 2c.

Nos. 152-159a Surcharged in Black

1977, Nov. 15 ***Perf. 13½x14***

B19 A41 6c + 1c multicolored .20 .20
B20 A42 6c + 1c multicolored .20 .20
B21 A41 7c + 1c multicolored .20 .20
B22 A42 7c + 1c multicolored .20 .20
B23 A41 15c + 1c multicolored .20 .20
B24 A42 15c + 1c multicolored .20 .20
B25 A41 20c + 1c multicolored .30 .30
B26 A42 20c + 1c multicolored .30 .30
a. Souvenir sheet of 8 1.60 1.60
Nos. B19-B26 (8) 1.80 1.80

Surtax was for child welfare. Stamps of No. B26a each surcharged 2c.

Easter Type of 1978
Souvenir Sheets

Paintings: No. B27, like No. 163. No. B28, like No. 164. No. B29, like No. 165.

1978, Mar. 17 Photo. ***Perf. 14***

B27 A44 50c + 5c multicolored .70 .70
B28 A44 50c + 5c multicolored .70 .70
B29 A44 50c + 5c multicolored .70 .70

Nos. B27-B29 contain one stamp 33x25mm.

Christmas Type of 1978
Souvenir Sheet

1978, Dec. 4 Photo. ***Perf. 14½x13***

B30 Sheet of 4 2.25 2.25
a. A46 15c + 2c like #167 .30 .30
b. A46 17c + 2c like #168 .35 .35
c. A46 30c + 2c like #169 .55 .55
d. A46 35c + 2c like #170 .60 .60

Year of the Child Type
Souvenir Sheet

1979, Oct. 1 Photo. ***Perf. 14x13½***

B31 Sheet of 3 1.40 1.40
a. A48 30c + 3c like #173 .30 .30
b. A48 35c + 3c like #174 .35 .35
c. A48 65c + 3c like #175 .60 .60

Easter Type of 1980
Souvenir Sheet

Designs: No. B32 shows entire painting in continuous design. Nos. B32a-B32c similar to Nos. B183-185. Size of Nos. B32a-B32c: 25x50mm.

1980, Apr. 3 Photo. ***Perf. 13x13½***

B32 Sheet of 3 1.40 1.40
a. A50 20c + 2c multicolored .35 .35
b. A50 30c + 2c multicolored .45 .45
c. A50 35c + 2c multicolored .55 .55

Christmas Type of 1980
Souvenir Sheet

1980, Nov. 21 Photo. ***Perf. 13x13½***

B33 Sheet of 4 1.40 1.40
a. A53 15c + 2c like #208 .20 .20
b. A53 20c + 2c like #209 .30 .30
c. A53 25c + 2c like #210 .35 .35
d. A53 35c + 2c like #211 .45 .45

Easter Type of 1981
Souvenir Sheet

1981, Mar. 31 Photo. ***Perf. 13½***

B34 Sheet of 3 1.65 1.65
a. A54 30c + 2c like #212 .35 .35
b. A54 40c + 2c like #213 .50 .50
c. A54 50c + 2c like #214 .65 .65

Nos. 247-249 Surcharged

1981, Nov. 23 Photo. ***Perf. 13x13½***

B35 A56 60 + 5c multi .90 .90
B36 A56 80 + 5c multi 1.10 1.10
B37 A56 $1.40 + 5c multi 2.00 2.00
Nos. B35-B37 (3) 4.00 4.00

Intl. Year of the Disabled. Surtax was for the handicapped.

Soccer Type of 1981
Souvenir Sheet

1981, Nov. 30 ***Perf. 14***

B38 A57 Sheet of 8, multi 2.50 2.50

No. B38 contains stamps with 2c surtax similar to Nos. 250-253. Surtax was for local sports.

Nos. 400-404 Surcharged "NOVEMBER/21-24 1986/FIRST VISIT TO SOUTH/PACIFIC" and 10c in Silver

1986, Nov. 25 Litho. ***Perf. 13½***

B39 A79 75c + 10c multi 1.25 1.25
B40 A79 $1.35 + 10c multi 2.00 2.00
B41 A79 $1.95 + 10c multi 3.00 3.00
B42 A79 $2.75 + 10c multi 4.00 4.00
Nos. B39-B42 (4) 10.25 10.25

Souvenir Sheet

B43 Sheet of 4 13.00 13.00
a.-d. A79 $1.65 +10c on #404a-404d 3.25 3.25

State visit of Pope John Paul II.
For surcharges see Nos. B51-B54.

Nos. 394-395, 397 and 400-403 Surcharged "HURRICANE RELIEF/ + 50c" in Silver or Black

1987, Apr. 29 Litho. ***Perf. 13½, 14***

B44 A79 75c + 50c #400 2.00 2.00
B45 A77 $1 + 50c #394 (B) 2.50 2.50
B46 A79 $1.35 + 50c #401 3.00 3.00
B47 A79 $1.95 + 50c #402 3.25 3.25
B48 A78 $2 + 50c #397 3.25 3.25
B49 A77 $2.75 + 50c #395 (B) 4.25 4.25
B50 A79 $2.75 + 50c #403 4.25 4.25
Nos. B44-B50 (7) 22.50 22.50

Nos. B39-B42 Surcharged "HURRICANE RELIEF / +50c" in Silver

1987, Apr. 29 Litho. ***Perf. 13½***

B51 A79 75c + 50c No. B39 2.00 2.00
B52 A79 $1.35 + 50c No. B40 2.50 2.50
B53 A79 $1.95 + 50c No. B41 3.00 3.00
B54 A79 $2.75 + 50c No. B42 3.50 3.50
Nos. B51-B54 (4) 11.00 11.00

Souvenir Sheet
No. 523 Surcharged "CHILDREN'S/CHARITIES" in Silver

1998, Nov. 19 Litho. ***Perf. 14***

B55 A108 $4 + $1 multicolored 6.25 6.25

AIR POST STAMPS

Capt. Bligh Type of 1974

1974, Sept. 9 Litho. ***Perf. 13***

Size: 46x26mm

C1 A27 10c Bligh and "Bounty" .55 .55
C2 A27 10c "Bounty" at sea .55 .55
C3 A27 25c Bligh and "Bounty" 1.25 1.25
C4 A27 25c Chart, 1856 1.25 1.25
C5 A27 30c Cook and "Resolution" 1.60 1.60
C6 A27 30c Maps 1.60 1.60
Nos. C1-C6 (6) 6.80 6.80

Stamps of same denomination printed se-tenant in sheets of 20. See note after No. 101.

OFFICIAL STAMPS

Nos. 83-90, 92-95, 150-151 Overprinted or Surcharged in Black, Silver or Gold **O.H.M.S.**

1978-79 Photo. ***Perf. 13x13½***

O1 A25 1c multi .20 .20
O2 A25 2c multi .20 .20
O3 A25 3c multi .20 .20
O4 A25 4c multi (G) .20 .20
O5 A25 5c multi .20 .20
O6 A25 8c multi .20 .20
O7 A25 10c multi .20 .20
O8 A25 15c on 60c multi .20 .20
O9 A25 18c on 60c multi .25 .25
O10 A25 20c multi (G) .30 .25
O11 A40 50c multi .75 .70
O12 A25 60c multi .90 .80
O13 A25 $1 multi 1.40 1.25
O14 A26 $2 multi 3.00 2.75
O15 A40 $4 on $1 multi (S) 6.00 5.50
O16 A26 $5 multi 7.25 6.50
Nos. O1-O16 (16) 21.45 19.60

Overprint on 4c, 20c, $1 diagonal.
Issued: #O14-O16, 2/20/79; others, 11/3/78.

Stamps of 1983-84 Ovptd. or Surcharged in Green

O.H.M.S.

or Gold (#O29-O32)

75c

O.H.M.S.

1985, Aug. 9 *Perf. 14, 13x13½*

O17	A66	2c No. 322	.20	.20
O18	A66	5c No. 324	.20	.20
O19	A66	10c No. 325	.20	.20
O20	A66	12c No. 326	.20	.20
O21	A66	18c No. 327	.20	.20
O22	A66	20c on 24c No. 328	.20	.20
O23	A66	30c No. 329	.35	.35
O24	A66	40c on 36c No. 330	.45	.45
O25	A66	50c No. 332	.55	.55
O26	A66	55c on 48c No. 331	.65	.65
O27	A66	60c No. 333	.70	.70
O28	A66	65c on 72c No. 334	.75	.75
O29	A61	75c on 48c No. 276	.85	.85
O30	A61	75c on 48c No. 277	.85	.85
O31	A61	75c on 48c No. 278	.85	.85
O32	A61	75c on 48c No. 279	.85	.85
a.		Block of 4, Nos. O29-O32	3.50	3.50
O33	A66	80c on 96c No. 335	.90	.90
		Nos. O17-O33 (17)	8.95	8.95

Nos. 336-341, 246C-246D Overprinted or Surcharged Like Nos. O17-O28, O33 in Metallic Green or Blue

1986, Oct. 1 *Perf. 14*

O34	A66	$3 multi	3.00	3.00
O35	A66	$4.20 multi	4.25	4.25
O36	A66	$5.60 multi	5.75	5.75
O37	A66	$9.60 multi	10.00	10.00

1988-91 *Perf. 14*

O38	A66	$1.20 multi	1.50	1.50
O39	A66	$2.10 multi	2.50	2.50

Perf. 13½

O40	A55	$14 on $4 (B)	17.50	17.50
O41	A55	$18 on $5 (B)	22.50	22.50
		Nos. O34-O41 (8)	67.00	67.00

Issue dates: July 2, 1991; others, June 15.

AJMAN

äj-ˈmán

LOCATION — Oman Peninsula, Arabia, on Persian Gulf
GOVT. — Sheikdom under British Protection
AREA — 100 sq. mi.
POP. — 4,400
CAPITAL — Ajman

Ajman is one of six Persian Gulf sheikdoms to join the United Arab Emirates, which proclaimed its independence Dec. 2, 1971. See United Arab Emirates.

100 Naye Paise = 1 Rupee

Catalogue values for all unused stamps in this country are for Never Hinged items.

Sheik Rashid bin Humaid al Naimi and Arab Stallion A1

Designs: 2np, 50np, Regal angelfish. 3np, 70np, Camel. 4np, 1r, Angelfish. 5np, 1.50r, Green turtle. 10np, 2r, Jewelfish. 15np, 3r, White storks. 20np, 5r, White-eyed gulls. 30np, 10r, Lanner falcon. 40np as 1np.

Photo. & Litho.

1964 **Unwmk.** *Perf. 14*

Size: 35x22mm

1	A1	1np gold & multi	.20	.20
2	A1	2np gold & multi	.20	.20
3	A1	3np gold & multi	.20	.20
4	A1	4np gold & multi	.20	.20
5	A1	5np gold & multi	.20	.20
6	A1	10np gold & multi	.20	.20
7	A1	15np gold & multi	.20	.20
8	A1	20np gold & multi	.20	.20
9	A1	30np gold & multi	.20	.20

Size: 42x27mm

10	A1	40np gold & multi	.20	.20
11	A1	50np gold & multi	.25	.20
12	A1	70np gold & multi	.25	.20
13	A1	1r gold & multi	.40	.20
14	A1	1.50r gold & multi	.50	.20
15	A1	2r gold & multi	.75	.20

Size: 53x33½mm

16	A1	3r gold & multi	1.00	.20
17	A1	5r gold & multi	1.50	.40
18	A1	10r gold & multi	3.25	.75
		Nos. 1-18 (18)	9.90	4.35

Issued: #1-9, 6/20; #10-15, 9/7; #16-18, 11/4.

Pres. and Mrs. John F. Kennedy with Caroline — A2

Pres. Kennedy: 10np, As a boy in football uniform. 15np, Diving. 50np, As navy lieutenant, receiving Navy and Marine Corps Medal from Capt. Frederic L. Conklin. 1r, Sailing with Jacqueline Kennedy. 2r, With Eleanor Roosevelt. 5r, With Lyndon B. Johnson and Hubert H. Humphrey. 10r, Portrait.

1964, Dec. 15 **Photo.** *Perf. 13½x14*

19	A2	10np grn & red lil	.20	.20
20	A2	15np Prus bl & vio	.20	.20
21	A2	50np org brn & dk bl	.20	.20
22	A2	1r brn & Prus grn	.45	.20
23	A2	2r red lil & dp ol	.80	.20
24	A2	3r grn & red brn	1.25	.20
25	A2	5r vio & brn	2.00	.30
26	A2	10r dk bl & red brn	5.00	.70
		Nos. 19-26 (8)	10.10	2.20

John F. Kennedy (1917-63). A souvenir sheet contains one each of Nos. 23-26.

Runners at Start — A3

10np, 1.50r, Boxing. 25np, 2r, Judo. 50np, 5r, Gymnast on vaulting horse. 1r, 3r, Sailing yacht.

1965, Jan. 12 **Photo.** *Perf. 13½x14*

27	A3	5np red brn, brt pink & Prus grn	.20	.20
28	A3	10np dk ol grn, bl gray & red brn	.20	.20
29	A3	15np dk vio, grn & sep	.20	.20
30	A3	25np bl sal pink & blk	.20	.20
31	A3	50np mar, bl & ind	.20	.20
32	A3	1r dk grn, lil & ultra	.35	.20
33	A3	1.50r lil, grn & brn	.55	.20
34	A3	2r red org, bis & dk bl	.75	.20
35	A3	3r dk brn, grnsh bl & lil	1.00	.25
36	A3	5r grn, yel & red brn	2.00	.40
		Nos. 27-36 (10)	5.65	2.25

18th Olympic Games, Tokyo, Oct. 10-25, 1964. A souvenir sheet contains four stamps similar to Nos. 33-36 in changed colors.

Stanley Gibbons Catalogue, 1865, US No. 1X2 — A4

Designs: 10np, Austria, Scarlet Mercury 1856. 15np, British Guiana 1c, 1856. 25np, Canada 12p, 1851. 50np, Hawaii 2c, 1851. 1r, Mauritius 2p, 1847. 3r, Switzerland, Geneva 10c, 1843. 5r, Tuscany 31, 1860. 5np, 15np, 50np and 3r show first edition of Stanley Gibbons Catalogue; 10np, 25np, 1r and 5r show 1965 Elizabethan Catalogue.

1965, May 6 **Unwmk.** *Perf. 13*

37	A4	5np multi	.20	.20
38	A4	10np multi	.20	.20
39	A4	15np multi	.20	.20
40	A4	25np multi	.20	.20
41	A4	50np multi	.20	.20
42	A4	1r multi	.45	.20
43	A4	3r multi	.75	.20
a.		Souv. sheet of 4, #38-39, 42-43	2.00	
44	A4	5r multi	1.25	.30
a.		Souv. sheet of 4, #37, 40-41, 44	2.25	
		Nos. 37-44 (8)	3.45	1.70

Gibbons Catalogue Cent. Exhib., London, Feb. 17-20. Nos. 43a and 44a for 125th anniv. of 1st postage stamp. Sheets exist imperf.

Stamps of Ajman were replaced in 1972 by those of United Arab Emirates.

AIR POST STAMPS

Type of Regular Issue, 1964

Designs: 15np, Arab stallion. 25np, Regal angelfish. 35np, Camel. 50np, Angelfish. 75np, Green turtle. 1r, Jewelfish. 2r, White storks. 3r, White-eyed gulls. 5r, Lanner falcon.

Photo. & Litho.

1965 **Unwmk.** *Perf. 14*

Size: 42x25½mm

C1	A1	15np silver & multi	.20	.20
C2	A1	25np silver & multi	.20	.20
C3	A1	35np silver & multi	.20	.20
C4	Al	50np silver & multi	.20	.20
C5	A1	75np silver & multi	.20	.20
C6	A1	1r silver & multi	.40	.20

Size: 53x33½mm

C7	A1	2r silver & multi	.75	.20
C8	A1	3r silver & multi	2.00	.20
C9	A1	5r silver & multi	3.25	.30
		Nos. C1-C9 (9)	7.40	1.90

Issue dates: #C1-C6, Nov. 15, C7-C9, Dec 18.

AIR POST OFFICIAL STAMPS

Type of Regular Issue, 1964

Designs: 75np, Jewelfish. 2r, White storks. 3r, White-eyed gulls. 5r, Lanner falcon.

Photo. & Litho.

1965, Dec. 18 **Unwmk.** *Perf. 14*

Size: 42x25½mm

CO1	A1	75np gold & multi	.35	.20

Size: 53x33½mm

CO2	A1	2r gold & multi	1.00	.20
CO3	A1	3r gold & multi	1.50	.20
CO4	A1	5r gold & multi	3.00	.35
		Nos. CO1-CO4 (4)	5.85	.95

OFFICIAL STAMPS

Type of Regular Issue, 1964

25np, Arab stallion. 40np, Regal angelfish. 50np, Camel. 75np, Angelfish. 1r, Green turtle.

Photo. & Litho.

1965, Dec. 1 **Unwmk.** *Perf. 14*

Size: 42x25½mm

O1	A1	25np gold & multi	.20	.20
O2	A1	40np gold & multi	.20	.20
O3	A1	50np gold & multi	.20	.20
O4	A1	75np gold & multi	.20	.20
O5	A1	1r gold & multi	.25	.20
		Nos. O1-O5 (5)	1.05	1.00

ALAOUITES

ˈal-au-ˌwītz

LOCATION — A division of Syria, in Western Asia
GOVT. — Under French Mandate
AREA — 2,500 sq. mi.
POP. — 278,000 (approx. 1930)
CAPITAL — Latakia

This territory became an independent state in 1924, although still administered under the French Mandate. In 1930 it was renamed Latakia and Syrian stamps overprinted "Lattaquie" superseded the stamps of Alaouites. For these and subsequent issues see Latakia and Syria.

100 Centimes = 1 Piaster

Issued under French Mandate

Stamps of France Surcharged:

ALAOUITES 0 P. 25 العلويين ١/٤ الغرش	ALAOUITES 2 PIASTRES العلويين غروش ٢
Nos. 1-6, 16-18	Nos. 7-15, 19-21

1925 **Unwmk.** *Perf. 14x13½*

1	A16	10c on 2c vio brn	1.10	1.10
2	A22	25c on 5c orange	.90	.90
3	A20	75c on 15c gray grn	1.75	1.75
4	A22	1p on 20c red brn	1.00	1.00
5	A22	1.25p on 25c blue	1.40	1.40
6	A22	1.50p on 30c red	4.50	4.50
7	A22	2p on 35c violet	1.10	1.10
8	A18	2p on 40c red & pale bl	2.25	2.25
9	A18	2p on 45c grn & bl	4.50	4.50
10	A18	3p on 60c vio & ultra	3.00	3.00
11	A20	3p on 60c lt vio	4.50	4.50
12	A20	4p on 85c vermilion	1.00	1.00
13	A18	5p on 1fr cl & ol grn	3.00	3.00
14	A18	10p on 2fr org & pale bl	4.50	4.50
15	A18	25p on 5fr bl & buff	5.50	5.50
		Nos. 1-15 (15)	40.00	40.00

For overprints see Nos. C1-C4.

Same Surcharges on Pasteur Stamps of France

16	A23	50c on 10c green	1.00	1.00
17	A23	75c on 15c green	1.00	1.00
18	A23	1.50p on 30c red	1.00	1.00
19	A23	2p on 45c red	1.50	1.50
20	A23	2.50p on 50c blue	1.50	1.50
21	A23	4p on 75c blue	2.00	2.00
		Nos. 16-21 (6)	8.00	8.00

Stamps of Syria, 1925, Overprinted in Red, Black or Blue:

ALAOUITES العلوين	ALAOUITES العلويين
On A3, A5	On A4

1925, Mar. 1 *Perf. 12½, 13½*

25	A3	10c dk violet (R)	.30	.30
a.		Double overprint	15.00	15.00
26	A4	25c olive black (R)	.60	.60
a.		Inverted overprint	10.00	10.00
b.		Blue overprint	20.00	20.00
27	A4	50c yellow green	.45	.45
a.		Inverted overprint	10.00	10.00
b.		Blue overprint	20.00	20.00
c.		Red overprint	17.50	17.50
28	A4	75c brown orange	.50	.50
a.		Inverted overprint	9.00	9.00
29	A5	1p magenta	.75	.75
30	A4	1.25p deep green	.55	.55
a.		Red overprint	17.50	17.50
31	A4	1.50p rose red (Bl)	.55	.55
a.		Inverted overprint	10.00	10.00
b.		Black overprint	20.00	20.00
32	A4	2p dk brown (R)	.55	.55
a.		Blue overprint	25.00	25.00
33	A4	2.50p pck blue (R)	1.00	1.00
a.		Black overprint	25.00	25.00
34	A4	3p orange brown	.55	.55
a.		Inverted overprint	6.50	6.50
b.		Blue overprint	25.00	25.00
35	A4	5p violet	.70	.70
a.		Red overprint	25.00	25.00
36	A4	10p violet brown	1.00	1.00
37	A4	25p ultra (R)	2.50	2.50
		Nos. 25-37 (13)	10.00	10.00

For overprints see Nos. C5-C19.

Stamps of Syria, 1925, Surcharged in Black or Red:

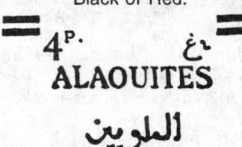

4P. غ
ALAOUITES
العلويين

Nos. 38-42

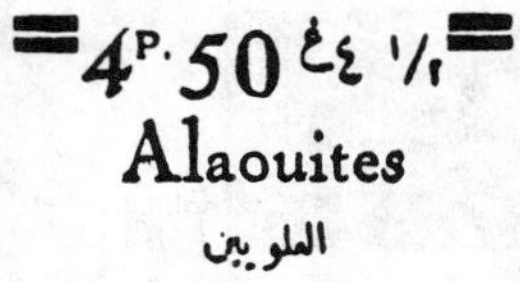

Nos. 43-45

1926

No.	Type	Description	Unused	Used
38	A4	3.50p on 75c brn org	.75	.60
a.		Surcharged on face and back	5.00	4.50
39	A4	4p on 25c ol blk (R)	1.00	.60
40	A4	6p on 2.50p pck bl (R)	.80	.60
41	A4	12p on 1.25p dp grn	.70	.60
a.		Inverted surcharge	10.00	10.00
42	A4	20p on 1.25p dp grn	1.25	1.10
43	A4	4.50p on 75c brn org	2.50	1.25
a.		Inverted surcharge	25.00	
44	A4	7.50p on 2.50p pck bl	2.00	1.25
45	A4	15p on 25p ultra	3.50	2.00
		Nos. 38-45 (8)	12.50	8.00

For overprint see No. C21.

Syria #199 Ovptd. like #25 in Red

1928

No.	Type	Description	Unused	Used
46	A3	5c on 10c dk violet	.30	.30
a.		Double surcharge	13.00	

Syria Nos. 178 and 174 Surcharged like Nos. 43-45 in Red

No.	Type	Description	Unused	Used
47	A4	2p on 1.25p dp green	6.00	3.50
48	A4	4p on 25c olive black	3.25	2.50

For overprint see No. C20.

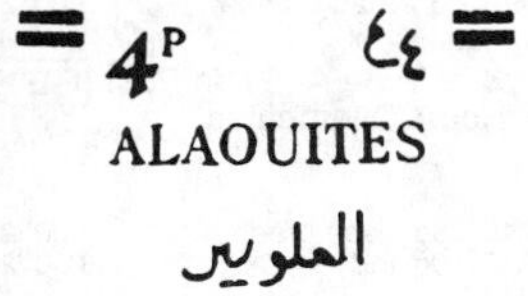

No.	Type	Description	Unused	Used
49	A4	4p on 25c olive black	35.00	30.00
a.		Double impression		
		Nos. 46-49 (4)	44.55	36.30

AIR POST STAMPS

Nos. 8, 10, 13 & 14 with Additional Overprint in Black

1925, Jan. 1 Unwmk. Perf. 14x13½

No.	Type	Description	Unused	Used
C1	A18	2p on 40c	3.50	3.50
a.		Overprint reversed	60.00	
C2	A18	3p on 60c	5.25	5.25
a.		Overprint reversed	60.00	60.00
C3	A18	5p on 1fr	3.50	3.50
C4	A18	10p on 2fr	3.50	3.50
		Nos. C1-C4 (4)	15.75	15.75

Nos. 32, 34, 35 & 36 With Additional Overprint in Green

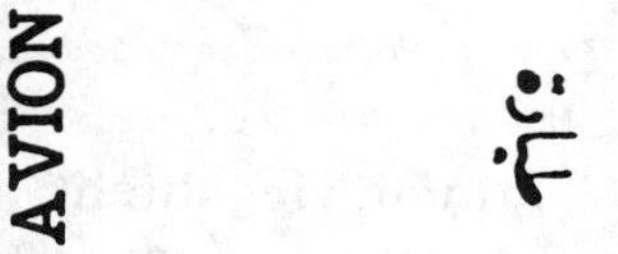

1925, Mar. 1 Perf. 13½

No.	Type	Description	Unused	Used
C5	A4	2p dark brown	1.00	1.00
C6	A4	3p orange brown	1.00	1.00
C7	A4	5p violet	1.00	1.00
C8	A4	10p violet brown	1.00	1.00
		Nos. C5-C8 (4)	4.00	4.00

Nos. 32, 34, 35 & 36 With Additional Overprint in Red

1926, May 1

No.	Type	Description	Unused	Used
C9	A4	2p dark brown	1.40	1.40
C10	A4	3p orange brown	1.40	1.40
C11	A4	5p violet	1.40	1.40
C12	A4	10p violet brown	1.40	1.40
		Nos. C9-C12 (4)	5.60	5.60

No. C9 has the original overprint in black.

Double or inverted overprints, original or plane, are known on most of Nos. C9-C12. Value, $8-$10.

The red plane overprint was also applied to Nos. C5-C8. These are believed to have been essays, and were not regularly issued.

Nos. 27, 29, and 37 With Additional Overprint of Airplane in Red or Black

1929, June-July

No.	Type	Description	Unused	Used
C17	A4	50c yel grn (R)	.75	.75
a.		Plane overprint double	15.00	
b.		Plane ovpt. on face and back	11.00	
c.		Pair with plane overprint tete beche	35.00	
C18	A5	1p magenta (Bk)	2.75	2.75
C19	A4	25p ultra (R)	17.50	10.00
a.		Plane overprint inverted	60.00	60.00
		Nos. C17-C19 (3)	21.00	13.50

Nos. 47 and 45 With Additional Overprint of Airplane in Red

1929-30

No.	Type	Description	Unused	Used
C20	A4	2p on 1.25p ('30)	1.25	1.25
a.		Surcharge inverted	4.00	
b.		Double surcharge	3.50	
C21	A4	15p on 25p (Bk + R)	19.00	14.00
a.		Plane overprint inverted	35.00	35.00

POSTAGE DUE STAMPS

Postage Due Stamps of France, 1893-1920, Surcharged Like No. 1 (Nos. J1-J2) or No. 7 (Nos. J3-J5)

1925 Unwmk. Perf. 14x13½

No.	Type	Description	Unused	Used
J1	D2	50c on 10c choc	1.90	1.90
J2	D2	1p on 20c ol grn	1.90	1.90
J3	D2	2p on 30c red	1.90	1.90
J4	D2	3p on 50c vio brn	1.90	1.90
J5	D2	5p on 1fr red brn, *straw*	1.90	1.90
		Nos. J1-J5 (5)	9.50	9.50

Postage Due Stamps of Syria, 1925, Overprinted Like No. 26 (Type D5) or No. 25 (Type D6) in Black, Blue or Red

1925 Perf. 13½

No.	Type	Description	Unused	Used
J6	D5	50c brown, *yel*	.60	.60
J7	D6	1p vio, *rose* (Bl)	.60	.60
a.		Black overprint	9.00	9.00
b.		Double overprint (Bk + Bl)	14.00	14.00
J8	D5	2p blk, *blue* (R)	1.00	1.00
J9	D5	3p blk, *red org*	1.40	1.40
J10	D5	5p blk, *bl grn* (R)	1.90	1.90
		Nos. J6-J10 (5)	5.50	5.50

The stamps of Alaouites were superseded in 1930 by those of Latakia.

ALBANIA

al-'bā-nē-ə

LOCATION — Southeastern Europe
GOVT. — Republic
AREA — 11,101 sq. mi.
POP. — 3,364,571 (1999 est.)
CAPITAL — Tirana

After the outbreak of World War I, the country fell into a state of anarchy when the Prince and all members of the International Commission left Albania. Subsequently General Ferrero in command of Italian troops declared Albania an independent country. A constitution was adopted and a republican form of government was instituted which continued until 1928 when, by constitutional amendment, Albania was declared to be a monarchy. The President of the republic, Ahmed Zogu, became king of the new state. Many unlisted varieties or surcharges and lithographed labels are said to have done postal duty in Albania and Epirus during this unsettled period.

In March 1939, Italy invaded Albania. King Zog fled but did not abdicate. The King of Italy acquired the crown.

Germany occupied Albania from September, 1943, until late 1944 when it became an independent state. The People's Republic began in January, 1946.

40 Paras = 1 Piaster = 1 Grossion
100 Centimes = 1 Franc (1917)
100 Qintar = 1 Franc
100 Qintar (Qindarka) = 1 Lek (1947)

Catalogue values for unused stamps in this country are for Never Hinged items, beginning with Scott 458 in the regular postage section, Scott B34 in the semi-postal section, and Scott C67 in the airpost section.

Watermarks

Wmk. 125-Lozenges

Wmk. 220-Double Headed Eagle

Stamps of Turkey Handstamped

Handstamped on Issue of 1908

Perf. 12, 13½ and Compound

1913, June Unwmk.

No.	Type	Description	Unused	Used
1	A19	2½pi violet brown	550.00	375.00

With Additional Overprint in Carmine ب

No.	Type	Description	Unused	Used
2	A19	10pa blue green	250.00	200.00

The eagle handstamp was applied to other Turkish stamps of 1908: 25pi green and 50 pi red brown. The 5pa ocher, Albania No. 4, was surcharged "2 paras." These three stamps were retained by officials. Values, $2,250, $5,500, $375.

Handstamped on Issue of 1909

No.	Type	Description	Unused	Used
4	A21	5pa ocher	200.00	200.00
5	A21	10pa blue green	200.00	135.00
6	A21	20pa car rose	160.00	125.00
7	A21	1pi ultra	135.00	135.00
8	A21	2pi blue black	250.00	225.00
10	A21	5pi dark violet	500.00	450.00
11	A21	10pi dull red	2,000.	2,000.

For surcharge see No. 19.

With Additional Overprint in Blue or Carmine ب

No.	Type	Description	Unused	Used
14	A21	20pa car rose (Bl)	550.00	575.00
15	A21	1pi brt blue (C)	900.00	900.00

Handstamped on Newspaper Stamp of 1911

No.	Type	Description	Unused	Used
17	A21	2pa olive green	200.00	175.00

Handstamped on Postage Due Stamp of 1908

No.	Type	Description	Unused	Used
18	A19	1pi black, *dp rose*	1600.	1550.

No. 18 was used for regular postage.

No. 6 Surcharged With New Value

No.	Type	Description	Unused	Used
19	A21	10pa on 20pa car rose	750.00	700.00

The overprint on #1-19 was handstamped and is found inverted, double, etc.

Nos. 6, 7 and 8 exist with the handstamp in red, blue or violet, but these varieties are not known to have been regularly issued.

Excellent counterfeits exist of Nos. 1 to 19.

A1

1913, July *Imperf.*

Handstamped on White Laid Paper Without Eagle and Value

No.	Type	Description	Unused	Used
20	A1	(1pi) black	140.00	*275.00*
		Cut to shape	65.00	65.00
a.		Sewing machine perf.	200.00	175.00

Counterfeits exist.

1913, Aug.

Value Typewritten in Violet With Eagle

No.	Type	Description	Unused	Used
21	A1	10pa violet	8.00	6.00
22	A1	20pa red & black	9.00	7.50
23	A1	1gr black	9.00	9.00
24	A1	2gr blue & violet	10.00	8.50
25	A1	5gr violet & blue	14.00	12.00
26	A1	10gr blue	14.00	12.00
		Nos. 21-26 (6)	64.00	55.00

Nos. 21-26 exist with the eagle inverted or omitted and with numerous errors in the figures of value and the spelling of the word "grosh."

A2

Skanderbeg (George Castriota) — A3

1913, Nov. *Perf. 11½*

Handstamped on White Laid Paper Eagle and Value in Black

No.	Type	Description	Unused	Used
27	A2	10pa green	3.00	2.00
b.		Eagle and value in green	25.00	
c.		10pa red (error)	20.00	20.00
d.		10pa violet (error)	20.00	20.00
29	A2	20pa red	4.00	3.00
b.		20pa green (error)	20.00	20.00
30	A2	30pa violet	4.00	3.00
a.		30pa ultramarine (error)	20.00	20.00
b.		30pa red (error)	20.00	20.00
31	A2	1gr ultramarine	5.00	4.00
a.		1gr green (error)	20.00	20.00
b.		1gr black (error)	20.00	20.00
c.		1gr violet (error)	20.00	20.00
33	A2	2gr black	8.00	7.00
a.		2gr violet (error)	20.00	20.00
b.		2gr blue (error)	20.00	20.00
		Nos. 27-33 (5)	24.00	19.00

The stamps of this issue are known with eagle or value inverted or omitted.

1st anniv. of Albanian independence.

Counterfeits exist.

1913, Dec. Typo. *Perf. 14*

No.	Type	Description	Unused	Used
35	A3	2q orange brn & buff	1.00	1.00
36	A3	5q green & blue grn	1.00	1.00
37	A3	10q rose red	1.00	1.00
38	A3	25q dark blue	1.00	1.00
39	A3	50q violet & red	3.00	2.00
40	A3	1fr deep brown	7.00	*6.00*
		Nos. 35-40 (6)	14.00	*12.00*

For overprints and surcharges see Nos. 41-52, 105, J1-J9.

Nos. 35-40 Handstamped in Black or Violet

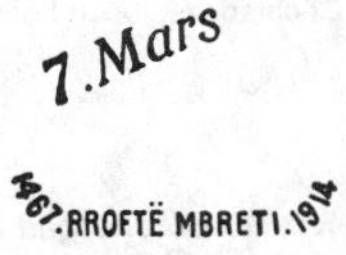

1914, Mar. 7

No.	Type	Description	Unused	Used
41	A3	2q orange brn & buff	20.00	*18.00*
42	A3	5q grn & bl grn (V)	20.00	*18.00*
43	A3	10q rose red	20.00	*18.00*
44	A3	25q dark blue (V)	20.00	*18.00*
45	A3	50q violet & red	20.00	*18.00*
46	A3	1fr deep brown	20.00	*18.00*
		Nos. 41-46 (6)	120.00	*108.00*

Issued to celebrate the arrival of Prince Wilhelm zu Wied on Mar. 7, 1914.

Nos. 35-40 Surcharged in Black:

5 • PARA • (a) — 1 GROSH (b)

1914, Apr. 2

47	A3 (a) 5pa on 2q	1.10	1.10
48	A3 (a) 10pa on 5q	1.10	1.10
49	A3 (a) 20pa on 10q	2.00	1.50
50	A3 (b) 1gr on 25q	2.50	2.00
51	A3 (b) 2gr on 50q	2.50	2.00
52	A3 (b) 5gr on 1fr	13.00	11.00
	Nos. 47-52 (6)	22.20	18.70

For overprints see Nos. 105, J6-J9.

Inverted Surcharge

47a	A3 (a) 5pa on 2q	5.00	5.00
48a	A3 (a) 10pa on 5q	5.00	5.00
49a	A3 (a) 20pa on 10q	5.00	5.00
50a	A3 (b) 1gr on 25q	6.50	6.50
51a	A3 (b) 2gr on 50q	7.50	7.50
52b	A3 (b) 5gr on 1fr	21.00	21.00
	Nos. 47a-52b (6)	50.00	50.00

Korce (Korytsa) Issues

A4

1914 Handstamped *Imperf.*

52A	A4 10pa violet & red	90.00	90.00
c.	10pa black & red	90.00	90.00
53	A4 25pa violet & red	90.00	90.00
a.	25pa black & red	150.00	150.00

Nos. 52A-53a originally were handstamped directly on the cover, so the paper varies. Later they were also produced in sheets; these are rarely found. Nos. 52A-53a were issued by Albanian military authorities.

Counterfeits exist of No. 53.

A5

A6

1917 Typo. & Litho. *Perf. 11½*

54	A5 1c dk brown & grn	9.00	6.50
55	A5 2c red & green	9.00	6.50
56	A5 3c gray grn & grn	9.00	6.50
57	A5 5c green & black	7.00	4.25
58	A5 10c rose red & black	7.00	4.25
59	A5 25c blue & black	7.00	4.25
60	A5 50c violet & black	8.50	6.00
61	A5 1fr brown & black	8.50	6.00
	Nos. 54-61 (8)	65.00	44.25

1917-18

62	A6 1c dk brown & grn	2.75	2.50
63	A6 2c red brown & grn	2.75	2.50
a.	"CTM" for "CTS"	30.00	30.00
64	A6 3c black & green	2.75	2.50
a.	"CTM" for "CTS"	30.00	30.00
65	A6 5c green & black	2.75	2.75
66	A6 10c dull red & black	2.75	2.75
67	A6 50c violet & black	7.50	6.00
68	A6 1fr red brn & black	10.00	8.00
	Nos. 62-68 (7)	31.25	27.00

Counterfeits abound of Nos. 54-68, 80-81.

No. 65 Surcharged in Red

QARKU
I
KORÇËS
25 CTS

1918

80	A6 25c on 5c green & blk	55.00	45.00

A7

1918

81	A7 25c blue & black	35.00	30.00

General Issue

A8

A9

Handstamped in Rose or Blue — XV I MCMXIX

1919 *Perf. 12½*

84	A8 (2)q on 2h brown	4.25	4.25
85	A8 5q on 16h green	4.25	4.25
86	A8 10q on 8h rose (Bl)	4.25	4.25
87	A8 25q on 64h blue	4.25	4.25
88	A9 25q on 64h blue	200.00	200.00
89	A8 50q on 32h violet	4.25	4.25
90	A8 1fr on 1.28k org, *bl*	6.00	6.00
	Nos. 84-90 (7)	227.25	227.25

See Nos. J10-J13. Compare with types A10-A14. For overprints see Nos 91-104.

Handstamped in Rose or Blue

1919, Jan. 16

91	A8 (2)q on 2h brown	8.50	8.50
92	A8 5q on 16h green	8.50	8.50
93	A8 10q on 8h rose (Bl)	8.50	8.50
94	A8 25q on 64h blue	26.00	26.00
95	A9 25q on 64h blue	21.00	21.00
96	A8 50q on 32h violet	8.50	8.50
97	A8 1fr on 1.28k org, *bl*	8.50	8.50
	Nos. 91-97 (7)	89.50	89.50

Handstamped in Violet

1919

98	A8 (2)q on 2h brown	10.00	10.00
99	A8 5q on 16h green	10.00	10.00
100	A8 10q on 8h rose	10.00	10.00
101	A8 25q on 64h blue	10.00	10.00
102	A9 25q on 64h blue	100.00	90.00
103	A8 50q on 32h violet	10.00	10.00
104	A8 1fr on 1.28k org, *bl*	10.00	10.00
	Nos. 98-104 (7)	160.00	150.00

No. 50 Overprinted in Violet

SHKODER • 1919

1919 *Perf. 14*

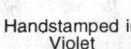

105	A3 1gr on 25q blue	5.00	*5.00*

A10

A11

1919, June 5 *Perf. 11½, 12½*

106	A10 10q on 2h brown	3.50	3.50
107	A11 15q on 8h rose	3.50	3.50
108	A11 20q on 16h green	3.50	3.50
109	A10 25q on 64h blue	3.50	3.50
110	A11 50q on 32h violet	3.50	3.50
111	A11 1fr on 96h orange	3.50	3.50
112	A10 2fr on 1.60k vio, *buff*	14.00	14.00
	Nos. 106-112 (7)	35.00	35.00

Nos. 106-108, 110 exist with inverted surcharge.

A12

A13

Black or Violet Surcharge

1919

113	A12 10q on 8h car	3.50	3.50
114	A12 15q on 8h car (V)	3.50	3.50
115	A13 20q on 16h green	3.50	3.50
116	A13 25q on 35h violet	3.50	3.50
117	A13 50q on 64h blue	9.25	9.25
118	A13 1fr on 96h orange	4.75	4.75
119	A12 2fr on 1.60k vio, *buff*	7.00	7.00
	Nos. 113-119 (7)	35.00	35.00

A14

A15

Overprinted in Blue or Black Without New Value

1920 *Perf. 12½*

120	A14 1q gray (Bl)	22.50	22.50
121	A14 10q rose (Bk)	1.75	2.75
a.	Double overprint	24.00	*27.50*
122	A14 20q brown (Bl)	11.00	11.00
123	A14 25q blue (Bk)	110.00	*110.00*
124	A14 50q brown vio (Bk)	14.00	16.00
	Nos. 120-124 (5)	159.25	*162.25*

Counterfeit overprints exist of Nos. 120-128.

Surcharged with New Value

125	A14 2q on 10q rose (R)	4.25	4.25
126	A14 5q on 10q rose (G)	4.25	4.25
127	A14 25q on 10q rose (Bl)	4.25	4.25
128	A14 50q on 10q rose (Br)	4.25	4.25
	Nos. 125-128 (4)	17.00	17.00

Stamps of type A14 (Portrait of the Prince zu Wied) were not placed in use without overprint or surcharge.

Post Horn Overprinted in Black

1920 *Perf. 14x13*

129	A15 2q orange	3.75	3.25
130	A15 5q deep green	6.25	6.00
131	A15 10q red	11.00	11.00
132	A15 25q light blue	20.00	11.00
133	A15 50q gray green	4.25	4.00
134	A15 1fr claret	4.25	4.00
	Nos. 129-134 (6)	49.50	39.25

Type A15 was never placed in use without post horn or "Besa" overprint.

Stamps of Type A15 (No Post Horn) Overprinted

1921

135	A15 2q orange	3.25	3.25
136	A15 5q deep green	4.50	4.50
137	A15 10q red	7.75	7.75
138	A15 25q light blue	17.50	14.00
139	A15 50q gray green	5.75	5.75
140	A15 1fr claret	4.75	4.75
	Nos. 135-140 (6)	43.50	40.00

For surcharge & overprints see #154, 156-157.

Stamps of these types, and with "TAKSE" overprint, were unauthorized and never placed in use. They are common.

Gjirokaster A18

Korcha — A19

Designs: 5q, Kanina. 10q, Berati. 25q, Bridge at Vezirit. 50q, Rozafat. 2fr, Dursit.

1923 Typo. *Perf. 12½, 11½*

147	A18 2q orange	.60	.60
148	A18 5q yellow green	.50	.50
149	A18 10q carmine	.50	.50
150	A18 25q dark blue	.50	.50
151	A18 50q dark green	.50	.50
152	A19 1fr dark violet	.65	.65
153	A19 2fr olive green	1.75	1.75
	Nos. 147-153 (7)	5.00	5.00

For overprints & surcharges see #158-185, B1-B8.

No. 135 Surcharged — Q 1

1922 *Perf. 14x13*

154	A15 1q on 2q orange	3.00	3.00

Stamps of Type A15 (No Post Horn) Overprinted — BESA

1922

156	A15 5q deep green	3.00	2.50
157	A15 10q red	3.00	2.50

Mbledhje Kushtetuese

Nos. 147-151 Overprinted (top line in Black; diamond in Violet)

1924, Jan. *Perf. 12½*

158	A18 2q red orange	4.00	3.75
159	A18 5q yellow green	4.00	3.75
160	A18 10q carmine	4.00	3.75
161	A18 25q dark blue	4.00	3.75
162	A18 50q dark green	4.00	3.75
	Nos. 158-162 (5)	20.00	18.75

The words "Mbledhje Kushtetuese" are in taller letters on the 25q than on the other values. Opening of the Constituent Assembly.

Counterfeits of Nos. 158 and 161 abound.

No. 147 Surcharged

= →1← =

1924

163	A18 1q on 2q red orange	2.25	2.25

Nos. 163, 147-152 Overprinted

Triumf' i legalitetit

24 Dhetuer 1924

1924

164	A18 1q on 2q orange	1.75	2.50
165	A18 2q orange	1.75	2.50
166	A18 5q yellow green	1.75	2.50
167	A18 10q carmine	1.75	2.50
168	A18 25q dark blue	1.75	2.50
169	A18 50q dark green	1.75	2.50
170	A19 1fr dark violet	1.75	2.50
	Nos. 164-170 (7)	12.25	17.50

Issued to celebrate the return of the Government to the Capital after a revolution.

Nos. 163, 147-152 Overprinted

Republika Shqiptare

21 Kallnduer 1925

1925

171	A18 1q on 2q orange	1.75	2.50
172	A18 2q orange	1.75	2.50
173	A18 5q yellow green	1.75	2.50
174	A18 10q carmine	1.75	2.50

175 A18 25q dark blue		1.75	2.50
176 A18 50q dark green		1.75	2.50
177 A19 1fr dark violet		1.75	2.50
Nos. 171-177 (7)		12.25	17.50

Proclamation of the Republic, Jan. 21, 1925. The date "1921" instead of "1925" occurs once in each sheet of 50.
Counterfeits exist.

Nos. 163, 147-153 Overprinted

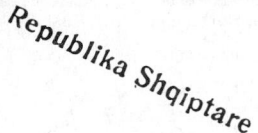

Republika Shqiptare

1925

178 A18 1q on 2q orange	.55	.75
a. Inverted overprint	7.00	7.00
179 A18 2q orange	.55	.75
180 A18 5q yellow green	.55	.75
a. Inverted overprint	7.00	7.00
181 A18 10q carmine	.55	.75
182 A18 25q dark blue	.55	.75
183 A18 50q dark green	.55	.75
184 A19 1fr dark violet	.65	.90
185 A19 2fr olive green	.65	.90
Nos. 178-185 (8)	4.60	6.30

Counterfeits exist.

President Ahmed Zogu
A25 A26

1925 *Perf. 13½, 13½x13*

186 A25 1q orange	.20	.20
187 A25 2q red brown	.20	.20
188 A25 5q green	.20	.20
189 A25 10q rose red	.20	.20
190 A25 15q gray brown	1.50	1.50
191 A25 25q dark blue	.20	.20
192 A25 50q blue green	.55	.55
193 A26 1fr red & ultra	.95	.95
194 A26 2fr green & orange	.95	.95
195 A26 3fr brown & violet	1.50	1.50
196 A26 5fr violet & black	3.75	3.75
Nos. 186-196 (11)	10.20	10.20

No. 193 in ultramarine and brown, and No. 194 in gray and brown were not regularly issued. Value, both $15.
For overprints & surcharges see #197-209, 238-248.

Nos. 186-196 Overprinted in Various Colors

1927

197 A25 1q orange (V)	.60	.40
198 A25 2q red brn (G)	.25	.20
199 A25 5q green (R)	1.25	.20
200 A25 10q rose red (Bl)	.25	.20
201 A25 15q gray brn (G)	7.50	7.50
202 A25 25q dk blue (R)	.60	.20
203 A25 50q blue grn (Bl)	.60	.20
204 A26 1fr red & ultra (Bk)	1.25	.20
205 A26 2fr green & org (Bk)	1.25	.20
206 A26 3fr brown & vio (Bk)	2.00	.55
207 A26 5fr violet & blk (Bk)	3.00	.95
Nos. 197-207 (11)	18.55	10.80

No. 200 exists perf. 11.
For surcharges see Nos. 208-209, 238-240.

Nos. 200, 202 Surcharged in Black or Red

═ 5 ═

1928

208 A25 1q on 10q rose red	.40	.30
a. Inverted surcharge	3.75	3.75
209 A25 5q on 25q dk blue (R)	.40	.30
a. Inverted surcharge	3.75	3.75

King Zog I
A27 A28
Black Overprint

1928 *Perf. 14x13½*

210 A27 1q orange brown	2.25	2.25
211 A27 2q slate	2.25	2.25
212 A27 5q blue green	2.25	2.25
213 A27 10q rose red	2.25	2.25
214 A27 15q bister	12.00	12.00
215 A27 25q deep blue	1.75	1.75
216 A27 50q lilac rose	2.25	2.25

Red Overprint

Perf. 13½x14

217 A28 1fr blue & slate	2.50	2.50
Nos. 210-217 (8)	27.50	27.50

Compare with types A29-A32.

A29 A30

Black or Red Overprint

1928 *Perf. 14x13½*

218 A29 1q orange brown	8.25	8.25
219 A29 2q slate (R)	8.25	8.25
220 A29 5q blue green	7.00	7.00
221 A29 10q rose red	4.50	4.50
222 A29 15q bister	4.75	4.75
223 A29 25q deep blue (R)	4.75	4.75
224 A29 50q lilac rose	5.25	5.25

Perf. 13½x14

225 A30 1fr blue & slate (R)	7.75	7.75
226 A30 2fr green & slate (R)	9.50	9.50
Nos. 218-226 (9)	60.00	60.00

Proclamation of Ahmed Zogu as King of Albania.

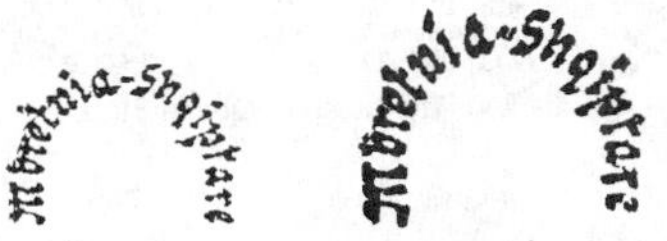

A31 A32

Black Overprint

1928 *Perf. 14x13½*

227 A31 1q orange brown	.35	.35
228 A31 2q slate	.35	.25
229 A31 5q blue green	2.25	.35
230 A31 10q rose red	.35	.25
231 A31 15q bister	9.00	8.00
232 A31 25q deep blue	.35	.25
233 A31 50q lilac rose	.60	.25

Perf. 13½x14

234 A32 1fr blue & slate	1.25	1.10
235 A32 2fr green & slate	1.25	1.25
236 A32 3fr dk red & ol bis	3.50	1.75
237 A32 5fr dull vio & gray	4.50	4.50
Nos. 227-237 (11)	23.75	18.30

The overprint reads "Kingdom of Albania."

Mbr. Shqiptare

Nos. 203, 202, 200 Surcharged in Black

■ 5 ■

1929 *Perf. 13½x13, 11½*

238 A25 1q on 50q blue green	.35	.35
239 A25 5q on 25q dark blue	.35	.35
240 A25 15q on 10q rose red	.55	.50
Nos. 238-240 (3)	1.25	1.20

RROFT-MBRETI

Nos. 186-189, 191-194 Overprinted in Black or Red

8X1929.

1929 *Perf. 11½, 13½*

241 A25 1q orange	4.00	4.00
242 A25 2q red brown	4.00	4.00
243 A25 5q green	4.00	4.00
244 A25 10q rose red	4.00	4.00
245 A25 25q dark blue	4.00	4.00
246 A25 50q blue green (R)	4.75	4.75
247 A26 1fr red & ultra	7.00	7.00
248 A26 2fr green & orange	8.75	8.75
Nos. 241-248 (8)	40.50	40.50

34th birthday of King Zog. The overprint reads "Long live the King."

Lake Butrinto — A33 King Zog I — A34

Zog Bridge A35 Ruin at Zog Manor A36

Perf. 14, 14½

1930, Sept. 1 Photo. Wmk. 220

250 A33 1q slate	.20	.20
251 A33 2q orange red	.20	.20
252 A34 5q yellow green	.20	.20
253 A34 10q carmine	.20	.20
254 A34 15q dark brown	.20	.20
255 A34 25q dark ultra	.20	.20
256 A33 50q slate green	.30	.30
257 A35 1fr violet	.75	.75
258 A35 2fr indigo	.85	.85
259 A36 3fr gray green	1.90	1.90
260 A36 5fr orange brown	3.25	3.25
Nos. 250-260 (11)	8.25	8.25

2nd anniversary of accession of King Zog I.
For overprints see Nos. 261-270, 299-309, J39. For surcharges see Nos. 354-360.

Nos. 250-259 Overprinted in Black

1 1
9 9
2 3
4=24Dhetuer=4

1934, Dec. 24

261 A33 1q slate	2.00	2.00
262 A33 2q orange red	2.00	2.00
263 A34 5q yellow green	2.00	2.00
264 A34 10q carmine	2.00	2.00
265 A34 15q dark brown	2.00	2.00
266 A34 25q dark ultra	2.00	2.00
267 A33 50q slate green	2.00	2.00
268 A35 1fr violet	4.50	4.50
269 A35 2fr indigo	9.00	9.00
270 A36 3fr gray green	12.50	12.50
Nos. 261-270 (10)	40.00	40.00

Tenth anniversary of the Constitution.

Allegory of Death of Skanderbeg A37 Albanian Eagle in Turkish Shackles A38

5q, 25q, 40q, 2fr, Eagle with wings spread.

1937 Unwmk. *Perf. 14*

271 A37 1q brown violet	.20	.20
272 A38 2q brown	.20	.20
273 A38 5q lt green	.25	.25
274 A37 10q olive brown	.30	.30
275 A38 15q rose red	.40	.40
276 A38 25q blue	.70	.70
277 A37 50q deep green	.95	.95
278 A38 1fr violet	1.60	1.60
279 A38 2fr orange brown	4.25	4.25
Nos. 271-279 (9)	8.85	8.85

Souvenir Sheet

280 Sheet of 3	13.00	12.00
a. A37 20q red violet	2.50	2.50
b. A38 30q olive brown	2.50	2.50
c. A38 40q red	2.50	2.50

25th anniv. of independence from Turkey, proclaimed Nov. 26, 1912.

Queen Geraldine and King Zog — A40

1938 *Perf. 14*

281 A40 1q slate violet	.20	.20
282 A40 2q red brown	.20	.20
283 A40 5q green	.20	.20
284 A40 10q olive brown	.35	.35
285 A40 15q rose red	.60	.60
286 A40 25q blue	.85	.85
287 A40 50q Prus green	2.50	2.50
288 A40 1fr purple	5.25	5.25
Nos. 281-288 (8)	10.15	10.15

Souvenir Sheet

289 Sheet of 4	18.00	18.00
a. A40 20q dark red violet	1.75	1.75
b. A40 30q brown olive	1.75	1.75

Wedding of King Zog and Countess Geraldine Apponyi, Apr. 27, 1938.
No. 289 contains 2 each of Nos. 289a, 289b.

Queen Geraldine A42 National Emblems A43

Designs: 10q, 25q, 30q, 1fr, King Zog.

1938

290 A42 1q dp red violet	.20	.20
291 A43 2q red orange	.20	.20
292 A42 5q deep green	.20	.20
293 A42 10q red brown	.20	.20
294 A42 15q deep rose	.55	.55
295 A42 25q deep blue	.70	.70
296 A43 50q gray black	1.75	1.75
297 A42 1fr slate green	6.00	6.00
Nos. 290-297 (8)	9.80	9.80

Souvenir Sheet

298 Sheet of 3	18.00	18.00
b. A43 20q Prussian green	2.00	2.00
c. A42 30q deep violet	2.00	2.00

10th anniv. of royal rule. They were on sale for 3 days (Aug. 30-31, Sept. 1) only, during which their use was required on all mail.
No. 298 contains Nos. 294, 298b, 298c.

Issued under Italian Dominion

Nos. 250-260 Overprinted in Black

Mbledhja Kushtetuëse 12-IV-1939 XVII

1939 Wmk. 220 *Perf. 14*

299 A33 1q slate	.20	.20
300 A33 2q orange red	.20	.20
301 A34 5q yellow green	.20	.20
302 A34 10q carmine	.40	.40
303 A34 15q dark brown	.40	.40
304 A34 25q dark ultra	.60	.60
305 A33 50q slate green	.90	.90
306 A35 1fr violet	1.75	1.75
307 A35 2fr indigo	2.50	2.50
308 A36 3fr gray green	5.00	5.00
309 A36 5fr orange brown	7.00	7.00
Nos. 299-309 (11)	19.15	19.15

Resolution adopted by the Natl. Assembly, Apr. 12, 1939, offering the Albanian Crown to Italy.

Native Costumes
A46 A47 A48

King Victor Emmanuel III
A49 A50

Native Costume
A51

Monastery
A52

Designs: 2fr, Bridge at Vezirit. 3fr, Ancient Columns. 5fr, Amphitheater.

1939 Unwmk. Photo. *Perf. 14*

310	A46	1q blue gray	.20	.20
311	A47	2q olive green	.20	.20
312	A48	3q golden brown	.20	.20
313	A49	5q green	.20	.20
314	A50	10q brown	.20	.20
315	A50	15q crimson	.25	.20
316	A50	25q sapphire	.40	.25
317	A50	30q brt violet	.55	.35
318	A51	50q dull purple	.70	.35
319	A49	65q red brown	1.00	1.00
320	A52	1fr myrtle green	1.25	1.25
321	A52	2fr brown lake	3.00	3.00
322	A52	3fr brown black	5.75	5.75
323	A52	5fr gray violet	12.00	12.00
		Nos. 310-323 (14)	25.90	25.15

For overprints and surcharges see Nos. 331-353.

King Victor Emmanuel III — A56

1942 Photo.

324	A56	5q green	.20	.20
325	A56	10q brown	.35	.35
326	A56	15q rose red	.55	.55
327	A56	25q blue	1.25	1.25
328	A56	65q red brown	1.90	1.90
329	A56	1fr myrtle green	3.50	3.50
330	A56	2fr gray violet	7.75	7.75
		Nos. 324-330 (7)	15.50	15.50

Conquest of Albania by Italy, 3rd anniv.

No. 311 Surcharged in Black **1 QIND**

331	A47	1q on 2q olive green	1.00	1.00

Issued under German Administration

Stamps of 1939 Overprinted in Carmine or Brown **14 Shtator 1943**

1943

332	A47	2q olive green	1.10	1.40
333	A48	3q golden brown	1.10	1.40
334	A49	5q green	1.10	1.40
335	A50	10q brown	1.10	1.40
336	A50	15q crimson (Br)	1.10	1.40
337	A50	25q sapphire	1.10	1.40
338	A50	30q brt violet	1.10	1.40
339	A49	65q red brown	1.25	2.25
340	A52	1fr myrtle green	7.75	10.00
341	A52	2fr brown lake	10.50	*20.00*
342	A52	3fr brown black	45.00	*52.50*

Surcharged with New Values

343	A48	1q on 3q gldn brn	1.10	1.40
344	A49	50q on 65q red brn	1.25	2.25
		Nos. 332-344 (13)	74.55	*98.20*

Proclamation of Albanian independence.

The overprint "14 Shtator 1943" on Nos. 324 to 328 is private and fraudulent.

Independent State

Nos. 312 to 317 and 319 to 321 Surcharged with New Value and Bars in Black or Carmine, and:

QEVERIJA
DEMOKRAT.
E SHQIPERISE
22-X-1944

1945

345	A48	30q on 3q gldn brn	3.50	3.50
346	A49	40q on 5q green	3.50	3.50
347	A50	50q on 10q brown	3.50	3.50
348	A50	60q on 15q crimson	3.50	3.50
349	A50	80q on 25q saph (C)	3.50	3.50
350	A50	1fr on 30q brt vio	3.50	3.50
351	A49	2fr on 65q red brn	3.50	3.50
352	A52	3fr on 1fr myr grn	3.50	3.50
353	A52	5fr on 2fr brn lake	3.50	3.50
		Nos. 345-353 (9)	31.50	31.50

"DEMOKRATIKE" is not abbreviated on Nos. 352 and 353.

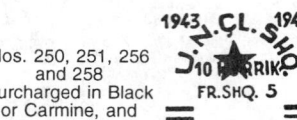

Nos. 250, 251, 256 and 258 Surcharged in Black or Carmine, and

1943 U.N.ÇL.SHQ. 1945
10 KORRIK
FR.SHQ. 5

1945 Wmk. 220

354	A33	30q on 1q slate	1.25	1.25
355	A33	60q on 1q slate	1.50	1.50
356	A33	80q on 1q slate	1.75	1.75
357	A33	1fr on 1q slate	2.50	2.50
358	A33	2fr on 2q org red	3.25	3.25
359	A33	3fr on 50q sl grn	8.50	8.50
360	A35	5fr on 2fr indigo	11.00	11.00
		Nos. 354-360 (7)	29.75	29.75

Albanian Natl. Army of Liberation, 2nd anniv.

The surcharge on No. 360 is condensed to fit the size of the stamp.

Country House, Labinot — A57

40q, 60q, Bridge at Berat. 1fr, 3fr, Permet.

Perf. 11½

1945, Nov. 28 Unwmk. Typo.

361	A57	20q bluish green	.20	.20
362	A57	30q deep orange	.40	.40
363	A57	40q brown	.40	.40
364	A57	60q red violet	.60	.60
365	A57	1fr rose red	1.25	1.25
366	A57	3fr dark blue	6.00	6.00
		Nos. 361-366 (6)	8.85	8.85

Counterfeits: lithographed; genuine: typographed.

For overprints and surcharges see Nos. 367-378, 418-423, B28-B33.

Nos. 361 to 366 Overprinted in Black

ASAMBLEJA
KUSHTETUESE
10 KALLHUER 1946

1946

367	A57	20q bluish green	.60	.60
368	A57	30q deep orange	.60	.60
369	A57	40q brown	.95	.95
370	A57	60q red violet	1.75	1.75
371	A57	1fr rose red	4.75	4.75
372	A57	3fr dark blue	7.50	7.50
		Nos. 367-372 (6)	16.15	16.15

Convocation of the Constitutional Assembly, Jan. 10, 1946.

People's Republic

Nos. 361 to 366 Overprinted in Black

REPUBLIKA POPULLORE
E
SHQIPERISE

1946 *Perf. 11*

373	A57	20q bluish green	.75	.75
374	A57	30q deep orange	1.25	1.25
375	A57	40q brown	1.75	1.75
376	A57	60q red violet	2.75	2.75
377	A57	1fr rose red	5.00	5.00
378	A57	3fr dark blue	8.50	8.50
		Nos. 373-378 (6)	20.00	20.00

Proclamation of the Albanian People's Republic.

For surcharges see Nos. 418-423.

Globe, Dove and Olive Branch — A60

Perf. 11½, Imperf.

1946, Mar. 8 Typo.

Denomination in Black

379	A60	20q lilac & dull red	.20	.30
380	A60	40q dp lilac & dull red	.35	.50
381	A60	50q violet & dull red	.50	.75
382	A60	1fr lt blue & red	.80	1.00
383	A60	2fr dk blue & red	1.60	2.00
		Nos. 379-383 (5)	3.45	4.55

International Women's Congress.

Counterfeits exist.

Athletes with Shot and Indian Club — A61

Perf. 11½

1946, Oct. 6 Litho. Unwmk.

384	A61	1q grnsh black	6.00	6.00
385	A61	2q green	6.00	6.00
386	A61	5q brown	6.00	6.00
387	A61	10q crimson	6.00	6.00
388	A61	20q ultra	6.00	6.00
389	A61	40q rose violet	6.00	6.00
390	A61	1fr deep orange	10.00	10.00
		Nos. 384-390 (7)	46.00	46.00

Balkan Games, Tirana, Oct. 6-13.

Qemal Stafa — A62

1947, May 5 *Perf. 12½x11½*

391	A62	20q brn & yel brn	2.50	3.00
392	A62	28q dk blue & blue	2.50	3.00
393	A62	40q brn blk & gray brn	2.50	3.00
a.		Souvenir sheet, #391-393	6.50	6.50
		Nos. 391-393 (3)	7.50	9.00

5th anniv. of the death of Qemal Stafa.

Young Railway Laborers A64

1947, May 16 *Perf. 11½*

395	A64	1q brn blk & gray brn	1.25	.60
396	A64	4q dk green & green	1.25	.60
397	A64	10q blk brn & bis brn	1.25	.60
398	A64	15q dk red & red	1.50	.60
399	A64	20q indigo & bl gray	2.00	.90
400	A64	28q dk blue & blue	3.00	.90
401	A64	40q brn vio & rose vio	7.75	4.25
402	A64	68q dk brn & org brn	12.00	7.75
		Nos. 395-402 (8)	30.00	16.20

Issued to publicize the construction of the Durres Elbasan Railway by Albanian youths.

The 4q, 20q, 28q and 40q exist perf 13x12½.

Citizens Led by Hasim Zeneli — A65

Enver Hoxha and Vasil Shanto — A66

Vojo Kushi — A68

Inauguration of Vithkuq Brigade A67

1947, July 10 Litho.

403	A65	16q brn org & red brn	3.25	3.25
404	A66	20q org brn & dk brn	3.25	3.25
405	A67	28q blue & dk blue	3.50	3.50
406	A68	40q lilac & dk brn	5.00	5.00
		Nos. 403-406 (4)	15.00	15.00

4th anniv. of the formation of Albania's army, July 10, 1943.

Conference Building Ruins, Peza — A69

Disabled Soldiers — A70

1947, Sept. 16

407	A69	2 l red violet	2.25	2.00
408	A69	2.50 l deep blue	2.25	2.00

Peza Conf., Sept. 16, 1942, 5th anniv.

1947, Nov. 17 *Perf. 12½x11½*

408A	A70	1 l red	3.50	3.50

Disabled War Veterans Cong., Nov. 14-20, 1947.

A71

A73

Designs: 2 l, Banquet. 2.50 l, Peasants rejoicing.

Perf. 11½x12½, 12½x11½

1947, Nov. 17 Unwmk.

409	A71	1.50 l dull violet	2.50	2.50
410	A71	2 l brown	2.50	2.50
411	A71	2.50 l blue	2.50	2.50
412	A73	3 l rose red	2.50	2.50
		Nos. 409-412 (4)	10.00	10.00

Agrarian reform law of Nov. 17, 1946, 1st anniv.

Burning Farm Buildings A74

Designs: 2.50 l, Trench scene. 5 l, Firing line. 8 l, Winter advance. 12 l, Infantry column.

1947, Nov. 29 ***Perf. 11½x12½***

413 A74	1.50 l	red	1.60	1.60
414 A74	2.50 l	rose brown	2.00	2.00
415 A74	5 l	blue	2.50	2.50
416 A74	8 l	purple	4.00	4.00
417 A74	12 l	brown	6.00	6.00
		Nos. 413-417 (5)	16.10	16.10

3rd anniv. of Albania's liberation.

Nos. 373 to 378 Surcharged with New Value and Bars in Black

1948, Feb. 22 ***Perf. 11***

418 A57	50q	on 30q deep org	.25	.25
419 A57	1 l	on 20q bluish grn	.50	.50
420 A57	2.50 l	on 60q red vio	1.00	1.00
421 A57	3 l	on 1fr rose red	1.25	1.25
422 A57	5 l	on 3fr dark blue	2.25	2.25
423 A57	12 l	on 40q brown	4.75	4.75
		Nos. 418-423 (6)	10.00	10.00

The two bars consist of four type squares each set close together.

Map, Train and Construction Workers A75

1948, June 1 **Litho.** ***Perf. 11½***

424 A75	50q	dk car rose	1.10	.55
425 A75	1 l	lt green & blk	1.25	.55
426 A75	1.50 l	deep rose	1.25	.55
427 A75	2.50 l	org brn & dk brn	1.25	.55
428 A75	5 l	dull blue	2.00	1.10
429 A75	8 l	salmon & dk brn	4.75	2.00
430 A75	12 l	red vio & dk vio	6.50	2.25
431 A75	20 l	olive gray	12.50	5.00
		Nos. 424-431 (8)	30.60	12.55

Issued to publicize the construction of the Durres-Tirana Railway.

Marching Soldiers A76

Design: 8 l, Battle scene.

1948, July 10

432 A76	2.50 l	yellow brown	1.25	1.25
433 A76	5 l	dark blue	1.75	1.75
434 A76	8 l	violet gray	3.25	3.25
		Nos. 432-434 (3)	6.25	6.25

5th anniv. of the formation of Albania's army.

Bricklayer, Flag, Globe and "Industry" A77

Map and Soldier A78

1949, May 1 **Photo.** ***Perf. 12½x12***

435 A77	2.50 l	olive brown	.30	.30
436 A77	5 l	blue	.70	.70
437 A77	8 l	violet brown	1.10	1.10
		Nos. 435-437 (3)	2.10	2.10

Issued to publicize Labor Day, May 1, 1949.

1949, July 10 **Unwmk.**

438 A78	2.50 l	brown	.50	.50
439 A78	5 l	light ultra	.75	.75
440 A78	8 l	brown orange	1.50	1.50
		Nos. 438-440 (3)	2.75	2.75

6th anniv. of the formation of Albania's army.

Enver Hoxha A79

Albanian Citizen and Spasski Tower, Kremlin A80

1949, Oct. 16 **Engr.** ***Perf. 12½***

441 A79	50q	purple	.20	.20
442 A79	1 l	dull green	.20	.20
443 A79	1.50 l	car lake	.20	.20
444 A79	2.50 l	brown	.30	.20
445 A79	5 l	violet blue	.65	.20
446 A79	8 l	sepia	1.10	.90
447 A79	12 l	rose lilac	2.50	1.50
448 A79	20 l	gray blue	5.00	2.50
		Nos. 441-448 (8)	10.15	5.90

Perf. 12½x12

1949, Sept. 10 **Photo.**

449 A80	2.50 l	orange brown	.50	.50
450 A80	5 l	deep ultra	1.00	1.00

Albanian-Soviet friendship.

Albanian Soldier and Flag — A81

Battle Scene — A82

1949, Nov. 29 **Unwmk.** ***Perf. 12***

451 A81	2.50 l	brown	.25	.25
452 A82	3 l	dark red	.50	.50
453 A81	5 l	violet	.60	.60
454 A82	8 l	black	1.75	1.75
		Nos. 451-454 (4)	3.10	3.10

Fifth anniversary of Albania's liberation.

Joseph V. Stalin — A83

Symbols of UPU and Postal Transport — A84

1949, Dec. 21

455 A83	2.50 l	dark brown	.45	.55
456 A83	5 l	violet blue	1.25	1.25
457 A83	8 l	rose brown	2.00	2.25
		Nos. 455-457 (3)	3.70	4.05

70th anniv. of the birth of Joseph V. Stalin.

Canceled to Order

Beginning in 1950, Albania sold some issues in sheets canceled to order. Values in second column when much less than unused are for "CTO" copies. Postally used stamps are valued at slightly less than, or the same as, unused.

Catalogue values for unused stamps in this section, from this point to the end of the section, are for Never Hinged items.

1950, July 1 **Photo.** ***Perf. 12x12½***

458 A84	5 l	blue	2.25	1.25
459 A84	8 l	rose brown	3.25	1.75
460 A84	12 l	sepia	4.00	2.25
		Nos. 458-460 (3)	9.50	5.25

75th anniv. (in 1949) of the UPU.

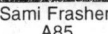

Sami Frasheri A85

Arms and Albanian Flags A86

Authors: 2.50 l, Andon Zako. 3 l, Naim Frasheri. 5 l, Kostandin Kristoforidhi.

1950, Nov. 5 ***Perf. 14***

461 A85	2 l	dark green	.70	.15
462 A85	2.50 l	red brown	.95	.20
463 A85	3 l	brown carmine	1.40	.25
464 A85	5 l	deep blue	2.00	.60
		Nos. 461-464 (4)	5.05	1.20

"Jubilee of the Writers of the Renaissance."

1951, Jan. 11 **Engr.** ***Perf. 14x13½***

465 A86	2.50 l	brown carmine	1.10	.25
466 A86	5 l	deep blue	2.00	.50
467 A86	8 l	sepia	3.00	1.00
		Nos. 465-467 (3)	6.10	1.75

5th anniv. of the formation of the Albanian People's Republic.

Skanderbeg A87

Enver Hoxha and Congress of Permet A88

1951, Mar. 1

468 A87	2.50 l	brown	.75	.25
469 A87	5 l	violet	1.50	.50
470 A87	8 l	olive bister	2.50	1.00
		Nos. 468-470 (3)	4.75	1.75

483rd anniv. of the death of George Castriota (Skanderbeg).

1951, May 24 **Photo.** ***Perf. 12***

471 A88	2.50 l	dark brown	.45	.20
472 A88	3 l	rose brown	.70	.30
473 A88	5 l	violet blue	1.10	.50
474 A88	8 l	rose lilac	1.90	.80
		Nos. 471-474 (4)	4.15	1.80

Congress of Permet, 7th anniversary.

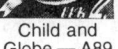

Child and Globe — A89

Weighing Baby — A90

1951, July 16

475 A89	2 l	green	1.00	.30
476 A90	2.50 l	brown	1.50	.40
477 A90	3 l	red	2.00	.50
478 A89	5 l	blue	3.00	.80
		Nos. 475-478 (4)	7.50	2.00

Intl. Children's Day, June 1, 1951.

Enver Hoxha and Birthplace of Albanian Communist Party — A91

1951, Nov. 8 **Photo.** ***Perf. 14***

479 A91	2.50 l	olive brown	.30	.25
480 A91	3 l	rose brown	.45	.35
481 A91	5 l	dark slate blue	.70	.60
482 A91	8 l	black	1.00	.85
		Nos. 479-482 (4)	2.45	2.05

Albanian Communist Party, 10th anniv.

Battle Scene — A92

Designs: 5 l, Schoolgirl, "Agriculture and Industry." 8 l, Four portraits.

1951, Nov. 28 ***Perf. 12x12½***

483 A92	2.50 l	brown	.40	.20
484 A92	5 l	blue	.65	.40
485 A92	8 l	brown carmine	1.40	.75
		Nos. 483-485 (3)	2.45	1.35

Albanian Communist Youth Org., 10th anniv.

Albanian Heroes (Haxhija, Lezhe, Giyebegej, Mezi and Dedej) — A93

Nos. 486-489 each show five "Heroes of the People"; No. 490 shows two (Stafa and Shanto).

1950, Dec. 25 **Unwmk.** ***Perf. 14***

486 A93	2 l	dark green	.60	.20
487 A93	2.50 l	purple	.80	.20
488 A93	3 l	scarlet	1.25	.25
489 A93	5 l	brt blue	1.75	.35
490 A93	8 l	olive brown	4.50	1.00
		Nos. 486-490 (5)	8.90	2.00

6th anniv. of Albania's liberation.

Tobacco Factory, Shkoder — A94

Composite, Lenin Hydroelectric Plant — A95

Designs: 1 l, Canal. 2.50 l, Textile factory. 3 l, "8 November" Cannery. 5 l, Motion Picture Studio, Tirana. 8 l, Stalin Textile Mill, Tirana. 20 l, Central Hydroelectric Dam.

1953, Aug. 1 ***Perf. 12x12½, 12½x12***

491 A94	50q	red brown	.20	.20
492 A94	1 l	dull green	.20	.20
493 A94	2.50 l	brown	.60	.20
494 A94	3 l	rose brown	.85	.20
495 A94	5 l	blue	1.25	.20
496 A94	8 l	brown olive	2.25	.20
497 A95	12 l	deep plum	3.50	.35
498 A94	20 l	slate blue	6.25	.50
		Nos. 491-498 (8)	15.10	2.05

Liberation Scene — A96

1954, Nov. 29 ***Perf. 12x12½***

499 A96	50q	brown violet	.20	.20
500 A96	1 l	olive green	.25	.20
501 A96	2.50 l	yellow brown	.65	.20
502 A96	3 l	carmine rose	.80	.20
503 A96	5 l	gray blue	1.10	.20
504 A96	8 l	rose brown	2.00	.55
		Nos. 499-504 (6)	5.00	1.55

10th anniversary of Albania's liberation.

School — A97

Pandeli Sotiri, Petro Nini Luarasi, Nuci Naci — A98

1956, Feb. 23 **Unwmk.**

505 A97 2 l rose violet .35 .20
506 A98 2.50 l lt green .50 .20
507 A98 5 l ultra 1.10 .20
508 A97 10 l brt grnsh blue 2.25 .35
Nos. 505-508 (4) 4.20 .95

Opening of the 1st Albanian school, 70th anniv.

Flags — A99

Designs: 5 l, Labor Party headquarters, Tirana. 8 l, Marx and Lenin.

1957, June 1 Engr. ***Perf. 11½x11***

509 A99 2.50 l brown .45 .20
510 A99 5 l lt violet blue .90 .20
511 A99 8 l rose lilac 2.00 .20
Nos. 509-511 (3) 3.35 .60

Albania's Labor Party, 15th anniv.

Congress Emblem A100

1957, Oct. 4 Unwmk. ***Perf. 11½***

512 A100 2.50 l gray brown .50 .20
513 A100 3 l rose red .70 .20
514 A100 5 l dark blue .90 .20
515 A100 8 l green 1.60 .30
Nos. 512-515 (4) 3.70 .90

4th Intl. Trade Union Cong., Leipzig, Oct. 4-15.

Lenin and Cruiser "Aurora" A101

1957, Nov. 7 Litho. ***Perf. 10½***

516 A101 2.50 l violet brown .45 .20
517 A101 5 l violet blue .95 .20
518 A101 8 l gray 1.25 .30
Nos. 516-518 (3) 2.65 .70

40th anniv. of the Russian Revolution.

Albanian Fighter Holding Flag A102

Naum Veqilharxhj A103

1957, Nov. 28 ***Perf. 10½***

519 A102 1.50 l magenta .40 .20
520 A102 2.50 l brown .60 .20
521 A102 5 l blue 1.00 .20
522 A102 8 l green 2.00 .30
Nos. 519-522 (4) 4.00 .90

Proclamation of independence, 45th anniv.

1958, Feb. 1 **Unwmk.**

523 A103 2.50 l dark brown .50 .20
524 A103 5 l violet blue 1.00 .20
525 A103 8 l rose lilac 2.00 .30
Nos. 523-525 (3) 3.50 .70

160th anniv. of the birth of Naum Veqilharxhj, patriot and writer.

Buying Sets
It is often less expensive to purchase complete sets than individual stamps that make up the set.

Luigi Gurakuqi A104

Soldiers A105

1958, Apr. 15 Photo. ***Perf. 10½***

526 A104 1.50 l dark green .30 .20
527 A104 2.50 l brown .40 .20
528 A104 5 l blue .75 .20
529 A104 8 l sepia 1.50 .20
Nos. 526-529 (4) 2.95 .80

Transfer of the ashes of Luigi Gurakuqi.

1958, July 10 **Litho.**

2.50 l, 11 l, Airman, sailor, soldier and tank.

530 A105 1.50 l blue green .20 .20
531 A105 2.50 l dark red brown .30 .20
532 A105 8 l rose red .95 .20
533 A105 11 l bright blue 1.50 .25
Nos. 530-533 (4) 2.95 .85

15th anniversary of Albanian army.

Cerciz Topulli and Mihal Grameno — A106

Buildings and Tree — A107

1958, July 1

534 A106 2.50 l dk olive bister .35 .20
535 A107 3 l green .45 .20
536 A106 5 l blue .75 .20
537 A107 8 l red brown 1.25 .20
Nos. 534-537 (4) 2.80 .80

50th anniversary, Battle of Mashkullore.

Ancient Amphitheater and Goddess of Butrinto A108

1959, Jan. 25 Litho. ***Perf. 10½***

538 A108 2.50 l redsh brown .65 .20
539 A108 6.50 l lt blue green 1.60 .20
540 A108 11 l dark blue 2.50 .40
Nos. 538-540 (3) 4.75 .80

Cultural Monuments Week.

Frederic Joliot-Curie and World Peace Congress Emblem A109

Basketball A110

1959, July 1 **Unwmk.**

541 A109 1.50 l carmine rose 1.00 .20
542 A109 2.50 l rose violet 1.75 .30
543 A109 11 l blue 5.00 1.50
Nos. 541-543 (3) 7.75 2.00

10th anniv. of the World Peace Movement.

1959, Nov. 20 ***Perf. 10½***

Sports: 2.50 l, Soccer, 5 l, Runner. 11 l, Man and woman runners with torch and flags.

544 A110 1.50 l bright violet .40 .20
545 A110 2.50 l emerald .55 .20
546 A110 5 l carmine rose 1.50 .25
547 A110 11 l ultra 4.00 1.75
Nos. 544-547 (4) 6.45 2.40

1st Albanian Spartacist Games.

Fighter and Flags A111

Mother and Child, UN Emblem A112

Designs: 2.50 l, Miner with drill standing guard. 3 l, Farm woman with sheaf of grain. 6.50 l, Man and woman in laboratory.

1959, Nov. 29

548 A111 1.50 l brt carmine .50 .20
549 A111 2.50 l red brown .70 .20
550 A111 3 l brt blue green .90 .20
551 A111 6.50 l bright red 2.00 .25
a. Souvenir sheet 6.00 6.00
Nos. 548-551 (4) 4.10 .85

15th anniversary of Albania's liberation.

No. 551a contains one each of Nos. 548-551, imperf. and all in bright carmine. Inscribed ribbon frame of sheet and frame lines for each stamp are blue green.

1959, Dec. 5 **Unwmk.**

552 A112 5 l lt grnsh blue 3.00 .55
a. Miniature sheet 4.00 4.00

10th anniv. (in 1958) of the signing of the Universal Declaration of Human Rights.

No. 552a contains one imperf. stamp similar to No. 552; ornamental border.

Woman with Olive Branch A113

Alexander Moissi A114

1960, Mar. 8 Litho. ***Perf. 10½***

553 A113 2.50 l chocolate .45 .20
554 A113 11 l rose carmine 2.00 .30

50th anniv. of Intl. Women's Day, Mar. 8.

1960, Apr. 20

555 A114 3 l deep brown .35 .20
556 A114 11 l Prus green 1.40 .25

80th anniversary of the birth of Alexander Moissi (Moisiu) (1880-1935), German actor.

Lenin A115

School Building A116

1960, Apr. 22

557 A115 4 l Prus blue 1.60 .20
558 A115 11 l lake 3.50 .20

90th anniversary of birth of Lenin.

1960, May 30 Litho. ***Perf. 10½***

559 A116 5 l green 1.25 .20
560 A116 6.50 l plum 1.25 .20

1st Albanian secondary school, 50th anniv.

Soldier on Guard Duty — A117

Liberation Monument, Tirana, Family and Policeman — A118

1960, May 12 Unwmk. ***Perf. 10½***

561 A117 1.50 l carmine rose .30 .20
562 A117 11 l Prus blue 1.60 .20

15th anniversary of the Frontier Guards.

1960, May 14

563 A118 1.50 l green .30 .20
564 A118 8.50 l brown 1.60 .25

15th anniversary of the People's Police.

Congress Site — A119

Pashko Vasa — A120

1960, Mar. 25

565 A119 2.50 l sepia .25 .20
566 A119 7.50 l dull blue 1.00 .25

40th anniversary, Congress of Louchnia.

1960, May 5

Designs: 1.50 l, Jani Vreto. 6.50 l, Sami Frasheri. 11 l, Page of statutes of association.

567 A120 1 l gray olive .35 .20
568 A120 1.50 l brown .50 .20
569 A120 6.50 l blue 1.10 .20
570 A120 11 l rose red 2.00 .20
Nos. 567-570 (4) 3.95 .80

80th anniv. (in 1959) of the Association of Albanian Authors.

Albanian Fighter and Cannon A121

TU-104 Plane, Clock Tower, Tirana, and Kremlin, Moscow A122

1960, Aug. 2 Litho. ***Perf. 10½***

571 A121 1.50 l olive brown .40 .20
572 A121 2.50 l maroon .50 .20
573 A121 5 l dark blue 1.25 .20
Nos. 571-573 (3) 2.15 .60

Battle of Viona (against Italian troops), 40th anniv.

1960, Aug. 18

574 A122 1 l redsh brown .40 .20
575 A122 7.50 l brt grnsh blue 1.50 .35
576 A122 11.50 l gray 2.75 .60
Nos. 574-576 (3) 4.65 1.15

TU-104 flights, Moscow-Tirana, 2nd anniv.

Rising Sun and Federation Emblem A123

Ali Kelmendi A124

1960, Nov. 10 Unwmk. ***Perf. 10½***

577 A123 1.50 l ultra .30 .20
578 A123 8.50 l red 1.10 .20

Intl. Youth Federation, 15th anniv.

1960, Dec. 5 Litho. ***Perf. 10½***

579 A124 1.50 l pale gray grn .30 .20
580 A124 11 l dull rose lake .70 .20

Ali Kelmendi, communist leader, 60th birthday.

Flags of Russia and Albania and Clasped Hands
A125

Marx and Lenin
A126

1961, Jan. 10 Unwmk. *Perf. 10½*

581 A125 2 l violet .30 .20
582 A125 8 l dull red brown .70 .20

15th anniv. of the Albanian-Soviet Friendship Society.

1961, Feb. 13 Litho.

583 A126 2 l rose red .30 .20
584 A126 8 l violet blue 1.10 .20

Fourth Communist Party Congress.

Man from Shkoder
A127

Otter
A128

Costumes: 1.50 l, Woman from Shkoder. 6.50 l, Man from Lume. 11 l, Woman from Mirdite.

1961, Apr. 28 *Perf. 10½*

585 A127 1 l slate .35 .20
586 A127 1.50 l dull claret .60 .20
587 A127 6.50 l ultra 1.90 .20
588 A127 11 l red 3.25 .35
Nos. 585-588 (4) 6.10 .95

1961, June 25 Unwmk. *Perf. 10½*

Designs: 6.50 l, Badger. 11 l, Brown bear.

589 A128 2.50 l grayish blue 2.00 .25
590 A128 6.50 l blue green 4.50 .50
591 A128 11 l dark red brown 8.00 .85
Nos. 589-591 (3) 14.50 1.60

Dalmatian Pelicans
A129

Cyclamen
A130

1961, Sept. 30 *Perf. 14*

592 A129 1.50 l shown 2.00 .20
593 A129 7.50 l Gray herons 4.00 .40
594 A129 11 l Little egret 6.00 .60
Nos. 592-594 (3) 12.00 1.20

1961, Oct. 27 Litho.

595 A130 1.50 l shown 2.00 .20
596 A130 8 l Forsythia 3.50 .20
597 A130 11 l Lily 4.50 .40
Nos. 595-597 (3) 10.00 .80

Milosh G. Nikolla — A131

Flag with Marx and Lenin — A132

1961, Oct. 30 *Perf. 14*

598 A131 50q violet brown .30 .20
599 A131 8.50 l Prus green 1.25 .25

50th anniv. of the birth of Milosh Gjergi Nikolla, poet.

1961, Nov. 8

600 A132 2.50 l vermilion .50 .20
601 A132 7.50 l dull red brown 1.00 .25

20th anniv. of the founding of Albania's Communist Party.

Worker, Farm Woman and Emblem
A133

Yuri Gagarin and Vostok 1
A134

1961, Nov. 23 Unwmk. *Perf. 14*

602 A133 2.50 l violet blue .50 .20
603 A133 7.50 l rose claret 1.00 .30

20th anniv. of the Albanian Workers' Party.

1962, Feb. 15 Unwmk. *Perf. 14*

604 A134 50q blue .35 .20
605 A134 4 l red lilac 1.60 .20
606 A134 11 l dk slate grn 3.25 .65
Nos. 604-606 (3) 5.20 1.05

1st manned space flight, made by Yuri A. Gagarin, Soviet astronaut, Apr. 12, 1961.
Nos. 604-606 were overprinted with an over-all yellow tint and with "POSTA AJRORE" (Air Mail) in maroon in 1962. Value, set $50.

Petro Nini Luarasi
A135

Malaria Eradication Emblem
A136

1962, Feb. 28 Litho.

607 A135 50q Prus blue .25 .20
608 A135 8.50 l olive gray 1.50 .25

50th anniv. (in 1961) of the death of Petro Nini Luarasi, Albanian patriot.

1962, Apr. 30 Unwmk. *Perf. 14*

609 A136 1.50 l brt green .20 .20
610 A136 2.50 l brown red .20 .20
611 A136 10 l red lilac .55 .25
612 A136 11 l blue .90 .35
Nos. 609-612 (4) 1.85 1.00

WHO drive to eradicate malaria.
Souvenir sheets, perf. and imperf., contain one each of Nos. 609-612. Value $20 each.
Nos. 609-612 imperf., value, set $14.

Camomile
A137

Woman Diver
A138

Medicinal plants.

1962, May 10

613 A137 50q shown .20 .20
614 A137 8 l Linden .75 .25
615 A137 11.50 l Garden sage 1.75 .50
Nos. 613-615 (3) 2.70 .95

Value, imperf. set $12.

1962, May 31 *Perf. 14*

2.50 l, Pole vault. 3 l, Mt. Fuji & torch, horiz. 9 l, Woman javelin thrower. 10 l, Shot putting.

616 A138 50q brt grnsh bl & blk .20 .20
617 A138 2.50 l gldn brn & sepia .20 .20
618 A138 3 l blue & gray .40 .20
619 A138 9 l rose car & dk brn 1.10 .25
620 A138 10 l olive & blk 1.25 .30
Nos. 616-620 (5) 3.15 1.15

1964 Olympic Games, Tokyo. Value, imperf. set $25. A 15 l (like 3 l) exists in souv. sheet, perf. and imperf.

Globe and Orbits — A139

Dog Laika and Sputnik 2 — A140

Designs: 1.50 l, Rocket to the sun. 20 l, Lunik 3 photographing far side of the moon.

1962, June Unwmk. *Perf. 14*

621 A139 50q violet & org .20 .20
622 A140 1 l blue grn & brn .35 .20
623 A140 1.50 l yellow & ver .50 .20
624 A139 20 l magenta & bl 3.50 .80
Nos. 621-624 (4) 4.55 1.40

Russian space explorations.
#621-624 exist imperforate in changed colors.
Two miniature sheets exist, containing one 14-lek picturing Sputnik 1. The perforated 14-lek is yellow and brown; the imperf. red and brown.

Soccer Game, Map of South America — A141

2.50 l, 15 l, Soccer game and globe as ball.

1962, July Litho.

625 A141 1 l org & dk pur .20 .20
626 A141 2.50 l emer & bluish grn .25 .20
627 A141 6.50 l lt brn & pink .90 .20
628 A141 15 l bluish grn & mar 1.50 .35
Nos. 625-628 (4) 2.85 .95

Issued to commemorate the World Soccer Championships, Chile, May 30-June 17.
Exist imperforate in changed colors.
Two miniature sheets exist, each containing a single 20-lek in design similar to A141. The perf. sheet is brown and green; the imperf., brown and orange.

Map of Europe and Albania
A142

Woman of Dardhe
A143

Designs: 1 l, 2.50 l, Map of Adriatic Sea and Albania and Roman statue.

1962, Aug.

630 A142 50q multicolored .40 .35
631 A142 1 l ultra & red 1.00 .80
632 A142 2.50 l blue & red 3.00 2.50
633 A142 11 l multicolored 6.00 5.00
Nos. 630-633 (4) 10.40 8.65

Tourist propaganda. Imperforates in changed colors exist.
Miniature sheets containing a 7 l and 8 l stamp, perf. and imperf., exist.

1962, Sept.

Regional Costumes: 1 l, Man from Devoll. 2.50 l, Woman from Lunxheri. 14 l, Man from Gjirokaster.

635 A143 50q car, bl & pur .20 .20
636 A143 1 l red brn & ocher .20 .20
637 A143 2.50 l vio, yel grn & blk .65 .20
638 A143 14 l red brn & pale grn 2.25 .50
Nos. 635-638 (4) 3.30 1.10

Value, imperf. set $18.

Chamois
A144

Ismail Qemali
A145

Animals: 1 l, Lynx, horiz. 1.50 l, Wild boar, horiz. 15 l, 20 l, Roe deer.

1962, Oct. 24 Unwmk. *Perf. 14*

639 A144 50q sl grn & dk pur .60 .20
640 A144 1 l orange & blk 1.10 .20
641 A144 1.50 l red brn & blk 1.50 .20
642 A144 15 l yel ol & red brn 7.75 1.00
Nos. 639-642 (4) 10.95 1.60

Miniature Sheet

643 A144 20 l yel ol & red brn 50.00 50.00

Imperfs. in changed colors, value #639-642 $25, #643 $25.

1962, Dec. 28 Litho.

Designs: 1 l, Albania eagle. 16 l, Eagle over fortress formed by "RPSH."

644 A145 1 l red & red brn .30 .20
645 A145 3 l org brn & blk .55 .20
646 A145 16 l dk car rose & blk 3.50 .50
Nos. 644-646 (3) 4.35 .90

50th anniv. of independence. Imperfs. in changed colors, value, set $12.50.

Monument of October Revolution
A146

Henri Dunant, Cross, Globe and Nurse
A147

1963, Jan. 5 Unwmk. *Perf. 14*

647 A146 5 l shown .50 .20
648 A146 10 l Lenin statue 1.25 .25

October Revolution (Russia, 1917), 45th anniv.

1963, Jan 25 Unwmk. *Perf. 14*

649 A147 1.50 l rose lake, red & blk .25 .20
650 A147 2.50 l lt bl, red & blk .30 .20
651 A147 6 l emerald, red & blk .75 .25
652 A147 10 l dull yel, red & blk 1.40 .35
Nos. 649-652 (4) 2.70 1.00

Cent. of the Geneva Conf., which led to the establishment of the Intl. Red Cross in 1864.
Imperfs. in changed colors, value, set $20.

Stalin and Battle of Stalingrad
A148

Andrian G. Nikolayev
A149

1963, Feb. 2

653 A148 8 l dk green & slate 4.00 .50

Battle of Stalingrad, 20th anniv. See #C67.

1963, Feb. 28 **Litho.**

Designs: 7.50 l, Vostoks 3 and 4 and globe, horiz. 20 l, Pavel R. Popovich. 25 l, Nikolayev, Popovich and globe with trajectories.

654 A149 2.50 l vio bl & sepia .40 .20
655 A149 7.50 l lt blue & blk .75 .20
656 A149 20 l violet & sepia 2.25 .70
Nos. 654-656 (3) 3.40 1.10

Miniature Sheet

657 A149 25 l vio bl & sepia 12.00 12.00

1st group space flight of Vostoks 3 and 4, Aug. 11-15, 1962. Imperfs. in changed colors, value #654-656 $12, #657 $12.

"Albania" Decorating Police Officer — A150

Polyphylla Fullo — A151

1963, Mar. 20 **Unwmk.** ***Perf. 14***

658 A150 2.50 l crim, mag & blk .40 .20
659 A150 7.50 l org ver, dk red & blk 1.40 .25

20th anniversary of the security police.

1963, Mar. 20

Beetles: 1.50 l, Lucanus cervus. 8 l, Procerus gigas. 10 l, Cicindela Albanica.

660 A151 50q ol grn & brn .25 .20
661 A151 1.50 l blue & brn .55 .20
662 A151 8 l dl rose & blk vio 2.75 1.10
663 A151 10 l brt citron & blk 3.00 1.25
Nos. 660-663 (4) 6.55 2.75

1913 Stamp and Postmark A152

Design: 10 l, Stamps of 1913, 1937 and 1962.

1963, May 5

664 A152 5 l yel, buff, bl & blk .70 .25
665 A152 10 l car rose, grn & blk 1.40 .45

50th anniversary of Albanian stamps.

Boxer — A153

Crested Grebe — A154

Designs: 3 l, Basketball baskets. 5 l, Volleyball. 6 l, Bicyclists. 9 l, Gymnast. 15 l, Hands holding torch, and map of Japan.

1963, May 25 ***Perf. 13½***

666 A153 2 l yel, blk & red brn .25 .20
667 A153 3 l ocher, brn & bl .35 .20
668 A153 5 l gray bl, red brn & brn .60 .20
669 A153 6 l gray, dk gray & grn .80 .25
670 A153 9 l rose, red brn & bl 1.50 .30
Nos. 666-670 (5) 3.50 1.15

Miniature Sheet

671 A153 15 l lt bl, car, blk & brn 9.00 9.00

1964 Olympic Games in Tokyo. Value, imperfs. #666-670 $7.50, #671 $8.

1963, Apr. 20 **Litho.** ***Perf. 14***

Birds: 3 l, Golden eagle. 6.50 l, Gray partridges. 11 l, Capercaillie.

672 A154 50q multicolored .20 .20
673 A154 3 l multicolored 1.10 .25
674 A154 6.50 l multicolored 2.50 .55
675 A154 11 l multicolored 4.00 .85
Nos. 672-675 (4) 7.80 1.85

Soldier and Building A155

2.50 l, Soldier with pack, ship, plane. 5 l, Soldier in battle. 6 l, Soldier, bulldozer.

1963, July 10 **Unwmk.** ***Perf. 12***

676 A155 1.50 l brick red, yel & blk .30 .20
677 A155 2.50 l bl, ocher & brn .40 .20
678 A155 5 l bluish grn, gray & blk .90 .20
679 A155 6 l red brn, buff & bl 1.25 .25
Nos. 676-679 (4) 2.85 .85

Albanian army, 20th anniversary.

Maj. Yuri A. Gagarin A156

Designs: 5 l, Maj. Gherman Titov. 7 l, Maj. Andrian G. Nikolayev. 11 l, Lt. Col. Pavel R. Popovich. 14 l, Lt. Col. Valeri Bykovski. 20 l, Lt. Valentina Tereshkova.

1963, July 30

Portraits in Yellow and Black

680 A156 3 l brt purple .45 .20
681 A156 5 l dull blue .65 .20
682 A156 7 l gray .90 .20
683 A156 11 l deep claret 1.50 .35
684 A156 14 l blue green 2.25 .55
685 A156 20 l ultra 3.25 1.00
Nos. 680-685 (6) 9.00 2.50

Man's conquest of space. Value, imperf. set $18.

Volleyball — A157

1963, Aug. 31 ***Perf. 12x12½***

686 A157 2 l shown .20 .20
687 A157 3 l Weight lifting .35 .20
688 A157 5 l Soccer .65 .20
689 A157 7 l Boxing .80 .25
690 A157 8 l Rowing 1.50 .30
Nos. 686-690 (5) 3.50 1.15

European championships. Imperfs. in changed colors, value set $16.

Papilio Podalirius A158

1963, Sept. 29 **Litho.**

Various Butterflies and Moths in Natural Colors

691 A158 1 l red .20 *.20*
692 A158 2 l blue .75 *.20*
693 A158 4 l dull lilac 1.25 *.25*
694 A158 5 l pale green 2.25 *.40*
695 A158 8 l bister 2.75 *.55*
696 A158 10 l light blue 4.50 *.70*
Nos. 691-696 (6) 11.70 *2.30*

Oil Refinery, Cerrik — A159

Flag and Shield — A160

2.50 l, Food processing plant, Tirana, horiz. 30 l, Fruit canning plant. 50 l, Tannery, horiz.

1963, Nov. 15 **Unwmk.** ***Perf. 14***

697 A159 2.50 l rose red, *pnksh* .40 .20
698 A159 20 l slate grn, *grnsh* 1.40 .20
699 A159 30 l dull pur, *grysh* 3.25 .50
700 A159 50 l ocher, *yel* 3.50 .75
Nos. 697-700 (4) 8.55 1.65

Industrial development in Albania.

1963, Nov. 24 ***Perf. 12½x12***

701 A160 2 l grnsh bl, blk, ocher & red .35 .20
702 A160 8 l blue, blk, ocher & red 1.00 .50

1st Congress of Army Aid Assn.

Chinese, Caucasian and Negro Men A161

1963, Dec. 10 ***Perf. 12x11½***

703 A161 3 l bister & blk .50 .20
704 A161 5 l bister & ultra .95 .20
705 A161 7 l bister & vio 1.50 .30
Nos. 703-705 (3) 2.95 .70

15th anniv. of the Universal Declaration of Human Rights.

Slalom Ascent A162

Lenin A163

Designs: 50q, Bobsled, horiz. 6.50 l, Ice hockey, horiz. 12.50 l, Women's figure skating. No. 709A, Ski jumper.

1963, Dec. 25 ***Perf. 14***

706 A162 50q grnsh bl & blk .20 .20
707 A162 2.50 l red, gray & blk .30 .20
708 A162 6.50 l yel, blk & gray .75 .20
709 A162 12.50 l red, blk & yel grn 1.75 .50
Nos. 706-709 (4) 3.00 1.10

Miniature Sheet

709A A162 12.50 l multi 10.00 7.50

9th Winter Olympic Games, Innsbruck, Jan. 29-Feb. 9, 1964. Imperfs. in changed colors, value #706-709 $25, #709A $30.

1964, Jan. 21 ***Perf. 12½x12***

710 A163 5 l gray & bister .35 .20
711 A163 10 l gray & ocher .65 .30

40th anniversary, death of Lenin.

Hurdling A164

Fish A165

Designs: 3 l, Track, horiz. 6.50 l, Rifle shooting, horiz. 8 l, Basketball.

Perf. 12½x12, 12x12½

1964, Jan. 30 **Litho.**

712 A164 2.50 l pale vio & ultra .30 .20
713 A164 3 l lt grn & red brn .45 .20
714 A164 6.50 l blue & claret .90 .20
715 A164 8 l lt blue & ocher 1.25 .20
Nos. 712-715 (4) 2.90 .80

1st Games of the New Emerging Forces, GANEFO, Jakarta, Indonesia, Nov. 10-22, 1963.

1964, Feb. 26 **Unwmk.** ***Perf. 14***

716 A165 50q Sturgeon .20 .20
717 A165 1 l Gilthead .20 .20
718 A165 1.50 l Striped mullet .40 .20
719 A165 2.50 l Carp .60 .20
720 A165 6.50 l Mackerel 1.60 .40
721 A165 10 l Lake Ohrid trout 3.00 .50
Nos. 716-721 (6) 6.00 1.70

Wild Animals A166

1964, Mar. 28 ***Perf. 12½x12***

722 A166 1 l Red Squirrel .20 .20
723 A166 1.50 l Beech marten .20 .20
724 A166 2 l Red fox .50 .20
725 A166 2.50 l Hedgehog .55 .20
726 A166 3 l Hare .65 .20
727 A166 5 l Jackal 1.10 .25
728 A166 7 l Wildcat 1.60 .35
729 A166 8 l Wolf 2.00 .50
Nos. 722-729 (8) 6.80 2.10

Lighting Olympic Torch — A167

Designs: 5 l, Torch and globes. 7 l, 15 l, Olympic flag and Mt. Fuji. 10 l, National Stadium, Tokyo.

1964, May 18 ***Perf. 12x12½***

730 A167 3 l lt yel grn, yel & buff .25 .20
731 A167 5 l red & vio blue .35 .20
732 A167 7 l lt bl, ultra & yel .55 .20
733 A167 10 l orange, bl & vio .75 .25
Nos. 730-733 (4) 1.90 .85

Miniature Sheet

734 A167 15 l lt bl, ultra & org 12.50 12.50

18th Olympic Games, Tokyo, Oct. 10-25, 1964. No. 734 contains one 49x62mm stamp. Imperfs. in changed colors, value #730-733 $11, #734 $14.

See No. 745.

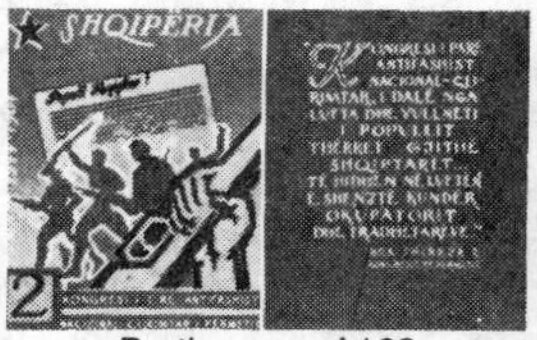

Partisans — A168

Designs: 5 l, Arms of Albania. 8 l, Enver Hoxha.

Perf. 12½x12

1964, May 24 **Litho.** **Unwmk.**

735 A168 2 l orange, red & blk .50 .20
736 A168 5 l multicolored 1.25 .20
737 A168 8 l red brn, blk & red 2.50 .20
Nos. 735-737 (3) 4.25 .60

20th anniv. of the Natl. Anti-Fascist Cong. of Liberation, Permet, May 24, 1944. The label attached to each stamp, without perforations between, carries a quotation from the 1944 Congress.

Albanian Flag and Revolutionists A169

Full Moon A170

Perf. 12½x12

1964, June 10 **Litho.** **Unwmk.**

738 A169 2.50 l red & gray .20 .20
739 A169 7.50 l lilac rose & gray .60 .20

Albanian revolution of 1924, 40th anniv.

1964, June 27 *Perf. 12x12½*

Designs: 5 l, New moon. 8 l, Half moon. 11 l, Waning moon. 15 l, Far side of moon.

740	A170	1 l purple & yel	.25	.20
741	A170	5 l violet & yel	.60	.20
742	A170	8 l blue & yel	1.10	.30
743	A170	11 l green & yel	1.75	.45
		Nos. 740-743 (4)	3.70	1.15

Miniature Sheet

Perf. 12 on 2 sides

744	A170	15 l ultra & yel	12.50	12.50

No. 744 contains one stamp, size: 35x36mm, perforated at top and bottom. Imperfs. in changed colors, value #740-743 $12.50, #744 $12.50.

No. 733 with Added Inscription: "Rimini 25-VI-64"

1964 *Perf. 12x12½*

745	A167	10 l orange, bl & vio	3.50	3.00

"Toward Tokyo 1964" Phil. Exhib. at Rimini, Italy, June 25-July 6.

Wren — A171

Birds: 1 l, Penduline titmouse. 2.50 l, Green woodpecker. 3 l, Tree creeper. 4 l, Nuthatch. 5 l, Great titmouse. 6 l, Goldfinch. 18 l, Oriole.

1964, July 31 *Perf. 12x12½*

746	A171	50q multi	.20	.20
747	A171	1 l orange & multi	.20	.20
748	A171	2.50 l multi	.25	.20
749	A171	3 l blue & multi	.35	.20
750	A171	4 l yellow & multi	.45	.20
751	A171	5 l blue & multi	.55	.20
752	A171	6 l lt vio & multi	.80	.30
753	A171	18 l pink & multi	2.25	.85
		Nos. 746-753 (8)	5.05	2.35

Running and Gymnastics A172

Sport: 2 l, Weight lifting, judo. 3 l, Equestrian, bicycling. 4 l, Soccer, water polo. 5 l, Wrestling, boxing. 6 l, Pentathlon, hockey. 7 l, Swimming, sailing. 8 l, Basketball, volleyball. 9 l, Rowing, canoeing. 10 l, Fencing, pistol shooting. 20 l, Three winners.

Perf. 12x12½

1964, Sept. 25 **Litho.** **Unwmk.**

754	A172	1 l lt bl, rose & emer	.20	.20
755	A172	2 l bis brn, bluish grn & vio	.20	.20
756	A172	3 l vio, red org & ol bis	.20	.20
757	A172	4 l grnsh bl, ol & ultra	.20	.20
758	A172	5 l grnsh bl, car & pale lil	.30	.20
759	A172	6 l dk bl, org & lt bl	.35	.20
760	A172	7 l dk bl, lt ol & org	.35	.20
761	A172	8 l emerald, gray & yel	.50	.20
762	A172	9 l bl, yel & lil rose	.65	.30
763	A172	10 l brt grn, org brn & yel grn	1.60	.50
		Nos. 754-763 (10)	4.55	2.40

Miniature Sheet

Perf. 12

764	A172	20 l violet & lemon	20.00	10.00

18th Olympic Games, Tokyo, Oct. 10-25. No. 764 contains one stamp, size: 41x68mm. Imperfs. in changed colors, value #754-763 $12.50, #764 $12.50.

Arms of People's Republic of China — A173

Mao Tse-tung and Flag A174

1964, Oct. 1 *Perf. 11½x12, 12x11½*

765	A173	7 l black, red & yellow	2.00	.30
766	A174	8 l black, red & yellow	3.00	.40

People's Republic of China, 15th anniv.

Karl Marx A175

Jeronim de Rada A176

Designs: 5 l, St. Martin's Hall, London. 8 l, Friedrich Engels.

1964, Nov. 5 *Perf. 12x11½*

767	A175	2 l red, lt vio & blk	.55	.20
768	A175	5 l gray blue	1.10	.20
769	A175	8 l ocher, blk & red	2.25	.30
		Nos. 767-769 (3)	3.90	.70

Centenary of First Socialist International.

1964, Nov. 15 *Perf. 12½x11½*

770	A176	7 l slate green	1.10	.30
771	A176	8 l dull violet	1.60	.35

Birth of Jeronim de Rada, poet, 150th anniv.

Arms of Albania — A177

Factories A178

Designs: 3 l, Combine harvester. 4 l, Woman chemist. 10 l, Hands holding Constitution, hammer and sickle.

Perf. 11½x12, 12x11½

1964, Nov. 29

772	A177	1 l multicolored	.35	.20
773	A178	2 l red, yel & vio bl	.45	.20
774	A178	3 l red, yel & brn	.85	.20
775	A178	4 l red, yel & gray grn	1.00	.20
776	A177	10 l red, bl & blk	1.65	.45
		Nos. 772-776 (5)	4.30	1.25

20th anniversary of liberation.

Planet Mercury — A179

Planets: 2 l, Venus and rocket. 3 l, Earth, moon and rocket. 4 l, Mars and rocket. 5 l, Jupiter. 6 l, Saturn. 7 l, Uranus. 8 l, Neptune. 9 l, Pluto. 15 l, Solar system and rocket.

1964, Dec. 15 *Perf. 12x12½*

777	A179	1 l yellow & pur	.20	.20
778	A179	2 l multicolored	.20	.20
779	A179	3 l multicolored	.20	.20
780	A179	4 l multicolored	.25	.20
781	A179	5 l yel, dk pur & brn	.45	.20
782	A179	6 l lt grn, vio brn & yel	.60	.20
783	A179	7 l yellow & grn	.70	.20
784	A179	8 l yellow & vio	.85	.25
785	A179	9 l lt grn, yel & blk	1.25	.35
		Nos. 777-785 (9)	4.70	2.00

Miniature Sheet

Perf. 12 on 2 sides

786	A179	15 l car, bl, yel & grn	17.50	17.50

No. 786 contains one stamp, size: 62x51mm, perforated at top and bottom. Imperfs. in changed colors. Value #777-785, $15; #786, $17.50.

European Chestnut A180

Symbols of Industry A181

1965, Jan. 25 *Perf. 11½x12*

787	A180	1 l shown	.20	.20
788	A180	2 l Medlars	.25	.20
789	A180	3 l Persimmon	.50	.20
790	A180	4 l Pomegranate	.55	.20
791	A180	5 l Quince	.80	.20
792	A180	10 l Orange	1.60	.35
		Nos. 787-792 (6)	3.90	1.35

1965, Feb. 20

Designs: 5 l, Books, triangle and compass. 8 l, Beach, trees and hotel.

793	A181	2 l blk, car rose & pink	*1.75*	.40
794	A181	5 l yel, gray & blk	*3.50*	.85
795	A181	8 l blk, vio bl & lt bl	*5.75*	1.60
		Nos. 793-795 (3)	*11.00*	2.85

Professional trade associations, 20th anniv.

Water Buffalo A182

Various designs: Water buffalo.

1965, Mar. *Perf. 12x11½*

796	A182	1 l lt yel grn, yel & brn blk	.35	.20
797	A182	2 l lt bl, dk gray & blk	.85	.20
798	A182	3 l yellow, brn & grn	1.10	.20
799	A182	7 l brt grn, yel & brn blk	2.75	.35
800	A182	12 l pale lil, dk brn & ind	4.00	.65
		Nos. 796-800 (5)	9.05	1.60

Mountain View, Valbona — A183

1.50 l, Seashore. 3 l, Glacier and peak. 4 l, Gorge. 5 l, Mountain peaks. 9 l, Lake and hills.

1965, Mar. **Litho.** *Perf. 12*

801	A183	1.50 l multi	1.40	.20
802	A183	2.50 l multi	1.75	.20
803	A183	3 l multi, vert.	2.75	.25
804	A183	4 l multi, vert.	3.00	.40
805	A183	5 l multi	5.00	.50
806	A183	9 l multi	8.00	.75
		Nos. 801-806 (6)	21.90	2.30

Frontier Guard A184

Small-bore Rifle Shooting, Prone A185

1965, Apr. 25 **Unwmk.**

807	A184	2.50 l lt blue & multi	.85	.20
808	A184	12.50 l lt ultra & multi	3.50	.90

20th anniversary of the Frontier Guards.

1965, May 10

Designs: 2 l, Rifle shooting, standing. 3 l, Target over map of Europe, showing Bucharest. 4 l, Pistol shooting. 15 l, Rifle shooting, kneeling.

809	A185	1 l lil, car rose, blk & brn	.20	.20
810	A185	2 l bl, blk, brn & vio bl	.35	.20
811	A185	3 l pink & car rose	.45	.20
812	A185	4 l bis, blk & vio brn	.60	.20
813	A185	15 l brt grn, brn & vio brn	2.25	.50
		Nos. 809-813 (5)	3.85	1.30

European Shooting Championships, Bucharest.

ITU Emblem, Old and New Communications Equipment A186

Col. Pavel Belyayev A187

1965, May 17 *Perf. 12½x12*

814	A186	2.50 l brt grn, blk & lil rose	.50	.20
815	A186	12.50 l vio, blk & brt bl	3.25	.30

Centenary of the ITU.

1965, June 15 *Perf. 12*

Designs: 2 l, Voskhod II. 6.50 l, Lt. Col. Alexei Leonov. 20 l, Leonov floating in space.

816	A187	1.50 l lt blue & brn	.20	.20
817	A187	2 l dk bl, lt vio & lt ultra	.20	.20
818	A187	6.50 l lilac & brn	.70	.20
819	A187	20 l chlky bl, yel & blk	1.90	.35
		Nos. 816-819 (4)	3.00	.95

Miniature Sheet

Perf. 12 on 2 sides

820	A187	20 l brt bl, org & blk	6.00	6.00

Space flight of Voskhod II and 1st man walking in space, Lt. Col. Alexei Leonov. No. 820 contains one stamp, size: 51x59½mm, perforated at top and bottom. Imperf., brt grn background, value $6.

Marx and Lenin — A188

Mother and Child — A189

1965, June 21 *Perf. 12*

821	A188	2.50 l dk brn, red & yel	.85	.20
822	A188	7.50 l sl grn, org ver & buff	2.25	.25

6th Conf. of Postal Ministers of Communist Countries, Peking, June 21-July 15.

Perf. 12½x12, 12x12½

1965, June 29 Litho. Unwmk.

Designs: 2 l, Pioneers. 3 l, Boy and girl at play, horiz. 4 l, Child on beach. 15 l, Girl with book.

823 A189 1 l brt bl, rose lil & blk .20 .20
824 A189 2 l salmon, vio & blk .35 .20
825 A189 3 l green, org & vio .50 .20
826 A189 4 l multicolored .70 .20
827 A189 15 l lil rose, brn & ocher 2.25 .40
Nos. 823-827 (5) 4.00 1.20

Issued for International Children's Day.

Statue of Magistrate A190

Flowers A191

Designs: 1 l, Amphora. 2 l, Illyrian armor. 3 l, Mosaic, horiz. 15 l, Torso, Apollo statue.

1965, July 20 ***Perf. 12***

828 A190 1 l lt ol, org & brn .20 .20
829 A190 2 l gray grn, grn & brn .25 .20
830 A190 3 l tan, brn, car & lil .50 .20
831 A190 4 l green, bis & brn .70 .20
832 A190 15 l gray & pale claret 1.75 .65
Nos. 828-832 (5) 3.40 1.45

1965, Aug. 11 ***Perf. 12½x12***

833 A191 1 l Fuchsia .20 .20
834 A191 2 l Cyclamen .30 .20
835 A191 3 l Tiger lily .50 .20
836 A191 3.50 l Iris .60 .20
837 A191 4 l Dahlia .70 .20
838 A191 4.50 l Hydrangea .80 .20
839 A191 5 l Rose 1.00 .20
840 A191 7 l Tulips 1.90 .30
Nos. 833-840 (8) 6.00 1.70

Nos. 698-700 Surcharged New Value and Two Bars

1965, Aug. 16 ***Perf. 14***

841 A159 5q on 30 l .20 .20
842 A159 15q on 30 l .30 .20
843 A159 25q on 50 l .45 .20
844 A159 80q on 50 l .90 .20
845 A159 1.10 l on 20 l 1.50 .30
846 A159 2 l on 20 l 2.75 .60
Nos. 841-846 (6) 6.10 1.70

White Stork — A192

"Homecoming," by Bukurosh Sejdini — A193

Migratory Birds: 20q, Cuckoo. 30q, Hoopoe. 40q, European bee-eater. 50q, European nightjar. 1.50 l, Quail.

1965, Aug. 31 ***Perf. 12***

847 A192 10q yellow, blk & gray .20 .20
848 A192 20q brt pink, blk & dk bl .35 .20
849 A192 30q violet, blk & bis .65 .20
850 A192 40q emer, blk yel & org 1.40 .20
851 A192 50q ultra, brn & red brn 1.60 .25
852 A192 1.50 l bis, red brn & dp org 4.50 .75
Nos. 847-852 (6) 8.70 1.80

1965, Sept. 26 Litho. ***Perf. 12x12½***

853 A193 25q olive black 1.75 .20
854 A193 65q blue black 4.25 .35
855 A193 1.10 l black 6.50 .60
Nos. 853-855 (3) 12.50 1.15

Second war veterans' meeting.

Hunting — A194

Oleander — A195

1965, Oct. 6 Litho. Unwmk.

856 A194 10q Capercaillie .25 .20
857 A194 20q Deer .40 .20
858 A194 30q Pheasant .70 .20
859 A194 40q Mallards 1.10 .20
860 A194 50q Boar 1.25 .25
861 A194 1 l Rabbit 3.75 .55
Nos. 856-861 (6) 7.45 1.60

1965, Oct. 26 ***Perf. 12½x12***

Flowers: 20q, Forget-me-nots. 30q, Pink. 40q, White water lily. 50q, Bird's foot. 1 l, Corn poppy.

862 A195 10q brt bl, grn & car rose .20 .20
863 A195 20q org red, bl, brn & grn .40 .20
864 A195 30q vio, car rose & grn .60 .20
865 A195 40q emerald, yel & blk .80 .20
866 A195 50q org brn, yel & grn 1.00 .20
867 A195 1 l yel grn, blk & rose red 2.00 .70
Nos. 862-867 (6) 5.00 1.70

Hotel Turizmi, Fier — A196

Freighter "Teuta" — A197

Buildings: 10q, Hotel, Peshkopi. 15q, Sanatorium, Tirana. 25q, Rest home, Pogradec. 65q, Partisan Sports Arena, Tirana. 80q, Rest home, Mali Dajt. 1.10 l, Culture House, Tirana. 1.60 l, Hotel Adriatik, Durres. 2 l, Migjeni Theater, Shkoder. 3 l, Alexander Moissi House of Culture, Durres.

1965, Oct. ***Perf. 12x12½***

868 A196 5q blue & blk .20 .20
869 A196 10q ocher & blk .20 .20
870 A196 15q dull grn & blk .20 .20
871 A196 25q violet & blk .20 .20
872 A196 65q lt brn & blk .70 .20
873 A196 80q yel grn & blk .90 .20
874 A196 1.10 l lilac & blk 1.25 .20
875 A196 1.60 l lt vio bl & blk 1.90 .35
876 A196 2 l dull rose & blk 2.50 .50
877 A196 3 l gray & blk 4.00 .70
Nos. 868-877 (10) 12.05 2.95

1965, Nov. 16

Ships: 20q, Raft. 30q, Sailing ship, 19th cent. 40q, Sailing ship, 18th cent. 50q, Freighter "Vlora." 1 l, Illyric galleys.

878 A197 10q brt grn & dk grn .20 .20
879 A197 20q ol bis & dk grn .20 .20
880 A197 30q lt & dp ultra .35 .20
881 A197 40q vio & dp vio .60 .20
882 A197 50q pink & dk red .75 .20
883 A197 1 l bister & brn 1.50 .45
Nos. 878-883 (6) 3.60 1.45

Brown Bear A198

Basketball and Players A199

Various Albanian bears. 50q, 55q, 60q, horiz.

1965, Dec. 7 ***Perf. 11½x12***

884 A198 10q bister & dk brn .30 .20
885 A198 20q pale brn & dk brn .40 .20
886 A198 30q bis, dk brn & car .65 .20
887 A198 35q pale brn & dk brn .80 .20
888 A198 40q bister & dk brn 1.25 .20
889 A198 50q bister & dk brn 1.50 .20
890 A198 55q bister & dk brn 1.50 .30
891 A198 60q pale brn, dk brn & car 1.75 .45
Nos. 884-891 (8) 8.15 1.95

1965, Dec. 15 Litho. ***Perf. 12½x12***

Designs: 10q, Games' emblem (map of Albania and basket). 30q, 50q, Players with ball (diff. designs). 1.40 l, Basketball medal on ribbon.

892 A199 10q blue, yel & car .20 .20
893 A199 20q rose lil, lt brn & blk .35 .20
894 A199 30q bis, lt brn, red & blk .45 .20
895 A199 50q lt grn, lt brn & blk .95 .20
896 A199 1.40 l rose, blk, brn & yel 1.75 .50
Nos. 892-896 (5) 3.70 1.30

7th Balkan Basketball Championships, Tirana, Dec. 15-19.

Arms of Republic and Smokestacks — A200

Designs (Arms and): 10q, Book. 30q, Wheat. 60q, Book, hammer and sickle. 80q, Factories.

1966, Jan. 11 Litho. ***Perf. 11½x12***

Coat of Arms in Gold

897 A200 10q crimson & brn .20 .20
898 A200 20q blue & vio bl .20 .20
899 A200 30q org yel & brn .35 .20
900 A200 60q yel grn & brt grn .50 .20
901 A200 80q crimson & brn 1.10 .25
Nos. 897-901 (5) 2.35 1.05

Albanian People's Republic, 20th anniv.

Cow — A201

Perf. 12½x12, 12x12½

1966, Feb. 25

902 A201 10q shown .20 .20
903 A201 20q Pig .35 .20
904 A201 30q Ewe & lamb .45 .20
905 A201 35q Ram .65 .20
906 A201 40q Dog .95 .20
907 A201 50q Cat, vert. 1.00 .20
908 A201 55q Horse, vert. 1.25 .25
909 A201 60q Ass, vert. 1.50 .30
Nos. 902-909 (8) 6.35 1.75

Soccer Player and Map of Uruguay A202

Andon Zako Cajupi A203

5q, Globe in form of soccer ball. 15q, Player, map of Italy. 20q, Goalkeeper, map of France. 25q, Player, map of Brazil. 30q, Player, map of Switzerland. 35q, Player, map of Sweden. 40q, Player, map of Chile. 50q, Player, map of Great Britain. 70q, World Championship cup & ball.

1966, Mar. 20 Litho. ***Perf. 12***

910 A202 5q gray & dp org .20 .20
911 A202 10q lt brn, bl & vio .20 .20
912 A202 15q cit, dk bl & brt bl .20 .20
913 A202 20q org, vio bl & brt bl .25 .20
914 A202 25q salmon & sepia .30 .20
915 A202 30q lt yel grn & brn .30 .20
916 A202 35q lt ultra & emer .35 .20
917 A202 40q pink & brown .55 .20
918 A202 50q pale grn, mag & rose red .55 .20
919 A202 70q gray, brn, yel & blk .70 .25
Nos. 910-919 (10) 3.60 2.05

World Cup Soccer Championship, Wembley, England, July 11-30.

1966, Mar. 27 Unwmk.

920 A203 40q bluish blk .50 .20
921 A203 1.10 l dark green 1.50 .20

Andon Zako Cajupi, poet, birth centenary .

Painted Lady — A204

WHO Headquarters, Geneva, and Emblem — A205

Designs: 20q, Blue dragonfly. 30q, Cloudless sulphur butterfly. 35q, 40q, Splendid dragonfly. 50q, Machaon swallow-tail. 55q, Sulphur butterfly. 60q, Whitemarbled butterfly.

1966, Apr. 21 Litho. ***Perf. 11½x12***

922 A204 10q multicolored .25 .20
923 A204 20q yellow & multi .40 .20
924 A204 30q yellow & multi .65 .20
925 A204 35q sky blue & multi .80 .20
926 A204 40q multicolored .85 .20
927 A204 50q rose & multi 1.10 .20
928 A204 55q multicolored 1.25 .20
929 A204 60q multicolored 2.00 .20
Nos. 922-929 (8) 7.30 1.60

Perf. 12x12½, 12½x12

1966, May 3 Litho.

Designs (WHO Emblem and): 35q, Ambulance and stretcher bearers, vert. 60q, Albanian mother and nurse weighing infant, vert. 80q, X-ray machine and hospital.

930 A205 25q lt blue & blk .30 .20
931 A205 35q salmon & ultra .55 .20
932 A205 60q lt grn, bl & red .90 .20
933 A205 80q yel, bl, grn & lt brn 1.25 .25
Nos. 930-933 (4) 3.00 .85

Inauguration of the WHO Headquarters, Geneva.

Bird's Foot Starfish — A206

Designs: 25q, Starfish. 35q, Brittle star. 45q, But-thorn starfish. 50q, Starfish. 60q, Sea cucumber. 70q, Sea urchin.

1966, May 10 ***Perf. 12x12½***

934 A206 15q multicolored .25 .20
935 A206 25q multicolored .45 .20
936 A206 35q multicolored .65 .20
937 A206 45q multicolored .90 .20
938 A206 50q multicolored 1.10 .20
939 A206 60q multicolored 1.25 .20
940 A206 70q multicolored 1.90 .35
Nos. 934-940 (7) 6.50 1.55

Luna 10 — A207

30q, 80q, Trajectory of Luna 10, earth & moon.

1966, June 10 ***Perf. 12x12½***

941	A207	20q blue, yel & blk	.35	.20
942	A207	30q yel grn, blk & bl	.45	.20
943	A207	70q vio, yel & blk	.90	.20
944	A207	80q yel, vio, grn & blk	1.25	.20
		Nos. 941-944 (4)	2.95	.80

Launching of the 1st artificial moon satellite, Luna 10, Apr. 3, 1966.

Jules Rimet Cup and Soccer A208

Designs: Various scenes of soccer play.

1966, July 12 Litho. ***Perf. 12x12½***

Black Inscriptions

945	A208	10q ocher & lilac	.20	.20
946	A208	20q lt blue & cit	.20	.20
947	A208	30q brick red & Prus bl	.25	.20
948	A208	35q lt ultra & rose	.30	.20
949	A208	40q yel grn & lt red brn	.35	.20
950	A208	50q lt red brn & yel grn	.60	.20
951	A208	55q rose lil & yel grn	.65	.20
952	A208	60q dp rose & ocher	1.25	.25
		Nos. 945-952 (8)	3.80	1.65

World Cup Soccer Championship, Wembley, England, July 11-30.

Water Level Map of Albania — A209

30q, Water measure & fields. 70q, Turbine & pylon. 80q, Hydrological decade emblem.

1966, July ***Perf. 12½x12***

953	A209	20q brick red, blk & org	.30	.20
954	A209	30q emer, blk & lt brn	.50	.20
955	A209	70q brt violet & blk	1.10	.25
956	A209	80q brt bl, org, yel & blk	1.25	.30
		Nos. 953-956 (4)	3.15	.95

Hydrological Decade (UNESCO), 1965-74.

Greek Turtle — A210

Designs: 15q, Grass snake. 25q, European pond turtle. 30q, Wall lizard. 35q, Wall gecko. 45q, Emerald lizard. 50q, Slowworm. 90q, Horned viper (or sand viper).

1966, Aug. 10 Litho. ***Perf. 12½x12***

957	A210	10q gray & multi	.20	.20
958	A210	15q yellow & multi	.20	.20
959	A210	25q ultra & multi	.30	.20
960	A210	30q multicolored	.45	.20
961	A210	35q multicolored	.60	.20
962	A210	45q multicolored	.70	.25
963	A210	50q orange & multi	.80	.30
964	A210	90q lilac & multi	1.75	.55
		Nos. 957-964 (8)	5.00	2.10

Persian Cat A211

Cats: 10q, Siamese, vert. 15q, European tabby, vert. 25q, Black kitten. 60q, 65q, 80q, Various Persians.

Perf. 12x12½, 12½x12

1966, Sept. 20 **Litho.**

965	A211	10q multicolored	.20	.20
966	A211	15q blk, sepia & car	.25	.20
967	A211	25q blk, dk & lt brn	.30	.20
968	A211	45q blk, org & yel	.60	.20
969	A211	60q blk, brn & yel	.75	.20
970	A211	65q multicolored	.90	.20
971	A211	80q blk, gray & yel	1.50	.30
		Nos. 965-971 (7)	4.50	1.50

Pjeter Budi, Writer — A212

1966, Oct. 5 ***Perf. 12x12½***

972	A212	25q buff & slate grn	.25	.20
973	A212	1.75 l gray & dull claret	1.75	.45

UNESCO Emblem A213

Designs (UNESCO Emblem and): 15q, Open book, rose and school. 25q, Male folk dancers. 1.55 l, Jug, column and old building.

1966, Oct. 20 Litho. ***Perf. 12***

974	A213	5q lt gray & multi	.20	.20
975	A213	15q dp blue & multi	.25	.20
976	A213	25q gray & multi	.50	.20
977	A213	1.55 l multi	2.00	.50
		Nos. 974-977 (4)	2.95	1.10

20th anniv. of UNESCO.

Hand Holding Book with Pictures of Marx, Engels, Lenin and Stalin A214

Hammer and Sickle, Party Emblem in Sunburst A215

Designs: 25q, Map of Albania, hammer and sickle, symbols of agriculture and industry. 65q, Symbolic grain and factories. 95q, Fists holding rifle, spade, axe, sickle and book.

1966, Nov. 1 Litho. ***Perf. 11½x12***

978	A214	15q vermilion & gold	.35	.20
979	A214	25q multicolored	.55	.20
980	A214	65q brn, brn org & gold	1.25	.20
981	A214	95q yellow & multi	1.90	.35
		Nos. 978-981 (4)	4.05	.95

Albanian Communist Party, 5th Cong.

1966, Nov. 8

Designs: 25q, Partisan and sunburst. 65q, Steel worker and blast furnace. 95q, Combine harvester, factories, and pylon.

982	A215	15q orange & multi	.30	.20
983	A215	25q red & multi	.40	.20
984	A215	65q multicolored	1.10	.20
985	A215	95q blue & multi	1.50	.35
		Nos. 982-985 (4)	3.30	.95

25th anniv. of the founding of the Albanian Workers Party.

Russian Wolfhound — A216

Dogs: 15q, Sheep dog. 25q, English setter. 45q, English springer spaniel. 60q, Bulldog. 65q, Saint Bernard. 80q, Dachshund.

1966 Litho. ***Perf. 12½x12***

986	A216	10q green & multi	.20	.20
987	A216	15q multicolored	.30	.20
988	A216	25q lilac & multi	.40	.20
989	A216	45q rose & multi	.75	.35
990	A216	60q brown & multi	1.00	.40
991	A216	65q ultra & multi	1.10	.45
992	A216	80q blue grn & multi	1.50	.50
		Nos. 986-992 (7)	5.25	2.30

Ndre Mjeda A217

Proclamation A218

1966 ***Perf. 12½x12***

993	A217	25q brt bl & dk brn	.50	.20
994	A217	1.75 l brt grn & dk brn	2.00	.65

Birth Centenary of the priest Ndre Mjeda.

1966 ***Perf. 11½x12, 12x11½***

Designs: 10q, Banner, man and woman holding gun and axe, horiz. 1.85 l, man with axe and banner and partisan with gun.

995	A218	5q lt brn, red & blk	.20	.20
996	A218	10q red, blk, gray & bl	.20	.20
997	A218	1.85 l red, blk & salmon	1.50	.30
		Nos. 995-997 (3)	1.90	.70

25th anniv. of the Albanian Communist Party.

Golden Eagle — A219

Birds of Prey: 15q, European sea eagle. 25q, Griffon vulture. 40q, Common sparrowhawk. 50q, Osprey. 70q, Egyptian vulture. 90q, Kestrel.

1966, Dec. 20 Litho. ***Perf. 11½x12***

998	A219	10q gray & multi	.20	.20
999	A219	15q multicolored	.25	.20
1000	A219	25q citron & multi	.45	.20
1001	A219	40q multicolored	.80	.20
1002	A219	50q multicolored	.95	.25
1003	A219	70q yellow & multi	1.40	.35
1004	A219	90q multicolored	1.90	.45
		Nos. 998-1004 (7)	5.95	1.85

Hake A220

Fish: 15q, Red mullet. 25q, Opah. 40q, Atlantic wolf fish. 65q, Lumpfish. 80q, Swordfish. 1.15 l, Shorthorn sculpin.

1967, Jan. Photo. ***Perf. 12x11½***

Fish in Natural Colors

1005	A220	10q blue	.20	.20
1006	A220	15q lt yellow grn	.25	.20
1007	A220	25q Prus blue	.35	.20
1008	A220	40q emerald	.85	.20
1009	A220	65q brt blue grn	.95	.25
1010	A220	80q blue	1.40	.35
1011	A220	1.15 l brt green	1.75	.60
		Nos. 1005-1011 (7)	5.75	2.00

White Pelican A221

Designs: Various groups of pelicans.

1967, Feb. 22 Litho. ***Perf. 12***

1012	A221	10q pink & multi	.20	.20
1013	A221	15q pink & multi	.25	.20
1014	A221	25q pink & multi	.55	.20
1015	A221	50q pink & multi	1.00	.20
1016	A221	2 l pink & multi	3.75	.75
		Nos. 1012-1016 (5)	5.75	1.55

Camellia A222

Flowers: 10q, Chrysanthemum. 15q, Hollyhock. 25q, Flowering Maple. 35q, Peony. 65q, Gladiolus. 80q, Freesia. 1.15 l, Carnation.

Unwmk.

1967, Apr. 12 Litho. ***Perf. 12***

Flowers in Natural Colors

1017	A222	5q pale brown	.20	.20
1018	A222	10q lt lilac	.20	.20
1019	A222	15q gray	.25	.20
1020	A222	25q ultra	.40	.20
1021	A222	35q lt blue	.70	.20
1022	A222	65q lt blue grn	1.00	.20
1023	A222	80q lt bluish gray	1.50	.25
1024	A222	1.15 l dull yellow	2.00	.40
		Nos. 1017-1024 (8)	6.25	1.85

A223

Rose — A224

Design: Congress emblem and power station.

1967, Apr. 24 Litho. ***Perf. 12***

1025	A223	25q multi	.25	.20
1026	A223	1.75 l multi	2.25	.45

Cong. of the Union of Professional Workers, Tirana, Apr. 24.

1967, May 15 ***Perf. 12x12½***

Various Roses in Natural Colors.

1027	A224	5q blue gray	.20	.20
1028	A224	10q brt blue	.20	.20
1029	A224	15q rose violet	.20	.20
1030	A224	25q lemon	.35	.20
1031	A224	35q brt grnsh blue	.45	.20
1032	A224	65q gray	.85	.20
1033	A224	80q brown	1.10	.25
1034	A224	1.65 l gray green	2.50	.45
		Nos. 1027-1034 (8)	5.85	1.90

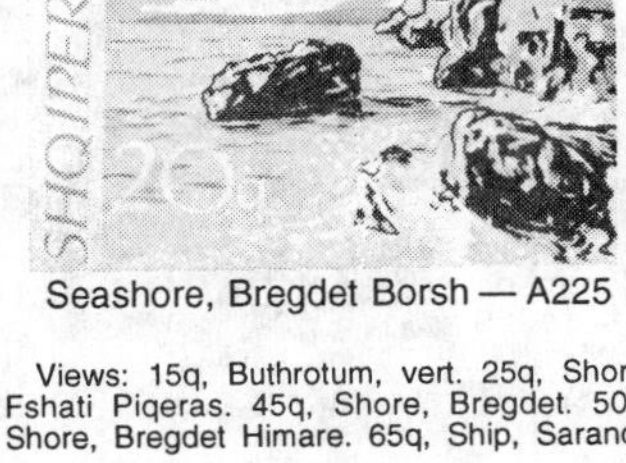

Seashore, Bregdet Borsh — A225

Views: 15q, Buthrotum, vert. 25q, Shore, Fshati Piqeras. 45q, Shore, Bregdet. 50q, Shore, Bregdet Himare. 65q, Ship, Sarande

(Santi Quaranta). 80q, Shore, Dhermi. 1 l, Sunset, Bregdet, vert.

Perf. 12x12½, 12½x12

1967, June 10

1035	A225	15q multicolored	.20	.20
1036	A225	20q multicolored	.25	.20
1037	A225	25q multicolored	.30	.20
1038	A225	45q multicolored	.80	.20
1039	A225	50q multicolored	.90	.20
1040	A225	65q multicolored	1.25	.20
1041	A225	80q multicolored	1.40	.25
1042	A225	1 l multicolored	1.90	.35
		Nos. 1035-1042 (8)	7.00	1.80

Fawn A226

Roe Deer: 20q, Stag, vert. 25q, Doe, vert. 30q, Young stag and doe. 35q, Doe and fawn. 40q, Young stag, vert. 65q, Stag and doe, vert. 70q, Running stag and does.

Perf. 12½x12, 12x12½

1967, July 20 **Litho.**

1043	A226	15q multicolored	.35	.20
1044	A226	20q multicolored	.35	.20
1045	A226	25q multicolored	.55	.20
1046	A226	30q multicolored	.65	.20
1047	A226	35q multicolored	.80	.20
1048	A226	40q multicolored	1.10	.20
1049	A226	65q multicolored	1.60	.30
1050	A226	70q multicolored	1.60	.35
		Nos. 1043-1050 (8)	7.00	1.85

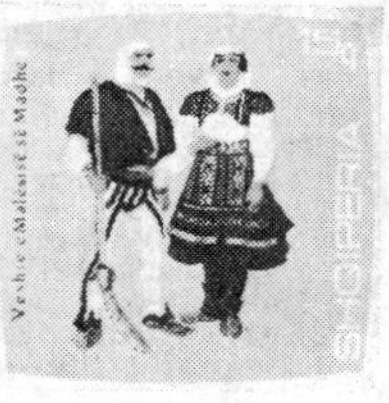
Man and Woman from Madhe A227

Regional Costumes: 20q, Woman from Zadrimes. 25q, Dancer and drummer, Kukesit. 45q, Woman spinner, Dardhes. 50q, Farm couple, Myseqese. 65q, Dancer with tambourine, Tirana. 80q, Man and woman, Dropullit. 1 l, Piper, Laberise.

1967, Aug. 25 ***Perf. 12***

1051	A227	15q tan & multi	.20	.20
1052	A227	20q lt yellow grn	.20	.20
1053	A227	25q multicolored	.20	.20
1054	A227	45q sky blue & multi	.35	.20
1055	A227	50q lemon & multi	.55	.25
1056	A227	65q pink & multi	.60	.35
1057	A227	80q multicolored	.80	.40
1058	A227	1 l gray & multi	1.10	.55
		Nos. 1051-1058 (8)	4.00	2.35

Fighters and Newspaper — A228

Designs: 75q, Printing plant, newspapers and microphone. 2 l, People holding newspaper.

1967, Aug. 25 ***Perf. 12½x12***

1059	A228	25q multicolored	.40	.20
1060	A228	75q pink & multi	.85	.20
1061	A228	2 l multicolored	2.25	.35
		Nos. 1059-1061 (3)	3.50	.75

Issued for the Day of the Press.

Street Scene, by Kolé Idromeno A229

Hakmarrja Battalion, by Sali Shijaku — A230

Designs: 20q, David, fresco by Onufri, 16th century, vert. 45q, Woman's head, ancient mosaic, vert. 50q, Men on horseback from 16th century icon, vert. 65q, Farm Women, by Zef Shoshi. 80q, Street Scene, by Vangjush Mio. 1 l, Bride, by Kolé Idromeno, vert.

Perf. 12, 12x12½, (A230)

1967, Oct. 25 **Litho.**

1062	A229	15q multicolored	.40	.20
1063	A229	20q multicolored	.45	.20
1064	A230	25q multicolored	.55	.20
1065	A229	45q multicolored	1.10	.20
1066	A229	50q multicolored	1.40	.20
1067	A230	65q multicolored	1.60	.20
1068	A230	80q multicolored	2.00	.25
1069	A230	1 l multicolored	2.50	.30
		Nos. 1062-1069 (8)	10.00	1.75

Lenin at Storming of Winter Palace A231

Rabbit A232

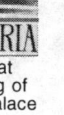

Designs: 15q, Lenin and Stalin, horiz. 50q, Lenin and Stalin addressing meeting. 1.10 l, Storming of the Winter Palace, horiz.

1967, Nov. 7 ***Perf. 12***

1070	A231	15q red & multi	.25	.20
1071	A231	25q slate grn & blk	.55	.20
1072	A231	50q brn, blk & brn vio	.85	.20
1073	A231	1.10 l lilac, gray & blk	2.75	.25
		Nos. 1070-1073 (4)	4.40	.85

50th anniv. of the Russian October Revolution.

1967, Nov. 25

Designs: Various hares and rabbits. The 15q, 25q, 35q, 40q and 1 l are horizontal.

1074	A232	15q orange & multi	.20	.20
1075	A232	20q brt yel & multi	.20	.20
1076	A232	25q lt brn & multi	.25	.20
1077	A232	35q multicolored	.35	.20
1078	A232	40q yellow & multi	.65	.20
1079	A232	50q pink & multi	.75	.20
1080	A232	65q multicolored	1.25	.30
1081	A232	1 l lilac & multi	2.00	.45
		Nos. 1074-1081 (8)	5.65	1.95

University, Torch and Book — A233

1967 **Litho.** ***Perf. 12***

1082	A233	25q multi	.25	.20
1083	A233	1.75 l multi	1.40	.30

10th anniv. of the founding of the State University, Tirana.

Coat of Arms and Soldiers A234

Designs: 65q, Arms, Factory, grain, flag, gun and radio tower. 1.20 l, Arms and hand holding torch.

1967 ***Perf. 12x11½***

1084	A234	15q multi	.20	.20
1085	A234	65q multi	.55	.20
1086	A234	1.20 l multi	1.00	.20
		Nos. 1084-1086 (3)	1.75	.60

25th anniversary of the Democratic Front.

Turkey — A235

Designs: 20q, Duck. 25q, Hen. 45q, Rooster. 50q, Guinea fowl. 65q, Goose, horiz. 80q, Mallard, horiz. 1 l, Chicks, horiz.

Perf. 12x12½, 12½x12

1967, Nov. 25 **Photo.**

1087	A235	15q gold & multi	.25	.20
1088	A235	20q gold & multi	.25	.20
1089	A235	25q gold & multi	.30	.20
1090	A235	45q gold & multi	.50	.20
1091	A235	50q gold & multi	.75	.20
1092	A235	65q gold & multi	.95	.20
1093	A235	80q gold & multi	1.75	.30
1094	A235	1 l gold & multi	2.25	.40
		Nos. 1087-1094 (8)	7.00	1.90

Skanderbeg A236

Designs: 10q, Arms of Skanderbeg. 25q, Helmet and sword. 30q, Kruje Castle. 35q, Petreles Castle. 65q, Berati Castle. 80q, Skanderbeg addressing national chiefs. 90q, Battle of Albulenes.

1967, Dec. 10 Litho. ***Perf. 12x12½***

Medallion in Bister and Dark Brown

1095	A236	10q gold & violet	.20	.20
1096	A236	15q gold & rose car	.20	.20
1097	A236	25q gold & vio bl	.20	.20
1098	A236	30q gold & dk blue	.25	.20
1099	A236	35q gold & maroon	.35	.20
1100	A236	65q gold & green	.60	.20
1101	A236	80q gold & gray brn	.95	.20
1102	A236	90q gold & ultra	1.75	.20
		Nos. 1095-1102 (8)	4.50	1.60

500th anniv. of the death of Skanderbeg (George Castriota), national hero.

Ice Hockey — A237

Designs: 15q, 2 l, Winter Olympics emblem. 30q, Women's figure skating. 50q, Slalom. 80q, Downhill skiing. 1 l, Ski jump.

1967-68

1103	A237	15q multicolored	.20	.20
1104	A237	25q multicolored	.20	.20
1105	A237	30q multicolored	.20	.20
1106	A237	50q multicolored	.30	.20
1107	A237	80q multicolored	.60	.20
1108	A237	1 l multicolored	.85	.25
		Nos. 1103-1108 (6)	2.35	1.25

Miniature Sheet

Imperf

1109	A237	2 l red, gray & brt bl ('68)	6.00	6.00

10th Winter Olympic Games, Grenoble, France, Feb. 6-18.

Nos. 1103-1108 issued Dec. 29, 1967.

Skanderbeg Monument, Kruje — A238

Designs: 10q, Skanderbeg monument, Tirana. 15q, Skanderbeg portrait, Uffizi Galleries, Florence. 25q, engraved portrait of Gen. Tanush Topia. 35q, Portrait of Gen. Gjergj Arianti, horiz. 65q, Portrait bust of Skanderbeg by O. Paskali. 80q, Title page of "The Life of Skanderbeg." 90q, Skanderbeg battling the Turks, painting by S. Rrota, horiz.

Perf. 12x12½, 12½x12

1968, Jan. 17 **Litho.**

1110	A238	10q multicolored	.20	.20
1111	A238	15q multicolored	.25	.20
1112	A238	25q blk, yel & lt bl	.35	.20
1113	A238	30q multicolored	.40	.20
1114	A238	35q lt vio, pink & blk	.65	.20
1115	A238	65q multicolored	1.00	.20
1116	A238	80q pink, blk & yel	1.25	.20
1117	A238	90q beige & multi	1.75	.25
		Nos. 1110-1117 (8)	5.85	1.65

500th anniv. of the death of Skanderbeg (George Castriota), national hero.

Carnation A239

1968, Feb. 15 ***Perf. 12***

Various Carnations in Natural Colors

1118	A239	15q green	.20	.20
1119	A239	20q dk brown	.20	.20
1120	A239	25q brt blue	.20	.20
1121	A239	50q gray olice	.30	.20
1122	A239	80q bluish gray	.75	.20
1123	A239	1.10 l violet gray	1.00	.25
		Nos. 1118-1123 (6)	2.65	1.25

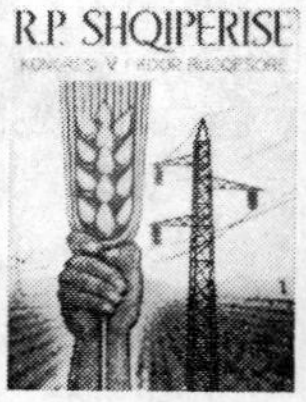

"Electrification" A240

65q, Farm tractor, horiz. 1.10 l, Cow & herd.

1968, Mar. 5 **Litho.** ***Perf. 12***

1124	A240	25q multi	.25	.20
1125	A240	65q multi	.70	.20
1126	A240	1.10 l multi	1.00	.20
		Nos. 1124-1126 (3)	1.95	.60

Fifth Farm Cooperatives Congress.

Goat A241

Various goats. 15q, 20q, 25q are vertical.

Perf. 12x12½, 12½x12

1968, Mar. 25

1127	A241	15q multi	.20	.20
1128	A241	20q multi	.20	.20
1129	A241	25q multi	.20	.20
1130	A241	30q multi	.30	.20
1131	A241	40q multi	.40	.20
1132	A241	50q multi	.45	.20

1133 A241 80q multi .80 .20
1134 A241 1.40 l multi 2.00 .35
Nos. 1127-1134 (8) 4.55 1.75

Zef N. Jubani A242

Physician and Hospital A243

1968, Mar. 30 ***Perf. 12***
1135 A242 25q yellow & choc .25 .20
1136 A242 1.75 l lt violet & blk 1.10 .30

Sesquicentennial of the birth of Zef N. Jubani, writer and scholar.

Perf. 12½x12, 12x12½
1968, Apr. 7 **Litho.**

Designs (World Health Organization Emblem and): 65q, Hospital and microscope, horiz. 1.10 l, Mother feeding child.

1137 A243 25q green & claret .20 .20
1138 A243 65q black, yel & bl .55 .20
1139 A243 1.10 l black & dp org .80 .20
Nos. 1137-1139 (3) 1.55 .60

20th anniv. of WHO.

Scientist A244

Women: 15q, Militia member. 60q, Farm worker. 1 l, Factory worker.

1968, Apr. 14 ***Perf. 12***
1140 A244 15q ver & dk red .35 .20
1141 A244 25q blue grn & grn .50 .20
1142 A244 60q dull yel & brn .80 .20
1143 A244 1 l lt vio & vio 2.00 .30
Nos. 1140-1143 (4) 3.65 .90

Albanian Women's Organization, 25th anniv.

Karl Marx — A245

Designs: 25q, Marx lecturing to students. 65q, "Das Kapital," "Communist Manifesto" and marching crowd. 95q, Full-face portrait.

1968, May 5 **Litho.** ***Perf. 12***
1144 A245 15q gray, dk bl & bis .25 .20
1145 A245 25q brn vio, dk brn & dl yel .50 .20
1146 A245 65q gray, blk, brn & car 1.25 .20
1147 A245 95q gray, ocher & blk 2.00 .35
Nos. 1144-1147 (4) 4.00 .95

Karl Marx, 150th birth anniversary.

Heliopsis A246

Flowers: 20q, Red flax. 25q, Orchid. 30q, Gloxinia. 40q, Turk's-cap lily. 80q, Amaryllis. 1.40 l, Red magnolia.

1968, May 10 ***Perf. 12x12½***
1148 A246 15q gold & multi .20 .20
1149 A246 20q gold & multi .20 .20
1150 A246 25q gold & multi .20 .20
1151 A246 30q gold & multi .20 .20
1152 A246 40q gold & multi .45 .20
1153 A246 80q gold & multi .55 .20
1154 A246 1.40 l gold & multi .85 .30
Nos. 1148-1154 (7) 2.65 1.50

Proclamation of Prizren A247

25q, Abdyl Frasheri. 40q, House in Prizren.

1968, June 10 **Litho.** ***Perf. 12***
1155 A247 25q emerald & blk .20 .20
1156 A247 40q multicolored .45 .20
1157 A247 85q yellow & multi .85 .25
Nos. 1155-1157 (3) 1.50 .65

League of Prizren against the Turks, 90th anniv.

Shepherd, by A. Kushi — A248

Paintings from Tirana Art Gallery: 20q, View of Tirana, by V. Mio, horiz. 25q, Mountaineer, by G. Madhi. 40q, Refugees, by A. Buza. 80q, Guerrillas of Shahin Matrakut, by S. Xega. 1.50 l, Portrait of an Old Man, by S. Papadhimitri. 1.70 l, View of Scutari, by S. Rrota. 2.50 l, Woman in Scutari Costume, by Z. Colombi.

1968, June 20 ***Perf. 12x12½***
1158 A248 15q gold & multi .20 .20
1159 A248 20q gold & multi .20 .20
1160 A248 25q gold & multi .25 .20
1161 A248 40q gold & multi .45 .20
1162 A248 80q gold & multi .75 .20
1163 A248 1.50 l gold & multi 1.25 .25
1164 A248 1.70 l gold & multi 1.50 .50
Nos. 1158-1164 (7) 4.60 1.75

Miniature Sheet
Perf. 12½xImperf.
1165 A248 2.50 l multi 2.00 .90

No. 1165 contains one stamp, size: 50x71mm.

Soldier and Guns — A249

Designs: 25q, Sailor and warships. 65q, Aviator and planes, vert. 95q, Militiamen and woman.

1968, July 10 **Litho.** ***Perf. 12***
1166 A249 15q multicolored .30 .20
1167 A249 25q multicolored .45 .20
1168 A249 65q multicolored 1.25 .20
1169 A249 95q multicolored 2.50 .20
Nos. 1166-1169 (4) 4.50 .80

25th anniversary of the People's Army.

Squid — A250

Designs: 20q, Crayfish. 25q, Whelk. 50q, Crab. 70q, Spiny lobster. 80q, Shore crab. 90q, Norway lobster.

1968, Aug. 20
1170 A250 15q multicolored .20 .20
1171 A250 20q multicolored .20 .20
1172 A250 25q multicolored .25 .20
1173 A250 50q multicolored .45 .20
1174 A250 70q multicolored .70 .25
1175 A250 80q multicolored .90 .30
1176 A250 90q multicolored 1.25 .35
Nos. 1170-1176 (7) 3.95 1.70

Women's Relay Race — A251

Sport: 20q, Running. 25q, Women's discus. 30q, Equestrian. 40q, High jump. 50q, Women's hurdling. 80q, Soccer. 1.40 l, Woman diver. 2 l, Olympic stadium.

1968, Sept. 23 **Photo.** ***Perf. 12***
1177 A251 15q multicolored .20 .20
1178 A251 20q multicolored .20 .20
1179 A251 25q multicolored .20 .20
1180 A251 30q multicolored .20 .20
1181 A251 40q multicolored .25 .20
1182 A251 50q multicolored .35 .20
1183 A251 80q multicolored .55 .20
1184 A251 1.40 l multicolored .95 .35
Nos. 1177-1184 (8) 2.90 1.75

Souvenir Sheet
Perf. 12½ Horizontally
1185 A251 2 l multicolored 2.25 .75

19th Olympic Games, Mexico City, Oct. 12-27. No. 1185 contains one rectangular stamp, size: 64x54mm. Value of imperfs., #1177-1184 $7, #1185 $5.

Enver Hoxha — A252

1968, Oct. 16 **Litho.** ***Perf. 12***
1186 A252 25q blue gray .35 .20
1187 A252 35q rose brown .50 .20
1188 A252 80q violet .90 .35
1189 A252 1.10 l brown 1.10 .50
Nos. 1186-1189 (4) 2.85 1.25

Souvenir Sheet
Imperf
1190 A252 1.50 l rose red, bl vio & gold *55.00 40.00*

60th birthday of Enver Hoxha, First Secretary of the Central Committee of the Communist Party of Albania.

Book and Pupils A253

1968, Nov. 14 **Photo.**
1191 A253 15q maroon & slate grn .45 .20
1192 A253 85q gray olive & sepia 2.75 .20

60th anniv. of the Congress of Monastir, Nov. 14-22, 1908, which adopted a unified Albanian alphabet.

Waxwing — A254

Birds: 20q, Rose-colored starling. 25q, Kingfishers. 50q, Long-tailed tits. 80q, Wallcreeper. 1.10 l, Bearded tit.

1968, Nov. 15 **Litho.**
Birds in Natural Colors
1193 A254 15q lt blue & blk .20 .20
1194 A254 20q bister & blk .20 .20
1195 A254 25q pink & blk .30 .20
1196 A254 50q lt yel grn & blk .35 .20
1197 A254 80q bis brn & blk .80 .20
1198 A254 1.10 l pale green & blk 1.00 .25
Nos. 1193-1198 (6) 2.85 1.25

Mao Tse-tung — A255

1968, Dec. 26 **Litho.** ***Perf. 12½x12***
1199 A255 25q gold, red & blk .40 .20
1200 A255 1.75 l gold, red & blk 2.00 .30

75th birthday of Mao Tse-tung, Chairman of the Communist Party of the People's Republic of China.

Adem Reka and Crane — A256

Portraits: 10q, Pjeter Lleshi and power lines. 15q, Mohammed Shehu and Myrteza Kepi. 25q, Shkurte Vata and women railroad workers. 65q, Agron Elezi, frontier guard. 80q, Ismet Bruçaj and mountain road. 1.30 l, Fuat Cela, blind revolutionary.

1969, Feb. 10 **Litho.** ***Perf. 12x12½***
1201 A256 5q multicolored .20 .20
1202 A256 10q multicolored .20 .20
1203 A256 15q multicolored .20 .20
1204 A256 25q multicolored .20 .20
1205 A256 65q multicolored .40 .20
1206 A256 80q multicolored .75 .20
1207 A256 1.30 l multicolored 1.25 .20
Nos. 1201-1207 (7) 3.20 1.40

Issued to honor a contemporary heroine and heroes.

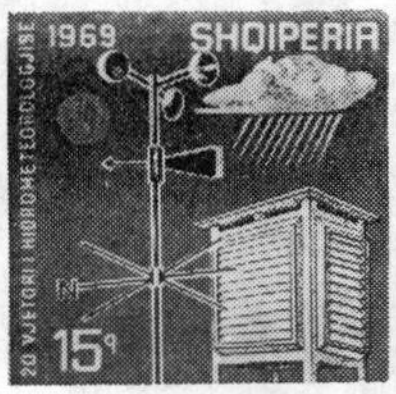
Meteorological Instruments A257

Designs: 25q, Water gauge. 1.60 l, Radar, balloon and isobars.

1969, Feb. 25 *Perf. 12*

1208 A257 15q multicolored .25 .20
1209 A257 25q ultra, org & blk .45 .20
1210 A257 1.60 l rose vio, yel & blk 2.50 .25
Nos. 1208-1210 (3) 3.20 .65

20th anniv. of Albanian hydrometeorology.

Partisans, 1944, by F. Haxmiu — A258

Paintings: 5q, Student Revolutionists, by P. Mele, vert. 65q, Steel Mill, by C. Ceka. 80q, Reconstruction, by V. Kilica. 1.10 l, Harvest, by N. Jonuzi. 1.15 l, Terraced Landscape, by S. Kaceli. 2 l, Partisans' Meeting.

Perf. 12x12½, 12½x12

1969, Apr. 25 **Litho.**

Size: 31½x41½mm

1211 A258 5q buff & multi .20 .20

Size: 51½x30½mm

1212 A258 25q buff & multi .20 .20

Size: 40½x32mm

1213 A258 65q buff & multi .35 .20

Size: 51½x30½mm

1214 A258 80q buff & multi .65 .20
1215 A258 1.10 l buff & multi .70 .20
1216 A258 1.15 l buff & multi .95 .20
Nos. 1211-1216 (6) 3.05 1.20

Miniature Sheet

Imperf

Size: 111x90mm

1217 A258 2 l ocher & multi 1.75 1.75

Leonardo da Vinci, Self-portrait A259

Designs (after Leonardo da Vinci): 35q, Lilies. 40q, Design for a flying machine, horiz. 1 l, Portrait of Beatrice. No. 1222, Portrait of a Noblewoman. No. 1223, Mona Lisa.

Perf. 12x12½, 12½x12

1969, May 2 **Litho.**

1218 A259 25q gold & sepia .20 .20
1219 A259 35q gold & sepia .40 .20
1220 A259 40q gold & sepia .45 .20
1221 A259 1 l gold & multi 1.25 .20
1222 A259 2 l gold & sepia 2.25 .55
Nos. 1218-1222 (5) 4.55 1.35

Miniature Sheet

Imperf

1223 A259 2 l gold & multi 3.25 2.25

Leonardo da Vinci (1452-1519), painter, sculptor, architect and engineer.

First Congress Meeting Place A260

Designs: 1 l, Albanian coat of arms. 2.25 l, Two partisans with guns and flag.

1969, May 24 *Perf. 12*

1224 A260 25q lt grn, blk & red .35 .20
1225 A260 2.25 l multi 2.50 .85

Souvenir Sheet

1226 A260 1 l gold, bl, blk & red *30.00 12.50*

25th anniversary of the First Anti-Fascist Congress of Permet, May 24, 1944.

Albanian Violet — A261

Designs: Violets and Pansies.

1969, June 30 **Litho.** *Perf. 12x12½*

1227 A261 5q gold & multi .20 .20
1228 A261 10q gold & multi .20 .20
1229 A261 15q gold & multi .20 .20
1230 A261 20q gold & multi .20 .20
1231 A261 25q gold & multi .35 .20
1232 A261 80q gold & multi .50 .30
1233 A261 1.95 l gold & multi 1.40 .65
Nos. 1227-1233 (7) 3.05 1.95

Plum, Fruit and Blossoms A262

Designs: Blossoms and Fruits.

1969, Aug. 10 **Litho.** *Perf. 12*

1234 A262 10q shown .20 .20
1235 A262 15q Lemon .20 .20
1236 A262 25q Pomegranate .30 .20
1237 A262 50q Cherry .60 .20
1238 A262 80q Peach .95 .20
1239 A262 1.20 l Apple 1.75 .35
Nos. 1234-1239 (6) 4.00 1.35

Basketball — A263

Designs: 10q, 80q, 2.20 l, Various views of basketball game. 25q, Hand aiming ball at basket and map of Europe, horiz.

1969, Sept. 15 **Litho.** *Perf. 12*

1240 A263 10q multi .20 .20
1241 A263 15q buff & multi .20 .20
1242 A263 25q blue & multi .25 .20
1243 A263 80q multi .65 .20
1244 A263 2.20 l multi 1.60 .50
Nos. 1240-1244 (5) 2.90 1.30

16th European Basketball Championships, Naples, Italy, Sept. 27-Oct. 5.

Runner A264

Designs: 5q, Games' emblem. 10q, Woman gymnast. 20q, Pistol shooting. 25q, Swimmer at start. 80q, Bicyclist. 95q, Soccer.

1969, Sept. 30

1245 A264 5q multicolored .20 .20
1246 A264 10q multicolored .20 .20
1247 A264 15q multicolored .20 .20
1248 A264 20q multicolored .30 .20
1249 A264 25q multicolored .40 .20
1250 A264 80q multicolored .80 .20
1251 A264 95q multicolored 1.25 .20
Nos. 1245-1251 (7) 3.35 1.40

Second National Spartakiad.

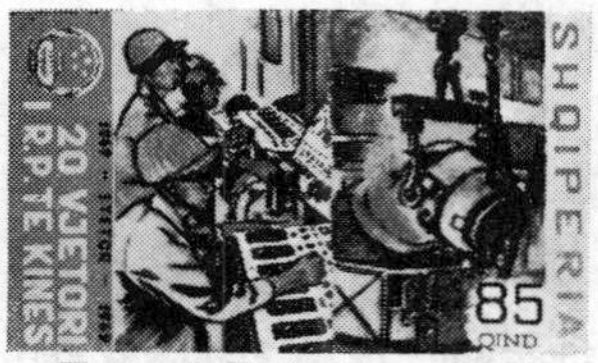

Electronic Technicians, Steel Ladle — A265

Designs: 25q, Mao Tse-tung with microphones, vert. 1.40 l, Children holding Mao's red book, vert.

1969, Oct. 1 **Litho.** *Perf. 12*

1252 A265 25q multi .40 .20
1253 A265 85q multi 1.00 .20
1254 A265 1.40 l multi 1.60 .30
Nos. 1252-1254 (3) 3.00 .70

People's Republic of China, 20th anniv.

Enver Hoxha — A266

Designs: 80q, Pages from Berat resolution. 1.45 l, Partisans with flag.

1969, Oct. 20 **Litho.** *Perf. 12*

1255 A266 25q multicolored .20 .20
1256 A266 80q gray & multi .50 .20
1257 A266 1.45 l ocher & multi .80 .30
Nos. 1255-1257 (3) 1.50 .70

25th anniv. of the 2nd reunion of the Natl. Antifascist Liberation Council, Berat.

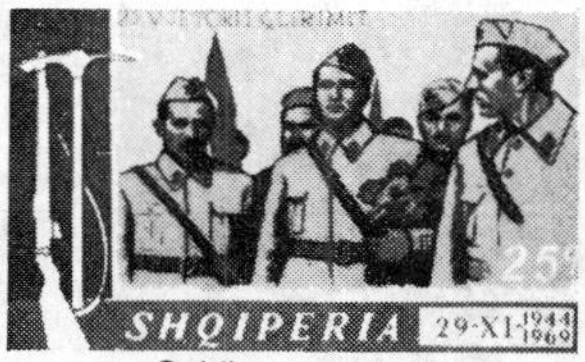

Soldiers — A267

Designs: 30q, Oil refinery. 35q, Combine harvester. 45q, Hydroelectric station and dam. 55q, Militia woman, man and soldier. 1.10 l, Dancers and musicians.

1969, Nov. 29

1258 A267 25q multi .25 .20
1259 A267 30q multi .25 .20
1260 A267 35q multi .25 .20
1261 A267 45q multi .30 .20
1262 A267 55q multi .80 .20
1263 A267 1.10 l multi 1.60 .20
Nos. 1258-1263 (6) 3.45 1.20

25th anniv. of the socialist republic.

Joseph V. Stalin, (1879-1953), Russian Political Leader — A268

1969, Dec. 21 **Litho.** *Perf. 12*

1264 A268 15q lilac .20 .20
1265 A268 25q slate blue .20 .20
1266 A268 1 l brown .75 .20
1267 A268 1.10 l violet blue 1.25 .20
Nos. 1264-1267 (4) 2.40 .80

Head of Woman — A269

Greco-Roman Mosaics: 25q, Geometrical floor design, horiz. 80q, Bird and tree, horiz. 1.10 l, Floor with birds and grapes, horiz. 1.20 l, Fragment with corn within oval design.

1969, Dec. 25 *Perf. 12½x12*

1268 A269 15q gold & multi .20 .20
1269 A269 25q gold & multi .20 .20
1270 A269 80q gold & multi .45 .20
1271 A269 1.10 l gold & multi .70 .20
1272 A269 1.20 l gold & multi .95 .30
Nos. 1268-1272 (5) 2.50 1.10

Cancellation of 1920 — A270

Design: 25q, Proclamation and congress site.

1970, Jan. 21 **Litho.** *Perf. 12*

1273 A270 25q red, gray & blk .20 .20
1274 A270 1.25 l dk grn, yel & blk 1.25 .20

Congress of Louchnia, 50th anniversary.

Worker, Student and Flag A271

1970, Feb. 11 *Perf. 12½x12*

1275 A271 25q red & multi .20 .20
1276 A271 1.75 l red & multi 1.25 .25

Vocational organizations in Albania, 25th anniv.

Turk's-cap Lily A272

Lilies: 5q, Cernum, vert. 15q, Madonna, vert. 25q, Royal, vert. 1.10 l, Tiger. 1.15 l, Albanian.

Perf. 11½x12, 12x11½

1970, Mar. 10 **Litho.**

1277 A272 5q multi .20 .20
1278 A272 15q multi .20 .20
1279 A272 25q multi .30 .20
1280 A272 80q multi .75 .20
1281 A272 1.10 l multi 1.10 .25
1282 A272 1.15 l multi 1.40 .25
Nos. 1277-1282 (6) 3.95 1.25

Lenin A273

Designs (Lenin): 5q, Portrait, vert. 25q, As volunteer construction worker. 95q, Addressing crowd. 1.10 l, Saluting, vert.

1970, Apr. 22 Litho. *Perf. 12*

1283	A273	5q	multi	.20	.20
1284	A273	15q	multi	.20	.20
1285	A273	25q	multi	.20	.20
1286	A273	95q	multi	.60	.20
1287	A273	1.10 l	multi	1.10	.20
			Nos. 1283-1287 (5)	2.30	1.00

Centenary of birth of Lenin (1870-1924).

Frontier Guard A274

1970, Apr. 25

1288	A274	25q	multi	.45	.20
1289	A274	1.25 l	multi	2.50	.20

25th anniversary of Frontier Guards.

Soccer Players — A275

Designs: 5q, Jules Rimet Cup and globes. 10q, Aztec Stadium, Mexico City. 25q, Defending goal. 65q, 80q, No. 1296, Two soccer players in various plays. No. 1297, Mexican horseman and volcano Popocatepetl.

1970, May 15 Litho. *Perf. 12½x12*

1290	A275	5q	multicolored	.20	.20
1291	A275	10q	multicolored	.20	.20
1292	A275	15q	multicolored	.20	.20
1293	A275	25q	lt green & multi	.20	.20
1294	A275	65q	pink & multi	.30	.20
1295	A275	80q	lt blue & multi	.55	.20
1296	A275	2 l	yellow & multi	1.50	.25
			Nos. 1290-1296 (7)	3.15	1.45

Souvenir Sheet

Perf 12 x Imperf

1297	A275	2 l	multicolored	2.25	.80

World Soccer Championships for the Jules Rimet Cup, Mexico City, May 31-June 21, 1970. No. 1297 contains one large horizontal stamp. Nos. 1290-1297 exist imperf.

UPU Headquarters and Monument, Bern — A276

1970, May 30 Litho. *Perf. 12½x12*

1298	A276	25q	ultra, gray & blk	.20	.20
1299	A276	1.10 l	orange, buff & blk	.65	.20
1300	A276	1.15 l	green, gray & blk	.90	.25
			Nos. 1298-1300 (3)	1.75	.65

Inauguration of the new UPU Headquarters in Bern.

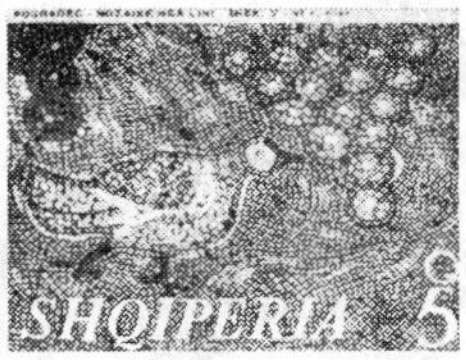

Bird and Grapes Mosaic A277

Mosaics, 5th-6th centuries, excavated near Pogradec: 10q, Waterfowl and grapes. 20q, Bird and tree stump. 25q, Bird and leaves. 65q, Fish. 2.25 l, Peacock, vert.

1970, July 10 *Perf. 12½x12, 12x12½*

1301	A277	5q	multi	.20	.20
1302	A277	10q	multi	.20	.20
1303	A277	20q	multi	.20	.20
1304	A277	25q	multi	.30	.20
1305	A277	65q	multi	.55	.20
1306	A277	2.25 l	multi	1.75	.35
			Nos. 1301-1306 (6)	3.20	1.35

Fruit Harvest and Dancers A278

Designs: 25q, Contour-plowed fields and conference table. 80q, Cattle and newspapers. 1.30 l, Wheat harvest.

1970, Aug. 28 Litho. *Perf. 12x11½*

1307	A278	15q	brt violet & blk	.20	.20
1308	A278	25q	dp blue & blk	.20	.20
1309	A278	80q	dp brown & blk	.60	.20
1310	A278	1.30 l	org brn & blk	.90	.20
			Nos. 1307-1310 (4)	1.90	.80

25th anniv. of the agrarian reform law.

Attacking Partisans — A279

Designs: 25q, Partisans with horses and flag. 1.60 l, Partisans.

1970, Sept. 3 *Perf. 12*

1311	A279	15q	org brn & blk	.20	.20
1312	A279	25q	brn, yel & blk	.20	.20
1313	A279	1.60 l	dp grn & blk	1.25	.30
			Nos. 1311-1313 (3)	1.65	.70

50th anniversary of liberation of Vlona.

Miners, by Nexhmedin Zajmi — A280

Paintings from the National Gallery, Tirana: 5q, Bringing in the Harvest, by Isuf Sulovari, vert. 15q, The Activists, by Dhimitraq Trebicka, vert. 65q, Instruction of Partisans, by Hasan Nallbani. 95q, Architectural Planning, by Vilson Kilica. No. 1319, Woman Machinist, by Zef Shoshi, vert. No. 1320, Partisan Destroying Tank, by Sali Shijaku, vert.

Perf. 12½x12, 12x12½

1970, Sept. 25 Litho.

1314	A280	5q	multicolored	.20	.20
1315	A280	15q	multicolored	.20	.20
1316	A280	25q	multicolored	.20	.20
1317	A280	65q	multicolored	.25	.20
1318	A280	95q	multicolored	.45	.20
1319	A280	2 l	multicolored	1.75	.30
			Nos. 1314-1319 (6)	3.05	1.30

Miniature Sheet

Imperf

1320	A280	2 l	multicolored	1.50	.95

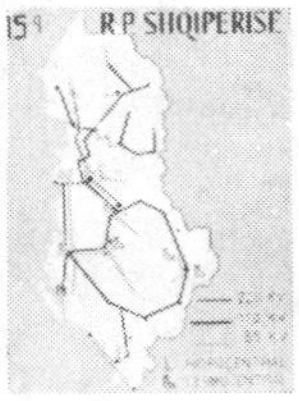

Electrification Map of Albania — A281

Designs: 25q, Light bulb, hammer and sickle emblem, map of Albania and power graph. 80q, Linemen at work. 1.10 l, Use of electricity on the farm, in home and business.

1970, Oct. 25 Litho. *Perf. 12*

1321	A281	15q	multi	.20	.20
1322	A281	25q	multi	.20	.20
1323	A281	80q	multi	.70	.20
1324	A281	1.10 l	multi	1.00	.20
			Nos. 1321-1324 (4)	2.10	.80

Albanian village electrification completion.

Friedrich Engels — A282

Designs: 1.10 l, Engels as young man. 1.15 l, Engels addressing crowd.

1970, Nov. 28 Litho. *Perf. 12x12½*

1325	A282	25q	bister & dk bl	.20	.20
1326	A282	1.10 l	bister & dp claret	.60	.20
1327	A282	1.15 l	bister & dk ol grn	.70	.25
			Nos. 1325-1327 (3)	1.50	.65

150th anniv. of the birth of Friedrich Engels (1820-95), German socialist, collaborator with Karl Marx.

Ludwig van Beethoven — A283

Designs: 5q, Birthplace, Bonn. 25q, 65q, 1.10 l, various portraits. 1.80 l, Scene from Fidelio, horiz.

1970, Dec. 16 Litho. *Perf. 12*

1328	A283	5q	dp plum & gold	.20	.20
1329	A283	15q	brt rose lil & sil	.20	.20
1330	A283	25q	green & gold	.20	.20
1331	A283	65q	magenta & sil	.30	.20
1332	A283	1.10 l	dk blue & gold	.60	.25
1333	A283	1.80 l	black & sil	1.40	.45
			Nos. 1328-1333 (6)	2.90	1.50

Ludwig van Beethoven (1770-1827), composer.

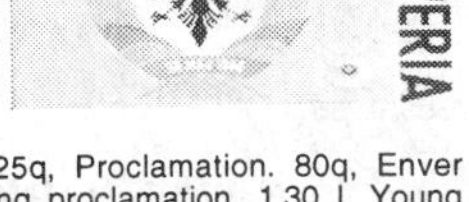

Coat of Arms A284

Designs: 25q, Proclamation. 80q, Enver Hoxha reading proclamation. 1.30 l, Young people and proclamation.

1971, Jan. 11 Litho. *Perf. 12*

1334	A284	15q	lt bl, gold, blk & red	.20	.20
1335	A284	25q	rose lil, blk, gold & gray	.20	.20
1336	A284	80q	emerald, blk & gold	.55	.20
1337	A284	1.30 l	yel org, blk & gold	.85	.25
			Nos. 1334-1337 (4)	1.80	.85

Declaration of the Republic, 25th anniv.

"Liberty" A285

Black Men A286

Designs: 50q, Women's brigade. 65q, Street battle, horiz. 1.10 l, Execution, horiz.

Perf. 12x11½, 11½x12

1971, Mar. 18 Litho.

1338	A285	25q	dk bl & bl	.20	.20
1339	A285	50q	slate green	.35	.20
1340	A285	65q	dk brn & chestnut	.50	.20
1341	A285	1.10 l	purple	.75	.20
			Nos. 1338-1341 (4)	1.80	.80

Centenary of the Paris Commune.

1971, Mar. 21 *Perf. 12x12½*

1.10 l, Men of 3 races. 1.15 l, Black protest.

1342	A286	25q	blk & bis brn	.20	.20
1343	A286	1.10 l	blk & rose car	.60	.20
1344	A286	1.15 l	blk & ver	.70	.20
			Nos. 1342-1344 (3)	1.50	.60

Intl. year against racial discrimination.

Tulip — A287

Horseman, by Dürer — A288

Designs: Various tulips.

1971, Mar. 25

1345	A287	5q	multi	.20	.20
1346	A287	10q	yellow & multi	.20	.20
1347	A287	15q	pink & multi	.20	.20
1348	A287	20q	lt blue & multi	.20	.20
1349	A287	25q	multi	.25	.20
1350	A287	80q	multi	.50	.20
1351	A287	1 l	multi	.75	.20
1352	A287	1.45 l	citron & multi	1.10	.25
			Nos. 1345-1352 (8)	3.40	1.65

Perf. 11½x12, 12x11½

1971, May 15 Litho.

Art Works by Dürer: 15q, Three peasants. 25q, Dancing peasant couple. 45q, The bagpiper. 65q, View of Kalkrebut, horiz. 2.40 l, View of Trent, horiz. 2.50 l, Self-portrait.

1353	A288	10q	black & pale grn	.20	.20
1354	A288	15q	black & pale lil	.20	.20
1355	A288	25q	black & pale bl	.25	.20
1356	A288	45q	black & pale rose	.40	.20
1357	A288	65q	black & multi	.60	.20
1358	A288	2.40 l	black & multi	2.25	.35
			Nos. 1353-1358 (6)	3.90	1.35

Miniature Sheet

Imperf

1359	A288	2.50 l	multi	3.00	.80

Albrecht Dürer (1471-1528), German painter and engraver.

Satellite Orbiting Globe — A289

Designs: 1.20 l, Government Building, Tirana, and Red Star emblem. 2.20 l, like 60q, 2.50 l, Flag of People's Republic of China forming trajectory around globe.

1971, June 10 Litho. *Perf. 12x12½*

1360 A289	60q purple & multi	.40	.20
1361 A289	1.20 l ver & multi	1.00	.25
1362 A289	2.20 l green & multi	1.60	.45

Imperf

1363 A289	2.50 l vio blk & multi	2.50	.90
Nos. 1360-1363 (4)		5.50	1.80

Space developments of People's Republic of China.

Mao Tse-tung — A290

Designs: 1.05 l, House where Communist Party was founded, horiz. 1.20 l, Peking crowd with placards, horiz.

1971, July 1 *Perf. 12x12½, 12½x12*

1364 A290	25q silver & multi	.30	.20
1365 A290	1.05 l silver & multi	.95	.20
1366 A290	1.20 l silver & multi	1.25	.25
Nos. 1364-1366 (3)		2.50	.65

50th anniv. of Chinese Communist Party.

Crested Titmouse — A291

1971, Aug. 15 Litho. *Perf. 12½x12*

1367 A291	5q shown	.20	.20
1368 A291	10q European serin	.20	.20
1369 A291	15q Linnet	.20	.20
1370 A291	25q Firecrest	.20	.20
1371 A291	45q Rock thrush	.40	.20
1372 A291	60q Blue tit	.60	.25
1373 A291	2.40 l Chaffinch	2.00	.60
a.	Block of 7, #1367-1373 + label	3.00	3.00

Continuous design with bird's nest label at upper left.

Olympic Rings and Running — A292

Designs (Olympic Rings and): 10q, Hurdles. 15q, Canoeing. 25q, Gymnastics. 80q, Fencing. 1.05 l, Soccer. 2 l, Runner at finish line. 3.60 l, Diving, women's.

1971, Sept. 15

1374 A292	5q green & multi	.20	.20
1375 A292	10q multicolored	.20	.20
1376 A292	15q blue & multi	.20	.20
1377 A292	25q violet & multi	.20	.20
1378 A292	80q lilac & multi	.35	.20
1379 A292	1.05 l multicolored	.45	.20
1380 A292	3.60 l multicolored	2.50	.50
Nos. 1374-1380 (7)		4.10	1.70

Souvenir Sheet

Imperf

1381 A292	2 l brt blue & multi	2.50	.75

20th Olympic Games, Munich, Aug. 26-Sept. 10, 1972.

Workers with Flags A293

Designs: 1.05 l, Party Headquarters, Tirana, and Red Star. 1.20 l, Rifle, star, flag and "VI," vert.

1971, Nov. 1 *Perf. 12*

1382 A293	25q gold, sil, red & bl	.20	.20
1383 A293	1.05 l gold, sil, red & bl	.65	.20
1384 A293	1.20 l gold, sil, red & blk	.80	.25
Nos. 1382-1384 (3)		1.65	.65

6th Congress of Workers' Party.

Factories and Workers A294

Designs: 80q, "XXX" and flag, vert. 1.55 l, Enver Hoxha and flags.

1971, Nov. 8

1385 A294	15q gold, sil, lil & yel	.20	.20
1386 A294	80q gold, sil & red	.70	.20
1387 A294	1.55 l gold, sil, red & brn	1.40	.25
Nos. 1385-1387 (3)		2.30	.65

30th anniversary of Workers' Party.

Construction Work, by M. Fushekati — A295

Contemporary Albanian Paintings: 5q, Young Man, by R. Kuci, vert. 25q, Partisan, by D. Jukniu, vert. 80q, Fliers, by S. Kristo. 1.20 l, Girl in Forest, by A. Sadikaj. 1.55 l, Warriors with Spears and Shields, by S. Kamberi. 2 l, Freedom Fighter, by I. Lulani.

Perf. 12x12½, 12½x12

1971, Nov. 20

1388 A295	5q gold & multi	.20	.20
1389 A295	15q gold & multi	.20	.20
1390 A295	25q gold & multi	.20	.20
1391 A295	80q gold & multi	.40	.20
1392 A295	1.20 l gold & multi	.90	.20
1393 A295	1.55 l gold & multi	1.10	.25
Nos. 1388-1393 (6)		3.00	1.25

Miniature Sheet

Imperf

1394 A295	2 l gold & multi	2.25	.70

Young Workers' Emblem — A296

1971, Nov. 23 *Perf. 12x12½*

1395 A296	15q lt blue & multi	.20	.20
1396 A296	1.35 l grnsh gray & multi	1.10	.25

Albanian Young Workers' Union, 30th anniv.

"Halili and Hajria" Ballet — A297

Scenes from "Halili and Hajria" Ballet: 10q, Brother and sister. 15q, Hajria before Sultan Suleiman. 50q, Hajria and husband. 80q, Execution of Halili. 1.40 l, Hajria killing her husband.

1971, Dec. 27 *Perf. 12½x12*

1397 A297	5q silver & multi	.20	.20
1398 A297	10q silver & multi	.20	.20
1399 A297	15q silver & multi	.20	.20
1400 A297	50q silver & multi	.45	.20
1401 A297	80q silver & multi	.70	.20
1402 A297	1.40 l silver & multi	1.10	.35
Nos. 1397-1402 (6)		2.85	1.35

Albanian ballet Halili and Hajria after drama by Kol Jakova.

Biathlon and Olympic Rings — A298

Designs (Olympic Rings and): 10q, Sledding. 15q, Ice hockey. 20q, Bobsledding. 50q, Speed skating. 1 l, Slalom. 2 l, Ski jump. 2.50 l, Figure skating, pairs.

1972, Feb. 10

1403 A298	5q lt olive & multi	.20	.20
1404 A298	10q lt violet & multi	.20	.20
1405 A298	15q multicolored	.20	.20
1406 A298	20q pink & multi	.20	.20
1407 A298	50q lt blue & multi	.30	.20
1408 A298	1 l ocher & multi	.75	.20
1409 A298	2 l lilac & multi	1.50	.35
Nos. 1403-1409 (7)		3.35	1.55

Souvenir Sheet

Imperf

1410 A298	2.50 l blue & multi	2.25	.50

11th Winter Olympic Games, Sapporo, Japan, Feb. 3-13.

Wild Strawberries A299

Wild Fruits and Nuts: 10q, Blackberries. 15q, Hazelnuts. 20q, Walnuts. 25q, Strawberry-tree fruit. 30q, Dogwood berries. 2.40 l, Rowan berries.

1972, Mar. 20 Litho. *Perf. 12*

1411 A299	5q lt grn & multi	.20	.20
1412 A299	10q yellow & multi	.20	.20
1413 A299	15q lt vio & multi	.20	.20
1414 A299	20q pink & multi	.20	.20
1415 A299	25q multi	.25	.20
1416 A299	30q multi	.35	.20
1417 A299	2.40 l multi	1.75	.45
Nos. 1411-1417 (7)		3.15	1.65

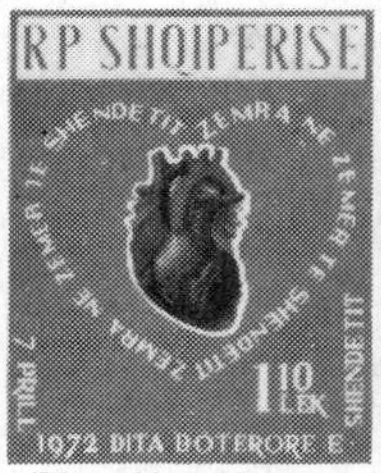

"Your Heart is your Health" A300

Worker and Student A301

World Health Day: 1.20 l, Cardiac patient and electrocardiogram.

1972, Apr. 7 *Perf. 12x12½*

1418 A300	1.10 l multicolored	.55	.20
1419 A300	1.20 l rose & multi	.70	.25

Perf. 11½x12½

1972, Apr. 24 Litho.

7th Trade Union Cong., May 8: 2.05 l, Assembly Hall, dancers and emblem.

1420 A301	25q multi	.25	.20
1421 A301	2.05 l blue & multi	1.50	.40

Qemal Stafa A302

Designs: 15q, Memorial flame. 25q, Monument "Spirit of Defiance," vert.

1972, May 5 *Perf. 12½x12, 12x12½*

1422 A302	15q gray & multi	.20	.20
1423 A302	25q sal rose, blk & gray	.20	.20
1424 A302	1.90 l dull yel & blk	1.10	.30
Nos. 1422-1424 (3)		1.50	.70

30th anniversary of the murder of Qemal Stafa and of Martyrs' Day.

Camellia A303

Designs: Various camellias.

1972, May 10 *Perf. 12x12½*

Flowers in Natural Colors

1425 A303	5q lt blue & blk	.20	.20
1426 A303	10q citron & blk	.20	.20
1427 A303	15q grnsh gray & blk	.20	.20
1428 A303	25q pale sal & blk	.20	.20
1429 A303	45q gray & blk	.30	.20
1430 A303	50q sal pink & blk	.45	.20
1431 A303	2.50 l bluish gray & blk	1.90	.75
Nos. 1425-1431 (7)		3.45	1.95

High Jump — A304

Designs (Olympic and Motion Emblems and): 10q, Running. 15q, Shot put. 20q, Bicycling. 25q, Pole vault. 50q, Hurdles, women's. 5q, Hockey. 2 l, Swimming. 2.50 l, Diving, women's.

1972, June 30 Litho. *Perf. 12½x12*

1432	A304	5q	multicolored	.20	.20
1433	A304	10q	lt brn & multi	.20	.20
1434	A304	15q	lt lil & multi	.20	.20
1435	A304	20q	multicolored	.20	.20
1436	A304	25q	lt vio & multi	.20	.20
1437	A304	50q	lt grn & multi	.40	.20
1438	A304	75q	multicolored	.80	.20
1439	A304	2 l	multicolored	1.50	.30
			Nos. 1432-1439 (8)	3.70	1.70

Miniature Sheet

Imperf

1440	A304	2.50 l	multi	1.50	.85

20th Olympic Games, Munich, Aug. 26-Sept. 11. Nos. 1432-1439 each issued in sheets of 8 stamps and one label (3x3) showing Olympic rings in gold.

Autobus A305

Designs: 25q, Electric train. 80q, Ocean liner Tirana. 1.05 l, Automobile. 1.20 l, Trailer truck.

1972, July 25 Litho. *Perf. 12*

1441	A305	15q	org brn & multi	.20	.20
1442	A305	25q	gray & multi	.20	.20
1443	A305	80q	dp grn & multi	.40	.20
1444	A305	1.05 l	multi	.55	.20
1445	A305	1.20 l	multi	.65	.20
			Nos. 1441-1445 (5)	2.00	1.00

Arm Wrestling A306

Folk Games: 10q, Piggyback ball game. 15q, Women's jumping. 25q, Rope game (srum). 90q, Leapfrog. 2 l, Women throwing pitchers.

1972, Aug. 18

1446	A306	5q	multi	.20	.20
1447	A306	10q	lt bl & multi	.20	.20
1448	A306	15q	rose & multi	.20	.20
1449	A306	25q	lt bl & multi	.20	.20
1450	A306	90q	ocher & multi	.65	.20
1451	A306	2 l	lt grn & multi	1.25	.25
			Nos. 1446-1451 (6)	2.70	1.25

1st National Festival of People's Games.

Mastheads — A307

30th Press Day: 25q, Printing press. 1.90 l, Workers reading paper.

1972, Aug. 25

1452	A307	15q	lt bl & blk	.20	.20
1453	A307	25q	red, grn & blk	.20	.20
1454	A307	1.90 l	lt vio & blk	1.25	.35
			Nos. 1452-1454 (3)	1.65	.75

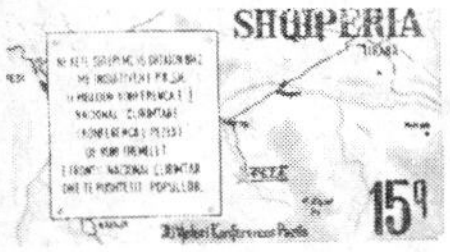

Map of Peza Area, Memorial Tablet A308

1972, Sept. 16

1455	A308	15q	shown	.20	.20
1456	A308	25q	Guerrillas with flag	.30	.20
1457	A308	1.90 l	Peza Conference memorial	1.75	.35
			Nos. 1455-1457 (3)	2.25	.75

30th anniversary, Conference of Peza.

Partisans, by Sotir Capo — A309

Paintings: 10q, Woman, by Ismail Lulani, vert. 15q, "Communists," by Lec Shkreli, vert. 20q, View of Nendorit, 1941, by Sali Shijaku, vert. 50q, Woman with Sheaf, by Zef Shoshi, vert. 1 l, Landscape with Children, by Dhimitraq Trebicka. 2 l, Women on Bicycles, by Vilson Kilica. 2.30 l, Folk Dance, by Abdurrahim Buza.

Perf. 12½x12, 12x12½

1972, Sept. 25 Litho.

1458	A309	5q	gold & multi	.20	.20
1459	A309	10q	gold & multi	.20	.20
1460	A309	15q	gold & multi	.20	.20
1461	A309	20q	gold & multi	.20	.20
1462	A309	50q	gold & multi	.35	.20
1463	A309	1 l	gold & multi	.70	.20
1464	A309	2 l	gold & multi	1.50	.35
			Nos. 1458-1464 (7)	3.35	1.55

Miniature Sheet

Imperf

1465	A309	2.30 l	gold & multi	2.00	.80

No. 1465 contains one 41x68mm stamp.

Congress Emblem — A310

Design: 2.05 l, Young worker with banner.

1972, Oct. 23 Litho. *Perf. 12*

1466	A310	25q	silver, red & gold	.20	.20
1467	A310	2.05 l	silver & multi	1.65	.45

Union of Working Youth, 6th Congress.

Hammer and Sickle A311

Ismail Qemali A312

Design: 1.20 l, Lenin as orator.

1972, Nov. 7 Litho. *Perf. 11½x12*

1468	A311	1.10 l	multi	.55	.20
1469	A311	1.20 l	multi	.60	.25

55th anniv. of the Russian October Revolution.

Perf. 12x11½, 11½x12

1972, Nov. 29

Designs: 15q, Albanian fighters, horiz. 65q, Rally, horiz. 1.25 l, Coat of arms.

1470	A312	15q	red, brt bl & blk	.20	.20
1471	A312	25q	yel, blk & red	.20	.20
1472	A312	65q	red, sal & blk	.50	.20
1473	A312	1.25 l	dl red & blk	.95	.25
			Nos. 1470-1473 (4)	1.85	.85

60th anniv. of independence.

Cock, Mosaic A313

Mosaics, 2nd-5th centuries, excavated near Buthrotium and Apollonia: 10q, Bird, vert. 15q, Partridges, vert. 25q, Warrior's legs. 45q, Nymph riding dolphin, vert. 50q, Fish, vert. 2.50 l, Warrior with helmet.

Perf. 12½x12, 12x12½

1972, Dec. 10

1474	A313	5q	silver & multi	.20	.20
1475	A313	10q	silver & multi	.20	.20
1476	A313	15q	silver & multi	.20	.20
1477	A313	25q	silver & multi	.20	.20
1478	A313	45q	silver & multi	.20	.20
1479	A313	50q	silver & multi	.30	.20
1480	A313	2.50 l	silver & multi	1.25	.40
			Nos. 1474-1480 (7)	2.55	1.60

Nicolaus Copernicus A314

Designs: 10q, 25q, 80q, 1.20 l, Various portraits of Copernicus. 1.60 l, Heliocentric solar system.

1973, Feb. 19 Litho. *Perf. 12x12½*

1481	A314	5q	lilac rose & multi	.20	.20
1482	A314	10q	dull olive & multi	.20	.20
1483	A314	25q	multicolored	.20	.20
1484	A314	80q	lt violet & multi	.60	.20
1485	A314	1.20 l	blue & multi	.85	.25
1486	A314	1.60 l	gray & multi	1.25	.35
			Nos. 1481-1486 (6)	3.30	1.40

500th anniversary of the birth of Nicolaus Copernicus (1473-1543), Polish astronomer.

Flowering Cactus — A315

Designs: Various flowering cacti.

1973, Mar. 25 Litho. *Perf. 12*

1487	A315	10q	multicolored	.20	.20
1488	A315	15q	multicolored	.20	.20
1489	A315	20q	beige & multi	.20	.20
1490	A315	25q	gray & multi	.20	.20
1491	A315	30q	beige & multi	.30	.20
1492	A315	65q	gray & multi	.75	.20
1493	A315	80q	multicolored	.95	.20
1494	A315	2 l	multicolored	2.50	.30
a.			Block of 8, #1487-1494	5.00	3.00
			Nos. 1487-1494 (8)	5.30	1.70

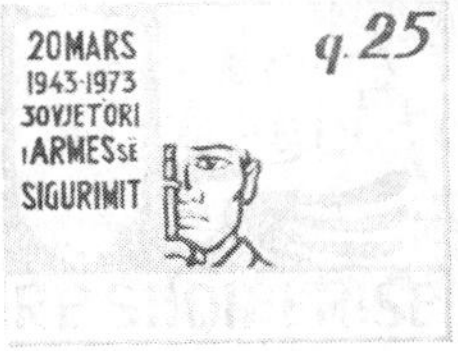

Guard and Factories A316

Design: 1.80 l, Guard and guards with prisoner.

1973, Mar. 20 Litho. *Perf. 12½x12*

1495	A316	25q	ultra & blk	.30	.20
1496	A316	1.80 l	dk red & multi	1.40	.40

30th anniv. of the State Security Branch.

Common Tern A317

Sea Birds: 15q, White-winged black terns, vert. 25q, Black-headed gull, vert. 45q, Great black-headed gull. 80q, Slender-billed gull, vert. 2.40 l, Sandwich terns.

1973, Apr. 30 *Perf. 12½x12, 12x12½*

1497	A317	5q	gold & multi	.20	.20
1498	A317	15q	gold & multi	.20	.20
1499	A317	25q	gold & multi	.30	.20
1500	A317	45q	gold & multi	.35	.20
1501	A317	80q	gold & multi	.80	.20
1502	A317	2.40 l	gold & multi	2.50	.50
			Nos. 1497-1502 (6)	4.35	1.50

Letters, 1913 Cancellation and Post Horn — A318

Design: 1.80 l, Mailman, 1913 cancel.

1973, May, 5 Litho. *Perf. 12x11½*

1503	A318	25q	red & multi	.40	.20
1504	A318	1.80 l	red & multi	2.50	.50

60th anniversary of Albanian stamps.

Farmer, Worker, Soldier A319

Design: 25q, Woman and factory, vert.

1973, June 4 *Perf. 12*

1505	A319	25q	carmine rose	.25	.20
1506	A319	1.80 l	yel, dp org & blk	1.50	.45

7th Congress of Albanian Women's Union.

Creation of General Staff, by G. Madhi — A320

Designs: 40q, "August 1949," sculpture by Sh. Haderi, vert. 60q, "Generation after Generation," sculpture by H. Dule, vert. 80q, "Defend Revolutionary Victories," by M. Fushekati.

1973, July 10 Litho. *Perf. 12½x12*

1507	A320	25q	gold & multi	*3.25*	.20
1508	A320	40q	gold & multi	*5.00*	.20
1509	A320	60q	gold & multi	*7.50*	.25
1510	A320	80q	gold & multi	*9.25*	.25
			Nos. 1507-1510 (4)	*25.00*	.90

30th anniversary of the People's Army.

"Electrification," by S. Hysa — A321

Albanian Paintings: 10q, Woman Textile Worker, by N. Nallbani. 15q, Gymnasts, by M. Fushekati. 50q, Aviator, by F. Stamo. 80q, Fascist Prisoner, by A. Lakuriqi. 1.20 l, Workers with Banner, by P. Mele. 1.30 l, Farm Woman, by Zef Shoshi. 2.05 l, Battle of Tenda, by F. Haxhiu. 10q, 50q, 80q, 1.20 l, 1.30 l, vertical.

Perf. 12½x12, 12x12½

1973, Aug. 10

1511	A321	5q	gold & multi	.20	.20
1512	A321	10q	gold & multi	.20	.20
1513	A321	15q	gold & multi	.20	.20
1514	A321	50q	gold & multi	.25	.20
1515	A321	80q	gold & multi	.55	.20
1516	A321	1.20 l	gold & multi	.90	.20
1517	A321	1.30 l	gold & multi	.95	.20
			Nos. 1511-1517 (7)	3.25	1.40

Souvenir Sheet

Imperf

1518	A321	2.05 l	multi	2.25	.65

Mary Magdalene, by Caravaggio A322

Paintings by Michelangelo da Caravaggio: 10q, The Lute Player, horiz. 15q, Self-portrait. 50q, Boy Carrying Fruit and Flowers. 80q, Still Life, horiz. 1.20 l, Narcissus. 1.30 l, Boy Peeling Apple. 2.05 l, Man with Feathered Hat.

Perf. 12x12½, 12½x12

1973, Sept. 28

1519	A322	5q	gold & multi	.20	.20
1520	A322	10q	gold & multi	.20	.20
1521	A322	15q	gold, blk & gray	.20	.20
1522	A322	50q	gold & multi	.25	.20
1523	A322	80q	gold & multi	.60	.20
1524	A322	1.20 l	gold & multi	.80	.25
1525	A322	1.30 l	gold & multi	.90	.25
			Nos. 1519-1525 (7)	3.15	1.50

Souvenir Sheet

Imperf

1526	A322	2.05 l	multi	3.75	.60

Michelangelo da Caravaggio (Merisi; 1573?-1609), Italian painter. No. 1526 contains one stamp, size: 63x73mm.

Soccer — A323

Designs: 5q-1.25 l, Various soccer scenes. 2.05 l, Ball in goal and list of cities where championships were held.

1973, Oct. 30 Litho. *Perf. 12½x12*

1527	A323	5q	multi	.20	.20
1528	A323	10q	multi	.20	.20
1529	A323	15q	multi	.20	.20
1530	A323	20q	multi	.20	.20
1531	A323	25q	multi	.20	.20
1532	A323	90q	multi	.65	.20
1533	A323	1.20 l	multi	.95	.20
1534	A323	1.25 l	multi	1.10	.20
			Nos. 1527-1534 (8)	3.70	1.60

Minature Sheet

Imperf

1535	A323	2.05 l	multi	2.00	.60

World Soccer Cup, Munich 1974.

Weight Lifter — A324

Designs: Various stages of weight lifting. 1.20 l, 1.60 l, horiz.

1973, Oct. 30 Litho. *Perf. 12*

1536	A324	5q	multi	.20	.20
1537	A324	10q	multi	.20	.20
1538	A324	25q	multi	.20	.20
1539	A324	90q	multi	.55	.20
1540	A324	1.20 l	multi	.45	.20
1541	A324	1.60 l	multi	.95	.20
			Nos. 1536-1541 (6)	2.55	1.20

Weight Lifting Championships, Havana, Cuba.

Ballet — A325

Harvester Combine — A326

Designs: 5q, Cement factory, Kavaje. 10q, Ali Kelmendi truck factory and tank cars, horiz. 25q, "Communication." 35q, Skiers and hotel, horiz. 60q, Resort, horiz. 80q, Mountain lake. 1 l, Mao Tse-tung textile mill. 1.20 l, Steel workers. 2.40 l, Welder and pipe. 3 l, Skanderbeg Monument, Tirana. 5 l, Roman arches, Durres.

Perf. 12½x12, 12x12½

1973-74 Litho.

1543	A325	5q	gold & multi	.20	.20
1544	A325	10q	gold & multi	.20	.20
1545	A325	15q	gold & multi	.20	.20
1545A	A326	20q	gold & multi	.20	.20
1546	A326	25q	gold & multi	.20	.20
1547	A326	35q	gold & multi	.20	.20
1548	A326	60q	gold & multi	.35	.20
1549	A326	80q	gold & multi	.50	.20
1549A	A326	1 l	gold & multi	.45	.20
1549B	A326	1.20 l	gold & multi	.75	.20
1549C	A326	2.40 l	gold & multi	1.50	.35
1550	A326	3 l	gold & multi	1.75	.35
1551	A326	5 l	gold & multi	2.75	.60
			Nos. 1543-1551 (13)	9.25	3.30

Issue dates: Nos. 1545-1546, 1549-1550, Dec. 5, 1973; others, 1974.

Mao Tse-tung — A327

80th birthday of Mao Tse-tung: 1.20 l, Mao Tse-tung addressing crowd.

1973, Dec. 26 *Perf. 12*

1552	A327	85q	gold, red & sepia	.80	.20
1553	A327	1.20 l	gold, red & sepia	1.25	.20

Old Man and Dog, by Gericault — A328

Paintings by Jean Louis André Theodore Gericault: 10q, Horse's Head. 15q, Male Model. 25q, Head of Black Man. 1.20 l, Self-portrait. 2.05 l, Raft of the Medusa, horiz. 2.20 l, Battle of the Giants.

Perf. 12x12½, 12½x12

1974, Jan. 18 Litho.

1554	A328	10q	gold & multi	.20	.20
1555	A328	15q	gold & multi	.20	.20
1556	A328	20q	gold & multi	.20	.20
1557	A328	25q	gold & blk	.25	.20
1558	A328	1.20 l	gold & multi	.90	.20
1559	A328	2.20 l	gold & multi	1.75	.35
			Nos. 1554-1559 (6)	3.50	1.35

Souvenir Sheet

Imperf

1560	A328	2.05 l	gold & multi	1.50	.45

No. 1560 contains one 87x78mm stamp.

Lenin, by Pandi Mele — A329

Designs: 25q, Lenin with Sailors on Cruiser Aurora, by Dhimitraq Trebicka, horiz. 1.20 l, Lenin, by Vilson Kilica.

1974, Jan. 21 *Perf. 12½x12, 12x12½*

1561	A329	25q	gold & multi	.20	.20
1562	A329	60q	gold & multi	.50	.20
1563	A329	1.20 l	gold & multi	1.10	.25
			Nos. 1561-1563 (3)	1.80	.65

50th anniv. of the death of Lenin.

Swimming Duck, Mosaic — A330

Designs: Mosaics from the 5th-6th Centuries A.D., excavated near Buthrotium, Pogradec and Apollonia.

1974, Feb. 20 Litho. *Perf. 12½x12*

1564	A330	5q	shown	.20	.20
1565	A330	10q	Bird and flower	.20	.20
1566	A330	15q	Vase and grapes	.20	.20
1567	A330	25q	Duck	.20	.20
1568	A330	40q	Donkey and bird	.30	.20
1569	A330	2.50 l	Sea horse	1.50	.35
			Nos. 1564-1569 (6)	2.60	1.35

Soccer — A331

Various scenes from soccer. 2.05 l, World Soccer Cup & names of participating countries.

1974, Apr. 25 Litho. *Perf. 12½x12*

1570	A331	10q	gold & multi	.20	.20
1571	A331	15q	gold & multi	.20	.20
1572	A331	20q	gold & multi	.20	.20
1573	A331	25q	gold & multi	.20	.20
1574	A331	40q	gold & multi	.30	.20
1575	A331	80q	gold & multi	.55	.20
1576	A331	1 l	gold & multi	.85	.25
1577	A331	1.20 l	gold & multi	1.10	.35
			Nos. 1570-1577 (8)	3.60	1.80

Souvenir Sheet

Imperf

1578	A331	2.05 l	gold & multi	2.50	.90

World Cup Soccer Championship, Munich, June 13-July 7. No. 1578 contains one stamp (60x60mm) with simulated perforations. Nos. 1570-1577 exist imperf, No. 1578 with simulated perfs omitted.

Arms of Albania, Soldier — A332

Design: 1.80 l, Soldier and front page of 1944 Congress Book.

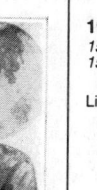

1974, May 24 Litho. *Perf. 12*

1579	A332	25q	multicolored	.20	.20
1580	A332	1.80 l	multicolored	1.25	.25

30th anniversary of the First Anti-Fascist Liberation Congress of Permet.

Medicinal Plants — A333

40q, 80q, 2.20 l, horiz.

1974, May 5 *Perf. 12x12½*

1581	A333	10q	Bittersweet	.20	.20
1582	A333	15q	Arbutus	.20	.20
1583	A333	20q	Lilies of the valley	.20	.20
1584	A333	25q	Autumn crocus	.20	.20
1585	A333	40q	Borage	.25	.20
1586	A333	80q	Soapwort	.85	.20
1587	A333	2.20 l	Gentian	1.90	.40
			Nos. 1581-1587 (7)	3.80	1.60

Revolutionaries with Albanian Flag — A334

1.80 l, Portraits of 5 revolutionaries, vert.

Perf. 12½x12, 12x12½

1974, June 10

1588	A334	25q	red, blk & lil	.20	.20
1589	A334	1.80 l	yel, red & blk	.80	.25

50th anniversary Albanian Bourgeois Democratic Revolution.

European Redwing — A335

Designs: Songbirds; Nos. 1597-1600 vert.

Perf. 12½x12, 12x12½

1974, July 15 Litho.

1594	A335	10q	shown	.20	.20
1595	A335	15q	European robin	.20	.20
1596	A335	20q	Greenfinch	.20	.20
1597	A335	25q	Bullfinch	.20	.20
1598	A335	40q	Hawfinch	.35	.20
1599	A335	80q	Blackcap	.85	.20
1600	A335	2.20 l	Nightingale	1.90	.45
			Nos. 1594-1600 (7)	3.90	1.65

Globe — A336

Cent. of UPU: 1.20 l, UPU emblem. 2.05 l, Jet over globe.

1974, Aug. 25 Litho. *Perf. 12x12½*

1601	A336	85q	green & multi	.80	.20
1602	A336	1.20 l	vio & ol grn	1.25	.20

Miniature Sheet

Imperf

1603	A336	2.05 l	blue & multi	12.00	12.00

Widows, by Sali Shijaku — A337

Albanian Paintings: 15q, Drillers, by Danish Jukniu, vert. 20q, Workers with Blueprints, by Clirim Ceka. 25q, Call to Action, by Spiro Kristo, vert. 40q, Winter Battle, by Sabaudin Xhaferi. 80q, Comrades, by Clirim Ceka, vert. 1 l, Aiding the Partisans, by Guri Madhi. 1.20 l, Teacher with Pupils, by Kleo Nini Brezat. 2.05 l, Comrades in Arms, by Guri Madhi.

Perf. 12½x12, 12x12½

1974, Sept. 25

1604	A337	10q silver & multi	.20	.20
1605	A337	15q silver & multi	.20	.20
1606	A337	20q silver & multi	.20	.20
1607	A337	25q silver & multi	.20	.20
1608	A337	40q silver & multi	.40	.20
1609	A337	80q silver & multi	.75	.20
1610	A337	1 l silver & multi	.95	.20
1611	A337	1.20 l silver & multi	1.00	.20
		Nos. 1604-1611 (8)	3.90	1.60

Miniature Sheet

Imperf

1612	A337	2.05 l silver & multi	2.00	.40

Crowd on Tien An Men Square A338

Design: 1.20 l, Mao Tse-tung, vert.

1974, Oct. 1 *Perf. 12*

1613	A338	85q gold & multi	.80	.20
1614	A338	1.20 l gold & multi	1.25	.20

25th anniversary of the proclamation of the People's Republic of China.

Women's Volleyball A339

Designs (Spartakiad Medal and): 15q, Women hurdlers. 20q, Women gymnasts. 25q, Mass exercises in Stadium. 40q, Weight lifter. 80q, Wrestlers. 1 l, Military rifle drill. 1.20 l, Soccer.

1974, Oct. 9 *Perf. 12x12½*

1615	A339	10q multi	.20	.20
1616	A339	15q multi	.20	.20
1617	A339	20q multi	.20	.20
1618	A339	25q gray & multi	.20	.20
1619	A339	40q multi	.20	.20
1620	A339	80q multi	.45	.20
1621	A339	1 l multi	.50	.20
1622	A339	1.20 l tan & multi	.60	.20
		Nos. 1615-1622 (8)	2.55	1.60

National Spartakiad, Oct. 9-17.

View of Berat — A340

Designs: 80q, Enver Hoxha addressing Congress, bas-relief, horiz. 1 l, Hoxha and leaders leaving Congress Hall.

Perf. 12x12½, 12½x12

1974, Oct. 20 **Litho.**

1623	A340	25q rose car & blk	.30	.20
1624	A340	80q yel, brn & blk	.60	.20
1625	A340	1 l dp lilac & blk	.90	.20
		Nos. 1623-1625 (3)	1.80	.60

30th anniversary of 2nd Congress of Berat.

Anniversary Emblem, Factory Guards — A341

35q, Chemical industry. 50q, Agriculture. 80q, Arts. 1 l, Atomic diagram & computer. 1.20 l, Youth education. 2.05 l, Crowd & History Book.

1974, Nov. 29 **Litho.** *Perf. 12½x12*

1626	A341	25q green & multi	.20	.20
1627	A341	35q ultra & multi	.20	.20
1628	A341	50q brown & multi	.25	.20
1629	A341	80q multicolored	.40	.20
1630	A341	1 l violet & multi	.45	.20
1631	A341	1.20 l multicolored	.50	.20
		Nos. 1626-1631 (6)	2.00	1.20

Miniature Sheet

Imperf

1632	A341	2.05 l gold & multi	2.00	.50

30th anniv. of liberation from Fascism.

Artemis, from Apolloni A342

1974, Dec. 25 **Photo.** *Perf. 12x12½*

1633	A342	10q shown	.20	.20
1634	A342	15q Zeus statue	.20	.20
1635	A342	20q Poseidon statue	.20	.20
1636	A342	25q Illyrian helmet	.20	.20
1637	A342	40q Amphora	.20	.20
1638	A342	80q Agrippa	.50	.20
1639	A342	1 l Demosthenes	.60	.20
1640	A342	1.20 l Head of Bilia	.70	.20
		Nos. 1633-1640 (8)	2.80	1.60

Miniature Sheet

Imperf

1641	A342	2.05 l Artemis & amphora	2.00	.60

Archaeological discoveries in Albania.

Workers and Factories A343

Design: 25q, Handshake, tools and book, vert.

1975, Feb. 11 **Litho.** *Perf. 12*

1642	A343	25q brown & multi	.20	.20
1643	A343	1.80 l yellow & multi	1.10	.30

Albanian Trade Unions, 30th anniversary.

Chicory A344

1975, Feb. 15

1644	A344	5q shown	.20	.20
1645	A344	10q Houseleek	.20	.20
1646	A344	15q Columbine	.20	.20
1647	A344	20q Anemone	.20	.20
1648	A344	25q Hibiscus	.20	.20
1649	A344	30q Gentian	.20	.20
1650	A344	35q Hollyhock	.20	.20
1651	A344	2.70 l Iris	1.20	.40
		Nos. 1644-1651 (8)	2.60	1.80

Protected flowers.

Jesus, from Doni Madonna A345

Works by Michelangelo: 10q, Slave, sculpture. 15q, Head of Dawn, sculpture. 20q, Awakening Giant, sculpture. 25q, Cumaenian Sybil, Sistine Chapel. 30q, Lorenzo di Medici, sculpture. 1.20 l, David, sculpture. 2.05 l, Self-portrait. 3.90 l, Delphic Sybil, Sistine Chapel.

1975, Mar. 20 **Litho.** *Perf. 12x12½*

1652	A345	5q gold & multi	.20	.20
1653	A345	10q gold & multi	.20	.20
1654	A345	15q gold & multi	.20	.20
1655	A345	20q gold & multi	.20	.20
1656	A345	25q gold & multi	.20	.20
1657	A345	30q gold & multi	.20	.20
1658	A345	1.20 l gold & multi	.35	.20
1659	A345	3.90 l gold & multi	1.50	.50
		Nos. 1652-1659 (8)	3.05	1.90

Miniature Sheet

Imperf

1660	A345	2.05 l gold & multi	1.10	.50

Michelangelo Buonarroti (1475-1564), Italian sculptor, painter and architect.

Two-wheeled Cart — A346

Albanian Transportation of the Past: 5q, Horseback rider. 15q, Lake ferry. 20q, Coastal three-master. 25q, Phaeton. 3.35 l, Early automobile on bridge.

1975, Apr. 15 **Litho.** *Perf. 12½x12*

1661	A346	5q bl grn & multi	.20	.20
1662	A346	10q ol & multi	.20	.20
1663	A346	15q lil & multi	.20	.20
1664	A346	20q multi	.20	.20
1665	A346	25q multi	.20	.20
1666	A346	3.35 l ocher & multi	1.50	.50
		Nos. 1661-1666 (6)	2.50	1.50

Guard at Frontier Stone — A347

Guardsman and Militia — A348

1975, Apr. 25 *Perf. 12*

1667	A347	25q multi	.20	.20
1668	A348	1.80 l multi	1.10	.20

30th anniversary of Frontier Guards.

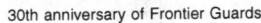

Posting Illegal Poster — A349

Designs: 60q, Partisans in battle. 1.20 l, Partisan killing German soldier, and Albanian coat of arms.

1975, May 9 *Perf. 12½x12*

1669	A349	25q multi	.20	.20
1670	A349	60q multi	.25	.20
1671	A349	1.20 l red & multi	.75	.25
		Nos. 1669-1671 (3)	1.20	.65

30th anniversary of victory over Fascism.

European Widgeons — A350

Waterfowl: 10q, Red-crested pochards. 15q, White-fronted goose. 20q, Northern pintails. 25q, Red-breasted merganser. 30q, Eider ducks. 35q, Whooper swan. 2.70 l, Shovelers.

1975, June 15 **Litho.** *Perf. 12*

1672	A350	5q brt blue & multi	.20	.20
1673	A350	10q yel grn & multi	.20	.20
1674	A350	15q brt rose lil & multi	.20	.20
1675	A350	20q bl grn & multi	.20	.20
1676	A350	25q multicolored	.20	.20
1677	A350	30q multicolored	.20	.20
1678	A350	35q orange & multi	.20	.20
1679	A350	2.70 l multi	1.60	.35
		Nos. 1672-1679 (8)	3.00	1.75

Shyqyri Kanapari, by Musa Qarri — A351

Albanian Paintings: 10q, Woman Saving Children in Sea, by Agim Faja. 15q, "November 28, 1912" (revolution), by Petrit Ceno, horiz. 20q, "Workers Unite," by Sali Shijaku. 25q, The Partisan Shota Galica, by Ismail Lulani. 30q, Victorious Resistance Fighters, 1943, by Nestor Jonuzi. 80q, Partisan Couple in Front of Red Flag, by Vilson Halimi. 2.05 l, Dancing Procession, by Abdurahim Buza. 2.25 l, Republic Day Celebration, by Fatmir Haxhiu, horiz.

Perf. 12x12½, 12½x12

1975, July 15 **Litho.**

1680	A351	5q gold & multi	.20	.20
1681	A351	10q gold & multi	.20	.20
1682	A351	15q gold & multi	.20	.20
1683	A351	20q gold & multi	.20	.20
1684	A351	25q gold & multi	.20	.20
1685	A351	30q gold & multi	.20	.20
1686	A351	80q gold & multi	.35	.20
1687	A351	2.25 l gold & multi	1.25	.30
		Nos. 1680-1687 (8)	2.80	1.70

Miniature Sheet

Imperf

1688	A351	2.05 l gold & multi	1.65	.50

Nos. 1680-1687 issued in sheets of 8 stamps and gold center label showing palette and easel.

Farmer Holding Reform Law — A352

Design: 2 l, Produce and farm machinery.

1975, Aug. 28 ***Perf. 12***

1689	A352	15q multicolored	.20	.20
1690	A352	2 l multicolored	1.10	.35

Agrarian reform, 30th anniversary.

Alcynonium Palmatum A353

Corals: 10q, Paramuricea chamaeleon. 20q, Coralium rubrum. 25q, Eunicella covalini. 3.70 l, Cladocora cespitosa.

1975, Sept. 25 **Litho.** ***Perf. 12***

1691	A353	5q blue, ol & blk	.20	.20
1692	A353	10q blue & multi	.20	.20
1693	A353	20q blue & multi	.20	.20
1694	A353	25q blue & blk	.20	.20
1695	A353	3.70 l blue & blk	2.00	.50
		Nos. 1691-1695 (5)	2.80	1.30

Bicycling A354

Designs (Montreal Olympic Games Emblem and): 10q, Canoeing. 15q, Fieldball. 20q, Basketball. 25q, Water polo. 30q, Hockey. 1.20 l, Pole vault. 2.05 l, Fencing. 2.15 l, Montreal Olympic Games emblem and various sports.

1975, Oct. 20 **Litho.** ***Perf. 12½***

1696	A354	5q multi	.20	.20
1697	A354	10q multi	.20	.20
1698	A354	15q multi	.20	.20
1699	A354	20q multi	.20	.20
1700	A354	25q multi	.20	.20
1701	A354	30q multi	.20	.20
1702	A354	1.20 l multi	.40	.20
1703	A354	2.05 l multi	.85	.25
		Nos. 1696-1703 (8)	2.45	1.65

Miniature Sheet

Imperf

1704	A354	2.15 l org & multi	2.75	1.75

21st Olympic Games, Montreal, July 18-Aug. 8, 1976. Nos. 1696-1703 exist imperf.

Power Lines Leading to Village — A355

Designs: 25q, Transformers and insulators. 80q, Dam and power station. 85q, Television set, power lines, grain and cogwheel.

1975, Oct. 25 ***Perf. 12x12½***

1705	A355	15q ultra & yel	.20	.20
1706	A355	25q brt vio & pink	.20	.20
1707	A355	80q lt grn & gray	.40	.20
1708	A355	85q ocher & brn	.40	.20
		Nos. 1705-1708 (4)	1.20	.80

General electrification, 5th anniversary.

Child, Rabbit and Teddy Bear Planting Tree — A356

Fairy Tales: 10q, Mother fox. 15q, Ducks in school. 20q, Little pigs building house. 25q, Animals watching television. 30q, Rabbit and bear at work. 35q, Working and playing ants. 2.70 l, Wolf in sheep's clothes.

1975, Dec. 25 **Litho.** ***Perf. 12½x12***

1709	A356	5q black & multi	.20	.20
1710	A356	10q black & multi	.20	.20
1711	A356	15q black & multi	.20	.20
1712	A356	20q black & multi	.20	.20
1713	A356	25q black & multi	.20	.20
1714	A356	30q black & multi	.20	.20
1715	A356	35q black & multi	.20	.20
1716	A356	2.70 l black & multi	1.25	.30
		Nos. 1709-1716 (8)	2.65	1.70

Arms, People, Factories A357

Design: 1.90 l, Arms, government building, celebrating crowd.

1976, Jan. 11 **Litho.** ***Perf. 12***

1717	A357	25q gold & multi	.20	.20
1718	A357	1.90 l gold & multi	.85	.25

30th anniversary of proclamation of Albanian People's Republic.

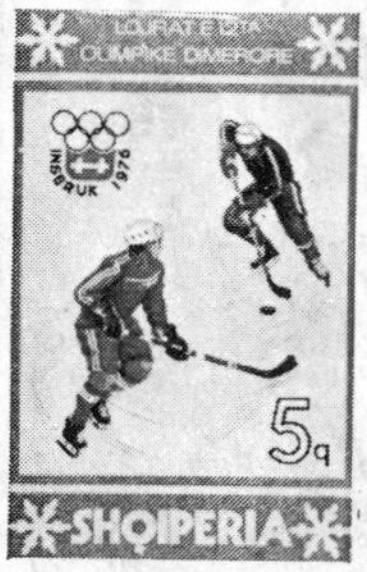

Ice Hockey, Olympic Games' Emblem — A358

Designs: 10q, Speed skating. 15q, Biathlon. 50q, Ski jump. 1.20 l, Slalom. 2.15 l, Figure skating, pairs. 2.30 l, One-man bobsled.

1976, Feb. 4

1719	A358	5q silver & multi	.20	.20
1720	A358	10q silver & multi	.20	.20
1721	A358	15q silver & multi	.20	.20
1722	A358	50q silver & multi	.25	.20
1723	A358	1.20 l silver & multi	.60	.20
1724	A358	2.30 l silver & multi	1.40	.35
		Nos. 1719-1724 (6)	2.85	1.35

Miniature Sheet

Perf. 12 on 2 sides x Imperf.

1725	A358	2.15 l silver & multi	1.90	.80

12th Winter Olympic Games, Innsbruck, Austria, Feb. 4-15.

Meadow Saffron — A359

Medicinal Plants: 10q, Deadly night-shade. 15q, Yellow gentian. 20q, Horse chestnut. 70q, Shield fern. 80q, Marshmallow. 2.30 l, Thorn apple.

1976, Apr. 10 **Litho.** ***Perf. 12x12½***

1726	A359	5q black & multi	.20	.20
1727	A359	10q black & multi	.20	.20
1728	A359	15q black & multi	.20	.20
1729	A359	20q black & multi	.20	.20
1730	A359	70q black & multi	.25	.20
1731	A359	80q black & multi	.45	.20
1732	A359	2.30 l black & multi	1.25	.35
		Nos. 1726-1732 (7)	2.75	1.55

Bowl and Spoon — A360

15q, Flask, vert. 20q, Carved handles, vert. 25q, Pistol and dagger. 80q, Wall hanging, vert. 1.20 l, Earrings and belt buckle. 1.40 l, Jugs, vert.

1976 **Litho.** ***Perf. 12½x12, 12x12½***

1733	A360	10q lilac & multi	.20	.20
1734	A360	15q gray & multi	.20	.20
1735	A360	20q multi	.20	.20
1736	A360	25q car & multi	.20	.20
1737	A360	80q yellow & multi	.35	.20
1738	A360	1.20 l multi	.50	.20
1739	A360	1.40 l tan & multi	.65	.25
		Nos. 1733-1739 (7)	2.30	1.45

Natl. Ethnographic Conf., Tirana, June 28.
For surcharge see No. 1873.

Founding of Cooperatives, by Zef Shoshi — A361

Paintings: 10q, Going to Work, by Agim Zajmi, vert. 25q, Crowd Listening to Loudspeaker, by Vilson Kilica. 40q, Woman Welder, by Sabaudin Xhaferi, vert. 50q, Factory, by Isuf Sulovari, vert. 1.20 l, 1942 Revolt, by Lec Shkreli, vert. 1.60 l, Coming Home from Work, by Agron Dine. 2.05 l, Honoring a Young Pioneer, by Andon Lakuriqi.

Perf. 12½x12, 12x12½

1976, Aug. 8 **Litho.**

1740	A361	5q gold & multi	.20	.20
1741	A361	10q gold & multi	.20	.20
1742	A361	25q gold & multi	.20	.20
1743	A361	40q gold & multi	.20	.20
1744	A361	50q gold & multi	.20	.20
1745	A361	1.20 l gold & multi	.50	.20
1746	A361	1.60 l gold & multi	.75	.30
		Nos. 1740-1746 (7)	2.25	1.50

Miniature Sheet

Perf. 12 on 2 sides x Imperf.

1747	A361	2.05 l gold & multi	1.10	.45

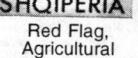

Red Flag, Agricultural Symbols — A362

Enver Hoxha, Partisans and Albanian Flag — A363

Design: 1.20 l, Red flag and raised pickax.

1976, Nov. 1

1748	A362	25q multi	.20	.20
1749	A362	1.20 l multi	.80	.20

7th Workers Party Congress.

1976, Oct. 28 ***Perf. 12x12½***

1.90 l, Demonstrators with Albanian flag.

1750	A363	25q multi	.20	.20
1751	A363	1.90 l multi	1.00	.30

Anti-Fascist demonstrations, 35th anniv.

Attacking Partisans, Meeting House — A364

Designs (Red Flag and): 25q, Partisans, pickax and gun. 80q, Workers, soldiers, pickax and gun. 1.20 l, Agriculture and industry. 1.70 l, Dancers, symbols of science and art.

1976, Nov. 8 **Litho.** ***Perf. 12x12½***

1752	A364	15q gold & multi	.20	.20
1753	A364	25q gold & multi	.20	.20
1754	A364	80q gold & multi	.30	.20
1755	A364	1.20 l gold & multi	.50	.20
1756	A364	1.70 l gold & multi	1.00	.20
		Nos. 1752-1756 (5)	2.20	1.00

35th anniv. of 1st Workers Party Cong.

Young Workers and Track A365

Design: 1.25 l, Young soldiers and Albanian flag.

1976, Nov. 23 ***Perf. 12***

1757	A365	80q yellow & multi	.55	.20
1758	A365	1.25 l carmine & multi	.75	.20

Union of Young Communists, 35th anniv.

"Cuca e Maleve" Ballet A366

Designs: Scenes from ballet "Mountain Girl."

1976, Dec. 14 ***Perf. 12***

1759	A366	10q gold & multi	.20	.20
1760	A366	15q gold & multi	.20	.20
1761	A366	20q gold & multi	.20	.20
1762	A366	25q gold & multi	.20	.20
1763	A366	80q gold & multi	.55	.20
1764	A366	1.20 l gold & multi	.75	.20
1765	A366	1.40 l gold & multi	.95	.25
		Nos. 1759-1765 (7)	3.05	1.45

Miniature Sheet

Perf. 12 on 2 sides x Imperf.

1766 A366 2.05 l gold & multi 1.75 .45

Bashtoves Castle A367

Albanian Castles: 15q, Gjirokastres. 20q, Ali Pash Tepelenes. 25q, Petreles. 80q, Beratit. 1.20 l, Durresit. 1.40 l, Krujes.

1976, Dec. 30 Litho. *Perf. 12*

1767 A367 10q black & dull bl .20 .20
1768 A367 15q black & grn .20 .20
1769 A367 20q black & gray .20 .20
1770 A367 25q black & brn .20 .20
1771 A367 80q black & rose .40 .20
1772 A367 1.20 l black & vio .45 .20
1773 A367 1.40 l black & brn red .90 .20
Nos. 1767-1773 (7) 2.55 1.40

Skanderbeg's Shield and Spear — A368

Skanderbeg's Weapons: 80q, Helmet, sword and scabbard. 1 l, Halberd, quiver with arrows, crossbow and spear.

1977, Jan. 28 Litho. *Perf. 12*

1774 A368 15q silver & multi .50 .20
1775 A368 80q silver & multi 2.25 .20
1776 A368 1 l silver & multi 3.25 .25
Nos. 1774-1776 (3) 6.00 .65

Skanderbeg (1403-1468), national hero.

Ilia Oiqi, Messenger in Storm — A369

Modern Heroes: 10q, Ilia Dashi, sailor in battle. 25q, Fran Ndue Ivanaj, fisherman in storm. 80q, Zeliha Allmetaj, woman rescuing child. 1 l, Ylli Zaimi, rescuing goats from flood. 1.90 l, Isuf Plloci, fighting forest fire.

1977, Feb. 28 Litho. *Perf. 12x12½*

1777 A369 5q brown & multi .20 .20
1778 A369 10q ultra & multi .20 .20
1779 A369 25q blue & multi .20 .20
1780 A369 80q ocher & multi .50 .20
1781 A369 1 l brown & multi .80 .20
1782 A369 1.90 l brown & multi 1.40 .20
Nos. 1777-1782 (6) 3.30 1.20

Polyvinylchloride Plant, Vlore — A370

6th Five-year plan: 25q, Naphtha fractioning plant, Ballsh. 65q, Hydroelectric station and dam, Fjerzes. 1 l, Metallurgical plant and blast furance, Elbasan.

1977, Mar. 29 Litho. *Perf. 12½x12*

1783 A370 15q silver & multi .20 .20
1784 A370 25q silver & multi .30 .20
1785 A370 65q silver & multi .65 .20
1786 A370 1 l silver & multi 1.10 .20
Nos. 1783-1786 (4) 2.25 .80

Qerime Halil Galica — A371

Victory Monument, Tirana — A372

Design: 1.25 l, Qerime Halil Galica "Shota" and father Azem Galica.

1977, Apr. 20 Litho. *Perf. 12*

1787 A371 80q dark red .65 .20
1788 A371 1.25 l gray blue 1.10 .20

"Shota" Galica, communist fighter.

1977, May 5 Litho. *Perf. 12*

Designs (Red Star and): 80q, Clenched fist, Albanian flag. 1.20 l, Bust of Qemal Stafa and poppies.

1789 A372 25q multi .30 .20
1790 A372 80q multi .90 .20
1791 A372 1.20 l multi 1.50 .20
Nos. 1789-1791 (3) 2.70 .60

35th anniversary of Martyrs' Day.

Physician Visiting Farm, Mobile Clinic — A373

Designs: 10q, Cowherd and cattle ranch. 20q, Militia woman helping with harvest, rifle and combine. 80q, Modern village, highway and power lines. 2.95 l, Tractor and greenhouses.

1977, June 18

1792 A373 5q multi .20 .20
1793 A373 10q multi .20 .20
1794 A373 20q multi .20 .20
1795 A373 80q multi .40 .20
1796 A373 2.95 l multi 2.50 .40
Nos. 1792-1796 (5) 3.50 1.20

"Socialist transformation of the villages."

Armed Workers, Flag and Factory — A374

1.80 l, Workers with proclamation and flags.

1977, June 20

1797 A374 25q multi .20 .20
1798 A374 1.80 l multi 1.25 .20

9th Labor Unions Congress.

Kerchief Dance — A375

Designs: Various folk dances.

1977, Aug. 20 Litho. *Perf. 12*

1799 A375 5q multi .20 .20
1800 A375 10q multi .20 .20
1801 A375 15q multi .20 .20
1802 A375 25q multi .20 .20
1803 A375 80q multi .30 .20
1804 A375 1.20 l multi .60 .20
1805 A375 1.55 l multi .75 .25
Nos. 1799-1805 (7) 2.45 1.45

Miniature Sheet

Perf. 12 on 2 sides x Imperf.

1806 A375 2.05 l multi 1.25 .40

See Nos. 1836-1840, 1884-1888.

Attack A376

Designs: 25q, Enver Hoxha addressing Army. 80q, Volunteers and riflemen. 1 l, Volunteers, hydrofoil patrolboat and MiG planes. 1.90 l, Volunteers and Albanian flag.

1977, July 10 Litho. *Perf. 12*

1807 A376 15q gold & multi .20 .20
1808 A376 25q gold & multi .20 .20
1809 A376 80q gold & multi .45 .20
1810 A376 1 l gold & multi .70 .20
1811 A376 1.90 l gold & multi 1.25 .25
Nos. 1807-1811 (5) 2.80 1.05

"One People-One Army."

Armed Workers, Article 3 of Constitution A377

Design: 1.20 l, Symbols of farming and fertilizer industry, Article 25 of Constitution.

1977, Oct.

1812 A377 25q red, gold & blk .25 .20
1813 A377 1.20 l red, gold & blk .95 .20

New Constitution.

Picnic — A378

Film Frames: 15q, Telephone lineman in winter. 25q, Two men and a woman. 80q, Workers. 1.20 l, Boys playing in street. 1.60 l, Harvest.

1977, Oct. 25 Litho. *Perf. 12½x12*

1814 A378 10q blue green .20 .20
1815 A378 15q multi .20 .20
1816 A378 25q black .20 .20
1817 A378 80q multi .55 .20
1818 A378 1.20 l deep claret .95 .20
1819 A378 1.60 l multi 1.25 .20
Nos. 1814-1819 (6) 3.35 1.20

Albanian films.

Farm Workers in Field, by V. Mio A379

Paintings by V. Mio: 10q, Landscape in Snow. 15q, Grazing Sheep under Walnut Tree in Spring. 25q, Street in Korce. 80q, Horseback Riders on Mountain Pass. 1 l, Boats on Shore. 1.75 l, Tractors Plowing Fields. 2.05 l, Self-portrait.

1977, Dec. 25 Litho. *Perf. 12½x12*

1820 A379 5q gold & multi .20 .20
1821 A379 10q gold & multi .20 .20
1822 A379 15q gold & multi .20 .20
1823 A379 25q gold & multi .20 .20
1824 A379 80q gold & multi .40 .20
1825 A379 1 l gold & multi .45 .20
1826 A379 1.75 l gold & multi .80 .20
Nos. 1820-1826 (7) 2.45 1.40

Miniature Sheet

Imperf.; Perf. 12 Horiz. between Vignette and Value Panel

1827 A379 2.05 l gold & multi 2.00 .35

Pan Flute — A380

Albanian Flag, Monument and People — A381

Folk Musical Instruments: 25q, Single-string goat's-head fiddle. 80q, Woodwind. 1.20 l, Drum. 1.70 l, Bagpipe. Background shows various woven folk patterns.

1978, Jan. 20 *Perf. 12x12½*

1828 A380 15q multi .20 .20
1829 A380 25q multi .25 .20
1830 A380 80q multi .70 .20
1831 A380 1.20 l multi 1.10 .20
1832 A380 1.70 l multi 1.50 .20
Nos. 1828-1832 (5) 3.75 1.00

1978 *Perf. 12½x12, 12x12½*

Designs: 25q, Ismail Qemali and fighters, horiz. 1.65 l, People dancing around Albanian flag, horiz.

1833 A381 15q multi .20 .20
1834 A381 25q multi .25 .20
1835 A381 1.65 l multi 1.50 .20
Nos. 1833-1835 (3) 1.95 .60

65th anniversary of independence.

Folk Dancing Type of 1977

Designs: Various dances.

1978, Feb. 15 Litho. *Perf. 12*

1836 A375 5q multi .20 .20
1837 A375 25q multi .20 .20
1838 A375 80q multi .35 .20
1839 A375 1 l multi .50 .20
1840 A375 2.30 l multi 1.00 .25
Nos. 1836-1840 (5) 2.25 1.05

Nos. 1836-1840 have white background around dancers, Nos. 1799-1805 have pinkish shadows.

Tractor Drivers, by Dhimitraq Trebicka A382

Working Class Paintings: 80q, Steeplejack, by Spiro Kristo. 85q, "A Point in the Discussion," by Skender Milori. 90q, Oil rig crew, by Anesti Cini, vert. 1.60 l, Metal workers, by Ramadan Karanxha. 2.20 l, Political discussion, by Sotiraq Sholla.

1978, Mar. 25 Litho. *Perf. 12*

1841 A382 25q multi .20 .20
1842 A382 80q multi .35 .20
1843 A382 85q multi .35 .20
1844 A382 90q multi .40 .20
1845 A382 1.60 l multi .80 .25
Nos. 1841-1845 (5) 2.10 1.05

Miniature Sheet

Perf. 12 on 2 sides x Imperf.

1846 A382 2.20 l multi 1.75 .40

Woman with Rifle and Pickax A383

1.95 l, Farm & Militia women, industrial plant.

1978, June 1 Litho. *Perf. 12*

1847 A383 25q gold & red .25 .20
1848 A383 1.95 l gold & red 1.40 .25

8th Congress of Women's Union.

Children and Flowers — A384

Designs: 10q, Children with rifle, ax, book and flags. 25q, Dancing children in folk costume. 1.80 l, Children in school.

1978, June 1 **Litho.**

1849	A384	5q multi	.20	.20
1850	A384	10q multi	.20	.20
1851	A384	25q multi	.25	.20
1852	A384	1.80 l multi	1.50	.20
		Nos. 1849-1852 (4)	2.15	.80

International Children's Day.

Spirit of Skanderbeg as Conqueror — A385

Designs: 10q, Battle at Mostar Bridge. 80q, Marchers and Albanian flag. 1.20 l, Riflemen in winter battle. 1.65 l, Abdyl Frasheri (1839-1892). 2.20 l, Rifles, scroll and pen, League building. 2.60 l, League headquarters, Prizren.

1978, June 10 **Litho.** ***Perf. 12***

1853	A385	10q multi	.20	.20
1854	A385	25q multi	.20	.20
1855	A385	80q multi	.25	.20
1856	A385	1.20 l multi	.55	.20
1857	A385	1.65 l multi	.85	.20
1858	A385	2.60 l multi	1.00	.30
		Nos. 1853-1858 (6)	3.05	1.30

Miniature Sheet

Perf. 12 on 2 sides x Imperf.

1859	A385	2.20 l multi	2.00	.35

Centenary of League of Prizren.

Guerrillas and Flag, 1943 — A386

Designs: 25q, Soldier, sailor, airman, militiaman, horiz. 1.90 l, Members of armed forces, civil guards, and Young Pioneers.

1978, July 10 ***Perf. 11½x12½***

1860	A386	5q multi	.20	.20
1861	A386	25q multi	.45	.20
1862	A386	1.90 l multi	3.25	.20
		Nos. 1860-1862 (3)	3.90	.60

35th anniversary of People's Army.

Woman with Machine Carbine — A387

Kerchief Dance — A388

Designs: 25q, Man with target rifle, horiz. 95q, Man shooting with telescopic sights, horiz. 2.40 l, Woman target shooting with pistol.

Perf. 12½x12, 12x12½

1978, Sept. 20 **Litho.**

1863	A387	25q black & yel	.20	.20
1864	A387	80q orange & blk	.35	.20
1865	A387	95q red & blk	.50	.20
1866	A387	2.40 l carmine & blk	1.10	.30
		Nos. 1863-1866 (4)	2.15	.90

32nd National Rifle-shooting Championships, Sept. 20.

1978, Oct. 6 ***Perf. 12***

Designs: 15q, Musicians. 25q, Fiddler with single-stringed instrument. 80q, Dancers, men. 1.20 l, Saber dance. 1.90 l, Singers, women.

1867	A388	10q multi	.20	.20
1868	A388	15q multi	.20	.20
1869	A388	25q multi	.20	.20
1870	A388	80q multi	.30	.20
1871	A388	1.20 l multi	.60	.20
1872	A388	1.90 l multi	.95	.25
		Nos. 1867-1872 (6)	2.45	1.25

National Folklore Festival.

See Nos. 2082-2085, 2289-2290.

No. 1736 Surcharged with New Value, 2 Bars and "RICCIONE 78"

1978 **Litho.** ***Perf. 12½x12***

1873	A360	3.30 l on 25q multi	5.00	1.10

Riccione 78 Philatelic Exhibition.

Enver Hoxha — A389

1978, Oct. 16 **Litho.** ***Perf. 12x12½***

1874	A389	80q red & multi	.30	.20
1875	A389	1.20 l red & multi	.45	.20
1876	A389	2.40 l red & multi	.90	.25
		Nos. 1874-1876 (3)	1.65	.65

Miniature Sheet

Perf. 12½ on 2 sides x Imperf.

1877	A389	2.20 l red & multi	1.75	.40

70th birthday of Enver Hoxha, First Secretary of Central Committee of the Communist Party of Albania.

Woman and Wheat — A390

Designs: 25q, Woman with egg crates. 80q, Shepherd and sheep. 2.60 l, Milkmaid and cows.

1978, Dec. 15 ***Perf. 12x12½***

1878	A390	15q multicolored	.20	.20
1879	A390	25q multicolored	.35	.20
1880	A390	80q multicolored	.90	.20
1881	A390	2.60 l multicolored	2.50	.50
		Nos. 1878-1881 (4)	3.95	1.10

Dora d'Istria — A391

Tower House — A392

Design: 1.10 l, Full portrait of Dora d'Istria, author; birth sesquicentennial.

1979, Jan. 22 **Litho.** ***Perf. 12***

1882	A391	80q lt grn & blk	.70	.20
1883	A391	1.10 l vio brn & blk	.80	.20

Costume Type of 1977

Designs: Various folk dances.

1979, Feb. 25

1884	A375	15q multi	.20	.20
1885	A375	25q multi	.20	.20
1886	A375	80q multi	.40	.20
1887	A375	1.20 l multi	.50	.20
1888	A375	1.40 l multi	.75	.25
		Nos. 1884-1888 (5)	2.05	1.05

#1884-1888 have white background. Denomination in UL on #1885, in UR on #1802; LL on #1886, UL on #1803.

1979, Mar. 20

Traditional Houses: 15q, Stone gallery house, horiz. 80q, House with wooden galleries, horiz. 1.20 l, Galleried tower house. 1.40 l, 1.90 l, Tower houses, diff.

1889	A392	15q multi	.20	.20
1890	A392	25q multi	.20	.20
1891	A392	80q multi	.40	.20
1892	A392	1.20 l multi	.50	.20
1893	A392	1.40 l multi	.75	.25
		Nos. 1889-1893 (5)	2.05	1.05

Miniature Sheet

Perf. 12 on 2 sides x Imperf.

1894	A392	1.90 l multi	1.50	.40

See Nos. 2015-2018.

Soldier, Factories, Wheat A393

1.65 l, Soldiers, workers and coat of arms.

1979, May 14 **Litho.** ***Perf. 12***

1895	A393	25q multi	.45	.20
1896	A393	1.65 l multi	2.00	.20

Congress of Permet, 35th anniversary.

Albanian Flag — A394

1979, June 4

1897	A394	25q multi	.50	.20
1898	A394	1.65 l multi	2.50	.20

5th Congress of Albanian Democratic Front.

Vasil Shanto, (1913-44) A395

Alexander Moissi, (1880-1935), Actor — A396

Design: 25q, 90q, Qemal Stafa (1921-42).

1979

1899	A395	15q multi	.20	.20
1900	A395	25q multi	.20	.20
1901	A395	60q multi	.60	.20
1902	A396	80q multi	.80	.20
1903	A395	90q multi	.80	.20
1904	A396	1.10 l multi, diff.	1.00	.20
		Nos. 1899-1904 (6)	3.60	1.20

Shanto and Stafa, anti-Fascist fighters.

Issued: type A396, Apr. 2; type A395, May 5.

For similar design see A410.

Winter Campaign, by Arben Basha — A397

Paintings of Military Scenes by: 25q, Ismail Lulani. 80q, Myrteza Fushekati. 1.20 l, Muhamet Deliu. 1.40 l, Jorgji Gjikopulli. 1.90 l, Fatmir Haxhiu.

1979, July 15 **Litho.** ***Perf. 12½x12***

1905	A397	15q multi	.20	.20
1906	A397	25q multi	.20	.20
1907	A397	80q multi	.35	.20
1908	A397	1.20 l multi	.60	.20
1909	A397	1.40 l multi	.65	.25
		Nos. 1905-1909 (5)	2.00	1.05

Miniature Sheet

Perf. 12 on 2 sides x Imperf.

1910	A397	1.90 l multi	1.75	.40

Athletes Surrounding Flag A398

Literary Society Headquarters A399

1979, Oct. 1 **Litho.** ***Perf. 12***

1911	A398	15q shown	.20	.20
1912	A398	25q Shooting	.20	.20
1913	A398	80q Dancing	.25	.20
1914	A398	1.20 l Soccer	.50	.20
1915	A398	1.40 l High jump	.65	.25
		Nos. 1911-1915 (5)	1.80	1.05

Liberation Spartakiad, 35th anniversary.

1979, Oct. 12

Albanian Literary Society Centenary: 25q, Seal and charter. 80q, Founder. 1.55 l, 1879 Headquarters. 1.90 l, Founders.

1916	A399	25q multi	.20	.20
1917	A399	80q multi	.40	.20
1918	A399	1.20 l multi	.60	.20
1919	A399	1.55 l multi	.75	.20
		Nos. 1916-1919 (4)	1.95	.80

Miniature Sheet

Perf. 12½ on 2 sides x Imperf.

1920	A399	1.90 l multi	2.00	.40

Congress Statute, Coat of Arms — A400

1979, Oct. 20 **Photo.** ***Perf. 12x12½***

1921	A400	25q multi	.50	.20
1922	A400	1.65 l multi	2.50	.25

2nd Congress of Berat, 35th anniversary.

Children Entering School, Books — A401

1979 **Litho.** ***Perf. 12½x12***

1923	A401	5q shown	.20	.20
1924	A401	10q Communications	.20	.20
1925	A401	15q Steel workers	.20	.20

1926 A401 20q Dancers, instruments .20 .20
1927 A401 25q Newspapers, radio, television .20 .20
1928 A401 60q Textile worker .40 .20
1929 A401 80q Armed forces .55 .20
1930 A401 1.20 l Industry .80 .20
1931 A401 1.60 l Transportation 1.00 .30
1932 A401 2.40 l Agriculture 1.50 .35
1932A A401 3 l Medicine 1.90 .50
Nos. 1923-1932A (11) 7.15 2.75

Workers and Factory A402

Worker, Red Flag and: 80q, Hand holding sickle and rifle. 1.20 l, Red star and open book. 1.55 l, Open book and cogwheel.

1979, Nov. 29
1933 A402 25q multi .20 .20
1934 A402 80q multi .20 .20
1935 A402 1.20 l multi .50 .20
1936 A402 1.55 l multi .60 .20
Nos. 1933-1936 (4) 1.50 .80

35th anniversary of independence.

Joseph Stalin — A403

Design: 1.10 l, Stalin on dais, horiz.

1979, Dec. 21 Litho. *Perf. 12*
1937 A403 80q red & dk bl .75 .20
1938 A403 1.10 l red & dk bl 1.00 .20

Joseph Stalin (1879-1953), birth centenary.

Fireplace and Pottery, Korcar A404

Home Furnishings: 80q, Cupboard bed, dagger, pistol, ammunition pouch, Shkodar. 1.20 l, Stool, pot, chair, Mirdit. 1.35 l, Chimney, dagger, jacket, Gjirokaster.

1980, Feb. 27 Litho. *Perf. 12*
1939 A404 25q multi .20 .20
1940 A404 80q multi .35 .20
1941 A404 1.20 l multi .55 .20
1942 A404 1.35 l multi .60 .30
Nos. 1939-1942 (4) 1.70 .90

See Nos. 1985-1988.

Pipe, Painted Flask A405

1980, Mar. 4
1943 A405 25q shown .20 .20
1944 A405 80q Leather handbags .35 .20
1945 A405 1.20 l Carved eagle, embroidered rug .55 .20
1946 A405 1.35 l Lace .60 .30
Nos. 1943-1946 (4) 1.70 .90

Prof. Aleksander Xhuvanit Birth Centenary — A406

1980, Mar. 14
1947 A406 80q multi .55 .20
1948 A406 1 l multi .70 .20

Revolutionaries on Horseback — A407

Insurrection at Kosove, 70th Anniversary: 1 l, Battle scene.

1980, Apr. 4
1949 A407 80q red & black .60 .20
1950 A407 1 l red & black .75 .20

Soldiers and Workers Laboring to Aid the Stricken Populations, by D. Jukinui and I. Lulani — A408

1980, Apr. 15 Litho. *Perf. 12½*
1951 A408 80q lt blue & multi .60 .20
1952 A408 1 l lt blue grn & multi .75 .20

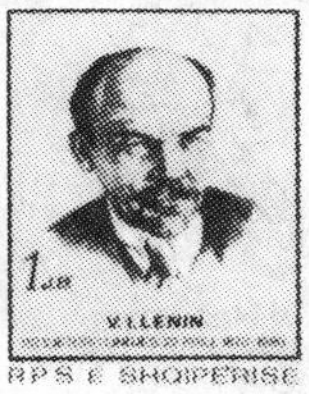

Lenin, 110th Birth Anniversary — A409

1980, Apr. 22
1953 A409 80q multi .90 .20
1954 A409 1 l multi 1.10 .20

Misto Mame and Ali Demi, War Martyrs A410

War Martyrs: 80q, Sadik Staveleci, Vojo Kusji, Hoxhi Martini. 1.20 l, Bule Naipi, Persefoni Kokedhima. 1.35 l, Ndoc Deda, Hydajet Lezha, Naim Gyylbegu, Ndoc Mazi, Ahmed Haxha.

1980, May 5
1955 A410 25q multi .20 .20
1956 A410 80q multi .40 .20
1957 A410 1.20 l multi .55 .20
1958 A410 1.35 l multi .70 .30
Nos. 1955-1958 (4) 1.85 .90

See Nos. 2012A-2012D, 2025-2028, 2064-2067, 2122-2125, 2171-2174, 2207-2209.

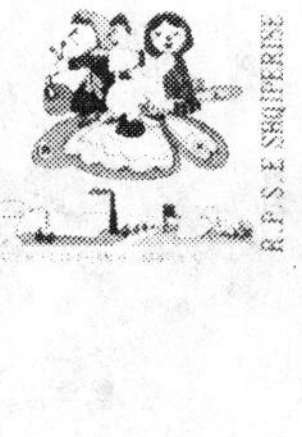

Scene from "Mirela" A411

1980, June 7
1959 A411 15q shown .20 .20
1960 A411 25q The Scribbler .20 .20
1961 A411 80q Circus Bears .35 .20
1962 A411 2.40 l Waterdrops 1.00 .35
Nos. 1959-1962 (4) 1.75 .95

Carrying Iron Castings in the Enver Hoxha Tractor Combine, by S. Shijaku and M. Fushekati — A412

Paintings (Gallery of Figurative Paintings, Tirana): 80q, The Welder, by Harilla Dhima. 1.20 l, Steel Erectors, by Petro Kokushta. 1.35 l, Pandeli Lena, 1.80 l Communists, by Vilson Kilica.

1980, July 22
1963 A412 25q multi .20 .20
1964 A412 80q multi .35 .20
1965 A412 1.20 l multi .50 .20
1966 A412 1.35 l multi .65 .25
Nos. 1963-1966 (4) 1.70 .85

Souvenir Sheet
1967 A412 1.80 l multi 1.40 .40

Gate, Parchment Miniature, 11th Cent. — A413

Bas reliefs of the Middle Ages: 80q, Eagle, 13th cent. 1.20 l, Heraldic lion, 14th cent. 1.35 l, Pheasant, 14th cent.

1980, Sept. 27 Litho. *Perf. 12*
1968 A413 25q gold & blk .20 .20
1969 A413 80q gold & blk .25 .20
1970 A413 1.20 l gold & blk .45 .20
1971 A413 1.35 l gold & blk .55 .25
Nos. 1968-1971 (4) 1.45 .85

Divjaka National Park — A414

1980, Nov. 6 Photo.
1972 A414 80q shown .50 .20
1973 A414 1.20 l Lura .85 .25
1974 A414 1.60 l Thethi 1.10 .25
Nos. 1972-1974 (3) 2.45 .70

Souvenir Sheet
Perf. 12½
1975 A414 1.80 l Llogara Park 2.00 .75

Citizens, Flag and Arms of Albania A415

1981, Jan. 11 Litho. *Perf. 12*
1976 A415 80q shown .50 .20
1977 A415 1 l People's Party Headquarters, Tirana .75 .25

35th anniversary of the Republic.

Child's Bed — A416

1981, Mar. 20 Litho. *Perf. 12*
1978 A416 25q shown .20 .20
1979 A416 80q Wooden bucket, brass bottle .35 .20
1980 A416 1.20 l Shoes .55 .25
1981 A416 1.35 l Jugs .60 .30
Nos. 1978-1981 (4) 1.70 .95

A417

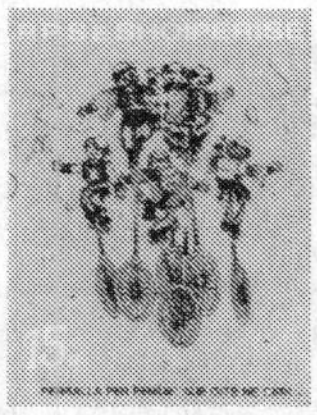

A419

1981, Apr. 20
1982 A417 80q Soldiers .40 .20
1983 A417 1 l Sword combat .60 .25

Souvenir Sheet
Perf. 12½ Vert.
1984 A417 1.80 l Soldier with pistol 1.25 .80

Battle of Shtimje centenary.

Home Furnishings Type of 1980

1981, Feb. 25 Litho. *Perf. 12*
1985 A404 25q House interior, Labara .20 .20
1986 A404 80q Labara, diff. .35 .20
1987 A404 1.20 l Mat .55 .25
1988 A404 1.35 l Dibres .55 .30
Nos. 1985-1988 (4) 1.65 .95

1981, June *Perf. 12*

Designs: Children's circus.

1989 A419 15q multi .20 .20
1990 A419 25q multi .20 .20
1991 A419 80q multi .35 .20
1992 A419 2.40 l multi 1.00 .60
Nos. 1989-1992 (4) 1.75 1.20

Soccer Players A420

1982 World Cup Soccer Elimination Games: Various soccer players.

1981, Mar. 31 Litho. *Perf. 12*
1993 A420 25q multi .25 .20
1994 A420 80q multi 1.90 .40
1995 A420 1.20 l multi 2.75 .65
1996 A420 1.35 l multi 3.50 .80
Nos. 1993-1996 (4) 8.40 2.05

Allies, by S. Hysa A421

Paintings: 80q, Warriors, by A. Buza. 1.20 l, Rallying to the Flag, Dec. 1911, by A. Zajmi, vert. 1.35 l, My Flag is My Heart, by L. Cefa, vert. 1.80 l, Circling the Flag in a Common Cause, by N. Vasia.

1981, July 10 *Perf. 12½x12*
1997 A421 25q multi .20 .20
1998 A421 80q multi .35 .20
1999 A421 1.20 l multi .50 .25
2000 A421 1.35 l multi .55 .30
Nos. 1997-2000 (4) 1.60 .95

Souvenir Sheet
2001 A421 1.80 l multi 1.40 .85

No. 2001 contains one stamp, size: 55x55mm.

Rifleman
A422

1981, Aug. 30 *Perf. 12*

2002	A422	25q	shown	.20	.20
2003	A422	80q	Weight lifting	.40	.20
2004	A422	1.20 l	Volleyball	.55	.25
2005	A422	1.35 l	Soccer	.65	.35
			Nos. 2002-2005 (4)	1.80	1.00

Albanian Workers' Party, 8th Congress
A423

1981, Nov. 1

2006	A423	80q	Flag, star	.30	.20
2007	A423	1 l	Flag, hammer & sickle	.40	.25

Albanian Workers' Party, 40th Anniv. — A424

Communist Youth Org., 40th Anniv. — A425

1981, Nov. 8

2008	A424	80q	Symbols of industrialization	.35	.25
2009	A424	2.80 l	Fist, emblem	1.25	.70

Souvenir Sheet

2010	A424	1.80 l	Enver Hoxha, Memoirs	2.00	.85

1981, Nov. 23

2011	A425	80q	Star, ax, map	.65	.20
2012	A425	1 l	Flags, star	.85	.25

War Martyrs Type of 1980

Portraits: 25q, Perlat Rexhepi (1919-42) and Branko Kadia (1921-42). 80q, Xheladin Beqiri (1908-44) and Hajdar Dushi (1916-44). 1.20 l, Koci Bako (1905-41), Vasil Laci (1923-41) and Mujo Ulqinaku (1898-1939). 1.35 l, Mine Peza (1875-1942) and Zoja Cure (1920-44).

1981, May 5 **Litho.** *Perf. 12*

2012A	A410	25q	silver & multi	.20	.20
2012B	A410	80q	gold & multi	.75	.40
2012C	A410	1.20 l	silver & multi	1.25	.55
2012D	A410	1.35 l	gold & multi	1.40	.60
			Nos. 2012A-2012D (4)	3.60	1.75

Fan S. Noli, Writer, Birth Centenary — A426

1982, Jan. 6 **Litho.** *Perf. 12*

2013	A426	80q	lt ol grn & gold	.40	.20
2014	A426	1.10 l	lt red brn & gold	.60	.25

Traditional Houses Type of 1979

1982, Feb. *Perf. 12½x12½*

2015	A392	25q	Bulqize	.30	.20
2016	A392	80q	Lebush	.35	.20
2017	A392	1.20 l	Bicaj	.55	.30
2018	A392	1.55 l	Klos	.80	.40
			Nos. 2015-2018 (4)	2.00	1.10

TB Bacillus Centenary
A428

1982, Mar. 24 *Perf. 12*

2019	A428	80q	Globe	1.00	.25
2020	A428	1.10 l	Koch	1.40	.35

Albanian League House, Prizren, by K. Buza — A429

Kosova Landscapes: 25q, Castle at Prizrenit, by G. Madhi. 1.20 l, Mountain Gorge at Rogove, by K. Buza. 1.55 l, Street of the Hadhji at Zekes, by G. Madhi. 25q, 1.20 l, 1.55 l vert.

Perf. 12x12½, 12½x12

1982, Apr. 15 **Litho.**

2021	A429	25q	multi	.20	.20
2022	A429	80q	multi	.50	.20
2023	A429	1.20 l	multi	.70	.20
2024	A429	1.55 l	multi	1.00	.30
			Nos. 2021-2024 (4)	2.40	.90

War Martyr Type of 1980

Designs: 25q, Hibe Palikuqi, Liri Gero. 80q, Mihal Duri, Kajo Karafili. 1.20 l, Fato Dudumi, Margarita Tutulani, Shejnaze Juka. 1.55 l, Memo Meto, Gjok Doci.

1982, May *Perf. 12*

2025	A410	25q	multi	.20	.20
2026	A410	80q	multi	.35	.20
2027	A410	1.20 l	multi	.60	.30
2028	A410	1.55 l	multi	.85	.45
			Nos. 2025-2028 (4)	2.00	1.15

Loading Freighter — A430

Children's Paintings.

1982, June 15 *Perf. 12½x12*

2029	A430	15q	shown	.20	.20
2030	A430	80q	Forest	.55	.20
2031	A430	1.20 l	City	.90	.30
2032	A430	1.65 l	Park	1.25	.45
			Nos. 2029-2032 (4)	2.90	1.15

9th Congress of Trade Unions
A431

1982, June 6 **Litho.** *Perf. 12*

2033	A431	80q	Workers, factories	.80	.20
2034	A431	1.10 l	Emblem, flag	1.10	.25

Alpine Village Festival, by Danish Jukniu
A432

Industrial Development Paintings: 80q, Hydroelectric Station Builders, by Ali Miruku. 1.20 l, Steel Workers, by Clirim Ceka. 1.55 l, Oil drillers, by Pandeli Lena. 1.90 l, Trapping the Furnace, by Jorgji Gjikopulli.

1982, July *Perf. 12½*

2035	A432	25q	multi	.20	.20
2036	A432	80q	multi	.50	.20
2037	A432	1.20 l	multi	.75	.20
2038	A432	1.55 l	multi	1.00	.30
			Nos. 2035-2038 (4)	2.45	.90

Souvenir Sheet
Perf. 12

2039	A432	1.90 l	multi	1.75	.40

No. 2039 contains one 54x48mm stamp.

Communist Party Newspaper "Voice of the People," 40th Anniv. — A432a

1982, Aug. 25 **Litho.** *Perf. 12*

2039A	A432a	80q	Newspapers		
2039B	A432a	1.10 l	Paper, press		

40th Anniv. of Democratic Front — A433

1982, Sept. 16 *Perf. 12*

2040	A433	80q	Glory to the Heroes of Peza Monument	.80	.20
2041	A433	1.10 l	Marchers	1.10	.25

8th Youth Congress
A434

Handmade Shoulder Bags
A435

1982, Oct. 4

2042	A434	80q	multi	.80	.20
2043	A434	1.10 l	multi	1.10	.25

1982, Nov.

2044	A435	25q	Rug, horiz.	.20	.20
2045	A435	80q	shown	.40	.20
2046	A435	1.20 l	Wooden pots, bowls, horiz.	.60	.20
2047	A435	1.55 l	Jug	.80	.30
			Nos. 2044-2047 (4)	2.00	.90

70th Anniv. of Independence — A436

1982, Nov. 28

2048	A436	20q	Ishamil Qemali	.20	.20
2049	A436	1.20 l	Partisans	.60	.20
2050	A436	2.40 l	Partisans, diff.	1.25	.40
			Nos. 2048-2050 (3)	2.05	.80

Souvenir Sheet

2051	A436	1.90 l	Independence Monument, Tirana	1.75	.40

Dhermi Beach
A437

1982, Dec. 20

2052	A437	25q	shown	.20	.20
2053	A437	80q	Sarande	.50	.20
2054	A437	1.20 l	Ksamil	.75	.25
2055	A437	1.55 l	Lukove	1.00	.35
			Nos. 2052-2055 (4)	2.45	1.00

Handkerchief Dancers — A438

Folkdancers.

1983, Feb. 20 **Litho.** *Perf. 12*

2056	A438	25q	shown	.20	.20
2057	A438	80q	With kerchief, drum	.40	.20
2058	A438	1.20 l	With guitar, flute, tambourine	.60	.25
2059	A438	1.55 l	Women	.80	.35
			Nos. 2056-2059 (4)	2.00	1.00

A439

A440

1983, Mar. 14 **Litho.** *Perf. 12*

2060	A439	80q	multi	1.10	.20
2061	A439	1.10 l	multi	1.50	.25

Karl Marx (1818-83).

1983, Apr. 20

2062	A440	80q	Electricity generation	.40	.20
2063	A440	1.10 l	Gas & oil production	.55	.25

Energy development.

War Martyr Type of 1980

Designs: 25q, Asim Zeneli (1916-43), Nazmi Rushiti (1919-42). 80q, Shyqyri Ishmi (1922-42), Shyqyri Alimerko (1923-43), Myzafer Asqeriu (1918-42). 1.20 l, Qybra Sokoli (1924-44), Qeriba Derri (1905-44), Ylbere Bilibashi (1928-44). 1.55 l, Themo Vasi (1915-43), Abaz Shehu (1905-42).

1983, May 5 **Litho.** *Perf. 12*

2064	A410	25q	multi	.20	.20
2065	A410	80q	multi	.40	.20
2066	A410	1.20 l	multi	.60	.25
2067	A410	1.55 l	multi	.80	.35
			Nos. 2064-2067 (4)	2.00	1.00

Women's Union, 9th Congress
A441

1983, June 1 **Litho.** *Perf. 12x12½*

2068	A441	80q	red & gold	.85	.20
2069	A441	1.10 l	blue & gold	1.10	.25

Bicycling
A442

1983, June 20 *Perf. 12*

2070	A442	25q	shown	.20	.20
2071	A442	80q	Chess	.40	.20
2072	A442	1.20 l	Gymnastics	.60	.25
2073	A442	1.55 l	Wrestling	.80	.35
			Nos. 2070-2073 (4)	2.00	1.00

40th Anniv. of People's Army — A443

1983, July 10

2074 A443 20q Armed services .20 .20
2075 A443 1.20 l Soldier, gun barrels .85 .25
2076 A443 2.40 l Factory guard, crowd 1.60 .50
Nos. 2074-2076 (3) 2.65 .95

Sunny Day, by Myrteza Fushekati A444

Paintings: 80q, Messenger of the Grasp, by Niko Progi. 1.20 l, 29 November 1944, by Harilla Dhimo. 1.55 l, Fireworks, by Pandi Mele. 1.90 l, Partisan Assault, by Sali Shijaku and M. Fushekati.

1983, Aug. 28 Litho. *Perf. 12½x12*

2077 A444 25q multi .20 .20
2078 A444 80q multi .40 .20
2079 A444 1.20 l multi .60 .25
2080 A444 1.55 l multi .80 .35
Nos. 2077-2080 (4) 2.00 1.00

Souvenir Sheet

Perf. 12

2081 A444 1.90 l multi 4.00 .50

Folklore Festival Type of 1978

Gjirokaster Folklore Festival: folkdances.

1983, Oct. 6 Litho. *Perf. 12*

2082 A388 25q Sword dance .20 .20
2083 A388 80q Kerchief dance .50 .20
2084 A388 1.20 l Shepherd flautists .75 .25
2085 A388 1.55 l Garland dance 1.00 .35
Nos. 2082-2085 (4) 2.45 1.00

World Communications Year — A446

1983, Nov. 10

2086 A446 60q multi .40 .20
2087 A446 1.20 l multi .85 .25

75th Birthday of Enver Hoxha — A447

1983, Oct. 16 Litho. *Perf. 12½*

2088 A447 80q multi .40 .20
2089 A447 1.20 l multi .60 .25
2090 A447 1.80 l multi .90 .40
Nos. 2088-2090 (3) 1.90 .85

Souvenir Sheet

Perf. 12

2091 A447 1.90 l multi 1.40 .50

The Right to a Joint Triumph, by J. Keraj A448

Era of Skanderbeg in Figurative Art: 80q, The Heroic Center of the Battle of Krujes, by N. Bakalli. 1.20 l, The Rights of the Enemy after our Triumph, by N. Progri. 1.55 l, The Discussion at Lezhes, by B. Ahmeti. 1.90 l, Victory over the Turks, by G. Madhi.

1983, Dec. 10 *Perf. 12½x12*

2092 A448 25q multi .20 .20
2093 A448 80q multi .60 .20
2094 A448 1.20 l multi .90 .25
2095 A448 1.55 l multi 1.25 .35
Nos. 2092-2095 (4) 2.95 1.00

Souvenir Sheet

Perf. 12

2096 A448 1.90 l multi 2.25 .50

Greco-Roman Ruins of Illyria — A449

1983, Dec. 28 *Perf. 12*

2097 A449 80q Amphitheater, Buthroxtum .65 .20
2098 A449 1.20 l Colonnade, Apollonium .95 .25
2099 A449 1.80 l Vaulted gallery, amphitheater at Epidamnus 1.40 .40
Nos. 2097-2099 (3) 3.00 .85

Archeological Discoveries A450

Designs: Apollo, 3rd cent. 25q, Tombstone, Korce, 3rd cent. 80q, Apollo, diff. 1st cent. 1.10 l, Earthenware pot (child's head), Tren, 1st cent. 1.20 l, Man's head, Dyrrah, 2.20 l, Eros with Dolphin, statue Bronze Dyrrah, 3rd cent.

1984, Feb. 25 *Perf. 12x12½*

2100 A450 15q multi .20 .20
2101 A450 25q multi .20 .20
2102 A450 80q multi .40 .20
2103 A450 1.10 l multi .55 .20
2104 A450 1.20 l multi .60 .25
2105 A450 2.20 l multi 1.10 .50
Nos. 2100-2105 (6) 3.05 1.55

Clock Towers — A451

1984, Mar. 30 Litho. *Perf. 12*

2106 A451 15q Gjirokaster .20 .20
2107 A451 25q Kavaje .20 .20
2108 A451 80q Elbasan .40 .20
2109 A451 1.10 l Tirana .55 .20
2110 A451 1.20 l Peqin .60 .25
2111 A451 2.20 l Kruje 1.10 .50
Nos. 2106-2111 (6) 3.05 1.55

40th Anniv. of Liberation A452

1984, Apr. 20 Litho. *Perf. 12*

2112 A452 15q Student & microscope .20 .20
2113 A452 25q Guerrilla with flag .20 .20
2114 A452 80q Children with flag .40 .20
2115 A452 1.10 l Soldier .55 .20
2116 A452 1.20 l Workers with flag .60 .25
2117 A452 2.20 l Militia at dam 1.10 .50
Nos. 2112-2117 (6) 3.05 1.55

Children — A453

1984, May Litho. *Perf. 12*

2118 A453 15q Children reading .20 .20
2119 A453 25q Young pioneers .25 .20
2120 A453 60q Gardening .60 .20
2121 A453 2.80 l Kite flying 2.75 .60
Nos. 2118-2121 (4) 3.80 1.20

War Martyr Type of 1980

Designs: 15q, Manush Almani, Mustafa Matohiti, Kastriot Muco. 25q, Zaho Koka, Reshit Collaku, Maliq Muco. 1.20 l, Lefter Talo, Tom Kola, Fuat Babani. 2.20 l, Myslysm Shyri, Dervish Hexali, Skender Caci.

1984, May 5 Litho. *Perf. 12*

2122 A410 15q multi .20 .20
2123 A410 25q multi .20 .20
2124 A410 1.20 l multi .95 .30
2125 A410 2.20 l multi 1.75 .60
Nos. 2122-2125 (4) 3.10 1.30

A454 A455

1984, May 24 Litho. *Perf. 12*

2126 A454 80q Enver Hoxha .80 .20
2127 A454 1.10 l Resistance fighter 1.25 .30

40th anniv. of Permet Congress.

1984, June 12 Litho. *Perf. 12*

2128 A455 15q Goalkeeper .20 .20
2129 A455 25q Referee .20 .20
2130 A455 1.20 l Map of Europe .90 .45
2131 A455 2.20 l Field diagram 1.75 .90
Nos. 2128-2131 (4) 3.05 1.75

European soccer championships.

Freedom Came, by Myrteza Fushekati A456

Paintings, Tirana Gallery of Figurative Art: 25q, Morning, by Zamir Mati, vert. 80q, My Darling, by Agim Zajmi, vert. 2.60 l, For the Partisans, by Arben Basha. 1.90 l, Eagle, by Zamir Mati, vert.

1984, June 12 *Perf. 12½*

2132 A456 15q multi .20 .20
2133 A456 25q multi .25 .20
2134 A456 80q multi .80 .25
2135 A456 2.60 l multi 2.75 .80
Nos. 2132-2135 (4) 4.00 1.45

Souvenir Sheet

Perf. 12 Horiz.

2136 A456 1.90 l multi 3.00 .60

Flora — A457

1984, Aug. 20 Litho. *Perf. 12*

2137 A457 15q Moraceae L. .35 .20
2138 A457 25q Plantaginaceae L. .60 .20
2139 A457 1.20 l Hypericaceae L. 2.75 .60
2140 A457 2.20 l Leontopodium alpinum 5.25 1.10
Nos. 2137-2140 (4) 8.95 2.10

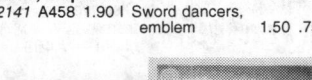

AUSIPEX '84, Melbourne, Sept. 21-30 — A458

Perf. 12 Horiz.

1984, Sept. 21 Litho.

2141 A458 1.90 l Sword dancers, emblem 1.50 .75

A459 A460

Forestry, logging, UNFAO emblem.

1984, Sept. 25 *Perf. 12*

2142 A459 15q Beech trees, transport .20 .20
2143 A459 25q Pine forest, logging cable .20 .20
2144 A459 1.20 l Firs, sawmill .90 .45
2145 A459 2.20 l Forester clearing woods 1.75 .90
Nos. 2142-2145 (4) 3.05 1.75

1984, Oct. 13 *Perf. 12½*

2146 A460 1.20 l View of Gjirokaster 2.00 .45

EURPHILA '84, Rome.

5th National Spartakiad — A461

1984, Oct. 19 *Perf. 12*

2147 A461 15q Soccer .20 .20
2148 A461 25q Women's track & field .20 .20
2149 A461 80q Weight lifting .60 .30
2150 A461 2.20 l Pistol shooting 1.75 .90
Nos. 2147-2150 (4) 2.75 1.60

Souvenir Sheet

Perf. 12 Horiz.

2151 A461 1.90 l Opening ceremony, red flags 2.00 .75

November 29 Revolution, 40th Anniv. A462

1984, Nov. 29 *Perf. 12*

2152 A462 80q Industrial reconstruction 1.25 .30
2153 A462 1.10 l Natl. flag, partisans 1.65 .40

Souvenir Sheet

Perf. 12 Horiz.

2154 A462 1.90 l Gen. Enver Hoxha reading 1944 declaration 2.00 .75

Archaeological Discoveries from Illyria — A463

Designs: 15q, Iron Age water container. 80q, Terra-cotta woman's head, 6th-7th cent. B.C. 1.20 l, Aphrodite, bust, 3rd cent. B.C. 1.70 l, Nike, A.D. 1st-2nd cent. bronze statue.

1985, Feb. 25 *Perf. 12x12½*

2155 A463 15q multi .20 .20
2156 A463 80q multi .80 .40
2157 A463 1.20 l multi 1.10 .55
2158 A463 1.70 l multi 1.75 .85
Nos. 2155-2158 (4) 3.85 2.00

Hysni Kapo (1915-1980), Natl. Labor Party Leader — A464

1985, Mar. 4 *Perf. 12*

2159 A464 90q red & blk .85 .45
2160 A464 1.10 l chlky bl & blk 1.10 .55

OLYMPHILEX '85, Lausanne — A465

1985, Mar. 18

2161 A465 25q Women's track & field .25 .20
2162 A465 60q Weight lifting .60 .30
2163 A465 1.20 l Soccer 1.10 .55
2164 A465 1.50 l Women's pistol shooting 1.25 .65
Nos. 2161-2164 (4) 3.20 1.70

Johann Sebastian Bach — A466

1985, Mar. 31

2165 A466 80q Portrait, manuscript 2.00 .40
2166 A466 1.20 l Eisenach, birthplace 3.00 .55

Gen. Enver Hoxha (1908-1985) A467

1985, Apr. 11 *Perf. 12½*

2167 A467 80q multicolored .80 .40

Souvenir Sheet

Imperf

2168 A467 1.90 l multicolored 2.00 1.00

Natl. Frontier Guards, 40th Anniv. A468

1985, Apr. 25 *Perf. 12*

2169 A468 25q Guardsman, family .35 .20
2170 A468 80q At frontier post 1.10 .40

War Martyrs Type of 1980

Cameo portraits: 25q, Mitro Xhani (1916-44), Nimete Progonati (1929-44), Kozma Nushi (1909-44). 40q, Ajet Xhindoli (1922-43), Mustafa Kacaci (1903-44), Estref Caka Osaja (1919-44). 60q, Celo Sinani (1929-44), Lt. Ambro Andoni (1920-44), Meleq Gosnishti (1913-44). 1.20 l, Thodhori Mastora (1920-44), Fejzi Micoli (1919-45), Hysen Cino (1920-44).

1985, May 5

2171 A410 25q multi .25 .20
2172 A410 40q multi .40 .20
2173 A410 60q multi .60 .30
2174 A410 1.20 l multi 1.25 .55
Nos. 2171-2174 (4) 2.50 1.25

Victory over Fascism A469

Designs: 25q, Rifle, red flag, inscribed May 9. 80q, Hand holding rifle, globe, broken swastika.

1985, May 9

2175 A469 25q multi .65 .20
2176 A469 80q multi 2.00 .40

End of World War II, 40th anniv.

Primary School, by Thoma Malo A470

Paintings, Tirana Gallery of Figurative Art: 80q, The Heroes, by Hysen Devolli, vert. 90q, In Our Days, by Angjelin Dodmasej, vert. 1.20 l, Going Off to Sow, by Ksenofon Dilo. 1.90 l, Foundry Workers, by Mikel Gurashi.

1985, June 25 *Perf. 12½*

2177 A470 25q multi .25 .20
2178 A470 80q multi .80 .40
2179 A470 90q multi .85 .45
2180 A470 1.20 l multi 1.10 .55
Nos. 2177-2180 (4) 3.00 1.60

Souvenir Sheet

Perf. 12 Horiz.

2181 A470 1.90 l multi 2.00 1.00

Basketball Championships, Spain — A471

Fruits — A472

Various plays.

1985, July 20 **Litho.** *Perf. 12*

2182 A471 25q dull bl & blk .25 .20
2183 A471 80q dull grn & blk .80 .40
2184 A471 1.20 l dl vio & blk 1.10 .60
2185 A471 1.60 l dl rose & blk 1.50 .75
Nos. 2182-2185 (4) 3.65 1.95

1985, Aug. 20

2186 A472 25q Oranges .25 .20
2187 A472 80q Plums .80 .40
2188 A472 1.20 l Apples 1.10 .60
2189 A472 1.60 l Cherries 1.50 .75
Nos. 2186-2189 (4) 3.65 1.95

Architecture A473

1985, Sept. 20

2190 A473 25q Kruja .25 .20
2191 A473 80q Gjirokastra .80 .40
2192 A473 1.20 l Berati 1.10 .60
2193 A473 1.60 l Shkodera 1.50 .75
Nos. 2190-2193 (4) 3.65 1.95

Natl. Folk Theater Festival — A474

Various scenes from folk plays.

1985, Oct. 6

2194 A474 25q multi .25 .20
2195 A474 80q multi .80 .40
2196 A474 1.20 l multi 1.10 .60
2197 A474 1.60 l multi 1.50 .75

Size: 56x82mm

Imperf

2198 A474 1.90 l multi 3.50 1.90
Nos. 2194-2198 (5) 7.15 3.85

Socialist People's Republic, 40th Anniv. — A475

1986, Jan. 11 **Litho.** *Perf. 12½*

2199 A475 25q Natl. crest, vert. .70 .20
2200 A475 80q Proclamation, 1946 2.25 .40

A476

A477

Designs: 25q, Dam, River Drin, Melgun. 80q, Bust of Enver Hoxha, dam power house.

1986, Feb. 20 *Perf. 12*

2201 A476 25q multi 1.25 .20
2202 A476 80q multi 3.75 .40

Enver Hoxha hydro-electric power station, Koman.

1986, Mar. 20 **Litho.** *Perf. 12*

Flowers.

2203 A477 25q Gymnospermium shqipetarum .35 .20
2204 A477 1.20 l Leucojum valentinum 1.90 .60
a. Pair, #2203-2204 2.25 1.00

No. 2204a sold only in booklets of 2; exists imperf.

A478

Famous Men — A479

Designs: 25q, Maxim Gorky, Russian author. 80q, Andre Marie Ampere, French physicist. 1.20 l, James Watt, English inventor of modern steam engine. 2.40 l, Franz Liszt, Hungarian composer.

1986, Apr. 20

2205 Strip of 4 4.40 2.20
a. A478 25q dull red brown .25 .20
b. A478 80q dull violet .75 .40
c. A478 1.20 l blue green 1.10 .60
d. A478 2.40 l dull lilac rose 2.25 .90

Size: 88x72mm

Imperf

2206 A479 1.90 l multi 1.75 .88

No. 2206 has central area picturing Gorky, Ampere, Watt and Liszt, perf. 12½.

War Martyrs Type of 1980

Portraits: 25q, Ramiz Aranitasi (1923-43), Inajete Dumi (1924-44) and Laze Nuro Ferraj (1897-1944). 80q, Dine Kalenja (1919-44), Kozma Naska (1921-44), Met Hasa (1929-44) and Fahri Ramadani (1920-44). 1.20 l, Hiqmet Buzi (1927-44), Bajram Tusha (1922-42), Mumin Selami (1923-42) and Hajrfdin Bylyshi (1923-42).

1986, May 5 ***Perf. 12***

2207 A410 25q multi .65 .20
2208 A410 80q multi 2.25 .40
2209 A410 1.20 l multi 3.00 .55
Nos. 2207-2209 (3) 5.90 1.15

A480

1986 World Cup Soccer Championships, Mexico — A481

1986, May 31 **Litho.** ***Perf. 12***

2210 A480 25q Globe, world cup .25 .20
2211 A480 1.20 l Player, soccer ball 1.25 .60

Size: 97x64mm

Imperf

2212 A481 1.90 l multi 1.75 .90
Nos. 2210-2212 (3) 3.25 1.70

No. 2212 has central label, perf. 12½.

Transportation Workers' Day, 40th Anniv. — A482

1986, Aug. 10 **Litho.** ***Perf. 12***

2213 A482 1.20 l multi 3.00 .60

Prominent Albanians A483

Designs: 30q, Naim Frasheri (1846-1900), poet. 60q, Ndre Mjeda (1866-1937), poet. 90q, Petro Nini Luarasi (1865-1911), poet, journalist. 1 l, Andon Zako Cajupi (1866-1930), poet. 1.20 l, Millosh Gjergj Nikolla Migjeni (1911-1938), novelist. 2.60 l, Urani Rumbo (1884-1936), educator.

1986, Sept. 20 **Litho.** ***Perf. 12***

2214 A483 30q multi .30 .20
2215 A483 60q multi .60 .30
2216 A483 90q multi .90 .45
2217 A483 1 l multi .95 .50
2218 A483 1.20 l multi 1.10 .60
2219 A483 2.60 l multi 2.50 1.25
Nos. 2214-2219 (6) 6.35 3.30

Albanian Workers' Party, 9th Congress, Tirana A484

1986, Nov. 3 **Litho.** ***Perf. 12***

2220 A484 30q multi 1.90 .25

A485

A486

Albanian Workers' Party, 45th Anniv.: 30q, Handstamp, signature of Hoxha. 1.20 l, Marx, Engels, Lenin and Stalin, party building.

1986, Nov. 8

2221 A485 30q multi .60 .20
2222 A485 1.20 l multi 2.25 .60

1986, Nov. 29 ***Perf. 12x12½***

Statue of Mother Albania.

2223 A486 10q peacock blue .20 .20
2224 A486 20q henna brn .20 .20
2225 A486 30q vermilion .30 .20
2226 A486 50q dk olive bis .50 .25
2227 A486 60q lt olive grn .60 .30
2228 A486 80q rose .80 .40
2229 A486 90q ultra .90 .45
2230 A486 1.20 l green 1.10 .60
2231 A486 1.60 l red vio 1.50 .75
2232 A486 2.20 l myrtle grn 2.00 1.10
2233 A486 3 l brn org 2.75 1.40
2234 A486 6 l yel bister 5.50 2.25
Nos. 2223-2234 (12) 16.35 8.10

For surcharges see Nos. 2435-2439.

Artifacts A487

Designs: 30q, Head of Aesoulapius, 5th cent. B.C. Byllis, marble. 80q, Aphrodite, 3rd cent. B.C., Fier, terracotta. 1 l, Pan, 3rd-2nd cent, B.C., Byllis, bronze. 1.20 l, Jupiter, A.D. 2nd cent., Tirana, limestone.

1987, Feb. 20

2235 A487 30q multi .30 .20
2236 A487 80q multi .75 .40
2237 A487 1 l multi .95 .45
2238 A487 1.20 l multi 1.10 .60
Nos. 2235-2238 (4) 3.10 1.65

1st Albanian School, Cont. — A488

Famous Men — A489

Gun, quill pen, bock of the alphabet and: 30q, Monument, vert. 80q, School, Korca. 1.20 l, Students.

1987, Mar. 7 ***Perf. 12***

2239 A488 30q multi .35 .20
2240 A488 80q multi .85 .40
2241 A488 1.20 l multi 1.25 .60
Nos. 2239-2241 (3) 2.45 1.20

1987, Apr. 20

Designs: 30q, Victor Hugo, French author. 80q, Galileo Galilei, Italian mathematician, philosopher. 90q, Charles Darwin, British biologist. 1.30 l, Miguel Cervantes, Spanish novelist.

2242 A489 30q multi .30 .20
2243 A489 80q multi .75 .40
2244 A489 90q multi .90 .45
2245 A489 1.30 l multi 1.25 .80
Nos. 2242-2245 (4) 3.20 1.85

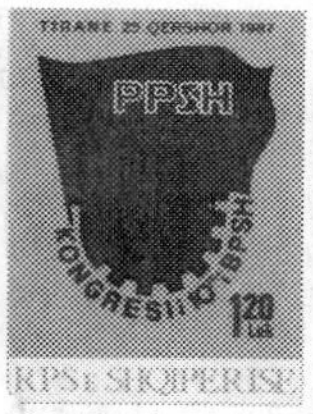

World Food Day — A490

10th Trade Unions Cong. — A491

1987, May 20

2246 A490 30q Forsythia europaea .30 .20
2247 A490 90q Moltkia doerfleri .85 .45
2248 A490 2.10 l Wulfenia baldacii 2.00 1.00
Nos. 2246-2248 (3) 3.15 1.65

1987, June 25

2249 A491 1.20 l multi 2.25 .60

Sowing, by Bujar Asllani — A492

Paintings in the Eponymous Museum, Tirana: 30q, The Sustenance of Industry, by Myrteza Fushekati, vert. 80q, The Gifted Partisan, by Skender Kokobobo, vert. 1.20 l, At the Forging Block, by Clirim Ceka.

Perf. 12x12½, 12½x12

1987, July 20 **Litho.**

2250 A492 30q multi .30 .20
2251 A492 80q multi .80 .40
2252 A492 1 l shown 1.00 .50
2253 A492 1.20 l multi 1.25 .60
Nos. 2250-2253 (4) 3.35 1.70

A493

OLYMPHILEX '87, Rome, Aug. 29-Sept. 6 — A494

Illustration A494 reduced.

1987, Aug. 29 **Litho.** ***Perf. 12½***

2254 A493 30q Hammer throw .30 .20
2255 A493 90q Running .90 .45
2256 A493 1.10 l Shot put 1.25 .60

Size: 85x60mm

2257 A494 1.90 l Runner, globe 2.00 1.00
Nos. 2254-2257 (4) 4.45 2.25

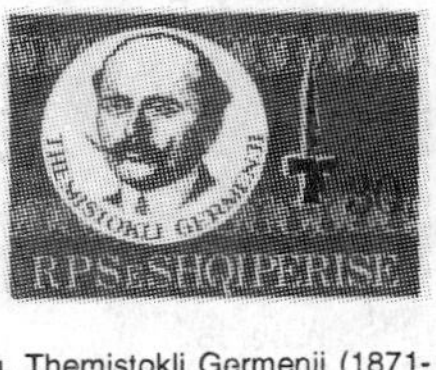

Famous Men — A495

Designs: 30q, Themistokli Germenji (1871-1917), author, politician. 80q, Bajram Curri (1862-1925), founder of the Albanian League. 90q, Aleks Stavre Drenova (1872-1947), poet. 1.30 l, Gjerasim D. Qiriazi (1861-1894), teacher, journalist.

1987, Sept. 30 ***Perf. 12***

2258 A495 30q multi .30 .20
2259 A495 80q multi .80 .40
2260 A495 90q multi .90 .45
2261 A495 1.30 l multi 1.25 .65
Nos. 2258-2261 (4) 3.25 1.70

Albanian Labor Party Congress, Tirana A496

1987, Oct. 22 **Litho.** ***Perf. 12***

2262 A496 1.20 l multi 1.90 .60

Natl. Independence, 75th Anniv. — A497

Postal Administration, 75th Anniv. — A498

1987, Nov. 27

2263 A497 1.20 l State flag 1.90 .60

1987, Dec. 5

2264 A498 90q P.O. emblem 2.00 .45
2265 A498 1.20 l State seal 2.50 .60

Art & Literature — A499

WHO, 40th Anniv. — A500

Portraits: 30q, Lord Byron (1788-1824), English Poet. 1.20 l, Eugene Delacroix (1798-1863), French painter.

1988, Mar. 10

2266 A499 30q org brn & blk 1.00 .20
2267 A499 1.20 l pale vio & blk 4.00 .60

1988, Apr. 7

2268 A500 90q multi 2.00 .45
2269 A500 1.20 l multi 2.50 .60

Flowers — A501

1988, May 20

Booklet Stamps

2270 A501 30q *Sideritis raeseri* .75 .20
2271 A501 90q *Lunaria telekiana* 2.25 .45
2272 A501 2.10 l *Sanguisorba albanica* 5.50 1.10
a. Bklt. pane of 3, plus label 8.50
Nos. 2270-2272 (3) 8.50 1.75

10th Women's Federation Congress A502

1988, June 6
2273 A502 90q blk, red & dark org 2.50 .45

European Soccer Championships — A503

Various athletes.
1.90 l, Goalie designs of Nos. 2274-2276.

1988, June 10
2274 A503 30q multicolored .30 .20
2275 A503 80q multicolored .80 .40
2276 A503 1.20 l multicolored 1.25 .60

Size: 79x68mm
Imperf
2277 A503 1.90 l multicolored 1.90 .95
Nos. 2274-2277 (4) 4.25 2.15

Migjeni (1911-1938), Poet — A507

1988, Aug. 26 Litho. *Perf. 12*
2285 A507 90q silver & brown 2.50 .50

Ballads A508

1988, Sept. 5
2286 A508 30q Dede Skurra 1.00 .20
2287 A508 90q Omeri Iri 3.00 .50
2288 A508 1.20 l Gjergj Elez Alia 4.00 .65
Nos. 2286-2288 (3) 8.00 1.35

Folklore Festival Type of 1978

1988, Oct. 6
2289 A388 30q Kerchief Dance 1.25 .20
2290 A388 1.20 l Dancers with raised arm 4.75 .65

Enver Hoxha Museum A510

Perf. 12x12½, 12½x12
1988, Oct. 16 Litho.
2291 A510 90q Portrait, vert. 1.10 .35
2292 A510 1.20 l shown 1.40 .50

Enver Hoxha (1908-1985), Communist leader.

Locomotives, Map Showing Rail Network — A512

1989, Feb. 28 Litho. *Perf. 12½x12*
2295 A512 30q 1947 .20 .20
2296 A512 90q 1949 .65 .35
2297 A512 1.20 l 1978 .85 .40
2298 A512 1.80 l 1985 1.25 .65
2299 A512 2.40 l 1988 1.60 .85
Nos. 2295-2299 (5) 4.55 2.45

Archaeological Treasures — A513

30q, Illyrian grave. 90q, Warrior on horseback.

1989, Mar. 10 Litho. *Perf. 12*
2300 A513 30q blk & tan .20 .20
2301 A513 90q blk & dl grn .65 .35
2302 A513 2.10 l shown 1.50 .75
Nos. 2300-2302 (3) 2.35 1.30

Folklore A514

1989, Apr. 5 Litho. *Perf. 12x12½*
2303 A514 30q multicolored .20 .20
2304 A514 80q multi, diff. .55 .30
2305 A514 1 l multi, diff. .70 .35
2306 A514 1.20 l multi, diff. .85 .45
Nos. 2303-2306 (4) 2.30 1.30

Flowers — A515

Famous People — A516

Designs: 30q, *Aster albanicus.* 90q, *Orchis x paparisti.* 2.10 l, *Orchis albanica.*

1989, May 10 *Perf. 12*
2307 A515 30q multicolored .20 .20
2308 A515 90q multicolored .65 .35
2309 A515 2.10 l multicolored 1.50 .75
Nos. 2307-2309 (3) 2.35 1.30

1989, June 3

Designs: 30q, Johann Strauss the Younger (1825-1899), composer. 80q, Marie Curie (1867-1934), chemist. 1 l, Federico Garcia Lorca (1898-1936), poet. 1.20 l, Albert Einstein (1879-1955), physicist.

2310 A516 30q gold & blk brn .20 .20
2311 A516 80q gold & blk brn .60 .30
2312 A516 1 l gold & blk brn .75 .35
2313 A516 1.20 l gold & blk brn .85 .45
Nos. 2310-2313 (4) 2.40 1.30

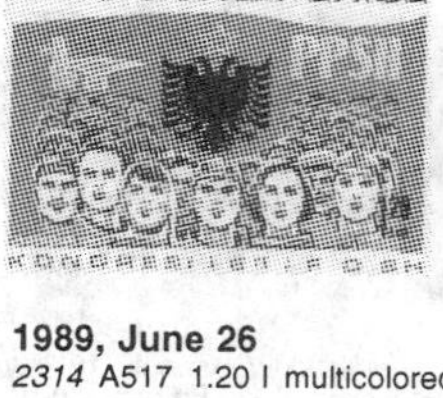

6th Congress of Albanian Democratic Front A517

1989, June 26
2314 A517 1.20 l multicolored 1.50 .65

French Revolution, Bicent. — A518

90q, Storming of the Bastille. 1.20 l, Statue.

1989, July 7 Litho. *Perf. 12½*
2315 A518 90q multicolored .75 .40
2316 A518 1.20 l shown 1.00 .50

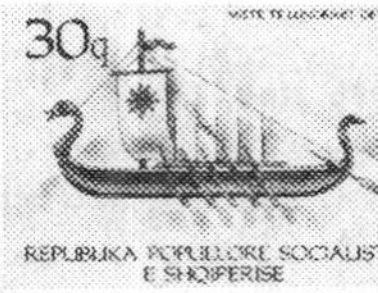

Illyrian Ship — A519

1989, July 25 *Perf. 12*
2317 A519 30q shown .25 .20
2318 A519 80q Caravel .60 .30
2319 A519 90q 3-masted schooner .65 .35
2320 A519 1.30 l Modern cargo ship 1.00 .50
Nos. 2317-2320 (4) 2.50 1.35

A520

A521

Famous Men: 30q, Pjeter Bogdani (1625-1689), writer. 80q, Gavril Dara (1826-1889), poet. 90q, Thimi Mitko (1820-1890), writer. 1.30 l, Kole Idromeno (1860-1939), painter.

1989, Aug. 30 Litho. *Perf. 12*
2321 A520 30q multicolored .30 .20
2322 A520 80q multicolored .80 .40
2323 A520 90q multicolored .90 .45
2324 A520 1.30 l multicolored 1.25 .65
Nos. 2321-2324 (4) 3.25 1.70

1989, Sept. 29
2325 A521 90q shown .70 .35
2326 A521 1.20 l Workers .95 .50

First Communist International, 125th anniv.

Spartakiad Games A522

1989, Oct. 27 *Perf. 12x12½*
2327 A522 30q Gymasnastics .20 .20
2328 A522 80q Soccer .55 .30
2329 A522 1 l Cycling .70 .35
2330 A522 1.20 l Running .85 .45
Nos. 2327-2330 (4) 2.30 1.30

Miniature Sheet

45th Anniv. of Liberation — A523

1989, Nov. 29 *Perf. 12x12½*
2331 Sheet of 4 2.50 1.25
a. A523 30q Revolutionary .20 .20
b. A523 80q "45" .55 .30
c. A523 1 l Coat of arms .70 .35
d. A523 1.20 l Workers .85 .45

Rupicapra Rupicapra — A524

1990, Mar. 15 *Perf. 12*
2332 A524 10q Two adults .20 .20
2333 A524 30q Adult, kid .30 .20
2334 A524 80q Adult .80 .40
2335 A524 90q Adult head .90 .45
a. Block of 4, #2332-2335 2.10 1.10

World Wildlife Fund.

Tribal Masks — A525

1990, Apr. 4 *Perf. 12x12½*
2336 A525 30q shown .30 .20
2337 A525 90q multi, diff. .95 .50
2338 A525 1.20 l multi, diff. 1.25 .65
2339 A525 1.80 l multi, diff. 1.90 .95
Nos. 2336-2339 (4) 4.40 2.30

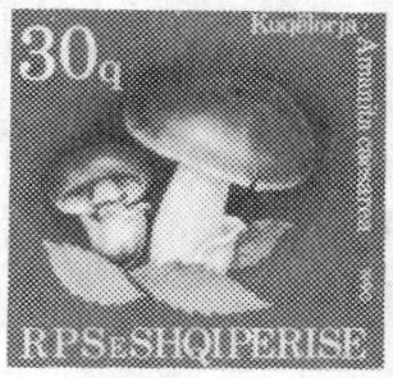

Mushrooms A526

1990, Apr. 28 Litho. *Perf. 12*
2340 A526 30q Amanita caesarea .25 .20
2341 A526 90q Lepiota procera .75 .40
2342 A526 1.20 l Boletus edulis 1.00 .50
2343 A526 1.80 l Clathrus cancelatus 1.50 .75
Nos. 2340-2343 (4) 3.50 1.85

First Postage Stamp, 150th Anniv. A527

1990, May 6 *Perf. 12*
2344 A527 90q shown .95 .50
2345 A527 1.20 l Post rider 1.25 .60
2346 A527 1.80 l Carriage 1.75 .95
a. Bklt. pane of 3, #2344-2346 + label 4.25
Nos. 2344-2346 (3) 3.95 2.05

World Cup Soccer, Italy — A528

1990, June Litho. *Perf. 12*
2347 A528 30q multicolored .50 .25
2348 A528 90q multi, diff. 1.40 .75
2349 A528 1.20 l multi, diff. 2.00 1.00

Size: 80x63mm

Imperf

2350 A528 3.30 l multi, diff. 5.30 2.65
Nos. 2347-2350 (4) 9.20 4.65

Vincent Van Gogh, Death Cent. A529

Self portraits and: 30q, Details from various paintings. 90q, Woman in field. 2.10 l, Asylum. 2.40 l, Self-portrait.

1990, July 27

2351 A529 30q multicolored .50 .25
2352 A529 90q multicolored 1.40 .75
2353 A529 2.10 l multicolored 3.50 1.75

Size: 87x73mm

Imperf

2354 A529 2.40 l multicolored 1.90 .95
Nos. 2351-2354 (4) 7.30 3.70

Albanian Folklore — A530

Scenes from medieval folktale of "Gjergj Elez Alia": 30q, Alia lying wounded. 90q, Alia being helped onto horse. 1.20 l, Alia fighting Bajloz. 1.80 l, Alia on horseback over severed head of Bajloz.

1990, Aug. 30 ***Perf. 12½x12***

2355 A530 30q multicolored .50 .25
2356 A530 90q multicolored 1.40 .70
2357 A530 1.20 l multicolored 2.00 .95
2358 A530 1.80 l multicolored 3.00 1.50
Nos. 2355-2358 (4) 6.90 3.40

Founding of Berat, 2400th Anniv. A531

Designs: 30q, Xhamia E Plumbit. 90q, Kisha E Shen Triadhes. 1.20 l, Ura E Beratit. 1.80 l, Onufri-Piktor Mesjetar. 2.40 l, Nikolla-Piktor Mesjetar.

1990, Sept. 20 ***Perf. 12½***

2359 Block of 5 + 4 labels 4.25 2.10
a. A531 30q multi .20 .20
b. A531 90q multi .65 .30
c. A531 1.20 l multi .70 .35
d. A531 1.80 l multi 1.25 .65
e. A531 2.40 l multi 1.40 .70

No. 2359 was sold in souvenir folders for 9.90 l.

Illyrian Heroes — A532

1990, Oct. 20 ***Perf. 12***

2360 A532 30q Pirroja .50 .25
2361 A532 90q Teuta 1.40 .70
2362 A532 1.20 l Bato 2.00 .95
2363 A532 1.80 l Bardhyli 3.00 1.50
Nos. 2360-2363 (4) 6.90 3.40

Intl. Literacy Year — A533

1990, Oct. 30

2364 A533 90q lt bl & multi 1.40 .70
2365 A533 1.20 l pink & multi 2.00 .95

Albanian Horseman by Eugene Delacroix A534

Designs: 1.20 l, Albanian Woman by Camille Corot. 1.80 l, Skanderbeg by unknown artist.

1990, Nov. 30 ***Perf. 12x12½***

2366 A534 30q multicolored .50 .25
2367 A534 1.20 l multicolored 1.90 .95
2368 A534 1.80 l multicolored 3.00 1.50
Nos. 2366-2368 (3) 5.40 2.70

Isa Boletini (1864-1916), Freedom Fighter — A535

1991, Jan. 23 Litho. ***Perf. 12x12½***

2369 A535 90q Portrait .65 .30
2370 A535 1.20 l shown .90 .45

Pierre Auguste Renoir (1841-1919), Painter — A537

Paintings: 30q, Girl Reading, 1876, vert. 90q, The Swing, 1876, vert. 1.20 l, Boating Party, 1868-1869. 1.80 l, Flowers and grapes, 1878. 3 l, Self-portrait.

1991, Feb. 25 ***Perf. 12½x12***

2373 A537 30q multicolored .20 .20
2374 A537 90q multicolored .65 .30
2375 A537 1.20 l multicolored .90 .45
2376 A537 1.80 l multicolored 1.25 .65

Size: 95x75mm

Imperf

2377 A537 3 l multicolored 4.75 2.50
Nos. 2373-2377 (5) 7.75 4.10

Flowers — A538

1991, Mar. 30 ***Perf. 12***

2378 A538 30q Cistus albanicus .50 .25
2379 A538 90q Trifolium pilczii 1.40 .75
2380 A538 1.80 l Lilium albanicum 3.00 1.50
Nos. 2378-2380 (3) 4.90 2.50

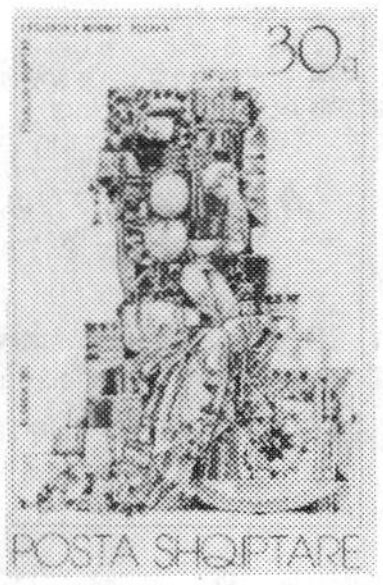

Legend of Rozafa — A539

Various scenes from legend.

1991, Sept. 30 Litho. ***Perf. 12x12½***

2381 A539 30q multicolored .50 .25
2382 A539 90q multicolored 1.40 .70
2383 A539 1.20 l multicolored 2.00 .95
2384 A539 1.80 l multicolored 3.00 1.50
Nos. 2381-2384 (4) 6.90 3.40

For surcharge see No. 2586.

Wolfgang Amadeus Mozart, Death Bicent. — A540

1991, Oct. 5 Litho. ***Perf. 12***

2385 A540 90q Conducting .70 .35
2386 A540 1.20 l Portrait .90 .45
2387 A540 1.80 l Playing piano 1.40 .70

Size: 89x70mm

Imperf

2388 A540 3 l Medal, score 4.00 4.00
Nos. 2385-2388 (4) 7.00 5.50

Airplanes A541

Designs: 30q, Glider, Otto Lilienthal, 1896. 80q, Avion III, Clement Ader, 1897. 90q, Flyer, Wright Brothers, 1903. 1.20 l, Concorde. 1.80 l, Tupolev 114. 2.40 l, Dornier 31 E.

1992, Jan. 27 Litho. ***Perf. 12½x12***

2389 A541 30q multicolored .50 .25
2390 A541 80q multicolored 1.25 .65
2391 A541 90q multicolored 1.40 .70
2392 A541 1.20 l multicolored 2.00 .95
2393 A541 1.80 l multicolored 3.00 1.50
2394 A541 2.40 l multicolored 4.00 2.00
Nos. 2389-2394 (6) 12.15 6.05

No. 2393 misidentifies a Tupolev 144.

Explorers — A542

1992, Jan. 10

2395 A542 30q Bering .50 .25
2396 A542 90q Columbus 1.40 .70
2397 A542 1.80 l Magellan 3.00 1.50
Nos. 2395-2397 (3) 4.90 2.45

1992 Winter Olympics, Albertville A543

1992, Feb. 15 Litho. ***Perf. 12½***

2398 A543 30q Ski jumping .25 .20
2399 A543 90q Cross country skiing .70 .35
2400 A543 1.20 l Pairs figure skating .95 .50
2401 A543 1.80 l Luge 1.40 .70
Nos. 2398-2401 (4) 3.30 1.70

For surcharge see No. 2598.

Participation of Albania in Conference on Security and Cooperation in Europe, Berlin (1991) — A544

1992, Mar. 31 Litho. ***Perf. 12½x12***

2402 A544 90q shown *.95 .95*
2403 A544 1.20 l Flags, map *1.25 1.25*
a. Pair, #2402-2403 *2.25 2.25*

Dated 1991. Issued in sheets containing 2 #2403a, 3 each #2402-2403 + 2 labels.

Albanian Admission to CEPT — A545

1992, Apr. 25 Litho. ***Perf. 12½***

2404 A545 90q Envelopes, CEPT emblem .90 .90
2405 A545 1.20 l shown 1.25 1.25
a. Pair, #2404-2405 2.25 2.25

Issued in sheets containing 2 #2405a, 3 each #2404-2405 and 2 labels.

Martyrs' Day — A546

1992, May 5 ***Perf. 12x12½***

2406 A546 90q Freedom flame, vert. *1.00 1.00*

Perf. 12½x12

2407 A546 4.10 l Flowers *4.50 4.50*

European Soccer Championships, Sweden'92 — A547

Various stylized designs of soccer plays.

1992, June 10 Litho. *Perf. 12*

2408 A547 30q green & lt grn .20 .20
2409 A547 90q blue & pink .25 .25
2410 A547 10.80 l henna & tan 3.00 3.00

Size: 90x70mm

Imperf

2411 A547 5 l tan, lt green & pink 1.40 1.40
Nos. 2408-2411 (4) 4.85 4.85

1992 Summer Olympics, Barcelona A548

1992, June 14 Litho. *Perf. 12*

2412 A548 30q Tennis *.35 .35*
2413 A548 90q Baseball *1.00 1.00*
2414 A548 1.80 l Table tennis *2.00 2.00*

Size: 90x70mm

Imperf

2415 A548 5 l Torch bearer *1.50 1.50*
Nos. 2412-2415 (4) *4.85 4.85*

United Europe A549

1992, July 10 Litho. *Perf. 12*

2416 A549 1.20 l multicolored .90 .45

Horses A550

1992, Aug. 10 Litho. *Perf. 12*

2417 A550 30q Native .20 .20
2418 A550 90q Nonius .25 .25
2419 A550 1.20 l Arabian, vert. .35 .35
2420 A550 10.60 l Haflinger, vert. *2.75 2.75*
Nos. 2417-2420 (4) *3.55 3.55*

Discovery of America, 500th Anniv. A551

Map of North and South America and: 60q, Columbus, sailing ships. 3.20 l, Columbus meeting natives.

1992, Aug. 20

2421 A551 60q blk, bl & gray .25 .25
2422 A551 3.20 l blk, brn & gray 1.25 1.25

Size: 90x70mm

Imperf

2423 A551 5 l Map, Columbus

A552 A553

Mother Theresa, infant.

1992, Oct. 4 Litho. *Perf. 12x12½*

2424 A552 40q fawn .20 .20
2425 A552 60q brown .20 .20
2426 A552 1 l violet .20 .20
2427 A552 1.80 l gray .25 .25
2428 A552 2 l red .30 .30
2429 A552 2.40 l green .35 .35
2430 A552 3.20 l blue .50 .50
2431 A552 5.60 l rose violet 1.00 1.00
2432 A552 7.20 l olive 1.10 1.10
2433 A552 10 l orange brown 1.50 1.50
Nos. 2424-2433 (10) 5.60 5.60

See Nos. 2472-2476.

1993, Apr. 25 Litho. *Perf. 12*

2434 A553 16 l multicolored *2.50 2.50*

Visit of Pope John Paul II.

POSTA SHQIPTARE

Nos. 2223-2226, 2229 Surcharged

■ 3 Lekë

1993, May 2 Litho. *Perf. 12x12½*

2435 A486 3 l on 10q .60 .60
2436 A486 6.50 l on 20q 1.25 1.25
2437 A486 13 l on 30q 2.50 2.50
2438 A486 20 l on 90q 4.00 4.00
2439 A486 30 l on 50q 5.75 5.75
Nos. 2435-2439 (5) 14.10 14.10

Lef Nosi (1873-1945), Minister of Posts — A554

1993, May 5 Litho. *Perf. 12*

2440 A554 6.50 l olive brown & bister .90 .90

First Albanian postage stamps, 80th anniv.

Europa A555

Contemporary paintings by: 3 l, A. Zajmi, vert. 7 l, E. Hila. 20 l, B. Ahmeti-Peizazh.

1993, May 28 Litho. *Perf. 12*

2441 A555 3 l multicolored .55 .55
2442 A555 7 l multicolored 1.25 1.25

Size: 116x122mm

2443 A555 20 l multicolored 3.75 3.75
Nos. 2441-2443 (3) 5.55 5.55

1993 Mediterranean Games, France — A556

1993, June 20 Litho. *Perf. 12*

2444 A556 3 l Running .55 .55
2445 A556 16 l Kayaking 3.00 3.00
2446 A556 21 l Cycling 3.75 3.75

Size: 111x78mm

Imperf

2447 A556 20 l Mediterranean map 3.50 3.50
Nos. 2444-2447 (4) 10.80 10.80

Frang Bardhi, Author, 350th Death Anniv. — A557

1993, Aug. 20 Litho. *Perf. 12x12½*

2448 A557 6.50 l shown 1.10 1.10

Size: 89x101mm

Imperf

2449 A557 20 l Writing at desk 3.50 3.50

A558 A559

1994, July 17 Litho. *Perf. 12*

2450 A558 42 l shown 1.50 1.50
2451 A558 68 l Mascot, ball, US map 2.50 2.50

1994 World Cup Soccer Championships, US.

1994, Dec. 31 Litho. *Perf. 14*

European Inventors, Discoveries: 50 l, Gjovalin Gjadri, engineer. 100 l, Karl von Ghega, Austrian engineer. 150 l, Sketch of road project.

2452 A559 50 l multicolored 2.00 2.00
2453 A559 100 l multicolored 4.00 4.00

Size: 50x70mm

Imperf

2454 A559 150 l multicolored 6.00 6.00
Nos. 2452-2454 (3) 12.00 12.00

Europa (#2454).

Ali Pasa of Tepelene (Lion of Janina) (1744-1822) A560

1995, Jan. 28 *Perf. 14*

2455 A560 60 l shown 2.50 2.50

Size: 70x50mm

Imperf

2456 A560 100 l Tepelene Palace 4.00 4.00

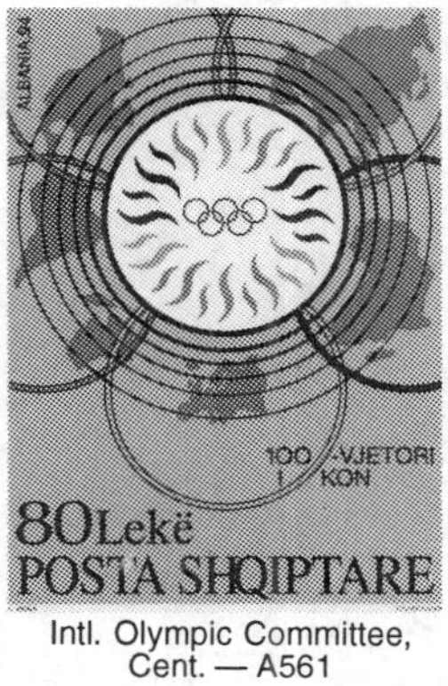

Intl. Olympic Committee, Cent. — A561

1995, Feb. 2 *Imperf.*

2457 A561 80 l multicolored 3.25 3.25

Karl Benz (1844-1929), Automobile Pioneer — A562

Designs: 5 l, Automobile company emblem, Benz. 10 l, Modern Mercedes Benz automobile. 60 l, First four-wheel Benz 1886 motor car. 125 l, Pre-war Mercedes touring car.

1995, Jan. 21 Litho. *Perf. 14*

2458 A562 5 l multicolored .20 .20
2459 A562 10 l multicolored .30 .30
2460 A562 60 l multicolored 1.60 1.60
2461 A562 125 l multicolored 3.50 3.50
Nos. 2458-2461 (4) 5.60 5.60

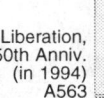

Liberation, 50th Anniv. (in 1994) A563

1995, Jan. 28 Litho. *Perf. 14*

2462 A563 50 l black, gray & red 2.00 2.00

Dated 1994.

Miniature Sheet

Albania '93 — A564

Composers: a, 3 l, Wagner. b, 6.50 l, Grieg. c, 11 l, Gounod. d, 20 l, Tchaikovsky.

1995, Jan. 26 *Perf. 12*

2463 A564 Sheet of 4, #a.-d. 2.00 2.00

Veskopoja Academy, 250th Anniv. — A565

Buildings of Veskopoja.

1995, Feb. 2

2464 A565 42 l multicolored 1.50 1.50
2465 A565 68 l multicolored 2.50 2.50
 a. Pair, #2464-2465 4.00 4.00

Bleta Apricula — A566 Peace & Freedom — A567

1995, Aug. 20 Litho. *Perf. 12*

2466 A566 5 l On flower .20 .20
2467 A566 10 l Honeycomb, bee .40 .40
2468 A566 25 l Emerging from cell of honeycomb 1.00 1.00
Nos. 2466-2468 (3) 1.60 1.60

1995, Aug. 10 *Perf. 13½x14*

Stylized hands reaching for: 50 l, Olive branch. 100 l, Peace dove.
150 l, Stylized person.

2469 A567 50 l multicolored 1.50 1.50
2470 A567 100 l multicolored 3.25 3.25

Size: 80x60mm

Imperf

2471 A567 150 l multicolored 4.75 4.75
Nos. 2469-2471 (3) 9.50 9.50

Europa.

Mother Teresa Type of 1992

1994-95 Litho. *Perf. 12x12½*

2472 A552 5 l violet .25 .25
2473 A552 18 l orange .85 .85
2474 A552 20 l rose lilac .95 .95
2475 A552 25 l green 1.10 1.10
2476 A552 60 l olive 2.75 2.75
Nos. 2472-2476 (5) 5.90 5.90

Issued: 20 l, 1994; 60 l, 1995; others, 7/94.

Arctic Explorers — A568

Designs: a, Fridtjof Nansen (1861-1930), Norway. b, James Cook (1728-79), England. c, Roald Amundsen (1872-1928), Norway. d, Robert F. Scott (1872-1928), Great Britain.

1995, Sept. 14 Litho. *Perf. 13½x14*

2477 A568 25 l Block of 4, #a.-d. 4.25 4.25

UN, 50th Anniv. A569

1995, Sept. 14 Litho. *Perf. 14x13½*

2478 A569 2 l shown .20 .20
2479 A569 100 l like #2478, flags streaming to right 4.25 4.25

Poets — A570

1995 *Perf. 13½x14*

2480 A570 25 l Pol Elyar 1.10 1.10
2481 A570 50 l Sergej Esnin 2.25 2.25
a. Pair, #2480-2481 3.50 3.50

Entry into Council of Europe A571

Designs: 25 l, Doves flying from headquarters, Strasbourg. 85 l, Albanian eagle over map of Europe.

1995 *Perf. 14x13½*

2482 A571 25 l multicolored 1.10 1.10
2483 A571 85 l multicolored 3.75 3.75

For surcharge see No. 2583

Jan Kukuzeli, Composer A572

Stylized figure: 18 l, Writing. 20 l, Holding hand to head. 100 l, Holding up scroll of paper.

1995, Oct. 17 *Perf. 13½x14*

2484 A572 18 l multicolored .85 .85
2485 A572 20 l multicolored .95 .95

Size: 74x74mm

2486 A572 100 l multicolored 4.50 4.50
Nos. 2484-2486 (3) 6.30 6.30

World Tourism Organization, 20th Anniv. — A573

Stylized designs: 18 l, Church, saint holding scroll. 20 l, City, older buildings. 42 l, City, modern buildings.

1995, Oct. 17

2487 A573 18 l multicolored 1.00 1.00
2488 A573 20 l multicolored 1.10 1.10
2489 A573 42 l multicolored 2.50 2.50
Nos. 2487-2489 (3) 4.60 4.60

Fables of Jean de la Fontaine (1621-95) A574

Designs: 2 l, Raptor, turtle, wolf, goose, mouse, lion, rats. 3 l, Crow, goose, dog, foxes. 25 l, Insect, doves, frogs.
60 l, Drawings of Da la Fontaine, animals, birds.

1995, Aug. 20 Litho. *Perf. 14x13½*

2490 A574 2 l multicolored .20 .20
2491 A574 3 l multicolored .20 .20
2492 A574 25 l multicolored .95 .95

Imperf

Size: 73x56mm

2493 A574 60 l multicolored 2.70 2.70
Nos. 2490-2493 (4) 4.05 4.05

Folklore Festival, Berat — A575

Motion Pictures, Cent. — A576

Stylized designs: 5 l, Men's choir. 50 l, Costumed woman seated in chair.

1995, Oct. 17 Litho. *Perf. 13½x14*

2494 A575 5 l multicolored .20 .20
2495 A575 50 l multicolored 2.25 2.25

1995, Nov. 17

2496 A576 10 l Louis Lumiere .45 .45
2497 A576 85 l Auguste Lumiere 3.75 3.75
a. Pair, #2496-2497 4.20 4.20

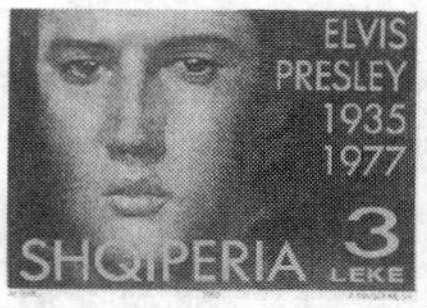

Elvis Presley (1935-77) A577

1995, Nov. 20 Litho. *Perf. 14x13½*

2498 A577 3 l orange & multi .20 .20
2499 A577 60 l green & multi 2.50 2.50

A578

A579

1995, Nov. 25 *Perf. 13½x14*

2500 A578 10 l 1925 Bank notes .45 .45
2501 A578 25 l 1995 Bank notes 1.10 1.10

National Bank, 70th anniv.

1995, Nov. 27 Litho. *Perf. 13½x14*

2502 A579 5 l shown .20 .20
2503 A579 50 l Maiden planting tree 2.25 2.25

Democracy, 5th anniv.

A580

Mother Teresa — A581

Designs: 25 l, Soccer ball, British flag, map of Europe, stadium. 100 l, Soccer ball, player.

1996, June 4 *Perf. 14*

2504 A580 25 l multicolored 1.10 1.10
2505 A580 100 l multicolored 4.50 4.50

Euro '96, European Soccer Championships, Great Britain.

1996, May 5 *Perf. 13½x14*

2506 A581 25 l blue & multi 1.10 1.10
2507 A581 100 l red & multi 4.50 4.50

Size: 52x74mm

Imperf

2508 A581 150 l Mother Teresa, diff. 6.75 6.75
Nos. 2506-2508 (3) 12.35 12.35

Europa. For overprints see Nos. 2551, 2582.

GSM Cellular Telephone Transmission A582

Designs: 10 l, Satellite transmitting signals. 60 l, Uses for cellular telephone, vert.

Perf. 13x13½, 13½x13

1996, Aug. 1 Litho.

2509 A582 10 l multicolored .45 .45
2510 A582 60 l multicolored 2.50 2.50

1996 Summer Olympic Games, Atlanta — A583

Stylized designs.

1996, Aug. 3 Litho. *Perf. 13x14*

2511 A583 5 l Runners .20 .20
2512 A583 25 l Throwers 1.00 1.00
2513 A583 60 l Jumpers 2.40 2.40

Size: 52x37mm

Imperf

2514 A583 100 l Emblem, US flag 4.00 4.00
Nos. 2511-2514 (4) 7.60 7.60

Gottfried Wilhelm Leibniz (1646-1716), Mathematician — A584

85 l, René Descartes (1596-1650), mathematician.

1996, Sept. 20 Litho. *Perf. 14*

2515 A584 10 l multicolored .40 .40
2516 A584 85 l multicolored 3.50 3.50

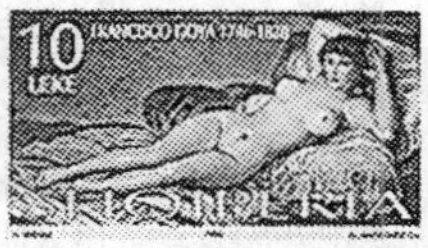

Paintings by Francisco Goya (1746-1828) A585

Designs: 10 l, The Naked Maja. 60 l, Dona Isabel Cobos de Porcel. 100 l, Self portrait.

1996, Sept. 25 *Perf. 14x13½*

2517 A585 10 l multicolored .40 .40
2518 A585 60 l multicolored 2.50 2.50

Souvenir Sheet

2519 A585 100 l multicolored 4.00 4.00

Religious Engravings A586

UNICEF, 50th Anniv. A587

Designs: a, 5 l, Book cover showing crucifixion, angels. b, 25 l, Medallion of crucifixion. c, 85 l, Book cover depicting life of Christ.

1996, Nov. 5 *Perf. 13x13½*

2520 A586 Block of 3, #a.-c. + label 4.75 4.75

1996, Nov. 11 *Perf. 13½*

Children's paintings: 5 l, Fairy princess. 10 l, Doll, sun. 25 l, Sea life. 50 l, House, people.

2521 A587 5 l multicolored .20 .20
2522 A587 10 l multicolored .45 .45
2523 A587 25 l multicolored 1.10 1.10
2524 A587 50 l multicolored 2.25 2.25
Nos. 2521-2524 (4) 4.00 4.00

Gjergj Fishta (1871-1940), Writer, Priest
A588

Omar Khayyam
A589

1996, Dec. 20 *Perf. 13½x14*

2525 A588 10 l shown .40 .40
2526 A588 60 l Battle scene, portrait 2.50 2.50

1997, Mar. 6 *Perf. 14*

2527 A589 20 l shown .70 .70
2528 A589 50 l Portrait, diff. 1.75 1.75

A590 A591

1997, Mar. 20 *Perf. 14x14½*

2529 A590 20 l Portrait .70 .70
2530 A590 60 l Printing press 2.15 2.15
a. Pair, #2529-2530 2.85 2.85

Johannes Gutenberg (1397?-1468).

1997, May 5 Litho. *Perf. 13x14*

The Azure Eye (Stories and Legends): 30 l, Dragon on rock looking at warrior, donkey. 100 l, Dragon drinking water from pond, warrior.

2531 A591 30 l multicolored 1.25 1.25
2532 A591 100 l multicolored 4.00 4.00

Europa.

A592 A593

1997, Apr. 10 *Perf. 14*

2533 A592 10 l Pelicanus Crispus .40 .40
2534 A592 80 l Pelicans, diff. 3.00 3.00
a. Pair, #2533-2534 3.40 3.40

No. 2534a is a continuous design.

1997, June 25 Litho. *Perf. 14*

2535 A593 10 l black & dark brown .40 .40
2536 A593 25 l black & blue black 1.00 1.00

Souvenir Sheet

2537 A593 80 l gray brown 2.90 2.90

Faik Konica (1875-1942), writer and politician.

No. 2537 contains one 22x26mm stamp.

A594

Skanderbeg — A595

1997 Mediterranean Games, Bari: 20 l, Man running. 30 l, Woman running, 3-man canoe. 100 l, Man breaking finish line, silhouettes of man and woman.

1997, June 13

2538 A594 20 l Man running .75 .75
2539 A594 30 l Woman running, canoe 1.10 1.10

Size: 52x74mm

Imperf

2540 A594 100 l multicolored 3.60 3.60

1997, Aug. 25 Litho. *Perf. 13*

2541 A595 5 l red brn & red .20 .20
2542 A595 10 l dp ol & ol .40 .40
2543 A595 20 l dp green & grn .80 .80
2544 A595 25 l dp mag & red lil 1.00 1.00
2545 A595 30 l dk violet & vio 1.25 1.25
2546 A595 50 l black 2.00 2.00
2547 A595 60 l brown & lt brn 2.40 2.40
2548 A595 80 l dk brown & brn 3.25 3.25
2549 A595 100 l dk red brown & red brn 4.00 4.00
2550 A595 110 l dark blue 4.25 4.25
Nos. 2541-2550 (10) 19.55 19.55

No. 2507 Ovptd. in Silver "HOMAZH / 1910-1997"

1997 *Perf. 13½x14*

2551 A581 100 l red & multi 6.50 6.50

Religious Manuscripts
A596

Albanian Codex: a, 10 l, 11th cent. b, 25 l, 6th cent. c, 60 l, 6th cent., diff.

1997, Nov. 15 Litho. *Perf. 13x14*

2552 A596 Block of 3, #a.-c. + label 3.50 3.50

See No. 2575.

Post and Telecommunications Administration, 85th Anniv. — A597

1997, Dec. 4 *Perf. 13½*

2553 A597 10 l multi .40 .40
2554 A597 30 l multi, diff. 1.10 1.10

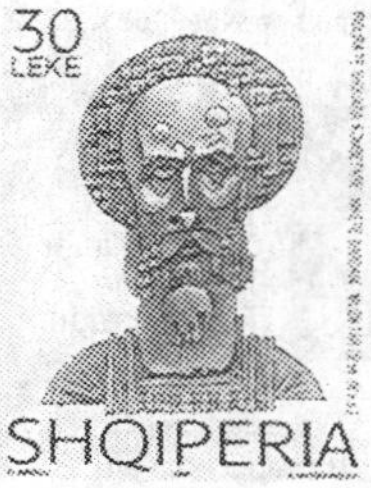

A598 A599

1998, Mar. 25 Litho. *Perf. 14*

2555 A598 30 l red brown & multi .75 .75
2556 A598 100 l tan & multi 2.75 2.75
a. Pair, #2555-2556 3.50 3.50

Nikete Dardani, musician.

1998, Apr. 15

Legends of Pogradecit: a, 30 l, Old man seated at table. b, 50 l, Three Graces. c, 60 l, Two women, fountain. d, 80 l, Iceman.

2557 A599 Block of 4, #a.-d. 5.50 5.50

A600 A601

1998, May 5 Litho. *Perf. 13x14*

2558 A600 60 l shown 1.50 1.50
2559 A600 100 l multi, diff. 2.50 2.50

Size: 50x72mm

Imperf

2560 A600 150 l multi, diff. 3.75 3.75

Europa (folk festivals).

1998, June 10 Litho. *Perf. 13½x13*

Albanian League of Prizren, 120th anniv.: a, 30 l, Abdyl Frasheri. b, 50 l, Sulejman Vokshi. c, 60 l, Iljaz Pashe Dibra. d, 80 l, Ymer Prizreni.

2561 A601 Block of 4, #a.-d. 5.50 5.50

1998 World Cup Soccer Championships, France — A602

Perf. 13½

1998, June 10

Stylized soccer players.

2562 A602 60 l multicolored 1.50 1.50
2563 A602 100 l multicolored 2.50 2.50

Size: 50x73mm

Imperf

2564 A602 120 l Mascot 3.00 3.00

European Youth Greco-Roman Wrestling Championships, Albania — A603

1998, July 5 *Perf. 13½*

2565 A603 30 l shown .75 .75
2566 A603 60 l Wrestlers, diff. 1.50 1.50
a. Pair, #2565-2566 2.25 2.25

Eqerem Cabej (1908-1980), Albanian Etymologist — A604

1998, Aug. 7 *Perf. 14*

2567 A604 60 l yel brn & multi 1.50 1.50
2568 A604 80 l brown red & multi 2.00 2.00
a. Pair, #2567-2568 3.50 3.50

Paul Gauguin (1848-1903)
A605

Paintings (details): 60 l, The Vision after the Sermon. 80 l, Ea Haere Ia Oe.

120 l, Stylized design to resemble self-portrait.

1998, Sept. 10 *Perf. 13½*

2569 A605 60 l multicolored 1.50 1.50
2570 A605 80 l multicolored 2.00 2.00
a. Pair, #2569-2570 3.50 3.50

Size: 50x73mm

Imperf

2571 A605 120 l multicolored 3.00 3.00

Epitaph of Gllavenica, 14th Cent. Depiction of Christ
A606

Designs: 30 l, Entire cloth showing artwork. 80 l, Closer view.

100 l, Upper portion of cloth, vert.

1998, Oct. 5 *Perf. 14½x14*

2572 A606 30 l multicolored .75 .75
2573 A606 80 l multicolored 2.00 2.00

Souvenir Sheet

Perf. 13

2574 A606 100 l multicolored 2.50 2.50

No. 2574 contains one 25x29mm stamp.

Religious Manuscripts Type of 1997

Illustrations from Purple Codex, Gold Codex: a, 30 l, Manuscript, columns on sides, arched top. b, 50 l, Manuscript cover with embossed pictures of icons. c, 80 l, Manuscript picturing cathedral, birds.

1998, Oct. 15 *Perf. 13x14*

2575 A596 Block of 3, #a.-c. + label 4.00 4.00

Mikel Koliqi (1902-97), First Albanian Cardinal — A607

1998, Nov. 28 *Perf. 14*

2576 A607 30 l shown .75 .75
2577 A607 100 l Portrait, facing 2.50 2.50
a. Pair, #2576-2577 3.25 3.25

Mother Teresa (1910-97)
A608

Diana, Princess of Wales (1961-97)
A609

Perf. 14x13½, 13½x14

1998, Sept. 5 Photo.

2578 A608 60 l With child, horiz. 1.50 1.50
2579 A608 100 l shown 2.50 2.50

See Italy Nos. 2254-2255.

1998, Aug. 31 Litho. *Perf. 13½*

2580 A609 60 l shown 1.50 1.50
2581 A609 100 l With Mother Teresa 2.50 2.50

No. 2508 Ovptd. in Blue

1998, Oct. 23 Litho. ***Imperf.***

2582 A581 150 l multicolored 6.25 6.25

No. 2482 Surcharged

1999, Apr. 20 Litho. *Perf. 14x13½*
2583 A571 150 l on 25 l multi 2.25 2.25

Famous Americans A610

a, Washington. b, Lincoln. c. Martin Luther King, Jr.

1999, Mar. 15 *Perf. 14*
2584 A610 150 l Block of 3, #a.-c. + label 6.25 6.25

Monacus Albiventris A611

Seals: a, 110 l, One looking left, one looking right. b, 150 l, Both looking right. c, 110 l, Mirror image of #2585b. d, 150 l, Mirror image of #2585a.

1999, Apr. 10
2585 A611 Sheet of 4, #a.-d. 7.50 7.50

No. 2382 Surcharged

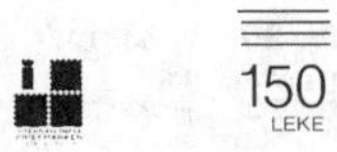

1999, Apr. 24 Litho. *Perf. 12x12¼*
2586 A539 150 l on 90 l multi 4.00 4.00

IBRA '99, Nuremburg.

A612

A613

Perf. 13½x13¾
1999, Apr. 25 Litho.
2587 A612 10 l blue & multi .25 .25
2588 A612 100 l green & multi 2.50 2.50

Souvenir Sheet
Perf. 13
2589 A612 250 l green & multi 6.75 6.75

NATO, 50th anniv. No. 2589 contains one 30x50mm stamp.

1999, Apr. 30 Litho. *Perf. 13x13¾*

Cartoon mouse: a, 80 l, Writing. b, 110 l, Holding chin. c, 150 l, Wearing bow tie. d, 60 l, Pointing.

2590 A613 Strip of 4, #a.-d. 10.50 10.50

Animated films.

Europa A614

1999, May 1 Litho. *Perf. 13¾x13*
2591 A614 90 l Thethi Park 2.40 2.40
2592 A614 310 l Lura Park 8.25 8.25

Illyrian Coins A615

Designs: a, 200 l, Kings of Illyria - Monumiou c. 300-280 BC cow suckling calf, square containing double stellate pattern, and Epidamos-Dyrrachium c. 623 BC, square with double stellate. b, 20 l, Damastion c. 395-380 BC siver drachm portable ingot, Byllis c. 238-168 BC AE13 serpent entwined around cornucopia, Skodra after 168 BC, AE17 war galley, and other war galley coin. c, 10l, Epirote Republic before 238 BC silver tetraobol with jugate busts of Zeus and Dione on obverse and thunderbolt within oak wreath reverse.
310 l, Kings of Illyria - Genthos c. 197-168 BC head wearing kausia.

1999, June 1 Litho. *Perf. 13¾x13¼*
2593 A615 Strip of 3, #a.-c. 6.25 6.25

Souvenir Sheet
Perf. 13
2594 A615 310 l multicolored 8.50 8.50

Charlie Chaplin — A616

Designs: 30 l, Holding cigarette. 50 l, Tipping hat. 250 l, Dancing.

1999, June 20 Litho. *Perf. 14x14¼*
2595 A616 30 l multicolored .75 .75
2596 A616 50 l multicolored 1.25 1.25
2597 A616 250 l multicolored 6.75 6.75
a. Booklet pane, 2 each #2595-2597, perf. 14¼ vert. 17.50
Complete booklet 17.50
Nos. 2595-2597 (3) 8.75 8.75

In No. 2597a, the 30 l stamps are at the ends of the pane and the 250 l stamps are in the middle.

No. 2398 Surcharged

150
LEKE

1999, July 2 Litho. *Perf. 12½*
2598 A543 150 l on 30q multi 4.25 4.25

PhilexFrance 99.

First Manned Moon Landing, 30th Anniv. — A618

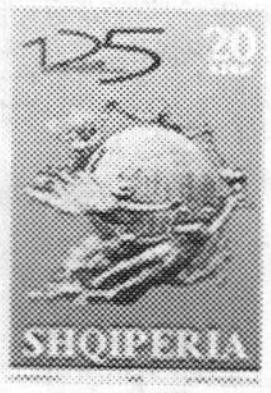

UPU, 125th Anniv. — A619

No. 2601: a, 30 l, Astronaut, earth. b, 150 l, Lunar Module. c, 300 l, Astronaut, flag. 280 l, Lift-off.

1999, July 25 Litho. *Perf. 13¼x14*
2601 A618 Strip of 3, #a.-c 13.00 13.00

Souvenir Sheet
Perf. 13
2602 A618 280 l multicolored 7.25 7.25

No. 2602 contains one 25x29mm stamp.

1999, Aug. 1 Litho. *Perf. 14x14¼*

Background colors: a, 20 l, aquamarine and brown. b, 60 l, bister and dark blue.

2603 A619 Pair, #a.-b. 2.10 2.10

SEMI-POSTAL STAMPS

Nos. 148-151 Surcharged in Red and Black

+
5 qind.

1924, Nov. 1
B1 A18 5q + 5q yel grn 5.00 6.50
B2 A18 10q + 5q carmine 5.00 6.50
B3 A18 25q + 5q dark blue 5.00 6.50
B4 A18 50q + 5q dark grn 5.00 6.50
Nos. B1-B4 (4) 20.00 26.00

Nos. B1 to B4 with Additional Surcharge in Red and Black

+ 5 qind.

1924
B5 A18 5q + 5q + 5q yel grn 5.00 6.50
B6 A18 10q + 5q + 5q car 5.00 6.50
B7 A18 25q + 5q + 5q dk bl 5.00 6.50
B8 A18 50q + 5q + 5q dk grn 5.00 6.50
Nos. B5-B8 (4) 20.00 26.00

Issued under Italian Dominion

Nurse and Child — SP1

Unwmk.
1943, Apr. 1 Photo. *Perf. 14*
B9 SP1 5q + 5q dark grn .25 .25
B10 SP1 10q + 10q olive brn .25 .25
B11 SP1 15q + 10q rose red .35 .35
B12 SP1 25q + 15q saphire .50 .50
B13 SP1 30q + 20q violet .60 .60
B14 SP1 50q + 25q dk org .75 .75
B15 SP1 65q + 30q grnsh blk 1.10 1.10
B16 SP1 1fr + 40q chestnut 2.50 2.50
Nos. B9-B16 (8) 6.30 6.30

The surtax was for the control of tuberculosis.
For surcharges see Nos. B24-B27.

Issued under German Administration

War Victims SP2

1944, Sept. 22
B17 SP2 5q + 5(q) dp grn 2.10 2.75
B18 SP2 10q + 5(q) dp brn 2.10 2.75
B19 SP2 15q + 5(q) car lake 2.10 2.75
B20 SP2 25q + 10(q) dp blue 2.10 2.75
B21 SP2 1fr + 50q dk olive 2.10 2.75
B22 SP2 2fr + 1(fr) purple 2.10 2.75
B23 SP2 3fr + 1.50(fr) dk org 2.10 2.75
Nos. B17-B23 (7) 14.70 19.25

Surtax for victims of World War II.

Independent State

Nos. B9 to B12 Surcharged in Carmine

1945, May 4 Unwmk. *Perf. 14*
B24 SP1 30q +15q on 5q+5q 1.75 1.75
B25 SP1 50q +25q on 10q+10q 1.75 1.75
B26 SP1 1fr +50q on 15q+10q 5.00 5.00
B27 SP1 2fr +1fr on 25q+15q 8.75 8.75
Nos. B24-B27 (4) 17.25 17.25

The surtax was for the Albanian Red Cross.

People's Republic

Nos. 361 to 366 Overprinted in Red (cross) and Surcharged in Black

KONGRESI
K.K.SH.
24-25-11-46
+0.10

1946, July 16 ***Perf. 11***

B28	A57	20q + 10q bluish grn	6.50	6.50
B29	A57	30q + 15q dp org	6.50	6.50
B30	A57	40q + 20q brown	6.50	6.50
B31	A57	60q + 30q red vio	6.50	6.50
B32	A57	1fr + 50q rose red	6.50	6.50
B33	A57	3fr + 1.50fr dk bl	6.50	6.50
		Nos. B28-B33 (6)	39.00	39.00

To honor and benefit the Congress of the Albanian Red Cross.

Counterfeits: lithographed; genuine: typographed.

Catalogue values for unused stamps in this section, from this point to the end of the section, are for Never Hinged items.

SP3

SP4

First Aid and Red Cross: 25q+5q, Nurse carrying child on stretcher. 65q+25q, Symbolic blood transfusion. 80q+40q, Mother and child.

1967, Dec. 1 **Litho.** ***Perf. 11½x12***

B34	SP3	15q + 5q blk, red & brn	.90	.45
B35	SP3	25q + 5q multi	1.00	.60
B36	SP3	65q + 25q multi	3.00	.65
B37	SP3	80q + 40q multi	5.00	1.50
		Nos. B34-B37 (4)	9.90	3.20

6th congress of the Albanian Red Cross.

1996, Aug. 5 **Litho.** ***Perf. 13½x13***

B38	SP4	50 l +10 l multi	2.50	2.50

Albanian Red Cross, 75th anniv.

AIR POST STAMPS

Airplane Crossing Mountains AP1

Wmk. 125

1925, May 30 **Typo.** ***Perf. 14***

C1	AP1	5q green	.50	.50
C2	AP1	10q rose red	.50	.50
C3	AP1	25q deep blue	.450	.50
C4	AP1	50q dark green	1.00	1.00
C5	AP1	1fr dk vio & blk	1.90	1.90
C6	AP1	2fr ol grn & vio	3.00	3.00
C7	AP1	3fr brn org & dk grn	5.25	5.25
		Nos. C1-C7 (7)	16.65	12.65

Nos. C1-C7 exist imperf.

For overprint see Nos. C8-C28.

Nos. C1-C7 Overprinted

Rep. Shqiptare

1927, Jan. 18

C8	AP1	5q green	3.00	3.00
a.		Dbl. overprint, one invtd.	35.00	
C9	AP1	10q rose red	3.00	3.00
a.		Inverted overprint	30.00	
b.		Dbl. overprint, one invtd.	35.00	
C10	AP1	25q deep blue	1.60	1.60
C11	AP1	50q dark grn	1.60	1.60
a.		Inverted overprint	30.00	
C12	AP1	1fr dk vio & blk	1.60	1.60
a.		Inverted overprint	30.00	
b.		Double overprint	30.00	
C13	AP1	2fr ol grn & vio	1.60	1.60
C14	AP1	3fr brn org & dk grn	2.75	2.75
		Nos. C8-C14 (7)	15.15	15.15

Nos. C1-C7 Overprinted

REP. SHQYPTARE
Fluturim' i I-ar
Vlonë--Brindisi
21. IV. 1928

1928, Apr. 21

C15	AP1	5q green	1.50	1.50
a.		Inverted overprint	20.00	
C16	AP1	10q rose red	1.50	1.50
C17	AP1	25q deep blue	1.50	1.50
C18	AP1	50q dark green	2.50	2.50
C19	AP1	1fr dk vio & blk	19.00	19.00
C20	AP1	2fr ol grn & vio	19.00	19.00
C21	AP1	3fr brn org & dk grn	19.00	19.00
		Nos. C15-C21 (7)	64.00	64.00

First flight across the Adriatic, Valona to Brindisi, Apr. 21, 1928.

The variety "SHQYRTARE" occurs once in the sheet for each value. Value 3 times normal.

Nos. C1-C7 Overprinted in Red Brown

Mbr. Shqiptare

1929, Dec. 1

C22	AP1	5q green	3.50	3.50
C23	AP1	10q rose red	3.50	3.50
C24	AP1	25q deep blue	3.75	3.75
C25	AP1	50q dk grn	17.50	17.50
C26	AP1	1fr dk vio & blk	165.00	165.00
C27	AP1	2fr ol grn	165.00	165.00
C28	AP1	3fr brn org & dk grn	165.00	165.00
		Nos. C22-C28 (7)	523.25	523.25

Excellent counterfeits exist.

King Zog and Airplane over Tirana AP2

AP3

1930, Oct. 8 **Photo.** **Unwmk.**

C29	AP2	5q yellow green	.35	.30
C30	AP2	15q rose red	.45	.40
C31	AP2	20q slate blue	.60	.55
C32	AP2	50q olive green	.80	.75
C33	AP3	1fr dark blue	1.75	1.65
C34	AP3	2fr olive brown	5.50	5.25
C35	AP3	3fr purple	7.50	7.00
		Nos. C29-C35 (7)	16.95	15.90

For overprints and surcharges see Nos. C36-C45.

Nos. C29-C35 Overprinted

TIRANE-ROME
6 KORRIK 1931

1931, July 6

C36	AP2	5q yellow grn	2.00	2.00
a.		Double overprint	65.00	
C37	AP2	15q rose red	2.00	2.00
C38	AP2	20q slate blue	2.00	2.00
C39	AP2	50q olive grn	2.00	2.00
C40	AP3	1fr dark blue	15.00	15.00
C41	AP3	2fr olive brn	15.00	15.00
C42	AP3	3fr purple	15.00	15.00
a.		Inverted overprint	175.00	
		Nos. C36-C42 (7)	53.00	53.00

1st air post flight from Tirana to Rome.

Only a very small part of this issue was sold to the public. Most of the stamps were given to the Aviation Company to help provide funds for conducting the service.

Issued under Italian Dominion

Nos. C29-C30 Overprinted in Black

Mbledhja
Kushtetuëse
12-IV-1939
XVII

1939, Apr. 19 **Unwmk.** ***Perf. 14***

C43	AP2	5q yel green	1.25	1.10
C44	AP2	15q rose red	1.25	1.10

No. C32 With Additional Surcharge

C45	AP2	20q on 50q ol grn	2.00	2.00
a.		Inverted overprint		
		Nos. C43-C45 (3)	4.50	4.20

See note after No. 309.

King Victor Emmanuel III and Plane over Mountains AP4

1939, Aug. 4 **Photo.**

C46	AP4	20q brown	13.00	4.00

Shepherds AP5

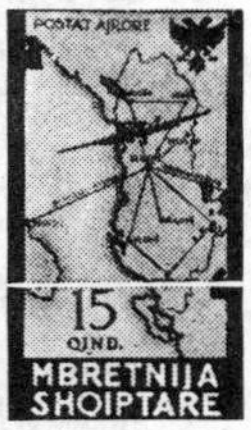

Map of Albania Showing Air Routes — AP6

Designs: 20q, Victor Emmanuel III and harbor view. 50q, Woman and river valley. 1fr, Bridge at Vezirit. 2fr, Ruins. 3fr, Women waving to plane.

1940, Mar. 20 **Unwmk.**

C47	AP5	5q green	.25	.25
C48	AP6	15q rose red	.25	.25
C49	AP5	20q deep blue	.25	.25
C50	AP6	50q brown	.65	.65
C51	AP5	1fr myrtle green	1.25	1.25
C52	AP6	2fr brown black	4.25	4.25
C53	AP6	3fr rose violet	10.00	10.00
		Nos. C47-C53 (7)	16.90	16.90

People's Republic

Vuno-Himare AP12

Albanian Towns: 1 l, 10 l, Rozafat-Shkoder. 2 l, 20 l, Keshtjelle-Butrinto.

1950, Dec. 15 **Engr.** ***Perf. 12½x12***

C54	AP12	50q gray black	.25	.25
C55	AP12	1 l red brown	.25	.25
C56	AP12	2 l ultra	.45	.45
C57	AP12	5 l deep green	.95	.95
C58	AP12	10 l deep blue	2.25	2.25
C59	AP12	20 l purple	5.75	5.75
		Nos. C54-C59 (6)	9.90	9.90

Nos. C56-C58 Surcharged with New Value and Bars in Red or Black

1952-53

C60	AP12	50q on 2 l (R)	40.00	40.00
C61	AP12	50q on 5 l	10.00	5.00
C62	AP12	2.50 l on 5 l (R)	60.00	60.00
C63	AP12	2.50 l on 10 l	10.00	5.00
		Nos. C60-C63 (4)	120.00	110.00

Issued: #C60, C62, 12/26/52; #C61, C63, 3/14/53.

Catalogue values for unused stamps in this section, from this point to the end of the section, are for Never Hinged items.

Banner with Lenin, Map of Stalingrad and Tanks — AP13

1963, Feb. 2 **Litho.** ***Perf. 14***

C67	AP13	7 l grn & dp car	3.00	.60

20th anniversary, Battle of Stalingrad.

Sputnik and Sun AP14

Designs: 3 l, Lunik 4. 5 l, Lunik 3 photographing far side of the Moon. 8 l, Venus space probe. 12 l, Mars 1.

1963, Oct. 31 **Unwmk.** ***Perf. 12***

C68	AP14	2 l org, yel & blk	.25	.30
C69	AP14	3 l multi	.50	.30
C70	AP14	5 l rose lil, yel & blk	.90	.45
C71	AP14	8 l multi	1.25	.85
C72	AP14	12 l blue & org	2.25	2.50
		Nos. C68-72 (5)	5.15	4.40

Russian interplanetary explorations.

Nos. C68 and C71 Overprinted: "Riccione 23-8-1964"

1964, Aug. 23

C73	AP14	2 l org, yel & blk	8.00	3.50
C74	AP14	8 l multicolored	12.00	5.25

Intl. Space Exhib. in Riccione, Italy.

Plane over Berat AP15

1975, Nov. 25 **Litho.** ***Perf. 12***

C75	AP15	20q multi	.20	.20
C76	AP15	40q Gjirokaster	.20	.20
C77	AP15	60q Sarande	.20	.20
C78	AP15	90q Durres	.50	.20
C79	AP15	1.20 l Kruje	.75	.20
C80	AP15	2.40 l Boga	1.60	.35
C81	AP15	4.05 l Tirana	2.50	.70
		Nos. C75-C81 (7)	5.95	2.05

SPECIAL DELIVERY STAMPS

Issued under Italian Dominion

King Victor Emmanuel III — SD1

1940 **Unwmk.** **Photo.** ***Perf. 14***

E1	SD1	25q bright violet	.40	.40
E2	SD1	50q red orange	1.25	1.50

Issued under German Administration

No. E1 Overprinted in Carmine

14
Shtator
1943

1943

E3	SD1	25q bright violet	15.00	17.50

Proclamation of Albanian independence.

POSTAGE DUE STAMPS

Nos. 35-39 Handstamped in Various Colors

T
TAKSË

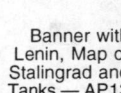

1914, Feb. 23 Unwmk. *Perf. 14*

J1	A3	2q org brn & buff (Bl)	6.00	1.60
J2	A3	5q green (R)	6.00	2.50
J3	A3	10q rose red (Bl)	8.00	1.60
J4	A3	25q dark blue (R)	10.00	1.60
J5	A3	50q vio & red (Bk)	14.00	5.00
		Nos. J1-J5 (5)	44.00	12.30

The two parts of the overprint are handstamped separately. Stamps exist with one or both handstamps inverted, double, omitted or in wrong color.

Nos. 48-51 Overprinted in Black TAKSË

1914, Apr. 16

J6	A3 (a)	10pa on 5q green	2.75	2.25
J7	A3 (a)	20pa on 10q rose red	2.75	2.25
J8	A3 (b)	1gr on 25q blue	2.75	2.25
J9	A3 (b)	2gr on 50q vio & red	2.75	2.25
		Nos. J6-J9 (4)	11.00	9.00

Same Design as Regular Issue of 1919, Overprinted

1919, Feb. 10 *Perf. 11½, 12½*

J10	A8	(4)q on 4h rose	5.00	4.50
J11	A8	(10)q on 10k red, *grn*	5.00	4.50
J12	A8	20q on 2k org, *gray*	5.00	4.50
J13	A8	50q on 5k brn, *yel*	5.00	4.50
		Nos. J10-J13 (4)	20.00	18.00

Fortress at Scutari — D3

D5

Post Horn Overprinted in Black

1920, Apr. 1 *Perf. 14x13*

J14	D3	4q olive green	.40	.40
J15	D3	10q rose red	.85	.85
J16	D3	20q bister brn	.85	.85
J17	D3	50q black	2.00	2.00
		Nos. J14-J17 (4)	4.10	4.10

1922 *Perf. 12½, 11½*

Background of Red Wavy Lines

J23	D5	4q black, *red*	1.00	1.00
J24	D5	10q black, *red*	1.00	1.00
J25	D5	20q black, *red*	1.00	1.00
J26	D5	50q black, *red*	1.00	1.00
		Nos. J23-J26 (4)	4.00	4.00

Same Overprinted in White — Repubblika Shqiptare

1925

J27	D5	4q black, *red*	1.00	1.00
J28	D5	10q black, *red*	1.00	1.00
J29	D5	20q black, *red*	1.00	1.00
J30	D5	50q black, *red*	1.00	1.00
		Nos. J27-J30 (4)	4.00	4.00

The 10q with overprint in gold was a trial printing. It was not put in use.

D7

Coat of Arms — D8

Overprinted "QINDAR" in Red

1926, Dec. 24 *Perf. 13½x13*

J31	D7	10q dark blue	.25	.20
J32	D7	20q green	.50	.40
J33	D7	30q red brown	.80	.60
J34	D7	50q dark brown	1.25	1.00
		Nos. J31-J34 (4)	2.80	2.20

Wmk. Double Headed Eagle (220)

1930, Sept. 1 Photo. *Perf. 14, 14½*

J35	D8	10q dark blue	4.75	4.75
J36	D8	20q rose red	1.25	1.25
J37	D8	30q violet	1.25	1.25
J38	D8	50q dark green	1.50	1.50
		Nos. J35-J38 (4)	8.75	8.75

Nos. J36-J38 exist with overprint "14 Shtator 1943" (see Nos. 332-344) which is private and fraudulent on these stamps.

No. 253 Overprinted **Taksë**

1936 *Perf. 14*

J39	A34	10q carmine	3.50	4.75

Issued under Italian Dominion

Coat of Arms — D9

1940 Unwmk. Photo. *Perf. 14*

J40	D9	4q red orange	*22.50*	*18.00*
J41	D9	10q bright violet	*22.50*	*18.00*
J42	D9	20q brown	*22.50*	*18.00*
J43	D9	30q dark blue	*22.50*	*18.00*
J44	D9	50q carmine rose	*22.50*	*18.00*
		Nos. J40-J44 (5)	*112.50*	*90.00*

ALEXANDRETTA

ˌa-lig-(ˌ)zan-ˈdre-tə

LOCATION — A political territory in northern Syria, bordering on Turkey
GOVT. — French mandate
AREA — 10,000 sq. mi. (approx.)
POP. — 270,000 (approx.)

Included in the Syrian territory mandated to France under the Versailles Treaty, the name was changed to Hatay in 1938. The following year France returned the territory to Turkey in exchange for certain concessions. See Hatay.

100 Centimes = 1 Piaster

Stamps of Syria, 1930-36, Overprinted or Surcharged in Black or Red:

Sandjak d'Alexandrette — a

SANDJAK D'ALEXANDRETTE — b

Sandjak d'Alexandrette — c

Sandjak d'Alexandrette 2P50 — d

POSTES *Sandjak d'Alexandrette* 12P50 — e

1938 Unwmk. *Perf. 12x12½*

1	A6 (a)	10c vio brn	.40	.40
2	A6 (a)	20c brn org	.50	.50
		Perf. 13½		
3	A9 (b)	50c vio (R)	.60	.60
4	A10 (b)	1p bis brn	.70	.70
5	A9 (b)	2p dk vio (R)	.90	.90
6	A13 (b)	3p yel grn (R)	1.75	1.75
7	A10 (b)	4p yel org	1.75	1.75
8	A16 (b)	6p grnsh blk (R)	2.00	2.00
9	A18 (b)	25p vio brn	6.50	6.50
10	A15 (c)	75c org red	.70	.70
11	A10 (d)	2.50p on 4p yel org	1.20	1.20
12	AP2 (e)	12.50p on 15p org red	3.00	3.00
		Nos. 1-12 (12)	20.00	20.00

Issue dates: #1-9, Apr. 14, #10-12, Sept. 2.

Nos. 4, 7, 10-12 Overprinted in Black

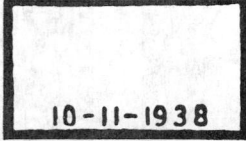

10-11-1938

1938, Nov. 10

13	A15	75c	30.00	30.00
14	A10	1p	20.00	18.00
15	A10	2.50p on 4p	12.50	11.00
16	A10	4p	15.00	13.50
17	AP2	12.50p on 15p	30.00	30.00
		Nos. 13-17 (5)	107.50	102.50

Death of Kemal Ataturk, pres. of Turkey.

AIR POST STAMPS

Air Post Stamps of Syria, 1937, Overprinted Type "b" in Red or Black

1938, Apr. 14 Unwmk. *Perf. 13*

C1	AP14	½p dark vio (R)	.75	.75
C2	AP15	1p black (R)	.35	.35
C3	AP14	2p blue grn (R)	1.50	1.50
C4	AP15	3p deep ultra	1.75	1.75
C5	AP14	5p rose lake	4.50	4.50
C6	AP15	10p red brown	5.00	5.00
C7	AP14	15p lake brown	5.75	5.75
C8	AP15	25p dk blue (R)	7.50	7.50
		Nos. C1-C8 (8)	27.10	27.10

POSTAGE DUE STAMPS

Postage Due Stamps of Syria, 1925-31, Ovptd. Type "b" in Black or Red

1938, Apr. 14 Unwmk. *Perf. 13½*

J1	D5	50c brown, *yel*	1.25	1.25
J2	D6	1p violet, *rose*	1.50	1.50
J3	D5	2p blk, *blue* (R)	2.00	2.00
J4	D5	3p blk, *red org*	3.75	3.75
J5	D5	5p blk, *bl grn* (R)	6.00	6.00
J6	D7	8p blk, *gray bl* (R)	7.00	7.00
		Nos. J1-J6 (6)	21.50	21.50

On No. J2, the overprint is vertical, reading up, other denominations, horizontal.

Stamps of Alexandretta were discontinued in 1938 and replaced by those of Hatay.

ALGERIA

al-ˈjir-ē-ə

LOCATION — North Africa
GOVT. — Republic
AREA — 919,595 sq. mi.
POP. — 29,300,000 (1998 est.)
CAPITAL — Algiers

The former French colony of Algeria became an integral part of France on Sept. 1, 1958, when French stamps replaced Algerian stamps. Algeria became an independent country July 3, 1962.

100 Centimes = 1 Franc
100 Centimes = 1 Dinar (1964)

Catalogue values for unused stamps in this country are for Never Hinged items, beginning with Scott 109 in the regular postage section, Scott B27 in the semi-postal section, Scott C1 in the airpost section, Scott CB1 in the airpost semi-postal section, and Scott J25 in the postage due section.

Stamps of France Overprinted in Red, Blue or Black:

ALGÉRIE — a

ALGÉRIE — b

ALGÉRIE — c

ALGÉRIE — d

1924-26 Unwmk. *Perf. 14x13½*

1	A16(a)	1c dk gray (R)	.20	.20
2	A16(a)	2c violet brn	.20	.20
3	A16(a)	3c orange	.20	.20
4	A16(a)	4c yel brn (Bl)	.20	.20
5	A22(a)	5c orange (Bl)	.20	.20
6	A16(a)	5c green ('25)	.40	.30
7	A23(a)	10c green	.30	.20
b.		Booklet pane of 10	6.00	
8	A22(a)	10c green ('25)	.50	.20
9	A20(a)	15c slate grn	.20	.20
10	A23(a)	15c green ('25)	.60	.20
11	A22(a)	15c red brn (Bl) ('26)	.20	.20
12	A22(a)	20c red brn (Bl)	.25	.20
13	A22(a)	25c blue (R)	.20	.20
a.		Booklet pane of 10	50.00	
14	A23(a)	30c red (Bl)	.90	.20
15	A22(a)	30c cerise ('25)	.70	.50
a.		"ALGERIE" double	135.00	
16	A22(a)	30c lt bl (R) ('25)	.30	.20
a.		Booklet pane of 10	42.50	
17	A22(a)	35c violet	.30	.20
18	A18(b)	40c red & pale bl	.30	.20
19	A22(a)	40c ol brn (R) ('25)	.75	.50
20	A18(b)	45c grn & bl (R)	.40	.30
a.		Double overprint	210.00	
21	A23(a)	45c red (Bl) ('25)	.60	.20
22	A23(a)	50c blue (R)	.20	.20
23	A20(a)	60c lt violet	.20	.20
a.		Inverted overprint		*2150.*
24	A20(a)	65c rose (Bl)	.35	.20
25	A23(a)	75c blue (R)	.60	.30
a.		Double overprint	190.00	
26	A20(a)	80c ver ('26)	.90	.40
27	A20(a)	85c ver (Bl)	.60	.20
28	A18(b)	1fr cl & ol grn	1.00	.30
29	A22(a)	1.05fr ver ('26)	1.00	.40
30	A18(c)	2fr org & pale bl	1.00	.55
31	A18(b)	3fr vio & bl ('26)	3.00	.80
32	A18(d)	5fr bl & buff (R)	8.00	4.75
		Nos. 1-32 (32)	24.75	13.30

No. 15 was issued precanceled only. Values for precanceled stamps in first column are for those which have not been through the post and have original gum. Values in second column are for postally used, gumless stamps.

For surcharges see Nos. 75, P1.

Street in Kasbah, Algiers — A1

Mosque of Sidi Abd-er-Rahman — A2

La Pêcherie Mosque — A3

Marabout of Sidi Yacoub — A4

1926-39 Typo. *Perf. 14x13½*

33	A1	1c olive	.20	.20
34	A1	2c red brown	.20	.20
35	A1	3c orange	.20	.20
36	A1	5c blue green	.20	.20
37	A1	10c brt violet	.20	.20
a.		Booklet pane of 10	3.25	
38	A2	15c orange brn	.20	.20
39	A2	20c green	.20	.20
40	A2	20c deep rose	.20	.20
41	A2	25c blue grn	.20	.20
42	A2	25c blue ('27)	.40	.20
43	A2	25c vio bl ('39)	.20	.20
44	A2	30c blue	.25	.20
45	A2	30c bl grn ('27)	.80	.30
46	A2	35c dp violet	1.00	.65
47	A2	40c olive green	.20	.20
a.		Booklet pane of 10	2.25	
48	A3	45c violet brn	.25	.20
49	A3	50c blue	.25	.20
a.		Booklet pane of 10	3.50	
50	A3	50c dk red ('30)	.20	.20
a.		Booklet pane of 10	4.75	
51	A3	60c yellow grn	.20	.20
52	A3	65c blk brn ('27)	1.25	.85
53	A1	65c ultra ('38)	.25	.20
a.		Booklet pane of 10	1.75	
54	A3	75c carmine	.30	.25
55	A3	75c blue ('29)	2.25	.20
56	A3	80c orange red	.45	.25
57	A3	90c red ('27)	5.00	2.75
58	A4	1fr gray grn & red brn	.65	.20
59	A3	1.05fr lt brown	.55	.30
60	A3	1.10fr mag ('27)	5.00	1.75
61	A4	1.25fr dk bl & ultra	1.00	.80
62	A4	1.50fr dk bl & ultra ('27)	2.25	.20

63	A4	2fr Prus bl & blk brn	1.90	.20
64	A4	3fr violet & org	3.25	.65
65	A4	5fr red & violet	6.00	2.00
66	A4	10fr ol brn & rose ('27)	40.00	20.00
67	A4	20fr vio & grn ('27)	5.00	4.00
		Nos. 33-67 (35)	80.65	38.95

Type A4, 50c blue and rose red, inscribed "CENTENAIRE-ALGERIE" is France No. 255.

See design A24. For stamps and types surcharged see Nos. 68-74, 131, 136, 187, B1-B13, J27, P2.

Stamps of 1926 Surcharged with New Values

1927

68	A2	10c on 35c dp violet	.20	.20
69	A2	25c on 30c blue	.20	.20
70	A2	30c on 25c blue grn	.20	.20
71	A3	65c on 60c yel grn	.75	.35
72	A3	90c on 80c org red	.50	.20
73	A3	1.10fr on 1.05fr lt brn	.30	.20
74	A4	1.50fr on 1.25fr dk bl & ultra	1.25	.45
		Nos. 68-74 (7)	3.40	1.80

Bars cancel the old value on #68, 69, 73, 74.

No. 4 Surcharged

5c

1927

75	A16	5c on 4c yellow brown	.75	.25

Bay of Algiers A5

1930, May 4 Engr. *Perf. 11, 12½*

78	A5	10fr red brown	9.50	7.50
a.		Imperf., pair	25.00	

Cent. of Algeria and for Intl. Phil. Exhib. of North Africa, May, 1930.

One copy of No. 78 was sold with each 10fr admission.

Travel across the Sahara — A6

Arch of Triumph, Lambese A7

Admiralty Building, Algiers — A8

Kings' Tombs near Touggourt A9

El-Kebir Mosque, Algiers A10

The values of stamps in less than very fine condition generally are less than catalogue value.

Oued River at Colomb-Bechar A11

Sidi Bon Medine Cemetery at Tlemcen A13

View of Ghardaia A12

1936-41 Engr. *Perf. 13*

79	A6	1c ultra	.20	.20
80	A11	2c dk violet	.20	.20
81	A7	3c dk blue grn	.20	.20
82	A12	5c red violet	.20	.20
83	A8	10c emerald	.20	.20
84	A9	15c red	.20	.20
85	A13	20c dk blue grn	.20	.20
86	A10	25c rose vio	.32	.20
87	A12	30c yellow grn	.28	.20
88	A9	40c brown vio	.20	.20
89	A13	45c deep ultra	.65	.40
90	A8	50c red	.40	.20
91	A6	65c red brn	2.50	1.75
92	A6	65c rose car ('37)	.35	.20
93	A6	70c red brn ('39)	.20	.20
94	A11	75c slate bl	.20	.20
95	A7	90c henna brn	.65	.45
96	A10	1fr brown	.20	.20
97	A8	1.25fr lt violet	.35	.20
98	A8	1.25fr car rose ('39)	.30	.20
99	A11	1.50fr turq blue	.90	.20
99A	A11	1.50fr rose ('40)	.35	.20
100	A12	1.75fr henna brn	.20	.20
101	A7	2fr dk brown	.20	.20
102	A6	2.25fr yellow grn	8.00	6.50
103	A12	2.50fr dk ultra ('41)	.30	.25
104	A13	3fr magenta	.25	.20
105	A10	3.50fr pck blue	1.90	1.40
106	A8	5fr slate blue	.30	.20
107	A11	10fr henna brn	.30	.20
108	A9	20fr turq blue	.60	.35
		Nos. 79-108 (31)	21.30	15.90

See Nos. 124-125, 162.

Nos. 82 and 100 with surcharge "E. F. M. 30frs" (Emergency Field Message) were used in 1943 to pay cable tolls for US and Canadian servicemen.

For other surcharges see Nos. 122, B27.

Catalogue values for unused stamps in this section, from this point to the end of the section, are for Never Hinged items.

Algerian Pavilion — A14

1937 *Perf. 13*

109	A14	40c brt green	.40	.35
110	A14	50c rose carmine	.25	.20
111	A14	1.50fr blue	.60	.25
112	A14	1.75fr brown black	.65	.50
		Nos. 109-112 (4)	1.90	1.30

Paris International Exposition.

Constantine in 1837 — A15

1937

113	A15	65c deep rose	.30	.20
114	A15	1fr brown	3.25	.50
115	A15	1.75fr blue green	.25	.20
116	A15	2.15fr red violet	.20	.20
		Nos. 113-116 (4)	4.00	1.10

Taking of Constantine by the French, cent.

Ruins of a Roman Villa — A16

1938

117	A16	30c green	.50	.30
118	A16	65c ultra	.20	.20
119	A16	75c rose violet	.55	.40
120	A16	3fr carmine rose	1.40	1.40
121	A16	5fr yellow brown	2.25	2.25
		Nos. 117-121 (5)	4.90	4.55

Centenary of Philippeville.

No. 90 Surcharged in Black

0,25

1938

122	A8	25c on 50c red	.20	.20
a.		Double surcharge	35.00	30.00
b.		Inverted surcharge	20.00	18.00

Types of 1936

1939

Numerals of Value on Colorless Background

124	A7	90c henna brown	.20	.20
125	A10	2.25fr blue green	.20	.20

For surcharge see No. B38.

American Export Liner Unloading Cargo — A17

1939

126	A17	20c green	.65	.65
127	A17	40c red violet	.65	.50
128	A17	90c brown black	.35	.20
129	A17	1.25fr rose	2.25	.80
130	A17	2.25fr ultra	.65	.60
		Nos. 126-130 (5)	4.55	2.75

New York World's Fair.

Type of 1926, Surcharged in Black

1F

Two types of surcharge:
I - Bars 6mm
II - Bars 7mm

1939-40 *Perf. 14x13½*

131	A1	1fr on 90c crimson (I)	.20	.20
a.		Booklet pane of 10		
b.		Double surcharge (I)	35.00	
c.		Inverted surcharge (I)	22.50	
d.		Pair, one without surch. (I)	*800.00*	
e.		Type II ('40)	1.50	.20
f.		Inverted surcharge (II)	27.50	
g.		Pair, one without surch. (II)	*800.00*	

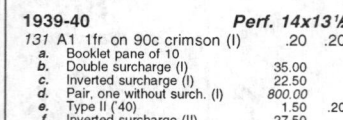

View of Algiers — A18

1941 Typo.

132	A18	30c ultra	.20	.20
133	A18	70c sepia	.20	.20
134	A18	1fr carmine rose	.20	.20
		Nos. 132-134 (3)	.60	.60

See No. 163.

Marshal Pétain
A19 A20

1941 Engr. *Perf. 13*

135	A19	1fr dark blue	.30	.20

For stamp and type surcharged see #B36-B37.

No. 53 Surcharged in Black with New Value and Bars

1941 *Perf. 14x13½*

136	A1	50c on 65c ultra	.30	.20
a.		Booklet pane of 10		
b.		Inverted surcharge	21.00	
c.		Pair, one without surch.	52.50	

1942 *Perf. 14x13*

137	A20	1.50fr orange red	.20	.20

Four other denominations of type A20 exist (4, 5, 10, 20fr), but were not placed in use.

Constantine A21

Oran A22

Arms of Algiers — A23

Engraver's Name at Lower Left

1942-43 Photo. *Perf. 12*

138	A21	40c dark vio ('43)	.20	.20
139	A22	60c rose ('43)	.20	.20
140	A21	1.20fr yel grn ('43)	.20	.20
141	A23	1.50fr car rose	.20	.20
142	A22	2fr sapphire	.20	.20
143	A21	2.40fr rose ('43)	.20	.20
144	A23	3fr sapphire	.20	.20
145	A21	4fr blue ('43)	.20	.20
146	A22	5fr yel grn ('43)	.20	.20
		Nos. 138-146 (9)	1.80	1.80

For type surcharged see No. 166.

Imperforates

Nearly all of Algeria Nos. 138-285, B39-B96, C1-C12 and CB1-CB3 exist imperforate. See note after France No. 395.

Without Engraver's Name

1942-45 Typo. *Perf. 14x13½*

147	A23	10c dull brn vio ('45)	.20	.20
148	A22	30c dp bl grn ('45)	.20	.20
149	A21	40c dull brn vio ('45)	.20	.20
150	A22	60c rose ('45)	.20	.20
151	A21	70c deep bl ('45)	.20	.20
152	A23	80c dk bl grn ('43)	.25	.25
153	A21	1.20fr dp bl grn ('45)	.20	.20
154	A23	1.50fr brt rose ('43)	.20	.20
155	A22	2fr dp blue ('45)	.20	.20
156	A21	2.40fr rose ('45)	.30	.25
157	A23	3fr dp blue ('45)	.20	.20
158	A22	4.50fr brown vio	.20	.20
		Nos. 147-158 (12)	2.55	2.50

For surcharge see No. 190.

La Pêcherie Mosque — A24

1942 Typo.

159	A24	50c dull red	.20	.20
a.		Booklet pane of 10	2.75	

1942 Photo. *Perf. 12*

160	A24	40c gray green	.20	.20
161	A24	50c red	.20	.20

Types of 1936-41, Without "RF"

1942 Engr. *Perf. 13*

162 A11 1.50fr rose .30 .20

Typo. *Perf. 14x13½*

163 A18 30c ultra .20 .20

"One Aim Alone - Victory"
A25 A26

1943 Litho. *Perf. 12*

164 A25 1.50fr deep rose .20 .20
165 A26 1.50fr dark blue .20 .20

Type of 1942-3 Surcharged with New Value in Black

1943 Photo.

166 A22 2fr on 5fr red orange .20 .20
a. Surcharge omitted 140.00

Summer Palace, Algiers
A27

1944, Dec. 1 Litho.

167 A27 15fr slate .80 .80
168 A27 20fr lt blue grn .60 .40
169 A27 50fr dk carmine .60 .50
170 A27 100fr deep blue 1.50 1.25
171 A27 200fr dull bis brn 2.50 1.40
Nos. 167-171 (5) 6.00 4.35

Marianne A28 Gallic Cock A29

1944-45

172 A28 10c gray .20 .20
173 A28 30c red violet .20 .20
174 A29 40c rose car ('45) .20 .20
175 A28 50c red .20 .20
176 A28 80c emerald .20 .20
177 A29 1fr green ('45) .20 .20
178 A28 1.20fr rose lilac .20 .20
179 A28 1.50fr dark blue .20 .20
a. Double impression 20.00
180 A29 2fr red .20 .20
a. Double impression 22.50
181 A29 2fr dk brown ('45) .20 .20
182 A28 2.40fr rose red .20 .20
183 A28 3fr purple .20 .20
184 A29 4fr ultra ('45) .20 .20
185 A28 4.50fr olive blk .30 .25
186 A29 10fr grnsh blk ('45) .50 .35
Nos. 172-186 (15) 3.40 3.20

No. 38 Surcharged in Black **0f.30**

1944 *Perf. 14x13½*

187 A2 30c on 15c orange brn .20 .20
a. Inverted surcharge 10.00 4.00

This stamp exists precanceled only. See note below No. 32.

No. 154 Surcharged "RF" and New Value

1945

190 A23 50c on 1.50fr brt rose .20 .20
a. Inverted surcharge 15.00

Stamps of France, 1944, Overprinted Type "a" of 1924 in Black

1945-46

191 A99 80c yellow grn .20 .20
192 A99 1fr grnsh blue .20 .20
193 A99 1.20fr violet .20 .20
194 A99 2fr violet brown .25 .20
195 A99 2.40fr carmine rose .25 .20
196 A99 3fr orange .25 .20
Nos. 191-196 (6) 1.35 1.20

Same Overprint on Stamps of France, 1945-47, in Black, Red or Carmine

1945-47

197 A145 40c lilac rose .20 .20
198 A145 50c violet bl (R) .20 .20
199 A146 60c brt ultra (R) .25 .20
200 A146 1fr rose red ('47) .20 .20
201 A146 1.50fr rose lilac ('47) .20 .20
202 A147 2fr myr grn (R) ('46) .20 .20
203 A147 3fr deep rose .20 .20
204 A147 4.50fr ultra (C) ('47) .55 .20
205 A147 5fr lt green ('46) .20 .20
206 A147 10fr ultra .50 .25
Nos. 197-206 (10) 2.70 2.05

Same Overprint on France No. 383 and New Value Surcharged in Black

1946

207 A99 2fr on 1.50fr henna brn .20 .20
a. Without "2F" 110.00

Same Overprint on France Nos. 562 and 564, in Carmine or Blue

1947

208 A153 10c dp ultra & blk (C) .25 .25
209 A155 50c brown, yel & red (Bl) .30 .30

Constantine A30 Algiers A31

Arms of Oran — A32

Perf. 14x13½

1947-49 Unwmk. Typo.

210 A30 10c dk grn & brt red .20 .20
211 A31 50c black & orange .20 .20
212 A32 1fr ultra & yellow .20 .20
213 A30 1.30fr blk & grnsh bl .55 .35
214 A31 1.50fr pur & org yel .20 .20
215 A32 2fr blk & brt grn .20 .20
216 A30 2.50fr blk & brt red .35 .30
217 A31 3fr vio brn & grn .20 .20
218 A32 3.50fr lt grn & rose lil .20 .20
219 A30 4fr dk brn & brt grn .20 .20
220 A31 4.50fr ultra & scar .20 .20
221 A31 5fr blk & grnsh bl .20 .20
222 A32 6fr brown & scarlet .25 .20
223 A32 8fr choc & ultra ('48) .20 .20
224 A30 10fr car & choc ('48) .35 .20
225 A31 15fr black & red ('49) .35 .20
Nos. 210-225 (16) 4.05 3.45

See Nos. 274-280, 285.

Peoples of the World — A33

1949, Oct. 24 Engr. *Perf. 13*

226 A33 5fr green 1.00 .80
227 A33 15fr scarlet 1.00 .80
228 A33 25fr ultra 2.50 2.50
Nos. 226-228 (3) 4.50 4.10

75th anniv. of the UPU.

Grapes A34 Apollo of Cherchell A35

Designs: 25fr, Dates. 40fr, Oranges and lemons.

1950, Feb. 25

229 A34 20fr multicolored 1.25 .35
230 A34 25fr multicolored 1.40 .40
231 A34 40fr multicolored 2.75 .80
Nos. 229-231 (3) 5.40 1.55

1952 Unwmk. *Perf. 13*

Designs: 12fr, 18fr, Isis statue, Cherchell. 15fr, 20fr, Child with eagle.

240 A35 10fr gray black .25 .20
241 A35 12fr orange brn .35 .20
242 A35 15fr deep blue .25 .20
243 A35 18fr rose red .35 .25
244 A35 20fr deep green .35 .20
245 A35 30fr deep blue .65 .35
Nos. 240-245 (6) 2.20 1.40

War Memorial, Algiers A38 Fossilized Nautilus A39

Phonolite Dike — A40

1952, Apr. 11

246 A38 12fr dark green .50 .35

Issued to honor the French Africa Army.

1952, Aug. 11

247 A39 15fr brt crimson .85 .60
248 A40 30fr deep ultra .90 .65

19th Intl. Geological Cong., Algiers, Sept. 8-15.

French and Algerian Soldiers and Camel — A41

1952, Nov. 30

249 A41 12fr chestnut brown .75 .50

50th anniv. of the establishment of the Sahara Companies.

Eugène Millon — A42

François C. Maillot A43 Oranges A44

Portrait: 50fr, Alphonse Laveran.

Unwmk.

1954, Jan. 4 Engr. *Perf. 13*

250 A42 25fr dk grn & choc 1.10 .20
251 A43 40fr org brn & brn car 1.75 .60
252 A42 50fr ultra & indigo 1.75 .20
Nos. 250-252 (3) 4.60 1.00

Military Health Service.

1954, May 8

253 A44 15fr indigo & blue .70 .40

3rd Intl. Cong. on Agronomy, Algiers, 1954.

Type of France, 1954 Overprinted type "a" in Black

Unwmk.

1954, June 6 Engr. *Perf. 13*

254 A240 15fr rose carmine .55 .45

Liberation of France, 10th anniversary.

Darguinah Hydroelectric Works A45 Patio of Bardo Museum A46

1954, June 19

255 A45 15fr lilac rose .65 .45

Opening of Darguinah hydroelectric works.

1954 Typo. *Perf. 14x13½*

257 A46 12fr red brn & brn org .60 .25
258 A46 15fr dk blue & blue .60 .25

See Nos. 267-271.

Type of France, 1954, Overprinted type "a" in Carmine

1954 Engr. *Perf. 13*

260 A247 12fr dark green .50 .45

150th anniv. of the 1st Legion of Honor awards at Camp de Boulogne.

St. Augustine — A47

1954, Nov. 11

261 A47 15fr chocolate .75 .65

1600th anniv. of the birth of St. Augustine.

Aesculapius Statue and El Kattar Hospital, Algiers A48

1955, Apr. 3 Unwmk. *Perf. 13*

262 A48 15fr red .50 .35

Issued to publicize the 30th French Congress of Medicine, Algiers, April 3-6, 1955.

Chenua Mountain and View of Tipasa A49

1955, May 31

263 A49 50fr brown carmine .50 .20

2000th anniv. of the founding of Tipasa.

Type of France, 1955 Overprinted type "a" in Red

1955, June 13

264 A251 30fr deep ultra .60 .45

Rotary Intl., 50th anniv.

Marianne
A50

Great Kabylia
Mountains
A51

Perf. 14x13½

1955, Oct. 3 Typo. Unwmk.

265 A50 15fr carmine .50 .25

See No. 284.

1955, Dec. 17 Engr. *Perf. 13*

266 A51 100fr indigo & ultra 2.00 .20

Bardo Type of 1954,
"Postes" and "Algerie" in White

Perf. 14x13½

1955-57 Unwmk. Typo.

267 A46 10fr dk brown & lt brown .25 .20
268 A46 12fr red brn & brn org ('56) .20 .20
269 A46 18fr crimson & ver ('57) .45 .20
270 A46 20fr grn & yel grn ('57) .35 .25
271 A46 25fr purple & brt purple .50 .20
Nos. 267-271 (5) 1.75 1.05

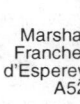

Marshal
Franchet
d'Esperey
A52

1956, May 25 Engr. *Perf. 13*

272 A52 15fr sapphire & indigo .70 .60

Birth cent. of Marshal Franchet d'Esperey.

Marshal
Jacques
Leclerc
A53

1956, Nov. 29

273 A53 15fr red brown & sepia .50 .50

Death of Marshal Leclerc.
For type surcharged see No. B90.

Type of 1947-49 and

Arms of Bône — A54

Arms: 2fr, Tizi-Quzou. 3fr, Mostaganem. 5fr, Tlemcen. 10fr, Setif. 12fr, Orleansville.

1956-58 Typo. *Perf. 14x13½*

274 A54 1fr green & ver .25 .20
275 A54 2fr ver & ultra ('58) .45 .25
276 A54 3fr ultra & emer ('58) .45 .25
277 A54 5fr ultra & yellow .25 .20
278 A31 6fr red & grn ('57) .45 .30
279 A54 10fr dp cl & emer ('58) .50 .30
280 A54 12fr ultra & red ('58) .50 .30
Nos. 274-280 (7) 2.85 1.80

Nos. 275 and 279 are inscribed "Republique Francaise." See No. 285.

View of
Oran — A55

1956-58 Engr. *Perf. 13*

281 A55 30fr dull purple .45 .20
282 A55 35fr car rose ('58) .75 .45

Electric Train
Crossing
Bridge
A56

1957, Mar. 25

283 A56 40fr dk blue grn & emer .60 .20

Marianne Type of 1955
Inscribed "Algerie" Vertically

Perf. 14x13½

1957, Dec. 2 Typo. Unwmk.

284 A50 20fr ultra .40 .20

Arms Type of 1947-49 Inscribed
"Republique Francaise"

1958, July

285 A31 6fr red & green 10.00 10.00

Independent State

France Nos. 939, 968, 945-946 and 1013 Overprinted "EA" and Bars, Handstamped or Typographed, in Black or Red

1962, July 2

286 A336 10c brt green .25 .20
a. Typographed overprint .30 .20
287 A349 25c lake & gray .20 .20
a. Handstamped overprint .25 .20
288 A339 45c brt vio & ol gray 3.50 3.00
a. Handstamped overprint *15.00* *10.00*
289 A339 50c sl grn & lt claret 5.00 3.00
a. Handstamped overprint *15.00* *12.00*
290 A372 1fr dk bl, sl & bis 2.75 1.00
a. Handstamped overprint *3.50* *1.50*
Nos. 286-290 (5) 11.70 7.40

Post offices were authorized to overprint their stock of these 5 French stamps. The size of the letters was specified as 3x6mm each, but various sizes were used. The post offices had permission to make their own rubber stamps. Typography, pen or pencil were also used. Many types exist. Colors of handstamped overprints include black, red, blue, violet. "EA" stands for Etat Algérien.

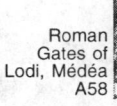

Mosque,
Tlemcen — A57

Roman
Gates of
Lodi, Médéa
A58

Designs: 5c, Kerrata Gorge. 10c, Dam at Foum el Gherza. 95c, Oil field, Hassi Messaoud.

1962, Nov. 1 Engr. *Perf. 13*

291 A57 5c Prus grn, grn & choc .20 .20
292 A58 10c ol blk & dk bl .20 .20
293 A57 25c sl grn, brn & ver .40 .20
294 A57 95c dk bl, blk & bis 1.50 .55
295 A58 1fr green & blk 1.50 1.10
Nos. 291-295 (5) 3.80 2.25

The designs of Nos. 291-295 are similar to French issues of 1959-61 with "Republique Algerienne" replacing "Republique Francaise."

Flag, Rifle, Olive
Branch — A59

Design: Nos. 300-303, Broken chain and rifle added to design A59.

1963, Jan. 6 Litho. *Perf. 12½*

Flag in Green and Red

296 A59 5c bister brown .25 .20
297 A59 10c blue .25 .20
298 A59 25c vermilion 1.50 .20
299 A59 95c violet 1.25 .45
300 A59 1fr green 1.00 .20
301 A59 2fr brown 2.50 .45
302 A59 5fr lilac 4.00 1.25
303 A59 10fr gray 14.00 7.00
Nos. 296-303 (8) 24.75 9.95

Nos. 296-299 for the successful revolution and Nos. 300-303 the return of peace.

Men of
Various
Races,
Wheat
Emblem and
Globe — A60

1963, Mar. 21 Engr. *Perf. 13*

304 A60 25c maroon, dl grn & yel .30 .25

FAO "Freedom from Hunger" campaign.

Map of Algeria
and Emblems
A61

Physicians from
13th Century
Manuscript
A62

1963, July 5 Unwmk. *Perf. 13*

305 A61 25c bl, dk brn, grn & red .40 .25

1st anniv. of Algeria's independence.

1963, July 29 Engr.

306 A62 25c brn red, grn & bis 1.00 .35

2nd Congress of the Union of Arab physicians.

Orange and
Blossom
A63

Scales and Scroll
A64

1963 *Perf. 14x13*

307 A63 8c gray grn & org .65 .65
308 A63 20c slate & org red .75 .75
309 A63 40c grnsh bl & org 1.00 1.00
310 A63 55c ol grn & org red 2.00 2.00
Nos. 307-310 (4) 4.40 4.40

Nos. 307-310 issued precanceled only. See note below No. 32.

1963, Oct. 13 Unwmk. *Perf. 13*

311 A64 25c blk, grn & rose red .40 .25

Issued to honor the new constitution.

Guerrillas
A65

Centenary
Emblem
A66

1963, Nov. 1

312 A65 25c dk brn, yel grn & car .55 .25

9th anniversary of Algerian revolution.

1963, Dec. 8 Photo. *Perf. 12*

313 A66 25c lt vio bl, yel & dk red .55 .30

Centenary of International Red Cross.

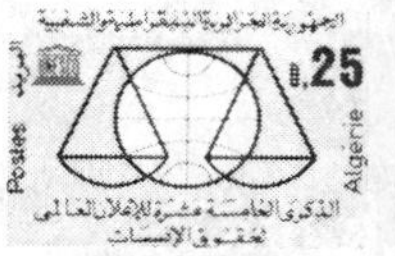

UNESCO Emblem,
Scales and Globe
A67

Workers
A68

1963, Dec. 16 Unwmk. *Perf. 12*

314 A67 25c lt blue & blk .55 .25

15th anniv. of the Universal Declaration of Human Rights.

1964, May 1 Engr. *Perf. 13*

315 A68 50c dull red, red org & bl .90 .50

Issued for the Labor Festival.

Map of Africa
and
Flags — A69

1964, May 25 Unwmk. *Perf. 13*

316 A69 45c blue, orange & car .55 .30

Africa Day on the 1st anniv. of the Addis Ababa charter on African unity.

Ramses II Battling the Hittites (from
Abu Simbel) — A70

Design: 30c, Two statues of Ramses II.

1964, June 28 Engr. *Perf. 13*

317 A70 20c choc, red & vio bl .55 .30
318 A70 30c brn, red & grnsh bl .65 .40

UNESCO world campaign to save historic monuments in Nubia.

A71

A72

5, 25, 85c, Tractors. 10, 30, 65c, Men working with lathe. 12, 15, 45c, Electronics center & atom symbol. 20, 50, 95c, Draftsman & bricklayer.

1964-65 Typo. *Perf. 14x13½*

319 A71 5c red lilac .20 .20
320 A71 10c brown .20 .20
321 A71 12c emerald ('65) .40 .20
322 A71 15c dk blue ('65) .25 .20
323 A71 20c yellow .40 .20
324 A71 25c red .50 .20
325 A71 30c purple ('65) .40 .20
326 A71 45c rose car .50 .20
327 A71 50c ultra .60 .20
328 A71 65c orange .80 .20
329 A71 85c green 1.40 .25
330 A71 95c car rose 1.75 .30
Nos. 319-330 (12) 7.40 2.55

For surcharges see Nos. 389, 424.

1964, Aug. 30 Engr. *Perf. 13*

331 A72 85c Communications tower 1.50 .75

Inauguration of the Hertzian cable telephone line Algiers-Annaba.

Industrial & Agricultural Symbols — A73

Gas Flames and Pipes — A74

1964, Sept. 26 Typo. *Perf. 13½x14*

332 A73 25c lt ultra, yel & red	.60	.45

1st Intl. Fair at Algiers, Sept. 26-Oct. 11.

1964, Sept. 27

333 A74 30c violet, blue & yel	.45	.35

Arzew natural gas liquification plant opening.

Planting Trees A75

Children and UNICEF Emblem A76

1964, Nov. 29 Unwmk.

334 A75 25c slate grn, yel & car	.30	.20

National reforestation campaign.

1964, Dec. 13 *Perf. 13½x14*

335 A76 15c pink, vio bl & lt grn	.25	.20

Issued for Children's Day.

Decorated Camel Saddle — A77

1965, May 29 Typo. *Perf. 13½x14*

336 A77 20c blk, red, emer & brn	.25	.20

Handicrafts of Sahara.

ICY Emblem A78

1965, Aug. 29 Engr. *Perf. 13*

337 A78 30c blk, mar & bl grn	.45	.30
338 A78 60c blk, brt bl & bl grn	.85	.40

International Cooperation Year, 1965.

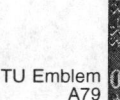

ITU Emblem A79

1965, Sept. 19

339 A79 60c purple, emer & buff	.45	.30
340 A79 95c dk brn, mar & buff	.65	.35

Cent. of the ITU.

Musicians A80

Miniatures by Mohammed Racim: 60c, Two female musicians. 5d, Algerian princess and antelope.

1965, Dec. 27 Photo. *Perf. 11½*

341 A80 30c multicolored	.70	.55
342 A80 60c multicolored	1.10	.70
343 A80 5d multicolored	8.00	5.25
Nos. 341-343 (3)	9.80	6.50

Bulls, Painted in 6000 B.C. — A81

Wall Paintings from Tassili-N-Ajjer, c. 6000 B.C.: No. 345, Shepherd, vert. 2d, Fleeing ostriches. 3d, Two girls, vert.

1966, Jan. 29 Photo. *Perf. 11½*

344 A81 1d brn, bis & red brn	2.75	1.90
345 A81 1d gray, blk, ocher & dk brn	2.75	1.90
346 A81 2d brn, ocher & red brn	6.50	3.00
347 A81 3d buff, blk, ocher & brn red	8.00	4.25
Nos. 344-347 (4)	20.00	11.05

See Nos. 365-368.

Pottery — A82

Handicrafts from Great Kabylia: 50c, Weaving, woman at loom, horiz. 70c, Jewelry.

1966, Feb. 26 Engr. *Perf. 13*

348 A82 40c Prus bl, brn red & blk	.30	.25
349 A82 50c dk red, ol & ocher	.40	.30
350 A82 70c vio bl, blk & red	.65	.40
Nos. 348-350 (3)	1.35	.95

Weather Balloon, Compass Rose and Anemometer A83

1966, Mar. 23 Engr. Unwmk.

351 A83 1d claret, brt bl & grn	.85	.40

World Meteorological Day.

Book, Grain, Cogwheel and UNESCO Emblem — A84

Design: 60c, Grain, cogwheel, book and UNESCO emblem.

1966, May 2 Typo. *Perf. 13x14*

352 A84 30c yellow bis & blk	.25	.20
353 A84 60c dk red, gray & blk	.40	.25

Literacy as basis for development.

WHO Headquarters, Geneva — A85

1966, May 30 Engr. *Perf. 13*

354 A85 30c multicolored	.35	.30
355 A85 60c multicolored	.70	.40

Inauguration of the WHO Headquarters, Geneva.

Algerian Scout Emblem A86

Arab Jamboree Emblem A87

1966, July 23 Photo. *Perf. 12x12½*

356 A86 30c multicolored	.65	.50
357 A87 1d multicolored	1.75	1.25

No. 356 commemorates the 30th anniv. of the Algerian Mohammedan Boy Scouts. No. 357, the 7th Arab Boy Scout Jamboree, held at Good Daim, Libya, Aug. 12.

Map of Palestine and Victims A88

Abd-el-Kader A89

1966, Sept. 26 Typo. *Perf. 10½*

358 A88 30c red & black	.80	.40

Deir Yassin Massacre, Apr. 9, 1948.

1966, Nov. 2 Photo. *Perf. 11½*

359 A89 30c multicolored	.40	.20
360 A89 95c multicolored	1.10	.35

Transfer from Damascus to Algiers of the ashes of Abd-el-Kader (1807?-1883), Emir of Mascara. See Nos. 382-387.

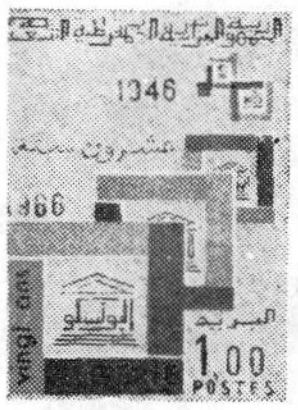

UNESCO Emblem — A90

1966, Nov. 19 Typo. *Perf. 10½*

361 A90 1d multicolored	1.00	.35

20th anniv. of UNESCO.

Horseman A91

Miniatures by Mohammed Racim: 1.50d, Woman at her toilette. 2d, The pirate Barbarossa in front of the Admiralty.

1966, Dec. 17 Photo. *Perf. 11½*
Granite Paper

362 A91 1d multicolored	3.25	1.40
363 A91 1.50d multicolored	4.25	2.00
364 A91 2d multicolored	7.00	3.50
Nos. 362-364 (3)	14.50	6.90

Wall Paintings Type of 1966

Wall Paintings from Tassili-N-Ajjer, c. 6000 B.C.: 1d, Cow. No. 366, Antelope. No. 367, Archers. 3d, Warrior, vert.

1967, Jan. 28 Photo. *Perf. 11½*

365 A81 1d brn, bis & dl vio	2.75	1.90
366 A81 2d brn, ocher & red brn	5.00	3.25
367 A81 2d brn, yel & red brn	5.00	3.25
368 A81 3d blk, gray, yel & red brn	7.75	5.00
Nos. 365-368 (4)	20.50	13.40

Bardo Museum A92

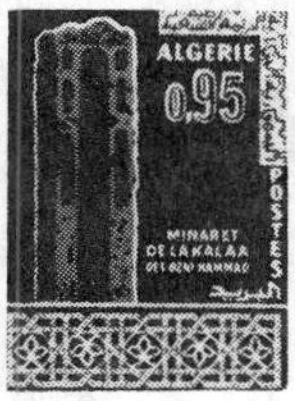

La Kalaa Minaret — A93

Design: 1.30d, Ruins at Sedrata.

1967, Feb. 27 Photo. *Perf. 13*

369 A92 35c multicolored	.20	.20
370 A93 95c multicolored	.45	.30
371 A92 1.30d multicolored	.75	.40
Nos. 369-371 (3)	1.40	.90

Moretti and International Tourist Year Emblem A94

Design: 70c, Tuareg riding camel, Tassili, and Tourist Year Emblem, vert.

1967, Apr. 29 Litho. *Perf. 14*

372 A94 40c multi	.50	.25
373 A94 70c multi	1.00	.35

International Tourist Year, 1967.

Spiny-tailed Agamid — A95

Designs: 20c, Ostrich, vert. 40c, Slender-horned gazelle, vert. 70c, Fennec.

1967, June 24 Photo. *Perf. 11½*

374 A95 5c bister & blk	.60	.50
375 A95 20c ocher, blk & pink	1.25	.80
376 A95 40c ol bis, blk & red brn	2.00	1.00
377 A95 70c gray, blk & dp org	3.50	2.00
Nos. 374-377 (4)	7.35	4.30

Dancers — A96

Typographed and Engraved

1967, July 4 ***Perf. 10½***
378 A96 50c gray vio, yel & blk .45 .35

National Youth Festival.

Map of the Mediterranean and Sport Scenes — A97

1967, Sept. 2 Typo. ***Perf. 10½***
379 A97 30c black, red & blue .25 .20

Issued to publicize the 5th Mediterranean Games, Tunis, Sept. 8-17.

Skiers — A98

Olympic Emblem and Sports A99

1967, Oct. 21 Engr. ***Perf. 13***
380 A98 30c brt blue & ultra .35 .20
381 A99 95c brn org, pur & brt grn .80 .55

Issued to publicize the 10th Winter Olympic Games, Grenoble, Feb. 6-18, 1968.

Abd-el-Kader Type of 1966

Lithographed, Photogravure

1967-71 ***Perf. 13½, 11½***
382 A89 5c dull pur ('68) .20 .20
383 A89 10c green .85 .35
383A A89 10c sl grn (litho., '69) .20 .20
383B A89 25c orange ('71) .20 .20
384 A89 30c black ('68) .50 .20
385 A89 30c lt violet ('68) .75 .30
386 A89 50c rose claret .65 .20
387 A89 70c violet blue .85 .25
Nos. 382-387 (8) 4.20 1.90

No. 383, 50c and 70c, issued Nov. 13, 1967, are on granite paper, photo. The 5c, No.383A, 25c and 30c are litho., perf. 13½; others, perf. 11½.

The three 1967 stamps (No. 383, 50c, 70c) have numerals thin, narrow and close together; the Arabic inscription at lower right is 2mm high. The 5 litho. stamps are redrawn, with numerals thicker and spaced more widely; Arabic at lower right 3mm high.

Boy Scouts Holding Jamboree Emblem A100

1967, Dec. 23 Engr. ***Perf. 13***
388 A100 1d multicolored 1.00 .80

12th Boy Scout World Jamboree, Farragut State Park, Idaho, Aug. 1-9.

No. 324 Surcharged

1967 Typo. ***Perf. 14x13½***
389 A71 30c on 25c red .50 .20

Mandolin — A101

1968, Feb. 17 Photo. ***Perf. 12½x13***
390 A101 30c shown .35 .25
391 A101 40c Lute .40 .25
392 A101 1.30d Rebec 1.40 .65
Nos. 390-392 (3) 2.15 1.15

Nememcha Rug — A102

Algerian Rugs: 70c, Guergour. 95c, Djebel-Amour. 1.30d, Kalaa.

1968, Apr. 13 Photo. ***Perf. 11½***
393 A102 30c multi .75 .75
394 A102 70c multi 1.50 1.50
395 A102 95c multi 2.00 2.00
396 A102 1.30d multi 2.50 2.50
Nos. 393-396 (4) 6.75 6.75

Human Rights Flame A103

1968, May 18 Typo. ***Perf. 10½***
397 A103 40c blue, red & yel .40 .30

International Human Rights Year, 1968.

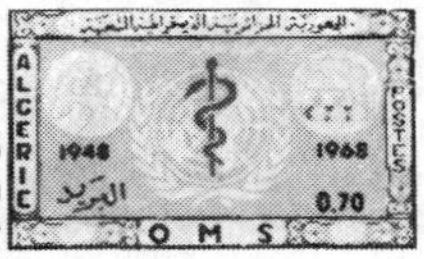
WHO Emblem A104

1968, May 18
398 A104 70c blk, lt bl & yel .55 .30

20th anniv. of the WHO.

Welder A105

Athletes, Olympic Flame and Rings A106

1968, June 15 Engr. ***Perf. 13***
399 A105 30c gray, brn & ultra .25 .20

Algerian emigration to Europe.

Perf. 12½x13, 13x12½

1968, July 4 Photo.

50c, Soccer player. 1d, Mexican pyramid, emblem, Olympic flame, rings & athletes, horiz.

400 A106 30c green, red & yel .35 .30
401 A106 50c rose car & multi .60 .30
402 A106 1d dk grn, org, brn & red 1.10 .65
Nos. 400-402 (3) 2.05 1.25

19th Olympic Games, Mexico City, Oct. 12-27.

Scouts and Emblem A107

Barbary Sheep A108

1968, July 4 ***Perf. 13***
403 A107 30c multicolored .50 .20

8th Arab Boy Scout Jamboree, Algiers, 1968.

1968, Oct. 19 Photo. ***Perf. 11½***
404 A108 40c shown .50 .25
405 A108 1d Red deer 1.25 .60

Hunting Scenes, Djemila A109

"Industry" A110

Design: 95c, Neptune's chariot, Timgad, horiz. Both designs are from Roman mosaics.

Perf. 12½x13, 13x12½

1968, Nov. 23 Photo.
406 A109 40c gray & multi .35 .25
407 A109 95c gray & multi .85 .50

1968, Dec. 14 ***Perf. 11½***

Designs: No. 409, Miner with drill. 95c, "Energy" (circle and rays).

408 A110 30c dp orange & sil .25 .20
409 A110 30c brown & multi .25 .20
410 A110 95c silver, red & blk .75 .35
Nos. 408-410 (3) 1.25 .75

Issued to publicize industrial development.

Opuntia Ficus Indica — A111

Flowers: 40c, Carnations. 70c, Roses. 95c, Bird-of-paradise flower.

1969, Jan. Photo. ***Perf. 11½***

Flowers in Natural Colors

411 A111 25c pink & blk .55 .25
412 A111 40c yellow & blk .65 .35
413 A111 70c gray & blk 1.25 .45
414 A111 95c brt blue & blk 2.00 .80
Nos. 411-414 (4) 4.45 1.85

See Nos. 496-499.

Irrigation Dam at Djorf Torba-Oued Guir — A112

Design: 1.50d, Truck on Highway No. 51 and camel caravan.

1969, Feb. 22 Photo. ***Perf. 11½***
415 A112 30c multi .25 .20
416 A112 1.50d multi 1.25 .65

Public works in the Sahara.

Mail Coach A113

1969, Mar. 22 Photo. ***Perf. 11½***
417 A113 1d multicolored 1.10 .60

Issued for Stamp Day, 1969.

Capitol, Timgad — A114

Design: 1d, Septimius Temple, Djemila, horiz.

1969, Apr. 5 Photo. ***Perf. 13x12½***
418 A114 30c gray & multi .35 .20
419 A114 1d gray & multi .85 .35

Second Timgad Festival, Apr. 4-8.

ILO Emblem A115

Arabian Saddle A116

1969, May 24 Photo. ***Perf. 11½***
420 A115 95c dp car, yel & blk 1.00 .40

50th anniv. of the ILO.

1969, June 28 Photo. ***Perf. 12x12½***

Algerian Handicrafts: 30c, Bookcase. 60c, Decorated copper plate.

Granite Paper

421 A116 30c multicolored .30 .20
422 A116 60c multicolored .55 .25
423 A116 1d multicolored 1.00 .45
Nos. 421-423 (3) 1.85 .90

No. 321 Surcharged 0,20

1969 Typo. *Perf. 14x13½*
424 A71 20c on 12c emerald .25 .20

Pan-African Culture Festival Emblem — A117

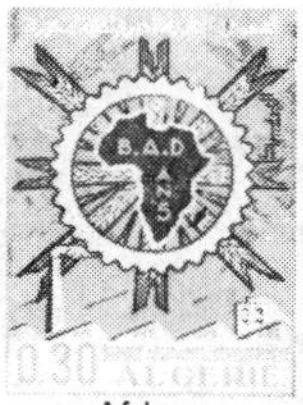

African Development Bank Emblem — A118

1969, July 19 Photo. *Perf. 12½*
425 A117 30c multicolored .35 .20

Issued to commemorate the First Pan-African Culture Festival, Algiers, July 21-Aug. 1.

1969, Aug. 23 Typo. *Perf. 10½*
426 A118 30c dull blue, yel & blk .35 .20

5th anniversary of the African Development Bank.

Astronauts and Landing Module on Moon — A119

Perf. 12½x11½
1969, Aug. 23 Photo.
427 A119 50c gold & multi .60 .35

Man's 1st landing on the moon, July 20, 1969. US astronauts Neil A. Armstrong and Col. Edwin E. Aldrin, Jr., with Lieut. Col. Michael Collins piloting Apollo 11.

Algerian Women, by Dinet — A120

1.50d, The Watchmen, by Etienne Dinet.

1969, Nov. 29 Photo. *Perf. 14½*
428 A120 1d multi 1.75 .90
429 A120 1.50d multi 2.75 1.40

Mother and Child — A121

1969, Dec. 27 Photo. *Perf. 11½*
430 A121 30c multicolored .35 .25

Issued to promote mother and child protection.

Agricultural Growth Chart, Tractor and Dam — A122

Designs: 30c, Transportation and development. 50c, Abstract symbols of industrialization.

1970, Jan. 31 Photo. *Perf. 12½*
Size: 37x23mm
431 A122 25c dk brn, yel & org .20 .20

Litho. *Perf. 14*
Size: 49x23mm
432 A122 30c blue & multi .25 .20

Photo. *Perf. 12½*
Size: 37x23mm
433 A122 50c rose lilac & blk .30 .20
Nos. 431-433 (3) .75 .60

Four-Year Development Plan.

Old and New Mail Delivery A123

Spiny Lobster A124

1970, Feb. 28 Photo. *Perf. 11½*
Granite Paper
434 A123 30c multicolored .30 .20

Issued for Stamp Day.

1970, Mar. 28

Designs: 40c, Mollusks. 75c, Retepora cellulosa. 1d, Red coral.

435 A124 30c ocher & multi .35 .20
436 A124 40c multicolored .50 .25
437 A124 75c ultra & multi .90 .35
438 A124 1d lt blue & multi 1.25 .50
Nos. 435-438 (4) 3.00 1.30

Oranges, EXPO '70 Emblem — A125

Designs (EXPO '70 Emblem and): 60c, Algerian pavilion. 70c, Grapes.

1970, Apr. 25 Photo. *Perf. 12½x12*
439 A125 30c lt blue, grn & org .50 .20
440 A125 60c multicolored .65 .20
441 A125 70c multicolored 1.00 .35
Nos. 439-441 (3) 2.15 .75

EXPO '70 International Exhibition, Osaka, Japan, Mar. 15-Sept. 13, 1970.

Olives, Oil Bottle — A126

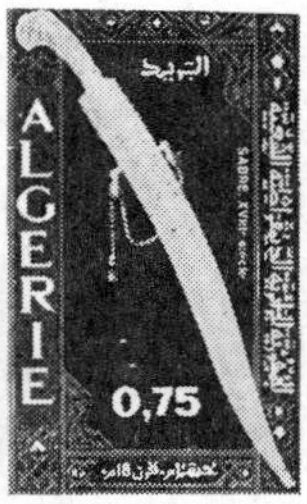

Saber — A127

1970, May 16 Photo. *Perf. 12½x12*
442 A126 1d yellow & multi 1.00 .65

Olive Year, 1969-1970.

Common Design Types pictured following the introduction.

UPU Headquarters Issue
Common Design Type
1970, May 30 *Perf. 13*
Size: 36x26mm
443 CD133 75c multicolored .50 .40

1970, June 27 Photo. *Perf. 12½*

Designs: 40c, Guns, 18th century, horiz. 1d, Pistol, 18th century, horiz.

444 A127 40c yellow & multi .65 .25
445 A127 75c red & multi .80 .40
446 A127 1d multicolored 1.25 .50
Nos. 444-446 (3) 2.70 1.15

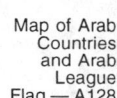

Map of Arab Countries and Arab League Flag — A128

Typographed and Engraved
1970, July 25 *Perf. 10½*
447 A128 30c grn, ocher & lt bl .30 .20

25th anniversary of the Arab League.

Lenin — A129

1970, Aug. 29 Litho. *Perf. 11½x12*
448 A129 30c brown & buff .25 .20

Lenin (1870-1924), Russian communist leader.

Exhibition Hall and Algiers Fair Emblem — A130

1970, Sept. 11 Engr. *Perf. 14x13½*
449 A130 60c lt olive green .40 .30

New Exhibition Hall for Algiers International Fair.

Education Year Emblem, Blackboard, Atom Symbol — A131

Koran Page — A132

1970, Oct. 24 Photo. *Perf. 14*
450 A131 30c pink, blk, gold & lt bl .25 .20
451 A132 3d multicolored 2.50 1.50

Issued for International Education Year.

Great Mosque, Tlemcen A133

Design: 40c, Ketchaoua Mosque, Algiers, vert. 1d, Mosque, Sidi-Okba, vert.

1970-71 Litho. *Perf. 14*
456 A133 30c multicolored .20 .20
457 A133 40c sepia & lemon ('71) .25 .20
458 A133 1d multicolored .65 .30
Nos. 456-458 (3) 1.10 .70

Symbols of the Arts — A134

1970, Dec. 26 Photo. *Perf. 13x12½*
459 A134 1d grn, lt grn & org .80 .45

Main Post Office, Algiers A135

1971, Jan. 23 *Perf. 11½*
460 A135 30c multicolored .30 .20

Stamp Day, 1971.

Hurdling A136

40c, Vaulting, vert. 75c, Basketball, vert.

1971, Mar. 7 Photo. *Perf. 11½*
461 A136 20c lt blue & slate .25 .20
462 A136 40c lt ol grn & slate .35 .35
463 A136 75c salmon pink & slate .65 .50
Nos. 461-463 (3) 1.25 1.05

Mediterranean Games, Izmir, Turkey, Oct. 1971.

Symbolic Head — A137

1971, Mar. 27 ***Perf. 12½***

464 A137 60c car rose, blk & sil .30 .20

Intl. year against racial discrimination.

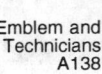

Emblem and Technicians A138

1971, Apr. 24 Photo. ***Perf. 12½x12***

465 A138 70c claret, org & bluish blk .40 .30

Founding of the Institute of Technology.

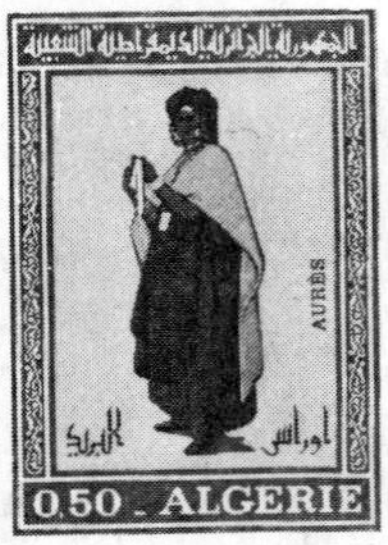

Woman from Aurès — A139

Regional Costumes: 70c, Man from Oran. 80c, Man from Algiers. 90c, Woman from Amour Mountains.

1971, Oct. 16 ***Perf. 11½***

466 A139 50c gold & multi	1.50	.65
467 A139 70c gold & multi	1.75	1.00
468 A139 80c gold & multi	2.25	1.10
469 A139 90c gold & multi	2.50	1.25
Nos. 466-469 (4)	8.00	4.00

See Nos. 485-488, 534-537.

UNICEF Emblem, Birds and Plants — A140

1971, Dec. 6 ***Perf. 11½***

470 A140 60c multicolored .55 .30

25th anniv. of UNICEF.

Lion of St. Mark A141

Design: 1.15d, Bridge of Sighs, Venice, vert.

1972, Jan. 24 Litho. ***Perf. 12***

471 A141 80c multi	.60	.35
472 A141 1.15d multi	.90	.50

UNESCO campaign to save Venice.

Javelin A142

Book and Book Year Emblem A143

Designs: 25c, Bicycling, horiz. 60c, Wrestling. 1d, Gymnast on rings.

1972, Mar. 25 Photo. ***Perf. 11½***

473 A142 25c maroon & multi	.30	.20
474 A142 40c ocher & multi	.35	.25
475 A142 60c ultra & multi	.40	.40
476 A142 1d rose & multi	1.00	.50
Nos. 473-476 (4)	2.05	1.35

20th Olympic Games, Munich, Aug. 26-Sept. 11.

1972, Apr. 15

477 A143 1.15d bister, brn & red .65 .50

International Book Year 1972.

Mailmen A144

Flowers A145

1972, Apr. 22

478 A144 40c gray & multi .25 .20

Stamp Day 1972.

1972, May 27

479 A145 50c Jasmine	.65	.30
480 A145 60c Violets	.75	.35
481 A145 1.15d Tuberose	1.50	.55
Nos. 479-481 (3)	2.90	1.20

Olympic Stadium, Chéraga A146

1972, June 10

482 A146 50c gray, choc & grn .60 .30

New Day, Algerian Flag — A147

1972, July 5

483 A147 1d green & multi .65 .40

10th anniversary of independence.

Festival Emblem — A148

Mailing a Letter — A149

1972, July 5 Litho. ***Perf. 10½***

484 A148 40c grn, dk brn & org .25 .20

1st Arab Youth Festival, Algiers, July 5-11.

Costume Type of 1971

Regional Costumes: 50c, Woman from Hoggar. 60c, Kabyle woman. 70c, Man from Mzab. 90c, Woman from Tlemcen.

1972, Nov. 18 Photo. ***Perf. 11½***

485 A139 50c gold & multi	.80	.70
486 A139 60c gold & multi	1.10	.90
487 A139 70c gold & multi	1.25	1.10
488 A139 90c gold & multi	1.75	1.25
Nos. 485-488 (4)	4.90	3.95

1973, Jan. 20 Photo. ***Perf. 11***

489 A149 40c orange & multi .40 .20

Stamp Day.

Ho Chi Minh, Map of Viet Nam — A150

1973, Feb. 17 Photo. ***Perf. 11½***

490 A150 40c multicolored .75 .50

To honor the people of Viet Nam.

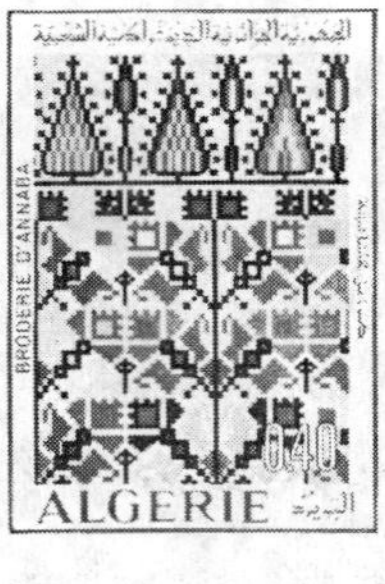

Embroidery from Annaba A151

Designs: 60c, Tree of Life pattern from Algiers. 80c, Constantine embroidery.

1973, Feb. 24

491 A151 40c gray & multi	.75	.40
492 A151 60c blue and multi	1.00	.60
493 A151 80c dk red, gold & blk	1.50	.80
Nos. 491-493 (3)	3.25	1.80

Stylized Globe and Wheat — A152

1973, Mar. 26 Photo. ***Perf. 11½***

494 A152 1.15d brt rose lil, org & grn .75 .40

World Food Program, 10th anniversary.

Soldier and Flag A153

1973, Apr. 23 Photo. ***Perf. 14x13½***

495 A153 40c multicolored .25 .20

Honoring the National Service.

Flower Type of 1969

Flowers: 30c, Opuntia ficus indica. 40c, Roses. 1d, Carnations. 1.15d, Bird-of-paradise flower.

1973, May 21 Photo. ***Perf. 11½***

Flowers in Natural Colors

496 A111 30c pink & blk	.40	.20
497 A111 40c gray & blk	.50	.20
498 A111 1d yellow & multi	.90	.40
499 A111 1.15d multi	1.25	.50
Nos. 496-499 (4)	3.05	1.30

For overprints and surcharges see #518-519, 531.

OAU Emblem — A154

1973, May 28 Photo. ***Perf. 12½x13***

500 A154 40c multicolored .40 .20

Org. for African Unity, 10th anniv.

Desert and Fruitful Land, Farmer and Family A155

1973, June 18 ***Perf. 11½***

501 A155 40c gold & multi .50 .40

Agricultural revolution.

Map of Africa, Scout Emblem — A156

1973, July 16 Litho. ***Perf. 10½***

502 A156 80c purple 1.00 .50

24th Boy Scout World Conference (1st in Africa), Nairobi, Kenya, July 16-21.

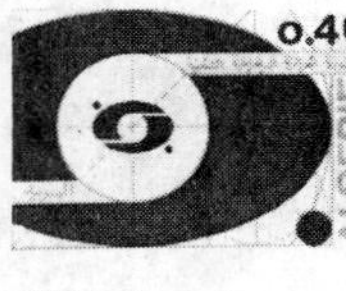

Algerian PTT Emblem A157

1973, Aug. 6 ***Perf. 14***

503 A157 40c blue & orange .25 .20

Adoption of new emblem for Post, Telegraph and Telephone System.

Conference Emblem — A158

Perf. 13½x12½

1973, Sept. 5 Photo.

504 A158 40c dp rose & multi .20 .20
505 A158 80c blue grn & multi .50 .25

4th Summit Conference of Non-aligned Nations, Algiers, Sept. 5-9.

Port of Skikda A159

1973, Sept. 29 Photo. *Perf. 11½*

506 A159 80c ocher, blk & ultra .50 .25

New port of Skikda.

Young Workers — A160

1973, Oct. 22 Photo. *Perf. 13*

507 A160 40c multicolored .25 .20

Voluntary work service.

Arms of Algiers A161

1973, Dec. 22 Photo. *Perf. 13*

508 A161 2d gold & multi 1.60 1.10

Millennium of Algiers.

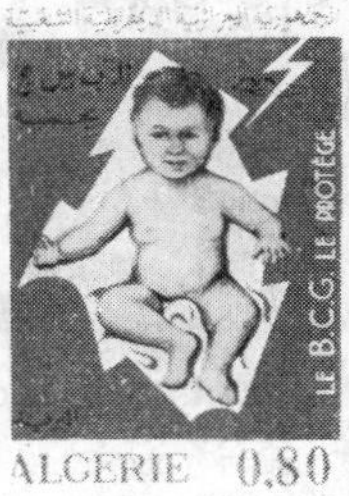

Infant — A162

1974, Jan. 7 Litho. *Perf. 10½x11*

509 A162 80c orange & multi .60 .35

Fight against tuberculosis.

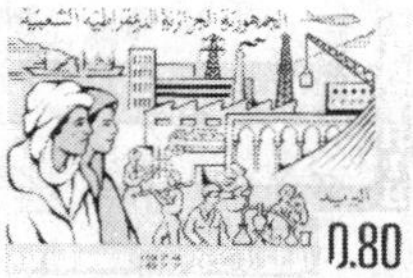

Man and Woman, Industry and Transportation — A163

1974, Feb. 18 Photo. *Perf. 11½*

510 A163 80c multicolored .50 .20

Four-year plan.

A164

1974, Feb. 25 Photo. *Perf. 11½*

511 A164 1.50d multi 1.10 .65

Millennium of the birth of abu-al-Rayhan al-Biruni (973-1048), philosopher and mathematician.

Map and Colors of Algeria, Tunisia, Morocco A165

1974, Mar. 4 Photo. *Perf. 13*

512 A165 40c gold & multi .30 .20

Maghreb Committee for Coordination of Posts and Telecommunications.

Hand Holding Rifle A166

Mother and Children A167

1974, Mar. 25 *Perf. 11½*

513 A166 80c red & black .30 .20

Solidarity with the struggle of the people of South Africa.

1974, Apr. 8 *Perf. 13½*

514 A167 85c multicolored .35 .25

Honoring Algerian mothers.

Village A168

Designs: 80c, Harvest. 90c, Tractor and sun. Designs after children's drawings.

1974, June 15

Size: 45x26mm

515 A168 70c multicolored .40 .20

Size: 48x33mm

516 A168 80c multicolored .50 .30
517 A168 90c multicolored .60 .40
Nos. 515-517 (3) 1.50 .90

Nos. 498-499 Overprinted "FLORALIES/1974"

1974, June 22 Photo. *Perf. 11½*

518 A111 1d multi .65 .35
519 A111 1.15d multi .70 .40

1974 Flower Show.

Stamp Vending Machine — A169

1974, Oct. 7 Photo. *Perf. 13*

520 A169 80c multicolored .40 .20

Stamp Day 1974.

UPU Emblem and Globe A170

1974, Oct. 14 *Perf. 14*

521 A170 80c multicolored .50 .30

Centenary of Universal Postal Union.

"Revolution" — A171

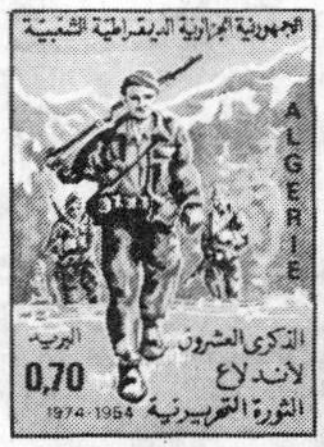

Soldiers and Mountains A172

Raising New Flag A173

Design: 1d, Algerian struggle for independence (people, sun and fields).

1974, Nov. 4 Photo. *Perf. 14*

522 A171 40c multicolored .30 .20
523 A172 70c multicolored .40 .20
524 A173 95c multicolored .50 .25
525 A171 1d multicolored .60 .30
Nos. 522-525 (4) 1.80 .95

20th anniv. of the start of the revolution.

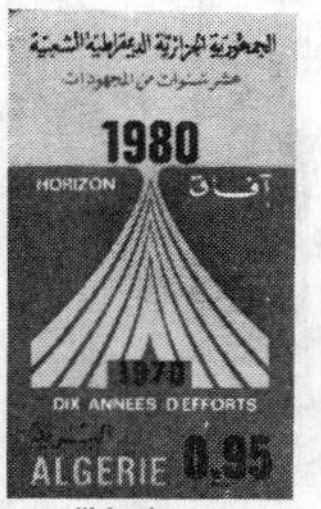

"Horizon 1980" — A174

Ewer and Basin — A175

1974, Nov. 23 Photo. *Perf. 13*

526 A174 95c ocher, dk red & blk .55 .25

10-year development plan, 1971-1980.

1974, Dec. 21 *Perf. 11½*

527 A175 50c shown .25 .20
528 A175 60c Coffee pot .30 .20
529 A175 95c Sugar bowl .45 .30
530 A175 1d Bath tub .50 .35
Nos. 527-530 (4) 1.50 1.05

17th century Algerian copperware.

No. 497 Surcharged with New Value and Heavy Bar

1975, Jan. 4

531 A111 50c on 40c multi .50 .40

Mediterranean Games' Emblem — A176

1975, Jan. 27 *Perf. 13½*

532 A176 50c purple, yel & grn .30 .20
533 A176 1d orange, bl & mar .60 .25

Mediterranean Games, Algiers, 1975.

Costume Type of 1971

Regional Costumes: No. 534, Woman from Hoggar. No. 535, Woman from Algiers. No. 536, Woman from Oran. No. 537, Man from Tlemcen.

1975, Feb. 22 Photo. *Perf. 11½*

534 A139 1d gold & multi .90 .80
535 A139 1d gold & multi .90 .80
536 A139 1d gold & multi .90 .80
537 A139 1d gold & multi .90 .80
Nos. 534-537 (4) 3.60 3.20

Map of Arab Countries, ALO Emblem A177

1975, Mar. 10 Litho. *Perf. 10½x11*

538 A177 50c red brown .25 .20

Arab Labor Organization, 10th anniversary.

Blood Transfusion A178

1975, Mar. 15 *Perf. 14*

539 A178 50c car rose & multi .30 .20

Blood donation and transfusions.

Post Office, Al-Kantara
A179

Policeman and Map of Algeria
A180

1975, May 10 Photo. *Perf. 11½*
Granite Paper

540 A179 50c multicolored .25 .20

Stamp Day 1975.

1975, June 1 Photo. *Perf. 13*

541 A180 50c multicolored .75 .40

Natl. Security and 10th Natl. Police Day.

Ground Receiving Station
A181

Designs: 1d, Map of Algeria with locations of radar sites, transmission mast and satellite. 1.20d, Main and subsidiary stations.

1975, June 28 Photo. *Perf. 13*

542 A181 50c blue & multi .30 .20
543 A181 1d blue & multi .55 .20
544 A181 1.20d blue & multi .60 .25
Nos. 542-544 (3) 1.45 .65

National satellite telecommunications network.

Revolutionary with Flag — A182

1975, Aug. 20 Photo. *Perf. 11½*

545 A182 1d multicolored .50 .25

August 20th Revolutionary Movement (Skikda), 20th anniversary.

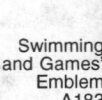

Swimming and Games' Emblem
A183

Perf. 13x13½, 13½x13

1975, Aug. 23 Photo.

546 A183 25c shown .20 .20
547 A183 50c Judo, map .25 .20
548 A183 70c Soccer, vert. .50 .20
549 A183 1d Running, vert. .55 .25
550 A183 1.20d Handball, vert. .70 .40
 a. Souv. sheet of 5, #546-550, perf 13 4.50 4.50
Nos. 546-550 (5) 2.20 1.25

7th Mediterranean Games, Algiers, 8/23-9/46.

No. 550a sold for 4.50d. Exists imperf., same value.

Setif, Guelma, Kherrata — A184

1975 Litho. *Perf. 13½x14*

551 A184 5c orange & blk .20 .20
552 A184 10c emerald & brn .20 .20
553 A184 25c dl blue & blk .20 .20
554 A184 30c lemon & blk .20 .20
555 A184 50c brt grn & blk .25 .20
556 A184 70c fawn & blk .35 .20
557 A184 1d vermilion & blk .50 .25
Nos. 551-557 (7) 1.90 1.45

30th anniv. of victory in World War II.

Issue dates: 50c, 1d, Nov. 3; others, Dec. 17.

For surcharge see No. 611.

Map of Maghreb and APU Emblem
A185

1975, Nov. 20 Photo. *Perf. 11½*

558 A185 1d multicolored .55 .30

10th Cong. of Arab Postal Union, Algiers.

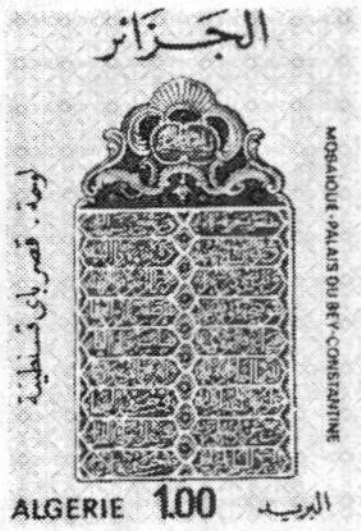

Mosaic, Bey Constantine's Palace — A186

Dey-Alger Palace — A187

Famous buildings: 2d, Prayer niche, Medersa Sidi-Boumediene, Tlemcen.

1975, Dec. 22

559 A186 1d lt blue & multi .60 .25
560 A186 2d buff & multi 1.10 .60
561 A187 2.50d buff & blk 1.60 .90
Nos. 559-561 (3) 3.30 1.75

Al-Azhar University
A188

Perf. 11½x12½

1975, Dec. 29 Litho.

562 A188 2d multicolored 1.10 .60

Millennium of Al-Azhar University.

Red-billed Firefinch — A189

Birds: 1.40d, Black-headed bush shrike, horiz. 2d, Blue tit. 2.50d, Blackbellied sandgrouse, horiz.

1976, Jan. 24 Photo. *Perf. 11½*

563 A189 50c multi .35 .20
564 A189 1.40d multi .85 .55
565 A189 2d multi 1.10 .65
566 A189 2.50d multi 1.50 .90
Nos. 563-566 (4) 3.80 2.30

See Nos. 595-598.

Telephones 1876 and 1976 — A190

Map of Africa with Angola and its Flag — A191

1976, Feb. 23 Photo. *Perf. 13½x13*

567 A190 1.40d rose, dk & lt bl .65 .40

Centenary of first telephone call by Alexander Graham Bell, Mar. 10, 1876.

1976, Feb. 23 *Perf. 11½*

568 A191 50c brown & multi .25 .20

Algeria's solidarity with the People's Republic of Angola.

A192

A193

Sahraoui flag and child, map of former Spanish Sahara.

1976, Mar. 15 Photo. *Perf. 11½*

569 A192 50c multicolored .25 .20

Algeria's solidarity with Sahraoui Arab Democratic Republic, former Spanish Sahara.

1976, Mar. 22

570 A193 1.40d Mailman .60 .30

Stamp Day 1976.

Microscope, Slide with TB Bacilli, Patients
A194

1976, Apr. 26 *Perf. 13x13½*

571 A194 50c multicolored .40 .20

Fight against tuberculosis.

"Setif, Guelma, Kherrata" — A195

1976, May 24 Photo. *Perf. 13½x13*

572 A195 50c blue & yellow .35 .20
 a. Booklet pane of 6 4.75
 b. Booklet pane of 10 4.00

No. 572 was issued in booklets only.

Ram's Head over Landscape
A196

People Holding Torch, Map of Algeria
A197

1976, June 17 Photo. *Perf. 11½*

573 A196 50c multicolored .40 .20

Livestock breeding.

1976, June 29 Photo. *Perf. 14x13½*

574 A197 50c multicolored .25 .20

National Charter.

Palestine Map and Flag — A198

Map of Africa — A199

1976, July 12 *Perf. 11½*
Granite Paper

575 A198 50c multicolored 2.00 1.00

Solidarity with the Palestinians.

1976, Oct. 3 Litho. *Perf. 10½x11*

576 A199 2d dk blue & multi 1.00 .50

2nd Pan-African Commercial Fair, Algiers.

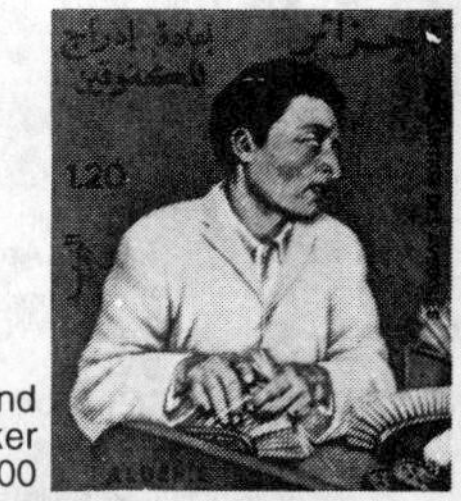

Blind Brushmaker
A200

The Blind, by Dinet
A201

1976, Oct. 23 Photo. *Perf. 14½*

577 A200 1.20d blue & multi .65 .35
578 A201 1.40d gold & multi 1.50 .75

Rehabilitation of the blind.

"Constitution 1976" — A202

1976, Nov. 19 Photo. *Perf. 11½*
579 A202 2d multicolored 1.00 .55

New Constitution.

Soldiers Planting Seedlings — A203

1976, Nov. 25 Litho. *Perf. 12*
580 A203 1.40d multicolored .75 .35

Green barrier against the Sahara.

Ornamental Border and Inscription A204

1976, Dec. 18 Photo. *Perf. 11½*
Granite Paper
581 A204 2d multicolored 1.25 .75

Re-election of Pres. Houari Boumediene. See No. 627.

Map with Charge Zones and Dials A205

People and Buildings A206

1977, Jan. 22 *Perf. 13*
582 A205 40c silver & multi .30 .20

Inauguration of automatic national and international telephone service.

1977, Jan. 29 Photo. *Perf. 11½*
583 A206 60c on 50c multi .35 .20

2nd General Population and Buildings Census. No. 583 was not issued without the typographed red brown surcharge, date, and bars.

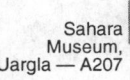

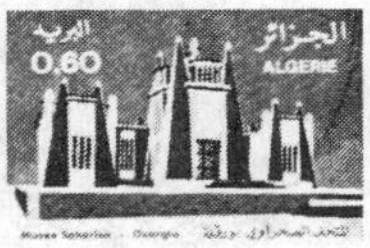

Sahara Museum, Uargla — A207

1977, Feb. 12 Litho. *Perf. 14*
584 A207 60c multicolored .35 .20

El-Kantara Gorge — A208

Perf. 12½x13½
1977, Feb. 19 Photo.
585 A208 20c green & yellow .20 .20
  a. Bklt. pane, 3 #585, 4 #586 + label 8.00
  b. Bklt. pane, 5 #585, 2 #587 + label 6.50
586 A208 60c brt lilac & yel .20 .20
587 A208 1d brown & yellow .40 .20
  Nos. 585-587 (3) .80 .60

National Assembly — A209

1977, Feb. 27 *Perf. 11½*
588 A209 2d multicolored 1.00 .60

People and Flag — A210

Soldier and Flag — A211

Perf. 13½, 11½ (3d)
1977, Mar. 12 Photo.
589 A210 2d multicolored 1.25 .40
590 A211 3d multicolored 1.75 .65

Solidarity with the peoples of Zimbabwe (Rhodesia), 2d; Namibia, 3d.

Winter, Roman Mosaic A212

The Seasons from Roman Villa, 2nd century A.D.: 1.40d, Fall. 2d, Summer. 3d, Spring.

1977, Apr. 21 Photo. *Perf. 11½*
Granite Paper
591 A212 1.20d multi .95 .50
592 A212 1.40d multi 1.25 .55
593 A212 2d multi 1.65 .95
594 A212 3d multi 2.50 1.60
  a. Souv. sheet of 4, #591-594, perf., imperf. 10.00 10.00
  Nos. 591-594 (4) 6.35 3.60

No. 594a sold for 8d.

Bird Type of 1976

Birds: 60c, Tristram's warbler. 1.40d, Moussier's redstart, horiz. 2d, Temminck's horned lark, horiz. 3d, Eurasian hoopoe.

1977, May 21 Photo. *Perf. 11½*
595 A189 60c multi .75 .25
596 A189 1.40d multi 1.25 .40
597 A189 2d multi 1.75 .65
598 A189 3d multi 2.50 1.10
  Nos. 595-598 (4) 6.25 2.40

Horseman — A213

Design: 5d, Attacking horsemen, horiz.

1977, June 25 Photo. *Perf. 11½*
599 A213 2d multicolored 1.75 .75
600 A213 5d multicolored 3.50 2.00

Flag Colors, Games Emblem — A214

Wall Painting, Games Emblem A215

1977, Sept. 24 Photo. *Perf. 11½*
601 A214 60c multi .35 .25
602 A215 1.40d multi .80 .45

3rd African Games, Algiers 1978.

Village and Tractor A216

1977, Nov. 12 *Perf. 14x13*
603 A216 1.40d multi .90 .65

Socialist agricultural village.

Almohades Dirham, 12th Century — A217

Ancient Coins: 1.40d, Almohades coin, 12th century. 2d, Almoravides dinar, 11th century.

1977, Dec. 17 Photo. *Perf. 11½*
604 A217 60c ultra, sil & blk .50 .35
605 A217 1.40d green, gold & brn 1.10 .50
606 A217 2d red brn, gold & brn 1.50 .90
  Nos. 604-606 (3) 3.10 1.75

Flowering Trees — A218

1978, Feb. 11 Photo. *Perf. 11½*
607 A218 60c Cherry .35 .25
608 A218 1.20d Peach .85 .50
609 A218 1.30d Almond .85 .50
610 A218 1.40d Apple .90 .55
  Nos. 607-610 (4) 2.95 1.80

No. 555 Surcharged with New Value and Bar

1978, Feb. 11 Litho. *Perf. 13½x14*
611 A184 60c on 50c .50 .20

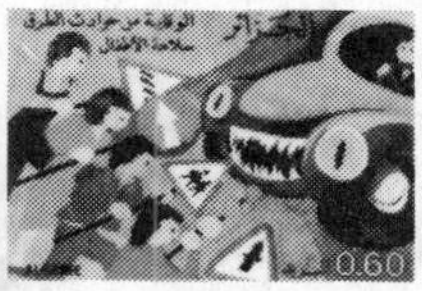

Children with Traffic Signs and Car — A219

1978, Apr. 29 Photo. *Perf. 11½*
612 A219 60c multicolored .30 .20

Road safety and protection of children.

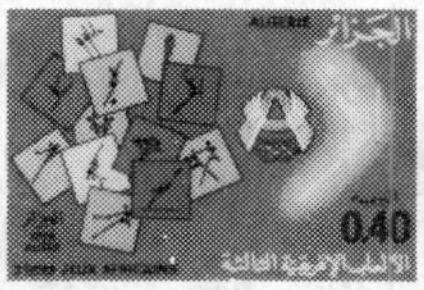

Sports and Games Emblems A220

Designs (Games Emblem and): 60c, Rower, vert. 1.20d, Flag colors. 1.30d, Fireworks, vert. 1.40d, Map of Africa and dancers, vert.

1978, July 13 Photo. *Perf. 11½*
613 A220 40c mul .20 .20
614 A220 60c multi .30 .20
615 A220 1.20d multi .60 .30
616 A220 1.30d multi .60 .35
617 A220 1.40d multi .65 .35
  Nos. 613-617 (5) 2.35 1.40

3rd African Games, Algiers, July 13-28.

TB Patient Returning to Family — A221

1978, Oct. 5 Photo. *Perf. 13½x14*
618 A221 60c multicolored .35 .20

Anti-tuberculosis campaign.

Holy Kaaba — A222

1978, Oct. 28 Photo. *Perf. 11½*
619 A222 60c multicolored .30 .20

Pilgrimage to Mecca.

National Servicemen Building Road — A223

1978, Nov. 4
620 A223 60c multicolored .30 .20

African Unity Road from El Goleah to In Salah, inauguration.

Fibula
A224

Pres. Boumediene
A225

Jewelry: 1.35d, Pendant. 1.40d, Ankle ring.

1978, Dec. 21 Photo. *Perf. 12x11½*

621 A224 1.20d multi .65 .30
622 A224 1.35d multi .70 .30
623 A224 1.40d multi 1.10 1.10
Nos. 621-623 (3) 2.45 1.70

1979, Jan. 7 Photo. *Perf. 12x11½*

624 A225 60c green, red & brown .30 .20

Houari Boumediene, pres. of Algeria 1965-1978.

Torch and Books
A226

1979, Jan. 27 Photo. *Perf. 11½*

625 A226 60c multicolored .30 .20

Natl. Front of Liberation Party Cong.

Pres. Boumediene — A227

1979, Feb. 4 Photo. *Perf. 11½*

626 A227 1.40d multi .65 .30

40 days after death of Pres. Houari Boumediene.

Ornamental Type of 1976

Proclamation of new President.

1979, Feb. 10

627 A204 2d multicolored 1.00 .35

Election of Pres. Chadli Bendjedid.

A229

A230

1979, Apr. 18 Photo. *Perf. 11½*

628 A229 60c multicolored .30 .20

Sheik Abdul-Hamid Ben Badis (1889-1940).

1979, May 19 Photo. *Perf. 13½x14*

Designs: 1.20d, Telephone dial, map of Africa. 1.40d, Symbolic Morse key and waves.

629 A230 1.20d multi .55 .20
630 A230 1.40d multi .60 .25

Telecom '79 Exhib., Geneva, Sept. 20-26.

Harvest, IYC Emblem
A231

Design: 1.40d, Dancers and IYC emblem, vert.

Perf. 11½x11, 11x11½

1979, June 21

631 A231 60c multi .40 .20
632 A231 1.40d multi .60 .45

International Year of the Child.

A232

A233

1979, Oct. 20 Photo. *Perf. 11½*

633 A232 1.40d Nuthatch .90 .40

1979, Nov. 1 Photo. *Perf. 12½*

Designs: 1.40d, Flag, soldiers and workers. 3d, Revolutionaries and emblem.

634 A233 1.40d multi .90 .25

Size: 37x48mm

Perf. 11½

635 A233 3d multi 2.25 .65

November 1 revolution, 25th anniversary.

Hegira, 1500 Anniv.
A234

1979, Dec. 2 Photo. *Perf. 11½*

636 A234 3d multicolored 1.25 .65

Camels, Lion, Men and Slave — A235

Dionysian Procession (Setif Mosaic): 1.35d, Elephants, tigers and women. Men in tiger-drawn cart. No. 639a has continuous design.

1980, Feb. 16 Photo. *Perf. 11½*

Granite Paper

637 A235 1.20d multi .55 .20
638 A235 1.35d multi .60 .35
639 A235 1.40d multi .65 .55
a. Strip of 3, #637-639 1.80 1.25

Science Day — A236

1980, Apr. 19 Photo. *Perf. 12*

640 A236 60c multicolored .30 .20

Dam and Workers
A237

1980, June 17 Photo. *Perf. 11½*

641 A237 60c multicolored .30 .20

Extraordinary Congress of the National Liberation Front Party.

Olympic Sports, Moscow '80 Emblem
A238

1980, June 28

642 A238 50c Flame, rings, vert. .25 .20
643 A238 1.40d shown .65 .35

22nd Summer Olympic Games, Moscow, July 19-Aug. 3.

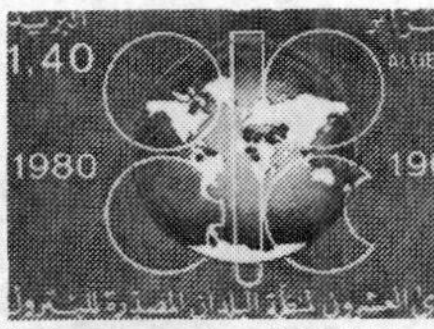

20th Anniversary of OPEC — A239

Perf. 11x10½, 10½x11

1980, Sept. 15 Engr.

644 A239 60c Men holding OPEC emblem, vert. .30 .20
645 A239 1.40d shown .65 .35

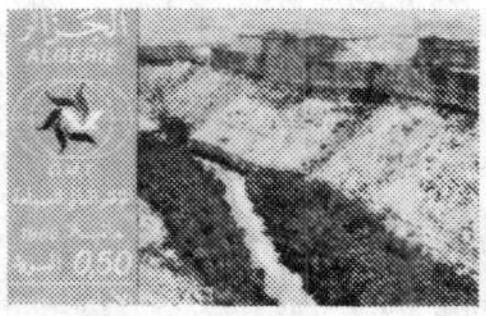

Aures Valley
A240

1980, Sept. 25 Litho. *Perf. 13½x14*

646 A240 50c shown .25 .20
647 A240 1d El Oued Oasis .40 .20
648 A240 1.40d Tassili Rocks .60 .25
649 A240 2d View of Algiers .90 .40
Nos. 646-649 (4) 2.15 1.05

World Tourism Conf., Manila, Sept. 27.

Avicenna (980-1037), Philosopher and Physician
A241

1980, Oct. 25 Photo. *Perf. 12*

650 A241 2d multicolored 1.50 .75

Ruins of El Asnam
A242

1980, Nov. 13 Photo. *Perf. 12*

651 A242 3d multicolored 1.25 .45

Earthquake relief.

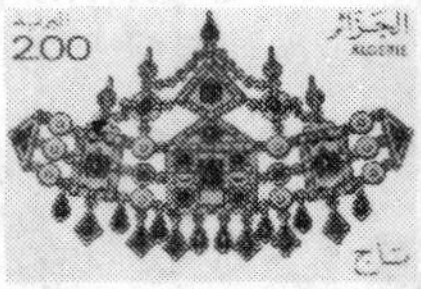

Crown
A243

1980, Dec. 20 Photo. *Perf. 12*

Granite Paper

652 A243 60c Necklace, vert. .30 .20
653 A243 1.40d Earrings, bracelet, vert. .60 .30
654 A243 2d shown .80 .45
Nos. 652-654 (3) 1.70 .95

See Nos. 705-707.

1980-1984 Five-Year Plan — A244

1981, Jan. 29 Litho. *Perf. 14*

655 A244 60c multicolored .25 .20

Basket Weaving — A245

1981, Feb. 19 Photo. *Perf. 12½*

Granite Paper

656 A245 40c shown .20 .20
657 A245 60c Rug weaving .30 .20
658 A245 1d Coppersmith .40 .20
659 A245 1.40d Jeweler .60 .30
Nos. 656-659 (4) 1.50 .90

Cedar Tree — A246

Arbor Day: 1.40d, Cypress tree, vert.

1981, Mar. 19 Photo. *Perf. 12*

Granite Paper

660 A246 60c multi .30 .20
661 A246 1.40d multi .60 .30

Mohamed Bachir el Ibrahimi (1869-1965) A247

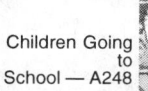

Children Going to School — A248

1981, Apr. 16
Granite Paper

662 A247 60c multicolored .25 .20
663 A248 60c multicolored .25 .20

Science Day.

12th International Hydatidological Congress, Algiers — A249

1981, Apr. 23 ***Perf. 14x13½***

664 A249 2d multicolored .80 .30

13th World Telecommunications Day — A250

1981, May 14 Photo. ***Perf. 14x13½***

665 A250 1.40d multi .60 .20

Disabled People and Hand Offering Flower — A251

Perf. 12½x13, 13x12½
1981, June 20 **Litho.**

666 A251 1.20d Symbolic globe, vert. .55 .20
667 A251 1.40d shown .60 .20

Intl. Year of the Disabled.

Papilio Machaon A252

1981, Aug. 20 Photo. ***Perf. 11½***
Granite Paper

668 A252 60c shown .25 .20
669 A252 1.20d Rhodocera rhamni .55 .20
670 A252 1.40d Charaxes jasius .60 .25
671 A252 2d Papilio podalirius .80 .40
Nos. 668-671 (4) 2.20 1.05

Monk Seal — A253

1981, Sept. 17 ***Perf. 14x13½***

672 A253 60c shown .25 .20
673 A253 1.40d Macaque .60 .35

World Food Day — A254

Cave Drawings of Tassili — A255

1981, Oct. 16 Photo. ***Perf. 14x14½***

674 A254 2d multicolored .65 .35

1981, Nov. 21 ***Perf. 11½***

Designs: Various cave drawings. 1.60d, 2d horiz.

675 A255 60c multi .30 .20
676 A255 1d multi .50 .20
677 A255 1.60d multi .75 .35
678 A255 2d multi .90 .40
Nos. 675-678 (4) 2.45 1.15

Galley, 17-18th Cent. A256

1981, Dec. 17 Photo. ***Perf. 11½***

679 A256 60c shown .40 .20
680 A256 1.60d Ship, diff. .90 .35

1982 World Cup Soccer A257

Designs: Various soccer players.

Perf. 13x12½x 12½x13
1982, Feb. 25 **Litho.**

681 A257 80c multi, vert. .35 .20
682 A257 2.80d multi 1.10 .50

TB Bacillus Centenary A258

1982, Mar. 20 Photo. ***Perf. 14½x14***

683 A258 80c multi .35 .20

Painted Stand A259

1982, Apr. 24 Photo. ***Perf. 11½***
Granite Paper

684 A259 80c Mirror, vert. .30 .20
685 A259 2d shown .75 .40

Size: 48x33mm

686 A259 2.40d Chest .90 .55
Nos. 684-686 (3) 1.95 1.15

Djamaael Djadid Mosque, Algiers — A260

1982, May 15 Litho. ***Perf. 14***

687 A260 80c shown .30 .20
688 A260 2.40d Sidi Boumediene Mosque, Tlemcen .80 .50
689 A260 3d Garden of Dey, Algiers 1.00 .55
Nos. 687-689 (3) 2.10 1.25

See Nos. 731-734, 745-747, 774, 778-783.

Callitris Articulata — A261

Independence, 20th Anniv. — A262

Designs: Medicinal plants.

1982, May 27 Photo. ***Perf. 11½***
Granite Paper

690 A261 50c shown .25 .20
691 A261 80c Artemisia herba-alba .30 .20
692 A261 1d Ricinus communis .60 .20
693 A261 2.40d Thymus fontanesii 1.10 .45
Nos. 690-693 (4) 2.25 1.05

1982, July 5
Granite Paper

694 A262 50c Riflemen .20 .20
695 A262 80c Soldiers, horiz. .35 .20
696 A262 2d Symbols, citizens, horiz. .80 .45
Nos. 694-696 (3) 1.35 .85

Souvenir Sheet

697 A262 5d Emblem 2.25 2.25

No. 697 contains one 32x39mm stamp.

Soummam Congress A263

1982, Aug. 20 **Litho.**

698 A263 80c Congress building .35 .20

Scouting Year — A264

1982, Oct. 21 **Photo.**
Granite Paper

699 A264 2.80d multi 1.00 .45

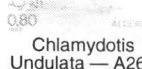

Palestinian Child — A265

Chlamydotis Undulata — A266

1982, Nov. 25 Litho. ***Perf. 10½***

700 A265 1.60d multi 3.00 .75

Perf. 15x14, 14x15
1982, Dec. 23 **Photo.**

Protected birds. 50c, 2d horiz.

701 A266 50c Geronticus eremita .40 .20
702 A266 80c shown .65 .20
703 A266 2d Aguila rapax 1.25 .40
704 A266 2.40d Gypaetus barbatus 1.75 .45
Nos. 701-704 (4) 4.05 1.25

Jewelry Type of 1980

1983, Feb. 10 ***Perf. 11½***
Granite Paper

705 A243 50c Picture frame .20 .20
706 A243 1d Flaska .35 .25
707 A243 2d Brooch, horiz. .65 .45
Nos. 705-707 (3) 1.20 .90

A267

A268

1983, Mar. 17 **Photo.**
Granite Paper

708 A267 80c Abies numidica, vert. .25 .20
709 A267 2.80d Acacia raddiana .75 .60

Intl. Arbor Day.

Perf. 12x12½, 12½x12
1983, Apr. 21 **Photo.**

Various minerals. 1.20d, 2.40d horiz.

Granite Paper

710 A268 70c multi .30 .20
711 A268 80c multi .35 .20
712 A268 1.20d multi .50 .30
713 A268 2.40d multi 1.00 .60
Nos. 710-713 (4) 2.15 1.30

30th Anniv. of Intl. Customs Cooperation Council A269

1983, May 14 Photo. ***Perf. 11½***
Granite Paper

714 A269 80c multi .35 .20

Emir Abdelkader Death Centenary — A270

1983, May 22 Photo. ***Perf. 12***
Granite Paper

715 A270 4d multi 1.60 .75

A271

A272

Local mushrooms.

1983, July 21 ***Perf. 14x15***

716 A271 50c Amanita muscaria .25 .20
717 A271 80c Amanita phalloides .50 .25
718 A271 1.40d Pleurotus eryngii 1.00 .50
719 A271 2.80d Tefezia leonis 2.25 1.00
Nos. 716-719 (4) 4.00 1.95

1983, Sept. 1 Photo. ***Perf. 11½***

720 A272 80c multi .35 .20

ibn-Khaldun, historian, philosopher.

World Communications Year — A273

Perf. 11½x12½

1983, Sept. 22 Litho.

721 A273 80c Post Office, Algiers .35 .20
722 A273 2.40d Telephone, circuit box 1.00 .40

Goat and Tassili Mountains A274

1983, Oct. 20 Litho. ***Perf. 12½x13***

723 A274 50c shown .20 .20
724 A274 80c Tuaregs in native costume .30 .20
725 A274 2.40d Animals, rock painting 1.00 .40
726 A274 2.80d Rock formation 1.00 .60
Nos. 723-726 (4) 2.50 1.40

Sloughi Dog — A275

Perf. 14x14½, 14½x14

1983, Nov. 24 Photo.

727 A275 80c shown .60 .40
728 A275 2.40d Sloughi, horiz. 1.50 .75

Natl. Liberation Party, 5th Congress — A276

1983, Dec. 19 Photo. ***Perf. 11½***

729 A276 80c Symbols of development .35 .25

Souvenir Sheet

730 A276 5d Emblem 3.00 2.50

No. 730 contains one 32x38mm stamp.

View Type of 1982

1984, Jan. 26 Litho. ***Perf. 14***

731 A260 10c View of Oran, 1830 .20 .20
732 A260 1d Sidi Abderahman and Taalibi Mosques .40 .20
733 A260 2d Bejaia, 1830 .80 .35
734 A260 4d Constantine, 1830 2.00 .60
Nos. 731-734 (4) 3.40 1.35

See Nos. 745-747, 781, 783.

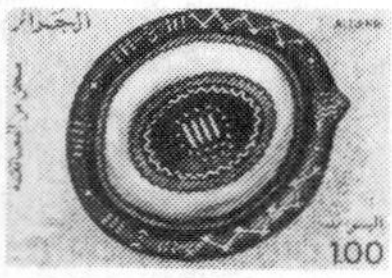
Pottery A278

Perf. 11½x12, 12x11½

1984, Feb. 23 Photo.

Granite Paper

735 A278 80c Jug, vert. .35 .20
736 A278 1d Platter .50 .25
737 A278 2d Oil lamp, vert. 1.00 .45
738 A278 2.40d Pitcher 1.50 .60
Nos. 735-738 (4) 3.35 1.50

Fountains of Old Algiers A279

1984 Summer Olympics A280

Various fountains.

1984, Mar. 22 Photo. ***Perf. 11½***

Granite Paper

739 A279 50c multi .20 .20
740 A279 80c multi .35 .20
741 A279 2.40d multi 1.00 .60
Nos. 739-741 (3) 1.55 1.00

1984, May 19 Photo. ***Perf. 11½***

Granite Paper

742 A280 1d multi .45 .30

Brown Stallion A281

1984, June 14 Photo. ***Perf. 11½***

Granite Paper

743 A281 80c shown .35 .20
744 A281 2.40d White mare 1.00 .60

View Type of 1982

1984 Litho. ***Perf. 14***

745 A260 5c Mustapha Pacha .20 .20
746 A260 20c Bab Azzoun .20 .20
746A A260 30c Algiers .20 .20
746B A260 40c Kolea .20 .20
746C A260 50c Algiers .20 .20
747 A260 70c Mostaganem .35 .20
Nos. 745-747 (6) 1.35 1.20

Issued: #745, 746, 747, 7/19; #746A-746C, 10/20.

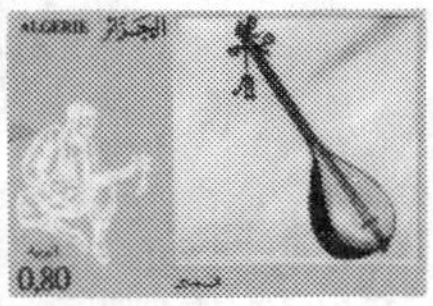
Lute A282

Native musical instruments.

1984, Sept. 22 Litho. ***Perf. 15x14***

748 A282 80c shown .20 .20
749 A282 1d Drum .25 .20
750 A282 2.40d Fiddle .60 .35
751 A282 2.80d Bagpipe .70 .40
Nos. 748-751 (4) 1.75 1.15

30th Anniv. of Algerian Revolution — A284

1984, Nov. 3 Photo. ***Perf. 11½x12***

757 A284 80c Partisans .20 .20

Souvenir Sheet

758 A284 5d Algerian flags, vert. 2.00 1.00

M'Zab Valley A285

1984, Dec. 15 ***Perf. 15x14, 14x15***

759 A285 80c Map of valley .20 .20
760 A285 2.40d Town of M'Zab, vert. .50 .30

18th and 19th Century Metalware — A286

1985, Jan. 26 Photo. ***Perf. 11½***

761 A286 80c Coffee pot .20 .20
762 A286 2d Bowl, horiz. .50 .25
763 A286 2.40d Covered bowl .65 .30
Nos. 761-763 (3) 1.35 .75

Fish A287

1985, Feb. 23 Photo. ***Perf. 15x14***

764 A287 50c Thunnus thynnus .20 .20
765 A287 80c Sparus aurata .20 .20
766 A287 2.40d Epinephelus guaza .60 .30
767 A287 2.80d Mustelus mustelus .65 .35
Nos. 764-767 (4) 1.65 1.05

National Games — A288

1985, Mar. 28 ***Perf. 11½x12***

Granite Paper

768 A288 80c Doves, emblem .20 .20

Environmental Conservation — A289

1985, Apr. 25 ***Perf. 13½***

769 A289 80c Stylized trees .20 .20
770 A289 1.40d Stylized waves .35 .20

View Type of 1982 and

The Casbah A290

View of Constantine A290a

Street Scene in Algiers — A290b

Designs: 2.50d, Djamaael Djadid Mosque, Algiers. 2.90d, like #746. 5d, like #746A. 1.50d, like #746B. 4.20d, like #764.

Perf. 13½x12½, 13 (#774, 4.20d),
Perf. 13½x14 (#775)
Perf. 14½x14 (2d)

Photo., Litho. (2d, 6,20d, 7.50d, #775)

1985-94

771 A290 20c dk blue & buff .20 .20
772 A290 80c sage grn & buff .20 .20
773 A290a 1d dk olive grn .50 .25
a. Bklt. pane of 5 + label 2.50
774 A260 1.50d dull red .55 .30
775 A290b 1.50d red brown & brn .25 .20
a. Booklet pane of 6 1.50
776 A290b 2d dk blue & lt blue .20 .20
a. Booklet pane of 5 + label .95
777 A290 2.40d chestnut & buff .60 .30
a. Bklt. pane of 5 (20c, 3 80c, 2.40d) + label 1.40
778 A260 2.50d bluish green 1.00 .50
779 A260 2.90d slate 1.15 .60
780 A260 4.20d gray green 1.60 .85
781 A260 5d deep bister & black 2.00 1.00

Perf. 14

782 A260 6.20d like #731 1.00 .50
783 A260 7.50d like #745 1.25 .65
Nos. 771-783 (13) 10.50 5.75

Nos. 771-772, 777 issued only in booklet panes.

Issued: 20c, 80c, 2.40d, 6/1/85; 1d, 1/26/89; 2.50d, 2.90d, 5d, 2/23/89; #774, 4.20d, 3/21/91; #775, 5/20/92; 6.20d, 7.50d, 4/22/92; 2d, 10/21/93; #776a, 10/21/94.

See No. 1010.

UN, 40th Anniv. — A291

Natl. Youth Festival — A292

1985, June 26 Photo. ***Perf. 14***

784 A291 1d Dove, emblem, 40 .25 .20

1985, July 5 Litho. ***Perf. 13½***

785 A292 80c multicolored .25 .20

Intl. Youth Year — A293

1985, July 5

786 A293 80c Silhouette, globe, emblem, vert. .25 .20
787 A293 1.40d Doves, globe .45 .20

World Map, OPEC — A294

Perf. 12½x13

1985, Sept. 14 **Photo.**

788 A294 80c multicolored .25 .20

Organization of Petroleum Exporting Countries, 25th anniv.

Family Planning A295

El-Meniaa Township A296

1985, Oct. 3 **Litho.** ***Perf. 14***

789 A295 80c Mother and sons .20 .20
790 A295 1.40d Weighing infant .35 .20
791 A295 1.70d Breast-feeding .45 .20
Nos. 789-791 (3) 1.00 .60

1985, Oct. 24 **Engr.** ***Perf. 13***

792 A296 80c Chetaibi Bay, horiz. .20 .20
793 A296 2d shown .50 .25
794 A296 2.40d Bou Noura Town, horiz. .65 .30
Nos. 792-794 (3) 1.35 .75

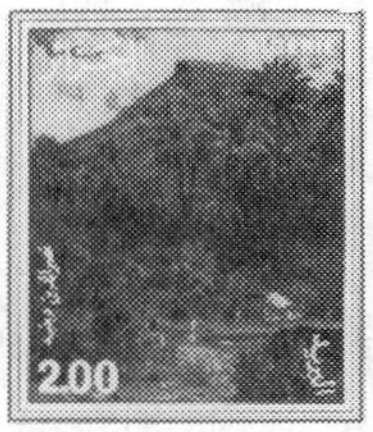
The Palm Grove, by N. Dinet — A297

1985, Nov. 21 **Photo.** ***Perf. 11½x12***
Granite Paper

795 A297 2d multi .50 .25
796 A297 3d multi, diff. .85 .40

Tapestries A298

Various designs.

1985, Dec. 19
Granite Paper

797 A298 80c multi .20 .20
798 A298 1.40d multi .40 .20
799 A298 2.40d multi .60 .30
800 A298 2.80d multi .75 .40
Nos. 797-800 (4) 1.95 1.10

Wildcats A299

1986, Jan. 23 ***Perf. 12x11½, 11½x12***
Granite Paper

801 A299 80c Felis margarita .50 .20
802 A299 1d Felis caracal .70 .20
803 A299 2d Felis sylvestris 1.40 .80
804 A299 2.40d Felis serval, vert. 1.90 .95
Nos. 801-804 (4) 4.50 2.15

UN Child Survival Campaign A300

Algerian General Worker's Union, 30th Anniv. A301

1986, Feb. 13 **Litho.** ***Perf. 13½***

805 A300 80c Oral vaccine .25 .20
806 A300 1.40d Mother, child, sun .60 .25
807 A300 1.70d Three children 1.00 .35
Nos. 805-807 (3) 1.85 .80

1986, Feb. 24 ***Perf. 12½***
Granite Paper

808 A301 2d multi .50 .25

National Charter A302

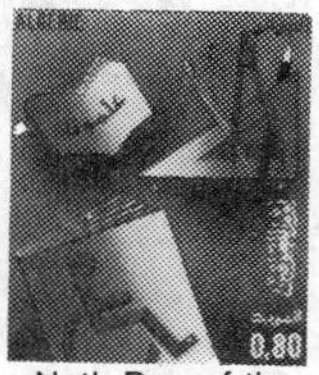
Natl. Day of the Disabled A303

1986, Mar. 6 **Photo.** ***Perf. 11½***
Granite Paper

809 A302 4d multi 1.00 .45

1986, Mar. 15 ***Perf. 12½x13***

810 A303 80c multi .20 .20

A304

A305

1986, Apr. 17 **Litho.** ***Perf. 14x15***

811 A304 80c multi .20 .20

Anti-Tuberculosis campaign.

1986, Apr. 24 ***Perf. 14***

812 A305 2d Soccer ball, sombrero .50 .25
813 A305 2.40d Soccer players .65 .30

1986 World Cup Soccer Championships, Mexico.

Inner Courtyards A306

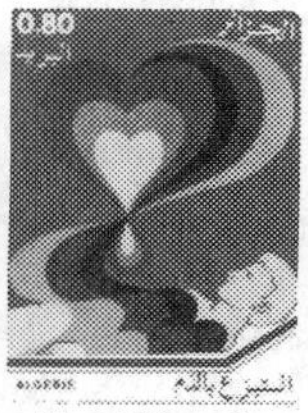
Blood Donation Campaign A307

1986, May 15 **Photo.** ***Perf. 11½***
Granite Paper

814 A306 80c multi .20 .20
815 A306 2.40d multi, diff. .65 .30
816 A306 3d multi, diff. .80 .40
Nos. 814-816 (3) 1.65 .90

1986, June 26 **Litho.** ***Perf. 13½***

817 A307 80c multi .25 .20

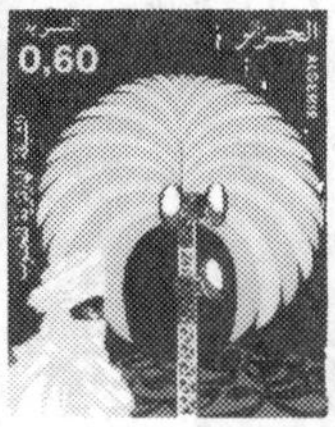
Southern District Radio Communication Inauguration A308

1986, July ***Perf. 13***

818 A308 60c multi .20 .20

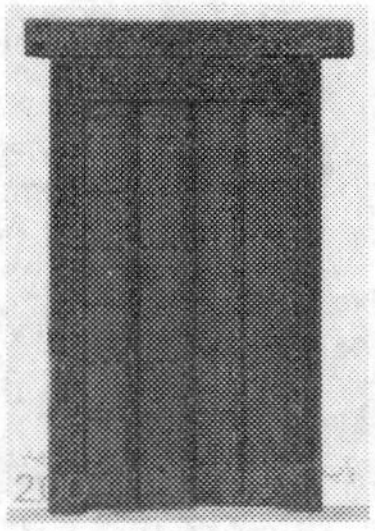
Mosque Gateways A309

Perf. 12x11½

1986, Sept. 27 **Photo.**
Granite Paper

819 A309 2d Door .50 .25
820 A309 2.40d Ornamental arch .65 .30

Intl. Peace Year — A310

Perf. 13½x14½

1986, Oct. 16 **Photo.**

821 A310 2.40d multi .65 .30

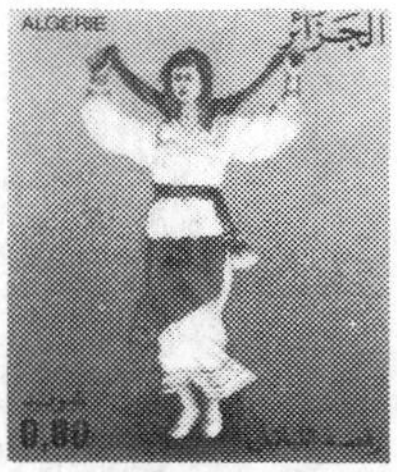
Folk Dancing A311

1986, Nov. 22 **Litho.** ***Perf. 14x13½***

822 A311 80c Woman, scarf .25 .20
823 A311 2.40d Woman, diff. .65 .30
824 A311 2.80d Man, sword .70 .40
Nos. 822-824 (3) 1.60 .90

Flowers — A312

1986, Dec. 18 **Photo.** ***Perf. 14***

825 A312 80c Narcissus tazetta .25 .20
826 A312 1.40d Iris unguicularis .40 .20
827 A312 2.40d Capparis spinosa .65 .30
828 A312 2.80d Gladiolus segetum .70 .40
Nos. 825-828 (4) 2.00 1.10

See Nos. 936-938.

Abstract Paintings by Mohammed Issia Khem A313

Perf. 11½x12, 12x11½

1987, Jan. 29 **Litho.**

829 A313 2d Man and woman, vert. .65 .35
830 A313 5d Man and books 1.60 .80

Jewelry from Aures A314

1987, Feb. 27 **Photo.** ***Perf. 12***
Granite Paper

831 A314 1d Earrings .35 .20
832 A314 1.80d Bracelets .60 .30
833 A314 2.90d Nose rings 1.00 .50
834 A314 3.30d Necklace 1.10 .55
Nos. 831-834 (4) 3.05 1.55

Nos. 831-833 vert.

Petroglyphs, Atlas — A315

1987, Mar. 26 **Litho.** ***Perf. 12x11½***
Granite Paper

835 A315 1d Man and woman .35 .20
836 A315 2.90d Goat 1.00 .50
837 A315 3.30d Horse, bull 1.10 .60
Nos. 835-837 (3) 2.45 1.30

Syringe as an Umbrella — A316

1987, Apr. 7 ***Perf. 11½***
Granite Paper

838 A316 1d multi .35 .20

Child Immunization Campaign, World Health Day.

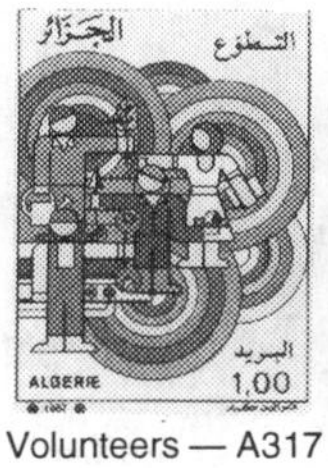
Volunteers — A317

Third General Census — A318

1987, Apr. 23 ***Perf. 10½***

839 A317 1d multi .35 .20

1987, May 21 ***Perf. 13½***

840 A318 1d multi .35 .20

Algerian Postage, 25th Anniv. — A319

War Orphans' Fund label (1fr + 9fr) of 1962.

1987, July 5 Photo. *Perf. 11½x12*
Granite Paper
841 A319 1.80d multi .60 .30

A320

A321

1987, July 5
Granite Paper
842 A320 1d multi .35 .20
Souvenir Sheet
843 A321 5d multi 1.75 1.60
Natl. independence, 25th anniv.

Amateur Theater Festival, Mostaganem A322

1987, July 20 *Perf. 12x11½*
Granite Paper
844 A322 1d Actors on stage .35 .20
845 A322 1.80d Theater .60 .30
a. Pair, #844-845 1.00 .50
No. 845a has continuous design.

Mediterranean Games, Latakia — A323

1987, Aug. 6 *Perf. 13x12½, 12½x13*
846 A323 1d Discus .35 .20
847 A323 2.90d Tennis, vert. 1.00 .50
848 A323 3.30d Team handball 1.50 .55
Nos. 846-848 (3) 2.85 1.25

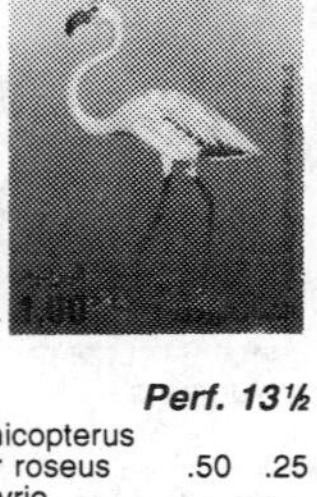

Birds — A324

1987 Litho. *Perf. 13½*
849 A324 1d Phoenicopterus ruber roseus .50 .25
850 A324 1.80d Porphyrio porphyrio .90 .50
851 A324 2.50d Elanus caeruleus 1.25 .65
852 A324 2.90d Milvus milvus 1.50 .75
Nos. 849-852 (4) 4.15 2.15

Agriculture A325

Perf. 10½x11, 11x10½
1987, Nov. 26 Litho.
853 A325 1d Planting .35 .20
854 A325 1d Reservoir .35 .20
855 A325 1d Harvesting crop, vert. .35 .20
856 A325 1d Produce, vert. .35 .20
Nos. 853-856 (4) 1.40 .80

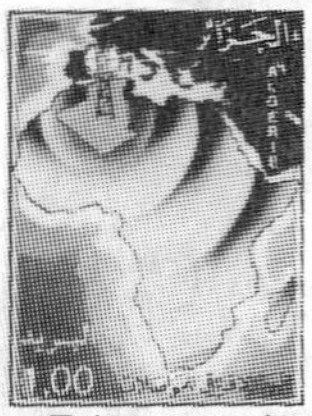

African Telecommunications Day — A326

1987, Dec. 7 *Perf. 10½*
857 A326 1d multi .35 .20

Transportation — A327

1987, Dec. 18 Litho. *Perf. 10½x11*
858 A327 2.90d shown 1.00 .50
859 A327 3.30d Diesel train 1.10 .55

Algerian Universities A328

Various campuses.

Perf. 10½x11, 11x10½
1987, Dec. 26
860 A328 1d shown .35 .20
861 A328 2.50d multi, diff. 1.00 .40
862 A328 2.90d multi, diff. 1.50 .50
863 A328 3.30d multi, diff., vert. 1.75 .55
Nos. 860-863 (4) 4.60 1.65

Intl. Rural Development Fund, 10th Anniv. A329

1988, Jan. 27 *Perf. 10½x11*
864 A329 1d multi .50 .25

Autonomy of State-owned Utilities — A330

1988, Feb. 27 Litho. *Perf. 11x10½*
865 A330 1d multi .50 .25

Intl. Women's Day — A331

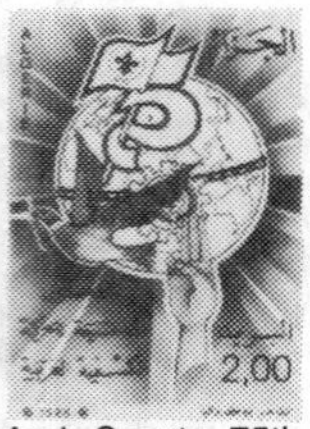

Arab Scouts, 75th Anniv. — A332

1988, Mar. 10 Litho. *Perf. 11x10½*
866 A331 1d multi .50 .25

1988, Apr. 7 Litho. *Perf. 10½*
867 A332 2d multi .95 .50

1988 Summer Olympics, Seoul — A333

Hot Springs — A334

1988, July 23 Litho. *Perf. 10½*
868 A333 2.90d multi 1.40 .70

1988, July 16
869 A334 1d shown .50 .25
870 A334 2.90d Caverns, horiz. 1.40 .70
871 A334 3.30d Gazebo, fountain, horiz. 1.60 .80
Nos. 869-871 (3) 3.50 1.75

World Wildlife Fund — A335

Barbary apes, *Macaca sylvanus.*

1988, Sept. 17 Litho. *Perf. 10½*
872 A335 50c Adult .25 .20
873 A335 90c Family .45 .25
874 A335 1d Close-up, vert. .50 .25
875 A335 1.80d Seated on branch, vert. .90 .45
Nos. 872-875 (4) 2.10 1.15

Intl. Literacy Day — A336

WHO, 40th Anniv. — A337

1988, Sept. 10 Photo. *Perf. 10½*
876 A336 2.90d multi 1.40 .70

1988, Oct. 15
877 A337 2.90d multi 1.40 .70

Fight Apartheid A338

1988, Nov. 19 Litho. *Perf. 10½x11*
878 A338 2.50d multi 1.25 .60

Natl. Front Congress — A339

1988, Nov. 29 *Perf. 11x10½*
879 A339 1d multi .50 .25

Agriculture A340

1988, Dec. 24 *Perf. 10½*
880 A340 1d Irrigation .50 .25
881 A340 1d Orchard, fields, livestock .50 .25

Natl. Goals — A342

Airports — A343

1989, Mar. 9 Litho. *Perf. 11½*
Granite Paper
886 A342 1d shown .50 .25
887 A342 1d Ancient fort .50 .25
888 A342 1d Telecommunications .50 .25
889 A342 1d Modern buildings .50 .25
Nos. 886-889 (4) 2.00 1.00
Nos. 887-889 horiz.

Perf. 10½x11, 11x10½
1989, Mar. 23
890 A343 2.90d Oran Es Senia, horiz. 1.25 .70
891 A343 3.30d Tebessa, horiz. 1.50 .80
892 A343 5d shown 2.25 1.25
Nos. 890-892 (3) 5.00 2.75

Development of the South — A344

1989, Apr. 24 Litho. *Perf. 13½*
893 A344 1d Irrigation .45 .25
894 A344 1.80d Building .90 .45
895 A344 2.50d Fossil fuel extraction, vert. 1.25 .60
Nos. 893-895 (3) 2.60 1.30

Eradicate Locusts A345

1989, May 25 *Perf. 10½*
896 A345 1d multi .50 .25

National Service — A346

1989, May 11 Litho. *Perf. 13½*

897 A346 2d multicolored .80 .40

1st Moon Landing, 20th Anniv. A347

4d, Astronaut, lunar module, Moon's surface.

1989, July 23 Litho. *Perf. 13½*

898 A347 2.90d shown 1.00 .55
899 A347 4d multi, vert. 1.40 .75

Interparliamentary Union, Cent. — A348

1989, Sept. 4 *Perf. 10½*

900 A348 2.90d gold, brt rose lil & blk 1.10 .55

Produce A349

1989, Sept. 23 Litho. *Perf. 11½*
Granite Paper

901 Strip of 3 4.00 2.00
a. A349 2d multi, diff. .75 .40
b. A349 3d multi, diff. 1.10 .55
c. A349 5d shown 2.00 1.00

Fish — A350

1989, Oct. 27 Litho. *Perf. 13½*

902 A350 1d *Sarda sarda* .30 .20
903 A350 1.80d *Zeus faber* .50 .35
904 A350 2.90d *Pagellus bogaraveo* .90 .55
905 A350 3.30d *Xiphias gladius* 1.00 .65
Nos. 902-905 (4) 2.70 1.75

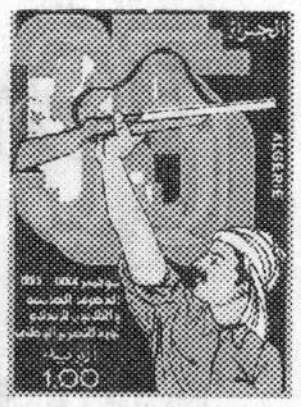

Algerian Revolution, 35th Anniv. — A351

1989, Nov. 4 Litho. *Perf. 13½*

906 A351 1d multicolored .40 .20

African Development Bank, 25th Anniv. A352

Mushrooms A353

1989, Nov. 18 *Perf. 10½*

907 A352 1d multicolored .40 .20

1989, Dec. 16 *Perf. 13½*

908 A353 1d *Boletus satanas* .30 .20
909 A353 1.80d *Psalliota xanthoderma* .60 .35
910 A353 2.90d *Lepiota procera* 1.00 .55
911 A353 3.30d *Lactarius deliciosus* 1.10 .65
Nos. 908-911 (4) 3.00 1.75

A354

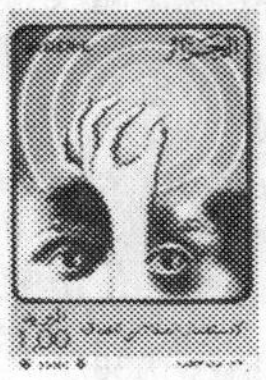

A355

1990, Jan. 18 Litho. *Perf. 10½*

912 A354 1d multicolored .40 .20

Pan-African Postal Union, 10th anniv.

1990, Feb. 22 Litho. *Perf. 14*

913 A355 1d Energy conservation .25 .20

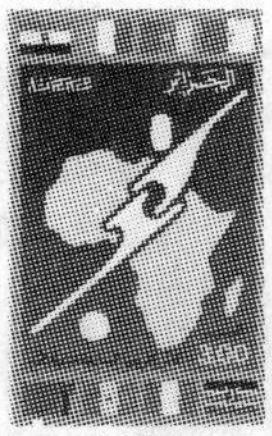

A356

A357

1990, Mar. 2 Photo. *Perf. 11½*

914 A356 3d multicolored .65 .30

African Soccer Championships.

1990, May 17 Litho. *Perf. 13½*

917 A357 2.90d shown .75 .40
918 A357 5d Trophy 1.25 .65

World Cup Soccer Championships, Italy.

Rural Electrification — A358

1990, June 21

919 A358 2d multicolored .50 .25

Youth A359

Youth Holding Rainbow — A360

1990, July 6 *Perf. 13½*

920 A359 2d multicolored .50 .25
921 A360 3d multicolored .75 .35

Maghreb Arab Union — A361

1990 *Perf. 14x13½*

922 A361 1d multicolored .40 .20

Vocations A362

1990, Apr. 26 Litho. *Perf. 12½*

923 A362 2d Craftsmen .75 .40
924 A362 2.90d Auto mechanics 1.10 .60
925 A362 3.30d Deep sea fishing 1.25 .65
Nos. 923-925 (3) 3.10 1.65

Organization of Petroleum Exporting Countries (OPEC), 30th Anniv. A363

1990 *Perf. 13½*

926 A363 2d multicolored .75 .40

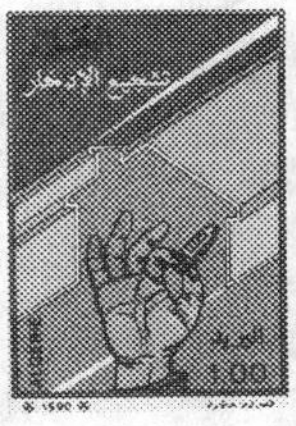

Savings Promotion — A364

1990, Oct. 31 Litho. *Perf. 14*

927 A364 1d multicolored .20 .20

Namibian Independence — A365

1990, Nov. 8

928 A365 3d multicolored .60 .50

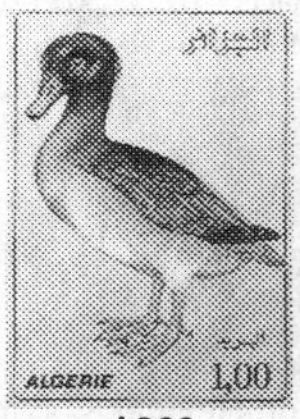

A366

A367

Farm animals.

1990, Nov. 29 *Perf. 13½*

929 A366 1d Duck .35 .20
930 A366 2d Rabbit, horiz. .65 .40
931 A366 2.90d Turkey 1.00 .60
932 A366 3d Rooster, horiz. 1.00 .60
Nos. 929-932 (4) 3.00 1.80

1990, Dec. 11

933 A367 1d multicolored .25 .20

Anti-French Riots, 30th anniv.

A368

A369

1990, Dec. 20 *Perf. 14*

934 A368 1d multicolored .25 .20

Fight against respiratory diseases.

1991, Feb. 24 Litho. *Perf. 13½*

935 A369 1d multicolored .25 .20

Constitution, 2nd anniv.

Flower Type of 1986

1991, May 23 Litho. *Perf. 13½*
Size: 26x36mm

936 A312 2d Jasminum fruticans .60 .30
937 A312 4d Dianthus crinitus 1.10 .65
938 A312 5d Cyclamen africanum 1.50 .85
Nos. 936-938 (3) 3.20 1.80

Children's Drawings A370

1991, June 3 Litho. *Perf. 13½*

939 A370 3d shown 1.00 .50
940 A370 4d Children playing 1.25 .65

Maghreb Arab Union Summit — A371

1991, June 10
941 A371 1d multicolored .30 .20

Geneva Convention on Refugees, 40th Anniv. — A372

Perf. 14½x13½
1991, July 28 **Litho.**
942 A372 3d multicolored 1.00 .50

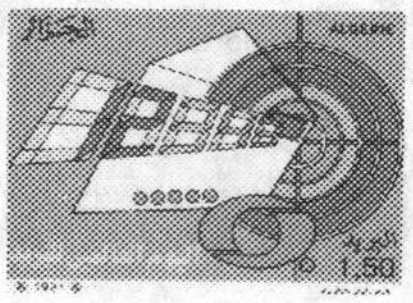

Postal Service A373

1991, Oct. 12 ***Perf. 14***
943 A373 1.50d shown .55 .25
944 A373 4.20d Expo emblem, vert. 1.50 .75

Telecom '91, 6th World Forum and Exposition on Telecommunications, Geneva, Switzerland (No. 944).

Butterflies A374

1991, Nov. 21 **Litho.** ***Perf. 11½***
Granite Paper
945 A374 2d Zerynthia rumina .30 .20
946 A374 4d Melitaea didyma .65 .30
947 A374 6d Vanessa atalanta 1.00 .50
948 A374 7d Nymphalis polychloros 1.10 .55
Nos. 945-948 (4) 3.05 1.55

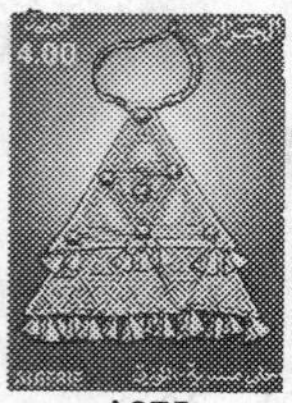

A375

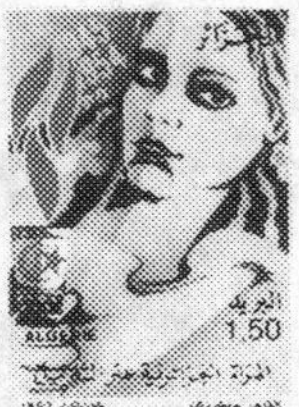

A376

1991, Dec. 21 ***Perf. 12***
Granite Paper
949 A375 3d Necklace .40 .25
950 A375 4d Jewelry of Southern Tuaregs .60 .30
951 A375 5d Brooch .70 .40
952 A375 7d Rings, horiz. 1.00 .55
Nos. 949-952 (4) 2.70 1.50

1992, Mar. 8 **Litho.** ***Perf. 14***
953 A376 1.50d Algerian Women .20 .20

Gazelles A377

Designs: 1.50d, Gazella dorcas. 6.20d, Gazella cuvieri. 8.60d, Gazella dama.

1992, May 13 ***Perf. 14½x13***
954 A377 1.50d multicolored .25 .20
955 A377 6.20d multicolored .95 .50
956 A377 8.60d multicolored 1.25 .65
Nos. 954-956 (3) 2.45 1.35

1992 Summer Olympics, Barcelona A379

1992, June 24 **Litho.** ***Perf. 14***
958 A379 6.20d Runners 1.00 .55

A381

A382

1992, July 7 **Litho.** ***Perf. 14***
960 A381 5d multicolored .90 .45

Independence, 30th anniv.

1992, Sept. 23 **Litho.** ***Perf. 14***

Designs: Medicinal plants.

961 A382 1.50d Ajuga iva .20 .20
962 A382 5.10d Rhamnus alaternus .60 .35
963 A382 6.20d Silybum marianum .70 .40
964 A382 8.60d Lavandula stoechas 1.00 .55
Nos. 961-964 (4) 2.50 1.50

Post Office Modernization A383

1992, Oct. 10 **Litho.** ***Perf. 14***
965 A383 1.50d multicolored .20 .20

Marine Life — A384

Designs: 1.50d, Hippocampus hippocampus. 2.70d, Caretta caretta. 6.20d, Muraena helena. 7.50d, Palinurus elephas.

1992, Dec. 23
966 A384 1.50d multicolored .20 .20
967 A384 2.70d multicolored .35 .20
968 A384 6.20d multicolored .85 .40
969 A384 7.50d multicolored 1.00 .50
Nos. 966-969 (4) 2.40 1.30

Pres. Mohammad Boudiaf (1919-92) — A385

1992, Nov. 3 **Litho.** ***Perf. 11½***
Granite Paper
970 A385 2d green & multi .30 .20
971 A385 8.60d blue & multi 1.10 .55

Coins A386

1992, Dec. 16 **Litho.** ***Perf. 11½***
Granite Paper
972 A386 1.50d Numidia, 2nd cent. BC .20 .20
973 A386 2d Dinar, 14th cent. .30 .20
974 A386 5.10d Dinar, 11th cent. .65 .35
975 A386 6.20d Abdelkader, 19th cent. .85 .40
Nos. 972-975 (4) 2.00 1.15

Door Knockers A387

Flowering Trees A388

1993, Feb. 17 **Litho.** ***Perf. 14***
976 A387 2d Algiers .30 .20
977 A387 5.60d Constantine .75 .40
978 A387 8.60d Tlemcen 1.10 .60
Nos. 976-978 (3) 2.15 1.20

Perf. 12x11½, 11½x12
1993, Mar. 17
Granite Paper
979 A388 4.50d Neflier (medlar), horiz. .50 .30
980 A388 8.60d Cognassier (quince) 1.00 .60
981 A388 11d Abricotier (apricot) 1.25 .75
Nos. 979-981 (3) 2.75 1.65

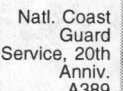

Natl. Coast Guard Service, 20th Anniv. A389

1993, Apr. 3 **Litho.** ***Perf. 14***
982 A389 2d multicolored .30 .20

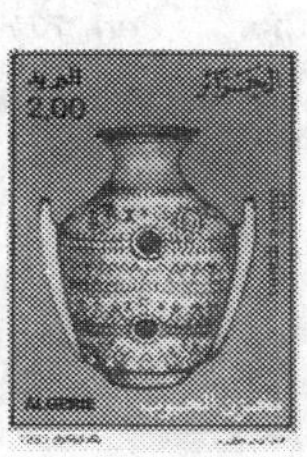

Traditional Grain Processing — A390

1993, May 19 **Litho.** ***Perf. 14***
983 A390 2d Container .25 .20
984 A390 5.60d Millstone .75 .40
985 A390 8.60d Press 1.00 .55
Nos. 983-985 (3) 2.00 1.15

Royal Mausoleums A391

1993, June 16 **Litho.** ***Perf. 14***
986 A391 8.60d Mauretania 1.10 .60
987 A391 12d El Khroub 1.60 .80

Ports A392

1993, Oct. 20 **Litho.** ***Perf. 14x13½***
988 A392 2d Annaba .20 .20
989 A392 8.60d Arzew 1.00 .55

Varanus Griseus A393

Design: 2d, Chamaeleo vulgaris, vert.

Perf. 13½x14, 14x13½
1993, Nov. 20
990 A393 2d multicolored .25 .20
991 A393 8.60d multicolored 1.10 .55

Tourism A394

1993, Dec. 18 **Litho.** ***Perf. 14x13½***
992 A394 2d Tipaza .20 .20
993 A394 8.60d Kerzaz .80 .40

A395

Chahid Day — A396

1994, Jan. 2 ***Perf. 13½x14***
994 A395 2d multicolored .20 .20

SONATRACH (Natl. Society for Research, Transformation, and Commercialization of Hydrocarbons), 30th anniv.

1994, Feb. 18 **Litho.** ***Perf. 13½x14***
995 A396 2d multicolored .20 .20

1994 World Cup Soccer Championships, US — A397

1994, Mar. 16 ***Perf. 14x13½***
996 A397 8.60d multicolored .80 .40

A398

Ancient Petroglyphs A399

Orchids: 5.60d, Orchis simia lam. 8.60d, Ophrys lutea cavan. 11d, Ophrys apifera huds.

1994, Apr. 20 Litho. *Perf. 11½*
Granite Paper

997 A398 5.60d multicolored .55 .30
998 A398 8.60d multicolored .85 .40
999 A398 11d multicolored 1.10 .55
Nos. 997-999 (3) 2.50 1.25

1994, May 21 Litho. *Perf. 13x14*

1000 A399 3d Inscriptions .35 .20
1001 A399 10d Man on horse 1.25 .60

A400

A401

1994, June 25

1002 A400 12d multicolored 1.25 .65

Intl. Olympic Committee, cent.

1994, July 13

1003 A401 3d multicolored .35 .20

World Population Day.

Views of Algiers Type of 1992

Design: 3d, like #775.

1994, July 13 Litho. *Perf. 14*

1010 A290b 3d dk blue & lt blue .35 .20

This is an expanding set. Number may change.

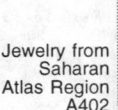

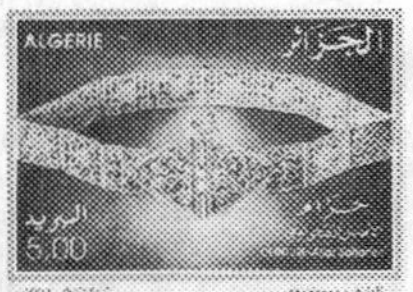

Jewelry from Saharan Atlas Region A402

Perf. 13½x14, 14x13½

1994, Oct. 18 Litho.

1019 A402 3d Fibules, vert. .20 .20
1020 A402 5d Belt .25 .20
1021 A402 12d Bracelets .55 .30
Nos. 1019-1021 (3) 1.00 .70

A403

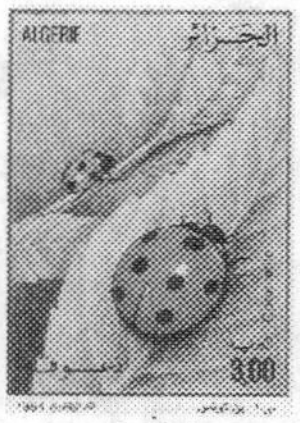

A404

1994, Nov. 3 Litho. *Perf. 13½x14*

1022 A403 3d multicolored .40 .20

Algerian Revolution, 40th anniv.

1994, Nov. 16 Litho. *Perf. 13½x14*

1023 A404 3d Ladybugs .20 .20
1024 A404 12d Beetles .55 .30

Fight Against AIDS A405

1994, Dec. 1 Litho. *Perf. 14x13½*

1025 A405 3d multicolored .38 .20

Folk Dances — A406

Minerals — A407

1994, Dec. 17 Litho. *Perf. 13½x14*

1026 A406 3d Algeroise .20 .20
1027 A406 10d Constantinoise .50 .25
1028 A406 12d Alaoui .55 .30
Nos. 1026-1028 (3) 1.25 .75

1994, Sept. 21

1029 A407 3d Gres lite-erode .20 .20
1030 A407 5d Cipolin .25 .20
1031 A407 10d Marne a turitella .50 .25
Nos. 1029-1031 (3) .95 .65

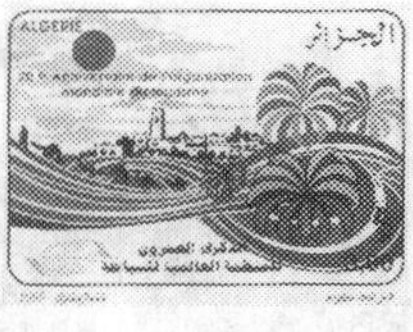

World Tourism Organization, 20th Anniv. A408

1995, Jan. 28 Litho. *Perf. 14x13½*

1032 A408 3d multicolored .35 .20

Honey Bees — A409

Flowers — A410

Perf. 13½x14, 14x13½

1995, Feb. 22

1033 A409 3d shown .35 .20
1034 A409 13d On flower, horiz. 1.50 .75

1995, Mar. 29 Photo. *Perf. 11½*
Granite Paper

1035 A410 3d Dahlias .25 .20
1036 A410 10d Zinnias 1.00 .55
1037 A410 13d Lilacs 1.25 .75
Nos. 1035-1037 (3) 2.50 1.50

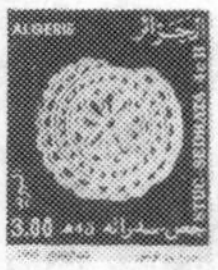

Decorative Stonework — A411

Various patterns.

1995, Apr. 19 *Perf. 14*

1039 A411 3d brown .35 .20
1040 A411 4d green .45 .25
1041 A411 5d deep claret .55 .30
Nos. 1039-1041 (3) 1.35 .75

This is an expanding set. Numbers may change.

End of World War II, 50th Anniv. A413

1995, May 3 *Perf. 14x13½*

1048 A413 3d multicolored .35 .20

Souvenir Sheet

VE Day, 50th Anniv. — A414

Illustration reduced.

1995, May 10 Litho. *Perf. 13½x14*

1049 A414 13d multicolored 1.50 .85

Volleyball, Cent. A415

Environmental Protection A416

1995, June 14

1050 A415 3d multicolored .40 .20

1995, June 5

1051 A416 3d Air, water pollution .35 .20
1052 A416 13d Air pollution 1.50 .85

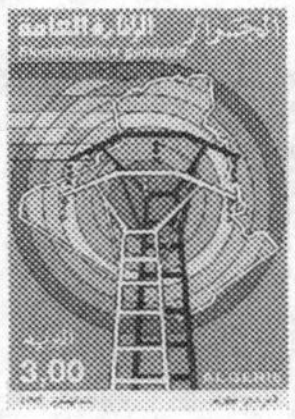

General Electrification A417

1995, July 5 Litho. *Perf. 13½x14*

1053 A417 3d multicolored .45 .20

UN, 50th Anniv. A418

1995, Oct. 24 *Perf. 14x13½*

1054 A418 13d multicolored 2.00 1.00

Pottery — A419

10d, Pot, Lakhdaria. 20d, Pitcher, Aokas. 21d, Jar, Larbaa Nath Iraten. 30d, Vase, Ouadhia.

1995, Nov. 14 Litho. *Perf. 14*

1055 A419 10d dark brown 1.50 .75
1056 A419 20d dull maroon 3.00 1.50
1057 A419 21d golden brown 3.25 1.60
1058 A419 30d dark rose brown 4.50 2.25
Nos. 1055-1058 (4) 12.25 6.10

Aquatic Birds — A420

1995, Dec. 20 Litho. *Perf. 14x13½*

1059 A420 3d Tadorna tadorna .40 .20
1060 A420 5d Gallinago gallinago .70 .35

1996 Summer Olympics, Atlanta A421

1996, Jan. 24 Litho. *Perf. 14x13½*

1061 A421 20d multicolored 2.50 1.25

Touareg Leather Crafts A422

Perf. 14x13½, 13½x14

1996, Feb. 14 Litho.

1062 A422 5d shown .60 .40
1063 A422 16d Saddle bag, vert. 2.25 1.00

Pasteur Institute of Algeria — A423

1996, Mar. 20 Litho. *Perf. 13½x14*

1064 A423 5d multicolored .75 .40

Youm El Ilm — A424

Designs: 16d, Dove, stylus, vert. 23d, Open book showing pencil, stylus, compass, satellite in earth orbit, vert.

Perf. 14x13½,13½x14

1996, Apr. 16 Litho.

1065 A424 5d multicolored .50 .40
1066 A424 16d multicolored 2.00 1.00
1067 A424 23d multicolored 3.00 1.50
Nos. 1065-1067 (3) 5.50 2.90

Minerals A425

Mineral, region: 10d, Iron, Djebel-Ouenza. 20d, Gold, Tirek-Amesmessa.

1996, May 6 Litho. *Perf. 14x13½*

1068 A425 10d multicolored .75 .25
1069 A425 20d multicolored 2.00 .60

Butterflies A426

Designs: 5d, Pandoriana pandora. 10d, Coenonympha pamphilus. 20d, Cynthia cardui. 23d, Melanargia galathea.

1996, June 12 Litho. *Perf. 11½*

Granite Paper

1070 A426 5d multicolored .30 .20
1071 A426 10d multicolored .75 .20
1072 A426 20d multicolored 1.50 .35
1073 A426 23d multicolored 2.00 .40
Nos. 1070-1073 (4) 4.55 1.15

Civil Protection A427

Designs: 5d, Giving medical aid, ambulance. 23d, Prevention of natural disasters, vert.

Perf. 14x13½, 13½x14

1996, Oct. 9 Litho.

1074 A427 5d multicolored .40 .20
1075 A427 23d multicolored 1.25 .40

World Day Against Use of Illegal Drugs A428

1996, June 26 Litho. *Perf. 14x13½*

1076 A428 5d multicolored .40 .20

UNICEF, 50th Anniv. — A429

Stylized designs: 5d, Two children, wreath, pencils, flowers. 10d, Five children, pencil, key, flower, flag, hypodermic.

1996, Nov. 20 Litho. *Perf. 13½x14*

1077 A429 5d multicolored .30 .20
1078 A429 10d multicolored .50 .20

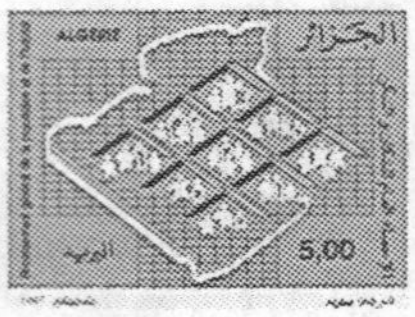

4th General Census A430

1997, Feb. 12 Litho. *Perf. 14x13½*

1079 A430 5d multicolored .20 .20

A431 A432

1997, Feb. 27 *Perf. 13½x14*

1080 A431 5d multicolored .20 .20

Protest at Ouargla, 35th anniv.

1996, Dec. 18 Litho. *Perf. 13½x14*

Interior Courts of Algerian Dwellings: 5d, Palace of Hassan Pasha. 10d, Khedaouj El-Amia, Algiers. 20d, Palace of Light. 30d, Abdellatif Villa.

1081 A432 5d multicolored .20 .20
1082 A432 10d multicolored .35 .20
1083 A432 20d multicolored .70 .35
1084 A432 30d multicolored 1.10 .55
Nos. 1081-1084 (4) 2.35 1.30

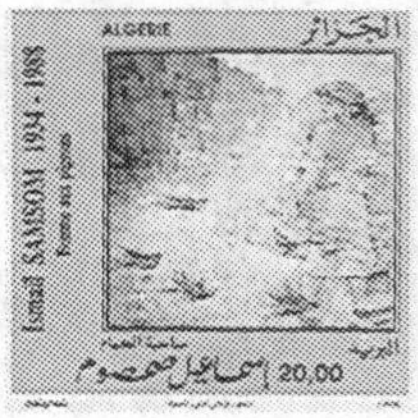

Paintings by Ismail Samson (1934-88) A433

20d, Woman with Pigeons. 30d, Interrogation.

1996, Dec. 25 *Perf. 14*

1085 A433 20d multicolored 1.00 .35
1086 A433 30d multicolored 1.50 .55

Victory Day, 35th Anniv. A434

1997, Mar. 19 *Perf. 14x13½*

1087 A434 5d multicolored .20 .20

Flowers — A435

Designs: 5d, Ficaria verna. 16d, Lonicera arborea. 23d, Papaver rhoeas.

1997, Apr. 23 Litho. *Perf. 13½x14*

1088 A435 5d multicolored .20 .20
1089 A435 16d multicolored .55 .30
1090 A435 23d multicolored .80 .40
Nos. 1088-1090 (3) 1.55 .90

World Day to Stop Smoking A436

Legislative Elections A437

1997, May 31 Litho. *Perf. 13½x14*

1091 A436 5d multicolored .20 .20

1997, June 4

1092 A437 5d multicolored .20 .20

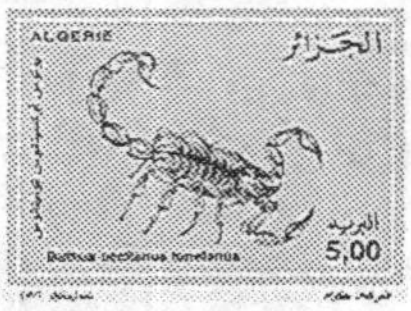

Scorpions A438

Designs: 5d, Buthus occitanus tunetanus. 10d, Androctonus australis hector.

1997, June 18 *Perf. 14x13½*

1093 A438 5d multicolored .20 .20
1094 A438 10d multicolored .35 .20

Natl. Independence, 35th Anniv. — A439

Designs: 5d, Crowd celebrating, flags. 10d, Doves, broken chain, "35," flag.

1997, July 5 Litho. *Perf. 14x13½*

1095 A439 5d multicolored .20 .20

Souvenir Sheet

Perf. 14

1096 A439 10d multicolored .35 .20

No. 1096 contains one 30x40mm stamp.

A440 A441

Wood Carvings: 5d, Inscription, Nedroma Mosque. 23d, Door, Ketchaoua Mosque.

1997, Jan. 15 Litho. *Perf. 13½x14*

1097 A440 5d multicolored .20 .20
1098 A440 23d multicolored .80 .40

1997, Aug. 17 Litho. *Perf. 13½x14*

1099 A441 5d multicolored .20 .20

Moufdi Zakaria (1908-77), poet.

Textile Patterns A442

1997, Sept. 17 Litho. *Perf. 14*

1100 A442 3d Dokkali .20 .20
1101 A442 5d Tellis .20 .20
1102 A442 10d Bou-Taleb .35 .20
1103 A442 20d Ddil .70 .35
Nos. 1100-1103 (4) 1.45 .95

Natl. Police Force, 25th Anniv. A443

1997, Oct. 6 *Perf. 14x13½*

1104 A443 5d multicolored .20 .20

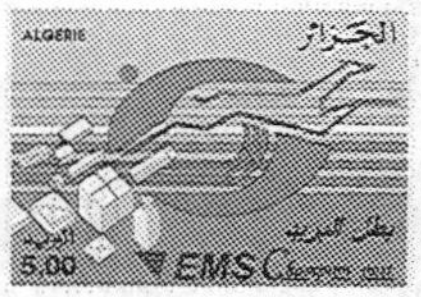

Express Mail Service A444

1997, Oct. 9

1105 A444 5d multicolored .20 .20

Local Elections — A445

1997, Oct. 23 *Perf. 13½x14*

1106 A445 5d multicolored .20 .20

Lighthouses A446

Perf. 14x13½, 13½x14

1997, Nov. 5 Litho.

1107 A446 5d Tenes .20 .20
1108 A446 10d Cape Caxine, vert. .35 .20

New Airpost Service, 1st Anniv. A447

1997, Nov. 17 *Perf. 14x13½*

1109 A447 5d multicolored .20 .20

Shells A448

Designs: 5d, Chlamys varia. 10d, Bolinus brandaris. 20d, Hinia reticulata, vert.

Perf. 14x13½, 13½x14

1997, Dec. 17 Litho.

1110 A448 5d multicolored .20 .20
1111 A448 10d multicolored .35 .20
1112 A448 20d multicolored .70 .35
Nos. 1110-1112 (3) 1.25 .75

A449

A450

1997, Dec. 25 *Perf. 13½x14*
1113 A449 5d multicolored .20 .20

Election of the Natl. Council.

1997, Dec. 30 Litho. *Perf. 13½x14*

Completion of Government Reforms: a, Natl. flag, people, book, ballot box. b, People, open book, torch. c, Ballot box. d, Flag, rising sun, flower. e, Ballots, building, flag.

1114 A450 5d Strip of 5, #a.-e. .85 .45

Bombing of Sakiet Sidi Youcef, 40th Anniv. A451

1998, Feb. 8 Litho. *Perf. 14x13½*
1115 A451 5d multicolored .20 .20

National Archives A452

1998, Feb. 16
1116 A452 5d multicolored .20 .20

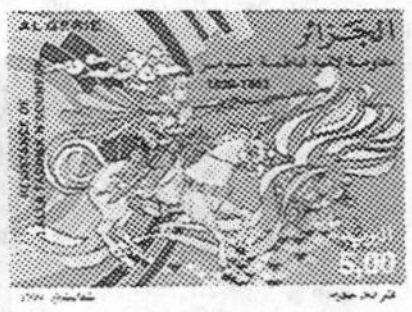
Intl. Women's Day — A453

1998, Mar. 8 Litho. *Perf. 14x13½*
1117 A453 5d multicolored .20 .20

SEMI-POSTAL STAMPS

Regular Issue of 1926 Surcharged in Black or Red

+10c ☪

1927 Unwmk. *Perf. 14x13½*

B1	A1	5c +5c bl grn	.50	.50
B2	A1	10c +10c lilac	.50	.50
B3	A2	15c +15c org brn	.50	.50
B4	A2	20c +20c car rose	.50	.50
B5	A2	25c +25c bl grn	.50	.50
B6	A2	30c +30c lt bl	.50	.50
B7	A2	35c +35c dp vio	.55	.55
B8	A2	40c +40c ol grn	.60	.60
B9	A3	50c +50c dp bl (R)	.60	.60
a.		Double surcharge	200.00	200.00
B10	A3	80c +80c red org	.60	.60
B11	A4	1fr +1fr gray grn & red brn	.65	.65
B12	A4	2fr +2fr Prus bl & blk brn	15.00	15.00
B13	A4	5fr +5fr red & vio	21.00	21.00
		Nos. B1-B13 (13)	42.00	42.00

The surtax was for the benefit of wounded soldiers. Government officials speculated in this issue.

Railroad Terminal, Oran — SP1

Ruins at Djemila SP2

Mosque of Sidi Abd-er-Rahman SP3

Designs: 10c+10c, Rummel Gorge, Constantine. 15c+15c, Admiralty Buildings, Algiers. 25c+25c, View of Algiers. 30c+30c, Trajan's Arch, Timgad. 40c+40c, Temple of the North, Djemila. 75c+75c Mansourah Minaret, Tlemcen. 1f+1f, View of Ghardaia. 1.50f+1.50f, View of Tolga. 2f+2f, Tuareg warriors. 3f+3f, Kasbah, Algiers.

1930 Engr. *Perf. 12½*

B14	SP1	5c +5c orange	5.00	5.00
B15	SP1	10c +10c ol grn	5.00	5.00
B16	SP1	15c +15c dk brn	5.00	5.00
B17	SP1	25c +25c black	5.00	5.00
B18	SP1	30c +30c dk red	5.00	5.00
B19	SP1	40c +40c ap grn	5.00	5.00
B20	SP2	50c +50c ultra	5.00	5.00
B21	SP2	75c +75c red pur	5.00	5.00
B22	SP2	1fr +1fr org red	5.00	5.00
B23	SP2	1.50fr +1.50fr deep ultra	5.00	5.00
B24	SP2	2fr +2fr dk car	5.00	5.00
B25	SP2	3fr +3fr dk grn	5.00	5.00
B26	SP3	5fr +5fr grn & car	12.00	12.00
a.		Center inverted	450.00	
		Nos. B14-B26 (13)	72.00	72.00

Centenary of the French occupation of Algeria. The surtax on the stamps was given to the funds for the celebration.

Nos. B14-B26 exist imperf. Value, set in pairs, $350.

Catalogue values for unused stamps in this section, from this point to the end of the section, are for Never Hinged items.

No. 102 Surcharged in Red

1918-11 Nov.-1938
0.65 + 0.35

1938 *Perf. 13*
B27 A6 65c +35c on 2.25fr yel grn .50 .40

20th anniversary of Armistice.

René Caillié, Charles Lavigerie and Henri Duveyrier SP14

1939 Engr.

B28	SP14	30c +20c dk bl grn	1.00	.60
B29	SP14	90c +60c car rose	1.25	.65
B30	SP14	2.25fr +75c ultra	6.75	6.25
B31	SP14	5fr +5fr brn blk	14.00	14.00
		Nos. B28-B31 (4)	23.00	21.50

Pioneers of the Sahara.

French and Algerian Soldiers SP15

1940 Photo. *Perf. 12*

B32	SP15	1fr +1fr bl & car	.50	.40
B33	SP15	1fr +2fr brn rose & blk	.50	.40
B34	SP15	1fr +4fr dp grn & red	.70	.60
B35	SP15	1fr +9fr brn & car	1.00	1.00
		Nos. B32-B35 (4)	2.70	2.40

The surtax was used to assist the families of mobilized men.

Type of Regular Issue, 1941 Surcharged in Carmine

+ 4f

1941 Engr. *Perf. 13*
B36 A19 1fr +4fr black .20 .20

No. 135 Surcharged in Carmine

SECOURS NATIONAL + 4f

B37 A19 1fr +4fr dark blue .20 .20

The surtax was for National Relief.

No. 124 Surcharged in Black "+60c"

1942
B38 A7 90c +60c henna brn .20 .20
a. Double surcharge 55.00

The surtax was used for National Relief. The stamp could also be used as 1.50 francs for postage.

Mother and Child — SP16

1943, Dec. 1 Litho. *Perf. 12*

B39	SP16	50c +4.50fr brt pink	.50	.25
B40	SP16	1.50fr +8.50fr lt grn	.50	.25
B41	SP16	3fr +12fr dp bl	.50	.25
B42	SP16	5fr +15fr vio brn	.50	.25
		Nos. B39-B42 (4)	2.00	1.00

The surtax was for the benefit of soldiers and prisoners of war.

Planes over Fields SP17

Unwmk.
1945, July 2 Engr. *Perf. 13*
B43 SP17 1.50fr +3.50fr lt ultra, red org & blk .25 .25

The surtax was for the benefit of Algerian airmen and their families.

France No. B192 Overprinted Type "a" of 1924 in Black

1945
B44 SP146 4fr +6fr dk vio brn .35 .20

The surtax was for war victims of the P.T.T.

Overprinted in Blue on Type of France, 1945

1945, Oct. 15
B45 SP150 2fr +3fr dk brn .40 .40

For Stamp Day.

Overprinted in Blue on Type of France, 1946

1946, June 29
B46 SP160 3fr +2fr red .45 .45

For Stamp Day.

Children Playing by Stream SP18

Girl SP19

Athlete SP20

Repatriated Prisoner and Bay of Algiers SP21

1946, Oct. 2 Engr. *Perf. 13*

B47	SP18	3fr +17fr dark grn	.65	.65
B48	SP19	4fr +21fr red	.65	.65
B49	SP20	8fr +27fr rose lilac	2.75	2.75
B50	SP21	10fr +35fr dark blue	.70	.70
		Nos. B47-B50 (4)	4.75	4.75

Type of France, 1947, Overprinted type "a" of 1924 in Carmine

1947, Mar. 15
B51 SP172 4.50fr +5.50fr dp ultra .40 .40

For Stamp Day.

Same on Type of France, 1947, Surcharged Like No. B36 in Carmine

1947, Nov. 13
B52 A173 5fr +10fr dk Prus grn .55 .40

Type of France, 1948, Overprinted in Dark Green — f

ALGÉRIE

1948, Mar. 6
B53 SP176 6fr +4fr dk grn .55 .45

For Stamp Day.

Type of France, 1948, Overprinted type "a" of 1924 in Blue and New Value

1948, May
B54 A176 6fr +4fr red .55 .35

Battleship Richelieu and the Admiralty, Algiers SP22

Aircraft Carrier Arromanches SP23

Unwmk.
1949, Jan. 15 Engr. *Perf. 13*
B55 SP22 10fr +15fr dp blue 4.50 4.50
B56 SP23 18fr +22fr red 4.50 4.50

The surtax was for naval charities.

Type of France, 1949, Overprinted in Blue — g

ALGÉRIE

1949, Mar. 26
B57 SP180 15fr +5fr lilac rose 1.25 1.10

For Stamp Day, Mar. 26-27.

Type of France, 1950, Overprinted type "f" in Green

1950, Mar. 11
B58 SP183 12fr +3fr blk brn 1.25 1.10

For Stamp Day, Mar. 11-12.

Foreign Legionary — SP24

1950, Apr. 30
B59 SP24 15fr +5fr dk grn 1.10 1.10

Charles de Foucauld and Gen. J. F. H. Laperrine SP25

1950, Aug. 21 Unwmk. *Perf. 13*
B60 SP25 25fr +5fr brn ol & brn blk 3.00 3.00

50th anniversary of the presence of the French in the Sahara.

Emir Abd-el-Kader and Marshal T. R. Bugeaud SP26

1950, Aug. 21
B61 SP26 40fr +10fr dk brn & blk brn 3.00 3.00

Unveiling of a monument to Emir Abd-el-Kader at Cacheron.

Col. Colonna d'Ornano and Fine Arts Museum, Algiers SP27

1951, Jan. 11
B62 SP27 15fr +5fr blk brn, vio brn & red brn .65 .65

Death of Col. Colonna d'Ornano, 10th anniv.

Type of France, 1951, Overprinted type "a" of 1924 in Black

1951, Mar. 10
B63 SP186 12fr +3fr brown .85 .85

For Stamp Day.

Type of France, 1952, Overprinted type "g" in Dark Blue

1952, Mar. 8 Unwmk. *Perf. 13*
B64 SP190 12fr +3fr dk bl 1.25 1.25

For Stamp Day.

French Military Medal — SP28

Unwmk.
1952, July 5 Engr. *Perf. 13*
B65 SP28 15fr +5fr grn, yel & brn 1.75 1.25

Centenary of the creation of the French Military Medal.

Type of France 1952, Surcharged type "g" and Surtax in Black

1952, Sept. 15
B66 A222 30fr +5fr dp ultra 1.40 1.25

10th anniv. of the defense of Bir-Hakeim.

View of El Oued SP29

Design: 12fr+3fr, View of Bou-Noura.

1952, Nov. 15 Engr.
B67 SP29 8fr +2fr ultra & red 1.25 1.10
B68 SP29 12fr +3fr red 2.25 1.90

The surtax was for the Red Cross.

Type of France, 1953, Overprinted type "a" of 1924 in Black

1953, Mar. 14 Engr.
B69 SP193 12fr +3fr purple 1.00 .90

For Stamp Day. Surtax for Red Cross.

Victory of Cythera — SP30

Unwmk.
1953, Dec. 18 Engr. *Perf. 13*
B70 SP30 15fr +5fr blk brn & brn .65 .60

The surtax was for army welfare work.

Type of France, 1954, Overprinted type "a" of 1924 in Black

1954, Mar. 20 Unwmk. *Perf. 13*
B71 SP196 12fr +3fr scarlet .75 .65

For Stamp Day.

Soldiers and Flags SP31

Foreign Legionary SP32

1954, Mar. 27
B72 SP31 15fr +5fr dk brn .65 .50

The surtax was for old soldiers.

1954, Apr. 30
B73 SP32 15fr +5fr dk grn 1.25 1.00

The surtax was for the welfare fund of the Foreign Legion.

Nurses and Verdun Hospital, Algiers SP33

15fr+5fr, J. H. Dunant & ruins at Djemila.

1954, Oct. 30
B74 SP33 12fr +3fr indigo & red 2.00 1.75
B75 SP33 15fr +5fr pur & red 2.50 2.00

The surtax was for the Red Cross.

Earthquake Victims and Ruins SP34

First Aid SP35

Design: #B80-B81, Removing wounded.

1954, Dec. 5
B76 SP34 12fr +4fr dk vio brn 1.00 1.00
B77 SP34 15fr +5fr dp bl 1.00 1.00
B78 SP35 18fr +6fr lil rose 1.75 1.75
B79 SP35 20fr +7fr violet 1.75 1.75
B80 SP35 25fr +8fr rose brn 2.00 2.00
B81 SP35 30fr +10fr brt bl grn 2.00 2.00
Nos. B76-B81 (6) 9.50 9.50

The surtax was for victims of the Orleansville earthquake disaster of September 1954.

Type of France, 1955, Overprinted type "a" of 1924 in Black

1955, Mar. 19
B82 SP199 12fr +3fr dp ultra 1.00 1.00

For Stamp Day, Mar. 19-20.

Women and Children SP36

Cancer Victim SP37

1955, Nov. 5
B83 SP36 15fr +5fr blue & indigo .60 .60

The tax was for war victims.

1956, Mar. 3 Unwmk. *Perf. 13*
B84 SP37 15fr +5fr dk brn .75 .50

The surtax was for the Algerian Cancer Society. The male figure in the design is Rodin's "Age of Bronze."

Type of France, 1956, Overprinted type "a" of 1924 in Black

1956, Mar.
B85 SP202 12fr +3fr red .90 .60

For Stamp Day, Mar. 17-18.

Foreign Legion Rest Home SP38

1956, Apr. 29
B86 SP38 15fr +5fr dk bl grn .90 .90

Honoring the French Foreign Legion.

Type of France, 1957, Overprinted type "f" in Black

1957, Mar. 16 Engr. *Perf. 13*
B87 SP204 12fr +3fr dull purple .70 .70

For Stamp Day and to honor the Maritime Postal Service.

Fennec SP39

Design: 15fr+5fr, Stork flying over roofs.

1957, Apr. 6
B88 SP39 12fr +3fr red brn & red 3.75 3.75
B89 SP39 15fr +5fr sepia & red 3.75 3.75

The surtax was for the Red Cross.

Type of Regular Issue, 1956 Surcharged in Dark Blue

18 JUIN 1940
+ 5F

1957, June 18
B90 A53 15fr +5fr scar & rose red .95 .95

17th anniv. of General de Gaulle's appeal for a Free France.

The Giaour, by Delacroix — SP40

On the Banks of the Oued, by Fromentin SP41

Design: 35fr+10fr, Dancer, by Chasseriau.

Unwmk.
1957, Nov. 30 Engr. *Perf. 13*
B91 SP40 15fr +5fr dk car 3.75 3.75
B92 SP41 20fr +5fr grn 3.75 3.75
B93 SP40 35fr +10fr dk bl 3.75 3.75
Nos. B91-B93 (3) 11.25 11.25

Surtax for army welfare organizations.

Type of France Overprinted type "f" in Blue

1958, Mar. 15 Unwmk. *Perf. 13*
B94 SP206 15fr +5fr org brn .75 .75

For Stamp Day.

Bird-of-Paradise Flower — SP42

Arms & Marshal's Baton — SP43

1958, June 14 Engr. *Perf. 13*
B95 SP42 20fr +5fr grn, org & vio 2.25 2.25

The surtax was for Child Welfare.

1958, July 20
B96 SP43 20fr +5fr ultra, car & grn 1.00 1.00

Marshal de Lattre Foundation.

Independent State

Clasped Hands, Wheat, Olive Branch SP44

Burning Books SP45

1963, May 27 Unwmk. *Perf. 13*
B97 SP44 50c +20c sl grn, brt grn & car .80 .60

Surtax for the Natl. Solidarity Fund.

1965, June 7 Engr. *Perf. 13*
B98 SP45 20c +5c ol grn, red & blk .50 .40

Issued to commemorate the burning of the Library of Algiers, June 7, 1962.

Soldiers and Woman Comforting Wounded Soldier — SP46

1966, Aug. 20 Photo. *Perf. 11½*
B99 SP46 30c +10c multi 1.25 .70
B100 SP46 95c +10c multi 1.75 1.10

Day of the Moudjahid (Moslem volunteers).

Red Crescent, Boy and Girl — SP47

1967, May 27 Litho. *Perf. 14*
B101 SP47 30c +10c brt grn, brn & car .45 .35

Algerian Red Crescent Society.

Flood Victims — SP48

Design: 95c+25c, Rescuing flood victims.

1969, Nov. 15 Typo. *Perf. 10½*
B102 SP48 30c +10c dl bl, sal & blk .45 .35

Litho.
B103 SP48 95c +25c multi 1.00 .65

Red Crescent Flag — SP49

1971, May 17 Engr. *Perf. 10½*
B104 SP49 30c +10c slate grn & car .35 .30

Algerian Red Crescent Society.

Intl. Children's Day — SP50

1989, June 1 Litho. *Perf. 10½x11*
B105 SP50 1d +30c multi .65 .50

Surtax for child welfare.

Solidarity with Palestinians SP51

1990, Dec. 9 Litho. *Perf. 10½x11*
B106 SP51 1d +30c multi .50 .30

Natl. Solidarity with Education — SP52

1995, Sept. 20 Litho. *Perf. 13x14*
B107 SP52 3d +50c multi .50 .25

AIR POST STAMPS

Catalogue values for unused stamps in this section are for Never Hinged items.

Plane over Algiers Harbor AP1

Two types of 20fr:
Type I - Monogram "F" without serifs. "POSTE" indented 3mm.
Type II - Monogram "F" with serifs. "POSTE" indented 4½mm.

Unwmk.

1946, June 20 Engr. *Perf. 13*
C1 AP1 5fr red .25 .20
C2 AP1 10fr deep blue .25 .20
C3 AP1 15fr deep green .45 .20
C4 AP1 20fr brown (II) .25 .20
C4A AP1 20fr brown (I) 100.00 65.00
C5 AP1 25fr violet .55 .20
C6 AP1 40fr gray black .75 .20
Nos. C1-C4,C5-CC6 (6) 2.50 1.20

For surcharges see Nos. C7, CB1-CB2.

No. C1 Surcharged in Black **— 10 %**

1947, Jan. 18
C7 AP1 (4.50fr) on 5fr red .25 .20

Storks over Mosque — AP2

Plane over Village AP3

1949-53
C8 AP2 50fr green 2.00 .25
C9 AP3 100fr brown 1.75 .25
C10 AP2 200fr bright red 4.00 3.00
C11 AP3 500fr ultra ('53) 14.00 10.00
Nos. C8-C11 (4) 21.75 13.50

Beni Bahdel Dam — AP4

1957, July 1 Unwmk. *Perf. 13*
C12 AP4 200fr dark red 3.25 .75

Caravelle over Ghardaia — AP5

Designs: 2d, Caravelle over El Oued. 5d, Caravelle over Tipasa.

1967-68 Engr. *Perf. 13*
C13 AP5 1d lil, org brn & emer 1.00 .50
C14 AP5 2d brt bl, org brn & emer 2.50 1.25
C15 AP5 5d brt bl, grn & org brn ('68) 6.00 2.75
Nos. C13-C15 (3) 9.50 4.50

Plane over Casbah, Algiers — AP6

Designs: 3d, Plane over Oran. 4d, Plane over Rhumel Gorge.

1971-72 Photo. *Perf. 12½*
C16 AP6 2d grysh blk & multi 1.60 .80
C17 AP6 3d violet & blk 2.50 1.40
C18 AP6 4d blk & multi 3.25 1.75
Nos. C16-C18 (3) 7.35 3.95

Issued: 2d, 6/12/71; 3d, 4d, 2/28/72.

Storks and Plane — AP7

1979, Mar. 24 Photo. *Perf. 11½*
C19 AP7 10d multi 4.00 1.60

Plane Approaching Coastal City — AP8

1991, Apr. 26 Litho. *Perf. 13½*
C20 AP8 10d shown 3.00 1.50
C21 AP8 20d Plane over city 6.00 3.00

Plane Over Djidjelli Corniche — AP9

1993, Sept. 25 Engr. *Perf. 13½x14*
C22 AP9 50d blue, green & brown 6.25 3.25

AIR POST SEMI-POSTAL STAMPS

Catalogue values for unused stamps in this section are for Never Hinged items.

No. C2 Surcharged in Carmine

‡
18 Juin 1940
+10Fr.

1947, June 18 *Perf. 13*
CB1 AP1 10fr +10fr deep blue .75 .60

7th anniv. of Gen. Charles de Gaulle's speech in London, June 18, 1940.

No. C1 Surcharged in Blue

‡
18 JUIN 1940
+10 Fr.

1948, June 18
CB2 AP1 5fr +10fr red .70 .60

8th anniv. of Gen. Charles de Gaulle's speech in London, June 18, 1940.

Monument, Clock Tower and Plane — SPAP1

1949, Nov. 10 Engr. Unwmk.
CB3 SPAP1 15fr +20fr dk brn 3.50 3.50

25th anniv. of Algeria's 1st postage stamps.

POSTAGE DUE STAMPS

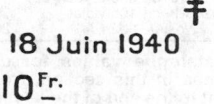

D1

D2

Perf. 14x13½

1926-27 Typo. Unwmk.
J1 D1 5c light blue .20 .20
J2 D1 10c dk brn .20 .20
J3 D1 20c olive grn .20 .20
J4 D1 25c car rose .35 .35
J5 D1 30c rose red .20 .20
J6 D1 45c blue grn .50 .50
J7 D1 50c brn vio .20 .20
J8 D1 60c green ('27) 1.25 .30
J9 D1 1fr red brn, *straw* .20 .20
J10 D1 2fr lil rose ('27) .20 .20
J11 D1 3fr deep blue ('27) .20 .20
Nos. J1-J11 (11) 3.70 2.75

See Nos. J25-J26, J28-J32. For surcharges, see Nos. J18-J20.

1926-27
J12 D2 1c olive grn .20 .20
J13 D2 10c violet .40 .20
J14 D2 30c bister .25 .20
J15 D2 60c dull red .20 .20
J16 D2 1fr brt vio ('27) 11.00 1.75
J17 D2 2fr lt bl ('27) 7.50 .65
Nos. J12-J17 (6) 19.55 3.20

See note below France No. J51.
For surcharges, see Nos. J21-J24.

Stamps of 1926 Surcharged

1927
J18 D1 60c on 20c olive grn .90 .25
J19 D1 2fr on 45c blue grn 1.10 .65
J20 D1 3fr on 25c car rose .75 .25
Nos. J18-J20 (3) 2.75 1.15

Recouvrement Stamps of 1926 Surcharged **10c**

1927-32
J21 D2 10c on 30c bis ('32) 2.25 1.50
J22 D2 1fr on 1c olive grn .65 .60
J23 D2 1fr on 60c dl red ('32) 11.00 .25
J24 D2 2fr on 10c violet 6.25 6.25
Nos. J21-J24 (4) 20.15 8.60

Catalogue values for unused stamps in this section, from this point to the end of the section, are for Never Hinged items.

Type of 1926, Without "R F"

1942 Typo. *Perf. 14x13½*
J25 D1 30c dark red .20 .20
J26 D1 2fr magenta .20 .20

Type of 1926 Surcharged in Red **T 0.50**

1944 *Perf. 14x13½*
J27 A2 50c on 20c yel grn .20 .20
a. Inverted surcharge 3.50
b. Double surcharge 9.50

No. J27 was issued precanceled only. See note after No. 32.

Type of 1926

1944 Litho. *Perf. 12*
J28 D1 1.50fr brt rose lilac .30 .20
J29 D1 2fr greenish blue .30 .20
J30 D1 5fr rose carmine .30 .20
Nos. J28-J30 (3) .90 .60

Type of 1926

1947 Typo. *Perf. 14x13½*
J32 D1 5fr green .60 .45

France Nos. J80-J81 Overprinted Type "a" of 1925 in Carmine or Black

1947
J33 D5 10c sepia (C) .20 .20
J34 D5 30c bright red violet .20 .20

D3

Perf. 14x13

1947-55 Unwmk. Engr.
J35 D3 20c red .20 .20
J36 D3 60c ultra .22 .20
J37 D3 1fr dk org brn .20 .20
J38 D3 1.50fr dull green .40 .40
J39 D3 2fr red .20 .20
J40 D3 3fr violet .20 .20
J41 D3 5fr ultra ('49) .20 .20
J42 D3 6fr black .20 .20
J43 D3 10fr lil rose .20 .20
J44 D3 15fr ol grn ('55) .45 .45
J45 D3 20fr brt grn .22 .20
J46 D3 30fr red org ('55) .40 .40
J47 D3 50fr indigo ('51) .95 .95
J48 D3 100fr brt bl ('53) 4.00 3.50
Nos. J35-J48 (14) 8.04 7.50

Independent State

France Nos. J93-J97 Overprinted "EA" in Black like Nos. 286-290

Perf. 14x13½

1962, July 2 Typo. Unwmk.

Handstamped Overprint
J49 D6 5c bright pink 2.25 1.60
J50 D6 10c red orange 2.25 1.40
J51 D6 20c olive bister 2.25 1.40
J52 D6 50c dark green 3.00 2.75
J53 D6 1fr deep green 4.25 4.00
Nos. J49-J53 (5) 14.00 11.15

Typographed Overprint
J49a D6 5c bright pink 6.00 6.00
J50a D6 10c red orange 6.00 6.00
J51a D6 20c olive bister 5.50 5.50
J52a D6 50c dark green 14.00 14.00
J53a D6 1fr deep green 25.00 25.00
Nos. J49a-J53a (5) 56.50 56.50

See note after No. 290.

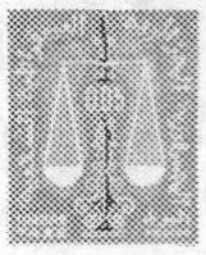
Scales — D4

Grain — D5

1963, June 25 *Perf. 14x13½*
J54 D4 5c car rose & blk .20 .20
J55 D4 10c olive & car .20 .20
J56 D4 20c ultra & blk .20 .20
J57 D4 50c bister brn & grn .50 .30
J58 D4 1fr lilac & org .85 .50
Nos. J54-J58 (5) 1.95 1.40

#J58 Surcharged with New Value & 3 Bars

1968, Mar. 28 Typo. *Perf. 14x13½*
J59 D4 60c on 1fr lilac & org .40 .30

1972-93 Litho. *Perf. 13½x14*
J60 D5 10c bister .20 .20
J61 D5 20c deep brown .20 .20
J62 D5 40c orange .20 .20
J63 D5 50c dk vio blue .20 .20
J64 D5 80c dk olive gray .40 .20
J65 D5 1d green .45 .25
J66 D5 2d blue .95 .40
J67 D5 3d violet .45 .20
J68 D5 4d lilac rose .60 .30
Nos. J60-J68 (9) 3.65 2.15

Issued: 3d, 4d, 1/21/93; others, 10/21/72.

NEWSPAPER STAMPS

Nos. 1 and 33 Surcharged in Red **½ centime**

1924-26 Unwmk. *Perf. 14x13½*
P1 A16 ½c on 1c dk gray .20 .20
a. Triple surcharge 87.50
P2 A1 ½c on 1c olive ('26) .20 .20

ALLENSTEIN

'a-lən-ˌshtīn

LOCATION — In East Prussia
AREA — 4,457 sq. mi.
POP. — 540,000 (estimated 1920)
CAPITAL — Allenstein

Allenstein, a district of East Prussia, held a plebiscite in 1920 under the Versailles Treaty, voting to join Germany rather than Poland. Later that year, Allenstein became part of the German Republic.

100 Pfennig = 1 Mark

Stamps of Germany, 1906-20, Overprinted **PLÉBISCITE OLSZTYN ALLENSTEIN**

Perf. 14, 14½, 14x14½, 14½x14

1920 Wmk. 125
1 A16 5pf green .20 .20
2 A16 10pf carmine .20 .20
3 A22 15pf dk vio .20 .20
4 A22 15pf vio brn 6.50 6.50
5 A16 20pf bl vio .25 .25
6 A16 30pf org & blk, *buff* .40 .30
7 A16 40pf lake & blk .30 .25
8 A16 50pf pur & blk, *buff* .30 .25
9 A16 75pf grn & blk .35 .20
10 A17 1m car rose .75 .80
a. Double overprint 375.00 600.00
11 A17 1.25m green .70 1.00
a. Double overprint 475.00 1,000.
12 A17 1.50m yel brn .70 1.00
13 A21 2.50m lilac rose 1.40 4.00
14 A19 3m blk vio 1.75 1.25
a. Double overprint 350.00 925.00
b. Inverted overprint 375.00 600.00
Nos. 1-14 (14) 13.80 16.10
Set, never hinged 24.00

Overprinted

15 A16 5pf green .20 .25
16 A16 10pf carmine .20 .25
17 A22 15pf dark vio .20 .20
18 A22 15pf vio brn 30.00 25.00
19 A16 20pf blue vio .20 .20
20 A16 30pf org & blk, *buff* .40 .35
21 A16 40pf lake & blk .40 .35
22 A16 50pf pur & blk, *buff* .20 .20
23 A16 75pf grn & blk .20 .20
24 A17 1m car rose .75 .65
a. Inverted overprint 550.00 750.00
25 A17 1.25m green .70 .70
26 A17 1.50m yel brn .70 .70
27 A21 2.50m lilac rose 1.50 2.00
28 A19 3m blk vio 1.00 1.00
a. Inverted overprint 350.00 550.00
b. Double overprint 325.00 550.00
Nos. 15-28 (14) 36.60 37.70
Set, never hinged 75.00

The 40pf carmine rose (Germany No. 124) exists with this oval overprint, but it is doubtful whether it was regularly issued. Value $250.

ANDORRA

an-'dor-ə

LOCATION — On the southern slope of the Pyrenees Mountains between France and Spain.
GOVT. — Co-principality
AREA — 179 sq. mi.
POP. — 72,766 (July 1, 1996)
CAPITAL — Andorra la Vella

Andorra is subject to the joint control of France and the Spanish Bishop of Urgel and pays annual tribute to both. The country has no monetary unit of its own, the peseta and franc both being in general use.

100 Centimos = 1 Peseta
100 Centimes = 1 Franc

Catalogue values for unused stamps in the Spanish Administration for this country are for Never Hinged items, beginning with Scott 50 in the regular postage section and Scott C2 in the airpost section; for the French Administration of this country, Never Hinged items begin at Scott 78 for regular postage, Scott B1 for the semi-postal section, Scott C1 for the airpost section, and Scott J21 for the postage due section.

SPANISH ADMINISTRATION

A majority of the Spanish Andorra stamps issued to about 1950 are poorly centered. The very fine examples that are valued will be somewhat off center. Very poorly centered examples (perfs cutting design) sell for less. Well centered stamps are scarce and sell for approximately twice the values shown.

Stamps of Spain, 1922-26, Overprinted in Red or Black **:-: CORREOS :-: ANDORRA**

Perf. 14, 13½x12½, 12½x11½

1928 Unwmk.
1 A49 2c olive green .35 .30

Control Numbers on Back
2 A49 5c car rose (Bk) .45 .30
3 A49 10c green .45 .35
4 A49 15c slate blue 2.00 2.00
5 A49 20c violet 2.25 2.00
6 A49 25c rose red (Bk) 2.00 2.00
7 A49 30c black brown 10.00 8.25
8 A49 40c deep blue 10.00 5.75
9 A49 50c orange (Bk) 10.00 7.50
10 A49a 1p blue blk 12.00 12.50
11 A49a 4p lake (Bk) 80.00 90.00
12 A49a 10p brown (Bk) 140.00 140.00
Nos. 1-12 (12) 269.50 270.95
Set, never hinged 395.35

Counterfeit overprints exist.

La Vall
A1

St. Juan de Caselles
A2

St. Julia de Loria
A3

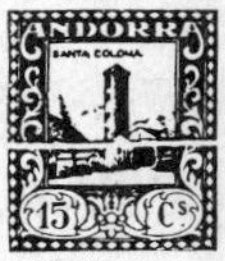
St. Coloma
A4

General Council — A5

1929, Nov. 25 Engr. *Perf. 14*
13 A1 2c olive green 1.00 .50

Control Numbers on Back
14 A2 5c carmine lake 2.25 1.25
15 A3 10c yellow green 2.25 2.50
16 A4 15c slate green 2.25 2.50
17 A3 20c violet 2.25 2.50
18 A4 25c carmine rose 5.50 5.50
19 A1 30c olive brown 100.00 100.00
20 A2 40c dark blue 4.50 2.75
21 A3 50c deep orange 4.50 3.50
22 A5 1p slate 11.00 11.00
23 A5 4p deep rose 65.00 65.00
24 A5 10p bister brown 75.00 85.00
Nos. 13-24 (12) 275.50 282.00
Set, never hinged 344.75

Nos. 13-24 exist imperforate.

1931-38

Perf. 11½
13a A1 2c 4.00 1.25

Control Numbers on Back
14a A2 5c 7.00 5.25
15a A3 10c 7.00 3.00
16a A4 15c 20.00 16.00
17a A3 20c 9.00 7.00
18a A4 25c 6.50 4.00
19a A1 30c ('33) 100.00 55.00
20a A2 40c ('35) 10.00 8.00
22a A5 1p ('38) 25.00 16.00
b. Control number omitted 1,400.
Set, never hinged 250.00

Without Control Numbers

1936-43 *Perf. 11½x11*
25 A1 2c red brown ('37) 2.00 1.00
26 A2 5c dark brown 2.00 1.00
27 A3 10c blue green 9.00 4.00
a. 10c yellow green 72.50 60.00
28 A4 15c blue green ('37) 4.00 3.50
29 A3 20c violet 6.00 3.50
30 A4 25c deep rose ('37) 2.00 3.00
31 A1 30c carmine 3.00 2.75
31A A2 40c dark blue 600.00 —
Never hinged 750.00
32 A1 45c rose red ('37) 3.00 1.75
33 A3 50c deep orange 7.00 4.00
34 A1 60c deep blue ('37) 5.00 3.50
35 A5 4p deep rose ('43) 35.00 35.00
36 A5 10p bister brn ('43) 35.00 45.00
Nos. 25-31,32-36 (12) 113.00 108.00
Set, never hinged 153.25

Nos. 26, 28, 32 exist imperforate.

Edelweiss
A6

Provost
A7

Coat of
Arms — A8

Plaza of
Ordino — A9

Chapel of
Meritxell
A10

Map
A11

1948-53 Unwmk. Photo. *Perf. 12½*

37	A6	2c dark olive grn ('51)	.40	.70
38	A6	5c deep orange ('53)	.40	.70
39	A6	10c deep blue ('53)	.45	.70

Engr. *Perf. 9½x10*

40	A7	20c brown vio	6.50	3.00
41	A7	25c org, perf. 12½ ('53)	4.75	2.25
42	A8	30c dk slate grn	8.50	3.50
43	A9	50c deep green	10.00	5.00
44	A10	75c dark blue	15.00	5.00
45	A9	90c dp car rose	6.50	4.00
46	A10	1p brt orange ver	10.00	5.00
47	A8	1.35p dk blue vio	6.50	6.00

Perf. 10

48	A11	4p ultra ('53)	10.00	10.00
49	A11	10p dk violet brn ('51)	21.00	10.00
		Nos. 37-49 (13)	100.00	55.85
		Set, never hinged	130.00	

Catalogue values for unused stamps in this section, from this point to the end of the section, are for Never Hinged items.

Bridge of St.
Anthony — A12

Madonna of
Meritxell, 8th
Century — A13

Designs: 70c, Aynos pasture. 1p, View of Canillo. 2p, St. Coloma. 2.50p, Arms of Andorra. 3p, Old Andorra, horiz. 5p, View of Ordino, horiz.

1963-64 Unwmk. Engr. *Perf. 13*

50	A12	25c dk gray & sepia	.20	.20
51	A12	70c dk sl grn & brn blk	.20	.20
52	A12	1p slate & dull pur	.30	.20
53	A12	2p violet & dull pur	.30	.20
54	A12	2.50p rose claret	.80	.60
55	A12	3p blk & grnsh gray	1.40	.60
56	A12	5p dk brn & choc	2.00	1.10
57	A13	6p sepia & car	3.00	1.10
		Nos. 50-57 (8)	8.20	4.20

Issued: 25c-2p, 7/20/63; 2.50p-6p, 2/29/64.

Narcissus — A14

Encamp
Valley — A15

1966, June 10 Engr. *Perf. 13*

58	A14	50c shown	.20	.20
59	A14	1p Pinks	.20	.20
60	A14	5p Jonquils	1.10	.55
61	A14	10p Hellebore	2.50	.65
		Nos. 58-61 (4)	4.00	1.60

Common Design Types
pictured following the introduction.

Europa Issue 1972
Common Design Type

1972, May 2 Photo. *Perf. 13*
Size: 25½x38mm

62	CD15	8p multicolored	110.00	70.00

1972, July 4 Photo. *Perf. 13*

Tourist publicity: 1.50p, Massana (village). 2p, Skiing on De La Casa Pass. 5p, Pessons Lake, horiz.

63	A15	1p multicolored	.20	.20
64	A15	1.50p multicolored	.70	.55
65	A15	2p multicolored	1.75	.55
66	A15	5p multicolored	2.25	.90
		Nos. 63-66 (4)	4.90	2.20

Butterfly
Stroke
A16

Design: 2p, Volleyball, vert.

1972, Oct. Photo. *Perf. 13*

67	A16	2p lt blue & multi	.20	.20
68	A16	5p multicolored	.30	.20

20th Olympic Games, Munich, Aug. 26-Sept. 11.

St. Anthony
Singers
A17

1972, Dec. 5 Photo. *Perf. 13*

69	A17	1p shown	.20	.20
70	A17	1.50p Les Caramelles (boys' choir)	.20	.20
71	A17	2p Nativity scene	.20	.20
72	A17	5p Man holding giant cigar, vert	.50	.20
73	A17	8p Hermit of Meritxell, vert	.70	.35
74	A17	15p Marratxa dancers	1.60	.50
		Nos. 69-74 (6)	3.40	1.65

Andorran customs. No. 71 is for Christmas.

Europa Issue 1973
Common Design Type and

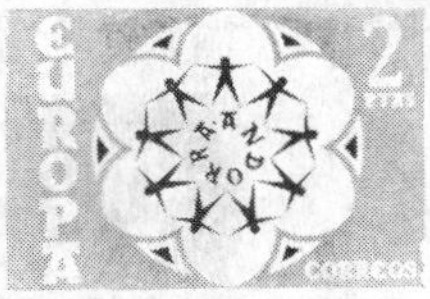

Symbol of
Unity
A18

1973, Apr. 30 Photo. *Perf. 13*

75	A18	2p ultra, red & blk	.20	.20

Size: 37x25mm

76	CD16	8p tan, red & blk	.70	.30

Nativity — A19

Virgin of
Ordino — A20

Christmas: 5p, Adoration of the Kings. Designs are from altar panels of Meritxell Parish Church.

1973, Dec. 14 Photo. *Perf. 13*

77	A19	2p multicolored	.20	.20
78	A19	5p multicolored	.65	.40

1974, Apr. 29 Photo. *Perf. 13*

Europa: 8p, Les Banyes Cross.

79	A20	2p multicolored	1.10	.40
80	A20	8p slate & brt blue	3.50	1.10

Cupboard — A21

Crowns of Virgin
and Child of
Roser — A22

1974, July 30 Photo. *Perf. 13*

81	A21	10p multicolored	1.60	.50
82	A22	25p dark red & multi	4.00	1.65

UPU
Monument,
Bern — A23

1974, Oct. 9 Photo. *Perf. 13*

83	A23	15p multicolored	1.25	.55

Centenary of Universal Postal Union.

Nativity
A24

Christmas: 5p, Adoration of the Kings.

1974, Dec. 4 Photo. *Perf. 13*

84	A24	2p multicolored	.50	.20
85	A24	5p multicolored	1.75	.45

Mail Delivery,
Andorra, 19th
Century — A25

12th Century
Painting, Ordino
Church — A26

1975, Apr. 4 Photo. *Perf. 13*

86	A25	3p multicolored	.30	.20

Espana 75 International Philatelic Exhibition, Madrid, Apr. 4-13.

1975, Apr. 28 Photo. *Perf. 13*

Design: 12p, Christ in Glory, 12th century Romanesque painting, Ordino church.

87	A26	3p multicolored	1.25	.35
88	A26	12p multicolored	2.25	.60

Urgel Cathedral
and
Document — A27

1975, Oct. 4 Photo. *Perf. 13*

89	A27	7p multicolored	.90	.50

Millennium of consecration of Urgel Cathedral, and Literary Festival 1975.

Nativity,
Ordino
A28

Christmas: 7p, Adoration of the Kings, Ordino.

1975, Dec. 3 Photo. *Perf. 13*

90	A28	3p multicolored	.20	.20
91	A28	7p multicolored	.40	.25

Caldron and
CEPT
Emblem
A29

Slalom and
Montreal
Olympic
Emblem
A30

Europa: 12p, Chest and CEPT emblem, horiz.

1976, May 3 Photo. *Perf. 13*

92	A29	3p bister & multi	.20	.20
93	A29	12p yellow & multi	.60	.20

1976, July 9 Photo. *Perf. 13*

Design: 15p, One-man canoe and Montreal Olympic emblem, horiz.

94	A30	7p multicolored	.20	.20
95	A30	15p multicolored	.40	.25

21st Olympic Games, Montreal, Canada, July 17-Aug. 1.

Nativity
A31

Christmas: 25p, Adoration of the Kings. Wall paintings in La Massana Church.

1976, Dec. 7 Photo. *Perf. 13*

96	A31	3p multicolored	.20	.20
97	A31	25p multicolored	.40	.25

View of Ansalonge — A32

Europa: 12p, Xuclar, valley, mountains.

1977, May 2 Litho. *Perf. 13*

98 A32 3p multicolored .20 .20
99 A32 12p multicolored .45 .25

Cross of Terme — A33

Map of Post Offices — A34

Christmas: 12p, Church of St. Miguel d'Engolasters.

1977, Dec. 2 Photo. *Perf. 13x12½*

100 A33 5p multicolored .30 .25
101 A33 12p multicolored .70 .50

Souvenir Sheet

Designs: 10p, Mail delivery. 20p, Post Office, 1928. 25p, Andorran coat of arms.

1978, Mar. 31 Photo. *Perf. 13x13½*

102 Sheet of 4 .85 .85
a. A34 5p multicolored .20 .20
b. A34 10p multicolored .20 .20
c. A34 20p multicolored .25 .25
d. A34 25p multicolored .30 .30

Spanish postal service in Andorra, 50th anniv.

La Vall — A35

Europa: 12p, St. Juan de Caselles.

1978, May 2 *Perf. 13*

103 A35 5p multicolored .20 .20
104 A35 12p multicolored .25 .20

Crown, Bishop's Mitre and Staff A36

1978, Sept. 24 Photo. *Perf. 13*

105 A36 5p brown, car & yel .35 .20

700th anniversary of the signing of treaty establishing Co-Principality of Andorra.

Holy Family — A37

Young Woman — A38

Christmas: 25p, Adoration of the Kings. Both designs after frescoes in the Church of St. Mary d'Encamp.

1978, Dec. 5 Photo. *Perf. 13*

106 A37 5p multicolored .20 .20
107 A37 25p multicolored .35 .20

1979, Feb. 14 Photo. *Perf. 13*

Designs: 5p, Young man. 12p, Bridegroom and bride riding mule.

108 A38 3p multicolored .20 .20
109 A38 5p multicolored .20 .20
110 A38 12p multicolored .20 .20
Nos. 108-110 (3) .60 .60

Old Mail Truck A39

Europa: 12p, Stampless covers of 1846 & 1854.

1979, Apr. 30 Engr. *Perf. 13*

111 A39 5p yel grn & dk blue .20 .20
112 A39 12p dk red & violet .25 .20

Children Holding Hands A40

1979, Oct. 18 Photo. *Perf. 13*

113 A40 19p multicolored .35 .20

International Year of the Child.

St. Coloma's Church — A41

Christmas: 25p, Agnus Dei roundel, St. Coloma's Church.

1979, Nov. 28 Photo. *Perf. 13½*

114 A41 8p multicolored .20 .20
115 A41 25p multicolored .35 .25

Bishop Pere d'Arg A42

Bishops of Urgel: 5p, Josep Caixal. 13p, Joan Benlloch.

1979, Dec. 27 Engr.

116 A42 1p dk blue & brown .20 .20
117 A42 5p rose lake & purple .20 .20
118 A42 13p brown & dk green .20 .20
Nos. 116-118 (3) .60 .60

See Nos. 132-133, 159, 175, C4.

Antoni Fiter, Magistrate — A43

Europa: 19p, Francesc Cairat, magistrate.

1980, Apr. 28 Photo. *Perf. 13x13½*

119 A43 8p bister, blk & brn .20 .20
120 A43 19p lt green & blk .30 .20

Boxing, Moscow '80 Emblem A44

1980, July 23 Photo. *Perf. 13½x13*

121 A44 5p Downhill skiing .20 .20
122 A44 8p shown .20 .20
123 A44 50p Target shooting .70 .50
Nos. 121-123 (3) 1.10 .90

12th Winter Olympic Games, Lake Placid, NY, Feb. 12-24 (5p); 22nd Summer Olympic Games, Moscow, July 19-Aug. 3.

Nativity A45

1980, Dec. 12 Litho. *Perf. 13*

124 A45 10p Nativity, vert. .20 .20
125 A45 22p shown .35 .20

Christmas 1980.

Children Dancing at Santa Anna Feast A46

Europa: 30p, Going to church on Aplec de la Verge de Canolich Day.

1981, May 7 Photo. *Perf. 13*

126 A46 12p multicolored .20 .20
127 A46 30p multicolored .40 .25

50th Anniv. of Police Force A47

1981, July 2 Photo. *Perf. 13½x13*

128 A47 30p multicolored .40 .20

Intl. Year of the Disabled A48

1981, Oct. 8 Photo. *Perf. 13½*

129 A48 50p multicolored .65 .30

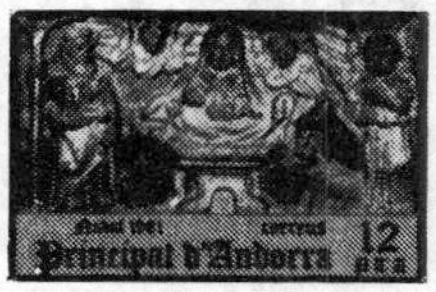

Christmas 1981 — A49

Designs: Encamp Church retable.

1981, Dec. 3 Photo. *Perf. 13½*

130 A49 12p Nativity .20 .20
131 A49 30p Adoration .40 .20

Bishops of Urgel Type of 1979

1981, Dec. 12 Engr. *Perf. 13½*

132 A42 7p Salvador Casanas .20 .20
133 A42 20p Josep de Boltas .30 .20

Natl. Arms — A51

1982, Feb. 17 Photo. *Perf. 13x13½*

134 A51 1p bright pink .20 .20
135 A51 3p bister brown .20 .20
136 A51 7p red orange .20 .20
137 A51 12p lake .20 .20
138 A51 15p ultra .20 .20
139 A51 20p blue green .25 .20
140 A51 30p crimson rose .35 .20

Perf. 13½x12½

1982, Sept. 30 Engr.

Size: 25½x30½mm

141 A51 50p dark green .80 .20
142 A51 100p dark blue 1.60 .50
Nos. 134-142 (9) 4.00 2.10

For type A51 without "PTA" see #192-198.

Europa 1982 — A52

1982, May 12 Photo. *Perf. 13*

143 A52 14p New Reforms, 1866, vert. .20 .20
144 A52 33p Reform of Institutions, 1981 .45 .25

1982 World Cup — A53

Designs: Various soccer players.

1982, June 13 Photo. *Perf. 13x13½*

145 A53 14p multicolored .45 .45
146 A53 33p multicolored 1.00 1.00
a. Pair, #145-146 + label 1.50 1.50

A54

A55

Anniversaries: 9p, Permanent Spanish and French delegations, cent. 14p, 50th anniv. of Andorran stamps. 23p, St. Francis of Assisi (1182-1226). 33p, Anyos Pro-Vicarial District membership centenary (Relacio sobre la Vall de Andorra titlepage).

1982, Sept. 7 Engr. *Perf. 13*

147 A54 9p dk blue & brown .20 .20
148 A54 14p black & green .50 .20
149 A54 23p dk blue & brown .30 .20
150 A54 33p black & olive grn .60 .45
Nos. 147-150 (4) 1.60 1.05

Perf. 13x13½, 13½x13

1982, Dec. 9 Photo.

Christmas: 14p, Madonna and Child, Andorra la Vieille Church, vert. 33p, El Tio de Nadal (children in traditional costumes striking hollow tree).

151 A55 14p multicolored .20 .20
152 A55 33p multicolored .45 .25

Europa 1983 A56

1983, June 7 Photo. *Perf. 13*

153 A56 16p La Cortinada Church, architect, 12th cent. .20 .20
154 A56 38p Water mill, 16th cent. .55 .40

Local Mushrooms — A57

1983, July 20 Photo. ***Perf. 13x12½***
155 A57 16p Lactarius sanguifluus 1.25 .50

See Nos. 165, 169, 172.

Universal Suffrage, 50th Anniv. A58

Photogravure and Engraved

1983, Sept. 6 ***Perf. 13***
156 A58 10p multicolored .20 .20

Visit of Monsignor Jacinto Verdaguer Bishop and Co-Prince A59

1983, Sept. 6
157 A59 50p multicolored .80 .45

Christmas 1983 — A60

Saint Cerni de Nagol, Romanesque fresco, Church of San Cerni de Nagol.

1983, Nov. 24 Photo. ***Perf. 13½***
158 A60 16p multicolored .30 .20

Bishops of Urgel Type of 1979

1983, Dec. 7 Engr. ***Perf. 13***
159 A42 26p Joan J. Laguarda Fenollera .35 .20

1984 Winter Olympics A62

1984, Feb. 17 Litho. ***Perf. 13½x14***
160 A62 16p Ski jumping .35 .20

ESPANA '84 — A63

1984, Apr. 27 Photo. ***Perf. 13***
161 A63 26p Emblems .35 .20

Europa (1959-84) A64

1984, May 5 Engr.
162 A64 16p brown .25 .20
163 A64 38p blue .60 .35

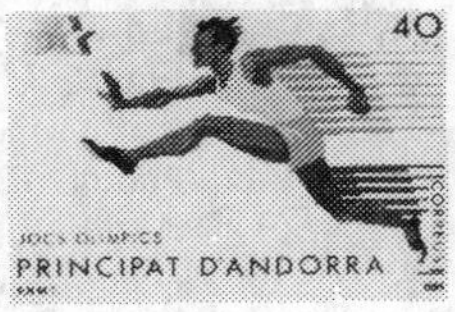

1984 Summer Olympics A65

1984, Aug. 9 Litho. ***Perf. 13½x14***
164 A65 40p Running .60 .35

Mushroom Type of 1983

Perf. 13x12½

1984, Sept. 27 Photo.
165 A57 11p Morchella esculenta *10.00* 1.50

Christmas 1984 A66

1984, Dec. 6 Photo. ***Perf. 13½***
166 A66 17p Nativity carving .30 .20

Europa 1985 A67

18p, Mossen Enric Arfany, composer, natl. hymn score. 45p, Musician Playing Viol, Romanesque fresco detail, La Cortinada Church, vert.

1985, May 3 Engr. ***Perf. 13½***
167 A67 18p dk vio, grn & chocolate .25 .20
168 A67 45p green & chocolate .75 .25

Mushroom Type of 1983

Perf. 13½x12½

1985, Sept. 19 Photo.
169 A57 30p Gyromitra esculenta .50 .25

Pal Village — A68

1985, Nov. 7 Engr. ***Perf. 13½***
170 A68 17p brt ultra & dk blue .30 .20

Christmas 1985 — A69

Fresco: Angels Playing Trumpet and Psaltery, St. Bartholomew Chapel.

1985, Dec. 11 Photo. ***Perf. 13½x13***
171 A69 17p multicolored .30 .20

Mushroom Type of 1983

Perf. 13½x12½

1986, Apr. 10 Photo.
172 A57 30p Marasmius oreades .50 .25

Europa 1986 — A70

1986, May 5 Engr. ***Perf. 13***
173 A70 17p Water .25 .20
174 A70 45p Soil and air .70 .25

Bishops of Urgel Type of 1979

1986, Sept. 11 Engr. ***Perf. 13½***
175 A42 35p Justi Guitart .50 .20

A72

A73

Santa Roma de Les Bons Church bell.

1986, Dec. 11 Litho. ***Perf. 14***
176 A72 19p multicolored .30 .20

Christmas.

1987, Mar. 27 Photo. ***Perf. 14***

Contemporary Natl. Coat of Arms.

177 A73 48p multicolored .70 .40

Visit of the co-princes: the Bishop of Urgel and president of France, September 26, 1986.

Europa 1987 A74

Modern architecture: 19p, Meritxell Sanctuary interior. 48p, Sanctuary exterior, vert.

1987, May 15 Engr. ***Perf. 14x13½***
178 A74 19p dark blue & brown .25 .20
179 A74 48p dark blue & brown .70 .25

Souvenir Sheet

1992 Summer Olympics, Barcelona A75

20p, House of the Valleys. 50p, Bell tower, Chapel of the Archangel Michael, and torchbearer.

1987, July 20 Photo. ***Perf. 14***
180 Sheet of 2 4.00 4.00
a. A75 20p multicolored 1.10 1.10
b. A75 50p multicolored 2.75 2.75

Local Mushrooms — A76

1987, Sept. 11 ***Perf. 13½x12½***
181 A76 100p Boletus edulis 1.40 .60

Christmas A77

Design: Detail from a Catalan manuscript, De Nativitat, by R. Llull.

1987, Nov. 18 Litho. ***Perf. 14***
182 A77 20p multicolored .30 .20

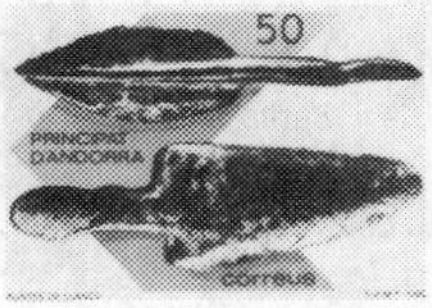

Lance and Arrowhead (Bronze Age) — A78

1988, Mar. 25 Photo. ***Perf. 14***
183 A78 50p multicolored .75 .30

Europa 1988 — A79

Pyrenean Mastiff — A80

Transport and communications: 20p, Les Bons, a medieval road. 45p, Trader and pack mules, early 20th cent.

1988, May 5 Engr. ***Perf. 14x13½***
184 A79 20p dark blue & dark red .25 .20
185 A79 45p dark blue & dark red .60 .25

1988, July 26 Litho. ***Perf. 14x13½***
186 A80 20p multicolored .30 .20

Bishop of Urgel and Seigneur of Caboet Confirming Co-Principality, 700th Anniv. — A81

1988, Oct. 24 Litho. ***Perf. 14x13½***
187 A81 20p gold, blk & int blue .30 .20

Christmas 1988 A82

1988, Nov. 30 Litho. ***Perf. 14x13½***
188 A82 20p multicolored .30 .20

Arms Type of 1982 Without "PTA"

1988, Dec. 2 Photo. ***Perf. 13x13½***
192 A51 20p brt blue green .30 .20

Size: 25x30½mm

Perf. 13½x12½

Engr.

194 A51 50p grnsh black .75 .30
196 A51 100p dark blue 1.50 .50
198 A51 500p dark brown 7.75 2.50
Nos. 192-198 (4) 10.30 3.50

This is an expanding set. Numbers will change if necessary.

Europa 1989
A83

Perf. 14x13½, 13½x14

1989, May 8 Litho. & Engr.

200 A83 20p Leapfrog, vert. .30 .20
201 A83 45p Tug of war .60 .25

Santa Roma Church, Les Bons
A84

Litho. & Engr.

1989, June 20 *Perf. 13½x14*

202 A84 50p blk, dp blue & grn blue .65 .25

Anniv. Emblem — A85

Christmas — A86

1989, Oct. 26 Litho. *Perf. 14x13½*

203 A85 20p multicolored .30 .20

Intl. Red Cross and Red Crescent societies, 125th annivs.; Year for the Protection of Human Life.

1989, Dec. 1

204 A86 20p *The Immaculate Conception* .30 .20

Europa 1990
A87

Post offices.

Perf. 13½x14, 14x13½

1990, May 17 Photo.

205 A87 20p shown .30 .20
206 A87 50p Post office, vert. .70 .30

Gomphidius Rutilus — A88

1990, June 21 Litho. *Perf. 13x13½*

207 A88 45p multicolored .70 .35

Plandolit House — A89

Christmas — A90

Litho. & Engr.

1990, Oct. 17 *Perf. 13x12½*

208 A89 20p brown & org yel .35 .20

1990, Nov. 26 Litho. *Perf. 14x13½*

209 A90 25p lake, brn & bister .40 .20

4th Games of the Small European States
A91

1991, Apr. 29 Photo. *Perf. 13½x14*

210 A91 25p Discus .40 .20
211 A91 45p High jump, runner .75 .35

Europa — A92

Perf. 14x13½, 13½x14

1991, May 10 Litho.

212 A92 25p Olympus-1 satellite .45 .20
213 A92 55p Olympus-1, horiz. .95 .45

A93

Christmas — A94

1991, Sept. 20 Litho. *Perf. 13x12½*

214 A93 45p Macrolepiota Procera .70 .35

1991, Nov. 29 Photo. *Perf. 14x13½*

215 A94 25p multicolored .40 .20

Woman Carrying Water Pails
A95

1992, Feb. 14 Photo. *Perf. 13½x14*

216 A95 25p multicolored .40 .20

Discovery of America, 500th Anniv.
A96

Perf. 14x13½, 13½x14

1992, May 8 Photo.

217 A96 27p Santa Maria, vert. .50 .20
218 A96 45p King Ferdinand .80 .35

Europa.

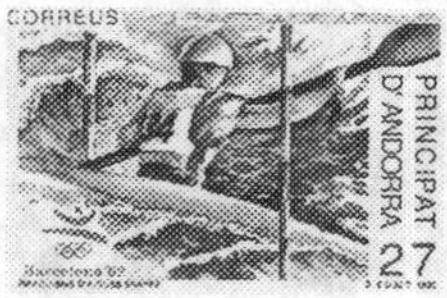

1992 Summer Olympics, Barcelona
A97

1992, July 22 Photo. *Perf. 13½x14*

219 A97 27p Kayak .65 .30

Nativity Scene, by Fra Angelico — A98

1992, Nov. 18 Photo. *Perf. 14*

220 A98 27p multicolored .50 .20

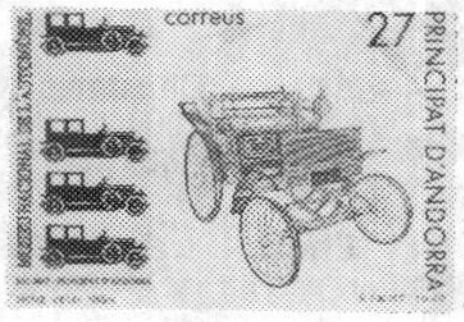

Natl. Automobile Museum
A99

Litho. & Engr.

1992, Sept. 10 *Perf. 13½x14*

221 A99 27p 1894 Benz .50 .30

Cantharellus Cibarius — A100

1993, Mar. 25 Photo. *Perf. 13½x14*

222 A100 28p multicolored .65 .30

Contemporary Paintings — A101

Europa: 28p, Upatream, by John Alan Morrison. 45p, Rhythm, by Angel Calvente, vert.

Perf. 13½x14, 14x13½

1993, May 20 Litho.

223 A101 28p multicolored .65 .30
224 A101 45p multicolored 1.10 .50

A102

A103

1993, Sept. 23 Litho. *Perf. 14*

225 A102 28p multicolored .70 .30

Art and Literature Society, 25th anniv.

Litho. & Engr.

1993, Nov. 25 *Perf. 14x13½*

226 A103 28p Christmas .70 .30

Souvenir Sheet

Constitution, 1st Anniv. — A104

1994, Mar. 14 Photo. *Perf. 14*

227 A104 29p multicolored .75 .75

Sir Alexander Fleming (1881-1955), Co-discoverer of Penicillin — A105

1994, May 6 Photo. *Perf. 13½x14*

228 A105 29p Portrait .75 .75
229 A105 55p AIDS virus 1.50 1.50

Europa.

Hygrophorus Gliocyclus — A106

1994, Sept. 27 Photo. *Perf. 14*

230 A106 29p multicolored .75 .75

Christmas — A107

1994, Nov. 29 Photo. *Perf. 14x13½*

231 A107 29p multicolored .75 .75

Nature Conservation in Europe — A108

1995, Mar. 23 Photo. *Perf. 14*

232 A108 30p Farm in valley .80 .80
233 A108 60p Stone fence, valley 1.60 1.60

Europa
A109

1995, May 8 Photo. *Perf. 14*

234 A109 60p multicolored 1.60 1.60

Christmas — A110

1995, Nov. 8 Photo. *Perf. 14*
235 A110 30p Flight to Egypt .80 .80

Entrance Into Council of Europe A111

1995, Nov. 10
236 A111 30p multicolored .80 .80

Mushrooms A112

1996, Apr. 30 Photo. *Perf. 14*
237 A112 30p Ramaria aurea .80 .80
238 A112 60p Tuber melanosporum 1.60 1.60

Isabelle Sandy (1884-1975), Writer — A113

1996, May 7
239 A113 60p brown & violet 1.75 1.75
Europa.

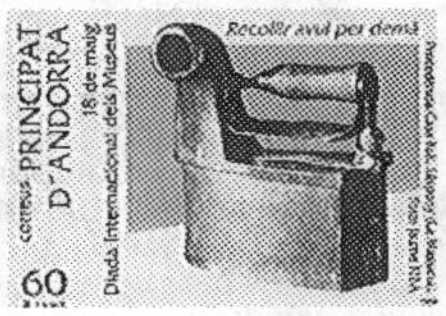

Intl. Museum Day A114

Design: Antique coal-heated iron.

1996, Sept. 12 Photo. *Perf. 14*
240 A114 60p multicolored .95 .95

Christmas A115

The Annunciation, by Andrew Martin, 1753, St. Eulalia d'Encamp Church.

1996, Nov. 26 Photo. *Perf. 14*
241 A115 30p multicolored .45 .45

Museums of Andorra A116

Early bicycles designed by: 32p, Karl Drais, 1818. 65p, Pierre Michaux, 1861.

1997, Apr. 28 Photo. *Perf. 14*
242 A116 32p multicolored .45 .45
243 A116 65p multicolored .90 .90
See Nos. 248-249.

A117

UNESCO — A118

Europa (Stories and Legends): Hikers watching family of bears crossing over river on fallen tree.

1997, May 6 Photo. *Perf. 14*
244 A117 65p multicolored .90 .90

1997, Sept. 30 Photo. *Perf. 14*
245 A118 32p multicolored .45 .45

Christmas — A119

1997, Nov. 25 Photo. *Perf. 14*
246 A119 32p multicolored .45 .45

1998 Winter Olympic Games, Nagano A120

1998, Feb. 23 Photo. *Perf. 14*
247 A120 35p Slalom skier .45 .45

Museums of Andorra Type of 1997

Early bicycles: 35p, Kangaroo, 1878. 70p, Hirondelle, 1889.

1998, Apr. 24 Photo. *Perf. 13½x14*
248 A116 35p multicolored .45 .45
249 A116 70p multicolored .90 .90

Harlequins, Canillas Carnival A121

1998, May 22 Photo. *Perf. 14*
250 A121 70p multicolored .95 .95
Europa.

Manual Digest, 250th Anniv. — A122

1998, Sept. 30 Photo. *Perf. 14*
251 A122 35p multicolored .50 .50

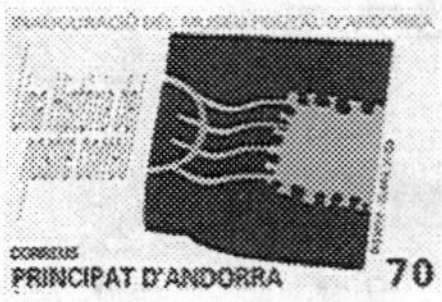

Inauguration of the Postal Museum of Andorra A123

1998, Nov. 19 Photo. *Perf. 14*
252 A123 70p multicolored 1.00 1.00

Christmas A124

1998, Nov. 26
253 A124 35p multicolored .50 .50

Museums of Andorra A125

Early bicycles designed by: 35p, Salvo, 1878, vert. 70p, Rudge, 1883.

1999, Jan. 29 Photo. *Perf. 14*
254 A125 35p multicolored .50 .50
255 A125 70p multicolored 1.00 1.00

Council of Europe, 50th Anniv. A126

1999, Apr. 29 Photo. *Perf. 14*
256 A126 35p multicolored .45 .45

Incles Valley A127

1999, May 6
257 A127 70p multicolored .90 .90
Europa.

Tansporting Mail on Horseback A128

1999, Feb. 18 Photo. *Perf. 14*
258 A128 35p black & sepia .50 .50

Restoration of Casa Rull, Sispony, La Massana A129

Perf. 13½x14
1999, Sept. 22 Photo.
259 A129 35p multicolored .45 .45

Christmas A130

St. Coloma's Church A131

1999, Nov. 10 Engr. *Perf. 14x13½*
260 A130 35p orange brn & brn .45 .45

1999, Nov. 12 Photo.
261 A131 35p multicolored .45 .45
European heritage.

AIR POST STAMPS

AP1

Unwmk.
1951, June 27 Engr. *Perf. 11*
C1 AP1 1p dark violet brown 22.50 5.00

Catalogue values for unused stamps in this section, from this point to the end of the section, are for Never Hinged items.

AP2

AP3

Litho. & Engr.
1983, Oct. 20 *Perf. 13*
C2 AP2 20p brown & bis brn .30 .20

Jaime Sansa Nequi, Episcopal Church official.

1984, Oct. 25 Photo. *Perf. 13*
C3 AP3 20p multicolored .35 .25
Pyrenees Art Center.

Bishops of Urgel Type of 1979
1985, June 13 Engr. *Perf. 13½*
C4 A42 20p Ramon Iglesias .35 .20

SPECIAL DELIVERY STAMPS

Special Delivery Stamp of Spain, 1905 Overprinted

CORREOS

ANDORRA

1928 Unwmk. *Perf. 14*
Without Control Number on Back
E1 SD1 20c red 62.50 *65.00*
Never hinged 80.00

With Control Number on Back
E2 SD1 20c pale red 40.00 *45.00*
Never hinged 50.00

Eagle over Mountain Pass — SD2

1929 *Perf. 14*
With Control Number on Back

E3	SD2	20c scarlet	18.00	18.00
		Never hinged	22.50	

Perf 11½ examples are numbered A000.000 and are specimens.

1937 *Perf. 11½x11*
Without Control Number on Back

E4	SD2	20c red	6.75	6.50
		Never hinged	7.50	

Arms and Squirrel — SD3

1949 Unwmk. Engr. *Perf. 10x9½*

E5	SD3	25c red	4.00	4.00

FRENCH ADMINISTRATION

Stamps and Types of France, 1900-1929, Overprinted **ANDORRE**

Perf. 14x13½
1931, June 16 **Unwmk.**

1	A16	1c gray	.55	.55
a.		Double overprint	1000.	1000.
2	A16	2c red brown	.60	.70
3	A16	3c orange	.60	.70
4	A16	5c green	1.00	1.25
5	A16	10c lilac	1.50	1.75
6	A22	15c red brown	3.00	3.00
7	A22	20c red violet	4.00	4.00
8	A22	25c yellow brn	5.00	4.00
9	A22	30c green	4.00	4.00
10	A22	40c ultra	6.75	6.75
11	A20	45c lt violet	7.25	7.25
12	A20	50c vermilion	6.25	6.00
13	A20	65c gray green	11.00	12.75
14	A20	75c rose lilac	14.50	14.75
15	A22	90c red	17.50	17.50
16	A20	1fr dull blue	21.00	20.00
17	A22	1.50fr light blue	25.00	25.00

Overprinted **ANDORRE**

18	A18	2fr org & pale bl	17.00	17.50
19	A18	3fr brt vio & rose	60.00	62.50
20	A18	5fr dk bl & buff	100.00	100.00
21	A18	10fr grn & red	195.00	210.00
22	A18	20fr mag & grn	250.00	275.00
		Nos. 1-22 (22)	751.50	794.95

See No. P1 for ½c on 1c gray.
Nos. 9, 15 and 17 were not issued in France without overprint.

Chapel of Meritxell A50

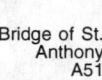

Bridge of St. Anthony A51

St. Miguel d'Engolasters A52

Gorge of St. Julia A53

Old Andorra A54

1932-43 Engr. *Perf. 13*

23	A50	1c gray blk	.30	.25
24	A50	2c violet	.40	.40
25	A50	3c brown	.30	.30
26	A50	5c blue green	.40	.40
27	A51	10c dull lilac	.65	.60
28	A50	15c deep red	1.00	1.00
29	A51	20c lt rose	6.25	4.50
30	A52	25c brown	2.25	2.25
31	A51	25c brn car ('37)	4.50	6.50
32	A51	30c emerald	1.75	1.50
33	A51	40c ultra	5.00	4.25
34	A51	40c brn blk ('39)	.65	.60
35	A51	45c lt red	6.00	5.00
36	A51	45c bl grn ('39)	3.00	2.50
37	A52	50c lilac rose	6.50	5.00
38	A51	50c lt vio ('39)	3.00	2.50
38A	A51	50c grn ('40)	1.40	1.40
39	A51	55c lt vio ('38)	9.50	6.00
40	A51	60c yel brn ('38)	.60	.50
41	A52	65c yel grn	35.00	35.00
42	A51	65c blue ('38)	6.50	5.50
43	A51	70c red ('39)	1.25	1.00
44	A52	75c violet	3.25	2.50
45	A51	75c ultra ('39)	2.50	2.25
46	A51	80c green ('38)	13.00	9.50
46A	A51	80c bl grn ('40)	.25	.30
47	A53	90c deep rose	3.25	2.25
48	A53	90c dk grn ('39)	2.25	2.25
49	A53	1fr blue grn	9.50	6.00
50	A53	1fr scarlet ('38)	15.00	15.00
51	A53	1fr dp ultra ('39)	.25	.25
51A	A53	1.20fr brt vio ('42)	.25	.25
52	A50	1.25fr rose car ('33)	35.00	25.00
52A	A50	1.25fr rose ('38)	3.00	1.40
52B	A53	1.30fr sepia ('40)	.25	.25
53	A54	1.50fr ultra	8.25	7.50
53A	A53	1.50fr crim ('40)	.25	.25
54	A53	1.75fr violet ('33)	80.00	80.00
55	A53	1.75fr dk bl ('38)	30.00	22.50
56	A53	2fr red violet	3.75	3.50
56A	A50	2fr rose red ('40)	1.00	.65
56B	A50	2fr dk bl grn ('42)	.25	.20
57	A50	2.15fr dk vio ('38)	40.00	27.50
58	A50	2.25fr ultra ('39)	4.00	3.00
58A	A50	2.40fr red ('42)	.25	.20
59	A50	2.50fr gray blk ('39)	4.00	3.00
59A	A50	2.50fr dp ultra ('40)	1.40	1.25
60	A53	3fr orange brn	3.75	3.50
60A	A50	3fr red brn ('40)	.30	.25
60B	A50	4fr sl bl ('42)	.30	.25
60C	A50	4.50fr dp vio ('42)	.75	.75
61	A54	5fr brown	.40	.35
62	A54	10fr violet	.45	.40
62B	A54	15fr dp ultra ('42)	.50	.40
63	A54	20fr rose lake	.50	.40
63A	A51	50fr turq bl ('43)	1.00	.50
		Nos. 23-63A (56)	365.05	310.50

A 20c ultra exists. Value $12,500.

No. 37 Surcharged with Bars and New Value in Black

1935, Sept. 25

64	A52	20c on 50c lil rose	13.00	11.00
a.		Double surcharge	2,000.	

Coat of Arms
A55 A56

1936-42 *Perf. 14x13*

65	A55	1c black ('37)	.20	.20
66	A55	2c blue	.20	.20
67	A55	3c brown	.20	.20
68	A55	5c rose lilac	.20	.20
69	A55	10c ultra ('37)	.20	.20
70	A55	15c red violet	.55	.55
71	A55	20c emerald ('37)	.20	.20
72	A55	30c cop red ('38)	.30	.30
72A	A55	30c blk brn ('42)	.20	.20
73	A55	35c Prus grn ('38)	30.00	30.00
74	A55	40c cop red ('42)	.20	.20
75	A55	50c Prus grn ('42)	.20	.20
76	A55	60c turq bl ('42)	.20	.20
77	A55	70c vio ('42)	.20	.20
		Nos. 65-77 (14)	33.05	33.05

Catalogue values for unused stamps in this section, from this point to the end of the section, are for Never Hinged items.

1944

78	A56	10c violet	.20	.20
79	A56	30c deep magenta	.20	.20
80	A56	40c dull blue	.20	.20
81	A56	50c orange red	.20	.20
82	A56	60c black	.20	.20
83	A56	70c brt red violet	.20	.20
84	A56	80c blue green	.20	.20
		Nos. 78-84 (7)	1.40	1.40

See No. 114.

St. Jean de Caselles A57

La Maison des Vallees A58

Old Andorra A59

Provost A60

1944-47 *Perf. 13*

85	A57	1fr brown violet	.35	.20
86	A57	1.20fr blue	.20	.20
87	A57	1.50fr red	.35	.20
88	A57	2fr dk blue grn	.20	.20
89	A58	2.40fr rose red	.30	.20
90	A58	2.50fr rose red ('46)	4.50	1.40
91	A58	3fr sepia	.20	.20
92	A58	4fr ultra	.35	.20
93	A59	4.50fr brown blk	.35	.20
94	A58	4.50fr dk bl grn ('47)	7.00	3.50
95	A59	5fr ultra	.30	.20
96	A59	5fr Prus grn ('46)	.55	.30
97	A59	6fr rose car ('45)	.40	.20
98	A59	10fr Prus green	.20	.20
99	A59	10fr ultra ('46)	.30	.20
100	A60	15fr rose lilac	.65	.25
101	A60	20fr deep blue	.75	.45
102	A60	25fr lt rose red ('46)	4.50	2.25
103	A60	40fr dk green ('46)	4.50	3.00
104	A60	50fr sepia	2.00	1.10
		Nos. 85-104 (20)	27.95	14.65

1948-49

105	A58	4fr lt blue grn	1.00	.80
106	A59	6fr violet brn	.50	.40
107	A59	8fr indigo	1.50	1.25
108	A59	12fr bright red	1.00	.90
109	A59	12fr blue grn ('49)	1.10	.90
110	A59	15fr crimson ('49)	.60	.50
111	A60	18fr deep blue	3.75	2.00
112	A60	20fr dark violet	3.00	2.25
113	A60	25fr ultra ('49)	2.00	1.50
		Nos. 105-113 (9)	14.45	10.50

1949-51 *Perf. 14x13, 13*

114	A56	1fr deep blue	1.25	.75
115	A57	3fr red ('51)	6.00	5.00
116	A57	4fr sepia	3.00	2.50
117	A58	5fr emerald	3.50	3.00
118	A58	5fr purple ('51)	6.00	5.00
119	A58	6fr blue grn ('51)	5.00	4.50
120	A58	8fr brown	1.50	1.00
121	A59	15fr blk brn ('51)	6.50	5.00
122	A59	18fr rose red ('51)	17.50	12.00
123	A60	30fr ultra ('51)	30.00	12.00
		Nos. 114-123 (10)	80.25	50.75

Les Escaldres Spa — A61

St. Coloma Belfry A62

Designs: 15fr-25fr, Gothic cross. 30fr-75fr, Village of Les Bons.

1955-58 Unwmk. Engr. *Perf. 13*

124	A61	1fr dk gray bl	.20	.20
125	A61	2fr dp green	.20	.20
126	A61	3fr red	.25	.20
127	A61	5fr chocolate	.25	.20
128	A62	6fr dk bl grn	.50	.40
129	A62	8fr rose brown	.50	.45
130	A62	10fr brt violet	.80	.55
131	A62	12fr indigo	.90	.60
132	A61	15fr red	1.25	.85
133	A61	18fr blue grn	1.25	.85
134	A61	20fr dp purple	1.90	1.50
135	A61	25fr sepia	2.25	1.50
136	A62	30fr deep blue	26.00	16.00
137	A62	35fr Prus bl ('57)	10.00	6.75
138	A62	40fr dk green	27.50	18.00
139	A62	50fr cerise	3.50	2.25
140	A62	65fr purple ('58)	9.50	5.75
141	A62	70fr chestnut ('57)	6.50	5.75
142	A62	75fr violet blue	45.00	32.50
		Nos. 124-142 (19)	138.25	94.50

Issued: 35fr, 70fr, 8/19; 65fr, 2/10; others, 2/15.

Coat of Arms — A63

Gothic Cross, Meritxell — A64

Designs: 65c, 85c, 1fr, Pond of Engolasters.

1961, June 19 Typo. *Perf. 14x13*

143	A63	5c brt green & blk	.20	.20
144	A63	10c red, pink & blk	.20	.20
145	A63	15c blue & black	.20	.20
146	A63	20c yellow & brown	.20	.20

Engr. *Perf. 13*

147	A64	25c violet, bl & grn	.25	.25
148	A64	30c mar, ol grn & brn	.30	.30
149	A64	45c indigo, bl & grn	13.00	6.50
150	A64	50c pur, lt brn & ol grn	1.00	1.00
151	A64	65c bl, ol & brn	17.50	14.00
152	A64	85c rose lil, vio bl & brn	17.50	14.00
153	A64	1fr grnsh bl, ind & brn	1.00	1.00
		Nos. 143-153 (11)	51.35	37.85

See Nos. 161-166A.

Imperforates

Most stamps of Andorra, French Administration, from 1961 onward exist imperforate in issued and trial colors, and also in small presentation sheets in issued colors.

Telstar and Globe Showing Andover and Pleumeur-Bodou — A65

1962, Sept. 29 **Engr.**

154	A65	50c ultra & purple	1.00	1.00

1st television connection of the US and Europe through the Telstar satellite, July 11-12.

"La Sardane" A66

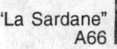

Charlemagne Crossing Andorra — A67

1fr, Louis le Debonnaire giving founding charter.

1963, June 22 Unwmk. *Perf. 13*

155 A66 20c lil rose, cl & ol grn 3.00 2.75
156 A67 50c sl grn & dk car rose 5.00 4.50
157 A67 1fr red brn, ultra & dk grn 7.50 7.00
Nos. 155-157 (3) 15.50 14.25

Old Andorra Church and Champs-Elysées Palace — A68

1964, Jan. 20 Engr.

158 A68 25c blk, grn & vio brn 1.00 .75

"PHILATEC," Intl. Philatelic and Postal Techniques Exhib., Paris, June 5-21, 1964.

Bishop of Urgel and Seigneur of Caboet Confirming Co-Principality, 1288 — A69

Design: 60c, Napoleon re-establishing Co-principality, 1806.

1964, Apr. 25 Engr. *Perf. 13*

159 A69 60c dk brn, red brn & sl grn 10.00 10.00
160 A69 1fr brt bl, org brn & blk 10.00 10.00

Arms Type of 1961

1964, May 16 Typo. *Perf. 14x13*

161 A63 1c dk blue & gray .25 .20
162 A63 2c black & orange .25 .20
163 A63 12c purple, emer & yel .40 .30
164 A63 18c black, lil & pink .40 .30
Nos. 161-164 (4) 1.30 1.00

Scenic Type of 1961

Designs: 40c, 45c, Gothic Cross, Meritxell. 60c, 90c, Pond of Engolasters.

1965-71 Engr. *Perf. 13*

165 A64 40c dk brn, org brn & sl grn .50 .50
165A A64 45c vio bl, ol bis & slate .90 .75
166 A64 60c org brn & dk brn .60 .60
166A A64 90c ultra, bl grn & bister .50 .50
Nos. 165-166A (4) 2.50 2.35

Issued: 40c, 60c, Apr. 24, 1965. 45c, June 13, 1970. 90c, Aug. 28, 1971.

Syncom Satellite over Pleumeur-Bodou Station — A70

Andorra House, Paris — A71

1965, May 17 Unwmk.

167 A70 60c dp car, lil & bl 3.50 3.25

Cent. of the ITU.

1965, June 5

168 A71 25c dk bl, org brn & ol gray .90 .75

Ski Lift — A72

Design: 25c, Chair lift, vert.

1966, Apr. 2 Engr. *Perf. 13*

169 A72 25c brt bl, grn & dk brn .90 .80
170 A72 40c mag, brt ultra & sep 1.25 1.10

Winter sports in Andorra.

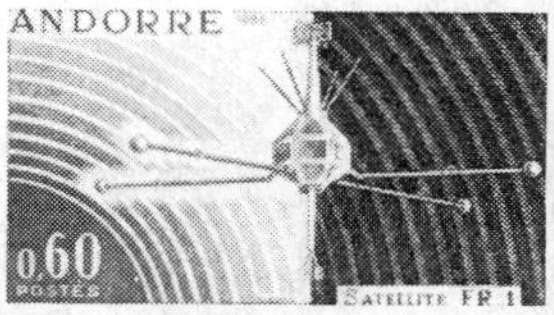

FR-1 Satellite — A73

1966, May 7 *Perf. 13*

171 A73 60c brt bl, grn & dk grn 1.40 1.40

Issued to commemorate the launching of the scientific satellite FR-1, Dec. 6, 1965.

Common Design Types pictured following the introduction.

Europa Issue, 1966
Common Design Type

1966, Sept. 24 Engr. *Perf. 13*
Size: 21½x35½mm

172 CD9 60c brown 2.75 2.00

Folk Dancers, Sculpture by Josep Viladomat — A74

Telephone Encircling the Globe — A75

1967, Apr. 29 Engr. *Perf. 13*

173 A74 30c ol grn, dp grn & slate .60 .45

Cent. (in 1966) of the New Reform, which reaffirmed and strengthened political freedom in Andorra.

Europa Issue, 1967
Common Design Type

1967, Apr. 29
Size: 22x36mm

174 CD10 30c bluish blk & lt bl 1.75 1.50
175 CD10 60c dk red & brt pink 2.75 2.00

1967, Apr. 29

176 A75 60c dk car, vio & blk 1.00 .75

Automatic telephone service.

Injured Father at Home — A76

1967, Sept. 23 Engr. *Perf. 13*

177 A76 2.30fr ocher, dk red brn & brn red 7.00 4.00

Introduction of Social Security System.

Jesus in Garden of Gethsemane — A77

Designs (from 16th century frescoes in La Maison des Vallees): 30c, The Kiss of Judas. 60c, The Descent from the Cross (Pieta).

1967, Sept. 23

178 A77 25c black & red brn .45 .35
179 A77 30c purple & red lilac .70 .45
180 A77 60c indigo & Prus blue 1.25 .80
Nos. 178-180 (3) 2.40 1.60

See Nos. 185-187.

Downhill Skier — A78

1968, Jan. 27 Engr. *Perf. 13*

181 A78 40c org, ver & red lil .70 .55

10th Winter Olympic Games, Grenoble, France, Feb. 6-18.

Europa Issue, 1968
Common Design Type

1968, Apr. 27 Engr. *Perf. 13*
Size: 36x22mm

182 CD11 30c gray & brt bl 4.00 2.50
183 CD11 60c brown & lilac 6.00 3.00

High Jump — A79

1968, Oct. 12 Engr. *Perf. 13*

184 A79 40c brt blue & brn 1.00 .75

19th Olympic Games, Mexico City, Oct. 12-27.

Fresco Type of 1967

Designs (from 16th century frescoes in La Maison des Vallees): 25c, The Scourging of Christ. 30c, Christ Carrying the Cross. 60c, The Crucifixion. (All horiz.)

1968, Oct. 12

185 A77 25c dk grn & gray grn .50 .50
186 A77 30c dk brown & lilac .90 .90
187 A77 60c dk car & vio brn 1.25 1.25
Nos. 185-187 (3) 2.65 2.65

Europa Issue, 1969
Common Design Type

1969, Apr. 26 Engr. *Perf. 13*

188 CD12 40c rose car, gray & dl bl 4.50 2.00
189 CD12 70c indigo, dl red & ol 7.00 4.00

10th anniv. of the Conf. of European Postal and Telecommunications Administrations.

Kayak on Isère River — A80

Drops of Water and Diamond — A80a

1969, Aug. 2 Engr. *Perf. 13*

190 A80 70c dk sl grn, ultra & ind 2.00 2.00

Intl. Canoe & Kayak Championships, Bourg-Saint-Maurice, Savoy, July 31-Aug. 6.

1969, Sept. 27 Engr. *Perf. 13*

191 A80a 70c blk, dp ultra & grnsh bl 4.00 4.00

European Water Charter.

St. John, the Woman and the Dragon — A81

The Revelation (From the Altar of St. John, Caselles): 40c, St. John Hearing Voice from Heaven on Patmos. 70c, St. John and the Seven Candlesticks.

1969, Oct. 18

192 A81 30c brn, dp pur & brn red .60 .60
193 A81 40c gray, dk brn & brn ol .80 .80
194 A81 70c dk red, maroon & brt rose lilac 1.50 1.50
Nos. 192-194 (3) 2.90 2.90

See Nos. 199-201, 207-209, 214-216.

Field Ball — A82

Shot Put — A83

1970, Feb. 21 Engr. *Perf. 13*

195 A82 80c multi 1.75 1.25

Issued to publicize the 7th International Field Ball Games, France, Feb. 26-Mar. 8.

Europa Issue, 1970
Common Design Type

1970, May 2 Engr. *Perf. 13*
Size: 36x22mm

196 CD13 40c orange 4.00 2.00
197 CD13 80c violet blue 8.00 4.00

1970, Sept. 11 Engr. *Perf. 13*

198 A83 80c bl & dk brn 1.50 1.25

1st European Junior Athletic Championships, Colombes, France, Sept. 11-13.

Altar Type of 1969

The Revelation (from the Altar of St. John, Caselles): 30c, St. John recording angel's message. 40c, Angel erecting column symbolizing faithful in heaven. 80c, St. John's trial in kettle of boiling oil.

1970, Oct. 24

199 A81 30c dp car, dk brn & brt pur .70 .70
200 A81 40c violet & slate grn .85 .85
201 A81 80c ol, dk bl & car rose 1.75 1.75
Nos. 199-201 (3) 3.30 3.30

Ice Skating A84

1971, Feb. 20 **Engr.** ***Perf. 13***

202 A84 80c dk red, red lil & pur 2.00 1.25

World Figure Skating Championships, Lyons, France, Feb. 23-28.

Capercaillie — A85

Nature protection: No. 204, Brown bear.

1971, Apr. 24 **Photo.** ***Perf. 13***

203 A85 80c multicolored 3.25 2.25

Engr.

204 A85 80c blue, grn & brn 3.25 2.25

Europa Issue, 1971

Common Design Type

1971, May 8 **Engr.** ***Perf. 13***

Size: 35½x22mm

205 CD14 50c rose red 5.50 3.00
206 CD14 80c lt blue green 8.50 4.00

Altar Type of 1969

The Revelation (from the Altar of St. John, Caselles): 30c, St. John preaching, Rev. 1:3. 50c, "The Sign of the Beast . . ." Rev. 16:1-2. 90c, The Woman, Rev. 17:1.

1971, Sept. 18

207 A81 30c dl grn, ol & brt grn .70 .70
208 A81 50c rose car, org & ol brn .90 .90
209 A81 90c blk, dk pur & bl 1.50 1.50
Nos. 207-209 (3) 3.10 3.10

Europa Issue 1972

Common Design Type

1972, Apr. 29 **Photo.** ***Perf. 13***

Size: 21½x37mm

210 CD15 50c brt mag & multi 5.00 3.00
211 CD15 90c multicolored 7.00 4.50

Golden Eagle — A86

1972, May 27 **Engr.**

212 A86 60c dk grn, olive & plum 3.50 2.00

Nature protection.

Shooting A87

1972, July 8

213 A87 1fr dk purple 2.00 1.50

20th Olympic Games, Munich, Aug. 26-Sept. 11.

Altar Type of 1969

The Revelation (from the Altar of St. John, Caselles): 30c, St. John, bishop and servant. 50c, Resurrection of Lazarus. 90c, Angel with lance and nails.

1972, Sept. 16 **Engr.** ***Perf. 13***

214 A81 30c dk ol, gray & red lil .70 .70
215 A81 50c vio blue & slate 1.00 1.00
216 A81 90c dk Prus bl & sl grn 1.50 1.50
Nos. 214-216 (3) 3.20 3.20

De Gaulle as Coprince of Andorra — A88

90c, De Gaulle in front of Maison des Vallées.

1972, Oct. 23 **Engr.** ***Perf. 13***

217 A88 50c violet blue 1.25 1.25
218 A88 90c dk carmine 1.75 1.75
a. Pair, #217-218 + label 3.00 3.00

Visit of Charles de Gaulle to Andorra, 5th anniv.

See Nos. 399-400.

Europa Issue 1973

Common Design Type

1973, Apr. 28 **Photo.** ***Perf. 13***

Size: 36x22mm

219 CD16 50c violet & multi 5.50 2.75
220 CD16 90c dk red & multi 8.50 3.00

Virgin of Canolich A89

1973, June 16 **Engr.** ***Perf. 13***

221 A89 1fr ol, Prus bl & vio 1.50 1.50

Lily — A90

Blue Titmouse — A91

Designs: 45c, Iris. 50c, Columbine. 65c, Tobacco. No. 226, Pinks. No. 227, Narcissuses.

1973-74 **Photo.** ***Perf. 13***

222 A90 30c car rose & multi .35 .35
223 A90 45c yel grn & multi .25 .25
224 A90 50c buff & multi 1.25 1.25
225 A90 65c gray & multi .35 .35
226 A90 90c ultra & multi .80 .80
227 A90 90c grnsh bl & multi .70 .70
Nos. 222-227 (6) 3.70 3.70

See Nos. 238-240.

1973-74 **Photo.** ***Perf. 13***

Nature protection: 60c, Citril finch and mistletoe. 80c, Eurasian bullfinch. 1fr, Lesser spotted woodpecker.

228 A91 60c buff & multi 3.25 3.00
229 A91 80c gray & multi 2.25 2.00
230 A91 90c gray & multi 2.25 2.00
231 A91 1fr yel grn & multi 2.25 2.00
Nos. 228-231 (4) 10.00 9.00

Europa Issue 1974

Virgin of Pal — A92

Design: 90c, Virgin of Santa Coloma. Statues are polychrome 12th century carvings by rural artists.

1974, Apr. 27 **Engr.** ***Perf. 13***

232 A92 50c multicolored 5.00 3.75
233 A92 90c multicolored 10.00 5.00

Arms of Andorra and Cahors Bridge — A93

Mail Box, Chutes and Globe — A94

1974, Aug. 24 **Engr.** ***Perf. 13***

234 A93 1fr blue, vio & org 1.00 .60

First anniversary of meeting of the co-princes of Andorra: Pres. Georges Pompidou of France and Msgr. Juan Marti Alanis, Bishop of Urgel.

1974, Oct. 5 **Engr.** ***Perf. 13***

235 A94 1.20fr multi 1.10 1.00

Centenary of Universal Postal Union.

Coronation of St. Marti, 16th Century — A95

Europa: 80c, Crucifixion, 16th cent., vert.

Perf. 11½x13, 13x11½

1975, Apr. 26 **Photo.**

236 A95 80c gold & multi 6.00 3.50
237 A95 1.20fr gold & multi 7.50 4.00

Flower Type of 1973

Designs: 60c, Gentian. 80c, Anemone. 1.20fr, Autumn crocus.

1975, May 10 **Photo.** ***Perf. 13***

238 A90 60c olive & multi .30 .30
239 A90 80c brt rose & multi .70 .70
240 A90 1.20fr green & multi .75 .75
Nos. 238-240 (3) 1.75 1.75

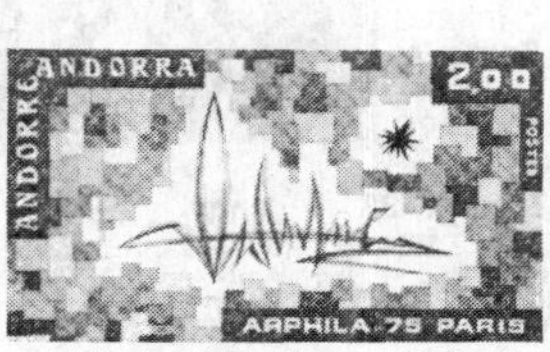

Abstract Design — A96

1975, June 7 **Engr.** ***Perf. 13***

241 A96 2fr bl, magenta & emer 1.50 1.50

ARPHILA 75 International Philatelic Exhibition, Paris, June 6-16.

A97

A98

1975, Aug. 23 **Engr.** ***Perf. 13***

242 A97 80c violet bl & blk .75 .75

Georges Pompidou (1911-74), pres. of France and co-prince of Andorra (1969-74).

1975, Nov. 8 **Engr.** ***Perf. 13***

243 A98 1.20fr Costume, IWY Emblem 1.00 .75

International Women's Year.

Skier and Snowflake A99

1976, Jan. 31 **Engr.** ***Perf. 13***

244 A99 1.20fr multicolored 1.00 .75

12th Winter Olympic Games, Innsbruck, Austria, Feb. 4-15.

Telephone and Satellite — A100

1976, Mar. 20 **Engr.** ***Perf. 13***

245 A100 1fr multicolored .80 .80

Centenary of first telephone call by Alexander Graham Bell, Mar. 10, 1976.

Catalan Forge A101

Europa: 1.20fr, Lacemaker.

1976, May 8 **Engr.** ***Perf. 13***

246 A101 80c multi 1.50 1.10
247 A101 1.20fr multi 2.50 1.65

Thomas Jefferson A102

Trapshooting A103

1976, July 3 **Engr.** ***Perf. 13***

248 A102 1.20fr multi 1.00 .75

American Bicentennial.

1976, July 17 **Engr.** ***Perf. 13***

249 A103 2fr multi 1.50 1.00

21st Olympic Games, Montreal, Canada, July 17-Aug. 1.

Meritxell Sanctuary and Old Chapel — A104

1976, Sept. 4 Engr. Perf. 13
250 A104 1fr multi .75 .65

Dedication of rebuilt Meritxell Church, Sept. 8, 1976.

Apollo A105

Ermine A106

Design: 1.40fr, Morio butterfly.

1976, Oct. 16 Photo. Perf. 13
251 A105 80c black & multi 1.75 1.25
252 A105 1.40fr salmon & multi 2.25 1.65

Nature protection.

1977, Apr. 2 Photo. Perf. 13
253 A106 1fr vio bl, gray & blk 1.50 1.50

Nature protection.

St. Jean de Caselles A107

Manual Digest, 1748, Arms of Andorra A108

Europa: 1.40fr, Sant Vicens Castle.

1977, Apr. 30 Engr. Perf. 13
254 A107 1fr multi 1.75 .90
255 A107 1.40fr multi 2.25 1.40

1977, June 11 Engr. Perf. 13
256 A108 80c grn, bl & brn .75 .65

Establishment of Institute of Andorran Studies.

St. Romanus of Caesarea A109

1977, July 23 Engr. Perf. 12½x13
257 A109 2fr multi 1.25 1.00

Design from altarpiece in Church of St. Roma de les Bons.

General Council Chamber A110

Guillem d'Arény Plandolit — A111

1977, Sept. 24 Engr. Perf. 13
258 A110 1.10fr multi 2.00 1.00
259 A111 2fr car & dk brn 1.25 1.00

Andorran heritage. Guillem d'Arény Plandolit started Andorran reform movement in 1866.

Squirrel A112

Flag and Valira River Bridge A113

1978, Mar. 18 Engr. Perf. 13
260 A112 1fr multi .90 .50

1978, Apr. 8
261 A113 80c multi .50 .40

Signing of the treaty establishing the Co-Principality of Andorra, 700th anniv.

Pal Church A114

Europa: 1.40fr, Charlemagne's Castle, Charlemagne on horseback, vert.

1978, Apr. 29 Engr. Perf. 13
262 A114 1fr multi 2.00 1.65
263 A114 1.40fr multi 3.00 2.25

Virgin of Sispony A115

1978, May 20 Engr. Perf. 12x13
264 A115 2fr multi 1.25 1.00

Visura Tribunal A116

1978, June 24 Engr. Perf. 13
265 A116 1.20fr multi .75 .40

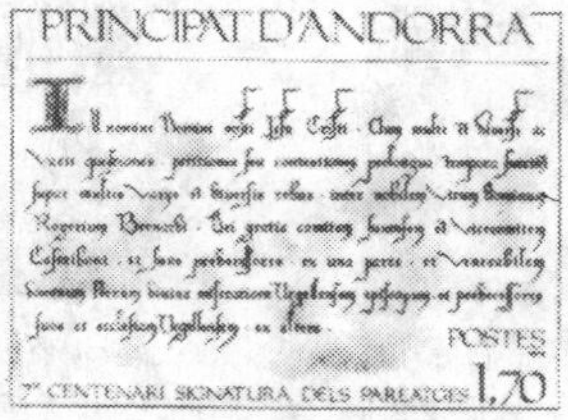

Preamble of 1278 Treaty — A117

1978, Sept. 2 Engr. Perf. 13x12½
266 A117 1.70fr multi .75 .40

700th anniversary of the signing of treaty establishing Co-Principality of Andorra.

Pyrenean Chamois A118

White Partridges A119

1979, Mar. 26 Engr. Perf. 13
267 A118 1fr multi .50 .35

1979, Apr. 9 Photo. Perf. 13
268 A119 1.20fr multi .75 .60

Nature protection. See Nos. 288-289.

French Mailman, 1900 — A120

Europa: 1.70fr, 1st French p.o. in Andorra.

1979, Apr. 28 Engr. Perf. 13
269 A120 1.20fr multi 1.10 .90
270 A120 1.70fr multi 1.65 1.10

Falcon, Pre-Roman Painting A121

1979, June 2 Engr. Perf. 12½x13
271 A121 2fr multi 1.00 .75

A122

A123

Child with Lambs, Church, IYC emblem.

1979, July 7 Photo. Perf. 13
272 A122 1.70fr multi .75 .40

International Year of the Child.

1979, Sept. 29 Engr. Perf. 13

Bas-relief, Trobada monument.

273 A123 2fr multi 1.00 .75

700th anniversary of Co-Principality of Andorra

Judo Hold — A124

Farm House, Cortinada — A125

1979, Nov. 24 Engr. Perf. 13
274 A124 1.30fr multi .75 .40

World Judo Championships, Paris, Dec. 1979.

1980, Jan. 26 Engr. Perf. 13
275 A125 1.10fr multi .40 .30

Cross-Country Skiing — A126

1980, Feb. 9
276 A126 1.80fr ultra & lil rose 1.25 .75

13th Winter Olympic Games, Lake Placid, NY, Feb. 12-24.

A128

A129

1980, Aug. 30 Engr. Perf. 13
278 A128 1.20fr multi .50 .30

World Bicycling championships.

1980, Apr. 26 Engr. Perf. 13

Europa: 1.30fr, Charlemagne (742-814). 1.80fr, Napoleon I (1769-1821).

279 A129 1.30fr multi .50 .35
280 A129 1.80fr gray grn & brn .75 .50

Pyrenees Lily — A130

1980 Photo.
281 A130 1.10fr Dog-toothed violet .50 .30
282 A130 1.30fr shown .55 .35

Nature protection. Issue dates: 1.10fr, June 21, 1.30fr, May 17.

De La Vall House, 400th Anniversary of Restoration A131

1980, Sept. 6 **Engr.**
283 A131 1.40fr multi .45 .35

Angel, Church of St. Cerni de Nagol, Pre-Romanesque Fresco — A132

1980, Oct. 27 ***Perf. 13x12½***
284 A132 2fr multi .75 .60

Bordes de Mereig Mountain Village A133

1981, Mar. 21 **Engr.** ***Perf. 13***
285 A133 1.40fr bl gray & dk brn .50 .40

Europa Issue 1981

Ball de l'Ossa, Winter Game A134

1981, May 16 **Engr.**
286 A134 1.40fr shown .65 .45
287 A134 2fr El Contrapas dance .80 .60

Bird Type of 1979

1981, June 20 **Photo.**
288 A119 1.20fr Phylloscopus bonelli .60 .30
289 A119 1.40fr Tichodroma muraria .60 .40

World Fencing Championship, Clermont-Ferrand, July 2-13 — A135

1981, July 4 **Engr.**
290 A135 2fr bl & blk .65 .35

St. Martin, 12th Cent. Tapestry — A136

1981, Sept. 5 **Engr.** ***Perf. 12x13***
291 A136 3fr multi 1.00 .75

Andorra, French Administration, stamps can be mounted in the annually supplemented Scott Monaco and French Andorra album.

Intl. Drinking Water Decade A137

Intl. Year of the Disabled A138

1981, Oct. 17 ***Perf. 13***
292 A137 1.60fr multi .50 .30

1981, Nov. 7
293 A138 2.30fr multi .75 .65

Europa 1982 — A139

1982, May 8 **Engr.** ***Perf. 13***
294 A139 1.60fr Creation of Andorran govt., 1982 .50 .40
295 A139 2.30fr Land Council, 1419 .75 .50

1982 World Cup — A140

Designs: Various soccer players. Nos. 296-297 se-tenant with label showing natl. arms.

1982, June 12 **Engr.** ***Perf. 13***
296 A140 1.60fr red & dk brn .50 .40
297 A140 2.60fr red & dk brn .75 .55

Souvenir Sheet

No. 52 — A141

1982, Aug. 21 **Engr.**
298 A141 5fr blk & rose car 1.40 1.40

1st Andorran Stamp Exhib., Aug. 21-Sept. 19.

Horse, Roman Wall Painting — A142

1982, Sept. 4 **Photo.** ***Perf. 13x12½***
299 A142 3fr multi 1.00 .80

Wild Cat — A143

1982, Oct. 9 **Engr.** ***Perf. 13***
300 A143 1.80fr shown .60 .40
301 A143 2.60fr Pine trees .75 .55

TB Bacillus Centenary A144

St. Thomas Aquinas (1225-74) A145

1982, Nov. 13
302 A144 2.10fr Koch, lungs .65 .50

1982, Dec. 4
303 A145 2fr multi .75 .50

Manned Flight Bicentenary A146

1983, Feb. 26 **Engr.**
304 A146 2fr multi .65 .50

Nature Protection A147

1983, Apr. 16 **Engr.** ***Perf. 13***
305 A147 1fr Birch trees .30 .20
306 A147 1.50fr Trout .50 .35

See Nos. 325-326.

Europa 1983 A148

Catalane Gold Works.

1983, May 7 **Engr.** ***Perf. 13***
307 A148 1.80fr Exterior .60 .40
308 A148 2.60fr Interior .80 .50

30th Anniv. of Customs Cooperation Council A149

1983, May 14
309 A149 3fr Letter of King Louis XIII 1.25 .80

First Arms of Valleys of Andorra A150

1983, Sept. 3 **Engr.** ***Perf. 13***
310 A150 5c olive grn & red .20 .20
311 A150 10c grn & olive grn .20 .20
312 A150 20c brt pur & red .20 .20
313 A150 30c brn vio & red .20 .20
314 A150 40c dk bl & ultra .20 .20
315 A150 50c gray & red .20 .20
316 A150 1fr deep magenta .30 .20
317 A150 2fr org red & red brn .50 .30
318 A150 5fr dk brn & red 1.00 .75
Nos. 310-318 (9) 3.00 2.45

See Nos. 329-335, 380-385, 464-465.

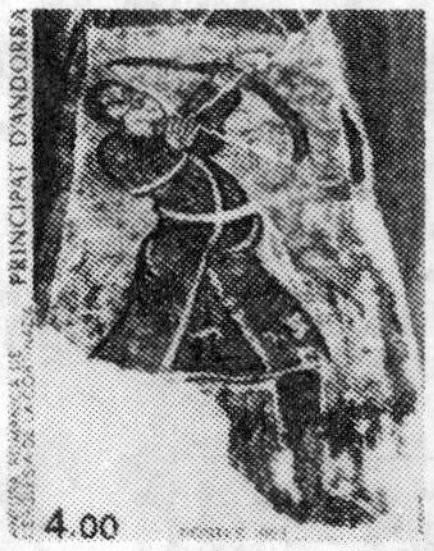

Painting, Cortinada Church A151

1983, Sept. 24 ***Perf. 12x13***
319 A151 4fr multi 1.25 .80

Plandolit House — A152

1983, Oct. 15 **Photo.** ***Perf. 13***
320 A152 1.60fr dp ultra & brn .50 .35

1984 Winter Olympics A153

1984, Feb. 18 **Engr.**
321 A153 2.80fr multicolored .80 .60

Pyrenees Region Work Community (Labor Org.) — A154

1984, Apr. 28 **Engr.** ***Perf. 13***
322 A154 3fr brt blue & sepia 1.00 .65

Europa (1959-84) A155

1984, May 5 **Engr.**
323 A155 2fr brt grn .75 .40
324 A155 2.80fr rose car 1.00 .60

Nature Protection Type of 1983

1984, July 7 **Engr.** ***Perf. 13***
325 A147 1.70fr Chestnut tree .65 .40
326 A147 2.10fr Walnut tree .80 .50

Pyrenees Art Center A155a

1984, Sept. 7 **Engr.**
327 A155a 3fr multi 1.00 .75

Romanesque Fresco, Church of St. Cerni de Nagol — A156

1984, Nov. 17 *Perf. 12x13*
328 A156 5fr multi 1.75 1.25

First Arms Type of 1983

1984-87 Engr. *Perf. 13*
329 A150 1.90fr emerald .65 .20
330 A150 2.20fr red orange .75 .20
a. Bklt. pane, 2 #329, 6 #330 6.25
331 A150 3fr bl grn & red brn .75 .45
332 A150 4fr brt org & brn 1.15 .85
333 A150 10fr brn org & blk 2.50 1.50
334 A150 15fr grn & dk grn 4.25 3.25
335 A150 20fr brt bl & red brn 5.25 3.00
Nos. 329-335 (7) 15.30 9.45

Nos. 329-330 issued in booklets only.
Issued: 3fr, 20fr, 12/1/84; 10fr, 2/9/85; 4fr, 15fr, 4/19/86; 1.90fr, 2.20fr, 3/28/87.

Saint Julia Valley A157

1985, Apr. 13 **Engr.**
336 A157 2fr multi .80 .45

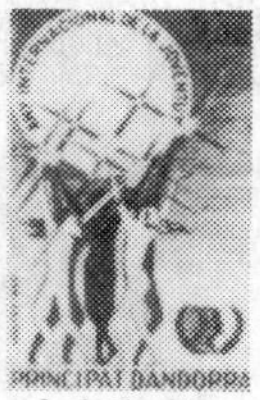

Europa 1985 — A158

Intl. Youth Year — A159

1985, May 4 **Engr.**
337 A158 2.10fr Le Val D'Andorre .95 .55
338 A158 3fr Instruments 1.40 .75

1985, June 8 **Engr.**
339 A159 3fr multi .90 .60

Wildlife Conservation A160

1985, Aug. 3 **Photo.**
340 A160 1.80fr Anas platyrhynchos .65 .40
341 A160 2.20fr Carduelis carduelis .85 .45

Two Saints, Medieval Fresco in St. Cerni de Nagol Church A161

1985, Sept. 14 Engr. *Perf. 12½x13*
342 A161 5fr multi 1.50 1.10

Postal Museum Inauguration A162

1986, Mar. 22 Engr. *Perf. 13*
343 A162 2.20fr like No. 269 .80 .20

Europa 1986 A163

1986, May 3 Engr. *Perf. 13*
344 A163 2.20fr Ansalonga 1.00 .35
345 A163 3.20fr Isard 1.75 .50

1986 World Cup Soccer Championships, Mexico — A164

1986, June 14
346 A164 3fr multi .90 .20

Angonella Lake A165

1986, June 28
347 A165 2.20fr multi .65 .20

Manual Digest Frontispiece, 1748 — A166

1986, Sept. 6 **Engr.**
348 A166 5fr chnt brn, gray ol & blk 1.65 .30

Intl. Peace Year — A167

1986, Sept. 29
349 A167 1.90fr bl gray & grnsh bl .65 .20

A168 A169

1986, Oct. 18 Engr. *Perf. 13½x13*
350 A168 1.90fr St. Vicenc D'Enclar .75 .20

1987, Mar. 27 Litho. *Perf. 12½x13*
351 A169 2.20fr Contemporary natl. coat of arms 1.50 .20

Visit of the French co-prince.

Europa 1987 A170

1987, May 2 Engr. *Perf. 13*
352 A170 2.20fr Meritxell Sanctuary 1.00 .30
353 A170 3.40fr Pleta D'Ordino 1.50 .50

Ransol Village — A171

1987, June 13 **Photo.**
354 A171 1.90fr multicolored 1.00 .20

Nature A172

1987, July 4
355 A172 1.90fr Cavall rogenc 1.10 .20
356 A172 2.20fr Graellsia isabellae 1.40 .20

Aryalsu, Romanesque Painting, La Cortinada Church — A173

Litho. & Engr.

1987, Sept. 5 *Perf. 12½x13*
357 A173 5fr multi 2.00 .35

Hiker Looking at Map — A174

1987, Sept. 19 Engr. *Perf. 13*
358 A174 2fr olive, grn & dark brn vio .80 .20

Medieval Iron Key, La Cortinada A175

1987, Oct. 17 **Litho.**
359 A175 3fr multi 1.10 .20

Andorran Coat of Arms — A176

Booklet Stamp

1988, Feb. 6 Engr. *Perf. 13*
360 A176 2.20fr red .80 .20
a. Bklt. pane of 10 8.00

See Nos. 388-389B.

Shoemaker's Last from Roc de l'Oral — A177

1988, Feb. 13 **Photo.**
361 A177 3fr multi 1.25 .30

Rugby A178

1988, Mar. 19 Engr. *Perf. 13½x13*
362 A178 2.20fr emer grn, Prus grn & brn .95 .20

Europa 1988 — A179

Hot Springs, Escaldes — A180

Transport and communication: 2.20fr, Broadcast tower. 3.60fr, Computer graphics.

1988, May 2 Engr. *Perf. 13*
363 A179 2.20fr multicolored .90 .20
364 A179 3.60fr multicolored 1.40 .35

1988, May 14 **Engr.**
365 A180 2.20fr Prus blue, org brn & emer .85 .20

Tor D'Ansalonga Farmhouse, Ansalonga Pass — A181

1988, June 13 **Engr.**
366 A181 2fr multi .75 .20

Sheepdog — A182

1988, July 2 **Photo.**
367 A182 2fr shown .90 .20
368 A182 2.20fr Hare 1.10 .20

Roman Fresco, 8th Cent., St. Steven's Church, Andorre-La-Vieille — A183

1988, Sept. 3 **Engr.** ***Perf. 13x12½***
369 A183 5fr multicolored 1.75 .40

French Revolution, Bicent. — A184

1989, Jan. 1 **Litho.** ***Perf. 13***
370 A184 2.20fr red & vio bl .85 .20

Poble de Pal Village A185

1989, Mar. 4 **Engr.** ***Perf. 13***
371 A185 2.20fr indigo & lilac .80 .20

Europa 1989 A186

Children's games.

1989, June 9 **Engr.** ***Perf. 13***
372 A186 2.20fr Human tower .80 .20
373 A186 3.60fr The handkerchief 1.40 .30

Red Cross A187

1989, May 6
374 A187 3.60fr multi 1.25 .25

Visigothic-Merovingian Age Cincture from a Column, St. Vicenc D'Anclar — A188

1989, June 3 **Photo.**
375 A188 3fr multi 1.00 .20

Wildlife A189

1989, Sept. 18 **Engr.** ***Perf. 13***
376 A189 2.20fr Wild boar .90 .20
377 A189 3.60fr Newt 1.40 .40

Scene of Salome from the Retable of St. Michael of Mosquera, Encamp — A190

1989, Oct. 16 ***Perf. 13x13½***
378 A190 5fr multi 1.50 .30

La Margineda Bridge A191

1990, Feb. 26 **Engr.** ***Perf. 13***
379 A191 2.30fr multi .80 .20

Tourism.

Arms Types of 1983 and 1988

1990-93 **Engr.** ***Perf. 13***
380 A150 2.10fr green .80 .20
381 A150 2.20fr green 1.50 .50
382 A150 2.30fr vermilion .85 .20
383 A150 2.40fr green .90 .30
384 A150 2.50fr vermilion 1.75 .55
385 A150 2.80fr vermilion 1.00 .30
Nos. 380-385 (6) 6.80 2.05

Booklet Stamps
Perf. 13
386 A176 2.30fr red .85 .20
a. Booklet pane of 5 4.25
387 A176 2.50fr vermilion 1.75 .55
a. Booklet pane of 5 8.50
388 A176 2.80fr red 1.00 .30
c. Booklet pane of 5 5.00
Nos. 386-388 (3) 3.60 1.05

Issued: 2.20fr, #384, 10/28/91; #387, 10/21/91; 2.40fr, 2.80fr, 8/9/93; 2.10fr, 2.30fr, 1990.

Llorts Mines A193

1990, Apr. 21 **Engr.** ***Perf. 12½x13***
390 A193 3.20fr multicolored 1.25 .25

Europa A194

Designs: 2.30fr, Early post office. 3.20fr, Modern post office.

1990, May 5 ***Perf. 13***
391 A194 2.30fr blk & scar .95 .20
392 A194 3.20fr scar & vio 1.40 .25

Otter A195

1990, May 25 ***Perf. 12x13***
393 A195 2.30fr Roses, vert. .95 .20
394 A195 3.20fr shown 1.40 .25

Censer of St. Roma of Les Bons A196

1990, June 25 ***Perf. 12½x13***
395 A196 3fr multicolored 1.10 .30

Tobacco Drying Sheds, Les Bons A197

1990, Sept. 15 **Engr.** ***Perf. 12½x13***
396 A197 2.30fr multi .85 .20

St. Coloma (Detail) A198

1990, Oct. 8 ***Perf. 12½x13***
397 A198 5fr multi 2.00 .75

Coin from Church of St. Eulalia d'Encamp A199

1990, Oct. 27 **Litho.** ***Perf. 13***
398 A199 3.20fr multi 1.10 .40

De Gaulle Type of 1972 Dated 1990

1990, Oct. 23 **Engr.** ***Perf. 13***
399 A88 2.30fr vio bl 1.00 .35
400 A88 3.20fr dk car 1.40 .55
a. Pair, #399-400 + label 2.40 .85

Birth centenary of De Gaulle.

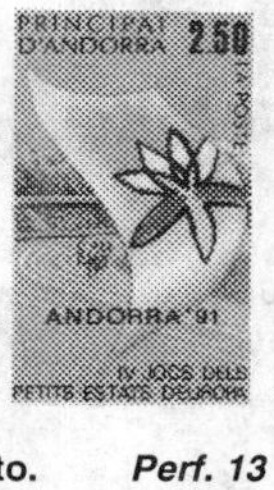

4th Games of the Small European States — A200

1991, Apr. 8 **Photo.** ***Perf. 13***
401 A200 2.50fr multicolored .90 .30

Chapel of St. Roma Dels Vilars A201

1991, Mar. 9 **Engr.** ***Perf. 13***
402 A201 2.50fr multicolored .90 .30

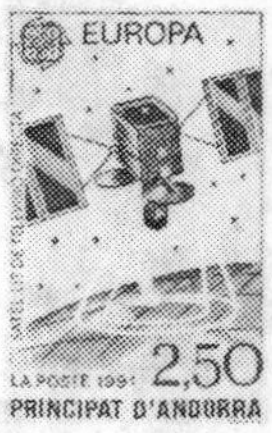

Europa — A202

1991, Apr. 27 ***Perf. 13x12½, 12½x13***
403 A202 2.50fr TV satellite .90 .30
404 A202 3.50fr Telescope, horiz. 1.25 .45

Bottles from Tombs of St. Vincenc d'Enclar A203

1991, May 11 **Photo.** ***Perf. 13***
405 A203 3.20fr multicolored 1.25 .40

Farm Animals A204

1991, June 22 **Engr.** ***Perf. 13***
406 A204 2.50fr Sheep .90 .30
407 A204 3.50fr Cow 1.25 .40

Petanque World Championships — A205

1991, Sept. 14 **Engr.** ***Perf. 13***
408 A205 2.50fr multicolored .90 .30

Wolfgang Amadeus Mozart, Death Bicent. A206

1991, Oct. 5
409 A206 3.40fr multicolored 1.40 .45

Virgin and Child of St. Julia and St. Germa A207

1991, Nov. 16 **Engr.** ***Perf. 12½x13***
410 A207 5fr multicolored 2.00 .65

1992 Winter Olympics, Albertville — A208

1992, Feb. 10 Litho. *Perf. 13*

411 A208 2.50fr Slalom skiing .95 .30
412 A208 3.40fr Figure skating 1.25 .40
a. Pair, #411-412 + label 2.25 .70

Church of St. Andrew of Arinsal A209

1992, Mar. 21 Engr. *Perf. 12x13*

413 A209 2.50fr black & tan 1.10 .35

Discovery of America, 500th Anniv. A210

1992, Apr. 25 *Perf. 13*

414 A210 2.50fr Columbus' fleet .90 .30
415 A210 3.40fr Landing in New World 1.25 .40

Europa.

1992 Summer Olympics, Barcelona A211

European Globeflower A212

1992, June 8 Litho. *Perf. 13*

416 A211 2.50fr Kayaking 1.00 .35
417 A211 3.40fr Shooting 1.40 .45
a. Pair, #416-417 + label 2.40 .80

1992, July 6

Design: 3.40fr, Vulture, horiz.

418 A212 2.50fr multicolored 1.00 .35
419 A212 3.40fr multicolored 1.40 .45

Martyrdom of St. Eulalia A213

1992, Sept. 14 Photo. *Perf. 13*

420 A213 4fr multicolored 1.50 .50

Sculpture by Mauro Staccioli A214

1992, Oct. 5 Engr. *Perf. 12½x13*

421 A214 5fr multicolored 2.00 .70

Ordino Arcalis '91.

Tempest in a Tea Cup, by Dennis Oppenheim — A215

1992, Nov. 14 Engr. *Perf. 13x12½*

422 A215 5fr multicolored 2.00 .70

Skiing in Andorra — A216

Ski resorts: No. 423: a, 2.50fr, Soldeu El Tarter. b, 3.40fr, Arinsal.

No. 424: a, 2.50fr, Pas de la Casa-Grau Roig. b, 2.50fr, Ordino Arcalis. c, 3.40fr, Pal.

1993, Mar. 13 Litho. *Perf. 13*

423 A216 Pair, #a.-b. + label 2.25 .75
424 A216 Strip of 3, #a.-c. 3.25 1.00

Sculptures — A217

Europa: 2.50fr, "Estructures Autogeneradores," by Jorge du Bon, vert. 3.40fr, Sculpture, "Fisicromia per Andorra," by Carlos Cruz-Diez.

1993, May 15 Engr. *Perf. 12½x13*

425 A217 2.50fr multicolored 1.00 .35

Litho.

Perf. 14x13½

426 A217 3.40fr multicolored 1.40 .45

Butterflies A218

1993, June 28 Litho. *Perf. 13*

427 A218 2.50fr Polymmatus icarus .95 .30
428 A218 4.20fr Nymphalidae 1.50 .50

Tour de France Bicycle Race — A219

1993, July 20 Litho. *Perf. 13*

429 A219 2.50fr multicolored .90 .30

Andorra School, 10th Anniv. A220

1993, Sept. 20 Litho. *Perf. 13*

430 A220 2.80fr multicolored 1.00 .35

Un Lloc Paga, by Michael Warren A221

1993, Oct. 18 Engr. *Perf. 12½x13*

431 A221 5fr blue & black 1.75 .60

Sculpture, by Erik Dietman A222

1993, Nov. 8 Engr. *Perf. 12½x13*

432 A222 5fr multicolored 1.75 .60

1994 Winter Olympics, Lillehammer A223

1994, Feb. 21 Litho. *Perf. 13*

433 A223 3.70fr multicolored 1.25 .45

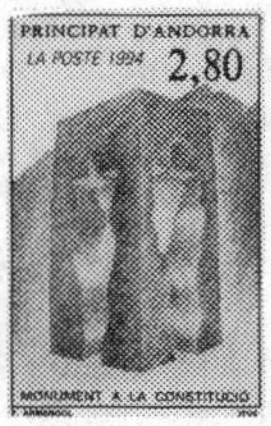

1st Anniversary of the Constitution — A224

Designs: 2.80fr, Monument, by Emili Armengol. 3.70fr, Stone tablet with inscription.

1994, Mar. 15 Litho. *Perf. 13*

434 A224 2.80fr multicolored 1.00 .35
435 A224 3.70fr multicolored 1.40 .50
a. Pair, #434-435 + label 2.40 .85

European Discoveries A225

Europa: 2.80fr, Discovery of AIDS virus. 3.70fr, Radio diffusion.

1994, May 9 Litho. *Perf. 13*

436 A225 2.80fr multicolored 1.10 .35
437 A225 3.70fr multicolored 1.50 .50

1994 World Cup Soccer Championships, US — A226

1994, June 20

438 A226 3.70fr multicolored 1.50 .50

Tourist Sports — A227

#439, Mountain climbing. #440, Fishing. #441, Horseback riding. #442, Mountain biking.

1994, July 11

439 A227 2.80fr multicolored 1.10 .35
440 A227 2.80fr multicolored 1.10 .35
a. Pair, #439-440 + label 2.20 .70
441 A227 2.80fr multicolored 1.10 .35
442 A227 2.80fr multicolored 1.10 .35
a. Pair, #441-442 + label 2.20 .70
Nos. 439-442 (4) 4.40 1.40

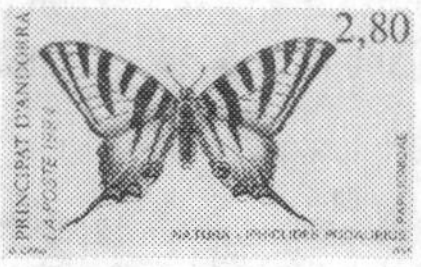

Butterflies A228

1994, Sept. 5 Litho. *Perf. 13*

443 A228 2.80fr Iphiclides podalirus 1.10 .35
444 A228 4.40fr Aglais urticae 1.75 .60

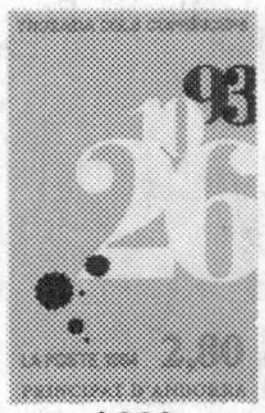

A229 A230

1994, Oct. 22 Litho. *Perf. 13*

445 A229 2.80fr multicolored 1.25 .40

Meeting of the Co-Princes, 1st anniv.

1995, Feb. 27 Litho. *Perf. 13*

446 A230 2.80fr multicolored 1.25 .40

European Nature Conservation Year

1995 World Cup Rugby Championships — A231

1995, Apr. 24 Litho. *Perf. 13*
447 A231 2.80fr multicolored 1.25 .40

Peace & Freedom A232

Europa: 2.80fr, Dove with olive branch. 3.70fr, Flock of doves.

1995, May 2
448 A232 2.80fr multicolored 1.25 .40
449 A232 3.70fr multicolored 1.60 .50

Caritas in Andorra, 15th Anniv. A233

1995, May 15 Litho. *Perf. 13*
450 A233 2.80fr multicolored 1.25 1.00

Caldea Health Spa — A234

1995, June 26 Litho. *Perf. 13*
451 A234 2.80fr multicolored 1.25 1.00

Ordino Natl. Auditorium A235

1995, July 10 Litho. & Engr.
452 A235 3.70fr black & buff 1.60 1.25

Virgin of Meritxell — A236

1995, Sept. 11 Litho. *Perf. 14*
453 A236 4.40fr multicolored 1.90 1.50

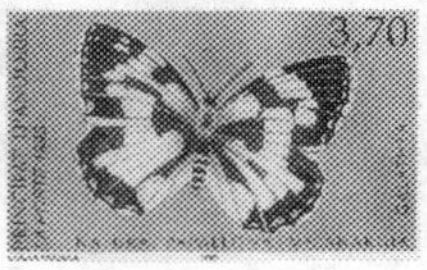

Protection of Nature A237

Butterflies: 2.80fr, Papallona llimonera, vert. 3.70fr, Papallona melanargia galathea.

1995, Sept. 25 *Perf. 13*
454 A237 2.80fr multicolored 1.25 1.00
455 A237 3.70fr multicolored 1.60 1.25

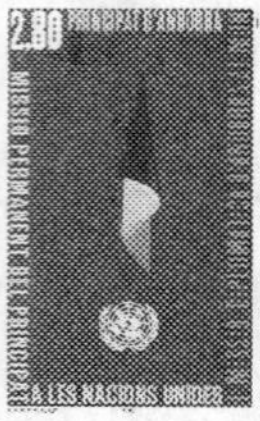

UN, 50th Anniv. — A238

1995, Oct. 21 Litho. *Perf. 13*
456 A238 2.80fr Flag, emblem 1.25 1.00
457 A238 3.70fr Emblem, "50," flag 1.60 1.25
a. Pair, #456-457 + label 3.00 3.00

Andorra's Entrance into Council of Europe A239

1995, Nov. 4
458 A239 2.80fr multicolored 1.25 1.00

World Skiing Championships, Ordino Arcalis — A240

1996, Jan. 29 Litho. *Perf. 13*
459 A240 2.80fr multicolored 1.25 1.25

Basketball in Andorra — A241

1996, Jan. 29 Litho. *Perf. 13*
460 A241 3.70fr multicolored 1.60 1.60

Our Lady of Meritxell Special School, 25th Anniv. A242

1996, Feb. 17 Litho. *Perf. 13*
461 A242 2.80fr multicolored 1.20 1.20

Songbirds A243

1996, Mar. 25
462 A243 3fr Pit riog 1.30 1.30
463 A243 3.80fr Mallarenga carbonera 1.60 1.60

First Arms Type of 1983

1996, Apr. 17 Engr. *Perf. 13*
464 A150 2.70fr green 1.20 1.20
465 A150 3fr red 1.40 1.40

Cross of St. James d'Engordany — A244

1996, Apr. 20 Litho.
466 A244 3fr multicolored 1.40 1.40

Censar of St. Eulalia d'Encamp A245

1996, Apr. 20
467 A245 3.80fr multicolored 1.75 1.75

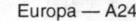

Europa — A246 Chess — A247

1996, May 6
468 A246 3fr Ermessenda de Castellbo 1.40 1.40

1996, June 8 Litho. *Perf. 13*
469 A247 4.50fr multicolored 2.00 2.00

1996 Summer Olympic Games, Atlanta A248

1996, June 29 Litho. *Perf. 13*
470 A248 3fr multicolored 1.25 1.25

Arms of the Community of Canillo — A249

Serpentine Die Cut 7 Vert.

1996, June 10 Litho.

Self-Adhesive

471 A249 (3fr) multicolored 1.75 1.75

Natl. Children's Choir, 5th Anniv. A250

1996, Sept. 14 *Perf. 13*
472 A250 3fr multicolored 1.40 1.40

Livestock Fair — A251

1996, Oct. 26 Engr. *Perf. 12x13*
473 A251 3fr multicolored 1.25 1.25

Churches A252

#474, St. Romá de Les Bons. #475, St. Coloma.

1996, Nov. 16 Litho. *Perf. 13*
474 A252 6.70fr multicolored 2.75 2.75
475 A252 6.70fr multicolored 2.75 2.75

A253 A254

1997, Jan. 7 Litho. *Perf. 13*
476 A253 3fr multicolored 1.25 1.25

Pres. Francois Mitterrand (1916-96).

Sawtooth Die Cut 7 Vert. x Straight Die Cut

1997, Feb. 24 Litho.

Self-Adhesive

477 A254 (3fr) Arms of Encamp 1.25 1.25
a. Booklet pane of 10 12.50

By its nature, No. 477a is a complete booklet. The peelable paper backing serves as a booklet cover.

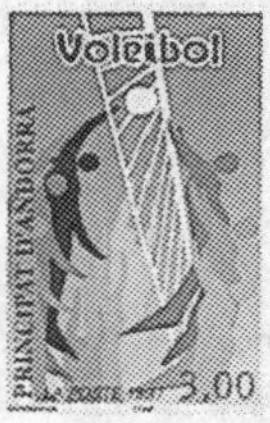

A255 A256

1997, Mar. 22 *Perf. 13*
478 A255 3fr Volleyball 1.25 1.25

1997, May 12 Litho. *Perf. 13*
479 A256 3fr "The White Lady" 1.25 1.25

Europa (Stories and Legends).

Oreneta Cuablanca A257

1997, May 31 Litho. *Perf. 13*
480 A257 3.80fr multicolored 1.60 1.60

Paintings of Mills — A258

1997, Sept. 15 Litho. *Perf. 13*
481 A258 3fr Cal Pal, vert. 1.15 1.15
482 A258 4.50fr Mas d'en Sole 1.75 1.75

Religious Artifacts A259

Designs: 3fr, Monstrance of St. Iscle and St. Victoria. 15.50fr, Altar piece of St. Pierre d'Alxirivall.

1997, Oct. 27

483 A259 3fr multicolored 1.10 1.10
484 A259 15.50fr multicolored 5.75 5.75
a. Pair, #483-484 + label 6.90 6.90

Legends — A260

Designs: No. 485, Legend of Meritxell. No. 486, The cross of seven arms. 3.80fr, The fountain of Esmelicat.

1997, Nov. 22 Litho. *Perf. 13*

485 A260 3fr multicolored 1.10 1.10
486 A260 3fr multicolored 1.10 1.10
487 A260 3.80fr multicolored 1.40 1.40
a. Strip of 3, #485-487 3.60 3.60

Monaco Intl. Philatelic Exhibition — A261

1997, Nov. 28 Litho. *Perf. 13*

488 A261 3fr Chapel of St. Miguel d'Engolasters 1.10 1.10

Happy Anniversary A262

1998 Winter Olympic Games, Nagano A263

1998, Jan. 3 Litho. *Perf. 13*

489 A262 3fr Juggling candles 1.10 1.10

1998, Feb. 14

490 A263 4.40fr multicolored 1.75 1.75

Arms of Ordino — A264

Serpentine Die Cut Vert.

1998, Mar. 7 Litho.

Booklet Stamp

Self-Adhesive

491 A491 (3fr) multicolored 1.10 1.10
a. Booklet pane of 10 11.00
Complete booklet, #491a 11.00

See No. 504.

Mesa de Vila Church — A265

1998, Mar. 28 *Perf. 13*

492 A265 4.50fr multicolored 1.75 1.75

Rotary Club of Andorra, 20th Anniv. A265a

1998, Apr. 11

493 A265a 3fr multicolored 1.10 1.10

Finch A266

1998 Litho. *Perf. 13*

494 A266 3.80fr multicolored 1.40 1.40

1998 World Cup Soccer Championships, France — A267

1998, June 6 Litho. *Perf. 13*

495 A267 3fr multicolored 1.10 1.10

For overprint see No. 499.

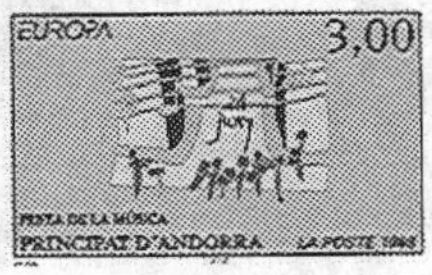

Music Festival A268

1998, June 20 Litho. *Perf. 13*

496 A268 3fr multicolored 1.10 1.10

Europa.

Expo '98, Lisbon A269

1998, July 6

497 A269 5fr multicolored 1.75 1.75

Chalice, House of the Valleys — A270

1998, Sept. 19 Litho. *Perf. 13*

498 A270 4.50fr multicolored 1.60 1.60

No. 495 Ovptd. "FINAL / FRANCA/BRASIL / 3-0"

1998, Nov. 16

499 A267 3fr multicolored 1.10 1.10

Early Maps of Andorra A271

1998, Nov. 16

500 A271 3fr 1717, vert. 1.10 1.10
501 A271 15.50fr 1777 5.75 5.75

Inauguration of the Postal Museum A272

1998, Nov. 19 Litho. *Perf. 13*

502 A272 3fr multicolored 1.10 1.10

Manual Digest, 250th Anniv. A273

1998, Dec. 7

503 A273 3.80fr multicolored 1.40 1.40

Arms Type of 1998

Serpentine Die Cut Vert.

1999, Jan. 18

Booklet Stamp

Self-Adhesive

504 A264 (3fr) La Massana 1.10 1.10
a. Booklet pane of 10 11.00

No. 504a is a complete booklet.

Recycling A274

1999, Mar. 13 Litho. *Perf. 13*

505 A274 5fr multicolored 1.75 1.75

Sorteny Valley — A275

Illustration reduced.

1999, Apr. 10

506 A275 3fr multicolored 1.10 1.10

Europa.

Council of Europe, 50th Anniv. A276

1999, May 5 Litho. *Perf. 13*

507 A276 3.80fr multicolored 1.40 1.40

A277

A278

1999, May 15

508 A277 2.70fr 1st Stage Coach 1.00 1.00

1999, June 10 Photo. *Perf. 13*

509 A278 4.50fr multicolored 1.75 1.75

1999 European National Soccer Championships.

PhilexFrance 99 — A279

1999, July 2 Litho. *Perf. 13x13¼*

510 A279 3fr multicolored 1.10 1.10

Historic View of Pal — A280

Perf. 13x13¼, 13¼x13

1999, July 10 Litho.

511 A280 3fr shown 1.10 1.10
512 A280 3fr Different view, vert. 1.10 1.10

International Federation of Photographic Art, 50th Anniv. — A281

1999, July 24 Litho. *Perf. 13*

513 A281 4.40fr multicolored 1.60 1.60

Chest With Six Locks — A283

1999, Oct. 9 Litho. *Perf. 13x13¼*

515 A283 6.70fr multicolored 2.40 2.40

SEMI-POSTAL STAMP

Catalogue values for unused stamps in this section are for Never Hinged items.

Virgin of St. Coloma — SP1

Unwmk.

1964, July 25 Engr. *Perf. 13*

B1	SP1	25c + 10c multi	20.00	20.00

The surtax was for the Red Cross.

AIR POST STAMPS

Catalogue values for unused stamps in this section are for Never Hinged items.

Chamois AP1

Unwmk.

1950, Feb. 20 Engr. *Perf. 13*

C1	AP1	100fr indigo	65.00	45.00

East Branch of Valira River — AP2

1955-57

C2	AP2	100fr dark green	8.50	6.50
C3	AP2	200fr cerise	17.50	14.00
C4	AP2	500fr deep blue ('57)	90.00	65.00
		Nos. C2-C4 (3)	116.00	85.50

D'Inclès Valley — AP3

1961-64 Unwmk. *Perf. 13*

C5	AP3	2fr red, ol gray & claret	1.00	.65
C6	AP3	3fr bl, mar & slate grn	1.25	1.25
C7	AP3	5fr rose lil & red org	2.00	1.75
C8	AP3	10fr bl grn & slate grn	3.75	3.50
		Nos. C5-C8 (4)	8.00	7.15

Issued: 10fr, 4/25/64; others, 6/19/61.

POSTAGE DUE STAMPS

Postage Due Stamps of France, 1893-1931, Overprinted

ANDORRE

On Stamps of 1893-1926

1931-33 Unwmk. *Perf. 14x13½*

J1	D2	5c blue	1.00	1.00
J2	D2	10c brown	1.00	1.00
J3	D2	30c rose red	.40	.40
J4	D2	50c violet brn	1.00	1.00
J5	D2	60c green	10.00	10.00
J6	D2	1fr red brn, *straw*	.50	.50
J7	D2	2fr brt violet	6.00	6.00
J8	D2	3fr magenta	1.10	1.10
		Nos. J1-J8 (8)	21.00	21.00

On Stamps of 1927-31

J9	D4	1c olive grn	1.25	1.25
J10	D4	10c rose	2.75	2.75
J11	D4	60c red	16.00	16.00
J12	D4	1fr Prus grn ('32)	65.00	65.00
J13	D4	1.20fr on 2fr bl	50.00	50.00
J14	D4	2fr ol brn ('33)	140.00	140.00
J15	D4	5fr on 1fr vio	65.00	65.00
		Nos. J9-J15 (7)	340.00	340.00

D5

D6

1935-41 Typo.

J16	D5	1c gray grn	2.25	1.25
J17	D6	5c lt bl ('37)	3.75	*4.50*
J18	D6	10c brn ('41)	3.00	*4.50*
J19	D6	2fr vio ('41)	6.00	3.25
J20	D6	5fr red org ('41)	11.00	3.25
		Nos. J16-J20 (5)	26.00	16.75

Catalogue values for unused stamps in this section, from this point to the end of the section, are for Never Hinged items.

Wheat Sheaves — D7

1943-46 *Perf. 14x13½*

J21	D7	10c sepia	1.00	1.00
J22	D7	30c brt red vio	1.50	1.50
J23	D7	50c blue grn	1.75	1.75
J24	D7	1fr brt ultra	.80	.80
J25	D7	1.50fr rose red	5.75	5.75
J26	D7	2fr turq blue	1.50	1.50
J27	D7	3fr brown org	2.75	2.75
J28	D7	4fr dp vio ('45)	4.50	4.50
J29	D7	5fr brt pink	4.50	4.50
J30	D7	10fr red org ('45)	5.75	5.75
J31	D7	20fr olive brn ('46)	6.00	6.00
		Nos. J21-J31 (11)	35.80	35.80

Inscribed: "Timbre Taxe"

1946-53

J32	D7	10c sepia ('46)	1.10	1.10
J33	D7	1fr ultra	.75	.75
J34	D7	2fr turq blue	1.00	1.00
J35	D7	3fr orange brn	2.00	2.00
J36	D7	4fr violet	2.75	2.75
J37	D7	5fr brt pink	1.75	1.75
J38	D7	10fr red orange	2.75	2.75
J39	D7	20fr olive brn	6.25	6.25
J40	D7	50fr dk green ('50)	16.50	16.50
J41	D7	100fr dp green ('53)	87.50	87.50
		Nos. J32-J41 (10)	122.35	122.35

Inscribed: "Timbre Taxe"

1961, June 19 *Perf. 14x13½*

J42	D7	5c rose pink	3.00	3.00
J43	D7	10c red orange	6.00	6.00
J44	D7	20c olive	9.00	9.00
J45	D7	50c dark slate green	15.00	15.00
		Nos. J42-J45 (4)	33.00	33.00

D8

D9

1964-71 Typo. *Perf. 14x13½*

J46	D8	5c Centaury ('65)	.20	.20
J47	D8	10c Gentian ('65)	.20	.20
J48	D8	15c Corn poppy	.20	.20
J49	D8	20c Violets ('71)	.20	.20
J50	D8	30c Forget-me-not	.20	.20
J51	D8	40c Columbine ('71)	.20	.20
J52	D8	50c Clover ('65)	.30	.30
		Nos. J46-J52 (7)	1.50	1.50

1985, Oct. 21 Engr. *Perf. 13*

J53	D9	10c Holly	.20	.20
J54	D9	20c Blueberries	.20	.20
J55	D9	30c Raspberries	.20	.20
J56	D9	40c Bilberries	.20	.20
J57	D9	50c Blackberries	.20	.20
J58	D9	1fr Broom	.35	.30
J59	D9	2fr Rosehips	.65	.35
J60	D9	3fr Nightshade	1.00	.60
J61	D9	4fr Nabiu	1.40	.75
J62	D9	5fr Strawberries	1.75	.95
		Nos. J53-J62 (10)	6.15	3.95

NEWSPAPER STAMP

France No. P7 Overprinted **ANDORRE**

1931 Unwmk. *Perf. 14x13½*

P1	A16	½c on lc gray	.75	.75

ANGOLA

aŋ-ˈgō-lə

LOCATION — S.W. Africa between Zaire and Namibia.
GOVT. — Republic
AREA — 481,351 sq. mi.
POP. — 11,177,537 (1999 est.)
CAPITAL — Luanda

Angola was a Portuguese overseas territory until it became independent November 11, 1975, as the People's Republic of Angola.

1000 Reis = 1 Milreis
100 Centavos = 1 Escudo (1913, 1954)
100 Centavos = 1 Angolar (1932)
10 Lweys = 1 Kwanza (1977)

Catalogue values for unused stamps in this country are for Never Hinged items, beginning with Scott 328 in the regular postage section, Scott C26 in the airpost section, Scott J31 in the postage due section, and Scott RA7 in the postal tax section.

Watermark

Wmk. 232-Maltese Cross

Portuguese Crown — A1

Perf. 12½, 13½

1870-77 Typo. Unwmk.

1	A1	5r black	3.50	1.10
a.		Perf. 13½	9.00	3.25
2	A1	10r yellow	22.50	10.00
3	A1	20r bister	3.75	2.00
a.		Perf. 13½	65.00	50.00
4	A1	25r red	10.00	3.00
a.		25r rose	10.00	2.00
c.		25r rose, perf. 14	225.00	75.00
d.		Perf. 13½	20.00	8.00
5	A1	40r blue ('77)	150.00	75.00
6	A1	50r green	50.00	15.00
a.		Perf. 13½	225.00	65.00
7	A1	100r lilac	3.50	2.00
a.		Perf. 12½	8.00	4.00
8	A1	200r orange ('77)	3.50	2.00
a.		Perf. 12½	4.00	1.75
9	A1	300r choc ('77)	3.75	3.00
a.		Perf. 12½	10.00	4.75

1881-85

10	A1	10r green ('83)	4.00	1.50
a.		Perf. 12½	20.00	2.25
11	A1	20r carmine rose ('85)	9.00	5.00
12	A1	25r violet ('85)	4.00	2.00
a.		Perf. 13½	6.00	2.75
13	A1	40r buff ('82)	5.00	2.00
a.		Perf. 12½	6.00	2.00
15	A1	50r blue	12.00	1.75
a.		Perf. 13½	20.00	1.75
		Nos. 10-15 (5)	34.00	12.25

Two types of numerals are found on #2, 11, 13, 15.

The cliche of 40r in plate of 20r error, was discovered before the stamps were issued. All copies were defaced by a blue pencil mark.

In perf. 12½, Nos. 1-4, 4a and 6, as well as 7a, were printed in 1870 on thicker paper and 1875 on normal paper. Stamps of the earlier printing sell for 2 to 5 times more than those of the 1875 printing.

Some reprints of the 1870-85 issues are on a smooth white chalky paper, ungummed and perf. 13½.

Other reprints of these issues are on thin ivory paper with shiny white gum and clear-cut perf. 13½.

King Luiz — A2

King Carlos — A3

1886 Embossed *Perf. 12½*

16	A2	5r black	3.50	2.50
a.		Perf. 13½	11.50	8.50
17	A2	10r green	3.50	2.50
a.		Perf. 13½	13.00	7.25
18	A2	20r rose	10.00	6.25
a.		Perf. 13½	12.50	6.50
19	A2	25r red violet	7.50	1.50
20	A2	40r chocolate	8.00	5.00
21	A2	50r blue	10.50	2.00
22	A2	100r yellow brn	14.00	6.00
23	A2	200r gray violet	18.00	10.00
24	A2	300r orange	20.00	12.00
		Nos. 16-24 (9)	95.00	47.75

For surcharges see #61-69, 172-174, 208-210.

Reprints of 5r, 20r & 100r have cleancut perf. 13½.

1893-94 Typo. *Perf. 11½, 12½, 13½*

25	A3	5r yellow	1.00	.85
26	A3	10r redsh violet	2.00	.90
27	A3	15r chocolate	2.75	1.25
28	A3	20r lavender	2.75	1.25
29	A3	25r green	1.25	1.00
a.		Perf. 12½	4.00	2.00
30	A3	50r light blue	3.25	1.25
a.		Perf. 13½	5.00	2.75
31	A3	75r carmine	6.00	3.50
a.		Perf. 11½	8.00	6.25
32	A3	80r lt green	7.50	3.50
33	A3	100r brown, *buff*	6.75	3.50
a.		Perf. 11½	50.00	32.50
34	A3	150r car, *rose*	12.00	10.00
35	A3	200r dk blue, *lt bl*	14.00	11.00
36	A3	300r dk blue, *sal*	15.00	11.00
		Nos. 25-36 (12)	74.25	49.00

For surcharges see Nos. 70-81, 175-179, 213-216, 234.

No. P1 Surcharged in Blue

1894, Aug.

37	N1	25r on 2½r brown	80.00	22.50

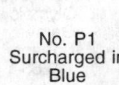

King Carlos — A5

1898-1903 *Perf. 11½*

Name and Value in Black except 500r

38	A5	2½r gray	.20	.20
39	A5	5r orange	.20	.20
40	A5	10r yellow grn	.20	.20
41	A5	15r violet brn	1.50	.70

42 A5 15r gray green ('03) .65 .50
43 A5 20r gray violet .25 .20
44 A5 25r sea green 1.00 .40
45 A5 25r car ('03) .50 .20
46 A5 50r blue 1.60 .35
47 A5 50r brown ('03) 3.00 2.00
48 A5 65r dull blue ('03) 10.00 7.00
49 A5 75r rose 4.50 1.60
50 A5 75r red violet ('03) 1.25 .90
51 A5 80r violet 4.50 2.00
52 A5 100r dk blue, *blue* .90 .65
53 A5 115r org brn, *pink* ('03) 9.00 6.50
54 A5 130r brn, *straw* ('03) 9.00 6.50
55 A5 150r brn, *straw* 8.00 5.00
56 A5 200r red vio, *pink* 2.25 1.00
57 A5 300r dk blue, *rose* 3.25 3.25
58 A5 400r dull bl, *straw* ('03) 4.00 2.50
59 A5 500r blk & red, *bl* ('01) 3.50 3.00
60 A5 700r vio, *yelsh* ('01) 14.00 10.00
Nos. 38-60 (23) 83.25 54.85

For surcharges and overprints see Nos. 83-102, 113-117, 159-171, 181-183, 217-218, 221-225.

Stamps of 1886-94 Surcharged in Black or Red

65 RÉIS

Two types of surcharge:
I - 3mm between numeral and REIS.
II - 4½mm spacing.

1902 ***Perf. 12½***
61 A2 65r on 40r choc 4.50 3.50
62 A2 65r on 300r org, I 4.50 3.50
a. Type II 32.50 25.00
63 A2 115r on 10r green 4.00 3.25
a. Inverted surcharge
b. Perf. 13½ 18.00 17.00
64 A2 115r on 200r gray vio 4.00 2.75
65 A2 130r on 50r blue 6.50 4.75
66 A2 130r on 100r brown 5.00 3.00
67 A2 400r on 20r rose 60.00 30.00
a. Perf. 13½ 60.00 45.00
68 A2 400r on 25r violet 9.00 6.00
69 A2 400r on 5r black (R) 8.00 6.25
a. Double surcharge
Nos. 61-69 (9) 105.50 63.00

For surcharges see Nos. 172-174, 208-210.

Perf. 11½, 12½, 13½
70 A3 65r on 5r yel, I 4.00 2.75
a. Type II 10.00 10.00
71 A3 65r on 10r red vio, I 3.25 2.25
a. Type II 13.00 5.25
b. Perf. 11½, type I 8.75 5.25
c. Perf. 11½, type II 3.50 2.50
72 A3 65r on 20r lav 5.00 3.00
a. Type II 6.50 6.00
73 65r on 25r green 4.00 2.50
a. Perf. 11½ 9.25 7.25
74 A3 115r on 80r lt grn 6.00 4.00
75 A3 115r on 100r brn, *buff* 6.00 3.50
a. Perf. 13½ 9.25 6.50
76 A3 115r on 150r car, *rose* 8.50 5.25
a. Perf. 13½ 10.00 6.00
77 A3 130r on 15r choc 3.50 2.00
78 A3 130r on 75r carmine 3.50 2.25
a. Perf. 13½ 14.00 11.50
79 A3 130r on 300r dk bl, *sal* 9.00 6.50
80 A3 400r on 50r lt bl 3.00 2.75
81 A3 400r on 200r bl, *bl* 3.00 3.25
a. Perf. 13½ 21.00 8.75
82 N1 400r on 2½r brn 1.75 1.10
a. Type II 2.50 2.25
Nos. 70-82 (13) 60.50 41.10

For surcharges see #175-180, 211-216, 234-235.

Reprints of Nos. 65, 67, 68 and 69 have clean-cut perforation 13½.

Stamps of 1898 Overprinted — a

PROVISORIO

1902 ***Perf. 11½***
83 A5 15r brown 1.25 .60
84 A5 25r sea green 1.00 .35
85 A5 50r blue 1.75 .85
86 A5 75r rose 3.00 2.00
Nos. 83-86 (4) 7.00 3.80

For surcharge see No. 116.

No. 48 Surcharged in Black

50 RÉIS

1905
87 A5 50r on 65r dull blue 3.00 1.25

For surcharge see No. 183.

Stamps of 1898-1903 Overprinted in Carmine or Green — b

REPUBLICA

1911
88 A5 2½r gray .20 .20
89 A5 5r orange yel .20 .20
90 A5 10r light green .25 .20
91 A5 15r gray green .25 .20
92 A5 20r gray violet .25 .20
93 A5 25r car (G) .25 .20
94 A5 50r brown 1.50 .90
95 A5 75r lilac 2.50 2.50
96 A5 100r dk blue, *bl* 2.50 2.50
97 A5 115r org brn, *pink* 1.00 .60
98 A5 130r brn, *straw* 1.00 .60
99 A5 200r red lil, *pnksh* 1.00 .60
100 A5 400r dull bl, *straw* 1.50 .65
101 A5 500r blk & red, *bl* 1.25 .65
102 A5 700r violet, *yelsh* 1.75 .70
Nos. 88-102 (15) 15.40 10.90

Inverted and double overprints of Nos. 88-102 were made intentionally.

For surcharges see Nos. 217-218, 221-222, 224.

King Manuel II — A6

Ceres — A7

Overprinted in Carmine or Green

1912 ***Perf. 11½x12***
103 A6 2½r violet .25 .50
104 A6 5r black .25 .50
105 A6 10r gray green .35 .30
106 A6 20r carmine (G) .35 .30
107 A6 25r violet brown .35 .30
108 A6 50r dk blue .60 .50
109 A6 75r bister brown .65 1.00
110 A6 100r brown, *lt green* 1.60 .70
111 A6 200r dk green, *salmon* 1.10 .70
112 A6 300r black, *azure* 1.10 .70
Nos. 103-112 (10) 6.60 5.50

For surcharges see Nos. 219-220, 226-227.

No. 91 Surcharged with New Values as 5

1912, June ***Perf. 11½***
113 A5 2½r on 15r gray green 2.25 2.25
114 A5 5r on 15r gray green 1.75 1.50
115 A5 10r on 15r gray green 1.75 1.50
Nos. 113-115 (3) 5.75 5.25

Inverted and double surcharges of Nos. 113-115 were made intentionally.

Nos. 86 and 50 Surcharged "25" in Black and Overprinted in Violet — c

REPUBLICA

1912
116 A5 25r on 75r rose 70.00 50.00
117 A5 25r on 75r red violet 2.75 1.50
a. "REUPBLICA" 22.50 20.00
b. "25" omitted 27.50 25.00
c. "REPUBLICA" omitted 32.50 27.50

1914-26 Typo. ***Perf. 12x11½, 15x14***

Name and Value in Black
118 A7 ¼c olive brown .20 .20
a. Inscriptions inverted 6.00
119 A7 ½c black .20 .20
120 A7 1c blue green .20 .20
121 A7 1c yel grn ('22) .20 .20
122 A7 1½c lilac brown .20 .20
123 A7 2c carmine .20 .20
124 A7 2c gray ('25) .30 1.00
125 A7 2½c lt violet .20 .20
126 A7 3c orange ('21) .20 .60
127 A7 4c dull rose ('21) .20 .20
128 A7 4½c gray ('21) .20 .80
130 A7 5c blue .20 .20
131 A7 6c lilac ('21) .20 .20
132 A7 7c ultra ('21) .20 .20
133 A7 7½c yellow brn .20 .20
134 A7 8c slate .20 .20
135 A7 10c orange brn .20 .20
136 A7 12c olive brn ('21) .35 .25
137 A7 12c dp green ('25) .20 .20
138 A7 15c plum .75 .20
139 A7 15c brown rose ('21) .20 .20
140 A7 20c yel green .25 .20
141 A7 24c ultra ('25) 1.25 .75
142 A7 25c choc ('25) 1.25 .75
143 A7 30c brown, *green* 2.00 2.00
144 A7 30c gray grn ('21) .75 .20
145 A7 40c brown, *pink* 3.50 2.00
146 A7 40c turq blue ('21) .75 .20
147 A7 50c orange, *sal* 6.00 4.25
148 A7 50c lt violet ('25) 1.50 .20
149 A7 60c dk blue ('22) 1.25 .20
150 A7 60c dp rose ('26) 40.00 40.00
151 A7 80c pink ('22) 1.25 .20
152 A7 1e green, *blue* 3.50 2.25
153 A7 1e rose ('22) 2.25 .20
154 A7 1e dp blue ('25) 4.00 3.00
155 A7 2e dk violet ('22) 1.25 .50
156 A7 5e buff ('25) 15.00 2.25
157 A7 10e pink ('25) 22.50 10.00
158 A7 20e pale turq ('25) 50.00 35.00
Nos. 118-158 (40) 163.25 110.20

Two kinds of paper, chalky-surfaced paper and ordinary, were used for Nos. 118-120, 122-123, 125, 130, 133-135, 138 and 140. Those on coated paper sell unused for 10 to 40 times the values listed; used for about 5 to 20 times.

All but #143, 145, 147 come perf 12x11½. All but #124, 137, 141-142, 146, 148, 151, 153-154, 156-158 come perf 15x14.

For surcharges see Nos. 228-229, 236-239.

Stamps of 1898-1903 Overprinted type "c" in Red or Green
On Stamps of 1898-1903

1914 ***Perf. 11½, 12***
159 A5 10r yel green (R) 3.25 2.75
160 A5 15r gray green (R) 3.25 2.75
161 A5 20r gray violet (G) .80 1.00
163 A5 75r red violet (G) .80 1.00
164 A5 100r blue, *blue* (R) 1.25 1.25
165 A5 115r org brn, *pink* (R) 67.50
167 A5 200r red vio, *pnksh* (G) .90 .50
169 A5 400r dl bl, *straw* (R) 40.00 30.00
170 A5 500r blk & red, *bl* (R) 5.00 3.00
171 A5 700r vio, *yelsh* (G) 15.00 12.00

Inverted and double overprints were made intentionally. No. 165 was not regularly issued. Red overprints on the 20r, 75r, 200r were not regularly issued. The 130r was not regularly issued without surcharge (No. 225).

On Nos. 63-65, 74-76, 78-79, 82

Perf. 11½, 12½, 13½
172 A2 115r on 10r (R) 30.00 20.00
a. Perf. 13½ 30.00 20.00
173 A2 115r on 200r (R) 35.00 20.00
174 A2 130r on 50r (R) 35.00 20.00
175 A3 115r on 80r (R) 100.00 75.00
176 A3 115r on 100r (R) 250.00 150.00
177 A3 115r on 150r (G) 165.00 125.00
178 A3 130r on 75r (G) 1.75 1.65
179 A3 130r on 300r (R) 4.00 3.25
a. Perf. 12½ 7.00 4.50
180 N1 400r on 2½r (R) .40 .40
a. Perf. 11½ 1.65 1.25
Nos. 172-180 (9) 621.15 415.30

Overprinted PROVISORIO

On Stamps of 1902

Perf. 11½, 12
181 A5 50r blue (R) .90 .60
182 A5 75r rose (G) 2.75 2.00

On No. 87
183 A5 50r on 65r dull blue (R) 2.50 2.50
Nos. 181-183 (3) 6.15 5.10

Inverted and double surcharges of Nos. 181-183 were made intentionally.

Common Design Types pictured following the introduction.

Vasco da Gama Issue of Various Portuguese Colonies

Common Design Types CD20-CD27 Surcharged

REPUBLICA
ANGOLA
¼ C.

On Stamps of Macao

1913 ***Perf. 12½ to 16***
184 ¼c on ½a blue grn 4.00 4.00
185 ½c on 1a red 3.00 3.00
186 1c on 2a red violet 3.00 3.00
187 2½c on 4a yel green 2.00 2.00
188 5c on 8a dk blue 2.00 2.00
189 7½c on 12a vio brn 5.50 5.50
190 10c on 16a bister brn 4.00 4.00
191 15c on 24a bister 4.00 4.00
Nos. 184-191 (8) 27.50 27.50

On Stamps of Portuguese Africa

Perf. 14 to 15
192 ¼c on 2½r blue grn .75 .75
193 ½c on 5r red .75 .75
194 1c on 10r red violet .75 .75
195 2½c on 25r yel grn .75 .75
196 5c on 50r dk blue .75 .75
197 7½c on 75r vio brn 2.50 2.50
198 10c on 100r bister brn 1.25 1.25
199 15c on 150r bister 1.75 1.75
Nos. 192-199 (8) 9.25 9.25

On Stamps of Timor
200 ¼c on ½a blue grn 2.00 2.00
201 ½c on 1a red 2.00 2.00
202 1c on 2a red vio 2.00 2.00
203 2½c on 4a yel grn 2.00 2.00
204 5c on 8a dk blue 2.00 2.00
205 7½c on 12a vio brn 3.00 3.00
206 10c on 16a bis brn 2.00 2.00
207 15c on 24a bister 2.00 2.00
Nos. 200-207 (8) 17.00 17.00
Nos. 184-207 (24) 53.75 53.75

Provisional Issue of 1902 Overprinted in Carmine

REPUBLICA

1915 ***Perf. 11½, 12½, 13½***
208 A2 115r on 10r green 1.00 2.00
209 A2 115r on 200r gray vio .90 2.00
210 A2 130r on 100r brown .70 2.00
211 A3 115r on 80r lt green 1.10 2.00
212 A3 115r on 100r brn, *buff* .90 2.00
a. Perf. 11½ 17.00 17.00
213 A3 115r on 150r car, *rose* 1.75 2.00
214 A3 130r on 15r choc .65 2.00
a. Perf. 12½ 7.00 7.00
215 A3 130r on 75r carmine 1.50 1.75
216 A3 130r on 300r dk bl, *sal* 1.10 1.75
Nos. 208-216 (9) 9.60 17.50

Stamps of 1911-14 Surcharged in Black:

½ C.

½ C. d e

On Stamps of 1911

1919 ***Perf. 11½***
217 A5 (d) ½c on 75r red lilac 1.50 2.00
218 A5 (d) 2½c on 100r blue, *grysh* 1.75 2.00

On Stamps of 1912

Perf. 11½x12
219 A6 (e) ½c on 75r bis brn .65 .65
220 A6 (e) 2½c on 100r brn, *lt grn* .85 .40

On Stamps of 1914
221 A5 (d) ½c on 75r red lil .65 .40
222 A5 (d) 2½c on 100r bl, *grysh* .70 .60
Nos. 217-222 (6) 6.10 6.05

Inverted and double surcharges were made for sale to collectors.

Nos. 163, 98 and Type of 1914 Surcharged with New Values and Bars in Black

1921
223 A5 (c) 00.5c on 75r 350.00 350.00
224 A5 (b) 4c on 130r (#98) .70 .70
225 A5 (c) 4c on 130r brn, *straw* 2.75 2.50

Nos. 109 and 108 Surcharged with New Values and Bars in Black
226 A6 00.5c on 75c .85 .85
227 A6 1c on 50r .75 .65

Nos. 133 and 138 Surcharged with New Values and Bars in Black

228 A7	00.5c on 7½c	.70	.60
229 A7	04c on 15c	1.10	1.10
	Nos. 224-229 (6)	6.85	6.40

The 04c surcharge exists on the 15c brown rose, perf 12x11½, No. 139.

Nos. 81-82 Surcharged

República

40 C.

1925 *Perf. 12½*

234 A3	40c on 400r on 200r bl, *bl*	.80	.65
a.	Perf. 13½	3.25	2.25
235 N1	40c on 400c on 2½r brn	.60	.60
a.	Perf. 13½	.60	.60

Nos. 150-151, 154-155 Surcharged

70 C.

1931 *Perf. 11½*

236 A7	50c on 60c deep rose	1.10	.80
237 A7	70c on 80c pink	2.25	1.00
238 A7	70c on 1e deep blue	2.00	1.10
239 A7	1.40e on 2e dark violet	2.00	1.10
	Nos. 236-239 (4)	7.35	4.00

Ceres — A14

Perf. 12x11½

1932-46 Typo. Wmk. 232

243	A14	1c bister brn	.20	.20
244	A14	5c dk brown	.20	.20
245	A14	10c dp violet	.20	.20
246	A14	15c black	.20	.20
247	A14	20c gray	.20	.20
248	A14	30c myrtle grn	.25	.20
249	A14	35c yel grn ('46)	4.50	2.00
250	A14	40c dp orange	.25	.20
251	A14	45c lt blue	.85	.65
252	A14	50c lt brown	.20	.20
253	A14	60c olive grn	.30	.20
254	A14	70c orange brn	.65	.20
255	A14	80c emerald	.25	.20
256	A14	85c rose	2.00	2.00
257	A14	1a claret	.65	.20
258	A14	1.40a dk blue	4.50	1.10
258A	A14	1.75a dk blue ('46)	6.00	1.10
259	A14	2a dull vio	2.25	.35
260	A14	5a pale yel grn	3.00	.50
261	A14	10a olive bis	10.00	.90
262	A14	20a orange	17.50	2.00
		Nos. 243-262 (21)	54.20	13.00

For surcharges see Nos. 263-267, 271-273, 294A-300, J31-J36.

Surcharged with New Value and Bars

5½mm between bars and new value.

1934

263 A14	10c on 45c lt bl	1.25	.70
264 A14	20c on 85c rose	1.10	.70
265 A14	30c on 1.40a dk bl	1.10	.70
266 A14	70c on 2a dl vio	1.50	1.10
267 A14	80c on 5a pale yel grn	2.25	1.00
	Nos. 263-267 (5)	7.20	4.20

See Nos. 294A-300.

Nos. J26, J30 Surcharged in Black

CORREIOS

5 CENTAVOS

1935 Unwmk. *Perf. 11½*

268 D2	5c on 6c lt brown	.90	.60
269 D2	30c on 50c gray	.90	.60
270 D2	40c on 50c gray	.90	.60
	Nos. 268-270 (3)	2.70	1.80

No. 255 Surcharged in Black

0,15 Cent.

1938 Wmk. 232 *Perf. 12x11½*

271 A14	5c on 80c emerald	.40	*1.00*
272 A14	10c on 80c emerald	.50	*1.75*
273 A14	15c on 80c emerald	.65	*2.50*
	Nos. 271-273 (3)	1.55	*5.25*

Vasco da Gama Issue
Common Design Types

Engr.; Name & Value Typo. in Black
Perf. 13½x13

1938, July 26 Unwmk.

274 CD34	1c gray green	.20	.20
275 CD34	5c orange brn	.20	.20
276 CD34	10c dk carmine	.20	.20
277 CD34	15c dk violet brn	.20	.20
278 CD34	20c slate	.20	.20
279 CD35	30c rose violet	.25	.20
280 CD35	35c brt green	.35	.20
281 CD35	40c brown	.25	.20
282 CD35	50c brt red vio	.25	.20
283 CD36	60c gray black	.35	.20
284 CD36	70c brown vio	.30	.20
285 CD36	80c orange	.30	.20
286 CD36	1a red	.30	.20
287 CD37	1.75a blue	.85	.30
288 CD37	2a brown car	1.50	.30
289 CD37	5a olive grn	3.00	.30
290 CD38	10a blue vio	6.50	.60
291 CD38	20a red brown	15.00	1.10
	Nos. 274-291 (18)	30.20	5.20

For surcharges see Nos. 301-304.

Marble Column and Portuguese Arms with Cross — A20

1938, July 29 *Perf. 12½*

292 A20	80c blue green	1.00	.95
293 A20	1.75a deep blue	5.00	1.00
294 A20	20a dk red brown	14.00	11.00
	Nos. 292-294 (3)	20.00	12.95

Visit of the President of Portugal to this colony in 1938.

Stamps of 1932 Surcharged with New Value and Bars

8mm between bars and new value.

1941-45 Wmk. 232 *Perf. 12x11½*

294A A14	5c on 80c emer ('45)	.25	.20
295 A14	10c on 45c lt blue	.65	.55
296 A14	15c on 45c lt blue	1.00	.70
297 A14	20c on 85c rose	.65	.55
298 A14	35c on 85c rose	.65	.55
299 A14	50c on 1.40a dk blue	.65	.55
300 A14	60c on 1a claret	5.75	4.00
	Nos. 294A-300 (7)	9.60	7.10

Nos. 285 to 287 Surcharged with New Values and Bars in Black or Red

1945 Unwmk. *Perf. 13½x13*

301 CD36	5c on 80c org	.30	.20
302 CD36	50c on 1a red	.60	.20
303 CD37	50c on 1.75a bl (R)	.40	.20
304 CD37	50c on 1.75a bl	.60	.20
	Nos. 301-304 (4)	1.90	.80

Sao Miguel Fort, Luanda — A21

John IV — A22

Designs: 10c, Our Lady of Nazareth Church, Luanda. 50c, Salvador Correia de Sa e Bene vides. 1a, Surrender of Luanda. 1.75a, Diogo Cao. 2a, Manuel Cerveira Pereira. 5a, Stone Cliffs, Yelala. 10a, Paulo Dias de Novais. 20a, Massangano Fort.

Perf. 14½

1948, May Unwmk. Litho.

305 A21	5c dk violet	.20	.20
306 A21	10c dk brown	.25	.20
307 A22	30c blue grn	.20	.20
308 A22	50c vio brown	.20	.20
309 A21	1a carmine	.35	.20
310 A22	1.75a slate blue	.65	.20
311 A22	2a green	.65	.20
312 A21	5a gray black	1.00	.35
313 A22	10a rose lilac	2.00	.35
314 A21	20a gray blue	5.00	1.10
a.	Sheet of 10, #305-314	40.00	40.00
	Nos. 305-314 (10)	10.50	3.20

300th anniv. of the restoration of Angola to Portugal. No. 314a sold for 42.50a.

Lady of Fatima Issue
Common Design Type

1948, Dec.

315 CD40	50c carmine	.65	.50
316 CD40	3a ultra	2.00	1.00
317 CD40	6a red orange	7.00	2.50
318 CD40	9a dp claret	17.00	3.00
	Nos. 315-318 (4)	26.65	7.00

Our Lady of the Rosary at Fatima, Portugal.

Chiumbe River — A24

Black Rocks — A25

Designs: 50c, View of Luanda. 2.50a, Sa da Bandeira. 3.50a, Mocamedes. 15a, Cubal River. 50a, Duke of Bragança Falls.

1949 Unwmk. *Perf. 13½*

319	A24	20c dk slate blue	.20	.20
320	A25	40c black brown	.20	.20
321	A24	50c rose brown	.20	.20
322	A24	2.50a blue violet	1.10	.25
323	A24	3.50a slate gray	1.10	.25
323A	A24	15a dk green	8.25	1.50
324	A24	50a dp green	22.50	3.75
		Nos. 319-324 (7)	33.55	6.35

Sailing Vessel — A26

UPU Symbols — A27

1949, Aug. *Perf. 14*

325 A26	1a chocolate	4.00	.35
326 A26	4a dk Prus green	10.00	.85

Centenary of founding of Mocamedes.

1949, Oct.

327 A27	4a dk grn & lt grn	3.50	1.50

75th anniv. of the UPU.

Catalogue values for unused stamps in this section, from this point to the end of the section, are for Never Hinged items.

Stamp of 1870 — A28

1950, Apr. 2 *Perf. 11½x12*

328 A28	50c yellow green	.80	.25
329 A28	1a fawn	.80	.25
330 A28	4a black	3.25	.70
a.	Sheet of 3, #328-330	7.50	7.50
	Nos. 328-330 (3)	4.85	1.20

Angola's first philatelic exhibition, marking the 80th anniversary of Angola's first stamps.

No. 330a contains Nos. 328, 329 (inverted), 330, perf. 11½ and sold for 6.50a. All copies carry an oval exhibition cancellation in the margin but the stamps were valid for postage.

Holy Year Issue
Common Design Types

1950, May *Perf. 13x13½*

331 CD41	1a dull rose vio	.35	.20
332 CD42	4a black	3.00	.35

Dark Chanting Goshawk A31

European Bee Eater A32

10c, Racquet-tailed roller. 15c, Bataleur eagle. 50c, Giant kingfisher. 1a, Yellow-fronted barbet. 1.50a, Openbill (stork). 2a, Southern ground hornbill. 2.50a, African skimmer. 3a, Shikra. 3.50a, Denham's bustard. 4a, African golden oriole. 4.50a, Long-tailed shrike. 5a, Red-shouldered glossy starling. 6a, Sharp-tailed glossy starling. 7a, Red-shouldered widow bird. 10a, Half-colored kingfisher. 12.50a, White-crowned shrike. 15a, White-winged babbling starling. 20a, Yellow-billed hornbill. 25a, Amethyst starling. 30a, Orange-breasted shrike. 40a, Secretary bird. 50a, Rosy-faced lovebird.

Photogravure and Lithographed

1951 Unwmk. *Perf. 11½*

Birds in Natural Colors

333 A31	5c lt blue	.20	*.50*
334 A32	10c aqua	.20	.20
335 A32	15c salmon pink	.30	*1.00*
336 A32	20c pale yellow	.50	.25
337 A31	50c gray blue	.30	.20
338 A31	1a lilac	.30	.20
339 A31	1.50a gray buff	.40	.20
340 A31	2a cream	.40	.20
341 A32	2.50a gray	.40	.20
342 A32	3a lemon yel	.40	.20
343 A31	3.50a lt gray	.40	.20
344 A31	4a rose buff	1.25	.20
345 A32	4.50a rose lilac	1.25	.20
346 A31	5a green	6.25	.20
347 A31	6a blue	6.25	.55
348 A31	7a orange	6.25	.75
349 A31	10a lilac rose	40.00	1.10
350 A32	12.50a slate gray	8.50	1.75
351 A31	15a pale olive	8.50	1.75
352 A31	20a pale bis brn	45.00	4.50
353 A31	25a lilac rose	25.00	2.50
354 A32	30a pale salmon	25.00	3.00
355 A31	40a yellow	50.00	3.75
356 A31	50a turquoise	110.00	14.00
	Nos. 333-356 (24)	337.05	37.60

Holy Year Extension Issue
Common Design Type

1951, Oct. Litho. *Perf. 14*

357 CD43	4a orange	1.25	.50

Sheets contain alternate vertical rows of stamps and labels bearing quotations from Pope Pius XII or the Patriarch Cardinal of Lisbon.

Medical Congress Issue
Common Design Type

Design: Medical examination

1952, June *Perf. 13½*

358 CD44	1a vio blue & brn blk	.40	.20

Head of Christ — A35

1952, Oct. Unwmk. *Perf. 13*

359 A35	10c dk blue & buff	.20	.20
360 A35	50c dk ol grn & gray	.20	.20
361 A35	2a rose vio & cream	1.25	.20
	Nos. 359-361 (3)	1.65	.60

Exhibition of Sacred Missionary Art, Lisbon, 1951.

Leopard
A36

Sable Antelope
A37

Animals: 20c, Elephant. 30c, Eland. 40c, African crocodile. 50c, Impala. 1a, Mountain zebra. 1.50a, Sitatunga. 2a, Black rhinoceros. 2.30a, Gemsbok. 2.50a, Lion. 3a, Buffalo. 3.50a, Springbok. 4a, Brindled gnu. 5a, Hartebeest. 7a, Wart hog. 10a, Defassa waterbuck. 12.50a, Hippopotamus. 15a, Greater kudu. 20a, Giraffe.

1953, Aug. 15 ***Perf. 12½***

362	A36	5c	multicolored	.20	.20
363	A37	10c	multicolored	.20	.20
364	A37	20c	multicolored	.20	.20
365	A37	30c	multicolored	.20	.20
366	A36	40c	multicolored	.20	.20
367	A37	50c	multicolored	.20	.20
368	A37	1a	multicolored	.20	.20
369	A37	1.50a	multicolored	.20	.20
370	A36	2a	multicolored	.20	.20
371	A37	2.30a	multicolored	.25	.20
372	A37	2.50a	multicolored	.30	.20
373	A36	3a	multicolored	.30	.20
374	A37	3.50a	multicolored	.20	.20
375	A37	4a	multicolored	6.00	.25
376	A37	5a	multicolored	.35	.20
377	A37	7a	multicolored	.75	.25
378	A37	10a	multicolored	1.25	.20
379	A37	12.50a	multicolored	4.00	1.75
380	A37	15a	multicolored	4.00	1.25
381	A37	20a	multicolored	5.00	.35
			Nos. 362-381 (20)	24.20	6.85

Stamp of Portugal and Arms of Colonies — A38

1953, Nov. **Photo.** ***Perf. 13***
Stamp and Arms Multicolored

382 A38 50c gray & dark gray .55 .35

Cent. of Portugal's 1st postage stamps.

Map and Plane — A39

Typographed and Lithographed
1954, May 27 ***Perf. 13½***

383	A39	35c	multicolored	.20	.20
384	A39	4.50e	multicolored	.70	.30

Visit of Pres. Francisco H C. Lopes.

Sao Paulo Issue
Common Design Type

1954 **Litho.**

385 CD46 1e bister & gray .32 .20

Map of Angola — A41

Artur de Paiva — A42

1955, Aug. **Unwmk.** ***Perf. 13½***

386	A41	5c	multicolored	.20	.20
387	A41	20c	multicolored	.20	.20
388	A41	50c	multicolored	.20	.20
389	A41	1e	multicolored	.20	.20
390	A41	2.30e	multicolored	.30	.20
391	A41	4e	multicolored	.50	.20
392	A41	10e	multicolored	.50	.20
393	A41	20e	multicolored	1.00	.20
			Nos. 386-393 (8)	3.10	1.60

For overprints see Nos. 593, 598, 604.

1956, Oct. 9 ***Perf. 13½x12½***

394 A42 1e blk, dk bl & ocher .20 .20

Cent. of the birth of Col. Artur de Paiva.

Man of Malange
A43

Jose M. Antunes
A44

Various Costumes in Multicolor; Inscriptions in Black Brown

1957, Jan. 1 **Photo.** ***Perf. 11½***
Granite Paper

395	A43	5c	gray	.20	.20
396	A43	10c	orange yel	.20	.20
397	A43	15c	lt blue grn	.20	.20
398	A43	20c	pale rose vio	.20	.20
399	A43	30c	brt rose	.20	.20
400	A43	40c	blue gray	.20	.20
401	A43	50c	pale olive	.20	.20
402	A43	80c	lt violet	.20	.20
403	A43	1.50e	buff	1.00	.20
404	A43	2.50e	lt yel grn	1.00	.20
405	A43	4e	salmon	.50	.20
406	A43	10e	salmon pink	1.00	.25
			Nos. 395-406 (12)	5.10	2.45

1957, Apr. ***Perf. 13½***

407 A44 1e aqua & brown .65 .20

Birth cent. of Father Jose Maria Antunes.

Fair Emblem, Globe and Arms — A45

1958, July **Litho.** ***Perf. 12x11½***

408 A45 1.50e multicolored .25 .20

World's Fair, Brussels, Apr. 17-Oct. 19.

Tropical Medicine Congress Issue
Common Design Type

Design: Securidaca longipedunculata.

1958, Dec. 15 ***Perf. 13½***

409 CD47 2.50e multicolored 1.10 .70

Medicine Man — A47

Welwitschia Mirabilis — A48

Designs: 1.50e, Early government doctor. 2.50e, Modern medical team.

1958, Dec. 18 ***Perf. 11½x12***

410	A47	1e	blue blk & brown	.20	.20
411	A47	1.50e	gray, blk & brown	.50	.20
412	A47	2.50e	multicolored	.75	.40
			Nos. 410-412 (3)	1.45	.80

75th anniversary of the Maria Pia Hospital, Luanda.

1959, Oct. 1 **Litho.** ***Perf. 14½***
Various Views of Plant and Various Frames

413	A48	1.50e	lt brown, grn & blk	.55	.45
414	A48	2.50e	multicolored	.85	.50
415	A48	5e	multicolored	1.10	.75
416	A48	10e	multicolored	2.75	1.00
			Nos. 413-416 (4)	5.25	2.70

Centenary of discovery of Welwitschia mirabilis, desert plant.

Map of West Africa, c. 1540, by Jorge Reinel — A49

1960, June 25 ***Perf. 13½***

417 A49 2.50e multicolored .20 .20

500th anniv. of the death of Prince Henry the Navigator.

Distributing Medicines — A50

Girl of Angola — A51

1960, Oct. **Litho.** ***Perf. 14½***

418 A50 2.50e multicolored .30 .20

10th anniv. of the Commission for Technical Co-operation in Africa South of the Sahara (C.C.T.A.).

1961, Nov. 30 **Unwmk.** ***Perf. 13***

Various portraits.

419	A51	10c	multicolored	.20	.20
420	A51	15c	multicolored	.20	.20
421	A51	30c	multicolored	.20	.20
422	A51	40c	multicolored	.20	.20
423	A51	60c	multicolored	.20	.20
424	A51	1.50e	multicolored	.20	.20
425	A51	2e	multicolored	.60	.20
426	A51	2.50e	multicolored	.85	.20
427	A51	3e	multicolored	2.00	.20
428	A51	4e	multicolored	.90	.20
429	A51	5e	multicolored	.70	.20
430	A51	7.50e	multicolored	.90	.45
431	A51	10e	multicolored	.70	.25
432	A51	15e	multicolored	.65	.40
432A	A51	25e	multicolored	1.90	.65
432B	A51	50e	multicolored	3.25	1.00
			Nos. 419-432B (16)	13.65	4.95

Sports Issue
Common Design Type

Sports: 50c, Flying. 1e, Rowing. 1.50e, Water polo. 2.50e, Hammer throwing. 4.50e, High jump. 15e, Weight lifting.

1962, Jan. 18 ***Perf. 13½***
Multicolored Design

433	CD48	50c	lt blue	.20	.20
434	CD48	1e	olive bister	.70	.20
435	CD48	1.50e	salmon	.35	.20
436	CD48	2.50e	lt green	.40	.20
437	CD48	4.50e	pale blue	.35	.25
438	CD48	15e	yellow	1.50	.65
			Nos. 433-438 (6)	3.50	1.70

For overprint see No. 608.

Anti-Malaria Issue
Common Design Type

Design: Anopheles funestus.

1962, April **Litho.** ***Perf. 13½***

439 CD49 2.50e multicolored .60 .35

Gen. Norton de Matos — A54

Locusts — A56

1962, Aug. 8 **Unwmk.** ***Perf. 14½***

440 A54 2.50e multicolored .30 .20

50th anniv. of the founding of Nova Lisboa.

1963, June 2 **Litho.** ***Perf. 14***

447 A56 2.50e multicolored .40 .20

15th anniv. of the Intl. Anti-Locust Organ.

Arms of Luanda
A57

Vila de Santo Antonio do Zaire — A58

Coats of Arms (Provinces and Cities): 10c, Massangano. 15c, Sanza-Pombo. 25c, Ambriz. 30c, Muxima. 40c, Ambrizete. 50c, Carmona. 60c, Catete. 70c, Quibaxe. No. 458, Maquelo do Zombo. 1e, Salazar. 1.20e, Bembe. No. 461, Malanje. No. 462, Caxito. 1.80e, Dondo. 2e, Henrique de Carvalho. No. 465, Moçamedes. No. 466, Damba. 3e, Novo Redondo. 3.50e, S. Salvador do Congo. 4e, Cuimba. 5e, Luso. 6.50e, Negage. 7e, Quitexe. 7.50e, S. Filipe de Benguela. 8e, Mucaba. 9e, 31 de Janeiro. 10e, Lobito. 11e, Nova Caipemba. 12.50e, Gabela. 14e, Songo. 15e Sá da Bandeira. 17e, Quimbele. 17.50e, Silva Porto. 20e, Nova Lisboa. 22.50e, Cabinda. 25e, Noqui. 30e, Serpa Pinto. 35e, Santa Cruz. 50e, General Freire.

1963 ***Perf. 13½***
Arms in Original Colors; Red and Violet Blue Inscriptions

448	A57	5c	tan	.20	.20
449	A57	10c	lt blue	.20	.20
450	A58	15c	salmon	.20	.20
451	A58	20c	olive	.20	.20
452	A58	25c	lt blue	.20	.20
453	A57	30c	buff	.20	.20
454	A58	40c	gray	.20	.20
455	A57	50c	lt green	.20	.20
456	A58	60c	brt yellow	.20	.20
457	A58	70c	dull rose	.20	.20
458	A57	1e	pale lilac	.30	.20
459	A58	1e	dull yellow	.20	.20
460	A58	1.20e	rose	.20	.20
461	A57	1.50e	pale salmon	.60	.20
462	A58	1.50e	lt green	.40	.20
463	A58	1.80e	yel olive	.25	.20
464	A57	2e	lt yel green	.30	.20
465	A57	2.50e	lt gray	1.50	.20
466	A58	2.50e	dull blue	1.25	.20
467	A57	3e	yel olive	.45	.20
468	A57	3.50e	gray	.50	.20
469	A58	4e	citron	.35	.20
470	A57	5e	citron	.40	.25
471	A58	6.50e	tan	.40	.25
472	A58	7e	rose lilac	.45	.25
473	A57	7.50e	pale lilac	.55	.30
474	A58	8e	lt aqua	.45	.30
475	A58	9e	yellow	.60	.30
476	A57	10e	dp salmon	.70	.35
477	A58	11e	dull yel grn	.70	.55
478	A57	12.50e	pale blue	.90	.45
479	A58	14e	lt gray	.90	.45
480	A57	15e	lt blue	1.00	.45
481	A58	17e	pale blue	1.10	.70
482	A57	17.50e	dull yellow	1.50	1.00
483	A57	20e	lt aqua	1.50	.70
484	A57	22.50e	gray	1.50	1.00
485	A58	25e	citron	1.50	.70
486	A57	30e	yellow	2.00	1.25
487	A58	35e	grysh blue	2.00	1.50
488	A58	50e	dp yellow	3.00	1.25
			Nos. 448-488 (41)	29.45	16.40

Pres. Américo Rodrigues Thomaz — A59

1963, Sept. 16 **Litho.**

489 A59 2.50e multicolored .50 .30

Visit of the President of Portugal.

Airline Anniversary Issue
Common Design Type

1963, Oct. 5 **Unwmk.** ***Perf. 14½***

490 CD50 1e lt blue & multi .25 .20

Cathedral of Sá da Bandeira A61

Malange Cathedral A62

Churches: 20c, Landana. 30c, Luanda Cathedral. 40c, Gabela. 50c, St. Martin's Chapel, Baia dos Tigres. 1.50e, St. Peter, Chibia. 2e, Church of Our Lady, Benguela. 2.50e, Church of Jesus, Luanda. 3e, Camabatela. 3.50e, Mission, Cabinda. 4e, Vila Folgares. 4.50e, Church of Our Lady, Lobito. 5e, Church of Cabinda. 7.50e, Cacuso Church, Malange. 10e, Lubango Mission. 12.50e, Huila Mission. 15e, Church of Our Lady, Luanda Island.

1963, Nov. 1 Litho.
Multicolored Design and Inscription

491	A61	10c	gray blue	.20	.20
492	A61	20c	pink	.20	.20
493	A61	30c	lt blue	.20	.20
494	A61	40c	tan	.20	.20
495	A61	50c	lt green	.20	.20
496	A62	1e	buff	.20	.20
497	A61	1.50e	lt vio blue	.20	.20
498	A62	2e	pale rose	.20	.20
499	A61	2.50e	gray	.20	.20
500	A62	3e	buff	.20	.20
501	A61	3.50e	olive	.25	.20
502	A62	4e	buff	.25	.20
503	A62	4.50e	pale blue	.40	.25
504	A61	5e	tan	.50	.25
505	A62	7.50e	gray	.60	.35
506	A61	10e	dull yellow	.75	.40
507	A62	12.50e	bister	1.00	.80
508	A62	15e	pale gray vio	2.50	.70
			Nos. 491-508 (18)	8.25	5.15

National Overseas Bank Issue
Common Design Type

Design: Antonio Teixeira de Sousa.

1964, May 16 ***Perf. 13½***
509 CD51 2.50e multicolored .40 .25

Commerce Building and Arms of Chamber of Commerce A64

1964, Nov. Litho. ***Perf. 12***
510 A64 1e multicolored .20 .20

Luanda Chamber of Commerce centenary.

ITU Issue
Common Design Type

1965, May 17 Unwmk. ***Perf. 14½***
511 CD52 2.50e gray & multi .70 .25

Plane over Luanda Airport — A65

Harquebusier, 1539 — A66

1965, Dec. 3 Litho. ***Perf. 13***
512 A65 2.50e multicolored .25 .20

25th anniv. of DTA, Direccao dos Transportes Aereos.

1966, Feb. 25 Litho. ***Perf. 14½***

50c, Harquebusier, 1539. 1e, Harquebusier, 1640. 1.50e, Infantry officer, 1777. 2e, Standard bearer, infantry, 1777. 2.50e, Infantry soldier, 1777. 3e, Cavalry officer, 1783. 4e, Cavalry soldier, 1783. 4.50e, Infantry officer, 1807. 5e, Infantry soldier, 1807. 6e, Cavalry officer, 1807. 8e, Cavalry soldier, 1807. 9e, Infantry soldier, 1873.

513	A66	50c	multicolored	.20	.20
514	A66	1e	multicolored	.20	.20
515	A66	1.50e	multicolored	.20	.20
516	A66	2e	multicolored	.20	.20
517	A66	2.50e	multicolored	.20	.20
518	A66	3e	multicolored	.20	.20
519	A66	4e	multicolored	.40	.25
520	A66	4.50e	multicolored	.40	.25
521	A66	5e	multicolored	.60	.20
522	A66	6e	multicolored	.75	.50
523	A66	8e	multicolored	1.25	.85
524	A66	9e	multicolored	1.50	1.00
			Nos. 513-524 (12)	6.10	4.25

National Revolution Issue
Common Design Type

Design: St. Paul's Hospital and Commercial and Industrial School.

1966, May 28 Litho. ***Perf. 12***
525 CD53 1e multicolored .20 .20

Emblem of Holy Ghost Society — A68

1966 Litho. ***Perf. 13***
526 A68 1e blue & multi .20 .20

Centenary of the Holy Ghost Society.

Navy Club Issue
Common Design Type

Designs: 1e, Mendes Barata and cruiser Dom Carlos I. 2.50e, Capt. Augusto de Castilho and corvette Mindelo.

1967, Jan. 31 Litho. ***Perf. 13***
527 CD54 1e multicolored .40 .20
528 CD54 2.50e multicolored .65 .20

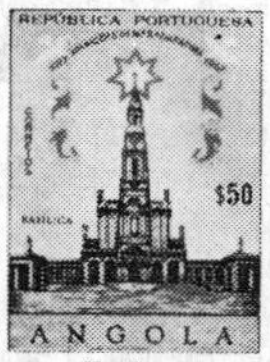

Fatima Basilica — A70

Angola Map, Manuel Cerveira Pereira — A71

1967, May 13 Litho. ***Perf. 12½x13***
529 A70 50c multicolored .20 .20

50th anniv. of the apparition of the Virgin Mary to 3 shepherd children at Fatima.

1967, Aug. 15 Litho. ***Perf. 12½x13***
530 A71 50c multicolored .20 .20

350th anniv. of the founding of Benguela.

Administration Building, Carmona — A72

1967 Litho. ***Perf. 12***
531 A72 1e multicolored .20 .20

50th anniv. of the founding of Carmona.

Military Order of Valor — A73

Our Lady of Hope — A74

50c, Ribbon of the Three Orders. 1.50e, Military Order of Avis. 2e, Military Order of Christ. 2.50e, Military Order of St. John of Espada. 3e, Order of the Empire. 4e, Order of Prince Henry. 5e, Order of Benemerencia. 10e, Order of Public Instruction. 20e, Order for Industrial & Agricultural Merit.

1967, Oct. 31 ***Perf. 14***

532	A73	50c	lt gray & multi	.20	.20
533	A73	1e	lt green & multi	.20	.20
534	A73	1.50e	yellow & multi	.20	.20
535	A73	2e	multicolored	.20	.20
536	A73	2.50e	multicolored	.20	.20
537	A73	3e	lt olive & multi	.20	.20
538	A73	4e	gray & multi	.20	.20
539	A73	5e	multicolored	.25	.20
540	A73	10e	lilac & multi	.40	.25
541	A73	20e	lt blue & multi	1.00	.55
			Nos. 532-541 (10)	3.05	2.40

1968, Apr. 22 Litho. ***Perf. 14***

Designs: 1e, Belmonte Castle, horiz. 1.50e, St. Jerome's Convent. 2.50e, Cabral's Armada.

542	A74	50c	yellow & multi	.20	.20
543	A74	1e	gray & multi	.25	.20
544	A74	1.50e	lt blue & multi	.40	.20
545	A74	2.50e	buff & multi	.60	.20
			Nos. 542-545 (4)	1.45	.80

500th anniv. of the birth of Pedro Alvares Cabral, navigator who took possession of Brazil for Portugal.

Francisco Inocencio de Souza Coutinho — A75

1969, Jan. 7 Litho. ***Perf. 14***
546 A75 2e multicolored .25 .20

Founding of Novo Redondo, 200th anniv.

Admiral Coutinho Issue
Common Design Type

Design: Adm. Gago Coutinho and his first ship.

1969, Feb. 17 Litho. ***Perf. 14***
547 CD55 2.50e multicolored .30 .20

Compass Rose A77

Portal of St. Jeronimo's Monastery A79

1969, Aug. 29 Litho. ***Perf. 14***
548 A77 1e multicolored .20 .20

500th anniv. of the birth of Vasco da Gama (1469-1524), navigator.

Administration Reform Issue
Common Design Type

1969, Sept. 25 Litho. ***Perf. 14***
549 CD56 1.50e multicolored .20 .20

1969, Dec. 1 Litho. ***Perf. 14***
550 A79 3e multicolored .20 .20

500th anniv. of the birth of King Manuel I.

Angolasaurus Bocagei — A80

Fossils and Minerals: 1e, Ferrometeorite. 1.50e, Dioptase crystals. 2e, Gondwanidium. 2.50e, Diamonds. 3e, Estromatolite. 3.50e, Procarcharodon megalodon. 4e, Microceratodus angolensis. 4.50e, Moscovite. 5e, Barite. 6e, Nostoceras. 10e, Rotula orbiculus angolensis.

1970, Oct. 31 Litho. ***Perf. 13***

551	A80	50c	tan & multi	.20	.20
552	A80	1e	multicolored	.20	.20
553	A80	1.50e	multicolored	.20	.20
554	A80	2e	multicolored	.20	.20
555	A80	2.50e	lt gray & multi	.20	.20
556	A80	3e	multicolored	.20	.20
557	A80	3.50e	blue & multi	.30	.20
558	A80	4e	lt gray & multi	.30	.20
559	A80	4.50e	gray & multi	.30	.20
560	A80	5e	gray & multi	.30	.20
561	A80	6e	pink & multi	.60	.20
562	A80	10e	lt blue & multi	.75	.35
			Nos. 551-562 (12)	3.75	2.55

Marshal Carmona Issue
Common Design Type

1970, Nov. 15 ***Perf. 14***
563 CD57 2.50e multicolored .25 .20

Arms of Malanje, Cotton Boll and Field — A82

1970, Nov. 20 ***Perf. 13***
564 A82 2.50e multicolored .25 .20

Centenary of the municipality of Malanje.

Mail Ships and Angola No. 1 A83

4.50e, Steam locomotive and Angola No. 4.

1970, Dec. 1 ***Perf. 13½***
565 A83 1.50e multicolored .30 .20
566 A83 4.50e multicolored .65 .25

Cent. of stamps of Angola. See No. C36. For overprint see No. 616B.

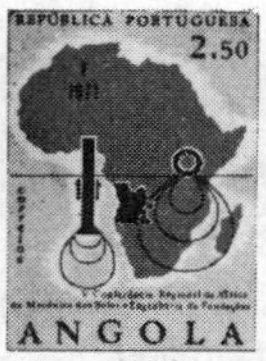

Map of Africa, Diagram of Seismic Tests — A84

Galleon on Congo River — A85

1971, Aug. 22 Litho. ***Perf. 13***
567 A84 2.50e multicolored .20 .20

5th Regional Conference of Soil and Foundation Engineers, Luanda, Aug. 22-Sept. 5.

1972, May 25 Litho. ***Perf. 13***
568 A85 1e emerald & multi .20 .20

4th centenary of the publication of The Lusiads by Luiz Camoens.

Olympic Games Issue
Common Design Type

1972, June 20 ***Perf. 14x13½***
569 CD59 50c multicolored .20 .20

Lisbon-Rio de Janeiro Flight Issue
Common Design Type

1972, Sept. 20 Litho. ***Perf. 13½***
570 CD60 1e multicolored .20 .20

WMO Centenary Issue
Common Design Type

1973, Dec. 15 Litho. ***Perf. 13***
571 CD61 1e dk gray & multi .20 .20

Radar Station A89

1974, June 25 Litho. *Perf. 13*
572 A89 2e multicolored .25 .20

Establishment of satellite communications network via Intelsat among Portugal, Angola and Mozambique.
For overprint see No. 616A

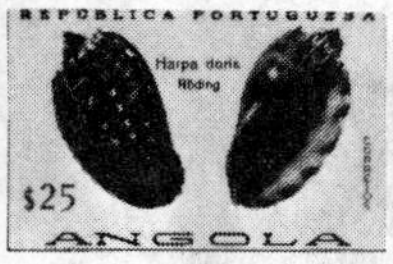
Harpa Doris — A90

Designs: Sea shells.

1974, Oct. 25 Litho. *Perf. 12x12½*
573 A90 25c shown .20 .20
574 A90 30c Murex melanamathos .20 .20
575 A90 50c Venus foliaceo lamellosa .20 .20
576 A90 70c Lathyrus filosus .20 .20
577 A90 1e Cymbium cisium .20 .20
578 A90 1.50e Cassis tesselata .20 .20
579 A90 2e Cypraea stercoraria .20 .20
580 A90 2.50e Conus prometheus .20 .20
581 A90 3e Strombus latus .20 .20
582 A90 3.50e Tympanotonus fuscatus .20 .20
583 A90 4e Cardium costatum .25 .20
584 A90 5e Natica fulminea .25 .20
585 A90 6e Lyropecten nodosus .30 .20
586 A90 7e Tonna galea .75 .25
587 A90 10e Donax rugosus .90 .30
588 A90 25e Cymatium trigonum 1.50 .40
589 A90 30e Olivancilaria acuminata 2.50 .75
590 A90 35e Semifusus morio 2.50 .75
591 A90 40e Clavatula lineata 3.00 1.00
592 A90 50e Solarium granulatum 4.00 1.50
Nos. 573-592 (20) 17.95 7.55

For overprints see Nos. 605-607, 617-630.

No. 386 Overprinted in Blue: "1974 / FILATELIA / JUVENIL"

1974, Dec. 21 Litho. *Perf. 13½*
593 A41 5c multicolored .20 .20

Youth philately.

Republic

Star and Hand Holding Rifle — A91

1975, Nov. 11 Litho. *Perf. 13x13½*
594 A91 1.50e red & multi .20 .20

Independence in 1975.

Diquiche Mask — A92

Design: 3e, Bui ou Congolo mask.

1976, Feb. 6 *Perf. 13½*
595 A92 50c lt blue & multi .20 .20
596 A92 3e multicolored .20 .20

Workers — A93

President Agostinho Neto — A94

1976, May 1 Litho. *Perf. 12*
597 A93 1e red & multi .20 .20

International Workers' Day.

No. 392 Overprinted Bar and: "DIA DO SELO / 15 Junho 1976 / REP. POPULAR / DE"

1976, June 15 Litho. *Perf. 13½*
598 A41 10e multicolored .40 .25

Stamp Day.

1976, Nov. 11 Litho. *Perf. 13*
599 A94 50c yel & dk brown .20 .20
600 A94 2e lt gray & plum .20 .20
601 A94 3e gray & indigo .20 .20
602 A94 5e buff & brown .20 .20
603 A94 10e tan & sepia .40 .20
a. Souv. sheet of 1, imperf. 2.00 1.25
Nos. 599-603 (5) 1.20 1.00

First anniversary of independence.

Nos. 393, 588-589, 592 Overprinted with Bar over Republica Portuguesa and: "REPUBLICA POPULAR DE"

1977, Feb. 9 *Perf. 13½, 12x12½*
604 A41 20e multicolored 1.25 .25
605 A90 25e multicolored 1.75 .35
606 A90 30e multicolored 2.50 .50
607 A90 50e multicolored 4.00 .75
Nos. 604-607 (4) 9.50 1.85

Overprint in 3 lines on No. 604, in 2 lines on others.

No. 438 Overprinted with Bar over Republica Portuguesa and: "S. Silvestre / 1976 / Rep. Popular / de"

1976, Dec. 31 *Perf. 13½*
608 CD48 15e multicolored 3.50 .25

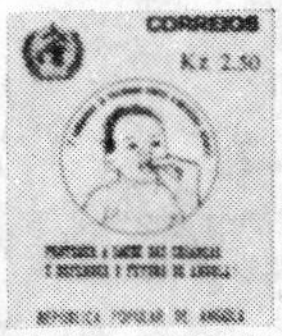
Child and WHO Emblem — A95

Map of Africa, Flag of Angola — A96

1977 Litho. *Perf. 10½*
609 A95 2.50k blk & lt blue .20 .20

Campaign for vaccination against poliomyelitis.

Anti-Apartheid Emblem — A97

1979, June 20 Litho. *Perf. 13½*
611 A97 1k multicolored .20 .20

Anti-Apartheid Year.

Human Rights Emblem A98

Child Flowers, Globe, IYC Emblem A99

1979, June 15 Litho. *Perf. 13½*
612 A98 2.50k multicolored .20 .20

Declaration of Human Rights, 30th anniv. (in 1975).

1980, May 1 Litho. *Perf. 14x14½*
613 A99 3.50k multicolored .20 .20

International Year of the Child (1979).

Running, Moscow '80 Emblem A100

5th Anniv. of Independence A101

1980, Dec. 15 Litho. *Perf. 13½*
614 A100 9k shown .30 .20
615 A100 12k Swimming, horiz. .40 .20

22nd Summer Olympic Games, Moscow, July 19-Aug. 3.

1980, Nov. 11
616 A101 5.50k multicolored .20 .20

Nos. 572, 566 Overprinted with Bar and: "REPUBLICA POPULAR / DE"

1980-81 Litho. *Perf. 13½x13*
616A A89 2e multi (bar only) .50
616B A83 4.50e multicolored 1.00

Issue dates: 2e, May 17, 1981, 4.50e, June 15. See No. C37.

Nos. 577-580, 582-591 Overprinted with Black Bar over "Republica Portuguesa"

1981, June 15 Litho. *Perf. 12x12½*
617 A90 1e multicolored
618 A90 1.50e multicolored
619 A90 2e multicolored
620 A90 2.50e multicolored
621 A90 3.50e multicolored
622 A90 4e multicolored
623 A90 5e multicolored
624 A90 6e multicolored
625 A90 7e multicolored
626 A90 10e multicolored
627 A90 25e multicolored
628 A90 30e multicolored
629 A90 35e multicolored
630 A90 40e multicolored
Nos. 617-630 (14) 15.00 8.00

Man Walking with Canes, Tchibinda Ilunga Statue — A102

1981, Sept. 5 Litho. *Perf. 13½*
631 A102 9k multicolored .30 .20

Turipex '81 tourism exhibition.

M.P.L.A. Workers' Party Congress A103

1980, Dec. 23 Litho. *Perf. 14*
632 A103 50 l Millet .20 .20
633 A103 5k Coffee .20 .20
634 A103 7.50k Sunflowers .25 .20
635 A103 13.50k Cotton .40 .20
636 A103 14k Oil .45 .25
637 A103 16k Diamonds .45 .25
Nos. 632-637 (6) 1.95 1.30

People's Power A104

Natl. Heroes' Day A105

1980, Nov. 11
638 A104 40k lt blue & blk 1.25 .40

1980, Sept. 17 *Perf. 14x13½*
639 A105 4.50k Former Pres. Neto .20 .20
640 A105 50k Neto, diff. 1.50 .65

Soweto Uprising, 5th Anniv. A106

1981
641 A106 4.50k multicolored .20 .20

2nd Central African Games A107

1981, Sept. 3 Litho. *Perf. 13½*
642 A107 50 l Bicycling, tennis .20 .20
643 A107 5k Judo, boxing .20 .20
644 A107 6k Basketball, volleyball .25 .20
645 A107 10k Handball, soccer .40 .25
Nos. 642-645 (4) 1.05 .85

Souvenir Sheet

Imperf

646 A107 15k multicolored 2.00

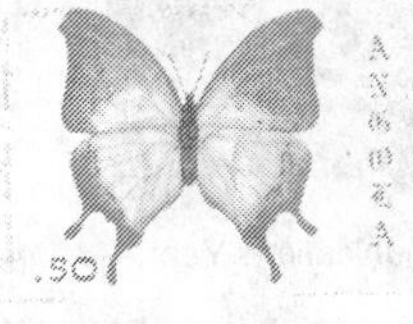
Charaxes Kahldeni A108

1982, Feb. 26 Litho. *Perf. 13½*
647 A108 50 l shown .20 .20
648 A108 1k Abantis zambesiaca .20 .20
649 A108 5k Catacroptera cloanthe .20 .20
650 A108 9k Myrina ficedula, vert. .40 .20
651 A108 10k Colotis danae .40 .20
652 A108 15k Acraea acrita .55 .25
653 A108 100k Precis hierta 2.75 1.25
a. Souvenir sheet 2.00 1.00
Nos. 647-653 (7) 4.70 2.50

No. 653a contains Nos. 647-653, imperf., and sold for 30k (stamps probably not valid individually).

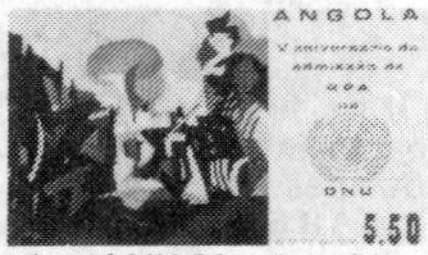

5th Anniv. of UN Membership — A109

5.50k, The Silence of the Night, by Musseque Catambor. 7.50k, Cotton picking, Catete.

1982, Sept. 22 **Litho.**

654 A109 5.50k multicolored .20 .20
655 A109 7.50k multicolored .25 .20

20th Anniv. of Engineering Laboratory A110

1982, Dec. 21 **Litho.** ***Perf. 14***

656 A110 9k Lab .25 .20
657 A110 13k Worker, vert. .40 .20
658 A110 100k Equipment, vert. 3.25 1.25
Nos. 656-658 (3) 3.90 1.65

Local Flowers A111

1983, Feb. 18 ***Perf. 13½***

659 A111 5k Dichrostachys glomerata .20 .20
660 A111 12k Amblygonocarpus obtusangulus .40 .20
661 A111 50k Albizzia versicolor 2.00 .65
Nos. 659-661 (3) 2.60 1.05

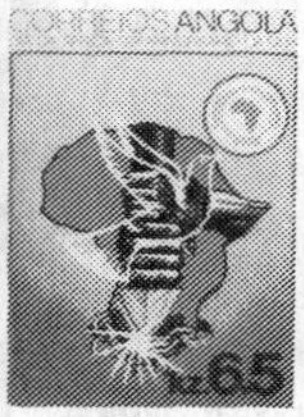

Women's Org., First Congress — A112

Africa Day — A113

1983 **Litho.** ***Perf. 13½***

662 A112 20k multicolored .80 .80

1983, June 30 ***Perf. 13***

663 A113 6.5k multi .25 .25

World Communications Year — A114

1983, June 30 **Litho.** ***Perf. 13½***

664 A114 6.5k M'pungi .25 .25
665 A114 12k Mondu .40 .40

BRASILIANA '83 Stamp Exhibition, Rio de Janeiro, July 29-Aug. 7 — A115

Crop-eating insects.

1983, July 29 **Litho.** ***Perf. 13***

666 A115 4.5k Antestiopsis lineaticollis .20 .20
667 A115 6.5k Stephanoderes hampei ferr. .25 .25
668 A115 10k Zonocerus variegatus .40 .40
Nos. 666-668 (3) .85 .85

25th Anniv. of Economic Commission for Africa A116

1983, Aug. 2

669 A116 10k Map, emblem .40 .40

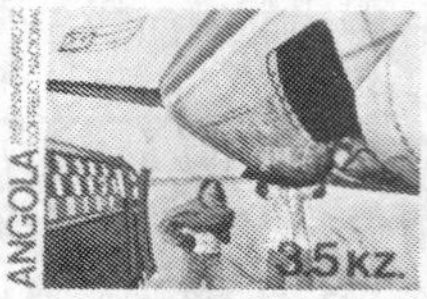

185th Anniv. of Post Office A117

1983, Dec. 7 **Litho.** ***Perf. 13½***

670 A117 50 l Mail collection, vert. .20 .20
671 A117 3.5k Unloading mail plane .20 .20
672 A117 5k Sorting mail .20 .20
673 A117 15k Mailing letter, vert. .60 .60
674 A117 30k Post office box delivery 1.25 1.25
a. Min. sheet of 3, #671-672, 674 4.00 4.00
Nos. 670-674 (5) 2.45 2.45

No. 674a sold for 100k.

Local Butterflies A118

1984, Jan. 20 **Litho.** ***Perf. 13½***

675 A118 50 l Parasa karschi .20 .20
676 A118 1k Diaphone angolensis .20 .20
677 A118 3.5k Choeropasis jucunda .20 .20
678 A118 6.5k Hespagarista rendalli .25 .25
679 A118 15k Euchromia guineensis .60 .60
680 A118 17.5k Mazuca roseistriga .70 .70
681 A118 20k Utetheisa callima .85 .85
Nos. 675-681 (7) 3.00 3.00

A119

A120

1984, Apr. 11 **Litho.** ***Perf. 13½***

682 A119 30k multicolored 1.25 1.25

First Natl. Worker's Union Congress, Apr. 11-16 .

1984, Oct. 24 **Litho.** ***Perf. 13½***

Local birds.

683 A120 10.50k Bucorvos leadbeateri .45 .40
684 A120 14k Gypohicax angolensis .55 .50
685 A120 16k Ardea goliath .60 .50
686 A120 19.50k Pelicanus onocrotalus .80 .75
687 A120 22k Platelea alba .90 .90
688 A120 26k Balearica pavonnia 1.00 1.00
Nos. 683-688 (6) 4.30 4.05

Local Animals A121

1984, Nov. 12

689 A121 1k Tragelephus strepsicerus .20 .20
690 A121 4k Antidorcos marsupialis angolerusis .20 .20
691 A121 5k Pan troglodytes .20 .20
692 A121 10k Sycerus caffer .40 .40
693 A121 15k Hippotragus niger variani .60 .60
694 A121 20k Orycteropus afer .80 .80
695 A121 25k Crocuta crocuta 1.00 1.00
Nos. 689-695 (7) 3.40 3.40

Angolese Monuments A122

1985, Feb. 21 **Litho.** ***Perf. 13½***

696 A122 5k San Pedro da Barra .25 .25
697 A122 12.5k Nova Oeiras .55 .55
698 A122 18k M'Banza Kongo .80 .80
699 A122 26k Massangano 1.10 1.10
700 A122 39k Escravatura Museum 1.60 1.60
Nos. 696-700 (5) 4.30 4.30

United Workers' Party, 25th Anniv. A123

1985, May **Litho.** ***Perf. 12***

701 A123 77k XXV, red flags 1.50 1.50

Printed in sheets of 5.

A124

A125

1985, May

702 A124 1k Flags .20 .20
703 A124 11k Oil drilling platform, Cabinda .25 .25
704 A124 57k Conference 1.10 1.10
a. Strip of 3, #702-704 1.40 1.40

Southern African Development Council, 5th anniv.

Lithographed and Typographed

1985, July 5 ***Perf. 11***

Medicinal plants.

705 A125 1k Lonchocarpus sericeus .20 .20
706 A125 4k Gossypium .20 .20
707 A125 11k Cassia occidentalis .25 .25
708 A125 25.50k Gloriosa superba .50 .50
709 A125 55k Cochlospermum angolensis 1.10 1.10
Nos. 705-709 (5) 2.25 2.25

ARGENTINA '85 exhibition.

5th Natl. Heroes Day — A126

Natl. flag and: 10.50k, Portrait of Agostinho Neto, party leader. 36.50k, Neto working.

1985 **Litho.** ***Perf. 13½***

710 A126 10.50k multicolored .20 .20
711 A126 36.50k multicolored .70 .70

Ministerial Conference of Non-Aligned Countries, Luanda — A127

1985, Sept. 4 **Photo.** ***Perf. 11***

712 A127 35k multicolored 1.50 1.50

UN, 40th Anniv. A128

1985, Oct. 29 **Litho.** ***Perf. 11***

713 A128 12.50k multicolored .55 .55

Industry and Natural Resources A129

1985, Nov. 11

714 A129 50 l Cement Factory .20 .20
715 A129 5k Logging .25 .25
716 A129 7k Quartz .30 .30
717 A129 10k Iron mine .45 .45
a. Souvenir sheet of 4, #714-717, imperf. 1.00 1.00
Nos. 714-717 (4) 1.20 1.20

Natl. independence, 10th anniv.

2nd Natl. Workers' Party Congress (MPLA) A130

1985, Nov. 28 ***Perf. 13½***

718 A130 20k multicolored .85 .85

Demostenes de Almeida Clington Races, 30th Anniv. — A131

Various runners.

1985, Dec. 13

719 A131 50 l multicolored .20 .20
720 A131 5k multicolored .25 .25
721 A131 6.50k multicolored .30 .30
722 A131 10k multicolored .40 .40
Nos. 719-722 (4) 1.15 1.15

1986 World Cup Soccer Championships, Mexico — A132

Map, soccer field and various plays.

1986, May 6 Litho. *Perf. 11½x11*

723	A132	50 l	multi	.20	.20
724	A132	3.50k	multi	.20	.20
725	A132	5k	multi	.25	.25
726	A132	7k	multi	.30	.30
727	A132	10k	multi	.45	.45
728	A132	18k	multi	.85	.85
			Nos. 723-728 (6)	2.25	2.25

Struggle Against Portugal, 25th Anniv. A133

1986, May 6 *Perf. 11x11½*

729 A133 15k multicolored .65 .65

First Man in Space, 25th Anniv. A134

1986, Aug. 21 Litho. *Perf. 11x11½*

730	A134	50 l	Skylab, US	.20	.20
731	A134	1k	Spacecraft	.20	.20
732	A134	5k	A. Leonov space-walking	.25	.25
733	A134	10k	Lunokhod on Moon	.40	.40
734	A134	13k	Apollo-Soyuz link-up	.60	.60
			Nos. 730-734 (5)	1.65	1.65

Admission of Angola to UN, 10th Anniv. — A135

1986, Dec. 1 Litho. *Perf. 11x11½*

735 A135 22k multi .90 .90

Liberation Movement, 30th Anniv. — A136

Angolese at work, fighting and: No. 736a, "1956." No. 736b, Congress emblem, "1980." No. 736c, Labor Party emblem, "1985."

1986, Dec. 3 *Perf. 11½x11*

736 A136 Strip of 3 .65 .65
a.-c. 5k any single .20 .20

Agostinho Neto University, 10th Anniv. A137

1986, Dec. 30 Litho. *Perf. 11x11½*

737	A137	50 l	Mathematics	.20	.20
738	A137	1k	Law	.20	.20
739	A137	10k	Medicine	.45	.45
			Nos. 737-739 (3)	.85	.85

Tribal Hairstyles — A138

1987, Apr. 15 Litho. *Perf. 11½x11*

740	A138	1k	Ouioca	.20	.20
741	A138	1.50k	Luanda	.20	.20
742	A138	5k	Humbe	.20	.20
743	A138	7k	Muila	.20	.20
744	A138	20k	Muila, diff.	.45	.45
745	A138	30k	Dilolo	.70	.70
			Nos. 740-745 (6)	1.95	1.95

Landscapes A139 — Lenin A140

Perf. 11½x12, 12x11½

1987, July 7 Litho.

746	A139	50 l	Pambala Shore	.20	.20
747	A139	1.50k	Dala Waterfalls	.20	.20
748	A139	3.50k	Black Stones	.20	.20
749	A139	5k	Cuango River	.20	.20
750	A139	10k	Launda coast	.25	.25
751	A139	20k	Hills of Leba	.50	.50
			Nos. 746-751 (6)	1.55	1.55

Nos. 746-747, 749 and 751 horiz.

1987, Nov. 25 *Perf. 12x12½*

752 A140 15k multi .60 .60

October Revolution, Russia, 70th anniv.

2nd Congress of the Organization of Angolan Women (OMA) — A141

1988, May 30 Litho. *Perf. 13x13½*

753 A141 2k shown .20 .20
754 A141 10k Soldier, nurse, technician, student .35 .35

Victory Carnival, 10th Anniv. — A142

Various carnival scenes.

1988, June 15 Litho. *Perf. 13½x13*

755 A142 5k shown .20 .20
756 A142 10k multi, diff. .35 .35

Augusto N'Gangula (1956-1968), Youth Pioneer Killed by Portuguese Colonial Army — A143

Agostinho Neto Pioneers' Organization (OPA), 25th Anniv. — A144

1989, Oct. 2 Litho. *Perf. 12x11½*

757 A143 12k multicolored .40 .40
758 A144 15k multicolored .50 .50

Pioneer Day.

10th Natl. Soccer Championships, Benguela, May 1 — A145

1989, Oct. 16

759	A145	5k	shown	.20	.20
760	A145	5k	Luanda, 3 years	.20	.20
761	A145	5k	Luanda, 5 years	.20	.20
			Nos. 759-761 (3)	.60	.60

Intl. Fund for Agricultural Development, 10th Anniv. — A146

1990, Feb. 15 Litho. *Perf. 11½x12*

762 A146 10k multicolored .70 .70

Ingombotas' Houses A147

Architecture: 2k, Alta Train Station. 5k, National Museum of Anthropology. 15k, Ana Joaquina Palace. 23k, Iron Palace. 36k, Meteorological observatory, vert. 50k, People's Palace.

Perf. 12x11½, 11½x12

1990, Feb. 20

763	A147	1k	shown	.20	.20
764	A147	2k	multicolored	.20	.20
765	A147	5k	multicolored	.35	.35
766	A147	15k	multicolored	1.00	1.00
767	A147	23k	multicolored	1.50	1.50
768	A147	36k	multicolored	2.25	2.25
769	A147	50k	multicolored	3.25	3.25
			Nos. 763-769 (7)	8.75	8.75

Luanda and Benguela Railways A148

Various maps and locomotives.

1990, Mar. 1 *Perf. 12x11½*

770	A148	5k	shown	.35	.35
771	A148	12k	Garrat T (left)	.80	.80
772	A148	12k	Garrat T (right)	.80	.80
a.			Pair, #771-772	1.60	1.60
773	A148	14k	Mikado	.95	.95
			Nos. 770-773 (4)	2.90	2.90

Souvenir Sheet

774 A148 25k Diesel electric 2.35 2.35

No. 772a has a continuous design.

Southern Africa Development Coordinating Conf. (SADCC), 10th Anniv. A149

1990, Apr. 1 Litho. *Perf. 14*

775 A149 5k shown *1.25 1.25*
776 A149 9k Floating oil rig *2.50 2.50*

Pan-African Postal Union (PAPU), 10th Anniv. A150

1990, Apr. 6

777 A150 4k shown .75 .75
778 A150 10k Simulated stamp, map 1.50 1.50

Paintings by Raul Indipwo A151

1990, Apr. 24

779 A151 6k *Tres Gracas* .40 .40
780 A151 9k *Muxima*, vert. .65 .65

Stamp World London 90.

Hippotragus Niger Variani, Adult Male and Female — A152

1990, May 9 *Perf. 14x13½*

781	A152	5k	Adult male	.35	.35
782	A152	5k	shown	.35	.35
783	A152	5k	Adult female	.35	.35
784	A152	5k	Female, calf	.35	.35
			Nos. 781-784 (4)	1.40	1.40

World Wildlife Fund. Various combinations available in blocks or strips of four.

Rosa de Porcelana — A153

1990, June 2 Litho. *Perf. 14*

785	A153	5k	shown	.35	.35
786	A153	8k	Cravo burro	.55	.55
787	A153	10k	Alamandra	.70	.70
			Nos. 785-787 (3)	1.60	1.60

Souvenir Sheet

788 A153 40k Hibiscus 2.70 2.70

Belgica '90.

20-Cent Minimum Value
The minimum value for a single stamp is 20 cents. This value reflects the costs of handling inexpensive stamps.

Miniature Sheet

Intl. Literacy Year — A154

Various animals and forest scenes.

1990, July 26 Litho. *Perf. 14*

789 Sheet of 30 2.25 2.25
a. A154 1k any single .20 .20
790 A154 5k Zebra .35 .35
791 A154 5k Butterfly .35 .35
792 A154 5k Horse .35 .35
a. Block of 3, #790-792 + label 1.05 1.05

People's Assembly, 10th Anniv. A155

1990, Nov. 11 *Perf. 14*

793 A155 10k multicolored .70 .70

3rd Natl. Labor Congress — A156

1990 Litho. *Perf. 13½*

794 A156 14k multicolored 1.35 1.35

War of Independence, 30th Anniv. — A157

Uniforms.

1991, Feb. 28 Litho. *Perf. 14*

795 A157 6k Machete, 1961 .40 .40
a. Perf. 13½ vert. .40 .40
796 A157 6k Rifle, 1962-63 .40 .40
a. Perf. 13½ vert. .40 .40
797 A157 6k Rifle, 1968 .40 .40
a. Perf. 13½ vert. .40 .40
798 A157 6k Automatic rifle, 1972 .40 .40
a. Perf. 13½ vert. .40 .40
b. Bklt. pane of 4, #795a-798a 1.70
Nos. 795-798 (4) 1.60 1.60

Musical Instruments A158

Designs: a, Marimba. b, Mucupela. c, Ngoma la Txina. d, Kissange.

1991, Apr. 5 Litho. *Perf. 14*

799 A158 6k Block or strip of 4, #799a-799d 1.70 1.70

Tourism A159

Designs: 3k, Iona National Park. 7k, Kalandula Waterfalls. 35k, Lobito Bay. 60k, Weltwitschia Mirabilis plant.

1991, June 25 Litho. *Perf. 14*

800 A159 3k multi .20 .20
801 A159 7k multi .25 .25
802 A159 35k multi 1.10 1.10
803 A159 60k multi 2.00 2.00
Nos. 800-803 (4) 3.55 3.55

Dogs A160

1991, July 5 Litho. *Perf. 14*

804 A160 5k Kabir of dembos .20 .20
805 A160 7k Ombua .25 .25
806 A160 11k Kabir massongo .40 .40
807 A160 12k Kawa tchowe .40 .40
Nos. 804-807 (4) 1.25 1.25

1992 Summer Olympics, Barcelona A161

1991, July 26 *Perf. 13*

808 A161 4k Judo .20 .20
809 A161 6k Sailing .20 .20
810 A161 10k Running .35 .35
811 A161 100k Swimming 3.40 3.40
Nos. 808-811 (4) 4.15 4.15

Navigation Aids — A162

1991, Nov. 8 Litho. *Perf. 12*

812 A162 5k Quadrant .20 .20
813 A162 15k Astrolabe .50 .50
814 A162 20k Cross-staff .70 .70
815 A162 50k Portolano 1.75 1.75
Nos. 812-815 (4) 3.15 3.15

Iberex '91.

Rays A163

1992, Mar. 30 Litho. *Perf. 14*

816 A163 40k Myliobatis aquila .20 .20
817 A163 50k Aetobatus narinari .20 .20
818 A163 66k Manta birostris .25 .25
819 A163 80k Raja miraletus .30 .30
Nos. 816-819 (4) .95 .95

Souvenir Sheet

Perf. 13½

820 A163 25k Manta birostris, diff. .20 .20

Quioca Masks — A164

1992, Apr. 30 Litho. *Perf. 13½*

821 A164 60k Kalelwa .20 .20
822 A164 100k Mukixe Wa Kino .40 .40
823 A164 150k Cikunza .55 .55
824 A164 250k Mukixi Wa Mbwesu .90 .90
Nos. 821-824 (4) 2.05 2.05

See Nos. 854-857, 868-871, 883-886, 895-898.

Medicinal Plants — A165

Designs: 200k, Ptaeroxylon obliquum. 300k, Spondias mombin. 500k, Parinari curatellifolia. 600k, Cochlospermum angolense.

1992, May 8 *Perf. 14*

825 A165 200k brown & pale yel .75 .75
826 A165 300k brown & pale yel 1.10 1.10
827 A165 500k brown & pale yel 1.90 1.90
828 A165 600k brown & pale yel 2.20 2.20
a. Block or strip of 4, #825-828 5.90 5.90

Evangelization of Angola, 500th Anniv. — A166

1992, May 10 *Perf. 13½*

829 A166 150k King, missionaries .55 .55
830 A166 420k Ruins of M'banza Congo 1.50 1.50
831 A166 470k Maxima Church 1.75 1.75
832 A166 500k Faces of people 1.90 1.90
Nos. 829-832 (4) 5.70 5.70

Traditional Houses — A167

Perf. 14, 13½ Vert. (#832A)

1992, May 22

832A A167 150k Dimbas 1.25 1.25
b. Bklt. pane of 4, #832A, 833a-835a 5.00
833 A167 330k Cokwe 1.25 1.25
a. Perf. 13½ vert. 1.25 1.25
834 A167 360k Mbali 1.40 1.40
a. Perf. 13½ vert. 1.40 1.40
835 A167 420k Ambwelas 1.60 1.60
a. Perf. 13½ vert. 1.60 1.60
836 A167 500k Upper Zambezi 1.90 1.90
Nos. 832A-836 (5) 7.40 7.40

Expo '92, Seville.

Agapornis Roseicollis A168

1992, June 2 *Perf. 12x11½*

837 A168 150k Two birds on branch .55 .55
838 A168 200k Birds feeding .75 .75
839 A168 250k Hand holding bird .90 .90
840 A168 300k Bird on perch 1.10 1.10
a. Strip of 4, #837-840 3.35 3.35

Expo '92, Seville.

Souvenir Sheet

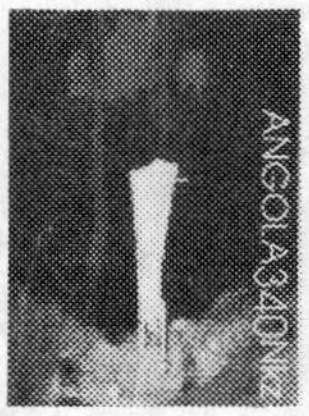

Visit of Pope John Paul II to Angola — A169

Abstract paintings: a, 340k, The Crucifixion. b, 370k, The Resurrection.

1992, June 4 Litho. *Perf. 13½*

841 A169 Sheet of 2, #a.-b. + 2 labels 1.75 1.75

1992 Summer Olympics, Barcelona A170

1992, July 30 *Perf. 14*

842 A170 120k Hurdles .30 .30
843 A170 180k Cycling .50 .50
844 A170 240k Roller hockey .65 .65
845 A170 360k Basketball 1.00 1.00
Nos. 842-845 (4) 2.45 2.45

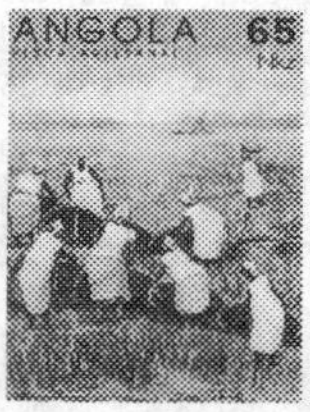

Native Fishing — A171

1992, Aug. 5 *Perf. 11½x12*

846 A171 65k Building traps .20 .20
847 A171 90k Using nets .25 .25
848 A171 100k Laying traps .30 .30
849 A171 120k Fisherman in boats .35 .35
Nos. 846-849 (4) 1.10 1.10

Souvenir Sheet

Discovery of America, 500th Anniv. — A172

1992, Sept. 18 Litho. *Perf. 12*

850 A172 500k multicolored 1.40 1.40

Genoa '92.

First Free Elections in Angola — A173

Designs: 120k, People voting. 150k, Map, ballot box, peace doves. 200k, People, dove, hand dropping ballot into ballot box.

1992, Oct. 27 Litho. *Perf. 11½x12*
851 A173 120k multicolored .30 .30
852 A173 150k multicolored .40 .40
853 A173 200k multicolored .55 .55
Nos. 851-853 (3) 1.25 1.25

Quioca Mask Type of 1992

1992, Nov. 6 *Perf. 13½*
854 A164 72k Cihongo .30 .30
855 A164 80k Mbwasu .35 .35
856 A164 120k Cinhanga .45 .45
857 A164 210k Kalewa .80 .80
Nos. 854-857 (4) 1.90 1.90

Inauguration of Express Mail Service A174

1992, Dec. 14 Litho. *Perf. 12x11½*
858 A174 450k Truck 1.10 1.10
859 A174 550k Airplane 1.25 1.25

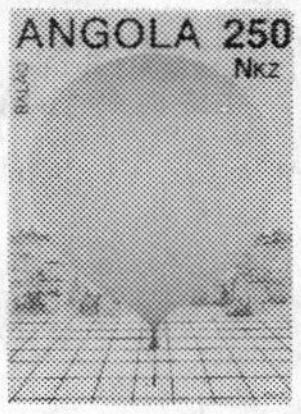

Meteorological Instruments A175

1993, Mar. 23 Litho. *Perf. 11½x12*
860 A175 250k Weather balloon .60 .60
861 A175 470k Actinometer 1.10 1.10
862 A175 500k Rain gauge 1.25 1.25
Nos. 860-862 (3) 2.95 2.95

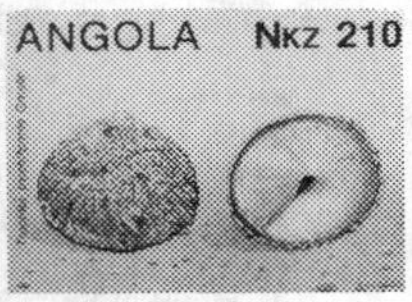

Seashells A176

1993, Apr. 6 *Perf. 12x11½*
863 A176 210k Trochita trochiformis .50 .50
864 A176 330k Strombus latus .75 .75
865 A176 400k Aporrhais pesgallinae .95 .95
866 A176 500k Fusos aff. albinus 1.25 1.25
Nos. 863-866 (4) 3.45 3.45

Souvenir Sheet

867 A176 1000k Pusionella nifat 2.25 2.25

Quioca Art Type of 1992

1993, June 7 Litho. *Perf. 12*
868 A164 72k Men with vehicles .20 .20
869 A164 210k Cavalier .45 .45
870 A164 420k Airplane .90 .90
871 A164 600k Men carrying stretcher 1.25 1.25
Nos. 868-871 (4) 2.80 2.80

Flowering Plants — A177

1993, June 28 *Perf. 11½x12*
872 A177 360k Sansevieria cylindrica .75 .75
873 A177 400k Euphorbia tirucalli .85 .85
874 A177 500k Opuntia ficus-indica 1.10 1.10
875 A177 600k Dracaena aubryana 1.25 1.25
Nos. 872-875 (4) 3.95 3.95

Souvenir Sheet

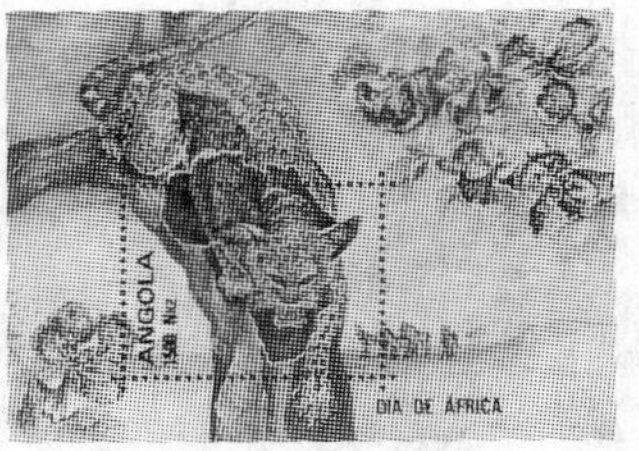

Africa Day — A178

1993, May 31 *Perf. 12*
876 A178 1500k Leopard 3.15 3.15

Tribal Pipes — A179

1993, Aug. 16 Litho. *Perf. 11½x12*
877 A179 72k Vimbundi .20 .20
878 A179 200k Vimbundi, diff. .45 .45
879 A179 420k Mutopa .90 .90
880 A179 600k Pexi 1.25 1.25
Nos. 877-880 (4) 2.80 2.80

Souvenir Sheet

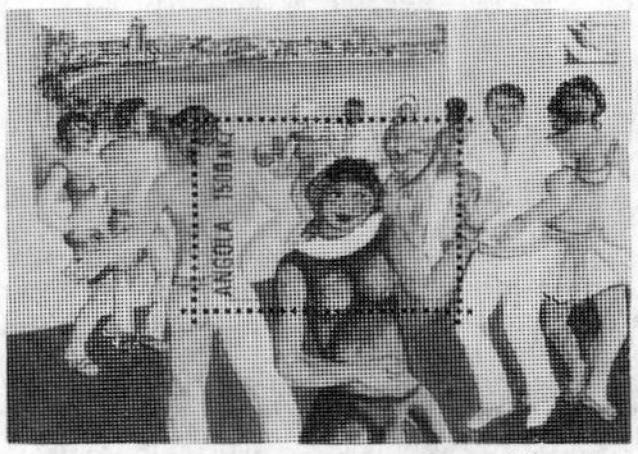

Union of Portuguese Speaking Capitals — A180

1993, July 30 *Perf. 12x11½*
881 A180 1500k multicolored 3.25 3.25

Turtles — A181

Designs: a, 180k, Chelonia mydas (b). b, 450k, Eretmochelys imbricata. c, 550k, Dermochelys coriacea. d, 630k, Caretta caretta.

1993, July 9 Litho. *Perf. 12½x12*
882 A181 Block of 4, #a.-d. 3.50 3.50

Quioca Art Type of 1992

1993, Sept. 1 Litho. *Perf. 12*
883 A164 300k Leopard .65 .65
884 A164 600k Malhado 1.25 1.25
885 A164 800k Birds 1.60 1.60
886 A164 1000k Chickens 2.00 2.00
Nos. 883-886 (4) 5.50 5.50

Mushrooms A182

A183

1993, Dec. 5 Litho. *Perf. 12*
887 A182 300k Tricholoma georgii .55 .55
a. Perf. 11½ vert. .55 .55
888 A182 500k Amanita phalloides .95 .95
a. Perf. 11½ vert. .95 .95
889 A182 600k Amanita vaginata 1.10 1.10
a. Perf. 11½ vert. 1.10 1.10
890 A182 1000k Macrolepiota procera 1.90 1.90
a. Perf. 11½ vert. 1.90 1.90
b. Booklet pane of 4, #887a-890a 4.50
Nos. 887-890 (4) 4.50 4.50

1994, Jan. 10 Litho. *Perf. 12*

Natl. Culture Day: 500k, Cinganji, wood carving of dancer. 1000k, Ohunya yo soma, staff with woman's face. 1200k, Ongende, sculpture of man on donkey. 2200k, Upi, corn pestle.

891 A183 500k multicolored .45 .45
892 A183 1000k multicolored .90 .90
893 A183 1200k multicolored 1.10 1.10
894 A183 2200k multicolored 2.00 2.00
Nos. 891-894 (4) 4.45 4.45

Hong Kong '94.

Quioca Art Type of 1992

1994, Feb. 21 Litho. *Perf. 12*
895 A164 500k Bird on flower .30 .30
896 A164 2000k Plant with roots 1.25 1.25
897 A164 2500k Feto 1.60 1.60
898 A164 3000k Plant 2.00 2.00
Nos. 895-898 (4) 5.15 5.15

Social Responsibilities of AIDS — A184

Designs: 500k, Mass of people. 1000k, Witchdoctor receiving AIDS through needle, people being educated. 3000k, Stylized man, woman.

1994, May 5 Litho. *Perf. 12*
899 A184 500k multicolored .35 .35
900 A184 1000k multicolored .65 .65
901 A184 3000k multicolored 2.00 2.00
Nos. 899-901 (3) 3.00 3.00

1994 World Cup Soccer Championships, US — A185

1994, June 17 *Perf. 14*
902 A185 500k Large arrows, small ball .30 .30
903 A185 700k Small arrows, large ball .45 .45
904 A185 2200k Ball in goal 1.50 1.50
905 A185 2500k Ball, foot 1.60 1.60
Nos. 902-905 (4) 3.85 3.85

Dinosaurs A186

1994, Aug. 16 Litho. *Perf. 12*
906 A186 1000k Brachiosaurus .20 .20
907 A186 3000k Spinosaurus .55 .55
908 A186 5000k Ouranosaurus .90 .90
909 A186 10,000k Lesothosaurus 1.90 1.90
Nos. 906-909 (4) 3.55 3.55

Souvenir Sheet

910 A186 19,000k Lesothosaurus, map of Africa 3.50 3.50

PHILAKOREA '94, SINGPEX '94. No. 910 contains one 44x34mm stamp.

Tourism A187

1994, Sept. 27 Litho. *Perf. 12x11½*
911 A187 2000k Birds .20 .20
912 A187 4000k Wild animals .35 .35
913 A187 8000k Native women .75 .75
914 A187 10,000k Native men .90 .90
Nos. 911-914 (4) 2.20 2.20

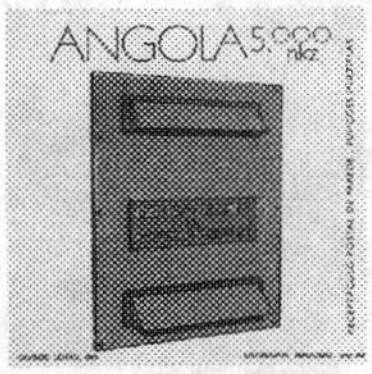

Post Boxes — A188

Designs: 5000k, Letters, bundled mail wall box. 7500k, Wall box for letters. 10,000k, Pillar box. 21,000k, Multi-function units.

1994, Oct. 7 *Perf. 14½*
915 A188 5000k multicolored .45 .45
916 A188 7500k multicolored .70 .70
917 A188 10,000k multicolored .90 .90
918 A188 21,000k multicolored 1.90 1.90
Nos. 915-918 (4) 3.95 3.95

Cotton Pests — A189

Insects: 5000k, Heliothis armigera. 6000k, Bemisia tabasi. 10,000k, Dysdercus. 27,000k, Spodoptera exigua.

1994, Nov. 11 Litho. *Perf. 14*
919 A189 5000k multicolored .45 .45
920 A189 6000k multicolored .55 .55
921 A189 10,000k multicolored .95 .95
922 A189 27,000k multicolored 2.50 2.50
Nos. 919-922 (4) 4.45 4.45

Intl. Olympic Committee, Cent. A190

1994, Dec. 15
923 A190 27,000k multicolored 2.75 2.75

Tribal Culture A191

Designs: 10,000k. Rubbing sticks to start fire. 15,000k, Extracting sap from tree. 20,000k, Smoking tribal pipe. 25,000k, Shooting bow & arrow. 28,000k, Mothers, children. 30,000k, Cave art.

1995, Jan. 6 Litho. *Perf. 14*

924 A191 10,000k multicolored .40 .40
925 A191 15,000k multicolored .65 .65
926 A191 20,000k multicolored .85 .85
927 A191 25,000k multicolored 1.00 1.00
928 A191 28,000k multicolored 1.10 1.10
929 A191 30,000k multicolored 1.25 1.25
Nos. 924-929 (6) 5.25 5.25

Traditional Ceramics A192

Designs: No. 930, Pitcher with bust of a woman as stopper. No. 931, Cone-shaped vase. No. 932, Bird-shaped vase. No. 933, Pitcher with bust of a man as stopper.

1995, Jan. 2 Litho. *Perf. 14½*

930 A192 (2) 2nd class natl.
931 A192 (1) 1st class natl.
932 A192 (2) 2nd class intl.
933 A192 (1) 1st class intl.
Nos. 930-933 (4) 3.25

Rotary Intl., 90th Anniv. A193

a, Immunizing boy against polio. b, Medical examination. c, Immunizing girl against polio.
No. 936, Dove over map.

1995, Feb. 23 Litho. *Perf. 14*

934 Strip of 3 2.25 2.25
a.-c. A193 27,000k any single .75 .75
935 Strip of 3 2.25 2.25
a.-c. A193 27,000k any single .75 .75

Souvenir Sheet

936 A193 81,000k multicolored 4.00 4.00
a. English inscription 4.00 4.00

No. 934 has Portuguese inscriptions. No. 935 has English inscriptions. Both were issued in sheets of 9 stamps.
No. 936 contains Portuguese inscription in sheet margin.

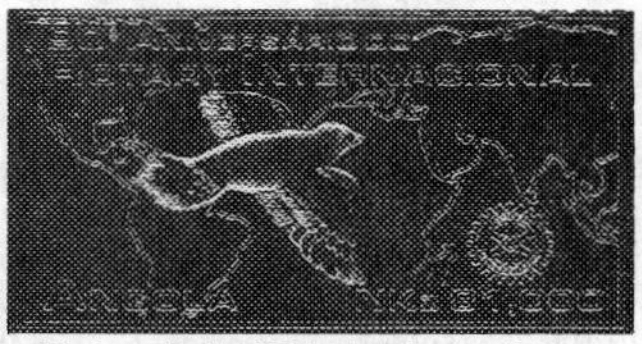

Rotary Intl., 90th Anniv. — A194

Illustration reduced.

Litho. & Embossed

1995, Feb. 23 *Perf. 11½x12*

937 A194 81,000k gold

World Telecommunications Day — A195

Designs: No. 938, 1957 Sputnik 1. No. 939, Shuttle, Intelsat satellite.

1995 Litho. *Perf. 14*

938 A195 27,000k multicolored 1.50 1.50
939 A195 27,000k multicolored 1.50 1.50
a. Souvenir sheet, #938-939 3.00 3.00

Independence, 20th Anniv. — A196

1995, Nov. 11 Litho. *Perf. 14*

940 A196 2900k multicolored 1.50 1.50

4th World Conference on Women, Beijing — A197

Designs: 375k, Women working in fields. 1106k, Woman teaching, girls with book. 1265k, Woman in industry, career woman. 2900k, Woman in native headdress, vert.
1500k, Native mother, children, vert.

1996, Jan. 29 Litho. *Perf. 14*

941 A197 375k multicolored .20 .20
942 A197 1106k multicolored .40 .40
943 A197 1265k multicolored .45 .45
944 A197 2900k multicolored 1.00 1.00
Nos. 941-944 (4) 2.05 2.05

Souvenir Sheet

945 A197 1500k multicolored .50 .50

UN Assistance Programs — A198

Designs: 200k, Boy, highlift moving supplies. 1265k, Supply ship arriving. No. 948, Two high lifts. No. 949, Tractor-trailer traveling past vultures, native girl.
No. 950, Man, ship.

1996 Litho. *Perf. 14*

946 A198 200k multicolored .20 .20
947 A198 1265k multicolored .50 .50
948 A198 2583k multicolored 1.00 1.00
949 A198 2583k multicolored 1.00 1.00
Nos. 946-949 (4) 2.70 2.70

Souvenir Sheet

950 A198 1265k multicolored .50 .50

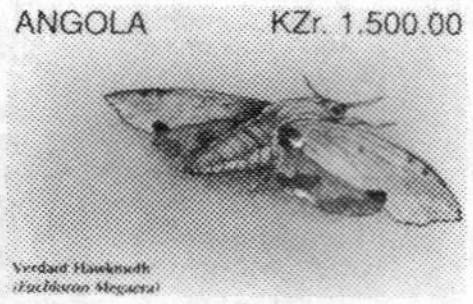

Flora and Fauna A199

1500k, Verdant hawkmoth. 4400k, Water lily. 5100k, Panther toad. 6000k, African wild dog.
1500k: a, Western honey buzzard. b, Bateleuer. c, Common kestrel.
4400k; d, Red-crested turaco. e, Giraffe. f, Elephant.
5100k: g, Hippopotamus. h, Cattle egret. i, Lion.
6000k: j, Helmeted turtle. k, African pygmy goose. l, Egyptian plover.
12,000k, Spotted hyena.

1996, Apr. 20 Litho. *Perf. 14*

951-954 A199 Set of 4 1.00 1.00
955 A199 Sheet of 12, #a.-l. 4.00 4.00

Souvenir Sheet

956 A199 12,000k multicolored .80 .80

Sheets of 12

Birds — A200

Fowl: No. 957a, California quail. b, Greater prairie chicken. c, Painted quail. d, Golden pheasant. e, Roulroul partridge. f, Ceylon sourfowl. g, Himalayan snowcock. h, Temminicks tragopan. i, Lady Amherst's pheasant. j, Great curassow. k, Red-legged partridge. l, Impeyan pheasant.
Hummingbirds: No. 958a, Anna's. b, Blue-throated. c, Broad-tailed. d, Costa's. e, White-eared. f, Calliope. g, Violet-crowned. h, Rufous. i, Crimson topaz. j, Broad-billed. k, Frilled coquette. l, Ruby-throated.
No. 959, Ring-necked pheasant. No. 960, Racquet-tail hummingbird.

1996, Apr. 20

957-958 A200 5500k #a.-l., each 4.25 4.25

Souvenir Sheets

959-960 A200 12,000k each .80 .80

Lubrapex '96 — A201

Wild animals: a, 180k, Lions attacking zebra. b, 450k, Zebras, lions, diff. c, 180k, Zebras grazing, lions stalking. d, 450k, Panthera leo. e, 550k, Cheetah. f, 630k, Cheetah running. g, 550k, Cheetah chasing antilope. h, 630k, Cheetah attacking antelope. i, 180k, Antilope (gnu) being attacked by wild dogs. j, 450k, Antelope, wild dogs. k, 180k, Pack of wild dogs. l, 450k, Licaon pictus. m, 550k, Panthera pardus. n, 630k, Oryx. o, 550k, Oryx, diff. p, 630k, Leopard attacking oryx.

1996, Apr. 27

961 A201 Sheet of 16, #a.-p. 6.00 6.00

Sheets of 6

Ships A202

Designs: No. 962a, Styrbjorn, Sweden, 1789. b, Constellation, US, 1797. c, Taureau, France, 1865. d, Bomb Ketch, France, 1682. e, Sardegna, Italy, 1881. f, HMS Glasgow, England, 1867.
No. 963a, Essex, US, 1812. b, HMS Inflexible, England, 1881. c, HMS Minotaur, England, 1863. d, Napoleon, France, 1854. e, Sophia Amalia, Denmark, 1650. f, Massena, France, 1887.
No. 964, HMS Tremendous, England, 1806, vert. No. 965, Royal Prince, England, 1666.

1996, May 4

962-963 A202 6000k #a.-f., each 2.50 2.50

Souvenir Sheets

964-965 A202 12,000k each .80 .80

UN, 50th Anniv. (in 1995) A203

Designs: No. 966, Boys pumping water. No. 967, Man, woman with girl.
8000k, Unloading supplies from ship.

1996, Apr. 27 Litho. *Perf. 14*

966 A203 3500k multicolored 1.00 1.00
967 A203 3500k multicolored 1.00 1.00

Souvenir Sheet

968 A203 8000k multicolored 1.00 1.00

Sonangol, 20th Anniv. A204

Face in traditional mask, costume, native birds, and: No. 969, Oil derricks. No. 970, Oil storage tanks, ship. 2500k, Refinery equipment. 5000k, Cargo shipment, jet.

1996, May 12

969 A204 1000k multicolored .20 .20
970 A204 1000k multicolored .20 .20
971 A204 2500k multicolored .25 .25
972 A204 5000k multicolored .55 .55
Nos. 969-972 (4) 1.20 1.20

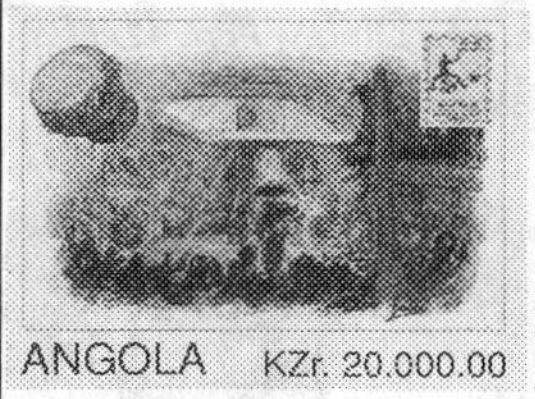

Brapex '96 A205

#973, Slaves in hold. #974, Slaves fleeing ship as it's overturned. #975, Slave boats approaching ship. #976, Slaves talking with captain.
50,000k, like #975.

1996, Oct. 19 Litho. *Perf. 14*

973 A205 20,000k multicolored 1.25 1.25
974 A205 20,000k multicolored 1.25 1.25
975 A205 30,000k multicolored 1.90 1.90
976 A205 30,000k multicolored 1.90 1.90
Nos. 973-976 (4) 6.30 6.30

Souvenir Sheet

977 A205 50,000k multicolored 3.25 3.25

Churches — A206

Designs: 5,000k, Mission, Huila. No. 979, Church of the Nazarene. No. 980, Church of Our Lady of Pó Pulo. 25,000k, St. Adriáo Church.

1996, Dec. 6 Litho. *Perf. 14*

978 A206 5,000k multicolored .30 .30
979 A206 10,000k multicolored .65 .65
980 A206 10,000k multicolored .65 .65
981 A206 25,000k multicolored 1.60 1.60
Nos. 978-981 (4) 3.20 3.20

1996 Summer Olympic Games, Atlanta A207

1996, Dec. 9

982 A207 5,000k Handball, vert. .30 .30
983 A207 10,000k Swimming .65 .65
984 A207 25,000k Track & field, vert. 1.60 1.60
985 A207 35,000k Shooting 2.25 2.25
Nos. 982-985 (4) 4.80 4.80

Souvenir Sheet

986 A207 65,000k Basketball 4.00 4.00

From this point the value of Angolan currency is in question.

MPLA (Liberation Movement), 40th Anniv. — A208

1996, Dec. 10 Litho. *Perf. 14*

987 A208 30,000k Dolphins, map *1.75 1.75*

Trains A209

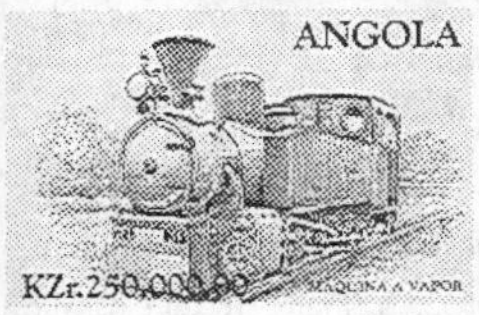

Trains A209a

No. 988: a, AVE, Spain. b, Bullet Train, Japan. c, GM F7 Warbonnet, US. d, Deltic, Great Britain. e, Eurostar, France/Great Britain. f, ETR 450, Italy.

No. 989: a, Class E1300, Morocco. b, ICE, Germany. c, X2000, Sweden. d, TGV Duplex, France.

No. 989E: f, Steam engine. g, Garrat. h, General Electric.

No. 990, Canadian Pacific 4-4-0, Canada. No. 991, Via Rail Canadian, Canada.

1997, May 29 Litho. *Perf. 14*

Sheets of 6, 4 or 3

988 A209 100,000k #a.-f. *6.00 6.00*
989 A209 140,000k #a.-d. *6.00 6.00*
989E A209a 250,000k Sheet of 3, #f.-h. *5.75 5.75*

Souvenir Sheets

Perf. 13½

990-991 A209 110,000k each *4.00 4.00*

Nos. 990-991 contain one 38x50 or 50x38mm stamp, respectively.

PACIFIC 97.

Horses A210

No. 992: a, Thoroughbred. b, Palomino, appaloosa. c, Arabians. d, Arabian colt. e, Thoroughbred colt. f, Mustang. g, Mustang, diff. h, Furioso.

No. 993: a, Thoroughbred. b, Arabian, palomino. c, Arabian, chincoteague. d, Pintos. e, Przewalski's horse. f, Thoroughbred colt. g, Arabians. h, New forest pony.

No. 994: a, Selle Francais. b, Fjord. c, Percheron. d, Italian heavy draft. e, Shagya Arab. f, Avelignese. g, Czechoslovakian warmblood. h, New forest pony.

215,000k, Thoroughbreds. 220,000k, Thoroughbreds, diff.

1997, July 5 Litho. *Perf. 14*

Sheets of 8

992 A210 100,000k #a.-h. *4.00 4.00*
993 A210 120,000k #a.-h. *5.00 5.00*
994 A210 140,000k #a.-h. *5.50 5.50*

Souvenir Sheets

995 A210 215,000k multicolored *4.00 4.00*
996 A210 220,000k multicolored *4.00 4.00*

PACIFIC 97.

Angola stamps can be mounted in the Scott Portuguese Colonies album part 1, Portugal albums part 2-5 and Portuguese Colonies supplements.

1998 World Cup Soccer Championships, France — A211

Winners holding World Cup trophy: No. 997: a, Uruguay, 1930. b, Germany, 1954. c, Brazil, 1970. d, Argentina, 1986. e, Brazil, 1994.

Winning team pictures: No. 998a, Germany, 1954. b, Uruguay, 1958. c, Italy, 1938. d, Brazil, 1962. e, Brazil, 1970. f, Uruguay, 1930.

220,000k, Angolan team members standing. 250,000k, 1997 Angolan team picture.

1997, July 5 Litho. *Perf. 14*

Sheets of 5 or 6

997 A211 100,000k #a.-e. + label *5.00 5.00*
998 A211 100,000k #a.-f. *6.00 6.00*

Souvenir Sheets

999 A211 220,000k multicolored *3.50 3.50*
1000 A211 250,000k multicolored *4.00 4.00*

ENSA (Security System), 20th Anniv. — A212

"Star" emblem, and stylized protection of "egg:" #1001, Industry. #1002, Recreation. #1003, Homes, shelters. #1004, Accident prevention.

350,000k, Emblem.

1998 Litho. *Perf. 13½*

1001-1004 A212 240,000k Set of 4 *7.50 7.50*

Souvenir Sheet

Perf. 13½x13

1005 A212 350,000k multicolored *2.75 2.75*

No. 1005 contains one 60x40mm stamp.

GURN (Natl. Unity & Reconciliation Government), 1st Anniv. — A213

Emblem, portion of country map and: 100,000k, a, Sea, swordfish, ships, oil derrick. b, Sea, ships, swordfish. c, Sea, swordfish, ships, mining car on railroad track. d, Sea, power lines.

200,000k: e, Train on track, antelope. f, Mining cars on track, tractor pulling cart. g, Railroad track across rivers, tractor plowing. h, Power lines. i, UR corner of map, crystals. j, Train on track. k, Elephant, tree. l, Trunk of tree, bottom edge of map.

1998

1006 A213 Sheet of 12, #a.-l. 15.00 15.00

Souvenir Sheet

Education in Angola — A214

Illustration reduced.

1998

1007 A214 400,000k multicolored *3.25 3.25*

Diana, Princess of Wales (1961-97) — A215

Various portraits, color of sheet margin: No. 1008, pale green. No. 1009, pale yellow. 400,000k, Wearing protective clothing.

1998, May 21 Litho. *Perf. 14*

Sheets of 6

1008-1009 A215 100,000k #a.-f., each *4.75 4.75*

Souvenir Sheet

1010 A215 400,000k multicolored *3.25 3.25*

See No. 1028.

Expo '98, Lisbon A216

Marine life: No. 1011, 100,000k, Anemones. No. 1012, 100,000k, Sea urchin. No. 1013, 100,000k, Sea horses. No. 1014, 100,000k, Coral (Caravela). No. 1015, 240,000k, Sea slug. No. 1016, 240,000k, Worms (Tunicados).

1998, May 21 *Perf. 13½*

1011-1016 A216 Set of 6 7.00 7.00

Butterflies A217

No. 1017: a, Metamorpha stelene. b, Papilio glaucus. c, Danaus plexippus. d, Catonephele numili. e, Plebejus argus. f, Hypolimnas bolina.

No. 1018: a, Terinos terpander. b, Bematistes aganice. c, Hebomoia glaucippe. d, Colias eurytheme. e, Pereute leucodrosime. f, Lycaena dispar.

No. 1019, horiz.: a, Dynastor napolean. b, Zeuxidia amethystus. c, Battus philenor. d, Phoebis philea. e, Danaus chrysippus. f, Glaucopsyche alexis.

No. 1020, Euphaedra neophron. No. 1021, Thecla betulae, horiz. No. 1022, Uraneis ucubis, armillaria staminea.

1998, May 21 *Perf. 14*

Sheets of 6

1017-1019 A217 120,000k #a.-f., each *6.00 6.00*

Souvenir Sheets

1020-1022 A217 250,000k each *4.00 4.00*

Cats and Dogs A218

Cats: No. 1023a, British tortoiseshell. b, Chinchilla. c, Russian blue. d, Black Persian (longhair). e, British red tabby. f, Birman.

Dogs: No. 1024a, West Highland terrier. b, Irish setter. c, Dachshund. d, St. John water dog. e, Shetland sheep dog. f, Dalmatian.

No. 1025, Turkish van (swimming cat). No. 1026, Labrador retriever.

1998, May 21 Litho. *Perf. 14x13½*

Sheets of 6

1023-1024 A218 140,000k #a.-f., each *6.75 6.75*

Souvenir Sheets

1025-1026 A218 500,000k each *4.00 4.00*

Wild Animals A219

100,000k: a, Panthera leo. b, Hippopotamus amphibius. c, Loxodonta africana. d, Giraffa camelopardalis.

220,000k: e, Syncerus caffer-caffer. f, Gorilla gorilla. g, Ceratotherim simum. h, Oryx gazella.

1998, July 24 Litho. *Perf. 14*

1027 A219 Sheet of 8, #a.-h. 10.00 10.00

Diana, Princes of Wales Type of 1998

Pictures showing Diana's campaign to ban land mines: a, With girl. b, With two boys. c, Wearing protective clothing.

1998, Aug. 31 Litho. *Perf. 14*

1028 A215 150,000k Strip of 3, #a.-c. *4.75 4.75*

No. 1028 was issued in sheets of 6 stamps.

Intl. Year of the Ocean — A220

Marine life: No. 1029a, Pagurites. b, Callinectes marginatus. c, Thais forbesi. d, Ostrea tulipa. e, Balanus amohitrite. f, Uca tangeri.

No. 1030: a, Littorina angulifera. b, Semifusus morio. c, Thais coronata. d, Cerithium atratum (red branch). e, Ostrea tulipa. f, Cerithium atratum (green branch).

No. 1031, Goniopsis, horiz. No. 1032, Unidentified shell.

1998, Sept. 4

Sheets of 6

1029 A220 100,000k #a.-f. *3.00 3.00*
1030 A220 170,000k #a.-f. *5.00 5.00*

Souvenir Sheets

1031-1032 A220 300,000k each *4.00 4.00*

Souvenir Sheet

Battle Against Polio in Angola — A221

Illustration reduced.

1998, Aug. 28 Litho. *Perf. 13½*

1033 A221 500,000k multicolored *2.50 2.50*

Traditional Boats A222

Designs: No. 1034, 250,000k, Boat, Bimba. No. 1035, 250,000k, Canoe with sail, Ndongo. 500,000k, Constructing boat, Ndongo.

1998, Sept. 4 *Perf. 14*
1034-1036 A222 Set of 3 5.00 5.00

Titanic A223

Views of Titanic: a, Under tow. b, Stern. c, Starboard side at night. d, At dock.

1998, Sept. 4
1037 A223 350,000k Sheet of 4, #a.-d. *7.00 7.00*

#1037c is 76x30mm, #1037d is 38x61mm.

Angolan Food A224

Various vegetables, fruits: #1038, 100,000k, 4 fruits. #1039, 100,000k, Squash sliced in half. #1040, 120,000k, Ears of corn. #1041, 120,000k, Green beans. #1042, 140,000k, Fruit with red seeds sliced in half. #1043, 140,000k, Sliced bananas.

1998
1038-1043 A224 Set of 6 5.50 5.50

Portugal '98.

Airplanes — A225

No. 1044, IL-62 M. No. 1045, B737 100.

No. 1046: a, Ultralight. b, Gyroplane. c, Business jet. d, onvertible plane (e). e, Chuterplane (a, b, d). f, Twin rotors (e). g, Skycrane. h, Aerospatiale Concorde (i). i, Flying boat.

No. 1047: a, Pedal power (b). b, Sail plane (a, e). c, Aerobatic (f). d, Hang gliding (g). e, Balloon (h). f, Glidercraft (e, i). g, Model airplane. h, Air racing (i). i, Solar cells.

No. 1048, Boeing 777. No. 1049, Columbia Space Shuttle, vert. No. 1049A, Boeing 737-200. No. 1049B, Boeing 747-300.

1998-99 **Litho.** *Perf. 14*
1044 A225 200,000k multicolored *1.50 1.50*
1045 A225 200,000k multicolored *1.50 1.50*

Sheets of 9
1046 A225 150,000k #a.-i. *4.50 4.50*
1047 A225 250,000k #a.-i. *6.00 6.00*

Souvenir Sheets
1048-1049B A225 1,000,000k ea *5.00 5.00*

Nos. 1048-1049B each contain one 85x28mm stamp.

Issued: Nos. 1049A-1049B, 3/25/99; others 12/24/98.

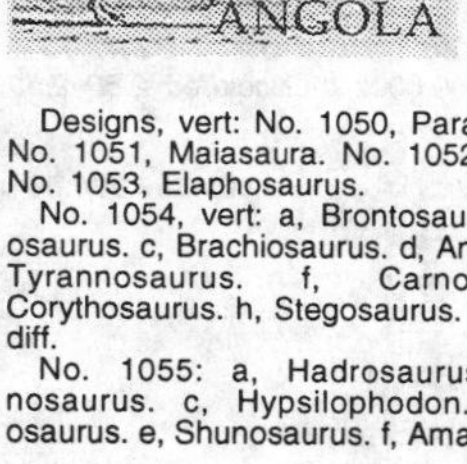

Dinosaurs A226

Designs, vert: No. 1050, Parasaurolophus. No. 1051, Maiasaura. No. 1052, Iguanodon. No. 1053, Elaphosaurus.

No. 1054, vert: a, Brontosaurus. b, Plateosaurus. c, Brachiosaurus. d, Anatosaurus. e, Tyrannosaurus. f, Carnotaurus. g, Corythosaurus. h, Stegosaurus. i, Iguanodon, diff.

No. 1055: a, Hadrosaurus. b, Ouranosaurus. c, Hypsilophodon. d, Brachiosaurus. e, Shunosaurus. f, Amargasaurus. g, Tuojiangosaurus. h, Monoclonius. i, Struthiosaurus.

No. 1056, Triceratops, vert. No. 1057, Tyrannosaurus, vert.

1998, Dec. 28
1050-1053 A226 120,000k Set of 4 *6.00 6.00*

Sheets of 9
1054-1055 A226 120,000k #a.-i., each *7.50 7.50*

Souvenir Sheets
1056-1057 A226 550,000k each *2.00 2.00*

World Wildlife Fund — A227

Lesser flamingo: a, Facing left. b, Body facing forward. c, Head and neck. d, With wings spread.

1999 **Litho.** *Perf. 14*

Strip of 4
1058 A227 300,000k #a.-d. *3.25 3.25*

No. 1058 was issued in sheets of 16 stamps.

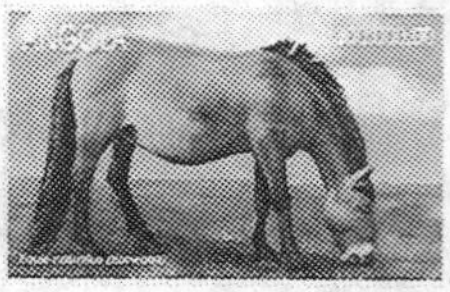
Fauna A228

Designs: No. 1059, Equis caballus przewalski. No. 1060, Sphenisciformes, vert. No. 1061, Haliaeetus leucocephalus, vert. No. 1062, Anodorhynchus hyacinthinus.

No. 1063: a, Vulpes velox hebes. b, Odocoileus. c, Pongo pygmaeus. d, Leontopitecus rosalia. e, Panthera tigris. f, Tragelaphus eurycerus.

No. 1064: a, Tremarctos ornatus. b, Aphelocoma. c, Otus insularis. d, Balaeniceps rex. e, Lepidochelys kempii. f, Lutra canadensis.

No. 1065, Ailuropoda melanoleuca, vert. No. 1066, Ursus arctos horribilis.

1999
1059-1062 A228 300,000k Set of 4 *9.25 9.25*

Sheets of 6
1063-1064 A228 300,000k #a.-f., each *6.00 6.00*

Souvenir Sheets
1065-1066 A228 1,000,000k each *4.00 4.00*

Flora and Fauna A229

Designs: 5000k, Hippopotamus amphibus. 10,000k, Aleunia aurantia. 15,000k, Large water bird. 20,000k, Gnu. 25,000k, Mycena alcalina. 50,000k, Small bird. 100,000k, Acinonyx jubatus. 125,000k, Surcopon imbricatum. 150,000k, Bird in water. 200,000k, Ceratotherium simum. 250,000k, Stropharia aeruginosa. 300,000k, Bird eating insect.

1999 **Litho.** *Perf. 14*

1067	A229	5000k multi	.20	.20
1068	A229	10,000k multi	.20	.20
1069	A229	15,000k multi	.25	.25
1070	A229	20,000k multi	.35	.35
1071	A229	25,000k multi	.40	.40
1072	A229	50,000k multi	.85	.85
1073	A229	100,000k multi	1.60	1.60
1074	A229	125,000k multi	2.00	2.00
1075	A229	150,000z multi	2.50	2.50
1076	A229	200,000k multi	3.25	3.25
1077	A229	250,000k multi	4.25	4.25
1078	A229	300,000k multi	5.00	5.00
		Nos. 1067-1078 (12)	20.85	20.85

Nos. 1073, 1076 are incorrectly inscribed.
The status of Nos. 1067-1078 is in question.

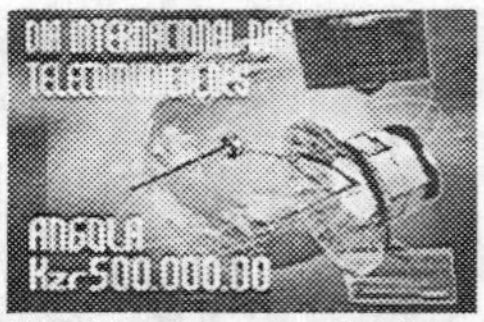

World Telecommunications Day — A230

1999, May 17 **Litho.** *Perf. 14*
1079 A230 500,000k multi *.50 .50*

Souvenir Sheet

Waterfalls — A231

a, Andulo. b, Chiumbo. c, Ruacaná. d, Coemba.

1999, June 5 **Sheet of 4**
1080 A231 500,000k #a.-d. *2.00 2.00*

A232

African Men's Basketball Championships - No. 1081: a, Poster. b, Basketball, hoop, tan background. c, Basketball, hoop, green background. d, Welwitschia plant holding basketball.

2,500,000k, Similar to No. 1081c.

1999, July 29 *Perf. 13½*

Sheet of 4
1081 A232 1,500,000k #a.-d. *3.00 3.00*

Souvenir Sheet

Perf. 13x13½
1082 A232 2,500,000k multi *2.00 2.00*

No. 1082 contains one 40x30mm stamp.

A233

1999, Aug. 17 *Perf. 14*
1083 A233 1,000,000k multi *.80 .80*

Southern African Development Community. Issued in sheets of 4.

A234

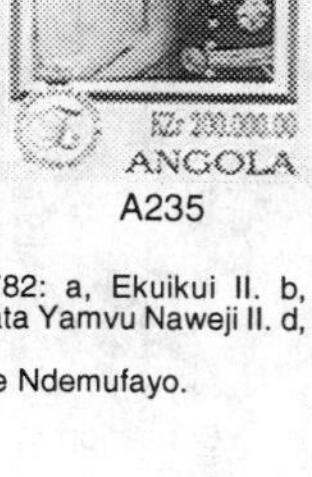

A235

Tribal kings - No. 782: a, Ekuikui II. b, Mvemba Nzinga. c, Mwata Yamvu Naweji II. d, Njinga Mbande.

1,000,000k, Mandume Ndemufayo.

1999, Sept. 17 **Sheet of 4**
1084 A234 500,000k #a.-d. *2.00 2.00*

Souvenir Sheet
1085 A234 1,000,000k multi *1.00 1.00*

1999, Sept. 17 **Litho.** *Perf. 14*

Queen Mother (b. 1900) - No. 1086: a, With King George VI. b, Wearing brooch. c, Wearing tiara. d, Wearing hat.

500,000k, Wearing academic gown.

Sheet of 4
1086 A235 200,000k #a.-d. *6.00 6.00*

Souvenir Sheet

Perf. 13¾
1087 A235 500,000k multi *3.75 3.75*

No. 1087 contains one 38x51mm stamp.

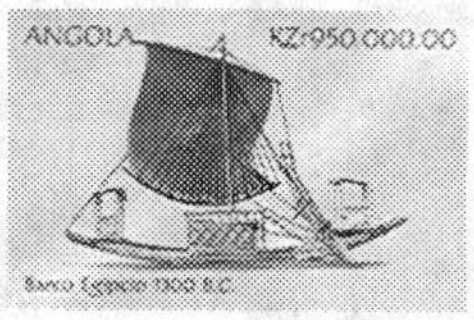

Ships A236

No. 1088: a, Egyptian bark, 1300 B.C. b, Flemish carrack, 1480. c, Beagle, 1830. d, North Star, 1852. e, Fram, 1892. f, Unyon Maru, 1909. g, Juan Sebastian de Elcano, 1927. h, Tovarishch, 1933.

No. 1089: a, Bucentauro, 1728. b, Clermont, 1807. c, Savannah, 1819. d, Dromedary, 1844. e, Iberia, 1881. f, S.S. Gluckauf, 1886. g, City of Paris, 1888. h, Mauretania, 1906.

No. 1090: a, Gloire, 1859. b, L'Ocean, 1868. c, Dandalo, 1876, stern of HMS Dreadnought, 1906. d, Bow of Dreadnought. e, Bismarck, 1939, stern of USS Cleveland, 1946. f, Bow of Cleveland. g, USS Boston, 1942, stern of USS Long Beach, 1959. h, Bow of Long Beach.

No. 1091, Chinese junk. No. 1092, Madre de Deus, 1609. No. 1093, Catamaran, 1861. No. 1094, Natchez, 1870.

1999, Sept. 23 **Litho.** *Perf. 14*

Sheets of 8
1088-1090 A236 950,000k #a.-h., each *6.00 6.00*

Souvenir Sheets
1091-1094 A236 5,000,000k each *3.00 3.00*

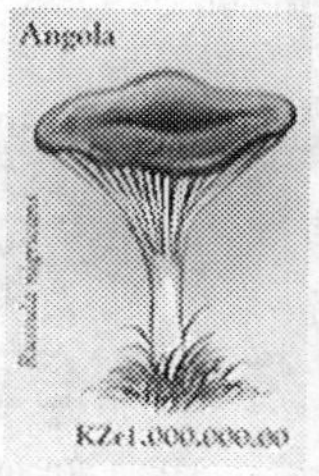

Mushrooms A237

No. 1103: a, Russula nigricans. b, Boletus granulatus. c, Mycena strobilinoides. d, Amanita caesarea. e, Amanita muscaria. f, Boletus, crocipodius. g, Russula virescens. h, Lactarius deliciosus.

No. 1104, Psalliota haemorrhoidaria.

1999, Sept. 23 **Litho.** *Perf. 14*
1103 A237 1,000,000k Sheet of 8, #a.-h. 6.50 6.50

Souvenir Sheet
1104 A237 5,000,000k multi 3.00 3.00

Numbers have been reserved for additional stamps in this set.

A238

First Manned Moon Landing, 30th Anniv. A239

No. 1107: a, Astronaut spacewalking. b, Mariner 8. c, Viking 10. d, GINGA satellite. e, Soyuz 19. f, Voyager.
No. 1108, vert.: a, Space telescope. b, Space shuttle Atlantis. c, Uhuru satellite. d, Mir space station. e, Gemini 7. f, Venera 7.
No. 1109: a, Mercury, Venus. b, Jupiter. c, Neptune, Pluto. d, Earth, Mars. e, Saturn. f, Uranus.
No. 1110: a, Explorer 17. b, Intelsat 4A. c, GOES-D Satellite. d, Intelsat 2. e, Navstar. f, S.M.S.
No. 1111, Lunar rover, vert. No. 1112, Apollo 17 astronaut on moon, vert. No. 1113, Neil Armstrong, vert. No. 1114, Space shuttle Columbia. No. 1115, SBS-4, vert.

Perf. 13¾ (A238), 14 (A239)

1999, Nov. 15 Litho.

Sheets of 6

1107-1108	A238	3,500,000k #a.-f.	7.25	7.25
1109-1110	A239	3,500,000k #a.-f.	7.25	7.25

Souvenir Sheets

1111-1112	A238	6,000,000k ea	1.60	1.60
1113-1115	A239	12,000,000k ea	3.25	3.25

Hokusai Paintings — A240

No. 1116: a, Night attack. b, Usigafuchi No Kudan. c, Drawing of man and bowl. d, Wildlife. e, Pheasant. f, People on bridge.
No. 1117: a, Tree and shoreline. b, Kabuki theater. c, Hen. d, Cooper. e, Trip to Enoshima. f, Sumida River landscape.
No. 1118, Yama-uba and Kintori, vert. No. 1119, Woman, vert.

1999, Dec. 13 Litho. *Perf. 13¾*

Sheets of 6, #a.-f.

1116-1117	A240	3,500,000k ea	4.50	4.50

Souvenir Sheets

1118-1119	A240	12,000,000k ea	4.00	4.00

On Dec. 13, the date of issue of these stamps, Angola devalued its currency, with approximately 1,000,000k being worth 1k after the devaluation.

SEMI-POSTAL STAMPS

Angolan Red Cross — SP1

1991, Sept. 19 Litho. *Perf. 14*

B1	SP1	20k +5k Mother and child	.85	.85
B2	SP1	40k +5k Zebra and foal	1.50	1.50

AIR POST STAMPS

Common Design Type

Perf. 13½x13

1938, July 26 Engr. Unwmk.

Name and Value in Black

C1	CD39	10c scarlet	.20	.20
C2	CD39	20c purple	.25	.20
C3	CD39	50c orange	.20	.20
C4	CD39	1a ultra	.40	.20
C5	CD39	2a lilac brn	.85	.20
C6	CD39	3a dk green	2.25	.25
C7	CD39	5a red brown	3.25	.35
C8	CD39	9a rose carmine	4.25	1.10
C9	CD39	10a magenta	5.50	1.10
		Nos. C1-C9 (9)	17.15	3.80

No. C7 exists with overprint "Exposicao Internacional de Nova York, 1939-1940" and Trylon and Perisphere.

AP2

Planes Circling Globe — AP3

1947, Aug. Litho. *Perf. 10½*

C10	AP2	1a red brown	6.25	1.60
C11	AP2	2a yellow grn	6.25	1.60
C12	AP2	3a orange	8.00	1.60
C13	AP2	3.50a orange	10.00	4.00
C14	AP2	5a olive grn	90.00	15.00
C15	AP2	6a rose	90.00	17.50
C16	AP2	9a red	275.00	200.00
C17	AP2	10a green	175.00	60.00
C18	AP2	20a blue	175.00	60.00
C19	AP2	50a black	400.00	200.00
C20	AP2	100a yellow	750.00	600.00
		Nos. C10-C20 (11)	1,985.	1,161.

1949, May 1 Photo. *Perf. 11½*

C21	AP3	1a henna brown	.20	.20
C22	AP3	2a red brown	.40	.20
C23	AP3	3a plum	.65	.20
C24	AP3	6a dull green	2.00	.40
C25	AP3	9a violet brown	3.00	1.00
		Nos. C21-C25 (5)	6.25	2.00

Catalogue values for unused stamps in this section, from this point to the end of the section, are for Never Hinged items.

Cambambe Dam — AP4

Designs: 1.50e, Oil refinery, vert. 3e, Salazar Dam. 4e, Capt. Teófilo Duarte Dam. 4.50e, Craveiro Lopes Dam. 5e, Cuango Dam. 6e, Quanza River Bridge. 7e, Capt. Teófilo Duarte Bridge. 8.50e, Oliveira Salazar Bridge. 12.50e, Capt. Silva Carvalho Bridge.

Perf. 11½x12, 12x11½

1965, July 12 Litho. Unwmk.

C26	AP4	1.50e multicolored	1.00	.20
C27	AP4	2.50e multicolored	.60	.20
C28	AP4	3e multicolored	1.00	.20
C29	AP4	4e multicolored	.40	.20
C30	AP4	4.50e multicolored	.40	.20
C31	AP4	5e multicolored	.65	.20
C32	AP4	6e multicolored	.65	.20
C33	AP4	7e multicolored	1.00	.20
C34	AP4	8.50e multicolored	1.25	.55
C35	AP4	12.50e multicolored	1.50	.65
		Nos. C26-C35 (10)	8.45	2.80

Stamp Centenary Type

Design: 2.50e, Boeing 707 jet & Angola #2.

1970, Dec. 1 Litho. *Perf. 13½*

C36	A83	2.50e multicolored	.45	.20
a.		Souv. sheet of 3, #565-566, C36	2.50	2.50

No. C36a sold for 15e.

No. C36 Overprinted with Bar and: "REPUBLICA POPULAR / DE"

1980, June 15 Litho. *Perf. 13½*

C37	A83	2.50e multicolored	.20	

POSTAGE DUE STAMPS

D1

D2

1904 Unwmk. Typo. *Perf. 11½x12*

J1	D1	5r yellow grn	.25	.20
J2	D1	10r slate	.25	.20
J3	D1	20r yellow brn	.35	.30
J4	D1	30r orange	.60	.60
J5	D1	50r gray brown	.60	.60
J6	D1	60r red brown	4.00	2.50
J7	D1	100r lilac	1.75	1.60
J8	D1	130r dull blue	1.75	1.60
J9	D1	200r carmine	4.00	3.00
J10	D1	500r gray violet	4.00	3.00
		Nos. J1-J10 (10)	17.55	13.60

Postage Due Stamps of 1904 Overprinted in Carmine or Green

REPUBLICA

1911

J11	D1	5r yellow grn	.20	.20
J12	D1	10r slate	.20	.20
J13	D1	20r yellow brn	.20	.20
J14	D1	30r orange	.30	.30
J15	D1	50r gray brown	.30	.30
J16	D1	60r red brown	.60	.60
J17	D1	100r lilac	.60	.60
J18	D1	130r dull blue	.60	.60
J19	D1	200r carmine (G)	.60	.60
J20	D1	500r gray violet	.70	.70
		Nos. J11-J20 (10)	4.30	4.30

1921 *Perf. 11½*

J21	D2	½c yellow green	.20	.20
J22	D2	1c slate	.20	.20
J23	D2	2c orange brown	.20	.20
J24	D2	3c orange	.20	.20
J25	D2	5c gray brown	.20	.20
J26	D2	6c lt brown	.20	.20
J27	D2	10c red violet	.20	.20
J28	D2	13c dull blue	.20	.20
J29	D2	20c carmine	.20	.20
J30	D2	50c gray	.20	.20
		Nos. J21-J30 (10)	2.00	2.00

For surcharges see Nos. 268-270.

Catalogue values for unused stamps in this section, from this point to the end of the section, are for Never Hinged items.

Stamps of 1932 Surcharged in Black

= =
PORTEADO
10
Centavos

1948 Wmk. 232 *Perf. 12x11½*

J31	A14	10c on 20c gray	.20	.20
J32	A14	20c on 30c myrtle grn	.20	.20
J33	A14	30c on 50c lt brown	.45	.45
J34	A14	40c on 1a claret	.45	.45
J35	A14	50c on 2a dull vio	.90	.45
J36	A14	1a on 5a pale yel grn	1.25	1.00
		Nos. J31-J36 (6)	3.45	2.75

Common Design Type

Photogravure and Typographed

1952 Unwmk. *Perf. 14*

Numeral in Red, Frame Multicolored

J37	CD45	10c red brown	.20	.20
J38	CD45	30c olive green	.20	.20
J39	CD45	50c chocolate	.20	.20
J40	CD45	1a dk vio blue	.20	.20
J41	CD45	2a red brown	.20	.20
J42	CD45	5a black brown	.35	.35
		Nos. J37-J42 (6)	1.35	1.35

NEWSPAPER STAMP

N1

Perf. 11½, 12½, 13½

1893 Typo. Unwmk.

P1	N1	2½r brown	1.00	.70

No. P1 was also used for ordinary postage.
For surcharges see Nos. 37, 82, 180, 235.

POSTAL TAX STAMPS

Pombal Issue

Common Design Types

1925, May 8 Unwmk. *Perf. 12½*

RA1	CD28	15c lilac & black	.35	.25
RA2	CD29	15c lilac & black	.35	.25
RA3	CD30	15c lilac & black	.35	.25
		Nos. RA1-RA3 (3)	1.05	.75

"Charity" PT1

Coat of Arms PT2

1929 Litho. *Perf. 11*

Without Gum

RA4	PT1	50c dark blue	2.00	.70

1939 Without Gum *Perf. 10½*

RA5	PT2	50c turq green	1.75	.20
RA6	PT2	1a red	3.25	1.50

A 1.50a, type PT2, was issued for fiscal use.

Catalogue values for unused stamps in this section, from this point to the end of the section, are for Never Hinged items.

Old Man PT3

Mother and Child PT4

Designs: 1e, Boy. 1.50e, Girl.

Imprint: "Foto-Lito-E.G.A.-Luanda"

1955 Unwmk. *Perf. 13*

Heads in dark brown

RA7	PT3	50c dk ocher	.20	.20
RA8	PT3	1e orange ver	.75	.40
RA9	PT3	1.50e brt yel grn	.50	.25
		Nos. RA7-RA9 (3)	1.45	.85

A 2.50e, type PT3 showing an old woman, was issued for revenue use.
See Nos. RA16, RA19-RA21, RA25-RA27.

No. RA7 Surcharged with New Values and two Bars in Red or Black

1957-58

Head in dark brown

RA11	PT3	10c on 50c dk ocher (R)	.25	.25
RA12	PT3	10c on 50c dk ocher ('58)	.20	.20
RA13	PT3	30c on 50c dk ocher	.25	.25
		Nos. RA11-RA13 (3)	.70	.70

1959 Litho. *Perf. 13*

Design: 30c, Boy and girl.

RA14	PT4	10c orange & blk	.20	.20
RA15	PT4	30c slate & blk	.20	.20

Type of 1955 Redrawn

Design: 1e, Boy.

1961, Nov. ***Perf. 13***

RA16	PT3	1e salmon pink & dk brn	.20	.20

Denomination in italics.

Yellow, White and Black Men — PT5

1962, July 1 Typo. ***Perf. 10½***

Without Gum

RA17	PT5	50c multicolored	.65	.65
RA18	PT5	1e multicolored	.35	.35

Issued for the Provincial Settlement Committee (Junta Provincial do Povoamento). The tax was used to promote Portuguese settlement in Angola, and to raise educational and living standards of recent immigrants.

Denominations higher than 1e were used for revenue purposes.

Head Type of 1955
Without Imprint

Designs: 50c, Old man. 1e, Boy. 1.50e, Girl.

1964-65 Litho. ***Perf. 11½***

Heads in dark brown

RA19	PT3	50c orange	.20	.20
RA20	PT3	1e dull red org ('65)	.20	.20
RA21	PT3	1.50e yel grn ('65)	.25	.25
		Nos. RA19-RA21 (3)	.65	.65

No. RA20 is second redrawing of 1e, with bolder lettering and denomination in gothic. Space between "Assistencia" and denomination on RA19-RA21 is ½mm; on 1955 issue space is 2mm.

Map of Angola, Industrial and Farm Workers — PT6

1965, Sept. 1 Litho. ***Perf. 13***

RA22	PT6	50c multicolored	.35	.20
RA23	PT6	1e multicolored	.35	.25

The 2e was used for revenue purposes.

Head Type of 1955
Imprint: "I.N.A." or "INA" (1e)

Designs: 50c, Old man. 1e, Boy. 1.50e, Girl.

1966

Heads in dark brown

RA25	PT3	50c dull orange	.20	.20
RA26	PT3	1e dull brick red	.20	.20
RA27	PT3	1.50e lt yel grn	.35	.20
		Nos. RA25-RA27 (3)	.75	.60

Woman Planting Tree — PT7

1972 Litho. ***Perf. 13***

RA28	PT7	50c shown	.20	.20
RA29	PT7	1e Workers	.20	.20
RA30	PT7	2e Produce	.20	.20
		Nos. RA28-RA30 (3)	.60	.60

POSTAL TAX DUE STAMPS

Pombal Issue

Common Design Types

1925, May 8 Unwmk. ***Perf. 12½***

RAJ1	CD28	30c lilac & black	.50	*1.25*
RAJ2	CD29	30c lilac & black	.50	*1.25*
RAJ3	CD30	30c lilac & black	.50	*1.25*
		Nos. RAJ1-RAJ3 (3)	1.50	*3.75*

See note after Portugal No. RAJ4.

ANGRA

'aŋ-grə

LOCATION — An administrative district of the Azores, consisting of the islands of Terceira, Sao Jorge and Graciosa.
GOVT. — A district of Portugal
AREA — 275 sq. mi.
POP. — 70,000 (approx.)
CAPITAL — Angra do Heroismo

1000 Reis = 1 Milreis

King Carlos
A1 A2

1892-93 Typo. Unwmk. ***Perf. 12½***

1	A1	5r yellow	3.00	1.25
a.		Perf. 11½	6.50	4.00
b.		Perf. 13½	2.75	1.25
2	A1	10r redsh violet	3.00	1.25
a.		Perf. 13½	3.75	2.00
3	A1	15r chocolate	3.50	2.00
a.		Perf. 13½	3.75	2.00
4	A1	20r lavender	5.00	2.00
a.		Perf. 13½	5.00	2.00
5	A1	25r green	4.50	.50
a.		Perf. 13½	7.00	2.50
b.		Perf. 11½	5.00	.90
7	A1	50r blue	7.75	3.00
a.		Perf. 13½	10.00	4.50
8	A1	75r carmine	9.00	3.50
9	A1	80r yellow green	10.00	7.00
10	A1	100r brown, *yel*, perf. 13½ ('93)	35.00	10.00
a.		Perf. 12½	140.00	95.00
11	A1	150r car, *rose* ('93)	50.00	25.00
a.		Perf. 13½	60.00	37.50
12	A1	200r dk blue, *bl* ('93)	50.00	25.00
a.		Perf. 13½	60.00	37.50
13	A1	300r dk blue, *sal* ('93)	50.00	25.00
a.		Perf. 13½	60.00	37.50

Reprints of 50r, 150r, 200r and 300r, made in 1900, are perf. 11½ and ungummed. Value, each $7.50. Reprints of all values, made in 1905, have shiny white gum and clean-cut perf. 13½.

1897-1905 ***Perf. 11½***

Name and Value in Black except Nos. 26 and 35

14	A2	2½r gray	.65	.35
15	A2	5r orange	.65	.35
a.		Diagonal half used as 2½r on cover		*22.50*
16	A2	10r yellow grn	.70	.40
17	A2	15r brown	8.50	3.50
18	A2	15r gray grn ('99)	.90	.45
19	A2	20r gray violet	1.50	.90
20	A2	25r sea green	2.75	.90
21	A2	25r car rose ('99)	.70	.40
22	A2	50r dark blue	5.00	1.25
23	A2	50r ultra ('05)	12.50	8.00
24	A2	65r slate bl ('98)	1.00	.40
25	A2	75r rose	3.00	1.00
26	A2	75r gray brn & car, *straw* ('05)	16.00	*19.00*
27	A2	80r violet	1.50	1.00
28	A2	100r dk blue, *bl*	2.50	1.25
29	A2	115r org brn, *pink* ('98)	2.50	1.40
30	A2	130r gray brn, *straw* ('98)	2.50	1.40
31	A2	150r lt brn, *straw*	2.50	1.40
32	A2	180r sl, *pnksh* ('98)	3.00	2.00
33	A2	200r red vio, *pnksh*	5.00	2.75
34	A2	300r blue, *rose*	7.50	4.00
35	A2	500r blk & red, *bl*	16.00	10.00
a.		Perf. 12½	21.00	12.50
		Nos. 14-35 (22)	96.85	62.10

Azores stamps were used in Angra from 1906 to 1931, when they were superseded by those of Portugal.

ANGUILLA

aŋ-gwi-lə

LOCATION — In the West Indies southeast of Puerto Rico
GOVT. — British territory
AREA — 60 sq. mi.
POP. — 10,663 (est. 1997)
CAPITAL — The Valley

Anguilla separated unilaterally from the Associated State of St. Kitts-Nevis-Anguilla in 1967, formalized in 1980 following direct United Kingdom intervention some years before. A British Commissioner exercises executive authority.

100 Cents = 1 Dollar

Catalogue values for all unused stamps in this country are for Never Hinged items.

St. Kitts-Nevis Nos. 145-160 Overprinted

[redacted]

Independent Anguilla
On Type A14

[redacted]

Independent Anguilla
On Type A15

Wmk. 314

1967, Sept. 4 Photo. ***Perf. 14***

1	A14	½c blue & dk brn	25.00	22.50
2	A15	1c multicolored	25.00	7.00
3	A14	2c multicolored	25.00	2.00
4	A14	3c multicolored	25.00	5.00
5	A15	4c multicolored	25.00	6.00
6	A15	5c multicolored	100.00	20.00
7	A15	6c multicolored	50.00	10.00
8	A15	10c multicolored	25.00	7.50
9	A14	15c multicolored	55.00	12.00
10	A15	20c multicolored	85.00	20.00
11	A14	25c multicolored	70.00	22.50
12	A15	50c multicolored	*2,000.*	*500.00*
13	A14	60c multicolored	*2,500.*	*900.00*
14	A14	$1 multicolored	*1,600.*	*425.00*
15	A15	$2.50 multicolored	*1,600.*	*325.00*
16	A14	$5 multicolored	*1,300.*	*325.00*
		Nos. 1-16 (16)	*9,510.*	*2,609.*

Counterfeit overprints exist.

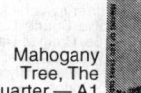

Mahogany Tree, The Quarter — A1

Designs: 2c, Sombrero Lighthouse. 3c, St. Mary's Church. 4c, Valley Police Station. 5c, Old Plantation House, Mt. Fortune. 6c, Valley Post Office. 10c, Methodist Church, West End. 15c, Wall-Blake Airport. 20c, Plane over Sandy Ground. 25c, Island Harbor. 40c, Map of Anguilla. 60c, Hermit crab and starfish. $1, Hibiscus. $2.50, Coconut harvest. $5, Spiny lobster.

Perf. 12½x13

1967-68 Litho. Unwmk.

17	A1	1c orange & multi	.20	.20
18	A1	2c gray green & blk	.20	.20
19	A1	3c emerald & blk	.20	.20
20	A1	4c brt blue & blk	.20	.20
21	A1	5c lt blue & multi	.20	.20
22	A1	6c ver & black	.20	.20
23	A1	10c multicolored	.20	.20
24	A1	15c multicolored	.20	.20
25	A1	20c multicolored	.20	.20
26	A1	25c multicolored	.30	.30
27	A1	40c blue & multi	.45	.45
28	A1	60c yellow & multi	.65	.65
29	A1	$1 lt green & multi	1.25	1.25
30	A1	$2.50 multicolored	3.25	3.25
31	A1	$5 multicolored	6.00	6.00
		Nos. 17-31 (15)	13.70	13.70

Issued: 1c, 5c, 10c, 20c, 25c, 40c, 11/27/67; 3c, 4c, 15c, 60c, $1, $5, 2/10/68; 2c, 6c, $2.50, 3/21/68.

For overprints see Nos. 53-67, 78-82.

Sailboats A2

Designs: 15c, Boat building. 25c, Schooner Warspite. 40c, Yacht Atlantic Star.

1968, May 11 ***Perf. 14***

32	A2	10c rose & multi	.25	.20
33	A2	15c olive & multi	.40	.20
34	A2	25c lilac rose & multi	.65	.40
35	A2	40c dull blue & multi	1.10	.75
		Nos. 32-35 (4)	2.40	1.55

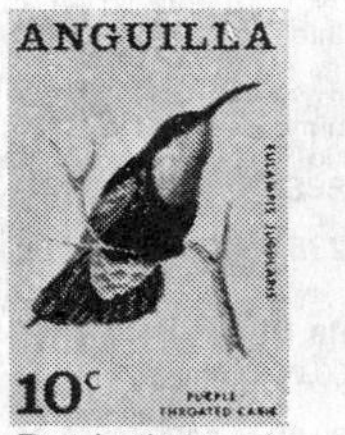

Purple-throated Carib — A3 Girl Guide Badge — A4

Anguillan Birds: 15c, Bananaquit. 25c, Black-necked stilt, horiz. 40c, Royal tern, horiz.

1968, July 8

36	A3	10c dull yel & multi	.45	.20
37	A3	15c yel green & multi	.60	.20
38	A3	25c multicolored	1.75	.75
39	A3	40c multicolored	2.00	1.00
		Nos. 36-39 (4)	4.80	2.15

1968, Oct. 14 ***Perf. 13x13½, 13½x13***

Designs: 10c, Girl Guide badge, horiz. 25c, Badge and Headquarters, horiz. 40c, Merit Badges.

40	A4	10c lt green & multi	.20	.20
41	A4	15c lt blue & multi	.25	.20
42	A4	25c multicolored	.55	.45
43	A4	40c multicolored	.75	.50
		Nos. 40-43 (4)	1.75	1.35

Anguillan Girl Guides, 35th anniversary.

Three Kings — A5

Christmas: 10c, Three Kings seeing Star, vert. 15c, Holy Family, vert. 40c, Shepherds seeing Star. 50c, Holy Family and donkey.

1968, Nov. 18

44	A5	1c lilac rose & black	.20	.20
45	A5	10c blue & black	.20	.20
46	A5	15c brown & black	.20	.20
47	A5	40c brt ultra & black	.60	.40
48	A5	50c green & black	.90	.75
		Nos. 44-48 (5)	2.10	1.75

Bagging Salt — A6

Salt Industry: 15c, Packing salt. 40c, Salt pond. 50c, Loading salt.

1969, Jan. 4 ***Perf. 13***

49	A6	10c red & multi	.20	.20
50	A6	15c lt blue & multi	.20	.20
51	A6	40c emerald & multi	.55	.50
52	A6	50c purple & multi	.65	.60
		Nos. 49-52 (4)	1.60	1.50

Nos. 17-31 Overprinted: "INDEPENDENCE/JANUARY, 1969"

1969, Jan. 9 ***Perf. 12½x13***

53	A1	1c orange & multi	.20	.20
54	A1	2c gray green & blk	.20	.20
55	A1	3c emerald & blk	.20	.20
56	A1	4c brt blue & blk	.20	.20
57	A1	5c lt blue & multi	.20	.20
58	A1	6c vermilion & blk	.20	.20
59	A1	10c multicolored	.20	.20

60	A1	15c	multicolored	.20	.20
61	A1	20c	multicolored	.25	.25
62	A1	25c	multicolored	.35	.35
63	A1	40c	blue & multi	.50	.50
64	A1	60c	yellow & multi	.70	.70
65	A1	$1	lt green & multi	1.25	1.25
66	A1	$2.50	multicolored	3.00	3.00
67	A1	$5	multicolored	6.25	6.25
			Nos. 53-67 (15)	13.90	13.90

Crucifixion, School of Quentin Massys — A7

Easter: 40c, The Last Supper, ascribed to Roberti.

1969, Mar. 31 Litho. *Perf. 13½*

68	A7	25c	multicolored	.30	.20
69	A7	40c	multicolored	.50	.25

Amaryllis A8

1969, June 10 *Perf. 14*

70	A8	10c	shown	.20	.20
71	A8	15c	Bougainvillea	.35	.30
72	A8	40c	Hibiscus	.75	.60
73	A8	50c	Cattleya orchid	1.00	.80
			Nos. 70-73 (4)	2.30	1.90

Turban and Star Shells A9

Sea Shells: 15c, Spiny oysters. 40c, Scotch, royal and smooth bonnets. 50c, Triton trumpet.

1969, Sept. 22

74	A9	10c	multicolored	.30	.20
75	A9	15c	multicolored	.40	.30
76	A9	40c	multicolored	.75	.50
77	A9	50c	multicolored	1.00	.75
			Nos. 74-77 (4)	2.45	1.75

Nos. 17, 25-28 Overprinted "CHRISTMAS 1969" and Various Christmas Designs

1969, Oct. 27 *Perf. 12½x13*

78	A1	1c	orange & multi	.20	.20
79	A1	20c	multicolored	.25	.20
80	A1	25c	multicolored	.35	.30
81	A1	40c	blue & multi	.75	.60
82	A1	60c	yellow & multi	1.50	1.00
			Nos. 78-82 (5)	3.05	2.30

Red Goatfish A10

Designs: 15c, Blue-striped grunts. 40c, Mutton grouper. 50c, Banded butterfly-fish.

1969, Dec. 1 *Perf. 14*

83	A10	10c	multicolored	.25	.20
84	A10	15c	multicolored	.35	.25
85	A10	40c	multicolored	1.00	.75
86	A10	50c	multicolored	1.25	1.00
			Nos. 83-86 (4)	2.85	2.20

Morning Glory — A11

1970, Feb. 23

87	A11	10c	shown	.20	.20
88	A11	15c	Blue petrea	.30	.25
89	A11	40c	Hibiscus	1.00	.75
90	A11	50c	Flamboyant	1.25	1.00
			Nos. 87-90 (4)	2.75	2.20

The Way to Calvary, by Tiepolo — A12

Easter: 20c, Crucifixion, by Masaccio, vert. 40c, Descent from the Cross, by Rosso Fiorentino, vert. 60c, Jesus Carrying the Cross, by Murillo.

1970, Mar. 26 *Perf. 13½*

91	A12	10c	multicolored	.20	.20
92	A12	20c	multicolored	.25	.20
93	A12	40c	multicolored	.35	.30
94	A12	60c	multicolored	.50	.40
			Nos. 91-94 (4)	1.30	1.10

Anguilla Map, Scout Badge A13

Designs: 15c, Cub Scouts practicing first aid. 40c, Monkey bridge. 50c, Scout Headquarters, The Valley, and Lord Baden-Powell.

1970, Aug. 10 *Perf. 13*

95	A13	10c	multicolored	.20	.20
96	A13	15c	multicolored	.30	.25
97	A13	40c	multicolored	.75	.60
98	A13	50c	multicolored	1.00	.75
			Nos. 95-98 (4)	2.25	1.80

Anguilla Boy Scouts, 40th anniversary.

Boat Building A14

Designs: 2c, Road construction. 3c, Blowing Point dock. 4c, Radio announcer. 5c, Cottage Hospital extension. 6c, Valley secondary school. 10c, Hotel extension. 15c, Sandy Ground. 20c, Supermarket and movie house. 25c, Bananas and mangoes. 40c, Wall-Blake airport. 60c, Sandy Ground jetty. $1, Administration building. $2.50, Cow and calf. $5, Sandy Hill Bay.

1970, Nov. 23 Litho. *Perf. 14*

99	A14	1c	multicolored	.20	.20
100	A14	2c	multicolored	.20	.20
101	A14	3c	multicolored	.20	.20
102	A14	4c	multicolored	.20	.20
103	A14	5c	multicolored	.20	.20
104	A14	6c	multicolored	.20	.20
105	A14	10c	multicolored	.20	.20
106	A14	15c	multicolored	.25	.25
107	A14	20c	multicolored	.30	.30
108	A14	25c	multicolored	.35	.35
109	A14	40c	multicolored	.60	.60
110	A14	60c	multicolored	.90	.90
111	A14	$1	multicolored	1.50	1.50
112	A14	$2.50	multicolored	3.50	3.50
113	A14	$5	multicolored	7.25	7.25
			Nos. 99-113 (15)	16.05	16.05

Adoration of the Shepherds, by Guido Reni — A15

Christmas: 20c, Virgin and Child, by Benozzo Gozzoli. 25c, Nativity, by Botticelli. 40c, Santa Margherita Madonna, by Mazzola. 50c, Adoration of the Kings, by Tiepolo.

1970, Dec. 11 *Perf. 13½*

114	A15	1c	multicolored	.20	.20
115	A15	20c	multicolored	.25	.20
116	A15	25c	multicolored	.30	.25
117	A15	40c	multicolored	.50	.40
118	A15	50c	multicolored	.55	.50
			Nos. 114-118 (5)	1.80	1.55

Angels Weeping over the Dead Christ, by Guercino — A16

Easter: 10c, Ecce Homo, by Correggio, vert. 15c, Christ Appearing to St. Peter, by Carracci, vert. 50c, The Supper at Emmaus, by Caravaggio.

1971, Mar. 29

119	A16	10c	pink & multi	.20	.20
120	A16	15c	lt blue & multi	.25	.20
121	A16	40c	yel green & multi	.50	.40
122	A16	50c	violet & multi	.60	.50
			Nos. 119-122 (4)	1.55	1.30

Hypolimnas Misippus A17

Butterflies: 15c, Junonia lavinia. 40c, Agraulis vanillae. 50c, Danaus plexippus.

1971, June 21 *Perf. 14x14½*

123	A17	10c	multicolored	.75	.70
124	A17	15c	multicolored	1.00	.90
125	A17	40c	multicolored	1.90	1.75
126	A17	50c	multicolored	2.25	2.00
			Nos. 123-126 (4)	5.90	5.35

Magnanime and Aimable in Battle — A18

Ships: 15c, HMS Duke and Agamemnon against Glorieux. 25c, HMS Formidable and Namur against Ville de Paris. 40c, HMS Canada. 50c, HMS St. Albans and wreck of Hector.

1971, Aug. 30 Litho. *Perf. 14*

127	A18	10c	multicolored	.35	.35
128	A18	15c	multicolored	.60	.65
129	A18	25c	multicolored	1.25	1.40
130	A18	40c	multicolored	2.00	2.25
131	A18	50c	multicolored	2.75	3.00
a.			Strip of 5, #127-131	7.25	7.25

West Indies sea battles.

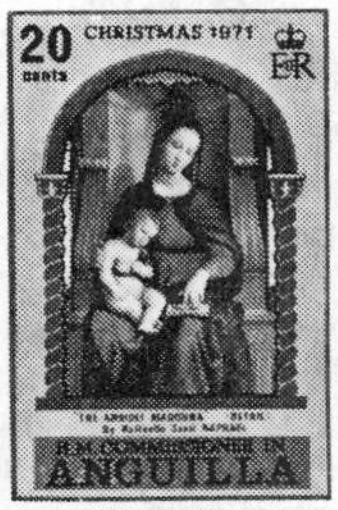

Ansidei Madonna, by Raphael — A19

Christmas: 25c, Mystic Nativity, by Botticelli. 40c, Virgin and Child, School of Seville, inscribed Murillo. 50c, Madonna of the Iris, ascribed to Dürer.

1971, Nov. 29 *Perf. 14x13½*

132	A19	20c	green & multi	.25	.25
133	A19	25c	blue & multi	.30	.30
134	A19	40c	lilac rose & multi	.50	.60
135	A19	50c	violet & multi	.65	.75
			Nos. 132-135 (4)	1.70	1.90

Map of Anguilla and St. Maarten, by Jefferys, 1775 — A20

Jesus Buffeted, Stained-glass Window — A21

Maps of Anguilla by: 15c, Samuel Fahlberg, 1814. 40c, Thomas Jefferys, 1775, horiz. 50c, Capt. E. Barnett, 1847, horiz.

1972, Jan. 24 *Perf. 14x13½, 13½x14*

136	A20	10c	lt blue & multi	.20	.20
137	A20	15c	lt green & multi	.35	.25
138	A20	40c	lt green & multi	.75	.50
139	A20	50c	lt ultra & multi	1.00	.75
			Nos. 136-139 (4)	2.30	1.70

1972, Mar. 14 *Perf. 14x13½*

Easter (19th cent. Stained-glass Windows, Bray Church): 15c, Jesus Carrying the Cross. 25c, Crucifixion. 40c, Descent from the Cross. 50c, Burial.

140	A21	10c	multicolored	.20	.20
141	A21	15c	multicolored	.25	.25
142	A21	25c	multicolored	.35	.35
143	A21	40c	multicolored	.75	.75
144	A21	50c	multicolored	.90	.90
a.			Strip of 5, #140-144	2.50	2.50

Spear Fishing A22

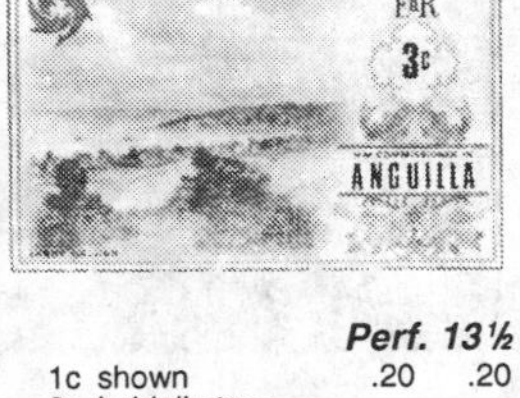

Sandy Ground A23

1972-75 *Perf. 13½*

145	A22	1c	shown	.20	.20
146	A23	2c	Loblolly tree, vert.	.20	.20
147	A23	3c	shown	.20	.20
148	A23	4c	Ferry, Blowing Point, vert.	.20	.20
149	A23	5c	Agriculture	.20	.20
150	A23	6c	St. Mary's Church, vert.	.20	.20
151	A23	10c	St. Gerard's Church	.20	.20

152	A22	15c	Cottage Hospital	.30	.30
153	A23	20c	Public Library	.35	.35
154	A23	25c	Sunset, Blowing Point	.50	.50
155	A22	40c	Boat building	.75	.75
156	A22	60c	Hibiscus	1.25	1.25
157	A23	$1	Man-o-war bird	2.50	2.50
158	A23	$2.50	Frangipani	5.75	5.75
159	A23	$5	Brown pelican	11.00	11.00
160	A22	$10	Green-back turtle	27.50	27.50
			Nos. 145-160 (16)	51.30	51.30

Issued: $10, 5/20/75; others 10/30/72.
For overprints see Nos. 229-246.

Common Design Types pictured following the introduction.

Silver Wedding Issue, 1972

Common Design Type

Design: Queen Elizabeth II, Prince Philip, schooner and dolphin.

Perf. 14x14½

1972, Nov. 20 Photo. Wmk. 314

161	CD324	25c olive & multi	1.10	1.25
162	CD324	40c maroon & multi	1.40	1.75

Flight into Egypt — A24

Perf. 13½

1972, Dec. 4 Litho. Unwmk.

163	A24	1c	shown	.20	.20
164	A24	20c	Star of Bethlehem	.25	.30
165	A24	25c	Nativity	.30	.35
166	A24	40c	Three Kings	.40	.45
167	A24	50c	Adoration of the Kings	.60	.70
a.			Vert. strip of 4, #164-167	2.00	2.00
			Nos. 163-167 (5)	1.75	2.00

Christmas.

Betrayal of Jesus — A25

1973, Mar. 26

168	A25	1c	shown	.20	.20
169	A25	10c	Man of Sorrow	.20	.20
170	A25	20c	Jesus Carrying Cross	.25	.25
171	A25	25c	Crucifixion	.30	.30
172	A25	40c	Descent from Cross	.40	.45
173	A25	50c	Resurrection	.50	.60
a.			Souvenir sheet of 6	1.75	1.75
b.			Vert. strip of 5, #169-173	1.75	1.75
			Nos. 168-173 (6)	1.85	2.00

Easter. #173a contains 6 stamps similar to #168-173 with bottom panel in lilac rose.

Santa Maria A26

1973, Sept. 10

174	A26	1c	shown	.20	.20
175	A26	20c	Old West Indies map	.50	.50
176	A26	40c	Map of voyages	1.25	1.25
177	A26	70c	Sighting land	2.00	1.75
178	A26	$1.20	Columbus landing	4.00	3.50
a.			Souvenir sheet of 5, #174-178	8.00	9.00
b.			Horiz. strip of 4, #175-178	8.00	8.00
			Nos. 174-178 (5)	7.95	7.20

Discovery of West Indies by Columbus.

Princess Anne's Wedding Issue

Common Design Type

1973, Nov. 14 Wmk. 314 *Perf. 13½*

179	CD325	60c blue grn & multi	.25	.20
180	CD325	$1.20 lilac & multi	.50	.40

Wedding of Princess Anne and Capt. Mark Phillips, Nov. 14, 1973.

Adoration of the Shepherds, by Guido Reni — A27

Paintings: 10c, Virgin and Child, by Filippino Lippi. 20c, Nativity, by Meester Van de Brunswijkse Diptiek. 25c, Madonna of the Meadow, by Bellini. 40c, Virgin and Child, by Cima. 50c, Adoration of the Kings, by Geertgen Tot Sint Jans.

1973, Dec. 2 Unwmk.

181	A27	1c multicolored	.20	.20
182	A27	10c multicolored	.20	.20
183	A27	20c multicolored	.20	.20
184	A27	25c multicolored	.25	.25
185	A27	40c multicolored	.30	.30
186	A27	50c multicolored	.50	.50
a.		Souvenir sheet of 6, #181-186	1.75	1.75
b.		Horiz. strip of 5, #182-186	1.75	1.75
		Nos. 181-186 (6)	1.65	1.65

Christmas.

Crucifixion, by Raphael — A28

Easter (Details from Crucifixion by Raphael): 15c, Virgin Mary and St. John. 20c, The Two Marys. 25c, Left Angel. 40c, Right Angel. $1, Christ on the Cross.

1974, Mar. 30

187	A28	1c lilac & multi	.20	.20
188	A28	15c gray & multi	.20	.20
189	A28	20c salmon & multi	.20	.20
190	A28	25c yel green & multi	.25	.25
191	A28	40c orange & multi	.30	.30
192	A28	$1 lt blue & multi	.50	.50
a.		Souvenir sheet of 6, #187-192	1.75	2.00
b.		Vert. strip of 5, #188-192	1.75	1.75
		Nos. 187-192 (6)	1.65	1.65

Churchill Making Victory Sign — A29

Designs: 20c, Roosevelt, Churchill, American and British flags. 25c, Churchill broadcasting during the war. 40c, Blenheim Palace. 60c, Churchill Statue and Parliament. $1.20, Chartwell.

1974, June 24

193	A29	1c multicolored	.20	.20
194	A29	20c multicolored	.20	.20
195	A29	25c multicolored	.25	.25
196	A29	40c multicolored	.35	.35
197	A29	60c multicolored	.50	.50
198	A29	$1.20 multicolored	1.00	1.00
a.		Souvenir sheet of 6, #193-198	2.75	3.00
b.		Horiz. strip of 5, #194-198	2.75	2.75
		Nos. 193-198 (6)	2.50	2.50

Sir Winston Spencer Churchill (1874-1965).

UPU Emblem, Map of Anguilla — A30

1974, Aug. 27

199	A30	1c black & ultra	.20	.20
200	A30	20c black & orange	.20	.20
201	A30	25c black & yellow	.20	.20
202	A30	40c black & brt lilac	.30	.30
203	A30	60c black & lt green	.35	.35
204	A30	$1.20 black & blue	.60	.60
a.		Souvenir sheet of 6	2.25	2.50
b.		Horiz. strip of 5, #200-204	1.90	1.90
		Nos. 199-204 (6)	1.85	1.85

UPU, centenary. No. 204a contains one each of Nos. 199-204 with second row (40c, 60c, $1.20) perf. 15 at bottom.

Fishermen Seeing Star — A31

Christmas: 20c, Nativity. 25c, King offering gift. 40c, Star over map of Anguilla. 60c, Family looking at star. $1.20, Two angels with star and "Peace."

1974, Dec. 16 Litho. *Perf. 14½*

205	A31	1c brt blue & multi	.20	.20
206	A31	20c dull grn & multi	.20	.20
207	A31	25c gray & multi	.20	.20
208	A31	40c car & multi	.25	.30
209	A31	60c dp blue & multi	.40	.45
210	A31	$1.20 ultra & multi	.50	.75
a.		Souvenir sheet of 6, #205-210	2.00	2.25
b.		Horiz. strip of 5, #206-210	1.75	1.75
		Nos. 205-210 (6)	1.75	2.10

Virgin Mary, St. John, Mary Magdalene — A32

Paintings from Isenheim Altar, by Matthias Grunewald: 10c, Crucifixion. 15c, John the Baptist. 20c, St. Sebastian and Angels. $1, Burial of Christ, horiz. $1.50, St. Anthony, the Hermit.

1975, Mar. 25 *Perf. 13½*

211	A32	1c multicolored	.20	.20
212	A32	10c multicolored	.20	.20
213	A32	15c multicolored	.20	.20
214	A32	20c multicolored	.20	.20
215	A32	$1 multicolored	.50	.60
216	A32	$1.50 multicolored	.70	.90
a.		Souvenir sheet of 6	2.00	2.25
b.		Horiz. strip of 5, #212-216	2.00	2.00
		Nos. 211-216 (6)	2.00	2.30

Easter. No. 216a contains 6 stamps similar to Nos. 211-216 with simulated perforations.

Statue of Liberty, N.Y. Skyline — A33

Designs: 10c, Capitol, Washington, D.C. 15c, Congress voting independence. 20c, Washington, map and his battles. $1, Boston Tea Party. $1.50, Bicentennial emblem, historic U.S. flags.

1975, Nov. 10

217	A33	1c multicolored	.20	.20
218	A33	10c multicolored	.20	.20
219	A33	15c multicolored	.20	.20
220	A33	20c multicolored	.20	.20
221	A33	$1 multicolored	.70	.60
222	A33	$1.50 multicolored	1.00	.75
a.		Souvenir sheet of 6	2.75	3.25
b.		Horiz. strip of 5, #218-222	2.50	2.25
		Nos. 217-222 (6)	2.50	2.15

American Bicentennial. No. 222a contains one each of Nos. 217-222 with second row (20c, $1, $1.50) perf. 15 at bottom.

Virgin and Child with St. John, by Raphael — A34

Paintings, Virgin and Child by: 10c, Cima. 15c, Dolci. 20c, Durer. $1, Bellini. $1.50, Botticelli.

1975, Dec. 8 *Perf. 14x13½*

223	A34	1c ultra & multi	.20	.20
224	A34	10c Prus blue & multi	.20	.20
225	A34	15c plum & multi	.20	.20
226	A34	20c car rose & multi	.20	.20
227	A34	$1 brt grn & multi	.75	.65
228	A34	$1.50 blue grn & multi	1.00	.90
a.		Souvenir sheet of 6, #223-228	4.00	4.00
b.		Horiz. strip of 5, #224-228	2.40	2.40
		Nos. 223-228 (6)	2.55	2.35

Christmas.

Nos. 145-146, 148, 150-160 Overprinted "NEW CONSTITUTION 1976"

1976 Litho. *Perf. 13½*

229	A22	1c	#145	.20	*.25*
230	A22	2c	on 1c #145	.20	*.25*
231	A23	2c	#146	2.00	.85
232	A22	3c	on 40c #155	.50	.20
233	A23	4c	#148	.75	.75
234	A22	5c	on 40c #155	.20	*.25*
235	A23	6c	#150	.20	*.25*
236	A23	10c	on 20c #153	.20	*.25*
237	A23	10c	#151	2.00	1.50
238	A22	15c	#152	.20	*.50*
239	A23	20c	#153	.25	*.30*
240	A23	25c	#154	.25	*.30*
241	A22	40c	#155	.75	.45
242	A22	60c	#156	.50	.50
243	A23	$1	#157	5.00	1.25
244	A23	$2.50	#158	2.00	1.50
245	A23	$5	#159	6.50	5.00
246	A22	$10	#160	8.00	*9.00*
			Nos. 229-246 (18)	29.70	*23.35*

Flowering Trees — A35

1976, Feb. 16 *Perf. 13½x14*

247	A35	1c	Almond	.20	.20
248	A35	10c	Clusia rosea	.20	.20
249	A35	15c	Calabash	.20	.20
250	A35	20c	Cordia	.20	.20
251	A35	$1	Papaya	.75	.75
252	A35	$1.50	Flamboyant	1.00	1.00
a.			Souvenir sheet of 6, #247-252	2.75	2.75
b.			Horiz. strip of 5, #248-252	2.25	2.25
			Nos. 247-252 (6)	2.55	2.55

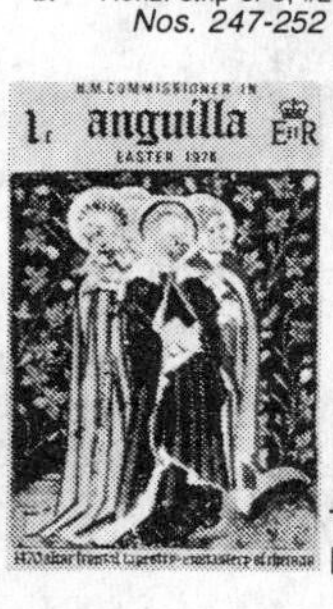

The Three Marys — A36

Designs: 10c, Crucifixion. 15c, Two soldiers. 20c, Annunciation. $1, Altar tapestry, 1470, Monastery of Rheinau, Switzerland, horiz. $1.50, "Noli me Tangere" (Jesus and Mary Magdalene). Designs of vertical stamps show details from tapestry shown on $1 stamp.

1976, Apr. 5 ***Perf. 14x13½, 13½x14***

253 A36	1c multicolored	.20	.20
254 A36	10c multicolored	.20	.20
255 A36	15c multicolored	.20	.20
256 A36	20c multicolored	.30	.30
257 A36	$1 multicolored	1.00	1.00
258 A36	$1.50 multicolored	1.40	1.40
a.	Souvenir sheet of 6	3.25	3.25
b.	Horiz. strip of 5, #254-258	3.00	3.00
	Nos. 253-258 (6)	3.30	3.30

Easter. No. 258a contains 6 stamps similar to Nos. 253-258 with simulated perforations.

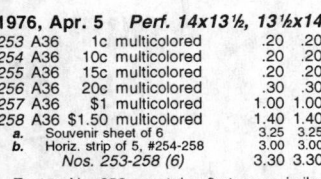

Le Desius and La Vaillante Approaching Anguilla — A37

Sailing Ships: 3c, Sailboat leaving Anguilla for Antigua to get help. 15c, HMS Lapwing in battle with frigate Le Desius and brig La Vaillante. 25c, La Vaillante aground off St. Maarten. $1, Lapwing. $1.50, Le Desius burning.

1976, Nov. 8 **Litho.** ***Perf. 13½x14***

259 A37	1c multicolored	.20	.20
260 A37	3c multicolored	.75	.25
261 A37	15c multicolored	1.00	.30
262 A37	25c multicolored	1.25	.50
263 A37	$1 multicolored	2.50	2.25
264 A37	$1.50 multicolored	3.25	3.00
a.	Souvenir sheet of 6, #259-264	8.50	8.50
b.	Strip of 5, #260-264	8.50	8.50
	Nos. 259-264 (6)	8.95	6.50

Bicentenary of Battle of Anguilla between French and British ships.

Christmas Carnival — A38

Children's Paintings: 3c, 3 children dreaming of Christmas gifts. 15c, Caroling. 25c, Candlelight procession. $1, Going to Church on Christmas Eve. $1.50, Airport, coming home for Christmas.

1976, Nov. 22

265 A38	1c multicolored	.20	.20
266 A38	3c multicolored	.20	.20
267 A38	15c multicolored	.20	.20
268 A38	25c multicolored	.20	.20
269 A38	$1 multicolored	.65	.65
270 A38	$1.50 multicolored	.85	.75
a.	Souvenir sheet of 6, #265-270	2.50	*2.75*
b.	Strip of 5, #266-270	2.00	1.75
	Nos. 265-270 (6)	2.30	2.20

Christmas. For overprints and surcharges see Nos. 305-310a.

Prince Charles and HMS Minerva, 1973 — A39

Designs: 40c, Prince Philip landing at Road Bay, 1964. $1.20, Homage to Queen at Coronation. $2.50, Coronation regalia and map of Anguilla.

1977, Feb. 9

271 A39	25c multicolored	.20	.20
272 A39	40c multicolored	.20	.20
273 A39	$1.20 multicolored	.40	.35
274 A39	$2.50 multicolored	.75	.70
a.	Souvenir sheet of 4, #271-274	1.50	2.00
	Nos. 271-274 (4)	1.55	1.45

25th anniv. of reign of Queen Elizabeth II. For overprints see Nos. 297-300.

Yellow-crowned Night Heron — A40

Designs: 2c, Great barracuda. 3c, Queen conch. 4c, Spanish bayonet (Yucca). 5c, Trunkfish. 6c, Cable and telegraph building. 10c, American sparrow hawk. 15c, Ground orchids. 20c, Parlorfish. 22c, Lobster fishing boat. 35c, Boat race. 50c Sea bean (flowers). $1, Sandy Island with palms. $2.50, Manchineel (fruit). $5, Ground lizard. $10, Red-billed tropic bird.

1977-78 **Litho.** ***Perf. 13½x14***

275 A40	1c multicolored	.25	*.40*
276 A40	2c multicolored	.25	*.75*
277 A40	3c multicolored	.75	*1.10*
278 A40	4c multicolored	.30	.20
279 A40	5c multicolored	1.25	.20
280 A40	6c multicolored	.25	.20
281 A40	10c multicolored	3.00	1.25
282 A40	15c multicolored	2.25	1.25
283 A40	20c multicolored	1.75	.50
284 A40	22c multicolored	.30	.40
285 A40	35c multicolored	1.00	.50
286 A40	50c multicolored	.65	.35
287 A40	$1 multicolored	1.00	.50
288 A40	$2.50 multicolored	2.00	2.00
289 A40	$5 multicolored	5.00	4.00
290 A40	$10 multicolored	11.00	8.00
	Nos. 275-290 (16)	31.00	21.60

Issued: #275-280, 290, 4/18/77; others 2/20/78.

For overprints and surcharges see Nos. 319-324, 337-342, 387-390, 402-404, 407-415, 417-423.

Crucifixion, by Quentin Massys — A41

Easter (Paintings): 3c, Betrayal of Christ, by Ugolino. 22c, Way to Calvary, by Ugolino. 30c, The Deposition, by Ugolino. $1, Resurrection, by Ugolino. $1.50, Crucifixion, by Andrea del Castagno.

1977, Apr. 25

291 A41	1c multicolored	.20	.20
292 A41	3c multicolored	.20	.20
293 A41	22c multicolored	.25	.25
294 A41	30c multicolored	.30	.30
295 A41	$1 multicolored	.75	.75
296 A41	$1.50 multicolored	1.10	1.10
a.	Souvenir sheet of 6, #291-296	2.75	2.75
b.	Strip of 5, #292-296	2.75	2.75
	Nos. 291-296 (6)	2.80	2.80

Nos. 271-274, 274a Overprinted: "ROYAL VISIT/TO WEST INDIES"

1977, Oct. 26 **Litho.** ***Perf. 13½x14***

297 A39	25c multicolored	.20	.20
298 A39	40c multicolored	.20	.20
299 A39	$1.20 multicolored	.50	*.60*
300 A39	$2.50 multicolored	1.00	*1.25*
a.	Souvenir sheet of 4	1.75	2.00
	Nos. 297-300 (4)	1.90	*2.25*

Visit of Queen Elizabeth II to West Indies.

Suzanne Fourment in Velvet Hat, by Rubens — A42

Rubens Paintings: 40c, Helena Fourment with her Children. $1.20, Rubens with his wife. $2.50, Marchesa Brigida Spinola-Doria.

1977, Nov. 1 ***Perf. 14x13½***

301 A42	25c black & multi	.20	.20
302 A42	40c black & multi	.20	.20
303 A42	$1.20 multicolored	.75	.75
304 A42	$2.50 black & multi	1.50	1.50
a.	Souvenir sheet of 4, #301-304	3.00	3.00
	Nos. 301-304 (4)	2.65	2.65

Peter Paul Rubens, 400th birth anniv. Nos. 301-304 printed in sheets of 5 stamps and blue label with Rubens' portrait.

Nos. 265-270b Overprinted 1977 and Surcharged

1977, Nov. 7 ***Perf. 13½x14***

305 A38	1c multicolored	.20	.20
306 A38	5c on 3c multi	.20	.20
307 A38	12c on 15c multi	.20	.20
308 A38	18c on 25c multi	.20	.20
309 A38	$1 multicolored	.65	.65
310 A38	$2.50 on $1.50 multi	1.75	1.75
a.	Souvenir sheet of 6, #305-310	3.75	3.75
b.	Strip of 5, #306-310	3.00	3.00
	Nos. 305-310 (6)	3.20	3.20

Christmas. Stamps and souvenir sheets have "1976" and old denomination obliterated with variously shaped rectangles.

Nos. 301-304a Ovptd. in Gold: "EASTER 1978"

1978, Mar. 6 ***Perf. 14x13½***

311 A42	25c black & multi	.20	.20
312 A42	40c black & multi	.25	.25
313 A42	$1.20 black & multi	.65	.65
314 A42	$2.50 black & multi	1.40	1.40
a.	Souvenir sheet of 4, #311-314	2.50	2.50
	Nos. 311-314 (4)	2.50	2.50

Buckingham Palace — A43

Designs: 50c, Coronation procession. $1.50, Royal family on balcony. $2.50, Royal coat of arms.

1978, Apr. 6 ***Perf. 14***

315 A43	22c multicolored	.20	.20
316 A43	50c multicolored	.20	.20
317 A43	$1.50 multicolored	.35	.45
318 A43	$2.50 multicolored	.50	.70
a.	Souvenir sheet of 4, #315-318	2.00	2.00
	Nos. 315-318 (4)	1.25	1.55

25th anniv. of coronation of Queen Elizabeth II.

#315-318 each exist in a booklet pane of 2.

Nos. 284-285 and 288 Ovptd. and Surcharged: "VALLEY / SECONDARY / SCHOOL / 1953-1978"

1978, Aug. 14 **Litho.** ***Perf. 13½x14***

319 A40	22c multicolored	.20	.20
320 A40	35c multicolored	.25	.20
321 A40	$1.50 on $2.50 multi	1.25	1.25
	Nos. 319-321 (3)	1.70	1.65

Valley Secondary School, 25th anniv. Surcharge on No. 321 includes heavy bar over old denomination.

Nos. 286-287, 289 Ovptd. and Surcharged: "ROAD / METHODIST / CHURCH / 1878-1978"

1978, Aug. 14

322 A40	50c multicolored	.40	.40
323 A40	$1 multicolored	.75	.75
324 A40	$1.20 on $5 multi	1.00	1.00
	Nos. 322-324 (3)	2.15	2.15

Road Methodist Church, centenary. Surcharge on No. 324 includes heavy bar over old denomination.

Mother and Child A44

Christmas: 12c, Christmas masquerade. 18c, Christmas dinner. 22c, Serenade. $1, Star over manger. $2.50, Family going to church.

1978, Dec. 11 **Litho.** ***Perf. 13½***

325 A44	5c multicolored	.20	.20
326 A44	12c multicolored	.20	.20
327 A44	18c multicolored	.20	.20
328 A44	22c multicolored	.20	.20
329 A44	$1 multicolored	.50	.50
330 A44	$2.50 multicolored	1.00	1.00
a.	Souvenir sheet of 6, #325-330	2.75	2.00
	Nos. 325-330 (6)	2.30	2.30

Type A44 in Changed Colors with IYC Emblem and Inscription.

1979, Jan. 15 **Litho.** ***Perf. 13½***

331 A44	5c multicolored	.20	.20
332 A44	12c multicolored	.20	.20
333 A44	18c multicolored	.20	.20
334 A44	22c multicolored	.20	.20
335 A44	$1 multicolored	.50	.50
336 A44	$2.50 multicolored	1.00	1.00
a.	Souvenir sheet of 4, #331-336	3.50	3.50
	Nos. 331-336 (6)	2.30	2.30

Intl. Year of the Child. For overprint, see No. 416

18 CENTS

Nos. 275-278, 280-281 Surcharged

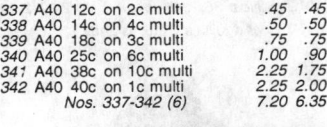

1979, Feb. 8 **Litho.** ***Perf. 13½x14***

337 A40	12c on 2c multi	*.45*	*.45*
338 A40	14c on 4c multi	*.50*	*.50*
339 A40	18c on 3c multi	*.75*	*.75*
340 A40	25c on 6c multi	*1.00*	*.90*
341 A40	38c on 10c multi	*2.25*	*1.75*
342 A40	40c on 1c multi	*2.25*	*2.00*
	Nos. 337-342 (6)	*7.20*	*6.35*

Valley Methodist Church A45

Church Interiors: 12c, St. Mary's Anglican Church, The Valley. 18c, St. Gerard's Roman Catholic Church, The Valley. 22c, Road Methodist Church. $1.50, St. Augustine's Anglican Church, East End. $2.50, West End Methodist Church.

1979, Mar. 30 **Litho.** ***Perf. 14***

343 A45	5c multicolored	.20	.20
344 A45	12c multicolored	.20	.20
345 A45	18c multicolored	.20	.20
346 A45	22c multicolored	.20	.20
347 A45	$1.50 multicolored	.90	.90
348 A45	$2.50 multicolored	1.25	1.25
a.	Souvenir sheet of 6	2.75	2.75
b.	Strip of 6, #343-348	2.50	2.50

Easter. No. 348a contains Nos. 343-348 in 2 horizontal rows of 3.

US No. C3a A46

Designs: No. 350, Cape of Good Hope #1. No. 351, Penny Black. No. 352, Germany #C36. No. 353, US #245. No. 354, Great Britain #93.

1979, Apr. 23 **Litho.** ***Perf. 14***

349 A46	1c multicolored	.20	.20
350 A46	1c multicolored	.20	.20
351 A46	22c multicolored	.20	.20
352 A46	35c multicolored	.20	.20
353 A46	$1.50 multicolored	.75	.75
354 A46	$2.50 multicolored	1.10	1.10
a.	Souvenir sheet of 6, #349-353	2.50	2.50
	Nos. 349-354 (6)	2.65	2.65

Sir Rowland Hill (1795-1879), originator of penny postage.

Wright's Flyer A — A47

History of Aviation: 12c, Louis Bleriot landing at Dover, 1909. 18c, Vickers Vimy, 1919. 22c, Spirit of St. Louis, 1927. $1.50, LZ127 Graf Zeppelin, 1928. $2.50, Concorde, 1979.

1979, May 21 **Litho.** ***Perf. 14***

355 A47	5c multicolored	.20	.20
356 A47	12c multicolored	.20	.20
357 A47	18c multicolored	.25	.20
358 A47	22c multicolored	.25	.20

359 A47 $1.50 multicolored .90 .90
360 A47 $2.50 multicolored 1.90 1.90
a. Souvenir sheet of 6, #355-360 4.00 3.75
Nos. 355-360 (6) 3.70 3.60

Map of Anguilla, Map and View of Sombrero Island A48

Map of Anguilla, Map and View of: 12c, Anguillita Island. 18c, Sandy Island. 25c, Prickly Pear Cays. $1, Dog Island. $2.50, Scrub Island.

1979 Litho. *Perf. 14*
361 A48 5c multicolored .20 .20
362 A48 12c multicolored .20 .20
363 A48 18c multicolored .20 .20
364 A48 25c multicolored .20 .20
365 A48 $1 multicolored .40 .40
366 A48 $2.50 multicolored 1.00 1.00
a. Souvenir sheet of 6, #361-366 3.50 3.50
Nos. 361-366 (6) 2.20 2.20

Anguilla's Outer Islands.

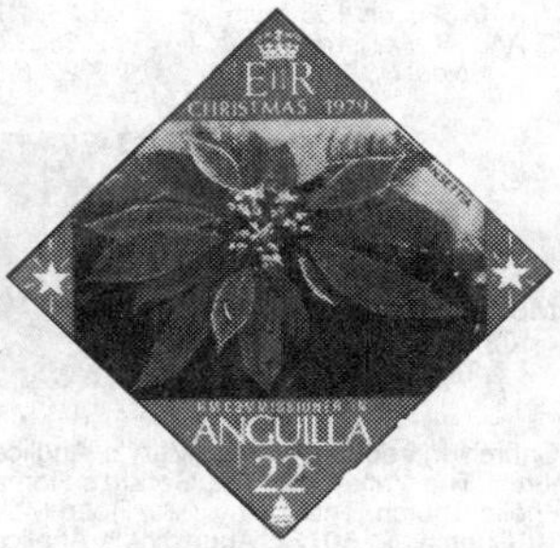

Red Poinsettia — A49

1979, Oct. 22 Litho. *Perf. 14½*
367 A49 22c shown .20 .20
368 A49 35c Kalanchoe .20 .20
369 A49 $1.50 Cream poinsettia .85 .75
370 A49 $2.50 White poinsettia 1.50 1.25
a. Souvenir sheet of 4, #367-370 3.00 3.00
Nos. 367-370 (4) 2.75 2.40

Christmas.

Booths and Frames A50

50c, Earls Court Exhibition Hall. $1.50, Penny Black, Great Britain #2. $2.50, Exhibition emblem.

1979, Dec. 10 Litho. *Perf. 13, 14½*
371 A50 35c multicolored .20 .20
372 A50 50c multicolored .20 .20
373 A50 $1.50 multicolored .75 .75
374 A50 $2.50 multicolored 1.00 1.00
a. Souvenir sheet of 4, #371-374 3.25 3.25
Nos. 371-374 (4) 2.15 2.15

London 1980 Intl. Stamp Exhibition, May 6-14, 1980.

Lake Placid and Olympic Rings — A51

Olympic Rings and: 18c, Ice Hockey. 35c, Figure skating. 50c, Bobsledding. $1, Ski jump. $2.50, Luge.

1980, Jan. Litho. *Perf. 13½, 14½*
375 A51 5c multicolored .20 .20
376 A51 18c multicolored .20 .20
377 A51 35c multicolored .20 .20
378 A51 50c multicolored .20 .20
379 A51 $1 multicolored .35 .35
380 A51 $2.50 multicolored .60 .60
a. Souvenir sheet of 6, #375-380 2.25 2.25
Nos. 375-380 (6) 1.75 1.75

13th Winter Olympic Games, Lake Placid, NY, Feb. 12-24.

Salt Field A52

1980, Apr. 14 Litho. *Perf. 14*
381 A52 5c shown .20 .20
382 A52 12c Tallying salt .20 .20
383 A52 18c Unloading salt flats .20 .20
384 A52 22c Storage pile .20 .20
385 A52 $1 Bagging and grinding .40 .40
386 A52 $2.50 Loading onto boats .90 .90
a. Souvenir sheet of 6, #381-386 2.00 2.00
Nos. 381-386 (6) 2.10 2.10

Salt industry.

Nos. 281, 288 Overprinted: "50th Anniversary / Scouting 1980"

1980, Apr. 16 *Perf. 13½x14*
387 A40 10c multicolored 1.10 .40
388 A40 $2.50 multicolored 2.00 1.75

Nos. 283, 289 Overprinted: "75th Anniversary / Rotary 1980" and Rotary Emblem

1980, Apr. 16 *Perf. 13½x14*
389 A40 20c multicolored .90 .40
390 A40 $5 multicolored 2.75 2.50

Rotary International, 75th anniversary.

Big Ben, Great Britain #643, London 1980 Emblem — A53

Designs: $1.50, Canada #756. $2.50, Statue of Liberty, US #1632.

1980, May
391 A53 50c multicolored .75 .75
392 A53 $1.50 multicolored 1.00 1.00
393 A53 $2.50 multicolored 1.50 1.50
a. Souvenir sheet of 3, #391-393 3.50 3.50
Nos. 391-393 (3) 3.25 3.25

London 1980 International Stamp Exhibition, May 6-14.

Queen Mother Elizabeth, 80th Birthday — A54

1980, Aug. 4 Litho. *Perf. 14*
394 A54 35c multicolored .50 .20
395 A54 50c multicolored .75 .30
396 A54 $1.50 multicolored 1.25 .90
397 A54 $3 multicolored 3.00 1.75
a. Souvenir sheet of 4, #394-397 6.00 6.00
Nos. 394-397 (4) 5.50 3.15

> *Anguilla stamps can be mounted in the annual Scott Anguilla supplement.*

Pelicans — A55

1980, Nov. 10 Litho. *Perf. 14*
398 A55 5c shown .50 .20
399 A55 22c Great gray herons 1.25 .25
400 A55 $1.50 Swallows 2.25 1.50
401 A55 $3 Hummingbirds 3.00 2.00
a. Souvenir sheet of 4, #398-401 11.00 9.00
Nos. 398-401 (4) 7.00 3.95

Christmas. For overprints see #405-406.

Nos. 275, 278, 280-290, 334, 400-401 Overprinted: "SEPARATION 1980"

Perf. 13½x14, 14 (A55)

1980, Dec. 18 Litho.
402 A40 1c #275 .20 .20
403 A40 2c on 4c #278 .20 .20
404 A40 5c on 15c #282 .20 .20
405 A55 5c on $1.50 #400 .20 .20
406 A55 5c on $3 #401 .20 .20
407 A40 10c #281 .20 .20
408 A40 12c on $1 #287 .20 .20
409 A40 14c on $2.50 #288 .20 .20
410 A40 15c #282 .20 .20
411 A40 18c on $5 #289 .20 .20
412 A40 20c #283 .20 .20
413 A40 22c #284 .20 .20
414 A40 25c on 15c #282 .20 .20
415 A40 35c #285 .25 .25
416 A44 38c on 22c #334 .30 .30
417 A40 40c on 1c #275 .30 .30
418 A40 50c #286 .40 .40
419 A40 $1 #287 .65 .65
420 A40 $2.50 #288 1.50 2.00
421 A40 $5 #289 3.75 4.00
422 A40 $10 #290 7.50 8.00
423 A40 $10 on 6c #280 7.50 8.00
Nos. 402-423 (22) 24.75 26.50

Petition for Separation, 1825 — A56

1980, Dec. 18 *Perf. 14*
424 A56 18c shown .20 .20
425 A56 22c Referendum ballot, 1967 .20 .20
426 A56 35c Airport blockade, 1967 .25 .25
427 A56 50c Anguilla flag .30 .30
428 A56 $1 Separation celebration, 1980 .50 .50
a. Souvenir sheet of 5, #424-428 1.50 1.60
Nos. 424-428 (5) 1.45 1.45

Separation from St. Kitts-Nevis.

Nelson's Dockyard, by R. Granger Barrett A57

Ship Paintings: 35c, Agamemnon, Vanguard, Elephant, Captain and Victory, by Nicholas Pocock. 50c, Victory, by Monamy Swaine. $3, Battle of Trafalgar, by Clarkson Stanfield. $5, Lord Nelson, by L.F. Abbott and Nelson's arms.

1981, Mar. 2 Litho. *Perf. 14*
429 A57 22c multicolored 1.25 .75
430 A57 35c multicolored 1.50 1.00
431 A57 50c multicolored 2.00 1.25
432 A57 $3 multicolored 2.50 1.75
Nos. 429-432 (4) 7.25 4.75

Souvenir Sheet

433 A57 $5 multicolored 4.50 4.50

Lord Horatio Nelson (1758-1805), 175th death anniversary (1980).

Minnie Mouse — A58

Easter: Various Disney characters in Easter outfits.

1981, Mar. 30 Litho. *Perf. 13½*
434 A58 1c multicolored .20 .20
435 A58 2c multicolored .20 .20
436 A58 3c multicolored .20 .20
437 A58 5c multicolored .20 .20
438 A58 7c multicolored .20 .20
439 A58 9c multicolored .20 .20
440 A58 10c multicolored .20 .20
441 A58 $2 multicolored 1.50 1.50
442 A58 $3 multicolored 2.00 2.00
Nos. 434-442 (9) 4.90 4.90

Souvenir Sheet

443 A58 $5 multicolored 5.50 5.50

Prince Charles, Lady Diana, St. Paul's Cathedral A59

1981, June 15 Litho. *Perf. 14*
444 A59 50c shown .20 .25
a. Souvenir sheet of 2 .30 .30
b. Wmk. 380 .30 .30
c. Booklet pane of 4 #444b 1.25 1.25
445 A59 $2.50 Althorp .45 .60
a. Souvenir sheet of 2 1.60 1.60
446 A59 $3 Windsor Castle .55 .75
a. Souvenir sheet of 2 2.00 2.00
b. Wmk. 380 2.00 2.00
c. Booklet pane of 4 #446b 8.00 8.00
Nos. 444-446 (3) 1.20 1.60

Souvenir Sheet

447 A59 $5 Buckingham Palace 2.00 2.00

Royal Wedding. Nos. 444a-446a contain stamps in different colors.

Boys Climbing Tree A60

1981 Litho. *Perf. 14*
448 A60 5c shown .20 .20
449 A60 10c Boys sailing boats .25 .25
450 A60 15c Children playing instruments .35 .35
451 A60 $3 Children with animals 2.50 2.50
Nos. 448-451 (4) 3.30 3.30

Souvenir Sheet

452 A60 $4 Boys playing soccer, vert. 5.00 5.00

UNICEF, 35th anniv.
Issued: 5c-15c, July 31; $3-$4, Sept. 30.

"The Children were Nestled all Snug in their Beds" — A61

Christmas: Scenes from Walt Disney's The Night Before Christmas.

1981, Nov. 2 Litho. *Perf. 13½*
453 A61 1c multicolored .20 .20
454 A61 2c multicolored .20 .20
455 A61 3c multicolored .20 .20

456 A61 5c multicolored .20 .20
457 A61 7c multicolored .20 .20
458 A61 10c multicolored .20 .20
459 A61 12c multicolored .20 .20
460 A61 $2 multicolored 3.00 1.75
461 A61 $3 multicolored 3.00 2.25
Nos. 453-461 (9) 7.40 5.40

Souvenir Sheet

462 A61 $5 multicolored 6.00 6.00

Red Grouper — A62

1982, Jan. 1 Litho. *Perf. 14*

463 A62 1c shown .20 *.60*
464 A62 5c Ferries, Blowing Point .35 *.60*
465 A62 10c Racing boats .25 *.60*
466 A62 15c Majorettes .25 *.60*
467 A62 20c Launching boat, Sandy Hill .45 *.60*
468 A62 25c Coral 1.50 .60
469 A62 30c Little Bay cliffs .35 *.75*
470 A62 35c Fountain Cave 1.50 .80
471 A62 40c Sandy Isld. .35 *.75*
472 A62 45c Landing, Sombrero .60 *.80*
473 A62 50c on 45c, #472 .60 .35
474 A62 60c Seine fishing 3.75 2.25
475 A62 75c Boat race, Sandy Ground 1.00 *1.75*
476 A62 $1 Bagging lobster, Island Harbor 2.75 1.75
477 A62 $5 Pelicans 17.00 10.00
478 A62 $7.50 Hibiscus 13.00 11.00
479 A62 $10 Queen triggerfish 15.00 12.00
Nos. 463-479 (17) 58.90 45.80

For overprints and surcharges see Nos. 507-510, 546A-546D, 578-582, 606-608, 640-647.

Easter — A63

Princess Diana, 21st Birthday — A64

Designs: Butterflies on flowers.

1982, Apr. 5

480 A63 10c Zebra, anthurium .50 .20
481 A63 35c Caribbean buckeye 1.25 .35
482 A63 75c Monarch, allamanda 1.50 .75
483 A63 $3 Red rim, orchid 2.25 2.25
Nos. 480-483 (4) 5.50 3.55

Souvenir Sheet

484 A63 $5 Flambeau, amaryllis 4.25 4.25

1982, May 17

Designs: Portraits, 1961-1981.

485 A64 10c 1961 .20 .20
486 A64 30c 1968 .20 .20
487 A64 40c 1970 .25 .25
488 A64 60c 1974 .40 .40
489 A64 $2 1981 1.40 1.40
490 A64 $3 1981 2.00 2.00
a. Souvenir sheet of 6, #485-490 4.50 4.50
Nos. 485-490 (6) 4.45 4.45

Souvenir Sheet

491 A64 $5 1981 5.00 5.00

For overprints see Nos. 639A-639G.

1982 World Cup — A65

Designs: Various Disney characters playing soccer.

1982, Aug. 3 Litho. *Perf. 11*

492 A65 1c multicolored .20 .20
493 A65 3c multicolored .20 .20
494 A65 4c multicolored .20 .20
495 A65 5c multicolored .20 .20
496 A65 7c multicolored .20 .20
497 A65 9c multicolored .20 .20
498 A65 10c multicolored .20 .20
499 A65 $2.50 multicolored 2.50 2.25
500 A65 $3 multicolored 2.50 2.25
Nos. 492-500 (9) 6.40 5.90

Souvenir Sheet

Perf. 14

501 A65 $5 multicolored 7.00 7.00

Scouting Year A66

1982, July 5

502 A66 10c Pitching tent .60 .50
503 A66 35c Marching band 1.00 .75
504 A66 75c Sailing 1.50 1.25
505 A66 $3 Flag bearers 4.00 3.00
Nos. 502-505 (4) 7.10 5.50

Souvenir Sheet

506 A66 $5 Camping 6.00 6.00

Nos. 465, 474-475, 477 Overprinted: "COMMONWEALTH / GAMES 1982"

1982, Oct. 18 Litho. *Perf. 14*

507 A62 10c multicolored .20 .20
508 A62 60c multicolored .55 .55
509 A62 75c multicolored .75 .75
510 A62 $5 multicolored 4.00 4.00
Nos. 507-510 (4) 5.50 5.50

12th Commonwealth Games, Brisbane, Australia, Sept. 30-Oct. 9.

Christmas — A67

Scenes from Walt Disney's Winnie the Pooh.

1982, Nov. 29

511 A67 1c multicolored .20 .20
512 A67 2c multicolored .20 .20
513 A67 3c multicolored .20 .20
514 A67 5c multicolored .25 .20
515 A67 7c multicolored .25 .20
516 A67 10c multicolored .25 .20
517 A67 12c multicolored .35 .25
518 A67 20c multicolored .60 .50
519 A67 $5 multicolored 6.00 5.00
Nos. 511-519 (9) 8.30 6.95

Souvenir Sheet

520 A67 $5 multicolored 7.50 7.50

Commonwealth Day (Mar. 14) — A68

1983, Feb. 28 Litho. *Perf. 14*

521 A68 10c Carnival procession .20 .20
522 A68 35c Flags .50 .50
523 A68 75c Economic cooperation 1.00 1.00
524 A68 $2.50 Salt pond 4.00 4.00
Nos. 521-524 (4) 5.70 5.70

Souvenir Sheet

525 A68 $5 Map showing Commonwealth 4.50 4.00

Easter — A69

Ten Commandments.

1983, Mar. 31 Litho. *Perf. 14*

526 A69 1c multicolored .20 .20
527 A69 2c multicolored .20 .20
528 A69 3c multicolored .20 .20
529 A69 10c multicolored .25 .20
530 A69 35c multicolored .55 .30
531 A69 60c multicolored 1.00 .50
532 A69 75c multicolored 1.10 .55
533 A69 $2 multicolored 2.75 2.00
534 A69 $2.50 multicolored 3.00 2.00
535 A69 $5 multicolored 4.75 3.00
Nos. 526-535 (10) 14.00 9.15

Souvenir Sheet

536 A69 $5 Moses Taking Tablets 4.00 4.00

Local Turtles and World Wildlife Fund Emblem — A70

1983, Aug. 10 Litho. *Perf. 13½*

537 A70 10c Leatherback *2.00 1.00*
538 A70 35c Hawksbill *4.00 2.00*
539 A70 75c Green *5.50 2.75*
540 A70 $1 Loggerhead *6.50 3.25*
Nos. 537-540 (4) *18.00 9.00*

Souvenir Sheet

541 A70 $5 Leatherback, diff. *11.00 5.50*

1983, Aug. 10 Litho. *Perf. 12*

537a A70 10c Leatherback *2.00 1.00*
538a A70 35c Hawksbill *7.00 3.50*
539a A70 75c Green *9.00 4.50*
540a A70 $1 Loggerhead *11.00 5.50*
Nos. 537a-540a (4) *29.00 14.50*

Manned Flight Bicentenary — A71

1983, Aug. 22 *Perf. 14*

542 A71 10c Montgolfiere, 1783 .35 .25
543 A71 60c Blanchard & Jeffries, 1785 1.00 .60
544 A71 $1 Giffard's airship, 1852 1.50 1.00
545 A71 $2.50 Lilienthal's glider, 1890 2.25 1.75
Nos. 542-545 (4) 5.10 3.60

Souvenir Sheet

546 A71 $5 Wright Brothers' plane, 1909 4.00 4.00

Nos. 465, 471, 476-477 Overprinted: 150TH ANNIVERSARY / ABOLITION OF SLAVERY ACT

1983, Oct. 24 Litho. *Perf. 14*

546A A62 10c Racing boats .20 .20
546B A62 40c Sandy Isld. .40 .35
546C A62 $1 Bagging lobster, Island Harbor 1.00 .90
546D A62 $5 Pelicans 4.75 4.50
Nos. 546A-546D (4) 6.35 5.95

Jiminy Cricket — A72

Designs: Various Disney productions.

1983, Nov. 14 *Perf. 13½*

547 A72 1c shown .20 .20
548 A72 2c Jiminy Cricket, kettle .20 .20
549 A72 3c Jiminy Cricket, toys .20 .20
550 A72 4c Mickey and Morty .20 .20
551 A72 5c Scrooge McDuck .20 .20
552 A72 6c Minnie and Goofy .20 .20
553 A72 10c Goofy and Elf .20 .20
554 A72 $2 Scrooge McDuck, diff. 3.00 2.25
555 A72 $3 Disney characters 3.50 2.50
Nos. 547-555 (9) 7.90 6.15

Souvenir Sheet

556 A72 $5 Scrooge McDuck 7.50 7.50

Boys' Brigade Centenary — A73

1983, Sept. 12 Litho. *Perf. 14*

557 A73 10c Anguilla company, banner .25 .25
558 A73 $5 Marching with drummer 4.25 4.25
a. Souvenir sheet of 2, #557-558 4.00 4.00

1984 Olympics, Los Angeles — A74

Mickey Mouse Competing in Decathlon.

1984, Feb. 20 Litho. *Perf. 14*

559 A74 1c 100-meter run .20 .20
560 A74 2c Long jump .20 .20
561 A74 3c Shot put .20 .20
562 A74 4c High jump .20 .20
563 A74 5c 400-meter run .20 .20
564 A74 6c Hurdles .20 .20
565 A74 10c Discus .20 .20
566 A74 $1 Pole vault 2.50 2.50
567 A74 $4 Javelin 4.50 4.50
Nos. 559-567 (9) 8.40 8.40

Souvenir Sheet

568 A74 $5 1500-meter run 8.00 8.00

1984, Apr. 24 *Perf. 12½x12*

559a A74 1c .20 .20
560a A74 2c .20 .20
561a A74 3c .20 .20
562a A74 4c .20 .20
563a A74 5c .20 .20
564a A74 6c .20 .20
565a A74 10c .20 .20
566a A74 $1 3.00 3.00
567a A74 $4 5.50 5.50
Nos. 559a-567a (9) 9.90 9.90

Souvenir Sheet

568a A74 $5 With Olympic rings emblem 8.00 8.00

Nos. 559a-567a inscribed with Olympic rings emblem. Printed in sheets of 5 plus label.

Easter — A75

Ceiling and Wall Frescoes, La Stanze della Segnatura, by Raphael (details).

1984, Apr. 19 Litho. Perf. 13½x14

569 A75 10c Justice .20 .20
570 A75 25c Poetry .30 .30
571 A75 35c Philosophy .40 .40
572 A75 40c Theology .40 .40
573 A75 $1 Abraham & Paul 1.10 1.10
574 A75 $2 Moses & Matthew 2.25 2.25
575 A75 $3 John & David 3.00 3.00
576 A75 $4 Peter & Adam 3.50 3.50
Nos. 569-576 (8) 11.15 11.15

Souvenir Sheet

577 A75 $5 Astronomy 4.50 4.50

Nos. 463, 469, 477-479 Surcharged

1984 Litho. Perf. 14

578 A62 25c on $7.50 #478 .45 .45
579 A62 35c on 30c #469 .50 .50
580 A62 60c on 1c #463 .55 .55
581 A62 $2.50 on $5 #477 2.25 2.25
582 A62 $2.50 on $10 #479 1.75 1.75
Nos. 578-582 (5) 5.50 5.50

Issue dates: 25c, May 17, others, Apr. 24.

Ausipex '84 A76

Australian stamps.

1984, July 16 Litho. Perf. 13½

583 A76 10c No. 2 .40 .40
584 A76 75c No. 18 1.25 1.25
585 A76 $1 No. 130 1.75 1.75
586 A76 $2.50 No. 178 2.25 2.25
Nos. 583-586 (4) 5.65 5.65

Souvenir Sheet

587 A76 $5 Nos. 378, 379 5.50 5.50

Slavery Abolition Sesquicentennial — A77

Abolitionists and Vignettes: 10c, Thomas Fowell Buxton, planting sugar cane. 25c, Abraham Lincoln, cotton field. 35c, Henri Christophe, armed slave revolt. 60c, Thomas Clarkson, addressing Anti-Slavery Society. 75c, William Wilberforce, Slave auction. $1, Olaudah Equiano, slave raid on Benin coast. $2.50, General Gordon, slave convoy in Sudan. $5, Granville Sharp, restraining ship captain from boarding slave.

1984, Aug. 1 Perf. 12

588 A77 10c multicolored .20 .20
589 A77 25c multicolored .35 .35
590 A77 35c multicolored .50 .50
591 A77 60c multicolored .65 .65
592 A77 75c multicolored .90 .90
593 A77 $1 multicolored 1.00 1.00
594 A77 $2.50 multicolored 2.00 2.00
595 A77 $5 multicolored 4.00 4.00
a. Miniature sheet of 8, #588-595 9.50 9.50
Nos. 588-595 (8) 9.60 9.60

For overprints see Nos. 688-695a.

Christmas — A78

Various Disney characters and celebrations.

Perf. 14, 12½x12 ($2)

1984, Nov. 12 Litho.

596 A78 1c multicolored .20 .20
597 A78 2c multicolored .20 .20
598 A78 3c multicolored .20 .20
599 A78 4c multicolored .20 .20
600 A78 5c multicolored .20 .20
601 A78 10c multicolored .20 .20
602 A78 $1 multicolored 2.75 2.50
603 A78 $2 multicolored 3.50 3.25
604 A78 $4 multicolored 5.50 5.00
Nos. 596-604 (9) 12.95 11.95

Souvenir Sheet

605 A78 $5 multicolored 7.50 7.50

Nos. 464-465, 477 Overprinted or Surcharged: "U.P.U. CONGRESS / HAMBURG 1984"

1984, Aug. 13

606 A62 5c #464 .30 .20
607 A62 20c on 10c #465 .45 .30
608 A62 $5 #477 6.00 4.00
Nos. 606-608 (3) 6.75 4.50

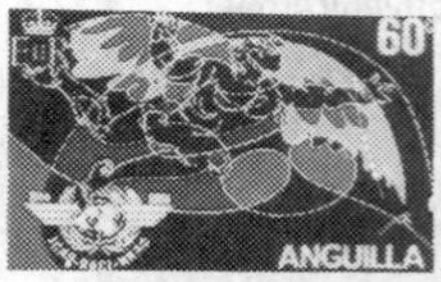

Intl. Civil Aviation Org., 40th Anniv. A79

1984, Dec. 3 Litho. Perf. 14

609 A79 60c Icarus, by Hans Erni .75 .75
610 A79 75c Sun Princess, by Sadiou Diouf 1.00 1.00
611 A79 $2.50 Anniv. emblem, vert. 2.50 2.50
Nos. 609-611 (3) 4.25 4.25

Souvenir Sheet

612 A79 $5 Map of the Caribbean 4.50 4.50

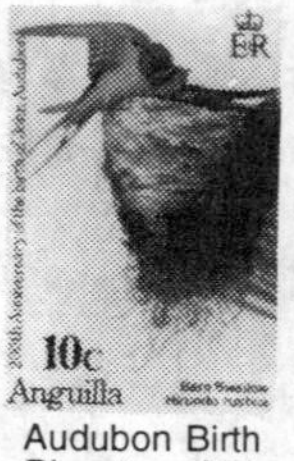

Audubon Birth Bicent. — A80

Queen Mother 85th Birthday — A81

Illustrations by artist and naturalist J. J. Audubon (1785-1851).

1985, Apr. 30 Litho. Perf. 14

613 A80 10c Hirundo rustica .60 .50
614 A80 60c Mycteria americana 1.10 1.00
615 A80 75c Sterna dougallii 1.10 1.00
616 A80 $5 Pandion haliaetus 4.25 3.75
Nos. 613-616 (4) 7.05 6.25

Souvenir Sheets

617 A80 $4 Vireo solitarus, horiz. 3.75 3.75
618 A80 $4 Piranga ludoviciana, horiz. 3.75 3.75

1985, July 2

Photographs: 10c, Visiting the children's ward at King's College Hospital. $2, Inspecting Royal Marine Volunteer Cadets at Deal. $3, Outside Clarence House in London. $5, In an open carriage at Ascot.

619 A81 10c multicolored .20 .20
620 A81 $2 multicolored 1.25 1.25
621 A81 $3 multicolored 1.90 1.90
Nos. 619-621 (3) 3.35 3.35

Souvenir Sheet

622 A81 $5 multicolored 3.25 3.25

Nos. 619-621 printed in sheetlets of 5.

Birds A82

1985-86 Litho. Perf. 13½x14

623 A82 5c Brown pelican 1.00 1.00
624 A82 10c Turtle dove 1.00 1.00
625 A82 15c Man-o-war 1.00 1.00
626 A82 20c Antillean crested hummingbird 1.00 1.00
627 A82 25c White-tailed tropicbird 1.25 1.25
628 A82 30c Caribbean elaenia 1.25 1.25
629 A82 35c Black-whiskered vireo 5.50 5.00
629A A82 35c Lesser Antillean bullfinch ('86) 1.25 1.25
630 A82 40c Yellow-crowned night heron 1.25 1.25
631 A82 45c Pearly-eyed thrasher 1.25 1.25
632 A82 50c Laughing bird 1.25 1.25
633 A82 65c Brown booby 1.25 1.25
634 A82 80c Gray kingbird 2.00 2.75
635 A82 $1 Audubon's shearwater 2.00 2.75
636 A82 $1.35 Roseate tern 1.50 2.75
637 A82 $2.50 Bananaquit 4.50 6.00
638 A82 $5 Belted kingfisher 3.75 7.00
639 A82 $10 Green heron 6.50 9.00
Nos. 623-639 (18) 38.50 48.00

Issued: 25c, 65c, $1.35, $5, 7/22; 45c, 50c, 80c, $1, $10, 9/30; 5c-20c, 30c, #629, 40c, $2.50, 11/11; #629A, 3/10.

For overprints and surcharges see Nos. 678-682, 713-716, 723-739, 750-753, 764-767.

Nos. 485-491 Overprinted "PRINCE HENRY / BIRTH 15.9.84."

1985, Oct. 31 Litho. Perf. 14

639A A64 10c multicolored .20 .20
639B A64 30c multicolored .20 .20
639C A64 40c multicolored .30 .30
639D A64 60c multicolored .45 .45
639E A64 $2 multicolored 1.50 1.50
639F A64 $3 multicolored 4.25 4.25
h. Souv. sheet of 6, #639A-639F 4.80 4.80
Nos. 639A-639F (6) 6.90 6.90

Souvenir Sheet

639G A64 $5 multicolored 3.50 3.50

Nos. 464, 469 and 477 Ovptd. with Anniversary Emblem and "GIRL GUIDES 75th ANNIVERSARY / 1910-1985"

1985, Oct. 14 Litho. Perf. 14

640 A62 5c multicolored .20 .20
641 A62 30c multicolored .40 .30
642 A62 75c multicolored .55 .50
643 A62 $5 multicolored 6.00 5.00
Nos. 640-643 (4) 7.15 6.00

Nos. 465 and 470 Overprinted or Surcharged with Organization Emblem and "80th ANNIVERSARY ROTARY 1985."

1985, Nov. 18

644 A62 10c multicolored .20 .20
645 A62 35c on 30c multi .30 .30

Nos. 476, 469 Surcharged or Ovptd. with Emblem, Text and "INTERNATIONAL YOUTH YEAR"

1985, Nov. 18

646 A62 $1 multicolored 1.00 1.00
647 A62 $5 on 30c multi 4.50 4.50

Brothers Grimm — A83

Christmas: Disney characters in Hansel and Gretel.

1985, Nov. 11 Litho. Perf. 14

648 A83 5c multicolored .20 .20
649 A83 50c multicolored .75 .70
650 A83 90c multicolored 1.25 1.10
651 A83 $4 multicolored 3.50 3.25
Nos. 648-651 (4) 5.70 5.25

Souvenir Sheet

652 A83 $5 multicolored 6.25 6.25

Mark Twain (1835-1910), Author — A84

Disney characters in Huckleberry Finn.

1985, Nov. 11

653 A84 10c multicolored .30 .30
654 A84 60c multicolored 1.10 1.10
654A A84 $1 multicolored 1.75 1.75
655 A84 $3 multicolored 3.50 3.50
Nos. 653-655 (4) 6.65 6.65

Souvenir Sheet

656 A84 $5 multicolored 6.75 6.75

Christmas. No. 654A printed in sheets of 8.

Statue of Liberty Centennial A85

1985, Nov. 25

657 A85 10c Danmark, Denmark .55 .65
658 A85 20c Eagle, USA .75 .90
659 A85 60c Amerigo Vespucci, Italy 1.40 1.50
660 A85 75c Sir Winston Churchill, G.B. 1.40 1.50
661 A85 $2 Nippon Maru, Japan 2.00 2.25
662 A85 $2.50 Gorch, Germany 2.25 2.50
Nos. 657-662 (6) 8.35 9.30

Souvenir Sheet

663 A85 $5 Statue of Liberty, vert. 7.25 6.00

Easter — A86

Stained glass windows.

1986, Mar. 27 Litho. Perf. 14

664 A86 10c multicolored .25 .25
665 A86 25c multicolored .45 .45
666 A86 45c multicolored .80 .80
667 A86 $4 multicolored 4.00 4.00
Nos. 664-667 (4) 5.50 5.50

Souvenir Sheet

668 A86 $5 multi, horiz. 6.25 6.25

A87

Halley's Comet A88

Designs: 5c, Johannes Hevelius (1611-1687), Mayan temple observatory. 10c, US Viking probe landing on Mars, 1976. 60c, Theatri Cosmicum (detail), 1668. $4, Sighting, 1835. $5, Comet over Anguilla.

1986, Mar. 24

669	A87	5c	multicolored	.25	.25
670	A87	10c	multicolored	.30	.30
671	A87	60c	multicolored	1.00	1.00
672	A87	$4	multicolored	4.00	4.00
			Nos. 669-672 (4)	5.55	5.55

Souvenir Sheet

673	A88	$5	multicolored	5.25	5.25

Queen Elizabeth II, 60th Birthday
Common Design Type

1986, Apr. 21

674	CD339	20c	Inspecting guards, 1946	.20	.20
675	CD339	$2	Garter Ceremony, 1985	1.75	1.75
676	CD339	$3	Trooping the color	2.50	2.50
			Nos. 674-676 (3)	4.45	4.45

Souvenir Sheet

677	CD339	$5	Christening, 1926	4.50	4.50

Nos. 623, 631, 635, 637 and 639 Ovptd. "AMERIPEX 1986"

1986, May 22 ***Perf. 13½x14***

678	A82	5c	multicolored	.45	.45
679	A82	45c	multicolored	.75	.75
680	A82	$1	multicolored	1.40	1.40
681	A82	$2.50	multicolored	2.50	2.50
682	A82	$10	multicolored	6.50	6.50
			Nos. 678-682 (5)	11.60	11.60

Wedding of Prince Andrew and Sarah Ferguson — A89

1986, July 23 Litho. ***Perf. 14, 12***

683	A89	10c	Couple	.20	.25
684	A89	35c	Andrew	.25	.30
685	A89	$2	Sarah	1.50	1.75
686	A89	$3	Couple, diff.	2.25	2.75
			Nos. 683-686 (4)	4.20	5.05

Souvenir Sheet

687	A89	$6	Westminster Abbey	7.00	7.00

Nos. 588-595 Ovptd. "INTERNATIONAL / YEAR OF / PEACE"

1986, Sept. 29 Litho. ***Perf. 12***

688	A77	10c	multicolored	.30	.30
689	A77	25c	multicolored	.50	.50
690	A77	35c	multicolored	.60	.60
691	A77	60c	multicolored	.90	.90
692	A77	75c	multicolored	1.10	1.10
693	A77	$1	multicolored	1.25	1.25
694	A77	$2.50	multicolored	2.25	2.25
695	A77	$5	multicolored	3.50	3.50
a.			Miniature sheet of 8, #688-695	12.50	12.50
			Nos. 688-695 (8)	10.40	10.40

Ships A90

1986, Nov. 29 Litho. ***Perf. 14***

696	A90	10c	Trading Sloop	.75	.75
697	A90	45c	Lady Rodney	1.25	1.25
698	A90	80c	West Derby	1.75	1.75
699	A90	$3	Warspite	3.50	3.50
			Nos. 696-699 (4)	7.25	7.25

Souvenir Sheet

700	A90	$6	Boat Race Day, vert.	10.00	10.00

Christmas.

Discovery of America, 500th Anniv. (in 1992) — A91

Dragon Tree — A92

5c, Christopher Columbus, astrolabe. 10c, Aboard ship. 35c, Santa Maria. 80c, Ferdinand, Isabella. $4, Indians. No. 707, Caribbean manatee.

1986, Dec. 22

701	A91	5c	multi	.30	*.35*
702	A91	10c	multi	.50	*.55*
703	A91	35c	multi	1.25	*1.40*
704	A91	80c	multi, horiz.	1.50	*1.75*
705	A91	$4	multi	3.25	*3.50*
			Nos. 701-705 (5)	6.80	*7.55*

Souvenir Sheets

706	A92	$5	shown	6.50	6.50
707	A92	$5	multi, horiz.	6.50	6.50

Butterflies A93

1987, Apr. 14 Litho. ***Perf. 14***

708	A93	10c	Monarch	.75	.75
709	A93	80c	White peacock	2.25	2.25
710	A93	$1	Zebra	2.50	2.50
711	A93	$2	Caribbean buckeye	4.00	4.00
			Nos. 708-711 (4)	9.50	9.50

Souvenir Sheet

712	A93	$6	Flambeau	9.00	9.00

Easter.

Nos. 629A, 631, 634 and 639 Ovptd. with CAPEX '87 Emblem in Red

1987, May 25 Litho. ***Perf. 13½x14***

713	A82	35c	on No. 629A	.75	*.80*
714	A82	45c	on No. 631	.85	*.90*
715	A82	80c	on No. 634	1.25	*1.40*
716	A82	$10	on No. 639	7.00	*7.50*
			Nos. 713-716 (4)	9.85	10.60

Separation from St. Kitts and Nevis, 20th Anniv. — A94

Designs: 10c, Old goose iron, electric iron. 35c, Old East End School, Albena Lake-Hodge Comprehensive College. 45c, Old market place, People's Market. 80c, Old ferries and modern ferry at Blowing Point. $1, Old and new cable and wireless offices. $2, Public meeting at Burrowes Park, House of Assembly.

1987, May 25 ***Perf. 14***

717	A94	10c	multicolored	.20	.20
718	A94	35c	multicolored	.30	.30
719	A94	45c	multicolored	.35	.35
720	A94	80c	multicolored	.65	.65
721	A94	$1	multicolored	.80	.80
722	A94	$2	multicolored	1.75	1.75
a.			Souvenir sheet of 6, #717-722	5.25	5.25
			Nos. 717-722 (6)	4.05	4.05

Nos. 623, 625-628, 629A-639 Ovptd. "20 YEARS OF PROGRESS / 1967-1987" in Red or Surcharged in Red & Black

1987, Sept. 4 Litho. ***Perf. 13½x14***

723	A82	5c	No. 623	.75	*.80*
724	A82	10c	on 15c No. 625	.75	*.80*
725	A82	15c	No. 625	1.00	*1.10*
726	A82	20c	No. 626	1.00	*1.10*
727	A82	25c	No. 627	1.00	*1.10*
728	A82	30c	No. 628	1.00	*1.10*
729	A82	35c	No. 629A	1.00	*1.10*
730	A82	40c	No. 630	1.00	*1.10*
731	A82	45c	No. 631	1.00	*1.10*
732	A82	50c	No. 632	1.00	*1.10*
733	A82	65c	No. 633	1.40	*1.50*
734	A82	80c	No. 634	1.50	*1.60*
735	A82	$1	No. 635	1.60	*1.75*
736	A82	$1.35	No. 636	2.00	*2.25*
737	A82	$2.50	No. 637	2.25	*2.50*
738	A82	$5	No. 638	3.50	*3.75*
739	A82	$10	No. 639	6.00	*6.50*
			Nos. 723-739 (17)	27.75	*30.25*

Cricket World Cup A95

Various action scenes.

1987, Oct. 5 ***Perf. 14***

740	A95	10c	multicolored	.65	.60
741	A95	35c	multicolored	1.10	1.00
742	A95	45c	multicolored	1.25	1.10
743	A95	$2.50	multicolored	3.00	2.75
			Nos. 740-743 (4)	6.00	5.45

Souvenir Sheet

744	A95	$6	multicolored	8.00	*8.50*

Sea Shells, Crabs A96

1987, Nov. 2

745	A96	10c	West Indian top shell	.50	.50
746	A96	35c	Ghost crab	.80	.80
747	A96	50c	Spiny Caribbean vase	1.50	1.50
748	A96	$2	Great land crab	2.50	2.50
			Nos. 745-748 (4)	5.30	5.30

Souvenir Sheet

749	A96	$6	Queen conch	7.00	*7.50*

Christmas.

Nos. 629A, 635-636 and 639 Ovptd. "40TH WEDDING ANNIVERSARY / H.M. QUEEN ELIZABETH II / H.R.H. THE DUKE OF EDINBURGH" in Scarlet

1987, Dec. 14 Litho. ***Perf. 13½x14***

750	A82	35c	multicolored	.30	.30
751	A82	$1	multicolored	.70	.75
752	A82	$1.35	multicolored	1.00	1.00
753	A82	$10	multicolored	7.00	7.50
			Nos. 750-753 (4)	9.00	9.55

Easter (Lilies) — A97

1988 Summer Olympics, Seoul — A98

1988, Mar. 28 Litho. ***Perf. 14***

754	A97	30c	Crinum erubescens	.30	.30
755	A97	45c	Hymenocallis caribaea	.40	.40
756	A97	$1	Crinum macowanii	.90	.90
757	A97	$2.50	Hemerocallis fulva	2.25	2.25
			Nos. 754-757 (4)	3.85	3.85

Souvenir Sheet

758	A97	$6	Lilium longiflorum	5.00	*5.50*

1988, July 25 Litho. ***Perf. 14***

759	A98	35c	4x100-Meter relay	.30	.25
760	A98	45c	Windsurfing	.45	.40
761	A98	50c	Tennis	1.10	1.00
762	A98	80c	Basketball	2.00	1.75
			Nos. 759-762 (4)	3.85	3.40

Souvenir Sheet

763	A98	$6	Women's 200 meters	5.00	*6.00*

Nos. 629A, 634-635 and 637 Ovptd. "H.R.H. PRINCESS / ALEXANDRA'S / VISIT NOVEMBER 1988"

1988, Dec. 14 Litho. ***Perf. 13½x14***

764	A82	35c	multicolored	.75	*.60*
765	A82	80c	multicolored	1.25	*1.40*
766	A82	$1	multicolored	1.50	*1.60*
767	A82	$2.50	multicolored	2.50	*2.75*
			Nos. 764-767 (4)	6.00	*6.35*

Marine Life A99

1988, Dec. 5 Litho. ***Perf. 14***

768	A99	35c	Common sea fan	.35	.35
769	A99	80c	Coral crab	.75	.75
770	A99	$1	Grooved brain coral	1.00	1.00
771	A99	$1.60	Old wife	1.75	1.75
			Nos. 768-771 (4)	3.85	3.85

Souvenir Sheet

772	A99	$6	West Indies spiny lobster	5.00	5.00

Christmas.

Lizards A100

1989, Feb. 20 Litho. ***Perf. 13½x14***

773	A100	45c	Wood slave	.50	.35
774	A100	80c	Slippery back	.75	.70
775	A100	$2.50	Iguana	2.25	*2.75*
			Nos. 773-775 (3)	3.50	*3.80*

Souvenir Sheet

776	A100	$6	Tree lizard	4.75	*5.00*

Easter — A101

Paintings: 35c, Christ Crowned with Thorns, by Hieronymous Bosch (c. 1450-1516. 80c, Christ Bearing the Cross, by David. $1, The Deposition, by David. $1.60, Pieta, by Rogier van der Weyden (1400-1464). $6, Crucified Christ with the Virgin Mary and Saints, by Raphael.

1989, Mar. 23 Litho. ***Perf. 14x13½***

777	A101	35c	multicolored	.30	*.35*
778	A101	80c	multicolored	.60	*.70*
779	A101	$1	multicolored	.75	.75
780	A101	$1.60	multicolored	1.25	*1.75*
			Nos. 777-780 (4)	2.90	*3.55*

Souvenir Sheet

781	A101	$6	multicolored	4.75	*5.50*

University of the West Indies, 40th Anniv. — A102

1989, Apr. 24 Litho. *Perf. 14x13½*
782 A102 $5 Coat of arms 4.00 *4.50*

Nos. 634-636 and 638 Ovptd. "20th / ANNIVERSARY / MOON / LANDING"

1989, July 3 Litho. *Perf. 13½X14*
783 A82 80c multicolored .60 .60
784 A82 $1 multicolored .75 .75
785 A82 $1.35 multicolored 1.00 1.00
786 A82 $5 multicolored 3.75 3.75
Nos. 783-786 (4) 6.10 6.10

Christmas — A103

Well-known and historic houses.

1989, Dec. 4 Litho. *Perf. 13½x14*
787 A103 5c Lone Star, 1930 .20 .20
788 A103 35c Whitehouse, 1906 .30 .30
789 A103 45c Hodges House .35 .35
790 A103 80c Warden's Place .60 .60
Nos. 787-790 (4) 1.45 1.45

Souvenir Sheet
791 A103 $6 Wallblake House, 1787 4.50 4.50

Fish A104

1990, Apr. 2 Litho. *Perf. 13½x14*
792 A104 5c Blear eye .20 .20
793 A104 10c Redman .20 .20
794 A104 15c Speckletail .20 .20
795 A104 25c Grunt .20 .20
796 A104 30c Amber jack .20 .20
797 A104 35c Red hind .25 .25
798 A104 40c Goatfish .30 .30
799 A104 45c Old wife .35 .35
800 A104 50c Butter fish .40 .40
801 A104 65c Shell fish .50 .50
802 A104 80c Yellowtail snapper .60 .60
803 A104 $1 Katy .75 .75
804 A104 $1.35 Mutton grouper 1.00 1.00
805 A104 $2.50 Doctor fish 1.90 1.90
806 A104 $5 Angelfish 3.75 3.75
807 A104 $10 Barracuda 7.50 7.50
Nos. 792-807 (16) 18.30 18.30

Nos. 792-793, 797 exist inscribed 1992. For overprints and surcharge see #821-824, 849.

Easter — A105

1990, Apr. 2 *Perf. 14x13½*
811 A105 35c Last Supper .25 .25
812 A105 45c Trial .35 .35
813 A105 $1.35 Calvary 1.00 1.00
814 A105 $2.50 Empty tomb 1.90 1.90
Nos. 811-814 (4) 3.50 3.50

Souvenir Sheet
815 A105 $6 The Resurrection 4.50 4.50

See Nos. 834-838.

Cape of Good Hope #7 A106

Stamps of Great Britain and exhibition emblem: 25c, #1, vert. 50c, #2, vert. $2.50, #93. $6, #1-2.

1990, Apr. 30 *Perf. 14*
816 A106 25c multicolored .20 .20
817 A106 50c multicolored .35 .35
818 A106 $1.50 shown 1.10 1.10
819 A106 $2.50 multicolored 1.90 1.90
Nos. 816-819 (4) 3.55 3.55

Souvenir Sheet
820 A106 $6 multicolored 4.50 4.50

Stamp World London '90, Penny Black 150th anniv.

Nos. 803-806 Overprinted:
a. EXPO '90
b. 1990 INTERNATIONAL / LITERACY YEAR
c. WORLD CUP FOOTBALL / CHAMPIONSHIPS 1990
d. 90TH BIRTHDAY / H.M. THE QUEEN MOTHER

1990, Sept. 24 Litho. *Perf. 13½x14*
821 A104(a) $1 Katy .75 .75
822 A104(b) $1.35 Mutton grouper 1.00 1.00
823 A104(c) $2.50 Doctor fish 1.90 1.90
824 A104(d) $5 Angelfish 3.75 3.75
Nos. 821-824 (4) 7.40 7.40

Christmas — A107

Birds.

1990, Dec. 3 *Perf. 14*
825 A107 10c Laughing gull .20 .20
826 A107 35c Brown booby .35 .35
827 A107 $1.50 Bridled tern 1.40 1.40
828 A107 $3.50 Brown pelican 3.50 3.50
Nos. 825-828 (4) 5.45 5.45

Souvenir Sheet
829 A107 $6 Least tern 7.00 7.00

Flags A108

1991, Nov. 5 Litho. *Perf. 13½x14*
830 A108 50c Mermaid .40 .40
831 A108 80c New Anguilla official .60 .60
832 A108 $1 Three dolphins .75 .75
833 A108 $5 Governor's official 3.75 3.75
Nos. 830-833 (4) 5.50 5.50

Nos. 811-815 Inscribed or Overprinted "1991"

1991, Apr. 30 Litho. *Perf. 14x13½*
834 A105 35c like #811 .25 .25
835 A105 45c like #812 .35 .35
836 A105 $1.35 like #813 1.00 1.00
837 A105 $2.50 like #814 1.90 1.90
Nos. 834-837 (4) 3.50 3.50

Souvenir Sheet
838 A105 $6 like #815 7.75 7.75

Easter. "1990" obliterated by black bar in souvenir sheet margin.

Christmas — A109

Perf. 14x13½, 13½x14
1991, Dec. Litho.
839 A109 5c Angel, vert. .20 .20
840 A109 35c Santa, vert. .25 .25
841 A109 80c shown .60 .60
842 A109 $1 Palm trees, poinsettias .75 .75
Nos. 839-842 (4) 1.80 1.80

Souvenir Sheet
843 A109 $5 Homes, holly 3.75 3.75

Easter A110

Designs: 35c, Church, angels holding palms, vert. 45c Church, angels singing, vert. 80c, Village. $1, People going to church, vert. $5, People at beach, sailboats.

1992 Litho. *Perf. 14*
844 A110 35c multicolored .30 .30
845 A110 45c multicolored .40 .40
846 A110 80c multicolored .70 .70
847 A110 $1 multicolored .85 .85
848 A110 $5 multicolored 4.25 4.25
Nos. 844-848 (5) 6.50 6.50

No. 796 Surcharged **$1.60**

1992, June 10 Litho. *Perf. 13½x14*
849 A104 $1.60 on 30c #796 1.40 1.40

No. 849 inscribed "1992."

Independence, 25th Anniv. — A111

1992, Aug. 10 Litho. *Perf. 14*
850 A111 80c Official seal, flag .60 .60
851 A111 $1 Official seal .70 .70
852 A111 $1.60 Flags, airport 1.25 1.25
853 A111 $2 First seal 1.40 1.40
Nos. 850-853 (4) 3.95 3.95

Souvenir Sheet
854 A111 $10 #1, 8-11, 15-16 8.50 8.50

No. 854 contains one 85x85mm stamp.

Sailboat Racing — A112

Designs: 20c, On course. 35c, Stylized boat poster. 45c, Start of race. No. 858, Blue Bird, 1971, vert. No. 859, Construction plans for Blue Bird, vert. $1, Stylized boat poster, diff. $6, Like Nos. 855 & 857.

Perf. 13½x14, 14x13½
1992, Oct. 12 Litho.
855 A112 20c multicolored .20 .20
856 A112 35c multicolored .25 .25
857 A112 45c multicolored .35 .35
858 A112 80c multicolored .55 .55
859 A112 80c multicolored .55 .55
a. Pair, #858-859 1.10 1.10
860 A112 $1 multicolored .70 .70
Nos. 855-860 (6) 2.60 2.60

Souvenir Sheet
861 A112 $6 multicolored 4.55 4.55

No. 861 contains one 96x31mm stamp.

Discovery of America, 500th Anniv. A113

1992, Dec. 15 Litho. *Perf. 14*
862 A113 80c Landfall .70 .70
863 A113 $1 Columbus, vert. .85 .85
864 A113 $2 Fleet 1.75 1.75
865 A113 $3 Pinta 2.50 2.50
Nos. 862-865 (4) 5.80 5.80

Souvenir Sheet
866 A113 $6 Map of voyage, vert. 5.00 5.00

Christmas A114

Various Christmas trees and: 20c, Mucka Jumbie on stilts. 70c, Masquerading house to house. $1.05, Christmas baking, old oven style. $2.40, $5, Collecting presents.

1992, Dec. 7
867 A114 20c multicolored .20 .20
868 A114 70c multicolored .60 .60
869 A114 $1.05 multicolored .90 .90
870 A114 $2.40 multicolored 2.00 2.00
Nos. 867-870 (4) 3.70 3.70

Souvenir Sheet
871 A114 $5 Sheet of 1 + 3 labels 4.25 4.25

Labels on No. 871 are similar to Nos. 867-869, but without denomination.

Easter — A115

Children's drawings: 20c, Kite flying. 45c, Cliff top village service. 80c, Morning devotion on Sombrero. $1.50, Hilltop church service. $5, Good Friday kites.

1993, Mar. 29 Litho. *Perf. 14*
872 A115 20c multicolored .20 .20
873 A115 45c multicolored .40 .40
874 A115 80c multicolored .65 .65
875 A115 $1.50 multicolored 1.25 1.25
Nos. 872-875 (4) 2.50 2.50

Souvenir Sheet
876 A115 $5 multicolored 4.25 4.25

No. 876 contains one 42x56mm stamp.

Native Industries A116

1993, June 23 Litho. *Perf. 14*

877 A116 20c Salt .20 .20
878 A116 80c Tobacco .65 .65
879 A116 $1 Cotton .80 .80
880 A116 $2 Sugar cane 1.60 1.60
Nos. 877-880 (4) 3.25 3.25

Souvenir Sheet

881 A116 $6 Fishing 4.75 4.75

Coronation of Queen Elizabeth II, 40th Anniv. — A117

Designs: 80c, Lord Great Chamberlain presents the spurs of chivalry. $1, The benediction. $2, Queen Elizabeth II, coronation photograph. $3, St. Edward's Crown. $6, Queen, Prince Philip in Gold State Coach.

1993, Aug. 16 Litho. *Perf. 14*

882 A117 80c multicolored .65 .65
883 A117 $1 multicolored .80 .80
884 A117 $2 multicolored 1.75 1.75
885 A117 $3 multicolored 2.50 2.50
Nos. 882-885 (4) 5.70 5.70

Souvenir Sheet

886 A117 $6 multicolored 4.75 4.75

Anguilla Carnival — A118

1993, Aug. 23 Litho. *Perf. 14*

887 A118 20c Pan musician .20 .20
888 A118 45c Pirates .35 .35
889 A118 80c Stars .65 .65
890 A118 $1 Playing mas .80 .80
891 A118 $2 Masqueraders 1.75 1.75
892 A118 $3 Commandos 2.50 2.50
Nos. 887-892 (6) 6.25 6.25

Souvenir Sheet

893 A118 $5 Carnival fantasy 4.00 4.00

Christmas — A119

Mail Delivery — A120

Traditional Christmas customs: 20c, Mucka Jumbies. 35c, Serenaders. 45c, Baking. $3, Five-fingers Christmas tree. $4, Mucka Jumbies and serenaders.

1993, Dec. 7 Litho. *Perf. 14x13½*

894 A119 20c multicolored .20 .20
895 A119 35c multicolored .30 .30
896 A119 45c multicolored .40 .40
897 A119 $3 multicolored 2.50 2.50
Nos. 894-897 (4) 3.40 3.40

Souvenir Sheet

Perf. 14

898 A119 $4 multicolored 3.50 3.50

No. 898 contains one 54x42mm stamp.

1993, Feb. 11 Litho. *Perf. 14*

Designs: 20c, Traveling Branch mail van, Sandy Ground, horiz. 45c, Mail boat, Betsy R, The Forest. 80c, Old post office, horiz. $1, Mail by jeep, Island Harbor. $4, New post office, 1993, horiz.

899 A120 20c multicolored .20 .20
900 A120 45c multicolored .40 .40
901 A120 80c multicolored .70 .70
902 A120 $1 multicolored .85 .85
903 A120 $4 multicolored 3.50 3.50
Nos. 899-903 (5) 5.65 5.65

Royal Visits — A121

Easter — A122

1994, Feb. 18

904 A121 45c Princess Alexandra .35 .35
905 A121 50c Princess Alice .45 .45
906 A121 80c Prince Philip .70 .70
907 A121 $1 Prince Charles .85 .85
908 A121 $2 Queen Elizabeth II 1.75 1.75
a. Souvenir sheet of 4, #904-908 4.00 4.00
Nos. 904-908 (5) 4.10 4.10

1994, Apr. 6 Litho. *Perf. 14x15*

Stained glass windows: 20c, Crucifixion. 45c, Empty tomb. 80c, Resurrection. $3, Risen Christ with disciples.

909 A122 20c multicolored .20 .20
910 A122 45c multicolored .40 .40
911 A122 80c multicolored .75 .75
912 A122 $3 multicolored 2.75 2.75
Nos. 909-912 (4) 4.10 4.10

Christmas — A123

Designs: 20c, Adoration of the shepherds. 30c, Magi, shepherds. 35c, The Annunciation. 45c, Nativity Scene. $2.40, Flight into Egypt.

1994, Nov. 22 Litho. *Perf. 14*

913 A123 20c multicolored .20 .20
914 A123 30c multicolored .30 .30
915 A123 35c multicolored .35 .35
916 A123 45c multicolored .45 .45
917 A123 $2.40 multicolored 2.50 2.50
Nos. 913-917 (5) 3.80 3.80

1994 World Cup Soccer Championships, US — A124

Soccer player and: 20c, Pontiac Silverdome, Detroit. 70c, Foxboro Stadium, Boston. $1.80, RFK Memorial Stadium, Washington. $2.40, Soldier Field, Chicago. $6, Two players.

1994, Oct. 3 Litho. *Perf. 13½x14*

918 A124 20c multicolored .20 .20
919 A124 70c multicolored .65 .65
920 A124 $1.80 multicolored 1.60 1.60
921 A124 $2.40 multicolored 1.90 1.90
Nos. 918-921 (4) 4.35 4.35

Souvenir Sheet

922 A124 $6 multicolored 5.50 5.50

Easter A125

Turtle dove: 45c, One on tree branch. 50c, One on nest, one on branch. $5, Mother with young.

1995, Apr. 10 Litho. *Perf. 14*

923 A125 20c multicolored .20 .20
924 A125 45c multicolored .40 .40
925 A125 50c multicolored .45 .45
926 A125 $5 multicolored 4.75 4.75
Nos. 923-926 (4) 5.80 5.80

UN, 50th Anniv. A126

Secretaries general and: 20c, Trygve Lie (1946-53), general assembly. 80c, UN flag, UN headquarters with "50" (no portrait). $1, Dag Hammarskjold (1953-61), charter, U Thant (1961-71). $5, UN complex, New York, vert. (no portrait).

Perf. 13½x14, 14x13½

1995, June 26 Litho.

927 A126 20c multicolored .20 .20
928 A126 80c multicolored .75 .75
929 A126 $1 multicolored .95 .95
930 A126 $5 multicolored 4.75 4.75
Nos. 927-930 (4) 6.65 6.65

Caribbean Development Bank, 25th Anniv. — A127

Designs: 45c, Emblem, map of Anguilla. $5, Local headquarters along waterfront.

1995, Aug. 15 Litho. *Perf. 13½x14*

931 A127 45c multicolored .45 .45
932 A127 $5 multicolored 5.00 5.00
a. Pair, #931-932 5.45 5.45

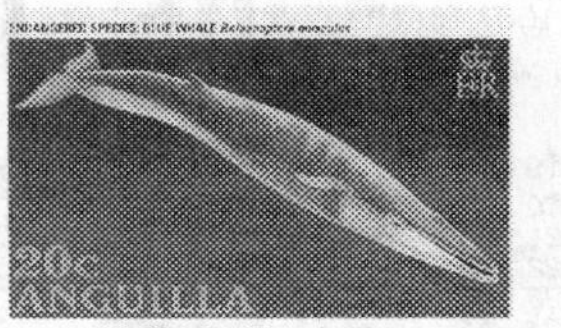

Whales — A128

Perf. 13½x14, 14x13½

1995, Nov. 24 Litho.

933 A128 20c Blue whale .20 .20
934 A128 45c Right whale, vert. .40 .40
935 A128 $1 Sperm whale .90 .90
936 A128 $5 Humpback whale 4.25 4.25
Nos. 933-936 (4) 5.75 5.75

Christmas A129

1995, Dec. 12 *Perf. 14½*

937 A129 10c Palm tree .20 .20
938 A129 25c Fish net floats .20 .20
939 A129 45c Sea shells .40 .40
940 A129 $5 Fish 4.25 4.25
Nos. 937-940 (4) 5.05 5.05

Corals A130

1996, June 21 Litho. *Perf. 14x14½*

941 A130 20c Deep water gorgonia .20 .20
942 A130 80c Common sea fan .70 .70
943 A130 $5 Venus sea fern 4.25 4.25
Nos. 941-943 (3) 5.15 5.15

A131

A132

1996 Summer Olympic Games, Atlanta: 20c, Running. 80c, Javelin, wheelchair basketball. $1, High jump. $3.50, Olympic torch, Greek, US flags.

1996, Dec. 12 Litho. *Perf. 14*

944 A131 20c multicolored .20 .20
945 A131 80c multicolored .65 .65
946 A131 $1 multicolored .80 .80
947 A131 $3.50 multicolored 2.75 2.75
Nos. 944-947 (4) 4.40 4.40

1996, Dec. 12

Battle for Anguilla, bicent.: 60c, Sandy Hill Fort, HMS Lapwing. 75c, French troops destroy church, horiz. $1.50, HMS Lapwing defeats Valiant, Decius, horiz. $4, French troops land, Rendezvous Bay.

948 A132 60c multicolored .50 .50
949 A132 75c multicolored .60 .60
950 A132 $1.50 multicolored 1.25 1.25
951 A132 $4 multicolored 3.25 3.25
Nos. 948-951 (4) 5.60 5.60

Fruits and Nuts A133

1997, Apr. 30 Litho. *Perf. 14*

952 A133 10c Gooseberry .20 .20
953 A133 20c West Indian cherry .20 .20
954 A133 40c Tamarind .35 .35
955 A133 50c Pommesurette .40 .40
956 A133 60c Sea almond .50 .50
957 A133 75c Sea grape .65 .65
958 A133 80c Banana .70 .70
959 A133 $1 Genip .85 .85
960 A133 $1.10 Coco plum .90 .90
961 A133 $1.25 Pope 1.00 1.00
962 A133 $1.50 Papaya 1.25 1.25
963 A133 $2 Sugar apple 1.75 1.75
964 A133 $3 Soursop 2.50 2.50
965 A133 $4 Pomegrante 3.25 3.25
966 A133 $5 Cashew 4.25 4.25
967 A133 $10 Mango 8.25 8.25
Nos. 952-967 (16) 27.00 27.00

Iguanas — A134

World Wildlife Fund: a, 20c, Baby iguanas emerging from eggs, juvenile iguana. b, 50c, Adult on rock. c, 75c, Two iguanas on tree limbs. d, $3, Adult up close, adult on tree branch.

1997, Oct. 13 Litho. *Perf. 13½x14*

968 A134 Strip of 4, #a.-d. 4.00 4.00

Diana, Princess of Wales (1961-67) — A135

Designs: a, 15c, In red & white. b, $1, In yellow. c, $1.90, Wearing tiara. d, $2.25, Wearing blouse with Red Cross emblem.

1998, Apr. 14 Litho. *Perf. 14*

969	A135	Strip of 4, #a.-d.	4.00	4.00

No. 969 was issued in sheets of 16 stamps.

Fountain Cavern Carvings A136

Designs: 30c, Rainbow Deity (Juluca). $1.25, Lizard. $2.25, Solar Chieftan. $2.75, Creator.

1997, Nov. 17 Litho. *Perf. 14x14½*

970	A136	30c multicolored	.25	.25
971	A136	$1.25 multicolored	1.10	1.10
972	A136	$2.25 multicolored	1.90	1.90
973	A136	$2.75 multicolored	2.25	2.25
		Nos. 970-973 (4)	5.50	5.50

1998 Intl. Arts Festival A137

Paintings: 15c, "Treasure Island." 30c, "Posing in the Light." $1, "Pescadores de Anguilla." $1.50, "Fresh Catch." $1.90, "The Bell Tower of St. Mary's."

1998, Aug. 24 Litho. *Perf. 14*

974	A137	15c multi	.20	.20
975	A137	30c multi, vert.	.25	.25
976	A137	$1 multi, vert.	.80	.80
977	A137	$1.50 multi	1.25	1.25
978	A137	$1.90 multi, vert.	1.50	1.50
		Nos. 974-978 (5)	4.00	4.00

Christmas A138

Paintings of "Hidden beauty of Anguilla:" 15c, Woman cooking over open fire, girl seated on steps. $1, Person looking over fruits and vegetables. $1.50, Underwater scene. $3, Cacti growing along shore.

1998

979	A138	15c multicolored	.20	.20
980	A138	$1 multicolored	.80	.80
981	A138	$1.50 multicolored	1.25	1.25
982	A138	$3 multicolored	2.40	2.40
		Nos. 979-982 (4)	4.65	4.65

Royal Air Force, 80th Anniv. A139

Designs: 30c, Sopwith Camel, Bristol F2B. $1, Supermarine Spitfire II, Hawker Hurricane Mk1. $1.50, Avro Lancaster. $1.90, Harrier GR7, Panavia Tornado F3.

1998 Litho. *Perf. 13½*
Granite Paper (No. 983)

983	A139	30c multicolored	.25	.25
984	A139	$1 multicolored	.80	.80
985	A139	$1.50 multicolored	1.25	1.25
986	A139	$1.90 multicolored	1.50	1.50
		Nos. 983-986 (4)	3.80	3.80

ANJOUAN

'an-jü-wän

LOCATION — One of the Comoro Islands in the Mozambique Channel between Madagascar and Mozambique.
GOVT. — Former French colony.
AREA — 89 sq. mi.
POP. — 20,000 (approx. 1912)
CAPITAL — Mossamondu

See Comoro Islands.

100 Centimes = 1 Franc

Navigation and Commerce — A1

Perf. 14x13½

1892-1907 Typo. Unwmk.
Name of Colony in Blue or Carmine

1	A1	1c black, *blue*	.85	.80
2	A1	2c brown, *buff*	1.25	1.10
3	A1	4c claret, *lav*	2.00	1.50
4	A1	5c green, *grnsh*	3.50	3.00
5	A1	10c blk, *lavender*	4.25	2.50
6	A1	10c red ('00)	17.50	12.50
7	A1	15c bl, quadrille paper	4.25	3.25
8	A1	15c gray, *lt gray* ('00)	9.00	6.50
9	A1	20c red, *green*	4.50	3.25
10	A1	25c black, *rose*	5.00	4.75
11	A1	25c blue ('00)	8.00	8.00
12	A1	30c brn, *bister*	12.50	10.00
13	A1	35c blk, *yel* ('06)	5.75	4.50
14	A1	40c red, *straw*	24.00	15.00
15	A1	45c blk, *gray grn* ('07)	80.00	77.50
16	A1	50c car, *rose*	25.00	17.00
17	A1	50c brn, *azure* ('00)	16.00	9.00
18	A1	75c vio, *orange*	25.00	15.00
19	A1	1fr brnz grn, *straw*	55.00	42.50
		Nos. 1-19 (19)	303.35	237.65

Perf. 13½x14 stamps are counterfeits.

Issues of 1892-1907 Surcharged in Black or Carmine **05 10**

1912

20	A1	5c on 2c brn, *buff*	.50	.50
21	A1	5c on 4c claret, *lav* (C)	.50	.50
22	A1	5c on 15c blue (C)	.50	.50
23	A1	5c on 20c red, *green*	.50	.50
24	A1	5c on 25c blk, *rose* (C)	.50	.50
25	A1	5c on 30c brn, *bis* (C)	.50	.50
26	A1	10c on 40c red, *straw*	.70	.70
27	A1	10c on 45c blk, *gray grn* (C)	.85	.85
28	A1	10c on 50c car, *rose*	1.90	1.90
29	A1	10c on 75c vio, *org*	1.40	1.40
30	A1	10c on 1fr brnz grn, *straw*	1.40	1.40
		Nos. 20-30 (11)	9.25	9.25

Nos. 21-23, 30 exist in pairs, one without surcharge. Value, $550 each.

Two spacings between the surcharged numerals are found on Nos. 20-30.

Nos. 20-30 were available for use in Madagascar and the Comoro archipelago.

The stamps of Anjouan were superseded by those of Madagascar, and in 1950 by those of Comoro Islands.

ANNAM AND TONKIN

a-'nam and 'tän-'kin

LOCATION — In French Indo-China bordering on the China Sea on the east and Siam on the west.
GOVT. — French Protectorate
AREA — 97,503 sq. mi.
POP. — 14,124,000 (approx. 1890)
CAPITAL — Annam: Hue; Tonkin: Hanoi

For administrative purposes, the Protectorates of Annam, Tonkin, Cambodia, Laos and the Colony of Cochin-China were grouped together and were known as French Indo-China.

100 Centimes = 1 Franc

Catalogue values for unused stamps are for examples without gum as most stamps were issued in that condition.

Stamps of French Colonies, 1881-86 Handstamped Surcharged in Black:

A & T 1   A & T 5

Perf. 14x13½

1888, Jan. 21 Unwmk.

1	A9	1c on 2c brn, *buff*	22.50	20.00
a.		Inverted surcharge	100.00	100.00
b.		Sideways surcharge	100.00	100.00
2	A9	1c on 4c claret, *lav*	17.50	14.00
a.		Inverted surcharge	100.00	100.00
b.		Double surcharge	125.00	125.00
c.		Sideways surcharge	100.00	100.00
3	A9	5c on 10c blk, *lav*	17.50	15.00
a.		Inverted surcharge	100.00	100.00
b.		Double surcharge	125.00	125.00

Hyphen between "A" and "T"

7	A9	1c on 2c brn, *buff*	225.00	200.00
a.		Inverted surcharge	450.00	
8	A9	1c on 4c claret, *lav*	350.00	350.00
9	A9	5c on 10c blk, *lav*	160.00	160.00

A 5c on 2c was prepared but not issued. Value $6,500.

In these surcharges there are different types of numerals and letters.

There are numerous other errors in the placing of the surcharges, including double one inverted, double both inverted, double one sideways, pair #1, 7, and pair one without surcharge. Such varieties command substantial premiums.

These stamps were superseded in 1892 by those of Indo-China.

ANTIGUA

an-'tēg-(w)ə

LOCATION — In the West Indies, southeast of Puerto Rico
GOVT. — Independent state
AREA — 171 sq. mi.
POP. — 64,246 (est. 1999)
CAPITAL — St. John's

Antigua was one of the presidencies of the former Leeward Islands colony until becoming a Crown Colony in 1956. It became an Associated State of the United Kingdom in 1967 and an independent nation on November 1, 1981, taking the name of Antigua and Barbuda.

Antigua stamps were discontinued in 1890 and resumed in 1903. In the interim, stamps of Leeward Islands were used. Between 1903-1956, stamps of Antigua and Leeward Islands were used concurrently.

12 Pence = 1 Shilling
20 Shillings = 1 Pound
100 Cents = 1 Dollar (1951)

Catalogue values for unused stamps in this country are for Never Hinged items, beginning with Scott 96.

Watermarks

Wmk. 5- Star

Values for unused stamps are for examples with original gum as defined in the catalogue introduction. Any exceptions will be noted. Very fine examples of Nos. 1-8, 11, 18-20 will have perforations touching the design on at least one frameline due to the narrow spacing of the stamps on the plates. Stamps with perfs clear of the framelines on all four sides are extremely scarce and will command higher prices.

Queen Victoria
A1 A2

Rough Perf. 14-16

1862 Engr. Unwmk.

1	A1	6p blue green	1,000.	650.
a.		Perf. 11-13	*5,250.*	
b.		Perf. 11-13x14-16	*2,750.*	
c.		Perf. 11-13 compound with 14-16	*3,000.*	

There is a question whether Nos. 1a-1c ever did postal duty.

Values for No. 1 are for stamps with perfs. cutting into the design. Values for No. 1b are for copies without gum.

1863-67 Wmk. 5

2	A1	1p lilac rose	110.00	32.50
a.		Vert. pair, imperf. btwn.	*15,000.*	
3	A1	1p vermilion ('67)	375.00	27.50
a.		Horiz. pair, imperf. btwn.	*16,000.*	
4	A1	6p green	375.00	30.00
a.		6p yellow green	*3,750.*	70.00
b.		Pair, imperf. between	—	

1872 Wmk. 1 *Perf. 12½*

5	A1	1p lake	100.00	27.50
6	A1	1p vermilion	140.00	27.50
7	A1	6p blue green	550.00	11.00
		Nos. 5-7 (3)	790.00	66.00

1873-79 *Perf. 14*

8	A1	1p lake	95.00	12.50
a.		Half used as ½p on cover		*2,750.*

Typo.

9	A2	2½p red brown ('79)	600.00	175.00
10	A2	4p blue ('79)	300.00	18.00

Engr.

11	A1	6p blue green ('76)	300.00	13.50

1882-86 Typo. Wmk. 2

12	A2	½p green	2.75	10.00
13	A2	2½p red brown	125.00	47.50
14	A2	2½p ultra ('86)	8.25	*55.00*
15	A2	4p blue	275.00	18.00
16	A2	4p brown org ('86)	2.25	*3.25*
17	A2	1sh violet ('86)	175.00	125.00

Engr.

18	A1	1p carmine ('84)	1.50	*2.75*
19	A1	6p deep green	60.00	*125.00*

No. 18 was used for a time in St. Christopher and is identified by the "A12" cancellation.

1884 *Perf. 12*

20	A1	1p rose red	50.00	17.00

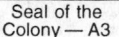

Seal of the Colony — A3

King Edward VII — A4

1903 Typo. Wmk. 1 Perf. 14

21	A3	½p blue grn & blk	3.00	4.75
a.		Bluish paper ('09)	100.00	100.00
22	A3	1p car & black	4.75	.90
a.		Bluish paper ('09)	90.00	90.00
23	A3	2p org brn & vio	5.75	22.50
24	A3	2½p ultra & black	7.50	13.00
25	A3	3p ocher & gray green	9.00	19.00
26	A3	6p black & red vio	26.00	45.00
27	A3	1sh violet & ultra	37.50	45.00
28	A3	2sh pur & gray green	62.50	80.00
29	A3	2sh6p red vio & blk	20.00	45.00
30	A4	5sh pur & gray green	65.00	90.00
		Nos. 21-30 (10)	241.00	365.15

The 2½p, 1sh and 5sh exist on both ordinary and chalky paper.

1908-15 Wmk. 3

31	A3	½p green	2.10	3.50
32	A3	1p carmine	4.25	1.75
a.		1p scarlet ('15)	4.50	2.75
33	A3	2p org brn & dull vio ('12)	3.50	24.00
34	A3	2½p ultra	9.00	14.00
35	A3	3p ocher & grn ('12)	6.00	17.50
36	A3	6p blk & red vio ('11)	7.00	32.50
37	A3	1sh vio & ultra	14.00	62.50
38	A3	2sh vio & green ('12)	55.00	75.00
		Nos. 31-38 (8)	100.85	230.75

Nos. 33, 35-38 are on chalky paper.
For overprints see Nos. MR1-MR3.

George V — A6

St. John's Harbor — A7

1913

41	A6	5sh violet & green	70.00	110.00

1921-29 Wmk. 4

42	A7	½p green	1.20	.20
43	A7	1p rose red	.95	.20
44	A7	1p dp violet ('23)	2.20	1.40
45	A7	1½p orange ('22)	1.90	6.50
46	A7	1½p rose red ('26)	3.50	1.75
47	A7	1½p fawn ('29)	1.90	.55
48	A7	2p gray	1.50	.75
49	A7	2½p ultra	3.00	5.00
50	A7	2½p orange ('23)	1.50	16.00

Chalky Paper

51	A7	3p violet, *yel* ('25)	3.75	8.00
52	A7	6p vio & red vio	2.75	6.25
53	A7	1sh black, *emer* ('29)	5.75	7.50
54	A7	2sh vio & ultra, *blue* ('27)	9.50	50.00
55	A7	2sh6p blk & red, *blue* ('27)	16.00	22.50
56	A7	3sh grn & vio ('22)	22.50	72.50
57	A7	4sh blk & red ('22)	45.00	57.50
		Nos. 42-57 (16)	122.90	256.60

Wmk. 3

Chalky Paper

58	A7	3p violet, *yel*	3.50	10.50
59	A7	4p black & red, *yel* ('22)	1.40	4.75
60	A7	1sh black, *emerald*	3.50	7.00
61	A7	2sh vio & ultra, *bl*	10.50	17.50
62	A7	2sh6p blk & red, *bl*	12.00	42.50
63	A7	5sh grn & red, *yel* ('22)	8.00	40.00
64	A7	£1 vio & black, *red* ('22)	225.00	275.00
		Nos. 58-64 (7)	263.90	397.25

Old Dockyard, English Harbour — A8

Govt. House, St. John's — A9

Nelson's "Victory," 1805 — A10

Sir Thomas Warner's Ship, 1632 — A11

Perf. 12½

1932, Jan. 27 Engr. Wmk. 4

67	A8	½p green	1.75	5.25
68	A8	1p scarlet	2.40	4.00
69	A8	1½p lt brown	3.00	4.00
70	A9	2p gray	3.50	14.00
71	A9	2½p ultra	3.50	8.00
72	A9	3p orange	4.50	11.50
73	A10	6p violet	12.50	11.50
74	A10	1sh olive green	16.75	24.00
75	A10	2sh6p claret	37.50	45.00
76	A11	5sh red brn & black	100.00	110.00
		Nos. 67-76 (10)	185.40	237.25

Tercentenary of the colony.

Common Design Types pictured following the introduction.

Silver Jubilee Issue

Common Design Type

1935, May 6 Perf. 13½x14

77	CD301	1p car & blue	2.00	1.50
78	CD301	1½p gray blk & ultra	2.50	1.25
79	CD301	2½p blue & brn	5.00	4.00
80	CD301	1sh brt vio & ind	9.50	12.50
		Nos. 77-80 (4)	19.00	19.25
		Set, never hinged	27.50	

Coronation Issue

Common Design Type

1937, May 12 Perf. 11x11½

81	CD302	1p carmine	.45	.75
82	CD302	1½p brown	.55	.85
83	CD302	2½p deep ultra	1.10	1.50
		Nos. 81-83 (3)	2.10	3.10
		Set, never hinged	2.75	

English Harbour — A14

Nelson's Dockyard — A15

Fort James — A16

St. John's Harbor — A17

1938-48 Engr. Perf. 12½

84	A14	½p green	.20	.90
85	A15	1p red	1.50	1.60
86	A15	1½p brown violet	1.75	1.25
87	A14	2p dark gray	.25	.50
88	A15	2½p deep ultra	.35	.75
89	A16	3p pale orange	.30	.80
90	A17	6p purple	.65	.80
91	A17	1sh brown & blk	1.90	1.00
92	A16	2sh6p deep claret	15.00	7.50
93	A17	5sh grayish ol grn	10.00	6.50
94	A15	10sh red vio ('48)	11.00	24.00
95	A16	£1 Prus blue ('48)	17.00	30.00
		Nos. 84-95 (12)	59.90	75.60
		Set, never hinged	82.50	

See Nos. 107-113, 115-116, 118-121, 136-142, 144-145.
For overprint see Nos. 125-126.

Catalogue values for unused stamps in this section, from this point to the end of the section, are for Never Hinged items.

Peace Issue

Common Design Type

1946, Nov. 1 Wmk. 4 Perf. 13½x14

96	CD303	1½p brown	.30	.30
97	CD303	3p deep orange	.30	.30

Silver Wedding Issue

Common Design Types

1949, Jan. 3 Photo. Perf. 14x14½

98	CD304	2½p bright ultra	.40	1.00

Engraved; Name Typographed

Perf. 11½x11

99	CD305	5sh dk brown olive	7.50	9.00

UPU Issue

Common Design Types

Perf. 13½, 11x11½

1949, Oct. 10 Wmk. 4

Engr.; Name Typo. on 3p and 6p

100	CD306	2½p deep ultra	.40	.50
101	CD307	3p orange	1.40	1.60
102	CD308	6p purple	1.75	1.75
103	CD309	1sh red brown	2.00	2.00
		Nos. 100-103 (4)	5.55	5.85

University Issue

Common Design Types

Perf. 14x14½

1951, Feb. 16 Engr. Wmk. 4

104	CD310	3c chocolate & blk	.40	.40
105	CD311	12c purple & blk	.60	.65

Coronation Issue

Common Design Type

1953, June 2 Perf. 13½x13

106	CD312	2c dk green & blk	.50	.75

Types of 1938 with Portrait of Queen Elizabeth II

Martello Tower — A24

Perf. 13x13½, 13½x13

1953-56 Wmk. 4

107	A16	½c dk red brn ('56)	.20	.25
108	A14	1c gray	.25	.50
109	A15	2c deep green	.25	.20
110	A15	3c yellow & blk	.30	.20
111	A14	4c rose red (shades)	.75	.20
112	A15	5c dull vio & blk	1.50	.30
113	A16	6c orange	1.10	.20
114	A24	8c deep blue	1.25	.20
115	A17	12c violet	1.25	.20
116	A17	24c chocolate & blk	1.50	.20
117	A24	48c dp bl & rose lil	4.00	1.50
118	A16	60c claret	4.50	.50
119	A17	$1.20 olive green	1.50	.50
120	A15	$2.40 magenta	5.00	6.00
121	A16	$4.80 greenish blue	7.50	10.00
		Nos. 107-121 (15)	30.85	20.95

See #143. For overprint see #125-126.

West Indies Federation

Common Design Type

Perf. 11½x11

1958, Apr. 22 Engr. Wmk. 314

122	CD313	3c green	.35	.20
123	CD313	6c blue	.90	1.25
124	CD313	12c carmine rose	1.65	.75
		Nos. 122-124 (3)	2.90	2.20

Nos. 110 and 115 Overprinted in Red or Black: "Commemoration Antigua Constitution 1960"

Perf. 13x13½, 13½x13

1960, Jan. 1 Wmk. 4

125	A15	3c yellow & black	.20	.20
126	A17	12c violet (Blk)	.20	.20

Constitutional reforms effective Jan. 1, 1960.

Lord Nelson and Nelson's Dockyard A26

Perf. 11½x11

1961, Nov. 14 Wmk. 314

127	A26	20c brown & lilac	.60	.65
128	A26	30c dk blue & green	1.00	1.10

Completion of the restoration of Lord Nelson's headquarters, English Harbour.

Stamp of 1862 and Royal Mail Steam Packet in English Harbour A27

1962, Aug. 1 Engr. Perf. 13

129	A27	3c dull green & pur	.20	.20
130	A27	10c dull green & ultra	.20	.20
131	A27	12c dull green & blk	.30	.30
132	A27	50c dull grn & brn org	1.50	1.50
		Nos. 129-132 (4)	2.20	2.20

Centenary of first Antigua postage stamp.

Freedom from Hunger Issue

Common Design Type

Perf. 14x14½

1963, June 4 Photo. Wmk. 314

133	CD314	12c green	.40	.40

Red Cross Centenary Issue

Common Design Type

1963, Sept. 2 Litho. Perf. 13

134	CD315	3c black & red	.20	.25
135	CD315	12c ultra & red	1.10	1.25

Types of 1938-53 with Portrait of Queen Elizabeth II

Perf. 13x13½, 13½x13

1963-65 Engr. Wmk. 314

136	A16	½c brown ('65)	.30	.30
137	A14	1c gray ('65)	.30	.30
138	A15	2c deep green	.20	.20
139	A15	3c orange yel & blk	.20	.20
140	A14	4c brown red	.35	.35
141	A15	5c dull vio & black	.35	.35
142	A16	6c orange	.40	.40
143	A24	8c deep blue	.45	.45
144	A17	12c violet	.85	.50
145	A17	24c choc & black	1.75	.75
		Nos. 136-145 (10)	5.15	3.80

For surcharge see No. 152.

Shakespeare Issue

Common Design Type

Perf. 14x14½

1964, Apr. 23 Photo. Wmk. 314

151	CD316	12c red brown	.35	.20

No. 144 Surcharged with New Value and Bars

Perf. 13½x13

1965, Apr. 1 Engr. Wmk. 314

152	A17	15c on 12c violet	.35	.35

ITU Issue

Common Design Type

Perf. 11x11½

1965, May 17 Litho. Wmk. 314

153	CD317	2c blue & ver	.20	.20
154	CD317	50c orange & vio bl	1.75	1.50

Intl. Cooperation Year Issue

Common Design Type

1965, Oct. 25 Perf. 14½

155	CD318	4c blue grn & claret	.20	.20
156	CD318	15c lt vio & green	.70	.50

Churchill Memorial Issue

Common Design Type

1966, Jan. 24 Photo. Perf. 14

Design in Black, Gold and Carmine Rose

157	CD319	½c bright blue	.20	.20
158	CD319	4c green	.20	.20
159	CD319	25c brown	.85	.50
160	CD319	35c violet	1.40	1.00
		Nos. 157-160 (4)	2.65	1.90

Royal Visit Issue

Common Design Type

1966, Feb. 4 Litho. Perf. 11x12

Portraits in Black

161	CD320	6c violet blue	1.25	.90
162	CD320	15c dark car rose	2.00	1.10

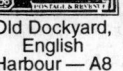

World Cup Soccer Issue
Common Design Type

1966, July 1 Wmk. 314 *Perf. 14*

163 CD321	6c	multicolored	.20	.25
164 CD321	35c	multicolored	.65	.25

WHO Headquarters Issue
Common Design Type

1966, Sept. 20 *Perf. 14*

165 CD322	2c	multicolored	.20	.20
166 CD322	15c	multicolored	.75	.35

Nelson's Dockyard A35

Designs: 1c, Old post office, St. John's. 2c, Health Center. 3c, Teachers' Training College. 4c, Martello Tower, Barbuda. 5c, Ruins of officers quarters, Shirley Heights. 6c, Government House, Barbuda. 10c, Princess Margaret School. 15c, Air terminal. 25c, General post office. 35c, Clarence House. 50c, Government House. 75c, Administration building. $1, Court House, St. John's. $2.50, Magistrates' Court. $5, St. John's Cathedral.

Perf. 11½x11

1966, Nov. 1 Engr. Wmk. 314

167 A35	½c	green & blue	.20	.20
168 A35	1c	purple & rose	.20	.25
169 A35	2c	slate & org	.20	.25
170 A35	3c	rose red & blk	.20	.25
171 A35	4c	dull vio & brn	.20	.20
172 A35	5c	vio bl & olive	.20	.20
a.		Booklet pane of 4 ('68)	.40	
173 A35	6c	dp org & pur	.20	.20
174 A35	10c	brt grn & rose red	.20	.20
a.		Booklet pane of 4 ('68)	1.00	
175 A35	15c	brn & blue	1.00	.20
a.		Booklet pane of 4 ('68)	1.25	
176 A35	25c	slate & brn	.45	.20
177 A35	35c	dp rose & sep	1.00	.60
178 A35	50c	green & black	.90	1.50
179 A35	75c	Prus bl & vio blue	1.10	1.75
180 A35	$1	dp rose & olive	4.50	2.00
181 A35	$2.50	black & rose	3.75	5.50
182 A35	$5	ol grn & dl vio	5.50	6.50
		Nos. 167-182 (16)	19.80	20.00

For surcharge see No. 231.

1969 *Perf. 13½*

167a	A35	½c	.20	*.40*
168a	A35	1c	.20	*.50*
169a	A35	2c	.20	*.30*
170a	A35	3c	.20	*.20*
171a	A35	4c	.20	*.20*
172b	A35	5c	.20	*.20*
173a	A35	6c	.20	*.50*
174b	A35	10c	.20	*.20*
175b	A35	15c	.30	*.30*
176a	A35	25c	.50	*.20*
177a	A35	35c	.60	*.75*
178a	A35	50c	.95	*2.00*
180a	A35	$1	2.00	*3.00*
181a	A35	$2.50	5.50	*6.00*
182a	A35	$5	19.00	*24.00*
		Nos. 167a-182a (15)	30.45	*38.75*

UNESCO Anniversary Issue
Common Design Type

1966, Dec. 1 Litho. *Perf. 14*

183 CD323	4c	"Education"	.20	.20
184 CD323	25c	"Science"	.40	.20
185 CD323	$1	"Culture"	2.00	*3.00*
		Nos. 183-185 (3)	2.60	*3.40*

Independent State

Flag of Antigua, Spiny Lobster, Maps of Antigua and Barbuda A37

Designs: 15c, 35c, Flag of Antigua. 25c, Flag and Premier's Office Building.

1967, Feb. 27 Photo. *Perf. 14*

186 A37	4c	multicolored	.20	.20
187 A37	15c	multicolored	.20	.20
188 A37	25c	multicolored	.25	*.30*
189 A37	35c	multicolored	.30	*.50*
		Nos. 186-189 (4)	.95	*1.20*

Antigua's independence, Feb. 27, 1967.

Gilbert Memorial Church, Antigua — A38

Designs: 25c, Nathaniel Gilbert's House. 35c, Map of the Caribbean and Central America.

Perf. 14x13½

1967, May 18 Photo. Wmk. 314

190 A38	4c	brt red & black	.20	.20
191 A38	25c	emerald & black	.30	.30
192 A38	35c	ultra & black	.40	.40
		Nos. 190-192 (3)	.90	.90

Attainment of autonomy by the Methodist Church in the Caribbean and the Americas, and the opening of headquarters near St. John's, Antigua, May 1967.

Antiguan and British Royal Arms — A39

1967, July 21 *Perf. 14½x14*

193 A39	15c	dark green & multi	.20	.20
194 A39	35c	deep blue & multi	.45	.30

Granting of a new coat of arms to the State of Antigua; 300th anniv. of the Treaty of Breda.

Sailing Ship, 17th Century A40

Design: 6c, 35c, Map of Barbuda from Jan Blaeu's Atlas, 1665.

Perf. 11½x11

1967, Dec. 14 Engr. Wmk. 314

195 A40	4c	dark blue	.20	.20
196 A40	6c	deep plum	.20	*.75*
197 A40	25c	green	.30	.20
198 A40	35c	black	.50	.30
		Nos. 195-198 (4)	1.20	*1.45*

Resettlement of Barbuda, 300th anniv.

Dow Hill Antenna — A41

Designs: 15c, Antenna and rocket blasting off. 25c, Nose cone orbiting moon. 50c, Reentry of space capsule.

Perf. 14½x14

1968, Mar. 29 Photo. Wmk. 314

199 A41	4c	dk blue, org & black	.20	.20
200 A41	15c	dk blue, org & black	.20	.20
201 A41	25c	dk blue, org & black	.25	.20
202 A41	50c	dk blue, org & black	.45	.45
		Nos. 199-202 (4)	1.10	1.05

Dedication of the Dow Hill tracking station in Antigua for the NASA Apollo project.

Beach and Sailfish A42

Designs: ½c, 50c, Limbo dancer, flames and dancing girls. 15c, Three girls on a beach and water skier. 35c, Woman scuba diver, corals and fish.

1968, July 1 Photo. *Perf. 14*

203 A42	½c	red & multi	.20	.20
204 A42	15c	sky blue & multi	.20	.20
205 A42	25c	blue & multi	.30	.20
206 A42	35c	brt blue & multi	.35	.20
207 A42	50c	multicolored	.60	*.90*
		Nos. 203-207 (5)	1.65	*1.70*

Issued for tourist publicity.

St. John's Harbor, 1768 A43

St. John's Harbor: 15c, 1829. 25c, Map of deep-sea harbor, 1968. 35c, Dock, 1968. 2c, Like $1.

Engr. & Litho.; Engr. ($1)

1968, Oct. 31 Wmk. 314 *Perf. 13*

208 A43	2c	dp car & lt blue	.20	*.30*
209 A43	15c	sepia & yel grn	.20	.20
210 A43	25c	dk blue & yel	.40	.20
211 A43	35c	dp green & sal	.45	.20
212 A43	$1	black	1.50	*2.00*
		Nos. 208-212 (5)	2.75	*2.90*

Opening of St. John's deep-sea harbor.

Mace and Parliament A44

Mace and: 15c, Mace bearer. 25c, House of Representatives, interior. 50c, Antigua coat of arms and great seal.

1969, Feb. 3 Photo. *Perf. 12½*

213 A44	4c	crimson & multi	.20	.20
214 A44	15c	crimson & multi	.20	.20
215 A44	25c	crimson & multi	.30	.20
216 A44	50c	crimson & multi	.60	*1.50*
		Nos. 213-216 (4)	1.30	*2.10*

300th anniversary of Antigua Parliament.

CARIFTA Cargo — A45

Design: 4c, 15c, Ship, plane and trucks, horiz.

Perf. 13½x13, 13x13½

1969, Apr. 14 Litho. Wmk. 314

217 A45	4c	blk & brt lilac rose	.20	.20
218 A45	15c	blk & brt grnsh blue	.20	.25
219 A45	25c	bister & black	.20	.25
220 A45	35c	tan & black	.35	.40
		Nos. 217-220 (4)	.95	1.10

1st anniv. of CARIFTA (Caribbean Free Trade Area).

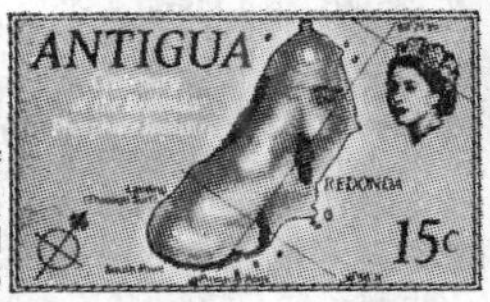

Map of Redonda Island A46

25c, View of Redonda from the sea & seagulls.

1969, Aug. 1 Photo. *Perf. 13x13½*

221 A46	15c	ultra & multi	.25	.20
222 A46	25c	multicolored	.40	.20
223 A46	50c	salmon & multi	1.10	*1.50*
		Nos. 221-223 (3)	1.75	*1.90*

Centenary of Redonda phosphate industry.

Adoration of the Kings, by Gugliemo Marcillat A47

Christmas: 10c, 50c, Holy Family, by anonymous German artist, 15th century.

1969, Oct. 15 Litho. *Perf. 13x14*

224 A47	6c	bister brn & multi	.20	.20
225 A47	10c	fawn & multi	.20	.20
226 A47	35c	gray olive & multi	.35	.20
227 A47	50c	gray blue & multi	.60	.50
		Nos. 224-227 (4)	1.35	1.10

Arms of Antigua — A48

Coil Stamps

Perf. 14½x14

1970, Jan. 30 Photo. Wmk. 314

228 A48	5c	bright blue	.20	.20
a.		Wmk. 373 ('77)	9.00	9.00
229 A48	10c	bright green	.20	.25
230 A48	25c	deep magenta	.45	.50
a.		Wmk. 373 ('77)	16.00	16.00
		Nos. 228-230 (3)	.85	.95

No. 176 Surcharged 20¢

1970, Jan. 2 Engr. *Perf. 11½x11*

231 A35	20c on 25c	slate & brown	.35	.20

Sikorsky S-38 — A49

Aircraft: 20c, Dornier DO-X. 35c, Hawker Siddeley 748. 50c, Douglas C-124C Globemaster II. 75c, Vickers VC 10.

1970, Feb. 16 Litho. *Perf. 14½*

232 A49	5c	brt green & multi	.20	.20
233 A49	20c	ultra & multi	.35	.20
234 A49	35c	blue grn & multi	.60	.20
235 A49	50c	blue & multi	.90	.75
236 A49	75c	vio blue & multi	1.50	1.75
		Nos. 232-236 (5)	3.55	3.10

40th anniversary of air service.

Dickens and Scene from "Pickwick Papers" A50

Charles Dickens (1812-1870), English novelist and Scene from: 5c, "Nicholas Nickleby." 35c, "Oliver Twist." $1, "David Copperfield."

Wmk. 314

1970, May 19 Litho. *Perf. 14*

237 A50	5c	olive & sepia	.20	.20
238 A50	20c	aqua & sepia	.25	.20
239 A50	35c	violet & sepia	.30	.20
240 A50	$1	scarlet & sepia	1.00	.80
		Nos. 237-240 (4)	1.75	1.40

Carib Indian and War Canoe — A51

Ships: 1c, Columbus and "Nina." 2c, Sir Thomas Warner's arms and sailing ship. 3c, Viscount Hood and "Barfleur." 4c, Sir George Rodney and "Formidable." 5c, Capt. Horatio Nelson and "Boreas." 6c, King William IV and "Pegasus." 10c, Blackbeard (Edward Teach) and pirate ketch. 15c, Capt. Cuthbert Collingwood and "Pelican." 20c, Admiral Nelson and "Victoria." 25c, Paddle steamer "Solent" and Steam Packet Company emblem. 35c, King George V and corvette "Canada." 50c, Cruiser "Renown" and royal badge. 75c, S.S. "Federal Maple" and maple leaf. $1, Racing yacht "Sol-Quest" and Gallant 53 class emblem. $2.50, Missile destroyer "London" and her emblem. $5, Tug "Pathfinder" and arms of Antigua.

Wmk. 314 Sideways

1970, Aug. 19 Litho. *Perf. 14*

241	A51	½c ocher & multi	.20	.20
242	A51	1c Prus bl & multi	.20	.20
243	A51	2c yel grn & multi	.20	.20
244	A51	3c ol bis & multi	.20	.20
245	A51	4c bl gray & multi	.20	.20
246	A51	5c fawn & multi	.20	.20
247	A51	6c rose lil & multi	.20	.20
248	A51	10c brn org & multi	.25	.20
249	A51	15c ultra & multi	.40	.25
250	A51	20c ol grn & multi	.35	.20
251	A51	25c olive & multi	.40	.20
252	A51	35c dull red brn & multi	.70	.35
253	A51	50c lt brn & multi	.95	.55
254	A51	75c beige & multi	1.25	.75
255	A51	$1 Prus green & multi	1.75	1.10
256	A51	$2.50 gray & multi	5.00	2.75
257	A51	$5 yel & multi	10.00	7.00
		Nos. 241-257 (17)	22.45	14.75

1972-74 Wmk. 314 Upright

241a	A51	½c	.20	.25
242a	A51	1c	.20	.50
244a	A51	3c	.20	.40
245a	A51	4c	.20	1.00
246a	A51	5c	.20	.20
247a	A51	6c	.20	1.50
248a	A51	10c	.20	.20
249a	A51	15c	1.60	.50
254a	A51	75c	3.25	2.00
255a	A51	$1	3.60	1.60
256a	A51	$2.50	6.00	*7.50*
257a	A51	$5	6.75	*10.50*
		Nos. 241a-257a (12)	22.60	*26.15*

For surcharge see No. 368.

1975, Jan. 21 Wmk. 373

257b	A51	$5 yellow & multi	12.00	*13.00*

Nativity, by Albrecht Dürer — A52

Private, 4th West India Regiment, 1804 — A53

Christmas: 10c, 50c, Adoration of the Magi, by Albrecht Dürer.

Engr. & Litho.

1970, Oct. 28 *Perf. 13½x14*

258	A52	3c brt grnsh blue & blk	.20	.20
259	A52	10c pink & plum	.20	.20
260	A52	35c brick red & black	.35	.20
261	A52	50c lilac & violet	.60	.60
		Nos. 258-261 (4)	1.35	1.20

Perf. 14x13½

1970, Dec. 1 Litho. Wmk. 314

Military Uniforms: ½c, Drummer Boy, 4th King's Own Regiment, 1759. 20c, Grenadier Company Officer, 60th Regiment, The Royal American, 1809. 35c, Light Company Officer, 93rd Regiment, The Sutherland Highlanders, 1826-1834. 75c, Private, 3rd West India Regiment, 1851.

262	A53	½c lake & multi	.20	.20
263	A53	10c brn org & multi	.40	.40
264	A53	20c Prus grn & multi	.70	.70
265	A53	35c dl pur & multi	1.40	1.40
266	A53	75c dk ol grn & multi	3.75	3.75
a.		Souv. sheet of 5, #262-266 + label	8.25	8.25
		Nos. 262-266 (5)	6.45	6.45

See #274-278, 283-287, 307-311, 329-333.

Market Woman Voting — A54

Voting by: 20c, Businessman. 35c, Mother (and child). 50c, Workman.

Perf. 14½x14

1971, Feb. 1 Photo. Wmk. 314

267	A54	5c brown	.20	.20
268	A54	20c olive black	.20	.20
269	A54	35c rose magenta	.20	.20
270	A54	50c violet blue	.35	.35
		Nos. 267-270 (4)	.95	.95

Adult suffrage, 20th anniversary.

Last Supper, from The Small Passion, by Dürer — A55

Woodcuts by Albrecht Dürer: 35c, Crucifixion from Eichstaff Missal. 75c, Resurrection from The Great Passion.

Perf. 14x13½

1971, Apr. 7 Litho. Wmk. 314

271	A55	5c gray, red & black	.20	.20
272	A55	35c gray, violet & black	.25	.25
273	A55	75c gray, gold & black	.55	.55
		Nos. 271-273 (3)	1.00	1.00

Easter.

Military Uniform Type of 1970

Military Uniforms: ½c, Private, Suffolk Regiment, 1704. 10c, Grenadier, South Staffordshire, 1751. 20c, Fusilier, Royal Northumberland, 1778. 35c, Private, Northamptonshire. 1793, 75c, Private, East Yorkshire, 1805.

1971, July 12 Litho. Wmk. 314

274	A53	½c gray grn & multi	.20	.20
275	A53	10c bluish blk & multi	.30	.25
276	A53	20c dk pur & multi	.50	.30
277	A53	35c dk ol & multi	1.00	.35
278	A53	75c brown & multi	2.00	3.25
a.		Souvenir sheet of 5, #274-278 + label	6.75	7.50
		Nos. 274-278 (5)	4.00	4.35

Virgin and Child, by Veronese — A56

Christmas: 5c, 50c, Adoration of the Shepherds, by Bonifazio Veronese.

1971, Oct. 4 *Perf. 14x13½*

279	A56	3c multicolored	.20	.20
280	A56	5c multicolored	.20	.20
281	A56	35c multicolored	.45	.25
282	A56	50c multicolored	.70	.50
		Nos. 279-282 (4)	1.55	1.15

Uniform Type of 1970

Military Uniforms: ½c, Officer, King's Own Borderers Regiment, 1815. 10c, Sergeant, Buckinghamshire Regiment, 1837. 20c, Private, South Hampshire Regiment, 1853. 35c, Officer, Royal Artillery, 1854. 75c, Private, Worcestershire Regiment, 1870.

1972, July 1

283	A53	½c ol brn & multi	.20	.20
284	A53	10c dp grn & multi	.35	.20
285	A53	20c brt vio & multi	.70	.25
286	A53	35c mar & multi	1.25	.40
287	A53	75c dk vio bl & multi	2.50	*3.50*
a.		Souvenir sheet of 5, #283-287 + label	8.00	*9.00*
		Nos. 283-287 (5)	5.00	*4.55*

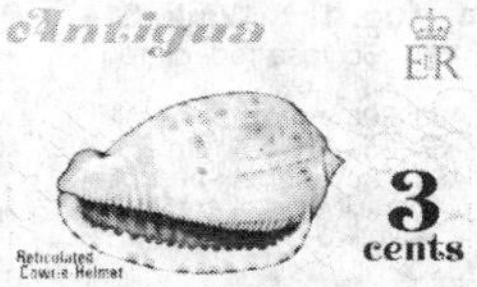

Reticulated Helmet Cowrie — A57

Sea Shells: 5c, Measled cowrie. 35c, West Indian fighting conch. 50c, Hawkwing conch.

1972, Aug. 1 *Perf. 14½x14*

288	A57	3c multicolored	.20	.20
289	A57	5c ver & multi	.35	.20
290	A57	35c lt vio & multi	1.20	.25
291	A57	50c rose red & multi	2.25	*3.00*
		Nos. 288-291 (4)	4.00	*3.65*

St. John's Cathedral, 1745-1843 A58

Christmas: 50c, Interior of St. John's. 75c, St. John's rebuilt.

1972, Nov. 6 Litho. *Perf. 14*

292	A58	35c org brn & multi	.35	.20
293	A58	50c vio & multi	.60	.60
294	A58	75c multicolored	1.00	*1.50*
a.		Souv. sheet of 3, #292-294, perf. 15	3.25	*4.00*
		Nos. 292-294 (3)	1.95	*2.30*

Silver Wedding Issue, 1972

Common Design Type

1972, Nov. 20 Photo. *Perf. 14x14½*

295	CD324	20c ultra & multi	.25	.25
296	CD324	35c steel blue & multi	.40	.40

Map of Antigua, Batsman Driving Ball — A60

Designs: 35c, Batsman and wicketkeeper. $1, Emblem of Rising Sun Cricket Club.

1972, Dec. 15 *Perf. 13½x14*

297	A60	5c multicolored	.25	.25
298	A60	35c multicolored	1.10	.50
299	A60	$1 multicolored	2.75	*3.25*
a.		Souvenir sheet of 3, #297-299	5.00	*6.00*
		Nos. 297-299 (3)	4.10	*4.00*

Rising Sun Cricket Club, St. John's, 50th anniv.

Map of Antigua and Yacht — A61

1972, Dec. 29 *Perf. 14½*

300	A61	35c shown	.30	.30
301	A61	50c Racing yachts	.35	.35
302	A61	75c St. John's G.P.O.	.65	.50
303	A61	$1 Statue of Liberty	1.00	.50
a.		Souvenir sheet of 2, #301, 303	2.00	*2.50*
		Nos. 300-303 (4)	2.30	1.65

Opening of Antigua and Barbuda Information Office in New York City.

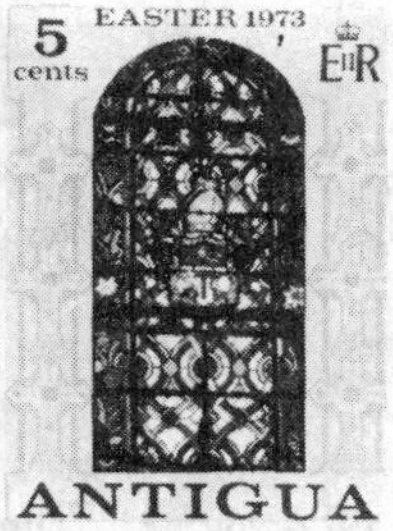

Window with Episcopal Coat of Arms — A62

Stained glass windows from Cathedral of St. John: 35c, Crucifixion. 75c, Arm of Rt. Rev. D.G. Davis, 1st bishop of Antigua.

1973, Apr. 16 Litho. *Perf. 13½*

304	A62	5c yellow & multi	.20	.20
305	A62	35c brt lilac & multi	.25	.20
306	A62	75c blue & multi	.55	.60
		Nos. 304-306 (3)	1.00	1.00

Easter.

Uniform Type of 1970

Military Uniforms: ½c, Private, Col. Zacharia Tiffin's Regiment, 1701. 10c, Private, 63rd Regiment, 1759. 20c, Officer, 35th Sussex Regiment, 1828. 35c, Private, 2nd West India Regiment, 1853. 75c, Sergeant, Princess of Wales Regiment, Hertfordshire, 1858.

Perf. 14x13½

1973, July 1 Wmk. 314

307	A53	½c dp ultra & multi	.20	.20
308	A53	10c rose lilac & multi	.20	.20
309	A53	20c gray & multi	.35	.25
310	A53	35c multicolored	.60	.25
311	A53	75c multicolored	1.60	1.25
a.		Souvenir sheet of 5	3.50	3.00
		Nos. 307-311 (5)	2.95	2.15

No. 311a contains one each of Nos. 307-311 and label with coat of arms and date.

Butterfly Costumes — A63

Designs: 20c, Carnival revelers. 35c, Costumed group. 75c, Carnival Queen.

Perf. 13½x14

1973, July 30 Unwmk.

312	A63	5c multicolored	.20	.20
313	A63	20c multicolored	.20	.20
314	A63	35c multicolored	.35	.20
315	A63	75c multicolored	.90	.90
a.		Souvenir sheet of 4, #312-315	2.00	*2.50*
		Nos. 312-315 (4)	1.65	1.50

Carnival, July 29-Aug. 7.

Virgin of the Porridge, by David — A64

Christmas: 5c, Adoration of the Kings, by Stomer. 20c, Virgin of the Grand Duke, by Raphael. 35c, Nativity with God the Father and Holy Ghost, by Tiepolo. $1, Madonna and Child, by Murillo.

Perf. 14½

1973, Oct. 15 Photo. Unwmk.

316	A64	3c brt blue & multi	.20	.20
317	A64	5c emerald & multi	.20	.20
318	A64	20c gold & multi	.25	.20
319	A64	35c violet & multi	.45	.20
320	A64	$1 red & multi	1.25	1.25
a.		Souvenir sheet of 5, #316-320	3.00	*3.50*
		Nos. 316-320 (5)	2.35	2.05

Princess Anne and Mark Phillips — A65

Design: $2, different border.

1973, Nov. 14 Litho. Perf. 13½

321	A65	35c dull ultra & multi	.20	.20
322	A65	$2 yel grn & multi	.90	.90
a.		Souvenir sheet of 2, #321-322	1.00	1.00

Wedding of Princess Anne and Capt. Mark Phillips.

Nos. 321-322 were issued in sheets of 5 plus label.

Nos. 321-322 and 322a Overprinted Vertically: "HONEYMOON / VISIT / DECEMBER 16th / 1973"

1973, Dec. 15 Litho. Perf. 13½

323	A65	35c multicolored	.20	.20
324	A65	$2 multicolored	.90	.90
a.		Souvenir sheet of 2, #323-324	1.50	1.50

Visit of Princess Anne and Mark Phillips to Antigua, Dec. 16. Same overprint in sheet margins of Nos. 323-324 and 324a.

Arms of Antigua and U.W.I. A66

Designs: 20c, Dancers. 35c, Antigua campus. 75c, Chancellor Sir Hugh Wooding.

1974, Feb. 18 Wmk. 314

325	A66	5c multicolored	.20	.20
326	A66	20c multicolored	.20	.20
327	A66	35c multicolored	.25	.20
328	A66	75c multicolored	.55	.65
		Nos. 325-328 (4)	1.20	1.25

University of the West Indies, 24th anniv.

Uniform Type of 1970

Military Uniforms: ½c, Officer, 59th Foot, 1797. 10c, Gunner, Royal Artillery, 1800. 20c, Private, 1st West India Regiment, 1830. 35c, Officer, Gordon Highlanders, 1843. 75c, Private, Royal Welsh Fusiliers, 1846.

1974, May 1 Perf. 14x13½

329	A53	½c dull grn & multi	.20	.20
330	A53	10c ocher & multi	.20	.20
331	A53	20c multicolored	.30	.20
332	A53	35c gray bl & multi	.50	.20
333	A53	75c dk gray & multi	1.10	1.50
a.		Souvenir sheet of 5, #329-333	2.75	2.25
		Nos. 329-333 (5)	2.30	2.30

English Mailman and Coach, Helicopter — A67

UPU, Cent.: 1c, English bellman, 1846; Orinoco mailboat, 1851; telecommunications satellite. 2c, English mailtrain guard, 1852; Swiss post passenger bus, 1906; Italian hydrofoil. 5c, Swiss messenger, 16th century; Wells Fargo coach, 1800; Concorde. 20c, German position, 1820; Japanese mailmen, 19th century; carrier pigeon. 35c, Contemporary Antiguan mailman; radar station; aquaplane. $1, Medieval French courier; American train, 1884; British Airways jet.

1974, July 15 Litho. Perf. 14½

334	A67	½c multicolored	.20	.20
335	A67	1c multicolored	.20	.20
336	A67	2c multicolored	.20	.20
337	A67	5c multicolored	.20	.20
338	A67	20c multicolored	.30	.20
339	A67	35c multicolored	.65	.25
340	A67	$1 multicolored	1.60	1.50
a.		Souvenir sheet of 7, #334-340 + label, perf. 13	3.25	2.50
		Nos. 334-340 (7)	3.35	2.75

For surcharges see Nos. 365-367.

Traditional Steel Band A68

Carnival 1974 (Steel Bands): 5c, Traditional players, vert. 35c, Modern steel band. 75c, Modern players, vert.

1974, Aug. 1, Wmk. 314 Perf. 14

341	A68	5c rose red, dk red & blk	.20	.20
342	A68	20c ocher, brn & blk	.20	.20
343	A68	35c yel grn, grn & blk	.25	.20
344	A68	75c dl bl, dk bl & blk	.50	.75
a.		Souvenir sheet of 4, #341-344	1.50	2.00
		Nos. 341-344 (4)	1.15	1.35

Soccer — A69

Designs: Games' emblem and soccer.

1974, Sept. 23 Unwmk. Perf. 14½

345	A69	5c multicolored	.20	.20
346	A69	35c multicolored	.30	.20
347	A69	75c multicolored	.60	.60
348	A69	$1 multicolored	.90	1.00
a.		Souvenir sheet of 4	2.25	2.25
		Nos. 345-348 (4)	2.00	2.00

World Cup Soccer Championship, Munich, June 13-July 7. Nos. 345-348 issued in sheets of 5 plus label showing Soccer Cup. No. 348a contains one each of Nos. 345-348, perf. 13½, and 2 labels.

For overprints and surcharges see Nos. 361-364.

Winston Churchill (1874-1965) at Harrow A70

Designs: 35c, St. Paul's during bombing and Churchill portrait. 75c, Churchill's coat of arms and catafalque. $1, Churchill during Boer war, warrant for arrest and map of his escape route.

1974, Oct. 20 Unwmk. Perf. 14½

349	A70	5c multicolored	.20	.20
350	A70	35c multicolored	.25	.20
351	A70	75c multicolored	.60	.90
352	A70	$1 multicolored	.80	1.25
a.		Souvenir sheet of 4, #349-352	2.00	2.75
		Nos. 349-352 (4)	1.85	2.55

Virgin and Child, by Giovanni Bellini — A71

Christmas: Paintings of the Virgin and Child.

1974, Nov. 18 Litho. Perf. 14½

353	A71	½c shown	.20	.20
354	A71	1c Raphael	.20	.20
355	A71	2c Van der Weyden	.20	.20
356	A71	3c Giorgione	.20	.20
357	A71	5c Andrea Mantegna	.20	.20
358	A71	20c Alvise Vivarini	.25	.20
359	A71	35c Bartolommeo Montagna	.35	.20
360	A71	75c Lorenzo Costa	.75	1.00
a.		Souvenir sheet of 4, #357-360, perf. 13½	1.50	2.00
		Nos. 353-360 (8)	2.35	2.40

Nos. 346-348 Overprinted and No. 344 Surcharged and Overprinted: "EARTHQUAKE / RELIEF"

1974, Oct. 16 Litho. Perf. 14½, 14

361	A69	35c multicolored	.20	.20
362	A69	75c multicolored	.50	.50
363	A69	$1 multicolored	.75	.60
364	A68	$5 on 75c multi	3.75	4.00
		Nos. 361-364 (4)	5.20	5.30

Earthquake of Oct. 8, 1974.

Nos. 338-340 and 254a Surcharged with New Value and Two Bars

1974-75 Wmk. 314 Perf. 14½

365	A67	50c on 20c	.50	.75
366	A67	$2.50 on 35c	2.25	3.00
367	A67	$5 on $1	4.50	5.50
		Perf. 14		
368	A51	$10 on 75c	8.75	8.75
		Nos. 365-368 (4)	16.00	18.00

Carib War Canoe, English Harbour A72

Designs (Nelson's Dockyard): 15c, Raising ship, 1770. 35c, Lord Nelson and "Boreas." 50c, Yachts arriving for Sailing Week, 1974. $1, "Anchorage" in Old Dockyard, 1970.

1975, Mar. 17 Unwmk. Perf. 14½

369	A72	5c multicolored	.20	.20
370	A72	15c multicolored	.30	.20
371	A72	35c multicolored	.50	.25
372	A72	50c multicolored	.75	.75
373	A72	$1 multicolored	1.50	1.75
		Nos. 369-373 (5)	3.25	3.15

Souvenir Sheet

Perf. 13½

373A	A72	Sheet of 5, #369-373	4.00	3.00

Stamps in No. 373A are 43x28mm.

Lady of the Valley Church A73

Churches of Antigua: 20c, Gilbert Memorial. 35c, Grace Hill Moravian. 50c, St. Phillip's. $1, Ebenezer Methodist.

1975, May 19 Litho. Perf. 14½

374	A73	5c multicolored	.20	.20
375	A73	20c multicolored	.20	.20
376	A73	35c multicolored	.25	.25
377	A73	50c multicolored	.40	.40
378	A73	$1 multicolored	.70	1.00
a.		Souvenir sheet of 3, #376-378, perf. 13½	2.00	2.75
		Nos. 374-378 (5)	1.75	2.05

Antigua, Senex's Atlas, 1721, and Hevelius Sextant, 1640 A74

Maps of Antigua: 20c, Jeffery's Atlas, 1775, and 18th century engraving of ship. 35c, Barbuda and Antigua, 1775 and 1975. $1, St. John's and English Harbour, 1973.

1975, July 21 Wmk. 314

379	A74	5c multicolored	.20	.25
380	A74	20c multicolored	.30	.25
381	A74	35c multicolored	.50	.25
382	A74	$1 multicolored	1.50	2.00
a.		Souvenir sheet of 4, #379-382	2.50	2.00
		Nos. 379-382 (4)	2.50	2.75

Bugler and Sunset A75

Nordjamb 75 Emblem and: 20c, Black and white Scouts, tents and flags. 35c, Lord Baden-Powell and tents. $2, Dahomey dancers.

Unwmk.

1975, Aug. 26 Litho. Perf. 14

383	A75	15c multicolored	.25	.20
384	A75	20c multicolored	.35	.20
384	A75	35c multicolored	.50	.25
386	A75	$2 multicolored	2.50	2.25
a.		Souvenir sheet of 4, #383-386	4.25	4.50
		Nos. 383-386 (4)	3.60	2.90

Nordjamb 75, 14th Boy Scout Jamboree, Lillehammer, Norway, July 29-Aug. 7.

Eurema Elathea A76

Butterflies: 1c, Danaus plexippus. 2c, Phoebis philea. 5c, Marpesia petreus thetys. 20c, Eurema proterpia. 35c, Papilio polydamas. $2, Vanessa cardui.

1975, Oct. 30 Litho. Perf. 14

387	A76	½c multicolored	.20	.20
388	A76	1c multicolored	.20	.20
389	A76	2c multicolored	.20	.20
390	A76	5c multicolored	.20	.20
391	A76	20c multicolored	.40	.35
392	A76	35c multicolored	.75	.60
393	A76	$2 multicolored	4.25	4.50
a.		Miniature sheet of 4, #390-393	6.25	7.00
		Nos. 387-393 (7)	6.20	6.75

Virgin and Child, by Correggio — A77

Christmas: Virgin and Child paintings.

1975, Nov. 17 Unwmk.

394	A77	½c shown	.20	.20
395	A77	1c El Greco	.20	.20
396	A77	2c Durer	.20	.20
397	A77	3c Antonello	.20	.20
398	A77	5c Bellini	.20	.20
399	A77	10c Durer	.20	.20
400	A77	35c Bellini	.35	.20
401	A77	$2 Durer	1.50	1.50
a.		Souvenir sheet of 4, #398-401	2.50	2.50
		Nos. 394-401 (8)	3.05	2.90

West Indies Team A78

Designs: 5c, Batsman I.V.A. Richards and cup, vert. 35c, Bowler A.M.E. Roberts and cup, vert.

1975, Dec. 15 Litho. Perf. 14

402	A78	5c multicolored	.20	.20
403	A78	35c multicolored	.80	.50
404	A78	$2 multicolored	3.25	4.00
		Nos. 402-404 (3)	4.25	4.70

World Cricket Cup, victory of West Indies team.

Antillean Crested Hummingbird — A79

Irrigation System, Diamond Estate — A80

Designs: 1c, Imperial parrot. 2c, Zenaida dove. 3c, Loggerhead kingbird. 4c, Red-necked pigeon. 5c, Rufous-throated solitaire. 6c, Orchid tree. 10c, Bougainvillea. 15c, Geiger tree. 20c, Flamboyant. 25c, Hibiscus. 35c, Flame of the Woods. 50c, Cannon at Fort James. 75c, Premier's Office. $1, Potworks Dam. $5, Government House. $10, Coolidge International Airport.

1976, Jan. 19 Litho. *Perf. 15*

405	A79	½c multicolored	.20	.35
406	A79	1c multicolored	.20	.35
407	A79	2c multicolored	.20	.35
408	A79	3c multicolored	.20	.40
409	A79	4c multicolored	.20	.40
410	A79	5c multicolored	.20	.20
411	A79	6c multicolored	.20	.40
412	A79	10c multicolored	.20	.20
413	A79	15c multicolored	.20	.20
414	A79	20c multicolored	.20	.20
415	A79	25c multicolored	.20	.20
416	A79	35c multicolored	.25	.25
417	A79	50c multicolored	.35	.35
418	A79	75c multicolored	.50	.60
419	A79	$1 multicolored	.70	.80

Perf. 13½x14

420	A80	$2.50 rose & multi	1.50	*2.50*
421	A80	$5 lilac & multi	3.25	*4.50*
422	A80	$10 multicolored	6.75	*8.00*
		Nos. 405-422 (18)	15.50	*20.25*

Nos. 405-422 exist inscribed "1978."
For overprints see Nos. 607-617.

Privates, Clark's Illinois Regiment — A81

1c, Riflemen, Pennsylvania Militia. 2c, Decorated American powder horn. 5c, Water bottle of Maryland troops. 35c, "Liberty Tree" and "Rattlesnake" flags. $1, American privateer Montgomery. $2.50, Congress Flag. $5, Continental Navy sloop Ranger.

1976, Mar. 17 Litho. *Perf. 14½*

423	A81	½c multicolored	.20	.20
424	A81	1c multicolored	.20	.20
425	A81	2c multicolored	.20	.20
426	A81	5c multicolored	.20	.20
427	A81	35c multicolored	.35	.20
428	A81	$1 multicolored	.75	.25
429	A81	$5 multicolored	3.75	4.00
		Nos. 423-429 (7)	5.65	5.25

Souvenir Sheet

Perf. 13

430	A81	$2.50 multicolored	3.00	3.50

American Bicentennial.

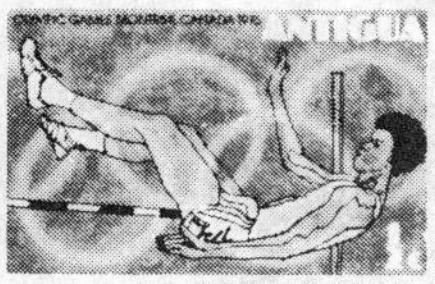

High Jump, Olympic Rings A82

Olympic Rings and: 1c, Boxing. 2c, Pole vault. 15c, Swimming. 30c, Running. $1, Bicycling. $2, Shot put.

1976, July 12 Litho. *Perf. 14½*

431	A82	½c yellow & multi	.20	.20
432	A82	1c purple & multi	.20	.20
433	A82	2c emerald & multi	.20	.20
434	A82	15c brt blue & multi	.20	.20
435	A82	30c olive & multi	.30	.20
436	A82	$1 orange & multi	.75	.25
437	A82	$2 red & multi	1.50	1.75
a.		Souvenir sheet of 4	3.00	*3.50*
		Nos. 431-437 (7)	3.35	3.00

21st Olympic Games, Montreal, Canada, July 17-Aug. 1. No. 437a contains one each of Nos. 434-437, perf. 13½.

Water Skiing A83

Water Sports: 1c, Sailfish sailing. 2c, Snorkeling. 20c, Deep-sea fishing. 50c, Scuba diving. $2, Swimming.

1976, Aug. 26 *Perf. 14*

438	A83	½c yel grn & multi	.20	.20
439	A83	1c sepia & multi	.20	.20
440	A83	2c gray & multi	.20	.20
441	A83	20c multicolored	.20	.20
442	A83	50c brt vio & multi	.35	.40
443	A83	$2 lt gray & multi	1.10	1.25
a.		Souvenir sheet of 3, #441-443	2.00	2.50
		Nos. 438-443 (6)	2.25	2.45

French Angelfish — A84

1976, Oct. 4 Litho. *Perf. 13½x14*

444	A84	15c shown	.20	.20
445	A84	30c Yellowfish grouper	.30	.25
446	A84	50c Yellowtail snappers	.65	.35
447	A84	90c Shy hamlet	1.10	.75
		Nos. 444-447 (4)	2.25	1.55

The Annunciation A85

Christmas: 10c, Flight into Egypt. 15c, Three Kings. 50c, Shepherds and star. $1, Kings presenting gifts to Christ Child.

1976, Nov. 15 Litho. *Perf. 14*

448	A85	8c multicolored	.20	.20
449	A85	10c multicolored	.20	.20
450	A85	15c multicolored	.20	.20
451	A85	50c multicolored	.35	.40
452	A85	$1 multi	.65	.75
		Nos. 448-452 (5)	1.60	1.75

Mercury and UPU Emblem A86

Designs: 1c, Alfred Nobel, symbols of prize categories. 10c, Viking spacecraft. 50c, Vivi Richards (batsman) and Andy Roberts (bowler). $1, Alexander G. Bell, telephones, 1876 and 1976. $2, Schooner Freelance.

1976, Dec. 28 Litho. *Perf. 14*

453	A86	½c multicolored	.20	.20
454	A86	1c multicolored	.20	.20
455	A86	10c multicolored	.20	.20
456	A86	50c multicolored	1.25	.65
457	A86	$1 multicolored	.50	1.00
458	A86	$2 multicolored	.90	1.75
a.		Souvenir sheet of 4, #455-458	4.00	5.00
		Nos. 453-458 (6)	3.25	4.00

Special 1976 Events: UN Postal Admin., 25th anniv. (½c); Nobel Prize, 75th anniv. (1c); Viking Space Mission to Mars (10c); World Cricket Cup victory (50c); Telephone cent. ($1); Operation Sail, American Bicent. ($2).

Royal Family — A87

Designs: 30c, Elizabeth II and Prince Philip touring Antigua. 50c, Queen enthroned. 90c, Queen wearing crown. $2.50, Queen and Prince Charles. $5, Queen and Prince Philip.

1977, Feb. 7 *Perf. 13½x14*

459	A87	10c multicolored	.20	.20
460	A87	30c multicolored	.20	.20
461	A87	50c multicolored	.25	.25
462	A87	90c multicolored	.50	.35
463	A87	$2.50 multicolored	1.25	1.50
		Nos. 459-463 (5)	2.40	2.50

Souvenir Sheet

464	A87	$5 multicolored	3.00	3.25

25th anniv. of the reign of Queen Elizabeth II.

Nos. 459-463 were printed in sheets of 40. Sheets of 5 plus label, perf. 12, probably were not sold by the Antigua Post Office.

A booklet of self-adhesive stamps contains one pane of six roulетted and die cut 50c stamps in design of 90c, and one pane of one die cut $5. Stamps have changed colors. Panes have marginal inscriptions.

For overprints see Nos. 477-482.

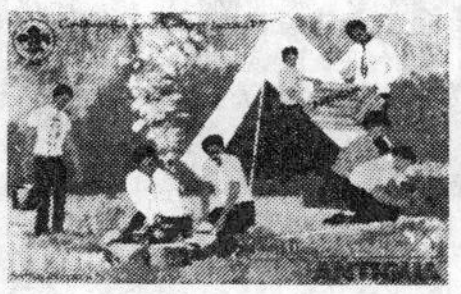

Scouts Camping A88

Boy Scout Emblem and: 1c, Scouts on hike. 2c, Rock climbing. 10c, Cutting logs. 30c, Map and compass reading. 50c, First aid. $2, Scouts on raft.

1977, May 23 Litho. *Perf. 14*

465	A88	½c multicolored	.20	.20
466	A88	1c multicolored	.20	.20
467	A88	2c multicolored	.20	.20
468	A88	10c multicolored	.20	.20
469	A88	30c multicolored	.25	.20
470	A88	50c multicolored	.45	.35
471	A88	$2 multicolored	1.50	1.75
a.		Souvenir sheet of 3, #469-471	2.75	2.75
		Nos. 465-471 (7)	3.00	3.10

Caribbean Boy Scout Jamboree, Jamaica.

Carnival Queen Holding Horseshoe — A89

Designs: 30c, Carnival Queen in feather costume. 50c, Butterfly costume. 90c, Carnival Queen with ornaments. $1, Carnival King and Queen.

1977, July 18 Litho. *Perf. 14*

472	A89	10c multicolored	.20	.20
473	A89	30c multicolored	.20	.20
474	A89	50c multicolored	.25	.25
475	A89	90c multicolored	.50	.40
476	A89	$1 multicolored	.60	.55
a.		Souvenir sheet of 4, #473-476	1.75	*2.25*
		Nos. 472-476 (5)	1.75	1.60

21st Summer Carnival.

Nos. 459-464 Overprinted: "ROYAL VISIT / 28th OCTOBER 1977"

Perf. 13½x14, 12

1977, Oct. 17 Litho.

477	A87	10c multicolored	.20	.20
478	A87	30c multicolored	.20	.20
479	A87	50c multicolored	.20	.20
480	A87	90c multicolored	.40	.35
481	A87	$2.50 multicolored	1.25	1.00
		Nos. 477-481 (5)	2.25	1.95

Souvenir Sheet

482	A87	$5 multicolored	3.00	3.25

Visit of Queen Elizabeth II, Oct. 28.

Virgin and Child, by Cosimo Tura — A90

Virgin and Child by: 1c, $2, Carlo Crivelli (different). 2c, 25c, Lorenzo Lotto (different). 8c, Jacopo da Pontormo. 10c, Tura.

1977, Nov. 15 Litho. *Perf. 14*

483	A90	½c multicolored	.20	.20
484	A90	1c multicolored	.20	.20
485	A90	2c multicolored	.20	.20
486	A90	8c multicolored	.20	.20
487	A90	10c multicolored	.20	.20
488	A90	25c multicolored	.20	.20
489	A90	$2 multicolored	1.00	.75
a.		Souvenir sheet of 4, #486-489	1.50	*2.00*
		Nos. 483-489 (7)	2.20	1.95

Christmas.

Pineapple A91

10th anniv. of Statehood: 15c, Flag of Antigua. 50c, Police band. 90c, Prime Minister V. C. Bird. $2, Coat of Arms.

1977, Dec. 28 Litho. *Perf. 13x13½*

490	A91	10c multicolored	.20	.20
491	A91	15c multicolored	.20	.20
492	A91	50c multicolored	.75	.40
493	A91	90c multicolored	.35	.40
494	A91	$2 multicolored	.50	.60
a.		Souv. sheet of 4, #491-494, perf. 14	2.00	1.75
		Nos. 490-494 (5)	2.00	1.80

Wright Glider III, 1902 A92

Designs: 1c, Flyer I in air, 1903. 2c, Weight and derrick launch system and Wright engine, 1903. 10c, Orville Wright, vert. 50c, Flyer III, 1905. 90c, Wilbur Wright, vert. $2, Wright Model B, 1910. $2.50, Flyer I, 1903, on ground.

1978, Mar. 28 *Perf. 14*

495	A92	½c multicolored	.20	.20
496	A92	1c multicolored	.20	.20
497	A92	2c multicolored	.20	.20
498	A92	10c multicolored	.20	.20
499	A92	50c multicolored	.25	.20
500	A92	90c multicolored	.50	.30
501	A92	$2 multicolored	1.10	.90
		Nos. 495-501 (7)	2.65	2.20

Souvenir Sheet

502	A92	$2.50 multicolored	2.00	*3.00*

1st powered flight by Wright brothers, 75th anniv.

Sunfish Regatta A93

Sailing Week 1978: 50c, Fishing and work boat race. 90c, Curtain Bluff race. $2, Powerboat rally. $2.50, Guadeloupe-Antigua race.

1978, Apr. 29 Litho. *Perf. 14½*

503 A93	10c multicolored	.20	.20
504 A93	50c multicolored	.30	.25
505 A93	90c multicolored	.50	.35
506 A93	$2 multicolored	1.10	1.25
	Nos. 503-506 (4)	2.10	2.05

Souvenir Sheet

507 A93	$2.50 multicolored	2.25	2.50

Elizabeth II and Prince Philip — A94

Designs: 30c, Coronation. 50c, State coach. 90c, Elizabth II and Archbishop. $2.50, Elizabeth II. $5, Elizabeth II, Prince Philip, Prince Charles and Princess Anne as children.

1978, June 2 Litho. *Perf. 14, 12*

508 A94	10c multicolored	.20	.20
509 A94	30c multicolored	.20	.20
510 A94	50c multicolored	.20	.20
511 A94	90c multicolored	.40	.25
512 A94	$2.50 multicolored	1.25	1.25
	Nos. 508-512 (5)	2.25	2.10

Souvenir Sheet

513 A94	$5 multicolored	3.00	3.00

25th anniv. of coronation of Queen Elizabeth II.

Nos. 508-512 were printed in sheets of 50 (2 panes of 25), perf. 14, and in sheets of 3 plus label, perf. 12, with frames in changed colors.

Glass Coach A95

Royal Coaches: 50c, Irish state coach. $5, Coronation coach.

1978, June 2 Litho. *Imperf.*

Self-adhesive

514	Souvenir booklet	5.50	
a.	A95 Bklt. pane, 3 each 25c, 50c	1.65	
b.	A95 Bklt. pane, 1 $5	3.50	

25th anniversary of coronation of Queen Elizabeth II. No. 514 contains 2 booklet panes printed on peelable paper backing showing royal processions.

Soccer — A96

Purple Wreath — A97

Designs: Various soccer scenes. Stamps in souvenir sheet horizontal.

1978, Aug. 18 Litho. *Perf. 15*

515 A96	10c multicolored	.20	.20
516 A96	15c multicolored	.20	.20
517 A96	$3 multicolored	2.00	1.75
	Nos. 515-517 (3)	2.40	2.15

Souvenir Sheet

518	Sheet of 4	2.50	2.50
a.	A96 25c multicolored	.20	.20
b.	A96 30c multicolored	.25	.25
c.	A96 50c multicolored	.40	.40
d.	A96 $2 multicolored	1.75	1.50

11th World Cup Soccer Championship, Argentina, June 1-25.

1978, Oct. Litho. *Perf. 14*

519 A97	25c shown	.20	.20
520 A97	50c Sunflowers	.30	.20
521 A97	90c Frangipani	.60	.30
522 A97	$2 Passionflower	1.50	1.25
	Nos. 519-522 (4)	2.60	1.95

Souvenir Sheet

523 A97	$2.50 Red hibiscus	2.25	2.50

St. Ildefonso Receiving Chasuble, by Rubens — A98

Christmas: 25c, Flight of St. Barbara, by Rubens. $2, Holy Family, by Sebastiano del Piombo. $4, Annunciation, by Rubens.

1978, Oct. 30 Litho. *Perf. 14*

524 A98	8c multicolored	.20	.20
525 A98	25c multicolored	.20	.20
526 A98	$2 multicolored	1.50	1.25
	Nos. 524-526 (3)	1.90	1.65

Souvenir Sheet

527 A98	$4 multicolored	4.00	4.25

Antigua No. 2 — A99

Crucifixion, by Durer — A100

Designs: 50c, Great Britain Penny Black, 1840. $1, Woman posting letter in pillar box, and coach. $2, Mail train, ship, plane and Concorde. $2.50, Rowland Hill.

1979, Feb. 12 Litho. *Perf. 14*

528 A99	25c multicolored	.20	.20
529 A99	50c multicolored	.20	.20
530 A99	$1 multicolored	.40	.25
531 A99	$2 multicolored	.85	.50
	Nos. 528-531 (4)	1.65	1.15

Souvenir Sheet

532 A99	$2.50 multicolored	1.40	1.50

Sir Rowland Hill (1795-1879), originator of penny postage.

Nos. 528-531 were printed in sheets of 50 (2 panes of 25), perf. 14, and in sheets of 5 plus label, perf. 12, with frames in changed colors.

For overprints, see Nos. 571A-571D.

1979, Mar. 15

Designs (after Dürer): 10c, Deposition. $2.50, Crucifixion. $4, Man of Sorrows.

533 A100	10c multicolored	.20	.20
534 A100	50c multicolored	.30	.25
535 A100	$4 multicolored	2.25	1.75
	Nos. 533-535 (3)	2.75	2.20

Souvenir Sheet

536 A100	$2.50 multicolored	1.60	1.60

Easter.

Child Playing with Sailboat — A101

IYC emblem, child's hand holding toy: 50c, Rocket. 90c, Automobile. $2, Train. $5, Plane.

1979, Apr. 9 Litho. *Perf. 14*

537 A101	25c multicolored	.20	.20
538 A101	50c multicolored	.25	.20
539 A101	90c multicolored	.50	.35
540 A101	$2 multicolored	1.25	1.10
	Nos. 537-540 (4)	2.20	1.85

Souvenir Sheet

541 A101	$5 multicolored	3.75	3.75

International Year of the Child.

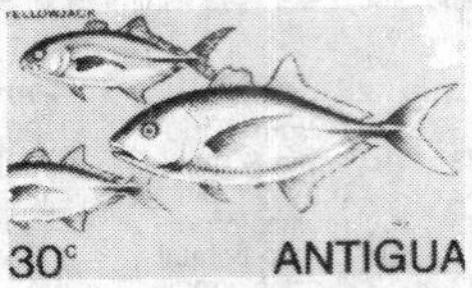

Yellowjacks — A102

Sport Fish: 50c, Bluefin tunas. 90c, Sailfish. $2.50, Barracuda. $3, Wahoos.

1979, May Litho. *Perf. 14½*

542 A102	30c multicolored	.25	.25
543 A102	50c multicolored	.40	.30
544 A102	90c multicolored	.60	.40
545 A102	$3 multicolored	2.00	1.50
	Nos. 542-545 (4)	3.25	2.45

Souvenir Sheet

546 A102	$2.50 multicolored	2.00	1.75

Capt. Cook and his Birthplace at Marton — A103

Holy Family — A104

Capt. James Cook (1728-1779) and: 50c, HMS Endeavour. 90c, Marine timekeeper. $2.50, HMS Resolution. $3, Landing at Botany Bay.

1979, July 2 Litho. *Perf. 14*

547 A103	25c multicolored	.40	.30
548 A103	50c multicolored	.50	.40
549 A103	90c multicolored	.50	.55
550 A103	$3 multicolored	1.75	*2.50*
	Nos. 547-550 (4)	3.15	*3.75*

Souvenir Sheet

551 A103	$2.50 multicolored	2.00	1.75

1979, Oct. 1 Litho. *Perf. 14*

Stained-glass Windows: 25c, Flight into Egypt. 50c, Shepherd and star. $3, Angel with trumpet. $4, Three Kings offering gifts.

552 A104	8c multicolored	.20	.20
553 A104	25c multicolored	.20	.20
554 A104	50c multicolored	.25	.30
555 A104	$4 multicolored	2.00	*2.50*
	Nos. 552-555 (4)	2.65	*3.20*

Souvenir Sheet

Perf. 12x12½

556 A104	$3 multicolored	2.00	*2.75*

Christmas.

Javelin, Olympic Rings — A105

1980, Feb. 7 Litho. *Perf. 14*

557 A105	10c shown	.20	.20
558 A105	25c Running	.30	.20
559 A105	$1 Pole vault	.60	.50
560 A105	$2 Hurdles	1.00	1.40
	Nos. 557-560 (4)	2.10	2.30

Souvenir Sheet

561 A105	$3 Boxing, horiz.	1.75	2.00

22nd Summer Olympic Games, Moscow, July 19-Aug. 3.

Disney Characters and IYC Emblem A106

Designs: Transportation scenes. ½c, 2c, 3c, 4c, 5c, $1, $2.50, horiz.

1980, Mar. 24 Litho. *Perf. 11*

562 A106	½c Mickey, plane	.20	.20
563 A106	1c Donald, car	.20	.20
564 A106	2c Goofy driving taxi	.20	.20
565 A106	3c Mickey, Minnie in sidecar	.20	.20
566 A106	4c Huey, Dewey and Louie	.20	.20
567 A106	5c Grandma Duck	.20	.20
568 A106	10c Mickey in jeep	.20	.20
569 A106	$1 Chip and Dale sailing	1.00	1.25
570 A106	$4 Donald on train	3.50	*4.50*
	Nos. 562-570 (9)	5.90	*7.15*

Souvenir Sheet

571 A106	$2.50 Goofy in glider	5.50	4.00

Nos. 528-531 in Changed Colors Overprinted "LONDON 1980"

1980, May 6 Litho. *Perf. 12*

571A A99	25c multicolored	.20	.20
571B A99	50c multicolored	.25	.30
571C A99	$1 multicolored	.60	.65
571D A99	$2 multicolored	1.10	1.40
	Nos. 571A-571D (4)	2.15	2.55

London '80 Intl. Stamp Exhib., May 6-14.

Birth of Venus, by Botticelli — A106a

Designs: 10c, David, by Donatello, vert. 50c, Reclining Couple, sarcophagus, Cerveteri. 90c, The Garden of Earthly Delights, by Hieronymus Bosch. $1, Portinari Altarpiece, by Hugo van der Goes. $4, Eleanora of Toledo and her Son Giovanni de Medici, by Bronzino, vert. $5, The Holy Family, by Rembrandt.

Perf. 13½x14, 14x13½

1980, June 23 Litho.

572 A106a	10c multicolored	.20	.20
573 A106a	30c multicolored	.25	.20
574 A106a	50c multicolored	.35	.30
575 A106a	90c multicolored	.45	.45
576 A106a	$1 multicolored	.50	.50
577 A106a	$4 multicolored	2.75	3.00
	Nos. 572-577 (6)	4.50	4.65

Souvenir Sheet

Perf. 14

578 A106a	$5 multicolored	3.50	3.00

Anniversary Emblem, Intl. Headquarters, Evanston, IL — A107

1980, July 21 Litho. *Perf. 14*

579 A107	3c shown	.25	.25
580 A107	50c Antigua club banner	.30	.35
581 A107	90c Map of Antigua	.50	.60
582 A107	$3 Paul. P. Harris, emblem	2.00	*2.75*
	Nos. 579-582 (4)	3.05	*3.95*

Souvenir Sheet

583 A107	$5 Emblems, Antigua flags	3.00	*3.75*

Rotary International, 75th anniv.

Queen Mother Elizabeth, 80th Birthday — A108

1980, Sept. 15

584 A108 10c multicolored .20 .20
585 A108 $2.50 multicolored 1.65 *2.00*

Souvenir Sheet
Perf. 12

586 A108 $3 multicolored 1.75 *2.50*

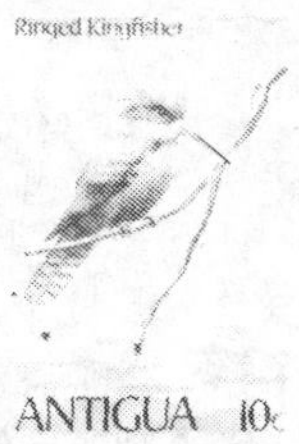

Ringed Kingfisher — A109

1980, Nov. 3 Litho. *Perf. 14*

587 A109 10c shown .50 *.25*
588 A109 30c Plain pigeon .75 *.40*
589 A109 $1 Green-throated carib 1.00 *1.00*
590 A109 $2 Black-necked stilt 2.00 *2.75*
Nos. 587-590 (4) 4.25 *4.40*

Souvenir Sheet

591 A109 $2.50 Roseate tern 3.50 3.00

Sleeping Beauty and the Prince — A110

Christmas: Various scenes from Walt Disney's Sleeping Beauty. $4 vert.

1980, Dec. 23 *Perf. 11, 13½x14 ($4)*

592 A110 ½c multicolored .20 .20
593 A110 1c multicolored .20 .20
594 A110 2c multicolored .20 .20
595 A110 4c multicolored .20 .20
596 A110 8c multicolored .20 .20
597 A110 10c multicolored .20 .20
598 A110 25c multicolored .25 .25
599 A110 $2 multicolored 1.75 1.75
600 A110 $2.50 multicolored 2.25 2.25
Nos. 592-600 (9) 5.45 5.45

Souvenir Sheet

601 A110 $4 multicolored 3.00 2.00

Sugar-cane Railway Diesel Locomotive No. 15 — A111

1981, Jan. 12 *Perf. 14*

602 A111 25c shown .20 .20
603 A111 50c Narrow-gauge steam locomotive .35 .40
604 A111 90c Diesels #1, #10 .60 .65
605 A111 $3 Hauling sugar-cane 2.00 2.25
Nos. 602-605 (4) 3.15 3.50

Souvenir Sheet

606 A111 $2.50 Sugar factory, train yard 1.90 1.90

Nos. 411-412, 414-422 Overprinted: "INDEPENDENCE 1981"

1981, Mar. 31 Litho.

607 A79 6c multicolored .20 .20
608 A79 10c multicolored .20 .20
609 A79 20c multicolored .20 .20
610 A79 25c multicolored .20 .20
611 A79 35c multicolored .20 .20
612 A79 50c multicolored .35 .35
613 A79 75c multicolored .55 .55
614 A79 $1 multicolored .65 .65
615 A80 $2.50 multicolored 1.50 1.50
616 A80 $5 multicolored 3.00 *3.50*
617 A80 $10 multicolored 5.50 *6.75*
Nos. 607-617 (11) 12.55 *14.30*

Pipes of Pan, by Picasso — A112

Paintings by Pablo Picasso (1881-1973): 50c, Seated Harlequin. 90c, Paulo as Harlequin. $4, Mother and Child. $5, Three Musicians.

1981, May 5 Litho. *Perf. 14*

618 A112 10c multicolored .20 .20
619 A112 50c multicolored .35 .35
620 A112 90c multicolored .60 .60
621 A112 $4 multicolored 2.50 2.50
Nos. 618-621 (4) 3.65 3.65

Souvenir Sheet
Perf. 14x14½

622 A112 $5 multicolored 3.25 *3.75*

Royal Wedding Issue
Common Design Type

1981, June 16 Litho. *Perf. 14*

623 CD331 25c Couple .20 .20
624 CD331 50c Glamis Castle .30 .30
625 CD331 $4 Charles 2.50 2.50
Nos. 623-625 (3) 3.00 3.00

Souvenir Sheet

626 CD331 $5 Glass coach 3.00 3.00
627 CD331 Booklet 9.00
a. Pane of 6 (2x25c, 2x$1, 2x$2), Charles 5.00
b. Pane of 1, $5, Couple 4.00

No. 627 contains imperf., self-adhesive stamps.

Nos. 623-625 also printed in sheets of 5 plus label, perf. 12 in changed colors.

For surcharges see Nos. 792, 795, 802, 805.

Campfire Sing A113

1981, Oct. 28 Litho. *Perf. 15*

628 A113 10c Irene Joshua .20 .20
629 A113 50c shown .30 .25
630 A113 90c Sailing .60 .50
631 A113 $2.50 Milking cow 1.50 *1.75*
Nos. 628-631 (4) 2.60 2.70

Souvenir Sheet

632 A113 $5 Flag raising 3.50 2.25

Girl Guides, 50th anniv.

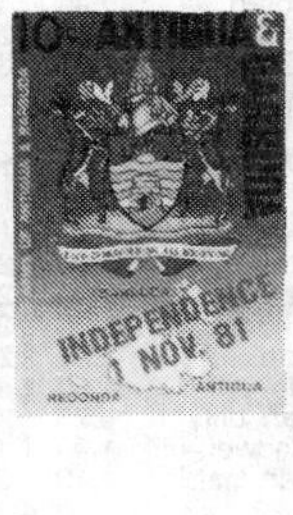

Independence A114

A115

1981, Nov. 1 Litho. *Perf. 15*

633 A114 10c Arms .20 .20
634 A114 50c Flag .35 .25
635 A114 90c Prime Minister Bird .60 .60
636 A114 $2.50 St. John's Cathedral, horiz. 1.50 *2.50*
Nos. 633-636 (4) 2.65 *3.55*

Souvenir Sheet

637 A114 $5 Map 3.25 2.75

No. 637 contains one 41x41mm stamp.

1981, Nov. 16

Christmas (Virgin and Child Paintings by): 8c, Holy Night, by Jacques Stella (1596-1657). 30c Julius Schnorr von Carolfeld (1794-1872). $1, Alonso Cano (1601-1667). $3, Lorenzo de Credi (1459-1537). $5, Holy Family, by Pieter von Avoni (1600-1652).

638 A115 8c multicolored .20 .20
639 A115 30c multicolored .25 .20
640 A115 $1 multicolored .65 *.75*
641 A115 $3 multicolored 1.75 *3.25*
Nos. 638-641 (4) 2.85 *4.40*

Souvenir Sheet

642 A115 $5 multicolored 3.25 *5.00*

Intl. Year of the Disabled A116

1981, Dec. 1 Litho. *Perf. 15*

643 A116 10c Swimming .20 .20
644 A116 50c Discus .25 .35
645 A116 90c Archery .55 .60
646 A116 $2 Baseball 1.40 *1.50*
Nos. 643-646 (4) 2.40 *2.65*

Souvenir Sheet

647 A116 $4 Basketball 2.75 1.75

1982 World Cup Soccer A117

Designs: Various soccer players.

1982, Apr. 15 Litho. *Perf. 14*

648 A117 10c multicolored .20 .20
649 A117 50c multicolored .35 .25
650 A117 90c multicolored .60 .50
651 A117 $4 multicolored 2.50 2.50
Nos. 648-651 (4) 3.65 3.45

Souvenir Sheet

652 A117 $5 multicolored 3.50 *4.00*

Also issued in sheetlets of 5 + label in changed colors, perf. 12.

A118

A119

1982, June 17 Litho. *Perf. 14½*

653 A118 10c A-300 Airbus .20 .20
654 A118 50c Hawker-Siddeley 748 .40 .40
655 A118 90c De Havilland Twin Otter DCH6 .65 .65
656 A118 $2.50 Britten-Norman Islander 1.75 1.75
Nos. 653-656 (4) 3.00 3.00

Souvenir Sheet

657 A118 $5 Jet, horiz. 3.50 *4.00*

Coolidge Intl. Airport opening.

1982, June 28 Litho. *Perf. 14½*

658 A119 10c Cordia, vert. .20 .20
659 A119 50c Golden spotted mongoose .35 .30
660 A119 90c Corallita, vert. .60 .60
661 A119 $3 Bulldog bats 2.00 *3.00*
Nos. 658-661 (4) 3.15 *4.10*

Souvenir Sheet

662 A119 $5 Caribbean monk seals 3.50 *4.25*

Charles Darwin's death centenary.

Princess Diana Issue
Common Design Type

1982, July 1 Litho. *Perf. 14½x14*

663 CD332 90c Greenwich Palace .60 .60
664 CD332 $1 Wedding .75 .75
665 CD332 $4 Diana 3.00 3.00
Nos. 663-665 (3) 4.35 4.35

Souvenir Sheet

666 CD332 $5 Diana, diff. 4.50 4.25

For overprints and surcharges see Nos. 672-675, 797, 799, 803, 806.

Scouting Year A120

Designs: Independence Day celebration.

1982, July 15 *Perf. 14*

667 A120 10c Decorating buildings .20 .20
668 A120 50c Helping woman .35 .30
669 A120 90c Princess Margaret .60 .50
670 A120 $2.20 Cub Scout giving directions 1.60 *2.25*
Nos. 667-670 (4) 2.75 *3.25*

Souvenir Sheet

671 A120 $5 Baden-Powell 3.50 3.25

Nos. 663-666 Overprinted: "ROYAL BABY / 21.6.82"

1982, Aug. 30 Litho. *Perf. 14½x14*

672 CD332 90c multicolored .70 .70
673 CD332 $1 multicolored .80 .80
674 CD332 $4 multicolored 3.25 2.50
Nos. 672-674 (3) 4.75 4.00

Souvenir Sheet

675 CD332 $5 multicolored 4.00 4.00

For surcharges see Nos. 798, 800, 804, 807.

Roosevelt Driving by "The Little White House" A121

1982, Sept. 20 *Perf. 15*

676 A121 10c shown .20 .20
677 A121 25c Washington as blacksmith .25 .20
678 A121 45c Churchill, Roosevelt, Stalin .80 .25
679 A121 60c Washington crossing Delaware, vert. .80 .25
680 A121 $1 Roosevelt on train, vert. 1.00 .90
681 A121 $3 Roosevelt, vert. 1.25 *1.75*
Nos. 676-681 (6) 4.30 *3.55*

Souvenir Sheets

682 A121 $4 Washington, vert. 2.75 2.50
683 A121 $4 Eleanor and Franklin 2.75 2.50

George Washington's 250th birth anniv. and Franklin D. Roosevelt's birth centenary.

Christmas — A122

Raphael Paintings.

1982, Nov. Litho. *Perf. 14*
684 A122 10c Annunciation .20 .20
685 A122 30c Adoration of the Magi .20 .20
686 A122 $1 Presentation at the Temple .75 .75
687 A122 $4 Coronation of the Virgin 2.75 *3.00*
Nos. 684-687 (4) 3.90 *4.15*

Souvenir Sheet
688 A122 $5 Marriage of the Virgin 3.25 3.00

500th Birth Anniv. of Raphael A123

1983, Jan. 28. Litho. *Perf. 14½*
689 A123 45c Galatea taking Reins of Dolphins, vert. .35 *.40*
690 A123 50c Sea Nymphs carried by Tritons, vert. .40 *.45*
691 A123 60c Winged Angel Steering Dolphins .45 *.50*
692 A123 $4 Cupids Shooting Arrows 2.75 *3.00*
Nos. 689-692 (4) 3.95 *4.35*

Souvenir Sheet
693 A123 $5 Galatea 3.25 3.50

A124

1983, Mar. 14 *Perf. 14*
694 A124 25c Pineapple crop .20 .20
695 A124 45c Carnival .35 .40
696 A124 60c Tourists, sailboat .45 .50
697 A124 $3 Control Tower 2.00 2.50
Nos. 694-697 (4) 3.00 3.60

Commonwealth Day.

World Communications Year — A125

1983, Apr. 5 Litho. *Perf. 14*
698 A125 15c TV screen, camera .20 .20
699 A125 50c Police radio, car 1.25 .75
700 A125 60c Long distance phone call 1.25 .75
701 A125 $3 Dish antenna, planets 2.25 2.25
Nos. 698-701 (4) 4.95 3.95

Souvenir Sheet
702 A125 $5 Comsat satellite 3.50 4.00

Imperforates

Quantities of imperforates of Nos. 745-749, 755-759, 819, 821, 810, 811, 815, 909, 935, 936, 961 and possibly others, became available when the printer was liquidated.

Bottlenose Dolphin — A126

1983, May 9 Litho. *Perf. 15*
703 A126 15c shown .40 .20
704 A126 50c Finback whale .75 .60
705 A126 60c Bowhead whale .80 .60
706 A126 $3 Spectacled porpoise 2.00 2.25
Nos. 703-706 (4) 3.95 3.65

Souvenir Sheet
707 A126 $5 Unicorn whale 3.50 2.50

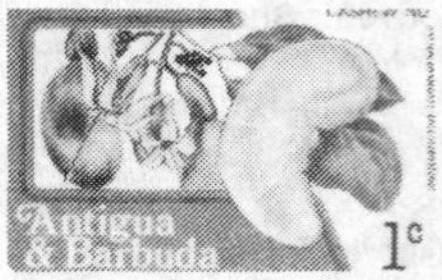

Cashew Nut A127

1983, July 11 *Perf. 14*
708 A127 1c shown .20 *.30*
709 A127 2c Passion fruit .20 *.30*
710 A127 3c Mango .20 *.30*
711 A127 5c Grapefruit .20 .20
712 A127 10c Pawpaw .30 .20
713 A127 15c Breadfruit .35 .20
714 A127 20c Coconut .35 .20
715 A127 25c Oleander .40 .20
716 A127 30c Banana .40 .25
717 A127 40c Pineapple .45 .25
718 A127 45c Cordcia .50 .35
719 A127 50c Cassia .55 .40
720 A127 60c Poui .65 .50
721 A127 $1 Frangipani 1.00 .75
722 A127 $2 Flamboyant 1.50 1.50
723 A127 $2.50 Lemon 2.00 2.50
724 A127 $5 Lignum vitae 3.50 5.00
725 A127 $10 Arms 6.50 8.00
Nos. 708-725 (18) 19.25 *21.40*

1985 *Perf. 12½x12*
708a A127 1c .20 *.30*
709a A127 2c .20 *.30*
710a A127 3c .20 *.30*
711a A127 5c .20 .20
712a A127 10c .25 .20
713a A127 15c .35 .20
714a A127 20c .40 .20
715a A127 25c .40 .20
716a A127 30c .50 .25
717a A127 40c .50 .25
718a A127 45c .65 .30
719a A127 50c .80 .30
720a A127 60c .80 .65
721a A127 $1 1.50 .75
722a A127 $2 1.50 1.65
723a A127 $2.50 1.75 2.00
724a A127 $5 3.00 *5.00*
725a A127 $10 5.50 *8.00*
Nos. 708a-725a (18) 18.70 *21.05*

Issue dates: $2-$5, Dec; others Mar.

Manned Flight Bicentenary A128

1983, Aug. 15 *Perf. 15*
726 A128 30c Dornier DoX .50 .25
727 A128 50c Supermarine S-6B .60 .40
728 A128 60c Curtiss F9C, USS Akron .75 .65
729 A128 $4 Pro Juventute balloon 2.00 *3.00*
Nos. 726-729 (4) 3.85 *4.30*

Souvenir Sheet
730 A128 $5 Graf Zeppelin 3.25 *4.00*

Christmas — A129

Raphael Paintings: 10c, 30c, $1, $4, Sybils and Angels details. $5, Vision of Ezekiel.

1983, Oct. 4 Litho. *Perf. 14*
731 A129 10c Angel flying with scroll .20 .20
732 A129 30c Angel, diff. .25 .20
733 A129 $1 Inscribing tablet .75 .65
734 A129 $4 Angel showing tablet 3.00 *3.25*
Nos. 731-734 (4) 4.20 *4.30*

Souvenir Sheet
735 A129 $5 multicolored 3.75 4.25

Methodist Church, Anniv. — A130

1984 Olympics, Los Angeles — A131

Designs: 15c, John Wesley founder of Methodism. 50c, Nathaniel Gilbert, Antiguan founder. 60c, St. John's Methodist Church Steeple. $3, Ebenezer Methodist Church.

1983, Nov. Litho. *Perf. 14*
736 A130 15c multicolored .20 .20
737 A130 50c multicolored .35 .25
738 A130 60c multicolored .45 .40
739 A130 $3 multicolored 2.00 *3.00*
Nos. 736-739 (4) 3.00 *3.85*

1984, Jan. Litho. *Perf. 15*
740 A131 25c Discus .20 .20
741 A131 50c Gymnastics .30 .20
742 A131 90c Hurdling .60 *.65*
743 A131 $3 Bicycling 2.00 *2.25*
Nos. 740-743 (4) 3.10 *3.30*

Souvenir Sheet
744 A131 $5 Volleyball, horiz. 3.25 *4.00*

Booker Vanguard A132

1984, June 4 Litho. *Perf. 15*
745 A132 45c shown .50 .30
746 A132 50c Canberra .60 .45
747 A132 60c Yachts .75 .55
748 A132 $4 Fairwind 1.50 *3.00*
Nos. 745-748 (4) 3.35 *4.30*

Souvenir Sheet
749 A132 $5 Man-of-war, vert. 3.25 *4.00*

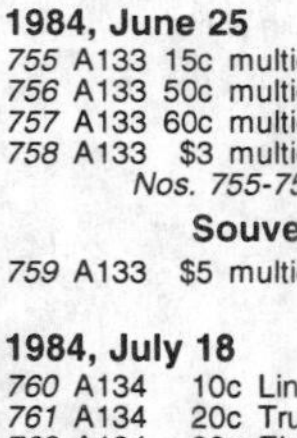

Local Flowers A133

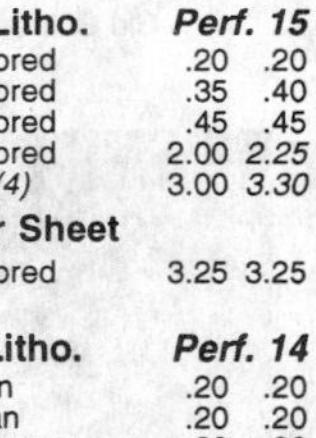

US Presidents A134

1984, June 25 Litho. *Perf. 15*
755 A133 15c multicolored .20 .20
756 A133 50c multicolored .35 .40
757 A133 60c multicolored .45 .45
758 A133 $3 multicolored 2.00 *2.25*
Nos. 755-758 (4) 3.00 *3.30*

Souvenir Sheet
759 A133 $5 multicolored 3.25 3.25

1984, July 18 Litho. *Perf. 14*
760 A134 10c Lincoln .20 .20
761 A134 20c Truman .20 .20
762 A134 30c Eisenhower .20 .20
763 A134 40c Reagan .25 .20
764 A134 90c Lincoln, diff. .50 .40
765 A134 $1.10 Truman, diff. .75 .75
766 A134 $1.50 Eisenhower, diff. 1.00 *1.10*
767 A134 $2 Reagan, diff. 1.10 *1.25*
Nos. 760-767 (8) 4.20 *4.30*

Slavery Abolition Sesquicentennial — A135

1984, Aug. 1
768 A135 40c Moravian Mission .50 .30
769 A135 50c Antigua Courthouse, 1823 .55 .35
770 A135 60c Sugar cane planting .60 .45
771 A135 $3 Boiling House, Delaps' Estate 2.00 *2.50*
Nos. 768-771 (4) 3.65 *3.60*

Souvenir Sheet
772 A135 $5 Willoughby Bay 3.25 3.25

Song Birds — A136

1984, Aug. 15 *Perf. 15*
773 A136 40c Rufous-sided towhee .80 .50
774 A136 50c Parula warbler .90 .75
775 A136 60c House wren 1.00 1.00
776 A136 $2 Ruby-crowned kinglet 1.25 *2.00*
777 A136 $3 Yellow-shafted flicker 1.75 *3.00*
Nos. 773-777 (5) 5.70 *7.25*

Souvenir Sheet
778 A136 $5 Yellow-breasted chat 3.50 *5.00*

AUSIPEX '84 — A137

The Blue Dancers, by Degas — A137a

1984, Sept. 21 *Perf. 15*
779 A137 $1 Grass skiing 1.00 1.00
780 A137 $5 Australian rules football 3.00 *3.75*

Souvenir Sheet
781 A137 $5 Boomerang 3.50 *4.00*

1984, Oct. Litho. *Perf. 15*

Paintings by Correggio: 25c, Virgin and Infant with Angels and Cherubs. 60c, The Four Saints. 90c, Saint Catherine. $3, The Campori Madonna. #790, St. John the Baptist.

Paintings by Degas: 50c, The Pink Dancers. 70c, Two Dancers. $4, Dancers at the Bar. #791, Folk Dancers.

782 A137a 15c multicolored .20 .20
783 A137a 25c multicolored .20 .20
784 A137a 50c multicolored .40 .40
785 A137a 60c multicolored .45 .45
786 A137a 70c multicolored .50 .50
787 A137a 90c multicolored .60 .65
788 A137a $3 multicolored 2.00 *2.25*
789 A137a $4 multicolored 2.75 *3.00*
Nos. 782-789 (8) 7.10 *7.65*

Souvenir Sheets
790 A137a $5 multicolored 3.50 3.50
791 A137a $5 multi, horiz. 3.50 3.50

Nos. 623-626, 663-666, 672-675, 694-697 Surcharged in Black or Gold

1984, June *Perf. 14, 14½x14*
792 CD331 $2 on 25c #623 1.50 1.50
793 CD334 $2 on 25c #694 1.50 1.50
794 CD334 $2 on 45c #695 1.50 1.50
795 CD331 $2 on 50c #624 1.50 1.50
796 CD334 $2 on 60c #696 1.50 1.50
797 CD332 $2 on 90c #663 (G) 1.50 1.50
798 CD332 $2 on 90c #672 (G) 1.50 1.50

799 CD332 $2 on $1 #664 (G) 1.50 1.50
800 CD332 $2 on $1 #673 (G) 1.50 1.50
801 CD334 $2 on $3 #697 1.50 1.50
802 CD331 $2 on $4 #625 1.50 1.50
803 CD332 $2 on $4 #665 (G) 1.50 1.50
804 CD332 $2 on $4 #674 (G) 1.50 1.50
Nos. 792-804 (13) 19.50 19.50

Souvenir Sheets

805 CD331 $2 on $5 #626 1.50 1.50
806 CD332 $2 on $5 #666 1.50 1.50
807 CD332 $2 on $5 #675 1.50 1.50

Nos. 797-800, 803-804 exist with silver surcharge.

Christmas 1984 and 50th Anniv. of Donald Duck — A138

Scenes from various Donald Duck comics.

1984, Nov. Litho. *Perf. 11*

808 A138 1c multicolored .20 .20
809 A138 2c multicolored .20 .20
810 A138 3c multicolored .20 .20
811 A138 4c multicolored .20 .20
812 A138 5c multicolored .20 .20
813 A138 10c multicolored .20 .20
814 A138 $1 multicolored 1.50 1.00
815 A138 $2 multicolored 2.25 2.25
816 A138 $5 multicolored 3.25 *3.75*
Nos. 808-816 (9) 8.20 8.20

Souvenir Sheets

Perf. 14

817 A138 $5 multi, horiz. 4.50 *5.50*
818 A138 $5 Donald on beach 4.50 *5.50*

20th Century Leaders A139

1984, Nov. 19 Litho. *Perf. 15*

819 A139 60c John F. Kennedy (1917-1963), vert. .50 *.65*
820 A139 60c Winston Churchill (1874-1965), vert. .50 *.65*
821 A139 60c Mahatma Gandhi (1869-1948), vert. .50 *.65*
822 A139 60c Mao Tse-Tung (1883-1976), vert. .50 *.65*
823 A139 $1 Kennedy in Berlin .60 *.80*
824 A139 $1 Churchill in Paris .60 *.80*
825 A139 $1 Gandhi in Great Britain .60 *.80*
826 A139 $1 Mao in Peking .60 *.80*
Nos. 819-826 (8) 4.40 *5.80*

Souvenir Sheet

827 A139 $5 Flags of Great Britain, India, China, USA 3.75 2.00

Statue of Liberty Centennial A140

1985, Jan. 7

828 A140 25c Torch on display, 1885 .20 .20
829 A140 30c Restoration, 1984-1986, vert. .20 .20
830 A140 50c Bartholdi supervising construction, 1876 .30 .30
831 A140 90c Statue on Liberty Island .65 .65
832 A140 $1 Dedication Ceremony, 1886, vert. .70 .70
833 A140 $3 Operation Sail, 1976, vert. 2.00 *2.25*
Nos. 828-833 (6) 4.05 *4.30*

Souvenir Sheet

834 A140 $5 Port of New York 3.50 3.50

Traditional Scenes A141

1985, Jan. 21

835 A141 15c Ceramics, Arawak pot shard .20 .20
836 A141 50c Tatooing, body design .35 .40
837 A141 60c Harvesting Manioc, god Yocahu .45 .50
838 A141 $3 Caribs in battle, war club 2.00 *2.25*
Nos. 835-838 (4) 3.00 *3.35*

Souvenir Sheet

839 A141 $5 Tainos worshiping 3.25 *3.50*

Invention of the Motorcycle, Cent. A142

1985, Mar. 7 *Perf. 14*

840 A142 10c Triumph 2HP Jap, 1903 .30 .20
841 A142 30c Indian Arrow, 1949 .50 .25
842 A142 60c BMW R100RS, 1976 .75 .60
843 A142 $4 Harley Davidson Model II, 1916 2.50 *3.00*
Nos. 840-843 (4) 4.05 *4.05*

Souvenir Sheet

844 A142 $5 Laverda Jota, 1975 3.75 *4.25*

John J. Audubon, 200th Birth Anniv. A143

1985, Mar. 25 *Perf. 14*

845 A143 90c Horned grebe .80 .70
846 A143 $1 Least petrel .90 .75
847 A143 $1.50 Great blue heron 1.10 *1.25*
848 A143 $3 Double-crested cormorant 1.75 *3.00*
Nos. 845-848 (4) 4.55 *5.70*

Souvenir Sheet

849 A143 $5 White-tailed tropic bird, vert. 3.50 2.75

See Nos.910-914.

Butterflies A144

1985, Apr. 16 *Perf. 14*

850 A144 25c Polygrapha cyanea .40 .20
851 A144 60c Leodonta dysoni 1.00 .50
852 A144 95c Junea doraete 1.25 .60
853 A144 $4 Prepona xenagoras 2.75 3.50
Nos. 850-853 (4) 5.40 4.80

Souvenir Sheet

854 A144 $5 Caerois gerdrudtus 4.25 *5.00*

Cessna 172 — A145

1985, Apr. 30

855 A145 30c shown .40 .20
856 A145 90c Fokker DVII .90 .40
857 A145 $1.50 Spad VII 1.25 1.10
858 A145 $3 Boeing 747 1.75 *2.50*
Nos. 855-858 (4) 4.30 *4.20*

Souvenir Sheet

859 A145 $5 Twin Otter, Coolidge Intl. Airport 3.25 *4.00*

40th anniv. of the ICAO. Nos. 855, 858-859 show the ICAO and UN emblems.

Maimonides (1135-1204), Judaic Philosopher and Physician — A146

1985, June 17 Litho. *Perf. 14*

860 A146 $2 yellow green 1.35 1.25

Souvenir Sheet

861 A146 $5 deep brown 3.00 2.00

Intl. Youth Year A147

1985, July 1

862 A147 25c Agriculture .20 .20
863 A147 50c Hotel management .25 .30
864 A147 60c Environmental studies .30 .50
865 A147 $3 Windsurfing 2.25 *3.00*
Nos. 862-865 (4) 3.00 *4.00*

Souvenir Sheet

866 A147 $5 Youths, national flag 3.25 3.50

Queen Mother, 85th Birthday — A148

Designs: 90c, $1, Attending a church service. No. 867A, $1.50, Touring the London Gardens, children in a sandpit. $2.50, $3, Photograph (1979). $5, With Prince Edward at the wedding of Prince Charles and Lady Diana Spencer.

Perf. 14, 12x12½ (90c, $1, $3)

1985, July 15

866A A148 90c multi ('86) .65 .65
867 A148 $1 multi .75 .75
867A A148 $1 multi ('86) .75 .75
868 A148 $1.50 multi 1.10 1.10
869 A148 $2.50 multi 1.75 1.75
869A A148 $3 multi ('86) 2.00 2.00
Nos. 866A-869A (6) 7.00 7.00

Souvenir Sheet

870 A148 $5 multicolored 3.25 3.25

Nos. 866A, 867A, 869A issued in sheets of 5 plus label on Jan. 13, 1986.

Marine Life — A149

Johann Sebastian Bach — A150

1985, Aug. 1 *Perf. 14*

871 A149 15c Fregata magnificens .30 .20
872 A149 45c Diploria labyrinthiformis .50 .25
873 A149 60c Oreaster reticulatus .55 .45
874 A149 $3 Gymnothorax moringa 1.75 *2.25*
Nos. 871-874 (4) 3.10 *3.15*

Souvenir Sheet

875 A149 $5 Acropora palmata 3.25 3.25

1985, Aug. 26 Litho. *Perf. 14*

876 A150 25c Bass trombone .30 .20
877 A150 50c English horn .50 .30
878 A150 $1 Violino piccolo .65 .35
879 A150 $3 Bass rackett 1.75 *1.90*
Nos. 876-879 (4) 3.20 *2.75*

Souvenir Sheet

880 A150 $5 Portrait 3.25 3.50

Girl Guides, 75th Anniv. A151

Public service and growth-oriented activities.

1985, Sept. 10

881 A151 15c Public service .40 .20
882 A151 45c Guides meeting .50 .40
883 A151 60c Lord and Lady Baden-Powell .75 .50
884 A151 $3 Nature study 1.75 *2.25*
Nos. 881-884 (4) 3.40 *3.35*

Souvenir Sheet

885 A151 $5 Barn swallow 3.25 3.25

State Visit of Elizabeth II, Oct. 24 — A152

1985, Oct. 24 Litho. *Perf. 14½*

886 A152 60c National flags .55 .45
887 A152 $1 Elizabeth II, vert. .75 .75
888 A152 $4 HMY Britannia 2.25 *3.00*
Nos. 886-888 (3) 3.55 *4.20*

Souvenir Sheet

889 A152 $5 Map of Antigua 3.25 3.25

Mark Twain — A153

Disney characters in Roughing It.

1985, Nov. 4 *Perf. 14*

890 A153 25c Cowboys and Indians .30 .20
891 A153 50c Canoeing .50 .30
892 A153 $1.10 Pony Express .90 1.00
893 A153 $1.50 Buffalo hunt in Missouri 1.10 *1.50*
894 A153 $2 Nevada silver mine 1.75 *2.25*
Nos. 890-894 (5) 4.55 *5.25*

Souvenir Sheet

895 A153 $5 Stagecoach on Kansas plains 4.50 4.50

Jacob and Wilhelm Grimm, Fabulists and Philologists — A154

Disney characters in Spindle, Shuttle and Needle.

1985, Nov. 11

896 A154 30c multicolored .40 .25
897 A154 60c multicolored .50 .40
898 A154 70c multicolored .60 .45
899 A154 $1 multicolored 1.25 1.10
900 A154 $3 multicolored 2.50 3.00
Nos. 896-900 (5) 5.25 5.20

Souvenir Sheet

900A A154 $5 multicolored 4.50 4.50

UN 40th Anniv. A155

Stamps of UN and portraits: 40c, No. 18 and Benjamin Franklin. $1, No. 391 and George Washington Carver, agricultural chemist. $3, No. 299 and Charles Lindbergh. $5, Marc Chagall, artist, vert.

1985, Nov. 18 **Perf. 13½x14**

901 A155 40c multicolored .40 .30
902 A155 $1 multicolored .75 .75
903 A155 $3 multicolored 1.75 2.25
Nos. 901-903 (3) 2.90 3.30

Souvenir Sheet
Perf. 14x13½

904 A155 $5 multicolored 3.25 2.50

Christmas — A156

Religious paintings: 10c, Madonna and Child, by De Landi. 25c, Madonna and Child, by Bonaventura Berlingheiri (d. 1244). 60c, The Nativity, by Fra Angelico (1400-1455). $4, Presentation in the Temple, by Giovanni di Paolo Grazia (c.1403-1482). $5, The Nativity, by Antoniazzo Romano.

1985, Dec. 30 **Perf. 15**

905 A156 10c multicolored .20 .20
906 A156 25c multicolored .40 .20
907 A156 60c multicolored .55 .45
908 A156 $4 multicolored 2.00 3.00
Nos. 905-908 (4) 3.15 3.85

Souvenir Sheet

909 A156 $5 multicolored 3.25 3.50

Audubon Type of 1985

Illustrations of North American ducks.

1986, Jan. 6 **Perf. 12½x12**

910 A143 60c Mallard .70 .50
911 A143 90c Dusky duck .80 .65
912 A143 $1.50 Common pintail 1.10 1.50
913 A143 $3 Widgeon 1.50 2.25
Nos. 910-913 (4) 4.10 4.90

Souvenir Sheet
Perf. 14

914 A143 $5 Common eider 3.25 2.50

1986 World Cup Soccer Championships, Mexico — A157

1986, Mar. 17 **Litho.** **Perf. 14**

915 A157 30c shown .40 .20
916 A157 60c Heading the ball .60 .35
917 A157 $1 Referee .75 .60
918 A157 $4 Goal 2.25 3.00
Nos. 915-918 (4) 4.00 4.15

Souvenir Sheet

919 A157 $5 Action 3.25 2.75

Nos. 916-917 vert.
For overprints see Nos. 963-967.

A158

Halley's Comet A159

Designs: 5c, Edmond Halley, Greenwich Observatory. 10c, Me 163B Komet. German WWII fighter plane. 60c, Montezuma sighting comet, 1517. $4, Pocahontas saving Capt. John Smith's life, 1607 sighting as sign for Powhatan Indians to raid Jamestown. $5, Comet over Antigua.

1986, Mar. 24

920 A158 5c multicolored .20 .20
921 A158 10c multicolored .20 .20
922 A158 60c multicolored .75 .35
923 A158 $4 multicolored 2.25 2.50
Nos. 920-923 (4) 3.40 3.25

Souvenir Sheet

924 A159 $5 multicolored 3.50 3.50

For overprints see Nos. 973-977.

Queen Elizabeth II, 60th Birthday
Common Design Type

1986, Apr. 21

925 CD339 60c Wedding, 1947 .60 .65
926 CD339 $1 Trooping the color 1.00 1.10
927 CD339 $4 Visiting Scotland 2.75 3.00
Nos. 925-927 (3) 4.35 4.75

Souvenir Sheet

928 CD339 $5 Held by Queen Mary, 1927 3.50 4.50

Boats — A160

1986, May 15

929 A160 30c Tugboat .25 .20
930 A160 60c Fishing boat .45 .35
931 A160 $1 Sailboat 2056 .75 .60
932 A160 $4 Lateen-rigged sailboat 2.50 3.00
Nos. 929-932 (4) 3.95 4.15

Souvenir Sheet

933 A160 $5 Boatbuilding 3.50 4.50

AMERIPEX '86 — A161

American trains.

1986, May 22 **Perf. 15**

934 A161 25c Hiawatha .50 .20
935 A161 50c Grand Canyon .60 .40
936 A161 $1 Powhattan Arrow .75 .90
937 A161 $3 Empire State 1.50 2.50
Nos. 934-937 (4) 3.35 4.00

Souvenir Sheet

938 A161 $5 Daylight 3.50 5.50

Wedding of Prince Andrew and Sarah Ferguson
Common Design Type

1986, July 23 **Perf. 14**

939 CD340 45c Couple .35 .35
940 CD340 60c Prince Andrew .45 .45
941 CD340 $4 Princes Andrew, Philip 2.75 3.50
Nos. 939-941 (3) 3.55 4.30

Souvenir Sheet

942 CD340 $5 Couple, diff. 3.25 3.50

Conch Shells — A162

1986, Aug. 6 **Litho.** **Perf. 15**

943 A162 15c Say fly-specked cerith .25 .20
944 A162 45c Gmelin smooth scotch bonnet .55 .35
945 A162 60c Linne West Indian crown conch .65 .65
946 A162 $3 Murex ciboney 2.25 3.50
Nos. 943-946 (4) 3.70 4.70

Souvenir Sheet

947 A162 $5 Atlantic natica 3.50 3.75

Flowers A163

1986, Aug. 25 **Litho.** **Perf. 15**

948 A163 10c Water lily .20 .20
949 A163 15c Queen of the night .20 .20
950 A163 50c Cup of gold .50 .50
951 A163 60c Beach morning glory .75 .75
952 A163 70c Golden trumpet .85 .85
953 A163 $1 Air plant .90 1.10
954 A163 $3 Purple wreath 1.75 2.50
955 A163 $4 Zephyr lily 2.00 3.25
Nos. 948-955 (8) 7.15 9.35

Souvenir Sheets

956 A163 $4 Dozakie 2.50 3.00
957 A163 $5 Four o'clock 3.25 3.75

Fungi — A164

1986, Sept. 15

958 A164 10c Hygrocybe occidentalis scarletina .40 .20
959 A164 50c Trogia buccinalis .60 .35
960 A164 $1 Collybia subpruinosa .90 .75
961 A164 $4 Leucocoprinus brebissonii 2.50 2.50
Nos. 958-961 (4) 4.40 3.80

Souvenir Sheet

962 A164 $5 Pyrrhoglossum pyrrhum 3.50 3.50

Nos. 915-919 Ovptd. "WINNERS Argentina 3 W. Germany 2" in Gold in 2 or 3 lines

1986, Sept. 15 **Perf. 14**

963 A157 30c multicolored .20 .20
964 A157 60c multicolored .30 .45
965 A157 $1 multicolored .75 .75
966 A157 $4 multicolored 2.75 3.00
Nos. 963-966 (4) 4.00 4.40

Souvenir Sheet

967 A157 $5 multicolored 3.25 3.25

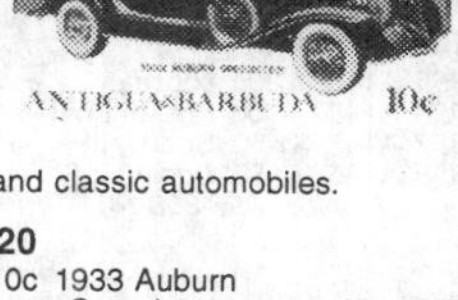

Automobile, Cent. A165

Carl Benz and classic automobiles.

1986, Oct. 20

968 A165 10c 1933 Auburn Speedster .20 .20
968A A165 15c 1986 Mercury Sable .20 .20
969 A165 50c 1959 Cadillac .40 .25
970 A165 60c 1950 Studebaker .50 .35
970A A165 70c 1939 Lagonda V-12 .60 .50
970B A165 $1 1930 Adler Standard .75 .60
970C A165 $3 1956 DKW 2.00 2.00
971 A165 $4 1936 Mercedes 500K 2.75 2.75
Nos. 968-971 (8) 7.40 6.85

Souvenir Sheets

972 A165 $5 1921 Mercedes Knight 3.50 3.25
972A A165 $5 1896 Daimler 3.50 3.25

Nos. 920-924 Ovptd. with Halley's Comet Emblem in Black or Silver

1986, Oct. 22 **Litho.** **Perf. 14**

973 A158 5c multicolored .20 .20
974 A158 10c multicolored .20 .20
975 A158 60c multicolored .45 .30
976 A158 $4 multicolored 3.00 2.75
Nos. 973-976 (4) 3.85 3.45

Souvenir Sheet

977 A159 $5 multicolored (S) 3.75 3.75

Christmas — A166

Disney characters as children.

1986, Nov. 4 **Perf. 11**

978 A166 25c Mickey .30 .25
979 A166 30c Mickey, Minnie .35 .30
980 A166 40c Aunt Matilda, Goofy .40 .35
981 A166 60c Goofy, Pluto .50 .55
982 A166 70c Pluto, Donald, Daisy .60 .65
983 A166 $1.50 Stringing popcorn 1.25 2.00
984 A166 $3 Grandma Duck, Minnie 2.25 2.75
985 A166 $4 Donald, Pete 2.75 3.25
Nos. 978-985 (8) 8.40 10.10

Souvenir Sheets
Perf. 14

986 A166 $5 Playing with presents 3.50 3.50
987 A166 $5 Reindeer 3.50 3.50

Nos. 985 printed in sheets of 8.

Coat of Arms — A167

Natl. Flag — A168

1986, Nov. 25 **Litho.** **Perf. 14x14½**

988 A167 10c bright blue .20 .20
989 A168 25c orange .25 .25

Marc Chagall (1887-1985), Artist — A169

Designs: No. 990, The Profile, 1957. No. 991, Portrait of the Artist's Sister, 1910. No. 992, Bride with Fan, 1911. No. 993, David in Profile, 1914. No. 994, Fiancee with Bouquet, 1977. No. 995, Self-portrait with Brushes, 1909. No. 996, The Walk, 1973. No. 997, Candles, 1938. No. 998, Fall of Icarus, 1975. No. 999, Myth of Orpheus, 1977.

1987, Mar. 30 Litho. *Perf. 13½x14*
990 A169 10c multicolored .20 .20
991 A169 30c multicolored .25 .20
992 A169 40c multicolored .30 .30
993 A169 60c multicolored .35 .35
994 A169 90c multicolored .60 .60
995 A169 $1 multicolored .65 .65
996 A169 $3 multicolored 2.00 *2.25*
997 A169 $4 multicolored 2.75 *3.00*

Size: 110x95mm

Imperf
998 A169 $5 multicolored 3.25 3.25
999 A169 $5 multicolored 3.25 3.25
Nos. 990-999 (10) 13.60 14.05

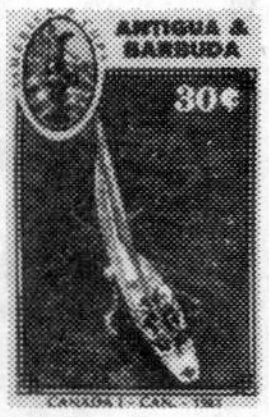

A170

America's Cup A171

1987, Feb. 5 *Perf. 15*
1000 A170 30c Canada I, 1981 .25 .20
1001 A170 60c Gretel II, 1970 .30 .35
1002 A170 $1 Sceptre, 1958 .70 .75
1003 A170 $3 Vigilant, 1893 1.50 *2.25*
Nos. 1000-1003 (4) 2.75 *3.55*

Souvenir Sheet
1004 A171 $5 Australia II, Liberty, 1983 2.75 3.50

Fish, World Wildlife Fund A172

Marine Birds A173

1987, Feb. 23 Litho. *Perf. 14*
1005 A172 15c Bridled burrfish .50 .20
1006 A173 30c Brown noddy .90 .25
1007 A172 40c Nassau grouper .65 .30
1008 A173 50c Laughing gull 1.25 .50
1009 A172 60c French angelfish .90 .50
1010 A172 $1 Porkfish .90 .60
1011 A173 $2 Royal tern 1.75 1.65
1012 A173 $3 Sooty tern 2.00 2.00
Nos. 1005-1012 (8) 8.85 6.00

Souvenir Sheets
1013 A172 $5 Banded butterfly fish 5.00 5.00
1014 A173 $5 Brown booby 5.00 5.00

The 30c, 50c, $2, $3 and Nos. 1013-1014 do not picture the WWF emblem.

For overprints see Nos. 1137-1139A.

Statue of Liberty, Cent. A174

Photographs by Peter B. Kaplan.

1987, Apr. 20 *Perf. 14*
1015 A174 15c Lee Iacocca .20 .20
1016 A174 30c Statue at dusk .25 .25
1017 A174 45c Crown, head .45 .45
1018 A174 50c Iacocca, torch .50 .50
1019 A174 60c Crown observatory .50 .50
1020 A174 90c Interior restoration .70 .70
1021 A174 $1 Head .80 .80
1022 A174 $2 Statue at sunset 1.65 *1.75*
1023 A174 $3 Men on scaffold, flag 1.75 *2.50*
1024 A174 $5 Statue at night 3.00 *4.00*
Nos. 1015-1024 (10) 9.80 *11.65*

Nos. 1015-1018, 1021-1022, 1024 vert.

A175

Transportation Innovations — A175a

1987, Apr. 19 *Perf. 15*
1025 A175 10c Spirit of Australia, 1978 .20 .20
1026 A175a 15c Siemens' Electric locomotive, 1879 .30 .20
1027 A175 30c USS Triton, 1960 .30 .20
1028 A175a 50c Trevithick, 1801 .35 .30
1029 A175 60c USS New Jersey, 1942 .40 .35
1030 A175a 70c Draisine bicycle, 1818 .40 .40
1031 A175 90c SS United States, 1952 .60 .60
1032 A175a $1.50 Cierva C-4, 1923 .75 *1.50*
1033 A175a $2 Curtiss NC-4, 1919 .90 *1.60*
1034 A175 $3 Queen Elizabeth II, 1969 1.50 *1.75*
Nos. 1025-1034 (10) 5.70 *7.10*

Reptiles and Amphibians — A176

1987, June 15 *Perf. 14*
1035 A176 30c Eleutherodactylus martinicensis .35 .20
1036 A176 60c Thecadactylus bapicauda .50 .45
1037 A176 $1 Anolis bimaculatus leachi .70 .60
1038 A176 $3 Geochelone carbonaria 1.75 *2.25*
Nos. 1035-1038 (4) 3.30 *3.50*

Souvenir Sheet
1039 A176 $5 Ameiva griswoldi 3.25 3.25

Entertainers — A177

1987, May 11
1040 A177 15c Grace Kelly .30 .20
1041 A177 30c Marilyn Monroe .60 .25
1042 A177 45c Orson Welles .30 .20
1043 A177 50c Judy Garland .30 .20
1044 A177 60c John Lennon .75 .35
1045 A177 $1 Rock Hudson .50 .35
1046 A177 $2 John Wayne .75 .70
1047 A177 $3 Elvis Presley 2.00 1.25
Nos. 1040-1047 (8) 5.50 3.50

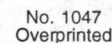

No. 1047 Overprinted

1987, Sept. 9 Litho. *Perf. 14*
1047A A177 $3 multicolored 2.50 2.50

1988 Summer Olympics, Seoul A178

1987, Mar. 23
1048 A178 10c Basketball .20 .20
1049 A178 60c Fencing .50 .25
1050 A178 $1 Women's gymnastics .70 .70
1051 A178 $3 Soccer 1.75 *2.50*
Nos. 1048-1051 (4) 3.15 *3.65*

Souvenir Sheet
1052 A178 $5 Boxing glove 3.25 *3.50*

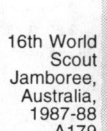

16th World Scout Jamboree, Australia, 1987-88 A179

1987, Nov. 2 Litho. *Perf. 15*
1053 A179 10c Campfire, red kangaroo .30 .20
1054 A179 60c Kayaking, blue-winged kookaburra .75 .45
1055 A179 $1 Obstacle course, ring-tailed rock wallaby .75 .50
1056 A179 $3 Field kitchen, koalas 1.25 *2.25*
Nos. 1053-1056 (4) 3.05 *3.40*

Souvenir Sheet
1057 A179 $5 Flags 3.25 3.25

US Constitution Bicent. — A180

Designs: 15c, Virginia House of Burgesses exercising right of freedom of speech. 45c, Connecticut state seal. 60c, Delaware state seal. $4, Gouverneur Morris (1752-1816), principal writer of the Constitution, vert. $5, Roger Sherman (1721-1793), jurist and statesman, vert.

1987, Nov. 16 Litho. *Perf. 14*
1058 A180 15c multicolored .20 .20
1059 A180 45c multicolored .25 *.30*
1060 A180 60c multicolored .35 *.40*
1061 A180 $4 multicolored 2.25 *2.75*
Nos. 1058-1061 (4) 3.05 *3.65*

Souvenir Sheet
1062 A180 $5 multicolored 3.25 3.25

Christmas — A181

A182

Paintings: 45c, Madonna and Child, by Bernardo Daddi (1290-1355). 60c, Joseph, detail from The Nativity, by Sano Di Pietro (1406-1481). $1, Mary, detail from Di Pietro's The Nativity. $4, Music-making Angel, by Melozzo Da Forli (1438-1494). $5, The Flight into Egypt, by Di Pietro.

1987, Dec. 1
1063 A181 45c multicolored .30 .20
1064 A181 60c multicolored .45 .30
1065 A181 $1 multicolored .75 .70
1066 A181 $4 multicolored 2.25 *3.00*
Nos. 1063-1066 (4) 3.75 *4.20*

Souvenir Sheet
1067 A181 $5 multicolored 3.25 3.25

1988, Feb. 8 Litho. *Perf. 14*
1068 A182 25c Wedding portrait .20 .20
1069 A182 60c Elizabeth II, c. 1970 .45 *.50*
1070 A182 $2 Christening of Charles, 1948 1.25 *1.50*
1071 A182 $3 Elizabeth II, c. 1980 1.75 *2.00*
Nos. 1068-1071 (4) 3.65 *4.20*

Souvenir Sheet
1072 A182 $5 Royal family, c. 1951 3.25 3.25

40th wedding anniv. of Queen Elizabeth II and Prince Philip.

Tropical Birds A183

1988, Mar. 1
1073 A183 10c Great blue heron, vert. .25 .20
1074 A183 15c Ringed kingfisher .25 .20
1075 A183 50c Bananaquit .50 .40
1076 A183 60c Purple gallinule .50 .45
1077 A183 70c Blue-hooded euphonia .60 .55
1078 A183 $1 Caribbean parakeet, vert. .75 .65
1079 A183 $3 Troupial 2.50 2.25
1080 A183 $4 Hummingbird 2.50 *3.00*
Nos. 1073-1080 (8) 7.85 7.70

Souvenir Sheets
1081 A183 $5 Roseate flamingo, vert. 3.25 3.25
1082 A183 $5 Brown pelicans, vert. 3.25 3.25

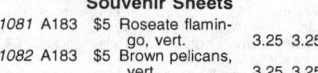

Salvation Army — A184

1988, Mar. 7
1083 A184 25c Day-care, Antigua .30 .25
1084 A184 30c Penicillin inoculation, Indonesia .30 .25
1085 A184 40c Day-care Center, Bolivia .40 .30
1086 A184 45c Rehabilitation, India .40 .30
1087 A184 50c Training the blind, Kenya .45 *.50*
1088 A184 60c Infant care, Ghana .45 *.50*
1089 A184 $1 Job training, Zambia .75 *.90*
1090 A184 $2 Food distribution, Sri Lanka 1.25 *1.75*
Nos. 1083-1090 (8) 4.30 *4.75*

Souvenir Sheet
1091 A184 $5 General Eva Burrows 3.25 3.25

A185

Discovery of America, 500th Anniv. (in 1992)
A186

Anniv. emblem and: 10c, Fleet. 30c, View of fleet in harbor from Paino Indian village. 45c, Caravel anchored in harbor, Paino village. 60c, Columbus, 3 Indians in canoe. 90c, Indian, parrot, Columbus. $1, Columbus in longboat. $3, Spanish guard, fleet in harbor. $4, Ships under full sail. No. 1100, Stone cross given to Columbus by Queen Isabella. No. 1101, Gold exelente.

1988, Mar. 14 Litho. *Perf. 14*

1092	A185	10c	multicolored	.30	.20
1093	A185	30c	multicolored	.30	.20
1094	A185	45c	multicolored	.35	.25
1095	A185	60c	multicolored	.35	.30
1096	A185	90c	multicolored	.70	.50
1097	A185	$1	multicolored	.70	.70
1098	A185	$3	multicolored	1.25	1.25
1099	A185	$4	multicolored	1.50	*2.00*
			Nos. 1092-1099 (8)	5.45	5.40

Souvenir Sheets

1100	A186	$5	multicolored	3.25	3.25
1101	A186	$5	multicolored	3.25	3.25

Paintings by Titian
A187

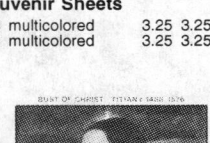

Details: 30c, Bust of Christ. 40c, Scourging of Christ. 45c, Madonna in Glory with Saints. 50c, The Averoldi Polyptych. $1, Christ Crowned with Thorns. $2, Christ Mocked. $3, Christ and Simon of Cyrene. $4, Crucifixion with Virgin and Saints. No. 1110, Ecce Homo. No. 1111, Noli Me Tangere.

1988, Apr. 11 Litho. *Perf. 13½x14*

1102	A187	30c	shown	.35	.25
1103	A187	40c	multicolored	.40	.30
1104	A187	45c	multicolored	.40	.30
1105	A187	50c	multicolored	.45	.45
1106	A187	$1	multicolored	.75	.75
1107	A187	$2	multicolored	1.25	*1.40*
1108	A187	$3	multicolored	2.00	*2.25*
1109	A187	$4	multicolored	2.25	*2.50*
			Nos. 1102-1109 (8)	7.85	*8.20*

Souvenir Sheets

1110	A187	$5	multicolored	3.25	*3.75*
1111	A187	$5	multicolored	3.25	*3.75*

Sailing Week
A188

1988, Apr. 18 *Perf. 15*

1112	A188	30c	Canada I, 1980	.20	.20
1113	A188	60c	Gretel II, Australia, 1970	.50	*.55*
1114	A188	$1	Sceptre, GB, 1958	.80	*.85*
1115	A188	$3	Vigilant, US, 1893	1.75	*3.00*
			Nos. 1112-1115 (4)	3.25	*4.60*

Souvenir Sheet

1116	A188	$5	Australia II, 1983	3.25	*4.25*

Walt Disney Animated Characters and Epcot Center, Walt Disney World — A189

1988, May 3 *Perf. 14x13½, 13½x14*

1116A	A189	1c	like 25c	.20	.20
1116B	A189	2c	like 30c	.20	.20
1116C	A189	3c	like 40c	.20	.20
1116D	A189	4c	like 60c	.20	.20
1116E	A189	5c	like 70c	.20	.20
1116F	A189	10c	like $1.50	.20	.20
1117	A189	25c	The Living Seas	.20	.20
1118	A189	30c	World of Motion	.25	.25
1119	A189	40c	Spaceship Earth	.25	.25
1120	A189	60c	Universe of Energy	.30	.30
1121	A189	70c	Journey to Imagination	.40	.40
1122	A189	$1.50	The Land	1.25	1.25
1123	A189	$3	Communicore	2.25	2.25
1124	A189	$4	Horizons	2.50	2.50
			Nos. 1116A-1124 (14)	8.60	8.60

Souvenir Sheets

1125	A189	$5	Epcot Center	3.50	*3.75*
1126	A189	$5	The Contemporary Resort Hotel	3.50	*3.75*

30c, 40c, $1.50, $3 and No. 1126 are vert.

Flowering Trees
A190 A191

1988, May 16 *Perf. 14*

1127	A190	10c	Jacaranda	.30	.20
1128	A190	30c	Cordia	.35	.25
1129	A190	50c	Orchid tree	.50	.50
1130	A190	90c	Flamboyant	.60	.60
1131	A190	$1	African tulip tree	.75	.75
1132	A190	$2	Potato tree	1.50	*1.75*
1133	A190	$3	Crepe myrtle	2.00	*2.25*
1134	A190	$4	Pitch apple	2.50	*3.00*
			Nos. 1127-1134 (8)	8.50	*9.30*

Souvenir Sheets

1135	A191	$5	Cassia	3.25	*3.50*
1136	A191	$5	Chinaberry	3.25	*3.50*

Nos. 1011-1012, 1014 and 1013 Ovptd. in Black for Philatelic Exhibitions

a Praga '88

b INDEPENDENCE 40

c FINLANDIA 88

d OLYMPHILEX '88

1988, May 9 Litho. *Perf. 14*

1137	A173 (a)	$2	multicolored	1.25	*1.50*
1138	A173 (b)	$3	multicolored	2.00	*2.25*

Souvenir Sheets

1139	A173 (c)	$5	multicolored	3.25	3.25
1139A	A172 (d)	$5	multicolored	3.25	3.25

1988 Summer Olympics, Seoul
A192

1988, June 10

1140	A192	40c	Gymnastic rings, vert.	.30	.30
1141	A192	60c	Weight lifting, vert.	.45	.45
1142	A192	$1	Water polo	.70	*.75*
1143	A192	$3	Boxing	1.75	*2.25*
			Nos. 1140-1143 (4)	3.20	*3.75*

Souvenir Sheet

1144	A192	$5	Torch-bearer, vert.	3.25	*3.75*

Butterflies
A193

1988-90 Litho. *Perf. 14*

1145	A193	1c	Monarch	.20	.20
1146	A193	2c	Jamaican clearwing	.20	.20
1147	A193	3c	Yellow-barred ringlet	.25	.25
1148	A193	5c	Cracker	.35	.35
1149	A193	10c	Jamaican mestra	.40	.25
1150	A193	15c	Mimic	.50	.25
1151	A193	20c	Silver spot	.60	.25
1152	A193	25c	Zebra	.60	.25
1153	A193	30c	Fiery sulphur	.60	.25
1154	A193	40c	Androgeus swallowtail	.65	.25
1155	A193	45c	Giant brimstone	.65	.25
1156	A193	50c	Orbed sulphur	.75	.35
1157	A193	60c	Blue-backed skipper	.80	.45
1158	A193	$1	Common white skipper	.70	.60
1159	A193	$2	Baracoa skipper	1.25	*1.75*
1160	A193	$2.50	Mangrove skipper	2.25	*2.50*
1161	A193	$5	Silver king	2.75	*3.50*
1161A	A193	$10	Pygmy skipper	4.00	*4.50*
1162	A193	$20	Parides lycimenes	12.50	*14.00*
			Nos. 1145-1162 (19)	30.00	*30.40*

Issued: $20, Feb. 19, 1990; others, Aug. 29.
This is an expanding set. Numbers will change if necessary.

John F. Kennedy
A194

1988, Nov. 22 Litho. *Perf. 14*

1162A	A194	1c	like 30c	.20	.20
1162B	A194	2c	like $4	.20	.20
1162C	A194	3c	like $1	.20	.20
1162D	A194	4c	like 60c	.20	.20
1163	A194	30c	First family	.25	.20
1164	A194	60c	Motorcade, Mexico	.45	.40
1165	A194	$1	Funeral procession	.70	*.70*
1166	A194	$4	Aboard PT109	2.25	*2.50*
			Nos. 1162A-1166 (8)	4.45	*4.60*

Souvenir Sheet

1167	A194	$5	Taking Oath of Office	3.25	*3.75*

Miniature Sheet

Christmas, Mickey Mouse 60th Anniv. — A195

Walt Disney characters: No. 1168a, Morty and Ferdie. No. 1168b, Goofy. No. 1168c, Chip-n-Dale. No. 1168d, Huey and Dewey. No. 1168e, Minnie Mouse. No. 1168f, Pluto. No. 1168g, Mickey Mouse. No. 1168h, Donald Duck and Louie. No. 1169, Goofy driving Mickey and Minnie in a horse-drawn carriage. No. 1170, Characters on roller skates, caroling.

1988, Dec. 1 *Perf. 13½x14, 14x13½*

1168	A195		Sheet of 8	6.00	6.00
a.-h.		$1	any single	.75	.75

Souvenir Sheets

1169	A195	$7	multicolored	5.00	5.00
1170	A195	$7	multi, horiz.	5.00	5.00

1988, Dec. 1 Litho. *Perf. 14*

1171	A195	10c	like No. 1168e	.20	.20
1172	A195	25c	like No. 1168f	.20	.20
1173	A195	30c	like No. 1168g	.25	.25
1174	A195	70c	like No. 1168h	.50	.50
			Nos. 1171-1174 (4)	1.15	1.15

Arawak Indian Whip Dance — A196

UPAE and discovery of America emblems and: a, Five adults. b, Eight adults. c, Seven adults. d, Three adults, three children.

1989, May 16 Litho. *Perf. 14*

1175			Strip of 4	4.50	4.50
a.-d.	A196	$1.50	any single	1.10	1.10

Souvenir Sheet

1176	A196	$6	Arawak chief	4.50	4.50

Discovery of America 500th anniv. (in 1992), pre-Columbian societies and customs.

Jet Flight, 50th Anniv.
A197

Various jet aircraft.

1989, May 29 Litho. *Perf. 14x13½*

1177	A197	10c	DeHavilland Comet 4	.20	.20
1178	A197	30c	Messerschmitt Me262	.25	.20
1179	A197	40c	Boeing 707	.25	.30
1180	A197	60c	Canadair F-86 Sabre	.30	.25
1181	A197	$1	Lockheed F-104 Starfighter	.40	.35
1182	A197	$2	McDonnell Douglas DC-10	.80	*1.00*
1183	A197	$3	Boeing 747	1.00	*1.10*
1184	A197	$4	McDonnell F-4 Phantom	1.00	*1.10*
			Nos. 1177-1184 (8)	4.20	*4.50*

Souvenir Sheets

1185	A197	$7	Grumman F-14 Tomcat	4.75	*5.00*
1186	A197	$7	Concorde	4.75	*5.00*

Caribbean Cruise Ships
A198

1989, June 20 Litho. *Perf. 14*

1187	A198	25c	TSS *Festivale*	.20	.20
1188	A198	45c	M.S. *Southward*	.30	.20
1189	A198	50c	M.S. *Sagafjord*	.40	.20
1190	A198	60c	MTS *Daphne*	.45	.30
1191	A198	75c	M.V. *Cunard Countess*	.55	.45
1192	A198	90c	M.S. *Song of America*	.70	.65
1193	A198	$3	M.S. *Island Princess*	2.00	*2.25*
1194	A198	$4	S.S. *Galileo*	2.00	*2.25*
			Nos. 1187-1194 (8)	6.60	*6.50*

Souvenir Sheets

1195	A198	$6	S.S. *Norway*	4.25	*4.75*
1196	A198	$6	S.S. *Oceanic*	4.25	*4.75*

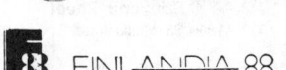

Paintings by Hiroshige — A199

Designs: 25c, *Fish Swimming by Duck Half-submerged in Stream.* 45c, *Crane and Wave.* 50c, *Sparrows and Morning Glories.* 60c, *Crested Blackbird and Flowering Cherry.* $1, *Great Knot Sitting among Water Grass.* $2, *Goose on a Bank of Water.* $3, *Black Paradise Flycatcher and Blossoms.* $4, *Sleepy Owl Perched on a Pine Branch.* No. 1205, *Bullfinch Flying Near a Clematis Branch.* No. 1206, *Tit-mouse on a Cherry Branch.*

1989, July 3 — ***Perf. 14x13½***

1197 A199 25c multicolored .45 .20
1198 A199 45c multicolored .55 .35
1199 A199 50c multicolored .60 .35
1200 A199 60c multicolored .70 .45
1201 A199 $1 multicolored .80 .60
1202 A199 $2 multicolored 1.75 1.75
1203 A199 $3 multicolored 2.00 2.00
1204 A199 $4 multicolored 2.00 2.00
Nos. 1197-1204 (8) 8.85 7.70

Souvenir Sheets

1205 A199 $5 multicolored 3.25 3.25
1206 A199 $5 multicolored 3.25 3.25

Hirohito (1901-1989) and enthronement of Akihito as emperor of Japan.

PHILEXFRANCE '89 — A200

Walt Disney characters, French landmarks: 1c, Helicopter over the Seine. 2c, Arc de Triomphe. 3c, Painting Notre Dame Cathedral. 4c, Entrance to the Metro. 5c, Fashion show. 10c, Follies. No. 1213, Shopping stalls on the Seine. $6, Sidewalk cafe, Left Bank. No. 1215, Hot air balloon *Ear Force One.* No. 1216, Dining.

1989, July 7 — ***Perf. 14x13½***

1207 A200 1c multicolored .20 .20
1208 A200 2c multicolored .20 .20
1209 A200 3c multicolored .20 .20
1210 A200 4c multicolored .20 .20
1211 A200 5c multicolored .20 .20
1212 A200 10c multicolored .20 .20
1213 A200 $5 multicolored 3.25 *3.75*
1214 A200 $6 multicolored 3.75 *4.00*
Nos. 1207-1214 (8) 8.20 *8.95*

Souvenir Sheets

1215 A200 $5 multicolored 3.25 3.25
1216 A200 $5 multicolored 3.25 3.25

1990 World Cup Soccer Championships, Italy — A201

Natl. flag, various actions of a defending goalie.

1989, Aug. 21 — ***Perf. 14***

1217 A201 15c multicolored .45 .20
1218 A201 25c multicolored .50 .20
1219 A201 $1 multicolored 1.00 .75
1220 A201 $4 multicolored 2.00 *3.50*
Nos. 1217-1220 (4) 3.95 *4.65*

Souvenir Sheets

1221 A201 $5 2 players, horiz. 3.25 *3.50*
1222 A201 $5 3 players, horiz. 3.25 *3.50*

For overprints see Nos. 1344-1349.

Mushrooms — A202

1989, Oct. 12 — **Litho.** — ***Perf. 14***

1223 A202 10c Lilac fairy helmet .20 .20
1224 A202 25c Rough psathyrella, vert. .25 .20
1225 A202 50c Golden tops .60 .40
1226 A202 60c Blue cap, vert. .60 .45
1227 A202 75c Brown cap, vert. .75 .55
1228 A202 $1 Green gill, vert. 1.00 .75
1229 A202 $3 Red pinwheel 2.00 *2.50*
1230 A202 $4 Red chanterelle 2.00 *2.50*
Nos. 1223-1230 (8) 7.40 *7.55*

Souvenir Sheets

1231 A202 $6 Slender stalk 4.25 4.00
1232 A202 $6 Paddy straw mushroom 4.25 4.00

Nos. 1224, 1226-1228, 1231 vert.

Wildlife A203

1989, Oct. 19 — **Litho.** — ***Perf. 14***

1233 A203 25c Hutia .30 .25
1234 A203 45c Caribbean monk seal .75 .40
1235 A203 60c Mustache bat, vert. .50 .45
1236 A203 $4 Manatee, vert. 1.50 *2.25*
Nos. 1233-1236 (4) 3.05 *3.35*

Souvenir Sheet

1237 A203 $5 West Indies giant rice rat 3.25 *3.75*

American Philatelic Soc. Emblem, Stamps on Stamps and Walt Disney Characters Promoting Philately A204

Designs: 1c, Israel #150, printing press. 2c, Italy #1238, first day cancel. 3c, US #143L4, Pony Express recruits. 4c, Denmark #566, early radio broadcast. 5c, German Democratic Republic #702, television. 10c, Great Britain #1, stamp collector. $4, Japan #1414, integrated circuits. $6, Germany #B667, boom box. No. 1246, US #1355, C3a, and Jenny biplane over Disneyland, horiz. No. 1247, US #940, 1421 and stamps for the wounded.

1989, Nov. 2 — ***Perf. 13½x14, 14x13½***

1238 A204 1c multicolored .20 .20
1239 A204 2c multicolored .20 .20
1240 A204 3c multicolored .20 .20
1241 A204 4c multicolored .20 .20
1242 A204 5c multicolored .20 .20
1243 A204 10c multicolored .20 .20
1244 A204 $4 multicolored 3.00 *3.25*
1245 A204 $6 multicolored 4.00 *4.25*
Nos. 1238-1245 (8) 8.20 *8.70*

Souvenir Sheets

1246 A204 $5 multicolored 3.50 *3.75*
1247 A204 $5 multicolored 3.50 *3.75*

Locomotives and Walt Disney Characters — A205

Perf. 14x13½, 13½x14

1989, Nov. 17

1248 A205 25c John Bull, 1831 .50 .50
1249 A205 45c Atlantic, 1832 .60 .50
1250 A205 50c William Crook's, 1861 .60 .50
1251 A205 60c Minnetonka, 1869 .70 .65
1252 A205 $1 Thatcher Perkins, 1863 .75 .75
1253 A205 $2 Pioneer, 1848 1.50 *2.00*
1254 A205 $3 Peppersass, 1869 1.75 *2.50*
1255 A205 $4 Gimbels Flyer 2.00 *2.50*
Nos. 1248-1255 (8) 8.40 *9.90*

Souvenir Sheets

1256 A205 $6 #6100 Class S-1 & 1835 Thomas Jefferson 4.25 *4.50*
1257 A205 $6 Jupiter & #119 4.25 *4.50*

New York World's Fair, 50th anniv., and World Stamp Expo '89, Washington, DC.

1st Moon Landing, 20th Anniv. A206

1989, Nov. 24 — **Litho.** — ***Perf. 14***

1258 A206 10c Apollo 11 liftoff .20 .20
1259 A206 45c Aldrin walking on Moon .35 .20
1260 A206 $1 *Eagle* ascending from Moon .70 .60
1261 A206 $4 Recovery after splashdown 2.75 *3.25*
Nos. 1258-1261 (4) 4.00 *4.25*

Souvenir Sheet

1262 A206 $5 Armstrong 3.50 *3.75*

Nos. 1258-1259 and 1262, vert.

Souvenir Sheet

Smithsonian Institution, Washington, DC — A207

1989, Nov. 17 — **Litho.** — ***Perf. 14***

1263 A207 $4 multicolored 3.00 3.00

World Stamp Expo '89.

Christmas — A208

Religious paintings: 10c, *The Small Cowper Madonna.* 25c, *Madonna of the Goldfinch.* 30c, *The Alba Madonna.* 50c, *Bologna Altarpiece* (attendant). 60c, *Bologna Altarpiece* (heralding angel). 70c, *Bologna Altarpiece* (archangel). $4, *Bologna Altarpiece* (saint holding ledger). No. 1271, *Madonna of Foligno.* No. 1272, *The Marriage of the Virgin.* No. 1273, *Bologna Altarpiece* (Madonna and Child).

Bologna Altarpiece by Giotto. Other paintings by Raphael.

1989, Dec. 11 — **Litho.** — ***Perf. 14***

1264 A208 10c multicolored .20 .20
1265 A208 25c multicolored .20 .20
1266 A208 30c multicolored .20 .20
1267 A208 50c multicolored .45 .35
1268 A208 60c multicolored .50 .40
1269 A208 70c multicolored .55 .45
1270 A208 $4 multicolored 2.75 *3.00*
1271 A208 $5 multicolored 3.50 *4.00*
Nos. 1264-1271 (8) 8.35 *8.80*

Souvenir Sheets

1272 A208 $5 multicolored 3.50 *4.00*
1273 A208 $5 multicolored 3.50 *4.00*

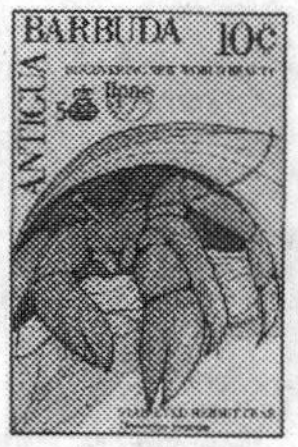

America Issue — A210

Orchids — A211

UPAE, discovery of America 500th anniv. emblems and marine life: 10c, Star-eyed hermit crab. 20c, Spiny lobster. 25c, Magnificent banded fanworm. 45c, Cannonball jellyfish. 60c, Red-spiny sea star. $2, Peppermint shrimp. $3, Coral crab. $4, Branching fire coral. No. 1283, Common sea fan. No. 1284, Portuguese man-of-war.

1990, Mar. 26 — **Litho.** — ***Perf. 14***

1275 A210 10c multicolored .20 .20
1276 A210 20c multicolored .20 .20
1277 A210 25c multicolored .25 .25
1278 A210 45c multicolored .45 .45
1279 A210 60c multicolored .70 .70
1280 A210 $2 multicolored 1.75 *2.00*
1281 A210 $3 multicolored 2.00 *2.25*
1282 A210 $4 multicolored 2.50 *2.75*
Nos. 1275-1282 (8) 8.05 *8.80*

Souvenir Sheets

1283 A210 $5 multicolored 3.50 *4.00*
1284 A210 $5 multicolored 3.50 *4.00*

1990, Apr. 17 — ***Perf. 14***

1285 A211 15c *Vanilla mexicana* .35 .25
1286 A211 45c *Epidendrum ibaguense* .50 .25
1287 A211 50c *Epidendrum secundum* .55 .30
1288 A211 60c *Maxillaria conferta* .60 .35
1289 A211 $1 *Oncidium altissimum* .90 .70
1290 A211 $2 *Spiranthes lanceolata* 1.25 *1.50*
1291 A211 $3 *Tonopsis utricularioides* 1.75 *2.25*
1292 A211 $5 *Epidendrum nocturnum* 3.50 *3.75*
Nos. 1285-1292 (8) 9.40 *9.35*

Souvenir Sheets

1293 A211 $6 *Octomeria graminifolia* 4.00 *4.50*
1294 A211 $6 *Rodriguezia lanceolata* 4.00 *4.50*

EXPO '90, Osaka.

Fish A212

1990, May 21 — ***Perf. 14***

1295 A212 10c Flamefish .35 .35
1296 A212 15c Coney .40 .35
1297 A212 50c Squirrelfish .60 .45
1298 A212 60c Sergeant major .60 .45
1299 A212 $1 Yellowtail snapper .85 .65
1300 A212 $2 Rock beauty 1.50 *1.75*
1301 A212 $3 Spanish hogfish 2.00 *2.25*
1302 A212 $4 Striped parrotfish 2.00 *2.25*
Nos. 1295-1302 (8) 8.30 *8.50*

Souvenir sheets

1303 A212 $5 Blackbar soldierfish 3.50 *4.00*
1304 A212 $5 Foureye butterflyfish 3.50 *4.00*

Victoria and Elizabeth II — A213

1990, May 3 Litho. *Perf. 15x14*

1305 A213 45c green .60 .30
1306 A213 60c bright rose .70 .50
1307 A213 $5 bright ultra 3.25 *4.00*
Nos. 1305-1307 (3) 4.55 *4.80*

Souvenir Sheet

1308 A213 $6 black 4.25 *4.75*

Penny Black, 150th anniv.

Royal Mail Transport — A214

Designs: 50c, Steam packet *Britannia*, 1840. 75c, Railway mail car, 1892. $4, *Centaurus* seaplane, 1938. $6, Subway, 1927.

1990, May 3 *Perf. 13½*

1309 A214 50c red & deep green .55 .30
1310 A214 75c red & vio brn .75 .70
1311 A214 $4 red & brt ultra 3.00 *3.75*
Nos. 1309-1311 (3) 4.30 *4.75*

Souvenir Sheet

1312 A214 $6 red & black 4.25 *4.75*

Stamp World London '90.

Miniature Sheet

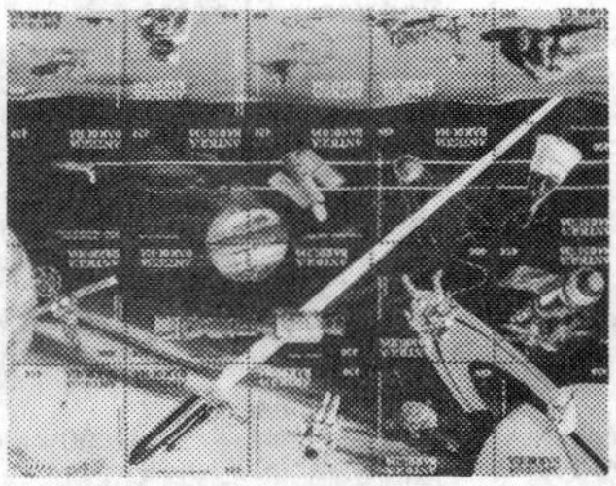
Space Achievements — A215

Designs: a, *Voyager 2* passing Saturn. b, *Pioneer 11* photographing Saturn. c, Manned maneuvering unit. d, *Columbia* space shuttle. e, Splashdown of Apollo 10 command module. f, *Skylab*. g, Ed White space walking, Gemini 4 mission. h, Apollo module, Apollo-Soyuz mission. i, Soyuz module, Apollo-Soyuz mission. j, *Mariner 1* passing Venus. k, Gemini 4 module. l, *Sputnik*. m, Hubble Space Telescope. n, X-15 rocket plane. o, Bell X-1 breaking sound barrier. p, Astronaut, Apollo 17 mission. r, American lunar rover. r, Lunar module, Apollo 14 mission. s, First men on the Moon, Apollo 11 mission. t, Lunokhod, Soviet lunar rover.

1990, June 11 Litho. *Perf. 14*

1313 A215 Sheet of 20 6.75 6.75
a.-t. 45c any single .30 .30

Mickey Production Studios — A216

Walt Disney characters in Hollywood: 45c, Minnie Mouse reading script. 50c, Director Mickey Mouse, take 1 of Minnie. 60c, Make-up artist Daisy Duck. $1, Clarabelle as Cleopatra. $2, Mickey, Goofy, Donald Duck. $3, Goofy destroying set. $4, Mickey, Donald editing film. No. 1322, Mickey directs surfing film. No. 1323, Minnie, Daisy, Clarabelle in musical.

1990, Sept. 3 Litho. *Perf. 14x13½*

1314 A216 25c shown .25 .20
1315 A216 45c multicolored .45 .20
1316 A216 50c multicolored .55 .25
1317 A216 60c multicolored .60 .30
1318 A216 $1 multicolored .80 .60
1319 A216 $2 multicolored 1.50 1.75
1320 A216 $3 multicolored 2.00 2.25
1321 A216 $4 multicolored 2.00 2.25
Nos. 1314-1321 (8) 8.15 7.80

Souvenir Sheets

1322 A216 $5 multicolored 3.50 3.50
1323 A216 $5 multicolored 3.50 3.50

A217

A218

1990, Aug. 27 Litho. *Perf. 14*

1324 A217 15c multicolored .20 .20
1325 A217 35c multi, diff. .30 .20
1326 A217 75c multi, diff. .55 .55
1327 A217 $3 multi, diff. 2.00 2.50
Nos. 1324-1327 (4) 3.05 3.45

Souvenir Sheet

1328 A217 $6 multi, diff. 4.00 4.50

Queen Mother, 90th birthday.

1990, Oct. 1 Litho. *Perf. 14*

1329 A218 50c 20-Kilometer Walk .55 .30
1330 A218 75c Triple jump .70 .65
1331 A218 $1 10,000 meter run .90 .85
1332 A218 $5 Javelin 3.00 4.25
Nos. 1329-1332 (4) 5.15 6.05

Souvenir Sheet

1333 A218 $6 Opening ceremony, Los Angeles, 1984 4.25 *5.50*

1992 Summer Olympics, Barcelona.

Intl. Literacy Year
A219

Walt Disney characters in scenes from books by Charles Dickens: 15c, Huey and Dewey, Christmas Stories. 45c, Donald Duck, Bleak House. 50c, Dewey, Bad Pete, Oliver Twist. 60c, Daisy Duck, Old Curiosity Shop. $1, Little Nell. $2, Scrooge McDuck, Pickwick Papers. $3, Mickey and Minnie Mouse, Dombey and Son. $5, Minnie, Our Mutual Friend. No. 1342, Mickey and friends, David Copperfield. No. 1343, Pinocchio, Oliver Twist.

1990, Oct. 15 Litho. *Perf. 14*

1334 A219 15c multicolored .20 .20
1335 A219 45c multicolored .35 .35
1336 A219 50c multicolored .40 .40
1337 A219 60c multicolored .45 .45
1338 A219 $1 multicolored .70 .70
1339 A219 $2 multicolored 1.25 1.75
1340 A219 $3 multicolored 1.75 2.25
1341 A219 $5 multicolored 2.50 3.00
Nos. 1334-1341 (8) 7.60 9.10

Souvenir Sheets

1342 A219 $6 multicolored 4.25 4.50
1343 A219 $6 multicolored 4.25 4.50

Nos. 1217-1222 Overprinted **Winners West Germany 1 Argentina 0**

1990, Nov. 11

1344 A201 15c multicolored .40 .20
1345 A201 25c multicolored .40 .20
1346 A201 $1 multicolored 1.00 1.00
1347 A201 $4 multicolored 2.50 3.25
Nos. 1344-1347 (4) 4.30 4.65

Souvenir Sheets

1348 A201 $5 on #1221 3.50 3.75
1349 A201 $5 on #1222 3.50 3.75

Overprint on Nos. 1348-1349 is 32x13mm.

Birds — A220

1990, Nov. 19

1350 A220 10c Pearly-eyed thrasher .30 .30
1351 A220 25c Purple-throated carib .35 .35
1352 A220 50c Common yellow-throat .40 .40
1353 A220 60c American kestrel .70 .70
1354 A220 $1 Yellow-bellied sapsucker .75 .75
1355 A220 $2 Purple gallinule 1.75 2.00
1356 A220 $3 Yellow-crowned night heron 2.25 2.50
1357 A220 $4 Blue-hooded euphonia 2.25 2.50
Nos. 1350-1357 (8) 8.75 9.50

Souvenir Sheets

1358 A220 $6 Brown pelican 4.25 4.75
1359 A220 $6 Frigate bird 4.25 4.75

Christmas — A221

Paintings: 25c, Madonna and Child with Saints by del Piombo. 30c, Virgin and Child with Angels by Grunewald, vert. 40c, Holy Family and a Shepherd by Titian. 60c, Virgin and Child by Fra Filippo Lippi, vert. $1, Jesus, St. John and Two Angels by Rubens. $2, Adoration of the Shepherds by Catena. $4, Adoration of the Magi by Giorgione. $5, Virgin and Child Adored by a Warrior by Catena. No. 1368, Allegory of the Blessings of Jacob by Rubens, vert. No. 1369, Adoration of the Magi by Fra Angelico, vert.

Perf. 14x13½, 13½x14

1990, Dec. 10 Litho.

1360 A221 25c multicolored .25 .20
1361 A221 30c multicolored .30 .20
1362 A221 40c multicolored .40 .25
1363 A221 60c multicolored .55 .35
1364 A221 $1 multicolored .75 .60
1365 A221 $2 multicolored 1.60 1.75
1366 A221 $4 multicolored 2.75 3.00
1367 A221 $5 multicolored 2.75 3.00
Nos. 1360-1367 (8) 9.35 9.35

Souvenir Sheets

1368 A221 $6 multicolored 4.25 4.50
1369 A221 $6 multicolored 4.25 4.50

Peter Paul Rubens (1577-1640), Painter — A222

Entire paintings or different details from: 25c, Rape of the Daughters of Leucippus. 45c, $2, $4, Bacchanal. 50c, $1, $3, Rape of the Sabine Women. 60c, Battle of the Amazons. No. 1378, Rape of Hippodameia. No. 1379, Battle of the Amazons.

1991, Jan. 21 Litho. *Perf. 14*

1370 A222 25c multicolored .45 .30
1371 A222 45c multicolored .65 .45
1372 A222 50c multicolored .70 .50
1373 A222 60c multicolored .75 .65
1374 A222 $1 multicolored .90 .90
1375 A222 $2 multicolored 1.25 1.50
1376 A222 $3 multicolored 2.00 2.25
1377 A222 $4 multicolored 2.75 3.00
Nos. 1370-1377 (8) 9.45 9.55

Souvenir Sheets

1378 A222 $6 multicolored 4.25 4.50
1379 A222 $6 multicolored 4.25 4.50

World War II Milestones — A223

Designs: 10c, US troops enter Germany, Sept. 11, 1944. 15c, All axis forces surrender in North Africa, May 12, 1943. 25c, US troops invade Kwajalein, Jan. 31, 1944. 45c, Roosevelt and Churchill meet in Casablanca, Jan. 14, 1943. 50c, Marshal Badoglio signs agreement with allies, Sept. 1, 1943. $1, Mountbatten appointed Supreme Allied Commander, Southeast Asia Command, Aug. 25, 1943. $2, Major Greek tactical victory, Koritza, Nov. 22, 1940. $4, Britain and USSR sign mutual assistance pact, July 12, 1941. $5, Operation Torch, Nov. 8, 1942. No. 1389, Japanese attack on Pearl Harbor, Dec. 7, 1941. No. 1390, American bombing attack on Schweinfurt, Oct. 14, 1943.

1991, Mar. 11 Litho. *Perf. 14*

1380 A223 10c multicolored .25 .25
1381 A223 15c multicolored .30 .20
1382 A223 25c multicolored .35 .35
1383 A223 45c multicolored .70 .50
1384 A223 50c multicolored .60 .45
1385 A223 $1 multicolored .75 .65
1386 A223 $2 multicolored 1.50 1.75
1387 A223 $4 multicolored 2.25 2.50
1388 A223 $5 multicolored 2.25 2.50
Nos. 1380-1388 (9) 8.95 9.15

Souvenir Sheets

1389 A223 $6 multicolored 4.25 4.50
1390 A223 $6 multicolored 4.25 4.50

Cog Railways of the World A224

Designs: 25c, Prince Regent, Middleton Colliery, 1812. 30c, Snowdon Mountain Railway, Wales. 40c, 1st Railcar at Hell Gate, Manitou and Pike's Peak Railway. 60c, PNKA Rack Railway, Amberawa, Java. $1, Green Mountain Railway, Mt. Desert Island, Maine, 1883. $2, Cog locomotive, Pike's Peak, 1891. $4, Vitznau-Rigi Cog Railway, Lake Lucerne. $5, Leopoldina Railway, Brazil. No. 1399, Electric Cog Donkey Engines, Panama Canal. No. 1400, Gornergratbahn, 1st electric cog railway in Switzerland, vert.

1991, Mar. 18 Litho. *Perf. 14*

1391 A224 25c multicolored .20 .20
1392 A224 30c multicolored .25 .25
1393 A224 40c multicolored .30 .30
1394 A224 60c multicolored .45 .45
1395 A224 $1 multicolored 1.00 .75
1396 A224 $2 multicolored 1.75 1.50
1397 A224 $4 multicolored 3.00 3.00
1398 A224 $5 multicolored 3.00 3.75
Nos. 1391-1398 (8) 9.95 10.20

Souvenir Sheets

1399 A224 $6 multicolored 4.25 4.25
1400 A224 $6 multicolored 4.25 4.25

Butterflies A225

1991, Apr. 15 Litho. *Perf. 14*

1401 A225 10c Zebra .20 .20
1402 A225 35c Southern daggertail .25 .25
1403 A225 50c Red anartia .40 .40
1404 A225 75c Malachite .55 .55
1405 A225 $1 Polydamas swallowtail .70 .75
1406 A225 $2 Orion 1.25 1.50
1407 A225 $4 Mimic 2.75 3.00
1408 A225 $5 Cracker 3.25 3.75
Nos. 1401-1408 (8) 9.35 10.40

Souvenir Sheets

Caterpillars

1409 A225 $6 Monarch, vert. 4.25 4.25
1410 A225 $6 Painted lady, vert. 4.25 4.25

Voyages of Discovery A226

Designs: 10c, Hanno, Phoenicia, c. 450 B.C. 15c, Pytheas, Greece, 325 B.C. 45c, Eric the Red, Viking, A.D. 985. 60c, Leif Erikson, Viking, A.D. 1000. $1, Scylax, Greece, A.D. 518. $2, Marco Polo, A.D. 1259. $4, Queen Hatshepsut, Egypt, 1493 B.C. $5, St. Brendan, Ireland, 500 A.D. No. 1419, Columbus, bareheaded. No. 1420, Columbus, wearing hat.

1991, Apr. 22

1411 A226 10c multicolored .20 .20
1412 A226 15c multicolored .20 .20
1413 A226 45c multicolored .35 .35
1414 A226 60c multicolored .45 .45
1415 A226 $1 multicolored .70 .75
1416 A226 $2 multicolored 1.25 1.50
1417 A226 $4 multicolored 2.50 3.00
1418 A226 $5 multicolored 3.00 3.75
Nos. 1411-1418 (8) 8.65 10.20

Souvenir Sheets

1419 A226 $6 multicolored 4.00 4.00
1420 A226 $6 multicolored 4.00 4.00

Discovery of America, 500th anniv. (in 1992).

Paintings by Vincent Van Gogh A227

Designs: 5c, Portrait of Camille Roulin. 10c, Portrait of Armand Roulin. 15c, Young Peasant Woman with Straw Hat Sitting in the Wheat. 25c, Portrait of Adeline Ravoux. 30c, The Schoolboy (Camille Roulin). 40c, Portrait of Doctor Gachet. 50c, Portrait of a Man. 75c, Two Children. $2, Portrait of Postman Joseph Roulin. $3, The Seated Zouave. $4, L'arlesienne: Madame Ginoux with Books. No. 1432, Self Portrait, November/December 1888. No. 1433, Flowering Garden. No. 1434, Farmhouse in Provence. $6, The Bridge at Trinquetaille.

1991, May 13 ***Perf. 13½***

1421 A227 5c multicolored .20 .20
1422 A227 10c multicolored .20 .20
1423 A227 15c multicolored .20 .20
1424 A227 25c multicolored .20 .20
1425 A227 30c multicolored .25 .25
1426 A227 40c multicolored .30 .30
1427 A227 50c multicolored .35 .35
1428 A227 75c multicolored .55 .55
1429 A227 $2 multicolored 1.25 1.50
1430 A227 $3 multicolored 2.00 2.25
1431 A227 $4 multicolored 2.50 3.00
1432 A227 $5 multicolored 3.00 3.75
Nos. 1421-1432 (12) 11.00 12.75

Size: 102x76mm

Imperf

1433 A227 $5 multicolored 3.50 3.50
1434 A227 $5 multicolored 3.50 3.50
1435 A227 $6 multicolored 4.25 4.25

Phila Nippon '91 — A228

Walt Disney characters demonstrating Japanese martial arts: 10c, Mickey as champion sumo wrestler, vert. 15c, Goofy using tonfa. 45c, Ninja Donald in full field dress. 60c, Mickey using weapon in kung fu, vert. $1, Goofy tries kendo, vert. $2, Mickey, Donald demonstrating special technique of aikido. $4, Mickey flips Donald with judo throw. $5, Mickey demonstrates yabusame (target shooting from running horse), vert. No. 1444, Mickey using karate. No. 1445, Mickey demonstrating tamashiwara (powerbreaking), vert.

Perf. 13½x14, 14x13½

1991, June 29 **Litho.**

1436 A220 10c multicolored .20 .20
1437 A228 15c multicolored .20 .20
1438 A228 45c multicolored .35 .35
1439 A220 60c multicolored .45 .45
1440 A228 $1 multicolored .70 .75
1441 A220 $2 multicolored 1.25 1.50
1442 A220 $4 multicolored 2.50 3.00
1443 A228 $5 multicolored 3.00 3.75
Nos. 1436-1443 (8) 8.65 10.20

Souvenir Sheets

1444 A228 $6 multicolored 4.25 4.25
1445 A228 $6 multicolored 4.25 4.25

Royal Family Birthday, Anniversary

Common Design Type

1991, July 8 **Litho.** ***Perf. 14***

1446 CD347 10c multicolored .20 .20
1447 CD347 15c multicolored .20 .20
1448 CD347 20c multicolored .20 .20
1449 CD347 40c multicolored .30 .30
1450 CD347 $1 multicolored .70 .75
1451 CD347 $2 multicolored 1.25 1.50
1452 CD347 $4 multicolored 2.50 3.00
1453 CD347 $5 multicolored 3.00 3.75
Nos. 1446-1453 (8) 8.35 9.90

Souvenir Sheets

1454 CD347 $4 Elizabeth, Philip 2.75 2.75
1455 CD347 $4 Charles, Diana, sons 2.75 2.75

10c, 40c, $1, $5, No. 1455, Charles and Diana, 10th wedding anniversary. Others, Queen Elizabeth II, 65th birthday.

Walt Disney Characters Playing Golf A229

Designs: 10c, Daisy Duck teeing off. 15c, Goofy using 3-Wood. 45c, Mickey using 3-Iron. 60c, Mickey missing ball using 6-Iron. $1, Donald trying 8-Iron to get out of pond. $2, Minnie using 9-Iron. $4, Donald digging hole with sand wedge. $5, Goofy trying new approach with putter. No. 1464, Grandma Duck using pitching wedge. No. 1465, Mickey cheering Minnie as she uses her 5-Wood, horiz.

Perf. 13½x14, 14x13½

1991, Aug. 7 **Litho.**

1456 A229 10c multicolored .20 .20
1457 A229 15c multicolored .20 .20
1458 A229 45c multicolored .35 .35
1459 A229 60c multicolored .45 .45
1460 A229 $1 multicolored .70 .75
1461 A229 $2 multicolored 1.25 1.50
1462 A229 $4 multicolored 2.50 3.00
1463 A229 $5 multicolored 3.00 3.75
Nos. 1456-1463 (8) 8.65 10.20

Souvenir Sheets

1464 A229 $6 multicolored 4.25 4.25
1465 A229 $6 multicolored 4.25 4.25

1992 Summer Olympics, Barcelona A230

Archie Comics, 50th anniv.: 10c, Moose receiving gold medal. 25c, Archie, Veronica, Mr. Lodge, polo match, horiz. 40c, Archie & Betty, fencing. 60c, Archie, women's volleyball. $1, Archie, tennis. $2, Archie, marathon race. $4, Archie, judging women's gymnastics, horiz. $5, Archie, Betty, Veronica, basketball. No. 1474, Archie, soccer. No. 1475, Archie, Betty, baseball, horiz.

Perf. 13½x14, 14x13½

1991, Aug. 19

1466 A230 10c multicolored .20 .20
1467 A230 25c multicolored .20 .20
1468 A230 40c multicolored .30 .30
1469 A230 60c multicolored .45 .45
1470 A230 $1 multicolored .75 .75
1471 A230 $2 multicolored 1.50 1.50
1472 A230 $4 multicolored 3.00 3.00
1473 A230 $5 multicolored 3.75 3.75
Nos. 1466-1473 (8) 10.15 10.15

Souvenir Sheets

1474 A230 $6 multicolored 4.50 4.50
1475 A230 $6 multicolored 4.50 4.50

Charles de Gaulle, Birth Cent. A231

Charles de Gaulle: 10c, and Pres. Kennedy, families, 1961. 15c, and Pres. Roosevelt, 1945, vert. 45c, and Chancellor Adenauer, 1962, vert. 60c, Liberation of Paris, 1944, vert. $1, Crossing the Rhine, 1945. $2, In Algiers, 1944. $4, and Pres. Eisenhower, 1960. $5, Returning from Germany, 1968, vert. No. 1484, and Churchill at Casablanca, 1943. No. 1485, and Citizens.

1991, Sept. 11 **Litho.** ***Perf. 14***

1476 A231 10c multicolored .20 .20
1477 A231 15c multicolored .20 .20
1478 A231 45c multicolored .35 .35
1479 A231 60c multicolored .45 .45
1480 A231 $1 multicolored .70 .75
1481 A231 $2 multicolored 1.25 1.50
1482 A231 $4 multicolored 2.50 3.00
1483 A231 $5 multicolored 3.00 3.75
Nos. 1476-1483 (8) 8.65 10.20

Souvenir Sheets

1484 A231 $6 multicolored 4.25 4.25
1485 A231 $6 multicolored 4.25 4.25

Independence, 10th Anniv. — A232

Designs: 10c, Island maps, government building. $6, Old P. O., St. Johns, #1 & #635.

1991, Oct. 28

1486 A232 10c multicolored .20 .20

Souvenir Sheet

1487 A232 $6 multicolored 4.25 4.25

No. 1487 contains one 50x38mm stamp.

Miniature Sheet

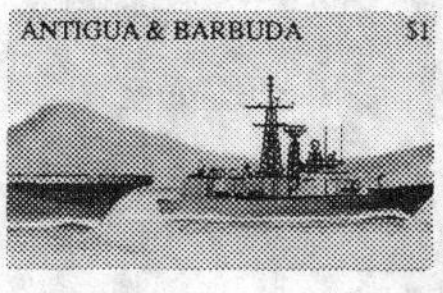

Attack on Pearl Harbor, 50th Anniv. A233

Designs: No. 1488a, Bow of Nimitz class carrier, Ticonderoga class cruiser. b, Tourist boat to Arizona Memorial. c, USS Arizona Memorial. d, Aircraft salute to missing men. e, White tern. f, Japanese Kate torpedo bombers. g, Japanese Zero fighters. h, Battleship row in flames. i, USS Nevada breaking out. j, Zeros returning to carriers.

1991, Dec. 9 ***Perf. 14½x15***

1488 A233 $1 Sheet of 10, #a.-j. 7.50 7.50

Inscription for No. 1488f incorrectly describes torpedo bombers as Zekes.

3rd Antigua Methodist Cub Scout Pack, 60th Anniv. A234

Designs: $2, Lord Robert Baden-Powell, scouts, vert. $3.50, Scouts around campfire. $5, Antigua & Barbuda flag, Jamboree emblem, vert.

1991, Dec. 9 ***Perf. 14***

1489 A234 75c multicolored .60 .60
1490 A234 $2 multicolored 1.25 1.50
1491 A234 $3.50 multicolored 2.25 2.75
Nos. 1489-1491 (3) 4.10 4.85

Souvenir Sheet

1492 A234 $5 multicolored 3.25 3.25

17th World Scout Jamboree, Korea.

Wolfgang Amadeus Mozart, Death Bicent. A235

Portrait of Mozart and: $1.50, Scene from opera, Don Giovanni. $4, St. Peter's Cathedral, Salzburg.

1991, Dec. 9

1493 A235 $1.50 multicolored 1.10 1.10
1494 A235 $4 multicolored 2.50 3.00

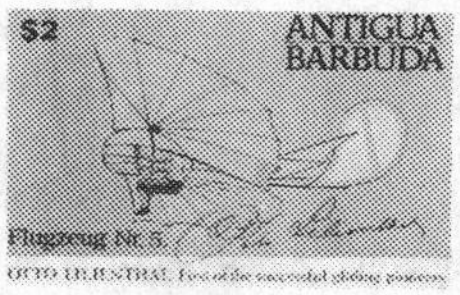

Anniversaries and Events — A236

Designs: $2, Otto Lilienthal's glider No. 5. $2.50, Locomotive cab, vert.

1991, Dec. 9 **Litho.** ***Perf. 14***

1495 A236 $2 multicolored 1.25 1.50
1496 A236 $2.50 multicolored 1.60 1.90

First glider flight, cent. (No. 1495). Trans-Siberian Railway, cent. (No. 1496). Numbers have been reserved for additional values in this set.

Brandenburg Gate, Bicent. — A237

Designs: 25c, Demonstrators in autos, German flag. $2, Statue. $3, Portions of decorative frieze.

1991, Dec. 9 **Litho.** ***Perf. 14***

1499 A237 25c multicolored .20 .20
1500 A237 $2 multicolored 1.25 1.50
1501 A237 $3 multicolored 2.00 2.25
Nos. 1499-1501 (3) 3.45 3.95

Souvenir Sheet

1502 A237 $4 multicolored 3.00 3.00

Christmas A238

Paintings by Fra Angelico: 10c, The Annunciation. 30c, Nativity. 40c, Adoration of the Magi. 60c, Presentation in the Temple. $1, Circumcision. $3, Flight into Egypt. $4, Massacre of the Innocents. $5, Christ Teaching in the Temple. No. 1511, Adoration of the Magi, diff. No. 1512, Adoration of the Magi (Cook Tondo).

1991, Dec. 12 ***Perf. 12***

1503 A238 10c multicolored .20 .20
1504 A238 30c multicolored .25 .25
1505 A238 40c multicolored .30 .30

1506 A238 60c multicolored .45 .45
1507 A238 $1 multicolored .70 .75
1508 A238 $3 multicolored 2.00 2.25
1509 A238 $4 multicolored 2.50 3.00
1510 A238 $5 multicolored 3.00 3.75
Nos. 1503-1510 (8) 9.40 10.95

Souvenir Sheets

1511 A238 $6 multicolored 4.25 4.25
1512 A238 $6 multicolored 4.25 4.25

Queen Elizabeth II's Accession to the Throne, 40th Anniv.

Common Design Type

Queen Elizabeth II and various island scenes.

1992, Feb. 6 Litho. *Perf. 14*

1513 CD348 10c multicolored .20 .20
1514 CD348 30c multicolored .20 .20
1515 CD348 $1 multicolored .70 .75
1516 CD348 $5 multicolored 3.00 3.75
Nos. 1513-1516 (4) 4.10 4.90

Souvenir Sheets

1517 CD348 $6 Beach 4.25 4.25
1518 CD348 $6 Flora 4.25 4.25

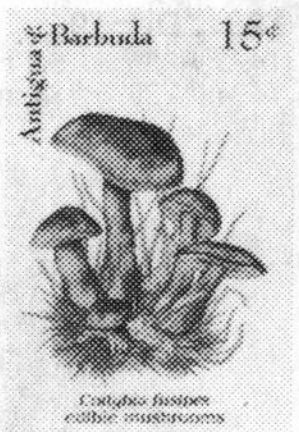

Mushrooms — A239

1992 Litho. *Perf. 14*

1519 A239 10c Amanita caesarea .20 .20
1520 A239 15c Collybia fusipes .20 .20
1521 A239 30c Boletus aereus .20 .20
1522 A239 40c Laccaria amethystina .30 .30
1523 A239 $1 Russula virescens .70 .75
1524 A239 $2 Tricholoma auratum 1.25 1.50
1525 A239 $4 Calocybe gambosa 2.50 3.00
1526 A239 $5 Panus tigrinus 3.00 3.75
Nos. 1519-1526 (8) 8.35 9.90

Souvenir Sheet

1527 A239 $6 Auricularia auricula 4.25 4.25
1528 A239 $6 Clavariadelphus truncatus 4.25 4.25

Issued: 10c, 30c, $1, $5, #1528, May 18; others, Mar.

Disney Characters at Summer Olympics, Barcelona A240

Designs: 10c, Mickey presenting gold medal to mermaid for swimming. 15c, Dewey and Huey watching Louie in kayak. 30c, Uncle McScrooge, Donald yachting. 50c, Donald, horse trying water polo. $1, Big Pete weight lifting. $2, Donald, Goofy fencing. $4, Mickey, Donald playing volleyball. $5, Goofy vaulting over horse. No. 1537, Mickey playing basketball, horiz. No. 1538, Minnie Mouse on uneven parallel bars, horiz. No. 1539, Mickey, Goofy, and Donald judging Minnie's floor exercise, horiz. No. 1540, Mickey running after soccer ball.

1992, Mar. 16 *Perf. 13*

1529 A240 10c multicolored .20 .20
1530 A240 15c multicolored .20 .20
1531 A240 30c multicolored .20 .20
1532 A240 50c multicolored .40 .40
1533 A240 $1 multicolored .70 .75
1534 A240 $2 multicolored 1.25 1.50
1535 A240 $4 multicolored 2.50 3.00
1536 A240 $5 multicolored 3.00 3.75
Nos. 1529-1536 (8) 8.45 10.00

Souvenir Sheets

1537-1540 A240 $6 each 4.25 4.25

Dinosaurs A241

1992, Apr. 6 *Perf. 14*

1541 A241 10c Pteranodon .20 .20
1542 A241 15c Brachiosaurus .20 .20
1543 A241 30c Tyrannosaurus rex .20 .20
1544 A241 50c Parasaurolophus .40 .40
1545 A241 $1 Deinonychus .70 .75
1546 A241 $2 Triceratops 1.25 1.50
1547 A241 $4 Protoceratops 2.50 3.00
1548 A241 $5 Stegosaurus 3.00 3.75
Nos. 1541-1548 (8) 8.45 10.00

Souvenir Sheets

1549 A241 $6 Apatosaurus 4.25 4.25
1550 A241 $6 Allosaurus 4.25 4.25

Nos. 1541-1544 are vert.

Easter — A242

Paintings: 10c, Supper at Emmaus, by Caravaggio. 15c, The Vision of St. Peter, by Francisco de Zurbaran. 30c, $1, Christ Driving the Money Changers from the Temple, by Tiepolo (detail on $1). 40c, Martyrdom of St. Bartholomew (detail), by Jusepe de Ribera. $2, Crucifixion (detail), by Albrecht Altdorfer. $4, $5, The Deposition (diff. detail), by Fra Angelico. No. 1559, Crucifixion, by Albrecht Altdorfer, vert. No. 1560, The Last Supper, by Vicente Juan Masip.

1992 *Perf. 14x13½*

1551 A242 10c multicolored .20 .20
1552 A242 15c multicolored .20 .20
1553 A242 30c multicolored .20 .20
1554 A242 40c multicolored .30 .30
1555 A242 $1 multicolored .70 .75
1556 A242 $2 multicolored 1.25 1.50
1557 A242 $4 multicolored 2.50 3.00
1558 A242 $5 multicolored 3.00 3.75
Nos. 1551-1558 (8) 8.35 9.90

Souvenir Sheet

Perf. 13½x14

1559 A242 $6 multicolored 4.25 4.25
1560 A242 $6 multicolored 4.25 4.25

Spanish Art — A243

Designs: 10c, The Miracle at the Well, by Alonso Cano. 15c, The Poet Luis de Gongora y Argote, by Velazquez. 30c, The Painter Francisco Goya, by Vincente Lopez Portana. 40c, Maria de Las Nieves Michaela Fourdiniere, by Luis Paret y Alcazar. $1, Charles III Eating before His Court, by Paret y Alcazar, horiz. $2, A Rain Shower in Granada, by Antonio Munoz Degrain, horiz. $4, Sarah Bernhardt, by Santiago Rusinol y Prats. $5, The Hermitage Garden, by Joaquin Mir Trinxet. No. 1569, Olympus: Battle with the Giants, by Francisco Bayeu y Subias. No. 1570, The Ascent of Monsieur Boucle's Montgolfier Balloon in the Gardens of Aranjuez, by Antonio Carnicero.

1992, May 11

1561 A243 10c multicolored .20 .20
1562 A243 15c multicolored .20 .20
1563 A243 30c multicolored .20 .20
1564 A243 40c multicolored .30 .30
1565 A243 $1 multicolored .70 .75
1566 A243 $2 multicolored 1.25 1.50
1567 A243 $4 multicolored 2.50 3.00
1568 A243 $5 multicolored 3.00 3.75

Size: 120x95mm

Imperf

1569 A243 $6 multicolored 3.75 4.50
1570 A243 $6 multicolored 3.75 4.50
Nos. 1561-1570 (10) 15.85 18.90

Granada '92.

Discovery of America, 500th Anniv. — A244

Designs: 15c, San Salvador Island. 30c, Martin Alonzo Pinzon, captain of Pinta. 40c, Columbus, signature, coat of arms. $1, Pinta. $2, Nina. $4, Santa Maria. No. 1577, Sea monster. No. 1578, Map, sailing ship.

1992, May 25 Litho. *Perf. 14*

1571 A244 15c multicolored .20 .20
1572 A244 30c multicolored .20 .20
1573 A244 40c multicolored .30 .30
1574 A244 $1 multicolored .70 .75
1575 A244 $2 multicolored 1.25 1.50
1576 A244 $4 multicolored 2.50 3.00
Nos. 1571-1576 (6) 5.15 5.95

Souvenir Sheets

1577 A244 $6 multicolored 4.25 4.25
1578 A244 $6 multicolored 4.25 4.25

World Columbian Stamp Expo '92, Chicago.

Hummel Figurines — A245

Wanderers: 15c, No. 1587a, Boy sitting on rock pointing to flower in cap. 30c, No. 1587b, Girl sitting on fence. 40c, No. 1587c, Boy holding binoculars. 50c, No. 1587d, Boy carrying umbrella. $1, No. 1588a, Two boys looking up at direction marker. $2, No. 1588b, Boy carrying basket on back, walking with stick. $4, No. 1588c, Two girls, goat. $5, No. 1588d, Boy carrying walking stick.

1993, Jan. 6 Litho. *Perf. 14*

1579 A245 15c multicolored .20 .20
1580 A245 30c multicolored .20 .20
1581 A245 40c multicolored .30 .30
1582 A245 50c multicolored .40 .40
1583 A245 $1 multicolored .70 .75
1584 A245 $2 multicolored 1.25 1.50
1585 A245 $4 multicolored 2.50 3.00
1586 A245 $5 multicolored 3.00 3.75
Nos. 1579-1586 (8) 8.55 10.10

Souvenir Sheets of 4

1587 A245 $1.50 #a.-d. 4.25 4.25
1588 A245 $1.50 #a.-d. 4.25 4.25

Hummingbirds and Flowers — A246

Designs: 10c, Antillean crested, wild plantain. 25c, Green mango, parrot's plantain. 45c, Purple-throated carib, lobster claws. 60c, Antillean mango, coral plant. $1, Vervain, cardinal's guard. $2, Rufous breasted hermit, heliconia. $4, Blue-headed, red ginger. $5, Green-throated carib, ornamental banana. No. 1597, Bee, jungle flame. No. 1598, Western streamertails, bignonia.

1992, Aug. 10 Litho. *Perf. 14*

1589 A246 10c multicolored .20 .20
1590 A246 25c multicolored .20 .20
1591 A246 45c multicolored .35 .35
1592 A246 60c multicolored .45 .45
1593 A246 $1 multicolored .70 .75
1594 A246 $2 multicolored 1.25 1.50
1595 A246 $4 multicolored 2.50 3.00
1596 A246 $5 multicolored 3.00 3.75
Nos. 1589-1596 (8) 8.65 10.20

Souvenir Sheets

1597 A246 $6 multicolored 6.75 6.75
1598 A246 $6 multicolored 6.75 6.75

Genoa '92.

Discovery of America, 500th Anniv. — A247

1992 Litho. *Perf. 14½*

1599 A247 $1 Coming ashore .75 .75
1600 A247 $2 Natives, ships 1.25 1.50

Organization of East Caribbean States.

Souvenir Sheet

Madison Square Garden, NYC — A248

1992 Litho. *Perf. 14*

1601 A248 $6 multicolored 5.00 5.00

Postage Stamp Mega-Event, Jacob Javits Center, New York City.

Elvis Presley (1935-1977) — A249

Various pictures of Elvis Presley.

1992 *Perf. 13½x14*

1602 A249 $1 Sheet of 9, #a.-i. 7.00 7.00

Inventors and Pioneers A250

Designs: 10c, Ts'ai Lun, paper. 25c, Igor I. Sikorsky, 4-engine airplane. 30c, Alexander Graham Bell, telephone. 40c, Johannes Gutenberg, printing press. 60c, James Watt, steam engine. $1, Anton van Leeuwenhoek, microscope. $4, Louis Braille, Braille printing. $5, Galileo, telescope. No. 1607, Phonograph. No. 1608, Steamboat.

1992, Oct. 19 Litho. *Perf. 14*

1603 A250 10c multicolored .20 .20
1604 A250 25c multicolored .20 .20
1605 A250 30c multicolored .25 .25
1605A A250 40c multicolored .40 .40
1605B A250 60c multicolored .45 .45
1605C A250 $1 multicolored .75 .75
1605D A250 $4 multicolored 3.00 3.00
1606 A250 $5 multicolored 3.75 3.75
Nos. 1603-1606 (8) 9.00 9.00

Souvenir Sheet

1607	A250	$6 multicolored	4.00	4.00
1608	A250	$6 multicolored	4.00	4.00

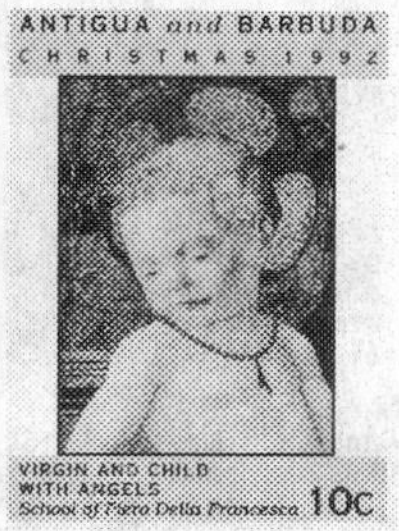

Christmas A251

Details from Paintings: 10c, Virgin and Child with Angels, by School of Piero Della Francesca. 25c, Madonna Degli Alberelli, by Giovanni Bellini. 30c, Madonna and Child with St. Anthony Abbot and St. Sigismund, by Neroccio di Landi. 40c, Madonna and the Grand Duke, by Raphael. 60c, The Nativity, by George de la Tour. $1, Holy Family, by Jacob Jordaens. $4, Madonna and Child Enthroned, by Margaritone. $5, Madonna and Child on a Curved Throne, by Byzantine artist. No. 1617, Madonna and Child, by Domenico Ghirlandaio (both names misspelled). No. 1618, The Holy Family, by Pontormo.

1992 **Perf. 13½x14**

1609	A251	10c multicolored	.20	.20
1610	A251	25c multicolored	.20	.20
1611	A251	30c multicolored	.25	.25
1612	A251	40c multicolored	.30	.30
1613	A251	60c multicolored	.45	.45
1614	A251	$1 multicolored	.75	.75
1615	A251	$4 multicolored	3.00	3.00
1616	A251	$5 multicolored	3.75	3.75
		Nos. 1609-1616 (8)	8.90	8.90

Souvenir Sheet

1617	A251	$6 multicolored	4.50	4.50
1618	A251	$6 multicolored	4.50	4.50

A252

A253

Anniversaries and Events: 10c, Cosomonauts. 40c, Graf Zeppelin, Goodyear blimp. 45c, Right Rev. Daniel C. Davis, St. John's Cathedral. 75c, Konrad Adenauer. $1, Bus Mosbacher, Weatherly. $1.50, Rain forest. No. 1625, Felis tigris. No. 1626, Flag, emblems, plant. No. 1627, Women acting on stage. $2.25, Women carrying baskets of food on their heads. $3, Lions Club emblem, club member. No. 1630, West German, NATO flags. No. 1631, China's Long March Booster Rocket. No. 1632, Dr. Hugo Eckener. No. 1633, The Hindenburg. No. 1634, Brandenburg Gate, German flag. No. 1635, Monarch butterfly. No. 1636, Hermes Shuttle, Columbus Space Station.

1992 **Litho.** **Perf. 14**

1619	A252	10c multicolored	.20	.20
1620	A252	40c multicolored	.30	.30
1621	A253	45c multicolored	.35	.35
1622	A252	75c multicolored	.60	.60
1623	A252	$1 multicolored	.75	.75
1624	A252	$1.50 multicolored	1.10	1.10
1625	A252	$2 multicolored	1.50	1.50
1626	A253	$2 multicolored	1.50	1.50
1627	A253	$2 multicolored	1.50	1.50
1628	A252	$2.25 multicolored	1.75	1.75
1629	A252	$3 multicolored	2.25	2.25
1630	A252	$4 multicolored	3.00	3.00
1631	A252	$4 multicolored	3.00	3.00
1632	A252	$6 multicolored	4.50	4.50
		Nos. 1619-1632 (14)	22.30	22.30

Souvenir Sheets

1633-1636	A252	$6 each	4.50	4.50

Intl. Space Year (#1619, 1631, 1636). Count Zeppelin, 75th anniv. of death (#1620, 1632-1633). Diocese of Northeast Caribbean and Aruba District, 150th anniv. (#1621). Konrad Adenauer, 25th anniv. of death (#1622, 1630, 1634). 1962 winner of America's Cup (#1623). Earth Summit, Rio (#1624-1625, 1635). Inter-American Institute for Cooperation on Agriculture, 50th anniv. (#1626). Cultural Development, 40th anniv. (#1627). WHO Intl. Conf. on Nutrition, Rome (#1628). Lions Club, 75th anniv. (#1629).

Issued: #1619, 1621-1623, 1626-1631, 1634, 1636, Nov.; #1624-1625, 1635, Dec. 14.

Euro Disney, Paris — A254

Disney characters: 10c, Golf course. 25c, Davy Crockett Campground. 30c, Cheyenne Hotel. 40c, Santa Fe Hotel. $1, New York Hotel. $2, In car, map showing location. $4, Pirates of the Caribbean. $5, Adventureland. No. 1645, Mickey Mouse on map with star, vert. No. 1646, Roof turret at entrance, Mickey Mouse in uniform. No. 1646A, Mickey Mouse, colored spots on poster, vert. No. 1646B, Mickey on poster, vert., diff.

1992-93 **Litho.** **Perf. 14x13½**

1637	A254	10c multicolored	.20	.20
1638	A254	25c multicolored	.20	.20
1639	A254	30c multicolored	.25	.25
1640	A254	40c multicolored	.30	.30
1641	A254	$1 multicolored	.75	.75
1642	A254	$2 multicolored	1.50	1.50
1643	A254	$4 multicolored	3.00	3.00
1644	A254	$5 multicolored	3.75	3.75
		Nos. 1637-1644 (8)	9.95	9.95

Souvenir Sheets

Perf. 13½x14

1645-1646B	A254	$6 each	4.50	4.50

Issued: #1638-1639, 1642-1643, 1646-1646B, 2/22/93; others, 12/1992.

Miniature Sheets

Louvre Museum, Bicent. A255

Details or entire paintings, by Peter Paul Rubens: No. 1647a, Destiny of Marie de' Medici. b, Birth of Marie de'Medici. c, Marie's Education. d, Destiny of Marie de'Medici, diff. e, Henry IV Receives the Portrait. f, The Meeting at Lyons. g, The Marriage. h, The Birth of Louis XIII.

No. 1648a, The Capture of Juliers. b, The Exchange of Princesses. c, The Happiness of the Regency. d, The Majority of Louis XIII. e, The Flight from Blois. f, The Treaty of Angouleme. g, The Peace of Angers. h, The Queen's Reconciliation with Her Son.

$6, Helene Fourment Au Carosse.

1993, Mar. 22 **Litho.** **Perf. 12**

Sheets of 8 + Label

1647	A255	$1 #a.-h.	6.00	6.00
1648	A255	$1 #a.-h.	6.00	6.00

Souvenir Sheet

Perf. 14½

1649	A255	$6 multicolored	4.50	4.50

No. 1649 contains one 55x88mm stamp.

Flowers — A256

1993, Mar. 15 **Litho.** **Perf. 14**

1650	A256	15c Cardinal's guard	.20	.20
1651	A256	25c Giant granadilla	.20	.20
1652	A256	30c Spider flower	.25	.25
1653	A256	40c Gold vine	.30	.30
1654	A256	$1 Frangipani	.75	.75
1655	A256	$2 Bougainvillea	1.50	1.50
1656	A256	$4 Yellow oleander	3.00	3.00
1657	A256	$5 Spicy jatropha	3.75	3.75
		Nos. 1650-1657 (8)	9.95	9.95

Souvenir Sheets

1658	A256	$6 Bird lime tree	4.50	4.50
1659	A256	$6 Fairy lily	4.50	4.50

Endangered Species — A257

Designs: No. 1660a, St. Lucia parrot. b, Cahow. c, Swallow-tailed kite. d, Everglades kite. e, Imperial parrot. f, Humpback whale. g, Puerto Rican plain pigeon. h, St. Vincent parrot. i, Puerto Rican parrot. j, Leatherback turtle. k, American crocodile. l, Hawksbill turtle.

No. 1662, West Indian manatee.

1993, Apr. 5

1660	A257	$1 Sheet of 12, #a.-l.	9.00	9.00

Souvenir Sheets

1661	A257	$6 like #1660f	4.50	4.50
1662	A257	$6 multicolored	4.50	4.50

Philatelic Publishing Personalities — A258

Portrait, stamp: No. 1663, J. Walter Scott (1842-1919), US "#C3a," Antigua #1. No. 1664, Theodore Champion, France #8, Antigua #1. No. 1665, E. Stanley Gibbons (1856-1913), cover of his first price list and catalogue, Antigua #1. No. 1666, Hugo Michel (1866-1944), Bavaria #1, Antigua #1. No. 1667, Alberto (1877-1944) and Giulio (1902-1987) Bolaffi, Sardinia #1, Great Britain #3. No. 1668, Richard Borek (1874-1947), Brunswick #24, Bavaria #1.

Front pages, Mekeel's Weekly Stamp News: No. 1669a, Jan. 7, 1890. b, Feb. 12, 1993.

1993, June 14

1663	A258	$1.50 multicolored	1.10	1.10
1664	A258	$1.50 multicolored	1.10	1.10
1665	A258	$1.50 multicolored	1.10	1.10
1666	A258	$1.50 multicolored	1.10	1.10
1667	A258	$1.50 multicolored	1.10	1.10
1668	A258	$1.50 multicolored	1.10	1.10
		Nos. 1663-1668 (6)	6.60	6.60

Souvenir Sheet of 2

1669	A258	$3 #a.-b.	4.50	4.50

Mekeel's Weekly Stamp News, cent. (in 1891; #1669).

Miniature Sheets

Coronation of Queen Elizabeth II, 40th Anniv. A259

Coronation: 1670a, 30c, Official photograph. b, 40c, Crown of Queen Elizabeth, the Queen Mother. c, $2, Dignataries attending ceremony. d, $4, Queen, Prince Edward.

$6, Portrait, by Denis Fildes.

First decade, 1953-1963: No. 1671a, Wedding photograph of Princess Margaret and Antony Armstrong-Jones. b, Queen opening Parliament, Prince Philip. c, Queen holding infant. d, Royal family. e, Queen Elizabeth II, formal portrait. f, Queen, Charles de Gaulle. g, Queen, Pope John XXIII. h, Queen inspecting troops.

Second decade, 1963-1973: No. 1672a, Investiture of Charles as Prince of Wales. b, Queen opening Parliament, Prince Philip, diff. c, Queen holding infant, diff. d, Queen, Prince Philip, children. e, Wearing blue robe, diadem. f, Prince Philip, Queen seated. g, Prince Charles, Queen at microphone. h, Queen conversing, model airplane.

Third decade, 1973-1983: No. 1673a, Wedding photograph of Prince Charles and Princess Diana. b, Queen opening Parliament, Prince Philip, diff. c, Princess Diana with infant. d, Princess Anne with infant. e, Portrait of Queen. f, Queen waving, Prince Philip. g, Queen, Pope John Paul II. h, Wedding portrait of Mark Phillips and Princess Anne.

Fourth decade, 1983-1993: No. 1674a, Wedding photograph of Sarah Ferguson and Prince Andrew. b, Queen opening Parliament, Prince Philip, diff. c, Princess Diana holding infant, diff. d, Sarah Ferguson, infant. e, Queen wearing blue dress. f, Queen waving from carriage, Prince Philip. g, Queen wearing military uniform. h, Queen Mother.

1993, June 2 **Litho.** **Perf. 13½x14**

1670	A259	Sheet, 2 each #a.-d.	10.00	10.00

Sheets of 8

1671	A259	$1 #a.-h. + label	6.00	6.00
1672	A259	$1 #a.-h. + label	6.00	6.00
1673	A259	$1 #a.-h. + label	6.00	6.00
1674	A259	$1 #a.-h. + label	6.00	6.00

Souvenir Sheet

Perf. 14

1675	A259	$6 multicolored	4.50	4.50

No. 1675 contains one 28x42mm stamp.

Wedding of Japan's Crown Prince Naruhito and Masako Owada A260

Cameo photos of couple and: 40c, Crown Prince. $3, Princess.

$6, Princess wearing white coat, vert.

1993, Aug. 16 **Litho.** **Perf. 14**

1676	A260	40c multicolored	.30	.30
1677	A260	$3 multicolored	2.25	2.25

Souvenir Sheet

1678	A260	$6 multicolored	4.50	4.50

Picasso (1881-1973) — A261

Paintings: 30c, Cat and Bird, 1939. 40c, Fish on a Newspaper, 1957. $5, Dying Bull, 1934. $6, Woman with a Dog, 1953.

1993, Aug. 16 Litho. *Perf. 14*

1679 A261 30c multicolored .25 .25
1680 A261 40c multicolored .30 .30
1681 A261 $5 multicolored 4.00 4.00
Nos. 1679-1681 (3) 4.55 4.55

Souvenir Sheet

1682 A261 $6 multicolored 4.50 4.50

Copernicus (1473-1543) A262

Designs: 40c, Astronomical devices. $4, Photograph of supernova. $5, Copernicus.

1993, Aug. 16

1683 A262 40c multicolored .30 .30
1684 A262 $4 multicolored 3.25 3.25

Souvenir Sheet

1685 A262 $5 multicolored 3.75 3.75

Willy Brandt (1913-1992), German Chancellor — A263

Designs: 30c, Helmut Schmidt, George Leber, Brandt. $4, Brandt, newspaper headlines. $6, Brandt at Warsaw Ghetto Memorial, 1970.

1993, Aug. 16

1686 A263 30c multicolored .25 .25
1687 A263 $4 multicolored 3.25 3.25

Souvenir Sheet

1688 A263 $6 multicolored 4.50 4.50

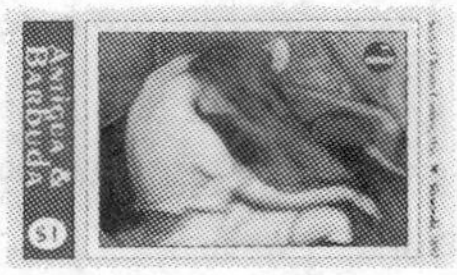

Polska '93 A264

Paintings: $1, Study of a Woman Combing Her Hair, by Wladyslaw Slewinski, 1897. $3, Artist's Wife with Cat, by Konrad Kryzanowski, 1912. $6, General Confusion, by S. I. Witkiewicz, 1930, vert.

1993, Aug. 16

1689 A264 $1 multicolored .80 .80
1690 A264 $3 multicolored 2.50 2.50

Souvenir Sheet

1691 A264 $6 multicolored 4.50 4.50

Inauguration of Pres. William J. Clinton — A265

Designs: $5, Pres. Clinton driving car. $6, Pres. Clinton, inauguration ceremony, vert.

1993, Aug. 16

1692 A265 $5 multicolored 4.00 4.00

Souvenir Sheet

1693 A265 $6 multicolored 4.50 4.50

No. 1693 contains one 43x57mm stamp.

Antigua stamps can be mounted in the annual Scott Antigua supplement.

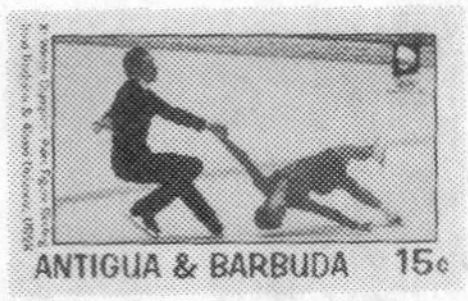

1994 Winter Olympics, Lillehammer, Norway — A266

15c, Irina Rodnina, Alexei Ulanov, gold medalists, pairs figure skating, 1972. $5, Alberto Tomba, gold medal, giant slalom, 1988, 1992. $6, Yvonne van Gennip, Andrea Ehrig, gold, bronze medalists, speedskating, 1988.

1993, Aug. 16

1694 A266 15c multicolored .20 .20
1695 A266 $5 multicolored 4.00 4.00

Souvenir Sheet

1696 A266 $6 multicolored 4.50 4.50

1994 World Cup Soccer Championships, US — A267

English soccer players: No. 1697, Gordon Banks. No. 1698, 1709, Bobby Moore. No. 1699, Peter Shilton. No. 1700, Nobby Stiles. No. 1701, Bryan Robson. No. 1702, Geoff Hurst. No. 1703, Gary Lineker. No. 1704, Bobby Charlton. No. 1705, Martin Peters. No. 1706, John Barnes. No. 1707, David Platt. No. 1708, Paul Gascoigne. No. 1710, Player holding 1990 Fair Play Winners Trophy.

1993, July 30 Litho. *Perf. 14*

1697-1708 A267 $2 Set of 12 18.00 18.00

Souvenir Sheets

1709 A267 $6 multicolored 4.50 4.50
1710 A267 $6 multicolored 4.50 4.50

Nos. 1697-1708 issued in sheets of five plus label identifying player.

Aviation Anniversaries — A268

Designs: 30c, Dr. Hugo Eckener, Dr. Wm. Beckers, zeppelin over Lake George, NY. No. 1712, Chicago Century of Progress Exhibition seen from zeppelin. No. 1713, George Washington, Blanchard's balloon, vert. No. 1714, Gloster E.28/39, first British jet plane. $4, Pres. Wilson watching take-off of first scheduled air mail plane. No. 1716, Hindenburg over Ebbets Field, Brooklyn, NY, 1937. No. 1717, Gloster Meteor in combat. No. 1718, Eckener, vert. No. 1719, Alexander Hamilton, Pres. Washington, John Jay, gondola of Blanchard's balloon. No. 1720, PBY-5.

1993, Oct. 11

1711 A268 30c multicolored .20 .20
1712 A268 40c multicolored .30 .30
1713 A268 40c multicolored .30 .30
1714 A268 40c multicolored .30 .30
1715 A268 $4 multicolored 3.00 3.00
1716 A268 $5 multicolored 3.75 3.75
1717 A268 $5 multicolored 3.75 3.75
Nos. 1711-1717 (7) 11.60 11.60

Souvenir Sheets

1718 A268 $6 multicolored 4.50 4.50
1719 A268 $6 multicolored 4.50 4.50
1720 A268 $6 multicolored 4.50 4.50

Dr. Hugo Eckener, 125th anniv. of birth (#1711-1712, 1716, 1718). First US balloon flight, bicent. (#1713, 1715, 1719). Royal Air Force, 75th anniv. (#1714, 1717, 1720).

No. 1720 contains one 57x43mm stamp.

Mickey Mouse Movie Posters A269

Nos. 1721-1729: 10c, The Musical Farmer, 1932. 15c, Little Whirlwind, 1941. 30c, Pluto's Dream House, 1940. 40c, Gulliver Mickey, 1934. 50c, Alpine Climbers, 1936. $1, Mr. Mouse Takes a Trip, 1940. $2, The Nifty Nineties, 1941. $4, Mickey Down Under, 1948. $5, The Pointer, 1939.

#1730, The Simple Things, 1953. #1731, The Prince and the Pauper, 1990.

1993, Oct. 25 Litho. *Perf. 13½x14*

1721-1729 A269 Set of 9 12.00 12.00

Souvenir Sheets

1730-1731 A269 $6 each 4.50 4.50

St. John's Lodge #492, 150th Anniv. A270

Designs: 10c, W.K. Heath, Grand Inspector 1961-82, vert. 30c, Present Masonic Hall. 40c, 1st Masonic Hall. 60c, J.L.E. Jeffery, Grand Inspector 1953-61, vert.

1993, Aug. 16 Litho. *Perf. 14*

1732-1735 A270 Set of 4 1.10 1.10

First Ford Engine and Benz's First 4-Wheel Car, Cent. A271

30c, Lincoln Continental. 40c, 1914 Mercedes racing car. $4, 1966 Ford GT40. $5, 1954 Mercedes Benz gull wing coupe, street version. No. 1740, Mustang emblem. No. 1741, US #1286A, Germany #471.

1993, Oct. 11 Litho. *Perf. 14*

1736-1739 A271 Set of 4 7.00 7.00

Souvenir Sheets

1740-1741 A271 $6 each 4.50 4.50

Christmas — A272

Nos. 1742-1750, Disney characters in The Nutcracker: 10c, 15c, 20c, 30c, 40c, 50c, 60c, $3, $6. 1751, Minnie and Mickey. No. 1752, Mickey, vert.

1993, Nov. 8 *Perf. 14x13½, 13½x14*

1742-1750 A272 Set of 9 8.50 8.50

Souvenir Sheets

1751-1752 A272 $6 each 4.50 4.50

Fine Art — A273

Paintings by Rembrandt: No. 1753, 15c, Hannah and Samuel. 30c, Isaac & Rebecca (The Jewish Bride). 40c, Jacob Wrestling with the Angel. $5, Moses with the Tablets of the Law.

Paintings by Matisse: No. 1754, 15c, Guitarist. 60c, Interior with a Goldfish Bowl. $1, Portrait of Mlle. Yvonne Landsberg. $4, The Toboggan, Plate XX from Jazz. No. 1761, The Blinding of Samson by the Philistines, by Rembrandt. No. 1762, The Three Sisters, by Matisse.

1993, Nov. 22 *Perf. 13½x14*

1753-1760 A273 Set of 8 9.00 9.00

Souvenir Sheets

1761-1762 A273 $6 each 4.50 4.50

A274

Hong Kong '94 A275

Stamps, fishing boats at Shau Kei Wan: No. 1763, Hong Kong #370, bow of boat. No. 1764, Stern of boat, #1300.

Museum of Qin figures, Shaanxi Province, Tomb of Qin First Emperor: No. 1765a, Inside museum. b, Cavalryman, horse. c, Warriors in battle formation. d, Painted bronze horses, chariot. e, Pekingese dog (not antiquity). f, Chin warrior figures, horses.

1994, Feb. 18 Litho. *Perf. 14*

1763 A274 40c multicolored .30 .30
1764 A274 40c multicolored .30 .30
a. Pair, #1763-1764 .60 .60

Miniature Sheet

1765 A275 40c Sheet of 6, #a.-f. 1.75 1.75

Nos. 1763-1764 issued in sheets of 5 pairs. No. 1764a is a continuous design.

New Year 1994 (Year of the Dog) (#1765e).

Hong Kong '94 — A276

Disney characters: 10c, Mickey's "Pleasure Junk." 15c, Mandarin Minnie. 30c, Donald, Daisy journey by house boat. 50c, Mickey, Birdman of Mongkok. $1, Pluto encounters a good-luck dog. $2, Minnie, Daisy celebrate Bun Festival. $4, Goofy, the noodle maker. $5, Goofy pulls Mickey in a rickshaw.

No. 1774, Mickey celebrating New Year with Dragon Dance, horiz. No. 1775, View of Hong Kong Harbor, horiz.

1994, Feb. 18 Litho. *Perf. 13½x14*

1766-1773 A276 Set of 8 10.00 10.00

Souvenir Sheets
Perf. 14x13½

1774-1775 A276 $5 each 3.75 3.75

Miniature Sheets of 8

Sierra Club, Cent. — A277

No. 1776: a, Bactrian camel, emblem UR. b, Bactrian camel, emblem UL. c, African elephant, emblem UL. d, African elephant, emblem UR. e, Leopard, blue background. f, Leopard, emblem UR. g, Leopard, emblem UL. h, Club emblem.

No. 1777: a, Sumatran rhinoceros, lying on ground. b, Sumatran rhinoceros, looking straight ahead. c, Ring-tailed lemur standing. d, Ring-tailed lemur sitting on branch. e, Red-fronted brown lemur on branch. f, Red-fronted brown lemur. g, Red-fronted brown lemur, diff.

No. 1778, Sumatran rhinoceros, horiz. No. 1779, Ring-tailed lemur, horiz. No. 1780, Bactrian camel, horiz. No. 1781, African elephant, horiz.

1994, Mar. 1 Litho. *Perf. 14*

1776 A277 $1.50 #a.-h. 9.00 9.00
1777 A277 $1.50 #a.-g, #1776h 9.00 9.00

Souvenir Sheets

1778-1781 A277 $1.50 each 1.10 1.10

Miniature Sheets

New Year 1994 (Year of the Dog) A278

Small breeds of dogs: No. 1782a, West highland white terrier. b, Beagle. c, Scottish terrier. d, Pekingese. e, Dachshund. f, Yorkshire terrier. g, Pomeranian. h, Poodle. i, Shetland sheepdog. j, Pug. k, Shih tzu. l, Chihuahua.

Large breeds of dogs: No. 1783a, Mastiff. b, Border collie. c, Samoyed. d, Airedale terrier. e, English setter. f, Rough collie. g, Newfoundland. h, Weimaraner. i, English springer spaniel. j, Dalmatian. k, Boxer. l, Old English sheepdog.

No. 1784, Welsh corgi. No. 1785, Labrador retriever.

1994, Apr. 5 *Perf. 14*

1782 A278 50c Sheet of 12, #a.-l. 4.50 4.50
1783 A278 75c Sheet of 12, #a.-l. 6.75 6.75

Souvenir Sheets

1784-1785 A278 $6 each 4.50 4.50

Orchids A279

Butterflies A280

Designs: 10c, Spiranthes lanceolata. 20c, Ionopsis utricularioides. 30c, Tetramicra canaliculata. 50c, Oncidium picturatum. $1, Epidendrum difforme. $2, Epidendrum ciliare. $4, Epidendrum ibaguense. $5, Epidendrum nocturnum.

No. 1794, Encyclia cochleata. No. 1795, Rodriguezia lanceolata.

1994, Apr. 11 *Perf. 14*

1786-1793 A279 Set of 8 10.00 10.00

Souvenir Sheets

1794-1795 A279 $6 each 4.50 4.50

1994, June 27 *Perf. 14*

Designs: 10c, Monarch. 15c, Florida white. 30c, Little sulphur. 40c, Troglodyte. $1, Common long-tail skipper. $2, Caribbean buckeye. $4, Polydamas swallowtail. $5, Zebra.

#1804, Cloudless sulphur. #1805, Hanno blue.

1796-1803 A280 Set of 8 10.00 10.00

Souvenir Sheets

1804-1805 A280 $6 each 4.50 4.50

Miniature Sheet of 9

Marine Life — A281

Designs: No. 1806a, Bottlenose dolphin. b, Killer whale (a). c, Spinner dolphin (b). d, Ocean sunfish (a). e, Caribbean reef shark, short fin pilot whale (d, f). f, Butterfly fish. g, Moray eel. h, Trigger fish. i, Red lobster (h).

#1807, Blue marlin, horiz. #1808, Sea horse.

1994, July 21 Litho. *Perf. 14*

1806 A281 50c a.-i. 3.50 3.50

Souvenir Sheets

1807-1808 A281 $6 each 4.50 4.50

Intl. Year of the Family A282

1994, Aug. 4

1809 A282 90c multicolored .70 .70

D-Day, 50th Anniv. A283

Designs: 40c, Short Sunderland attacks U-boat. $2, Lockheed P-38 Lightning attacks train. $3, B-26 Marauders of 9th Air Force.

$6, Hawker Typhoon Fighter Bombers.

1994, Aug. 4

1810-1812 A283 Set of 3 4.25 4.25

Souvenir Sheet

1813 A283 $6 multicolored 4.50 4.50

A284

Intl. Olympic Committee, Cent. — A285

Designs: 50c, Edwin Moses, US, hurdles, 1984. $1.50, Steffi Graf, Germany, tennis, 1988. $6, Johann Olav Koss, Norway, speed skating, 1994.

1994, Aug. 4

1814 A284 50c multicolored .40 .40
1815 A284 $1.50 multicolored 1.10 1.10

Souvenir Sheet

1816 A285 $6 multicolored 4.50 4.50

English Touring Cricket, Cent. A286

35c, M.A. Atherton, England, Wisden Trophy. 75c, I.V.A. Richards, Leeward Islands, vert. $1.20, R.B. Richardson, Leeward Islands, Wisden Trophy.

$3, First English team, 1895.

1994, Aug. 4

1817-1819 A286 Set of 3 1.75 1.75

Souvenir Sheet

1820 A286 $3 multicolored 2.25 2.25

Miniature Sheets of 6

First Manned Moon Landing, 25th Anniv. A287

No. 1821: a, Edwin E. Aldrin, Jr. b, First footprint on Moon. c, Neil A. Armstrong. d, Aldrin descending to lunar surface. e, Aldrin deploys ALSET. f, Aldrin, US flag, Tranquility Base.

No. 1822: a, Scientific research, Tranquility Base. b, Plaque on Moon. c, Eagle ascending to docking. d, Command module in lunar orbit. e, US No. C76 made from die carried to Moon. f, Pres. Nixon, Apollo 11 crew.

$6, Armstrong, Aldrin, Postmaster General Blount.

1994, Aug. 4

1821-1822 A287 $1.50 #a.-f. 6.75 6.75

Souvenir Sheet

1823 A287 $6 multicolored 4.50 4.50

A288

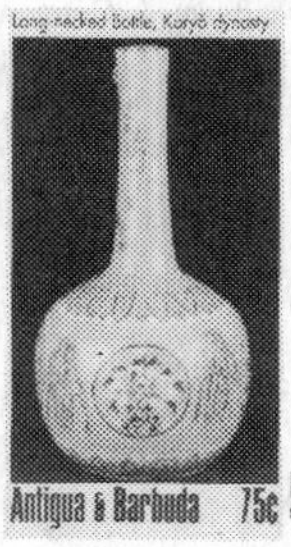

PHILAKOREA '94 — A289

40c, Entrance bridge, Songgwangsa Temple. 90c, Song-op Folk Village, Cheju. $3, Panoramic view, Port Sogwip'o.

Ceramics, Koryo & Choson Dynasties: No. 1827a, Long-necked bottle. b, Jar. c, Jar, diff. d, Ewer in form of bamboo shoot. e, Jar, diff. f, Pear-shaped bottle. g, Porcelain jar with dragon design. h, Porcelain jar with bonsai design.

$4, Ox, ox herder, vert.

1994, Aug. 4 *Perf. 14, 13½ (#1827)*

1824-1826 A288 Set of 3 3.50 3.50

Miniature Sheet of 8

1827 A289 75c #a.-h. 6.00 6.00

Souvenir Sheet

1828 A288 $4 multicolored 3.00 3.00

Miniature Sheets of 8

Stars of Country & Western Music — A290

No. 1829: a, Patsy Cline. b, Tanya Tucker. c, Dolly Parton. d, Anne Murray. e, Tammy Wynette. f, Loretta Lynn. g, Reba McEntire. h, Skeeter Davis.

No. 1830a, Travis Tritt. b, Dwight Yoakam. c, Billy Ray Cyrus. d, Alan Jackson. e, Garth Brooks. f, Vince Gill. g, Clint Black. h, Eddie Rabbit.

No. 1831: a, Hank Snow. b, Gene Autry. c, Jimmie Rogers. d, Ernest Tubb. e, Eddy Arnold. f, Willie Nelson. g, Johnny Cash. h, George Jones.

No. 1832, Kitty Wells, horiz. No. 1833, Hank Williams, Sr. No. 1834, Hank Williams, Jr.

1994, Aug. 18 Litho. *Perf. 14*

1829-1831 A290 75c #a.-h, each 4.50 4.50

Souvenir Sheets

1832-1834 A290 $6 each 4.50 4.50

1994 World Cup Soccer Championships, US — A291

Designs: 15c, Hugo Sanchez, Mexico. 35c, Juergen Klinsman, Germany. 65c, Antigua player. $1.20, Cobi Jones, US. $4, Roberto Baggio, Italy. $5, Bwalya Kalusha, Zambia.

No. 1841, FIFA World Cup Trophy, vert. No. 1842, Maldive Islands player, vert.

1994, Sept. 19

1835-1840 A291 Set of 6 8.50 8.50

Souvenir Sheets

1841-1842 A291 $6 each 4.50 4.50

Order of the Caribbean Community — A292

First award recipients: 65c, Sir Shridath Ramphal, statesman, Guyana. 90c, William Demas, economist, Trinidad & Tobago. $1.20, Derek Walcott, writer, St. Lucia.

1994, Sept. 26

1843-1845 A292 Set of 3 2.00 2.00

Herman E. Sieger (1902-54) A293

Germany #C35, Graf Zeppelin, Sieger.

1994 Litho. *Perf. 14*

1846 A293 $1.50 multicolored 1.25 1.25

Birds A294

Designs: 10c, Magnificent frigate birds. 15c, Bridled quail dove. 30c, Magnificent frigate bird hatchling. 40c, Purple-throated carib, vert. No. 1851, $1, Antigua broad-wing hawk, vert. No. 1852, $1, Magnificent frigate bird, vert. $3, Magnificent frigate bird, white head. $4, Yellow warbler.

No. 1855, West Indian Whistling duck. No. 1856, Magnificent frigate bird, diff., vert.

1994, Dec. 12 Litho. *Perf. 14*

1847-1854 A294 Set of 8 7.50 7.50

Souvenir Sheets

1855-1856 A294 $6 each 4.50 4.50

World Wildlife Fund (#1847, 1849, 1852-1853).

Christmas A295

Paintings of Madonnas: 15c, The Virgin and Child by the Fireside, by Robert Campin. 35c, The Reading Madonna, by Giorgione. 40c, Madonna and Child, by Giovanni Bellini. 45c, The Litta Madonna, by da Vinci. 65c, The Virgin and Child Under the Apple Tree, by Lucas Cranach the Elder. 75c, Madonna and Child, by Master of the Female Half-Lengths. $1.20, An Allegory of the Church, by Alessandro Allori. $5, Madonna and Child Wreathed with Flowers, by Jacob Jordaens.

No. 1865, The Virgin Enthroned with Child, by Bohemian Master. No. 1866, Madonna and Child with (painting's) Commissioners, by Palma Vecchio.

1994, Dec. 12 *Perf. 13½x14*

1857-1864 A295 Set of 8 6.75 6.75

Souvenir Sheets

1865-1866 A295 $6 each 4.50 4.50

Birds — A296

Designs: 15c, Magnificent frigate bird. 25c, Blue-hooded euphonia. 35c, Meadowlark. 40c, Red-billed tropic bird. 45c, Greater flamingo. 60c, Yellow-faced grassquit. 65c, Yellow-billed cuckoo. 70c, Purple-throated carib. 75c, Bananaquit. 90c, Painted bunting. $1.20, Red-legged honeycreeper. $2, Jacana. $5, Greater antillean bullfinch. $10, Caribbean elaenia. $20, Trembler.

1994 *Perf. 14½x14*

1867	A296	15c multicolored	.20	.20
1868	A296	25c multicolored	.20	.20
1869	A296	35c multicolored	.25	.25
1870	A296	40c multicolored	.60	.60
1871	A296	45c multicolored	.35	.35
1872	A296	60c multicolored	.45	.45
1873	A296	65c multicolored	.45	.45
1874	A296	70c multicolored	.50	.50
1875	A296	75c multicolored	.55	.55
1876	A296	90c multicolored	.70	.70
1877	A296	$1.20 multicolored	.90	.90
1878	A296	$2 multicolored	1.50	1.50
1879	A296	$5 multicolored	4.50	4.50
1880	A296	$10 multicolored	7.50	7.50
1881	A296	$20 multicolored	15.00	15.00
		Nos. 1867-1881 (15)	33.65	33.65

Prehistoric Animals — A297

Designs, vert: 15c, Pachycephalosaurus. 20c, Afrovenator. 65c, Centrosaurus. 90c, Pentaceratops. $1.20, Tarbosaurus. $5, Styracosaur.

No. 1888a, Kronosaur. b, Ichthyosaur. c, Plesiosaur. d, Archelon. e, Two tyrannosaurs. f, One tyrannosaur. g, One parasaurolophus. h, Two parasaurolophuses. i, Oviraptor. j, Protoceratops with eggs. k, Pteranodon, protoceratops. l, Protoceratops.

#1889, Carnotaurus. #1890, Corythosaurus.

1995, May 15 Litho. *Perf. 14*

1882-1887 A297 Set of 6 6.25 6.25

Miniature Sheet of 12

1888 A297 75c #a.-l. 6.75 6.75

Souvenir Sheets

1889-1890 A297 $6 each 4.50 4.50

1996 Summer Olympics, Atlanta — A298

Gold medalists: 15c, Al Oerter, US, discus. 20c, Greg Louganis, US, diving. 65c, Naim Suleymanoglu, Turkey, weight lifting. 90c, Louise Ritter, US, high jump. $1.20, Nadia Comaneci, Romania, gymnastics. $5, Olga Boldarenko, USSR, 10,000-meter run.

No. 1897, Lutz Hessilch, Germany, 1000-meter sprint cycling, vert. No. 1898, US team, eight-oared shell, 800-, 1500-meters.

1995, June 6 Litho. *Perf. 14*

1891-1896 A298 Set of 6 6.00 6.00

Souvenir Sheets

1897-1898 A298 $6 each 4.50 4.50

Miniature Sheets of 6 or 8

End of World War II, 50th Anniv. A299

No. 1899: a, Chiang Kai-Shek. b, Gen. MacArthur. c, Gen. Chennault. d, Brigadier Orde C. Wingate. e, Gen. Stillwell. f, Field Marshall William Slim.

No. 1900: a, Map of Germany showing battle plan. b, Tanks, infantry advance. c, Red Army at gates of Berlin. d, German defenses smashed. e, Airstrikes on Berlin. f. German soldiers give up. g, Berlin falls to Russians. h, Germany surrenders.

$3, Plane, ship, Adm. Chester Nimitz. $6, Gen. Konev at command post outside Berlin, vert.

1995, July 20

1899 A299 $1.20 #a.-f. + label 5.50 5.50

1900 A299 $1.20 #a.-h. + label 7.25 7.25

Souvenir Sheets

1901 A299 $3 multicolored 2.25 2.25

1902 A299 $6 multicolored 4.50 4.50

UN, 50th Anniv. — A300

FAO, 50th Anniv. — A301

No. 1903: a, 75c, Earl of Halifax, signatures. b, 90c, Virginia Gildersleeve. c, $1.20, Harold Stassen.

$6, Franklin D. Roosevelt.

1995, July 20 Litho. *Perf. 14*

1903 A300 Strip of 3, #a.-c. 2.25 2.25

Souvenir Sheet

1904 A300 $6 multicolored 4.50 4.50

No. 1903 is a continuous design.

1995, July 20

Street market scene: No. 1905a, 75c, Two women, bananas. b, 90c, Women, crates, produce. c, $1.20, Women talking, one with box of food on head.

$6, Tractor.

1905 A301 Strip of 3, #a.-c. 2.25 2.25

Souvenir Sheet

1906 A301 $6 multicolored 4.50 4.50

No. 1905 is a continuous design.

Rotary Intl., 90th Anniv. — A302

1995, July 20

1907 A302 $5 shown 3.75 3.75

Souvenir Sheet

1908 A302 $6 Natl. flag, Rotary emblem 4.50 4.50

Queen Mother, 95th Birthday A303

No. 1909: a, Drawing. b, White & dark pink hat. c, Formal portrait. d, Blue green hat, dress.

No. 1910, Light blue dress, pearls.

1995, July 20 *Perf. 13½x14*

1909 A303 $1.50 Strip or block of 4, #a.-d. 4.50 4.50

Souvenir Sheet

1910 A303 $6 multicolored 4.50 4.50

No. 1909 was issued in sheets of 2 each.

Miniature Sheet of 12

Ducks — A304

No. 1911: a, Ring-necked duck. b, Ruddy duck. c, Green-winged teal (d). d, Wood duck. e, Hooded merganser (f). f, Lesser scaup (g). g, West Indian tree duck (h, k, l). h, Fulvous whistling duck (l). i, Bahama pintail. j, Shoveler (i). k, Masked duck (l). l, American widgeon.

$6, Blue-winged teal.

1995, Aug. 31 Litho. *Perf. 14*

1911 A304 75c #a.-l. 6.75 6.75

Souvenir Sheet

1912 A304 $6 multicolored 4.50 4.50

Bees A305

Designs: 90c, Mining bee. $1.20, Solitary bee. $1.65, Leaf-cutter. $1.75, Honey bee.

$6, Solitary mining bee.

1995, Sept. 7

1913-1916 A305 Set of 4 4.25 4.25

Souvenir Sheet

1917 A305 $6 multicolored 4.50 4.50

Miniature Sheet of 12

Domestic Cats — A306

Designs: a, Somali. b, Persian. c, Devon rex. d, Turkish angora. e, Himalayan. f, Maine coon. g, Nonpedigree. h, American wirehair. i, British shorthair. j, American curl. k, Black nonpedigree. l, Birman.

$6, Siberian, vert.

1995, Sept. 7

1918 A306 45c #a.-l. 4.00 4.00

Souvenir Sheet

1919 A306 $6 multicolored 4.50 4.50

Miniature Sheet

Tourism A307

Stylized paintings depicting: a, Caring. b, Marketing. c, Working. d, Enjoying life.

1995, July 31 Litho. *Perf. 14*

1920 A307 $2 Sheet of 4, #a.-d. 6.00 6.00

Greenbay Moravian Church, 150th Anniv. — A308

20c, 1st structure, wood & stone. 60c, 1st stone, concrete building, 3/67. 75c, $2, Present structure. 90c, John A. Buckley, 1st minister of African descent. $1.20, John Ephraim Knight, longest serving minister. $6, Front of present structure.

1995, Sept. 4

1921-1926 A308 Set of 6 4.25 4.25

Souvenir Sheet

1927 A308 $6 multicolored 4.50 4.50

Miniature Sheet of 12

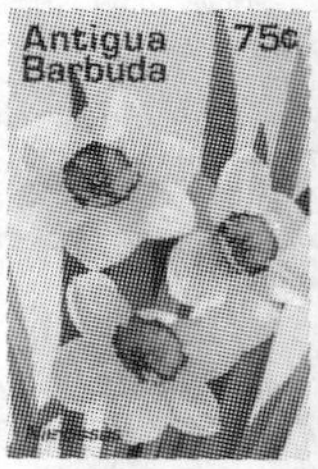

Flowers — A309

No. 1928: a, Narcissus. b, Camellia. c, Iris. d, Tulip. e, Poppy. f, Peony. g, Magnolia. h, Oriental lily. i, Rose. j, Pansy. k, Hydrangea. l, Azaleas.

$6, Bird of paradise, calla lily.

1995, Sept. 7

1928 A309 75c #a.-l. 6.75 6.75

Souvenir Sheet

1929 A309 $6 multicolored 4.50 4.50

1995 Boy Scout Jamboree, Holland — A310

Tents - #1930: a, Explorer. b, Camper. c, Wall.
#1931: a, Trail tarp. b, Miner's. c, Voyager.
#1932, Scout with camping equipment, vert.
#1933, Scout making camp fire.

1995, Oct. 5

Strip of 3

1930-1931 A310 $1.20 #a.-c, ea 2.75 2.75

Souvenir Sheets

1932-1933 A310 $6 each 4.50 4.50

For overprints see Nos. 1963-1966.

Trains A311

Designs: 35c, Gabon. 65c, Canadian. 75c, US. 90c, British high-speed. $1.20, French high-speed. No. 1939, American high-speed (Amtrak).

No. 1940: a, Australian diesel. b, Italian high-speed. c, Thai diesel. d, US steam. e, South African steam. f, Natal steam. g, US war train. h, British steam. i, British steam, diff.

No. 1941, Australian diesel, vert. No. 1942, Asian steam, vert.

1995, Oct. 23 Litho. *Perf. 14*

1934-1939 A311 Set of 6 7.50 7.50

Miniature Sheet of 9

1940 A311 $1.20 #a.-i. 8.25 8.25

Souvenir Sheets

1941-1942 A311 $6 each 4.50 4.50

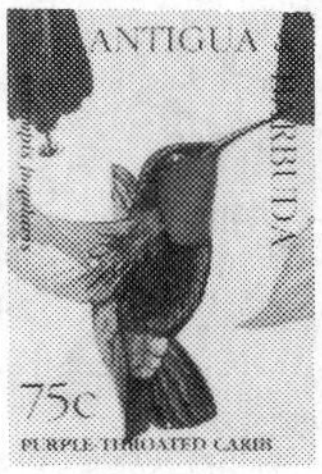

Birds — A312

No. 1943: a, Purple-thoated carib. b, Antillean crested hummingbird. c, Bananaquit (d). d, Mangrove cuckoo. e, Troupial. f, Green-throated carib (e, g). g, Yellow warbler (h). h, Blue-hooded Euphonia. i, Scally-breasted thrasher. j, Burrowing owl (i). k, Caribbean crackle (k). l, Adelaide's warbler.

$6, Purple gallinule.

1995

Miniature Sheet of 12

1943 A312 75c #a.-l. 6.75 6.75

Souvenir Sheet

1944 A312 $6 multicolored 4.50 4.50

Miniature Sheets of 9

Nobel Prize Fund Established, Cent. — A313

Recipients: No. 1945a, S.Y. Agnon, literature, 1966. b, Kipling, literature, 1907. c, Aleksandr Solzhenitsyn, literature, 1970. d, Jack Steinberger, physics, 1988. e, Andrei Sakharov, peace, 1975. f, Otto Stern, physics, 1943. g, Steinbeck, literature, 1962. h, Nadine Gordimer, literature, 1991. i, Faulkner, literature, 1949.

No. 1946: a, Hammarskjold, peace, 1961. b, Georg Wittig, chemistry, 1979. c, Wilhelm Ostwald, chemistry, 1909. d, Koch, physiology or medicine, 1945. e, Karl Ziegler, chemistry, 1963. f, Fleming, physiology or medicine, 1945. g, Hermann Staudinger, chemistry, 1953. h, Manfred Eigen, chemistry, 1967. i, Arno Penzias, physics, 1978.

No. 1947, Elie Wiesel, peace, 1986, vert. No. 1948, Dalai Lama, peace, 1989, vert.

1995, Nov. 8

1945-1946 A313 $1 #a.-i. + label, each 6.75 6.75

Souvenir Sheets

1947-1948 A313 $6 each 4.50 4.50

Christmas A314

Details or entire paintings: 15c, Rest on the Flight into Egypt, by Veronese. 35c, Madonna with The Child, by Van Dyck. 65c, Sacred Conversation Piece, by Veronese. 75c, Vision of Saint Anthony, by Van Dyck. 90c, The Virgin and the Infant, by Van Eyck. No. 1954, The Immaculate Conception, by Tiepolo.

$5, Christ Appearing to His Mother, by Van Der Weyden. No. 1956, Infant Jesus and the Young St. John, by Murillo.

1995, Dec. 18 Litho. *Perf. 13½x14*

1949-1954 A314 Set of 6 6.75 6.75

Souvenir Sheets

1955 A314 $5 multicolored 3.75 3.75
1956 A314 $6 multicolored 4.50 4.50

Miniature Sheet

Elvis Presley (1935-77) A315

Nos. 1957-1958, Various portraits depicting Presley's life.

1995, Dec. 8 *Perf. 14*

1957 A315 $1 Sheet of 9, #a.-i. 6.75 6.75

Souvenir Sheet

1958 A315 $6 multicolored 4.50 4.50

John Lennon (1940-80), Entertainer — A316

45c, 50c, 65c, 75c, Various portraits of Lennon.

1995, Dec. 8

1959-1962 A316 Set of 4 1.75 1.75

Souvenir Sheet

1962A A316 $6 like 75c 4.50 4.50

Nos. 1959-1962 were each issued in miniature sheets of 16.

No. 1962A has a continuous design.

Nos. 1930-1933 Ovptd. 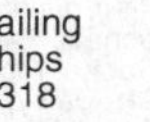

1995, Dec. 14

Strip of 12

1963-1964 A310 $1.20 #a.-c., ea 2.75 2.75

Souvenir Sheets

1965-1966 A310 $6 each 4.50 4.50

Size and location of overprint varies.

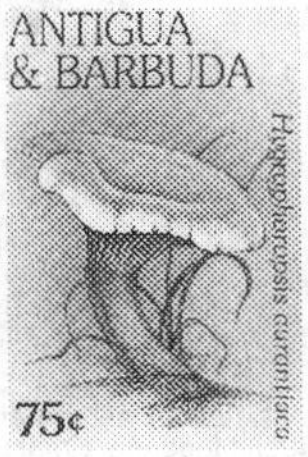

Mushrooms A317

Designs: No. 1967a, Hygrophoropsis aurantiaca. b, Hygrophorus bakerensis. c, Hygrophorus conicus. d, Hygrophorus miniatus.

No. 1968a, Suillus brevipes. b, Suillus luteus. c, Suillus granulatus. d, Suillus caerulescens.

No. 1969, Conocybe filaris. No. 1970, Hygrocybe flavescens.

1996, Apr. 22 Litho. *Perf. 14*

Strip of 4

1967-1968 A317 75c #a.-d., ea 2.25 2.25

Souvenir Sheets

1969-1970 A317 $6 each 4.50 4.50

#1967-1968 were each issued in sheets of 12 stamps.

Sailing Ships A318

Designs: 15c, Resolution. 25c, Mayflower. 45c, Santa Maria. No. 1970D, 75c, Aemilia, Holland, 1630. No. 1970E, 75c, Sovereign of the Seas, England, 1637. 90c, HMS Victory, England, 1765.

Battleships: No. 1971: a, Aemila, Holland, 1630. b, Sovereign of the Seas, England, 1637. c, Royal Louis, France, 1692. d, HMS Royal George, England, 1715. e, Le Protecteur, France, 1761. f, HMS Victory, England, 1765.

Ships of exploration: No. 1972: a, Santa Maria. b, Victoria. c, Golden Hinde. d, Mayflower. e, Griffin. f, Resolution.

No. 1973, Grande Hermine. No. 1974, USS Constitution, 1797.

1996, Apr. 25

1970A-1970F A318 Set of 6 2.50 2.50

Sheets of 6

1971 A318 $1.20 #a.-f. 5.50 5.50
1972 A318 $1.50 #a.-f. 6.75 6.75

Souvenir Sheets

1973-1974 A318 $6 each 4.50 4.50

1996 Summer Olympics, Atlanta — A319

Designs: 65c, Florence Griffith Joyner, women's track, vert. 75c, Olympic Stadium, Seoul, 1988. 90c, Allison Jolly, yachting. $1.20, 2000m Tandem cycling.

Medalists: No. 1979a, Wolfgang Nordwig, pole vault. b, Shirley Strong, women's 100m hurdles. c, Sergei Bubka, pole vault. d, Filbert Bayi, 3000m steeplechase. e, Victor Saneyev, triple jump. f, Silke Renk, women's javelin. g, Daley Thompson, decathlon. h, Bob Richards, pole vault. i, Parry O'Brien, shot put.

Diving medalists: No. 1980a, Ingrid Kramer, women's platform. b, Kelly McCormick, women's springboard. c, Gary Tobian, men's springboard. d, Greg Louganis, men's diving. e, Michelle Mitchell, women's platform. f, Zhou Jihong, women's platform. g, Wendy Wyland, women's platform. h, Xu Yanmei, women's platform. i, Fu Mingxia, women's platform.

$5, Bill Toomey, decathlon. $6, Mark Lenzi, men's springboard.

1996, May 6

1975-1978 A319 Set of 4 2.50 2.50

Sheets of 9

1979-1980 A319 90c #a.-i., each 6.25 6.25

Souvenir Sheets

1981 A319 $5 multicolored 3.75 3.75
1982 A319 $6 multicolored 4.50 4.50

Sea Birds A320

No. 1983: a, Black skimmer. b, Black-capped petrel. c, Sooty tern. d, Royal tern.

No. 1984 a, Pomarina jaegger. b, White-tailed tropicbird. c, Northern gannet. d, Laughing gull.

$5, Great frigatebird. $6, Brown pelican.

1996, May 13

Vertical Strip of 4

1983-1984 A320 75c #a.-d., ea 2.25 2.25

Souvenir Sheets

1985 A320 $5 multicolored 3.75 3.75
1986 A320 $6 multicolored 4.50 4.50

Nos. 1983-1984 were each issued in sheets of 12 stamps with each strip in sheet having a different order.

Disney Characters In Scenes from Jules Verne's Science Fiction Novels — A321

Designs: 1c, Around the World in Eighty Days. 2c, Journey to the Center of the Earth. 5c, Michel Strogoff. 10c, From the Earth to the Moon. 15c, Five Weeks in a Balloon. 20c, Around the World in Eighty Days, diff. $1, The Mysterious Island. $2, From the Earth to the Moon, diff. $3, Captain Grant's Children. $5, Twenty Thousand Leagues Under the Sea.

No. 1997, Twenty Thousand Leagues Under the Sea, diff. No. 1998, Journey to the Center of the Earth, diff.

1996, June 6 Litho. *Perf. 14x13½*

1987-1996 A321 Set of 10 8.75 8.75

Souvenir Sheets

1997-1998 A321 $6 each 4.50 4.50

Bruce Lee (1940-73), Martial Arts Expert — A322

Various portraits.

1996, June 13 *Perf. 14*

1999 A322 75c Sheet of 9, #a.-i. 5.25 5.25

Souvenir Sheet

2000 A322 $5 multicolored 3.75 3.75

China '96 (#1999).

Queen Elizabeth II, 70th Birthday A323

Designs: a, In blue dress, pearls. b, Carrying bouquet of flowers. c, In uniform.
$6, Painting as younger woman.

1996, July 17 *Perf. 13½x14*

2001 A323 $2 Strip of 3, #a.-c. 4.50 4.50

Souvenir Sheet

2002 A323 $6 multicolored 4.50 4.50

No. 2001 was issued in sheets of 9 stamps.

Traditional Cavalry — A324

a, Ancient Egyptian. b, 13th cent. English. c, 16th cent. Spanish. d, 18th cent. Chinese.
$6, 19th cent. French.

1996, July 24 **Litho.** *Perf. 14*

2003 A324 60c Block of 4, #a.-d. 1.75 1.75

Souvenir Sheet

2004 A324 $6 multicolored 4.50 4.50

No. 2003 was issued in sheets of 16 stamps.

A325 A326

UNICEF, 50th Anniv.: 75c, Girl. 90c, Children. $1.20, Woman holding baby. $6, Girl, diff.

1996, July 30

2005-2007 A325 Set of 3 2.00 2.00

Souvenir Sheet

2008 A325 $6 multicolored 4.50 4.50

1996, July 30

Site, flower: 75c, Tomb of Zachariah, verbascum sinuatum. 90c, Pool of Siloam, hyacinthus orientalis. $1.20, Hurva Synagogue, ranunculus asiaticus.
$6, Model of Herod's Temple.

2009-2011 A326 Set of 3 2.25 2.25

Souvenir Sheet

2012 A326 $6 multicolored 4.50 4.50

Jerusalem, 3000th anniv.

Radio, Cent. — A327

Entertainers: 65c, Kate Smith. 75c, Dinah Shore. 90c, Rudy Vallee. $1.20, Bing Crosby.
$6, Jo Stafford.

1996, July 30

2013-2016 A327 Set of 4 2.75 2.75

Souvenir Sheet

2017 A327 $6 multicolored 4.50 4.50

Christmas A328

Details or entire paintings, by Filippo Lippi: 60c, Madonna Enthroned. 90c, Adoration of the Child and Saints. $1, Annunciation. $1.20, Birth of the Virgin. $1.60, Adoration of the Child. $1.75, Madonna and Child.
No. 2024, Madonna and Child, diff. No. 2025, Circumcision.

1996, Nov. 25 *Perf. 13½x14*

2018-2023 A328 Set of 6 5.25 5.25

Souvenir Sheets

2024-2025 A328 $6 each 4.50 4.50

Disney Pals — A329

1c, Goofy, Wilbur. 2c, Donald, Goofy. 5c, Donald, Panchito, Jose Carioca. 10c, Mickey, Goofy. 15c, Dale, Chip. 20c, Pluto, Mickey. $1, Daisy, Minnie at ice cream shop. $2, Daisy, Minnie. $3, Gus Goose, Donald.
No. 2035, Donald, vert. No. 2036, Goofy.

1997, Feb. 17 **Litho.** *Perf. 14x13½*

2026-2034 A329 Set of 9 5.00 5.00

Souvenir Sheets

Perf. 13½x14, 14x13½

2035-2036 A329 $6 each 4.50 4.50

Salute to Broadway A330

Stars, show: No. 2037: a, Robert Preston, The Music Man. b, Michael Crawford, Phantom of the Opera. c, Zero Mostel, Fiddler on the Roof. d, Patti Lupone, Evita. e, Raul Julia, Threepenny Opera. f, Mary Martin, South Pacific. g, Carol Channing, Hello Dolly. h, Yul Brynner, The King and I. i, Julie Andrews, My Fair Lady.
$6, Mickey Rooney, Sugar Babies.

1997 *Perf. 14*

2037 A330 $1 Sheet of 9, #a.-i. 6.80 6.80

Souvenir Sheet

2038 A330 $6 multicolored 4.50 4.50

Butterflies A331

Designs: 90c, Charaxes porthos. $1.20, Aethiopana honorius. $1.60, Charaxes hadrianus. $1.75, Precis westermanni.
No. 2043: a, Charaxes protoclea. b, Byblia ilithyia. c, Black-headed tchagra (bird). d, Charaxes nobilis. e, Pseudacraea boisduvali. f, Charaxes smaragdalis. g, Charaxes lasti. h, Pseudacraea poggei. i, Graphium colonna.
No. 2044a, Carmine bee-eater (bird). b, Pseudacraea eurytus. c, Hypolimnas monteironis. d, Charaxes anticlea. e, Graphium leonidas. f, Graphium illyris. g, Nepheronia argia. h, Graphium policenes. i, Papilio dardanus.
No. 2045, Euxanthe tiberius, horiz. No. 2046, Charaxes lactitinctus, horiz. No. 2047, Euphaedra neophron.

1997, Mar. 10

2039-2042 A331 Set of 4 4.00 4.00

Sheets of 9

2043-2044 A331 $1.10 #a.-i., ea 7.50 7.50

Souvenir Sheets

2045-2047 A331 $6 each 4.50 4.50

UNESCO, 50th Anniv. — A332

World Heritage Sites: 60c, Convent of the Companions of Jesus, Morelia, Mexico. 90c, Fortress, San Lorenzo, Panama, vert. $1, Canaima Natl. Park, Venezuela, vert. $1.20, Huascarán Natl. Park, Peru, vert. $1.60, Church of San Francisco, Guatemala, vert. $1.75, Santo Domingo, Dominican Republic, vert.
No. 2054, vert: a-c, Guanajuato, Mexico. d, Jesuit missions of the Chiquitos, Bolivia. e, Huascarán Natl. Park, Peru. f, Jesuit missions, La Santisima, Paraguay. g, Cartagena, Colombia. h, Old Havana fortification, Cuba.
No. 2055: a, Tikal Natl. Park, Guatemala. b, Rio Platano Reserve, Honduras. c, Ruins of Copán, Honduras. d, Church of El Carmen, Antigua, Guatemala. e, Teotihuacán, Mexico.
No. 2056, Teotihuacán, Mexico, diff. No. 2057, Tikal Natl. Park, Guatemala, diff.

1997, Apr. 10 **Litho.** *Perf. 14*

2048-2053 A332 Set of 6 5.25 5.25

Sheets of 8 or 5

2054 A332 $1.10 #a.-h. + label 6.75 6.75

2055 A332 $1.65 #a.-e. + label 6.25 6.25

Souvenir Sheets

2056-2057 A332 $6 each 4.50 4.50

Fauna — A333

No. 2058: a, Red bishop. b, Yellow baboon. c, Superb starling. d, Ratel. e, Hunting dog. f, Serval.
No. 2059: a, Okapi. b, Giant forest squirrel. c, Masked weaver. d, Common genet. e, Yellow-billed stork. f, Red-headed agama.
No. 2060, Malachite kingfisher. No. 2061, Gray crowned crane. No. 2062, Bat-eared fox.

1997, Apr. 24

Sheets of 6

2058 A333 $1.20 #a.-f. 5.50 5.50

2059 A333 $1.65 #a.-f. 7.50 7.50

Souvenir Sheets

2060-2062 A333 $6 each 4.50 4.50

Charlie Chaplin (1889-1977), Comedian, Actor — A334

Various portraits.

1997, Feb. 24 **Litho.** *Perf. 14*

2063 A334 $1 Sheet of 9, #a.-i. 6.75 6.75

Souvenir Sheet

2064 A334 $6 multicolored 4.50 4.50

Paul P. Harris (1868-1947), Founder of Rotary, Intl. — A335

Designs: $1.75, Service above self, James Grant, Ivory Coast, 1994, portrait of Harris.
$6, Group study exchange, New Zealand.

1997, June 12 **Litho.** *Perf. 14*

2065 A335 $1.75 multicolored 1.25 1.25

Souvenir Sheet

2066 A335 $6 multicolored 4.50 4.50

Heinrich von Stephan (1831-97) A336

Portrait of Von Stephan and: No. 2067: a, Kaiser Wilhelm I. b, UPU emblem. c, Pigeon Post.
$6, Von Stephan, Basel messenger, 1400's.

1997, June 12

2067 A336 $1.75 Sheet of 3, #a.-c. 4.00 4.00

Souvenir Sheet

2068 A336 $6 multicolored 4.50 4.50

PACIFIC 97.

Queen Elizabeth II, Prince Philip, 50th Wedding Anniv. A337

No. 2069: a, Queen. b, Royal arms. c, Queen, Prince in royal attire. d, Queen, King riding in open carriage. e, Balmoral Castle. f, Prince Philip.
$6, Early portrait of Queen, King in royal attire.

1997, June 12

2069 A337 $1 Sheet of 6, #a.-f. 4.50 4.50

Souvenir Sheet

2070 A337 $6 multicolored 4.50 4.50

Grimm's Fairy Tales A338

Scenes from "Cinderella:" No. 2071: a, Mother, stepsisters. b, Cinderella, fairy godmother. c, Cinderella, Prince Charming.
$6, Prince trying shoe on Cinderella.

1997, June 13 *Perf. 13½x14*
2071 A338 $1.75 Sheet of 3, #a.-c. 4.00 4.00

Souvenir Sheet

2072 A338 $6 multicolored 4.50 4.50

Chernobyl Disaster, 10th Anniv. A339

Designs: $1.65, UNESCO. $2, Chabad's Children of Chernobyl.

1997, June 12
2073 A339 $1.65 multicolored 1.25 1.25
2074 A339 $2 multicolored 1.50 1.50

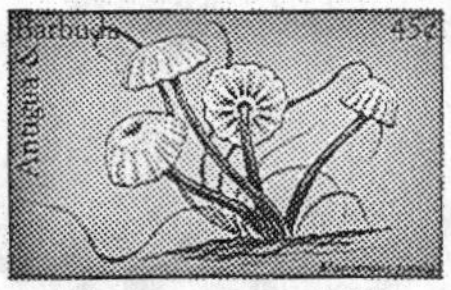

Mushrooms — A340

Designs: 45c, Marasmius rotula. 65c, Cantharellus cibarius. 70c, Lepiota cristata. 90c, Auricularia mesenterica. $1, Pholiota alnicola. $1.65, Leccinum aurantiacum.
No. 2081: a, Entoloma serrulatum. b, Panaeolus sphinctrinus. c, Volvariella bombycina. d, Conocybe percincta. e, Pluteus cervinus. f, Russula foetens.
No. 2082, Panellus serotinus. No. 2083, Amanita cothurnata.

1997, Aug. 12 **Litho.** *Perf. 14*
2075-2080 A340 Set of 6 4.00 4.00

Sheets of 6

2081 A340 $1.75 #a.-f. 8.00 8.00

Souvenir Sheets

2082-2083 A340 $6 each 4.50 4.50

Orchids — A341

Designs: 45c, Odontoglossum cervantesii. 65c, Medford star. 75c, Motes resplendent. 90c, Debutante. $1, Apple blossom. $2, Dendrobium.
No. 2090: a, Angel lace. b, Precious stones. c, Orange theope butterfly. d, Promenaea xanthina. e, Lycaste macrobulbon. f, Amesiella philippinensis. g, Machu Picchu. h, Zuma urchin.
No. 2091: a, Sophia Martin. b, Dogface butterfly. c, Mini purple. d, Showgirl. e, Mem. Dorothy Bertsch. f, Black II. g, Leeanum. h, Paphiopedilum macranthum.
No. 2092, Seine. No. 2093, Paphiopedilum gratrixianum.

1997, Aug. 19 **Litho.** *Perf. 14*
2084-2089 A341 Set of 6 4.25 4.25

Sheets of 8

2090-2091 A341 $1.65 #a.-h., each 5.00 5.00

Souvenir Sheets

2092-2093 A341 $6 each 4.50 4.50

1998 World Cup Soccer Championships, France — A342

Designs: 60c, Maradona, Argentina, 1986. 75c, Fritzwalter, W. Germany, 1954. 90c, Zoff, Italy, 1982. $1.20, Moore, England, 1966. $1.65, Alberto, Brazil, 1970. $1.75, Matthäus, W. Germany.
No. 2100, vert: a, Ademir, Brazil, 1950. b, Eusebio, Portugal, 1966. c, Fontaine, France, 1958. d, Schillaci, Italy, 1990. e, Leonidas, Brazil, 1938. f, Stabile, Argentina, 1930. g, Nejedly, Czechoslovakia, 1934. h, Muller, W. Germany, 1970.
No. 2101, Players, W. Germany, 1990. No. 2102, Bebeto, Brazil, vert.

1997, Oct. 6 **Litho.** *Perf. 14*
2094-2099 A342 Set of 6 6.00 6.00

Sheet of 8 + Label

2100 A342 $1 #a.-h. 6.00 6.00

Souvenir Sheets

2101-2102 A342 $6 each 4.50 4.50

Domestic Animals A343

Dogs: No. 2103: a, Dachshund. b, Staffordshire terrier. c, Sharpei. d, Beagle. e, Norfolk terrier. f, Golden retriever.
Cats: No. 2104: a, Scottish fold. b, Japanese bobtail. c, Tabby manx. d, Bicolor American shorthair. e, Sorrel abyssinian. f, Himalayan blue point.
No. 2105, Siberian husky, vert. No. 2106, Red tabby American shorthair kitten, vert.

1997, Oct. 27 **Litho.** *Perf. 14*

Sheets of 6

2103-2104 A343 $1.65 #a.-f., ea 7.50 7.50

Souvenir Sheets

2105-2106 A343 $6 each 4.50 4.50

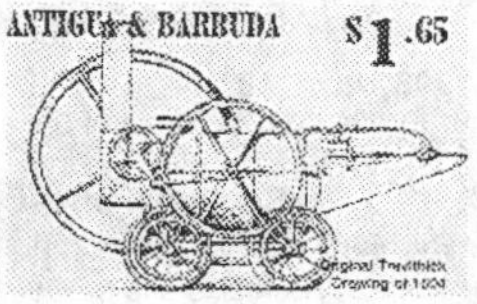

Early Trains A344

No. 2107: a, Original Trevithick drawing, 1804. b, "Puffing Billy," William Hedley, 1860. c, Crampton locomotive, Northern Railway, France, 1858. d, Twenty-five ton locomotive, Lawrence Machine Shop, 1860's. e, First locomotive, "Mississippi," built in England. f, "Coppernob," locomotive by Edward Bury, Furness Railway.
No. 2108: a, "Jenny Lind," by David Joy for E.B. Wilson. b, "Atlantic" type locomotive, by Schenectady Locomotive Works, 1899. c, British built tank engine, Japan, by Kisons of Leeds, 1881. d, Express freight locomotive, 4-8-2 type, Pennsylvania Railroad. e, Four-cylinder locomotive, by Karl Golsdorf, Austria. f, "E" series 0-10-0 locomotive, produced by Lugansk Works, Russia, 1930.
No. 2109, "Patente" George Stephenson, 1843. No. 2110, Brunel's Trestle, Lynher River.

1997, Nov. 10

Sheets of 6

2107-2108 A344 $1.65 #a.-f., ea 7.50 7.50

Souvenir Sheets

2109-2110 A344 $6 each 4.50 4.50

Christmas A345

Entire paintings or details: 15c, The Angel Leaving Tobias and His Family, by Rembrandt. 25c, The Resurrection, by Martin Knoller. 60c, Astronomy, by Raphael. 75c, Music-making Angel, by Melozzo da Forli. 90c, Amor, by Parmigianino. $1.20, Madonna and Child with Saints John the Baptist, Anthony, Stephen and Jerome, by Rosso Fiorentino.
No. 2117, The Portinari Altarpiece, by Hugo Van Der Goes. No. 2118, The Wedding of Tobiolo, by Gianantonio and Francesco Guardi.

1997, Dec. 2 **Litho.** *Perf. 14*
2111-2116 A345 Set of 6 5.25 5.25

Souvenir Sheets

2117-2118 A345 $6 each 4.50 4.50

Diana, Princess of Wales (1961-97) — A346

Various portraits, color of sheet margin: No. 2119, Pale green. No. 2120, Pale pink.
No. 2121, With her sons (in margin). No. 2122, With Pope John Paul II (in margin).

1998, Jan. 19 **Litho.** *Perf. 14*

Sheets of 6

2119-2120 A346 $1.65 #a.-f., each 7.50 7.50

Souvenir Sheets

2121-2122 A346 $6 each 4.50 4.50

Fish A347

Designs: 75c, Yellow damselfish. 90c, Barred hamlet. $1, Jewelfish. $1.20, Bluehead wrasse. $1.50, Queen angelfish. $1.75, Queen triggerfish.
No. 2129: a, Jack-knife fish. b, Cuban hogfish. c, Sergeant major. d, Neon goby. e, Jawfish. f, Flamefish.
No. 2130: a, Rock beauty. b, Yellowtail snapper. c, Creole wrasse. d, Slender filefish. e, Squirrel fish. f, Fairy basslet.
No. 2131, Black-capped gramma. No. 2132, Porkfish.

1998, Feb. 19
2123-2128 A347 Set of 6 5.50 5.50

Sheets of 6

2129-2130 A347 $1.65 #a.-f., each 7.50 7.50

Souvenir Sheets

2131-2132 A347 $6 each 4.50 4.50

Cedar Hall Moravian Church, 175th Anniv. — A348

Designs: 20c, First church, manse, 1822-40. 45c, Cedar Hall School, 1840. 75c, Hugh A. King, former minister. 90c, Present structure. $1.20, Water tank, 1822. $2, Former manse demolished, 1978.
$6, Present structure, diff.

1998, Mar. 16 **Litho.** *Perf. 14*
2133-2138 A348 Set of 6 4.25 4.25

Souvenir Sheet

2139 A348 $6 multicolored 4.50 4.50

No. 2139 contains one 50x37mm stamp.

Lighthouses — A349

Lighthouse, location: 45c, Trinity, Europa Point, Gibraltar, vert. 65c, Tierra Del Fuego, Argentina. 75c, Point Loma, California, US. 90c, Groenpoint, South Africa, vert. $1, Youghal, County Cork, Ireland, vert. $1.20, Launceston, Tasmania, Australia, vert. $1.65, Point Abino, Ontario, Canada. $1.75, Great Inagua, Bahamas.
$6, Capa Hatteras, North Carolina, US.

1998, Apr. 20
2140-2147 A349 Set of 8 6.50 6.50

Souvenir Sheet

2148 A349 $6 multi, vert. 4.50 4.50

Winnie the Pooh — A350

No. 2149: a, Pooh, Tigger in January. b, Pooh, Piglet in February. c, Piglet in March. d, Tigger, Pooh, Piglet in April. e, Kanga, Roo in May. f, Pooh, Owl in June.
No. 2150: a, Pooh, Eeyore, Tigger, Piglet in July. b, Pooh, Piglet in August. c, Christopher Robin in September. d, Eeyore in October. e, Pooh, Rabbit in November. f, Pooh, Piglet in December.
No. 2151, Pooh, Rabbit holding blanket, Spring. No. 2152, Pooh holding hand to mouth, Summer. No. 2153, Pooh holding rake, Fall. No. 2154, Eeyore, Pooh, Winter.

1998, May 11 **Litho.** *Perf. 13½x14*

Sheets of 6

2149-2150 A360 $1 #a.-f., each 4.50 4.50

Souvenir Sheet

2151-2154 A350 $6 each 4.50 4.50

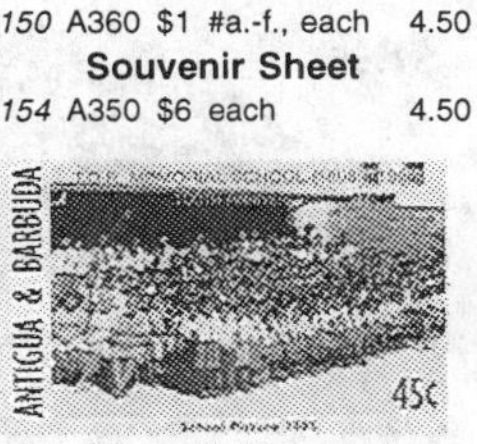

Thomas Oliver Robinson Memorial High School, Cent. A351

Designs: 20c, $6, Nellie Robinson (1880-1972), founder, vert. 45c, School picture, 1985. 65c, Former building, 1930-49. 75c, Students with present headmistress, Natalie Hurst. 90c, Ina Loving (1908-96), educator, vert. $1.20, Present building, 1950.

1998, July 23 Litho. *Perf. 14*
2155-2160 A351 Set of 6 3.25 3.25

Souvenir Sheet

2161 A351 $6 multicolored 4.50 4.50

No. 2161 is a continuous design.

Intl. Year of the Ocean A352

Marine life, "20,000 Leagues Under the Sea:" No. 2162: a, Spotted eagle ray. b, Manta ray. c, Hawksbill turtle. d, Jellyfish. e, Queen angelfish. f, Octopus. g, Emperor angelfish. h, Regal angelfish. i, Porkfish. j, Raccoon butterfly fish. k, Atlantic barracuda. l, Sea horse. m, Nautilus. n, Trumpet fish. o, White tip shark. p, Spanish galleon. q, Black tip shark. r, Long-nosed butterfly fish. s, Green moray eel. t, Captain Nemo. u, Treasure chest. v, Hammerhead shark. w, Divers. x, Lion fish. y, Clown fish.

Wildlife and birds: No. 2163: a, Maroon tailed conure. b, Cocoi heron. c, Common tern. d, Rainbow lorikeet. e, Saddleback butterfly fish. f, Goatfish, cat shark. g, Blue shark, stingray. h, Majestic snapper. i, Nassau grouper. j, Black-cap gramma, blue tang. k, Stingrays. l, Stingrays, giant starfish.

#2164, Fiddler ray. #2165, Humpback whale.

1998, Aug. 17
2162 A352 40c Sheet of 25, #a.-y. 7.50 7.50
2163 A352 75c Sheet of 12, #a.-l. 6.75 6.75

Souvenir Sheets

2164-2165 A352 $6 each 4.50 4.50

Ships A353

No. 2166: a, Savannah. b, Viking ship. c, Greek warship.

No. 2167: a, Clipper. b, Dhow. c, Fishing cat.

No. 2168, Dory, vert. No. 2169, Baltimore clipper. No. 2170, English warship, 13th cent.

1998, Aug. 18 *Perf. 14x14½*

Sheets of 3

2166-2167 A353 $1.75 #a.-c., each 4.00 4.00

Souvenir Sheets

Perf. 14

2168-2170 A353 $6 each 4.50 4.50

CARICOM, 25th Anniv. A354

1998, Aug. 20 Litho. *Perf. 13½*
2171 A354 $1 multicolored .75 .75

Antique Automobiles — A355

No. 2172: a, 1911 Torpedo. b, 1913 Mercedes 22. c, 1920 Rover. d, 1956 Mercedes Benz. e, 1934 Packard V12. f, 1924 Opel.

Fords: No. 2173: a, 1896. b, 1903 Model A. c, 1928 Model T. d, 1922 Model T. e, 1929 Blackhawk. f, 1934 Sedan. #2174, 1908. #2175, 1929.

1998, Sept. 1 *Perf. 14*

Sheets of 6

2172-2173 A355 $1.65 #a.-f., each 7.50 7.50

Souvenir Sheets

2174-2175 A355 $6 each 4.50 4.50

Nos. 2174-2175 each contain one 60x40mm stamp.

Aircraft A356

No. 2176: a, NASA Space Shuttle. b, Saab Grippen. c, Eurofighter EF2000. d. Sukhoi SU 27. e, Northrop B-2. f, Lockheed F-117 Nighthawk.

No. 2177: a, Lockheed-Boeing General Dynamics Yf-22. b, Dassault-Breguet Rafale BO 1. c, MiG 29. d, Dassault-Breguet Mirage 2000D. e, Rockwell B-1B Lancer. f, McDonnell-Douglas C-17A.

No. 2178, Sukhoi SU 35. No. 2179, F18 Hornet.

1998, Sept. 21

Sheets of 6

2176-2177 A356 $1.65 #a.-f., each 7.50 7.50

Souvenir Sheets

2178-2179 A356 $6 each 4.50 4.50

Famous People of the 20th Cent. — A357

Diana, Princess of Wales (1961-97) — A358

Inventors and their inventions: No. 2180: a, Rudolf Diesel (1858-1913). b, Internal combustion, diesel engines. c, Zeppelin war balloon, Intrepid. d, Ferdinand von Zeppelin (1838-1917). e, Wilhelm Conrad Röntgen (1845-1923). f, X-ray machine. g, Saturn rocket. h, Wernher von Braun (1912-77).

No. 2181: a, Carl Benz (1844-1929). b, Internal combustion engine, automobile. c, Atomic bomb. d, Albert Einstein. e, Leopold Godowsky, Jr. (1901-83) and Leopold Damrosch Mannes (1899-1964). f, Kodachrome film. g, First turbo jet airplane. h, Hans Pabst von Ohain (1911-98).

No. 2182, Hans Geiger (1882-1945), inventor of the Geiger counter. No. 2183, William Shockley (1910-89), developer of transistors.

1998, Nov. 10 Litho. *Perf. 14*

Sheets of 8

2180-2181 A357 $1 #a.-h., each 6.00 6.00

Souvenir Sheets

2182-2183 A357 $6 each 4.50 4.50

Nos. 2180b-2180c, 2180f-2180g, 2181b-2181c, 2181f-2181g are 53x38mm.

1998, Nov. 18
2184 A358 $1.20 multicolored .90 .90

No. 2184 was issued in sheets of 6.

Gandhi — A359

Picasso — A360

Portraits: 90c, Up close, later years. $1, Seated with hands clasped. $1.20, Up close, early years. $1.65, Primary school, Rajkot, age 7. $6, Wwith stick, walking with boy (in margin).

1998, Nov. 18
2185-2188 A359 Set of 4 2.75 2.75

Souvenir Sheet

2189 A359 $6 multicolored 2.25 2.25

1998, Nov. 18

Paintings: $1.20, Figures on the Seashore, 1931, horiz. $1.65, Three Figures Under a Tree, 1907. $1.75, Two Women Running on the Beach, 1922, horiz.

$6, Bullfight, 1900, horiz.

2190-2192 A360 Set of 3 3.50 3.50

Souvenir Sheet

2193 A360 $6 multicolored 4.50 4.50

1998 World Scouting Jamboree, Chile A361

90c, Handshake. $1, Scouts hiking. $1.20, Sign.

$6, Lord Baden-Powell.

1998, Oct. 8 Litho. *Perf. 14*
2194-2196 A361 Set of 3 2.50 2.50

Souvenir Sheet

2197 A361 $6 multicolored 4.50 4.50

Organization of American States, 50th Anniv. — A362

1998, Nov. 18 *Perf. 13½*
2198 A362 $1 multicolored .75 .75

Enzo Ferrari (1898-1988), Automobile Manufacturer — A363

No. 2199: a, Top view of Dino 246 GT-GTS. b, Front view of Dino 246 GT-GTS. c, 1977 365 GT4 BB.

$6, Dino 246 GT-GTS.

1998, Nov. 18 *Perf. 14*
2199 A363 $1.75 Sheet of 3, #a.-c. 4.00 4.00

Souvenir Sheet

2200 A363 $6 multicolored 4.50 4.50

No. 2200 contains one 92x35mm stamp.

Royal Air Force, 80th Anniv. A364

No. 2201: a, McDonnell Douglas Phantom FGR1. b, Sepecat Jaguar GR1A. c, Panavia Tornado F3. d, McDonnell Douglas Phantom FGR2.

No. 2202, Eurofighter 2000, Hurricane. No. 2203, Hawk, biplane.

1998, Nov. 18
2201 A364 $1.75 Sheet of 4, #a.-d. 4.00 4.00

Souvenir Sheets

2202-2203 A364 $6 each 4.50 4.50

Sea Birds A365

Designs: 15c, Brown pelican. 25c, Dunlin. 45c, Atlantic puffin. 90c, Pied cormorant.

No. 2208: a, King eider. b, Inca tern. c, Dovekie. d, Ross's bull. e, Brown noddy. f, Marbled murrelet. g, Northern gannet. h, Razorbill. i, Long-tailed jaeger. j, Black guillemot. k, Whimbrel. l, Oystercatcher.

No. 2209, Rhynchops niger. No. 2210, Diomedea exulans.

1998, Nov. 24
2204-2207 A365 Set of 4 1.25 1.25
2208 A365 75c Sheet of 12, #a.-l. 6.75 6.75

Souvenir Sheets

2209-2210 A365 $6 each 4.50 4.50

Christmas A366

Dogs with Christmas decorations: 15c, Border collie. 25c, Dalmatian. 65c, Weimaraner. 75c, Scottish terrier. 90c, Long-haired dachshund. $1.20, Golden retriever. $2, Pekingese.

No. 2218, Dalmatian, diff. No. 2219, Jack Russell terrier.

1998, Dec. 10
2211-2217 A366 Set of 7 4.50 4.50

Souvenir Sheet

2218-2219 A366 $6 each 4.50 4.50

Disney Characters in Water Sports A367

Water skiing - No. 2220: a, Goofy, maroon skis. b, Mickey. c, Goofy, Mickey. d, Donald. e, Goofy, blue skis. f, Minnie.

Surfing - No. 2221: a, Goofy running with board. b, Mickey. c, Donald holding board. d, Donald, riding board. e, Minnie. f, Goofy in water.

Sailing & sailboarding - No. 2221G: h, Mickey wearing cap. i, Mickey, Goofy, counterbalancing boat. j, Goofy sailboarding. k, Mickey, seagull overhead. l, Goofy puffing at sail. m, Mickey sailboarding.

No. 2222, Mickey. No. 2223, Minnie. No. 2224, Goofy. No. 2225, Donald.

1999, Jan. 11 Litho. *Perf. 13½x14*

Sheets of 6

2220-2221 A367 $1 #a.-f., each 4.50 4.50
2221G A367 $1 #h.-m. 4.50 4.50

Souvenir Sheets

2222-2225 A367 $6 each 4.50 4.50

Mickey Mouse, 70th anniv.

Hell's Gate Steel Orchestra, 50th Anniv. — A368

Designs: 20c, Nelson's Dockyard, 1996. 60c, Holiday Inn, Rochester, New York, 1992. 75c, Early years, 1950. 90c, World's Fair, 1964, Eustace Henry (AKA Manning). $1.20, Alston Henry playing double tenor.

No. 2231, like #2229, vert. No. 2232, The early years, vert.

1999, Feb. 1 Litho. *Perf. 14*
2226-2230 A368 Set of 5 2.75 2.75

Souvenir Sheets
2231-2232 A368 $4 each 3.00 3.00

Flowers A369

Designs, vert: 60c, Tulip. 75c, Fuschia. $1.20, Calla lily. $1.65, Sweet pea.

No. 2237: a, Morning glory. b, Geranium. c, Blue hibiscus. d, Marigolds. e, Sunflower. f, Impatiens. g, Petunia. h, Pansy. i, Saucer magnolia.

No. 2238: a, Primrose. b, Bleeding heart. c, Pink dogwood. d, Peony. e, Rose. f, Hellebores. g, Lily. h, Violet. i, Cherry blossoms.

No. 2239, Lily, vert. no. 2240, Zinnias, vert.

1999, Apr. 19 Litho. *Perf. 14*
2233-2236 A369 Set of 4 3.25 3.25

Sheets of 9
2237 A369 90c #a.-i. 6.00 6.00
2238 A369 $1 #a.-i. 6.75 6.75

Souvenir Sheets
2239-2240 A369 $6 each 4.50 4.50

Elle Macpherson, Model — A370

Various portraits.

1999, Apr. 26 *Perf. 13½*
2241 A370 $1.20 Sheet of 8, #a.-h. 7.25 7.25

Australia '99 World Stamp Expo.

John Glenn's Space Flight A371

Space Exploration A372

John Glenn, 1962 - No. 2242: a, Climbing into Mercury Capsule. b, Formal portrait. c, Having helmet adjusted. d, Entering pressure chamber.

No. 2243: a, Luna 2. b, Mariner 2. c, Giotto space probe. d, Rosat. e, Intl. Ultraviolet Explorer. f, Ulysses Space Probe.

No. 2244: a, Mariner 10. b, Luna 9. c, Advanced X-ray Astrophysics Facility. d, Magellan Spacecraft. e, Pioneer-Venus 2. f, Infra-red Astronomy Satellite.

No. 2245, Salyut 1, horiz. No. 2246, MIR, horiz.

1999, May 6 Litho. *Perf. 14*
2242 A371 $1.75 Sheet of 4, #a.-d. 5.25 5.25

Sheets of 6
2243-2244 A372 $1.65 #a.-f., each 7.50 7.50

Souvenir Sheets
2245-2246 A372 $6 each 4.50 4.50

Nos. 2245-2246 are incorrectly inscribed.

Prehistoric Animals — A373

Designs: 65c, Brachiosaurus. 75c, Oviraptor, vert. $1, Homotherium. $1.20, Macrauchenia, vert.

No. 2251: a, Leptictidium. b, Ictitherium. c, Plesictis. d, Hemicyon. e, Diacodexis. f, Stylinodon. g, Kanuites. h, Chriacus. i, Argyrolagus.

No. 2252: a, Struthiomimus. b, Corythosaurus. c, Dsungaripterus. d, Compognathus. e, Prosaurolophus. f, Montanoceratops. g, Stegosaurus. h, Deinonychus. i, Ouranosaurus.

No. 2253, Pteranodon. No. 2254, Eurhinodelphus.

1999, May 26
2247-2250 A373 Set of 4 3.50 3.50

Sheets of 9
2251-2252 A373 $1.65 #a.-i., each 11.50 11.50

Souvenir Sheets
2253-2254 A373 $6 each 4.50 4.50

Illustrations on Nos. 2247-2248 are switched.

IBRA'99, World Stamp Exhibition, Nuremberg — A374

Exhibition emblem, Leipzig-Dresden Railway and: No. 2255, $1, Caroline Islands #19. No. 2257, $1.65, Caroline Islands #4.

Emblem, Gölsdorf 4-4-0 and: No. 2256, $1.20, Caroline Islands #16. No. 2258, $1.90, Caroline Islands #8, #10.

$6, Registered label on cover.

Illustration reduced.

1999, June 24 Litho. *Perf. 14*
2255-2258 A374 Set of 4 4.50 4.50

Souvenir Sheet
2259 A374 $6 multicolored 5.00 5.00

Paintings by Hokusai (1760-1849) — A375

Details or entire paintings: No. 2260: a, Asakusa Honganji. b, Dawn at Isawa in Kai Province. c, Samurai with Bow and Arrow (bows level). d, Samurai with Bow and Arrow (bows at different angles). e, Kajikazawa in Kai Province. f, A Great Wave.

No. 2261: a, People on the Balcony of the Sazaido. b, Nakahara in Sagami Province. c, Defensive Positions (2 men). d, Defensive Positions (3 men). e, Mount Fuji in Clear Weather. f, Nihonbashi in Edo.

No. 2262, Cotenyama At Shinagawa on Tokaido Highway, vert. No. 2263, A Netsuke Workshop, vert.

1999, June 24

Sheets of 6
2260-2261 A375 $1.65 #a.-f., each 7.50 7.50

Souvenir Sheets
2262-2263 A375 $6 each 4.50 4.50

Johann Wolfgang von Goethe (1749-1832), Poet — A376

No. 2264: a, Three archangels in "Faust." b, Portraits of Goethe and Friedrich von Schiller (1759-1805). c, Faust reclining in landscape with spirits.

$6, Profile portrait of Goethe.

1999, June 24 Litho. *Perf. 14*
2264 A376 $1.75 Sheet of 3, #a.-c. 4.00 4.00

Souvenir Sheet
2265 A376 $6 multicolored 4.50 4.50

Souvenir Sheets

Philexfrance '99, World Philatelic Exhibition — A377

Locomotives: #2266, Crampton 1855-69. #2267, 232-U1 4-Cylinder Compound 4-6-4, 1949.

Illustration reduced.

1999, June 24 *Perf. 13¾*
2266 A377 $6 multicolored 4.50 4.50
2267 A377 $6 multicolored 4.50 4.50

A378 A379

Wedding of Prince Edward and Sophie Rhys-Jones - No. 2268: a, Sophie. b. Sophie, Edward. c, Edward.

$6, Horse and carriage, couple.

1999, June 24 *Perf. 13½*
2268 A378 $3 Sheet of 3, #a.-c. 6.75 6.75

Souvenir Sheet
2269 A378 $6 multicolored 4.50 4.50

1999, May 25 Litho. *Perf. 14½x14*

Various white kittens: 35c, 45c, 60c, 75c, 90c, $1.

No. 2276: a, One holding paw on another. b, Black & white. c, White kitten, black kitten. d, One with yarn. e, Two in basket. f, One looking up.

No. 2277: a, One playing with red yarn. b, Two long-haired. c, Yellow tabby. d, One with mouse. e, Yellow tabby on pillow. f, Black & gray tabby.

No. 2278, Tabby cat carrying kitten. No. 2279, Yellow kitten in tree.

2270-2275 A379 Set of 6 3.00 3.00

Sheets of 6
2276-2277 A379 $1.65 #a.-f., each 7.50 7.50

Souvenir Sheets
2278-2279 A379 $6 each 4.50 4.50

Australia '99, World Stamp Expo (#2276-2279).

A380 A381

UN Rights of the Child Convention, 10th Anniv. - No. 2280: a, Three children. b, Adult hand taking child's hand, silhouette of mother holding infant. c, UN Building, member flags, dove.

$6, Dove.

1999, June 22 *Perf. 14*
2280 A380 $3 Sheet of 3, #a.-c. 6.75 6.75

Souvenir Sheet
2281 A380 $6 multicolored 4.50 4.50

1999, June 24 Litho. *Perf. 13x11*

Boats and ships: 25c, Missa Ferdie. 45c, Sailboats. 60c, Jolly Roger Pirate Ship. 90c, $4, Freewinds. $1.20, Monarch of the Seas.

2282-2286 A381 Set of 5 2.60 2.60
2286a Souvenir sheet, #2282-2286 2.60 2.60

Souvenir Sheet
Perf. 13¾
2287 A381 $4 multicolored 3.00 3.00

No. 2287 contains one 51x38mm stamp.

A382

Butterflies: 65c, Fiery jewel. 75c, Hewitson's blue hairstreak. $1.20, Scarce bamboo page, horiz. $1.65, Paris peacock, horiz.

No. 2292, horiz.: a, California dog face. b, Small copper. c, Zebra swallowtail. d, White M hairstreak. e, Old world swallowtail. f, Buckeye. g, Apollo. h, Sonoran blue. i, Purple emperor.

No. 2293, Monarch. No. 2294, Cairns birdwing, horiz.

1999, Aug. 16 *Perf. 14*
2288-2291 A382 Set of 4 3.25 3.25
2292 A382 $1 Sheet of 9, #a.-i. 6.75 6.75

Souvenir Sheets
2293-2294 A382 $6 each 4.50 4.50

Christmas A383

15c, Madonna and child in a Wreath of Flowers by Peter Paul Rubens. 25c, Shroud of Christ Held by Two Angels, by Albrecht Dürer. 45c, Madonna and Child Enthroned Between Two Saints, by Raphael. 60c, Holy Family with

the Lamb, by Raphael. $2, The Transfiguration, by Raphael. $4, Three Putti Holding a Coat of Arms, by Dürer.
$6, The Coronation of the Holy St. Catherine, by Rubens.

1999, Nov. 22 Litho. *Perf. 13¾*

2295-2300	A383 Set of 6	5.50	5.50

Souvenir Sheet

2301	A383 $6 multicolored	4.50	4.50

WAR TAX STAMPS

No. 31 and Type A3 Overprinted in Black or Red **WAR STAMP**

1916-18 Wmk. 3 *Perf. 14*

MR1	A3 ½p green	.60	*1.40*
MR2	A3 ½p green (R) ('17)	1.00	*1.70*
MR3	A3 1½p orange ('18)	.60	*.85*
	Nos. MR1-MR3 (3)	2.20	*3.95*

ARGENTINA

ˌär-jən-ˈtē-nə

LOCATION — In South America
GOVT. — Republic
AREA — 1,084,120 sq. mi.
POP. — 36,737,664 (est. 1999)
CAPITAL — Buenos Aires

100 Centavos = 1 Peso (1858, 1992)
100 Centavos = 1 Austral (1985)

Catalogue values for unused stamps in this country are for Never Hinged items, beginning with Scott 587 in the regular postage section, Scott B12 in the semi-postal section, Scott C59 in the airpost section, Scott CB1 in the airpost semi-postal section and Scott O79 in the officials section.

Watermarks

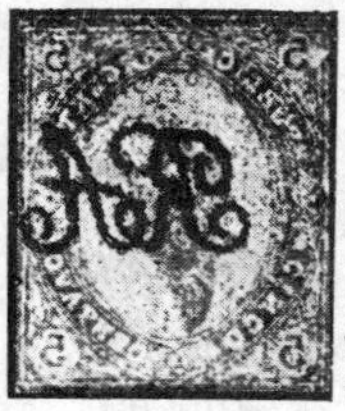
Wmk. 84- Italic RA

Wmk. 85- Small Sun, 4 ½mm

Wmk. 86- Large Sun, 6mm

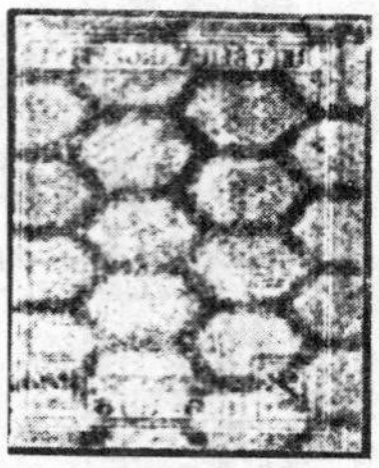
Wmk. 87- Honeycomb

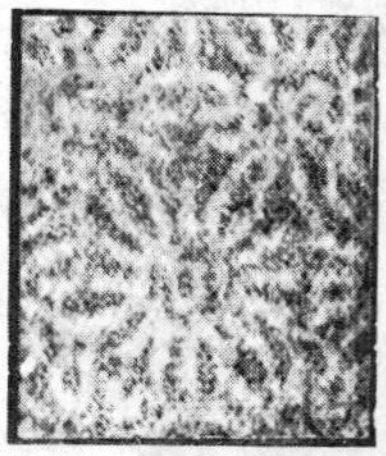
Wmk. 88- Multiple Suns

Wmk. 89- Large Sun

In this watermark the face of the sun is 7mm in diameter, the rays are heavier than in the large sun watermark of 1896-1911 and the watermarks are placed close together, so that parts of several frequently appear on one stamp. This paper was intended to be used for fiscal stamps and is usually referred to as "fiscal sun paper."

Wmk. 90- RA in Sun

In 1928 watermark 90 was slightly modified, making the diameter of the Sun 9mm instead of 10mm. Several types of this watermark exist.

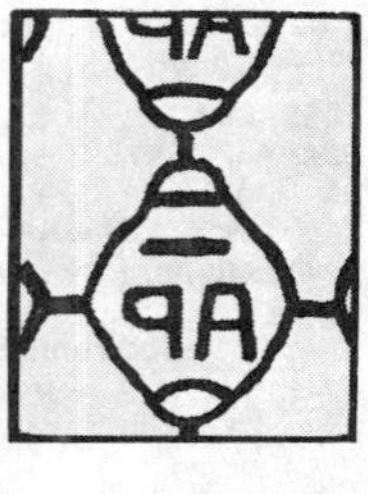
Wmk. 205- AP in Oval

The letters "AP" are the initials of "AHORRO POSTAL." This paper was formerly used exclusively for Postal Savings stamps.

Wmk. 287- Double Circle and Letters in Sheet

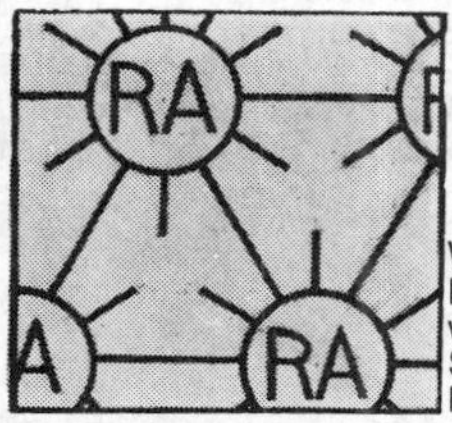
Wmk. 288- RA in Sun with Straight Rays

Wmk. 365- Argentine Arms, "Casa de Moneda de la Nacion" & "RA" Multiple

Values for Unused
Unused values for Nos. 5-17 are for examples without gum. Examples with original gum command higher prices. Unused values of Nos. 1-4B and stamps after No. 17 are for examples with original gum as defined in the catalogue introduction.

Argentine Confederation

Symbolical of the Argentine Confederation
A1 A2

Unwmk.

1858, May 1 Litho. *Imperf.*

1	A1 5c red	1.50	*24.00*
a.	Colon after "5"	1.75	*32.50*
b.	Colon after "V"	1.75	*32.50*
2	A1 10c green	2.50	*57.50*
f.	Diagonal half used as 5c on cover		*800.00*
3	A1 15c blue	16.00	*160.00*
c.	One-third used as 5c on cover		*6,500.*
	Nos. 1-3 (3)	20.00	*241.50*

There are nine varieties of Nos. 1, 2 and 3. Counterfeits and forged cancellations of Nos. 1-3 are plentiful.

1860, Jan.

4	A2 5c red	3.25	*72.50*
4A	A2 10c green	7.00	
4B	A2 15c blue	25.00	
	Nos. 4-4B (3)	35.25	

Nos. 4A and 4B were never placed in use. Some compostitions of Nos. 4-4B contain 8 different types across the sheet. Other settings exist with minor variations. Counterfeits and forged cancellations of Nos. 4-4B are plentiful.

Argentine Republic

Seal of the Republic — A3

Broad "C" in "CENTAVOS," Accent on "U" of "REPUBLICA"

1862, Jan. 11

5	A3 5c rose	40.00	37.50
a.	5c rose lilac	87.50	35.00
6	A3 10c green	140.00	65.00
b.	Diagonal half used as 5c on cover		*4,750.*
7	A3 15c blue	275.00	225.00
a.	Without accent on "U"	*7,000.*	*3,000.*
b.	Tete beche pair	*100,000.*	*100,000.*
i.	15c ultramarine	425.00	325.00
j.	Diagonal third used as 5c on cover		*5,000.*

Only one used example of No. 7b is known. It has faults. Two unused examples are known. One is sound with origional gum, the other is in a block, without gum, and has tiny faults.

Broad "C" in "CENTAVOS," No Accent on "U"

1863

7C	A3 5c rose	18.00	21.00
d.	5c rose lilac	100.00	110.00
e.	Worn plate (rose)	200.00	52.50
7F	A3 10c yellow green	350.00	140.00
g.	10c olive green	*500.00*	250.00
k.	10c green, ribbed paper	425.00	200.00
l.	Worn plate (green)	325.00	150.00
m.	Worn plate (olive green)	425.00	165.00

Narrow "C" in "CENTAVOS," No Accent on "U"

1864

7H	A3 5c rose red	160.00	32.50

The so-called reprints of 10c and 15c are counterfeits. They have narrow "C" and straight lines in shield. Nos. 7C and 7H have been extensively counterfeited.

Rivadavia Issue

Bernardino Rivadavia
A4 A5

Rivadavia — A6

1864-67 Engr. Wmk. 84 *Imperf.*
Clear Impressions

8	A4 5c brown rose	*1,300.*	*160.*
a.	5c orange red ('67)	*1,500.*	*160.*
9	A5 10c green	*2,000.*	*1,200.*
10	A6 15c blue	*7,250.*	*4,000.*

Perf. 11½
Dull to Worn Impressions

11	A4	5c brown rose ('65)	30.00	12.00
11B	A4	5c lake	77.50	17.50
12	A5	10c green	80.00	30.00
a.		Half used as 5c on cover		1,100.
c.		Horiz. pair, imperf vert.		1,750.
13	A6	15c blue	275.00	110.00

1867-72 Unwmk. *Imperf.*

14	A4	5c carmine ('72)	250.	65.
15	A4	5c rose	200.	100.
15A	A5	10c green	4,000.	4,000.
16	A6	15c blue	2,250.	1,750.

Nos. 15A-16 issued without gum.

1867 *Perf. 11½*

17	A4	5c carmine	350.00	150.00

Nos. 14, 15 and 17 exist with part of papermaker's wmk. "LACROIX FRERES."

Rivadavia
A7

Manuel Belgrano
A8

Jose de San Martin — A9

Groundwork of Horizontal Lines

1867-68 *Perf. 12*

18	A7	5c vermilion	200.00	10.00
18A	A8	10c green	30.00	4.50
b.		Diag. half used as 5c on cover		750.00
19	A9	15c blue	65.00	15.00

Groundwork of Crossed Lines

20	A7	5c vermilion	10.50	.65
21	A9	15c blue	92.50	12.00

See Nos. 27, 33-34, 39 and types A19, A33, A34, A37. For surcharges and overprints see Nos. 30-32, 41-42, 47-51, O6-O7, O26.

Gen. Antonio G. Balcarce
A10

Mariano Moreno
A11

Carlos Maria de Alvear — A12

Gervasio Antonio Posadas — A13

Cornelio Saavedra — A14

1873

22	A10	1c purple	5.00	2.00
a.		1c gray violet	6.25	2.00
23	A11	4c brown	4.75	.40
a.		4c red brown	17.00	2.00
24	A12	30c orange	100.00	15.00
a.		Vert. pair, imperf horiz.	4,000.	
25	A13	60c black	100.00	4.75
26	A14	90c blue	25.00	2.25
		Nos. 22-26 (5)	234.75	24.40

For overprints see Nos. O5, O12-O14, O19-O21, O25, O29.

1873

Laid Paper

27	A8	10c green	200.00	20.00

Nos.18, 18A Surcharged in Black

Nos. 30-31

No. 32

1877, Feb.

Wove Paper

30	A7	1c on 5c vermilion	47.50	15.00
a.		Inverted surcharge	350.00	200.00
31	A7	2c on 5c vermilion	92.50	60.00
a.		Inverted surcharge	700.00	500.00
32	A8	8c on 10c green	125.00	30.00
b.		Inverted surcharge	500.00	425.00
		Nos. 30-32 (3)	265.00	105.00

Varieties also exist with double and triple surcharges, surcharge on reverse, 8c on No. 27, all made clandestinely from the original cliches of the surcharges.

Forgeries of these surcharges include the inverted and double varieties.

1876-77 *Rouletted*

33	A7	5c vermilion	150.00	60.00
34	A7	8c lake ('77)	25.00	.35

Belgrano
A17

Dalmacio Vélez Sarsfield
A18

San Martín — A19

1878 *Rouletted*

35	A17	16c green	8.00	1.10
36	A18	20c blue	10.00	3.00
37	A19	24c blue	17.00	3.00
		Nos. 35-37 (3)	35.00	7.10

See No. 56. For overprints see Nos. O9-O10, O15-O17, O22, O28.

Vicente Lopez — A20

Alvear — A21

1877-80 *Perf. 12*

38	A20	2c yellow green	4.25	.90
39	A7	8c lake ('80)	4.25	.35
a.		8c brown lake	27.50	.35
40	A21	25c lake ('78)	22.50	6.00
		Nos. 38-40 (3)	31.00	7.25

For overprints see Nos. O4, O11, O18, O24.

No. 18 Surcharged in Black

½ (PROVISORIO)
Large "P" Wide "V"

½ (PROVISORIO)
Small "P" Narrow "V"

1882

41	A7	½c on 5c ver	1.50	1.50
a.		Double surcharge	80.00	80.00
b.		Inverted surcharge	20.00	20.00
c.		"PROVISORIO" omitted	80.00	80.00
d.		Fraction omitted	50.00	
e.		"PROVISOBIO"	30.00	30.00
f.		Pair, one without surcharge	200.00	
g.		Small "P" in "PROVISORIO"	2.50	2.50
h.		As "a," small "P" in "PROVISORIO"	32.50	32.50
i.		As "b," small "P" in "PROVISORIO"	40.00	40.00
j.		As "d," small "P" in "PROVISORIO"	15.00	15.00

Perforated across Middle of Stamp

42	A7	½c on 5c ver	3.00	3.00
a.		"PROVISORIO"	40.00	40.00
b.		Large "P" in "PROVISORIO"	30.00	22.50

A23

1882 Typo. *Perf. 12*

43	A23	½c brown	1.40	.80
a.		Imperf., pair	40.00	40.00
44	A23	1c red, perf. 14	3.50	1.00
a.		Perf. 12	9.00	4.25
45	A23	12c ultra	55.00	8.75
a.		Perf. 14	45.00	8.75

Engr.

46	A23	12c grnsh blue, perf. 14	125.00	11.00
		Nos. 43-46 (4)	184.90	21.55

See type A29. For overprints see Nos. O2, O8, O23, O27.

No. 21 Surcharged in Red:

1884 ½
a

1 c 1884
b

CUATRO Centavos 1884
c

1884 Engr. *Perf. 12*

47	A9 (a)	½c on 15c blue	2.00	1.50
a.		Groundwork of horiz. lines	100.00	80.00
b.		Inverted surcharge	27.50	20.00
48	A9 (b)	1c on 15c blue	16.00	13.00
a.		Groundwork of horiz. lines	10.00	6.00
b.		Inverted surcharge	80.00	55.00
c.		Double surcharge	40.00	32.50
d.		Triple surcharge	350.00	

Nos. 20-21 Surcharged in Black

49	A7 (a)	½c on 5c ver	4.00	3.00
a.		Inverted surcharge	150.00	110.00
b.		Date omitted	150.00	—
c.		Pair, one without surcharge	375.00	
d.		Double surcharge	550.00	
50	A9 (a)	½c on 15c blue	10.00	8.00
a.		Groundwork of horiz. lines	30.00	25.00
b.		Inverted surcharge	70.00	55.00
c.		Pair, one without surcharge	325.00	
51	A7 (c)	4c on 5c ver	10.00	6.00
a.		Inverted surcharge	25.00	20.00
b.		Double surcharge	325.00	200.00
c.		Pair, one without surcharge but with "4" in manuscript	550.00	350.00
d.		Pair, one without surcharge	250.00	
		Nos. 47-51 (5)	42.00	31.50

A29

1884-85 Engr. *Perf. 12*

52	A29	½c red brown	.90	.45
a.		Horiz. pair, imperf vert.	300.00	250.00
53	A29	1c rose red	5.25	.45
a.		Horiz. pair, imperf vert.	300.00	250.00
54	A29	12c grnsh blue ('85)	30.00	1.25
a.		12c deep blue	25.00	1.25
b.		Horiz. pair, imperf vert.	300.00	250.00
		Nos. 52-54 (3)	36.15	2.15

For overprints see Nos. O1, O3, O9.

San Martin Type of 1878

1887 Engr.

56	A19	24c blue	17.50	1.40

Justo Jose de Urquiza
A30

Lopez
A31

Miguel Juarez Celman
A32

Rivadavia (Large head)
A33

Rivadavia (Small head)
A34

Domingo F. Sarmiento
A35

Nicolas Avellaneda
A36

San Martin
A37

Julio A. Roca
A37a

Belgrano
A37b

Manuel Dorrego
A38

Moreno
A39

Bartolome Mitre — A40

CINCO CENTAVOS.
A33 - Shows collar on left side only.
A34 - Shows collar on both sides. Lozenges in background larger and clearer than in A33.

1888-90 Litho. *Perf. 11½*

57	A30	½c blue	.50	.45
b.		Vert. pair, imperf. horiz.	120.00	65.00
c.		Horiz. pair, imperf. vert.	120.00	65.00
58	A31	2c yellow green	9.25	6.00
b.		Vert. pair, imperf. horiz.	80.00	
c.		Horiz. pair, imperf. vert.	200.00	
59	A32	3c blue green	1.75	.60
b.		Horiz. pair, imperf. vert.	80.00	
c.		Horiz. pair, imperf. btwn.	100.00	
d.		Vert. pair, imperf. btwn.	25.00	
60	A33	5c carmine	8.00	.75
b.		Vert. pair, imperf. horiz.	100.00	
61	A34	5c carmine	11.00	1.25
b.		Vert. pair, imperf. btwn.		
c.		Vert. pair, imperf. horiz.		400.00
62	A35	6c red	25.00	15.00
b.		Vert. pair, imperf. btwn.	80.00	
c.		Perf. 12	52.50	42.50
63	A36	10c brown	15.00	1.10
64	A37	15c orange	15.00	1.60
d.		Vert. pair, imperf. between		600.00
64A	A37a	20c green	12.00	1.25
64B	A37b	25c purple	15.00	1.60
65	A38	30c chocolate	21.00	2.50
b.		30c reddish chocolate brown	400.00	80.00
c.		Horiz. pair, imperf. between	400.00	325.00

66	A39	40c slate, perf. 12	25.00	3.00
a.		Perf. 11½	80.00	16.00
b.		Horiz. pair, imperf. btwn. (#66)		600.00
67	A40	50c blue	100.00	8.25
		Nos. 57-67 (13)	258.50	43.35

In this issue there are several varieties of each value, the difference between them being in the relative position of the head to the frame.

Imperf., Pairs

57a	A30	½c	75.00	60.00
58a	A31	2c	55.00	
59a	A32	3c	35.00	25.00
61a	A34	5c		*100.00*
62a	A35	6c	*55.00*	
63a	A36	10c	*55.00*	
64c	A37	15c		*200.00*
65a	A38	30c	*275.00*	*200.00*

Urquiza A41

Velez Sarsfield A42

Miguel Juarez Celman A43

Rivadavia (Large head) A44

Sarmiento A45

Juan Bautista Alberdi A46

1888-89 Engr. *Perf. 11½, 11½x12*

68	A41	½c ultra	.30	.20
a.		Vert. pair, imperf. horiz.	—	—
b.		Imperf., pair	30.00	—
69	A42	1c brown	.85	.20
a.		Vert. pair, imperf. horiz.	65.00	
b.		Vert. pair, imperf. btwn.	—	
c.		Imperf., pair	30.00	
d.		Horiz. pair, imperf. btwn.	100.00	
70	A43	3c blue green	2.50	.70
71	A44	5c rose	2.75	.20
a.		Imperf., pair	40.00	—
72	A45	6c blue black	1.40	.55
b.		Perf. 11½x12	12.50	3.00
73	A46	12c blue	5.50	1.75
a.		Imperf., pair	30.00	
b.		bluish paper	8.00	2.00
c.		Perf. 11½	8.25	3.25
		Nos. 68-73 (6)	13.30	3.60

#69-70 exist with papermakers' watermarks.

See No. 77, types A50, A61. For surcharges see Nos. 83-84.

Jose Maria Paz A48

Santiago Derqui A49

Rivadavia (Small head) A50

Avellaneda A51

Moreno A53

Mitre A54

Posadas — A55

1890 Engr. *Perf. 11½*

75	A48	¼c green	.20	.20
76	A49	2c violet	.85	.20
a.		2c purple	.85	.20
b.		2c slate	1.25	.30
c.		Horiz. pair, imperf. btwn.	25.00	
d.		Imperf., pair	35.00	
e.		Perf. 11½x12	5.00	.25
77	A50	5c carmine	1.90	.20
a.		Imperf., pair	50.00	25.00
b.		Perf. 11½x12	5.00	.30
c.		Vert. pair, imperf. btwn.	75.00	60.00
d.		Horiz. pair, imperf. btwn.	75.00	60.00
78	A51	10c brown	1.60	.25
b.		Imperf., pair	150.00	—
c.		Vert. pair, imperf. btwn.	225.00	
80	A53	40c olive green	5.00	.80
a.		Imperf., pair	40.00	
b.		Horiz. pair, imperf. btwn.		*250.00*
81	A54	50c orange	4.00	.80
a.		Imperf., pair	60.00	
b.		Perf. 11½x12	4.25	1.10
82	A55	60c black	15.00	2.75
a.		Imperf., pair	—	—
b.		Vert. pair, imperf. btwn.	125.00	100.00
		Nos. 75-82 (7)	28.55	5.20

Type A50 differs from type A44 in having the head smaller, the letters of "Cinco Centavos" not as tall, and the curved ornaments at sides close to the first and last letters of "Republica Argentina."

Lithographed Surcharge on No. 73 in Black or Red

1890 *Perf. 11½x12*

83	A46	¼c on 12c blue	.40	.40
a.		Perf. 11½	35.00	25.00
b.		Double surcharge	75.00	35.00
c.		Inverted surcharge	80.00	
84	A46	¼c on 12c blue (R)	.40	.40
a.		Double surcharge	52.50	52.50
b.		Perf. 11½	7.00	2.00

Surcharge is different on #83 and 84.

Nos. 83-84 exist as pairs, one without surcharge. These were privately produced.

Rivadavia A57

Jose de San Martin A58

Gregorio Araoz de Lamadrid — A59

Admiral Guillermo Brown — A60

1891 Engr. *Perf. 11½*

85	A57	8c carmine rose	1.25	.20
a.		Imperf., pair	75.00	
86	A58	1p deep blue	40.00	5.75
87	A59	5p ultra	200.00	16.00
88	A60	20p green	300.00	45.00
		Nos. 85-88 (4)	541.25	66.95

A 10p brown and a 50p red were prepared but not issued. Values: 10p $1,500 for fine, 50p $1,000 with rough or somewhat damaged perfs.

Velez Sarsfield — A61

"Santa Maria," "Nina" and "Pinta" — A62

1890 *Perf. 11½*

89	A61	1c brown	.80	.40
b.		Horiz. pair, imperf. btwn.		*550.00*

Type A61 is a re-engraving of A42. The figure "1" in each upper corner has a short horizontal serif instead of a long one pointing downward. In type A61 the first and last letters of "Correos y Telegrafos" are closer to the curved ornaments below than in type A42. Background is of horizontal lines (cross-hatching on No. 69).

1892, Oct. 12 Wmk. 85 *Perf. 11½*

90	A62	2c light blue	6.00	3.00
a.		Double impression	190.00	
91	A62	5c dark blue	8.50	5.00

Discovery of America, 400th anniv. Counterfeits of Nos. 90-91 are litho.

Rivadavia A63

Belgrano A64

San Martin — A65

Perf. 11½, 12 and Compound

1892-95 Wmk. 85

92	A63	½c dull blue	.30	.20
a.		½c bright ultra	50.00	25.00
93	A63	1c brown	.35	.20
94	A63	2c green	.35	.20
95	A63	3c orange ('95)	1.00	.20
96	A63	5c carmine	1.50	.20
b.		5c green (error)	350.00	350.00
98	A64	10c carmine rose	10.00	.40
99	A64	12c deep blue ('93)	7.00	.40
100	A64	16c gray	12.50	.55
101	A64	24c gray brown	12.50	.55
b.		Perf. 12	25.00	7.00
102	A64	50c blue green	18.00	.55
b.		Perf. 12	25.00	2.75
103	A65	1p lake ('93)	10.00	.70
a.		1p red brown	17.50	5.00
104	A65	2p dark green	21.00	2.25
a.		Perf. 12	77.50	27.50
105	A65	5p dark blue	37.50	2.75
		Nos. 92-105 (13)	132.00	9.15

The high values of this and succeeding issues are frequently punched with the word "INUTILIZADO," parts of the letters showing on each stamp. These punched stamps sell for only a small fraction of the catalogue values.

Reprints of No. 96b have white gum. The original stamp has yellowish gum. Value $125.

Imperf., Pairs

92b	A63	½c	55.00	—
93a	A63	1c	55.00	—
94a	A63	2c	25.00	—
96a	A63	5c	25.00	—
98a	A64	10c	55.00	—
99a	A64	12c	55.00	—
100a	A64	16c	55.00	—
101a	A64	24c	55.00	—
102a	A64	50c	55.00	—
103b	A65	1p	60.00	—
105a	A65	5p	140.00	—

Nos. 102a, 103b and 105a exist only without gum; the other imperfs are found with or without gum, and values are the same for either condition.

Vertical Pairs, Imperf. Between

92c	A63	½c	125.00	
93b	A63	1c	100.00	
94b	A63	2c	50.00	
95a	A63	3c	250.00	
96c	A63	5c	45.00	50.00
98b	A64	10c	100.00	
99b	A64	12c	100.00	

Horizontal Pairs, Imperf. Between

93c	A63	1c	110.00	
94c	A63	2c	55.00	
96d	A63	5c	55.00	45.00
98c	A64	10c	110.00	

1896-97 Wmk. 86

106	A63	½c slate	.50	.20
a.		½c gray blue	.50	.20
b.		½c indigo	.50	.20
107	A63	1c brown	.50	.20
108	A63	2c yellow green	.60	.20
109	A63	3c orange	.60	.20
110	A63	5c carmine	.60	.20
a.		Imperf., pair	100.00	
111	A64	10c carmine rose	8.00	.20
112	A64	12c deep blue	4.00	.20
a.		Imperf., pair	—	
113	A64	16c gray	10.00	.80
114	A64	24c gray brown	10.50	1.25
a.		Imperf., pair	100.00	—
115	A64	30c orange ('97)	10.00	.60
116	A64	50c blue green	10.00	.60
117	A64	80c dull violet	18.00	.80
118	A65	1p lake	25.00	.75
119	A65	1p20c black ('97)	10.00	3.50
120	A65	2p dark green	15.00	7.00
121	A65	5p dark blue	90.00	10.00
a.		Perf. 12	325.00	90.00
		Nos. 106-121 (16)	213.30	26.70

Vertical Pairs, Imperf. Between

106c	A63	½c	200.00	
107a	A63	1c	125.00	
108a	A63	2c	125.00	
109a	A63	3c	200.00	
110b	A63	5c	125.00	125.00
112b	A64	12c	125.00	100.00

Horizontal Pairs, Imperf. Between

107b	A63	1c	125.00	
108b	A63	2c	125.00	
110c	A63	5c	125.00	80.00
111a	A64	10c	125.00	
112c	A64	12c	125.00	

Allegory, Liberty Seated
A66 A67

Perf. 11½, 12 and Compound

1899-1903

122	A66	½c yellow brown	.20	.20
123	A66	1c green	.20	.20
124	A66	2c slate	.20	.20
125	A66	3c orange ('01)	.85	.20
126	A66	4c yellow ('03)	1.50	.20
127	A66	5c carmine rose	.20	.20
128	A66	6c black ('03)	1.00	.40
129	A66	10c dark green	1.50	.30
130	A66	12c dull blue	1.00	.50
131	A66	12c olive grn ('01)	1.00	.50
132	A66	15c sea green ('01)	2.75	.50
132B	A66	15c dull blue ('01)	3.00	.50
133	A66	16c orange	7.50	3.75
134	A66	20c claret	2.00	.20
135	A66	24c violet	3.50	.70
136	A66	30c rose	7.50	.40
137	A66	30c vermilion ('01)	3.75	.40
a.		30c scarlet	50.00	2.50
138	A66	50c brt blue	4.75	.40
139	A67	1p bl & blk, perf. 11½	14.00	.65
a.		Center inverted	*1,500.*	*650.00*
b.		Perf. 12	250.00	125.00
140	A67	5p orange & blk	57.50	7.00
		Punch cancellation		1.50
a.		Center inverted	*2,750.*	—
141	A67	10p green & blk	50.00	9.25
		Punch cancellation		1.75
a.		Center inverted	*3,500.*	
		Punch cancellation		675.00
142	A67	20p red & black	200.00	21.00
		Punch cancellation		1.75
a.		Center invtd.(punch cancel)		*2,000.*
		Nos. 122-142 (22)	363.90	47.65

Imperf., Pairs

122a	A66	½c	30.00	
123a	A66	1c	45.00	
124a	A66	2c	15.00	
125a	A66	3c	250.00	
127a	A66	5c	15.00	
128a	A66	6c	45.00	
129a	A66	10c	45.00	
132a	A66	15c	45.00	

Vertical Pairs, Imperf. Between

122b	A66	½c	10.00	10.00
123b	A66	1c	10.00	10.00
124b	A66	2c	5.00	5.00
125b	A66	3c	200.00	150.00
126a	A66	4c	250.00	200.00
127b	A66	5c	5.00	3.00
128b	A66	6c	12.00	10.00
129b	A66	10c	75.00	
132c	A66	15c	12.00	10.00

Horizontal Pairs, Imperf. Between

122c	A66	½c	30.00	20.00
123c	A66	1c	50.00	20.00
124c	A66	2c	10.00	5.00
125c	A66	3c	225.00	150.00
126b	A66	4c	275.00	
127c	A66	5c	10.00	5.00
128c	A66	6c	17.50	10.00
129c	A66	10c	17.50	10.00
132d	A66	15c	35.00	20.00
138a	A66	50c	160.00	

River Port of Rosario A68

1902, Oct. 26 Perf. 11½, 11½x12

143 A68 5c deep blue 4.50 2.50
a. Imperf., pair 95.00
b. Vert. pair, imperf. btwn. 95.00
c. Horiz. pair, imperf. btwn. 75.00

Completion of port facilities at Rosario.

San Martin
A69 A70

1908-09 Typo. Perf. 13½, 13½x12½

144 A69 ½c violet .20 .20
145 A69 1c brnsh buff .20 .20
146 A69 2c chocolate .55 .20
147 A69 3c green .70 .30
148 A69 4c redsh violet 1.40 .30
149 A69 5c carmine .30 .20
150 A69 6c olive bister .80 .25
151 A69 10c gray green 1.50 .20
152 A69 12c yellow buff .40 .40
153 A69 12c dk blue ('09) 1.25 .20
154 A69 15c apple green 1.75 .85
155 A69 20c ultra 1.25 .20
156 A69 24c red brown 3.25 .60
157 A69 30c dull rose 5.00 .60
158 A69 50c black 4.75 .40
159 A70 1p sl bl & pink 11.00 1.75
Nos. 144-159 (16) 34.30 6.85

The 1c blue was not issued. Value $250.

Wmk. 86 appears on ½, 1, 6, 20, 24 and 50c. Other values have similar wmk. with wavy rays.

Stamps lacking wmk. are from outer rows printed on sheet margin.

Pyramid of May — A71

Nicolas Rodriguez Pena and Hipolito Vieytes — A72

Meeting at Pena's Home — A73

3c, Miguel de Azcuenaga (1754-1833) & Father Manuel M. Alberti (1763-1811). 4c, Viceroy's house & Fort Buenos Aires. 5c, Cornelio Saavedra (1759-1829). 10c, Antonio Luis Beruti (1772-1842) & French distributing badges. 12c, Congress building. 20c, Juan Jose Castelli (1764-1812) & Domingo Matheu (1765-1831). 24c, 1st council. 30c, Manuel Belgrano (1770-1820) & Juan Larrea (1782-1847). 50c, 1st meeting of republican government, May 25, 1810. 1p, Mariano Moreno (1778-1811) & Juan Jose Paso (1758-1833). 5p, Oath of the Junta. 10p, Centenary Monument. 20p, Jose Francisco de San Martin (1778-1850).

Inscribed "1810 1910"
Various Frames

1910, May 1 Engr. Perf. 11½

160 A71 ½c bl & gray bl .30 .20
161 A72 1c blue grn & blk .30 .20
b. Horiz. pair, imperf. btwn. 65.00
162 A73 2c olive & gray .20 .20
163 A72 3c green .70 .20
164 A73 4c dk blue & grn .70 .25
165 A71 5c carmine .40 .20
166 A73 10c yel brn & blk 1.75 .20
167 A73 12c brt blue 1.40 .25
168 A72 20c gray brn & blk 3.25 .35
169 A73 24c org brn & bl 1.75 .90
170 A72 30c lilac & blk 1.75 .65
171 A71 50c carmine & blk 4.50 .90
172 A72 1p brt blue 10.00 3.50
173 A73 5p orange & vio 70.00 30.00
Punch cancel 2.50
174 A71 10p orange & blk 90.00 65.00
Punch cancel 3.00
175 A71 20p dp blue & ind 150.00 90.00
Punch cancel 4.50
Nos. 160-175 (16) 337.00 193.00

Centenary of the republic.

Center Inverted

160a A71 ½c 750.00
161a A72 1c 750.00
162a A73 2c 800.00
164a A73 4c 500.00
167a A73 12c 650.00
171a A71 50c 650.00
173a A73 5p 650.00

Domingo F. Sarmiento A87

Agriculture A88

1911, May 15 Typo. Perf. 13½

176 A87 5c gray brn & blk .75 .50

Domingo Faustino Sarmiento (1811-88), pres. of Argentina, 1868-74.

Wmk. 86, without Face

1911 Engr. Perf. 12

Size: 19x25mm

177 A88 5c vermilion .40 .20
178 A88 12c deep blue 5.00 .20
Set value .25

Wmk. 86, with Face

1911 Typo. Perf. 13½x12½

Size: 18x23mm

179 A88 ½c violet .20 .20
180 A88 1c brown ocher .20 .20
181 A88 2c chocolate .20 .20
a. Perf. 13½ 4.25 1.75
b. Imperf., pair 26.00
182 A88 3c green .40 .20
183 A88 4c brown violet .35 .25
184 A88 10c gray green .50 .20
185 A88 20c ultra 4.25 1.00
186 A88 24c red brown 5.25 3.50
187 A88 30c claret 1.75 .50
188 A88 50c black 8.00 .85
Nos. 179-188 (10) 21.10 7.10

The 5c dull red is a proof. In this issue Wmk. 86 comes: straight rays (4c, 20c, 24c) and wavy rays (2c). All other values exist with both forms.

Wmk. 87 (Horiz. or Vert.)

1912-14 Perf. 13½x12½

189 A88 ½c violet .20 .20
190 A88 1c ocher .20 .20
191 A88 2c chocolate .30 .20
192 A88 3c green .60 .20
193 A88 4c brown violet .60 .20
194 A88 5c red .20 .20
195 A88 10c deep green 1.40 .20
196 A88 12c deep blue 1.40 .20
197 A88 20c ultra 8.00 .70
198 A88 24c red brown 3.25 1.60
199 A88 30c claret 8.00 .60
200 A88 50c black 5.00 .60
Nos. 189-200 (12) 29.15 5.10

See Nos. 208-212. For overprints see Nos. OD1-OD8, OD47-OD54, OD102-OD108, OD146-OD152, OD183-OD190, OD235-OD241, OD281-OD284, OD318-OD323.

Perf. 13½

189a A88 ½c .80 .25
190a A88 1c .80 .25
191a A88 2c .80 .20
192a A88 3c 35.00 16.00
193a A88 4c 1.60 .70
194a A88 5c .30 .20
196a A88 12c 3.25 .80
197a A88 20c 5.00 .70
Nos. 189a-197a (8) 47.55 19.10

A89

1912-13 Perf. 13½

201 A89 1p dull bl & rose 6.00 1.00
Punch cancel .30
202 A89 5p slate & ol grn 19.00 6.00
Punch cancel .60
203 A89 10p violet & blue 75.00 9.00
Punch cancel 1.40
204 A89 20p blue & claret 175.00 60.00
Punch cancel 2.00
Nos. 201-204 (4) 275.00 76.00

1915 Unwmk. Perf. 13½x12½

208 A88 1c ocher .50 .20
209 A88 2c chocolate .50 .20
212 A88 5c red .50 .20
Nos. 208-212 (3) 1.50 .60

Only these denominations were printed on paper without watermark.

Other stamps of the series are known unwatermarked but they are from the outer rows of sheets the other parts of which are watermarked.

Francisco Narciso de Laprida A90

Declaration of Independence A91

Jose de San Martin
A92 A92a

Perf. 13½, 13½x12½

1916, July 9 Litho. Wmk. 87

215 A90 ½c violet .20 .20
216 A90 1c buff .25 .20

Perf. 13½x12½

217 A90 2c chocolate .20 .20
218 A90 3c green .45 .20
219 A90 4c red violet .65 .20

Perf. 13½

220 A91 5c red .30 .20
a. Imperf., pair 40.00
221 A91 10c gray green 1.50 .20
222 A92 12c blue .65 .20
223 A92 20c ultra 1.00 .25
224 A92 24c red brown 1.60 .75
225 A92 30c claret 1.60 .35
226 A92 50c gray black 3.25 .45
227 A92a 1p slate bl & red 9.25 4.00
Punch cancel .50
a. Imperf., pair 325.00
228 A92a 5p black & gray grn 110.00 40.00
Punch cancel 3.25
229 A92a 10p violet & blue 110.00 75.00
Punch cancel 2.50
230 A92a 20p dull blue & cl 160.00 67.50
Punch cancel 1.00
a. Imperf., pair 650.00
Nos. 215-230 (16) 400.90 189.90

Cent. of Argentina's declaration of independence of Spain, July 9, 1816.

The watermark is either vert. or horiz. on Nos. 215-220, 222; only vert. on No. 221, and only horiz. on Nos. 223-230.

For overprints see #OD9, OD55-OD56, OD109, OD153, OD191-OD192, OD285, OD324.

A93

A94

A94a

Juan Gregorio Pujol — A95

1917 Perf. 13½, 13½x12½

231 A93 ½c violet .20 .20
232 A93 1c buff .25 .20
233 A93 2c brown .25 .20
234 A93 3c lt green .75 .20
235 A93 4c red violet .80 .40
236 A93 5c red .25 .20
a. Imperf., pair 14.00
237 A93 10c gray green 1.50 .20

Perf. 13½

238 A94 12c blue 1.00 .20
239 A94 20c ultra 1.50 .20
240 A94 24c red brown 4.50 2.00
241 A94 30c claret 4.50 .60
242 A94 50c gray black 4.00 .60
243 A94a 1p slate bl & red 4.00 .35
244 A94a 5p black & gray grn 20.00 3.00
Punch cancel 1.50
245 A94a 10p violet & blue 47.50 9.25
Punch cancel 1.00
246 A94a 20p dull bl & claret 77.50 15.00
Punch cancel .80
a. Center inverted 1,200. 875.00
Nos. 231-246 (16) 168.50 32.80

The watermark is either vert. or horiz. on Nos. 231-236, 238; only vert. on No. 237, and only horiz. on Nos. 239-246.

1918, June 15 Litho. Perf. 13½

247 A95 5c bister & gray .70 .25

Cent. of the birth of Juan G. Pujol (1817-61), lawyer and legislator.

Perf. 13½, 13½x12½

1918-19 Unwmk.

248 A93 ½c violet .20 .20
249 A93 1c buff .20 .20
a. Imperf., pair 14.00
250 A93 2c brown .20 .20
251 A93 3c lt green .25 .20
252 A93 4c red violet .25 .20
253 A93 5c red .20 .20
254 A93 10c gray green 1.10 .20

Perf. 13½

255 A94 12c blue 1.25 .20
256 A94 20c ultra 1.60 .20
257 A94 24c red brown 2.00 .50
258 A94 30c claret 2.50 .30
259 A94 50c gray black 5.50 .25
Nos. 248-259 (12) 15.25 2.85

The stamps of this issue sometimes show letters of papermakers' watermarks.

There were two printings, in 1918 and 1923, using different ink and paper.

1920 Wmk. 88 Perf. 13½, 13½x12½

264 A93 ½c violet .20 .20
265 A93 1c buff .25 .20
266 A93 2c brown .25 .20
267 A93 3c green 1.50 .30
268 A93 4c red violet 2.00 1.25
269 A93 5c red .40 .20
270 A93 10c gray green 3.25 .20

Perf. 13½

271 A94 12c blue 1.75 .20
272 A94 20c ultra 2.50 .20
274 A94 30c claret 8.25 .70
275 A94 50c gray black 5.00 .90
Nos. 264-275 (11) 25.35 4.55

See #292-300, 304-307A, 310-314, 318, 322.

For overprints see Nos. OD10-OD20, OD57-OD71, OD74, OD110-OD121, OD154-OD159, OD161-OD162, OD193-OD207, OD209-OD211, OD242-OD252, OD254-OD255, OD286-OD290, OD325-OD328, OD330.

Belgrano's Mausoleum A96

Creation of Argentine Flag A97

Gen. Manuel Belgrano — A98

1920, June 18 Perf. 13½

280 A96 2c red .35 .20
a. Perf. 13½x12½ .35 .20
281 A97 5c rose & blue .40 .20
282 A98 12c green & blue .75 .75
Nos. 280-282 (3) 1.50 1.15

Belgrano (1770-1820), Argentine general, patriot and diplomat.

Gen. Justo Jose de Urquiza A99

Bartolome Mitre A100

1920, Nov. 11
283 A99 5c gray blue .25 .20

Gen. Justo Jose de Urquiza (1801-70), pres. of Argentina, 1854-60. See No. 303.

1921, June 26 **Unwmk.**
284 A100 2c violet brown .25 .20
285 A100 5c light blue .25 .20

Bartolome Mitre (1821-1906), pres. of Argentina, 1862-65.

Allegory, Pan-America — A101

1921, Aug. 25 ***Perf. 13½***
286 A101 3c violet .55 .30
287 A101 5c blue .80 .20
288 A101 10c vio brown 1.40 .35
289 A101 12c rose 2.00 .75
Nos. 286-289 (4) 4.75 1.60

Inscribed "Buenos Aires-Agosto de 1921" A102

Inscribed "Republica Argentina" A103

1921, Oct. ***Perf. 13½x12½***
290 A102 5c rose .30 .20
a. Perf. 13½ 1.25 .20
291 A103 5c rose 1.50 .20
a. Perf. 13½ 2.50 .20

1st Pan-American Postal Cong., Buenos Aires, Aug., 1921.
See Nos. 308-309, 319. For overprints see Nos. OD72, OD160, OD208, OD253, OD329.

1920 Wmk. 89 ***Perf. 13½, 13½x12½***
292 A93 ½c violet 2.00 .75
293 A93 1c buff 5.00 .75
294 A93 2c brown 3.00 .75
297 A93 5c red 4.00 .50
298 A93 10c gray green 4.00 .40

Perf. 13½
299 A94 12c blue 3,000. 125.00
300 A94 20c ultra 12.00 .75
Nos. 292-298,300 (6) 30.00 3.90

1920
303 A99 5c gray blue 350.00 225.00

Perf. 13½, 13½x12½

1922-23 **Wmk. 90**
304 A93 ½c violet .20 .20
305 A93 1c buff .20 .20
306 A93 2c brown .20 .20
307 A93 3c green .45 .30
307A A93 4c red violet 3.75 1.00
308 A102 5c rose 2.25 .20
309 A103 5c red 1.50 .20
310 A93 10c gray green 4.75 .30

Perf. 13½
311 A94 12c blue .85 .20
312 A94 20c ultra 1.25 .20
313 A94 24c red brown 9.25 4.50
314 A94 30c claret 5.50 .50
Nos. 304-314 (12) 30.15 8.00

Paper with Gray Overprint RA in Sun
Perf. 13½, 13½x12½

1922-23 **Unwmk.**
318 A93 2c brown 3.00 1.00
319 A103 5c red 2.00 .30

Perf. 13½
322 A94 20c ultra 15.00 1.50
Nos. 318-322 (3) 20.00 2.80

San Martín
A104 A105
With Period after Value

1923, May **Litho.** **Wmk. 90**
323 A104 ½c red violet .20 .20
324 A104 1c buff .30 .20
325 A104 2c dark brown .30 .20
326 A104 3c lt green .30 .20
327 A104 4c red brown .30 .20
328 A104 5c red .30 .20
329 A104 10c dull green 2.50 .20
330 A104 12c deep blue .40 .20
331 A104 20c ultra 1.00 .20
332 A104 24c lt brown 2.50 1.50
333 A104 30c claret 7.75 .60
334 A104 50c black 4.00 .35

Without Period after Value

Wmk. 87 ***Perf. 13½***
335 A105 1p blue & red 4.00 .20
336 A105 5p gray lilac & grn 16.00 1.75
Punch cancel .60
337 A105 10p claret & blue 55.00 10.50
Punch cancel 1.00
338 A105 20p slate & brn lake 90.00 30.00
Punch cancel .60
a. Center inverted
Nos. 323-338 (16) 184.85 46.70

Nos. 335-338 and 353-356 canceled with round or oval killers in purple (revenue cancellations) sell for one-fifth to one-half as much as postally used copies.
For overprints see Nos. 399-404.

Design of 1923
Without Period after Value
Perf. 13½, 13½x12½

1923-24 **Litho.** **Wmk. 90**
340 A104 ½c red violet .20 .20
341 A104 1c buff .20 .20
342 A104 2c dk brown .20 .20
343 A104 3c green .20 .20
a. Imperf., pair 8.00
344 A104 4c red brown .40 .20
345 A104 5c red .20 .20
346 A104 10c dull green .30 .20
347 A104 12c deep blue .50 .20
348 A104 20c ultra .65 .20
349 A104 24c lt brown 1.60 .70
350 A104 25c purple .80 .20
351 A104 30c claret 1.60 .20
352 A104 50c black 1.60 .20
353 A105 1p blue & red 2.00 .20
354 A105 5p dk violet & grn 15.00 .75
Punch cancel .20
355 A105 10p claret & blue 32.50 3.25
Punch cancel .20
356 A105 20p slate & lake 47.50 7.50
Punch cancel .20
Nos. 340-356 (17) 105.45 14.80

1931-33

Typographed
343b A104 3c 1.40 .25
345a A104 5c 2.50 .20
346a A104 10c 4.00 .20
347a A104 12c 8.50 1.50
348a A104 20c 32.50 1.60
350a A104 25c 20.00 .75
351a A104 30c 15.00 .40
Nos. 343b-351a (7) 83.90 4.90

The typographed stamps were issued only in coils and have a rough impression with heavy shading about the eyes and nose. Nos. 343 and 346 are known without watermark.
Nos. 341-345, 347-349, 351a may be found in pairs, one with period.
See note after No. 338. See Nos. 362-368. For overprints see Nos. OD21-OD33, OD75-OD87, OD122-OD133, OD163-OD175, OD212-OD226, OD256-OD268, OD291-OD304, OD331-OD345.

Rivadavia — A106

1926, Feb. 8 ***Perf. 13½***
357 A106 5c rose .40 .20

Presidency of Bernardino Rivadavia, cent.

Rivadavia A108

San Martin A109

General Post Office, 1926 — A110

General Post Office, 1826 — A111

1926, July 1 ***Perf. 13½x12½***
358 A108 3c gray green .20 .20
359 A109 5c red .20 .20

Perf. 13½
360 A110 12c deep blue .90 .20
361 A111 25c chocolate 1.60 .20
a. "1326" for "1826" 6.00 .75
Nos. 358-361 (4) 2.90 .80

Centenary of the Post Office.
For overprints see Nos. OD34, OD88, OD134, OD227-OD228, OD269, OD305, OD346.

Type of 1923-31 Issue
Without Period after Value

1927 Wmk. 205 ***Perf. 13½x12½***
362 A104 ½c red violet .25 .25
a. Pelure paper 1.75 1.50
363 A104 1c buff .25 .25
364 A104 2c dark brown .25 .20
a. Pelure paper .35 .20
365 A104 5c red .30 .20
a. Period after value 3.50 1.90
b. Pelure paper .40 .20
366 A104 10c dull green 4.50 2.25
367 A104 20c ultra 18.00 2.25

Perf. 13½
368 A105 1p blue & red 35.00 7.00
Nos. 362-368 (7) 58.55 12.40

Arms of Argentina and Brazil — A112

Wmk. RA in Sun (90)

1928, Aug. 27 ***Perf. 12½x13***
369 A112 5c rose red 1.00 .25
370 A112 12c deep blue 1.50 .50

Cent. of peace between the Empire of Brazil and the United Provinces of the Rio de la Plata.

Allegory, Discovery of the New World A113

"Spain" and "Argentina" A114

"America" Offering Laurels to Columbus — A115

1929, Oct. 12 **Litho.** ***Perf. 13½***
371 A113 2c lilac brown .85 .25
372 A114 5c light red .85 .20
373 A115 12c dull blue 2.00 .75
Nos. 371-373 (3) 3.70 1.20

Discovery of America by Columbus, 437th anniv.

Spirit of Victory Attending Insurgents A116

March of the Victorious Insurgents A117

Perf. 13½x12½ (A116), 12½x13 (A117)

1930
374 A116 ½c violet gray .20 .20
375 A116 1c myrtle green .20 .20
376 A117 2c dull violet .25 .20
377 A116 3c green .30 .25
378 A116 4c violet .25 .25
379 A116 5c rose red .20 .20
380 A116 10c gray black .70 .35
381 A117 12c dull blue .50 .25
382 A117 20c ocher .50 .25
383 A117 24c red brown 2.25 1.50
384 A117 25c green 2.50 1.50
385 A117 30c deep violet 4.50 2.00
386 A117 50c black 6.25 2.50
387 A117 1p sl bl & red 11.00 10.00
388 A117 2p black & org 22.50 10.00
389 A117 5p dull grn & blk 65.00 40.00
390 A117 10p dp red brn & dull blue 90.00 42.50
391 A117 20p yel grn & dl bl 225.00 100.00
392 A117 50p dk grn & vio 600.00 450.00
Nos. 374-390 (17) 207.10 112.15

Revolution of 1930.
Nos. 387-392 with oval (parcel post) cancellation sell for less.
For overprint see No. 405.

1931 ***Perf. 12½x13***
393 A117 ½c red violet .20 .20
394 A117 1c gray black 1.25 .50
395 A117 3c green .60 .30
396 A117 4c red brown .35 .25
397 A117 5c red .20 .20
a. Plane omitted, top left corner 3.00 1.60
398 A117 10c dull green 1.25 .30
Nos. 393-398 (6) 3.85 1.75

Revolution of 1930.

Stamps of 1924-25 Overprinted in Red or Green

-6-
Septiembre
1930 - 1931

1931, Sept. 6 ***Perf. 13½, 13½x12½***
399 A104 3c green .20 .20
400 A104 10c dull green .60 .60
401 A104 30c claret (G) 3.25 3.25
402 A104 50c black 3.25 3.25

Overprinted in Blue

1930
Septiembre
6
1931

403 A105 1p blue & red 3.75 3.25
404 A105 5p dk violet & grn 70.00 20.00

No. 388 Overprinted in Blue

6 Septiembre 1931

Perf. 12½x13
405 A117 2p black & orange 13.00 9.00
Nos. 399-405 (7) 94.05 39.55

1st anniv. of the Revolution of 1930.
See Nos. C30-C34.

Refrigeration Compressor — A118

Perf. 13½x12½

1932, Aug. 29 **Litho.**

406	A118	3c green	.40	.25
407	A118	10c scarlet	1.25	.20
408	A118	12c gray blue	3.25	1.25
		Nos. 406-408 (3)	4.90	1.70

6th Intl. Refrigeration Congress.

Port of La Plata — A119

Pres. Julio A. Roca — A120

Municipal Palace — A121

Cathedral of La Plata — A122

Dardo Rocha — A123

Perf. 13½x13, 13x13½ (10c)

1933, Jan.

409	A119	3c green & dk brn	.35	.30
410	A120	10c orange & dk vio	.50	.20
411	A121	15c dk blue & dp blue	3.50	1.75
412	A122	20c violet & yel brn	1.60	1.00
413	A123	30c dk grn & vio brn	14.00	5.50
		Nos. 409-413 (5)	19.95	8.75

50th anniv. of the founding of the city of La Plata, Nov. 19th, 1882.

Christ of the Andes — A124

Buenos Aires Cathedral A125

1934, Oct. 1 ***Perf. 13x13½, 13½x13***

414	A124	10c rose & brown	.70	.20
415	A125	15c dark blue	1.40	.45

32nd Intl. Eucharistic Cong., Oct. 10-14.

"Liberty" with Arms of Brazil and Argentina A126

Symbolical of "Peace" and "Friendship" A127

1935, May 15 ***Perf. 13x13½***

416	A126	10c red	.85	.25
417	A127	15c blue	1.60	.50

Visit of Pres. Getulio Vargas of Brazil.

Belgrano A128

Sarmiento A129

Urquiza A130

Louis Braille A131

San Martin A132

Brown A133

Moreno A134

Alberdi A135

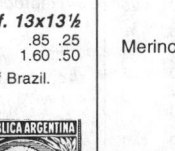

Nicolas Avellaneda A136

Rivadavia A137

Mitre A138

Bull (Cattle Breeding) A139

Martin Güemes A140

Agriculture A141

Merino Sheep (Wool) A142

Sugar Cane A143

Oil Well (Petroleum) A144

Map of South America A145 A146

Fruit A147

Iguacu Falls (Scenic Wonders) A148

Grapes (Vineyards) A149

Cotton A150

Two types of A140:
Type I - Inscribed Juan Martin Guemes.
Type II - Inscribed Martin Güemes.

Perf. 13, 13½x13, 13x13½

1935-51 **Litho.** **Wmk. 90**

418	A128	½c red violet	.20	.20
419	A129	1c buff	.20	.20
a.		Typo.	.20	.20
420	A130	2c dark brown	.20	.20
421	A131	2½c black ('39)	.20	.20
422	A132	3c green	.20	.20
423	A132	3c lt gray ('39)	.20	.20
424	A134	3c lt gray ('46)	.20	.20
425	A133	4c lt gray	.20	.20
426	A133	4c sage green ('39)	.20	.20
427	A134	5c yel brn, typo.	.20	.20
a.		Tete beche pair, typo.	4.50	2.25
b.		Booklet pane of 8, typo.		
c.		Booklet pane of 4, typo.		
d.		Litho.	1.40	.20
428	A135	6c olive green	.20	.20
429	A136	8c orange ('39)	.20	.20
430	A137	10c car, typo.	.30	.20
431	A137	10c brown ('42)	.20	.20
a.		Typo.	.40	.20
432	A138	12c brown	.20	.20
433	A138	12c red ('39)	.20	.20
434	A139	15c slate bl ('36)	.85	.20
435	A139	15c pale ultra ('39)	.50	.20
436	A140	15c lt gray bl (II) ('42)	37.50	1.75
437	A140	20c lt ultra (I)	.60	.20
438	A140	20c lt ultra (II) ('36)	.35	.20
439	A140	20c bl gray (II) ('39)	.35	.20
439A	A139	20c dk bl & pale bl, ('42) 22x33mm	.85	.20
440	A139	20c blue ('51)	.20	.20
a.		Typo.	.20	.20
441	A141	25c carmine ('36)	.20	.20
442	A142	30c org brn ('36)	.50	.20
443	A143	40c dk violet ('36)	.40	.20
444	A144	50c red & org ('36)	.35	.20
445	A145	1p brn blk & lt bl ('36)	17.00	.70
446	A146	1p brn blk & lt bl ('37)	7.00	.20
a.		Chalky paper	42.50	.85
447	A147	2p brn lake & dk ultra ('36)	.85	.20
448	A148	5p ind & ol grn ('36)	6.00	.30
449	A149	10p brn lake & blk	35.00	2.00
450	A150	20p bl grn & brn ('36)	47.50	7.50
		Nos. 418-450 (34)	159.30	18.05

See Nos. 485-500, 523-540, 659, 668. For overprints see Nos. O37-O41, O43-O51, O53-O56, O58-O78, O108, O112, OD35-OD46, OD89-OD101, OD135-OD145, OD176-OD182C, OD229-OD234F, OD270-OD280, OD306-OD317, OD347-OD357.

No. 439A exists with attached label showing medallion. Value $42.50 unused, $22.50 used.

Souvenir Sheet

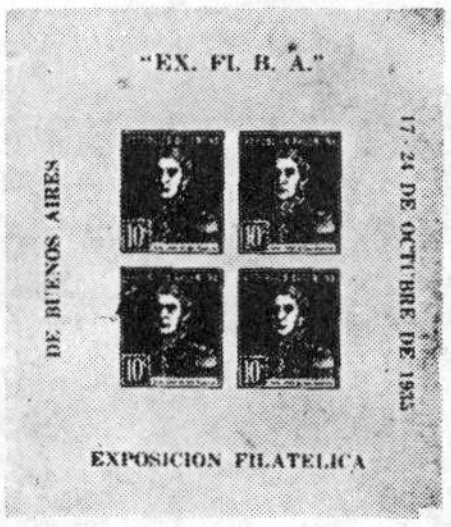

A151

Without Period after Value

1935, Oct. 17 **Litho.** ***Imperf.***

452	A151	Sheet of 4	52.50	30.00
a.		10c dull green	7.00	4.00

Phil. Exhib. at Buenos Aires, Oct. 17-24, 1935. The stamps were on sale during the 8 days of the exhibition only. Sheets measure 83x101mm.

Plaque — A152

1936, Dec. 1 ***Perf. 13x13½***

453	A152	10c rose	.50	.25

Inter-American Conference for Peace.

Domingo Faustino Sarmiento A153

"Presidente Sarmiento" A154

1938, Sept. 5

454 A153	3c sage green	.20	.20
455 A153	5c red	.20	.20
456 A153	15c deep blue	.60	.20
457 A153	50c orange	1.75	1.00
	Nos. 454-457 (4)	2.75	1.60

50th anniv. of the death of Domingo Faustino Sarmiento, pres., educator and author.

1939, Mar. 16

458 A154	5c greenish blue	.35	.20

Final voyage of the training ship "Presidente Sarmiento."

Allegory of the UPU — A155

Coat of Arms — A157

Post Office, Buenos Aires — A156

Iguacu Falls — A158

Bonete Hill, Nahuel Huapi Park — A159

Allegory of Modern Communications A160

Argentina, Land of Promise A161

Lake Frias, Nahuel Huapi Park — A162

Perf. 13x13½, 13½x13

1939, Apr. 1 **Photo.**

459 A155	5c rose carmine	.20	.20
460 A156	15c grnsh black	.40	.25
461 A157	20c brt blue	.40	.20
462 A158	25c dp blue grn	.85	.40
463 A159	50c brown	1.60	.65
464 A160	1p brown violet	1.90	.80
465 A161	2p magenta	8.75	5.25
466 A162	5p purple	35.00	16.00
	Nos. 459-466 (8)	49.10	23.75

Universal Postal Union, 11th Congress.

Souvenir Sheets

A163

A164

1939, May 12 **Wmk. 90** ***Imperf.***

467 A163	Sheet of 4	6.00	4.25
a.	5c rose carmine (A155)	1.25	.75
b.	20c bright blue (A157)	1.25	.75
c.	25c deep blue green (A158)	1.25	.75
d.	50c brown (A159)	1.25	.75
468 A164	Sheet of 4	6.00	4.25

Issued in four forms:

a.	Unsevered horizontal pair of sheets, type A163 at left, A164 at right	15.00	15.00
b.	Unsevered vertical pair of sheets, type A163 at top, A164 at bottom	15.00	15.00
c.	Unsevered block of 4 sheets, type A163 at left, A164 at right	52.50	52.50
d.	Unsevered block of 4 sheets, type A163 at top, A164 at bottom	52.50	52.50

11th Cong. of the UPU and the Argentina Intl. Phil. Exposition (C.Y.T.R.A.).
No. 468 contains Nos. 467a-467d.

Family and New House — A165

Perf. 13½x13

1939, Oct. 2 **Litho.** **Wmk. 90**

469 A165	5c bluish green	.25	.20

1st Pan-American Housing Congress.

Bird Carrying Record A166

Head of Liberty and Arms of Argentina A167

Record and Winged Letter — A168

1939, Dec. 11 **Photo.** ***Perf. 13***

470 A166	1.18p indigo	15.00	7.00
471 A167	1.32p bright blue	15.00	7.00
472 A168	1.50p dark brown	50.00	27.50
	Nos. 470-472 (3)	80.00	41.50

These stamps were issued for the recording and mailing of flexible phonograph records.

Map of the Americas — A169

1940, Apr. 14 ***Perf. 13x13½***

473 A169	15c ultramarine	.40	.20

50th anniv. of the Pan American Union.

Souvenir Sheet

Reproductions of Early Argentine Stamps — A170

Wmk. RA in Sun (90)

1940, May 25 **Litho.** ***Imperf.***

474 A170	Sheet of 5	9.50	5.50
a.	5c dark blue (Corrientes A2)	1.10	.70
b.	5c red (Argentina A1)	1.10	.70
c.	5c dark blue (Cordoba #1)	1.10	.70
d.	5c red (Argentina A3)	1.10	.70
e.	10c dark blue (Buenos Aires A1)	1.10	.70

100th anniv. of the first postage stamp.

General Domingo French and Colonel Antonio Beruti — A171

1941, Feb. 20 ***Perf. 13½x13***

475 A171	5c dk gray blue & lt blue	.30	.20

Issued in honor of General French and Colonel Beruti, patriots.

Marco M. de Avellaneda A172

Statue of Gen. Julio Roca A173

1941, Oct. 3 ***Perf. 13x13½***

476 A172	5c dull slate blue	.30	.20

Marco M. de Avellaneda, (1814-41), Army leader and martyr.

1941, Oct. 19 **Photo.** **Wmk. 90**

477 A173	5c dark olive green	.30	.20

Dedication of a monument to Lt. Gen. Julio Argentino Roca (1843-1914).

Carlos Pellegrini and Bank of the Nation — A174

1941, Oct. 26 ***Perf. 13½x13***

478 A174	5c brown carmine	.30	.20

Founding of the Bank of the Nation, 50th anniv.

Gen. Juan Lavalle — A175

1941, Dec. 5 ***Perf. 13x13½***

479 A175	5c bright blue	.30	.20

Gen. Juan Galo de Lavalle (1797-1841).

National Postal Savings Bank — A176

1942, Apr. 5 **Litho.** ***Perf. 13½x13***

480 A176	1c pale olive	.20	.20

Jose Manuel Estrada — A177

1942, July 13 ***Perf. 13x13½***

481 A177	5c brown violet	.30	.20

Jose Estrada (1842-1894), writer and diplomat.

No. 481 exists with label, showing medallion, attached. Value, pair $10.

Types of 1935-51

Perf. 13, 13x13½, 13½x13

1942-50 **Litho.** **Wmk. 288**

485 A128	½c brown violet	4.75	1.00
486 A129	1c buff ('50)	.20	.20
487 A130	2c dk brown ('50)	.20	.20
488 A132	3c lt gray	16.00	1.25
489 A134	3c lt gray ('49)	.20	.20
490 A137	10c red brown ('49)	.20	.20
491 A138	12c red	.20	.20
492 A140	15c lt gray blue (II)	.30	.20
493 A139	20c dk sl bl & pale bl	1.25	.20
494 A141	25c dull rose ('49)	.60	.20
495 A142	30c orange brn ('49)	1.25	.20
496 A143	40c violet ('49)	8.00	.20
497 A144	50c red & org ('49)	8.00	.20
498 A146	1p brn blk & lt bl	6.50	.20
499 A147	2p brn lake & bl ('49)	13.00	.75
500 A148	5p ind & ol grn ('49)	50.00	4.50
	Nos. 485-500 (16)	110.65	9.90

No. 493 measures 22x33mm.

Post Office, Buenos Aires A178

Proposed Columbus Lighthouse A179

Inscribed: "Correos y Telegrafos."

1942, Oct. 5 **Litho.** ***Perf. 13***

503 A178	35c lt ultra	2.75	.20

See Nos. 541-543.

1942, Oct. 12 **Wmk. 288**

504 A179	15c dull blue	3.00	.20

Wmk. 90

505 A179	15c dull blue	60.00	5.00

450th anniv. of the discovery of America by Columbus.

Jose C. Paz — A180

Books and Argentine Flag — A181

1942, Dec. 15 **Wmk. 288**
506 A180 5c dark gray .35 .20

Cent. of the birth of Jose C. Paz, stateman and founder of the newspaper La Prensa.

1943, Apr. 1 **Litho.** ***Perf. 13***
507 A181 5c dull blue .20 .20

1st Book Fair of Argentina.

Arms of Argentina Inscribed "Honesty, Justice, Duty" — A182

1943-50 **Wmk. 288** ***Perf. 13***
Size: 20x26mm
508 A182 5c red ('50) 2.50 .20
Wmk. 90
509 A182 5c red .25 .20
a. 5c dull red, unsurfaced paper 3.00 .20
510 A182 15c green .70 .20
Perf. 13x13½
Size: 22x33mm
511 A182 20c dark blue 1.10 .20
Nos. 508-511 (4) 4.55 .80

Change of political organization, June 4, 1943.

Independence House, Tucuman A183

Liberty Head and Savings Bank A184

1943-51 **Wmk. 90** ***Perf. 13***
512 A183 5c blue green .90 .20
Wmk. 288
513 A183 5c blue green ('51) .35 .20

Restoration of Independence House.

1943, Oct. 25 **Wmk. 90**
514 A184 5c violet brown .20 .20
Wmk. 288
515 A184 5c violet brown 37.50 3.00

1st conference of National Postal Savings.

Port of Buenos Aires in 1800 — A185

1943, Dec. 11 **Wmk. 90**
516 A185 5c gray black .20 .20

Day of Exports.

Warship, Merchant Ship and Sailboat A186

Arms of Argentine Republic A187

1944, Jan. 31 ***Perf. 13***
517 A186 5c blue .20 .20

Issued to commemorate Sea Week.

1944, June 4
518 A187 5c dull blue .20 .20

1st anniv. of the change of political organization in Argentina.

St. Gabriel A188

Cross at Palermo A189

1944, Oct. 11
519 A188 3c yellow green .20 .20
520 A189 5c deep rose .20 .20

Fourth national Eucharistic Congress.

Allegory of Savings A190

Reservists A191

1944, Oct. 24
521 A190 5c gray .20 .20

20th anniv. of the National Savings Bank.

1944, Dec. 1
522 A191 5c blue .20 .20

Day of the Reservists.

Types of 1935-51
Perf. 13x13½, 13½x13
1945-47 **Litho.** **Unwmk.**
523 A128 ½c brown vio ('46) .20 .20
524 A129 1c yellow brown .20 .20
525 A130 2c sepia .20 .20
526 A132 3c lt gray (San Martin) .40 .20
527 A134 3c lt gray (Moreno) ('46) .20 .20
528 A135 6c olive grn ('47) .20 .20
529 A137 10c brown ('46) 1.25 .20
530 A140 15c lt gray bl (II) .75 .20
531 A139 20c dk sl bl & pale bl 1.25 .20
532 A141 25c dull rose .45 .20
533 A142 30c orange brown .35 .20
534 A143 40c violet 1.25 .20
535 A144 50c red & orange 1.25 .20
536 A146 1p brown blk & lt bl 1.60 .20
537 A147 2p brown lake & bl 8.00 .25
538 A148 5p ind & ol grn ('46) 45.00 2.50
539 A149 10p dp cl & int blk 5.50 .90
540 A150 20p bl grn & brn ('46) 5.75 .90
Nos. 523-540 (18) 73.80 7.35

No. 531 measures 22x33mm.

Post Office Type Inscribed:
"Correos y Telecommunicaciones"

1945 **Unwmk.** ***Perf. 13x13½***
541 A178 35c lt ultra 1.25 .20
Wmk. 90
542 A178 35c lt ultra 1.25 .20
Wmk. 288
543 A178 35c lt ultra .35 .20
Nos. 541-543 (3) 2.85 .60

Bernardino Rivadavia
A192 A193

Mausoleum of Rivadavia A194

Perf. 13½x13
1945, Sept. 1 **Litho.** **Unwmk.**
544 A192 3c blue green .20 .20
545 A193 5c rose .20 .20
546 A194 20c blue .30 .20
Nos. 544-546 (3) .70 .60

Cent. of the death of Bernardino Rivadavia, Argentina's first president.

No. 546 exists with mute label attached. The pair sells for four times the price of the single stamp.

San Martin A195

Monument to Army of the Andes, Mendoza A196

1945-46 **Wmk. 90** **Typo. or Litho.**
547 A195 5c carmine .20 .20
a. Litho. ('46) .20 .20
Wmk. 288
548 A195 5c carmine, litho. 125.00 20.00
Unwmk.
549 A195 5c carmine ('46) .50 .20
a. Litho. ('46) .20 .20

For overprints see Nos. O42, O57.

1946, Jan. 14 **Litho.** ***Perf. 13½x13***
550 A196 5c violet brown .20 .20

Issued to honor the Unknown Soldier of the War for Independence.

A197

A198

1946, Apr. 12
551 A197 5c Franklin D. Roosevelt .20 .20

1946, June 4 ***Perf. 13x13½***

Liberty Administering Presidential Oath.

552 A198 5c blue .20 .20

Inauguration of Pres. Juan D. Perón, 6/4/46.

Argentina Receiving Popular Acclaim A199

1946, Oct. 17 ***Perf. 13½x13***
553 A199 5c rose violet .20 .20
554 A199 10c blue green .25 .20
555 A199 15c dark blue .50 .20
556 A199 50c red brown .70 .30
557 A199 1p carmine rose 1.40 .70
Nos. 553-557 (5) 3.05 1.60

First anniversary of the political organization change of Oct. 17, 1945.

Coin Bank and World Map — A200

1946, Oct. 31 **Unwmk.**
558 A200 30c dk rose car & pink .60 .20

Universal Day of Savings, October 31, 1946.

Argentine Industry A201

International Bridge Connecting Argentina and Brazil A202

1946, Dec. 6 ***Perf. 13x13½***
559 A201 5c violet brown .20 .20

Day of Argentine Industry, Dec. 6.

1947, May 21 **Litho.** ***Perf. 13½x13***
560 A202 5c green .20 .20

Opening of the Argentina-Brazil International Bridge, May 21, 1947.

Map of Argentine Antarctic Claims A203

Justice A204

1947-49 **Unwmk.** ***Perf. 13x13½***
561 A203 5c violet & lilac .35 .20
562 A203 20c dk car rose & rose .70 .20
Wmk. 90
563 A203 20c dk car rose & rose 2.00 .20
Wmk. 288
564 A203 20c dk car rose & rose ('49) 2.00 .20
Nos. 561-564 (4) 5.05 .80

1st Argentine Antarctic mail, 43rd anniv.

1947, June 4 **Unwmk.**
565 A204 5c brn vio & pale yel .20 .20

1st anniversary of the Peron government.

Icarus Falling — A205

1947, Sept. 25 ***Perf. 13½x13***
566 A205 15c red violet .20 .20

Aviation Week.

Training Ship Presidente Sarmiento — A206

1947, Oct. 5 ***Perf. 13x13½***
567 A206 5c blue .20 .20

50th anniv. of the launching of the Argentine training frigate "Presidente Sarmiento."

Cervantes and Characters from Don Quixote
A207

Perf. 13½x13

1947, Oct. 12 Photo. Wmk. 90

568 A207 5c olive green .20 .20

400th anniv. of the birth of Miguel de Cervantes Saavedra, playwright and poet.

Gen. Jose de San Martin — A208

Perf. 13½x13

1947-49 Unwmk. Litho.

569 A208 5c dull green .20 .20

Wmk. 288

570 A208 5c dull green ('49) .20 .20

Transfer of the remains of Gen. Jose de San Martin's parents.

School Children — A209

Statue of Araucanian Indian — A210

1947-49 Unwmk. *Perf. 13x13½*

571 A209 5c green .20 .20

Wmk. 90

574 A209 20c brown .35 .20

Wmk. 288

575 A209 5c green ('49) .35 .20

Nos. 571-575 (3) .90 .60

Argentine School Crusade for World Peace.

1948, May 21 Wmk. 90

576 A210 25c yellow brown .30 .20

American Indian Day, Apr. 19.

Cap of Liberty A211

Manual Stop Signal A212

1948, July 16

577 A211 5c ultra .20 .20

Revolution of June 4, 1943, 5th anniv.

1948, July 22

578 A212 5c chocolate & yellow .20 .20

Traffic Safety Day, June 10.

Argentina stamps can be mounted in the Scott annual Argentina supplement.

Post Horn and Oak Leaves A213

Argentine Farmers A214

1948, July 22 Unwmk.

579 A213 5c lilac rose .20 .20

200th anniversary of the establishment of regular postal service on the Plata River.

Perf. 13x13½

1948, Sept. 20 Wmk. 288

580 A214 10c red brown .20 .20

Agriculture Day, Sept. 8, 1948.

Liberty and Symbols of Progress — A215

Perf. 13x13½

1948, Nov. 23 Photo. Wmk. 287

581 A215 25c red brown .20 .20

3rd anniversary of President Juan D. Peron's return to power, October 17, 1945.

Souvenir Sheets

A216

15c, Mail coach. 45c, Buenos Aires in 18th cent. 55c, 1st train, 1857. 85c, Sailing ship, 1767.

1948, Dec. 21 Unwmk. *Imperf.*

582 A216 Sheet of 4 3.00 3.00

a. 15c dark green .45 .45

b. 45c orange brown .45 .45

c. 55c lilac brown .45 .45

d. 85c ultramarine .45 .45

A217

Designs: 85c, Domingo de Basavilibaso (1709-75). 1.05p, Postrider. 1.20p, Sailing ship, 1798. 1.90p, Courier in the Andes, 1772.

583 A217 Sheet of 4 14.00 11.00

a. 85c brown 3.00 2.50

b. 1.05p dark green 3.00 2.50

c. 1.20p dark blue 3.00 2.50

d. 1.90p red brown 3.00 2.50

200th anniversary of the establishment of regular postal service on the Plata River.

Winged Wheel — A218

Perf. 13½x13

1949, Mar. 1 Wmk. 288

584 A218 10c blue .25 .20

Railroad nationalization, 1st anniv.

Liberty A219

1949, June 20 Engr. Wmk. 90

585 A219 1p red & red violet .40 .20

Ratification of the Constitution of 1949.

Allegory of the UPU A220

1949, Nov. 19

586 A220 25c dk grn & yel grn .25 .20

75th anniv. of the UPU.

Catalogue values for unused stamps in this section, from this point to the end of the section, are for Never Hinged items.

Gen. Jose de San Martin — A221

San Martin at Boulogne sur Mer A222

Mausoleum of San Martin — A223

Designs: 20c, 50c, 75c, Different Portraits of San Martin. 1p, House where San Martin died.

Engr., Photo. (25c, 1p, 2p)

1950, Aug. 17 Wmk. 90 *Perf. 13½*

587 A221 10c indigo & dk pur .20 .20

588 A221 20c red brn & dk brn .20 .20

589 A222 25c brown .20 .20

590 A221 50c dk green & ind .40 .20

591 A221 75c choc & dk grn .40 .20

a. Souv. sheet of 4, #587, 588, 590, 591, imperf. 1.25 .80

592 A222 1p dark green .85 .25

593 A223 2p dp red lilac .70 .35

Nos. 587-593 (7) 2.95 1.60

Death cent. of General Jose de San Martin.

Map Showing Antarctic Claims — A224

1951, May 21 Litho. *Perf. 13x13½*

594 A224 1p choc & lt blue .70 .20

For overprint see No. O52.

Pegasus and Train A225

Communications Symbols — A226

Design: 25c, Ship and dolphin.

1951, Oct. 17 Photo. *Perf. 13½*

595 A225 5c dark brown .20 .20

596 A225 25c Prus green .25 .20

597 A226 40c rose brown .30 .20

Nos. 595-597 (3) .75 .60

Close of Argentine Five Year Plan.

Woman Voter and "Argentina" A227

1951, Dec. 14 *Perf. 13½x13*

598 A227 10c brown violet .20 .20

Granting of women's suffrage.

Eva Peron

A228 A229

Litho. or Engraved (#605)

1952, Aug. 26 Wmk. 90 *Perf. 13*

599 A228 1c orange brown .20 .20

600 A228 5c gray .20 .20

601 A228 10c rose lilac .20 .20

602 A228 20c rose pink .20 .20

603 A228 25c dull green .20 .20

604 A228 40c dull violet .20 .20

605 A228 45c deep blue .20 .20

606 A228 50c dull brown .20 .20

Photo.

607 A229 1p dark brown .25 .20
608 A229 1.50p deep green 1.50 .20
609 A229 2p brt carmine .45 .20
610 A229 3p indigo .75 .20
Nos. 599-610 (12) 4.55 2.40

For overprints see Nos. O79-O85.

Inscribed: "Eva Peron"

1952-53 ***Perf. 13x13½***

611 A229 1p dark brown .30 .20
612 A229 1.50p deep green 1.10 .20
613 A229 2p brt car ('53) 1.10 .20
614 A229 3p indigo 2.75 .20

Engr.

Perf. 13½x13

Size: 30x40mm

615 A229 5p red brown 2.75 .35
616 A228 10p red 7.00 1.40
617 A229 20p green 11.00 4.00
618 A228 50p ultra 20.00 10.00
Nos. 611-618 (8) 46.00 16.55

For overprints see Nos. O86-O93.

Indian Funeral Urn — A230

1953, Aug. 28 Photo. ***Perf. 13x13½***

619 A230 50c blue green .20 .20

Founding of Santiago del Estero, 400th anniv.

Rescue Ship "Uruguay" A231

1953, Oct. 8 ***Perf. 13½***

620 A231 50c ultra .85 .20

50th anniv. of the rescue of the Antarctic expedition of Otto C. Nordenskjold.

Planting Argentine Flag in the Antarctic — A232

1954, Jan. 20 Engr. ***Perf. 13½x13***

621 A232 1.45p blue 1.25 .20

50th anniv. of Argentina's 1st antarctic p.o. and the establishing of the La Hoy radio p.o. in the South Orkneys.

Wired Communications A233

Television A234

Perf. 13x13½, 13½x13

1954, Apr. Photo. Wmk. 90

622 A233 1.50p shown .35 .25
623 A233 3p Radio 1.10 .30
624 A234 5p shown 1.40 .55
Nos. 622-624 (3) 2.85 1.10

Intl. Plenipotentiary Conf. of Telecommunications, Buenos Aires, 1952.

Pediment, Buenos Aires Stock Exchange A235

1954, July 13 ***Perf. 13½x13***

625 A235 1p dark green .30 .20

Cent. of the establishment of the Buenos Aires Stock Exchange.

Eva Peron — A236

1954 Wmk. 90

626 A236 3p dp car rose 1.25 .25

Wmk. 288

627 A236 3p dp car rose 225.00 40.00

2nd anniv. of the death of Eva Peron.

Jose de San Martin A237

Wheat A238

Industry A238a

Eva Peron Foundation Building A239

Cliffs of Humahuaca — A240

Gen. Jose de San Martin — A241

Designs: 50c, Buenos Aires harbor. 1p, Cattle ranch (Ganaderia). 3p, Nihuil Dam. 5p, Iguacu Falls, vert. 20p, Mt. Fitz Roy, vert.

Engraved (#632, 638-642), Photogravure (#634-637)

Perf. 13½, 13x13½ (80c), 13½x13 (#639, 641-642)

1954-59 Wmk. 90

628 A237 20c brt red, typo. .20 .20
629 A237 20c red, litho. ('55) .60 .20
630 A237 40c red, litho. ('56) .20 .20
631 A237 40c brt red, typo. ('55) .25 .20
632 A239 50c blue ('56) .20 .20
633 A239 50c bl, litho. ('59) .20 .20
634 A238 80c brown .25 .20
635 A239 1p brown ('58) .25 .20
636 A238a 1.50p ultra ('58) .20 .20
637 A239 2p dk rose lake .30 .20
638 A239 3p violet brn ('56) .30 .20
639 A240 5p gray grn ('55) 5.25 .20
a. Perf. 13½ 6.50 .20
640 A240 10p yel grn ('55) 3.75 .20
641 A240 20p dull vio ('55) 7.75 .20
a. Perf. 13½ 9.50 .20
642 A241 50p ultra & ind ('55) 7.75 .20
a. Perf. 13½ 7.75 .20
Nos. 628-642 (15) 27.45 3.00

See Nos. 699-700. For similar designs inscribed "Republica Argentina" see Nos. 823-827, 890, 935, 937, 940, 990, 995, 1039, 1044, 1048.

For overprints see Nos. O94-O106, O142, O153-O157.

Allegory — A242

1954, Aug. 26 Typo. ***Perf. 13½***

643 A242 1.50p slate black .65 .20

Cent. of the establishment of the Buenos Aires Grain Exchange.

Clasped Hands and Congress Medal — A243

1955, Mar. 21 Photo. ***Perf. 13½x13***

644 A243 3p red brown .80 .20

Issued to publicize the National Productivity and Social Welfare Congress.

Allegory of Aviation A244

Argentina Breaking Chains A245

1955, June 18 Wmk. 90 ***Perf. 13½***

645 A244 1.50p olive gray .65 .20

Commercial aviation in Argentina, 25th anniv.

1955, Oct. 16 Litho.

647 A245 1.50p olive green .30 .20

Liberation Revolution of Sept. 16, 1955.

Army Navy and Air Force Emblems A246

Perf. 13½x13

1955, Dec. 31 Photo. Wmk. 90

648 A246 3p blue .40 .20

"Brotherhood of the Armed Forces."

A247

A248

1956, Feb. 3 ***Perf. 13½***

649 A247 1.50p Justo Jose de Urquiza .30 .20

Battle of Caseros, 104th anniversary.

1956, July 28 Engr. ***Perf. 13½x13***

650 A248 2p Coin and die .30 .20

75th anniversary of the Argentine Mint.

1856 Stamp of Corrientes A249

Juan G. Pujol — A250

Design: 2.40p, Stamp of 1860-78.

1956, Aug. 21

651 A249 40c dk grn & blue .20 .20
652 A249 2.40p brn & lil rose .30 .20

Photo.

653 A250 4.40p brt blue .65 .20
a. Souv. sheet of 3, #651-653, imperf. 2.25 2.00
Nos. 651-653 (3) 1.15 .60

Centenary of Argentine postage stamps.

No. 653a for the Argentine stamp cent. and Philatelic Exhib. for the Cent. of Corrientes Stamps, Oct. 12-21. The 4.40p is photo., the other two stamps and border litho. Colors of 40c and 2.40p differ slightly from engraved stamps.

Felling Trees, La Pampa A251

Maté Herb and Gourd, Misiones A252

Design: 1p, Cotton plant and harvest, Chaco.

1956, Sept. 1 ***Perf. 13½***

654	A251	50c ultra	.20	.20
655	A251	1p magenta	.20	.20
656	A252	1.50p green	.25	.20
		Nos. 654-656 (3)	.65	.60

Elevation of the territories of La Pampa, Chaco and Misiones to provinces.

"Liberty"
A253

Florentino Ameghino
A254

Perf. 13½

1956, Sept. 15 **Wmk. 90** **Photo.**

657 A253 2.40p lilac rose .30 .20

1st anniv. of the Revolution of Liberation.

1956, Nov. 30

658 A254 2.40p brown .30 .20

Issued to honor Florentino Ameghino (1854-1911), anthropologist.

For overprint see No. O110.

Adm. Brown Type of 1935-51

1956 **Litho.** ***Perf. 13***

Two types:

I. Bust touches upper frame line of name panel at bottom.

II. White line separates bust from frame line.

Size: 19½-20½x26-27mm

659	A133	20c dull purple (I)	.20	.20
	a.	Type II	.20	.20
	b.	Size 19½x25¼mm (I)	.20	.20

For overprint see No. O108.

Benjamin Franklin
A255

1956, Dec. 22 **Photo.** ***Perf. 13½***

660 A255 40c intense blue .30 .20

250th anniv. of the birth of Benjamin Franklin.

Frigate "Hercules"
A256

Guillermo Brown
A257

1957, Mar. 2

661	A256	40c brt blue	.20	.20
662	A257	2.40p gray black	.35	.20
		Nos. 661-662,C63-C65 (5)	1.20	1.00

Admiral Guillermo (William) Brown (1777-1857), founder of the Argentine navy.

20-Cent Minimum Value

The minimum catalogue value is 20 cents. Separating se-tenant pieces into individual stamps does not increase the value of the stamps since demand for the separated stamps may be small.

Roque Saenz Pena (1851-1914)
A258

Church of Santo Domingo, 1807
A259

1957, Apr. 1

663 A258 4.40p grnsh gray .45 .20

Roque Saenz Pena, pres. 1910-14.

For overprint see No. O111.

1957, July 6 **Wmk. 90**

664 A259 40c brt blue green .20 .20

150th anniv. of the defense of Buenos Aires.

"La Portena"
A260

1957, Aug. 31 **Wmk. 90** ***Perf. 13½***

665 A260 40c pale brown .20 .20

Centenary of Argentine railroads.

Esteban Echeverria
A261

"Liberty"
A262

1957, Sept. 2 ***Perf. 13x13½***

666 A261 2p claret .25 .20

Esteban Echeverria (1805-1851), poet.

For overprint see No. O109.

1957, Sept. 28 ***Perf. 13½***

667 A262 40c carmine rose .20 .20

Constitutional reform convention.

Portrait Type of 1935-51

1957, Oct. 28 **Litho.** ***Perf. 13½***

Size: 16½x22mm

668 A128 5c Jose Hernandez .20 .20

For overprint see No. O112.

Oil Derrick and Hands Holding Oil — A263

Perf. 13½

1957, Dec. 21 **Wmk. 90** **Photo.**

669 A263 40c bright blue .20 .20

50th anniv. of the national oil industry.

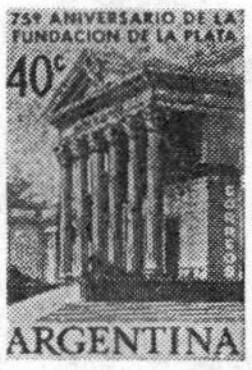

Museum, La Plata — A264

1958, Jan. 11

670 A264 40c dark gray .20 .20

City of La Plata, 75th anniversary.

A265

A266

40c, Locomotive & arms of Argentina & Bolivia. 1p, Map of Argentine-Bolivian boundary & plane.

1958, Apr. 19 **Wmk. 90** ***Perf. 13½***

671	A265	40c slate & dp car	.30	.20
672	A266	1p dark brown	.30	.20

Argentine-Bolivian friendship. No. 671 for the opening of the Jacuiba-Santa Cruz railroad; No. 672, the exchange of presidential visits.

Symbols of the Republic
A267

Flag Monument
A268

1958, Apr. 30 **Photo. & Engr.**

673	A267	40c multicolored	.20	.20
674	A267	1p multicolored	.20	.20
675	A267	2p multicolored	.25	.20
		Nos. 673-675 (3)	.65	.60

Transmission of Presidential power.

1958, June 21 **Litho.** **Wmk. 90**

676 A268 40c blue & violet bl .20 .20

1st anniv. of the Flag Monument of Rosario.

Map of Antarctica
A269

Stamp of Cordoba and Mail Coach
A270

1958, July 12 ***Perf. 13½***

677 A269 40c car rose & blk .50 .20

International Geophysical Year, 1957-58.

1958, Oct. 18

678	A270	40c pale blue & slate	.20	.20
		Nos. 678,C72-C73 (3)	.65	.60

Contenary of Cordoba postage stamps.

"Slave" by Michelangelo and UN Emblem — A271

Engraved and Lithographed

1959, Mar. 14 **Wmk. 90** ***Perf. 13½***

679 A271 40c violet brn & gray .20 .20

10th anniv. (in 1958) of the signing of the Universal Declaration of Human Rights.

Orchids and Globe — A272

1959, May 23 **Photo.** ***Perf. 13½***

680 A272 1p dull claret .25 .20

1st International Horticulture Exposition.

Pope Pius XII
A273

William Harvey
A274

1959, June 20 **Engr.** ***Perf. 13½***

681 A273 1p yellow & black .20 .20

Pope Pius XII, 1876-1958.

1959, Aug. 8 **Litho.** **Wmk. 90**

1p, Claude Bernard. 1.50p, Ivan P. Pavlov.

682	A274	50c green	.20	.20
683	A274	1p dark red	.20	.20
684	A274	1.50p brown	.25	.20
		Nos. 682-684 (3)	.65	.60

21st Intl. Cong. of Physiological Sciences, Buenos Aires.

Type of 1958 and

Domestic Horse
A275

Jose de San Martin
A276

Tierra del Fuego — A277

Inca Bridge, Mendoza
A278

Ski Jumper
A279

Mar del Plata
A280

Designs: 10c, Cayman. 20c, Llama. 50c, Puma. No. 690, Sunflower. 3p, Zapata Slope, Catamarca. 12p, 23p, 25p, Red Quebracho tree. 20p, Nahuel Huapi Lake. 22p, "Industry" (cogwheel and factory).

Two overall paper sizes for 1p, 5p:

I - 27x37½mm or 37½x27mm.

II - 27x39mm or 39x27mm.

Perf. 13x13½

1959-70 Litho. Wmk. 90

685	A275	10c slate green	.20	.20
686	A275	20c dl red brn ('61)	.20	.20
687	A275	50c bister ('60)	.20	.20
688	A275	50c bis, typo. ('60)	.20	.20
689	A275	1p rose red	.20	.20

Perf. 13½

690	A278	1p brn, photo., I ('61)	.20	.20
a.		Paper II ('69)	.20	.20
690B	A278	1p brown, I	.65	.20
691	A276	2p rose red ('61)	.25	.20
692	A276	2p red, typo. (19½ x 26mm) ('61)	.30	.20
a.		Redrawn (19½ x 25mm)	4.75	.20
693	A277	3p dk bl, photo. ('60)	.20	.20
694	A276	4p red, typo ('62)	.20	.20
694A	A276	4p red ('62)	.40	.20
695	A277	5p gray brn, photo., I	.40	.20
e.		5p dark brown, paper II ('70)	6.25	.20
695A	A276	8p ver ('65)	1.25	.20
695B	A276	8p red, typo. ('65)	.30	.20
695C	A276	10p ver ('66)	.65	.20
695D	A276	10p red, typo. ('66)	.50	.20

Photo.

696	A278	10p lt red brn ('60)	.50	.20
697	A278	12p dk brn vio ('62)	.80	.20
697A	A278	12p dk brn, litho. ('64)	8.00	.20
698	A278	20p Prus grn ('60)	2.75	.20
698A	A276	20p red, typo. ('67)	.25	.20
699	A238a	22p ultra ('62)	1.50	.20
700	A238a	22p ultra, litho. ('62)	24.00	.20
701	A278	23p green ('65)	4.75	.20
702	A278	25p dp vio ('66)	1.25	.20
703	A278	25p pur, litho. ('66)	6.25	.20
704	A279	100p blue ('61)	5.00	.20
705	A280	300p dp vio ('62)	2.75	.20
		Nos. 685-705 (29)	64.10	5.80

See Nos. 882-887, 889, 892, 923-925, 928-930, 938, 987-989, 991.

For overprints and surcharges see Nos. 1076, C82-C83, O113-O118, O122-O124, O126-O141, O143-O145, O163.

The 300p remained on sale as a 3p stamp after the 1970 currency exchange.

Symbolic Sailboat A281

Child Playing with Doll A282

1959, Oct. 3 Litho. *Perf. 13½*
706 A281 1p blk, red & bl .20 .20

Red Cross sanitary education campaign.

1959, Oct. 17
707 A282 1p red & blk .20 .20

Issued for Mother's Day, 1959.

Buenos Aires 1p Stamp of 1859 — A283

1959, Nov. 21 Wmk. 90 *Perf. 13½*
708 A283 1p gray & dk bl .20 .20

Issued for the Day of Philately.

Bartolomé Mitre and Justo José de Urquiza A284

1959, Dec. 12 Photo. *Perf. 13½*
709 A284 1p purple .20 .20

Treaty of San Jose de Flores, centenary.

WRY Emblem A285

Abraham Lincoln A286

1960, Apr. 7 Litho. Wmk. 90
710 A285 1p bister & car .20 .20
711 A285 4.20p apple grn & dp claret .30 .20

World Refugee Year, July 1, 1959-June 30, 1960. See No. B25.

1960, Apr. 14 Photo. *Perf. 13½*
712 A286 5p ultra .40 .20

Sesquicentennial (in 1959) of the birth of Abraham Lincoln.

Cornelio Saavedra and Cabildo, Buenos Aires — A287

"Cabildo" and: 2p, Juan José Paso. 4.20p, Manuel Alberti and Miguel Azcuénaga. 10.70p, Juan Larrea and Domingo Matheu.

Perf. 13½

1960, May 28 Wmk. 90 Photo.

713	A287	1p rose lilac	.20	.20
714	A287	2p bluish grn	.20	.20
715	A287	4.20p gray & grn	.25	.20
716	A287	10.70p gray & ultra	.45	.20
		Nos. 713-716,C75-C76 (6)	1.65	1.20

150th anniversary of the May Revolution. Souvenir sheets are Nos. C75a and C76a.

Luis Maria Drago A288

Juan Bautista Alberdi A289

1960, July 8
717 A288 4.20p brown .25 .20

Ccentenary of the birth of Dr. Luis Maria Drago, statesman and jurist.

1960, Sept. 10 Wmk. 90 *Perf. 13½*
718 A289 1p green .20 .20

150th anniversary of the birth of Juan Bautista Alberdi, statesman and philosopher.

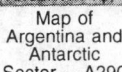

Map of Argentina and Antarctic Sector — A290

Caravel and Emblem — A291

1960, Sept. 24 Litho. *Perf. 13½*
719 A290 5p violet .85 .25

National census of 1960.

1960, Oct. 1 Photo.

720	A291	1p dk olive grn	.20	.20
721	A291	5p brown	.45	.20
		Nos. 720-721,C78-C79 (4)	1.25	.80

8th Congress of the Postal Union of the Americas and Spain.

Virgin of Luján, Patroness of Argentina A292

Argentine Boy Scout Emblem A293

1960, Nov. 12 Wmk. 90 *Perf. 13½*
722 A292 1p dark blue .20 .20

First Inter-American Marian Congress.

1961, Jan. 17 Litho.
723 A293 1p car rose & blk .30 .20

International Patrol Encampment of the Boy Scouts, Buenos Aires.

"Shipment of Cereals," by Quinquela Martin A294

1961, Feb. 11 Photo. *Perf. 13½*
724 A294 1p red brown .30 .20

Export drive: "To export is to advance."

Naval Battle of San Nicolás A295

Mariano Moreno by Juan de Dios Rivera A296

1961, Mar. 2 *Perf. 13½*
725 A295 2p gray .30 .20

Naval battle of San Nicolas, 150th anniv.

1961, Mar. 25 *Perf. 13½*
726 A296 2p blue .20 .20

Mariano Moreno (1778-1811), writer, politician, member of the 1810 Junta.

Emperor Trajan Statue — A297

Rabindranath Tagore — A298

1961, Apr. 11
727 A297 2p slate green .20 .20

Visit of Pres. Giovanni Gronchi of Italy to Argentina, April 1961.

1961, May 13 Photo. *Perf. 13½*
728 A298 2p purple, *grysh* .20 .20

Centenary of the birth of Rabindranath Tagore, Indian poet.

San Martin Statue, Madrid — A299

1961, May 24 Wmk. 90
729 A299 1p olive gray .20 .20

Unveiling of a statue of General José de San Martin in Madrid.

Manuel Belgrano A300

1961, June 17 *Perf. 13½*
730 A300 2p violet blue .20 .20

Erection of a monument by Hector Rocha, to General Manuel Belgrano in Buenos Aires.

Explorers, Sledge and Dog Team — A301

1961, Aug. 19 Photo. Wmk. 90
731 A301 2p black .70 .25

10th anniversary of the General San Martin Base, Argentine Antarctic.

Spanish Conquistador and Sword — A302

Sarmiento Statue by Rodin, Buenos Aires — A303

1961, Aug. 19 Litho.
732 A302 2p red & blk .20 .20

First city of Jujuy, 400th anniversary.

1961, Sept. 9 Photo.
733 A303 2p violet .20 .20

Domingo Faustino Sarmiento (1811-88), political leader and writer.

Symbol of World Town Planning A304

1961, Nov. 25 Litho. *Perf. 13½*
734 A304 2p ultra & yel .20 .20

World Town Planning Day, Nov. 8.

Manuel Belgrano Statue, Buenos Aires
A305

Grenadier, Flag and Regimental Emblem
A306

1962, Feb. 24 **Photo.**
735 A305 2p Prus blue .20 .20

150th anniversary of the Argentine flag.

1962, Mar. 31 **Wmk. 90** ***Perf. 13½***
736 A306 2p carmine rose .20 .20

150th anniversary of the San Martin Grenadier Guards regiment.

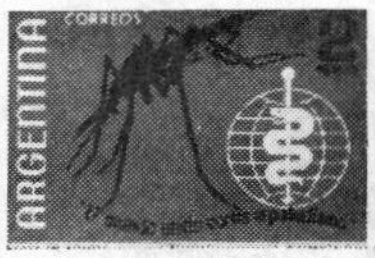

Mosquito and Malaria Eradication Emblem
A307

1962, Apr. 7 **Litho.**
737 A307 2p vermilion & blk .20 .20

WHO drive to eradicate malaria.

Church of the Virgin of Lujà>n
A308

Bust of Juan Jufrè
A309

1962, May 12 ***Perf. 13½***
738 A308 2p org brn & blk .20 .20

75th anniversary of the pontifical coronation of the Virgin of Lujan.

1962, June 23 **Photo.**
739 A309 2p Prus blue .20 .20

Founding of San Juan, 4th cent.

"Soaring into Space"
A310

Juan Vucetich
A311

1962, Aug. 18 **Litho.** ***Perf. 13½***
740 A310 2p maroon, blk & bl .20 .20

Argentine Air Force, 50th anniversary.

1962, Oct. 6 **Photo.** **Wmk. 90**
741 A311 2p green .20 .20

Juan Vucetich (1864-1925), inventor of the Argentine system of fingerprinting.

Domingo F. Sarmiento
A312

February 20th Monument, Salta
A313

Design: 4p, Jose Hernandez.

1962-66 **Photo.** ***Perf. 13½***
742 A312 2p deep green .65 .20

Litho.

742A A312 2p lt green ('64) .55 .20

Photo.

742B A312 4p dull red ('65) .45 .20

Litho.

742C A312 4p rose red ('66) .60 .20
Nos. 742-742C (4) 2.25 .80

See No. 817-819. For overprints see Nos. O119-O121, O125, O149.

1963, Feb. 23 **Photo.** **Wmk. 90**
743 A313 2p dark green .20 .20

150th anniversary of the Battle of Salta, War of Independence.

Gear Wheels — A314

1963, Mar. 16 **Litho.** ***Perf. 13½***
744 A314 4p gray, blk & brt rose .20 .20

Argentine Industrial Union, 75th anniv.

National College, Buenos Aires — A315

Child Draining Cup — A316

1963, Mar. 16 **Wmk. 90**
745 A315 4p dull org & blk .20 .20

National College of Buenos Aires, cent.

1963, Apr. 6
746 A316 4p multicolored .20 .20

FAO "Freedom from Hunger" campaign.

Frigate "La Argentina," 1817, by Emilio Biggeri — A317

1963, May 18 **Photo.**
747 A317 4p bluish green .30 .20

Issued for Navy Day, May 17.

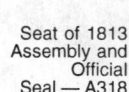

Seat of 1813 Assembly and Official Seal — A318

1963, July 13 **Litho.** ***Perf. 13½***
748 A318 4p lt blue & blk .20 .20

150th anniversary of the 1813 Assembly.

Battle of San Lorenzo, 1813
A319

1963, Aug. 24
749 A319 4p grn & blk, *grnsh* .20 .20

Sesquicentennial of the Battle of San Lorenzo.

Queen Nefertari Offering Papyrus Flowers, Abu Simbel — A320

1963, Sept. 14 ***Perf. 13½***
750 A320 4p ocher, blk & bl grn .30 .20

Campaign to save the historic monuments in Nubia.

Government House, Buenos Aires — A321

1963, Oct. 12 **Wmk. 90** ***Perf. 13½***
751 A321 5p rose & brown .20 .20

Inauguration of President Arturo Illia.

"Science"
A322

Francisco de las Carreras, Supreme Court Justice
A323

1963, Oct. 16 **Litho.**
752 A322 4p org brn, bl & blk .20 .20

10th Latin-American Neurosurgery Congress.

1963, Nov. 23 **Photo.** ***Perf. 13½***
753 A323 5p bluish green .20 .20

Centenary of judicial power.

Blackboards
A324

1963, Nov. 23 **Litho.**
754 A324 5p red, blk & bl .20 .20

Issued to publicize "Teachers for America" through the Alliance for Progress program.

Kemal Atatürk
A325

"Payador" by Juan Carlos Castagnino
A326

1963, Dec. 28 **Photo.** ***Perf. 13½***
755 A325 12p dark gray .30 .20

25th anniversary of the death of Kemal Atatürk, president of Turkey.

1964, Jan. 25 **Litho.**
756 A326 4p ultra, blk & lt bl .30 .20

Fourth National Folklore Festival.

Maps of South Georgia, South Orkney and South Sandwich Islands
A327

4p, Map of Argentina & Antarctic claims, vert.

1964, Feb. 22 **Wmk. 90** ***Perf. 13½***

Size: 33x22mm

757 A327 2p lt & dk bl & bister 1.25 .25

Size: 30x40mm

758 A327 4p lt & dk bl & ol grn 1.75 .30
Nos. 757-758,C92 (3) 4.75 1.25

Argentina's claim to Antarctic territories, 60th anniv.

Jorge Newbery in Cockpit
A328

1964, Feb. 23 **Photo.**
759 A328 4p deep green .20 .20

Newbery, aviator, 50th death anniv.

John F. Kennedy — A329

José Brochero by José Cuello — A330

1964, Apr. 14 **Engr.** **Wmk. 90**
760 A329 4p claret & dk bl .35 .20

President John F. Kennedy (1917-63).

1964, May 9 **Photo.** ***Perf. 13½***
761 A330 4p light sepia .20 .20

50th anniversary of the death of Father Jose Gabriel Brochero.

Soldier of Patricios Regiment A331

1964, May 29 **Litho.** **Wmk. 90**
762 A331 4p blk, ultra & red .40 .20

Issued for Army Day. Later Army Day stamps, inscribed "Republica Argentina," are of type A340a.

Pope John XXIII — A332

1964, June 27 **Engr.**
763 A332 4p orange & blk .25 .20

Issued in memory of Pope John XXIII.

University of Cordoba Arms — A333

Pigeons and UN Building, NYC — A334

1964, Aug. 22 **Litho.** **Wmk. 90**
764 A333 4p blk, ultra & yel .20 .20

350th anniv. of the University of Cordoba.

1964, Oct. 24 ***Perf. 13½***
765 A334 4p dk blue & lt blue .20 .20

Issued for United Nations Day.

Joaquin V. Gonzalez A335

Julio Argentino Roca A336

1964, Nov. 14 **Photo.**
766 A335 4p dk rose carmine .20 .20

Centenary (in 1963) of the birth of Joaquin V. Gonzalez, writer.

1964, Dec. 12 ***Perf. 13½***
767 A336 4p violet blue .20 .20

General Julio A. Roca, (1843-1914), president of Argentina, (1880-86, 1898-1904).

Market at Montserrat Square, by Carlos Morel — A337

1964, Dec. 19 **Photo.**
768 A337 4p sepia .30 .20

19th century Argentine painter Carlos Morel.

Icebreaker General San Martin — A338

Girl with Piggy Bank — A339

Design: 2p, General Belgrano Base, Antarctica.

1965 ***Perf. 13½***
769 A338 2p dull purple .40 .20
770 A338 4p ultra .50 .20

Issued to publicize the national territory of Tierra del Fuego, Antarctic and South Atlantic Isles.

Issue dates: 4p, Feb. 27; 2p, June 5.

1965, Apr. 3 **Litho.**
771 A339 4p red org & blk .20 .20

National Postal Savings Bank, 50th anniv.

Sun and Globe — A340

1965, May 29
772 A340 4p blk, org & dl bl .25 .20
Nos. 772,C98-C99 (3) 1.65 .90

International Quiet Sun Year, 1964-65.

Hussar of Pueyrredon Regiment A340a

Ricardo Rojas (1882-1957) A341

1965, June 5 **Wmk. 90** ***Perf. 13½***
773 A340a 8p dp ultra, blk & red .50 .20

Issued for Army Day. See Nos. 796, 838, 857, 893, 944, 958, 974, 1145.

1965, June 26 **Photo.**

Portraits: No. 775, Ricardo Guiraldes (1886-1927). No. 776, Enrique Larreta (1873-1961). No. 777, Leopoldo Lugones (1874-1938). No. 778, Roberto J. Payro (1867-1928).

774 A341 8p brown .35 .20
775 A341 8p brown .35 .20
776 A341 8p brown .35 .20
777 A341 8p brown .35 .20
778 A341 8p brown .35 .20
Nos. 774-778 (5) 1.75 1.00

Issued to honor Argentine writers. Printed se-tenant in sheets of 100 (10x10); 2 horizontal rows of each design with Guiraldes in top rows and Rojas in bottom rows.

Hipolito Yrigoyen A342

1965, July 3 **Litho.**
779 A342 8p pink & black .20 .20

Hipolito Yrigoyen (1852-1933), president of Argentina 1916-22, 1928-30.

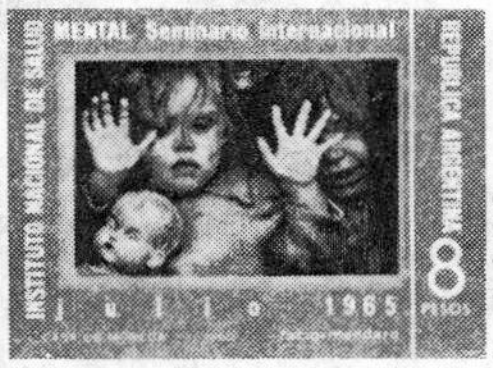

Children Looking Through Window A343

1965, July 24 **Photo.**
780 A343 8p salmon & blk .25 .20

International Seminar on Mental Health.

Child's Funerary Urn and 16th Century Map A344

1965, Aug. 7 **Litho.**
781 A344 8p lt grn, dk red, brn & ocher .30 .20

City of San Miguel de Tucuman, 400th anniv.

Cardinal Cagliero A345

Dante Alighieri A346

1965, Aug. 21 **Photo.**
782 A345 8p violet .20 .20

Juan Cardinal Cagliero (1839-1926), missionary to Argentina and Bishop of Magida.

1965, Sept. 16 **Wmk. 90** ***Perf. 13½***
783 A346 8p light ultra .30 .20

Dante Alighieri (1265-1321), Italian poet.

Clipper "Mimosa" and Map of Patagonia A347

1965, Sept. 25 **Litho.**
784 A347 8p red & black .30 .20

Centenary of Welsh colonization of Chubut, and the founding of the city of Rawson.

Map of Buenos Aires, Cock and Compass Emblem of Federal Police — A348

1965, Oct. 30 **Photo.** ***Perf. 13½***
785 A348 8p carmine rose .30 .20

Issued for Federal Police Day.

Child's Drawing of Children A349

1965, Nov. 6 **Litho.** **Wmk. 90**
786 A349 8p lt yel grn & blk .30 .20

Public education law, 81st anniversary.

Church of St. Francis, Catamarca A350

Ruben Dario A351

1965, Dec. 8
787 A350 8p org yel & red brn .20 .20

Brother Mamerto de la Asuncion Esquiu, preacher, teacher and official of 1885 Provincial Constitutional Convention.

Litho. and Photo.

1965, Dec. 22 ***Perf. 13½***
788 A351 15p bl vio, *gray* .20 .20

Ruben Dario (pen name of Felix Ruben Garcia Sarmiento, 1867-1916), Nicaraguan poet, newspaper correspondent and diplomat.

"The Orange Seller" A352

Pueyrredon Paintings: No. 790, "Stop at the Grocery Store." No. 791, "Landscape at San Fernando" (sailboats). No. 792, "Bathing Horses at River Plata."

1966, Jan. 29 **Photo.** ***Perf. 13½***
789 A352 8p bluish green .70 .40
790 A352 8p bluish green .70 .40
791 A352 8p bluish green .70 .40
792 A352 8p bluish green .70 .40
a. Block of 4, #789-792 + 2 labels 2.80 1.60

Prilidiano Pueyrredon (1823-1870), painter.

Sun Yat-sen, Flags of Argentina and China — A353

1966, Mar. 12 **Wmk. 90** ***Perf. 13½***
793 A353 8p dk red brown .70 .25

Dr. Sun Yat-sen (1866-1925), founder of the Republic of China.

Souvenir Sheet

Rivadavia Issue of 1864 — A354

Wmk. 90

1966, Apr. 20 Litho. *Imperf.*

794 A354 Sheet of 3 .95 .95
a. 4p gray & red brown .20 .20
b. 5p gray & green .20 .20
c. 8p gray & dark blue .20 .20

2nd Rio de la Plata Stamp Show, Buenos Aires, Mar. 16-24.

People of Various Races and WHO Emblem A355

1966, Apr. 23 *Perf. 13½*

795 A355 8p brown & blk .30 .20

Opening of the WHO Headquarters, Geneva.

Soldier Type of 1965

Army Day: 8p, Cavalryman, Guemes Infernal Regiment.

1966, May 28 Litho.

796 A340a 8p multicolored .55 .30

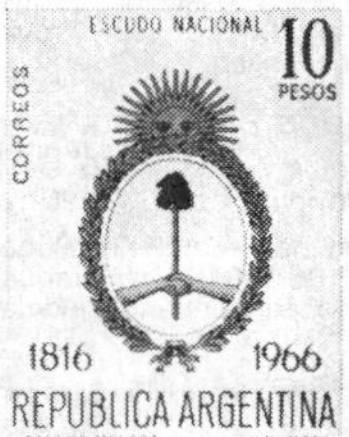

Coat of Arms — A356

Arms: a, Buenos Aires. b, Federal Capital. c, Catamarca. d, Cordoba. e, Corrientes. f, Chaco. g, Chubut. h, Entre Rios. i, Formosa. j, Jujuy. k, La Pampa. l, La Rioja. m, Mendoza. n, Misiones. o, Neuquen. p, Salta. q, San Juan. r, San Luis. s, Santa Cruz. t, Santa Fe. u, Santiago del Estero. v, Tucuman. w, map of Rio Negro. x, map of Tierra del Fuego, Antarctica. y, South Atlantic Islands.

1966, July 30 Wmk. 90 *Perf. 13½*

797 Sheet of 25 40.00
a.-y. A356 10p black & multi 1.00 .65

150th anniv. of Argentina's Declaration of Independence.

Three Crosses, Caritas Emblem A357

1966, Sept. 10 Litho. *Perf. 13½*

798 A357 10p ol grn, blk & lt bl .25 .20

Caritas, charity organization.

Hilario Ascasubi (1807-75) — A358

Portraits: #800, Estanislao del Campo (1834-80). #801, Miguel Cane (1851-1905). #802, Lucio V. Lopez (1848-94). #803, Rafael Obligado (1851-1920). #804, Luis Agote (1868-1954), M.D. #805, Juan B. Ambrosetti (1865-1917), naturalist and archaeologist. #806, Miguel Lillo (1862-1931), botanist and chemist. #807, Francisco P. Moreno (1852-1919), naturalist and paleontologist. #808, Francisco J. Muñiz (1795-1871), physician.

1966 Photo. Wmk. 90

799 A358 10p dk blue green .40 .35
800 A358 10p dk blue green .40 .35
801 A358 10p dk blue green .40 .35
802 A358 10p dk blue green .40 .35
803 A358 10p dk blue green .40 .35
804 A358 10p deep violet .40 .35
805 A358 10p deep violet .40 .35
806 A358 10p deep violet .40 .35
807 A358 10p deep violet .40 .35
808 A358 10p deep violet .40 .35
Nos. 799-808 (10) 4.00 3.50

Nos. 799-803 issued Sept. 17 to honor Argentine writers. Printed se-tenant in sheets of 100 (10x10); 2 horizontal rows of each portrait. Nos. 804-808 issued Oct. 22 to honor Argentine scientists; 2 horizontal rows of each portrait. Scientists set has value at upper left, frame line with rounded corners.

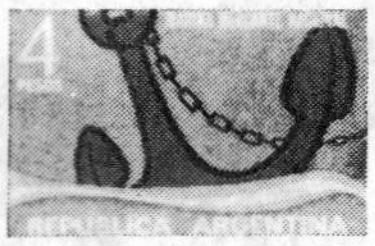

Anchor — A359

1966, Oct. 8 Litho.

809 A359 4p multicolored .25 .20

Argentine merchant marine.

Flags and Map of the Americas — A360

Argentine National Bank — A361

1966, Oct. 29 *Perf. 13½*

810 A360 10p gray & multi .25 .20

7th Conference of American Armies.

1966, Nov. 5 Photo.

811 A361 10p brt blue green .20 .20

75th anniv. of the Argentine National Bank.

La Salle Monument and College, Buenos Aires — A362

1966, Nov. 26 Litho. *Perf. 13½*

812 A362 10p brown org & blk .20 .20

75th anniv. of the Colegio de la Salle, Buenos Aires, and to honor Saint Jean Baptiste de la Salle (1651-1719), educator.

Map of Argentine Antarctica and Expedition Route — A363

1966, Dec. 10 Wmk. 90

813 A363 10p multicolored .70 .45

1965 Argentine Antarctic expedition, which planted the Argentine flag on the South Pole. See No. 851.

Juan Martin de Pueyrredon A364

Gen. Juan de Las Heras A365

1966, Dec. 17 Photo. *Perf. 13½*

814 A364 10p dull red brn .20 .20

Issued to honor Juan Martin de Pueyrredon (1777-1850), Governor of Cordoba and of the United Provinces of the River Plata.

1966, Dec. 17 Engr.

815 A365 10p black .20 .20

Issued to honor Gen. Juan Gregorio de Las Heras (1780-1866), Peruvian field marshal and aide-de-camp to San Martin.

Inscribed "Republica Argentina" Types of 1955-61 and

Guillermo Brown — A366

Trout Leaping in National Park — A366a

Designs: 6p, Jose Hernandez. 50p, Gen. Jose de San Martin. 500p, Red deer in forest.

Two overall paper sizes for 6p, 50p (No. 827) and 90p:
I - 27x37½mm
II - 27x39mm

Perf. 13½

1965-68 Wmk. 90 Photo.

817 A366 6p rose red, litho, I ('67) 1.25 .20
818 A366 6p rose red ('67) 2.25 .20
819 A366 6p brn, 15x22mm ('68) .20 .20
823 A238a 43p dk car rose 6.25 .20
824 A238a 45p brn ('66) 4.25 .20
825 A238a 45p brn, litho ('67) 7.00 .20
826 A241 50p dk bl, 29x40mm 7.00 .20
827 A241 50p dk bl, 22x31½mm, I ('67) 4.75 .20
a. Paper II 2.75 .20
828 A366 90p ol bis, I ('67) 3.00 .20
a. Paper II 12.00 .20

Engr.

829 A495 500p yellow grn ('66) 1.40 .30
829A A366a 1,000p vio bl ('68) 5.50 1.25
Nos. 817-829A (11) 42.85 3.35

The 500p and 1,000p remained on sale as 5p and 10p stamps after the 1970 currency exchange.

See Nos. 888, 891, 939, 941, 992, 1031, 1040, 1045-1047. For surcharge and overprints see Nos. 1077, O153-O158, O162.

Pre-Columbian Pottery — A367

1967, Feb. 18 Litho. *Perf. 13½*

830 A367 10p multicolored .30 .20

20th anniv. of UNESCO.

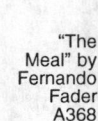

"The Meal" by Fernando Fader A368

1967, Feb. 25 Photo. Wmk. 90

831 A368 10p red brown .30 .20

Issued in memory of the Argentine painter Fernando Fader (1882-1935).

Col. Juana Azurduy de Padilla (1781-1862), Soldier — A369

Schooner "Invencible," 1811 — A370

Famous Argentine Women: #833, Juana Manuela Gorriti, writer. #834, Cecilia Grierson (1858-1934), physician. #835, Juana Paula Manso (1819-75), writer and educator. #836, Alfonsina Storni (1892-1938), writer and educator.

1967, May 13 Photo. *Perf. 13½*

832 A369 6p dark brown .30 .20
833 A369 6p dark brown .30 .20
834 A369 6p dark brown .30 .20
835 A369 6p dark brown .30 .20
836 A369 6p dark brown .30 .20
Nos. 832-836 (5) 1.50 1.00

Printed se-tenant in sheets of 100 (10x10); 2 horizontal rows of each portrait.

1967, May 20 Litho.

837 A370 20p multicolored .85 .35

Issued for Navy Day.

Soldier Type of 1965

Army Day: 20p, Highlander (Arribeños Corps).

1967, May 27

838 A340a 20p multicolored .70 .30

Souvenir Sheet

Manuel Belgrano and José Artigas — A371

1967, June 22 *Imperf.*

839 A371 Sheet of 2 .40 .40
a. 6p gray & brown .20 .20
b. 22p brown & gray .25 .25

Third Rio de la Plata Stamp Show, Montevideo, Uruguay, June 18-25.

Peace Dove and Valise
A372

PADELAI Emblem
A373

1967, Aug. 5 Litho. *Perf. 13½*

840	A372	20p multicolored	.25	.20

Issued for International Tourist Year 1967.

1967, Aug. 12 Litho.

841	A373	20p multicolored	.25	.20

75th anniv. of the Children's Welfare Association (Patronato de la Infancia-PADELAI).

Stagecoach and Modern City — A374

1967, Sept. 23 Wmk. 90 *Perf. 13½*

842	A374	20p rose, yel & blk	.25	.20

Centenary of Villa Maria, Cordoba.

San Martin by Ibarra — A375

"Battle of Chacabuco" by P. Subercaseaux — A376

1967, Sept. 30 Litho.

843	A375	20p blk brn & pale yel	.55	.20

Engr.

844	A376	40p blue black	.85	.20

Battle of Chacabuco, 150th anniversary.

Exhibition Rooms — A377

1967, Oct. 11 Photo.

845	A377	20p blue gray	.20	.20

Government House Museum, 10th anniv.

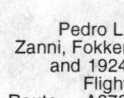

Pedro L. Zanni, Fokker and 1924 Flight Route — A378

1967, Oct. 21 Litho. *Perf. 13½*

846	A378	20p multicolored	.30	.20

Issued for Aviation Week and to commemorate the 1924 flight of the Fokker seaplane "Province of Buenos Aires" from Amsterdam, Netherlands, to Osaka, Japan.

Training Ship General Brown, by Emilio Biggeri
A379

1967, Oct. 28 Wmk. 90

847	A379	20p multicolored	.85	.35

Issued to honor the Military Naval School.

Ovidio Lagos and Front Page — A380

St. Barbara — A381

1967, Nov. 11 Photo.

848	A380	20p sepia	.20	.20

Centenary of La Capital, Rosario newspaper.

1967, Dec. 2 *Perf. 13½*

849	A381	20p rose red	.30	.20

St. Barbara, patron saint of artillerymen.

Portrait of his Wife, by Eduardo Sivori — A382

1968, Jan. 27 Photo. *Perf. 13½*

850	A382	20p blue green	.30	.20

Eduardo Sivori (1847-1918), painter.

Antarctic Type of 1966 and

Admiral Brown Scientific Station
A383

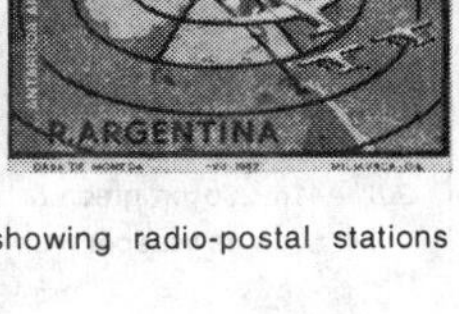

Planes over Map of Antarctica
A384

6p, Map showing radio-postal stations 1966-67.

1968, Feb. 17 Litho. Wmk. 90

851	A363	6p multicolored	.45	.20
852	A383	20p multicolored	.60	.25
853	A384	40p multicolored	1.00	.30
		Nos. 851-853 (3)	2.05	.75

Issued to publicize Argentine research projects in Argentine Antarctica.

The Annunciation, by Leonardo da Vinci — A385

Man in Wheelchair and Factory — A386

1968, Mar. 23 Photo. *Perf. 13½*

854	A385	20p lilac rose	.20	.20

Issued for the Day of the Army Communications System and its patron saint, Gabriel.

1968, Mar. 23 Litho.

855	A386	20p green & black	.20	.20

Day of Rehabilitation of the Handicapped.

Children and WHO Emblem — A387

1968, May 11 Wmk. 90 *Perf. 13½*

856	A387	20p dk vio bl & ver	.20	.20

20th anniv. of WHO.

Soldier Type of 1965

Army Day: 20p, Uniform of First Artillery Regiment "General Iriarte."

1968, June 8 Litho.

857	A340a	20p multicolored	.75	.25

Frigate "Libertad," Painting by Emilio Biggeri
A388

1968, June 15 Wmk. 90

858	A388	20p multicolored	.75	.25

Issued for Navy Day.

Guillermo Rawson and Old Hospital
A389

1968, July 20 Photo. *Perf. 13½*

859	A389	6p olive bister	.20	.20

Cent. of Rawson Hospital, Buenos Aires.

Student Directing Traffic for Schoolmates
A390

1968, Aug. 10 Litho. *Perf. 13½*

860	A390	20p lt bl, blk, buff & car	.20	.20

Traffic safety and education.

O'Higgins Joining San Martin at Battle of Maipu, by P. Subercaseaux — A391

1968, Aug. 15 Engr.

861	A391	40p bluish black	.65	.30

Sesquicentennial of the Battle of Maipu.

Osvaldo Magnasco (1864-1920), Lawyer, Professor of Law and Minister of Justice — A392

1968, Sept. 7 Photo. *Perf. 13½*

862	A392	20p brown	.25	.20

Grandmother's Birthday, by Patricia Lynch — A393

The Sea, by Edgardo Gomez — A394

1968, Sept. 21 Litho.

863	A393	20p multicolored	.25	.20
864	A394	20p multicolored	.25	.20

The designs were chosen in a competition among kindergarten and elementary school children.

Mar del Plata at Night — A395

1968, Oct. 19 Litho. *Perf. 13½*

865	A395	20p black, ocher & bl	.25	.20
		Nos. 865,C113-C114 (3)	1.30	.70

4th Plenary Assembly of the Intl. Telegraph and Telephone Consultative Committee, Mar del Plata, Sept. 23-Oct. 25.

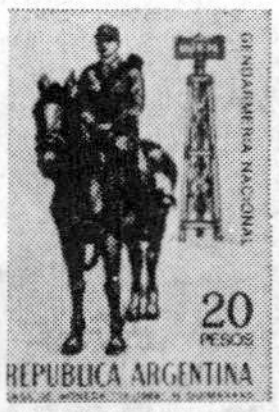

Frontier Gendarme
A396

Patrol Boat
A397

1968, Oct. 26

866	A396	20p multicolored	.30	.20
867	A397	20p blue, vio bl & blk	.30	.20

No. 866 honors the Gendarmery; No. 867 the Coast Guard.

Aaron de Anchorena and Pampero Balloon
A398

1968, Nov. 2 **Photo.**
868 A398 20p blue & multi .30 .20

22nd Aeronautics and Space Week.

St. Martin of Tours, by Alfredo Guido — A399

1968, Nov. 9 **Litho.**
869 A399 20p lilac & dk brn .20 .20

St. Martin of Tours, patron saint of Buenos Aires.

Municipal Bank Emblem
A400

1968, Nov. 16
870 A400 20p multicolored .20 .20

90th anniv. of the Buenos Aires Municipal Bank.

Anniversary Emblem
A401

1968, Dec. 14 **Wmk. 90** ***Perf. 13½***
871 A401 20p car rose & dk grn .20 .20

25th anniversary of ALPI (Fight Against Polio Association).

Shovel and State Coal Fields Emblem
A402

Pouring Ladle and Army Manufacturing Emblem
A403

1968, Dec. 21 **Litho.**
872 A402 20p orange, bl & blk .25 .20
873 A403 20p dl vio, dl yel & blk .25 .20

Issued to publicize the National Coal and Steel industry at the Rio Turbio coal fields and the Zapla blast furnaces.

Woman Potter, by Ramon Gomez Cornet — A404

1968, Dec. 21 **Photo.** ***Perf. 13½***
874 A404 20p carmine rose .50 .40

Centenary of the Witcomb Gallery.

View of Buenos Aires and Rio de la Plata by Ulrico Schmidl
A405

1969, Feb. 8 **Litho.** **Wmk. 90**
875 A405 20p yellow, blk & ver .50 .35

Ulrico Schmidl (c. 1462-1554) who wrote "Journey to the Rio de la Plata and Paraguay."

Types of 1955-67

Designs: 50c, Puma. 1p, Sunflower. 3p, Zapata Slope, Catamarca. 5p, Tierra del Fuego. 6p, José Hernandez. 10p, Inca Bridge, Mendoza. 50p, José de San Martin. 90p, Guillermo Brown. 100p, Ski jumper.

Photo.; Litho. (50c, 3p, 10p)

1969-70 **Wmk. 365** ***Perf. 13½***
882 A275 50c bister ('70) .70 .20
883 A277 5p brown 1.25 .20
884 A279 100p blue 26.00 1.40

Unwmk.

885 A278 1p brown ('70) .65 .20
886 A277 3p dk blue ('70) .65 .20
a. Wmk. 90 5.25 .35
887 A277 5p brown ('70) .75 .20
888 A366 6p red brn, 15x22mm ('70) 1.25 .20
889 A278 10p dull red ('70) .50 .20
a. Wmk. 90 475.00 47.50
890 A241 50p dk bl, 22x31½mm ('70) 1.75 .20
891 A366 90p ol brn, 22x32mm ('70) 3.50 .20
892 A279 100p blue ('70) 9.00 .30
Nos. 882-892 (11) 46.00 3.50

For surcharges see Nos. 1076-1077.

Soldier Type of 1965

Army Day: 20p, Sapper (gastador) of Buenos Aires Province, 1856.

Wmk. 365

1969, May 31 **Litho.** ***Perf. 13½***
893 A340a 20p multicolored .85 .35

Frigate Hercules, by Emilio Biggeri — A406

1969, May 31
894 A406 20p multicolored 1.00 .30

Issued for Navy Day.

"All Men are Equal"
A407

ILO Emblem
A408

1969, June 28 **Wmk. 90**
895 A407 20p black & ocher .20 .20

International Human Rights Year.

1969, June 28 **Litho.** **Wmk. 365**
896 A408 20p lt green & multi .20 .20

50th anniv. of the ILO.

Pedro N. Arata (1849-1922), Chemist
A409

Radar Antenna, Balcarce Station and Satellite
A410

Portraits: No. 898, Miguel Fernandez (1883-1950), zoologist. No. 899, Angel P. Gallardo (1867-1934), biologist. No. 900, Cristobal M. Hicken (1875-1933), botanist. No. 901, Eduardo Ladislao Holmberg, M.D. (1852-1937), natural scientist.

1969, Aug. 9 **Wmk. 365** ***Perf. 13½***
897 A409 6p Arata .40 .20
898 A409 6p Fernandez .40 .20
899 A409 6p Gallardo .40 .20
900 A409 6p Hicken .40 .20
901 A409 6p Holmberg .40 .20
Nos. 897-901 (5) 2.00 1.00

Argentine scientists. See No. 778 note.

1969, Aug. 23 **Wmk. 99**
902 A410 20p yellow & blk .30 .20

Communications by satellite through Intl. Telecommunications Satellite Consortium (INTELSAT). See No. C115.

Nieuport 28, Flight Route and Map of Buenos Aires Province
A411

1969, Sept. 13 **Litho.** **Wmk. 90**
903 A411 20p multicolored .30 .20

50th anniv. of the first Argentine airmail service from El Palomar to Mar del Plata, flown Feb. 23-24, 1919, by Capt. Pedro L. Zanni.

Military College Gate and Emblem
A412

1969, Oct. 4 **Wmk. 365** ***Perf. 13½***
904 A412 20p multicolored .30 .20

Cent. of the National Military College, El Palomar (Greater Buenos Aires).

Gen. Angel Pacheco
A413

La Farola, Logotype of La Prensa
A414

1969, Nov. 8 **Photo.** **Wmk. 365**
905 A413 20p deep green .25 .20

Gen. Angel Pacheco (1795-1869).

1969, Nov. 8 **Litho.** ***Perf. 13½***

#907, Bartolomé Mitre & La Nacion logotype.

906 A414 20p orange, yel & blk .70 .25
907 A414 20p brt green & blk .70 .25

Cent. of newspapers La Prensa and La Nacion.

Julian Aguirre — A415

Musicians: No. 909, Felipe Boero. No. 910, Constantino Gaito. No. 911, Carlos Lopez Buchardo. No. 912, Alberto Williams.

Wmk. 365

1969, Dec. 6 **Photo.** ***Perf. 13½***
908 A415 6p Aguirre .55 .30
909 A415 6p Boero .55 .30
910 A415 6p Gaito .55 .30
911 A415 6p Buchardo .55 .30
912 A415 6p Williams .55 .30
Nos. 908-912 (5) 2.75 1.50

Argentine musicians. See No. 778 note.

Lt. Benjamin Matienzo and Nieuport Plane
A416

1969, Dec. 13 **Litho.**
913 A416 20p multicolored .55 .35

23rd Aeronautics and Space Week.

High Power Lines and Map
A417

Design: 20p, Map of Santa Fe Province and schematic view of tunnel.

1969, Dec. 13
914 A417 6p multicolored .50 .20
915 A417 20p multicolored 1.00 .20

Completion of development projects: 6p for the hydroelectric dams on the Limay and Neuquen Rivers, the 20p the tunnel under Rio Grande from Sante Fe to Parana.

Lions Emblem
A418

1969, Dec. 20 **Wmk. 365** ***Perf. 13½***
916 A418 20p black, emer & org .60 .25

Argentine Lions Intl. Club, 50th anniv.

Madonna and Child, by Raul Soldi — A419

1969, Dec. 27 **Litho.**
917 A419 20p multicolored .70 .30

Christmas 1969.

Manuel Belgrano, by Jean Gericault — A420

The Creation of the Flag, Bas-relief by Jose Fioravanti — A421

Perf. 13½

1970, July 4 Unwmk. Photo.

918 A420 20c deep brown .35 .20

Litho. *Perf. 12½*

919 A421 50c bister, blk & bl .85 .50

Gen. Manuel Belgrano (1770-1820), Argentine patriot.

San Jose Palace A422

1970, Aug. 9 Litho. *Perf. 13½*

920 A422 20c yellow grn & multi .25 .20

Cent. of the death of Gen. Justo Jose de Urquiza (1801-70), pres. of Argentina, 1854-60.

Schooner "Juliet" A423

1970, Aug. 8 Unwmk.

921 A423 20c multicolored 1.00 .40

Issued for Navy Day.

Receiver of 1920 and Waves A424

1970, Aug. 29

922 A424 20c lt blue & multi .30 .20

50th anniv. of Argentine broadcasting.

Types of 1955-67 Inscribed "Republica Argentina" and Types A425, A426

Belgrano A425

Lujan Basilica A426

Designs: 1c, Sunflower. 3c, Zapata Slope, Catamarca. 5c, Tierra del Fuego. 8c, No. 931, Belgrano. 10c, Inca Bridge, Mendoza. 25c, 50c, 70c, Jose de San Martin. 65c, 90c, 1.20p, San Martin. 1p, Ski jumper. 1.15p, 1.80p, Adm. Brown.

1970-73 Photo. Unwmk. *Perf. 13½*

923	A278	1c dk green ('71)	.20	.20
924	A277	3c car rose ('71)	.20	.20
925	A277	5c blue ('71)	.20	.20
926	A425	6c deep blue	.20	.20
927	A425	8c green ('72)	.20	.20
928	A278	10c dull red ('71)	.40	.20
929	A278	10c brn, litho. ('71)	.50	.20
930	A278	10c orange brn ('72)	.45	.20
931	A425	10c brown ('73)	.20	.20
932	A426	18c yel & dk brn, litho ('73)	.20	.20
933	A425	25c brown ('71)	.30	.20
934	A425	50c scarlet ('72)	1.25	.20
935	A241	65c brn, 22x31½mm, paper II ('71)	.65	.20
936	A425	70c dk blue ('73)	.30	.20
937	A241	90c emer, 22x31½mm ('72)	3.25	.20
938	A279	1p brn, 22½x29½mm ('71)	1.90	.20
939	A366	1.15p dk bl, 22½x32mm ('71)	1.10	.20
940	A241	1.20p org, 22x31½mm ('73)	1.10	.20
941	A366	1.80p brown ('73)	1.10	.20
		Nos. 923-941 (19)	13.70	3.80

The imprint "Casa de Moneda de la Nacion" (in capitals) appears on 3c, 5c, Nos. 928-929; 65c, 90c, 1p, 1.20p.

On type A425 only the 6c is inscribed "Ley 18.188" below denomination.

Fluorescent paper was used in printing the 25c, 50c, and 70c. The 3c, 5c, 8c, No. 931 and 65c were issued on both ordinary and fluorescent paper.

See Nos. 987-996, 1032-1038, 1042-1043, 1089-1107. For overprint and surcharge see Nos. 1010, 1078.

Soldier Type of 1965

20c, Galloping messenger of Field Army, 1879.

1970, Oct. 17 Litho. *Perf. 13½*

944 A340a 20c multicolored .80 .25

Dome of Cathedral of Cordoba — A430

1970, Nov. 7 Unwmk.

945 A430 50c gray & blk .80 .20

Bishopric of Tucuman, 400th anniv. See #C131.

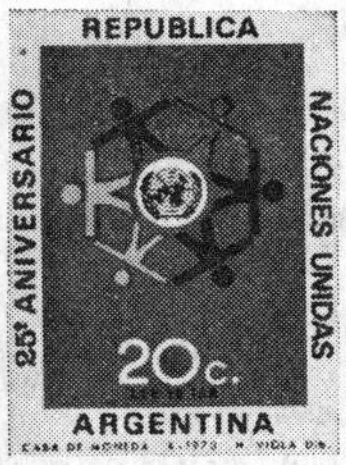

People Around UN Emblem — A431

1970, Nov. 7

946 A431 20c tan & multi .20 .20

25th anniversary of the United Nations.

State Mint and Medal A432

1970, Nov. 28 Unwmk. *Perf. 13½*

947 A432 20c gold, grn & blk .20 .20

Inauguration of the State Mint Building, 25th anniversary.

St. John Bosco and Dean Funes College A433

1970, Dec. 19 Litho.

948 A433 20c olive & blk .20 .20

Honoring the work of the Salesian Order in Patagonia.

Nativity, by Horacio Gramajo Gutierrez — A434

1970, Dec. 19

949 A434 20c multicolored .55 .35

Christmas 1970.

Argentine Flag, Map of Argentine Antarctica A435

1971, Feb. 20 Litho. *Perf. 13½*

950 A435 20c multicolored 1.25 .50

Argentine South Pole Expedition, 5th anniv.

Phosphorescent Sorting Code and Albert Einstein — A436

1971, Apr. 30 Unwmk. *Perf. 13½*

951 A436 25c multicolored .50 .30

Electronics in postal development.

Symbolic Road Crossing A437

1971, May 29 Litho.

952 A437 25c blue & blk .25 .20

Inter-American Regional Meeting of the Intl. Federation of Roads, Buenos Aires, Mar. 28-31.

Elias Alippi — A438

Actors: No. 954, Juan Aurelio Casacuberta. No. 955, Angelina Pagano. No. 956, Roberto Casaux. No. 957, Florencio Parravicini. See No. 778 note.

1971, May 29 Litho.

953	A438	15c Alippi	.35	.20
954	A438	15c Casacuberta	.35	.20
955	A438	15c Pagano	.35	.20
956	A438	15c Casaux	.35	.20
957	A438	15c Parravicini	.35	.20
		Nos. 953-957 (5)	1.75	1.00

Soldier Type of 1965

Army Day, May 29: Artilleryman, 1826.

1971, July 3 Unwmk. *Perf. 13½*

958 A340a 25c multicolored 1.25 .50

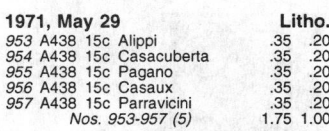

Bilander "Carmen," by Emilio Biggeri A439

1971, July 3

959 A439 25c multicolored 1.25 .25

Navy Day

Peruvian Order of the Sun A440

1971, Aug. 28

960 A440 31c multicolored .30 .20

Sesquicentennial of Peru's independence.

Güemes in Battle, by Lorenzo Gigli A441

No. 962, Death of Güemes, by Antonio Alice.

1971, Aug. 28

Size: 39x29mm

961 A441 25c multicolored .50 .30

Size: 84x29mm

962 A441 25c multicolored .50 .30

Sesquicentennial of the death of Martin Miguel de Güemes, leader in Gaucho War, Governor and Captain General of Salta Province.

Stylized Tulip — A442

1971, Sept. 18

963 A442 25c tan & multi .25 .20

3rd Intl. and 8th Natl. Horticultural Exhib.

Father Antonio Saenz, by Juan Gut — A443

1971, Sept. 18
964 A433 25c gray & multi .25 .20

Sesquicentennial of University of Buenos Aires, and to honor Father Antonio Saenz, first Chancellor and Rector.

Fabricaciones Militares Emblem — A444

1971, Oct. 16 Unwmk. *Perf. 13½*
965 A444 25c brn, gold, bl & blk .25 .20

30th anniv. of military armament works.

Cars and Trucks A445

Design: 65c, Tree converted into paper.

1971, Oct. 16
966 A445 25c dull bl & multi .50 .20
967 A445 65c green & multi 1.25 .50
Nos. 966-967,C134 (3) 2.35 .95

Nationalized industries.

Luis C. Candelaria and his Plane, 1918 A446

1971, Nov. 27
968 A446 25c multicolored .25 .20

25th Aeronautics and Space Week.

Observatory and Nebula of Magellan — A447

1971, Nov. 27
969 A447 25c multicolored .25 .20

Cordoba Astronomical Observatory, cent.

Christ in Majesty — A448

1971, Dec. 18 Litho.
970 A448 25c blk & multi .25 .20

Christmas 1971. Design is from a tapestry by Horacio Butler in Basilica of St. Francis, Buenos Aires.

Mother and Child, by J. C. Castagnino A449

1972, May 6 Unwmk. *Perf. 13½*
971 A449 25c fawn & black .25 .20

25th anniv. (in 1971) of UNICEF.

Mailman's Bag A450

1972, Sept. 2 Litho. *Perf. 13½*
972 A450 25c lemon & multi .20 .20

Bicentenary of appointment of first Argentine mailman.

Adm. Brown Station, Map of Antarctica A451

1972, Sept. 2
973 A451 25c blue & multi .70 .35

10th anniv. (in 1971) of Antarctic Treaty.

Soldier Type of 1965

Army Day: 25c, Sergeant, Negro and Mulatto Corps, 1806-1807.

1972, Sept. 23
974 A340a 25c multicolored .75 .35

Brigantine "Santisima Trinidad" A452

1972, Sept. 23
975 A452 25c multicolored .75 .35

Navy Day. See No. 1006.

A453

A454

1972, Sept. 30 Litho. *Perf. 13½*
976 A453 45c Oil pump .90 .20

50th anniv. of the organ. of the state oil fields (Yacimientos Petroliferos Fiscales).

1972, Sept. 30
977 A454 25c Sounding balloon .25 .20

Cent. of Natl. Meteorological Service.

Trees and Globe — A455

1972, Oct. 14 *Perf. 13x13½*
978 A455 25c bl, blk & lt bl .70 .20

7th World Forestry Congress, Buenos Aires, Oct. 4-18.

Arms of Naval School, Frigate "Presidente Sarmiento" — A456

1972, Oct. 14
979 A456 25c gold & multi .65 .35

Centenary of Military Naval School.

Early Balloon and Plane, Antonio de Marchi — A457

Bartolomé Mitre — A458

1972, Nov. 4 *Perf. 13½*
980 A457 25c multicolored .25 .20

Aeronautics and Space Week, and in honor of Baron Antonio de Marchi (1875-1934), aviation pioneer.

1972, Nov. 4 Engr.
981 A458 25c dark blue .20 .20

Pres. Bartolome Mitre (1821-1906), writer, historian, soldier.

Flower and Heart — A459

1972, Dec. 2 Litho. *Perf. 13½*
982 A459 90c lt bl, ultra & blk .60 .35

"Your heart is your health," World Health Day.

"Martin Fierro," by Juan C. Castignano A460

"Spirit of the Gaucho," by Vicente Forte A461

1972, Dec. 2 Litho. *Perf. 13½*
983 A460 50c multicolored .30 .20
984 A461 90c multicolored .65 .35

Intl. Book Year 1972, and cent. of publication of the poem, Martin Fierro, by Jose Hernandez (1834-86).

Iguacu Falls and Tourist Year Emblem — A462

1972, Dec. 16 *Perf. 13x13½*
985 A462 45c multicolored .30 .20

Tourism Year of the Americas.

King, Wood Carving, 18th Century — A463

1972, Dec. 16 *Perf. 13½*
986 A463 50c multicolored .50 .25

Christmas 1972.

Types of 1955-73 Inscribed "Republica Argentina" and

Moon Valley, San Juan Province — A463a

Designs: 1c, Sunflower. 5c, Tierra del Fuego. 10c, Inca Bridge, Mendoza. 50c, Lujan Basilica. 65c, 22.50p, San Martin. 1p, Ski jumper. 1.15p, 4.50p, Guillermo Brown. 1.80p, Manuel Belgrano.

Litho.; Photo. (1c, 65c, 1p)
Perf. 13½, 12½ (1.80p)

1972-75 Wmk. 365

987	A278	1c	dk green	.20	.20
988	A277	5c	dark blue	.20	.20
989	A278	10c	bister brn	.20	.20
989A	A426	50c	dull pur ('75)	.20	.20
990	A241	65c	gray brown	3.25	.20
991	A279	1p	brown	1.40	.20
992	A366	1.15p	dk gray bl	1.40	.20
993	A425	1.80p	blue ('75)	.20	.20
994	A366	4.50p	green ('75)	.65	.20
995	A241	22.50p	vio bl ('75)	1.40	.20
996	A463a	50p	multi ('75)	2.75	.30
	Nos. 987-996 (11)			11.85	2.30

Paper size of 1c is 27½x39mm; others of 1972, 37x27, 27x37mm.
Size of 22.50p, 50p: 26½x38½mm.
See Nos. 1050, 1108.

Cock (Symbolic of Police) — A464

First Coin of Bank of Buenos Aires — A465

1973, Feb. 3 Litho. Unwmk.
997 A464 50c lt green & multi .30 .20

Sesqui. of Federal Police of Argentina.

1973, Feb. 3 *Perf. 13½*
998 A465 50c purple, yel & brn .20 .20

Sesquicentennial of the Bank of Buenos Aires Province.

DC-3 Planes Over Antarctica A466

1973, Apr. 28 Litho. *Perf. 13½*
999 A466 50c lt blue & multi 1.50 .60

10th anniversary of Argentina's first flight to the South Pole.

Rivadavia's Chair, Argentine Arms and Colors — A467

1973, May 19 Litho. *Perf. 13½*
1000 A467 50c multicolored .25 .20

Inauguration of Pres. Hector J. Campora, May 25, 1973.

San Martin, by Gil de Castro — A468

San Martin and Bolivar A469

1973, July 7 Litho. *Perf. 13½*
1001 A468 50c lt green & multi .35 .20
1002 A469 50c yellow & multi .35 .20

Gen. San Martin's farewell to the people of Peru and his meeting with Simon Bolivar at Guayaquil July 26-27, 1822.

Eva Peron A470

1973, July 26 Litho. *Perf. 13½*
1003 A470 70c black, org & bl .20 .20

Maria Eva Duarte de Peron (1919-1952), political leader.

House of Viceroy Sobremonte, by Hortensia de Virgilion — A471

1973, July 28 *Perf. 13x13½*
1004 A471 50c blue & multi .20 .20

400th anniversary of the city of Cordoba.

Woman, by Lino Spilimbergo A472

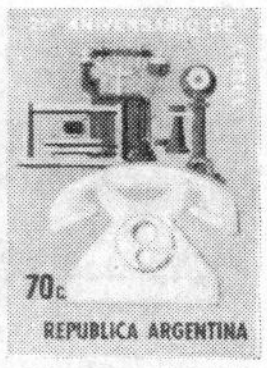

New and Old Telephones A473

1973, Aug. 28 Litho. *Perf. 13½*
1005 A472 70c multicolored .70 .20

Philatelists' Day. See Nos. B60-B61.

Ship Type of 1972

Navy Day: 70c, Frigate "La Argentina."

1973, Oct. 27 Litho. *Perf. 13½*
1006 A452 70c multicolored .60 .35

1973, Oct. 27
1007 A473 70c brt blue & multi .40 .20

25th anniv. of natl. telecommunications system.

Plume Made of Flags of Participants A474

1973, Nov. 3 *Perf. 13½*
1008 A474 70c yellow bis & multi .25 .20

12th Cong. of Latin Notaries, Buenos Aires.

No. 940 Overprinted

TRANSMISION DEL MANDO PRESIDENCIAL
12 OCTUBRE 1973

1973, Nov. 30 Photo.
1010 A241 1.20p orange .85 .20

Assumption of presidency by Juan Peron, Oct. 12.

Virgin and Child, Window, La Plata Cathedral A476

Christmas: 1.20p, Nativity, by Bruno Venier, b. 1914.

1973, Dec. 15 Litho. *Perf. 13½*
1011 A476 70c gray & multi .35 .20
1012 A476 1.20p black & multi .70 .35

The Lama, by Juan Batlle Planas — A477

Paintings: 50c, Houses in Boca District, by Eugenio Daneri, horiz. 90c, The Blue Grotto, by Emilio Pettoruti, horiz.

1974, Feb. 9 Litho. *Perf. 13½*
1013 A477 50c multicolored .30 .20
1014 A477 70c multicolored .35 .20
1015 A477 90c multicolored .60 .30
Nos. 1013-1015,B64 (4) 1.55 .95

Argentine painters.

Mar del Plata A478

1974, Feb. 9
1016 A478 70c multicolored .30 .20

Centenary of Mar del Plata.

Weather Symbols A479

Justo Santa Maria de Oro A480

1974, Mar. 23 Litho. *Perf. 13½*
1017 A479 1.20p multicolored .35 .20

Cent. of intl. meteorological cooperation.

1974, Mar. 23
1018 A480 70c multicolored .20 .20

Bicentenary of the birth of Brother Justo Santa Maria de Oro (1772-1836), theologian, patriot, first Argentine bishop.

Belisario Roldan (1873-1922), Writer — A481

1974, June 29 Photo. Unwmk.
1019 A481 70c bl & brn .20 .20

Poster with Names of OAS Members A482

1974, June 29 Litho.
1020 A482 1.38p multicolored .20 .20

Organization of American States, 25th anniv.

ENCOTEL Emblem — A483

1974, Aug. 10 Litho. *Perf. 13*
1021 A483 1.20p blue, gold & blk .40 .20

ENCOTEL, Natl. Post and Telegraph Press.

Flags of Argentina, Bolivia, Brazil, Paraguay, Uruguay — A484

1974, Aug. 16 *Perf. 13½*
1022 A484 1.38p multicolored .25 .20

6th Meeting of Foreign Ministers of Rio de la Plata Basin Countries.

El Chocon Hydroelectric Complex, Limay River — A485

Somisa Steel Mill, San Nicolas — A486

Gen. Belgrano Bridge, Chaco-Corrientes — A487

Perf. 13½, 13x13½ (4.50p)

1974, Sept. 14
1023 A485 70c multicolored .40 .20
1024 A486 1.20p multicolored .60 .35
1025 A487 4.50p multicolored 2.00 .50
Nos. 1023-1025 (3) 3.00 1.05

Development projects.

Brigantine Belgrano, by Emilio Biggeri A488

1974, Oct. 26 Litho. *Perf. 13½*
1026 A488 1.20p multicolored .60 .30

Departure into exile in Chile of General San Martin, Sept. 22, 1822.

Alberto R. Mascias and Bleriot Plane — A489

1974, Oct. 26 **Unwmk.**
1027 A489 1.20p multicolored .50 .25

Air Force Day, Aug. 10, and to honor Alberto Roque Garcias (1878-1951), aviation pioneer.
Exists with wmk. 365.

Hussar, 1812, by Eleodoro Marenco A490

1974, Oct. 26
1028 A490 1.20p multicolored .50 .25

Army Day.

Post Horn and Flags A491

1974, Nov. 23 **Unwmk.** ***Perf. 13½***
1029 A491 2.65p multicolored .85 .20

Centenary of Universal Postal Union.
Exists with wmk. 365.

Franciscan Monastery A492

1974, Nov. 23 **Litho.**
1030 A492 1.20p multicolored .40 .20

400th anniversary, city of Santa Fe.

Trout Type of 1968

1974 **Engr.** **Unwmk.**
1031 A366a 1000p vio bl 3.25 .80

Due to a shortage of 10p stamps a quantity of this 1,000p was released for use as 10p.

Types of 1954-73 Inscribed "Republica Argentina" and

Red Deer in Forest — A495

Congress Building A497

Designs: 30c, 60c, 1.80p, Manuel Belgrano. 50c, Lujan Basilica. No. 1036, 2p, 6p, San Martin (16x22½mm). 2.70p, 7.50p, 22.50p, San Martin (22x31½mm). 4.50p, 13.50p, Guillermo Brown. 10p, Leaping trout.

1974-76 **Unwmk.** **Photo.** ***Perf. 13½***

1032	A425	30c	brown vio	.20	.20
1033	A426	50c	blk & brn red	.20	.20
1034	A426	50c	bister & bl	.20	.20
1035	A425	60c	ocher	.20	.20
1036	A425	1.20p	red	.30	.20
1037	A425	1.80p	deep blue	.20	.20
1038	A425	2p	dark purple	.20	.20
1039	A241	2.70p	dk bl, 22x31½mm	.25	.20
1040	A366	4.50p	green	.85	.20
1041	A495	5p	yellow green	.40	.20
1042	A425	6p	red orange	.20	.20
1043	A425	6p	emerald	.20	.20
1044	A241	7.50p	grn, 22x31½mm	.85	.20
1045	A366a	10p	violet blue	1.00	.20
1046	A366	13.50p	scar, 16x22½mm	.85	.20
1047	A366	13.50p	scar, 22x31½mm	.85	.20
1048	A241	22.50p	dp bl, 22x31½mm	.75	.20
1049	A497	30p	yel & dk red brn	1.10	.20
1050	A463a	50p	multicolored	1.50	.20
			Nos. 1032-1050 (19)	10.30	3.80

Nos. 1033-1035, 1037-1038, 1042-1044, 1046-1048 issued in 1976, No. 1050 in 1976.
Fluorescent paper was used in printing No. 1036, 2p, Nos. 1044 and 1047. The 30p was issued on both ordinary and fluorescent paper.
See No. 829. For type of A495 overprinted see No. 1144.

Miniature Sheet

A498

1974, Dec. 7 **Litho.** ***Perf. 13½***
1052 A498 Sheet of 6 3.50 2.75

a.	1p Mariano Necochea	.25
b.	1.20p Jose de San Martin	.25
c.	1.70p Manuel Isidoro Suarez	.35
d.	1.90p Juan Pascual Pringles	.40
e.	2.70p Latin American flags	.65
f.	4.50p Jose Felix Bogado	1.10

Sesqui. of Battles of Junin and Ayacucho.

Dove, by Vito Campanella — A499

St. Anne, by Raul Soldi — A500

1974, Dec. 21 **Litho.** ***Perf. 13½***
1053 A499 1.20p multicolored .50 .20
1054 A500 2.65p multicolored .75 .30

Christmas 1974.

Boy Looking at Stamp — A501

1974, Dec. 21
1055 A501 1.70p black & yel .40 .20

World Youth Philately Year.

Space Monsters, by Raquel Forner A502

Argentine modern art: 4.50p, Dream, by Emilio Centurion.

1975, Feb. 22 **Litho.** ***Perf. 13½***
1056 A502 2.70p multi .90 .25
1057 A502 4.50p multi 1.75 .40

Indian Woman and Cathedral, Catamarca — A503

Tourist Publicity: #1059, Carved chancel and street scene. #1060, Grazing cattleand monastery yard. #1061, Painted pottery and power station. #1062, Farm cart and colonial mansion. #1063, Perito Moreno glacier and spinning mill. #1064, Lake Lapataia and scientific surveyor. #1065, Los Alerces National Park and oil derrick.

1975 **Litho.** **Unwmk.** ***Perf. 13½***

1058	A503	1.20p	shown	.25	.20
1059	A503	1.20p	Jujuy	.25	.20
1060	A503	1.20p	Salta	.25	.20
1061	A503	1.20p	Santiago del Estero	.25	.20
1062	A503	1.20p	Tucuman	.25	.20
1063	A503	6p	Santa Cruz	.50	.20
1064	A503	6p	Tierra del Fuego	.50	.20
1065	A503	6p	Chubut	.50	.20
			Nos. 1058-1065 (8)	2.75	1.60

Issue dates: 1.20p, Mar. 8; 6p, Dec. 20.

"We Have Been Inoculated" A504

1975, Apr. 26 **Unwmk.** ***Perf. 13½***
1066 A504 2p multi .45 .25

Children's inoculation campaign (child's painting).

Hugo A. Acuña and South Orkney Station — A505

Designs: No. 1068, Francisco P. Moreno and Lake Nahuel Huapi. No. 1069, Lt. Col. Luis Piedra Buena and cutter, Luisito. No. 1070, Ensign José M. Sobral and Snow Hill House. No. 1071, Capt. Carlos M. Moyano and Cerro del Toro (mountain).

1975, June 28 **Litho.** ***Perf. 13***

1067	A505	2p	grnsh bl & multi	.25	.20
1068	A505	2p	yel grn & multi	.25	.20
1069	A505	2p	lt vio & multi	.25	.20
1070	A505	2p	gray bl & multi	.25	.20
1071	A505	2p	pale grn & multi	.25	.20
			Nos. 1067-1071 (5)	1.25	1.00

Pioneers of Antarctica.

Frigate "25 de Mayo" A506

1975, Sept. 27 **Unwmk.** ***Perf. 13½***
1072 A506 6p multi .40 .25

Navy Day 1975.

Eduardo Bradley and Balloon — A507

1975, Sept. 27 **Wmk. 365**
1073 A507 6p multi .40 .25

Air Force Day.

Declaration of Independence, by Juan M. Blanes — A508

1975, Oct. 25
1074 A508 6p multi .30 .20

Sesquicentennial of Uruguay's declaration of independence.

Flame A509

1975, Oct. 17 **Unwmk.**
1075 A509 6p gray & multi .30 .20

Loyalty Day, 30th anniversary of Pres. Peron's accession to power.

Nos. 886, 891 and 932 Surcharged

REVALORIZADO
6 c.

REVALORIZADO
30 c

REVALORIZADO
5 pesos

Lithographed, Photogravure

1975
1076 A277 6c on 3p .20 .20
1077 A366 30c on 90p .20 .20
1078 A426 5p on 18c .35 .20
Nos. 1076-1078 (3) .75 .60

Issued: 6c, 10/30; 30c, 11/20; 5p, 10/24.
The 6c also exists on No. 886a.

International Bridge, Flags of Argentina and Uruguay — A510

1975, Oct. 25 Litho. Wmk. 365

1081 A510 6p multi		.35	.20

Opening of bridge connecting Colon, Argentina, and Paysandu, Uruguay.

Post Horn, Surcharged A511

1975, Nov. 8

1082 A511 10p on 20c multi		.45	.20

Introduction of postal code. Not issued without surcharge.

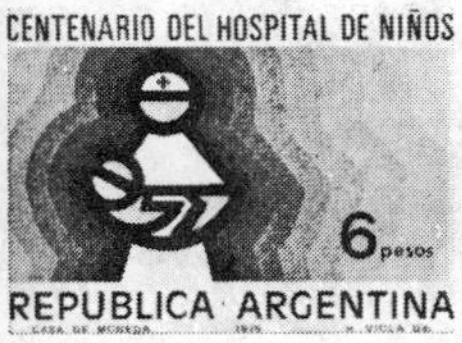

Nurse Holding Infant A512

1975, Dec. 13 Litho. *Perf. 13½*

1083 A512 6p multi		.45	.20

Children's Hospital, centenary.

Nativity, Nueva Pompeya Church — A513

1975, Dec. 13 Litho. Unwmk.

1084 A513 6p multi		.30	.20

Christmas 1975.

Types of 1970-75 and

Church of St. Francis, Salta — A515

Designs: 3p, No. 1099, 60p, 90p, Manuel Belgrano. 12p, 15p, 20p, 30p, No. 1100, 100p, 110p, 120p, 130p, San Martin. 15p, 70p, Guillermo Brown. 300p, Moon Valley (lower inscriptions italic). 500p, Adm. Brown Station, Antarctica.

1976-78 Photo. Unwmk. *Perf. 13½*

1089 A425	3p slate	.20	.20
1090 A425	12p rose red	.25	.20

Perf. 12½x13

Litho. Wmk. 365

1091 A425	12p rose red	.20	.20
1092 A425	12p emerald	.20	.20

Perf. 13½

Photo. Unwmk.

1093 A425	12p emer ('77)	.20	.20
1094 A425	15p rose red	.20	.20
1095 A425	15p vio bl ('77)	.20	.20
1097 A425	20p rose red ('77)	.35	.20
1098 A425	30p rose red ('77)	.35	.20
1099 A425	40p dp grn	.50	.20
1100 A425	40p rose red ('77)	.35	.20
1101 A425	60p dk bl ('77)	.70	.20
1102 A425	70p dk bl ('77)	.85	.20
1103 A425	90p emer ('77)	1.00	.30
1104 A425	100p red	.75	.25
1105 A425	110p rose red ('78)	.50	.20
1106 A425	120p rose red ('78)	.60	.20
1107 A425	130p rose red ('78)	.70	.25

Litho.

1108 A463a	300p multi	3.50	1.50
1109 A515	500p multi ('77)	8.25	1.40
1110 A515	1000p multi ('77)	10.00	2.00
	Nos. 1089-1110 (21)	29.85	8.70

Fluorescent paper was used in printing both 12p rose red, 15p rose red, 20p, 30p, 40p rose red, 100p, 110p, 120p, 130p. No. 1099 and the 300p were issued on both ordinary and fluorescent paper.

300p and 500p exist with wmk. 365.

See Nos. B73-B74.

A516

1976 Photo. Unwmk. *Perf. 13½*

1112 A516	12c gray & blk	.20	.20
1113 A516	50c gray & grn	.20	.20
1114 A516	1p red & blk	.20	.20
1115 A516	4p bl & blk	.20	.20
1116 A516	5p org & blk	.20	.20
1117 A516	6p dp brn & blk	.20	.20
1118 A516	10p gray & vio bl	.25	.20
1119 A516	27p lt grn & blk	.50	.20
1120 A516	30p lt bl & blk	.90	.20
1121 A516	45p yel & blk	.90	.20
1122 A516	50p dl grn & blk	1.25	.20
1123 A516	100p brt grn & red	1.60	.25

Perf. 13x12½

1976 Litho. Wmk. 365

1124 A516	5p org & blk	.20	.20
1125 A516	27p lt grn & blk	.50	.20
1126 A516	45p yel & blk	1.25	.20
	Nos. 1112-1126 (15)	8.55	3.05

The 1p, 6p, 10p, 50p and No. 1116 were issued on both ordinary and fluorescent paper.

Jet and Airlines Emblem — A517

Perf. 13x13½

1976, Apr. 24 Litho. Unwmk.

1130 A517 30p bl, lt bl & dk bl		1.00	.20

Argentine Airlines, 25th anniversary.

Frigate Heroina and Map of Falkland Islands — A518

1976, Apr. 26

1131 A518 6p multi		1.00	.40

Argentina's claim to Falkland Islands.

Louis Braille — A519

Wmk. 365

1976, May 22 Engr. *Perf. 13½*

1132 A519 19.70 dp bl		.30	.20

Sesquicentennial of the invention of the Braille system of writing for the blind by Louis Braille (1809-1852).

Private, 7th Infantry Regiment A520

1976, May 29 Litho. Unwmk.

1133 A520 12p multi		.40	.20

Army Day.

Schooner Rio de la Plata, by Emilio Biggeri A521

1976, June 19

1134 A521 12p multi		.40	.20

Navy Day.

Dr. Bernardo Houssay A522

Argentine Nobel Prize Winners: 15p, Luis F. Leloir, chemistry, 1970. 20p, Carlos Saavedra Lamas, peace, 1936. Bernardo Houssay, medicine and physiology, 1947.

1976, Aug. 14 Litho. *Perf. 13½*

1135 A522	10p org & blk	.25	.20
1136 A522	15p yel & blk	.30	.20
1137 A522	20p ocher & blk	.45	.25
	Nos. 1135-1137 (3)	1.00	.65

Rio de la Plata International Bridge — A523

1976, Sept. 18 Litho. *Perf. 13½*

1138 A523 12p multi		.30	.20

Inauguration of International Bridge connecting Puerte Unzue, Argentina, and Fray Bentos, Uruguay.

Pipelines and Cooling Tower, Gen. Mosconi Plant A524

1976, Nov. 20 Litho. *Perf. 13½*

1139 A524 28p multi		.40	.20

Pablo Teodoro Fels and Bleriot Monoplane, 1910 — A525

1976, Nov. 20

1140 A525 15p multi		.30	.20

Air Force Day.

Nativity A526

1976, Dec. 18 Litho. *Perf. 13½*

1141 A526 20p multi		.65	.30

Christmas. Painting by Edith Chiapetto.

Water Conference Emblem — A527

1977, Mar. 19 Litho. *Perf. 13½*

1142 A527 70p multi		.70	.25

UN Water Conf., Mar del Plata, Mar. 14-25.

Dalmacio Velez Sarsfield A528

1977, Mar. 19 Engr.

1143 A528 50p blk & red brn		.70	.30

Dalmacio Velez Sarsfield (1800-1875), author of Argentine civil code.

100 PESOS

150°. ANIV. DEL CORREO NACIONAL DEL URUGUAY

Red Deer Type of 1974 Surcharged

1977, July 30 Photo. *Perf. 13½*

1144 A495 100p on 5p brn		1.40	.35

Sesquicentennial of Uruguayan postal service. Not issued without surcharge.

Soldier, 16th Lancers — A529

1977, July 30

1145 A529 30p multi		.40	.20

Army Day.

Schooner Sarandi, by Emilio Biggeri
A530

1977, July 30
1146 A530 30p multi .40 .25

Navy Day.

Soccer Games' Emblem — A531

70p, Argentina '78 emblem, flags & soccer field.

1977, May 14
1147 A531 30p multi .40 .20
1148 A531 70p multi .85 .40

11th World Cup Soccer Championship, Argentina, June 1-25, 1978.

The Visit, by Horacio Butler
A532

Consecration, by Miguel P. Caride — A533

1977, Mar. 26 **Litho.**
1149 A532 50p multi .50 .25
1150 A533 70p multi .65 .40

Argentine artists.

Sierra de la Ventana — A534

Views: No. 1152, Civic Center, Santa Rosa. No. 1153, Skiers, San Martin de los Andes. No. 1154, Boat on Lake Fonck, Rio Negro.

1977, Oct. 8 **Litho.** ***Perf. 13x13½***
1151 A534 30p multi .30 .20
1152 A534 30p multi .30 .20
1153 A534 30p multi .30 .20
1154 A534 30p multi .30 .20
Nos. 1151-1154 (4) 1.20 .80

Guillermo Brown, by R. del Villar — A535

1977, Oct. 8 ***Perf. 13½***
1155 A535 30p multi .40 .25

Adm. Guillermo Brown (1777-1857), leader in fight for independence, bicentenary of birth.

Jet
A536

Double-decker, 1926 — A537

1977 **Litho.** ***Perf. 13½***
1156 A536 30p multi .25 .20
1157 A537 40p multi .30 .20

50th anniversary of military plane production (30p); Air Force Day (40p).
Issue dates: 30p, Dec. 3; 40p, Nov. 26.

Adoration of the Kings — A538

1977, Dec. 17
1158 A538 100p multi 1.00 .30

Christmas 1977.

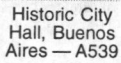

Historic City Hall, Buenos Aires — A539

Chapel of Rio Grande Museum, Tierra del Fuego — A540

Designs: 5p, 20p, La Plata Museum. 10p, Independence Hall, Tucuman. 40p, City Hall, Salta, vert. No. 1165, City Hall, Buenos Aires. 100p, Columbus Theater, Buenos Aires. 200p, flag Monument, Rosario. 280p, 300p, Chapel of Rio Grande Museum, Tierra del Fuego. 480p, 520p, 800, Ruins of Jesuit Mission Church of San Ignacio, Misiones. 500p, Candonga Chapel, Cordoba. 1000p, G.P.O., Buenos Aires. 2000p, Civic Center, Bariloche, Rio Negro.

Three types of 10p: I. Nine vertical window bars; small imprint "E. MILIAVACA Dib." II. Nine bars; large imprint "E. MILIAVACA DIB." III. Redrawn; 5 bars; large imprint.

1977-81 **Photo.** **Unwmk.** ***Perf. 13½***
Size: 32x21mm, 21x32mm

1159 A540 5p gray & blk .20 .20
1160 A540 10p lt ultra & blk, I .20 .20
a. Type II .20 .20
1161 A540 10p lt bl & blk, III .20 .20
1162 A540 20p citron & blk, litho. .20 .20
1163 A540 40p gray bl & blk .25 .20
1164 A539 50p yel & blk .30 .20
1165 A540 50p citron & blk .20 .20
1166 A540 100p org & blk, litho. .35 .20
a. Wmk. 365 92.50 24.00
1167 A540 100p red org & blk .20 .20
1168 A540 100p turq & blk .20 .20
1169 A539 200p lt bl & blk .50 .25
1170 A540 280p rose & blk 14.00 .20
1171 A540 300p lemon & blk .95 .20
1172 A540 480p org & blk 1.75 .25
1173 A540 500p yel grn & blk 1.75 .20
1174 A540 520p org & blk 1.75 .30
1175 A540 800p rose lil & blk 2.25 .30
1176 A540 1000p lem bis & blk 2.50 .40
1177 A540 1000p gold & blk, 40x29mm 3.75 .40
1178 A540 2000p multi 2.25 .40
Nos. 1159-1178 (20) 33.75 4.90

#1161, 1163, 1165, 1167, 1169, 1171, 1173, 1176, 1177 were issued on both ordinary and fluorescent paper. No. 1174 was issued only on fluorescent paper. All others were issued only on ordinary paper.

Issued: #1164, 5/30/77; 280p, 12/15/77; #1160, 3/14/78; 480p, 5/22/78; 5p, 7/25/78; 20p, 500p, 9/8/78; #1166, 9/20/78; #1177, 9/28/78; 520p, 9/30/78; 300p, 10/5/78; 40p, 12/1/78; #1161/79; #1165, 1/8/79; 800p, 3/20/79; #1167, 4/25/79; 200p, 6/23/79; #1176, 12/15/79; 2000p, 6/25/80; #1168, 5/26/81.

For overprints see Nos. 1253, 1315.

Soccer Games' Emblem
A544

1978, Feb. 10 **Photo.** ***Perf. 13½***
1179 A544 200p yel grn & bl .85 .30

11th World Cup Soccer Championship, Argentina, June 1-25. Exists with wmk. 365.

View of El Rio, Rosario — A545

Designs (Argentina '78 Emblem and): 100p, Rio Tercero Dam, Cordoba. 150p, Cordillera Mountains, Mendoza. 200p, City Center, Mar del Plata. 300p, View of Buenos Aires.

1978, May 6 **Litho.** ***Perf. 13***
1180 A545 50p multi .20 .20
1181 A545 100p multi .30 .20
1182 A545 150p multi .50 .20
1183 A545 200p multi .50 .25
1184 A545 300p multi 1.10 .30
Nos. 1180-1184 (5) 2.60 1.15

Sites of 11th World Cup Soccer Championship, June 1-25.

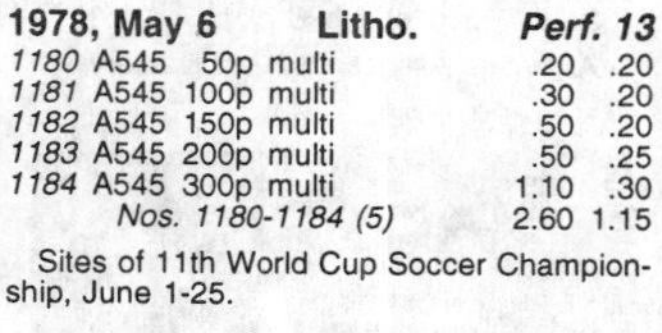

Children — A546

1978, May 20
1185 A546 100p multi .35 .20

50th anniversary of Children's Institute.

Labor Day, by B. Quinquela Martin — A547

Design: No. 1187, Woman's torso, sculpture by Orlando Pierri.

1978, May 20 ***Perf. 13½***
1186 A547 100p multi .35 .20
1187 A547 100p multi .35 .20

Argentina, Hungary, France, Italy and Emblem — A548

Stadium
A549

Teams and Argentina '78 Emblem: 200p, Poland, Fed. Rep. of Germany, Tunisia, Mexico. 300p, Austria, Spain, Sweden, Brazil. 400p, Netherlands, Iran, Peru, Scotland.

1978 **Litho.** ***Perf. 13***
1188 A548 100p multi .30 .20
1189 A548 200p multi .65 .20
1190 A548 300p multi .95 .25
1191 A548 400p multi 1.25 .30
Nos. 1188-1191 (4) 3.15 .95

Souvenir Sheet
Lithographed and Engraved
Perf. 13½

1192 A549 700p buff & blk 2.50 1.40

11th World Cup Soccer Championship, Argentina, June 1-25. Issued: Nos. 1188-1191, June 6, No. 1192, June 3.

Stadium Type of 1978 Inscribed in Red: "ARGENTINA / CAMPEON"

Lithographed and Engraved
1978, Sept. 2 ***Perf. 13½***
1193 A549 1000p bulf, blk & red 3.25 1.40

Argentina's victory in 1978 Soccer Championship. No. 1193 has margin similar to No. 1192 with Rimet Cup emblem added in red.

Young Tree Nourished by Old Trunk, UN Emblem — A550

1978 Sept. 2 **Litho.**
1194 A550 100p multi .35 .25

Technical Cooperation among Developing Countries Conf., Buenos Aires, Sept. 1978.

Emblems of Buenos Aires and Bank — A551

1978, Sept. 16

1195 A551 100p multi .35 .25

Bank of City of Buenos Aires, centenary.

General Savio and Steel Production — A552

1978, Sept. 16

1196 A552 100p multi .35 .25

Gen. Manuel N. Savio (1892-1948), general manager of military heavy industry.

San Martin — A553

1978, Oct. **Engr.**

1197 A553 2000p grnsh blk 6.25 1.10

1979 **Wmk. 365**

1198 A553 2000p grnsh blk 4.75 .35

Gen Jose de San Martin (1778-1850), soldier and statesman. See No. 1292.

Globe and Argentine Flag — A554

1978, Oct. 7 **Litho.** ***Perf. 13½***

1199 A554 200p multi .70 .30

12th Intl. Cancer Cong., Buenos Aires, Oct. 5-11.

Chessboard, Queen and Pawn — A555

1978, Oct. 7

1200 A555 200p multi 2.00 .65

23rd National Chess Olympics, Buenos Aires, Oct. 25-Nov. 12.

Correct Positioning of Stamps A557

Design: 50p, Use correct postal code number.

1978 **Photo.** ***Perf. 13½***

1201 A557 20p ultra .20 .20
1203 A557 50p carmine .25 .20

No. 1201 issued on both ordinary and fluorescent paper.

A558

A559

1978-82 **Photo.** ***Perf. 13½***

1204	A558	150p bl & ultra	.35	.20
1205	A558	180p bl & ultra	.45	.20
1206	A558	200p bl & ultra	.30	.20
1207	A559	240p ol bis & bl ('79)	.40	.20
1208	A559	260p blk & lt bl ('79)	.40	.20
1209	A559	290p blk & lt bl ('79)	.45	.20
1210	A559	310p mag & bl ('79)	.50	.20
1211	A559	350p ver & bl ('79)	.65	.20
1212	A559	450p ultra & bl	.50	.20
1213	A559	600p grn & bl ('80)	.70	.25
1214	A559	700p blk & bl ('80)	.70	.25
1215	A559	800p red & bl ('81)	.65	.20
1216	A559	1100p gray & bl ('81)	.90	.20
1217	A559	1500p blk & bl ('81)	.35	.20
1218	A559	1700p grn & bl ('82)	.45	.20
		Nos. 1204-1218 (15)	7.75	3.10

No. 1204 issued on fluorescent and ordinary paper. No. 1206 issued only on fluorescent paper.

For overprint see No. 1338.

Balsa "24" A561

Ships: 200p, Tug Legador. 300p, River Parana tug No. 34. 400p, Passenger ship Ciudad de Parana.

1978, Nov. 4 **Litho.** ***Perf. 13½***

1220	A561 100p multi	.25	.20
1221	A561 200p multi	.50	.20
1222	A561 300p multi	.70	.30
a.	Pair, #1221-1222	1.25	
1223	A561 400p multi	.95	.40
a.	Pair, #1220, 1223	1.25	
	Nos. 1220-1223 (4)	2.40	1.10

20th anniversary of national river fleet. Issued on fluorescent paper.

View and Arms of Bahia Blanca A562

1978, Nov. 25 **Litho.** ***Perf. 13½***

1224 A562 20p multi .50 .20

Sesquicentennial of Bahia Blanca.

"Spain," (Queen Isabella and Columbus) by Arturo Dresco — A563

1978, Nov. 25

1225 A563 300p multi 2.75 .30

Visit of King Juan Carlos and Queen Sofia of Spain to Argentina, Nov. 26.

Virgin and Child, San Isidro Cathedral A564

1978, Dec. 16

1226 A564 200p gold & multi .55 .30

Christmas 1978.

Slope at Chacabuco, by Pedro Subercaseaux — A565

Painting: 1000p, The Embrace of Maipu (San Martin and O'Higgins), by Pedro Subercaseaux, vert.

1978, Dec. 16 **Litho.** ***Perf. 13½***

1227 A565 500p multi 1.00 .25
1228 A565 1000p multi 2.00 .40

José de San Martin, 200th birth anniversary.

Adolfo Alsina A566

Design: No. 1230, Mariano Moreno.

1979, Jan. 20

1229 A566 200p lt bl & blk .30 .20
1230 A566 200p yel red & blk .30 .20

Adolfo Alsina (1828-1877), political leader, vice-president; Mariano Moreno (1778-1811), lawyer, educator, political leader.

Argentina No. 37 and UPU Emblem A567

1979, Jan. 20

1231 A567 200p multi .25 .20

Centenary of Argentina's UPU membership.

Still-life, by Carcova A568

Painting: 300p, The Laundresses, by Faustino Brughetti.

1979, Mar. 3

1232 A568 200p multi .45 .20
1233 A568 300p multi .60 .20

Ernesto de la Carcova (1866-1927) and Faustino Brughetti (1877-1956), Argentine painters.

A569

A570

1979, Mar. 3

1234 A569 200p Balcarce Earth station .55 .25

Third Inter-American Telecommunications Conference, Buenos Aires, March 5-9.

1979

1235 A570 30p Stamp collecting .20 .20

Printed on ordinary and fluorescent paper.

European Olive — A571

Laurel and Regimental Emblem — A572

1979, June 2 **Litho.** ***Perf. 13½***

1236	A571 100p shown	.25	.20
1237	A571 200p Tea	.55	.25
1238	A571 300p Sorghum	.85	.40
1239	A571 400p Common flax	1.10	.55
	Nos. 1236-1239 (4)	2.75	1.40

1979, June 9

1240 A572 200p gold & multi .40 .25

Founding of Subteniente Berdina Village in memory of Sub-lieutenant Rodolfo Hernan Berdina, killed by terrorists in 1975.

"75" and Automobile Club Emblem A573

1979, June 9

1241 A573 200p gold & multi .40 .20

Argentine Automobile Club, 75th anniv.

Exchange Building and Emblem A574

1979, June 9

1242 A574 200p bl, blk & gold .40 .20

Grain Exchange, 125th anniversary.

Cavalry Officer, 1817 — A575

1979, July 7 Litho. *Perf. 13½*
1243 A575 200p multi 1.00 .30

Army Day.

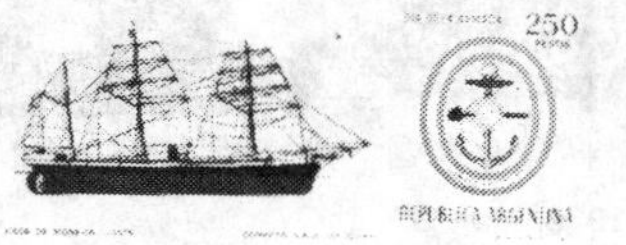

Corvette Uruguay and Navy Emblem — A576

#1245, Hydrographic service ship & emblem.

1979 *Perf. 13*
1244 A576 250p multi .85 .35
1245 A576 250p multi .85 .35

Navy Day; Cent. of Naval Hydrographic Service. Issued: #1244, July 28; #1245, July 7.

Tree and Man — A577

1979, July 28 *Perf. 13½*
1246 A577 250p multi .60 .25

Protection of the Environment Day, June 5.

"Spad" Flying over Andes, and Vicente Almandos Almonacid A578

1979, Aug. 4
1247 A578 250p multi .70 .25

Air Force Day.

Gen. Julio A. Roca Occupying Rio Negro, by Juan M. Blanes A579

1979, Aug. 4
1248 A579 250p multi .70 .25

Conquest of Rio Negro Desert, centenary.

> *The Scott Catalogue value is a retail value; that is, what you could expect to pay for the stamp in a grade of Very Fine. The value listed reflects recent actual dealer selling prices.*

Rowland Hill — A580

1979, Sept. 29 Litho. *Perf. 13½*
1249 A580 300p gray red & blk .55 .25

Sir Rowland Hill (1795-1879), originator of penny postage.

Viedma Navarez Monument A581

1979, Sept. 29
1250 A581 300p multi .60 .25

Viedma and Carmen de Patagones towns, bicentenary.

Pope Paul VI — A582

Design: No. 1252, Pope John Paul I.

1979, Oct. 27 Engr. *Perf. 13½*
1251 A582 500p black 1.00 .30
1252 A582 500p sepia 1.00 .30

No. 1169 Overprinted in Red: "75 ANIV. / SOCIEDAD/ FILATELICA / DE ROSARIO"

1979, Nov. 10 Photo. *Perf. 13½*
1253 A539 200p lt bl & blk .60 .20

Rosario Philatelic Society, 75th anniversary.

A583

A584

1979, Nov. 10 Litho.
1254 A583 300p multi .70 .30

Frontier resettlement.

1979, Dec. 1 Litho. *Perf. 13½*
1255 A584 300p multi .70 .30

Military Geographic Institute centenary.

Christmas 1979 A585

1979, Dec. 1
1256 A585 300p multi .55 .25

General Mosconi Birth Centenary — A586

1979, Dec. 15 Engr. *Perf. 13½*
1257 A586 1000p blk & bl 1.50 .25

Rotary Emblem and Globe A587

1979, Dec. 29 Litho.
1258 A587 300p multi 1.75 .35

Rotary International, 75th anniversary.

Child and IYC Emblem — A588

Family, by Pablo Menicucci A589

1979, Dec. 29
1259 A588 500p lt bl & sepia .75 .20
1260 A589 1000p multi 1.50 .25

International Year of the Child.

Microphone, Waves, ITU Emblem — A590

1980, Mar. 22 Litho. *Perf. 13x13½*
1261 A590 500p multi .95 .25

Regional Administrative Conference on Broadcasting by Hectometric Waves for Area 2, Buenos Aires, Mar. 10-29.

Guillermo Brown — A591

1980 Engr. *Perf. 13½*
1262 A591 5000p black 4.50 .20

See No. 1372.

Argentine Red Cross Centenary — A592

1980, Apr. 19 Litho. *Perf. 13½*
1263 A592 500p multi .50 .20

OAS Emblem A593

1980, Apr. 19
1264 A593 500p multi .55 .25

Day of the Americas, Apr. 14.

Dish Antennae, Balcarce — A594

1980, Apr. 26 Litho. & Engr.
1265 A594 300p shown .40 .20
1266 A594 300p Hydroelectric Station, Salto Grande .40 .20
1267 A594 300p Bridge, Zarate-Brazo Largo .40 .20
Nos. 1265-1267 (3) 1.20 .60

Capt. Hipolito Bouchard, Frigate "Argentina" — A595

1980, May 31 Litho. *Perf. 13x13½*
1268 A595 500p multicolored .70 .30

Navy Day.

"Villarino," San Martin, by Theodore Gericault — A596

1980, May 31
1269 A596 500p multicolored .70 .30

Return of the remains of Gen. Jose de San Martin to Argentina, centenary.

Buenos Aires Gazette, 1810, Signature A597

1980, June 7 *Perf. 13½*
1270 A597 500p multicolored .55 .25

Journalism Day.

Miniature Sheet

Coaches in Victoria Square — A598

1980 June 14

1271 Sheet of 14 9.00 9.00
a. A598 500p any single .60 .60

Buenos Aires, 400th anniv. No. 1271 shows ceramic mural of Victoria Square by Rodolfo Franco in continuous design. See No. 1285.

Gen. Pedro Aramburu A599

1980, July 12 Litho. *Perf. 13½*

1272 A599 500p yel & blk .55 .25

Gen. Pedro Eugenio Aramburu (1903-1970), provisional president, 1955.

Army Day A600

1980, July 12

1273 A600 500p multicolored .85 .30

Gen. Juan Gregorio de Las Heras (1780-1866), Hero of 1817 War of Independence — A601

Grandees of Argentina Bicentenary: No. 1275, Rivadavia. No. 1276, Brig. Gen Jose Matias Zapiola (1780-1874), naval commander and statesman.

1980, Aug. 2 Litho. *Perf. 13½*

1274 A601 500p tan & blk .55 .25
1275 A601 500p multicolored .55 .25
1276 A601 500p lt lilac & blk .55 .25
Nos. 1274-1276 (3) 1.65 .75

Avro "Gosport" Biplane, Maj. Francisco de Artega — A602

1980, Aug. 16 *Perf. 13*

1277 A602 500p multicolored .70 .25

Air Force Day. Artega (1882-1930) was first director of Military Aircraft Factory where Avro "Gosport" was built (1927).

University of La Plata, 75th Anniversary — A603

1980, Aug. 16 *Perf. 13½*

1278 A603 500p multi .55 .25

Souvenir Sheets

Emperor Penguin — A604

South Orkneys Argentine Base A605 A606

No. 1279 (A604): a, shown. b, Bearded penguin. c, Adelie penguins. d, Papua penguins. e, Sea elephants. f, A605 shown. g, A606 shown. h, Fur seals. i, Giant petrels. j, Blue-eyed cororants. k, Stormy petrels. m, Anarctic doves.

1980, Sept. 27 Litho. *Perf. 13½*

1279 Sheet of 12 11.00 11.00
a.-m. A604 500p, any single .75 .60
1280 Sheet of 12 11.00 11.00
a. A605 500p Puerto Soledad .75 .60
b. A606 500p Different view .75 .60

75th anniv. of Argentina's presence in the South Orkneys and 150th anniv. of political and military command in the Falkland Islands. Nos. 1279-1280 each contain 12 stamps (4x3) with landscape designs in center of sheets. Silhouettes of Argentine exploration ships in margins. #1280 contains #1279a-1279e, 1279h-1279m, 1280a-1280b.

Anti-smoking Campaign A608

1980, Oct. 11

1282 A608 700p multi .90 .25

National Census — A609

1980, Sept.

1283 A609 500p blk & bl 1.00 .20

Madonna and Child (Congress Emblem) A610

1980, Oct. 1 Litho.

1284 A610 700p multi .85 .20

National Marian Cong., Mendoza, Oct. 8-12

Mural Type of 1980
Miniature Sheet

1980, Oct. 25

1285 Sheet of 14 9.00 9.00
a. A598 500p, any single .60 .50

Buenos Aires, 400th anniv./Buenos Aires '80 Stamp Exhib., Oct. 24-Nov. 2. No. 1285 shows ceramic mural Arte bajo la Ciudad by Alfredo Guido in continuous design.

Technical Military Academy, 50th Anniversary A611

Amateur Radio Operation A612

1980, Nov. 1

1286 A611 700p multi .75 .20

1980, Nov. 1

1287 A612 700p multi .75 .20

Medal — A613

Lujan Cathedral Floor Plan — A614

1980, Nov. 29 Litho. *Perf. 13½*

1288 A613 700p multi .75 .25
1289 A614 700p olive & brn .75 .25

Christmas 1980. 150th anniv. of apparition of Holy Virgin to St. Catherine Laboure, Paris (No. 1288), 350th anniv. of apparition at Lujan.

150th Death Anniversary of Simon Bolivar — A615

1980, Dec. 13

1290 A615 700p multi .75 .25

Soccer Gold Cup Championship, Montevideo, 1980 — A616

1981, Jan. 3 Litho.

1291 A616 1000p multi 1.10 .25

San Martin Type of 1978

1981, Jan. 20 Engr. *Perf. 13½*

1292 A553 10,000p dark blue 7.25 .20

Landscape in Lujan, by Marcos Tiglio A617

Paintings: No. 1304, Expansion of Light along a Straight Line, by Miguel Angel Vidal, vert.

1981, Apr. 11 Litho.

1303 A617 1000p multi .85 .30
1304 A617 1000p multi .85 .30

Intl. Sports Medicine Congress, June 7-12 — A618

1981, June 6 Litho. *Perf. 13½*

1305 A618 1000p bl & dk brn .75 .20

Esperanza Base, Antarctica — A619

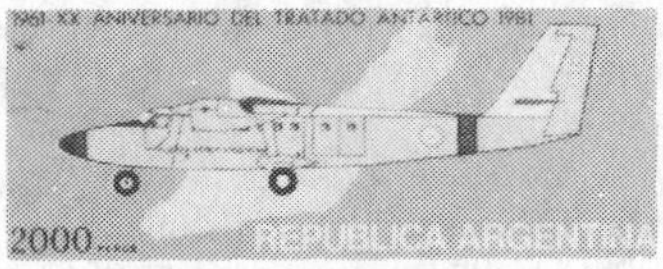

Cargo Plane, Map of Vice-Commodore Marambio Island — A620

Perf. 13½, 13x13½ (No. 1308)

1981, June 13

1306 A619 1000p shown 1.40 .40
1307 A619 2000p Almirante Irizar 2.50 .55
1308 A620 2000p shown 2.50 .85
Nos. 1306-1308 (3) 6.40 1.80

Antarctic Treaty 20th anniv.

Antique Pistols (Military Club Centenary) A621

1981, June 27 *Perf. 13½*

1309 A621 1000p Club building .80 .20
1310 A621 2000p shown .80 .20

Gen. Juan A. Alvarez de Arenales (1770-1831) A622

Famous Men: No. 1312, Felix G. Frias (1816-1881), writer. No. 1313, Jose E. Uriburu (1831-1914), statesman.

1981, Aug. 8 Litho. *Perf. 13½*

1311 A622 1000p multi .70 .20
1312 A622 1000p multi .70 .20
1313 A622 1000p multi .70 .20
Nos. 1311-1313 (3) 2.10 .60

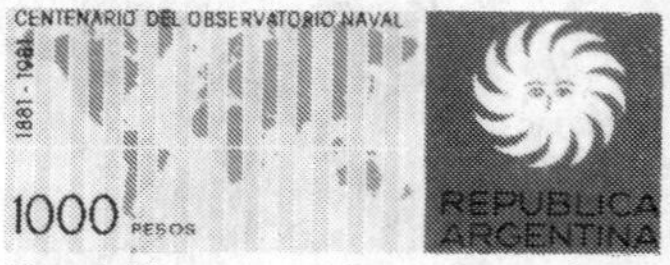

Naval Observatory Centenary — A623

1981, Aug. 15 Litho. *Perf. 13x13½*
1314 A623 1000p multi .75 .25

No. 1176 Overprinted in Red: "50 ANIV. DE LA ASOCIACION / FILATELICA Y NUMISMATICA / DE BAHIA BLANCA"

1981, Aug. 15 Photo. *Perf. 13½*
1315 A540 1000p lem & blk 1.90 .25

50th anniv. of Bahia Blanca Philatelic and Numismatic Society.

St. Cayetano, Stained-glass Window, Buenos Aires — A624

1981, Sept. 5 Litho. *Perf. 13½*
1316 A624 1000p multi .70 .20

St. Cayetano, founder of Teatino Order, 500th birth anniv.

Pablo Castaibert (1883-1909) and his Monoplane (Air Force Day) — A625

1981, Sept. 5 *Perf. 13x13½*
1317 A625 1000p multi .65 .20

Intl. Year of the Disabled A626

1981, Sept. 10 *Perf. 13½*
1318 A626 1000p multi .65 .20

22nd Latin-American Steelmakers' Congress, Buenos Aires, Sept. 21-23 — A627

1981, Sept. 19
1319 A627 1000p multi .65 .20

Army Regiment No. 1 (Patricios), 175th Anniv. — A628

1981, Oct. 10 Litho. *Perf. 13½*
1320 A628 1500p Natl. arms .45 .20
1321 A628 1500p shown .45 .20
a. Pair, #1320-1321 .90 .30

A629

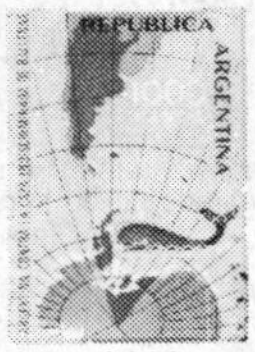

A630

San Martin as artillery Captain in Battle of Bailen, 1808.

1981, Oct. 5
1322 Sheet of 8 + 4 labels 4.75 1.75
a. A629 1000p multi .35 .20
b. A629 1500p multi .50 .20

Espamer '81 Intl. Stamp Exhib. (Americas, Spain, Portugal), Buenos Aires, Nov. 13-22.
No. 1322 contains 2 each se-tenant pairs with label between.

1981, Oct. 5
1323 A630 1000p multi 2.25 .30

Anti-indiscriminate whaling.

Espamer '81 Emblem and Ship — A631

1981
1324 A631 1300p multi .55 .20

No. 1324 Overprinted in Blue: "CURSO SUPERIOR DE ORGANIZACIONES DE FILATELICOS-UPAE-BUENOS AIRES-1981"

1981, Nov. 7 Photo. *Perf. 13½*
1325 A631 1300p multi 1.25 .20

Postal Administration philatelic training course.

Soccer Players — A632

Designs: Soccer players.

1981, Nov. 13 Litho.
1326 Sheet of 4 + 2 labels 7.25 7.25
a. A632 1000p multi .25 .25
b. A632 3000p multi .65 .65
c. A632 5000p multi 1.10 1.10
d. A632 15,000p multi 3.25 3.25

Espamer '81.

"Peso" Coin Centenary A633

1981, Nov. 21
1327 A633 2000p Patacon, 1881 .40 .20
1328 A633 3000p Argentine Oro, 1881 .60 .20

Christmas 1981 — A634

1981, Dec. 12
1329 A634 1500p multi .85 .25

Traffic Safety A635

1981, Dec. 19 Litho.
1330 A635 1000p Observe traffic lights, vert. .75 .40
1331 A635 2000p Drive carefully, vert. .75 .40
1332 A635 3000p Cross at white lines .75 .40
1333 A635 4000p Don't shine headlights 1.50 .40
Nos. 1330-1333 (4) 3.75 1.60

Francisco Luis Bernardez, Ciuda Laura — A636

Writers and title pages from their works: 2000p, Lucio V. Mansilla, Excursion a los indios ranqueles. 3000p, Conrado Nale Roxlo, El Grillo. 4000p, Victoria Ocampo, Sur.

1982, Mar. 20 Litho.
1334 A636 1000p shown .60 .20
1335 A636 2000p multi .85 .20
1336 A636 3000p multi 1.25 .30
1337 A636 4000p multi 1.75 .30
Nos. 1334-1337 (4) 4.45 1.00

No. 1218 Overprinted: "LAS / MALVINAS / SON/ ARGENTINAS"

1982, Apr. 17 Photo. *Perf. 13½*
1338 A559 1700p green & blue .50 .20

Argentina's claim on Falkland Islds.

Robert Koch — A637

American Airforces Commanders' 22nd Conf. — A638

1982, Apr. 17 Litho. Wmk. 365
1339 A637 2000p multi .50 .25

TB bacillus centenary and 25th Intl. Tuberculosis Conference.

1982, Apr. 17
1340 A638 2000p multi .70 .30

Stone Carving, City Founder's Signature (Don Hernando de Lerma) A639

1982, Apr. 17
1341 A639 2000p multi .70 .30

Souvenir Sheet

1342 A639 5000p multi 2.00 2.00

City of Salta, 400th anniv. No. 1342 contains one 43x30mm stamp.

Naval Center Centenary — A640

1982, Apr. 24 *Perf. 13x13½*
1343 A640 2000p multi .70 .30

Chorisia Speciosa — A641

1982 Unwmk. Photo. *Perf. 13½*
1344 A641 200p Zinnia peruviana .20 .20
1345 A641 300p Ipomoea purpurea .20 .20
1346 A641 400p Tillandsia aeranthos .20 .20
1347 A641 500p shown .20 .20
1348 A641 800p Oncidium bifolium .20 .20
1349 A641 1000p Erythrina crista-galli .20 .20
1350 A641 2000p Jacaranda mimosi-folia .22 .20
1351 A641 3000p Bauhinia candicans .30 .20
1352 A641 5000p Tecoma stans .50 .20
1353 A641 10,000p Tabebuia ipe 1.10 .22
1354 A641 20,000p Passiflora coerulea 2.25 .35
1355 A641 30,000p Aristolochia littoralis 3.25 .50
1356 A641 50,000p Oxalis en-neaphylla 5.25 .70
Nos. 1344-1356 (13) 14.07 3.57

Nos. 1344-1346, 1348-1350 issued on fluorescent paper. Nos. 1353-1356 issued on ordinary paper. Others issued on both fluorescent and ordinary paper.
Issue dates: 500p, 2000p, 5000p, 10,000p, May 22. 200p, 300p, 1000p, 20,000p, Sept. 25. 400p, 800p, 30,000p, 50,000p, Dec. 4. 3000p, Dec. 18.
See Nos. 1429-1443A, 1515-1527, 1683-1691. For overprint see No. 1382.

10th Death Anniv. of Gen. Juan C. Sanchez A641a

1982, May 29 Litho. Wmk. 365
1364 A641a 5000p grn & blk .90 .30

Luis Venet, First Commander — A641b

1982, June 12
1365 A641b 5000p org & blk 1.10 .45

Size: 83x28mm

1366 A641b 5000p Map .75 .30
a. Pair, Nos. 1365-1366 2.00 2.00

153rd Anniv. of Malvinas Political and Military Command District.

Visit of Pope John Paul II — A641c

1982, June 12
1367 A641c 5000p multi 1.75 .55

Organ Grinder, by Aldo Severi (b. 1928) — A641d

3000p, Still Life, by Santiago Cogorno (b. 1915).

1982, July 3 Wmk. 365
1368 A641d 2000p shown .25 .20
1369 A641d 3000p multi .40 .20

Guillermo Brown Type of 1980 and:

Jose de San Martin — A641e

Litho. and Engr.
1982 Unwmk. *Perf. 13½*
1372 A591 30,000p blk & bl 3.25 .65
1376 A641e 50,000p sepia & car 6.50 .85

Issue dates: 30,000p, June; 50,000p, July.

Scouting Year A641f

Wmk. 365
1982, Aug. 7 Litho. *Perf. 13½*
1380 A641f 5000p multi 1.25 .20

Alconafta Fuel Campaign A641g

1982, Aug. 7 Wmk. 365
1381 A641g 2000p multi .30 .20

No. 1352 Overprinted: "50 ANIVERSARIO SOCIEDAD FILATELICA DE TUCUMAN"

1982, Aug. 7 Photo. Unwmk.
1382 A641 5000p multi 1.50 1.25

Rio III Central Nuclear Power Plant, Cordoba A642

Wmk. 365
1982, Sept. 4 Litho. *Perf. 13½*
1383 A642 2000p shown .30 .20
1384 A642 2000p Control room .30 .20

Namibia Day — A643

1982, Sept. 4
1385 A643 5000p Map .75 .20

Formosa Cathedral A644

Churches and Cathedrals of the Northeast: 2000p, Our Lady of Itati, Corrientes, vert. 3000p, Resistencia Cathedral, Chaco, vert. 10,000p, St. Ignatius Church ruins, Misiones.

1982, Sept. 18 Litho. & Engr.
1386 A644 2000p dk grn & blk .25 .20
1387 A644 3000p dk brn & brn .35 .20
1388 A644 5000p dk bl & brn .60 .20
1389 A644 10,000p dp org & blk 1.10 .35
Nos. 1386-1389 (4) 2.30 .95

Tension Sideral, by Mario Alberto Agatiello — A645

Sculpture (Espamer '81 and Juvenex '82 Exhibitions): 3000p, Sugerencia II, by Eduardo Mac Entyre. 5000p, Storm, by Carlos Silva.

1982, Oct. 2 Litho. *Perf. 13½*
1390 A645 2000p multi .25 .20
1391 A645 3000p multi .45 .20
1392 A645 5000p multi .60 .20
Nos. 1390-1392 (3) 1.30 .60

Sante Fe Bridge A646

1982, Oct. 16 Litho. & Engr.
1393 A646 2000p bl & blk .40 .20

2nd Southern Cross Games, Santa Fe and Rosario, Nov. 26-Dec. 5.

10th World Men's Volleyball Championship — A647

1982, Oct. 16 Litho. Wmk. 365
1394 A647 2000p multi .25 .20
1395 A647 5000p multi .50 .20

Los Andes Newspaper Centenary — A648

Design: Army of the Andes Monument, Hill of Glory, Mendoza.

1982, Oct. 30
1396 A648 5000p multi .50 .20

A649 A650

1982, Oct. 30 Wmk. 365
1397 A649 5000p Signs .55 .25

50th Anniv. of Natl. Roads, Administration.

1982, Nov. 20 Litho.

La Plata City Cent.: No. 1400: a, Cathedral, diff. b, Head, top. c, Observatory. d, City Hall, diff. e, Head, bottom. f, University.

1398 A650 5000p Cathedral .75 .20
1399 A650 5000p City Hall .75 .20
1400 Sheet of 6 2.25 1.00
a.-f. A650 2500p any single .30 .20

Well, Natl. Hydrocarbon Congress Emblem — A651

1982, Nov. 20
1401 A651 5000p multi .50 .20

Oil Discovery, Comodoro Rivadavia, 75th anniv.

Jockey Club of Buenos Aires Centenary — A652

Christmas 1982 — A653

#1403, Carlos Pellegrini, first president.

1982, Dec. 4 Litho.
1402 A652 5000p Emblem .50 .20
1403 A652 5000p multi .50 .20

1982, Dec. 18 *Perf. 13½*
1404 A653 3000p St. Vincent de Paul 1.50 .20

Size: 29x38mm

1405 A653 5000p St. Francis of Assisi 1.25 .20

Pedro B. Palacios (1854-1917), Writer — A654

Writers: 2000p, Leopoldo Marechal (1900-1970). 3000p, Delfina Bunge de Galvez (1881-1952). 4000p, Manuel Galvez (1882-1962). 5000p, Evaristo Carriego (1883-1912).

1983, Mar. 26 Litho. *Perf. 13½*
1406 A654 1000p multi .20 .20
1407 A654 2000p multi .25 .20
1408 A654 3000p multi .30 .20
1409 A654 4000p multi .40 .20
1410 A654 5000p multi .55 .20
a. Strip of 5, #1406-1410 1.75 1.00

Recovery of the Malvinas (Falkland Islands) — A655

1983, Apr. 9 Litho. *Perf. 13½*
1411 A655 20,000p Map, flag .60 .30

Telecommunications Systems — A656

1983, Apr. 16 Wmk. 365
1412 A656 5000p SITRAM .75 .20
1413 A656 5000p RED ARPAC .75 .20

Naval League Emblem — A657

1983, May 14 Litho. *Perf. 13½*
1414 A657 5000p multi .35 .20

Navy Day and 50th anniv. of Naval League.

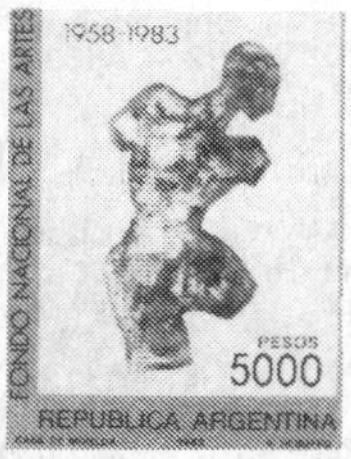

Allegory, by Victor Rebuffo — A658

1983, May 14
1415 A658 5000p multi .35 .20

Natl. Arts Fund, 25th Anniv.

75th Anniv. of Colon Opera House, Buenos Aires — A659

1983, May 28 Wmk. 365
1416 A659 5000p Main hall .70 .20
1417 A659 10000p Stage 1.00 .20

Protected Species A660

1983, July 2 Litho. *Perf. 13½*

1418	A660	1p	Chrysocyon brachtyurus	.30	.20
1419	A660	1.50p	Ozotocerus bezoarticus	.50	.20
1420	A660	2p	Myrmecophaga tridactyla	.55	.20
1421	A660	2.50p	Leo onca	.65	.20
			Nos. 1418-1421 (4)	2.00	.80

City of Catamarca, 300th Anniv. — A661

Foundation of the City of Catamarca, by Luis Varela Lezana (1900-1982).

1983, July 16 Litho. *Perf. 13½*
1422 A661 1p multi .30 .20

Mamerto Esquiu (1826-1883) A662

1983, July 16
1423 A662 1p multi .30 .20

Bolivar, by Herrera Toro — A663

Bolivar, Engraving by Kepper — A664

Perf. 13 (A663), 13½ (A664)

1983 Unwmk.

1424	A663	1p	multi	.30	.20
1425	A664	2p	black	.60	.20
1426	A664	10p	San Martin	3.00	1.50
			Nos. 1424-1426 (3)	3.90	1.90

Issue dates: 1p, 2p, July 23. 10p, Aug. 20.
See Nos. 1457-1462B.

Gen. Toribio de Luzuriaga (1782-1842) A665

1983, Aug. 20 Litho. *Perf. 13½*
1427 A665 1p multi .30 .20

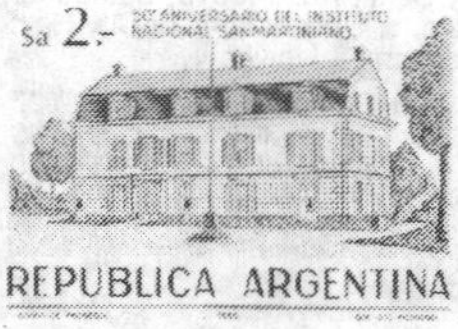

50th Anniv. of San Martin National Institute A666

1983, Aug. 20 Engr. Unwmk.
1428 A666 2p sepia .60 .20

Flower Type of 1982 in New Currency

1983-85 Photo. *Perf. 13½*

1429	A641	5c	like #1347	.20	.20
1430	A641	10c	like #1349	.20	.20
1431	A641	20c	like #1350	.20	.20
1432	A641	30c	like #1351	.20	.20
1433	A641	40c	Eichhornia crassipes	.20	.20
1434	A641	50c	like #1352	.20	.20
1435	A641	1p	like #1353	.20	.20
1435A	A641	1.80p	Mutisia retusa	.20	.20
1436	A641	2p	like #1354	.25	.20
1437	A641	3p	like #1355	.30	.20
1438	A641	5p	like #1356	.55	.20
1439	A641	10p	Alstroemeria aurantiaca	1.10	.80
1440	A641	20p	like #1345	.55	.20
1441	A641	30p	Embothrium coccineum	3.50	2.50
1442	A641	50p	like #1346	1.10	.40
1443	A641	100p	like #1348	1.60	.50
1443A	A641	300p	Cassia carnaval	.80	.25
			Nos. 1429-1443A (17)	11.35	6.85

Issue dates: 20p, Aug. 27, 1984; 50p, Oct. 19, 1984; 100p, Dec. 1984; 300p, June 15, 1985.

Nos. 1429, 1433, 1435A issued on fluorescent paper. Nos. 1443, 1443A issued on ordinary paper. Others issued on both ordinary and fluorescent paper.

For overprint and surcharge see #1489, 1530.

Intl. Rotary South American Regional Conference, Buenos Aires, Sept. 25-28 — A667

1983, Sept. 24 Litho.
1444 A667 1p multi .55 .25

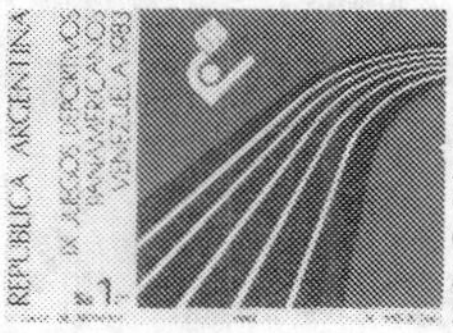

9th Pan American Games, Caracas, Aug. 13-28 A668

1983, Sept. 24
1445 A668 1p Track .30 .20
1446 A668 2p Emblem .65 .30

World Communications Year — A669

1983, Oct. 8 *Perf. 13½*
1447 A669 2p multi .60 .25

Squash Peddler by Antonio Berni (1905-1981) A670

2p, Figure in Yellow by Luis Seoane (1910-79).

1983, Oct. 15 *Perf. 13½*
1448 A670 1p multi .30 .20
1449 A670 2p multi .50 .25

World Communications Year — A671

Designs: 1p, Wagon, 18th cent. 2p, Post chaise, 19th cent. 4p, Steam locomotive, 1857. 5p, Tramway, 1910.

1983, Nov. 19 Litho. *Perf. 13½*

1450	A671	1p	multi	.20	.20
1451	A671	2p	multi	.25	.20
1452	A671	4p	multi	.50	.20
1453	A671	5p	multi	.65	.25
			Nos. 1450-1453 (4)	1.60	.85

A672 A673

1983, Nov. 26 Litho. *Perf. 12½x12*
1454 A672 2p General Post Office .40 .20

World Communications Year.

1983, Dec. 10 Photo. *Perf. 13½*
1455 A673 2p Coin, 1813 .30 .20

Return to elected government.

Eudyptes Crestatus A674

Designs: b, Diomedea exulans. c, Diomedea melanophris. d, Eudyptes chrysolophus. e, Luis Piedra Buena. f, Carlos Maria Moyano. g, Luis Py. h, Augusto Lasserre. i, Phoebetria palpebrata. j, Hydrurga leptonyx. k, Lobodon carcinophagus. l, Leptonychotes weddelli.

1983, Dec. 10 Litho.
1456 Sheet of 12 4.50 2.25
a.-l. A674 2p any single .35 .20

Southern pioneers and fauna. Margin depicts various airplanes and emblems.

Bolivar Type of 1983

Famous men: 10p, Angel J. Carranza (1834-99), historian. No. 1458, 500p, Guillermo Brown. No. 1459, Estanislao del Campo (1834-80), poet. 30p, Jose Hernandez (1834-86), author. 40p, Vicente Lopez y Planes (1784-1856), poet and patriot. 50p, San Martin. 200p, Belgrano.

1983-85 Litho. & Engr. *Perf. 13½*

1457	A664	10p	pale bl & dk bl	.20	.20
1458	A664	20p	dk bl & blk	2.75	1.40
1459	A664	20p	dl brn ol & ol blk	.20	.20
1460	A664	30p	pale bl & bluish blk	.20	.20
1461	A664	40p	lt bl grn & blk	.20	.20
1462	A664	50p	Prus & choc	1.10	.25
1462A	A664	200p	int bl & blk	3.00	.95
1462B	A664	500p	brn & int bl	1.50	.30
			Nos. 1457-1462B (8)	9.15	3.70

Issue dates: #1458, Oct. 6, 1983. 10p, #1459, 30p, 40p, Mar. 23, 1985. 50p, Apr. 23, 1985. 200p, Nov. 2, 1985. 500p, May 2, 1985.

Christmas 1983 A675

Nativity Scenes: 2p, Tapestry, by Silke. 3p, Stained-glass window, San Carlos de Bariloche's Wayn Church, vert.

1983, Dec. 17 Litho. *Perf. 13½*
1463 A675 2p multi .30 .20
1464 A675 3p multi .55 .30

Centenary of El Dia Newspaper A676

1984, Mar. 24 **Litho.**

1465 A676 4p Masthead, printing roll .40 .20

Alejandro Carbo Teachers' College Centenary — A677

1984, June 2 **Litho.** ***Perf. 13½***

1466 A677 10p Building .40 .25

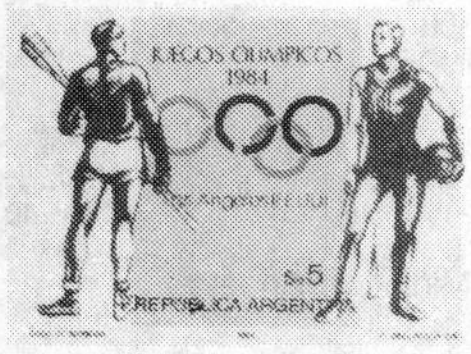

1984 Olympics A678

#1468, Weightlifting, discus, shot put. #1469, Javelin, fencing. #1470, Bicycling, swimming.

1984, July 28 **Litho.** ***Perf. 13½***

1467 A678 5p shown .25 .20
1468 A678 5p multicolored .25 .20
1469 A678 10p multicolored .45 .25
1470 A678 10p multicolored .45 .25
Nos. 1467-1470 (4) 1.40 .90

Rosario Stock Exchange Centenary A679

1984, Aug. 11

1471 A679 10p multicolored .45 .25

Wheat A680

1984, Aug. 11

1472 A680 10p shown .50 .25
1473 A680 10p Corn .50 .25
1474 A680 10p Sunflower .50 .25
Nos. 1472-1474 (3) 1.50 .75

18th FAO Regional Conference for Latin America and Caribbean (No. 1472); 3rd Natl. Corn Congress (No. 1473); World Food Day (No. 1474).

Wildlife Protection A681

1984, Sept. 22 **Litho.** ***Perf. 13½***

1475 A681 20p Hippocamelus bisulcus .40 .20
1476 A681 20p Vicugna vicugna .40 .20
1477 A681 20p Aburria jacutinga .40 .20
1478 A681 20p Mergus octosetaceus .40 .20
1479 A681 20p Podiceps gallardoi .40 .20
Nos. 1475-1479 (5) 2.00 1.00

First Latin American Theater Festival, Cordoba, Oct. — A682

1984, Oct. 13 **Litho.** ***Perf. 13½***

1480 A682 20p Mask .25 .20

Intl. Eucharistic Congress, 50th Anniv. A683

Design: Apostles' Communion, by Fra Angelico.

1984, Oct. 13

1481 A683 20p multicolored .30 .20

Glaciares Natl. Park (UNESCO World Heritage List) A684

1984, Nov. 17 **Litho.**

1482 A684 20p Sea .25 .20
1483 A684 30p Glacier .40 .20

City of Puerto Deseado Centenary A685

1984, Nov. 17 ***Perf. 13½***

1484 A685 20p shown .30 .20
1485 A685 20p Ushuaia centenary .30 .20

Childrens' Paintings, Christmas 1984 A686

1984, Dec. 1 **Litho.** ***Perf. 13½***

1486 A686 20p Diego Aguero .30 .20
1487 A686 30p Leandro Ruiz .60 .20
1488 A686 50p Maria Castillo, vert. .60 .20
Nos. 1486-1488 (3) 1.50 .60

No. 1439 Overprinted

1984, Dec. 1 **Photo.** ***Perf. 13½***

1489 A641 10p multicolored .25 .25

Buenos Aires Philatelic Center, 50th anniv.

Vista Del Jardin Zoologico, by Fermin Eguia — A687

Paintings: No. 1491, El Congreso Iluminado, by Francisco Travieso. No. 1492, Galpones (La Boca), by Marcos Borio.

1984, Dec. 15 ***Perf. 13½***

1490 A687 20p multi .30 .20
1491 A687 20p multi, vert. .30 .20
1492 A687 20p multi, vert. .30 .20
Nos. 1490-1492 (3) .90 .60

Gen. Martin Miguel de Guemes (1785-1821) — A688

1985, Mar. 23 **Litho.** ***Perf. 13½***

1493 A688 30p multicolored .25 .20

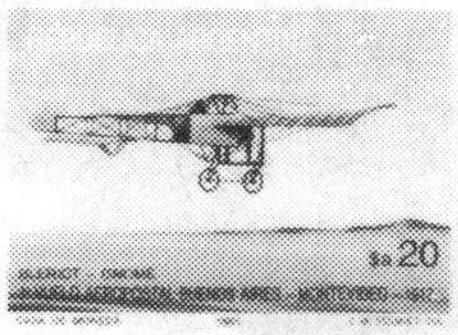

ARGENTINA '85 Exhibition — A689

First airmail service from: 20p, Buenos Aires to Montevideo, 1917. 40p, Cordoba to Villa Dolores, 1925. 60p, Bahia Blanca to Comodoro Rivadavia, 1929. 80p, Argentina to Germany, 1934. 100p, naval service to the Antarctic, 1952.

1985, Apr. 27

1494 A689 20p Bleriot Gnome .20 .20
1495 A689 40p Junker F-13L .30 .20
1496 A689 60p Latte 25 .50 .20
1497 A689 80p L.Z. 127 Graf Zeppelin .65 .30
1498 A689 100p Consolidated PBY Catalina .85 .40
Nos. 1494-1498 (5) 2.50 1.30

Central Bank, 50th Anniv. A690

1985, June 1

1499 A690 80p Bank Bldg., Buenos Aires .55 .20

Jose A. Ferreyra (1889-1943), Director of Munequitas Portenas — A691

Famous directors and their films: No. 1501, Leopoldo Torre Nilsson (1924-1978), scene from Martin Fierro.

1985, June 1

1500 A691 100p shown .60 .20
1501 A691 100p multi .60 .20

Carlos Gardel (1890-1935), Entertainer A692

Paintings: No. 1502, Gardel playing the guitar on stage, by Carlos Alonso (b. 1929). No. 1503, Gardel in a wide-brimmed hat, by Hermegildo Sabat (b. 1933). No. 1504, Portrait of Gardel in an ornamental frame, by Aldo Severi (b. 1928) and Martiniano Arce (b. 1939).

1985, June 15

1502 A692 200p multi .95 .45
1503 A692 200p multi .95 .45
1504 A692 200p multi .95 .45
Nos. 1502-1504 (3) 2.85 1.35

The Arrival, by Pedro Figari A693

A Halt on the Plains, by Prilidiano Pueyrredon — A693a

Oil paintings (details): 30c, The Wagon Square, by C. B. de Quiros. Ilustration A693a is reduced.

1985, July 6 **Litho.** ***Perf. 13½***

1505 A693 20c multi 1.00 .25
1506 A693 30c multi 1.25 .25

Souvenir Sheet

Perf. 12

1507 A693a Sheet of 2 2.50 2.50
a. 20c Pilgrims, vert. .30 .30
b. 30c Wagon .40 .40

ARGENTINA '85. No. 1507 contains 2 30x40mm stamps. See No. 1542.

Buenos Aires to Montevideo, 1917 Teodoro Fels Flight A694

Historic flight covers: #1509, Villa Dolores to Cordoba, 1925. #1510, Buenos Aires to France, 1929 St. Exupery flight. #1511, Buenos Aires to Bremerhaven, 1934 Graf Zeppelin flight. #1512, First Antarctic flight, 1952.

1985, July 13 ***Perf. 12x12½***

1508 A694 10c emer & multi .40 .20
1509 A694 10c ultra & multi .40 .20
1510 A694 10c lt choc & multi .40 .20
1511 A694 10c chnt & multi .40 .20
1512 A694 10c ap grn & multi .40 .20
Nos. 1508-1512 (5) 2.00 1.00

ARGENTINA '85.

Illuminated Fruit, by Fortunato Lacamera (1887-1951) — A695

Paintings: 20c, Woman with Bird, by Juan del Prete, vert.

1985, Sept. 7 ***Perf. 13½***

1513	A695	20c multi	.85	.30
1514	A695	30c multi	1.00	.30

Flower Types of 1982-85

Designs: 1a, Begonia micranthera var. hieronymi. 5a, Gymnocalycium bruchii.

1985-88 Photo. ***Perf. 13½***

1515	A641	½c like #1356	.20	.20
1516	A641	1c like #1439	.20	.20
1517	A641	2c like #1345	.20	.20
1518	A641	3c like #1441	.20	.20
1519	A641	5c like #1346	.25	.20
1520	A641	10c like #1348	.35	.20
1521	A641	20c like #1347	.70	.20
1522	A641	30c like #1443A	1.10	.25
1523	A641	50c like #1344	1.75	.35
1524	A641	1a multi	3.50	.65
1525	A641	2a like #1351	.40	.20
1526	A641	5a multi	6.75	3.00

Size: 15x23mm

1527	A641	8½c like #1349	.30	.20
		Nos. 1515-1527 (13)	15.90	6.05

Issue dates: ½c, 1c, Dec. 16. 2c, 8½c, 30c, Sept. 18. 3c, 5c, 10c, 50c, 1a, Sept. 7. 20c, Oct. 17. 5a, Mar. 21, 1987. 2a, Dec. 5, 1988.

No. 1435 Surcharged

1986, Nov. 4 Photo. ***Perf. 13½***

1530	A641	10c on 1p No. 1435	.20	.20

Folk Musical Instruments A699

1985, Sept. 14 Litho. ***Perf. 13½***

1531	A699	20c Frame drum	.55	.25
1532	A699	20c Long flute	.55	.25
1533	A699	20c Jew's harp	.55	.25
1534	A699	20c Pan flutes	.55	.25
1535	A699	20c Musical bow	.55	.25
		Nos. 1531-1535 (5)	2.75	1.25

Juan Bautista Alberdi (1810-1884), Historian, Politician A700

Famous men: Nicolas Avellaneda (1836-1885), President in 1874. 30c, Fr. Luis Beltran (1784-1827), military and naval engineer. 40c, Ricardo Levene (1885-1959), historian, author.

1985, Oct. 5

1536	A700	10c multi	.25	.20
1537	A700	20c multi	.45	.25
1538	A700	30c multi	.65	.30
1539	A700	40c multi	1.10	.45
		Nos. 1536-1539 (4)	2.45	1.20

Type of 1985 and

Skaters A701

Deception, by J. H. Rivoira — A702

1985, Oct. 19 Litho. ***Perf. 13½***

1540	A701	20c multi	.35	.30
1541	A702	30c multi	.50	.50

Size: 147x75mm

Imperf

1542	A693a	1a multi	1.90

IYY. No. 1542 is inscribed in silver with the UN 40th anniversary and IYY emblems.

Provincial Views — A703

Designs: No. 1543, Rock Window, Buenos Aires. No. 1544, Forclaz Windmill, Entre Rios. No. 1545, Lake Potrero de los Funes, San Luis. No. 1546, Mission church, north-east province. No. 1547, Penguin colony, Punta Tombo, Chubut. No. 1548, Water Mirrors, Cordoba.

1985, Nov. 23 ***Perf. 13½***

1543	A703	10c multi	.25	.25
1544	A703	10c multi	.25	.25
1545	A703	10c multi	.25	.25
1546	A703	10c multi	.25	.25
1547	A703	10c multi	.25	.25
1548	A703	10c multi	.25	.25
		Nos. 1543-1548 (6)	1.50	1.50

Christmas 1985 — A704

Designs: 10c, Birth of Our Lord, by Carlos Cortes. 20c, Christmas, by Hector Viola.

1985, Dec. 7

1549	A704	10c multi	.25	.20
1550	A704	20c multi	.50	.45

Natl. Campaign for the Prevention of Blindness — A705

1985, Dec. 7

1551	A705	10c multi	.25	.20

Rio Gallegos City, Cent. — A716

1985, Dec. 21 Litho. ***Perf. 13½***

1552	A716	10c Church	.25	.20

Natl. Grape Harvest Festival, 50th Anniv. A717

1986, Mar. 15

1553	A717	10c multi	.25	.20

Historical Architecture in Buenos Aires — A718

Designs: No. 1554, Valentin Alsina House, Italian Period, 1860-70. No. 1555, House on Cerrito Street, French influence, 1880-1900. No. 1556, House on the Avenida de Mayo y Santiago del Estero, Art Nouveau, 1900-10. No. 1557, Customs Building, academic architecture, 1900-15. No. 1558, Isaac Fernandez Blanco Museum, house of architect Martin Noel, natl. restoration, 1910-30. Nos. 1554-1556 vert.

1986, Apr. 19

1554	A718	20c multi	.40	.30
1555	A718	20c multi	.40	.30
1556	A718	20c multi	.40	.30
1557	A718	20c multi	.40	.30
1558	A718	20c multi	.40	.30
		Nos. 1554-1558 (5)	2.00	1.50

Antarctic Bases, Pioneers and Fauna — A719

Designs: a, Base, Jubany. b, Arctocephalus gazella. c, Otaria byronia. d, Gen. Belgrano Base. e, Daption capensis. f, Diomedia melanophris. g, Apterodytes patagonica. h, Macronectes giganteus. i, Hugo Alberto Acuna (1885-1953). j, Spheniscus magellanicus. k, Gallinago gallinage. l, Capt. Agustin del Castillo (1855-89).

1986, May 31

1559		Sheet of 12	9.00	9.00
a.-l.		A719 10c any single	.75	.75

Famous People — A720

Statuary, Buenos Aires — A721

#1560, Dr. Alicia Moreau de Justo, human rights activist. #1561, Dr. Emilio Ravignani (1886-1954), historian. #1562, Indira Gandhi.

1986, July 5 Litho. ***Perf. 13½***

1560	A720	10c multi	.40	.25
1561	A720	10c multi	.40	.25
1562	A720	30c multi	1.25	.65
		Nos. 1560-1562 (3)	2.05	1.15

1986, July 5

Designs: 20c, Fountain of the Nereids, by Dolores Lola Mora (1866-1936). 30c, Lamenting at Work, by Rogelio Yrurtia (1879-1950), horiz.

1563	A721	20c multi	.50	.45
1564	A721	30c multi	.80	.65

Famous Men — A722

Designs: No. 1565, Francisco N. Laprida (1786-1829), politician. No. 1566, Estanislao Lopez (1786-1838), brigadier general. No. 1567, Francisco Ramirez (1786-1821), general.

1986, Aug. 9 Litho. ***Perf. 13***

1565	A722	20c dl yel, brn & blk	.40	.40
1566	A722	20c dl yel, brn & blk	.40	.40
1567	A722	20c dl yel, brn & blk	.40	.40
		Nos. 1565-1567 (3)	1.20	1.20

Fr. Ceferino Namuncura (1886-1905) A723

1986, Aug. 30 ***Perf. 13½***

1568	A723	20c multi	.60	.40

Miniature Sheets

Natl. Team Victory, 1986 World Cup Soccer Championships, Mexico — A724

Designs: No. 1569a-1569d, Team. Nos. 1569e-1569h, Shot on goal. Nos. 1570a-1570d, Action close-up. Nos. 1570e-1570h, Diego Maradona holding soccer cup.

1986, Nov. 8 Litho. ***Perf. 13½***

1569	A724	Sheet of 8	9.25	12.00
a.-h.		75c any single	1.15	1.50
1570	A724	Sheet of 8	9.25	12.00
a.-h.		75c any single	1.15	1.50

San Francisco (Cordoba), Cent. — A725

1986, Nov. 8

1571	A725	20c Municipal Building	.50	.45

Trelew City (Chubut), Cent. A726

1986, Nov. 22 Litho. ***Perf. 13½***

1572	A726	20c Old railroad station, 1865	.50	.45

Mutualism Day — A727

1986, Nov. 22
1573 A727 20c multi .60 .45

Christmas — A728

Designs: 20c, Naif retable, by Aniko Szabo (b. 1945). 30c, Everyone's Tree, by Franca Delacqua (b. 1947).

1986, Dec. 13 Litho. *Perf. 13½*
1574 A728 20c multicolored .50 .35
1575 A728 30c multicolored .60 .35

Santa Rosa de Lima, 400th Birth Anniv. — A729

Rio Cuarto Municipal Building — A730

1986, Dec. 13
1576 A729 50c multicolored 1.75 .75

1986, Dec. 20
1577 A730 20c shown .40 .25
1578 A730 20c Court Building, Cordoba .40 .25

Rio Cuarto City, bicent. Court Building, Cordoba, 50th anniv.

Antarctic Treaty, 25th Anniv. — A731

1987, Mar. 7 Litho. *Perf. 13½*
1579 A731 20c Marine biologist .35 .20
1580 A731 30c Ornithologist .60 .25

Souvenir Sheet
Perf. 12

1581 Sheet of 2 1.00 .50
a. A731 20c like No. 1579 .40 .20
b. A731 30c like No. 1580 .55 .25

No. 1581 contains 2 stamps, size: 40x50mm.

Natl. Mortgage Bank, Cent. A732

1987, Mar. 21 *Perf. 13½*
1582 A732 20c multicolored .65 .45

Natl. Cooperative Associations Movement — A733

1987, Mar. 21
1583 A733 20c multicolored .65 .45

Second State Visit of Pope John Paul II — A734

Engr., Litho. (No. 1585)
1987, Apr. 4 *Perf. 13½*
1584 A734 20c shown .35 .25
1585 A734 80c Papal blessing 1.40 .70

Souvenir Sheet
Perf. 12

1586 A734 1a like 20c 2.25 2.25

No. 1586 contains one 40x50mm stamp.

Intl. Peace Year A735

30c, Pigeon, abstract sculpture by Victor Kaniuka.

1987, Apr. 11 Litho.
1587 A735 20c multicolored .35 .20
1588 A735 30c multicolored .55 .35

Low Handicap World Polo Championships A736

Design: Polo Players, painting by Alejandro Moy.

1987, Apr. 11
1589 A736 20c multicolored .75 .20

Miniature Sheet

ICOM '86 — A737

Designs: a, Emblem. b, Family crest, National History Museum, Buenos Aires. c, St. Bartholomew, Enrique Larreta Museum of Spanish Art, Buenos Aires. d, Zoomorphic club, Patagonian Museum, San Carlos de Bariloche. e, Supplication, anthropomorphic sculpture, Natural Sciences Museum, La Plata. f, Wrought iron lattice from the house of J. Urquiza, president of the Confederation of Argentina, Entre Rios History Museum, Parana. g, St. Joseph, 18th cent. wood figurine, Northern History Museum, Salta. h, Funerary urn, Provincial Archaeological Museum, Santiago del Estero.

1987, May 30
1590 Sheet of 8 3.50 3.50
a.-h. A737 25c any single .40 .30

Intl. Council of Museums, 14th general conf.

Natl. College of Monserrat, Cordoba, 300th Anniv. — A738

1987, July 4 *Imperf.*
1591 A738 1a multicolored 1.40 1.40

Monserrat '87 Philatelic Exposition.

Fight Drug Abuse A739

Design: The Proportions of Man, by da Vinci.

1987, Aug. 15 *Perf. 13½*
1592 A739 30c multicolored .45 .20

Famous Men A740

Portraits and quotations: 20c, Jorge Luis Borges (1899-1986), writer. 30c, Armando Discepolo (1887-1971), playwright. 50c, Carlos A. Pueyrredon (1887-1962), professor, Legion of Honor laureate.

1987, Aug. 15
1593 A740 20c multicolored .30 .20
1594 A740 30c multicolored .50 .25
1595 A740 50c multicolored .75 .35
Nos. 1593-1595 (3) 1.55 .80

Pillar Boxes
A741 A742

1987 Photo. *Perf. 13½*
1596 A741 (30c) yel, blk & dark red .80 .30
1597 A742 (33c) lt blue grn, blk & yel .85 .35

Issue dates: (30c), June 8; (33c), July 13.

The Sower, by Julio Vanzo A743

1987, Sept. 12
1598 A743 30c multicolored .35 .20

Argentine Agrarian Federation, 75th anniv.

10th Pan American Games, Indianapolis, Aug. 7-25 — A744

1987, Sept. 26
1599 A744 20c Basketball .25 .20
1600 A744 30c Rowing .35 .20
1601 A744 50c Yachting .55 .20
Nos. 1599-1601 (3) 1.15 .60

Children Playing Doctor, WHO Emblem A745

1987, Oct. 7
1602 A745 30c multi .35

Vaccinate every child campaign.

Heroes of the Revolution A746

Signing of the San Nicolas Accord, 1852, by Rafael del Villar A747

Independence anniversaries and historic events: No. 1603, Maj.-Col. Ignacio Alvarez Thomas (1787-1857). No. 1604, Col. Manuel Crispulo Bernabe Dorrego (1787-1829). No. 1606, 18th cent. Spanish map of the Falkland Isls., administered by Jacinto de Altolaguirre.

1987, Oct. 17
1603 A746 25c shown .30 .20
1604 A746 25c multi .30 .20
1605 A747 50c shown .55 .30
1606 A747 50c multi .55 .30
Nos. 1603-1606 (4) 1.70 1.00

Museum established in the House of the San Nicholas Accord, 50th anniv. (#1605); Jacinto de Altolaguirre (1754-1787), governor the Malvinas Isls. for the King of Spain (#1606).

Celedonio Galvan Moreno, 1st Director
A748

1987, Nov. 21

1607 A748 50c multicolored .55 .40

Postas Argentinas magazine, 50th anniv.

LRA National Radio, Buenos Aires, 50th Anniv. — A749

1987, Nov. 21

1608 A749 50c multicolored .55 .40

Natl. Philatelic Society, Cent.
A750

1987, Nov. 21

1609 A750 1a Jose Marco del Pont 1.10 .55

Christmas
A751

Tapestries: 50c, *Navidad*, by Alisia Frega. 1a, *Vitral*, by Silvina Trigos.

1987, Dec. 5

1610 A751 50c multicolored .55 .20
1611 A751 1a multicolored 1.10 .55

Natl. Parks — A752

1987, Dec. 19 ***Perf. 13x13½***

1612 A752 50c Baritu .55 .35
1613 A752 50c Nahuel Huapi .55 .35
1614 A752 50c Rio Pilcomayo .55 .35
1615 A752 50c Tierra del Fuego .55 .35
1616 A752 50c Iguacu .55 .35
Nos. 1612-1616 (5) 2.75 1.75

See Nos. 1647-1651, 1715-1719, 1742-1746.

Landscapes in Buenos Aires Painted by Jose Cannella — A753

1988-89 **Litho.** ***Perf. 13½***

1617 A753 5a Caminito 2.00 1.10
1618 A753 10a Viejo Almacen 4.00 2.25
1618A A753 10a like No. 1618 1.10 .50
1618B A753 50a like No. 1617 1.10 .50
c. Wmk 365 *125.00*
Nos. 1617-1618B (4) 8.20 4.35

No. 1618 inscribed "Viejo Almacen"; No. 1618A inscribed "El Viejo Almacen."

Issue dates: 5a, #1618, 3/15; #1618A, 10/20; 50a, 5/30/89.

For overprint see No. 1635.

Minstrel in a Tavern, by Carlos Morel
A754

Paintings: No. 1620, Interior of Curuzu, by Candido Lopez.

1988, Mar. 19 **Litho.** ***Perf. 13½***

1619 A754 1a shown .60 .30
1620 A754 1a multicolored .60 .30

See Nos. 1640-1641.

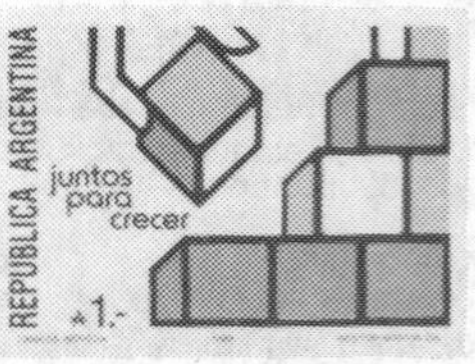

Argentine-Brazilian Economic Cooperation and Integration Program for Mutual Growth — A755

1988, Mar. 19

1621 A755 1a multicolored .50 .25

Cities of Alta Gracia and Corrientes, 400th Annivs.
A756

1988, Apr. 9 **Litho.** ***Perf. 13½***

1622 A756 1a Alta Gracia Church .75 .40
1623 A756 1a Chapel of St. Anne, Corrientes .75 .40

Labor Day — A757

Grain Carriers, a tile mosaic by Alfredo Guido, Line D of Nueve de Julio station, Buenos Aires subway: a, (UL). b, (UR). c, (LL). d, (LR).

1988, May 21

1624 A757 Block of 4 2.00 2.00
a.-d. 50c any single .50 .50

1988 Summer Olympics, Seoul — A758

1988, July 16 **Litho.** ***Perf. 13½***

1625 A758 1a Running .30 .20
1626 A758 2a Soccer .75 .30
1627 A758 3a Field hockey 1.10 .50
1628 A758 4a Tennis 1.40 .65
Nos. 1625-1628 (4) 3.55 1.65

Mendoza Bank, Cent.
A759

Natl. Gendarmerie, Cent. — A760

1988, Aug. 13

1629 A759 2a multicolored .65 .45
1630 A760 2a multicolored .65 .45

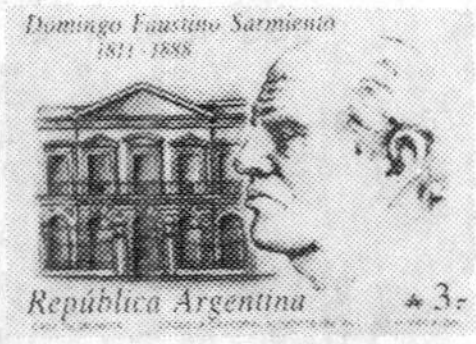

Sarmiento and Cathedral School to the North, Buenos Aires
A761

1988, Sept. 10 **Litho.** ***Perf. 13½***

1631 A761 3a multicolored .65 .45

Domingo Faustino Sarmiento (1811-1888), educator, politician.

St. Cayetano, Patron of Workers — A762

El Amor, by Antonio Berni, Pacific Gallery, Buenos Aires — A763

1988, Sept. 10 **Litho.**

1632 A762 2a multicolored .45 .45
1633 A762 3a Our Lady of Carmen, Cuyo .70 .70

Souvenir Sheet

Perf. 12

1634 A763 5a multicolored 1.00 1.00

Liniers Philatelic Circle and the Argentine Western Philatelic Institution (IFADO), 50th annivs.

No. 1634 contains one 40x30mm stamp.

No. 1617 Ovptd. with Congress Emblem and:
"XXI CONGRESO
DE LA SOCIEDAD
INTERNACIONAL
DE UROLOGIA"

1988, Oct. 29 **Litho.** ***Perf. 13½***

1635 A753 5a multicolored *3.50* .40

21st Congress of the Intl. Urology Soc.

Tourism
A763a

1988, Nov. 1 **Litho.** ***Perf. 13½***

1635A A763a 3a Purmamarca, Jujuy .50 .25

Size: 28½x38mm

1635B A763a 20a Ushuaia 3.35 1.60

Buenos Aires Subway, 75th Anniv.
A764

1988, Dec. 17 **Litho.** ***Perf. 13½***

1636 A764 5a Train, c. 1913 1.10 .55

Christmas
A765

Frescoes in Ucrania Cathedral, Buenos Aires: No. 1637, *Virgin Patron.* No. 1638, *Virgin of Tenderness.*

1988, Dec. 17

1637 A765 5a multicolored 1.25 .50
1638 A765 5a multicolored 1.25 .50

St. John Bosco (1815-1888), Educator, and Church in Ushuaia — A766

1989, Apr. 8 **Litho.** ***Perf. 13½***

1639 A766 5a multicolored .30 .20

Dated 1988.

Art Type of 1988

Paintings: No. 1640, *Blancos*, by Fernando Fader (1882-1935). No. 1641, *Rincon de los Areneros*, by Justo Lynch (1870-1953).

1989, Apr. 8

1640 A754 5a multicolored .50 .20
1641 A754 5a multicolored .50 .20

Holy Week
A767

Sculpture and churches: No. 1642, *The Crown of Thorns,* Calvary of Tandil, and Church of Our Lady Carmelite, Tandil. No. 1643, *Jesus the Nazarene* and Metropolitan Cathedral, Buenos Aires. No. 1644, *Jesus Encounters His Mother* (scene of the crucifixion), La Quebrada Village, San Luis. No. 1645, *Our Lady of Sorrow* and Church of Humahuaca, Jujuy.

1989, Apr. 22 Litho. *Perf. 13½*

1642 A767 2a multicolored	.20	.20
1643 A767 2a multicolored	.20	.20
1644 A767 3a multicolored	.30	.20
1645 A767 3a multicolored	.30	.20
Nos. 1642-1645 (4)	1.00	.80

Printed in sheets of 16+4 labels containing blocks of 4 of each design. Labels picture Jesus's arrival in Jerusalem (Palm Sunday).

Prevent Alcoholism — A768

1989, Apr. 22

1646 A768 5a multicolored .30 .20

Natl. Park Type of 1987

1989, May 6 *Perf. 13x13½*

1647 A752 5a Lihue Calel	.70	.20
1648 A752 5a El Palmar	.70	.20
1649 A752 5a Calilegua	.70	.20
1650 A752 5a Chaco	.70	.20
1651 A752 5a Los Glaciares	.70	.20
Nos. 1647-1651 (5)	3.50	1.00

Admission of Argentina to the ITU, Cent. A769

1989, May 6 *Perf. 13½*

1652 A769 10a multicolored .45 .20

World Model Aircraft Championships — A770

1989, May 27 Litho. *Perf. 13½*

1653 A770 5a F1A glider	.20	.20
1654 A770 5a F1B rubber band motor	.20	.20
1655 A770 10a F1C gas motor	.35	.20
Nos. 1653-1655 (3)	.75	.60

French Revolution, Bicent. — A771

Designs: 10a, "All men are born free and equal." 15a, French flag and *La Marianne*, by Gandon. 25a, *Liberty Guiding the People*, by Delacroix.

1989, July 1 Litho. *Perf. 13½*

1656 A771 10a shown	.20	.20
1657 A771 15a multicolored	.20	.20

Souvenir Sheet

Perf. 12

1658 A771 25a multicolored .25 .20

No. 1658 contains one 40x30mm stamp.

The Republic, a Bronze Bust in the Congreso de la Nacion, Buenos Aires — A772

1989, Aug. 12 Litho. *Perf. 13½*

1659 A772 300a on 50a multi .75 .50

Peaceful transition of power (presidential office). Not issued without surcharge.

Immigration to Argentina — A773

1989, Aug. 19 *Perf. 13½*

1660 A773 150a S.S. *Weser,* 1889	.65	.35
1661 A773 200a Immigrant hotel, 1889	.75	.45

Souvenir Sheet

Perf. 12

1662 Sheet of 2	1.60	1.60
a. A773 150a like No. 1660	.65	.35
b. A773 200a like No. 1661	.75	.45

No. 1662 contains 40c30mm stamps.

Famous Men A774

Designs: No. 1663, Fr. Guillermo Furlong (1889-1974), historian, and title page of *The Jesuits.* No. 1664, Dr. Gregorio Alvarez (1889-1986), physician, and title page of *Canto a Chos Malal.* 200a, Brig.-Gen. Enrique Martinez (1789-1870) and lithograph *La Batalla de Maipu,* by Teodoro Gericault.

1989, Oct. 7 Litho. *Perf. 13½*

1663 A774 150a multicolored	.35	.20
1664 A774 150a multicolored	.35	.20
1665 A774 200a multicolored	.35	.20
Nos. 1663-1665 (3)	1.05	.60

America Issue — A775

Emblem of the Postal Union of the Americas and Spain (PUAS) and pre-Columbian art from Catamarca Province: 200a, Wooden mask from Atajo, Loma Morada. 300a, Urn of the Santa Maria Culture (Phase 3) from Punta de Balastro, Santa Maria Department.

1989, Oct. 14

1666 A775 200a multicolored	.50	.35
1667 A775 300a multicolored	.75	.50

Federal Police Week — A776

Children's drawings: No. 1668, Diego Molinari, age 13. No. 1669, Carlos Alberto Sarago, age 8. No. 1670, Roxana Andrea Osuna, age 7. No. 1671, Pablo Javier Quaglia, age 9.

1989, Oct. 28 Litho. *Perf. 13½*

1668 A776 100a multi	.25	.20
1669 A776 100a multi	.25	.20
1670 A776 150a multi	.40	.20
1671 A776 150a multi	.40	.20
Nos. 1668-1671 (4)	1.30	.80

Battle of Vuelta de Obligado, 1845 — A777

(Illustration reduced.)

1989, Dec. 2 Litho. *Perf. 13x13½*

1672 A777 300a multicolored .40 .20

Paintings A778

Cristo de los Cerros, Sculpture by Chipo Cespedes A779

1989, Dec. 2 *Perf. 13½*

1673 A778 200a Gato Frias	.35	.20
1674 A778 200a Maria Carballido	.35	.20
1675 A779 300a shown	.35	.20
Nos. 1673-1675 (3)	1.05	.60

Christmas.

Buenos Aires Port, Cent. — A780

(Illustration reduced.)

1990, Mar. 3 Litho. *Perf. 13½*

1676 A780 Strip of 4	7.50	2.50
a.-d. 200a any single	1.25	.65

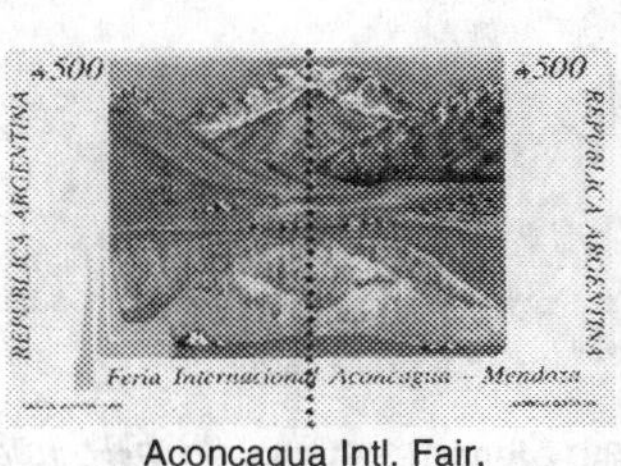

Aconcagua Intl. Fair, Mendoza — A781

Design: Aconcagua mountain, Los Horcones Lagoon and fair emblem.

(Illustration reduced.)

1990, Mar. 3

1677 A781 Pair	2.00	1.00
a.-b. 500a any single	1.00	.50

Natl. Savings and Insurance Fund, 75th Anniv. A782

1990, May 5 Litho. *Perf. 13½*

1678 A782 1000a multicolored .35 .20

Miniature Sheet

1990 World Cup Soccer Championships, Italy — A783

Designs: a, Athlete's torso (striped jersey). b, Athlete's torso (solid jersey). c, Players' feet, soccer ball. d, Player (knee to waist).

1990, May 5

1679 Sheet of 4	5.00	5.00
a.-d. A783 2500a multicolored	1.00	1.00

Carlos Pellegrini, Commercial High School Founder, Cent. — A784

1990, June 2 Litho. *Perf. 13½*

1680 A784 2000a multicolored .30 .20

Youth Against Drugs A785

1990, June 2

1681 A785 2000a multicolored .30 .20

Intl. Literacy Year A786

1990, July 14 Litho. *Perf. 13½*

1682 A786 2000a multicolored .30 .20

Flower Type of 1982 in New Currency

1989-90 Photo. *Perf. 13½*

1683 A641 10a like #1433 .20 .20
1684 A641 20a like #1435A .20 .20
1685 A641 50a like #1354 .20 .20
1686 A641 100a like #1439 .20 .20
1687 A641 300a like #1345 .40 .20
1688 A641 500a like #1441 .65 .35
1689 A641 1000a like #1355 .20 .20
1690 A641 5000a like #1349 1.00 .70
1691 A641 10,000a like #1350 1.50 1.00
Nos. 1683-1691 (9) 4.55 3.25

Issued: 20a, 100a, 300a, 500a, 8/1/89; 10a, 8/24/89; 50a, 8/30/89; 1000, 3/8/90; 5000a, 4/6/90; 10,000a, 7/2/90.

World Basketball Championships A787

1990, Aug. 11 Litho. *Perf. 13½*

1703 A787 2000a multicolored 2.00 1.50

Souvenir Sheet

Perf. 12

1704 A787 5000a Jump ball 3.75 2.75

Postal Union of the Americas and Spain, 14th Congress A788

1990, Sept. 15 Litho. *Perf. 13½*

1705 A788 3000a Arms, seal 1.50 .75
1706 A788 3000a Sailing ships 1.50 .75
1707 A788 3000a Modern freighter 1.50 .75
1708 A788 3000a Van, cargo plane 1.50 .75
Nos. 1705-1708 (4) 6.00 3.00

America Issue A789

1990, Oct. 13

1709 A789 3000a Iguacu Falls, hamelia erecta 1.50 .60
1710 A789 3000a Puerto Deseado, elephant seal 1.50 .60

Natl. Parks Type of 1987

1990, Oct. 27 *Perf. 13x13½*

1715 A752 3000a Lanin 1.50 .65
1716 A752 3000a Laguna Blanca 1.50 .65
1717 A752 3000a Perito Moreno 1.50 .65
1718 A752 3000a Puelo 1.50 .65
1719 A752 3000a El Rey 1.50 .65
Nos. 1715-1719 (5) 7.50 3.25

Stamp Day A790

1990, Oct. 27 *Perf. 13½*

1720 A790 3000a multicolored 1.50 .60

Salvation Army, Cent. A793

Designs: No. 1722, Natl. University of the Littoral, Santa Fe, cent.

1990, Dec. 1 Litho. *Perf. 13½*

1721 A793 3000a multicolored 1.75 1.00
1722 A793 3000a multicolored 1.75 1.00
a. Pair, #1721-1722 + label 3.75 2.25

Miniature Sheets

Christmas — A794

Stained glass windows: No. 1723, The Immaculate Conception. No. 1724, The Nativity. No. 1725, Presentation of Jesus at the Temple.

1990, Dec. 1 *Perf. 13½x13*

Sheets of 4

1723 A794 3000a #a.-d. 6.00 6.00
1724 A794 3000a #a.-d. 6.00 6.00
1725 A794 3000a #a.-d. 6.00 6.00

Landscapes — A795

Paintings: No. 1726, Los Sauces, by Atilio Malinverno. No. 1727, Paisaje, by Pio Collivadino, vert.

1991, May 4 Litho. *Perf. 13½*

1726 A795 4000a multicolored 1.00 .85
1727 A795 4000a multicolored 1.00 .85

Return of Remains of Juan Manuel de Rosas (1793-1877) A796

1991, June 1 Litho. *Perf. 13½*

1728 A796 4000a multicolored 1.00 .85

Swiss Confederation, 700th Anniv. — A797

1991, Aug. 3 Litho. *Perf. 13½*

1729 A797 4000a multicolored .95 .80

Miniature Sheet

Cartoons A798

Designs: a, Hernan, the Corsair by Jose Luis Salinas. b, Don Fulgencio by Lino Palacio. c, Medical Rules of Salerno by Oscar Esteban Conti. d, Buenos Aires Undershirt by Alejandro del Prado. e, Girls! by Jose A.G. Divito. f, Langostino by Eduardo Carlos Ferro. g, Mafalda by Joaquin Salvador Lavoro. h, Mort Cinder by Alberto Breccia.

1991, Aug. 3

1730 A798 4000a Sheet of 8, #a.-h. 7.75 7.50

City of La Rioja, 400th Anniv. — A799

1991, Sept. 14 Litho. *Perf. 13½*

1731 A799 4000a multicolored 1.00 .85

First Balloon Flight over the Andes, 75th Anniv. — A800

Illustration reduced.

1991, Sept. 14

1732 A800 4000a multicolored 1.00 .85

America Issue A801

Designs: No. 1733, Magellan's caravel, Our Lady of Victory. No. 1734, Ships of Juan Diaz de Solis.

1991, Nov. 9 Litho. *Perf. 13½*

1733 A801 4000a multicolored 1.00 .80
1734 A801 4000a multicolored 1.00 .80

Anniversaries — A802

Designs: a, J. Enrique Pestalozzi, founder of newspaper, Daily Argentinian. b, Leandro N. Alem, founder of Radical People's Party. c, Man with rifle, emblem of Argentine Federal Shooting Club. d, Dr. Nicasio Etchepareborda, emblem of College of Odontology. e, Dalmiro Huergo, emblem of Graduate School of Economics.

1991, Nov. 30

1735 A802 4000a Strip of 5, #a.-e. 5.00 4.00

Christmas A803

Stained glass windows from Our Lady of Lourdes Basilica, Buenos Aires: Nos. 1736a-1736b, Top and bottom portions of Virgin of the Valley, Catamarca. Nos. 1736c-1736d, Top and bottom portions of Virgin of the Rosary of the Miracle, Cordoba.

1991, Nov. 30

1736 A803 4000a Block of 4, #a.-d. 5.00 3.50

Famous Men A804

Designs: a, Gen. Juan de Lavalle (1797-1841), Peruvian medal of honor. b, Brig. Gen. Jose Maria del Rosario Siriaco Paz (1791-1854), medal. c, Marco Manuel de Avellaneda (1813-1841), lawyer. d, Guillermo Enrique Hudson (1841-1922), author.

1991, Dec. 14 Litho. *Perf. 13½*

1737 A804 4000a Block of 4, #a.-d. 5.00 3.50

Birds — A805

1991, Dec. 28

1738 A805 4000a Pterocnemia pennata 1.25 .85
1739 A805 4000a Morphnu guianensis 1.25 .85
1740 A805 4000a Ara chloroptera 1.25 .85
Nos. 1738-1740 (3) 3.75 2.55

Miniature Sheet

Arbrafex '92, Argentina-Brazil Philatelic Exhibition A806

Traditional costumes: a, Gaucho, woman. b, Gaucho, horse. c, Gaucho in store. d, Gaucho holding lariat.

1992 Litho. *Perf. 13½*
1741 A806 38c Sheet of 4, #a.-d. 3.00 3.00

Natl. Parks Type of 1987

1992, Apr. 4 Litho. *Perf. 13x13½*
1742 A752 38c Alerces .75 .55
1743 A752 38c Formosa Nature Reserve .75 .55
1744 A752 38c Petrified Forest .75 .55
1745 A752 38c Arrayanes .75 .55
1746 A752 38c Laguna de los Pozuelos .75 .55
Nos. 1742-1746 (5) 3.75 2.75

Mushrooms — A807

1992-94 Photo. *Perf. 13½*
1748 A807 10c Psilocybe cubensis .20 .20
1749 A807 25c Coprinus atramentarius .50 .35
a. Wmk. 365 30.00 30.00
1750 A807 38c like #1748 .75 .55
1751 A807 48c like #1749 .95 .65
1752 A807 50c Suillus granulatus 1.00 .70
1753 A807 51c Morchella esculenta 1.00 .70
1754 A807 61c Amanita muscaria 1.25 .85
1755 A807 68c Coprinus comatus 1.25 .85
1756 A807 1p like #1754 2.00 1.40
1757 A807 1.25p like #1752 2.50 1.75
1758 A807 1.77p Stropharia oeruginosa 3.50 2.50
1759 A807 2p like #1753 4.00 2.75
Nos. 1748-1759 (12) 18.90 13.25

No. 1758 not issued without overprint "Centro Filatelico de Neuquen y Rio Negro 50th Aniversario."

Issued: 38c, 4/4/92; 48c, 51c, 61c, 8/1/92; 1.77p, 11/7/92; 25c, 50c, 8/17/93; 1p, 2p, 8/26/93; 10c, 1/11/94; 68c, 1.25p, 10/10/92; #1749a, 1997.

See design A838.

Falkland Islands War, 10th Anniv. A808

1992, May 2 Litho. *Perf. 13½*
1767 A808 38c Pucara 1A-58 .75 .55
1768 A808 38c Cruiser Gen. Belgrano .75 .55
1769 A808 38c Soldier and truck .75 .55
Nos. 1767-1769 (3) 2.25 1.65

Miniature Sheet

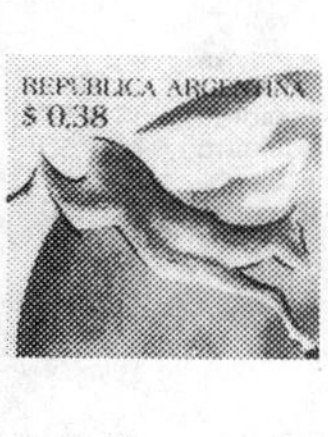

Preserve the Environment A809

a, Deer. b, Geese. c, Butterflies. d, Whale.

1992, June 6 Litho. *Perf. 12*
1770 A809 38c Sheet of 4, #a.-d. 3.00 3.00

Paintings by Florencio Molina Campos A810

1992, June 6 *Perf. 13½*
1771 A810 38c A La Sombra .75 .55
1772 A810 38c Tiléforo Areco, vert. .75 .55

Famous Men A811

Designs: No. 1773, Gen. Lucio N. Mansilla (1792-1871). No. 1774, Jose Manuel Estrada (1842-1894), writer. No. 1775, Brig. Gen. Jose I. Garmendia (1842-1915).

1992, July 4 Litho. *Perf. 13½*
1773 A811 38c multicolored .75 .55
1774 A811 38c multicolored .75 .55
1775 A811 38c multicolored .75 .55
Nos. 1773-1775 (3) 2.25 1.65

Fight Against Drugs — A812

1992, Aug. 1 *Perf. 13½x13*
1776 A812 38c multicolored .75 .55

Col. Jose M. Calaza, 140th Birth Anniv. A813

1992, Sept. 5 Litho. *Perf. 13½*
1777 A813 38c multicolored .75 .55

Discovery of America, 500th Anniv. — A814

Designs: a, Columbus, castle, ship. b, Native drawings, Columbus.

1992, Oct. 10 Litho. *Perf. 13½*
1778 A814 38c Pair, #a.-b. 1.50 1.50

Argentine Film Posters — A815

1992, Nov. 7 Litho. *Perf. 13½*
1779 A815 38c Dios Se Lo Pague, 1948 .75 .55
1780 A815 38c Las Aguas Bajan Turbias, 1952 .75 .55
1781 A815 38c Un Guapo Del 900, 1960 .75 .55
1782 A815 38c La Tregua, 1974 .75 .55
1783 A815 38c La Historia Oficial, 1984 .75 .55
Nos. 1779-1783 (5) 3.75 2.75

Christmas A816

1992, Nov. 28
1784 A816 38c multicolored .75 .55

Miniature Sheet

Iberoprenfil '92 — A817

Lighthouses: a, Punta Mogotes. b, Rio Negro. c, San Antonio. d, Cabo Blanco.

1992, Dec. 5
1785 A817 38c Sheet of 4, #a.-d. 3.00 3.00

Fight Against AIDS
A818 A819

1992, Dec. 12 Litho. *Perf. 13½*
1786 A818 10c multicolored .20 .20
1787 A819 26c multicolored .55 .40

Intl. Space Year A820

1992, Dec. 19
1788 A820 38c multicolored .75 .55

Souvenir Sheet

Miraculous Lord Crucifix, 400th Anniv. of Arrival in America — A821

1992, Dec. 26 *Perf. 12*
1789 A821 76c multicolored 1.50 1.50

Jujuy City, 400th Anniv. — A822

1993, Apr. 24 Litho. *Perf. 13½*
1790 A822 38c multicolored .75 .55

Argentina Soccer Assoc., Cent. A823

1993, Mar. 27
1791 A823 38c multicolored .75 .55

Souvenir Sheet

Intl. Philatelic Exhibitions — A824

Designs: a, 38c, City Hall, Poznan, Poland. b, 48c, Statue of Christ the Redeemer, Rio de Janeiro, Brazil. c, 76c, Royal Palace, Bangkok, Thailand.

1993, May 8 Litho. *Perf. 12*
1792 A824 Sheet of 3, #a.-c. 3.25 3.25

Polska '93 (#1792a), Brasiliana '93 (#1792b), Bangkok '92 (#1792c).

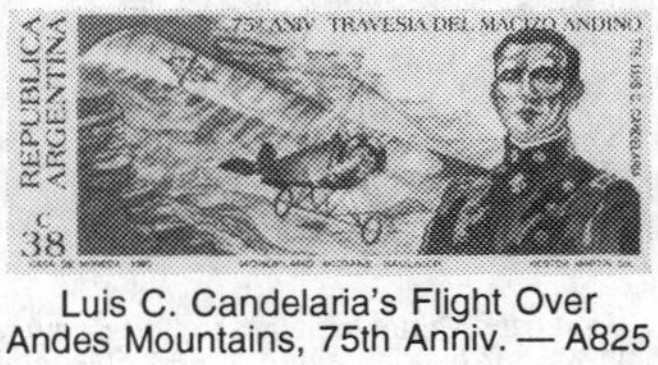

Luis C. Candelaria's Flight Over Andes Mountains, 75th Anniv. — A825

1993, June 26 Litho. *Perf. 13x13½*
1793 A825 38c multicolored .75 .55

Illustration reduced.

Order of San Martin, 50th Anniv. — A826

National History Academy, Cent. — A827

1993, May 29 ***Perf. 13½***

1794 A826 38c multicolored	.75	.55
1795 A827 38c multicolored	.75	.55

Armed Forces Memorial Day — A828

1993, June 12

1796 A828 38c Natl. Gendarmerie	.75	.55
1797 A828 38c Coast Guard	.75	.55

Paintings A829

#1798, Old House, by Norberto Russo. #1799, Pa'las Casas, by Adriana Zaefferer.

1993, Aug. 14 Litho. ***Perf. 13½***

1798 A829 38c multicolored	.75	.55
1799 A829 38c multicolored	.75	.55

Pato — A830

1993, Aug. 28 Litho. ***Perf. 12***

1800 A830 1p multicolored	2.00	1.40

Nut-Bearing Trees — A831

#1801, Enterolobium contortisiliquum. #1802, Prosopis alba. #1803, Magnolia grandiflora. #1804, Erythrina falcata. Illustration reduced.

1993, Sept. 25 Litho. ***Perf. 13x13½***

1801 A831 75c multicolored	1.50	1.00
1802 A831 75c multicolored	1.50	1.00
1803 A831 1.50p multicolored	3.00	2.00
1804 A831 1.50p multicolored	3.00	2.00
Nos. 1801-1804 (4)	9.00	6.00

America Issue A832

Whales: 50c, Eubalaena australis. 75c, Cephalorhynchus commersonii.

1993, Oct. 9 ***Perf. 13½***

1805 A832 50c multicolored	1.00	.70
1806 A832 75c multicolored	1.50	1.10

Miniature Sheet

Christmas, New Year — A833

Denomination at: a, UL. b, UR. c, LL. d, LR.

1993, Dec. 4 Litho. ***Perf. 13½***

1807 A833 75c Sheet of 4, #a.-d.	6.00	6.00

Cave of the Hands, Santa Cruz — A834

1993, Dec. 18

1808 A834 1p multicolored	2.00	1.40

New Emblem, Argentine Postal Service — A835

Illustration reduced.

1994, Jan. 8 ***Perf. 11½***

1809 A835 75c multicolored	1.50	1.00

A836

1994 World Cup Soccer Championships, US — A837

Players from: 25c, Germany, 1990. 50c, Brazil, 1970. 75c, 1.50p, Argentina, 1986. 1p, Italy, 1982.

1994, June 11 Litho. ***Perf. 13½***

1810 A836 25c multicolored	.50	.20
1811 A836 50c multicolored	1.00	.70
1812 A836 75c multicolored	1.50	1.00
1813 A836 1p multicolored	2.00	1.40
Nos. 1810-1813 (4)	5.00	3.30

Souvenir Sheet

Perf. 12

1814 A836 1.50p multicolored	3.00	3.00

No. 1814 contains one 40x50mm stamp with continuous design.

Nos. 1810-1813 issued in sheets containing a block of 4 of each stamp + 4 labels.

1994, July 23 ***Perf. 13½***

Drawings of championships by: No. 1815, Julian Lisenberg. No. 1816, Matias Taylor, vert. No. 1817, Torcuato S. Gonzalez Agote, vert. No. 1818, Maria Paula Palma.

1815 A837 75c multicolored	1.50	1.00
1816 A837 75c multicolored	1.50	1.00
1817 A837 75c multicolored	1.50	1.00
1818 A837 75c multicolored	1.50	1.00
Nos. 1815-1818 (4)	6.00	4.00

A838

Molothrus Badius — A838a

1994-95 Litho. ***Perf. 13½***

1819 A838	10c like #1748	.20	.20
1820 A838	25c like #1749	.50	.35
1823 A838	50c like #1752	1.00	.70
1828 A838	1p like #1754	2.00	1.40
1832 A838	2p like #1753	4.00	2.75
1835 A838a	9.40p multicolored	19.00	13.00
Nos. 1819-1835 (6)		26.70	18.40

See design A807.

Issued: 10c, 25c, 50c, 1p, 2p, 6/14/94; 9.40p, 4/12/95.

This is an expanding set. Numbers may change.

Wildlife of Falkland Islands A839

Designs: 25c, Melanodera melanodera. 50c, Pygoscelis papua. 75c, Tachyeres brachypterus. 1p, Mirounga leonina.

1994, Aug 6

1839 A839 25c multicolored	.50	.35
1840 A839 50c multicolored	1.00	.70
1841 A839 75c multicolored	1.50	1.00
1842 A839 1p multicolored	2.00	1.40
Nos. 1839-1842 (4)	5.00	3.45

City of San Luis, 400th Anniv. — A840

1994, Aug. 20

1843 A840 75c multicolored	1.50	1.00

Province of Tierra del Fuego, Antarctica and South Atlantic Islands — A841

1994, Aug. 20

1844 A841 75c multicolored	1.50	1.00

Argentine Inventors — A842

Designs: No. 1845, Ladislao Jose Biro (1899-1985), ball point pen. No. 1846, Raul Pateras de Pescara (1890-1966), helicopter. No. 1847, Quirino Cristiani (1896-1984), animated drawings. No. 1848, Enrique Finochietto (1881-1948), surgical instruments.

1994, Oct. 1

1845 A842 75c multicolored	1.50	1.00
1846 A842 75c multicolored	1.50	1.00
1847 A842 75c multicolored	1.50	1.00
1848 A842 75c multicolored	1.50	1.00
a. Block of 4, #1845-1848	6.00	6.00

Issued in sheets containing 4 #1848a + 4 labels.

UNICEF Christmas A843

1994, Nov. 26 Litho. ***Perf. 11½***

1849 A843 50c shown	1.00	.70
1850 A843 75c Bell, bulb, star, diff.	1.50	1.00

Take Care of Our Planet A844

Children's paintings: No. 1851, Boy, girl holding earth, vert. No. 1852, Children outdoors, vert. No. 1853, World as house. No. 1854, People around "world" table.

1994, Dec. 3 ***Perf. 13½***

1851 A844 25c multicolored	.50	.35
1852 A844 25c multicolored	.50	.35
1853 A844 50c multicolored	1.00	.70
1854 A844 50c multicolored	1.00	.70
Nos. 1851-1854 (4)	3.00	2.10

Christmas — A845

1994, Dec. 10
1855 A845 50c Annunciation 1.00 .70
1856 A845 75c Madonna & Child 1.50 1.00

Nos. 1855-1856 each issued in sheets of 20 + 5 labels.

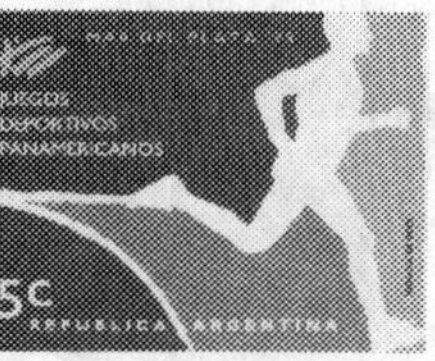

12th Pan American Games, Mar del Plata — A846

1995 Litho. *Perf. 13½*
1857 A846 75c Running 1.50 1.00
1858 A846 75c Cycling 1.50 1.00
1859 A846 75c Diving 1.50 1.00
1860 A846 1.25p Gymnastics, vert. 2.50 1.75
1861 A846 1.25p Soccer, vert. 2.50 1.75
Nos. 1857-1861 (5) 9.50 6.50

Issued: No. 1857, 2/18; others, 3/11.

Natl. Constitution — A847

Design: 75c, Natl. Congress Dome, woman from statue The Republic Triumphant.

1995, Apr. 8
1862 A847 75c multicolored 1.50 1.00

21st Intl. Book Fair — A848

Illustration reduced.

1995, Apr. 8
1863 A848 75c multicolored 1.50 1.00

Birds A849

1995 Litho. *Perf. 13½*
1876 A849 5p Carduelis magellanica 10.00 7.00
1880 A849 10p Zonotrichia capensis 20.00 14.00

Issued: 5p, 10p, 5/23/95. This is an expanding set. Numbers may change.

A850

1995, Mar. 25 Litho. *Die Cut*
Self-Adhesive
1883A A850 25c multicolored .50 .35
1884 A850 75c multicolored 1.50 1.00
a. Booklet pane, 2 #1883A, 6 #1884 12.50
Complete booklet, #1884a 12.50
b. Booklet pane, 4 #1883A, 12 #1884 25.00
Complete booklet, #1884b 25.00

Argentine Engineers' Center, Cent. — A851

1995, June 3 *Perf. 13½*
1885 A851 75c multicolored 1.50 1.00

Jose Marti (1853-95) — A852

#1887, Antonio Jose de Sucre (1795-1830).

1995, Aug. 12 Litho. *Perf. 13½*
1886 A852 1p multicolored 2.00 1.40
1887 A852 1p multicolored 2.00 1.40

Fauna — A853

1995, Sept. 1 Litho. *Perf. 13½*
1888 A853 5c Ostrich .20 .20
1889 A853 25c Penguin .50 .35
1890 A853 50c Toucan 1.00 .70
1891 A853 75c Condor 1.50 1.00
1892 A853 1p Owl 2.00 1.40
1893 A853 2p Bigua 4.00 2.75
1894 A853 2.75p Tero 5.50 3.75

Booklet Stamps
Perf. 13½ on 2 or 3 Sides
1895 A853 25c Alligator .50 .35
1896 A853 50c Fox 1.00 .70
1897 A853 75c Anteater 1.50 1.00
1898 A853 75c Deer 1.50 1.00
1899 A853 75c Whale 1.50 1.00
a. Booklet pane, 1 each Nos. 1889-1891, 1895-1899 9.00
Complete booklet, #1899a 9.00
Nos. 1888-1899 (12) 20.70 14.20

See Nos. 1958, 2004-2004A.

Native Heritage A854

a, Cave drawings, shifting sands. b, Stone mask. c, Anthropomorphous vessel. d, Woven textile.

1995, Sept. 9
1900 A854 75c Block of 4, #a.-d. 6.00 6.00

Sunflower, Postal Service Emblem — A855

1995, Oct. 7
1901 A855 75c multicolored 1.50 1.00

Juan D. Peron (1895-1974) — A856

1995, Oct. 7
1902 A856 75c lt ol bis & dk bl 1.50 1.00

Miniature Sheet

Anniversaries — A857

Annivs: a, UN, 50th. b, ICAO, 50th (in 1994). c, FAO, 50th. d, ILO, 75th (in 1994).

1995, Oct. 14 *Perf. 12*
1903 A857 75c Sheet of 4, #a.-d. 6.00 6.00

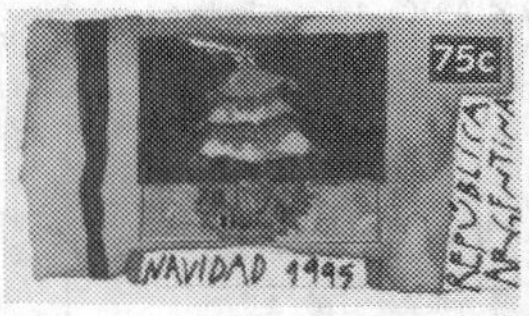

Christmas and New Year — A858

Designs: Nos. 1904, 1908, Christmas tree, presents. No. 1905, "1996." No. 1906, Champagne glasses. No. 1907, Present.

1995, Nov. 25 Litho. *Perf. 13½*
1904 A858 75c multicolored 1.50 1.00

Booklet Stamps
Perf. 13½ on 1 or 2 Sides
1905 A858 75c multicolored 1.50 1.00
1906 A858 75c multicolored 1.50 1.00
1907 A858 75c multicolored 1.50 1.00
1908 A858 75c multicolored 1.50 1.00
a. Booklet pane, #1905-1908 + label 6.00
Complete booklet, #1908a 6.00
Nos. 1904-1908 (5) 7.50 5.00

No. 1908a is a continuous design. Ribbon extends from edge to edge on #1908 and stops at edge of package on #1905.

Miniature Sheet

Motion Pictures, Cent. — A859

Black and white film clips, director: a, The Battleship Potemkin, Sergei Eisenstein (Soviet Union). b, Casablanca, Michael Curtiz (US). c, Bicycle Thief, Vittorio De Sica (Italy). d, Limelights, Charles Chaplin (England). e, The 400 Blows, Francois Truffaut (France). f, Chronicle of the Lonely Child, Leonardo Favio (Argentina).

1995, Dec. 2 *Perf. 13½*
1909 A859 75c Sheet of 6, #a.-f. 9.00 9.00

The Sky — A860

1995, Dec. 16 *Perf. 13½ on 3 Sides*
Booklet Stamps
1910 A860 25c Dirigible .50 .35
1911 A860 25c Kite .50 .35
1912 A860 25c Hot air balloon .50 .35
1913 A860 50c Balloons 1.00 .70
1914 A860 50c Paper airplane 1.00 .70
1915 A860 75c Airplane 1.50 1.00
1916 A860 75c Helicopter 1.50 1.00
1917 A860 75c Parachute 1.50 1.00
a. Booklet pane, #1910-1917 + label 8.00
Complete booklet, No. 1917a 8.00

Nos. 1910-1917 do not appear in Scott number order in No. 1917a, which has a continuous design.

America Issue — A861

Postal vehicles from Postal &Telegraph Museum: #1918, Horse & carriage. #1919, Truck.

1995, Dec. 16 *Perf. 13½*
1918 A861 75c multicolored 1.50 1.00
1919 A861 75c multicolored 1.50 1.00

Olympic Games, Cent. A862

1996, Mar. 30 Litho. *Perf. 13½*
1920 A862 75c Running 1.50 1.00
1921 A862 1p Discus 2.00 1.40

Physicians — A863

Designs: a, Francisco J. Muniz (1795-1871). b, Ricardo Gutierrez (1838-96). c, Ignacio Pirovano (1844-95). d, Esteban L. Maradona (1895-1995).

1996, Apr. 20 Litho. *Perf. 12*
1922 A863 50c Sheet of 4 4.00 4.00
a.-d. Any single 1.00 1.00

Jerusalem, 3000th Anniv. — A864

7th cent. mosaic maps of city, denomination at: No. 1923, LL. No. 1924, LR.

1996, May 18 Litho. *Perf. 13½*

1923	A864	75c multicolored	1.50	1.00
1924	A864	75c multicolored	1.50	1.00
a.		Pair, #1923-1924	3.00	3.00

No. 1924a is a continuous design and was issued in sheets of 8 + 4 labels.

Endangered Fauna — A865

1996, June 15 Litho. *Perf. 13½*

1925	A865	75c Capybara	1.50	1.00
1926	A865	75c Guanaco	1.50	1.00
a.		Pair, #1925-1926	3.00	3.00

America Issue.

Summer Olympic Games — A866

Designs: 75c, Torch bearer, Buenos Aires, candidate for 2004 Games. 1p, Men's eight with coxswain, Atlanta, 1996.

1996, July 6

1927	A866	75c multicolored	1.50	1.00
1928	A866	1p multicolored	2.00	1.40

National Parks — A867

Wildlife, national park: No. 1929, Mountain turkey, Diamante. No. 1930, Parrot, San Antonio Nature Reserve. No. 1931, Deer, Otamendi Natl. Reserve. No. 1932, Rabbit, El Leoncito Nature Reserve.
Illustration reduced.

1996, Aug. 24 Litho. *Perf. 13x13½*

1929	A867	75c multicolored	1.50	1.00
1930	A867	75c multicolored	1.50	1.00
1931	A867	75c multicolored	1.50	1.00
1932	A867	75c multicolored	1.50	1.00
		Nos. 1929-1932 (4)	6.00	4.00

Central Post Office, Buenos Aires — A868

1996, Oct. 5 Litho. *Die Cut*
Self-Adhesive
Size: 25x35mm

1933	A868	75c multicolored	1.50	1.50

Vignette of No. 1933 is broken by circular and rectangular die cut areas to guard against reuse.
See Nos. 1983-1984.

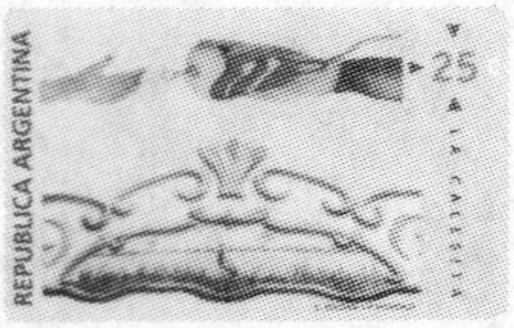

Carousel Figures — A869

#1934, Hand-carved decorative ornaments. #1935, Child on carousel horse. #1936, Carousel. #1937, Heads of horses. #1938, Child in airplane. #1939, Carousel pig. #1940, Boy in car.

1996, Oct. 5 *Perf. 13½ Horiz.*
Booklet Stamps

1934	A869	25c multicolored	.50	.50
1935	A869	25c multicolored	.50	.50
1936	A869	25c multicolored	.50	.50
1937	A869	50c multicolored	1.00	1.00
1938	A869	50c multicolored	1.00	1.00
1939	A869	50c multicolored	1.00	1.00
1940	A869	75c multicolored	1.50	1.50
a.		Booklet pane, #1934-1940	6.00	
		Complete booklet, #1940a	6.00	

Sequence of stamps in No. 1940a: No. 1940, 1934, 1937, 1935, 1938, 1936, 1939.

Port Belgrano Naval Base, Cent. — A870

Designs: 25c, LST "San Antonio." 50c, Corvette *Rosales.* 75c, Destroyer *Hercules.* 1p, Aircraft carrier, "25th of May."

1996-97 Litho. *Perf. 13½*

1941	A870	25c multicolored	.50	.50
1942	A870	50c multicolored	1.00	1.00
1943	A870	75c multicolored	1.50	1.50
1944	A870	1p multicolored	2.00	2.00
		Nos. 1941-1944 (4)	5.00	5.00

Issued: 25c, 1p, 10/5/96; 50c, 75c, 2/1/97.

Christmas A871

Tapestries: 75c, Nativity, by Gladys Angelica Rinaldi, vert. 1p, Candles, by Norma Bonet de Maekawa.

1996, Nov. 30 Litho. *Perf. 13½*

1945	A871	75c multicolored	1.50	1.50
1946	A871	1p multicolored	2.00	2.00

Exploration of Antarctica — A872

Designs: 75c, Melchior Base. 1.25p, Icebreaker ARA Alte. Irizar.

1996, Nov. 30

1947	A872	75c multicolored	1.50	1.50
1948	A872	1.25p multicolored	2.50	2.50

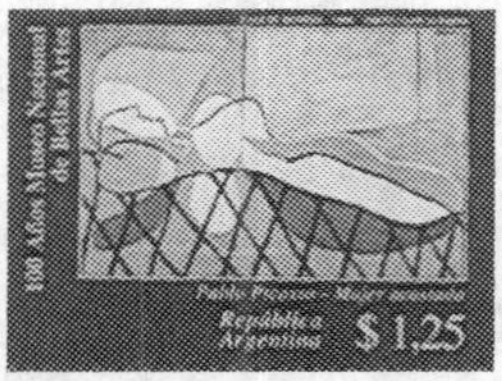

National Gallery, Cent. — A873

Paintings of women by: 75c, Paul Gauguin, vert. No. 1950, Edouard Monet, vert. No. 1951, Amedeo Modigiliani, vert. 1.25p, Pablo Picasso.

1996, Dec. 14

1949	A873	75c multicolored	1.50	1.50
1950	A873	1p multicolored	2.00	2.00
1951	A873	1p multicolored	2.00	2.00
1952	A873	1.25p multicolored	2.50	2.50
		Nos. 1949-1952 (4)	8.00	8.00

Mining Industry — A874

1997, Feb. 1 Litho. *Perf. 13½*

1953	A874	75c Granite	1.50	1.50
1954	A874	1.25p Borax	2.50	2.50

Traditional Costumes — A875

1997, Feb. 22 Litho. *Perf. 13½*

1955	A875	75c multicolored	1.50	1.50

America issue.

Repatriation of the Curved Sword of Gen. San Martin, Cent. — A876

1997, Mar. 15 Litho. *Perf. 13½*

1956	A876	75c multicolored	1.50	1.50

29th Youth Rugby World Championships — A877

1997, Mar. 22

1957	A877	75c multicolored	1.50	1.50

Fauna Type of 1995

1997, Feb. 22 Litho. *Perf. 13½*

1958	A853	10c Reddish sandpiper	.20	.20

Buenos Aires-Rio de Janeiro Regatta, 50th Anniv. — A879

1997, Apr. 5 Litho. *Perf. 13½*

1960	A879	75c Fortuna II	1.50	1.50

Natl. History Museum, Cent. A880

1997, May 17

1961	A880	75c multicolored	1.50	1.50

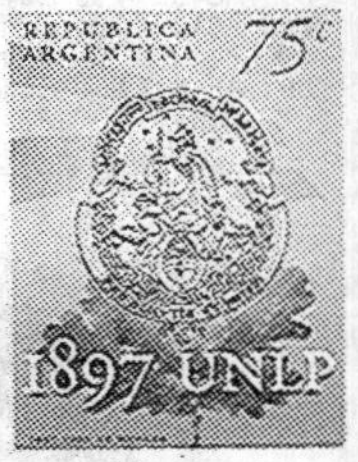

La Plata Natl. University, Cent. — A881

1997, May 17

1962	A881	75c multicolored	1.50	1.50

Lighthouses A882

Designs: a, Cabo Virgenes. b, Isla Pingüino. c, San Juan de Salvamento. d, Punta Delgada.

1997, May 31

1963	A882	75c Sheet of 4, #a.-d.	6.00	6.00

Ramón J. Cárcano (1860-1946), Developer of Postal and Telegraph System A883

1997, May 31

1964	A883	75c multicolored	1.50	1.50

Buenos Aires, Candidate for 2004 Summer Olympics — A884

1997, June 21

1965	A884	75c multicolored	1.50	1.50

First Electric Tram in Buenos Aires, Cent. — A885

Designs: a, Lacroze Suburban Service Tram Co, 1912. b, Lacroze Urban Service Tram Co., 1907. c, Anglo Argentina Tram Co., 1930. d, Buenos Aires City Transportation Corp., 1942. e, Military Manufacture Tram, 1956. f, South Electric Tram, 1908.

1997, July 12

Sheet of 6

1966 A885 75c #a.-f. + 2 labels 9.00 9.00

Monument to Joaquín V. González (1863-1923), La Rioja — A886

1997, Aug. 9

1967 A886 75c multicolored 1.50 1.50

Musicians and Composers A887

Paintings: No. 1968, Alberto Ginastera (1916-83), by Carlos Nine. No. 1969, Astor Piazzolla (1921-92), by Carlos Alonso. No. 1970, Anibal Troilo (1914-75), by Hermenegildo Sabat. No. 1971, Atahualpa Yupanqui (b. 1908), by Luis Scafati.

1997, Aug. 9

1968 A887 75c multicolored 1.50 1.50
1969 A887 75c multicolored 1.50 1.50
1970 A887 75c multicolored 1.50 1.50
1971 A887 75c multicolored 1.50 1.50
Nos. 1968-1971 (4) 6.00 6.00

Argentine Authors — A888

#1972, Jorge Luis Borges (1899-1986), maze. #1973, Julio Cortázar (1914-84), hop scotch game.

1997, Aug. 30 Litho. *Perf. 13*

1972 A888 1p multicolored 2.00 2.00
1973 A888 1p multicolored 2.00 2.00

Women's Political Rights Law, 50th Anniv. A889

1997, Sept. 6 Litho. *Perf. 13½*

1974 A889 75c Eva Perón 1.50 1.50

Mercosur (Common Market of Latin America) A890

1997, Sept. 27 Litho. *Perf. 13½*

1975 A890 75c multicolored 1.50 1.50

See Bolivia #1019, Brazil #2646, Paraguay #2564, Uruguay #1681.

Launching of Frigate President Sarmiento, Cent. — A891

No. 1976, Painting of ship by Hugo Leban. No. 1977: a, Ship. b, Ship's figurehead, vert.

1997, Oct. 4

1976 A891 75c multicolored 1.50 1.50

Souvenir Sheet

Perf. 12

1977 A891 75c Sheet of 2, #a.-b. 3.00 3.00

No. 1977 contains two 40x30mm stamps.

Ernesto "Che" Guevara (1928-67) A892

1997, Oct. 18

1978 A892 75c multicolored 1.50 1.50

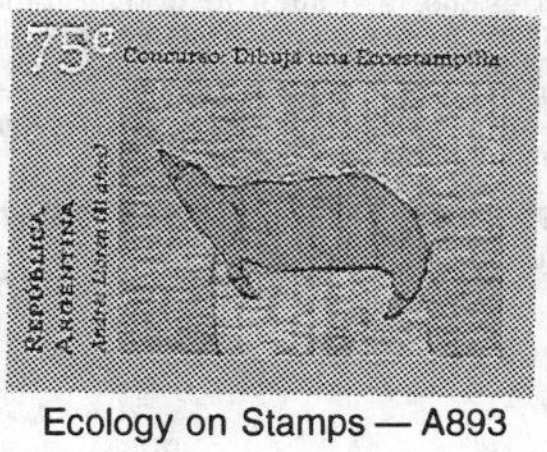

Ecology on Stamps — A893

Children's drawings: No. 1979, Animal, by J. Chiapparo, vert. No. 1980, Vicuna, by L.L. Portal, vert. No. 1981, Seal, by A. Lloren. No. 1982, Bird in flight, by J. Saccone.

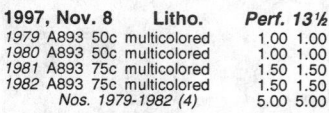

1997, Nov. 8 Litho. *Perf. 13½*

1979 A893 50c multicolored 1.00 1.00
1980 A893 50c multicolored 1.00 1.00
1981 A893 75c multicolored 1.50 1.50
1982 A893 75c multicolored 1.50 1.50
Nos. 1979-1982 (4) 5.00 5.00

Central Post Office, Buenos Aires, Type of 1996

1997, July 24 Litho. *Die Cut*

Self-Adhesive

Size: 23x35mm

1983 A868 25c multicolored .50 .50
1984 A868 75c multicolored 1.50 1.50
a. Booklet pane, 2 #1983, 6 #1984 10.00
Complete booklet, #1984a 10.00

Nos. 1983-1984 are broken at both the top and bottom of each stamp by three lines of wavy die cutting.

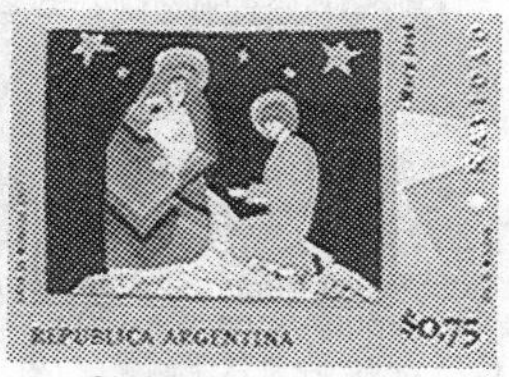

Christmas — A893a

Nativity scene tapestries by: #1984B, 1984G, Mary José. #1984C, Elena Aguilar. #1984D, Silvia Pettachi. #1984E, Ana Escobar. #1984F, Alejandra Martinez. #1984H, Nidia Martinez.

1997, Nov. 22 Litho. *Perf. 13½*

1984B A893a 75c multicolored 1.50 1.50

Booklet Stamps

Self-Adhesive

Size: 44x27mm

Die Cut

1984C A893a 25c multicolored .50 .50
1984D A893a 25c multicolored .50 .50
1984E A893a 50c multicolored 1.00 1.00
1984F A893a 50c multicolored 1.00 1.00
1984G A893a 75c multicolored 1.50 1.50
1984H A893a 75c multicolored 1.50 1.50
i. Booklet pane, #1984C-1984H 6.00

Nos. 1984C-1984H are broken at upper right by three die cut chevrons.

Mother Teresa (1910-97) A893b

1997, Dec. 27

1984J A893b 75c multicolored 1.50 1.50

Dr. Bernardo A. Houssay (1887-1971), 1947 Nobel Prize Winner in Medicine — A894

1998, Jan. 31 Litho. *Perf. 13½*

1985 A894 75c multicolored 1.50 1.50

First Ascension of Mount Aconcagua, Cent. — A895

Illustration reduced.

1998, Feb. 14 *Perf. 12*

1986 A895 1.25p multicolored 2.50 2.50

Founding of San Martin de los Andes, Cent. A896

1998, Mar. 14 Litho. *Perf. 13½*

1987 A896 75c multicolored 1.50 1.50

Regimental Quarters of Gen. San Martin's Mounted Grenadiers A897

Designs: a, Statue. b, Large jar with painting of San Martin. c, Regimental seal. d, Regimental quarters.

1998, Mar. 21 Litho. *Perf. 13½*

1988 A897 75c Block of 4, #a.-d. 6.00 6.00

Protection of the Ozone A898

1998, Mar. 28 Litho. *Perf. 13½*

1989 A898 75c multicolored 1.50 1.50

America Issue — A899

Letter carriers: #1990, Wearing white uniform. #1991, Carrying letter bag with shoulder strap.

1998, Apr. 4

1990 A899 75c multicolored 1.50 1.50
1991 A899 75c multicolored 1.50 1.50

Characters from Stories by Maria Elena Walsh — A900

#1992, El Reino Del Reves. #1993, Zoo Loco. #1994, Dailan Kifki. #1995, Manuelita.

1998, Apr. 17 Litho. *Die Cut*
Booklet Stamps
Self-Adhesive

1992 A900 75c multicolored 1.50 1.50
1993 A900 75c multicolored 1.50 1.50
1994 A900 75c multicolored 1.50 1.50
1995 A900 75c multicolored 1.50 1.50
a. Complete booklet, #1992-1995 6.00

Historic Chapels A901

#1996, San Pedro de Fiambalá, Catamarca. #1997, Huacalera, Jujuy. #1998, Santo Domingo, La Rioja. #1999, Tumbaya, Jujuy.

1998, Apr. 25 Litho. *Perf. 13x13½*

1996 A901 75c multicolored 1.50 1.50
1997 A901 75c multicolored 1.50 1.50
1998 A901 75c multicolored 1.50 1.50
1999 A901 75c multicolored 1.50 1.50
Nos. 1996-1999 (4) 6.00 6.00

White Helmets, A Commitment to Humanity — A902

1998, May 23 Litho. *Perf. 13½*

2000 A902 1p multicolored 2.00 2.00

Beginning with No. 2001, many Argentine stamps are inscribed "Correo Official," but are not official stamps.

1998 World Cup Soccer Championships, France — A903

Stylized players representing: a, Argentina. b, Croatia. c, Jamaica. d, Japan.

1998, May 30

2001 A903 75c Block of 4, #a.-d. 6.00 6.00

Journalist's Day — A904

1998, June 20

2002 A904 75c multicolored 1.50 1.50

Creation of Argentine Postal System, 250th Anniv. — A905

a, Corrientes design A2, peso coin. b, Building, post box.

1998, June 27

2003 A905 75c Pair, #a.-b. 3.00 3.00

Fauna Type of 1995

1998 Litho. *Die Cut*
Self-Adhesive (#2004)

2004 A853 60c Picaflor 1.25 1.25

Perf. 13½

2004A A853 3.25p Tero 6.50 6.50

#2004 is broken at bottom right by 5 lines of wavy die cutting. Issued: 60c, 12/12; 3.25p, 7/22.

Ruins, Mission St. Ignacio — A906

1998, July 25 Litho. *Perf. 13½*

2005 A906 75c multicolored 1.50 1.50

Mercosur.

Cattle A907

1998, Aug. 1

2006 A907 25c Brahman .50 .50
2007 A907 25c Aberdeen-Angus .50 .50
2008 A907 50c Hereford 1.00 1.00
2009 A907 50c Criolla 1.00 1.00
2010 A907 75c Holland-Argentina 1.50 1.50
2011 A907 75c Shorthorn 1.50 1.50
Nos. 2006-2011 (6) 6.00 6.00

Deception Island Base, Antarctica, 50th Anniv. — A908

1998, Aug. 15 Litho. *Perf. 14½*

2012 A908 75c multicolored 1.50 1.50

State of Israel, 50th Anniv. A909

1998, Sept. 5 Litho. *Perf. 13½*

2013 A909 75c multicolored 1.50 1.50

Argentine-Japan Friendship Treaty, Cent. — A910

1998, Oct. 3

2014 A910 75c multicolored 1.50 1.50

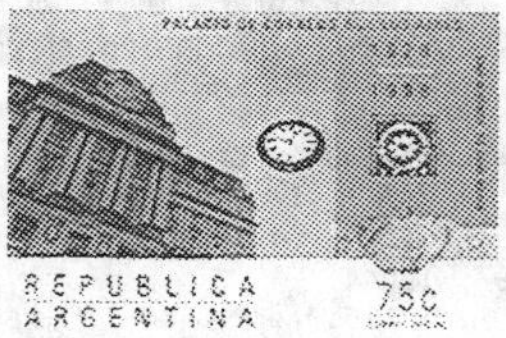

Post Office Building, Buenos Aires, 70th Anniv. — A911

Designs: No. 2015, Building, clock, tile. No. 2016, Column ornamentation, tile, bench.

1998, Oct. 3

2015 A911 75c multicolored 1.50 1.50
2016 A911 75c multicolored 1.50 1.50
a. Pair, #2015-2016 3.00 3.00

Cartoons A912

Designs: a, Patoruzu, by Quinterno. b, Matias, by Sendra. c, Clemente, by Caloi. d, El Eternauta, by Oesterheld and López. e, Loco Chavez, by Trillo and Altuna. f, Inodoro Pereyra, by Fontanarrosa. g, Tia Vicenta, by Landrú. h, Gaturro, by Nik.

1998, Oct. 17 Litho. *Perf. 13¾x13¼*

2017 A912 75c Sheet of 8, #a.-h. 12.00 12.00

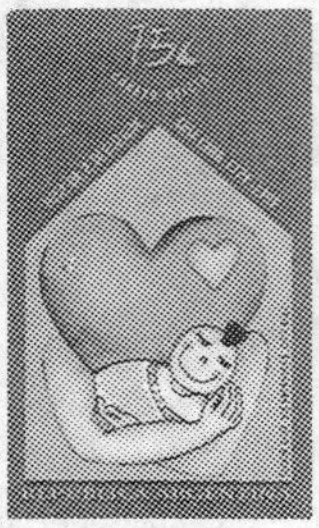

Dr. Pedro de Elizalde's Children's Hospital, 220th Anniv. — A913

1998, Oct. 24 Litho. *Perf. 13½*

2025 A913 15c multicolored .30 .30

Raoul Wallenberg (1912-47), Humanitarian — A914

1998, Nov. 21

2026 A914 75c multicolored 1.50 1.50

Espamer '98 — A915

25c, Spanish flags, arms. 75c, 18th cent. schooner. 75c+75c, Brigantine, gray sails. 1.25p+1.25p, Brigantine, white sails.

1998, Nov. 21 *Die Cut*
Booklet Stamps
Self-Adhesive

2027 A915 25c multicolored .50 .50
2028 A915 75c multicolored 1.50 1.50
2029 A915 75c +75c multi 3.00 3.00
2030 A915 1.25p +1.25p multi 5.00 5.00
a. Booklet pane, #2027-2030 10.00

Nos. 2027-2030 are broken at top right of each stamp by four lines of wavy die cutting. No. 2030a is a complete booklet.

Organization of American States, 50th Anniv. — A916

1998, Nov. 28 *Perf. 13½*

2031 A916 75c multicolored 1.50 1.50

Dinosaurs of Argentina — A917

Designs: a, Eoraptor. b, Gasparinisaura. c, Giganotosaurus. d, Patagosaurus.

1998, Nov. 28

2032 A917 75c Sheet of 4, #a.-d. 6.00 6.00

Christmas A918

1998, Dec. 5
2033 A918 75c multicolored 1.50 1.50

Newspaper El Liberal, Cent. A919

1998, Dec. 5
2034 A919 75c Juan A. Figueroa 1.50 1.50

La Nueva Provincia, Daily Newspaper, Cent. A920

1998, Dec. 12
2035 A920 75c Enrique Julio 1.50 1.50

Universal Declaration of Human Rights, 50th Anniv. — A921

1998, Dec. 12
2036 A921 75c multicolored 1.50 1.50

Holocaust Memorial, Cathedral of Buenos Aires A922

1998, Dec. 12
2037 A922 75c multicolored 1.50 1.50

National Fund for the Arts, 40th Anniv. — A925

1999, Mar. 6 Litho. *Perf. 13½*
2042 A925 75c multicolored 1.50 1.50

Intl. Year of the Ocean (in 1998) A926

1999, Mar. 6
2043 A926 50c Penguin, vert. 1.00 1.00
2044 A926 75c Dolphins 1.50 1.50

Postmen — A927

Designs: 25c, Early postman, city scene. 50c, Early postman, people on bicycles, factory. 75c, Modern postman, city buildings.

1998-99 Litho. *Die Cut*
Self-Adhesive
2045 A927 25c multicolored .50 .50
2046 A927 75c multicolored 1.50 1.50
a. Strip of 4, 1 #2045, 3 #2046 5.00

Booklet Stamps
Serpentine Die Cut
2047 A927 25c multicolored .50 .50
2048 A927 75c multicolored 1.50 1.50
a. Booklet pane, 2 #2047, 6 #2048 10.00
Complete booklet, #2048a 10.00

Size: 21x27mm
Die Cut
2049 A927 25c multicolored .50 .50
2050 A927 50c multicolored 1.00 1.00
2051 A927 75c multicolored 1.50 1.50
a. Booklet pane, 2 each #2049-2051 6.00
Complete booklet, #2051a 6.00

Nos. 2045-2048 are broken at lower right by five lines of wavy die cutting. Nos. 2049-2051 are broken in center by five wavy lines of die cutting. Nos. 2045-2046 have darker vignettes than #2047-2048.

Issued: Nos. 2045-2048, 12/9/98. Nos. 2049-2051, 2/2/99.

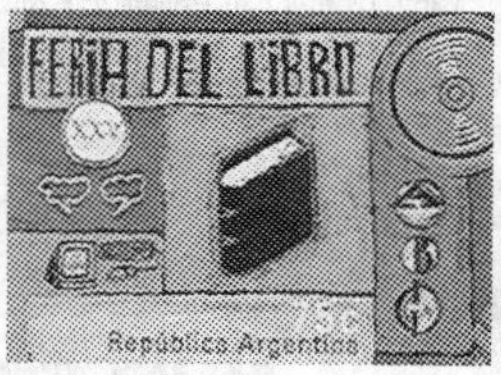

25th Book Fair A928

Designs: a, Book. b, Obelisk, readers.

Perf. 13¾x13½
1999, Apr. 17 Litho.
2052 A928 75c Pair, a.-b. 1.50 1.50

Argentine Rugby Union, Cent. — A929

75c, Player, balls. 1.50p, Old, modern players.

Perf. 13¾x13½
1999, Apr. 24 Litho.
2054 A929 75c multicolored 1.50 1.50

Souvenir Sheet
2055 A929 1.50p multi + 3 labels 3.00 3.00

Cafes of Buenos Aires — A930

Designs: a, Mug, Giralda Dairy. b, Two glasses, Homero Manzi Cafe. c, Hat hanging on rack, Ideal Sweet Shop. d, Cup and saucer, Tortoni Cafe.

Serpentine Die Cut
1999, Apr. 30 Litho.
Self-Adhesive
2056 Booklet pane of 4 6.00
a. A930 25c multicolored .50 .50
b.-c. A930 75c multi, each 1.50 1.50
d. A930 1.25p multicolored 2.50 2.50
Complete booklet, #2056 6.00

Argentine Olympic Committee, 75th Anniv. — A931

1999, May 15 *Perf. 14x13¼*
2057 A931 75c Pierre de Coubertin 1.50 1.50

Enrico Caruso (1873-1921), Opera Singer — A932

Designs: a, Portrait of Caruso. b, Singer, various musical instruments. c, Outside of Colon Theatre, Buenos Aires. d, Scene from opera, "El Matrero."

1999, May 15 *Perf. 13½*
2058 A932 75c Sheet of 4, #a.-d. 6.00 6.00

Famous Women A933

Designs: a, Rosario Vera Penaloza (1873-1950), educator. b, Julieta Lanteri (1862-1932), physician.

1999, June 5 *Perf. 14x13¼*
2059 A933 75c Pair, #a.-b. 3.00 3.00

Souvenir Sheets

Paintings from Natl. Museum of Art, Buenos Aires — A934

No. 2060: a, Anarchy of Year 20, by Luis Felipe Noé. b, Retrato de L.E.S., by Carlos Alonso.

No. 2061: a, Typical Orchestra, by Antonio Berni. b, Untitled, (Woman seated), by Aída Carballo.

Illustration reduced.

1999, June 5 *Perf. 14*
Sheets of 2
2060-2061 A934 75c #a.-b., each 3.00 3.00

No. 2060b is 40x40mm, No. 2061a, 70x50mm, No. 2061b, 40x50mm.

Carrier Pigeon A935

1999, June 12 *Perf. 13¾x13½*
2062 A935 75c multicolored 1.50 1.50

Maps — A936

1999, June 12 *Die Cut*
Self-Adhesive
2063 A936 35c Local highway .70 .70
2064 A936 40c City street .80 .80
2065 A936 50c Regional highway 1.00 1.00
Nos. 2063-2065 (3) 2.50 2.50

Nos. 2063-2065 are broken at lower left by five wavy lines of die cutting.

Dogs A937

Designs: a, 25c, Boxer. b, 25c, English sheepdog. c, 50c, Collie. d, 50c, St. Bernard. e, 75c, German shepherd. f, 75c, Siberian husky.

1999, July 24 Litho. *Perf. 13½*
2066 A937 Sheet of 6, #a.-f. 6.00 6.00

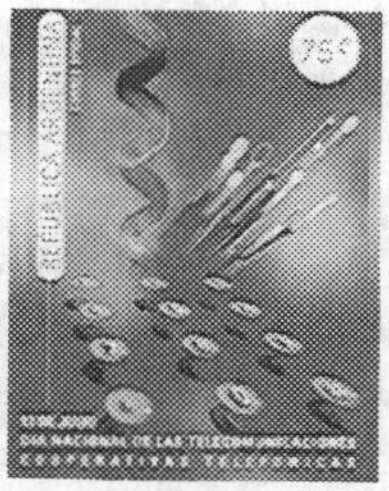

Natl. Telecommunications Day — A938

1999, July 24 *Perf. 13½x13¾*
2067 A938 75c multicolored 1.50 1.50

Justo José de Urquiza School, Concepcion del Uruguay, 150th Anniv. A939

1999, Aug. 7 ***Perf. 13¾x13½***

2068 A939 75c multicolored	1.50	1.50

Otto Krause Technical School, Buenos Aires, Cent. — A940

1999, Aug. 7 ***Perf. 13½x13¾***

2069 A940 75c multicolored	1.50	1.50

Bethlehem 2000 Project — A941

1999, Aug. 21 ***Perf. 13½***

2070 A941 75c multicolored	1.50	1.50

America Issue, A New Millennium Without Arms — A942

Perf. 13½x13¾, 13¾x13½

1999, Aug. 21

2071 A942 75c shown	1.50	1.50
2072 A942 75c Tree of hands, vert.	1.50	1.50

National Parks — A943

Parks and animals: No. 2073, Mburucuyá, coypu. No. 2074, Quebrada de Los Condoritos, condor. No. 2075, San Guillermo, vicuna. No. 2076, Sierra de las Quijadas, puma. No. 2077, Talampaya, gray fox.

Illustration reduced.

1999, Sept. 25 Litho. ***Perf. 14x13½***

2073 A943 50c multicolored	1.00	1.00
2074 A943 50c multicolored	1.00	1.00
2075 A943 50c multicolored	1.00	1.00
2076 A943 75c multicolored	1.50	1.50
2077 A943 75c multicolored	1.50	1.50
Nos. 2073-2077 (5)	6.00	6.00

SEMI-POSTAL STAMPS

Samuel F. B. Morse — SP1

Globe — SP2

Landing of Columbus — SP5

Map of Argentina — SP6

Designs: 10c+5c, Alexander Graham Bell. 25c+15c, Rowland Hill.

Wmk. RA in Sun (90)

1944, Jan. 5 Litho. ***Perf. 13***

B1 SP1 3c +2c lt vio & sl bl	.35	.25
B2 SP2 5c +5c dl red & sl bl	.65	.20
B3 SP1 10c +5c org & slate bl	1.25	.70
B4 SP1 25c +15c red brn & sl bl	1.75	1.10
B5 SP5 1p +50c lt grn & sl bl	8.00	7.25
Nos. B1-B5 (5)	12.00	9.50

The surtax was for the Postal Employees Benefit Association.

1944, Feb. 17 Wmk. 90 ***Perf. 13***

B6 SP6 5c +10c ol yel & slate	.75	.50
B7 SP6 5c +50c vio brn & slate	3.25	2.00
B8 SP6 5c +1p dl org & slate	9.00	6.50
B9 SP6 5c +20p dp bl & slate	22.50	15.00
Nos. B6-B9 (4)	35.50	24.00

The surtax was for the victims of the San Juan earthquake.

Souvenir Sheets

National Anthem and Flag — SP7

Illustration reduced.

1944, July 17 ***Imperf.***

B10 SP7 5c +1p vio brn & lt bl	1.90	1.90
B11 SP7 5c +50p bl blk & lt bl	350.00	250.00

Surtax for the needy in the provinces of La Rioja and Catamarca.

Catalogue values for unused stamps in this section, from this point to the end of the section, are for Never Hinged items.

Stamp Designing — SP8

1950, Aug. 26 Photo. ***Perf. 13½***

B12 SP8 10c +10c violet	.25	.25
Nos. B12,CB1-CB5 (6)	20.45	15.65

Argentine Intl. Philatelic Exhibition, 1950.

Poliomyelitis Victim — SP9

1956, Apr. 14 ***Perf. 13½x13***

B13 SP9 20c +30c slate	.30	.20

The surtax was for the poliomyelitis fund. Head in design is from Correggio's "Antiope," Louvre.

Stamp of 1858 and Mail Coach on Raft — SP10

Designs: 2.40p+1.20p, Album, magnifying glass and stamp of 1858. 4.40p+2.20p, Government seat of Confederation, Parana.

1958, Mar. 29 Litho. ***Perf. 13½***

B14 SP10 40c +20c brt grn & dl pur	.30	.25
B15 SP10 2.40p +1.20p ol gray & bl	.40	.25
B16 SP10 4.40p +2.20p lt bl & dp claret	.60	.40
Nos. B14-B16,CB8-CB12 (8)	5.80	4.55

Surtax for Intl. Centennial Philatelic Exhibition, Paraná, Entre Rios, Apr. 19-27.

View of Flooded Land — SP11

1958, Oct. 4 Photo. ***Perf. 13½***

B17 SP11 40c +20c brown	.20	.20
Nos. B17,CB13-CB14 (3)	1.25	1.15

The surtax was for flood victims in the Buenos Aires district.

Child Receiving Blood — SP12

Runner — SP13

1958, Dec. 20 Litho. Wmk. 90

B18 SP12 1p +50c blk & rose red	.20	.20

The surtax went to the Anti-Leukemia Foundation.

1959, Sept. 5 ***Perf. 13½***

Designs: 50c+20c, Basketball players, vert. 1p+50c, Boxers, vert.

B19 SP13 20c +10c emer & blk	.20	.20
B20 SP13 50c +20c yel & blk	.20	.20
B21 SP13 1p +50c mar & blk	.20	.20
Nos. B19-B21,CB15-CB16 (5)	1.60	1.35

3rd Pan American Games, Chicago, Aug. 27-Sept. 7, 1959.

Condor — SP14

Birds: 50c+20c, Fork-tailed flycatchers. 1p+50c, Magellanic woodpecker.

1960, Feb. 6

B22 SP14 20c +10c dk bl	.20	.20
B23 SP14 50c +20c dp vio bl	.20	.20
B24 SP14 1p +50c brn & buff	.20	.20
Nos. B22-B24,CB17-CB18 (5)	1.35	1.15

The surtax was for child welfare work. See Nos. B30, CB29.

Souvenir Sheet

Uprooted Oak Emblem — SP15

1960, Apr. 7 Wmk. 90 ***Imperf.***

B25 SP15 Sheet of 2	1.25	1.25
a. 1p + 50c bister & carmine	.55	.55
b. 4.20p + 2.10p apple grn & dp claret	.55	.55

WRY, July 1, 1959-June 30, 1960.

The surtax was for aid to refugees.

Jacaranda — SP16

Flowers: 1p+1p, Passionflower. 3p+3p, Orchid. 5p+5p, Tabebuia.

1960, Dec. 3 Photo. ***Perf. 13½***

B26 SP16 50c +50c deep blue	.20	.20
B27 SP16 1p +1p bluish grn	.20	.20
B28 SP16 3p +3p henna brn	.30	.25
B29 SP16 5p +5p dark brn	.50	.35
Nos. B26-B29 (4)	1.20	1.00

"TEMEX 61" (Intl. Thematic Exposition).

For overprints see Nos. B31-B34.

Type of 1960

Bird: 4.20p+2.10p, Blue-eyed shag.

1961, Feb. 25 Wmk. 90 ***Perf. 13½***

B30 SP14 4.20p +2.10p chestnut brn	.50	.30

Surtax for child welfare work. See #CB29.

Nos. B26-B29 Overprinted in Black, Brown, Blue or Red: "14 DE ABRIL DIA DE LAS AMERICAS"

1961, Apr. 15

B31 SP16 50c +50c deep blue	.20	.20
B32 SP16 1p +1p bluish grn (Brn)	.20	.20
B33 SP16 3p +3p henna brn (Bl)	.30	.25
B34 SP16 5p +5p dk brn (R)	.50	.40
Nos. B31-B34 (4)	1.20	1.05

Day of the Americas, Apr. 14.

Cathedral, Cordoba — SP17

Stamp of 1862 — SP18

Flight into Egypt, by Ana Maria Moncalvo — SP19

Design: 10p+10p, Cathedral, Buenos Aires.

Perf. 13½

1961, Oct. 21 Wmk. 90 Photo.

B35 SP17 2p +2p rose claret .25 .20
B36 SP18 3p +3p green .30 .20
B37 SP17 10p +10p brt blue .90 .50
a. Souvenir sheet of 3 1.75 1.10
Nos. B35-B37 (3) 1.45 .90

1962 International Stamp Exhibition.

No. B37a contains three imperf. stamps similar to Nos. B35-B37 in dark blue.

1961, Dec. 16 Litho.

B38 SP19 2p +1p lilac & blk brn .20 .20
B39 SP19 10p +5p light & deep claret .50 .20

The surtax was for child welfare.

Chalk-browed Mockingbird SP20

Soccer SP21

Design: 12p+6p, Rufous-collared sparrow.

1962, Dec. 29 ***Perf. 13½***

B40 SP20 4p +2p bis, brn & bl grn .90 .60
B41 SP20 12p +6p gray, yel, grn & brn 1.50 1.10

The surtax was for child welfare. See Nos. B44, B47, B48-B50, CB32, CB35-CB36.

1963, May 18 ***Perf. 13½***

B42 SP21 4p +2p multi .25 .20
B43 SP21 12p +6p Horseman-ship .45 .35
a. Dark carmine (jacket) omitted
Nos. B42-B43,CB31 (3) 1.25 1.05

4th Pan American Games, Sao Paulo.

Bird Type of 1962

Design: Vermilion flycatcher.

1963, Dec. 21 Litho.

B44 SP20 4p +2p blk, red, org & grn .60 .30

The surtax was for child welfare. See No. CB32.

Fencers — SP22

Design: 4p+2p, National Stadium, Tokyo, horiz.

1964, July 18 Wmk. 90 ***Perf. 13½***

B45 SP22 4p +2p red, ocher & brn .20 .20
B46 SP22 12p +6p bl grn & blk .40 .30
Nos. B45-B46,CB33 (3) 1.10 1.00

18th Olympic Games, Tokyo, Oct. 10-25, 1964. See No. CB33.

Bird Type of 1962

Design: Red-crested cardinal.

1964, Dec. 23 Litho.

B47 SP20 4p +2p dk bl, red & grn .60 .30

The surtax was for child welfare. See #CB35.

Bird Type of 1962
Inscribed "R. ARGENTINA"

Designs: 8p+4p, Lapwing. 10p+5p, Scarlet-headed marshbird, horiz. 20p+10p, Amazon kingfisher.

1966-67 ***Perf. 13½***

B48 SP20 8p +4p blk, ol, brt grn & red .80 .35
B49 SP20 10p +5p blk, bl, org & grn .80 .55
B50 SP20 20p +10p blk, yel, bl & pink .40 .35
Nos. B48-B50,CB36,CB38-CB39 (6) 4.30 3.25

The surtax was for child welfare.

Issue dates: 8p+4p, Mar. 26, 1966. 10p+5p, Jan. 14, 1967. 20p+10p, Dec. 23, 1967.

Grandmother's Birthday, by Patricia Lynch; Lions Emblem — SP23

Perf. 12½x13½

1968, Dec. 14 Litho. Wmk. 90

B51 SP23 40p + 20p multi .45 .40

1st Lions Intl. Benevolent Phil. Exhib. Surtax for the Children's Hospital Benevolent Fund.

White-faced Tree Duck — SP24

1969, Sept. 20 Wmk. 365 ***Perf. 13½***

B52 SP24 20p + 10p multi .50 .35

Surtax for child welfare. See No. CB40.

Slender-tailed Woodstar (Hummingbird) SP25

1970, May 9 Wmk. 365 ***Perf. 13½***

B53 SP25 20c + 10c multi .45 .40

The surtax was for child welfare. See Nos. CB41, B56-B59, B62-B63.

Dolphinfish — SP26

1971, Feb. 20 Unwmk. ***Perf. 12½***

Size: 75x15mm

B54 SP26 20c + 10c multi .50 .45

Surtax for child welfare. See No. CB42.

Children with Stamps, by Mariette Lydis — SP27

1971, Dec. 18 Litho. ***Perf. 13½***

B55 SP27 1p + 50p multi .50 .30

2nd Lions Intl. Solidarity Stamp Exhib.

Bird Type of 1970

Birds: 25c+10c, Saffron finch. 65c+30c, Rufous-bellied thrush, horiz.

1972, May 6 Unwmk. ***Perf. 13½***

B56 SP25 25c + 10c multi .30 .20
B57 SP25 65c + 30c multi .45 .30

Surtax was for child welfare.

Bird Type of 1970

Birds: 50c+25c, Southern screamer (chaja). 90c+45c, Saffron-cowled blackbird, horiz.

1973, Apr. 28

B58 SP25 50c + 25c multi .50 .30
B59 SP25 90c + 45c multi .70 .50

Surtax was for child welfare.

Painting Type of Regular Issue

Designs: 15c+15c, Still Life, by Alfredo Guttero, horiz. 90c+90c, Nude, by Miguel C. Victorica, horiz.

1973, Aug. 28 Litho. ***Perf. 13½***

B60 A472 15c + 15c multi .30 .20
B61 A472 90c + 90c multi 1.00 .70

Bird Type of 1970

Birds: 70c+30c, Blue seed-eater. 1.20p+60c, Hooded siskin.

1974, May 11 Litho. ***Perf. 13½***

B62 SP25 70c + 30c multi .50 .35
B63 SP25 1.20p + 60c multi .75 .40

Surtax was for child welfare.

Painting Type of 1974

Design: 70c+30c, The Lama, by Juan Batlle Planas.

1974, May 11 Litho. ***Perf. 13½***

B64 A477 70c + 30c multi .30 .25

PRENFIL-74 UPU, Intl. Exhib. of Phil. Periodicals, Buenos Aires, Oct. 1-12.

Plushcrested Jay — SP28

Designs: 13p+6.50p, Golden-collared macaw. 20p+10p, Begonia. 40p+20p, Teasel.

1976, June 12 Litho. ***Perf. 13½***

B65 SP28 7p + 3.50p multi .20 .20
B66 SP28 13p + 6.50p multi .30 .20
B67 SP28 20p + 10p multi .50 .30
B68 SP28 40p + 20p multi .95 .50
Nos. B65-B68 (4) 1.95 1.20

Argentine philately.

Telegraph, Communications Satellite — SP29

Designs: 20p+10p, Old and new mail trucks. 60p+30p, Old, new packet boats. 70p+35p, Biplane and jet.

1977, July 16 Litho. ***Perf. 13½***

B69 SP29 10p + 5p multi .30 .20
B70 SP29 20p + 10p multi .50 .60
B71 SP29 60p + 30p multi 1.00 .85
B72 SP29 70p + 35p multi 1.25 .85
Nos. B69-B72 (4) 3.05 2.50

Surtax was for Argentine philately.

No. B70 exists with wmk. 365.

Church of St. Francis Type, 1977,
Inscribed: "EXPOSICION ARGENTINA '77"

1977, Aug. 27

B73 A515 160p + 80p multi 2.50 2.00

Surtax was for Argentina '77 Philatelic Exhibition. Issued in sheets of 4.

No. B73 Overprinted with Soccer Cup Emblem

1978, Feb. 4 Litho. ***Perf. 13½***

B74 A515 160p + 80p multi 4.50 4.25
a. Souvenir sheet of 4 20.00 19.00

11th World Cup Soccer Championship, Argentina, June 1-25.

Spinus Magellanicus SP30

Birds: #B76, Variable seedeater. #B77, Yellow thrush. #B78, Pyrocephalus rubineus. #B79, Great kiskadee.

1978, Aug. 5 Litho. ***Perf. 13½***

B75 SP30 50p + 50p multi .90 .60
B76 SP30 100p + 100p multi 1.10 .90
B77 SP30 150p + 150p multi 1.40 1.25
B78 SP30 200p + 200p multi 1.75 1.75
B79 SP30 500p + 500p multi 8.50 7.25
Nos. B75-B79 (5) 13.65 11.75

ARGENTINA '78, Inter-American Philatelic Exhibition, Buenos Aires, Oct. 27-Nov. 5. Nos. B75-B79 issued in sheets of 4 with marginal inscriptions commemorating Exhibition and 1978 Soccer Championship.

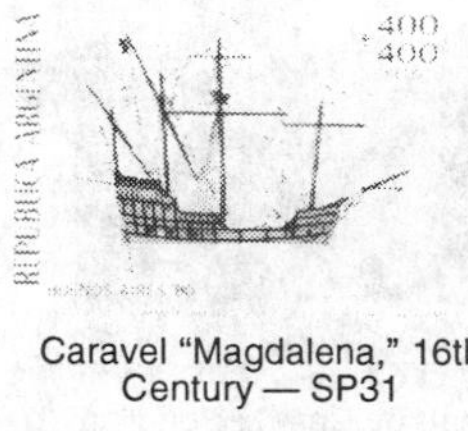

Caravel "Magdalena," 16th Century — SP31

Sailing Ships: 500+500p, 3 master "Rio de la Plata," 17th cent. 600+600p, Corvette "Descubierta," 18th cent. 1500+1500p, Naval Academy yacht "A.R.A. Fortuna," 1979.

1979, Sept. 8 Litho. ***Perf. 13½***

B80 SP31 400p +400p multi 4.00 2.25
B81 SP31 500p +500p multi 4.75 2.50
B82 SP31 600p +600p multi 6.00 3.25
B83 SP31 1500p +1500p multi 15.00 8.00
Nos. B80-B83 (4) 29.75 16.00

Buenos Aires '80, International Philatelic Exhibition, Oct. 24-Nov. 2, 1980. Issued in sheets of 4.

Purmamarca Church — SP32

Churches: 200p + 100p, Molinos. 300p + 150p, Animana. 400p + 200p, San Jose de Lules.

1979, Nov. 3 Litho. *Perf. 13½*

B84 SP32 100p + 50p multi .25 .20
B85 SP32 200p + 100p multi .45 .20
B86 SP32 300p + 150p multi .60 .20
B87 SP32 400p + 200p multi .90 .25
Nos. B84-B87 (4) 2.20 .85

Buenos Aires No. 3, Exhibition and Society Emblems — SP33

Argentine Stamps: 750p+750p, type A580. 1000p+1000p, No. 91. 2000p+2000p, type A588.

1979, Dec. 15 Litho. *Perf. 13½*

B88 SP33 250p + 250p multi .90 .70
B89 SP33 750p + 750p multi 2.25 1.75
B90 SP33 1000p + 1000p multi 3.00 2.50
B91 SP33 2000p + 2000p multi 6.00 5.00
Nos. B88-B91 (4) 12.15 9.95

PRENFIL '80, Intl. Philatelic Literature and Publications Exhib., Buenos Aires, Nov. 7-16, 1980.

Minuet, by Carlos E. Pellegrini SP34

Paintings: 700p+350p, Media Cana, by Carlos Morel. 800p+400p, Cielito, by Pellegrini. 1000p+500p, El Gato, by Juan Leon Palliere.

1981, July 11 Litho. *Perf. 13½*

B92 SP34 500p + 250p multi .70 .35
B93 SP34 700p + 350p multi 1.00 .70
B94 SP34 800p + 400p multi 1.10 .90
B95 SP34 1000p + 500p multi 1.40 1.25
Nos. B92-B95 (4) 4.20 3.20

Espamer '81 Intl. Stamp Exhib. (Americas, Spain, Portugal), Buenos Aires, Nov. 13-22.

Canal, by Beatrix Bongliani (b. 1933) — SP35

Tapestries: 1000p+500p, Shadows, by Silvia Sieburger, vert. 2000p+1000p, Interpretation of a Rectangle, by Silke R. de Haupt, vert. 4000p+2000p, Tilcara, by Tana Sachs.

1982, July 31 Litho. *Perf. 13½*

B96 SP35 1000p + 500p multi .20 .20
B97 SP35 2000p + 1000p multi .40 .40
B98 SP35 3000p + 1500p multi .60 .60
B99 SP35 4000p + 2000p multi .80 .80
Nos. B96-B99 (4) 2.00 2.00

Boy Playing Marbles — SP36

1983, July 2 Litho. *Perf. 13½*

B100 SP36 20c + 10c shown .20 .20
B101 SP36 30c + 15c Jumping rope .45 .20
B102 SP36 50c + 25c Hopscotch .85 .20
B103 SP36 1p + 50c Flying kites 1.10 .50
B104 SP36 2p + 1p Spinning top 1.60 .65
Nos. B100-B104 (5) 4.20 1.75

Surtax was for natl. philatelic associations. See Nos. B106-B110.

Compass, 15th Cent. — SP37

ARGENTINA '85 Intl. Stamp Show: b, Arms of Spain, Argentina. c, Columbus' arms. d-f, Columbus' arrival at San Salvador Island. Nos. B105d-B105f in continuous design; ships shown on singles range in size, left to right, from small to large. Surtax was for exhibition.

1984, Apr. 28 Litho. *Perf. 13½*

B105 Block of 6 3.75 3.75
a.-f. SP37 5p + 2.50p, any single .50 .25

Children's Game Type of 1983

1984, July 7 Litho. *Perf. 13½*

B106 SP36 2p + 1p Blind Man's Buff .20 .20
B107 SP36 3p + 1.50p The Loop .30 .25
B108 SP36 4p + 2p Leap Frog .35 .30
B109 SP36 5p + 2.50p Rolling the loop .45 .35
B110 SP36 6p + 3p Ball Mold .55 .45
Nos. B106-B110 (5) 1.85 1.55

Butterflies — SP38

1985, Nov. 9 Litho. *Perf. 13½*

B111 SP38 5c + 2c Rothschildia jacobaeae .75 .20
B112 SP38 10c + 5c Heliconius erato phyllis .75 .40
B113 SP38 20c + 10c Precis evarete hilaris 1.00 .75
B114 SP38 25c + 13c Cyanopepla pretiosa 1.50 1.00
B115 SP38 40c + 20c Papilio androgeus 2.00 1.50
Nos. B111-B115 (5) 6.00 3.85

Children's Drawings — SP39

1986, Aug. 30 Litho.

B116 SP39 5c + 2c N. Pastor .20 .20
B117 SP39 10c + 5c T. Valleistein .35 .35
B118 SP39 20c + 10c J.M. Flores .60 .60
B119 SP39 25c + 13c M.E. Pezzuto .75 .75
B120 SP39 40c + 20c E. Diehl 1.10 1.10
Nos. B116-B120 (5) 3.00 3.00

Surtax for natl. philatelic associations.

Miniature Sheets

Fresh-water Fish — SP40

No. B121: a, Metynnis maculatus. b, Cynolebias nigripinnis. c, Leporinus solarii. d, Aphyocharax rathbuni. e, Corydoras aeneus. f, Thoracocharax securis. g, Cynolebias melanotaenia. h, Cichlasoma facetum.

No. B122: a, Tetragonopterus argenteus. b, Hemigrammus caudovittatus. c, Astyanax bimaculatus. d, Gymnocorymbus ternetzi. e, Hoplias malabaricus. f, Aphyocharax rubripinnis. g, Apistogramma agassizi. h, Pyrrhulina rachoviana.

1987, June 27

B121 Sheet of 8 2.00 1.75
a.-h. SP40 10c +5c, any single .25 .20
B122 Sheet of 8 4.00 3.50
a.-h. SP40 20c +10c, any single .50 .40

PRENFIL '88, Intl. Philatelic Literature and Media Exhibition, Buenos Aires, Nov. 25-Dec. 2 — SP41

Locomotives and railroad car: No. B123, Yatay locomotive, 1888. No. B124, FCCA electric passenger car, 1914. No. B125, B-15 locomotive, 1942. No. B126, GT-22 No. 200 locomotive, 1988.

1988, June 4 Litho. *Perf. 13½*

B123 SP41 1a +50c multi .65 .50
B124 SP41 1a +50c multi .65 .50
B125 SP41 1a +50c multi .65 .50
B126 SP41 1a +50c multi .65 .50
Nos. B123-B126 (4) 2.60 2.00

Nos. B123-B125 each issued in sheets of 4.

Horses SP42

Paintings: No. B127, *The Waiting*, by Gustavo Solari. No. B128, *Mare and Foal*, by E. Castro. No. B129, *Saint Isidor*, by Castro. No. B130, *At Lagoon's Edge*, by F. Romero Carranza. No. B131, *Under the Tail*, by Castro.

1988, Oct. 29 Litho. *Perf. 13½*

B127 SP42 2a +1a multi .70 .50
B128 SP42 2a +1a multi .70 .50
B129 SP42 2a +1a multi .70 .50
B130 SP42 2a +1a multi .70 .50
B131 SP42 2a +1a multi .70 .50
Nos. B127-B131 (5) 3.50 2.50

PRENFIL '88 — SP43

Covers of philatelic magazines.

1988, Nov. 26 Litho. *Perf. 13½*

B132 SP43 1a +1a *Cronaca Filatelica*, Italy .40 .30
B133 SP43 1a +1a *CO-FI*, Brazil .40 .30
B134 SP43 1a +1a *References de la Poste*, France .40 .30
B135 SP43 2a +2a *Postas Argentinas* .65 .50
Nos. B132-B135 (4) 1.85 1.40

Souvenir Sheet

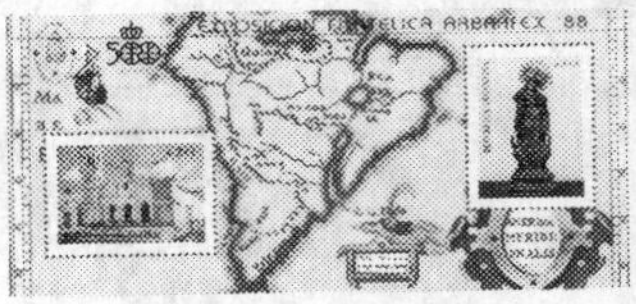
ARBRAPEX '88 — SP44

Designs: No. B136a, *Candel Delivery at San Ignacio*, by Leonie Matthis, Cornelio Saavedra Museum, Buenos Aires. No. B136b, *Immaculate Conception*, a statue in the Isaac Fernandez Blanco Museum, Buenos Aires.

1988, Nov. 26 *Perf. 12*

B136 SP44 Sheet of 2 1.60 1.25
a. 2a +2a multi .65 .50
b. 3a +3a multi .95 .70

Fish SP45

#B137, *Diplomystes viedmensis*. #B138, *Haplochiton taeniatus*. #B139, *Percichthys trucha*. #B140, *Galaxias platei*. #B141, *Salmo fario*.

1989, June 24 Litho. *Perf. 13½*

B137 SP45 10a +5a multi .25 .20
B138 SP45 10a +5a multi .25 .20
B139 SP45 10a +5a multi .25 .20
B140 SP45 10a +5a multi .25 .20
B141 SP45 10a +5a multi .25 .20
Nos. B137-B141 (5) 1.25 1.00

Printed in sheets of 4.

Discovery of America 500th Anniv. (in 1992) and ESPAMER '90 — SP46

Documents and chronicles: No. B142, Columbus's coat of arms, *Book of Privileges* title page. No. B143, Illustration from *New Chronicle and Good Government*, by Guaman Poma de Ayala. No. B144, Illustration from *Discovery and Conquest of Peru*, by Pedro de Cieza de Leon. No. B145, Illustration from *Travel to the River Plate*, by Ulrico Schmidl.

1989, Sept. 16 Litho. *Perf. 13½*
Yellow, Rose Violet & Black

B142 SP46 100a +50a .90 .80
B143 SP46 150a +50a .90 .80
B144 SP46 200a +100a .90 .80
B145 SP46 250a +100a .90 .80
Nos. B142-B145 (4) 3.60 3.20

Insects — SP47

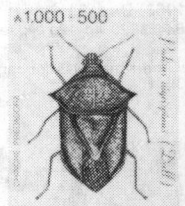

Designs: No. B146, *Podisus nigrispinus*. No. B147, *Adalia bipunctata*. No. B148, *Nabis punctipennis*. No. B149, *Hippodamia convergens*. No. B150, *Calleida suturalis*.

1990, June 30 Litho. *Perf. 13½*

B146 SP47 1000a +500a multi	1.00	.85
B147 SP47 1000a +500a multi	1.00	.85
B148 SP47 1000a +500a multi	1.00	.85
B149 SP47 1000a +500a multi	1.00	.85
B150 SP47 1000a +500a multi	1.00	.85
Nos. B146-B150 (5)	5.00	4.25

Printed in sheets of 4.

Souvenir Sheet

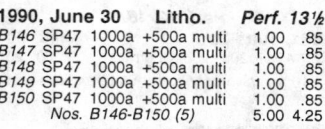

First Natl. Exposition of Aerophilately — SP48

Designs: a, Lieut. Marcos A. Zar, Macchi seaplane. b, Capt. Antonio Parodi, Ansaldo SVA biplane. (Illustration reduced).

1990, July 14 Litho. *Perf. 12*

B151 Sheet of 2	6.00	5.00
a. SP48 2000a +2000a multi	3.00	2.50
b. SP48 3000a +3000a multi	3.00	2.50

Souvenir Sheet

1992 Summer Olympics, Barcelona SP49

Designs: a, Shot put. b, High jump. c, Hurdles. d, Pole vault.

1990, Dec. 15 Litho. *Perf. 13½*

B152 Sheet of 4	9.00	9.00
a.-d. SP49 2000a +2000a multi	2.25	2.25

Espamer '91 Philatelic Exhibition.
See No. B155.

Souvenir Sheet

Discovery of America, 500th Anniv. (in 1992) — SP50

Voyage of Alesandro Malaspina, 1789-1794: a, Sailing ship. b, Malaspina. c, Indian, hut. d, Indian, horse, artist drawing.

1990, Oct. 13 Litho. *Perf. 13½*

B153 Sheet of 4	6.00	6.00
a.-d. SP50 2000a +1000a, any single	1.50	1.50

Espamer '91, Buenos Aires.

Souvenir Sheet

Race Cars and Drivers — SP51

Designs: a, Juan Manuel Fangio. b, Juan Manuel Bordeu. c, Carlos Alberto Reutemann. d, Oscar and Juan Galvez.

1991 Litho. *Perf. 13½*

B154 SP51 Sheet of 4	4.75	4.75
a.-d. 2500a +2500a, any single	1.25	1.25

Espamer '91.

Souvenir Sheet

1992 Summer Olympics Type of 1990

Women's gymnastics routines: a, Floor exercise. b, Uneven parallel bars. c, Balance beam. d, Rhythmic gymnastics.

1991, June 29 Litho. *Perf. 13½*

B155 Sheet of 4	4.75	4.75
a.-d. SP49 2500a +2500a, any single	1.25	1.25

Espamer '91.

Iberoprenfil '92 — SP52

Designs: No. B156, Castor missile. No. B157, Satellite LUSAT 1.

1991, Dec. 28 Litho. *Perf. 13½*

B156 SP52 4000a +4000a multi	2.00	1.75
B157 SP52 4000a +4000a multi	2.00	1.75

Dinosaurs SP53

1992, May 2 Litho. *Perf. 13½*

B158 SP53 38c +38c Carnotaurus	1.50	1.50
B159 SP53 38c +38c Amargasaurus	1.50	1.50

Iberoprenfil '92, Buenos Aires — SP54

Paintings by Raul Soldi (b. 1905): No. B160, The Fiesta. No. B161, Church of St. Anne of Glew.

1992, Sept. 5 Litho. *Perf. 13½*

B160 SP54 76c +76c multi	3.00	3.00
B161 SP54 76c +76c multi	3.00	3.00

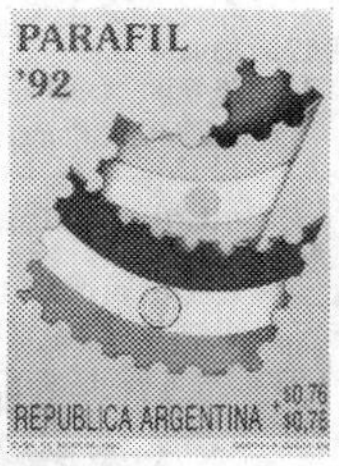

Parafil '92 — SP55

1992, Nov. 21 Litho. *Perf. 13½*

B162 SP55 76c +76c multi	3.00	3.00

2nd Argentine-Paraguayan Philatelic Exhibition, Buenos Aires.

Souvenir Sheet

Birds — SP56

a, Egretta thula. b, Amblyramphus holosericeus. c, Paroaria coronata. d, Chloroceryle amazona.

1993, July 17 Litho. *Perf. 13½*

B163 SP56 38c +38c Sheet of 4	6.00	6.00

Souvenir Sheet

Latin American Air Post Philatelic Exhibition — SP57

Designs: a, 25c+25c, Antoine de Saint-Exupery (1940-44), pilot, author. b, 75c+75c, "The Little Prince," vert. Illustration reduced.

1995, June 3 Litho. *Perf. 12*

B164 SP57 Sheet of 2, #a.-b.	4.00	4.00

For overprint see No. B180.

Souvenir Sheet

Exploration of Antarctica — SP58

75c+25c, Transport ship ARA Bahia Aguirre. 1.25p+75c, Argentine Air Force Hercules C-130.

1995, July 8

B165 SP58 Sheet of 2, #a.-b.	6.00	6.00

Aerofila '96 SP59

Historic airplanes, pilots: No. B166, "Plus ultra," Ramón Franco Bahamonde (1896-1938). No. B167, 14 Bis, Alberto Santos-Dumont (1873-1932). No. B168, Spirit of St. Louis, Charles A. Lindbergh (1902-1974). No. B169, Buenos Aires, Eduardo A. Olivero (1896-1966).

1996, July 13 Litho. *Perf. 13½*

B166 SP59 25c +25c multi	1.00	1.00
B167 SP59 25c +25c multi	1.00	1.00
B168 SP59 50c +50c multi	2.00	2.00
B169 SP59 50c +50c multi	2.00	2.00
Nos. B166-B169 (4)	6.00	6.00

Ceramic Murals from Buenos Aires Subway — SP60

1996, Sept. 21 Litho. *Perf. 13½*

B170 SP60 1p +50c Dragon	3.00	3.00
B171 SP60 1.50p +1p Bird	5.00	5.00

MEVIFIL '97, 1st Intl. Exhibition of Audio-Visual and Philatelic Information Media — SP61

Designs: No. B172, France Type A1. No. B173, Spain Type A3. No. B174, Argentina Type A4. No. B175, Buenos Aires Type A1.

1997, May 10 Litho. *Perf. 13½*

B172 SP61 50c +50c multi	2.00	2.00
B173 SP61 50c +50c multi	2.00	2.00
B174 SP61 50c +50c multi	2.00	2.00
B175 SP61 50c +50c multi	2.00	2.00
a. Block of 4, #B172-B175	8.00	8.00

Issued in sheets of 16 stamps + 4 labels.

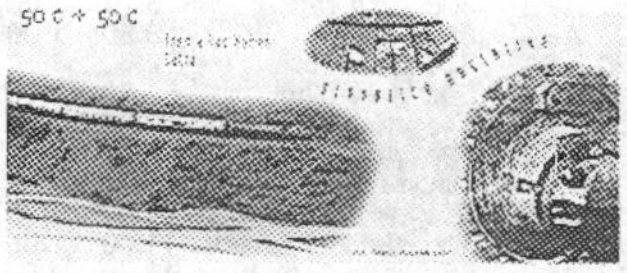

Trains — SP62

Designs: No. B176, Las Nubes (Train to the Clouds), Salta. No. B177, Historical train, Buenos Aires. No. B178, Old Patagonian Express, Rio Negro-Chubut. No. B179, Southern Fueguino Railway, Tierra Del Fuego. Illustration reduced.

1997, Sept. 6 Litho. *Perf. 13*

B176 SP62 50c +50c multi	2.00	2.00
B177 SP62 50c +50c multi	2.00	2.00
B178 SP62 50c +50c multi	2.00	2.00
B179 SP62 50c +50c multi	2.00	2.00
Nos. B176-B179 (4)	8.00	8.00

No. B164 Ovptd. in Red Violet in Sheet Margin:

1997, Sept. 27 Litho. *Perf. 12*

B180 SP57 Sheet of 2, #a.-b.	4.00	4.00

AIR POST STAMPS

Airplane Circles the Globe — AP1

Eagle — AP2

Wings Cross the Sea — AP3

Condor on Mountain Crag — AP4

Perforations of Nos. C1-C37 vary from clean-cut to rough and uneven, with many skipped perfs.

Perf. 13x13½, 13½x13

1928, Mar. 1 Litho. Wmk. 90

C1	AP1	5c	lt red	1.25	.50
C2	AP1	10c	Prus blue	2.25	1.00
C3	AP2	15c	lt brown	2.25	.80
C4	AP1	18c	lilac gray	3.00	2.75
a.			18c brown lilac	3.25	2.75
b.			Double impression	*375.00*	
C5	AP2	20c	ultra	2.25	.80
C6	AP2	24c	deep blue	3.50	2.75
C7	AP3	25c	brt violet	3.50	1.50
C8	AP3	30c	rose red	5.25	1.00
C9	AP4	35c	rose	3.50	1.00
C10	AP1	36c	bister brn	2.50	1.50
C11	AP4	50c	gray black	4.00	.50
C12	AP2	54c	chocolate	3.50	2.00
C13	AP2	72c	yellow grn	4.75	2.00
a.			Double impression	*300.00*	
C14	AP3	90c	dk brown	9.00	1.75
C15	AP3	1p	slate bl & red	11.00	.65
C16	AP3	1.08p	rose & dk bl	16.00	4.50
C17	AP4	1.26p	dull vio & grn	20.00	8.00
C18	AP4	1.80p	blue & lil rose	20.00	8.00
C19	AP4	3.60p	gray & blue	42.50	19.00
			Nos. C1-C19 (19)	160.00	60.00

The watermark on No. C4a is larger than on the other stamps of this set, measuring 10mm across Sun.

Zeppelin First Flight

Air Post Stamps of 1928 Overprinted in Blue

"ZEPPELIN" 1er VUELO 1930

1930, May

C20	AP2	20c	ultra	10.00	5.00
C21	AP4	50c	gray black	20.00	10.00
a.			Inverted overprint	*475.00*	
C22	AP3	1p	slate bl & red	21.00	10.00
a.			Inverted overprint	*650.00*	
C23	AP4	1.80p	blue & lil rose	55.00	25.00
C24	AP4	3.60p	gray & blue	150.00	70.00
			Nos. C20-C24 (5)	256.00	120.00

Overprinted in Green

C25	AP2	20c	ultra	10.00	6.00
C26	AP4	50c	gray black	12.50	9.00
C27	AP3	90c	dark brown	10.00	6.00
C28	AP3	1p	slate bl & red	20.00	12.50
C29	AP4	1.80p	blue & lil rose	600.00	400.00
a.			Thick paper	*850.00*	
			Nos. C25-C29 (5)	652.50	433.50

Air Post Stamps of 1928 Overprinted in Red or Blue

1930 6 Septiembre -1931-
On AP1-AP2

6 de Septiembre 1930 — 1931
On AP3-AP4

1931

C30	AP1	18c	lilac gray	2.00	1.50
C31	AP2	72c	yellow green	14.00	10.50
C32	AP3	90c	dark brown	14.00	10.50
C33	AP4	1.80p	bl & lil rose (Bl)	30.00	22.50
C34	AP4	3.60p	gray & blue	57.50	40.00
			Nos. C30-C34 (5)	117.50	85.00

1st anniv. of the Revolution of 1930.

Zeppelin Issue

Nos. C1, C4, C4a, C14 Overprinted in Blue or Red

GRAF ZEPPELIN 1932
On AP1

GRAF ZEPPELIN 1932
On AP3

1932, Aug. 4

C35	AP1	5c	lt red (Bl)	3.00	2.00
C36	AP1	18c	lilac gray (R)	12.50	9.00
a.			18c brown lilac (R)	100.00	60.00
C37	AP3	90c	dark brown (R)	32.50	26.00
			Nos. C35-C37 (3)	48.00	37.00

Plane and Letter — AP5

Mercury — AP6

Plane in Flight — AP7

Perf. 13½x13, 13x13½

1940, Oct. 23 Photo. Wmk. 90

C38	AP5	30c	deep orange	5.00	.20
C39	AP6	50c	dark brown	7.50	.20
C40	AP5	1p	carmine	1.75	.20
C41	AP7	1.25p	deep green	.50	.20
C42	AP5	2.50p	bright blue	1.25	.20
			Nos. C38-C42 (5)	16.00	1.00

Plane and Letter — AP8

Mercury and Plane — AP9

Perf. 13½x13, 13x13½

1942, Oct. 6 Litho. Wmk. 90

C43	AP8	30c	orange	.20	.20
C44	AP9	50c	dull brn & buff	.40	.20

See Nos. C49-C52, C57, C61.

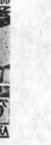

Plane over Iguaçu Falls — AP10

Plane over the Andes — AP11

Perf. 13½x13

1946, June 10 Unwmk.

C45	AP10	15c	dull red brn	.25	.20
C46	AP11	25c	gray green	.20	.20

See Nos. C53-C54.

Allegory of Flight AP12

Astrolabe — AP13

Perf. 13½x13, 13x13½

1946, Sept. 25 Litho. Unwmk.

Surface-Tinted Paper

C47	AP12	15c	sl grn, *pale grn*	.55	.20
C48	AP13	60c	vio brn, *ocher*	.55	.35

Types of 1942

1946-48 Unwmk. *Perf. 13½x13*

C49	AP8	30c	orange	1.40	.20
C50	AP9	50c	dull brn & buff	2.50	.20
C51	AP8	1p	carmine ('47)	1.25	.20
C52	AP8	2.50p	brt blue ('48)	5.50	.75
			Nos. C49-C52 (4)	10.65	1.35

Types of 1946

1948 Wmk. 90

C53	AP10	15c	dull red brn	.20	.20
C54	AP11	25c	gray green	.25	.20

Atlas (National Museum, Naples) — AP14

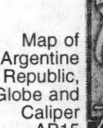

Map of Argentine Republic, Globe and Caliper AP15

Perf. 13½x13, 13x13½

1948-49 Photo. Wmk. 288

C55	AP14	45c	dk brown ('49)	.35	.20
C56	AP15	70c	dark green	.50	.25

4th Pan-American Reunion of Cartographers, Buenos Aires, Oct.-Nov., 1948.

Mercury Type of 1942

1949 Litho. *Perf. 13x13½*

C57	AP9	50c	dull brn & buff	.40	.20

Marksmanship Trophy — AP16

1949, Nov. 4 Photo.

C58	AP16	75c	brown	.75	.20

World Rifle Championship, 1949.

Catalogue values for unused stamps in this section, from this point to the end of the section, are for Never Hinged items.

Douglas DC-3 and Condor AP17

Perf. 13x13½

1951, June 20 Wmk. 90

C59	AP17	20c	dk olive grn	.20	.20

10th anniversary of the State air lines.

Douglas DC-6 and Condor — AP18

1951, Oct. 17 *Perf. 13½*

C60	AP18	20c	blue	.20	.20

End of Argentine 5-year Plan.

Plane-Letter Type of 1942

1951 Litho. *Perf. 13½x13*

C61	AP8	1p	carmine	.40	.20

Jesus by Leonardo da Vinci (detail, "Virgin of the Rocks") — AP19

Perf. 13½x13

1956, Sept. 29 Photo. Wmk. 90

C62	AP19	1p	dull purple	.35	.20

Issued to express the gratitude of the children of Argentina to the people of the world for their help against poliomyelitis.

Battle of Montevideo AP20

Leonardo Rosales and Tomas Espora — AP21

Guillermo Brown — AP22

AP23

1957, Mar. 2 *Perf. 13½*

C63	AP20	60c	blue gray	.20	.20
C64	AP21	1p	brt pink	.20	.20
C65	AP22	2p	brown	.25	.20
			Nos. C63-C65 (3)	.65	.60

Cent. of the death of Admiral Guillermo Brown, founder of the Argentine navy.

1957, Aug. 16

Map of Americas and Arms of Buenos Aires.

C66	AP23	2p	rose violet	.40	.20

Issued to publicize the Inter-American Economic Conference in Buenos Aires.

AP24

AP25

1957, Aug. 31 Wmk. 90 *Perf. 13½*
C67 AP24 60c Modern jlcomotive .20 .20

Centenary of Argentine railroads.

1957, Sept. 14
C68 AP25 1p Globe, Flag,Compass Rose .20 .20
C69 AP25 2p Key .30 .20

1957 International Congress for Tourism.

Birds Carrying Letters AP26

1957, Nov. 6
C70 AP26 1p bright blue .20 .20

Issued for Letter Writing Week, Oct. 6-12.

Early Plane — AP27

1958, May 31 *Perf. 13½*
C71 AP27 2p maroon .20 .20

50th anniversary of the Argentine Aviation Club.

Stamp Anniv. Type

Designs: 80c, Stamp of Buenos Aires and view of the Plaza de la Aduana. 1p, Stamp of 1858 and "The Post of Santa Fe."

1958 Litho. *Perf. 13½*
C72 A270 80c pale bis & sl bl .20 .20
C73 A270 1p red org & dk bl .25 .20

Centenary of the first postage stamps of Buenos Aires and the Argentine Confederation.

Issue dates: 80c, Oct. 18; 1p, Aug. 23.

Comet Jet over World Map AP29

1959, May 16 *Perf. 13½*
C74 AP29 5p black & olive .35 .20

Inauguration of jet flights by Argentine Airlines.

Type of Regular Issue, 1960.

"Cabildo" and: 1.80p, Mariano Moreno. 5p, Manuel Belgrano and Juan Jose Castelli.

Perf. 13½
1960, May 28 Wmk. 90 Photo.
C75 A287 1.80p red brown .20 .20
a. Souvenir sheet of 3 .65 .40
C76 A287 5p buff & purple .35 .20
a. Souvenir sheet of 3 1.25 .80

Souvenir sheets are imperf. No. C75a contains one No. C75 and 1p and 2p resembling Nos. 713-714; stamps in reddish brown. No. C76a contains one No. C76 and 4.20p and 10.70p resembling Nos. 715-716; stamps are in green.

Symbolic of New Provinces — AP30

1960, July 8 Litho.
C77 AP30 1.80p dp car & blue .20 .20

Elevation of the territories of Chubut, Formosa, Neuquen, Rio Negro and Santa Cruz to provinces.

Type of Regular Issue, 1960

1960, Oct. 1 Photo. *Perf. 13½*
C78 A291 1.80p rose lilac .20 .20
C79 A291 10.70p brt grnsh blue .40 .20

UNESCO Emblem AP31

1962, July 14 Litho.
C80 AP31 13p ocher & brown .40 .25

15th anniv. of UNESCO.

Mail Coach — AP32

1962, Oct. 6 Wmk. 90 *Perf. 13½*
C81 AP32 5.60p gray brn & blk .20 .20

Mailman's Day, Sept. 14, 1962.

No. 695 and Type of 1959 Surcharged in Green

AEREO
5 60
PESOS

1962, Oct. 31 Photo.
C82 A277 5.60p on 5p brown .30 .20
C83 A277 18p on 5p brn, *grnsh* 1.00 .20

UPAE Emblem AP33

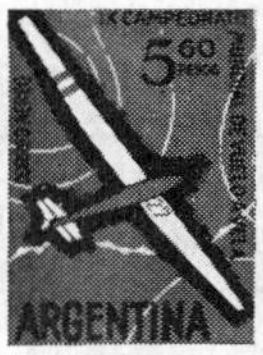

Skylark AP34

1962, Nov. 24 Photo. *Perf. 13½*
C84 AP33 5.60p dark blue .20 .20

50th anniv. of the founding of the Postal Union of the Americas and Spain, UPAE.

1963, Feb. 9 Litho.

Design: 11p, Super Albatros.

C85 AP34 5.60p blue & black .20 .20
C86 AP34 11p blue, blk & red .30 .20

9th World Gliding Championships.

Symbolic Plane — AP35

1963-65 Wmk. 90 *Perf. 13½*
C87 AP35 5.60p dk pur, car & brt grn .40 .20
C88 AP35 7p black & bis ('64) .55 .20
C88A AP35 7p black & bis ('65) 4.00 .55
C89 AP35 11p blk, dk pur & grn .55 .25
C90 AP35 18p dk pur, red & vio bl 1.10 .35
C91 AP35 21p brown, red & gray 1.40 .55
Nos. C87-C91 (6) 8.00 2.10

"Argentina" reads down on No. C88, up on No. C88A. See Nos. C101-C104, C108-C111, C123-C126, C135-C141. For overprint and surcharges see Nos. C96, C146-C150.

Type of Regular Issue, 1964

18p, Map of Falkland Islands (Islas Malvinas).

1964, Feb. 22 *Perf. 13½*
Size: 33x22mm
C92 A327 18p lt & dk bl & ol grn 1.75 .70

UPU Monument, Bern, and UN Emblem — AP36

1964, May 23 Engr. *Perf. 13½*
C93 AP36 18p red & dk brown .50 .25

15th UPU Cong., Vienna, Austria, May-June 1964.

Discovery of America, Florentine Woodcut — AP37

1964, Oct. 10 Litho.
C94 AP37 13p tan & black .35 .30

Day of the Race, Columbus Day.

Lt. Matienzo Base, Antarctica AP38

1965, Feb. 27 Photo. *Perf. 13½*
C95 AP38 11p salmon pink .50 .20

Issued to publicize the national territory of Tierra del Fuego, Antarctic and South Atlantic Isles.

No. C88A Overprinted in Silver: "PRIMERS / JORNADAS FILATELICAS / RIOPLATENSES"

1965, Mar. 17 Litho.
C96 AP35 7p black & bister .25 .20

1st Rio de la Plata Stamp Show, sponsored jointly by the Argentine and Uruguayan Philatelic Associations, Montevideo, Mar. 19-28.

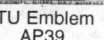

ITU Emblem AP39

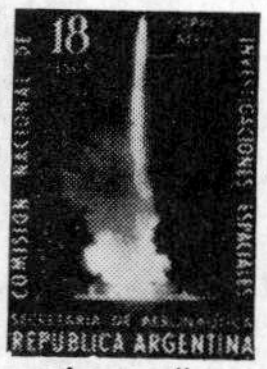

Ascending Rocket AP40

1965, May 11 Wmk. 90 *Perf. 13½*
C97 AP39 18p slate, blk & red .40 .25

Centenary of the ITU.

1965, May 29 Photo. *Perf. 13½*

Design: 50p, Earth with trajectories and magnetic field, horiz.

C98 AP40 18p vermilion .40 .20
C99 AP40 50p dp violet blue 1.00 .50

6th Symposium on Space Research, held in Buenos Aires, and to honor the Natl. Commission of Space Research.

Type of 1963-65 Inscribed "Republica Argentina" Reading Down

1965, Oct. 13 Litho. Wmk. 90
C101 AP35 12p dk car rose & brn 1.40 .20
C102 AP35 15p vio blue & dk red .85 .25
C103 AP35 27.50p dk bl grn & gray 1.40 .40
C104 AP35 30.50p dk brown & dk bl 2.00 .60
Nos. C101-C104 (4) 5.65 1.45

Argentine Antarctica Map and Centaur Rocket — AP41

1966, Feb. 19 *Perf. 13½*
C105 AP41 27.50p bl, blk & dp org 1.00 .75

Launchings of sounding balloons and of a Gamma Centaur rocket in Antarctica during February, 1965.

Sea Gull and Southern Cross AP42

1966, May 14 *Perf. 13½*
C106 AP42 12p Prus blue, blk & red .30 .20

50th anniv. of the Naval Aviation School.

Blériot Plane Flown by Fels, 1917 — AP43

1967, Sept. 2 Litho. *Perf. 13½*
C107 AP43 26p olive, bl & blk .25 .20

Flight by Theodore Fels from Buenos Aires to Montevideo, Sept. 2, 1917, allegedly the 1st intl. airmail flight.

Type of 1963-65 Inscribed "Republica Argentina" Reading Down

1967, Dec. 20 *Perf. 13½*
C108 AP35 26p brown .60 .25
C109 AP35 40p violet 4.50 .30
C110 AP35 68p blue green 3.00 .45
C111 AP35 78p ultra 1.25 .60
Nos. C108-C111 (4) 9.35 1.60

Vito Dumas and Ketch "Legh II"
AP44

1968, July 27 **Litho.** **Wmk. 90**

C112 AP44 68p bl, blk, red & vio bl .65 .40

Issued to commemorate Vito Dumas's one-man voyage around the world in 1943.

Type of Regular Issue and

Assembly Emblem
AP45

Design: 40p, Globe and map of South America.

1968, Oct. 19 **Litho.** ***Perf. 13½***

C113 A395 40p brt pink, lt bl & blk .40 .20
C114 AP45 68p bl, lt bl, gold & blk .65 .30

4th Plenary Assembly of the Intl. Telegraph and Telephone Consultative Committee, Mar del Plata, Sept. 23-Oct. 25.

Radar Antenna, Balcarce Station — AP46

Perf. 13½

1969, Aug. 23 **Wmk. 90** **Photo.**

C115 AP46 40p blue gray .70 .25

Communications by satellite through Intl. Telecommunications Consortium (INTELSAT).

Atucha Nuclear Center
AP47

1969, Dec. 13 **Litho.** **Wmk. 365**

C116 AP47 26p blue & multi 1.40 .80

Completion of Atucha Nuclear Center.

Type of 1963-65 Inscribed "Republica Argentina" Reading Down

1969-71 ***Perf. 13½***

C123 AP35 40p violet 5.00 .30
C124 AP35 68p dk blue grn ('70) 2.00 .60

Unwmk.

C125 AP35 26p yellow brn ('71) .30 .20
C126 AP35 40p violet ('71) 2.75 .40
Nos. C123-C126 (4) 10.05 1.50

Old Fire Engine and Fire Brigade Emblem
AP48

1970, Aug. 8 **Litho.** **Unwmk.**

C128 AP48 40c green & multi .55 .30

Centenary of the Fire Brigade.

Education Year Emblem — AP49

1970, Aug. 29 ***Perf. 13½***

C129 AP49 68c blue & blk .40 .25

Issued for International Education Year.

Fleet Leaving Valparaiso, by Antonio Abel
AP50

1970, Oct. 17 **Litho.** ***Perf. 13½***

C130 AP50 26c multicolored 1.00 .35

150th anniv. of the departure for Peru of the liberation fleet from Valparaiso, Chile.

Sumampa Chapel
AP51

1970, Nov. 7 **Photo.**

C131 AP51 40c multicolored .95 .35

Bishopric of Tucuman, 400th anniversary.

Buenos Aires Planetarium — AP52

1970, Nov. 28 **Litho.** ***Perf. 13½***

C132 AP52 40c multicolored .60 .25

Jorge Newbery and Morane Saulnier Plane
AP53

1970, Dec. 19

C133 AP53 26c bl, blk, yel & grn .40 .25

24th Aeronautics and Space Week.

Industries Type of Regular Issue

Design: 31c, Refinery.

1971, Oct. 16 **Litho.** ***Perf. 13½***

C134 A445 31c red, blk & yel .60 .25

Type of 1963-65 Inscribed "Republica Argentina" Reading Down

1971-74 **Unwmk.**

C135 AP35 45c brown 3.25 .20
C136 AP35 68c red .50 .20
C137 AP35 70c vio blue ('73) .80 .20
C138 AP35 90c emerald ('73) 1.90 .20
C139 AP35 1.70p blue ('74) .50 .25
C140 AP35 1.95p emerald ('74) .50 .30
C141 AP35 2.65p dp claret ('74) .50 .40
Nos. C135-C141 (7) 7.95 1.75

Fluorescent paper was used for Nos. C135-C136, C138-C141. The 70c was issued on both papers.

Don Quixote, Drawing by Ignacio Zuloaga — AP54

1975, Apr. 26 **Photo.** ***Perf. 13½***

C145 AP54 2.75p yellow, blk & red .60 .35

Day of the Race and for Espana 75 Intl. Philatelic Exhibition, Madrid, Apr. 4-13.

No. C87 Surcharged **100 PESOS**

1975, Sept. 15 **Litho.** **Wmk. 90**

C146 AP35 9.20p on 5.60p .90 .20
C147 AP35 19.70p on 5.60p 1.25 .45
C148 AP35 100p on 5.60p 5.50 2.25
Nos. C146-C148 (3) 7.65 2.90

No. C87 Surcharged **REVALORIZADO 9 20 PESOS**

1975, Oct. 15

C149 AP35 9.20p on 5.60p .70 .30
C150 AP35 19.70p on 5.60p 1.25 .60

Argentine State Airline, 50th Anniv.
AP55

1990, Sept. 15 **Litho.** ***Perf. 13½***

C151 AP55 2500a Junkers JU52-3M 1.25 .90
C152 AP55 2500a Grumman SA-16 1.25 .90
C153 AP55 2500a Fokker F-27 1.25 .90
C154 AP55 2500a Fokker F-28 1.25 .90
Nos. C151-C154 (4) 5.00 3.60

AIR POST SEMI-POSTAL STAMPS

Catalogue values for unused stamps in this section are for Never Hinged items.

Philatelic Exhibition Type

Designs: 45c+45c, Stamp engraving. 70c+70c, Proofing stamp die. 1p+1p, Sheet of stamps. 2.50p+2.50p, The letter. 5p+5p, Gen. San Martin.

Perf. 13½

1950, Aug. 26 **Wmk. 90** **Photo.**

CB1 SP8 45c + 45c violet bl .40 .25
CB2 SP8 70c + 70c dark brown .55 .40
a. Souv. sheet of 3, #B12, CB1, CB2, imperf. 3.00 3.00
CB3 SP8 1p + 1p cerise 1.50 1.50
CB4 SP8 2.50p + 2.50p ol gray 8.50 6.00
CB5 SP8 5p + 5p dull green 9.25 7.25
Nos. CB1-CB5 (5) 20.20 15.40

Argentine Intl. Philatelic Exhib., 1950.

Pieta by Michelangelo
SPAP2

1951, Dec. 22 ***Perf. 13½x13***

CB6 SPAP2 2.45p +7.55p grnsh blk 21.00 14.00

Surtax as for the Eva Peron Foundation.

Flower and Child's Head
SPAP3

Stamp of 1858
SPAP4

1958, Mar. 15 ***Perf. 13½***

CB7 SPAP3 1p +50c deep claret .30 .30

Surtax for National Council for Children.

1958, Mar. 29 **Litho.** **Wmk. 90**

CB8 SPAP4 1p + 50c gray ol & bl .40 .30
CB9 SPAP4 2p + 1p rose lilac & vio .50 .40
CB10 SPAP4 3p + 1.50p green & brown .60 .50
CB11 SPAP4 5p + 2.50p gray ol & car rose 1.00 .85
CB12 SPAP4 10p + 5p gray ol & brn 2.00 1.60
Nos. CB8-CB12 (5) 4.50 3.65

The surtax was for the Intl. Centennial Philatelic Exhibition, Buenos Aires, Apr. 19-27.

Type of Semi-Postal Issue, 1958

Designs: 1p+50c, Flooded area. 5p+2.50p, House and truck under water.

1958, Oct. 4 **Photo.** ***Perf. 13½***

CB13 SP11 1p + 50c dull purple .25 .20
CB14 SP11 5p + 2.50p grnsh blue .80 .75

The surtax was for victims of a flood in the Buenos Aires district.

Type of Semi-Postal Issue, 1959

1959, Sept. 5 **Litho.** ***Perf. 13½***

CB15 SP13 2p + 1p Rowing .40 .25
CB16 SP13 3p + 1.50p Woman diver .60 .50

Type of Semi-Postal Issue, 1960

Birds: 2p+1p, Rufous tinamou. 3p+1.50p, Rhea.

1960, Feb. 6 ***Perf. 13½***

CB17 SP14 2p + 1p rose car & sal .30 .20
CB18 SP14 3p + 1.50p slate green .45 .35

The surtax was for child welfare work.
See No. CB29.

Buenos Aires Market Place, 1810
SPAP5

Seibo, National Flower
SPAP6

6p+3p, Oxcart water carrier. 10.70p+5.30p, Settlers landing. 20p+10p, The Fort.

1960, Aug. 20 **Photo.** **Wmk. 90**

CB19 SPAP5 2 + 1p rose brown .20 .20
CB20 SPAP5 6 + 3p gray .35 .25
CB21 SPAP5 10.70 + 5.30p blue .60 .35

CB22 SPAP5 20 + 10p bluish grn 1.00 .85
Nos. CB19-CB22 (4) 2.15 1.65

Inter-American Philatelic Exhibition EFIMAYO 1960, Buenos Aires, Oct. 12-24, held to for the sesquicentennial of the May Revolution of 1910.
For overprints see Nos. CB25-CB28.

1960, Sept. 10 ***Perf. 13½***

10.70p+5.30p, Copihue, Chile's national flower.

CB23 SPAP6 6 + 3p lilac rose .35 .30
CB24 SPAP6 10.70 + 5.30p vermilion .50 .40

The surtax was for earthquake victims in Chile.

Nos. CB19-CB22 Overprinted: "DIA DE LAS NACIONES UNIDAS 24 DE OCTUBRE"

1960, Oct. 8

CB25 SPAP5 2 + 1p rose brown .20 .20
CB26 SPAP5 6 + 3p gray .30 .30
CB27 SPAP5 10.70 + 5.30p blue .50 .40
CB28 SPAP5 20 + 10p bluish green .85 .75
Nos. CB25-CB28 (4) 1.85 1.65

United Nations Day, Oct. 24, 1960.

Type of Semi-Postal Issue, 1960

Design: Emperor penguins.

1961, Feb. 25 Photo. Wmk. 90

CB29 SP14 1.80p + 90c gray .30 .20

The surtax was for child welfare work.

Stamp of 1862 — SPAP7

Crutch, Olympic Torch and Rings — SPAP8

1962, May 19 **Litho.**

CB30 SPAP7 6.50p + 6.50p Prus bl & grnsh bl .70 .65

Opening of the "Argentina 62" Philatelic Exhibition, Buenos Aires, May 19-29.

Type of Semi-Postal Issue, 1963

1963, May 18 Wmk. 90 ***Perf. 13½***

CB31 SP21 11p + 5p Bicycling .55 .50

Type of Semi-Postal Issue, 1962

1963, Dec. 21 ***Perf. 13½***

CB32 SP20 11p + 5p Great kiskadee .70 .60

The surtax was for child welfare.

Type of Semi-Postal Issue, 1964

1964, July 18 **Litho.**

CB33 SP22 11p + 5p Sailboat .50 .50

1964, Sept. 19 Litho. ***Perf. 13½***

CB34 SPAP8 18p + 9p bluish grn, blk, red & yel .60 .60

13th "Olympic" games for the handicapped, Tokyo, 1964.

Bird Type of Semi-Postal Issue, 1962

1964, Dec. 23 Litho. Wmk. 90

CB35 SP20 18p + 9p Chilean swallow .90 .75

The surtax was for child welfare.

Bird Type of Semi-Postal Issue, 1962, Inscribed "R. ARGENTINA"

Design: Rufous ovenbird.

1966, Mar. 26 ***Perf. 13½***

CB36 SP20 27.50p + 12.50p bl, ocher, yel & grn .80 .70

The surtax was for child welfare.

Coat of Arms — SPAP9

1966, June 25 Litho. ***Perf. 13½***

CB37 SPAP9 10p + 10p yellow & multi 1.75 1.40

ARGENTINA '66 Philatelic Exhibition held in connection with the sesquicentennial celebration of the Declaration of Independence, Buenos Aires, July 16-23. The surtax was for the Exhibition. Issued in sheets of 4.

Bird Type of Semi-Postal Issue, 1962, Inscribed "R. ARGENTINA"

Designs: 15p+7p, Blue and yellow tanager. 26p+13p, Toco toucan.

1967 Litho. Wmk. 90

CB38 SP20 15p + 7p blk, bl, grn & yel 1.00 .90
CB39 SP20 26p + 13p blk, org, yel & bl .50 .40

The surtax was for child welfare.
Issue dates: 15p+7p, Jan. 14. 26p+13p, Dec. 23.

Bird Type of Semi-Postal Issue, 1969

Design: 26p+13p, Lineated woodpecker.

1969, Sept. 20 Wmk. 365 ***Perf. 13½***

CB40 SP24 26p + 13p multi .50 .40

The surtax was for child welfare.

Bird Type of Semi-Postal Issue, 1970

Design: 40c+20c, Chilean flamingo.

1970, May 9 Litho. Wmk. 365

CB41 SP25 40c + 20c multi .45 .40

The surtax was for child welfare.

Fish Type of Semi-Postal Issue, 1971

Design: Pejerrey (atherinidae family).

1971, Feb. 20 Unwmk. ***Perf. 12½***
Size: 75x15mm

CB42 SP26 40c + 20c lt blue & multi .40 .40

The surtax was for child welfare.

OFFICIAL STAMPS

Regular Issues Overprinted in Black

OFICIAL

1884-87 Unwmk. ***Perf. 12, 14***

O1 A29 ½c brown 12.00 10.00
O2 A23 1c red 8.00 6.00
b. Perf. 12 40.00 30.00
O3 A29 1c red .50 .35
b. Double overprint 35.00 35.00
O4 A20 2c green .50 .35
b. Double overprint 35.00 35.00
O5 A11 4c brown .50 .35
O6 A7 8c lake .50 .35
O7 A8 10c green 40.00 25.00
O8 A23 12c ultra (#45) 6.50 4.00
a. Perf. 14 325.00 125.00
O9 A29 12c grnsh blue .80 .60
O10 A19 24c blue 1.00 .85
O11 A21 25c lake 16.00 12.50
O12 A12 30c orange 32.50 20.00
O13 A13 60c black 20.00 12.50
O14 A14 90c blue 20.00 15.00
b. Double overprint 50.00 45.00
Nos. O1-O14 (14) 158.80 107.85

Inverted Overprint

O1a A29 ½c 16.00 12.50
O2a A23 1c Perf. 14 50.00 40.00
c. Perf. 12 32.50 30.00
O3a A29 1c 1.50 1.00
O4a A20 2c 65.00 40.00
O5a A11 4c 40.00 32.50
O6a A7 8c 60.00 60.00
O8b A23 12c Perf. 12 12.50
O9a A29 12c 125.00 65.00
O10a A19 24c 2.75 1.60
O13a A13 60c 90.00 50.00
O14a A14 90c 50.00 40.00

1884 ***Rouletted***

O15 A17 16c green 1.75 1.00
a. Double overprint 15.00 —
b. Inverted overprint 125.00
O16 A18 20c blue 8.00 7.00
a. Inverted overprint 60.00 40.00
O17 A19 24c blue 1.25 1.00
a. Inverted overprint 4.00 2.50
b. Double ovpt., one inverted 250.00 —
Nos. O15-O17 (3) 11.00 9.00

Overprinted Diagonally in Red

1885 ***Perf. 12***

O18 A20 2c green 2.00 1.50
a. Inverted overprint 40.00 32.50
O19 A11 4c brown 2.00 1.25
a. Inverted overprint 40.00 30.00
b. Double overprint 50.00 —
O20 A13 60c black 20.00 16.00
O21 A14 90c blue 200.00 150.00

1885 ***Rouletted***

O22 A19 24c blue 17.50 12.50

On all of these stamps, the overprint is found reading both upwards and downwards.
Counterfeits exist of No. O21 overprint and others.

Regular Issues Handstamped Horizontally in Black

OFICIAL

1884 ***Perf. 12, 14***

O23 A23 1c red 50.00 17.00
a. Perf. 12 150.00 100.00
O24 A20 2c green, diagonal overprint 25.00 15.00
a. Horizontal overprint 150.00 125.00
O25 A11 4c brown 10.00 7.50
O26 A7 8c lake 10.00 10.00
O27 A23 12c ultra 27.50 20.00

Overprinted Diagonally

O28 A19 24c bl, rouletted 20.00 14.00
O29 A13 60c black 15.00 10.00

Counterfeit overprints exist.

Liberty Head — O1

Perf. 11½, 12 and Compound

1901, Dec. 1 **Engr.**

O31 O1 1c gray .20 .20
b. Vert. pair, imperf. horiz. 50.00
c. Horiz. pair, imperf. vert. 50.00
O32 O1 2c orange brown .30 .20
O33 O1 5c red .40 .20
b. Vert. pair, imperf. horiz. 50.00
O34 O1 10c dark green .45 .20
O35 O1 30c dark blue 4.00 1.00
O36 O1 50c orange 1.60 1.00
Nos. O31-O36 (6) 6.95 2.80

Imperf, Pairs

O31a O1 1c 40.00
O32a O1 2c 40.00
O33a O1 5c 50.00
O34a O1 10c 40.00
O35a O1 30c 65.00
O36a O1 50c 50.00

Regular Stamps of 1935-51 Overprinted in Black

SERVICIO
OFICIAL
c

Perf. 13x13½, 13½x13, 13

1938-54 Wmk. RA in Sun (90)

O37 A129 1c buff ('40) .20 .20
O38 A130 2c dk brn ('40) .20 .20
O39 A132 3c grn ('39) .20 .20
O40 A132 3c lt gray ('39) .20 .20
O41 A134 5c yel brn .20 .20
O42 A195 5c car ('53) .20 .20
O43 A137 10c carmine .20 .20
O44 A137 10c brn ('39) .20 .20
O45 A140 15c lt gray bl, type II ('47) .20 .20
O46 A139 15c slate blue .50 .20
O47 A139 15c pale ultra ('39) .20 .20
O48 A139 20c blue ('53) .30 .20
O49 A141 25c carmine .20 .20
a. Overprint 11mm .20 .20
O49B A143 40c dk violet .90 .20
O50 A144 50c red & org .20 .20
a. Overprint 11mm .25 .20
O51 A146 1p brn blk & lt bl ('40) .20 .20
a. Overprint 11mm
O52 A224 1p choc & lt bl ('51) .20 .20
a. Overprint 11mm .20 .20

O53 A147 2p brn lake & dk ultra (ovpt. 11mm) ('54) .70 .20
Nos. O37-O53 (18) 5.20 3.60

Overprinted in Black on Stamps and Types of 1945-47

Perf. 13x13½, 13½x13

1945-46 **Unwmk.**

O54 A130 2c sepia 2.75 .40
O55 A134 3c lt gray 2.25 .30
O56 A134 5c yel brn .65 .20
O57 A195 5c dp car .20 .20
O58 A137 10c brown .20 .20
a. Double overprint
O59 A140 15c lt gray bl, type II .20 .20
O61 A141 25c dull rose .20 .20
O62 A144 50c red & org .55 .20
O63 A146 1p brn blk & lt bl .20 .20
O64 A147 2p brn lake & bl .40 .20
O65 A148 5p ind & ol grn .20 .20
O66 A149 10p dp cl & int blk .45 .20
O67 A150 20p bl grn & brn 1.00 .30
Nos. O54-O67 (13) 9.25 3.00

Overprinted in Black on Stamps and Types of 1942-50

Perf. 13, 13x13½

1944-51 **Wmk. 288**

O73 A134 3c lt gray 1.10 .50
O74 A134 5c yellow brown .25 .20
O75 A137 10c red brown .20 .20
O76 A140 15c lt gray bl, type II .25 .20
O77 A144 50c red & org (overprint 11 mm) 1.50 .50
O78 A146 1p brn blk & lt bl (overprint 11mm) 1.75 .35
Nos. O73-O78 (6) 5.05 1.95

Catalogue values for unused stamps in this section, from this point to the end of the section, are for Never Hinged items.

Nos. 600-606 Overprinted in Black

SERVICIO OFICIAL
d

1953 Wmk. 90 ***Perf. 13***

O79 A228 5c gray .20 .20
O80 A228 10c rose lilac .20 .20
O81 A228 20c rose pink .20 .20
O82 A228 25c dull green .20 .20
O83 A228 40c dull violet .20 .20
O84 A228 45c deep blue .20 .20
O85 A228 50c dull broen .20 .20

SERVICIO OFICIAL
e

SERVICIO OFICIAL
f

Nos. 611-617 Overprinted Type "e" in Blue

Perf. 13x13½, 13½x13

O86 A229 1p dk brown .20 .20
O87 A229 1.50p dp green .30 .20
O88 A229 2p brt carmine .20 .20
O89 A229 3p indigo .55 .25

Size: 30x40mm

O90 A229 5p red brown .60 .45
O91 A228 10p red 2.75 1.75
O92 A229 20p green 30.00 20.00
Nos. O79-O92 (14) 36.00 24.45

No. 612 Overprinted Type "f" in Blue

O93 A229 1.50p dp grn 1.00 .30

Regular Issues of 1954-59 Variously Overprinted in Black or Blue

S. OFICIAL
g

SERVICIO OFICIAL
h

Perf. 13½, 13x13½, 13½x13

1955-61 Litho. Wmk. 90

O94 A237(c) 20c red (#629) .20 .20
O95 A237(d) 20c red (#629) .20 .20
O96 A237(d) 40c red, ovpt. 15mm (#630) .20 .20

Engr.

O97 A239(g) 50c bl (#632) .20 .20

Photo.

O98 A239(h) 1p brn (#635) .20 .20
O99 A239(e) 1p brn (Bl, #635) .20 .20

O100 A239(e) 1p brn (Bk, #635) .20 .20

Engr.

O101 A239(h) 3p vio brn (#638) .20 .20
O102 A240(h) 5p gray grn (#639) .30 .20
O103 A240(e) 10p yel grn (#640) .50 .20
O104 A240(f) 20p dl vio (#641) .75 .30
O105 A240(h) 20p dl vio (#641) .75 .25
O106 A241(e) 50p ultra & ind (#642) 1.10 .20
Nos. O94-O106 (13) 5.00 2.75

The overprints on Nos. O99-O100 and O103-O104 are horizontal; that on No. O109 is vertical. On No. O106 overprint measures 23mm.

Issue dates: No. O102, 1957. Nos. O97, O101, O103, O105, 1958. Nos. O98-O99, O104, 1959. No. O100, 1960. No. O106, 1961.

No. 659 Overprinted Type "d"

1957 Wmk. 90 Litho. *Perf. 13*

O108 A133 20c dl pur (ovpt. 15mm) .20 .20

Nos. 666, 658 and 663 Variously Overprinted

1957 Photo. *Perf. 13x13½, 13½*

O109 A261(g) 2p claret .20 .20
O110 A254(e) 2.40p brown .20 .20
O111 A258(c) 4.40p grnsh gray .25 .20
Nos. O109-O111 (3) .65 .60

Nos. 668, 685-687, 690-691, 693-705, 742, 742C and Types of 1959-65 Overprinted in black, Blue or Red Types "e," "g," or

S. OFICIAL — i
S. OFICIAL — j
S. OFICIAL — k
S. OFICIAL — m
S. OFICIAL — n

Lithographed; Photogravure

1960-68 *Perf. 13x13½, 13½*

O112 A128(g) 5c buff (vert. ovpt.) .20 .20
O113 A275(j) 10c sl grn .20 .20
O114 A275(j) 20c dl red brn .20 .20
O115 A275(i) 50c bister .20 .20
O116 A278(k) 1p brn .20 .20
O117 A278(j) 1p brn, photo. (vert. ovpt.) .20 .20
O117A A278(j) 1p brn, litho., (down) .20 .20
O118 A276(j) 2p rose red .20 .20
O119 A312(m) 2p dp grn (down) .25 .20
O120 A312(j) 2p brt grn (up) .20 .20
O121 A312(j) 2p grn litho. (down) .25 .20
O122 A277(e) 3p dk bl (horiz.) .20 .20
O123 A277(j) 3p dk blue .20 .20
O124 A276(j) 4p red, litho. .20 .20
O125 A312(j) 4p rose red, litho. (down) .20 .20
O126 A277(e) 5p brn (Bl) (horiz.) .25 .20
O127 A277(e) 5p brn (Bk) (horiz.) .25 .20
O128 A277(j) 5p sepia .20 .20
O129 A277(e) 5p sepia (horiz. ovpt.) .20 .20
O130 A276(j) 8p red .20 .20
O131 A278(i) 10p lt red brn .45 .20
O132 A276(j) 10p vermilion .20 .20
O133 A278(j) 10p brn car (up) .20 .20
O134 A278(m) 12p dk brn vio .35 .20
O135 A278(k) 20p Prus grn .50 .20
O136 A278(j) 20p Prus grn (up) .40 .20
O137 A276(j) 20p red, litho. .35 .20
O138 A276(m) 20p red, litho. .25 .20
O139 A278(j) 23p grn (vert. ovpt.) .50 .20
O140 A278(j) 25p dp vio, photo. (R) (up) .50 .20
O141 A278(j) 25p pur, litho. (R) (down) .50 .20
O142 A241(n) 50p dk blue 1.10 .20
O143 A279(m) 100p bl (horiz. ovpt.) 1.10 .35
O144 A279(m) 100p blue (up) 1.10 .35
O145 A280(m) 300p dp violet 2.25 .60
Nos. O112-O145 (35) 13.95 7.70

The "m" overprint measures 15½mm on 2p; 14½mm on 12p, 100p and 300p; 13mm on 20p.

Issue dates: Nos. O122, O127, O135, 1961. Nos. O122-O114, O116, O118, 1962. No. O124, 1963. Nos. O119, O134, O143, 1964. Nos. O117, O125, O130, O139, O144, 1965. Nos. O120, O128, O132-O133, O136, O140, O142, O145, 1966. Nos. O121, O129, O137-O138, O141, 1967. No. O117A, 1968.

Nos. 699, 823-825, 827-829, and Type of 1962 Overprinted in Black or Red Types "j," "m," or "o"

SERVICIO OFICIAL — o

Inscribed: "Republica Argentina"

Litho., Photo., Engr.

1964-67 Wmk. 90 *Perf. 13½*

O149 A312(j) 6p rose red (down) .25 .20
O153 A238a(m) 22p ultra .50 .20
O154 A238a(j) 43p dk car rose (down) .75 .20
O155 A238a(j) 45p brn, photo. (up) .75 .20
O156 A238a(j) 45p brn, litho. (up) 1.10 .20
O157 A241(j) 50p dk bl (up) (R) 2.25 .20
O158 A366(j) 90p ol bis (up) 2.75 .20
O162 A495(o) 500p yel grn 3.50 .80
Nos. O149-O162 (8) 11.85 2.20

Issued: No. O153, 1964; No. O155, 1966; Nos. O149, O156-O162, 1967.

Type of 1959-67 Ovptd. Type "j"

1969 Litho. Wmk. 365 *Perf. 13½*

O163 A276 20p vermilion .20 .20

Beginning with No. 2001, many Argentine stamps are inscribed "Correo Official," but are not official stamps.

OFFICIAL DEPARTMENT STAMPS

Regular Issues of 1911-37 Overprinted in Black

M. A. — Type I
M. A. — Type II

Ministry of Agriculture (M. A.)

Type I

1913-37

On Stamp of 1911

OD1 A88 2c #181 .20 .20

On Stamps of 1912-14

OD2 A88 1c #190 .20 .20
OD3 A88 2c #191 .20 .20
OD4 A88 5c #194 .30 .20
OD5 A88 12c #196 .20 .20
Nos. OD2-OD5 (4) .90 .80

On Stamps of 1915-16

OD6 A88 1c #208 .20 .20
OD7 A88 2c #209 .20 .20
OD8 A88 5c #212 .20 .20
OD9 A91 5c #220 .20 .20
Nos. OD6-OD9 (4) .80 .80

On Stamp of 1917

OD10 A94 12c #238 .30 .20

On Stamps of 1918-19

OD11 A93 1c #249 .20 .20
OD12 A93 2c #250 .20 .20
OD13 A93 5c #253 .20 .20
OD14 A94 12c #255 .20 .20
OD15 A94 20c #256 .20 .20
Nos. OD10-OD15 (6) 1.30 1.20

On Stamps of 1920

OD16 A93 1c #265 .30 .25
OD17 A93 2c #266 .50 .25
OD18 A93 5c #269 .20 .20
Nos. OD16-OD18 (3) 1.00 .70

On Stamps of 1922-23

OD19 A94 12c #311 1.00 .40
OD20 A94 20c #312 25.00

On Stamps of 1923

OD21 A104 1c #324 .20 .20
OD22 A104 2c #325 .25 .20
OD23 A104 5c #328 .20 .20
OD24 A104 12c #330 .20 .20
OD25 A104 20c #331 .20 .20
Nos. OD21-OD25 (5) 1.05 1.00

On Stamps of 1923-31

OD26 A104 1c #341 .20 .20
OD27 A104 2c #342, I .20 .20
a. Type II 1.50 .75
OD28 A104 3c #343 .20 .20
OD29 A104 5c #345, II .20 .20
a. Type I .20 .20
OD30 A104 10c #346, II .20 .20
a. Type I .20 .20
OD31 A104 12c #347 .20 .20
OD32 A104 20c #348, I .20 .20
a. Type II .20 .20
OD33 A104 30c #351 .20 .20
Nos. OD26-OD33 (8) 1.60 1.60

On Stamp of 1926

OD34 A110 12c #360 .20 .20

Type II

On Stamps of 1935-37

OD35 A129 1c #419 .20 .20
OD36 A130 2c #420 .20 .20
OD37 A132 3c #422 .20 .20
OD38 A134 5c #427 .20 .20
OD39 A137 10c #430 .20 .20
OD40 A139 15c #434 .50 .20
OD41 A140 20c #437 .30 .20
OD42 A140 20c #438 .20 .20
OD43 A141 25c #441 .25 .20
OD44 A142 30c #442 .20 .20
OD45 A145 1p #445 2.50 1.50
OD46 A146 1p #446 .50 .25
Nos. OD35-OD46 (12) 5.45 3.75

Ministry of War (M. G.)

Type I

On Stamp of 1911

OD47 A88 2c #181 .20 .20

On Stamps of 1912-14

OD48 A88 1c #190 .20 .20
OD49 A88 2c #191 .75 .20
OD50 A88 5c #194 .20 .20
OD51 A88 12c #196 .20 .20
Nos. OD48-OD51 (4) 1.35 .80

On Stamps of 1915-16

OD52 A88 1c #208 6.00 .75
OD53 A88 2c #209 .60 .20
OD54 A88 5c #212 .75 .20
OD55 A91 5c #220 1.00 .25
OD56 A92 12c #222 1.00 .35
Nos. OD52-OD56 (5) 9.35 1.75

On Stamps of 1917

OD57 A93 1c #232 .30 .20
OD58 A93 2c #233 .40 .20
OD59 A93 5c #236 .30 .20
OD60 A94 12c #238 .60 .20
Nos. OD57-OD60 (4) 1.60 .80

On Stamps of 1918-19

OD61 A93 1c #249 .20 .20
OD62 A93 2c #250 .20 .20
OD63 A93 5c #253 .20 .20
OD64 A94 12c #255 .40 .20
OD65 A94 20c #256 1.25 .20
Nos. OD61-OD65 (5) 2.25 1.00

On Stamps of 1920

OD66 A93 2c #266 .40 .20
OD67 A93 5c #269 .40 .20
OD68 A94 12c #271 .35 .20
Nos. OD66-OD68 (3) 1.15 .60

On Stamp of 1920

OD69 A94 12c #299 2.00 .25

On Stamps of 1922-23

OD70 A93 1c #305 .75 .20
OD71 A93 2c #306 1.50 .45
OD72 A103 5c #309 .75 .20
OD73 A94 20c #312 .30 .20
Nos. OD70-OD73 (4) 3.30 1.05

On Stamp of 1922-23

OD74 A93 2c #318 5.00 .50

On Stamps of 1923

OD75 A104 1c #324 .20 .20
OD76 A104 2c #325 .20 .20
OD77 A104 5c #328 .20 .20
OD78 A104 12c #330 .20 .20
OD79 A104 20c #331 1.00 .20
Nos. OD75-OD79 (5) 1.80 1.00

On Stamps of 1923-31

OD80 A104 1c #341 1.25 .45
OD81 A104 2c #342 .20 .20
OD82 A104 3c #343, I .20 .20
a. Type II .40 .20
OD83 A104 5c #345, I .20 .20
a. Type II .20 .20
OD84 A104 10c #346, II .20 .20
a. Type I .60 .20
OD85 A104 20c #348, I .20 .20
a. Type II .40 .20
OD86 A104 30c #351, II .20 .20
a. Type I 1.00 .20
OD87 A105 1p #353 2.00 .30
Nos. OD80-OD87 (8) 4.45 1.95

On Stamp of 1926

OD88 A109 5c #359 .60 .20

Type II

On Stamps of 1935-37

OD89 A129 1c #419 .20 .20
OD90 A130 2c #420 .20 .20
OD91 A132 3c #422 .20 .20
OD92 A134 5c #427 .20 .20
OD93 A137 10c #430 .20 .20
OD94 A139 15c #434 .25 .20
OD95 A140 20c #437 1.00 .20
OD96 A140 20c #438 .25 .20
OD97 A141 25c #441 .20 .20
OD98 A142 30c #442 .20 .20
OD99 A144 50c #444 .25 .20
OD100 A145 1p #445 1.25 .50
OD101 A146 1p #446 .50 .25
Nos. OD89-OD101 (13) 4.90 2.95

Ministry of Finance (M. H.)

Type I

On Stamp of 1911

OD102 A88 2c #181 .20 .20

On Stamps of 1912-14

OD103 A88 1c #190 .20 .20
OD104 A88 2c #191 .20 .20
OD105 A88 5c #194 .20 .20
OD106 A88 12c #196 .20 .20
Nos. OD103-OD106 (4) .80 .80

On Stamps of 1915-16

OD107 A88 2c #209 .20 .20
OD108 A88 5c #212 .20 .20
OD109 A91 5c #220 .20 .20
Nos. OD107-OD109 (3) .60 .60

On Stamps of 1917

OD110 A93 2c #233 .20 .20
OD111 A93 5c #236 1.25 .20
OD112 A94 12c #238 .20 .20
Nos. OD110-OD112 (3) 1.65 .60

On Stamps of 1918-19

OD113 A93 2c #250 25.00
OD114 A93 5c #253 .20 .20
OD115 A94 12c #255 .45 .20
OD116 A94 20c #256 .45 .20

On Stamps of 1920

OD117 A93 1c #265 .75 .45
OD118 A93 2c #266 1.25 .45
OD119 A93 5c #269 .30 .20
OD120 A94 12c #271 .60 .20
Nos. OD117-OD120 (4) 2.90 1.30

On Stamp of 1922-23

OD121 A94 20c #312 12.50 2.50

On Stamps of 1923

OD122 A104 1c #324 .75 .40
OD123 A104 2c #325 .20 .20
OD124 A104 5c #328 .20 .20
OD125 A104 12c #330 .20 .20
OD126 A104 20c #331 .20 .20
Nos. OD122-OD126 (5) 1.55 1.20

On Stamps of 1923-31

OD127 A104 3c #343 7.00 1.50
OD128 A104 5c #345 .20 .20
OD129 A104 10c #346 .20 .20
OD130 A104 12c #347 7.00 3.75
OD131 A104 20c #348, I .20 .20
a. Type II .35 .20
OD132 A104 30c #351 .25 .20
OD133 A105 1p #353 .40 .20
Nos. OD127-OD133 (7) 15.25 6.25

On Stamp of 1926

OD134 A110 12c #360 12.50 12.50

Type II

On Stamps of 1935-37

OD135 A129 1c #419 .20 .20
OD136 A130 2c #420 .20 .20
OD137 A132 3c #422 .20 .20
OD138 A134 5c #427 .20 .20
OD139 A137 10c #430 .20 .20
OD140 A139 15c #434 .45 .20
OD141 A140 20c #437 .20 .20
OD142 A140 20c #438 .20 .20
OD143 A142 30c #442 .20 .20
OD144 A145 1p #445 2.00 1.00
OD145 A146 1p #446 .50 .25
Nos. OD135-OD145 (11) 4.55 3.05

Ministry of the Interior (M. I.)

Type I

On Stamp of 1911

OD146 A88 2c #181 .25 .20

On Stamps of 1912-14

OD147 A88 1c #190 .20 .20
OD148 A88 2c #191 .20 .20
OD149 A88 5c #194 .20 .20
OD150 A88 12c #196 .20 .20
Nos. OD146-OD150 (5) 1.05 1.00

On Stamps of 1915-17

OD151 A88 2c #209 .80 .30
OD152 A88 5c #212 .75 .20
OD153 A91 5c #220 .60 .20
OD154 A93 5c #236 1.50 .20
Nos. OD151-OD154 (4) 3.65 .90

On Stamps of 1918-19

OD155 A93 2c #250 .20 .20
OD156 A93 5c #253 .20 .20

On Stamps of 1920

OD157 A93 1c #265 3.75 1.25
OD158 A93 5c #269 .75 .35

On Stamps of 1922-23

OD159 A93 2c #306 12.50 12.50
OD160 A103 5c #309 3.50 1.25
OD161 A94 12c #311 1.25 .40
OD162 A94 20c #312 1.25 .40
Nos. OD159-OD162 (4) 18.50 14.55

On Stamps of 1923

OD163 A104 1c #324 .20 .20
OD164 A104 2c #325 .20 .20
OD165 A104 5c #328 .20 .20
OD166 A104 12c #330 2.00 2.00
OD167 A104 20c #331 .75 .20
Nos. OD163-OD167 (5) 3.35 2.80

On Stamps of 1923-31

OD168 A104 1c #341 .20 .20
OD169 A104 2c #342 .20 .20
OD170 A104 3c #343, II .20 .20
a. Type I 1.25 .30
OD171 A104 5c #345, I .20 .20
a. Type II .20 .20
OD172 A104 10c #346, II .20 .20
OD173 A104 12c #347 .30 .20
OD174 A104 20c #348, II .20 .20
a. Type I .75 .20
OD175 A104 30c #351 .20 .20
Nos. OD168-OD175 (8) 1.70 1.60

Type II
On Stamps of 1935-37

OD176 A129 1c #419 .20 .20
OD177 A130 2c #420 .20 .20
OD178 A132 3c #422 .20 .20
OD178A A134 5c #427 .20 .20
OD179 A137 10c #430 .20 .20
OD180 A139 15c #434 .30 .20
OD181 A140 20c #437 .75 .20
OD182 A140 20c #438 .20 .20
OD182A A142 30c #442 .20 .20
OD182B A145 1p #445 2.00 1.00
OD182C A146 1p #446 .50 .25
Nos. OD176-OD182C (11) 4.95 3.05

Ministry of Justice and Instruction (M. J. I.)
Type I
On Stamp of 1911

OD183 A88 2c #181 1.25 .20

On Stamps of 1912-14

OD184 A88 1c #190 1.50 .20
OD185 A88 2c #191 1.00 .20
OD186 A88 5c #194 .45 .20
OD187 A88 12c #196 .45 .20
Nos. OD184-OD187 (4) 3.40 .80

On Stamps of 1915-17

OD188 A88 1c #208 .30 .20
OD189 A88 2c #209 .30 .20
OD190 A88 5c #212 1.00 .20
OD191 A91 5c #220 .25 .20
OD192 A92 12c #222 .75 .20
Nos. OD188-OD192 (5) 2.60 1.00

On Stamps of 1917

OD193 A93 1c #232 .25 .20
OD194 A93 2c #233 .75 .20
OD195 A93 5c #236 .25 .20
OD196 A94 12c #238 17.50 5.00
Nos. OD193-OD196 (4) 18.75 5.60

On Stamps of 1918-19

OD197 A93 1c #249 .20 .20
OD198 A93 2c #250 .20 .20
OD199 A93 5c #253 .20 .20
OD200 A94 12c #255 .20 .20
OD201 A94 20c #256 .50 .20
Nos. OD197-OD201 (5) 1.30 1.00

On Stamps of 1920

OD202 A93 1c #265 .25 .20
OD203 A93 2c #266 .20 .20
OD204 A93 5c #269 .20 .20
OD205 A94 12c #271 .40 .20
Nos. OD202-OD205 (4) 1.05 .80

On Stamps of 1922-23

OD206 A93 1c #305 .25 .20
OD207 A93 2c #306 1.50 .50
OD208 A103 5c #309 .25 .20
OD209 A94 12c #311 10.00 1.75
OD210 A94 20c #312 1.50 .30
Nos. OD206-OD210 (5) 13.50 2.95

On Stamp of 1922-23

OD211 A93 2c #318 2.50 2.50

On Stamps of 1923

OD212 A104 1c #324 .20 .20
OD213 A104 2c #325 .20 .20
OD214 A104 5c #328 .20 .20
OD215 A104 12c #330 .20 .20
OD216 A104 20c #331 .50 .20
Nos. OD212-OD216 (5) 1.30 1.00

On Stamps of 1923-31

OD217 A104 ½c #340 2.00 .75
OD218 A104 1c #341, I .20 .20
a. Type II .20 .20
OD219 A104 2c #342 .20 .20
OD220 A104 3c #343, I .20 .20
a. Type II .20 .20
OD221 A104 5c #345, I .20 .20
a. Type II .20 .20
OD222 A104 10c #346, II .20 .20
a. Type I .30 .20
OD223 A104 12c #347, I .20 .20
a. Type II .30 .20
OD224 A104 20c #348, I .20 .20
a. Type II .20 .20
OD225 A104 30c #351 .20 .20
OD226 A105 1p #353 .40 .50
Nos. OD217-OD226 (10) 4.00 2.85

On Stamps of 1926

OD227 A109 5c #359 .20 .20
OD228 A110 12c #360 .20 .20

Type II
On Stamps of 1935-37

OD229 A129 1c #419 .20 .20
OD230 A130 2c #420 .20 .20
OD231 A132 3c #422 .20 .20
OD232 A134 5c #427 .20 .20
OD233 A137 10c #430 .20 .20
OD234 A139 15c #434 .45 .20
OD234A A140 20c #437 .20 .20
OD234B A140 20c #438 .20 .20
OD234C A141 25c #441 .20 .20
OD234D A142 30c #442 .20 .20
OD234E A145 1p #445 1.00 .60
OD234F A146 1p #446 .30 .20
Nos. OD229-OD234F (12) 3.55 2.80

Ministry of Marine (M. M.)
Type I
On Stamp of 1911

OD235 A88 2c #181 .20 .20

On Stamps of 1912-14

OD236 A88 1c #190 .20 .20
OD237 A88 2c #191 .20 .20
OD238 A88 5c #194 2.00 .20
OD239 A88 12c #196 .20 .20
Nos. OD236-OD239 (4) 2.60 .80

On Stamps of 1915-16

OD240 A88 2c #209 .60 .20
OD241 A88 5c #212 .40 .20

On Stamps of 1917

OD242 A93 1c #232 .20 .20
OD243 A93 2c #233 .20 .20
OD244 A93 5c #236 .20 .20
Nos. OD242-OD244 (3) .60 .60

On Stamps of 1918-19

OD245 A93 1c #249 .20 .20
OD246 A93 2c #250 .20 .20
OD247 A93 5c #253 .25 .20
OD248 A94 12c #255 .25 .20
OD249 A94 20c #256 3.00 .35
Nos. OD245-OD249 (5) 3.90 1.15

On Stamps of 1920

OD250 A93 1c #265 .20 .20
OD251 A93 2c #266 .20 .20
OD252 A93 5c #269 .25 .20
Nos. OD250-OD252 (3) .65 .60

On Stamps of 1922-23

OD253 A103 5c #309 1.00 .20
OD254 A94 12c #311 7.00 7.00
OD255 A94 20c #312 7.00 1.50
Nos. OD253-OD254 (2) 8.00 7.20

On Stamps of 1923

OD256 A104 1c #324 .20 .20
OD257 A104 2c #325 .20 .20
OD258 A104 5c #328 .35 .20
OD259 A104 12c #330 .65 .20
OD260 A104 20c #331 .65 .20
Nos. OD256-OD260 (5) 2.05 1.00

On Stamps of 1923-31

OD261 A104 1c #341 .75 .25
OD262 A104 2c #342 .20 .20
OD263 A104 3c #343 .60 .20
OD264 A104 5c #345, I .20 .20
a. Type II .60 .20
OD265 A104 10c #346 .60 .20
OD266 A104 20c #348, II .60 .20
a. Type I .75 .20
OD267 A104 30c #351 1.00 .20
OD268 A105 1p #353 11.00 3.00
Nos. OD261-OD268 (8) 14.95 4.45

On Stamp of 1926

OD269 A109 5c #359 .50 .20

Type II
On Stamps of 1935-37

OD270 A129 1c #419 .20 .20
OD271 A130 2c #420 .20 .20
OD272 A132 3c #422 .20 .20
OD273 A134 5c #427 .25 .20
OD274 A137 10c #430 .25 .20
OD275 A139 15c #434 .30 .20
OD276 A140 20c #437 .40 .20
OD277 A140 20c #438 .30 .20
OD278 A142 30c #442 .25 .20
OD279 A145 1p #445 3.25 1.00
OD280 A146 1p #446 .75 .25
Nos. OD270-OD280 (11) 6.30 3.05

Ministry of Public Works (M. O. P.)
Type I
On Stamp of 1911

OD281 A88 2c #181 .30 .20

On Stamps of 1912-14

OD282 A88 1c #190 .30 .20
OD283 A88 5c #194 .20 .20
OD284 A88 12c #196 1.50 .35
Nos. OD282-OD284 (3) 2.00 .75

On Stamps of 1916-19

OD285 A91 5c #220 10.00 1.00
OD286 A94 12c #238 25.00
OD287 A94 20c #256 25.00

On Stamps of 1920

OD288 A93 2c #266 6.00 2.50
OD289 A93 5c #269 2.00 .20
OD290 A94 12c #271 20.00 6.00
Nos. OD288-OD290 (3) 28.00 8.70

On Stamps of 1923

OD291 A104 1c #324 .40 .20
OD292 A104 2c #325 .30 .20
OD293 A104 5c #328 .40 .20
OD294 A104 12c #330 .60 .20
OD295 A104 20c #331 1.00 .20
Nos. OD291-OD295 (5) 2.70 1.00

On Stamps of 1923-31

OD296 A104 1c #341 .20 .20
OD297 A104 2c #342 .20 .20
OD298 A104 3c #343 .20 .20
OD299 A104 5c #345, I .20 .20
a. Type II .20 .20
OD300 A104 10c #346 .20 .20
OD301 A104 12c #347 9.00 1.25
OD302 A104 20c #348, I .20 .20
a. Type II 2.50 .50
OD303 A104 30c #351 .40 .20
OD304 A105 1p #353 20.00 6.00
Nos. OD296-OD304 (9) 30.60 8.65

On Stamp of 1926

OD305 A109 5c #359 .60 .20

Type II
On Stamps of 1935-37

OD306 A129 1c #419 .20 .20
OD307 A130 2c #420 .20 .20
OD308 A132 3c #422 .20 .20
OD309 A134 5c #427 .20 .20
OD310 A137 10c #430 .30 .20
OD311 A139 15c #434 .60 .20
OD312 A140 20c #437 .75 .20
OD313 A140 20c #438 .20 .20
OD314 A142 30c #442 .20 .20
OD315 A144 50c #444 .20 .20
OD316 A145 1p #445 2.00 1.00
OD317 A146 1p #446 .50 .25
Nos. OD306-OD317 (12) 5.55 3.25

Ministry of Foreign Affairs and Religion (M. R. C.)
Type I
On Stamp of 1911

OD318 A88 2c #181 5.00 1.25

On Stamps of 1912-14

OD319 A88 1c #190 .20 .20
OD320 A88 2c #191 .20 .20
OD321 A88 5c #194 .40 .20
OD322 A88 12c #196 1.50 .25
Nos. OD319-OD322 (4) 2.30 .85

On Stamps of 1915-19

OD323 A88 5c #212 .40 .20
OD324 A91 5c #220 .20 .20
OD325 A94 20c #256 2.00 .75
Nos. OD323-OD325 (3) 2.60 1.15

On Stamps of 1920

OD326 A93 1c #265 .40 .20
OD327 A93 5c #269 .20 .20

On Stamps of 1922-23

OD328 A93 2c #306 9.00 3.50
OD329 A103 5c #309 27.50
OD330 A93 10c #311 22.50
Nos. OD328-OD330 (3) 59.00

On Stamps of 1923

OD331 A104 1c #324 .20 .20
OD332 A104 2c #325 .20 .20
OD333 A104 5c #328 .20 .20
OD334 A104 12c #330 .20 .20
OD335 A104 20c #331 .20 .20
Nos. OD331-OD335 (5) 1.00 1.00

On Stamps of 1923-31

OD336 A104 ½c #340 1.00 .50
OD337 A104 1c #341 .20 .20
OD338 A104 2c #342 .20 .20
OD339 A104 3c #343 .20 .20
OD340 A104 5c #345 .20 .20
OD341 A104 10c #346, II .20 .20
a. Type I 1.50 .20
OD342 A104 12c #347 .20 .20
OD343 A104 20c #348, I .20 .20
a. Type II .20 .20
OD344 A104 30c #351, I .20 .20
a. Type II .20 .20
OD345 A105 1p #353 .40 .20
Nos. OD336-OD346 (11) 3.20 2.50

On Stamp of 1926

OD346 A110 12c #360 .20 .20

Type II
On Stamps of 1935-37

OD347 A129 1c #419 .20 .20
OD348 A130 2c #420 .20 .20
OD349 A132 3c #422 .20 .20
OD350 A134 5c #427 .20 .20
OD351 A137 10c #430 .20 .20
OD352 A139 15c #434 .20 .20
OD353 A140 20c #437 .20 .20
OD354 A140 20c #438 .20 .20
OD355 A142 30c #442 .20 .20
OD356 A145 1p #445 2.50 1.25
OD357 A146 1p #446 1.00 .50
Nos. OD347-OD357 (11) 5.30 3.55

BUENOS AIRES

The central point of the Argentine struggle for independence. At intervals Buenos Aires maintained an independent government but after 1862 became a province of the Argentine Republic.

8 Reales = 1 Peso

> Values of Buenos Aires Nos. 1-8 vary according to condition. Quotations are for fine copies. Very fine to superb specimens sell at much higher prices, and inferior or poor copies sell at reduced values, depending on the condition of the individual specimen.
> Nos. 1-8 were issued without gum.

Steamship — A1

1858 Unwmk. Typo. *Imperf.*

1 A1 1 (in) pesos lt brn 350. 250.
2 A1 2 (dos) pesos blue 175. 140.
b. Diagonal half used as 1p on cover 7,500.
3 A1 3 (tres) pesos grn 1,500. 750.
a. 3p dark green 1,800. 825.
4 A1 4 (cuatro) pesos ver 4,750. 1,750.
a. Half used as 2p on cover 15,000.
5 A1 5 (cinco) pesos org 4,250. 1,400.
a. 5p ocher 4,250. 1,400.
b. 5p olive yellow 4,250. 1,400.

Issued: #2-5, Apr. 29; #1, Oct. 26.

1858, Oct. 26

6 A1 4 (cuatro) reales brown 250. 200.
a. 4r gray brown 250. 200.
b. 4r yellow brown 250. 200.

1859, Jan. 1

7 A1 1 (in) pesos blue 160. 225.
a. 1p indigo 200. 250.
b. Impression on reverse of stamp in blue 3,000.
c. Double impression 250. 300.
d. Tete beche pair 65,000.
e. Half used as 4r on cover 7,500.
8 A1 1 (to) pesos blue 350. 225.

Nos. 1, 2, 3 and 7 have been reprinted on very thick, hand-made paper. The same four stamps and No. 8 have been reprinted on thin, hard, white wove paper.

Counterfeits of Nos. 1-8 are plentiful.

Liberty Head — A2

1859, Sept. 3

9 A2 4r green, *bluish* 250.00 160.00
10 A2 1p blue 35.00 17.50
11 A2 2p vermilion 350.00 150.00
a. 2p red 300.00 125.00

Both clear and rough impressions of these stamps may be found. They have generally been called Paris and Local prints, respectively, but the opinion now obtains that the differences are due to the impression and that they do not represent separate issues. Values are for fine impressions. Rough or blurred impressions sell for less.

Many shades exist of Nos. 1-11.

1862, Oct. 4

12 A2 1p rose 200.00 100.00
13 A2 2p blue 350.00 75.00

All three values have been reprinted in black, brownish black, blue and red brown on thin hard white paper. The 4r has also been reprinted in green on bluish paper.
Values are for fine impressions. Rough or blurred impressions sell for less.

CORDOBA

A province in the central part of the Argentine Republic.

100 Centavos = 1 Peso

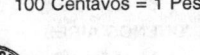

Arms of Cordoba — A1

Unwmk.
1858, Oct. 28 Litho. *Imperf.*
Laid Paper

1 A1 5c blue 125.
2 A1 10c black *2,500.*

Cordoba stamps were printed on laid paper, but stamps from edges of the sheets sometimes do not show any laid lines and appear to be on wove paper. Counterfeits are plentiful.

CORRIENTES

The northeast province of the Argentine Republic.

1 Real M(oneda) C(orriente) =
12½ Centavos M.C. = 50 Centavos
100 Centavos Fuertes = 1 Peso Fuerte

Nos. 1-2 were issued without gum. Nos. 3-8 were issued both with and without gum (values the same).

Ceres
A1 A2

Unwmk.
1856, Aug. 21 Typo. *Imperf.*

1 A1 1r black, *blue* 85.00 *110.00*

No. 1 used is valued with pen cancellation.

Pen Stroke Through "Un Real"

1860, Feb. 8

2 A1 (3c) black, *blue* 350.00 *175.00*

No. 2 used is valued with pen cancellation.

1860-78

3 A2 (3c) black, *blue* 9.50 *30.00*
4 A2 (2c) blk, *yel grn* ('64) 37.50 37.50
a. (2c) black, *blue green* 92.50 *110.00*
5 A2 (2c) blk, *yel* ('67) 7.50 *19.00*
6 A2 (3c) blk, *dk bl* ('71) 3.00 *19.00*
7 A2 (3c) blk, *rose red* ('76) 100.00 50.00
a. (3c) black, *lil rose* ('75) 135.00 80.00
8 A2 (3c) blk, *dk rose* ('79) 8.00 *32.50*
a. (3c) black, *red vio* ('77) 60.00 35.00
Nos. 3-8 (6) 165.50 188.00

Pen canceled examples of Nos. 3-8 sell for much less.

Printed from settings of 8 varieties, 3 or 4 impressions constituting a sheet. Some impressions were printed inverted and tete beche pairs may be cut from adjacent impressions.

From Jan. 1 to Feb. 24, 1864, No. 4 was used as a 5 centavos stamp but copies so used can only be distinguished when they bear dated cancellations.

The reprints show numerous spots and small defects which are not found on the originals. They are printed on gray blue, dull blue, gray green, dull orange and light magenta papers.

ARMENIA

är-ˈmē-nē-ə

LOCATION — South of Russia bounded by Georgia, Azerbaijan, Iran and Turkey
GOVT. — Republic
AREA — 11,490 sq. mi.
POP. — 3,409,234 (est. 1999)
CAPITAL — Yerevan

With Azerbaijan and Georgia, Armenia made up the Transcaucasian Federation of Soviet Republics.

Stamps of Armenia were replaced in 1923 by those of Transcaucasian Federated Republics.

With the breakup of the Soviet Union on Dec. 26, 1991, Armenia and ten former Soviet republics established the Commonwealth of Independent States.

100 Kopecks = 1 Ruble
100 Luma = 1 Dram (1993)

Catalogue values for unused stamps in this country are for Never Hinged items, beginning with Scott 430 in the regular postage section.

Counterfeits abound of all overprinted and surcharged stamps.

Watermark

Diamonds
Wmk. 171

Perforations
Perforations are the same as the basic Russian stamps.

National Republic
Russian Stamps of 1902-19 Handstamped

At least thirteen types exist of both framed and unframed overprints ("a" and "c"). The device is the Armenian "H," initial of Hayasdan (Armenia). Inverted and double overprints are found.

Surcharged K 60 K

Type I - Without periods (two types).
Type II - Periods after 1st "K" and "60."

Black Surcharge

1919 Unwmk. *Perf. 14x14½*

1 A14 60k on 1k orange (II) 2.50 .40
a. Imperf. (I) 1.00 .25
b. Imperf. (II) 1.00 .25

Violet Surcharge

2 A14 60k on 1k orange (II) .50 .50

Handstamped in Violet — a

Perf.

6 A15 4k carmine 2.00 2.00
7 A14 5k claret, imperf. 7.50 7.50
a. Perf. 5.00 5.00
9 A14 10k on 7k lt blue 5.00 1.25
10 A11 15k red brn & bl 3.00 .25
11 A8 20k blue & car 2.00 1.00
13 A11 35k red brn & grn 3.50 3.50
14 A8 50k violet & green 3.50 3.50
15 A14 60k on 1k orange (II) 2.00 2.00
a. Imperf. (I) 1.90 2.00
b. Imperf. (II) 8.50 9.00
18 A13 5r dk bl, grn & pale bl 3.50 4.25
a. Imperf. 1.00 1.00
19 A12 7r dk green & pink 1.75 2.00
20 A13 10r scarlet, yel & gray 1.75 2.00

Handstamped in Black

31 A14 2k green, imperf. 1.00 .20
a. Perf. 5.00 4.25
32 A14 3k red, imperf. 1.00 .20
a. Perf. 5.00 2.00
33 A15 4k carmine .20 .20
34 A14 5k claret 1.00 .20
a. Imperf. 5.00 5.00
36 A15 10k dark blue 2.00 .65
37 A14 10k on 7k lt blue .50 .20
38 A11 15k red brn & bl .50 .20
a. Imperf. 3.00 3.00
39 A8 20k blue & car 1.00 .20
40 A11 25k green & gray vio 1.00 .20
41 A11 35k red brn & grn 1.00 .20
42 A8 50k violet & green 1.00 .20
43 A14 60k on 1k orange (II) 2.50 2.50
43A A11 70k brown & org 1.00 .30
b. Imperf. .50 .30
44 A9 1r pale brn, dk brn & org 1.50 .30
a. Imperf. .50 .50
45 A12 3½r mar & lt grn, imperf. 5.00 .65
a. Perf. 5.00 .85
46 A13 5r dk bl, grn & pale bl .60 .65
a. Imperf. 6.00 1.00
47 A12 7r dk green & pink 6.00 1.10
48 A13 10r scar, yel & gray *50.00* 1.00

Handstamped in Violet — c

Unwmk. *Perf.*
Wove Paper

62 A14 2k green, imperf. .40 .40
a. Perf. 4.50 4.50
63 A14 3k red, imperf. .25 .25
a. Perf. 3.00 2.75
64 A15 4k carmine .50 .50
65 A14 5k claret 3.00 .40
a. Imperf. 3.00 .60
67 A15 10k dark blue 1.00 .85
68 A14 10k on 7k lt bl 1.00 .65
69 A11 15k red brn & bl 2.50 2.50
70 A8 20k blue & car .40 .40
71 A11 25k grn & gray vio 1.00 1.00
72 A11 35k red brn & grn 1.50 1.50
73 A8 50k violet & grn .50 .50
74 A14 60k on 1k org (II) 2.50 2.00
a. Imperf. (I) 1.65 1.65
b. Imperf. (II) 2.00 2.00
75 A9 1r pale brn, dk brn & org .60 .60
a. Imperf. 1.50 1.50
76 A12 3½r mar & lt grn, imperf. .75 .75
a. Perf. 1.00 1.00
77 A13 5r dk bl, grn & pale bl, imperf. 5.00 5.00
a. Perf. 4.00 4.00
78 A12 7r dk green & pink 7.50 7.50
79 A13 10r scar, yel & gray 2.25 1.90

Imperf

85 A11 70k brown & org 5.00 2.00

Handstamped in Black
Perf.

90 A14 1k orange 10.00 4.50
a. Imperf. 10.00 6.00
91 A14 2k green, imperf. 1.00 .20
a. Perf. 7.50 2.50
92 A14 3k red, imperf. 1.00 .20
a. Perf. 10.00 2.75
93 A15 4k carmine .50 .50
94 A14 5k claret 1.00 .20
a. Imperf. 3.00 .60
95 A14 7k light blue 15.00 15.00
96 A15 10k dark blue 12.00 12.00
97 A14 10k on 7k lt bl .20 .20
98 A11 15k red brn & bl .20 .20
99 A8 20k blue & car .20 .20
100 A11 25k grn & gray vio .50 .20
101 A11 35k red brn & grn .20 .20
102 A8 50k violet & grn .20 .20
102A A14 60k on 1k org, imperf. (I) .30 .30
b. Imperf. (II) .50 .50
c. Perf. (II) 2.50 1.25
103 A9 1r pale brn, dk brn & org 1.00 1.00
a. Imperf. .75 .75
104 A12 3½r maroon & lt grn 4.00 .50
a. Imperf. 5.00 .30
105 A13 5r dk bl, grn & pale bl 2.50 2.50
a. Imperf. 2.50 2.50
106 A12 7r dk green & pink 3.00 2.50
107 A13 10r scar, yel & gray 7.00 3.50

Imperf

113 A11 70k brown & org 1.00 .25

Handstamped in Violet or Black:

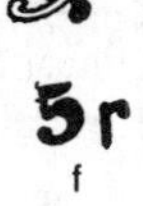

f

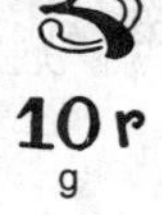

g

Violet Surcharge, Type f

1920 *Perf.*

120 A14 3r on 3k red, imperf. .85 .85
a. Perf. 2.50 2.50
121 A14 5r on 3k red 3.75 3.25
122 A15 5r on 4k car 10.00 8.00
123 A14 5r on 5k claret, imperf. 10.00 10.00
a. Perf. 10.00 8.00
124 A15 5r on 10k dk blue 10.00 8.00
125 A14 5r on 10k on 7k lt bl 10.00 8.00
126 A8 5r on 20k bl & car

Imperf

127 A14 5r on 2k green 7.00 7.00
128 A11 5r on 35k red brn & grn 7.00 7.00

Black Surcharge, Type f or Type g (#130)
Perf.

130 A14 1r on 1k orange .50 .50
a. Imperf. .75 .75
131 A14 3r on 3k red .20 .20
a. Imperf. .20 .20
132 A15 3r on 4k carmine 3.00 3.00
133 A14 5r on 2k green, imperf. .20 .20
a. Perf. 2.00 2.00
134 A14 5r on 3k red 5.00 5.00
a. Imperf. 2.50 2.50
135 A15 5r on 4k carmine .40 .40
a. Imperf. 4.75 4.75
136 A14 5r on 5k claret .50 .50
a. Imperf. .50 .50
137 A14 5r on 7k lt blue 2.00 2.00
138 A15 5r on 10k dk blue .50 .50
139 A14 5r on 10k on 7k lt bl .50 .50
140 A11 5r on 14k bl & rose 2.00 2.00
141 A11 5r on 15k red brn & blue .50 .50
a. Imperf. 2.00 2.00
142 A8 5r on 20k bl & car .50 .50
a. Imperf. 10.00 10.00
143 A11 5r on 20k on 14k bl & rose 12.00 12.00
144 A11 5r on 25k grn & gray vio 12.00 12.00

Black Surcharge, Type g or Type f (#148A, 151)

145 A14 10r on 1k org, imperf. .90 .90
a. Perf. *225.00 225.00*
146 A14 10r on 3k red *175.00 175.00*
147 A14 10r on 5k claret 15.00 15.00
a. Imperf. 6.00
148 A8 10r on 20k bl & car 15.00 15.00
148A A11 10r on 25k grn & gray vio 8.00 8.00
149 A11 10r on 25k grn & gray vio 5.00 5.00
a. Imperf. 8.00 8.00
150 A11 10r on 35k red brn & grn .50 .50
151 A8 10r on 50k brn vio & grn 1.75 1.75
152 A8 10r on 50k brn vio & grn .45 .45
152A A11 10r on 70k brn & org, imperf. 3.00 3.00
b. Perf. *200.00 200.00*
152C A8 25r on 20k bl & car 4.00 4.00
153 A11 25r on 25k grn & gray vio 2.00 2.00
154 A11 25r on 35k red brn & grn 2.00 2.00
a. Imperf. 3.50 3.50
155 A8 25r on 50k vio & grn 4.00 4.00
a. Imperf. 5.00 5.00
156 A11 25r on 70k brn & org 8.00 8.00
a. Imperf. 5.00 5.00
157 A9 50r on 1r pale brn, dk brn & org, imperf. 1.00 1.00
a. Perf. 5.00 5.00
158 A13 50r on 5r dk bl, grn & lt bl 10.00 10.00
a. Imperf. 10.00 10.00
159 A12 100r on 3½r mar & lt grn 7.00 7.00
a. Imperf. 7.00 7.00
160 A13 100r on 5r dk bl, grn & pale bl 10.00 10.00
a. Imperf. 7.00 7.00
161 A12 100r on 7r dk grn & pink 10.00 10.00
a. Imperf. 35.00 35.00
162 A13 100r on 10r scar, yel & gray 10.00 10.00

Wmk. Wavy Lines (168)
Perf. 11½
Vertically Laid Paper

163 A12 100r on 3½r blk & gray *100.00 100.00*
164 A12 100r on 7r blk & yel *100.00 100.00*

1920 Unwmk. *Imperf.*

Wove Paper

166 A14 (g) 1r on 60k on 1k org (I) 12.00 12.00
168 A14 (f) 5r on 1k orange 9.00 9.00
173 A11 (f) 5r on 35k red brn & grn 2.50 2.50
177 A11 (g) 50r on 70k brn & org 5.00 5.00
179 A12 (g) 50r on 3½r mar & lt grn 2.00 2.00
181 A9 (g) 100r on 1r pale brn, dk brn & org 4.00 4.00

Romanov Issues Surcharged Type g or Type f (#185-187, 190)

On Stamps of 1913

1920 *Perf. 13½*

184 A16 1r on 1k brn org 10.00 10.00
185 A18 3r on 3k rose red 15.00 15.00
186 A19 5r on 4k dull red 10.00 10.00
187 A22 5r on 14k blue grn 60.00 60.00
187A A19 10r on 4k dull red 30.00
187B A26 10r on 35k gray vio & dk grn
187C A19 25r on 4k dull red 10.00 10.00
188 A26 25r on 35k gray vio & dk grn 2.75 2.75
189 A28 25r on 70k yel grn & brn 2.75 2.75
190 A31 50r on 3r dk violet 2.00 2.00
190A A16 100r on 1k brn org 100.00 100.00
190B A17 100r on 2k green 100.00 100.00
191 A30 100r on 2r brown 10.50 10.50
192 A31 100r on 3r dk vio 10.50 10.50

On Stamps of 1915, Type g

Thin Cardboard

Inscriptions on Back

Perf. 12

193 A21 100r on 10k blue 3.00
194 A23 100r on 15k brown 3.00
195 A24 100r on 20k ol grn 3.00

On Stamps of 1916, Type f

Perf. 13½

196 A20 5r on 10k on 7k brown 5.00 5.00
197 A22 5r on 20k on 14k bl grn 8.00 8.00

Surch. Type f or Type g (#204-205A, 207-207C, 210-211) over Type c

Type c in Violet

Perf.

200 A15 5r on 4k carmine 1.00 1.00
201 A15 5r on 10k dk blue 1.00 1.00
202 A11 5r on 15k red brn & bl 2.00 2.00
203 A8 5r on 20k blue & car 1.75 1.75
204 A11 10r on 25k grn & gray vio 1.50 1.50
205 A11 10r on 35k red brn & grn 3.00 3.00
205A A8 10r on 50k brn vio & grn 3.50 3.50
206 A8 25r on 50k brn vio & grn *150.00 150.00*
207 A9 50r on 1r pale brn, dk brn & org, imperf. 3.50 3.50
a. Perf. 25.00 25.00
207B A12 100r on 3½r mar & lt grn 30.00
207C A12 100r on 7r dk grn & pink 9.00

Imperf

208 A14 5r on 2k green 25.00 25.00
209 A14 5r on 5k claret 25.00 25.00
210 A11 25r on 70k brn & org 5.50 5.50
211 A13 100r on 5r dk bl, grn & pale bl 1.00 1.00

Surcharged Type g or Type f (212-213, 215, 219-219A, 221-222) over Type c

Type c in Black

Perf.

212 A14 5r on 7k lt bl *150.00 150.00*
213 A14 5r on 10k on 7k lt bl 5.00 5.00
214 A11 5r on 15k red brn & bl .50 .50
215 A8 5r on 20k blue & car 3.00 3.00
215A A11 10r on 5r on 25k grn & gray vio 5.00 5.00
216 A11 10r on 35k red brn & grn .50 .50
217 A8 10r on 50k brn vio & grn 1.00 1.00
217A A9 50r on 1r pale brn, dk brn & org 1.00 1.00
b. Imperf. 1.10 1.10
217C A12 100r on 3½r mar & lt grn 1.50 1.50
218 A13 100r on 5r dk bl, grn & pale bl 10.00 10.00
a. Imperf. 1.75 1.75
219 A12 100r on 7r dk grn & pink 15.00 15.00
219A A13 100r on 10r scar, yel & gray 10.00 10.00

Imperf

220 A14 1r on 60k on 1k org (I) 20.00 20.00
221 A14 5r on 2k green .80 .80
222 A14 5r on 5k claret 3.00 3.00
223 A11 10r on 70k brn & org 2.00 2.00
224 A11 25r on 70k brn & org 2.00 2.00

Surcharged Type g or Type f (#233) over Type a

Type a in Violet

Imperf

231 A9 50r on 1r pale brn, dk brn & org *140.00 140.00*
232 A13 100r on 5r dk bl, grn & pale bl 10.50

Type a in Black

Perf.

233 A8 5r on 20k blue & car .80 .80
233A A11 10r on 25k grn & gray vio *55.00 55.00*
234 A11 10r on 35k red brn & grn .90 .90
235 A12 100r on 3½r mar & lt grn 1.25 1.25
a. Imperf. 1.50 1.50

Imperf

237 A14 5r on 2k green 125.00 125.00
237A A11 10r on 70k brn & org

Surcharged Type a and New Value

Type a in Violet

Perf.

238 A11 10r on 15k red brn & blue .80 .80

Type a in Black

239 A8 5r on 20k blue & car 3.00 3.00
239A A8 10r on 20k blue & car 3.00 3.00
239B A8 10r on 50k brn red & grn 7.50

Imperf

240 A12 100r on 3½r mar & lt grn 1.90 1.90

Surcharged Type c and New Value

Type c in Black

1920 *Perf.*

241 A15 5r on 4k red 1.75 1.75
242 A11 5r on 15k red brn & bl 1.00 1.00
243 A8 10r on 20k blue & car 1.75 1.75
243A A11 10r on 25k grn & gray vio 1.00 1.00
244 A11 10r on 35k red brn & grn 1.00 1.00
a. With additional surch. "5r" 1.50 1.50
245 A12 100r on 3½r mar & lt grn 1.50 1.50

Imperf

247 A14 3r on 3k red 4.75 4.75
248 A14 5r on 2k green .30 .30
249 A9 50r on 1r pale brn, dk brn & org .90 .90

Type c in Violet

249A A14 5r on 2k green 6.50

Postal Savings Stamps Surcharged

A1

A2

A3

Perf. 14½x15

Wmk. 171

250 A1 60k on 1k red & buff 50.00 50.00
251 A2 1r on 1k red & buff 5.00 5.00
252 A3 5r on 5k green & buff 7.25 7.25
253 A3 5r on 10k brown & buff 30.00 3.00

Russian Semi-Postal Stamps of 1914-18 Surcharged with Armenian Monogram and New Values like Regular Issues

On Stamps of 1914

Unwmk. *Perf.*

255 SP5 25r on 1k red brn & dk grn, *straw* 60.00 60.00
256 SP6 25r on 3k mar & gray grn, *pink* 60.00 60.00
257 SP7 50r on 7 dk brn & dk grn, *buff* 20.00 20.00
258 SP5 100r on 1k red brn & dk grn, *straw* 25.00 25.00
259 SP6 100r on 3k mar & gray grn, *pink* 25.00 25.00
260 SP7 100r on 7k dk brn & dk grn, *buff* 25.00 25.00

On Stamps of 1915-19

261 SP5 25r on 1k org brn & gray 75.00 75.00
262 SP6 25r on 3k car & gray 30.00 30.00
263 SP8 50r on 10k dk bl & brn 25.00 25.00
264 SP5 100r on 1k org brn & gray 3.25 3.50
265 SP8 100r on 10k dk bl & brn 3.25 3.50

These surcharged semi-postal stamps were used for ordinary postage.

A set of 10 stamps in the above designs, and in a third design showing a woman quilling, was prepared in 1920, but not issued. Value of set, $4. Exist with "SPECIMEN" overprint and imperf. Reprints exist.

Soviet Socialist Republic

Hammer and Sickle — A7

Mythological Monster — A8

Symbols of Soviet Republics on Designs from old Armenian Manuscripts — A9

Ruined City of Ani — A10

Mythological Monster — A11

Armenian Soldier — A12

Soviet Symbols, Armenian Designs — A14

Mythological Monster — A13

Mt. Alagöz and Plain of Shirak A15

Fisherman on River Aras — A16

Post Office in Erevan and Mt. Ararat A17

Ruin in City of Ani — A18

Street in Erevan — A19

Lake Sevan and Sevan Monastery — A20

Mythological Subject from old Armenian Monument — A21

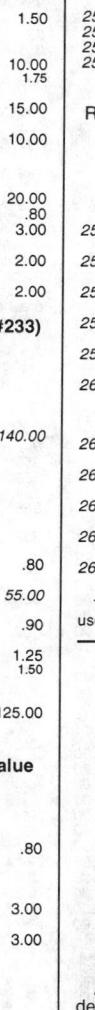

Mt. Ararat A22

1921 Unwmk. *Perf. 11½, Imperf.*

278	A7	1r	gray green	.30	
279	A8	2r	slate gray	.30	
280	A9	3r	carmine	.30	
281	A10	5r	dark brown	.30	
282	A11	25r	gray	.30	.20
283	A12	50r	red	.20	
284	A13	100r	orange	.20	
285	A14	250r	dark blue	.20	
286	A15	500r	brown vio	.20	
287	A16	1000r	sea green	.25	
288	A17	2000r	bister	.75	
289	A18	5000r	dark brown	.60	
290	A19	10,000r	dull red	.60	
291	A20	15,000r	slate blue	.60	
292	A21	20,000r	lake	.60	
293	A22	25,000r	gray blue	1.25	
294	A22	25,000r	brown olive	6.50	
			Nos. 278-294 (17)	13.45	

Except the 25r, Nos. 278-294 were not regularly issued and used. Counterfeits exist.

For surcharges see Nos. 347-390.

Russian Stamps of 1909-17 Surcharged

Wove Paper

Lozenges of Varnish on Face

1921, Aug. *Perf. 13½*

295	A9	5000r on 1r	*10.00*	
296	A12	5000r on 3½r	*10.00*	
297	A13	5000r on 5r	*10.00*	
298	A12	5000r on 7r	*10.00*	
299	A13	5000r on 10r	*10.00*	
		Nos. 295-299 (5)	*50.00*	

Nos. 295-299 were not officially issued. Counterfeits abound.

Mt. Ararat and Soviet Star
A23 A24

Soviet Symbols — A25

Crane — A26

Peasant — A27

Harpy — A28

Peasant Sowing — A29

Soviet Symbols — A30

Forging — A31

Plowing A32

1922 *Perf. 11½*

300	A23	50r green & red	.50	
301	A24	300r slate bl & buff	.60	
302	A25	400r blue & pink	.60	
303	A26	500r vio & pale lil	.60	
304	A27	1000r dull bl & pale bl	.60	
305	A28	2000r black & gray	.85	
306	A29	3000r black & grn	.85	
307	A30	4000r black & lt brn	.85	
308	A31	5000r black & dull red	.75	
309	A32	10,000r black & pale rose	.75	
a.		Tête bêche pair	35.00	
		Nos. 300-309 (10)	6.95	

Nos. 300-309 were not issued without surcharge.

Stamps of types A23 to A32, printed in other colors than Nos. 300 to 309, are essays.

Nos. 300-309 with Handstamped Surcharge of New Values in Rose, Violet or Black

1922

310	10,000 on 50r (R)	*8.50*	*11.00*
311	10,000 on 50r (V)	*8.50*	*11.00*
312	10,000 on 50r	*8.50*	*11.00*
313	15,000 on 300r (R)	*8.50*	*14.00*
314	15,000 on 300r (V)	*8.50*	*14.00*
315	15,000 on 300r	*8.50*	*14.00*
316	25,000 on 400r (V)	*8.50*	*14.00*
317	25,000 on 400r	*8.50*	*14.00*
318	30,000 on 500r (R)	*10.00*	*17.00*
319	30,000 on 500r (V)	*10.00*	*17.00*
320	30,000 on 500r	*10.00*	*17.00*
321	50,000 on 1000r (R)	*8.50*	*14.00*
322	50,000 on 1000r (V)	*8.50*	*14.00*
323	50,000 on 1000r	*8.50*	*14.00*
324	75,000 on 3000r	*11.00*	*20.00*
325	100,000 on 2000r (R)	*20.00*	*20.00*
326	100,000 on 2000r (V)	*20.00*	*20.00*
327	100,000 on 2000r	*20.00*	*20.00*
328	200,000 on 4000r (V)	*22.50*	*22.50*
329	200,000 on 4000r	*22.50*	*22.50*
330	300,000 on 5000r (V)	*30.00*	*45.00*
331	300,000 on 5000r	*30.00*	*45.00*
332	500,000 on 10,000r (V)	*30.00*	*30.00*
333	500,000 on 10,000r	*30.00*	*30.00*
	Nos. 310-333 (24)	*359.50*	*471.00*

Goose — A33

Armenian Woman at Well — A35

Armenian Village Scene A34

Mt. Ararat — A36

Mt. Ararat A37

New Values in Gold Kopecks, Handstamped Surcharge in Black

1922 *Imperf.*

334	A33	1(k) on 250r rose	12.50	12.50
335	A33	1(k) on 250r gray	20.00	20.00
336	A34	2(k) on 500r rose	8.00	8.00
337	A34	3(k) on 500r gray	8.00	8.00
338	A35	4(k) on 1000r rose	8.00	8.00
339	A35	4(k) on 1000r gray	15.00	15.00
340	A36	5(k) on 2000r gray	8.00	8.00
341	A36	10(k) on 2000r rose	8.00	8.00
342	A37	15(k) on 5000r rose	52.50	52.50
343	A37	20(k) on 5000r gray	8.00	8.00
		Nos. 334-343 (10)	148.00	148.00

Nos. 334-343 were issued for postal tax purposes.

Nos. 334-343 exist without surcharge but are not known to have been issued in that condition. Counterfeits exist of both sets.

Regular Issue of 1921 Handstamped with New Values in Black or Red Short, Thick Numerals

1922 *Imperf.*

347	A8	2(k) on 2r (R)	50.00	50.00
350	A11	4(k) on 25r (R)	30.00	30.00
353	A13	10(k) on 100r (R)	20.00	20.00
354	A14	15(k) on 250r	10.00	10.00
355	A15	20(k) on 500r	15.00	15.00
a.		With "k" written in red	10.00	10.00
357	A22	50(k) on 25,000r bl (R)	12.00	12.00
358	A22	50(k) on 25,000r brn ol (R)	9.00	9.00
359	A22	50(k) on 25,000r brn ol		
		Nos. 347-358 (7)	146.0	146.00

Perf. 11½

360	A7	1(k) on 1r, imperf.	*25.00*	*25.00*
a.		Perf.	*15.00*	*15.00*
361	A7	1(k) on 1r (R)	*35.00*	*35.00*
a.		Imperf.	*40.00*	*40.00*
362	A8	2(k) on 2r, imperf.	*40.00*	*40.00*
a.		Perf.	*40.00*	*40.00*
363	A15	2(k) on 500r	*35.00*	*35.00*
a.		Imperf.	*50.00*	*50.00*
364	A15	2(k) on 500r (R)	9.00	9.00
365	A11	4(k) on 25r, imperf.	*25.00*	*25.00*
a.		Perf.	*25.00*	*25.00*
366	A12	5(k) on 50r, imperf.	1.75	1.75
a.		Perf.	*2.50*	*2.50*
367	A13	10(k) on 100r	*20.00*	*20.00*
a.		Imperf.	*20.00*	*20.00*
368	A21	35(k) on 20,000r, imperf.	*50.00*	*50.00*
a.		With "k" written in violet	*50.00*	*50.00*
b.		Perf.	*65.00*	*65.00*
c.		As "a," perf.	*65.00*	*65.00*
d.		With "kop" written in violet, imperf.		
		Nos. 360-368 (9)	*240.75*	*240.75*

Manuscript Surcharge in Red

Perf. 11½

371	A14	1k on 250r dk bl	*40.00*	*40.00*

Handstamped in Black or Red

Tall, Thin Numerals

Imperf

377	A11	4(k) on 25r (R)	4.25	4.25
379	A13	10(k) on 100r	10.00	10.00
380	A15	20(k) on 500r	6.00	6.00
381	A22	50k on 25,000r bl	*75.00*	*75.00*
a.		Surcharged "50" only	50.00	50.00
382	A22	50k on 25,000r bl (R)	12.00	12.00
382A	A22	50k on 25,000r brn ol	24.00	24.00
		Nos. 377-382A (6)	*131.25*	*131.25*

On Nos. 381, 382 and 382A the letter "k" forms part of the surcharge.

Perf. 11½

383	A7	1(k) on 1r (R)	*50.00*	*50.00*
a.		Imperf.		
384	A14	1(k) on 250r	1.75	1.75
385	A15	2(k) on 500r	8.00	8.00
a.		Imperf.	20.00	20.00
386	A15	2(k) on 500r (R)	20.00	20.00
387	A9	3(k) on 3r	20.00	20.00
a.		Imperf.	20.00	20.00
388	A21	3(k) on 20,000r, imperf.	10.00	10.00
a.		Perf.	50.00	50.00
389	A11	4(k) on 25r	2.50	2.50
a.		Imperf.	4.25	4.25
390	A12	5(k) on 50r, imperf.	*10.00*	*10.00*
a.		Perf.	*15.00*	*15.00*
		Nos. 383-390 (8)	*122.25*	*122.25*

Catalogue values for unused stamps in this section, from this point to the end of the section, are for Never Hinged items.

Mt. Ararat — A45

a, 20k. b, 2r. c, 5r.

1992, May 28 Litho. *Perf. 14*

430	A45	Strip of 3, #a.-c.	3.00	3.00

Souvenir Sheet

431	A45	7r Eagle & Mt. Ararat	37.50	37.50

AT & T Communications System in Armenia — A45a

1992, July 1 Litho. *Perf. 13x13½*

431A	A45a	50k multicolored	3.50	3.50

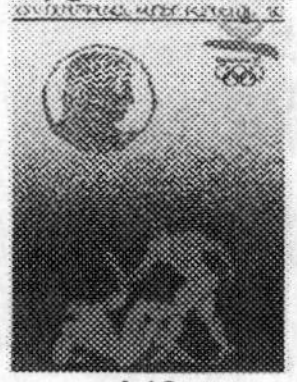
A46

A47

1992 Summer Olympics, Barcelona: a, 40k, Ancient Greek wrestlers. b, 3.60r, Boxing. c, 5r, Weight lifting. d, 12r, Gymnastics.

1992, July 25 Litho. *Perf. 14*

432	A46	Strip of 4, #a.-d.	3.50	3.50

1992-93 Litho. *Perf. 14½, 15x14½*

20k, Natl. flag. 1r, Goddess Waroubini, Orgov radio telescope. 2r, Yerevan Airport. No. 436, Goddess Anahit. No. 437, Runic message, 7th cent B.C. 5r, UPU emblem. 20r, Silver cup.

433	A47	20k multicolored	.20	.20
434	A47	1r gray green	.20	.20
435	A47	2r blue	.30	.30
436	A47	3r brown	.50	.50
437	A47	3r bronze	.20	.20
438	A47	5r brown black	.75	.75
439	A47	20r gray	.20	.20
		Nos. 433-439 (7)	2.35	2.35

No. 435 is airmail. See Nos. 464-471, 521-524.

Issued: #436, 20k, 2r, 5r, 8/25/92; others, 5/12/93.

Religious Artifacts — A50

Yerevan '93 — A52

David of Sassoun, by Hakop Kojoian — A50a

Scenic Views — A51

1993, May 23 Litho. *Perf. 14*

448 A50	40k Marker	.25	.20
449 A50	80k Gospel page	.35	.25
450 A50	3.60r Bas-relief, 13th cent.	1.25	1.10
451 A50	5r Icon of the Madonna	1.90	1.75
	Nos. 448-451 (4)	3.75	3.30

Souvenir Sheet

Perf. 14x13½

451A A50a 12r multicolored 6.75 6.00

1993, May 24 *Perf. 14*

Designs (illustration reduced): 40k, Garni Canyon, vert. 80k, Shaki Waterfall, Zangezur, vert. 3.60r, Arpa River Canyon, vert. 5r, Lake Sevan. 12r, Mount Aragats.

452 A51	40k multicolored	.20	.20
453 A51	80k multicolored	.20	.20
454 A51	3.60r multicolored	.50	.50
455 A51	5r multicolored	.65	.65
456 A51	12r multicolored	1.65	1.65
	Nos. 452-456 (5)	3.20	3.20

1993, May 25 *Perf. 14½*

457 A52 10r multicolored .50 .50
a. Min. sheet of 6 + 2 labels 4.25

For surcharges see Nos. 485-486.

Souvenir Sheet

Noah's Descent from Mt. Ararat, by Hovhannes Aivazovsky — A52

1993, May 24 Litho. *Perf. 14½*

458 A52 7r multicolored *2.50 2.50*

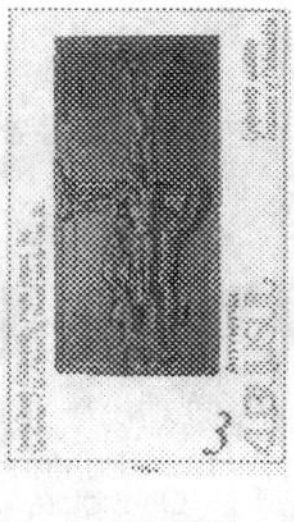
Religious Relics, Echmiadzin — A53

Designs: 3r, Wooden panel, descent from cross, 9th cent. 5r, Gilded silver reliquary for Holy Cross of Khotakerats. 12r, Cross depicting right hand of St. Karapet, 14th cent. 30r, Reliquary for arm of St. Thaddeus the Apostle, 17th cent. 50r, Gilded silver vessel for consecrated ointment, 1815.

1994, Aug. 4 Litho. *Perf. 14x14½*

459 A53	3d multicolored	*.20*	*.20*
460 A53	5d multicolored	*.20*	*.20*
461 A53	12d multicolored	*.30*	*.30*
462 A53	30d multicolored	*.80*	*.80*
463 A53	50d multicolored	*1.25*	*1.25*
	Nos. 459-463 (5)	*2.75*	*2.75*

Artifacts and Landmarks Type of 1993

Gods of Van (Urartu): 10 l, Shivini, god of the sun. 50 l, Tayshaba, god of elements. 10d, Khaldi, supreme god.
25d, Natl. arms.

1994 *Perf. 14½*

464 A47	10 l black & brown	*.20*	*.20*
465 A47	50 l black & red brown	*.20*	*.20*
469 A47	10d black & gray	*.50*	*.50*
471 A47	25d red & bister	*1.25*	*1.25*
	Nos. 464-471 (4)	*2.15*	*2.15*

Issued: 10 l, 50 l, 10d, 25d, 8/4/94.
This is an expanding set. Numbers may change.

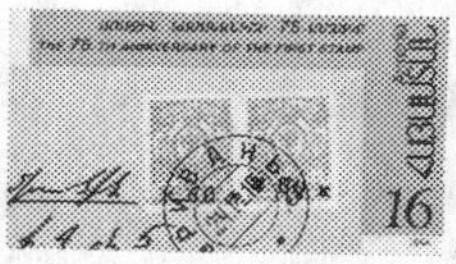
A54

1994, Dec. 31 Litho. *Perf. 14½x14*

479 A54 16d No. 1a .45 .45

First Armenian postage stamp, 75th anniv.

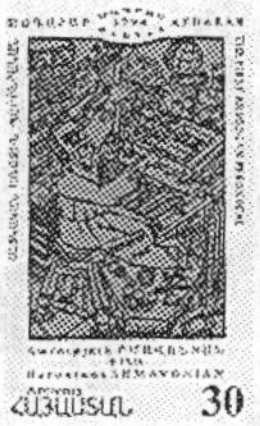
A54a

A54b

1994, Dec. 30 Litho. *Perf. 14x14½*

480 A54a 30d Early printing press .50 .50

First Armenian periodical, 170th anniv.

1994, Dec. 30 Litho. *Perf. 14x14½*

481 A54b 30d Natl. arms, stadium .55 .55

Natl. Olympic Committee.

Armenia stamps can be mounted in the annual Scott Armenia supplement.

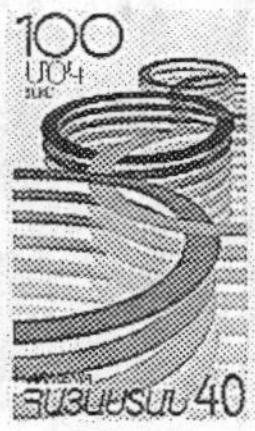
A54c

A54d

1994, Dec. 30 Litho. *Perf. 14x14½*

482 A54c 40d Olympic rings .75 .75

Intl. Olympic Committee, Cent.

1994, Dec. 31 Litho. *Perf. 14x14½*

483 A54d 50d multi + label .85 .85

Ervand Otian (1869-1926)

A54e

1994, Dec. 31 Litho. *Perf. 14½x14*

484 A54e 50d multi + label .85 .85

Levon Shant (1869-1951).

No. 457 Surcharged in Blue or Red Brown

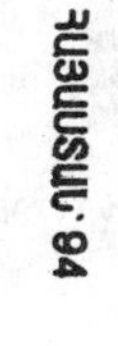
40
a

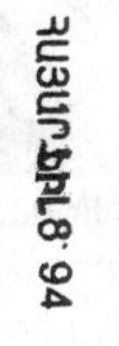
40
b

1994, Sept. 10 Litho. *Perf. 14*

485 A52(a)	40d on 10r (Bl)	1.65	1.65
486 A52(b)	40d on 10r (RB)	1.65	1.65

Yerevan '94.

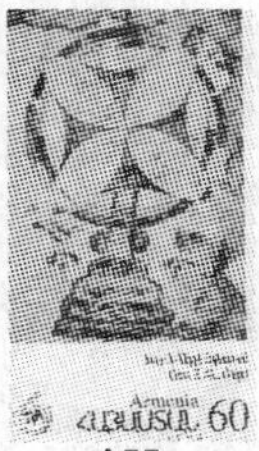
A55

A56

Christianity in Armenia: 60d, Cross, 10th-11th cent. No. 488, Kings Abgar & Trdat, 1836. No. 489, St. Bartholomew, St. Thaddeus. 80d, St. Gregory, the Illuminator. 90d, Baptism of the Armenian people, 1892. 400d, Plan of Echmiadzin, c. 1660, engr. by Jakob Peeters.

1995, Apr. 3 Litho. *Perf. 14x15*

487 A55	60d multicolored	.55	.55
488 A55	70d multicolored	.65	.65
489 A55	70d multicolored	.65	.65
490 A55	80d multicolored	.75	.75
491 A55	90d multicolored	.85	.85
	Nos. 487-491 (5)	3.45	3.45

Souvenir Sheet

492 A55 400d multicolored 4.00 4.00

Nos. 488-489 are 45x44mm.

1995, Apr. 3

493 A56 150d gray & black 1.25 1.25

Vazgen I (1908-94), Catholikos of All Armenians.

Armenia Fund A57

1995, Apr. 27 *Perf. 15x14*

494 A57 90d multicolored .80 .80

UN, 50th Anniv. A58

1995, Apr. 28

495 A58 90d multicolored .80 .80

Cultural Artifacts — A59

Designs: 30d, Black polished pottery, 14th-13th cent. B.C. 60d, Silver cup, 5th cent. B.C. 130d, Gohar carpet, 1700 A.D.

1995, Apr. 27 *Perf. 15x14*

496 A59	30d multicolored	.30	.30
497 A59	60d multicolored	.50	.50
498 A59	130d multicolored	1.25	1.25
	Nos. 496-498 (3)	2.05	2.05

Birds — A60

1995, Apr. 27 *Perf. 14*

499 A60	40d Milvus milvus	.50	.50
500 A60	60d Aquila chrysaetos	.75	.75

End of World War II, 50th Anniv. A61

Designs: No. 501, P. Kitsook, 408th Armenian Rifle Division. No. 502, A. Sargissin, N. Safarian, 89th Taman Armenian Triple Order-Bearer Division. No. 503, B. Chernikov, N. Tavartkeladze, V. Penkovsky, 76th Armenian Alpine Rifle Red Banner (51st Guards) Division. No. 504, S. Zakian, H. Babayan, I. Lyudnikov, 390th Armenian Rifle Division. No. 505, A. Vasillian, M. Dobrovolsky, Y. Grechany, G. Sorokin, 409th Armenian Rifle Division.

No. 506, vert.: a, Marshal Hovhannes Baghramian. b, Adm. Hovhannes Issakov. c, Marshal Hamazasp Babajanian. d, Marshal Sergey Khoudyakov.

No. 507: Return of the Hero, by Mariam Aslamazian.

1995, Sept. 30 Litho. *Perf. 15x14*

501 A61	60d multicolored	.45	.45
502 A61	60d multicolored	.45	.45
503 A61	60d multicolored	.45	.45
504 A61	60d multicolored	.45	.45
505 A61	60d multicolored	.45	.45
	Nos. 501-505 (5)	2.25	2.25

Miniature Sheet

Perf. 15x14½

506 A61 60d Sheet of 4, #a.-d. 3.00 3.00

Souvenir Sheet

Perf. 15x14

507 A61 300d multicolored 3.75 3.75

Authors
A62

Designs: No. 508, Ghevond Alishan (1820-1901). No. 509, Gregor Artsruni (1845-92), vert. No. 510, Franz Werfel (1890-1945).

1995, Oct. 5 Litho. *Perf. 15x14*

508 A62 90d blue & black .75 .75
509 A62 90d multicolored .75 .75
510 A62 90d blue & maroon .75 .75
Nos. 508-510 (3) 2.25 2.25

Nos. 508-510 issued with se-tenant label.

A64

Prehistoric artifacts: 40d, Four-wheeled carriages, 15th cent. BC, horiz. 60d, Bronze model of geocentric solar system, 11-10th cent. BC. 90d, Tombstone, Red Tufa, 7-6th cent. BC.

1995, Dec. 5 *Perf. 14½x15, 15x14½*

512 A64 40d multicolored .25 .25
513 A64 60d multicolored .60 .60
514 A64 90d multicolored .90 .90
Nos. 512-514 (3) 1.75 1.75

A65

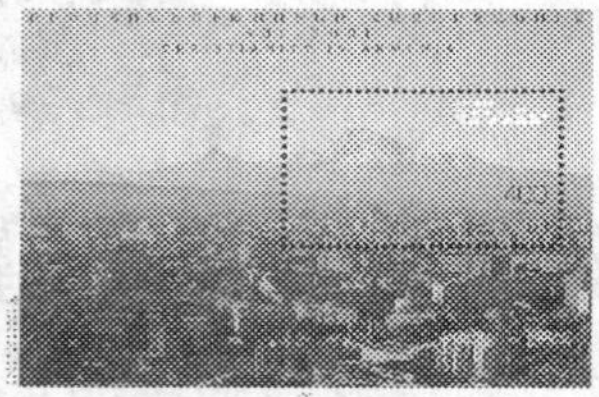

Christianity in Armenia — A66

Views of Yerevan: 60d, Brandy distillery, wine cellars. 80d, Abovian Street. 90d, Sports and concert complex. 100d, Baghramian Avenue. 120d, Republic Square.
400d, Panoramic photograph of Yerevan.

1995, Dec. 5 *Perf. 15x14*

515 A65 60d salmon & black .35 .35
516 A65 80d pale orange & black .45 .45
517 A65 90d buff & black .50 .50

Size: 61x24mm

518 A65 100d pale yellow bis & blk .85 .85
519 A65 120d dull orange & black 1.10 1.10
Nos. 515-519 (5) 3.25 3.25

Souvenir Sheet

520 A66 400d multicolored 3.50 3.50

No. 464 Surcharged in Green, Red, Blue Violet, or Red Brown

1996, Mar. 30 Litho. *Perf. 14½*

521 A47 40d on 10l (G) 1.00 1.00
522 A47 100d on 10l (R) 2.50 2.50
523 A47 150d on 10l (BV) 3.50 3.50
524 A47 200d on 10l (RB) 5.00 5.00
Nos. 521-524 (4) 12.00 12.00

Alexsandre Griboyedov (1795-1829), Writer — A67

1996, Apr. 24 Litho. *Perf. 14x14½*

525 A67 90d multicolored .70 .70

No. 525 is printed se-tenant with label.

Khrimian Hayrik (1820-1907), Catholicos of All Armenians — A68

1996, Apr. 30 *Perf. 14½x14*

526 A68 90d brown & blue .70 .70

No. 526 is printed se-tenant with label.

Admiral Lazar Serbryakov (1795-1862) — A69

1996, Apr. 30

527 A69 90d multicolored .70 .70

No. 527 is printed se-tenant with label.

Armenian Red Cross, 75th Anniv. — A70

1996, May 3 *Perf. 14x14½*

528 A70 60d multicolored .45 .45

Motion Pictures, Cent. A71

1996, May 3 *Perf. 14½x14*

529 A71 60d multicolored .45 .45

Endangered Fauna — A72

1996, May 3 *Perf. 14*

530 A72 40d Carpa aegagrus .30 .30
531 A72 60d Panthera pardus .45 .45

1996 Summer Olympics, Atlanta — A73

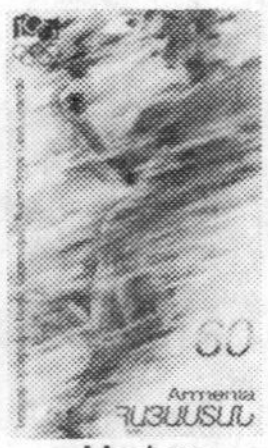

Modern Olympic Games, Cent. — A74

Designs: a, 40d, Cyclist. b, 60d, Athletic event. c, 90d, Wrestling.

1996, July 25

532 A73 Strip of 3, #a.-c. 1.25 1.25

1996, July 25 *Perf. 14x14½*

533 A74 60d multicolored .45 .45

Fridtjof Nansen (1861-1930), Arctic Explorer — A75

1996, May 20 Litho. *Perf. 14x14½*

534 A75 90d multicolored .60 .60

32nd Chess Olympiad, Yerevan — A76

#535, Petrosian-Botvinnik, World Championship match, Moscow, 1963. #536, Kasparov-Karpov, World Championship Match, Leningrad, 1986. #537, G. Kasparian, first prize winner, Contest of the Shakhmati v SSSR magazine, 1939. #538, 32nd Chess Olympiad, Yerevan.

1996, Sept. 15 Litho. *Perf. 14*

535 A76 40d multicolored .35 .35
536 A76 40d multicolored .35 .35
537 A76 40d multicolored .35 .35
538 A76 40d multicolored .35 .35
a. Booklet pane, #535-538 *1.50*
Complete booklet, 2 #538a *3.00*
Nos. 535-538 (4) 1.40 1.40

No. 538a issued 9/24.

Tigran Petrosian, World Chess Champion, Chess House, Yerevan — A77

1996, Sept. 20 *Perf. 14x15*

539 A77 90d multicolored .75 .75

Capra Aegagrus A78

World Wildlife Fund: 70d, Two running. 100d, One standing. 130d, One holding head down. 350d, Two facing forward.

1996, Oct. 20 Litho. *Perf. 14½x14*

540 A78 70d multicolored .40 .40
541 A78 100d multicolored .50 .50
542 A78 130d multicolored .75 .75
543 A78 350d multicolored 2.00 2.00
a. Block of 4, #540-543 3.75 3.75
b. Booklet pane, 2 #543a 7.50
Complete booklet, #543b 7.50

Issued in sheets of 16 stamps.

Christianity in Armenia, 1700th Anniv. — A79

Armenian churches: No. 544, St. Catherine Church, St. Petersburg, 1780. No. 545, Church of the Holy Mother, Kishinev, 1803. No. 546, Church of the Holy Mother, Samarkand, 1903. No. 547, Armenian Church, Lvov, 1370. No. 548, St. Hripsime Church, Yalta, 1913.
500d, Church of St. Gevorg of Etchmiadzin, Tbilisi, 1805.

1996 Litho. *Perf. 14x15*

544 A79 100d multicolored .50 .50
545 A79 100d multicolored .50 .50
546 A79 100d multicolored .50 .50
547 A79 100d multicolored .50 .50
548 A79 100d multicolored .50 .50
Nos. 544-548 (5) 2.50 2.50

Souvenir Sheet

549 A79 500d multicolored 2.50 2.50

First Armenian Printing Press, Etchmiadzin, 225th Anniv. — A80

1997, Mar. 26 Litho. *Perf. 15x14*

550 A80 70d multicolored .35 .35

Armenian Entertainers — A81

#551, Folk singer, Jivani (1846-1909). #552, Arno Babajanian (1921-83), composer, vert.

1997, Mar. 26 *Perf. 15x14, 14x15*

551 A81 90d multicolored .45 .45
552 A81 90d multicolored .45 .45

Paintings from Natl. Gallery of Armenia A82

#553, "One of my Dreams," by Eghishe Tadevossian. #554, "Countryside," by Gevorg Bashinjaghian. #555, "Portrait of Natalia Tehumian," by Hakob Hovnatanian. #556, "Salomé," by Vardges Sureniants.

1997, May 28 Litho. *Perf. 15x14*

553 A82 150d multi .70 .70
554 A82 150d multi .70 .70
555 A82 150d multi, vert. .70 .70
556 A82 150d multi, vert. .70 .70
Nos. 553-556 (4) 2.80 2.80

See Nos. 573-575.

Rouben Mamulian (1897-1987), Motion Picture Director — A83

1997, Oct. 8 Litho. *Perf. 15x14*
557 A83 150d multicolored .70 .70

Moscow '97, World Philatelic Exhibition — A84

1997, Oct. 17 *Perf. 14x15*
558 A84 170d St. Basil's Cathedral .80 .80

Eghishe Charents (1897-1937), Poet — A85

1997, Oct. 19 *Perf. 15x14*
559 A85 150d multicolored .70 .70

A86

A87

Europa (Stories and Legends): 170d, Hayk, the Progenitor of the Armenians. 250d, Vahagn, the Dragon Slayer.

1997, Oct. 18 *Perf. 14x15*
560 A86 170d multicolored .80 .80
561 A86 250d multicolored 1.15 1.15

1997, Dec. 19 Litho. *Perf. 14*
562 A87 40d Iris lycotis .20 .20
563 A87 170d Iris elegantissima .85 .85

Religious Buildings A88

Christmas A89

#564, San Lazzaro, the Mekhitarian Congregation, Venice. #565, St. Gregory the Illuminator Cathedral, Anthelias. #566, St. Khach Armenian Church, Rostov upon Don. #567, St. James Monastery, Jerusalem. #568, Nercissian School, Tbilisi.
500d, Lazarian Seminary, Moscow.

1997, Dec. 22 *Perf. 15x14, 14x15*
564 A88 100d multi, horiz. .50 .50
565 A88 100d multi .50 .50
566 A88 100d multi .50 .50
567 A88 100d multi, horiz. .50 .50

Size: 60x21mm
568 A88 100d multi, horiz. .50 .50
Nos. 564-568 (5) 2.50 2.50

Souvenir Sheet
569 A88 500d multicolored 2.50 2.50

Christianity in Armenia, 1700th anniv. (in 2001).

1997, Dec. 26 *Perf. 14x15*
570 A89 40d multicolored .25 .25

Diana, Princess of Wales (1961-97) A90

1998, Apr. 8 Litho. *Perf. 15x14*
571 A90 250d multicolored 1.00 1.00

No. 571 was issued in sheets of 5 + label.

Karabakh Movement, 10th Anniv. — A91

1998, Feb. 20 Litho. *Perf. 13½x14*
572 A91 250d multicolored 1.00 1.00

Paintings from Natl. Gallery of Armenia Type of 1997

#573, "Tartar Women's Dance," by Alexander Bazhbeouk-Melikian. #574, "Family. Generations," by Yervand Kochar. #575, "Spring in Our Yard," by Haroutiun Kalents.

1998, Feb. 21 *Perf. 15x14, 14x15*
573 A82 150d multi .65 .65
574 A82 150d multi, vert. .65 .65
575 A82 150d multi, vert. .65 .65
Nos. 573-575 (3) 1.95 1.95

1998 World Cup Soccer Championships, France — A92

1998, June 10 Litho. *Perf. 14x15*
576 A92 250d multicolored 1.10 1.10

National Holidays and Festivals A93

Europa: 170d, Couple jumping over fire, Trndez. 250d, Girls taking part in traditional ceremony, Ascension Day.

1998, June 24 Litho. *Perf. 15x14*
577 A93 170d multicolored .80 .80
578 A93 250d multicolored 1.25 1.25

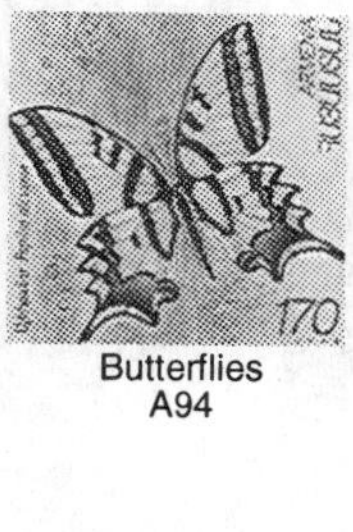

Butterflies A94

National Costumes A95

1998, June 26 *Perf. 14*
579 A94 170d Papilio alexanor .80 .80
580 A94 250d Rethera komarovi 1.25 1.25

1998, July 16 Litho. *Perf. 14x13½*
581 A95 170d Ayrarat .75 .75
582 A95 250d Vaspurakan 1.10 1.10

See Nos. 591-592.

Christianity in Armenia, 1700th Anniv. (in 2001) — A96

Churches: a, St. Forty Children's, 1958, Milan. b, St. Sargis, London, 1923. c, St. Vardan Cathedral, 1968, New York. d, St. Hovannes Cathedral, 1902, Paris. e, St. Gregory the Illuminator Cathedral, 1938, Buenos Aires.

1998, Sept. 25 Litho. *Perf. 11½*
583 A96 100d Sheet of 5, #a.-e. 2.40 2.40

Memorial to Armenian Earthquake Victims — A97

1998, Sept. 26 *Perf. 15x14*
584 A97 250d multicolored 1.10 1.10

No. 584 was issued in sheets of 8 + 2 labels.

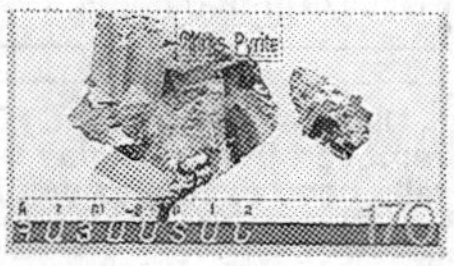

Minerals A98

1998, Oct. 23
585 A98 170d Pyrite .75 .75
586 A98 250d Agate 1.10 1.10

Valery Bryusov (1873-1924), Writer — A99

1998, Dec. 1 *Perf. 14x15*
587 A99 90d multicolored .45 .45

Souvenir Sheet

Sergei Parajanov, Film Director, 75th Birth Anniv. — A100

Illustration reduced.

1999, Apr. 19 Litho. *Perf. 14x14¾*
588 A100 500d multicolored 2.25 2.25
a. IBRA 99 emblem in margin 2.25 2.25

State Reserves A101

1999, Apr. 22 *Perf. 14¾x14¼*
589 A101 170d Khosrov .80 .80
590 A101 250d Kilijan 1.25 1.25

Europa.

National Costumes Type of 1998

1999, Apr. 20 Litho. *Perf. 14x13½*
591 A95 170d Karin .80 .80
592 A95 250d Zangezour 1.25 1.25

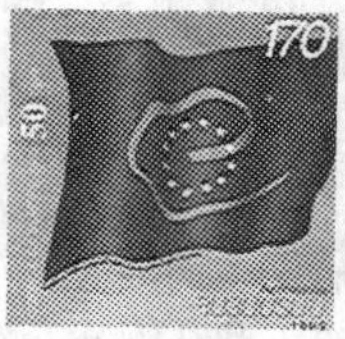

Council of Europe, 50th Anniv. — A102

1999, June 12
593 A102 170d multicolored .80 .80

Cilician Ships A103

1999, Aug. 12 Litho. *Perf. 14¾x14*

Sail Colors

594 A103 170d orange & blue .80 .80
595 A103 250d red & white 1.25 1.25

With PhilexFrance 99 Emblem at LR

596 A103 250d red & white 1.25 1.25
Nos. 594-596 (3) 3.30 3.30

Domesticated Animals — A104

1999, Aug. 19 *Perf. 13¼x13¾*

597 A104 170d Armenian gampr dog .80 .80
598 A104 250d Van cat 1.25 1.25

With China 1999 World Philatelic Exhibition Emblem at LR

599 A104 250d Van cat 1.25 1.25
Nos. 597-599 (3) 3.30 3.30

Souvenir Sheet

First Pan-Armenian Games — A105

Illustration reduced.

1999, Aug. 28 *Perf. 14¾x14*

600 A105 250d multicolored 2.10 2.10

Souvenir Sheet

Christianity in Armentia, 1700th Anniv. (in 2001) A106

Churches: a, St. Gregory the Illuminator, Cairo. b, St. Gregory the Illuminator, Singapore. c, St. Khach, Suceava, Romania. d, St. Savior, Worcester, Mass. e, Church of the Holy Mother, Madras, India.

1999, Aug. Litho. *Perf. 13¼x13¾*

601 A106 70d Sheet of 5, #a.-e. + label 1.60 1.60

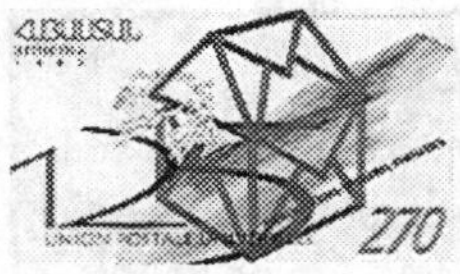

UPU, 125th Anniv. A107

1999, Oct. *Perf. 14¾x14¼*

602 A107 270d multicolored 1.40 1.40

AIR POST STAMPS

AP1

AP2

Design: 90d, Artiom Katsian (1886-1943), world record holding pilot on range and altitude in 1909.

1995, Dec. 5 Litho. *Perf. 14x15*

C1 AP1 90d multicolored *.75 .75*

1996, Apr. 30 Litho. *Perf. 14x14½*

C2 AP2 90d multicolored *.70 .70*

Nelson Stepanian (1913-44), WWII fighter ace.

ARUBA

ə-'rü-bə

LOCATION — West Indies, north of Venezuela
AREA — 78 sq. mi.
POP. — 67,014
CAPITAL — Oranjestad

On Jan. 1, 1986 Aruba, formerly part of Netherlands Antilles, achieved a separate status within the Kingdom of the Netherlands.

100 Cents = 1 Gulden

Catalogue values for all unused stamps in this country are for Never Hinged items.

Used values are for CTO or stamps removed from first day covers. Postally used examples sell for more.

Traditional House — A1

Perf. 14x13

1986-87 Litho. Unwmk.

1	A1	5c	shown	.20	.20
2	A1	15c	King William III Tower	.20	.20
3	A1	20c	Loading crane	.20	.20
4	A1	25c	Lighthouse	.20	.20
5	A1	30c	Snake	.30	.25
6	A1	35c	Owl	.30	.25
7	A1	45c	Shell	.30	.25
8	A1	55c	Frog	.40	.35
9	A1	60c	Water skier	.50	.45
10	A1	65c	Net fishing	.60	.55
11	A1	75c	Music box	.60	.55
12	A1	85c	Pre-Columbian bisque pot	.65	.60
13	A1	90c	Bulb cactus	.70	.65
14	A1	100c	Grain	.75	.70
15	A1	150c	Watapana tree	1.25	1.10
16	A1	250c	Aloe plant	2.10	1.90
			Nos. 1-16 (16)	9.25	8.40

Issued: 5c, 30c, 60c, 150c, 1/1; 15c, 35c, 65c, 250c, 2/5; 20c, 45c, 75c, 100c, 4/7/87; 25c, 55c, 85c, 90c, 7/17/87.

Independence A2

1986, Jan. 1 *Perf. 14x13, 13x14*

18 A2 25c Map .35 .30
19 A2 45c Coat of arms, vert. .60 .55
20 A2 55c Natl. anthem, vert. .70 .65
21 A2 100c Flag 1.00 .90
Nos. 18-21 (4) 2.65 2.40

Intl. Peace Year — A3

1986, Aug. 29 Litho. *Perf. 14x13*

22 A3 60c shown .60 .55
23 A3 100c Barbed wire .90 .80

Princess Juliana and Prince Bernhard, 50th Wedding Anniv. — A4

1987, Jan. 7 Photo. *Perf. 13x14*

24 A4 135c multicolored 1.25 1.10

State Visit of Queen Beatrix and Prince Claus of the Netherlands A5

1987, Feb. 16 Litho. *Perf. 14x13*

25 A5 55c shown .50 .45
26 A5 60c Prince William-Alexander .55 .50

Tourism — A6

1987, June 5 Litho.

27 A6 60c Beach and sea .75 .70
28 A6 100c Rock and cacti 1.25 1.10

Aloe Vera Plant — A7

Coins — A8

1988, Jan. 27 Litho. *Perf. 13x14*

29 A7 45c Field .45 .40
30 A7 60c Plant .60 .55
31 A7 100c Harvest 1.00 .90
Nos. 29-31 (3) 2.05 1.85

1988, Mar. 16 Litho. *Perf. 13x14*

32 A8 25c 25-cent .30 .25
33 A8 55c 50-cent .55 .50
34 A8 65c 5 and 10-cent .75 .70
35 A8 150c 1-florin 1.60 1.40
Nos. 32-35 (4) 3.20 2.85

Love Issue — A9

A10

1988, May 4

36 A9 70c shown .60 .55
37 A9 135c Seashells, coastal scenery 1.25 1.10

1988, Aug. 24

38 A10 35c shown .40 .35
39 A10 100c Emblems 1.00 .90

Aruba, the 162nd member of the Intl. Olympic Committee (35c), 1988 Summer Olympics, Seoul (100c).

Carnival A11

1989, Jan. 5 *Perf. 14x13*

40 A11 45c Two children .45 .40
41 A11 60c Girl .60 .55
42 A11 100c Entertainer 1.00 .90
Nos. 40-42 (3) 2.05 1.85

Maripampun, *Omphalophalmum Rubrum* — A12

1989, Mar. 16 Litho. *Perf. 14x13*

43 A12 35c Leaves .35 .30
44 A12 55c Pods .55 .50
45 A12 200c Blossom 1.75 1.60
Nos. 43-45 (3) 2.65 2.40

New Year 1990 — A13

UPU — A14

Dande band members playing instruments or singing: 25c, Violin, tambor, cuatro, marimba. 70c, Lead singer, guitar. 150c, Accordion, urri, guitar.

1989, Nov. 16 Litho. *Perf. 13x14*

46 A13 25c multicolored .25 .20
47 A13 70c multicolored .60 .55
48 A13 150c multicolored 1.25 1.10
Nos. 46-48 (3) 2.10 1.85

1989, June 8 Litho. *Perf. 13x14*

49 A14 250c multicolored 2.25 2.00

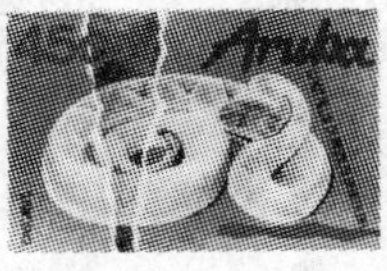

Crotalus durissus unicolor A15

1989, Aug. 24 *Perf. 14x13*

50 A15 45c shown .45 .40
51 A15 55c multi, diff. .50 .45
52 A15 60c multi, diff. .65 .60
Nos. 50-52 (3) 1.60 1.45

Snake species in danger of extinction.

Man Living in Harmony with Nature — A16

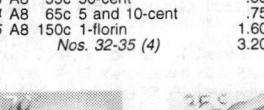

1990, Feb. 7 ***Perf. 13x14, 14x13***

53	A16	45c The land	.45	.40
54	A16	55c shown	.55	.50
55	A16	100c The sea	1.00	.90
		Nos. 53-55 (3)	2.00	1.80

Environmental protection. #53, 55 horiz.

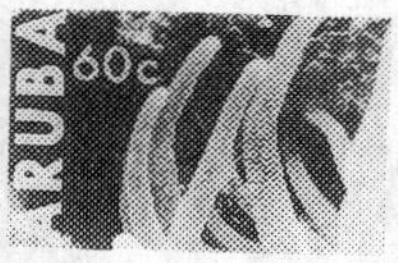

Marine Life — A17

Designs: 60c, Giant caribbean anemone, Pederson's cleaning shrimp. 70c, Queen angelfish, red and orange coral. 100c, Banded coral shrimp, fire sponge, yellow boring sponge.

1990, Apr. 4 **Litho.** ***Perf. 14x13***

56	A17	60c multicolored	.65	.60
57	A17	70c multicolored	.75	.70
58	A17	100c multicolored	1.10	1.00
		Nos. 56-58 (3)	2.50	2.30

A18

A19

1990, May 30 **Litho.** ***Perf. 13x14***

59	A18	35c multicolored	.30	.25
60	A18	200c Character trade-mark	1.75	1.60

World Cup Soccer Championships, Italy.

1990, Sept. 12

61	A19	45c Tools	.40	.35
62	A19	60c Stone figure	.60	.55
63	A19	100c Jar	1.00	.90
		Nos. 61-63 (3)	2.00	1.80

Archeological discoveries.

Landscapes A20

1991, Jan. 31 **Litho.** ***Perf. 14x13***

64	A20	55c Seashore	.55	.50
65	A20	65c Desert	.65	.60
66	A20	100c Cactus, ocean view	1.00	.90
		Nos. 64-66 (3)	2.20	2.00

Working Women — A21

Medicinal Plants — A22

Designs: 35c, Taking care of others. 70c, Housewife. 100c, Women in society.

1991, Mar. 28 **Litho.** ***Perf. 13x14***

67	A21	35c multicolored	.35	.30
68	A21	70c multicolored	.75	.70
69	A21	100c multicolored	1.00	.90
		Nos. 67-69 (3)	2.10	1.90

Style of inscriptions varies.

1991, May 29

70	A22	65c Ocimum sanctum	.60	.55
71	A22	75c Jatropha gossypifolia	.70	.65
72	A22	95c Croton flavens	.90	.80
		Nos. 70-72 (3)	2.20	2.00

A23

A24

Aruban Handicrafts: 35c, Fish net, wood float, wooden needle. 250c, Straw hat, hat block.

1991, July 31 **Litho.** ***Perf. 13x14***

73	A23	35c lt bl, dk bl & blk	.40	.35
74	A23	250c pink, lil rose & blk	2.75	2.50

1991, Nov. 29 **Litho.** ***Perf. 13x14***

75	A24	35c Toucan	.35	.30
76	A24	70c People shaking hands	.65	.60
77	A24	100c Windmill	1.00	.90
		Nos. 75-77 (3)	2.00	1.80

Welcome to Aruba.

Aruba Postal Service, Cent. — A25

Designs: 60c, Government decree, 1892, vert. 75c, First post office. 80c, Current post office.

Perf. 13x14, 14x13

1992, Jan. 31 **Litho.**

78	A25	60c multicolored	.60	.55
79	A25	75c multicolored	.75	.70
80	A25	80c multicolored	.85	.75
		Nos. 78-80 (3)	2.20	2.00

Equality Day — A26

1992, Mar. 25 **Litho.** ***Perf. 14x13***

81	A26	100c People of five races	.90	.80
82	A26	100c Woman, man, scales	.90	.80

Discovery of America, 500th Anniv. — A27

1992, July 30 **Litho.** ***Perf. 13x14***

83	A27	30c Columbus	.30	.25
84	A27	40c Sailing ship	.40	.35
85	A27	50c Natives, map	.55	.50
		Nos. 83-85 (3)	1.25	1.10

Natural Bridges in Aruba — A28

Designs: 70c, Seroe Colorado Bridge, south coast. 80c, Natural Bridge, north coast.

1992, Nov. 30 **Litho.** ***Perf. 14x13***

86	A28	70c multicolored	.70	.65
87	A28	80c multicolored	.80	.70

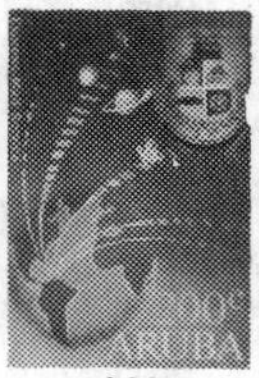

A29

A30

1993, Jan. 29 **Litho.** ***Perf. 13x14***

88	A29	200c multicolored	2.00	2.00

Express mail service.

1993, Mar. 31 **Litho.** ***Perf. 13x14***

Various rock formations found in Districts of Ayo and Casibari.

89	A30	50c multicolored	.55	.55
90	A30	60c multicolored	.60	.60
91	A30	100c multicolored	1.00	1.00
		Nos. 89-91 (3)	2.15	2.15

Folklore — A31

Sailing Sports — A32

40c, String instruments, drum. 70c, Traditional music & games. 80c, Dera Gai song lyrics.

1993, May 28 **Litho.** ***Perf. 13x14***

92	A31	40c multicolored	.40	.40
93	A31	70c multicolored	.70	.70
94	A31	80c multicolored	.80	.80
		Nos. 92-94 (3)	1.90	1.90

1993, July 30 **Litho.** ***Perf. 13x14***

95	A32	50c Sailboating	.50	.50
96	A32	65c Land sailing	.65	.65
97	A32	75c Wind surfing	.75	.75
		Nos. 95-97 (3)	1.90	1.90

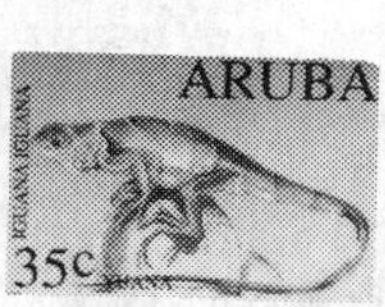

Iguana Iguana — A33

Perf. 14x13, 13x14

1993, Sept. 1 **Litho.**

98	A33	35c Young	.35	.35
99	A33	60c Almost grown	.60	.60
100	A33	100c Mature, vert.	1.00	1.00
		Nos. 98-100 (3)	1.95	1.95

Burrowing Owl — A34

Perf. 14x13, 13x14

1994, Jan. 28 **Litho.**

101	A34	5c Two adults	.20	.20
102	A34	10c Two adults, young	.20	.20
103	A34	35c Adult with prey, vert.	.45	.45
104	A34	40c Adult, vert.	.50	.50
		Nos. 101-104 (4)	1.35	1.35

World Wildlife Fund.

A35

A36

Intl. Olympic Committee, Cent.: 90c, Baron Pierre de Coubertin (1863-1937), founder of modern Olympics.

1994, Mar. 29 **Litho.** ***Perf. 13x14***

105	A35	50c multicolored	.50	.50
106	A35	90c multicolored	.95	.95

1994, July 7 **Litho.** ***Perf. 13x14***

107	A36	65c shown	.65	.65
108	A36	150c Mascot, soccer ball	1.50	1.50

1994 World Cup Soccer Championships, US.

Wild Fruit — A37

Designs: 40c, Malpighia punicifolia. 70c, Cordia sebestena. 85c, Pithecellobium unguis-cati. 150c, Coccoloba uvifera.

1994, Sept. 28 **Litho.** ***Perf. 13x14***

109	A37	40c multicolored	.40	.40
110	A37	70c multicolored	.75	.75
111	A37	85c multicolored	.90	.90
112	A37	150c multicolored	1.50	1.50
		Nos. 109-112 (4)	3.55	3.55

Architectural Landmarks A38

Designs: 35c, Government building, 1888. 60c, Ecury residence, 1929, vert. 100c, Protestant Church, 1846, vert.

1995, Jan. 27 **Litho.** ***Perf. 14x13***

113	A38	35c multicolored	.35	.35

Perf. 13x14

114	A38	60c multicolored	.65	.65
115	A38	100c multicolored	1.00	1.00
		Nos. 113-115 (3)	2.00	2.00

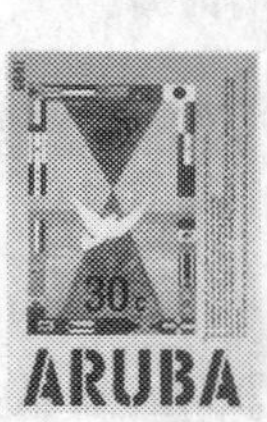

UN, 50th Anniv. — A39

Interpaso Horses — A40

Designs: 30c, Flags, sea, UN emblem, dove, text from UN charter. 200c, World with flags, doves, UN emblem.

1995, Mar. 29 **Litho.** ***Perf. 13x14***

116	A39	30c multicolored	.30	.30
117	A39	200c multicolored	2.00	2.00

1995, May 26 ***Perf. 14x13, 13x14***

Designs: 25c, 10-time champion Casanova II, ribbons, horiz. 75c, Paso Fino, horiz. 80c, Horse doing figure 8. 90c, Girl on horse.

118	A40	25c multicolored	.25	.25
119	A40	75c multicolored	.70	.70
120	A40	80c multicolored	.75	.75
121	A40	90c multicolored	.85	.85
		Nos. 118-121 (4)	2.55	2.55

Vegetables — A41

1995, July 28 Litho. *Perf. 13x14*

122 A41 25c Vigna sinensis .25 .25
123 A41 50c Cucumis anguria .50 .50
124 A41 70c Hibiscus esculentus .70 .70
125 A41 85c Cucurbita moschata .80 .80
Nos. 122-125 (4) 2.25 2.25

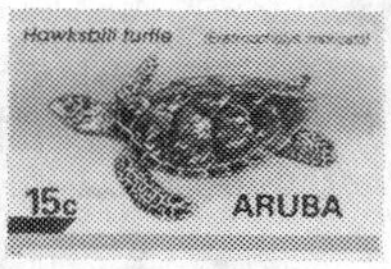

Turtles — A42

1995, Sept. 27 Litho. *Perf. 14x13*

126 A42 15c Hawksbill .20 .20
127 A42 50c Green .55 .55
128 A42 95c Loggerhead .90 .90
129 A42 100c Leatherback 1.00 1.00
Nos. 126-129 (4) 2.65 2.65

Separate Status, 10th Anniv. — A43

Statesmen and politicians: No. 130, Jan Hendrik Albert Eman (1887-1957). No. 131, Juan Enrique Irausquin (1904-62). No. 132, Cornelis Albert Eman (1916-67). No. 133, Gilberto Francois Croes (1938-85).

1996, Jan. 1 Litho. *Perf. 13x14*

130 A43 100c multicolored 1.00 1.00
131 A43 100c multicolored 1.00 1.00
132 A43 100c multicolored 1.00 1.00
133 A43 100c multicolored 1.00 1.00
Nos. 130-133 (4) 4.00 4.00

The 1986 date on No. 133 is in error.

America Issue — A44

National dresswear: 65c, Woman wearing long, full dress, apron, vert. 70c, Man wearing hat, bow tie, white shirt, black pants, vert. 100c, Couple dancing.

Perf. 13x14, 14x13

1996, Mar. 25 Litho.

134 A44 65c multicolored .75 .75
135 A44 70c multicolored .80 .80
136 A44 100c multicolored 1.10 1.10
Nos. 134-136 (3) 2.65 2.65

1996 Summer Olympic Games, Atlanta A45

1996, May 28 Litho. *Perf. 14x13*

137 A45 85c Runners 1.10 1.10
138 A45 130c Cyclist 1.60 1.60

A46

A47

Famous Women: No. 139, Livia (Mimi) Ecury (1920-91), nurse. No. 140, Lolita Euson (1914-94), poet. No. 141, Laura Wernet-Paskel (1911-62), teacher.

1996, Sept. 27 Litho. *Perf. 13x14*

139 A46 60c multicolored .70 .70
140 A46 60c multicolored .70 .70
141 A46 60c multicolored .70 .70
Nos. 139-141 (3) 2.10 2.10

1997, Jan. 23 Litho. *Perf. 13x14*

Year of Papiamento 1997: 50c, Sign promoting use of Papiamento language, children playing on beach, people in water, boat. 140c, "Papiamento," sunrise.

142 A47 50c multicolored .55 .55
143 A47 140c multicolored 1.60 1.60

Mailman on Bicycle, 1936-57 A48

America issue: 70c, Mailman handing mail to woman, jeep, 1957-88. 80c, Mailman on motor scooter placing mail in mailbox, 1995.

1997, Mar. 27 Litho. *Perf. 14x13*

144 A48 60c multicolored .70 .70
145 A48 70c multicolored .80 .80
146 A48 80c multicolored .90 .90
Nos. 144-146 (3) 2.40 2.40

Aruban Architectrue A49

30c, Decorated cunucu house. 65c, Steps with "popchi's." 100c, Arends's Building, vert.

1997, May 22 Litho. *Perf. 14x13*

147 A49 30c multicolored .40 .40
148 A49 65c multicolored .80 .80

Perf. 13x14

149 A49 100c multicolored 1.25 1.25
Nos. 147-149 (3) 2.45 2.45

Marine Life — A50

Designs: a, Marlin jumping out of water, lighthouse. b, Dolphin jumping out of water, trees, plants on beach. c, Iguana on rock, beach. d, Dolphin, fish. e, Two dolphins, fish. f, Fish, turtles, owl on beach. g, Various fish among coral. h, Diver, shipwreck, fish, coral. i, Various fish.

1997, May 29 Litho. *Perf. 12½x13*

150 A50 90c Sheet of 9, #a.-i. 10.00 10.00

PACIFIC 97.

Cruise Tourism A51

Designs: 35c, Ship at pier, tourists walking toward ship. 50c, Ship with gangway lowered, tourists. 150c, Ship out to sea, small boat.

1997, July 24 Litho. *Perf. 14x13*

151 A51 35c multicolored .40 .40
152 A51 50c multicolored .55 .55
153 A51 150c multicolored 1.60 1.60
Nos. 151-153 (3) 2.55 2.55

Aruban Wild Flowers A52

50c, Erythrina velutina. 60c, Cordia dentata. 70c, Tabebuia billbergii. 130c, Guaiacum officinale.

1997, Sept. 25

154 A52 50c multicolored .55 .55
155 A52 60c multicolored .70 .70
156 A52 70c multicolored .80 .80
157 A52 130c multicolored 1.50 1.50
Nos. 154-157 (4) 3.55 3.55

Fort Zoutman, Bicent. — A53

1998, Jan. 13 Litho. *Perf. 14x13*

158 A53 30c sepia & multi .35 .35
159 A53 250c gray & multi 3.00 3.00

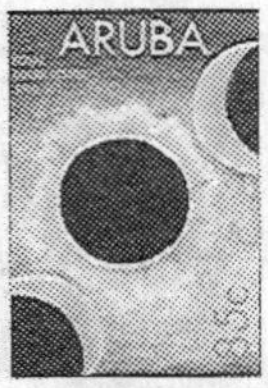

Total Solar Eclipse, 1998 — A54

1998, Feb. 26 Litho. *Perf. 13x14*

160 A54 85c shown 1.10 1.10
161 A54 100c Map, track of eclipse 1.25 1.25

Native Birds — A55

50c, Mimus gilvus. 60c, Falco sparverius. 70c, Icterus icterus. 150c, Coereba flaveola.

Perf. 14x13, 13x14

1998, July 10 Litho.

162 A55 50c multi .55 .55
163 A55 60c multi, vert. .70 .70
164 A55 70c multi, vert. .80 .80
165 A55 150c multi 1.75 1.75
Nos. 162-165 (4) 3.80 3.80

World Stamp 1998 — A56

1998, Sept. 8 Litho. *Perf. 14x13*

166 A56 225c multicolored 2.50 2.50

Endangered Animals — A57

Equus asinus: 40c, Two standing on hill. 65c, Three standing, rocks, cacti, tree. 100c, Adult, foal standing among rocks, cacti.

1999, Jan. 29 Litho. *Perf. 14x13*

167 A57 40c multicolored .45 .45
168 A57 65c multicolored .75 .75
169 A57 100c multicolored 1.10 1.10
Nos. 167-169 (3) 2.30 2.30

Cacti — A58

Designs: 50c, Opuntia wentiana. 60c, Lemaireocereus griseus. 70c, Cephalocereus lanuginosus. 75c, Cephalocereus lanuginosus (in bloom).

1999, Mar. 31 Litho. *Perf. 14x13*

170 A58 50c multicolored .55 .55
171 A58 60c multicolored .70 .70
172 A58 70c multicolored .80 .80
173 A58 75c multicolored .90 .90
Nos. 170-173 (4) 2.95 2.95

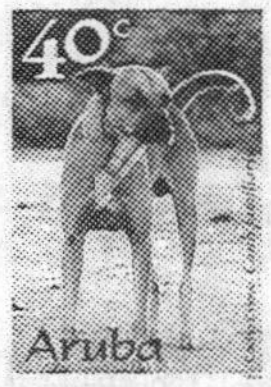

Dogs — A59

Various dogs, background: 40c, Trees. 60c, Cactus, aloe plant, rocks. 80c, Tree, sea. 165c, Sky, clouds.

1999, May 31 Litho. *Perf. 12¾x14*

174 A59 40c multicolored .45 .45
175 A59 60c multicolored .70 .70
176 A59 80c multicolored .90 .90
177 A59 165c multicolored 1.90 1.90
Nos. 174-177 (4) 3.95 3.95

Discovery of Aruba, 500th Anniv. — A60

1999, Aug. 9 Litho. *Perf. 14x13*

178 A60 150c shown 1.75 1.75
179 A60 175c Abstract paintings 2.00 2.00
a. Souvenir sheet, #178-179 3.75 3.75

Natl. Library, 50th Anniv. — A61

1999, Aug. 20

180 A61 70c shown .80 .80
181 A61 100c Original building 1.10 1.10

Christmas — A62

Die Cut Perf. 13x13½

1999, Dec. 1 Litho.

Self-Adhesive Coil Stamps

182 A62 40c Magi on shore .45 .45
183 A62 70c Magi in desert .80 .80
184 A62 100c Holy Family 1.10 1.10
Nos. 182-184 (3) 2.35 2.35

SEMI-POSTAL STAMPS

Surtax for child welfare organizations unless otherwise stated.

Solidarity SP1

1986, May 7 Litho. *Perf. 14x13*

B1 SP1 30c + 10c shown .30 .30
B2 SP1 35c + 15c Three ropes .55 .55
B3 SP1 60c + 25c One rope .75 .75
Nos. B1-B3 (3) 1.60 1.60

Surtax for social and cultural projects.

SP2

1986, Oct. 29 Litho. *Perf. 14x13*

B4	SP2	45c + 20c Boy, caterpillar	.65	.65
B5	SP2	70c + 25c Boy, cocoon	.90	.90
B6	SP2	100c + 40c Girl, butterfly	1.40	1.40
		Nos. B4-B6 (3)	2.95	2.95

Christmas
SP3

1987, Oct. 27 Litho. *Perf. 14x13*

B7	SP3	25c +10c Boy on beach	.45	.45
B8	SP3	45c +20c Drawing Christmas tree	.65	.65
B9	SP3	70c +30c Child, creche figures	1.00	1.00
		Nos. B7-B9 (3)	2.10	2.10

Solidarity
SP4

YMCA emblem in various geometric designs.

1988, Aug. 3 Litho. *Perf. 14x13*

B10	SP4	45c +20c shown	.60	.60
B11	SP4	60c +25c multi, diff.	.80	.80
B12	SP4	100c +50c multi, diff.	1.40	1.40
		Nos. B10-B12 (3)	2.80	2.80

11th YMCA world council.
Surtax for social and cultural projects.

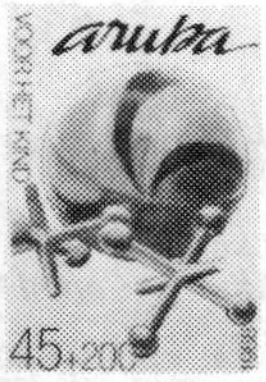

Children's
Toys — SP5

1988, Oct. 26 *Perf. 13x14*

B13	SP5	45c +20c Jacks	.60	.60
B14	SP5	70c +30c Top	.95	.95
B15	SP5	100c +50c Kite	1.40	1.40
		Nos. B13-B15 (3)	2.95	2.95

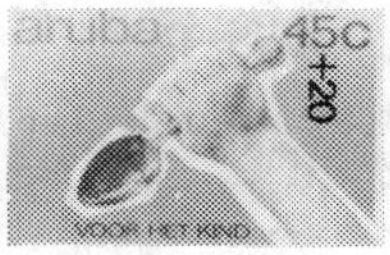

Children
SP6

1989, Oct. 26 *Perf. 14x13*

B16	SP6	45c +20c Baby spoon	.60	.60
B17	SP6	60c +30c Chasing a ball	.75	.75
B18	SP6	100c +50c Adult & child holding hands	1.25	1.25
		Nos. B16-B18 (3)	2.60	2.60

Solidarity
SP7

1990, July 25

B19	SP7	55c +25c shown	1.00	1.00
B20	SP7	100c +50c Family, house	1.75	1.75

Surtax for social and cultural projects.

SP8

SP9

Christmas song.

1990, Oct. 24 Litho. *Perf. 13x14*

B21	SP8	45c +20c Wind surfboards	.70	.70
B22	SP8	60c +30c shown	.90	.90
B23	SP8	100c +50c Kites, lizard	1.50	1.50
		Nos. B21-B23 (3)	3.10	3.10

1991, Oct. 25 Litho. *Perf. 13x14*

Literacy: 45c+25c, Discovery of reading. 60c+35c, Pointing to letter. 100c+50c, Child reading.

B24	SP9	45c +25c multi	.70	.70
B25	SP9	60c +35c multi	.90	.90
B26	SP9	100c +50c multi	1.50	1.50
		Nos. B24-B26 (3)	3.10	3.10

Solidarity
SP10

55c+30c, Girl scouts, flag & emblem. 100c+50c, Hand holding cancer fund emblem, people.

1992, May 27 Litho. *Perf. 14x13*

B27	SP10	55c +30c multi	.80	.80
B28	SP10	100c +50c multi	1.50	1.50

Surtax for social and cultural projects.

Postal Services of Aruba, Cent. — SP11

Designs: 50c+30c, Heart. 70c+35c, Airplane, letters. 100c+55c, Pigeon with letter in beak, vert.

1992, Oct. 30 Litho. *Perf. 14x13*

B29	SP11	50c +30c multi	.90	.90
B30	SP11	70c +35c multi	1.10	1.10

Perf. 13x14

B31	SP11	100c +50c multi	1.60	1.60
		Nos. B29-B31 (3)	3.60	3.60

Youth Foreign Study Programs
SP12

Abstract designs of: 50c+30c, Landscapes. 75c+40c, Young man, scenes of other countries, vert. 100c+50c, Integrating cultures.

1993, Oct. 27 *Perf. 14x13, 13x14*

B32	SP12	50c +30c multi	.80	.80
B33	SP12	75c +40c multi	1.10	1.10
B34	SP12	100c +50c multi	1.50	1.50
		Nos. B32-B34 (3)	3.40	3.40

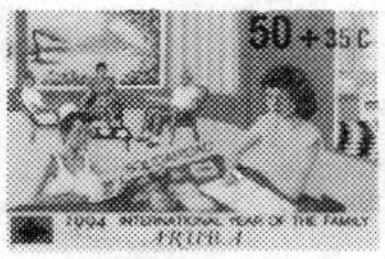

Intl. Year of the Family
SP13

Designs: 50c+35c, Family seated, reading, studying. 100c+50c, Family playing in front of house.

1994, May 30 Litho. *Perf. 14x13*

B35	SP13	50c +35c multi	.90	.90
B36	SP13	100c +50c multi	1.50	1.50

Surtax for social and cultural projects.

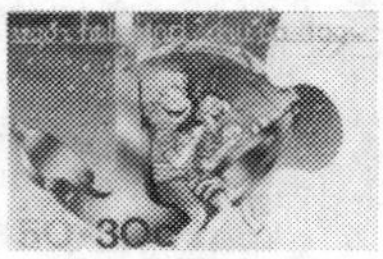

SP14

Designs: 50c+30c, Children on anchor with umbrella. 80c+35c, Children inside Sun. 100c+50c, Child riding owl.

1994, Oct. 27 Litho. *Perf. 14x13*

B37	SP14	50c +30c multi	.80	.80
B38	SP14	80c +35c multi	1.25	1.25
B39	SP14	100c +50c multi	1.50	1.50
		Nos. B37-B39 (3)	3.55	3.55

SP15

SP16

Children's drawings: 50c+25c, Children with balloons, house. 70c+35c, Three people with picnic basket on sunny day. 100c+50c, People gardening on sunny day.

1995, Oct. 26 Litho. *Perf. 13x14*

B40	SP15	50c +25c multi	.70	.70
B41	SP15	70c +35c multi	1.00	1.00
B42	SP15	100c +50c multi	1.40	1.40
		Nos. B40-B42 (3)	3.10	3.10

1996, July 26 Litho. *Perf. 13x14*

El Sol Naciente Lodge, 75th Anniv.: 60c+30c, Masonic emblems. 100c+ 50c, Columns, terrestrial and celestial globes.

B43	SP16	60c +30c multi	1.10	1.10
B44	SP16	100c +50c multi	1.90	1.90

Surtax for social and cultural projects.

SP17

Cartoons: 50c+25c, Mother, baby rabbit waiting at school bus stop. 70c+35c, Mother, baby owl, outside school. 100c+50c, Children flying kite.

1996, Oct. 24 Litho. *Perf. 14x13*

B45	SP17	50c +25c multi	.95	.95
B46	SP17	70c +35c multi	1.25	1.25
B47	SP17	100c +50c multi	1.90	1.90
		Nos. B45-B47 (3)	4.10	4.10

SP18

Designs: 50c+25c, Girl sitting among aloe plants. 70c+35c, Boy, butterfly, cactus, vert. 100c+50c, Girl swimming under water, fish, coral.

Perf. 14x13, 13x14

1997, Oct. 23 Litho.

B48	SP18	50c +25c multi	.85	.85
B49	SP18	70c +35c multi	1.25	1.25
B50	SP18	100c +50c multi	1.60	1.60
		Nos. B48-B50 (3)	3.70	3.70

SP19

Service Organizations: 60c+30c, Globe, emblem of Lions Intl., wheelchair balanced on map of Aruba. 100c+50c, Child reading book, emblem of Rotary Intl., woman in rocking chair.

1998, May 29 Litho. *Perf. 14x13*

B51	SP19	60c +30c multi	1.20	1.20
B52	SP19	100c +50c multi	2.00	2.00

Surtax for social and cultural projects.

SP20

Designs: 50c+25c, Girl performing traditional ribbon dance. 80c+40c, Boy playing a cuarta. 100c+50c, Two boys playing basketball.

1998, Oct. 22 Litho. *Perf. 13x14*

B53	SP20	50c +25c multi	.85	.85
B54	SP20	80c +40c multi	1.25	1.25
B55	SP20	100c +50c multi	1.75	1.75
		Nos. B53-B55 (3)	3.85	3.85

SP21

Designs: 60c+30c, Child on beach with man with fishing net. 80c+40c, Adult reading to children. 100c+50c, Mother, child, vert.

Perf. 14x13, 13x14

1999, Oct. 21 Litho.

B56	SP21	60c +30c multi	1.00	1.00
B57	SP21	80c +40c multi	1.40	1.40
B58	SP21	100c +50c multi	1.75	1.75
		Nos. B56-B58 (3)	4.15	4.15

ASCENSION

ə-ˈsen(t)-shən

LOCATION — An island in the South Atlantic Ocean, 900 miles from Liberia
GOVT. — A part of the British Crown Colony of St. Helena
AREA — 34 sq. mi.
POP. — 1,117 (1993)

In 1922 Ascension was placed under the administration of the Colonial Office and annexed to the British Crown Colony of St. Helena. The only post office is at Georgetown.

12 Pence = 1 Shilling
20 Shillings = 1 Pound
100 Pence = 1 Pound (1971)

Catalogue values for unused stamps in this country are for Never Hinged items, beginning with Scott 50.

Stamps and Types of St. Helena, 1912-22 Overprinted in Black or Red

ASCENSION

1922 Wmk. 4 *Perf. 14*

1	A9	½p	green & blk	3.50	*10.00*
2	A10	1p	green	4.00	*10.50*
3	A10	1½p	rose red	13.00	*47.50*
4	A9	2p	gray & blk	12.00	11.00
5	A9	3p	ultra	11.00	*14.00*
6	A10	8p	dl vio & blk	24.00	*42.50*
7	A10	2sh	ultra & blk, *blue*	75.00	*115.00*
8	A10	3sh	vio & blk	110.00	*150.00*

Wmk. 3

9	A9	1sh	blk, *gray grn* (R)	27.50	*42.50*
			Nos. 1-9 (9)	280.00	*443.00*

Seal of Colony — A3

1924-27 Typo. Wmk. 4 Perf. 14
Chalky Paper

10	A3	½p black & gray	2.75	*10.00*
11	A3	1p green & blk	4.50	*6.00*
12	A3	1½p rose red	6.50	*25.00*
13	A3	2p bluish gray & gray	9.75	5.00
14	A3	3p ultra	6.75	*10.00*
15	A3	4p blk & gray, *yel*	42.50	*70.00*
16	A3	5p ol & lil ('27)	9.50	*18.50*
17	A3	6p rose lil & gray	42.50	*75.00*
18	A3	8p violet & gray	12.50	*37.50*
19	A3	1sh brown & gray	17.00	*42.50*
20	A3	2sh ultra & gray, *blue*	50.00	*80.00*
21	A3	3sh blk & gray, *blue*	75.00	*85.00*
		Nos. 10-21 (12)	279.25	*464.50*

View of Georgetown — A4

Map of Ascension — A5

Sooty Tern Breeding Colony A9

Designs: 1½p, Pier at Georgetown. 3p, Long Beach. 5p, Three Sisters. 5sh, Green Mountain.

1934, July 2 Engr.

23	A4	½p violet & blk	.85	.75
24	A5	1p lt grn & blk	1.60	1.25
25	A4	1½p red & black	1.60	*2.10*
26	A5	2p org & black	1.60	*2.40*
27	A4	3p ultra & blk	1.60	1.40
28	A4	5p blue & black	2.10	*3.00*
29	A5	8p dk brn & blk	4.00	*4.50*
30	A9	1sh carmine & blk	17.50	6.00
31	A5	2sh6p violet & blk	32.50	*45.00*
32	A4	5sh brown & blk	52.50	*65.00*
		Nos. 23-32 (10)	115.85	*131.40*

Common Design Types pictured following the introduction.

Silver Jubilee Issue
Common Design Type

1935, May 6 Perf. 11x12

33	CD301	1½p car & dk blue	3.25	*7.00*
34	CD301	2p blk & ultra	10.00	*20.00*
35	CD301	5p ind & grn	16.00	*22.50*
36	CD301	1sh brn vio & indigo	22.50	*25.00*
		Nos. 33-36 (4)	51.75	*74.50*

25th anniv. of the reign of King George V.

Coronation Issue
Common Design Type

1937, May 19 Perf. 13½x14

37	CD302	1p deep green	.45	.45
38	CD302	2p deep orange	1.25	.70
39	CD302	3p bright ultra	1.25	.90
		Nos. 37-39 (3)	2.95	2.05
		Set, never hinged	3.50	

Georgetown — A11

Designs: 1p, 2p, 4p, Green Mountain. 1½p, 2sh6p, Pier at Georgetown. 3p, 5sh, Long Beach. 6p, 10sh, Three Sisters.

1938-49 Perf. 13½
Center in Black

40	A11	½p violet, perf. 13 ('44)	.35	*1.75*
		Never hinged	.65	
a.		Perf. 13½	1.75	1.25
		Never hinged	3.50	
41	A11	1p green	19.00	7.50
		Never hinged	37.50	
41A	A11	1p org yel, perf. 13 ('42)	.25	*.55*
		Never hinged	.45	
b.		Perf. 14 ('49)	.35	*15.00*
		Never hinged	.65	
c.		Perf. 13½	6.50	*8.50*
		Never hinged	13.50	
42	A11	1½p red, perf. 13 ('44)	.40	*.75*
		Never hinged	.80	
a.		Perf. 14 ('49)	1.40	*12.00*
		Never hinged	2.75	
b.		Perf. 13½	1.75	1.40
		Never hinged	3.50	
43	A11	2p orange, perf. 13 ('44)	.40	.40
		Never hinged	.75	
a.		Perf. 14 ('49)	2.00	*32.50*
		Never hinged	3.00	
b.		Perf. 13½	1.60	1.00
		Never hinged	3.25	
44	A11	3p ultra	55.00	25.00
		Never hinged	95.00	
44A	A11	3p black, perf. 13 ('44)	.35	*.80*
		Never hinged	.65	
c.		Perf. 13½('40)	7.50	.90
		Never hinged	16.00	
44B	A11	4p ultra, perf. 13 ('44)	2.25	*3.00*
		Never hinged	4.25	
d.		Perf. 13½	6.00	3.00
		Never hinged	13.00	
45	A11	6p gray blue	4.50	1.25
		Never hinged	8.50	
a.		Perf. 13 ('44)	4.50	4.50
		Never hinged	8.50	

Perf. 13

46	A11	1sh dk brown ('44)	3.25	2.00
		Never hinged	4.50	
a.		Perf. 13½	6.75	1.40
		Never hinged	14.00	
47	A11	2sh6p car ('44)	17.00	*30.00*
		Never hinged	32.50	
a.		Perf. 13½	20.00	7.00
		Never hinged	37.50	
48	A11	5sh yel brn ('44)	25.00	25.00
		Never hinged	45.00	
a.		Perf. 13½	55.00	7.00
		Never hinged	110.00	
49	A11	10sh red vio ('44)	45.00	*52.50*
		Never hinged	62.50	
a.		Perf. 13½	60.00	45.00
		Never hinged	125.00	

See Nos. 54-56.

Catalogue values for unused stamps in this section, from this point to the end of the section, are for Never Hinged items.

Peace Issue
Common Design Type
Perf. 13½x14

1946, Oct. 21 Engr. Wmk. 4

50	CD303	2p deep orange	.40	*.50*
51	CD303	4p deep blue	.40	.30

Silver Wedding Issue
Common Design Types

1948, Oct. 20 Photo. Perf. 14x14½

52	CD304	3p black	.50	.50

Engraved; Name Typographed
Perf. 11½x11

53	CD305	10sh red violet	42.50	40.00

Type of 1938

Designs: 1p, Three Sisters. 1½p, Georgetown Pier. 2p, Green Mountain.

Perf. 13

1949, June 1 Engr. Wmk. 4

54	A11	1p green & black	.45	.40

Perf. 14

55	A11	1½p lilac rose & blk	.55	.75
a.		Perf. 13	.50	*6.00*
b.		1½p carmine & black	7.00	4.75
56	A11	2p red & black	.75	.75
		Nos. 54-56 (3)	1.75	1.90

Issue date: No. 55a, Feb. 25, 1953.

UPU Issue
Common Design Types
Engr.; Name Typo. on Nos. 58, 59

1949, Oct. 10 Perf. 13½, 11x11½

57	CD306	3p rose carmine	1.40	1.25
58	CD307	4p indigo	3.25	2.50
59	CD308	6p olive	3.50	3.00
60	CD309	1sh slate	6.25	6.00
		Nos. 57-60 (4)	14.40	12.75

3sa

Coronation Issue
Common Design Type

1953, June 2 Engr. Perf. 13½x13

61	CD312	3p gray & black	1.50	1.50

Reservoir A16

Designs: 1p, Map of Ascension. 1½p, Georgetown. 2p, Map showing Ascension between South America and Africa and cable lines. 2½p, Mountain road. 3p, Yellow-billed tropic bird. 4p, Longfinned tuna. 6p, Waves. 7p, Young green turtles. 1sh, Land crab. 2sh6p, Sooty tern (wideawake). 5sh, Perfect Crater. 10sh, View from Northwest.

1956, Nov. 19 Wmk. 4 Perf. 13
Center in Black

62	A16	½p brown	.20	.20
63	A16	1p lilac rose	.35	.30
64	A16	1½p orange	.35	.25
65	A16	2p carmine	.55	.35
66	A16	2½p orange brown	.65	.55
67	A16	3p blue	.90	.50
68	A16	4p turq blue	.85	.85
69	A16	6p dark blue	1.10	1.10
70	A16	7p olive	1.40	1.40
71	A16	1sh scarlet	1.90	1.50
72	A16	2sh6p brown violet	19.00	11.00
73	A16	5sh bright green	25.00	16.00
74	A16	10sh purple	50.00	30.00
		Nos. 62-74 (13)	102.25	64.00

Brown Booby — A17

Birds: 1½p, Black tern. 2p, Fairy tern. 3p, Red-billed tropic bird in flight. 4½p, Brown noddy. 6p, Sooty tern. 7p, Frigate bird. 10p, Blue-faced booby. 1sh, Yellow-billed tropic bird. 1sh6p, Red-billed tropic bird. 2sh6p, Madeiran storm petrel. 5sh, Red-footed booby (brown phase). 10sh, Frigate birds. £1, Red-footed booby (white phase).

Perf. 14x14½

1963, May 23 Photo. Wmk. 314

75	A17	1p multicolored	.20	.20
a.		Booklet pane of 4	.30	
76	A17	1½p multicolored	.20	.20
a.		Booklet pane of 4	.50	
b.		Blue omitted	70.00	
77	A17	2p multicolored	.20	.20
a.		Booklet pane of 4	1.10	
78	A17	3p multicolored	.20	.20
a.		Booklet pane of 4	1.25	
79	A17	4½p multicolored	.25	.20
80	A17	6p multicolored	.35	.25
a.		Booklet pane of 4	3.25	
81	A17	7p multicolored	.35	.30
82	A17	10p multicolored	.50	.40
83	A17	1sh multicolored	.55	.50
84	A17	1sh6p multicolored	1.10	1.00
a.		Booklet pane of 4	6.25	
85	A17	2sh6p multicolored	2.75	2.50
86	A17	5sh multicolored	5.50	5.00
87	A17	10sh multicolored	12.50	10.00
88	A17	£1 multicolored	22.50	20.00
		Nos. 75-88 (14)	47.15	40.95

Freedom from Hunger Issue
Common Design Type

1963, June 4 Wmk. 314

89	CD314	1sh6p car rose	3.00	2.50

Red Cross Centenary Issue
Common Design Type

1963, Sept. 2 Litho. Perf. 13

90	CD315	3p black & red	.90	.90
91	CD315	1sh6p ultra & red	6.00	6.00

ITU Issue
Common Design Type
Perf. 11x11½

1965, May 17 Litho. Wmk. 314

92	CD317	3p mag & violet	.60	.60
93	CD317	6p grnsh bl & brn org	1.60	1.60

Intl. Cooperation Year Issue
Common Design Type

1965, Oct. 25 Wmk. 314 Perf. 14½

94	CD318	1p bl grn & claret	.40	.30
95	CD318	6p lt vio & green	1.60	1.50

Churchill Memorial Issue
Common Design Type

1966, Jan. 24 Photo. Perf. 14
Design in Black, Gold and Carmine Rose

96	CD319	1p bright blue	.35	.25
97	CD319	3p green	1.25	.85
98	CD319	6p brown	1.60	1.40
99	CD319	1sh6p violet	5.00	4.00
		Nos. 96-99 (4)	8.20	6.50

World Cup Soccer Issue
Common Design Type

1966, July 1 Litho. Perf. 14

100	CD321	3p multicolored	.70	.55
101	CD321	6p multicolored	1.40	2.25

WHO Headquarters Issue
Common Design Type

1966, Sept. 20 Litho. Perf. 14

102	CD322	3p multicolored	1.25	1.00
103	CD322	1sh6p multicolored	3.25	3.00

Apollo Satellite Station, Ascension — A18

Wmk. 314

1966, Nov. 7 Photo. Perf. 14

104	A18	4p purple & black	.20	.20
105	A18	8p blue grn & blk	.20	.20
106	A18	1sh3p brn ol & blk	.30	.20
107	A18	2sh6p brt grnsh blue & black	.60	.40
		Nos. 104-107 (4)	1.30	1.00

Opening of the Apollo communications satellite-earth station, part of the US Apollo program.

UNESCO Anniversary Issue
Common Design Type

1967, Jan. 3 Litho. Perf. 14

108	CD323	3p "Education"	.70	.65
109	CD323	6p "Science"	2.00	1.75
110	CD323	1sh6p "Culture"	5.00	5.00
		Nos. 108-110 (3)	7.70	7.40

BBC Emblem A19

Photo.; Gold Impressed

1967, Dec. 1 Wmk. 314 Perf. 14½

111	A19	1p ultra & gold	.20	.20
112	A19	3p dk green & gold	.20	.20
113	A19	6p brt purple & gold	.20	.20
114	A19	1sh6p brt red & gold	.50	.50
		Nos. 111-114 (4)	1.10	1.10

Opening of the British Broadcasting Company's South Atlantic Relay Station on Ascension Island.

Human Rights Flame and Chain — A20

Perf. 14½x14

1968, July 8 Litho. Wmk. 314

115	A20	6p org, car & blk	.20	.20
116	A20	1sh6p gray, mag & blk	.30	.25
117	A20	2sh6p brt grn, plum & blk	.60	.50
		Nos. 115-117 (3)	1.10	.95

International Human Rights Year.

Blackfish A21

Fish: No. 119, Sailfish. 6p, Oldwife. 8p, Leather jacks. 1sh6p, Yellowtails. 1sh9p, Tuna. 2sh3p, Mako sharks. 2sh11p, Rock hind (jack).

Perf. 13x12½

1968-69 Wmk. 314 Litho.

118	A21	4p brt grnsh bl & blk	.25	.20
119	A21	4p red & multi	.30	.25
120	A21	6p yel olive & multi	.40	.35
121	A21	8p brt rose lil & multi	.55	.40
122	A21	1sh6p brown & multi	1.75	1.40
123	A21	1sh9p emer & multi	1.00	.85
124	A21	2sh3p ocher & multi	1.60	1.10
125	A21	2sh11p dp org & multi	3.25	2.00
		Nos. 118-125 (8)	9.10	6.55

Issue dates: No. 119, 6p, 1sh6p, 2sh11p, Mar. 3, 1969; others, Oct. 23, 1968.

See Nos. 130-133.

Arms of R.N.S. Rattlesnake — A22

Coats of Arms of Royal Naval Ships: 9p, Weston. 1sh9p, Undaunted. 2sh3p, Eagle.

Perf. 14x14½

1969, Oct. 1 Photo. Wmk. 314

126	A22	4p multicolored	.25	.25
127	A22	9p multicolored	.50	.50
128	A22	1sh9p multicolored	1.25	1.25
129	A22	2sh3p multicolored	1.75	1.75
a.		Min. sheet of 4, #126-129	6.75	5.75
		Nos. 126-129 (4)	3.75	3.75

See Nos. 134-137, 152-159, 166-169.

Fish Type of 1968

Deep-sea fish: 4p, Wahoo. 9p, Coalfish. 1sh9p, Dolphinfishes. 2sh3p, Soldierfish.

1970, Apr. 6 Litho. *Perf. 14*

130	A21	4p bluish grn & multi	.55	.35
131	A21	9p org & multi	.90	.60
132	A21	1sh9p ultra & multi	1.75	1.40
133	A21	2sh3p gray & multi	3.25	2.00
		Nos. 130-133 (4)	6.45	4.35

Naval Arms Type of 1969

4p, Penelope. 9p, Carlisle. 1sh6p, Amphion. 2sh6p, Magpie.

Perf. 12½x12

1970, Sept. 7 Photo. Wmk. 314

134	A22	4p ultra, gold & blk	.25	.25
135	A22	9p lt bl, blk, gold & red	.50	.50
136	A22	1sh6p grnsh bl, gold & blk	1.25	1.25
137	A22	2sh6p lt grnsh bl, gold & blk	2.00	2.00
a.		Miniature sheet of 4, #134-137	7.50	6.00
		Nos. 134-137 (4)	4.00	4.00

Decimal Currency Issue

Tycho Brahe's Observatory, Quadrant and Supernova, 1572 — A23

Man into Space: ½p, Chinese rocket, 1232, vert. 1p, Medieval Arab astronomers, vert. 2p, Galileo, his telescope and drawing of moon, 1609. 2½p, Isaac Newton, telescope and apple. 3½p, Harrison's chronometer and ship, 1735. 4½p, First American manned orbital flight (Project Mercury, 1962, vert.). 5p, Reflector of Palomar telescope and ring nebula in Lyra, Messier 57. 7½p, Jodrell Bank telescope. 10p, Mariner 7, 1969, and telescopic view of Mars. 12½p, Sputnik 2 and dog Laika, 1957. 25p, Astronaut walking in space, 1965 (Gemini 4; vert.). 50p, US astronauts and moon landing module, 1969. £1, Future space research station.

1971, Feb. 15 Litho. *Perf. 14½*

138	A23	½p multicolored	.20	.20
a.		Booklet pane of 4	.50	
139	A23	1p multicolored	.20	.20
a.		Booklet pane of 4	.75	
140	A23	1½p multicolored	.20	.20
a.		Booklet pane of 4	1.00	
141	A23	2p multicolored	.20	.20
a.		Booklet pane of 4	1.90	
142	A23	2½p multicolored	.35	.35
a.		Booklet pane of 4	2.50	
143	A23	3½p multicolored	.45	.45
a.		Booklet pane of 4	3.50	
144	A23	4½p multicolored	.60	.60
145	A23	5p multicolored	.65	.65
146	A23	7½p multicolored	.75	.75
147	A23	10p multicolored	1.00	1.00
148	A23	12½p multicolored	1.40	1.40
149	A23	25p multicolored	2.50	2.50
150	A23	50p multicolored	5.25	5.25
151	A23	£1 multicolored	10.00	10.00
		Nos. 138-151 (14)	23.75	23.75

For overprints see Nos. 189-191.

Arms of H.M.S. Phoenix — A24

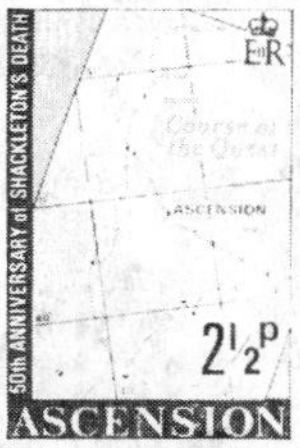

Course of Quest — A25

Coats of Arms of Royal Naval Ships: 4p, Milford. 9p, Pelican. 15p, Oberon.

1971, Nov. 15 Photo. *Perf. 13½x13*

152	A24	2p gold & multi	.20	.20
153	A24	4p gold & multi	.40	.40
154	A24	9p gold & multi	1.10	1.10
155	A24	15p gold & multi	2.25	2.25
a.		Souvenir sheet of 4, #152-155	7.00	7.00
		Nos. 152-155 (4)	3.95	3.95

Naval Arms Type of 1969

1½p, Lowestoft. 3p, Auckland. 6p, Nigeria. 17½p, Bermuda.

1972, May 22 Litho. *Perf. 14x14½*

156	A22	1½p bl, gold & blk	.20	.20
157	A22	3p grnsh bl, gold & blk	.45	.45
158	A22	6p grn, gold, blk & bl	.90	.90
159	A22	17½p lil, gold, blk & red	2.75	2.75
a.		Miniature sheet of 4, #156-159	5.00	5.00
		Nos. 156-159 (4)	4.30	4.30

1972, Aug. 2 *Perf. 14*

Designs: 4p, Shackleton and "Quest", horiz. 7½p, Shackleton's cabin and Quest in pack ice, horiz. 11p, Shackleton statue, London, and memorial cairn, South Georgia.

160	A25	2½p multicolored	.30	.30
161	A25	4p multicolored	.50	.50
162	A25	7½p multicolored	1.00	1.00
163	A25	11p multicolored	1.60	1.60
a.		Souvenir sheet of 4, #160-163	4.25	4.25
		Nos. 160-163 (4)	3.40	3.40

Sir Ernest Henry Shackleton (1874-1922), explorer of Antarctica.

Silver Wedding Issue, 1972

Common Design Type

Design: Queen Elizabeth II, Prince Philip, land crab and shark.

1972, Nov. 20 Photo. *Perf. 14x14½*

164	CD324	2p violet & multi	.20	.20
165	CD324	16p car rose & multi	.75	.75

Naval Arms Type of 1969

2p, Birmingham. 4p, Cardiff. 9p, Penzance. 13p, Rochester.

1973, May 28 Litho. Wmk. 314

166	A22	2p blue & multi	.60	.45
167	A22	4p yel grn & multi	1.50	1.10
168	A22	9p lt blue & multi	3.00	2.25
169	A22	13p violet & multi	4.25	3.75
a.		Min. sheet of 4, #166-169	18.00	18.00
		Nos. 166-169 (4)	9.35	7.55

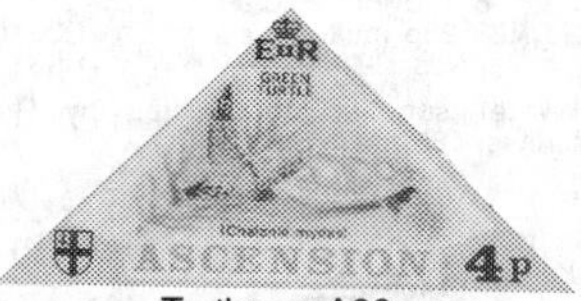

Turtles — A26

1973, Aug. 28 *Perf. 13½*

170	A26	4p Green	1.75	1.10
171	A26	9p Loggerhead	3.50	2.25
172	A26	12p Hawksbill	5.50	3.50
		Nos. 170-172 (3)	10.75	6.85

Light Infanty Marine Sergeant, 1900 — A27

Uniforms (Royal Marines): 6p, Private, 1816. 12p, Officer, Light Infantry, 1880. 20p, Color Sergeant, Artillery, 1910.

1973, Oct. 31 *Perf. 14½*

173	A27	2p multicolored	.50	.50
174	A27	6p lt green & multi	1.75	1.75
175	A27	12p lt blue & multi	3.50	3.50
176	A27	20p lt lilac & multi	6.00	6.00
		Nos. 173-176 (4)	11.75	11.75

Departure of the Royal Marines from Ascension, 50th anniv.

Princess Anne's Wedding Issue

Common Design Type

1973, Nov. 14 *Perf. 14*

177	CD325	2p ocher & multi	.20	.20
178	CD325	18p multicolored	.65	.65

Letter and UPU Emblem A29

UPU Cent.: 9p, Emblem and Mercury.

Wmk. 314

1974, Mar. 27 Litho. *Perf. 14½*

179	A29	2p multicolored	.20	.20
180	A29	9p vio blue & multi	.70	.70

Young Churchill and Blenheim Palace A30

25p, Churchill and UN Headquarters, NYC.

1974, Nov. 30 Litho. Unwmk.

181	A30	5p slate grn & multi	.20	.20
182	A30	25p purple & multi	.80	.80
a.		Souvenir sheet of 2, #181-182	2.00	1.75

Sir Winston Churchill (1874-1965).

Skylab over Photograph of Ascension Taken by Skylab 3 — A31

Skylab Space Station: 18p, Command module and photo of Ascension from Skylab 4.

1975, Mar. 20 Wmk. 314 *Perf. 14½*

183	A31	2p multicolored	.20	.20
184	A31	18p multicolored	1.00	1.00

US Air Force C-141A Starlifter — A32

Aircraft: 5p, Royal Air Force C-130 Hercules. 9p, Vickers VC-10. 24p, U.S. Air Force C-5A Galaxy.

Perf. 13½x14

1975, June 19 Litho. Wmk. 314

185	A32	2p multicolored	.25	.25
186	A32	5p multicolored	.60	.60
187	A32	9p multicolored	1.10	1.10
188	A32	24p multicolored	3.00	3.00
a.		Souvenir sheet of 4, #185-188	10.00	10.00
		Nos. 185-188 (4)	4.95	4.95

Wideawake Airfield, Ascension Island.

Nos. 144, 148-149 Overprinted **APOLLO-SOYUZ LINK 1975**

1975, Aug. Litho. *Perf. 14½*

189	A23	4½p multicolored	.20	.20
190	A23	12½p multicolored	.40	.40
191	A23	25p multicolored	.95	.95
		Nos. 189-191 (3)	1.55	1.55

Apollo Soyuz space test project (Russo-American cooperation), launching July 15; link-up, July 17.

HMS Peruvian and Zenobia Arriving Oct. 22, 1815 A33

Designs: 5p, Water Supply, Dampiers Drip. 9p, First Landing, Oct. 1815. 15p, The Garden on Green Mountain. All designs after paintings by Isobel McManus.

1975, Oct. 22 Wmk. 373 *Perf. 14½*

192	A33	2p lt blue & multi	.20	.20
193	A33	5p lt blue & multi	.30	.20
194	A33	9p red & multi	.45	.40
195	A33	15p red & multi	.90	.75
		Nos. 192-195 (4)	1.85	1.55

British occupation, 160th anniv.

Canaries A34

Designs: 2p, Fairy tern, vert. 3p, Waxbills. 4p, Black noddy, vert. 5p, Brown noddy. 6p, Common mynah. 7p, Madeira storm petrels, vert. 8p, Sooty terns. 9p, White booby, vert. 10p, Red-footed booby. 15p, Red-throated francolin, vert. 18p, Brown booby, vert. 25p, Red-billed bo'sun bird. 50p, Yellow-billed bo'sun bird. £1, Ascension frigatebird, vert. £2, Boatswain Island Bird Sanctuary and birds.

Perf. 14x14½, 14½x14

1976, Apr. 26 Litho. Wmk. 373

Size: 35x27mm, 27x35mm

196	A34	1p multicolored	.20	.20
197	A34	2p multicolored	.20	.20
198	A34	3p multicolored	.20	.20
199	A34	4p multicolored	.20	.20
200	A34	5p multicolored	.20	.20
201	A34	6p multicolored	.20	.20
202	A34	7p multicolored	.25	.20
203	A34	8p multicolored	.30	.20
204	A34	9p multicolored	.40	.25
205	A34	10p multicolored	.45	.25
206	A34	15p multicolored	.65	.40
207	A34	18p multicolored	.85	.50
208	A34	25p multicolored	1.25	.65
209	A34	50p multicolored	2.25	1.25
210	A34	£1 multicolored	3.25	2.75

Perf. 13½

Size: 46x33mm

211	A34	£2 multicolored	6.50	5.25
		Nos. 196-211 (16)	17.35	12.90

Great Britain Type A1 with Ascension Cancel — A35

9p, Ascension No. 1, vert. 25p, Freighter Southampton Castle.

1976, May 4 *Perf. 13½x14, 14x13½*

212	A35	5p lt brn, car & blk	.20	.20
213	A35	9p gray grn, grn & blk	.30	.30
214	A35	25p blue & multi	.95	.95
		Nos. 212-214 (3)	1.45	1.45

Festival of Stamps 1976. See Tristan da Cunha #208a for souvenir sheet that contains one each of Ascension #214, St. Helena #297 and Tristan da Cunha #208.

US Base A36

Designs: 9p, NASA Station, Devil's Ashpit. 25p, Viking satellite landing on Mars.

Wmk. 373

1976, July 4 Litho. *Perf. 13½*

215	A36	8p black & multi	.40	.40
216	A36	9p black & multi	.50	.50
217	A36	25p black & multi	1.10	1.10
		Nos. 215-217 (3)	2.00	2.00

American Bicentennial. No. 215 also for the 20th anniv. of Bahamas Long Range Proving Ground (extension) Agreement.

Queen in Coronation Coach — A37

Designs: 8p, Prince Philip on Ascension Island, 1957, vert. 12p, Queen leaving Buckingham Palace in coronation coach.

Perf. 14x13½, 13½x14

1977, Feb. 7 Litho. Wmk. 373

218	A37	8p multicolored	.20	.20
219	A37	12p multicolored	.30	.25
220	A37	25p multicolored	.60	.55
		Nos. 218-220 (3)	1.10	1.00

Reign of Queen Elizabeth II, 25th anniv.

Ascension stamps can be mounted in the Scott British Africa album and the Scott Ascension supplement.

Water Pipe in Tunnel — A38

5p, Breakneck Valley wells. 12p, Break tank in pipe line, horiz. 25p, Dam & reservoir, horiz.

1977, June 27 Litho. *Perf. 14½*

221	A38	3p multicolored	.20	.20
222	A38	5p multicolored	.20	.20
223	A38	12p multicolored	.50	.50
224	A38	25p multicolored	1.00	1.00
		Nos. 221-224 (4)	1.90	1.90

Water supplies constructed by Royal Marines, 1832 and 1881.

Mars Bay Site, 1877 A39

Designs: 8p, Mars Bay and instrument sites. 12p, Prof. and Mrs. Gill before their tent. 25p, Map of Ascension.

Perf. 13½x14

1977, Oct. 3 Litho. Wmk. 373

225	A39	3p multicolored	.20	.20
226	A39	8p multicolored	.30	.25
227	A39	12p multicolored	.50	.45
228	A39	25p multicolored	1.00	.85
		Nos. 225-228 (4)	2.00	1.75

Centenary of visit of Prof. David Gill (1843-1914), astronomer, to Ascension.

Elizabeth II Coronation Anniversary Issue

Souvenir Sheet

Common Design Types

Unwmk.

1978, May 21 Litho. *Perf. 15*

229	Sheet of 6	2.50	2.50
a.	CD326 25p Lion of England	.40	.40
b.	CD327 25p Elizabeth II	.40	.40
c.	CD328 25p Green turtle	.40	.40

No. 229 contains 2 se-tenant strips of Nos. 229a-229c, separated by horizontal gutter with commemorative and descriptive inscriptions and showing central part of coronation procession with coach.

East Crater (Broken Tooth) — A40

Volcanoes: 5p, Hollands Crater (Hollow Tooth). 12p, Bears Back. 15p, Green Mountain. 25p, Two Boats village.

1978, Sept. 4 Litho. *Perf. 14½*

230	A40	3p multicolored	.20	.20
231	A40	5p multicolored	.20	.20
232	A40	12p multicolored	.45	.45
233	A40	15p multicolored	.55	.55
234	A40	25p multicolored	.90	.90
a.		Souvenir sheet, 2 each #230-234	4.50	4.50
b.		Strip of 5, #230-234	2.25	2.25

No. 234b shows panoramic view of volcanic terrain.

Resolution A41

Capt. Cook's voyages: 8p, Cook's chronometer. 12p, Green turtle. 25p, Cook after Flaxman/Wedgwood medallion.

Litho.; Litho. & Engr. (25p)

1979, Jan. 8 *Perf. 11*

235	A41	3p multicolored	.20	.20
236	A41	8p multicolored	.30	.25
237	A41	12p multicolored	.55	.40
238	A41	25p multicolored	1.10	.85
		Nos. 235-238 (4)	2.15	1.70

St. Mary's Church, Georgetown — A42

Designs: 12p, Old map of Ascension Island. 50p, Ascension, by Rembrandt.

Wmk. 373

1979, May 24 Litho. *Perf. 14½*

239	A42	8p multicolored	.20	.20
240	A42	12p multicolored	.25	.25
241	A42	50p multicolored	.95	.95
		Nos. 239-241 (3)	1.40	1.40

Ascension Day.

Landing Cable at Comfortless Cove — A43

Eastern Telegraph Co., 80th anniv.: 8p, Cable Ship Anglia. 12p, Map showing cables across the Atlantic, vert. 15p, Cable-laying ship. 25p, Cable and earth station.

1979, Sept. 15

242	A43	3p rose car & black	.20	.20
243	A43	8p dk yel grn & black	.20	.20
244	A43	12p yel bister & black	.30	.30
245	A43	15p violet & black	.35	.35
246	A43	25p deep org & black	.55	.55
		Nos. 242-246 (5)	1.60	1.60

Ascension No. 45 — A44

1979, Dec. 17 Wmk. 373 *Perf. 14*

247	A44	3p shown	.20	.20
248	A44	8p No. 73	.20	.20
249	A44	12p No. 14	.20	.20
250	A44	50p Hill portrait, vert.	.85	.85
		Nos. 247-250 (4)	1.45	1.45

Sir Rowland Hill (1795-1879), originator of penny postage.

Anogramma Ascensionis A45

1980, Feb. 18 Litho. *Perf. 14½*

251	A45	3p shown	.20	.20
252	A45	6p Xiphopteris ascensionense	.20	.20
253	A45	8p Sporobolus caespitosus	.20	.20
254	A45	12p Sporobolus durus, vert.	.25	.25
255	A45	18p Dryopteris ascensionis, vert.	.40	.40
256	A45	24p Marattia purpurascens, vert.	.50	.50
		Nos. 251-256 (6)	1.75	1.75

17th Century Bottle Post, London 1980 Emblem A46

1980, May 1 Wmk. 373 *Perf. 14*

257	A46	8p shown	.20	.20
258	A46	12p 36-gun frigate, 19th century	.25	.25
259	A46	15p "Garth Castle," 1863	.30	.30
260	A46	50p "St. Helena," Lockheed C141	.85	.85
a.		Souvenir sheet of 4, #257-260	2.00	2.00
		Nos. 257-260 (4)	1.60	1.60

London 1980 Intl. Stamp Exhib., May 6-14.

Queen Mother Elizabeth Birthday

Common Design Type

1980, Aug. 11 Litho. *Perf. 14*

261	CD330	15p multicolored	.40	.40

Lubbock's Yellowtail A47

1980, Sept. 15 Litho. *Perf. 13½x14*

262	A47	3p shown	.20	.20
263	A47	10p Resplendent angelfish	.30	.30
264	A47	25p Hedgehog butterflyfish	.70	.70
265	A47	40p Marmalade razorfish	1.10	1.10
		Nos. 262-265 (4)	2.30	2.30

Tortoisen, by Thomas Maxon A48

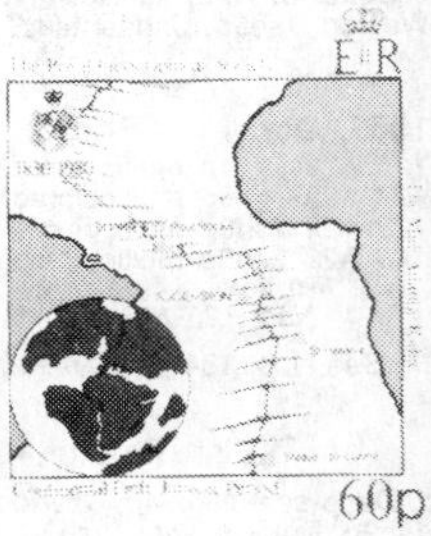

Map of South Atlantic Ridge and Contintental Drift — A49

15p, Wideawake Fair, by Linton Palmer, 1866.

1980, Nov. 17 *Perf. 13½, 14 (60p)*

266	A48	10p multicolored	.20	.20
267	A48	15p multicolored	.35	.35
268	A49	60p multicolored	1.25	1.25
		Nos. 266-268 (3)	1.80	1.80

Royal Geographical Soc., 50th anniv.

Green Mountain Farm, 1881 — A50

Designs: 15p, Two Boats, 1881. 20p, Green Mountain and Two Boats farms, 1981. 30p, Green Mountain Farm, 1981.

1981, Feb. 15 Litho. *Perf. 14*
269 A50 12p multicolored .20 .20
270 A50 15p multicolored .30 .30
271 A50 20p multicolored .35 .35
272 A50 30p multicolored .65 .65
Nos. 269-272 (4) 1.50 1.50

Cable and Wireless Earth Station A51

1981, Apr. 27 Litho. *Perf. 14*
273 Sheet of 10 3.75 3.75
a. A51 15p multicolored .35 .35

Flight of Columbia space shuttle. Gutter contains story of Ascension and space shuttle; margin shows craft and dish antenna.

Poinsettia A52

1981, May 11 Wmk. 373 *Perf. 13½*
274 A52 1p shown .20 .20
275 A52 2p Clustererd wax flower .20 .20
276 A52 3p Kolanchoe, vert. .20 .20
277 A52 4p Yellow pops .20 .20
278 A52 5p Camel's foot creeper .20 .20
279 A52 8p White oleander .20 .20
280 A52 10p Ascension lily, vert. .25 .25
281 A52 12p Coral plant, vert. .30 .30
282 A52 15p Yellow allamanda .40 .40
283 A52 20p Ascention euphorbia .50 .50
284 A52 30p Flame of the forest, vert. .85 .85
285 A52 40p Bougainvillea 1.00 1.00

Size: 42x53mm

286 A52 50p Solanum 1.25 1.25
287 A52 £1 Ladies petticoat 2.75 2.75
288 A52 £2 Red hibiscus 5.25 5.25
Nos. 274-288 (15) 13.75 13.75

Nos. 275-276, 280, 282-283 and 287 also issued inscribed 1982.

For overprints see Nos. 321-322.

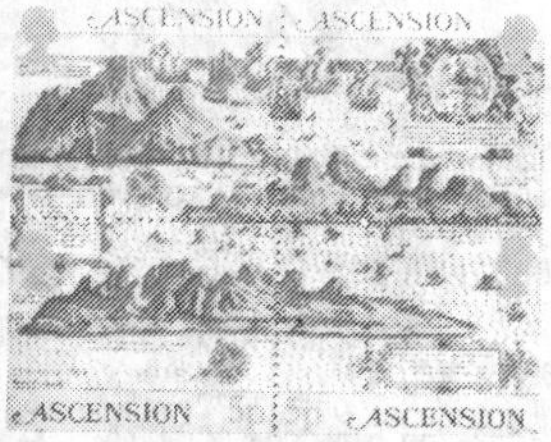

Linschoten's Map of Ascension, 1599 (Illustration reduced) — A53

Maxwell's Map of Ascension, 1793 — A54

Designs: Old maps of Ascension.

1981, May 22 *Perf. 14½*
289 A53 Sheet of 4 .60 .60
a.-d. 5p any single .20 .20
290 A54 10p shown .25 .25
291 A54 12p Maxwell, 1793, diff. .35 .35
292 A54 15p Eckberg & Chapman, 1811 .40 .40
293 A54 40p Campbell, 1819 1.10 1.10
Nos. 289-293 (5) 2.70 2.70

Royal Wedding Issue
Common Design Type

1981, July 22 Wmk. 373 *Perf. 14*
294 CD331 10p Bouquet .20 .20
295 CD331 15p Charles .30 .30
296 CD331 50p Couple 1.00 1.00
Nos. 294-296 (3) 1.50 1.50

Nos. 294-296 each se-tenant with label.

Man Shining Cannon — A55

1981, Sept. 14 Litho. *Perf. 14*
297 A55 5p shown .20 .20
298 A55 10p Mountain climbing .20 .20
299 A55 15p First aid treatment .35 .35
300 A55 40p Duke of Edinburgh .80 .80
Nos. 297-300 (4) 1.55 1.55

Duke of Edinburgh's Awards, 25th anniv.

Scouting Year A56

1982, Feb. 22 Litho. *Perf. 14*
301 A56 10p Parallel rope walking .25 .25
302 A56 15p 1st Ascension scout flag .40 .40
303 A56 25p Radio operators .55 .55
304 A56 40p Baden-Powell .75 .75
a. Souvenir sheet of 4 2.25 2.25
Nos. 301-304 (4) 1.95 1.95

No. 304a contains stamps in designs of Nos. 301-304 (30x30mm, perf. 14½, diamond-shape).

Sesquicentennial of Charles Darwin's Visit — A57

1982, Apr. 19
305 A57 10p Portrait .25 .25
306 A57 12p Pistols .35 .35
307 A57 15p Rock crab .40 .40
308 A57 40p Beagle 1.10 1.10
Nos. 305-308 (4) 2.10 2.10

40th Anniv. of Wideawake Airfield — A58

1982, June 15 Litho. *Perf. 14*
309 A58 5p Fairey Swordfish .60 .60
310 A58 10p North American B25C Mitchell .80 .80
311 A58 15p Boeing EC-135N Aria 1.10 1.10
312 A58 50p Lockheed Hercules 1.60 1.60
Nos. 309-312 (4) 4.10 4.10

Princess Diana Issue
Common Design Type
Perf. 14½x14

1982, July 1 Wmk. 373
313 CD333 12p Arms .30 .30
314 CD333 15p Diana .40 .40
315 CD333 25p Wedding .60 .60
316 CD333 50p Portrait 1.25 1.25
Nos. 313-316 (4) 2.55 2.55

Christmas and 50th Anniv. of BBC Overseas Broadcasting — A59

Anniv. Emblem and: 5p, Bush House (London headquarters). 10p, Atlantic relay station. 25p, Lord Reith, first director general. 40p, King George V delivering Christmas address, 1932.

1982, Dec. 20 Litho. *Perf. 14*
317 A59 5p multicolored .20 .20
318 A59 10p multicolored .30 .30
319 A59 25p multicolored .70 .70
320 A59 40p multicolored 1.10 1.10
Nos. 317-320 (4) 2.30 2.30

Nos. 282-283 Overprinted: "1st PARTICIPATION/COMMONWEALTH GAMES 1982"

1982 Litho. *Perf. 13½*
321 A52 15p multicolored .40 .40
322 A52 20p multicolored .50 .50

12th Commonwealth Games, Brisbane, Australia, Sept. 30-Oct. 9.

A60

1983, Mar. 1 *Perf. 14*
323 A60 7p Marasmius echinosphaerus .25 .25
324 A60 12p Chlorophyllum molybdites .45 .45
325 A60 15p Leucocoprinus cepaestipes .55 .55
326 A60 20p Lycoperdon marginatum .75 .75
327 A60 50p Marasmiellus distantifolius 1.75 1.75
Nos. 323-327 (5) 3.75 3.75

View of Georgetown A61

1983, May 12 Litho. *Perf. 14*
328 A61 12p shown .30 .30
329 A61 15p Farm, Green Mountain .30 .30
330 A61 20p Boatswain Bird Isld. .45 .45
331 A61 60p Telemetry Hill 1.10 1.10
Nos. 328-331 (4) 2.15 2.15

See Nos. 359-362.

Manned Flight Bicentenary — A62

Military Aircraft.

1983, Aug. 1 Wmk. 373 *Perf. 14*
332 A62 12p Wessex Five helicopter .75 .75
333 A62 15p Vulcan B2 .85 .85
334 A62 20p Nimrod MR2P 1.00 1.00
335 A62 60p Victor K2 1.75 1.75
Nos. 332-335 (4) 4.35 4.35

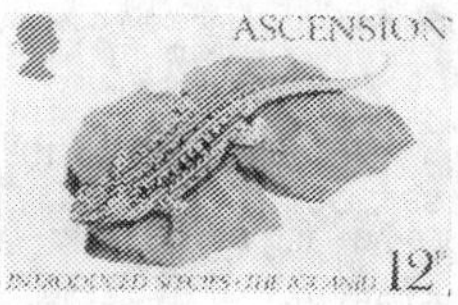

Introduced Species A63

1983, Sept. Litho. Wmk. 373
336 A63 12p Iguanid .30 .30
337 A63 15p Rabbit .40 .40
338 A63 20p Cat .50 .50
339 A63 60p Donkey 1.50 1.50
Nos. 336-339 (4) 2.70 2.70

Tellina Antonii Philippi A64

1983, Nov. 28 Litho. *Perf. 14½*
340 A64 7p shown .20 .20
341 A64 12p Nodipecten nodosus .35 .35
342 A64 15p Cypraea lurida oceanica .45 .45
343 A64 20p Nerita ascensionis gmelin .60 .60
344 A64 50p Micromelo undatus 1.50 1.50
Nos. 340-344 (5) 3.10 3.10

St. Helena Colony, 150th Anniv. — A65

Designs: First issue inscribed Ascension instead of overprinted.

1984, Jan. 10 Litho. *Perf. 14*
345 A65 12p No. 3 .30 .30
346 A65 15p No. 4 .40 .40
347 A65 20p No. 6 .50 .50
348 A65 60p No. 9 1.50 1.50
Nos. 345-348 (4) 2.70 2.70

Souvenir Sheet

Visit of Prince Andrew — A66

1984, Apr. 10 *Perf. 14½x14*
349 Sheet of 2 2.25 2.25
a. A66 12p Andrew .25 .25
b. A66 70p In naval uniform 1.75 1.75

Lloyd's List Issue
Common Design Type

1984, May 28
351 CD335 12p Naval semaphore .25 .25
352 CD335 15p "Southampton Castle" .35 .35
353 CD335 20p Pier Head .45 .45
354 CD335 70p Dane 1.50 1.50
Nos. 351-354 (4) 2.55 2.55

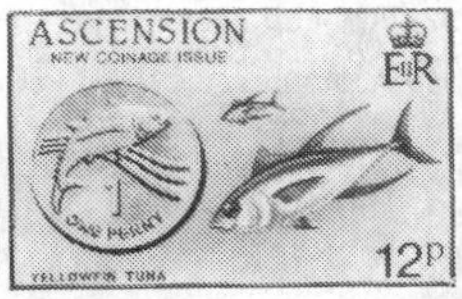

1984 Coins and Wildlife A67

1984, June *Perf. 14*
355 A67 12p One penny, yellowfin tuna .45 .45
356 A67 15p Two pence, donkeys .60 .60
357 A67 20p Fifty pence, green turtle .70 .70

358 A67 70p One pound, sooty terns 1.75 1.75
Nos. 355-358 (4) 3.50 3.50

View Type of 1983

1984, Oct. Litho. Wmk. 373

359 A61 12p Devil's Riding School .25 .25
360 A61 15p St. Mary's Church .35 .35
361 A61 20p Two Boats Village .50 .50
362 A61 70p Ascension Isld. 1.75 1.75
Nos. 359-362 (4) 2.85 2.85

Trees — A68

1985, Mar. 8 Litho. *Perf. 14½x14*

363 A68 7p Bermuda cypress .50 .50
364 A68 12p Norfolk Island pine .55 .55
365 A68 15p Screwpine .65 .65
366 A68 20p Eucalyptus .80 .80
367 A68 65p Spore tree 2.00 2.00
Nos. 363-367 (5) 4.50 4.50

Military Firearms A69

Large guns and insignia: 12p, Thirty-two pounder small bore muzzle loader, c. 1820; Royal Marines hat plate, c. 1816. 15p, Seven-inch rifled muzzle loader, c. 1866; royal cipher. 20p, Seven-pounder rifled muzzle loader, c. 1877; Royal Artillery badge. 70p, HMS Hood 5.5-inch gun; ship crest.

1985, July 21 Wmk. 373 *Perf. 14½*

368 A69 12p multicolored .65 .65
369 A69 15p multicolored .75 .75
370 A69 20p multicolored .80 .80
371 A69 70p multicolored 2.25 2.25
Nos. 368-371 (4) 4.45 4.45

Queen Mother 85th Birthday
Common Design Type

Designs: 12p, With Duke of York, Balmoral, 1924. 15p, With Princes Andrew and Edward. 20p, At Ascot. 70p, Christening of Prince Henry, Windsor Castle. 75p, Leaving the QEII, 1968.

Perf. 14½x14

1985, June 7 Wmk. 384

372 CD336 12p multicolored .25 .25
373 CD336 15p multicolored .30 .30
374 CD336 20p multicolored .40 .40
375 CD336 70p multicolored 1.40 1.40
Nos. 372-375 (4) 2.35 2.35

Souvenir Sheet

376 CD336 75p multicolored 1.60 1.50

Intl. Youth Year, Girl Guides 75th Anniv. — A70

1985, Oct. 4 Wmk. 373

377 A70 12p Guides' banner .65 .65
378 A70 15p First aid .75 .75
379 A70 20p Camping .85 .85
380 A70 70p Lady Baden-Powell 2.50 2.50
Nos. 377-380 (4) 4.75 4.75

Wildflowers A71

Halley's Comet A72

Wmk. 384

1985, Dec. 6 Litho. *Perf. 14*

381 A71 12p Clerodendrum fragrans .40 .40
382 A71 15p Shell ginger .45 .45
383 A71 20p Cape daisy .60 .60
384 A71 70p Ginger lily 1.75 1.75
Nos. 381-384 (4) 3.20 3.20

1986, Mar. 7

Designs: 12p, Newton's reflector telescope. 15p, Edmond Halley, Old Greenwich Observatory. 20p, Short's Gregorian telescope, comet, 1759. 70p, ICE space probe, Ascension satellite tracking station.

385 A72 12p multicolored .55 .55
386 A72 15p multicolored .65 .65
387 A72 20p multicolored .70 .70
388 A72 70p multicolored 2.00 2.00
Nos. 385-388 (4) 3.90 3.90

Queen Elizabeth II 60th Birthday
Common Design Type

Designs: 7p, Infant photograph, 1926. 15p, 1st worldwide Christmas broadcast, 1952. 20p, Garter Ceremony, Windsor Castle, 1983. 35p, Royal Tour, New Zealand, 1981. £1, Visiting Crown Agents' offices, 1983.

1986, Apr. 21 *Perf. 14x14½*

389 CD337 7p scarlet, blk & sil .20 .20
390 CD337 15p ultra, blk & sil .25 .25
391 CD337 20p green & multi .35 .35
392 CD337 35p violet & multi .65 .65
393 CD337 £1 rose vio & multi 1.75 1.75
Nos. 389-393 (5) 3.20 3.20

For overprints see Nos. 431-435.

AMERIPEX '86 — A73

1986, May 22 *Perf. 14½*

394 A73 12p No. 183 .35 .35
395 A73 15p No. 260 .45 .45
396 A73 20p No. 215 .55 .55
397 A73 70p No. 310 2.00 2.00
Nos. 394-397 (4) 3.35 3.35

Souvenir Sheet

398 A73 75p Statue of Liberty, New York Harbor 2.25 2.25

Statue of Liberty, cent.

Royal Wedding Issue, 1986
Common Design Type

Designs: 15p, Couple kissing. 35p, Andrew in navy uniform, helicopter.

Wmk. 384

1986, July 23 Litho. *Perf. 14*

399 CD338 15p multicolored .45 .45
400 CD338 35p multicolored 1.00 1.00

Ships A74

1986, Oct. 14 Wmk. 384 *Perf. 14½*

401 A74 1p Ganymede, c. 1811 .20 .20
402 A74 2p Kangaroo, c. 1811 .20 .20
403 A74 4p Trinculo, c. 1811 .20 .20
404 A74 5p Daring, c. 1811 .20 .20
405 A74 9p Thais, c. 1811 .30 .30
406 A74 10p Pheasant, 1819 .35 .35
407 A74 15p Myrmidon, 1819 .45 .45
408 A74 18p Atholl, 1825 .55 .55
409 A74 20p Medina, 1830 .60 .60
410 A74 25p Saracen, 1840 .80 .80
411 A74 30p Hydra, c. 1845 .90 .90
412 A74 50p Sealark, 1840 1.40 1.40
413 A74 70p Rattlesnake, 1868 1.90 1.90
414 A74 £1 Penelope, 1889 3.00 3.00
415 A74 £2 Monarch, 1897 6.00 6.00
Nos. 401-415 (15) 17.05 17.05

For surcharges see Nos. 502-504.

Edible Bush Fruits A75

1987, Jan. 29 *Perf. 14*

416 A75 12p Cape gooseberry .35 .35
417 A75 15p Prickly pear .45 .45
418 A75 20p Guava .60 .60
419 A75 70p Loquat 2.00 2.00
Nos. 416-419 (4) 3.40 3.40

1st Manned Space Flight, 25th Anniv. — A76

Military Uniforms, 1815-20 — A77

1987, Mar. 30

420 A76 15p Ignition .45 .45
421 A76 18p Lift-off .55 .55
422 A76 25p Reentry .70 .70
423 A76 £1 Splashdown 3.00 3.00
Nos. 420-423 (4) 4.70 4.70

Souvenir Sheet

424 A76 70p Friendship 7 capsule 2.25 2.25

1987, June 29

Designs: a, Captains in full dress, 1st landing on Ascenion. b, Surgeon and sailors at campsite. c, Seaman returning from Dampier's Drip with water supply. d, Midshipman at lookout post. e, Commander and surveyor.

425 Strip of 5 4.00 4.00
a.-e. A77 25p multicolored .80 .80

See Nos. 458, 474, 482, 507.

Butterflies A78

1987, Aug. 10 *Perf. 14½*

426 A78 15p Painted lady .60 .60
427 A78 18p Monarch .75 .75
428 A78 25p Diadem 1.00 1.00
429 A78 £1 Long-tailed blue 3.75 3.75
Nos. 426-429 (4) 6.10 6.10

See Nos. 436-439, 459-462.

Birds — A79

Designs: a, Ascension frigatebirds (males). b, Brown booby, frigatebird, white boobies. c, Frigatebird, white booby. d, Ascension frigatebirds (females). e, Adult frigatebird feeding young.

1987, Oct. 8 Wmk. 373 *Perf. 14*

430 Strip of 5 6.00 6.00
a.-e. A79 25p any single 1.25 1.25

No. 430 has continuous design.
See No. 453.

Nos. 389-393 Ovptd. "40TH WEDDING ANNIVERSARY" in Silver

Perf. 14x14½

1987, Dec. 9 Litho. Wmk. 384

431 CD337 7p scar, blk & sil .20 .20
432 CD337 15p ultra, blk & sil .40 .40
433 CD337 20p green & multi .60 .60
434 CD337 35p violet & multi 1.00 1.00
435 CD337 £1 rose vio & multi 2.75 2.75
Nos. 431-435 (5) 4.95 4.95

40th wedding anniv. of Queen Elizabeth II and Prince Philip.

Insects Type of 1987

1988, Jan. 18 *Perf. 14½*

436 A78 15p Field cricket .60 .60
437 A78 18p Bush cricket .75 .75
438 A78 25p Ladybug 1.00 1.00
439 A78 £1 Burnished brass moth 4.00 4.00
Nos. 436-439 (4) 6.35 6.35

Capt. William Bate (d. 1838), 1st Garrison Commander and Colonial Founder of Ascension
A80

Designs: 9p, Bate's Memorial, St. Mary's Church. 15p, Commodore's Cottage, Cross Hill. 18p, North East or Bate's Cottage, 1833. 25p, Landmarks on map. 70p, Bate and 3 soldiers.

1988, Apr. 14 Litho. *Perf. 14*

440 A80 9p multicolored .35 .35
441 A80 15p multicolored .55 .55
442 A80 18p multicolored .65 .65
443 A80 25p multicolored .90 .90
444 A80 70p multicolored 2.25 2.25
Nos. 440-444 (5) 4.70 4.70

Australia Bicentennial Emblem and Ships Named HMS Resolution — A81

1988, June 23 Litho. *Perf. 14*

445 A81 9p 3-Masted square-rigger, 1667 .35 .35
446 A81 18p 3-Masted square-rigger, 1772 .65 .65
447 A81 25p Navy cruiser, 1892 .90 .90
448 A81 65p Battleship, 1916 2.25 2.25
Nos. 445-448 (4) 4.15 4.15

Australia bicentennial.

Nos. 445-448 Overprinted

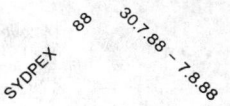

SYDPEX 88 30.7.88 – 7.8.88

Wmk. 384

1988, July 30 Litho. *Perf. 14*

449 A81 9p multicolored .35 .35
450 A81 18p multicolored .65 .65
451 A81 25p multicolored .90 .90
452 A81 65p multicolored 2.25 2.25
Nos. 449-452 (4) 4.15 4.15

SYDPEX '88, July 30-Aug. 7.

Bird Type of 1987

Behaviors of the wideawake tern, Sterna fuscata: a, Two adults, flock overhead. b, Nesting (two birds). c, Nesting (three birds). d, Adult and young. e, Tern flapping its wings.

1988, Aug. 15 *Perf. 14*
453 Strip of 5 6.00 6.00
a.-e. A79 25p any single 1.25 1.25

No. 453 has continuous design.

Lloyds of London, 300th Anniv.
Common Design Type

Designs: 8p, Lloyd's Coffee House, Tower Street, 1688. 18p, Cable ship Alert, horiz. 25p, Satellite recovery in space, horiz. 65p, Ship Good Hope Castle on fire off Ascension, 1973.

Wmk. 373

1988, Oct. 17 Litho. *Perf. 14*
454 CD341 8p multicolored .30 .30
455 CD341 18p multicolored .60 .60
456 CD341 25p multicolored .85 .85
457 CD341 65p multicolored 2.25 2.25
Nos. 454-457 (4) 4.00 4.00

Military Uniforms Type of 1987

Uniforms of the Royal Marines: a, Marines arrive in Ascension (marines), 1821. b, Semaphore station (officer, marine), 1829. c, Octagonal tank (sergeant), 1831. d, Water pipe tunnel (officers), 1833. e, Constructing barracks (officer), 1834.

1988, Nov. 21
458 Strip of 5 5.00 5.00
a.-e. A77 25p multicolored 1.00 1.00

Insect Type of 1987

Wmk. 384

1989, Jan. 16 Litho. *Perf. 14½*
459 A78 15p Plume moth .60 .60
460 A78 18p Green bottle .70 .70
461 A78 25p Weevil .95 .95
462 A78 £1 Paper wasp 3.75 3.75
Nos. 459-462 (4) 6.00 6.00

Land Crabs, Gecarcinus Lagostoma — A82

1989, Apr. 17
463 A82 15p multi .50 .50
464 A82 18p multi, diff. .65 .65
465 A82 25p multi, diff. .90 .90
466 A82 £1 multi, diff. 3.50 3.50
Nos. 463-466 (4) 5.55 5.55

Miniature Sheet

467 Sheet of 4 5.50 5.50
a. A82 15p like No. 463 .50 .50
b. A82 18p like No. 464 .65 .65
c. A82 25p like No. 465 .85 .85
d. A82 £1 like No. 466 3.50 3.50

Vignettes of Nos. 467a-467d do not have frame.

Moon Landing, 20th Anniv.
Common Design Type

Apollo 7: 15p, Tracking Station, Ascension Is. 18p, Launch, Cape Kennedy. 25p, Mission emblem. 70p, Expended Saturn IVB stage. £1, Lunar landing profile for the Apollo 11 mission.

1989, July 20 *Perf. 14x13½*
Size of Nos. 469-470: 29x29mm
468 CD342 15p multicolored .45 .45
469 CD342 18p multicolored .55 .55
470 CD342 25p multicolored .75 .75
471 CD342 70p multicolored 2.10 2.10
Nos. 468-471 (4) 3.85 3.85

Souvenir Sheet

472 CD342 £1 multicolored 3.00 3.00

Souvenir Sheet

A83

1989, July 7 *Perf. 14x13½*
473 A83 75p Emblems, No. 60 2.50 2.50

Miniature Sheet

World Stamp Expo '89, Washington, DC, and PHILEXFRANCE '89, Paris — A84

The Statue of Liberty and scenes from the centenary celebrations, 1986: a, Operation Sail. b, Face. c, Upper body. d, Three crown points. e, Ships in harbor, view of lower Manhattan. f, Ship in port, New York City.

1989, Aug. 21 **Wmk. 373**
474 Sheet of 6 2.75 2.75
a.-f. A84 15p any single .45 .45

Devil's Ashpit Tracking Station A85

1989, Sept. 30 Wmk. 384 *Perf. 14*
475 Sheet, 5 each #a.-b. 6.75 6.75
a. A85 18p shown .55 .55
b. A85 25p US space shuttle launch .80 .80

Termination of NASA tracking operations, begun in 1965, at the station.

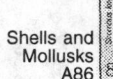

Shells and Mollusks A86

Wmk. 384

1989, Nov. 6 Litho. *Perf. 14*
476 A86 8p *Strombus latus* .30 .30
477 A86 18p *Tonna galea* .65 .65
478 A86 25p *Harpa doris* .85 .85
479 A86 £1 *Charonia variegata* 3.25 3.25
Nos. 476-479 (4) 5.05 5.05

Donkeys — A87

Perf. 14 on 3 Sides

1989, Nov. 17 Litho. Wmk. 384

Booklet Stamps

480 A87 18p shown .50 .50
a. Booklet pane of 6 3.00
481 A87 25p Green turtle .75 .75
a. Booklet pane of 4 3.00

No. 480a sold for £1.

Military Type of 1987

Royal Navy equipment, c. 1815-1820: a, Seaman's pistol, hat, cutlass. b, Midshipman's belt buckle, button, sword, hat. c, Surgeon's hat, sword, instrument chest. d, Captain's hat, telescope, sword. e, Admiral's epaulet, megaphone, hat, pocket.

1990, Feb. 12 Litho. *Perf. 14*
482 Strip of 5 4.75 4.75
a.-e. A77 25p any single .95 .95

World Wildlife Fund — A88

Frigate birds *(Fregata aquila)*: 9p, Family group. 10p, Chick. 11p, Male in flight. 15p, Female and immature in flight.

Perf. 14½x14

1990, Mar. 5 Litho. Wmk. 373
483 A88 9p multicolored *1.25* 1.00
484 A88 10p multicolored *1.50* 1.25
485 A88 11p multicolored *1.75* 1.50
486 A88 15p multicolored *2.50* 2.00
Nos. 483-486 (4) 7.00 5.75

Great Britain Nos. 1-2 A89

Exhibition emblem and: 18p, Early Ascension cancellations. 25p, Unloading mail at Wideawake Airfield. £1, Main P.O., Royal Mail van.

1990, May 3 Litho. *Perf. 14*
487 A89 9p shown .30 .30
488 A89 18p multicolored .60 .60
489 A89 25p multicolored .85 .85
490 A89 £1 multicolored 3.25 3.25
Nos. 487-490 (4) 5.00 5.00

Penny Black 150th anniv., Stamp World London '90.

Queen Mother, 90th Birthday
Common Design Types

1990, Aug. 4 Wmk. 384 *Perf. 14x15*
491 CD343 25p Portrait, 1940 .85 .85

Perf. 14½

492 CD344 £1 King, Queen with soldiers 3.25 3.25

Garth Castle, 1910 — A90

Designs: 18p, RMS St. Helena, 1982. 25p, Launching new RMS St. Helena, 1989. 70p, Duke of York launching new RMS St. Helena. £1, New RMS St. Helena.

Wmk. 373

1990, Sept. 13 Litho. *Perf. 14½*
493 A90 9p multicolored .35 .35
494 A90 18p multicolored .65 .65
495 A90 25p multicolored .90 .90
496 A90 70p multicolored 2.50 2.50
Nos. 493-496 (4) 4.40 4.40

Souvenir Sheet

497 A90 £1 multicolored 3.50 3.50

See St. Helena Nos. 535-539, Tristan da Cunha Nos. 482-486.

Christmas A91

Sculpture (8p) and paintings of Madonna and Child by: 8p, Felici. 18p, Unknown artist. 25p, Gebhard. 65p, Gritti.

1990, Oct. 24 *Perf. 14*
498 A91 8p multicolored .30 .30
499 A91 18p multicolored .65 .65
500 A91 25p multicolored .90 .90
501 A91 65p multicolored 3.25 3.25
Nos. 498-501 (4) 5.10 5.10

Nos. 410, 412 & 414 Ovptd. in Silver BRITISH FOR 175 YEARS

1991, Feb. 5 Wmk. 384 *Perf. 14½*
502 A74 25p on #410 1.00 1.00
503 A74 50p on #412 2.00 2.00
504 A74 £1 on #414 4.00 4.00
Nos. 502-504 (3) 7.00 7.00

Elizabeth & Philip, Birthdays
Common Design Types

1991, June 18
505 CD345 25p multicolored .80 .80
506 CD346 25p multicolored .80 .80
a. Pair, #505-506 + label 1.60 1.60

Military Uniforms Type of 1987

Royal Marines Equipment 1821-1844: a, Officer's shako, epaulettes, belt plate, button. b, Officer's cap, sword, epaulettes, belt plate. c, Drum Major's shako with cords, staff. d, Sergeant's shako, chevrons, belt plate, canteen. e, Drummer's drum, sticks, shako.

1991, Aug. 1 Wmk. 373 *Perf. 14*
507 A77 25p Strip of 5, #a.-e. 4.00 4.00

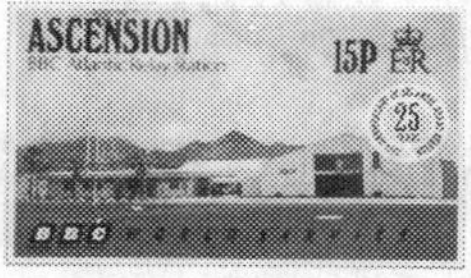

Atlantic Relay Station, 25th Anniv. A92

Designs: 15p, BBC Atlantic relay station. 18p, English Bay transmitters. 25p, Satellite receiving station, vert. 70p, Antenna support tower, vert.

1991, Sept. 17 Wmk. 384 *Perf. 14½*
508 A92 15p multicolored .50 .50
509 A92 18p multicolored .60 .60
510 A92 25p multicolored .85 .85
511 A92 70p multicolored 2.50 2.50
Nos. 508-511 (4) 4.45 4.45

Christmas — A93

Designs: 8p, St. Mary's Church, exterior. 18p, St. Mary's Church, interior. 25p, Grotto of Our Lady of Ascension, exterior. 65p, Grotto of Our Lady of Ascension, interior.

1991, Oct. 1 *Perf. 14*
512 A93 8p multicolored .30 .30
513 A93 18p multicolored .60 .60
514 A93 25p multicolored .85 .85
515 A93 65p multicolored 2.25 2.25
Nos. 512-515 (4) 4.00 4.00

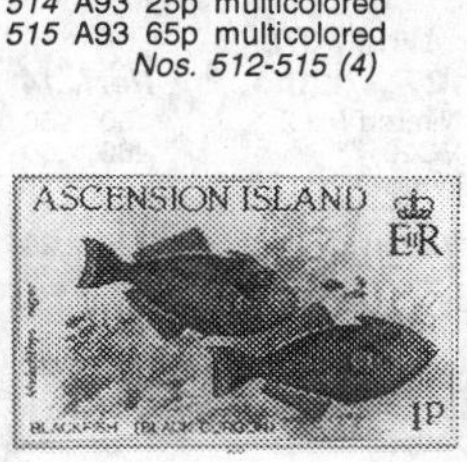

Fish A94

Wmk. 373

1991, Dec. 10 Litho. *Perf. 14*

516 A94	1p	Blackfish	.20	.20
517 A94	2p	Five finger	.20	.20
518 A94	4p	Resplendent angelfish	.20	.20
519 A94	5p	Silver fish	.20	.20
520 A94	9p	Gurnard	.30	.30
521 A94	10p	Blue dad	.35	.35
522 A94	15p	Cunning fish	.50	.50
523 A94	18p	Grouper	.60	.60
524 A94	20p	Moray eel	.65	.65
525 A94	25p	Hardback soldierfish	.85	.85
526 A94	30p	Blue marlin	1.00	1.00
527 A94	50p	Wahoo	1.65	1.65
528 A94	70p	Yellowfin tuna	2.25	2.25
529 A94	£1	Blue shark	3.25	3.25
530 A94	£2.50	Bottlenose dolphin	8.50	8.50
		Nos. 516-530 (15)	20.70	20.70

Queen Elizabeth II's Accession to the Throne, 40th Anniv.

Common Design Type

Wmk. 373

1992, Feb. 6 Litho. *Perf. 14*

531 CD349	9p	multicolored	.30	.30
532 CD349	15p	multicolored	.50	.50
533 CD349	18p	multicolored	.60	.60
534 CD349	25p	multicolored	.85	.85
535 CD349	70p	multicolored	2.25	2.25
		Nos. 531-535 (5)	4.50	4.50

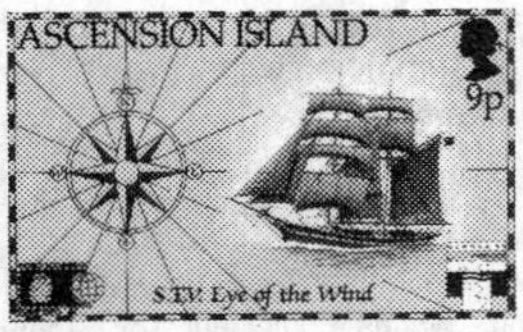

Discovery of America, 500th Anniv. — A95

Wmk. 373

1992, Feb. 18 Litho. *Perf. 14*

536 A95	9p	STV Eye of the Wind	.30	.30
537 A95	18p	STV Soren Larsen	.60	.60
538 A95	25p	Pinta, Santa Maria, & Nina	.85	.85
539 A95	70p	Columbus, Santa Maria	2.25	2.25
		Nos. 536-539 (4)	4.00	4.00

World Columbian Stamp Expo '92, Chicago and Genoa '92 Intl. Philatelic Exhibitions.

Wideawake Airfield, 50th Anniv. — A96

Wmk. 373

1992, May 5 Litho. *Perf. 14*

540 A96	15p	Control tower	.50	.50
541 A96	18p	Nose hangar	.60	.60
542 A96	25p	Construction work	.85	.85
543 A96	70p	Laying fuel pipeline	2.25	2.25
		Nos. 540-543 (4)	4.20	4.20

Ascension's Participation in Falkland Islands' Liberation, 10th Anniv. — A97

#548a, 15p + 3p like #544. b, 18p + 4p like #545. c, 25p + 5p like #546. d, 65p + 13p like #547.

Wmk. 373

1992, June 12 Litho. *Perf. 14*

544 A97	15p	Nimrod Mk.2	.50	.50
545 A97	18p	VC10	.60	.60
546 A97	25p	Wessex HU Mk.5 helicopter	.85	.85
547 A97	65p	Vulcan B2	2.25	2.25
		Nos. 544-547 (4)	4.20	4.20

Souvenir Sheet

548 A97	Sheet of 4, #a.-d.	5.00	5.00

Surtax for Soldiers', Sailors' and Airmen's Families Association.

Christmas A98

Children's drawings: 8p, Snowman, rocks, candle. 18p, Underwater Santa, Christmas tree. 25p, Hello, bells. 65p, Nativity Scene, angel.

Wmk. 384

1992, Oct. 13 Litho. *Perf. 14*

549 A98	8p	multicolored	.30	.30
550 A98	18p	multicolored	.70	.70
551 A98	25p	multicolored	.95	.95
552 A98	65p	multicolored	2.50	2.50
		Nos. 549-552 (4)	4.45	4.45

Yellow Canary — A99

Wmk. 373

1993, Jan. 12 Litho. *Perf. 14½*

553 A99	15p	Singing male	.45	.45
554 A99	18p	Adult male, female	.55	.55
555 A99	25p	Young calling for food	.80	.80
556 A99	70p	Mixed flock	2.25	2.25
		Nos. 553-556 (4)	4.05	4.05

Royal Air Force, 75th Anniv.

Common Design Type

Designs: 20p, Sopwith Snipe. No. 558, Supermarine Southampton. 30p, Avro Anson. 70p, Vickers Wellington 1C.

No. 561a, Westland Lysander. b, Gloster Meteor. c, DeHavilland Comet. d, British Aerospace Nimrod.

Wmk. 373

1993, Apr. 1 Litho. *Perf. 14*

557 CD350	20p	multicolored	.60	.60
558 CD350	25p	multicolored	.70	.70
559 CD350	30p	multicolored	.85	.85
560 CD350	70p	multicolored	2.25	2.25
		Nos. 557-560 (4)	4.40	4.40

Souvenir Sheet

561 CD350	25p	Sheet of 4, #a.-d.	3.00	3.00

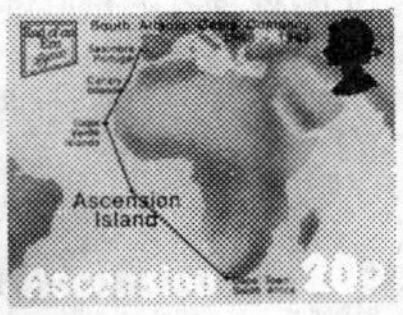

South Atlantic Cable Company, 25th Anniv. A100

Designs: 20p, Map showing cable route. 25p, Cable ship laying cable. 30p, Map of Ascension. 70p, Cable ship off Ascension.

Perf. 14x14½

1993, June 8 Litho. Wmk. 384

562 A100	20p	multicolored	.60	.60
563 A100	25p	multicolored	.75	.75
564 A100	30p	multicolored	.90	.90
565 A100	70p	multicolored	2.00	2.00
		Nos. 562-565 (4)	4.25	4.25

Flowers A101

Perf. 14x14½

1993, Aug. 3 Litho. Wmk. 384

566 A101	20p	Lantana camara	.60	.60
567 A101	25p	Moonflower	.75	.75
568 A101	30p	Hibiscus	.90	.90
569 A101	70p	Frangipani	2.00	2.00
		Nos. 566-569 (4)	4.25	4.25

Christmas — A102

Designs: 12p, Child mailing Christmas card. 20p, Mail loaded onto Tristar. 25p, Plane in flight. 30p, Mail unloaded at Wideawake Airfield. 65p, Child reading card, Georgetown.

Perf. 14½x14

1993, Oct. 19 Litho. Wmk. 373

570 A102	12p	multicolored	.35	.35
571 A102	20p	multicolored	.60	.60
572 A102	25p	multicolored	.75	.75
573 A102	30p	multicolored	.90	.90
574 A102	65p	multicolored	2.00	2.00
a.		Souvenir sheet of 5, #570-574	4.50	4.50
		Nos. 570-574 (5)	4.60	4.60

Stamps from No. 574a show a continuous design, while Nos. 570-574 have white borders on sides.

Prehistoric Aquatic Reptiles — A103

1994, Jan. 25 Wmk. 373 *Perf. 14*

575 A103	12p	Ichthyosaurus	.35	.35
576 A103	20p	Metriorhynchus	.60	.60
577 A103	25p	Mosasaurus	.75	.75
578 A103	30p	Elasmosaurus	.90	.90
579 A103	65p	Plesiosaurus	1.90	1.90
		Nos. 575-579 (5)	4.50	4.50

Ovptd. with Hong Kong '94 Emblem

1994, Feb. 18

580 A103	12p	on #575	.35	.35
581 A103	20p	on #576	.60	.60
582 A103	25p	on #577	.75	.75
583 A103	30p	on #578	.90	.90
584 A103	65p	on #579	1.90	1.90
		Nos. 580-584 (5)	4.50	4.50

Green Turtle A104

Designs: 20p, Four on beach. 25p, Crawling in sand. No. 587, Crawling from sea. 65p, Swimming.

No. 589a, Side view, crawling from sea. b, Digging nest. c, Hatchlings heading to sea. d, Digging nest, diff.

1994, Mar. 22

585 A104	20p	multicolored	.60	.60
586 A104	25p	multicolored	.75	.75
587 A104	30p	multicolored	.90	.90
588 A104	65p	multicolored	1.90	1.90
		Nos. 585-588 (4)	4.15	4.15

Souvenir Sheet

589 A104	30p	Sheet of 4, #a.-d.	3.50	3.50

Civilian Ships A105

Ships serving during Falkland Islands War, 1982: 20p, Tug Yorkshireman. 25p, Minesweeper support ship RMS St. Helena. 30p, Oil tanker British ESK. 65p, Cruise liner Uganda, hospital ship.

1994, June 14

590 A105	20p	multicolored	.60	.60
591 A105	25p	multicolored	.75	.75
592 A105	30p	multicolored	.90	.90
593 A105	65p	multicolored	1.90	1.90
		Nos. 590-593 (4)	4.15	4.15

Sooty Tern A106

1994, Aug. 16

594 A106	20p	Chick	.60	.60
595 A106	25p	Juvenile	.75	.75
596 A106	30p	Brooding adult	.90	.90
597 A106	65p	Displaying male	1.90	1.90
		Nos. 594-597 (4)	4.15	4.15

Souvenir Sheet

598 A106	£1	Dread	3.00	3.00

Christmas A107

Donkeys: 12p, Mare with foal. 20p, Young adult. 25p, Foal. 30p, Adult, egrets. 65p, Adult.

1994, Oct. 11 *Perf. 14x14½*

599 A107	12p	multicolored	.40	.40
600 A107	20p	multicolored	.60	.60
601 A107	25p	multicolored	.75	.75
602 A107	30p	multicolored	.95	.95
603 A107	65p	multicolored	2.00	2.00
		Nos. 599-603 (5)	4.70	4.70

Flowers A108

Designs: 20p, Leonurus japonicus, vert. 25p, Periwinkle. 30p, Four o'clock, vert. 65p, Blood flower.

1995, Jan. 10 *Perf. 14*

604 A108	20p	multicolored	.60	.60
605 A108	25p	multicolored	.75	.75
606 A108	30p	multicolored	.95	.95
607 A108	65p	multicolored	2.00	2.00
		Nos. 604-607 (4)	4.30	4.30

Island Scenes, c. 1895 A109

Designs: 12p, Horse-drawn wagon, Two Boats, Green Mountain. 20p, Island stewards' store. 25p, Royal Navy headquarters, barracks. 30p, Police office. 65p, Pier head.

1995, Mar. 7 Wmk. 384 *Perf. 14½*

608 A109	12p	sepia	.35	.35
609 A109	20p	sepia	.60	.60
610 A109	25p	sepia	.75	.75
611 A109	30p	sepia	.90	.90
612 A109	65p	sepia	2.00	2.00
		Nos. 608-612 (5)	4.60	4.60

End of World War II, 50th Anniv.

Common Design Types

Designs: 20p, 5.5-inch guns taken from HMS Hood, 1941. 25p, Fairey Swordfish, first aircraft to land at Ascension. 30p, HMS Dorsetshire patrolling South Atlantic. 65p, HMS Devonshire patrolling South Atlantic.

£1, Reverse of War Medal, 1939-45.

1995, May 8 Wmk. 373 *Perf. 14*

613 CD351	20p	multicolored	.60	.60
614 CD351	25p	multicolored	.75	.75
615 CD351	30p	multicolored	.90	.90
616 CD351	65p	multicolored	2.00	2.00
		Nos. 613-616 (4)	4.25	4.25

Souvenir Sheet

617 CD352	£1	multicolored	3.00	3.00

Butterflies
A110

1995, Sept. 1 **Wmk. 384**
618 A110 20p Long-tailed blue .60 .60
619 A110 25p Painted lady .75 .75
620 A110 30p Diadem .90 .90
621 A110 65p African monarch 2.00 2.00
Nos. 618-621 (4) 4.25 4.25

Souvenir Sheet

622 A110 £1 Red admiral 3.00 3.00

Singapore '95 (#622).

Christmas
A111

Designs based on children's drawings: 12p, Santa on boat. 20p, Santa on wall. 25p, Santa in chimney. 30p, Santa on dolphin. 65p, South Atlantic run.

1995, Oct. 10 **Wmk. 373**
623 A111 12p multicolored .35 .35
624 A111 20p multicolored .60 .60
625 A111 25p multicolored .75 .75
626 A111 30p multicolored .90 .90
627 A111 65p multicolored 2.00 2.00
Nos. 623-627 (5) 4.60 4.60

Mollusks
A112

12p, Cypraea lurida. 25p, Cypraea spurca. 30p, Harpa doris. 65p, Umbraculum umbraculum.

Wmk. 384

1996, Jan. 10 **Litho.** ***Perf. 14***
628 A112 12p multicolored .35 .35
629 A112 25p multicolored .75 .75
630 A112 30p multicolored .90 .90
631 A112 65p multicolored 2.00 2.00
a. Strip of 4, #628-631 4.00 4.00

Queen Elizabeth II, 70th Birthday
Common Design Type

Various portraits of Queen, scenes of Ascension: 20p, St. Marys Church. 25p, The Residency. 30p, Roman Catholic Grotto. 65p, The Exiles Club.

Wmk. 384

1996, Apr. 22 **Litho.** ***Perf. 13½***
632 CD354 20p multicolored .65 .65
633 CD354 25p multicolored .80 .80
634 CD354 30p multicolored 1.00 1.00
635 CD354 65p multicolored 2.00 2.00
Nos. 632-635 (4) 4.45 4.45

CAPEX
'96
A113

Island transport: 20p, US Army Jeep. 25p, 1924 Citreon 7.5HP two seater. 30p, 1930 Austin Ten-four Tourer. 65p, Series 1 Land Rover.

Wmk. 384

1996, June 8 **Litho.** ***Perf. 14***
636 A113 20p multicolored .65 .65
637 A113 25p multicolored .80 .80
638 A113 30p multicolored 1.00 1.00
639 A113 65p multicolored 2.00 2.00
Nos. 636-639 (4) 4.45 4.45

Birds and Their
Young — A114

1p, Madeiran storm petrel. 2p, Red-billed tropicbird. 4p, Indian mynah. 5p, House sparrow. 7p, Common waxbill. 10p, White tern. 12p, Francolin. 15p, Brown noddy. 20p, Yellow canary. 25p, Black noddy. 30p, Red-footed booby. 40p, Yellow-billed tropicbird. 65p, Brown booby. £1, Masked booby. £2, Sooty tern. £3, Ascension frigate bird.

Wmk. 373

1996, Aug. 12 **Litho.** ***Perf. 13***
640 A114 1p multicolored .20 .20
641 A114 2p multicolored .20 .20
642 A114 4p multicolored .20 .20
643 A114 5p multicolored .20 .20
644 A114 7p multicolored .20 .20
645 A114 10p multicolored .30 .30
646 A114 12p multicolored .35 .35
647 A114 15p multicolored .45 .45
648 A114 20p multicolored .60 .60
649 A114 25p multicolored .70 .70
650 A114 30p multicolored .90 .90
651 A114 40p multicolored 1.10 1.10
652 A114 65p multicolored 1.90 1.90
a. Sheet of 1, perf. 14 2.10 2.10
653 A114 £1 multicolored 3.00 3.00
a. Souvenir sheet of 1 3.25 3.25
654 A114 £2 multicolored 6.00 6.00
655 A114 £3 multicolored 9.00 9.00
Nos. 640-655 (16) 25.30 25.30

No. 652a for Hong Kong '97. Issued 2/3/97.
No. 653a for return of Hong Kong to China. Issued 7/1/97.

BBC Atlantic Relay Station, 30th Anniv.
A115

Various views of relay station: 20p, 25p, Towers. 30p, Towers, buildings. 65p, Satellite dish, towers, beach.

1996, Sept. 9 **Wmk. 384** ***Perf. 14***
656 A115 20p multicolored .65 .65
657 A115 25p multicolored .80 .80
658 A115 30p multicolored 1.00 1.00
659 A115 65p multicolored 2.00 2.00
Nos. 656-659 (4) 4.45 4.45

Christmas
A116

Santa Claus: 12p, On satellite dish. 20p, Playing golf. 25p, By beach. 30p, On RAF Tristar. 65p, Aboard RMS St. Helena.

Perf. 14x14½

1996, Sept. 23 **Litho.** **Wmk. 373**
660 A116 12p multicolored .40 .40
661 A116 20p multicolored .65 .65
662 A116 25p multicolored .80 .80
663 A116 30p multicolored 1.00 1.00
664 A116 65p multicolored 2.00 2.00
Nos. 660-664 (5) 4.85 4.85

UNICEF, 50th anniv.

A117 A118

Wmk. 373

1997, Jan. 7 **Litho.** ***Perf. 14½***
665 A117 20p Date palm .65 .65
666 A117 25p Mauritius hemp .80 .80
667 A117 30p Norfolk Island pine 1.00 1.00
668 A117 65p Dwarf palm 2.00 2.00
Nos. 665-668 (4) 4.45 4.45

Hong Kong '97.

Wmk. 373

1997, Apr. 1 **Litho.** ***Perf. 14½***

Flag, ship or aircraft: 12p, Great Britain Red Ensign, tanker Maserk Ascension. 25p, RAF Ensign, Tristar. 30p, NASA emblem, Space Shuttle Atlantis. 65p, Royal Navy White Ensign, HMS Northumberland.

669 A118 12p multicolored .40 .40
670 A118 25p multicolored .80 .80
671 A118 30p multicolored .95 .95
672 A118 65p multicolored 2.00 2.00
Nos. 669-672 (4) 4.15 4.15

Herbs
A119

Designs: a, Solanum sodomaeum. b, Ageratum conyzoides. c, Leonurus sibricus. d, Cerastium vulgatum. e, Commelina diffusa.

Perf. 14x14½

1997, June 7 **Litho.** **Wmk. 373**
673 A119 30p Strip of 5, #a.-e. 5.00 5.00

A120 Birds — A121

Queen Elizabeth II and Prince Philip, 50th Wedding Anniv.: No. 674, Queen Elizabeth II. No. 675, Prince Philip playing polo. No. 676, Queen petting horse. No. 677, Prince Philip. No. 678, Prince Philip, Queen Elizabeth II. No. 679, Prince Harry, Prince William riding horses.

£1.50, Queen Elizabeth, Prince Philip riding in open carriage.

Wmk. 384

1997, July 10 **Litho.** ***Perf. 13½***
674 A120 20p multicolored .65 .65
675 A120 20p multicolored .65 .65
a. Pair, #674-675 1.40 1.40
676 A120 25p multicolored .85 .85
677 A120 25p multicolored .85 .85
a. Pair, #676-677 1.75 1.75
678 A120 30p multicolored 1.00 1.00
679 A120 30p multicolored 1.00 1.00
a. Pair, #678-679 2.00 2.00
Nos. 674-679 (6) 5.00 5.00

Souvenir Sheet

680 A120 £1.50 multicolored 4.75 4.75

Perf. 14 on 3 Sides

1997, Sept. 1 **Litho.** **Wmk. 373**

Booklet Stamps

681 A121 15p like #644 .50 .50
682 A121 35p like #648 1.10 1.10
a. Booklet pane, 2 ea #681-682 3.25
Complete booklet, #682a 3.25

Game
Fish — A122

Perf. 14x14½

1997, Sept. 3 **Litho.** **Wmk. 373**
683 A122 12p Black marlin .40 .40
684 A122 20p Atlantic sailfish .65 .65
685 A122 25p Swordfish .80 .80
686 A122 30p Wahoo .95 .95
687 A122 £1 Yellowfin tuna 3.25 3.25
Nos. 683-687 (5) 6.05 6.05

A123 A124

St. Mary's Church (Christmas): 15p, Interior view. 35p, Stained glass window, Madonna and Child. 40p, Stained glass window, Falklands, 1982. 50p, Stained glass window.

Wmk. 384

1997, Oct. 1 **Litho.** ***Perf. 14***
688 A123 15p multicolored .50 .50
689 A123 35p multicolored 1.10 1.10
690 A123 40p multicolored 1.25 1.25
691 A123 50p multicolored 1.75 1.75
Nos. 688-691 (4) 4.60 4.60

Wmk. 373

1998, Feb. 10 **Litho.** ***Perf. 14***

Insects: 15p, Cactoblastis cactorum. 35p, Teleonemia scrupulosa. 40p, Neltumius arizonensis. 50p, Algarobius prosopis.

692 A124 15p multicolored .50 .50
693 A124 35p multicolored 1.10 1.10
694 A124 40p multicolored 1.25 1.25
695 A124 50p multicolored 1.60 1.60
Nos. 692-695 (4) 4.45 4.45

Diana, Princess of Wales (1961-97)
Common Design Type

Designs: a, In polka-dotted dress. b, In yellow blouse. c, With longer hair style. d, Holding flowers.

Perf. 14½x14

1998, Mar. 31 **Litho.** **Wmk. 373**
696 CD355 35p Sheet of 4, #a.-d. 5.25 5.25

No. 696 sold for £1.40 + 20p, with surtax from international sales being donated to the Princess Diana Memorial Fund and surtax from national sales being donated to designated local charity.

Royal Air Force, 80th Anniv.
Common Design Type of 1993
Re-inscribed

15p, Fairey Fawn. 35p, Vickers Vernon. 40p, Supermarine Spitfire F-22. 50p, Bristol Britannia C2.

No. 701: a, Blackburn Kangaroo. b, SE5a. c, Curtiss Kittyhawk III. d, Boeing Fortress II (B-17).

Wmk. 384

1998, Apr. 1 **Litho.** ***Perf. 14***
697 CD350 15p multicolored .70 .70
698 CD350 35p multicolored 1.60 1.60
699 CD350 40p multicolored 1.90 1.90
700 CD350 50p multicolored 2.25 2.25
Nos. 697-700 (4) 6.45 6.45

Souvenir Sheet

701 CD350 50p Sheet of 4, #a.-d. 6.75 6.75

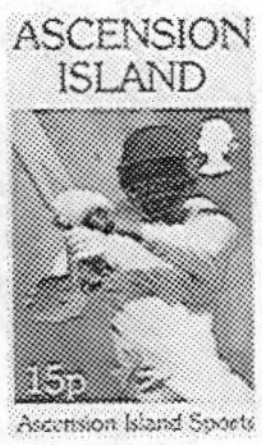

Birds — A125 Island Sports — A126

Wmk. 373

1998, June 15 **Litho.** ***Perf. 14***
702 A125 15p Swallow .50 .50
703 A125 25p House martin .80 .80
704 A125 35p Cattle egret 1.10 1.10
705 A125 40p Swift 1.25 1.25
706 A125 50p Allen's gallinule 1.60 1.60
Nos. 702-706 (5) 5.25 5.25

Wmk. 373

1998, Aug. 17 Litho. *Perf. 14*

707	A126	15p Cricket	.50	.50
708	A126	35p Golf	1.10	1.10
709	A126	40p Soccer	1.25	1.25
710	A126	50p Trapshooting	1.60	1.60
		Nos. 707-709 (3)	2.85	2.85

Christmas A127

Designs: 15p, Children's nativity play. 35p, Santa arriving on Ascension. 40p, Santa arriving at a party. 50p, Carol singers.

Wmk. 373

1998, Oct. 1 Litho. *Perf. 14*

711	A127	15p multicolored	.50	.50
712	A127	35p multicolored	1.10	1.10
713	A127	40p multicolored	1.25	1.25
714	A127	50p multicolored	1.60	1.60
		Nos. 711-714 (4)	4.45	4.45

World War II Aircraft A128

Designs: 15p, Curtiss C-46 Commando. 35p, Douglas C-47 Dakota. 40p, Douglas C-54 Skymaster. 50p, Consolidated Liberator Mk.V.
£1.50, Consolidated Liberator LB-30.

Wmk. 373

1999, Jan. 20 Litho. *Perf. 14*

715	A128	15p multicolored	.50	.50
716	A128	35p multicolored	1.10	1.10
717	A128	40p multicolored	1.25	1.25
718	A128	50p multicolored	1.60	1.60
		Nos. 715-718 (4)	4.45	4.45

Souvenir Sheet

719	A128	£1.50 multicolored	4.75	4.75

Winston Churchill, 125th birth anniv.

Australia '99, World Stamp Expo A129

Union Castle Mail Ships: 15p, SS Glengorm Castle. 35p, SS Gloucester Castle. 40p, SS Durham Castle. 50p, SS Garth Castle.
£1, HMS Endeavour.

Perf. 14½x14

1999, Mar. 5 Litho. Wmk. 373

720	A129	15p multicolored	.50	.50
721	A129	35p multicolored	1.10	1.10
722	A129	40p multicolored	1.25	1.25
723	A129	50p multicolored	1.60	1.60
		Nos. 720-723 (4)	4.45	4.45

Souvenir Sheet

724	A129	£1 multicolored	3.25	3.25

World Wildlife Fund — A130

Fairy tern: No. 725, Two on branch. No. 726, One on branch. No. 727, Two in flight. No. 728, Adult feeding chick.

Wmk. 384

1999, Apr. 27 Litho. *Perf. 14½*

725	A130	10p multicolored	.35	.35
726	A130	10p multicolored	.35	.35
727	A130	10p multicolored	.35	.35
728	A130	10p multicolored	.35	.35
a.		Sheet of 16, 4 each #725-728	5.75	5.75
		Nos. 725-728 (4)	1.40	1.40

Wedding of Prince Edward and Sophie Rhys-Jones

Common Design Type

Perf. 13¾x14

1999, June 19 Litho. Wmk. 384

729	CD356	50p Separate portraits	1.60	1.60
730	CD356	£1 Couple	3.25	3.25

1st Manned Moon Landing, 30th Anniv.

Common Design Type

Designs: 15p, Command and service modules. 35p, Moon from Apollo 11. 40p, Devil's Ashpit Tracking Station. 50p, Lunar module lifts off moon.
£1.50, Looking at earth from moon.

Perf. 14x13¾

1999, July 20 Litho. Wmk. 384

731	CD357	15p multicolored	.50	.50
732	CD357	35p multicolored	1.10	1.10
733	CD357	40p multicolored	1.25	1.25
734	CD357	50p multicolored	1.60	1.60
		Nos. 731-734 (4)	4.45	4.45

Souvenir Sheet

Perf. 14

735	CD357	£1.50 multicolored	4.75	4.75

No. 735 contains one 40mm circular stamp.

Queen Mother's Century

Common Design Type

Queen Mother: 15p, With King George VI, Winston Churchill. 35p, With Prince Charles. 40p, At Clarence House, 88th birthday. 50p, With drummers at Clarence House.
£1.50, With Titanic.

Wmk. 384

1999, Aug. 20 Litho. *Perf. 13½*

736	CD358	15p multicolored	.50	.50
737	CD358	35p multicolored	1.10	1.10
738	CD358	40p multicolored	1.25	1.25
739	CD358	50p multicolored	1.75	1.75
		Nos. 736-739 (4)	4.60	4.60

Souvenir Sheet

740	CD358	£1.50 black	5.00	5.00

Christmas A131

Wmk. 384

1999, Oct. 6 Litho. *Perf. 13¾*

741	A131	15p 3 children	.50	.50
742	A131	35p 2 children, hats	1.10	1.10
743	A131	40p 2 children, bed	1.25	1.25
744	A131	50p 4 children	1.75	1.75
		Nos. 741-744 (4)	4.60	4.60

Cable and Wireless, Cent. A132

Perf. 13¼x13¾

1999, Dec. 13 Litho. Wmk. 373

745	A132	15p CS Anglia	.50	.50
746	A132	35p CS Cambria	1.10	1.10
747	A132	40p Map	1.25	1.25
748	A132	50p CS Colonia	1.60	1.60
		Nos. 745-748 (4)	4.45	4.45

Souvenir Sheet

749	A132	£1.50 CS Seine	5.00	5.00

POSTAGE DUE STAMPS

Outline Map of Ascension — D1

1986 Litho. *Perf. 15x14*

J1	D1	1p beige & brown	.20	.20
J2	D1	2p orange & brown	.20	.20
J3	D1	5p org ver & brn	.20	.20
J4	D1	7p violet & black	.20	.20
J5	D1	10p ultra & black	.25	.25
J6	D1	25p pale green & blk	.60	.60
		Nos. J1-J6 (6)	1.65	1.65

AUSTRALIAN STATES

NEW SOUTH WALES

'nü sauth 'wā(ə)lz

LOCATION — Southeast coast of Australia in the South Pacific Ocean
GOVT. — British Crown Colony
AREA — 309,432 sq. mi.
POP. — 1,500,000 (estimated, 1900)
CAPITAL — Sydney

In 1901 New South Wales united with five other British colonies to form the Commonwealth of Australia. Stamps of Australia are now used.

12 Pence = 1 Shilling
20 Shillings = 1 Pound

Watermarks

Wmk. 12- Crown and Single-lined A

Wmk. 13- Large Crown and Double-lined A

Wmk. 49- Double-lined Numerals Corresponding with the Value

Wmk. 50- Single-lined Numeral

Wmk. 51- Single-lined Numeral

Wmk. 52- Single-lined Numeral

Wmk. 53- 5/-

Wmk. 54- Small Crown and NSW

Wmk. 55- Large Crown and NSW

Wmk. 56- NSW

Wmk. 57- 5/- NSW in Diamond

Wmk. 58- 20/- NSW in Circle

Wmk. 70- V and Crown

Wmk. 199- Crown and A in Circle

Values for unused stamps are for examples with original gum as defined in the catalogue introduction except for Nos. 1-20 which are rarely found with gum and are valued without gum. Very fine examples of Nos. 35-100, F3-F5, J1-J10 and O1-O40 will have perforations touching the framelines or design on one or more sides due to the narrow spacing of the stamps on the plates and imperfect perforation methods. Stamps with perfs clear of the design on all four sides are scarce and will command higher prices.

Seal of the Colony
A1 A2

A1 has no clouds. A2 has clouds added to the design, except in pos. 15.

1850 Unwmk. Engr. *Imperf.*

1 A1 1p red, *yelsh wove* 4,000. 400.
b. 1p red, *bluish wove* 4,000. 350.
2 A2 1p red, *yelsh wove* 2,500. 275.
b. 1p red, *yellowish laid* 4,000. 450.
c. 1p red, *bluish wove* 2,500. 275.
e. 1p red, *bluish laid*
f. Hill unshaded 4,250. 450.
g. No clouds 4,250. 450.
h. No trees 4,250. 450.

Twenty-five varieties.

Stamps from early impressions of the plate sell at considerably higher prices.

No. 1 was reproduced by the collotype process in a souvenir sheet distributed at the London International Stamp Exhibition 1950. The paper is white.

Plate I — A3

Plate II — A4

Plate I: Vertically lined background.

Plate I re-touched: Lines above and below "POSTAGE" and "TWO PENCE" deepened. Outlines of circular band around picture also deepened.

Plate II (First re-engraving of Plate I): Horizontally lined background; the bale on the left side is dated and there is a dot in the star in each corner.

Plate II retouched: Dots and dashes added in lower spandrels.

Plate I

Late (worn plate) Impressions

3 A3 2p blue, *yelsh wove* 1,600. 150.
a. Early impressions 4,500. 350.

Twenty-four varieties.

Plate I, Retouched

4 A3 2p blue, *yelsh wove* 2,750. 250.

Twelve varieties.

Plate II

Late (worn plate) Impressions

5 A4 2p blue, *yelsh wove* 1,750. 175.
a. 2p blue, *bluish wove* 1,750. 175.
b. 2p blue, *grayish wove* 1,750. 175.
c. "CREVIT" omitted — 350.
d. Pick and shovel omitted — 275.
e. No whip 3,250. 225.
h. Early impressions 4,000. 225.

Plate II, Retouched

5F A4 2p blue, *bluish wove* 2,250. 200.
g. No whip — 275.
i. "CREVIT" omitted — 375.

Eleven varieties.

Plate III
A5

Plate IV
A6

Plate III (Second re-engraving of Plate I): The bale is not dated and, with the exception of Nos. 7, 10 and 12, it is single-lined. There are no dots in the stars.

Plate IV (Third re-engraving of Plate I): The bale is double-lined and there is a circle in the center of each star.

1850-51

6 A5 2p blue, *grayish wove* 2,100. 175.
a. Fan with 6 segments — 350.
b. Double-lined bale — 225.
c. No whip — 250.
7 A6 2p blue, *bluish wove* ('51) 2,250. 150.
a. 2p ultra, *white laid* 2,750. 150.
b. 2p blue, *grayish wove* 2,250. 150.
c. Fan with 6 segments — 200.
d. No clouds — 200.

Twenty-four varieties.

Plate V — A7

A8

Plate V (Fourth re-engraving of Plate I): There is a pearl in the fan-shaped ornament below the central design.

1850-51

8 A7 2p blue, *grayish wove* ('51) 2,250. 165.
a. 2p ultra, *white laid* 3,250. 275.
b. Fan with 6 segments — 250.
c. Pick and shovel omitted — 250.
9 A8 3p green, *bluish wove* 2,250. 200.
a. 3p green, *yellowish wove* 3,750. 225.
b. 3p green, *yellowish laid* 4,500. 400.
c. 3p green, *bluish laid* 4,500. 400.
d. No whip 2,500. 300.

Twenty-four varieties of #8, twenty-five of #9.

Queen Victoria
A9 A10

TWO PENCE
Plate I - Background of wavy lines.
Plate II - Stars in corners.
Plate III (Plate I re-engraved) - Background of crossed lines.

SIX PENCE
Plate I - Background of fine lines.
Plate II (Plate I re-engraved) - Background of coarse lines.

1851 Yellowish Wove Paper

10 A9 1p carmine 1,650. 250.00
b. No leaves to right of "SOUTH" *3,250.* 365.00
c. Two leaves to right of "SOUTH" *3,250.* 425.00
d. "WALE" *3,250.* 425.00
11 A9 2p ultra, Plate I 750.00 90.00

1852 Bluish Laid Paper

12 A9 1p carmine 3,000. 400.
a. No leaves to right of "SOUTH" 500.
b. Two leaves to right of "SOUTH" 600.
c. "WALE" 600.

1852-55

Bluish or Grayish Wove Paper

13 A9 1p red 750.00 125.00
a. 1p carmine 1,000. 140.00
b. No leaves to right of "SOUTH" 200.00
c. Two leaves to right of "SOUTH" 250.00
d. "WALE" 200.00
14 A9 2p blue, Plate I 300.00 30.00
a. 2p ultramarine 325.00 30.00
b. 2p slate 425.00 30.00
15 A10 2p blue, Plate II ('53) 900.00 87.50
a. "WAEES" *2,300.* 450.00
16 A9 2p blue, Plate III ('55) 425.00 55.00
17 A9 3p green 900.00 140.00
a. 3p emerald 1,300. 100.00
b. "WACES" 2,300. 325.00
18 A9 6p brown, Plate I 2,000. 250.00
a. 6p black brown 2,000. 225.00
b. "WALLS" 4,250. 425.00
19 A9 6p brown, Plate II 2,000. 250.00
a. 6p bister brown 2,000. 225.00
20 A9 8p yellow ('53) 3,600. 500.00
a. 8p orange 3,600. 550.00
b. No leaves to right of "SOUTH" 900.00

The plates of the 1, 2, 3 and 8p each contained 50 varieties and those of the 6p 25 varieties.

The 2p, plate II, 6p, plate II, and 8p have been reprinted on grayish blue wove paper. The reprints of the 2p have the spandrels and background much worn. Most of the reprints of the 6p have no floreate ornaments to the right and left of "South". On all the values the wreath has been retouched.

Type of 1851 and:

A11

A12

A13

A14

1854-55 Wmk. 49

23 A9 1p orange 125.00 13.00
a. No leaves to right of "SOUTH" 275.00 60.00
b. Two leaves to right of "SOUTH" 400.00 100.00
c. "WALE" 400.00 125.00
24 A9 2p blue 100.00 10.00
a. 2p ultramarine 100.00 10.00
25 A9 3p green 150.00 25.00
a. "WACES" 80.00
b. Watermarked "2" 500.00

Value for No. 25b is for copy with the design cut into.

26 A11 5p green 800.00 375.00
27 A12 6p sage green 425.00 32.50
28 A12 6p brown 450.00 32.50
a. Watermarked "8" 1,650. 85.00
29 A12 6p gray 325.00 30.00
a. Watermarked "8" 1,650. 80.00
30 A13 8p orange ('55) 4,750. 1,000.
a. 8p yellow 4,750. 1,000.
31 A14 1sh pale red brown 650.00 75.00
a. 1sh red 650.00 75.00
b. Watermarked "8" 2,000. 150.00

See Nos. 38-42, 56, 58, 65, 67.

Nos. 38-42 exist with wide margins. Copies with perforations trimmed are often offered as Nos. 26, 30, and 30a.

A15

A16

1856

32 A15 1p red 90.00 16.00
a. 1p orange 90.00 16.00
b. Printed on both sides *2,250.*
33 A15 2p blue 110.00 5.00
a. Watermarked "1" 5,000.
b. Watermarked "5" 550.00 25.00
c. Watermarked "8"
34 A15 3p green 750.00 80.00
a. 3p yellow green 725.00 75.00
b. Watermarked "2" *4,000.*
Nos. 32-34 (3) 950.00 101.00

The two known copies of No. 33c are in museums. Both are used.

The 1p has been reprinted in orange on paper watermarked Small Crown and NSW, and the 2p in deep blue on paper watermarked single lined "2." These reprints are usually overprinted "SPECIMEN."

See Nos. 34C-37, 54, 63, 90.

1859 Litho.

34C A15 2p light blue 625.00

1860-63 Engr. Wmk. 49 *Perf. 13*

35 A15 1p red 55.00 8.00
a. 1p orange 100.00 8.00
b. Perf. 12x13 2,000.
c. Perf. 12 90.00 15.00
36 A15 2p blue, perf. 12 100.00 10.00
a. Watermarked "1" 3,500.
c. Perf. 12x13 2,600. 250.00
37 A15 3p blue green 50.00 9.00
a. 3p yellow green 50.00 9.00
b. 3p deep green 50.00 10.00
c. Watermarked "6" 60.00 12.50
d. Perf. 12 600.00 45.00
38 A11 5p dark green 40.00 12.50
a. 5p yellow green 50.00 21.00
b. Perf. 12 165.00 42.50
39 A12 6p brown, perf. 12 275.00 45.00
a. 6p gray, perf. 12 275.00 45.00
40 A12 6p violet 60.00 5.00
a. 6p aniline lilac 950.00 150.00
b. Watermarked "5" 360.00 30.00
c. Watermarked "12" 240.00 20.00
e. Perf. 12 275.00 30.00
41 A13 8p yellow 140.00 40.00
a. 8p orange 150.00 35.00
b. Perf. 12 2,100. 550.00
42 A14 1sh rose 65.00 8.00
a. 1sh carmine 55.00 5.75
c. Perf. 12 400.00 50.00
Nos. 35-42 (8) 785.00 137.50

1864 Wmk. 50 *Perf. 13*

43 A15 1p red 45.00 15.00

1861-80 Wmk. 53 *Perf. 13*

44 A16 5sh dull violet 250.00 40.00
a. 5sh purple 225.00 30.00
b. 5sh dull violet, perf. 12 1,650. 400.00
c. 5sh purple, perf. 12 250.00 50.00
d. 5sh purple, perf. 10 250.00 42.50
e. 5sh purple, perf. 12x10 450.00 65.00

See No. 101. For overprint see No. O11.

Reprints are perf. 10 and overprinted "REPRINT" in black.

New South Wales stamps can be mounted in the Scott Australia album.

A17

A18

1862-65 Typo. Unwmk. *Perf. 13*

45 A17 1p red ('65) 72.50 35.00
a. Perf. 14 72.50 55.00
46 A18 2p blue 30.00 2.50
a. Perf. 14 60.00 17.50

1863-64 Wmk. 50 *Perf. 13*

47 A17 1p red 21.00 .90
a. Watermarked "2" 95.00 10.50
48 A18 2p blue 10.00 .35
a. Watermarked "1" 135.00 5.00

1862 Wmk. 49 *Perf. 13*

49 A18 2p blue 50.00 8.50
a. Watermarked "5" 135.00 18.00
b. Perf. 12x13 600.00
c. Perf. 12 165.00 16.00

See Nos. 52-53, 61-62, 70-76.

A19

A20

1867, Sept. Wmk. 51, 52 *Perf. 13*

50 A19 4p red brown 30.00 3.25
a. Imperf.
51 A20 10p lilac 11.00 3.50
a. Imperf.
b. Horiz. pair, imperf. between 600.00

See Nos. 55, 64, 91, 97, 117, 129.

A21

A22

A23

Typo.; Engr. (3p, 5p, 8p)

1871-84 Wmk. 54 *Perf. 13*

52 A17 1p red 4.50 .20
a. Perf. 10 400.00 15.00
b. Perf. 13x10 15.00 .20
c. Horiz. pair imperf. between
53 A18 2p blue 7.00 .20
a. Imperf.
b. Horiz. pair, imperf. vert. *800.00*
c. Perf. 10 400.00 21.00
d. Perf. 13x10 4.50 .20
e. Perf. 12x13
f. Perf. 11x12 30.00
54 A15 3p green ('74) 21.00 1.75
a. Perf. 11 225.00 150.00
b. Perf. 12 *500.00* 250.00
c. Perf. 10x12 175.00 35.00
d. Perf. 12x11 135.00 50.00
e. Perf. 10 70.00 4.50
f. Perf. 13x10 135.00 13.00
55 A19 4p red brown ('77) 40.00 5.00
a. Perf. 10 300.00 50.00
b. Perf. 13x10 75.00 2.50
56 A11 5p dk grn, perf. 10 ('84) 15.00 7.50
a. Imperf.
b. Perf. 12 325.00 135.00
c. Perf. 10x12 24.00 9.00
d. Perf. 13x10
57 A21 6p lilac ('72) 35.00 .75
a. Imperf.
b. Perf. 13x10 50.00 1.75
c. Perf. 10 325.00 15.00
58 A13 8p yellow ('77) 90.00 16.00
a. Imperf.
b. Perf. 10 325.00 21.00
c. Perf. 13x10 225.00 18.00
59 A22 9p on 10p red brown, perf. 12 (Bk) 14.00 3.00
a. Double surcharge, blk & bl 195.00
b. Perf. 10x12 375.00 300.00
c. Perf. 10 12.00 3.25
d. Perf. 12x11 18.00 5.75
e. Perf. 11x12 18.00 5.75
f. Perf. 13 24.00 2.75
g. Perf. 11 40.00 7.25
h. Perf. 10x11 50.00 12.00
60 A23 1sh black ('76) 75.00 1.50
a. Imperf.
b. Perf. 13x10 275.00 3.25

c. Perf. 10 550.00 12.00
d. Perf. 11
Nos. 52-60 (9) 301.50 35.90

The surcharge on #59 measures 15mm.
See #66, 68. For overprints see #O1-O10.

Typo.; Engr. (3p, 5p, 8p)

1882-91 Wmk. 55 *Perf. 11x12*

61 A17 1p red 5.00 .20
a. Perf. 10 9.00 .20
b. Perf. 10x13 120.00 5.00
c. Perf. 10x12 325.00 85.00
d. Perf. 12x11 150.00
e. Perf. 10x11 *600.00* 150.00
f. Perf. 11 200.00
g. Perf. 13 135.00
62 A18 2p blue 5.00 .20
a. Perf. 10 12.00 .20
b. Perf. 13x10 90.00 2.50
c. Perf. 13 600.00 135.00
d. Perf. 12x10 325.00 70.00
e. Perf. 11 135.00
f. Perf. 12x11 135.00
g. Perf. 11x10 600.00 135.00
h. Perf. 12 275.00
63 A15 3p green 4.75 .35
a. Imperf., pair 200.00
b. Vert. pair, imperf. btwn. 225.00
c. Imperf. vert., pair
d. Double impression
e. Perf. 10 7.25 .35
f. Perf. 11 7.25 .35
g. Perf. 12 8.00 .35
h. Perf. 12x11 8.00 .40
i. Perf. 10x12 210.00 12.50
m. Perf. 10x11 20.00 1.25
n. Perf. 12x10 100.00 3.50
64 A19 4p red brown 27.50 1.40
a. Perf. 10 27.50 1.65
b. Perf. 10x12 150.00
c. Perf. 12 40.00
65 A11 5p dk blue green 7.25 .70
a. Imperf., pair 225.00
b. Perf. 11 13.00 .75
c. Perf. 10 13.00 .80
d. Perf. 12 13.00 .80
e. Perf. 10x12
f. 5p green, perf. 12x11 7.50 .75
g. 5p green, perf. 11x10 42.50 2.00
h. 5p green, perf. 12x10 75.00 3.25
i. 5p green, perf. 10x11 37.50 3.75
j. 5p green, perf. 11 3.75
66 A21 6p lilac, perf. 10 30.00 .75
a. Horiz. pair, imperf. between 825.00
b. Perf. 10x12 30.00 .75
c. Perf. 11x12 32.50 1.25
d. Perf. 12 95.00 2.75
e. Perf. 11x10 60.00 .75
f. Perf. 11 95.00 6.00
g. Perf. 10x13 325.00
67 A13 8p yellow, perf. 10 100.00 15.00
a. Perf. 11 90.00 13.00
b. Perf. 12 120.00 18.00
c. Perf. 10x12 100.00 22.50
68 A23 1sh black 60.00 .75
a. Perf. 10x13 12.00
b. Perf. 10 55.00 .75
c. Perf. 11 225.00 12.00
d. Perf. 10x12
Nos. 61-68 (8) 239.50 19.35

Nos. 63 and 65 exist with two types of watermark 55 - spacings of 1mm or 2mm between crown and NSW.

See No. 90. For surcharges and overprints see Nos. 92-94, O12-O19.

The 1, 2, 4, 6, 8p and 1sh have been reprinted on paper watermarked Large Crown and NSW. The 1, 2, 4p and 1sh are perforated 11x12, the 6p is perforated 10 and the 8p 11. All are overprinted "REPRINT," the 1sh in red and the others in black.

Perf. 11x12

1886-87 Typo. Wmk. 56

Bluish Revenue Stamp Paper

70 A17 1p scarlet 11.00 2.50
a. Perf. 10 18.00 4.50
71 A18 2p dark blue 15.00 4.50
a. Perf. 10 65.00 9.00

For overprint, see No. O20.

A24

Perf. 12 (#73-75), 12x10 (#72, 75A) and Compound

1885-86

"POSTAGE" in Black

72 A24 5sh green & vio 450.00 65.00
a. Perf. 10
73 A24 10sh rose & vio 1,250. 240.00
74 A24 £1 rose & vio 2,750. 1,000.
a. Perf. 13 2,100.

"POSTAGE" in Blue

Bluish Paper

75 A24 10sh rose & vio 175.00 35.00
b. Perf. 10 750.00 165.00

c. Perf. 12x11 375.00 *150.00*

White Paper

75A A24 £1 rose & vio 3,750. *1,750.*

For overprints, see Nos. O21-O23.

The 5sh with black overprint and the £1 with blue overprint have been reprinted on paper watermarked NSW. They are perforated 12x10 and are overprinted "REPRINT" in black.

1894 White Paper

"POSTAGE" in Blue

76 A24 10sh rose & violet 175.00 30.00
a. Double overprint

See No. 108B.

View of Sydney — A25

Emu — A26

Captain Cook — A27

Victoria and Coat of Arms — A28

Lyrebird A29

Kangaroo A30

1888-89 Wmk. 55 *Perf. 11x12*

77 A25 1p violet 3.50 .20
a. Perf. 12 4.50 .20
b. Perf. 12x11½ 16.00 .20
78 A26 2p blue 3.00 .20
a. Imperf., pair 125.00
b. Perf. 12 7.50 .20
c. Perf. 12x11½ 13.00 .20
79 A27 4p brown 9.00 .75
a. Perf. 12x11½ 15.00 .75
b. Perf. 12 15.00 .75
c. Perf. 11 450.00 135.00
d. Imperf.
80 A28 6p carmine rose 22.50 1.25
a. Perf. 12 15.00 1.25
b. Perf. 12x11½ 35.00 1.75
81 A29 8p red violet 11.00 .75
a. Perf. 12 9.00 1.50
b. Perf. 12x11½ 12.00 1.50
82 A30 1sh vio brown ('89) 14.00 .75
a. Imperf., pair 725.00
b. Perf. 12x11½ 16.00 .75
c. Perf. 12 24.00 .75
Nos. 77-82 (6) 63.00 3.90

First British settlement in Australia, cent.
For overprints see Nos. O24-O29.

1888 Wmk. 56 *Perf. 11x12*

83 A25 1p violet 11.00 1.40
84 A26 2p blue 65.00 6.75

See #104B-106C, 113-115, 118, 125-127, 130.

Map of Australia — A31

Governors Capt. Arthur Phillip (above) and Lord Carrington — A32

1888-89 Wmk. 53 *Perf. 10*

85 A31 5sh violet ('89) 240.00 55.00
86 A32 20sh ultra 375.00 175.00

See #88, 120. For overprints see #O30-O31.

1890 Wmk. 57 *Perf. 10*

87 A31 5sh violet 200.00 17.50
a. Perf. 11 200.00 22.50
b. Perf. 10x11 225.00 17.50
c. Perf. 12 360.00 25.00

Perf. 11x12

Wmk. 58

88 A32 20sh ultra 225.00 75.00
a. Perf. 11 250.00 57.50
b. Perf. 10 250.00 77.50
c. Perf. 12 350.00 135.00

For overprints see Nos. O32-O33.

"Australia" A33

Victoria A37

1890, Dec. 22 Wmk. 55 *Perf. 11x12*

89 A33 2½p ultra 2.00 .38
a. Perf. 12 11.50 .38
b. Perf. 12x11½ 67.50 *50.00*

For overprint see No. O35.

Type of 1856

1891 Engr. Wmk. 52 *Perf. 10*

90 A15 3p green 10.00 15.00
a. Double impression

Type of 1867

1893 Typo. *Perf. 11*

91 A20 10p lilac 15.00 6.00
a. Perf. 10 16.00 7.50
b. Perf. 11x10 or 10x11 24.00 12.00
c. Perf. 12x11 175.00 24.00

Types of 1862-84 Surcharged in Black:

SEVEN-PENCE

Halfpenny
a

HALFPENNY
b

1891, Jan. 5 Wmk. 55 *Perf. 11x12*

92 A17(a) ½p on 1p gray 1.25 1.25
a. Imperf.
b. Surcharge omitted
c. Double surcharge
93 A21(b) 7½p on 6p brown 3.50 1.65
a. Perf. 10 5.00 1.25
b. Perf. 11 5.00 1.25
c. Perf. 12 5.00 1.75
d. Perf. 10x12 4.25 1.75

Perf. 12x11½

94 A23(b) 12½p on 1sh red 6.00 4.00
a. Perf. 11x12 12.00 4.00
b. Perf. 10 12.00 4.00
c. Perf. 11 9.00 4.00
d. Perf. 12 10.00 4.00
Nos. 92-94 (3) 10.75 6.90

For overprints see Nos. O34, O36-O37.

1892

95 A37 ½p slate 1.25 .20
a. Perf. 12x11½ 1.25 .20
b. Perf. 12 1.25 .20
c. Perf. 10 27.50 .90
d. Perf. 10x12 150.00 10.50
e. Perf. 11 165.00 9.00

See #102, 109, 121. For overprint see #O38.

Types of 1867-71

1897 *Perf. 11x12*

96 A22 9p on 10p red brn (Bk) 8.00 3.25
a. 9p on 10p org brn (Bk) 8.00 3.25
b. Surcharge omitted 125.00
c. Double surcharge 125.00 100.00
d. Perf. 11 11.00 7.50
e. Perf. 12 9.00 7.50
97 A20 10p violet 12.00 5.50
a. Perf. 12x11½ 12.00 5.50
b. Perf. 11 13.00 6.00
c. Perf. 12 13.00 6.00

The surcharge on No. 96 measures 13½mm.
For overprints see Nos. O39-O40.

Seal A38

Victoria A39

A40

ONE PENNY:

Die I - The first pearl in the crown at the left is merged into the arch, the shading under the fleur-de-lis is indistinct, and the "s" of "WALES" is open.

Die II - The first pearl is circular, the vertical shading under the fleur-de-lis is clear, and the "s" of "WALES" not so open.

2½ PENCE:

Die I - There are 12 radiating lines in the star on the Queen's breast.

Die II - There are 16 radiating lines in the star. The eye is nearly full of color.

1897 *Perf. 12*

98 A38 1p rose red (II) 2.50 .20
a. Die I, perf. 11x12 3.00 .20
b. Imperf., pair 75.00
c. Imperf. horiz., pair 600.00
d. Die I, perf. 12x11½ 4.50 .20
e. Die I, perf. 12 7.50 .60
f. Die II, perf. 12x11½ 2.00 .20
g. Die II, perf. 11x12 3.00 .20
99 A39 2p deep blue 2.25 .20
a. Perf. 11x12 2.75 .20
b. Perf. 12x11½ 2.75 .20
100 A40 2½p dp purple (II) 4.25 1.10
a. Die I, perf. 12x11 6.50 1.10
b. Die I, perf. 11 7.50 1.90
c. Die I, perf. 11½x12 10.50 1.10
d. Die II, perf. 11x12 4.25 1.10
e. Die II, perf. 11½x12 8.00 1.10
Nos. 98-100 (3) 9.00 1.50

Sixtieth year of Queen Victoria's reign.
See Nos. 103-104, 110-112, 122-124.

Type of 1861

1897 Engr. Wmk. 53 *Perf. 11*

101 A16 5sh red violet 75.00 15.00
a. Horiz. pair, imperf. btwn. *3,000.*
b. Perf. 11x12 or 12x11 80.00 19.00
c. Perf. 12 90.00 15.00

Perf. 12x11½, 11½x12

1899, Oct. Typo. Wmk. 55

HALF PENNY:
Die I - Narrow "H" in "HALF."

102 A37 ½p blue green (I) 1.00 .20
a. Imperf., pair 60.00 45.00
103 A39 2p ultra 1.25 .20
a. Imperf., pair 55.00
104 A40 2½p dk blue (II) 2.50 .35
a. Imperf., pair 90.00
104B A27 4p org brown 9.00 .50
c. Imperf. pair 300.00
105 A28 6p emerald 37.50 3.25
a. Imperf., pair 235.00
106 A28 6p orange 11.00 .75
a. 6p yellow 14.00 .75
b. Imperf., pair 195.00
106C A29 8p magenta 9.00 2.00
Nos. 102-106C (7) 71.25 7.25

Lyrebird A41

"Australia" A42

1903 *Perf. 12x11½*

107 A41 2sh6p blue green 42.50 14.00

See Nos. 119, 131.

1903 Wmk. 70 *Perf. 12½*

108 A42 9p org brn & ultra 10.00 2.75
a. Perf. 11 750.00 425.00

See No. 128.

Type of 1885-86

1904 Wmk. 56 *Perf. 11*

Chalky Paper

"POSTAGE" in Blue

108B A24 10sh brt rose & violet 175.00 25.00
c. Perf. 12x11 140.00 25.00
d. Perf. 12 140.00 25.00

The watermark (NSW) of No. 108B is 20x7mm, with rounded angles in "N" and "W." On No. 75, the watermark is 21x7mm, with sharp angles in the "N" and "W."

HALF PENNY:
Die II - Wide "H" in "HALF."

Perf. 11, 11x12½, 12x11½ and Compound

1905-06 Wmk. 12

109 A37 ½p blue grn (II) 1.25 .40
a. ½p blue green (I) 2.75 .40
b. Booklet pane of 12
110 A38 1p car rose (II) 1.25 .20
a. Booklet pane of 6
b. Booklet pane of 12

111 A39 2p deep ultra 1.50 .20
112 A40 2½p dk blue (II) 2.50 .40
113 A27 4p org brown 8.25 .75
114 A28 6p orange 11.50 .75
a. 6p yellow 13.00 .75
b. Perf. 11 250.00
115 A29 8p magenta 16.00 1.50
117 A20 10p violet 12.50 2.25
118 A30 1sh vio brown 15.00 .75
119 A41 2sh6p blue green 27.50 12.00

Wmk. 199

120 A32 20sh ultra 200.00 75.00
Nos. 109-115,117-120 (11) 297.25 94.20

1906-07 **Wmk. 13**

121 A37 ½p green (I) 5.00 2.00
122 A38 1p rose (II) 6.00 1.50
123 A39 2p ultra 6.00 1.50
124 A40 2½p blue (II) 70.00
125 A27 4p org brown 15.00 10.00
126 A28 6p orange 40.00 25.00
127 A29 8p red violet 50.00 30.00
128 A42 9p org brn & ultra, perf. 12x12½ ('06) 8.00 2.00
a. Perf. 11 65.00 55.00
129 A20 10p violet 100.00
130 A30 1sh vio brown 50.00 20.00
131 A41 2sh6p blue green 100.00 75.00
Nos. 121-131 (11) 450.00
Nos. 121-123,125-128,130-131 (9) 167.00

Portions of some of the sheets on which the above are printed show the watermark "COMMONWEALTH OF AUSTRALIA." Stamps may also be found from portions of the sheet without watermark.

SEMI-POSTAL STAMPS

Allegory of Charity
SP1 SP2

Illustrations reduced.

1897, June **Wmk. 55** ***Perf. 11***

B1 SP1 1p (1sh) grn & brn 35.00 25.00
B2 SP2 2½p (2sh6p) rose, bl & gold 225.00 250.00

Diamond Jubilee of Queen Victoria.

The difference between the postal and face values of these stamps was donated to a fund for a home for consumptives.

REGISTRATION STAMPS

Queen Victoria — R1

Unwmk.

1856, Jan. 1 **Engr.** ***Imperf.***

F1 R1 (6p) orange & blue 600.00 150.00
F2 R1 (6p) red & blue 575.00 150.00
a. Frame printed on back 2,750. 1,350.

1860 ***Perf. 12, 13***

F3 R1 (6p) orange & blue 280.00 30.00
F4 R1 (6p) red & blue 265.00 30.00

Nos. F1 to F4 exist also on paper with papermaker's watermark in sheet.

1863 **Wmk. 49**

F5 R1 (6p) red & blue 75.00 15.00

Fifty varieties.

Nos. F1-F2 were reprinted on thin white wove unwatermarked paper and on thick yellowish wove unwatermarked paper; the former are usually overprinted "SPECIMEN."

No. F4 was reprinted on thin white wove unwatermarked paper; perf. 10 and overprinted "REPRINT" in black.

POSTAGE DUE STAMPS

D1

Perf. 10, 11, 11½, 12 and Compound

1891-92 **Typo.** **Wmk. 55**

J1 D1 ½p green, perf 10 3.25 1.50
J2 D1 1p green 4.00 .75
a. Perf. 12 20.00 3.75
J3 D1 2p green 5.00 .75
a. Perf. 10x12 17.00 4.00
J4 D1 3p green 10.00 2.50
J5 D1 4p green 10.00 .75
J6 D1 6p green, perf 10 15.00 2.25
J7 D1 8p green, perf 10 70.00 10.00
J8 D1 5sh green, perf 10 165.00 25.00
a. Perf. 11 225.00 85.00
J9 D1 10sh green, perf 12x10 225.00 50.00
a. Perf. 10 365.00
J10 D1 20sh green, perf 12x10 300.00
a. Perf. 10 350.00 70.00
b. Perf. 12 350.00
Nos. J1-J10 (10) 807.25 93.50

Nos. J1-J5 exist on both ordinary and chalky paper.

Used values for Nos. J8-J10 are for c-t-o copies.

OFFICIAL STAMPS

Regular Issues Overprinted in Black or Red **O S**

Perf. 10, 11, 12, 13 and Compound

1879-80 **Wmk. 54**

O1 A17 1p red 9.25 3.00
a. Perf. 10 325.00 45.00
b. Perf. 10x13 22.50 5.25
O2 A18 2p blue *15.00* 3.50
a. Perf. 11x12 250.00
b. Perf. 10 250.00 45.00
O3 A15 3p green (R) 300.00
O4 A15 3p green 225.00 65.00
a. Watermarked "6" 500.00
b. Double overprint
O5 A19 4p red brown 225.00 11.50
a. Perf. 10x13 300.00 14.00
O6 A11 5p dark green 24.00 13.00
O7 A21 6p lilac 300.00 10.00
a. Perf. 10 65.00
b. Perf. 10x13
O8 A13 8p yellow (R) *1,000.* 200.00
O9 A13 8p yellow 22.50
a. Perf. 10 375.00 115.00
O10 A23 1sh black (R) 300.00 11.00
a. Perf. 10 24.00
b. Perf. 10x13 30.00

1880 **Wmk. 53**

O11 A16 5sh lilac, perf. 11 265.00 75.00
a. Double overprint
b. Perf. 10 375.00 150.00
c. Perf. 12x10 325.00 130.00
d. Perf. 13 465.00 82.50
e. Perf. 10x12

1881 **Wmk. 55**

O12 A17 1p red 6.00 .75
a. Perf. 10x13 225.00
O13 A18 2p blue 6.50 1.00
a. Perf. 10x13 360.00 100.00
O14 A15 3p green 6.00 1.65
a. Double overprint
b. Perf. 12 240.00 130.00
c. Perf. 11
O15 A19 4p red brown 11.00 2.25
a. Perf. 10x12 90.00
b. Perf. 12 360.00 225.00
O16 A11 5p dark green 12.00 5.00
a. Perf. 12 140.00
b. Perf. 10x12 400.00 130.00
O17 A21 6p lilac 22.50 4.00
a. Perf. 12 60.00
b. Perf. 11x12 72.50 16.00
O18 A13 8p yellow 27.50 9.50
a. Double overprint
b. Perf. 12 240.00 50.00
O19 A23 1sh black (R) 27.50 *5.00*
a. Double overprint
b. Perf. 10x13 70.00
c. Perf. 11
Nos. O12-O19 (8) 119.00 29.15

Beware of other red overprints on watermark 55 stamps.

1881 **Wmk. 56**

O20 A17 1p red 32.50 10.00

1887-90

O21 A24 10sh on #75 *350.00*
O22 A24 £1 on #75A *3,250. 3,250.*

No. 75 Overprinted **O S**

1889

O23 A24 10sh rose & vio *1,950. 600.00*
a. Perf. 10 *3,500. 2,250.*

Overprinted **O S**

1888-89 **Wmk. 55**

O24 A25 1p violet 1.50 .20
a. Overprinted "O" only
O25 A26 2p blue 1.50 .20
O26 A27 4p red brown 6.00 1.50
O27 A28 6p carmine 8.00 2.00
O28 A29 8p red lilac 14.00 4.00
O29 A30 1sh vio brown 14.00 2.00
a. Double overprint
Nos. O24-O29 (6) 45.00 9.90

Wmk. 53

O30 A31 5sh violet (R) *700.00 450.00*
O31 A32 20sh ultra *1,250.*

1890 **Wmk. 57**

O32 A31 5sh violet *150.00* 60.00
a. Perf. 12 625.00

Wmk. 58

O33 A32 20sh ultra *2,000.*

Centenary of the founding of the Colony (Nos. O24-O33).

1891 **Wmk. 55**

O34 A17(a) ½p on 1p gray & black 47.50 14.00
a. Double overprint
O35 A33 2½p ultra 7.00 3.25
O36 A21(b) 7½p on 6p brn & black 35.00 12.00
O37 A23(b) 12½p on 1sh red & black 60.00 32.50
Nos. O34-O37 (4) 149.50 61.75

1892

O38 A37 ½p gray 5.50 4.00

1894 **Wmk. 54**

O39 A22 9p on 10p red brn 300.00 350.00

Wmk. 52

O40 A20 10p lilac, perf. 10 225.00 200.00
a. Perf. 11x10 350.00 325.00

The official stamps became obsolete on Dec. 31, 1894. In Aug., 1895, sets of 32 varieties of "O.S." stamps, together with some envelopes and postal cards, were placed on sale at the Sydney post office at £2 per set. These sets contained most of the varieties listed above and a few which are not known in the original issues.

An obliteration consisting of the letters G.P.O. or N.S.W. in three concentric ovals was lightly applied to the center of each block of four stamps. It is understood that the earlier stamps and many of the overprints were reprinted to make up these sets.

QUEENSLAND

ˈkwēnz-ˌland

LOCATION — Northeastern part of Australia
GOVT. — British Crown Colony
AREA — 670,500 sq. mi.
POP. — 498,129 (1901)
CAPITAL — Brisbane

Originally a part of New South Wales, Queensland was constituted a separate colony in 1859. It was one of the six British Colonies that united in 1901 to form the Commonwealth of Australia.

12 Pence = 1 Shilling
20 Shillings = 1 Pound

Values for unused stamps are for examples with original gum as defined in the catalogue introduction. Very fine examples of Nos. 4-73, 84-125, 128-140, and F1-F3b will have perforations touching the design on at least one or more sides due to the narrow spacing of the stamps on the plates. Stamps with perfs clear of the design on all four sides are scarce and will command higher prices.

Watermarks

Wmk. 5- Small Star

Wmk. 6- Large Star

Wmk. 12- Crown and Single-lined A

Wmk. 13- Crown and Double-lined A

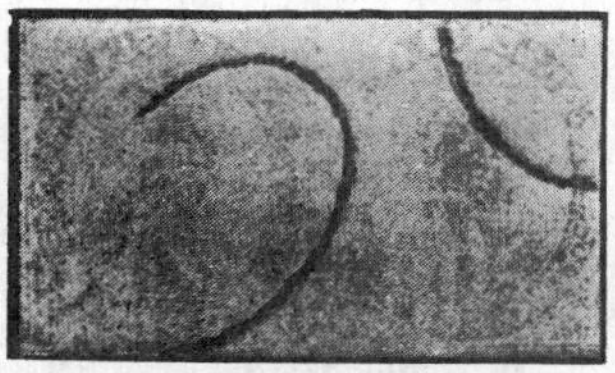

Wmk. 65- "Queensland Postage Stamps" in Sheet in Script Capitals

Wmks. 66 & 67- "Queensland" in Large Single-lined Roman Capitals in the Sheet and Short-pointed Star to Each Stamp (Stars Vary Slightly in Size and Shape)

Wmk. 68- Crown and Q

Wmk. 69- Large Crown and Q

There are two varieties of the watermark 68, differing slightly in the position and shape of the crown and the tongue of the "Q."

Wmk. 70- V and Crown

Queen Victoria — A1

Wmk. 6

1860, Nov. 1 Engr. *Imperf.*

1	A1	1p deep rose	3,000.	750.
2	A1	2p deep blue	6,250.	2,250.
3	A1	6p deep green	4,250.	750.

Clean-Cut Perf. 14 to 16

4	A1	1p deep rose	1,750.	225.
5	A1	2p deep blue	475.	100.
6	A1	6p deep green	475.	60.

Clean-Cut Perf. 14 to 16

1860-61 Wmk. 5

6A	A1	2p blue	525.00	100.00
b.		Horiz. pair, imperf. vert		875.00
6D	A1	3p brown ('61)	275.00	50.00
6E	A1	6p deep green	550.00	50.00
6F	A1	1sh gray violet	475.00	65.00

Regular Perf. 14

6H	A1	1p rose	125.00	35.00
6I	A1	2p deep blue	325.00	50.00

Rough Perf. 14 to 16

7	A1	1p deep rose	80.00	35.00
8	A1	2p blue	90.00	35.00
9	A1	3p brown ('61)	55.00	30.00
a.		Horiz. pair, imperf. vert.	2,000.	
10	A1	6p deep green	150.00	25.00
a.		6p yellow green	200.00	25.00
11	A1	1sh dull violet	400.00	85.00

Thick Yellowish Paper

Square Perf. 12½ to 13

1862-67 Unwmk.

12	A1	1p Indian red	325.00	70.00
13	A1	1p orange ('63)	60.00	15.00
a.		Perf. 13, round holes ('67)	60.00	15.00
b.		Horiz. pair, imperf. between		
c.		Imperf., pair	—	525.00
14	A1	2p deep blue	40.00	17.00
a.		2p pale blue	90.00	30.00
b.		Perf. 13, round holes ('67)	90.00	30.00
c.		Imperf., pair	—	500.00
e.		Horiz. pair, imperf. between	—	*900.00*
f.		Vert. pair, imperf. between	*1,200*	
15	A1	3p brown ('63)	55.00	30.00
a.		Imperf.		
b.		Perf. 13, round holes ('67)		
16	A1	6p yellow grn ('63)	80.00	15.00
a.		6p green	125.00	25.00
b.		Perf. 13, round holes ('67)	125.00	25.00
c.		Imperf., pair	—	500.00
d.		Horiz. pair, imperf. between	—	950.00
17	A1	1sh gray ('63)	125.00	25.00
b.		Imperf. horizontally		
c.		Horiz. pair, imperf. between	—	950.00
d.		Perf. 13, round holes ('67)		

White Wove Paper

1865 Wmk. 5 *Rough Perf. 13*

18	A1	1p orange	55.00	20.00
a.		Horiz. pair, imperf. vert.	425.00	
19	A1	2p light blue	50.00	16.00
a.		Vert. pair, imperf. horiz.	900.00	
b.		Half used as 1p on cover		2,000.
20	A1	6p yellow green	135.00	24.00
		Nos. 18-20 (3)	240.00	60.00

Perf. 13, Round Holes

1866 Wmk. 65

21	A1	1p orange vermilion	160.00	25.00
22	A1	2p blue	55.00	18.00
b.		Diagonal half used as 1p on cover		—

1866 Unwmk. Litho. *Perf. 13*

23	A1	4p lilac	90.00	18.00
a.		4p slate	140.00	20.00
24	A1	5sh pink	225.00	50.00
b.		Vert. pair, imperf between	—	725.00

Wmk. 66, 67

1868-74 Engr. *Perf. 13*

25	A1	1p orange ('71)	45.00	5.00
26	A1	2p blue	45.00	2.50
27	A1	3p grnsh brn ('71)	85.00	5.00
a.		3p brown	87.50	3.50
b.		3p olive brown	87.50	3.50
28	A1	6p yel green ('71)	125.00	8.50
a.		6p deep green	175.00	11.00
30	A1	1sh grnsh gray ('72)	375.00	40.00
31	A1	1sh violet ('74)	200.00	20.00

Perf. 12

32	A1	1p orange	275.00	35.00
33	A1	2p blue		37.50
34	A1	3p brown	275.00	150.00
35	A1	6p deep green	900.00	50.00
36	A1	1sh violet	—	50.00

Perf. 13x12

36A	A1	1p orange		250.00
37	A1	2p blue	*1,500.*	100.00
37A	A1	3p brown		*1,250.*

The reprints are perforated 13 and the colors differ slightly from those of the originals.

1868-75 Wmk. 68 *Perf. 13*

38	A1	1p orange	45.00	5.00
39	A1	1p rose ('74)	50.00	9.00
40	A1	2p blue	35.00	2.50
b.		Imperf., pair	315.00	
41	A1	3p brown ('75)	65.00	14.00
42	A1	6p yel green ('69)	100.00	7.50
a.		6p apple green	135.00	10.00
b.		6p deep green	125.00	10.00
43	A1	1sh violet ('75)	*150.00*	26.00
		Nos. 38-43 (6)	*445.00*	64.00

No. 40 exists in vert. pair, imperf. btwn.

1876-78 *Perf. 12*

44	A1	1p orange	35.00	3.00
a.		Imperf.	300.00	
45	A1	1p rose	45.00	11.00
46	A1	2p blue	22.50	1.50
a.		Imperf.		
47	A1	3p brown	60.00	10.00
48	A1	6p yellow green	125.00	5.00
a.		6p apple green	135.00	4.75
b.		6p deep green	135.00	4.75
49	A1	1sh violet	42.50	5.00
		Nos. 44-49 (6)	330.00	35.50

#44, 49 exist in vertical pairs, imperf. between.

Perf. 13x12

49B	A1	1p orange		165.00
49C	A1	2p blue	*1,800.*	200.00
49D	A1	4p yellow		
49E	A1	6p deep green		200.00

The reprints are perforated 12 and are in paler colors than the originals.

1879 Unwmk. *Perf. 12*

50	A1	6p pale emerald	200.00	25.00
a.		Horiz. pair, imperf. vert.		650.00

A2

A3

1875-81 Litho. Wmk. 68 *Perf. 13*

50B	A1	4p yellow ('75)	800.00	42.50

Perf. 12

51	A1	4p buff ('76)	600.00	22.50
a.		4p yellow	600.00	22.50
52	A1	2sh pale blue ('81)	60.00	12.00
a.		2sh deep blue	67.50	12.00
b.		Imperf.		
53	A2	2sh6p lt red ('81)	110.00	30.00
54	A1	5sh orange brn ('81)	150.00	27.50
a.		5sh fawn	150.00	27.50
55	A1	10sh brown ('81)	325.00	110.00
a.		Imperf., pair	550.00	
56	A1	20sh rose ('81)	650.00	90.00
		Nos. 50B-56 (7)	2,695.	334.50

Nos. 53-56, 62-64, 74-83 with pen (revenue) cancellations removed are often offered as unused.

1879-81 Typo. Wmk. 68 *Perf. 12*

57	A3	1p rose red	9.50	1.50
a.		1p red orange	9.50	1.75
b.		1p brown orange	30.00	5.50
c.		"QOEENSLAND"	110.00	32.50
d.		Imperf.		
e.		Vert. pair, imperf. horiz.		90.00
58	A3	2p gray blue	22.50	.70
a.		2p deep ultra	27.50	.80
b.		Imperf.		
c.		"PENGE"		70.00
d.		"TW" joined	25.00	1.10
e.		Vert. pair, imperf. horiz.	450.00	
59	A3	4p orange yellow	100.00	10.00
a.		Imperf.		
60	A3	6p yellow green	55.00	5.00
a.		Imperf.		
61	A3	1sh pale violet ('81)	50.00	5.00
a.		1sh deep violet	45.00	3.75
		Nos. 57-61 (5)	237.00	22.20

The stamps of type A3 were electrotyped from plates made up of groups of four types, differing in minor details. Two dies were used for the 1p and 2p, giving eight varieties for each of those values.

Nos. 59-60 exist imperf. vertically.

For surcharge see No. 65.

Moire on Back

1878-79 Unwmk.

62	A3	1p brown org ('79)	400.00	60.00
a.		"QOEENSLAND"		2,000.
63	A3	2p deep ultra ('79)	500.00	30.00
a.		"PENGE"	4,750.	725.00
64	A1	1sh red violet	100.00	47.50
		Nos. 62-64 (3)	1,000.	137.50

No. 57b Surcharged Vertically in Black

Half-penny

1881 Wmk. 68

65	A3	½p on 1p brn org	175.00	95.00
a.		"QOEENSLAND"	1,000.	825.00

A4

A5

1882-83 Typo. *Perf. 12*

66	A4	1p pale red	5.75	.20
a.		1p rose	5.75	.20
b.		Imperf. pair	30.00	30.00
67	A4	2p gray blue	9.00	.20
a.		2p deep ultra	9.00	.20
b.		Imperf.		
68	A4	4p yellow ('83)	20.00	1.00
a.		"PENGE"	125.00	45.00
b.		Imperf., pair		150.00
69	A4	6p yellow green	10.00	.70
70	A4	1sh violet ('83)	12.00	1.00
		Nos. 66-70 (5)	56.75	3.10

There are eight minor varieties of the 1p, twelve of the 2p and four each of the other values. On the 1p there is a period after "PENNY." On all values the lines of shading on the neck extend from side to side.

Compare design A4 with A6, A10, A11, A15, A16.

1883 *Perf. 9½x12*

71	A4	1p rose	160.00	25.00
72	A4	2p gray blue	350.00	55.00
73	A4	1sh pale violet	225.00	30.00
		Nos. 71-73 (3)	735.00	110.00

Beware of faked perfs.

See Nos. 94, 95, 100.

Wmk. 68 Twice Sideways

1882-85 Engr. *Perf. 12*

Thin Paper

74	A5	2sh ultra	60.00	18.00
75	A5	2sh6p vermilion	50.00	22.50
76	A5	5sh car rose ('85)	50.00	25.00
77	A5	10sh brown	95.00	42.50
78	A5	£1 dark green ('83)	165.00	75.00
		Nos. 74-78 (5)	420.00	183.00

The 2sh, 5sh and £1 exist imperf.

There are two varieties of the watermark on Nos. 74-78, as in the 1879-81 issue.

Copies with revenue cancels sell for $3.25-6.50.

1886 Wmk. 69 *Perf. 12*

Thick Paper

79	A5	2sh ultra	100.00	35.00
80	A5	2sh6p vermilion	40.00	22.50
81	A5	5sh car rose	37.50	30.00
82	A5	10sh dark brown	100.00	40.00
83	A5	£1 dark green	175.00	60.00
		Nos. 79-83 (5)	452.50	187.50

High value stamps with cancellations removed are offered as unused.

Copies with revenue cancels sell for $3.25-6.50.

See Nos. 126-127, 141-144.

A6

Redrawn

1887-89 Typo. Wmk. 68 *Perf. 12*

84	A6	1p orange	4.50	.20
a.		Imperf., pair	40.00	60.00
85	A6	2p gray blue	9.00	.20
a.		2p deep ultra	11.50	.25
86	A6	2sh red brown ('89)	65.00	20.00

Perf. 9½x12

88	A6	2p deep ultra	*250.00*	110.00
		Nos. 84-88 (4)	*328.50*	130.40

The 1p has no period after the value.

In the redrawn stamps the shading lines on the neck are not completed at the left, leaving an irregular white line along that side.

Variety "LA" joined exists on Nos. 84-86, 88, 90, 91, 93, 97, 98, 102.

On No. 88 beware of faked perfs.

A7

A8

1890-92 *Perf. 12½, 13*

89	A7	½p green	4.50	.30
90	A6	1p orange red	3.00	.20
91	A6	2p gray blue	5.00	.20
92	A8	2½p rose carmine	11.00	.35
93	A6	3p brown ('92)	9.00	2.00
94	A4	4p orange	15.00	1.25
a.		4p yellow	16.00	1.25
b.		"PENGE"	65.00	27.50
95	A4	6p green	11.00	2.00
96	A6	2sh red brown	40.00	8.25
		Nos. 89-96 (8)	98.50	14.55

The ½p and 3p exist imperf.

1895 Wmk. 69 *Perf. 12½, 13*

Thick Paper

98	A6	1p orange	3.50	.50
99	A6	2p gray blue	3.50	.50

Perf. 12

100	A4	1sh pale violet	17.00	3.75
		Nos. 98-100 (3)	24.00	4.75

Queensland stamps can be mounted in the Scott Australia album.

A9

A10

Moiré on Back

1895 Unwmk. *Perf. 12½, 13*

101 A9	½p green		1.90	1.90
a.	Without moire		55.00	
102 A6	1p orange		2.25	2.25
a.	"PE" missing			

Wmk. 68

103 A9	½p green	2.25	.35
a.	½p deep green	1.65	.35
b.	Printed on both sides	60.00	
104 A10	1p orange	2.50	.20
105 A10	2p gray blue	3.25	.25

Wmk. 69

Thick Paper

106 A9	½p green	1.90	1.90

1895-96 Unwmk. Thin Paper

Crown and Q Faintly Impressed

107 A9	½p green	2.75	.80
108 A10	1p orange	4.00	1.10
108A A6	2p gray blue	11.00	

A11

A12

A13

1895-96 Wmk. 68

109 A11	1p red	8.50	.20
110 A12	2½p rose	9.00	1.75
111 A13	5p violet brown	12.50	1.75
111A A11	6p yellow green		

A14

A15

A16

A17

A18

A19

TWO PENCE:

Type I - Point of bust does not touch frame.

Type II - First redrawing. The top of the crown, the chignon and the point of the bust touch the frame. The forehead is completely shaded.

Type III - Second redrawing. The top of crown does not touch the frame, though the chignon and the point of the bust do. The forehead and the bridge of the nose are not shaded.

1897-1900 *Perf. 12½, 13*

112 A14	½p deep green	3.50	2.00
a.	Perf. 12		150.00
113 A15	1p red	1.50	.20
a.	Perf. 12	1.75	.20
114 A16	2p gray blue (I)	2.00	.20
a.	Perf. 12		6.00
115 A17	2½p rose	17.00	6.25
116 A17	2½p violet, *blue*	8.50	.70
117 A15	3p brown	8.00	.70
118 A15	4p bright yellow	8.00	.70
119 A18	5p violet brown	7.50	1.25
120 A15	6p yellow green	9.00	.70
121 A19	1sh lilac	13.00	1.65
a.	1sh light violet	16.00	1.65
122 A19	2sh turq blue	32.50	6.00
	Nos. 112-122 (11)	110.50	20.35

1898 *Serrated Roulette 13*

123 A15	1p scarlet	5.00	2.00
a.	Serrated and perf. 13	6.00	3.00
b.	Serrated in black	10.00	10.00
c.	Serrated without color and in black	9.00	9.00
d.	Same as "b," and perf. 13	85.00	
e.	Same as "c," and perf. 13	110.00	

Victoria — A20

"Australia" — A21

1899 Typo. *Perf. 12, 12½, 13*

124 A20	½p blue green	1.00	.25

Unwatermarked stamps are proofs.

1903 Wmk. 70 *Perf. 12½*

NINE PENCE:
Type I- "QUEENSLAND" 18x1½mm.
Type II- "QUEENSLAND" 17½x1¼mm.

125 A21	9p org brn & ultra, type II	12.00	3.00
a.	Type I	13.00	3.50

See No. 128.

Type of 1882

Perf. 12, 12½, 13

1906 Litho. Wmk. 68

126 A5	5sh rose	150.00	82.50
127 A5	£1 dark green	500.00	150.00

1907 Typo. Wmk. 13 *Perf. 12½*

128 A21	9p yel brn & ultra, type I	15.00	3.00
a.	Type II	27.50	4.25
b.	Perf. 11, type II		240.00

1907 Wmk. 68 *Perf. 12½, 13*

129 A16	2p ultra, type II	9.00	1.25
129A A18	5p dark brown	9.00	1.90
b.	5p olive brown	9.00	1.90

1907-09 Wmk. 12

130 A20	½p deep green	1.25	.30
131 A15	1p red	1.25	.20
a.	Imperf., pair	200.00	
132 A16	2p ultra, type II	7.50	.20
133 A16	2p ultra, type III	2.25	.20
134 A15	3p pale brown	10.00	1.00
135 A15	4p bright yellow	12.00	2.75
136 A15	4p gray black ('09)	12.00	1.65
137 A18	5p brown	8.50	1.65
a.	5p olive brown	12.50	3.25
138 A15	6p yellow green	12.00	2.50
139 A19	1sh violet	15.00	3.75
140 A19	2sh turquoise bl	35.00	9.00

Wmk. 12 Sideways

Litho.

141 A5	2sh6p deep orange	50.00	37.50
142 A5	5sh rose	55.00	37.50
143 A5	10sh dark brown	100.00	35.00
144 A5	£1 blue green	225.00	135.00
	Nos. 130-144 (15)	546.75	268.20

POSTAL FISCAL STAMPS

Authorised for postal use from Jan. 1, 1880. Authorization withdrawn July 1, 1892.

Used values are for examples with postal cancellations used from Jan. 1, 1880 through June 30, 1892.

Beware of copies with a pen cancellation removed and a fake postmark added.

Queen Victoria
PF1 PF2

1866-74 Engr. Unwmk. *Perf. 13*

AR1	PF1	1p blue	30.00	8.00
AR2	PF1	6p violet	30.00	*35.00*
AR3	PF1	1sh green	35.00	10.00
AR4	PF1	2sh brown	100.00	50.00
AR5	PF1	2sh 6p red	100.00	37.50
AR6	PF1	5sh yellow	300.00	75.00
AR7	PF1	6sh yellow		
AR8	PF1	10sh yellow green	400.00	*175.00*
AR9	PF1	20sh rose	500.00	*175.00*

Wmk. 68

AR10	PF1	1p blue	20.00	20.00
AR11	PF1	6p violet	27.50	*30.00*
AR12	PF1	6p blue	27.50	17.50
AR13	PF1	1sh green	35.00	17.50
AR14	PF1	2sh brown	100.00	35.00
AR15	PF1	5sh yellow	300.00	75.00
AR16	PF1	10sh yellow green	400.00	*110.00*
AR17	PF1	20sh rose	500.00	*175.00*

1872-73 Wmk. 69 *Perf. 13*

AR18	PF2	1p lilac	12.00	8.00
AR19	PF2	6p brown	25.00	12.50
AR20	PF2	1sh green	35.00	15.00
AR21	PF2	2sh blue	50.00	12.50
AR22	PF2	2sh 6p vermilion	75.00	30.00
AR23	PF2	5sh orange brn	125.00	30.00
AR24	PF2	10sh brown	300.00	*85.00*
AR25	PF2	20sh rose	500.00	*150.00*

Perf. 12

AR26	PF2	1p lilac	12.00	8.00
AR27	PF2	6p brown	25.00	12.50
AR28	PF2	2sh blue	50.00	12.50
AR29	PF2	2sh 6p vermilion	75.00	30.00
AR30	PF2	5sh orange brn	125.00	30.00
AR31	PF2	10sh brown	300.00	*85.00*
AR32	PF2	20sh rose	500.00	*150.00*

Unwmk.

Perf. 13

AR33	PF2	1p lilac	15.00	10.00
AR34	PF2	6p lilac	75.00	37.50
AR35	PF2	6p brown	25.00	12.50
AR36	PF2	1sh green	35.00	15.00
AR37	PF2	2sh blue	55.00	60.00
AR38	PF2	2sh 6p vermilion	100.00	40.00
AR39	PF2	5sh orange brn	150.00	50.00
AR40	PF2	10sh brown	300.00	100.00
AR41	PF2	20sh rose	500.00	125.00

Perf. 12

AR42	PF2	1p lilac	15.00	10.00
AR43	PF2	6p lilac	90.00	50.00
AR44	PF2	6p brown	50.00	40.00
AR45	PF2	1sh green	35.00	15.00
AR46	PF2	2sh blue	55.00	60.00
AR47	PF2	2sh 6p vermilion	100.00	40.00
AR48	PF2	5sh orange brn	150.00	50.00
AR49	PF2	10sh brown	300.00	100.00
AR50	PF2	20sh rose	500.00	125.00

Queen Victoria — PF3

1878-79 Engr. Unwmk. *Perf. 12*

AR51	PF3	1p violet	50.00	15.00

Wmk. 68

AR52	PF3	1p violet	20.00	10.00

SEMI-POSTAL STAMPS

Queen Victoria, Colors and Bearers — SP1

SP2

Perf. 12, 12½

1900, June 19 Wmk. 68

B1 SP1	1p red lilac	90.00	90.00
B2 SP2	2p deep violet	225.00	210.00

These stamps were sold at 1sh and 2sh respectively. The difference was applied to a patriotic fund in connection with the Boer War.

REGISTRATION STAMPS

R1

Clean-Cut Perf. 14 to 16

1861 Wmk. 5 Engr.

F1 R1	(6p) olive yellow	400.00	75.00
a.	Horiz. pair, imperf. vert.		*4,500.*

Rough Perf. 14 to 16

F2 R1	(6p) dull yellow	50.00	35.00

1864 *Perf. 12½ to 13*

F3 R1	(6p) golden yellow	80.00	40.00
a.	Imperf.		
b.	Double impression		900.00

The reprints are watermarked with a small truncated star and perforated 12.

SOUTH AUSTRALIA

'sauth o-'strāl-yə

LOCATION — Central part of southern Australia
GOVT. — British Colony
AREA — 380,070 sq. mi.
POP. — 358,346 (1901)
CAPITAL — Adelaide

South Australia was one of the six British colonies that united in 1901 to form the Commonwealth of Australia.

12 Pence = 1 Shilling
20 Shillings = 1 Pound

Values for unused stamps are for examples with original gum as defined in the catalogue introduction. Very fine examples of Nos. 10-60 and O1-O60 will have perforations slightly cutting into the framelines or design on one or more sides due to the narrow spacing of the stamps on the plates. Stamps with perfs clear on all sides are scarce to rare and will command higher to substantially higher prices.

South Australia stamps can be mounted in the Scott Australia album.

Watermarks

Wmk. 6- Star with Long Narrow Points

Wmk. 7- Star with Short Broad Points

Wmk. 70- Crown and V

Wmk. 72- Crown and SA

Wmk. 73- Crown and SA, Letters Close

Wmk. 74- Crown and Single-lined A

Queen Victoria — A1

1855-56 Engr. Wmk. 6 *Imperf.*
London Print

1 A1 1p dark green 2,750. 375.
2 A1 2p dull carmine 600. 80.
3 A1 6p deep blue 2,500. 150.
4 A1 1sh violet ('56) *4,500.*

No. 4 was never put in use. Nos. 1 and 3 without watermark are proofs.

1856-59 Local Print

5 A1 1p deep yel grn ('58) *6,000.* 550.00
a. 1p yellow green ('58) — 550.00
6 A1 2p blood red 1,500. 80.00
a. Printed on both sides
b. 2p orange red ('56) — 90.00
7 A1 2p pale red ('57) 700.00 60.00
a. Printed on both sides *650.00*
8 A1 6p slate blue ('57) 2,500. 175.00
9 A1 1sh orange ('57) 4,750. 350.00
a. Printed on both sides
b. 1sh red orange — 375.00

1858-59 *Rouletted*

10 A1 1p yellow grn ('59) 475.00 45.00
a. Horiz. pair, imperf. between
b. 1p pale yellow green 500.00 50.00
11 A1 2p pale red ('59) 125.00 22.50
a. Printed on both sides
12 A1 6p slate blue 375.00 27.50
13 A1 1sh orange ('59) 1,250. 35.00
c. Printed on both sides *1,400.*

See Nos. 14-16, 19-20, 25-26, 28-29, 32, 35-36, 41-43, 47, 51-52, 69-70, 73, 113, 118. For overprints see Nos. O1-O2, O5, O7, O9, O11-O13, O17, O20, O27, O30, O32, O39-O40, O42, O52, O76, O85.

A2

A3

Surcharge on #22-24, 34, 49-50

TEN PENCE

1860-69 *Rouletted*

14 A1 1p dull blue green 50.00 22.50
a. 1p deep green 250.00 65.00
b. 1p bright green 250.00 65.00
15 A1 1p sage green 72.50 27.50
16 A1 2p vermilion ('62) 50.00 4.00
a. Horiz. pair, imperf. btwn. 700.00 350.00
b. Rouletted and perf. all around *700.00*
c. Printed on both sides 500.00
18 A2 4p dull violet ('67) 75.00 17.00
19 A1 6p grnsh blue ('63) 65.00 3.75
20 A1 6p dull blue 85.00 3.75
a. 6p sky blue 125.00 6.50
b. 6p Prussian blue 750.00 50.00
c. Horiz. pair, imperf. between 850.00
d. 6p ultramarine 60.00 3.75
e. Horiz. pair, imperf. btwn. (#20f) — 425.00
f. 6p indigo blue — 60.00
g. Rouletted and perf. all around (#20f) — *350.00*
21 A3 9p gray lilac ('69) 55.00 9.00
a. Double impression
c. Rouletted and perf. all around *1,750.* *275.00*
22 A3 10p on 9p red orange (Bl) ('66) 125.00 25.00
23 A3 10p on 9p yel (Bl) ('67) 165.00 21.00
24 A3 10p on 9p yel (Blk) ('69) 1,300. 32.50
a. Inverted surcharge — *2,750.*
c. Printed on both sides — 1,100.
d. Rouletted x perf. 10 —
24E A1 1sh red brown 135.00 13.00
f. Vert. pair, imperf. btwn. — 1,250.
25 A1 1sh lake brown ('65) 135.00 13.00
a. Horiz. pair, imperf. btwn. — 425.00
26 A1 1sh brown ('63) 140.00 16.00
a. 1sh chestnut ('64) 150.00 12.00
27 A2 2sh carmine ('67) 165.00 27.50
a. Horiz. pair, imperf. btwn. — 1,000.

There are six varieties of the surcharge "TEN PENCE" in this and subsequent issues.

Nos. 16b, 20g, 21c, 28a, 32c, 33a are rouletted remainders that were later perforated.

See Nos. 31, 33, 46, 48, 53, 63, 68, 72, 74, 112, 113B, 119-120. For overprints see Nos. O4, O6, O8, O10, O16, O18, O21, O26, O29, O31, O33, O37-O38, O41B, O43, O53. For surcharges see Nos. 34, 44-45, 49-50, 59, 67, 71, O19, O28, O36, O41. Compare with design A6a.

1867-72 *Perf. 11½ to 12½xRoulette*

28 A1 1p blue green 225.00 32.50
a. Rouletted and perf. all around 650.00
29 A1 1p yellow green 140.00 20.00
31 A2 4p dull violet ('68) 1,500. 110.00
a. 4p purple ('69) — 110.00
32 A1 6p Prus blue 450.00 21.00
a. 6p sky blue 500.00 17.50
b. Printed on both sides
c. Rouletted and perf. all around 300.00
d. 6p indigo blue ('69) 475.00 25.00
33 A3 9p gray lilac ('72) 275.00
34 A3 10p on 9p yel (Bl) ('68) 800.00 35.00
a. Printed on both sides — 500.00
35 A1 1sh chestnut ('68) 275.00 30.00
36 A1 1sh lake brown ('69) 275.00 25.00

#44-45 **3-PENCE**

Perf. 10, 11½, 12½ and Compound
1867-74

41 A1 1p yellow green 45.00 17.50
42 A1 1p blue green 60.00 12.50
a. Printed on both sides
43 A1 2p vermilion 1,250.
44 A2 3p on 4p dp bl (Blk) ('70) 60.00 5.50
a. 3p on 4p ultra, black surcharge 125.00 5.50
b. Surcharge omitted *20,000.* *5,000.*
c. Double surcharge 4,500.
d. Surcharged on both sides 3,250.
45 A2 3p on 4p sl bl (Red) ('70) 425.00 32.50
46 A2 4p dull violet 60.00 9.00
47 A1 6p dark blue 90.00 8.00
a. 6p sky blue 350.00 9.25
b. Imperf. vert., pair

48 A3 9p red lilac ('72) 47.50 5.00
a. 9p violet 115.00 5.50
b. 9p red violet 115.00 5.50
c. Printed on both sides 350.00
49 A3 10p on 9p yel (Bl) ('68) 1,500. 26.00
50 A3 10p on 9p yel (Blk) ('69) 150.00 21.00
51 A1 1sh deep brown 150.00 12.00
52 A1 1sh red brown 100.00 12.00
a. 1sh chestnut 125.00 12.50
53 A2 2sh carmine 60.00 7.50
a. Printed on both sides 400.00
b. Horiz. pair, imperf. vert.

See Nos. 67, O14, O28, O36.

A6

A6a

1868 Typo. Wmk. 72 *Rouletted*

54 A6a 2p orange red 65.00 4.00
a. Imperf.
b. Printed on both sides 275.00
c. Horiz. pair, imperf. btwn. 275.00

1869 *Perf. 11½ to 12½xRoulette*

55 A6a 2p orange red 150.00

1870 *Perf. 10xRoulette*

56 A6a 2p orange red 350.00 30.00

Perf. 10, 11½, 12½ and Compound
1868-75

57 A6 1p blue green ('75) 24.00 4.50
58 A6a 2p orange red 13.00 1.00
a. Printed on both sides 200.00
b. Horiz. pair, imperf. vert.

Engr.

59 A3 10p on 9p yellow (Bl) *1,500.*

1869 Typo. Wmk. 6 *Rouletted*

60 A6a 2p orange red 65.00 11.50
a. Imperf.
b. Printed on both sides

Perf. 11½ to 12½xRoulette

61 A6a 2p orange red 125.00

Perf. 11½ to 12½

61B A6a 2p orange red

See Nos. 62, 64-66, 97-98, 105-106, 115-116, 133-134, 145-146. For overprints see Nos. O3, O22-O25, O34-O35, O44-O47, O55-O56, O62-O63, O68-O69, O74, O78-O79. For surcharges see Nos. 75, O49.

1871 Wmk. 70 *Perf. 10*

62 A6a 2p orange red 75.00 16.00

Engr.

63 A2 4p dull violet 2,250. 350.00
a. Printed on both sides

Copies of the 4p from edge of sheet sometimes lack watermark.

Perf. 10, 11½, 12½ and Compound
1876-80 Typo. Wmk. 73

64 A6 1p green 6.00 .50
65 A6a 2p orange 4.25 .50
66 A6a 2p blood red ('80) 225.00 7.50
Nos. 64-66 (3) 235.25 8.50

See #97-98, 105-106, 115-116, 133-134, 145-146.

8 PENCE
No. 71

HALF-
PENNY
No. 75

1876-84 Engr. Wmk. 7

67 A2 3p on 4p ultra (Blk) 65.00 17.50
a. 3p on 4p deep blue 15.00
b. Double surcharge *1,500.*
68 A2 4p reddish violet 50.00 5.50
a. 4p dull violet 60.00 9.00
69 A1 6p deep blue 65.00 4.50
a. Horiz. pair, imperf. vert.
b. Imperf.
70 A1 6p pale ultra ('84) 40.00 2.25
71 A3 8p on 9p bister brn 65.00 5.50
a. 8p on 9p yellow brown 57.50 2.50
b. 8p on 9p gray brown ('80) 52.50 4.00
d. Double surcharge 380.00
72 A3 9p rose lilac 12.00 5.50
a. Printed on both sides 300.00

73 A1 1sh red brown 37.50 3.25
a. 1sh brown 40.00 2.50
b. Horiz. pair, imperf. btwn. 300.00
74 A2 2sh carmine 35.00 4.50
a. Horiz. pair, imperf. vert. *400.00*
b. Imperf., pair

For overprint see No. O41.

1882 Wmk. 73 *Perf. 10*
Black Surcharge

75 A6 ½p on 1p green 10.50 4.00

A9

A10

A11

A12

Perf. 10, 11½, 12½ and Compound
1883-90 Typo.

76 A9 ½p chocolate brown 2.25 .25
a. ½p red brown ('89) 2.25 .25
b. ½p bister brown 3.50 .25
78 A10 3p deep green ('86) 6.50 .75
a. 3p olive green ('90) 11.00 1.50
79 A11 4p violet ('90) 7.75 1.75
80 A12 6p blue ('87) 7.75 1.00
Nos. 76-80 (4) 24.25 3.75

See Nos. 96, 100-101, 104, 108-109, 111. For overprints see Nos. O50-O51, O54, O58, O60-O61, O64, O66-O67, O71, O73, O75, O81-O82. For surcharges see Nos. 94-95, 99, O48, O57, O59.

A13

1886-96 *Perf. 10, 11½ to 12½*

81 A13 2sh6p violet 27.50 6.50
82 A13 5sh rose 40.00 16.00
83 A13 10sh green 100.00 25.00
84 A13 15sh buff 200.00 140.00
85 A13 £1 blue 165.00 60.00
86 A13 £2 red brown 475.00 150.00
87 A13 50sh rose red 600.00 200.00
88 A13 £3 olive green 825.00
89 A13 £4 lemon 1,000.
90 A13 £5 gray *2,700.*
90A A13 £5 brown ('96) *2,600.*
91 A13 £10 bronze *3,000.* *700.00*
92 A13 £15 silver *6,500.*
93 A13 £20 lilac *8,250.*

For overprints see Nos. O83-O84.

2½d.
#94, 99

5D.
#95

Perf. 10, 11½x12½ and Compound
1891
Brown Surcharge

94 A11 2½p on 4p green 8.00 1.40
a. "½" nearer the "2" 30.00 20.00
b. Pair, imperf. between 375.00
c. Fraction bar omitted 90.00 80.00

Carmine Surcharge

95 A12 5p on 6p red brown 17.00 6.00
a. No period after "D" 165.00

See #99. For overprints see #O48, O57, O59.

Many stamps of the issues of 1855-91 have been reprinted; they are all on paper watermarked Crown and SA, letters wide apart, and are overprinted "REPRINT."

1893 Typo. *Perf. 15*

96 A9 ½p brown 3.00 .20
a. Horiz. pair, imperf. between 125.00
b. Pair, perf. 12 between and perf. 15 around 195.00 50.00
97 A6 1p green 4.00 .20
98 A6a 2p orange 6.50 .20
a. Vert. pair, imperf. between 225.00
99 A11 2½p on 4p green 12.00 1.65
a. "½" nearer the "2" 40.00 35.00
b. Fraction bar omitted
100 A11 4p gray violet 13.00 2.00
101 A12 6p blue 32.50 4.25
Nos. 96-101 (6) 71.00 8.50

Kangaroo, Palm — A16

Coat of Arms — A17

1894, Mar. 1

102 A16 2½p blue violet 13.00 1.50
103 A17 5p dull violet 15.00 2.50

See Nos. 107, 110, 117, 135-136, 147, 151. For overprints see Nos. O65, O70, O72, O80.

1895-97 *Perf. 13*

104 A9 ½p pale brown 3.00 .25
105 A6 1p green 5.25 .50
a. Vert. pair, imperf. between
106 A6a 2p orange 4.25 .20
107 A16 2½p blue violet 7.50 .35
108 A10 3p olive green ('97) 5.00 .30
109 A11 4p bright violet 6.50 .35
110 A17 5p dull violet 7.00 .35
111 A12 6p blue 8.00 .40
Nos. 104-111 (8) 46.50 2.70

Some authorities regard the so-called redrawn 1p stamps with thicker lettering (said to have been issued in 1897) as impressions from a new or cleaned plate.

Perf. 11½, 12½, Clean-Cut, Compound

1896 Engr. Wmk. 7

112 A3 9p lilac rose 12.50 6.50
113 A1 1sh dark brown 26.00 5.50
a. Horiz. pair, imperf. vert.
c. Vert. pair, imperf. btwn. 180.00
113B A2 2sh carmine 32.50 8.00
Nos. 112-113B (3) 71.00 20.00

Adelaide Post Office — A18

1899 Typo. Wmk. 73 *Perf. 13*

114 A18 ½p yellow green 1.75 .25
115 A6 1p carmine 3.00 .20
a. 1p scarlet 2.75 .50
116 A6a 2p purple 2.25 .25
117 A16 2½p dark blue 7.00 .75
Nos. 114-117 (4) 14.00 1.45

See #132, 144. For overprint see #O77.

Perf. 11½, 12½

1901 Engr. Wmk. 72

118 A1 1sh dark brown 24.00 16.00
a. 1sh red brown 24.00 10.00
b. Horiz. pair, imperf. vert.
119 A2 2sh carmine 27.50 15.00

1902

120 A3 9p magenta 20.00 20.00

A19

A20

Perf. 11½, 12½ and Compound

1902-03 Typo. Wmk. 73

121 A19 3p olive green 4.75 .75
122 A19 4p red orange 7.50 1.50
123 A19 6p blue green 6.50 1.50
124 A19 8p ultra (value 19mm long) 8.50 2.25
124A A19 8p ultra (value 16½mm long) ('03) 13.00 3.00
b. "EIGNT" 900.00 *3,000.*
125 A19 9p claret 8.50 2.25
a. Pair, imperf. between 300.00
126 A19 10p org buff 11.00 3.50
127 A19 1sh brown ('03) 12.00 3.00
a. Horiz. or vert. pair, imperf. btwn. 700.00
128 A19 2sh6p purple 32.50 9.00
129 A19 5sh rose 75.00 52.50
130 A19 10sh green ('03) 110.00 65.00
131 A19 £1 blue 275.00 150.00
Nos. 121-131 (12) 564.25 294.25

1904 *Perf. 12x11½*

132 A18 ½p yellow green 3.00 .60
133 A6 1p rose 6.50 .60
134 A6a 2p purple 6.50 .60
135 A16 2½p dark blue 14.00 1.50
136 A17 5p dull violet 11.00 1.75
Nos. 132-136 (5) 41.00 5.05

1904-08 *Perf. 12 and 12x11½*

137 A20 6p blue green 8.25 1.75
138 A20 8p ultra ('06) 11.50 2.25
139 A20 9p claret 8.00 1.65
139A A20 10p org buff ('07) 20.00 5.25
b. Pair, imperf. between 325.00 225.00
140 A20 1sh brown 12.00 2.00
a. Pair, imperf. between 250.00
141 A20 2sh6p purple ('05) 55.00 8.25
142 A20 5sh scarlet 55.00 32.50
142B A20 10sh green ('08) 140.00 125.00
143 A20 £1 deep blue 200.00 140.00
Nos. 137-143 (9) 509.75 318.65

See Nos. 148-150, 152-157.

1906-12 Wmk. 74

144 A18 ½p green 1.50 .20
145 A6 1p carmine 1.50 .20
146 A6a 2p purple 2.50 .20
a. Horiz. pair, imperf. between
147 A16 2½p dk blue ('11) 10.50 1.50
148 A20 3p ol grn (value 19mm long) 6.50 1.25
a. Horiz. pair, imperf. between
149 A20 3p ol grn (value 17mm long) ('09) 8.50 1.50
150 A20 4p red orange 9.75 1.75
151 A17 5p dull vio ('08) 8.50 2.00
152 A20 6p blue grn ('07) 7.50 1.10
a. Vert. pair, imperf. between 240.00
153 A20 8p ultra ('09) 15.00 5.50
154 A20 9p claret 15.00 3.00
a. Vert. pair, imperf. between 195.00
b. Horiz. pair, imperf. between 225.00
155 A20 1sh brown 11.00 3.00
a. Pair, imperf. between 175.00
156 A20 2sh6p purple ('09) 32.50 10.50
157 A20 5sh lt red ('12) 82.50
Nos. 144-157 (14) 212.75 31.70

OFFICIAL STAMPS

For Departments

Regular Issues Overprinted in Red, Black or Blue:

A. (Architect), A. G. (Attorney General), A. O. (Audit Office), B. D. (Barracks Department), B. G. (Botanical Gardens), B. M. (Bench of Magistrates), C. (Customs), C. D. (Convict Department), C. L. (Crown Lands), C. O. (Commissariat Officer), C. S. (Chief Secretary), C. Sgn. (Colonial Surgeon), C. P. (Commissioner of Police), C. T. (Commissioner of Titles), D. B. (Destitute Board), D. R. (Deed Registry), E. (Engineer), E. B. (Education Board),

G. P. (Government Printer), G. S. (Government Storekeeper), G. T. (Goolwa Tramway), G. F. (Gold Fields), H. (Hospital), H. A. (House of Assembly), I. A. (Immigration Agent), I. E. (Intestate Estates), I. S. (Inspector of Sheep), L. A. (Lunatic Asylum), L. C. (Legislative Council), L. L. (Legislative Library), L. T. (Land Titles), M. (Military), M. B. (Marine Board), M. R. (Manager of Railways), M. R. G. (Main Roads Gambierton), N. T. (Northern Territory),

O. A. (Official Assignee), P. (Police), P. A. (Protector of Aborigines), P. O. (Post Office), P. S. (Private Secretary), P. W. (Public Works), R. B. (Road Board), R. G. (Registrar General of Births, &c.), S. (Sheriff), S. C. (Supreme Court), S.G. (Surveyor General), S. M. (Stipendiary Magistrate), S. T. (Superintendent of Telegraph), T. (Treasurer), T. R. (Titles Registry), V. (Volunteers), V. A. (Valuator), V. N. (Vaccination), W. (Waterworks).

1868-74 Wmk. 6 *Rouletted*

O1 A1 1p green
O2 A1 2p pale red
O3 A6a 2p vermilion
O4 A2 4p dull violet
O5 A1 6p slate blue
O6 A3 9p gray lilac
O7 A1 1sh brown
O8 A2 2sh carmine

Perf. 11½ to 12½ x Roulette

O9 A1 1p green
O10 A2 4p dull violet
O11 A1 6p blue
O12 A1 1sh brown

Perf. 10, 11½, 12½ and Compound

O13 A1 1p green
O14 A2 3p on 4p slate blue (Red)
O16 A2 4p dull violet
O17 A1 6p deep blue
O18 A3 9p violet
O19 A3 10p on 9p yellow (Blk)
O20 A1 1sh brown
O21 A2 2sh carmine

Rouletted

Wmk. 72

O22 A6a 2p orange

Perf. 10 x Roulette

O23 A6a 2p orange

Perf. 10, 11½, 12½ and Compound

O24 A6a 2p orange

Wmk. 70

Perf. 10

O25 A6a 2p orange
O26 A2 4p dull violet

For General Use

Overprinted in Black **O.S.**

Perf. 10, 11½, 12½ and Compound

1874 Wmk. 6

O27 A1 1p green — *450.00*
a. Printed on both sides
O28 A2 3p on 4p ultra 150.00
a. No period after "S" 375.00
O29 A2 4p dull violet 27.50 9.50
a. Inverted overprint
b. No period after "S" 25.00
c. Perf. 10 1,650. 400.00
O30 A1 6p deep blue 55.00 9.50
a. No period after "S" 22.50
O31 A3 9p violet 250.00 60.00
a. No period after "S" 300.00
O32 A1 1sh red brown 55.00 16.00
a. Double overprint 27.50
b. No period after "S" 110.00 40.00
O33 A2 2sh carmine 67.50 14.00
a. Double overprint
b. No period after "S" 32.50

1874-75 Wmk. 72

O34 A6 1p blue green 100.00 27.50
a. Inverted overprint
O35 A6a 2p orange 14.00 1.40

1876-86 Wmk. 7

O36 A2 3p on 4p ultra
O37 A2 4p dull violet 100.00 17.00
O38 A2 4p reddish vio 37.50 3.00
a. Double overprint
b. Inverted overprint
c. Dbl. ovpt., one inverted
O39 A1 6p dark blue 62.50 5.00
a. Double overprint 37.50
b. Inverted overprint
O40 A1 6p ultramarine 57.50 4.50
a. Double overprint
b. Inverted overprint
O41 A3 8p on 9p yel brn 425.00 125.00
a. Double overprint 750.00
O41B A3 9p violet *4,000.*
O42 A1 1sh red brown 45.00 5.00
a. Inverted overprint 150.00 75.00
b. Double overprint
O43 A2 2sh carmine 110.00 8.00
a. Double overprint 70.00
b. Inverted overprint 75.00

1880-91 Wmk. 73

O44 A6 1p blue green 11.00 .50
a. Inverted overprint 22.50
b. Double overprint 35.00 20.00
c. Dbl. ovpt., one inverted
O45 A6 1p yellow green 12.00 .50
O46 A6a 2p orange 11.00 .25
a. Inverted overprint 10.00
b. Double overprint 70.00 25.00
c. Overprinted sideways
d. Dbl. ovpt., one inverted
e. Dbl. ovpt., both inverted 57.50
O47 A6a 2p blood red 52.50 5.00
O48 A11 2½p on 4p green 35.00 9.50
a. "½" nearer the "2" 75.00
b. Double overprint
c. Pair, one without ovpt.
Nos. O44-O48 (5) 121.50 15.75

1882-90 *Perf. 10*

O49 A6 ½p on 1p green 25.00 8.00
a. Inverted overprint
O50 A11 4p violet 21.00 1.90
O51 A12 6p blue 12.00 1.25
a. Double overprint
Nos. O49-O51 (3) 58.00 11.15

Overprinted in Black **O.S.**

Perf. 10, 11½, 12½ and Compound

1891 Wmk. 7

O52 A1 1sh red brown 42.50 3.50
O53 A2 2sh carmine 100.00 10.00
a. Double overprint

1891-95 Wmk. 73

O54 A9 ½p brown 12.00 2.50
O55 A6 1p blue green 12.00 .30
a. Double overprint 80.00
O56 A6a 2p orange 12.00 .30
O57 A11 2½p on 4p green 45.00 2.75
a. "½" nearer the "2" 52.50 18.00
b. Inverted overprint 100.00
O58 A11 4p violet 17.50 1.25
a. Double overprint
O59 A12 5p on 6p red brn 55.00 2.50
O60 A12 6p blue 9.75 .75
a. Double overprint
Nos. O54-O60 (7) 163.25 10.35

1893 *Perf. 15*

O61 A9 ½p brown 15.00 1.75
O62 A6 1p green 11.00 .30
O63 A6a 2p orange 12.00 .20
a. Inverted overprint 18.00
b. Double overprint 32.50
O64 A11 4p gray violet 65.00 1.75
a. Double overprint 21.00
O65 A17 5p dull violet 80.00 4.50
O66 A12 6p blue 20.00 .70
Nos. O61-O66 (6) 203.00 9.20

1896 *Perf. 13*

O67 A9 ½p brown 12.50 1.75
a. Triple overprint
O68 A6 1p green 16.00 .20
O69 A6a 2p orange 11.00 .20
O70 A16 2½p blue violet 60.00 1.40
O71 A11 4p brt violet 65.00 1.75
a. Double overprint 30.00 40.00
O72 A17 5p dull violet 60.00 4.25
O73 A12 6p blue 25.00 .90
Nos. O67-O73 (7) 249.50 10.45

On No. O67a, one overprint is upright, two sideways.

Same Overprint in Dark Blue

1891-95 *Perf. 10*

O74 A6 1p green 150.00 15.00
O75 A12 6p blue

Black Overprint

Perf. 11½, 12½, Clean-Cut

1897 Wmk. 7

O76 A1 1sh brown 40.00 4.50
a. Double overprint

Overprinted in Black **O. S.**

1900 Wmk. 73 *Perf. 13*

O77 A18 ½p yellow green 10.00 1.75
O78 A6 1p carmine rose 11.50 .20
a. Inverted overprint
b. Double overprint
O79 A6a 2p purple 11.50 .20
a. Inverted ovpt. 40.00
O80 A16 2½p dark blue 82.50 1.40
a. Inverted overprint 30.00
O81 A11 4p violet 65.00 .70
a. Inverted overprint 125.00
O82 A12 6p blue 20.00 .70
Nos. O77-O82 (6) 200.50 4.95

1901 *Perf. 10*

O83 A13 2sh6p violet *2,000. 2,000.*
O84 A13 5sh rose *2,250. 2,250.*

On Nos. O77-O82 the letters "O.S." are 11½mm apart; on Nos. O83-O84, 14½mm apart.

Overprinted in Black **O.S.**

1903 Wmk. 72 *Perf. 11½, 12½*

O85 A1 1sh red brown 40.00 25.00

Many of the official stamps are found with one or both the periods after "O.S." missing. This occurs more often in the later than in the earlier issues.

TASMANIA

taz-ˈmā-nē-ə

LOCATION — An island off the southeastern coast of Australia
GOVT. — British Colony
AREA — 26,215 sq. mi.
POP. — 172,475 (1901)
CAPITAL — Hobart

Tasmania was one of the six British colonies that united in 1901 to form the Commonwealth of Australia. The island was originally named Van Diemen's Land by its discoverer, Abel Tasman, the present name having been adopted in 1853. Stamps of Australia are now used.

12 Pence = 1 Shilling
20 Shillings = 1 Pound

Watermarks

Wmk. 6- Large Star

Wmk. 49- Double-lined Numeral

Wmk. 75- Double-lined Numeral

Wmk. 50- Single-lined "2"

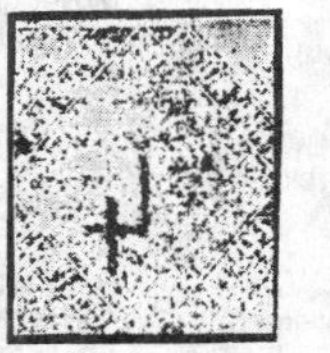
Wmk. 51- Single-lined "4"

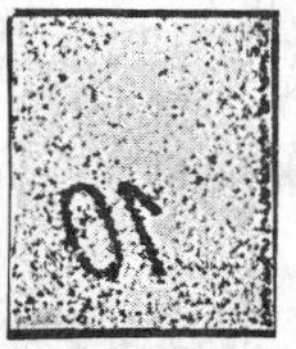
Wmk. 52- Single-lined "10"

Wmk. 70- V and Crown

Wmk. 13- Crown & Double-lined A

Wmk. 76- TAS

Wmk. 77- TAS

Tasmania stamps can be mounted in the Scott Australia album.

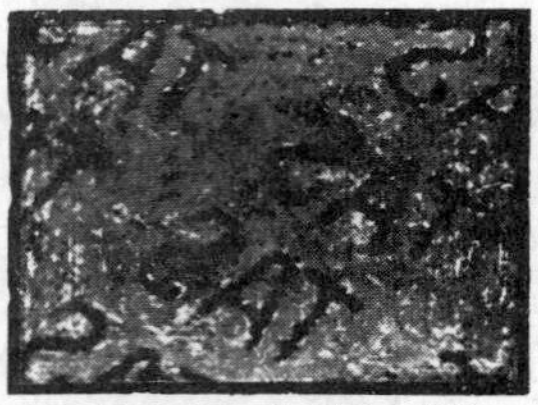
Wmk. 78- Multiple TAS

Values for unused stamps are for examples with original gum as defined in the catalogue introduction except for Nos. 1-2a and 10 which are valued without gum as few examples exist with any remaining original gum. Very fine examples of Nos. 17-75a will have perforations touching the design on one or more sides due to the narrow spacing of the stamps on the plates. Stamps with perfs clear of the design on all four sides are scarce and command higher prices.

Queen Victoria
A1 A2

Unwmk.

1853, Nov. 1 Engr. *Imperf.*
1 A1 1p blue 3,250. 750.00
2 A2 4p red orange 2,000. 300.00
 a. 4p yellow orange 2,250. 300.00
 Cut to shape 15.00

Twenty-four varieties of each.

The 4p on vertically laid paper is believed to be a proof. Value, unused, $6,250.

The reprints are made from defaced plates and show marks across the face of each stamp. They are on thin and thick, unwatermarked paper and thin cardboard; only the first are perforated. Nearly all the reprints of Tasmania may be found with and without the overprint "REPRINT."

Nos. 1-47A with pen or revenue cancellations sell for a small fraction of the price of postally used specimens. Copies are found with pen cancellation removed.

Queen Victoria — A3

1855 Wmk. 6 Wove Paper
4 A3 1p dark carmine 6,000. 825.00
5 A3 2p green 1,800. 500.00
 a. 2p deep green 1,800. 600.00
6 A3 4p deep blue 1,250. 85.00

1856-57 Unwmk.
7 A3 1p pale red 6,000. 500.00
8 A3 2p emerald ('57) 7,250. 700.00
9 A3 4p blue ('57) 650.00 85.00

1856 Pelure Paper
10 A3 1p brown red 3,000. 600.00

1857 Wmk. 139, 49, 75
11 A3 1p carmine 80.00 15.00
 a. 1p orange red 85.00 15.00
 b. 1p brown red 275.00 17.00
 c. Double impression 165.00
12 A3 2p sage green 130.00 42.50
 a. 2p yellow green 250.00 55.00
 b. 2p green — 30.00
13 A3 4p pale blue 100.00 13.00
 b. Printed on both sides —
 Nos. 11-13 (3) 310.00

See #17-19, 23-25, 29-31, 35-37, 39-41, 45-47A.

A4

A4a

1858
14 A4 6p gray lilac 125.00 50.00
 a. 6p red violet 600.00 150.00
 b. Double impression 200.00
15 A4 6p blue gray 325.00 70.00
16 A4a 1sh vermilion 500.00 55.00
 Nos. 14-16 (3) 950.00 175.00

No. 15 watermarked large star was not regularly issued.

1864 *Rouletted*
17 A3 1p carmine 375.00 125.00
 a. 1p brick red 180.00
18 A3 2p yellow grn 375.00
19 A3 4p blue 180.00
21 A4 6p gray lilac 225.00
22 A4a 1sh vermilion 625.00

1864-69 *Perf. 10*
23 A3 1p brick red 50.00 19.00
 a. 1p carmine 50.00 19.00
 b. 1p orange red 50.00 19.00
24 A3 2p yellow green 275.00 65.00
 a. 2p sage green 375.00 150.00
25 A3 4p blue 125.00 9.00
 a. Double impression 100.00
26 A4 6p lilac 140.00 12.50
 a. 6p red lilac 375.00 55.00
27 A4 6p slate blue 190.00 20.00
28 A4a 1sh vermilion 100.00 17.50
 a. Horiz. pair, imperf. vert.
 Nos. 23-28 (6) 880.00 143.00

1864-69 *Perf. 12, 12½*
29 A3 1p carmine 24.00 6.00
 a. 1p orange red 40.00 16.00
 b. 1p brick red 42.50 22.50
 c. Double impression
 d. Wmkd. "2" 950.00
 As "d," pen cancel 125.00
30 A3 2p yellow green 130.00 35.00
 a. 2p dark green 200.00 35.00
 b. 2p sage green 250.00 100.00
31 A3 4p blue 65.00 11.00

Perf. 11½, 12½
32 A4 6p red lilac 25.00 11.00
 a. 6p purple 75.00 21.00
 b. 6p violet 110.00 17.50
 d. Horiz. pair, imperf. vert.
 e. Double impression 100.00
33 A4 6p slate blue, perf. 12½ 250.00 65.00
34 A4a 1sh vermilion 90.00 27.50
 a. Double impression 165.00
 b. Horiz. pair, imperf. vert.
 Nos. 29-34 (6) 584.00 155.50

The reprints are on unwatermarked paper, perforated 11½, and on thin cardboard, imperforate and perforated.

Pin-perf. 5½ to 9½, 13½ to 14½
1867
35 A3 1p carmine 350.00 77.50
36 A3 2p yellow green 275.00
37 A3 4p blue 165.00
38 A4 6p gray 150.00
38A A4 6p red lilac 450.00
38B A4a 1sh vermilion —

Oblique Roulette
39 A3 1p carmine 675.00 275.00
40 A3 2p yellow green 400.00
41 A3 4p blue 325.00
42 A4 6p gray 550.00
43 A4 6p red lilac 575.00
44 A4a 1sh vermilion 750.00

1868 *Serrate Perf. 19*
45 A3 1p carmine 225.00 100.00
46 A3 2p yellow green 175.00
47 A3 4p blue 650.00 110.00
47A A3 6p purple 500.00

Queen Victoria — A5

1870-71 Typo. Wmk. 50 *Perf. 11½*
48 A5 2p blue green 35.00 3.25
 a. Imperf., pair
 b. Perf. 12 45.00 5.00
 d. 2p blue green 80.00 6.50
 e. As "d," perf. 12 40.00 5.00

See Nos. 49-75, 98, 108-109.

Wmk. 51
49 A5 1p rose ('71) 60.00 20.00
 a. Imperf., pair 600.00 215.00
50 A5 4p blue 725.00 300.00

Wmk. 52
51 A5 1p rose 40.00 9.00
 a. Imperf. pair 265.00 250.00
 c. Perf. 11½ 1,000.
52 A5 10p black 20.00 17.00
 a. Imperf. pair 120.00
 b. Perf. 11½ 25.00 20.00

The reprints are on unwatermarked paper. The 4p has also been reprinted on thin cardboard, imperf and perf.

1871-76 Wmk. 76 *Perf. 11½*
53 A5 1p rose 4.50 .60
 a. Imperf.
 c. Perf. 12 65.00 9.00
53B A5 1p vermilion ('73) 250.00 95.00
54 A5 2p deep green ('72) 12.00 .60
 a. 2p yellow green 120.00 1.25
 b. 2p blue green 45.00 .60
 c. Imperf. pair 120.00
 d. 2p green, perf. 12 450.00 135.00
 e. Double impression
55 A5 3p brown 37.50 4.50
 a. 3p purple brown 37.50 4.50
 b. As "a," imperf. pair 325.00
56 A5 3p red brown ('71) 37.50 4.50
 a. 3p indian red 35.00 4.50
 b. Imperf. pair 120.00
 c. Vert. pair, imperf. horiz.
 d. Perf. 12 85.00 21.00
57 A5 4p dull yellow ('76) 40.00 7.50
 a. Perf. 12 225.00 15.00
58 A5 9p blue 20.00 7.50
 a. Imperf. pair 120.00
 b. Perf. 12 40.00 40.00
59 A5 5sh bright violet 125.00 37.50
 a. Imperf.
 b. Horiz. pair, imperf. vert.
 c. Perf. 12 175.00 150.00
 Pen cancel .30
 Nos. 53-59 (8) 526.50 157.70

The reprints are on unwatermarked paper, the 5sh has also been reprinted on thin cardboard; all are perforated.

1878 Wmk. 77 *Perf. 14*
60 A5 1p rose 4.50 .60
61 A5 2p deep green 4.50 .60
62 A5 8p violet brown 15.00 4.50
 Nos. 60-62 (3) 24.00 5.70

The 8p has been reprinted on thin unwatermarked paper, perforated 11½.

1880-83 *Perf. 12, 11½*
63 A5 3p indian red, perf. 12 9.00 2.00
 a. Imperf. pair 85.00
 b. Horiz. pair, imperf. between 600.00
 c. Perf. 11½ 10.50 3.00
64 A5 4p lem, perf. 11½ ('83) 40.00 7.50
 a. 4p olive yellow, perf. 11½ 95.00 21.00
 b. Printed on both sides 210.00
 c. Imperf.
 d. 4p deep yellow, perf. 12 75.00 22.50

Type of 1871 Surcharged in Black **Halfpenny**

1889 *Perf. 14*
65 A5 ½p on 1p carmine 9.00 1.75
 a. "al" sideways in surcharge 825.00 *500.00*

No. 65 has been reprinted on thin cardboard, perforated 12, with the surcharge "Halfpenny" 19mm long.

1889-96 *Perf. 11½*
66 A5 ½p red orange 2.25 .70
 a. ½p yellow orange 2.25 .70
 b. Perf. 12 2.00 .85
67 A5 1p dull red 8.25 2.00
 a. 1p vermilion 5.00 2.00
68 A5 1p car, perf. 12 8.25 3.25
 a. 1p pink, perf. 12 27.50 5.00
 b. 1p salmon rose, perf. 12 8.25 3.25
 c. Imperf. pair 92.50 92.50

Perf. 12
69 A5 4p bister ('96) 18.00 8.25
70 A5 9p chalky bl ('96) 10.00 3.25
 Nos. 66-70 (5) 46.75 17.45

1891 Wmk. 76 *Perf. 11½*
71 A5 ½p orange 16.00 8.25
 a. ½p brown orange 16.00 8.25
 b. Imperf. pair 75.00
 c. Perf. 12 35.00 9.25
72 A5 1p salmon rose 21.00 11.50
 a. 1p carmine, perf. 12 40.00 20.00
73 A5 4p ol bis, perf. 12 15.00 6.50
 Nos. 71-73 (3) 52.00 26.25

See Nos. 98, 108-109.

Surcharged in Black **d. 2½**

1891 Wmk. 77 *Perf. 11½*

Surcharge 14mm High

74	A5	2½p on 9p lt blue	6.00	6.50
a.		Dbl. surcharge, one invtd.	210.00	200.00
b.		Imperf. pair	135.00	

Perf. 12

Surcharge 15mm High

75	A5	2½p on 9p lt blue	5.50	5.00
a.		Surcharged in blue		

No. 74 has been reprinted on thin unwatermarked paper, imperforate. There is also a reprint on thin cardboard, in deep ultramarine, with surcharge 16½mm high, and perforated 12.

A8

A9

1892-99 Typo. *Perf. 14*

76	A8	½p orange & vio	.85	.35
77	A9	2½p magenta	2.50	.65
78	A8	5p pale bl & brn	3.50	1.40
79	A8	6p blue vio & blk	3.50	1.50
80	A8	10p red brn & grn ('99)	6.75	5.50
81	A8	1sh rose & green	4.50	1.50
82	A8	2sh6p brown & blue	25.00	8.00
83	A8	5sh brn vio & red	37.50	17.00
84	A8	10sh brt vio & brn	75.00	45.00
85	A8	£1 green & yel	475.00	225.00
		Nos. 76-85 (10)	634.10	305.90

No. 80 shows the numeral on white tablet.

See #99, 110-111. For overprint see #AR35.

Lake Marion
A10

Mt. Wellington
A11

View of
Hobart — A12

Tasman's
Arch — A13

Spring River, Port
Davey — A14

Russell
Falls — A15

Mt. Gould and
Lake St.
Clair — A16

Dilston
Falls — A17

1899-1900 Engr. Wmk. 78 *Perf. 14*

86	A10	½p dark green	5.00	1.75
87	A11	1p carmine	5.00	.60
88	A12	2p violet	5.50	.45
89	A13	2½p dark blue	11.00	5.00
90	A14	3p dark brown	8.50	1.75
91	A15	4p ocher	16.00	2.25
92	A16	5p ultramarine	16.00	7.50
93	A17	6p lake	20.00	6.50
		Nos. 86-93 (8)	87.00	25.80

See Nos. 94-97, 102-107, 114-117.

Perf. 11, 12½, 11x12½

1902-03 Litho., Typo. Wmk. 70

94	A10	½p green	2.25	.30
95	A11	1p carmine	5.50	.20
96	A11	1p dull red	5.00	.20
97	A12	2p violet	3.25	.20
98	A5	9p blue	9.00	3.00
a.		9p ultramarine	225.00	
b.		9p indigo	90.00	
c.		Perf. 11	7.25	3.50
99	A8	1sh rose & green	12.00	3.75
a.		Perf. 11	27.50	27.50
		Nos. 94-99 (6)	37.00	7.65

Nos. 94, 97 are litho., Nos. 96, 98-99 typo. No. 95 was printed both ways.

No. 78 Surcharged in Black **1½d.**

1904 Wmk. 77 *Perf. 14*

100	A8	1½p on 5p blue & brn	1.75	1.25

Perf. 11, 12, 12½ and Compound

1905-08 Typo. Wmk. 13

102	A10	½p dull green	2.00	.20
a.		Booklet pane of 12		
103	A11	1p carmine	2.00	.20
a.		Booklet pane of 18		
104	A12	2p violet	3.50	.20
105	A14	3p dark brown	7.00	2.00
106	A15	4p ocher	13.00	2.25
107	A17	6p lake	40.00	5.00
108	A5	8p violet brown	19.00	5.00
109	A5	9p blue	8.00	3.00
110	A8	1sh rose & green	13.00	2.50
111	A8	10sh brt vio & brn	100.00	62.50
a.		Perf. 11	175.00	
		Nos. 102-111 (10)	207.50	82.85

Nos. 104-107 also printed litho.

1911 Redrawn

114	A12	2p bright violet	3.50	.30
115	A15	4p dull yellow	16.00	8.00
116	A17	6p lake	17.00	8.00
		Nos. 114-116 (3)	36.50	16.30

The redrawn 2p measures 33½x25mm instead of 32½x24½mm. There are many slight changes in the clouds and other parts of the design.

The 4p is much lighter, especially the waterfall and trees above it. This appears to be a new or cleaned plate rather than a redrawn one.

In the redrawn 6p there are more colored lines in the waterfall and the river and more white dots in the trees.

No. 114 Surcharged in Red **ONE PENNY**

1912

117	A12	1p on 2p bright violet	.85	.50

POSTAL FISCAL STAMPS

Authorised for postal use by Act of November 1, 1882. Authorization withdrawn Nov. 30, 1900.

Used values are for examples with postal cancellations used from Nov. 1, 1882 through Nov. 30, 1900.

Beware of copies with a pen cancelation removed and a fake postmark added.

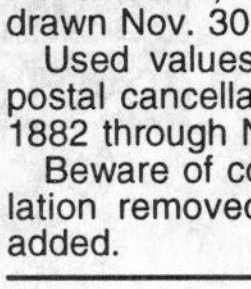
PF1

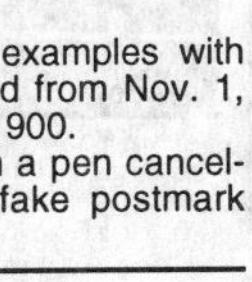
PF2

St. George and the Dragon
PF3 PF4

1863-64 Engr. Wmk. 139 *Imperf.*

AR1	PF1	3p green	75.00	50.00
AR2	PF2	2sh 6p carmine	80.00	50.00
AR3	PF3	5sh green	75.00	55.00
AR4	PF3	5sh brown	200.00	*150.00*
AR5	PF4	10sh orange	175.00	*150.00*

For overprint see No. AR32.

Perf. 10

AR6	PF1	3p green	40.00	22.50
AR7	PF2	2sh 6p carmine	50.00	
AR8	PF3	5sh brown	75.00	
AR9	PF4	10sh orange	42.50	

Perf. 12

AR10	PF1	3p green	45.00	27.50
AR11	PF2	2sh 6p carmine	45.00	35.00
AR12	PF3	5sh green	32.50	27.50
AR13	PF3	5sh brown	80.00	
AR14	PF4	10sh orange	35.00	27.50

Perf. 12½

AR15	PF1	3p green	80.00	
AR16	PF2	2sh 6p carmine	80.00	
AR17	PF3	5sh brown	100.00	
AR18	PF4	10sh orange	70.00	

Perf. 11½

AR19	PF1	3p green		
AR20	PF2	2sh 6p carmine	42.50	32.50
AR21	PF3	5sh green	32.50	22.50
AR22	PF4	10sh orange	55.00	40.00

Wmk. 77

Perf. 12

AR23	PF2	2sh 6p carmine	20.00	15.00

For overprint see No. AR33.

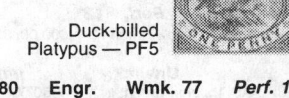

Duck-billed
Platypus — PF5

1880 Engr. Wmk. 77 *Perf. 14*

AR24	PF5	1p slate	12.50	4.00
AR25	PF5	3p brown	12.50	3.00
AR26	PF5	6p lilac	65.00	2.50
AR27	PF5	1sh rose	75.00	6.00

For overprints see Nos. AR28-AR31.

Nos. AR24-AR27, AR2, AR23, 85 Overprinted "REVENUE"

1900, Nov. 15

AR28	PF5	1p slate	20.00	
AR29	PF5	3p brown	20.00	*20.00*
AR30	PF5	6p lilac	60.00	
AR31	PF5	1sh rose	100.00	
AR32	PF2	2sh 6p car (#AR2)		
AR33	PF2	2sh 6p car (#AR23)	200.00	
AR34	PF4	10sh orange		
AR35	A8	£1 grn & yel (#85)	200.00	*150.00*

Nos. AR28-AR35 were not supposed to be postally used. Because of imprecise terminology postal use was permitted until all postal use of revenues ceased on Nov. 30, 1900.

Other denominations and watermarks were overprinted after postal use was no longer allowed.

VICTORIA

vik-ˈtōr-ē-ə

LOCATION — In the extreme southeastern part of Australia
GOVT. — British Colony
AREA — 87,884 sq. mi.
POP. — 1,201,341 (1901)
CAPITAL — Melbourne

Victoria was one of the six former British colonies which united on Jan. 1, 1901, to form the Commonwealth of Australia.

12 Pence = 1 Shilling
20 Shillings = 1 Pound

Unused values for Nos. 1-16 are for stamps without gum as these stamps are seldom found with original gum. Otherwise, unused values are for stamps with original gum as defined in the catalogue introduction.

Very fine examples of all rouletted, perforated and serrate perforated stamps from Nos. 9-109 and F2 will have roulettes, perforations or serrate perforations touching the design. Examples clear on four sides range from scarce to rare and will command higher prices.

Watermarks

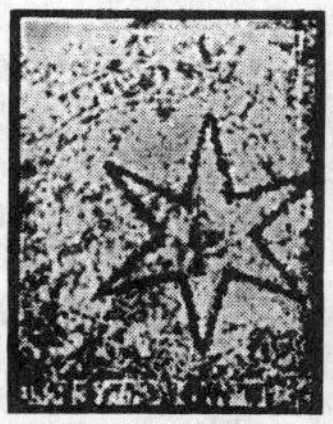
Wmk. 6- Large Star

Wmk. 80

Wmk. 50

Wmk. 80a

Wmk. 81

Wmk. 139

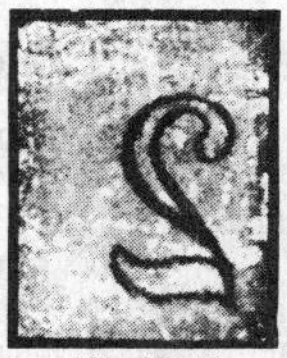
Wmk. 49

Wmk. 75

Wmk. 70- V and Crown

Wmk. 13- Crown & Double-lined A

Queen
Victoria
A1

Victoria on
Throne
A2

1850 Litho. Unwmk. *Imperf.*

1	A1	1p dull red	875.00	90.00
a.		1p vermilion	600.00	125.00
2	A1	1p rose	375.00	75.00
a.		1p pink	400.00	85.00
3	A1	3p blue	600.00	45.00
a.		3p light blue	550.00	45.00
4	A1	3p indigo	625.00	50.00
		Nos. 1-4 (4)	2,475.	260.00

Nos. 1-4 exist with and without frame line.

THREE TYPES OF 2p:
Type I - Border, two sets of nine wavy lines crisscrossing. Background, 22 groups of wavy triple lines below "VICTORIA."
Type II - Border, same. Background, 15 groups of wavy triple lines below "VICTORIA."
Type III - Border, two sets of five wavy lines crisscrossing. Background, same as type II.

5	A1	2p lilac, I	*3,000.*	300.00
a.		2p brn lilac, I	*3,750.*	325.00
6	A1	2p brn lilac, II	1,000.	90.00
a.		2p gray lilac, II	1,000.	90.00
7	A1	2p brn lilac, III	875.00	80.00
a.		2p gray lilac, III	875.00	90.00
b.		Value omitted, III		2,500.
8	A1	2p yel brn, III	650.00	55.00

Rouletted 7

9	A1	1p vermilion		*2,250.*
10	A1	3p blue		140.00
a.		3p deep blue	1,600.	190.00

Perf. 12

12	A1	3p blue	*2,000.*	125.00
a.		3p deep blue	*2,000.*	125.00

1852 Engr. *Imperf.*

14	A2	2p reddish brown	160.00	35.00

#14 was reprinted on paper with watermark 70, imperf. & perf. 12½, overprinted "REPRINT."

1854 Litho.

15	A2	2p gray brown	220.00	35.00
16	A2	2p brown lilac	200.00	30.00
a.		2p red lilac	250.00	35.00

Fifty varieties.

A3

A4

1854-58 Typo.

17	A3	6p orange	175.00	25.00
a.		6p red orange	225.00	27.50

See Nos. 19-20, 22-24A, 26-28

Lithographed

18	A4	1sh blue	450.00	20.00

See Nos. 21, 25.

Typographed

19	A3	2sh green	1,100.	125.00

1857-58 *Rouletted 7, 9½*

20	A3	6p orange	525.00	60.00

Lithographed

21	A4	1sh blue	1,500.	90.00

Typographed

22	A3	2sh green ('58)	*4,000.*	225.00

Small Serrate Perf. 19

23	A3	6p orange	*1,200.*	100.00

Large Serpentine Perf. 10½

24	A3	6p orange	800.00	75.00

Serrate x Serpentine Perf.

24A	A3	6p orange		125.00

1859 Litho. *Perf. 12*

25	A4	1sh blue	180.00	14.00

Typographed

26	A3	2sh green	260.00	37.50

1861 Wmk. "SIX PENCE" (80)

27	A3	6p black	260.00	57.50

Wmk. Single-lined "2" (50)

1864 *Perf. 12, 13*

28	A3	2sh blue, *green*	250.00	8.50

A5

Wmk. Large Star (6)

1856, Oct. Engr. *Imperf.*

29	A5	1p green	125.00	30.00

1858 *Rouletted 5½-6½*

30	A5	6p blue	125.00	7.00

Nos. 29 and 30 have been reprinted on paper watermarked V and Crown. They are imperforate and overprinted "REPRINT."

A6

A7

1857-61 Typo. *Imperf.*

31	A6	1p yellow green	100.00	15.00
a.		Printed on both sides		*900.00*
32	A6	4p vermilion	275.00	15.00
a.		Printed on both sides		*900.00*
33	A6	4p rose	200.00	11.50

Rouletted 7 to 9½

34	A6	1p yellow green	325.00	125.00
35	A6	4p rose	525.00	40.00

Perf. 12

36	A6	1p yellow green	600.00	325.00

Unwmk. *Imperf.*

37	A6	1p blue green	350.00	15.00
38	A6	2p lilac	275.00	15.00
39	A6	4p rose	*500.00*	40.00

Copies of No. 39 printed in dull carmine on thin paper are regarded as printer's waste and of little value. They are also found printed on both sides.

Rouletted 7 to 9½

40	A6	1p blue green	300.00	10.00
a.		1p yellow green	400.00	32.50
b.		Horiz. pair, imperf. btwn.		*1,000.*
41	A6	2p lilac	—	225.00
42	A6	4p rose	300.00	8.00
a.		Horiz. pair, imperf. btwn.		*1,000.*

Perf. 12

43	A6	1p blue green	160.00	10.00
a.		1p yellow green	200.00	15.00
b.		Horiz. pair, imperf. btwn.		*650.00*
44	A6	2p lilac		90.00
45	A6	4p rose	180.00	5.00
b.		Vert. pair, imperf. btwn.		

Serrate Perf. 19

45A	A6	2p lilac	600.00	250.00

Laid Paper

Imperf

46	A6	4p rose	600.00	22.50

Rouletted 5 to 7

47	A6	2p violet	150.00	5.00
a.		2p brown lilac	225.00	8.00
b.		2p dark lilac	200.00	8.00
48	A6	4p rose	160.00	5.25

Perf. 12

49	A6	1p green	240.00	14.00
50	A6	4p rose	150.00	11.00

Wove Paper

1860 Wmk. Value in Words (80)

51	A6	1p yellow green	60.00	8.00
a.		Wmk. "FOUR PENCE" (error)		*2,000.*
52	A6	2p gray lilac	140.00	7.50
a.		2p brown lilac	400.00	24.00

Wmk. "THREE PENCE" (80)

53	A6	2p gray lilac	240.00	10.00

Single-lined "2" (50)

54	A6	2p lilac	160.00	16.00
a.		2p gray lilac	160.00	16.00
b.		2p brown lilac	160.00	16.00
c.		As "b," wmkd. single-lined "6"		*4,500.*

1860 Unwmk. Laid Paper

56	A7	3p deep blue	360.00	45.00

Wmk. Value in Words (80)

Perf. 11½ to 12

1860-62 Wove Paper

57	A7	3p blue	175.00	10.00
58	A7	3p claret	175.00	35.00
a.		Perf. 13	190.00	40.00
59	A7	4p rose	175.00	4.50
60	A7	6p orange	*3,000.*	325.00
61	A7	6p black	250.00	8.00

Wmk. "FIVE SHILLINGS" (80)

62	A7	4p rose	1,500.	20.00

Wmk. Single-lined "4" (80a)

1863 *Imperf.*

63	A7	4p rose	—	*135.00*

Rouletted

64	A7	4p rose	*2,400.*	200.00

Perf. 11½ to 12

65	A7	4p rose	100.00	8.00

1863 Unwmk. *Perf. 12*

66	A7	4p rose	450.00	10.50

A8

A9

1861-63 Wmk. 80 *Perf. 11½ to 12*

67	A8	1p green	90.00	9.00
68	A9	6p black	175.00	7.50

Wmk. Double-lined "1" (139)

69	A8	1p green	200.00	13.00

Wmk. Single-lined Figures (50)

70	A8	1p green	45.00	6.50
71	A9	6p black	175.00	6.50

The 1p and 6p of 1861-63 are known on paper without watermark but were probably impressions on the margins of watermarked sheets.

A10

A11

A12

A13

Wmk. Single-lined Figures (50, 80a, 81)

1863-67 *Perf. 11½ to 13*

74	A10	1p green	70.00	4.00
a.		Double impression		900.00
75	A10	2p gray lilac	75.00	4.00
a.		2p violet	50.00	2.75
76	A10	4p rose	110.00	3.00
a.		Double impression		900.00
77	A11	6p blue	87.50	3.00
78	A10	8p orange	300.00	50.00
79	A12	10p brn, *rose*	150.00	4.50
80	A13	1sh blue, *blue*	150.00	3.00
		Nos. 74-80 (7)	942.50	71.50

See Nos. 81-82, 84-96, 99-101, 108-112, 115-119, 124-126, 144, 188. Compare type A11 with type A54.

A14

Wmk. Double-lined "1" (139)

81	A10	1p green	95.00	5.00
82	A10	2p gray lilac	250.00	8.00
83	A14	3p lilac	200.00	35.00
84	A11	6p blue	65.00	6.00
		Nos. 81-84 (4)	610.00	54.00

See Nos. 97, 113, 155, 186. Compare type A14 with type A51.

Wmk. Double-lined "2" (49)

85	A11	6p blue		*3,250.*

Wmk. Single-lined "4" (80a)

86	A10	1p green	150.00	11.00
87	A10	2p gray lilac	200.00	7.00
88	A11	6p blue		*1,500.*

Wmk. Double-lined "4" (75)

89	A10	1p green	1,300.	145.00
90	A10	2p gray lilac	200.00	6.00
91	A10	4p rose	225.00	7.00
92	A11	6p blue	325.00	18.00

Wmk. Single-lined "6" (50)

93	A10	1p green	250.00	20.00
94	A10	2p gray lilac	225.00	5.75

Wmk. Single-lined "8" (50)

95	A10	1p green	225.00	15.00
96	A10	2p gray lilac	250.00	7.50
97	A14	3p lilac	200.00	30.00
99	A12	10p slate	600.00	120.00

Wmk. "SIX PENCE" (80)

100	A10	1p green	750.00	21.00
101	A11	6p blue	350.00	15.00

All values of the 1864-67 series except the 3p and 8p are known on unwatermarked paper. They are probably varieties from watermarked sheets which have been so placed on the printing press that some of the stamps escaped the watermark.

One copy of the 2p gray lilac, type A10, is reported to exist with only "PENCE" of watermark 80 showing. Some believe this is part of the "SIX PENCE" watermark.

1870 Wmk. "THREE PENCE" (80)

108	A11	6p blue	225.00	6.25

Wmk. "FOUR PENCE" (80)

109	A11	6p blue	500.00	40.00

A15

1867-78 Wmk. (70) *Perf. 11½ to 13*

110 A10 1p green 60.00 2.00
111 A10 2p lilac 85.00 3.25
a. 2p gray lilac 62.50 2.00
112 A10 2p lilac, *lilac* 90.00 10.00
113 A14 3p red lilac 300.00 18.00
a. 3p lilac 350.00 20.00
114 A14 3p orange 22.50 2.00
a. 3p yellow 62.50 2.00
115 A10 4p rose 90.00 3.50
116 A11 6p blue 25.00 2.50
117 A11 6p ultra 27.50 2.50
a. 6p lilac blue 62.50 2.25
118 A10 8p brn, *rose* 125.00 5.00
119 A13 1sh bl, *blue* 250.00 10.00
120 A15 5sh bl, *yel* 1,700. 450.00
121 A15 5sh bl & rose 160.00 15.00
a. Without blue line under crown 140.00 15.00
122 A15 5sh ultra & rose 175.00 20.00

See #126, 144, 188. For surcharge see #124.
For additional stamps of type A15, see No. 191. Compare type A15 with type A58.

A16

A19

1870 ***Perf. 13***

123 A16 2p lilac 40.00 2.00
a. Perf. 12 40.00 1.25

No. 110 Surcharged in Red

½ ½
HALF

1873, July 19 ***Perf. 13, 12***

124 A10 ½p on 1p green 35.00 10.00

No. 79 Surcharged in Blue

9 9
NINEPENCE

1871 Wmk. Single-lined "10" (81)

125 A12 9p on 10p brn, *rose* 375.00 11.00
a. Double surcharge *1,200.*

1873-78 Typo.

126 A10 8p brown, *rose* ('78) 125.00 6.50
127 A19 9p brown, *rose* 125.00 6.50

For additional stamps of type A19, see Nos. 128-129, 174-175. Compare type A19 with type A55.

1875 Wmk. V and Crown (70)

128 A19 9p brown, *rose* 140.00 11.00

No. 128 Surcharged in Black

8d 8d
EIGHTPENCE

1876

129 A19 8p on 9p brn, *rose* 175.00 14.00

A21

A22

A23

A24

A25

1873-81 ***Perf. 13, 12***

130 A21 ½p rose ('74) 5.50 .35
131 A21 ½p rose, *rose* ('78) 20.00 8.00
132 A22 1p grn ('75) 15.00 1.00
133 A22 1p grn, *gray* ('78) 90.00 60.00
134 A22 1p grn, *yel* ('78) 60.00 15.00
135 A23 2p violet 15.00 .25
136 A23 2p vio, *grnsh* ('78) 125.00 15.00
137 A23 2p vio, *buff* ('78) 125.00 15.00
137A A23 2p vio, *lil* ('78) 340.00
138 A24 1sh bl, *bl* ('76) 55.00 4.00
139 A25 2sh bl, *grn* ('81) 175.00 20.00

See Nos. 140, 156A-159, 184, 189-190. Compare type A21 with type A46, A24 with A56, A25 with A57.

1878

Double-lined Outer Oval

140 A23 2p violet 20.00 .25
a. Imperf., pair 400.00
b. Pair, imperf. btwn.

A26

A27

A28

1881-83 ***Perf. 12½***

141 A26 1p green ('83) 14.00 .90
142 A27 2p brown 27.50 .25
143 A27 2p lilac 12.00 .20
144 A10 4p car rose 200.00 2.75
145 A28 4p car rose 40.00 1.50
Nos. 141-145 (5) 293.50 5.60

See Nos. 156, 185, 187. Compare type A26 with type A47, A27 with A49, A28 with A52.

A29

A30

A31

A32

A33

A34

1884-86

146 A29 ½p rose 6.00 .40
147 A30 1p green 6.00 .20
148 A31 2p violet 4.75 .20
a. 2p lilac rose 10.50 .20
149 A30 3p bister 8.00 .50
a. 3p ocher 6.50 .50
150 A32 4p magenta 32.50 2.25
a. 4p violet (error) *4,000.* 400.00
151 A30 6p gray blue 42.50 1.40
a. 6p ultramarine 35.00 1.40
152 A33 8p rose, *rose* 22.50 4.50
153 A34 1sh blue, *yel* 47.50 3.25
154 A33 2sh olive, *grn* 22.50 2.00
Nos. 146-154 (9) 192.25 14.70

See Nos. 177-178, 192A. Compare types A31-A32 with types A37-A38.

Nos. 114, 145, 138-139 Overprinted "STAMP / DUTY" Vertically in Blue or Black

1885

155 A14 3p orange (Bl) 60.00 21.00
156 A28 4p car rose (Bl) 50.00 12.50
156A A24 1sh bl, *bl* (Bl) 1,250.
157 A24 1sh bl, *bl* (Bk) 95.00 22.50
158 A25 2sh bl, *grn* (Bk) 75.00 20.00
Nos. 155-156,157-158 (4) 280.00 76.00

Reprints of 4p and 1sh have brighter colors than originals. They lack the overprint "REPRINT."

A35

A36

A37

A38

A39

A40

1886-87 ***Perf. 12½***

159 A35 ½p lilac 16.00 3.00
160 A35 ½p rose 4.50 .20
160A A35 ½p scarlet 5.00 .20
161 A36 1p green 5.00 .20
162 A37 2p violet 3.00 .20
a. 2p red lilac 2.00 .20
b. Imperf.
163 A38 4p red 6.00 .60
164 A39 6p blue 7.50 .40
165 A39 6p ultra 7.50 .20
166 A40 1sh lilac brown 22.50 1.50
Nos. 159-166 (9) 77.00 6.50

See No. 180.

A41

A42

1889

167 A41 1sh6p blue 110.00 62.50
168 A41 1sh6p orange 15.00 4.00

Southern Cross
A43

Queen Victoria
A44

1890-95 ***Perf. 12½***

169 A42 1p org brn 2.25 .20
a. 1p chocolate brown 2.75 .20
170 A42 1p yel brn 2.00 .20
171 A42 1p brn org, *pink* ('91) 1.65 .50
172 A43 2½p brn red, *yel* 6.00 .50
173 A44 5p choc ('91) 7.00 .50
174 A19 9p green ('92) 20.00 5.00
175 A19 9p rose red 13.00 1.50
a. 9p rose ('95) 13.00 1.50
176 A40 1sh deep claret 15.00 .50
a. 1sh red brown 13.00 .40
b. 1sh maroon 20.00 1.00
177 A33 2sh yel grn 25.00 10.00
178 A33 2sh emerald 20.00 6.00
Nos. 169-178 (10) 111.90 24.90

In 1891 many stamps of the early issues were reprinted. They are on paper watermarked V and Crown, perforated 12, 12½, and overprinted "REPRINT."
See Nos. 181, 183, 192. Compare type A43 with type A50, A44 with A53.

A45

1897

179 A45 1½p yellow green 4.00 1.75

See No. 182. Compare type A45 with type A48.

1899

180 A35 ½p emerald 5.00 .20
181 A42 1p brt rose 4.00 .20
182 A45 1½p red, *yel* 2.75 1.50
183 A43 2½p dark blue 6.50 1.25
Nos. 180-183 (4) 18.25 3.15

1901

184 A21 ½p blue green 1.90 .50
a. "VICTCRIA" 65.00 25.00
185 A27 2p violet 4.50 .20
186 A14 3p brown org 14.00 1.50
187 A28 4p bister 25.00 5.00
188 A11 6p emerald 9.00 2.75
189 A24 1sh orange yel 35.00 10.00
190 A25 2sh blue, *rose* 40.00 11.00
191 A15 5sh rose red & bl 60.00 20.00
Nos. 184-191 (8) 189.40 50.95

1901

192 A42 1p olive green 6.50 5.00
192A A30 3p sage green 21.00 12.00

Nos. 192-192A were available for postal use until June 30, 1901, and thereafter restricted to revenue use.

A46 A47

A48

A49

A50

A51

A52

A53

A54

A55

A56

A57

A58

1901 *Perf. 11, 12½ and Compound*

193 A46 ½p blue green 1.50 .20
194 A47 1p rose red 1.25 .20
a. 1p rose 1.25 .20
195 A48 1½p red, *yellow* 2.25 .50
a. Perf. 11 50.00 32.50
196 A49 2p violet 2.75 .20
197 A50 2½p blue 3.25 .20
198 A51 3p brown org 6.00 .30
199 A52 4p bister 6.00 .35

200	A53	5p chocolate	5.25	.25
201	A54	6p emerald	8.00	.50
202	A55	9p rose	10.00	.75
203	A56	1sh org yel	11.50	.75
204	A57	2sh blue, *rose*	21.00	2.25
205	A58	5sh rose red & bl	65.00	12.50
a.		5sh carmine & blue	65.00	9.00
		Nos. 193-205 (13)	143.75	18.95

See Nos. 209-229, 232.

King Edward VII
A59 A60

1901-05

206 A59	£1 deep rose	325.00	125.00
a.	Perf. 11 ('05)	325.00	140.00
208 A60	£2 dk blue ('02)	750.00	275.00
a.	Perf. 11 ('05)	850.00	600.00

See Nos. 230-231.

1903 **Redrawn**

209 A56 1sh yellow	15.00	1.40
a. 1sh orange	13.00	1.40

No. 209 has the network lighter than No. 203. In the latter the "P" and "E" of "POSTAGE" are in a position more nearly horizontal than on No. 209.

Perf. 11, 12x12½, 12½, 12½x11

1905-10 **Wmk. 13**

218	A46 ½p blue green	1.25	.60
219	A47 1p rose red	1.00	.20
a.	1p carmine rose	2.00	.20
220	A49 2p violet	3.25	.20
a.	2p purple	3.25	.20
221	A50 2½p blue	3.50	.25
222	A51 3p brown org	4.50	.30
a.	3p dull yellow	5.25	.25
223	A52 4p bister	6.50	.40
224	A53 5p chocolate	6.00	.30
225	A54 6p emerald	8.25	.50
226	A55 9p orange brown	10.00	1.10
a.	9p brown rose	13.00	1.10
227	A55 9p car rose	10.00	1.10
228	A56 1sh yellow ('08)	10.00	1.00
229	A58 5sh org red & ultra	62.50	12.50
a.	5sh rose red & ultra	70.00	12.50
230	A59 £1 pale red ('07)	325.00	110.00
a.	£1 rose ('10)	325.00	100.00
231	A60 £2 dull blue	750.00	300.00
	Nos. 218-229 (12)	126.75	18.45

No. 220 Surcharged in Red **ONE PENNY**

1912, July 1

232 A49 1p on 2p violet	.32	.20

POSTAL FISCAL STAMPS

On Jan. 1, 1884, all postage and fiscal stamps were made available for either purpose. Fiscal stamp became invalid after June 30, 1901.

Used values are for examples with postal cancellations used from Jan. 1, 1884 through June 30, 1901.

Beware of copies with a pen cancellation removed and a fake postmark added.

Stamps inscribed "Stamp Duty" that were issued primarily in postal rates in the normal postage stamp size are listed in the postage section (Nos. 146-178, 180-183, 192-192A). The stamps meeting primarily fiscal rates and in the larger fiscal stamp size, are listed here in the Postal-Fiscal section.

Victoria stamps can be mounted in the Scott Australia album.

Stamps Inscribed "Stamp Statute"

Victoria — PF1

Coat of Arms — PF2

PF3

3p, denomination in center. Frames differ on design PF1.

Wmk. V and Crown (70)

1870-83 **Typo.** ***Perf. 13***

AR1	PF1 1p green	17.50	17.50
	Revenue cancel		2.00
a.	Perf. 12½	30.00	30.00
AR2	PF1 3p lilac	125.00	100.00
	Revenue cancel		45.00
AR3	PF1 4p red	125.00	75.00
	Revenue cancel		45.00
AR4	PF1 6p blue	50.00	15.00
	Revenue cancel		5.00
a.	Perf. 12	50.00	15.00
	Revenue cancel		5.00
AR5	PF1 1sh blue, *blue*	45.00	17.50
	Revenue cancel		6.00
a.	Perf. 12	50.00	22.50
	Revenue cancel		6.00
b.	Perf. 12½	45.00	17.50
	Revenue cancel		6.00
c.	Wmk. 50, perf. 13	40.00	17.50
	Revenue cancel		6.00
d.	Wmk. 50, perf. 12	65.00	22.50
	Revenue cancel		7.00
AR6	PF1 2sh blue, *grn*	65.00	42.50
	Revenue cancel		12.50
a.	Perf. 12	65.00	50.00
	Revenue cancel		12.50
b.	Wmk. 50, perf. 13	75.00	55.00
	Revenue cancel		12.50
c.	Wmk. 50, perf. 12	75.00	55.00
	Revenue cancel		12.50
AR7	PF2 2sh 6p orange, *yel*	125.00	55.00
	Revenue cancel		30.00
a.	Perf. 12	125.00	75.00
	Revenue cancel		30.00
b.	Perf. 12½	—	75.00
	Revenue cancel		30.00
AR8	PF1 5sh blue, *yel*	150.00	50.00
	Revenue cancel		30.00
a.	Perf. 12	175.00	
b.	Perf. 12½	150.00	50.00
	Revenue cancel		30.00
AR9	PF1 10sh brown, *rose*	600.00	125.00
	Revenue cancel		50.00
a.	Perf. 12		
b.	Wmk. 50, perf. 13	600.00	125.00
	Revenue cancel		50.00
c.	Wmk. 50, perf. 12		
AR10	PF1 £1 lilac, *yel*	350.00	100.00
	Revenue cancel		40.00
a.	Perf. 12	350.00	100.00
	Revenue cancel		40.00
b.	Perf. 12½	350.00	100.00
	Revenue cancel		40.00
AR11	PF3 £5 black, *grn*	3,000.	300.00
	Revenue cancel		70.00
a.	Perf. 12		
b.	Perf. 12½	3,000.	300.00
	Revenue cancel		70.00

Nos. AR1-AR12 distributed for postal use from Jan. 1, 1884 through Apr. 23, 1884.

No. AR1 Surcharged "½d/HALF"

1879-96

AR12	PF1 ½p on 1p green	75.00	50.00
	Revenue cancel		20.00

Stamps Inscribed "Stamp Duty"

PF4

PF5

PF6

PF7

PF8

PF9

PF10

PF11

PF12

PF13

PF14

PF15

PF16

PF17

PF18

PF23

PF19

PF24

PF20

PF25

PF21

PF26

PF22

PF27

PF28

Wmk. V and Crown (70)

1879-96 **Litho.** ***Perf. 13***

AR13	PF4 1p green	50.00	10.00
	Revenue cancel		4.00
a.	Perf. 12	50.00	10.00
	Revenue cancel		4.00
b.	Perf. 12½		
AR14	PF8 1sh 6p pink	130.00	20.00
	Revenue cancel		8.00
a.	Perf. 12	—	27.50
	Revenue cancel		8.00
b.	Perf. 12½		
AR15	PF11 3sh violet, *blue*	350.00	27.50
	Revenue cancel		8.00
a.	Perf. 12	—	40.00
	Revenue cancel		8.00
b.	Perf. 12½		
AR16	PF12 4sh orange	80.00	17.50
	Revenue cancel		4.00
a.	Perf. 12	80.00	17.50
	Revenue cancel		4.00
b.	Perf. 12½		
AR17	PF4 6sh green	250.00	27.50
	Revenue cancel		8.00
a.	Perf. 12½		
AR18	PF15 10sh brown, *pink*	350.00	60.00
	Revenue cancel		30.00
a.	Perf. 12		
b.	Perf. 12½		
AR19	PF16 15sh lilac	1,000.	125.00
	Revenue cancel		40.00
AR20	PF17 £1 orange	400.00	65.00
	Revenue cancel		15.00
a.	Perf. 12½	400.00	
AR21	PF18 £1 5sh pink	850.00	150.00
	Revenue cancel		100.00
AR22	PF19 £1 10sh olive	900.00	100.00
	Revenue cancel		40.00
AR23	PF20 35sh lilac	3,500.	
	Revenue cancel		200.00
AR24	PF21 £2 blue	—	90.00
	Revenue cancel		15.00
AR25	PF22 45sh violet	1,500.	125.00
	Revenue cancel		35.00
AR26	PF23 £5 rose	1,250.	275.00
	Revenue cancel		70.00
AR27	PF24 £6 blue, *pink*	—	500.00
	Revenue cancel		100.00
AR28	PF25 £7 violet, *blue*	—	500.00
	Revenue cancel		100.00

AR29	PF26	£8 scarlet, *yel*	—	650.00
		Revenue cancel		110.00
AR30	PF27	£9 green, *grn*	—	650.00
		Revenue cancel		110.00

Typo.

AR31	PF4	1p green	30.00	10.00
		Revenue cancel		4.00
a.		Perf. 12	30.00	10.00
		Revenue cancel		4.00
b.		Perf. 12½		
AR32	PF5	1p brown	8.00	2.00
		Revenue cancel		.75
a.		Perf. 12	8.00	3.00
		Revenue cancel		.75
b.		Perf. 12½		
AR33	PF6	6p blue	40.00	6.00
		Revenue cancel		2.50
a.		Perf. 12	50.00	6.00
		Revenue cancel		2.50
b.		Perf. 12½		
AR34	PF7	1sh blue, *blue*	65.00	6.00
		Revenue cancel		2.50
a.		Perf. 12	65.00	6.00
		Revenue cancel		2.50
b.		Perf. 12½	65.00	6.00
		Revenue cancel		2.50
AR35	PF7	1sh blue, *yel,* perf 12½	90.00	20.00
		Revenue cancel		10.00
AR36	PF8	1sh 6p pink	150.00	25.00
		Revenue cancel		10.00
AR37	PF9	2sh blue, *grn*	100.00	15.00
		Revenue cancel		7.50
a.		Perf. 12	125.00	17.50
		Revenue cancel		7.50
b.		Perf. 12½	—	20.00
		Revenue cancel		7.50
AR38	PF10	2sh 6p orange, perf 12½	80.00	12.50
		Revenue cancel		2.00
AR39	PF11	3sh violet, *bl,* perf 12½	200.00	22.50
		Revenue cancel		7.50
AR40	PF11	3sh bister	60.00	17.50
		Revenue cancel		7.50
AR41	PF12	4sh org, perf 12½	90.00	10.00
		Revenue cancel		2.50
AR42	PF13	5sh claret, *yel*	55.00	6.00
		Revenue cancel		2.00
a.		Perf. 12	70.00	12.50
		Revenue cancel		2.00
b.		Perf. 12½	55.00	12.50
		Revenue cancel		2.00
AR43	PF13	5sh car rose	85.00	10.00
		Revenue cancel		4.00
AR44	PF14	6sh green	90.00	25.00
		Revenue cancel		8.00
AR45	PF15	10sh brn, *pink*	—	60.00
		Revenue cancel		30.00
a.		Perf. 12		
b.		Perf. 12½		
AR46	PF15	10sh green	110.00	17.50
		Revenue cancel		10.00
AR47	PF16	15sh brown	350.00	45.00
		Revenue cancel		8.00
AR48	PF17	£1 orange, *yel,* perf 12½	375.00	65.00
		Revenue cancel		15.00
a.		Perf. 12	650.00	80.00
		Revenue cancel		15.00
AR49	PF18	£1 5sh pink	1,000.	90.00
		Revenue cancel		50.00
AR50	PF19	£1 10sh olive	700.00	80.00
		Revenue cancel		30.00
AR51	PF21	£2 blue	850.00	80.00
		Revenue cancel		15.00
a.		Perf. 12	—	100.00
		Revenue cancel		15.00
AR52	PF22	45sh gray lilac	2,500.	100.00
		Revenue cancel		30.00
AR53	PF23	£5 rose, perf. 12	—	250.00
		Revenue cancel		75.00
a.		perf. 12½	—	400.00
		Revenue cancel		100.00
AR54	PF28	£10 lilac	2,000.	100.00
		Revenue cancel		35.00
a.		Perf. 12	1,750.	110.00
		Revenue cancel		35.00

Nos. AR49-AR52, AR54, used, are valued cto.

PF29

PF30

PF31

Wmk. V and Crown (70)

1879-1900 Engr. *Perf. 12½*

AR55	PF29	£25 green	—	500.00
		Revenue cancel		65.00
a.		Perf. 13		
b.		Perf. 12		
AR56	PF30	£50 violet	—	500.00
		Revenue cancel		75.00
a.		Perf. 13		
AR57	PF31	£100 red	—	475.00
		Revenue cancel		125.00
a.		Perf. 13		
b.		Perf. 12		
		Revenue cancel		125.00

Typo.

AR58	PF29	£25 green	—	110.00
a.		Lithographed		
		Revenue cancel		50.00
AR59	PF30	£50 violet	—	150.00
a.		Lithographed		
		Revenue cancel		70.00
AR60	PF31	£100 red	—	225.00
a.		Lithographed		
		Revenue cancel		100.00

Nos. AR55-AR60, used, are valued cto.

PF32

1887-90 Typo.

AR61	PF32	£5 claret & ultra	*1,250.*	100.00
		Revenue cancel		25.00
AR62	PF32	£6 blue & yel	*1,500.*	125.00
		Revenue cancel		30.00
AR63	PF32	£7 blk & red	*1,750.*	150.00
		Revenue cancel		40.00
AR64	PF32	£8 orange & lilac	*1,900.*	175.00
		Revenue cancel		45.00
AR65	PF32	£9 red & green	*2,000.*	200.00
		Revenue cancel		50.00

Nos. AR61-AR65, used, are valued cto.

SEMI-POSTAL STAMPS

SP1

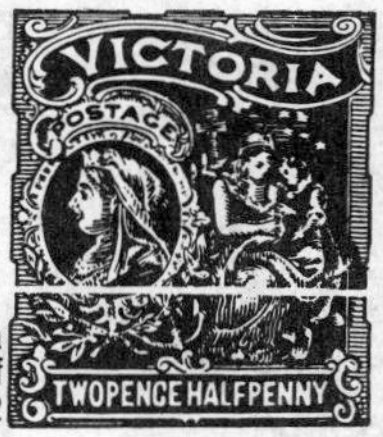

Queen Victoria and Figure of Charity — SP2

Wmk. V and Crown (70)

1897, Oct. Typo. *Perf. 12½*

B1	SP1	1p deep blue	15.00	18.00
B2	SP2	2½p red brown	110.00	110.00

These stamps were sold at 1sh and 2sh6p respectively. The premium was given to a charitable institution.

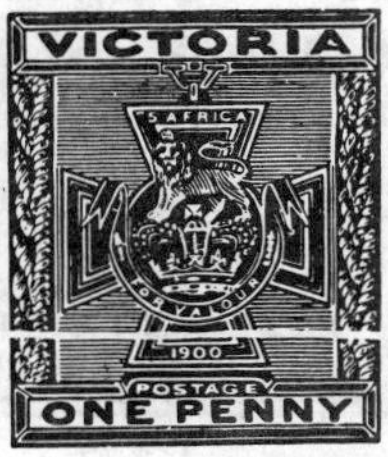

Victoria Cross — SP3

Scout Reporting SP4

1900

B3	SP3	1p brown olive	70.00	70.00
B4	SP4	2p emerald	140.00	140.00

These stamps were sold at 1sh and 2sh respectively. The premium was given to a patriotic fund in connection with the South African War.

REGISTRATION STAMPS

R1

Unwmk.

1854, Dec. 1 Typo. *Imperf.*

F1	R1	1sh rose & blue	1,000.	100.00

1857 *Rouletted 7*

F2	R1	1sh rose & blue	5,000.	150.00

LATE FEE STAMP

LF1

Unwmk.

1855, Jan. 1 Typo. *Imperf.*

I1	LF1	6p lilac & green	650.00	150.00

POSTAGE DUE STAMPS

D1

Wmk. V and Crown (70)

1890 Typo. *Perf. 12½*

J1	D1	½p claret & blue	2.00	1.65
J2	D1	1p claret & blue	3.25	1.25
J3	D1	2p claret & blue	5.00	1.50
J4	D1	4p claret & blue	6.00	1.75
J5	D1	5p claret & blue	5.50	1.65
J6	D1	6p claret & blue	6.25	1.50
J7	D1	10p claret & blue	60.00	32.50
J8	D1	1sh claret & blue	35.00	5.00
J9	D1	2sh claret & blue	92.50	42.50
J10	D1	5sh claret & blue	140.00	90.00
		Nos. J1-J10 (10)	355.50	179.30

1891

J11	D1	½p lake & blue	2.50	2.00
J12	D1	1p brown red & blue	4.25	1.25
J13	D1	2p brown red & blue	4.25	.90
J14	D1	4p lake & blue	6.50	4.50
		Nos. J11-J14 (4)	17.50	8.65

1894

J15	D1	½p bl grn & rose	1.65	1.40
J16	D1	1p bl grn & rose	.70	.35
J17	D1	2p bl grn & rose	1.50	.30
J18	D1	4p bl grn & rose	3.50	1.25
J19	D1	5p bl grn & rose	4.00	2.25
J20	D1	6p bl grn & rose	4.00	2.50
J21	D1	10p bl grn & rose	10.00	8.50
J22	D1	1sh bl grn & rose	5.00	2.75
J23	D1	2sh green & rose	60.00	20.00
J24	D1	5sh green & rose	100.00	35.00
		Nos. J15-J24 (10)	190.35	74.30

1906 Wmk. 13

J25	D1	½p yel grn & rose	1.65	1.65
J26	D1	1p yel grn & rose	3.00	.65
J27	D1	2p yel grn & rose	6.50	1.50
J28	D1	4p yel grn & rose	13.00	10.00
		Nos. J25-J28 (4)	24.15	13.80

A 5p with wmk. 13 exists but was not issued.

WESTERN AUSTRALIA

ˈwes-tərn o-ˈstrāl-yə

LOCATION — Western part of Australia, occupying about a third of that continent

GOVT. — British Colony

AREA — 975,920 sq. mi.

POP. — 184,124 (1901)

CAPITAL — Perth

Western Australia was one of the six British colonies that united on January 1, 1901, to form the Commonwealth of Australia.

12 Pence = 1 Shilling

20 Shillings = 1 Pound

Unused values for Nos. 1-10 are for stamps without gum as these stamps are seldom found with original gum. Otherwise, unused values are for stamps with original gum as defined in the catalogue introduction.

Very fine examples of all rouletted and perforated stamps from Nos. 6-34 have roulettes or perforations touching the design. Examples clear on all four sides range from scarce to rare and will command higher prices.

Watermarks

Wmk. 82- Swan

Wmk. 83- Crown and W A

Wmk. 70- V and Crown

Wmk. 13- Crown & Double-lined A

Wmk. 74- Crown and Single-lined A

Swan

A1 A2

1854-57 Engr. Wmk. 82 *Imperf.*

1 A1 1p black 750. 190.

Litho.

2 A2 2p brown, *red* ('57) 1,300. 425.
a. 2p brown, *deep red* ('57) 1,500. 475.
b. Printed on both sides 1,500. 750.

See Nos. 4, 6-7, 9, 14-39, 44-52, 54, 59-61. For surcharges see Nos. 41, 55-56.

A3 A4

3 A3 4p blue 275. 150.
a. Frame inverted 60,000.
As "a," cut to shape 16,000.
b. 4p slate blue 1,000. 575.
4 A2 6p bronze ('57) 3,000. 600.
5 A4 1sh pale brown 400. 225.
a. 1sh dark brown 500. 375.
b. 1sh dark red brown 800. 400.
c. 1sh pale red brown 1,800.

Engraved
Rouletted

6 A1 1p black 1,750. 500.

Lithographed

7 A2 2p brown, *red* ('57) 3,250. 1,200.
a. Printed on both sides
8 A3 4p blue 1,400. 600.
9 A2 6p bronze ('57) 3,500. 1,000.
10 A4 1sh brown 2,000. 700.

The 2p, 4p and 6p are known with pin-perforation but this is believed to be unofficial.

1860 Engr. *Imperf.*

14 A1 2p vermilion 100.00 87.50
a. 2p pale orange 95.00 60.00
15 A1 4p blue 300.00 *800.00*
16 A1 6p dull green 1,100. 600.00

Rouletted

17 A1 2p vermilion 600.00 200.00
a. 2p pale orange 600.00 200.00
18 A1 4p deep blue 2,500. —
19 A1 6p dull green — 400.00

1861 *Clean-Cut Perf. 14 to 16*

20 A1 1p rose 330.00 80.00
a. Imperf.
21 A1 2p blue 70.00 25.00
a. Imperf., pair
b. Horiz. pair, imperf. vert.
22 A1 4p vermilion 265.00 150.00
a. Imperf.
23 A1 6p purple brn 175.00 35.00
a. Imperf.
24 A1 1sh green 300.00 45.00
a. Imperf.

Rough Perf. 14 to 16

24B A1 1p rose 200.00 27.50
24C A1 6p pur brn, *bluish* 750.00 50.00
24D A1 1sh deep green 1,200. 350.00

Perf. 14

25 A1 1p rose 140.00 45.00
25A A1 2p blue 70.00 30.00
25B A1 4p vermilion 200.00 100.00

Unwmk. *Perf. 13*

26 A1 1p lake 40.00 5.50
28 A1 6p violet 90.00 32.50

1865-79 Wmk. 1 *Perf. 12½*

29 A1 1p bister 40.00 2.00
30 A1 1p yel ocher 60.00 5.50
31 A1 2p yellow 45.00 .60
a. 2p lilac (error) ('79) *7,500.* *3,750.*
32 A1 4p carmine 50.00 5.50
a. Double impression *6,000.*
33 A1 6p violet 62.50 6.00
a. 6p lilac 130.00 6.00
b. 6p red lilac 120.00 6.00
c. Double impression
34 A1 1sh bright green 85.00 10.50
a. 1sh sage green 200.00 18.00
Nos. 29-34 (6) 342.50 30.10

1872-78 *Perf. 14*

35 A1 1p bister 50.00 2.00
36 A1 1p yellow ocher 40.00 .50
37 A1 2p yellow 40.00 .40
38 A1 4p carmine 200.00 65.00
39 A1 6p lilac 80.00 4.00
Nos. 35-39 (5) 410.00 71.90

A5 A8

1872 Typo.

40 A5 3p red brown 26.00 3.75
a. 3p brown 26.00 3.75

See #53, 92. For surcharges see #57, 69-72A.

No. 31 Surcharged in Green ONE PENNY

1875 Engr. *Perf. 12½*

41 A1 1p on 2p yellow 200.00 45.00
a. Pair, one without surcharge
b. "O" of "ONE" omitted
c. Triple surcharge

Forged surcharges exist.

1882 Wmk. 2 *Perf. 12*

44 A1 1p ocher yellow 85.00 1.65
46 A1 2p yellow 110.00 1.10
47 A1 4p carmine 160.00 27.50
48 A1 6p pale violet 275.00 27.50
Nos. 44-48 (4) 630.00 57.75

1882 *Perf. 14*

49 A1 1p ocher yellow 14.00 .20
50 A1 2p yellow 18.00 .20
51 A1 4p carmine 72.50 11.50
52 A1 6p pale violet 80.00 2.50
a. 6p violet 47.50 2.50

Typographed

53 A5 3p red brown 8.50 .70
a. 3p brown 12.50 .45
Nos. 49-53 (5) 193.00 15.10

1883 Engr. *Perf. 12x14*

54 A1 1p ocher yellow 1,650. 300.00

Nos. 44 and 49 Surcharged in Red $\frac{1}{2}$

1884 *Perf. 12*

55 A1 ½p on 1p ocher yel 9.00 12.00

Perf. 14

56 A1 ½p on 1p ocher yel 13.00 15.00

No. 40 Surcharged in Green **1d.**

1885 Typo. Wmk. 1

57 A5 1p on 3p red brown 27.50 8.50
a. 1p on 3p brown 12.00 6.00
b. "1" with straight top 27.50 11.00

Wmk. Crown and C A (2)

1885 Typo. *Perf. 14*

58 A8 ½p green 2.00 .20

See No. 89.

1888 Engr.

59 A1 1p rose 12.00 .70
60 A1 2p slate 30.00 2.00
61 A1 4p red brown 82.50 18.00
Nos. 59-61 (3) 124.50 20.70

A9 A10

A11 A12

1890-93 Typo.

62 A9 1p carmine rose 10.00 .20
63 A10 2p slate 14.00 .20
64 A11 2½p blue 6.00 .80
65 A12 4p orange brown 6.00 .80
66 A12 5p bister 8.25 1.00
67 A12 6p violet 14.00 .80
68 A12 1sh olive green 16.00 2.25
Nos. 62-68 (7) 74.25 6.05

See Nos. 73-74, 76, 80, 90, 94.

Nos. 40 and 53a Surcharged in Green **ONE PENNY**

1893 Wmk. Crown and C C (1)

69 A5 1p on 3p red brown 11.00 5.00
a. 1p on 3p brown 11.00 3.25
b. Double surcharge *725.00*

Wmkd. Crown and C A (2)

70 A5 1p on 3p brown 40.00 9.00

Nos. 40a and 53a Surcharged in Green **Half-penny**

1895 Wmk. Crown and C C (1)

71 A5 ½p on 3p brown 7.00 3.00
a. Double surcharge *700.00*

Green and Red Surcharge

72 A5 ½p on 3p brown 125.00

Wmk. Crown and C A (2)

72A A5 ½p on 3p brown 75.00

After the supply of paper watermarked Crown and C C was exhausted, No. 72A was printed. Ostensibly this was to provide samples for Postal Union distribution, but a supply for philatelic demands was also made.

Types of 1890-93 and

A15

1899-1901 Typo. Wmk. 83

73 A9 1p carmine rose 3.50 .20
74 A10 2p yellow 9.00 .20
75 A15 2½p blue ('01) 6.00 .20
Nos. 73-75 (3) 18.50 .60

A16 A17

A18 A19

A20 A21

A22 Southern Cross — A23

Queen Victoria

A24 A25

Perf. 12½, 12x12½

1902-05 Wmk. 70

76 A9 1p carmine rose 6.50 .20
a. 1p salmon
b. Perf. 11 100.00 5.00
c. Perf. 12½x11 180.00
77 A16 2p yellow 3.25 .20
a. Perf. 11 125.00 5.50
b. Perf. 12½x11 220.00
79 A17 4p orange brn 6.00 .80
a. Perf. 11 375.00 110.00
80 A12 5p olive bis ('05) 72.50 40.00
a. Perf. 11 45.00 21.00
81 A18 8p pale yel grn 20.00 2.75
82 A19 9p orange 27.50 4.00
b. Perf. 11 60.00 40.00
83 A20 10p red 27.50 5.50
84 A21 2sh red, *yel* 42.50 8.25
a. Perf. 11 125.00 55.00
85 A22 2sh6p dk bl, *rose* 40.00 7.75
86 A23 5sh blue green 70.00 19.00
87 A24 10sh violet 175.00 60.00
88 A25 £1 brown org 475.00 225.00
Nos. 76-88 (12) 965.75 373.45

Perf. 12½, 12x12½

1905-12 Wmk. 13

89 A8 ½p dp green ('10) 2.25 .35
90 A9 1p rose 3.00 .20
e. Perf. 11 13.00 2.50
f. Perf. 12½x11 200.00 82.50
91 A16 2p yellow 3.00 .20
a. Perf. 11 11.00 4.50
b. Perf. 12½x11 230.00 95.00
92 A5 3p brown 6.50 .40
a. Perf. 11 12.00 2.75
b. Perf. 12½x11 265.00 82.50
93 A17 4p orange brn 8.00 1.50
a. 4p bister brown 8.00 1.50
b. Perf. 11 465.00 90.00
94 A12 5p olive bis 10.00 .70
a. Perf. 11 25.00 8.50
95 A18 8p pale yel grn ('12) 16.00 17.00
96 A19 9p orange 21.00 3.00
b. Perf. 11 65.00 55.00
97 A20 10p red orange 21.00 10.00
98 A23 5s blue green 140.00 40.00
Nos. 89-98 (10) 230.75 73.35

For surcharge see No. 103.

A26 A27

1906-07 Wmk. 83 *Perf. 14*

99 A26 6p bright violet 18.00 .70
100 A27 1sh olive green 25.00 6.00

1912 Wmk. 74 *Perf. 11½x12*

101	A26	6p bright violet	11.00	3.00
102	A27	1sh gray green	22.50	4.00
a.		Perf. 12½		

No. 91 Surcharged **ONE PENNY**

1912 Wmk. 13 *Perf. 12½*

103	A16	1p on 2p yellow	.75	.40

Stamps of Western Australia were replaced by those of Australia.

POSTAL FISCAL STAMPS

Postal use of the 1p telegraph stamp was authorized beginning Oct. 25, 1886.

Used values are for examples with postal cancellations.

Beware of copies with a pen cancellation removed and a fake postmark added.

PF1

PF2

1886 Wmk. 1 *Perf. 14*

AR1	PF1	1p bister	30.00	6.00
		Perf. 12½		
AR2	PF1	1p bister	27.50	4.00

The 6p is known postally used but was not authorized.

Authorized for postal use by the Post and Telegraph Act of Sept. 5, 1893 were the current revenue stamps through the 1sh value.

Beware of copies with a pen cancellation removed and a fake postmark added.

Because the Act specified current stamps, postally used examples from the provisional issue of of 1881 are not included here.

1882 Wmk. 2 *Perf. 14*

AR3	PF2	1p purple	10.00	1.50
AR4	PF2	2p purple	100.00	35.00
AR5	PF2	3p purple	35.00	2.25
AR6	PF2	6p purple	40.00	4.00
AR7	PF2	1sh purple	75.00	5.50
		Wmk. 83		
AR8	PF2	1p purple	6.50	1.50
AR9	PF2	3p purple	27.50	2.25
AR10	PF2	6p purple	27.50	2.50
AR11	PF2	1sh purple	75.00	10.00

Nos. AR7, AR11 have a rectangular outer frame and a circular frame around the swan.

Higher values are known with postal cancels, some postally used, but these were not authorized.

AUSTRALIA

o-'strāl-yə

LOCATION — Oceania, south of Indonesia, bounded on the west by the Indian Ocean
GOVT. — Self-governing dominion of the British Commonwealth
AREA — 2,967,909 sq. mi.
POP. — 17,892,423 (1996)
CAPITAL — Canberra

Australia includes the former British colonies of New South Wales, Victoria, Queensland, South Australia, Western Australia and Tasmania.

12 Pence = 1 Shilling
20 Shillings = 1 Pound
100 Cents = 1 Dollar (1966)

Catalogue values for unused stamps in this country are for Never Hinged items, beginning with Scott 197 in the regular postage section, Scott C6 in the air post section, Scott J71 in the postage due section, and all of the Australian Antarctic Territory.

Watermarks

Wmk. 8- Wide Crown and Wide A

Wmk. 9- Wide Crown and Narrow A

Wmk. 10- Narrow Crown and Narrow A

Wmk. 11- Multiple Crown and A

Wmk. 12- Crown and Single-lined A

Wmk. 13- Large Crown and Double-lined A

Wmk. 55- Large Crown and NSW

Wmk. 203- Small Crown and A Multiple

Wmk. 228- Small Crown and C of A Multiple

Kangaroo and Map — A1

Die I - The inside frameline has a break at left, even with the top of the letters of the denomination.

Die II - The frameline does not show a break.

Die III - The left inside frameline shows a break parallel to the face of the kangaroo.

Die IV - As Die III, with a break in the top outside frameline above the "ST" of "AUSTRALIA." The upper right inside frameline has an incomplete corner.

Dies are only indicated when there are more than one for any denomination.

1913 Typo. Wmk. 8 *Perf. 11½, 12*

1	A1	½p green	5.50	2.50
		Never hinged	10.00	
2	A1	1p car, die I	6.75	.65
		Never hinged	11.50	
h.		Die II	12.50	.90
		Never hinged	22.50	
3	A1	2p gray	22.50	4.00
		Never hinged	40.00	
4	A1	2½p dark blue	25.00	12.00
		Never hinged	40.00	
5	A1	3p ol bis, die I	45.00	8.50
		Never hinged	80.00	
a.		Die II	150.00	47.50
		Never hinged	*300.00*	
6	A1	4p orange	47.50	21.00
		Never hinged	100.00	
7	A1	5p orange brown	40.00	30.00
		Never hinged	110.00	
8	A1	6p ultra (II)	45.00	18.00
		Never hinged	125.00	
b.		Die III	*1,000.*	*300.00*
9	A1	9p purple	42.50	22.50
		Never hinged	110.00	
10	A1	1sh blue green	45.00	13.50
		Never hinged	175.00	
11	A1	2sh brown	150.00	75.00
		Never hinged	500.00	
12	A1	5sh yellow & gray	250.00	140.00
		Never hinged	650.00	
13	A1	10sh pink & gray	600.00	425.00
		Never hinged	1,600.	
14	A1	£1 ultra & brown	1,300.	1,000.
		Never hinged	2,750.	
15	A1	£2 dp rose & blk	2,250.	1,550.
		Nos. 1-12 (12)	724.75	347.65

On No. 4 "2½d" is colorless in solid blue background.

See Nos. 38-59, 96-102, 121-129, 206.

King George V
A2

Kookaburra (Kingfisher)
A3

1913-14 Unwmk. Engr. *Perf. 11*

17	A2	1p carmine	4.25	4.25
		Never hinged	5.75	
a.		Vert. pair, imperf. between	*2,000.*	
18	A3	6p lake brown ('14)	70.00	35.00
		Never hinged	150.00	

See No. 95.

A4

ONE PENNY

Die I - Normal die, having outside the oval band with "AUSTRALIA" a white line and a heavy colored line.

Die Ia - As die I with a small white spur below the right serif at foot of the "1" in left tablet.

Die II - A heavy colored line between two white lines back of the emu's neck. A white scratch crossing the vertical shading lines at the lowest point of the bust.

TWO PENCE

Die I - The numeral "2" is thin. The upper curve is 1mm. across and a very thin line connects it with the foot of the figure.

Die II - The "2" is thicker than in die I. The top curve is 1½mm across and a strong white line connects it with the foot of the figure. There are thin vertical lines across the ends of the groups of short horizontal lines at each side of "TWO PENCE."

THREE PENCE

Die I - The ends of the thin horizontal lines in the background run into the solid color of the various parts of the design. The numerals are thin and the letters of "THREE PENCE" are thin and irregular.

Die II - The oval about the portrait, the shields with the numerals, etc., are outlined by thin white lines which separate them from the horizontal background lines. The numerals are thick and the letters of "THREE PENCE" are heavy and regular.

FIVE PENCE

Die I - The top of the flag of the "5" is slightly curved.

Die II - The top of the flag of the "5" is flat. There are thin white vertical lines across the ends of the short horizontal lines at each side of "FIVE PENCE."

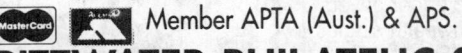

1914-24 Typo. Wmk. 9 *Perf. 14*

19 A4 ½p emerald ('15) 2.50 .40
Never hinged 4.50
a. Thin "½" at right 1,400. 700.00
20 A4 ½p orange ('23) 2.50 1.25
Never hinged 3.50
21 A4 1p red (I) 4.25 .20
Never hinged 7.50
a. 1p carmine rose (I) 8.25 .80
Never hinged 20.00
b. 1p red (Ia) 375.00 4.75
Never hinged 500.00
c. 1p carmine (II) ('18) 60.00 30.00
Never hinged 95.00
d. 1p scar (I), rough paper 18.00 2.00
e. 1p rose red (Ia), rough paper 250.00 20.00
f. 1p brt rose (Ia), rough paper 375.00 50.00
22 A4 1p vio (I) ('22) 4.50 .60
Never hinged 8.00
a. 1p red violet 6.50 1.50
Never hinged 10.00
23 A4 1p green (I) ('24) 3.50 .20
Never hinged 4.50
24 A4 1½p choc ('18) 5.00 .20
Never hinged 8.00
a. 1½p red brown 5.50 .20
Never hinged 14.00
b. 1½p black brown 4.50 .25
Never hinged 7.50
25 A4 1½p emerald ('23) 3.50 .20
Never hinged 4.00
26 A4 1½p scarlet ('24) 2.50 .20
Never hinged 3.50
27 A4 2p brn org (I) ('20) 10.00 .25
Never hinged 17.00
a. 2p orange (I) ('20) 12.00 .30
Never hinged 19.00
b. Booklet pane of 6
28 A4 2p red (I) ('22) 7.50 .20
Never hinged 14.00
29 A4 2p red brn (I) ('24) 15.00 3.75
Never hinged 25.00
30 A4 3p ultra (I) ('24) 25.00 2.25
Never hinged 35.00
31 A4 4p orange ('15) 70.00 2.25
Never hinged 40.00
a. 4p yellow 110.00 16.00
Never hinged 250.00
32 A4 4p violet ('21) 17.50 13.00
Never hinged 25.00
33 A4 4p lt ultra ('22) 45.00 4.50
Never hinged 60.00
34 A4 4p ol bis ('24) 27.50 4.00
Never hinged 37.50
35 A4 4½p violet ('24) 22.50 4.00
Never hinged 35.00
36 A4 5p org brn (I) ('15) 18.00 3.00
Never hinged 45.00
37 A4 1sh4p lt blue ('20) 65.00 19.00
Never hinged 100.00
Nos. 19-37 (19) 351.25 59.45

See Nos. 60-76, 113-120, 124.

1915 *Perf. 11½, 12*

38 A1 2p gray 45.00 11.00
Never hinged 95.00
39 A1 2½p dark blue 45.00 15.00
Never hinged 110.00
40 A1 6p ultra (II) 125.00 19.00
Never hinged 275.00
a. Die III 900.00 250.00
41 A1 9p violet 125.00 32.50
Never hinged 275.00
42 A1 1sh blue green 125.00 20.00
Never hinged 325.00
43 A1 2sh brown 400.00 90.00
Never hinged 900.00
44 A1 5sh yellow & gray 700.00 225.00
Never hinged 1,500.
Nos. 38-44 (7) 1,565. 412.50

1915-24 Wmk. 10

45 A1 2p gray (I) 20.00 5.00
Never hinged 40.00
a. Die II, shiny paper 35.00 8.00
46 A1 2½p dark blue 20.00 7.50
Never hinged 40.00
a. "1" of fraction omitted 10,000. 3,500.
47 A1 3p olive bister (I) 20.00 3.50
Never hinged 35.00
a. Die II 80.00 25.00
b. 3p lt olive (IV) 35.00 10.00
48 A1 6p ultra (II) 45.00 7.00
Never hinged 90.00
a. 6p chalky blue (III) 65.00 7.00
c. 6p ultra (IV) 50.00 6.00
49 A1 6p yel brn (IV, '23) 20.00 2.50
Never hinged 40.00
50 A1 9p lilac (III) 35.00 6.00
Never hinged 55.00
a. 9p violet (II) 35.00 6.00
Never hinged 55.00
51 A1 1sh blue grn (II, '16) 35.00 4.50
Never hinged 55.00
b. Die IV 35.00 3.00
52 A1 2sh brown ('16) 150.00 15.00
Never hinged 350.00
53 A1 2sh vio brn (II, '24) 50.00 20.00
Never hinged 100.00
54 A1 5sh yel & gray ('18) 180.00 80.00
Never hinged 350.00
55 A1 10sh brt pink & gray ('17) 400.00 150.00
Never hinged 750.00
56 A1 £1 ultra & brn ('16) 1,250. 700.00
Never hinged 2,500.
a. £1 ultra & brn org ('16) 1,300. 700.00
57 A1 £1 gray (IV, '24) 450.00 275.00
Never hinged 750.00
58 A1 £2 dp rose & blk ('19) 2,250. 1,250.
Never hinged 3,000.
59 A1 £2 rose & vio brn ('24) 1,750. 1,200.
Never hinged 2,750.
Nos. 45-54 (10) 575.00 151.00

Perf. 14, 14½, 14½x14

1918-23 Wmk. 11

60 A4 ½p emerald 3.00 1.00
Never hinged 4.25
a. Thin "½" at right 110.00 45.00
61 A4 1p rose (I) 25.00 9.00
Never hinged 32.50
62 A4 1p dl grn (I) ('24) 6.00 6.00
Never hinged 9.00
63 A4 1½p choc ('19) 5.00 1.00
Never hinged 11.00
a. 1½p red brown ('19) 8.00 1.00
Never hinged 15.00
Nos. 60-63 (4) 39.00 17.00

1924 Unwmk. *Perf. 14*

64 A4 1p green (I) 4.25 3.75
Never hinged 5.50
65 A4 1½p carmine 4.25 3.00
Never hinged 6.75

Perf. 14, 13½x12½

1926-30 Wmk. 203

66 A4 ½p orange 1.40 1.00
Never hinged 3.00
a. Perf. 14 ('27) 6.50 5.25
Never hinged 8.50
67 A4 1p green (I) 1.50 .40
Never hinged 3.00
a. 1p green (Ia) 47.50 60.00
Never hinged 65.00
b. Perf. 14 2.75 .45
Never hinged 4.50
68 A4 1½p rose red ('27) 2.75 .20
Never hinged 3.50
c. Perf. 14 ('26) 6.00 .65
Never hinged 12.00
69 A4 1½p red brn ('30) 4.00 2.00
Never hinged 8.00
70 A4 2p red brn (II, '28) 7.00 4.00
Never hinged 10.50
a. Perf. 14 (I, '27) 27.50 20.00
Never hinged 40.00
71 A4 2p red (II) ('30) 4.00 .20
Never hinged 12.50
a. 2p red (I) ('30) 5.00 1.65
Never hinged 12.00
c. Unwmkd. (II) ('31) 1,500. 1,000.
72 A4 3p ultra (I) 30.00 10.00
Never hinged 55.00
a. 3p ultra (II) ('29) 17.50 2.00
Never hinged 30.00
b. Perf. 14 20.00 4.50
Never hinged 37.50
73 A4 4p ol bis ('29) 16.00 2.00
Never hinged 32.50
a. Perf. 14 ('28) 42.50 22.50
Never hinged 85.00
74 A4 4½p dk vio ('27) 17.00 3.75
Never hinged 25.00
a. Perf. 13½x12½ ('28) 47.50 13.00
Never hinged 67.50
75 A4 5p brn buff (II) ('30) 17.50 4.50
Never hinged 32.50
76 A4 1sh4p pale turq bl ('28) 85.00 20.00
Never hinged 175.00
a. Perf. 14 ('27) 125.00 67.50
Never hinged 300.00
Nos. 66-76 (11) 186.15 48.05

For surcharges & overprints see #106-107, O3-O4.

Parliament House, Canberra — A5

Unwmk.

1927, May 9 Engr. *Perf. 11*

94 A5 1½p brown red .45 .20
Never hinged .85
a. Vert. pair, imperf. btwn. 2,750. 2,500.

Opening of Parliament House at Canberra.

Melbourne Exhibition Issue

Kookaburra Type of 1914

1928, Oct. 29

95 A3 3p deep blue 3.75 3.00
Never hinged 5.25
a. Pane of 4 125.00 150.00
Never hinged 190.00

No. 95a was issued at the Melbourne Intl. Phil. Exhib. No marginal inscription. Printed in sheets of 60 stamps (15 panes). No. 95 was printed in sheets of 120 and issued Nov. 2 throughout Australia.

Kangaroo-Map Type of 1913

Perf. 11½, 12

1929-30 Wmk. 203 Typo.

96 A1 6p brown 21.00 5.00
Never hinged 30.00
97 A1 9p violet 30.00 5.00
Never hinged 70.00
98 A1 1sh blue green 27.50 4.50
Never hinged 65.00
99 A1 2sh red brown 60.00 12.50
Never hinged 140.00
100 A1 5sh yel & gray 190.00 60.00
Never hinged 325.00
101 A1 10sh pink & gray 350.00 275.00
Never hinged 600.00
102 A1 £2 dl red & blk ('30) 1,800. 425.00
Never hinged 3,750.
Nos. 96-102 (7) 2,478. 787.00

For overprint see No. O5.

Black Swan — A6

Capt. Charles Sturt — A7

Unwmk.

1929, Sept. 28 Engr. *Perf. 11*

103 A6 1½p dull red .75 .75
Never hinged 1.40

Centenary of Western Australia.

1930, June 2

104 A7 1½p dark red .40 .20
Never hinged .45
105 A7 3p dark blue 3.50 3.00
Never hinged 6.00

Capt. Charles Sturt's exploration of the Murray River, cent.

Nos. 68 and 74a surcharged

FIVE

PENCE

1930 Wmk. 203 *Perf. 13½x12½*

106 A4 2p on 1½p rose red .75 .25
Never hinged 1.50
107 A4 5p on 4½p dark violet 5.00 5.00
Never hinged 10.00

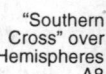

"Southern Cross" over Hemispheres A8

Perf. 11, 11½

1931, Mar. 19 Unwmk.

111 A8 2p dull red .75 .20
Never hinged 1.10
112 A8 3p blue 4.75 3.25
Never hinged 8.00
Nos. 111-112,C2 (3) 13.00 10.95

Trans-oceanic flights (1928-1930) of Sir Charles Edward Kingsford-Smith (1897-1935).
See #C3 for similar design. For overprints see #CO1, O1-O2.

Types of 1913-23 Issues

Perf. 13½x12½

1931-36 Typo. Wmk. 228

113 A4 ½p orange ('32) 2.50 1.65
Never hinged 3.00
114 A4 1p green (I) 1.50 .20
Never hinged 2.25
115 A4 1½p red brn ('36) 6.00 4.50
Never hinged 8.00
116 A4 2p red (II) 1.75 .20
Never hinged 2.50
117 A4 3p ultra (II) ('32) 17.50 .30
Never hinged 25.00
118 A4 4p ol bis ('33) 17.50 .45
Never hinged 26.00
120 A4 5p brn buff (II) ('32) 12.00 .30
Never hinged 20.00

Perf. 11½, 12; 13½x12½ (1sh4p)

121 A1 6p yel brn ('36) 16.00 11.00
Never hinged 25.00
122 A1 9p violet ('32) 16.50 2.00
Never hinged 40.00
124 A4 1sh4p lt blue ('32) 60.00 6.00
Never hinged 135.00
125 A1 2sh red brn ('35) 4.00 .90
Never hinged 6.00
126 A1 5sh yel & gray ('32) 125.00 18.00
Never hinged 250.00
127 A1 10sh pink & gray ('32) 325.00 100.00
Never hinged 650.00
128 A1 £1 gray ('35) 450.00 165.00
Never hinged 650.00
129 A1 £2 dl rose & blk ('34) 2,000. 350.00
Never hinged 3,000.
Nos. 113-129 (15) 3,055. 660.50

For redrawn 2sh see No. 206. For overprints see Nos. O6-O11.

Sydney Harbor Bridge — A9

Unwmk.

1932, Mar. 14 Engr. *Perf. 11*

130 A9 2p red 1.90 .50
Never hinged 2.25
131 A9 3p blue 4.00 3.00
Never hinged 6.75
132 A9 5sh gray green 350.00 200.00
Never hinged 575.00

Wmk. 228

Perf. 10½

Typo.

133 A9 2p red 1.65 .80
Never hinged 2.75

Opening of the Sydney Harbor Bridge on Mar. 19, 1932.
Value for 5sh, used, is for CTO copies.
For overprints see Nos. O12-O13.

Kookaburra A14

Male Lyrebird A16

1932, June 1 *Perf. 13½x12½*

139 A14 6p light brown 15.00 .50
Never hinged 25.00

1932, Feb. 15 Unwmk. *Perf. 11*
Size: 21½x25mm

141 A16 1sh green 37.50 .75
Never hinged 75.00

See #175, 300. For overprint see #O14.

YarraYarra Tribesman, Yarra River and View of Melbourne A17

Wmk. 228

1934, July 2 Engr. *Perf. 10½*

142 A17 2p vermilion 1.10 .30
Never hinged 1.75
a. Perf. 11½ 3.75 .75
Never hinged 6.50
143 A17 3p blue 2.75 2.50
Never hinged 5.25
a. Perf. 11½ 4.25 2.50
Never hinged 6.50
144 A17 1sh black 40.00 16.00
Never hinged 67.50
a. Perf. 11½ 40.00 20.00
Never hinged 72.50
Nos. 142-144 (3) 43.85 18.80

Centenary of Victoria.

Merino Sheep — A18

1934, Nov. 1 *Perf. 11½*

147 A18 2p copper red 2.50 .20
Never hinged 3.50
148 A18 3p dark blue 8.50 4.50
Never hinged 12.00
149 A18 9p dark violet 35.00 25.00
Never hinged 67.50
Nos. 147-149 (3) 46.00 29.70

Capt. John Macarthur (1767-1834), "father of the New South Wales woolen industry."
There are two types of the 2p.

Cenotaph in Whitehall, London A19

George V on His Charger "Anzac" A20

1935, Mar. 18 *Perf. 13½x12½*

150 A19 2p red .65 .20
Never hinged .90

Perf. 11

151 A19 1sh black 40.00 25.00
Never hinged 70.00

Anzacs' landing at Gallipoli, 20th anniv.

1935, May 2 *Perf. 11½*

152 A20 2p red .40 .20
Never hinged .70
153 A20 3p blue 3.00 2.25
Never hinged 7.50
154 A20 2sh violet 37.50 30.00
Never hinged 70.00
Nos. 152-154 (3) 40.90 32.45

25th anniv. of the reign of King George V.

Amphitrite Joining Cables between Australia and Tasmania A21

1936, Apr. 1

157 A21 2p red .35 .20
Never hinged .45
158 A21 3p dark blue 3.25 2.00
Never hinged 4.75

Australia/Tasmania telephone link.

Proclamation Tree and View of Adelaide, 1936 — A22

1936, Aug. 3

159 A22 2p red .40 .20
Never hinged 1.10
160 A22 3p dark blue 3.25 3.25
Never hinged 5.00
161 A22 1sh green 12.00 6.00
Never hinged 20.00
Nos. 159-161 (3) 15.65 9.45

Centenary of South Australia.

Gov. Arthur Phillip at Sydney Cove — A23

1937, Oct. 1 *Perf. 13x13½*

163 A23 2p red .90 .20
Never hinged 1.90
164 A23 3p ultra 2.75 1.65
Never hinged 4.50
165 A23 9p violet 16.00 11.00
Never hinged 25.00
Nos. 163-165 (3) 19.65 12.85

150th anniversary of New South Wales.

Kangaroo A24

Queen Elizabeth A25

King George VI
A26 A27

Koala A28

Merino Sheep A29

Kookaburra (Kingfisher) A30

Platypus A31

Queen Elizabeth and King George VI in Coronation Robes
A32 A33

King George VI and Queen Elizabeth — A34

Two Types of A25 and A26:
Type I - Highlighted background. Lines around letters of Australia Postage and numerals of value.
Type II - Background of heavy diagonal lines without the highlighted effect. No lines around letters and numerals.

Perf. 13½x14, 14x13½

1937-46 Engr. Wmk. 228

166 A24 ½p org, perf. 15x14 ('42) .20 .20
Never hinged 1.00
a. Perf. 13½x14 ('38) .70 .25
Never hinged 1.25
167 A25 1p emerald (I) .20 .20
Never hinged 1.00
168 A26 1½p dull red brn (II) 3.00 1.75
Never hinged 4.50
a. Perf. 15x14 ('41) 4.25 3.50
Never hinged 6.25
169 A26 2p scarlet (I) .30 .20
Never hinged 1.00
170 A27 3p ultramarine 12.00 .60
Never hinged 30.00
a. 3p dp ultra, thin paper ('38) 20.00 .80
Never hinged 50.00
171 A28 4p grn, perf. 15x14 ('42) .85 .20
Never hinged 1.25
a. Perf. 13½x14 ('38) 2.50 .90
Never hinged 5.00
172 A29 5p pale rose vio, perf. 14x15 ('46) 1.25 .50
Never hinged 2.00
a. Perf. 14x13½ ('38) 2.50 .55
Never hinged 4.00
173 A30 6p vio brn, perf. 15x14 ('42) .60 .20
Never hinged 1.50
a. Perf. 13½x14 5.25 .85
Never hinged 15.00
b. 6p chocolate, perf. 15x14 1.00 .20
Never hinged 1.50
174 A31 9p sep, perf. 14x15 ('43) 1.75 .20
Never hinged 2.50
a. Perf. 14x13½ ('38) 3.75 .90
Never hinged 7.25
175 A16 1sh gray grn, perf. 15x14 ('41) 1.10 .20
Never hinged 1.50
a. Perf. 13½x14 22.50 2.00
Never hinged 47.50
176 A27 1sh4p magenta ('38) 1.50 .50
Never hinged 2.00

Perf. 13½

177 A32 5sh dl red brn ('38) 5.00 2.50
Never hinged 7.50
178 A33 10sh dl gray vio ('38) 30.00 13.00
Never hinged 45.00
179 A34 £1 bl gray ('38) 60.00 27.50
Never hinged 90.00
Nos. 166-179 (14) 117.75 47.75

No. 175 measures 17½x21½mm.
See #223A, 293, 295, 298, 300. For surcharge & overprints see #190, M1, M4-M5, M7.

1938-42 *Perf. 15x14*

180 A25 1p emerald (II) .55 .25
181 A25 1p dl red brn (II) ('41) .50 .20
181B A26 1½p bl grn (II) ('41) .60 .20
182 A26 2p scarlet (II) .60 .20
182B A26 2p red vio (II) ('41) .20 .20
183 A27 3p dk ultra ('40) 15.00 .75
Never hinged 30.00
183A A27 3p dk vio brn ('42) .20 .20
Nos. 180-183A (7) 17.65 2.00
Set, never hinged 40.00

No. 183 differs from Nos. 170-170a in the shading lines on the king's left eyebrow which go downward, left to right, instead of the reverse. Also, more of the left epaulette shows.
For surcharges & overprint see #188-189, M3.

Coil Perforation

A special perforation was applied to stamps intended for use in coils to make separation easier. It consists of small and large holes (2 small, 10 large, 2 small) on the stamps' narrow side. Some of the stamps so perforated were sold in sheets.
This coil perforation may be found on Nos. 166, 181, 182, 182B, 193, 215, 223A, 231, 257, 315-316, 319, 319a and others.

Nurse, Sailor, Soldier and Aviator — A35

Perf. 13½x13

1940, July 15 Engr. Wmk. 228

184 A35 1p green 1.00 .20
Never hinged 2.00
185 A35 2p red 1.00 .20
Never hinged 2.00
186 A35 3p ultra 4.00 3.00
Never hinged 7.00
187 A35 6p chocolate 12.50 10.00
Never hinged 21.00
Nos. 184-187 (4) 18.50 13.40

Australia's participation in WWII.

No. 182 Surcharged in Blue 2½d

1941, Dec. 10 *Perf. 15x14*

188 A26 2½p on 2p red .20 .20
Never hinged .25

No. 183 Surcharged in Blue and Yellow 3½d

189 A27 3½p on 3p dk ultra .40 .35
Never hinged .50

No. 172a Surcharged in Purple 5½d

Perf. 14x13½

190 A29 5½p on 5p pale rose violet 4.00 4.00
Never hinged 4.75
Nos. 188-190 (3) 4.60 4.55

Queen Elizabeth
A36 A37

King George VI
A38 A39

George VI and Blue Wrens — A40

Emu — A41

1942-44 Engr. *Perf. 15x14*

191 A36 1p brown vio ('43) .20 .20
192 A37 1½p green .20 .20
193 A38 2p lt rose vio ('44) .20 .20
194 A39 2½p red .20 .20
195 A40 3½p ultramarine .20 .20
196 A41 5½p indigo .35 .20
Nos. 191-196 (6) 1.35 1.20
Set, never hinged 1.75

See #224-225. For overprint see #M2.

Catalogue values for unused stamps in this section, from this point to the end of the section, are for Never Hinged items.

Duke and Duchess of Gloucester — A42

1945, Feb. 19 Engr. *Perf. 14½*

197 A42 2½p brown red .20 .20
198 A42 3½p bright ultra .25 .25
199 A42 5½p indigo .25 .25
Nos. 197-199 (3) .70 .70

Inauguration of the Duke of Gloucester as Governor General.

Official Crest and Inscriptions — A43

Dove and Australian Flag
A44

Angel of Peace; "Motherhood" and "Industry"
A45

1946, Feb. 18 Wmk. 228 *Perf. 14½*

200 A43 2½p carmine .20 .20
201 A44 3½p deep ultra .20 .25
202 A45 5½p deep yellow green .40 .35
Nos. 200-202 (3) .80 .80

End of WWII. See #1456-1458.

Sir Thomas Mitchell and Map of Queensland
A46

1946, Oct. 14

203 A46 2½p dark carmine .20 .20
204 A46 3½p deep ultra .20 .25
205 A46 1sh olive green .80 .35
Nos. 203-205 (3) 1.20 .80

Sir Thomas Mitchell's exploration of central Queensland, cent.

Kangaroo-Map Type of 1913 Redrawn

1945, Dec. Typo. *Perf. 11½*

206 A1 2sh dk red brown 4.50 2.50

The R and A of AUSTRALIA are separated at the base and there is a single line between the value tablet and "Two Shillings." On No. 125 the tail of the R touches the A, while two lines appear between value tablet and "Two Shillings." There are many other minor differences in the design.

For overprint see No. M6.

John Shortland — A47

Pouring Steel — A48

Loading Coal — A49

1947, Sept. Engr. *Perf. 14½x14*

207 A47 2½p brown red .30 .20

Perf. 14½

208 A48 3½p deep blue .25 .30
209 A49 5½p deep green .35 .30
Nos. 207-209 (3) .90 .80

150th anniv. of the discovery of the Hunter River estuary, site of Newcastle by Lieut. John Shortland. By error the 2½p shows his father, Capt. John Shortland.

Princess Elizabeth — A50

Perf. 14x14½

1947, Nov. 20 Wmk. 228

210 A50 1p brown violet .20 .20

See No. 215.

Hereford Bull
A51

Crocodile
A52

1948, Feb. 16 *Perf. 14½*

211 A51 1sh3p violet brown 1.90 .70
212 A52 2sh chocolate 2.50 .20

See No. 302.

William J. Farrer — A53

Design: No. 214, Ferdinand von Mueller.

1948 *Perf. 14½x14*

213 A53 2½p red .20 .20
214 A53 2½p dark red .20 .20

William J. Farrer (1845-1906), wheat researcher, and Ferdinand von Mueller (1825-1896), German-born botanist.

Issue dates: #213, July 12. #214, Sept. 13.

Elizabeth Type of 1947

1948, Aug. Unwmk. *Perf. 14x14½*

215 A50 1p brown violet .20 .20

Scout in Uniform
A55

Arms of Australia
A56

1948, Nov. 15 Engr. Wmk. 228

216 A55 2½p brown red .20 .20

Pan-Pacific Scout Jamboree, Victoria, Dec. 29, 1948 to Jan. 9, 1949. See No. 249.

1949-50 Wmk. 228 *Perf. 14x13½*

218 A56 5sh dark red 4.00 .20
219 A56 10sh red violet 21.00 .40
220 A56 £1 deep blue 35.00 3.25
221 A56 £2 green ('50) 140.00 15.00
Nos. 218-221 (4) 200.00 18.85

Henry Lawson
A57

Outback Mail Carrier and Plane
A58

Perf. 14½x14

1949, June 17 Unwmk.

222 A57 2½p rose brown .20 .20

Henry Hertzberg Lawson (1867-1922), author and poet.

1949, Oct. 10

223 A58 3½p violet blue .25 .20

UPU, 75th anniv.

Types of 1938, 1942-44 & A59

Aborigine
A59

John Forrest
A60

1948-50 Unwmk. *Perf. 14½x14*

223A A24 ½p orange ('49) .20 .20
224 A37 1½p green ('49) .25 .20
225 A38 2p lt rose violet .30 .20

Wmk. 228

226 A59 8½p dark brown ('50) .50 .35
Nos. 223A-226 (4) 1.25 .95

Issue dates: 2p, Dec., ½p, Sept., 1½p, Aug. 29, 8½p, Aug. 14.

See Nos. 248, 303.

1949, Nov. 28 Wmk. 228

227 A60 2½p brown red .20 .20

Forrest (1847-1918), explorer & statesman.

New South Wales
A61

Victoria
A62

First stamp designs.

Perf. 14½x14

1950, Sept. 27 Unwmk.

228 A61 2½p rose brown .25 .20
229 A62 2½p rose brown .25 .20
a. Pair, #228-229 .65 .40

Cent. of Australian adhesive postage stamps. Issued in sheets of 160 stamps containing alternate copies of Nos. 228 and 229.

Elizabeth
A63

George VI
A64

A65

A66

1950-51 Engr. Unwmk.

230 A63 1½p deep green .30 .20
231 A63 2p yellow grn ('51) .20 .20
232 A64 2½p violet brn ('51) .20 .20
233 A64 3p dull green ('51) .30 .20
Nos. 230-233 (4) 1.00 .80

Issue dates: 1½p, June 19, 2p, Mar. 28, 2½p, May 23, 3p, Nov. 14.

1950-52 Wmk. 228

234 A64 2½p red .20 .20
235 A64 3p red ('51) .20 .20
236 A65 3½p red brown ('51) .30 .20
237 A65 4½p scarlet ('52) .40 .35
238 A65 6½p choc ('52) .30 .30
238A A65 6½p blue green ('52) .40 .20
239 A66 7½p deep blue ('51) .45 .30
Nos. 234-239 (7) 2.25 1.75

Issued: 2½p, 4/12; 3p, 2/28; 7½p, 10/31; 3½p, 11/28; 4½p, #238, 2/20; #238A, 4/9.

Sir Edmund Barton
A67

Duke of York Opening First Federal Parliament
A68

Designs: No. 241, Sir Henry Parkes. 1sh6p, Parliament House, Canberra.

Perf. 14½x14

1951, May 1 Engr. Unwmk.

240 A67 3p carmine .40 .20
241 A67 3p carmine .40 .20
a. Pair, #240, 241 .80 .65
242 A68 5½p deep blue .40 .65
243 A68 1sh6p red brown 1.25 .90
Nos. 240-243 (4) 2.45 1.95

Founding of the Commonwealth of Australia, 50th anniv.

Edward Hammond Hargraves
A69

King George VI
A70

Design: No. 245, Charles Joseph Latrobe (1801-1875), first governor of Victoria.

1951, July 2

244 A69 3p rose brown .25 .20
245 A69 3p rose brown .25 .20
a. Pair, #244, 245 .65 .65

Discovery of gold in Australia, cent. (No. 244); Establishment of representative government in Victoria, cent. (No. 245). Sheets contain alternate rows of Nos. 244 and 245.

1952, Mar. 19 Wmk. 228 *Perf. 14½*

247 A70 1sh½p slate blue 1.65 .25

Aborigine Type of 1950 Redrawn

Size: 20½x25mm

248 A59 2sh6p dark brown 3.25 .25

Portrait as on A59; lettering altered and value repeated at lower left. See No. 303.

Scout Type of 1948
Dated "1952-53"

Perf. 14x14½

1952, Nov. 19 Wmk. 228

249 A55 3½p red brown .20 .20

Pan-Pacific Scout Jamboree, Greystanes, Dec. 30, 1952, to Jan. 9, 1953.

Modern Dairy, Butter Production — A71

Perf. 14½

1953, Feb. 11 Unwmk. Typo.

250 A71 3p shown .75 .20
251 A71 3p Wheat .75 .20
252 A71 3p Beef .75 .20
a. Strip of 3, #250-252 6.50 6.50
253 A71 3½p shown .75 .20
254 A71 3½p Wheat .75 .20
255 A71 3½p Beef .75 .20
a. Strip of 3, #253-255 4.50 *4.50*
Nos. 250-255 (6) 4.50 1.20

Both the 3p and 3½p were printed in panes of 50 stamps: 17 Butter, 17 Wheat and 16 Beef. The stamps were issued to encourage food production.

Queen Elizabeth II — A72

Perf. 14½x14

1953-54 Unwmk. Engr.

256 A72 1p purple .20 .20
256A A72 2½p deep blue ('54) .25 .20
257 A72 3p dark green .25 .20

Wmk. 228

258 A72 3½p dark red .25 .20
258B A72 6½p orange ('54) .90 .20
Nos. 256-258B (5) 1.85 1.00

Issue dates: 3½p, Apr. 21. 3p, June 17. 1p, Aug. 19. 2½p, 6½p, June 23.
See Nos. 292 and 296.

Coronation Issue

Queen Elizabeth II A73

1953, May 25 Unwmk.

259 A73 3½p rose red .25 .20
260 A73 7½p violet .70 .45
261 A73 2sh dull green 2.25 1.10
Nos. 259-261 (3) 3.20 1.75

Boy and Girl with Calf — A74

1953, Sept. 3 *Perf. 14½*

262 A74 3½p dp green & red brn .25 .20

Official establishment of Young Farmers' Clubs, 25th anniv.

Lieut. Gov. David Collins A75

Tasmania Stamp of 1853 A77

Sullivan Cove, Hobart A76

#264, Lieut. Gov. William Paterson (facing left).

1953, Sept. 23 *Perf. 14½x14*

263 A75 3½p red brown .35 .20
264 A75 3½p red brown .35 .20
a. Pair, #263-264 1.25 1.10
265 A76 2sh green 4.25 3.25
Nos. 263-265 (3) 4.95 3.65

Settlement in Tasmania, 150th anniv. Sheets contain alternate rows of Nos. 263 and 264.

1953, Nov. 11 *Perf. 14½*

266 A77 3p red .20 .20

Tasmania's first postage stamps, cent.

Elizabeth II and Duke of Edinburgh — A78

Elizabeth II — A79

Telegraph Pole and Key — A80

1954, Feb. 2 *Perf. 14½x14, 14x14½*

267 A78 3½p rose red .20 .20
268 A79 7½p purple .35 .75
269 A78 2sh green 1.50 1.00
Nos. 267-269 (3) 2.05 1.95

Visit of Queen Elizabeth II and the Duke of Edinburgh, 1954.

1954, Apr. 7 Engr. *Perf. 14*

270 A80 3½p dark red .25 .20

Inauguration of the telegraph in Australia, cent.

Red Cross and Globe — A81

Swan — A82

1954, June 9 *Perf. 14½x14*

271 A81 3½p deep blue & red .20 .20

Australian Red Cross Society.

1954, Aug. 2 Unwmk. *Perf. 14½*

274 A82 3½p black .20 .20

Western Australia's first postage stamp, cent.

Diesel and Early Steam Locomotives A83

1954, Sept. 13 *Perf. 14x14½*

275 A83 3½p red brown .20 .20

Centenary of Australian railroads.

Antarctic Flora and Fauna and Map A84

Olympic Circles and Arms of Melbourne A85

1954, Nov. 17 *Perf. 14*

276 A84 3½p black .20 .20

Australia's interest in the Antarctic continent.

1954, Dec. 1

277 A85 2sh dark blue 2.00 1.50

16th Olympic Games to be held in Melbourne Nov.-Dec. 1956. See No. 286.

Globe, Flags and Rotary Emblem — A86

1955, Feb. 23 *Perf. 14x14½*

278 A86 3½p carmine .20 .20

Rotary International, 50th anniv.

Elizabeth II — A87

Top of US Monument, Canberra — A88

1955, Mar. 9 Wmk. 228 *Perf. 14½*

279 A87 1sh½p dk gray blue 3.50 .25

See No. 301.

1955, May 4 Unwmk. *Perf. 14x14½*

280 A88 3½p deep ultra .20 .20

Friendship between Australia and the US.

Cobb and Company Mail Coach — A89

1955, July 6 *Perf. 14½x14*

281 A89 3½p dark brown .20 .20
282 A89 2sh brown 2.50 1.90

Pioneers of Australia's coaching era.

World Map, YMCA Emblem A90

Engr. and Typo.

1955, Aug. 10 *Perf. 14*

283 A90 3½p Prus green & red .20 .20

Centenary of YMCA.

Florence Nightingale and Modern Nurse A91

Queen Victoria A92

1955, Sept. 21 Engr. *Perf. 14x14½*

284 A91 3½p red violet .20 .20

Centenary of Florence Nightingale's work in the Crimea and of the founding of modern nursing.

1955, Oct. 17 *Perf. 14½*

285 A92 3½p green .20 .20

South Australia's first postage stamps, cent.

Olympic Type of 1954

1955, Nov. 30 Unwmk. *Perf. 14*

286 A85 2sh deep green 2.25 1.50

16th Olympic Games at Melbourne, Nov. 22-Dec. 8, 1956.

Queen Victoria, Queen Elizabeth II and Badges of Victoria, New South Wales and Tasmania A93

1956, Sept. 26 *Perf. 14½x14*

287 A93 3½p brown carmine .25 .20

Centenary of responsible government in Victoria, New South Wales and Tasmania.

Melbourne Coat of Arms — A94

Southern Cross, Olympic Torch — A95

Collins Street, Melbourne A96

Design: 2sh, Melbourne across Yarra River.

1956, Oct. 31 Engr. *Perf. 14½, 14*

288 A94 4p dark carmine .20 .20
289 A95 7½p ultramarine .60 .45

Photo.

Perf. 14x14½

290 A96 1sh multicolored .85 .45

Perf. 12x11½

Granite Paper

291 A96 2sh multicolored 1.60 1.00
Nos. 288-291 (4) 3.25 2.10

16th Olympic Games, Melbourne, 11/22-12/8.

A lithographed souvenir sheet incorporating reproductions of Nos. 288-291 in reduced size was of private origin and not postally valid.

Types of 1938-55 and

Queen Elizabeth II — A97

Perf. 14½x14, 14x15, 15x14, 14½

1956-57 Engr. Unwmk.

292 A72	3½p	dark red	1.00	.20
293 A28	4p	green	1.65	.20
294 A97	4p	claret ('57)	.30	.20
a.		Booklet pane of 6 ('57)	7.50	
295 A30	6p	brown violet	2.75	.20
296 A72	6½p	orange	1.75	.20
297 A97	7½p	violet ('57)	3.00	.40
298 A31	9p	sepia	9.00	.55
299 A97	10p	gray blue ('57)	2.75	.20
300 A16	1sh	gray green	6.00	.30
301 A87	1sh7p	redsh brn ('57)	4.50	.30
302 A52	2sh	chocolate	12.00	.25
303 A59	2sh6p	brown ('57)	9.00	.25
		Nos. 292-303 (12)	53.70	3.25

No. 300 measures 17½x21½mm. No. 303 measures 20½x25mm and is the redrawn type of 1952.

Issued: 3½p, 7/2; 2sh, 7/21; #293, 6p, 8/18; 6½p, Sept. 9p, 1sh, 12/13; 2sh6p, 1/30; 10p, 3/6; #294, 1sh7p, 3/13; 7½p, 11/13.

South Australia Coat of Arms — A99

1957, Apr. 17 Unwmk. *Perf. 14½*

304 A99 4p brown red .20 .20

Centenary of responsible government in South Australia.

There are two types of No. 304.

Caduceus and Map of Australia A100

1957, Aug. 21 *Perf. 14½x14*

305 A100 7p violet blue .60 .20

Royal Flying Doctor Service of Australia.

Star of Bethlehem and Praying Child — A101

1957, Nov. 6 Engr.

306 A101 3½p dull rose .25 .20
307 A101 4p pale purple .25 .20

Christmas.

Canberra War Memorial, Sailor and Airman A102

Design: No. 309, As No. 308 with soldier and service woman. Printed in alternate rows in sheet.

1958, Feb. 10 Unwmk.

308 A102 5½p brown carmine 1.25 .75
309 A102 5½p brown carmine 1.25 .75
a. Pair, #308-309 3.50 3.50

Sir Charles Kingsford-Smith and "Southern Cross" — A103

1958, Aug. 27 *Perf. 14x14½*

310 A103 8p brt violet blue 1.00 .90

1st air crossing of the Tasman Sea, 30th anniv. See New Zealand No. 321.

Broken Hill Mine A104

Nativity A105

1958, Sept. 10 *Perf. 14½x14*

311 A104 4p brown .25 .20

Broken Hill mining field, 75th anniv.

1958, Nov. 5 *Perf. 14½x15*

312 A105 3½p dark red .20 .20
313 A105 4p dark purple .25 .20

Christmas.

A106

A107

A109

A108

A110

Platypus A111

Tasmanian Tiger A112

Flannel Flower A113

Aboriginal Stockman Cutting Out a Steer A114

Designs: 3p, Queen Elizabeth II facing right. 6p, Banded anteater. 8p, Tiger cat. 9p, Kangaroos. 11p, Rabbit bandicoot. 1sh6p, Christmas bells (flower). 2sh3p, Wattle (flower). 2sh5p, Banksia (flower). 3sh, Waratah (flower).

FIVE PENCE

Die I - Four short lines inside "5" at right of ball; six short lines left of ball; full length line above ball is seventh from bottom. Odd numbered horizontal rows in each sheet are in Die I.

Die II - Five short lines inside "5" at right of ball; seven at left; full length line above ball is eighth from bottom. Even numbered horizontal rows in each sheet are in Die II.

Perf. 14½x14, 14x14½, 14½

1959-64 Engr. Unwmk.

314	A106	1p	dull violet	.25	.20
315	A107	2p	red brown	.35	.20
316	A108	3p	bluish green	.25	.20
317	A108	3½p	dark green	.45	.20
318	A109	4p	carmine	.35	.20
a.			Booklet pane of 6	25.00	
319	A110	5p	dark blue (I)	.65	.20
a.			5p dark blue (II)	.65	.20
b.			Booklet pane of 6 ('60)	12.00	
320	A111	6p	chocolate	.65	.20
321	A111	8p	red brown	.60	.20
322	A111	9p	brown black	2.50	.20
323	A111	11p	dark blue	.95	.20
324	A111	1sh	slate green	3.75	.20
325	A112	1sh2p	dk purple	1.50	.20
326	A113	1sh6p	red, *yellow*	2.50	.60
327	A113	2sh	dark blue	2.50	.20
328	A113	2sh3p	green, *yel*	2.50	.20
328A	A113	2sh3p	yellow grn	7.50	1.00
329	A113	2sh5p	brown, *yellow*	8.75	.40
330	A113	3sh	crimson	3.50	.35

Wmk. 228

331	A114	5sh	red brown	25.00	1.00
			Nos. 314-331 (19)	64.50	6.15

Issued: 1p, 4p, 2/2; 3½p, 3/18; 2sh, 4/8; 3p, 5/20; 3sh, 7/15; 1sh, #328, 9/9; 5p, 10/1; 9p, 10/21; 1sh6p, 2/3/60; 2sh5p, 3/16/60; 8p, 5/11/60; 6p, 9/30/60; 11p, 5/3/61; 5sh, 7/26/61; 2p, 1sh2p, 3/21/62; #328A, 10/28/64.

Luminescent Printings

Paper with an orange red phosphorescence (surface coating), was used for some printings of the Colombo Plan 1sh, No. 340, the Churchill 5p, No. 389, and several regular postage stamps. These include 2p, 3p, 6p, 8p, 9p, 11p, 1sh2p, 1sh6p and 2sh3p (Nos. 315, 316, 365, 367, 321, 368, 323, 325, 369, 328A).

Stamps printed only on phosphorescent paper include the Monash 5p, Hargrave 5p, ICY 2sh3p and Christmas 5p (Nos. 388, 390-393) and succeeding commemoratives; the 2sh, 2sh6p and 3sh regular birds (Nos. 370, 372, 373); and most of the regular series in decimal currency.

Ink with a phosphorescent content was used in printing most of the 5p red, No. 366, almost all of the 5p red booklets, No. 366a, most of the decimal 4c regular, No. 397, and its booklet pane, No. 397a, and all of No. 398.

Postmaster Isaac Nichols Boarding Vessel to Receive Mail — A115

1959, Apr. 22 *Perf. 14½x14*

332 A115 4p dark gray blue .25 .20

First post office, Sydney, 150th anniv.

Parliament House, Brisbane, and Queensland Arms — A116

1959, June 5 *Perf. 14x14½*

333 A116 4p dk green & violet .25 .20

Cent. of Queensland self-government.

Approach of the Magi — A117

1959, Nov. 4 *Perf. 15x14½*

334 A117 5p purple .25 .20

Christmas.

Girl Guide and Lord Baden-Powell A118

1960, Aug. 18 *Perf. 14½x14*

335 A118 5p dark blue .30 .20

50th anniversary of the Girl Guides.

The Overlanders by Sir Daryl Lindsay — A119

Melbourne Cup and Archer, 1861 Winner — A120

1960, Sept. 21 *Perf. 14½*

336 A119 5p lilac rose .30 .20

Exploration of Australia's Northern Territory, cent.

1960, Oct. 12 Unwmk.

337 A120 5p sepia .30 .20

Centenary of the Melbourne Cup.

Queen Victoria A121

Open Bible and Candle A122

1960 Nov. 2 Engr. *Perf. 14½*

338 A121 5p dark green .20 .20

Centenary of the first Queensland stamps.

1960, Nov. 9 Unwmk.

339 A122 5p maroon .20 .20

Christmas; beginning of 350th anniv. year of the publication of the King James translation of the Bible.

Colombo Plan Emblem — A123

1961, June 30 *Perf. 14x14½*

340 A123 1sh red brown .75 .20

Colombo Plan for the peaceful development of South East Asia countries, 10th anniv.

Dame Nellie Melba, by Sir Bertram Mackennal — A124

1961, Sept. 20 *Perf. 14½*

341 A124 5p deep blue .30 .20

Dame Nellie Melba, singer, birth cent.

Page from Book of Hours, 15th Century A125

John McDouall Stuart A126

1961, Nov. 8 *Perf. 14½x14*

342 A125 5p reddish brown .30 .20

Christmas; end of the 350th anniv. year of the publication of the King James translation of the Bible.

1962, July 25 Unwmk. *Perf. 14½*

345 A126 5p carmine .30 .20

First south-north crossing of Australia by John McDouall Stuart, cent.

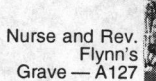

Nurse and Rev. Flynn's Grave — A127

1962, Sept. 5 Photo. Perf. 13½

346 A127 5p multicolored .30 .20
a. Red omitted *275.00*

Australian Inland Mission founded by Rev. John Flynn, 50th anniv.

Woman and Globe A128

Madonna and Child A129

1962, Sept. 26 Engr. Perf. 14x14½

347 A128 5p dark green .30 .20

World Conf. of the Associated Country Women of the World, Melbourne, Oct. 2-12.

1962, Oct. 17 Perf. 14½

348 A129 5p deep violet .30 .20

Christmas.

View of Perth and Kangaroo Paw — A130

Arms of Perth — A131

1962, Nov. 1 Photo. Perf. 14

349 A130 5p multicolored .30 .20
a. Red omitted *450.00*

Perf. 14½x14

350 A131 2sh3p emer, blk, red & ultra 4.00 4.00

British Empire and Commonwealth Games, Perth, Nov. 22-Dec. 1.

Elizabeth II — A132

Elizabeth II and Prince Philip — A133

1963, Feb. 18 Engr. Perf. 14½

351 A132 5p dark green .30 .20
352 A133 2sh3 red brown 4.00 4.00

Visit of Elizabeth II and Prince Philip.

Walter Burley Griffin and Arms of Canberra A134

Red Cross Centenary Emblem A135

1963, Mar. 8 Unwmk. Perf. 14½x14

353 A134 5p dark green .35 .20

50th anniv. of Canberra; Walter Burley Griffin, American architect, who laid out plan for Canberra.

1963, May 8 Photo. Perf. 13½x13

354 A135 5p dk blue, red & gray .35 .20

Centenary of the International Red Cross.

Explorers Blaxland, Lawson and Wentworth Looking West from Mt. York — A136

1963, May 28 Engr. Perf. 14½x14

355 A136 5p dark blue .30 .20

1st crossing of the Blue Mts., 150th anniv.

Globe, Ship, Plane and Map of Australia A137

1963, Aug. 28 Unwmk.

356 A137 5p red .35 .20

Importance of exports to Australian economy.

Elizabeth II — A138

Black-backed Magpie and Eucalyptus — A139

Abel Tasman and Ship A144

George Bass, Whaleboat A145

Designs: 6p, Yellow-tailed thornbill, horiz. 1sh6p, Galah on tree stump. 2sh, Golden whistler. 2sh5p, Blue wren and bracken fern. 2sh6p, Scarlet robin, horiz. 3sh, Straw-necked ibis. 5sh, William Dampier and "Roebuck" sailing ship. 7sh6p, Capt. James Cook. 10sh, Matthew Flinders and three-master "Investigator." £2, Admiral Philip Parker King.

Perf. 15x14

1963-65 Unwmk. Engr.

365 A138 5p green .25 .20
a. Booklet pane of 6 ('64) 20.00
b. Pair, imperf. btwn. 3.75 3.75
366 A138 5p red .25 .20
a. Booklet pane of 6 25.00

Photo.

Perf. 13½

367 A139 6p multicolored .45 .20
a. Vert. pair, imperf. btwn.
368 A139 9p multicolored 2.50 1.90
369 A139 1sh6p multicolored 1.25 1.10
370 A139 2sh multicolored 2.50 .30
371 A139 2sh5p multicolored 8.25 2.25
372 A139 2sh6p multicolored 3.75 1.50
a. Red omitted *1,000.*
373 A139 3sh multicolored 2.50 1.25

Engr.

Perf. 14½x14, 14½x15

374 A144 4sh violet blue 3.75 .55

Wmk. 228

375 A145 5sh red brown 5.25 1.25
376 A144 7sh6p olive green 24.00 15.00
377 A144 10sh deep claret 30.00 7.25
378 A145 £1 purple 50.00 22.50
379 A145 £2 brown black 100.00 90.00
Nos. 365-379 (15) 234.70 145.45

No. 365a was printed in sheets of 288 which were sold intact by the Philatelic Bureau. These sheets have been broken to obtain pairs and blocks which are imperf. between (see No. 365b).

Issued: #365, 4sh, 10/9/63; 10sh, £1, 2/26/64; 9p, 1sh6p, 2sh5p, 3/11/64; 6p, 8/19/64; 7sh6p, £2, 8/26/64; 5sh, 11/25/64; 2sh, 2sh6p, 3sh, 4/21/65; #366, 6/30/65.

See Nos. 400-401, 406-417, 1727-1728.

Star of Bethlehem — A146

1963, Oct. 25 Unwmk. Perf. 14½

380 A146 5p blue .20 .20

Christmas.

Cable Around World and Under Sea — A147

1963, Dec. 3 Photo. Perf. 13½

381 A147 2sh3p gray, ver, blk & blue 6.00 4.25

Opening of the Commonwealth Pacific (telephone) cable service (COMPAC).

See New Zealand No. 364.

Bleriot 60 Plane, 1914 — A148

1964, July 1 Engr. Perf. 14½x14

382 A148 5p olive green .20 .20
383 A148 2sh3p red 5.25 4.25

50th anniv. of the first air mail flight in Australia; Maurice Guillaux, aviator.

Child Looking at Nativity Scene — A149

1964, Oct. 21 Photo. Perf. 13½

384 A149 5p bl, blk, red & buff .20 .20
a. Red omitted — *375.00*
b. Black omitted *375.00*

Christmas.

No. 384a used is valued on cover. The red ink can be removed from No. 384 by bleaching.

"Simpson and His Donkey" by Wallace Anderson — A150

1965, Apr. 14 Engr. Perf. 14x14½

385 A150 5p olive bister .20 .20
386 A150 8p dark blue 1.25 .90
387 A150 2sh3p rose claret 4.50 4.00
Nos. 385-387 (3) 5.95 5.10

50th anniv. of the landing of the Australian and New Zealand Army Corps (ANZAC) at Gallipoli, Turkey, Apr. 25, 1915. Private John Simpson Kirkpatrick saved the lives of many wounded soldiers. The statue erected in his honor stands in front of Melbourne's Shrine of Remembrance.

Radio Mast and Satellite Orbiting Earth A151

Winston Churchill A152

1965, May 10 Photo. Perf. 13½

388 A151 5p multicolored .20 .20
a. Black ("5d" and pylon) omitted *650.00*

ITU, cent.

1965, May 24

389 A152 5p lt blue, gray & blk .25 .20

Sir Winston Spencer Churchill (1874-1965), statesman and WWII leader.

See New Zealand No. 371.

John Monash and Transmission Tower — A153

Lawrence Hargrave and Sketch for 1902 Seaplane — A154

1965, June 23 Photo. Perf. 13½

390 A153 5p red, yel, blk & lt brn .25 .20

Birth cent. of General Sir John Monash (1865-1931), soldier, Vice-Chancellor of University of Melbourne and chairman of the Victoria state electricity commission.

1965, Aug. 4 Unwmk. Perf. 13½

391 A154 5p multicolored .25 .20
a. Purple (5d) omitted *190.00*

50th anniv. of the death of Lawrence Hargrave (1850-1915), aviation pioneer.

ICY Emblem A155

Nativity A156

1965, Sept. 1 Photo. Perf. 13½

392 A155 2sh3p lt blue & green 2.75 2.50

International Cooperation Year.

1965, Oct. 20 Unwmk. Perf. 13½

393 A156 5p multicolored .30 .20
a. Gold omitted *300.00*
b. Ultramarine omitted 325.00

Christmas.

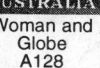

Types of 1963-65 and

Elizabeth II — A157

Humbug Fish — A158

Designs: No. 400, Yellow-tailed thornbill, horiz. 6c, blue-faced honeyeater, horiz. 8c, Coral fish. 9c, Hermit crab. 10c Anemone fish. 13c, Red-necked avocet. 15c, Galah on tree stump. 20c, Golden whistler. 24c Azure kingfisher, horiz. 25c, Scarlet robin, horiz. 30c Straw-necked ibis. 40c Abel Tasman and ship. 50c, William Dampier and "Roebuck" sailing ship. 75c, Capt. James Cook. $1, Matthew Flinders and three-master "Investigator." $2, George Bass and whaleboat. $4, Admiral Philip Parker King.

Perf. 14½x14 (A157); 13½ (A158, A139)

Engr. (A157), Photo. (A158, A139)

1966-71

394 A157 1c red brown .25 .20
395 A157 2c olive green .50 .20
396 A157 3c Prus green .65 .20
397 A157 4c red .20 .20
a. Booklet pane of 5 + label 30.00
398 A157 5c on 4c red ('67) .75 .20
a. Booklet pane of 5 + label ('67) 5.50
399 A157 5c dk blue ('67) 1.00 .20
a. Booklet pane of 5 + label 11.00
400 A139 5c lt grn, blk, brn & yel .20 .20
401 A139 6c gray, blk, lem & bl .55 .25
401A A157 6c orange ('70) .20 .20
402 A158 7c brn, ver, blk & gray 1.00 .20
402A A157 7c dp rose lilac ('71) .20 .20
403 A158 8c multicolored 1.10 .20
404 A158 9c multicolored 1.50 .20
405 A158 10c lt brn, blk, org & bl 1.10 .25
406 A139 13c lt bl grn, blk, gray & red 2.00 .50
a. Red omitted 400.00
b. Gray omitted 400.00
407 A139 15c lt grn, blk, gray & rose 3.50 .40
a. Gray omitted 1,500.
408 A139 20c pink, blk, yel & gray 5.75 .20
a. Yellow omitted 350.00
409 A139 24c tan, blk, vio bl & org 1.10 .55
410 A139 25c gray, grn, blk & red 3.75 .20
a. Red omitted 750.00
411 A139 30c lt grn, buff, blk & red 19.00 .40
a. Red omitted *575.00*

Engr.

Perf. 14½x14, 14½x15

412 A144 40c violet blue 13.50 .30
413 A145 50c brown red 17.00 .20
414 A144 75c olive green 1.00 1.00
415 A144 $1 deep claret 2.50 .30
a. Perf 15x14 75.00 15.00
416 A145 $2 purple 7.50 1.10
417 A145 $4 sepia 5.50 4.50
Nos. 394-417 (26) 91.30 12.55

No. 398 issued in booklets only.

Booklet panes of 10 of No. 399, and of 5 No. 400, are torn from sheets. They were issued for the use of "Australian Defence Forces," as the covers read, in Viet Nam.

Issued: #398, 399, 9/29/67; #401A, 9/28/70; #402A, 10/1/71; #415a, 1973; others, 2/14/66.

Coil Stamps

1966-67 Photo. *Perf. 15 Horiz.*

418 A157 3c emerald, blk & buff .40 .35
419 A157 4c org red, blk & buff .60 .20
420 A157 5c blue, black & buff .75 .20
Nos. 418-420 (3) 1.75 .75

Issued: 5c, Sept. 29, 1967; others, Feb. 14, 1966.

Rescue A159

1966 July 6 Photo. *Perf. 13½*

421 A159 4c blue, ultra & black .25 .20

Royal Life Saving Society, 75th anniv.

Adoration of the Shepherds A160

1966, Oct. 19 Photo. *Perf. 13½*

422 A160 4c olive & black .25 .20

Christmas.

Dutch Sailing Ship, 17th Century A161

Hands Reaching for Bible A162

1966, Oct. 24 Photo. *Perf. 13½*

423 A161 4c bl, blk, dp org & gold .25 .20

350th anniv. of Dirk Hartog's discovery of the Australian west coast, and his landing on the island named after him.

1967, Mar. 7 Photo. *Perf. 13½*

424 A162 4c multicolored .25 .20

British and Foreign Bible Soc., 150th anniv.

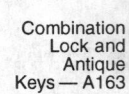

Combination Lock and Antique Keys — A163

1967, Apr. 5 Photo. *Perf. 13½*

425 A163 4c emerald, blk & lt blue .25 .20

150th anniv. of banking in Australia (Bank of New South Wales).

Lions Intl., 50th Anniv. — A164

1967, June 7 Photo. *Perf. 13½*

426 A164 4c ultra, black & gold .25 .20

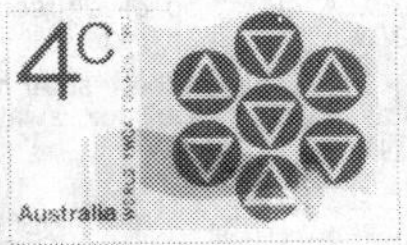

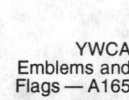

YWCA Emblems and Flags — A165

1967, Aug. 21 Photo. *Perf. 13½*

427 A165 4c dk blue, lt bl & lilac .25 .20

World Council Meeting of the YWCA, Monash University, Victoria, Aug. 14-Sept. 1.

Seated Women Symbolizing Obstetrics and Gynecology, Female Symbol A166

1967, Sept. 20 Photo. *Perf. 13½*

428 A166 4c lilac, dk blue & blk .25 .20

5th World Congress of Gynecology and Obstetrics, Sydney, Sept. 23-30.

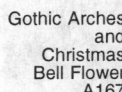

Gothic Arches and Christmas Bell Flower A167

Cross, Stars of David and Yin Yang Forming Mandala — A168

1967 Photo. *Perf. 13½*

429 A167 5c multicolored .25 .20
430 A168 25c multicolored 2.25 2.25

Christmas.

Issue dates: 5c, Oct. 18; 25c, Nov. 27.

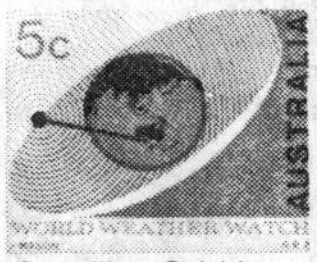

Satellite Orbiting Earth A169

Satellite and Antenna, Moree, N.S.W. A170

Design: 20c, World weather map connecting Washington, Moscow and Melbourne, and computer and teleprinter tape spools.

1968, Mar. 20 Photo. *Perf. 13½*

431 A169 5c dull yel, red, bl & dk blue .25 .20
432 A169 20c blue, blk & red 3.00 3.00
433 A170 25c Prus blue, blk & lt green 3.50 3.50
Nos. 431-433 (3) 6.75 6.70

Use of satellites for weather observations and communications.

Kangaroo Paw, Western Australia A171

Sturt's Desert Rose, Northern Territory A171a

State Flowers: 13c, Pink heath, Victoria. 15c, Tasmanian blue gum, Tasmania. 20c, Sturt's desert pea, South Australia. 25c, Cooktown orchid, Queensland. 30c, Waratah, New South Wales.

1968, July 10 Photo. *Perf. 13½*

Flowers in Natural Colors

434 A171 6c bister & dk brn .30 .20
435 A171 13c lt grnsh blue .40 .20
436 A171 15c dk brn & yel 1.50 .25
437 A171 20c lemon & black 5.25 .20
438 A171 25c light ultra 3.75 .20
439 A171 30c chocolate 1.10 .20
Nos. 434-439 (6) 12.30 1.25

Coil Stamps

1970-75 *Perf. 14½ Horiz.*

Designs: 5c, Golden wattle, national flower. 7c, 10c, Sturt's desert pea.

439A A171a 2c dk grn & multi .20 .20
i. Lettering and value bolder .20 .20
439B A171a 4c gray & multi .50 .40
439C A171a 5c gray & multi .20 .20
439D A171a 6c gray & multi 1.10 .50
h. Green omitted 300.00
439E A171a 7c blk, red & grn .35 .20
f. Green omitted 150.00
439G A171a 10c blk, red & grn .30 .20
Nos. 439A-439G (6) 2.65 1.70

Issued: 4c, 5c, 4/27; 6c, 10/28; 2c, 7c, 10/1/71; 10c, 1/15/75; #439Ai, 11/73.

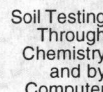

Soil Testing Through Chemistry and by Computer A172

Hippocrates and Hands Holding Hypodermic A173

1968, Aug. 6 Photo. *Perf. 13½*

440 A172 5c multicolored .25 .20
441 A173 5c multicolored .25 .20

9th Intl. Congress of Soil Science, University of Adelaide, Aug. 6-16 (No. 440); General Assembly of World Medical Associations, Sydney, Aug. 6-9 (No. 441). Nos. 440-441 printed in sheets of 100 in two separate panes of 50 connected by a gutter. Each sheet contains 10 gutter pairs.

Runner and Aztec Calendar Stone A174

Symbolic House and Money A175

Design: 25c, Aztec calendar stone and Mexican flag, horiz.

1968, Oct. 2

442 A174 5c multicolored .20 .20
443 A174 25c multicolored 2.25 2.00

19th Olympic Games, Mexico City, Oct. 12-27. Nos. 442-443 printed in sheets of 100 in two separate panes of 50 connected by a gutter. Each sheet contains 10 gutter pairs.

1968, Oct. 16

444 A175 5c multicolored .25 .20

11th Triennial Congress of the Intl. Union of Building Societies and Savings Associations, Sydney, Oct. 20-27.

View of Bethlehem and Church Window — A176

1968, Oct. 23 Photo. *Perf. 13½*

445 A176 5c lt bl, red, grn & gold .20 .20
a. Red omitted 350.00

Christmas.

Edgeworth David (1858-1934), Geologist A177

Sir Edmund Barton (1849-1920) A178

Reginald C. and John R. Duigan, Aviators — A179

Famous Australians: No. 447, Caroline Chisholm (1808-1877), social worker and reformer. No. 448, Albert Namatjira (1902-

1959), aborigine, artist. No. 449, Andrew Barton (Banjo) Paterson (1864-1941), poet and writer.

1968, Nov. 6 Engr. *Perf. 15x14*

446 A177 5c green, *greenish* .80 .20
a. Booklet pane of 5 + label 4.00
447 A177 5c purple, *pink* .80 .20
a. Booklet pane of 5 + label 4.00
448 A177 5c dark brown, *buff* .80 .20
a. Booklet pane of 5 + label 4.00
449 A177 5c indigo, *lt blue* .80 .20
a. Booklet pane of 5 + label 4.00
Nos. 446-449 (4) 3.20 .80

1969, Oct. 22 Engr. *Perf. 15x14*

Prime Ministers: No. 451, Alfred Deakin (1856-1919). No. 452, John C. Watson (1867-1941). No.453, Sir George H. Reid (1845-1918).

450 A178 5c indigo, *greenish* .80 .20
a. Booklet pane of 5 + label 4.00
451 A178 5c indigo, *greenish* .80 .20
a. Booklet pane of 5 + label 4.00
452 A178 5c indigo, *greenish* .80 .20
a. Booklet pane of 5 + label 4.00
453 A178 5c indigo, *greenish* .80 .20
a. Booklet pane of 5 + label 4.00
Nos. 450-453 (4) 3.20 .80

1970, Nov. 16 Engr. *Perf. 15x14*

Famous Australians: No. 455, Lachlan Macquarie (1761-1824), Governor of New South Wales. No. 456, Adam Lindsay Gordon (1833-1870), poet. No. 457, Edward John Eyre (1815-1901), explorer.

454 A179 6c dark blue .80 .20
a. Booklet pane of 5 + label 4.00
455 A179 6c dark brown, *salmon* .80 .20
a. Booklet pane of 5 + label 4.00
456 A179 6c magenta, *brt pink* .80 .20
a. Booklet pane of 5 + label 4.00
457 A179 6c brown red, *salmon* .80 .20
a. Booklet pane of 5 + label 4.00
Nos. 454-457 (4) 3.20 .80

Nos. 446-457 were issued in booklet panes only; all stamps have 1 or 2 straight edges.

Macquarie Lighthouse A180

Perf. 14½x13½

1968, Nov. 27 Engr.

458 A180 5c indigo, *buff* .35 .20

Macquarie Lighthouse, Outer South Head, Sydney, 150th anniv.

Surveyor George W. Goyder and Assistants, 1869; Building in Darwin, 1969 — A181

1969, Feb. 5 Photo. *Perf. 13½*

459 A181 5c black brn & dull yel .20 .20

First permanent settlement of the Northern Territory of Australia, cent.

Melbourne Harbor Scene — A182

1969, Feb. 26 Photo. *Perf. 13½*

460 A182 5c dull blue & multi .20 .20

6th Biennial Conference of the Intl. Assoc. of Ports and Harbors, Melbourne, March 3-8.

Overlapping Circles A183

1969, June 5 Photo. *Perf. 13½*

461 A183 5c gray, vio bl, bl & gold .20 .20

ILO, 50th anniv.

Sugar Cane — A184

Designs (Primary industries): 15c, Eucalyptus (timber). 20c, Wheat. 25c, Ram, ewe and lamb (wool).

1969, Sept. 17 *Perf. 13½x13*

462 A184 7c blue & multi .75 .75
463 A184 15c emerald & multi 3.75 3.50
464 A184 20c org brn & multi 1.40 .60
465 A184 25c gray, black & yel 1.25 .70
Nos. 462-465 (4) 7.15 5.55

Nativity A185

Tree of Life A186

Perf. 13½x13, 13x13½

1969, Oct. 15 Photo.

466 A185 5c multicolored .20 .20
467 A186 25c multicolored 2.75 2.75

Christmas.

Vickers Vimy Flown by Ross Smith, England to Australia A187

Designs: No. 469, B.E. 2E plane, automobile and spectators. No. 470, Ford truck and surveyors Lieuts. Hudson Fysh and P.J. McGinness.

1969, Nov. 12 *Perf. 13x13½*

468 A187 5c bl, blk, cop red & ol .60 .35
469 A187 5c bl, blk, cop red & ol .60 .35
470 A187 5c cop red, black & ol .60 .35
a. Strip of 3, #468-470 3.50 3.00
Nos. 468-470 (3) 1.80 1.05

50th anniv. of the first England to Australia flight by Capt. Ross Smith and Lieut. Keith Smith.

Nos. 468-470 are printed se-tenant with various combinations possible.

Diesel Locomotive and New Track Linking Melbourne, Sydney and Brisbane with Perth — A188

1970, Feb. 11 Photo. *Perf. 13x13½*

471 A188 5c multicolored .25 .20

Completion of the standard gauge railroad between Sydney and Perth.

EXPO '70 Australian Pavilion A189

Design: 20c, Southern Cross and Japanese inscription: "From the country of the south with warm feeling."

1970, Mar. 16 Photo. *Perf. 13x13½*

472 A189 5c bl, blk, red & brnz .25 .20
473 A189 20c red & black 1.00 .45

EXPO '70 Intl. Exhib., Osaka, Japan, Mar. 15-Sept. 13.

Queen Elizabeth II and Prince Philip — A190

Australian Flag — A191

1970, Mar. 31

474 A190 5c yel bister & black .25 .20
475 A191 30c vio blue & multi 2.25 2.00

Visit of Queen Elizabeth II, Prince Philip and Princess Anne to Australia.

Steer, Alfalfa and Native Spear Grass — A192

1970, Apr. 13 Photo. *Perf. 13x13½*

476 A192 5c emerald & multi .25 .20

11th Intl. Grasslands Congress, Surfers Paradise, Queensland, Apr. 13-23.

Capt. James Cook and "Endeavour" — A193

Designs: No. 478, Sextant and "Endeavour." No. 479, "Endeavour," landing party and kangaroo. No. 480, Daniel Charles Solander, Sir Joseph Banks, Cook, map and botanical drawing. No. 481, Cook taking possession with Union Jack; "Endeavour" and coral. 30c, Cook, "Endeavour," sextant, kangaroo and aborigines.

1970, Apr. 20 *Perf. 13½x13*

Size: 24x35½mm

477 A193 5c org brn & multi .50 .20
478 A193 5c org brn & multi .50 .20
479 A193 5c org brn & multi .50 .20
480 A193 5c org brn & multi .50 .20
481 A193 5c org brn & multi .50 .20
a. Strip of 5, #477-481 2.50 2.50

Size: 62x29mm

482 A193 30c org brn & multi 3.50 3.50
a. Souv. sheet of 6, #477-482, imperf. 11.00 11.00
Nos. 477-482 (6) 6.00 4.50

Cook's discovery and exploration of the eastern coast of Australia, 200th anniv.

No. 481a has continuous design.

No. 482a with brown marginal overprint "Souvenir Sheet ANPEX 1970. . ." is of private origin.

Snowy Mountains Hydroelectric Project A194

Designs: 8c, Ord River hydroelectric project (dam, cotton plant and boll). 9c, Bauxite and aluminum production (mine, conveyor belt and aluminum window frame). 10c, Oil and natural gas (off-shore drilling rig and pipelines).

1970, Aug. 31 Photo. *Perf. 13x13½*

483 A194 7c multicolored 1.65 .40
484 A194 8c multicolored .25 .20
485 A194 9c multicolored .25 .20
486 A194 10c multicolored 1.10 .20
Nos. 483-486 (4) 3.25 1.00

Australian economic development.

Flame Symbolizing Democracy and Freedom of Speech — A195

1970, Oct. 2 Photo. *Perf. 13½x13*

487 A195 6c green & multi .25 .20

16th Commonwealth Parliamentary Assoc. Conference, Canberra, Oct. 2-9.

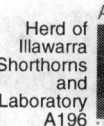

Herd of Illawarra Shorthorns and Laboratory A196

1970, Oct. 7 *Perf. 13x13½*

488 A196 6c multicolored .25 .20

18th Intl. Dairy Cong., Sydney, Oct. 12-16.

Madonna and Child, by William Beasley A197

UN Emblem, Dove and Symbols A198

1970, Oct. 14 *Perf. 13½x13*

489 A197 6c multicolored .25 .20

Christmas.

1970, Oct. 19

490 A198 6c blue & multi .25 .20

25th anniversary of the United Nations.

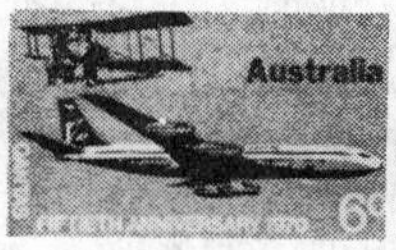

Qantas Boeing 707, and Avro 504 — A199

Design: 30c, Sunbeam Dyak powered Avro 504 on ground and Qantas Boeing 707 in the air.

1970, Nov. 2 *Perf. 13x13½*

491 A199 6c multicolored .20 .20
492 A199 30c multicolored 1.40 1.40

Qantas, Australian overseas airlines, 50th anniv.

Japanese Noh Actor, Australian Dancer and Chinese Opera Character — A200

Designs: 15c, Chinese pipe and trumpet, Australian aboriginal didgeridoo, Thai fiddle, Indian double oboe and Tibetan drums. 20c, Red Sea dhow, Chinese junk, Australian lifeguard's surfboat, Malaysian and South Indian river boats.

1971, Jan. 6 Photo. *Perf. 13½x13*

493 A200 7c multicolored	.60	.20
494 A200 15c multicolored	1.50	1.10
495 A200 20c multicolored	1.50	.80
Nos. 493-495 (3)	3.60	2.10

Link between Australia and Asia; 28th Intl. Congress of Orientalists, Canberra, Jan. 6-12.

Southern Cross A201

1971, Apr. 21 Photo. *Perf. 13x13½*

496 A201 6c multicolored	.25	.20

Australian Natives Assoc., cent.

Symbolic Market Graphs — A202

Rotary Emblem — A203

1971, May 5 *Perf. 13½x13*

497 A202 6c silver & multi	.25	.20

Centenary of Sydney Stock Exchange.

1971, May 17 *Perf. 13x13½*

498 A203 6c multicolored	.25	.20

First Intl. Rotary Convention held in Australia, Sydney, May 16-20.

DH-9A, Australian Mirage Jet Fighters A204

RSPCA Centenary A205

1971, June 9 *Perf. 13½x13*

499 A204 6c multicolored	.35	.20

Royal Australian Air Force, 50th anniv.

1971, July 5 Photo. *Perf. 13½x13*

Designs: 12c, Man and lamb (animal science). 18c, Kangaroo (fauna conservation). 24c, Seeing eye dog (animals' aid to man).

500 A205 6c blk, brown & org	.25	.20
501 A205 12c blk, dk grn & yel	.75	.20
502 A205 18c brown & multi	.95	.30
503 A205 24c blue & multi	1.25	.50
Nos. 500-503 (4)	3.20	1.20

Royal Society for Prevention of Cruelty to Animals in Australia, cent.

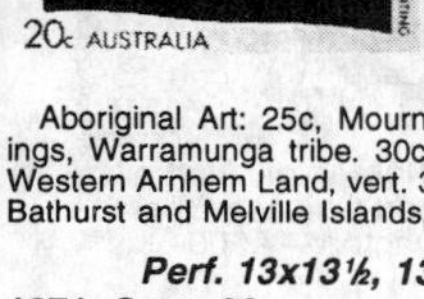

Longnecked Tortoise, Painted on Bark — A206

Aboriginal Art: 25c, Mourners' body paintings, Warramunga tribe. 30c, Cave painting, Western Arnhem Land, vert. 35c, Graveposts, Bathurst and Melville Islands, vert.

Perf. 13x13½, 13½x13

1971, Sept. 29

504 A206 20c multicolored	.65	.25
505 A206 25c multicolored	.65	.45
506 A206 30c multicolored	.90	.35
507 A206 35c multicolored	.65	.40
Nos. 504-507 (4)	2.85	1.45

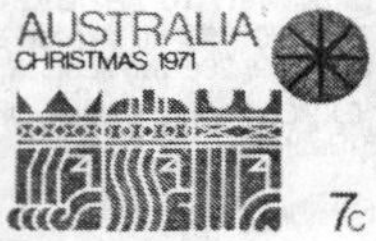

Three Kings and Star — A207

1971, Oct. 13 Photo. *Perf. 13½x13*

508 Block of 7	50.00	
a. A207 7c brt grn, dk bl (Kings) & lil	9.00	.30
b. A207 7c lil, red brn, grn & dk bl	6.25	.20
c. A207 7c red brown & lilac	1.75	.20
d. A207 7c lilac, red brn & brt grn	2.75	.20
e. A207 7c red brown & dark blue	3.00	.20
f. A207 7c lilac, green & dk blue	20.00	1.40
g. A207 7c brt grn, dk bl & lilac (Kings)	3.50	.20

Christmas. Nos. 508a-508g printed se-tenant in sheets of 50. Each sheet contains 2 green crosses formed by 4 No. 508g and three No. 508a.

Andrew Fisher (1862-1928) A208

Cameo Brooch A209

Prime Ministers: No. 515, Joseph Cook (1860-1947). No. 516, William Morris Hughes (1864-1952). No. 517, Stanley Melbourne Bruce (1883-1967).

1972, Mar. 8 Engr. *Perf. 15x14*

514 A208 7c dark blue	.60	.20
a. Booklet pane of 5 + label	3.00	
515 A208 7c dark red	.60	.20
a. Booklet pane of 5 + label	3.00	
516 A208 7c dark blue	.60	.20
a. Booklet pane of 5 + label	3.00	
517 A208 7c dark red	.60	.20
a. Booklet pane of 5 + label	3.00	
Nos. 514-517 (4)	2.40	.80

Nos. 514-517 were issued in booklets only; all stamps have one or two straight edges.

1972, Apr. 18 Photo. *Perf. 13½*

518 A209 7c multicolored	.25	.20

Country Women's Assoc., 50th anniv.

Apple and Banana A210

1972, June 14

519 A210 20c shown	1.50	1.50
520 A210 25c Rice	2.25	2.25
521 A210 30c Fish	2.25	2.25
522 A210 35c Cattle	5.25	5.25
Nos. 519-522 (4)	11.25	11.25

Worker in Sheltered Workshop — A211

18c, Amputee assembling electrical circuit, horiz. 24c, Boy wearing Toronto splint, playing ball.

1972, Aug. 2 *Perf. 13½x13*

523 A211 12c green & brown	.25	.20
524 A211 18c orange & olive	1.25	.20
525 A211 24c brown & ultra	.50	.20
Nos. 523-525 (3)	2.00	.60

Rehabilitation of the handicapped.

Overland Telegraph Line — A212

1972, Aug. 22 Photo. *Perf. 13x13½*

526 A212 7c dk red, blk & lemon	.25	.20

Centenary of overland telegraph line.

Athlete, Olympic Rings — A213

1972, Aug. 28 *Perf. 13½x13*

527 A213 7c shown	.20	.20
528 A213 7c Swimming	.20	.20
529 A213 7c Rowing	.20	.20
530 A213 35c Equestrian	4.50	4.00
Nos. 527-530 (4)	5.10	4.60

20th Olympic Games, Munich, Aug. 26-Sept. 11.

Abacus, Numerals, Computer Circuits A214

1972, Oct. 16 Photo. *Perf. 13x13½*

531 A214 7c multicolored	.20	.20

10th Intl. Congress of Accountants.

19th Cent. Combine Harvester A215

Perf. 13½x13, 13x13½

1972, Nov. 15 Photo.

532 A215 5c Pioneer family, vert.	.20	.20
533 A215 10c Water pump, vert.	.45	.20
534 A215 15c shown	.30	.20
535 A215 40c Pioneer house	.65	.20
536 A215 50c Cobb & Co. coach	1.10	.20
537 A215 60c Early Morse key, vert.	1.00	.45
538 A215 80c Paddle-wheel steamer	1.10	.45
Nos. 532-538 (7)	4.80	1.90

Australian pioneer life.

Jesus and Children — A216

Dove, Cross and "Darkness into Light" — A217

Metric Conversion, Mass — A218

Perf. 14½x14, 13½x13

1972, Nov. 29

539 A216 7c tan & multi	.35	.20
540 A217 35c blue & multi	7.50	7.50

Christmas.

1973, Mar. 7 Photo. *Perf. 14x14½*

Metric conversion: No. 542, Temperature, horiz. No. 543, Length. No. 544, Volume.

541 A218 7c pale vio & multi	.80	.20
542 A218 7c yellow & multi	.80	.20
543 A218 7c yel green & multi	.80	.20
544 A218 7c brt rose & multi	.80	.20
Nos. 541-544 (4)	3.20	.80

Conversion to metric system.

Stylized Caduceus and Laurel A219

1973, Apr. 4 Photo. *Perf. 14½x14*

545 A219 7c dk bl, emer & lil rose	.25	.20

WHO, 25th anniv.

Dame Mary Gilmore, Writer A220

Shipping Industry A221

Famous Australians: No. 547, William Charles Wentworth, explorer. No. 548, Sir Isaac Isaacs, lawyer, first Australian-born Governor-General. No. 549, Marcus Clarke, writer.

Engr. & Litho.

1973, May 16 *Perf. 15x14*

546 A220 7c bister & black	1.00	.20
547 A220 7c bister & black	1.00	.20
548 A220 7c black & violet	1.00	.20
549 A220 7c black & violet	1.00	.20
a. Block of 4, #546-549	4.00	1.00

1973, June 6 Photo. *Perf. 13½x13*

Designs: 25c, Iron ore and steel. 30c, Truck convoy (beef road). 35c, Aerial mapping.

550 A221 20c ultra & multi	1.75	1.40
551 A221 25c red & multi	1.50	1.50
552 A221 30c ol brn & multi	2.00	2.00
553 A221 35c olive & multi	2.75	2.75
Nos. 550-553 (4)	8.00	7.65

Australian economic development.

Banded Coral Shrimp A222

Chrysoprase A223

Helichrysum Thomsonii A223a

Wombat A224

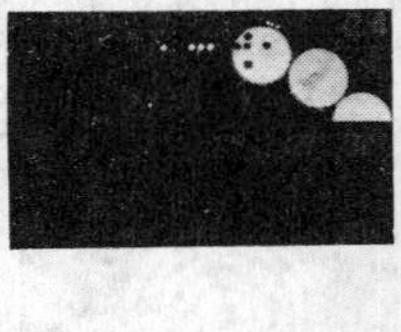

Radio Astronomy A225

Red Gums of the Far North, by Hans Heysen — A226

Coming South (Immigrants), by Tom Roberts — A226a

Paintings: $1, Sergeant of Light Horse, by George Lambert. No. 575, On the Wallaby Track. $4, Shearing the Rams, by Tom Roberts. No. 577, McMahon's Point, by Arthur Streeton. No. 578, Mentone.

Perf. 14x15, 15x14 (A222, A223, A223a); Perf. 14x14½ (A224); Perf. 13x13½ (A225, A226, $1)

1973-84 Photo.

554 A222	1c	shown	.20	.20
555 A222	2c	Fiddler crab	.20	.20
556 A222	3c	Coral crab	.20	.20
557 A222	4c	Mauve stinger	.20	.20
558 A223	6c	shown	.20	.20
559 A223	7c	Agate	.20	.20
560 A223	8c	Opal	.20	.20
561 A223	9c	Rhodonite	.20	.20
562 A223	10c	Star sapphire ('74)	.20	.20
563 A225	11c	Atomic absorption spectrophotometry ('75)	.55	.25
564 A223a	18c	shown ('75)	.50	.20
565 A224	20c	shown ('74)	.40	.20
566 A225	24c	shown ('75)	1.00	.40
567 A224	25c	Spiny anteater ('74)	1.25	.35
568 A224	30c	Brushtail possum ('74)	.70	.20
569 A225	33c	Immunology ('75)	1.00	1.00
570 A223a	45c	Callistemon teretifolius, horiz. ('75)	.65	.25
571 A225	48c	Oceanography ('75)	1.75	1.10
572 A224	75c	Feather-tailed glider ('74)	1.25	.75
573 A226a	$1	multi ('74)	1.50	.25
574 A226	$2	shown ('74)	2.75	.30
575 A226	$2	multi ('81)	2.50	.30
576 A226	$4	multi ('74)	4.00	2.25

Litho.

Perf. 14½

577 A226a	$5	multi ('79)	6.00	2.00
578 A226	$5	multi ('84)	5.00	1.25
579 A226a	$10	shown ('77)	10.00	3.25
		Nos. 554-579 (26)	42.60	16.10

Issued: 1c-9c, 7/11; 20c, 25c, 30c, 75c, 2/13; $1, #574, $4, 4/24; 10c, 10/16; 11c, 24c, 33c, 48c, 5/14; 18c, 45c, 8/27; $10, 10/19; #577, 3/14; #575, 6/17; #578, 4/4.

No. 560 Surcharged in Red = 9c

Perf. 15x14

580 A223 9c on 8c multi ('74) .20 .20

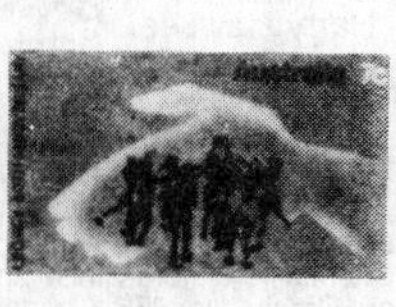

Hand Protecting Playing Children A227

1973, Sept. 5 Photo. ***Perf. 13x13½***

581 A227 7c bis brn, grn & plum .25 .20

50th anniv. of Legacy, an ex-servicemen's organization concerned with the welfare of widows and children of servicemen.

Baptism of Christ A228

The Good Shepherd A229

1973, Oct. 3 ***Perf. 14x14½***

582 A228 7c gold & multi .30 .20
a. Perf. 14x15 4.00 .60

Perf. 13½

583 A229 30c gold & multi 3.75 3.75

Christmas.

Buchanan's Hotel, Townsville A230

St. James' Church, Sydney A231

Designs: 7c, Opera House, Sydney. 40c, Como House, Melbourne.

1973, Oct. 17 Photo. ***Perf. 14½x14***

584 A230 7c lt blue & ultra .40 .20
a. Perf. 15x14 4.00 .80
585 A230 10c bister & black .60 .35

Perf. 13x13½, 13½x13

586 A230 40c dl pink, gray & blk .75 .75
587 A231 50c gray & multi 2.00 1.50
Nos. 584-587 (4) 3.75 2.80

Australian architecture; opening of the Sydney Opera House, Oct. 14, 1973 (No. 584).

Radio and Gramophone Speaker A232

1973, Nov. 21 Photo. ***Perf. 13½x13***

588 A232 7c dull blue, blk & brn .25 .20

Broadcasting in Australia, 50th anniv.

Supreme Court Judge on Bench A233

Australian Football A234

1974, May 15 Photo. ***Perf. 14x14½***

589 A233 7c multicolored .25 .20

150th anniv. of the proclamation of the Charter of Justice in New South Wales and Van Diemen's Land (Australia's Third Charter).

1974, July 24 Photo. ***Perf. 14x14½***

590 A234	7c	shown	.35	.20
591 A234	7c	Cricket	.35	.20
592 A234	7c	Golf	.35	.20
593 A234	7c	Surfing	.35	.20
594 A234	7c	Tennis	.35	.20
595 A234	7c	Bowls, horiz.	.35	.20
596 A234	7c	Rugby, horiz.	.35	.20
		Nos. 590-596 (7)	2.45	1.40

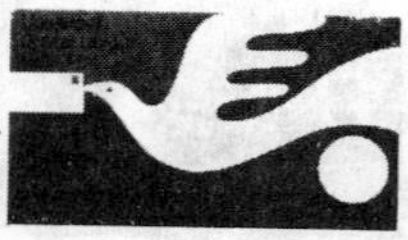

Carrier Pigeon A235

Designs: 30c, Carrier pigeons, vert.

1974, Oct. 9 Photo. ***Perf. 14½x14***

597 A235 7c multicolored .25 .20
a. Perf. 15x14 .75 .20

Perf. 13½x13

598 A235 30c multicolored 1.00 1.00

UPU, cent. A booklet containing a strip of 5 each of Nos. 597-598 was produced and sold for $4 Australian by the National Stamp Week Promotion Council with government approval.

William Charles Wentworth A236

Adoration of the Kings, by Dürer A237

Typo. & Litho.

1974, Oct. 9 ***Perf. 14x15***

599 A236 7c bister & black .35 .20
a. Perf. 14x14½ .90 .25

Sesquicentennial of 1st Australian independent newspaper. W. C. Wentworth and Dr. Robert Wardell were the editors and the "A" is type from masthead of "The Australian."

1974, Nov. 13 Engr. ***Perf. 14x14½***

Christmas: 35c, Flight into Egypt, by Albrecht Dürer.

600 A237 10c buff & black .22 .20
601 A237 35c buff & black .90 .90

Pre-school Education A238

Correspondence Schools — A239

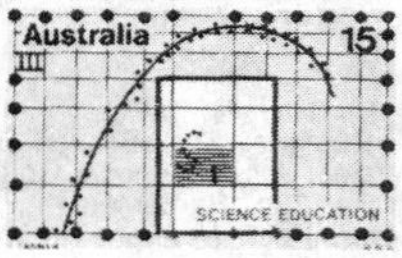

Science Education A240

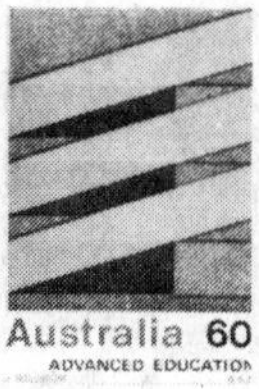

Advanced Education — A241

Perf. 13x13½, 13½x13

1974, Nov. 20 Photo.

602 A238	5c multicolored	.25	.20
603 A239	11c multicolored	.35	.25
604 A240	15c multicolored	.40	.30
605 A241	60c multicolored	1.00	.95
	Nos. 602-605 (4)	2.00	1.70

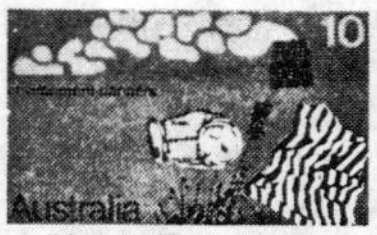

"Avoid Pollution" A242

"Road Safety" A243

Design: No. 607, "Avoid bush fires."

1975, Jan. 29 Photo. ***Perf. 14½x14***

606 A242 10c multicolored .30 .20
a. Perf. 15x14 7.50 3.75
607 A242 10c multicolored .30 .20
a. Perf. 15x14 1.50 1.00

Perf. 14x14½

608 A243 10c multicolored .30 .20
Nos. 606-608 (3) .90 .60

Environmental dangers.

Symbols of Womanhood, Sun, Moon A244

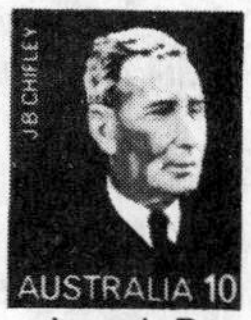

Joseph B. Chiefley (1885-1951) A245

1975, Mar. 12 Photo. ***Perf. 14x14½***

609 A244 10c dk vio blue & grn .25 .20

International Women's Year.

1975, Mar. 26

610 A245	10c shown	.20	.20
611 A245	10c John Curtin, 1885-1945	.20	.20
612 A245	10c Arthur W. Fadden, 1895-1973	.20	.20
613 A245	10c Joseph A. Lyons, 1879-1939	.20	.20
614 A245	10c Earle Page, 1880-1963	.20	.20
615 A245	10c John H. Scullin, 1876-1953	.20	.20
	Nos. 610-615 (6)	1.20	1.20

Australian Prime Ministers.

Australian Postal Commission A246

Design: No. 617, Australian Telecommunications Commission.

1975, July 1 Photo. ***Perf. 14½x14***

616 A246 10c red, black & gray .40 .20
a. Perf. 15x14 .50 .20
617 A246 10c yel, black & gray .40 .20
a. Pair, #616-617 .95 .75
b. Perf. 15x14 .50 .20
c. Pair, #616a, 617b 1.25 1.00

Formation of Australian Postal and Telecommunications Commissions. Printed checkerwise.

Edith Cowan, Judge and Legislator A247

Truganini, Last Tasmanian Aborigine A248

Portraits: No. 619, Louisa Lawson (1848-1920), journalist. No. 620, Ethel Florence

(Henry Handel) Richardson (1870-1946), novelist. No. 621, Catherine Spence (1825-1910), teacher, journalist, voting reformer. No. 622, Emma Constance Stone (1856-1902), first Australian woman physician.

1975, Aug. 6 Photo. *Perf. 14x14½*

618 A247 10c olive grn & multi .30 .30
a. Perf. 14x15 .35 .35
619 A247 10c yel bister & multi .30 .30
a. Perf. 14x15 .35 .35
620 A248 10c olive & multi .30 .30
a. Perf. 14x15 .35 .35
621 A248 10c gray & multi .30 .30
a. Perf. 14x15 .35 .35
622 A247 10c violet & multi .30 .30
a. Perf. 14x15 .35 .35
623 A248 10c brown & multi .30 .30
a. Perf. 14x15 .35 .35
Nos. 618-623 (6) 1.80 1.80

Famous Australian women.

Spirit House (PNG) and Sydney Opera House A249

Bird in Flight and Southern Cross A250

1975, Sept. 16 Photo. *Perf. 13½*

624 A249 18c multicolored .40 .20
625 A250 25c multicolored .75 .55

Papua New Guinea independence, Sept. 16, 1975.

Adoration of the Kings — A251

"The Light Shineth in the Darkness" — A252

1975, Oct. 29 Photo. *Perf. 14½x14*

626 A251 15c multicolored .30 .20
627 A252 45c silver & multi 1.50 1.50

Christmas.

Australian Coat of Arms — A253

Two Types of A253:
Type I - Kangaroo: eye is dot, right paw has 1 toe, left foot has 1 toe. Emu: feet have 1 toe.
Type II - Kangaroo: eye is line, right paw has 3 toes, left foot has 2 toes. Emu: feet have 2 toes.
Other differences exist.

1976, Jan. 5 Photo. *Perf. 14½x14*

628 A253 18c multicolored, type I .40 .20
a. Type II .75 .25

"Williams' Coffin" Telephone, 1878 — A254

1976, Mar. 10 Photo. *Perf. 13½*

629 A254 18c buff & multi .35 .20

Centenary of first telephone call by Alexander Graham Bell, Mar. 10, 1876.

John Oxley — A255

Designs: Australian explorers.

1976, June 9 Photo. *Perf. 13½*

630 A255 18c shown .25 .20
631 A255 18c Hamilton Hume and William Hovell .25 .20
632 A255 18c John Forrest .25 .20
633 A255 18c Ernest Giles .25 .20
634 A255 18c Peter Warburton .25 .20
635 A255 18c William Gosse .25 .20
Nos. 630-635 (6) 1.50 1.20

Survey Rule, Graph, Punched Tape — A256

1976, June 15 *Perf. 15x14*

636 A256 18c multicolored .30 .20

Commonwealth Scientific and Industrial Research Organization, 50th anniv.

Soccer Goalkeeper A257

Olympic Rings and: No. 638, Woman gymnast, vert. 25c, Woman diver, vert. 40c, Bicycling.

Perf. 13x13½, 13½x13

1976, July 14 Photo.

637 A257 18c multicolored .30 .20
638 A257 18c multicolored .30 .20
639 A257 25c multicolored .45 .40
640 A257 40c multicolored .65 .50
Nos. 637-640 (4) 1.70 1.30

21st Olympic Games, Montreal, Canada, July 17-Aug. 1.

Richmond Bridge, Tasmania A258

Mt. Buffalo, Victoria A259

Designs: 25c, Broken Bay, New South Wales. 35c, Wittenoom Gorge, Western Australia. 70c, Barrier Reef, Queensland. 85c, Ayers Rock, Northern Territory.

Perf. 14½x14, 14x14½

1976, Aug. 25 Photo.

641 A258 5c multicolored .25 .20
642 A258 25c multicolored .35 .20
643 A258 35c multicolored .30 .30
644 A259 50c multicolored .50 .25
645 A258 70c multicolored .60 .35
646 A258 85c multicolored 1.00 .80
Nos. 641-646 (6) 3.00 2.10

Blamire Young and Australia No. 59 — A260

1976, Sept. 27 Photo. *Perf. 13½*

647 A260 18c apple green & multi .35 .20

Miniature Sheet

648 Sheet of 4 1.65 1.50
a. A260 18c yellow & dark brown .35 .35
b. A260 18c rose, dk brown & yel .35 .35
c. A260 18c blue, dk brn, rose & yel .35 .35

Natl. Stamp Week, Sept. 27-Oct. 3. Blamire Young (1862-1935), designer of Australia's 1st issue. No. 648 shows different stages of 4-color printing. The 4th stamp in sheet is identical with No. 647.

Virgin and Child, after Simone Cantarini A261

Holly, Toy Koala, Christmas Tree and Decoration, Partridge A262

1976, Nov. 1 Photo. *Perf. 14½x14*

649 A261 15c brt car & lt blue .30 .20

Perf. 13½

650 A262 45c multicolored .80 .75

Christmas.

John Gould (1804-1881) Ornithologist A263

Violinists A264

Famous Australians: No. 652, Thomas Laby (1880-1946), nuclear scientist. No. 653, Sir Baldwin Spencer (1860-1929), anthropologist (aborigines). No. 654, Griffith Taylor (1880-1963), geographer and arctic explorer.

1976, Nov. 10 *Perf. 15x14*

651 A263 18c shown .30 .20
652 A263 18c Laby .30 .20
653 A263 18c Spencer .30 .20
654 A263 18c Taylor .30 .20
Nos. 651-654 (4) 1.20 .80

1977, Jan. 19 Photo. *Perf. 14x14½*

655 A264 20c shown .25 .20
656 A264 30c Dramatic scene .30 .20
657 A264 40c Dancer .55 .40
658 A264 60c Opera singer .70 .20
Nos. 655-658 (4) 1.80 1.00

Performing arts in Australia.

Elizabeth II A265

Wicket Keeper, Slip Fieldsman A266

Design: 45c, Elizabeth II and Prince Philip.

1977, Feb. 2

659 A265 18c multicolored .30 .20
660 A265 45c multicolored .75 .75

Reign of Queen Elizabeth II, 25th anniv.

1977, Mar. 9 Photo. *Perf. 13½*

Cricket match, 19th century: No. 662, Umpire and batsman. No. 663, Two fieldsmen. No. 664, Batsman and umpire. No. 665, Bowler and fieldsman. 45c, Batsman facing bowler.

661 A266 18c gray & multi .30 .25
662 A266 18c gray & multi .30 .25
663 A266 18c gray & multi .30 .25
664 A266 18c gray & multi .30 .25
665 A266 18c gray & multi .30 .25
a. Strip of 5, #661-665 1.50 1.50
666 A266 45c gray & multi .80 .80
Nos. 661-666 (6) 2.30 2.05

Parliament House, Canberra A267

1977, Apr. 13 *Perf. 14½x14*

667 A267 18c multicolored .40 .20

Parliament House, Canberra, 50th anniv.

Trade Union Workers A268

1977, May 9 Photo. *Perf. 13*

668 A268 18c multicolored .35 .20

Australian Council of Trade Unions (ACTU), 50th anniv.

Surfing Santa A269

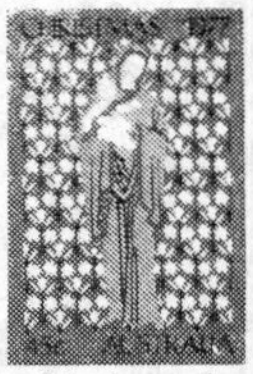

Virgin and Child A270

1977, Oct. 31 Photo. *Perf. 14x14½*

669 A269 15c multicolored .35 .20

Perf. 13½x13

670 A270 45c multicolored .75 .75

Christmas.

Australian Flag A271

1978, Jan. 26 Photo. *Perf. 13x13½*

671 A271 18c multicolored .35 .20

Australia Day, 190th anniversary of first permament settlement in New South Wales.

Harry Hawker and Sopwith "Camel" A272

Australian Aviators and their Planes: No. 673, Bert Hinkler and Avro Avian. No. 674, Charles Kingsford-Smith and Fokker "Southern Cross." No. 675, Charles Ulm and "Southern Cross."

1978, Apr. 19 Litho. *Perf. 15½*

672 A272 18c ultra & multi .30 .20
673 A272 18c blue & multi .30 .20
674 A272 18c orange & multi .30 .20
675 A272 18c yellow & multi .30 .20
a. Souv. sheet, 2 each #674-675, imperf. 1.65 1.65
Nos. 672-675 (4) 1.20 .80

No. 675a for 50th anniv. of first Trans-Pacific flight from Oakland, Cal., to Brisbane.

Beechcraft Baron Landing A273

1978, May 15 Photo. *Perf. 13½*
676 A273 18c multicolored .30 .20

Royal Flying Doctor Service, 50th anniv.

Illawarra Flame Tree A274

Sturt's Desert Rose, Map of Australia A275

Australian trees: 25c, Ghost gum. 40c, Grass tree. 45c, Cootamundra wattle.

1978, June 1
677 A274 18c multicolored .20 .20
678 A274 25c multicolored .60 .60
679 A274 40c multicolored .70 .70
680 A274 45c multicolored .65 .65
Nos. 677-680 (4) 2.15 2.15

1978, June 19 Litho. *Perf. 15½*
681 A275 18c multicolored .35 .20

Establishment of Government of the Northern Territory.

Hooded Dotterel — A276

Australian birds: 20c, Little grebe. 25c, Spur-wing Plover. 30c, Pied oystercatcher. 55c, Lotus bird.

1978 Photo. *Perf. 13½*
682 A276 5c multicolored .20 .20
683 A276 20c multicolored .25 .20
684 A276 25c multicolored .35 .20
685 A276 30c multicolored .40 .30
686 A276 55c multicolored .70 .50
Nos. 682-686 (5) 1.90 1.40

Issued: Nos. 683, 686, July 3; others, July 17. See Nos. 713-718, 732-739, 768.

Australia No. 95 on Album Page — A277

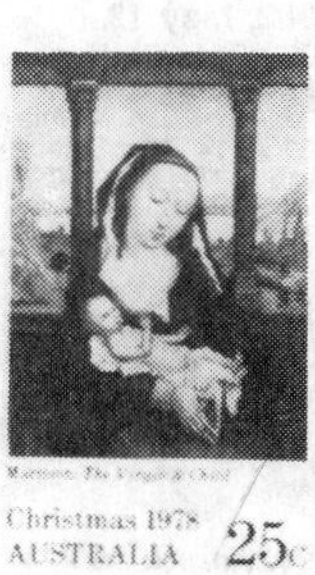

Virgin and Child, by Simon Marmion — A278

1978, Sept. 25 Litho. *Perf. 15½*
687 A277 20c multicolored .30 .20
a. Miniature sheet of 4 1.25 1.25

National Stamp Week; 50th anniv. of Melbourne Intl. Phil. Exhib., Oct. 1928.

1978 *Perf. 15*

Paintings from National Gallery, Victoria: 15c, Virgin and Child, after Van Eyck. 55c, Holy Family, by Perino del Vaga.

688 A278 15c multicolored .20 .20
689 A278 25c multicolored .50 .50
690 A278 55c multicolored .80 .80
Nos. 688-690 (3) 1.50 1.50

Christmas. Issued: 25c, Oct. 3, others, Nov. 1.

Tulloch A279

Race horses: 35c, Bernborough, vert. 50c, Phar Lap, vert. 55c, Peter Pan.

Perf. 15x14, 14x15
1978, Oct. 18 Photo.
691 A279 20c multicolored .25 .20
692 A279 35c multicolored .45 .45
693 A279 50c multicolored .65 .65
694 A279 55c multicolored .65 .65
Nos. 691-694 (4) 2.00 1.95

Australian horse racing.

Flag Raising at Sydney Cove — A280

1979, Jan. 26 Litho. *Perf. 15½*
695 A280 20c multicolored .35 .20

Australia Day, Jan. 26.

Passenger Steamer Canberra A281

Ferries and Murray River Steamers: 35c, M.V. Lady Denman. 50c, P.S. Murray River Queen. 55c, Hydrofoil Curl Curl.

1979, Feb. 14 Photo. *Perf. 13½*
696 A281 20c multicolored .30 .20
697 A281 35c multicolored .50 .40
698 A281 50c multicolored .75 .65
699 A281 55c multicolored .85 .85
Nos. 696-699 (4) 2.40 2.10

Port Campbell A282

Designs: Australian National Parks.

1979, Apr. 9 Litho. *Perf. 15½*
700 A282 20c shown .30 .20
701 A282 20c Uluru .30 .20
702 A282 20c Royal .30 .20
703 A282 20c Flinders Ranges .30 .20
704 A282 20c Namburg .30 .20
a. Strip of 5, #700-704 1.50
705 A282 20c Girraween, vert. .30 .20
706 A282 20c Mount Field, vert. .30 .20
a. Pair, #705-706 .60
Nos. 700-706 (7) 2.10 1.40

Double Fairlie A283

Australian steam locomotives: 35c, Puffing Billy. 50c, Pichi Richi. 55c, Zig Zag.

Perf. 13½, 15x14 (20c)
1979, May 16 Photo.
707 A283 20c multicolored .20 .20
708 A283 35c multicolored .40 .30
709 A283 50c multicolored .75 .60
710 A283 55c multicolored .80 .80
Nos. 707-710 (4) 2.15 1.90

"Black Swan" A284

1979, June 6 Photo. *Perf. 13½*
711 A284 20c multicolored .35 .20

150th anniversary of Western Australia.

Children Playing, IYC Emblem A285

1979, Aug. 13 Litho. *Perf. 13½x13*
712 A285 20c multicolored .30 .20

International Year of the Child.

Bird Type of 1978

Australian birds: 1c, Zebra finch. 2c, Crimson finch. 15c, Forest kingfisher, vert. 20c, Eastern yellow robin. 40c, Lovely wren, vert. 50c, Flame robin, vert.

1979, Sept. 17 Photo. *Perf. 13½*
713 A276 1c multicolored .20 .20
714 A276 2c multicolored .20 .20
715 A276 15c multicolored .30 .20
716 A276 20c multicolored .30 .20
717 A276 40c multicolored .50 .20
718 A276 50c multicolored .70 .20
Nos. 713-718 (6) 2.20 1.20

Christmas Letters, Flag-wrapped Parcels A286

Trout Fishing A287

Christmas: 15c, Nativity, icon. 55c, Madonna and Child, by Buglioni.

1979 Litho. *Perf. 13*
719 A286 15c multicolored .20 .20
720 A286 25c multicolored .30 .30
721 A286 55c multicolored .90 .90
Nos. 719-721 (3) 1.40 1.40

Issue dates: 25c, Sept. 24. Others, Nov. 1.

1979, Oct. 24 Photo. *Perf. 14x14½*

Sport fishing: 35c, Angler. 50c, Black marlin fishing. 55c, Surf fishing.

722 A287 20c multicolored .25 .20
723 A287 35c multicolored .45 .45
724 A287 50c multicolored .70 .45
725 A287 55c multicolored .75 .70
Nos. 722-725 (4) 2.15 1.80

Matthew Flinders, Map of Australia A288

1980, Jan. 23 Litho. *Perf. 13½*
726 A288 20c multicolored .30 .20

Australia Day, Jan. 28.

Dingo — A289

1980, Feb. 20 Litho. *Perf. 13½x13*
727 A289 20c shown .30 .20
728 A289 25c Border collie .35 .35
729 A289 35c Australian terrier .60 .40
730 A289 50c Australian cattle dog .80 .70
731 A289 55c Australian kelpie .65 .65
Nos. 727-731 (5) 2.70 2.30

Bird Type of 1978

Perf. 13½, 14x15 (22c), 13x12½ (28c, 60c)
1980 Litho., Photo. (22c)
732 A276 10c Golden-shoulder parrot, vert. .20 .20
a. Perf. 14½x14 1.25 .50
733 A276 22c White-tailed kingfisher, vert. .30 .20
734 A276 28c Rainbow bird, vert. .45 .20
735 A276 35c Regent bower bird, vert. .45 .20
736 A276 45c Masked woodswallow .95 .20
a. Perf. 14x14½ 4.00 2.00
737 A276 60c King parrot, vert. .75 .25
738 A276 80c Rainbow pitta 1.00 .40
739 A276 $1 Western magpie, vert. 1.25 .30
Nos. 732-739 (8) 5.35 1.95

Issued: #733, 734, 737, Mar. 31; others, July 1.

Queen Elizabeth II, 54th Birthday — A290

1980, Apr. 21 Litho. *Perf. 13x13½*
740 A290 22c multicolored .35 .20

Wanderer A291

High Court Building, Canberra A292

1980, May 7 Litho. *Perf. 13x13½*
741 Strip of 5 1.25 1.00
a. A291 22c shown .25 .20
b. A291 22c Stealing sheep .25 .20
c. A291 22c Squatter on horseback .25 .20
d. A291 22c Three troopers .25 .20
e. A291 22c Wanderer's ghost .25 .20

"Waltzing Matilda", poem by Andrew Barton Patterson (1864-1941). No. 741 in continuous design.

1980, May 19
742 A292 22c multicolored .35 .20

Opening of High Court of Australia Building, Canberra, May 26.

Salvation Army Officers A294

Perf. 13x13½, 13½x13
1980, Aug. 11
747 A294 22c shown .30 .20
748 A294 22c St. Vincent de Paul Society, vert. .30 .20
749 A294 22c Meals on Wheels, vert. .30 .20
750 A294 22c "Life. Be in it." (Joggers, bicyclists) .30 .20
Nos. 747-750 (4) 1.20 .80

Mailman c. 1900 A295

Holy Family, by Prospero Fontana A296

1980, Sept. 29 Litho. *Perf. 13x13½*

751	A295 22c Mailbox	.30	.20
752	A295 22c shown	.30	.20
753	A295 22c Mail truck	.30	.20
754	A295 22c Mailman, mailbox	.30	.20
755	A295 22c Mailman, diff.	.30	.20
a.	Souvenir sheet of 3	1.00	1.00
b.	Strip of 5, #751-755	1.50	1.00

Natl. Stamp Week, Sept. 29-Oct. 5. #755a contains stamps similar to #751, 753, 755.

1980 *Perf. 13x13½*

Christmas: 15c, Virgin Enthroned, by Justin O'Brien. 60c, Virgin and Child, by Michael Zuern the Younger, 1680.

756	A296 15c multicolored	.25	.20
757	A296 28c multicolored	.45	.45
758	A296 60c multicolored	.90	.65
	Nos. 756-758 (3)	1.60	1.30

Issued: 15c, 60c, Nov. 3; 28c, Oct. 1.

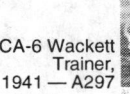

CA-6 Wackett Trainer, 1941 — A297

Designs: Australian military training planes.

1980, Nov. 19 *Perf. 13½x14*

759	A297 22c shown	.30	.25
760	A297 40c Winjeel, 1955	.60	.60
761	A297 45c Boomerang, 1944	.65	.50
762	A297 60c Nomad, 1975	1.00	.60
	Nos. 759-762 (4)	2.55	1.95

Bird Type of 1978

1980, Nov. 17 Litho. *Perf. 13½*

768	A276 18c Spotted catbird, vert.	.35	.20

Flag on Map of Australia A298

1981, Jan. 21

771	A298 22c multicolored	.35	.20

Australia Day, Jan. 21.

Jockey Darby Munro (1913-1966), by Tony Rafty — A299

Australian sportsmen (Caricatures by Tony Rafty): 35c, Victor Trumper (1877-1915), cricket batsman. 55c, Norman Brookes (1877-1968), tennis player. 60c, Walter Lindrum (1898-1960), billiards player.

1981, Feb. 18 *Perf. 14x13½*

772	A299 22c multicolored	.25	.20
773	A299 35c multicolored	.45	.45
774	A299 55c multicolored	.65	.65
775	A299 60c multicolored	.75	.75
	Nos. 772-775 (4)	2.10	2.05

Australia No. C2 and Cover A300

Perf. 13x13½, 13½x13

1981, Mar. 25 Litho.

776	A300 22c Australia No. C2, vert.	.30	.25
777	A300 60c shown	.90	.80

Australia-United Kingdom official airmail service, 50th anniv.

Map of Australia, APEX Emblem A301

1981, Apr. 6 Photo. *Perf. 13x13½*

778	A301 22c multicolored	.30	.20

50th anniv. of APEX (young men's service club).

Queen Elizabeth's Personal Flag of Australia A302

1981, Apr. 21 *Perf. 13*

779	A302 22c multicolored	.35	.20

Queen Elizabeth II, 55th birthday.

License Inspected, Forrest Creek, by S.T. Gill — A303

Gold Rush Era (Sketches by S.T. Gill): No. 781, Puddling. No. 782, Quality of Washing Stuff. No. 783, Diggers on Route to Deposit Gold.

1981, May 20 Photo. *Perf. 13x13½*

780	A303 22c multicolored	.30	.20
781	A303 22c multicolored	.30	.20
782	A303 22c multicolored	.30	.20
783	A303 22c multicolored	.30	.20
	Nos. 780-783 (4)	1.20	.80

Lace Monitor — A303a

Tasmanian Tiger — A304

Two Types of A304:

Type I - Indistinct line at right of ear, stripes even with base of tail.

Type II - Heavy line at right of ear, stripes longer.

1981-83 Litho.

784	A303a 1c shown	.20	.20
785	A303a 3c Corroboree frog	.20	.20
786	A304 5c Queensland hairy-nosed wombat, vert.	.20	.20
787	A303a 15c Eastern snake-necked tortoise	.20	.20
788	A304 24c shown, type I	.35	.20
a.	Type II	.35	.20
789	A304 25c Greater bilby, vert.	.35	.20
790	A303a 27c Blue Mountains tree frog	.35	.20
791	A304 30c Bridled nail-tailed wallaby, vert.	.35	.20
792	A303a 40c Smooth knob-tailed gecko	.45	.25
793	A304 50c Leadbeater's opossum	.75	.40
794	A304 55c Stick-nest rat, vert.	.75	.40
795	A303a 65c Yellow-faced whip snake	.80	.45
796	A303a 70c Crucifix toad	.90	.55
797	A303a 75c Eastern water dragon	.90	.55
798	A303a 85c Centralian blue-tongued lizard	1.00	.65
799	A303a 90c Freshwater crocodile	1.10	.70
800	A303a 95c Thorny devil	1.25	.75
	Nos. 784-800 (17)	10.10	6.30

Perfs: 1c, 70c, 85c, 95c, 13½; 3c, 15c, 27c, 40c, 50c, 65c, 75c, 90c, 12½x13; 5c, 25c, 30c, 55c, 13x12½; 24c, 13x13½.

Issued: 24c, 7/1/81; 5c, 25c, 30c, 50c, 55c, 7/15/81; 3c, 27c, 65c, 75c, 4/19/82; 15c, 40c, 90c, 6/16/82. 1c, 70c, 85c, 95c, 2/2/83.

1982-84 *Perf. 14x14½, 14½x14*

785a	A303a 3c ('84)	.30	.20
786a	A304 5c ('84)	.90	.20
787a	A303a 15c ('84)	.70	.25
789a	A304 25c ('83)	1.10	.20
790a	A303a 27c	.75	.25
792a	A303a 40c ('84)	2.00	.30
793a	A304 50c ('83)	1.25	.40
795a	A303a 65c ('84)	1.40	.60
797a	A303a 75c ('84)	1.50	.80
	Nos. 785a-797a (9)	9.90	3.20

Prince Charles and Lady Diana A305

1981, July 29 Litho. *Perf. 13*

804	A305 24c multicolored	.40	.20
805	A305 60c multicolored	1.15	.75

Royal Wedding.

Cortinarius Cinnabarinus A306

Intl. Year of the Disabled A307

Designs: Fungi.

1981, Aug. 19 Litho. *Perf. 13*

806	A306 24c shown	.25	.20
807	A306 35c Coprinus comatus	.40	.40
808	A306 55c Armillaria luteobubalina	.75	.60
809	A306 60c Cortinarius austrovenetus	.90	.80
	Nos. 806-809 (4)	2.30	2.00

1981, Sept. 16 *Perf. 14x13½*

810	A307 24c multicolored	.40	.20

Christmas Bush for His Adorning A308

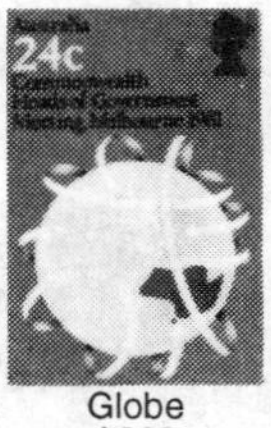

Globe A309

Christmas (Carols by William James and John Wheeler): 30c, The Silver Stars are in the Sky. 60c, Noeltime.

1981 Litho. *Perf. 13x13½*

811	A308 18c multicolored	.35	.20
812	A308 30c multicolored	.50	.35
813	A308 60c multicolored	1.25	1.00
	Nos. 811-813 (3)	2.10	1.55

Issue dates: 30c, Sept. 28; others, Nov. 2.

1981, Sept. 30

814	A309 24c multicolored	.35	.20
815	A309 60c multicolored	1.00	.90

Commonwealth Heads of Government Meeting, Melbourne, Sept. 30-Oct. 7.

Yacht — A310

1981, Oct. 14 Litho. *Perf. 13x13½*

816	A310 24c Ocean racer	.35	.20
817	A310 35c Lightweight sharpie	.50	.60
818	A310 55c 12-Meter	.75	.60
819	A310 60c Sabot	.90	.80
	Nos. 816-819 (4)	2.50	2.20

Australia Day, Jan. 26 A311

1982, Jan. 20 Litho. *Perf. 13x13½*

820	A311 24c multicolored	.40	.20

Sperm Whale — A312

Perf. 13x13½, 13½x13

1982, Feb. 17

821	A312 24c shown	.35	.20
822	A312 35c Southern right whale, vert.	.60	.60
823	A312 55c Blue whale, vert.	.90	.75
824	A312 60c Humpback whale	1.00	1.00
	Nos. 821-824 (4)	2.85	2.55

Elizabeth II, 56th Birthday — A313

Roses — A314

1982, Apr. 21 *Perf. 13½*

825	A313 27c multicolored	.40	.20

1982, May 19 *Perf. 13x13½*

826	A314 27c Marjorie Atherton	.30	.30
827	A314 40c Imp	.55	.50
828	A314 65c Minnie Watson	.80	.80
829	A314 75c Satellite	.90	.85
	Nos. 826-829 (4)	2.55	2.45

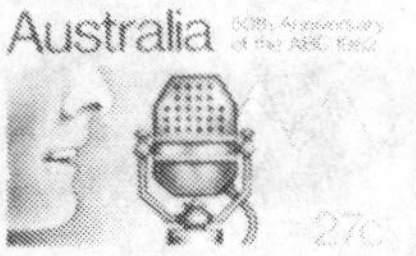

50th Anniv. of Australian Broadcasting Commission A315

1982, June 16 *Perf. 13½x13*

830	A315 27c Announcer, microphone	.45	.25
831	A315 27c Emblem	.45	.25
a.	Pair, #830-831	.90	.50

#830-831 se-tenant in continuous design.

Alice Springs Post Office, 1872 — A316

1982, Aug. 4 *Perf. 13½x14, 14x13½*

832	A316 27c shown	.30	.20
833	A316 27c Kingston, 1869	.30	.20
834	A316 27c York, 1893	.30	.20
835	A316 27c Flemington, 1890, vert.	.30	.20

836 A316 27c Forbes, 1881, vert. .30 .20
837 A316 27c Launceston, 1889, vert. .30 .20
838 A316 27c Rockhampton, 1892, vert. .30 .20
Nos. 832-838 (7) 2.10 1.40

Christmas — A317

1st Australian Christmas cards, 1881. 21c, horiz.

1982 Litho. *Perf. 14½*
839 A317 21c multicolored .25 .20
840 A317 35c multicolored .50 .30
841 A317 75c multicolored 1.00 .90
Nos. 839-841 (3) 1.75 1.40

Issue dates: 35c, Sept. 15; others, Nov. 1.

12th Commonwealth Games, Brisbane, Sept. 30-Oct. 9 — A318

1982, Sept. 22 Litho. *Perf. 14x14½*
842 A318 27c Archery .45 .20
843 A318 27c Boxing .45 .20
844 A318 27c Weightlifting .45 .20
a. Souvenir sheet of 3, #842-844 1.50 1.40
845 A318 75c Pole vault .90 .90
Nos. 842-845 (4) 2.25 1.50

Natl. Stamp Week A319

1982, Sept. 27 *Perf. 13x13½*
846 A319 27c No. 132 .40 .20

A320

A321

Design: Gurgurr (Moon Spirit), Bark Painting by Yirawala Gunwinggu Tribe.

1982, Oct. 12 *Perf. 14½*
847 A320 27c multicolored .40 .20

Opening of Natl. Gallery, Canberra.

Perf. 12½x13½
1982, Nov. 17 Photo.

Designs: Various eucalypts (gum trees).

848 A321 1c Pink-flowered marri .20 .20
849 A321 2c Gungurru .20 .20
850 A321 3c Red-flowering gum 1.00 .55
851 A321 10c Tasmanian blue gum 1.00 .60
852 A321 27c Forrest's marlock .75 .50
a. Bklt. pane of 9 + label (#850-851, 2 #848-849, 3 #852) 5.00
b. Bklt. pane (2 each #848-849, 852) 2.10
Nos. 848-852 (5) 3.15 2.05

Nos. 848-852 issued in booklets only.

Mimi Spirits Singing and Dancing, by David Milaybuma A322

Aboriginal Bark Paintings: Music and dance of the Mimi Spirits, Gunwinggu Tribe.

1982, Nov. 17 Litho. *Perf. 13½x14*
853 A322 27c shown .40 .25
854 A322 40c Lofty Nabardayal .65 .65
855 A322 65c Jimmy Galareya 1.00 .75
856 A322 75c Dick Nguleingulei Murrumurru 1.10 1.00
Nos. 853-856 (4) 3.15 2.65

Historic Fire Engines A323

1983, Jan. 12 *Perf. 13½x14*
857 A323 27c Shand Mason Steam, 1891 .40 .25
858 A323 40c Hotchkiss, 1914 .65 .65
859 A323 65c Ahrens-Fox PS2, 1929 1.00 1.00
860 A323 75c Merryweather Manual, 1851 1.10 1.00
Nos. 857-860 (4) 3.15 2.90

Australia Day — A324

1983, Jan. 26 Litho. *Perf. 14½*
861 A324 27c Sirius .45 .25
862 A324 27c Supply .45 .25
a. Pair, #861-862 .90 .75

A325

A326

1983, Feb. 2 *Perf. 14x13½*
863 A325 27c multicolored .40 .20

Australia-New Zealand Closer Economic Relationship agreement (ANZCER).

1983, Mar. 9 Litho. *Perf. 14½*
864 A326 27c Equality, dignity .45 .20
865 A326 27c Social justice, co-operation .45 .20
866 A326 27c Liberty, freedom .45 .20
867 A326 75c Peace, harmony 1.25 1.25
Nos. 864-867 (4) 2.60 1.85

Commonwealth day.

Queen Elizabeth II, 57th Birthday A327

1983, Apr. 20 *Perf. 14½*
868 A327 27c Britannia .40 .20

World Communications Year — A328

1983, May 18 Litho. *Perf. 13½x14*
869 A328 27c multicolored .45 .20

50th Anniv. of Australian Jaycees Youth Organization A329

1983, June 8
870 A329 27c multicolored .40 .20

St. John Ambulance Cent. A330

Regent Skipper A331

1983, June 8 *Perf. 13½x14*
871 A330 27c multicolored .40 .20

1983 *Perf. 13½, 14½x14 (30c)*
872 A331 4c shown .20 .20
873 A331 10c Cairn's birdwing .20 .20
874 A331 20c Macleay's swallowtail .30 .20
875 A331 27c Ulysses .45 .20
875A A331 30c Chlorinda hair-streak .50 .20
876 A331 35c Blue tiger .55 .20
877 A331 45c Big greasy .60 .20
878 A331 60c Wood white .85 .30
879 A331 80c Amaryllis azure 1.00 .40
880 A331 $1 Sword grass brown 1.25 .20
Nos. 872-880 (10) 5.90 2.30

Issue dates: 30c, Oct. 24; others, June 15.

The Sentimental Bloke, by C.J. Dennis, 1909 — A332

Folktale scenes: a, The bloke. b, Doreen - the intro. c, The stror at coot. d, Hitched. e, The mooch of life.

1983, Aug. 3 *Perf. 14½*
881 Strip of 5 1.75 1.50
a.-e. A332 27c multi, any single .35 .30

Kookaburra Bird Wearing Santa Hat — A333

1983 Litho. *Perf. 13½x14*
882 A333 24c Nativity .35 .35
883 A333 35c multicolored .50 .35
884 A333 85c Holiday beach scene 1.25 .60
Nos. 882-884 (3) 2.10 1.30

Christmas. Issued: #883, 9/14; #882, 884, 11/2.

Inland Explorers — A334

Clay sculptures by Dianne Quinn: No. 885, Ludwig Leichhardt (1813-48). No. 886, William John Wills (1834-61), Robert O'Hara Burke (1821-61). No. 887, Paul Edmund de Strzelecki (1797-1873). No. 888, Alexander Forrest (1849-1901).

1983, Sept. 26 *Perf. 14½*
885 A334 30c multicolored .35 .20
886 A334 30c multicolored .35 .20
887 A334 30c multicolored .35 .20
888 A334 30c multicolored .35 .20
Nos. 885-888 (4) 1.40 .80

Australia Day — A335

1984, Jan. 26 Litho. *Perf. 13½x14*
889 A335 30c Cooks' Cottage .30 .20

50th Anniv. of Official Air Mail Service — A336

Pilot Charles Ulm (1898-1934); his plane, "Faith in Australia," and different flight covers.

1984, Feb. 22 Litho. *Perf. 13½*
890 A336 45c Australia-New Zealand .75 .60
891 A336 45c Australia-Papua New Guinea .75 .60
a. Pair, #890-891 1.50 1.50

Thomson, 1898 — A337

Australian-made vintage cars: b, Tarrant, 1906. c, Australian Six, 1919. d, Summit, 1923. e, Chic, 1924.

1984, Mar. 14 *Perf. 14½*
892 Strip of 5 1.75 1.50
a.-e. A337 30c any single .35 .25

Queen Elizabeth II, 58th Birthday A338

1984, Apr. 18 *Perf. 14½*
893 A338 30c multicolored .30 .20

Clipper Ships — A339

1984, May 23 *Perf. 14x13½, 13½x14*
894 A339 30c Cutty Sark, 1869, vert. .35 .30
895 A339 45c Orient, 1853 .55 .55
896 A339 75c Sobraon, 1866 .90 .90
897 A339 85c Thermopylae, 1868, vert. 1.10 1.10
Nos. 894-897 (4) 2.90 2.85

Freestyle Skiing — A340

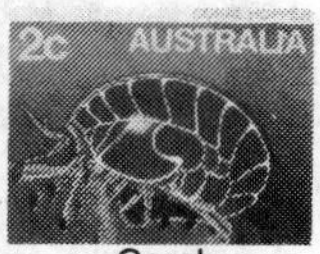

Coral Hopper — A341

1984, June 6 Litho. *Perf. 14½*

898 A340 30c shown .40 .20
899 A340 30c Slalom, horiz. .40 .20
900 A340 30c Cross-country, horiz. .40 .20
901 A340 30c Downhill .40 .20
Nos. 898-901 (4) 1.60 .80

Perf. 13½, 14x14½ (30c, 33c)

1984-86 Litho.

902 A341 2c shown .20 .20
903 A341 3c Jimble .20 .20
904 A341 5c Tasseled anglerfish .20 .20
905 A341 10c Stonefish .20 .20
906 A341 20c Red handfish .25 .20
907 A341 25c Orange-tipped cowrie .45 .25
908 A341 30c Choat's wrasse .55 .25
909 A341 33c Leafy sea dragon .45 .20
910 A341 40c Red velvet fish .55 .25
911 A341 45c Texile cone shell .65 .30
912 A341 50c Blue-lined surgeonfish .90 .50
913 A341 55c Bennett's nudibranch 1.00 .50
914 A341 60c Lionfish .85 .40
915 A341 65c Stingray .95 .40
916 A341 70c Blue-ringed octopus 1.00 .50
917 A341 80c Pineapple fish 1.15 .55
918 A341 85c Regal angelfish 1.50 .95
919 A341 90c Crab-eyed goby 1.20 .55
920 A341 $1 Crown of thorns starfish 1.50 .60
Nos. 902-920 (19) 13.75 7.20

Issued: 2c, 25c, 30c, 50c, 55c, 85c, June 18; 5c, 20c, 40c, 80c, 90c, June 12, 1985; 3c, 10c, 45c, 60c, 65c, 70c, $1, June 11, 1986.

1984 Summer Olympics A342

Event stages.

Perf. 13½x14, 14x13½

1984, July 25 Litho.

922 A342 30c Start (facing down) .45 .20
923 A342 30c Competing (facing right) .45 .20
924 A342 30c Finish, vert. .45 .20
Nos. 922-924 (3) 1.35 .60

Ausipex '84 A343

Christmas A344

Designs: No. 926a, Victoria #3. b, New South Wales #1. c, Tasmania #1. d, South Australia #1. e, Western Australia #1. f, Queensland #3.

1984 Litho. *Perf. 14½*

925 A343 30c No. 2 .45 .20

Souvenir Sheet

926 Sheet of 7 3.50 3.00
a.-f. A343 30c any single .50 .20

#926 contains #925, 926a-926f. Issue dates: #925, Aug. 22; #926, Sept. 21.

1984 Litho. *Perf. 14x13½*

927 A344 24c Angel and Child .30 .25
928 A344 30c Veiled Virgin and Child .35 .25
929 A344 40c Angel .50 .40
930 A344 50c Three Kings .65 .45
931 A344 85c Madonna and Child 1.10 1.00
Nos. 927-931 (5) 2.90 2.35

Stained-glass windows. Issue dates: 40c, Sept. 17; others, Oct. 30.

Australia stamps can be mounted in the Scott Australia album.

European Settlement Bicentenary A345

Settlement of Victoria Sesquicentenary A346

Design: No. 932, Bicentennial Emblem.

Rock paintings: No. 933, Stick figures, Cobar Region, New South Wales. No. 934, Bunjil's Cave, Grampians, Western Victoria. No. 935, Quinkan Gallery, Cape York, Queensland. No. 936, Wandjina Spirit and Snake Babies, Gibb River, Western Australia. No. 937, Rock Python, Western Australia. No. 938, Silver Barramundi, Kakadu Natl. Park, Northern Territory. 85c, Rock Possum, Kakadu Natl. Park.

1984, Nov. 7 Litho. *Perf. 14½*

932 A345 30c multicolored .40 .25
933 A345 30c multicolored .40 .25
934 A345 30c multicolored .40 .25
935 A345 30c multicolored .40 .25
936 A345 30c multicolored .40 .25
937 A345 30c multicolored .40 .25
938 A345 30c multicolored .40 .25
939 A345 85c multicolored 1.10 .60
Nos. 932-939 (8) 3.90 2.35

1984, Nov. 19

940 A346 30c Helmeted honeyeater .45 .20
941 A346 30c Leadbeater's possum .45 .20
a. Pair, #940-941 .90

Australia Day — A347

1985, Jan. 25 Litho.

942 A347 30c Musgrave Ranges, by Sidney Nolan .45 .20
943 A347 30c The Walls of China, by Russell Drysdale .45 .20
a. Pair, #942-943 .90

Intl. Youth Year — A348

1985, Feb. 13 Litho. *Perf. 14x13½*

944 A348 30c multicolored .40 .20

Royal Victorian Volunteer Artillery A349

District Nursing Service Centenary A350

Colonial military uniforms: b, Western Australian Pinjarrah Cavalry. c, New South Wales Lancers. d, New South Wales Contingent to the Sudan. e, Victorian Mounted Rifles.

1985, Feb. 25 *Perf. 14½*

945 Strip of 5 1.75 1.65
a.-e. A349 33c any single .35 .20

1985, Mar. 13

946 A350 33c multicolored .40 .20

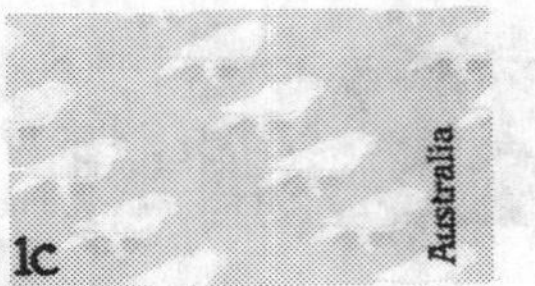

Australian Cockatoo — A351

Perf. 14 Horiz. on 1 or 2 sides

1985, Mar. 13

947 A351 1c apple grn, yel & buff .50 .50
948 A351 33c apple grn, yel, & lt grnsh blue .45 .20
a. Bklt. pane, 1 #947, 3 #948 2.75

Issued in booklets only.

A352

A353

1985, Apr. 10 *Perf. 13*

949 A352 33c Abel Tasman, explorer .55 .30
950 A352 33c The Eendracht .55 .30
951 A352 33c William Dampier .55 .30
952 A352 90c Globe and hand 1.50 .90
a. Souvenir sheet of 4, #949-952 3.50 2.00
Nos. 949-952 (4) 3.15 1.80

1985, Apr. 22 *Perf. 14x13½*

953 A353 33c Queen's Badge, Order of Australia .45 .20

Queen Elizabeth II, 59th birthday.

A354

A356

1985, May 15 Litho. *Perf. 14x13*

954 A354 33c Soil .45 .30
955 A354 50c Air .65 .50
956 A354 80c Water 1.00 .70
957 A354 90c Energy 1.10 .90
Nos. 954-957 (4) 3.20 2.40

Environmental conservation.

1985, July 17 Litho. *Perf. 14½*

Illustrations from classic children's books: a, Elves & Fairies, by Annie Rentoul. b, The Magic Pudding, text and illustrations by Norman Lindsay. c, Ginger Meggs, by James Charles Bancks. d, Blinky Bill, by Dorothy Wall. e, Snugglepot and Cuddlepie, by May Gibbs.

960 Strip of 5 1.75 1.25
a.-e. A356 33c any single .35 .20

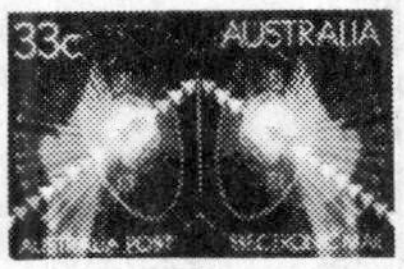

Electronic Mail — A357

1985, Sept. 18 Litho.

961 A357 33c multicolored .40 .20

Christmas A358

Angel in a ship, detail from a drawing by Albrecht Durer (1471-1528).

1985, Sept. 18 Litho.

962 A358 45c multicolored .45 .35

See Nos. 967-970.

Coastal Shipwrecks A359

Salvaged antiquities: 33c, Astrolabe from Batavia, 1629. 50c, German beardman (Bellarmine) jug from Vergulde Draeck, 1656. 90c, Wooden bobbins from Batavia, and scissors from Zeewijk, 1727. $1, Silver buckle from Zeewijk.

1985, Oct. 2 Litho. *Perf. 13*

963 A359 33c multicolored .40 .20
964 A359 50c multicolored .60 .60
965 A359 90c multicolored 1.10 1.00
966 A359 $1 multicolored 1.75 .80
Nos. 963-966 (4) 3.85 2.60

Christmas Type of 1985

Illustrations by Scott Hartshorne.

1985, Nov. 1 Litho. *Perf. 14*

967 A358 27c Angel with trumpet .30 .20
968 A358 33c Angel with bells .40 .25
969 A358 55c Angel with star .70 .65
970 A358 90c Angel with ornament 1.10 1.10
Nos. 967-970 (4) 2.50 2.20

Australia Day A360

AUSSAT A361

1986, Jan. 24 Litho. *Perf. 14½*

971 A360 33c Aboriginal painting .40 .20

1986, Jan. 24

Various communications satellites.

972 A361 33c multicolored .35 .20
973 A361 80c multicolored 1.15 .75

South Australia, Sesquicent. A362

1986, Feb. 12 *Perf. 13½x14*

974 A362 33c Sailing ship Buffalo .50 .20
975 A362 33c City Sign, sculpture by O.H. Hajek .50 .20
a. Pair, #974-975 1.00 .60

Cook's New Holland Expedition A363

1986, Mar. 12 *Perf. 13*

976 A363 33c Hibiscus merankensis .35 .25
977 A363 33c Banksia serrata .35 .25
978 A363 50c Dillenia alata .60 .60
979 A363 80c Corria reflexa .90 .70
980 A363 90c Parkinson 1.00 .90
981 A363 90c Banks 1.00 1.00
Nos. 976-981 (6) 4.20 3.70

Australian bicentennial. Sydney Parkinson (d. 1775), artist. Sir Joseph Banks (1743-1820), naturalist.

Halley's Comet A364

Elizabeth II, 60th Birthday A365

1986, Apr. 9 *Perf. 14x13½*
982 A364 33c Radio telescope, trajectory diagram .45 .20

1986, Apr. 21 *Perf. 14½*
983 A365 33c multicolored .45 .20

Horses A366

1986, May 21
984 A366 33c Brumbies .45 .25
985 A366 80c Stock horse mustering 1.10 .65
986 A366 90c Show-jumping 1.25 .95
987 A366 $1 Australian pony 1.40 .95
Nos. 984-987 (4) 4.20 2.80

Click Go the Shears, Folk Song — A366a

Lines from the song: b, Old shearer stands. c, Ringer looks around. d, Boss of the board. e, Tar-boy is there. f, Shearing is all over.

1986, July 21 Litho. *Perf. 14½*
987A Strip of 5 2.75 1.50
b.-f. A366a 33c, any single .55 .20

Amalgamated Shearers' Union, predecessor of the Australian Workers' Union, cent.

Australia Bicentennial A367

Settling of Botany Bay penal colony: No. 988, King George III, c. 1767, by A. Ramsay. No. 989, Lord Sydney, secretary of state, 1783-1789, by Gilbert Stuart. No. 990, Capt. Arthur Phillip, 1st penal colony governor, by F. Wheatley, 1786. $1, Capt. John Hunter, governor, 1795-1800, by W. B. Bennett, 1815.

1986, Aug. 6 Litho. *Perf. 13*
988 A367 33c multicolored .50 .30
989 A367 33c multicolored .50 .30
990 A367 33c multicolored .50 .30
991 A367 $1 multicolored 1.50 1.00
Nos. 988-991 (4) 3.00 1.90

Wildlife A368

Alpine Wildflowers A369

Designs: a, Red kangaroo. b, Emu. c, Koala. d, Kookaburra. e, Platypus.

1986, Aug. 13 *Perf. 14½x14*
992 Strip of 5 2.00 1.25
a.-e. A368 36c any single .40 .20

Rouletted 9½ Vert. on 1 or 2 sides
1986, Aug. 25
Booklet Stamps
993 A369 3c Royal bluebell .45 .45
994 A369 5c Alpine marsh marigold 1.00 1.00
995 A369 25c Mount Buffalo sunray 1.00 .75
996 A369 36c Silver snow daisy .90 .20
a. Bklt. pane, #993, #994, 2 #996 3.25
b. Bklt. pane, #993, #995, 2 #996 3.25
Nos. 993-996 (4) 3.35 2.40

Orchids A370

America's Cup Triumph '83 A371

1986, Sept. 18 *Perf. 14½*
997 A370 36c Elythranthera emarginata .50 .20
998 A370 55c Dendrobium nindii .80 .60
999 A370 90c Caleana major 1.40 1.00
1000 A370 $1 Thelymitra variegata 1.50 1.10
Nos. 997-1000 (4) 4.20 2.90

1986, Sept. 26 *Perf. 14x13½*
1001 A371 36c Australia II crossing finish line .60 .25
1002 A371 36c Trophy .60 .25
1003 A371 36c Boxing kangaroo .60 .25
Nos. 1001-1003 (3) 1.80 .75

Intl. Peace Year — A372

1986, Oct. 22 Litho. *Perf. 14x13½*
1004 A372 36c multicolored .50 .20

Christmas A373

Kindergarten nativity play: No. 1005, Holy Family, vert. No. 1006, Three Kings, vert. No. 1007, Angels. No. 1008a, Angels, peasants. No. 1008b, Holy Family, angels, vert. No. 1008c, Shepherd, angels, vert. No. 1008d, Three Kings. No. 1008e, Shepherds.

1986, Nov. 3 **Litho.**
1005 A373 30c multicolored .50 .20
a. Perf 14x13½ 1.00 .50
1006 A373 36c multicolored .60 .25
1007 A373 60c multicolored 1.00 .65
Nos. 1005-1007 (3) 2.10 1.10

Souvenir Sheet
1008 Sheet of 5 2.50 2.50
a.-e. A373 30c any single .50 .50

Perfs: Nos. 1005-1006, 1008c, 15x14½; Nos. 1007, 1008a 1008e, 14½x15. No. 1008b, 15x14½x15x15; 1008d, 14½x15x14½x14½.

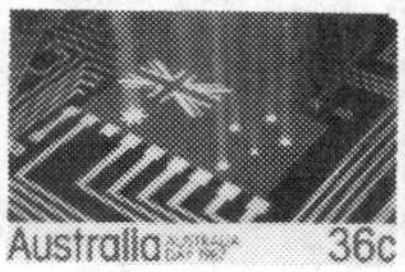

Australia Day — A374

1987, Jan. 23 Litho. *Perf. 13½x14*
1009 A374 36c Flag, circuit board .45 .20
1010 A374 36c Made in Australia campaign emblem .45 .20

America's Cup — A375

Fruits — A376

Views of yachts racing.

1987, Jan. 28 *Perf. 15x14½*
1011 A375 36c multicolored .40 .20
1012 A375 55c multicolored .60 .55
1013 A375 90c multicolored 1.10 .90
1014 A375 $1 multicolored 1.40 .95
Nos. 1011-1014 (4) 3.50 2.60

1987, Feb. 11 *Perf. 14x13½*
1015 A376 36c Melons, grapes .45 .30
1016 A376 65c Tropical fruit .80 .60
1017 A376 90c Pears, apples, oranges 1.10 .90
1018 A376 $1 Berries, peaches 1.25 .95
Nos. 1015-1018 (4) 3.60 2.75

Agricultural Shows — A377

1987, Apr. 10 Litho. *Perf. 14x13½*
1019 A377 36c Livestock .45 .20
1020 A377 65c Produce .80 .60
1021 A377 90c Carnival 1.10 .90
1022 A377 $1 Farmers 1.25 .95
Nos. 1019-1022 (4) 3.60 2.65

Queen Elizabeth II, 61st Birthday A378

1987, Apr. 21 *Perf. 13½x14*
1023 A378 36c multicolored .45 .20

First Fleet Leaving England A379

Continuous design: No. 1024a, Convicts awaiting transportation. b, Capt. Arthur Phillip, Mrs. Phillip, longboat on shore. c, Sailors relaxing and working. d, Longboats heading from and to fleet. 4e, Fleet in harbor.

No. 1025a, Longboat approaching Tenerife, The Canary Isls. b, Fishing in Tenerife Harbor. $1, Fleet, dolphins.

1987 *Perf. 13*
1024 Strip of 5 4.00 4.00
a.-e. A379 36c any single .80 .20
1025 Pair 1.00 1.00
a.-b. A379 36c any single .50 .20
1026 A379 $1 multicolored 1.50 1.50
Nos. 1024-1026 (3) 6.50 6.50

Australia bicent.; departure of the First Fleet, May 13, 1787; arrival at Tenerife, June 1787.

Issued: #1024, May 13; #1025-1026, June 3.

1987, Aug. 6

First Fleet arrives at Rio de Janeiro, Aug. 1787: a, Whale, storm in the Atlantic. b, Citrus grove. c, Market. d, Religious procession. e, Fireworks over harbor.

1027 Strip of 5 1.75 1.75
a.-e. A379 37c any single .35 .20

No. 1027 has a continuous design.

1987, Oct. 13

First Fleet arrives at Cape of Good Hope, Oct. 1787: No. 1028a, British officer surveys livestock and supplies, Table Mountain. No. 1028b, Ships anchored in Table Bay. No. 1029, Fishermen pull in nets as the Fleet approaches the Cape.

1028 Pair .90 .90
a.-b. A379 37c any single .45 .20
1029 A379 $1 multicolored 1.25 .50

No. 1028 has a continuous design.

1988, Jan. 26

Arrival of the First Fleet, Sydney Cove, Jan. 1788: a, Five aborigines on shore. b, Four aborigines on shore. c, Kangaroos. d, White cranes. e, Flag raising.

1030 Strip of 5 2.25 2.25
a.-e. A379 37c any single .45 .20

Printed se-tenant in a continuous design.

The Early Years: Sydney Cove and Parramatta Colonies A380

Details from panorama "View of Sydney from the East Side of the Cove," 1808, painted by convict artist John Eyre to illustrate The Present Picture of New South Wales, published in London in 1811, and paintings in British and Australian museums: a, Government House, 1790, Sydney, by midshipman George Raper. b, Government Farm, Parramatta, 1791, attributed to the Port Jackson Painter. c, Parramatta Road, 1796, attributed to convict artist Thomas Watling. d, The Rocks and Sydney Cove, 1800, an aquatint engraving by Edward Dayes. e, Sydney Hospital, 1803, by George William Evans, an explorer and surveyor-general of New South Wales. Printed se-tenant in a continuous design.

1988, Apr. 13 Litho. *Perf. 13*
1031 Strip of 5 2.50 2.50
a.-e. A380 37c any single .50 .20

Australia Bicentennial.

The Man from Snowy River, 1890, Ballad by A.B. Paterson — A381

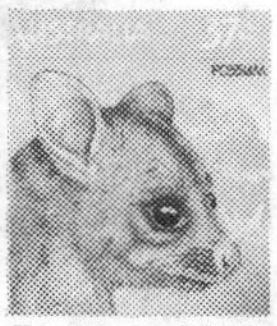
Fauna — A382

Excerpts: a, At the station. b, Mountain bred. c, Terrible descent. d, At their heels. e, Brought them back.

1987, June 24 *Perf. 14x13½*
1034 Strip of 5 2.25 2.25
a.-e. A381 36c any single .45 .30

Printed se-tenant in a continuous design.

1987, July 1 *Perf. 14½x14*

Designs: a, Possum. b, Cockatoo. c, Wombat. d, Rosella. e, Echidna.

1035 Strip of 5 1.75 1.75
a.-e. A382 37c any single .35 .20

Printed se-tenant in a continuous design.

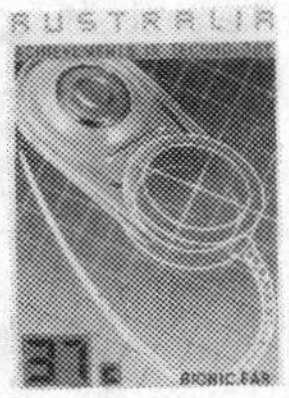
Technology — A383

1987, Aug. 19	***Perf. 14½***		
1036 A383 37c Bionic ear		.40	.20
1037 A383 53c Microchips		.55	.30
1038 A383 63c Robotics		.70	.35
1039 A383 68c Zirconia ceramics		.75	.35
Nos. 1036-1039 (4)		2.40	1.20

Children A384

1987, Sept. 16		
1040 A384 37c Crayfishing	.35	.20
1041 A384 55c Cat's cradle	.55	.30
1042 A384 90c Eating meat pies	.80	.45
1043 A384 $1 Playing with a joey	1.00	.50
Nos. 1040-1043 (4)	2.70	1.45

Christmas A385

Carolers: a, Woman, two girls. b, Man, two girls. c, Four children. d, Man, two women, boy. e, Six youths. 37c, three women, two men. Nos. 1044a-1044e are vert.

1987, Nov. 2 Litho. ***Perf. 14½***		
1044 Strip of 5	2.00	2.00
a.-e. A385 30c any single	.40	.20
Perf. 13½x14		
1045 A385 37c multicolored	.45	.20
1046 A385 63c shown	.80	.30
Nos. 1044-1046 (3)	3.25	2.50

Carols by Candlelight, Christmas Eve, Sidney Myer Bowl, Melbourne.

Aboriginal Crafts — A386

Designs: 3c, Spearthrower, Western Australia. 15c, Shield, New South Wales. No. 1049, Basket, Queensland. No. 1050, Bowl, Central Australia. No. 1051, Belt, Northern Territory.

Perf. 15½ Horiz.

1987, Oct. 13 **Photo.**		
1047 A386 3c multicolored	1.25	1.25
1048 A386 15c multicolored	1.90	1.25
1049 A386 37c multicolored	1.25	.35
a. Bklt. pane, 2 each #1047, #1049	4.50	
1050 A386 37c multicolored	1.25	.35
1051 A386 37c multicolored	1.25	.35
a. Bklt. pane, 1 #1048, 3 #1050, 2 #1051	9.00	
Nos. 1047-1051 (5)	6.75	3.55

Issued only in booklets.

Caricature of Australian Koala and American Bald Eagle — A387

1988, Jan. 26 ***Perf. 13***		
1052 A387 37c multicolored	.55	.20

Australia bicentennial. See No. 1086 and US No. 2370.

Living Together — A388

Cartoons.

1988 ***Perf. 14***		
1053 A388 1c Religion	.20	.20
1054 A388 2c Industry	.20	.20
1055 A388 3c Local government	.20	.20
1056 A388 4c Trade unions	.20	.20
1057 A388 5c Parliament	.20	.20
1058 A388 10c Transportation	.20	.20
1059 A388 15c Sports	.20	.15
1060 A388 20c Commerce	.30	.15
1061 A388 25c Housing	.35	.15
1062 A388 30c Welfare	.45	.20
1063 A388 37c Postal services	.55	.20
a. Booklet pane of 10	5.50	
1063B A388 39c Tourism	.55	.20
c. Booklet pane of 10	5.50	
1064 A388 40c Recreation	.60	.20
1065 A388 45c Health	.70	.25
1066 A388 50c Mining	.75	.30
1067 A388 53c Primary industry	.80	.30
1068 A388 55c Education	.85	.30
1069 A388 60c Armed Forces	.95	.35
1070 A388 63c Police	1.00	.35
1071 A388 65c Telecommunications	1.00	.35
1072 A388 68c The media	1.10	.40
1073 A388 70c Science and technology	1.10	.40
1074 A388 75c Visual arts	1.10	.45
1075 A388 80c Performing arts	1.25	.45
1076 A388 90c Banking	1.40	.50
1077 A388 95c Law	1.50	.55
1078 A388 $1 Rescue and emergency services	1.50	.55
Nos. 1053-1078 (27)	19.20	7.95

Issued: 1c, 2c, 3c, 5c, 30c, 40c, 55c, 60c, 63c, 65c, 68c, 75c, 95c, 3/16; 39c, 9/28; others, 2/17.

Queen Elizabeth II, 62nd Birthday A389

1988, Apr. 21 ***Perf. 14½***		
1079 A389 37c multicolored	.60	.20

EXPO '88, Brisbane, Apr. 30-Oct. 30 — A390

1988, Apr. 29 ***Perf. 13***		
1080 A390 37c multicolored	.60	.20

Opening of Parliament House, Canberra A391

1988, May 9 ***Perf. 14½***		
1081 A391 37c multicolored	.60	.20

Australia Bicentennial A392

Designs: No. 1082, Colonist, clipper ship. No. 1083, British and Australian parliaments, Queen Elizabeth II. No. 1084, Cricketer W.G. Grace. No. 1085, John Lennon (1940-1980), William Shakespeare (1564-1616) and Sydney Opera House. #1083a, 1085a have continuous design picturing flag of Australia.

1988, June 21 Litho. ***Perf. 13***		
1082 A392 37c multicolored	.80	.20
1083 A392 37c multicolored	.80	.20
a. Pair, #1082-1083	1.75	.75
1084 A392 $1 multicolored	2.25	.55
1085 A392 $1 multicolored	2.25	.55
a. Pair, #1084-1085	4.75	2.50
Nos. 1082-1085 (4)	6.10	1.50

See Great Britain Nos. 1222-1225.

Caricature Type of 1988

Design: Caricature of an Australian koala and New Zealand kiwi.

1988, June 21 Litho. ***Perf. 13½***		
1086 A387 37c multicolored	.60	.20

Australia bicentennial. See New Zealand No. 907.

"Dream" Lore on Art of the Desert A393

Aboriginal paintings from Papunya Settlement in the Flinders University Art Museum: 37c, Bush Potato Country, by Turkey Tolsen Tjupurrula with by David Corby Tjapaltjarri. 55c, Courtship Rejected, by Limpi Puntungka Tjapangati. 90c, Medicine Story, anonymous. $1, Ancestor Dreaming, by Tim Leura Tjapaltjarri.

1988, Aug. 1 Litho. ***Perf. 13***		
1087 A393 37c multicolored	.60	.20
1088 A393 55c multicolored	.90	.75
1089 A393 90c multicolored	1.50	.50
1090 A393 $1 multicolored	1.65	.55
Nos. 1087-1090 (4)	4.65	2.00

1988 Summer Olympics, Seoul — A394

1988, Sept. 14 ***Perf. 14½***		
1091 A394 37c Basketball	.60	.20
1092 A394 65c Running	1.10	.90
1093 A394 $1 Rhythmic gymnastics	1.65	.55
Nos. 1091-1093 (3)	3.35	1.65

34th Commonwealth Parliamentary Conference, Canberra A395

1988, Sept. 19		
1094 A395 37c Scepter and mace	.60	.20

Works in the Contemporary Decorative Arts Collection at the Natl. Gallery — A396

Roulette 9 Horiz.

1988, Sept. 28 **Litho.**		
1095 A396 2c "Australian Fetish," by Peter Tully	2.50	2.50
1096 A396 5c Vase by Colin Levy	2.50	2.50
1097 A396 39c Teapot by Frank Bauer	.75	.35
a. Bklt. pane of 3 (2c, 2 39c)	4.50	
b. Bklt. pane of 6 (5c, 5 39c)	6.25	
Nos. 1095-1097 (3)	5.75	5.35

Nos. 1095-1097 issued in booklets only.

Views — A397

1988, Oct. 17 Photo. ***Perf. 13***		
1098 A397 39c The Desert	.65	.25
1099 A397 55c The Top End	.90	.30
1100 A397 65c The Coast	1.10	.40
1101 A397 70c The Bush	1.10	.40
Nos. 1098-1101 (4)	3.75	1.35

Christmas A398

Children's design contest winning drawings: 32c, Nativity scene, by Danielle Hush, age 7. 39c, Koala wearing a Santa hat, by Kylie Courtney, age 6. 63c, Cockatoo wearing a Santa hat, by Benjamin Stevenson, age 10.

1988, Oct. 31 ***Perf. 13½x13***		
1102 A398 32c multicolored	.55	.20
1103 A398 39c multicolored	.65	.20
1104 A398 63c multicolored	1.10	.55
Nos. 1102-1104 (3)	2.30	.95

Sir Henry Parkes (1815-1896), Advocate of the Federation of the Six Colonies — A399

1989, Jan. 25 Litho. ***Perf. 14x13½***		
1105 A399 39c multicolored	.70	.20

Australia Day.

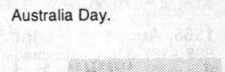

Sports — A400

1989, Feb. 13 ***Perf. 14x14½***		
1106 A400 1c Bowls	.20	.20
a. Perf. 13½x14 ('90)	.20	.20
1107 A400 2c Bowling	.20	.20
a. Perf. 13x13½ ('91)	.20	.20
1108 A400 3c Football	.20	.20
1109 A400 39c Fishing	.70	.20
a. Booklet pane of 10	7.00	
d. Perf. 13x13½ on 3 sides ('90)	.70	.20
e. Booklet pane of 10, #1109d	7.00	
1109B A400 41c Cycling	.60	.20
c. Booklet pane of 10	6.25	
1110 A400 55c Kite-flying	.95	.30
1111 A400 70c Cricket	1.25	.40
1112 A400 $1.10 Golf	1.95	.65

1990-94

1114 A400 5c Kayaking, canoeing .20 .20
  a. Perf. 13x13½ .20 .20
1115 A400 10c Windsurfing .20 .20
  a. Perf. 13x13½ .30 .20
1116 A400 20c Tennis .30 .20
  a. Perf. 13x13½ .30 .30
1117 A400 65c Rock climbing 1.00 .35
  a. Perf. 13x13½ 1.00 1.00
1118 A400 $1 Running 1.50 .55
  a. Perf. 13x13½ 3.75 2.00

Issued: #1114a, 1115a, 1116a, 1117a, 1118, 1/17/90; #1118a, 1/91; #1115, 1117, 2/92; #1116, 7/93; #1114, 3/94.

1990, Aug. 27

1119 A400 43c Skateboarding .65 .20
  a. Booklet pane of 10 6.75

Perf. 13½

1120 A400 $1.20 Hang-gliding 1.90 .50

1991, Aug. 22 ***Perf. 14x14½***

1121 A400 75c Netball 1.10 .40
1122 A400 80c Squash 1.25 .40
1123 A400 85c Diving 1.25 .40
1124 A400 90c Soccer 1.40 .45
  Nos. 1106-1124 (19) 16.80 6.20

For self-adhesive stamps see #1185-1186.

Botanical Gardens — A401

Designs: $2, Nooroo, New South Wales. $5, Mawarra, Victoria. $10, Palm House, Adelaide Botanical Garden. $20, A View of the Artist's House and Garden in Mills Plains, Van Diemen's Land by John Glover.

1989-90 Litho. & Engr. ***Perf. 14***

1132 A401 $2 multicolored 2.00 1.00
  a. Perf. 14x13½ ('91) 2.00 1.00
1133 A401 $5 multicolored 5.00 2.00
  a. Perf. 14x13½ 6.75 2.00
1134 A401 $10 multicolored 10.50 3.00

Perf. 14½x14

1135 A401 $20 multicolored 19.00 8.00
  Nos. 1132-1135 (4) 36.50 14.00

Issued: $10, 4/12; $2, $5, 9/13; $20, 8/15/90.

Sheep — A402

1989, Feb. 27 ***Perf. 13½x14***

1136 A402 39c Merino .55 .20
1137 A402 39c Poll Dorset .55 .20
1138 A402 85c Polwarth 1.25 .50
1139 A402 $1 Corriedale 1.40 .75
  Nos. 1136-1139 (4) 3.75 1.65

World Sheep and Wool Congress, Tasmania, Feb. 27-Mar. 6.

Queen Elizabeth II, 63rd Birthday — A403

1989, Apr. 21 Litho. ***Perf. 14½***

1140 A403 39c Statue by John Dowie .65 .20

Colonial Australia A404

Pastoral Era: a, Immigrant ship in port, c. 1835. b, Pioneer's hut, wool bales in dray. c, Squatter's homestead. d, Shepherds. e, Explorers.

1989, May 10

1141 Strip of 5 2.50 1.10
  a.-e. A404 39c any single .50 .20

Stars of Stage and Screen — A405

Performers and directors: 39c, Gladys Moncrieff and Roy Rene, the stage, 1920's. 85c, Charles Chauvel and Chips Rafferty, talking films. $1, Nellie Stewart and James Cassius Williamson, the stage, 1890's. $1.10, Lottie Lyell and Raymond Longford, silent films.

1989, July 12 Litho. ***Perf. 14½***

1142 A405 39c multicolored .50 .20
  a. Perf. 14x13½ ('90) 5.00 5.00
1143 A405 85c multicolored 1.00 1.00
1144 A405 $1 multicolored 1.25 .50
1145 A405 $1.10 multicolored 1.40 .55
  Nos. 1142-1145 (4) 4.15 2.25

Impressionist Paintings A406

Paintings by Australian artists: No. 1146, *Impression for Golden Summer,* by Sir Arthur Streeton. No. 1147, *All on a Summer's Day,* by Charles Conder, vert. No. 1148, *Petit Dejeuner,* by Frederick McCubbin. No. 1149, *Impression,* by Tom Roberts.

Perf. 13½x14, 14x13½

1989, Aug. 23 Litho.

1146 A406 41c shown .60 .20
1147 A406 41c multicolored .60 .20
1148 A406 41c multicolored .60 .20
1149 A406 41c multicolored .60 .20
  Nos. 1146-1149 (4) 2.40 .80

The Urban Environment — A407

1989, Sept. 1 Litho. ***Perf. 15½***

Booklet Stamps

1150 A407 41c Freeways .70 .70
1151 A407 41c Architecture .70 .70
1152 A407 41c Commuter train .70 .70
  a. Bklt. pane of 7, 2 each #1150, 1152 and 3 #1151 5.00
  Nos. 1150-1152 (3) 2.10 2.10

No. 1152a sold for $3.

Australian Youth Hostels, 50th Anniv. A408

1989, Sept. 13 ***Perf. 14½***

1153 A408 41c multicolored .65 .20

Street Cars — A409

Designs: No. 1154, Horse-drawn tram, Adelaide, 1878. No. 1155, Steam tram, Sydney, 1884. No. 1156, Cable car, Melbourne, 1886. No. 1157, Double-deck electric tram, Hobart, 1893. No. 1158, Combination electric tram, Brisbane, 1901.

1989, Oct. 11 Litho. ***Perf. 13½x14***

1154 A409 41c multicolored .65 .20
1155 A409 41c multicolored .65 .20
1156 A409 41c multicolored .65 .20
  a. Perf. 14½ on 3 sides 1.30 1.30
  b. Booklet pane of 10, #1156a 13.00
1157 A409 41c multicolored .65 .20
1158 A409 41c multicolored .65 .20
  Nos. 1154-1158 (5) 3.25 1.00

Purchase of booklet containing No. 1156b included STAMPSHOW '89 admission ticket and a Melbourne one-day transit pass. Sold for $8.

Christmas A410

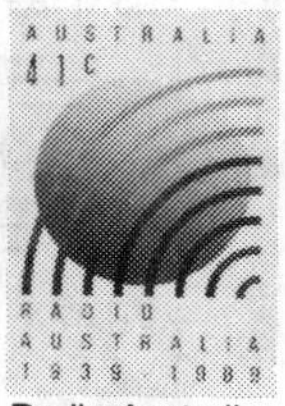

Radio Australia, 50th Anniv. A411

Illuminations: 36c, Annunciation, from the Nicholai Joseph Foucault Book of Hours, c. 1510-20. 41c, Annunciation to the Shepherds, from the Wharncliffe Hours, c. 1475. 80c, Adoration of the Magi, from Parisian Book of Hours, c. 1490-1500.

1989, Nov. 1 ***Perf. 14x13½***

1159 A410 36c multicolored .45 .20
  a. Booklet pane of 10 4.50

Perf. 15x14½

1160 A410 41c multicolored .55 .20
1161 A410 80c multicolored 1.00 .55
  Nos. 1159-1161 (3) 2.00 .95

1989, Nov. 1 ***Perf. 14x13½***

1162 A411 41c multicolored .65 .20

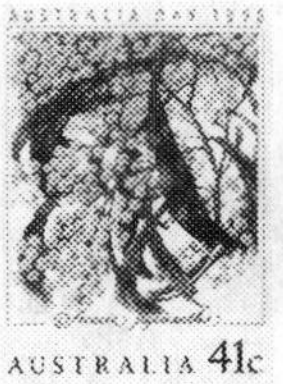

Australia Day A412

Special Occasions A413

1990, Jan. 17 Litho. ***Perf. 15x14½***

1163 A412 41c Golden wattle .65 .20

1990, Feb. 7 ***Perf. 14x13½***

1164 A413 41c Thinking of You .65 .20
  a. Booklet pane of 10 6.50
  b. Perf. 14½ on 3 sides .65 .20
  c. Booklet pane of 10, #1164b 6.50

See No. 1193.

Women Practicing Medicine in Australia, Cent. A414

1990, Feb. 7 ***Perf. 14½x15***

1165 A414 41c Constance Stone .65 .20

Dr. Constance Stone, Australia's first woman doctor.

A415

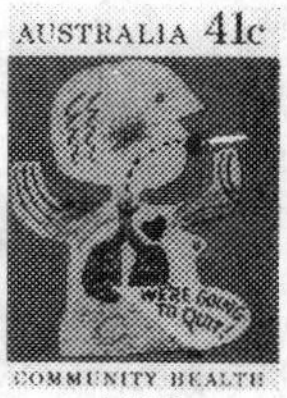

A416

Fauna of the High Country.

1990, Feb. 21 ***Perf. 14x13½***

1166 A415 41c Greater glider .55 .20
1167 A415 65c Spotted-tailed quoll .80 .55
1168 A415 70c Mountain pygmy-possum .90 .60
1169 A415 80c Brush-tailed rock-wallaby 1.00 .70
  Nos. 1166-1169 (4) 3.25 2.05

1990, Mar. 14

1170 A416 41c Quit smoking .55 .20
1171 A416 41c Don't drink and drive .55 .20
1172 A416 41c Eat right .55 .20
1173 A416 41c Medical check-ups .55 .20
  Nos. 1170-1173 (4) 2.20 .80

Community health.

A417

A418

Scenes from WW II, 1940-41: #1174, Anzacs at the front. #1175, Women working in factories, aircraft at the ready. 65c, Veterans and memorial parade. $1, Helicopters picking up wounded, cemetery. $1.10, Anzacs reading mail from home, 5 women watching departure of 2 ships.

1990, Apr. 12 Litho. ***Perf. 14½***

1174 A417 41c shown .55 .20
1175 A417 41c multicolored .55 .20
1176 A417 65c multicolored .80 .55
1177 A417 $1 multicolored 1.25 .65
1178 A417 $1.10 multicolored 1.40 .70
  Nos. 1174-1178 (5) 4.55 2.30

Australia and New Zealand Army Corps (ANZAC).

1990, Apr. 19 ***Perf. 14½***

1179 A418 41c multicolored .60 .20

Penny Black, 150th Anniv. A419

Stamps on stamps: a, New South Wales #44. b, South Australia #4. c, Tasmania #2. d, Victoria #120. e, Queensland #111A. f, Western Australia #3a.

1990, May 1 ***Perf. 13½x14***

1180 Block of 6 3.75 1.25
  a.-f. A419 41c any single .60 .20
  g. Souvenir sheet of 6 3.75 3.75

The Gold Rush — A420

a, Off to the diggings. b, The diggings. c, Panning for gold. d, Commissioner's tent. e, Gold escort.

1990, May 16 *Perf. 13*

1181 Strip of 5 2.50 2.50
a.-e. A420 41c any single .50 .20

Cooperation in Antarctic Research A421

1990, June 13 Litho. *Perf. 14½x14*

1182 A421 41c Glaciology .60 .20
1183 A421 $1.10 Krill (marine biology) 1.65 .55
a. Min. sheet of 2, #1182-1183 2.25 2.25

See Russia Nos. 5902-5903. For overprint see No. 1198.

Colonial Australia A422

Boom Time: a, Land boom. b, Building boom. c, Investment boom. d, Retail boom. e, Factory boom.

1990, July 12 Litho. *Perf. 13*

1184 Strip of 5 2.50 2.50
a.-e. A422 41c any single .50 .25

Sports Type of 1989

1990-91 Typo. *Die Cut Perf. 11½*

Self-Adhesive

1185 A400 41c Cycling .75 .65
1186 A400 43c Skateboarding .70 .20
a. Litho. .70 .20

Blue background has large dots on No. 1186 and smaller dots on No. 1186a. No. 1186 is on waxed paper backing printed with 0 to 4 koalas. No. 1186a is on plain paper backing printed with one kangaroo.

Issued: 41c, 5/16; #1186, 8/27; #1186a, 1991.

This is an expanding set. Numbers will change if necessary.

Salmon Gums by Robert Juniper — A423

Design: 43c, The Blue Dress by Brian Dunlop.

Perf. 15½ Vert.

1990, Sept. 3 Litho.

Booklet Stamps

1191 A423 28c multicolored .45 .30
a. Perf. 14½ vert. .45 .30
1192 A423 43c multicolored .65 .50
a. Bklt. pane, #1191, 4 #1192 3.25
b. Perf. 14½ vert. .65 .50
c. Booklet pane, #1191a, 4 #1192b 3.25

Thinking Of You Type

1990, Sept. 3 *Perf. 14½*

1193 A413 43c multicolored .50 .20
a. Booklet pane of 10 5.00

Christmas A424

1990, Oct. 31 *Perf. 14½*

1194 A424 38c Kookaburras .60 .20
a. Booklet pane of 10 6.25
1195 A424 43c Nativity, vert. .70 .20
1196 A424 80c Opossum 1.40 .60
Nos. 1194-1196 (3) 2.70 1.00

Local Government in Australia, 150th Anniv. — A425

1990, Oct. 31

1197 A425 43c Town Hall, Adelaide .70 .20

No. 1183a Ovptd. in Gold

NZ 1990

WORLD STAMP EXHIBITION
24 AUG - 2 SEPT 1990

1990 Litho. *Perf. 14½x14*

1198 A421 Miniature sheet of 2 3.75 3.75

Overprint applied to sheet margin only.

Flags — A426

1991, Jan. 10 Litho. *Perf. 14½*

1199 A426 43c National flag .55 .20
1200 A426 90c White ensign 1.10 .55
1201 A426 $1 Air Force ensign 1.25 .65
1202 A426 $1.20 Red ensign 1.40 .75
Nos. 1199-1202 (4) 4.30 2.15

Australia Day.

Water Birds A427

1991, Feb. 14

1203 A427 43c Black swan .55 .20
1204 A427 43c Black-necked stork, vert. .55 .20
1205 A427 85c Cape Barren goose, vert. 1.00 1.00
1206 A427 $1 Chestnut teal 1.10 .55
Nos. 1203-1206 (4) 3.20 1.95

Women's Wartime Services, 50th Anniv. A428

50th Anniversaries: No. 1208, Siege of Tobruk. $1.20, Australian War Memorial, Canberra.

1991, Mar. 14 Litho. *Perf. 14½*

1207 A428 43c shown .55 .20
1208 A428 43c multicolored .55 .20
1209 A428 $1.20 multicolored 1.40 .70
Nos. 1207-1209 (3) 2.50 1.10

Queen Elizabeth II's 65th Birthday — A429

1991, Apr. 11 Litho. *Perf. 14½*

1210 A429 43c multicolored .55 .20

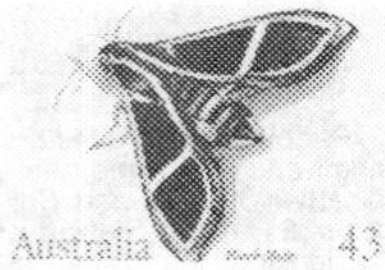

Insects A430

1991, Apr. 11

1211 A430 43c Hawk moth .55 .20
1212 A430 43c Cotton harlequin bug .55 .20
1213 A430 80c Leichhardt's grasshopper 1.00 .60
1214 A430 $1 Jewel beetle 1.10 .70
Nos. 1211-1214 (4) 3.20 1.70

Australian Photography, 150th Anniv. — A431

Designs: No. 1215a, Bondi, by Max Dupain, 1939. No. 1215b, Gears for the Mining Industry, Vickers Ruwolt Melbourne, by Wolfgang Sievers, 1967. 70c, Wheel of Youth, by Harold Cazneaux, 1929. $1.20, Teacup Ballet, by Olive Cotton, 1935.

1991, May 13 Litho. *Perf. 14½*

1215 Pair 1.10 .40
a.-b. A431 43c any single .55 .20
1216 A431 70c blk, olive & claret .90 .50
1217 A431 $1.20 blk, gray & Prus bl 1.40 .75
Nos. 1215-1217 (3) 3.40 1.65

Golden Days of Radio — A432

Pets — A433

1991, June 13 Litho. *Perf. 14½*

1218 A432 43c Music & variety shows .65 .20
1219 A432 43c Soap operas .65 .20
1220 A432 85c Quiz shows 1.25 1.25
1221 A432 $1 Children's stories 1.50 .65
Nos. 1218-1221 (4) 4.05 2.30

1991, July 25 Litho. *Perf. 14½*

1222 A433 43c Puppy .65 .20
1223 A433 43c Kitten .65 .20
1224 A433 70c Pony 1.10 .40
1225 A433 $1 Cockatoo 1.50 .60
Nos. 1222-1225 (4) 3.90 1.40

George Vancouver (1757-1798) and Edward John Eyre (1815-1901), Explorers — A434

1991, Sept. 26 Litho. *Perf. 14½*

1226 A434 $1.05 multicolored 1.60 .55
a. Souvenir sheet of 1 1.60 1.60
b. As "a," overprinted in gold 2.75 2.75

Vancouver's visit to Western Australia, 200th anniv. and Eyre's journey to Albany, Western Australia, 150th anniv.

No. 1226b overprinted in sheet margin with show emblem and: "PHILANIPPON / WORLD STAMP / EXHIBITION / TOKYO / 16-24 NOV 1991" followed by Japanese inscription.

Issue date: #1226b, Nov. 16.

Australian Literature of the 1890's A435

Designs: 43c, Seven Little Australians by Ethel Turner. 75c, On Our Selection by Steele Rudd. $1, Clancy of the Overflow by A.B. "Banjo" Paterson, vert. $1.20, The Drover's Wife by Henry Lawson, vert.

1991, Oct. 10

1227 A435 43c multicolored .65 .20
1228 A435 75c multicolored 1.10 .50
1229 A435 $1 multicolored 1.60 .65
1230 A435 $1.20 multicolored 1.90 .80
Nos. 1227-1230 (4) 5.25 2.15

Christmas A436

1991, Nov. 1

1231 A436 38c Shepherd .50 .20
a. Booklet pane of 20 10.00
1232 A436 43c Baby Jesus .55 .20
1233 A436 90c Wise man, camel 1.10 .45
Nos. 1231-1233 (3) 2.15 .85

Thinking of You — A437

1992, Jan. 2 Litho. *Perf. 14½x15*

1234 A437 45c Wildflowers .50 .25
a. Booklet pane of 10 5.00

Threatened Species — A438

Designs: No. 1235a, Parma wallaby. b, Ghost bat. c, Long-tailed dunnart. d, Little pygmy possum. e, Dusky hopping mouse. f, Squirrel glider.

1992, Jan. 2 Litho. *Perf. 14x14½*

1235 Block of 6 4.00 3.50
a.-f. A438 45c any single .65 .25

Die Cut

Perf. 11½

Self-Adhesive

Size: 31x22mm

1241 A438 45c like #1235a .65 .25
a. Typo. .65 .25
1242 A438 45c like #1235b .65 .25
a. Typo. .65 .25
1243 A438 45c like #1235c .65 .25
a. Typo. .65 .25
1244 A438 45c like #1235d .65 .25
a. Typo. .65 .25
1245 A438 45c like #1235e .65 .25
a. Typo. .65 .25
1246 A438 45c like #1235f .65 .25
a. Typo. .65 .25
b. Bklt. pane, 2 each #1241-1244, 1 each #1245-1246 6.25
c. Pane of 5, #1242-1246 3.25
d. Strip of 6, #1241-1246 4.00
e. Strip of 6, #1241a-1246a 4.00
f. #1246c overprinted 4.00
g. As "f," no die cutting 190.00

Litho. stamps are sharper in appearance than typo. stamps, most notably on the black lettering. Nos. 1246b and 1246c have tagging bars which make the right portion of the stamps appear toned.

No. 1246f - overprinted in Gold on sheet margin of No. 1246c with emblem of "WORLD COLUMBIAN / STAMP EXPO '92 / MAY 22-31, 1992 - CHICAGO." Issued in May.

See Nos. 1271-1293, 1406-1417.

Wetlands — A439

Perf. 14½ Horiz.

1992, Jan. 2 **Photo.**

Booklet Stamps

1247 A439 20c Noosa River, Queensland .55 .45
a. Perf. 14 horiz. .55
1248 A439 45c Lake Eildon, Victoria .55 .45
a. Bklt. pane, 1 #1247, 4 #1248 2.75
Complete booklet, #1248a 2.75
b. Perf. 14 horiz. .55
c. Bklt. pane, 1 #1247a, 4 #1248b 2.75
Complete booklet, #1248c 2.75

Sailing Ships A440

Perf. 14½x15, 15x14½

1992, Jan. 15 **Litho.**

1249 A440 45c Young Endeavour .70 .20
1250 A440 45c Britannia, vert. .70 .20
1251 A440 $1.05 Akarana, vert. 1.60 .60
1252 A440 $1.20 John Louis 1.75 .70
a. Sheet of 4, #1249-1252 4.75 4.75
b. As "a," overprinted 5.50 5.50
c. As "a," overprinted 7.50 7.50
Nos. 1249-1252 (4) 4.75 1.70

Australia Day. Discovery of America, 500th anniv. (No. 1252a).

Overprint in gold on sheet margin of No. 1252b contains emblem and "WORLD COLUMBIAN / STAMP EXPO '92 / MAY 22-31, 1992-CHICAGO." No. 1252b issued in May.

Overprint in gold on sheet margin of No. 1252c contains emblem and "GENOVA '92 / 18-27 SEPTEMBER." No. 1252c issued in Sept.

Australian Battles, 1942 — A441

1992, Feb. 19 **Litho.** ***Perf. 14½***

1253 A441 45c Bombing of Darwin .55 .20
1254 A441 75c Milne Bay .80 .60
1255 A441 75c Kokoda Trail .80 .60
1256 A441 $1.05 Coral Sea 1.25 .80
1257 A441 $1.20 El Alamein 1.40 .95
Nos. 1253-1257 (5) 4.80 3.15

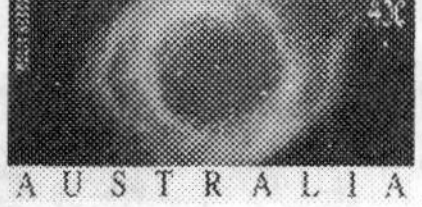

Intl. Space Year A442

1992, Mar. 19

1258 A442 45c Helix Nebula .65 .20
1259 A442 $1.05 The Pleiades 1.50 .65
1260 A442 $1.20 Spiral Galaxy NGC 2997 1.60 .70
a. Sheet of 3, #1258-1260 3.75 3.75
b. As "a," overprinted 5.00 5.00
Nos. 1258-1260 (3) 3.75 1.55

Overprint on sheet margin of No. 1260b contains emblem of "WORLD COLUMBIAN / STAMP EXPO '92 / MAY 22-31, 1992-CHICAGO." No. 1260b issued in May.

Queen Elizabeth II, 66th Birthday A443

1992, Apr. 9 ***Perf. 14x14½***

1261 A443 45c Wmk. 228 & #258 .65 .20

Vineyard Regions A444

Designs: No. 1262, Hunter Valley New South Wales. No. 1263, North Eastern Victoria. No. 1264, Barossa Valley South Australia. No. 1265, Coonawarra South Australia. No. 1266, Margaret River Western Australia.

1992, Apr. 9

1262 A444 45c multicolored .65 .20
1263 A444 45c multicolored .65 .20
1264 A444 45c multicolored .65 .20
1265 A444 45c multicolored .65 .20
1266 A444 45c multicolored .65 .20
Nos. 1262-1266 (5) 3.25 1.00

Land Care — A445

Designs: a, Salt action. b, Farm planning. c, Erosion control. d, Tree planting. e, Dune care.

1992, June 11 **Litho.** ***Perf. 14½x14***

1267 Strip of 5 2.75 2.25
a.-e. A445 45c Any single .55 .20

1992 Summer Olympics and Paralympics, Barcelona A446

1992, July 2 ***Perf. 14½***

1268 A446 45c Cycling .50 .20
1269 A446 $1.20 Weight lifting 1.40 .60
1270 A446 $1.20 High jump 1.40 .60
Nos. 1268-1270 (3) 3.30 1.40

Threatened Species Type of 1992

1992-98 **Litho.** ***Perf. 14x14½***

1271 A438 30c Saltwater crocodile .40 .20
1272 A438 35c Echidna .50 .20
1273 A438 40c Platypus .55 .20
1274 A438 45c Kangaroo .65 .20
1275 A438 45c Adult kangaroo with joey .65 .20
1276 A438 45c Two adult kangaroos .65 .20
a. Sheet of 3, #1274-1276 2.10 1.00
1277 A438 45c Four koalas .65 .20
1278 A438 45c Koala walking .65 .20
1279 A438 45c Koala in tree .65 .20
a. Block of 6, #1274-1279 4.00 1.40
b. Souvenir sheet of 6, #1274-1279 4.00 4.00
1280 A438 50c Koala .70 .25
1281 A438 60c Common brushtail possum .85 .30
1282 A438 70c Kookaburra .95 .35
a. "Australia 70c" in brown ('96) .95 .35
1283 A438 85c Pelican 1.25 .40
1284 A438 90c Eastern gray kangeroo 1.25 .40
1285 A438 95c Common wombat 1.40 .45
1286 A438 $1.20 Pink cockatoo 1.65 .55
a. "Australia $1.20" in brown ('98) 1.65 .55
1287 A438 $1.35 Emu 2.00 .65
Nos. 1271-1287 (17) 15.40 5.15

PHILAKOREA '94 (#1279b).

On No. 1279a Australia and denomination are orange, "KANGAROO" is 9mm lond, and date is 1½mm long. Date is 1mm long and "KANGAROO" 8mm long on Nos. 1279d and 1279f.

"Australia" and denominations on Nos. 1282, 1286 are in orange.

No. 1276a inscribed in sheet margin with "CHINA '96 - 9th Asian International Exhibition" in Chinese and English and exhibition emblems.

No. 1282a comes from 3 Koala or 1 Kangaroo and 1 Koala printing. No. 1286a comes from 1 Kangaroo printing.

Issued: 35c, 50c, 60c, 95c, 8/13; 40c, 70c, 90c, $1.20, 8/12/93; 30c, 85c, $1.35, 3/10/94; 45c, 5/12/94; #1279b, 8/94; #1282a, 3/96; #1276a, 5/18/96; #1286a, 12/98.

1996 **Litho.** ***Perf. 14x14½***

1274a A438 45c brown panel .60 .20
b. Bright orange panel .60 .20
1275a A438 45c brown panel .60 .20
b. Bright orange panel .60 .20
1276b A438 45c brown panel .60 .20
c. Bright orange panel .60 .20
1277a A438 45c brown panel .60 .20
b. Bright orange panel .60 .20
1278a A438 45c brown panel .60 .20
b. Bright orange panel .60 .20
1279c A438 45c brown panel .60 .20
d. Block of 6, #1274a-1275a, 1276b, 1277a-1278a, 1279c 4.00 1.40
e. Bright orange panel .60 .20
f. Block of 6, #1274b-1275b, 1276c, 1277b-1278b, 1279e 4.00 1.40

On No. 1279a Australia and denomination are orange, "KANGAROO" is 9mm lond, and date is 1½mm long. Date is 1mm long and "KANGAROO" 8mm long on Nos. 1279d and 1279f. No. 1279d comes from 2 Koala printing. No. 1279f comes from 3 Koala printing.

Die Cut Perf. 11

1994, May 12 **Litho.**

Self-Adhesive

1288 A438 45c like #1274 .65 .20
1289 A438 45c like #1275 .65 .20
1290 A438 45c like #1276 .65 .20
1291 A438 45c like #1277 .65 .20
1292 A438 45c like #1278 .65 .20
1293 A438 45c like #1279 .65 .20
a. Bklt. pane, #1290, 1293, 2 each #1288-1289, 1291-1292 6.50
b. Strip of 6, #1288-1293 4.00

Opening of Sydney Harbor Tunnel, August 29 — A447

Sydney Harbor Bridge and Tunnel: a, Left side. b, Right side.

1992, Aug. 28 **Litho.** ***Perf. 14½***

1296 A447 45c Pair, #a.-b. 1.25 .45
c. Pair, #d.-e., perf 15½ 1.25 .45

Buildings in Western Australia Goldfield Towns A448

#1297, Warden's Courthouse, Coolgardie. #1298, Post Office, Kalgoorlie. $1.05, York Hotel, Kalgoorlie. $1.20, Town Hall, Kalgoorlie.

1992, Sept. 17 **Litho.** ***Perf. 14x14½***

1297 A448 45c multicolored .50 .20
1298 A448 45c multicolored .50 .20
1299 A448 $1.05 multicolored 1.10 .50
1300 A448 $1.20 multicolored 1.25 .60
Nos. 1297-1300 (4) 3.35 1.50

Sheffield Shield Cricket Competition, Cent. — A449

Cricket match, 1890s: 45c, Bowler. $1.20, Batsman, wicket keeper.

1992, Oct. 15 **Litho.** ***Perf. 14½***

1301 A449 45c multicolored .60 .20
1302 A449 $1.20 multicolored 1.60 .55

Christmas A450

Designs: 40c, Children dressed as Mary and Joseph with baby carriage. 45c, Boy jumping from bed Christmas morning. $1, Boy and girl singing Christmas carol.

1992, Oct. 30 **Litho.** ***Perf. 14x14½***

1303 A450 40c multicolored .45 .45
a. Booklet pane of 20 9.00
1304 A450 45c multicolored .60 .20
1305 A450 $1 multicolored 1.25 .45
Nos. 1303-1305 (3) 2.30 1.10

Watercolor Paintings by Albert Namatjira A451

Designs: No. 1306a, Ghost Gum, Central Australia. b, Across the Plain to Mount Giles.

1993, Jan. 14 **Litho.** ***Perf. 14x15***

1306 A451 45c Pair, #a.-b. 1.25 .40

Australia Day.

Dreamings A452

Aboriginal paintings: 45c, Wild Onion Dreaming, by Pauline Nakamarra Woods. 75c, Yam Plants, by Jack Wunuwun, vert. 85c, Goose Egg Hunt, by George Milpurrurru, vert. $1, Kalumpiwarra-Ngulalintji, by Rover Thomas.

Perf. 14x14½, 14½x14

1993, Feb. 4 **Litho.**

1307 A452 45c red & multi .55 .20
1308 A452 75c org yel & multi .80 .30
1309 A452 85c buff & multi .90 .35
1310 A452 $1 salmon & multi 1.00 .45
Nos. 1307-1310 (4) 3.25 1.30

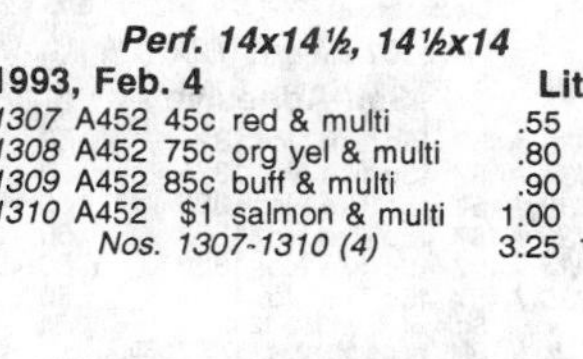

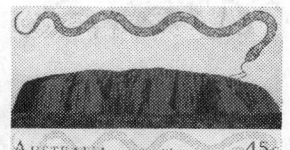

World Heritage Sites in Australia — A453

1993, Mar. 4 **Litho.** ***Perf. 14½x14***

1311 A453 45c Uluru (Ayers Rock) .55 .20
1312 A453 85c Fraser Island .90 .40
1313 A453 95c Shark Bay 1.00 .40
1314 A453 $2 Kakadu 2.00 .85
Nos. 1311-1314 (4) 4.45 1.85

See Nos. 1485-1488.

World War II Ships
A454

Designs: 45c, Cruiser HMAS Sydney II. 85c, Corvette HMAS Bathurst. $1.05, Destroyer HMAS Arunta. $1.20, Hospital Ship Centaur.

1993, Apr. 7 Litho. *Perf. 14x14½*

1315 A454 45c multicolored .55 .20
1316 A454 85c multicolored .90 .35
1317 A454 $1.05 multicolored 1.10 .60
1318 A454 $1.20 multicolored 1.40 .65
Nos. 1315-1318 (4) 3.95 1.80

A455

A456

1993, Apr. 7 *Perf. 14½x14*

1319 A455 45c multicolored .55 .20

Queen Elizabeth II, 67th birthday.

1993, May 7 Litho. *Perf. 14½x14*

Designs based on 19th century trade union banners: No. 1320, Baker, shoe maker. No. 1321, Stevedore, seamstresses. $1, Blacksmith, telephone operator, cook. $1.20, Carpenters.

1320 A456 45c multicolored .50 .20
1321 A456 45c multicolored .50 .20
1322 A456 $1 multicolored 1.00 .55
1323 A456 $1.20 multicolored 1.25 .65
Nos. 1320-1323 (4) 3.25 1.60

Working life in the 1890s.

Trains
A457

Designs: No. 1324, Centenary Special, Tasmania. No. 1325, Spirit of Progress. No. 1326, Western Endeavour. No. 1327, Silver City Comet. No. 1328, Kuranda Tourist Train. No. 1329, The Ghan.

1993, June 1 *Perf. 14x14½*

1324 A457 45c multicolored .60 .20
1325 A457 45c multicolored .60 .20
1326 A457 45c multicolored .60 .20
1327 A457 45c multicolored .60 .20
1328 A457 45c multicolored .60 .20
1329 A457 45c multicolored .60 .20
a. Block of 6, #1324-1329 3.75 2.75

Die Cut Perf. 12x11½

Self-Adhesive

1330 A457 45c like No. 1324 .60 .20
1331 A457 45c like No. 1325 .60 .20
1332 A457 45c like No. 1326 .60 .20
1333 A457 45c like No. 1327 .60 .20
1334 A457 45c like No. 1328 .60 .20
1335 A457 45c like No. 1329 .60 .20
a. Strip of 6, #1330-1335 3.75
b. Bklt. pane of 10, #1332, 1335, 2 each #1330-1331, 1333-1334 6.00

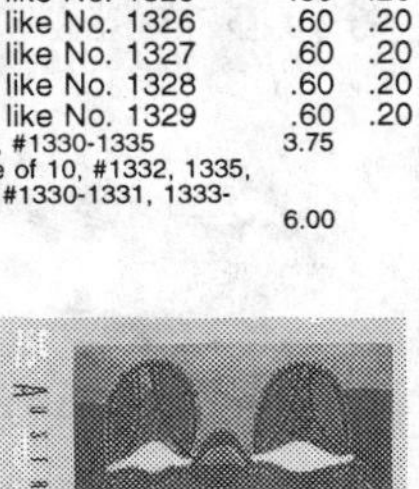

Aboriginal Art — A458

Aboriginal paintings: 45c, Black Cockatoo Feather, by Fiona Foley, vert. 75c, Ngarrgooroon Country, by Hector Jandany. $1, Ngak Ngak, by Ginger Riley. $1.05, Untitled work, by Robert Cole, vert.

Perf. 14½x14, 14x14½

1993, July 1 Litho.

1336 A458 45c henna brown & multi .60 .20
1337 A458 75c brown & multi 1.00 .30
1338 A458 $1 gray & multi 1.25 .55
1339 A458 $1.05 olive & multi 1.40 .60
Nos. 1336-1339 (4) 4.25 1.65

Dame Enid Lyons, MP, and Sen. Dorothy Tangney
A459

Design: No. 1340, Stylized globe, natl. arms, Inter-Parliamentary Conference emblem.

1993, Sept. 2 Litho. *Perf. 14½*

1340 A459 45c multicolored .60 .20
1341 A459 45c multicolored .60 .20
a. Pair, #1340-1341 1.20 .40

90th Inter-Parliamentary Union Conference (#1340). First women in Australian Federal Parliament, 50th anniv. (#1341). Nos. 1340-1341 printed in panes of 25 with 16 #1340 and 9 #1341. Panes with 16 #1341 and 9 #1340 were issued Nov. 19, but were available only through Philatelic Agency.

A460

A461

Dinosaurs: No. 1342, 1348, Ornithocheirus, horiz. No. 1343, 1349, Leaellynasaura. No. 1344, Allosaurus. No. 1345, Timimus. No. 1346, Muttaburrasaurus. No. 1347, Minmi, horiz.

1993, Oct. 1 *Perf. 14x14½, 14½x14*

1342 A460 45c multicolored .60 .20
1343 A460 45c multicolored .60 .20
1344 A461 45c multicolored .60 .20
1345 A461 45c multicolored .60 .20

Size: 29x50mm

1346 A461 75c multicolored .95 .35
1347 A461 $1.05 multicolored 1.40 .60
a. Souvenir sheet of 6, #1342-1347 4.75 4.75
b. As "a," overprinted 5.50 5.50
c. As "a," overprinted 5.50 5.50
Nos. 1342-1347 (6) 4.75 1.75

Self-Adhesive

Die Cut Perf. 11½

1348 A460 45c multicolored .60 .20
1349 A460 45c multicolored .60 .20
a. Bklt. pane, 5 each #1348-1349 6.00

Overprint in gold on sheet margin of No. 1347b contains "BANGKOK 1993" show emblem and "WORLD PHILATELIC / EXHIBITION / BANGKOK 1-10 OCTOBER 1993."

Overprint in gold on sheet margin of No. 1347c contains dinosaur and "Sydney / STAMP & COIN / SHOW / 15-17 October 1993."

Christmas — A462

1993, Nov. 1 Litho. *Perf. 14½x14*

1354 A462 40c Goodwill .50 .20
a. Booklet pane of 20 10.50
1355 A462 45c Joy .60 .20
1356 A462 $1 Peace 1.25 .45
Nos. 1354-1356 (3) 2.35 .85

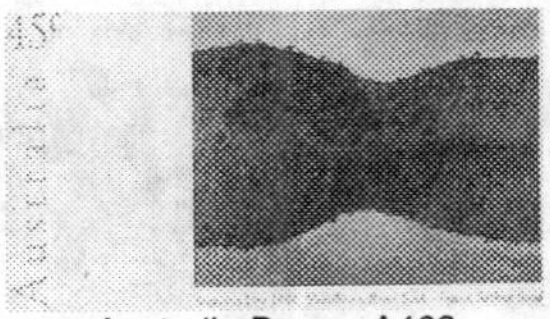

Australia Day — A463

Landscape paintings: 45c, Shoalhaven River Bank-Dawn, by Arthur Boyd. 85c, Wimmera (from Mt. Arapiles), by Sir Sidney Nolan. $1.05, Lagoon, Wimmera, by Nolan. $2, White Cockatoos in Paddock with Flame Trees, by Boyd, vert.

Perf. 14½x14, 14x14½

1994, Jan. 13 Litho.

1357 A463 45c multicolored .65 .20
1358 A463 85c multicolored 1.25 .40
1359 A463 $1.05 multicolored 1.50 .50
1360 A463 $2 multicolored 3.00 1.00
Nos. 1357-1360 (4) 6.40 2.10

See Nos. 1418-1421, 1476-1479, 1572-1574.

Royal Life Saving Society, Cent.
A464

1994, Jan. 20 Litho. *Perf. 14x14½*

1361 A464 45c Vigilance .55 .20
1362 A464 45c Education .55 .20
1363 A464 95c Drill 1.10 .45
1364 A464 $1.20 Fitness 1.40 .55
Nos. 1361-1364 (4) 3.60 1.40

Die Cut Perf. 11½

Self-Adhesive

1365 A464 45c like #1361 .65 .20
1366 A464 45c like #1362 .65 .20
a. Pair, #1365-1366 1.40
b. Booklet pane, 5 #1366a 7.00

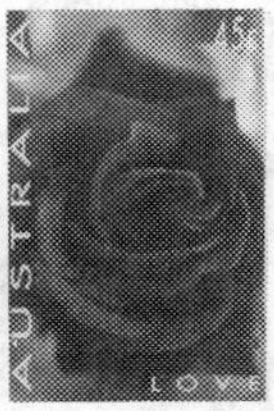

Thinking of You — A465

1994, Feb. 3 Litho. *Perf. 14½x14*

1367 A465 45c Rose .50 .20
1368 A465 45c Tulips .50 .20
1369 A465 45c Poppies .50 .20
a. Pair, #1368-1369 1.00 .40
b. Booklet pane, 5 #1369a 5.00
Nos. 1367-1369 (3) 1.50 .60

A466

A467

1994, Apr. 8 Litho. *Perf. 14½*

1370 A466 45c multicolored .50 .20

Queen Elizabeth II, 68th birthday.

1994, Apr. 8 *Perf. 14½x14*

1371 A467 95c multicolored 1.00 .45

Opening of Friendship Bridge, Thailand-Laos.

Intl. Year of the Family
A468

Children's paintings of their families: 45c, Bobbie Lea Blackmore. 75c, Kathryn Teoh. $1, Maree McCarthy.

1994, Apr. 14 Litho. *Perf. 14x14½*

1372 A468 45c multicolored .55 .20
1373 A468 75c multicolored .90 .35
1374 A468 $1 multicolored 1.25 .50
Nos. 1372-1374 (3) 2.70 1.05

Australian Women's Right to Vote, Cent. — A469

1994, June 9 Litho. *Perf. 14x14½*

1375 A469 45c multicolored .50 .20

Bunyips Folklore Creatures
A470

Types of Bunyips: No. 1376, Aboriginal legend. No. 1377, Nature Spirit. 90c, Berkeley's Creek. $1.35, Natural history.

1994, July 14 Litho. *Perf. 14x14½*

1376 A470 45c multicolored .55 .20
1377 A470 45c multicolored .55 .20
a. Pair, #1376-1377 1.00 .40
1378 A470 90c multicolored 1.00 .40
1379 A470 $1.35 multicolored 1.60 .65
Nos. 1376-1379 (4) 3.70 1.45

World War II Prime Ministers
A471

Designs: a, Robert Menzies. b, Arthur Fadden. c, John Curtin. d, Francis (Frank) Forde. e, Joseph Benedict (Ben) Chifley.

1994, Aug. 11

1380 Strip of 5 2.75 1.10
a.-e. A471 45c any single .55 .20

Aviation Pioneers — A472

Designs: No. 1381, Lawrence Hargrave, box kites. No. 1382, Ross and Keith Smith, Vickers Vimy. $1.35, Ivor McIntyre, Stanley Globe, Fairey IIID A10-3 seaplane. $1.80, Freda Thompson, DeHavilland Moth Major.

1994, Aug. 29 Engr. *Perf. 12*

1381 A472 45c multicolored .55 .20
1382 A472 45c multicolored .55 .20
1383 A472 $1.35 multicolored 1.60 .65
1384 A472 $1.80 multicolored 2.00 .85
Nos. 1381-1384 (4) 4.70 1.90

First England-Australia flight within 30-day time span (#1382). First aerial circumnavigation of Australia (#1383). First woman to fly solo from England-Australia (#1384).

Australian Zoo Animals
A473 A474

Perf. 14x14½, 14½x14

1994, Sept. 28 **Litho.**

1385 A473 45c Scarlet macaw .65 .20

1386 A473 45c Cheetah, vert. .65 .20

1387 A474 45c Fijian crested iguana .65 .20

1388 A474 45c Orangutan .65 .20

Size: 50x30mm

Perf. 14½x14

1389 A473 $1 Asian elephant 1.50 1.50

a. Souv. sheet of 5, #1385-1389, perf. 14½ 4.25 4.25

b. As "a," ovptd. 6.00 6.00

c. As "a," ovptd. 6.00 6.00

d. As "a," ovptd. 6.00 6.00

e. As "a," ovptd. 6.00 6.00

Nos. 1385-1389 (5) 4.10 2.30

Self-Adhesive

Die Cut Perf. 11½

1390 A473 45c like #1385 1.00 .25

1391 A473 45c like #1386 1.00 .25

a. Booklet pane, 6 #1390, 4 #1391 10.00

Overprint in gold on sheet margin:

No. 1389b, show emblem and "Brisbane Stamp Show Zoos / October 21-23, 1994."

No. 1389c, show emblem and "SYDNEY / STAMP / AND / COIN / SHOW / 30/9/94 TO 2/10/94."

No. 1389d, show emblem and "Stampshow '94 Melbourne October 27-30 / National/State Centennial Exhibition 1894-1994."

No. 1389e, show emblem and "STAMP SHOW 94 / Fremantle Convention Centre / 5-6 November 1994."

Christmas A475

Details from Adoration of the Magi, by Giovanni Toscani: 40c, Madonna and Child, vert. 45c, One of Magi, horse and groom. $1, Joseph receiving frankincense from Magi. $1.80, Entire painting.

1994, Oct. 31 **Litho.** ***Perf. 14½x14***

1392 A475 40c multicolored .60 .20

a. Booklet pane of 20 12.00

Complete booklet, #1392a 12.00

Perf. 14x14½

1393 A475 45c multicolored .70 .25

1394 A475 $1 multicolored 1.60 .40

Size: 50x30mm

1395 A475 $1.80 multicolored 2.75 .80

Nos. 1392-1395 (4) 5.65 1.65

50th Sydney-Hobart Yacht Race — A476

Designs: a, Yachts bow-on, Sydney Opera House, Harbor Bridge. b, Two yachts abeam.

1994, Oct. 31 ***Perf. 14½***

1396 Pair 1.40 .50

a.-b. A476 45c any single .70 .25

Self-Adhesive

Die Cut Perf. 11½

1397 A476 45c like #1396a 1.10 .25

1397A A476 45c like #1396b 1.10 .25

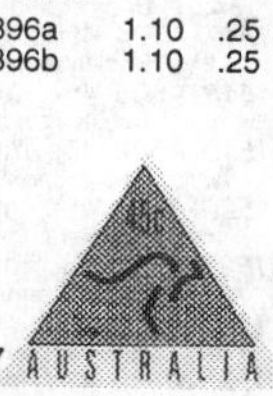

A477

Die Cut Perf. 17

1994, Nov. 2 **Litho.**

Self-Adhesive

Booklet Stamps

Background Color

1398 A477 45c bluish green .70 .25

1399 A477 45c blue .70 .25

1400 A477 45c purple .70 .25

1401 A477 45c yellow green .70 .25

1402 A477 45c pale yellow green .70 .25

1403 A477 45c pale red brown .70 .25

1404 A477 45c rose .70 .25

1405 A477 45c orange yellow .70 .25

a. Booklet pane of 20 14.00

Nos. 1398-1405 (8) 5.60 2.00

No. 1405a contains 3 each #1399, 1401, 1403, 1405 and 2 each #1398, 1400, 1402, 1404. No. 1405a was sold in ATM machines, at the Natl. Philatelic Center, and Australian Philatelic Bureau.

Threatened Species Type of 1992

Die Cut Perf. 11½

1994, Aug. **Litho.**

Self-Adhesive

Size: 53x31mm

1406 A438 45c like #1235a .70 .35

1407 A438 45c like #1235b .70 .35

1408 A438 45c like #1235c .70 .35

1409 A438 45c like #1235d .70 .35

1410 A438 45c like #1235e .70 .35

1411 A438 45c like #1235f .70 .35

a. Strip of 6, #1406-1411 4.25

Nos. 1406-1411 have computer-generated denomination and inscription "NPC" at bottom. Inscriptions "AUSTRALIA," animal name and "THREATENED SPECIES" appear beside design instead of above and below it as on No. 1235.

No. 1411a was issued with "PHILA KOREA" CODE.

Die Cut Perf. 11

1994, Nov. 17 **Litho.**

Self-Adhesive

Size: 40x27mm

1412 A438 45c like #1274 .70 .25

1413 A438 45c like #1275 .70 .25

1414 A438 45c like #1278 .70 .25

1415 A438 45c like #1279 .70 .25

1416 A438 45c like #1276 .70 .25

1417 A438 45c like #1277 .70 .25

Nos. 1412-1417 (6) 4.20 1.50

Nos. 1412-1417 have computer-generated denominations and location codes printed at bottom of each stamp. They differ from Nos. 1280-1282C in size and location of inscriptions.

Nos. 1412-1417 can be printed with denominations from 45c-$100. We have listed the 45c value with NPC (National Philatelic Center), which is available through the Australian Philatelic Bureau. Imprints for numerous shows and other purposes are known.

Australia Day Type of 1994

Paintings: No. 1418, Back Verandah, by Russell Drysdale. No. 1419, Skull Springs Country, by Guy Grey-Smith. $1.05, Outcamp, by Robert Juniper. $1.20, Kite Flying, by Ian Fairweather.

1995, Jan. 12 **Litho.** ***Perf. 15x14½***

1418 A463 45c multicolored .70 .25

1419 A463 45c multicolored .70 .25

1420 A463 $1.05 multicolored 1.60 .40

1421 A463 $1.20 multicolored 1.75 .45

Nos. 1418-1421 (4) 4.75 1.35

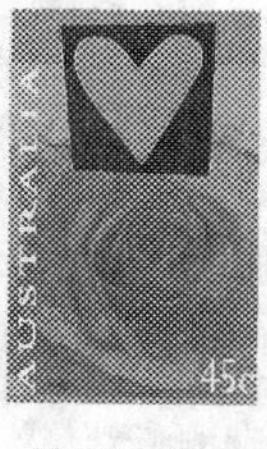

St. Valentine's Day — A478

Various designs: a, Red heart. b, Red & gold heart. c, Gold heart.

1995, Feb. 6 **Litho.** ***Perf. 14½x14***

1422 Strip of 3 2.10 .75

a.-c. A478 45c any single .70 .25

See No. 1480.

Endeavour A479

#1423: a, Captain Cook's Endeavour. b, Replica.

1995, Feb. 9 **Litho.** ***Perf. 14x14½***

1423 Pair 1.40 .50

a.-b. A479 45c any single .70 .25

Booklet Stamps

Size: 44x26mm

Perf. 14 Horiz.

1424 A479 20c like #1423a .30 .20

1425 A479 45c like #1423b .70 .25

a. Booklet pane, 1 #1424, 4 #1425 3.25

Complete booklet, #1425a 3.25

Natl. Trust, 50th Anniv. — A480

Designs: No. 1426a, Coalport plate, Regency style bracket clock. No. 1426b, 15th-16th cent. x-frame Italian style chair, 19th cent. Steiner doll. $1, Advance Australia teapot, neo-classical parian-ware statuette. $2, China urn, silver bowl.

1995, Mar. 16 **Engr.** ***Perf. 14x14½***

1426 Pair 1.40 .50

a.-b. A480 45c any single .70 .25

1427 A480 $1 red brown & blue 1.50 .50

1428 A480 $2 blue & green 3.00 1.00

Nos. 1426-1428 (3) 5.90 2.00

Opals — A481

1995, Apr. 5 **Litho.** ***Perf. 14½x14***

1429 A481 $1.20 Light opal 1.75 .90

1430 A481 $2.50 Black opal 3.75 1.90

Nos. 1429-1430 each contain a holographic image. Soaking in water may affect the hologram.

See Nos. 1554-1555.

A482

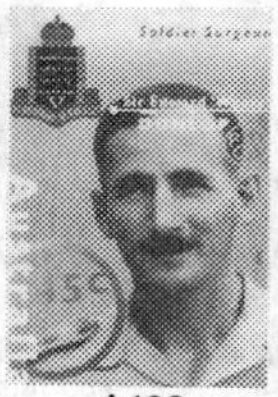

A483

1995, Apr. 20 **Litho.** ***Perf. 14½***

1431 A482 45c multicolored .65 .20

Queen Elizabeth II, 69th birthday.

1995, Apr. 20 **Litho.** ***Perf. 14½x14***

Famous Australians from World War II.

1432 A483 45c Sir Edward Dunlop .65 .25

1433 A483 45c Mrs. Jessie Vasey .65 .25

1434 A483 45c Tom Derrick .65 .25

1435 A483 45c Rawdon Hume Middleton .65 .25

a. Block of 4, #1432-1435 2.60 1.00

Self-Adhesive

Die Cut Perf. 11½

1436 A483 45c like #1432 .65 .20

1437 A483 45c like #1433 .65 .20

1438 A483 45c like #1434 .65 .20

1439 A483 45c like #1435 .65 .20

a. Booklet pane, 4 #1436, 2 each #1437-1439 6.50

b. Strip of 4, #1436-1439 3.00

Nos. 1432-1439 (8) 5.20 1.80

See Nos. 1452-1455.

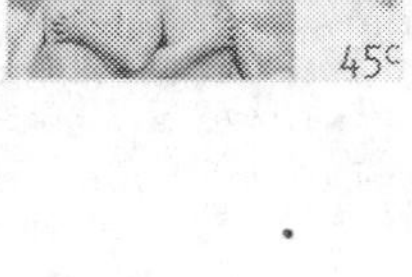

UN, 50th Anniv. A484

1995, May 11 **Litho.** ***Perf. 14x14½***

1440 A484 45c + label, multi .65 .20

a. Block of 4 + 4 labels 2.75 .90

No. 1440 was issued se-tenant with label in blocks of 4 + 4 labels in four designs. In alternating rows, labels appear on left or right side of stamp.

A485

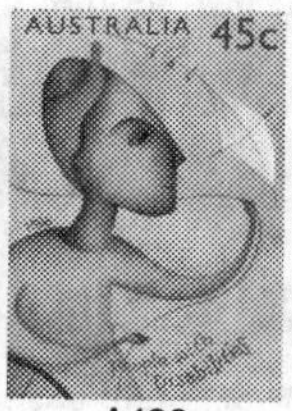

A486

Poster, scene from: No. 1441, The Story of the Kelly Gang, 1906. No. 1442, On Our Selection, 1932. No. 1443, Jedda, 1955. No. 1444, Picnic at Hanging Rock, 1970s. No. 1445, Strictly Ballroom, 1992.

1995, June 8 **Litho.** ***Perf. 14½x14***

1441 A485 45c multicolored .65 .25

1442 A485 45c multicolored .65 .25

1443 A485 45c multicolored .65 .25

1444 A485 45c multicolored .65 .25

1445 A485 45c multicolored .65 .25

a. Strip of 5, #1441-1445 3.25 1.25

Self-Adhesive

Die Cut Perf. 11½

1446 A485 45c like #1441 .65 .20

1447 A485 45c like #1442 .65 .20

1448 A485 45c like #1443 .65 .20

1449 A485 45c like #1444 .65 .20

1450 A485 45c like #1445 .65 .20

a. Strip of 5, #1446-1450 3.50

b. Booklet pane, 2 each #1446-1450 6.50

Motion Pictures, cent.

By its nature No. 1450b constitutes a complete booklet. The peelable backing serves as a booklet cover.

1995, July 13 **Litho.** ***Perf. 14½x14***

People with Disabilities: No. 1451a, Person flying kite from wheelchair. b, Blind person playing violin, guide dog.

1451 Pair 1.25 .95

a.-b. A486 45c any single .60 .20

Famous Australians from World War II Type of 1995

1995, Aug. 10 **Litho.** ***Perf. 14½x14***

1452 A483 45c Leon Goldsworthy .65 .25

1453 A483 45c Len Waters .65 .25

1454 A483 45c Ellen Savage .65 .25

1455 A483 45c Percy Collins .65 .25

a. Block of 4, #1452-1455 2.60 2.25

Peace Types of 1946

Perf. 14x14½, 14½x14

1995, Aug. 10 **Engr.**

1456 A43 45c red brown .65 .20

1457 A45 45c dark green .65 .20

1458 A44 $1.50 dark blue 2.25 2.00

Nos. 1456-1458 (3) 3.55 2.40

End of World War II, 50th anniv.

Wildlife A487

Designs: a, Koalas. b, Pandas.

1995, Sept. 1 **Litho.** ***Perf. 14***

1459 Pair 1.25 .95

a.-b. A487 45c any single .60 .20

c. Souv. sheet #1459a, perf. 11x11½ .60 .60

d. Souv. sheet #1459b, perf. 11x11½ .60 .60

e. #1459c Ovptd. in sheet margin 1.00 1.00

f. #1459d Ovptd. in sheet margin 1.00 1.00

Overprints read: No. 1459e: "AUSTRALIAN STAMP EXHIBITION." No. 1459f: "INTERNATIONAL STAMP & COIN EXPO. / BEIJING '95."

Issued: No. 1459f, 9/14/95.

See People's Republic of China Nos. 2597-2598.

Australian Medical Discoveries
A488

Designs: No. 1461a, Joseph Slattery, Thomas Lyle, Walter Filmer, x-ray pioneers. No. 1461b, Jean Macnamara, Macfarlane Burnet, viruses and immunology. No. 1461C, Fred Hollows, eye care, vert. $2.50, Howard Florey, co-discoverer of penicillin, vert.

1995, Sept. 7 ***Perf. 14x14½, 14½x14***

1461	Pair	1.25	.95
a.-b.	A488 45c any single	.60	.20
1461C	A488 45c multicolored	.60	.20
1461D	A488 $2.50 multicolored	3.75	1.50
	Nos. 1461-1461D (3)	5.60	2.65

No. 1461D exists in sheetlets of 10.

The World Down Under
A489

Designs: Nos. 1462a, 1465a, Flatback turtle. Nos. 1462b, 1465b, Flame angelfish, nudibranch. Nos. 1463a, 1465c, Potato cod, giant maori wrasse. Nos. 1463b, 1465d, Giant trevally. Nos. 1464a, 1465e, Black marlin. Nos. 1464b, 1465f, Mako & tiger sharks.

1995, Oct. 3 **Litho.** ***Perf. 14x14½***

1462	Pair	1.25	.80
a.-b.	A489 45c any single	.60	.20
1463	Pair	1.25	.80
a.-b.	A489 45c any single	.60	.20
1464	Pair	1.25	.80
a.-b.	A489 45c any single	.60	.20
	Nos. 1462-1464 (3)	3.75	2.40

Miniature Sheet of 6

1465	A489 45c #a.-f.	4.00	3.75
g.	Ovptd. in sheet margin	4.50	
h.	Ovptd. in sheet margin	4.50	
i.	Ovptd. in sheet margin	4.50	
j.	Ovptd. in sheet margin	4.50	
k.	Ovptd. in sheet margin	4.50	

Nos. 1462-1464 have pale blue border on three sides. No. 1465 is a continuous design and does not have the pale border. Fish on No. 1465 are printed with additional phosphor ink producing a glow-in-the-dark effect under ultraviolet light.

Overprints in gold in sheet margin of No. 1465 include show emblems and text:

No. 1465g: "ADELAIDE / STAMP AND / COLLECTIBLES / FAIR / 14/10/95 - / 15/10/95."

No. 1465h: "SYDNEY / CENTREPOINT 95 / STAMPSHOW."

No. 1465i: "Brisbane Stamp Show / 20-22 October 1995."

No. 1465j: "Melbourne Stamp & Coin Fair / 27-29 October 1995."

No. 1465k: "Swanpex WA / 28-29 October 1995."

Booklet Stamps
Self-Adhesive
Die Cut Perf. 11½

1466	A489 45c like #1462a	.65	.20
1467	A489 45c like #1462b	.65	.20
1468	A489 45c like #1463a	.65	.20
1469	A489 45c like #1463b	.65	.20
1470	A489 45c like #1464a	.65	.20
1471	A489 45c like #1464b	.65	.20
a.	Booklet pane, #1470-1471, 2 each #1466-1469	6.50	
b.	Strip of 6, #1466-1471	4.50	

By its nature, No. 1471a constitutes a complete booklet. The peelable backing serves as a booklet cover.

Christmas — A490

Stained glass windows, Our Lady Help of Christians Church, Melbourne: 40c, Madonna and Child. 45c, Angel carrying banner. $1, Three rejoicing angels.

1995, Nov. 1 **Litho.** ***Perf. 14½x14***

1472	A490 40c multicolored	.60	.30
1473	A490 45c multicolored	.65	.30
1474	A490 $1 multicolored	1.50	.75
	Nos. 1472-1474 (3)	2.75	1.35

Booklet Stamp
Self-Adhesive
Die Cut Perf. 11½

1475	A490 40c multicolored	.60	.30
a.	Booklet pane of 20	12.00	

Madonna and Child on No. 1475 are printed with additional phosphor ink giving parts of the stamp a rough texture.

By its nature, No. 1475a constitutes a complete booklet. The peelable backing serves as a booklet cover, which also contains 20 labels. The complete booklet is available with backing showing two different advertisements.

Australia Day Type of 1994

Paintings by Australian women: 45c, West Australian Banksia, by Margaret Preston, vert. 85c, The Babe is Wise, by Lina Bryans, vert. $1, The Bridge in Curve, by Grace Cossington Smith. $1.20, Beach Umbrellas, by Vida Lahey.

Perf. 14x14½, 14½x14

1996, Jan. 16 **Litho.**

1476	A463 45c multicolored	.65	.20
1477	A463 85c multicolored	1.25	.40
1478	A463 $1 multicolored	1.50	.50
1479	A463 $1.20 multicolored	1.75	.60
	Nos. 1476-1479 (4)	5.15	1.70

Heart and Roses
A491

1996, Jan. 30 ***Perf. 14x14½***

1480	A491 45c gold & multi	.65	.20

See No. 1422.

Military Aviation
A492

#1481, Firefly, Sea Fury. #1482, Beaufighter, Kittyhawk. #1483, Hornet. #1484, Kiowa.

1996, Feb. 26 **Litho.** ***Perf. 14x14½***

1481	A492 45c multicolored	.70	.20
1482	A492 45c multicolored	.70	.20
1483	A492 45c multicolored	.70	.20
1484	A492 45c multicolored	.70	.20
a.	Block of 4, #1481-1484	2.80	2.50

Australian World Heritage Sites Type of 1993

Designs: 45c, Tasmanian Wilderness. 75c, Willandra Lakes. 95c, Fossil Cave, Naracoorte. $1, Lord Howe Island.

1996, Mar. 14 **Litho.** ***Perf. 14½x14***

1485	A453 45c multicolored	.70	.20
1486	A453 75c multicolored	1.25	.40
1487	A453 95c multicolored	1.40	.45
1488	A453 $1 multicolored	1.50	.50
	Nos. 1485-1488 (4)	4.85	1.55

Indonesian Bear Cuscus — A493

Design: No. 1489, Australian Spotted Cuscus.

1996, Mar. 22

1489	A493 45c multicolored	.70	.20
1490	A493 45c multicolored	.70	.20
a.	Pair, Nos. 1489-1490	1.40	.95
b.	Souvenir sheet, No. 1490a	1.40	1.40

No. 1490a has continuous design.

nO. 1490B exists overprinted "WORLD PHILATELIC YOUTH EXHIBITION / PAMERAN FILATELI REMAJA DUNIA / INDONESIA '96." These were sold at the show, but apparently were never sold by the philatelic agency.

See Indonesia Nos. 1640-1642.

Queen Elizabeth II, 70th Birthday
A494

Litho. & Engr.

1996, Apr. 11 ***Perf. 14x14½***

1491	A494 45c multicolored	.70	.20

North Melbourne Kangaroos
A495

Brisbane Bears
A496

Sydney Swans — A497

Carlton Blues — A498

Adelaide Crows — A499

Fitzroy Lions — A500

Richmond Tigers — A501

St. Kilda Saints — A502

Melbourne Demons — A503

Collingwood Magpies — A504

Fremantle Dockers — A505

Footscray Bulldogs — A506

West Coast Eagles
A507

Essendon Bombers
A508

Geelong Cats — A509

Hawthorn Hawks — A510

1996, Apr. 23 **Litho.** ***Perf. 14½x14***

1492	A495 45c multicolored	.70	.50
1493	A496 45c multicolored	.70	.50
1494	A497 45c multicolored	.70	.50
1495	A498 45c multicolored	.70	.50
1496	A499 45c multicolored	.70	.50
1497	A500 45c multicolored	.70	.50
1498	A501 45c multicolored	.70	.50
1499	A502 45c multicolored	.70	.50
1500	A503 45c multicolored	.70	.50
1501	A504 45c multicolored	.70	.50
1502	A505 45c multicolored	.70	.50
1503	A506 45c multicolored	.70	.50
1504	A507 45c multicolored	.70	.50
1505	A508 45c multicolored	.70	.50
1506	A509 45c multicolored	.70	.50
1507	A510 45c multicolored	.70	.50
a.	Min. sheet of 16, #1492-1507	11.25	

Booklet Stamps
Self-Adhesive
Serpentine Die Cut 11½

1508	A495 45c multicolored	.70	.20
a.	Booklet pane of 10	7.00	
1509	A496 45c multicolored	.70	.20
a.	Booklet pane of 10	7.00	
1510	A497 45c multicolored	.70	.20
a.	Booklet pane of 10	7.00	
1511	A498 45c multicolored	.70	.20
a.	Booklet pane of 10	7.00	
1512	A499 45c multicolored	.70	.20
a.	Booklet pane of 10	7.00	
1513	A500 45c multicolored	.70	.20
a.	Booklet pane of 10	7.00	
1514	A501 45c multicolored	.70	.20
a.	Booklet pane of 10	7.00	
1515	A502 45c multicolored	.70	.20
a.	Booklet pane of 10	7.00	
1516	A503 45c multicolored	.70	.20
a.	Booklet pane of 10	7.00	
1517	A504 45c multicolored	.70	.20
a.	Booklet pane of 10	7.00	
1518	A505 45c multicolored	.70	.20
a.	Booklet pane of 10	7.00	
1519	A506 45c multicolored	.70	.20
a.	Booklet pane of 10	7.00	
1520	A507 45c multicolored	.70	.20
a.	Booklet pane of 10	7.00	
1521	A508 45c multicolored	.70	.20
a.	Booklet pane of 10	7.00	
1522	A509 45c multicolored	.70	.20
a.	Booklet pane of 10	7.00	
1523	A510 45c multicolored	.70	.20
a.	Booklet pane of 10	7.00	

By their nature, Nos. 1508a-1523a are complete booklets. The peelable paper backing serves as a booklet cover.

Australian Football League, cent.

Flora and Fauna — A511

Designs: 5c, Leadbeater's possum. 10c, Powerful owl. 20c, Saltwater crocodile, Kangkong flower. 25c, Northern dwarf tree frog, red lily. No. 1528, Little kingfisher. No. 1529, Jacana. No. 1530, Jabiru. No. 1531, Brolga. $1, Big greasy butterfly, water lily. $2, Blackwood wattle. $5, Mountain ash, fern. $10, Kakadu Wetlands during lightning storm, great egret, red lily.

1996-99 Litho. *Perf. 14x14½*

1524	A511 5c multi	.20	.20
1525	A511 10c multi	.20	.20
1526	A511 20c multi	.30	.20
1527	A511 25c multi	.40	.20
1528	A511 45c multi	.70	.20
1529	A511 45c multi	.70	.20
1530	A511 45c multi	.70	.20
1531	A511 45c multi	.70	.20
a.	Block of 4, #1528-1531	2.80	.80
b.	Souvenir sheet of 2, #1530-1531	1.20	
1532	A511 $1 multi	1.60	.40
1533	A511 $2 multi	3.25	1.00

Size: 30x50mm

1534	A511 $5 multi	8.00	2.60
1535	A511 $10 multi	15.00	4.00
a.	Souvenir sheet of 1	15.00	4.00
b.	As "a," ovptd. in sheet margin	15.00	4.00
	Nos. 1524-1535 (12)	31.75	9.60

Self-Adhesive

Serpentine Die Cut 11½

1536	A511 45c like #1529	.70	.20
1537	A511 45c like #1528	.70	.20
1538	A511 45c like #1531	.70	.20
1539	A511 45c like #1530	.70	.20
a.	Booklet pane, 3 ea #1536, #1538, 2 ea #1537, #1539	7.00	
b.	Strip of 4, #1536-1539	2.80	
h.	Sheet of 5, #1537-1539, 2 #1536	3.50	

Serpentine Die Cut 12½x13

1996-99 Litho *Perf. 14x14½*

1539C	A511 45c like #1529	.70	.20
1539D	A511 45c like #1528	.70	.20
1539E	A511 45c like #1531	.70	.20
1539F	A511 45c like #1530	.70	.20
g.	Strip of 4, #1539C-1539F	2.80	

Nos. 1536-1539 are booklet stamps.

No. 1531b is inscribed in sheet margin with Shanghai '97 emblem and "International Stamp & Coin Exposition Shanghai '97" in Chinese and English.

No. 1535b overprinted in silver in sheet margin with PACIFIC 97 emblem and "Australia Post Exhibition Sheet No. 4."

By its nature No. 1539a is a complete booklet. The peelable backing serves as a booklet cover.

Issued: 5c, 10c, $2, $5, 5/9/96; 20c, 25c, $1, $10, #1538a, 4/10/97; #1528-1531, 1536-1539, 6/2/97; #1531b, 11/17/97; #1539C-1539F, 11/13/99.

See Nos. 1734-1746E

Modern Olympic Games, Cent. A512

#1540, Edwin Flack, 1st Australian gold medalist, runners. #1541, Fanny Durack, 1st Australian woman gold medalist, swimmers. $1.05, Paralympics, Atlanta.

Litho. & Engr.

1996, June 6 *Perf. 14x14½*

1540	A512 45c multicolored	.70	.20
1541	A512 45c multicolored	.70	.20
a.	Pair, #1540-1541	1.40	.95
1542	A512 $1.05 multicolored	1.60	1.00
	Nos. 1540-1542 (3)	3.00	1.40

Transfer of Olympic Flag from Atlanta to Sydney A513

1996, July 22 Litho.

1543	A513 45c multicolored	.70	.20

Issued in sheets of 10.

Children's Book Council, 50th Anniv. A514

Covers from "Book of the Year" books: No. 1544, "Animalia." No. 1545, "Greetings from Sandy Beach." No. 1546, "Who Sank the Boat?" No. 1547, "John Brown, Rose and the Midnight Cat."

1996, July 4 Litho. *Perf. 14x14½*

1544	A514 45c multicolored	.70	.45
1545	A514 45c multicolored	.70	.45
1546	A514 45c multicolored	.70	.45
1547	A514 45c multicolored	.70	.45
a.	Block of 4, #1544-1547	2.80	2.50

Serpentine Die Cut 11½

Self-Adhesive

1548	A514 45c like #1544	.70	.20
1549	A514 45c like #1546	.70	.20
1550	A514 45c like #1547	.70	.20
1551	A514 45c like #1545	.70	.20
a.	Booklet pane, 4 #1548, 2 each #1549-1551	7.00	
b.	Strip of 4, #1548-1551	2.80	

By its nature, No. 1551a is a complete booklet. The peelable paper backing serves as a booklet cover.

National Council of Women, Cent. — A515

Designs: 45c, Margaret Windeyer (1866-1939), honorary life president. $1, Rose Scott (1847-1925), founding executive member.

1996, Aug. 8 Litho. *Perf. 14½x14*

1552	A515 45c claret & yellow	.70	.20
1553	A515 $1 blue & yellow	1.50	1.50

Gems Type of 1995

1996, Sept. 5 Litho. *Perf. 14½x14*

1554	A481 45c Pearl	.70	.20
1555	A481 $1.20 Diamond	1.90	1.90

No. 1555 contains a round foil design. Soaking in water may affect the design.

Arts Councils in Regional Australia A516

Silhouettes of performing artists, outdoor scene: 20c, Ballet dancer, violinist, field, bales, trees. 45c, Violinist, hand holding flower, dancer, tree in field.

Perf. 14 Horiz.

1996, Sept. 12 Litho.

Booklet Stamps

1556	A516 20c multicolored	.30	.20
1557	A516 45c multicolored	.70	.20
a.	Booklet pane, 1 #1556, 4 #1557	3.25	
	Complete booklet, #1557a	3.25	

Pets

A517 A518

1996-97 *Perf. 14x14½, 14½x14*

1558	A517 45c Cockatoo	.70	.20
1559	A517 45c Ducks, vert.	.70	.20
1560	A517 45c Dog, cat, vert.	.70	.20
a.	Pair, #1559-1560	1.40	.80
1561	A518 45c Dog, puppy	.70	.20
1562	A518 45c Kittens	.70	.20
a.	Pair, #1561-1562	1.40	.80

Size: 29x49mm

1563	A518 45c Pony mare, foal	.70	.20
a.	Souvenir sheet, #1558-1563	4.25	4.25
b.	As "a," ovptd.	4.25	4.25
c.	As "a," ovptd.	4.25	4.25
d.	As "a," ovptd.	4.25	4.25
e.	As "a," ovptd.	4.25	4.25
f.	As "a," ovptd.	4.25	4.25
g.	As "a," ovptd.	4.25	4.25
h.	As "a," ovptd.	4.25	4.25
	Nos. 1558-1563 (6)	4.20	1.20

Self-Adhesive

Serpentine Die Cut 11½

1564	A518 45c like #1561	.70	.20
1565	A518 45c like #1562	.70	.20
a.	Bklt. pane, 6 #1564, 4 #1565	7.00	

No. 1563a is a continuous design.

Overprints in gold on sheet margin: No. 1563b, show emblem and "10TH ASIAN INTERNATIONAL PHILATELIC EXHIBITION 1996" in Chinese and English. No. 1563c, pets emblem and, "ASDA CENTREPOINT '96 STAMP AND COIN SHOW / 5-7 October 1996." No. 1563d, pets emblem and "ST PETERS STAMP & COLLECTIBLE FAIR / 12-13 OCTOBER 1996." No. 1563e, pets emblem and "MELBOURNE '96 NATIONAL PHILATELIC EXHIBITION / 17-20 OCTOBER 1996." No. 1563f, pets emblem and "QUEENSLAND SPRING STAMP AND COIN SHOW / 25-27 OCTOBER 1996." No. 1563g, pets emblem and "SWANPEX '96 / 26-27 OCTOBER 1996." No. 1563h: Hong Kong '97 emblem and "11TH ASIAN INTERNATIONAL STAMP EXHIBITION / 12-16 FEBRUARY 1997."

By its nature, No. 1565a is a complete booklet. The peelable paper backing serves as a booklet cover.

Issued: Nos. 1558-1563, 1563a, 1564-1465, 10/1/96; Nos. 1563b-1563g, 10/3/96; No. 1563h, 2/12/97.

Baron Ferdinand von Mueller (1825-96), Botanist — A519

1996, Oct. 9 *Perf. 14*

1566	A519 $1.20 multicolored	1.90	1.00

See Germany No. 1949.

Christmas — A520

1996, Nov. 1 *Perf. 14½x14*

1567	A520 40c Madonna and Child	.65	.20
1568	A520 45c Wise man	.70	.20
1569	A520 $1 Shepherd boy, lamb	1.50	.30
	Nos. 1567-1569 (3)	2.85	.70

Self-Adhesive

Serpentine Die Cut 12

1570	A520 40c like #1567	.65	.20
a.	Booklet pane of 20	13.00	

By its nature, No. 1570a is a complete booklet. The peelable paper backing serves as a booklet cover.

Exploration of Australian Coast & Christmas Island by Willem de Vlamingh, 300th Anniv. — A521

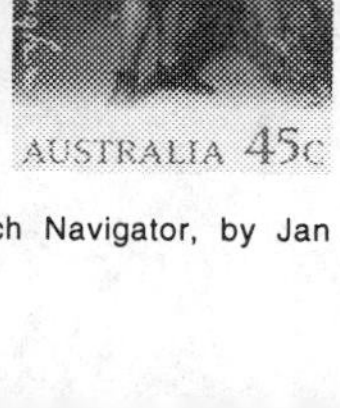

Portrait of a Dutch Navigator, by Jan Verkolje.

1996, Nov. 1 *Perf. 14x14½*

1571	A521 45c multicolored	.70	.20
a.	Pair, #1571 & Christmas Is. #404	1.40	.80

Australia Day Type of 1994

Paintings: 85c, Landscape '74, by Fred Williams. 90c, The Balcony 2, by Brett Whiteley. $1.20, Fire Haze at Gerringong, by Lloyd Rees.

1997, Jan. 16 Litho. *Perf. 14½x14*

1572	A463 85c multicolored	1.25	.40
1573	A463 90c multicolored	1.40	.45
1574	A463 $1.20 multicolored	1.90	.60
	Nos. 1572-1574 (3)	4.55	1.45

A522 A523

Sir Donald Bradman, cricketer.

1997, Jan. 23 Litho. *Perf. 14½*

1575	A522 45c Portrait	.70	.20
1576	A522 45c At bat	.70	.20
a.	Pair, No. 1575-1576	1.40	.80

See Nos. 1634-1646, 1719-1722.

1997, Jan. 29 *Perf. 14½x14*

1577	A523 45c Rose	.70	.20

Serpentine Die Cut 11½

Booklet Stamp

Self-Adhesive

1578	A523 45c like #1577	.70	.20
a.	Booklet pane of 10	7.00	

Greetings. By its nature, No. 1578a is a complete booklet. The peelable paper backing, which also contains 12 labels, serves as a booklet cover.

Classic Cars — A524

#1579, 1934 Ford Coupe Utility. #1580, 1948 GMH Holden 48-215 (FX). #1581, 1958 Austin Lancer. #1582, 1962 Chrysler Valiant R Series.

1997, Feb. 27 Litho. *Perf. 14x14½*

1579	A524 45c multicolored	.70	.20
a.	Booklet pane of 4	2.80	
1580	A524 45c multicolored	.70	.20
a.	Booklet pane of 4	2.80	
1581	A524 45c multicolored	.70	.20
a.	Booklet pane of 4	2.80	
1582	A524 45c multicolored	.70	.20
a.	Booklet pane of 4	2.80	
b.	Block of 4, #1579-1582	2.80	1.60
	Complete booklet, #1579a, 1580a, 1581a, 1582a	16.00	

Complete booklet contains 2 postal cards and 16 self-adhesive labels.

Serpentine Die Cut 12

Booklet Stamps

Self-Adhesive

1583	A524 45c like #1579	.70	.20
1584	A524 45c like #1580	.70	.20
1585	A524 45c like #1581	.70	.20
1586	A524 45c like #1582	.70	.20
a.	Booklet pane of 10, 2 ea #1583, 1585, 3 ea #1584, 1586	7.00	
b.	Strip of 4, #1583-1586	2.80	

By its nature, No. 1586a is a complete booklet. The peelable backing serves as a booklet cover. The backing for No. 1586b is inscribed with a 3x8mm black vertical box and "SNP CAMBEC."

Circuses in Australia, 150th Anniv. — A525

#1591, Queen of the Arena, May Wirth (1894-1978). #1592, Wizard of the Wire, Con Colleano (1899-1973). #1593, Clowns. #1594, Tumblers.

1997, Mar. 13 Litho. *Perf. 14½x14*

1591 A525 45c multicolored .70 .20
1592 A525 45c multicolored .70 .20
1593 A525 45c multicolored .70 .20
1594 A525 45c multicolored .70 .20
a. Block of 4, #1591-1594 2.80 1.60

Queen Elizabeth II, 71st Birthday, 50th Wedding Anniv. A526

1997, Apr. 17 Engr. *Perf. 14x14½*

1595 A526 45c Design A50 .70 .20

A527

A528

1997, Apr. 17 *Perf. 14½x14*

1596 A527 45c multicolored .70 .20

Lions Clubs of Australia, 50th anniv.

1997, May 8 Litho. *Perf. 14½x14*

Dolls and Teddy Bears: No. 1597, Doll wearing red hat. No. 1598, Bear standing. No. 1599, Doll wearing white dress holding teddy bear. No. 1600, Doll in brown outfit. No. 1601, Teddy bear seated.

1597 A528 45c multicolored .70 .20
1598 A528 45c multicolored .70 .20
1599 A528 45c multicolored .70 .20
1600 A528 45c multicolored .70 .20
1601 A528 45c multicolored .70 .20
a. Strip of 5, #1597-1601 3.50 2.00

Emergency Services A529

#1602, Disaster victim evacuated. #1603, Police rescue hiker. $1.05, Rapid response saves home. $1.20, Ambulance dash saves life.

1997, July 10 Litho. *Perf. 14x14½*

1602 A529 45c multicolored .70 .20
1603 A529 45c multicolored .70 .20
a. Pair, #1602-1603 1.40 .40
1604 A529 $1.05 multicolored 1.60 .50
1605 A529 $1.20 multicolored 1.80 .55
Nos. 1602-1605 (4) 4.80 1.45

Arrival of Merino Sheep in Australia, Bicent. A530

Designs: No. 1606, George Peppin, Junior (1827-76), breeder, Merino sheep. No. 1607, "Pepe" chair, uses of wool.

1997, Aug. 7 Litho. *Perf. 14x14½*

1606 A530 45c multicolored .70 .20
1607 A530 45c multicolored .70 .20
a. Pair, #1606-1607 1.40 .80

Scenes from "The Dreaming," Animated Stories for Children A531

Designs: 45c, Dumbi the Owl. $1, The Two Willy-Willies. $1.20, How Brolga Became a Bird. $1.80, Tuggan-Tuggan.

1997, Aug. 21 *Perf. 14½*

1608 A531 45c multicolored .70 .20
1609 A531 $1 multicolored 1.50 .40
1610 A531 $1.20 multicolored 1.75 .45
1611 A531 $1.80 multicolored 2.75 .70
Nos. 1608-1611 (4) 6.70 1.75

Prehistoric Animals — A532

Designs: No. 1612, Rhoetosaurus brownei. No. 1613, Mcnamaraspis kaprios. No. 1614, Ninjemys oweni. No. 1615, Paracyclotosaurus davidi. No. 1616, Woolungasaurus glendowerensis.

1997, Sept. 4 Litho. *Perf. 14½x14*

1612 A532 45c multicolored .65 .20
1613 A532 45c multicolored .65 .20
1614 A532 45c multicolored .65 .20
1615 A532 45c multicolored .65 .20
1616 A532 45c multicolored .65 .20
a. Strip of 5, #1612-1616 3.25 2.00

Printed in sheets of 10 stamps.

Nocturnal Animals
A533 A534

Perf. 14½x14, 14x14½

1997, Oct. 1 Litho.

1617 A533 45c Barking owl .65 .20
1618 A533 45c Spotted-tailed quoll .65 .20
a. Pair, #1617-1618 1.30 .80
1619 A534 45c Platypus .65 .20
1620 A534 45c Brown antechinus .65 .20
1621 A534 45c Dingo .65 .20
a. Strip of 3, #1619-1621 2.00 1.25

Size: 49x29mm

1622 A534 45c Yellow-bellied glider .65 .20
a. Souvenir sheet, #1617-1622 4.00 4.00
Nos. 1617-1622 (6) 3.90 1.20

No. 1622a is printed with additional phosphor ink revealing a glow-in-the-dark spider and web under ultraviolet light.

Size: 21x32mm

Serpentine Die Cut Perf. 11½

Self-Adhesive

1623 A533 45c like #1617 .65 .20
1624 A533 45c like #1618 .65 .20
a. Booklet pane, 5 each #1623-1624 6.50
b. Pair, #1623-1624 1.30

By its nature No. 1624a is a complete booklet. The peelable paper backing serves as a booklet cover.

Breast Cancer Awareness A535

1997, Oct. 27 Litho. *Perf. 14x14½*

1625 A535 45c multicolored .65 .20

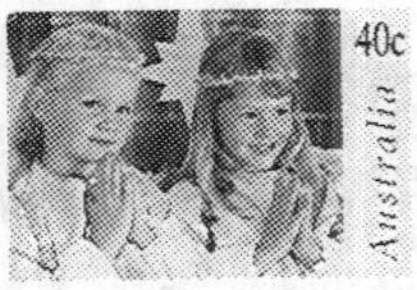

Christmas A536

Children in Christmas Nativity pageant: 40c, Angels. 45c, Mary holding Baby Jesus. $1, Three Wise Men.

1997, Nov. 3

1626 A536 40c multicolored .60 .20
1627 A536 45c multicolored .65 .20
1628 A536 $1 multicolored 1.40 .45
Nos. 1626-1628 (3) 2.65 .85

Booklet Stamps

Serpentine Die Cut Perf. 11½

Self-Adhesive

1629 A536 40c multicolored .60 .20
a. Booklet pane of 20 12.00

By its nature No. 1629a is a complete booklet. The peelable paper backing serves as a booklet cover, which also contains 20 labels.

Maritime Heritage A537

1998, Jan. 15 Litho. *Perf. 14½x14*

1630 A537 45c Flying Cloud .60 .20
a. Sheet of 10 6.00 2.00
1631 A537 85c Marco Polo 1.15 .35
a. Sheet of 2, #1631 perf. 13½ & Canada #1779, perf. 13 1.75 .85
1632 A537 $1 Chusan 1.30 .40
1633 A537 $1.20 Heather Belle 1.60 .50
Nos. 1630-1633 (4) 4.65 1.45

Australia '99 (#1630a). World Stamp Expo. (#1631a).
See Canada #1779a.
Issued: #1630a, 6/17/98; #1631a, 3/19/99.

Legends Type of 1997

Olympians: No. 1634: a, Betty Cuthbert. b, Cuthbert running. c, Herb Elliott. d, Elliott running. e, Dawn Fraser. f, Fraser swimming. g, Marjorie Jackson. h, Jackson running. i, Murray Rose. j, Rose swimming. k, Shirley Strickland. l, Strickland clearing hurdle.

1998, Jan. 21 *Perf. 14x14½*

Size: 34x27mm

1634 Sheet of 12 7.25 2.50
a.-l. A522 any single .60 .20

Booklet Stamps

Self-Adhesive

Serpentine Die Cut 11½

Size: 34x25mm

1635 A522 45c like #1634a .60 .20
1636 A522 45c like #1634b .60 .20
1637 A522 45c like #1634c .60 .20
1638 A522 45c like #1634d .60 .20
1639 A522 45c like #1634e .60 .20
1640 A522 45c like #1634f .60 .20
1641 A522 45c like #1634g .60 .20
1642 A522 45c like #1634h .60 .20
1643 A522 45c like #1634i .60 .20
1644 A522 45c like #1634j .60 .20
1645 A522 45c like #1634k .60 .20
1646 A522 45c like #1634l .60 .20
a. Booklet pane of 12, #1635-1646 7.25

By its nature, No. 1646a is a complete booklet. The peelable backing serves as a booklet cover.

Greetings — A538

1998, Feb. 12 Litho. *Perf. 14½x14*

1647 A538 45c Champagne roses .60 .20

Booklet Stamp

Self-Adhesive

Serpentine Die Cut 11½

1648 A538 45c like #1647 .60 .20
a. Booklet pane of 10 6.00

By its nature No. 1648a is a complete booklet. The peelable paper backing, which contains 12 labels, serves as a booklet cover.

Queen Elizabeth II, 72nd Birthday A539

1998, Apr. 9 Litho. *Perf. 14x14½*

1649 A539 45c multicolored .60 .20

Royal Australian Navy Fleet Air Arm, 50th Anniv. A540

1998, Apr. 9

1650 A540 45c multicolored .60 .20

Farming in Australia A541

Designs: No. 1651, Sheep for producing wool. No. 1652, Sheaves of wheat. No. 1653, Herding cattle on horseback. No. 1654, Harvesting sugar cane. No. 1655, Dairy cattle, man on motorcycle.

1998, Apr. 21

1651 A541 45c multicolored .60 .20
1652 A541 45c multicolored .60 .20
1653 A541 45c multicolored .60 .20
1654 A541 45c multicolored .60 .20
1655 A541 45c multicolored .60 .20
a. Strip of 5, #1651-1655 3.00 1.00

Booklet Stamps

Self-Adhesive

Serpentine Die Cut 11½

Size: 37x25mm

1656 A541 45c like #1651 .60 .20
1657 A541 45c like #1652 .60 .20
1658 A541 45c like #1653 .60 .20
1659 A541 45c like #1654 .60 .20
1660 A541 45c like #1655 .60 .20
a. Booklet pane, 2 each #1656-1660 6.00

The peelable backing of No. 1660a serves as a booklet cover.

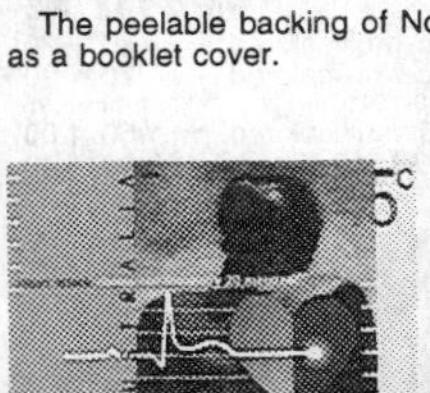

Heart Health A542

1998, May 4 Litho. *Perf. 14x14½*

1661 A542 45c multicolored .60 .20

Rock and Roll in Australia A543

a, "The Wild One," by Johnny O'Keefe, 1958. b, "Oh Yeah Uh Huh," by Col Joye and the Joye Boys, 1959. c, "He's My Blonde-headed Stompie Wompie Real Gone Surfer Boy," by Little Pattie, 1963. d, "Shakin' All Over," by Normie Rowe, 1965. e, "She's So Fine," by The Easybeats, 1965. f, "The Real Thing," by Russell Morris, 1969. g, "Turn Up Your Radio," by The Masters Apprentices, 1970. h, "Eagle Rock," by Daddy Cool, 1971. i, "Most People I Know Think That I'm Crazy," by Billy Thorpe & the Aztecs, 1972. j, "Horror Movie," by Skyhooks, 1974. k, "It's a Long Way to the Top," by AC/DC, 1975. l, "Howzat," by Sherbet, 1976.

1998, May 26

1662 A543 Sheet of 12 7.25 2.50
a.-l. 45c any single .60 .20

Coil Stamps
Self-Adhesive
Serpentine Die Cut 11½
Size: 37x25mm

1663 A543 45c like #1662a .60 .20
1664 A543 45c like #1662b .60 .20
1665 A543 45c like #1662c .60 .20
1666 A543 45c like #1662d .60 .20
1667 A543 45c like #1662e .60 .20
1668 A543 45c like #1662f .60 .20
1669 A543 45c like #1662g .60 .20
1670 A543 45c like #1662h .60 .20
1671 A543 45c like #1662i .60 .20
1672 A543 45c like #1662j .60 .20
1673 A543 45c like #1662k .60 .20
1674 A543 45c like #1662l .60 .20
a. Strip of 12 + label 7.25

Endangered Birds A544

World Wildlife Fund: #1675, Helmeted honeyeater. #1676, Orange-bellied parrot. #1677, Red-tailed black cockatoo. #1678, Gouldian finch.

1998, June 25 ***Perf. 14x14½***

1675 A544 5c multicolored .20 .20
1676 A544 5c multicolored .20 .20
a. Pair, #1675-1676 .20 .20
1677 A544 45c multicolored .60 .20
1678 A544 45c multicolored .60 .20
a. Pair, #1677-1678 1.20 .40

Performing and Visual Arts A545

Young people: No. 1679, Playing French horn. No. 1680, Dancing.

1998, July 16 Litho. ***Perf. 14x14½***

1679 A545 45c multicolored .60 .20
1680 A545 45c multicolored .60 .20
a. Pair, #1679-1680 1.20 .40

Orchids — A546

Designs: 45c, Phalaenopsis rosenstromii. 85c, Arundina graminifolia. $1, Grammatophyllum speciosum. $1.20, Dendrobium phalaenopsis.

1998, Aug. 6 Litho. ***Perf. 14½x14***

1681 A546 45c multicolored .60 .20
1682 A546 85c multicolored 1.00 .35
1683 A546 $1 multicolored 1.25 .40
1684 A546 $1.20 multicolored 1.50 .50
a. Souvenir sheet, #1681-1684 4.50 1.50
Nos. 1681-1684 (4) 4.35 1.45

See Singapore Nos. 858-861b.

The Teapot of Truth, by Cartoonist Michael Leunig A547

Designs: No. 1685, Angel carrying teapot, bird with flower. No. 1686, Birds perched on heart-shaped vine. No. 1687, Characters using their heads to pour tea into cup. $1, Stylized family. $1.20, Stylized teapot with face and legs.

1998, Aug. 13 ***Perf. 14x14½***

1685 A547 45c multicolored .60 .20
a. Booklet pane of 4 2.50
1686 A547 45c multicolored .60 .20
a. Booklet pane of 4 2.50
1687 A547 45c multicolored .60 .20
a. Booklet pane of 4 2.50

Size: 30x25mm

1688 A547 $1 multicolored 1.25 .40
a. Booklet pane of 2 2.50
1689 A547 $1.20 multicolored 1.50 .50
a. Booklet pane of 2 3.00
Complete booklet, #1685a, 1686a, 1687a, 1688a, 1689a, 1 postal card & 16 self-adhesive labels 14.00
Nos. 1685-1689 (5) 4.55 1.50

A548

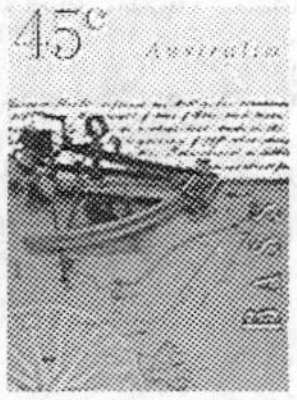

A549

Butterflies,

1998, Sept. 3 Litho. ***Perf. 14½x14***

1690 A548 45c Red lacewing .55 .20
1691 A548 45c Dull oakblue .55 .20
1692 A548 45c Meadow argus .55 .20
1693 A548 45c Ulysses .55 .20
1694 A548 45c Common red-eye .55 .20
a. Strip of 5, #1690-1694 2.75 1.00
b. Souvenir sheet of 5, #1690-1694 3.00 3.00

No. 1694b for China 1999 World Philatelic Exhibition. Issued 8/21/99.

Self-Adhesive
Serpentine Die Cut 11½

1695 A548 45c like #1690 .55 .20
1696 A548 45c like #1691 .55 .20
1697 A548 45c like #1692 .55 .20
1698 A548 45c like #1693 .55 .20
1699 A548 45c like #1694 .55 .20
a. Strip of 5, #1695-1699 2.75

1998, Sept. 10

#1700, Sextant, map of Bass Strait. #1701, Telescope, map of Van Diemen's Land (Tasmania).

1700 A549 45c multicolored .55 .20
1701 A549 45c multicolored .55 .20
a. Pair, #1700-1701 1.10 .40

Circumnavigation of Tasmania by George Bass (1771-c. 1803) and Matthew Flinders (1774-1814), bicent.

Marine Life
A550 A551

#1702, Fiery squid. #1703, Manta ray. #1704, Bottlenose dolphin. #1705, Weedy seadragon. #1706, Southern right whale. #1707, White pointer shark.

Perf. 14½x14, 14x14½

1998, Oct. 1 Litho.

1702 A550 45c multi .55 .20
1703 A550 45c multi, horiz. .55 .20
1704 A551 45c multi .55 .20
1705 A551 45c multi .55 .20
a. Pair, #1704-1705 1.10 .40

Size: 50x30mm

1706 A551 45c multi, horiz. .55 .20
1707 A551 45c multi .55 .20
a. Souvenir sheet, #1702-1707 3.30 1.20
Nos. 1702-1707 (6) 3.30 1.20

Booklet Stamps
Self-Adhesive
Serpentine Die Cut Perf. 11½

1708 A551 45c like #1704 .55 .20
1709 A551 45c like #1705 .55 .20
a. Booklet pane, 5 each #1708-1709 5.50

No. 1709a is a complete booklet. The peelable paper backing serves as a booklet cover. Nos. 1708-1709 also exist in coils.

Universal Declaration of Human Rights, 50th Anniv. — A552

1998, Oct. 22 Litho. ***Perf. 14½x14***

1712 A552 45c multicolored .60 .20

Christmas A553

40c, Magi. 45c, Nativity. $1, Journey to Bethlehem.

1998, Nov. 2 ***Perf. 14x14½***

1713 A553 40c multicolored .50 .20
1714 A553 45c multicolored .60 .20
1715 A553 $1 multicolored 1.25 .45
Nos. 1713-1715 (3) 2.35 .85

Booklet Stamp
Self-Adhesive
Serpentine Die Cut Perf. 11½

1716 A553 40c multicolored .50 .20
a. Booklet pane of 20 10.00

No. 1716a is a complete booklet.

Nationality and Citizenship Act, 50th Anniv. A554

1999, Jan. 14 Litho. ***Perf. 14x14½***

1717 A554 45c multicolored .55 .20

Die Cut Perf. 11¾
Self-Adhesive

1718 A554 45c multicolored .55 .20

Legends Type of 1997

Designs: Nos. 1719, 1721, Arthur Boyd, artist. Nos. 1720, 1722, "Nebuchadnezzar on Fire Falling over a Waterfall," by Boyd.

1999, Jan. 22 Litho. ***Perf. 14x14½***

1719 A522 45c multicolored .60 .20
1720 A522 45c multicolored .60 .20
a. Pair, #1719-1720 1.25 .40

Booklet Stamps
Self-Adhesive
Serpentine Die Cut Perf. 11½

1721 A522 45c multicolored .60 .20
1722 A522 45c multicolored .60 .20
a. Booklet pane, 5 each #1721-1722 6.00

No. 1722a is a complete booklet.

Love A555

1999, Feb. 4 ***Perf. 14x14½***

1723 A555 45c Red roses .60 .20

Booklet Stamp
Self-adhesive
Serpentine Die Cut Perf. 11½

1724 A555 45c like #1723 .60 .20
a. Booklet pane of 10 6.00

No. 1724a is a complete booklet.

Intl. Year of Older Persons A556

Designs: No. 1725, Woman walking with girl, man up close. No. 1726, Woman up close, man playing soccer with boy.

1999, Feb. 11 ***Perf. 14x14½***

1725 A556 45c multicolored .60 .20
1726 A556 45c multicolored .60 .20
a. Pair, #1725-1726 1.25 .40

Early Navigators Type of 1963

#1727: a, like #374. b, like #376. c, like #377.
#1728: a, like #375. b, like #379. c, like #378.

Perf. 14x14½, 14½x14

1999, Mar. 19 Litho.

1727 Sheet of 3 1.75 1.75
a.-c. A144 45c any single .55 .55
d. As #1727, imperf. 1.75 1.75
e. As #1727, perfin "A99" in sheet margin 1.75 1.75
1728 Sheet of 3 1.75 1.75
a.-c. A144 45c any single .55 .55
d. As #1728, imperf. 1.75 1.75
e. As #1728, perfin "A99" in sheet margin 1.75 1.75

Australia '99, World Stamp Expo.

Nos. 1727e-1728e were made from Nos. 1727d-1728d at Australia '99. Examples with the perforating and "A99" inverted were intentionally misperfed personally by patrons of the show.

Sailing Ships — A557 Olympic Torch — A558

1999, Mar. 19 ***Perf. 14½x14***

1729 A557 45c Polly Woodside .60 .20
a. Souvenir sheet of 2, #1729, Ireland #1169
1730 A557 85c Alma Doepel 1.10 .35
1731 A557 $1 Enterprize 1.25 .40
1732 A557 $1.05 Lady Nelson 1.40 .45

Australia '99, World Stamp Expo (#1729a).

No. 1729 was issued in sheets of 20 with a se-tenant label showing Australia '99 logo. Panes of 10 #1729 with labels were sold only at the show, where patrons could have their photos printed on the label.

1999, Mar. 22

1733 A558 $1.20 #289 1.60 .55

Flora & Fauna Type of 1963

Flowers: #1734, 1743, 1746B, Correa reflexa. #1735, 1744, 1746C, Hibbertia scandens. #1736, 1745, 1746D, Ipomoea pes-caprae. #1737, 1746, 1746E, Wahlenbergia stricta.

70c, Humpback whales, zebra volute. #1739, Brahminy kite, checkerboard helmet shell. #1740, Fraser Island, chambered nautilus. $1.05, Loggerhead turtle, baler. $1.20, White-bellied sea eagle, Campbell's stromb.

1999 Litho. *Perf. 14x14½*

1734 A511 45c multicolored .60 .20
1735 A511 45c multicolored .60 .20
1736 A511 45c multicolored .60 .20
1737 A511 45c multicolored .60 .20
a. Block of 4, #1734-1737 2.40 .80
1738 A511 70c multicolored .90 .30
1739 A511 90c multicolored 1.10 .40
1740 A511 90c multicolored 1.10 .40
a. Pair, #1739-1740 2.25 .80
1741 A511 $1.05 multicolored 1.40 .45
1742 A511 $1.20 multicolored 1.50 .50
Nos. 1734-1742 (9) 8.40 2.85

Booklet Stamps
Serpentine Die Cut 11
Self-Adhesive

1742A A511 45c like #1734 .60 .20
1742B A511 45c like #1735 .60 .20
1742C A511 45c like #1736 .60 .20
1742D A511 45c like #1737 .60 .20
e. Booklet pane, 3 each #1742A, 1742C, 2 each #1742B, 1742D 6.00

Die Cut perf. 12x12]¾

1743 A511 45c like #1734 .60 .20
1744 A511 45c like #1735 .60 .20
1745 A511 45c like #1736 .60 .20
1746 A511 45c like #1737 .60 .20
a. Booklet pane, 3 each #1743, 1745, 2 each #1744, #1746 6.00

Nos. 1742De, 1746a are complete booklets.

Coil Stamps
Serpentine Die Cut 11½

1746B A511 45c like #1734 .60 .20
1746C A511 45c like #1735 .60 .20
1746D A511 45c like #1736 .60 .20
1746E A511 45c like #1737 .60 .20
f. Strip of 4, #1746B-1746E 2.40

Issued: #1738-1742, 7/8; others, 4/8.

Queen Mother and Queen Elizabeth II — A559

1999, Apr. 15 *Perf. 14x14½*

1747 A559 45c multicolored .60 .20

Queen Elizabeth II, 73rd birthday.

Children's Television Programs — A560

Designs: #1748, 1753, "Here's Humphrey." #1749, 1754, "Bananas in Pajamas." #1750, 1755, "Mr. Squiggle." #1751, 1756, Teddy bears from "Play School." #1752, 1757, Clock, dog, boy from "Play School."

1999, May 6 Litho. *Perf. 14½x14*

1748 A560 45c multicolored .60 .20
1749 A560 45c multicolored .60 .20
1750 A560 45c multicolored .60 .20
1751 A560 45c multicolored .60 .20
1752 A560 45c multicolored .60 .20
a. Strip of 5, #1748-1752 3.00 1.00

Self-Adhesive
Serpentine Die Cut 11½x11¼

1753 A560 45c like #1748 .60 .20
1754 A560 45c like #1749 .60 .20
1755 A560 45c like #1750 .60 .20
1756 A560 45c like #1751 .60 .20
1757 A560 45c like #1752 .60 .20
a. Booklet pane, 2 each #1753-1757 6.00

No. 1757a is a complete booklet.

Perth Mint, Cent. A561

1999, May 13 Litho. *Perf. 14¼x14*

1758 A561 $2 gold & multi 2.50 1.25

Test Rugby in Australia, Cent. A562

#1759, 1763, Kicking ball, vert. #1760, 1764, Catching ball. $1, Diving with ball. $1.20, Being tackled.

1999, June 8 *Perf. 14½x14*

1759 A562 45c multi .60 .20
1760 A562 45c multi, vert. .60 .20
a. Pair, #1759-1760 1.20 .40

Perf. 14x14½

1761 A562 $1 multi 1.25 .40
1762 A562 $1.20 multi 1.50 .55

Serpentine Die Cut 11½
Self-Adhesive
Coil Stamps

1763 A562 45c like #1759 .60 .20
1764 A562 45c like #1760 .60 .20
a. Pair, #1763-1764 1.20

Snowy Mountains Hydroelectric Projects, 50th Anniv. — A563

#1765, Rock bolters at Tumut 2 Power Station Hall, driller at Tooma-Tumut Tunnel. #1766, English class for migrant workers at Cooma. #1767, Eucumbene Dam, Tumut 2 Tailwater Tunnel. #1768, Island Bend Dam, German carpenters.

1999, Aug. 12 Litho. *Perf. 14x14½*

1765 A563 45c multicolored .60 .20
1766 A563 45c multicolored .60 .20
1767 A563 45c multicolored .60 .20
1768 A563 45c multicolored .60 .20
a. Block of 4, #1765-1768 2.40 .80

Greetings — A564

A565

1999, Sept. 1 Litho. *Perf. 14½x14*

1773 A564 45c Teddy bear .60 .20
1774 A564 45c Birthday cake .60 .20
1775 A564 45c Roses, rings .60 .20
1776 A564 45c Pen, letter .60 .20
1777 A564 45c Christmas ornament .60 .20
1778 A564 $1 Koala 1.25 .40
Nos. 1773-1778 (6) 4.25 1.40

Nos. 1773-1778 each were printed with a se-tenant label at right in sheets of 20. Size of label is 24mm wide on No. 1777, 17mm on others. Labels were inscribed with phrases appropriate to the stamp design, or blank, upon which Australia Post printed photographs, sent to them through special orders.

1999, Sept. 14 Litho. *Perf. 14½x14*

1779 A565 45c multicolored .60 .20

2000 Olympic Games, Sydney.

Sydney Design 99, Intl. Design Congress A566

Designs: 45c, Australia Post emblem. 90c, Embryo chair. $1.35, Possum skin textile design. $1.50, Storey Hall, Royal Melbourne Institute of Technology.

1999, Sept. 16 Litho. *Perf. 14x14½*

1780 A566 45c multicolored .60 .20
1781 A566 90c multicolored 1.10 .40
1782 A566 $1.35 multicolored 1.75 .60
1783 A566 $1.50 multicolored 2.00 .65
Nos. 1780-1783 (4) 5.45 1.85

Pond Fauna — A567

Designs: Nos. 1784, 1790c, Roth's tree frog. Nos. 1785, 1790d, Dragonfly. Nos. 1786, 1790b, Sacred kingfisher. Nos. 1787, 1790f, Magnificent tree frog. Nos. 1788, 1790e, 1791, Northern dwarf tree frog. Nos. 1789, 1790a, 1792, Javelin frog.

1999, Oct. 1 Litho. *Perf. 14x14½*

1784 A567 45c multicolored .60 .20
1785 A567 45c multicolored .60 .20
a. Pair, #1784-1785 1.20 .40

Size: 26x38mm
Perf. 14½x14

1786 A567 45c multicolored .60 .20
1787 A567 45c multicolored .60 .20
a. Pair, #1786-1787 1.20 .40

Size: 24x30mm

1788 A567 50c multicolored .70 .25
1789 A567 50c multicolored .70 .25
a. Pair, #1788-1789 1.40 .50
Nos. 1784-1789 (6) 3.80 1.30

Souvenir Sheet
Perf. 14½

1790 A567 Sheet of 6, #a.-f 4.00 4.00

Booklet Stamps
Self-Adhesive
Size: 24x30mm
Serpentine Die Cut 11¼

1791 A567 50c multicolored .70 .25
1792 A567 50c multicolored .70 .25
a. Booklet pane, 5 each #1791-1792 7.00

No. 1790d has foil impression on dragonfly's wings.

No. 1792a is a complete booklet.

Numbers have been reserved for additional values in this set.

Christmas A568

1999, Nov. 1 *Perf. 14½x14*

1795 A568 40c Madonna and child, vert. .50 .20

Perf. 14x14½

1796 A568 $1 Tree 1.25 .40

Booklet Stamp
Self-Adhesive
Serpentine Die Cut 11¾

1797 A568 40c Like #1795 .50 .20
a. Booklet pane of 20 10.00

Celebrate 2000 — A569

1999, Nov. 1 Litho. *Perf. 14½x14*

1798 A569 45c multicolored .60 .20

No. 1798 has a holographic image. Soaking in water may affect hologram. No. 1798 printed with a se-tenant label at right in sheets of 20. Labels were inscribed "Celebrate 2000" or blank, upon which Australia Post printed photographs, sent to them through special orders.

AIR POST STAMPS

Airplane over Bush Lands — AP1

Unwmk.

1929, May 20 Engr. *Perf. 11*

C1 AP1 3p deep green 7.50 3.00
Never hinged 12.50
a. Booklet pane of 4 ('30) 125.00

Kingsford-Smith Type of 1931

1931, Mar. 19

C2 A8 6p gray violet 7.50 7.50
Never hinged 12.50

AP3

1931, Nov. 4

C3 AP3 6p olive brown 15.00 9.00
Never hinged 22.50

For overprint see No. CO1.

Mercury and Hemispheres AP4

1934, Dec. 1 *Perf. 11*

C4 AP4 1sh6p violet brown 30.00 1.75
Never hinged 75.00

Perf. 13x13½

1937, Oct. 22 **Wmk. 228**

C5 AP4 1sh6p violet brown 7.50 .25
Never hinged 12.50

Catalogue values for unused stamps in this section, from this point to the end of the section, are for Never Hinged items.

Mercury and Globe — AP5

1949, Sept. 1 *Perf. 14½*

C6 AP5 1sh6p sepia 1.75 .20

1956, Dec. 6 **Unwmk.**

C7 AP5 1sh6p sepia 16.00 .85

Super-Constellation over Globe — AP6

1958, Jan. 6 *Perf. 14½x14*

C8 AP6 2sh dark violet blue 2.50 1.75

Inauguration of Australian "Round the World" air service.

AIR POST OFFICIAL STAMP

No. C3 Overprinted **OS**

Perf. 11, 11½

1931, Nov. 17 **Unwmk.**

CO1 AP3 6p olive brown 25.00 *30.00*
Never hinged 40.00

Issued primarily for official use, but to prevent speculation, a quantity was issued for public distribution.

POSTAGE DUE STAMPS

Very fine examples of Nos. J1-J38 will have perforations touching the design on one or more sides due to the narrow spacing of the stamps on the plates. Stamps with perfs clear of the design on all four sides are scarce and will command higher prices.

D1

D2

1902 Typo. Wmk. 55 *Perf. 11½, 12*

J1 D1 ½p emerald 8.25 9.50
J2 D1 1p emerald 16.00 6.50
a. Perf. 11 *600.00 250.00*
J3 D1 2p emerald 20.00 7.75
J4 D1 3p emerald 30.00 10.00
J5 D1 4p emerald 35.00 10.00
J6 D1 6p emerald 45.00 19.00
J7 D1 8p emerald 125.00 110.00
J8 D1 5sh emerald 250.00 82.50
Nos. J1-J8 (8) 529.25 255.25

The 1p, 2p and 4p, type D1, exist also in perforations compounding 11 with 11½ & 12.

Perf. 11½, 12, 11 and 11 Compound with 11½, 12

1902-04

J9 D2 ½p emerald 7.25 8.25
a. Perf. 11 82.50 65.00
J10 D2 1p emerald 4.50 2.75
a. Perf. 11 110.00 37.50
J11 D2 2p emerald 15.00 3.50
J12 D2 3p emerald 55.00 8.75
J13 D2 4p emerald 50.00 6.00
J14 D2 5p emerald 50.00 16.00
a. Perf. 11 125.00 32.50
J15 D2 6p emerald 72.50 18.00
J16 D2 8p emerald 125.00 40.00
J17 D2 10p emerald 87.50 15.00
J18 D2 1sh emerald 57.50 14.00
a. Perf. 11 175.00 45.00
J19 D2 2sh emerald 110.00 25.00
J20 D2 5sh emerald 225.00 22.50
a. Perf. 11 375.00 150.00
J21 D2 10sh emerald *2,750. 1,050.*
J22 D2 20sh emerald *4,000. 1,900.*
Nos. J9-J20 (12) 859.25 179.75

Perf. 11½, 12 Compound with 11

1906 **Wmk. 12**

J23 D2 ½p emerald 14.00 10.00
J24 D2 1p emerald 30.00 5.50
a. Perf. 11 *650.00 250.00*
J25 D2 2p emerald 50.00 10.00
J26 D2 3p emerald 375.00 300.00
J27 D2 4p emerald 77.50 27.50
a. Perf. 11 *900.00 400.00*
J28 D2 6p emerald 225.00 22.50
Nos. J23-J28 (6) 771.50 375.50

1907 Wmk. 13 *Perf. 11½x11*

J29 D2 ½p emerald 45.00 45.00
J30 D2 1p emerald 72.50 45.00
J31 D2 2p emerald 165.00 100.00
J32 D2 4p emerald 225.00 125.00
J33 D2 6p emerald 325.00 140.00
Nos. J29-J33 (5) 832.50 455.00

D3

D4

Perf. 11 (2sh, 10sh, 20sh), 11½x11 (1sh, 5sh)

1908-09 **Wmk. 12**

J34 D3 1sh emer ('09) 125.00 16.00
J35 D3 2sh emerald *1,100. 500.00*
J36 D3 5sh emerald 225.00 52.50
J37 D3 10sh emerald *1,900. 1,750.*
J38 D3 20sh emerald *5,250. 5,000.*

Perf. 11, 12x12½, 12½, 14

1909 **Wmk. 13**

J39 D4 ½p green & car 8.75 3.50
J40 D4 1p green & car 11.00 1.65
J41 D4 2p green & car 14.00 1.90
J42 D4 3p green & car 22.50 6.50
J43 D4 4p green & car 25.00 3.75
J44 D4 6p green & car 22.50 3.50
J45 D4 1sh green & car 22.50 2.75
J46 D4 2sh green & car 82.50 14.00
J47 D4 5sh green & car 82.50 14.00
J48 D4 10sh green & car 350.00 300.00
J49 D4 £1 green & car 550.00 325.00
Nos. J39-J49 (11) 1,191. 676.55

1922-25 Wmk. 10 *Perf. 14, 11*

J50 D4 ½p grn & car ('23) 6.50 1.75
J51 D4 1p green & car 6.50 1.90
J52 D4 1½p yellow green & rose ('25) 3.75 3.25
J53 D4 2p green & car 8.00 3.75
J54 D4 3p green & car 15.00 2.75
J55 D4 4p green & car 19.00 2.25
J56 D4 6p green & car 22.50 13.00
Nos. J50-J56 (7) 81.25 28.65

1931-37 Wmk. 228 *Perf. 11, 14*

J57 D4 ½p yel green & rose ('34) 10.00 9.00
J58 D4 1p yel grn & rose 4.00 .75
J59 D4 2p yel grn & rose 4.00 .75
J60 D4 3p yel green & rose ('37) 125.00 42.50
J61 D4 4p yel green & rose ('34) 20.00 2.00
J62 D4 6p yel green & rose ('36) 350.00 300.00
J63 D4 1sh yel green & rose ('34) 50.00 17.50
Nos. J57-J63 (7) 563.00 372.50

D5

Engraved; Value Typo.

1938 *Perf. 14½x14*

J64 D5 ½p green & car .75 1.25
J65 D5 1p green & car 5.00 .50
J66 D5 2p green & car 4.50 .50
J67 D5 3p green & car 15.00 3.50
J68 D5 4p green & car 4.50 .25
J69 D5 6p green & car 45.00 17.50
J70 D5 1sh green & car 20.00 7.50
Nos. J64-J70 (7) 94.75 31.00

Catalogue values for unused stamps in this section, from this point to the end of the section, are for Never Hinged items.

Type of 1938
Value Tablet Redrawn

Original

Redrawn

Pence denominations: "D" has melon-shaped center in redrawn tablet. The redrawn 3p differs slightly, having semi-melon-shaped "D" center, with vertical white stroke half filling it.

1sh. 1938: Numeral "1" narrow, with six background lines above.

1sh. 1947: Numeral broader, showing more white space around dotted central ornament. Three lines above.

1946-57 **Wmk. 228**

J71 D5 ½p grn & car ('56) 2.75 1.40
J72 D5 1p grn & car ('47) 1.40 .25
J73 D5 2p green & car .85 1.00
J74 D5 3p green & car 4.50 .35
J75 D5 4p grn & car ('52) 5.50 .50
J76 D5 5p grn & car ('48) 8.25 1.25
J77 D5 6p grn & car ('47) 8.25 .65
J78 D5 7p grn & car ('53) 5.50 3.00
J79 D5 8p grn & car ('57) 13.50 11.50
J80 D5 1sh grn & car ('47) 13.50 1.25
Nos. J71-J80 (10) 64.00 21.15

1953-54

White Tablet, Carmine Numeral

J81 D5 1sh grn & car ('54) 9.00 5.00
J82 D5 2sh green & car 12.50 10.00
J83 D5 5sh green & car 17.50 2.50
Nos. J81-J83 (3) 39.00 17.50

Issued: 2sh, 5sh, Aug. 26; 1sh, Feb. 17.

Redrawn Type of 1947-57

Two Types of Some Pence Values:

Type I - Background lines touch numeral, "D" and period.

Type II - Lines do not touch numeral, etc.

Second engraving of 1sh has sharper and thicker lines.

The ½p type II has 7 dots under the "2."

The 8p type II has distinct lines in centers of "8" and between "8" and "D."

Engr.; Value Typo.

1958-60 Unwmk. *Perf. 14½x14*

J86 D5 ½p grn & car (II) 2.50 1.10
a. Six dots under the "2" 3.75 .95
J87 D5 1p grn & car (II) 2.50 .40
a. Type I 3.25 .40
J88 D5 3p grn & car (II) 2.50 .75
J89 D5 4p grn & car (I) 5.00 4.00
a. Type II ('59) 12.00 3.00
J90 D5 5p grn & car (I) 11.00 6.00
a. Type II ('59) 70.00 22.50
J91 D5 6p grn & car (II) 6.50 1.75
J92 D5 8p grn & car (II) 10.00 15.00
a. Indistinct lines 15.00 15.00
J93 D5 10p grn & car (II) 7.50 3.25

White Tablet, Carmine Numeral

J94 D5 1sh green & car 8.50 2.50
a. 2nd redrawing ('60) 9.00 .60
J95 D5 2sh grn & car 26.00 5.50
Nos. J86-J95 (10) 82.00 40.25

Issued: 1sh, 9/8/58; 10p, 12/9/59; 2sh, 3/8/60; 3p, 6p, 5/25/60; others, 2/27/58.

MILITARY STAMPS

Nos. 166, 191, 183A, 173, 175, 206 and 177 Overprinted in Black:

B.C.O.F. JAPAN 1946	**B.C.O.F. JAPAN 1946**	B. C. O. F. JAPAN 1946
a	b	c

Perf. 14½x14, 15x14, 11½, 13½x13

1946-47 **Wmk. 228**

M1 A24(a) ½p orange 2.75 2.75
Never hinged 3.50
M2 A36(b) 1p brown vio 2.25 2.25
Never hinged 3.00
a. Blue overprint 100.00 67.50
Never hinged 125.00
M3 A27(b) 3p dk vio brn 2.00 .75
Never hinged 2.75
M4 A30(a) 6p brn violet 5.00 5.00
Never hinged 6.50
M5 A16(a) 1sh gray green 7.50 7.50
Never hinged 10.00
M6 A1 (c) 2sh dk red brn 22.50 22.50
Never hinged 30.00
M7 A32(c) 5sh dl red brn 110.00 100.00
Never hinged 150.00
Nos. M1-M7 (7) 152.00 140.75

"B.C.O.F." stands for "British Commonwealth Occupation Force."

Forged overprints of Nos. M6-M7 exist.

Issued: #M1-M3, 10/11/46; #M4-M7, 5/8/47.

OFFICIAL STAMPS

Perforated Initials

In 1913-31, postage stamps were perforated "OS" for federal official use. The Scott Standard Catalogues do not list officials with perforated initials, but listings for these Australian stamps will be found in the Scott Classic Specialized Catalogue.

Overprinted Official stamps are comparatively more difficult to find well centered than the basic issues on which they are printed. This is because poorly centered sheets were purposely chosen to be overprinted.

Overprinted **OS**

On Regular Issue of 1931

1931, May 4 Unwmk. *Perf. 11, 11½*

O1 A8 2p dull red 60.00 22.50
O2 A8 3p blue 175.00 35.00

These stamps were issued primarily for official use but to prevent speculation a quantity was issued for public distribution.

Used values are for cto copies.

Counterfeit overprints exist.

On Regular Issues of 1928-32

1932 Wmk. 203 *Perf. 13½x12½*

O3 A4 2p red (II) 10.00 .90
O4 A4 4p olive bister 30.00 6.00

Perf. 11½, 12

O5 A1 6p brown 67.50 35.00

1932-33 Wmk. 228 *Perf. 13½x12½*

O6 A4 ½p orange 6.00 1.25
a. Inverted overprint *3,000. 1,500.*
O7 A4 1p green (I) 2.00 .75
O8 A4 2p red (II) 5.00 .60
a. Inverted overprint 2,250.
O9 A4 3p ultra (II) ('33) 14.00 7.50
O10 A4 5p brown buff 42.50 21.00
a. Wmk. 203 —

Perf. 11½, 12

O11 A1 6p yellow brown 35.00 25.00
a. Inverted overprint —
Nos. O6-O11 (6) 104.50 56.10

1932 Unwmk. *Perf. 11, 11½*

O12 A9 2p red 5.50 4.50
O13 A9 3p blue 18.00 18.00
O14 A16 1sh gray green 55.00 32.50
Nos. O12-O14 (3) 78.50 55.00

AUSTRALIAN ANTARCTIC TERRITORY

Catalogue values for all unused stamps in this section are for Never Hinged items.

All stamps are also valid for postage in Australia.

Edgeworth David, Douglas Mawson and A.F. McKay (1908-09 South Pole Expedition) — A1

Australian Explorers and Map of Antarctica — A2

Designs: 8p, Loading weasel (snow truck). 1sh, Dog team and iceberg, vert. 2sh3p, Emperor penguins and map, vert.

Perf. 14½, 14½x14, 14x14½

1957-59	**Engr.**	**Unwmk.**		
L1	A1	5p brown	.50	.20
L2	A2	8p dark blue	2.25	1.25
L3	A2	1sh dark green	4.00	2.10
L4	A2	2sh ultra ('57)	3.50	.35
L5	A2	2sh3p green	12.00	6.00
		Nos. L1-L5 (5)	22.25	9.90

Nos. L1 and L2 were printed as 4p and 7p stamps and surcharged typographically in black and dark blue before issuance.

Sizes of stamps: No. L2, 34x21mm; Nos. L3, L5, 21x34mm; No. L4, 43½x25½mm.

1961, July 5		***Perf. 14½***		
L6	A1	5p dark blue	1.10	.20

The denomination on No. L6 is not within a typographed circle, but is part of the engraved design.

Sir Douglas Mawson A3

Lookout and Iceberg A4

1961, Oct. 18				
L7	A3	5p dark green	.70	.20

50th anniv. of the 1911-14 Australian Antarctic Expedition.

Perf. 13½x13, 13x13½

1966-68	**Photo.**	**Unwmk.**		

Designs: 1c, Aurora australis and camera dome. 2c, Banding penguins. 5c, Branding of elephant seals. 7c, Measuring snow strata. 10c, Wind gauges. 15c, Weather balloon. 20c, Helicopter. 25c, Radio operator. 50c, Ice compression tests. $1, "Mock sun" (parahelion) and dogs. 20c, 25c, 50c and $1 horizontal.

L8	A4	1c multicolored	.55	.30
L9	A4	2c multicolored	1.00	.45
L10	A4	4c multicolored	1.10	.45
L11	A4	5c multicolored	1.75	1.25
L12	A4	7c multicolored	.55	.35
L13	A4	10c multicolored	2.50	.90
L14	A4	15c multicolored	3.25	3.25
L15	A4	20c multicolored	7.00	4.00
L16	A4	25c multicolored	4.00	4.25
L17	A4	50c multicolored	21.00	8.00
L18	A4	$1 multicolored	27.50	18.00
		Nos. L8-L18 (11)	70.20	41.20

Issued: 5c, 9/25/68; others, 9/28/66.

Nos. L8-L18 are on phosphorescent helecon paper. Fluorescent orange is one of the colors used in printing the 10c, 15c, 20c and 50c.

Sastrugi Snow Formation A5

1971, June 23	**Photo.**	***Perf. 13x13½***		
L19	A5	6c shown	.55	.55
L20	A5	30c Pancake ice	6.00	6.00

10th anniv. of the Antarctic Treaty pledging peaceful uses of and scientific cooperation in Antarctica.

Capt. Cook, Sextant, Azimuth Compass A6

Design: 35c, Chart of Cook's circumnavigation of Antarctica, and "Resolution."

Perf. 13x13½

1972, Sept. 13		**Photo.**		
L21	A6	7c bister & multi	2.00	.95
L22	A6	35c buff & multi	5.50	6.00

Bicentenary of Capt. James Cook's circumnavigation of Antarctica.

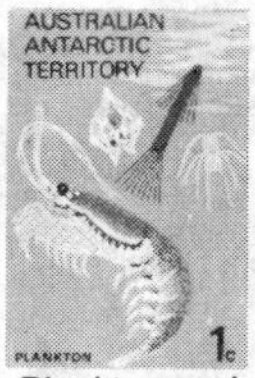

Plankton and Krill Shrimp — A7

Mawson's D.H. Gipsy Moth, 1931 — A8

Food Chain (Essential for Survival): 7c, Adelie penguin feeding on krill shrimp. 9c, Leopard seal pursuing fish, horiz. 10c, Killer whale hunting seals, horiz. 20c, Wandering albatross, horiz. $1, Sperm whale attacking giant squid.

Explorers' Aircraft: 8c, Rymill's DH Fox Moth returning to Barry Island. 25c, Hubert Wilkins Lockheed Vega, horiz. 30c, Lincoln Ellsworth's Northrop Gamma. 35c, Lars Christensen's Avro Avian and Framnes Mountains, horiz. 50c, Richard Byrd's Ford Tri-Motor dropping US flag over South Pole.

Perf. 13½x13, 13x13½

1973, Aug. 15				
L23	A7	1c multicolored	.20	.20
L24	A8	5c multicolored	.20	.20
L25	A7	7c multicolored	1.40	.60
L26	A8	8c multicolored	.30	.30
L27	A7	9c multicolored	.25	.25
L28	A7	10c multicolored	3.00	1.25
L29	A7	20c multicolored	.35	.35
L30	A8	25c multicolored	.35	.35
L31	A8	30c multicolored	.35	.35
L32	A8	35c multicolored	.30	.45
L33	A8	50c multicolored	1.25	.85
L34	A7	$1 multicolored	2.25	.85
		Nos. L23-L34 (12)	10.20	6.00

Adm. Byrd, Plane, Mountains A9

Design: 20c, Adm. Byrd, Floyd Bennett trimotored plane, map of Antarctica.

1979, June 20	**Litho.**	***Perf. 15½***		
L35	A9	20c multicolored	.50	.50
L36	A9	55c multicolored	1.00	.95

50th anniv. of first flight over South Pole by Richard Byrd (1888-1957).

"S.Y. Nimrod" A10

2c, 5c, 22c, 25c, 40c, 55c, $1 are vertical. No. L41 actually pictures the S.S. Morning.

Perf. 13½x13, 13x13½

1974-81		**Litho.**		
L37	A10	1c S.Y. Aurora	.20	.20
L38	A10	2c R.Y. Penola	.20	.20
L39	A10	5c M.V. Thala Dan	.20	.20
L40	A10	10c H.M.S. Challenger	.20	.20
L41	A10	15c shown	.95	.95
L42	A10	15c S.Y. Nimrod, stern view	.25	.20
L43	A10	20c R.R.S. Discovery II	.30	.30
L44	A10	22c R.Y.S. Terra Nova	.30	.30
L45	A10	25c S.S. Endurance	.40	.35
L46	A10	30c S.S. Fram	.50	.50
L47	A10	35c M.S. Nella Dan	.45	.45
L48	A10	40c M.S. Kista Dan	.50	.50
L49	A10	45c L'Astrolabe	.55	.55
L50	A10	50c S.S. Norvegia	.70	.70
L51	A10	55c S.Y. Discovery	.80	.80
L52	A10	$1 H.M.S. Resolution	1.25	.65
		Nos. L37-L52 (16)	7.75	7.05

A11

A12

1982, May 5	**Litho.**	***Perf. 14x13½***		
L53	A11	27c Mawson, landscape	.35	.35
L54	A11	75c Mawson, map	1.25	1.25

Sir Douglas Mawson (1882-1958), explorer.

1983, Apr. 6	**Litho.**	***Perf. 14½***		

Local Wildlife: a, Light-mantled sooty albatross. b, Macquarie Isld. shags. c, Elephant seals. d, Royal penguins. e, Antarctic prions.

L55		Strip of 5, multi	2.25	2.25
a.-e.		A12 27c, any single	.45	.45

12th Antarctic Treaty Consultative Meeting, Canberra, Sept. 13-27 — A13

1983, Sept. 7	**Litho.**	***Perf. 14½***		
L56	A13	27c multicolored	.40	.40

South Magnetic Pole Expedition, 75th Anniv. — A14

1984, Jan. 16				
L57	A14	30c Prismatic compass	.40	.40
L58	A14	85c Aneroid barometer	1.25	1.25

Dog Team, Mawson Station — A15

1984-87	**Litho.**	***Perf. 14½x15***		
L60	A15	2c Summer afternoon	.20	.20
L61	A15	5c shown	.20	.20
L62	A15	10c Evening	.20	.20
L63	A15	15c Prince Charles Mts.	.20	.20
L64	A15	20c Morning	.30	.30
L65	A15	25c Sea ice, iceberg	.40	.40
L66	A15	30c Mt. Coates	.50	.50
L67	A15	33c Iceberg Alley, Mawson	.50	.50
L68	A15	36c Winter evening	.50	.50
L69	A15	45c Brash ice, vert.	.65	.65
L70	A15	60c Midwinter shadows	.85	.85
L71	A15	75c Coastline	1.10	1.10
L72	A15	85c Landing field	1.35	1.35
L73	A15	90c Pancake ice, vert.	1.25	1.25
L74	A15	$1 Emperor penguins, Auster Rookery	1.50	1.50
		Nos. L60-L74 (15)	9.70	9.70

Issued: 5, 25, 30, 75, 85c, 7/18/84; 15, 33, 45, 90c, $1, 8/7/85; 2, 10, 20, 36, 60c, 3/11/87.

A16

A17

1986, Sept. 17	**Litho.**	***Perf. 14x13½***		
L75	A16	36c multicolored	.55	.55

Antarctic Treaty, 25th anniv.

1988, July 20	**Litho.**	***Perf. 13***		

Environment, Conservation and Technology: a, Hour-glass dolphins and the *Nella Dan*. b, Emperor penguins and Davis Station. c, Crabeater seal and helicopters. d, Adelie penguins and snow-ice transport vehicle. e, Gray-headed albatross and photographer.

L76		Strip of 5	3.10	1.20
a.-e.		A17 37c any single	.60	.20

Paintings by Sir Sidney Nolan (b. 1917) — A18

1989, June 14	**Litho.**	***Perf. 14x13½***		
L77	A18	39c *Antarctica*	.65	.65
L78	A18	39c *Iceberg Alley*	.65	.65
L79	A18	60c *Glacial Flow*	1.00	1.00
L80	A18	80c *Frozen Sea*	1.35	1.35
		Nos. L77-L80 (4)	3.65	3.65

Aurora Australis A19

Design: $1.20, Research ship Aurora Australis.

1991, June 20	**Litho.**	***Perf. 14½***		
L81	A19	43c multicolored	.65	.20
L82	A19	$1.20 multicolored	1.90	.65

Antarctic Treaty, 30th anniv. (No. L81).

Regional Wildlife A20

Perf. 14x14½, 14½x14

1992-93			**Litho.**		
L83	A20	45c	Adelie penguin	.60	.25
L84	A20	75c	Elephant seal	.95	.35
L85	A20	85c	Northern giant petrel	1.10	.40
L86	A20	95c	Weddell seal	1.25	.45
L86A	A20	$1	Royal penguins	1.25	.50
L87	A20	$1.20	Emperor penguin, vert.	1.50	.60
L88	A20	$1.40	Fur seals	1.65	.70
L89	A20	$1.50	King penguins, vert.	1.90	.75
			Nos. L83-L89 (8)	10.20	4.00

Issued: $1, $1.40, $1.50, 1/14/93; others, 5/14/92.

The Last Huskies A21

1994, Jan. 13 Litho. *Perf. 14½*

L90 A21	45c Dog up close, vert.	.65	.20
L91 A21	75c Sled team	1.10	.35
L92 A21	85c Dog seated, vert.	1.25	.40
L93 A21	$1.05 Three dogs	1.50	.50
	Nos. L90-L93 (4)	4.50	1.45

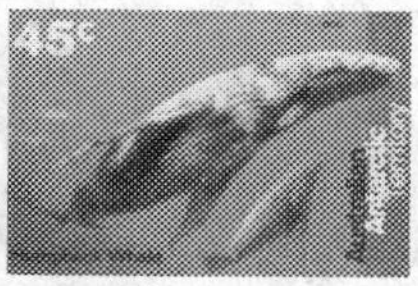

Whales & Dolphins A22

1995, June 15 Litho. *Perf. 14½*

L94 A22	45c Humpback whale	.65	.20
L95 A22	45c Hourglass dolphin, vert.	.65	.20
L96 A22	45c Minke whale, vert.	.65	.20
a.	Pair, #L95-L96	1.30	.45
L97 A22	$1 Killer whale	1.40	.50
a.	Souvenir sheet of 4, #L94-L97	3.50	3.50
b.	As "a," overprinted	3.50	3.50
c.	As "a," overprinted	3.50	3.50
	Nos. L94-L97 (4)	3.35	1.10

No. L97b is overprinted in gold in sheet margin with Singapore '95 emblem and: "Australia Post Exhibition Sheet No. 2," and, in both Chinese and English, with "Singapore 95 World Stamp Exhibition."

No. L97c is overprinted in gold in sheet margin with exhibition emblem, "Australian Post Exhibition Sheet No. 3" and "CAPEX '96 WORLD PHILATELIC EXHIBITION / EXPOSITION PHILATELIQUE MONDIALE"

Issued: #L97b, 9/1/95; #L97c, 6/15/96.

Landscapes, by Christian Clare Robertson — A23

#L98, Rafting sea ice. #L99, Shadow on the Plateau. $1, Ice cave. $1.20, Twelve Lake.

1996, May 16 Litho. *Perf. 14½x14*

L98 A23	45c multicolored	.70	.25
L99 A23	45c multicolored	.70	.25
a.	Pair, Nos. L98-L99	1.40	.50
L100 A23	$1 multicolored	1.60	.50
L101 A23	$1.20 multicolored	1.90	.60
	Nos. L98-L101 (4)	4.90	1.60

Australian Natl. Antarctic Research Expeditions, 50th Anniv. A24

Designs: No. L102, Apple field huts. No. L103, Inside an apple hut. 95c, Summer surveying. $1.05, Sea ice research. $1.20, Remote field camp.

1997, May 15 Litho. *Perf. 14x14½*

L102 A24	45c multicolored	.70	.20
L103 A24	45c multicolored	.70	.20
a.	Pair, #L102-L103	1.40	.40
L104 A24	95c multicolored	1.50	.45
L105 A24	$1.05 multicolored	1.65	.50
L106 A24	$1.20 multicolored	1.90	.55
	Nos. L102-L106 (5)	6.45	1.90

Modes of Transportion A25

Designs: No. L107, Snowmobile. No. L108, Ship, "Aurora Australis." $1, Helicopter airlifting a four-wheel drive ATV, vert. $2, Antarctic Hagglunds (rubber-tracked vehicles with fiberglass cabins), vert.

Perf. 14x14½, 14½x14

1998, Mar. 5 Litho.

L107 A25	45c multicolored	.60	.20
L108 A25	45c multicolored	.60	.20
a.	Pair, #L107-L108	1.20	.40
L109 A25	$1 multicolored	1.30	.45
L110 A25	$2 multicolored	2.60	.90
	Nos. L107-L110 (4)	5.10	1.75

Preservation of Huts used During Mawson's Antarctic Expedition — A26

#L111, Photograph of Mawson, sailing ship Aurora. #L112, Photograph, "Home of the Blizzard," by Frank Hurley. 90c, Photograph, "Huskie Team," by Xavier Mertz. $1.35, Huts restoration.

1999, May 13 Litho. *Perf. 14x14½*

L111 A26	45c multicolored	.60	.20
L112 A26	45c multicolored	.60	.20
a.	Pair, #L111-L112	1.25	.40
L113 A26	90c multicolored	1.25	.40
L114 A26	$1.35 multicolored	1.75	.60
	Nos. L111-L114 (4)	4.20	1.40

AUSTRIA

'os-trē-ə

LOCATION — Central Europe
GOVT. — Republic
AREA — 32,378 sq. mi.
POP. — 8,139,299 (1999 est.)
CAPITAL — Vienna

Before 1867 Austria was an absolute monarchy, which included Hungary and Lombardy-Venetia. In 1867 the Austro-Hungarian Monarchy was established, with Austria and Hungary as equal partners. After World War I, in 1918, the different nationalities established their own states and only the German-speaking parts remained, forming a republic under the name "Deutschosterreich" (German Austria), which was shortly again changed to "Austria." In 1938 German forces occupied Austria, which became part of the German Reich. After the liberation by Allied troops in 1945, an independent republic was re-established.

60 Kreuzer = 1 Gulden
100 Neu-Kreuzer = 1 Gulden (1858)
100 Heller = 1 Krone (1899)
100 Groschen = 1 Schilling (1925)

Catalogue values for unused stamps in this country are for Never Hinged items, beginning with Scott 432 in the regular postage section, Scott B165 in the semi-postal section, Scott C47 in the airpost section, Scott J175 in the postage due section, and Scott 4N1 in the AMG section.

Unused stamps without gum sell for about one-third or less of the values quoted.

Watermarks

Wmk. 91 - "BRIEF-MARKEN" In Double-lined Capitals Across the Middle of the Sheet

Wmk. 140 - Crown

Issues of the Austrian Monarchy (including Hungary)

Coat of Arms — A1

NINE KREUZER

Type I. One heavy line around coat of arms center. On the 9kr the top of "9" is about on a level with "Kreuzer" and not near the top of the label. Each cliche has the "9" in a different position.

Type IA. As type I, but with 1¼mm between "9" and "K."

Type II. One heavy line around coat of arms center. On the 9kr the top of "9" is much higher than the top of the word "Kreuzer" and nearly touches the top of the label.

Type III. As type II, but with two, thinner, lines around the center.

Wmk. K.K.H.M. in Sheet or Unwmk.
1850 Typo. *Imperf.*

The stamps of this issue were at first printed on a rough hand-made paper, varying in thickness and having a watermark in script letters K.K.H.M., the initials of Kaiserlich Königliches Handels-Ministerium (Imperial and Royal Ministry of Commerce), vertically in the gutter between the panes. Parts of these letters show on margin stamps in the sheet. From 1854 a thick, smooth machine-made paper without watermark was used.

Thin to Thick Paper

1	A1 1kr yellow	1,000.	70.00
a.	Printed on both sides	*1,900.*	130.00
b.	1kr orange	1,100.	100.00
c.	1kr brown orange	1,900.	375.00
2	A1 2kr black	1,000.	60.00
a.	Ribbed paper	—	*1,650.*
b.	2kr gray black	1,150.	70.00
d.	Half used as 1kr on cover		*25,000.*
3	A1 3kr red	350.00	3.00
a.	Ribbed paper	*1,900.*	95.00
b.	Laid paper	—	*9,000.*
c.	Printed on both sides		*7,500.*
4	A1 6kr brown	550.00	4.25
a.	Ribbed paper		*1,350.*
c.	Diagonal half used as 3kr on cover		*10,000.*
5	A1 9kr blue, type II	700.00	3.00
a.	9kr blue, type I	*1,150.*	7.50
b.	9kr blue, type IA	*13,500.*	*1,000.*
c.	Laid paper, type III		*6,750.*
d.	Printed on both sides, type II		*7,500.*

1854

Machine-made Paper, Type III

1d	A1	1kr yellow	*800.00*	70.00
2c	A1	2kr black	*725.00*	55.00
3e	A1	3kr red	*275.00*	2.10
f.		3kr red, type I	*2,150.*	27.50
4b	A1	6kr brown	*450.00*	3.50
5e	A1	9kr blue	*525.00*	2.25

In 1852-54, Nos. 1 to 5, rouletted 14, were used in Tokay and Homonna. A 12kr blue exists, but was not issued.

The reprints are type III in brighter colors, some on paper watermarked "Briefmarken" in the sheet.

For similar design see Lombardy-Venetia A1.

Emperor Franz Josef

A2 A3 A4

A5 A6

1858-59 Embossed *Perf. 14½*

Two Types of Each Value.

Type I. Loops of the bow at the back of the head broken, except the 2kr. In the 2kr, the "2" has a flat foot, thinning to the right. The frame line in the UR corner is thicker than the line below. In the 5kr the top frame line is unbroken.

Type II. Loops complete. Wreath projects further at top of head. In the 2kr, the "2" has a more curved foot of uniform thickness, with a shading line in the upper and lower curves. The frame line UR is thicker than the line below. In the 5kr the top frame line is broken.

6	A2 2kr yellow, type II	675.00	42.50
a.	2kr yellow, type I	1,750.	350.00
b.	2kr orange, type II	1,800.	225.00
c.	Half used as 1kr on cover		*25,000.*
7	A3 3kr black, type II	*1,900.*	175.00
a.	3kr black, type I	1,100.	225.00
8	A3 3kr green, type II ('59)	925.00	140.00
9	A4 5kr red, type II	225.00	.85
a.	5kr red, type I	350.00	11.50
b.	5kr red, type II with type I frame	400.00	20.00
10	A5 10kr brown, type II	550.00	2.50
a.	10kr brown, type I	625.00	27.50
b.	Half used as 5kr on cover		*11,000.*
11	A6 15kr blue, type II	525.00	1.90
a.	Type I	1,050.	12.50
b.	Half used as 7kr on cover		—

The reprints are of type II and are perforated 10½, 11, 12, 12½ and 13. There are also imperforate reprints of Nos. 6 to 8.

For similar designs see Lombardy-Venetia A2-A6.

Franz Josef — A7

Coat of Arms — A8

1860-61 Embossed *Perf. 14*

12	A7	2kr yellow	300.00	25.00
a.		Half used as 1kr on cover		*12,500.*
13	A7	3kr green	275.00	22.50
14	A7	5kr red	175.00	.75
15	A7	10kr brown	275.00	1.75
a.		Half used as 5kr on cover		*5,500.*
16	A7	15kr blue	275.00	1.00

The reprints are perforated 9, 9½, 10, 10½, 11, 11½, 12, 12½, 13 and 13½.

There are also imperforate reprints of the 2 and 3kr.

For similar design see Lombardy-Venetia A7. For overprints see Poland Nos. J11-J12.

1863

17	A8	2kr yellow	450.00	80.00
a.		Half used as 1kr on cover		*12,500.*
18	A8	3kr green	350.00	75.00
19	A8	5kr rose	300.00	7.00
20	A8	10kr blue	775.00	8.25
21	A8	15kr yellow brown	950.00	10.00

For similar design see Lombardy-Venetia A1.

Wmk. 91, or, before July 1864, Unwmkd.

1863-64 *Perf. 9½*

22	A8	2kr yellow ('64)	125.00	10.00
a.		Ribbed paper		325.00
b.		Half used as 1kr on cover		*12,500.*
23	A8	3kr green ('64)	125.00	10.00
24	A8	5kr rose	45.00	.40
a.		Ribbed paper		350.00
25	A8	10kr blue	140.00	2.50
a.		Half used as 5kr on cover		*11,000.*
26	A8	15kr yellow brown	140.00	1.50
		Nos. 22-26 (5)	575.00	24.40

The reprints are perforated 10½, 11½, 13 and 13½. There are also imperforate reprints of the 2 and 3kr.

Issues of Austro-Hungarian Monarchy

From 1867 to 1871 the independent postal administrations of Austria and Hungary used the same stamps.

A9

A10

5 kr:

Type I. In arabesques in lower left corner, the small ornament at left of the curve nearest the figure "5" is short and has three points at bottom.

Type II. The ornament is prolonged within the curve and has two points at bottom. The corresponding ornament at top of the lower left corner does not touch the curve (1872).

Type III. Similar to type II but the top ornament is joined to the curve (1881). Two different printing methods were used for the 1867-74 issues. The first produced stamps on which the hair and whiskers were coarse and thick, from the second they were fine and clear.

1867-72 Wmk. 91 Typo. *Perf. 9½*

Coarse Print

27	A9	2kr yellow	85.00	1.75
a.		Half used as 1kr on cover		*12,500.*
28	A9	3kr green	80.00	2.00
29	A9	5kr rose, type I	55.00	.20
a.		5kr rose, type II	50.00	.20
b.		Perf. 10½, type II	125.00	
c.		Cliché of 3kr in plate of 5kr		*52,500.*
30	A9	10kr blue	165.00	2.25
a.		Half used as 5kr on cover		*15,000.*
31	A9	15kr brown	140.00	4.25
32	A9	25kr lilac	20.00	12.50
b.		25kr brown violet	125.00	32.50

Perf. 12

33	A10	50kr light brown	27.50	*90.00*
a.		50kr pale red brown	275.00	100.00
b.		50kr brownish rose	325.00	175.00
c.		Pair, imperf. btwn., vert. or horizontal	700.00	*1,000.*

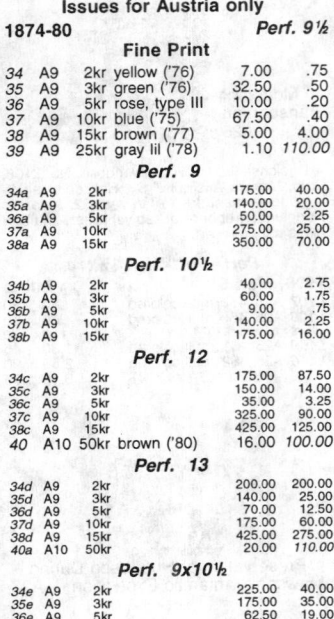

Issues for Austria only

1874-80 *Perf. 9½*

Fine Print

34	A9	2kr yellow ('76)	7.00	.75
35	A9	3kr green ('76)	32.50	.50
36	A9	5kr rose, type III	10.00	.20
37	A9	10kr blue ('75)	67.50	.40
38	A9	15kr brown ('77)	5.00	4.00
39	A9	25kr gray lil ('78)	1.10	*110.00*

Perf. 9

34a	A9	2kr	175.00	40.00
35a	A9	3kr	140.00	20.00
36a	A9	5kr	50.00	2.25
37a	A9	10kr	275.00	25.00
38a	A9	15kr	350.00	70.00

Perf. 10½

34b	A9	2kr	40.00	2.75
35b	A9	3kr	60.00	1.75
36b	A9	5kr	9.00	.75
37b	A9	10kr	140.00	2.25
38b	A9	15kr	175.00	16.00

Perf. 12

34c	A9	2kr	175.00	87.50
35c	A9	3kr	150.00	14.00
36c	A9	5kr	35.00	3.25
37c	A9	10kr	325.00	90.00
38c	A9	15kr	425.00	125.00
40	A10	50kr brown ('80)	16.00	*100.00*

Perf. 13

34d	A9	2kr	200.00	200.00
35d	A9	3kr	140.00	25.00
36d	A9	5kr	70.00	12.50
37d	A9	10kr	175.00	60.00
38d	A9	15kr	425.00	275.00
40a	A10	50kr	20.00	*110.00*

Perf. 9x10½

34e	A9	2kr	225.00	40.00
35e	A9	3kr	175.00	35.00
36e	A9	5kr	62.50	19.00
37e	A9	10kr	200.00	50.00

Various compound perforations exist.

Values are for stamps that do not show the watermark. Stamps showing the watermark often sell for more.

For similar designs see Offices in the Turkish Empire A1-A2.

A11

Perf. 9, 9½, 10, 10½, 11½, 12, 12½

1883

Inscriptions in Black

41	A11	2kr brown	5.50	.50
42	A11	3kr green	4.75	.30
43	A11	5kr rose	11.00	.25
a.		Vert. pair, imperf. btwn.	250.00	350.00
44	A11	10kr blue	4.25	.35
45	A11	20kr gray	55.00	3.25
46	A11	50kr red lilac	300.00	52.50

The last printings of Nos. 41-46 are watermarked "ZEITUNGS-MARKEN" instead of "BRIEF-MARKEN." Values are for stamps that do not show watermark. Stamps with watermarks that are identifiable as being from "BRIEF-MARKEN" sheets often sell for slightly more, while those with watermarks identifying stamps from "ZEITUNGS-MARKEN" sheets often sell for considerably more.

The 5kr has been reprinted in a dull red rose, perforated 10½.

For similar design see Offices in the Turkish Empire A3.

For surcharges see Offices in the Turkish Empire Nos. 15-19.

A12

A13

Perf. 9 to 13½, also Compound

1890-96 Unwmk.

Granite Paper

Numerals in black, Nos. 51-61

51	A12	1kr dark gray	1.25	.25
a.		Pair, imperf. between	160.00	350.00
52	A12	2kr light brown	.25	.25
53	A12	3kr gray green	.40	.25
a.		Pair, imperf. between	175.00	425.00
54	A12	5kr rose	.40	.25
a.		Pair, imperf. between	160.00	325.00
55	A12	10kr ultramarine	.75	.25
a.		Pair, imperf. between	200.00	425.00
56	A12	12kr claret	2.00	.35
a.		Pair, imperf. between	—	—
57	A12	15kr lilac	1.25	.35
a.		Pair, imperf. between	200.00	425.00
58	A12	20kr olive green	30.00	2.00
59	A12	24kr gray blue	2.00	1.25
a.		Pair, imperf. between	225.00	425.00
60	A12	30kr dark brown	2.50	.65
61	A12	50kr violet	5.00	7.50

Engr.

62	A13	1gld dark blue	1.50	2.25
63	A13	1gld pale lilac ('96)	35.00	3.50
64	A13	2gld carmine	3.50	12.50
65	A13	2gld gray green ('96)	15.00	27.50
		Nos. 51-65 (15)	100.80	59.10

Nearly all values of the 1890-1907 issues are found with numerals missing in one or more corners, some with numerals printed on the back.

For surcharges see Offices in the Turkish Empire Nos. 20-25, 28-31.

A14

Perf. 9 to 13½, also Compound

1891 Typo.

Numerals in black

66	A14	20kr olive green	2.25	.25
67	A14	24kr gray blue	4.50	.75
68	A14	30kr brown	2.25	.25
a.		Pair, imperf. between	225.00	350.00
b.		Perf. 9	100.00	32.50
69	A14	50kr violet	2.75	.40
		Nos. 66-69 (4)	11.75	1.65

For surcharges see Offices in the Turkish Empire Nos. 26-27.

A15

A16

A17

A18

Perf. 10½ to 13½ and Compound

1899

Without Varnish Bars

Numerals in black, Nos. 70-82

70	A15	1h lilac	.55	.20
b.		Imperf.	55.00	100.00
c.		Perf. 10½	15.00	4.50
d.		Numerals inverted	375.00	950.00
71	A15	2h dark gray	2.50	.50
72	A15	3h bister brown	5.00	.20
b.		"3" in lower right corner sideways		*1,100.*
73	A15	5h blue green	7.25	.20
c.		Perf. 10½	10.50	2.75
74	A15	6h orange	.40	.20
75	A16	10h rose	8.00	.20
b.		Perf. 10½	300.00	125.00
76	A16	20h brown	.60	.20
77	A16	25h ultramarine	50.00	.30
78	A16	30h red violet	14.50	2.25
b.		Horiz. pair, imperf. btwn.	275.00	—
80	A17	40h green	25.00	2.50
81	A17	50h gray blue	16.00	3.50
b.		All four "50's" parallel		*1,600.*
82	A17	60h brown	35.00	1.00
b.		Horiz. pair, imperf. btwn.	275.00	—
c.		Perf. 10½	50.00	1.50

Engr.

83	A18	1k carmine rose	2.25	.20
a.		1k carmine	5.00	.20
b.		Vert. pair, imperf. btwn.	275.00	300.00
84	A18	2k gray lilac	45.00	.40
a.		Vert. pair, imperf. btwn.	275.00	500.00
85	A18	4k gray green	4.00	10.00
		Nos. 70-85 (15)	216.05	21.85

For surcharges see Offices in Crete Nos. 1-7, Offices in the Turkish Empire Nos. 32-45.

1901 With Varnish Bars

70a	A15	1h lilac	1.75	.40
71a	A15	2h dark gray	1.75	.35
72a	A15	3h bister brown	.35	.20
73a	A15	5h blue green	.20	.20
74a	A15	6h orange	.20	.20
75a	A16	10h rose	.25	.20
76a	A16	20h brown	.65	.20
77a	A16	25h ultra	.85	.20
78a	A16	30h red violet	1.75	.90
79	A17	35h green	.85	.40
80a	A17	40h green	1.65	3.25

81a	A17	50h gray blue	4.00	6.75
82a	A17	60h brown	2.00	.65
		Nos. 70a-78a,79,80a-82a (13)	16.25	13.90

The diagonal yellow bars of varnish were printed across the face to prevent cleaning.

A19

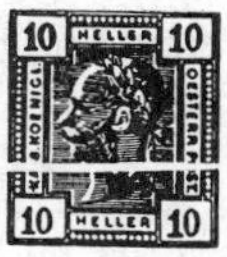

A20

A21

Perf. 12½ to 13½ and Compound

1905-07 **Typo.**

Colored Numerals

Without Varnish Bars

86	A19	1h lilac	.20	.35
87	A19	2h dark gray	.20	.20
88	A19	3h bister brown	.20	.20
89	A19	5h dk blue green	8.50	.20
90	A19	5h yellow grn ('06)	.40	.20
91	A19	6h deep orange	.40	.20
92	A20	10h carmine ('06)	.45	.20
93	A20	12h violet ('07)	1.00	.65
94	A20	20h brown ('06)	2.75	.20
95	A20	25h ultra ('06)	3.50	.35
96	A20	30h red violet ('06)	6.00	.25

Black Numerals

97	A20	10h carmine	10.50	.20
98	A20	20h brown	35.00	1.75
99	A20	25h ultra	32.50	1.75
100	A20	30h red violet	52.50	1.50

White Numerals

101	A21	35h green	2.25	.25
102	A21	40h deep violet	2.25	.75
103	A21	50h dull blue	2.75	2.25
104	A21	60h yellow brown	2.75	.60
105	A21	72h rose	2.75	1.60
		Nos. 86-105 (20)	166.85	13.65

For surcharges see Offices in Crete #8-14.

1904

With Varnish Bars

86a	A19	1h lilac	.50	.90
87a	A19	2h dark gray	1.60	.55
88a	A19	3h bister brown	1.75	.20
89a	A19	5h dk blue green	3.50	.20
91a	A19	6h deep orange	6.00	.30
97a	A20	10h carmine	2.00	.20
98a	A20	20h brown	27.50	.75
99a	A20	25h ultra	32.50	.75
100a	A20	30h red violet	40.00	1.50
101a	A21	35h green	32.50	.60
102a	A21	40h deep violet	30.00	3.50
103a	A21	50h dull blue	30.00	7.00
104a	A21	60h yellow brown	35.00	1.10
105a	A21	72h rose	1.10	1.10
		Nos. 86a-105a (14)	243.95	18.65

Stamps of the 1901, 1904 and 1905 issues perf. 9 or 10½, also compound with 12½, were not sold at any post office, but were supplied only to some high-ranking officials. This applies also to the contemporary issues of Austrian Offices Abroad.

Karl VI — A22

Franz Josef — A23

Schönbrunn Castle — A24

Franz Josef — A25

Designs: 2h, Maria Theresa. 3h, Joseph II. 5h, 10h, 25h, Franz Josef. 6h, Leopold II. 12h, Franz I. 20h, Ferdinand I. 30h, Franz Josef as youth. 35h, Franz Josef in middle age. 60h, Franz Josef on horseback. 1k, Franz Josef in royal robes. 5k, Hofburg, Vienna.

1908-13 **Typo.** ***Perf. 12½***

110	A22	1h gray black	.25	.20
111	A22	2h blue violet ('13)	.20	.45
a.		2h violet	.25	.20
112	A22	3h magenta	.20	.20
113	A22	5h yellow green	.20	.20
a.		Booklet pane of 6	25.00	
114	A22	6h buff	.60	.60
b.		6h orange brown ('13)	1.50	1.25
115	A22	10h rose	.20	.20
a.		Booklet pane of 6	75.00	
116	A22	12h scarlet	1.25	.80
117	A22	20h chocolate	1.60	.20
118	A22	25h ultra ('13)	1.40	.25
a.		25h deep blue	2.50	.25
119	A22	30h olive green	3.75	.25
120	A22	35h slate	2.25	.20

Engr.

121	A23	50h dark green	.65	.25
a.		Vert. pair, imperf. btwn.	190.00	275.00
b.		Horiz. pair, imperf. btwn.	190.00	275.00
122	A23	60h deep carmine	.35	.20
a.		Vert. pair, imperf. btwn.	275.00	325.00
b.		Horiz. pair, imperf. btwn.	275.00	325.00
123	A23	72h dk brown ('13)	1.75	.30
124	A23	1k purple	12.00	.20
a.		Vert. pair, imperf. btwn.	190.00	275.00
b.		Horiz. pair, imperf. btwn.	190.00	275.00
125	A24	2k lake & olive grn	18.00	.35
126	A24	5k bister & dk vio	35.00	4.00
127	A25	10k blue, bis & dp brn	165.00	50.00
		Nos. 110-127 (18)	244.65	58.85
		Set, never hinged	540.00	

Definitive set issued for the 60th year of the reign of Emperor Franz Josef.

The 1h-35h exist on both ordinary (1913) and chalk-surfaced (1908) paper.

All values exist imperforate. They were not sold at any post office, but presented to a number of high government officials. This applies also to all imperforate stamps of later issues, including semi-postals, etc., and those of the Austrian Offices Abroad.

Litho. forgeries of No. 127 exist.

For overprint and surcharge see #J47-J48. For similar designs see Offices in Crete A5-A6, Offices in the Turkish Empire A16-A17.

Birthday Jubilee Issue

Similar to 1908 Issue, but designs enlarged by labels at top and bottom bearing dates "1830" and "1910"

1910 **Typo.**

128	A22	1h gray black	4.00	6.25
129	A22	2h violet	5.00	7.75
130	A22	3h magenta	4.50	6.75
131	A22	5h yellow green	.20	.20
132	A22	6h buff	2.50	5.00
133	A22	10h rose	.20	.20
134	A22	12h scarlet	3.00	6.50
135	A22	20h chocolate	5.50	6.25
136	A22	25h deep blue	1.25	1.25
137	A22	30h olive green	3.25	4.50
138	A22	35h slate	3.25	4.50

Engr.

139	A23	50h dark green	4.50	8.00
140	A23	60h deep carmine	4.50	8.00
141	A23	1k purple	4.50	9.00
142	A24	2k lake & ol grn	125.00	190.00
143	A24	5k bister & dk vio	92.50	150.00
144	A25	10k blue, bis & dp brn	175.00	275.00
		Nos. 128-144 (17)	438.65	689.15
		Set, never hinged	736.00	

80th birthday of Emperor Franz Josef.
All values exist imperforate.
Litho. forgeries of Nos. 142-144 exist.

Austrian Crown — A37

Franz Josef — A38

Coat of Arms

A39 A40

1916-18 **Typo.**

145	A37	3h brt violet	.20	.20
146	A37	5h lt green	.20	.20
a.		Booklet pane of 6	14.00	
b.		Booklet pane of 4 + 2 labels	27.50	
147	A37	6h deep orange	.25	.65
148	A37	10h magenta	.20	.20
a.		Booklet pane of 6	27.50	
149	A37	12h light blue	.30	1.10
150	A38	15h rose red	.40	.20
a.		Booklet pane of 6	15.00	
151	A38	20h chocolate	3.25	.20
152	A38	25h blue	5.00	.40
153	A38	30h slate	4.50	.65
154	A39	40h olive green	.20	.20
155	A39	50h blue green	.20	.20
156	A39	60h deep blue	.20	.20
157	A39	80h orange brown	.20	.20
158	A39	90h red violet	.20	.20
159	A39	1k car, *yel* ('18)	.30	.20

Engr.

160	A40	2k dark blue	.55	.20
161	A40	3k claret	9.00	.90
162	A40	4k deep green	1.75	1.75
163	A40	10k deep violet	21.00	30.00
		Nos. 145-163 (19)	47.90	37.85
		Set, never hinged	107.00	

Stamps of type A38 have two varieties of the frame. Stamps of type A40 have various decorations about the shield.

Nos. 145-163 exist imperf. Value, set $400.

1917 **Ordinary Paper**

164	A40	2k light blue	.75	.50
165	A40	3k carmine rose	10.00	.75
166	A40	4k yellow green	1.10	1.10
167	A40	10k violet	90.00	70.00
		Nos. 164-167 (4)	101.85	72.35
		Set, never hinged	232.00	

Nos. 164-167 exist imperf. Value, set $250.

See Nos. 172-175 (granite paper). For overprints and surcharges see Nos. 181-199, C1-C3, J60-J63, N1-N5, N10-N19, N33-N37, N42-N51. Western Ukraine 2-7, 11-15, 19-28, 57-58, 85-89, 94-103, N3-N14, NJ13.

Emperor Karl I — A42

1917-18 **Typo.**

168	A42	15h dull red	.20	.20
a.		Booklet pane of 6	14.00	
169	A42	20h dk green ('18)	.20	.20
a.		20h green ('17)	.55	.20
170	A42	25h blue	.70	.20
171	A42	30h dull violet	.75	.20
		Nos. 168-171 (4)	1.85	.80
		Set, never hinged	5.80	

Nos. 168-171 exist imperf. Value, set $40.

For overprints and surcharges see Nos. N6-N9, N20, N38-N41, N52, N64. Western Ukraine 1, 8, 16-18, 90-93, N15-N18.

1918-19 **Engr.**

Granite Paper

172	A40	2k light blue	.20	.45
a.		Perf. 11½	450.00	525.00
		Never hinged, #172a	750.00	
173	A40	3k carmine rose	.25	1.10
174	A40	4k yellow green ('19)	4.00	13.50
175	A40	10k lt violet ('19)	7.50	16.00
		Nos. 172-175 (4)	11.95	31.05
		Set, never hinged	17.35	

Issues of the Republic

Austrian Stamps of 1916-18 Overprinted

1918-19 Unwmk. *Perf. 12½*

181	A37	3h bright violet	.20	.20
182	A37	5h light green	.20	.20
183	A37	6h deep orange	.20	.20
184	A37	10h magenta	.20	.20
185	A37	12h light blue	.25	*1.25*
186	A42	15h dull red	.20	*1.00*
187	A42	20h deep green	.20	.20
188	A42	25h blue	.20	.20
189	A42	30h dull violet	.20	.20
190	A39	40h olive green	.20	.20
191	A39	50h deep green	.45	*1.10*
192	A39	60h deep blue	.45	*1.75*
193	A39	80h orange brown	.20	.20
a.		Inverted overprint	200.00	
		Never hinged, #193a	275.00	
194	A39	90h red violet	.20	*.45*
195	A39	1k carmine, *yel*	.20	*.25*

Granite Paper

196	A40	2k light blue	.20	.20
a.		Pair, imperf. between	225.00	
		Never hinged, #196a	325.00	
b.		Perf. 11½	65.00	62.50
		Never hinged, #196b	100.00	
197	A40	3k carmine rose	.30	*.75*
198	A40	4k yellow green	.80	*1.90*
a.		Perf. 11½	16.00	25.00
		Never hinged, #198a	27.50	
199	A40	10k deep violet	7.25	*17.50*
		Nos. 181-199 (19)	12.10	*27.95*
		Set, never hinged	19.70	

Nos. 181, 182, 184, 187-191, 194, 197 and 199 exist imperforate.

Post Horn — A43

Coat of Arms — A44

Allegory of New Republic — A45

1919-20 Typo. *Perf. 12½*

Ordinary Paper

200	A43	3h gray	.20	.20
201	A44	5h yellow green	.20	.20
202	A44	5h gray ('20)	.20	.20
203	A43	6h orange	.20	*.45*
204	A44	10h deep rose	.20	.20
205	A44	10h red ('20)	.20	.20
a.		Thick grayish paper ('20)	.20	.20
206	A43	12h grnsh blue	.20	*.65*
207	A43	15h bister ('20)	.20	*.55*
a.		Thick grayish paper ('20)	.20	.20
208	A45	20h dark green	.20	.20
a.		20h yellow green	.20	.20
b.		As "a," thick grysh paper ('20)	.50	2.00
209	A44	25h blue	.20	.20
210	A43	25h violet ('20)	.20	.20
211	A45	30h dark brown	.20	.20
212	A45	40h violet	.20	.20
213	A45	40h lake ('20)	.20	.20
214	A44	45h olive green	.20	*.60*
215	A45	50h dark blue	.20	.20
a.		Thick grayish paper ('20)	.25	*.55*
216	A43	60h olive green ('20)	.20	.20
217	A44	1k carmine, *yel*	.20	.20
218	A44	1k light blue ('20)	.20	.20
		Nos. 200-218 (19)	3.80	5.25
		Set, never hinged	3.80	

All values exist imperf. (For regularly issued imperfs, see Nos. 227-235.)

For overprints and surcharge see Nos. B11-B19, B30-B38, J102, N21, N27, N53, N58, N65, N71.

Parliament Building A46

1919-20 Engr. *Perf. 12½, 11½*

Granite Paper

219	A46	2k vermilion & blk	.25	*.55*
a.		Center inverted	*3,500.*	
220	A46	2½k olive bis ('20)	.20	*.25*
221	A46	3k blue & blk brn	.20	.20
222	A46	4k carmine & blk	.20	.20
a.		Center inverted	*1,750.*	*1,400.*
223	A46	5k black ('20)	.20	.20
a.		Perf. 11½x12½	45.00	*67.50*
224	A46	7½k plum	.20	*.35*
a.		Perf. 11½	110.00	160.00
b.		Perf. 11½x12½	75.00	125.00
225	A46	10k olive grn & blk brn	.20	*.35*
a.		Perf. 11½x12½	125.00	175.00
b.		Perf. 11½	14.50	25.00
226	A46	20k lilac & red ('20)	.20	*.45*
a.		Center inverted	*10,500.*	*6,250.*
b.		Perf. 11½	62.50	110.00
		Nos. 219-226 (8)	1.65	*2.55*
		Set, never hinged	2.00	

A number of values exist imperforate between. Values, $300 to $400 a pair.

See No. 248. For overprints and surcharge see Nos. B23-B29, B43-B49, N30, N60, N74.

1920 Typo. *Imperf.*

Ordinary Paper

227	A44	5h yellow green	.20	*.45*
228	A44	5h gray	.20	.20
229	A44	10h deep rose	.20	.20
230	A44	10h red	.20	.20
231	A43	15h bister	.20	.20
232	A43	25h violet	.20	.20
233	A45	30h dark brown	.20	.20
234	A45	40h violet	.20	.20
235	A43	60h olive green	.20	.20
		Nos. 227-235 (9)	1.80	2.05
		Set, never hinged	1.80	

A47

A48

Arms

1920-21 Typo. *Perf. 12½*

Ordinary Paper

238	A47	80h rose	.20	.20
239	A47	1k black brown	.20	.20
241	A47	1½k green ('21)	.20	.20
242	A47	2k blue	.20	.20
243	A48	3k yel grn & dk grn ('21)	.20	*.25*
244	A48	4k red & claret ('21)	.20	.20
245	A48	5k vio & claret ('21)	.20	.20
246	A48	7½k yellow & brown ('21)	.20	*.25*
247	A48	10k ultra & blue ('21)	.20	*.20*
		Nos. 238-247 (9)	1.80	1.90
		Set, never hinged	1.80	

Nos. 238-245, 247 exist on white paper of good quality and on thick grayish paper of inferior quality; No. 246 only on white paper.

For overprints and surcharges see Nos. B20-B22, B39-B42, N22-N23, N31, N54-N55, N61-N62, N66-N67.

1921 Engr.

248	A46	50k dk violet, *yel*	.35	*.80*
		Never hinged	.60	
a.		Perf. 11½	15.00	*50.00*
		Never hinged	25.00	

Symbols of Agriculture A49

Symbols of Labor and Industry A50

1922-24 Typo. *Perf. 12½*

250	A49	½k olive bister	.20	*.60*
251	A50	1k brown	.20	.20
252	A50	2k cobalt blue	.20	.20
253	A49	2½k orange brown	.20	.20
254	A50	4k dull violet	.20	*1.00*
255	A50	5k gray green	.20	.20
256	A49	7½k gray violet	.20	.20
257	A50	10k claret	.20	.20
258	A49	12½k gray green	.20	.20
259	A49	15k bluish green	.20	.20
260	A49	20k dark blue	.20	.20
261	A49	25k claret	.20	.20
262	A50	30k pale gray	.20	.20
263	A50	45k pale red	.20	.20
264	A50	50k orange brown	.20	.20
265	A50	60k yellow green	.20	.20
266	A50	75k ultramarine	.20	.20
267	A50	80k yellow	.20	.20
268	A49	100k gray	.20	.20
269	A49	120k brown	.20	.20
270	A49	150k orange	.20	.20
271	A49	160k light green	.20	.20
272	A49	180k red	.20	.20
273	A49	200k pink	.20	.20
274	A49	240k dark violet	.20	.20
275	A49	300k light blue	.20	.20
276	A49	400k deep green	.85	.20
a.		400k gray green	.85	.30
277	A49	500k yellow	.20	.20
278	A49	600k slate	.20	.20
279	A49	700k brown ('24)	.70	.20
280	A49	800k violet ('24)	.80	*1.50*
281	A50	1000k violet ('23)	.55	.20
282	A50	1200k car rose ('23)	.35	*.45*
283	A50	1500k orange ('24)	1.00	.20
284	A50	1600k slate ('23)	2.75	2.75
285	A50	2000k deep blue ('23)	3.50	1.50
286	A50	3000k lt blue ('23)	11.00	1.75
287	A50	4000k dk bl, *bl* ('24)	5.00	2.10
		Nos. 250-287 (38)	32.10	17.65
		Set, never hinged	90.00	

Nos. 250-287 exist imperf. Value, set $500.

For overprints & surcharges see #N24-N26, N28-N29, N32, N56, N59, N63, N68-N70, N72-N73.

Symbols of Art and Science — A51

1922-24 Engr. *Perf. 12½*

288	A51	20k dark brown	.20	.20
a.		Perf. 11½	1.10	*1.25*
		Never hinged, #288a	1.60	
289	A51	25k blue	.20	.20
a.		Perf. 11½	1.00	*2.50*
		Never hinged, #289a	1.90	
290	A51	50k brown red	.20	.20
a.		Perf. 11½	2.25	*3.50*
		Never hinged, #290a	3.75	
b.		Vert. pair, imperf. btwn.	200.00	*250.00*
		Never hinged	250.00	
291	A51	100k deep green	.20	.20
a.		Perf. 11½	5.50	*7.00*
		Never hinged, #291a	8.00	
b.		Vert. pair, imperf. btwn.	—	*375.00*
292	A51	200k dark violet	.20	.20
a.		Perf. 11½	8.00	*13.50*
		Never hinged, #292a	12.00	
b.		Vert. pair, imperf. btwn.	300.00	
		Never hinged	375.00	
293	A51	500k dp orange	.20	*1.00*
294	A51	1000k blk vio, *yel*	.20	.20
a.		Perf. 11½	160.00	*250.00*
		Never hinged, #294a	400.00	
b.		Vert. pair, imperf. btwn.	250.00	
		Never hinged	300.00	
c.		Horiz. pair, imperf. btwn.	300.00	
		Never hinged	375.00	
295	A51	2000k olive grn, *yel*	.20	.20
a.		Vert. pair, imperf. btwn.	275.00	
		Never hinged	325.00	
296	A51	3000k claret brn ('23)	8.00	.65
297	A51	5000k gray black ('23)	1.50	1.50

Granite Paper

298	A51	10,000k red brown ('24)	3.25	*4.00*
		Nos. 288-298 (11)	14.35	8.55
		Set, never hinged	34.80	

On Nos. 281-287, 291-298 "kronen" is abbreviated to "k" and transposed with the numerals.

Nos. 288-298 exist imperf. Value, set $375.

Numeral A52

Fields Crossed by Telegraph Wires A53

White-Shouldered Eagle — A54

Church of Minorite Friars — A55

1925-27 Typo. *Perf. 12*

303	A52	1g dark gray	.20	.20
304	A52	2g claret	.35	.20
305	A52	3g scarlet	.70	.20
306	A52	4g grnsh blue ('27)	1.10	.20
307	A52	5g brown orange	1.50	.20
308	A52	6g ultramarine	1.25	.20
309	A52	7g chocolate	1.50	.20
310	A52	8g yellow green	5.75	.20
311	A53	10g orange	.35	.20
313	A53	15g red lilac	.35	.20
314	A53	16g dark blue	.35	.20
315	A53	18g olive green	1.10	.55
316	A54	20g dark violet	.35	.20
317	A54	24g carmine	.70	.40
318	A54	30g dark brown	.55	.20
319	A54	40g ultramarine	1.10	.20
320	A54	45g yellow brown	1.25	.20
321	A54	50g gray	1.50	.25
322	A54	80g turquoise blue	3.25	*4.50*

Perf. 12½

Engr.

323	A55	1s deep green	15.00	1.40
a.		1s light green	200.00	8.25
		Never hinged, #323a	625.00	
324	A55	2s brown rose	6.25	*10.00*
		Nos. 303-324 (21)	44.45	*20.10*
		Set, never hinged	137.50	

#303-305, 307-324 exist imperf. Value, set $400.

For type A52 surcharged see Nos. B118.

Güssing — A56

National Library, Vienna — A57

Designs: 15g, Hochosterwitz. 16g, 20g, Durnstein. 18g, Traunsee. 24g, Salzburg. 30g, Seewiesen. 40g, Innsbruck. 50g, Worthersee. 60g, Hohenems. 2s, St. Stephen's Cathedral, Vienna.

1929-30 Typo. *Perf. 12½*

Size: 25½x21½mm

326	A56	10g brown orange	.90	.20
327	A56	10g bister ('30)	.90	.20
328	A56	15g violet brown	.70	*1.25*
329	A56	16g dark gray	.25	.20
330	A56	18g blue green	.40	*.45*
331	A56	20g dark gray ('30)	.40	.20
332	A56	24g maroon	4.25	*6.00*
333	A56	24g lake ('30)	6.50	.45
334	A56	30g dark violet	4.25	.20
335	A56	40g dark blue	7.25	.20
336	A56	50g gray violet ('30)	27.50	.20
337	A56	60g olive green	22.50	.25

Engr.

Size: 21x26mm

338	A57	1s black brown	5.25	.25
a.		Horiz. pair, imperf. btwn.	225.00	
		Never hinged	300.00	
b.		Vert. pair, imperf. btwn.	225.00	
		Never hinged	300.00	
339	A57	2s dark green	9.25	8.75
a.		Horiz. pair, imperf. btwn.	225.00	
		Never hinged	300.00	
		Nos. 326-339 (14)	90.30	18.80
		Set, never hinged	288.90	

Type of 1929-30 Issue

Designs: 12g, Traunsee. 64g, Hohenems.

1932 *Perf. 12*

Size: 21x16½mm

340	A56	10g olive brown	.80	.20
341	A56	12g blue green	1.50	.20
342	A56	18g blue green	1.40	*2.10*
343	A56	20g dark gray	1.10	.20
344	A56	24g carmine rose	5.25	.20
345	A56	24g dull violet	3.50	.20
346	A56	30g dark violet	17.50	.20
347	A56	30g carmine rose	4.25	.20
a.		Vert. pair, imperf. btwn.	40.00	
		Never hinged, #347a	50.00	
348	A56	40g dark blue	19.00	.90
349	A56	40g dark violet	6.25	.30
350	A56	50g gray violet	24.00	.30
351	A56	50g dull blue	5.75	.30
352	A56	60g gray green	52.50	2.50
353	A56	64g gray green	12.00	.30
		Nos. 340-353 (14)	154.80	8.10
		Set, never hinged	504.00	

For overprints and surcharges see Nos. B87-B92, B119-B121.

Burgenland A67

Tyrol A68

Costumes of various districts: 3g, Burgenland. 4g, 5g, Carinthia. 6g, 8g, Lower Austria. 12g, 20g, Upper Austria. 24g, 25g, Salzburg.

30g, 35g, Styria. 45g, Tyrol. 60g, Vorarlberg bridal couple. 64g, Vorarlberg. 1s, Viennese family. 2s, Military.

1934-35 Typo. *Perf. 12*

354 A67 1g dark violet .20 .20
355 A67 3g scarlet .20 .20
356 A67 4g olive green .20 .20
357 A67 5g red violet .20 .20
358 A67 6g ultramarine .20 .25
359 A67 8g green .20 .20
360 A67 12g dark brown .20 .20
361 A67 20g yellow brown .20 .20
362 A67 24g grnsh blue .20 .20
363 A67 25g violet .20 .25
364 A67 30g maroon .20 .20
365 A67 35g rose carmine .30 .45

Perf. 12½

366 A68 40g slate gray .40 .25
367 A68 45g brown red .35 .20
368 A68 60g ultramarine .60 .35
369 A68 64g brown .75 .20
370 A68 1s deep violet .90 .55
371 A68 2s dull green 35.00 65.00

Designs Redrawn
Perf. 12 (6g), 12½ (2s)

372 A67 6g ultra ('35) .20 .20
373 A68 2s emerald ('35) 3.25 5.25
Nos. 354-373 (20) 43.95 74.75
Set, never hinged 108.00

The design of No. 358 looks as though the man's ears were on backwards, while No. 372 appears correctly.

On No. 373 there are seven feathers on each side of the eagle instead of five.

Nos. 354-373 exist imperf. Value, set $375.

For surcharges see Nos. B128-B131.

Dollfuss Mourning Issue

Engelbert Dollfuss — A85

1934-35 Engr. *Perf. 12½*

374 A85 24g greenish black .40 .30
Never hinged 1.25
375 A85 24g indigo ('35) .75 .70
Never hinged 2.50

"Mother and Child," by Joseph Danhauser — A86

"Madonna and Child," after Painting by Dürer — A87

1935, May 1

376 A86 24g dark blue .40 .20
Never hinged 1.00
a. Vert. pair, imperf. btwn. 200.00
Never hinged 250.00
b. Horiz. pair, imperf. btwn. 190.00
Never hinged 225.00

Mother's Day. Nos. 376-377 exist imperf. Value, each $150.

1936, May 5 Photo.

377 A87 24g violet blue .20 *.30*
Never hinged .55

Mother's Day.

Farm Workers — A88

Design: 5s, Factory workers.

1936, June Engr. *Perf. 12½*

378 A88 3s red orange 12.50 17.50
Never hinged 24.00
379 A88 5s brown black 30.00 42.50
Never hinged 45.00

Nos. 378-379 exist imperf. Value, set $210.

Engelbert Dollfuss — A90

Mother and Child — A91

1936, July 25

380 A90 10s dark blue 675.00 800.00
Never hinged 900.00

Second anniv. of death of Engelbert Dollfuss, chancellor. Exists imperf. Value, $1,750.

1937, May 5 Photo. *Perf. 12*

381 A91 24g henna brown .20 .25
Never hinged .55

Mother's Day. Exists imperf. Value, $140.

S.S. Maria Anna — A92

Steamships: 24g, Uranus, 64g, Oesterreich.

1937, June 9

382 A92 12g red brown .60 .35
383 A92 24g deep blue .60 .35
384 A92 64g dark green .60 *.80*
Nos. 382-384 (3) 1.80 *1.50*
Set, never hinged 5.00

Cent. of steamship service on Danube River. Exist imperf. Value, set $350.

First Locomotive, "Austria" — A95

Designs: 25g, Modern steam locomotive. 35g, Modern electric train.

1937, Nov. 22

385 A95 12g black brown .20 .20
386 A95 25g dark violet .65 *1.00*
387 A95 35g brown red 1.60 *2.25*
Nos. 385-387 (3) 2.45 *3.45*
Set, never hinged 6.90

Centenary of Austrian railways. Exist imperf. Value, set $90.

Rose and Zodiac Signs — A98

1937 Engr. *Perf. 13x12½*

388 A98 12g dark green .20 .20
389 A98 24g dark carmine .20 .20
Set, never hinged .40

For Use in Vienna, Lower Austria and Burgenland

Germany Nos. 509-511 and 511B Overprinted in Black

a

b

1945 Unwmk. *Perf. 14*

390 A115(a) 5pf dp yellow green .20 .20
391 A115(b) 6pf purple .20 .20
392 A115(a) 8pf red .20 .20
393 A115(b) 12pf carmine .20 .20
Nos. 390-393 (4) .80 .80
Set, never hinged .80

Nos. 390-393 exist with overprint inverted or double.

Germany No. 507, the 3pf, with overprint "a" was prepared, not issued, but sold to collectors after the definitive Republic issue had been placed in use. Value $30, hinged, $60, never hinged.

German Semi-Postal Stamps, #B207, B209, B210, B283 Surcharged in Black

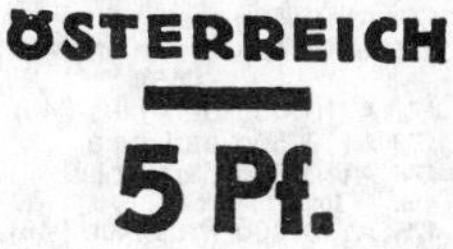

c

d

1945 *Perf. 14, 14x13½, 13½x14*

394 SP181(c) 5pf on 12pf + 88pf .50 1.50
395 SP184(d) 6pf on 6pf + 14pf 2.50 11.00
396 SP242(d) 8pf on 42pf + 108pf .50 1.50
397 SP183(d) 12pf on 3pf + 7pf .50 1.50
Nos. 394-397 (4) 4.00 15.50
Set, never hinged 10.00

The surcharges are spaced to fit the stamps.

Stamps of Germany, Nos. 509 to 511, 511B, 519 and 529 Overprinted

e

f

1945 Typo. *Perf. 14*
Size: 18½x22½mm

398 A115(e) 5pf dp yellow green .25 .45
399 A115(f) 5pf dp yellow green 4.00 *7.75*
400 A115(e) 6pf purple .20 *.35*
401 A115(e) 8pf red .20 *.35*
402 A115(e) 12pf carmine .20 *.35*

Engr.
Size: 21½x26mm

403 A115(e) 30pf olive green 6.25 *10.00*
a. Thin bar at bottom 15.00 *17.50*
a. Never hinged 25.00
404 A118(e) 42pf brt green 15.00 *32.50*
a. Thin bar at bottom 15.00 27.50
a. Never hinged 25.00
Nos. 398-404 (7) 26.10 *51.75*
Set, never hinged 55.00

On Nos. 403a and 404a, the bottom bar of the overprint is 2½mm wide, and, as the overprint was applied in two operations, "Osterreich" is usually not exactly centered in its diagonal slot. On Nos. 403 and 404, the bottom bar is 3mm wide, and "Osterreich" is always well centered.

Germany Nos. 524-527 (the 1m, 2m, 3m and 5m), overprinted with vertical bars and "Osterreich" similar to "e" and "f," were prepared, not issued, but sold to collectors after the definitive Republic issue had been placed in use. Value for set, $70 hinged, $150 ever hinged.

Counterfeits exist of Nos. 403-404, 403a-404a and 1m-5m overprints.

For Use in Styria

Stamps of Germany Nos. 506 to 511, 511A, 511B, 514 to 523 and 529 Overprinted in Black

1945 Unwmk. Typo. *Perf. 14*
Size: 18½x22½mm

405 A115 1pf gray black 1.50 3.00
406 A115 3pf lt brown 1.50 3.00
407 A115 4pf slate 5.00 10.00
408 A115 5pf dp yellow grn 1.00 2.00
409 A115 6pf purple .20 .30
410 A115 8pf red .70 1.60
411 A115 10pf dark brown 1.50 3.25
412 A115 12pf carmine .20 .30

Engr.

413 A115 15pf brown lake .75 1.75
414 A115 16pf pck green 14.00 18.00
415 A115 20pf blue 2.75 5.25
416 A115 24pf orange brown 10.00 18.00

Size: 22½x26mm

417 A115 25pf brt ultra 1.00 2.75
418 A115 30pf olive green 1.00 2.00
419 A115 40pf brt red violet 1.25 2.25
420 A118 42pf brt green 2.00 3.50
421 A115 50pf myrtle green 1.40 3.50
422 A115 60pf dk red brown 2.25 4.75
423 A115 80pf indigo 2.00 3.75
Nos. 405-423 (19) 50.00 88.95
Set, never hinged 110.00

Overprinted on Nos. 524-527
Perf. 12½, 14

424 A116 1m dk slate grn 7.50 *20.00*
a. Perf. 12½ 100.00
425 A116 2m violet 7.50 *25.00*
a. Perf. 14 12.00 *45.00*
426 A116 3m copper red 25.00 *55.00*
a. Perf. 14 125.00
427 A116 5m dark blue 225.00 *525.00*
a. Perf. 14 *575.00*
Nos. 424-427 (4) 265.00
Set, never hinged 450.00

On the preceding four stamps the innermost vertical lines are 10½mm apart; on the pfennig values 6½mm apart.

Counterfeits exist of Nos. 405-427 overprints.

Germany Nos. 524 to 527 Overprinted in Black

Perf. 14

428 A116 1m dk slate grn 10.50 *22.50*
429 A116 2m violet 10.50 *27.50*

Perf. 12½

430 A116 3m copper red 21.00 *60.00*
431 A116 5m dark blue 140.00 *450.00*
a. Perf. 14 *600.00*
Nos. 428-431 (4) 182.00
Set, never hinged 375.00

On the preceding four stamps, "Osterreich" is thinner, measuring 16mm. On the previous set of 23 values it measures 18mm.

Counterfeits exist of Nos. 428-431 overprints.

Catalogue values for unused stamps in this section, from this point to the end of the section, are for Never Hinged items.

For Use in Vienna, Lower Austria and Burgenland

Coat of Arms
A99 A100

Typographed or Lithographed

1945, July 3 Unwmk. *Perf. 14x13½*

Size: 21x25mm

432	A99	3pf brown	.20	.20
433	A99	4pf slate	.20	.20
434	A99	5pf dark green	.20	.20
435	A99	6pf deep violet	.20	.20
436	A99	8pf orange brown	.20	.20
437	A99	10pf deep brown	.20	.20
438	A99	12pf rose carmine	.20	.20
439	A99	15pf orange red	.20	.20
440	A99	16pf dull blue green	.20	.35

Perf. 14

Size: 24x28½mm

441	A99	20pf light blue	.20	.20
442	A99	24pf orange	.20	.20
443	A99	25pf dark blue	.20	.20
444	A99	30pf deep gray grn	.20	.20
445	A99	38pf ultramarine	.20	.20
446	A99	40pf brt red vio	.20	.20
447	A99	42pf sage green	.20	.20
448	A99	50pf blue green	.20	*.60*
449	A99	60pf maroon	.20	.20
450	A99	80pf dull lilac	.20	.20

Engr. *Perf. 14x13½*

451	A100	1m dark green	.20	*.60*
452	A100	2m dark purple	.20	*.60*
453	A100	3m dark violet	.20	*.60*
454	A100	5m brown red	.20	*.60*
		Nos. 432-454 (23)	4.60	*6.75*

Nos. 432, 433, 437, 439, 440, 443, 446, 448, 449 are typographed. Nos. 434, 435, 441, 442 are lithographed; the other values exist both ways.

For overprint see No. 604.

For General Use

Lermoos, Winter Scene
A101

The Prater Woods, Vienna
A105

Hochosterwitz, Carinthia
A106

Lake Constance
A110

Dürnstein, Lower Austria
A124

Designs: 4g, Eisenerz surface mine. 5g, Leopoldsberg, near Vienna. 6g, Hohensalzburg, Salzburg Province. 12g, Wolfgang See, near Salzburg. 15g, Forchtenstein Castle, Burgenland. 16g, Gesäuse Valley. 24g, Höldrichs Mill, Lower Austria. 25g, Oetz Valley Outlet, Tyrol. 30g, Neusiedler Lake, Burgenland. 35g, Belvedere Palace, Vienna. 38g, Langbath Lake. 40g, Mariazell, Styria. 42g, Traunkirchen. 45g, Hartenstein Castle. 50g, Silvretta Mountains, Vorarlberg. 60g, Railroad viaducts near Semmering. 70g, Waterfall of Bad-Gastein, Salzburg. 80g, Kaiser Mountains, Tyrol. 90g, Wayside Shrine, Tragöss, Styria. 2s, St. Christof am Arlberg, Tyrol. 3s, Heiligenblut, Carinthia. 5s, Schönbrunn, Vienna.

Perf. 14x13½

1945-46 Photo. Unwmk.

455	A101	3g sapphire	.20	.20
456	A101	4g dp orange ('46)	.20	.20
457	A101	5g dk carmine rose	.20	.20
458	A101	6g dk slate green	.20	.20
459	A105	8g golden brown	.20	.20
460	A106	10g dark green	.20	.20
461	A106	12g dark brown	.20	.20
462	A106	15g dk slate bl ('46)	.20	.20
463	A106	16g chnt brn ('46)	.20	.20

Perf. 13½x14

464	A110	20g dp ultra ('46)	.20	.20
465	A110	24g dp yellow grn ('46)	.20	.20
466	A110	25g gray black ('46)	.20	.20
467	A110	30g dark red	.20	.20
468	A110	35g brown red ('46)	.20	.20
469	A110	38g brown olive ('46)	.20	.20
470	A110	40g gray	.20	.20
471	A110	42g brown orange ('46)	.20	.20
472	A110	45g dark blue ('46)	.20	.25
473	A110	50g dark blue	.20	.20
474	A110	60g dark violet	.20	.20
	a.	Imperf., pair	50.00	60.00
475	A110	70g Prus blue ('46)	.20	.25
476	A110	80g brown	.20	.40
477	A110	90g Prussian green	1.10	1.10
478	A124	1s dk red brn ('46)	.75	.75
479	A124	2s blue gray ('46)	2.75	2.75
480	A124	3s dk slate grn ('46)	.75	.80
481	A124	5s dark red ('46)	1.50	1.75
		Nos. 455-481 (27)	11.25	11.85

See Nos. 486-488, 496-515. For overprints and surcharges see Nos. 492-493, B166, B280, B287.

No. 461 Overprinted in Carmine

1946, Sept. 26

482	A106	12g dark brown	.20	.20

Meeting of the Soc. for Cultural and Economic Relations with the USSR, Vienna, Sept. 26-29.

City Hall Park, Vienna
A128

Hochosterwitz, Carinthia
A129

Perf. 14x13½

1946-47 Photo. Unwmk.

483	A128	8g deep plum	.20	.20
484	A128	8g olive brown	.20	.20
	a.	8g dark olive green	.20	.20
485	A129	10g dk brn vio ('47)	.20	.20

Perf. 13½x14

486	A110	30g blue gray ('47)	.20	.20
487	A110	50g brown violet ('47)	.25	.25
488	A110	60g violet blue ('47)	2.00	1.10
		Nos. 483-488 (6)	3.05	2.15

See No. 502.

Franz Grillparzer
A130

Franz Schubert
A131

1947 Engr. *Perf. 14x13½*

489	A130	18g chocolate	.20	.20

Photo.

490	A130	18g dk violet brn	.20	.20

Death of Grillparzer, dramatic poet, 75th anniv.

A second printing of No. 490 on thicker paper has a darker frame and clearer delineation of the portrait.

Issue dates: #489, Feb. 10; #490, Mar. 31.

1947, Mar. 31 Engr.

491	A131	12g dark green	.20	.20

150th birth anniv. of Franz Schubert, musician and composer.

Nos. 469 and 463 Surcharged in Brown

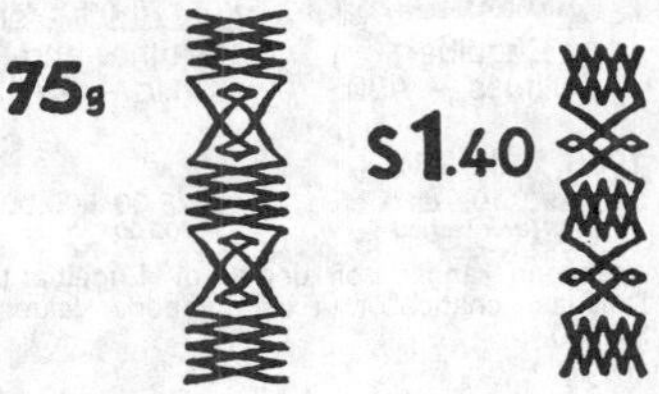

1947, Sept. 1 Photo. *Perf. 14*

492	A110	75g on 38g brown ol	.20	.80
493	A106	1.40s on 16g chnt brn	.20	.20

The surcharge on No. 493 varies from brown to black brown.

Symbols of Global Telegraphic Communication
A132

1947, Nov. 5 Engr. *Perf. 14x13½*

495	A132	40g dark violet	.20	.20

Centenary of the telegraph in Austria.

Scenic Type of 1946

1946, Aug. Photo. *Perf. 13½x14*

496	A124	1s dark brown	1.25	.50
497	A124	2s dark blue	7.00	2.75
498	A124	3s dark slate green	2.25	.75
499	A124	5s dark red	32.50	8.00
		Nos. 496-499 (4)	43.00	12.00

On Nos. 478 to 481 the upper and lower panels show a screen effect. On Nos. 496 to 499 the panels appear to be solid color.

Scenic Types of 1945-46

1947-48 Photo. *Perf. 14x13½*

500	A101	3g bright red	.20	.20
501	A101	5g bright red	.20	.20
502	A129	10g bright red	.20	.20
503	A106	15g brt red ('48)	1.40	1.25

Perf. 13½x14

504	A110	20g bright red	.50	.20
505	A110	30g bright red	.75	.20
506	A110	40g bright red	.75	.20
507	A110	50g bright red	1.00	.20
508	A110	60g brt red ('48)	6.50	1.25
509	A110	70g brt red ('48)	3.50	.20
510	A110	80g brt red ('48)	3.50	.20
511	A110	90g brt red ('48)	3.75	.25
512	A124	1s dark violet	.80	.20
513	A124	2s dark violet	1.10	.20
514	A124	3s dk violet ('48)	9.00	1.00
515	A124	5s dk violet ('48)	11.00	1.50
		Nos. 500-515 (16)	44.15	7.45

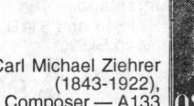

Carl Michael Ziehrer (1843-1922), Composer — A133

#517, Adalbert Stifter (1805-68), novelist. #518, Anton Bruckner (1824-96), composer. 60g, Friedrich von Amerling (1803-87), painter.

1948-49 Engr.

516	A133	20g dull green	.35	.20
517	A133	40g chocolate	5.00	2.50
518	A133	40g dark green	5.00	4.00
519	A133	60g rose brown	.65	.30
		Nos. 516-519 (4)	11.00	7.00

Issue dates: 20g, Jan. 21, No. 517, Sept. 6, No. 518, Sept. 3, 1949, 60g, Jan. 26.

Vorarlberg, Montafon Valley
A134

Costume of Vienna, 1850
A135

Designs (Austrian Costumes): 3g, Tyrol, Inn Valley. 5g, Salzburg, Pinzgau. 10g, Styria, Salzkammergut. 15g, Burgenland, Lutzmannsburg. 25g, Vienna, 1850. 30g, Salzburg, Pongau. 40g, Vienna, 1840. 45g, Carinthia, Lesach Valley. 50g, Vorarlberg, Bregenzer Forest. 60g, Carinthia, Lavant Valley. 70g, Lower Austria, Wachau. 75g, Styria, Salzkammergut. 80g, Styria, Enns Valley. 90g, Central Styria. 1s, Tyrol, Puster Valley. 1.20s, Lower Austria, Vienna Woods. 1.40s, Upper Austria, Inn District. 1.45s, Wilten. 1.50s, Vienna, 1853. 1.60s, Vienna, 1830. 1.70s, East Tyrol, Kals. 2s, Upper Austria. 2.20s, Ischl, 1820. 2.40s, Kitzbuhel. 2.50s, Upper Steiermark, 1850. 2.70s, Little Walser Valley. 3s, Burgenland. 3.50s, Lower Austria, 1850. 4.50s, Gail Valley. 5s, Ziller Valley. 7s, Steiermark, Sulm Valley.

Perf. 14x13½

1948-52 Unwmk. Photo.

520	A134	3g gray ('50)	.60	.50
521	A134	5g dark green ('49)	.25	.20
522	A134	10g deep blue	.25	.20
523	A134	15g brown	.60	.20
524	A134	20g yellow green	.20	.20
525	A134	25g brown ('49)	.20	.20
526	A134	30g dk car rose	2.50	.20
527	A134	30g dk violet ('50)	.60	.20
528	A134	40g violet	2.50	.20
529	A134	40g green ('49)	.20	.20
530	A134	45g violet blue	2.25	.40
531	A134	50g orange brn ('49)	.60	.20
532	A134	60g scarlet	.20	.20
533	A134	70g brt blue grn ('49)	.20	.20
534	A134	75g blue	3.75	.40
535	A134	80g carmine rose ('49)	.35	.20
536	A134	90g brown vio ('49)	22.50	.30
537	A134	1s ultramarine	4.00	.20
538	A134	1s rose red ('50)	62.50	.20
539	A134	1s dk green ('51)	.20	.20
540	A134	1.20s violet ('49)	.40	.20
541	A134	1.40s brown	2.50	.20
542	A134	1.45s dk carmine ('51)	1.00	.20
543	A134	1.50s ultra ('51)	.60	.20
544	A134	1.60s orange red ('49)	.20	.20
545	A134	1.70s violet blue ('50)	2.50	.55
546	A134	2s blue green	.40	.20
547	A134	2.20s slate ('52)	4.75	.20
548	A134	2.40s blue ('51)	1.00	.20
549	A134	2.50s brown ('52)	4.50	.20
550	A134	2.70s dk brown ('51)	.45	.45
551	A134	3s brown car ('49)	1.90	.20
552	A134	3.50s dull grn ('51)	9.75	.20
553	A134	4.50s brown vio ('51)	.60	.40
554	A134	5s dark red vio	1.00	.20
555	A134	7s olive ('52)	1.50	.20

Engr.

556	A135	10s gray ('50)	27.50	5.00
		Nos. 520-556 (37)	165.00	13.80

In 1958-59, 21 denominations of this set were printed on white paper, differing from the previous grayish paper with yellowish gum.

Pres. Karl Renner — A136

1948, Nov. 12 *Perf. 14x13½*

557	A136	1s deep blue	1.90	1.10

Founding of the Austrian Republic, 30th anniv. See Nos. 573, 636.

Franz Gruber and Josef Mohr — A137

1948, Dec. 18 ***Perf. 13½x14***
558 A137 60g red brown 4.25 4.00

130th anniv. of the hymn "Silent Night, Holy Night".

Symbolical of Child Welfare — A138

Johann Strauss, the Younger — A139

1949, May 14 Photo. ***Perf. 14x13½***
559 A138 1s bright blue 11.50 1.25

1st year of activity of UNICEF in Austria.

1949 **Engr.**

30g, Johann Strauss, the elder. #561, Johann Strauss, the younger. #562, Karl Millöcker.

560 A139 30g violet brown 2.25 1.60
561 A139 1s dark blue 2.75 1.10
562 A139 1s dark blue 12.00 6.25
Nos. 560-562 (3) 17.00 8.95

Johann Strauss, the elder (1804-49), Johann Strauss, the younger (1825-99), and Karl Millöcker (1842-1899), composers. See #574.

Esperanto Star, Olive Branches A140

St. Gebhard A141

1949, June 25 **Photo.**
563 A140 20g blue green 1.00 .50

Austrian Esperanto Congress at Graz.

1949, Aug. 6 **Engr.**
564 A141 30g dark violet 1.50 1.25

St. Gebhard (949-995), Bishop of Vorarlberg.

Letter, Roses and Post Horn — A142

UPU, 75th Anniv.: 60g, Plaque. 1s, "Austria," wings and monogram.

1949, Oct. 8 ***Perf. 13½x14***
565 A142 40g dark green 3.75 1.60
566 A142 60g dk carmine 3.75 1.60
567 A142 1s dk violet blue 6.50 4.75
Nos. 565-567 (3) 14.00 7.95

Moritz Michael Daffinger — A143

Andreas Hofer — A144

30g, Alexander Girardi. #569, Daffinger. #570, Hofer. #571, Josef Madersperger.

1950 **Unwmk.** ***Perf. 14x13½***
568 A144 30g dark blue 1.50 .75
569 A143 60g red brown 6.00 3.25
570 A144 60g dark violet 10.50 6.50
571 A144 60g purple 4.50 2.25
Nos. 568-571 (4) 22.50 12.75

Alexander Girardi (1850-1918), actor; Moritz Michael Daffinger (1790-1849), painter; Andreas Hofer (1767-1810), patriot; Josef Madersperger (1768-1850), inventor.

Issue dates: 30g, Dec. 5; No. 569, Jan. 25; No. 570, Feb. 20; No. 571, Oct. 2.

Austrian Stamp of 1850 — A146

1950, May 20 ***Perf. 14½***
572 A146 1s black, *straw* 1.60 .90

Centenary of Austrian postage stamps.

Renner Type of 1948, Frame and Inscriptions Altered

1951, Mar. 3
573 A136 1s black, *straw* 1.40 .20

In memory of Pres. Karl Renner, 1870-1950.

Strauss Type of 1949

Portrait: 60g, Joseph Lanner.

1951, Apr. 12
574 A139 60g dk blue green 3.50 1.10

150th birth anniv. of Joseph Lanner, composer.

Martin Johann Schmidt — A147

Boy Scout Emblem — A148

1951, June 28 **Engr.** ***Perf. 14x13½***
575 A147 1sh brown red 4.50 2.00

150th death anniv. of Martin Johann Schmidt, painter.

1951, Aug. 3 **Engr. and Litho.**
576 A148 1sh dk grn, ocher & pink 3.50 2.75

7th World Scout Jamboree, Bad Ischl-St. Wolfgang, Aug. 3-13, 1951.

Wilhelm Kienzl A149

Josef Schrammel A150

Design: 1s, Karl von Ghega.

1951-52 **Engr.** **Unwmk.**
577 A149 1s deep green ('52) 6.50 1.10
578 A149 1.50s indigo 3.00 .90
579 A150 1.50s violet blue ('52) 6.50 1.10
Nos. 577-579 (3) 16.00 3.10

Ghega (1802-60), civil engineer; Kienzl (1857-1941), composer; Schrammel (1852-95), composer. See #582.

Issued: 1s, Mar. 2; #578, Oct. 3; #579, Mar. 3.

Breakfast Pavilion, Schönbrunn A151

1952, May 24 ***Perf. 13½x14***
580 A151 1.50s dark green 5.75 1.00

Vienna Zoological Gardens, 200th anniv.

Globe as Dot Over "i" — A152

School Girl — A153

1952, July 1 ***Perf. 14x13½***
581 A152 1.50s dark blue 5.00 .65

Formation of the Intl. Union of Socialist Youth Camp, Vienna, July 1-10, 1952.

Type Similar to A150

Portrait: 1s, Nikolaus Lenau.

1952, Aug. 13
582 A150 1s deep green 6.00 1.10

Nikolaus Lenau, pseudonym of Nikolaus Franz Niembsch von Strehlenau (1802-50), poet.

1952, Sept. 6
583 A153 2.40s dp violet blue 9.00 1.75

Issued to stimulate letter-writing between Austrian and foreign school children.

Hugo Wolf — A154

Pres. Theodor Körner — A155

1953, Feb. 21 **Engr.** ***Perf. 14x13½***
587 A154 1.50s dark blue 6.00 .70

Hugo Wolf, composer, 50th death anniv.

1953, Apr. 24
588 A155 1.50s dk violet blue 6.00 .70

80th birthday of Pres. Theodor Körner. See Nos. 591, 614.

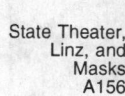

State Theater, Linz, and Masks A156

1953, Oct. 17 ***Perf. 13½x14***
589 A156 1.50s dark gray 14.00 1.50

State Theater at Linz, 150th anniv.

Child and Christmas Tree A157

Karl von Rokitansky A158

1953, Nov. 30 ***Perf. 14x13½***
590 A157 1s dark green 1.40 .20

See No. 597.

Type Similar to A155

Portrait: 1.50s, Moritz von Schwind.

1954, Jan. 21 ***Perf. 14x13½***
591 A155 1.50s purple 12.00 1.10

Moritz von Schwind, painter, 150th birth anniv.

1954, Feb. 19
592 A158 1.50s purple 14.00 1.40

Karl von Rokitansky, physician, 150th birth anniv. See No. 595.

Esperanto Star and Wreath A159

Engr. and Photo.

1954, June 5 ***Perf. 13½x14***
593 A159 1s dk brown & emer 4.50 .20

Esperanto movement in Austria, 50th anniv.

A160

A161

1954, Aug. 4 **Engr.** ***Perf. 14x13½***
594 A160 1s dark blue green 10.00 1.75

300th birth anniv. of Johann Michael Rottmayr von Rosenbrunn, painter.

Type Similar to A158

Portrait: 1.50s, Carl Auer von Welsbach.

1954, Aug. 4
595 A158 1.50s violet blue 30.00 1.50

25th death anniv. of Carl Auer von Welsbach (1858-1929), chemist.

1954, Oct. 2 **Unwmk.**

Organ, St. Florian Monastery and Cherub.

596 A161 1s brown 2.25 .20

2nd Intl. Congress for Catholic Church Music, Vienna, Oct. 4-10, 1954.

Christmas Type of 1953

1954, Nov. 30
597 A157 1s dark blue 2.75 .25

Arms of Austria and Official Publication A162

1954, Dec. 18 **Engr.**
598 A162 1s salmon & black 2.25 .20

Austria's State Printing Plant, 150th anniv., and Wiener Zeitung, government newspaper, 250th year of publication.

Parliament Building
A163

Designs: 1s, Western railroad station, Vienna. 1.45s, Letters forming flag. 1.50s, Public housing, Vienna. 2.40s, Limberg dam.

1955, Apr. 27 ***Perf. 13½x14***

599 A163 70g rose violet 1.50 .20
600 A163 1s deep ultra 5.50 .20
601 A163 1.45s scarlet 8.25 1.75
602 A163 1.50s brown 17.50 .20
603 A163 2.40s dk blue green 8.25 3.00
Nos. 599-603 (5) 41.00 5.35

10th anniv. of Austria's liberation.

Type of 1945 Overprinted in Blue **STAATSVERTRAG 1955**

1955, May 15 ***Perf. 14x13½***

604 A100 2s blue gray 2.00 .20

Signing of the state treaty with the US, France, Great Britain and Russia, May 15, 1955.

Workers of Three Races Climbing Globe
A164

1955, May 20 ***Perf. 13½x14***

605 A164 1s indigo 2.00 1.60

4th congress of the Intl. Confederation of Free Trade Unions, Vienna, May.

Burgtheater, Vienna
A165

Design: 2.40s, Opera House, Vienna.

1955, July 25

606 A165 1.50s light sepia 3.00 .20
607 A165 2.40s dark blue 4.00 1.25

Re-opening of the Burgtheater and Opera House in Vienna.

Symbolic of Austria's Desire to Join the UN — A166

1955, Oct. 24 **Unwmk.**

608 A166 2.40s green 14.00 1.40

Tenth anniversary of UN.

Wolfgang Amadeus Mozart — A167

Symbolic of Austria's Joining the UN — A168

1956, Jan. 21 ***Perf. 14x13½***

609 A167 2.40s slate blue 3.75 .50

200th birth anniv. of Wolfgang Amadeus Mozart, composer.

1956, Feb. 20

610 A168 2.40s chocolate 11.00 1.10

Austria's admission to the UN.

Globe Showing Energy of the Earth
A169

1956, May 8 ***Perf. 13½x14***

611 A169 2.40s deep blue 10.00 1.40

Fifth Intl. Power Conf., Vienna, June 17-23.

Map of Europe and City Maps — A170

J.B. Fischer von Erlach — A171

Photo. and Typo.

1956, June 8 ***Perf. 14x13½***

612 A170 1.45s lt grn blk & red 2.50 .50

23rd Intl. Housing and Town Planning Congress, Vienna, July 22-28.

1956, July 20 **Engr.**

613 A171 1.50s brown 1.25 1.10

300th birth anniv. of Johann Bernhard Fischer von Erlach, architect.

Körner Type of 1953

1957, Jan. 11

614 A155 1.50s gray black 1.50 1.25

Death of Pres. Theodor Körner.

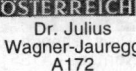

Dr. Julius Wagner-Jauregg
A172

Anton Wildgans
A173

1957, Mar. 7 ***Perf. 14x13½***

615 A172 2.40s brn violet 3.25 1.25

Birth cent. of Dr. Julius Wagner-Jauregg, psychiatrist.

1957, May 3 **Unwmk.**

616 A173 1s violet blue .30 .20

Anton Wildgans, poet, 25th death anniv.

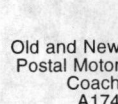

Old and New Postal Motor Coach
A174

1957, June 14 ***Perf. 13½x14***

617 A174 1s black, *yellow* .30 .20

Austrian Postal Motor Coach Service, 50th anniv.

Gasherbrum II and Glacier
A175

1957, July 27

618 A175 1.50s gray blue .35 .20

Austrian Karakorum Expedition, which climbed Mount Gasherbrum II on July 7, 1956.

A176

A177

Designs: 20g, Farmhouse at Mörbisch. 50g, Heiligenstadt, Vienna. 1s, Mariazell. 1.40s, County seat, Klagenfurt. 1.50s, Rabenhof Building, Erdberg, Vienna. 1.80s, The Mint, Hall, Tyrol. 2s, Christkindl Church. 3.40s, Steiner Gate, Krems. 4s, Vienna Gate, Hainburg. 4.50s, Schwechat Airport, Vienna. 5.50s, Chur Gate, Feldkirch. 6s, County seat, Graz. 6.40s, "Golden Roof," Innsbruck. 10s, Heidenreichstein Castle.

1957-61 **Litho.** ***Perf. 14x13½***

Size: 20x25mm

618A A176 20g violet blk ('61) .20 .20
619 A176 50g bluish black ('59) .20 .20

Engr.

620 A176 1s chocolate 1.25 .20

Typo.

621 A176 1s chocolate 1.75 .20

Litho.

622 A176 1s choc ('59) .90 .20
622A A176 1.40s brt greenish bl ('60) .30 .20
623 A176 1.50s rose lake ('58) .50 .20
624 A176 1.80s brt ultra ('60) .30 .20
625 A176 2s dull blue ('58) 6.00 .20
626 A176 3.40s yel grn ('60) .90 .80
627 A176 4s brt red lil ('60) .75 .20
627A A176 4.50s dl green ('60) 1.00 .50
628 A176 5.50s grnsh gray ('60) .55 .20
629 A176 6s brt vio ('60) 1.00 .20
629A A176 6.40s brt blue ('60) 1.00 .90

Engr.

Size: 22x28mm

630 A177 10s dk bl grn 3.00 .45
Nos. 618A-630 (16) 19.60 5.05

Of the three 1s stamps above, Nos. 620 and 621 have two names in imprint (designer H. Strohofer, engraver G. Wimmer). No. 622 has only Strohofer's name.

Values for Nos. 618A-624, 626-630 are for stamps on white paper. Most denominations also come on grayish paper with yellowish gum.

See Nos. 688-702.

1960-65 **Photo.** ***Perf. 14½x14***

Size: 17x21mm

630A A176 50g slate ('64) .20 .20

Size: 18x21½mm

630B A176 1s chocolate .20 .20

Size: 17x21mm

630C A176 1.50s dk car ('65) .20 .20
Nos. 630A-630C (3) .60 .60

Nos. 630A-630C issued in sheets and coils.

Graukogel, Badgastein — A180

1958, Feb. 1 **Engr.** ***Perf. 14x13½***

631 A180 1.50s dark blue .25 .20

Intl. Ski Federation Alpine championships, Badgastein, Feb. 2-7.

Plane over Map of Austria
A181

1958, Mar. 27 ***Perf. 13½x14***

632 A181 4s red .45 .20

Re-opening of Austrian Airlines.

Mother and Daughter
A182

Walther von der Vogelweide
A183

1958, May 8 **Unwmk.** ***Perf. 14x13½***

633 A182 1.50s dark blue .25 .20

Issued for Mother's Day.

1958, July 17 **Litho. and Engr.**

634 A183 1.50s multicolored .25 .20

3rd Austrian Song Festival, Vienna, July 17-20.

Oswald Redlich — A184

Giant "E" on Map — A185

1958, Sept. 17 **Engr.**

635 A184 2.40s ultramarine .45 .20

Prof. Oswald Redlich (1858-1944), historian, birth cent.

Renner Type of 1948

1958, Nov. 12

636 A136 1.50s deep green .45 .25

Austrian Republic, 40th anniv.

1959, Mar. 9

637 A185 2.40s emerald .35 .20

Idea of a United Europe.

Cigarette Machine and Trademark of Tobacco Monopoly
A186

Archduke Johann
A187

1959, May 8 **Unwmk.** ***Perf. 13½***

638 A186 2.40s dark olive bister .30 .20

Austrian tobacco monopoly, 175th anniv.

1959, May 11 ***Perf. 14x13½***

639 A187 1.50s deep green .25 .20

Archduke Johann of Austria, military leader and humanitarian, death cent.

Capercaillie
A188

Joseph Haydn
A189

Animals: 1.50s, Roe buck. 2.40s, Wild boar. 3.50s, Red deer, doe and fawn.

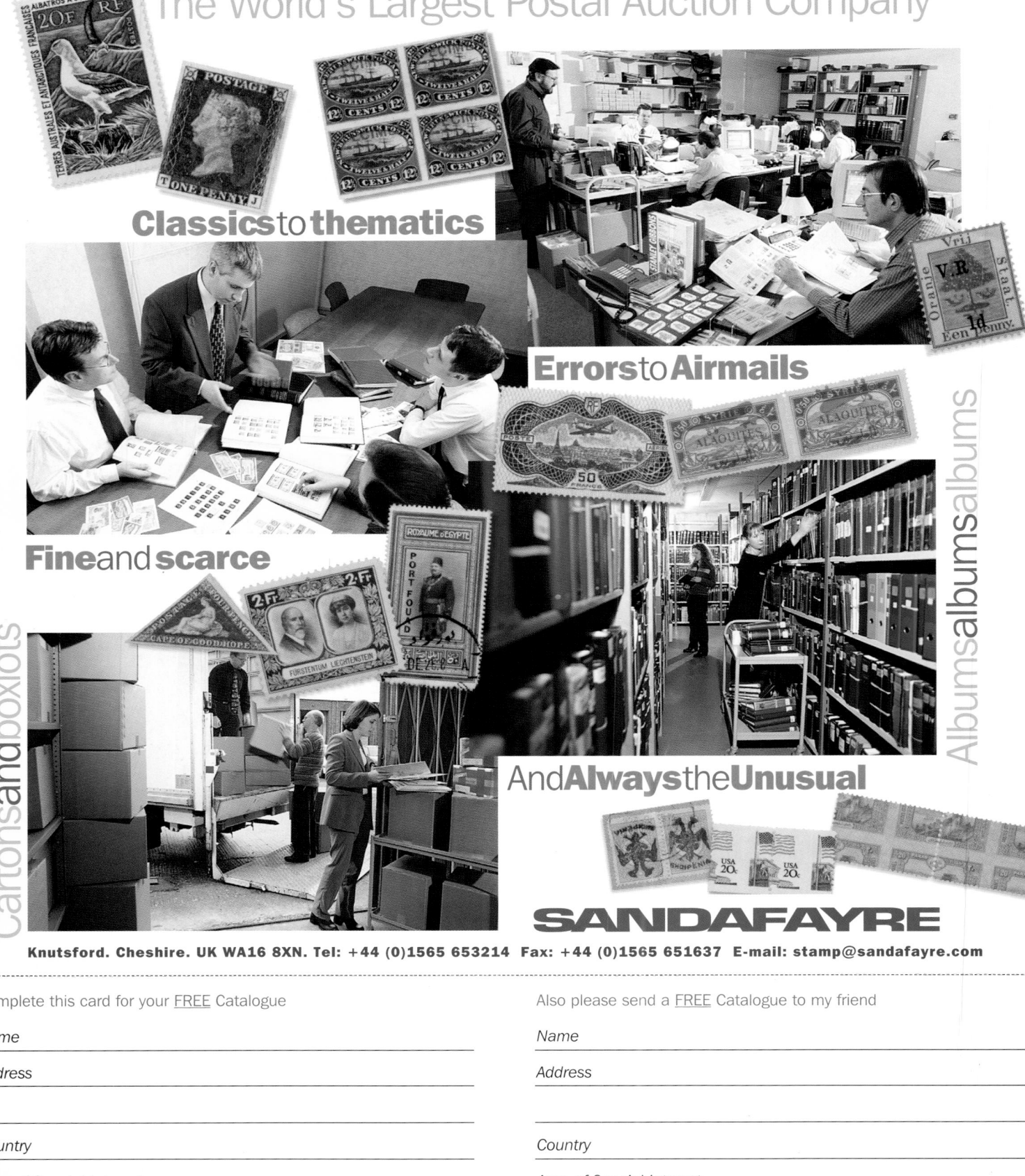

1959, May 20 **Engr.**

640 A188 1s rose violet .30 .20
641 A188 1.50s blue violet .65 .20
642 A188 2.40s dk bl green .45 .35
643 A188 3.50s dark brown .35 .20
Nos. 640-643 (4) 1.75 .95

Congress of the Intl. Hunting Council, Vienna, May 20-24.

1959, May 30 **Unwmk.**

644 A189 1.50s violet brown .45 .20

Joseph Haydn, composer, 150th death anniv.

Coat of Arms, Tyrol A190

Antenna, Zugspitze A191

1959, June 13 ***Perf. 14x13½***

645 A190 1.50s rose red .25 .20

Fight for liberation of Tyrol, 150th anniv.

1959, June 19 ***Perf. 13½***

646 A191 2.40s dk bl grn .30 .20

Inauguration of Austria's relay system.

Field Ball Player A192

Orchestral Instruments A193

1s, Runner. 1.80s, Gymnast on vaulting horse. 2s, Woman hurdler. 2.20s, Hammer thrower.

1959-70 **Engr.** ***Perf. 14x13½***

647 A192 1s lilac .20 .20
648 A192 1.50s blue green .50 .20
648A A192 1.80s carmine ('62) .45 .35
648B A192 2s rose lake ('70) .25 .20
648C A192 2.20s bluish blk ('67) .25 .20
Nos. 647-648C (5) 1.65 1.15

Litho. and Engr.

1959, Aug. 19 ***Perf. 14x13½***

649 A193 2.40s dull bl & blk .30 .20

World tour of the Vienna Philharmonic Orchestra.

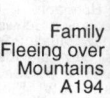

Family Fleeing over Mountains A194

1960, Apr. 7 **Engr.** ***Perf. 13½x14***

650 A194 3s Prussian green .65 .25

WRY, July 1, 1959-June 30, 1960.

President Adolf Schärf — A195

1960, Apr. 20 ***Perf. 14x13½***

651 A195 1.50s gray olive .65 .20

Pres. Adolf Scharf, 70th birthday.

Young Hikers and Hostel A196

1960, May 20 ***Perf. 13½x14***

652 A196 1s carmine rose .25 .20

Youth hiking; youth hostel movement.

Anton Eiselsberg A197

Gustav Mahler A198

Litho. and Engr.

1960, June 20 ***Perf. 14x13½***

653 A197 1.50s buff & dk brn .70 .20

Dr. Anton Eiselsberg, surgeon, birth cent.

1960, July 7 **Engr.**

654 A198 1.50s chocolate .70 .20

Gustav Mahler, composer, birth cent.

Jakob Prandtauer, Melk Abbey — A199

Gross Glockner Mountain Road — A200

1960, July 16 **Unwmk.**

655 A199 1.50s red brown .70 .20

Jakob Prandtauer, architect, 300th birth anniv.

1960, Aug. 3

656 A200 1.80s dark blue .70 .50

Gross Glockner Mountain Road, 25th anniv.

Ionic Capital — A201

1960, Aug. 29 ***Perf. 14x13½***

657 A201 3s black 1.40 .75

Europa: Idea of a United Europe.

Griffen, Carinthia A202

1960, Oct. 10 **Engr.** ***Perf. 13½x14***

658 A202 1.50s slate green .30 .20

40th anniv. of the plebiscite which kept Carinthia with Austria.

Flame and Broken Chain — A203

1961, May 8 **Unwmk.** ***Perf. 14x13½***

659 A203 1.50s scarlet .30 .20

Victims in Austria's fight for freedom.

First Austrian Mail Plane, 1918 — A204

1961, May 15 ***Perf. 13½x14***

660 A204 5s violet blue .70 .30

Airmail Phil. Exhib., LUPOSTA 1961, Vienna, May.

Transportation by Road, Rail and Waterway A205

Mountain Mower, by Albin Egger-Lienz A206

Engraved and Typographed

1961, May 29 ***Perf. 13½***

661 A205 3s rose red & olive .45 .30

13th European Conference of Transportation ministers, Vienna, May 29-31.

1961, June 12 **Engr.** ***Perf. 13½x14***

Designs: 1.50s, The Kiss, by August von Pettenkofen. 3s, Girl, by Anton Romako. 5s, Ariadne's Triumph, by Hans Makart.

Inscriptions in Red Brown

662 A206 1s rose lake .20 .20
663 A206 1.50s dull violet .25 .25
664 A206 3s olive green .75 .70
665 A206 5s blue violet .45 .40
Nos. 662-665 (4) 1.65 1.55

Society of Creative Artists, Künstlerhaus, Vienna, cent.

Sonnblick Mountain and Observatory A207

Mercury and Globe A208

1961, Sept. 1 ***Perf. 14x13½***

666 A207 1.80s violet blue .40 .30

Sonnblick meteorological observatory, 75th anniv.

1961, Sept. 18

667 A208 3s black .70 .40

Intl. Banking Congress, Vienna, Sept. 1961. English inscription listing UN financial groups.

Coal Mine Shaft — A209

Designs: 1.50s, Generator. 1.80s, Iron blast furnace. 3s, Pouring steel. 5s, Oil refinery.

1961, Sept. 15 **Engr.** ***Perf. 14x13½***

668 A209 1s black .20 .20
669 A209 1.50s green .25 .20
670 A209 1.80s dark car rose .55 .40
671 A209 3s bright lilac .70 .55
672 A209 5s blue .90 .70
Nos. 668-672 (5) 2.60 2.05

15th anniversary of nationalized industry.

Arms of Burgenland A210

Franz Liszt A211

1961, Oct. 9 **Engr. and Litho.**

673 A210 1.50s blk, yel & dk red .35 .20

Burgenland as part of the Austrian Republic, 40th anniv.

1961, Oct. 20 **Engr.**

674 A211 3s dark brown .55 .40

Franz Liszt, composer, 150th birth anniv.

Parliament A212

1961, Dec. 18 ***Perf. 13½x14***

675 A212 1s brown .20 .20

Austrian Bureau of Budget, 200th anniv.

Kaprun-Mooserboden Reservoir — A213

Hydroelectric Power Plants: 1.50s, Ybbs-Persenbeug dam and locks. 1.80s, Lünersee dam and reservoir. 3s, Grossraming dam. 4s, Bisamberg transformer plant. 6.40s, St. Andrä power plant.

1962, Mar. 26 **Unwmk.**

676 A213 1s violet blue .20 .20
677 A213 1.50s red lilac .25 .20
678 A213 1.80s green .40 .35
679 A213 3s brown .40 .35
680 A213 4s rose red .40 .35
681 A213 6.40s gray 1.25 1.10
Nos. 676-681 (6) 2.90 2.55

Nationalization of the electric power industry, 15th anniv.

Johann Nestroy
A214

Friedrich Gauermann
A215

1962, May 25 ***Perf. 14x13½***

682 A214 1s violet .20 .20

Johann Nepomuk Nestroy, Viennese playwright, author and actor, death cent.

1962, July 6 **Engr.**

683 A215 1.50s intense blue .20 .20

Friedrich Gauermann (1807-1862), landscape painter, death cent.

Scout Emblem and Handshake — A216

1962, Oct. 5

684 A216 1.50s dark green .35 .20

Austria's Boy Scouts, 50th anniv.

Lowlands Forest
A217

1.50s, Deciduous forest. 3s, Fir & larch forest.

1962, Oct. 12 ***Perf. 13½x14***

685	A217	1s greenish gray	.20	.20
686	A217	1.50s reddish brown	.25	.25
687	A217	3s dk slate green	.90	.70
		Nos. 685-687 (3)	1.35	1.15

Buildings Types of 1957-61

Designs: 30g, City Hall, Vienna. 40g, Porcia Castle, Spittal on the Drau. 60g, Tanners' Tower, Wels. 70g, Residenz Fountain, Salzburg. 80g, Old farmhouse, Pinzgau. 1s, Romanesque columns, Millstatt Abbey. 1.20s, Kornmesser House, Bruck on the Mur. 1.30s, Schatten Castle, Feldkirch, Vorarlberg. 2s, Dragon Fountain, Klagenfurt. 2.20s, Beethoven House, Vienna. 2.50s, Danube Bridge, Linz. 3s, Swiss Gate, Vienna. 3.50s, Esterhazy Palace, Eisenstadt. 8s, City Hall, Steyr. 20s, Melk Abbey.

1962-70 **Litho.** ***Perf. 14x13½***

Size: 20x25mm

688	A176	30g greenish gray	.50	.20
689	A176	40g rose red	.20	.20
690	A176	60g violet brown	.35	.20
691	A176	70g dark blue	.25	.20
692	A176	80g yellow brown	.35	.20
693	A176	1s brown ('70)	.20	.20
694	A176	1.20s red lilac	.40	.20
695	A176	1.30s green ('67)	.20	.20
696	A176	2s dk blue ('68)	.25	.20
697	A176	2.20s green	1.40	.20
698	A176	2.50s violet	.80	.20
699	A176	3s bright blue	.65	.20
700	A176	3.50s rose carmine	.80	.20
701	A176	8s claret ('65)	1.00	.20

Perf. 13½

Engr.

Size: 28x36½mm

702	A177	20s rose claret ('63)	2.50	.35
		Nos. 688-702 (15)	9.85	3.15

Values for Nos. 688-702 are for stamps on white paper. Some denominations also come on grayish paper with yellowish gum.

Electric Locomotive and Train of 1837
A218

Lithographed and Engraved

1962, Nov. 9 ***Perf. 13½x14***

703 A218 3s buff & black .90 .40

125th anniversary of Austrian railroads.

Postilions and Postal Clerk, 1863 — A219

Hermann Bahr — A220

1963, May 7 **Photo.** ***Perf. 14x13½***

704 A219 3s dk brn & citron .70 .40

First Intl. Postal Conference, Paris, cent.

Lithographed and Envraved

1963, July 19 ***Perf. 14x13½***

705 A220 1.50s blue & black .25 .20

Centenary of birth of Hermann Bahr, poet.

St. Florian Statue, Kefermarkt, Contemporary and Old Fire Engines — A221

1963, Aug. 30 **Unwmk.**

706 A221 1.50s brt rose & blk .25 .20

Austrian volunteer fire brigades, cent.

Factory, Flag and "ÖGB" on Map of Austria
A222

1963, Sept. 23 **Litho.** ***Perf. 13½x14***

707 A222 1.50s gray, red & dk brn .25 .20

5th Congress of the Austrian Trade Union Federation (ÖGB), Sept. 23-28.

Arms of Austria and Tyrol
A223

1963, Sept. 27 **Unwmk.**

708 A223 1.50s tan, blk, red & yel .25 .20

Tyrol's union with Austria, 600th anniv.

Prince Eugene of Savoy
A224

Centenary Emblem
A225

1963, Oct. 18 **Engr.** ***Perf. 14x13½***

709 A224 1.50s violet .25 .20

Prince Eugene of Savoy (1663-1736), Austrian general, 300th birth anniv.

1963, Oct. 25 **Engr. and Photo.**

710 A225 3s blk, sil & red .50 .20

Intl. Red Cross, cent.

Slalom
A226

Sports: 1.20s, Biathlon (skier with rifle). 1.50s, Ski jump. 1.80s, Women's figure skating. 2.20s, Ice hockey. 3s, Tobogganing. 4s, Bobsledding.

Photo. and Engr.

1963, Nov. 11 ***Perf. 13½x14***

711	A226	1s multi	.20	.20
712	A226	1.20s multi	.20	.20
713	A226	1.50s multi	.20	.20
714	A226	1.80s multi	.25	.20
715	A226	2.20s multi	.40	.25
716	A226	3s multi	.30	.20
717	A226	4s multi	.55	.35
		Nos. 711-717 (7)	2.10	1.60

9th Winter Olympic Games, Innsbruck, Jan. 29-Feb. 9, 1964.

Baroque Creche by Josef Thaddäus Stammel — A227

1963, Nov. 29 **Engr.** ***Perf. 14x13½***

718 A227 2s dark Prus green .25 .20

Flowers
A228

1964, Apr. 17 **Litho.** ***Perf. 14***

719	A228	1s Nasturtium	.20	.20
720	A228	1.50s Peony	.20	.20
721	A228	1.80s Clematis	.25	.20
722	A228	2.20s Dahlia	.35	.20
723	A228	3s Morning glory	.40	.25
724	A228	4s Hollyhock	.50	.35
		Nos. 719-724 (6)	1.90	1.40

Vienna Intl. Garden Show, Apr. 16-Oct. 11.

St. Mary Magdalene and Apostle — A229

Pallas Athena and National Council Chamber — A230

1964, May 21 **Engr.** ***Perf. 13½***

725 A229 1.50s bluish black .25 .20

Romanesque art in Austria. The 12th century stained-glass window is from the Weitensfeld Church, the bust of the Apostle from the portal of St. Stephen's Cathedral, Vienna.

Engr. and Litho.

1964, May 25 ***Perf. 14x13½***

726 A230 1.80s black & emer .30 .20

2nd Parliamentary and Scientific Conf., Vienna.

The Kiss, by Gustav Klimt
A231

1964, June 5 **Litho.** ***Perf. 13½***

727 A231 3s multicolored .35 .25

Re-opening of the Vienna Secession, a museum devoted to early 20th century art (art nouveau).

Brother of Mercy and Patient — A232

1964, June 11 **Engr.** ***Perf. 14x13½***

728 A232 1.50s dark blue .25 .20

Brothers of Mercy in Austria, 350th anniv.

"Bringing the News of Victory at Kunersdorf" by Bernardo Bellotto
A233

"The Post in Art": 1.20s, Changing Horses at Relay Station, by Julius Hörmann. 1.50s, The Honeymoon Trip, by Moritz von Schwind. 1.80s, After the Rain, by Ignaz Raffalt. 2.20s, Mailcoach in the Mountains, by Adam Klein. 3s, Changing Horses at Bavarian Border, by Friedrich Gauermann. 4s, Postal Sleigh (Truck) in the Mountains, by Adalbert Pilch. 6.40s, Saalbach Post Office, by Adalbert Pilch.

1964, June 15 ***Perf. 13½x14***

729	A233	1s rose claret	.20	.20
730	A233	1.20s sepia	.20	.20
731	A233	1.50s violet blue	.20	.20
732	A233	1.80s brt violet	.20	.20
733	A233	2.20s black	.20	.20
734	A233	3s dl car rose	.30	.20
735	A233	4s slate green	.35	.20
736	A233	6.40s dull claret	.80	.45
		Nos. 729-736 (8)	2.45	1.85

15th UPU Cong., Vienna, May-June 1964.

Workers — A234

1964, Sept. 4 ***Perf. 14x13½***

737 A234 1s black .20 .20

Centenary of Austrian Labor Movement.

Common Design Types pictured following the introduction.

Europa Issue, 1964
Common Design Type

1964, Sept. 14 Litho. *Perf. 12*
Size: 21x36mm

738 CD7 3s dark blue .50 .20

Emblem of Radio Austria and Transistor Radio Panel A235

1964, Oct. 1 Photo. *Perf. 13½*

739 A235 1s black brn & red .20 .20

Forty years of Radio Austria.

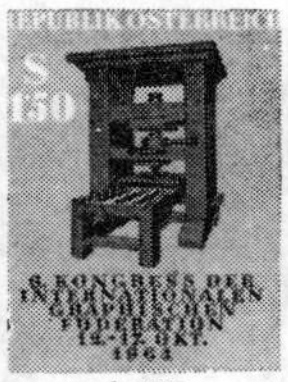

A236 A237

Litho. and Engr.

1964, Oct. 12 ***Perf. 14x13½***

740 A236 1.50s Old printing press .20 .20

6th Congress of the Intl. Graphic Federation, Vienna, Oct. 12-17.

Typo. and Engr.

1965, Apr. 20 ***Perf. 12***

Pres. Adolf Schärf and Scharf Student Center.

741 A237 1.50s bluish black .20 .20

Dr. Adolf Schärf (1890-1965), Pres. of Austria (1957-65).

Ruins and New Buildings — A238

1965, Apr. 27 Engr. *Perf. 14x13½*

742 A238 1.80s carmine lake .20 .20

Twenty years of reconstruction.

Oldest Seal of Vienna University A239 St. George, 16th Century Wood Sculpture A240

Photo. and Engr.

1965, May 10 ***Perf. 14x13½***

743 A239 3s gold & red .35 .20

University of Vienna, 600th anniv.

1965, May 17 Engr.

744 A240 1.80s bluish black .25 .20

Art of the Danube Art School, 1490-1540, exhibition, May-Oct. 1965. The stamp background shows an engraving by Albrecht Altdorfer.

ITU Emblem, Telegraph Key and TV Antenna A241 Ferdinand Raimund A242

1965, May 17 Unwmk.

745 A241 3s violet blue .35 .20

ITU, cent.

1965 Engr. *Perf. 14x13½*

Portraits: No. 746, Dr. Ignaz Philipp Semmelweis. No. 747, Bertha von Suttner. No. 749, Ferdinand Georg Waldmüller.

746	A242	1.50s violet	.30	.20
747	A242	1.50s bluish black	.30	.20
748	A242	3s dark brown	.55	.20
749	A242	3s greenish blk	.55	.20
		Nos. 746-749 (4)	1.70	.80

Semmelweis (1818-65), who discovered the cause of puerperal fever and introduced antisepsis into obstetrics (#746). 60th anniv. of the awarding of the Nobel Prize for Peace to von Suttner (1843-1914), pacifist and author (#747). Raimund (1790-1836), actor and playwright (#748). Waldmüller (1793-1865), painter (#749).

Issue dates: No. 746, Aug. 13; No. 747, Dec. 1; No. 748, June 1; No. 749, Aug. 23.

Dancers with Tambourines A243 Red Cross and Strip of Gauze A244

Design: 1.50s, Male gymnasts with practice bars.

1965, July 20 Photo. and Engr.

750 A243 1.50s gray & black .20 .20
751 A243 3s bister & blk .35 .25

4th Gymnaestrada, intl. athletic meet, Vienna, July 20-24.

1965, Oct. 1 Litho. *Perf. 14x13½*

752 A244 3s black & red .35 .20

20th Intl. Red Cross Conference, Vienna.

Austrian Flag and Eagle with Mural Crown — A245 Austrian Flag, UN Headquarters and Emblem — A246

1965, Oct. 7 Photo. and Engr.

753 A245 1.50s gold, red & blk .20 .20

50th anniv. of the Union of Austrian Towns.

Lithographed and Engraved

1965, Oct. 25 Unwmk. *Perf. 12*

754 A246 3s blk, brt bl & red .45 .20

Austria's admission to the UN, 10th anniv.

University of Technology, Vienna A247

1965, Nov. 8 Engr. *Perf. 13½x14*

755 A247 1.50s violet .20 .20

Vienna University of Technology, 150th anniv.

Map of Austria with Postal Zone Numbers — A248

1966, Jan. 14 Photo. *Perf. 12*

756 A248 1.50s yel, red & blk .20 .20

Introduction of postal zone numbers, Jan. 1, 1966.

PTT Building, Emblem and Churches of Sts. Maria Rotunda and Barbara A249 Maria von Ebner Eschenbach A250

Lithographed and Engraved

1966, Mar. 4 ***Perf. 14x13½***

757 A249 1.50s blk, *dull yellow* .20 .20

Headquarters of the Post and Telegraph Administration, cent.

1966, Mar. 11 Engr.

758 A250 3s plum .35 .20

50th death anniv. of Maria von Ebner Eschenbach (1830-1916), novelist and poet.

Ferris Wheel, Prater — A251

1966, Apr. 19 Engr. *Perf. 14x13½*

759 A251 1.50s slate green .20 .20

Opening of the Prater (park), Vienna, to the public by Emperor Joseph II, 200th anniv.

A252 A253

1966, May 6 Unwmk. *Perf. 12*

760 A252 3s dark brown .35 .20

Josef Hoffmann (1870-1956), architect, 10th death anniv.

Photo. and Engr.

1966, May 27 ***Perf. 14***

761 A253 1.50s Wiener Neustadt Arms .20 .20

Wiener Neustadt Art Exhib., centered around the time and person of Frederick III (1440-93).

Austrian Eagle and Emblem of National Bank A254

1966, May 27 ***Perf. 14***

762 A254 3s gray grn, dk brn & dk green .35 .20

Austrian National Bank, 150th anniv.

Puppy — A255 A256

Litho. and Engr.

1966, June 16 ***Perf. 12***

763 A255 1.80s yellow & black .25 .20

120th anniv. of the Vienna Humane Society.

1966, Aug. 17 Litho. *Perf. 13½*

Alpine Flowers: 1.50s, Columbine. 1.80s, Turk's cap. 2.20s, Wulfenia carinthiaca. 3s, Globeflowers. 4s, Fire lily. 5s, Pasqueflower.

Flowers in Natural Colors

764	A256	1.50s dark blue	.20	.20
765	A256	1.80s dark blue	.25	.20
766	A256	2.20s dark blue	.35	.20
767	A256	3s dark blue	.50	.30
768	A256	4s dark blue	.50	.35
769	A256	5s dark blue	.50	.35
		Nos. 764-769 (6)	2.30	1.60

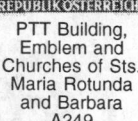

Fair Building A257

1966, Aug. 26 Engr. ***Perf. 13½x13***

770	A257	3s violet blue	.35	.20

First International Fair at Wels.

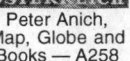

Peter Anich, Map, Globe and Books — A258

Sick Worker and Health Emblem — A259

1966, Sept. 1 ***Perf. 14x13½***

771	A258	1.80s black	.20	.20

Peter Anich (1723-1766), Tirolean cartographer and farmer, 200th death anniv.

1966, Sept. 19 Engr. and Litho.

772	A259	3s black & vermilion	.35	.20

15th Occupational Medicine Congress, Vienna, Sept. 19-24.

Theater Collection: "Eunuchus" by Terence from a 1496 Edition A260

Designs: 1.80s, Map Collection: Title page of Geographia Blavania (Cronus, Hercules and celestial sphere). 2.20s, Picture Archive and Portrait Collection: View of Old Vienna after a watercolor by Anton Stutzinger. 3s, Manuscript Collection: Illustration from the 15th century "Livre du Cuer d'Amours Espris" of the Duke René d'Anjou.

Photogravure and Engraved

1966, Sept. 28 ***Perf. 13½x14***

773	A260	1.50s multicolored	.20	.20
774	A260	1.80s multicolored	.20	.20
775	A260	2.20s multicolored	.25	.20
776	A260	3s multicolored	.30	.20
		Nos. 773-776 (4)	.95	.80

Austrian National Library.

Young Girl A261

Strawberries A262

Litho. and Engr.

1966, Oct. 3 ***Perf. 14x13½***

777	A261	3s light blue & black	.35	.20

"Save the Child" society, 10th anniv.

1966, Nov. 25 Photo. ***Perf. 13½x13***

778	A262	50g	shown	.20	.20
779	A262	1s	Grapes	.20	.20
780	A262	1.50s	Apple	.20	.20
781	A262	1.80s	Blackberries	.25	.20
782	A262	2.20s	Apricots	.25	.20
783	A262	3s	Cherries	.35	.25
			Nos. 778-783 (6)	1.45	1.25

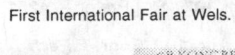

Coat of Arms of University of Linz — A263

Ice Skater, 1866 — A264

Photo. and Engr.

1966, Dec. 9 ***Perf. 14x13½***

784	A263	3s multi	.35	.20

Inauguration of the Universary of Linz, Oct. 8, 1966.

Photo. and Engr.

1967, Feb. 3 ***Perf. 14x13½***

785	A264	3s pale bl & dk bl	.35	.20

Centenary of Vienna Ice Skating Club.

Ballet Dancer A265

Karl Schönherr A266

1967, Feb. 15 Engr. ***Perf. 11½x12***

786	A265	3s deep claret	.35	.20
	a.	Perf. 12	1.25	1.10

"Blue Danube" waltz by Johann Strauss, cent.

1967, Feb. 24 Engr. ***Perf. 14x13½***

787	A266	3s gray brown	.35	.20

Dr. Karl Schönherr (1867-1943), poet, playwright and physician.

Ice Hockey Goalkeeper A267

Photogravure and Engraved

1967, Mar. 17 ***Perf. 13½x14***

788	A267	3s pale grn & dk bl	.35	.20

Ice Hockey Championships, Vienna, Mar. 18-29.

Violin, Organ and Laurel — A268

1967, Mar. 28 Engr. ***Perf. 13½***

789	A268	3.50s indigo	.40	.20

Vienna Philharmonic Orchestra, 125th anniv.

Motherhood, Watercolor by Peter Fendi — A269

1967, Apr. 28 Litho. ***Perf. 14***

790	A269	2s multicolored	.25	.20

Mother's Day.

Gothic Mantle Madonna A270

1967, May 19 Engr. ***Perf. 13½x14***

791	A270	3s slate	.35	.20

"Austrian Gothic," art exhibition, Krems, 1967. The Gothic wood carving is from Frauenstein in Upper Austria.

Medieval Gold Cross — A271

Swan, Tapestry by Oscar Kokoschka — A272

Litho. and Engr.

1967, June 9 ***Perf. 13½***

792	A271	3.50s Prus grn & multi	.40	.20

Salzburg Treasure Chamber; exhibition at Salzburg Cathedral, June 12-Sept. 15.

1967, June 9 Photo.

793	A272	2s multicolored	.25	.20

Nibelungen District Art Exhibition, Pöchlarn, celebrating the 700th anniversary of Pöchlarn as a city. The design is from the border of the Amor and Psyche tapestry at the Salzburg Festival Theater.

View and Arms of Vienna A273

Engraved and Photogravure

1967, June 12 ***Perf. 13x13½***

794	A273	3s black & red	.35	.20

10th Europa Talks, "Science and Society in Europe," Vienna, June 13-17.

Prize Bull "Mucki" A274

1967, Aug. 28 Engr. ***Perf. 13½***

795	A274	2s deep claret	.35	.20

Centenary of the Ried Festival and the Agricultural Fair.

Potato Beetle A275

Engraved and Photogravure

1967, Aug. 29 ***Perf. 13½x14***

796	A275	3s black & multi	.35	.20

6th Intl. Congress for Plant Protection, Vienna.

First Locomotive Used on Brenner Pass — A276

1967, Sept. 23 Photo. ***Perf. 12***

797	A276	3.50s tan & slate grn	.45	.20

Centenary of railroad over Brenner Pass.

Christ in Glory — A277

1967, Oct. 9 ***Perf. 13½***

798	A277	2s multicolored	.25	.20

Restoration of the Romanesque (11th century) frescoes in the Lambach monastery church.

Main Gate to Fair, Prater, Vienna A278

1967, Oct. 24 Photo. ***Perf. 13½x14***

799	A278	2s choc & buff	.25	.20

Congress of Intl. Trade Fairs, Vienna, Oct., 1967.

Medal Showing Minerva and Art Symbols A279

Frankfurt Medal for Reformation, 1717 A280

Litho. & Engr.

1967, Oct. 25 ***Perf. 13½***

800	A279	2s dk brn, dk bl & yel	.25	.20

Vienna Academy of Fine Arts, 275th anniv. The medal was designed by Georg Raphael Donner (1693-1741) and is awarded as an artist's prize.

1967, Oct. 31 Engr. ***Perf. 14x13½***

801	A280	3.50s blue black	.40	.20

450th anniversary of the Reformation.

Mountain Range and Stone Pines
A281

1967, Nov. 7 *Perf. 13½*
802 A281 3.50s green .40 .20

Centenary of academic study of forestry.

Land Survey Monument, 1770 — A282

St. Leopold, Window, Heiligenkreuz Abbey — A283

1967, Nov. 7 **Photo.**
803 A282 2s olive black .25 .20

150th anniversary of official land records.

1967, Nov. 15 **Engr. & Photo.**
804 A283 1.80s multicolored .25 .20

Margrave Leopold III (1075-1136), patron saint of Austria.

Tragic Mask and Violin — A284

Nativity from 15th Century Altar — A285

1967, Nov. 17 *Perf. 13½*
805 A284 3.50s bluish lil & blk .40 .20

Academy of Music and Dramatic Art, 150th anniv.

1967, Nov. 27 **Engr.** *Perf. 14x13½*
806 A285 2s green .25 .20

Christmas.

The design shows the late Gothic carved center panel of the altar in St. John's Chapel in Nonnberg Convent, Salzburg.

Innsbruck Stadium, Alps and FISU Emblem — A286

Camillo Sitte — A287

1968, Jan. 22 **Engr.** *Perf. 13½*
807 A286 2s dark blue .25 .20

Winter University Games under the auspices of FISU (Fédération Internationale du Sport Universitaire), Innsbruck, Jan. 21-28.

1968, Apr. 17 *Perf. 13½*
808 A287 2s black brown .25 .20

125th birth anniv. of Camillo Sitte (1843-1903), architect and city planner.

Mother and Child — A288

1968, May 7
809 A288 2s slate green .25 .20

Mother's Day.

Cup and Serpent Emblem — A289

1968, May 7 **Photo.**
810 A289 3.50s dp plum, gray & gold .40 .20

Bicentenary of the Veterinary College.

Bride with Lace Veil — A290

1968, May 24 **Engr.** *Perf. 12*
811 A290 3.50s blue black .40 .20

Embroidery industry of Vorarlberg, cent.

Horse Race
A291

1968, June 4 *Perf. 13½*
812 A291 3.50s sepia .40 .20

Centenary of horse racing at Freudenau, Vienna.

Dr. Karl Landsteiner
A292

Peter Rosegger
A293

1968, June 14 *Perf. 14x13½*
813 A292 3.50s dark blue .40 .20

Birth cent. of Dr. Karl Landsteiner (1868-1943), pathologist, discoverer of the four main human blood types.

1968, June 26
814 A293 2s slate green .25 .20

50th death anniv. of Peter Rosegger (1843-1918), poet and writer.

Angelica Kauffmann, Self-portrait
A294

Bronze Statue of Young Man, 1st Century B.C.
A295

1968, July 15 **Engr.** *Perf. 14x13½*
815 A294 2s intense black .25 .20

"Angelica Kauffmann and her Contemporaries," art exhibitions, Bregenz, July 28-Oct. 13, and Vienna, Oct. 22, 1968-Jan. 6, 1969.

1968, July 15 **Litho. & Engr.**
816 A295 2s grnsh gray & blk .25 .20

20 years of excavations on Magdalene Mountain, Carinthia.

Bishop, Romanesque Bas-relief — A296

1968, Sept. 20 **Engr.** *Perf. 14x13½*
817 A296 2s blue gray .25 .20

Graz-Seckau Bishopric, 750th anniv.

Koloman Moser — A297

Human Rights Flame — A298

Engr. & Photo.

1968, Oct. 18 *Perf. 12*
818 A297 2s black brn & ver .25 .20

50th death anniv. of Koloman Moser (1868-1918), stamp designer and painter.

1968, Oct. 18 **Photo.** *Perf. 14x13½*
819 A298 1.50s gray, dp car & dk green .30 .20

International Human Rights Year.

A299

A300

Designs: No. 820, Pres. Karl Renner and States' arms. No. 821, Coats of arms of Austria and Austrian states. No. 822, Article I of Austrian Constitution and States' coats of arms.

Engr. & Photo.

1968, Nov. 11 *Perf. 13½*
820 A299 2s black & multi .35 .30
821 A299 2s black & multi .35 .30
822 A299 2s black & multi .35 .30
Nos. 820-822 (3) 1.05 .90

50th anniversary of Republic of Austria.

1968, Nov. 29 **Engr.** *Perf. 14x13½*

Crèche, Memorial Chapel, Oberndorf-Salzburg.

823 A300 2s slate green .25 .20

Christmas; 150th anniv. of "Silent Night, Holy Night" hymn.

Angels, from Last Judgment by Troger (Röhrenbach-Greillenstein Chapel) — A301

Baroque Frescoes: No. 825, Vanquished Demons, by Paul Troger, Altenburg Abbey. No. 826, Sts. Peter and Paul, by Troger, Melk Abbey. No. 827, The Glorification of Mary, by Franz Anton Maulpertsch, Maria Treu Church, Vienna. No. 828, St. Leopold Carried into Heaven, by Maulpertsch, Ebenfurth Castle Chapel. No. 829, Symbolic figures from The Triumph of Apollo, by Maulpertsch, Halbthurn Castle.

Engr. & Photo.

1968, Dec. 11 *Perf. 13½x14*
824 A301 2s multicolored .30 .30
825 A301 2s multicolored .30 .30
826 A301 2s multicolored .30 .30
827 A301 2s multicolored .30 .30
828 A301 2s multicolored .30 .30
829 A301 2s multicolored .30 .30
Nos. 824-829 (6) 1.80 1.80

St. Stephen — A302

Statues in St. Stephen's Cathedral, Vienna: No. 831, St. Paul. No. 832, Mantle Madonna. No. 833, St. Christopher. No. 834, St. George and the Dragon. No. 835, St. Sebastian.

1969, Jan. 28 **Engr.** *Perf. 13½*
830 A302 2s black .30 .30
831 A302 2s rose claret .30 .30
832 A302 2s gray violet .30 .30
833 A302 2s slate blue .30 .30
834 A302 2s slate green .30 .30
835 A302 2s dk red brn .30 .30
Nos. 830-835 (6) 1.80 1.80

500th anniversary of Diocese of Vienna.

Parliament and Pallas Athena Fountain, Vienna
A303

1969, Apr. 8 **Engr.** *Perf. 13½*
836 A303 2s greenish black .25 .20

Interparliamentary Union Conf., Vienna, 4/7-13.

Europa Issue, 1969

Common Design Type

1969, Apr. 28 **Photo.** *Perf. 12*
837 CD12 2s gray grn, brick red & blue .25 .20

Council of Europe Emblem — A304

1969, May 5
838 A304 3.50s gray, ultra, blk & yel .45 .25

20th anniversary of Council of Europe.

Frontier Guards — A305

Engr. & Photo.

1969, May 14 *Perf. 12*
839 A305 2s sepia & red .25 .20

Austrian Federal Army.

Don Giovanni, by Mozart — A306

Cent. of Vienna Opera House: a, Don Giovanni, Mozart. b, Magic Flute, Mozart. c, Fidelio, Beethoven. d, Lohengrin, Wagner. e, Don Carlos, Verdi. f, Carmen, Bizet. g, Rosencavalier, Richard Strauss. h, Swan Lake, Ballet by Tchaikovsky.

1969, May 23 *Perf. 13½*
840 A306 Sheet of 8 4.00 4.00
a.-h. 2s, any single .35 .35

Centenary of Vienna Opera House.

No. 840 contains 8 stamps arranged around gold and red center label showing Opera House. Printed in sheets containing 4 Nos. 840 with wide gutters between.

A307

A308

Gothic armor of Maximilian I.

1969, June 4 **Engr.**
841 A307 2s bluish black .25 .20

Emperor Maximilian I Exhibition, Innsbruck, May 30-Oct. 5.

1969, June 16 **Photo.** *Perf. 13½*

Oldest Municipal Seal of Vienna.

842 A308 2s tan, red & black .25 .20

19th Cong. of the Intl. Org. of Municipalities, Vienna, June 1969.

A309

A310

Girl's head and village house.

Engraved and Photogravure

1969, June 16 *Perf. 13½x14*
843 A309 2s yel grn & sepia .25 .20

20th anniv. of the Children's Village Movement in Austria (SOS Villages).

1969, Aug. 22 **Photo.** *Perf. 13x13½*

Hands holding wrench, and UN emblem.

844 A310 2s deep green .25 .20

ILO, 50th anniv.

A311

A312

Austria's flag and shield circling the world.

Engraved and Lithographed

1969, Aug. 22 *Perf. 14x13½*
845 A311 3.50s slate & red .40 .20

Year of Austrians Living Abroad, 1969.

Engraved and Photogravure

1969, Sept. 26 *Perf. 13½*

Etchings: No. 846, Young Hare, by Dürer. No. 847, El Cid Killing a Bull, by Francisco de Goya. No. 848, Madonna with the Pomegranate, by Raphael. No. 849, The Painter, by Peter Brueghel. No. 850, Rubens' Son Nicolas, by Rubens. No. 851, Self-portrait, by Rembrandt. No. 852, Lady Reading, by Francois Guerin. No. 853, Wife of the Artist, by Egon Schiele.

Gray Frame, Buff Background

846 A312 2s black & brown .30 .30
847 A312 2s black .30 .30
848 A312 2s black .30 .30
849 A312 2s black .30 .30
850 A312 2s black & salmon .30 .30
851 A312 2s black .30 .30
852 A312 2s black & salmon .30 .30
853 A312 2s black .30 .30
Nos. 846-853 (8) 2.40 2.40

Etching collection in the Albertina, Vienna, 200th anniv.

President Franz Jonas — A313

1969, Oct. 3
854 A313 2s gray & vio blue .25 .20

70th birthday of Franz Jonas, Austrian Pres.

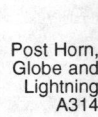

Post Horn, Globe and Lightning A314

1969, Oct. 17 *Perf. 13½x14*
855 A314 2s multicolored .25 .20

Union of Postal and Telegraph employees, 50th anniv.

Savings Box, about 1450 A315

Madonna, by Albin Egger-Lienz A316

1969, Oct. 31 **Photo.** *Perf. 13x13½*
856 A315 2s silver & slate green .25 .20

The importance of savings.

Engr. & Photo.

1969, Nov. 24 *Perf. 12*
857 A316 2s dp claret & pale yel .25 .20

Christmas.

Josef Schöffel A317

St. Klemens M. Hofbauer A318

1970, Feb. 6 **Engr.** *Perf. 14x13½*
858 A317 2s dull purple .25 .20

60th death anniv. of Josef Schöffel, (1832-1910), who saved the Vienna Woods.

Engraved and Photogravure

1970, Mar. 13 *Perf. 14x13½*
859 A318 2s dk brn & lt tan .25 .20

150th death anniv. St. Klemens Maria Hofbauer (1751-1820); Redemptorist preacher in Poland and Austria, canonized in 1909.

Chancellor Leopold Figl A319

Belvedere Palace, Vienna A320

1970, Apr. 27 **Engr.** *Perf. 13½*
860 A319 2s dark olive gray .25 .20
861 A320 2s dark rose brown .25 .20

25th anniversary of Second Republic.

A321

A322

1970, May 19 **Engr.** *Perf. 13½*
862 A321 2s Krimml waterfalls .30 .20

European Nature Conservation Year, 1970.

Litho. & Engr.

1970, June 5 *Perf. 13½*

St. Leopold on oldest seal of Innsbruck University.

863 A322 2s red & black .30 .20

Leopold Franzens University, Innsbruck, 300th anniv.

Organ, Great Hall, Music Academy — A323

Photo. & Engr.

1970, June 5 *Perf. 14*
864 A323 2s gold & deep claret .25 .20

Vienna Music Academy Building, cent.

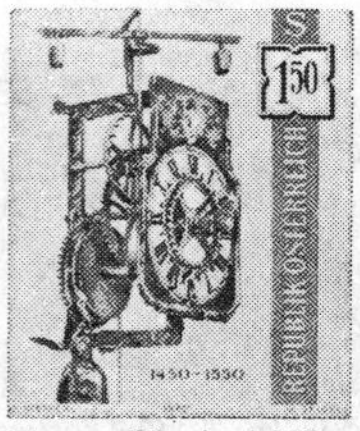

Tower Clock, 1450-1550 A324

The Beggar Student, by Carl Millöcker A325

Old Clocks from Vienna Horological Museum: #866, Lyre clock, 1790-1815. #867, Pendant clock 1600-50. #868, Pendant watch, 1800-30. #869, Bracket clock, 1720-60. #870, French column clock, 1820-50.

1970
865 A324 1.50s buff & sepia .25 .25
866 A324 1.50s greenish & grn .25 .25
867 A324 2s pale bl & dk bl .30 .30
868 A324 2s pale rose & lake .30 .30
869 A324 3.50s buff & brown .50 .50
870 A324 3.50s pale lil & brn vio .50 .50
Nos. 865-870 (6) 2.10 2.10

Issued: #865, 867, 869, 6/22; others, 10/23.

1970 **Photo & Engr.** *Perf. 13½*

Operettas: No. 872, Fledermaus, by Johann Strauss. No. 873, The Dream Waltz, by Oscar Strauss. No. 874, The Bird Seller, by Carl Zeller. No. 875, The Merry Widow, by Franz Lehar. No. 876, Two Hearts in Three-quarter Time, by Robert Stolz.

871 A325 1.50s pale grn & grn .25 .25
872 A325 1.50s yel & vio blue .25 .25
873 A325 2s pale rose & vio brn .30 .30
874 A325 2s pale grn & sep .30 .30
875 A325 3.50s pale bl & ind .50 .50
876 A325 3.50s beige & slate .50 .50
Nos. 871-876 (6) 2.10 2.10

Issued: #871, 873, 875, 7/3; others 9/11.

Bregenz Festival Stage — A326

1970, July 23 **Photo.**
877 A326 3.50s dark blue & buff .40 .20

25th anniversary of Bregenz Festival.

Salzburg Festival Emblem — A327

1970, July 27 *Perf. 14*
878 A327 3.50s blk, red, gold & gray .40 .20

50th anniversary of Salzburg Festival.

A328 A329

1970, Aug. 31 **Engr.**
879 A328 3.50s dark gray .45 .20

13th General Assembly of the World Veterans Federation, Aug. 28-Sept. 4. The head of St. John is from a sculpture showing the Agony in the Garden in the chapel of the Parish Church in Ried. It is attributed to Thomas Schwanthaler (1634-1702).

1970, Sept. 16 *Perf. 14x13½*
880 A329 2s chocolate .25 .20

Thomas Koschat (1845-1914), Carinthian composer of songs.

Mountain Scene A330

Perf. 14x13½

1970, Sept. 16 **Photo.**
881 A330 2s vio bl & pink .25 .20

Hiking and mountaineering in Austria.

Alfred Cossmann A331

Arms of Carinthia A332

1970, Oct. 2 Engr. *Perf. 14x13½*
882 A331 2s dark brown .25 .20

Alfred Cossmann (1870-1951), engraver.

Photo. & Engr.

1970, Oct. 2 *Perf. 14*
883 A332 2s ol, red, gold, blk & sil .25 .20

Carinthian plebiscite, 50th anniversary.

UN Emblem — A333

1970, Oct. 23 Litho. *Perf. 14x13½*
884 A333 3.50s lt blue & blk .50 .20

25th anniversary of the United Nations.

Adoration of the Shepherds, Carving from Garsten Vicarage A334

1970, Nov. 27 Engr. *Perf. 13½x14*
885 A334 2s dk violet blue .25 .20

Christmas.

Karl Renner A335

Beethoven, by Georg Waldmüller A336

1970, Dec. 14 Engr. *Perf. 14x13½*
886 A335 2s deep claret .25 .20

Karl Renner (1870-1950), Austrian Pres., birth cent.

Photo. & Engr.

1970, Dec. 16 *Perf. 13½*
887 A336 3.50s black & buff .50 .20

Ludwig van Beethoven (1770-1827), composer, birth bicentenary.

Enrica Handel-Mazzetti A337

1971, Jan. 11 Engr. *Perf. 14x13½*
888 A337 2s sepia .25 .20

Birth cent. of Enrica von Handel-Mazzetti (1871-1955), novelist and poet.

"Watch Out for Children!" A338

1971, Feb. 18 Photo. *Perf. 13½*
889 A338 2s blk, red brn & brt grn .25 .20

Traffic safety.

Saltcellar, by Benvenuto Cellini A339

Art Treasures: 1.50s, Covered vessel, made of prase, gold and precious stones, Florentine, 1580. 2s, Emperor Joseph I, ivory statue by Matthias Steinle, 1693.

Photo. & Engr.

1971, Mar. 22 *Perf. 14*
890 A339 1.50s gray & slate grn .20 .20
891 A339 2s gray & deep plum .25 .20
892 A339 3.50s gray, blk & bister .55 .35
Nos. 890-892 (3) 1.00 .75

Emblem of Austrian Wholesalers' Organization A340

1971, Apr. 16 Photo. *Perf. 13½*
893 A340 3.50s multicolored .45 .20

Intl. Chamber of Commerce, 23rd Congress, Vienna, Apr. 17-23.

Jacopo de Strada, by Titian — A341

Paintings in Vienna Museum: 2s, Village Feast, by Peter Brueghel, the Elder. 3.50s, Young Venetian Woman, by Albrecht Dürer.

1971, May 6 Engr. *Perf. 13½*
894 A341 1.50s rose lake .25 .20
895 A341 2s greenish black .25 .20
896 A341 3.50s deep brown .50 .35
Nos. 894-896 (3) 1.00 .75

Seal of Paulus of Franchenfordia, 1380 — A342

Photo. & Engr.

1971, May 6 *Perf. 13½x14*
897 A342 3.50s dk brn & bister .40 .20

Congress commemorating the centenary of the Austrian Notaries' Statute, May 5-8.

St. Matthew A343

August Neilreich A344

1971, May 27 *Perf. 12½x13½*
898 A343 2s brt rose lil & brn .25 .20

Exhibition of "1000 Years of Art in Krems." The statue of St. Matthew is from the Lentl Altar, created about 1520 by the Master of the Pulkau Altar.

1971, June 1 Engr. *Perf. 14x13½*
899 A344 2s brown .25 .20

August Neilreich (1803-71), botanist.

Singer with Lyre — A345

Photo. & Engr.

1971, July 1 *Perf. 13½x14*
900 A345 4s lt bl, vio bl & gold .50 .30

Intl. Choir Festival, Vienna, July 1-4.

Coat of Arms of Kitzbuhel — A346

1971, Aug. 23 *Perf. 14*
901 A346 2.50s gold & multi .35 .20

700th anniversary of the town of Kitzbuhel.

Vienna Stock Exchange — A347

1971, Sept. 1 Engr. *Perf. 13½x14*
902 A347 4s reddish brown .55 .20

Bicentenary of the Vienna Stock Exchange.

First and Latest Exhibition Halls A348

1971, Sept. 6 Photo. *Perf. 13½x13*
903 A348 2.50s dp rose lilac .35 .20

Vienna Intl. Fair, 50th anniv.

Trade Union Emblem A349

Arms of Burgenland A350

1971, Sept. 20 *Perf. 14x13½*
904 A349 2s gray, buff & red .25 .20

Austrian Trade Union Assoc., 25th anniv.

1971, Oct. 1
905 A350 2s dk bl, gold, red & blk .25 .20

50th anniv. of Burgenland joining Austria.

Marcus Car — A351

Photo. & Engr.

1971, Oct. 1 *Perf. 14*
906 A351 4s pale green & blk .50 .25

Austrian Automobile, Motorcycle and Touring Club, 75th anniv.

Europa Bridge — A352

1971, Oct. 8 Engr. *Perf. 14x13½*
907 A352 4s violet blue .50 .25

Opening of highway over Brenner Pass.

Styria's Iron Mountain A353

Designs: 2s, Austrian Nitrogen Products, Ltd., Linz. 4s, United Austrian Iron and Steel Works, Ltd. (VÖEST), Linz Harbor.

1971, Oct. 15 ***Perf. 13½***

908	A353	1.50s reddish brown	.25	.20
909	A353	2s bluish black	.30	.20
910	A353	4s dk slate grn	.45	.35
		Nos. 908-910 (3)	1.00	.75

25 years of nationalized industry.

High-speed Train on Semmering A354

Trout Fisherman A355

1971, Oct. 21 ***Perf. 14***

911 A354 2s claret .25 .20

Inter-city rapid train service.

1971, Nov. 15 ***Perf. 13½***

912 A355 2s dark red brn .25 .20

Erich Tschermak-Seysenegg A356

Infant Jesus as Savior, by Dürer A357

Photo. & Engr.

1971, Nov. 15 ***Perf. 14x13½***

913 A356 2s pale ol & dk pur .25 .20

Birth cent. of Dr. Erich Tschermak-Seysenegg (1871-1962), botanist.

1971, Nov. 26 ***Perf. 13½***

914 A357 2s gold & multi .25 .20

Christmas.

Franz Grillparzer, by Moritz Daffinger — A358

Fountain, Main Square, Friesach — A359

Litho. & Engr.

1972, Jan. 21 ***Perf. 14x13½***

915 A358 2s buff, gold & blk .30 .20

Death cent. of Franz Grillparzer (1791-1872), dramatic poet.

1972, Feb. 23 Engr. ***Perf. 14x13½***

Designs: 2s, Fountain, Heiligenkreuz Abbey. 2.50s, Leopold Fountain, Innsbruck.

916	A359	1.50s rose lilac	.25	.20
917	A359	2s brown	.25	.20
918	A359	2.50s olive	.30	.25
		Nos. 916-918 (3)	.80	.65

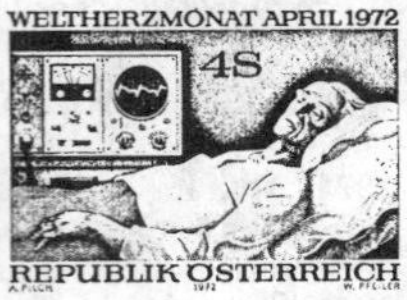

Cardiac Patient and Monitor A360

1972, Apr. 11 ***Perf. 13½x14***

919 A360 4s violet brown .55 .25

World Health Day.

A361

A362

Design: St. Michael's Gate, Royal Palace, Vienna.

1972, Apr. 11 ***Perf. 14x13½***

920 A361 4s violet blue .55 .25

Conference of European Post and Telecommunications Ministers, Vienna, Apr. 11-14.

Photo. & Engr.

1972, May 5 ***Perf. 14***

921 A362 2s Sculpture, Gurk Cathedral .30 .20

900th anniv. of Gurk (Carinthia) Diocese. The design is after the central column supporting the sarcophagus of St. Hemma in Gurk Cathedral.

City Hall, Congress Emblem — A363

1972, May 23 Litho. & Engr.

922 A363 4s red, blk & yel .55 .20

9th Intl. Congress of Public and Cooperative Economy, Vienna, May 23-25.

Power Line in Carnic Alps — A364

Designs: 2.50s, Power Station, Semmering. 4s, Zemm Power Station (lake in Zillertaler Alps).

1972, June 28 ***Perf. 13½x14***

923	A364	70g gray & violet	.20	.20
924	A364	2.50s gray & red brn	.30	.30
925	A364	4s gray & slate	.45	.45
		Nos. 923-925 (3)	.95	.95

Nationalization of the power industry, 25th anniv.

Runner with Olympic Torch — A365

St. Hermes, by Conrad Laib — A366

Engr. & Photo.

1972, Aug. 21 ***Perf. 14x13½***

926 A365 2s sepia & red .25 .20

Olympic torch relay from Olympia, Greece, to Munich, Germany, passing through Austria.

1972, Aug. 21 Engr.

927 A366 2s violet brown .25 .20

Exhibition of Late Gothic Art, Salzburg.

Pears A367

1972, Sept. ***Perf. 14***

928 A367 2.50s dk blue & multi .30 .20

World Congress of small plot Gardeners, Vienna, Sept. 7-10.

Souvenir Sheet

Spanish Walk — A368

1972, Sept. 12 ***Perf. 13½***

929	A368	Sheet of 6	2.75	2.75
a.		2s Spanish walk	.25	.25
b.		2s Piaffe	.25	.25
c.		2.50s Levade	.30	.30
d.		2.50s On long rein	.30	.30
e.		4s Capriole	.50	.50
f.		4s Courbette	.50	.50

400th anniv. of the Spanish Riding School in Vienna.

Arms of University of Agriculture A369

Church and Old University A370

Photo. & Engr.

1972, Oct. 17 ***Perf. 14x13½***

930 A369 2s black & multi .25 .20

University of Agriculture, Vienna, cent.

1972, Nov. 7 Engr.

931 A370 4s red brown .55 .20

Paris Lodron University, Salzburg, 350th anniv.

Carl Michael Ziehrer — A371

1972, Nov. 14

932 A371 2s rose claret .25 .20

50th death anniv. of Carl Michael Ziehrer (1843-1922), composer.

Virgin and Child, Wood, 1420-30 A372

Photo. & Engr.

1972, Dec. 1 ***Perf. 13½***

933 A372 2s olive & chocolate .25 .20

Christmas.

Racing Sleigh, 1750 A373

Designs: 2s, Coronation landau, 1824. 2.50s, Imperial state coach, 1763.

1972, Dec. 12

934	A373	1.50s pale gray & brn	.20	.20
935	A373	2s pale gray & sl grn	.30	.20
936	A373	2.50s pale gray & plum	.35	.25
		Nos. 934-936 (3)	.85	.65

Collection of historic state coaches and carriages in Schönbrunn Palace.

Map of Austrian Telephone System — A374

1972, Dec. 14 Photo. ***Perf. 14***

937 A374 2s yellow & blk .25 .20

Completion of automation of Austrian telephone system.

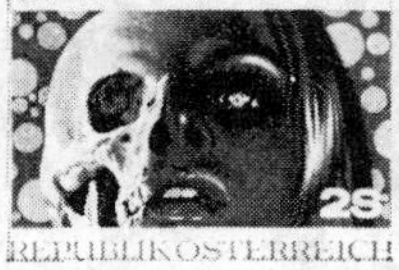

"Drugs are Death" A375

1973, Jan. 26 Photo. ***Perf. 13½x14***

938 A375 2s scarlet & multi 1.50 .45

Fight against drug abuse.

Alfons Petzold — A376

Theodor Körner — A377

1973, Jan. 26 Engr. ***Perf. 14x13½***

939 A376 2s reddish brn .25 .20

50th death anniv. of Alfons Petzold (1882-1923), poet.

Photo. & Engr.

1973, Apr. 24 ***Perf. 14x13½***
940 A377 2s gray & deep claret .25 .20

Theodor Korner (1873-1957), Austrian Pres., birth cent.

Douglas DC-9 — A378

1973, May 14 ***Perf. 13½x14***
941 A378 2s vio bl & rose red .30 .20

First intl. airmail service, Vienna to Kiev, Mar. 31, 1918, 55th anniv.; Austrian Aviation Corporation, 50th anniv.; Austrian Airlines, 15th anniv.

Otto Loewi A379

"Support" A380

1973, June 4 Engr. ***Perf. 14x13½***
942 A379 4s deep violet .55 .20

Birth cent. of Otto Loewi (1873-1961), pharmacologist, winner of 1936 Nobel prize.

1973, June 25
943 A380 2s dark blue .25 .20

Federation of Austrian Social Insurance Institutes, 25th anniv.

Europa Issue 1973

Post Horn and Telephone A381

1973, July 9 Photo. ***Perf. 14***
944 A381 2.50s ocher, blk & yel .30 .20

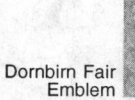

Dornbirn Fair Emblem A382

1973, July 27 ***Perf. 13½x14***
945 A382 2s multicolored .30 .20

Dornbirn Trade Fair, 25th anniversary.

Hurdles — A383

Leo Slezak — A384

1973, Aug. 13 Engr. ***Perf. 14x13½***
946 A383 4s gray olive .50 .20

23rd Intl. Military Pentathlon Championships, Wiener Neustadt, Aug. 13-18.

1973, Aug. 17 ***Perf. 14***
947 A384 4s dark brown .50 .20

Leo Slezak (1873-1946), operatic tenor.

Gate, Vienna Hofburg, and ISI Emblem — A385

Photogravure and Engraved

1973, Aug. 20 ***Perf. 14x13½***
948 A385 2s gray, dk brn & ver .25 .20

39th Congress of Intl. Statistical Institute, Vienna, Aug. 20-30.

Tegetthoff off Franz Josef Land, by Julius Prayer A386

1973, Aug. 30 Engr. ***Perf. 13½x14***
949 A386 2.50s Prussian grn .30 .20

Discovery of Franz Josef Land by an Austrian North Pole expedition, cent.

Academy of Science, by Canaletto A387

1973, Sept. 4
950 A387 2.50s violet .30 .20

Intl. meteorological cooperation, cent.

Arms of Viennese Tanners A388

Max Reinhardt A389

Photo. & Engr.

1973, Sept. 4 ***Perf. 14***
951 A388 4s red & multi .55 .20

13th Congress of the Intl. Union of Leather Chemists' Societies, Vienna, Sept. 1-7.

1973, Sept. 7 Engr. ***Perf. 13x13½***
952 A389 2s rose magenta .25 .20

Max Reinhardt (1873-1943), theatrical director and stage manager.

Trotter A390

1973, Sept. 28 ***Perf. 13½***
953 A390 2s green .30 .20

Centenary of Vienna Trotting Association.

Ferdinand Hanusch — A391

1973, Sept. 28 ***Perf. 14x13½***
954 A391 2s rose brown .25 .20

50th death anniv. of Ferdinand Hanusch (1866-1923), secretary of state.

Police Radio Operator A392

1973, Oct. 2 ***Perf. 13½x14***
955 A392 4s violet blue .50 .20

50th anniv. of Intl. Criminal Police Org. (INTERPOL).

Josef Petzval's Photographic Lens — A393

Litho. & Engr.

1973, Oct. 8 ***Perf. 14***
956 A393 2.50s blue & multi .30 .20

EUROPHOT Photographic Cong., Vienna.

Emperor's Spring, Hell Valley A394

Photo. & Engr.

1973, Oct. 23 ***Perf. 13½x14***
957 A394 2s sepia, blue & red .25 .20

Vienna's first mountain spring water supply system, cent.

Almsee, Upper Austria — A395

Hofburg and Prince Eugene Statue, Vienna — A395a

Designs: 50g, Farmhouses, Zillertal, Tirol. 1s, Kahlenbergerdorf. 1.50s, Bludenz, Vorarlberg. 2s, Inn Bridge, Alt Finstermunz. 2.50s, Murau, Styria. 3s, Bischofsmütze, Salzburg. 3.50s, Easter Church, Oberwart. 4.50s, Windmill, Retz. 5s, Aggstein Castle, Lower Austria. 6s, Lindauer Hut, Vorarlberg. 6.50s, Holy Cross Church, Villach, Carinthia. 7s, Falkenstein Castle, Carinthia. 7.50s, Hohensalzburg. 8s, Votive column, Reiteregg, Styria. 10s, Lake Neusiedl, Burgenland. 11s, Old Town, Enns. 16s, Openair Museum, Bad Tatzmannsdorf. 20s, Myra waterfalls.

Photo. & Engr.

1973-78 ***Perf. 13½x14***

Size: 23x29mm

Type A395

958	50g	gray & slate green	.20	.20
959	1s	brn & dk brown	.20	.20
960	1.50s	rose & brown	.25	.20
961	2s	gray bl & dk blue	.30	.20
962	2.50s	vio & dp violet	.35	.20
963	3s	lt ultra & vio blue	.45	.20
963A	3.50s	dl org & brown	.50	.20
964	4s	brt lil & pur	.55	.20
965	4.50s	brt grn & bl green	.60	.20
966	5s	lilac & vio	.65	.20
967	6s	dp rose & dk violet	.80	.20
968	6.50s	bl grn & indigo	.90	.20
969	7s	sage grn & sl green	.95	.20
970	7.50s	lil rose & claret	1.00	.25
971	8s	dl red & dp brown	1.10	.20
972	10s	gray grn & dk green	1.40	.20
973	11s	ver & dk carmine	1.60	.20
974	16s	bister & brown	2.25	.60
975	20s	ol bis & ol grn	2.75	1.25

Type A395a

976	50s	gray vio & vio bl	6.75	2.50
		Nos. 958-976 (20)	23.55	7.80

Issue dates: 1974, Nos. 960-963. 1975, Nos. 958-959, 967, 976. 1976, Nos. 965, 971, 973. 1977, Nos. 968, 970, 974-975. 1978, No. 963A. See Nos. 1100-1109.

Nativity — A396

Pregl — A397

1973, Nov. 30 ***Perf. 14***
977 A396 2s multicolored .30 .20

Christmas. Design from 14th century stained-glass window.

1973, Dec. 12 Engr. ***Perf. 14x13½***
978 A397 4s deep blue .50 .20

50th anniv. of the awarding of the Nobel prize for chemistry to Fritz Pregl (1869-1930).

Telex Machine A398

Hofmannsthal A399

1974, Jan. 14 Photo. ***Perf. 14x13½***
979 A398 2.50s ultramarine .30 .20

50th anniversary of Radio Austria.

1974, Feb. 1 Engr. ***Perf. 14***
980 A399 4s violet blue .50 .20

Birth cent. of Hugo Hofmannsthal (1874-1929), poet and playwright.

Anton Bruckner and Bruckner House A400

1974, Mar. 22 Engr. ***Perf. 14***
981 A400 4s brown .50 .20

Founding of Anton Bruckner House (concert hall), Linz, and birth of Anton Bruckner (1824-1896), composer, 150th anniv.

Vegetables A401

Photo. & Engr.

1974, Apr. 18 ***Perf. 14***
982 A401 2s shown .30 .20
983 A401 2.50s Fruits .35 .30
984 A401 4s Flowers .50 .50
Nos. 982-984 (3) 1.15 1.00

Intl. Garden Show, Vienna, Apr. 18-Oct. 14.

Seal of Judenburg A402

Karl Kraus A403

1974, Apr. 24 Photo. ***Perf. 14x13½***
985 A402 2s plum & multi .30 .20

750th anniversary of Judenburg.

1974, Apr. 6 **Engr.**
986 A403 4s dark red .50 .20

Karl Kraus (1874-1936), poet and satirist, birth cent.

St. Michael, by Thomas Schwanthaler A404

1974, May 3
987 A404 2.50s slate green .30 .20

Exhibition of the works by the Schwanthaler Family of sculptors, (1633-1848), Reichersberg am Inn, May 3-Oct. 13.

A405

A406

Europa: King Arthur, from tomb of Maximilian I

1974, May 8 ***Perf. 13½***
988 A405 2.50s ocher & slate blue .30 .20

Photo. & Engr.

1974, May 17 ***Perf. 14x13½***

De Dion Bouton motor tricycle.

989 A406 2s gray & vio brn .30 .20

Austrian Automobile Assoc., 75th anniv.

Satyr's Head, Terracotta A407

1974, May 22 ***Perf. 13½x14***
990 A407 2s org brn, gold & blk .30 .20

Exhibition, "Renaissance in Austria," Schallaburg Castle, May 22-Nov. 14.

Road Transport Union Emblem A408

Maulbertsch, Self-portrait A409

1974, May 24 Photo. ***Perf. 14x13½***
991 A408 4s deep orange & blk .50 .20

14th Congress of the Intl. Road Transport Union, Innsbruck.

1974, June 7 Engr. ***Perf. 14x13½***
992 A409 2s violet brown .25 .20

Franz Anton Maulbertsch (1724-96), painter, 250th birth anniv.

Gendarmes, 1824 and 1974 — A410

1974, June 7 Photo. ***Perf. 13½x14***
993 A410 2s red & multi .25 .20

125th anniversary of Austrian gendarmery.

Fencing A411

Photo. & Engr.

1974, June 14 ***Perf. 13½***
994 A411 2.50s red org & blk .30 .20

Transportation Symbols — A412

St. Virgil, Sculpture from Nonntal Church — A413

1974, June 18 Photo. ***Perf. 14x13½***
995 A412 4s lt ultra & multi .50 .20

European Conference of Transportation Ministers, Vienna, June 18-21.

1974, June 28 Engr. ***Perf. 13½x14***
996 A413 2s violet blue .25 .20

Consecration of the Cathedral of Salzburg by Scotch-Irish Bishop Feirgil (St. Virgil), 1200th anniv. Salzburg was a center of Christianization in the 8th century.

Franz Jonas and Austrian Eagle — A414

1974, June 28
997 A414 2s black .25 .20

Jonas (1899-1974), Austrian Pres., 1965-1974.

Franz Stelzhamer A415

Diver A416

1974, July 12 Engr. ***Perf. 14x13½***
998 A415 2s indigo .25 .20

Franz Stelzhamer (1802-1874), poet who wrote in Upper Austrian vernacular, death cent.

Photo. & Engr.

1974, Aug. 16 ***Perf. 13x13½***
999 A416 4s blue & sepia .50 .20

13th European Swimming, Diving and Water Polo Championships, Vienna, Aug. 18-25.

Ferdinand Ritter von Hebra — A417

1974, Sept. 10 Engr. ***Perf. 14x13½***
1000 A417 4s brown .50 .20

30th Meeting of the Assoc. of German-speaking Dermatologists, Graz, Sept. 10-14. Dr. von Hebra (1816-1880) was a founder of modern dermatology.

Arnold Schonberg A418

1974, Sept. 13 ***Perf. 13½x14***
1001 A418 2.50s purple .30 .20

Schönberg (1874-1951), composer.

Radio Station, Salzburg A419

1974, Oct. 1 Photo. ***Perf. 13½x14***
1002 A419 2s multicolored .25 .20

50th anniversary of Austrian broadcasting.

Edmund Eysler (1874-1949), Composer — A420

1974, Oct. 4 Engr. ***Perf. 14x13½***
1003 A420 2s dark olive .25 .20

Mailman, Mail Coach and Train, UPU Emblem A421

4s, Mailman, jet, truck, 1974, & UPU emblem.

1974, Oct. 9 Photo. ***Perf. 13½***
1004 A421 2s deep claret & lil .25 .20
1005 A421 4s dark blue & gray .50 .20

Centenary of Universal Postal Union.

Gauntlet Protecting Rose — A422

1974, Oct. 23 Photo. ***Perf. 13½x14***
1006 A422 2s multicolored .25 .20

Environment protection.

Austrian Sports Pool Emblem A423

1974, Oct. 23 Photo. ***Perf. 13½x14***
1007 A423 70g multicolored .20 .20

Austrian Sports Pool (lottery), 25th anniv.

Carl Ditters von Dittersdorf A424

Virgin and Child, Wood, c. 1600 A425

1974, Oct. 24 Engr. ***Perf. 14x13½***
1008 A424 2s Prussian green .25 .20

Von Dittersdorf (1739-1799), composer.

1974, Nov. 29 **Photo. & Engr.**
1009 A425 2s brown & gold .35 .20

Christmas.

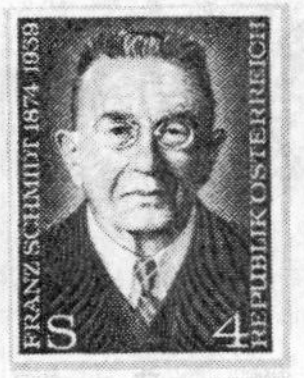

A426

A427

1974, Dec. 18
1010 A426 4s gray & black .55 .20

Franz Schmidt (1874-1939), composer.

Photo. & Engr.

1975, Jan. 24 ***Perf. 13½***
1011 A427 2.50s St. Christopher .40 .20

European Architectural Heritage Year. The design shows part of a wooden figure from central panel of the retable in the Kefermarkt Church, 1490-1497.

Safety Belt and Skeleton Arms — A428

Stained Glass Window, Vienna City Hall — A429

1975, Apr. 1 Photo. *Perf. 14x13½*
1012 A428 70g violet & multi .20 .20

Introduction of obligatory use of automobile safety belts.

1975, Apr. 2 *Perf. 14*
1013 A429 2.50s multicolored .30 .20

11th meeting of the Council of European Municipalities, Vienna, Apr. 2-5.

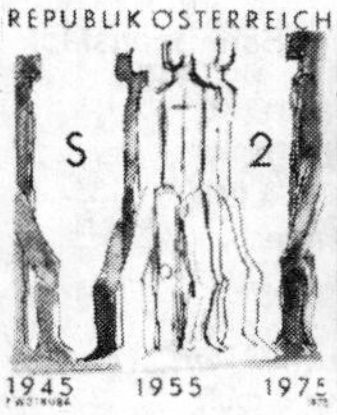

Austria as Mediator — A430

Forest — A431

1975, May 2 Litho. *Perf. 14*
1014 A430 2s blk & bister .30 .20

2nd Republic of Austria, 30th anniv.

1975, May 6 Engr.
1015 A431 2s green .35 .20

National forests, 50th anniversary.

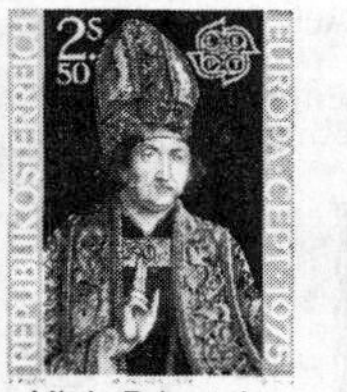

High Priest, by Michael Pacher A432

Gosaukamm Funicular A433

Europa Issue 1975

Photo. & Engr.

1975, May 27 *Perf. 14x13½*
1016 A432 2.50s black & multi .40 .20

Design is detail from painting "The Marriage of Joseph and Mary," by Michael Pacher (c. 1450-1500).

1975, June 23 *Perf. 14x13½*
1017 A433 2s slate & red .30 .20

4th Intl. Funicular Cong., Vienna, June 23-27.

Josef Misson and Mühlbach am Manhartsberg A434

1975, June 27 *Perf. 13½x14*
1018 A434 2s choc & redsh brn .25 .20

Josef Misson (1803-1875), poet who wrote in Lower Austrian vernacular, death cent.

Setting Sun and "P" — A435

1975, Aug. 27 Litho. *Perf. 14x13½*
1019 A435 1.50s org, blk & bl .20 .20

Austrian Assoc. of Pensioners 25th anniv. meeting, Vienna, Aug. 1975.

Ferdinand Porsche A436

Photo. & Engr.

1975, Sept. 3 *Perf. 13½x14*
1020 A436 1.50s gray & purple .25 .20

Ferdinand Porsche (1875-1951), engineer, developer of Porsche and Volkswagen cars, birth cent.

Leo Fall (1873-1925), Composer — A437

1975, Sept. 16 Engr. *Perf. 14x13½*
1021 A437 2s violet .25 .20

Judo Throw — A438

Heinrich Angeli — A439

1975, Oct. 20 Photo. *Perf. 14x13½*
1022 A438 2.50s gold & multi .30 .20

10th World Judo Championships, Vienna, Oct. 20-26.

1975, Oct. 21 Engr. *Perf. 14x13½*
1023 A439 2s rose lake .30 .20

Heinrich Angeli (1840-1925), painter, 50th death anniv.

Johann Strauss and Dancers A440

Photo. & Engr.

1975, Oct. 24 *Perf. 13½x14*
1024 A440 4s ocher & sepia .55 .20

Johann Strauss (1825-1899), composer.

Stylized Musician Playing a Viol — A441

Symbolic House — A442

1975, Oct. 30 *Perf. 14x13½*
1025 A441 2.50s silver & vio bl .35 .20

Vienna Symphony Orchestra, 75th anniv.

1975, Oct. 31 Photo.
1026 A442 2s multicolored .25 .20

Austrian building savings societies, 50th anniv.

Fan with "Hanswurst" Scene, 18th Century A443

1975, Nov. 14 Photo. *Perf. 13½x14*
1027 A443 1.50s green & multi .20 .20

Salzburg Theater bicentenary.

Virgin and Child, from 15th Century Altar A444

"The Spiral Tree," by Hundertwasser A445

Photo. & Engr.

1975, Nov. 28 *Perf. 13x13½*
1028 A444 2s gold & dull purple .25 .20

Christmas.

Photo., Engr. & Typo.

1975, Dec. 11 *Perf. 13½x14*
1029 A445 4s multicolored .65 .25

Austrian modern art. Friedenstreich Hundertwasser is the pseudonym of Friedrich Stowasser (b. 1928).

Old Burgtheater A446

No. 1030b, Grand staircase, new Burgtheater.

Perf. 14 (pane), 13½x14 (stamps)

1976, Apr. 8 Engr.

1030	Pane of 2 + label	1.10	1.10
a.	A446 3s violet blue	.30	.30
b.	A446 3s deep brown	.30	.30

Bicentenary of Vienna Burgtheater. Label (head of Pan) and inscription in vermilion.

Dr. Robert Barany (1876-1936), Winner of Nobel Prize for Medicine, 1914 — A447

Photo. & Engr.

1976, Apr. 22 *Perf. 14x13½*
1031 A447 3s blue & brown .45 .20

Ammonite A448

1976, Apr. 30 Photo. *Perf. 13½x14*
1032 A448 3s red & multi .45 .20

Vienna Museum of Natural History, Centenary Exhibition.

Carinthian Dukes' Coronation Chair — A449

Siege of Linz, 17th Century Etching — A450

Photo. & Engr.

1976, May 6 *Perf. 14x13½*
1033 A449 3s grnsh blk & org .45 .20

Millennium of Carinthia.

1976, May 14
1034 A450 4s blk & gray grn .55 .20

Upper Austrian Peasants' War, 350th anniv.

Skittles A451

1976, May 14 *Perf. 13½x14*
1035 A451 4s black & org .55 .20

11th World Skittles Championships, Vienna.

Duke Heinrich II, Stained-glass Window — A452

1976, May 14 *Perf. 14*
1036 A452 3s multicolored .45 .20

Babenberg Exhibition, Lilienfeld.

St. Wolfgang, from Pacher Altar — A453

1976, May 26 Engr. *Perf. 13½*
1037 A453 6s bright violet .75 .40

Intl. Art Exhibition at St. Wolfgang.

Europa Issue 1976

Tassilo Cup, Kremsmunster, 777 — A454

Photo. & Engr.

1976, Aug. 13 *Perf. 14x13½*
1038 A454 4s ultra & multi .60 .20

Timber Fair Emblem — A455

Constantin Economo, M.D. — A456

1976, Aug. 13 **Photo.**
1039 A455 3s green & multi .35 .20

Austrian Timber Fair, Klagenfurt, 25th anniv.

1976, Aug. 23 **Engr.**
1040 A456 3s dark red brown .35 .20

Dr. Economo (1876-1931), neurologist.

Administrative Court, by Salomon Klein — A457

1976, Oct. 25 **Engr.** *Perf. 13½x14*
1041 A457 6s deep brown .80 .30

Austrian Central Administrative Court, cent.

Souvenir Sheet

Coats of Arms of Austrian Provinces — A458

Millennium of Austria: a, Lower Austria. b, Upper Austria. c, Styria. d, Carinthia. e, Tyrol. f, Voralberg. g, Salzburg. h, Burgenland. i, Vienna.

Photo. & Engr.

1976, Oct. 25 *Perf. 14*
1042 Sheet of 9 3.00 3.00
a.-i. A458 2s any single .30 .30

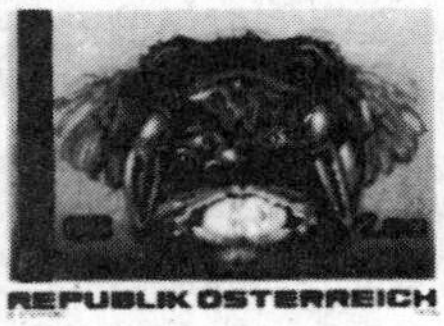
"Cancer" A459

1976, Nov. 17 **Photo.** *Perf. 14x13½*
1043 A459 2.50s multicolored .35 .20

Fight against cancer.

UN Emblem and Bridge — A460

1976, Nov. 17
1044 A460 3s blue & gold .45 .20

UN Industrial Development Org. (UNIDO), 10th anniv.

Punched Tape, Map of Europe — A461

1976, Nov. 17 *Perf. 14*
1045 A461 1.50s multicolored .20 .20

Austrian Press Agency (APA), 30th anniv.

Viktor Kaplan, Kaplan Turbine A462

Photo. & Engr.

1976, Nov. 26 *Perf. 13½x14*
1046 A462 2.50s multicolored .35 .20

Viktor Kaplan (1876-1934), inventor of Kaplan turbine, birth centenary.

Nativity, by Konrad von Friesach, c. 1450 A463

1976, Nov. 26 *Perf. 13½*
1047 A463 3s multicolored .40 .20

Christmas.

Augustin, the Piper — A464

Photo. & Engr.

1976, Dec. 29 *Perf. 13½*
1048 A464 6s multicolored .75 .25

Modern Austrian art.

Rainer Maria Rilke (1875-1926), Poet A465

Vienna City Synagogue A466

1976, Dec. 29 **Engr.** *Perf. 14x13½*
1049 A465 3s deep violet .40 .20

1976, Dec. 29 **Photo.** *Perf. 13½*
1050 A466 1.50s multicolored .20 .20

Sesquicentennial of Vienna City Synagogue.

Nikolaus Joseph von Jacquin (1727-1817), Botanist — A467

1977, Feb. 16 **Engr.** *Perf. 14x13½*
1051 A467 4s chocolate .55 .20

Oswald von Wolkenstein (1377-1445), Poet — A468

Photo. & Engr.

1977, Feb. 16 *Perf. 14*
1052 A468 3s multicolored .35 .20

Handball A469

1977, Feb. 25 **Photo.** *Perf. 13½x14*
1053 A469 1.50s multicolored .20 .20

World Indoor Handball Championships, Austria, Feb. 5-Mar. 6.

A470

A471

1977, Apr. 12 **Engr.** *Perf. 14x13½*
1054 A470 6s dk violet blue .70 .25

Alfred Kubin (1877-1959), illustrator and writer.

1977, Apr. 22 **Engr.** *Perf. 13½*

Designs: 2.50s, Great Spire, St. Stephen's Cathedral. 3s, Heathen Tower and Frederick's Gable. 4s, Interior view with Albertinian Choir.

1055 A471 2.50s dark brown .35 .20
1056 A471 3s dark blue .40 .25
1057 A471 4s rose lake .50 .35
Nos. 1055-1057 (3) 1.25 .80

Restoration and re-opening of St. Stephen's Cathedral, Vienna, 25th anniversary.

Fritz Hermanovsky-Orlando (1877-1954), Poet and Artist — A472

Photo. & Engr.

1977, Apr. 29 *Perf. 13½x14*
1058 A472 6s Prus green & gold .70 .25

IAEA Emblem A473

Arms of Schwanenstadt A474

1977, May 2 **Photo.** *Perf. 14*
1059 A473 3s brt bl, lt bl & gold .35 .20

Intl. Atomic Energy Agency (IAEA), 20th anniv.

1977, June 10 **Photo.** *Perf. 14x13½*
1060 A474 3s dk brown & multi .35 .20

Town of Schwanenstadt, 350th anniv.

Europa Issue 1977

Attersee, Upper Austria — A475

1977, June 10 **Engr.** *Perf. 14*
1061 A475 6s olive green .90 .30

Globe, by Vincenzo Coronelli, 1688 — A476

Photo. & Engr.

1977, June 29 *Perf. 14*
1062 A476 3s black & buff .35 .20

5th Intl. Symposium of the Coronelli World Fed. of Friends of the Globe, Austria, June 29-July 3.

Kayak Race — A477

1977, July 15 **Photo.** *Perf. 13½x14*
1063 A477 4s multicolored .50 .20

3rd Kayak Slalom White Water Race on Lieser River, Spittal.

The Good Samaritan, by Francesco Bassano — A478

1977, Sept. 16 Photo. & Engr.
1064 A478 1.50s brown & red .20 .20

Workers' Good Samaritan Org., 50th anniv.

Papermakers' Coat of Arms — A479

Man with Austrian Flag Lifting Barbed Wire — A480

1977, Oct. 10 ***Perf. 14x13½***
1065 A479 3s multicolored .35 .20

17th Conf. of the European Committee of Pulp and Paper Technology (EUCEPA), Vienna.

1977, Nov. 3 ***Perf. 14***
1066 A480 2.50s slate & red .35 .20

Honoring the martyrs for Austria's freedom.

"Austria," First Steam Locomotive in Austria — A481

Designs: 2.50s, Steam locomotive 214. 3s, Electric locomotive 1044.

Photo. & Engr.

1977, Nov. 17 ***Perf. 13½***

1067	A481	1.50s multicolored	.20	.20
1068	A481	2.50s multicolored	.40	.20
1069	A481	3s multicolored	.45	.20
		Nos. 1067-1069 (3)	1.05	.60

140th anniversary of Austrian railroads.

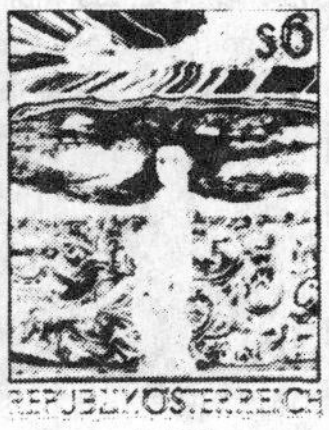

A482 A483

Virgin and Child, wood statue, Mariastein, Tyrol.

1977, Nov. 25 ***Perf. 14x13½***
1070 A482 3s multicolored .30 .20

Christmas.

1977, Dec. 2 ***Perf. 13½x14***

The Danube Maiden, by Wolfgang Hutter.

1071 A483 6s multicolored .75 .20

Modern Austrian art.

Egon Friedell (1878-1938), Writer and Historian A484

1978, Jan. 23 Photo. & Engr.
1072 A484 3s lt blue & blk .40 .20

Subway Train — A485

1978, Feb. 24 Photo. ***Perf. 13½x14***
1073 A485 3s multicolored .45 .20

New Vienna subway system.

Biathlon Competition A486

1978, Feb. 28 Photo. & Engr.
1074 A486 4s multicolored .45 .20

Biathlon World Championships, Hochfilzen, Tyrol, Feb. 28-Mar. 5.

Leopold Kunschak (1871-1953), Political Leader — A487

1978, Mar. 13 Engr. ***Perf. 14x13½***
1075 A487 3s violet blue .40 .20

Coyote, Aztec Feather Shield A488

1978, Mar. 13 Photo. ***Perf. 13½x14***
1076 A488 3s multicolored .40 .20

Ethnographical Museum, 50th anniv. exhibition.

Alpine Farm, Woodcut by Suitbert Lobisser — A489

1978, Mar. 23 Engr. ***Perf. 13½***
1077 A489 3s dark brown, *buff* .40 .20

Lobisser (1878-1943), graphic artist.

Capercaillie, Hunting Bag, 1730, and Rifle, 1655 — A490

Photo. & Engr.

1978, Apr. 28 ***Perf. 13½***
1078 A490 6s multicolored .75 .35

Intl. Hunting Exhibition, Marchegg.

Europa Issue 1978

Riegersburg, Styria — A491

1978, May 3 Engr.
1079 A491 6s deep rose lilac .75 .35

Parliament, Vienna, and Map of Europe — A492

Admont Pietà, c. 1410 — A493

1978, May 3 Photo. ***Perf. 14x13½***
1080 A492 4s multicolored .45 .20

3rd Interparliamentary Conference for European Cooperation and Security, Vienna.

1978, May 26 Photo. & Engr.
1081 A493 2.50s ocher & black .25 .20

Gothic Art in Styria Exhibition, St. Lambrecht, 1978.

Ort Castle, Gmunden — A494

1978, June 9
1082 A494 3s multicolored .30 .20

700th anniversary of Gmunden City.

Child with Flowers and Fruit — A495

Lehar and his Home, Bad Ischl — A496

Photo. & Engr.

1978, June 30 ***Perf. 14x13½***
1083 A495 6s gold & multi .85 .35

25 years of Social Tourism.

1978, July 14 Engr. ***Perf. 14x13½***
1084 A496 6s slate .75 .30

International Lehar Congress, Bad Ischl. Franz Lehar (1870-1948), operetta composer.

Congress Emblem A497

1978, Aug. 21 Photo. ***Perf. 13½x14***
1085 A497 1.50s black, red & yel .20 .20

Cong. of Intl. Fed. of Building Construction and Wood Workers, Vienna, Aug. 20-24.

Ottokar of Bohemia and Rudolf of Hapsburg A498

1978, Aug. 25 Photo. & Engr.
1086 A498 3s multicolored .35 .20

Battle of Durnkrut and Jedenspeigen (Marchfeld), which established Hapsburg rule in Austria, 700th anniversary.

First Documentary Reference to Villach, "ad pontem uillah" A499

1978, Sept. 8 Litho. ***Perf. 13½x14***
1087 A499 3s multicolored .35 .20

1100th anniversary of Villach, Carinthia.

Seal of Graz, 1440 — A500

Emperor Maximilian Fishing — A501

Photo. & Engr.

1978, Sept. 13 ***Perf. 14x13½***
1088 A500 4s multicolored .50 .25

850th anniversary of Graz.

1978, Sept. 15 ***Perf. 14x13½***
1089 A501 4s multicolored .50 .20

World Fishing Championships, Vienna, Sept. 1978.

"Aid to the Handicapped" — A502

1978, Oct. 2 Photo. ***Perf. 13½x14***
1090 A502 6s orange brn & blk .75 .30

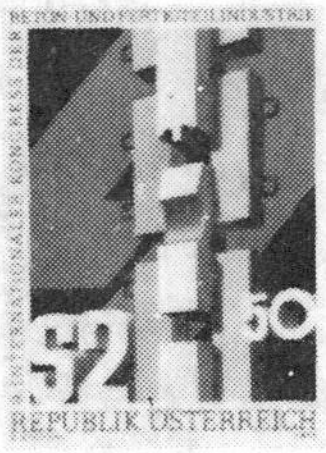

Symbolic Column — A503

1978, Oct. 9 Photo. *Perf. 13½*
1091 A503 2.50s orange, blk & gray .30 .20

9th Intl. Congress of Concrete and Prefabrication Industries, Vienna, Oct. 8-13.

Grace, by Albin Egger-Lienz A504

1978, Oct. 27 *Perf. 13½x14*
1092 A504 6s multicolored .75 .30

European Family Congress, Vienna, Oct. 26-29.

Lise Meitner (1878-1968), Physicist, and Atom Symbol — A505

1978, Nov. 7 Engr. *Perf. 14x13½*
1093 A505 6s dark violet .75 .30

Viktor Adler, by Anton Hanak A506

Photo. & Engr.

1978, Nov. 10 *Perf. 13½x14*
1094 A506 3s vermilion & black .40 .20

Viktor Adler (1852-1918), leader of Social Democratic Party, 60th death anniversary.

Franz Schubert, by Josef Kriehuber — A507

Virgin and Child, Wilhering Church — A508

1978, Nov. 17 Engr. *Perf. 14*
1095 A507 6s reddish brown .65 .35

Franz Schubert (1797-1828), composer.

Photo. & Engr.

1978, Dec. 1 *Perf. 12½x13½*
1096 A508 3s multicolored .35 .20

Christmas.

Archduke Johann Shelter, Grossglockner — A509

1978, Dec. 6 *Perf. 13½x14*
1097 A509 1.50s gold & dk vio bl .20 .20

Austrian Alpine Club, centenary.

A510 A511

Adam, by Rudolf Hausner.

1978, Dec. 6 Photo. *Perf. 13½x14*
1098 A510 6s multicolored .75 .35

Modern Austrian art.

1978, Dec. 6 *Perf. 14x13½*
1099 A511 6s Bound Hands .75 .30

Universal Declaration of Human Rights, 30th anniv.

Type of 1973

Designs: 20g, Freistadt, Upper Austria. 3s, Bishofsmutze, Salzburg. 4.20s, Hirschegg, Kleinwalsertal. 5.50s, Peace Chapel, Stoderzinken. 5.60s, Riezlern, Kleinwalsertal. 9s, Asten Carinthia. 12s, Kufstein Fortress. 14s, Weiszsee, Salzburg.

Photo. & Engr.

1978-83 *Perf. 13½x14*

Size: 23x29mm
1100 A395 20g vio bl & dk bl .20 .20

Size: 17x21mm
1102 A395 3s lt ultra & vio bl .45 .20

Size: 23x29mm
1104 A395 4.20s blk & grysh bl .55 .20
1105 A395 5.50s lilac & pur .75 .20
1106 A395 5.60s yel grn & ol grn .75 .20
1107 A395 9s rose & car 1.25 .45
1108 A395 12s ocher & vio brn 1.75 .20
1109 A395 14s lt green & green 2.00 .20
Nos. 1100-1109 (8) 7.70 1.85

Issued: 3s, 12/7/78; 4.20s, 6/22/79; 20g, 6/27/80; 12s, 10/3/80; 14s, 1/27/82; 5.50s, 5.60s, 7/1/82; 9s, 2/9/83.

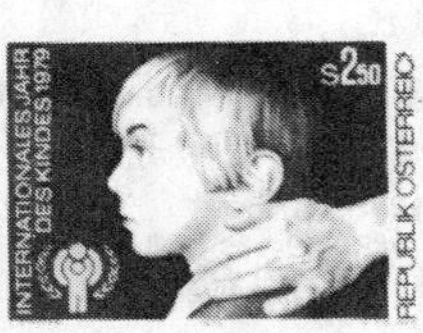

Child and IYC Emblem A512

Photo. & Engr.

1979, Jan. 16 *Perf. 14*
1110 A512 2.50s dk blue, blk & brn .30 .20

International Year of the Child.

CCIR Emblem A513

1979, Jan. 16 Photo. *Perf. 13½x14*
1111 A513 6s multicolored .75 .30

Intl. Radio Consultative Committee (CCIR) of the ITU, 50th anniv.

Air Rifle, Air Pistol and Club Emblem A514

Photo. & Engr.

1979, Mar. 7 *Perf. 13½*
1112 A514 6s multicolored .75 .30

Austrian Shooting Club, cent., and European Air Rifle and Air Pistol Championships, Graz.

Figure Skater — A515

1979, Mar. 7 Photo. *Perf. 14x13½*
1113 A515 4s multicolored .55 .25

World Ice Skating Championships, Vienna.

Steamer Franz I A516

Designs: 2.50s, Tugboat Linz. 3s, Passenger ship Theodor Körner.

1979, Mar. 13 Engr. *Perf. 13½*
1114 A516 1.50s violet blue .20 .20
1115 A516 2.50s sepia .30 .20
1116 A516 3s magenta .35 .20
Nos. 1114-1116 (3) .85 .60

1st Danube Steamship Company, 150th anniv.

Fashion Design, by Theo Zasche, 1900 — A517

Photo. & Engr.

1979, Mar. 26 *Perf. 13x13½*
1117 A517 2.50s multicolored .30 .20

50th Intl. Fashion Week, Vienna.

Wiener Neustadt Cathedral A518

1979, Mar. 27 Engr. *Perf. 13½*
1118 A518 4s violet blue .50 .25

Cathedral of Wiener Neustadt, 700th anniv.

Teacher and Pupils, by Franz A. Zauner — A519

Population Chart and Barock Angel — A520

Photo. & Engr.

1979, Mar. 30 *Perf. 14x13½*
1119 A519 2.50s multicolored .30 .20

Education of the deaf in Austria, 200th anniv.

1979, Apr. 6
1120 A520 2.50s multicolored .30 .20

Austrian Central Statistical Bureau, 150th anniv.

Laurenz Koschier A521

Diesel Motor A522

Europa Issue, 1979

1979, May 4
1121 A521 6s ocher & purple .80 .30

1979, May 4 Photo.
1122 A522 4s multicolored .45 .20

13th CIMAC Congress (Intl. Org. for Internal Combustion Machines).

Arms of Ried, Schärding and Braunau — A523

Photo. & Engr.

1979, June 1 *Perf. 14x13½*
1123 A523 3s multicolored .30 .20

200th anniversary of Innviertel District.

Flood and City — A524

1979, June 1 *Perf. 13½x14*
1124 A524 2.50s multicolored .30 .20

Control and eliminate water pollution.

Arms of Rottenmann A525

Jodok Fink A526

Photo. & Engr.

1979, June 22 *Perf. 14x13½*
1125 A525 3s multicolored .30 .20

700th anniversary of Rottenmann.

1979, June 29 Engr. *Perf. 14*
1126 A526 3s brown carmine .40 .20

Jodok Fink (1853-1929), governor of Vorarlberg.

Arms of Wels, Returnees' Emblem, "Europa Sail" — A527

1979, July 6 Photo. *Perf. 14x13½*
1127 A527 4s yellow grn & blk .45 .20

5th European Meeting of the Intl. Confederation of Former Prisoners of War, Wels, July 6-8.

Symbolic Flower, Conference Emblem — A528

1979, Aug. 20 Litho. *Perf. 14x13½*
1128 A528 4s turq blue .45 .20

UN Conf. for Science and Technology, Vienna, Aug. 20-31.

Donaupark, UNIDO and IAEA Emblems A529

1979, Aug. 24 Engr. *Perf. 13½x14*
1129 A529 6s grayish blue .75 .30

Opening of the Donaupark Intl. Center in Vienna, seat of the UN Industrial Development Org. (UNIDO) and the Intl. Atomic Energy Agency (IAEA).

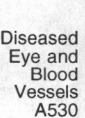

Diseased Eye and Blood Vessels A530

1979, Sept. 10 Photo. *Perf. 14*
1130 A530 2.50s multicolored .35 .20

10th World Congress of Intl. Diabetes Federation, Vienna, Sept. 9-14.

View of Stanz Valley through East Portal of Arlberg Tunnel A531

1979, Sept. 14 Photo. & Engr.
1131 A531 4s multicolored .45 .20

16th World Road Cong., Vienna, Sept. 16-21.

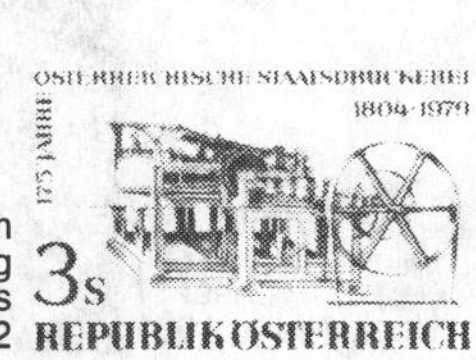

Steam Printing Press A532

Photo. & Engr.

1979, Sept. 18 *Perf. 13½x14*
1132 A532 3s multicolored .40 .20

Austrian Government Printing Office, 175th anniv.

Richard Zsigmondy (1865-1929), Chemist — A533

1979, Sept. 21 Engr. *Perf. 14x13½*
1133 A533 6s multicolored .75 .30

"Save Energy" A534

1979, Oct. 1 Photo. *Perf. 14x13½*
1134 A534 2.50s multicolored .30 .20

Festival and Convention Center, Bregenz (Model) — A535

1979, Oct. 1 Engr. *Perf. 14*
1135 A535 2.50s purple .30 .20

Lions International Emblem A536

1979, Oct. 11 Photo. & Engr.
1136 A536 4s multicolored .45 .25

25th Lions Europa Forum, Vienna, Oct. 11-13.

A537 A538

Photo. & Engr.

1979, Oct. 19 *Perf. 13½x14*
1137 A537 2.50s Wilhelm Exner .30 .20

Centenary of Technological Handicraft Museum, founded by Wilhelm Exner.

1979, Oct. 23 Litho. *Perf. 13½x14*

The Compassionate Christ, by Hans Fronius.

1138 A538 4s olive & ol blk .50 .25

Modern Austrian art.

Locomotive and Arms — A539

1979, Oct. 24 Photo. *Perf. 13½x14*
1139 A539 2.50s multicolored .30 .20

Raab-Odenburg-Ebenfurt railroad, cent.

August Musger — A540

Photo. & Engr.

1979, Oct. 30 *Perf. 14x13½*
1140 A540 2.50s bl gray & blk .30 .20

August Musger (1868-1929), developer of slow-motion film technique.

Nativity, St. Barbara's Church A541

1979, Nov. 30 *Perf. 13½x14*
1141 A541 4s multicolored .45 .25

Christmas.

Arms of Baden — A542

1980, Jan. 25 *Perf. 14*
1142 A542 4s multicolored .45 .25

Baden, 500th anniversary.

A543 A544

1980, Feb. 21 *Perf. 13½*
1143 A543 2.50s red & aqua .30 .20

Fight rheumatism.

1980, Feb. 21 Photo. *Perf. 14x13½*
1144 A544 4s dark blue & red .45 .25

Austrian exports.

Austrian Red Cross Centenary A545

1980, Mar. 14 Photo. *Perf. 13½x14*
1145 A545 2.50s multicolored .30 .20

Rudolph Kirchschlager A546

Photo. & Engr.

1980, Mar. 20 *Perf. 14x13½*
1146 A546 4s sepia & red .45 .25

Robert Hamerling (1830-1889), Poet A547

1980, Mar. 24 Engr. *Perf. 13½x14*
1147 A547 2.50s olive green .35 .20

Seal of Hallein — A548 Maria Theresa, by Andreas Moller — A549

Photo. & Engr.

1980, Apr. 30 *Perf. 14x13½*
1148 A548 4s red & black .45 .25

Hallein, 750th anniversary.

1980, May 13 Engr. *Perf. 13½*

Empress Maria Theresa (1717-1780) Paintings by: 4s, Martin van Meytens. 6s, Josef Ducreux.

1149 A549	2.50s	violet brown	.30	.25
1150 A549	4s	dark blue	.45	.40
1151 A549	6s	rose lake	.65	.65
Nos. 1149-1151 (3)			1.40	1.30

Flags of Austria and Four Powers — A550

1980, May 14 Photo. *Perf. 13½x14*
1152 A550 4s multicolored .45 .25

State Treaty, 25th anniversary.

St. Benedict, by Meinrad Guggenbichler A551

1980, May 16 Engr. *Perf. 14½*
1153 A551 2.50s olive green .30 .20

Congress of Benedictine Order of Austria.

Hygeia by Gustav Klimt — A552

1980, May 20 Photo. *Perf. 14*
1154 A552 4s multicolored .45 .25

Academic teaching of hygiene, 175th anniv.

Aflenz Ground Satellite Receiving Station Inauguration A553

1980, May 30 Photo. *Perf. 14*
1155 A553 6s multicolored .85 .30

Steyr, Etching, 1693 A554

Photo. & Engr.
1980, June 4 *Perf. 13½*
1156 A554 4s multicolored .45 .25

Millennium of Steyr.

Worker, Oil Drill Head — A555

1980, June 12
1157 A555 2.50s multicolored .30 .20

Austrian oil production, 25th anniversary.

Seal of Innsbruck, 1267 — A556

1980, June 23 *Perf. 13½x14½*
1158 A556 2.50s multicolored .35 .20

Innsbruck, 800th anniversary.

Duke's Hat — A557

Bible Illustration, Book of Genesis — A559

Leo Ascher (1880-1942), Composer A558

Perf. 14½x13½
1980, June 23 Photo.
1159 A557 4s multicolored .45 .20

800th anniversary of Styria as a Duchy.

1980, Aug. 18 Engr. *Perf. 14*
1160 A558 3s dark purple .45 .20

1980, Aug. 25 *Perf. 13½*
1161 A559 4s multicolored .45 .25

10th Intl. Cong. of the Org. for Old Testament Studies.

Europa Issue 1980

Robert Stolz (1880-1975), Composer — A560

1980, Aug. 25 Engr. *Perf. 14x13½*
1162 A560 6s red brown .85 .30

Old and Modern Bridges A561

1980, Sept. 1 Photo. *Perf. 13½*
1163 A561 4s multicolored .45 .25

11th Congress of the Intl. Assoc. for Bridge and Structural Engineering, Vienna.

Moon Figure, by Karl Brandstätter A562

Customs Service, Sesquicentennial A563

Photo. & Engr.
1980, Oct. 10 *Perf. 14x13½*
1164 A562 4s multicolored .45 .25

1980, Oct. 13 Photo.
1165 A563 2.50s multicolored .30 .20

Gazette Masthead, 1810 A564

1980, Oct. 23 Photo. *Perf. 13½*
1166 A564 2.50s multicolored .30 .20

Official Gazette of Linz, 350th anniversary.

Waidhofen Town Book Title Page, 14th Century — A565

Photo. & Engr.
1980, Oct. 24 *Perf. 14*
1167 A565 2.50s multicolored .30 .20

Waidhofen on Thaya, 750th anniversary.

Federal Austrian Army, 25th Anniversary A566

1980, Oct. 24 Photo. *Perf. 13½x14*
1168 A566 2.50s grnsh black & red .30 .20

Alfred Wegener A567

1980, Oct. 31 Engr.
1169 A567 4s violet blue .55 .25

Alfred Wegener (1880-1930), scientist, formulated theory of continental drift.

A568

A569

1980, Nov. 6 *Perf. 14x13½*
1170 A568 4s dark red brown .55 .25

Robert Musil (1880-1942), poet.

Photo. & Engr.
1980, Nov. 28 *Perf. 13½*

Nativity, stained glass window, Klagenfurt.

1171 A569 4s multicolored .55 .25

Christmas.

25th Anniversary of Social Security A570

1981, Jan. 19 Litho. *Perf. 13½x14*
1172 A570 2.50s multicolored .30 .20

Niebelungen Saga, 1926, by Dachauer A571

Machinist in Wheelchair A572

1981, Apr. 6 Engr. *Perf. 14x13½*
1173 A571 3s sepia .40 .20

Wilhelm Dachauer (1881-1951), artist and engraver.

1981, Apr. 6 Photo. & Engr.
1174 A572 6s multicolored .75 .35

Rehabilitation Intl., 3rd European Regional Conf.

Sigmund Freud — A573

Congress, Vienna — A574

1981, May 6 Engr.
1175 A573 3s rose violet .40 .20

Sigmund Freud (1856-1939), psychoanalyst.

1981, May 11 Photo.
1176 A574 4s multicolored .55 .25

A575

Europa — A576

Azzo (founder of House of Kuenringer) and his followers, bear-skin manuscript.

1981, May 15 Photo. & Engr.
1177 A575 3s multicolored .35 .20

Kuenringer Exhibition, Zwettl Monastery.

1981, May 22 Photo.
1178 A576 6s Maypole .80 .35

Telephone Service Centenary A577

Photo. and Engr.
1981 May 29 *Perf. 13½x14*
1179 A577 4s multicolored .45 .25

Seibersdorf Research Center, 25th Anniv. — A578

1981, June 29 Photo. *Perf. 13½*
1180 A578 4s multicolored .45 .25

The Frog King (Child's Drawing) A579

1981, June 29 *Perf. 13½x14*
1181 A579 3s multicolored .35 .20

Town Hall and Town Seal of 1250 — A580

Photo. & Engr.
1981, July 17 *Perf. 13½x14*
1182 A580 4s multicolored .45 .25

St. Veit an der Glan, 800th anniv.

Johann Florian Heller (1813-1871), Pioneer of Urinalysis — A581

1981, Aug. 31 *Perf. 14x13½*
1183 A581 6s red brown .75 .35

11th Intl. Clinical Chemistry Congress.

Ludwig Boltzmann (1844-1906), Physicist
A582

Scale
A583

1981, Sept. 4 Engr. *Perf. 14x13½*
1184 A582 3s dark green .45 .20

Photo. & Engr.

1981, Sept. 7 *Perf. 14*
1185 A583 6s multicolored .75 .35

Intl. Pharmaceutical Federation World Congress, Vienna, Sept. 6-11.

Otto Bauer, Politician, Birth Centenary
A584

Escher's Impossible Cube
A585

1981, Sept. 7 Photo. *Perf. 14x13½*
1186 A584 4s multicolored .45 .25

1981, Sept. 14
1187 A585 4s dk blue & brt blue .45 .25

10th Intl. Mathematicians' Cong., Innsbruck.

Kneeling Virgin, Detail of Coronation of Mary Altarpiece, St. Wolfgang, 500th Anniv. — A586

1981, Sept. 25 Engr. *Perf. 14x13½*
1188 A586 3s dark blue .35 .20

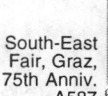

South-East Fair, Graz, 75th Anniv.
A587

Perf. 13½x14

1981, Sept. 25 Photo.
1189 A587 4s multicolored .45 .25

Holy Trinity, 12th Cent. Byzantine Miniature
A588

1981, Oct. 5
1190 A588 6s multicolored .75 .35

16th Intl. Byzantine Congress.

Hans Kelsen (1881-1973), Co-author of Federal Constitution
A589

1981, Oct. 9 Engr.
1191 A589 3s dark carmine .35 .20

Edict of Tolerance Bicen. — A590

Photo. & Engr.

1981, Oct. 9 *Perf. 14*
1192 A590 4s Joseph II .45 .25

World Food Day
A591

1981, Oct. 16 Photo. *Perf. 13½*
1193 A591 6s multicolored .75 .35

Between the Times, by Oscar Asboth
A592

1981, Oct. 22 Litho. *Perf. 13½x14*
1194 A592 4s multicolored .55 .25

Intl. Catholic Workers' Day — A593

Photo. & Engr.

1981, Oct. 23 *Perf. 14x13½*
1195 A593 3s multicolored .35 .20

Baron Josef Hammer-Purgstall, Founder of Oriental Studies, 125th Death Anniv. — A594

Photo. & Engr.

1981, Nov. 23 *Perf. 14*
1196 A594 3s multicolored .35 .20

Julius Raab (1891-1964), Politician
A595

1981, Nov. 27 Engr. *Perf. 13½*
1197 A595 6s rose lake .75 .35

Nativity, Corn Straw Figures
A596

1981, Nov. 27 Photo. & Engr.
1198 A596 4s multicolored .50 .20

Christmas.

Stefan Zweig (1881-1942), Poet — A597

1981, Nov. 27 Engr. *Perf. 14x13½*
1199 A597 4s dull violet .50 .20

800th Anniv. of St. Nikola on the Danube — A598

1981, Dec. 4 Photo. & Engr.
1200 A598 4s multicolored .55 .20

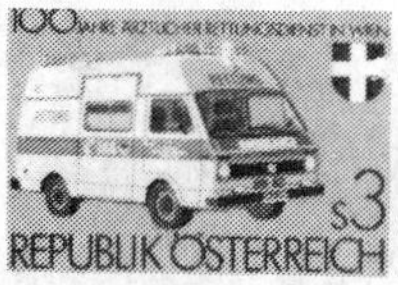

Vienna Emergency Medical Service Centenary
A599

1981, Dec. 9 Photo. *Perf. 13½x14*
1201 A599 3s multicolored .35 .20

Schladming-Haus Alpine World Skiing Championship
A600

1982, Jan. 27 *Perf. 14*
1202 A600 4s multicolored .45 .20

Dorotheum (State Auction Gallery), 275th Anniv. — A601

Photo. & Engr.

1982, Mar. 12 *Perf. 14*
1203 A601 4s multicolored .45 .20

A602

A603

1982, Mar. 19 Photo. *Perf. 14x13½*
1204 A602 5s multicolored .60 .30

Water Rescue Service, 25th anniv.

Photo. & Engr.

1982, Apr. 23 *Perf. 14x13½*
1205 A603 3s St. Severin .35 .20

St. Severin and the End of the Roman Era exhibition.

A604

A605

1982, May 4 *Perf. 14*
1206 A604 4s multicolored .55 .20

Intl. Kneipp Hydropathy Congress, Vienna.

1982, May 7
1207 A605 4s Printers' guild arms .55 .20

Printing in Austria, 500th anniv.

A606

A607

Design: Urine analysis, Canone di Avicenna manuscript.

1982, May 12 Photo.
1208 A606 6s multicolored .75 .35

5th European Urology Soc. Cong., Vienna.

1982, May 14 Photo. & Engr.
1209 A607 3s multicolored .35 .20

800th birth anniv. of St. Francis of Assisi.

A608

A609

1982, May 19 Engr. *Perf. 13½*
1210 A608 3s olive green .35 .20

Haydn and His Time Exhibition, Rohrau.

1982, May 25 Photo. *Perf. 14x13½*
1211 A609 7s multicolored .90 .40

25th World Milk Day.

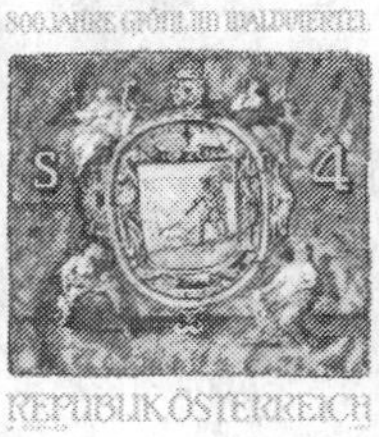

800th Anniv of Gfohl (Market Town) — A610

Photo. & Engr.

1982, May 28 *Perf. 14*
1212 A610 4s multicolored .45 .20

Tennis Player and Austrian Tennis Federation Emblem — A611

1982, June 11
1213 A611 3s multicolored .35 .20

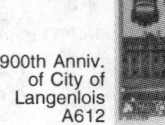

900th Anniv. of City of Langenlois A612

Photo. & Engr.

1982, June 11 *Perf. 13½x14*
1214 A612 4s multicolored .45 .20

800th Anniv. of City of Weiz A613

Ignaz Seipel (1876-1932), Statesman A614

1982, June 18 Photo. *Perf. 14x13½*
1215 A613 4s Arms .45 .20

1982, July 30 Engr. *Perf. 14x13½*
1216 A614 3s brown violet .35 .20

Europa Issue 1982

Sesquicentennial of Linz-Freistadt-Budweis Horse-drawn Railroad — A615

1982, July 30 *Perf. 13½*
1217 A615 6s brown .90 .35

Mail Bus Service, 75th Anniv. — A616

Rocket Lift-off — A617

1982, Aug. 6 Photo. *Perf. 14x13½*
1218 A616 4s multicolored .50 .20

1982, Aug. 9 *Perf. 14*
1219 A617 4s multicolored .50 .20

2nd UN Conference on Peaceful Uses of Outer Space, Vienna, Aug. 9-21.

Geodesists' Day — A618

Photo. & Engr.

1982, Sept. 1 *Perf. 13½x14*
1220 A618 3s Tower, Office of Standards .35 .20

Protection of Endangered Species — A619

1982, Sept. 9 *Perf. 14*
1221 A619 3s Bustard .45 .25
1222 A619 4s Beaver .60 .30
1223 A619 6s Capercaillie .90 .45
Nos. 1221-1223 (3) 1.95 1.00

10th Anniv. of Intl. Institute for Applied Systems Anaysis, Vienna A620

1982, Oct. 4 **Photo.**
1224 A620 3s Laxenburg Castle .35 .20

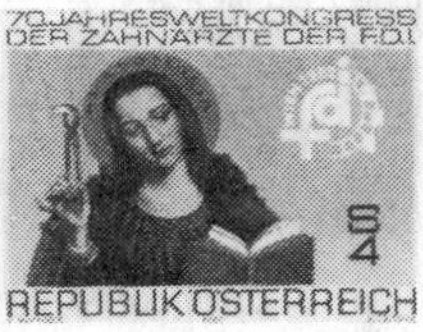

St. Apollonia (Patron Saint of Dentists) A621

1982, Oct. 11 **Photo. & Engr.**
1225 A621 4s multicolored .45 .20

70th Annual World Congress of Dentists.

Emmerich Kalman (1882-1953), Composer A622

1982, Oct. 22 Engr. *Perf. 13½*
1226 A622 3s dark blue .35 .20

Max Mell (1882-1971), Poet — A623

Christmas — A624

1982, Nov. 10 Photo. *Perf. 14x13½*
1227 A623 3s multicolored .35 .20

Photo. & Engr.

1982, Nov. 25 *Perf. 13½*

Design: Christmas crib, Damuls Church, Vorarlberg, 1630.

1228 A624 4s multicolored .45 .20

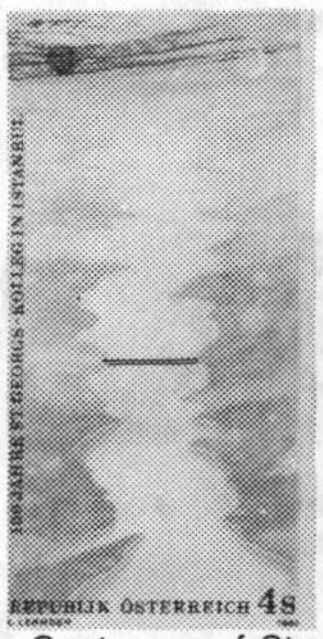

Centenary of St. George's College, Istanbul — A625

Portrait of a Girl, by Ernst Fuchs — A626

1982, Nov. 26 Litho. *Perf. 14*
1229 A625 4s Bosporus .45 .20

1982, Dec. 10 **Photo. & Engr.**
1230 A626 4s multicolored .45 .20

Postal Savings Bank Centenary A627

Photo. & Engr.

1983, Jan. 12 *Perf. 14*
1231 A627 4s Bank .55 .20

Hildegard Burjan (1883-1933), Founder of Caritas Socialis A628

1983, Jan. 28 **Engr.**
1232 A628 4s rose lake .55 .20

World Communications Year — A629

1983, Feb. 18 Photo. *Perf. 13½x14*
1233 A629 7s multicolored .95 .40

75th Anniv. Children's Friends Org. — A630

Photo. & Engr.

1983, Feb. 23 *Perf. 14x13½*
1234 A630 4s multicolored .55 .20

Josef Matthias Hauer (1883-1959), Composer A631

1983, Mar. 18 Engr. *Perf. 14*
1235 A631 3s deep lilac rose .40 .20

25th Anniv. of Austrian Airlines A632

1983, Mar. 31 Photo. *Perf. 13½x14*
1236 A632 6s multicolored .85 .35

Work Inspection Centenary A633

1983, Apr. 8 Photo. *Perf. 13½*
1237 A633 4s multicolored .55 .20

Upper Austria Millennium Provincial Exhibition A634

1983, Apr. 28 Photo. *Perf. 13½*
1238 A634 3s Wels Castle, by Matthaus Merian .40 .20

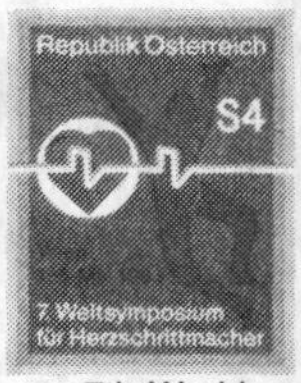

Gottweig Monastery, 900th Anniv. A635

7th World Pacemakers Symposium A636

Photo. & Engr.

1983, Apr. 29 *Perf. 13½*
1239 A635 3s multicolored .40 .20

1983, Apr. 29 Photo. *Perf. 14x13½*
1240 A636 4s multicolored .55 .20

Catholic Students' Org. — A637

1983, May 20 Photo. *Perf. 14*
1241 A637 4s multicolored .55 .20

Weitra, 800th Anniv. A638

Photo. & Engr.
1983, May 20 *Perf. 13½*
1242 A638 4s multicolored .55 .20

Granting of Town Rights to Hohenems, 650th Anniv. — A639

1983, May 27 Photo. *Perf. 14*
1243 A639 4s multicolored .55 .20

25th Anniv. of Stadthall, Vienna A640

1983, June 24 Photo. *Perf. 14*
1244 A640 4s multicolored .55 .20

Europa Issue 1983

A641 A642

1983, June 24 Engr. *Perf. 14x13½*
1245 A641 6s dark green .95 .35

Europa: Viktor Franz Hess (1883-1964), 1936 Nobel Prize winner in physics.

1983, July 1 Photo. *Perf. 13½*
1246 A642 5s multicolored .70 .30

Kiwanis Intl. Convention, Vienna, July 3-6.

7th World Congress of Psychiatry, Vienna — A643

1983, July 11 Photo. *Perf. 14*
1247 A643 4s Emblem, St. Stephen's Cathedral .55 .20

Baron Carl von Hasenauer (1833-1894), Architect A644

1983, July 20 Engr. *Perf. 13½x14*
1248 A644 3s Natural History Museum, Vienna .45 .20

27th Intl. Chamber of Commerce Professional Competition, Linz — A645

1983, Aug. 16 Photo.
1249 A645 4s Chamber building .55 .20

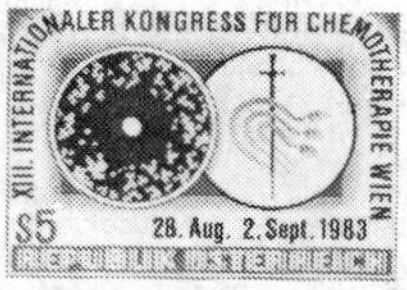

13th Intl. Chemotherapy Congress, Vienna, Aug. 28-Sept. 2 — A646

1983, Aug. 26
1250 A646 5s Penicillin test on cancer .70 .30

Catholics' Day — A647

Visit of Pope John Paul II — A648

1983, Sept. 9 Photo. *Perf. 14x13½*
1251 A647 3s multicolored .40 .20

Photo. & Engr.
1983, Sept. 9 *Perf. 13½*
1252 A648 6s multicolored .90 .35

Souvenir Sheet

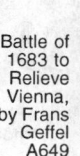

Battle of 1683 to Relieve Vienna, by Frans Geffel A649

1983, Sept. 9 *Perf. 14*
1253 A649 6s multicolored .95 .50

300th anniv. of Vienna's rescue from Turkey.

Vienna Rathaus Centenary — A650

1983, Sept. 23 *Perf. 13½x14*
1254 A650 4s multicolored .55 .20

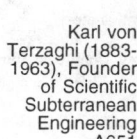

Karl von Terzaghi (1883-1963), Founder of Scientific Subterranean Engineering A651

1983, Oct. 3 Engr.
1255 A651 3s dark blue .40 .20

10th Trade Unions Federal Congress, Oct. 3-8 A652

1983, Oct. 3 Photo. *Perf. 13½*
1256 A652 3s black & red .40 .20

Evening Sun in Burgenland, by Gottfried Kumpf — A653

Photo. & Engr.
1983, Oct. 7 *Perf. 13½x14*
1257 A653 4s multicolored .55 .20

Modling-Hinterbruhl Electric Railroad Centenary — A654

1983, Oct. 21 Photo.
1258 A654 3s multicolored .40 .20

Provincial Museum of Upper Austria Sesquicentennial — A655

1983, Nov. 4 Photo. & Engr.
1259 A655 4s Francisco-Carolinum Museum .55 .20

Creche, St. Andreas Parish Church, Kitzbuhel A656

1983, Nov. 25 *Perf. 14*
1260 A656 4s multicolored .55 .20

Christmas.

Parliament Bldg. Vienna, 100th Anniv. — A657

1983, Dec. 2 Engr.
1261 A657 4s slate blue .55 .20

A658 A659

Altar picture, St. Nikola/Pram Church.

1983, Dec. 6 Photo. *Perf. 14x13½*
1262 A658 3s multicolored .40 .20

1983, Dec. 15 Engr. *Perf. 14½x13½*
1263 A659 6s dark red brn .90 .35

Wolfgang Pauli (1900-58), physicist, Nobel Prize winner.

Gregor Mendel (1822-1884), Genetics Founder — A660

Photo. & Engr.
1984, Jan. 5 *Perf. 13½*
1264 A660 4s multicolored .55 .20

Anton Hanak (1875-1934), Sculptor — A661

1984, Jan. 5
1265 A661 3s red brown & blk .40 .20

50th Anniv. of 1934 Uprising — A662

1984, Feb. 10 Photo. *Perf. 14*
1266 A662 4.50s Memorial, Woellersdorf .65 .30

Wernher von Reichersberg Family, Bas-relief, 15th Cent. — A663

Photo. & Engr.
1984, Apr. 25 *Perf. 14x13½*
1267 A663 3.50s brown & blue .50 .25

900th anniv. of Reichersberg Monastery.

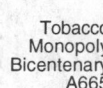

Tobacco Monopoly Bicentenary A665

1984, May 4 *Perf. 13½*
1269 A665 4.50s Cigar wrapper, tobacco plant .65 .30

1200th Anniv. of Kostendorf Municipality A666

1984, May 4
1270 A666 4.50s View, arms .65 .30

Automobile Engineers World Congress A667

1984, May 4 **Photo.** *Perf. 13½x14*
1271 A667 5s Wheel bearing cross-section .70 .30

Europa (1959-1984) A668

1984, May 4 *Perf. 13½*
1272 A668 6s multicolored .90 .35

A669

Aragonite — A670

Archduke Johann (1782-1859) by S. von Carolsfeld.

Photo. & Engr.

1984, May 11 *Perf. 14*
1273 A669 4.50s multicolored .65 .30

1984, May 11 *Perf. 13½*
1274 A670 3.50s multicolored .50 .20

Ore and Iron Provincial Exhibition.

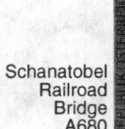

Era of Emperor Francis Joseph Exhibition A671

Design: Cover of Viribus Unitis, publ. by Max Herzig, 1898.

1984, May 18
1275 A671 3.50s red & gold .50 .20

A672

A673

Photo. & Engr.

1984, May 30 *Perf. 14x13½*
1276 A672 4.50s Tower, arms .65 .30

City of Vocklabruck, 850th anniv.

1984, June 1 *Perf. 13½*

Dionysius, Virinum mosaic.

1277 A673 3.50s multicolored .50 .20

Museum of Carinthia, centenary.

Erosion Prevention Systems Centenary A674

1984, June 5 **Engr.** *Perf. 14*
1278 A674 4.50s Stone reinforcement wall .65 .30

Tyrol Provincial Celebration, 1809-1984 — A675

Art Exhibition: Meeting of Imperial Troops with South Tyrolean Reserves under Andreas Hofer near Sterzing in April 1809, by Ludwig Schnorr von Carolsfeld, 1830.

Photo. & Engr.

1984, June 5 *Perf. 14x13½*
1279 A675 3.50s multicolored .50 .20

A676

A677

1984, June 5 **Engr.**
1280 A676 4s violet brown .55 .25

Ralph Benatzky (1884-1957), composer.

1984, June 22 **Photo.** *Perf. 14*
1281 A677 3.50s multicolored .50 .20

Christian von Ehrenfels (1859-1932), philosopher.

25th Anniv. of Minimundus (Model City) — A678

1984, June 22 *Perf. 13½x14*
1282 A678 4s Eiffel Tower, Tower of Pisa, ferris wheel .55 .25

Blockheide Eibenstein Nature Park A679

1984 **Photo. & Engr.**
1283 A679 4s shown .55 .25
1284 A679 4s Lake Neusiedl .55 .25

Issued: #1283, June 29; #1284, Aug. 13.
See Nos. 1349-1354, 1492-1496, 1744, 1777.

Monasteries and Abbeys — A679a

Designs: 3.50s, Geras Monastery, Lower Austria. 4s, Stams. 4.50s, Schlagl. 5s, Benedictine Abbey of St. Paul Levanttal. 6s, Rein-Hohenfurth.

1984-85 *Perf. 14*

1285	A679a 3.50s multicolored		.50	.20
1286	A679a 4s multicolored		.50	.20
1287	A679a 4.50s multicolored		.65	.30
1288	A679a 5s multicolored		.65	.30
1288A	A679a 6s multicolored		.90	.35
	Nos. 1285-1288A (5)		3.20	1.35

Issued: 3.50s, 4/27/84; 4s, 9/28/84; 4.50s, 5/18/84; 5s, 9/27/85; 6s, 10/4/84.
See Nos. 1361-1365, 1464A-1468.

Schanatobel Railroad Bridge A680

Railroad Anniversaries: 3.50s, Arlberg centenary. 4.50s, Tauern, 75th.

1984, July 6 *Perf. 14*
1289 A680 3.50s shown .50 .20
1290 A680 4.50s Falkenstein Bridge .65 .20

A681

A682

1984, July 6 **Photo.**
1291 A681 6s Johan Stuwer's balloon .90 .35

Balloon flight in Austria bicentenary.

1984, Aug. 31 **Photo. & Engr.**
1292 A682 7s Vienna Palace of Justice, emblem .95 .45

Intl. Lawyers' Congress, Vienna.

A683

A684

1984, Sept. 3 **Photo.**
1293 A683 6s Josef Hyrtl, anatomist .90 .35

7th European Anatomy Congress, Innsbruck, Sept. 3-7.

1984, Oct. 12
1294 A684 4s Window, by Karl Korab .55 .20

A685

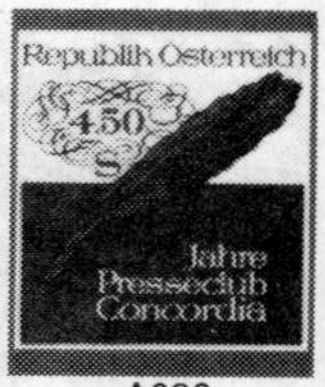

A686

1984, Oct. 18
1295 A685 3.50s Clock (Immset Uhr), 1555 .50 .20

Johannes of Gmunden, mathematician, 600th birth anniv.

1984, Nov. 9 **Photo.** *Perf. 13½*
1296 A686 4.50s Quill .65 .30

Concordia Press Club, 125th anniv.

Fanny Eissler, Dancer, Death Centenary — A687

1984, Nov. 23 **Photo. & Engr.**
1297 A687 4s multicolored .55 .30

Christmas A688

Design: Christ is Born, Aggsbacher Altar, Herzogenburg Monastery.

1984, Nov. 30 *Perf. 14*
1298 A688 4.50s multicolored .65 .20

A689

A690

1985, Jan. 4 *Perf. 14x13½*
1299 A689 3.50s Seal .50 .20

Karl Franzens University, Graz, 400th anniv.

1985, Jan. 15 **Engr.**
1300 A690 4.50s dk rose lake .60 .20

Dr. Lorenz Bohler, Surgeon, birth cent.

Nordic Events, Ski Championships, Seefeld — A691

1985, Jan. 17 **Photo.** *Perf. 13½*
1301 A691 4s Ski jumper, cross country racer .55 .20

Linz Diocese Bicentenary A692

1985, Jan. 25
1302 A692 4.50s Linz Cathedral interior .60 .20

Alban Berg (1885-1935), Composer — A693

1985, Feb. 8 **Engr.**
1303 A693 6s bluish black .80 .25

Vocational Training Inst., 25th Anniv. A694

1985, Feb. 15 **Photo.** ***Perf. 13½x14***
1304 A694 4.50s multicolored .60 .20

City of Bregenz, Bimillennium A695

1985, Feb. 22 ***Perf. 14x13½***
1305 A695 4s multicolored .55 .20

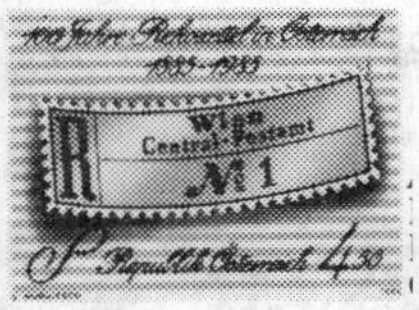

Austrian Registration Labels Cent. — A696

1985, Mar. 15 ***Perf. 13½x14***
1306 A696 4.50s Label, 1885 .60 .20

Josef Stefan (1835-1893), Physicist A697

Photo. & Engr.
1985, Mar. 22 ***Perf. 14x13½***
1307 A697 6s buff, dl red brn & dk brn .80 .25

A698 A699

St. Leopold 16th-17th cent. embroidery.

1985, Mar. 29
1308 A698 3.50s multicolored .50 .20

St. Leopold Exhibition, Klosterneuberg.

1985, Apr. 26 **Photo.**
1309 A699 4.50s multicolored .60 .20

Liberation from German occupation forces, 40th anniv.

Painter Franz von Defregger (1835-1921) A700

1985, Apr. 26
1310 A700 3.50s Fairy tale teller .50 .20

Europa Issue 1985

Johann Joseph Fux (1660-1741), Composer, Violin and Trombone A701

Photo. & Engr.
1985, May 3 ***Perf. 13½***
1311 A701 6s lil gray & dk brn .90 .25

Boheimkirchen (Market Town) Millennium — A702

1985, May 10 ***Perf. 14***
1312 A702 4.50s View, coat of arms .60 .20

A703 A704

Mercury staff, flags of member and affiliate nations.

1985, May 10 **Photo.** ***Perf. 13½***
1313 A703 4s multicolored .55 .20

European Free Trade Assoc., 25th anniv.

1985, May 15 **Photo. & Engr.**

Episcopal residence gate, St. Polten diocese arms.

1314 A704 4.50s multicolored .60 .20

St. Polten Diocese, bicentenary.

The Gumpp Family of Builders, Innsbruck — A705

Perf. 14½x13½
1985, May 17 **Photo.**
1315 A705 3.50s multicolored .50 .20

Garsten Market Town Millennium A706

Design: 17th century engraving by George Matthaus Fischer (1628-1696).

Photo. & Engr.
1985, June 7 ***Perf. 13½x14***
1316 A706 4.50s multicolored .60 .20

UN, 40th Anniv. A707

Perf. 13½x14½
1985, June 26 **Photo.**
1317 A707 4s multicolored .55 .20

Austrian membership, 30th anniv.

Intl. Assoc. for the Prevention of Suicide, 13th Congress A708

Photo. & Engr.
1985, June 28 ***Perf. 14***
1318 A708 5s brn, lt ap grn & yel .70 .30

Souvenir Sheet

Year of the Forest A709

1985, June 28 ***Perf. 13½***
1319 A709 6s Healthy and damaged woodland 1.00 .35

Kurhaus, Bad Ischl Operetta Activities Emblem A710

1985, July 5 ***Perf. 14***
1320 A710 3.50s multicolored .50 .20

Bad Ischl Festival, 25th anniv.

Intl. Competition of Fire Brigades, Vocklabruck A711

1985, July 18 **Photo.** ***Perf. 14x13½***
1321 A711 4.50s Fireman, emblem .60 .20

Grossglockner Alpine Motorway, 50th Anniv. — A712

Photo. & Engr.
1985, Aug. 2 ***Perf. 13½***
1322 A712 4s View of Fuschertorl .55 .20

World Chess Federation Congress, Graz — A713

1985, Aug. 28 **Photo.** ***Perf. 13½***
1323 A713 4s Checkered globe, emblem .55 .20

The Legendary Foundation of Konigstetten by Charlemagne, by Auguste Stephan, c. 1870 — A714

Photo. & Engr.
1985, Aug. 30 ***Perf. 14***
1324 A714 4.50s multicolored .60 .20

Konigstetten millennium.

Hofkirchen-Taufkirchen-Weibern Municipalities, 1200th Anniv. — A715

1985, Aug. 30 ***Perf. 13½x14***
1325 A715 4.50s View of Weiburn, municipal arms .60 .20

Dr. Adam Politzer (1835-1923), Physician A716

1985, Sept. 12 **Engr.** ***Perf. 14***
1326 A716 3.50s blue violet .50 .20

Politzer pioneered aural therapy for auditory disorders.

Intl. Assoc. of Forwarding Agents, World Congress, Vienna — A717

1985, Oct. 7 Photo. *Perf. 13½*
1327 A717 6s multicolored .85 .35

Carnival Figures Riding High Bicycles, By Paul Flora A718

Photo. & Engr.
1985, Oct. 25 *Perf. 14*
1328 A718 4s multicolored .55 .20

St. Martin on Horseback A719

1985, Nov. 8 Photo.
1329 A719 4.50s multicolored .60 .30

Eisenstadt Diocese, 25th anniv.

Creche, Marble Bas-relief, Salzburg — A720

Photo. & Engr.
1985, Nov. 29 *Perf. 13½*
1330 A720 4.50s gold, dl vio & buff .60 .30

Christmas.

Hanns Horbiger (1860-1931), Inventor — A721

1985, Nov. 29 *Perf. 14*
1331 A721 3.50s gold & sepia .50 .20

Aqueduct, Hundsau Brook, Near Gostling A722

1985, Nov. 29 *Perf. 13½x14½*
1332 A722 3.50s red, bluish blk & brt ultra .50 .20

Vienna Aqueduct, 75th anniv.

Chateau de la Muette, Paris Headquarters A723

1985, Dec. 13
1333 A723 4s sep, rose lil & gold .55 .25

Org. for Economic Cooperation and Development, 25th anniv.

Johann Bohm (1886-1959), Pres. Austrian Trade Fed. — A724

1986, Jan. 24 Photo. *Perf. 14*
1334 A724 4.50s blk, ver & grayish black .65 .30

Intl. Peace Year — A725

Perf. 13½x14½
1986, Jan. 24 Photo.
1335 A725 6s multicolored .85 .35

Digital Telephone Service Introduction A726

1986, Jan. 29 Photo.
1336 A726 5s Push-button keyboard .75 .30

Johann Georg Albrechtsberger (b. 1736), Composer — A727

Photo. & Engr.
1986, Jan. 31 *Perf. 13½x14½*
1337 A727 3.50s Klosterneuberg organ .50 .20

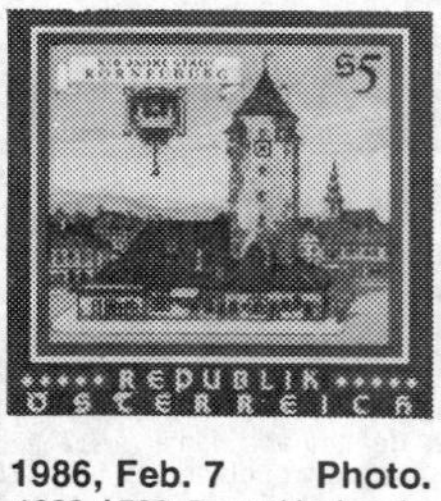

Korneuberg, 850th Anniv. A728

1986, Feb. 7 Photo. *Perf. 14*
1338 A728 5s multicolored .75 .30

A729

A730

Self-portrait, by Oskar Kokoschka (b.1886).

Perf. 14½x13½
1986, Feb. 28 Photo.
1339 A729 4s multicolored .60 .30

1986, Feb. 28 Photo. *Perf. 13x13½*
1340 A730 6s multicolored .85 .35

Admission to Council of Europe, 30th anniv.

Clemens Holzmeister (b. 1886), Architect, Salzburg Festival Theater, 1926 — A731

Photo. & Engr.
1986, Mar. 27 *Perf. 13½*
1341 A731 4s sepia & redsh brn .60 .30

3rd Intl. Geotextile Congress, Vienna A732

1986, Apr. 7 Photo. *Perf. 13½x14½*
1342 A732 5s multicolored .75 .30

Prince Eugen and Schlosshof Castle — A733

Photo. & Engr.
1986, Apr. 21 *Perf. 14*
1343 A733 4s multicolored .60 .30

Prince Eugen Exhibition, Schlosshof and Niederweiden.

St. Florian Monastery, Upper Austria A734

1986, Apr. 24
1344 A734 4s multicolored .60 .30

The World of Baroque provincial exhibition, St. Florian.

Herberstein Castle, Arms of Styria A735

1986, May 2 *Perf. 13½x14½*
1345 A735 4s multicolored .60 .30

Europa 1986 — A736

1986, May 2 *Perf. 13½*
1346 A736 6s Pasque flower .85 .45

Wagner, Scene from Opera Lohengrin — A737

1986, May 21
1347 A737 4s multicolored .60 .30

Intl. Richard Wagner Congress, Vienna.

Antimonite A738

1986, May 23 *Perf. 13½x14½*
1348 A738 4s multicolored .60 .30

Burgenland Provincial Minerals Exhibition.

Scenery Type of 1984

1986-89 Photo. & Engr. *Perf. 14*

1349 A679 5s Martinswall, Tyrol	.65	.35
1350 A679 5s Tschauko Falls, Carinthia	.65	.35
1351 A679 5s Dachstein Ice Caves	.80	.45
1352 A679 5s Gauertal, Montafon	.80	.45
1353 A679 5s Krimmler Waterfalls	.80	.60
1354 A679 5s Lusthauswasser	.80	.60
Nos. 1349-1354 (6)	4.50	2.80

Issued: #1351, 6/11/87; #1352, 8/21/87; #1353, 8/19/88; #1354, 9/1/89.

Waidhofen on Ybbs Township, 800th Anniv. A739

1986, June 20 Photo. *Perf. 13½*
1355 A739 4s multicolored .50 .30

Salzburg Local Railway, Cent. A740

1986, Aug. 8 Photo. *Perf. 14*
1356 A740 4s multicolored .55 .30

Seals of Dukes Leopold Of Austria, Otakar of Styria, and Georgenberg Church — A741

1986, Aug. 14 **Photo. & Engr.**
1357 A741 5s multicolored .70 .30

Georgenberg Treaty, 800th anniv.

Julius Tandler (1869-1936), Social Reformer — A742

1986, Aug. 22
1358 A742 4s multicolored .60 .30

Sonnblick Observatory, Cent. — A743

Photo. & Engr.
1986, Aug. 27 ***Perf. 13½x14½***
1359 A743 4s Observatory, 1886 .60 .30

Discovery of Mandrake Root — A744

1986, Aug. 27 ***Perf. 14½x13½***
1360 A744 5s multicolored .75 .30

European Assoc. for Anesthesiology, 7th cong.

Monasteries and Abbeys Type of 1984

Designs: 5.50s, St. Gerold's Provostry, Vorarlberg. 7s, Loretto Monastery, Burgenland. 7.50s, Dominican Convent, Vienna. 8s, Zwettl Monastery. 10s, Wilten Monastery.

1986-88 **Photo. & Engr.** ***Perf. 14***

1361	A679a	5.50s multicolored	.80	.60
1362	A679a	7s multicolored	1.10	.90
1363	A679a	7.50s multicolored	1.10	.85
1364	A679a	8s multicolored	1.40	1.00
1365	A679a	10s multicolored	1.75	1.25
		Nos. 1361-1365 (5)	6.15	4.60

Issued: 5.50s, 9/12/86; 7.50s, 10/3; 7s, 8/14/87; 8s, 5/27/88; 10s, 3/18/88.

A745 A746

Photo. & Engr.
1986, Sept. 3 ***Perf. 14***
1366 A745 4s multicolored .60 .30

Otto Stoessl (d. 1936), writer.

1986, Sept. 3 **Photo.**
1367 A746 4s Fireman, 1686 .60 .30

Vienna fire brigade, 300th anniv.

Silk Viennese Hunting Tapestry A747

Photo. & Engr.
1986, Sept. 3 ***Perf. 14***
1368 A747 5s multicolored .75 .40

Intl. conf. on Oriental Carpets, Vienna, Budapest.

A748 A749

Photo. & Engr.
1986, Oct. 10 ***Perf. 14***
1369 A748 5s Minister at pulpit .70 .40

Protestant Act, 25th anniv., and Protestant Patent of Franz Josef I ensuring religious equality, 125th anniv.

1986, Oct. 17 ***Perf. 13½x14***

Disintegration, by Walter Schmogner.

1370 A749 4s multicolored .60 .30

Franz Liszt, Composer, and Birthplace, Burgenland A750

1986, Oct. 17 ***Perf. 13½***
1371 A750 5s green & sepia .70 .40

Souvenir Sheet

European Security Conference, Vienna — A751

Illustration reduced.

1986, Nov. 4 ***Perf. 13½x14***
1372 A751 6s Vienna .95 .65

Strettweg Cart, 7th Cent. B.C. A752

Photo. & Engr.
1986, Nov. 26 ***Perf. 14***
1373 A752 4s multicolored .65 .30

Joanneum Styrian Land Museum, 175th anniv.

Christmas A753

Design: The Little Crib, bas-relief by Schwanthaler (1740-1810), Schlierbach Monastery.

1986, Nov. 28
1374 A753 5s gold & rose lake .80 .40

Federal Chamber of Commerce, 40th Anniv. — A754

1986, Dec. 2 **Photo.**
1375 A754 5s multicolored .80 .40

Industry A755

1986-91 ***Perf. 14x13½***

1376	A755	4s	Steel workers	.80	.30
1377	A755	4s	Office worker, computer	.80	.35
1378	A755	4s	Lab assistant	.80	.30
1378A	A755	4.50s	Textile worker	.75	.60
1379	A755	5s	Bricklayer	.80	.60
			Nos. 1376-1379 (5)	3.95	2.15

Issued: #1376, 12/4/86; #1377, 10/5/87; #1378, 10/21/88; 5s, 10/10/89; 4.50s, 10/11/91.

This is an expanding set. Numbers will change if necessary.

The Educated Eye, by Arnulf Rainer — A756

1987, Jan. 13 **Photo.** ***Perf. 13½x14***
1386 A756 5s multicolored .80 .40

Adult education in Vienna, cent.

The Large Blue Madonna, by Anton Faistauer (1887-1970) A757

Paintings: 6s, Self-portrait, 1922, by A. Paris Gutersloh (1887-1973).

1987, Jan. 29 ***Perf. 14***
1387 A757 4s multicolored .55 .20
1388 A757 6s multicolored .90 .40

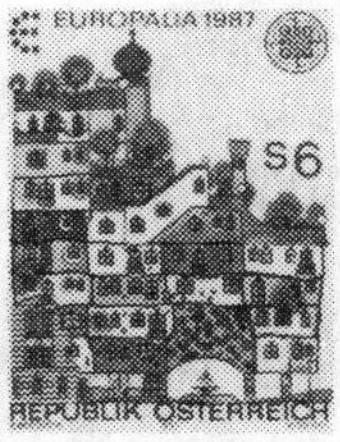

Europa 1987 — A758

Photo. & Engr.
1987, Apr. 6 ***Perf. 13½x14***
1389 A758 6s Hundertwasser House .95 .55

World Ice Hockey Championships, Vienna — A759

Perf. 13½x14½
1987, Apr. 17 **Photo.**
1390 A759 5s multicolored .80 .60

Opening of the Austria Center, Vienna A760

1987, Apr. 22
1391 A760 5s multicolored .80 .60

Salzburg City Charter, 700th Anniv. A761

1987, Apr. 24
1392 A761 5s multicolored .80 .60

A762 A763

Photo. & Engr.
1987, Apr. 29 ***Perf. 14***
1393 A762 4s Factory, 1920 .65 .50

Work-Men-Machines, provincial exhibition, Upper Austria.

1987, Apr. 29 **Photo.** ***Perf. 13½***
1394 A763 5s multicolored .80 .60

Equal rights for men and women.

A764 A765

Adele Block-Bauer I, abstract by Gustav Klimt.

Photo. & Engr.

1987, May 8 ***Perf. 13½***
1395 A764 4s multicolored .65 .50

The Era of Emperor Franz Joseph, provincial exhibition, Lower Austria.

1987, May 15 ***Perf. 14½x13½***
1396 A765 6s multicolored 1.00 .75

Arthur Schnitzler (1862-1931), poet.

Von Raitenau, View of Salzburg A766

1987, May 15 ***Perf. 14***
1397 A766 4s multicolored .65 .50

Prince Archbishop Wolf Dietrich von Raitenau, patron of baroque architecture in Salzburg, provincial exhibition.

Lace, Lustenau Municipal Arms A767

1987, May 22
1398 A767 5s multicolored .80 .60

Lustenau, 1100th anniv.

Souvenir Sheet

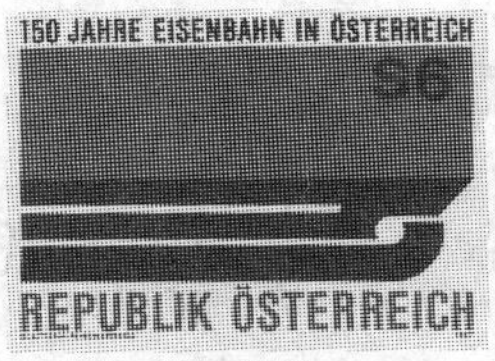

Austrian Railways Sesquicentenary — A768

1987, June 5 **Photo.** ***Perf. 13½***
1399 A768 6s multicolored 1.00 .75

8th Intl. Congress of Engravers, Vienna A769

Photo. & Engr.

1987, June 17 ***Perf. 14***
1400 A769 5s gray, gray brn & dull rose .80 .60

Dr. Karl Josef Bayer (1847-1904), Chemist — A770

Shipping on Achensee, Cent. — A771

1987, June 22 ***Perf. 14x13½***
1401 A770 5s multicolored .80 .60

Eighth Intl. Light Metals Congress, June 22-26, Leoben and Vienna; Bayer Technique for producing aluminum oxide from bauxite, cent.

1987, June 26 **Photo.**
1402 A771 4s multicolored .65 .50

A772

A773

1987, July 1
1403 A772 5s Palais Rottal, Vienna .80 .60

Ombudsmen's office, 10th anniv.

1987, Aug. 11 **Photo. & Engr.**
1404 A773 5s dull olive bister, choc & buff .80 .60

Dr. Erwin Schrodinger (1887-1961), 1933 Nobel laureate in physics.

Freistadt Exhibitions, 125th Anniv. A774

1987, Aug. 11 ***Perf. 14x14½***
1405 A774 5s multicolored .80 .60

Arbing, 850th Anniv. — A775

1987, Aug. 21 ***Perf. 13½***
1406 A775 5s multicolored .80 .60

1987 World Cycling Championships, Villach to Vienna — A776

1987, Aug. 25 ***Perf. 14***
1407 A776 5s multicolored .80 .60

World Congress of Savings Banks, Vienna A777

Perf. 13½x14½

1987, Sept. 9 **Photo.**
1408 A777 5s multicolored .80 .60

Johann Michael Haydn (1737-1806), Composer A778

Perf. 13½x14½

1987, Sept. 14 **Engr.**
1409 A778 4s dull violet .65 .50

Paul Hofhaymer (1459-1537), Composer A779

Photo. & Engr.

1987, Sept. 11 ***Perf. 14***
1410 A779 4s gold, blk & ultra .65 .50

Bearded Vulture — A780

1987, Sept. 25
1411 A780 4s multicolored .65 .50

Innsbruck Zoo, 25th anniv.

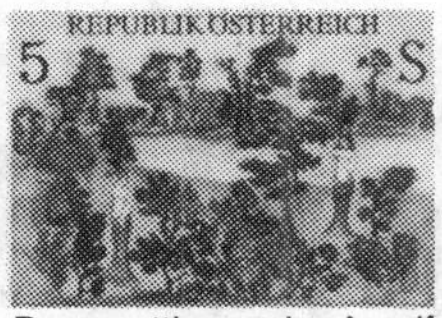

Baumgottinnen, by Arnulf Neuwirth — A781

1987, Oct. 9 ***Perf. 14x13½***
1412 A781 5s multicolored .80 .60

Modern Art.

Gambling Monopoly, 200th Anniv. — A782

Perf. 14½x13½

1987, Oct. 30 **Photo.**
1413 A782 5s Lottery drum .80 .60

Christoph Willibald Gluck (1714-1787), Composer A784

Photo. & Engr.

1987, Nov. 13 ***Perf. 14***
1415 A784 5s cream & blk .88 .65

Oskar Helmer (b. 1887), Politician — A785

1987, Nov. 13
1416 A785 4s multicolored .70 .50

Joseph Mohr (1792-1848) and Franz Gruber (1787-1863), Opening Bars of "Silent Night, Holy Night" — A786

1987, Nov. 27
1417 A786 5s multicolored .90 .65

Christmas.

A787

A788

Photo. & Engr.

1988, Jan. 12 ***Perf. 13½***
1418 A787 5s St. John Bosco, children .90 .65

Intl. Education Congress of Salesian Fathers.

Photo. & Engr.

1988, Feb. 19 ***Perf. 14½x13½***
1419 A788 6s multicolored 1.10 .80

Ernst Mach (1838-1916), physicist.

Village with Bridge (1904), by Franz von Zulow (1883-1963), Painter — A789

1988, Feb. 25 **Photo.** ***Perf. 14½x14***
1420 A789 4s multicolored .70 .50

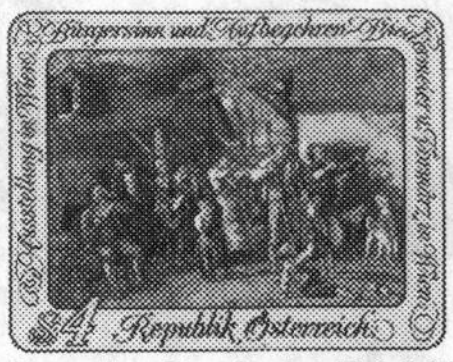

Biedermeier Provincial Exhibition, Vormarz in Vienna — A790

Painting: Confiscation, by Ferdinand Georg Waldmuller (1793-1865).

Photo. & Engr.

1988, Mar. 11 ***Perf. 14***
1421 A790 4s multicolored .70 .50

Anschluss of March 11, 1938 A791

1988, Mar. 11 **Photo.** ***Perf. 13½***
1422 A791 5s gray olive, brn blk & ver .85 .65

No. 2 Aigen Steam Locomotive, 1887 A792

1988, Mar. 22 ***Perf. 13½x14½***
1423 A792 4s shown .70 .50
1424 A792 5s Electric train, Josepsplatz .85 .65

Muhlkreis Railway, cent. (4s); Vienna Local Railway, cent. (5s).

World Wildlife Fund — A793

Photo. & Engr.

1988, Apr. 15 ***Perf. 13½x14***
1425 A793 5s Bee eater .90 .65

Styrian Provincial Exhibition on Glass and Coal, Barnbach A794

1988, Apr. 29 ***Perf. 13½***
1426 A794 4s Frosted glass .70 .50

Intl. Red Cross, 125th Anniv. — A795

1988, May 6 **Photo.** ***Perf. 14***
1427 A795 12s grn, brt red & blk 2.25 1.75

Gothic Silver Censer — A796

1988, May 6 **Photo. & Engr.**
1428 A796 4s multicolored .70 .50

Art and Monasticism at the Birth of Austria, lower Austrian provincial exhibition, Seitenstetten.

Europa 1988 A797

Communication and transportation.

1988, May 13 **Photo.**
1429 A797 6s multicolored 1.10 .80

Mattsee Monastery and Lion of Alz — A798

1988, May 18 **Photo. & Engr.**
1430 A798 4s multicolored .70 .50

Provincial exhibition at Mattsee Monastery: Bavarian Tribes in Salzburg.

Weinberg Castle A799

Perf. 13½x14½

1988, May 20 **Photo.**
1431 A799 4s multicolored .70 .50

Upper Austrian provincial exhibition: Weinberg Castle.

Odon von Horwath (1901-1938), Dramatist — A800

Photo. & Engr.

1988, June 1 ***Perf. 14½x13½***
1432 A800 6s olive bis & slate grn 1.10 .80

Stockerau Festival, 25th Anniv. — A801

1988, June 17 ***Perf. 14***
1433 A801 5s Stockerau Town Hall .80 .60

Tauern Motorway Opening — A802

1988, June 24 **Photo.** ***Perf. 13½x14***
1434 A802 4s multicolored .65 .50

Brixlegg, 1200th Anniv. A803

Photo. & Engr.

1988, July 1 ***Perf. 13½x14½***
1435 A803 5s multicolored .80 .60

View of Klagenfurt, Engraving by Matthaus Merian (1593-1650) A804

Photo. & Engr.

1988, Aug. 12 ***Perf. 14***
1436 A804 5s multicolored .80 .60

Carinthian Postal Service, 400th Anniv.

Brixen-im-Thale, 1200th Anniv. — A805

1988, Aug. 12
1437 A805 5s multicolored .80 .60

Feldkirchen, 1100th Anniv. — A806

1988, Sept. 2 ***Perf. 13½***
1438 A806 5s multicolored .80 .60

Feldbach, 800th Anniv. A807

1988, Sept. 15 **Photo. & Engr.**
1439 A807 5s multicolored .80 .60

Ansfelden, 1200th Anniv. — A808

1988, Sept. 23 ***Perf. 14***
1440 A808 5s multicolored .80 .60

Exports — A809

1988, Oct. 18 **Photo.** ***Perf. 14x13½***
1441 A809 8s multicolored 1.50 1.25

No. 1441 has a holographic image. Soaking in water may affect the hologram.

Vienna Concert Hall, 75th Anniv. A810

Photo. & Engr.

1988, Oct. 19 ***Perf. 13½***
1442 A810 5s multicolored .80 .60

The Watchmen, by Giselbert Hoke — A811

1988, Oct. 21 ***Perf. 14***
1443 A811 5s multicolored .80 .60

Social Democrats Unification Party Congress, Cent. — A812

1988, Nov. 11 **Photo.** ***Perf. 14½x14***
1444 A812 4s multicolored .65 .50

Leopold Schonbauer (1888-1963), Physician — A813

Photo. & Engr.

1988, Nov. 11 ***Perf. 14½x13½***
1445 A813 4s multicolored .65 .50

Christmas A814

Nativity painting from St. Barbara's Church.

1988, Nov. 25 ***Perf. 14***
1446 A814 5s multicolored .80 .60

Benedictine Monastery, Melk, 900th Anniv. A815

Design: Fresco by Paul Troger.

1989, Mar. 17 **Photo. & Engr.**
1447 A815 5s multicolored .80 .60

Madonna and Child, by Lucas Cranach (1472-1553) A816

Marianne Hainisch (1839-1936), Women's Rights Activist A817

1989, Mar. 17 ***Perf. 14½x13½***
1448 A816 4s multicolored .60 .50
Diocese of Innsbruck, 25th anniv.

1989, Mar. 24 ***Perf. 14x13½***
1449 A817 6s multicolored .95 .70

Glider Plane and Parachutist A818

1989, Mar. 31 **Photo.** ***Perf. 14***
1450 A818 6s multicolored 1.00 .75
World Gliding Championships, Wiener Neustadt, and World Parachuting Championships, Damuls.

Bruck an der Leitha Commune, 750th Anniv. — A819

Painting by Georg Matthaus Vischer (1628-1696).

1989, Apr. 21
1451 A819 5s multicolored .85 .60

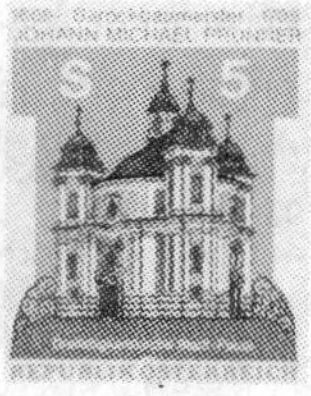

A820 A821

Die Malerei, 1904, by Rudolf Jettmar (1869-1939).

Perf. 14½x13½

1989, Apr. 21 **Photo.**
1452 A820 5s multicolored .85 .60

1989, Apr. 26 **Photo. & Engr.**
Holy Trinity Church, Stadl-Paura.
1453 A821 5s multicolored .85 .60
Michael Prunner (1669-1739), baroque architect.

A822 A823

Eduard Suess (1831-1914, structural geologist) portrait by J. Kriehuber (1800-1876) and map.

1989, Apr. 26
1454 A822 6s multicolored 1.00 .75

1989, Apr. 26
1455 A823 5s multicolored .85 .60
Ludwig Wittgenstein (1889-1951), philosopher.

Styrian Provincial Exhibition, Judenburg A824

Design: Judenberg, 17th cent., an engraving by Georg Matthaus Vischer.

1989, Apr. 28 ***Perf. 14x13½***
1456 A824 4s multicolored .70 .50

Industrial Technology Exhibition, Pottenstein — A825

1989, Apr. 28 **Photo.** ***Perf. 13½***
1457 A825 4s Steam engine .70 .50

Radstadt Township, 700th Anniv. A826

1989, May 3 **Photo.** ***Perf. 13½x14½***
1458 A826 5s multicolored .85 .60

Europa 1989 — A827

1989, May 5
1459 A827 6s Toy boat 1.00 .75

Monastery Church at Lambach, 900th Anniv. — A828

Photo. & Engr.

1989, May 19 ***Perf. 14***
1460 A828 4s multicolored .70 .50

Paddle Steamer *Gisela* A829

1989, May 19 **Photo.** ***Perf. 13½***
1461 A829 5s multicolored .85 .60
Shipping on the Traunsee, 150th anniv.

St. Andra im Lavanttal, 650th Anniv. A830

Period cityscape by Matthaus Merian.

1989, May 26 **Photo. & Engr.**
1462 A830 5s multicolored .85 .60

Richard Strauss (1864-1949), Composer — A831

Photo. & Engr.

1989, June 1 ***Perf. 14½x13½***
1463 A831 6s dark brn, gold & red brn 1.00 .75

Achensee Railway, Cent. A832

1989, June 8 **Photo.** ***Perf. 13½***
1464 A832 5s multicolored .85 .60

Monastery Type of 1984

Design: 50g, Vorau Abbey, Styria. 1s, Monastery of Mehrerau, Vorarlberg. 1.50s, Monastery of the German Order in Vienna. 2s, Bendictine Monastery, Michaelbeuern. 11s, Engelszell Abbey. 12s, Monastery of the Hospitalers, Eisenstadt. 17s, St. Peter, Salzburg. 20s, Wernberg Monastery.

1989-92 **Photo. & Engr.** ***Perf. 14***

1464A	A679a	50g	multi	.20	.20
1465	A679a	1s	multi	.20	.20
1465A	A679a	1.50s	multi	.30	.25
1466	A679a	2s	multi	.35	.25
1467	A679a	11s	multi	1.90	1.40
1467A	A679a	12s	multi	2.25	1.75
1468	A679a	17s	multi	2.75	2.00
1469	A679a	20s	multi	2.75	2.00
	Nos. 1464A-1469 (8)			10.70	8.05

Issued: 1s, 9/1/89; 17s, 6/29/89; 11s, 3/9/90; 50g, 10/12/90; 20s, 5/3/91; 2s, 9/27/91; 1.50s, 10/23/92; 12s, 6/17/92.

This is an expanding set. Numbers will change if necessary.

Interparliamentary Union, Cent. — A833

Photo. & Engr.

1989, June 30 ***Perf. 14***
1475 A833 6s Parliament, Vienna 1.00 .75

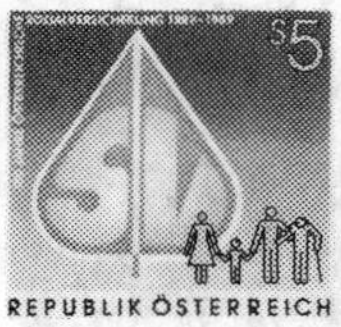

Social Security in Austria, Cent. — A834

1989, Aug. 1 **Photo.**
1476 A834 5s multicolored .70 .50

UN Offices in Vienna, 10th Anniv. A835

1989, Aug. 23
1477 A835 8s multicolored 1.10 .85

Wildalpen, 850th Anniv. A836

Photo. & Engr.

1989, Sept. 15 ***Perf. 13½x14***
1478 A836 5s Foundry, coat of arms .80 .60

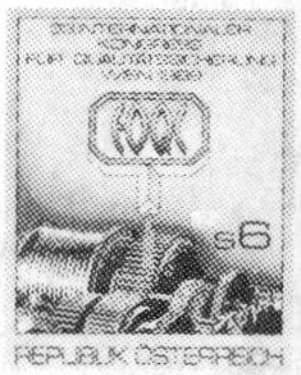

33rd Congress of the Association for Quality Assurance (EOQC) — A837

Perf. 14x13½

1989, Sept. 18 **Photo.**
1479 A837 6s multicolored .90 .70

14th World Congress of the Soc. for Criminal Law (AIDP) A838

Photo. & Engr.

1989, Oct. 2 ***Perf. 13½***
1480 A838 6s Justice Palace, Vienna .90 .70

Lebensbaum, by Ernst Steiner — A839

1989, Oct. 10 ***Perf. 13½x14***
1481 A839 5s multicolored .80 .60

A840 A841

Perf. 14½x13½

1989, Nov. 6 **Photo.**

1482 A840	4s Trakl		.60	.45
1483 A840	4s Anzengruber		.60	.45

Georg Trakl (1887-1914), expressionist poet; Ludwig Anzengruber (1839-1889), playwright and novelist.

1989, Nov. 10 **Photo. & Engr.**

1484 A841 6s multicolored .90 .70

Alfred Fried (1864-1921), pacifist and publisher awarded the Nobel peace prize for 1911 with Tobias Asser.

Parish Church Christ Child, by Johann Carl Reslfeld A842

1989, Dec. 1 ***Perf. 13½x14½***

1485 A842 5s multicolored .75 .60

Christmas.

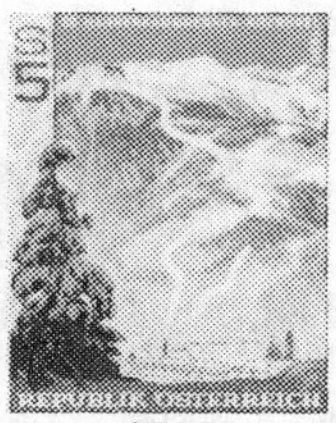

A843 A844

The Young Post Rider, an Engraving by Albrecht Durer

Photo. & Engr.

1990, Jan. 12 ***Perf. 14***

1486 A843 5s multicolored .80 .60

Postal communications in Europe, 500th anniv.

See Belgium No. 1332, Germany No. 1592, Berlin No. 9N584 and German Democratic Republic No. 2791.

Perf. 13½x14½

1990, Jan. 12 **Photo.**

1487 A844 5s multicolored .80 .60

Hahnenkamm alpine competition, Kitzbuhel, 50th anniv.

A845 A846

Perf. 14½x13½

1990, Jan. 17 **Photo.**

1488 A845 4.50s multicolored .70 .55

Salomon Sulzer (1804-90), cantor and composer.

1990, Jan. 22 **Photo. & Engr.**

1489 A846 6s claret & pale green .95 .70

Friedrich Emich (1860-1940), chemist.

Miniature from the *Market Book of Grein,* by Ulrich Schreier, c. 1490 A847

1990, Mar. 9 ***Perf. 14***

1490 A847 5s sepia, buff & gray .80 .60

City of Linz, 500th anniv.

University Seals — A848

1990, Apr. 6

1491 A848 5s multicolored .85 .65

625th Anniv. of Vienna University and 175th anniv. of Vienna Technical University.

Scenery Type of 1984

1990-97 ***Perf. 14***

1492 A679 5s Styrian Vineyards	.85	.65
1493 A679 5s Obir Caverns	.95	.70
1494 A679 5s Natural Bridge, Vorarlberg	.90	.75
1495 A679 6s Wilder Kaiser Mountain, Tyrol	1.25	.95
1496 A679 6s Peggau Cave, Styria	1.00	.80
1497 A679 6s Moorland, swamp, Heidenreichstein	1.25	1.00
1498 A679 6s Hohe Tauern Natl. Park	1.25	1.00
1499 A679 6s Nussberg Vineyards	1.00	.80
Nos. 1492-1499 (8)	8.45	6.65

Issued: #1492, 4/27; #1493, 3/26/91; #1494, 2/5/92; #1495, 2/19/93; #1496, 4/29/94; #1497, 5/19/95; #1498, 3/29/96; #1499, 2/21/97.

A849 A850

Church and municipal arms.

1990, Apr. 27 **Photo.** ***Perf. 14x13½***

1500 A849 7s multicolored 1.25 1.00

1200th anniv. of Anthering.

1990, Apr. 30 **Photo.** ***Perf. 13½***

1501 A850 4.50s multicolored .80 .60

Labor Day, cent.

Seckau Abbey, 850th Anniv. — A851 Ebene Reichenau Post Office — A852

1990, May 4 **Engr.** ***Perf. 14x13½***

1502 A851 4.50s bluish black .80 .60

1990, May 4 **Photo.** ***Perf. 13½x14***

1503 A852 7s multicolored 1.25 1.00

A853 A854

Self Portraits: 4.50s, Hans Makart (1840-84). 5s, Egon Schiele (1890-1918).

Photo. & Engr.

1990, May 29 ***Perf. 14***

1504 A853	4.50s multicolored	.80	.60
1505 A853	5s multicolored	.85	.65

1990, June 1 **Photo.** ***Perf. 14x13½***

1506 A854 4.50s multicolored .80 .60

Ferdinand Raimund (1790-1836), actor.

Christ Healing the Sick by Rembrandt — A855

Photo. & Engr.

1990, June 5 ***Perf. 14***

1507 A855 7s multicolored 1.25 1.00

2nd Intl. Christus Medicus Cong., Bad Ischl.

Hardegg, 700th Anniv. A856

Photo. & Engr.

1990, June 8 ***Perf. 13½x14***

1508 A856 4.50s multicolored .80 .60

Oberdrauburg, 750th Anniv. — A857

1990, June 8 **Photo.**

1509 A857 5s multicolored .85 .65

Gumpoldskirchen, 850th Anniv. — A858

Photo. & Engr.

1990, June 15 ***Perf. 13½***

1510 A858 5s multicolored .85 .65

Mathias Zdarsky (1856-1940), Alpine Skier — A859

1990, June 20 ***Perf. 14x13½***

1511 A859 5s multicolored .85 .65

Telegraph, 1880, Anton Tschechow, 1978 — A860

1990, June 28 **Photo.** ***Perf. 14***

1512 A860 9s multicolored 1.50 1.10

Modern shipbuilding in Austria, 150th anniv.

A861 A862

Photo. & Engr.

1990, Aug. 3 ***Perf. 14x13½***

1513 A861 5s gold & brown .85 .65

Joseph Friedrich Perkonig (1890-1959), poet.

Photo. & Engr.

1990, Aug. 30 ***Perf. 13½x14***

Herr des Regenbogens, by Robert Zeppel-Sperl.

1514 A862 5s gold & brown .85 .65

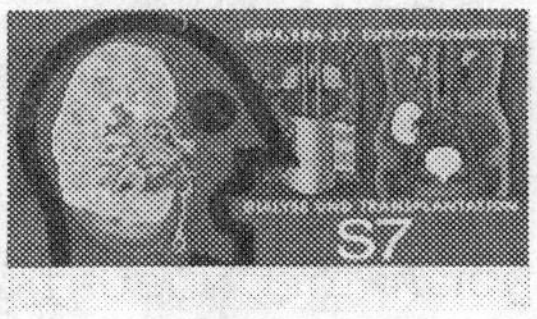

European Dialysis and Transplantation Society, 27th Congress — A863

1990, Sept. 4 **Photo.** ***Perf. 14***

1515 A863 7s multicolored 1.25 1.00

Franz Werfel (1890-1945), Writer — A864

Photo. & Engr.

1990, Sept. 11 ***Perf. 14x13½***

1516 A864 5s multicolored .95 .70

Austrian Forces in UN Peace Keeping Forces, 30th Anniv. A865

1990, Sept. 20 Photo. *Perf. 13½*
1517 A865 7s multicolored 1.25 1.00

Federal and State Arms A866

1990, Sept. 24 Photo. & Engr.
1518 A866 5s multicolored .95 .70

Federalism in Austria.

A867 A868

Photo & Engr.

1990, Oct. 22 *Perf. 14*
1519 A867 4.50s blk, bl grn & red .85 .65

Mining Univ., Leoben, 150th anniv.

Photo. & Engr.

1990, Nov. 8 *Perf. 14x13½*
1520 A868 4.50s multicolored .85 .65

Karl Freiherr von Vogelsang (1818-90), politician.

Metalworkers and Miners Trade Union, Cent. — A869

1990, Nov. 16 *Perf. 14*
1521 A869 5s multicolored .95 .70

3rd World Curling Championships A870

1990, Nov. 23 Photo. *Perf. 14x13½*
1522 A870 7s multicolored 1.40 1.00

Palmhouse at Schonbrunn A871

1990, Nov. 30 *Perf. 14*
1523 A871 5s multicolored .95 .70

A872 A873

Christmas: Altar in Klosterneuburg Abbey by the Master from Verdun.

Photo. & Engr.

1990, Nov. 23 *Perf. 13½*
1524 A872 5s multicolored .95 .70

Photo. & Engr.

1991, Jan. 15 *Perf. 14x13½*
1525 A873 4.50s multicolored .85 .65

Franz Grillparzer (1791-1872), dramatic poet.

A874 A875

1991, Jan. 21 *Perf. 13½*
1526 A874 5s multicolored .95 .70

Alpine Skiing World Championship, Saalbach-Hinterglemm.

1991, Jan. 21 Photo. *Perf. 14x13½*
1527 A875 5s multicolored .95 .70

Bruno Kreisky (1911-90), chancellor.

Friedrich Freiherr von Schmidt (1825-1891), Architect — A876

1991, Jan. 21 *Perf. 14*
1528 A876 7s multicolored 1.40 1.00

Visual Arts A877

Designs: 4.50s, Donner Fountain, Vienna, by Raphael Donner (1693-1741), sculptor. 5s, Kitzbuhel in Winter, by Alfons Walde (1891-1958), painter. 7s, Vienna Stock Exchange, Theophil Hansen (1813-1891), architect.

1991, Feb. 8

1529	A877	4.50s multicolored	.85	.65
1530	A877	5s multicolored	.95	.70
1531	A877	7s multicolored	1.40	1.00
		Nos. 1529-1531 (3)	3.20	2.35

See No. 1543.

Marie von Ebner Eschenbach (1830-1916), Poet — A878

1991, Mar. 12 Engr. *Perf. 13½x14½*
1532 A878 4.50s rose violet .85 .65

Miniature Sheet

Wolfgang Amadeus Mozart (1756-1791), Composer A879

Design: b, Magic Flute Fountain, Vienna.

1991, Mar. 22 *Perf. 13½*
1533 Sheet of 2 + label 1.75 1.25
a.-b. A879 5s any single .80 .60

Spittal an der Drau, 800th Anniv. A880

1991, Apr. 11 *Perf. 14*
1534 A880 4.50s multicolored .75 .60

Europa A881

1991, May 3 Photo. *Perf. 14*
1535 A881 7s ERS-1 satellite 1.10 .80

Garden Banquet by Anthony Bays A882

1991, May 10 Photo. *Perf. 13½*
1536 A882 5s multicolored .75 .60

Vorarlberg Provincial Exhibition, Hohenems.

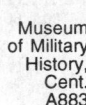

Museum of Military History, Cent. A883

Design: 7s, Interior of Museum of Art History.

Photo. & Engr.

1991, May 24 *Perf. 13½*
1537 A883 5s multicolored .95 .80
1538 A883 7s multicolored 1.25 1.00

Museum of Art History, Cent. (#1538).

Grein, 500th Anniv. A884

1991, May 24 Photo. *Perf. 14*
1539 A884 4.50s multicolored .90 .45

Tulln, 1200th Anniv. A885

1991, May 24 *Perf. 13½x14*
1540 A885 5s multicolored .95 .80

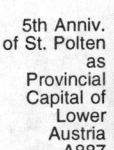

Completion of Karawanken Tunnels — A886

1991, May 31 *Perf. 14x13½*
1541 A886 7s multicolored 1.25 1.00

5th Anniv. of St. Polten as Provincial Capital of Lower Austria A887

1991, July 5 Photo. *Perf. 14*
1542 A887 5s multicolored .80 .65

Visual Arts Type of 1991

Design: 4.50s, Karlsplatz Station of Vienna Subway by Otto Wagner (1841-1918), Architect.

1991, July 12 Photo. & Engr.
1543 A877 4.50s multicolored .75 .60

Rowing and Junior Canoeing World Championships, Vienna — A888

1991, Aug. 20 Photo. *Perf. 13½x14*
1544 A888 5s multicolored .85 .70

European Congress of Radiologists A889

1991, Sept. 13 *Perf. 14*
1545 A889 7s multicolored 1.10 .95

Paracelsus (1493-1541), Physician — A890

1991, Sept. 27 ***Perf. 14x13½***
1546 A890 4.50s multicolored .75 .60

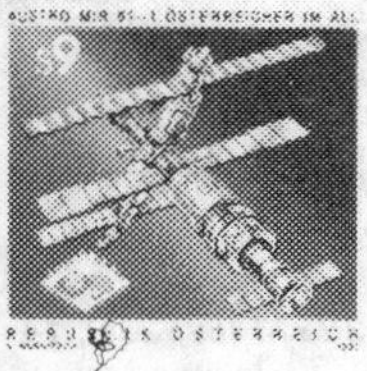

Joint Austrian-Soviet Space Mission — A891

1991, Oct. 2 ***Perf. 14***
1547 A891 9s multicolored 1.50 1.25

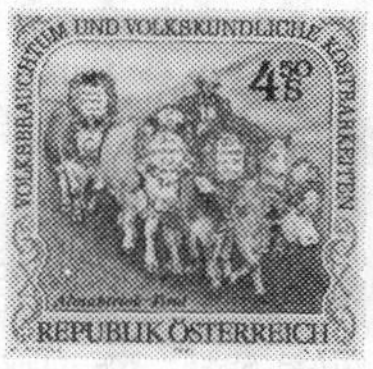

Austrian Folk Festivals A892

Designs: 4.50s, Almabtrieb, Tyrol. 5s, Winzerkrone, Vienna. 7s, Ernte-Monstranz, Styria.

1991, Oct. 4 **Photo. & Engr.**
1548 A892 4.50s multicolored .75 .60
1549 A892 5s multicolored .85 .70
1550 A892 7s multicolored 1.10 .95
Nos. 1548-1550 (3) 2.70 2.25

See Nos. 1577-1579, 1619-1621, 1633-1635, 1671-1673, 1694, 1705-1706, 1714, 1730, 1741, 1752-1753, 1762, 1778, 1799-1800.

The General by Rudolph Pointner — A893

Photo. & Engr.

1991, Oct. 11 ***Perf. 13½x14***
1551 A893 5s multicolored .85 .70

Birth of Christ, Baumgartenberg Church — A894

1991, Nov. 29
1552 A894 5s multicolored .85 .70

Christmas.

Julius Raab, Politician, Birth Cent. — A895

1991, Nov. 29 ***Perf. 14x13½***
1553 A895 4.50s red brn & brn .75 .60

1992 Winter and Summer Olympic Games A897

1992, Jan. 14 **Photo.** ***Perf. 14***
1555 A897 7s multicolored 1.25 1.00

Trade Union of Clerks in Private Enterprises, Cent. A898

1992, Jan. 14
1556 A898 5.50s multicolored .95 .80

A899 A900

1992, Jan. 29 ***Perf. 14x13½***
1557 A899 5s multicolored .90 .75

8th Natural Run Toboggan World Championships.

1992, Feb. 5 **Engr.** ***Perf. 14x13½***
1558 A900 5.50s brown .95 .80

George Saiko, Poet, birth cent.

Worker's Sports, Cent. — A901

1992, Feb. 5 **Photo.** ***Perf. 14***
1559 A901 5.50s multicolored .95 .80

Souvenir Sheet

Vienna Philharmonic Orchestra, 150th Anniv. — A902

Photo. & Engr.

1992, Mar. 27 ***Perf. 14***
1560 A902 5.50s multicolored .95 .80

Scientists — A903

Designs: 5s, Franz Joseph Muller von Reichenstein (1742-1825), discoverer of tellurium. 5.50s, Dr. Paul Kitaibel (1757-1817), botanist. 6s, Christian Johann Doppler (1803-1853), physicist. 7s, Richard Kuhn (1900-1967), chemist.

1992, Mar. 27 **Photo.**
1561 A903 5s multicolored .85 .70
1562 A903 5.50s multicolored .95 .80
1563 A903 6s multicolored 1.00 .85
1564 A903 7s multicolored 1.25 .95
Nos. 1561-1564 (4) 4.05 3.30

Railway Workers Union, Cent. A904

1992, Apr. 2 ***Perf. 14x13½***
1565 A904 5.50s black & red .95 .80

Norbert Hanrieder (1842-1913), Poet — A905

Photo. & Engr.

1992, Apr. 30 ***Perf. 14x13½***
1566 A905 5.50s purple & buff .95 .80

Carl Zeller (1842-1898) and Karl Millocker (1842-1899), Operetta Composers A906

Photo. & Engr.

1992, Apr. 30 ***Perf. 14***
1567 A906 6s multicolored 1.00 .85

LD Steel Mill, 40th Anniv. A907

1992, May 8 **Photo.** ***Perf. 14x13½***
1568 A907 5s multicolored .85 .70

Discovery of America, 500th Anniv. A908

Photo. & Engr.

1992, May 8 ***Perf. 14***
1569 A908 7s multicolored 1.25 .95

Europa.

Austro-Swiss Treaty on Regulation of Rhine River, Cent. A909

1992, May 8 **Photo.** ***Perf. 13½x14***
1570 A909 7s multicolored 1.25 .95

Protection of the Alps — A910

1992, May 22 ***Perf. 14x13½***
1571 A910 5.50s multicolored .95 .80

Dr. Anna Dengel (1892-1980), Physician A911

Sebastian Rieger (1867-1953), Poet A912

1992, May 22 **Photo. & Engr.**
1572 A911 5.50s multicolored .95 .80

1992, May 22 **Engr.**
1573 A912 5s red brown .85 .70

Lienz, 750th Anniv. A913

1992, June 17 **Photo.** ***Perf. 14x13½***
1574 A913 5s Town Hall .90 .70

Intl. Congress of Austrian Society of Surgeons A914

Photo. & Engr.

1992, June 17 ***Perf. 14***

1575 A914 6s multicolored 1.10 .90

Dr. Kurt Waldheim, President of Austria, 1986-92 — A915

1992, June 22 ***Perf. 14x13½***

1576 A915 5.50s multicolored .95 .75

Folk Festivals Type of 1991

Designs: 5s, Marksman's target, Lower Austria. 5.50s, Peasant's chest, Carinthia. 7s, Votive icon, Vorarlberg.

Photo. & Engr.

1992, Sept. 18 ***Perf. 14***

1577 A892 5s multicolored .90 .70
1578 A892 5.50s multicolored .95 .75
1579 A892 7s multicolored 1.25 1.00
Nos. 1577-1579 (3) 3.10 2.45

Marchfeld Canal — A917

1992, Oct. 9 Photo. ***Perf. 13½x14***

1580 A917 5s multicolored .90 .70

5th Intl. Ombudsman Conference, Vienna — A918

Photo & Engr.

1992, Oct. 9 ***Perf. 14***

1581 A918 5.50s multicolored .95 .75

The Clearance of Seawater, by Peter Pongratz A919

1992, Oct. 9

1582 A919 5.50s multicolored .95 .75

Academy of Fine Arts, 300th Anniv. — A920

Photo. & Engr.

1992, Oct. 23 ***Perf. 14***

1583 A920 5s red & blue 1.00 .85

Birth of Christ, by Johann Georg Schmidt A921

1992, Nov. 27 ***Perf. 14x13½***

1584 A921 5.50s multicolored 1.10 .90

Christmas.

Veit Koniger, Sculptor, Death Bicent. — A922

Photo. & Engr.

1992, Nov. 27 ***Perf. 14***

1585 A922 5s multicolored 1.00 .80

Herman Potocnik, Theoretician of Geosynchronous Satellite Orbit, Birth Cent. — A923

1992, Nov. 27 **Photo.**

1586 A923 10s multicolored 2.00 1.60

Famous Buildings A924

Designs: 5s, Statues and dome of Imperial Palace, Vienna, designed by Joseph Emanuel Fischer von Erlach. 5.50s, Kinsky Palace, designed by Lukas von Hildebrandt. 7s, Vienna State Opera, designed by Eduard van der Null and August Siccard von Siccardsburg.

1993, Jan. 22 **Photo. & Engr.**

1587 A924 5s multicolored 1.00 .80
1588 A924 5.50s multicolored 1.10 .90
1589 A924 7s multicolored 1.40 1.10
Nos. 1587-1589 (3) 3.50 2.80

Joseph Emanuel Fischer von Erlach, 300th birth anniv. (#1587). Johann Lukas von Hildebrandt, 325th birth anniv. (#1588). Eduard van der Null, August Siccard von Siccardsburg, 125th death anniv. (#1589).

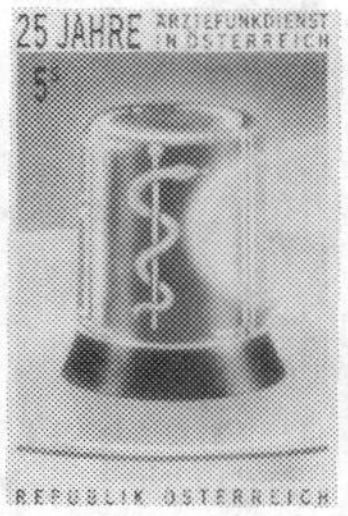

Radio Dispatched Medical Service, 25th Anniv. — A925

1993, Feb. 19 **Photo.**

1590 A925 5s multicolored 1.00 .80

Typewriter Made by Peter Mitterhofer (1822-1893) A926

1993, Feb. 19 ***Perf. 13½x14***

1591 A926 17s multicolored 3.50 2.75

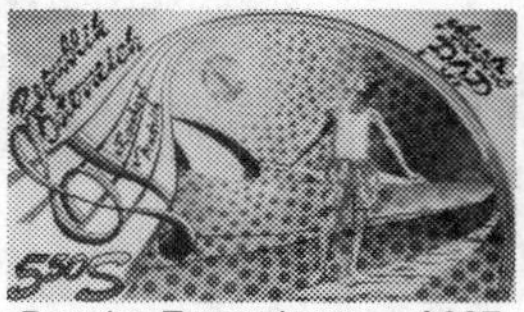

Popular Entertainers — A927

5.50s, Strada del Sole, by Rainhard Fendrich.

1993, Mar. 19 Photo. ***Perf. 14***

1592 A927 5.50s multicolored 1.00 .80

See Nos. 1626, 1639.

Charles Sealsfield (1793-1864), Writer A928

Photo. & Engr.

1993, Mar. 19 ***Perf. 13½x14***

1593 A928 10s multicolored 1.75 1.40

Rights of the Child — A930

1993, Apr. 16 Photo. ***Perf. 13½x14***

1595 A930 7s multicolored 1.25 1.00

Flying Harlequin, by Paul Flora — A931

1993, Apr. 16 **Photo. & Engr.**

1596 A931 7s multicolored 1.25 1.00

Europa.

Monastery of Admont — A932

Designs: 1s, Detail of abbesse's crosier, St. Gabriel Abbey, Styria. 5.50s, Death, wooden statue by Josef Stammel (1695-1765). 6s, Stained glass, Mariastern-Gwiggen Monastery. 7s, Marble lion, Franciscan Monastery, Salzburg. 8s, Gothic entry, Wilhering Monastery, Upper Austria. 7.50s, Cupola fresco, by Paul Troger, Monastery of Altenburg. 10s, Altarpiece, St. Peregrinus praying, Maria Luggau Monastery. 20s, Crosier, Fiecht Monastery. 26s, Sculpture of Mater Dolorosa, Franciscan Monastery, Schwaz, Tirol. 30s, Madonna of Scottish Order, Schottenstift Monastery, Vienna.

Perf. 14x13½, 13½x14 (8s, 26s), 14 (1s, 30s)

1993-95 **Photo. & Engr.**

1599 A932 1s multicolored .20 .20
1603 A932 5.50s green, black & yel 1.00 .80

Perf. 14

1606 A932 6s multicolored 1.10 .90
1606A A932 7s gray, blk & yel 1.25 1.00
1607 A932 7.50s brown, blk & bl 1.25 1.00
1608 A932 8s multicolored 1.60 1.25
1609 A932 10s multicolored 1.75 1.40
1613 A932 20s multicolored 3.50 1.75
1613A A932 26s multicolored 5.25 4.25
1614 A932 30s multicolored 5.50 4.50
Nos. 1599-1614 (10) 22.40 17.05

Issued: 5.50s, 4/16; 6s, 9/17; 20s, 10/8; 7.50s, 4/4/94; 10s, 8/26/94; 30s, 10/7/94; 7s, 11/18/94; 8s, 9/15/95; 26s, 10/6/95; 1s, 4/28/95.

This is an expanding set. Numbers may change.

Peter Rosegger (1843-1918), Writer — A933

1993, May 5 Photo. ***Perf. 14x13½***

1617 A933 5.50s green & black 1.00 .80

Lake Constance Steamer Hohentwiel A934

1993, May 5 **Photo.** ***Perf. 14***

1618 A934 6s multicolored 1.10 .85

See Germany No. 1786, Switzerland No. 931.

Folk Festivals Type of 1991

Designs: 5s, Corpus Christi Day Procession, Upper Austria. 5.50s, Blockdrawing, Burgenland. 7s, Cracking whip when snow is melting, Salzburg.

Photo. & Engr.

1993, June 11 ***Perf. 14***

1619 A892 5s multicolored .90 .70
1620 A892 5.50s multicolored 1.00 .80
1621 A892 7s multicolored 1.25 1.00
Nos. 1619-1621 (3) 3.15 2.50

UN Conference on Human Rights, Vienna — A935

1993, June 11 **Photo.**
1622 A935 10s multicolored 1.75 1.40

Franz Jagerstatter (1907-1943), Resistance Fighter — A936

1993, Aug. 6 **Photo.** ***Perf. 14x13½***
1623 A936 5.50s multicolored 1.00 .80

Schafberg Railway, Cent. — A937

1993, Aug. 6 ***Perf. 13½x14***
1624 A937 6s multicolored 1.10 .90

Self-portrait with Puppet, by Rudolf Wacker (1893-1939) A938

Photo. & Engr.

1993, Aug. 6 ***Perf. 14***
1625 A938 6s multicolored 1.10 .90

Popular Entertainers Type of 1993

Design: 5.50s, Granny, by Ludwig Hirsch.

1993, Sept. 3 **Photo.** ***Perf. 14***
1626 A927 5.50s multicolored 1.00 .80

Vienna Mens' Choral Society, 150th Anniv. A940

1993, Sept. 17 **Photo.** ***Perf. 14***
1627 A940 5s multicolored .90 .75

Easter, by Max Weiler A941

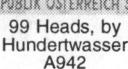

99 Heads, by Hundertwasser A942

Photo. & Engr.

1993, Oct. 8 ***Perf. 13½x14***
1628 A941 5.50s multicolored 1.00 .80

1993, Oct. 8
1629 A942 7s multicolored 1.25 1.00

Council of Europe Conference, Vienna.

Austrian Republic, 75th Anniv. — A943

Design: 5.50s, Statue of Pallas Athena.

Photo. & Engr.

1993, Nov. 12 ***Perf. 13½x14***
1630 A943 5.50s multicolored 1.00 .80

Trade Unions in Austria, Cent. A944

1993, Nov. 12 **Photo.** ***Perf. 14***
1631 A944 5.50s multicolored 1.00 .80

Birth of Christ, by Master of the Krainburger Altar — A945

Photo. & Engr.

1993, Nov. 26 ***Perf. 13½x14***
1632 A945 5.50s multicolored 1.00 .80

Christmas.

Folklore and Customs Type of 1991

Antiques: 5.50s, Dolls, cradle, Vorarlberg. 6s, Sled, Steiermark. 7s, Godparent's bowl, Upper Austria.

Photo. & Engr.

1994, Jan. 28 ***Perf. 14***
1633 A892 5.50s multicolored 1.00 .80
1634 A892 6s multicolored 1.10 .90
1635 A892 7s multicolored 1.25 1.00
Nos. 1633-1635 (3) 3.35 2.70

1994 Winter Olympics, Lillehammer, Norway — A946

1994, Feb. 9
1636 A946 7s multicolored 1.25 1.00

Vienna Mint, 800th Anniv. A947

1994, Feb. 18
1637 A947 6s multicolored 1.10 .90

Lying Lady, by Herbert Boeckl (1894-1966) — A948

1994, Mar. 18 **Photo.** ***Perf. 14x13½***
1638 A948 5.50s multicolored .95 .70

Popular Entertainers Type of 1993

Design: 6s, Rock Me Amadeus, by Falco.

1994, Mar. 18 ***Perf. 14***
1639 A927 6s multicolored 1.00 .80

Wiener Neustadt, 800th Anniv. — A949

1994, Mar. 18
1640 A949 6s multicolored 1.00 .80

Lake Rudolph, Teleki-Hohnel Expedition — A950

Photo. & Engr.

1994, May 27 ***Perf. 14x13½***
1641 A950 7s multicolored 1.25 1.00

Europa.

Daniel Gran, 300th Birth Anniv. A951

Fresco: 20s, Allegory of Theology, Jurisprudence and Medicine.

1994, May 27
1642 A951 20s multicolored 3.50 2.75

Carinthian Summer Festival, 25th Anniv. — A952

Design: 5.50s, Scene from The Prodigal Son.

Photo. & Engr.

1994, June 17 ***Perf. 14***
1643 A952 5.50s lake & gold .95 .75

Railway Centennials — A953

1994 **Photo. & Engr.** ***Perf. 14***
1647 A953 5.50s Gailtal .95 .75
1648 A953 6s Murtal 1.00 .80

Issued: 5.50s, 6s, 6/17/94.

Hermann Gmeiner, 75th Birth Anniv. — A954

1994, June 17 ***Perf. 14x13½***
1656 A954 7s multicolored 1.25 1.00

Karl Seitz (1869-1950) Politician A955

Karl Bohm (1894-1981), Conductor A956

1994, Aug. 12 **Photo.** ***Perf. 14***
1657 A955 5.50s multicolored 1.00 .80

Photo. & Engr.

1994, Aug. 26 ***Perf. 14x13½***
1658 A956 7s gold & dk blue 1.25 1.00

Ethnic Minorities in Austria — A957

1994, Sept. 9 **Photo.** ***Perf. 13½***
1659 A957 5.50s multicolored 1.00 .80

Franz Theodor Csokor (1885-1969), Writer — A958

Design: 7s, Joseph Roth (1894-1939), writer.

1994, Sept. 9 ***Perf. 14x13½***
1660 A958 6s multicolored 1.00 .80
1661 A958 7s multicolored 1.25 1.00

Coin Bank — A959

Modern Art — A960

Photo. & Engr.

1994, Oct. 7 *Perf. 14x13½*
1662 A959 7s multicolored 1.25 1.00

Savings banks in Austria, 175th anniv.

1994, Oct. 7 *Perf. 13½x14*

Design: 6s, "Head," by Franz Ringel.

1663 A960 6s multicolored 1.10 .90

Austrian Working Environment — A961

1994, Nov. 18 **Photo.** *Perf. 14*
1664 A961 6s Stewardess, child 1.10 .90

See Nos. 1690, 1703, 1736, 1773.

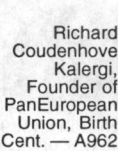

Richard Coudenhove Kalergi, Founder of PanEuropean Union, Birth Cent. — A962

Photo. & Engr.

1994, Nov. 18 *Perf. 13½*
1665 A962 10s multicolored 1.90 1.50

Birth of Christ, by Anton Wollenek A963

1994, Nov. 25 *Perf. 14*
1666 A963 6s multicolored 1.10 .90

Christmas.

Membership in European Union — A964

1995, Jan. 13 **Photo.** *Perf. 14*
1667 A964 7s multicolored 1.25 1.00

Adolf Loos (1870-1933), Architect A965

1995, Jan. 13
1668 A965 10s House, Vienna 1.90 1.50

Official Representation for Workers, 75th Anniv. — A966

1995, Feb. 24 *Perf. 14x13½*
1669 A966 6s multicolored 1.10 .90

Austrian Gymnastics and Sports Assoc., 50th Anniv. A967

1995, Feb. 24
1670 A967 6s multicolored 1.10 .90

Folklore and Customs Type of 1991

Designs: 5.50s, Belt, Gailtal, Carinthia. 6s, Vineyard watchman's costume, Vienna. 7s, Bonnet, Wachau, Lower Austria.

Photo. & Engr.

1995, Mar. 24 *Perf. 14*
1671 A892 5.50s multicolored 1.10 .90
1672 A892 6s multicolored 1.25 1.00
1673 A892 7s multicolored 1.40 1.10
Nos. 1671-1673 (3) 3.75 3.00

Second Republic, 50th Anniv. — A968

1995, Apr. 27
1674 A968 6s State seal 1.25 1.00

History of Mining & Industry A969

Design: Blast furnaces, old Heft ironworks.

1995, Apr. 28 *Perf. 13½x14*
1675 A969 5.50s multicolored 1.10 .90

Carinthian Provincial Exhibition.

Nature Lovers Club, Cent. — A970

1995, Apr. 28 *Perf. 14*
1676 A970 5.50s multicolored 1.10 .90

Europa — A971

1995, May 19 *Perf. 14*
1677 A971 7s multicolored 1.50 1.25

1995 Conference of Ministers of Transportation, Vienna — A972

1995, May 26 **Photo.** *Perf. 14*
1678 A972 7s multicolored 1.40 1.25

Bregenz Festival, 50th Anniv. A973

1995, June 9
1679 A973 6s multicolored 1.25 1.00

St. Gebhard (949-995) — A974

Design: Stained glass window, by Martin Hausle.

1995, June 9
1680 A974 7.50s multicolored 1.50 1.25

UN, 50th Anniv. — A975

1995, June 26 **Photo.** *Perf. 14*
1681 A975 10s multicolored 2.00 2.00

Josef Loschmidt (1821-95), Chemist — A976

Photo. & Engr.

1995, June 26 *Perf. 14x13½*
1682 A976 20s multicolored 4.00 4.00

A977

A978

Photo. & Engr.

1995, Aug. 18 *Perf. 13½x14*
1683 A977 6s multicolored 1.25 1.00

Salzburg Festival, 75th anniv.

1995, Aug. 18 *Perf. 14x13½*
1684 A978 6s buff, black & red 1.25 1.00

Kathe Leichter, resistance member, birth cent.

Europaisches Landschaftsbild, by Adolf Frohner — A979

1995, Aug. 18
1685 A979 6s multicolored 1.25 1.00

Operetta Composers A980

Designs: 6s, Franz von Suppe (1819-95), scene from "The Beautiful Galathea." 7s, Nico Dostal (b. 1895), scene from "The Hungarian Wedding."

1995, Sept. 15 *Perf. 14*
1686 A980 6s multicolored 1.25 1.00
1687 A980 7s multicolored 1.40 1.10

See Croatia No. 253.

University of Klagenfurt, 25th Anniv. — A981

1995, Oct. 6 **Photo.** *Perf. 14*
1688 A981 5.50s multicolored 1.10 .90

Values quoted in this catalogue are for stamps graded Very Fine and with no faults. An illustrated guide to grade is provided in the "Catalogue Information" section of the Introduction.

Carinthian Referendum, 75th Anniv. — A982

1995, Oct. 6 **Photo. & Engr.**
1689 A982 6s multicolored 1.25 1.00

Austria Working Environment Type of 1994

1995, Oct. 20
1690 A961 6s Post office official 1.25 1.00

Composers A983

Designs: 6s, Anton von Webern (1883-1945). 7s, Ludwig van Beethoven (1770-1827).

1995, Oct. 20 ***Perf. 13½x14***
1691 A983 6s orange & blue 1.25 1.00
1692 A983 7s orange & red 1.40 1.10

Christmas A984

Photo. & Engr.

1995, Dec. 1 ***Perf. 13½***
1693 A984 6s Christ Child 1.25 1.00

Folklore and Customs Type of 1991

Design: Roller and Scheller in "Procession of Masked Groups in Imst," Tyrol.

Photo. & Engr.

1996, Feb. 9 ***Perf. 14***
1694 A892 6s multicolored 1.25 1.00

Maria Theresa Academy, 250th Anniv. — A985

1996, Feb. 9
1695 A985 6s multicolored 1.25 1.00

1996 World Ski Jumping Championships A986

1996, Feb. 9 **Photo.**
1696 A986 7s multicolored 1.40 1.10

New Western Pier, Vienna Intl. Airport — A987

1996, Mar. 28 **Photo.** ***Perf. 14***
1697 A987 7s multicolored 1.40 1.10

A988 A989

6s, Mother with Child, by Peter Fendi (1796-1842). 7s, Self-portrait, by Leopold Kupelwieser (1795-1862).

1996, Mar. 29
1698 A988 6s multicolored 1.25 1.00
1699 A988 7s multicolored 1.40 1.10

Photo. & Engr.

1996, Apr. 26 ***Perf. 14***
1700 A989 5.50s Organ, music 1.15 .90

Anton Bruckner (1824-96), composer, organist.

Georg Matthäus Vischer, 300th Death Anniv. A990

1996, Apr. 26
1701 A990 10s Kollmitz Castle 2.00 1.50

City of Klagenfurt, 800th Anniv. A991

1996, May 3
1702 A991 6s Ancient square 1.25 1.00

Austrian Working Environment Type of 1994

1996, May 17
1703 A961 6s Chef, waitress 1.25 1.00

Paula von Preradovic, Author A992

1996, May 17 ***Perf. 13½x14***
1704 A992 7s black, gray & buff 1.40 1.10

Europa.

Folklore and Customs Type of 1991

Designs: 5.50s, Corpus Christi poles, Salzburg. 7s, Tyrolian riflemen.

Photo. & Engr.

1996, June 21 ***Perf. 14***
1705 A892 5.50s multicolored 1.00 .80
1706 A892 7s multicolored 1.25 1.00

1996 Summer Olympic Games, Atlanta — A993

1996, June 21
1707 A993 10s multicolored 1.90 1.50

Burgenland Province, 75th Anniv. A994

1996, Sept. 20
1708 A994 6s multicolored 1.10 .90

Austrian Mountain Rescue Service, Cent. — A995

1996, Sept. 27
1709 A995 6s multicolored 1.10 .90

Austria Millenium A996

Designs: a, Deed by Otto III. b, Empress Maria Theresa, Josef II. c, Duke Henry II. d, 1848 Revolution. e, Rudolf IV. f, Dr. Karl Renner, 1st Republic. g, Emperor Maximilian I. h, State Treaty of 1955, 2nd Republic. i, Imperial Crown of Rudolf II. j, Austria, Europe.

Photo. & Engr.

1996, Oct. 25 ***Perf. 14***
1710 Sheet of 10 19.00 19.00
a.-b. A996 6s any single 1.10 1.10
c.-f. A996 7s any single 1.25 1.25
g.-h. A996 10s any single 1.90 1.90
i.-j. A996 20s any single 3.80 3.80

Power Station, by Reinhard Artberg A997

1996, Nov. 22
1711 A997 7s multicolored 1.25 1.25

UNICEF, 50th Anniv. — A998

1996, Nov. 22 **Photo.**
1712 A998 10s multicolored 1.90 1.90

Christmas A999

1996, Nov. 29 **Photo. & Engr.**
1713 A999 6s multicolored 1.25 1.00

Folklore and Customs Type of 1991

Design: Epiphany Carol Singers, Burgenland.

Photo. & Engr.

1997, Jan. 17 ***Perf. 14***
1714 A892 7s multicolored 1.25 1.00

Theodor Kramer, Poet, Birth Cent. — A1000

1997, Jan. 17
1715 A1000 5.50s deep blue 1.00 .80

Austrian Academy of Sciences, 150th Anniv. — A1001

1997, Feb. 21 **Photo.** ***Perf. 14***
1716 A1001 10s multicolored 1.75 1.40

Austrian Electricity Board, 50th Anniv. A1002

1997, Mar. 21
1717 A1002 6s multicolored 1.00 .80

The Cruel Lady of Forchtenstein Castle, Burgenland
A1003

Erich Wolfgang Korngold (1897-1957), Composer
A1004

Photo. & Engr.

1997, Mar. 21 ***Perf. 14***
1718 A1003 7s multicolored 1.10 .95

See #1731, 1733, 1745-1746, 1763, 1775, 1794, 1802.

1997, Mar. 21

Design: Scene from opera, "The Dead City. "

1719 A1004 20s blue, black & gold 3.25 1.60

Vienna Rapid, Austrian Soccer Champions
A1005

1997, Apr. 25 **Photo.** ***Perf. 14***
1720 A1005 7s multicolored 1.25 1.00

See Nos. 1754, 1779.

Deer Feeding in Wintertime
A1006

1997, Apr. 25
1721 A1006 7s multicolored 1.25 1.00

See Nos. 1747, 1782.

St. Peter Canisius (1521-97)
A1007

1997, Apr. 25 ***Photo. & Engr.***
1722 A1007 7.50s Canisius Altar, Innsbruck 1.25 1.10

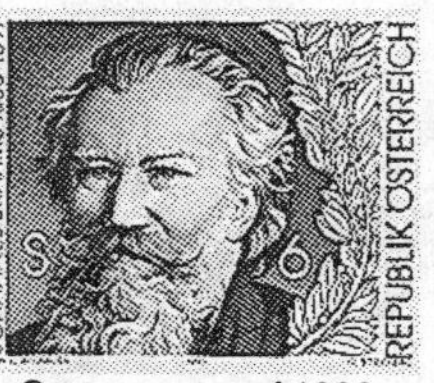

Composers — A1008

Designs: 6s, Johannes Brahms (1833-1897). 10s, Franz Schubert (1797-1828).

1997, May 9
1723 A1008 6s gold & violet blue 1.00 .80
1724 A1008 10s purple & gold 1.75 1.40

Stamp Day — A1009

1997, May 9 ***Perf. 13½***
1725 A1009 7s "A" and "E" 1.25 1.00

See Nos. B357-B362, 1765, 1791. The first letters will spell "Briefmarke," the second "Philatelie."

Child's View of "Town Band of Bremen"
A1010

1997, May 23 **Photo.**
1726 A1010 7s multicolored 1.25 1.00

Europa.

Technical Surveyance Assoc., 125th Anniv. — A1011

1997, June 13 **Photo.** ***Perf. 14***
1727 A1011 7s multicolored 1.40 1.15

Railways
A1012

Designs: 6s, Hochschneeberg Cog Railway. 7.50s, Wiener Neustadt-Odenburg Railway.

1997, June 13 **Photo. & Engr.**
1728 A1012 6s multicolored 1.20 .95
1729 A1012 7.50s multicolored 1.50 1.20

Folklore and Customs Type of 1991

Photo. & Engr.

1997, July 11 ***Perf. 14***
1730 A892 6.50s Marching band, Tyrol 1.25 1.00

Stories and Legends Type

Design: Dragon of Klagenfurt.

1997, July 11
1731 A1003 6.50s multicolored 1.25 1.00

Karl Heinrich Waggerl, Birth Cent. — A1013

1997, July 11
1732 A1013 7s multicolored 1.40 1.00

Stories and Legends Type of 1997

Design: Danube water nymph rescuing ferryman, Upper Austria.

Photo. & Engr.

1997, Sept. 19 ***Perf. 14***
1733 A1003 14s multicolored 2.75 2.10

1997 Orthopedics Congress, Vienna — A1014

1997, Sept. 19 **Photo.** ***Perf. 14***
1734 A1014 8s Adolph Lorenz 1.60 1.25

Vienna Agricultural University, 125th Anniv. — A1015

1997, Sept. 19
1735 A1015 9s multicolored 1.75 1.40

Austrian Working Environment Type of 1994

Photo. & Engr.

1997, Oct. 17 ***Perf. 14***
1736 A961 6.50s Nurse, patient 1.25 1.00

"House in Wind," by Helmut Schickhofer — A1016

1997, Oct. 17
1737 A1016 7s multicolored 1.40 1.00

Blind Persons Assocs. in Austria, Cent. — A1017

Photo. & Embossed

1997, Oct. 17
1738 A1017 7s multicolored 1.40 1.00

No. 1738 contains embossed Braille inscription.

A1018

A1019

Photo. & Engr.

1997, Oct. 31 ***Perf. 14x13½***
1739 A1018 7s multicolored 1.40 1.00

Dr. Thomas Klestil, Pres. of Austria, 65th birthday.

1997, Oct. 31 ***Perf. 14***
1740 A1019 7s multicolored 1.40 1.00

Oskar Werner (1922-84), actor.

Folklore and Customs Type of 1991

Upper Austria tower wind players, Steyr.

Photo. & Engr.

1997, Nov. 21 ***Perf. 14***
1741 A892 6.50s multicolored 1.25 1.00

Light For All Relief Organization, 25th Anniv. — A1020

1997, Nov. 28 **Photo.** ***Perf. 14***
1742 A1020 7s multicolored 1.40 1.00

Christmas
A1021

Photo. & Engr.

1997, Nov. 28 ***Perf. 14***
1743 A1021 7s Mariazell Madonna 1.40 1.00

Scenery Type of 1984

Kalkalpen Natl. Park, Upper Austria.

Photo. & Engr.

1998, Jan. 23 ***Perf. 14***
1744 A679 7s multicolored 1.10 .85

Stories and Legends Type of 1997

Designs: 9s, The Charming Augustin. 13s, Pied Piper from Korneuburg.

1998, Jan. 23
1745 A1003 9s multicolored 1.40 1.00
1746 A1003 13s multicolored 2.00 1.50

Hunting and Environment Type of 1997

1998, Feb. 6 **Photo.**
1747 A1006 9s Black cocks 1.40 1.00

1998 Winter Olympic Games, Nagano — A1022

1998, Feb. 6 **Photo. & Engr.**
1748 A1022 14s multicolored 2.25 1.60

Lithographic Printing, Bicent.
A1023

Portrait of Aloys Senefelder (1771-1834), inventor of lithography, on printing stone.

1998, Mar. 13 Litho. *Perf. 13½*
1749 A1023 7s multicolored 1.40 1.00

A1024

A1025

1998, Mar. 13 Photo. *Perf. 14*
1750 A1024 7s Poster 1.40 1.00

Joseph Binder (1898-1972), graphic artist.

1998, Mar. 13 Photo. & Engr.
1751 A1025 8s multicolored 1.60 1.25

Wiener Secession, cent. (Assoc. of Artists in Austria-Viennese Secession).

Folklore and Customs Type of 1991

Designs: 6.50s, Fiacre, Vienna. 7s, Samson figure, Palm Sunday Donkey Procession, Tyrol.

1998, Apr. 3
1752 A892 6.50s multicolored 1.25 .95
1753 A892 7s multicolored 1.40 1.00

Soccer Champions Type of 1997

1998, Apr. 17 Photo.
1754 A1005 7s Austria-Memphis Club 1.40 1.00

Salzburg Archdiocese, 1200th Anniv. — A1026

1998, Apr. 17 Photo. & Engr.
1755 A1026 7s multicolored 1.40 1.00

St. Florian, Patron Saint of Fire Brigades A1027

1998, Apr. 17 Photo.
1756 A1027 7s multicolored 1.40 1.00

Railway Centennials A1028

No. 1757, Ybbs Railway. No. 1758, Pöstlingberg Railway. No. 1759, Pinzgau Railway.

1998 Photo. & Engr. *Perf. 14*
1757 A1028 6.50s multicolored 1.25 1.00
1758 A1028 6.50s multicolored 1.25 1.00
1759 A1028 6.50s multicolored 1.25 1.00
Nos. 1757-1759 (3) 3.75 3.00

Issued: #1757, 5/15; #1758, 6/12; #1759, 7/17.

Ferdinandeum, Federal Museum of Tyrol, 175th Anniv. — A1029

1998, May 15
1760 A1029 7s multicolored 1.40 1.00

Vienna Festival Weeks — A1030

1998, May 15
1761 A1030 7s Townhall 1.40 1.00

Europa.

Folklore and Customs Type of 1991

Samson figure & the Zwergin, Lungau district, Salzburg.

1998, June 5
1762 A892 6.50s multicolored 1.25 1.00

Stories and Legends Type of 1997

Design: 25s, Saint Konrad collecting spring water in his handkerchief, Ems Castle.

1998, June 5
1763 A1003 25s multicolored 5.00 3.75

Christine Lavant, Poet, 25th Death Anniv. A1031

1998, June 5 Photo.
1764 A1031 7s multicolored 1.40 1.00

Stamp Day Type of 1997

Photo. & Engr.

1998, June 12 *Perf. 13½*
1765 A1009 7s "R" and "L" 1.40 1.00

See Nos. 1725, B357-B362. The first letters will spell "Briefmarke," the second "Philatelie."

Austrian Presidency of the European Union — A1032

1998, July 1 Photo. *Perf. 13½x14*
1766 A1032 7s multicolored 1.40 1.00

The People's Opera, Vienna, 50th Anniv. & Franz Lehar (1870-1948), Composer — A1033

1998, Sept. 10 Photo. *Perf. 14*
1767 A1033 6.50s multicolored 1.25 .85

Elizabeth, Empress of Austria (1837-98) A1034

1998, Sept. 10 Photo. & Engr.
1768 A1034 7s multicolored 1.40 .90

Vienna University for Commercial Sudies, Cent. — A1035

1998, Sept. 10 Photo.
1769 A1035 7s multicolored 1.40 .90

Hans Kudlich, Emancipator of Peasants, 175th Birth Anniv. — A1036

Photo. & Engr.

1998, Oct. 23 *Perf. 14*
1770 A1036 6.50s multicolored 1.25 .90

"My Garden," by Hans Staudacher A1037

1998, Oct. 23
1771 A1037 7s multicolored 1.25 .90

City of Eisenstadt, 350th Anniv. A1038

1998, Oct. 23
1772 A1038 7s multicolored 1.25 .90

Austrian Working Environment Type of 1994

Photo. & Engr.

1998, Nov. 6 *Perf. 14*
1773 A961 6.50s Reporter, photographer 1.10 .85

Christmas A1039

1423 Fresco from Tainach/Tinje Church, Carinthia.

1998, Nov. 27
1774 A1039 7s multicolored 1.25 .85

Stories and Legends Type of 1997

Design: The Dark Maiden of Hardegg Castle.

Photo. & Engr.

1999, Feb. 19 *Perf. 14*
1775 A1003 8s multicolored 1.25 .85

1999 Nordic Skiing World Championships, Mt. Dachstein, Ramsau — A1040

1999, Feb. 19
1776 A1040 7s multicolored 1.10 .85

Scenery Type of 1984

Bohemian Forest, Upper Austria.

Photo. & Engr.

1999, Mar. 19 *Perf. 14*
1777 A679 7s multicolored 1.10 .85

Folklore and Customs Type of 1991

Traditional walking pilgrimage to Mariazell.

1999, Mar. 19
1778 A892 6.50s multicolored 1.00 .75

Soccer Champions Type of 1997

Design: Soccer Club SK Puntigamer Sturm Graz.

1999, Apr. 16 Photo. *Perf. 14*
1779 A1005 7s multicolored 1.10 .85

Schönnbrun Palace, UNESCO World Heritage Site — A1041

Photo. & Engr.

1999, Apr. 16 *Perf. 14*
1780 A1041 13s multicolored 2.00 1.50

Austrian Patent Office, Cent. — A1042

1999, Apr. 16
1781 A1042 7s multicolored 1.10 .85

Hunting and Environment Type of 1997

1999, May 7 Litho. *Perf. 14*
1782 A1006 6.50s Partridges 1.00 .75

Austrian General Sport Federation, 50th Anniv. — A1043

1999, May 7 Engr. *Perf. 14*
1783 A1043 7s multicolored 1.10 .80

Council of Europe, 50th Anniv. A1044

1999, May 7 Photo. *Perf. 13½x14*
1784 A1044 14s multicolored 2.25 1.60

Karl Jenschke (1899-1969), Automobile Designer A1045

1999, May 28
1785 A1045 7s Steyr automobile 1.10 .80

Marble Relief of St. Martin — A1046

Photo. & Engr.
1999, May 28 *Perf. 14*
1786 A1046 8s multicolored 1.25 .95

See No. 1787.

Sculpture Type

Design: 9s, St. Anne, Mary and Jesus.

Photo. & Engr.
1999, Sept. 17 *Perf. 13¾*
1787 A1046 9s multicolored 1.40 1.10

Austrian Social Welfare Service, 125th Anniv. A1047

1999, June 4 Litho. *Perf. 13¾*
1788 A1047 7s multicolored 1.10 .80

Johann Strauss, the Younger (1825-99), Composer — A1048

Design: 8s, Johann Strauss, the Elder (1804-49).

1999, June 4 Photo. & Engr.
1789 A1048 7s multicolored 1.10 .80
1790 A1048 8s multicolored 1.25 .95

Stamp Day Type of 1997

1999, June 18 *Perf. 13½*
1791 A1009 7s "K" and "l" 1.10 .80

See Nos. 1725, 1765, B357-B362. The first letter of this stamp, and the others named, will spell "Briefmarke," the second "Philatelie."

Donau-Auen Natl. Park — A1049

1999, June 18 *Perf. 13¾*
1792 A1049 7s multicolored 1.10 .80

Europa.

Natl. Gendarmery, 150th Anniv. — A1050

1999, June 18
1793 A1050 7s multicolored 1.10 .80

Stories and Legends Type of 1997

Design: The Holy Notburga.

Photo. & Engr.
1999, Aug. 27 *Perf. 13¾x14*
1794 A1003 20s multicolored 3.25 2.50

Graz Opera House, 100th Anniv. — A1051

Photo. & Engr.
1999, Sept. 17 *Perf. 13¾*
1795 A1051 6.50s multicolored 1.00 .75

International Year of Older Persons — A1052

1999, Sept. 17 *Perf. 13¾*
1796 A1052 7s multicolored 1.10 .85

Federation of Austrian Trade Unions, 14th Congress A1053

1999, Oct. 15 Litho. *Perf. 13¾*
1797 A1053 6.50s multicolored 1.00 .75

"Caffee Girardi," by Wolfgang Herzig — A1054

Photo. & Engr.
1999, Oct. 22 *Perf. 13¾x14*
1798 A1054 7s multicolored 1.10 .85

Folklore & Customs Type of 1991

7s, The Pummerin, Bell in St. Stephen's Cathedral, Vienna. 8s, Pumpkin Festival, Lower Austria.

1999 Photo. & Engr. *Perf. 13¾*
1799 A892 7s multicolored 1.10 .85
1800 A892 8s multicolored 1.25 .95

Issued: 8s, 10/22; 7s, 11/12.

National Institute of Geology, 150th Anniv. A1055

Photo. & Engr.
1999, Nov. 12 *Perf. 13¾x14*
1801 A1055 7s multicolored 1.10 .85

Stories & Legends Type of 1997

Design: 32s, Discovery of Erzberg.

Photo. & Engr.
1999, Nov. 12 *Perf. 13¾x14*
1802 A1003 32s multicolored 5.00 3.75

Christmas A1056

Photo. & Engr.
1999, Nov. 26 *Perf. 13¾*
1803 A1056 7s Pinkafeld creche 1.10 .85

SEMI-POSTAL STAMPS

Issues of the Monarchy

Emperor Franz Josef — SP1

The Firing Step — SP2

Perf. 12½

1914, Oct. 4 Typo. Unwmk.
B1 SP1 5h green .20 *.30*
B2 SP1 10h rose .20 *.35*
Set, never hinged 1.10

Nos. B1-B2 were sold at an advance of 2h each over face value. Exist imperf.; value, set $50.

1915, May 1

Designs: 5h+2h, Cavalry. 10h+2h, Siege gun. 20h+3h, Battleship. 35h+3h, Airplane.

B3 SP2 3h + 1h violet brn .20 *.40*
B4 SP2 5h + 2h green .20 .20
B5 SP2 10h + 2h deep rose .20 .20
B6 SP2 20h + 3h Prus blue .45 *2.00*
B7 SP2 35h + 3h ultra 2.00 *4.25*
Nos. B3-B7 (5) 3.05 *7.05*
Set, never hinged 8.85

Exist imperf. Value, set $110.

Issues of the Republic

Kärnten

Types of Austria, 1919-20, Overprinted in Black

Abstimmung

1920, Sept. 16 *Perf. 12½*
B11 A44 5h gray, *yellow* .45 *1.10*
B12 A44 10h red, *pink* .35 *1.00*
B13 A43 15h bister, *yel* .25 *.75*
B14 A45 20h dark grn, *bl* .25 *.60*
B15 A43 25h violet, *pink* .25 *.65*
B16 A45 30h brown, *buff* 1.10 *2.50*
B17 A45 40h carmine, *yel* .25 *.70*
B18 A45 50h dark bl, *blue* .25 *.55*
B19 A43 60h ol grn, *azure* 1.10 *2.50*
B20 A47 80h red .30 *.65*
B21 A47 1k orange brown .35 *.75*
B22 A47 2k pale blue .35 *.80*

Granite Paper

Imperf

B23 A46 2½k brown red .35 *.90*
B24 A46 3k dk blue & green .45 *1.10*
B25 A46 4k carmine & violet .55 *1.25*
B26 A46 5k blue .55 *1.10*
B27 A46 7½k yellow green .60 *1.10*
B28 A46 10k gray grn & red .60 *1.25*
B29 A46 20k lilac & orange .65 *1.75*
Nos. B11-B29 (19) 9.00 *21.00*
Set, never hinged 15.00

Carinthia Plebiscite. Sold at three times face value for the benefit of the Plebiscite Propaganda Fund.

Nos. B11-B19 exist imperf. Value, set $125.

Hochwasser

Types of Regular Issues of 1919-21 Overprinted

1920

1921, Mar. 1 *Perf. 12½*
B30 A44 5h gray, *yellow* .25 *.45*
B31 A44 10h orange brown .25 *.45*
B32 A43 15h gray .25 *.45*
B33 A45 20h green, *yellow* .25 *.45*
B34 A43 25h blue, *yellow* .25 *.45*
B35 A45 30h violet, *bl* .45 *.90*
B36 A45 40h org brn, *pink* .50 *1.10*
B37 A45 50h green, *blue* 1.10 *2.00*
B38 A43 60h lilac, *yellow* .35 *.90*
B39 A47 80h pale blue .40 *.80*
B40 A47 1k red org, *blue* .35 *.75*
B41 A47 1½k green, *yellow* .20 *.40*
B42 A47 2k lilac brown .20 *.40*

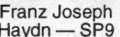

Overprinted **Hochwasser 1920**

B43 A46 2½k light blue .25 .45
B44 A46 3k ol grn & brn red .25 .45
B45 A46 4k lilac & orange .70 1.50
B46 A46 5k olive green .25 .55
B47 A46 7½k brown red .25 .65
B48 A46 10k blue & olive grn .25 .65
B49 A46 20k car rose & vio .45 1.00
Nos. B30-B49 (20) 7.20 14.75
Set, never hinged 12.75

Nos. B30-B49 were sold at three times face value, the excess going to help flood victims. Exists imperf. Value, set $175.

Franz Joseph Haydn — SP9

View of Bregenz — SP16

Musicians: 5k, Mozart. 7½k, Beethoven. 10k, Schubert. 25k, Anton Bruckner. 50k, Johann Strauss (son). 100k, Hugo Wolf.

1922, Apr. 24 Engr. *Perf. 12½*
B50 SP9 2½k brown, perf. 11½ 6.00 10.50
a. Perf. 12½ 7.25 12.00
B51 SP9 5k dark blue 1.10 1.50
B52 SP9 7½k black 1.40 2.50
a. Perf. 11½ 90.00 140.00
B53 SP9 10k dark violet 1.90 3.00
a. Perf. 11½ 2.50 5.25
B54 SP9 25k dark green 3.75 6.50
a. Perf. 11½ 4.25 8.25
B55 SP9 50k claret 2.00 3.00
B56 SP9 100k brown olive 7.00 8.75
a. Perf. 11½ 8.00 17.50
Nos. B50-B56 (7) 23.15 35.75
Set, never hinged 47.50

These stamps were sold at 10 times face value, the excess being given to needy musicians.

All values exist imperf. on both regular and handmade papers. Value, set $325.

A 1969 souvenir sheet without postal validity contains reprints of the 5k in black, 7½k in claret and 50k in dark blue, each overprinted "NEUDRUCK" in black at top. It was issued for the Vienna State Opera Centenary Exhibition.

1923, May 22 *Perf. 12½*

Designs: 120k, Mirabelle Gardens, Salzburg. 160k, Church at Eisenstadt. 180k, Assembly House, Klagenfurt. 200k, "Golden Roof," Innsbruck. 240k, Main Square, Linz. 400k, Castle Hill, Graz. 600k, Abbey at Melk. 1000k, Upper Belvedere, Vienna.

Various Frames
B57 SP16 100k dk green 2.75 5.00
B58 SP16 120k deep blue 2.50 5.00
B59 SP16 160k dk violet 2.50 5.00
B60 SP16 180k red violet 2.50 5.00
B61 SP16 200k lake 2.50 5.00
B62 SP16 240k red brown 2.50 5.00
B63 SP16 400k dark brown 2.50 5.00
B64 SP16 600k olive brn 2.75 5.00
B65 SP16 1000k black 4.00 5.00
Nos. B57-B65 (9) 24.50 45.00
Set, never hinged 55.50

Nos. B57-B65 were sold at five times face value, the excess going to needy artists.

All values exist imperf. on both regular and handmade papers. Value, set $325.

Feebleness SP25

Siegfried Slays the Dragon SP30

Designs: 300k+900k, Aid to industry. 500k+1500k, Orphans and widow. 600k+1800k, Indigent old man. 1000k+3000k, Alleviation of hunger.

1924, Sept. 6 Photo.
B66 SP25 100k + 300k yel green 3.25 3.25
B67 SP25 300k + 900k red brn 4.50 9.00
B68 SP25 500k + 1500k brn vio 4.50 9.00
B69 SP25 600k + 1800k pck bl 4.50 9.00
B70 SP25 1000k + 3000k brn org 7.50 12.50
Nos. B66-B70 (5) 24.25 42.75
Set, never hinged 45.75

The surtax was for child welfare and anti-tuberculosis work. Set exists imperf. Value, $325.

1926, Mar. 8 Engr.

Designs: 8g+2g, Gunther's voyage to Iceland. 15g+5g, Brunhild accusing Kriemhild. 20g+5g, Nymphs telling Hagen the future. 24g+6g, Rudiger von Bechelaren welcomes the Nibelungen. 40g+10g, Dietrich von Bern vanquishes Hagen.

B71 SP30 3g + 2g olive blk 1.10 .65
B72 SP30 8g + 2g indigo .25 .35
B73 SP30 15g + 5g dk claret .30 .35
B74 SP30 20g + 5g olive grn .45 .75
B75 SP30 24g + 6g dk violet .45 .75
B76 SP30 40g + 10g red brn 3.00 3.75
Nos. B71-B76 (6) 5.55 6.60
Set, never hinged 12.00

Nibelungen issue.

Nos. B71-B76 were printed in two sizes: 27½x28½mm and 28½x27½mm.

The surtax was for child welfare. Set exists imperf. Value, $250.

Pres. Michael Hainisch — SP36

Pres. Wilhelm Miklas — SP37

1928, Nov. 5
B77 SP36 10g dark brown 5.00 9.00
B78 SP36 15g red brown 5.00 9.00
B79 SP36 30g black 5.00 9.00
B80 SP36 40g indigo 5.00 9.00
Nos. B77-B80 (4) 20.00 36.00
Set, never hinged 31.00

Tenth anniversary of Austrian Republic. Sold at double face value, the premium aiding war orphans and children of war invalids.

Set exists imperf. Value $350.

1930, Oct. 4
B81 SP37 10g light brown 7.50 12.50
B82 SP37 20g red 7.50 12.50
B83 SP37 30g brown violet 7.50 12.50
B84 SP37 40g indigo 7.50 12.50
B85 SP37 50g dark green 7.50 12.50
B86 SP37 1s black brown 7.50 12.50
Nos. B81-B86 (6) 45.00 75.00
Set, never hinged 81.00

Nos. B81-B86 were sold at double face value. The excess aided the anti-tuberculosis campaign and the building of sanatoria in Carinthia.

Set exists imperf. Value, $425.

Regular Issue of 1929-30 Overprinted in Various Colors

CONVENTION WIEN 1931

1931, June 20
B87 A56 10g bister (Bl) 32.50 35.00
B88 A56 20g dk gray (R) 32.50 35.00
B89 A56 30g dk violet (Gl) 32.50 35.00
B90 A56 40g dk blue (Gl) 32.50 35.00
B91 A56 50g gray vio (O) 32.50 35.00
B92 A57 1s black brn (Bk) 32.50 35.00
Nos. B87-B92 (6) 195.00 210.00
Set, never hinged 465.00

Rotary convention, Vienna.

Nos. B87 to B92 were sold at double their face values. The excess was added to the beneficent funds of Rotary International.

Exists imperf.

Ferdinand Raimund — SP38

Poets: 20g, Franz Grillparzer. 30g, Johann Nestroy. 40g, Adalbert Stifter. 50g, Ludwig Anzengruber. 1s, Peter Rosegger.

1931, Sept. 12
B93 SP38 10g dark violet 12.00 17.50
B94 SP38 20g gray black 12.00 17.50
B95 SP38 30g orange red 12.00 17.50
B96 SP38 40g dull blue 12.00 17.50
B97 SP38 50g gray green 12.00 17.50
B98 SP38 1s yellow brown 12.00 17.50
Nos. B93-B98 (6) 72.00 105.00
Set, never hinged 114.00

Nos. B93-B98 were sold at double face value. The surtax aided unemployed young people.

Set exists imperf. Value, $425.

Chancellor Ignaz Seipel SP44

Ferdinand Georg Waldmüller SP45

1932, Oct. 12 *Perf. 13*
B99 SP44 50g ultra 9.00 17.50
Never hinged 16.00

Msgr. Ignaz Seipel, Chancellor of Austria, 1922-29. Sold at double face value, the excess aiding wounded veterans of World War I.

Exists imperf. Value, $150.

1932, Nov. 21

Artists: 24g, Moritz von Schwind. 30g, Rudolf von Alt. 40g, Hans Makart. 64g, Gustav Klimt. 1s, Albin Egger-Lienz.

B100 SP45 12g slate green 17.00 30.00
B101 SP45 24g dp violet 17.00 30.00
B102 SP45 30g dark red 17.00 30.00
B103 SP45 40g dark gray 17.00 30.00
B104 SP45 64g dark brown 17.00 30.00
B105 SP45 1s claret 17.00 30.00
Nos. B100-B105 (6) 102.00 180.00
Set, never hinged 156.00

Nos. B100 to B105 were sold at double their face values. The surtax was for the assistance of charitable institutions.

Set exists imperf. Value, $575.

Mountain Climbing SP51

Designs: 24g, Ski gliding. 30g, Walking on skis. 50g, Ski jumping.

1933, Jan. 9 Photo. *Perf. 12½*
B106 SP51 12g dark green 7.00 11.50
B107 SP51 24g dark violet 67.50 95.00
B108 SP51 30g brown red 12.50 17.50
B109 SP51 50g dark blue 67.50 95.00
Nos. B106-B109 (4) 154.50 219.00
Set, never hinged 295.00

Meeting of the Intl. Ski Federation, Innsbruck, Feb. 8-13.

These stamps were sold at double their face value. The surtax was for the benefit of "Youth in Distress."

#B106-B109 exist imperf. Value $1,200.

Stagecoach, after Painting by Moritz von Schwind — SP55

1933, June 23 Engr. *Perf. 12½*
Ordinary Paper
B110 SP55 50g deep ultra 150.00 190.00
Never hinged 225.00
a. Granite paper 300.00 425.00
Never hinged 450.00

Sheets of 25.

Nos. B110 and B110a exist imperf. Values $675 and $1,300.

Souvenir Sheet
Perf. 12
Granite Paper
B111 Sheet of 4 2,000. 2,750.
Never hinged 2,500.
a. SP55 50g deep ultra 375. 550.
Never hinged 525.

Intl. Phil. Exhib., Vienna, 1933. In addition to the postal value of 50g the stamp was sold at a premium of 50g for charity and of 1.60s for the admission fee to the exhibition.

Size of No. B111: 126x103mm.

A 50g dark red in souvenir sheet, with dark blue overprint ("NEUDRUCK WIPA 1965"), had no postal validity.

Even though the margins No. B111 have no gum, the sheet sells for a premium when definitely never hinged.

St. Stephen's Cathedral in 1683 SP56

Marco d'Aviano, Papal Legate SP57

Designs: 30g, Count Ernst Rudiger von Starhemberg. 40g, John III Sobieski, King of Poland. 50g, Karl V, Duke of Lorraine. 64g, Burgomaster Johann Andreas von Liebenberg.

1933, Sept. 6 Photo. *Perf. 12½*
B112 SP56 12g dark green 21.00 25.00
B113 SP57 24g dark violet 19.00 22.50
B114 SP57 30g brown red 19.00 22.50
B115 SP57 40g blue black 27.50 37.50
B116 SP57 50g dark blue 19.00 22.50
B117 SP57 64g olive brown 24.00 35.00
Nos. B112-B117 (6) 129.50 165.00
Set, never hinged 242.50

Deliverance of Vienna from the Turks, 250th anniv., and Pan-German Catholic Congress, Sept. 6, 1933.

The stamps were sold at double their face value, the excess being for the aid of Catholic works of charity.

Set exists imperf. Value, $850.

Types of Regular Issue of 1925-30 Surcharged:

+2g Winterhilfe
a

WINTERHILFE +6g
b

+50g WINTERHILFE
c

1933, Dec. 15
B118 A52(a) 5g + 2g olive grn .25 .55
B119 A56(b) 12g + 3g lt blue .25 .70
B120 A56(b) 24g + 6g brn orange .25 .60
B121 A57(c) 1s + 50g orange red 25.00 40.00
Nos. B118-B121 (4) 25.75 41.85
Set, never hinged 41.75

Winterhelp. Exists imperf. Value, set $525.

Anton Pilgram — SP62

Architects: 24g, J. B. Fischer von Erlach. 30g, Jakob Prandtauer. 40g, A. von Siccardsburg & E. van der Null. 60g, Heinrich von Ferstel. 64g, Otto Wagner.

1934, Dec. 2 Engr. *Perf. 12½*

Thick Yellowish Paper

B122	SP62	12g black	9.00	*15.00*
B123	SP62	24g dull violet	9.00	*15.00*
B124	SP62	30g carmine	9.00	*15.00*
B125	SP62	40g brown	9.00	*15.00*
B126	SP62	60g blue	9.00	*15.00*
B127	SP62	64g dull green	9.00	*15.00*
		Nos. B122-B127 (6)	54.00	*90.00*
		Set, never hinged	81.00	

Exist imperf. Value, set $425.

Nos. B124-B127 exist in horiz. pairs imperf. between. Value, each $160.

These stamps were sold at double their face value. The surtax on this and the following issues was devoted to general charity.

Types of Regular Issue of 1934 Surcharged in Black:

+50g

Winterhilfe +2g a

WINTERHILFE b

1935, Nov. 11 *Perf. 12, 12½*

B128	A67(a)	5g + 2g emerald	.45	*.90*
B129	A67(a)	12g + 3g blue	.75	*1.00*
B130	A67(a)	24g + 6g lt brown	.45	*.90*
B131	A68(b)	1s + 50g ver	24.00	*35.00*
		Nos. B128-B131 (4)	25.65	*37.80*
		Set, never hinged	45.35	

Winterhelp. Set exists imperf. Value, $125.

Prince Eugene of Savoy SP68

Slalom Turn SP74

Military Leaders: 24g, Field Marshal Laudon. 30g, Archduke Karl. 40g, Field Marshal Josef Radetzky. 60g, Admiral Wilhelm Tegetthoff. 64g, Field Marshal Franz Conrad Hotzendorff.

1935, Dec. 1 *Perf. 12½*

B132	SP68	12g brown	9.00	*14.00*
B133	SP68	24g dark green	9.00	*14.00*
B134	SP68	30g claret	9.00	*14.00*
B135	SP68	40g slate	9.00	*14.00*
B136	SP68	60g deep ultra	9.00	*14.00*
B137	SP68	64g dark violet	9.00	*14.00*
		Nos. B132-B137 (6)	54.00	*84.00*
		Set, never hinged	81.00	

These stamps were sold at double their face value. Set exists imperf. Value, $450.

1936, Feb. 20 Photo.

Designs: 24g, Jumper taking off. 35g, Slalom turn. 60g, Innsbruck view.

B138	SP74	12g Prus green	2.50	*3.00*
B139	SP74	24g dp violet	4.50	*4.50*
B140	SP74	35g rose car	22.50	*37.50*
B141	SP74	60g sapphire	22.50	*37.50*
		Nos. B138-B141 (4)	52.00	*82.50*
		Set, never hinged	90.50	

Ski concourse issue. These stamps were sold at twice face value. Set exists imperf. Value, $450.

St. Martin of Tours — SP78

Designs: 12g+3g, Medical clinic. 24g+6g, St. Elizabeth of Hungary. 1s+1s, "Flame of Charity."

1936, Nov. 2 Unwmk.

B142	SP78	5g + 2g dp green	.25	*.40*
B143	SP78	12g + 3g dp violet	.25	*.40*
B144	SP78	24g + 6g dp blue	.25	*.40*
B145	SP78	1s + 1s dk carmine	5.50	*11.00*
		Nos. B142-B145 (4)	6.25	*12.20*
		Set, never hinged	10.50	

Winterhelp. Set exists imperf. Value, $175.

Josef Ressel SP82

Nurse and Infant SP88

Inventors: 24g, Karl von Ghega. 30g, Josef Werndl. 40g, Carl Auer von Welsbach. 60g, Robert von Lieben. 64g, Viktor Kaplan.

1936, Dec. 6 Engr.

B146	SP82	12g dk brown	2.00	*4.50*
B147	SP82	24g dk violet	2.00	*4.50*
B148	SP82	30g dp claret	2.00	*4.50*
B149	SP82	40g gray violet	2.00	*4.50*
B150	SP82	60g vio blue	2.00	*4.50*
B151	SP82	64g dk slate green	2.00	*4.50*
		Nos. B146-B151 (6)	12.00	*27.00*
		Set, never hinged	24.00	

These stamps were sold at double their face value. Exists imperf. Value, set $350.

1937, Oct. 18 Photo.

12g+3g, Mother and child. 24g+6g, Nursing the aged. 1s+1s, Sister of Mercy with patient.

B152	SP88	5g + 2g dk green	.20	*.35*
B153	SP88	12g + 3g dk brown	.20	*.35*
B154	SP88	24g + 6g dk blue	.20	*.35*
B155	SP88	1s + 1s dk carmine	3.00	*6.75*
		Nos. B152-B155 (4)	3.60	*7.80*
		Set, never hinged	6.25	

Winterhelp. Set exists imperf. Value, $90.

Gerhard van Swieten SP92

The Dawn of Peace SP101

Physicians: 8g, Leopold Auenbrugger von Auenbrugg. 12g, Karl von Rokitansky. 20g, Joseph Skoda. 24g, Ferdinand von Hebra. 30g, Ferdinand von Arlt. 40g, Joseph Hyrtl. 60g, Theodor Billroth. 64g, Theodor Meynert.

1937, Dec. 5 Engr. *Perf. 12½*

B156	SP92	5g choc	1.90	*4.00*
B157	SP92	8g dk red	1.90	*4.00*
B158	SP92	12g brown blk	1.90	*4.00*
B159	SP92	20g dk green	1.90	*4.00*
B160	SP92	24g dk violet	1.90	*4.00*
B161	SP92	30g brown car	1.90	*4.00*
B162	SP92	40g dp olive grn	1.90	*4.00*
B163	SP92	60g indigo	1.90	*4.00*
B164	SP92	64g brown vio	1.90	*4.00*
		Nos. B156-B164 (9)	17.10	*36.00*
		Set, never hinged	29.25	

These stamps were sold at double their face value. Set exists imperf. Value, $550.

Catalogue values for unused stamps in this section, from this point to the end of the section, are for Never Hinged items.

1945, Sept. 10 Photo. *Perf. 14*

B165	SP101	1s + 10s dk green	.85	*1.40*

No. 467 Surcharged in Black

1946, June 25

B166	A110	30g + 20g dk red	3.00	*5.00*

First anniversary of United Nations.

Pres. Karl Renner SP102

1946 Engr. *Perf. 13½x14*

B167	SP102	1s + 1s dk slate grn	2.00	*4.00*
B168	SP102	2s + 2s dk blue vio	2.00	*4.00*
B169	SP102	3s + 3s dk purple	2.00	*4.00*
B170	SP102	5s + 5s dk violet brn	2.00	*4.00*
		Nos. B167-B170 (4)	8.00	*16.00*

See Nos. B185-B188.

Nazi Sword Piercing Austria SP103

Sweeping Away Fascist Symbols SP104

Designs: 8g+6g, St. Stephen's Cathedral in Flames. 12g+12g, Pleading hand in concentration camp. 30g+30g, Hand choking Nazi serpent. 42g+42g, Hammer breaking Nazi pillar. 1s+1s, Oath of allegiance. 2s+2s, Austrian eagle and burning swastika.

Unwmk.

1946, Sept. 16 Photo. *Perf. 14*

B171	SP103	5g + (3g) dk brown	.45	*.65*
B172	SP104	6g + (4g) dk slate grn	.30	*.55*
B173	SP104	8g + (6g) orange red	.30	*.55*
B174	SP104	12g + (12g) slate blk	.30	*.55*
B175	SP104	30g + (30g) violet	.30	*.55*
B176	SP104	42g + (42g) dull brn	.30	*.55*
B177	SP104	1s + 1s dk red	.45	*.65*
B178	SP104	2s + 2s dk car rose	.60	*.65*
		Nos. B171-B178 (8)	3.00	*4.70*

Anti-fascist propaganda.

Race Horse with Foal — SP111

Various Race Horses.

1946, Oct. 20 Engr. *Perf. 13½x14*

B179	SP111	16g + 16g rose brown	2.00	*3.00*
B180	SP111	24g + 24g dk purple	2.00	*3.00*
B181	SP111	60g + 60g dk green	2.00	*3.00*
B182	SP111	1s + 1s dk blue gray	2.00	*3.00*
B183	SP111	2s + 2s yel brown	2.00	*3.00*
		Nos. B179-B183 (5)	10.00	*15.00*

Austria Prize race, Vienna.

St. Ruprecht's Church, Vienna — SP116

1946, Oct. 30 *Perf. 14x13½*

B184	SP116	30g + 70g dark red	.35	*.70*

Founding of Austria, 950th anniv. The surtax aided the Stamp Day celebration.

Renner Type of 1946

Souvenir Sheets

1946, Sept. 5 *Imperf.*

B185	Sheet of 8	500.00	*900.00*
a.	SP102 1s+1s dk slate grn	55.00	*100.00*
B186	Sheet of 8	500.00	*900.00*
a.	SP102 2s+2s dk blue vio	55.00	*100.00*
B187	Sheet of 8	500.00	*900.00*
a.	SP102 3s+3s dark purple	55.00	*100.00*
B188	Sheet of 8	500.00	*900.00*
a.	SP102 5s+5s dk vio brown	55.00	*100.00*

1st anniv. of Austria's liberation. Sheets of 8 plus center label showing arms.

Statue of Rudolf IV the Founder SP118

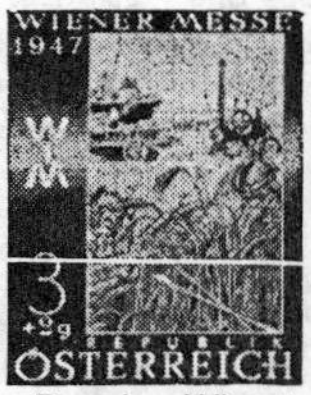

Reaping Wheat SP128

Designs: 5g+20g, Tomb of Frederick III. 6g+24g, Main pulpit. 8g+32g, Statue of St. Stephen. 10g+40g, Madonna of the Domestics statue. 12g+48g, High altar. 30g+1.20s, Organ, destroyed in 1945. 50g+1.80s, Anton Pilgram statue. 1s+5s, Cathedral from northeast. 2s+10s, Southwest corner of cathedral.

1946, Dec. 12 Engr. *Perf. 14x13½*

B189	SP118	3g + 12g brown	.25	*.50*
B190	SP118	5g + 20g dk vio brown	.25	*.50*
B191	SP118	6g + 24g dk blue	.25	*.50*
B192	SP118	8g + 32g dk green	.25	*.50*
B193	SP118	10g + 40g dp blue	.40	*.75*
B194	SP118	12g + 48g dk vio	.45	*.80*
B195	SP118	30g + 1.20s car	1.10	*1.90*
B196	SP118	50g + 1.80s dk bl	1.25	*2.00*
B197	SP118	1s + 5s brn vio	1.75	*3.25*
B198	SP118	2s + 10s vio brn	3.50	*7.50*
		Nos. B189-B198 (10)	9.45	*18.20*

The surtax aided reconstruction of St. Stephen's Cathedral, Vienna.

1947, Mar. 23 *Perf. 14x13½*

Designs: 8g+2g, Log raft. 10g+5g, Cement factory. 12g+8g, Coal mine. 18g+12g, Oil derricks. 30g+10g, Textile machinery. 35g+15g, Iron furnace. 60g+20g, Electric power lines.

B199	SP128	3g + 2g yel brown	.40	*.50*
B200	SP128	8g + 2g dk bl grn	.40	*.50*
B201	SP128	10g + 5g slate blk	.40	*.50*
B202	SP128	12g + 8g dark pur	.40	*.50*
B203	SP128	18g + 12g ol green	.40	*.50*
B204	SP128	30g + 10g deep cl	.40	*.50*
B205	SP128	35g + 15g crimson	.40	*.50*
B206	SP128	60g + 20g dk blue	.40	*.50*
		Nos. B199-B206 (8)	3.20	*4.00*

Vienna International Sample Fair, 1947.

Race Horse and Jockey SP136

1947, June 29 ***Perf. 13½x14***
B207 SP136 60g + 20g deep blue, *pale pink* .20 .20

Cup of Corvinus SP137 — Prisoner of War SP147

Designs: 8g+2g, Statue of Providence, Vienna. 10g+5g, Abbey at Melk. 12g+8g, Picture of a Woman, by Kriehuber. 18g+12g, Children at the Window, by Waldmuller. 20g+10g, Entrance, Upper Belvedere Palace. 30g+10g, Nymph Egeria, Schönbrunn Castle. 35g+15g, National Library, Vienna. 48g+12g, "Workshop of a Printer of Engravings," by Schmutzer. 60g+20g, Girl with Straw Hat, by Amerling.

1947, June 20 ***Perf. 14x13½***

B208 SP137 3g + 2g brown .30 *.40*
B209 SP137 8g + 2g dk blue grn .30 *.40*
B210 SP137 10g + 5g dp claret .30 *.40*
B211 SP137 12g + 8g dk purple .30 *.40*
B212 SP137 18g + 12g golden brn .30 *.40*
B213 SP137 20g + 10g sepia .30 *.40*
B214 SP137 30g + 10g dk yel grn .30 *.40*
B215 SP137 35g + 15g deep car .30 *.40*
B216 SP137 48g + 12g dk brn vio .30 *.40*
B217 SP137 60g + 20g dp blue .30 *.40*
Nos. B208-B217 (10) 3.00 *4.00*

1947, Aug. 30

Designs: 12g+8g, Prisoners' Mail, 18g+12g, Prison camp visitor. 35g+15g, Family reunion. 60g+20g, "Industry" beckoning. 1s+40g, Sower.

B218 SP147 8g + 2g dk green .20 *.30*
B219 SP147 12g + 8g dk vio brn .20 *.30*
B220 SP147 18g + 12g black brn .20 *.30*
B221 SP147 35g + 15g rose brn .20 *.30*
B222 SP147 60g + 20g dp blue .20 *.30*
B223 SP147 1s + 40g redsh brn .20 *.30*
Nos. B218-B223 (6) 1.20 *1.80*

Olympic Flame and Emblem SP153 — Laabenbach Bridge Neulengbach SP154

1948, Jan. 16 **Engr.**
B224 SP153 1s + 50g dark blue .35 .35

The surtax was used to help defray expenses of Austria's 1948 Olympics team.

1948, Feb. 18 ***Perf. 14x13½***

Designs: 20g+10g, Dam, Vermunt Lake. 30g+10g, Danube Port, Vienna. 40g+20g, Mining, Erzberg. 45g+20g, Tracks, Southern Railway Station, Vienna. 60g+30g, Communal housing project, Vienna. 75g+35g, Gas Works, Vienna. 80g+40g, Oil refinery. 1s+50g, Gesäuse Highway, Styria. 1.40s+70g, Parliament Building, Vienna.

B225 SP154 10g + 5g slate blk .20 .20
B226 SP154 20g + 10g lilac .20 .20
B227 SP154 30g + 10g dull grn .50 .50
B228 SP154 40g + 20g ol brn .20 .20
B229 SP154 45g + 20g dk blue .20 .20
B230 SP154 60g + 30g dk red .20 .20
B231 SP154 75g + 35g dk vio brn .20 .20
B232 SP154 80g + 40g vio brn .20 .20
B233 SP154 1s + 50g dp blue .20 .20
B234 SP154 1.40s + 70g dp car .50 .50
Nos. B225-B234 (10) 2.60 2.60

The surtax was for the Reconstruction Fund.

Violet — SP155 — Hans Makart — SP156

Designs: 20g+10g, Anemone. 30g+10g, Crocus. 40g+20g, Yellow primrose. 45g+20g, Pasqueflower. 60g+30g, Rhododendron. 75g+35g, Dogrose. 80g+40g, Cyclamen. 1s+50g, Alpine Gentian. 1.40s+70g, Edelweiss.

1948, May 14 **Engr. & Typo.**

B235 SP155 10g + 5g multi .35 .25
B236 SP155 20g + 10g multi .20 .20
B237 SP155 30g + 10g multi 2.50 2.00
B238 SP155 40g + 20g multi .50 .25
B239 SP155 45g + 20g multi .20 .20
B240 SP155 60g + 30g multi .20 .20
B241 SP155 75g + 35g multi .20 .20
B242 SP155 80g + 40g multi .30 .20
B243 SP155 1s + 50g multi .40 .30
B244 SP155 1.40s + 70g multi .65 .55
Nos. B235-B244 (10) 5.50 4.35

1948, June 15 **Unwmk.** **Engr.**

Designs: 20g+10g, Künstlerhaus, Vienna. 40g+20g, Carl Kundmann. 50g+25g, A. S. von Siccardsburg. 60g+30g, Hans Cannon. 1s+50g, William Unger. 1.40s+70g, Friedrich von Schmidt.

B245 SP156 20g + 10g dp yel green 6.25 5.00
B246 SP156 30g + 15g dark brown 3.00 1.90
B247 SP156 40g + 20g indigo 3.00 1.90
B248 SP156 50g + 25g dk vio 3.50 2.75
B249 SP156 60g + 30g dk red 3.50 2.75
B250 SP156 1s + 50g dk blue 6.25 5.00
B251 SP156 1.40s + 70g red brown 8.50 7.50
Nos. B245-B251 (7) 34.00 26.80

Kunstlerhaus, home of the leading Austrian Artists Association, 80th anniv.

St. Rupert — SP157 — Easter — SP158

Designs: 30g+15g, Cathedral and Fountain. 40g+20g, Facade of Cathedral. 50g+25g, Cathedral from South. 60g+30g, Abbey of St. Peter. 80g+40g, Inside Cathedral. 1s+50g, Salzburg Cathedral and Castle. 1.40s+70g, Madonna by Michael Pacher.

1948, Aug. 6 ***Perf. 14x13½***

B252 SP157 20g + 10g dp grn 6.00 5.50
B253 SP157 30g + 15g red brn 2.50 2.50
B254 SP157 40g + 20g sl blk 1.90 1.75
B255 SP157 50g + 25g choc .40 .40
B256 SP157 60g + 30g dk red .40 .40
B257 SP157 80g + 40g dk brn vio .40 .40
B258 SP157 1s + 50g dp blue .75 .50
B259 SP157 1.40s + 70g dk grn 1.50 1.25
Nos. B252-B259 (8) 13.85 12.70

The surtax was to aid in the reconstruction of Salzburg Cathedral.

1949, Apr. 13 **Unwmk.**

Designs: 60g+20g, St. Nicholas Day. 1s+25g, Birthday. 1.40s+35g, Christmas.

Inscribed: "Gluckliche Kindheit"

B260 SP158 40g + 10g brn vio 17.00 12.50
B261 SP158 60g + 20g brn red 17.00 12.50
B262 SP158 1s + 25g dp ultra 17.00 12.50
B263 SP158 1.40s + 35g dk grn 17.00 12.50
Nos. B260-B263 (4) 68.00 50.00

The surtax was for Child Welfare.

Arms of Austria, 1230 — SP159 — SP160

1949, Aug. 17 **Engr. & Photo.**
B264 SP159 40g + 10g 1230 7.00 6.00

Engraved and Typographed

B265 SP159 60g + 15g 1450 7.00 6.00
B266 SP159 1s + 25g 1600 7.00 6.00
B267 SP159 1.60s + 40g 1945 7.00 6.00
Nos. B264-B267 (4) 28.00 24.00

Surtax was for returned prisoners of war.

1949, Dec. 3 **Engr.**

Laurel Branch, Stamps and Magnifier

B268 SP160 60g + 15g dark red 2.25 1.50

Stamp Day, Dec. 3-4.

Arms of Austria and Carinthia SP161 — Carinthian with Austrian Flag SP162

Design: 1.70s+40g, Casting ballot.

1950, Oct. 10 **Photo.** ***Perf. 14x13½***

B269 SP161 60g + 15g 26.00 18.00
B270 SP162 1s + 25g 35.00 20.00
B271 SP162 1.70s + 40g 40.00 30.00
Nos. B269-B271 (3) 101.00 68.00

Plebiscite in Carinthia, 30th anniv.

Collector Examining Cover — SP163 — Miner and Mine — SP164

1950, Dec. 2 **Engr.**
B272 SP163 60g + 15g blue grn 8.50 6.00

Stamp Day.

1951, Mar. 10 **Unwmk.**

Designs: 60g+15g, Mason holding brick and trowel. 1s+25g, Bridge builder with hook and chain. 1.70s+40g, Electrician, pole and insulators.

B273 SP164 40g + 10g dark brown 13.00 11.00
B274 SP164 60g + 15g dk grn 13.00 11.00
B275 SP164 1s + 25g red brown 13.00 11.00
B276 SP164 1.70s + 40g vio bl 13.00 11.00
Nos. B273-B276 (4) 52.00 44.00

Issued to publicize Austrian reconstruction.

Laurel Branch and Olympic Circles SP165

1952, Jan. 26 ***Perf. 13½x14***
B277 SP165 2.40s + 60g grnsh black 15.00 13.00

The surtax was used to help defray expenses of Austria's athletes in the 1952 Olympic Games.

Cupid as Postman — SP166

1952, Mar. 10 ***Perf. 14x13½***
B278 SP166 1.50s + 35g dark brn car 17.50 16.00

Stamp Day.

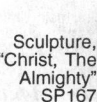

Sculpture, "Christ, The Almighty" SP167

1952, Sept. 6 ***Perf. 13½x14***
B279 SP167 1s + 25g grnsh gray 11.00 9.00

Austrian Catholic Conv., Vienna, Sept. 11-14.

Type of 1945-46 Overprinted in Gold

1953, Aug. 29 **Unwmk.**
B280 A124 1s + 25g on 5s dl bl 2.50 2.00

60th anniv. of labor unions in Austria.

Bummerlhaus Steyr SP168 — Globe and Philatelic Accessories SP169

Designs: 1s+25g, Johannes Kepler. 1.50s+40g, Lutheran Bible, 1st edition. 2.40s+60g, Theophil von Hansen. 3s+75g, Reconstructed Lutheran School, Vienna.

1953, Nov. 5 **Engr.** ***Perf. 14x13½***

B281 SP168 70g + 15g vio brn .30 .30
B282 SP168 1s + 25g dk gray blue .30 .30
B283 SP168 1.50s + 40g choc .90 .90
B284 SP168 2.40s + 60g dk grn 2.50 2.25

B285 SP168 3s + 75g dk pur 6.00 5.75
Nos. B281-B285 (5) 10.00 9.50

The surtax was used toward reconstruction of the Lutheran School, Vienna.

1953, Dec. 5
B286 SP169 1s + 25g chocolate 5.00 3.75

Stamp Day.

Type of 1945-46 with Denomination Replaced by Asterisks

Overprinted in Brown

LAWINENOPFER 1954

1s + 20g

1954, Feb. 19 ***Perf. 13½x14***
B287 A124 1s + 20g blue gray .20 .20

Surtax for aid to avalanche victims.

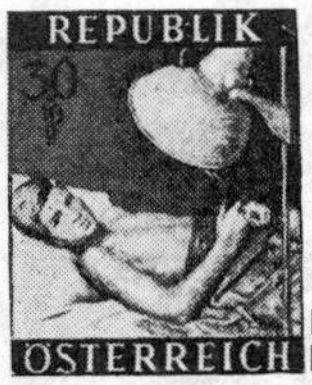

Patient Under Sun Lamp — SP170

Designs: 70g+15g, Physician using microscope. 1s+25g, Mother and children. 1.45s+35g, Operating room. 1.50s+35g, Baby on scale. 2.40s+60g, Nurse.

1954 **Engr.** ***Perf. 14x13½***
B288 SP170 30g + 10g purple 1.50 1.10
B289 SP170 70g + 15g dk brn .25 .25
B290 SP170 1s + 25g dk bl .30 .25
B291 SP170 1.45s + 35g dk bl green .45 .40
B292 SP170 1.50s + 35g dk red 5.00 4.50
B293 SP170 2.40s + 60g dk red brown 6.00 5.50
Nos. B288-B293 (6) 13.50 12.00

The surtax was for social welfare.

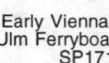

Early Vienna-Ulm Ferryboat SP171

1954, Dec. 4 ***Perf. 13½x14***
B294 SP171 1s + 25g dk gray grn 4.50 4.00

Stamp Day.

"Industry" Welcoming Returned Prisoner of War — SP172

1955, June 29
B295 SP172 1s + 25g red brn 2.00 1.50

Surtax for returned prisoners of war and relatives of prisoners not yet released.

Collector Looking at Album — SP173

Ornamental Shield and Letter — SP174

1955, Dec. 3 ***Perf. 14x13½***
B296 SP173 1s + 25g vio brn 3.00 2.75

Stamp Day. The surtax was for the promotion of Austrian philately.

1956, Dec. 1 **Engr.**
B297 SP174 1s + 25g scarlet 2.75 2.50

Stamp Day. See note after No. B296.

Arms of Austria, 1945 — SP175

Engr. & Typo.
1956, Dec. 21 ***Perf. 14x13½***
B298 SP175 1.50s + 50g on 1.60s + 40g gray & red .25 .20

The surtax was for Hungarian refugees.

New Post Office, Linz 2 — SP176

Design: 2.40s+60g, Post office, Kitzbuhel.

1957-58 **Engr.** ***Perf. 13½x14***
B299 SP176 1s + 25g dk sl grn 2.75 2.50
B300 SP176 2.40s + 60g blue .65 .60

Stamp Day. See note after B296. Issue dates: 1s, Nov. 30, 1957. 2.40s, Dec. 6, 1957. See No. B303.

Roman Carriage from Tomb at Maria Saal — SP177

Litho. & Engr.
1959, Dec. 5 ***Perf. 13½x14***
B301 SP177 2.40s + 60g pale lil & blk .55 .50

Stamp Day.

Progressive Die Proof under Magnifying Glass SP178

1960, Dec. 2 **Engr.** ***Perf. 13½x14***
B302 SP178 3s + 70g vio brn .85 .70

Stamp Day.

Post Office Type of 1957

Design: 3s+70g, Post Office, Rust.

1961, Dec. 1 **Unwmk.** ***Perf. 13½***
B303 SP176 3s + 70g dk bl grn .90 .70

Stamp Day. See note after No. B296.

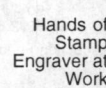

Hands of Stamp Engraver at Work SP179

1962, Nov. 30 ***Perf. 13½x14***
B304 SP179 3s + 70g dull pur 1.25 .90

Stamp Day.

Railroad Exit, Post Office Vienna 101 — SP180

1963, Nov. 29 **Litho. & Engr.**
B305 SP180 3s + 70g tan & blk .80 .80

Stamp Day.

View of Vienna, North SP181

Designs: Various view of Vienna with compass indicating direction.

1964, July 20 **Litho.** ***Perf. 13½x14***
B306 SP181 1.50s + 30g ("N") .20 .20
B307 SP181 1.50s + 30g ("NO") .20 .20
B308 SP181 1.50s + 30g ("O") .20 .20
B309 SP181 1.50s + 30g ("SO") .20 .20
B310 SP181 1.50s + 30g ("S") .20 .20
B311 SP181 1.50s + 30g ("SW") .20 .20
B312 SP181 1.50s + 30g ("W") .20 .20
B313 SP181 1.50s + 30g ("NW") .20 .20
Nos. B306-B313 (8) 1.60 1.60

Vienna Intl. Phil. Exhib. (WIPA 1965).

Post Bus Terminal, St. Gilgen, Wolfgangsee — SP182

1964, Dec. 4 **Unwmk.** ***Perf. 13½***
B314 SP182 3s + 70g multi .45 .45

Stamp Day.

Wall Painting, Tomb at Thebes — SP183

Development of Writing: 1.80s+50g, Cuneiform writing on stone tablet and man's head from Assyrian palace. 2.20s+60g, Wax tablet with Latin writing, Corinthian column. 3s+80g, Gothic writing on sealed letter, Gothic window from Munster Cathedral. 4s+1s, Letter with seal and postmark and upright desk. 5s+1.20s, Typewriter.

Litho. & Engr.
1965, June 4 ***Perf. 14x13½***
B315 SP183 1.50s + 40g multi .20 .20
B316 SP183 1.80s + 50g multi .20 .20
B317 SP183 2.20s + 60g multi .35 .35
B318 SP183 3s + 80g multi .20 .20
B319 SP183 4s + 1s multi .45 .45
B320 SP183 5s + 1.20s multi .60 .60
Nos. B315-B320 (6) 2.00 2.00

Vienna Intl. Phil. Exhib., WIPA, June 4-13.

Mailman Distributing Mail — SP184

1965, Dec. 3 **Engr.** ***Perf. 13½x14***
B321 SP184 3s + 70g blue grn .40 .35

Stamp Day.

Letter Carrier, 16th Century SP185

Letter Carrier, 16th Century Playing Card SP186

Litho. & Engr.
1966, Dec. 2 ***Perf. 13½***
B322 SP185 3s + 70g multi .40 .35

Stamp Day. Design is from Ambras Heroes' Book, Austrian National Library.

Engr. & Photo.
1967, Dec. 1 ***Perf. 13x13½***
B323 SP186 3.50s + 80g multi .40 .35

Stamp Day.

Mercury, Bas-relief from Purkersdorf SP187

Unken Post Station Sign, 1710 SP188

1968, Nov. 29 **Engr.** ***Perf. 13½***
B324 SP187 3.50s + 80g slate green .40 .35

Stamp Day.

Engr. & Photo.
1969, Dec. 5 ***Perf. 12***
B325 SP188 3.50s + 80g tan, red & blk .40 .35

Stamp Day. Design is from a watercolor by Friedrich Zeller.

Saddle, Bag, Harness and Post Horn — SP189

Engr. & Litho.
1970, Dec. 4 ***Perf. 13½x14***
B326 SP189 3.50s + 80g gray blk & yel .40 .35

Stamp Day.

"50 Years"
SP190

Engr. & Photo.

1971, Dec. 3 ***Perf. 13½***
B327 SP190 4s + 1.50s gold & red brn .60 .45

50th anniversary of the Federation of Austrian Philatelic Societies.

Local Post Carrier
SP191

Gabriel, by Lorenz Luchsperger, 15th Century
SP192

1972, Dec. 1 **Engr.** ***Perf. 14x13½***
B328 SP191 4s + 1s olive green .60 .45

Stamp Day.

1973, Nov. 30
B329 SP192 4s + 1s maroon .60 .45

Stamp Day.

Mail Coach Leaving Old PTT Building — SP193

1974, Nov. 29 **Engr.** ***Perf. 14x13½***
B330 SP193 4s + 2s violet blue .70 .70

Stamp Day.

Alpine Skiing, Women's
SP194

Designs: 1.50s+70g, Ice hockey. 2s+90g, Ski jump. 4s+1.90s, Bobsledding.

1975, Mar. 14 **Photo.** ***Perf. 13½x14***

B331 SP194	1s + 50g multi	.25	.25
B332 SP194	1.50s + 70g multi	.30	.30
B333 SP194	2s + 90g multi	.35	.35
B334 SP194	4s + 1.90s multi	.70	.70
	Nos. B331-B334 (4)	1.60	1.60

1975, Nov. 14

Designs: 70g+30g, Figure skating, pair. 2s+1s, Cross-country skiing. 2.50s+1s, Luge. 4s+2s, Biathlon.

B335 SP194 70g + 30g multi	.20	.20
B336 SP194 2s + 1s multi	.30	.30
B337 SP194 2.50s + 1s multi	.40	.40
B338 SP194 4s + 2s multi	.70	.70
Nos. B335-B338 (4)	1.60	1.60

12th Winter Olympic Games, Innsbruck, Feb. 4-15, 1976.

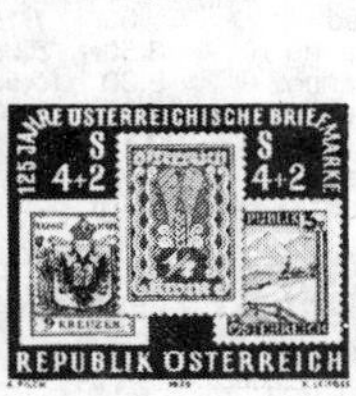

Austria Nos. 5, 250, 455 — SP195

Photo. & Engr.

1975, Nov. 28 ***Perf. 14***
B339 SP195 4s + 2s multi .65 .65

Stamp Day; 125th anniv. of Austrian stamps.

Postilion's Gala Hat and Horn
SP196

1976, Dec. 3 ***Perf. 13½x14***
B340 SP196 6s + 2s blk & lt vio .80 .80

Stamp Day.

Emanuel Herrmann
SP197

1977, Dec. 2 ***Perf. 14x13½***
B341 SP197 6s + 2s multi .80 .80

Stamp Day. Emanuel Herrmann (1839-1902), economist, invented postal card. Austria issued first postal card in 1869.

Post Bus, 1913
SP198

1978, Dec. 1 **Photo.** ***Perf. 13½x14***
B342 SP198 10s + 5s multi 1.40 1.40

Stamp Day.

Heroes' Square, Vienna
SP199

Photo. & Engr.

1979, Nov. 30 ***Perf. 13½***
B343 SP199 16s + 8s multi 2.75 2.50

No. B343 Inscribed "2. Phase"

1980, Nov. 21
B344 SP199 16s + 8s multi 2.75 2.50

Souvenir Sheet

1981, Feb. 20
B345 SP199 16s + 8s multi 3.00 2.50

WIPA 1981 Phil. Exhib., Vienna, May 22-31. No. B345 contains one stamp without inscription.

Mainz-Weber Mailbox, 1870 — SP200

1982, Nov. 26 **Photo. & Engr.**
B346 SP200 6s + 3s multi 1.00 1.00

Stamp Day.

Boy Examining Cover — SP201

Photo. & Engr.

1983, Oct. 21 ***Perf. 14***
B347 SP201 6s + 3s multi 1.10 1.10

Stamp Day. See Nos. B349-B352, B354-B355.

World Winter Games for the Handicapped — SP202

1984, Jan. 5 **Photo.** ***Perf. 13½x13***
B348 SP202 4s + 2s Downhill skier .75 .75

Stamp Day Type of 1983

Designs: No. B349, Seschemnofer III burial chamber detail, pyramid of Cheops, Gizeh. No. B350, Roman messenger on horseback. No. B351, Nuremberg messenger, 16th cent. No. B352, *The Postmaster* (detail), 1841, lithograph by Carl Schuster.

1984-87 **Photo. & Engr.** ***Perf. 14***

B349 SP201 6s + 3s multi	1.25	1.25
B350 SP201 6s + 3s multi	1.25	1.25
B351 SP201 6s + 3s multi	1.25	1.25
B352 SP201 6s + 3s multi	1.40	1.40
Nos. B349-B352 (4)	5.15	5.15

Issue: #B349, 11/30/84; #B350, 11/28/85; #B351, 11/28/86; #B352, 11/19/87.

4th World Winter Sports Championships for the Disabled, Innsbruck — SP203

1988, Jan. 15 **Photo.** ***Perf. 13½***
B353 SP203 5s + 2.50s multi 1.10 1.10

Stamp Day Type of 1983

Designs: No. B354, Railway mail car. No. B355, Hansa-Brandenburg CI mail plane.

1988-89 **Photo. & Engr.** ***Perf. 14***

B354 SP201 6s +3s multi	1.40	1.40
B355 SP201 6s +3s multi	1.40	1.40

Issued: #B354, Nov. 17; #B355, May 24, 1989.

Stamp Day — SP204

1990, May 25 **Photo.** ***Perf. 13½***
B356 SP204 7s +3s multi 1.75 1.75

SP205

Stamp Day — SP205a

1991, May 29 **Photo. & Engr.**
B357 SP205 7s +3s "B" & "P" 1.75 1.75

1992, May 22
B358 SP205 7s +3s "R" & "H" 1.75 1.75

1993, May 5
B359 SP205 7s +3s "I" & "I" 1.75 1.75

1994, May 27
B360 SP205 7s +3s "E" & "L" 1.75 1.75

1995, May 26
B361 SP205a 10s +5s "F" & "A" 3.00 3.00

1996, May 17
B362 SP205a 10s +5s "M" & "T" 3.00 3.00
Nos. B357-B362,1725,1765,1791 (9) 16.75 15.80

The first letters will spell "Briefmarke," the second "Philatelie."

For "A" & "E" see No. 1725; "R" & "L" No. 1765; "K" & "I" No. 1791.

Special Olympics Winter Games
SP206

1993, Mar. 19 **Photo.** ***Perf. 13½x14***
B367 SP206 6s +3s multi 1.75 1.75

Vienna Intl. Postage Stamp Exhibition (WIPA), 2000 — SP207

#B368, #5, postman on bicycle. #B369, #339, early mail truck. #B370, #525, airplane, service vehicles.

1997-99 **Photo. & Engr.** ***Perf. 14***

B368 SP207 27s +13s multi	6.75	6.75
B369 SP207 32s +13s multi	7.50	7.50
B370 SP207 32s +16s multi	7.50	7.50
Nos. B368-B370 (3)	21.75	21.75

Issued: #B368, 5/23; #B369, 11/6/98; #B370, 9/17/99.

AIR POST STAMPS

Issues of the Monarchy

FLUGPOST

Types of Regular Issue of 1916 Surcharged

2·50 K 2·50

1918, Mar. 30 **Unwmk.** ***Perf. 12½***

C1	A40 1.50k on 2k lilac	2.00	*3.75*
C2	A40 2.50k on 3k ocher	7.00	*16.00*
a.	Inverted surcharge	*1,100.*	
b.	Perf. 11½	325.00	*425.00*
c.	Perf. 12½x11½	27.50	*45.00*

Overprinted **FLUGPOST**

C3	A40	4k gray	5.00	11.00
		Nos. C1-C3 (3)	14.00	30.75
		Set, never hinged	24.50	

Set exists imperf. Value, $200.

Nos. C1-C3 also exist without surcharge or overprint. Value, set perf., $300; imperf., $275.

Nos. C1-C3 were printed on grayish and on white paper.

A 7k on 10k red brown was prepared but not regularly issued. Value, perf. or imperf., $300.

Issues of the Republic

Hawk — AP1

Wilhelm Kress — AP2

1922-24 Typo. *Perf. 12½*

C4	AP1	300k claret	.30	1.25
C5	AP1	400k green ('24)	4.50	12.50
C6	AP1	600k bister	.20	.55
C7	AP1	900k brn orange	.20	.55
		Engr.		
C8	AP2	1200k brn violet	.20	.55
C9	AP2	2400k slate	.20	.55
C10	AP2	3000k dp brn ('23)	2.50	3.50
C11	AP2	4800k dark bl ('23)	2.50	3.75
		Nos. C4-C11 (8)	10.60	23.20
		Set, never hinged	22.35	

Set exists imperf. Value, $250.

Plane and Pilot's Head — AP3

Airplane Passing Crane — AP4

1925-30 Typo. *Perf. 12½*

C12	AP3	2g gray brown	.35	.90
C13	AP3	5g red	.20	.30
a.		Horiz. pair, imperf. btwn.	250.00	
C14	AP3	6g dark blue	.80	1.40
C15	AP3	8g yel green	.90	1.60
C16	AP3	10g dp org ('26)	.90	1.60
a.		Horiz. pair, imperf. btwn.	250.00	
C17	AP3	15g red vio ('26)	.35	.80
a.		Horiz. pair, imperf. btwn.	300.00	
C18	AP3	20g org brn ('30)	10.00	6.25
C19	AP3	25g blk vio ('30)	3.75	7.50
C20	AP3	30g bister ('26)	7.00	8.25
C21	AP3	50g bl gray ('26)	12.50	12.50
C22	AP3	80g dk grn ('30)	1.90	3.50
		Photo.		
C23	AP4	10g orange red	.80	2.50
a.		Horiz. pair, imperf. btwn.	250.00	
C24	AP4	15g claret	.60	1.40
C25	AP4	30g brn violet	.70	2.50
C26	AP4	50g gray black	.75	2.75
C27	AP4	1s deep blue	6.00	6.25
C28	AP4	2s dark green	1.50	3.50
a.		Vertical pair, imperf. btwn.	250.00	
C29	AP4	3s red brn ('26)	42.50	52.50
C30	AP4	5s indigo ('26)	11.50	22.50
		Size: 25½x32mm		
C31	AP4	10s blk brown, *gray* ('26)	9.00	17.50
		Nos. C12-C31 (20)	112.00	156.00
		Set, never hinged	220.00	

Exists imperf. Value, set $800.

Airplane over Güssing Castle — AP5

Airplane over the Danube — AP6

Designs (each includes plane): 10g, Maria-Worth. 15g, Durnstein. 20g, Hallstatt. 25g, Salzburg. 30g, Upper Dachstein and Schladminger Glacier. 40g, Lake Wetter. 50g, Arlberg. 60g, St. Stephen's Cathedral. 80g, Church of the Minorites. 2s, Railroad viaduct, Carinthia. 3s, Gross Glockner mountain. 5s, Aerial railway. 10s, Seaplane and yachts.

1935, Aug. 16 Engr. *Perf. 12½*

C32	AP5	5g rose violet	.20	.40
C33	AP5	10g red orange	.20	.20
C34	AP5	15g yel green	.60	1.25
C35	AP5	20g gray blue	.20	.30
C36	AP5	25g violet brn	.20	.30
C37	AP5	30g brn orange	.20	.35
C38	AP5	40g gray green	.20	.35
C39	AP5	50g light sl bl	.20	.45
C40	AP5	60g black brn	.30	.65
C41	AP5	80g light brown	.35	.80
C42	AP6	1s rose red	.30	.70
C43	AP6	2s olive green	1.75	4.00
C44	AP6	3s yellow brn	7.00	15.00
C45	AP6	5s dark green	4.50	11.00
C46	AP6	10s slate blue	42.50	80.00
		Nos. C32-C46 (15)	58.70	115.75
		Set, never hinged	87.00	

Set exists imperf. Value, $275.

Catalogue values for unused stamps in this section, from this point to the end of the section, are for Never Hinged items.

Windmill, Neusiedler Lake Shore — AP20

Designs: 1s, Roman arch, Carnuntum. 2s, Town Hall, Gmund. 3s, Schieder Lake, Hinterstoder. 4s, Praegraten, Eastern Tyrol. 5s, Torsäule, Salzburg. 10s, St. Charles Church, Vienna.

1947 Unwmk. *Perf. 14x13½*

C47	AP20	50g black brown	.20	.20
C48	AP20	1s dark brn vio	.30	.25
C49	AP20	2s dark green	.35	.40
C50	AP20	3s chocolate	2.25	2.75
C51	AP20	4s dark green	1.40	2.00
C52	AP20	5s dark blue	1.40	2.00
C53	AP20	10s dark blue	.75	1.50
		Nos. C47-C53 (7)	6.65	9.10

Rooks AP27

Birds: 1s, Barn swallows. 2s, Blackheaded gulls. 3s, Great cormorants. 5s, Buzzard. 10s, Gray heron. 20s, Golden eagle.

1950-53 *Perf. 13½x14*

C54	AP27	60g dark bl vio	2.50	1.10
C55	AP27	1s dark vio blue ('53)	17.50	15.00
C56	AP27	2s dark blue	15.00	6.00
C57	AP27	3s dk slate green ('53)	100.00	65.00
C58	AP27	5s red brn ('53)	100.00	65.00
C59	AP27	10s gray vio ('53)	45.00	30.00
C60	AP27	20s brn blk ('52)	10.00	4.00
		Nos. C54-C60 (7)	290.00	186.10
		Set, hinged	180.00	

Value at lower left on Nos. C59 and C60.

No. C60 exists imperf.

Etrich "Dove" AP28

Designs: 3.50s, Twin-engine jet airliner. 5s, Four-engine jet airliner.

1968, May 31 Engr. *Perf. 13½x14*

C61	AP28	2s olive bister	.30	.25
C62	AP28	3.50s slate green	.50	.40
C63	AP28	5s dark blue	.75	.60
		Nos. C61-C63 (3)	1.55	1.25

IFA WIEN 1968 (International Air Post Exhibition), Vienna, May 30-June 4.

POSTAGE DUE STAMPS

Issues of the Monarchy

D1

D2

Perf. 10 to 13½

1894-95 Typo. Wmk. 91

J1	D1	1kr brown	1.60	1.40
a.		Perf. 13½	26.00	30.00
J2	D1	2kr brown ('95)	3.50	2.00
a.		Pair, imperf. btwn.	175.00	200.00
J3	D1	3kr brown	2.75	1.00
J4	D1	5kr brown	2.50	1.40
a.		Perf. 13½	16.00	15.00
b.		Pair, imperf. btwn.	160.00	175.00
J5	D1	6kr brown ('95)	2.50	5.00
J6	D1	7kr brown ('95)	.80	4.50
a.		Vert. pair, imperf. btwn.	250.00	300.00
b.		Horiz. pair, imperf. btwn.	275.00	—
J7	D1	10kr brown	4.00	.50
J8	D1	20kr brown	.80	4.50
J9	D1	50kr brown	35.00	55.00
		Nos. J1-J9 (9)	53.45	75.30

Values for Nos. J1-J9 are for stamps that do not show the watermark. Stamps showing the watermark often sell for more.

See Nos. J204-J231.

1899-1900 *Imperf.*

J10	D2	1h brown	.20	.40
J11	D2	2h brown	.25	.50
J12	D2	3h brown ('00)	.20	.40
J13	D2	4h brown	1.75	1.40
J14	D2	5h brown ('00)	2.25	1.10
J15	D2	6h brown	.30	.85
J16	D2	10h brown	.25	.40
J17	D2	12h brown	.40	2.25
J18	D2	15h brown	.40	1.40
J19	D2	20h brown	17.00	3.00
J20	D2	40h brown	.80	2.50
J21	D2	100h brown	4.00	2.25
		Nos. J10-J21 (12)	27.80	16.45

Perf. 10½, 12½, 13½ and Compound

J22	D2	1h brown	.55	.20
J23	D2	2h brown	.45	.20
J24	D2	3h brown ('00)	.40	.20
J25	D2	4h brown	.40	.20
J26	D2	5h brown ('00)	.40	.20
J27	D2	6h brown	.40	.20
J28	D2	10h brown	.45	.20
J29	D2	12h brown	.45	.65
J30	D2	15h brown	.70	.80
J31	D2	20h brown	.55	.30
J32	D2	40h brown	1.00	.75
J33	D2	100h brown	20.00	1.00
		Nos. J22-J33 (12)	25.75	4.90

Nos. J10-J33 exist on unwmkd. paper.

For surcharges see Offices in the Turkish Empire Nos. J1-J5.

D3

1908-13 Unwmk. *Perf. 12½*

J34	D3	1h carmine	1.00	1.00
J35	D3	2h carmine	.25	.25
J36	D3	4h carmine	.20	.20
J37	D3	6h carmine	.20	.20
J38	D3	10h carmine	.25	.20
J39	D3	14h carmine ('13)	3.25	1.75
J40	D3	20h carmine	4.75	.20
J41	D3	25h carmine ('10)	4.50	3.50
J42	D3	30h carmine	5.00	.20
J43	D3	50h carmine	7.50	.25
J44	D3	100h carmine	13.50	.45
		Nos. J34-J44 (11)	40.40	8.20

All values exist on ordinary paper, #J34-J38, J40, J42-J44 on chalky paper and #J34-J38, J40, J44 on thin ordinary paper. Values are for the least expensive stamp of the types. Some of the expensive types sell for considerably more.

All values exist imperf.

See Offices in the Turkish Empire type D3.

1911, July 16

J45	D3	5k violet	42.50	9.00
J46	D3	10k violet	175.00	2.75

Regular Issue of 1908 Overprinted or Surcharged in Carmine or Black:

PORTO
a

PORTO 15 15
b

1916, Oct. 21

J47	A22	1h gray (C)	.20	.20
a.		Pair, one without overprint	125.00	
J48	A22	15h on 2h vio (Bk)	.20	.35
		Set, never hinged	.40	

D4

D5

1916, Oct. 1

J49	D4	5h rose red	.20	.20
J50	D4	10h rose red	.20	.20
J51	D4	15h rose red	.20	.20
J52	D4	20h rose red	.20	.20
J53	D4	25h rose red	.30	.65
J54	D4	30h rose red	.20	.25
J55	D4	40h rose red	.20	.20
J56	D4	50h rose red	.90	1.50
J57	D5	1k ultramarine	.25	.20
a.		Horiz. pair, imperf. btwn.	325.00	350.00
J58	D5	5k ultramarine	1.60	1.40
J59	D5	10k ultramarine	2.25	.90
		Nos. J49-J59 (11)	6.50	5.90
		Set, never hinged	17.00	

Exists imperf. Value, set $80.

For overprints see J64-J74, Western Ukraine Nos. 54-55, NJ1-NJ6, Poland Nos. J1-J10.

Type of Regular Issue of 1916 Surcharged

PORTO

15 ✱ 15

1917

J60	A38	10h on 24h blue	1.10	.40
J61	A38	15h on 36h violet	.30	.20
J62	A38	20h on 54h orange	.20	.30
J63	A38	50h on 42h chocolate	.20	.20
		Nos. J60-J63 (4)	1.80	1.10
		Set, never hinged	5.00	

All values of this issue are known imperforate, also without surcharge, perforated and imperforate.

For overprints see Western Ukraine Nos. 57-58.

Issues of the Republic

Postage Due Stamps of 1916 Overprinted

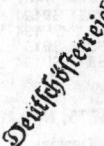

Deutschösterreich

1919

J64	D4	5h rose red	.20	.20
a.		Inverted overprint	225.00	225.00
J65	D4	10h rose red	.20	.20
J66	D4	15h rose red	.25	.35
J67	D4	20h rose red	.25	.35
J68	D4	25h rose red	8.75	13.50
J69	D4	30h rose red	.20	.25
J70	D4	40h rose red	.25	.60
J71	D4	50h rose red	.30	1.10
J72	D5	1k ultramarine	3.50	8.00
J73	D5	5k ultramarine	8.00	10.50
J74	D5	10k ultramarine	7.25	3.50
		Nos. J64-J74 (11)	29.15	38.55
		Set, never hinged	67.40	

Nos. J64, J65, J67 and J70 exist imperforate.

D6

D7

1920-21 *Perf. 12½*

J75	D6	5h bright red	.20	.30
J76	D6	10h bright red	.20	.20
J77	D6	15h bright red	.20	1.10
J78	D6	20h bright red	.20	.20
J79	D6	25h bright red	.20	.90
J80	D6	30h bright red	.20	.25
J81	D6	40h bright red	.20	.20
J82	D6	50h bright red	.20	.20
J83	D6	80h bright red	.20	.25
J84	D7	1k ultramarine	.20	.20
J85	D7	1½k ultra ('21)	.20	.20
J86	D7	2k ultra ('21)	.20	.20
J87	D7	3k ultra ('21)	.20	.50
J88	D7	4k ultra ('21)	.20	.55
J89	D7	5k ultramarine	.20	.20
J90	D7	8k ultra ('21)	.20	.60
J91	D7	10k ultramarine	.20	.25
J92	D7	20k ultra ('21)	.20	1.10
		Nos. J75-J92 (18)	3.60	7.40
		Set, never hinged	3.60	

Nos. J84 to J92 exist on white paper and on grayish white paper. They also exist imperf.; value, set $85.

Imperf

J93	D6	5h bright red	.20	.35
J94	D6	10h bright red	.20	.20
J95	D6	15h bright red	.20	.90
J96	D6	20h bright red	.20	.20
J97	D6	25h bright red	.20	.90
J98	D6	30h bright red	.20	.60
J99	D6	40h bright red	.20	.35
J100	D6	50h bright red	.20	.60
J101	D6	80h bright red	.20	.35
		Nos. J93-J101 (9)	1.80	4.45
		Set, never hinged	1.80	

No. 207a Surcharged in Dark Blue

Nachmarke

7½ K

1921, Dec. *Perf. 12½*

J102	A43	7½k on 15h bister	.20	.20
		Never hinged	.20	
a.		Inverted surcharge	250.00	350.00

D8

D9

D10

1922

J103	D8	1k reddish buff	.20	.20
J104	D8	2k reddish buff	.20	.25
J105	D8	4k reddish buff	.20	.50
J106	D8	5k reddish buff	.20	.25
J107	D8	7½k reddish buff	.20	.70
J108	D8	10k blue green	.20	.25
J109	D8	15k blue green	.20	.50
J110	D8	20k blue green	.20	.35
J111	D8	25k blue green	.20	.80
J112	D8	40k blue green	.20	.30
J113	D8	50k blue green	.20	.90
		Nos. J103-J113 (11)	2.20	5.00
		Set, never hinged	2.20	

Issue date: Nos. J108-J113, June 2.

1922-24

J114	D9	10k cobalt blue	.20	.30
J115	D9	15k cobalt blue	.20	.35
J116	D9	20k cobalt blue	.20	.45
J117	D9	50k cobalt blue	.20	.35
J118	D10	100k plum	.20	.20
J119	D10	150k plum	.20	.20
J120	D10	200k plum	.20	.20
J121	D10	400k plum	.20	.20
J122	D10	600k plum ('23)	.20	.35
J123	D10	800k plum	.20	.20
J124	D10	1,000k plum ('23)	.20	.20
J125	D10	1,200k plum ('23)	.20	2.50
J126	D10	1,500k plum ('24)	.20	.25
J127	D10	1,800k plum ('24)	1.50	5.25
J128	D10	2,000k plum ('23)	.30	.85
J129	D10	3,000k plum ('24)	5.75	12.00
J130	D10	4,000k plum ('24)	3.75	9.75
J131	D10	6,000k plum ('24)	3.75	16.00
		Nos. J114-J131 (18)	17.65	49.60
		Set, never hinged	38.00	

Value, Nos. J103-J131 imperf, $225.

D11

D12

1925-34 *Perf. 12½*

J132	D11	1g red	.20	.20
J133	D11	2g red	.20	.20
J134	D11	3g red	.20	.20
J135	D11	4g red	.20	.20
J136	D11	5g red ('27)	.20	.20
J137	D11	6g red	.20	.45
J138	D11	8g red	.20	.20
J139	D11	10g dark blue	.20	.20
J140	D11	12g dark blue	.20	.20
J141	D11	14g dark blue ('27)	.20	.20
J142	D11	15g dark blue	.20	.20
J143	D11	16g dark blue ('29)	.20	.20
J144	D11	18g dark blue ('34)	1.10	3.50
J145	D11	20g dark blue	.20	.20
J146	D11	23g dark blue	.25	.20
J147	D11	24g dark blue ('32)	1.10	.20
J148	D11	28g dark blue ('27)	.90	.30
J149	D11	30g dark blue	.20	.20
J150	D11	31g dark blue ('29)	1.10	.25
J151	D11	35g dark blue ('30)	1.10	.20
J152	D11	39g dark blue ('32)	1.40	.20
J153	D11	40g dark blue	1.25	1.75
J154	D11	60g dark blue	.85	1.10
J155	D12	1s dark green	5.50	1.10
J156	D12	2s dark green	27.50	3.50
J157	D12	5s dark green	77.50	30.00
J158	D12	10s dark green	45.00	4.25
		Nos. J132-J158 (27)	167.35	49.60
		Set, never hinged	422.00	

Issues of 1925-27 imperf, value, set $425.

Issued: 3g, 2s-10s, Dec; 5g, 28g, 1/1; 14g, June; 31g, 2/1; 35g, Jan; 24g, 39g, Sept; 16g, May; 18g, 6/25; others, 6/1.

Coat of Arms

D13 D14

1935, June 1

J159	D13	1g red	.20	.20
J160	D13	2g red	.20	.20
J161	D13	3g red	.20	.20
J162	D13	5g red	.20	.20
J163	D13	10g blue	.20	.20
J164	D13	12g blue	.20	.20
J165	D13	15g blue	.20	.40
J166	D13	20g blue	.20	.20
J167	D13	24g blue	.20	.20
J168	D13	30g blue	.20	.20
J169	D13	39g blue	.20	.20
J170	D13	60g blue	.75	.90
J171	D14	1s green	.75	.30
J172	D14	2s green	1.10	.70
J173	D14	5s green	2.50	2.50
J174	D14	10s green	3.75	.60
		Nos. J159-J174 (16)	11.05	7.40
		Set, never hinged	41.40	

On #J163-J170, background lines are horiz.

Nos. J159-J174 exist imperf. Value, set $125.

Catalogue values for unused stamps in this section, from this point to the end of the section, are for Never Hinged items.

D15

1945 Unwmk. Typo. *Perf. 10½*

J175	D15	1g vermilion	.20	.20
J176	D15	2g vermilion	.20	.20
J177	D15	3g vermilion	.20	.20
J178	D15	5g vermilion	.20	.20
J179	D15	10g vermilion	.20	.20
J180	D15	12g vermilion	.20	.20
J181	D15	20g vermilion	.20	.20
J182	D15	24g vermilion	.20	.20
J183	D15	30g vermilion	.20	.20
J184	D15	60g vermilion	.20	.20
J185	D15	1s violet	.20	.35
J186	D15	2s violet	.20	.45
J187	D15	5s violet	.20	.20
J188	D15	10s violet	.20	.20
		Nos. J175-J188 (14)	2.80	3.20

Issue dates: 1g-60g, Sept. 10, 1s-10s, Sept. 24.

Occupation Stamps of the Allied Military Government Overprinted in Black

PORTO

1946 *Perf. 11*

J189	OS1	3g deep orange	.35	.30
J190	OS1	5g bright green	.35	.30
J191	OS1	6g red violet	.35	.30
J192	OS1	8g rose pink	.35	.30
J193	OS1	10g light gray	.35	.30
J194	OS1	12g pale buff brown	.40	.30
J195	OS1	15g rose red	.40	.30
J196	OS1	20g copper brown	.40	.30
J197	OS1	25g deep blue	.40	.30
J198	OS1	30g bright violet	.40	.30
J199	OS1	40g light ultra	.40	.30
J200	OS1	60g light olive grn	.40	.30
J201	OS1	1s dark violet	.50	.40
J202	OS1	2s yellow	.50	.40
J203	OS1	5s deep ultra	.70	.60
		Nos. J189-J203 (15)	6.25	5.00

Nos. J189-J203 were issued by the Renner Government. Inverted overprints exist on about half of the denominations.

Issue dates: 3g-60g, Apr. 23, 1s-5s, May 20.

Type of 1894-95 Inscribed "Republik Osterreich"

1947 Typo. *Perf. 14*

J204	D1	1g chocolate	.20	.20
J205	D1	2g chocolate	.20	.20
J206	D1	3g chocolate	.20	.20
J207	D1	5g chocolate	.20	.20
J208	D1	8g chocolate	.20	.20
J209	D1	10g chocolate	.20	.20
J210	D1	12g chocolate	.20	.20
J211	D1	15g chocolate	.20	.20
J212	D1	16g chocolate	.20	.40
J213	D1	17g chocolate	.20	.40
J214	D1	18g chocolate	.20	.40
J215	D1	20g chocolate	.50	.20
J216	D1	24g chocolate	.30	.30
J217	D1	30g chocolate	.20	.20
J218	D1	36g chocolate	.50	.60
J219	D1	40g chocolate	.20	.20
J220	D1	42g chocolate	.50	.60
J221	D1	48g chocolate	.50	.60
J222	D1	50g chocolate	.55	.20
J223	D1	60g chocolate	.20	.20
J224	D1	70g chocolate	.20	.20
J225	D1	80g chocolate	3.75	1.75
J226	D1	1s blue	.20	.20
J227	D1	1.15s blue	2.50	.30
J228	D1	1.20s blue	3.00	1.00
J229	D1	2s blue	.40	.40
J230	D1	5s blue	.40	.40
J231	D1	10s blue	.40	.40
		Nos. J204-J231 (28)	16.50	10.55

Issue dates: 1g, 20g, 50g, 80g, 1.15s, 1.20s, Sept. 25, others, Aug. 14.

D16

D17

1949-57

J232	D16	1g carmine	.20	.20
J233	D16	2g carmine	.20	.20
J234	D16	4g carmine ('51)	1.00	.20
J235	D16	5g carmine	2.25	.25
J236	D16	8g carmine ('51)	2.75	1.50
J237	D16	10g carmine	.20	.20
J238	D16	20g carmine	.20	.20
J239	D16	30g carmine	.20	.20
J240	D16	40g carmine	.20	.20
J241	D16	50g carmine	.20	.20
J242	D16	60g carmine ('50)	7.50	.20
J243	D16	63g carmine ('57)	4.75	4.00
J244	D16	70g carmine	.20	.20
J245	D16	80g carmine	.20	.20
J246	D16	90g carmine ('50)	.20	.20
J247	D16	1s purple	.20	.20
J248	D16	1.20s purple	.35	.20
J249	D16	1.35s purple	.30	.20
J250	D16	1.40s purple ('51)	.45	.20
J251	D16	1.50s purple ('53)	.20	.20
J252	D16	1.65s purple ('50)	.40	.20
J253	D16	1.70s purple	.40	.20
J254	D16	2s purple	.35	.20
J255	D16	2.50s purple ('51)	.45	.20
J256	D16	3s purple ('51)	1.00	.20
J257	D16	4s purple ('51)	1.00	.40
J258	D16	5s purple	1.75	.20
J259	D16	10s purple	2.75	.20
		Nos. J232-J259 (28)	29.85	10.95

Issued: 60g, 90g, 1.65s, 8/7; 4g, 8g, 1.40s, 2.50s-4s, 12/4; 1.50s, 2/18; 63g, 4/30; others, 11/17.

1985-89 Photo. *Perf. 14*

Background Color

J260	D17	10g brt yel ('86)	.20	.20
J261	D17	20g pink ('86)	.20	.20
J262	D17	50g orange ('86)	.20	.20
J263	D17	1s lt blue ('86)	.20	.20
J264	D17	2s pale brn ('86)	.30	.20
J265	D17	3s violet ('86)	.40	.30
J266	D17	5s ocher	.60	.40
J267	D17	10s pale grn ('89)	1.50	1.10
		Nos. J260-J267 (8)	3.60	2.80

Issue dates: 5s, Dec. 12. 20g, 1s, 3s, Mar. 19. 10g, 50g, 2s, Oct. 3. 10s, June 30.

MILITARY STAMPS

Issues of the Austro-Hungarian Military Authorities for the Occupied Territories in World War I

See Bosnia and Herzegovina for similar designs inscribed "MILITARPOST" instead of "FELDPOST."

Stamps of Bosnia of 1912-14 Overprinted

K.U.K.

FELDPOST

1915 Unwmk. *Perf. 12½*

M1	A23	1h olive green	.20	.35
M2	A23	2h bright blue	.20	.35
M3	A23	3h claret	.20	.35
M4	A23	5h green	.20	.20
M5	A23	6h dark gray	.20	.35
M6	A23	10h rose carmine	.20	.20
M7	A23	12h deep ol grn	.25	.45
M8	A23	20h orange brn	.30	.55
M9	A23	25h ultramarine	.25	.45
M10	A23	30h orange red	2.75	5.25
M11	A24	35h myrtle grn	2.25	4.25
M12	A24	40h dark violet	2.25	4.25
M13	A24	45h olive brown	2.50	4.50
M14	A24	50h slate blue	2.25	4.25
M15	A24	60h brn violet	.30	3.25
M16	A24	72h dark blue	2.25	4.25
M17	A25	1k brn vio, *straw*	2.50	5.25
M18	A25	2k dk gray, *blue*	2.25	4.25
M19	A26	3k car, *green*	20.00	32.50
M20	A26	5k dk vio, *gray*	18.00	27.50
M21	A25	10k dk ultra, *gray*	160.00	200.00
		Nos. M1-M21 (21)	219.30	302.75
		Set, never hinged	330.00	

Exists imperf. Value, set $275.

Nos. M1-M21 also exist with overprint double, inverted and in red. These varieties were made by order of an official but were not regularly issued.

Emperor Franz Josef

M1 M2

Perf. 11½, 12½ and Compound

1915-17 Engr.

M22	M1	1h olive green	.20	.20
M23	M1	2h dull blue	.20	.20
M24	M1	3h claret	.20	.20
M25	M1	5h green	.20	.20
a.		Perf. 11½	42.50	60.00
b.		Perf. 11½x12½	55.00	100.00
c.		Perf. 12½x11½	77.50	110.00
M26	M1	6h dark gray	.20	.20
M27	M1	10h rose carmine	.20	.20
M28	M1	10h gray bl ('17)	.20	.20
M29	M1	12h dp olive grn	.20	.20
M30	M1	15h car rose ('17)	.20	.20
a.		Perf. 11½	7.00	15.00
M31	M1	20h orange brn	.30	.35
M32	M1	20h ol green ('17)	.30	.35
M33	M1	25h ultramarine	.20	.20
M34	M1	30h vermilion	.20	.35
M35	M1	35h dark green	.30	.50
M36	M1	40h dark violet	.30	.50
M37	M1	45h olive brown	.25	.50

M38	M1	50h myrtle green	.25	*.50*
M39	M1	60h brown violet	.25	*.50*
M40	M1	72h dark blue	.25	*.50*
M41	M1	80h org brn ('17)	.20	*.25*
M42	M1	90h magenta ('17)	.70	*1.10*
M43	M2	1k brn vio, *straw*	1.40	*2.10*
M44	M2	2k dk gray, *blue*	1.10	1.00
M45	M2	3k car, *green*	.80	*1.75*
M46	M2	4k dark violet, *gray* ('17)	.80	*2.75*
M47	M2	5k dk vio, *gray*	18.00	*27.50*
M48	M2	10k dk ultra, *gray*	2.75	*6.00*
		Nos. M22-M48 (27)	30.15	*48.50*
		Set, never hinged	63.40	

Nos. M22-M48 exist imperf. Value, set $125.

Emperor Karl I
M3 M4

1917-18 ***Perf. 12½***

M49	M3	1h grnsh blue ('18)	.20	.20
a.		Perf. 11½	3.25	*5.25*
M50	M3	2h red org ('18)	.20	.20
M51	M3	3h olive gray	.20	.20
a.		Perf. 11½	12.00	*19.00*
b.		Perf. 11½x12½	21.00	*35.00*
M52	M3	5h olive green	.20	.20
M53	M3	6h violet	.20	.20
M54	M3	10h orange brn	.20	.20
M55	M3	12h blue	.20	.20
a.		Perf. 11½	2.00	*4.25*
M56	M3	15h bright rose	.20	.20
M57	M3	20h red brown	.20	.20
M58	M3	25h ultramarine	.30	.30
M59	M3	30h slate	.20	.20
M60	M3	40h olive bister	.20	.20
a.		Perf. 11½	1.25	*2.10*
M61	M3	50h deep green	.20	.20
a.		Perf. 11½	5.00	*9.00*
M62	M3	60h car rose	.20	.20
M63	M3	80h dull blue	.20	.20
M64	M3	90h dk violet	.40	*.50*
M65	M4	2k rose, *straw*	.20	.20
a.		Perf. 11½	2.00	*3.50*
M66	M4	3k green, *blue*	.85	*1.75*
M67	M4	4k rose, *green*	13.50	*16.00*
a.		Perf. 11½	25.00	*35.00*
M68	M4	10k dl vio, *gray*	2.00	*4.25*
a.		Perf. 11½	10.00	*19.00*
		Nos. M49-M68 (20)	20.05	*25.80*
		Set, never hinged	35.00	

Nos. M49-M68 exist imperf. Value, set $45.

See No. M82. For surcharges and overprints see Italy Nos. N1-N19, Poland Nos. 30-40, Romania Nos. 1N1-1N17, Western Ukraine Nos. 34-53, 75-81.

Emperor Karl I — M5

1918 **Typo.** ***Perf. 12½***

M69	M5	1h grnsh blue	18.00
M70	M5	2h orange	9.00
M71	M5	3h olive gray	7.00
M72	M5	5h yellow green	.25
M73	M5	10h dark brown	.25
M74	M5	20h red	.25
M75	M5	25h blue	.70
M76	M5	30h bister	67.50
M77	M5	45h dark slate	67.50
M78	M5	50h deep green	45.00
M79	M5	60h violet	90.00
M80	M5	80h rose	45.00
M81	M5	90h brown violet	1.75

Engr.

M82	M4	1k ol bister, *blue*	.25
		Nos. M69-M82 (14)	352.90
		Set, never hinged	755.00

Nos. M69-M82 were on sale at the Vienna post office for a few days before the Armistice signing. They were never issued at the Army Post Offices. They exist imperf.; value, set $450.

For surcharges see Italy Nos. N20-N33.

MILITARY SEMI-POSTAL STAMPS

Emperor Karl I — MSP7

Empress Zita — MSP8

Perf. 12½x13

1918, July 20 **Unwmk.** **Typo.**

MB1	MSP7	10h gray green	.25	.55
MB2	MSP8	20h magenta	.25	.55
MB3	MSP7	45h blue	.25	.55
		Nos. MB1-MB3 (3)	.75	1.65
		Set, never hinged	2.10	

Nos. M69-M82 were on sale at the Vienna post office for a few days before the Armistice signing. They were never issued at the Army Post Offices. They exist imperf.; value, set $450. These stamps were sold at a premium of 10h each over face value. The surtax was for "Karl's Fund."

For overprints see Poland Nos. 27-29, Western Ukraine Nos. 31-33.

Exist imperf. Value, set $8.

MILITARY NEWSPAPER STAMPS

Mercury — MN1

1916 **Unwmk.** **Typo.** ***Perf. 12½***

MP1	MN1	2h blue	.20	*.20*
a.		Perf. 11½	1.40	*1.60*
b.		Perf. 12½x11½	150.00	*200.00*
MP2	MN1	6h orange	.50	*.80*
MP3	MN1	10h carmine	.60	*.80*
MP4	MN1	20h brown	.40	*.80*
a.		Perf. 11½	1.90	*5.00*
		Nos. MP1-MP4 (4)	1.70	*2.60*
		Set, never hinged	3.20	

Exist imperf. Values, Nos. MP2-MP3, $1 each, Nos. MP1, MP4, $18 each.

For surcharges see Italy Nos. NP1-NP4.

NEWSPAPER STAMPS

From 1851 to 1866, the Austrian Newspaper Stamps were also used in Lombardy-Venetia.

> Values for unused stamps 1851-67 are for fine copies with original gum. Specimens without gum sell for about a third or less of the figures quoted.

Issues of the Monarchy

Mercury — N1

Three Types

Type I - The "G" has no crossbar.

Type II - The "G" has a crossbar.

Type IIa - as type II but the rosette is deformed. Two spots of color in the "G."

1851-56 **Unwmk.** **Typo.** ***Imperf.***

Machine-made Paper

P1	N1	(0.6kr) bl, type IIa	125.00	70.00
a.		Blue, type I	160.00	85.00
b.		Ribbed paper	375.00	140.00
c.		Blue, type II	350.00	160.00
P2	N1	(6kr) yel, type I	*16,000.*	*7,000.*
P3	N1	(30kr) rose, type I	—	*9,000.*
P4	N1	(6kr) scar, type II ('56)	*37,500.*	*40,000.*

From 1852 No. P3 and from 1856 No. P2 were used as 0.6 kreuzer values.

Values for Nos. P2-P3 unused are for stamps without gum. Pale shades sell at considerably lower values.

Originals of Nos. P2-P3 are usually in pale colors and poorly printed. Values are for stamps clearly printed and in bright colors. Numerous reprints of Nos. P1-P4 were made between 1866 and 1904. Those of Nos. P2-P3 are always well printed and in much deeper colors. All reprints are in type I, but occasionally show faint traces of a crossbar on "G" of "ZEITUNGS."

N2

N3

Two Types of the 1858-59 Issue

Type I - Loops of the bow at the back of the head broken.

Type II - Loops complete. Wreath projects further at top of head.

1858-59 **Embossed**

P5	N2	(1kr) blue, type I	450.00	550.00
P6	N2	(1kr) lilac, type II ('59)	650.00	275.00

1861

P7	N3	(1kr) gray	140.00	140.00
a.		(1kr) gray lilac	350.00	200.00
b.		(1kr) deep lilac	1,500.	575.00

The embossing on the reprints of the 1858-59 and 1861 issues is not as sharp as on the originals.

N4

Wmk. 91, or, before July 1864, Unwmkd.

1863

P8	N4	(1.05kr) gray	35.00	13.00
a.		Tete beche pair	*18,000.*	
b.		(1.05kr) gray lilac	60.00	17.50

Values are for stamps that do not show the watermark. Stamps showing the watermark often sell for more.

The embossing of the reprints is not as sharp as on the originals.

Mercury
N5 N6

Three Types

Type I - Helmet not defined at back, more or less blurred. Two thick short lines in front of wing of helmet. Shadow on front of face not separated from hair.

Type II - Helmet distinctly defined. Four thin short lines in front of wing. Shadow on front of face clearly defined from hair.

Type III - Outer white circle around head is open at top (closed on types I and II). Greek border at top and bottom is wider than on types I and II.

1867-73 **Typo.** **Wmk. 91**

Coarse Print

P9	N5	(1kr) vio, type I	37.50	4.00
a.		(1kr) violet, type II ('73)	110.00	18.00

1874-76

Fine Print

P9B	N5	(1kr) violet, type III ('76)	.55	.20
c.		(1kr) gray lilac, type I ('76)	90.00	25.00
d.		(1kr) violet, type II	27.50	5.00
e.		Double impression, type III		175.00

Stamps of this issue, except No. P9c, exist in many shades, from gray to lilac brown and deep violet. Stamps in type III exist also privately perforated or rouletted.

1880

P10	N6	½kr blue green	4.50	.85

Nos. P9B and P10 also exist on thicker paper without sheet watermark and No. P10 exists with unofficial perforation.

N7

1899 **Unwmk.** ***Imperf.***

Without Varnish Bars

P11	N7	2h dark blue	.20	.20
P12	N7	6h orange	2.00	1.75
P13	N7	10h brown	.80	.75
P14	N7	20h rose	1.75	1.75
		Nos. P11-P14 (4)	4.75	4.45

1901

With Varnish Bars

P11a	N7	2h dark blue	.60	.20
P12a	N7	6h orange	8.50	*11.50*
P13a	N7	10h brown	10.50	6.75
P14a	N7	20h rose	19.00	*26.00*
		Nos. P11a-P14a (4)	38.60	*44.45*

Nos. P11 to P14 were re-issued in 1905.

Mercury
N8 N9

1908 ***Imperf.***

P15	N8	2h dark blue	.50	.20
a.		Tete beche pair	250.00	*300.00*
P16	N8	6h orange	2.50	.30
P17	N8	10h carmine	2.50	.30
P18	N8	20h brown	2.75	.25
		Nos. P15-P18 (4)	8.25	1.05

All values are found on chalky, regular and thin ordinary paper. They exist privately perforated.

1916 ***Imperf.***

P19	N9	2h brown	.20	.20
P20	N9	4h green	.30	.30
P21	N9	6h dark blue	.25	*.60*
P22	N9	10h orange	.35	.35
P23	N9	30h claret	.30	.30
		Nos. P19-P23 (5)	1.40	1.75
		Set, never hinged	2.80	

Issues of the Republic

Newspaper Stamps of 1916 Overprinted

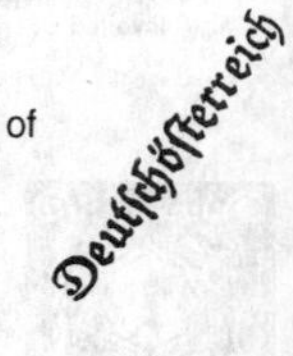

1919

P24	N9	2h brown	.20	.20
P25	N9	4h green	.25	*.70*
P26	N9	6h dark blue	.20	*.70*
P27	N9	10h orange	.25	*.90*
P28	N9	30h claret	.20	*.45*
		Nos. P24-P28 (5)	1.10	*2.95*
		Set, never hinged	1.70	

Mercury
N10 N11

1920-21 ***Imperf.***

P29	N10	2h violet	.20	.20
P30	N10	4h brown	.20	*.20*
P31	N10	5h slate	.20	.20
P32	N10	6h turq blue	.20	.20
P33	N10	8h green	.20	*.30*
P34	N10	9h yellow ('21)	.20	.20
P35	N10	10h red	.20	.20
P36	N10	12h blue	.20	*.30*
P37	N10	15h lilac ('21)	.20	.20
P38	N10	18h blue grn ('21)	.20	*.25*
P39	N10	20h orange	.20	*.25*
P40	N10	30h yellow brn ('21)	.20	.20
P41	N10	45h green ('21)	.20	*.35*
P42	N10	60h claret	.20	.20
P43	N10	72h chocolate ('21)	.20	*.45*
P44	N10	90h violet ('21)	.20	*.55*
P45	N10	1.20k red ('21)	.20	*.65*

P46 N10 2.40k yellow grn ('21) .20 *.55*
P47 N10 3k gray ('21) .20 *.40*
Nos. P29-P47 (19) 3.80 5.85
Set, never hinged 3.80

Nos. P37-P40, P42, P44 and P47 exist also on thick gray paper.

1921-22

P48 N11 45h gray .20 *.25*
P49 N11 75h brown org ('22) .20 *.35*
P50 N11 1.50k ol bister ('22) .20 *.50*
P51 N11 1.80k gray blue ('22) .20 *.55*
P52 N11 2.25k light brown .20 *.75*
P53 N11 3k dull green ('22) .20 *.55*
P54 N11 6k claret ('22) .20 *.65*
P55 N11 7.50k bister .20 *.85*
Nos. P48-P55 (8) 1.60 *4.45*
Set, never hinged 1.60

Nos. P24-P55 exist privately perforated.

NEWSPAPER TAX STAMPS

Values for unused stamps 1853-59 are for copies in fine condition with gum. Specimens without gum sell for about one-third or less of the figures quoted.

Issues of the Monarchy

NT1

NT2

Unwmk.

1853, Mar. 1 Typo. *Imperf.*

PR1 NT1 2kr green 1,300. 50.00

The reprints are in finer print than the more coarsely printed originals, and on a smooth toned paper.

Values for Nos. PR2-PR9 are for stamps that do not show the watermark. Stamps showing the watermark often sell for more.

Wmk. 91, or, before July 1864, Unwmkd.

1858-59

Two Types.

Type I - The banderol on the Crown of the left eagle touches the beak of the eagle.

Type II - The banderol does not touch the beak.

PR2 NT2 1kr blue, type II ('59) 30.00 5.50
a. 1kr blue, type I 625.00 140.00
b. Printed on both sides, type II —
PR3 NT2 2kr brown, type II ('59) 20.00 6.75
a. 2kr red brown, type II 350.00 140.00
PR4 NT2 4kr brn, type I 400.00 *1,000.*

Nos. PR2a, PR3a, and PR4 were printed only on unwatermarked paper. Nos. PR2 and PR3 exist on unwatermarked and watermarked paper.

Nos. PR2 and PR3 exist in coarse and (after 1874) in fine print, like the contemporary postage stamps.

The reprints of the 4kr brown are of type II and on a smooth toned paper.

Issue date: 4kr, Nov. 1.

See Lombardy-Venetia for the 1kr in black and the 2kr, 4fk in red.

NT3

NT4

1877 Redrawn

PR5 NT3 1kr blue 14.00 1.40
a. 1kr pale ultramarine *1,600.*
PR6 NT3 2kr brown 12.50 1.50

In the redrawn stamps the shield is larger and the vertical bar has eight lines above the white square and nine below, instead of five.

Nos. PR5 and PR6 exist also watermarked "WECHSEL" instead of "ZEITUNGS-MARKEN."

1890, June 1

PR7 NT4 1kr brown 9.00 1.00
PR8 NT4 2kr green 10.00 1.50

#PR5-PR8 exist with private perforation.

NT5

Perf. 13, 12½

1890, June 1 Wmk. 91

PR9 NT5 25kr carmine 100.00 *425.00*

Nos. PR1-PR9 did not pay postage, but were a fiscal tax, collected by the postal authorities on newspapers.

SPECIAL HANDLING STAMPS

(For Printed Matter Only)
Issues of the Monarchy

Mercury SH1

1916 Unwmk. *Perf. 12½*

QE1 SH1 2h claret, *yel* .60 *1.60*
QE2 SH1 5h dp green, *yel* .60 *1.60*
Set, never hinged 3.50

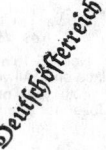

SH2

1917 *Perf. 12½*

QE3 SH2 2h claret, *yel* .20 .30
a. Pair, imperf. between 175.00 *250.00*
b. Perf. 11½x12½ 55.00 *95.00*
c. Perf. 12½x11½ 80.00 *150.00*
d. Perf. 11½ 1.10 *2.50*
QE4 SH2 5h dp green, *yel* .20 .30
a. Pair, imperf. between 160.00 *250.00*
b. Perf. 11½x12½ 45.00 *87.50*
c. Perf. 12½x11½ 70.00 *125.00*
d. Perf. 11½ 1.10 *2.50*
Set, never hinged .60

Nos. QE1-QE4 exist imperforate.

Issues of the Republic

Nos. QE3 and QE4 Overprinted

Deutschösterreich

1919

QE5 SH2 2h claret, *yel* .20 .20
a. Inverted overprint 325.00
b. Perf. 11½x12½ 5.25 *8.00*
c. Perf. 12½x11½ 65.00 *85.00*
d. Perf. 11½ .30 *.70*
QE6 SH2 5h deep green, *yel* .20 .20
a. Perf. 11½x12½ 2.25 *3.75*
b. Perf. 12½x11½ 25.00 *35.00*
c. Perf. 11½ .20 *.45*
Set, never hinged .40

Nos. QE5 and QE6 exist imperforate.

SH3

Dark Blue Surcharge

1921

QE7 SH3 50h on 2h claret, *yel* .20 *.20*
Never hinged .20
Never hinged .20

SH4

1922 *Perf. 12½*

QE8 SH4 50h lilac, *yel* .20 *.40*
Never hinged .20

#QE5-QE8 exist in vertical pairs, imperf between. No. QE8 exists imperf.

OCCUPATION STAMPS

Issued under Italian Occupation

Issued in Trieste

Austrian Stamps of 1916-18 Overprinted

Regno d'Italia
Venezia Giulia
3. XI. 18.

1918 Unwmk. *Perf. 12½*

N1 A37 3h bright vio 1.00 1.00
a. Double overprint 30.00 30.00
b. Inverted overprint 30.00 30.00
N2 A37 5h light grn 1.00 1.00
a. Inverted overprint 30.00 30.00
c. Double overprint 30.00
N3 A37 6h dp orange 1.40 1.40
N4 A37 10h magenta 4.00 2.50
a. Inverted overprint 30.00 30.00
N5 A37 12h light bl 2.00 2.00
a. Double overprint 30.00 30.00
N6 A42 15h dull red 1.00 1.00
a. Inverted overprint 30.00 30.00
b. Double overprint 30.00 30.00
N7 A42 20h dark green 1.00 1.00
a. Inverted overprint 30.00 30.00
c. Double overprint 67.50
N8 A42 25h deep blue 6.75 6.75
a. Inverted overprint 110.00 110.00
N9 A42 30h dl violet 2.00 2.00
N10 A39 40h olive grn 85.00 85.00
N11 A39 50h dark green 7.00 6.75
N12 A39 60h deep blue 19.00 18.00
N13 A39 80h orange brn 11.00 12.00
a. Inverted overprint —
N14 A39 1k car, *yel* 11.00 12.00
a. Double overprint 67.50
N15 A40 2k light bl 200.00 200.00
Never hinged 400.00
N16 A40 4k yellow grn 400.00 400.00
Never hinged 800.00

Handstamped

N17 A40 10k dp violet *25,000.* *25,000.*
Never hinged *27,500.*

Granite Paper

N18 A40 2k light blue 300.00
Never hinged 600.00
N19 A40 3k car rose 250.00 250.00
Never hinged 500.00
Nos. N1-N14 (14) 153.15 152.40
Set, never hinged, #N1-N14 295.00

Some authorities question the authenticity of No. N18. Counterfeits of Nos. N10, N15-N19 are plentiful.

Italian Stamps of 1901-18 Overprinted

Venezia
Giulia

Wmk. 140 *Perf. 14*

N20 A42 1c brown 1.50 *2.00*
a. Inverted overprint 20.00 20.00
N21 A43 2c orange brn 1.50 *2.00*
a. Inverted overprint 17.00 17.00
N22 A48 5c green .70 *1.00*
a. Inverted overprint 35.00 *35.00*
b. Double overprint 85.00
N23 A48 10c claret .70 *1.00*
a. Inverted overprint 47.50 *47.50*
b. Double overprint 85.00
N24 A50 20c brn orange .90 *1.10*
a. Inverted overprint 67.50 *67.50*
b. Double overprint 85.00 *85.00*
N25 A49 25c blue 1.00 *1.75*
a. Double overprint —
b. Inverted overprint 85.00 *85.00*
N26 A49 40c brown 8.00 *10.00*
a. Inverted overprint *35.00*
N27 A45 45c olive grn 2.50 *3.50*
a. Inverted overprint 95.00 *95.00*
N28 A49 50c violet 3.50 *4.75*
N29 A49 60c brown car 42.50 *55.00*
a. Inverted overprint —
b. Double overprint 190.00
N30 A46 1 l brn & green 14.50 *21.00*
a. Inverted overprint —
Nos. N20-N30 (11) 77.30 *103.10*
Set, never hinged 154.00

Italian Stamps of 1901-18 Surcharged

Venezia
Giulia
5 Heller

N31 A48 5h on 5c green 1.00 *1.50*
Never hinged 2.00
a. "5" omitted 85.00 *85.00*
b. Inverted surcharge 85.00 *85.00*
N32 A50 20h on 20c brn org 1.00 1.50
Never hinged 2.00
a. Double surcharge 85.00 *85.00*

Issued in the Trentino

Austrian Stamps of 1916-18 Overprinted

Regno d Italia
Trentino
3 nov 1918

1918 Unwmk. *Perf. 12½*

N33 A37 3h bright vio 4.00 3.00
a. Double overprint 67.50 *67.50*
b. Inverted overprint 55.00 *55.00*
N34 A37 5h light grn 3.50 1.75
a. "8 nov. 1918" *1,750.*
b. Inverted overprint 55.00 *55.00*
N35 A37 6h dp orange 50.00 40.00
N36 A37 10h magenta 3.50 2.00
a. "8 nov. 1918" 95.00 95.00
N37 A37 12h light blue 125.00 110.00
N38 A42 15h dull red 4.00 3.00
N39 A42 20h dark green 2.00 2.00
a. "8 nov. 1918" 110.00 *110.00*
b. Double overprint 67.50 67.50
c. Inverted overprint 22.50 22.50
N40 A42 25h deep blue 35.00 30.00
N41 A42 30h dl violet 12.00 10.00
N42 A39 40h olive grn 45.00 40.00
N43 A39 50h dark green 27.50 22.50
a. Inverted overprint 110.00 110.00
N44 A39 60h deep blue 40.00 35.00
a. Double overprint 110.00 *110.00*
N45 A39 80h orange brn 55.00 45.00
N46 A39 90h red violet 1,250. 1,000.
N47 A39 1k car, *yel* 55.00 45.00
N48 A40 2k light blue 375.00 275.00
N49 A40 4k yel green *1,750.* *1,500.*
N50 A40 10k dp violet —

Granite Paper

N51 A40 2k light blue *450.00*

Counterfeits of Nos. N33-N51 are plentiful.

Italian Stamps of 1901-18 Overprinted

Venezia
Tridentina

Wmk. 140 *Perf. 14*

N52 A42 1c brown 1.00 3.50
a. Inverted overprint 55.00 55.00
b. Double overprint 55.00
N53 A43 2c orange brn 1.00 3.50
a. Inverted overprint 55.00 55.00
N54 A48 5c green 1.00 3.50
a. Inverted overprint 55.00 55.00
b. Double overprint 55.00 55.00
N55 A48 10c claret 1.00 3.50
a. Inverted overprint 75.00 75.00
b. Double overprint 55.00 55.00
N56 A50 20c brn orange 1.00 3.50
a. Inverted overprint 75.00 75.00
N57 A49 40c brown 55.00 35.00
N58 A45 45c olive grn 25.00 35.00
a. Double overprint 140.00 *140.00*
N59 A49 50c violet 25.00 35.00
N60 A46 1 l brn & green 25.00 35.00
a. Double overprint 140.00 *140.00*
Nos. N52-N60 (9) 135.00 157.50

Italian Stamps of 1906-18 Surcharged

Venezia
Tridentina
5 Heller

N61 A48 5h on 5c green 1.00 *1.75*
N62 A48 10h on 10c claret 1.00 *1.75*
a. Inverted overprint 67.50 *67.50*
N63 A50 20h on 20c brn org 1.00 *1.75*
a. Double surcharge 67.50 *67.50*
Nos. N61-N63 (3) 3.00 *5.25*

General Issue

Italian Stamps of 1901-18 Surcharged

5
centesimi
di corona

1919

N64 A42 1c on 1c brown .90 *1.25*
a. Inverted surcharge 16.00 17.50
N65 A43 2c on 2c org brn .90 *1.25*
a. Double surcharge 175.00
b. Inverted surcharge 13.50 13.50
N66 A48 5c on 5c green .85 .45
a. Inverted surcharge 40.00 40.00
b. Double surcharge 67.50 67.50
N67 A48 10c on 10c claret .90 .45
a. Inverted surcharge 40.00 40.00
b. Double surcharge 67.50 *67.50*

N68 A50 20c on 20c brn org .90 .45
a. Double surcharge 87.50 *87.50*
N69 A49 25c on 25c blue .85 *1.00*
a. Double surcharge 87.50
N70 A49 40c on 40c brown .90 *2.00*
a. "ccrona" 100.00 *100.00*
N71 A45 45c on 45c ol grn .90 *2.00*
a. Inverted surcharge 110.00 110.00
N72 A49 50c on 50c violet .90 *2.00*
N73 A49 60c on 60c brn car .90 *3.00*
a. "00" for "60" 110.00 *110.00*

Surcharged **1 corona**

N74 A46 1cor on 1 l brn & grn 1.75 3.00
Nos. N64-N74 (11) 10.65 16.85

Surcharges similar to these but differing in style or arrangement of type were used in Dalmatia.

OCCUPATION SPECIAL DELIVERY STAMPS

Issued in Trieste

Special Delivery Stamp of Italy of 1903 Overprinted **Venezia Giulia**

1918 Wmk. 140 *Perf. 14*

NE1 SD1 25c rose red 30.00 37.50
Never hinged 60.00
a. Inverted overprint 125.00 125.00

General Issue

Special Delivery Stamps of Italy of 1903-09 Surcharged **25 centesimi di corona**

1919

NE2 SD1 25c on 25c rose 1.10 *1.75*
a. Double surcharge 67.50 *67.50*
NE3 SD2 30c on 30c bl & rose 1.50 *2.50*

OCCUPATION POSTAGE DUE STAMPS

Issued in Trieste

Postage Due Stamps of Italy, 1870-94, Overprinted **Venezia Giulia**

1918 Wmk. 140 *Perf. 14*

NJ1 D3 5c buff & mag .25 .45
a. Inverted overprint 13.50 13.50
b. Double overprint 150.00
NJ2 D3 10c buff & mag .35 .50
a. Inverted overprint 67.50 *67.50*
NJ3 D3 20c buff & mag .75 1.10
a. Double overprint 150.00
b. Inverted overprint 67.50 *67.50*
NJ4 D3 30c buff & mag 2.00 3.00
NJ5 D3 40c buff & mag 22.50 30.00
a. Inverted overprint 200.00 *200.00*
NJ6 D3 50c buff & mag 50.00 67.50
a. Inverted overprint 225.00 *250.00*
NJ7 D3 1 l bl & mag 150.00 200.00
Nos. NJ1-NJ7 (7) 225.85 302.55

General Issue

Postage Due Stamps of Italy, 1870-1903 Surcharged **5 centesimi di corona**

1919

Buff & Magenta

NJ8 D3 5c on 5c .50 .70
a. Inverted overprint 19.00 19.00
NJ9 D3 10c on 10c .50 .70
a. Center and surcharge invtd. 125.00 *125.00*
NJ10 D3 20c on 20c .70 1.00
a. Double overprint 140.00 *140.00*
NJ11 D3 30c on 30c .85 1.50
NJ12 D3 40c on 40c .85 1.50
NJ13 D3 50c on 50c .85 1.50

Surcharged **una corona**

NJ14 D3 1cor on 1 l bl & mag .85 1.50
NJ15 D3 2cor on 2 l bl & mag 45.00 80.00
NJ16 D3 5cor on 5 l bl & mag 45.00 80.00
Nos. NJ8-NJ16 (9) 95.10 168.40

A. M. G. ISSUE FOR AUSTRIA

Catalogue values for unused stamps in this section are for Never Hinged items.

Issued jointly by the Allied Military Government of the US and Great Britain, for civilian use in areas under American, British and French occupation. (Upper Austria, Salzburg, Tyrol, Vorarlberg, Styria and Carinthia).

OS1

1945 Unwmk. Litho. *Perf. 11*

4N1 OS1 1g aquamarine .25 .35
4N2 OS1 3g deep orange .25 .35
4N3 OS1 4g buff .25 .35
4N4 OS1 5g bright green .25 .35
4N5 OS1 6g red violet .35 .35
4N6 OS1 8g rose pink .25 .35
4N7 OS1 10g light gray .35 .35
4N8 OS1 12g pale buff brown .35 .35
4N9 OS1 15g rose red .35 .35
4N10 OS1 20g copper brown .35 .35
4N11 OS1 25g deep blue .25 .35
4N12 OS1 30g bright violet .25 .35
4N13 OS1 40g light ultra .25 .35
4N14 OS1 60g light olive grn .35 .35
4N15 OS1 1s dark violet .35 .45
4N16 OS1 2s yellow .35 .55
4N17 OS1 5s deep ultra .55 .75

For Nos. 4N2, 4N4-4N17 overprinted "PORTO" see Nos. J189-J203.

AUSTRIAN OFFICES ABROAD

These stamps were on sale and usable at all Austrian post-offices in Crete and in the Turkish Empire.

100 Centimes = 1 Franc

OFFICES IN CRETE

Used values are italicized for stamps often found with false cancellations.

Stamps of Austria of 1899-1901 Issue, Surcharged in Black:

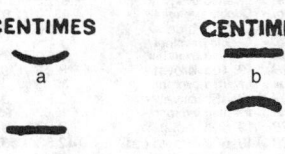

CENTIMES
a

CENTIMES
b

CENTIMES
c

FRANC
d

1903-04 Unwmk. *Perf. 12½, 13½*

On Nos. 73a, 75a, 77a, 81a

Granite Paper

With Varnish Bars

1 A15(a) 5c on 5h blue green 1.40 3.50
2 A16(b) 10c on 10h rose .80 *3.75*
3 A16(b) 25c on 25h ultra 30.00 22.50
4 A17(c) 50c on 50h gray blue 7.50 *110.00*

On Nos. 83, 83a, 84, 85

Without Varnish Bars

5 A18(d) 1fr on 1k car rose 2.00 *100.00*
a. 1fr on 1k carmine 4.00 —
b. Horiz. or vert. pair, imperf. between 175.00
6 A18(d) 2fr on 2k ('04) 8.50 *225.00*
7 A18(d) 4fr on 4k ('04) 10.50 *450.00*
Nos. 1-7 (7) 60.70

Surcharged on Austrian Stamps of 1904-05

1905

On Nos. 89, 97

Without Varnish Bars

8a A19(a) 5c on 5h blue green 35.00 35.00
9 A20(b) 10c on 10h car .70 *9.00*

On Nos. 89a, 97a, 99a, 103a

With Varnish Bars

8 A19(a) 5c on 5h bl grn 3.50 5.25
9a A20(b) 10c on 10h carmine 18.00 22.50
10 A20(b) 25c on 25h ultra .90 *95.00*
11 A21(b) 50c on 50h dl bl .90 *375.00*

Surcharged on Austrian Stamps and Type of 1906-07

1907 *Perf. 12½, 13½*

Without Varnish Bars

12 A19(a) 5c on 5h yel green (#90) .70 *3.50*
13 A20(b) 10c on 10h car (#92) 1.00 *27.50*
14 A20(b) 15c on 15h vio 1.10 *27.50*
Nos. 12-14 (3) 2.80 *58.50*

A5

A6

1908 Typo. *Perf. 12½*

15 A5 5c green, *yellow* .30 *.60*
16 A5 10c scarlet, *rose* .35 *.80*
17 A5 15c brown, *buff* .45 *4.50*
18 A5 25c dp blue, *blue* 10.50 5.00

Engr.

19 A6 50c lake, *yellow* 1.60 *22.50*
20 A6 1fr brown, *gray* 2.25 *30.00*
a. Vert pair, imperf. btwn. 200.00
Nos. 15-20 (6) 15.45 *63.40*

Nos. 15-18 are on paper colored on the surface only. All values exist imperforate.

60th year of the reign of Emperor Franz Josef, for permanent use.

Paper Colored Through

1914 Typo.

21 A5 10c rose, *rose* 1.50 *900.00*
22 A5 25c ultra, *blue* .60 *110.00*

Nos. 21 and 22 exist imperforate.

OFFICES IN THE TURKISH EMPIRE

From 1863 to 1867 the stamps of Lombardy-Venetia (Nos. 15 to 24) were used at the Austrian Offices in the Turkish Empire.

100 Soldi = 1 Florin
40 Paras = 1 Piaster

Values for unused stamps are for copies with gum. Specimens without gum sell for about one-third or less of the figures quoted.

Used values are italicized for stamps often found with false cancellations.

For similar designs in Kreuzers, see early Austria.

A1

A2

Two different printing methods were used, as in the 1867-74 issues of Austria. They may be distinguished by the coarse or fine lines of the hair and whiskers and by the paper, which is more transparent on the later issue.

1867 Typo. Wmk. 91 *Perf. 9½*

Coarse Print

1 A1 2sld orange 1.75 *22.50*
a. 2sld yellow 50.00 27.50
2 A1 3sld green 100.00 40.00
a. 3sld dark green 125.00 70.00
3 A1 5sld red 90.00 11.00
a. 5sld carmine 110.00 14.50
4 A1 10sld blue 95.00 1.75
a. 10sld light blue 110.00 2.50
b. 10sld dark blue 100.00 3.00
5 A1 15sld brown 16.00 6.50
a. 15sld dark brown 50.00 22.50
b. 15sld reddish brown 17.50 10.00
c. 15sld gray brown 45.00 9.00
6 A1 25sld violet 12.50 *30.00*
a. 25sld brown violet 16.00 *35.00*
b. 25sld gray lilac 50.00 *35.00*
7 A2 50sld brn, perf. 10½ 1.00 *42.50*
a. Perf. 12 80.00 *65.00*
b. Perf. 13 250.00
k. Perf. 9 25.00 *50.00*
l. 50sld pale red brn, perf. 12 55.00 60.00
m. Vert. pair, imperf. btwn. 300.00 *650.00*
n. Horiz. pair, imperf. btwn. 300.00 *750.00*
o. Perf. 10½x9 60.00 100.00

Perf. 9, 9½, 10½ and Compound

1876-83

Fine Print

7C A1 2sld yellow ('83) .20 *1,300.*
7D A1 3sld green ('78) 1.00 *20.00*
7E A1 5sld red ('78) .40 *15.00*
7F A1 10sld blue 65.00 1.00
7I A1 15sld org brn ('81) 9.00 *125.00*
7J A1 25sld gray lilac ('83) .50 *275.00*
Nos. 7C-7J (6) 76.10

The 10 soldi has been reprinted in deep dull blue, perforated 10½.

A3

1883 *Perf. 9½, 10, 10½*

8 A3 2sld brown .20 *110.00*
9 A3 3sld green 1.00 *25.00*
10 A3 5sld rose .20 *16.00*
11 A3 10sld blue .75 .50
12 A3 20sld gray, perf. 10 1.00 *60.00*
a. Perf. 9½ 5.00 6.75
13 A3 50sld red lilac 1.40 *16.00*
Nos. 8-13 (6) 4.55

No. 9 Surcharged **10 PARA 10**

10 PARAS ON 3 SOLDI:

Type I - Surcharge 16½mm across. "PARA" about ½mm above bottom of "10." 2mm space between "10" and "P"; 1½mm between "A" and "10." Perf. 9½ only.

Type II - Surcharge 15¼ to 16mm across. "PARA" on same line with figures or slightly higher or lower. 1½mm space between "10" and "P"; 1mm between "A" and "10." Perf. 9½ and 10.

1886 *Perf. 9½ and 10*

14 A3 10pa on 3sld green, type II .30 *5.50*
a. Surcharge type I 170.00 325.00
b. Inverted surcharge, type I *1,850.*

Same Surcharge on Austria Nos. 42-46

1888

15 A11 10pa on 3kr grn 3.00 7.50
a. "01 PARA 10" *400.00*
16 A11 20pa on 5kr rose .50 *7.25*
17 A11 1pi on 10kr blue 45.00 1.10
a. Perf. 13½ 225.00
b. Double surcharge 275.00
18 A11 2pi on 20kr gray 1.50 4.00
19 A11 5pi on 50kr vio 2.00 *15.00*
Nos. 15-19 (5) 52.00

Austria Nos. 52-55, 58, 61 Surcharged **10 PARA 10**

1890-92 Unwmk. *Perf. 9 to 13½*
Granite Paper

20 A12 8pa on 2kr brn ('92) .20 *.50*
a. Perf. 9½ 10.00 *13.50*
21 A12 10pa on 3kr green .65 .50
22 A12 20pa on 5kr rose .25 *.50*
23 A12 1pi on 10kr ultra .35 .20
24 A12 2pi on 20kr ol grn 5.50 *25.00*
25 A12 5pi on 50kr violet 11.00 *60.00*
Nos. 20-25 (6) 17.95

See note after Austria No. 65 on missing numerals, etc.

Austria Nos. 66, 69 Surcharged **2 PIASTER 2**

1891 *Perf. 10 to 13½*
26 A14 2pi on 20kr green 4.25 1.25
a. Perf. 9½ 110.00 70.00
27 A14 5pi on 50kr violet 2.50 2.50

Two types of the surcharge on No. 26 exist.

Austria Nos. 62-65 Surcharged **10 PIAST. 10**

1892 *Perf. 10½, 11½*
28 A13 10pi on 1gld blue 10.00 22.50
29 A13 20pi on 2gld car 12.00 35.00
a. Double surcharge

1896 *Perf. 10½, 11½, 12½*
30 A13 10pi on 1gld pale lilac 12.00 19.00
31 A13 20pi on 2gld gray grn 37.50 60.00

Austria Nos. 73, 75, 77, 81, 83-85 Surcharged

10 PARA 10 #32-35 **5 PIASTER 5** #36-38

Perf. 10½, 12½, 13½ and Compound
1900
Without Varnish Bars

32 A15 10pa on 5h bl grn 4.00 .80
33 A16 20pa on 10h rose 5.00 .75
b. Perf. 12½x10½ 250.00 85.00
34 A16 1pi on 25h ultra 3.00 .25
35 A17 2pi on 50h gray bl 7.25 3.25
36 A18 5pi on 1k car rose 1.00 .30
a. 5pi on 1k carmine 1.10 .90
b. Horiz. or vert. pair, imperf. btwn. 110.00
37 A18 10pi on 2k gray lil 2.50 2.25
38 A18 20pi on 4k gray grn 2.00 *6.00*
Nos. 32-38 (7) 24.75 *13.60*

In the surcharge on Nos. 37 and 38 "piaster" is printed "PIAST."

1901
With Varnish Bars

32a A15 10pa on 5h blue green 1.75 2.25
33a A16 20pa on 10h rose 2.25 *160.00*
34a A16 1pi on 25h ultra 1.50 .45
35a A17 2pi on 50h gray blue 3.25 5.25
Nos. 32a-35a (4) 8.75

A4

A5

A6

1906 *Perf. 12½ to 13½*
Without Varnish Bars

39 A4 10pa dark green 11.00 2.50
40 A5 20pa rose .80 .65
41 A5 1pi ultra .35 .25
42 A6 2pi gray blue .80 .65
Nos. 39-42 (4) 12.95 4.05

1903 With Varnish Bars

39a A4 10pa dark green 4.25 1.50
40a A5 20pa rose 2.25 .40
41a A5 1pi ultra 1.60 .25
42a A6 2pi gray blue 125.00 2.25

1907
Without Varnish Bars

43 A4 10pa yellow green .50 *1.25*
45 A5 30pa violet .50 *2.75*

A7

A8

1908 Typo. *Perf. 12½*
46 A7 10pa green, *yellow* .20 *.25*
47 A7 20pa scarlet, *rose* .25 .25
48 A7 30pa brown, *buff* .30 *.50*
49 A7 1pi deep bl, *blue* 11.00 .20
50 A7 60pa vio, *bluish* .55 *3.00*

Engr.
51 A8 2pi lake, *yellow* .35 .20
52 A8 5pi brown, *gray* .60 *.80*
53 A8 10pi green, *yellow* .80 *1.50*
54 A8 20pi blue, *gray* 1.50 *3.50*
Nos. 46-54 (9) 15.55 *10.20*

Nos. 46-50 are on paper colored on the surface only. 60th year of the reign of Emperor Franz Josef I, for permanent use. All values exist imperforate.

1913-14 Typo.
Paper Colored Through
57 A7 20pa rose, *rose* ('14) .70 *325.00*
58 A7 1pi ultra, *blue* .35 *.45*

Nos. 57 and 58 exist imperforate.

POSTAGE DUE STAMPS

Type of Austria D2 Surcharged **10 PARA**

Black Surcharge

1902 Unwmk. *Perf. 12½, 13½*
J1 D2 10pa on 5h green 1.10 2.75
J2 D2 20pa on 10h green 1.10 2.75
J3 D2 1pi on 20h green 1.75 3.25
J4 D2 2pi on 40h green 1.75 3.25
J5 D2 5pi on 100h green 2.75 2.75
Nos. J1-J5 (5) 8.45 14.75

Shades of Nos. J1-J5 exist, varying from yellowish green to dark green.

D3

1908 Typo. *Perf. 12½*
J6 D3 ¼pi green 2.50 5.50
J7 D3 ½pi green 1.40 *5.50*
J8 D3 1pi green 1.50 *5.50*
J9 D3 1½pi green .80 *11.00*
J10 D3 2pi green 1.75 *13.50*
J11 D3 5pi green 3.25 *8.00*
J12 D3 10pi green 16.00 *100.00*
J13 D3 20pi green 16.00 *110.00*
J14 D3 30pi green 13.00 11.50
Nos. J6-J14 (9) 56.20 *270.50*

Nos. J6-J14 exist in distinct shades of green and on thick chalky, regular and thin ordinary paper. Values are for the least expensive variety. No. J6-J14 exist imperforate.
Forgeries exist.

LOMBARDY-VENETIA

Formerly a kingdom in the north of Italy forming part of the Austrian Empire. Milan and Venice were the two principal cities. Lombardy was annexed to Sardinia in 1859, and Venetia to the kingdom of Italy in 1866.

100 Centesimi = 1 Lira
100 Soldi = 1 Florin (1858)

Unused examples without gum of Nos. 1-24 are worth approximately 20% of the values given, which are for stamps with original gum as defined in the catalogue introduction.

For similar designs in Kreuzers, see early Austria.

Coat of Arms — A1

15 CENTESIMI:
Type I- "5" is on a level with the "1." One heavy line around coat of arms center.
Type II- As type I, but "5" is a trifle sideways and is higher than the "1."
Type III- As type II, but two, thinner, lines around center.
45 CENTESIMI:
Type I- Lower part of "45" is lower than "Centes." One heavy line around coat of arms center. "45" varies in height and distance from "Centes."
Type II- One heavy line around coat of arms center. Lower part of "45" is on a level with lower part of "Centes."
Type III- As type II, but two, thinner, lines around center.

Wmk. K.K.H.M. in Sheet or Unwmkd.
1850 Typo. *Imperf.*
Thick to Thin Paper

1 A1 5c buff 2,500. 125.00
a. Printed on both sides 8,500. 225.00
b. 5c yellow 5,000. 425.00
c. 5c orange 2,600. 225.00
d. 5c lemon yellow 1,400.
3 A1 10c black 2,400. 125.00
a. 10c gray black 2,400. 125.00
4 A1 15c red, type III 1,200. 5.00
b. 15c red, type I 2,500. 20.00
c. Ribbed paper, type II — 750.00
d. Ribbed paper, type I 11,500. 190.00
f. 15c red, type II 1,300. 20.00
5 A1 30c brown 3,000. 12.50
a. Ribbed paper 5,000. 125.00
6 A1 45c blue, type III 10,500. 30.00
a. 45c blue, type I 11,000. 47.50
b. Ribbed paper, type I — 400.00
c. 45c blue, type II — 90.00

1854
Machine-made Paper, Type III
3c A1 10c black 6,250. 225.00
4g A1 15c pale red 700.00 3.50
5b A1 30c brown 3,250. 9.50
6d A1 45c blue 8,250. 42.50

See note about the paper of the 1850 issue of Austria. *The reprints are type III, in brighter colors.*

A2

A3

A4

A5

A6

Two Types of Each Value.
Type I- Loops of the bow at the back of the head broken.
Type II- Loops complete. Wreath projects further at top of head.

1858-62 Embossed *Perf. 14½*
7 A2 2s yel, type II 650.00 110.00
a. 2s yellow, type I 4,000. 600.00
8 A3 3s black, type II 6,500. 150.00
a. 3s black, type I 2,500. 275.00
b. Perf. 16, type I 1,100.
c. Perf. 15x16 or 16x15, type I *4,750.* 400.00
9 A3 3s grn, type II ('62) 550.00 100.00
10 A4 5s red, type II 275.00 5.00
a. 5s red, type I 875.00 12.50
b. Printed on both sides, type II *6,000.*
11 A5 10s brown, type II 2,000. 11.00
a. 10s brown, type I 500.00 42.50
12 A6 15s blue, type II 2,250. 24.00
a. 15s blue, type I 4,000. 100.00
b. Printed on both sides, type II *15,000.*

The reprints are of type II and are perforated 10½, 11, 11½, 12, 12½ and 13. There are also imperforate reprints of Nos. 7-9.

A7

A8

1861-62 *Perf. 14*
13 A7 5s red 2,750. 3.00
14 A7 10s brown ('62) 4,000. 30.00

The reprints are perforated 9, 9 ½, 10½, 11, 12, 12½ and 13. There are also imperforate reprints of the 2 and 3s.
The 2, 3 and 15s of this type exist only as reprints.

1863
15 A8 2s yellow 150.00 150.00
16 A8 3s green 2,250. 100.00
17 A8 5s rose 2,750. 15.00
18 A8 10s blue 5,000. 85.00
19 A8 15s yellow brown 3,500. 140.00

1864-65 Wmk. 91 *Perf. 9½*
20 A8 2s yellow ('65) 200.00 *500.00*
21 A8 3s green 30.00 21.00
22 A8 5s rose 4.50 3.00
23 A8 10s blue 30.00 9.00
24 A8 15s yellow brown 275.00 100.00

Nos. 15-24 reprints are perforated 10½ and 13. There are also imperforate reprints of the 2s and 3s.

NEWSPAPER TAX STAMPS

From 1853 to 1858 the Austrian Newspaper Tax Stamp 2kr green (No. PR1) was also used in Lombardy-Venetia, at the value of 10 centesimi.

NT1

Type I - The banderol of the left eagle touches the beak of the eagle.
Type II - The banderol does not touch the beak.

1858-59 Unwmk. Typo. *Imperf.*

PR1	NT1	1kr black, type I ('59)	3,200.	*3,200.*
PR2	NT1	2kr red, type II ('59)	325.00	60.00
PR3	NT1	4kr red, type I	*100,000.*	*3,500.*

No. PR2 exists with watermark 91.
The reprints are on a smooth toned paper and are all of type II.

AZERBAIJAN

ˌa-zər-ˌbī-ˈjän

(Azerbaidjan)

LOCATION — Southernmost part of Russia in Eastern Europe, bounded by Georgia, Dagestan, Caspian Sea, Iran and Armenia
GOVT. — A Soviet Socialist Republic
AREA — 33,430 sq. mi.
POP. — 7,908,224 (1999 est)
CAPITAL — Baku

With Armenia and Georgia, Azerbaijan made up the Transcaucasian Federation of Soviet Republics.

Stamps of Azerbaijan were replaced in 1923 by those of Transcaucasian Federated Republics. desc>With the breakup of the Soviet Union on Dec. 26, 1991, Azerbaijan and ten former Soviet republics established the Commonwealth of Independent States.

100 Kopecks = 1 Ruble
100 Giapiks = 1 Manat (1992)

Catalogue values for unused stamps in this country are for Never Hinged items, beginning with Scott 350 in the regular postage section.

National Republic

Standard Bearer
A1

Farmer at Sunset
A2

Baku — A3

Temple of Eternal Fires — A4

1919 Unwmk. Litho. *Imperf.*

1	A1	10k multicolored	.20	.30
2	A1	20k multicolored	.20	.30
3	A2	40k green, yellow & blk	.20	.30
4	A2	60k red, yellow & blk	.25	.30
5	A2	1r blue, yellow & blk	.35	.50
6	A3	2r red, bister & blk	.35	.50
7	A3	5r blue, bister & blk	.45	.85
8	A3	10r olive grn, bis & blk	.65	.95
9	A4	25r blue, red & black	1.10	*9.00*
10	A4	50r ol grn, red & black	1.40	1.75
		Nos. 1-10 (10)	5.15	*14.75*

The two printings of Nos. 1-10 are distinguished by the grayish or thin white paper. Both have yellowish gum. White paper copies are worth five times the above values.
For surcharges see Nos. 57-64, 75-80.

Soviet Socialist Republic

Symbols of Labor — A5

Oil Well — A6

Bibi Eibatt Oil Field — A7

Khan's Palace, Baku — A8

Globe and Workers
A9

Maiden's Tower, Baku
A10

Goukasoff House
A11

Blacksmiths
A12

Hall of Judgment, Baku — A13

1922

15	A5	1r gray green	.20	*.35*
16	A6	2r olive black	.50	*.50*
17	A7	5r gray brown	.20	*.35*
18	A8	10r gray	.50	*.65*
19	A9	25r orange brown	.20	*.40*
20	A10	50r violet	.20	*.40*
21	A11	100r dull red	.35	*.50*
22	A12	150r blue	.35	*.50*
23	A9	250r violet & buff	.35	*.50*
24	A13	400r dark blue	.35	*.50*
25	A12	500r gray vio & blk	.35	*.50*
26	A13	1000r dk blue & rose	.35	*.60*
27	A8	2000r blue & black	.35	*.50*
28	A7	3000r brown & blue	.35	*.50*
a.		Tete beche pair	15.00	15.00
29	A11	5000r black, *ol grn*	.60	*.75*
		Nos. 15-29 (15)	5.20	*7.50*

Counterfeits exist of Nos. 1-29. They generally sell for more than genuine copies.
For overprints and surcharges see Nos. 32-41, 43, 45-55, 65-72, 300-304, 307-333.

Nos. 15, 17, 23, 28, 27 Handstamped from Metal Dies in a Numbering Machine

15000

1922

32	A5	10,000r on 1r	8.00	8.00
33	A7	15,000r on 5r	9.50	*10.00*
34	A9	33,000r on 250r	5.00	5.00
35	A7	50,000r on 3000r	5.00	5.00
36	A8	66,000r on 2000r	11.00	10.00
		Nos. 32-36 (5)	38.50	38.00

Same Surcharges on Regular Issue and Semi-Postal Stamps of 1922

1922-23

36A	A7	500r on 5r	60.00	*67.50*
37	A6	1000r on 2r	15.00	15.00
38	A8	2000r on 10r	5.00	4.00
39	A8	5000r on 2000r	5.00	3.00
40	A11	15,000r on 5000r	12.00	10.00
41	A5	20,000r on 1r	10.00	9.00
42	SP1	25,000r on 500r	35.00	
43	A7	50,000r on 5r	12.50	12.50
44	SP2	50,000r on 1000r	26.00	
45	A11	50,000r on 5000r	5.00	4.50
45A	A8	60,000r on 2000r	12.50	*14.00*
46	A11	70,000r on 5000r	20.00	20.00
47	A6	100,000r on 2r	15.00	15.00
48	A8	200,000r on 10r	10.00	10.00
49	A9	200,000r on 25r	15.00	15.00
50	A7	300,000r on 3000r	5.00	5.00
51	A8	500,000r on 2000r	15.00	10.00

Revalued

52	A7	500r on #33	*200.00*	*200.00*
53	A11	15,000r on #46	*200.00*	*200.00*
54	A7	300,000r on #35	*200.00*	*200.00*
55	A8	500,000r on #36	*200.00*	*200.00*

The surcharged semi-postal stamps were used for regular postage.

Same Surcharges on Stamps of 1919

57	A1	25,000r on 10k	.70	*1.00*
58	A1	50,000r on 20k	.70	*1.00*
59	A2	75,000r on 40k	1.75	*2.50*
60	A2	100,000r on 60k	.70	*.95*
61	A2	200,000r on 1r	.70	*.95*
62	A3	300,000r on 2r	.95	*1.10*
63	A3	500,000r on 5r	1.00	*1.10*
64	A2	750,000r on 40k	3.50	*2.75*
		Nos. 57-64 (8)	10.00	*11.35*

Handstamped from Settings of Rubber Type in Black or Violet

100000 **200.000**
Nos. 65-66, 71-80 Nos. 67-70

On Stamps of 1922

65	A6	100,000r on 2r	12.00	12.00
66	A8	200,000r on 10r	13.00	*14.00*
67	A8	200,000r on 10r (V)	17.50	15.00
68	A9	200,000r on 25r (V)	15.00	11.00
a.		Black surcharge	26.00	*27.50*
69	A7	300,000r on 3000r (V)	25.00	25.00
70	A8	500,000r on 2000r (V)	20.00	20.00
a.		Black surcharge	27.50	*29.00*
72	A11	1,500,000r on 5000r (V)	16.00	15.00
a.		Black surcharge	16.00	15.00

On Stamps of 1919

75	A1	50,000r on 20k	1.00	
76	A2	75,000r on 40k	.65	
77	A2	100,000r on 60k	1.25	
78	A2	200,000r on 1r	.20	.20
79	A3	300,000r on 2r	1.00	
80	A3	500,000r on 5r	1.25	

Inverted and double surcharges of Nos. 32-80 sell for twice the normal price.
Counterfeits exist of Nos. 32-80.

Baku Province

Regular and Semi-Postal Stamps of 1922 Handstamped in Violet or Black

БАКИНСКОИ П. К.

The overprint reads "Bakinskoi P(ochtovoy) K(ontory)," meaning Baku Post Office.

1922 Unwmk. *Imperf.*

300	A5	1r gray green	*35.00*
301	A7	5r gray brown	*35.00*
302	A12	150r blue	*35.00*
303	A9	250r violet & buff	*35.00*
304	A13	400r dark blue	*35.00*
305	SP1	500r blue & pale blue	*35.00*
306	SP2	1000r brown & bister	*35.00*
307	A8	2000r blue & black	*35.00*
308	A7	3000r brown & blue	*35.00*
309	A11	5000r black, *ol grn*	*35.00*
		Nos. 300-309 (10)	*350.00*

Stamps of 1922 Handstamped in Violet

БАКИНСКАГО Г-П-Т.О.№1

Ovpt. reads: Baku Post, Telegraph Office No. 1.

1924

Overprint 24x2mm

312	A12	150r blue	*30.00*
313	A9	250r violet & buff	*30.00*
314	A13	400r dark blue	*30.00*
317	A8	2000r blue & black	*30.00*
318	A7	3000r brown & blue	*30.00*
319	A11	5000r black, *ol grn*	*30.00*

Overprint 30x3½mm

323	A12	150r blue	*30.00*
324	A9	250r violet & buff	*30.00*
325	A13	400r dark blue	*30.00*
328	A8	2000r blue & black	*30.00*
329	A7	3000r brown & blue	*30.00*
330	A11	5000r black, *ol grn*	*30.00*

Overprinted on Nos. 32-33, 35

331	A5	10,000r on 1r	*30.00*
332	A7	15,000r on 5r	*30.00*
333	A7	50,000r on 3000r	*30.00*
		Nos. 312-333 (15)	*450.00*

The overprinted semipostal stamps were used for regular postage.
A 24x2mm handstamp on #17, B1-B2, and 30x3½mm on #15, 17, B1-B2, was of private origin.

Catalogue values for unused stamps in this section, from this point to the end of the section, are for Never Hinged items.

Flag, Map — A20

Unwmk.

1992, Mar. 26 Litho. *Perf. 14*

350	A20	35k multicolored	*1.25*	1.25

Park — A21

1992, May 7 *Perf. 12*

351	A21	25g on 15k multicolored	.25	.25
a.		Booklet pane of 12	3.00	
		Complete booklet, #351a	3.00	
352	A21	35g on 15k multicolored	.30	.30
353	A21	50g on 15k multicolored	.40	.40
354	A21	1.50m on 15k multicolored	1.25	1.25
355	A21	2.50m on 15k multicolored	2.25	2.25
		Nos. 351-355 (5)	4.45	4.45

Nos. 351-355 are overprinted or sucharged on a National Park series prepared for the Soviet Union with one stamp for each republic. Not issued without surcharge. Value, $4.
For additional surcharges see Nos. 435, 501-504.

Azerbaijan stamps can be mounted in the annual Scott Russia album part 1 or Azerbaijan supplement.

Iran-Azerbaijan Telecommunications — A21a

1992 Photo. *Perf. 13x13½*
355A A21a 15g multicolored 1.60 1.60

See Iran No. 2544.
For surcharges see Nos. 403-406.

Horses A22

1993, Feb. 1 Litho. *Perf. 13*
356 A22 20g shown .20 .20
357 A22 30g Kabarda .20 .20
358 A22 50g Qarabair .20 .20
359 A22 1m Don .20 .20
360 A22 2.50m Yakut .45 .45
361 A22 5m Orlov 1.00 1.00
362 A22 10m Diliboz 2.00 2.00
Nos. 356-362 (7) 4.25 4.25

Perf. 12½
Souvenir Sheet
362A A22 8m Qarabag .65 .65

For overprints see Nos. 629-636.

Maiden's Tower — A23 Government Building — A24

1992-93 Litho. *Perf. 12½x12*
363 A23 10g blk & blue grn .20 .20
365 A23 20g black & red .20 .20
367 A23 50g black & blue grn .20 .20
368 A23 50g black & yellow .35 .35
370 A23 1m black & rose lilac .20 .20
372 A23 1.50m black & blue 1.00 1.00
373 A23 2.50m black & yellow .35 .35
374 A23 5m black & green .65 .65
Nos. 363-374 (8) 3.15 3.15

Issued: 10g, 20g, 1.50m, #367, Dec. 20; #368, 1m, 2.50m, 5m, June 20, 1993.
For surcharges see Nos. 550-557.
This is an expanding set. Numbers may change.

1993, Oct. 12 Litho. *Perf. 12½*
375 A24 25g yellow & black .20 .20
376 A24 30g green & black .20 .20
377 A24 50g blue & black .25 .25
378 A24 1m red & black .50 .50
Nos. 375-378 (4) 1.15 1.15

For surcharges see No. 407-414.

Flowers — A25

1993, Aug. 12 Litho. *Perf. 12½*
379 A25 25g Tulipa eichleri .20 .20
380 A25 50g Puschkinia scilloides .20 .20
381 A25 1m Iris elegantissima .20 .20
382 A25 1.50m Iris acutiloba .25 .25
383 A25 5m Tulipa florenskyii .80 .80
384 A25 10m Iris reticulata 1.50 1.50
Nos. 379-384 (6) 3.15 3.15

Souvenir Sheet
Perf. 13
385 A25 10m Muscari elecostomum 1.50 1.50

No. 385 contains one 32x40mm stamp.

Fish A26

25g, Acipenser guldenstadti. 50g, Acipenser stellatus. 1m, Rutilus frisii kutum. 1.50m, Rutilus rutilus caspicus. 5m, Salmo trutta caspius. No. 391, Alosa kessleri. #392, Huso huso.

1993, Aug. 27 *Perf. 12½*
386 A26 25g multicolored .20 .20
387 A26 50g multicolored .20 .20
388 A26 1m multicolored .20 .20
389 A26 1.50m multicolored .25 .25
390 A26 5m multicolored .80 .80
391 A26 10m multicolored 1.50 1.50
Nos. 386-391 (6) 3.15 3.15

Souvenir Sheet
Perf. 13
392 A26 10m multicolored 1.50 1.50

No. 392 contains one 40x32mm stamp.

Pres. Heydar A. Aliyev — A27

Design: No. 394, Map of Nakhichevan.

1993, Sept. 12 Litho. *Perf. 12½x13*
393 A27 25m multicolored 1.00 1.00
394 A27 25m multicolored 1.00 1.00
a. Pair, #393-394 2.00 2.00
b. Souv. sheet, #393-394, perf. 12 25.00
c. Souv. sheet, #393-394, perf. 12 4.00

Name on map spelled "Naxcivan" on #394c. It is spelled "Haxcivan" on #394-394b.
No. 394c issued Sept. 20, 1993.

Historic Buildings, Baku — A28

Style of tombs: 2m, Fortress, 13th-14th cent. 4m, Moorish gate, 15th cent. 8m, Oriental-style columns, 15th cent.

1994, Jan. 17 Litho. *Perf. 11*
395 A28 2m red, silver & black .20 .20
396 A28 4m green, silver & black .35 .35
397 A28 8m blue, silver & black .75 .75
Nos. 395-397 (3) 1.30 1.30

A29 A30

1994, Jan. 17 *Perf. 12½*
398 A29 5m Natl. Colors, Star, Crescent .45 .45
399 A29 8m Natl. coat of arms .75 .75

1994, Jan. 17 *Perf. 12½*
400 A30 10m multi + label .60 .60

Mohammed Fizuli (1494-1556), poet.

Mammed Amin Rasulzade (1884-1955), 1st President A31

Jalil Mamedkulizade, Writer, 125th Birth Anniv. — A32

1994, May 21 *Perf. 12½, 13 (#402)*
401 A31 15m black, yellow & brown 1.00 1.00
402 A32 20m black, blue & gold 1.00 1.00

No. 402 printed se-tenant with label.

No. 355A Surchaged

2 m.

1994, Jan. 18 Photo. *Perf. 13x13½*
403 A21a 2m on 15g .20 .20
404 A21a 20m on 15g .35 .35
405 A21a 25m on 15g .45 .45
406 A21a 50m on 15g 1.00 1.00
Nos. 403-406 (4) 2.00 2.00

5 m.

Nos. 375-378 Surcharged

1994, Feb. 22 Litho. *Perf. 12½*
407 A24 5m on 1m #375 .20 .20
408 A24 10m on 30g #377 .20 .20
409 A24 15m on 30g #377 .20 .20
a. Pair, #408-409 .30 .30
410 A24 20m on 50g #378 .25 .25
411 A24 25m on 1m #375 .30 .30
a. Pair, #407, 411 .45 .45
412 A24 40m on 50g #378 .40 .40
a. Pair, #410, 412 .65 .65
413 A24 50m on 25g #376 .50 .50
414 A24 100m on 25g #376 1.00 1.00
a. Pair, #413-414 1.50 1.50
Nos. 407-414 (8) 3.05 3.05

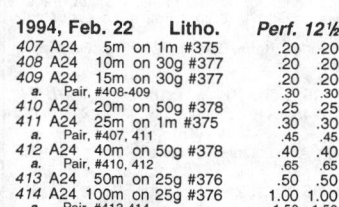

Baku Oil Fields — A33

Designs: 15m, Temple of Eternal Fires. 20m, Oil derricks. 25m, Early tanker. 50m, Ludwig Nobel, Robert Nobel, Petr Bilderling, Alfred Nobel.

1994, June 10 Photo. *Perf. 13*
415 A33 15m multicolored .30 .30
416 A33 20m multicolored .40 .40
417 A33 25m multicolored .45 .45
418 A33 50m multicolored 1.00 1.00
a. Souvenir sheet of 1 1.00 1.00
Nos. 415-418 (4) 2.15 2.15

See Turkmenistan Nos. 39-43.

Minerals — A34 Posthorn — A35

1994, June 15 Litho. *Perf. 13*
419 A34 5m Laumontite .30 .30
420 A34 10m Epidot calcite .55 .55
421 A34 15m Andradite .80 .80
422 A34 20m Amethyst 1.10 1.10
a. Souvenir sheet, #420-423 + 2 labels, perf. 12 2.75 2.75
Nos. 419-422 (4) 2.75 2.75

1994 Litho. *Perf. 12½*
426 A35 5m black & red .20 .20
427 A35 10m black & green .20 .20
428 A35 20m black & blue .20 .20
429 A35 25m black & yellow .25 .25
431 A35 40m black & brown .40 .40
Nos. 426-431 (5) 1.25 1.25

For surcharges see Nos. 487-489A.

400 м.

No. 351 Surcharged

25q

Unwmk.
1994, Oct. 17 Litho. *Perf. 12*
435 A21 400m on 25g multi .85 .85

Souvenir Sheet

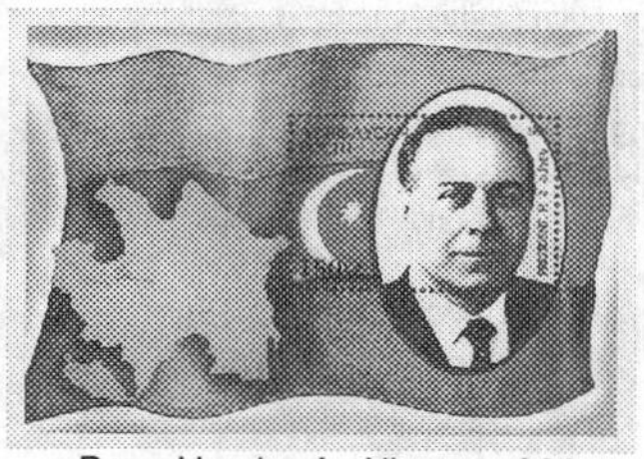

Pres. Heydar A. Aliyev — A36

Illustration reduced.

1994, Oct. 28 Litho. *Perf. 14*
436 A36 150m multicolored 2.25 2.25

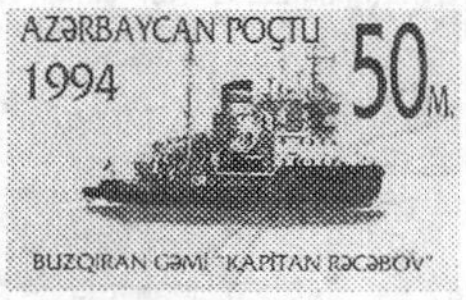

Ships of the Caspian Sea A37

Designs: a, Tugboat, "Captain Racebov." b, "Azerbaijan." c, Balt Ro Ro line, "Merkuri I." d, Tanker, "Tovuz." e, Tanker.

1994, Oct. 28
437 A37 50m Strip of 5, #a.-e. 1.75 1.75

Issued in sheets of 15 stamps. The background of the sheet shows a nautical chart, giving each stamp a different background.

1994 World Cup Soccer Championships, US — A38

Various soccer plays. Denominations: 5m, 10m, 20m, 25m, 30m, 50m, 80m.

1994, June 17 Litho. *Perf. 13*

438-444 A38 Set of 7		3.50	3.50

Souvenir Sheet

445 A38 100m multicolored		1.50	1.50

No. 445 contains one 32x40mm stamp and is a continuous design.

Dinosaurs — A39

Designs: 5m, Coelophysis, segisaurus. 10m, Pentaceratops, tyrannosaurids. 20m, Segnosaurus, oviraptor. 25m, Albertosaurus, corythosaurus. 30m, Iguanodons. 50m, Stegosaurus, allosaurus. 80m, Tyrannosaurus, saurolophus.
100m, Phobetor.

1994, Sept. 15

446-452 A39 Set of 7	3.50	3.50

Souvenir Sheet
Perf. 12½

453 A39 100m multicolored	1.50	1.50

No. 453 contains one 40x32mm stamp and is a continuous design.

Lyrurus Mlokosiewickzi — A40

a, 50m, Female on nest. b, 80m, Female on mountain cliff. c, 100m, 2 males. d, 120m, Male.

1994, Dec. 15 Litho. *Perf. 12½*

454 A40 Block of 4, #a.-d.	3.25	3.25

World Wildlife Fund.

Raptors A41

Designs: 10m, Haliaeetus albicilla. 15m, Aguila heliaca. 20m, Aguila rapax. 25m, Gypaetus barbatus, vert. 50m, Falco cherrug, vert.
100m, Aguila chrysaetos.

1994, Nov. 15 Litho. *Perf. 13*

458-462 A41 Set of 5	3.50	3.50

Souvenir Sheet
Perf. 12½

463 A41 100m multicolored	1.50	1.50

No. 463 contains one 40x32mm stamp and is a continuous design.

Cats A42

Designs: 10m, Felis libica, vert. 15m, Felis otocolobus, vert. 20m, Felis lyns, vert. 25m, Felis pardus. 50m, Panthera tigrus.
100m, Panthera tigrus adult and cub, vert.

1994, Dec. 14 *Perf. 13*

464-468 A42 Set of 5	3.50	3.50

Souvenir Sheet

469 A42 100m multicolored	1.50	1.50

No. 469 contains one 32x40mm stamp and is a continuous design.
For overprints see Nos. 637-642.

Butterflies A43

Designs: 10m, Parnassius apollo. 25m, Zegris menestho. 50m, Manduca atropos. 60m, Pararge adrastoides.

1995, Jan. 23 Litho. *Perf. 14*

470 A43 10m multicolored	.20	.20
471 A43 25m multicolored	.40	.40
472 A43 50m multicolored	.80	.80
473 A43 60m multicolored	1.00	1.00
a. Souvenir sheet of 4, #470-473	2.50	2.50
Nos. 470-473 (4)	2.40	2.40

Intl. Olympic Committee, Cent. — A44

Designs: No. 474, Pierre de Coubertin. No. 475, Discus. No. 476, Javelin.

1994, Dec. 15 Litho. *Perf. 12*

474-476 A44 100m Set of 3	2.00	2.00

A45 A46

1994 Winter Olympic medalists, Lillehammer: 10m, Aleksei Urnamov, Russia, figure skating, 25, Nancy Kerrigan, US, figure skating. 40m Bonnie Blair, US, speed skating, horiz. 50m, Takanori Kano, Japan, ski jumping, horiz. 80m, Philip Laros, Canada, freestyle skiing. 100m, Four-man bobsled, Germany.
200m, Katja Seizinger, skiing, Germany, vert.

1995, Feb. 10 Litho. *Perf. 14*

478-483 A45 Set of 6	2.00	2.00

Souvenir Sheet

484 A45 200m multicolored	1.75	1.75

1995, Feb. 21

Women in space: No. 485a, Mary Kliv, US. b, Valentina Tereshkova, Russia. c, Tamara Cernigan, US. d, Wendy Lourens, US.
No. 486a, Meg Jamison, US. b, Kitty Coleman, US. c, Ellen Sulman, US. d, M.I. Weber, US.

Miniature Sheets of 4

485-486 A46 100m each, #a.-d.	2.50

First manned moon landing, 25th anniv. (in 1994).

Nos. 426-428 Surcharged

100 M.

1995 Litho. *Perf. 12½*

487 A35 100m on 5m #426	.20	.20
488 A35 250m on 10m #427	.40	.40
488A A35 400m on 25m No. 429	.50	.50
489 A35 500m on 20m #428	.65	.65
489A A35 900m on 40m No. 431	1.10	1.10
Nos. 487-489A (5)	2.85	2.85

Issued: #488A, 7/7; #487-488, 489, 2/28.

Mushrooms — A47

Designs: 100m, Gymnopilus spectabilis. 250m, Fly agaris. 300m, Lepiota procera. 400m, Hygrophorus spectosus.
500m, Fly agaris, diff.

1995, Sept. 1 Litho. *Perf. 14*

490-493 A47 Set of 4	3.50	3.50

Souvenir Sheet

494 A47 500m multicolored	1.50	1.50

Singapore '95 — A48

Orchids: 100m, Paphiopedilum argus, paphiopedilum barbatum. 250m, Maxillaria picta. 300m, Laeliocattleya. 400m, Dendrobium nobile.
500m, Cattleya gloriette.

1995, Sept. 1

495-498 A48 Set of 4	3.50	3.50

Souvenir Sheet

499 A48 500m multicolored	1.50	1.50

UN, 50th Anniv. A49

Design: 250m, Azerbaijan Pres. Heydar A. Aliyev, UN Sec. Gen. Boutros Boutros-Ghali.

1995, Sept. 15

500 A49 250m multicolored	2.00	2.00

Nos. 352-355 Surcharged

200 M.

1995 Litho. *Perf. 12*

501 A21 200m on 2.50m #355	.30	.30
502 A21 600m on 35g #352	.85	.85
503 A21 800m on 50q #353	1.10	1.10
504 A21 1000m on 1.50m #354	1.40	1.40
Nos. 501-504 (4)	3.65	3.65

Uzeyir Hacibeyov (1885-1948) A50

Design: 400m, Oglu Iskenderov (1895-1965).

1995, June 30 Litho. *Perf. 12x12½*

505 A50 250m silver gray & black	.60	.60
506 A50 400m gold bister & brown	.90	.90

Balloons and Airships A51

100m, First hydrogen balloon, 1784. 150m, 1st motorized balloon, 1883. 250m, First elliptical balloon, 1784. 300m, 1st Scott Baldwin dirigible, 1904. 400m, US Marine balloon, 1917. 500m, Pedal-powered dirigible, 1909.
800m, 1st rigid dirigible designed by Hugo Eckener, 1924.

1995, July 20 Litho. *Perf. 13*

507 A51 100m multi, vert.	.20	.20
508 A51 150m multi, vert.	.30	.30
509 A51 250m multi	.45	.45
510 A51 300m multi	.55	.55
511 A51 400m multi	.75	.75
512 A51 500m multi	.90	.90
Nos. 507-512 (6)	3.15	3.15

Souvenir Sheet

513 A51 800m multicolored	1.50	1.50

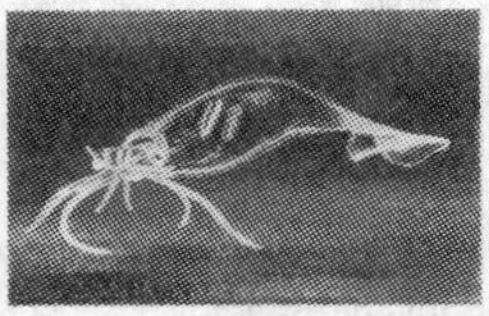

Marine Life A52

50m, Loligo vulgaris. 100m, Orchistoma pileus. 150m, Pegea confoederata. 250m, Polyorchis karafutoensis. 300m, Agalma okeni.
500m, Corolla spectabillis.

1995, June 2 Litho. *Perf. 13*

514 A52 50m multi	.20	.20
515 A52 100m multi	.40	.40
516 A52 150m multi	.50	.50
517 A52 250m multi, vert.	.90	.90
518 A52 300m multi, vert.	1.10	1.10
Nos. 514-518 (5)	3.10	3.10

Souvenir Sheet

519 A52 500m multicolored	1.50	1.50

Turtles A53

Designs: 50m, Chelus fimbriatus. 100m, Caretta caretta. 150m, Geochelone pardalis. 250m, Geochelone elegans. 300m, Testudo hermanni.
500m, Macroclemys temmincki.

1995, June 12 Litho. *Perf. 13*

520 A53 50m multicolored	.20	.20
521 A53 100m multicolored	.40	.40
522 A53 150m multicolored	.50	.50
523 A53 250m multicolored	.90	.90
524 A53 300m multicolored	1.10	1.10
Nos. 520-524 (5)	3.10	3.10

Souvenir Sheet

525 A53 500m multicolored	1.50	1.50

1998 World Cup Soccer Championships, France — A54

Various soccer plays.

1995, Sept. 30 Litho. *Perf. 12½*

526 A54 100m orange & multi	.40	.40
527 A54 150m green & multi	.60	.60
528 A54 250m yellow orange & multi	.90	.90
529 A54 300m yellow & multi	1.10	1.10
530 A54 400m blue & multi	1.50	1.50
Nos. 526-530 (5)	4.50	4.50

Souvenir Sheet
Perf. 13

531 A54 600m multicolored 2.25 2.25

Domestic Cats — A55

1995, Oct. 30 ***Perf. 12½***

532 A55 100m Persian .20 .20
533 A55 150m Chartreux .30 .30
534 A55 250m Somali .45 .45
535 A55 300m Longhair Scottish fold .55 .55
536 A55 400m Cumric .75 .75
537 A55 500m Turkish angora .90 .90
Nos. 532-537 (6) 3.15 3.15

Souvenir Sheet

538 A55 800m Birman 1.50 1.50

No. 538 contains one 32x40mm stamp.

Fauna and Flora — A56

Designs: 100m, Horse. 200m, Muscari elecostomum, vert. 250m, Huso huso. 300m, Aquila chrysaetos. 400m, Panthera tigrus. 500m, Lyrurus miokosiewickzi, facing right. 1000m, Lyrurus miokosiewickzi, facing left.

1995, Nov. 30

539 A56 100m multicolored .20 .20
540 A56 200m multicolored .30 .30
541 A56 250m multicolored .30 .30
542 A56 300m multicolored .40 .40
543 A56 400m multicolored .50 .50
544 A56 500m multicolored .60 .60
545 A56 1000m multicolored 1.50 1.50
Nos. 539-545 (7) 3.80 3.80

John Lennon (1940-80) A57

1995, Dec. 8 ***Perf. 14½***

546 A57 500m multicolored .60 .60

Issued in sheet of 16 plus label.

Miniature Sheet

Locomotives — A58

Designs: No. 547a, 4-4-0, America. b, J3 Hudson, US. c, 2-8-2. d, 2-6-2, Germany. e, 2-8-2, Germany. f, 2-6-2, Italy. g, G-C5, Japan. h, 2-10-2 QJ, China. i, 0-10-0, China.
500m, Electric passenger train, vert.

1996, Feb. 1 ***Perf. 14***

547 A58 100m Sheet of 9, #a.-i. 6.00 6.00

Souvenir Sheet

548 A58 500m multicolored 3.00 3.00

Dr. M. Topcubasov, Surgeon — A59

1996, Feb. 1

549 A59 300m multicolored 1.50 1.50

Nos. 363, 365, 367-368, 370, 372-374 Surcharged

250 м.

1995, Jan. 4 Litho. ***Perf. 12½x12***

550 A23 250m on 10g #363 .40 .40
551 A23 250m on 20g #365 .40 .40
552 A23 250m on 50g #368 .40 .40
553 A23 250m on 1.50m #372 .40 .40
554 A23 500m on 50g #367 .75 .75
555 A23 500m on 1m #370 .75 .75
556 A23 500m on 2.50m #373 .75 .75
557 A23 500m on 5m #374 .75 .75
Nos. 550-557 (8) 4.60 4.60

1996 Olympic Games, Atlanta A60

1996, Apr. 9 Litho. ***Perf. 14***

568 A60 50m Carl Lewis .20 .20
569 A60 100m Muhammed Ali .40 .40
570 A60 150m Li Ning .60 .60
571 A60 200m Said Aouita .80 .80
572 A60 250m Olga Korbut 1.00 1.00
573 A60 300m Nadia Comaneci 1.25 1.25
574 A60 400m Greg Louganis 1.50 1.50
Nos. 568-574 (7) 5.75 5.75

Souvenir Sheet

575 A60 500m Nazim Hüseynov, vert. 2.00 2.00

Husein Aliyev (1911-91), Artist — A61

Paintings: 100m, Water bird, swamp. 200m, Landscape.

1996, Apr. 16 Litho. ***Perf. 14***

576 A61 100m multicolored .75 .75
577 A61 200m multicolored 1.50 1.50
a. Pair, #576-577 + label 2.25 2.25

No. 577a issued in sheets of 6 stamps.

Resid Behbudov (1915-89), Singer — A62

1996, Apr. 22 ***Perf. 12½***

578 A62 100m multicolored 1.25 1.25

A63

A64

1996, Mar. 20

579 A63 250m multicolored 1.25 1.25

Novruz Bayrami, natl. holiday.

1996, May 28 Litho. ***Perf. 14***

580 A64 250m multicolored 1.25 1.25

Independence, 5th anniv.

A65

A66

1996, Apr. 22 Litho. ***Perf. 12½***

581 A65 100m multicolored 1.25 1.25

Yusif Memmedeliyev (1905-95), chemist.

1996, June 7 ***Perf. 14***

Jerusalem, 3000th Anniv.: a, 100m, Wailing Wall. b, 250m, Inside cathedral. c, 300m, Dome of the Rock.
500m, Windmill.

582 A66 Sheet of 3, #a.-c. 3.50 3.50

Souvenir Sheet

583 A66 500m multicolored 3.00 3.00

For overprints see Nos. 643-644.

Dogs A67

Designs: 50m, German shepherd. 100m, Basset hound. 150m, Collie. 200m, Bull terrier. 300m, Boxer. 400m, Cocker spaniel.
500m, Sharpei.

1996, June 18 ***Perf. 13***

584-589 A67 Set of 6 5.00 5.00

Souvenir Sheet

590 A67 500m multicolored 2.50 2.50

Birds — A68

Designs: 50m, Tetraenura regia. 100m, Coliuspasser macrourus. 150m, Oriolus xanthornus. 200m, Oriolus oriolus. 300m, Sturnus vulgaris. 400m, Serinus mozambicus.
500m, Merops apiaster.

1996, June 19 ***Perf. 13***

591-596 A68 Set of 6 5.00 5.00

Souvenir Sheet

597 A68 500m multicolored 2.50 2.50

Roses — A69

Designs: 50m, Burgundy. 100m, Virgo. 150m, Rose gaujard. 200m, Luna. 300m, Lady rose. 400m, Landora.
500m, Lougsor, horiz.

1996, June 19

598-603 A69 Set of 6 5.00 5.00

Souvenir Sheet

604 A69 500m multicolored 2.50 2.50

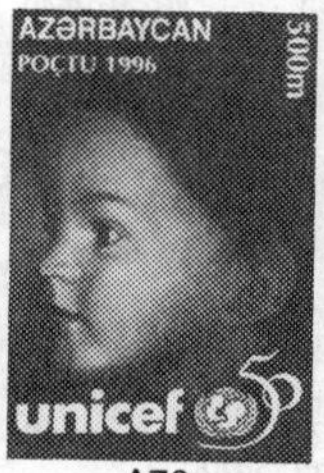

A70

A71

1996, July 8 Litho. ***Perf. 14***

605 A70 500m multicolored 1.25 1.25

UNICEF, 50th anniv.

1996, July 22

Competing teams: 100m, Spain, Bulgaria. 150m, Romania, France. 200m, Czech Republic, Germany. 250m, England, Israel. 300m, Croatia, Turkey. 400m, Italy, Russia.
500m, Trophy cup.

606-611 A71 Set of 6 3.25 3.25

Souvenir Sheet

612 A71 500m multicolored 1.50 1.50

Euro '96, European Soccer Championships, Great Britain.

Ships A72

Ship, home country: 100m, Chinese junk. 150m, Danmark, Denmark. 200m, Nippon Maru, Japan. 250m, Mircea, Romania. 300m, Kruzenshtern, Russia. 400m, Ariadne, Germany.
500m, Tovarishch, Russia, vert.

1996, Aug. 26 Litho. ***Perf. 14***

613-618 A72 Set of 6 4.00 4.00

Souvenir Sheet

619 A72 500m multicolored 3.00 3.00

For overprints see Nos. 645-651.

Baxram Gur Kills a Dragon, Sculpture — A73

1997, Mar. 6 Litho. ***Perf. 13½x13***

620 A73 250m black & yellow .45 .45
621 A73 400m black & vermilion .60 .60
622 A73 500m black & green .75 .75
623 A73 1000m black & purple 1.50 1.50
Nos. 620-623 (4) 3.30 3.30

See No. 671.

Famous Personalities — A74

Designs: No. 624, Mamed-Kerim Ogli Aliyev (1897-1962), politician. No. 625, Illyas Efendiyev (1914-96), writer. No. 626, Fatali Xan-Xoyskiy (1875-1920), politician. No. 627, Nariman Narimanov (1870-1925), politician, writer.

1997, Mar. 25 Litho. *Perf. 14*

Background Color

624 A74 250m tan	1.10	1.10
625 A74 250m gray blue	1.10	1.10
626 A74 250m pale red	1.10	1.10
627 A74 250m pale olive	1.10	1.10
Nos. 624-627 (4)	4.40	4.40

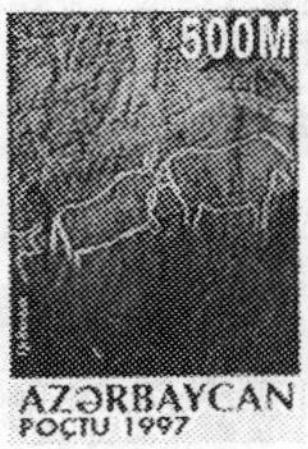

Qobustan Prehistoric Art — A75

Rock carvings: a, Oxen. b, Large horned animals. c, Six figures.

1997, May 19 Litho. *Perf. 14*

628 A75 500m Sheet of 3, #a.-c.	4.25	4.25

For overprint see No. 674.

#356-362A, 464-469 Ovptd. in Red

Red Cross

1997, June 2 Litho. *Perf. 13*

Denominations as Before

629-635 A22 Set of 7	*8.00*	*8.00*

Souvenir Sheet

636 A22 8m multicolored	*5.00*	*5.00*

Location of overprint varies. No. 636 is ovptd. both on stamp and in sheet margin.

1997, June 2

Denominations as Before

637-641 A42 Set of 5	*6.00*	*6.00*

Souvenir Sheet

642 A42 100m multicolored	*5.00*	*5.00*

Location of overprint varies. No. 642 is ovptd. both on stamp and in sheet margin.

Nos. 582-583, 613-619 Ovptd.

1997, June 2 *Perf. 14*

643 A66 Sheet of 3, #a.-c.	*5.00*	*5.00*

Souvenir Sheet

644 A66 500m multicolored	*5.00*	*5.00*

Size and location of overprint varies. Overprint appears both on stamp and in sheet margin.

1997, June 2 *Perf. 14*

Denominations as Before

645-650 A72 Set of 6	*5.00*	*5.00*

Souvenir Sheet

651 A72 500m multicolored	*5.00*	*5.00*

Location of overprint varies. No. 651 is ovptd. both on stamp and in sheet margin.

Grimm's Fairy Tales A76

Bremen Musical: No. 652: a, Dog. b, Dancing horse, cat. c, Rooster.
500m, Animals looking through window at treaure chest, man.

1997, July 1 *Perf. 13½x14*

652 A76 250m Sheet of 3, #a.-c.	2.00	2.00

Souvenir Sheet

653 A76 500m multicolored	1.40	1.40

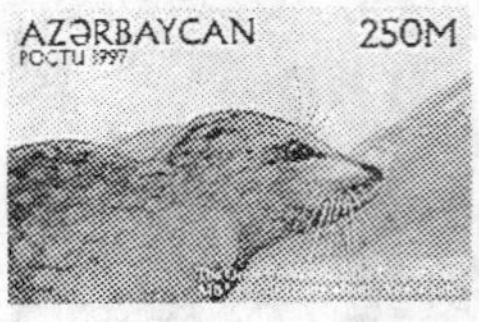

Caspian Seals A77

Designs: a, Seal looking right. b, Mountain top, seal looking forward. c, Seal, seagull. d, Seal looking left. e, Seal looking forward. f, Small seal.
500m, Mother nursing pup.

1997, July 1

654 A77 250m Sheet of 6, #a.-f.	4.25	4.25

Souvenir Sheet

655 A77 500m multicolored	1.40	1.40

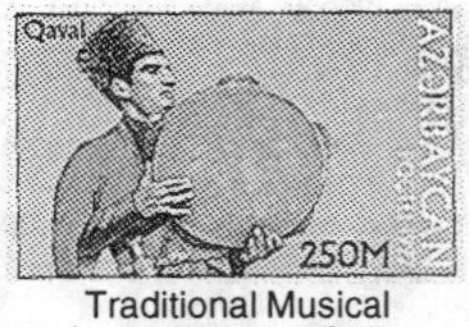

Traditional Musical Instruments — A77a

1997, Aug. 4 Litho. *Perf. 14*

656 A77a 250m Qaval	.75	.75
657 A77a 250m Tanbur	.75	.75
658 A77a 500m Cenq	1.50	1.50
Nos. 656-658 (3)	3.00	3.00

A78

A79

Azerbaijan Oil Industry: a, Early oil derricks, building. b, Off-shore oil drilling platform.

1997, Aug. 18 *Perf. 14½*

Souvenir Sheet

659 A78 500m Sheet of 2, #a.-b.	3.00	3.00

1997, Sept. 12 *Perf. 14x13½*

660 A79 250m Hagani Shirvany, poet	1.00	1.00

No. 660 was issued in sheets of 4 + 5 labels.

Mosques A80

#661, Ashaqi mechet Qovqar-agi, Shusha, 1874-75. #662, Momuna-Zatun, Naxcivan, 1187. #663, Taza-pir, Baku (1905-14).

1997, Sept. 18 Litho. *Perf. 14*

661 A80 250m multicolored	.85	.85
662 A80 250m multicolored	.85	.85
663 A80 250m multicolored	.85	.85
Nos. 661-663 (3)	2.55	2.55

H.C. Rasul Beyov (1917-1984), Communications Official — A81

1997, Oct. 6 Litho. *Perf. 14*

664 A81 250m multicolored	2.00	2.00

1998 World Cup Soccer Championships, France — A82

Winning team photos: No. 665: a, Italy, 1938. b, Argentina, 1986. c, Uruguay, 1980. d, Brazil, 1994. e, England, 1966. f, Germany, 1990.
1500m, Tofiq Bahramov, "Golden Whistle" prize winner, 1966, vert.

1997, Oct. 15

665 A82 250m Sheet of 6, #a.-f.	5.00	5.00

Souvenir Sheet

666 A82 1500m multicolored	4.00	4.00

A83

A84

Figure skaters: No. 667: a, Katarina Witt, Germany. b, Elvis Stojko, Canada. c, Midori Ito, Japan. d, Silhouettes of various winter sports against natl. flag. e, Hand holding Olympic torch. f, Kristi Yamaguchi, US. g, John Curry, England. h, Lu Chen, China.
No. 668, Gordeyeva and Grinkov, Russia.

1997 Litho. *Perf. 14*

667 A83 250m Sheet of 8, #a.-h.	2.50	2.50

Souvenir Sheet

668 A83 500m multicolored	.65	.65

1998 Winter Olympic Games, Nagano.

1998, Feb. 4 *Perf. 13½*

Diana, Princess of Wales (1961-97): No. 669, Wearing black turtleneck. No. 670, Wearing violet dress.

669 A84 400m multicolored	.50	.50
670 A84 400m multicolored	.50	.50

Nos. 669-670 were each issued in sheets of 6.

Sculpture Type of 1997

1998, Mar. 23 Litho. *Perf. 13½x13*

671 A73 100m black & bright pink	1.00	1.00

Hasan Aliyev, Ecologist, 90th Birth Anniv. A85

1998, Apr. 3 *Perf. 14*

672 A85 500m multicolored	1.00	1.00

Souvenir Sheet

Pres. Heydar Aliyev, 75th Birthday — A86

Illustration reduced.

1998, May 10 *Perf. 13½*

673 A86 500m multicolored	2.00	2.00

No. 628 Ovptd.

1998, May 13 *Perf. 14*

674 A75 500m Sheet of 3, #a.-c.	4.00	4.00

Additional inscription in sheet margin reads "ISRAEL 98 - WORLD STAMP EXHIBITION / TEL-AVIV 13-21 MAY 1998."

Musicians A87

#675, Gara Garayev. #676, Ashig Hasgar. #677, Sayid Mohammadhusein.

1998, June 7 Litho. *Perf. 14*

675 A87 250m multicolored	.50	.50
676 A87 250m multicolored	.50	.50
677 A87 250m multicolored	.50	.50
Nos. 675-677 (3)	1.50	1.50

Bul-Bul, Singer, Birth Cent. — A88

1998, July 7

678 A88 500m multicolored	1.00	1.00

Disney Characters at World Rapid Chess Championship A89

250m, Minnie, Mickey.
No. 679: a, Minnie, Mickey. b, Goofy. c, Donald. d, Pluto. e, Minnie. f, Daisy. g, Goofy, Donald. h, Mickey.
#680, Donald, Mickey. #681, Minnie, Mickey.

1998 ***Perf. 13½***

678A	A89	250m multicolored	.50	.50

Perf. 13½x14

679	A89	500m Sheet of 8, #a.-h.	8.00	8.00

Souvenir Sheets

680-681	A89	4000m each	8.00	8.00

Issued: 250m, 12/28; others, 11/13.

New Year Holiday A90

Europa: 1000m, Woman rolling dough. 3000m, Men performing at holiday festival.

1998, Dec. 29 Litho. ***Perf. 13x12½***

682	A90	1000m multicolored	.50	.50
683	A90	3000m multicolored	1.50	1.50

Nos. 682-683 Ovptd. 

1999, Apr. 27 Litho. ***Perf. 13x12½***

684	A90	1000m on #682	.50	.50
685	A90	3000m on #683	1.50	1.50

National Parks — A91

Europa: 1000m, Rose flamingo, Gizilagach Natl. Park. 3000m, Deer, Girkan Natl. Park.

1999, Apr. 28 ***Perf. 12½x12¾***

686	A91	1000m multicolored	.50	.50
687	A91	3000m multicolored	1.50	1.50

Towers — A92

Designs: 1000m, Dord Kundge, 14th cent. 3000m, Danravy, 13th cent.

1999, Aug. 3 Litho. ***Perf. 11¼x11¾***

688	A92	1000m black & blue	.45	.45
689	A92	3000m black & red	1.40	1.40

A93

A95

A94

Naxçivan Autonomous Republic, 75th anniv.: a, Pres. Heydar Aliyev, flag. b, Map of Naxçivan.

1999, Oct. 9 ***Perf. 12***

690	A93	1000m Pair, #a.-b.	.90	.90
c.		Souvenir sheet, pair, #a.-b.	.90	.90

1999, Oct. 20 ***Perf. 12½x12***

691	A94	250m multicolored	.20	.20

Gafar Gabbarli (1899-1934), playwright.

Souvenir Sheet

Perf. 14¾x14½ (a), 14½x13¾ (b-d)

1999, Oct. 30

80th anniv. of Azerbaijan postage stamps: a, #1. b, #3. c, #7. d, #10. b-d horiz.

692	A95	500m Sheet of 4, #a.-d.	1.00	1.00

SEMI-POSTAL STAMPS

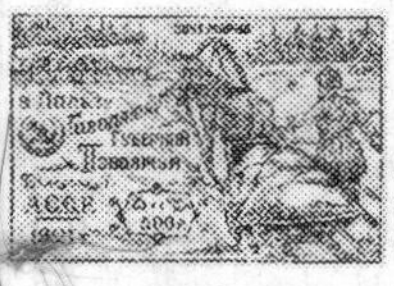

Carrying Food to Sufferers SP1

1922 Unwmk. ***Imperf.***

B1	SP1	500r blue & pale blue	.40	.75

For overprint and surcharge see Nos. 42, 305.

Widow and Orphans — SP2

1922

B2	SP2	1000r brown & bister	.50	1.25

Counterfeits exist.

For overprint and surcharge see Nos. 44, 306.

Russian stamps of 1909-18 were privately overprinted as above in red, blue or black by a group of Entente officers working with Russian soldiers returning from Persia. Azerbaijan was not occupied by the Allies. There is evidence that existing covers (some seemingly postmarked at Baku, dated Oct. 19, 1917, and at Tabriz, Russian Consulate, Apr. 25, 1917) are fakes.

AIR POST STAMP

Catalogue values for all stamps in this section are for never hinged items.

Eagle — AP1

1995, Oct. 16 Litho. ***Perf. 14***

C1	AP1	2200m multicolored	2.00	2.00

AZORES

'ā-ˌzōrz

LOCATION — Group of islands in the North Atlantic Ocean, due west of Portugal
GOVT. — Integral part of Portugal, former colony
AREA — 922 sq. mi.
POP. — 253,935 (1930)
CAPITAL — Ponta Delgada

Azores stamps were supplanted by those of Portugal in 1931.

1000 Reis = 1 Milreis
100 Centavos = 1 Escudo (1912)

See Portugal for other recent issues.

Stamps of Portugal Overprinted in Black or Carmine

AÇORES AÇORES
a

A second type of this overprint has a broad "O" and open "S."

1868 Unwmk. ***Imperf.***

1	A14	5r black	*3,250.*	*1,750.*
2	A14	10r yellow	*13,500.*	*7,500.*
3	A14	20r bister	250.00	125.00
4	A14	50r green	250.00	125.00
5	A14	80r orange	250.00	125.00
6	A14	100r lilac	250.00	125.00

The reprints are on thick chalky white wove paper, ungummed, and on thin ivory paper with shiny white gum. Value $20 each.

1868-70 ***Perf. 12½***

5 REIS:
Type I - The "5" at the right is 1mm from end of label.
Type II - The "5" is 1½mm from end of label.

7	A14	5r black (C)	70.00	50.00
8	A14	10r yellow	90.00	50.00
a.		Inverted overprint	*250.00*	*150.00*
9	A14	20r bister	70.00	45.00
10	A14	25r rose	70.00	8.00
a.		Inverted overprint	*200.00*	*200.00*
11	A14	50r green	200.00	140.00
12	A14	80r orange	200.00	140.00
13	A14	100r lilac	200.00	140.00
14	A14	120r blue	175.00	90.00
15	A14	240r violet	600.00	300.00

The reprints are on thick chalky white paper ungummed, perf 13½, and on thin ivory paper with shiny white gum, perf 13½. Value $10 each.

1871-75 ***Perf. 12½, 13½***

21	A15	5r black (C)	12.50	6.00
a.		Inverted overprint	*47.50*	*30.00*
23	A15	10r yellow	27.50	20.00
a.		Inverted overprint	*150.00*	*150.00*
24	A15	20r bister	25.00	19.00
25	A15	25r rose	16.00	3.00
a.		Inverted overprint	*100.00*	*100.00*
b.		Double overprint	35.00	25.00
c.		Perf. 14	165.00	55.00
d.		Dbl. impression of stamp	60.00	60.00
26	A15	50r green	80.00	30.00
27	A15	80r orange	110.00	50.00
28	A15	100r lilac	90.00	45.00
a.		Perf. 14	165.00	100.00
29	A15	120r blue	165.00	95.00
a.		Inverted overprint	*400.00*	*350.00*
30	A15	240r violet	800.00	500.00

Nos. 21-29 exist with overprint "b."

The reprints are of type "b." They are on thick chalky white paper ungummed, perf 13½, and also on thin white paper with shiny white gum and perforated 13½.

Overprinted in Black

AÇORES
b

1875-80

15 REIS:
Type I - The figures of value, 1 and 5, at the right in upper label are close together.
Type II - The figures of value at the right in upper label are spaced.

31	A15	10r blue green	175.00	100.00
32	A15	10r yellow green	100.00	60.00
33	A15	15r lilac brown	17.50	12.00
a.		Inverted overprint	*125.00*	
34	A15	50r blue	150.00	60.00
35	A15	150r blue	160.00	100.00
36	A15	150r yellow	200.00	175.00
37	A15	300r violet	80.00	50.00

The reprints have the same papers, gum and perforations as those of the preceding issue.

Black Overprint

1880 ***Perf. 12½, 13½***

38	A17	25r gray	125.00	30.00
39	A18	25r red lilac	50.00	6.00
a.		25r gray	50.00	6.00
b.		Double overprint		

Overprinted in Carmine or Black

1881-82

40	A16	5r black (C)	21.00	7.50
41	A23	25r brown ('82)	45.00	5.00
a.		Double overprint		
42	A19	50r blue	150.00	30.00
		Nos. 40-42 (3)	216.00	42.50

Reprints of Nos. 38, 39, 39a, 40 and 42 have the same papers, gum and perforations as those of preceding issues.

Overprinted in Red or Black

AÇORES
c

1882-85 ***Perf. 11½, 12½, 13½***

15, 20 REIS
Type I - The figures of value are some distance apart and close to the end of the label.
Type II - The figures are closer together and farther from the end of the label. On the 15 reis this is particularly apparent in the upper right figures.

43	A16	5r black (R)	25.00	10.00
44	A21	5r slate	15.00	3.00
a.		Double overprint	75.00	40.00
c.		Inverted overprint	60.00	40.00
45	A15	10r green	75.00	50.00
a.		Inverted overprint	200.00	150.00
46	A22	10r green	25.00	10.00
a.		Double overprint	90.00	50.00
47	A15	15r lilac brn	65.00	35.00
b.		Inverted overprint	125.00	100.00
48	A15	20r bister	90.00	50.00
a.		Inverted overprint	175.00	150.00
49	A15	20r carmine	125.00	80.00
a.		Double overprint	165.00	100.00
50	A23	25r brown	19.00	3.00
51	A15	50r blue	*2,500.*	*2,000.*
52	A24	50r blue	24.00	3.00
a.		Double overprint	100.00	100.00
53	A15	80r yellow	70.00	40.00
a.		80r orange	110.00	70.00
b.		Double overprint	175.00	125.00
54	A15	100r lilac	55.00	35.00
55	A15	150r blue	*1,000.*	*750.00*
56	A15	150r yellow	100.00	60.00
57	A15	300r violet	100.00	60.00

Reprints of the 1882-85 issues have the same papers, gum and perforations as those of preceding issues.

Red Overprint

58	A21	5r slate	20.00	4.00
59	A24a	500r black	160.00	110.00
60	A15	1000r black	125.00	85.00

1887 Black Overprint

61	A25	20r pink	25.00	10.00
a.		Inverted overprint	100.00	50.00
b.		Double overprint	50.00	40.00
62	A26	25r lilac rose	25.00	2.00
a.		Inverted overprint	100.00	50.00
b.		Double ovpt., one invtd.	100.00	50.00
63	A26	25r red violet	25.00	2.00
a.		Double overprint	60.00	40.00
64	A24a	500r red violet	125.00	75.00
a.		Perf. 13½	400.00	200.00
		Nos. 61-64 (4)	200.00	89.00

Nos. 58-64 inclusive have been reprinted on thin white paper with shiny white gum and perforated 13½.

Prince Henry the Navigator Issue

Portugal Nos. 97-109 Overprinted

AÇORES

1894, Mar. 4 ***Perf. 14***

65	A46	5r orange yel	3.00	2.00
a.		Inverted overprint	*45.00*	*45.00*
66	A46	10r violet rose	3.00	2.00
a.		Double overprint	50.00	40.00
b.		Inverted overprint	50.00	40.00
67	A46	15r brown	3.50	2.50
68	A46	20r violet	3.50	2.50
a.		Double overprint	50.00	40.00
69	A47	25r green	4.00	3.00
a.		Double overprint	*50.00*	*50.00*
b.		Inverted overprint	*50.00*	*50.00*
70	A47	50r blue	10.00	4.25
71	A47	75r dp carmine	20.00	6.00

72 A47 80r yellow grn 21.00 6.00
73 A47 100r lt brn, *pale buff* 21.00 5.00
a. Double overprint 100.00 75.00
74 A48 150r lt car, *pale rose* 30.00 10.00
75 A48 300r dk bl, *sal buff* 40.00 17.50
76 A48 500r brn vio, *pale lil* 60.00 25.00
77 A48 1000r gray blk, *yelsh* 125.00 45.00
a. Double overprint 500.00 400.00
Nos. 65-77 (13) 344.00 130.75

St. Anthony of Padua Issue

Portugal Nos. 132-146 Overprinted in Red or Black AÇORES

1895, June 13 ***Perf. 12***

78 A50 2½r black (R) 2.50 1.50
79 A51 5r brown yel 8.00 2.00
80 A51 10r red lilac 8.00 2.50
81 A51 15r red brown 12.50 4.00
82 A51 20r gray lilac 12.50 5.00
83 A51 25r green & vio 8.00 2.75
84 A52 50r blue & brn 25.00 14.00
85 A52 75r rose & brn 25.00 25.00
86 A52 80r lt green & brn 40.00 25.00
87 A52 100r choc & blk 50.00 25.00
88 A53 150r vio rose & bis 80.00 65.00
89 A53 200r blue & bis 100.00 60.00
90 A53 300r slate & bis 125.00 70.00
91 A53 500r vio brn & grn 200.00 100.00
92 A53 1000r violet & grn 400.00 200.00
Nos. 78-92 (15) 1,096. 601.75

7th cent. of the birth of Saint Anthony of Padua.

Common Design Types pictured following the introduction.

Vasco da Gama Issue

Common Design Types

1898, Apr. 1 ***Perf. 14, 15***

93 CD20 2½r blue green 3.00 .80
94 CD21 5r red 3.00 1.00
95 CD22 10r gray lilac 5.00 2.00
96 CD23 25r yellow green 5.00 2.00
97 CD24 50r dark blue 8.00 6.00
98 CD25 75r violet brown 16.00 9.00
99 CD26 100r bister brown 20.00 9.00
100 CD27 150r bister 32.50 18.00
Nos. 93-100 (8) 92.50 47.80

For overprints and surcharges see Nos. 141-148.

King Carlos — A28

King Manuel II — A29

1906 **Typo.** ***Perf. 11½x12***

101 A28 2½r gray .40 .20
a. Inverted overprint *25.00* *25.00*
102 A28 5r orange yel .40 .20
a. Inverted overprint *25.00* *25.00*
103 A28 10r yellow grn .40 .20
104 A28 20r gray vio .50 .30
105 A28 25r carmine .40 .20
106 A28 50r ultra 4.50 3.00
107 A28 75r brown, *straw* 1.50 *.80*
108 A28 100r dk blue, *bl* 1.50 *.90*
109 A28 200r red lilac, *pnksh* 1.50 *1.00*
110 A28 300r dk blue, *rose* 5.00 *3.25*
111 A28 500r black, *blue* 11.00 8.00
Nos. 101-111 (11) 27.10 18.05

"Acores" and letters and figures in the corners are in red on the 2½, 10, 20, 75 and 500r and in black on the other values.

1910, Apr. 1 ***Perf. 14x15***

112 A29 2½r violet .25 .20
113 A29 5r black .25 .20
114 A29 10r dk green .30 .25
115 A29 15r lilac brn .40 .50
116 A29 20r carmine .45 .45
117 A29 25r violet brn .25 .20
a. Perf. 11½ 1.25 .80
118 A29 50r blue 1.00 .70
119 A29 75r bister brn 1.75 1.25
120 A29 80r slate 1.75 1.25
121 A29 100r brown, *lt grn* 2.25 1.75
122 A29 200r green, *sal* 2.25 1.75
123 A29 300r black, *blue* 3.50 2.50
124 A29 500r olive & brown 7.00 7.00
125 A29 1000r blue & black 12.00 12.00
Nos. 112-125 (14) 33.40 30.00

The errors of color 10r black, 15r dark green, 25r black and 50r carmine are considered to be proofs.

Stamps of 1910 Overprinted in Carmine or Green

REPUBLICA

1910

126 A29 2½r violet .20 .20
a. Inverted overprint 9.00 9.00
127 A29 5r black .20 .20
a. Inverted overprint 9.00 9.00
128 A29 10r dk green .20 .20
a. Inverted overprint 9.00 9.00
129 A29 15r lilac brn .80 .65
a. Inverted overprint 9.00 9.00
130 A29 20r carmine (G) 1.00 .80
a. Inverted overprint 16.00 16.00
b. Double overprint 16.00 16.00
131 A29 25r violet brn .25 .20
a. Perf. 11½ 40.00 30.00
132 A29 50r blue .60 .50
133 A29 75r bister brn .35 .20
a. Double overprint 9.00 9.00
134 A29 80r slate .45 .35
135 A29 100r brown, *grn* .40 .25
136 A29 200r green, *sal* .60 *.60*
137 A29 300r black, *blue* 1.25 1.25
138 A29 500r olive & brn 1.25 *1.75*
139 A29 1000r blue & blk 3.50 *4.00*
Nos. 126-139 (14) 11.05 *11.15*

Vasco da Gama Issue Overprinted or Surcharged in Black:

REPUBLICA
d

REPUBLICA REPUBLICA

REIS 15 REIS 1$000
e f

1911 ***Perf. 14, 15***

141 CD20(d) 2½r blue green .35 .30
142 CD21(e) 15r on 5r red .20 .20
143 CD23(d) 25r yellow grn .40 .25
144 CD24(d) 50r dk blue 1.00 .70
145 CD25(d) 75r violet brn .60 .60
146 CD27(e) 80r on 150r bister .60 .60
147 CD26(d) 100r yellow brn .60 .60
a. Double surcharge 35.00 35.00
148 CD22(f) 1000r on 10r lilac 8.50 6.50
Nos. 141-148 (8) 12.25 9.75

Postage Due Stamps of Portugal Overprinted or Surcharged in Black "ACORES" and

REPUBLICA

REPUBLICA Rs 300 Rs

1911 ***Perf. 12***

149 D1 5r black .75 .35
150 D1 10r magenta 1.75 1.25
a. "Acores" double 20.00 20.00
151 D1 20r orange 2.00 2.00
152 D1 200r brn, *buff* 7.25 6.00
a. "Acores" inverted
153 D1 300r on 50r slate 7.25 6.00
154 D1 500r on 100r car, *pink* 7.25 6.00
Nos. 149-154 (6) 26.25 21.60

Ceres Issue of Portugal Overprinted in Black or Carmine

AÇORES

With Imprint

1912-31 ***Perf. 12x11½, 15x14***

155 A64 ¼c olive brown .20 .20
a. Inverted overprint 9.00
156 A64 ½c black (C) .20 .20
157 A64 1c deep green .55 .35
a. Inverted overprint 9.00
158 A64 1c deep brown ('18) .20 .20
a. Inverted overprint
159 A64 1½c choc ('13) .50 .40
a. Inverted overprint 9.00
160 A64 1½c deep green ('18) .35 .20
a. Inverted overprint
161 A64 2c carmine .30 .20
a. Inverted overprint 14.00
162 A64 2c orange ('18) .20 .20
a. Inverted overprint 18.00
163 A64 2½c violet .25 .20
164 A64 3c rose ('18) .20 .20
165 A64 3c dull ultra ('25) .20 .20
166 A64 3½c lt green ('18) .30 .20
167 A64 4c lt green ('19) .20 .20
168 A64 4c orange ('30) .25 .20
169 A64 5c dp blue .25 .20
170 A64 5c yellow brn ('18) .25 .20
171 A64 5c olive brn ('23) .20 .20
172 A64 5c black brn ('30) 2.75 2.50
173 A64 6c dull rose ('20) .20 .20
174 A64 6c choc ('25) .20 .20
175 A64 6c red brn ('31) .35 *.80*
176 A64 7½c yel brn 4.75 1.25
177 A64 7½c deep blue ('18) .60 .40
178 A64 8c slate ('13) .55 .20
179 A64 8c blue grn ('22) .25 .20
180 A64 8c orange ('25) .50 .25
181 A64 10c orange brown .30 .20
182 A64 12c blue gray ('20) 1.00 .70
183 A64 12c deep green ('22) .45 .35
184 A64 13½c chlky bl ('20) 1.00 *3.25*
185 A64 14c dk bl, *yel* ('20) 3.25 *6.00*
186 A64 15c plum ('13) .60 .60
187 A64 15c blk (R) ('23) .40 .40
188 A64 16c brt ultra ('24) 1.00 .40
189 A64 16c dp bl ('30) 2.00 *1.50*
190 A64 20c vio brn, *grn* ('13) 8.00 3.25
191 A64 20c choc ('20) .60 .20
192 A64 20c deep green ('23) .80 .80
a. Double overprint 15.00 15.00
193 A64 20c gray ('24) .60 .20
194 A64 24c grnsh bl ('21) .60 .40
195 A64 25c salmon ('23) .30 .20
196 A64 30c brn, *pink* ('13) 40.00 22.50
197 A64 30c brn, *yel* ('19) 4.00 2.25
198 A64 30c gray brn ('21) .80 .65
199 A64 32c dp green ('25) 4.00 1.00
200 A64 36c red ('21) .40 .20
201 A64 40c dp blue ('23) .75 .40
202 A64 40c black brn ('24) .20 .20
203 A64 40c brt green ('30) 1.50 .40
204 A64 48c brt rose ('24) 2.50 1.00
205 A64 48c dull pink ('31) 6.25 6.00
206 A64 50c org, *sal* ('13) 5.25 1.00
207 A64 50c yellow ('23) 1.25 1.00
208 A64 50c bister ('30) 2.50 1.75
209 A64 50c red brn ('31) 2.00 1.50
210 A64 60c blue ('21) 1.00 .70
211 A64 64c pale ultra ('24) 3.00 1.00
212 A64 64c brown rose ('31) 45.00 45.00
213 A64 75c dull rose ('23) 6.00 4.00
214 A64 75c car rose ('30) 2.00 1.25
215 A64 80c dull rose ('21) 1.25 .65
216 A64 80c violet ('24) 1.25 .90
217 A64 80c dk green ('31) 1.50 1.25
218 A64 90c chlky bl ('21) 2.00 .75
219 A64 96c dp rose ('26) 8.25 4.50
220 A64 1e dp grn, *bl* 4.75 1.50
221 A64 1e violet ('21) 2.00 .75
222 A64 1e gray vio ('24) 2.00 1.00
223 A64 1e brn lake ('30) 12.50 10.00
224 A64 1.10e yel brn ('21) 2.00 1.25
225 A64 1.20e yel grn ('21) 2.50 1.00
226 A64 1.20e buff ('24) 5.00 1.75
227 A64 1.25e dk blue ('30) 1.50 .75
228 A64 1.50e blk vio ('23) 3.00 1.75
229 A64 1.50e lilac ('25) 6.00 1.75
230 A64 1.60e dp bl ('25) 2.75 1.75
231 A64 2e slate grn ('21) 4.25 2.00
232 A64 2.40e apple grn ('26) 80.00 50.00
233 A64 3e lilac pink ('26) 80.00 55.00
234 A64 3.20e gray grn ('25) 10.00 4.50
235 A64 5e emerald ('24) 20.00 12.00
236 A64 10e pink ('24) 40.00 20.00
237 A64 20e pale turq ('25) 125.00 75.00
Nos. 155-237 (83) 581.55 369.80

For same overprint on surcharged stamps see Nos. 300-306. For same design without imprint see Nos. 307-313.

Castello-Branco Issue

Stamps of Portugal, 1925, Overprinted in Black or Red AÇORES

1925, Mar. 29 ***Perf. 12½***

238 A73 2c orange .20 *.50*
239 A73 3c green .20 *.50*
240 A73 4c ultra (R) .20 *.50*
241 A73 5c scarlet .20 *.50*
242 A74 10c pale blue .20 *.45*
243 A74 16c red orange .25 *.75*
244 A75 25c car rose .25 *.75*
245 A74 32c green .55 *.80*
246 A75 40c grn & blk (R) .25 *.75*
247 A74 48c red brn 1.25 *2.25*
248 A76 50c blue green .80 *2.25*
249 A76 64c orange brn 1.40 *2.25*
250 A76 75c gray blk (R) 1.00 *3.00*
251 A75 80c brown 1.00 *3.00*
252 A76 96c car rose 1.25 *3.00*
253 A77 1.50e dk bl, *bl* (R) 1.25 *2.25*
254 A75 1.60e indigo (R) 1.25 *2.25*
255 A77 2e dk grn, *grn* (R) 1.50 *3.00*
256 A77 2.40e red, *org* 2.00 *3.25*
257 A77 3.20e blk, *grn* (R) 3.00 *5.00*
Nos. 238-257 (20) 18.00 *37.00*

First Independence Issue

Stamps of Portugal, 1926, Overprinted in Red AÇÔRES

1926, Aug. 13 ***Perf. 14, 14½***

Center in Black

258 A79 2c orange .25 *.70*
259 A80 3c ultra .25 *.70*
260 A79 4c yellow grn .25 *.70*
261 A80 5c black brn .25 *.70*
262 A79 6c ocher .25 *.70*
263 A80 15c dk green .50 *.90*
264 A81 20c dull violet .50 *.90*
265 A82 25c scarlet .50 *.90*
266 A81 32c deep green .50 *.90*
267 A82 40c yellow brn .50 *.90*
268 A82 50c olive bis 1.25 *2.00*
269 A82 75c red brown 1.25 *2.00*
270 A83 1e black violet 1.75 *3.25*
271 A84 4.50e olive green 2.00 *6.75*
Nos. 258-271 (14) 10.00 *22.00*

The use of these stamps instead of those of the regular issue was obligatory on Aug. 13th and 14th, Nov. 30th and Dec. 1st, 1926.

Second Independence Issue

Same Overprint on Stamps of Portugal, 1927, in Red

1927, Nov. 29

Center in Black

272 A86 2c lt brown .25 *.70*
273 A87 3c ultra .25 *.70*
274 A86 4c orange .25 *.70*
275 A88 5c dk brown .25 *.70*
276 A89 6c orange brn .25 *.70*
277 A87 15c black brn .25 *.70*
278 A86 25c gray 1.00 *3.00*
279 A89 32c blue grn 1.00 *3.00*
280 A90 40c yellow grn 1.00 *3.00*
281 A90 96c red 2.50 *5.75*
282 A88 1.60e myrtle grn 2.50 *5.75*
283 A91 4.50e bister 4.50 *8.00*
Nos. 272-283 (12) 14.00 *32.70*

Third Independence Issue

Same Overprint on Stamps of Portugal, 1928, in Red

1928, Nov. 27

Center in Black

284 A93 2c lt blue .25 *.70*
285 A94 3c lt green .25 *.70*
286 A95 4c lake .25 *.70*
287 A96 5c olive grn .25 *.70*
288 A97 6c orange brn .25 *.70*
289 A94 15c slate .40 *1.25*
290 A95 16c dk violet .65 *2.25*
291 A93 25c ultra .65 *2.00*
292 A97 32c dk green .65 *2.00*
293 A96 40c olive brn .65 *2.00*
294 A95 50c red orange 1.25 *3.00*
295 A94 80c lt gray 1.25 *3.00*
296 A97 96c carmine 1.75 *6.00*
297 A96 1e claret 1.75 *6.00*
298 A93 1.60e dk blue 1.75 *6.00*
299 A98 4.50e yellow 4.00 *8.50*
Nos. 284-299 (16) 16.00 *45.50*

A31

A32

1929-30 *Perf. 12x11½, 15x14*
300 A31 4c on 25c pink ('30) .50 .35
301 A31 4c on 60c dp blue .50 .35
302 A31 10c on 25c pink 1.00 .40
303 A31 12c on 25c pink 1.00 .40
304 A31 15c on 25c pink .75 .60
305 A31 20c on 25c pink 1.00 .65
306 A31 40c on 1.10e yel brn 3.50 2.25
Nos. 300-306 (7) 8.25 5.00

Black or Red Overprint

1930 *Perf. 14*

Without Imprint at Foot

307 A32 4c orange .35 .40
308 A32 5c dp brown 1.50 1.00
309 A32 10c vermilion .80 .55
310 A32 15c black (R) .80 .55
311 A32 40c brt green .80 .55
312 A32 80c violet 11.00 8.75
313 A32 1.60e dk blue 1.75 1.00
Nos. 307-313 (7) 17.00 12.80

POSTAGE DUE STAMPS

D2

D3

Portugal Nos. J7-J13 Overprinted in Black

1904 **Unwmk.** *Perf. 12*
J1 D2 5r brown .45 *.65*
J2 D2 10r orange .45 *.65*
J3 D2 20r lilac .85 *1.10*
J4 D2 30r gray green 1.00 *1.10*
 a. Double overprint
J5 D2 40r gray violet 1.75 1.75
J6 D2 50r carmine 2.75 *3.00*
J7 D2 100r dull blue 4.25 *4.50*
Nos. J1-J7 (7) 11.50 *12.75*

Same Overprinted in Carmine or Green (Portugal Nos. J14-J20)

1911
J8 D2 5r brown .20 .20
J9 D2 10r orange .20 .20
J10 D2 20r lilac .20 .20
J11 D2 30r gray green .20 .20
J12 D2 40r gray violet .45 .45
J13 D2 50r carmine (G) 2.00 2.00
J14 D2 100r dull blue 1.25 1.25
Nos. J8-J14 (7) 4.50 4.50

Portugal Nos. J21-J27 Overprinted in Black

1918
J15 D3 ½c brown .20 .20
 a. Inverted overprint 4.00 4.00
 b. Double overprint 4.00 4.00
J16 D3 1c orange .20 .20
 a. Inverted overprint 4.00 4.00
 b. Double overprint 4.00 4.00
J17 D3 2c red lilac .20 .20
 a. Inverted overprint 4.00 4.00
 b. Double overprint 4.00 4.00
J18 D3 3c green .20 .20
 a. Inverted overprint 4.00 4.00
 b. Double overprint 4.00 4.00
J19 D3 4c gray .20 .20
 a. Inverted overprint 4.00 4.00
 b. Double overprint 4.00 4.00
J20 D3 5c rose .20 .20
 b. Double overprint 4.00 4.00
J21 D3 10c dark blue .20 .20
Nos. J15-J21 (7) 1.40 1.40

Stamps and Type of Portugal Postage Dues, 1921-27, Overprinted in Black

1922-24 *Perf. 11½x12*
J30 D3 ½c gray green ('23) .20 .20
J31 D3 1c gray green ('23) .20 .20
J32 D3 2c gray green ('23) .20 .20
J33 D3 3c gray green ('24) .35 .35
J34 D3 8c gray green ('24) .20 .20
J35 D3 10c gray green ('24) .40 .20
J36 D3 12c gray green ('24) .30 .20
J37 D3 16c gray green ('24) .50 .20
J38 D3 20c gray green 1.00 .50
J39 D3 24c gray green .50 .20
J40 D3 32c gray green ('24) .60 .20
J41 D3 36c gray green .75 .20
J42 D3 40c gray green ('24) 1.50 .50
J43 D3 48c gray green ('24) .75 .30
J44 D3 50c gray green 1.00 .50
J45 D3 60c gray green 2.00 .35
J46 D3 72c gray green 2.00 .35
J47 D3 80c gray green ('24) 3.00 1.40
J48 D3 1.20e gray green 3.00 1.40
Nos. J30-J48 (19) 18.45 7.65

NEWSPAPER STAMPS

Newspaper Stamps of Portugal, Nos. P1, P1a, Overprinted Types b & c in Black or Red and:

N3

Perf. 11½, 12½ and 13½

1876-88 **Unwmk.**
P1 N1 2½r (a) olive 11.00 3.50
 a. Inverted overprint
P2 N1 2½r (b) olive ('82) 5.00 1.00
 a. Inverted overprint
 b. Double overprint
P3 N3 2r black ('85) 5.00 2.00
 a. Inverted overprint
 b. Double overprint, one inverted
P4 N1 2½r (b) bister ('82) 5.00 1.00
 a. Double overprint
P5 N3 2r black (R) ('88) 15.00 10.00
Nos. P1-P5 (5) 41.00 17.50

Reprints of the newspaper stamps have the same papers, gum and perforations as reprints of the regular issues. Value $2 each.

PARCEL POST STAMPS

Portugal Nos. Q1-Q17 Overprinted Like Nos. 155-237 in Black or Red

1921-22 **Unwmk.** *Perf. 12*
Q1 PP1 1c lilac brown .20 .20
 a. Inverted overprint 4.00 4.00
Q2 PP1 2c orange .20 .20
 a. Inverted overprint 4.00 4.00
Q3 PP1 5c light brown .20 .20
 a. Inverted overprint 5.00 5.00
 b. Double overprint 5.00 5.00
Q4 PP1 10c red brown .25 .25
 a. Inverted overprint 5.00 5.00
 b. Double overprint 5.00 5.00
Q5 PP1 20c gray blue .30 .25
 a. Inverted overprint 5.00 5.00
 b. Double overprint 5.00 5.00
Q6 PP1 40c carmine .30 .30
 a. Double overprint 6.50 6.50
Q7 PP1 50c black (R) .55 .55
Q8 PP1 60c dark blue (R) .55 .55
Q9 PP1 70c gray brown 2.50 1.25
 a. Double overprint
Q10 PP1 80c ultra 2.50 1.25
Q11 PP1 90c light violet 2.50 1.25
Q12 PP1 1e light green 3.00 1.25
Q13 PP1 2e pale lilac 4.00 2.50
Q14 PP1 3e olive 6.00 3.25
Q15 PP1 4e ultra 7.00 5.00
Q16 PP1 5e gray 7.00 5.00
Q17 PP1 10e chocolate 20.00 13.00
Nos. Q1-Q17 (17) 57.05 36.25

POSTAL TAX STAMPS

These stamps represent a special fee for the delivery of postal matter on certain days in the year. The money derived from their sale is applied to works of public charity.

Nos. 114 and 157 Overprinted in Carmine **ASSISTENCIA**

1911-13 **Unwmk.** *Perf. 14x15*
RA1 A29 10r dark green .55 .40

The 20r of this type was for use on telegrams.

Perf. 15x14
RA2 A30 1c deep green 1.25 1.25

The 2c of this type was for use on telegrams.

Postal Tax Stamp of Portugal, No. RA4, Overprinted Like Nos. 155-237 in Black

1915 *Perf. 12*
RA3 PT2 1c carmine .20 .20

The 2c of this type was for use on telegrams.

Postal Tax Stamp of 1915 Surcharged **15 ctvs.**

1924
RA4 PT1 15c on 1c rose .75 *1.25*

Comrades of the Great War Issue

Postal Tax Stamps of Portugal, 1925, Overprinted **AÇORES**

1925, Apr. 8 *Perf. 11*
RA5 PT3 10c brown .40 .30
RA6 PT3 10c green .40 .30
RA7 PT3 10c rose .40 .30
RA8 PT3 10c ultra .40 .30
Nos. RA5-RA8 (4) 1.60 1.20

The use of Nos. RA5-RA11 in addition to the regular postage was compulsory on certain days. If the tax represented by these stamps was not prepaid, it was collected by means of Postal Tax Due Stamps.

In 1934-45, #RA5-RA11, RAJ1-RAJ4 were used for regular postage in Portugal.

Pombal Issue

Common Design Types

1925 *Perf. 12½*
RA9 CD28 20c dp green & black .35 .30
RA10 CD29 20c dp green & black .35 .30
RA11 CD30 20c dp green & black .35 .30
Nos. RA9-RA11 (3) 1.05 .90

POSTAL TAX DUE STAMPS

Postal Tax Due Stamp of Portugal Overprinted like Nos. RA5-RA8

1925, Apr. 8 **Unwmk.** *Perf. 11x11½*
RAJ1 PTD1 20c brown orange .40 .40

See note after No. RA8.

Pombal Issue

Common Design Types

1925, May 8 *Perf. 12½*
RAJ2 CD28 40c dp green & black .60 *4.00*
RAJ3 CD29 40c dp green & black .60 *4.00*
RAJ4 CD30 40c dp green & black .60 *4.00*
Nos. RAJ2-RAJ4 (3) 1.80 *12.00*

See note after No. RA8.
See Portugal for later issues.

BAHAMAS

bə-'hä-məs

LOCATION — A group of about 700 islands and 2,000 rocks in the West Indies, off the coast of Florida. Only 30 islands are inhabited.
GOVT. — Independent state in British Commonwealth
AREA — 5,382 sq. mi.
POP. — 283,705 (1999 est.)
CAPITAL — Nassau

The principal island, on which the capital is located, is New Providence. The Bahamas obtained internal self-government on January 7, 1964, and independence on July 10, 1973.

12 Pence = 1 Shilling
20 Shillings = 1 Pound
100 Cents = 1 Dollar (1966)

Catalogue values for unused stamps in this country are for Never Hinged items, beginning with Scott 130, and Scott C1 in the air post section.

Values for unused stamps are for examples with original gum as defined in the catalogue introduction. Very fine examples of Nos. 2-26 will have perforations touching the design or frameline on at least one side due to the narrow spacing of the stamps on the plates. Stamps with perfs clear of the design or framelines on all four sides are extremely scarce and will command higher prices.

Pen cancellations usually indicate revenue use. Such stamps sell for much less than postally canceled copies. Beware of stamps with revenue or pen cancellations removed and forged postal cancellations added.

Queen Victoria
A1 A2

1859-60 **Unwmk.** **Engr.** ***Imperf.***
1 A1 1p dull lake ('60) 50. *1,500.*
 a. 1p reddish lake *4,500.* *2,100.*
 b. 1p brownish lake *4,500.* *2,250.*

Most unused copies of #1 are remainders, and false cancellations are plentiful. #1a and 1b are on thicker paper than #1.

1861 ***Rough Perf. 14 to 16***
2 A1 1p lake 925. 275.
 a. Clean-cut perf. ('60) 2,100. 700.
3 A2 4p dull rose 1,600. 500.
 a. Imperf. between, pair *20,000.*
4 A2 6p gray lilac 3,000. 575.
 a. Pale lilac 3,250. 575.

1862 **Engr.** ***Perf. 11½, 12***
5 A1 1p lake 800. 175.
 a. Pair, imperf. between *5,000.*
6 A2 4p dull rose 3,000. 425.
7 A2 6p gray violet 4,750. 450.

No. 5a was not issued in the Bahamas. It is unique and faulty.

Nos. 5-7 exist with perf. 11½ or 12 compound with 11.

Perf. 13
8 A1 1p brown lake 600. 125.
 a. 1p carmine lake 625. 150.
9 A2 4p rose 2,750. 400.
10 A2 6p gray violet 3,250. 400.
 a. 6p dull violet 3,250. 500.

Queen Victoria — A3

1863-65 **Typo.** **Wmk. 1** ***Perf. 12½***
11 A1 1p lake 85.00 70.00
 a. 1p brown lake 85.00 70.00
 b. 1p rose lake 95.00 70.00
12 A1 1p vermilion 65.00 50.00
 a. 1p rose red 70.00 55.00
 b. 1p red 70.00 55.00
13 A2 4p rose 375.00 70.00
 a. 4p rose lake 400.00 90.00
 b. 4p bright rose 250.00 70.00
14 A2 6p dk violet 160.00 80.00
 a. 6p violet 250.00 100.00
 b. 6p rose lilac 5,500. *3,500.*
 c. 6p lilac 275.00 70.00
15 A3 1sh green ('65) 2,500. 325.00

For surcharge see No. 26.

1863-81 ***Perf. 14***
16 A1 1p vermilion 45.00 20.00
17 A1 1p car lake (anil.) 1,500.
18 A2 4p rose 400.00 50.00
 a. 4p deep rose ('76) 400.00 50.00
 b. 4p dull rose 1,750. 50.00
19 A3 1sh green ('80) 7.50 7.50
 a. 1shp dark green 120.00 45.00

Some copies of No. 16 show a light aniline appearance and care should be taken not to confuse these with No. 17. All known used copies of No. 17 bear fiscal cancels.

1882-98 **Wmk. 2**
20 A1 1p vermilion 350.00 65.00
21 A2 4p rose 800.00 65.00
22 A3 1sh green 30.00 17.50
23 A3 1sh blue grn ('98) 35.00 22.50

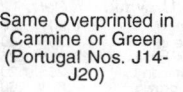

Perf. 12

24	A1	1p vermilion	40.00	22.50
25	A2	4p rose	500.00	60.00

No. 14a Surcharged in Black

FOURPENCE

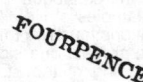

1883 Wmk. 1 Perf. 12½

26	A2	4p on 6p violet	675.	500.
a.		Inverted surcharge	7,250.	4,500.

The surcharge, being handstamped, is found in various positions. Counterfeit overprints exist.

Queen Victoria A5

Queen's Staircase A6

1884-90 Typo. Wmk. 2 Perf. 14

27	A5	1p carmine rose	5.00	2.00
a.		1p pale rose	45.00	10.00
28	A5	2½p ultra	8.25	2.00
a.		2½p dull blue	47.50	15.00
29	A5	4p yellow	8.25	5.00
30	A5	6p violet	5.00	25.00
31	A5	5sh olive green	60.00	70.00
32	A5	£1 brown	325.00	275.00
		Revenue cancellation		55.00
		Nos. 27-32 (6)	411.50	379.00

Cleaned fiscally used copies of No. 32 are often found with postmarks of small post offices added. Dangerous forged postmarks exist, especially dated "AU 29 94."

1901-03 Engr. Wmk. 1

33	A6	1p carmine & blk	5.50	4.00
34	A6	5p org & blk ('03)	10.00	40.00
35	A6	2sh ultra & blk ('03)	20.00	45.00
36	A6	3sh green & blk ('03)	22.50	47.50
		Nos. 33-36 (4)	58.00	136.50

See Nos. 48, 58-62, 71, 78, 81-82.

Edward VII A7

George V A8

1902 Wmk. 2 Typo.

37	A7	1p carmine rose	2.25	2.25
38	A7	2½p ultra	7.00	1.75
39	A7	4p orange	12.50	42.50
40	A7	6p bister brn	6.00	14.00
41	A7	1sh gray blk & car	16.00	42.50
42	A7	5sh violet & ultra	52.50	70.00
43	A7	£1 green & blk	325.00	350.00
		Nos. 37-43 (7)	421.25	523.00

Beware of forged postmarks, especially dated "2 MAR 10."

1906-11 Wmk. 3

44	A7	½p green	4.00	2.00
45	A7	1p car rose	19.00	2.00
46	A7	2½p ultra ('07)	19.00	21.00
47	A7	6p bister brn ('11)	35.00	50.00
		Nos. 44-47 (4)	77.00	75.00

1911-16 Engr.

48	A6	1p red & gray blk ('16)	3.50	2.40
a.		1p carmine & black	5.50	5.50

For overprints see Nos. B1-B2.

1912-19 Typo.

49	A8	½p green	.85	6.00
50	A8	1p car rose (aniline)	2.10	.45
50A	A8	2p gray ('19)	2.10	2.75
51	A8	2½p ultra	4.00	6.00
52	A8	4p orange	2.50	8.50
53	A8	6p bister brn	1.75	3.75

Chalky Paper

54	A8	1sh black & carmine	2.75	7.50
55	A8	5sh violet & ultra	32.50	57.50
56	A8	£1 dull grn & blk	225.00	275.00
		Nos. 49-56 (9)	273.55	367.45

1917-19 Engr.

58	A6	3p reddish pur, *buff*	4.25	4.25
59	A6	3p brown & blk ('19)	2.75	5.50
60	A6	5p violet & blk	3.50	10.00
61	A6	2sh ultra & black	22.50	40.00
62	A6	3sh green & black	42.50	45.00
		Nos. 58-62 (5)	75.50	104.75

Peace Commemorative Issue

King George V and Seal of Bahamas — A9

1920, Mar. 1 Engr. Perf. 14

65	A9	½p gray green	.85	3.75
66	A9	1p deep red	2.75	1.10
67	A9	2p gray	3.50	6.50
68	A9	3p brown	3.25	9.00
69	A9	1sh dark green	25.00	30.00
		Nos. 65-69 (5)	35.35	50.35

Types of 1901-12

Typo., Engr. (A6)

1921-34 Wmk. 4

70	A8	½p green ('24)	.45	.40
71	A6	1p car & black	.90	1.00
72	A8	1p car rose	1.00	.20
73	A8	1½p fawn ('34)	1.50	1.40
74	A8	2p gray ('27)	.90	2.75
75	A8	2½p ultra ('22)	.80	2.75
76	A8	3p violet, *yel* ('31)	5.50	15.00
77	A8	4p yellow ('24)	1.60	5.25
78	A6	5p red vio & gray blk ('29)	6.50	32.50
79	A8	6p bister brn ('22)	1.25	3.25
80	A8	1sh blk & red ('26)	3.25	8.00
81	A6	2sh ultra & blk ('22)	32.50	55.00
82	A6	3sh grn & blk ('24)	55.00	65.00
83	A8	5sh vio & ultra ('24)	30.00	47.50
84	A8	£1 grn & blk ('26)	160.00	275.00
		Nos. 70-84 (15)	301.15	515.00

The 3p, 1sh, 5sh and £1 are on chalky paper.

Seal of Bahamas — A10

1930, Jan. 2 Engr. Perf. 12

85	A10	1p red & black	1.50	2.50
86	A10	3p dp brown & blk	3.00	12.50
87	A10	5p dk vio & blk	3.50	12.50
88	A10	2sh ultra & black	20.00	37.50
89	A10	3sh dp green & blk	32.50	65.00
		Nos. 85-89 (5)	60.50	130.00

The dates on the stamps commemorate important events in the history of the colony. The 1st British occupation was in 1629. The Bahamas were ceded to Great Britain in 1729 and a treaty of peace was signed by that country, France and Spain.

Type of 1930 Issue Without Dates at Top

1931-46

90	A10	2sh ultra & black ('43)	4.75	2.50
a.		2sh ultra & slate purple	18.00	22.00
91	A10	3sh dp green & blk ('46)	3.75	1.90
a.		3sh deep grn & slate purple	27.50	22.50

Nos. 90a-91a are on thick paper with yellowish gum, Nos. 90-91 are on thin white paper with colorless gum.

For overprints see Nos. 126-127.

Common Design Types pictured following the introduction.

Silver Jubilee Issue

Common Design Type

1935, May 6 Perf. 13½x14

92	CD301	1½p car & blue	.65	1.60
93	CD301	2½p blue & brn	2.50	5.00
94	CD301	6p ol grn & lt bl	5.00	7.50
95	CD301	1sh brt vio & ind	6.50	7.25
		Nos. 92-95 (4)	14.65	21.35
		Set, never hinged	30.00	

Flamingos in Flight — A11

1935, May 22 Perf. 12½

96	A11	8p car & ultra	5.00	3.25
		Never hinged	8.50	

Coronation Issue

Common Design Type

1937, May 12 Perf. 13½x14

97	CD302	½p dp green	.20	.20
98	CD302	1½p brown	.25	.25
99	CD302	2½p brt ultra	.65	.65
		Nos. 97-99 (3)	1.10	1.10
		Set, never hinged	1.75	

George VI — A12

Sea Gardens, Nassau — A13

Fort Charlotte A14

Flamingos in Flight — A15

1938-46 Typo. Wmk. 4 Perf. 14

100	A12	½p green	.20	.65
101	A12	1p carmine	4.00	4.50
101A	A12	1p gray ('41)	.25	.50
102	A12	1½p red brown	.60	1.00
103	A12	2p gray	12.00	5.75
103B	A12	2p carmine ('41)	.35	.55
c.		"TWO PENCE" double		2,750.
104	A12	2½p ultra	1.90	2.00
104A	A12	2½p lt violet ('43)	.60	.65
b.		"2½ PENNY" double	2,000.	—
105	A12	3p lt violet	7.50	9.00
105A	A12	3p ultra ('43)	.45	.90

Engr.

Perf. 12½

106	A13	4p red org & blue	.60	.65
107	A14	6p blue & ol grn	.45	.65
108	A15	8p car & ultra	2.40	1.90

Typo.

Perf. 14

109	A12	10p yel org ('46)	.95	.60
110	A12	1sh black & bright red	3.25	.50
112	A12	5sh pur & ultra	11.00	9.00
113	A12	£1 bl grn & blk	37.50	42.50
		Nos. 100-113 (17)	84.00	81.30
		Set, never hinged	141.80	

#110-113 printed on chalky & ordinary paper.

See the Classic Specialized Catalogue for listings of shades.

See Nos. 154-156. For overprints see Nos. 116-125, 128-129.

No. 104 Surcharged in Black

3d.

1940, Nov. 28 Perf. 14

115	A12	3p on 2½p ultra	.30	.30
		Never hinged	.55	

Stamps of 1931-42 Overprinted in Black

1492
LANDFALL
OF
COLUMBUS
1942

1942, Oct. 12 Perf. 14, 12½, 12

116	A12	½p green	.20	.20
117	A12	1p gray	.20	.20
118	A12	1½p red brn	.20	.20
119	A12	2p carmine	.20	.20
120	A12	2½p lt violet	.20	.20
121	A12	3p ultra	.20	.20
122	A13	4p red org & blue	.25	.20
123	A14	6p blue & ol grn	.35	.25
124	A15	8p car & ultra	.45	.30
125	A12	1sh black & car	1.75	.40
126	A10	2sh dk ultra & blk	5.50	9.50
a.		2sh ultra & slate purple	7.50	15.00
127	A10	3sh dp grn & sl pur	3.00	9.00
a.		3sh deep green & black	19.00	17.00
128	A12	5sh lilac & ultra	8.50	9.00
129	A12	£1 green & black	20.00	30.00
		Nos. 116-129 (14)	41.00	59.85
		Set, never hinged	64.00	

450th anniv. of the discovery of America by Columbus.

Nos. 125, 128-129 printed on chalky and ordinary paper.

Two printings of the basic stamps were overprinted, the first with dark gum, the second with white gum.

Catalogue values for unused stamps in this section, from this point to the end of the section, are for Never Hinged items.

Peace Issue

Common Design Type

Perf. 13½x14

1946, Nov. 11 Engr. Wmk. 4

130	CD303	1½p brown	.20	.20
131	CD303	3p deep blue	.20	.20

Infant Welfare Clinic — A16

Designs: 1p, Modern agriculture. 1½p, Sisal. 2p, Native straw work. 2½p, Modern dairying. 3p, Fishing fleet. 4p, Out island settlement. 6p, Tuna fishing. 8p, Paradise Beach. 10p, Modern hotel. 1sh, Yacht racing. 2sh, Water skiing. 3sh, Shipbuilding. 5sh, Modern transportation. 10sh, Modern salt production. £1, Parliament Building.

1948, Oct. 11 Unwmk. Perf. 12

132	A16	½p orange	.20	.20
133	A16	1p olive green	.20	.20
134	A16	1½p olive bister	.35	.35
135	A16	2p vermilion	.25	.20
136	A16	2½p red brown	.65	.60
137	A16	3p brt ultra	.45	.45
138	A16	4p gray black	.45	.75
139	A16	6p emerald	.65	.75
140	A16	8p violet	.65	.75
141	A16	10p rose car	.70	.75
142	A16	1sh olive brn	1.25	1.10
143	A16	2sh claret	6.25	6.00
144	A16	3sh brt blue	6.25	6.00
145	A16	5sh purple	5.00	6.00
146	A16	10sh dk gray	5.00	7.00
147	A16	£1 red orange	10.00	12.00
		Nos. 132-147 (16)	38.30	43.10

300th anniv., in 1947, of the settlement of the colony.

Silver Wedding Issue

Common Design Type

Perf. 14x14½

1948, Dec. 1 Wmk. 4 Photo.

148	CD304	1½p red brown	.20	.20

Engr.; Name Typo.

Perf. 11½x11

149	CD305	£1 gray green	30.00	35.00

UPU Issue

Common Design Types

Engr.; Name Typo. on #151 & 152

1949, Oct. 10 Perf. 13½, 11x11½

150	CD306	2½p violet	.25	.25
151	CD307	3p indigo	.50	.50
152	CD308	6p blue gray	1.00	1.00
153	CD309	1sh rose car	1.75	1.75
		Nos. 150-153 (4)	3.50	3.50

George VI Type of 1938

Perf. 13½x14

1951-52 Wmk. 4 Typo.

154	A12	½p claret ('52)	.50	.20
a.		Wmk. 4a (error)	1,750.	
155	A12	2p green	.50	.40
156	A12	3p rose red ('52)	.70	3.00
		Nos. 154-156 (3)	1.70	3.60

Coronation Issue

Common Design Type

1953, June 3 Engr. Perf. 13½x13

157	CD312	6p blue & black	.60	.60

Infant Welfare Clinic A17

Designs: 1p, Modern Agriculture. 1½p, Out island settlement. 2p, Native strawwork. 3p, Fishing fleet. 4p, Water skiing. 5p, Modern dairying. 6p, Modern transportation. 8p, Paradise Beach. 10p, Modern hotels. 1sh, Yacht racing. 2sh, Sisal. 2sh6p, Shipbuilding. 5sh, Tuna fishing. 10sh, Modern salt production. £1, Parliament Building.

1954, Jan. 1 ***Perf. 11x11½***

158	A17	½p red org & blk	.20	.20
159	A17	1p org brn & ol grn	.20	.20
a.		Booklet pane of 4	.55	
160	A17	1½p black & blue	.20	.20
a.		Booklet pane of 4	.70	
161	A17	2p dk grn & brn org	.20	.20
a.		Booklet pane of 4	.70	
162	A17	3p dp car & blk	.20	.20
163	A17	4p lil rose & bl green	.30	.25
a.		Booklet pane of 4	1.75	
164	A17	5p dp ultra & brn	.65	*1.75*
165	A17	6p blk & aqua	.45	.25
a.		Booklet pane of 4	2.25	
166	A17	8p rose vio & blk	.50	.25
a.		Booklet pane of 4	2.50	
167	A17	10p ultra & blk	.55	.35
168	A17	1sh ol brn & ultra	.65	.50
169	A17	2sh blk & brn org	1.10	.75
170	A17	2sh6p dp bl & blk	2.50	1.10
171	A17	5sh dp org & emer	5.00	2.50
172	A17	10sh grnsh blk & black	7.00	5.00
173	A17	£1 vio & grnsh black	15.00	11.00
		Nos. 158-173 (16)	34.70	24.70

See No. 203. For types overprinted or surcharged see Nos. 181-182, 185-200, 202.

Queen Elizabeth II — A18

Wmk. 314

1959, June 10 **Engr.** ***Perf. 13***

174	A18	1p dk red & black	.20	.20
175	A18	2p green & black	.20	.20
176	A18	6p blue & black	.30	.30
177	A18	10p brown & black	.55	.55
		Nos. 174-177 (4)	1.25	1.25

Cent. of the 1st postage stamp of Bahamas.

Christ Church Cathedral, Nassau — A19

Perf. 14x13

1962, Jan. 30 **Photo.** **Unwmk.**

178	A19	8p shown	.60	.60
179	A19	10p Public library	.60	.60

Centenary of the city of Nassau.

Freedom from Hunger Issue

Common Design Type

Perf. 14x14½

1963, June 4 **Wmk. 314**

180	CD314	8p sepia	1.25	1.10
a.		"8d" and "BAHAMAS" omitted	875.00	

Nos. 166-167 Overprinted: "BAHAMAS TALKS/ 1962"

Perf. 11x11½

1963, July 15 **Engr.** **Wmk. 4**

181	A17	8p rose vio & black	1.00	.85
182	A17	10p ultra & black	1.75	1.60

Meeting of Pres. Kennedy and Prime Minister Harold Macmillan, Dec. 1962.

Red Cross Centenary Issue

Common Design Type

Wmk. 314

1963, Sept. 2 **Litho.** ***Perf. 13***

183	CD315	1p black & red	.20	.20
184	CD315	10p ultra & red	2.00	1.40

Type of 1954 Overprinted: "NEW CONSTITUTION/ 1964"

Designs as Before

Perf. 11x11½

1964, Jan. 7 **Engr.** **Wmk. 314**

185	A17	½p red org & blk	.20	.20
186	A17	1p org brn & ol green	.20	.20
187	A17	1½p black & blue	.20	.20
188	A17	2p dk grn & brn org	.20	.20
189	A17	3p dp car & blk	.20	.20
190	A17	4p lil rose & bl green	.20	.20
191	A17	5p dp ultra & brn	.20	.20
192	A17	6p blk & aqua	.25	.20
193	A17	8p rose vio & blk	.35	.30
194	A17	10p ultra & black	.45	.35
195	A17	1sh ol brn & ultra	.60	.45
196	A17	2sh blk & brn org	1.25	.95
197	A17	2sh6p dp bl & blk	1.50	1.25
198	A17	5sh dp org & emer	3.00	2.50
199	A17	10sh grnsh blk & black	5.50	4.75
200	A17	£1 vio & grnsh black	11.50	9.50
		Nos. 185-200 (16)	25.80	21.65

Shakespeare Issue

Common Design Type

Perf. 14x14½

1964, Apr. 23 **Photo.** **Wmk. 314**

201	CD316	6p greenish blue	.45	.35

Type of 1954 Surcharged with Olympic Rings, New Value and Bars

Perf. 11x11½

1964, Oct. 1 **Engr.** **Wmk. 314**

202	A17	8p on 1sh ol brn & ultra	.45	.45

18th Olympic Games, Tokyo, Oct. 10-25.

Queen Type of 1954

1964, Oct. 6 **Wmk. 314**

203	A17	2p dk grn & brn org	.50	.50

Out Island Regatta A21

Designs: ½p, Colony badge. 1½p, Princess Margaret Hospital. 2p, High School. 3p, Flamingo. 4p, Liner "Queen Elizabeth." 6p, Island development. 8p, Yachting. 10p, Public Square, Nassau. 1sh, Sea Garden, Nassau. 2sh, Cannons at Fort Charlotte. 2sh6p, Sea plane and jetliner. 5sh, 1914 Williamson film project and 1939 underwater post office. 10sh, Conch shell. £1, Columbus' flagship.

Engr. and Litho.

1965, Jan. 7 ***Perf. 13½x13***

204	A21	½p multi, *bluish*	.20	.20
205	A21	1p multi	.20	.20
a.		Booklet pane of 4	.40	
206	A21	1½p multi	.20	.20
a.		Booklet pane of 4	.45	
207	A21	2p multi	.20	.20
a.		Booklet pane of 4	.55	
208	A21	3p multi	.20	.20
209	A21	4p multi	.25	.20
a.		Booklet pane of 4	1.10	
210	A21	6p multi	.30	.20
a.		Booklet pane of 4	1.25	
211	A21	8p multi	.40	.30
a.		Booklet pane of 4	1.75	
212	A21	10p multi	.35	.20
213	A21	1sh multi, *grnsh*	.55	.25
214	A21	2sh multi, *grnsh*	1.10	.65
215	A21	2sh6p multi	1.50	.80
216	A21	5sh multi	3.00	1.60
217	A21	10sh multi	6.00	3.75
218	A21	£1 multi	12.00	7.25
		Nos. 204-218 (15)	26.45	16.20

Booklet panes were issued Mar. 23, 1965.

See Nos. 252-266. For surcharges see Nos. 221, 230-244.

ITU Issue

Common Design Type

Perf. 11x11½

1965, May 17 **Litho.** **Wmk. 314**

219	CD317	1p emerald & org	.20	.20
220	CD317	2sh lilac & olive	2.25	2.25

No. 211 Surcharged 9d

Engr. & Litho.

1965, July 12 ***Perf. 13½x13***

221	A21	9p on 8p multi	.60	.60

Intl. Cooperation Year Issue

Common Design Type

Wmk. 314

1965, Oct. 25 **Litho.** ***Perf. 14½***

222	CD318	½p blue grn & claret	.20	.20
223	CD318	1sh lt violet & grn	.85	.70

Churchill Memorial Issue

Common Design Type

1966, Jan. 24 **Photo.** ***Perf. 14***

224	CD319	½p multicolored	.20	.20
225	CD319	2p multicolored	.20	.20
226	CD319	10p multicolored	1.00	1.00
227	CD319	1sh multicolored	1.50	1.50
		Nos. 224-227 (4)	2.90	2.90

Royal Visit Issue

Common Design Type Inscribed "Royal Visit / 1966"

1966, Feb. 4 **Litho.** ***Perf. 11x12***

228	CD320	6p violet blue	.65	.65
229	CD320	1sh dk car rose	1.75	1.75

Nos. 204-218 Surcharged 2¢

Engr. & Litho.

Perf. 13½x13

1966, May 25 **Wmk. 314**

230	A21	1c on ½p multi	.20	.20
231	A21	2c on 1p multi	.20	.20
232	A21	3c on 2p multi	.20	.20
233	A21	4c on 3p multi	.20	.20
234	A21	5c on 4p multi	.20	.20
a.		Surch. omitted, vert. strip of 7-10	*3,000.*	
235	A21	8c on 6p multi	.20	.20
236	A21	10c on 8p multi	.25	.25
237	A21	11c on 1½p multi	.35	.25
238	A21	12c on 10p multi	.40	.30
239	A21	15c on 1sh multi	.50	.35
240	A21	22c on 2sh multi	.65	.40
241	A21	50c on 2sh6p multi	1.40	1.25
242	A21	$1 on 5sh multi	2.50	2.50
243	A21	$2 on 10sh multi	5.50	5.00
244	A21	$3 on £1 multi	8.00	7.50
		Nos. 230-244 (15)	20.75	19.00

The denominations are next to the bars instead of below on Nos. 232, 235-240; the length of the bars varies to cover old denomination.

No. 234a, if single, is identical with No. 209, but distinguishable if in vertical strip of 7 to 10. No. 234 was printed in sheets of 100 (10x10); No. 209 in sheets of 60 (10x6).

World Cup Soccer Issue

Common Design Type

1966, July 1 **Litho.** ***Perf. 14***

245	CD321	8c multicolored	.30	.30
246	CD321	15c multicolored	.60	.60

WHO Headquarters Issue

Common Design Type

1966, Sept. 20 **Litho.** ***Perf. 14***

247	CD322	11c multicolored	.50	.50
248	CD322	15c multicolored	.70	.70

UNESCO Anniversary Issue

Common Design Type

1966, Dec. 1 **Litho.** ***Perf. 14***

249	CD323	3c "Education"	.20	.20
250	CD323	15c "Science"	.65	.65
251	CD323	$1 "Culture"	3.25	3.25
		Nos. 249-251 (3)	4.10	4.10

Type of 1965

Values in Cents and Dollars

Engr. & Litho.

1967, May 25 ***Perf. 13½x13***

Designs: 1c, Colony badge. 2c, Out Island Regatta. 3c, High School. 4c, Flamingo. 5c, Liner "Oceanic." 8c, Island development. 10c, Yachting. 11c, Princess Margaret Hospital. 12c, Public Square, Nassau. 15c, Sea Garden, Nassau. 22c, Cannon at Fort Charlotte. 50c, Sea plane and jetliner. $1, 1914 Williamson film project and 1939 underwater post office. $2, Conch shell. $3, Columbus' flagship.

252	A21	1c brown & multi	.20	.20
253	A21	2c grn, slate & bl	.20	.20
254	A21	3c grn, indigo & vio	.20	.20
255	A21	4c ultra, blue & red	.20	.20
256	A21	5c pur, bl & indigo	.20	.20
257	A21	8c dk brn, bl & dl grn	.20	.20
258	A21	10c car rose, bl & pur	.25	.20
259	A21	11c bl, grn & rose red	.35	.25
260	A21	12c ol grn, bl & lt brn	.40	.20
261	A21	15c rose & multi	.50	.30
262	A21	22c rose red, brn & bl	.60	.40
263	A21	50c emer, ol & bl	1.40	.90
264	A21	$1 sep, brn org & dk blue	2.75	1.75
265	A21	$2 green & multi	5.50	4.25
266	A21	$3 pur, bl & brn org	8.50	6.75
		Nos. 252-266 (15)	21.45	16.20

Nos. 252-266 are on toned paper. Printings on very white, untinted paper appeared between late 1969 and May, 1971. Value, set $500.

Seal of Bahamas, Queen Elizabeth II and Lord Baden-Powell — A22

60th anniv. of world Scouting: 15c, Scout emblem and portraits as on 3c.

Perf. 14x13½

1967, Sept. 1 **Photo.** **Wmk. 314**

267	A22	3c multicolored	.25	.25
268	A22	15c multicolored	.85	.85

Human Rights Flame and Globe A23

Intl. Human Rights Year: 12c, Human rights flame and scales of justice. $1, Human rights flame and Seal of Bahamas.

1968, May 13 **Litho.** ***Perf. 14***

269	A23	3c multicolored	.20	.20
270	A23	12c multicolored	.50	.50
271	A23	$1 multicolored	2.25	2.25
		Nos. 269-271 (3)	2.95	2.95

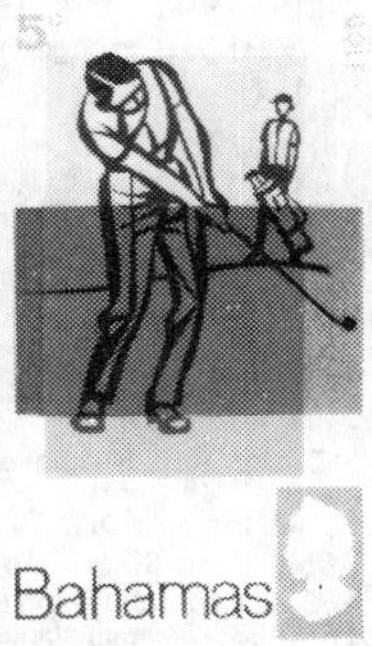

Golf — A24

Tourist Publicity: 11c, Yachting. 15c, Horse racing. 50c, Water skiing.

1968, Aug. 20 **Unwmk.** ***Perf. 13½***

272	A24	5c multicolored	.25	.25
273	A24	11c multicolored	.50	.50
274	A24	15c multicolored	.65	.65
275	A24	50c multicolored	2.25	2.25
		Nos. 272-275 (4)	3.65	3.65

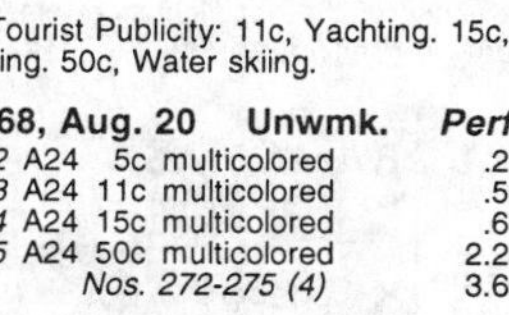

Olympic Monument and Sailboat — A25

Olympic Monument, San Salvador Island, Bahamas, and: 11c, Long jump. 50c, Running. $1, Sailing.

Perf. 14½x14

1968, Sept. 30 **Photo.**
276 A25 5c multicolored .20 .20
277 A25 11c multicolored .40 .40
278 A25 50c multicolored 1.60 1.60
279 A25 $1 multicolored 3.50 3.50
Nos. 276-279 (4) 5.70 5.70

19th Olympic Games, Mexico City, Oct. 12-27.

Legislative Building — A26

Designs: 10c, Bahamas mace and Big Ben, London, vert. 12c, Local straw market, vert. 15c, Horse-drawn surrey.

Perf. 14½

1968, Nov. 1 **Unwmk.** **Litho.**
280 A26 3c brt blue & multi .20 .20
281 A26 10c yel, blk & blue .40 .40
282 A26 12c brt rose & multi .45 .45
283 A26 15c green & multi .50 .50
Nos. 280-283 (4) 1.55 1.55

14th Commonwealth Parliamentary Conf., Nassau, Nov. 1-8.

$100 Coin with Queen Elizabeth II and Landing of Columbus — A27

Gold Coins with Elizabeth II on Obverse: 12c, $50 coin and Santa Maria flagship. 15c, $20 coin and Nassau Harbor Lighthouse. $1, $10 coin and Fort.

Engr. on Gold Paper

1968, Dec. 2 **Unwmk.** ***Perf. 13½***
284 A27 3c dark red .20 .20
285 A27 12c dark green .65 .65
286 A27 15c lilac .75 .75
287 A27 $1 black 4.50 2.50
Nos. 284-287 (4) 6.10 4.10

First gold coinage in the Bahamas.

Bahamas Postal Card and Airplane Wing A28

Design: 15c, Seaplane, 1929.

Perf. 14½x14

1969, Jan. 30 **Litho.** **Unwmk.**
288 A28 12c multicolored .90 .90
289 A28 15c multicolored 1.10 1.10

50th anniv. of the 1st flight from Nassau, Bahamas, to Miami, Fla., Jan. 30, 1919.

Game Fishing Boats A29

Designs: 11c, Paradise Beach. 12c, Sunfish sailboats. 15c, Parade on Rawson Square.

1969, Aug. 26 **Litho.** **Wmk. 314**
290 A29 3c multicolored .20 .20
291 A29 11c multicolored .60 .60
292 A29 12c multicolored .65 .65
293 A29 15c multicolored .80 .80
a. Souvenir sheet of 4, #290-293 4.25 4.25
Nos. 290-293 (4) 2.25 2.25

Tourist publicity.

Holy Family, by Nicolas Poussin — A30

Paintings: 3c, Adoration of the Shepherds, by Louis Le Nain. 12c, Adoration of the Kings, by Gerard David. 15c, Adoration of the Kings, by Vincenzo Foppa.

1969, Oct. 15 **Photo.** ***Perf. 12***
294 A30 3c red & multi .20 .20
295 A30 11c emerald & multi .60 .60
296 A30 12c ultra & multi .70 .70
297 A30 15c multicolored .90 .90
Nos. 294-297 (4) 2.40 2.40

Christmas.

Girl Guides, Globe and Flags — A31

Designs: 12c, Yellow elder and Brownie emblem. 15c, Ranger emblem.

1970, Feb. 23 **Wmk. 314** ***Perf. 14½***
298 A31 3c vio blue, yel & red .20 .20
299 A31 12c dk brn, grn & yel .60 .60
300 A31 15c vio bl, bluish grn & yel .80 .80
Nos. 298-300 (3) 1.60 1.60

60th anniversary of the Girl Guides.

Opening of UPU Headquarters, Bern — A32

1970, May 20 **Litho.** ***Perf. 14½***
301 A32 3c vermilion & multi .20 .20
302 A32 15c orange & multi .75 .75

Bus and Globe A33

Globe and: 11c, Train. 12c, Sailboat and ship. 15c, Plane.

1970, July 14 ***Perf. 13½x13***
303 A33 3c orange & multi .20 .20
304 A33 11c emerald & multi .65 .65
305 A33 12c multicolored .70 .70
306 A33 15c blue & multi 1.00 1.00
a. Souvenir sheet of 4, #303-306 9.00 9.00
Nos. 303-306 (4) 2.55 2.55

Issued to promote good will through world-wide travel and tourism.

People, Palms and Flamingo A34

15c, Red Cross Headquarters, Nassau & marlin.

1970, Aug. 18 ***Perf. 14x14½***
307 A34 3c multicolored .20 .20
308 A34 15c multicolored .80 .80

Centenary of British Red Cross Society.

Nativity by G. B. Pittoni — A35

Christmas: 11c, Holy Family, by Anton Raphael Mengs. 12c, Adoration of the Shepherds, by Giorgione. 15c, Adoration of the Shepherds, School of Seville.

Perf. 12½x13

1970, Nov. 3 **Litho.** **Wmk. 314**
309 A35 3c multicolored .20 .20
310 A35 11c red org & multi .55 .55
311 A35 12c emerald & multi .65 .65
312 A35 15c blue & multi .80 .80
a. Souv. sheet of 4, #309-312 + 3 labels 2.25 2.25
Nos. 309-312 (4) 2.20 2.20

International Airport A36

Designs: 2c, Breadfruit. 3c, Straw market. 4c, 6c, Hawksbill turtle. 5c, Grouper. 8c, Yellow elder. 10c, Bahamian sponge boat. 11c, Flamingos. 7c, 12c, Hibiscus. 15c, Bonefish. 18c, 22c, Royal poinciana. 50c, Post office, Nassau. $1, Pineapple, vert. $2, Crayfish, vert. $3, "Junkanoo" (costumed drummer), vert.

Wmk. 314 Upright (Sideways on $1, $2, $3)

1971 ***Perf. 14½x14, 14x14½***
313 A36 1c blue & multi .20 .20
314 A36 2c red & multi .20 .20
315 A36 3c lilac & multi .20 .20
316 A36 4c brown & multi .40 .40
317 A36 5c dp org & multi .30 .30
318 A36 6c brown & multi .20 .20
319 A36 7c green & multi .30 .30
320 A36 8c yel & multi .65 .40
321 A36 10c red & multi .40 .40
322 A36 11c red & multi .40 .40
323 A36 12c green & multi 1.10 1.10
324 A36 15c gray & multi .30 .30
325 A36 18c multicolored .40 .40
326 A36 22c green & multi 1.40 1.40
327 A36 50c multicolored 1.60 1.40
328 A36 $1 red & multi 3.50 2.75
329 A36 $2 blue & multi 6.75 5.50
330 A36 $3 vio bl & multi 10.00 8.75
Nos. 313-330 (18) 28.30 24.60

See Nos. 398-401, 426-443.

Wmk. 314 Sideways (Upright on $1, $2, $3)

1973
317a A36 5c .20 .20
320a A36 8c .25 .25
327a A36 50c 1.40 1.40
328a A36 $1 3.00 3.00
329a A36 $2 5.50 5.50
330a A36 $3 8.50 8.50
Nos. 317a-330a (6) 18.85 18.85

1976 **Wmk. 373**
313a A36 1c .20 .20
314a A36 2c .20 .20
315a A36 3c .20 .20
317b A36 5c .20 .20
320b A36 8c .20 .20
321a A36 10c .20 .20
327b A36 50c 1.25 1.25
328b A36 $1 2.50 2.50
329b A36 $2 4.75 4.75
330b A36 $3 7.50 7.50
Nos. 313a-330b (10) 17.20 17.20

Snowflake with Peace Signs A37

Christmas: 11c, "Peace on Earth" with doves. 15c, Christmas wreath around old Bahamas coat of arms. 18c, Star of Bethlehem over palms.

Perf. 14x14½

1971 **Photo.** **Wmk. 314**
331 A37 3c dp lil rose, gold & org .20 .20
332 A37 11c violet & gold .45 .45
333 A37 15c gold embossed & multi .65 .65
334 A37 18c brt bl, gold & vio bl .90 .90
a. Souv. sheet of 4, #331-334, perf. 15 2.50 2.50
Nos. 331-334 (4) 2.20 2.20

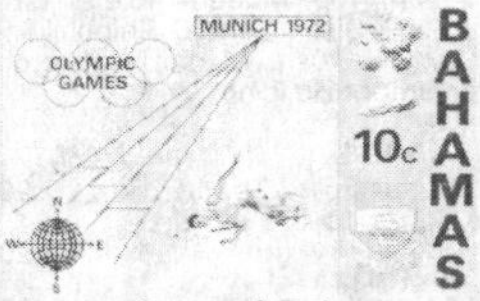

High Jump, Arms of Bahamas — A38

Olympic Rings, Compass, Arms of Bahamas and: 11c, Bicycling. 15c, Running. 18c, Sailing.

1972, June 27 **Litho.** ***Perf. 13x13½***
335 A38 10c lt violet & multi .40 .40
336 A38 11c ocher & multi .50 .50
337 A38 15c yel green & multi .70 .70
338 A38 18c blue & multi .95 .95
a. Souvenir sheet of 4, #335-338 3.25 *4.50*
Nos. 335-338 (4) 2.55 2.55

20th Olympic Games, Munich, Aug. 26-Sept. 10.

Shepherd and Star of Bethlehem — A39

Designs: 6c, Bells. 15c, Holly and monstrance. 20c, Poinsettia.

1972, Oct. 3 **Wmk. 314** ***Perf. 14***
339 A39 3c gold & multi .20 .20
340 A39 6c black & multi .30 .30
341 A39 15c black & multi .70 .70
342 A39 20c gold & multi .95 .95
a. Souvenir sheet of 4, #339-342 2.75 *3.25*
Nos. 339-342 (4) 2.15 2.15

Christmas. Gold on 15c is embossed.

Souvenir Sheet

Map of Bahama Islands — A40

1972, Nov. 1 **Litho.** ***Perf. 15***
343 A40 Sheet of 4 3.75 *4.75*
a. 11c blue & multi .35 .35
b. 15c blue & multi .45 .45
c. 18c blue & multi .55 .55
d. 50c blue & multi 1.50 1.50

Tourism Year of the Americas.

Silver Wedding Issue, 1972

Common Design Type

Design: Queen Elizabeth II, Prince Philip, mace and galleon.

Perf. 14x14½

1972, Nov. 13 **Photo.** **Wmk. 314**
344 CD324 11c car rose & multi .35 .35
345 CD324 18c violet & multi .55 .55

Weather Satellite, WMO Emblem A41

1973, Apr. 3 Litho. *Perf. 14*

346 A41 15c shown .65 .65
347 A41 18c Weather radar .90 .90

Intl. meteorological cooperation, cent.

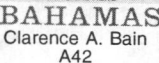

Clarence A. Bain
A42

Virgin in Prayer, by Sassoferrato
A43

Independence: 11c, New Bahamian coat of arms. 15c, New flag and Government House. $1, Milo B. Butler, Sr.

1973 Wmk. 314 *Perf. 14½x14*

348 A42 3c lilac & multi .20 .20
349 A42 11c lt blue & multi .30 .30
350 A42 15c lt green & multi .45 .45
351 A42 $1 yel & multi 2.25 2.25
a. Souvenir sheet of 4, #348-351 3.50 *4.50*
Nos. 348-351 (4) 3.20 3.20

Issued: #348-350, July 10; #351, 351a, Aug. 1.

1973, Oct. 16 Litho. *Perf. 14*

Christmas: 11c, Virgin and Child with St. John, by Filippino Lippi. 15c, Choir of Angels, by Marmion. 18c, The Two Trinities, by Murillo.

352 A43 3c blue & multi .20 .20
353 A43 11c multicolored .60 .60
354 A43 15c gray grn & multi .80 .80
355 A43 18c lil rose & multi 1.10 1.10
a. Souvenir sheet of 4, #352-355 2.75 *3.75*
Nos. 352-355 (4) 2.70 2.70

Agriculture, Science and Medicine — A44

18c, Symbols of engineering, art, and law.

1974, Feb. 5 Litho. *Perf. 13½x14*

356 A44 15c dull grn & multi .50 .50
357 A44 18 multicolored .65 .65

University of the West Indies, 25th anniv.

UPU Emblem
A45

Designs: 13c, UPU emblem, vert. 14c, UPU emblem. 18c, UPU monument, Bern, vert.

1974, Apr. 23 *Perf. 14*

358 A45 3c multicolored .20 .20
359 A45 13c multicolored .45 .45
360 A45 14c olive bis & multi .55 .55
361 A45 18c multicolored .80 .80
a. Souvenir sheet of 4, #358-361 1.90 *2.25*
Nos. 358-361 (4) 2.00 2.00

Centenary of Universal Postal Union.

Roseate Spoonbills, Trust Emblem — A46

Protected Birds (National Trust Emblem and): 14c, White-crowned pigeons. 21c, White-tailed tropic birds. 36c, Bahamian parrot.

1974, Sept. 10 Litho. *Perf. 14*

362 A46 13c multicolored .95 .70
363 A46 14c multicolored .95 .70
364 A46 21c multicolored 1.40 1.10
365 A46 36c multicolored 2.50 1.75
a. Souvenir sheet of 4, #362-365 7.50 *8.50*
Nos. 362-365 (4) 5.80 4.25

Bahamas National Trust, 15th anniv.

Holy Family, by Jacques de Stella
A47

Christmas: 10c, Virgin and Child, by Girolamo Romanino. 12c, Virgin and Child with St. John and St. Catherine, by Andrea Previtali. 21c, Virgin and Child with Angels, by Previtali.

1974, Oct. 29 Wmk. 314 *Perf. 13*

366 A47 8c black & multi .40 .40
367 A47 10c green & multi .50 .50
368 A47 12c red & multi .60 .60
369 A47 21c ultra & multi 1.00 1.00
a. Souvenir sheet of 4, #366-369 2.50 2.50
Nos. 366-369 (4) 2.50 2.50

Anteos Maerula
A48

1975, Feb. 4 Litho. *Perf. 14x13½*

370 A48 3c shown .30 .25
371 A48 14c Eurema nicippe 1.00 .70
372 A48 18c Papilio andraemon 1.25 1.00
373 A48 21c Euptoieta hegesia 1.50 1.40
a. Souvenir sheet of 4, #370-373 6.00 5.00
Nos. 370-373 (4) 4.05 3.35

Sheep Raising
A49

Designs: 14c, Electric reel fishing, vert. 18c, Growing food. 21c, Crude oil refinery, vert.

Unwmk.

1975, May 27 Litho. *Perf. 14*

374 A49 3c dull grn & multi .20 .20
375 A49 14c green & multi .50 .50
376 A49 18c brown & multi .65 .65
377 A49 21c vio bl & multi .75 .75
a. Souvenir sheet of 4, #374-377 2.25 2.25
Nos. 374-377 (4) 2.10 2.10

Economic diversification.

Rowena Rand, Staff and Chrismon
A50

Plant and IWY Emblem
A51

Wmk. 373

1975, July 22 Litho. *Perf. 14*

378 A50 14c multicolored .60 .60
379 A51 18c multicolored .80 .80

International Women's Year.

Adoration of the Shepherds, by Perugino — A52

Christmas: 8c, 18c, Adoration of the Kings, by Ghirlandaio. 21c, like 3c.

1975, Dec. 2 Litho. *Perf. 13½*

380 A52 3c dk green & multi .20 .20
381 A52 8c dk violet & multi .30 .30
382 A52 18c purple & multi .70 .70
383 A52 21c maroon & multi .85 .85
a. Souvenir sheet of 4, #380-383 2.25 2.25
Nos. 380-383 (4) 2.05 2.05

Telephones, 1876 and 1976 — A53

Designs: 16c, Radio-telephone link, Deleporte, Nassau (radar). 21c, Alexander Graham Bell. 25c, Communications satellite.

1976, Mar. 23 Litho. *Perf. 14*

384 A53 3c multicolored .20 .20
385 A53 16c multicolored .40 .40
386 A53 21c multicolored .50 .50
387 A53 25c multicolored .65 .65
Nos. 384-387 (4) 1.75 1.75

Centenary of first telephone call by Alexander Graham Bell, Mar. 10, 1876.

Bicycling and Olympic Rings — A54

Olympic Rings and: 16c, Long jump. 25c, Sailing. 40c, Boxing.

1976, July 13 Litho. *Perf. 14*

388 A54 8c magenta & blue .25 .25
389 A54 16c orange & brn .40 .40
390 A54 25c magenta & blue .60 .60
391 A54 40c orange & brn 1.10 1.10
a. Souvenir sheet of 4, #388-391 2.75 2.75
Nos. 388-391 (4) 2.35 2.35

21st Olympic Games, Montreal, Canada, July 17-Aug. 1.

John Murray, Earl of Dunmore
A55

Design: 16c, Map of US and Bahamas.

1976, June 1 Wmk. 373 *Perf. 14*

392 A55 16c multicolored .50 .50
393 A55 $1 multicolored 2.50 2.50
a. Souvenir sheet of 4, #393 10.00 10.00

American Bicentennial.

Virgin and Child, Filippo Lippi — A56

Christmas: 21c, Adoration of the Shepherds, School of Seville. 25c, Adoration of the Kings, by Vincenzo Foppa. 40c, Virgin and Child, by Vivarini.

1976, Oct. 19 Litho. *Perf. 14½x14*

394 A56 3c brt blue & multi .20 .20
395 A56 21c dp org & multi .60 .60
396 A56 25c emerald & multi .75 .75
397 A56 40c red lilac & multi 1.10 1.10
a. Souvenir sheet of 4, #394-397 2.75 2.75
Nos. 394-397 (4) 2.65 2.65

Type of 1971

Designs: 16c, Hibiscus. 21c, Breadfruit. 25c, Hawksbill turtle. 40c, Bahamian sponge boat.

1976, Nov. 2 Litho. Wmk. 373

398 A36 16c emerald & multi .55 .40
399 A36 21c vermilion & multi .65 *1.00*
400 A36 25c brown & multi .75 .50
401 A36 40c vermilion & multi 2.50 .75
Nos. 398-401 (4) 4.45 2.65

Elizabeth II Seated under Gold Canopy — A57

Designs: 16c, Coronation. 21c, Taking and signing of oath. 40c, Queen holding orb and scepter.

1977, Feb. 7 *Perf. 12*

402 A57 8c silver & multi .20 .20
403 A57 16c silver & multi .30 .30
404 A57 21c silver & multi .50 .50
405 A57 40c silver & multi 1.00 1.00
a. Souvenir sheet of 4, #402-405 3.00 *3.50*
Nos. 402-405 (4) 2.00 2.00

Reign of Queen Elizabeth II, 25th anniv.
For surcharges see Nos. 412-415. \

Featherduster — A58

Marine Life: 8c, Porkfish. 16c, Elkhorn coral. 21c, Soft coral and sponge.

1977, May 24 Litho. *Perf. 13½*

406 A58 3c multicolored .20 .20
407 A58 8c multicolored .30 .30
408 A58 16c multicolored .80 .80
409 A58 21c multicolored 1.00 1.00
a. Souvenir sheet of 4, #406-409, perf. 14½ 2.50 *3.00*
Nos. 406-409 (4) 2.30 2.30

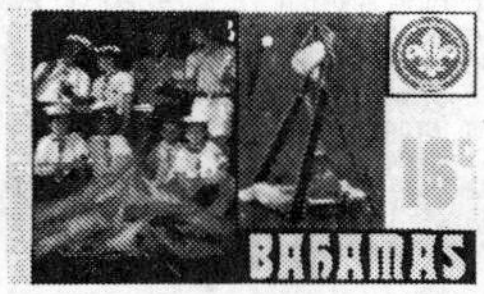

Campfire and Shower
A59

1977, Sept. 27 Litho. Wmk. 373

410 A59 16c shown .60 .50
411 A59 21c Boating .75 .60

6th Caribbean Jamboree, Kingston, Jamaica, Aug. 5-14.

Nos. 402-405a Overprinted: "Royal Visit / October 1977"

1977, Oct. 19 Litho. *Perf. 12*

412 A57 8c silver & multi .20 .20
413 A57 16c silver & multi .30 .30
414 A57 21c silver & multi .40 .40
415 A57 40c silver & multi .80 .80
a. Souvenir sheet of 4 2.25 *2.75*
Nos. 412-415 (4) 1.70 1.70

Caribbean visit of Queen Elizabeth II, Oct. 19-20.

Virgin and Child — A60

Nassau Public Library — A61

Crèche Figurines: 16c, Three Kings. 21c, Adoration of the Kings. 25c, Three Kings.

1977, Oct. 25 Litho. *Perf. 13½*
416 A60 3c gold & multi .20 .20
417 A60 16c gold & multi .40 .40
418 A60 21c gold & multi .50 .50
419 A60 25c gold & multi .60 .60
a. Souvenir sheet of 4, #416-419, perf. 14½ 1.90 1.90
Nos. 416-419 (4) 1.70 1.70

Christmas.

1978, Mar. 28 Litho. *Perf. 14½x14*

Architectural Heritage: 8c, St. Matthew's Church. 16c, Government House. 18c, The Hermitage, Cat Island.

420 A61 3c black & yel green .20 .20
421 A61 8c black & lt blue .20 .20
422 A61 16c black & lilac rose .30 .30
423 A61 18c black & salmon .35 .35
a. Souvenir sheet of 4, #420-423 1.10 1.10
Nos. 420-423 (4) 1.05 1.05

Scepter, St. Edward's Crown, Orb — A62

Perf. 14x13½
1978, June 27 Litho. Wmk. 373
424 A62 16c shown .30 .30
425 A62 $1 Elizabeth II 1.00 *1.10*
a. Souvenir sheet of 2, #424-425 2.25 2.25

Coronation of Queen Elizabeth II, 25th anniv.

Type of 1971

Designs as before and: 16c, Hibiscus. 25c, Hawksbill turtle.

Perf. 14½x14, 14x14½
1978, June Unwmk.
426 A36 1c blue & multi .20 .20
430 A36 5c dp org & multi .20 .20
436 A36 16c brt grn & multi .40 .40
439 A36 25c brown & multi .60 .60
440 A36 50c lemon & multi 1.10 1.10
441 A36 $1 lemon & multi 2.50 2.50
442 A36 $2 blue & multi 4.75 4.75
443 A36 $3 vio bl & multi 7.25 7.25
Nos. 426-443 (8) 17.00 17.00

Angels and Palms A63

Christmas: 5c, Coat of arms within wreath, and sailing ships.

Perf. 14x14½
1978, Nov. 14 Litho. Wmk. 373
444 A63 5c car, pink & gold .20 .20
445 A63 21c ultra, dk bl & gold .30 .30
a. Souvenir sheet of 2, #444-445 *2.50 2.50*

Baby Walking, IYC Emblem — A64

IYC Emblem and: 16c, Children playing leapfrog. 21c, Girl skipping rope. 25c, Building blocks with "IYC" and emblem.

Perf. 13½x13
1979, May 15 Litho. Wmk. 373
446 A64 5c multicolored .20 .20
447 A64 16c multicolored .25 .25
448 A64 21c multicolored .35 .35
449 A64 25c multicolored .40 .40
a. Souv. sheet of 4, #446-449, perf. 14 1.10 1.10
Nos. 446-449 (4) 1.20 1.20

International Year of the Child.

Rowland Hill and Penny Black — A65

Designs: 21c, Stamp printing press, 1840, and Bahamas No. 7. 25c, Great Britain No. 27 with 1850's Nassau cancellation, and Great Britain No. 29. 40c, Early mailboat and Bahamas No. 1.

1979, Aug. 14 *Perf. 13½x14*
450 A65 10c multicolored .20 .20
451 A65 21c multicolored .35 .35
452 A65 25c multicolored .40 .40
453 A65 40c multicolored .65 .65
a. Souvenir sheet of 4, #450-453 1.75 1.75
Nos. 450-453 (4) 1.60 1.60

Sir Rowland Hill (1795-1879), originator of penny postage.

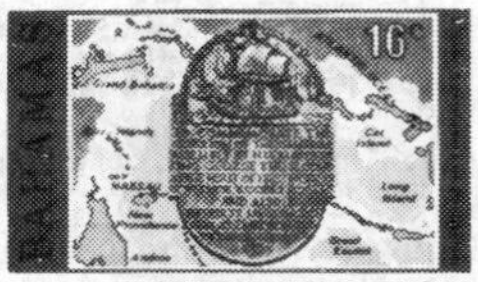

Commonwealth Plaque over Map of Bahamas — A66

Designs: 21c, Parliament buildings. 25c, Legislative chamber. $1, Senate chamber.

1979, Sept. 27 Litho. *Perf. 13½*
454 A66 16c multicolored .25 .25
455 A66 21c multicolored .35 .35
456 A66 25c multicolored .40 .40
457 A66 $1 multicolored 1.60 1.60
a. Souvenir sheet of 4, #454-457 2.75 2.75
Nos. 454-457 (4) 2.60 2.60

Parliament of Bahamas, 250th anniv.

Headdress — A67

Christmas: Goombay Carnival costumes.

1979, Nov. 6 Litho. *Perf. 13*
458 A67 5c multicolored .20 .20
459 A67 10c multicolored .20 .20
460 A67 16c multicolored .25 .25
461 A67 21c multicolored .30 .30
462 A67 25c multicolored .40 .40
463 A67 40c multicolored .60 .60
a. Souv. sheet of 6, 458-463, perf 13½ 2.00 2.00
Nos. 458-463 (6) 1.95 1.95

Columbus' Landing, 1492 A68

1980, July 9 Litho. *Perf. 15*
464 A68 1c shown .20 .20
465 A68 3c Blackbeard .20 .20
466 A68 5c Articles, 1647, Eleuthera map .20 .20
467 A68 10c Ceremonial mace .20 .20
468 A68 12c Col. Andrew Deveaux .25 .25
469 A68 15c Slave trading, Vendue House .30 .30
470 A68 16c Shipwreck salvage, 19th cent. .30 .30
471 A68 18c Blockade runner, 1860s .35 .35
472 A68 21c Bootlegging, 1919-1929 .40 .40
473 A68 25c Pineapple cultivation .25 .25
474 A68 40c Sponge clipping .75 .75
475 A68 50c Victoria & Colonial Hotels 1.00 1.00
476 A68 $1 Modern agriculture 2.00 2.00
477 A68 $2 Ship, jet 3.75 3.75
478 A68 $3 Central Bank, Arms 5.75 5.75
479 A68 $5 Prince Charles, Prime Minister Pindling 9.50 9.50
Nos. 464-479 (16) 25.40 25.40

For overprints and surcharges see Nos. 496-499, 532-535.

1985, Nov. 6 Wmk. 384
464a A68 1c .20 .20
465a A68 3c .20 .20
467a A68 10c .20 .20
473a A68 25c .50 .50
Nos. 464a-473a (4) 1.10 1.10

Virgin and Child, Straw Figures — A69

1980, Oct. 28 Litho. *Perf. 14½*
480 A69 5c shown .20 .20
481 A69 21c Three kings .35 .35
482 A69 25c Angel .40 .40
483 A69 $1 Christmas tree 1.60 1.60
a. Souvenir sheet of 4, #480-483 2.50 2.50
Nos. 480-483 (4) 2.55 2.55

Christmas.

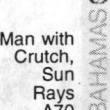

Man with Crutch, Sun Rays A70

1981, Feb. 10 Litho. *Perf. 14½*
484 A70 5c shown .20 .20
485 A70 $1 Man in wheelchair 1.60 1.60
a. Souvenir sheet of 2, #484-485 1.75 1.75

International Year of the Disabled.

Grand Bahama Tracking Station A71

Satellite Views: 20c, Bahamas, vert. 25c, Eleuthera. 50c, Andros and New Providence, vert.

Wmk. 373
1981, Apr. 21 Litho. *Perf. 13½*
486 A71 10c multicolored .20 .20
487 A71 20c multicolored .35 .35
488 A71 25c multicolored .45 .45
489 A71 50c multicolored .90 .90
a. Souvenir sheet of 4, #486-489 2.00 *2.75*
Nos. 486-489 (4) 1.90 1.90

Prince Charles and Lady Diana A72

Wmk. 373
1981, July 22 Litho. *Perf. 14½*
490 A72 30c shown .50 .50
491 A72 $2 Charles, Prime Minister 3.50 3.50
a. Souvenir sheet of 2, #490-491 5.00 *5.75*

Royal wedding.

Bahama Ducks — A73

Wmk. 373
1981, Aug. 25 Litho. *Perf. 14*
492 A73 5c shown .25 .25
493 A73 20c Reddish egrets 1.00 1.00
494 A73 25c Brown boobies 1.00 1.00
495 A73 $1 West Indian tree ducks 2.50 2.50
a. Souvenir sheet of 4, #492-495 5.25 5.25
Nos. 492-495 (4) 4.75 4.75

See Nos. 514-517.

Nos. 466-467, 473, 475 Overprinted: "COMMONWEALTH FINANCE MINISTERS' MEETING 21-23 SEPTEMBER 1981"

1981, Sept. Litho. *Perf. 15*
496 A68 5c multicolored .20 .20
497 A68 10c multicolored .20 .20
498 A68 25c multicolored .40 .40
499 A68 50c multicolored .85 .85
Nos. 496-499 (4) 1.65 1.65

World Food Day — A74

Perf. 13x13½
1981, Oct. 16 Wmk. 373
500 A74 5c Chickens .20 .20
501 A74 20c Sheep .40 .40
502 A74 30c Lobster .60 .60
503 A74 50c Pigs 1.00 1.00
a. Souvenir sheet of 4, #500-503 2.25 *2.75*
Nos. 500-503 (4) 2.20 2.20

Christmas — A75

Wmk. 373
1981, Nov. 23 Litho. *Perf. 14*
504 Sheet of 9 5.00 5.00
a. A75 5c Father Christmas .20 .20
b. A75 5c shown .20 .20
c. A75 5c St. Nicholas, Holland .20 .20
d. A75 25c Lussibruden, Sweden .40 .40
e. A75 25c Mother and child .40 .40
f. A75 25c King Wenceslas, Czechoslovakia .40 .40
g. A75 30c Mother and child .45 .45
h. A75 30c Mother and child standing .45 .45
i. A75 $1 Christkindl angel, Germany 1.75 1.75

TB Bacillus Centenary A76

1982, Feb. 3 Litho. *Perf. 14*
505 A76 5c Koch .20 .20
506 A76 16c X-ray .30 .30
507 A76 21c Microscopes .40 .40

508 A76 $1 Mantoux test 1.90 1.90
a. Souvenir sheet of 4, #505-508, perf. 14½ 3.50 4.00
Nos. 505-508 (4) 2.80 2.80

Flamingoes A77

Designs: a, Females. b, Males. c, Nesting. d, Juvenile birds. e, Immature birds. No. 509 in continuous design.

Wmk. 373

1982, Apr. 28 Litho. *Perf. 14*
509 Strip of 5, multicolored 4.00 4.00
a.-e. A77 25c any single .80 .80

Princess Diana Issue
Common Design Type

1982, July 1 Litho. *Perf. 14*
510 CD333 16c Arms .25 .25
511 CD333 25c Diana .40 .40
512 CD333 40c Wedding .60 .60
513 CD333 $1 Portrait 1.50 1.50
Nos. 510-513 (4) 2.75 2.75

Bird Type of 1981

Wmk. 373

1982, Aug. 18 Litho. *Perf. 14*
514 A73 10c Bat .20 .20
515 A73 16c Hutia .30 .30
516 A73 21c Racoon .35 .35
517 A73 $1 Dolphins 1.75 1.75
a. Souvenir sheet of 4, #514-517 3.25 3.25
Nos. 514-517 (4) 2.60 2.60

28th Commonwealth Parliamentary Conference A78

Perf. 14x13½

1982, Oct. 16 Litho. Wmk. 373
518 A78 5c Plaque .20 .20
519 A78 25c Assoc. arms .50 .50
520 A78 40c Natl. arms .80 .80
521 A78 50c House of Assembly 1.00 1.00
Nos. 518-521 (4) 2.50 2.50

Christmas — A79

Designs: 5c, Wesley Methodist Church, Baillou Hill Road. 12c, Centerville Seventh Day Adventist Church. 15c, Church of God of Prophecy, East Street. 21c, Bethel Baptist Church, Meeting Street. 25c, St. Francis Xavier Catholic Church, West Hill Street. $1, Holy Cross Anglican Church, Highbury Park.

1982, Nov. 3 *Perf. 14*
522 A79 5c multicolored .20 .20
523 A79 12c multicolored .25 .25
524 A79 15c multicolored .30 .30
525 A79 21c multicolored .40 .40
526 A79 25c multicolored .50 .50
527 A79 $1 multicolored 1.90 1.90
Nos. 522-527 (6) 3.55 3.55

A80

1983, Mar. 14 Litho.
528 A80 5c Lynden O. Pindling .20 .20
529 A80 25c Flags .40 .40
530 A80 35c Map .55 .55
531 A80 $1 Ocean liner 1.60 1.60
Nos. 528-531 (4) 2.75 2.75

Commonwealth Day.

Nos. 469-472 Surcharged

1983, Apr. 5 Litho. *Perf. 15*
532 A68 20c on 15c multi .35 .35
533 A68 31c on 21c multi .55 .55
534 A68 35c on 16c multi .65 .65
535 A68 80c on 18c multi 1.50 1.50
Nos. 532-535 (4) 3.05 3.05

30th Anniv. of Customs Cooperation Council A81

10th Anniv. of Independence A82

Perf. 14x13½

1983, May 31 Wmk. 373
536 A81 31c Officers, ship .50 .50
537 A81 $1 Officers, jet 1.60 1.60

1983, July 6 Litho. *Perf. 14*
538 A82 $1 Flag raising 1.50 1.50
a. Souvenir sheet, perf. 12 1.50 1.50

Local Butterflies A83

1983, Aug. 24 *Perf. 14½x14*
539 A83 5c Carters skipper .20 .20
540 A83 25c Giant southern white .90 .90
541 A83 31c Large orange sulphur 1.10 1.10
542 A83 50c Flambeau 1.75 1.75
a. Souvenir sheet of 4 4.25 4.25
Nos. 539-542 (4) 3.95 3.95

No. 542a contains Nos. 539-542, perf. 14 and perf. 14½x14.

American Loyalists Arrival Bicentenary — A84

Paintings by Alton Lowe.

1983, Sept. 28 *Perf. 14*
543 A84 5c Loyalist Dreams .20 .20
544 A84 31c New Plymouth, Abaco .55 .55
545 A84 35c New Plymouth Hotel .60 .60
546 A84 50c Island Hope .90 .90
a. Souvenir sheet of 4, #543-546 2.25 2.25
Nos. 543-546 (4) 2.25 2.25

Christmas — A85

125th Anniv. of Bahamas Stamps — A86

Children's designs: 5c, Christmas Bells, by Monica Pinder. 20c, The Flamingo by Cory Bullard. 25c, The Yellow Hibiscus with Christmas Candle by Monique A. Bailey. 31c, Santa goes a Sailing by Sabrina Seiler, horiz. 35c, Silhouette scene with palm trees by James Blake. 50c, Silhouette scene with Pelicans, by Erik Russell, horiz.

1983, Nov. 1 *Perf. 14*
547 A85 5c multicolored .20 .20
548 A85 20c multicolored .30 .30
549 A85 25c multicolored .40 .40
550 A85 31c multicolored .50 .50
551 A85 35c multicolored .60 .60
552 A85 50c multicolored .80 .80
Nos. 547-552 (6) 2.80 2.80

1984, Feb. 22 Litho. *Perf. 14*
553 A86 5c No. 3 .20 .20
554 A86 $1 No. 1 1.60 1.60

Lloyd's List Issue
Common Design Type

Wmk. 373

1984, Apr. 25 Litho. *Perf. 14½*
555 CD335 5c Trent .20 .20
556 CD335 31c Orinoco .55 .55
557 CD335 35c Nassau Harbor .60 .60
558 CD335 50c Container ship Oropesa .85 .85
Nos. 555-558 (4) 2.20 2.20

1984 Summer Olympics A87

1984, June 20 Litho. *Perf. 14x14½*
559 A87 5c Running .20 .20
560 A87 25c Discus .40 .40
561 A87 31c Boxing .50 .50
562 A87 $1 Basketball 1.60 1.60
a. Souvenir sheet of 4, #559-562 2.75 2.75
Nos. 559-562 (4) 2.70 2.70

Flags of Bahamas and Caribbean Community — A88

Wmk. 373

1984, July 4 Litho. *Perf. 14*
563 A88 50c multicolored .90 .90

Conference of Heads of Government of Caribbean Community, 5th Meeting.

Allen's Cay Iguana — A89

1984, Aug. 15 *Perf. 14*
564 A89 5c shown .20 .20
565 A89 25c Curly-tailed lizard .60 .60
566 A89 35c Greenhouse frog .80 .80
567 A89 50c Atlantic green turtle 1.00 1.00
a. Souvenir sheet of 4, #564-567 3.00 3.00
Nos. 564-567 (4) 2.60 2.60

25th Anniv. of Natl. Trust — A90

Christmas — A91

Wildlife: a, Calliphlox evelynae. b, Megaceryle alcyon, Eleutherodactylus planirostris. c, Phoebis sennae, Phoenicopterus ruber, Himantopus himantopus, Phoebus sennae. d, Urbanus proteus, Chelonia mydas. e, Pandion haliaetus.

Continuous design.

1984, Aug. 15 Litho. *Perf. 14*
568 Strip of 5 5.25 5.25
a.-e. A90 31c any single 1.10 1.10

1984, Nov. 7 Litho. *Perf. 13½x13*

Madonna and Child Paintings.

569 A91 5c Titian .20 .20
570 A91 31c Anais Colin .55 .55
571 A91 35c Elena Caula .60 .60
a. Souvenir sheet of 3, #569-571 1.40 1.40
Nos. 569-571 (3) 1.35 1.35

Girl Guides, 75th Anniv., Intl. Youth Year — A92

1985, Feb. 22 Litho. *Perf. 14*
572 A92 5c Brownies .20 .20
573 A92 25c Camping .40 .40
574 A92 31c Girl Guides .50 .50
575 A92 35c Rangers .55 .55
a. Souvenir sheet of 4, #572-575 1.60 1.60
Nos. 572-575 (4) 1.65 1.65

Audubon Birth Bicentenary — A93

Wmk. 373

1985, Apr. 24 Litho. *Perf. 14*
576 A93 5c Killdeer .20 .20
577 A93 31c Mourning dove, vert. .85 .85
578 A93 35c Mourning doves, diff., vert. .90 .90
579 A93 $1 Killdeers, diff. 2.50 2.50
Nos. 576-579 (4) 4.45 4.45

Queen Mother 85th Birthday
Common Design Type

Perf. 14½x14

1985, June 7 Litho. Wmk. 384
580 CD336 5c Portrait, 1927 .20 .20
581 CD336 25c At christening of Peter Phillips .40 .40
582 CD336 35c Portrait, 1985 .60 .60
583 CD336 50c Holding Prince Henry .85 .85
Nos. 580-583 (4) 2.05 2.05

Souvenir Sheet
584 CD336 $1.25 In a pony and trap 2.00 2.00

UN and UN Food and Agriculture Org., 40th Annivs. A94

Wmk. 373

1985, Aug. 26 Litho. *Perf. 14*
585 A94 25c Wheat, emblems .40 .40

Commonwealth Heads of Government Meeting, 1985 — A95

1985, Oct. 16 Wmk. 373 Perf. 14½

586 A95 31c Queen Elizabeth II .50 .50
587 A95 35c Flag, Commonwealth emblem .55 .55

Christmas A96

Paintings by Alton Roland Lowe: 5c, Grandma's Christmas Bouquet. 25c, Junkanoo Romeo and Juliet, vert. 31c, Bunce Girl, vert. 35c, Home for Christmas.

1985, Nov. 5 Perf. 13

588 A96 5c multicolored .20 .20
589 A96 25c multicolored .50 .50
590 A96 31c multicolored .60 .60
591 A96 35c multicolored .65 .65
a. Souv. sheet of 4, #588-591, perf. 14 1.90 1.90
Nos. 588-591 (4) 1.95 1.95

Queen Elizabeth II 60th Birthday
Common Design Type

Designs: 10c, Age 1, 1927. 25c, Coronation, Westminster Abbey, 1953. 35c, Giving speech, royal visit, Bahamas. 40c, At Djakova, Yugoslavia, state visit, 1972. $1, Visiting Crown Agents, 1983.

1986, Apr. 21 Wmk. 384 Perf. 14½

592 CD337 10c scar, blk & sil .20 *.25*
593 CD337 25c ultra & multi .35 *.45*
594 CD337 35c green & multi .45 *.60*
595 CD337 40c violet & multi .55 *.65*
596 CD337 $1 rose vio & multi 1.25 *1.75*
Nos. 592-596 (5) 2.80 *3.70*

AMERIPEX '86 — A97

1986, May 19 Perf. 14

597 A97 5c Nos. 464, 471 .20 .20
598 A97 25c Nos. 288-289 .45 .45
599 A97 31c No. 392 .55 .55
600 A97 50c No. 489a .90 .90
601 A97 $1 Statue of Liberty, vert. 1.75 1.75
a. Souvenir sheet of one 1.75 1.75
Nos. 597-601 (5) 3.85 3.85

Statue of Liberty, cent.

Royal Wedding Issue, 1986
Common Design Type

Designs: 10c, Formal engagement. $1, Andrew in dress uniform.

1986, July 23 Perf. 14½x14

602 CD338 10c multicolored .20 .20
603 CD338 $1 multicolored 1.60 1.60

Fish A98

1986-87 Wmk. 384 Perf. 14

604 A98 5c Rock beauty .20 .20
605 A98 10c Stoplight parrotfish .20 .20
606 A98 15c Jacknife fish .25 .25
607 A98 20c Flamefish .30 .30
608 A98 25c Swissguard basslet .35 .35
609 A98 30c Spotfin butterflyfish .40 .40
610 A98 35c Queen triggerfish .50 .50
611 A98 40c Four-eyed butterflyfish .55 .55
612 A98 45c Fairy basslet .65 .65
613 A98 50c Queen angelfish .70 .70
614 A98 60c Blue chromis .85 .85
615 A98 $1 Spanish hogfish 1.40 1.40
616 A98 $2 Harlequin bass 7.00 7.00
617 A98 $3 Blackbar soldierfish 6.50 6.50
618 A98 $5 Pygmy angelfish 7.25 7.25
618A A99 $10 Red hind ('87) 16.00 16.00
Nos. 604-618A (16) 43.10 43.10

Nos. 605, 608, 611-613, 615, 617-618 exist inscribed "1990." Nos. 611, 615, 616 "1988." Issue dates: $10, Jan. 2, others, Aug. 5.

1987, June 25 Wmk. 373

604a 5c .20 .20
605a 10c .20 .20
606a 15c .25 .25
611a 40c .55 .55
612a 45c .65 .65
613a 50c .70 .70
614a 60c .85 .85
615a $1 1.40 1.40
616a $2 2.75 2.75
Nos. 604a-616a (9) 7.55 7.55

Nos. 604a-616a dated 1987. No. 605a "1988." No. 604a "1989."

Christ Church Cathedral — A99

Wmk. 373

1986, Sept. 16 Litho. Perf. 14½

619 A99 10c View, 19th cent. .20 .20
620 A99 40c View, 1986 .65 .65
a. Souvenir sheet of 2, #619-620 .85 .85

City of Nassau, Diocese of Nassau and the Bahamas and Christ Church, 125th anniv.

Christmas, Intl. Peace Year — A100

Wmk. 384

1986, Nov. 4 Litho. Perf. 14

621 A100 10c Nativity .20 .20
622 A100 40c Flight to Egypt .65 .65
623 A100 45c Children praying .75 .75
624 A100 50c Exchanging gifts .80 .80
a. Souvenir sheet of 4, #621-624 2.50 2.50
Nos. 621-624 (4) 2.40 2.40

Pirates of the Caribbean A101

Map of the Bahamas A102

Wmk. 373

1987, June 2 Litho. Perf. 14½

625 A101 10c Anne Bonney .25 .25
626 A101 40c Blackbeard (d. 1718) .90 .90
627 A101 45c Capt. Edward England 1.00 1.00
628 A101 50c Capt. Woodes Rogers (c. 1679-1732) 1.25 1.25
Nos. 625-628 (4) 3.40 3.40

Souvenir Sheet

629 A102 $1.25 shown 2.75 2.75

Paintings of Lighthouses by Alton Roland Lowe A103

1987, Mar. 31 Wmk. 384

630 A103 10c Great Isaac .30 .30
631 A103 40c Bird Rock 1.25 1.25
632 A103 45c Castle Is. 1.50 1.50
633 A103 $1 Hole in the Wall 3.25 3.25
Nos. 630-633 (4) 6.30 6.30

Tourist Transportation A104

Ships: No. 634a, Cruise ship, sailboat. b, Cruise ships, tugboat, speedboat. c, Pleasure boat leaving harbor, sailboat. d, Pleasure boat docked, sailboats. e, Sailboats.

Aircraft: No. 635a, Bahamasair plane. b, Bahamasair and Pan Am aircraft. c, Aircraft, radar tower. d, Control tower, aircraft. e, Helicopter, planes.

1987, Aug. 26 Wmk. 373 Perf. 14

634 Strip of 5 3.75 3.75
a.-e. A104 40c any single .75 .75
635 Strip of 5 3.75 3.75
a.-e. A104 40c any single .75 .75

Orchids Painted by Alton Roland Lowe A105

1987, Oct. 20 Wmk. 384 Perf. 14½

636 A105 10c Cattleyopis lindenii .20 .20
637 A105 40c Encyclia lucayana .65 .65
638 A105 45c Encyclia hodgeana .75 .75
639 A105 50c Encyclia lleidae .80 .80
a. Souvenir sheet of 4, #636-639 2.50 2.50
Nos. 636-639 (4) 2.40 2.40

Christmas.

Discovery of America, 500th Anniv. (in 1992) — A106

10c, Ferdinand & Isabella. 40c, Columbus before the Talavera Committee. 45c, Lucayan village. 50c, Lucayan potters. $1.50, Map, c. 1500.

Perf. 14x14½

1988, Feb. 23 Litho. Wmk. 373

640 A106 10c multicolored .20 .20
641 A106 40c multicolored .65 .65
642 A106 45c multicolored .75 .75
643 A106 50c multicolored .80 .80
Nos. 640-643 (4) 2.40 2.40

Souvenir Sheet

644 A106 $1.50 multicolored 3.00 3.00

See #663-667, 688-692, 725-729, 749-753, 762.

World Wildlife Fund — A107

Whistling ducks, Dendrocygna arborea.

1988, Apr. 29 Perf. 14½

645 A107 5c Ducks in flight .75 .25
646 A107 10c Among marine plants 1.50 .50
647 A107 20c Adults, ducklings 3.00 1.00
648 A107 45c Wading 6.25 2.25
Nos. 645-648 (4) 11.50 4.00

Abolition of Slavery, 150th Anniv. A108

1988, Aug. 9 Perf. 14

649 A108 10c African hut .20 .20
650 A108 40c Basket weavers in hut, Grantstown .80 .80

1988 Summer Olympics, Seoul A109

Games emblem and details of painting by James Martin: 10c, Olympic flame, high jump, hammer throw, basketball and gymnastics. 40c, Swimming, boxing, weight lifting, fencing and running. 45c, Gymnastics, shot put and javelin. $1, Running, cycling and gymnastics.

Wmk. 384

1988, Aug. 30 Litho. Perf. 14

651 A109 10c multicolored .20 .20
652 A109 40c multicolored .80 .80
653 A109 45c multicolored .90 .90
654 A109 $1 multicolored 2.00 2.00
a. Souvenir sheet of 4, #651-654 4.00 4.00
Nos. 651-654 (4) 3.90 3.90

Lloyds of London, 300th Anniv.
Common Design Type

Designs: 10c, Lloyds List No. 560, 1740. 40c, Freeport Harbor, horiz. 45c, Space shuttle over the Bahamas, horiz. $1, Supply ship Yarmouth Castle on fire.

1988, Oct. 4 Wmk. 373

655 CD341 10c multicolored .20 .20
656 CD341 40c multicolored .80 .80
657 CD341 45c multicolored .90 .90
658 CD341 $1 multicolored 2.00 2.00
Nos. 655-658 (4) 3.90 3.90

Christmas Carols — A110

Designs: 10c, O' Little Town of Bethlehem. 40c, Little Donkey. 45c, Silent Night. 50c, Hark! The Herald Angels Sing.

1988, Nov. 21 Wmk. 384 Perf. 14½

659 A110 10c multicolored .20 .20
660 A110 40c multicolored .80 .80
661 A110 45c multicolored .90 .90
662 A110 50c multicolored 1.00 1.00
a. Souvenir sheet of 4, #659-662 2.90 2.90
Nos. 659-662 (4) 2.90 2.90

Discovery of America Type of 1988

Design: 10c, Columbus as chartmaker. 40c, Development of the caravel. 45c, Navigational tools. 50c, Arawak artifacts. $1.50, Caravel under construction, an illumination from the Nuremburg Chronicles, 15th cent.

Perf. 14½x14

1989, Jan. 25 Litho. Wmk. 373

663 A106 10c multicolored .20 .20
664 A106 40c multicolored .80 .80
665 A106 45c multicolored .90 .90
666 A106 50c multicolored 1.00 1.00
Nos. 663-666 (4) 2.90 2.90

Souvenir Sheet

667 A106 $1.50 multicolored 3.00 3.00

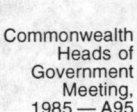

Hummingbirds
A111

Wmk. 384

1989, Mar. 29 Litho. *Perf. 14½*
668 A111 10c Cuban emerald .20 .20
669 A111 40c Ruby-throated .80 .80
670 A111 45c Bahama woodstar .90 .90
671 A111 50c Rufous 1.00 1.00
Nos. 668-671 (4) 2.90 2.90

Intl. Red Cross and Red Crescent Organizations, 125th Annivs. — A112

1989, May 31 *Perf. 14x14½*
672 A112 10c Water safety .20 .20
673 A112 $1 Dunant, Battle of Solferino 2.00 2.00

Moon Landing, 20th Anniv.
Common Design Type

Apollo 8: 10c, Apollo Communications System, Grand Bahama Is. 40c, James Lovell Jr., William Anders and Frank Borman. 45c, Mission emblem. $1, The Rising Earth (photograph). $2, Astronaut practicing lunar surface activities at Manned Spacecraft Center, Houston, in training for Apollo 11 mission.

1989, July 20 *Perf. 14x13½*
Size of Nos. 674-675: 29x29mm
674 CD342 10c multicolored .20 .20
675 CD342 40c multicolored .80 .80
676 CD342 45c multicolored .90 .90
677 CD342 $1 multicolored 2.00 2.00
Nos. 674-677 (4) 3.90 3.90

Souvenir Sheet
678 CD342 $2 multicolored 4.00 4.00

Christmas
A113

Designs: 10c, Church of the Nativity, Bethlehem. 40c, Basilica of the Annunciation, Nazareth. 45c, By the Sea of Galilee, Tabgha. $1, Church of the Holy Sepulcher, Jerusalem.

Perf. 14½x14
1989, Oct. 16 Wmk. 373
679 A113 10c multicolored .20 .20
680 A113 40c multicolored .80 .80
681 A113 45c multicolored .90 .90
682 A113 $1 multicolored 2.00 2.00
a. Souvenir sheet of 4, #679-682 4.00 4.00
Nos. 679-682 (4) 3.90 3.90

World Stamp Expo '89
A114

Expo emblem and: 10c, Earth, #359. 40c, UPU Headquarters, #301. 45c, US Capitol, #601. $1, Passenger jet, #150. $2, Washington, DC, on map.

1989, Nov. 17 Wmk. 384 *Perf. 14*
683 A114 10c multicolored .20 .20
684 A114 40c multicolored .80 .80
685 A114 45c multicolored .90 .90
686 A114 $1 multicolored 2.00 2.00
Nos. 683-686 (4) 3.90 3.90

Souvenir Sheet
Perf. 14½x14
687 A114 $2 multicolored 4.00 4.00

No. 687 contains one 31x38mm stamp.

Discovery of America Type of 1988

10c, Caravel launch. 40c, Provisioning ships. 45c, Shortening sails. 50c, Lucayan fishermen. $1.50, Columbus's fleet departing from Cadiz.

Perf. 14½x14
1990, Jan. 24 Litho. Wmk. 373
688 A106 10c multicolored .30 .25
689 A106 40c multicolored 1.25 1.00
690 A106 45c multicolored 1.50 1.25
691 A106 50c multicolored 1.75 1.50
Nos. 688-691 (4) 4.80 4.00

Souvenir Sheet
692 A106 $1.50 multicolored 5.00 5.00

Organization of American States, Cent. — A115

1990, Mar. 14 Wmk. 384 *Perf. 14*
693 A115 40c multicolored .80 .80

Souvenir Sheet

Stamp World London '90 — A116

Aircraft: a, Spitfire I. b, Hurricane IIc.

1990, May 3 Wmk. 384
694 A116 Sheet of 2 4.00 4.00
a.-b. $1 any single 2.00 2.00

For surcharge see No. B3.

Intl. Literacy Year
A117

10c, Teacher helping student. 40c, Children reading to each other. 50c, Children reading aloud.

1990, June 27 Wmk. 384 *Perf. 14*
695 A117 10c multicolored .20 .20
696 A117 40c multicolored .80 .80
697 A117 50c multicolored 1.00 1.00
Nos. 695-697 (3) 2.00 2.00

Queen Mother, 90th Birthday
Common Design Types

1990, Aug. 4 *Perf. 14x15*
698 CD343 40c Portrait, c. 1938 .80 .80

Perf. 14½
699 CD344 $1.50 At garden party, 1938 3.00 3.00

Bahamian Parrot — A118

1990, Sept. 26 Wmk. 373 *Perf. 14*
700 A118 10c shown .30 .25
701 A118 40c In flight 1.25 1.00
702 A118 45c Head 1.50 1.25
703 A118 50c On branch 1.75 1.50
Nos. 700-703 (4) 4.80 4.00

Souvenir Sheet
704 A118 $1.50 On branch, diff. 4.50 4.50

Christmas — A119

Birds — A120

Wmk. 373
1990, Nov. 5 Litho. *Perf. 13½*
705 A119 10c Angel appears to Mary .20 .20
706 A119 40c Nativity .80 .80
707 A119 45c Angel appears to shepherds .90 .90
708 A119 $1 Three kings 2.00 2.00
a. Souvenir sheet of 4, #705-708 3.90 3.90
Nos. 705-708 (4) 3.90 3.90

Wmk. 384
1991, Feb. 4 Litho. *Perf. 14*
709 A120 5c Green heron .20 .20
710 A120 10c Turkey vulture .20 .20
711 A120 15c Osprey .30 .30
712 A120 20c Clapper rail .40 .40
713 A120 25c Royal tern .50 .50
714 A120 30c Key West quail dove .60 .60
715 A120 40c Smooth-billed ani .80 .80
716 A120 45c Burrowing owl .90 .90
717 A120 50c Hairy woodpecker 1.00 1.00
718 A120 55c Mangrove cuckoo 1.10 1.10
719 A120 60c Bahama mockingbird 1.25 1.25
720 A120 70c Red-winged blackbird 1.40 1.40
721 A120 $1 Thick-billed vireo 2.00 2.00
722 A120 $2 Bahama yellowthroat 4.00 4.00
723 A120 $5 Stripe-headed tanager 10.00 10.00
724 A120 $10 Greater Antillean bullfinch 20.00 20.00
Nos. 709-724 (16) 44.65 44.65

Issued: $10, July 1; others, Feb. 4.

1993 Wmk. 373
710a 10c .20 .20
713a 25c .50 .50
714a 30c .60 .60
715a 40c .80 .80
718a 55c 1.10 1.10
723a $5 10.00 10.00
Nos. 710a-723a (6) 13.20 13.20

Nos. 710a-723a dated 1993. 40c, 55c exist dated 1995.
Issued: 40c, 12/31/93; others, 9/23/93.

Discovery of America Type of 1988

Designs: 15c, Columbus practices celestial navigation. 40c, The fleet in rough seas. 55c, Natives on the beach. 60c, Map of voyage. $1.50, Pinta's crew sights land.

Perf. 14½x14
1991, Apr. 9 Litho. Wmk. 384
725 A106 15c multicolored .30 .30
726 A106 40c multicolored .80 .80
727 A106 55c multicolored 1.10 1.10
728 A106 60c multicolored 1.25 1.25
Nos. 725-728 (4) 3.45 3.45

Souvenir Sheet
729 A106 $1.50 multicolored 3.00 3.00

Elizabeth & Philip, Birthdays
Common Design Types
Wmk. 384

1991, June 17 Litho. *Perf. 14½*
730 CD346 15c multicolored .30 .30
731 CD345 $1 multicolored 2.00 2.00
a. Pair, #730-731 + label 2.30 2.30

Hurricane Awareness — A121

Designs: 15c, Weather radar image of Hurricane Hugo. 40c, Anatomy of hurricane rotating around eye. 55c, Flooding caused by Hurricane David. 60c, Lockheed WP-3D Orion.

1991, Aug. 28 *Perf. 14*
732 A121 15c multicolored .30 .30
733 A121 40c multicolored .80 .80
734 A121 55c multicolored 1.10 1.10
735 A121 60c multicolored 1.25 1.25
Nos. 732-735 (4) 3.45 3.45

Christmas
A122

Designs: 15c, The Annunciation. 55c, Mary and Joseph traveling to Bethlehem. 60c, Angel appearing to shepherds. $1, Adoration of the Magi.

1991, Oct. 28 Wmk. 373 *Perf. 14*
736 A122 15c multicolored .30 .30
737 A122 55c multicolored 1.10 1.10
738 A122 60c multicolored 1.25 1.25
739 A122 $1 multicolored 2.00 2.00
a. Souvenir sheet of 4, #736-739 4.75 4.75
Nos. 736-739 (4) 4.65 4.65

Majority Rule, 25th Anniv.
A123

Designs: 15c, First Progressive Liberal Party cabinet. 40c, Signing of Independence Constitution. 55c, Handing over constitutional instrument, vert. 60c, First Bahamian Governor-General, Sir Milo Butler, vert.

Wmk. 373
1992, Jan. 10 Litho. *Perf. 14*
740 A123 15c multicolored .35 .35
741 A123 40c multicolored 1.00 1.00
742 A123 55c multicolored 1.25 1.25
743 A123 60c multicolored 1.50 1.50
Nos. 740-743 (4) 4.10 4.10

Queen Elizabeth II's Accession to the Throne, 40th Anniv.
Common Design Type
Wmk. 373

1992, Feb. 6 Litho. *Perf. 14*
744 CD349 15c multicolored .30 .30
745 CD349 40c multicolored .70 .70
746 CD349 55c multicolored 1.00 1.00
747 CD349 60c multicolored 1.10 1.10
748 CD349 $1 multicolored 1.90 1.90
Nos. 744-748 (5) 5.00 5.00

Discovery of America Type of 1988

Designs: 15c, Lucayans first sight of fleet. 40c, Approaching Bahamas coastline. 55c, Lucayans about to meet Columbus. 60c, Columbus gives thanks for safe arrival. $1.50, Monument to Columbus' landing.

Perf. 14½x14
1992, Mar. 17 Litho. Wmk. 384
749 A106 15c multicolored .30 .30
750 A106 40c multicolored .75 .75
751 A106 55c multicolored 1.00 1.00
752 A106 60c multicolored 1.10 1.10
Nos. 749-752 (4) 3.15 3.15

Souvenir Sheet
753 A106 $1.50 multicolored 2.75 2.75

Templeton, Galbraith and Hansberger Ltd. Building — A124

Wmk. 384

1992, Apr. 22 Litho. *Perf. 14½*

754 A124 55c multicolored 1.00 1.00

Templeton Prize for Progress in Religion, 20th Anniv.

1992 Summer Olympics, Barcelona — A125

Perf. 14½x14

1992, June 2 Wmk. 373

755 A125 15c Pole vault .30 .30
756 A125 40c Javelin .75 .75
757 A125 55c Hurdling 1.00 1.00
758 A125 60c Basketball 1.10 1.10
Nos. 755-758 (4) 3.15 3.15

Souvenir Sheet

759 A125 $2 Sailing 3.75 3.75

Intl. Conference on Nutrition — A126

Designs: 15c, Drought-affected earth, starving child. 55c, Hand holding plant, stalks of grain.

Perf. 14½x13

1992, Aug. 11 Litho. Wmk. 373

760 A126 15c multicolored .30 .30
761 A126 55c multicolored 1.00 1.00

Discovery of America Type of 1988

Souvenir Sheet

Perf. 14x13½

1992, Oct. 12 Litho. Wmk. 384

762 A106 $2 Coming ashore 3.75 3.75

Christmas — A127

1992, Nov. 2 Wmk. 373 *Perf. 14*

763 A127 15c The Annunciation .30 .30
764 A127 55c Nativity Scene 1.00 1.00
765 A127 60c Angel, shepherds 1.10 1.10
766 A127 70c The Magi 1.25 1.25
a. Souvenir sheet of 4, #763-766 3.75 3.75
Nos. 763-766 (4) 3.65 3.65

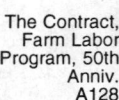

The Contract, Farm Labor Program, 50th Anniv. A128

Bahamian, American flags and: 15c, Silhouette of worker's head. 55c, Onions. 60c, Citrus fruits. 70c, Apples.

Perf. 14x14½

1993, Mar. 16 Litho. Wmk. 384

767 A128 15c multicolored .30 .30
768 A128 55c multicolored 1.00 1.00
769 A128 60c multicolored 1.10 1.10
770 A128 70c multicolored 1.25 1.25
Nos. 767-770 (4) 3.65 3.65

Royal Air Force, 75th Anniv.

Common Design Type

Designs: 15c, Westland Wapiti. 40c, Gloster Gladiator. 55c, DeHavilland Vampire. 70c, English Electric Lightning.

No. 775a, Avro Shackleton. b, Fairey Battle. c, Douglas Boston. d, DeHavilland DH9a.

Wmk. 373

1993, Apr. 1 Litho. *Perf. 14*

771 CD350 15c multicolored .25 .25
772 CD350 40c multicolored .70 .70
773 CD350 55c multicolored .95 .95
774 CD350 70c multicolored 1.25 1.25
Nos. 771-774 (4) 3.15 3.15

Souvenir Sheet

775 CD350 60c Sheet of 4, #a.-d. 4.50 4.50

Coronation of Queen Elizabeth II, 40th Anniv. A129

Wmk. 373

1993, June 2 Litho. *Perf. 13½*

776 A129 15c Nos. 424-425 .30 .30
777 A129 55c No. 157 1.00 1.00
778 A129 60c Nos. 402-403 1.10 1.10
779 A129 70c Nos. 404-405 1.25 1.25
Nos. 776-779 (4) 3.65 3.65

A130

A131

Natl. symbols: 15c, Lignum vitae. 55c, Yellow elder. 60c, Blue marlin. 70c, Flamingo.

1993, July 8 Litho. *Perf. 14*

780 A130 15c multicolored .30 .30
781 A130 55c multicolored 1.00 1.00
782 A130 60c multicolored 1.10 1.10
783 A130 70c multicolored 1.25 1.25
Nos. 780-783 (4) 3.65 3.65

Independence, 20th anniv.

1993, Sept. 8 Litho. *Perf. 14*

Wildflowers.

784 A131 15c Cordia .25 .25
785 A131 55c Seaside morning glory 1.10 1.10
786 A131 60c Poinciana 1.25 1.25
787 A131 70c Spider lily 1.40 1.40
Nos. 784-787 (4) 4.00 4.00

Christmas A132

1993, Nov. 1 Litho. *Perf. 14*

788 A132 15c Angel, Mary .30 .30
789 A132 55c Shepherds, angel 1.00 1.00
790 A132 60c Holy family 1.10 1.10
791 A132 70c Three wise men 1.25 1.25
Nos. 788-791 (4) 3.65 3.65

Souvenir Sheet

792 A132 $1 Madonna and Child 1.90 1.90

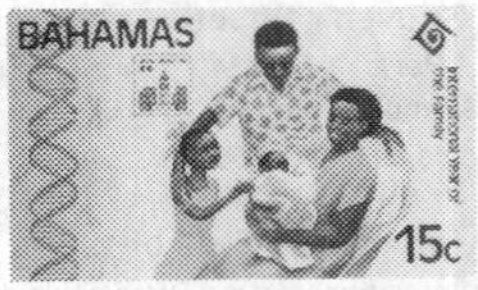

Intl. Year of the Family A133

Wmk. 384

1994, Feb. 18 Litho. *Perf. 13½*

793 A133 15c shown .30 .30
794 A133 55c Children studying 1.00 1.00
795 A133 60c Son, father fishing 1.10 1.10
796 A133 70c Children, grandmother 1.25 1.25
Nos. 793-796 (4) 3.65 3.65

Hong Kong '94.

Royal Visit — A134

Designs: 15c, Bahamas, United Kingdom flags. 55c, Royal Yacht Britannia. 60c, Queen Elizabeth II. 70c, Prince Philip, Queen.

Perf. 14x13½

1994, Mar. 7 Wmk. 373

797 A134 15c multicolored .30 .30
798 A134 55c multicolored 1.00 1.00
799 A134 60c multicolored 1.10 1.10
800 A134 70c multicolored 1.25 1.25
Nos. 797-800 (4) 3.65 3.65

Natl. Family Island Regatta, 40th Anniv. A135

Designs: 15c, 55c, 60c, 70c, Various sailing boats at sea. $2, Beached yacht, vert.

Wmk. 373

1994, Apr. 27 Litho. *Perf. 14*

801 A135 15c multicolored .30 .30
802 A135 55c multicolored 1.00 1.00
803 A135 60c multicolored 1.10 1.10
804 A135 70c multicolored 1.25 1.25
Nos. 801-804 (4) 3.65 3.65

Souvenir Sheet

805 A135 $2 multicolored 3.75 3.75

Intl. Olympic Committee, Cent. — A136

Flag, Olympic rings, and: 15c, Nos. 276-279, horiz. 55c, Nos. 388-391. 60c, Nos. 559-562, horiz. 70c, Nos. 755-758.

Wmk. 373

1994, May 31 Litho. *Perf. 14*

806 A136 15c multicolored .30 .30
807 A136 55c multicolored 1.00 1.00
808 A136 60c multicolored 1.10 1.10
809 A136 70c multicolored 1.25 1.25
Nos. 806-809 (4) 3.65 3.65

Souvenir Sheet

First Recipients of the Order of the Caribbean Community — A137

Illustration reduced.

Perf. 13x14

1994, July 5 Litho. Wmk. 373

810 A137 $2 multicolored 4.00 4.00

A138

A139

Butterfly, flower: 15c, Canna skipper, canna. 55c, Cloudless sulphur, cassia. 60c, White peacock, passion flower. 70c, Devillier's swallowtail, calico flower.

1994, Aug. 16 Litho. *Perf. 14*

811 A138 15c multicolored .25 .25
812 A138 55c multicolored 1.10 1.10
813 A138 60c multicolored 1.25 1.25
814 A138 70c multicolored 1.40 1.40
Nos. 811-814 (4) 4.00 4.00

1994, Sept. 13 *Perf. 13½x14*

Marine Life: a, Cuban hogfish, Spanish hogfish. b, Tomate, squirrelfish. c, French angelfish. d, Queen angelfish. e, Rock beauty.

$2, Rock beauty, queen angelfish.

815 A139 40c Strip of 5, #a.-e. 4.00 4.00

Souvenir Sheet

816 A139 $2 multicolored 4.00 4.00

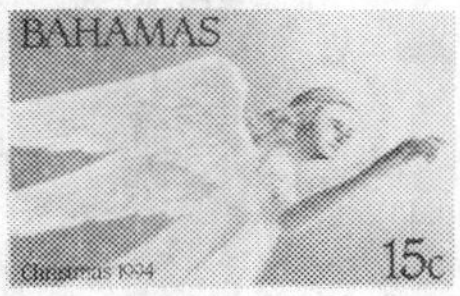

Christmas A140

Wmk. 384

1994, Oct. 31 Litho. *Perf. 14*

817 A140 15c Angel .25 .25
818 A140 55c Holy family 1.10 1.10
819 A140 60c Shepherds 1.25 1.25
820 A140 70c Magi 1.40 1.40
Nos. 817-820 (4) 4.00 4.00

Souvenir Sheet

821 A140 $2 Christ Child, vert. 3.75 3.75

College of the Bahamas, 20th Anniv. — A141

Designs: 15c, Lion. 70c, Queen Elizabeth II, college facade.

Wmk. 373

1995, Feb. 8 Litho. *Perf. 14*

822 A141 15c multicolored .30 .30
823 A141 70c multicolored 1.40 1.40

End of World War II, 50th Anniv.
Common Design Types

Designs: 15c, Bahamian soldiers on parade. 55c, Neutrality patrols flown by PBY-5A flying boats. 60c, Bahamian women in all three services. 70c, B-24 Liberator, Bahamians in RAF.
$2, Reverse of War Medal 1939-45.

Wmk. 373
1995, May 8 Litho. *Perf. 13½*
824 CD351 15c multicolored .25 .25
825 CD351 55c multicolored 1.10 1.10
826 CD351 60c multicolored 1.25 1.25
827 CD351 70c multicolored 1.40 1.40
Nos. 824-827 (4) 4.00 4.00

Souvenir Sheet
Perf. 14
828 CD352 $2 multicolored 4.00 4.00

Kirtland's Warbler — A142

Designs: No. 829a, 25c, Female feeding young. b, 25c Immature bird feeding, prior to migration. c, 15c, Female at nest. d, 15c, Singing male.
$2, Female on branch overlooking lake.

Wmk. 373
1995, June 7 Litho. *Perf. 13½*
829 A142 Strip of 4, #a.-d. 1.90 1.90

Souvenir Sheet
Perf. 13
830 A142 $2 multicolored 4.00 4.00

World Wildlife Fund (#829). No. 830 contains one 42x28mm stamp and has continuous design.

Tourism A143

Designs: 15c, Eleuthera Cliffs. 55c, Clarence Town, Long Island. 60c, Albert Lowe Museum. 70c, Yachting.

Wmk. 384
1995, July 18 Litho. *Perf. 14½*
831 A143 15c multicolored .25 .25
832 A143 55c multicolored 1.10 1.10
833 A143 60c multicolored 1.25 1.25
834 A143 70c multicolored 1.40 1.40
Nos. 831-834 (4) 4.00 4.00

FAO, 50th Anniv. A144

Designs: 15c, Pig, poultry farming. 55c, Horticultural methods. 60c, Healthy eating. 70c, Sustainable fishing.

Perf. 13½x13
1995, Sept. 5 Litho. Wmk. 373
835 A144 15c multicolored .25 .25
836 A144 55c multicolored 1.10 1.10
837 A144 60c multicolored 1.25 1.25
838 A144 70c multicolored 1.40 1.40
Nos. 835-838 (4) 4.00 4.00

UN, 50th Anniv.
Common Design Type

Designs: 15c, Sikorsky S-55, UNEF, Sinai, 1957. 55c, Ferret armored car, UNEF, Sinai, 1957. 60c, Fokker F-27, UNAMIC/UNTAC, Cambodia, 1991-93. 70c, Lockheed Hercules.

Wmk. 373
1995, Oct. 25 Litho. *Perf. 14*
839 CD353 15c multicolored .25 .25
840 CD353 55c multicolored 1.10 1.10
841 CD353 60c multicolored 1.25 1.25
842 CD353 70c multicolored 1.40 1.40
Nos. 839-842 (4) 4.00 4.00

Christmas A145

Designs: 15c, St. Agnes Anglican Church. 55c, Church of God. 60c, Sacred Heart Roman Catholic Church. 70c, Salem Union Baptist Church.

1995, Nov. 17
843 A145 15c multicolored .25 .25
844 A145 55c multicolored 1.10 1.10
845 A145 60c multicolored 1.25 1.25
846 A145 70c multicolored 1.40 1.40
Nos. 843-846 (4) 4.00 4.00

World AIDS Day A146

1995, Dec. 1
847 A146 25c Virus in blood .50 .50
848 A146 70c Scientific research 1.40 1.40

Shells A147

Designs: 5c, Sunrise tellin. 10c, Queen conch. 15c, Angular triton. 20c, True tulip. 25c, Reticulated cowrie-helmet. 30c, Sand dollar. 40c, Lace short-frond murex. 45c, Inflated sea biscuit. 50c, West Indian top shell (magpie). 55c, Spiny oyster. 60c, King helmet. 70c, Lion's paw. $1, Crown cone. $2, Atlantic partridge tun. $5, Wide-mouthed purpura. $10, Triton's trumpet.

1996 Litho. Wmk. 373 *Perf. 14*
849 A147 5c multicolored .20 .20
850 A147 10c multicolored .20 .20
851 A147 15c multicolored .30 .30
852 A147 20c multicolored .40 .40
853 A147 25c multicolored .50 .50
854 A147 30c multicolored .60 .60
855 A147 40c multicolored .80 .80
856 A147 45c multicolored .90 .90
857 A147 50c multicolored 1.00 1.00
858 A147 55c multicolored 1.10 1.10
859 A147 60c multicolored 1.25 1.25
860 A147 70c multicolored 1.40 1.40
a. Souvenir sheet of 1 1.40 1.40
861 A147 $1 multicolored 2.00 2.00
a. Souvenir sheet of 1 2.00 2.00
862 A147 $2 multicolored 4.00 4.00
863 A147 $5 multicolored 10.00 10.00
864 A147 $10 multicolored 20.00 20.00
Nos. 849-864 (16) 44.65 44.65

No. 860a issued 6/20/97 for return of Hong Kong to China.
No. 861a issued 2/3/97 for Hong Kong '97.
Nos. 850-851, 853, 861-864 exist dated "1997."
Nos. 849-853, 855, 857, 859, 861-864 exist dated "1999."
Issued: 5c, 10c, 15c, 20c, 25c, 30c, 40c, 45c, 50c, 55c, 60c, 70c, $1, $2, $5, 1/2/96.
See Nos. 962-964.

Radio, Cent. A148

Designs: 15c, East Goodwin Lightship, Marconi apparatus suspended from masthead. 55c, Arrest of Dr. Crippen, newspaper headline telling of wireless message from SS Montrose. 60c, SS Philadelphia, first readable transatlantic messages. 70c, Yacht Elettra, Guglielmo Marconi.
$2, SS Titantic, SS Carpathia.

1996, Feb. 4 Litho. *Perf. 13½*
865 A148 15c multicolored .25 .25
866 A148 55c multicolored 1.10 1.10
867 A148 60c multicolored 1.25 1.25
868 A148 70c multicolored 1.40 1.40
Nos. 865-868 (4) 4.00 4.00

Souvenir Sheet
869 A148 $2 multicolored 4.00 4.00

A149

A150

Wmk. 384
1996, June 25 Litho. *Perf. 13½*
870 A149 15c Swimming .25 .25
871 A149 55c Track 1.10 1.10
872 A149 60c Basketball 1.25 1.25
873 A149 70c Long jump 1.40 1.40
Nos. 870-873 (4) 4.00 4.00

Souvenir Sheet
874 A149 $2 Javelin, 1896 4.00 4.00

Modern Olympic Games, cent.

Wmk. 384
1996, Sept. 3 Litho. *Perf. 14*

Reptiles: 15c, Green anole. 55c, Fowl snake. 60c, Inagua freshwater turtle. 70c, Acklins rock iguana.

875 A150 15c multicolored .25 .25
876 A150 55c multicolored 1.10 1.10
877 A150 60c multicolored 1.25 1.25
878 A150 70c multicolored 1.40 1.40
a. Souvenir sheet, #875-878 4.00 4.00
Nos. 875-878 (4) 4.00 4.00

Environmental protection.

Christmas — A151

Designs: 15c, Angel Gabriel and Mary. 55c, Mary and Joseph. 60c, Shepherds. 70c, Magi.
$2, Prensentation at the Temple.

Wmk. 373
1996, Nov. 4 Litho. *Perf. 14*
879 A151 15c multicolored .25 .25
880 A151 55c multicolored 1.10 1.10
881 A151 60c multicolored 1.25 1.25
882 A151 70c multicolored 1.40 1.40
Nos. 879-882 (4) 4.00 4.00

Souvenir Sheet
883 A151 $2 multicolored 4.00 4.00

Archives Dept., 25th Anniv. — A152

Perf. 14½x14
1996, Dec. 9 Litho. Wmk. 384
884 A152 55c shown 1.10 1.10

Souvenir Sheet
Perf. 14x13½
885 A152 $2 Building, horiz. 4.00 4.00

Queen Elizabeth II and Prince Philip, 50th Wedding Anniv. — A153

Designs: No. 886, Queen. No. 887, Grenadier Guards. No. 888, Prince Philip. No. 889, Queen reviewing Grenadier Guards. No. 890, Prince holding trophy, Queen opening jewel box. No. 891, Prince on polo pony.
$2, Queen, Prince riding in open carriage, horiz.

Wmk. 373
1997, July 9 Litho. *Perf. 13*
886 A153 50c multicolored 1.00 1.00
887 A153 50c multicolored 1.00 1.00
a. Pair, #886-887 2.00 2.00
888 A153 60c multicolored 1.25 1.25
889 A153 60c multicolored 1.25 1.25
a. Pair, #888-889 2.50 2.50
890 A153 70c multicolored 1.40 1.40
891 A153 70c multicolored 1.40 1.40
a. Pair, #890-891 2.80 2.80
Nos. 886-891 (6) 7.30 7.30

Souvenir Sheet
892 A153 $2 multicolored 4.00 4.00

Intl. Year of the Reefs A154

Various pictures of marine life and coral.

Perf. 14x14½
1997, Sept. 3 Litho. Wmk. 384
893 A154 15c multicolored .25 .25
894 A154 55c multicolored 1.10 1.10
895 A154 60c multicolored 1.25 1.25
896 A154 70c multicolored 1.40 1.40
Nos. 893-896 (4) 4.00 4.00

Christmas — A155

Perf. 13x13½
1997, Oct. 6 Litho. Wmk. 373
897 A155 15c Angel .25 .25
898 A155 55c Madonna & Child 1.10 1.10
899 A155 60c Shepherd 1.25 1.25
900 A155 70c Magi 1.40 1.40
Nos. 897-900 (4) 4.00 4.00

Souvenir Sheet
901 A155 $2 Christ Child 4.00 4.00

Diana, Princess of Wales (1961-97)
Common Design Type

Various portraits: 902: a, 55c. b, 60c. c, 70c.

Perf. 14½x14
1998, Mar. 31 Litho. Wmk. 373
901A CD355 15c multicolored .30 .30

Sheet of 4
902 CD355 #a.-c., 901A 4.00 4.00

Organization of American States, 50th Anniv. — A156

Map of North and South America, national flags, and: 15c, "New Vision" paper. 55c, Building.

1998, Apr. 14 *Perf. 13½x14*
903 A156 15c multicolored .30 .30
904 A156 55c multicolored 1.10 1.10

University of the West Indies, 50th Anniv. — A157

1998, Apr. 14
905 A157 55c multicolored 1.10 1.10

Universal Declaration of Human Rights, 50th Anniv. — A158

1998, Apr. 14
906 A158 55c multicolored 1.10 1.10

Royal Air Force, 80th Anniv.
Common Design Type of 1993 Re-Inscribed

Designs: 15c, Handley Page Hyderabad. 55c, Hawker Demon. 60c, Gloster Meteor F.8. 70c, Lockheed Neptune MR.1.
No. 911: a, Sopwith Camel. b, Short 184. c, Supermarine Spitfire PR.19. d, North American Mitchell III.

1998, Apr. 1
907 CD350 15c multicolored .25 .25
908 CD350 55c multicolored 1.10 1.10
909 CD350 60c multicolored 1.25 1.25
910 CD350 70c multicolored 1.40 1.40
Nos. 907-910 (4) 4.00 4.00

Souvenir Sheet
911 CD350 50c Sheet of 4, #a.-d. 4.00 4.00

Independence, 25th Anniv. — A159

15c, Supreme Court Building. 55c, Nassau Library. 60c, Government House. 70c, Gregory Arch.
$2, Exuma-Family Island Regatta, George Town.

Wmk. 373
1998, July 10 Litho. *Perf. 13½*
912 A159 15c multicolored .30 .30
913 A159 55c multicolored 1.10 1.10
914 A159 60c multicolored 1.25 1.25
915 A159 70c multicolored 1.40 1.40
Nos. 912-915 (4) 4.05 4.05

Souvenir Sheet
916 A159 $2 multicolored 4.00 4.00

Castaway Cay, Disney Cruise Lines A160

1998, Aug. 1 *Perf. 14*
917 A160 55c Daytime 1.10 1.10
918 A160 55c Nighttime 1.10 1.10
a. Pair, #917-918 2.25 2.25
b. Booklet pane, 5 each #917-918 11.00
Complete booklet, #918b 11.00

MS Ryndam, Half Moon Cay — A161

1998, Aug. 19 *Perf. 13½x13*
919 A161 55c multicolored 1.10 1.10

Roses A162

Wmk. 373
1998, Sept. 8 Litho. *Perf. 14*
920 A162 55c Yellow cream 1.10 1.10
921 A162 55c Big red 1.10 1.10
922 A162 55c Seven sisters 1.10 1.10
923 A162 55c Barrel pink 1.10 1.10
924 A162 55c Island beauty 1.10 1.10
a. Booklet pane, 2 each #920-924 11.00
Complete booklet, #924a 11.00
Nos. 920-924 (5) 5.50 5.50

Souvenir Sheet
925 A162 55c like #924 1.10 1.10

No. 925 has parts of other roses extending into center left and upper left area of stamp.

Intl. Year of the Ocean A163

Wmk. 373
1998, Nov. 24 Litho. *Perf. 14*
926 A163 15c Killer whale .30 .30
927 A163 55c Tropical fish 1.10 1.10

Christmas A164

1998, Dec. 11
928 A164 15c The Annunciation .25 .25
929 A164 55c Shepherds, star 1.10 1.10
930 A164 60c Magi 1.25 1.25
931 A164 70c Flight into Egypt 1.40 1.40
Nos. 928-931 (4) 4.00 4.00

Souvenir Sheet
932 A164 $2 Nativity scene 4.00 4.00

Timothy Gibson, Composer of Natl. Anthem — A165

1998 Litho. Wmk. 373 *Perf. 13½*
933 A165 60c multicolored 1.25 1.25

Independence, 25th anniv.

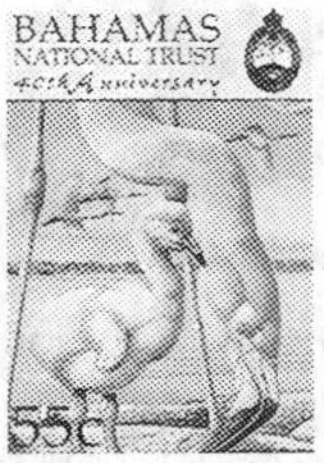

National Trust, 40th Anniv. — A166

Flamingos on the beach: a, One chick, adults. b, Two chicks, adults. c, One chick spreading wings, adults. d, Six in flight over others. e, Three ascending into flight.

Wmk. 384
1999, Feb. 9 Litho. *Perf. 14*
934 A166 55c Strip of 5, #a.-e. 5.50 5.50

No. 934 is a continuous design.
See Nos. 940, 961, 969.

Australia '99, World Stamp Expo — A167

Maritime history: 15c, Arawak Indians. 55c, Santa Maria. 60c, Blackbeard's ship, Queen Anne's Revenge. 70c, Banshee running Union blockade, US Civil War.
$2, American invasion of Fort Nassau, 1776.

Perf. 14x14½
1999, Mar. 9 Wmk. 373
935 A167 15c multicolored .30 .30
936 A167 55c multicolored 1.10 1.10
937 A167 60c multicolored 1.25 1.25
938 A167 70c multicolored 1.40 1.40
Nos. 935-938 (4) 4.05 4.05

Souvenir Sheet
939 A167 $2 multicolored 4.00 4.00

National Trust, 40th Anniv., Type of 1999

Marine life: a, Dolphin. b, Large fish, four in background. c, Several fish, coral. d, Turtle, fish, coral. e, Lobster, coral.

Wmk. 384
1999, Apr. 6 Litho. *Perf. 14*
940 A166 55c Strip of 5, #a.-e. 5.50 5.50

No. 940 is a continuous design.

Bahamas Historical Society, 40th Anniv. A168

1999, June 9 Litho. *Perf. 13*
941 A168 $1 multicolored 2.00 2.00

1st Manned Moon Landing, 30th Anniv.
Common Design Type

15c, Ascent module in assembly area. 65c, Apollo command & service module. 70c, Descent stage. 80c, Module turns to dock with service module.
$2, Looking at earth from moon.

Perf. 14x13¾
1999, July 20 Litho. Wmk. 384
942 CD357 15c multicolored .30 .30
943 CD357 65c multicolored 1.25 1.25
944 CD357 70c multicolored 1.40 1.40
945 CD357 80c multicolored 1.60 1.60
Nos. 942-945 (4) 4.55 4.55

Souvenir Sheet
Perf. 14
946 CD357 $2 multicolored 4.00 4.00

No. 946 contains one 40mm circular stamp 40mm.

UPU, 125th Anniv. A170

Wmk. 384
1999, Aug. 17 Litho. *Perf. 13½*
947 A170 15c Mail Packet Delaware .30 .30
948 A170 65c S.S. Atlantis 1.25 1.25
949 A170 70c M.V. Queen of Bermuda 1.40 1.40
950 A170 80c USS Saufley 1.60 1.60
Nos. 947-950 (4) 4.55 4.55

Queen Mother's Century
Common Design Type

Queen Mother: 15c, At Hertfordshire Hospital. 65c, With Princess Elizabeth. 70c, With Prince Andrew. 80c, With Irish Guards.
$2, With brother David and 1966 British World Cup team members.

Wmk. 373
1999, Aug. Litho. *Perf. 13½*
951 CD358 15c multicolored .30 .30
952 CD358 65c multicolored 1.25 1.25
953 CD358 70c multicolored 1.40 1.40
954 CD358 80c multicolored 1.60 1.60
Nos. 951-954 (4) 4.55 4.55

Souvenir Sheet
955 CD358 $2 multicolored 4.00 4.00

Environmental Protection — A171

15c, Turtle pond. 65c, Green turtles, limestone cliffs. 70c, Barracudas. 80c, Sea fans on reef.
$2, Atlantic bottlenose dolphin.

Bahamas stamps can be mounted in the annually supplemented Scott Bahamas album.

Wmk. 373

1999, Sept. 21 Litho. *Perf. 13¾*

956 A171 15c multicolored .30 .30
957 A171 65c multicolored 1.25 1.25
958 A171 70c multicolored 1.40 1.40
959 A171 80c multicolored 1.60 1.60
Nos. 956-959 (4) 4.55 4.55

Souvenir Sheet

960 A171 $2 multicolored 4.00 4.00

National Trust Type of 1999

Designs: a, Tern. b, Heron, c, Hummingbird, orange flower. d, Duck. e, Parrot.

Wmk. 384

1999, Oct. 8 Litho. *Perf. 14¼*

961 A166 65c Strip of 5, #a.-e. 6.50 6.50

Shell Type of 1996

1999 Litho. Wmk. 373 *Perf. 14*

962 A147 35c Like #854 .70 .70
963 A147 65c Like #856 1.25 1.25
964 A147 80c Like #858 1.60 1.60
Nos. 962-964 (3) 3.55 3.55

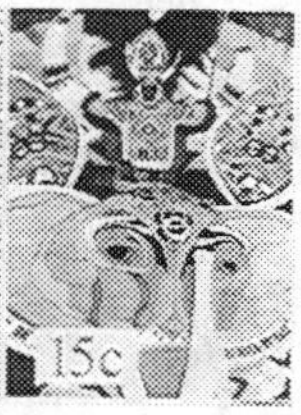

Christmas — A172

People in various Junkanoo costumes.

Perf. 14½x14¼

1999, Oct. 25 Litho. Wmk. 373

965 A172 15c multicolored .30 .30
966 A172 65c multicolored 1.25 1.25
967 A172 70c multicolored 1.40 1.40
968 A172 80c multicolored 1.60 1.60
Nos. 965-968 (4) 4.55 4.55

National Trust Type of 1999

Designs: a, Orchid. b, Rodent. c, Hummingbird, red flowers. d, Lizard. e, Hibiscus.

Wmk. 384

1999, Oct. 8 Litho. *Perf. 14¼*

969 A166 65c Strip of 5, #a.-e. 6.50 6.50

SEMI-POSTAL STAMPS

No. 48 Overprinted in Red

+
1.1.17.

1917, May 18 Wmk. 3 *Perf. 14*

B1 A6 1p car & black .40 *1.25*

Type of 1911 Overprinted in Red

WAR CHARITY 3.6.18.

1919, Jan. 1

B2 A6 1p red & black .40 *2.25*
a. Double overprint *3,500.*

This stamp was originally scheduled for release in 1918.

Souvenir Sheet

No. 694 Surcharged **HURRICANE RELIEF +$1**

Wmk. 384

1992, Nov. 16 Litho. *Perf. 14*

B3 A116 Sheet of 2, #a.-b. 8.00 8.00

AIR POST STAMPS

Catalogue values for all unused stamps in this section are for Never Hinged items.

Manned Flight Bicentenary — AP1

Airplanes.

Wmk. 373

1983, Oct. 13 Litho. *Perf. 14*

C1 AP1 10c Consolidated Catalina .20 .20
a. Without emblem ('85) .20 .20
b. Without emblem, wmk. 384 ('86) .20 .20
C2 AP1 25c Avro Tudor IV .40 .40
a. Without emblem ('85) .45 .45
b. Without emblem, wmk. 384 ('86) .45 .45
C3 AP1 31c Avro Lancastrian .55 .55
a. Without emblem ('85) .55 .55
C4 AP1 35c Consolidated Commodore .60 .60
a. Without emblem ('85) .65 .65
Nos. C1-C4 (4) 1.75 1.75

Aircraft AP2

1987, July 7

C5 AP2 15c Bahamasair Boeing 737 .25 .25
C6 AP2 40c Eastern Boeing 757 .65 .65
C7 AP2 45c Pan Am Airbus A300 B4 .75 .75
C8 AP2 50c British Airways Boeing 747 .85 .85
Nos. C5-C8 (4) 2.50 2.50

SPECIAL DELIVERY STAMPS

No. 34 Overprinted **SPECIAL DELIVERY**

1916 Wmk. 1 *Perf. 14*

E1 A6 5p orange & black 6.50 *27.50*
a. Double overprint *900.00 1,100.*
b. Inverted overprint *1,400. 1,400.*
c. Double ovpt., one invtd. *3,000. 3,000.*
d. Pair, one without overprint *12,500. 16,000.*

The No. E1 overprint exists in two types. Type I (illustrated) is much scarcer. Type II shows "SPECIAL" farther right, so that the letter "I" is slightly right of the vertical line of the "E" below it.

Type of Regular Issue of 1903 Overprinted **SPECIAL DELIVERY**

1917, July 2 Wmk. 3

E2 A6 5p orange & black .80 *4.25*

No. 60 Overprinted in Red **SPECIAL DELIVERY**

1918

E3 A6 5p violet & black .60 *1.40*

WAR TAX STAMPS

Stamps of 1912-18 Overprinted **WAR TAX**

1918, Feb. 21 Wmk. 3 *Perf. 14*

MR1 A8 ½p green 7.50 *30.00*
a. Double overprint *1,100. 1,100.*
b. Inverted overprint *1,200. 1,300.*
MR2 A8 1p car rose .80 *1.00*
a. Double overprint *1,250. 1,250.*
b. Inverted overprint *1,250. 1,300.*
MR3 A6 3p brown, *yel* 3.75 *4.00*
a. Inverted overprint *1,100. 1,100.*
b. Double overprint *1,100. 1,250.*
MR4 A8 1sh black & red 75.00 *110.00*
a. Double overprint *4,750.* —
Nos. MR1-MR4 (4) 87.05 *145.00*

Same Overprint on No. 48a

1918, July 10

MR5 A6 1p car & black 3.50 *5.50*
a. Double overprint *1,500. 1,600.*
b. Double ovpt., one invtd. *1,200.*
c. Inverted overprint *1,250. 1,300.*

Nos. 49-50, 54 Overprinted in Black or Red **WAR TAX**

MR6 A8 ½p green 1.00 *1.25*
MR7 A8 1p car rose .35 .25
a. Watermarked sideways 750.00
MR8 A8 1sh black & red (R) 6.00 2.50
Nos. MR6-MR8 (3) 7.35 4.00

Nos. 58-59 Overprinted **WAR TAX**

1918-19

MR9 A6 3p brown, *yel* .90 *3.25*
MR10 A6 3p brown & blk ('19) .90 *3.75*

Nos. 49-50, 54 Overprinted in Red or Black **WAR TAX**

1919, July 14

MR11 A8 ½p green (R) .30 *1.10*
MR12 A8 1p car rose 1.00 *1.40*
MR13 A8 1sh black & red (R) 8.50 *24.00*
Nos. MR11-MR13 (3) 9.80 *26.50*

No. 59 Overprinted **WAR TAX**

MR14 A6 3p brown & black .80 *5.25*

BAHRAIN

bä-ʹrān

LOCATION — An archipelago in the Persian Gulf, including the islands of Bahrain, Muharraq, Sitra, Nebi Saleh, Kasasifeh and Arad.
GOVT. — Independent sheikdom
AREA — 255 sq. mi.
POP. — 629,090 (1999 est.)
CAPITAL — Manama

Bahrain was a British-protected territory until it became an independent state on August 15, 1971.

12 Pies = 1 Anna
16 Annas = 1 Rupee
100 Naye Paise = 1 Rupee (1957)
1000 Fils = 1 Dinar (1966)

Catalogue values for unused stamps in this country are for Never Hinged items, beginning with Scott 62 in the regular postage section and Scott MR2 in the postal tax section.

Indian Postal Administration

Stamps of India, 1926-32, Overprinted in Black

BAHRAIN
a

Wmk. Multiple Stars (196)

1933, Aug. 10 *Perf. 14*

1 A46 3p gray 2.25 .40
2 A47 ½a green 6.75 3.00
3 A68 9p dark green 3.25 .85
4 A48 1a dark brown 6.00 .85
5 A69 1a3p violet 3.25 .65
6 A60 2a vermilion 8.50 7.00
7 A51 3a blue 17.00 *30.00*
8 A70 3a6p deep blue 3.00 .50
9 A61 4a olive green 16.00 *30.00*
10 A54 8a red violet 5.00 .90
11 A55 12a claret 6.50 1.50

Overprinted in Black

b **BAHRAIN**

12 A56 1r green & brown 14.00 7.50
13 A56 2r brn org & car rose 30.00 30.00
14 A56 5r dk violet & ultra 80.00 *110.00*
Nos. 1-14 (14) 201.50 *223.15*

Stamps of India, 1926-32, Overprinted Type "a" in Black

1934

15 A72 1a dark brown 7.50 .35
16 A51 3a carmine rose 4.25 .35
17 A52 4a olive green 3.50 .35
Nos. 15-17 (3) 15.25 1.05

India Nos. 138, 111, 111a Overprinted Type "a" in Black

1935-37 *Perf. 13½x14, 14*

18 A71 ½a green 3.50 .50
19 A49 2a vermilion 30.00 7.00
a. Small die ('37) 45.00 .25

India Stamps of 1937 Overprinted Type "a" in Black

1938-41 Wmk. 196 *Perf. 13½x14*

20 A80 3p slate 4.00 2.50
21 A80 ½a brown 1.75 .20
22 A80 9p green 1.40 *2.00*
23 A80 1a carmine 1.25 .20
24 A81 2a scarlet 3.75 .90
26 A81 3a yel grn ('41) 7.75 4.25
27 A81 3a6p ultra 2.50 *2.50*
28 A81 4a dk brn ('41) 67.50 45.00
30 A81 8a bl vio ('40) 80.00 35.00
31 A81 12a car lake ('40) 60.00 42.50

Overprinted Type "b" in Black

32 A82 1r brn & slate 1.50 1.25
33 A82 2r dk brn & dk vio 7.50 2.50
34 A82 5r dp ultra & dk grn 20.00 13.00
35 A82 10r rose car & dk vio ('41) 37.50 22.50
36 A82 15r dk grn & dk brn ('41) 26.00 *37.50*
37 A82 25r dk vio & bl vio ('41) 55.00 *65.00*
Nos. 20-37 (16) 377.40 276.80
Set, never hinged 525.00

India Stamps of 1941-43 Overprinted Type "a" in Black

1942-44 Wmk. 196 *Perf. 13½x14*

38 A83 3p slate .55 .45
39 A83 ½a rose vio ('44) 2.00 .75
40 A83 9p lt green ('43) 6.25 *8.75*
41 A83 1a car rose ('44) 2.00 .40
42 A84 1a3p bister ('43) 4.50 *10.00*
43 A84 1½a dk pur ('43) 2.75 2.75
45 A84 2a scarlet ('43) 2.00 1.25
46 A84 3a violet ('43) 7.50 3.25
47 A84 3½a ultra 2.00 *10.00*
48 A85 4a chocolate 1.10 1.00
49 A85 6a peacock blue 5.50 *6.25*
50 A85 8a blue vio ('43) 1.90 1.60
51 A85 12a car lake 2.75 2.75
Nos. 38-51 (13) 40.80 *49.20*
Set, never hinged 62.50

British Postal Administration

See Oman (Muscat) for similar stamps with surcharge of new value only.

Great Britain Nos. 258 to 263, 243 and 248 Surcharged in Black

BAHRAIN

c

½ ANNA

1948-49 Wmk. 251 *Perf. 14½x14*

52 A101 ½a on ½p green .25 *.40*
53 A101 1a on 1p vermilion .25 *.50*
54 A101 1½a on 1½p lt red brn .25 *.50*
55 A101 2a on 2p lt orange .25 .20
56 A101 2½a on 2½p ultra .30 *1.00*
57 A101 3a on 3p violet .25 .20
58 A102 6a on 6p rose lilac .25 .20
59 A103 1r on 1sh brown 1.00 .45

Great Britain Nos. 249A, 250 and 251A Surcharged in Black

BAHRAIN

2 RUPEES

Wmk. 259 *Perf. 14*

60 A104 2r on 2sh6p yel grn 3.25 *4.00*
61 A104 5r on 5sh dull red 4.50 *6.00*
61A A105 10r on 10sh ultra 37.50 37.50
Nos. 52-61A (11) 48.05 50.95
Set, never hinged 70.00

Surcharge bars at bottom on No. 61A.
Issued: 10r, 7/4/49; others, 4/1/48.

Catalogue values for unused stamps in this section, from this point to the end of the section, are for Never Hinged items.

Silver Wedding Issue

Great Britain Nos. 267 and 268 Surcharged in Black

BAHRAIN 2½ ANNAS

Perf. 14½x14, 14x14½

1948, Apr. 26 **Wmk. 251**

62 A109 2½a on 2½p .30 .20
63 A110 15r on £1 37.50 *45.00*

Three bars obliterate the original denomination on No. 63.

Olympic Issue

Great Britain Nos. 271 to 274 Surcharged "BAHRAIN" and New Value in Black

1948, July 29 *Perf. 14½x14*

64 A113 2½a on 2½p brt ultra .50 *.80*
a. Double surcharge 425.00 *525.00*
65 A114 3a on 3p dp vio .50 *1.50*
66 A115 6a on 6p red vio 1.25 *1.75*
67 A116 1r on 1sh dk brn 1.40 *1.75*
Nos. 64-67 (4) 3.65 *5.80*

A square of dots obliterates the original denomination on No. 67.

UPU Issue

Great Britain Nos. 276 to 279 Surcharged "BAHRAIN," New Value and Square of Dots in Black

1949, Oct. 10 Photo. *Perf. 14½x14*

68 A117 2½a on 2½p brt ultra .45 *1.50*
69 A118 3a on 3p brt vio .75 *2.00*
70 A119 6a on 6p red vio .70 *2.25*
71 A120 1r on 1sh brown 1.90 1.25
Nos. 68-71 (4) 3.80 *7.00*

Great Britain Nos. 280, 281, 283-285 Surcharged Type "c" in Black

1950-51 **Wmk. 251**

72 A101 ½a on ½p lt org .55 .50
73 A101 1a on 1p ultra 1.40 .20
74 A101 1½a on 1½p green 1.40 *6.75*
75 A101 2a on 2p lt red brn .55 .25
76 A101 2½a on 2½p ver 1.40 *6.75*
77 A102 4a on 4p ultra 1.40 1.25

Great Britain Nos. 286-288 Surcharged in Black

BAHRAIN

2 RUPEES

Perf. 11x12
Wmk. 259

78 A121 2r on 2sh6p green 20.00 4.75
79 A121 5r on 5sh dl red 15.00 3.25
80 A122 10r on 10sh ultra 25.00 6.00
Nos. 72-80 (9) 66.70 *29.70*

Longer bars, at lower right, on No. 80.
Issued: 4a, Nov. 2, 1950; others, May 3, 1951.

Stamps of Great Britain, 1952-54, Surcharged "BAHRAIN" and New Value in Black or Dark Blue

1952-54 Wmk. 298 *Perf. 14½x14*

81 A126 ½a on ½p red org ('53) .25 .25
a. "½" omitted 200.00 *225.00*
82 A126 1a on 1p ultra .25 .20
83 A126 1½a on 1½p grn .25 .25
84 A126 2a on 2p red brn .25 .25
85 A127 2½a on 2½p scar .55 .25
86 A127 3a on 3p dk pur (Dk Bl) .65 .25
87 A128 4a on 4p ultra 1.50 .75
88 A129 6a on 6p lil rose 1.25 .65
89 A132 12a on 1sh3p dk grn 4.00 1.50
90 A131 1r on 1sh6p dk bl 5.50 2.00
Nos. 81-90 (10) 14.45 6.35

Issued: #83, 85, 12/5; #81-82, 84, 8/31/53; #87, 89-90, 11/2/53; #86, 88, 1/18/54.

Six stamps of this design picturing Sheik Sulman bin Hamad Al Kalifah were for local use in 1953-57.
Six stamps of similar design (same sheik, "Bahrain" vertical at left) were issued in 1961 for local use.

Coronation Issue

Great Britain Nos. 313-316 Surcharged "BAHRAIN" and New Value in Black

Perf. 14½x14

1953, June 3 **Wmk. 298**

92 A134 2½a on 2½p scar 1.10 1.10
93 A135 4a on 4p brt ultra 1.75 1.75
94 A136 12a on 1sh3p dk grn 4.00 4.00
95 A137 1r on 1sh6p dk bl 5.25 5.25
Nos. 92-95 (4) 12.10 12.10

Squares of dots obliterate the original denominations on Nos. 94-95.

Great Britain Nos. 309-311 Surcharged "BAHRAIN" and New Value in Black

1955 Wmk. 308 Engr. *Perf. 11x12*

96 A133 2r on 2sh6p dk brn 3.00 1.25
97 A133 5r on 5sh crimson 9.50 4.00
98 A133 10r on 10sh brt ultra 20.00 6.50
Nos. 96-98 (3) 32.50 11.75

Three slightly different types of surcharge are found on the 2r; two on 5r and 10r.

Great Britain Nos. 317, 323, 325, 332-333 Surcharged "BAHRAIN" and New Value

Perf. 14½x14

1956-57 Wmk. 308 Photo.

99 A126 ½a on ½p red org .25 .20
100 A128 4a on 4p ultra 5.00 *6.25*
101 A129 6a on 6p lil rose .50 .40
102 A132 12a on 1sh3p dk green 6.25 *12.00*
103 A131 1r on 1sh6p dk bl ('57) 1.50 .75
Nos. 99-103 (5) 13.50 *19.60*

Great Britain Nos. 317-325, 328, 332 Surcharged "BAHRAIN" and New Value

1957, Apr. 1

104 A129 1np on 5p lt brown .20 .20
105 A126 3np on ½p red org .25 .25
106 A126 6np on 1p ultra .25 .25
107 A126 9np on 1½p green .25 .25
108 A126 12np on 2p red brn .30 .25
109 A127 15np on 2½p scar, type I .35 .20
a. Type II .40 *.50*
110 A127 20np on 3p dk pur .25 .20
111 A128 25np on 4p ultra .65 *1.00*
112 A129 40np on 6p lil rose .65 .35
113 A130 50np on 9p dp ol grn 1.75 1.75
114 A132 75np on 1sh3p dk grn 1.50 .55
Nos. 104-114 (11) 6.40 5.25

The arrangement of the surcharge varies on different values: there are three bars through value on No. 113.

Jubilee Jamboree Issue

Great Britain Nos. 334-336 Surcharged "BAHRAIN," New Value and Square of Dots in Black

Perf. 14½x14

1957, Aug. 1 Photo. Wmk. 308

115 A138 15np on 2½p scar .25 *.35*
116 A138 25np on 4p ultra .40 .40
117 A138 75np on 1sh3p dk grn .55 *.80*
Nos. 115-117 (3) 1.20 *1.55*

Great Britain No. 357 Surcharged "BAHRAIN/ NP 15 NP" in Black

1960 Wmk. 322 *Perf. 14½x14*

118 A127 15np on 2½p scar, type II 3.00 *7.25*

Sheik Sulman bin Hamad Al Khalifah
A1 A2

Perf. 14½x14

1960, July 1 Photo. Unwmk.

119 A1 5np lt ultra .20 .20
120 A1 15np orange .20 .20
121 A1 20np lt violet .20 .20
122 A1 30np olive bister .25 .20
123 A1 40np gray .30 .20
124 A1 50np emerald .30 .20
125 A1 75np red brown .60 .20

Engr.
Perf. 13x13½

126 A2 1r gray .90 .20
127 A2 2r carmine 1.75 .50
128 A2 5r ultra 4.50 1.75
129 A2 10r olive green 12.00 2.25
Nos. 119-129 (11) 21.20 6.10

Sheik Isa bin Sulman Al Khalifah — A3

Bahrain Airport — A4

Designs: 5r, 10r, Deep water jetty.

1964, Feb. 22 Photo. *Perf. 14½x14*

130 A3 5np ultra .20 .20
131 A3 15np orange .20 .20
132 A3 20np brt purple .20 .20
133 A3 30np brown olive .20 .20
134 A3 40np slate .20 .20
135 A3 50np emerald .30 .20
136 A3 75np chestnut .60 .25

Engr.
Perf. 13½x13

137 A4 1r black 1.00 .35
138 A4 2r rose red 5.00 .85
139 A4 5r violet blue 8.50 5.00
140 A4 10r dull green 14.00 5.00
Nos. 130-140 (11) 30.40 12.65

Bahrain Postal Administration

Sheik Isa bin Sulman Al Khalifah
A5

Sheik and Bahrain International Airport
A6

Pearl Divers — A7

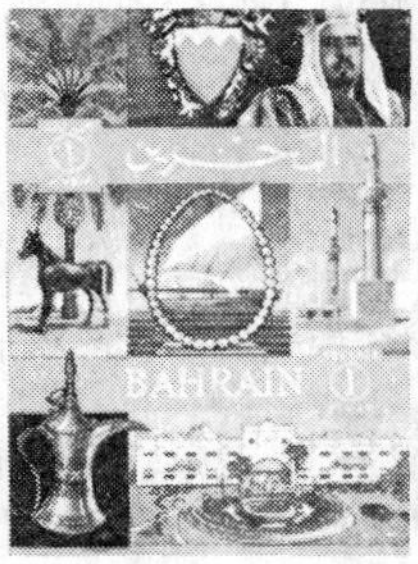

Bab al Bahrain, Suq Al-Khamis Mosque, Sheik, Emblem, etc. — A8

Designs: 50f, 75f, Pier, Mina Sulman harbor. 200f, Falcon and horse race. 500f, "Hospitality," pouring coffee and Sheik's Palace.

Perf. 14½x14

1966, Jan. 1 Photo. Unwmk.

141 A5 5f green .20 .20
142 A5 10f dark red .20 .20
143 A5 15f ultra .20 .20
144 A5 20f magenta .20 .20

Perf. 13½x14

145 A6 30f green & black .30 .20
146 A6 40f blue & black .35 .20
147 A6 50f dp car rose & blk .40 .25
148 A6 75f violet & black .60 .35

Perf. 14½x14

149 A7 100f dk blue & yel 1.00 .50
150 A7 200f dk green & org 3.00 1.00
151 A7 500f red brown & yel 6.25 2.50
152 A8 1d multicolored 12.50 5.00
Nos. 141-152 (12) 25.20 10.80

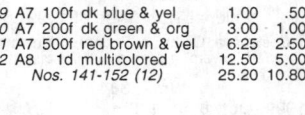

Produce, Date Palm, Ship, Truck and Plane
A9

Map of Bahrain and WHO Emblem
A10

1966, Mar. 28 Litho. *Perf. 13x13½*

153 A9 10f red & blue green .30 .30
154 A9 20f green & vio .65 .65
155 A9 40f olive bis & lt bl 1.25 1.25
156 A9 200f vio blue & pink 6.25 6.25
Nos. 153-156 (4) 8.45 8.45

6th Bahrain Trade Fair & Agricultural Show.

1968, June Unwmk. *Perf. 13½x14*

157 A10 20f gray & black .55 .55
158 A10 40f blue grn & black 1.40 1.40
159 A10 150f dp rose & black 5.50 5.50
Nos. 157-159 (3) 7.45 7.45

20th anniv. of the WHO.

Isa Town
A11

1968, Nov. 18 Litho. *Perf. 14½*

160 A11 50f shown 1.60 1.60
161 A11 80f Market 2.50 2.50
162 A11 120f Stadium 4.25 4.25
163 A11 150f Mosque 6.75 6.75
Nos. 160-163 (4) 15.10 15.10

Education Symbol — A12

1969, Apr. Litho. *Perf. 13*

164 A12	40f multicolored	1.25	1.25
165 A12	60f multicolored	2.00	2.00
166 A12	150f multicolored	4.25	4.25
	Nos. 164-166 (3)	7.50	7.50

50th anniversary of education in Bahrain.

Map of Arabian Gulf, Radar and Emblem A13

Designs: 40f, 150f, Radar installation and emblem of Cable & Wireless Ltd., vert.

Perf. 14x13½, 13½x14

1969, July 14 Litho.

167 A13	20f lt green & multi	1.00	1.00
168 A13	40f vio blue & multi	2.25	2.25
169 A13	100f ocher & multi	5.25	5.25
170 A13	150f rose lilac & multi	9.00	9.00
	Nos. 167-170 (4)	17.50	17.50

Opening of the satellite earth station (connected through the Indian Ocean satellite Intelsat III) at Ras Abu Jarjur, July 14.

Municipal Building, Arms and Map of Bahrain A14

1970, Feb. 23 Litho. *Perf. 12x12½*

171 A14	30f blue & multi	2.75	2.75
172 A14	150f multicolored	10.00	10.00

2nd Conf. of the Arab Cities' Org.

Copper Bull's Head A15

Conf. Emblem and: 80f, Gateway to Qalat al Bahrain, 7th cent. B.C. 120f, Aerial view of grave mounds, Bahrain. 150f, Dilmun seal, 2000 B.C.

1970, Mar. 1 Photo. *Perf. 14½*

173 A15	60f multicolored	2.00	2.00
174 A15	80f multicolored	2.25	2.25
175 A15	120f multicolored	3.50	3.50
176 A15	150f multicolored	4.25	4.25
	Nos. 173-176 (4)	12.00	12.00

3rd Intl. Asian Archaeological Conf., Bahrain.

Vickers VC 10, Big Ben and Minaret A16

1970, Apr. 5 Litho. *Perf. 14½x14*

177 A16	30f multicolored	.90	.90
178 A16	60f multicolored	1.90	1.90
179 A16	120f multicolored	6.25	6.25
	Nos. 177-179 (3)	9.05	9.05

1st flight to London from the Arabian Gulf Area by Gulf Aviation Company.

Intl. Education Year Emblem A17

120f, Education Year emblem & students.

1970, Nov. 1 Litho. *Perf. 14½x14*

180 A17	60f blk, blue & org	3.25	3.25
181 A17	120f multicolored	8.00	8.00

Independent State

Government House, Manama — A18

UN Emblem and Sails — A19

Designs: 30f, "Freedom" with dove and torch, and globe. 120f, 150f, Bahrain coat of arms.

1971, Oct. 2 Photo. *Perf. 14½x14*

182 A18	30f gold & multi	1.60	1.60
183 A18	60f gold & multi	3.25	3.25
184 A18	120f gold & multi	6.50	6.50
185 A18	150f gold & multi	8.25	8.25
	Nos. 182-185 (4)	19.60	19.60

Declaration of Bahrain independence, Aug. 15, 1971.

Perf. 14x14½, 14½x14

1972, Feb. 1 Litho.

Designs: 30f, 60f, Dhow with sails showing UN and Arab League emblems, horiz. 150f, as 120f.

186 A19	30f multicolored	2.50	2.50
187 A19	60f red, gray & multi	6.00	6.00
188 A19	120f dull blue & multi	12.50	12.50
189 A19	150f multicolored	14.00	14.00
	Nos. 186-189 (4)	35.00	35.00

Bahrain's admission to the Arab League and the United Nations.

"Your Heart is your Health" — A20

1972, Apr. 7 Litho. *Perf. 14½x14*

190 A20	30f black & multi	3.75	3.75
191 A20	60f gray & multi	7.50	7.50

World Health Day.

UN and FAO Emblems A21

1973, May 12 Litho. *Perf. 12½x13*

192 A21	30f org red, pur & grn	3.75	3.75
193 A21	60f ocher, brn & grn	6.50	6.50

World Food Programs, 10th anniversary.

People of Various Races, Human Rights Flame A22

1973, Nov. Litho. *Perf. 14x14½*

194 A22	30f blue, blk & brn	4.00	4.00
195 A22	60f lake, blk & brn	7.75	7.75

25th anniversary of the Universal Declaration of Human Rights.

Flour Mill — A23

60f, Intl. Airport. 120f, Sulmaniya Medical Center. 150f, ALBA aluminum smelting plant.

1973, Dec. 16 Photo. *Perf. 14½*

196 A23	30f multicolored	1.00	1.00
197 A23	60f multicolored	1.75	1.75
198 A23	120f multicolored	3.50	3.50
199 A23	150f multicolored	4.25	4.25
	Nos. 196-199 (4)	10.50	10.50

National Day.

Letters and UPU Emblem — A24

Carrier Pigeon and UPU Emblem A25

60f, UPU emblem & letters. 150f, Like 120f.

1974, Feb. 4 Litho. *Perf. 13½*

200 A24	30f blue & multi	1.00	1.00
201 A24	60f emerald & multi	1.75	1.75

Perf. 12½x13½

202 A25	120f ultra & multi	3.00	3.00
203 A25	150f yellow & multi	4.25	4.25
	Nos. 200-203 (4)	10.00	10.00

Bahrain's admission to UPU.

Traffic Signals — A26

1974, May 4 Litho. *Perf. 14½*

204 A26	30f org brown & multi	2.75	2.75
205 A26	60f brt blue & multi	6.25	6.25

International Traffic Day.

Jet, Globe, Mail Coach and UPU Emblem — A27

1974, Sept. 1 Photo. *Perf. 14x14½*

206 A27	30f multicolored	.80	.80
207 A27	60f multicolored	1.60	1.60
208 A27	120f multicolored	3.25	3.25
209 A27	150f multicolored	4.00	4.00
	Nos. 206-209 (4)	9.65	9.65

Centenary of Universal Postal Union.

National Day Emblem, Sitra Power Station — A28

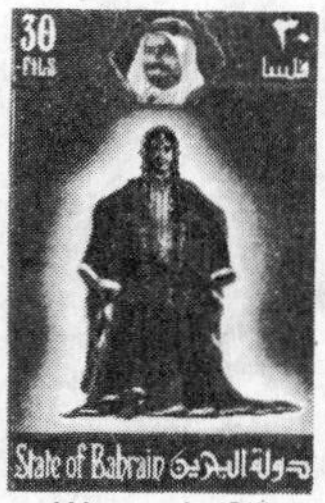

Woman's Silk Gown — A29

National Day: 120f, 150f, Bahrain dry dock.

1974, Dec. 16 Litho. *Perf. 14½*

210 A28	30f blue & multi	.90	.90
211 A28	60f green & multi	1.50	1.50
212 A28	120f lil rose & multi	3.50	3.50
213 A28	150f ver & multi	4.25	4.25
	Nos. 210-213 (4)	10.15	10.15

Photo.; Gold Embossed

1975, Feb. 1 *Perf. 14½x14*

Design: Various women's costumes.

214 A29	30f blue grn & multi	.70	.70
215 A29	60f vio blue & multi	1.10	1.10
216 A29	120f rose red & multi	2.75	2.75
217 A29	150f multicolored	3.50	3.50
	Nos. 214-217 (4)	8.05	8.05

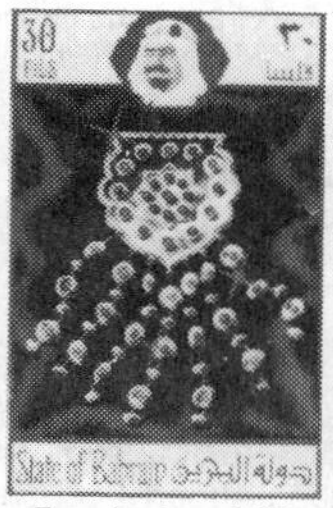

Pendant — A30

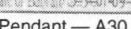

Woman Planting Flower, IWY Emblem — A31

Designs: Various jewelry.

1975, Apr. 1 Photo. *Perf. 14½x14*

218 A30	30f olive & multi	.60	.60
219 A30	60f dp pur & multi	1.40	1.40
220 A30	120f dp car & multi	2.75	2.75
221 A30	150f dp blue & multi	3.50	3.50
	Nos. 218-221 (4)	8.25	8.25

1975, July 28 Litho. *Perf. 14½*

60f, Educated woman holding IWY emblem.

222 A31	30f multicolored	1.50	1.50
223 A31	60f multicolored	3.50	3.50

International Women's Year.

Miniature Sheet

Arabian Stallion — A32

Arabian horses: a, Brown head. b, White mare. c, Mare and foal. d, White head. e, White mare. f, Mare and stallion. g, Bedouins on horseback. #224a, 224b, 224d are vert.

Perf. 14x14½, 14½x14

1975, Sept. 1 Photo.

224	Sheet of 8	52.50	32.50
a.-h.	A32 60f any single	5.25	3.50

Flag of Bahrain — A33

Map of Bahrain — A34

Sheik Isa — A35

1976-80 Litho. *Perf. 14½*

225	A33	5f red & ultra	.20	.20
226	A33	10f red & green	.20	.20
227	A33	15f red & black	.20	.20
228	A33	20f red & brown	.20	.20
228A	A34	25f gray & blk ('79)	.20	.20
229	A34	40f blue & black	.25	.25
229A	A34	50f yel grn & blk ('79)	.30	.30
230	A34	60f dl grn & blk ('77)	.35	.35
231	A34	80f rose lil & blk	.45	.45
232	A34	100f lt red brn & blk ('77)	.55	.55
233	A34	150f org & black	.85	.85
234	A34	200f yel & black	1.10	1.10

Engr.

Perf. 12x12½

235	A35	300f lt grn & grn	1.60	1.60
236	A35	400f pink & red brn	2.25	2.25
237	A35	500f lt bl & dk bl	2.75	2.75
238	A35	1d gray & sepia	5.50	5.00
239	A35	2d rose & vio ('80)	11.50	9.25
240	A35	3d buff & brn ('80)	17.00	14.00
		Nos. 225-240 (18)	45.45	39.70

A later printing of the 100f-200f, and possibly others, has a larger printers imprint at bottom.

Concorde at London Airport — A36

Designs: No. 245, Concorde at Bahrain Airport. No. 246, Concorde over London to Bahrain map. No. 247, Concorde on runway at night.

1976, Jan. 22 Photo. *Perf. 13x14*

244	A36	80f gold & multi	2.25	2.25
245	A36	80f gold & multi	2.25	2.25
246	A36	80f gold & multi	2.25	2.25
247	A36	80f gold & multi	2.25	2.25
a.		Souvenir sheet of 4	8.00	8.00
b.		Block of 4, #244-247	9.00	9.00

1st commercial flight of supersonic jet Concorde, London to Bahrain, Jan. 21. No. 247a contains 4 stamps with simulated perfs.

Soldier, Flag and Arms of Bahrain — A37

1976, Feb. 5 Litho. *Perf. 14½*

248	A37	40f yellow & multi	2.00	2.00
249	A37	80f lt blue & multi	4.00	4.00

Defense Force Day.

Sheik Isa, King Khalid, Bahrain and Saudi Flags A38

1976, Mar. 23 Litho. *Perf. 14½*

250	A38	40f gold & multi	1.75	1.75
251	A38	80f silver & multi	3.00	3.00

Visit of King Khalid of Saudi Arabia.

New Housing, Housing Ministry's Seal — A39

1976, Dec. 16 Litho. *Perf. 14½*

252	A39	40f rose & multi	1.60	1.60
253	A39	80f blue & multi	3.25	3.25

National Day.

APU Emblem A40

1977, Apr. 12 Litho. *Perf. 14½*

254	A40	40f silver & multi	1.50	1.50
255	A40	80f rose & multi	3.00	3.00

Arab Postal Union, 25th anniversary.

Miniature Sheet

Dogs on Beach and Dhow A41

Saluki dogs: b, Dog and camels. c, Dog and gazelles. d, Dog and Ruler's Palace. e, Dog's head. f, Heads of two dogs. g, Dog in dunes. h, Playing dogs.

1977, July Photo. *Perf. 14x14½*

256	Sheet of 8	28.00	28.00
a.-h.	A41 80f any single	2.75	2.75

Students and Candle A42

1977, Sept. 8 Litho. *Perf. 14½*

257	A42	40f multicolored	1.50	1.50
258	A42	80f multicolored	3.00	3.00

International Literacy Day.

Shipyard and Flags A43

1977, Dec. 16 Litho. *Perf. 14½*

259	A43	40f multicolored	1.50	1.50
260	A43	80f multicolored	3.00	3.00

Inauguration of Arab Shipbuilding and Repair Yard Co.

Antenna, ITU Emblem A44

1978, May 17 Litho. *Perf. 14½*

261	A44	40f yellow & multi	1.50	1.50
262	A44	80f silver & multi	3.00	3.00

10th World Telecommunications Day.

Ghanja Dhow A45

Dhows of the Arabian Gulf. #267-270 vertical.

Perf. 14x14½, 14½x14

1979, June 16 Photo.

263	A45	100f shown	3.25	3.25
264	A45	100f Zarook	3.25	3.25
265	A45	100f Shu'ai	3.25	3.25
266	A45	100f Jaliboot	3.25	3.25
267	A45	100f Baghla	3.25	3.25
268	A45	100f Sambuk	3.25	3.25
269	A45	100f Boom	3.25	3.25
270	A45	100f Kotia	3.25	3.25
a.		Block of 8, #263-270	26.00	26.00

Learning to Walk — A46

Hegira, 1,500th Anniv. — A47

IYC Emblem and: 100f, Hands surrounding girl, UN emblem.

1979 Litho. *Perf. 14½*

271	A46	50f multicolored	1.50	1.50
272	A46	100f multicolored	3.00	3.00

International Year of the Child.

1980 Photo. *Perf. 13x13½*

273	A47	50f multicolored	.65	.65
274	A47	100f multicolored	1.25	1.25
a.		Miniature sheet of 1	6.00	6.00
275	A47	150f multicolored	2.00	2.00
276	A47	200f multicolored	2.75	2.75
		Nos. 273-276 (4)	6.65	6.65

Falcon A48

Designs: Falcons.

Perf. 13½x14, 14x13½

1980, Nov. 1 Photo.

277	Block of 8	15.00	15.00
a.-h.	A48 100f any single	1.75	1.75

IYD Emblem, Sheik Isa — A49

1981, Mar. 21 Litho. *Perf. 14½*

278	A49	50f multicolored	1.60	1.60
279	A49	100f multicolored	3.25	3.25

International Year of the Disabled.

50th Anniversary of Electricity in Bahrain A50

1981, Apr. 26 Litho. *Perf. 14½*

280	A50	50f multicolored	1.60	1.60
281	A50	100f multicolored	3.25	3.25

Stone Cutting — A51

1981, July 1 Photo. *Perf. 14x13½*

282	A51	50f shown	.75	.75
283	A51	100f Pottery	1.25	1.25
284	A51	150f Weaving	2.75	2.75
285	A51	200f Basket making	3.00	3.00
		Nos. 282-285 (4)	7.75	7.75

Hegira (Pilgrimage Year) — A52

Designs: Various mosques.

1981, Oct. 1 Photo. *Perf. 14x13½*

286	A52	50f multicolored	.80	.80
287	A52	100f multicolored	1.60	1.60
288	A52	150f multicolored	2.25	2.25
289	A52	200f multicolored	3.25	3.25
		Nos. 286-289 (4)	7.90	7.90

Sheik Isa, 20th Anniv. of Coronation — A53

1981, Dec. 16 Photo. *Perf. 14x13½*

290	A53	15f multicolored	.25	.25
291	A53	50f multicolored	.80	.80
292	A53	100f multicolored	1.75	1.75
293	A53	150f multicolored	2.50	2.50
294	A53	200f multicolored	3.50	3.50
		Nos. 290-294 (5)	8.80	8.80

Wildlife in al Areen Park A54

Designs: a, Gazelle. b, Oryx. c, Dhub lizard. d, Arabian hares. e, Oryxes. f, Reems.

1982, Mar. 1 Photo. *Perf. 13½x14*

295	Sheet of 6	14.00	14.00
a.-f.	A54 100f any single	2.25	2.25

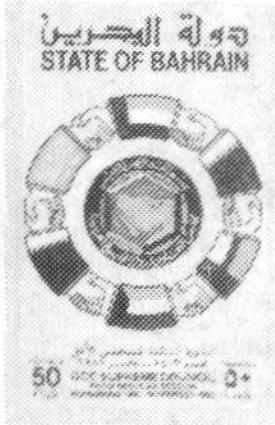

3rd Session of Gulf Supreme Council, Nov. — A55

1982, Nov. 9 Litho. *Perf. 14½*

296 A55 50f blue & multi .85 .85
297 A55 100f green & multi 2.25 2.25

Opening of Madinat Hamad Housing Development — A56

1983, Dec. 1 Litho. *Perf. 14½*

298 A56 50f multicolored .85 .85
299 A56 100f multicolored 2.25 2.25

Al Khalifa Dynasty Bicentenary — A57

Sheiks or Emblems: a, 500fr, Isa bin Sulman. b, Emblem (tan & multi). c, Isa bin Ali, 1869-1932. d, Hamad bin Isa, 1932-42. e, Sulman bin Hamad, 1942-61. f, Emblem (pale green & multi). g, Emblem (lemon & multi). h, Emblem (light blue & multi). i, Emblem (gray & multi).

1983, Dec. 16 Litho. *Perf. 14½*

300 Sheet of 9 9.00 9.00
a.-i. A57 100f any single .80 .80

Souvenir Sheet

301 A57 500f multicolored 8.50 8.50

No. 301 contains one stamp 60x38mm.

Gulf Co-operation Council Traffic Week — A58

1984, Apr. 30 Litho. *Perf. 14½*

302 A58 15f multicolored .30 .30
303 A58 50f multicolored 1.00 1.00
304 A58 100f multicolored 2.00 2.00
Nos. 302-304 (3) 3.30 3.30

1984 Summer Olympics A59

1984, Sept. 15 *Perf. 14½*

305 A59 15f Hurdles .25 .25
306 A59 50f Equestrian .80 .80
307 A59 100f Diving 1.60 1.60
308 A59 150f Fencing 2.00 2.00
309 A59 200f Shooting 3.50 3.50
Nos. 305-309 (5) 8.15 8.15

Postal Service Cent. A60

1984, Dec. 8 Photo. *Perf. 12x11½*

310 A60 15f multicolored .40 .40
311 A60 50f multicolored 1.25 1.25
312 A60 100f multicolored 2.25 2.25
Nos. 310-312 (3) 3.90 3.90

Miniature Sheet

Coastal Fish A61

1985, Feb. 10 Photo. *Perf. 13½x14*

313 Sheet of 10 12.00 12.00
a.-j. A61 100f any single 1.40 1.40

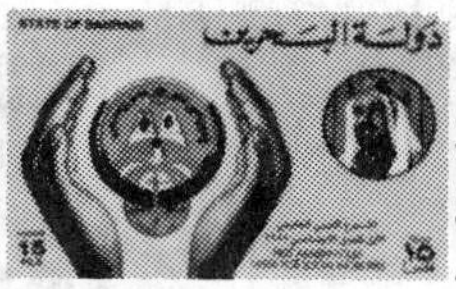

1st Arab Gulf States Week for Social Work A62

1985, Oct. 15 Litho. *Perf. 14½*

314 A62 15f multicolored .25 .25
315 A62 50f multicolored .85 .85
316 A62 100f multicolored 1.90 1.90
Nos. 314-316 (3) 3.00 3.00

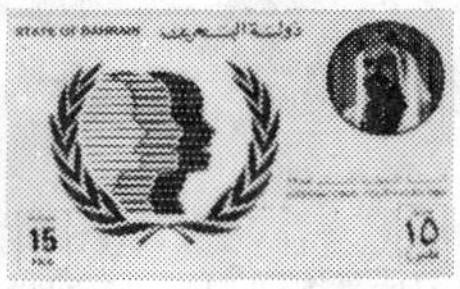

Intl. Youth Year A63

1985, Nov. 16

317 A63 15f multicolored .25 .25
318 A63 50f multicolored .85 .85
319 A63 100f multicolored 1.90 1.90
Nos. 317-319 (3) 3.00 3.00

Bahrain-Saudi Arabia Causeway Opening — A64

1986, Nov. Litho. *Perf. 14½*

320 A64 15f Causeway, aerial view .25 .25
321 A64 50f Island .85 .85
322 A64 100f Causeway 1.90 1.90
Nos. 320-322 (3) 3.00 3.00

Sheik Isa, 25th Anniv. as the Emir — A65

1986, Dec. 16

323 A65 15f multicolored .25 .25
324 A65 50f multicolored .85 .85
325 A65 100f multicolored 1.90 1.90
a. Souvenir sheet of 3, #323-325 5.50 5.50
Nos. 323-325 (3) 3.00 3.00

WHO, 40th Anniv. A66

1988, Apr. 30 Litho. *Perf. 14½*

326 A66 50f multicolored .50 .50
327 A66 150f multicolored 1.40 1.40

Opening of Ahmed Al Fateh Islamic Center A67

1988, June 2 Litho. *Perf. 14½*

328 A67 50f multicolored .50 .50
329 A67 150f multicolored 1.40 1.40

1988 Summer Olympics, Seoul A68

1988, Sept. 17 Litho. *Perf. 14½*

330 A68 50f Running .30 .30
331 A68 80f Equestrian .45 .45
332 A68 150f Fencing .80 .80
333 A68 200f Soccer 1.10 1.10
Nos. 330-333 (4) 2.65 2.65

Gulf Cooperation Council Supreme Council 9th Regular Session, Bahrain — A69

1988, Dec. 19 Litho. *Perf. 14½*

334 A69 50f multicolored .50 .50
335 A69 150f multicolored 1.40 1.40

Miniature Sheets

Camels — A70

No. 336: a, Close-up of head, rider in background. b, Camel kneeling at rest. c, Two adults, calf. d, Three adults. e, Camel facing right. f, Mount and rider (facing left).

No. 337: a, Man walking in front of camel, oil well. b, Man walking in front of camel. c, Oil well, camel's head. d, Mount and rider (facing forward). e, Mount and rider (facing right). f, Two dromedaries at a run. Nos. 337a-337f vert.

Perf. 13½x14, 14x13½

1989, June 15

336 Sheet of 6 6.00 6.00
a.-f. A70 150f any single 1.00 1.00
337 Sheet of 6 6.00 6.00
a.-f. A70 150f any single 1.00 1.00

Sheik Isa — A71

1989, Dec. 16 Litho. *Perf. 13½x14*

338 A71 25f multicolored .20 .20
339 A71 40f multicolored .25 .25
340 A71 50f multicolored .30 .30
341 A71 60f multicolored .35 .35
342 A71 75f multicolored .45 .45
343 A71 80f multicolored .50 .50
344 A71 100f multicolored .60 .60
345 A71 120f multicolored .75 .75
346 A71 150f multicolored .90 .90
347 A71 200f multicolored 1.25 1.25
a. Souvenir sheet of 10, #338-347 6.00 6.00
Nos. 338-347 (10) 5.55 5.55

Houbara (Bustard) — A72

Designs: a, Two birds facing right. b, Two birds facing each other. c, Chicks. d, Adult, chick. e, Adult, facing right, vert. f, In flight. g, Adult facing right. h, Chick, facing left, vert. i, Adult facing left. j, Adult male, close-up. k, Courtship display. l, Two birds facing left.

1990, Feb. 17 Photo. *Perf. 14*

348 Sheet of 12 11.00 11.00
a.-l. A72 150f any single .90 .90

Gulf Air, 40th Anniv. A73

1990, Mar. 24 Litho. *Perf. 14½*

360 A73 50f multicolored .30 .30
361 A73 80f multicolored .50 .50
362 A73 150f multicolored .95 .95
363 A73 200f multicolored 1.25 1.25
Nos. 360-363 (4) 3.00 3.00

Chamber of Commerce, 50th Anniv. — A74

1990, May 26

364 A74 50f multicolored .30 .30
365 A74 80f multicolored .50 .50
366 A74 150f multicolored .95 .95
367 A74 200f multicolored 1.25 1.25
Nos. 364-367 (4) 3.00 3.00

Intl. Literacy Year A75

1990, Sept. 8 Litho. *Perf. 14½*

368 A75 50f multicolored .30 .30
369 A75 80f multicolored .50 .50
370 A75 150f multicolored .95 .95
371 A75 200f multicolored 1.25 1.25
Nos. 368-371 (4) 3.00 3.00

Miniature Sheet

Indigenous Birds — A76

Designs: a, Galerida cristata. b, Upupa epops. c, Pycnonotus leucogenys. d, Streptopelia turtur. e, Streptopelia decaocto. f, Falco tinnunculus. g, Passer domesticus, horiz. h, Lanius excubitor, horiz. i, Psittacula krameri.

1991, Sept. 15 Litho. *Perf. 14½*

372 Sheet of 9 9.00 9.00
a.-i. A76 150f any single 1.10 1.10

See Nos. 382, 407.

Coronation of Sheik Isa, 30th Anniv. — A77

Design: Nos. 374, 376, 378, 380, 381a, Portrait at left, leaves.

Litho. & Embossed

1991, Dec. 16 ***Perf. 14½***

373 A77 50f multicolored .35 .35
374 A77 50f multicolored .35 .35
375 A77 80f multicolored .55 .55
376 A77 80f multicolored .55 .55
377 A77 150f multicolored 1.10 1.10
378 A77 150f multicolored 1.10 1.10
379 A77 200f multicolored 1.50 1.50
380 A77 200f multicolored 1.50 1.50
Nos. 373-380 (8) 7.00 7.00

Souvenir Sheet

Perf. 14x14½

381 Sheet of 2 7.50 7.50
a.-b. A77 500f any single 3.75 3.75

No. 381 contains 41x31mm stamps.

Miniature Sheet

Indigenous Birds Type of 1991

Designs: No. 382a, Ciconia ciconia. b, Merops apiaster. c, Sturnus vulgaris. d, Hypocolius ampelinus. e, Cuculus canorus. f, Turdus viscivorus. g, Coracias garrulus. h, Carduelis carduelis. i, Lanius collurio. j, Turdus iliacus, horiz. k, Motacilla alba, horiz. l, Oriolus oriolus, horiz. m, Erithacus rubecula. n, Luscinia luscinia. o, Muscicapa striata. p, Hirundo rustica.

1992, Mar. 21 **Litho.** ***Perf. 14½***

382 Sheet of 16 13.50 13.50
a.-p. A76 150f any single .80 .80

Miniature Sheet

Horse Racing A78

Designs: No. 383a, Horses leaving starting gate. b, Trainers leading horses. c, Horses racing around turn. d, Horses in stretch racing by flags. e, Two horses racing by grandstand. f, Five horses galloping. g, Two brown horses racing. h, Black horse, gray horse racing.

1992, May 22

383 Sheet of 8 7.25 7.25
a.-h. A78 150f any single .90 .90

1992 Summer Olympics, Barcelona — A79

1992, July 25 **Litho.** ***Perf. 14½***

384 A79 50f Equestrian .35 .35
385 A79 80f Running .60 .60
386 A79 150f Judo 1.10 1.10
387 A79 200f Cycling 1.40 1.40
Nos. 384-387 (4) 3.45 3.45

Bahrain Intl. Airport, 60th Anniv. A80

1992, Oct. 27 **Litho.** ***Perf. 14½***

388 A80 50f multicolored .35 .35
389 A80 80f multicolored .55 .55
390 A80 150f multicolored 1.00 1.00
391 A80 200f multicolored 1.25 1.25
Nos. 388-391 (4) 3.15 3.15

Children's Art — A81

Designs: 50f, Girl jumping rope, vert. 80f, Women in traditional dress, vert. 150f, Women stirring kettle. 200f, Fishermen.

1992, Nov. 28 **Litho.** ***Perf. 14½***

392 A81 50f multicolored .30 .30
393 A81 80f multicolored .50 .50
394 A81 150f multicolored .95 .95
395 A81 200f multicolored 1.25 1.25
Nos. 392-395 (4) 3.00 3.00

Inauguration of Expansion of Aluminum Bahrain — A82

Designs: 50f, Ore funicular. 80f, Smelting pot. 150f, Mill. 200f, Cylindrical aluminum ingots.

1992, Dec. 16

396 A82 50f multicolored .30 .30
397 A82 80f multicolored .50 .50
398 A82 150f multicolored .95 .95
399 A82 200f multicolored 1.25 1.25
Nos. 396-399 (4) 3.00 3.00

Bahrain Defense Force, 25th Anniv. A83

Designs: 50f, Artillery forces, vert. 80f, Fighters, tanks, and ship, vert. 150f, Frigate. 200f, Jet fighter.

Perf. 13½x13, 13x13½

1993, Feb. 5 **Litho.**

400 A83 50f multicolored .30 .30
401 A83 80f multicolored .50 .50
402 A83 150f multicolored .95 .95
403 A83 200f multicolored 1.25 1.25
Nos. 400-403 (4) 3.00 3.00

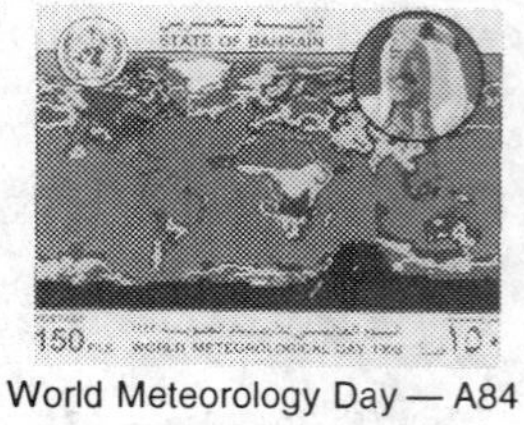

World Meteorology Day — A84

Designs: 50f, Satellite image of Bahrain, vert. 150f, Infrared satellite map of world. 200f, Earth, seen from space, vert.

1993, Mar. 23 **Litho.** ***Perf. 14½***

404 A84 50f multicolored .45 .45
405 A84 150f multicolored 1.40 1.40
406 A84 200f multicolored 1.75 1.75
Nos. 404-406 (3) 3.60 3.60

Bird Type of 1991

Miniature Sheet

Designs: a, Ardea purpurea. b, Gallinula chloropus. c, Phalacrocorax nigrogularis. d, Dromas ardeola. e, Alcedo atthis. f, Vanellus vanellus. g, Haematopus ostralegus, horiz. h, Nycticorax nycticorax. i, Sterna caspia, horiz. j, Arenaria interpres, horiz. k, Rallus aquaticus, horiz. l, Anas platyrhychos, horiz. m, Larus fuscus, horiz.

1993, May 22 **Litho.** ***Perf. 14½***

407 Sheet of 13 + 2 labels 11.00 11.00
a.-m. A76 150f any single .85 .85

Gazella Subgutturosa Marica — A85

1993, July 24 **Litho.** ***Perf. 14½***

408 A85 25f Calf .20 .20
409 A85 50f Female standing .30 .30
410 A85 50f Female walking .30 .30
411 A85 150f Male .95 .95
Nos. 408-411 (4) 1.75 1.75

World Wildlife Federation.

Wild Flowers — A86

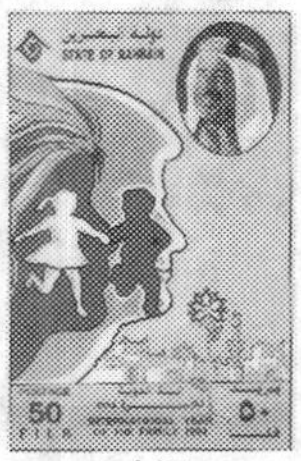

A87

Designs: a, Lycium shawii. b, Alhagi maurorum. c, Caparis spinosa. d, Cistanche phelypae. e, Asphodelus tenuifolius. f, Limonium axillare. g, Cynomorium coccineum. h, Calligonum polygonoides.

1993, Oct. 16 **Litho.** ***Perf. 13½x13***

412 A86 150f Sheet of 8, #a.-h. 6.50 6.50

1994, Jan. 22 **Litho.** ***Perf. 14½***

Background Color

413 A87 50f yellow .30 .30
414 A87 80f blue green .50 .50
415 A87 150f purple .95 .95
416 A87 200f blue 1.25 1.25
Nos. 413-416 (4) 3.00 3.00

Intl. Year of the Family.

A88

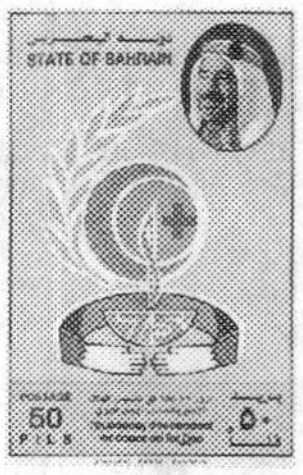

A89

Butterflies: No. 417a, Lepidochrysops arabicus. b, Ypthima bolanica. c, Eurema brigitta. d, Precis limnoria. e, Aglais urticae. f, Colotis protomedia. g, Salamis anacardii. h, Byblia ilithyia.

No. 418a, Papilio machaon. b, Agrodiaetus loewii. c, Vanessa cardui. d, Papilio demoleus. e, Hamanumida daedalus. f, Funonia orithya. g, Funonia chorimine. h, Colias croceus.

Perf. 13½x13, 13x13½

1994, Mar. 21 **Litho.**

417 A88 50f Sheet of 8, #a.-h. 2.50 2.50
418 A88 150f Sheet of 8, #a.-h. 7.50 7.50

No. 418 is horiz.

1994, May 8 **Litho.** ***Perf. 14½***

419 A89 50f lilac & multi .30 .30
420 A89 80f yellow & multi .50 .50
421 A89 150f salmon & multi .95 .95
422 A89 200f green blue & multi 1.25 1.25
Nos. 419-422 (4) 3.00 3.00

Intl. Red Cross & Red Crescent Societies, 75th anniv.

1994 World Cup Soccer Championships, US — A90

Designs: 50f, Goalkeeper. 80f, Heading ball. 150f, Dribbling ball. 200f, Slide tackle.

1994, June 17 **Litho.** ***Perf. 14***

423 A90 50f multicolored .30 .30
424 A90 80f multicolored .50 .50
425 A90 150f multicolored .95 .95
426 A90 200f multicolored 1.25 1.25
Nos. 423-426 (4) 3.00 3.00

Bahrain's First Satellite Earth Station, 25th Anniv. — A91

1994, July 14

427 A91 50f blue & multi .30 .30
428 A91 80f yellow & multi .50 .50
429 A91 150f violet & multi .95 .95
430 A91 200f pink, yellow & multi 1.25 1.25
Nos. 427-430 (4) 3.00 3.00

Education in Bahrain, 75th Anniv. — A92

1994, Nov. 19 **Litho.** ***Perf. 14½***

431 A92 50f yellow & multi .30 .30
432 A92 80f buff & multi .50 .50
433 A92 150f salmon & multi .95 .95
434 A92 200f pink & multi 1.25 1.25
Nos. 431-434 (4) 3.00 3.00

Gulf Cooperation Council Supreme Council, 15th Regular Session, Bahrain — A93

1994, Dec. 19 ***Perf. 14***

435 A93 50f blue green & multi .30 .30
436 A93 80f brown & multi .50 .50
437 A93 150f lilac rose & multi .95 .95
438 A93 200f blue & multi 1.25 1.25
Nos. 435-438 (4) 3.00 3.00

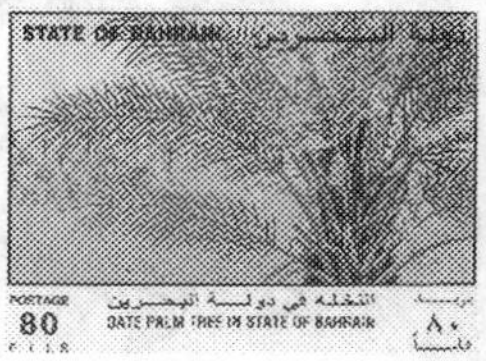

Date Palm A94

Designs: 80f, Flowering stage. 100f, Dates beginning to ripen. 200f, Dates up close. 250f, Trees from distance.

500f, Pitcher, basket of dates.

1995, Mar. 21 Litho. *Perf. 14*

439 A94 80f multicolored .50 .50
440 A94 100f multicolored .60 .60
441 A94 200f multicolored 1.25 1.25
442 A94 250f multicolored 1.50 1.50
Nos. 439-442 (4) 3.85 3.85

Souvenir Sheet

443 A94 500f multicolored 3.00 3.00

No. 443 contains one 65x48mm stamp.

Fight Against Polio — A95

1995, Apr. 22 Litho. *Perf. 13x13½*

444 A95 80f pink & multi .40 .40
445 A95 200f blue & multi 1.00 1.00
446 A95 250f lt brown & multi 1.40 1.40
Nos. 444-446 (3) 2.80 2.80

World Health Day.

1st Natl. Industries Exhibition A96

1995, May 15

447 A96 80f blue green & multi .40 .40
448 A96 200f lilac & multi 1.00 1.00
449 A96 250f lt brown & multi 1.40 1.40
Nos. 447-449 (3) 2.80 2.80

FAO, 50th Anniv. A97

Fields of various crops.

1995, June 17 Litho. *Perf. 14*

450 A97 80f lilac & multi .40 .40
451 A97 200f blue & multi 1.00 1.00
452 A97 250f lt pink & multi 1.40 1.40
Nos. 450-452 (3) 2.80 2.80

Arab League, 50th Anniv. — A98

1995, Sept. 14 Litho. *Perf. 14½*

453 A98 80f pink & multi .40 .40
454 A98 200f blue & multi 1.10 1.10
455 A98 250f yellow & multi 1.40 1.40
Nos. 453-455 (3) 2.90 2.90

UN, 50th Anniv. A99

1995, Oct. 24 Litho. *Perf. 14½*

456 A99 80f yellow & multi .40 .40
457 A99 100f green & multi .55 .55
458 A99 200f pink & multi 1.10 1.10
459 A99 250f blue & multi 1.40 1.40
Nos. 456-459 (4) 3.45 3.45

Miniature Sheet

Traditional Architecture — A100

Example of architecture, detail: a, Tower with balcony. b, Arched windows behind balcony. c, Double doors under arch. d, Four rows of square windows above row of arched windows. e, Door flanked by two windows. f, Three windows.

1995, Nov. 20 Litho. *Perf. 14½*

460 A100 200f Sheet of 6, #a.-f. 6.50 6.50

National Day — A101

1995, Dec. 16 Litho. *Perf. 14½*

461 A101 80f blue & multi .40 .40
462 A101 100f green & multi .55 .55
463 A101 200f violet & multi 1.10 1.10
464 A101 250f blue green & multi 1.40 1.40
Nos. 461-464 (4) 3.45 3.45

Public Library, 50th Anniv. — A102

1996, Mar. 23 Litho. *Perf. 14*

465 A102 80f pink & multi .40 .40
466 A102 200f green & multi 1.10 1.10
467 A102 250f blue & multi 1.40 1.40
Nos. 465-467 (3) 2.90 2.90

Pearl Diving — A103

Designs: 80f, Group of divers on ship, three in water. 100f, Five divers in water, ship. 200f, Diver underneath water. 250f, Diver being pulled up, underwater scene.

500f, Lantern, weight, scales, pearls, knife. Illustration reduced.

1996, May 8 Litho. *Perf. 14*

468 A103 80f multicolored .40 .40
469 A103 100f multicolored .55 .55
470 A103 200f multicolored 1.10 1.10
471 A103 250f multicolored 1.40 1.40
Nos. 468-471 (4) 3.45 3.45

Souvenir Sheet

Perf. 14½

472 A103 500f multicolored 2.75 2.75

No. 472 contains one 70x70mm stamp.

1996 Summer Olympics, Atlanta A104

1996, July 19 Litho. *Perf. 14*

473 A104 80f olive & multi .40 .40
474 A104 100f pink & multi .55 .55
475 A104 200f blue green & multi 1.10 1.10
476 A104 250f orange & multi 1.40 1.40
Nos. 473-476 (4) 3.45 3.45

Interpol, Intl. Criminal Police Organization — A105

1996, Sept. 25 Litho. *Perf. 14*

477 A105 80f blue & multi .40 .40
478 A105 100f yellow & multi .55 .55
479 A105 200f pink & multi 1.10 1.10
480 A105 250f green & multi 1.40 1.40
Nos. 477-480 (4) 3.45 3.45

Aluminum Production in Bahrain, 25th Anniv. — A106

1996, Nov. 20 Litho. *Perf. 14*

481 A106 80f bister & multi .40 .40
482 A106 100f orange & multi .55 .55
483 A106 200f blue & multi 1.10 1.10
484 A106 250f green & multi 1.40 1.40
Nos. 481-484 (4) 3.45 3.45

Accession to the Throne by Sheik Isa Bin Salman Al Khalifa, 35th Anniv. — A107

1996, Dec. 16

485 A107 80f gray & multi .40 .40
486 A107 100f green & multi .55 .55
487 A107 200f pink & multi 1.10 1.10
488 A107 250f blue & multi 1.40 1.40
Nos. 485-488 (4) 3.45 3.45

Bahrain Refinery, 60th Anniv. A108

1997, Jan. 15 Litho. *Perf. 14*

489 A108 80f red & multi .45 .45
490 A108 200f blue & multi 1.10 1.10
491 A108 250f yellow & multi 1.25 1.25
Nos. 489-491 (3) 2.80 2.80

Pure Strains of Arabian Horses, Amiri Stud A109

Designs: a, Musannaan, Al-Jellabieh, Rabdaan. b, Kuheilaan weld umm zorayr. c, Al-Jellaby. d, Musannaan. e, Kuheilaan aladiyat. f, Kuheilaan aafas. g, Al-Dhahma. h, Mlolshaan. i, Al-Kray. j, Krush. k, Al Hamdaany. l, Hadhfaan. m, Rabda. n, Al-Suwaitieh. o, Al-Obeyah. p, Al-Shuwaimeh. q, Al-Ma'anaghieh. r, Al-Tuwaisah. s, Wadhna. t, Al-Saqlawieh. u, Al-Shawafah.

1997, Apr. 23 Litho. *Perf. 14x14½*

492 A109 200f Sheet of 21, #a.-u. 22.50 22.50

9th Men's Junior World Volleyball Championship — A110

1997, Aug. 21 Litho. *Perf. 14x14½*

493 A110 80f brown & multi .45 .45
494 A110 100f green & multi .55 .55
495 A110 200f gray brown & multi 1.10 1.10
496 A110 250f blue & multi 1.25 1.25
Nos. 493-496 (4) 3.35 3.35

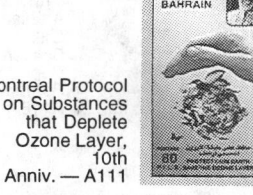

Montreal Protocol on Substances that Deplete Ozone Layer, 10th Anniv. — A111

1997, Sept. 16 Litho. *Perf. 14½*

497 A111 80f yellow & multi .45 .45
498 A111 100f purple & multi .55 .55
499 A111 200f red & multi 1.10 1.10
500 A111 250f green & multi 1.25 1.25
Nos. 497-500 (4) 3.35 3.35

Sheikh Isa Bin Salman Bridge A112

Designs: 80f, Pylon, supports. 200f, Center of bridge. 250f, 500f, Entire span.

1997, Dec. 28 Litho. *Perf. 13x13½*

501 A112 80f multicolored .45 .45
502 A112 200f multicolored 1.10 1.10

Size: 76x26mm

503 A112 250f multicolored 1.25 1.25
Nos. 501-503 (3) 2.80 2.80

Souvenir Sheet

504 A112 500f multicolored 2.75 2.75

Inuaguration of Urea Plant, GPIC (Refinery) Complex A113

Designs: 80f, View of plant from Persian Gulf. 200f, Plant facilities. 250f, Aerial view.

1998, Mar. 3 Litho. *Perf. 13x13½*

505 A113 80f multicolored	.45	.45
506 A113 200f multicolored	1.10	1.10
507 A113 250f multicolored	1.25	1.25
Nos. 505-507 (3)	2.80	2.80

World Health Organization, 50th Anniv. — A114

1998, May 11 Litho. *Perf. 14*

508 A114 80f orange & multi	.45	.45
509 A114 200f green & multi	1.10	1.10
510 A114 250f gray & multi	1.25	1.25
Nos. 508-510 (3)	2.80	2.80

1998 World Cup Soccer Championships, France — A115

Designs: 200f, Soccer balls, world maps, vert. 250f, Players, globe, vert.

1998, June 10

511 A115 80f multicolored	.45	.45
512 A115 200f multicolored	1.10	1.10
513 A115 250f multicolored	1.25	1.25
Nos. 511-513 (3)	2.80	2.80

14th Arabian Gulf Soccer Cup, Bahrain A116

Design: 200f, 250f, Soccer ball.

1998, Oct. 30 Litho. *Perf. 14*

514 A116 80f shown	.45	.45
515 A116 200f pale violet & multi	1.10	1.10
516 A116 250f bister & multi	1.25	1.25
Nos. 514-516 (3)	2.80	2.80

Grand Competition for Holy Koran Recitation A117

1999, Jan. 9 Litho. *Perf. 14*

517 A117 100f gray olive & multi	.55	.55
518 A117 200f yellow & multi	1.10	1.10
519 A117 250f green & multi	1.25	1.25
Nos. 517-519 (3)	2.90	2.90

Isa Bin Salman Al-Khalifa (1933-99), Emir of Bahrain — A118

Natl. flag, map and: 100f, 500f, Emir holding sword, vert. 250f, Portrait up close, vert.

Perf. 13¼ (#520, 522), 14¼ (#521)

1999, June 5 Litho.

520 A118 100f multicolored	.55	.55
521 A118 200f multicolored	1.10	1.10
522 A118 250f multicolored	1.25	1.25
Nos. 520-522 (3)	2.90	2.90

Souvenir Sheet

Perf. 14½x13

523 A118 500f multicolored	3.00	3.00

Nos. 520, 522 are 31x50mm. No. 523 contains one 67x102mm stamp.

Intl. Year of Older Persons A119

1999, Oct. 9 Litho. *Perf. 13x13½*

524 A119 100f multi	.55	.55
525 A119 200f multi, diff.	1.10	1.10
526 A119 250f multi, diff.	1.25	1.25
Nos. 524-526 (3)	2.90	2.90

WAR TAX STAMPS

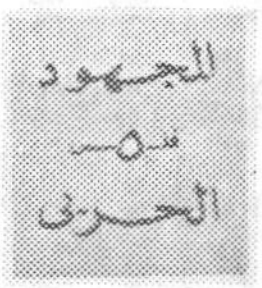

WT1

WT2

1973, Oct. 21 Litho. *Perf. 14½*

MR1 WT1 5f sky blue

> **Catalogue values for all unused stamps in this section, from this point to the end of the section, are for Never Hinged items.**

1974 Litho. *Perf. 14½*

MR2 WT2 5f light blue	1.75	.25
a. Perf. 14½x13½	2.50	

No. MR2a was issued around 1988.

BANGKOK

'baŋ-ˌkäk

LOCATION — Capital of Siam (Thailand)

Stamps were issued by Great Britain under rights obtained in the treaty of 1855. These were in use until July 1, 1885, when the stamps of Siam were designated as the only official postage stamps to be used in the kingdom.

100 Cents = 1 Dollar

Excellent counterfeits of Nos. 1-22 are plentiful.

Stamps of Straits Settlements Overprinted in Black **B**

1882 Wmk. 1 *Perf. 14*

1 A2 2c brown	*2,250.*	*1,200.*
2 A2 4c rose	*2,500.*	*1,200.*
a. Inverted overprint		
3 A6 5c brown violet	*300.00*	*150.00*
4 A2 6c violet	*225.00*	*125.00*
5 A3 8c yel orange	*2,000.*	160.00
6 A7 10c slate	*200.00*	*125.00*
7 A3 12c blue	*500.00*	*250.00*
8 A3 24c green	*650.00*	*125.00*
9 A4 30c claret	*40,000.*	*25,000.*
10 A5 96c olive gray	*4,000.*	*2,250.*

The existence of No. 2a is questioned.
See note after No. 20. No. 2 with two clear impressions: $6,000 used.

1882-83 Wmk. 2

11 A2 2c brown	*325.00*	*250.00*
12 A2 2c rose ('83)	*40.00*	*40.00*
a. Inverted overprint	*20,000.*	*10,000.*
b. Double overprint	*1,750.*	
c. Triple overprint	*10,000.*	
13 A2 4c rose	*400.00*	*250.00*
14 A2 4c brown ('83)	*60.00*	*60.00*
a. Double overprint	—	
15 A6 5c ultra ('83)	*160.00*	*160.00*
16 A2 6c violet ('83)	*100.00*	*100.00*
a. Double overprint		
17 A3 8c yel orange	*125.00*	*80.00*
a. Inverted overprint	*17,500.*	*10,000.*
18 A7 10c slate	*125.00*	*80.00*
a. Double overprint		
19 A3 12c violet brn ('83)	*175.00*	*140.00*
20 A3 24c green	*3,250.*	*2,250.*

Partial double overprints exist on a number of values of these issues. They sell for a modest premium over catalogue value depending on how much of the impression is present.

1883 Wmk. 1

21 A5 2c on 32c pale red	*2,250.*	*2,250.*

On Straits Settlements No. 9

1885 Wmk. 38

22 A7 32c on 2a yel (B+B)	*40,000.*	*50,000.*

BANGLADESH

ˌbäŋ-glə-ˈdesh

LOCATION — In southern, central Asia, touching India, Burma, and the Bay of Bengal
GOVT. — Republic in the British Commonwealth
AREA — 55,598 sq. mi.
POP. — 127,117,967 (1999 est.)
CAPITAL — Dhaka (Dacca)

Bangladesh, formerly East Pakistan, broke away from Pakistan in April 1971, proclaiming its independence. It consists of 14 former eastern districts of Bengal and the former Sylhet district of Assam province of India.

100 Paisas = 1 Rupee
100 Paisas (Poishas) = 1 Taka (1972)

> **Catalogue values for all unused stamps in this country are for Never Hinged items.**

Various stamps of Pakistan were handstamped locally for use in Bangladesh from March 26, 1971 until April 30, 1973.

Map of Bangladesh A1

Sheik Mujibur Rahman A2

Designs: 20p, "Dacca University Massacre." 50p, "A Nation of 75 Million People." 1r, Flag of Independence (showing map). 2r, Ballot box. 3r, Broken chain. 10r, "Support Bangladesh" and map.

Perf. 14x14½

1971, July 29 Litho. Unwmk.

1 A1 10p red, dk pur & lt bl	.20	.20
2 A1 20p bl, grn, red & yel	.20	.20
3 A1 50p dp org, gray & brn	.20	.20
4 A1 1r red, emer & yel	.20	.20
5 A1 2r lil rose, lt & dk bl	.40	.40
6 A1 3r blue, emer & grn	.50	.50
7 A2 5r dp org, tan & blk	1.00	1.00
8 A1 10r gold, dk bl & lil rose	1.60	1.60
Nos. 1-8 (8)	4.30	4.30

A set of 15 stamps of types A1 and A2 in new paisa-taka values and colors was rejected by Bangladesh officials and not issued. Bangladesh representatives in England released these stamps, which were not valid, on Feb. 1, 1972.

Imperfs of Nos. 1-8 were in the Format International liquidation. They are not errors.

Nos. 1-8 Overprinted in Black or Red

BANGLADESH
LIBERATED
বাংলাদেশের মুক্তি

1971, Dec. 20

9 A1 10p multicolored	.20	.20
10 A1 20p multicolored	.20	
11 A1 50p multicolored	.20	
12 A1 1r multicolored	.30	
13 A1 2r multicolored	.50	
14 A1 3r multicolored	.90	
15 A2 5r multicolored (R)	1.25	1.25
16 A1 10r multicolored	2.50	2.50
Nos. 9-16 (8)	6.05	

Liberation of Bangladesh.
The 10p, 5r and 10r were issued in Dacca, but Nos. 10-14 were not put on sale in Bangladesh.

Monument A3

"Independence" A4

1972, Feb. 21 Litho. *Perf. 13*

32 A3 20p green & rose	.70	.30

Language Movement Martyrs.

1972, Mar. 26 Photo. *Perf. 13*

33 A4 20p maroon & red	.20	.20
34 A4 60p dark blue & red	.30	.30
35 A4 75p purple & red	.30	.30
Nos. 33-35 (3)	.80	.80

First anniversary of independence.

Doves of Peace — A5

Flower Growing from Ruin — A6

1972, Dec. 16 Litho. *Perf. 13*

36 A5 20p ocher & multi	.20	.20
37 A5 60p lilac & multi	.30	.30
38 A5 75p yellow green & multi	.35	.35
Nos. 36-38 (3)	.85	.85

Victory Day, Dec. 16.

1973, Mar. 25 Litho. *Perf. 13*

39 A6 20p ocher & multi	.20	.20
40 A6 60p brown & multi	.40	.40
41 A6 1.35t violet blue & multi	1.00	1.00
Nos. 39-41 (3)	1.60	1.60

Martyrs of the war of liberation.

Embroidered Quilt — A7

Hilsa — A8

Court of Justice — A9

Designs: 3p, Jute field. 5p, Jack fruit. 10p, Farmer plowing with ox team. 20p, Hibiscus rosenensis. 25p, Tiger. 60p, Bamboo and water lilies. 75p, Women picking tea. 90p,

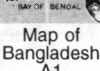

Handicraft. 2t, Collecting date palm juice, vert. 5t, Net fishing. 10t, Sixty-dome Mosque.

Perf. 14x14½, 14½x14

1973, Apr. 30 **Litho.**

Size: 21x28mm, 28x21mm

42	A7	2p black	.20	.20
43	A7	3p bright green	.20	.20
44	A7	5p light brown	.20	.20
45	A7	10p black	.20	.20
46	A7	20p olive	.70	.30
47	A7	25p red lilac	1.90	.60
48	A8	50p rose lilac	1.50	.50
49	A7	60p gray	.70	.25
50	A7	75p orange	1.25	.45
51	A7	90p red brown	1.25	.45

Taka Expressed as "TA"

Size: 35x22mm

52	A9	1t violet	3.50	1.25
53	A9	2t greenish gray	4.50	1.50
54	A9	5t grayish blue	6.00	2.00
55	A9	10t rose	6.50	2.25
		Nos. 42-55 (14)	28.60	10.35

See Nos. 82-85, 95-106, 165-176. For overprints see Nos. O1-O10, O13.

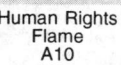

Human Rights Flame A10

Family, Chart, Map of Bangladesh A11

1973, Dec. 10 **Litho.** ***Perf. 13x13½***

56	A10	10p blue & multi	.20	.20
57	A10	1.25t violet & multi	.40	.40

25th anniversary of the Universal Declaration of Human Rights.

1974, Feb. 10 **Litho.** ***Perf. 13½***

58	A11	20p blue grn & multi	.20	.20
59	A11	25p brt blue & multi	.20	.20
60	A11	75p red & multi	.45	.45
		Nos. 58-60 (3)	.85	.85

First census in Bangladesh.
For overprints see Nos. 194-196.

Copernicus, Heliocentric System A12

Flag and UN Headquarters A13

1974, July 22 **Litho.** ***Perf. 13½***

61	A12	25p violet, blk & org	.20	.20
62	A12	75p emerald, blk & org	.60	.60

Nicolaus Copernicus (1473-1543), Polish astronomer.

1974, Sept. 25 **Litho.** ***Perf. 13½***

63	A13	25p lilac & multi	.20	.20
64	A13	1t blue & multi	.50	.50

Admission of Bangladesh to the UN.

A14

A15

Designs: 25p, 1.75t, UPU emblem. 1.25t, 5t, Mail runner. 25p, 1.25t, country and denomination appear on a yellow background, 1.75t, 5t, blue background.

1974, Oct. 9 ***Perf. 13½***

65	A14	25p multicolored	.20	.20
66	A14	1.25t multicolored	.20	.20
67	A14	1.75t multicolored	.35	.35
68	A14	5t multicolored	.95	.95
a.		Souv. sheet of 4, #65-68, imperf.	*35.00*	
		Nos. 65-68 (4)	1.70	1.70

1974, Nov. 4 **Litho.**

69	A15	25p Royal bengal tiger	.25	.25
70	A15	50p Tiger cub	1.25	1.25
71	A15	2t Swimming tiger	3.50	3.50
		Nos. 69-71 (3)	5.00	5.00

"Save the Tiger," World Wildlife Fund.

Type of 1973
Taka Expressed in Bengali

1974-75 ***Perf. 14½x14, 14x14½***

Size: 35x22mm

82	A9	1t violet	1.60	.20
83	A9	2t grayish green	2.50	1.00
84	A9	5t grayish blue ('75)	4.50	1.00
85	A9	10t rose ('75)	10.00	5.00
		Nos. 82-85 (4)	18.60	7.20

For overprints see Nos. O11-O12, O14.

Family A16

Children A17

Family A18

1974, Dec. 30 **Litho.** ***Perf. 14***

86	A16	25p ocher & multi	.20	.20
87	A17	70p claret & multi	.30	.30
88	A18	1.25t multicolored	.50	.50
		Nos. 86-88 (3)	1.00	1.00

Family planning. The numerals on No. 87 look like "90" but mean "70."

Betbunia Satellite Earth Station — A19

1975, June 14 **Litho.** ***Perf. 14***

89	A19	25p red, black & silver	.20	.20
90	A19	1t vio blue, blk & silver	.60	.60

Opening of Betbunia Satellite Earth Station.

Allegory, IWY Emblem A20

1975, Dec. 31 **Litho.** ***Perf. 15***

91	A20	50p rose & multi	.20	.20
92	A20	2t lt lilac & multi	.70	.70

International Women's Year.

Types of 1973 Redrawn

1976-77 **Litho.** ***Perf. 15x14½***

Size: 18x23mm, 23x18mm

95	A7	5p green	.20	.20
96	A7	10p black	.20	.20
97	A7	20p olive green	.20	.20
98	A7	25p rose lilac	.30	.20
99	A8	50p rose lilac	.45	.20
100	A7	60p gray	.60	.25
101	A7	75p olive	.70	*1.00*
102	A7	90p red brown	.90	.25

Taka Expressed in Bengali

Size: 32x20mm, 20x32mm

103	A9	1t violet	.95	.20
104	A9	2t greenish gray	6.50	.30
105	A9	5t grayish blue	4.00	2.00
106	A9	10t rose ('77)	9.00	2.00
		Nos. 95-106 (12)	24.00	7.00

For overprints see Nos. O16-O25.

Telephones, 1876 and 1976 — A21

Alexander Graham Bell — A22

1976, Mar. 10 **Litho.** ***Perf. 15***

107	A21	2.25t multicolored	.40	.40
108	A22	5t multicolored	1.00	1.00

Centenary of first telephone call by Alexander Graham Bell, Mar. 10, 1876.

Eye and Healthful Food — A23

1976, Apr. 7 **Litho.** ***Perf. 15***

109	A23	30p yellow & multi	.35	.35
110	A23	2.25t orange & multi	1.60	1.60

World Health Day: Foresight prevents blindness.

Liberty Bell — A24

Designs: 2.25t, Statue of Liberty, New York Skyline. 5t, Mayflower. 10t, Mt. Rushmore, presidents' heads.

1976, May 29 **Photo.** ***Perf. 13½x14***

111	A24	30p multicolored	.20	.20
112	A24	2.25t multicolored	.30	.30
113	A24	5t multicolored	.70	.70
114	A24	10t multicolored	1.40	1.40
a.		Souv. sheet of 4, #111-114, perf. 13	3.50	3.50
		Nos. 111-114 (4)	2.60	2.60

American Bicentennial. Sheet exists imperf.

Weaver, Chemist, Farmer, Student and Emblem — A25

1976, July 29 **Litho.** ***Perf. 15***

115	A25	30p multicolored	.20	.20
116	A25	2.25t multicolored	.75	.75

25th anniversary of Colombo Plan.
For overprint see No. 252.

Hurdles — A26

Montreal Olympic Emblem and: 30p, Running, horiz. 1t, High jump. 2.25t, Swimming, horiz. 3.50t, Gymnastics. 5t, Soccer.

1976, Nov. 29 **Litho.** ***Perf. 15***

117	A26	25p multicolored	.20	.20
118	A26	30p multicolored	.20	.20
119	A26	1t multicolored	.20	.20
120	A26	2.25t multicolored	.50	.50
121	A26	3.50t multicolored	.70	.70
122	A26	5t multicolored	1.10	1.10
		Nos. 117-122 (6)	2.90	2.90

21st Olympic Games, Montreal, Canada, July 17-Aug. 1.

Coronation Ceremony — A27

Designs: 2.25t, Queen Elizabeth II. 10t, Queen and Prince Philip.

1977, Feb. 7 ***Perf. 14x15***

123	A27	30p multicolored	.20	.20
124	A27	2.25t multicolored	.25	.25
125	A27	10t multicolored	.75	.75
a.		Souv. sheet of 3, #123-125, perf. 14½	1.50	1.50
		Nos. 123-125 (3)	1.20	1.20

25th anniv. of the reign of Elizabeth II.

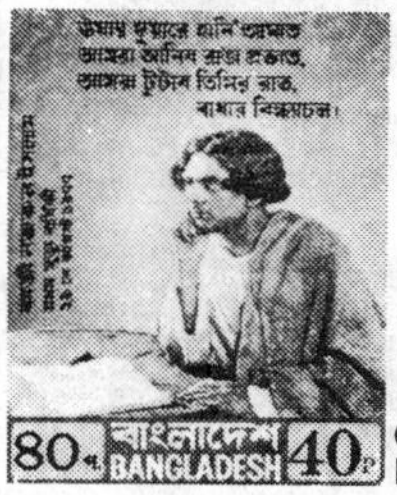

Qazi Nazrul Islam — A28

Nazrul A29

1977, Aug. 29 **Litho.** ***Perf. 14***

126	A28	40p lt green & black	.20	.20
127	A29	2.25t multicolored	.65	.65

Qazi Nazrul Islam (1899-1976), natl. poet.

Pigeon Carrying Letter A30

1977, Sept. 29 **Litho.** ***Perf. 14***

128	A30	30p multicolored	.20	.20
129	A30	2.25t multicolored	.60	.60

Asian-Oceanic Postal Union (AOPU), 15th anniversary.

Leopard A31

40p and 1t are vert.

1977, Nov. 9 Litho. *Perf. 13*

130 A31 40p Asiatic black bear .20 .20
131 A31 1t Axis deer .60 .60
132 A31 2.25t shown .70 .70
133 A31 3.50t Gayal .95 .95
134 A31 4t Elephant 1.50 1.50
135 A31 5t Bengal tiger 1.75 1.75
Nos. 130-135 (6) 5.70 5.70

Campfire, Tent, Scout Emblem — A32

Designs: 3.50t, Emblem, first aid, signaling, horiz. 5t, Scout emblem and oath.

1978, Jan. 22 Litho. *Perf. 13*

136 A32 40p multicolored .20 .20
137 A32 3.50t multicolored .90 .90
138 A32 5t multicolored 1.60 1.60
Nos. 136-138 (3) 2.70 2.70

1st National Boy Scout Jamboree, Jan. 22.
For overprint see No. 269.

Champac — A33

Flowers and Flowering Trees: 1t, Pudding pipe tree. 2.25t, Flamboyant tree. 3.50t, Water lilies. 4t, Butea. 5t, Anthocephalus indicus.

1978, Mar. 31 Litho. *Perf. 13*

139 A33 40p multicolored .20 .20
140 A33 1t multicolored .50 .50
141 A33 2.25t multicolored .85 .85
142 A33 3.50t multicolored 1.10 1.10
143 A33 4t multicolored 1.25 1.25
144 A33 5t multicolored 1.40 1.40
Nos. 139-144 (6) 5.30 5.30

For overprints see Nos. 259A-259F.

Crown, Scepter and Staff of State — A34

Designs: 3.50t, Royal family on balcony. 5t, Queen Elizabeth II and Prince Philip. 10t, Queen in coronation regalia, Westminster Abbey.

1978, May 20 *Perf. 14*

145 A34 40p multicolored .20 .20
146 A34 3.50t multicolored .20 .20
147 A34 5t multicolored .30 .30
148 A34 10t multicolored .55 .55
a. Souv. sheet of 4, #145-148, perf. 14½ 1.40 1.40
Nos. 145-148 (4) 1.25 1.25

Coronation of Queen Elizabeth II, 25th anniv.
For overprint see No. 228B.

Alan Cobham's DH50, 1926 — A35

Planes: 2.25t, Capt. Hans Bertram's Junkers W33 Atlantis, 1932-33. 3.50t, Wright brothers' plane. 5t, Concorde.

1978, June 15 Litho. *Perf. 13*

149 A35 40p multicolored .20 .20
150 A35 2.25t multicolored 1.25 1.25
151 A35 3.50t multicolored 1.90 1.90
152 A35 5t multicolored 2.50 2.50
Nos. 149-152 (4) 5.85 5.85

75th anniversary of powered flight.

Holy Kaaba, Mecca — A37

Design: 3.50t, Pilgrims at Mt. Arafat, horiz.

1978, Nov. 9 Litho. *Perf. 13*

154 A37 40p multicolored .20 .20
155 A37 3.50t multicolored .75 .75

Pilgrimage to Mecca.

Jasim Uddin, Poet A38

1979, Mar. 14 Litho. *Perf. 14*

156 A38 40p multicolored .40 .40

Rowland Hill — A39 Moulana Bhashani — A40

Hill and Stamps of Bangladesh: 3.50t, No. 1, horiz. 10t, No. 66, horiz.

1979, Aug. 27 Litho. *Perf. 14*

157 A39 40p multicolored .20 .20
158 A39 3.50t multicolored .35 .35
159 A39 10t multicolored 1.10 1.10
a. Souvenir sheet of 3, #157-159 2.75 2.75
Nos. 157-159 (3) 1.65 1.65

Sir Rowland Hill (1795-1879), originator of penny postage.

1979, Nov. 17 *Perf. 12½*

160 A40 40p multicolored .55 .55

Moulana Abdul Hamid Khan Bhashani (1880-1976), philosopher and statesman.

A41 A42

IYC Emblem and: 40p, Boys and Hoops. 3.50t, Boys flying kites. 5t, Children jumping.

1979, Dec. 17 Litho. *Perf. 14x14½*

161 A41 40p multicolored .20 .20
162 A41 3.50t multicolored .45 .45
163 A41 5t multicolored .65 .65
a. Souv. sheet of 3, #161-163, perf. 14½ 2.50 2.50
Nos. 161-163 (3) 1.30 1.30

International Year of the Child.

Type of 1973

Designs: 5p, Lalbag Fort. 10p, Fenchungan Fertilizer Factory, vert. 15p, Pineapple. 20p, Gas well. 25p, Jute on boat. 30p, Banana tree. 40p, Baitul Mukarram Mosque. 50p, Baitul Mukarram Mosque. 80p, Garh excavations. 1ta, Dotara (musical instrument.) 2t, Karnaphuli Dam.

1979-82 Photo. *Perf. 14½*

Size: 18x23mm, 23x18mm

165 A7 5p brown ('79) .20 .20
166 A7 10p Prus blue .20 .20
167 A7 15p yellow org ('81) .20 .20
168 A7 20p dk carmine ('79) .30 .20
169 A7 25p dk blue ('82) .35 .20
170 A7 30p lt olive grn ('80) .45 .20
171 A8 40p rose magenta ('79) .55 .20
172 A9 50p black & gray ('81) 1.25 .75
173 A7 80p dk brown ('80) .50 .20
174 A7 1t red lilac ('81) 2.50 .25
175 A7 2t brt ultra ('81) .75 .75
Nos. 165-175 (11) 7.25 3.35

For overprints see Nos. O27-O36.

1980, Feb. 23 Litho. *Perf. 14*

Rotary Intl., 75th Anniv.: 40p, Rotary emblem, diff.

179 A42 40p multicolored .20 .20
180 A42 5t ultra & gold .90 .90

For overprints see Nos. 285-286.

Canal Digging A43

1980, Mar. 27 Litho. *Perf. 14*

181 A43 40p multicolored .55 .55

Sher-e-Bangla A.K. Fazlul Huq (1873-1962), Natl. Leader — A44

1980, Apr. 27 Litho. *Perf. 14*

182 A44 40p multicolored .55 .55

Early Mail Transport, London 1980 Emblem — A45

1980, May 5

183 A45 1t shown .20 .20
184 A45 10t Modern mail transport 1.40 1.40
a. Souvenir sheet of 2, #183-184 1.75 1.75

London 80 Intl. Stamp Exhib., May 6-14.

Dome of the Rock — A46 Adult Education — A47

1980, Aug. 21 Litho. *Perf. 14½*

185 A46 50p violet rose .85 .85

For the families of Palestinians.

1980, Aug. 23 *Perf. 13½*

186 A47 50p multicolored .55 .55

Beach Scene A48

1980, Sept. 27 Litho. *Perf. 14*

187 A48 50p shown .20 .20
188 A48 5t Beach scene, diff. 1.40 1.40
a. Souvenir sheet of 2, #187-188 1.50 1.50
b. Pair, #187-188 1.50 1.50

World Tourism Conference, Manila, Sept. 27. No. 188b has continuous design.
For overprints see Nos. 243-244.

Hegira (Pilgrimage Year) — A49

1980, Nov. 11 Photo. *Perf. 14*

189 A49 50p multicolored .40 .40

A50 A51

Design: Deer and Boy Scout emblem.

1981, Jan. 1 Litho. *Perf. 14*

190 A50 50p multicolored .20 .20
191 A50 5t multicolored 1.40 1.40

5th Asia-Pacific and 2nd Bangladesh Scout Jamboree, 1980-1981.

1980, Dec. 9 Litho. *Perf. 14*

192 A51 50p multicolored .20 .20
193 A51 2t multicolored .55 .55

Begum Roquiah (1880-1932), educator.

Nos. 58-60 Overprinted:
2nd / CENSUS / 1981

1981, Mar. 6 *Perf. 13½*

194 A11 20p multicolored .20 .20
195 A11 25p multicolored .20 .20
196 A11 75p multicolored .35 .35
Nos. 194-196 (3) .75 .75

A52

A53

1981, Mar. 16 Litho. *Perf. 14*
197 A52 1t multicolored .20 .20
198 A52 15t multicolored 2.50 2.50
a. Souvenir sheet of 2, #197-198 3.25 3.25

Queen Mother Elizabeth, 80th birthday (1980).

1981, Mar. 26
199 A53 50p Citizen Holding Rifle & Flag .20 .20
200 A53 2t People, map .60 .60

10th anniversary of independence.

UN Conference on Least-developed Countries, Paris — A54

1981, Sept. 1 Litho. *Perf. 14x13½*
201 A54 50p multicolored .70 .70

Birth Centenary of Kemal Ataturk (First President of Turkey) — A55

1981, Nov. 10 Litho. *Perf. 14*
202 A55 50p Portrait .50 .50
203 A55 1t Portrait, diff. .70 .70

Intl. Year of the Disabled A56

1981, Dec. 26 Litho. *Perf. 14*
204 A56 50p Sign language, vert. .35 .35
205 A56 2t Amputee 1.10 1.10

World Food Day, Oct. 16 — A57

1981, Dec. 31 Litho. *Perf. 13½x14*
206 A57 50p multicolored .80 .80

A58

A59

1982, May 22 Litho. *Perf. 13½x14*
207 A58 50p Boat hauling rice straw .70 .70

10th Anniv. of UN Conf. on Human Environment.
For overprint see No. 281.

1982, Oct. 9
208 A59 50p multicolored .95 .95

Dr. Kazi Motahar Hossain, educator and statistician.

Scouting Year — A60

1982, Oct. 21 Litho. *Perf. 14*
209 A60 50p Emblem, knots .75 .75
210 A60 2t Baden-Powell, vert. 3.25 3.25

Capt. Mohiuddin Jahangir A61

Liberation Heroes (Tablet Color): b, Sepoy Hamidur Rahman (pale green). c, Sepoy Mohammed Mustafa Kamal (rose claret). d, Mohammad Ruhul Amin (yellow). e, M. Matiur Rahman (olive bister). f, Lance-Naik Munshi Abdur Rob (brown orange). g, Lance-Naik Nur Mouhammad (bright yellow green).

1982, Dec. 16 Litho. *Perf. 14*
211 Strip of 7 1.90 1.90
a.-g. A61 50p multicolored .25 .25

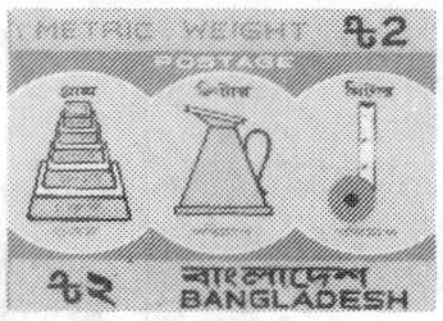
Metric System A62

1983, Jan. 10 Litho. *Perf. 14*
212 A62 50p Mail scale, vert. .60 .60
213 A62 2t Weights, measures 2.25 2.25

TB Bacillus Centenary — A63

1983, Feb. 20 Litho. *Perf. 14*
214 A63 50p Koch 1.00 1.00
215 A63 1t Slides, microscope 2.00 2.00

A64

1983, Mar. 14 Litho. *Perf. 14*
216 A64 1t Open stage theater .20 .20
217 A64 3t Boat race .20 .20
218 A64 10t Snake dance .60 .60
219 A64 15t Tea garden 1.00 1.00
Nos. 216-219 (4) 2.00 2.00

Commonwealth Day.

Jnantapash Shahidullah (1885-1969), Educator and Linguist — A65

1983, July 10 Litho. *Perf. 14*
220 A65 50p multicolored .95 .95

Birds A66

1983, Aug. 17 Litho. *Perf. 14*
221 A66 50p Copsychus saulari 1.25 .65
222 A66 2t Halcyon smyrnensis, vert. 2.00 2.00
223 A66 3.75t Dinopium benghalense, vert. 2.25 2.25
224 A66 5t Carina scutulota 3.00 3.00
a. Souvenir sheet of 4, #221-224 11.00 11.00
Nos. 221-224 (4) 8.50 7.90

No. 224a sold for 13t.

Local Fish — A67

1983, Oct. 31 Litho. *Perf. 14*
225 A67 50p Macrobrachium rosengergii .60 .25
226 A67 2t Stromateus cinereus 1.90 1.40
227 A67 3.75t Labeo rohita 2.25 1.75
228 A67 5t Anabas testudineus 2.75 2.25
a. Souv. sheet of 4, #225-228, imperf. 7.50 7.50
Nos. 225-228 (4) 7.50 5.65

No. 228a sold for 13t.

No. 148 Ovptd. "Nov. '83/Visit of Queen" in Red

1983, Nov. 14 Litho. *Perf. 14*
228B A34 10t multicolored 5.25 5.25

World Communications Year — A68

1983, Dec. 21 Litho. *Perf. 14*
229 A68 50p Messenger, vert. .20 .20
230 A68 5t Jet, train, ship, vert. 1.90 1.90
231 A68 10t Dish antenna, messenger 3.50 3.50
Nos. 229-231 (3) 5.60 5.60

Hall — A69

A70

1983, Dec. 5 Litho. *Perf. 14*
232 A69 50p Sangsad Bhaban .20 .20
233 A69 5t Shait Gumbaz 2.25 2.25

14th Islamic Foreign Ministers Conference.

Perf. 11½x12½, 12½x11½
1983, Dec. 21
234 A70 5p Mailboat .20 .20
235 A70 10p Dacca P.O. counter .20 .20
236 A70 15p IWTA Terminal .20 .20
237 A70 20p Sorting mail .20 .20
238 A70 25p Mail delivery .20 .20
239 A70 30p Postman at mailbox .20 .20
240 A70 50p Mobile post office .20 .20

Size: 30½x18½mm
Perf. 12x11½
241 A70 1t Kamalapur Railway Station .25 .25
242 A70 2t Zia Intl. Airport .50 .50
242A A70 5t Khulna P.O. 1.25 1.25
Nos. 234-242A (10) 3.40 3.40

Nos. 235-237, 239-242A horiz.
Nos. 234-240 reprinted on cream paper.
See #270-271. For overprints see #O37-O46, O48, O51-O52.

No. 188b Overprinted in English

First Bangladesh National Philatelic Exhibition 1984
50P ৫০প

or Bengali in Red

প্রথম বাংলাদেশ জাতীয় ডাকটিকিট প্রদর্শনী - ১৯৮৪
৳৫ ৳5

1984, Feb. 1 Litho. *Perf. 14*
243 A48 50p Beach Scene .25 .25
244 A48 5t Beach Scene, diff. 2.25 2.25
a. Pair, #243-244 2.50 2.50

1st Bangladesh Natl. Philatelic Exhibition, 1984. No. 244a has continuous design.

A71

1984, May 17 *Perf. 14½*
245 50p Girl examining stamp album .25 .25
246 7.50t Boy updating collection 2.00 2.00
a. Souvenir sheet of 2, #245-246 4.00 4.00
b. A71 Pair, #245-246 2.25 2.25
c. As "a," overprinted *9.25 9.25*

#246a sold for 10t.
Overprint in sheet margin of No. 246c reads: "SILVER JUBILEE / BANGLADESH POSTAGE STAMPS 1971-96."

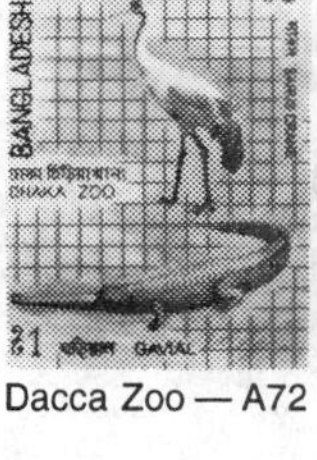
Dacca Zoo — A72

Postal Life Insurance, Cent. — A73

1984, July 17 Litho. *Perf. 14*

247 A72 1t Sarus crane, gavial	1.40	1.40
248 A72 2t Peafowl, royal Bengal tiger	2.75	2.75

1984, Dec. 3

249 A73 1t Chicken hawk, hen	.40	.40
250 A73 5t Beneficiaries	1.90	1.90

Abbasudin Ahmad, Bengali Singer — A74

1984, Dec. 24

251 A74 3t multicolored	1.10	1.10

No. 116 Ovptd. for KHULNAPEX '84 Stamp Exhibition

খুলনাপেক্স—৮৪

1984, Dec. 29 Litho. *Perf. 15*

252 A25 2.25t multicolored	1.10	1.10

1984 Summer Olympics, Los Angeles A75

1984, Dec. 31 *Perf. 14*

253 A75 1t Bicycling	1.25	.25
254 A75 5t Field hockey	2.50	2.50
255 A75 10t Volleyball	3.50	3.50
Nos. 253-255 (3)	7.25	6.25

Islamic Development Bank, 9th Annual Congress, Dacca — A76

1985, Feb. 2

256 A76 1t Farmer	.40	.40
257 A76 5t Four Asian races	1.90	1.90

UN Child Survival Campaign — A77

UN Decade for Women — A78

1985, Mar. 14

258 A77 1t Breastfeeding	.30	.30
259 A77 10t Growth monitoring	2.75	2.75

Nos. 139-144 Ovptd. in Bengali for Local Elections

উপজেলা নির্বাচন ১৯৮৫

1985, May 16 Litho. *Perf. 13*

259A A33 40p multicolored	.20	.20
259B A33 1t multicolored	.20	.20
259C A33 2.25t multicolored	.25	.25
259D A33 3.50t multicolored	.35	.35
259E A33 4t multicolored	.45	.45
259F A33 5t multicolored	.55	.55
Nos. 259A-259F (6)	2.00	2.00

1985, July 18 *Perf. 14*

260 A78 1t shown	.20	.20
261 A78 10t Technology	1.60	1.60

UN, 40th Anniv. A79

1985, Sept. 15

262 A79 1t UN building	.20	.20
263 A79 10t World map, natl. flag	1.25	1.25

11th anniv. of UN admission.

Intl. Youth Year — A80

1985, Nov. 2 Litho. *Perf. 14*

264 A80 1t Scissors, pencil	.20	.20
265 A80 5t Hammer, wrenches	.70	.70

Seven Doves, Council Emblem — A81

1985, Dec. 8 Litho. *Perf. 14*

266 A81 1t shown	.20	.20
267 A81 5t Flags, lotus blossom	.80	.80

1st South Asian Regional Council Summit, SARC, Dacca.

Shilpacharya Zainul Abedin (1914-1976), Founder, Dacca College of Art — A82

1985, Dec. 28

268 A82 3t multicolored	1.00	1.00

No. 138 Overprinted Reading Up

তৃতীয় বাংলাদেশ
জাতীয় জাম্বুরী
১৯৮৫-৮৬

1985, Dec. 29 *Perf. 13*

269 A32 5t multicolored	2.75	2.75

3rd Natl. Scout Jamboree.
The overprint comes in two types.

Postal Services Type of 1983-84

1986, Jan. 11 Litho. *Perf. 12x11½*

Size: 30½x19mm

270 A70 3t Sorting machine	.30	.30

Perf. 12x12½

Size: 33½x22½mm

271 A70 4t Chittagong Port	.55	.55

Issue dates: 3t, Jan. 11, 1986. 4t, Apr. 22, 1993.
For overprint see No. O46.
This is an expanding set. Numbers will change if necessary.

Fishing Net, by Safiuddin Ahmed A83

Paintings by Bengali artists: 5t, Happy Return, by Quamrul Hassan. 10t, Levelling the Plowed Field, by Zainul Abedin.

1986, Apr. 6 Litho. *Perf. 14*

275 A83 1t multicolored	.20	.20
276 A83 5t multicolored	.55	.55
277 A83 10t multicolored	1.10	1.10
Nos. 275-277 (3)	1.85	1.85

1986 World Cup Soccer Championships, Mexico — A84

1986, June 29 *Perf. 15x14*

278 A84 1t Stealing the ball	.30	.30
279 A84 10t Goal	3.00	3.00

Souvenir Sheet

Imperf

279A A84 20t multicolored	5.50	5.50

No. 279A contains one stamp 62x45mm with simulated perfs.

Gen. M.A.G. Osmani (1918-1984), Liberation Forces Commander-in-Chief — A85

1986, Sept. 10 Litho. *Perf. 14*

280 A85 3t multicolored	1.50	1.50

No. 207 Ovptd. SAARC SEMINAR '86

1986, Dec. 3 Litho. *Perf. 13½x14*

281 A58 50p on #207	*1.75*	*1.75*

Intl. Peace Year
A86 A87

1986, Dec. 25 Litho. *Perf. 12x12½*

282 A86 1t shown	.50	.25
283 A86 10t City ruins, flower	4.00	4.00

Souvenir Sheet

284 A87 20t shown	2.50	2.50

Nos. 179-180 Ovptd. or Surcharged "CONFERENCE FOR DEVELOPMENT '87"

1987, Jan. 12 *Perf. 14*

285 A42 1t on 40p multicolored	.20	.20
286 A42 5t multicolored	.65	.65

Language Movement, 35th Anniv. — A88

Illustration reduced.

1987, Feb. 21 *Perf. 12½x12*

287 A88 3t Protestors	1.00	1.00
288 A88 3t Memorial	1.00	1.00
a. Pair, Nos. 287-288	2.00	2.00

World Health Day — A89

Bengali New Year — A90

1987, Apr. 7 *Perf. 11½x12*

289 A89 1t Child immunization	*2.50*	*2.50*

See No. 318.

1987, Apr. 16 *Perf. 12x12½*

290 A90 1t Bengali script, embroidery	.20	.20
291 A90 10t shown	.75	.75

Jute Carpet A91

Exports: 1t, Jute shika (wall hanging, bowl-holder and mats), vert. 10t, Table lamp and shade, vert.

Perf. 12x12½, 12½x12

1987, May 18 Litho.

292 A91 1t multicolored	.20	.20
293 A91 5t shown	.35	.35
294 A91 10t multicolored	.75	.75
Nos. 292-294 (3)	1.30	1.30

Ustad Ayet Ali Khan (1884-1967), Composer, and Surbahar A92

1987, Sept. 8 *Perf. 12x12½*

295 A92 5t multicolored	.80	.80

Palanquin A93

Transportation.

1987, Oct. 24 Litho. *Perf. 12½x12*

296 A93 2t shown	.20	.20
297 A93 3t Bicycle rickshaw	.30	.30
298 A93 5t Paddle steamer	.55	.55
299 A93 7t Train	.75	.75
300 A93 10t Ox cart	1.25	1.25
Nos. 296-300 (5)	3.05	3.05

For overprint see No. 424.

Hossain Shahid Suhrawardy (1893-1963), Politician — A94

1987, Dec. 5 Litho. *Perf. 12x12½*

301 A94 3t multicolored .40 .40

Intl. Year of Shelter for the Homeless A95

1987, Dec. 15 *Perf. 12½x12*

302 A95 5t shown .50 .50
303 A95 5t Prosperous community .50 .50

Nos. 302-303 are printed se-tenant in a continuous design.

Natl. Democracy, 1st Anniv. — A96

Design: Pres. Hossain Mohammed Ershad addressing parliament.

1987, Dec. 31

304 A96 10t multicolored 1.90 1.90

Woman Tending Crop A97

1988, Jan. 26

305 A97 3t shown .35 .35
306 A97 5t Milking cow, village .50 .50

Intl. Fund for Agricultural Development (IFAD) Seminar on Loans for Women in Rural Areas.

1988 Summer Olympics, Seoul — A98

1988 Summer Games emblem and Sports: a, Basketball. b, Weight lifting. c, Women's tennis. d, Shooting. e, Boxing.

1988, Sept. 29 Litho. *Perf. 11½*

307 Strip of 5 3.00 3.00
a.-e. A98 5t any single .60 .60

Historical Sites A99

Designs: 1t, Shait Gumbaz Mosque (interior), Bagerhat. 4t, Paharpur Monastery. 5t, Kantanagar Temple, Dinajpur. 10t, Lalbag Fort, Dacca.

1988, Oct. 9 *Perf. 12½x12*

308 A99 1t multicolored .20 .20
309 A99 4t multicolored .20 .20
310 A99 5t multicolored .25 .25
311 A99 10t multicolored .50 .50
Nos. 308-311 (4) 1.15 1.15

Qudrat-i-Khuda (1900-1977), Scientist — A100

Asia Cup Cricket — A101

1988, Nov. 3 *Perf. 12x12½*

312 A100 5t multicolored .55 .55

1988, Nov. 27

313 Strip of 3 3.25 3.25
a. A101 1t Wicketkeeper .20 .20
b. A101 5t Batsman .95 .95
c. A101 10t Bowler 2.00 2.00

Intl. Red Cross and Red Crescent Organizations, 125th Annivs. — A102

1988, Oct. 26 Litho. *Perf. 12x12½*

314 A102 5t Emblems, Dunant .50 .50
315 A102 10t Blood donation 1.00 1.00

Dacca G.P.O., 25th Anniv. — A103

1988, Dec. 6 *Perf. 12*

316 A103 1t Exterior .20 .20
317 A103 5t Sales counter .65 .65

World Health Day Type of 1987

1988, Jan. 16 Litho. *Perf. 11½x12*

318 A89 25p Oral rehydration .70 .70

32nd Meeting of the Colombo Plan Consultative Committee, Dacca — A104

1988, Nov. 29 *Perf. 12x12½*

319 A104 3t multicolored .25 .25
320 A104 10t multicolored .75 .75

No. 191 Ovptd. ৫ম জাতীয় রোভার মুট ১৯৮৮-৮৯

1989, Dec. 29 Litho. *Perf. 14*

321 A50 5t multicolored 1.25 1.25

5th Natl. Rover Moot (Scouting).

No. 277 Ovptd. চতুর্থ দ্বিবার্ষিক এশীয় চারুকলা প্রদর্শনী বাংলাদেশ ১৯৮৯

1989, Mar. 1

322 A83 10t multicolored 1.10 1.10

4th Asiatic Exposition.

A106

A107

1989, Mar. 13 Litho. *Perf. 12x12½*

324 A106 10t multicolored .85 .85

Police academy, Sardah, 75th anniv.

1989, Mar. 7 Litho. *Perf. 12x12½*

Modernizing water supply services.

325 A107 10t multicolored .85 .85

12th Natl. Science & Technology Week.

A108

French Revolution, Bicent. — A109

Scenes from the revolution: 5t, Close-up of revolutionaries destroying the Bastille, vert. No. 326b, Liberty guiding the people. No. 326c, Women's march on Versailles, vert. No. 327a, Celebration of the Federation on the Champ de Mars. No. 327b, Storming of the Bastille. 25t, Montage of scenes, #326a-326c.

1989, July 12 *Perf. 14*

326 Sheet of 3 + label 2.25 2.25
a. A108 5t multicolored .45 .45
b.-c. A108 10t any single .90 .90

Perf. 14x15

327 Strip of 2 + label 2.25 2.25
a.-b. A109 17t any single 1.10 1.10

Size: 152x88mm

Imperf

328 A108 25t multicolored 2.25 2.25
Nos. 326-328 (3) 6.75 6.75

Labels picture the revolution anniv. emblem.

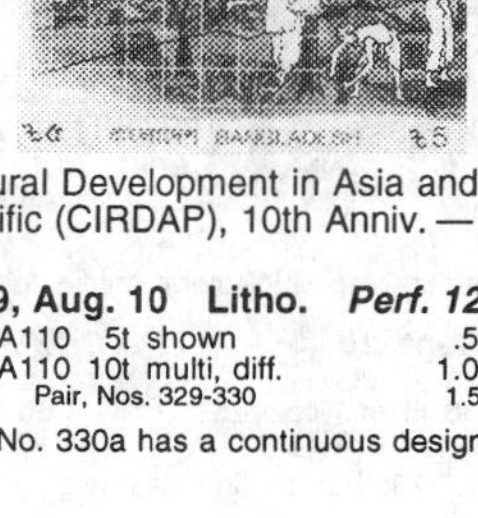

Rural Development in Asia and the Pacific (CIRDAP), 10th Anniv. — A110

1989, Aug. 10 Litho. *Perf. 12½x12*

329 A110 5t shown .50 .50
330 A110 10t multi, diff. 1.00 1.00
a. Pair, Nos. 329-330 1.50 1.50

No. 330a has a continuous design.

Child Survival A111

1989, Aug. 22

331 A111 1t shown .20 .20
332 A111 10t Women and children, diff. .90 .90

SOS Children's Village, 40th anniv.

Involvement of the Bangladesh Army in UN Peace-keeping Operations, 1st Anniv. — A112

1989, Sept. 12 *Perf. 12x12½*

333 A112 4t shown .65 .65
334 A112 10t Camp, two soldiers 1.60 1.60

2nd Asian Poetry Festival, Dacca — A113

1989, Nov. 17 Litho. *Perf. 12x12½*

335 A113 2t multicolored .20 .20
336 A113 10t multicolored .90 .90

State Printing Office A114

1989, Dec. 7 *Perf. 13½*

337 A114 10t multicolored 1.25 1.25

Bangladesh Television, 25th Anniv. — A115

1989, Dec. 25 Litho. *Perf. 12½x12*

338 A115 5t shown .50 .50
339 A115 10t Emblem, flowers, diff. 1.00 1.00

World Wildlife Fund A116

Various gavials, *(Gavialis gangeticus).*

1990, Jan. 31 Litho. *Perf. 14*

340 A116 50p shown .20 .20
341 A116 2t Reptile's jaws .55 .55
342 A116 4t 4 reptiles 1.00 1.00
343 A116 10t 2 reptiles resting 2.75 2.75
a. Block of 4, #340-343 4.50 4.50

A117

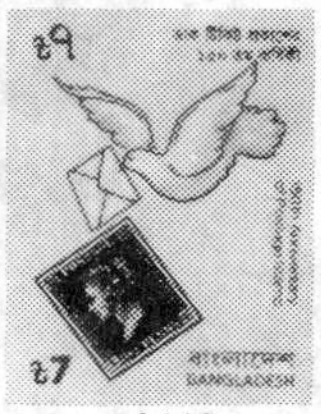
A118

1990, Feb. 2 *Perf. 14*
344 A117 6t multicolored .85 .85

Natl. Population Day.

1990, May 6 *Perf. 14*
345 A118 7t shown 1.60 1.60
346 A118 10t Penny Black, No. 230 2.50 2.50

Penny Black, 150th anniv.

Justice Syed Mahbub Murshed, (1911-1979) — A119

1990, Apr. 3 Litho. *Perf. 12½x12*
347 A119 5t multicolored 1.10 1.10

Intl. Literacy Year — A120

Design: 10t, Boy teaching girl to write.

1990, Apr. 10 *Perf. 12x12½*
348 A120 6t multicolored 1.40 1.40
349 A120 10t multicolored 2.00 2.00

Loading Cargo Plane — A121

Curzon Hall — A122

Fertilizer Plant — A123

Postal Academy, Rajshahi — A124

Salimullah Hall — A125

Bangla Academy — A126

1989-93 *Perf. 12x11½, 12, 12x12½*
350 A121 3t multicolored .20 .20
351 A122 5t gray blk & red brn .25 .25
352 A123 10t carmine .50 .50
353 A124 20t multicolored 1.10 1.10

Perf. 14½x14
354 A125 6t blue gray & yel .55 .55

Perf. 14x14½
355 A126 2t brown & green .20 .20
Nos. 350-355 (6) 2.80 2.80

Issue dates: 5t, Mar. 31. 3t, Apr. 30. 10t, 20t, July 8. 6t, Jan. 30, 1991. 2t, Dec. 3, 1993.
For overprints see Nos. O47A-O47B, O50.
This is an expanding set. Numbers will change.

World Cup Soccer Championships, Italy — A133

1990, June 12 Litho. *Perf. 14*
362 A133 8t shown 1.60 1.60
363 A133 10t Soccer player, diff. 2.25 2.25

Size: 115x79mm

Imperf
364 A133 25t Colosseum, soccer ball 6.00 6.00
Nos. 362-364 (3) 9.85 9.85

Fruits — A134

1990, July 16 *Perf. 12x12½*
365 A134 1t Mangifera indica .20 .20
366 A134 2t Psidium guayava .35 .35
367 A134 3t Citrullus vulgaris .50 .50
368 A134 4t Carica papaya .70 .70
369 A134 5t Artocarpus heterophyllus .90 .90
370 A134 10t Averrhoa carambola 1.75 1.75
Nos. 365-370 (6) 4.40 4.40

UN Conference on Least Developed Nations, Paris — A135

1990, Sept. 3 Litho. *Perf. 14*
371 A135 10t multicolored 1.90 1.90

Asia-Pacific Postal Training Center, 20th Anniv. — A136

Design: 6t, Map of Western Pacific, letters.

1990, Sept. 10 *Perf. 13½x14*
372 A136 2t shown .50 .50
373 A136 6t multicolored 1.50 1.50
a. Pair, #372-373 2.00 2.00

No. 373a has continuous design.

11th Asian Games, Beijing A137

1990, Sept. 22 *Perf. 14*
374 A137 2t Rowing .40 .40
375 A137 4t Kabaddi .85 .85
376 A137 8t Wrestling 1.75 1.75
377 A137 10t Badminton 2.00 2.00
Nos. 374-377 (4) 5.00 5.00

Lalan Shah, Poet — A138

1990, Oct. 17 Litho. *Perf. 14*
378 A138 6t multicolored 1.40 1.40

UN Development Program, 40th Anniv. — A139

1990, Oct. 24 Litho. *Perf. 14*
379 A139 6t multicolored 1.25 1.25

A139a

A140

1990, Nov. 29 Litho. *Perf. 14½x14*
379A A139a 2t brown .40 .40

Immunization program. See No. 560.

1990, Dec. 24 Litho. *Perf. 13½x12*

Butterflies.

380 A140 6t Danaus chrysippus 1.50 1.50
381 A140 6t Precis almana 1.50 1.50
382 A140 10t Ixias pyrene 2.50 2.50
383 A140 10t Danaus plexippus 2.50 2.50
a. Block of 4, #380-383 8.00 8.00

UN Decade Against Drugs A141

1991, Jan 1 Litho. *Perf. 14x13½*
384 A141 2t Drugs, map .75 .75
385 A141 4t shown 1.50 1.50

Third National Census — A142

1991, Mar. 12 Litho. *Perf. 14*
386 A142 4t multicolored .80 .80

Independence, 20th Anniv. — A143

Designs: a, Invincible Bangla statue. b, Freedom Fighter statue. c, Mujibnagar Memorial. d, Eternal flame. e, National Martyrs' Memorial.

1991, Mar. 26 *Perf. 13½*
387 A143 4t Strip of 5, #a.-e. 2.75 2.75

No. 387 printed in continuous design.

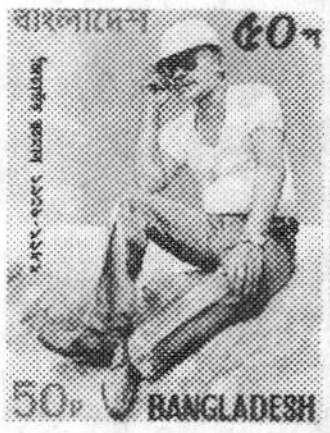

Pres. Ziaur Rahman, 10th Death Anniv.
A144 A145

1991, May 30 *Perf. 14*
388 A144 50p multicolored .20 .20
389 A145 2t multicolored .90 .90
a. Souvenir sheet of 2, #388-389 1.75 1.75

No. 389a sold for 10t.

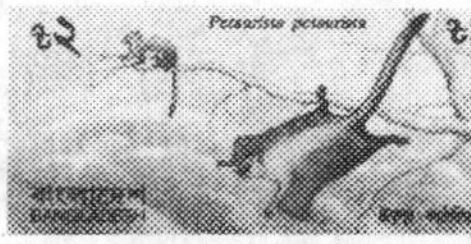
Endangered Animals — A146

1991, June 16 *Perf. 12*
390 A146 2t Petaurista petaurista .40 .40
391 A146 4t Presbytis entellus, vert. .75 .75
392 A146 6t Buceros bicornis, vert. 1.10 1.10
a. Pair, #391-392 1.85 1.85
393 A146 10t Manis crassicaudata 1.75 1.75
a. Pair, #390, 393 2.15 2.15
Nos. 390-393 (4) 4.00 4.00

Kaikobad (1857-1951), Poet — A147

1991, July 21 Litho. *Perf. 14*
394 A147 6t multicolored .85 .85

Rabindranath Tagore, Poet, 50th Anniv. of Death — A148

1991, Aug. 7
395 A148 4t multicolored .85 .85

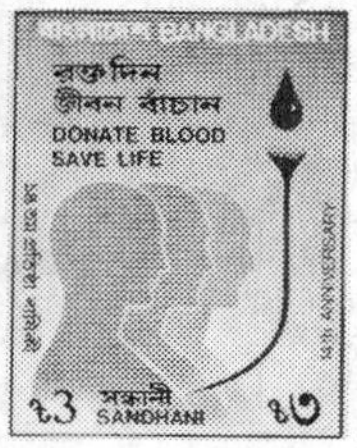

Blood and Eye Donations A149

1991, Sept. 19
396 A149 3t shown .60 .60
397 A149 5t Blind man and eye .95 .95

Sandhani, Medical Students Association, 14th anniversary.

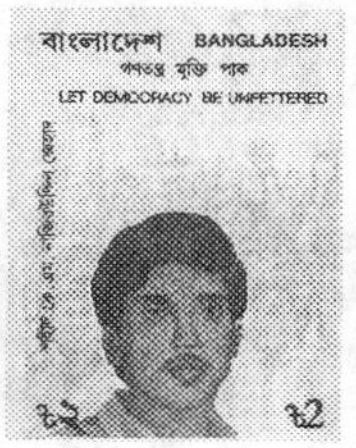

Shahid Naziruddin, Leader of Democratic Movement, 1st Anniv. of Death — A150

1991, Oct. 10
398 A150 2t multicolored .80 .80

Shaheed Noor Hossain, 4th Death Anniv. — A151

1991, Nov. 10 Litho. ***Perf. 14***
399 A151 2t multicolored .80 .80

Archaeological Treasures of Mainamati — A152

Designs: a, Bronze Stupa with images of Buddha. b, Bowl and pitcher. c, Ruins of Salban Vihara Monastery. d, Gold coins. e, Terra-cotta plaque.

1991, Nov. 26 Litho. ***Perf. 13½***
400 A152 4t Strip of 5, #a.-e. 4.00 4.00

Mass Uprising, First Anniv. A153

1991, Dec. 6 ***Perf. 14***
401 A153 4t multicolored .80 .80

Miniature Sheets

Independence, 20th Anniv. — A154

Martyred intellectuals who died in 1971 - No. 402: a, A.N.M. Munier Chowdhury. b, Ghyasuddin Ahmad. c, S.M.A. Rashidul Hasan. d, Muhammad Anwar Pasha. e, Dr. Md. Mortaza. f, Shahid Saber. g, Fazlur Rahman Khan. h, Ranada Prasad Saha. i, Adhyaksha Joges Chandra Ghose. j, Santosh Chandra Bhattacharyya.

No. 403: a, Dr. Gobinda Chandra Deb. b, A.N.M. Muniruzzaman. c, Mufazzal Haider Chaudhury. d, Dr. Abdul Alim Choudhury. e, Sirajuddin Hossain. f, Shahidulla Kaiser. g, Altaf Mahmud. h, Dr. Jyotirmay Guha Thakurta. i, Dr. Md. Abul Khair. j, Dr. Serajul Haque Khan.

No. 404: a, Dr. Mohammad Fazle Rabbi. b, Mir Abdul Quyyum. c, A.N.M. Golam Mostafa. d, Dhirendranath Dutta. e, S.A. Mannan (Ladu Bhai). f, Nizamuddin Ahmad. g, Abul Bashar Chowdhury. h, Selina Parveen. i, Dr. Abul Kalam Azad. j, Saidul Hassan.

No. 404K: l, LCDR. Moazzam Hussain. m, Muhammad Habibur Rahman. n, Khandoker Abu Taleb. o, Moshiur Rahman. p, Md. Abdul Muktadir. q, Nutan Chandra Sinha. r, Syed Nazmul Haque. s, Dr. Mohammed Amin Uddin. t, Dr. N.A.M. Faizul Mohee. u, Sukha Ranjan Somaddar.

1991-93 Litho. ***Perf. 13½***
Sheets of 10
402 A154 2t #a.-j. + 5 labels 1.90 1.90
403 A154 2t #a.-j. + 5 labels 1.90 1.90
404 A154 2t #a.-j. + 5 labels 1.90 1.90
Perf. 14½
404K A154 2t #l.-u. + 5 labels 3.00 3.00

Issued: #402-404, 12/14/91; #404K, 12/14/93.

See Nos. 470-471, 499-500, 534-535, 558-559, 568-569.

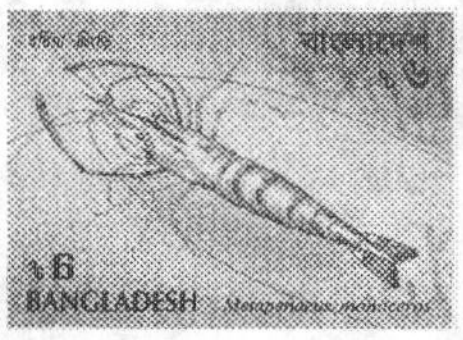

Shrimp A155

1991, Dec. 31 ***Perf. 14***
405 A155 6t Penaeus monodon 1.25 1.25
406 A155 6t Metapenaeus monoceros 1.25 1.25
a. Pair, #405-406 2.50 2.50

Shaheed Mirze Abu Raihan Jaglu, 5th Death Anniv. A156

1992, Feb. 8 Litho. ***Perf. 14x13½***
407 A156 2t multicolored *.95 .95*

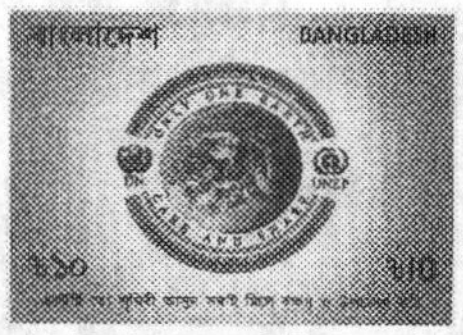

World Environment Day — A157

Design: 4t, Scenes of environmental protection and pollution control, vert.

1992, June 5 Litho. ***Perf. 14***
408 A157 4t multicolored .45 .45
409 A157 10t multicolored 1.10 1.10

Nawab Sirajuddaulah of Bengal (1733-1757) A158

1992, July 2 Litho. ***Perf. 14***
410 A158 10t multicolored 1.00 1.00

Syed Ismail Hossain Sirajee (1880-1931), Social Reformer A159

1992, July 17
411 A159 4t multicolored .80 .80

Tree Week — A160

1992, July 17 Litho. ***Perf. 14***
412 A160 2t Couple planting tree, horiz. .50 .50
413 A160 4t Birds, trees 1.00 1.00

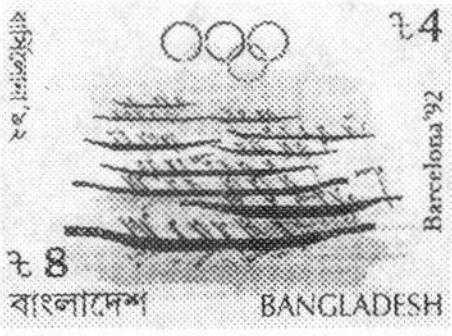

1992 Summer Olympics, Barcelona A161

Olympic rings and: a, 4t, Rowing. b, 6t, Hands holding Olympic torch. c, 10t, Peace doves. d, 10t, Clasped hands.

1992, July 25 Litho. ***Perf. 14***
414 A161 Block of 4, #a.-d. 2.75 2.75

The Star Mosque, 18th Cent. A162

1992, Oct. 29 Litho. ***Perf. 14½x14***
415 A162 10t multicolored 1.10 1.10

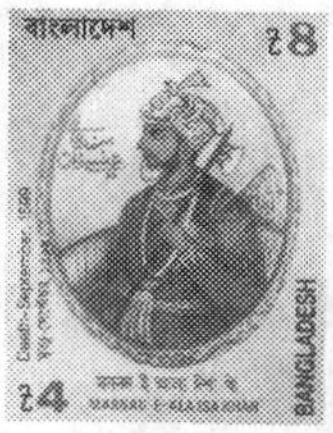

Masnad-E-Ala Isa Khan, 393rd Anniv. of Death — A163

1992, Sept. 15 ***Perf. 14x14½***
416 A163 4t multicolored .80 .80

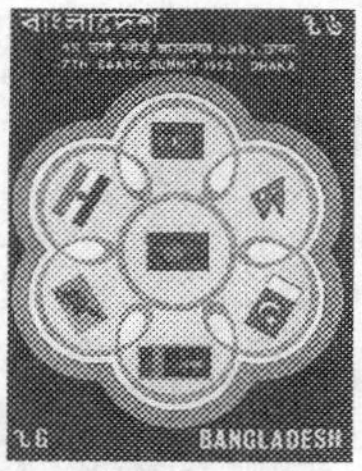

7th SAARC Summit, Dacca — A164

1992, Dec. 5
417 A164 6t Flags of members .50 .50
418 A164 10t Emblem .85 .85

1992 Bangladesh Natl. Philatelic Exhibition — A165

Designs: No. 419a, Elephant and mahout, ivory work, 19th cent. b, Post rider, mail box and postman delivering mail to villager.

1992, Sept. 26 ***Perf. 14½x14***
419 A165 10t Pair, #a.-b. + label 2.50 2.50
c. Souv. sheet, imperf. *2.75 2.75*

No. 419c contains one strip of No. 419 with simulated perforations and sold for 25t.

1992 Intl. Conference on Nutrition, Rome — A166

1992, Dec. 5
420 A166 4t multicolored .55 .55

Meer Nisar Ali Titumeer (1782-1831) — A167

1992, Nov. 19 Litho. ***Perf. 14½x14***
421 A167 10t multicolored 1.00 1.00

The lack of a value for a listed item does not necessarily indicate rarity.

Archaeological Relics, Mahasthan — A168

Relics from 3rd century B.C.-15th century A.D.: No. 422a, Terracotta seal and head. b, Terracotta hamsa. c, Terracotta Surya image. d, Gupta stone columns.

1992, Nov. 30 Litho. ***Perf. 14½x14***

422 A168 10t Strip of 4, #a.-d. 4.00 4.00

Canal Digging A169

a, Workers digging canal. b, Completed project.

1993, Mar. 31 Litho. ***Perf. 14½x14***

423 A169 2t Pair, #a.-b. 1.40 1.40

No. 300 Ovptd. বাংলাপেক্স '৯২ Banglapex '92

1992, Aug. 18 Litho. ***Perf. 12½x12***

424 A93 10t multicolored 1.10 1.10

Syed Abdus Samad (1895-1964), Soccer Player — A170

1993, Feb. 2 ***Perf. 14x14½***

425 A170 2t multicolored .80 .80

A171

1993, Apr. 14

426 A171 2t multicolored .70 .70

Completion of 14th cent. Bengali era.

Haji Shariat Ullah (1770-1839), Social Reformer, Religious and Political Leader — A172

1993, Mar. 10 Litho. ***Perf. 14x14½***

427 A172 2t multicolored .70 .70

World Health Day A173

1993, Apr. 7 ***Perf. 14½x14, 14x14½***

428 A173 6t Prevent accidents .75 .75

429 A173 10t Prevent violence, vert. 1.25 1.25

Compulsory Primary Education — A174

1993, May 26

430 A174 2t Slate, chalk, books .40 .40

431 A174 2t Hand writing, children, vert. .40 .40

Nawab Sir Salimullah (1871-1915), Social Reformer — A175

1993, June 7 Litho. ***Perf. 14½x14***

432 A175 4t multicolored .55 .55

Fishing Industry A176

1993, Aug. 15 Litho. ***Perf. 14½x14***

433 A176 2t multicolored .55 .55

Tomb of Sultan Ghiyasuddin Azam Shah — A177

1993, Dec. 30 Litho. ***Perf. 14½x14***

434 A177 10t multicolored 1.10 1.10

Scenic Views A178

Designs: No. 435, Sunderban. No. 436, Madhabkunda Waterfall, vert. No. 437, River, mountains, vert. No. 438, Beach, Kuakata.

1993, Oct. 30 ***Perf. 14½x14, 14x14½***

435 A178 10t multicolored 1.25 1.25

436 A178 10t multicolored 1.25 1.25

437 A178 10t multicolored 1.25 1.25

438 A178 10t multicolored 1.25 1.25

a. Souv. sheet of 4, #435-438, imperf. 5.50 5.50

Nos. 435-438 (4) 5.00 5.00

#438a sold for 50t and has simulated perfs.

6th Asian Art Biennial, Bangladesh A179

1993, Nov. 7 Litho. ***Perf. 14x14½***

439 A179 10t multicolored .85 .85

Foy's Lake A180

1993, Nov. 6 ***Perf. 14½x14***

440 A180 10t multicolored 1.10 1.10

Tourism month.

14th Asian Pacific, 5th Bangladesh Natl. Scout Jamboree A181

1994, Jan. 5 ***Perf. 14x14½***

441 A181 2t multicolored .55 .55

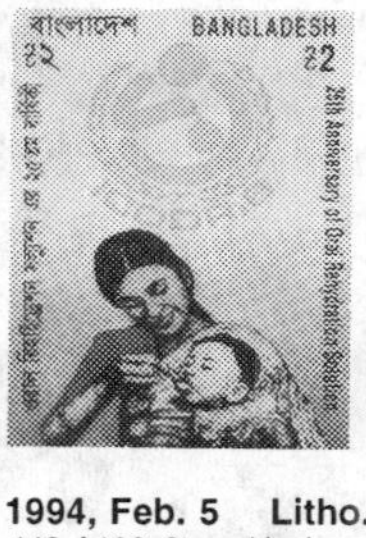

Oral Rehydration Solution, 25th Anniv. — A182

1994, Feb. 5 Litho. ***Perf. 13½x14***

442 A182 2t multicolored .55 .55

6th SAF Games, Dhaka A183

1993, Dec. 6 ***Perf. 14x13½, 13½x14***

443 A183 2t Shot put .30 .30

444 A183 4t Runners, vert. .65 .65

Mosques A184

Mosques: 4t, Interior, Chhota Sona, Nawabgonj. No. 446, Exterior, Chhota Sona. No. 447, Exterior, Baba Adam's, Munshigonj.

1994, Mar. 30 Litho. ***Perf. 14x13½***

445 A184 4t multicolored .30 .30

446 A184 6t multicolored .50 .50

447 A184 6t multicolored .50 .50

Nos. 445-447 (3) 1.30 1.30

For overprint see No. 509.

ILO, 75th Anniv. A185

Designs: 4t, People, oxen working in fields. 10t, Man rotating gearwheel, vert.

Perf. 14x13½, 13½x14

1994, Apr. 11 Litho.

448 A185 4t multicolored *.40 .40*

449 A185 10t multicolored *1.00 1.00*

Bangla Era, 15th Cent. — A186

1994, Apr. 14 ***Perf. 13½x14***

450 A186 2t multicolored *.55 .55*

Traditional Festivals A187

1994, May 12 ***Perf. 14x13½***

451 A187 4t Folk Festival *.40 .40*

452 A187 4t Baishakhi Festival *.40 .40*

Intl. Year of the Family — A188

1994, May 15 ***Perf. 13½x14***

453 A188 10t multicolored *1.50 1.50*

Tree Planting Campaign A189

1994, June 15 Litho. ***Perf. 13½x14***

454 A189 4t Family planting trees .55 .55

455 A189 6t Hands, seedlings .80 .80

1994 World Cup Soccer Championships, US — A190

Soccer player's uniform colors: a, Red, yellow & blue. b, Yellow, green, & red.

1994, June 17 Litho. *Perf. 14½*

456 A190 20t Pair, #a.-b. + label 4.25 4.25
Complete booklet, #456 *11.50*

Jamuna Multi-Purpose Bridge — A191

1994, July 24 *Perf. 14½x14*

457 A191 4t multicolored *.40 .40*

Birds — A192

Designs: 4t, Oriolus xanthornus. No. 459, Gallus gallus. No. 460, Dicrurus paradiseus. No. 461, Dendrocitta vagabunda.

1994, Aug. 31 *Perf. 14x14½*

458 A192 4t multicolored *.50 .50*
459 A192 6t multicolored *.75 .75*
460 A192 6t multicolored *.75 .75*
461 A192 6t multicolored *.75 .75*
a. Souvenir sheet, #458-461 *2.75 2.75*
Nos. 458-461 (4) *2.75 2.75*

No. 461a sold for 25t.

Dr. Mohammad Ibrahim (1911-89), Pioneer in Treatment of Diabetes — A193

1994, Sept. 6 Litho. *Perf. 14½x14*

462 A193 2t multicolored *.40 .40*

Nawab Faizunnessa Chowdhurani (1834-1903), Social Reformer A194

1994, Sept. 23 *Perf. 14x14½*

463 A194 2t multicolored *.40 .40*

12th Asian Games, Hiroshima, Japan — A195

1994, Oct. 2 *Perf. 14½x14*

464 A195 4t multicolored *.55 .55*

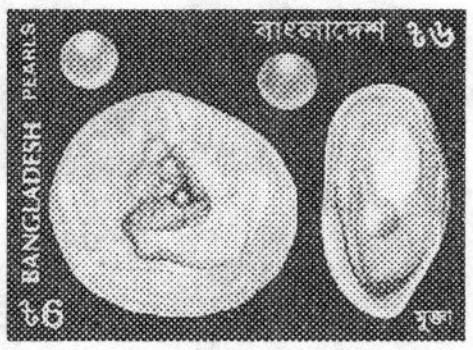

Shells A196

Designs: No. 465, White, pink pearls, oysters. No. 466, Snail, three other shells. No. 467, Scallop, other shells. No. 468, Spiral shaped shells, vert.

Perf. 14½x14, 14x14½

1994, Oct. 30 Litho.

465 A196 6t multicolored *.60 .60*
466 A196 6t multicolored *.60 .60*
467 A196 6t multicolored *.60 .60*
468 A196 6t multicolored *.60 .60*
Nos. 465-468 (4) *2.40 2.40*

Democracy Demonstration, Death of Dr. Shamsul Alam Khan Milon, 4th Anniv. — A197

1994, Nov. 27 *Perf. 14½x14*

469 A197 2t multicolored *.40 .40*

Martyred Intellectual Type of 1991
Miniature Sheets of 8

Martyred intellectuals who died in 1971: No. 470: a, Dr. Harinath Dey. b, Dr. Lt. Col. A.F. Ziaur Rahman. c, Mamum Mahmud. d, Mohsin Ali Dewan. e, Dr. Lt. Col. N.A.M. Jahangir. f, Shah Abdul Majid. g, Muhammad Akhter. h, Meherunnesa.

No. 471: a, Dr. Kasiruddin Talukder. b, Fazlul Haque Choudhury. c, Md. Shamsuzzaman. d, A.K.M. Shamsuddin. e, Lt. Mohammad Anwarul Azim. f, Nurul Amin Khan. g, Mohammad Sadeque. h, Md. Araz Ali.

1994, Dec. 14 *Perf. 14½*

470 A154 2t #a.-h. + 4 labels *1.25 1.25*
471 A154 2t #a.-h. + 4 lables *1.25 1.25*

Vegetables — A199

Perf. 14x14½, 14½x14

1994, Dec. 24

472 A199 4t Diplazium esculentum *.25 .25*
473 A199 4t Momordica charantia *.25 .25*
474 A199 6t Lagenaria siceraria *.50 .50*
475 A199 6t Trichosanthes dioica *.50 .50*
476 A199 10t Solanum melongena *.85 .85*
477 A199 10t Cucurbita maxima *.85 .85*
Nos. 472-477 (6) *3.20 3.20*

Nos. 472-476 are vert.

World Tourism Organization, 20th Anniv. — A200

1995, Jan. 2 *Perf. 14½x14*

478 A200 10t multicolored *.95 .95*

Intl. Trade Fair, Dhaka — A201

Designs: 4t, Trade products. 6t, Factories, emblems of industry.

1995, Jan. 7 Litho. *Perf. 14x14½*

479 A201 4t multicolored *.30 .30*
480 A201 6t multicolored *.60 .60*

Bangladesh Rifles, Bicent. — A202

1995, Jan. 10 Litho. *Perf. 14½x14*

481 A202 2t shown *.30 .30*
482 A202 4t Building, battalion *.60 .60*

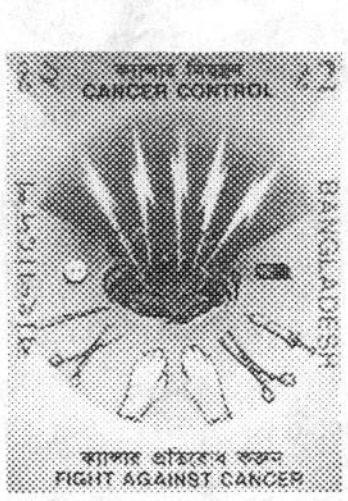

Fight Against Cancer A203

1995, Apr. 7 Litho. *Perf. 14x14½*

483 A203 2t multicolored *.40 .40*

Natl. Diabetes Awareness Day — A204

1995, Feb. 28 *Perf. 14*

484 A204 2t multicolored *.55 .55*

For overprint see No. O49.

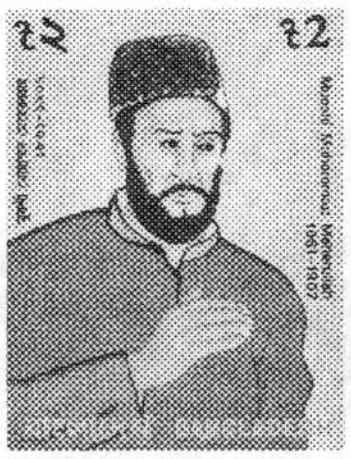

Munshi Mohammad Meherullah (1861-1907), Educator A205

1995, June 7 Litho. *Perf. 14x14½*

485 A205 2t multicolored *.55 .55*

FAO, 50th Anniv. — A206

1995, Oct. 16 Litho. *Perf. 14*

486 A206 10t multicolored *.90 .90*

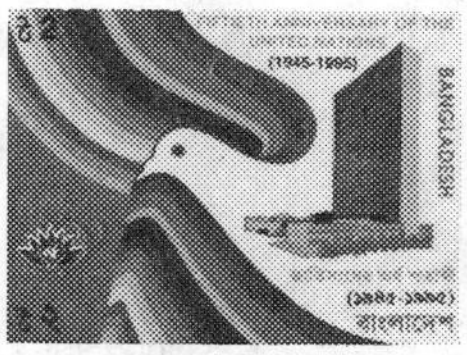

UN, 50th Anniv. A207

UN emblem, "50," and: 2t, Dove of peace, UN headquarters. No. 488, "1945," earth from space, "1995." No. 489, Hands of different nationalities clasping, UN headquarters.

1995, Oct. 24 *Perf. 14½x14*

487 A207 2t multicolored *.20 .20*
488 A207 10t multicolored *1.00 1.00*
489 A207 10t multicolored *1.00 1.00*
Nos. 487-489 (3) *2.20 2.20*

Flowers — A208

Designs: No. 490, Bombax ceiba. No. 491, Lagerstroemia speciosa. No. 492, Gloriosa superba. No. 493, Canna indica. No. 494, Bauhinia purpurea. No. 495, Passiflora incarnata.

1995, Oct. 9 *Perf. 14½x14, 14x14½*

490 A208 6t multicolored *.65 .65*
491 A208 6t multi, vert. *.65 .65*
492 A208 10t multi, vert. *1.00 1.00*
493 A208 10t multi, vert. *1.00 1.00*
494 A208 10t multi, vert. *1.00 1.00*
495 A208 10t multi, vert. *1.00 1.00*
Nos. 490-495 (6) *5.30 5.30*

18th Eastern Regional Conference on Tuberculosis and Respiratory Diseases, Dhaka — A209

1995, Oct. 29 Litho. *Perf. 14½x14*

497 A209 6t multicolored *.55 .55*

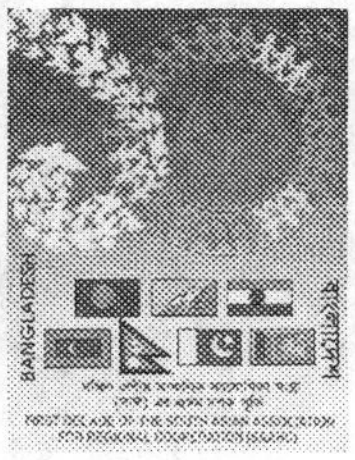

South Asian Assoc. for Regional Cooperation (SAARC), 10th Anniv. — A210

1995, Dec. 8 Litho. *Perf. 14x14½*

498 A210 2t multicolored *.70 .70*

Martyred Intellectual Type of 1991
Sheets of 8

Martyred intellectuals who died in 1971: No. 499a, Shaikh Habibur Rahman. b, Dr. Major Naimul Islam. c, Md. Shahidullah. d, Ataur Rahman Khan Khadim. e, A.B.M. Ashraful Islam Bhuiyan. f, Dr. Md. Sadat Ali. g, Sarafat Ali. h, M.A. Sayeed.

No. 500: a, Abdul Ahad. b, Lt. Col. Mohammad Abdul Qadir. c, Mozammel Hoque Chowdhury. d, Rafiqul Haider Chowdhury. e, Dr. Azharul Haque. f, A.K. Shamsuddin. g, Anudwaipayan Bhattacharjee. h, Lutfunnahar Helena.

1995, Dec. 14 Litho. *Perf. 14½x14*

499 A154 2t #a.-h. + 4 labels 1.50 1.50
500 A154 2t #a.-h. + 4 labels 1.50 1.50

Second Asian Pacific Community Development Scout Camp — A211

1995, Dec. 18 Litho. *Perf. 14x14½*

501 A211 2t multicolored .55 .55

Volleyball, Cent. — A212

1995, Dec. 25

502 A212 6t multicolored .55 .55

Traditional Costumes — A213

Designs: No. 503, Man in punjabi and lungi, vert. No. 504, Woman in sari, vert. No. 505, Christian bride and groom, vert. No. 506, Muslim bridal couple, vert. No. 507, Hindu bridal couple. No. 508, Buddhist bridal couple.

Perf. 14x14½, 14½x14

1995, Dec. 25

503 A213 6t multicolored .60 .60
504 A213 6t multicolored .60 .60
505 A213 10t multicolored 1.00 1.00
506 A213 10t multicolored 1.00 1.00
507 A213 10t multicolored 1.00 1.00
508 A213 10t multicolored 1.00 1.00
Nos. 503-508 (6) 5.20 5.20

No. 446 Ovptd. in Red

রাজশাহীপেক্স-৯৫

1995 Litho. *Perf. 14x13½*

509 A184 6t multicolored 1.50 1.50

This stamp was released for a brief period in 1995. Scott has recently received several copies of the stamp from various sources. Anyone with information about this stamp is asked to contact the New Issues Editor.

Shaheed Amanullah Mohammad Asaduzzaman (1942-69) A214

1996, Jan. 20 *Perf. 14x14½*

510 A214 2t multicolored .50 .50

1996 World Cup Cricket Championships — A215

Perf. 14x14½, 14½x14

1996, Feb. 14

511 A215 4t Pitching, vert. .60 .60
512 A215 6t At bat, vert. .85 .85
513 A215 10t shown 1.40 1.40
Nos. 511-513 (3) 2.85 2.85

Independence, 25th Anniv. — A216

Designs: No. 514, Natl. Martrys' Memorial. No. 515, Industrial development. No. 516, 1971 Destruction of war. No. 517, Educational development. No. 518, Development in communication. No. 519, Development in health.

1996, Mar. 26 Litho. *Perf. 14x14½*

514 A216 4t multicolored .35 .35
515 A216 4t multicolored .35 .35
516 A216 4t multicolored .35 .35
517 A216 4t multicolored .35 .35
518 A216 4t multicolored .35 .35
519 A216 4t multicolored .35 .35
Nos. 514-519 (6) 2.10 2.10

Michael Madhusudan Dutt (1824-73), Writer — A217

1996, June 29 Litho. *Perf. 14x14½*

520 A217 4t multicolored .60 .60

1996 Summer Olympic Games, Atlanta A218

1996, July 19 Litho. *Perf. 14*

521 A218 4t Gymnast, vert. .60 .60
522 A218 6t Judo, vert. .90 .90
523 A218 10t High jumper 1.40 1.40
524 A218 10t Runners 1.40 1.40
a. Souvenir sheet, #521-524 7.00 7.00
Nos. 521-524 (4) 4.30 4.30

No. 524a sold for 50t.

Sheikh Mujibur Rahman (1920-75), Prime Minister A219

Design: No. 527, Maulana Mohammad Akrum Khan (1868-1968).

1996 Litho. *Perf. 14x14½*

526 A219 4t multicolored .60 .60
527 A219 4t multicolored .60 .60

Issued: No. 526, 8/15/96, No. 527, 8/18/96.

Ustad Alauddin Khan (1862-1972), Musician A220

1996, Sept. 6 Litho. *Perf. 14x14½*

528 A220 4t multicolored .20 .20

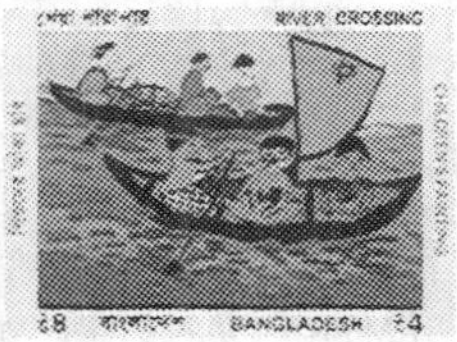

Children's Paintings A221

Perf. 14x14½, 14½x14

1996, Oct. 9 Litho.

529 A221 2t Kingfisher, vert. .45 .45
530 A221 4t River Crossing .95 .95

Jailed, 21st Death Anniv. — A222

a, Syed Nazrul Islam. b, Tajuddin Ahmad. c, M. Monsoor Ali. d, A.H.M. Quamaruzzaman.

1996, Nov. 3 Litho. *Perf. 14x14½*

531 A222 4t Block of 4, #a.-d. 2.00 2.00

UNICEF, 50th Anniv. — A223

Designs: 4t, Children receiving food, medicine, aid. 10t, Mother holding infant.

1996, Dec. 11

532 A223 4t multicolored .65 .65
533 A223 10t multicolored 1.60 1.60

Martyred Intellectual Type of 1991

Martyred intellectuals who died in 1971: No. 534: a, Dr. Jekrul Haque. b, Munshi Kabiruddin Ahmed. c, Md. Abdul Jabbar. d, Mohammad Amir. e, A.K.M. Shamsul Huq Khan. f, Dr. Siddique Ahmed. g, Dr. Soleman Khan. h, S.B.M. Mizanur Rahman.

No. 535: a, Aminuddin. b, Md. Nazrul Islam. c, Zahirul Islam. d, A.K. Lutfor Rahman. e, Afsar Hossain. f, Abul Hashem Mian. g, A.T.M. Alamgir. h, Baser Ali.

1996, Dec. 14 Litho. *Perf. 14½x14*

Sheets of 8

534 A154 2t #a.-h. + 4 labels 2.25 2.25
535 A154 2t #a.-h. + 4 labels 2.25 2.25

Victory Day, 25th Anniv. A224

Designs: 4t, People celebrating, natl. flag. 6t, Soldiers, monument, vert.

Perf. 14½x14, 14x14½

1996, Dec. 16

536 A224 4t multicolored .65 .65
537 A224 6t multicolored 1.00 1.00

Paul Harris (1868-1947), Founder of Rotary Intl. — A225

1997, Feb. 18 Litho. *Perf. 14x14½*

538 A225 4t multicolored .40 .40

Sheikh Mujibur Rahman's Mar. 7 Speech, 26th Anniv. — A226

1997, Mar. 7 *Perf. 12½*

539 A226 4t multicolored .40 .40

Sheikh Mujibur Rahman (1920-75) A227

1997, Mar. 17 *Perf. 14x14½*

540 A227 4t multicolored .40 .40

Heinrich von Stephan (1831-97) A229

1997, Apr. 8 Litho. *Perf. 14x14½*
542 A229 4t multicolored .40 .40

Livestock A230

1997, Apr. 10 Litho. *Perf. 14½x14*
543 A230 4t Goat .35 .35
544 A230 4t Sheep .35 .35
545 A230 6t Cow .50 .50
546 A230 6t Buffalo .50 .50
Nos. 543-546 (4) 1.70 1.70

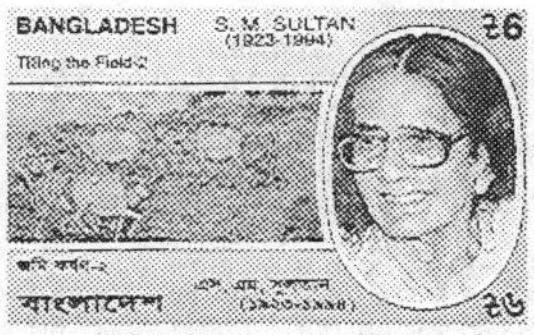

Paintings — A231

Designs: 6t, "Tilling the Field-2," by S.M. Sultan (1923-94). 10t, "Three Women," by Quamrul Hassan (1921-88).

1997, June 26 Litho. *Perf. 12½*
547 A231 6t multicolored .60 .60
548 A231 10t multicolored .95 .95

6th Intl. Cricket Council Trophy Championship, Malaysia — A232

1997, Sept. 4
549 A232 10t multicolored 1.00 1.00

Ancient Mosques A233

Designs: 4t, Kusumba Mosque, Naogaon, 1558. 6t, Atiya Mosque, Tangail, 1609. 10t, Bagha Mosque, Rajshahi, 1523.

1997, Sept. 4 Litho. *Perf. 14½x14*
550 A233 4t multicolored .25 .25
551 A233 6t multicolored .35 .35
552 A233 10t multicolored .60 .60
Nos. 550-552 (3) 1.20 1.20

Abdul Karim Sahitya Visharad (1871-1953), Scholar A234

1997, Oct. 11 *Perf. 14x14½*
553 A234 4t multicolored .25 .25

9th Asia-Pacific, 7th Bangladesh Rover Moot '97 — A235

1997, Oct. 25 *Perf. 14x14½*
554 A235 2t multicolored .35 .35

Armed Forces, 25th Anniv. A236

1997, Nov. 11 *Perf. 14½x14*
555 A236 2t multicolored .20 .20

East Bengal Regiment, 50th Anniv. — A237

1997
556 A237 2t multicolored .20 .20

Mohammad Mansooruddin (1904-87) A238

1997 *Perf. 14x14½*
557 A238 4t multicolored .25 .25

Martyred Intellectual Type of 1991
Sheets of 8 + 4 Labels

Martyred intellectuals who died in 1971: No. 558: a, Dr. Shamsuddin Ahmed. b, Mohammad Salimullah. c, Mohiuddin Haider. d, Abdur Rahim. e, Nitya Nanda Paul. f, Abdul Jabber. g, Dr. Humayun Kabir. h, Khaja Nizamuddin Bhuiyan.
No. 559: a, Gulam Hossain. b, Ali Karim. c, Md. Moazzem Hossain. d, Rafiqul Islam. e, M. Nur Hussain. f, Captain Mahmood Hossain Akonda. g, Abdul Wahab Talukder. h, Dr. Hasimoy Hazra.

1997, Dec. 14
558-559 A154 2t #a.-h., each 1.00 1.00

Immunization Type of 1990

1998, Jan. 22 *Perf. 14½x14*
560 A139a 1t green .20 .20

For overprint see No. O53.

Bulbul Chowdhury (1919-54), Dancer A239

1998 *Perf. 14x14½*
561 A239 4t multicolored .25 .25

Opening of the Bangabandhu Bridge — A240

Designs: 4t, East approach road. 6t, West approach road. 8t, River training works. 10t, Bangabandhu Bridge.

1998 *Perf. 14*
562 A240 4t multicolored .25 .25
563 A240 6t multicolored .35 .35
564 A240 8t multicolored .45 .45
565 A240 10t multicolored .55 .55
Nos. 562-565 (4) 1.60 1.60

1998 World Cup Soccer Championships, France — A241

1998
566 A241 6t Trophy .35 .35
567 A241 18t Player, trophy 1.00 1.00

Martyred Intellectural Type of 1991
Sheets of 8 + 4 Labels

Martyred intellectuals who died in 1971 - No. 568: a, Md. Khorshed Ali Sarker. b, Abu Yakub Mahfuz. c, S.M. Nurul Huda. d, Nazmul Hoque Sarker. e, Md. Taslim Uddin. f, Gulam Mostafa. g, A. H. Nurul Alam. h, Timir Kanti Dev.
No. 569: a, Altaf Hossain. b, Aminul Hoque. c, S.M. Fazlul Hoque. d, Mozammel Ali. e, Syed Akbar Hossain. f, Sk. Abdus Salam. g, Abdur Rahman. h, Dr. Shyamal Kanti Lala.

1998 Litho. *Perf. 14½x14*
568-569 A154 2t #a.-h., each .90 .90

OFFICIAL STAMPS

Nos. 42-47, 49-50, 52, 82-84 and 54 Overprinted in Black or Red **SERVICE**

Perf. 14x14½, 14½x14

1973-75 Litho.
O1 A7 2p black (R) .20 .20
O2 A7 3p brt green .20 .20
O3 A7 5p lt brown .20 .20
O4 A7 10p black (R) .20 .20
O5 A7 20p olive 1.10 .20
O6 A7 25p red lilac 3.00 .20
O8 A7 60p gray (R) 3.00 .20
O9 A7 75p orange ('74) 1.10 .25
O10 A9 1t violet (#52) 12.00 3.25
O11 A9 1t violet (#82) 2.25 .35
O12 A9 2t grayish grn ('74) 3.75 1.25
O13 A9 5t gray blue (#54) 5.25 4.50
O14 A9 5t grysh bl (#84) ('75) 6.50 5.00
Nos. O1-O14 (13) 38.75 16.00

Issue date: Apr. 30, 1973.

Nos. 95-101, 103-105 Overprinted "SERVICE" in Black or Red

1976 Litho. *Perf. 15x14½, 14½x15*
O16 A7 5p green .30 .30
O17 A7 10p black (R) .30 .30
O18 A7 20p olive .30 .30
O19 A7 25p rose .30 .30
O20 A8 50p rose lilac .40 .40
O21 A7 60p gray (R) .50 .50
O22 A7 75p olive .55 .55

Perf. 15
O23 A9 1t violet .85 .85
O24 A9 2t greenish gray 1.60 1.60
O25 A9 5t grayish blue 4.25 4.25
Nos. O16-O25 (10) 9.35 9.35

Nos. 165-169, 171-175 Ovptd. "SERVICE"

1979-82 Photo. *Perf. 14½*
O27 A7 5p brown .20 .20
O28 A7 10p Prussian blue .20 .20
O29 A7 15p yellow orange .20 .20
O30 A7 20p dk carmine .20 .20
O31 A7 25p dk blue ('82) .25 .25
O32 A9 40p rose magenta .45 .45
O33 A9 50p gray ('81) .55 .55
O34 A7 80p dark brown .80 .80
O35 A7 1t red lilac ('81) 1.10 1.10
O36 A7 2t brt ultra ('81) 1.90 1.90
Nos. O27-O36 (10) 5.85 5.85

#234-242, 271 Ovptd. "Service" in Red,
Diagonally Up on #O43A, 1t, 2t, 4t

1983-93 *Perf. 11½x12½, 12½x11½*
O37 A70 5p bluish green .20 .20
O38 A70 10p deep magenta .20 .20
O39 A70 15p blue .20 .20
O40 A70 20p dark gray .20 .20
O41 A70 25p slate .20 .20
O42 A70 30p gray brown .20 .20
O43 A70 50p yellow brown .20 .20
O43A A70 50p yellow brown .20 .20

Size: 30½x28½mm

Perf. 12x11½
O44 A70 1t ultramarine .30 .30
O45 A70 2t Prussian blue .60 .60

Perf. 12
O46 A70 4t blue 1.40 1.40
Nos. O37-O46 (11) 3.90 3.90

Issued: 4t, 7/27/92; #O43A, 1993(?); others, 12/21/83.

No. 350 Ovptd. "Service" Diagonally in Red

1994, July 16 Litho. *Perf. 12x11½*
O47A A122 3t multicolored 11.50 11.50

No. 354 Ovptd. in Red সার্ভিস

1992, Nov. 22 Litho. *Perf. 14½x14*
O47B A125 6t blue gray & yel 6.75 6.75

No. 241 Ovptd. in Red সার্ভিস

1992, Sept. 16 Litho. *Perf. 12x11½*
O48 A70 1t ultramarine .20 .20

No. 484 Ovptd. in Red সার্ভিস

1996 Litho. *Perf. 14*
O49 A204 2t multicolored 2.75 2.75

No. 351 Ovptd. in Blue সার্ভিস

1997? Litho. *Perf. 12*
O50 A122 5t multicolored .30 .30

Bengali overprint reads from top to bottom.

Nos. 235, 237 Ovptd. in Black or Red সার্ভিস

1997? *Perf. 12½x11½*
O51 A70 10p on #235 .65 .65
O52 A70 20p on #237 (R) 1.25 1.25

No. 560 Ovptd. in Red সার্ভিস

1998 Litho. *Perf. 14½x14*
O53 A139a 1t green .20 .20

BARBADOS

bär-ˈbā-ˌdōs

LOCATION — A West Indies island east of the Windwards
GOVT. — Independent state in the British Commonwealth
AREA — 166 sq. mi.
POP. — 266,100 (1997 est.)
CAPITAL — Bridgetown

The British colony of Barbados became an independent state on November 30, 1966.

4 Farthings = 1 Penny
12 Pence = 1 Shilling
20 Shillings = 1 Pound
100 Cents = 1 Dollar (1950)

Catalogue values for unused stamps in this country are for Never Hinged items, beginning with Scott 207 in the regular postage section, Scott B2 in the semi-postal section and Scott J1 in the postage due section.

Watermarks

Wmk. 5- Small Star

Wmk. 6- Large Star

Values for unused stamps are for examples with original gum as defined in the catalogue introduction. Very fine examples of Nos. 10-42a, 44-59a will have perforations touching the design on at least one side due to the narrow spacing of the stamps on the plates and imperfect perforation methods. Stamps with perfs clear of the design on all four sides are extremely scarce and will command higher prices.

Britannia
A1 A2

1852-55 Unwmk. Engr. *Imperf.*
Blued Paper

1 A1 (½p) deep green 100.00 *300.00*
a. (½p) yellow green *9,000.* 800.00
2 A1 (1p) dark blue 18.00 *70.00*
a. (1p) blue 22.00 *200.00*
3 A1 (2p) slate blue 15.00
a. (2p) grayish slate 225.00 *1,100.*
b. As "a," vert. half used as 1p on cover *6,750.*
4 A1 (4p) brown red ('55) 55.00 *300.00*
Nos. 1-4 (4) 188.00

No. 3 was not placed in use. Beware of color changelings of Nos. 2-3 that may resemble No. 3a. Certificates of authenticity are required for Nos. 3a and 3b.

1855-58
White Paper

5 A1 (½p) deep green ('58) 85.00 *200.00*
a. (½p) yellow green ('57) 450.00 110.00
6 A1 (1p) blue 21.00 *50.00*
a. (1p) pale blue 55.00 60.00

It is believed that the (4p) brownish red on white paper exists only as No. 17b.

1859
8 A2 6p rose red 600.00 110.00
9 A2 1sh black 140.00 70.00

Pin-perf. 14
10 A1 (½p) pale yel grn 2,500. 375.00
11 A1 (1p) blue 2,500. 150.00

Pin-perf. 12½
12 A1 (½p) pale yel grn 6,000. 550.
12A A1 (1p) blue *16,000.* 1,400.

1861 *Clean-Cut Perf. 14 to 16*
13 A1 (½p) dark blue grn 60.00 10.00
14 A1 (1p) pale blue 625.00 35.00
a. (1p) blue 725.00 35.00
b. Half used as ½p on cover *3,500.*

Rough Perf. 14 to 16
15 A1 (½p) green 9.00 9.00
a. (½p) blue green 65.00 75.00
b. Imperf., pair 500.00
16 A1 (1p) blue 24.00 1.50
a. Diagonal half used as ½p on cover *1,750.*
b. Imperf., pair 550.00
17 A1 (4p) rose red 60.00 25.00
a. (4p) brown red 100.00 32.50
b. As "a," imperf., pair 850.00
c. (4p) rose red, imperf., pair 750.00
18 A1 (4p) vermilion 175.00 60.00
a. Imperf., pair 850.00
19 A2 6p rose red 175.00 12.00
20 A2 6p orange ver 55.00 13.00
a. 6p vermilion 55.00 15.00
b. Imperf., pair 450.00 *800.00*
21 A2 1sh brownish black 35.00 5.00
b. Horiz. pair, imperf. btwn. *5,750.*
c. 1sh blue (error) *15,000.*

No. 21c was never placed in use. All copies are pen-marked (some have been removed) and have clipped perfs on one or more sides.

Perf. 11 to 13
22 A1 (½p) deep green *6,500.*
23 A1 (1p) blue *2,250.*

Nos. 22 and 23 were never placed in use.

1870 Wmk. 6 *Rough Perf. 14 to 16*
24 A1 (½p) green 75.00 10.00
a. Imperf., pair (#24) 675.00
b. (½p) yellow green 90.00 40.00
25 A1 (1p) blue 1,200. 30.00
a. Imperf., pair *1,500.*
26 A1 (4p) dull red 650.00 75.00
27 A2 6p vermilion 625.00 50.00
28 A2 1sh black 225.00 17.50

1871 Wmk. 5
29 A1 (1p) blue 75.00 3.00
30 A1 (4p) rose red 575.00 25.00
31 A2 6p vermilion 350.00 20.00
32 A2 1sh black 125.00 10.00

Clean-Cut Perf. 14½ to 16
33 A1 (1p) blue 200.00 3.00
a. Diagonal half used as ½p on cover *1,500.*
34 A2 6p vermilion 550.00 45.00
35 A2 1sh black 125.00 10.00

Perf. 11 to 13x14½ to 16
36 A1 (½p) blue green 225.00 25.00
37 A1 (4p) vermilion 450.00 75.00

1873 *Perf. 14*
38 A2 3p claret 475.00 110.00

Wmk. 6
Clean-Cut Perf. 14½ to 16
39 A1 (½p) blue green 175.00 17.50
40 A1 (4p) rose red 725.00 125.00
41 A2 6p vermilion 575.00 60.00
a. Imperf., pair 90.00 *1,500.*
b. Horiz. pair, imperf. btwn. *4,500.*
42 A2 1sh black 90.00 12.00
a. Horiz. pair, imperf. btwn. *4,500.*

Britannia — A3

1873 Wmk. 5 *Perf. 15½x15*
43 A3 5sh dull rose 1,100. 325.00

For surcharged bisects see Nos. 57-59.

1874 Wmk. 6 *Perf. 14*
44 A2 ½p blue green 17.50 7.50
45 A2 1p blue 67.50 3.00

Clean-Cut Perf. 14½ to 16
45A A2 1p blue *14,000.*

1875 Wmk. 1 *Perf. 12½*
46 A2 ½p yellow green 21.00 3.00
47 A2 4p scarlet 160.00 10.00
48 A2 6p orange 600.00 65.00
49 A2 1sh purple 450.00 17.50
Nos. 46-49 (4) 1,231. 95.50

1875-78 *Perf. 14*
50 A2 ½p yel green ('76) 6.00 1.75
51 A2 1p ultramarine 30.00 1.00
a. 1p gray blue 30.00 .75
b. Half used as ½p on cover 1,200.
c. Watermarked sideways 1,750.
52 A2 3p violet ('78) 80.00 10.00
53 A2 4p rose red 80.00 8.00
a. 4p scarlet 125.00 5.00
b. As "a," perf. 14x12½ *4,500.*
54 A2 4p lake 375.00 5.00
55 A2 6p chrome yel 100.00 3.25
a. 6p yellow 300.00 12.50
56 A2 1sh purple ('76) 125.00 5.00
a. 1sh violet 2,100. 45.00
b. 1sh dull mauve 275.00 4.00
c. Half used as 6p on cover *5,000.*

#48, 49, 55, 56 have the watermark sideways.

No. 53b was never placed in use.

A4

A5

Large Surcharge, ("1" 7mm High, "D" 2¾mm High)

1878 Wmk. 5 *Perf. 15½x15*
Slanting Serif
57 A4 1p on half of 5sh *4,000.* 650.
a. Unsevered pair *16,000.* *2,500.*
b. Unsevered horiz. pair, #57 + 58 *4,000.*
d. Unsevered horiz. pair, #57 + 58, imperf. between —
e. Unsevered horiz. pair, #57 + 59, imperf. between *25,000.* *8,500.*

Straight Serif
58 A4 1p on half of 5sh *4,750.* *950.*
a. Unsevered pair *4,250.*

Small Surcharge, ("1" 6mm, "D" 2½mm High)
59 A5 1p on half of 5sh *5,250.* *1,100.*
a. Unsevered pair *15,000.* *4,250.*

On Nos. 57, 58 and 59 the surcharge is found reading upwards or downwards.

The perforation, which divides the stamp into halves, measures 11½ to 13.

The old denomination has been cut off the bottom of the stamps.

Queen Victoria — A6

1882-85 Typo. Wmk. 2 *Perf. 14*
60 A6 ½p green 5.25 .80
61 A6 1p carmine rose 4.75 .50
a. 1p rose 30.00 1.50
b. Half used as ½p on cover 750.00
62 A6 2½p dull blue 52.50 .75
a. 2½p ultramarine 47.50 1.00
63 A6 3p magenta 3.00 *8.75*
a. 3p lilac 70.00 30.00
64 A6 4p slate 175.00 2.00
65 A6 4p brown ('85) 2.75 1.00
66 A6 6p olive gray 52.50 25.00
67 A6 1sh orange brown 17.00 18.00
68 A6 5sh bister 125.00 *175.00*
Nos. 60-68 (9) 437.75 *231.80*

No. 65 Surcharged in Black HALF-PENNY

1892
69 A6 ½p on 4p brown 1.00 2.00
a. Without hyphen 6.00 *11.00*
b. Double surcharge
c. Double surch., red & black 500.00 *1,200.*
d. As "c," without hyphen 1,500. 1,500.

Badge of Colony
A8 A9

1892-1903 Wmk. 2
70 A8 1f sl & car ('96) .85 .20
71 A8 ½p green .55 .20
72 A8 1p carmine rose 1.75 .20
73 A8 2p sl & org ('99) 5.25 1.50
74 A8 2½p ultramarine 8.75 .30
75 A8 5p olive brn 4.25 4.25
76 A8 6p vio & car 6.00 3.50
77 A8 8p org & ultra 2.25 *15.00*
78 A8 10p bl grn & car 4.50 *6.00*
79 A8 2sh6p slate & org 35.00 35.00
80 A8 2sh6p pur & grn ('03) 47.50 *75.00*
Nos. 70-80 (11) 116.65 *141.15*

See Nos. 90-101. For surcharge see No B1.

Victoria Jubilee Issue

1897 Wmk. 1
81 A9 1f gray & car 1.25 .30
82 A9 ½p gray green 1.75 .30
83 A9 1p carmine rose 2.00 .35
84 A9 2½p ultra 4.25 .70
85 A9 5p dk olive brn 8.50 *9.25*
86 A9 6p vio & car 12.00 *14.00*
87 A9 8p org & ultra 7.00 *15.00*
88 A9 10p bl grn & car 30.00 *35.00*
89 A9 2sh6p slate & org 35.00 *42.50*
Nos. 81-89 (9) 101.75 *117.40*

Bluish Paper
81a A9 1f gray & car 25.00 *30.00*
82a A9 ½p gray green 25.00 *30.00*
83a A9 1p carmine rose 35.00 *40.00*
84a A9 2½p ultra 37.50 *45.00*
85a A9 5p dk olive brn 225.00 *250.00*
86a A9 6p vio & car 100.00 *110.00*
87a A9 8p org & ultra 85.00 *100.00*
88a A9 10p bl grn & car 140.00 *150.00*
89a A9 2sh6p slate & org *90.00* *95.00*
Nos. 81a-89a (9) 762.50 *850.00*

Badge Type of 1892-1903

1904-10 Wmk. 3
90 A8 1f gray & car 3.50 1.25
91 A8 1f brown ('09) .90 .25
92 A8 ½p green 7.00 .20
93 A8 1p carmine rose 5.75 .20
94 A8 1p carmine ('09) 4.00 .20
95 A8 2p gray ('09) 4.00 *7.75*
96 A8 2½p ultramarine 4.00 .40
97 A8 6p vio & car 15.00 12.50
98 A8 6p dl vio & vio ('10) 5.00 *12.00*
99 A8 8p org & ultra 22.50 *52.50*
100 A8 1sh blk, *grn* ('10) 7.50 *12.00*
101 A8 2sh6p pur & green 27.50 *55.00*
Nos. 90-101 (12) 106.65 *154.25*

Nelson Centenary Issue

Lord Nelson Monument — A10

1906 Engr. Wmk. 1
102 A10 1f gray & black 2.00 .60
103 A10 ½p green & black 3.00 .40
104 A10 1p car & black 3.50 .30
105 A10 2p org & black 4.00 4.25
106 A10 2½p ultra & black 5.00 4.00
107 A10 6p lilac & black 15.00 *19.00*
108 A10 1sh rose & black 17.50 *32.50*
Nos. 102-108 (7) 50.00 *61.05*

See Nos. 110-112.

The "Olive Blossom" — A11

1906, Aug. 15 Wmk. 3
109 A11 1p blk, green & blue 8.00 1.25

Tercentenary of the 1st British landing.

Nelson Type of 1906

1907, July 6 Wmk. 3
110 A10 1f gray & black 2.50 2.00
111 A10 2p org & black 12.50 *15.00*
112 A10 2½p ultra & black 10.00 *12.50*
a. 2½p indigo & black 850.00 *1,200.*
Nos. 110-112 (3) 25.00 *29.50*

A12

A13

King George V — A14

1912 **Typo.**

116 A12 ¼p brown .40 .30
117 A12 ½p green 1.50 .20
a. Booklet pane of 6
118 A12 1p carmine 3.00 .20
a. 1p scarlet 10.00 1.00
b. Booklet pane of 6
119 A12 2p gray 1.60 *6.50*
120 A12 2½p ultramarine 1.00 .50
121 A13 3p violet, *yel* 1.00 *4.00*
122 A13 4p blk & scar, *yel* 1.00 *7.50*
123 A13 6p vio & red vio 6.00 5.00
124 A14 1sh black, *green* 4.00 *7.00*
125 A14 2sh vio & ultra, *bl* 24.00 *32.50*
126 A14 3sh grn & violet 47.50 37.50
Nos. 116-126 (11) 91.00 101.20

Seal of the Colony — A15

1916-18 **Engr.**

127 A15 ¼p brown .30 .25
128 A15 ½p green .75 .20
129 A15 1p red 1.00 .20
130 A15 2p gray 3.50 *10.00*
131 A15 2½p ultramarine .85 .75
132 A15 3p violet, *yel* 2.25 *2.50*
133 A15 4p red, *yel* .60 *5.00*
134 A15 4p red & black ('18) .85 *2.50*
135 A15 6p claret 1.50 *2.25*
136 A15 1sh black, *green* 3.50 *5.00*
137 A15 2sh violet, *blue* 15.00 8.50
138 A15 3sh dark violet 32.50 *70.00*
139 A15 3sh dk vio & grn ('18) 15.00 *30.00*
a. 3sh bright violet & green ('18) 140.00 *150.00*
Nos. 127-139 (13) 77.60 *137.15*

Nos. 134 and 139 are from a re-engraved die. The central medallion is not surrounded by a line and there are various other small alterations.

Victory Issue

Victory
A16 A17

1920, Sept. 9 **Wmk. 3**

140 A16 ¼p bister & black .25 *.55*
141 A16 ½p yel green & blk .80 .20
a. Booklet pane of 2
142 A16 1p org red & blk 2.25 .20
a. Booklet pane of 2
143 A16 2p gray & black 1.75 *4.25*
144 A16 2½p ultra & dk bl 2.40 *6.50*
145 A16 3p red lilac & blk 2.40 *3.25*
146 A16 4p gray grn & blk 2.40 *3.50*
147 A16 6p orange & blk 3.00 *6.50*
148 A17 1sh yel green & blk 7.50 *14.00*
149 A17 2sh brown & blk 17.00 *18.00*
150 A17 3sh orange & blk 20.00 *22.00*
Nos. 140-150 (11) 59.75 *78.95*

1921, Aug. 22 **Wmk. 4**

151 A16 1p orange red & blk 14.00 .20
Nos. 140-151 (12) 73.75 *79.15*

A18 A19

1921-24 **Wmk. 4**

152 A18 ¼p brown .20 .20
153 A18 ½p green .35 .20
154 A18 1p carmine .30 .20
155 A18 2p gray 1.00 .30
156 A18 2½p ultramarine .90 *1.50*
158 A18 6p claret 1.50 1.50
159 A18 1sh blk, *emer* ('24) 30.00 *32.50*
160 A18 2sh dk vio, *blue* 13.00 *17.50*
161 A18 3sh dark violet 13.00 *22.50*

Wmk. 3

162 A18 3p violet, *yel* .75 *1.50*
163 A18 4p red, *yel* .70 *3.00*
164 A18 1sh black, *green* 4.00 *10.00*
Nos. 152-164 (12) 65.70 *90.90*

1925-35 **Wmk. 4** ***Perf. 14***

165 A19 ¼p brown .20 .20
166 A19 ½p green .20 .20
a. Perf. 13½x12½ ('32) 1.25 .20
b. Booklet pane of 10
167 A19 1p carmine .20 .20
a. Perf. 13½x12½ ('32) .90 .30
b. Booklet pane of 10
168 A19 1½p org, perf. 13½x12½ ('32) .75 .60
a. Booklet pane of 6
b. Perf. 14 3.50 .80
169 A19 2p gray .50 *1.25*
170 A19 2½p ultramarine .50 .50
a. Perf. 13½x12½ ('32) 3.00 1.00
171 A19 3p vio brn, *yel* .60 .40
172 A19 3p red brn, *yel* ('35) 6.00 6.00
173 A19 4p red, *yel* .80 .80
174 A19 6p claret .80 .80
175 A19 1sh blk, *emerald* 1.50 *2.50*
a. Perf. 13½x12½ ('32) 15.00 10.00
176 A19 1sh brn blk, *yel grn* ('32) 4.25 *7.50*
177 A19 2sh violet, *bl* 5.00 4.00
178 A19 2sh6p car, *blue* ('32) 15.00 *17.50*
179 A19 3sh dark violet 8.00 *12.50*
Nos. 165-179 (15) 44.30 *54.95*

Charles I and George V — A20

1927, Feb. 17 ***Perf. 12½***

180 A20 1p carmine lake 1.00 .75

Tercentenary of the settlement of Barbados.

Common Design Types pictured following the introduction.

Silver Jubilee Issue
Common Design Type

1935, May 6 ***Perf. 11x12***

186 CD301 1p car & dk bl .20 .20
187 CD301 1½p blk & ultra 1.50 *2.00*
188 CD301 2½p ultra & brn 1.10 *1.25*
189 CD301 1sh brn vio & ind 7.50 7.50
Nos. 186-189 (4) 10.30 10.95
Set, never hinged 20.00

Coronation Issue
Common Design Type

1937, May 14 ***Perf. 13½x14***

190 CD302 1p carmine .20 .20
191 CD302 1½p brown .20 .20
192 CD302 2½p bright ultra .40 .40
Nos. 190-192 (3) .80 .80
Set, never hinged 1.00

A21

1938-47 ***Perf. 13-14 & Compound***

193 A21 ½p green .40 .20
b. Perf. 14 22.50 1.40
c. Booklet pane of 10
193A A21 ½p bister ('42) .20 .20
194 A21 1p carmine 1.75 .20
b. Perf. 13½x13 50.00 1.40
c. Booklet pane of 10
194A A21 1p green ('42) .20 .20
d. Perf. 13½x13 .30 .20
195 A21 1½p red orange .20 .20
c. Perf. 14 .60 .20
d. Booklet pane of 6
195A A21 2p rose lake ('41) 1.10 .50
195B A21 2p bright rose red ('43) .20 .20
e. Perf. 14 .20 .20
196 A21 2½p ultramarine .20 .20
197 A21 3p brown .20 .50
b. Perf. 14 .25 .20
197A A21 3p deep bl ('47) .20 .20
198 A21 4p black .20 .20
a. Perf. 14 .30 .30
199 A21 6p violet .20 .20
199A A21 8p red vio ('46) .65 .65
200 A21 1sh brn olive .50 .20
a. 1sh olive green 5.00 1.40
201 A21 2sh6p brown vio 2.75 .65
201A A21 5sh indigo ('41) 2.75 1.40
Nos. 193-201A (16) 11.70 5.90
Set, never hinged 25.00

For surcharge see No. 209.

Kings Charles I, George VI Assembly Chamber and Mace A22

Perf. 13½x14

1939, June 27 **Engr.** **Wmk. 4**

202 A22 ½p deep green .25 .20
203 A22 1p scarlet .25 .20
204 A22 1½p deep orange .35 .25
205 A22 2½p ultramarine .60 *.80*
206 A22 3p yellow brown .65 *.80*
Nos. 202-206 (5) 2.10 *2.25*
Set, never hinged 5.00

Tercentenary of the General Assembly.

Catalogue values for unused stamps in this section, from this point to the end of the section, are for Never Hinged items.

Peace Issue
Common Design Type

1946, Sept. 18

207 CD303 1½p deep orange .20 .20
208 CD303 3p brown .20 .20

Nos. 195e, 195B, Surcharged in Black — **ONE PENNY**

1947, Apr. 21 ***Perf. 14***

209 A21 1p on 2p brt rose red .55 .55
a. Double surcharge
b. Perf. 13½x13 .65 .65

Silver Wedding Issue
Common Design Types

Perf. 14x14½

1948, Nov. 24 **Photo.** **Wmk. 4**

210 CD304 1½p orange .20 .20

Engraved; Name Typographed

Perf. 11½x11

211 CD305 5sh dark blue 10.00 10.00

UPU Issue
Common Design Types

1949, Oct. 10 ***Perf. 13½, 11x11½***

212 CD306 1½p red orange .35 .35
213 CD307 3p indigo .55 .55
214 CD308 4p gray 1.00 1.00
215 CD309 1sh olive 1.40 1.40
Nos. 212-215 (4) 3.30 3.30

Dover Fort — A23

Admiral Nelson Statue — A24

Designs: 2c, Sugar cane breeding. 3c, Public buildings. 6c, Casting net. 8c, Intercolonial schooner. 12c, Flying Fish. 24c, Old Main Guard Garrison. 48c, Cathedral. 60c, Careenage. $1.20, Map. $2.40, Great Seal, 1660.

Perf. 11x11½ (A23), 13x13½ (A24)

1950, May 1 **Engr.** **Wmk. 4**

216 A23 1c slate .20 .20
217 A23 2c emerald .20 .20
218 A23 3c slate & brown .20 .20
219 A24 4c carmine .30 .30
220 A23 6c blue .35 .30
221 A23 8c choc & blue .60 .40
222 A23 12c olive & aqua 1.25 .75
223 A23 24c gray & red 1.50 1.00
224 A24 48c violet 4.00 2.75
225 A23 60c brn car & bl grn 2.50 *3.00*
226 A24 $1.20 olive & car 9.00 5.25
227 A23 $2.40 gray 21.00 13.00
Nos. 216-227 (12) 41.10 27.35

University Issue
Common Design Types

1951, Feb. 16 ***Perf. 14x14½***

228 CD310 3c turq bl & choc .20 .20
229 CD311 12c ol brn & turq bl .75 .75

Stamp of 1852 — A25

Perf. 13½

1952, Apr. 15 **Wmk. 4** **Engr.**

230 A25 3c slate bl & dp grn .20 .20
231 A25 4c rose pink & bl .25 .25
232 A25 12c emer & slate bl .40 .40
233 A25 24c gray blk & red brn .65 .65
Nos. 230-233 (4) 1.50 1.50

Centenary of Barbados postage stamps.

Coronation Issue
Common Design Type

1953, June 4 ***Perf. 13½x13***

234 CD312 4c red orange & black .20 .20

Harbor Police A26

Designs as in 1950 with portrait of Queen Elizabeth II. $2.40, Great Seal, 1660 ("E II R").

Perf. 11x11½ (horiz.), 13x13½ (vert.)

1953-57 **Engr.**

235 A23 1c slate ('53) .20 .20
236 A23 2c grnsh blue & deep org .20 .20
237 A23 3c emerald & blk .20 .20
238 A24 4c orange & gray .20 .20
239 A26 5c dp car & dp bl .20 .20
240 A23 6c red brown .20 .20
241 A23 8c brt blue & blk .30 .20
242 A23 12c brn ol & aqua .40 .20
243 A23 24c gray & red ('56) .55 .20
244 A24 48c violet ('56) 1.75 1.10
245 A23 60c brown car & blue grn ('56) 3.00 1.75
246 A24 $1.20 ol & car ('56) 5.25 3.25
247 A23 $2.40 gray ('57) 11.00 6.25
Nos. 235-247 (13) 23.45 14.15

See Nos. 257-264.

West Indies Federation
Common Design Type

Perf. 11½x11

1958, Apr. 23 **Wmk. 314**

248 CD313 3c green .20 .20
249 CD313 6c blue .40 .40
250 CD313 12c carmine rose .50 .50
Nos. 248-250 (3) 1.10 1.10

Deep Water Harbor, Bridgetown A27

1961, May 6 **Engr.** ***Perf. 11x11½***

251 A27 4c orange & black .20 .20
252 A27 8c ultra & black .30 .30
253 A27 24c black & pink .65 .65
Nos. 251-253 (3) 1.15 1.15

Deep Water Harbor at Bridgetown opening.

Scout Emblem and Map of Barbados — A28

Perf. 11½x11

1962, Mar. 9 **Wmk. 314**

254 A28 4c orange & black .20 .20
255 A28 12c gray & blue .30 .30
256 A28 $1.20 greenish gray & carmine rose 2.00 2.00
Nos. 254-256 (3) 2.50 2.50

50th anniv. of the founding of the Boy Scouts of Barbados.

Queen Types of 1953-57

Perf. 11x11½, 13x13½

1964-65 **Engr.** **Wmk. 314**

257 A23 1c slate .25 .25
258 A24 4c orange & gray .35 .35
259 A23 8c brt bl & blk ('65) .50 .45
260 A23 12c brn ol & aqua ('65) .60
261 A23 24c gray & red .60 .50
262 A24 48c violet 2.50 2.50
263 A23 60c brn car & bl grn 3.50 3.50
264 A23 $2.40 gray ('65) 5.50 5.50
Nos. 257-264 (8) 13.80
Nos. 257-259,261-264 (7) 13.05

The 12c was never put on sale in Barbados.

ITU Issue

Common Design Type

Perf. 11x11½

1965, May 17 **Litho.** **Wmk. 314**

265 CD317 2c lilac & ver .20 .20
266 CD317 48c yellow & gray 1.50 1.50

Sea Horse A29

Designs: 1c, Deep sea coral. 2c, Lobster. 4c, Sea urchin. 5c, Staghorn coral. 6c, Butterflyfish. 8c, File shell. 12c, Balloonfish. 15c, Angelfish. 25c, Brain coral. 35c, Brittle star. 50c, Flyingfish. $1, Queen conch shell. $2.50, Fiddler crab.

Wmk. 314 Upright

1965, July 15 **Photo.** ***Perf. 14x13½***

267 A29 1c dk blue, pink & black .20 .20
268 A29 2c car rose, sepia & orange .20 .20
269 A29 3c org, brn & sep *("Hippocampus")* .20 .20
270 A29 4c ol grn & dk bl .20 .20
a. Imperf., pair 450.00
271 A29 5c lil, brn & pink .20 .20
272 A29 6c greenish bl, yel & blk .20 .20
273 A29 8c ultra, orange, red & black .25 .20
274 A29 12c rose lil, yel & blk .40 .25
275 A29 15c red, yel & blk .75 .50
276 A29 25c yel brn & ultra 1.10 .80
277 A29 35c grn, rose brn & blk 1.75 1.00
278 A29 50c yel grn & ultra 2.75 1.60
279 A29 $1 gray & multi 5.50 4.00
280 A29 $2.50 lt bl & multi 12.00 10.00
Nos. 267-280 (14) 25.70 19.55

1966-69 **Wmk. 314 Sideways**

Design: $5, "Dolphin" (coryphaena hippurus).

267a A29 1c .20 .20
268a A29 2c ('67) .20 .20
269A A29 3c *("Hippocampus")* ('67) .20 .20
270b A29 4c .20 .20
271a A29 5c .20 .20
272a A29 6c ('67) .20 .20
273a A29 8c ('67) .25 .20
274a A29 12c ('67) .35 .20
275a A29 15c .50 .35
276a A29 25c .60 .55
277a A29 35c .85 .60
278a A29 50c 1.25 1.10
279a A29 $1 2.50 1.90
280a A29 $2.50 6.25 6.00
280B A29 $5 dk ol & multi ('69) 12.50 12.50
Nos. 267a-280B (15) 26.25 24.60

For surcharge see No. 327.

Churchill Memorial Issue

Common Design Type

1966, Jan. 24 **Wmk. 314** ***Perf. 14***

281 CD319 1c multicolored .20 .20
282 CD319 4c multicolored .20 .20
283 CD319 25c multicolored 1.00 1.00
284 CD319 35c multicolored 1.40 1.40
Nos. 281-284 (4) 2.80 2.80

Royal Visit Issue

Common Design Type

1966, Feb. 4 **Litho.** ***Perf. 11x12***

285 CD320 3c violet blue .20 .20
286 CD320 35c dark car rose 1.75 1.75

UNESCO Anniversary Issue

Common Design Type

1967, Jan. 6 **Litho.** ***Perf. 14***

287 CD323 4c "Education" .20 .20
288 CD323 12c "Science" .55 .55
289 CD323 25c "Culture" 1.40 1.40
Nos. 287-289 (3) 2.15 2.15

Arms of Barbados A30

Policeman and Anchor Monument A31

Designs: 25c, Hilton Hotel, horiz. 35c, Garfield Sobers, captain of Barbados and West Indies Cricket Team. 50c, Pine Hill Dairy, horiz.

1966, Dec. 2 **Unwmk.** **Photo.**

290 A30 4c multicolored .20 .20
291 A30 25c multicolored .35 .35
292 A30 35c multicolored .50 .50
293 A30 50c multicolored .75 .75
Nos. 290-293 (4) 1.80 1.80

Barbados' independence, Nov. 30, 1966.

1967, Oct. 16 **Litho.** ***Perf. 13½x14***

Designs: 25c, Policeman with telescope. 35c, Police motor launch, horiz. 50c, Policemen at Harbor Gate.

294 A31 4c multicolored .20 .20
295 A31 25c multicolored .30 .30
296 A31 35c multicolored .50 .50
297 A31 50c multicolored .80 .80
Nos. 294-297 (4) 1.80 1.80

Centenary of Bridgetown Harbor Police.
For surcharge see No. 322.

Independence Arch — A32

1st Anniv. of Independence: 4c, Sir Winston Scott, Governor-General, vert. 35c, Treasury Building. 50c, Parliament Building.

Perf. 14½x14, 14x14½

1967, Dec. 4 **Photo.** **Unwmk.**

298 A32 4c multicolored .20 .20
299 A32 25c multicolored .25 .25
300 A32 35c multicolored .40 .40
301 A32 50c multicolored .60 .60
Nos. 298-301 (4) 1.45 1.45

UN Building, Santiago, Chile A33

1968, Feb. 27 ***Perf. 14½x14***

302 A33 15c multicolored .20 .20

20th anniv. of the UN Economic Commission for Latin America.

Radar Antenna on Top of Old Sugar Mill, Sugar Cane — A34

Designs: 25c, Caribbean Meteorological Institute, Barbados, horiz. 50c, HARP gun used in High Altitude Research Program, at Paragon in Christ Church, Barbados.

Perf. 14x14½, 14½x14

1968, June 4 **Photo.** **Unwmk.**

303 A34 3c violet & multi .20 .20
304 A34 25c vermilion & multi .30 .30
305 A34 50c orange & multi .70 .70
Nos. 303-305 (3) 1.20 1.20

World Meteorological Day.

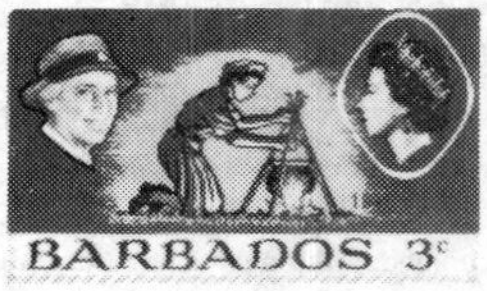

Girl Scout at Campfire, Lady Baden-Powell and Queen Elizabeth II — A35

Lady Baden-Powell, Queen Elizabeth II and: 25c, Pax Hill Headquarters. 35c, Girl Scout badge.

Perf. 14x14½

1968, Aug. 29 **Photo.** **Unwmk.**

306 A35 3c dp ultra, blk & gold .20 .20
307 A35 25c bluish green, black & gold .35 .35
308 A35 35c org yel, blk & gold .70 .70
Nos. 306-308 (3) 1.25 1.25

Barbados Girl Scouts' 50th anniv.

Human Rights Flame and Escape to Freedom A36

Designs: 4c, Human Rights flame, hands, and broken chain. 25c, Human Rights flame, family and broken chain.

Perf. 11x11½

1968, Dec. 10 **Litho.** **Unwmk.**

309 A36 4c violet, gray grn & red brown .20 .20
310 A36 25c org, blk & blue .40 .40
311 A36 35c greenish blue, blue, blk & org .55 .55
Nos. 309-311 (3) 1.15 1.15

International Human Rights Year.

In the Paddock A37

Horse Racing: 25c, "They're off!" 35c, On the flat. 50c, The Finish.

1969, Mar. 15 **Litho.** ***Perf. 14½***

312 A37 4c multicolored .20 .20
313 A37 25c multicolored .25 .25
314 A37 35c multicolored .35 .35
315 A37 50c multicolored .55 .55
a. Souvenir sheet of 4, #312-315 2.50 *3.00*
Nos. 312-315 (4) 1.35 1.35

Map of Caribbean — A38

Design: 12c, 50c, "Strength in Unity," horiz.

Perf. 14x14½, 14½x14

1969, May 6 **Photo.** **Wmk. 314**

316 A38 5c brown & multi .20 .20
317 A38 12c ultra & multi .20 .20
318 A38 25c green & multi .30 .30
319 A38 50c magenta & multi .65 .65
Nos. 316-319 (4) 1.35 1.35

1st anniv. of CARIFTA (Caribbean Free Trade Area).

ILO Emblem A39

Perf. 14x13

1969, Aug. 5 **Litho.** **Unwmk.**

320 A39 4c bl grn, brt grn & blk .20 .20
321 A39 25c red brn, brt mag & red .40 .40

50th anniv. of the ILO.

No. 294 Surcharged ONE CENT

1969, Aug. 30 ***Perf. 13½x14***

322 A31 1c on 4c multicolored .35 .35

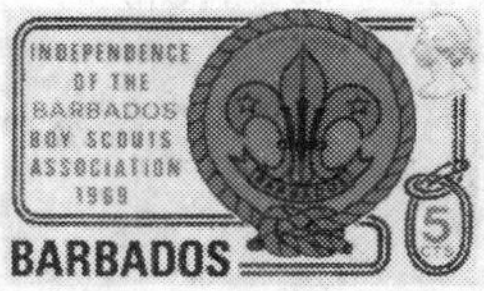

Barbados Boy Scout Emblem — A40

Designs: 25c, Sea Scouts rowing in Bridgetown harbor. 35c, Campfire. 50c, Various Scouts in front of National Headquarters and Training Center, Hazelwood.

Perf. 13½x13

1969, Dec. 16 **Litho.** **Unwmk.**

323 A40 5c multicolored .20 .20
324 A40 25c multicolored .50 .50
325 A40 35c multicolored .65 .65
326 A40 50c multicolored 1.00 1.00
a. Souvenir sheet of 4, #323-326 10.00 *12.00*
Nos. 323-326 (4) 2.35 2.35

Attainment of independence by the Barbados Boy Scout Assoc.

No. 271a Surcharged 4 X

Wmk. 314 Sideways

1970, Mar. 11 **Photo.** ***Perf. 14x13½***

327 A29 4c on 5c multicolored .20 .20

This locally applied surcharge exists in several variations: double, triple, on back, in pair with one missing, etc.

Lion at Gun Hill — A41

Barbados Museum A42

2c, Trafalgar Fountain. 3c, Montefiore Drinking Fountain. 4c, St. James' Monument. 5c, St. Ann's Fort. 6c, Old Sugar Mill, Morgan Lewis. 8c, Cenotaph. 10c, South Point Lighthouse. 15c, Sharon Moravian Church. 25c, George Washington House. 35c, St. Nicholas Abbey. 50c, Bowmanston Pumping Station. $1, Queen Elizabeth Hospital. $2.50, Modern sugar factory. $5, Seawell Intl. Airport.

Wmk. 314 Upright (A41), Sideways (A42)

Perf. 12½x13, 13x12½

1970, May 4 **Photo.**

328 A41	1c	blue grn & multi	.20	.20
329 A41	2c	crimson & multi	.20	.20
330 A41	3c	blue & multi	.20	.20
331 A41	4c	yellow & multi	.20	.20
332 A41	5c	dp org & multi	.20	.20
333 A41	6c	dull yel & multi	.20	.20
334 A41	8c	dp blue & multi	.20	.20
335 A41	10c	red & multi	.20	.20
336 A42	12c	ultra & multi	.20	.20
337 A42	15c	yellow & multi	.20	.20
338 A42	25c	orange & multi	.40	.40
339 A42	35c	pink & multi	.55	.55
340 A42	50c	bl grn & multi	.65	.65
341 A42	$1	emerald & multi	1.40	1.40
342 A42	$2.50	ver & multi	3.50	3.50
343 A42	$5	yellow & multi	6.50	6.50
		Nos. 328-343 (16)	15.00	15.00

Nos. 328-332, 334-343 were reissued in 1971 on glazed paper.

Wmk. 314 Sideways (A41), Upright (A42)

1972-74

331a A41	4c		.20	.20
332a A41	5c		.20	.20
333a A41	6c		.20	.20
334a A41	8c		.20	.20
335a A41	10c	('74)	.25	.25
336a A42	12c		.25	.25
337a A42	15c		.30	.30
338a A42	25c		.55	.55
339a A42	35c		.85	.85
340a A42	50c		1.25	1.25
341a A42	$1		2.50	2.50
342a A42	$2.50	('73)	6.50	6.50
343a A42	$5	('73)	13.00	13.00
		Nos. 331a-343a (13)	26.25	26.25

For surcharge, see No. 391.

Primary Education, UN and Education Year Emblems A43

Designs (UN and Education Year Emblems and): 5c, Secondary education (student with microscope). 25c, Technical education (men working with power drill). 50c, University building.

1970, June 26 **Litho.** ***Perf. 14***

344 A43	4c	multicolored	.20	.20
345 A43	5c	multicolored	.20	.20
346 A43	25c	multicolored	.35	.35
347 A43	50c	multicolored	.75	.75
		Nos. 344-347 (4)	1.50	1.50

UN, 25th anniv., and Intl. Education Year.

Minnie Root A44

Flowers: 1c, Barbados Easter lily, vert. 10c, Eyelash orchid. 25c, Pride of Barbados, vert. 35c, Christmas hope.

1970, Aug. 24 **Litho.** **Wmk. 314**

Flowers in Natural Colors

348 A44	1c	green	.20	.20
349 A44	5c	deep magenta	.20	.20
350 A44	10c	dark blue	.45	.25
351 A44	25c	brt orange brown	1.25	.55
352 A44	35c	blue	1.75	.90
a.		Souvenir sheet of 5	3.00	2.25
		Nos. 348-352 (5)	3.85	2.10

No. 352a contains 5 imperf. stamps similar to Nos. 348-352 with simulated perforations.

Christ Carrying Cross — A45

Easter: 10c, 50c, Resurrection, by Benjamin West, St. George's Anglican Church. 35c like 4c, Window from St. Margaret's Anglican Church, St. John.

1971, Apr. 7 **Wmk. 314** ***Perf. 14***

353 A45	4c	purple & multi	.20	.20
354 A45	10c	silver & multi	.20	.20
355 A45	35c	brt blue & multi	.50	.50
356 A45	50c	gold & multi	.80	.80
		Nos. 353-356 (4)	1.70	1.70

Sailfish Craft A46

Tourism: 5c, Tennis. 12c, Horseback riding. 25c, Water-skiing. 50c, Scuba diving.

1971, Aug. 17 ***Perf. 14x14½***

357 A46	1c	multicolored	.20	.20
358 A46	5c	multicolored	.20	.20
359 A46	12c	multicolored	.20	.20
360 A46	25c	multicolored	.50	.50
361 A46	50c	multicolored	1.00	1.00
		Nos. 357-361 (5)	2.10	2.10

Samuel Jackman Prescod — A47

1971, Sept. 26 ***Perf. 14***

362 A47	3c	orange & multi	.20	.20
363 A47	35c	ultra & multi	.65	.65

Samuel Jackman Prescod (1806-1871), 1st black member of Barbados Assembly.

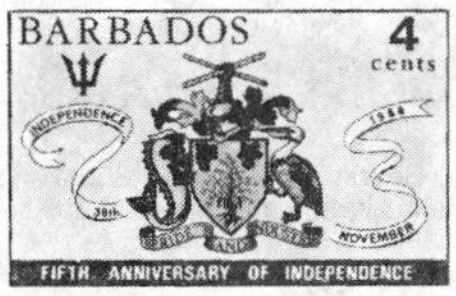

Coat of Arms A48

Designs: 15c, 50c, Flag and map of Barbados.

1971, Nov. 23

364 A48	4c	light blue & multi	.20	.20
365 A48	15c	multicolored	.30	.30
366 A48	25c	yel green & multi	.45	.45
367 A48	50c	blue & multi	.90	.90
		Nos. 364-367 (4)	1.85	1.85

5th anniv. of independence.

Telegraphy, 1872 and 1972 — A49

Designs: 10c, "Stanley Angwin" off St. Lawrence Coast. 35c, Earth station and Intelsat 4. 50c, Mt. Misery tropospheric scatter station.

1972, Mar. 28 **Litho.** ***Perf. 14***

368 A49	4c	purple & multi	.20	.20
369 A49	10c	emerald & multi	.25	.25
370 A49	35c	red & multi	.55	.55
371 A49	50c	orange & multi	.85	.85
		Nos. 368-371 (4)	1.85	1.85

Centenary of telecommunications to and from Barbados.

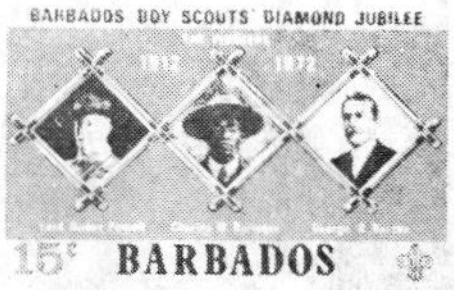

Lord Baden-Powell, Charles W. Springer, George B. Burton — A50

Designs: 5c, Map of Barbados and Combermere School, vert. 25c, Photograph of 1922 troop. 50c, Flags of various Boy Scout troops.

1972, Aug. 1

372 A50	5c	ultra & multi	.20	.20
373 A50	15c	ultra & multi	.40	.40
374 A50	25c	ultra & multi	.60	.60
375 A50	50c	ultra & multi	1.10	1.10
		Nos. 372-375 (4)	2.30	2.30

60th anniv. of Barbados Boy Scouts and 4th Caribbean Jamboree.

Bookmobile, Open Book — A51

Intl. Book Year: 15c, Visual aids truck. 25c, Central Library, Bridgetown. $1, Codrington College.

1972, Oct. 31 **Litho.** **Wmk. 314**

376 A51	4c	brt pink & multi	.20	.20
377 A51	15c	dull org & multi	.25	.25
378 A51	25c	buff & multi	.40	.40
379 A51	$1	lt violet & multi	1.90	1.90
		Nos. 376-379 (4)	2.75	2.75

Pottery Wheels A52

Barbados pottery industry: 15c, Kiln. 25c, Finished pottery, Chalky Mount. $1, Pottery on sale at market.

1973, Mar. 1 **Wmk. 314** ***Perf. 14***

380 A52	5c	dull red & multi	.20	.20
381 A52	15c	olive grn & multi	.20	.20
382 A52	25c	gray & multi	.35	.35
383 A52	$1	yellow & multi	1.40	1.40
		Nos. 380-383 (4)	2.15	2.15

First Flight in Barbados, Wright Box Kite, 1911 A53

Aircraft: 15c, First flight to Barbados, De Havilland biplane, 1928. 25c, Passenger plane, 1939. 50c, Vickers VC-10 over control tower, 1973.

1973, July 25 ***Perf. 12½x12***

384 A53	5c	blue & multi	.20	.20
385 A53	15c	vio blue & multi	.40	.40
386 A53	25c	multicolored	.65	.65
387 A53	50c	blue & multi	1.40	1.40
		Nos. 384-387 (4)	2.65	2.65

Chancellor Sir Hugh Wooding A54

Designs: 25c, Sherlock Hall, Cave Hill Campus. 35c, Cave Hill Campus.

1973, Dec. 11 ***Perf. 13x14***

388 A54	5c	dp orange & multi	.20	.20
389 A54	25c	red brown & multi	.40	.40
390 A54	35c	multicolored	.60	.60
		Nos. 388-390 (3)	1.20	1.20

25th anniv. of the Univ. of the West Indies.

No. 338a Surcharged **4c.**

1974, Apr. 30 **Photo.** ***Perf. 13x12½***

391 A42	4c	on 25c multi	.20	.20
a.		"4c." omitted	20.00	

Old Sailboat A55

Designs: 25c, Rowboat. 50c, Motor-powered fishing boat. $1, Trawler "Calamar."

1974, June 11 **Wmk. 314** ***Perf. 14***

392 A55	15c	blue & multi	.25	.25
393 A55	35c	multicolored	.50	.50
394 A55	50c	vio blue & multi	.70	.70
395 A55	$1	blue & multi	1.40	1.40
a.		Souvenir sheet of 4, #392-395	3.00	*3.75*
		Nos. 392-395 (4)	2.85	2.85

Fishing boats of Barbados.

Fire Orchid — A56

Orchids. 1c, 20c, 25c, $2.50, $5 horizontal.

Wmk. 314 Sideways; Upright (1c, 20c, 25c, $1, $10)

1974-77 **Photo.** ***Perf. 14***

396 A56	1c	Cattleya gaskelliana alba	.20	.20
397 A56	2c	shown	.20	.20
398 A56	3c	Rose Marie	.20	.20
399 A56	4c	Fiery red orchid	.20	.20
400 A56	5c	Schomburgkia humboltii	.20	.20
401 A56	8c	Dancing dolls	.20	.20
402 A56	10c	Spider orchids	.20	.20
403 A56	12c	Dendrobium aggregatum	.25	.20
404 A56	15c	Lady slippers	.40	.35
404C A56	20c	Spathoglottis	.45	.40
405 A56	25c	Eyelash	.75	.55
406 A56	35c	Bletia patula	.80	.65
406B A56	45c	Sunset Glow	1.10	.85
407 A56	50c	Sunset Glow	1.10	.85

Perf. 14½x14, 14x14½

408 A56	$1	Ascocenda red gem	2.00	1.50
409 A56	$2.50	Brassolaeliocattleya nugget	4.75	3.75

410 A56 $5 Caularthron bicornutum 9.50 8.00
411 A56 $10 Moon orchid 17.50 15.00
Nos. 396-411 (18) 40.00 33.50

Issued: 20c, 45c, 5/3/77; others, 9/16/74.
For surcharge see No. B2.

Wmk. 314 Upright; Sideways (1c, 25c, $1)

1976 ***Perf. 14***
396a A56 1c multicolored .20 .20
397a A56 2c multicolored .20 .20
398a A56 3c multicolored .20 .20
399a A56 4c multicolored .25 .20
402a A56 10c multicolored .45 .40
404a A56 15c multicolored .80 .70
405a A56 25c multicolored 1.00 .90
406a A56 35c multicolored 1.50 1.25

Perf. 14½x14
408a A56 $1 multicolored 4.00 3.50
Nos. 396a-408a (9) 8.60 7.55

1975 Wmk. 373 ***Perf. 14***
396b A56 1c multicolored .20 .20
397b A56 2c multicolored .20 .20
398b A56 3c multicolored .20 .20
399b A56 4c multicolored .25 .25
400b A56 5c multicolored .20 .20
402b A56 10c multicolored .20 .20
403b A56 12c multicolored .25 .25
404b A56 15c multicolored .50 .45
406c A56 45c multicolored 1.10 .90

Perf. 14½x14, 14x14½
408b A56 $1 multicolored 2.00 1.90
409b A56 $2.50 multicolored 5.00 4.50
410b A56 $5 multicolored 10.00 9.50
411b A56 $10 multicolored 18.00 18.00
Nos. 396b-411b (13) 38.10 36.75

UPU Emblem, Barbados No. 64 A57

Cent. of the UPU: 35c, Letters encircling globe. 50c, Barbados coat of arms. $1, Map of Barbados, sailing ship and jet.

1974, Oct. 9 Litho. ***Perf. 14½***
412 A57 8c brt rose, org & gray .20 .20
413 A57 35c red, blk, & ocher .45 .45
414 A57 50c vio blue, bl & sil .65 .65
415 A57 $1 ultra, blk & brn 1.25 1.25
a. Souvenir sheet of 4, #412-415 3.00 3.00
Nos. 412-415 (4) 2.55 2.55

Yacht Britannia off Barbados A58

Royal Visit, Feb. 1975: 35c, $1, Palms and sunset.

1975, Feb. 18
416 A58 8c brown & multi .20 .20
417 A58 25c blue & multi .40 .40
418 A58 35c purple & multi .60 .60
419 A58 $1 violet & multi 1.60 1.60
Nos. 416-419 (4) 2.80 2.80

St. Michael's Cathedral — A59

Designs: 15c, Bishop Coleridge. 50c, All Saint's Church. $1, St. Michael, stained glass window, St. Michael's Cathedral.

Wmk. 314

1975, July 29 Litho. ***Perf. 14***
420 A59 5c blue & multi .20 .20
421 A59 15c lilac & multi .20 .20
422 A59 50c green & multi .60 .60
423 A59 $1 multicolored 1.00 1.00
a. Souvenir sheet of 4, #420-423 2.25 2.75
Nos. 420-423 (4) 2.00 2.00

Anglican Diocese in Barbados, sesquicentennial.

Pony Float A60

Designs: 25c, Stiltsman (band and masqueraders). 35c, Maypole dancing. 50c, Cuban dancers.

1975, Nov. 18 Litho. Wmk. 373
424 A60 8c yellow & multi .20 .20
425 A60 25c buff & multi .30 .30
426 A60 35c ultra & multi .40 .40
427 A60 50c orange & multi .65 .65
a. Souvenir sheet of 4, #424-427 1.75 1.75
Nos. 424-427 (4) 1.55 1.55

Crop-over (harvest) festival.

Sailing Ship, 17th Cent. — A61

Coat of Arms — A62

350th Anniv. of 1st Settlement: 10c, Bearded fig tree and fruit. 25c, Ogilvy's 17th cent. map. $1, Capt. John Powell.

1975, Dec. 17 Wmk. 373 ***Perf. 13½***
428 A61 4c lt blue & multi .20 .20
429 A61 10c lt blue & multi .20 .20
430 A61 25c yellow & multi .55 .50
431 A61 $1 dk red & multi 1.90 1.60
a. Souvenir sheet of 4, #428-431 3.00 2.75
Nos. 428-431 (4) 2.85 2.50

Coil Stamps

1975, Dec. Unwmk. ***Perf. 15x14***
432 A62 5c light blue .20 .20
433 A62 25c violet .25 .25

Map of West Indies, Bats, Wicket and Ball — A63

Prudential Cup — A64

1976, July 7 Litho. ***Perf. 14***
438 A63 25c lt blue & multi .85 .50
439 A64 45c lilac rose & black 1.10 1.00

World Cricket Cup, won by West Indies Team, 1975.

Map of South Carolina settled by Barbadians — A65

American Bicentennial: 25c, George Washington and map of Bridge Town area. 50c, Declaration of Independence. $1, Masonic emblem and Prince Hall, founder and Grand Master of African Grand Lodge, Boston, 1790-1807.

1976, Aug. 17 Wmk. 373 ***Perf. 13½***
440 A65 15c multicolored .20 .20
441 A65 25c multicolored .35 .35
442 A65 50c multicolored .65 .65
443 A65 $1 multicolored 1.40 1.40
Nos. 440-443 (4) 2.60 2.60

Mailman with Bicycle A66

PO Act, 125th anniv.: 35c, Mailman on motor scooter. 50c, Cover with Barbados No. 2. $1, Mail truck.

1976, Oct. 19 Litho. ***Perf. 14***
444 A66 8c rose red, blk & bis .20 .20
445 A66 35c multicolored .40 .40
446 A66 50c vio blue & multi .60 .60
447 A66 $1 red & multi 1.10 1.10
Nos. 444-447 (4) 2.30 2.30

Coast Guard Vessels A67

Designs: 15c, Bank note, reverse, showing Barbados Parliament. 25c, National anthem by Van Roland Edwards (music) and Irvine Burgie (lyrics). $1, Independence Day parade.

1976, Nov. 30 ***Perf. 13x13½***
448 A67 5c multicolored .20 .20
449 A67 15c multicolored .20 .20
450 A67 25c yel, brown & blk .25 .25
451 A67 $1 multicolored 1.00 1.00
a. Souvenir sheet of 4, #448-451 2.00 2.00
Nos. 448-451 (4) 1.65 1.65

10th anniv. of independence.

Queen Knighting Garfield Sobers, 1957 Visit — A68

Designs: 50c, Queen arriving at Westminster Abbey. $1, Queen leaving coach.

1977, Feb. 7 ***Perf. 14x13½***
452 A68 15c silver & multi .20 .20
453 A68 50c silver & multi .55 .55
454 A68 $1 silver & multi 1.25 1.25
Nos. 452-454 (3) 2.00 2.00

25th anniv. of the reign of Queen Elizabeth II. See Nos. 467-469.

Underwater Park A69

Beauty of Barbados: 35c, Royal palms, vert. 50c, Underwater caves. $1, Stalagmite in Harrison's Cave, vert.

1977, May 3 Wmk. 373 ***Perf. 14***
455 A69 5c multicolored .20 .20
456 A69 35c multicolored .50 .50
457 A69 50c multicolored .65 .65
458 A69 $1 multicolored 1.40 1.40
a. Souvenir sheet of 4, #455-458 2.75 2.75
Nos. 455-458 (4) 2.75 2.75

House of Commons Maces — A70

Charles I Handing Charter to Carlisle — A71

Designs: 25c, Speaker's chair. 50c, Senate Chamber. $1, Sam Lord's Castle, horiz.

1977, Aug. 2 Litho. ***Perf. 13½***
459 A70 10c red brown & yel .20 .20
460 A70 25c slate grn & org .30 .30
461 A70 50c dk green, grn & yel .60 .60
462 A70 $1 dk & lt blue & org 1.10 1.10
Nos. 459-462 (4) 2.20 2.20

13th Regional Conference of Commonwealth Parliamentary Association.

Perf. 13½x13, 13x13½

1977, Oct. 11 Litho. Wmk. 373

Designs: 12c, Charter scroll. 45c, Charles I and Earl of Carlisle, horiz. $1, Map of Barbados, by Richard Ligon, 1657, horiz.

463 A71 12c buff & multi .20 .20
464 A71 25c buff & multi .30 .30
465 A71 45c buff & multi .55 .55
466 A71 $1 buff & multi 1.10 1.10
Nos. 463-466 (4) 2.15 2.15

350th anniv. of charter granting Barbados to the Earl of Carlisle.

Silver Jubilee Type, 1977, Inscribed: "ROYAL VISIT"

1977, Oct. 31 Unwmk. ***Roulette 5***
Self-adhesive
467 A68 15c silver & multi .20 .20
468 A68 50c silver & multi .60 .60
469 A68 $1 silver & multi 1.10 1.10
Nos. 467-469 (3) 1.90 1.90

Caribbean visit of Queen Elizabeth II. Printed on peelable paper backing inscribed in ultramarine multiple rows: "SILVER JUBILEE ROYAL VISIT BARBADOS." Printed with die-cut label inscribed in black "BEND & PEEL" attached at left of stamp. Sheets of 50 stamps and 50 labels.

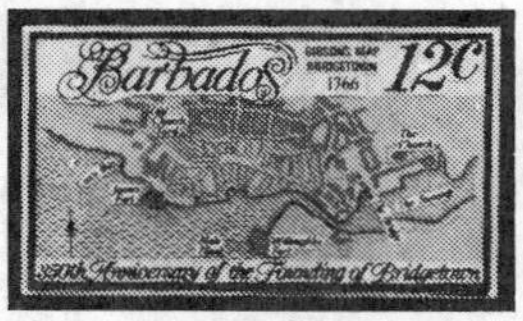

Gibson's Map of Bridgetown, 1766 — A72

25c, Bridgetown, engraving by S. Copens, 1695. 45c, Trafalgar Square, Bridgetown, drawing by J. M. Carter, 1835. $1, The Bridges, 1978.

Wmk. 373

1978, Mar. 1 Litho. ***Perf. 14½***
470 A72 12c gold & multi .20 .20
471 A72 25c gold & multi .25 .25
472 A72 45c gold & multi .45 .45
473 A72 $1 gold & multi .85 .85
Nos. 470-473 (4) 1.75 1.75

350th anniv. of founding of Bridgetown.

Elizabeth II Coronation Anniv. Issue
Souvenir Sheet
Common Design Types

1978, Apr. 21 Unwmk. ***Perf. 15***
474 Sheet of 6 3.00 3.00
a. CD326 50c Griffin of Edward III .50 .50
b. CD327 50c Elizabeth II .50 .50
c. CD328 50c Pelican .50 .50

No. 474 contains 2 se-tenant strips of Nos. 474a-474c, separated by horizontal gutter with commemorative and descriptive inscriptions and showing central part of coronation with coach.

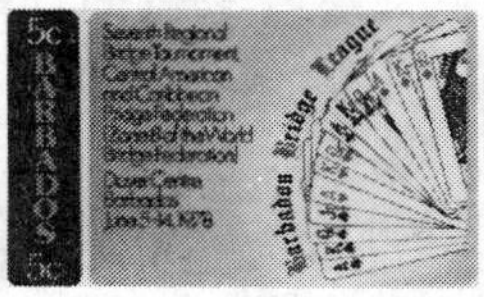

Freak Bridge Hand A73

Designs: 10c, World Bridge Fed. emblem. 45c, Central American and Caribbean Bridge Fed. emblem. $1, Map of Caribbean and cards.

Wmk. 373

1978, June 6 Litho. *Perf. 14½*

475 A73 5c multicolored .20 .20
476 A73 10c multicolored .20 .20
477 A73 45c multicolored .50 .50
478 A73 $1 multicolored 1.00 1.00
a. Souvenir sheet of 4, #475-478 1.50 1.50
Nos. 475-478 (4) 1.90 1.90

7th Regional Bridge Tournament, Dover Centre, Barbados, June 5-14.

Girl Guides' Camp — A74

Designs: 28c, Girl Guides helping children and handicapped. 50c, Badge with "60," vert. $1, Badge with initials, vert.

1978, Aug. 1 Litho. *Perf. 13½*

479 A74 12c multicolored .20 .20
480 A74 28c multicolored .30 .30
481 A74 50c multicolored .50 .50
482 A74 $1 multicolored 1.00 1.00
Nos. 479-482 (4) 2.00 2.00

Girl Guides of Barbados, 60th anniv.

Garment Industry A75

Industries of Barbados: 28c, Cooper, vert. 45c, Blacksmith, vert. 50c, Wrought iron industry.

1978, Nov. 14 Litho. *Perf. 14*

483 A75 12c multicolored .20 .20
484 A75 28c multicolored .30 .30
485 A75 45c multicolored .40 .40
486 A75 50c multicolored .50 .50
Nos. 483-486 (4) 1.40 1.40

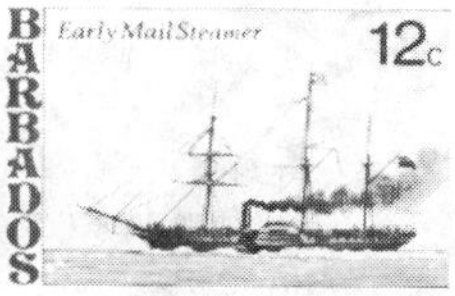

Early Mail Steamer A76

Ships: 25c, Q.E.II in Deep Water Harbour. 50c, Ra II (raft) nearing Barbados. $1, Early mail steamer.

1979, Feb. 8 Litho. *Perf. 13x13½*

487 A76 12c multicolored .20 .20
488 A76 25c multicolored .30 .30
489 A76 50c multicolored .50 .50
490 A76 $1 multicolored 1.00 1.00
Nos. 487-490 (4) 2.00 2.00

Barbados No. 235 A77

28c, Barbados #430, vert. 45c, Penny Black and Maltese postmark, vert. 50c, Barbados #21b.

Wmk. 373

1979, May 8 Litho. *Perf. 14*

491 A77 12c multicolored .20 .20
492 A77 28c multicolored .20 .20
493 A77 45c multicolored .30 .30
Nos. 491-493 (3) .70 .70

Souvenir Sheet

494 A77 50c multicolored .40 .40

Sir Rowland Hill (1795-1879), originator of penny postage.

Birds — A78

Launcher Transported through Barbados — A79

1979-81 Photo. Wmk. 373 *Perf. 14*

495 A78 1c Grass canaries .20 .20
496 A78 2c Rain birds .20 .20
497 A78 5c Sparrows .20 .20
498 A78 8c Frigate birds .20 .20
499 A78 10c Cattle egrets .20 .20
500 A78 12c Green gaulins .20 .20
501 A78 20c Hummingbirds .25 .20
502 A78 25c Ground doves .25 .25
503 A78 28c Blackbirds .30 .30
504 A78 35c Green-throated caribs .40 .40
505 A78 45c Wood doves .55 .55
506 A78 50c Ramiers .65 .65
506A A78 55c Black-breasted plover ('81) .80 .80
507 A78 70c Yellow breasts .80 .80
508 A78 $1 Pee whistlers 1.25 1.25
509 A78 $2.50 Christmas birds 3.25 3.25
510 A78 $5 Kingfishers 7.00 7.00
511 A78 $10 Red-seal coot 14.00 14.00
Nos. 495-511 (18) 30.70 30.65

Issue dates: 55c, Sept. 1; others, Aug. 7.
See #570-572. For surcharges see #563-565.

1979, Oct. 9 Photo.

Designs: 10c, Gun on landing craft, Foul Bay, horiz. 20c, Firing of 16-inch launcher by day. 28c, Bath Earth Station and Intelsat IV-A, horiz. 45c, Intelsat over Caribbean, horiz. 50c, Intelsat IV-A over Atlantic, and globe. $1, Lunar landing module, horiz.

512 A79 10c multicolored .20 .20
513 A79 12c multicolored .20 .20
514 A79 20c multicolored .20 .20
515 A79 28c multicolored .20 .20
516 A79 45c multicolored .30 .30
517 A79 50c multicolored .35 .35
Nos. 512-517 (6) 1.45 1.45

Souvenir Sheet

518 A79 $1 multicolored .85 .85

Space exploration. No. 518 commemorates 10th anniversary of first moon landing.

Family, IYC Emblem — A80

IYC Emblem and: 28c, Children holding hands and map of Barbados. 45c, Boy and teacher. 50c, Children playing. $1, Boy and girl flying kite.

1979, Nov. 27 Litho. *Perf. 14*

519 A80 12c multicolored .20 .20
520 A80 28c multicolored .20 .20
521 A80 45c multicolored .30 .30
522 A80 50c multicolored .35 .35
523 A80 $1 multicolored .65 .65
Nos. 519-523 (5) 1.70 1.70

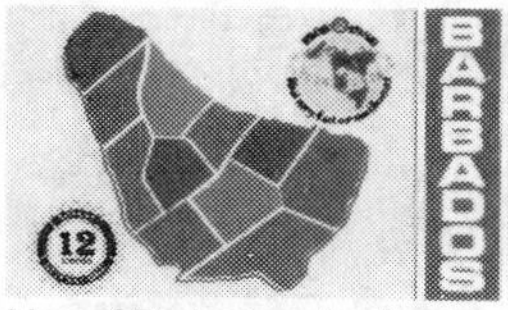

Map of Barbados, Anniversary Emblem — A81

Rotary Intl., 75th Anniv.: 28c, Map of district 404. 50c, 75th anniv. emblem. $1, Paul P. Harris, founder.

1980, Feb. 19 Litho. *Perf. 13½*

524 A81 12c multicolored .20 .20
525 A81 28c multicolored .20 .20
526 A81 50c multicolored .35 .35
527 A81 $1 multicolored .65 .65
Nos. 524-527 (4) 1.40 1.40

A82

A83

12c, Regiment volunteer, artillery company, 1909. 35c, Drum major. 50c, Sovereign's, regimental flags. $1, e, Women's corps.

Wmk. 373

1980, Apr. 8 Litho. *Perf. 14½*

528 A82 12c multicolored .20 .20
529 A82 35c multicolored .20 .20
530 A82 50c multicolored .35 .35
531 A82 $1 multicolored .65 .65
Nos. 528-531 (4) 1.40 1.40

Barbados Regiment, 75th anniv.

Souvenir Sheets

Wmk. 373

1980, May 6 Litho. *Perf. 14*

Early mailman, London 1980 emblem. The vignette is a different color for each stamp.

532 Sheet of 6 1.10 1.10
a.-f. A83 28c any single .20 .20
533 Sheet of 6 2.25 2.25
a.-f. A83 50c any single .35 .35

London 80 Intl. Stamp Exhib., May 6-14.

Underwater Scenes — A84

1980, Sept. 30 Litho. *Perf. 13½*

534 A84 12c multicolored .20 .20
535 A84 28c multicolored .25 .25
536 A84 50c multicolored .40 .40
537 A84 $1 multicolored .75 .75
a. Souvenir sheet of 4, #534-537 1.50 1.50
Nos. 534-537 (4) 1.60 1.60

Bathsheba Railroad Station — A85

1981, Jan. 13 Litho. *Perf. 14½*

538 A85 12c shown .20 .20
539 A85 28c Cab stand, The Green .20 .20
540 A85 45c Mule-drawn tram .30 .30
541 A85 70c Horse-drawn bus .50 .50
542 A85 $1 Fairchild St. railroad station .65 .65
Nos. 538-542 (5) 1.85 1.85

Visually Handicapped Girl at Typewriter — A86

1981, May 19 Litho. *Perf. 14*

543 A86 10c shown .20 .20
544 A86 25c Sign language alphabet, vert. .20 .20
545 A86 45c Blind people crossing street, vert. .30 .30
546 A86 $2.50 Baseball game 1.60 1.60
Nos. 543-546 (4) 2.30 2.30

International Year of the Disabled.

Royal Wedding Issue

Common Design Type

Wmk. 373

1981, July 22 Litho. *Perf. 13½*

547 CD331 28c Bouquet .20 .20
548 CD331 50c Charles .35 .35
549 CD331 $2.50 Couple 1.60 1.60
Nos. 547-549 (3) 2.15 2.15

4th Caribbean Arts Festival (CARIFESTA), July 19-Aug. 3 — A87

1981, Aug. 11 Litho. *Perf. 14½*

550 A87 15c Landship maneuver .20 .20
551 A87 20c Yoruba dancer .20 .20
552 A87 40c Tuk band .30 .30
553 A87 55c Frank Collymore (sculpture) .40 .40
554 A87 $1 Barbados Harbor (painting) .75 .75
Nos. 550-554 (5) 1.85 1.85

Hurricane Gladys, View from Apollo A88

1981, Sept. 29 Litho. *Perf. 14*

555 A88 35c Satellite view over Barbados .30 .30
556 A88 50c shown .40 .40
557 A88 60c Police watch .50 .50
558 A88 $1 Spotter plane .85 .85
Nos. 555-558 (4) 2.05 2.05

Harrison's Cave — A89

Perf. 14x14½

1981, Dec. 1 Litho. Wmk. 373

559 A89 10c Twin Falls .20 .20
560 A89 20c Rotunda Room Stream .20 .20
561 A89 55c Rotunda Room formation .35 .35
562 A89 $2.50 Cascade Pool 1.60 1.60
Nos. 559-562 (4) 2.35 2.35

Nos. 503, 505, 507 Surcharged

1982, Feb. 1 Photo. *Perf. 14*

563 A78 15c on 28c multi .20 .20
564 A78 40c on 45c multi .40 .40
565 A78 60c on 70c multi .60 .60
Nos. 563-565 (3) 1.20 1.20

Black Belly Sheep
A90

1982, Feb. 9 Litho.
566 A90 40c Ram .40 .40
567 A90 50c Ewe .50 .50
568 A90 60c Ewe, lambs .60 .60
569 A90 $1 Pair, map 1.00 1.00
Nos. 566-569 (4) 2.50 2.50

Bird Type of 1979
Wmk. 373

1982, Mar. 1 Photo. *Perf. 14*
570 A78 15c like #503 .20 .20
571 A78 40c like #506 .40 .40
572 A78 60c like #507 .60 .60
Nos. 570-572 (3) 1.20 1.20

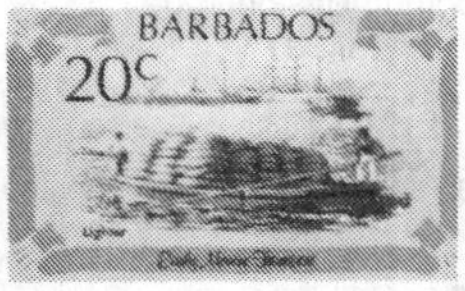

Early Marine Transport
A91

1982, Apr. 6 Litho. *Perf. 14½*
577 A91 20c Lighter .20 .20
578 A91 35c Rowboat .35 .35
579 A91 55c Speightstown schooner .55 .55
580 A91 $2.50 Inter-colonial schooner 2.50 2.50
Nos. 577-580 (4) 3.60 3.60

Visit of Pres. Ronald Reagan
A92

1982, Apr. 8 Litho. *Perf. 14*
581 A92 20c Barbados Flag, arms .20 .20
582 A92 20c US Flag, arms .20 .20
a. Pair, Nos. 581-582 .40 .40
583 A92 55c like #581 .55 .50
584 A92 55c like #582 .55 .50
a. Pair, Nos. 583-584 1.10 1.10
Nos. 581-584 (4) 1.50 1.40

Printed in sheets of 8 with gutter showing Pres. Reagan and Prime Minister Tom Adams.

Princess Diana Issue
Common Design Type

1982, July 1 Litho. *Perf. 14½*
585 CD333 20c Arms .20 .20
586 CD333 60c Diana .45 .45
587 CD333 $1.20 Wedding .90 .90
588 CD333 $2.50 Portrait 1.75 1.75
Nos. 585-588 (4) 3.30 3.30

Scouting Year — A93

Washington's 250th Birth Anniv. — A94

1982, Sept. 7 Wmk. 373 *Perf. 14*
589 A93 15c Helping woman .20 .20
590 A93 40c Sign, emblem, flag, horiz. .45 .45
591 A93 55c Religious service, horiz. .55 .55
592 A93 $1 Flags 1.00 1.00
Nos. 589-592 (4) 2.20 2.20

Souvenir Sheet
593 A93 $1.50 Laws 1.60 1.60

1982, Nov. 2 *Perf. 13½x13*
594 A94 10c Arms .20 .20
595 A94 55c Washington's house, Barbados .55 .55
596 A94 60c Taking command .60 .60
597 A94 $2.50 Taking oath 2.50 2.50
Nos. 594-597 (4) 3.85 3.85

A95

1983, Mar. 14 Litho. *Perf. 14*
598 A95 15c Map, globe .20 .20
599 A95 40c Beach .40 .40
600 A95 60c Sugar cane harvest .60 .60
601 A95 $1 Cricket game 1.00 1.00
Nos. 598-601 (4) 2.20 2.20

Commonwealth day.

Gulf Fritillary
A96

Perf. 13½x13
1983, Feb. 8 Litho. Wmk. 373
602 A96 20c shown .25 .25
603 A96 40c Monarch .45 .45
604 A96 55c Mimic .60 .60
605 A96 $2.50 Hanno Blue 3.00 3.00
Nos. 602-605 (4) 4.30 4.30

Manned Flight Bicentenary — A97

1983, June 14 Litho. *Perf. 14*
606 A97 20c US Navy dirigible .30 .30
607 A97 40c Douglas DC-3 .85 .85
608 A97 55c Vickers Viscount 1.25 1.25
609 A97 $1 Lockheed TriStar 2.50 2.50
Nos. 606-609 (4) 4.90 4.90

Nash 600, 1941
A98

1983, Aug. 9 Litho. *Perf. 14*
610 A98 25c shown .25 .25
611 A98 45c Dodge, 1938 .45 .45
612 A98 75c Ford Model AA, 1930 .75 .75
613 A98 $2.50 Dodge Four, 1918 2.50 2.50
Nos. 610-613 (4) 3.95 3.95

A99

A100

1983, Aug. 30 Litho. *Perf. 14*
614 A99 20c Players .20 .20
615 A99 65c Emblem, map .65 .65
616 A99 $1 Cup 1.00 1.00
Nos. 614-616 (3) 1.85 1.85

World Cup Table Tennis Championship.

1983, Nov. 1 *Perf. 14*

Christmas: 10c, 25c, Angel with lute, painting details. $2, The Virgin and Child, by Masaccio.

617 A100 10c multicolored .20 .20
618 A100 25c multicolored .25 .25

Souvenir Sheet
619 A100 $2 multicolored 2.00 2.00

Barbados Museum, Golden Jubilee
A101

Museum Paintings: 45c, by Richard Day. 75c, St. Ann's Garrison in Barbados by W.S. Hedges. $2.50, Needham's Point, Carlisle Bay.

1983, Nov. 1 *Perf. 14*
620 A101 45c multicolored .45 .45
621 A101 75c multicolored .75 .75
622 A101 $2.50 multicolored 2.50 2.50
Nos. 620-622 (3) 3.70 3.70

1984 Olympics, Los Angeles
A102

1984, Apr. 3 Litho. *Perf. 14*
623 A102 50c Track & field .50 .50
624 A102 65c Shooting .65 .65
625 A102 75c Sailing .75 .75
626 A102 $1 Bicycling 1.00 1.00
a. Souvenir sheet of 4, #623-626 3.00 3.00
Nos. 623-626 (4) 2.90 2.90

Lloyd's List Issue
Common Design Type

1984, Apr. 25 Litho. *Perf. 14½*
627 CD335 45c World map .45 .45
628 CD335 50c Bridgetown Harbor .50 .50
629 CD335 75c Philosopher .75 .75
630 CD335 $1 Sea Princess 1.00 1.00
Nos. 627-630 (4) 2.70 2.70

Souvenir Sheet

1984 UPU Congress
A103

1984, June 6 Litho. *Perf. 13½*
631 A103 $2 #213, UPU emblem 2.00 2.00

World Chess Fed., 60th Anniv.
A104

1984, Aug. 8 *Perf. 14x14½*
632 A104 25c Junior match .30 .30
633 A104 45c Knights .50 .50
634 A104 65c Queens .75 .75
635 A104 $2 Rooks 2.25 2.25
Nos. 632-635 (4) 3.80 3.80

Christmas — A105

1984, Oct. 24 Litho. *Perf. 14*
636 A105 50c Poinsettia .50 .50
637 A105 65c Snow-on-the-mountain .65 .65
638 A105 75c Christmas candle .75 .75
639 A105 $1 Christmas hope 1.00 1.00
Nos. 636-639 (4) 2.90 2.90

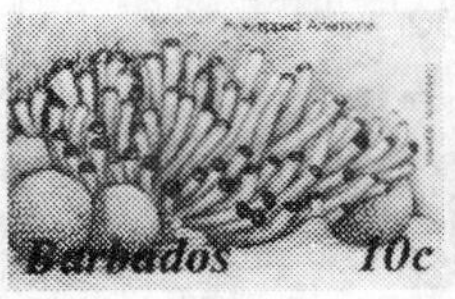

Marine Life
A106

1985 Litho. Wmk. 373 *Perf. 14*
640 A106 1c Bristle worm .20 .20
641 A106 2c Spotted trunk fish .20 .20
642 A106 5c Coney fish .20 .20
643 A106 10c Pink-tipped anemone .20 .20
645 A106 20c Christmas tree worm .30 .30
646 A106 25c Hermit crab .35 .35
648 A106 35c Animal flower .50 .50
649 A106 40c Vase sponge .60 .60
650 A106 45c Spotted moray .65 .65
651 A106 50c Ghost crab .75 .75
653 A106 65c Flaming tongue snail .95 .95
654 A106 75c Sergeant major fish 1.10 1.10
656 A106 $1 Caribbean warty anemone 1.50 1.50
657 A106 $2.50 Green turtle 3.75 3.75
658 A106 $5 Rock beauty 7.25 7.25
659 A106 $10 Elkhorn coral 15.00 15.00
Nos. 640-659 (16) 33.50 33.50

Issue dates: 10c, 20c, 25c, 50c, $2.50 and $5, Feb. 26; 5c, 35c, 40c, 65c and $10, Apr. 9; 1c, 2c, 45c, 75c and $1, May 7.
Exist inscribed "1987," etc.

1986 (?) Wmk. 384
640a A106 1c .20 .20
641a A106 2c .20 .20
642a A106 5c .20 .20
643a A106 10c .20 .20
645a A106 20c .30 .30
646a A106 25c .35 .35
648a A106 35c .45 .45
649a A106 40c .60 .60
650a A106 45c .65 .65
651a A106 50c .75 .75
653a A106 65c .95 .95
654a A106 75c 1.10 1.10
656a A106 $1 1.50 1.50
657a A106 $2.50 3.75 3.75
658a A106 $5 7.25 7.25
659a A106 $10 15.00 15.00
Nos. 640a-659a (16) 33.45 33.45

Some inscribed "1986." Also exist with "1987," "1988," and with no date.

Queen Mother 85th Birthday
Common Design Type

Perf. 14½x14
1985, June 7 Litho. Wmk. 384
660 CD336 25c At Buckingham Palace, 1930 .25 .25
661 CD336 65c With Lady Diana, 1981 .65 .65
662 CD336 75c At the docks .75 .75
663 CD336 $1 Holding Prince Henry 1.00 1.00
Nos. 660-663 (4) 2.65 2.65

Souvenir Sheet
664 CD336 $2 Opening the Garden Center, Syon House 2.00 2.00

Audubon Birth Bicentenary — A107

Illustrations of North American bird species. Nos. 666-668 vert.

Wmk. 373

1985, Aug. 6 Litho. *Perf. 14*
665 A107 45c Falco peregrinus .60 .60
666 A107 65c Dendroica discolor .90 .90
667 A107 75c Ardea herodias 1.10 1.10
668 A107 $1 Dendroica petechia 1.40 1.40
Nos. 665-668 (4) 4.00 4.00

Satellite Orbiting Earth
A108

1985, Sept. 10

669 A108 75c multicolored .75 .75

INTELSAT, Intl. Telecommunications Satellite Consortium, 20th anniv.

Royal Barbados Police, 150th Anniv. — A109

1985, Nov. 19

670 A109 25c Traffic Dept. .25 .25
671 A109 50c Police Band .50 .50
672 A109 65c Dog Force .65 .65
673 A109 $1 Mounted Police 1.00 1.00
Nos. 670-673 (4) 2.40 2.40

Souvenir Sheet

674 A109 $2 Band on parade, horiz. 2.00 2.00

Queen Elizabeth II 60th Birthday
Common Design Type

Designs: 25c, Age 2. 50c, Senate House opening, University College of the West Indies, Jamaica, 1953. 65c, With Prince Philip, Caribbean Tour, 1985. 75c, Banquet, state visit to Sao Paulo, Brazil, 1968. $2, Visiting Crown Agents, 1983.

Perf. 14x14½

1986, Apr. 21 Litho. Wmk. 384

675 CD337 25c scar, blk & sil .20 .20
676 CD337 50c ultra & multi .45 .45
677 CD337 65c green & multi .60 .60
678 CD337 75c violet & multi .70 .70
679 CD337 $2 rose vio & multi 1.90 1.90
Nos. 675-679 (5) 3.85 3.85

EXPO '86, Vancouver
A110

1986, May 2 *Perf. 14*

680 A110 50c Trans-Canada North Star .50 .50
681 A110 $2.50 Lady Nelson 2.50 2.50

AMERIPEX '86 — A111

1986, May 22 Wmk. 373

682 A111 45c No. 441 .45 .45
683 A111 50c No. 442 .50 .50
684 A111 65c No. 558 .65 .65
685 A111 $1 Nos. 583-584 1.00 1.00
Nos. 682-685 (4) 2.60 2.60

Souvenir Sheet

686 A111 $2 Statue of Liberty, NY Harbor 2.00 2.00

Statue of Liberty, cent.

Royal Wedding Issue, 1986
Common Design Type

Designs: 45c, Informal portrait. $1, Andrew in navy uniform.

Perf. 14½x14

1986, July 23 Litho. Wmk. 384

687 CD338 45c multicolored .45 .45
688 CD338 $1 multicolored 1.00 1.00

Electrification of Barbados, 75th Anniv.
A112

Designs: 10c, Transporting utility poles, 1923. 25c, Heathfield ladder, 1935, vert. 65c, Transport fleet, 1941. $2, Bucket truck, 1986, vert.

Wmk. 384

1986, Sept. 16 Litho. *Perf. 14*

689 A112 10c multicolored .20 .20
690 A112 25c multicolored .25 .25
691 A112 65c multicolored .65 .65
692 A112 $2 multicolored 2.00 2.00
Nos. 689-692 (4) 3.10 3.10

Christmas — A113

Church windows and flowers.

1986, Oct. 28 Wmk. 373

693 A113 25c Alpinia purpurata .25 .25
694 A113 50c Anthurium andraeanum .50 .50
695 A113 75c Heliconia rostrata .75 .75
696 A113 $2 Heliconia psittacorum 2.00 2.00
Nos. 693-696 (4) 3.50 3.50

Natl. Special Olympics, 10th Anniv. — A114

1987, Mar. 27 Wmk. 373 *Perf. 14*

697 A114 15c Shot put .20 .20
698 A114 45c Wheelchair race .45 .45
699 A114 65c Girl's long jump .65 .65
700 A114 $2 Emblem, creed 2.00 2.00
Nos. 697-700 (4) 3.30 3.30

CAPEX '87 — A115

1987, June 12

701 A115 25c Barn swallow .35 .35
702 A115 50c Yellow warbler .75 .75
703 A115 65c Audubon's shearwater .90 .90
704 A115 75c Black-whiskered vireo 1.10 1.10
705 A115 $1 Scarlet tanager 1.50 1.50
Nos. 701-705 (5) 4.60 4.60

Natl. Scouting Movement, 75th Anniv. — A116

1987, July 24 *Perf. 14x14½*

706 A116 10c Scout sign .20 .20
707 A116 25c Campfire .25 .25
708 A116 65c Merit badges, etc. .65 .65
709 A116 $2 Marching band 2.00 2.00
Nos. 706-709 (4) 3.10 3.10

Bridgetown Synagogue Restoration
A117

1987, Oct. 6 Wmk. 384 *Perf. 14½*

710 A117 50c Exterior .65 .65
711 A117 65c Interior .85 .85
712 A117 75c Ten Commandments, vert. 1.00 1.00
713 A117 $1 Marble laver, vert. 1.40 1.40
Nos. 710-713 (4) 3.90 3.90

Natl. Independence, 21st Anniv. — A118

E.W. Barrow (1920-87), Father of Independence
A119

Designs: 25c, Coat of arms and seal of the colony. 45c, Natl. flag and the Union Jack. 65c, Silver dollar and penny. $2, Old and new regimental flags and Queen Elizabeth's colors.

1987, Nov. 24 Litho. *Perf. 14½*

714 A118 25c multicolored .25 .25
715 A118 45c multicolored .45 .45
716 A118 65c multicolored .65 .65
717 A118 $2 multicolored 2.00 2.00
Nos. 714-717 (4) 3.35 3.35

Souvenir Sheet

718 A119 $1.50 multicolored 1.50 1.50

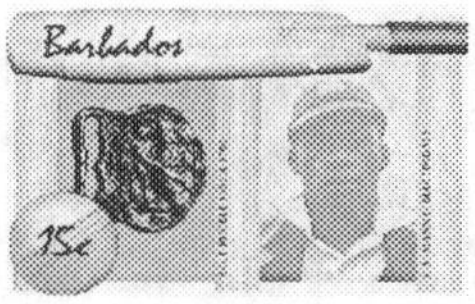

Cricket
A120

Bat, wicket posts, ball, 18th cent. belt buckle and batters: 15c, E.A. "Manny" Martindale. 45c, George Challenor. 50c, Herman C. Griffith. 75c, Harold Austin. $2, Frank Worrell.

1988 Litho. Wmk. 373 *Perf. 14*

719 A120 15c multicolored .20 .20
720 A120 45c multicolored .45 .45
720A A120 50c multicolored .50 .50
721 A120 75c multicolored .75 .75
722 A120 $2 multicolored 2.00 2.00
Nos. 719-722 (5) 3.90 3.90

The 50c was originally printed with the wrong photograph but was not issued. Copies of the error have appeared on the market.

Issued: No. 720A, July 11; others, June 6.

Barbados stamps can be mounted in the annual Scott Barbados supplement.

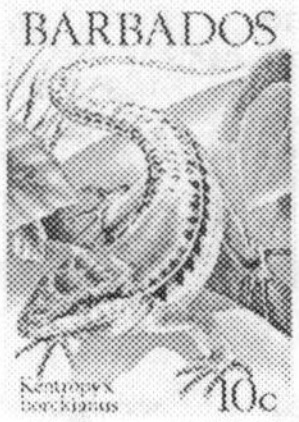

Lizards — A121

1988 Summer Olympics, Seoul — A122

1988, June 13

723 A121 10c Kentropyx borckianus .20 .20
724 A121 50c Hemidactylus mabouia .60 .60
725 A121 65c Anolis extremus .75 .75
726 A121 $2 Gymnophthalmus underwoodii 2.25 2.25
Nos. 723-726 (4) 3.80 3.80

Wmk. 373

1988, Aug. 2 Litho. *Perf. 14½*

727 A122 25c Cycling .25 .25
728 A122 45c Running .45 .45
729 A122 75c Swimming .75 .75
730 A122 $2 Yachting 2.00 2.00
a. Souvenir sheet of 4, #727-730 3.50 3.50
Nos. 727-730 (4) 3.45 3.45

Lloyds of London, 300th Anniv.
Common Design Type

Designs: 40c, Royal Exchange, 1774. 50c, Sugar mill (windmill), horiz. 65c, Container ship Author, horiz. $2, Sinking of the Titanic, 1912.

1988, Oct. 18 Litho. *Perf. 14*

731 CD341 40c multicolored .40 .40
732 CD341 50c multicolored .50 .50
733 CD341 65c multicolored .65 .65
734 CD341 $2 multicolored 2.00 2.00
Nos. 731-734 (4) 3.55 3.55

Harry Bayley Observatory, 25th Anniv.
A123

Designs: 25c, Observatory, crescent Moon, Venus and Harry Bayley. 65c, Observatory and constellations. 75c, Andromeda Galaxy and telescope. $2, Orion Constellation.

1988, Nov. 28 Wmk. 384 *Perf. 14½*

735 A123 25c multicolored .25 .25
736 A123 65c multicolored .65 .65
737 A123 75c multicolored .75 .75
738 A123 $2 multicolored 2.00 2.00
Nos. 735-738 (4) 3.65 3.65

Commercial Aviation, 50th Anniv. — A124

Designs: 25c, Caribbean Airline Liat BAe748. 65c, Pan American DC-8. 75c, Two British Airways Concordes, Grantley Adams Intl. Airport. $2, Two Caribbean Air Cargo Boeing 707-351c.

1989, Mar. 20 Litho. *Perf. 14*

739 A124 25c multicolored .25 .25
740 A124 65c multicolored .65 .65
741 A124 75c multicolored .75 .75
742 A124 $2 multicolored 2.00 2.00
Nos. 739-742 (4) 3.65 3.65

Parliament, 350th Anniv. — A125

1989, July 19 Litho. *Perf. 13½*

743 A125 25c Assembly chamber .25 .25
744 A125 50c The Speaker .50 .50
745 A125 75c Parliament, c. 1882 .75 .75
746 A125 $2.50 Queen in Parliament 2.50 2.50
Nos. 743-746 (4) 4.00 4.00

See No. 752.

Wildlife Preservation — A126

1989, Aug. 1 *Perf. 14x13½*

747 A126 10c Wild hare, vert. .20 .20
748 A126 50c Red-footed tortoise .80 .80
749 A126 65c Green monkey, vert. 1.00 1.00
750 A126 $2 Toad 3.00 3.00
Nos. 747-750 (4) 5.00 5.00

Souvenir Sheet

751 A126 $1 Mongoose, vert. 2.00 2.00

Parliament Anniv. Type of 1989
Souvenir Sheet

1989, Oct. 9 Wmk. 373 *Perf. 13½*

752 A125 $1 The Mace 1.00 1.00

35th Commonwealth Parliamentary Conf.

Wild Plants — A127

World Stamp Expo '89, Washington, DC — A128

1989-92 Wmk. 373 *Perf. 14½*

753 A127 2c Bread'n cheese .20 .20
754 A127 5c Scarlet cordia .20 .20
755 A127 10c Columnar cactus .20 .20
756 A127 20c Spiderlily .20 .20
757 A127 25c Rock balsam .25 .25
758 A127 30c Hollyhock .30 .30
758A A127 35c Red sage .35 .35
759 A127 45c Yellow shak-shak .45 .45
760 A127 50c Whitewood .50 .50
761 A127 55c Bluebell .55 .55
762 A127 65c Prickly sage .65 .65
763 A127 70c Seaside samphire .70 .70
764 A127 80c Flat-hand dildo .80 .80
764A A127 90c Herringbone .90 .90
765 A127 $1.10 Lent tree 1.10 1.10
766 A127 $2.50 Rodwood 2.50 2.50
767 A127 $5 Cowitch 5.00 5.00
768 A127 $10 Maypole 10.00 10.00
Nos. 753-768 (18) 24.85 24.85

Issue dates: 35c, 90c, June 9, 1992 (inscribed 1991). Others, Nov. 1.

Nos. 754-756, 763, 765 exist inscribed "1991."

For overprints see Nos. 788-790.

1990 Litho. Wmk. 384

753a A127 2c .20 .20
754a A127 5c .20 .20
755a A127 10c .20 .20
756a A127 20c .20 .20
757a A127 25c .25 .25
759a A127 45c .40 .40
760a A127 50c .45 .45
762a A127 65c .60 .60
766a A127 $2.50 2.25 2.25
767a A127 $5 4.50 4.50
768a A127 $10 9.00 9.00
Nos. 753a-768a (11) 18.25 18.25

Inscribed 1990.

1989, Nov. 17 Wmk. 384 *Perf. 14*

Water sports.

769 A128 25c Water skiing .25 .25
770 A128 50c Yachting .50 .50
771 A128 65c Scuba diving .65 .65
772 A128 $2.50 Surfing 2.50 2.50
Nos. 769-772 (4) 3.90 3.90

Horse Racing A129

Wmk. 373

1990, May 3 Litho. *Perf. 14*

773 A129 25c Bugler, jockeys .25 .25
774 A129 45c Parade ring .45 .45
775 A129 75c In the straight .75 .75
776 A129 $2 Winner, vert. 2.00 2.00
Nos. 773-776 (4) 3.45 3.45

Barbados No. 2 — A130

Stamps on stamps: No. 778, Barbados #61. 65c, Barbados #73. $2.50, Barbados #121. No. 781a, Great Britain #1. No. 781b, Barbados #108.

1990, May 3

777 A130 25c shown .25 .25
778 A130 50c multicolored .50 .50
779 A130 65c multicolored .65 .65
780 A130 $2.50 multicolored 2.50 2.50
Nos. 777-780 (4) 3.90 3.90

Souvenir Sheet

781 Sheet of 2 1.00 1.00
a.-b. A130 50c any single .50 .50

Stamp World London '90.

Queen Mother, 90th Birthday
Common Design Types

1990, Aug. 8 Wmk. 384 *Perf. 14x15*

782 CD343 75c At age 23 .75 .75

Perf. 14½

783 CD344 $2.50 Engagement portrait, 1923 2.50 2.50

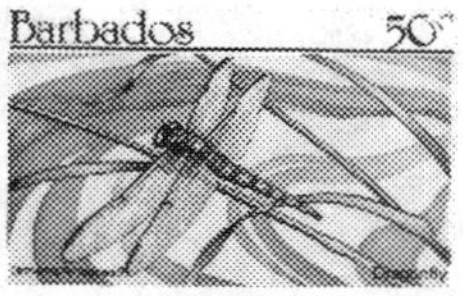

Insects A131

Wmk. 373

1990, Oct. 16 Litho. *Perf. 14*

784 A131 50c Dragonfly .50 .50
785 A131 65c Black hardback beetle .65 .65
786 A131 75c Green grasshopper .75 .75
787 A131 $2 God-horse 2.00 2.00
Nos. 784-787 (4) 3.90 3.90

Nos. 757, 764 and 766 Overprinted

VISIT OF
HRH THE
PRINCESS ROYAL
OCTOBER 1990

1990, Nov. 21 *Perf. 14½*

788 A127 25c on No. 757 .25 .25
789 A127 80c on No. 764 .80 .80
790 A127 $2.50 on No. 766 2.50 2.50
Nos. 788-790 (3) 3.55 3.55

Christmas — A132

1990, Dec. 4 *Perf. 14*

791 A132 20c Christmas star .20 .20
792 A132 50c Nativity scene .50 .50
793 A132 $1 Stained glass window 1.00 1.00
794 A132 $2 Angel 2.00 2.00
Nos. 791-794 (4) 3.70 3.70

Yellow Warbler A133

1991, Mar. 4

795 A133 10c shown .25 .25
796 A133 20c Male, female, nest .55 .55
797 A133 45c Female, chicks 1.25 1.25
798 A133 $1 Male, fledgling 2.75 2.75
Nos. 795-798 (4) 4.80 4.80

World Wildlife Fund.

Fishing A134

Perf. 13½x14, 14x13½

1991, June 18 Litho. Wmk. 373

799 A134 5c Daily catch, vert. .20 .20
800 A134 50c Line fishing .50 .50
801 A134 75c Cleaning fish .75 .75
802 A134 $2.50 Game fishing, vert. 2.50 2.50
Nos. 799-802 (4) 3.95 3.95

Freemasonry in Barbados, 250th Anniv. — A135

Designs: 25c, Masonic Building, Bridgetown. 65c, Compass and square. 75c, Royal arch jewel. $2.50, Columns, apron and centenary badge.

1991, Sept. 17 *Perf. 14*

803 A135 25c multicolored .25 .25
804 A135 65c multicolored .65 .65
805 A135 75c multicolored .75 .75
806 A135 $2.50 multicolored 2.50 2.50
Nos. 803-806 (4) 4.15 4.15

Butterflies A136

1991, Nov. 15 Wmk. 384

807 A136 20c Polydamus swallowtail .25 .25
808 A136 50c Long-tailed skipper, vert. .65 .65
809 A136 65c Cloudless sulphur .85 .85
810 A136 $2.50 Caribbean buckeye, vert. 3.25 3.25
Nos. 807-810 (4) 5.00 5.00

Souvenir Sheet

811 A136 $4 Painted lady 6.00 6.00

Phila Nippon '91.

Independence, 25th Anniv. — A137

Governor-General Dame Nita Barrow and: 10c, Students in classrom. 25c, Barbados Workers Union headquarters. 65c, Building industry. 75c, Agriculture. $1, Inoculations given at health clinic. $2.50, Gordon Greenidge, Desmond Haynes, cricket players (no portrait).

1991, Nov. 20 Wmk. 373

812 A137 10c multicolored .20 .20
813 A137 25c multicolored .25 .25
814 A137 65c multicolored .65 .65
815 A137 75c multicolored .75 .75
816 A137 $1 multicolored 1.00 1.00
Nos. 812-816 (5) 2.85 2.85

Souvenir Sheet

817 A137 $2.50 multi, vert. 2.40 2.50

Easter — A138

Wmk. 384

1992, Apr. 7 Litho. *Perf. 14*

818 A138 35c Christ carrying cross .35 .35
819 A138 70c Christ on cross .70 .70
820 A138 90c Christ taken down from cross .95 .95
821 A138 $3 Christ risen 3.00 3.00
Nos. 818-821 (4) 5.00 5.00

Flowering Trees A139

Perf. 14x13½

1992, June 9 Litho. Wmk. 373

822 A139 10c Cannon ball .20 .20
823 A139 30c Golden shower .30 .30
824 A139 80c Frangipani .80 .80
825 A139 $1.10 Flamboyant 1.10 1.10
Nos. 822-825 (4) 2.40 2.40

Orchids A140

Designs: 55c, Epidendrum "Costa Rica." 65c, Cattleya guttaca. 70c, Laeliacattleya "Splashing Around." $1.40, Phalaenopsis "Kathy Saegert."

1992, Sept. 8 *Perf. 13½x14*

826 A140 55c multicolored .55 .55
827 A140 65c multicolored .65 .65
828 A140 70c multicolored .70 .70
829 A140 $1.40 multicolored 1.40 1.40
Nos. 826-829 (4) 3.30 3.30

For overprints see Nos. 838-841.

Transport and Tourism A141

Designs: 5c, Mini Moke, Gun Hill Signal Station, St. George. 35c, Tour bus, Bathsheba Beach, St. Joseph. 90c, BWIA McDonnell Douglas MD 83, Grantley Adams Airport. $2,

Cruise ship Festivale, deep water harbor, Bridgetown.

Wmk. 373

1992, Dec. 15 Litho. *Perf. 14½*

830 A141 5c multicolored .20 .20
831 A141 35c multicolored .35 .35
832 A141 90c multicolored .90 .90
833 A141 $2 multicolored 2.00 2.00
Nos. 830-833 (4) 3.45 3.45

Cacti and Succulents — A142

Wmk. 373

1993, Feb. 9 Litho. *Perf. 14*

834 A142 10c Barbados gooseberry .20 .20
835 A142 35c Night-blooming cereus .40 .40
836 A142 $1.40 Aloe 1.40 1.40
837 A142 $2 Scrunchineel 2.00 2.00
Nos. 834-837 (4) 4.00 4.00

Nos. 826-829 Ovptd. "WORLD ORCHID CONFERENCE 1993" on 2 or 4 lines

Perf. 13½x14

1993, Apr. 1 Litho. Wmk. 373

838 A140 55c on #826 multi .55 .55
839 A140 65c on #827 multi .65 .65
840 A140 70c on #828 multi .70 .70
841 A140 $1.40 on #829 multi 1.40 1.40
Nos. 838-841 (4) 3.30 3.30

Royal Air Force, 75th Anniv.

Common Design Type

Designs: 10c, Hawker Hunter. 30c, Handley Page Victor. 70c, Hawker Typhoon. $3, Hawker Hurricane.

No. 846a, Armstrong Whitworth Siskin 3a. b, Supermarine S.6B. c, Supermarine Walrus. d, Hawker Hart.

1993, Apr. 1 *Perf. 14*

842 CD350 10c multicolored .20 .20
843 CD350 30c multicolored .30 .30
844 CD350 70c multicolored .70 .70
845 CD350 $3 multicolored 3.00 3.00
Nos. 842-845 (4) 4.20 4.20

Souvenir Sheet

846 CD350 50c Sheet of 4, #a.-d. 2.00 2.00

Cannon A143

Designs: 5c, 18-pounder Culverin, 1625, Denmark Fort. 45c, 6-pounder Commonwealth gun, 1649-1660, St. Ann's Fort. $1, 9-pounder Demi-culverin, 1691, The Main Guard. $2.50, 32-pounder Demi-cannon, 1693-94, Charles Fort.

Wmk. 373

1993, June 8 Litho. *Perf. 13*

847 A143 5c multicolored .20 .20
848 A143 45c multicolored .45 .45
849 A143 $1 multicolored 1.00 1.00
850 A143 $2.50 multicolored 2.50 2.50
Nos. 847-850 (4) 4.15 4.15

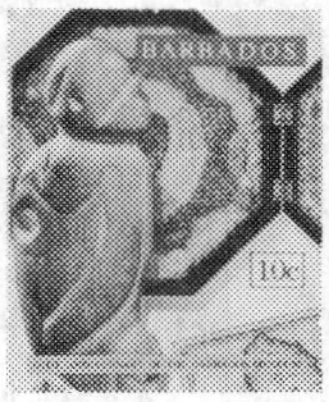

Barbados Museum, 60th Anniv. — A144

Designs: 10c, Shell box, carved figure. 75c, Map, print of three people. 90c, Silver cup, print of soldier. $1.10, Map.

Wmk. 373

1993, Sept. 14 Litho. *Perf. 14*

851 A144 10c multicolored .20 .20
852 A144 75c multicolored .75 .75
853 A144 90c multicolored .95 .95
854 A144 $1.10 multicolored 1.10 1.10
Nos. 851-854 (4) 3.00 3.00

A145

A146

Prehistoric Aquatic Reptiles: a, Plesiosaurus. b, Ichthyosaurus. c, Elasmosaurus. d, Mosasaurus. e, Archelon. Continuous design.

Wmk. 373

1993, Oct. 28 Litho. *Perf. 13*

855 A145 90c Strip of 5, #a.-e. 5.00 5.00

Wmk. 384

1994, Jan. 11 Litho. *Perf. 14*

856 A146 10c Cricket .20 .20
857 A146 35c Motor racing .35 .35
858 A146 50c Golf .50 .50
859 A146 70c Run Barbados 10k .70 .70
860 A146 $1.40 Swimming 1.40 1.40
Nos. 856-860 (5) 3.15 3.15

Sports & tourism.

No. 822 exists inscribed "1996"; Nos. 872-877, 880, 885 "1997."

Migratory Birds A147

Wmk. 373

1994, Feb. 18 Litho. *Perf. 14*

861 A147 10c Whimbrel .20 .20
862 A147 35c American golden plover .35 .35
863 A147 70c Ruddy turnstone .70 .70
864 A147 $3 Tricolored heron 3.00 3.00
Nos. 861-864 (4) 4.25 4.25

Hong Kong '94.

1st UN Conference of Small Island Developing States — A148

1994, Apr. 25 *Perf. 14x14½*

865 A148 10c Bathsheba .20 .20
866 A148 65c Pico Tenneriffe .65 .65
867 A148 90c Ragged Point Lighthouse .90 .90
868 A148 $2.50 Consett Bay 2.50 2.50
Nos. 865-868 (4) 4.25 4.25

Order of the Caribbean Community — A149

First award recipients: No. 869, Sir Shridath Ramphal, statesman, Guyana. No. 870, Derek Walcott, writer, Nobel Laureate, St. Lucia. No. 871, William Demas, economist, Trinidad and Tobago.

Wmk. 373

1994, July 4 Litho. *Perf. 14*

869 A149 70c multicolored .70 .70
870 A149 70c multicolored .70 .70
871 A149 70c multicolored .70 .70
Nos. 869-871 (3) 2.10 2.10

Ships A150

Designs: 5c, Dutch Flyut, 1695. 10c, Geestport, 1994. 25c, HMS Victory, 1805. 30c, Royal Viking Queen, 1994. 35c, HMS Barbados, 1945. 45c, Faraday, 1924. 50c, USCG Hamilton, 1974. 65c, HMCS Saguenay, 1939. 70c, Inanda, 1928. 80c, HMS Rodney, 1944. 90c, USS John F. Kennedy, 1982. $1.10, William & John, 1627. $5, USCG Champlain, 1931. $10, Artist, 1877.

Wmk. 373

1994, Aug. 16 Litho. *Perf. 14*

872 A150 5c multicolored .20 .20
873 A150 10c multicolored .20 .20
874 A150 25c multicolored .25 .25
875 A150 30c multicolored .30 .30
876 A150 35c multicolored .35 .35
877 A150 45c multicolored .45 .45
878 A150 50c multicolored .50 .50
879 A150 65c multicolored .65 .65
880 A150 70c multicolored .70 .70
881 A150 80c multicolored .80 .80
882 A150 90c multicolored .90 .90
883 A150 $1.10 multicolored 1.10 1.10
884 A150 $5 multicolored 5.00 5.00
885 A150 $10 multicolored 10.00 10.00
Nos. 872-885 (14) 21.40 21.40

Nos. 872-885 are not dated. Nos. 872-877, 880, 882, 885 exist inscribed "1997." Nos. 872-873, 877, 880 exist inscribed "1998." Nos. 873, 877, 885 exist inscribed "1999."

1996 Wmk. 384

872a A150 5c .20 .20
873a A150 10c .20 .20
875a A150 30c .30 .30
876a A150 35c .35 .35
877a A150 45c .45 .45
878a A150 50c .50 .50
879a A150 65c .65 .65
880a A150 70c .70 .70
881a A150 80c .80 .80
882a A150 90c .90 .90
883a A150 $1.10 1.10 1.10
884a A150 $5 5.00 5.00
Nos. 872a-884a (12) 11.15 11.15

Inscribed (1996."

Issued: Nos. 875a-877a, 879a-882a, 9/1/96; others, May.

West India Regiment, Bicent. — A151

Designs: 30c, 2nd Regiment, 1860. 50c, 4th Regiment, Light Company, 1795. 70c, 3rd Regiment, drum major, 1860. $1, 5th Regiment, undress, working dress, 1815. $1.10, 1st, 2nd Regiments, Review Order, 1874.

Perf. 15x14

1995, Feb. 21 Litho. Wmk. 373

886 A151 30c multicolored .30 .30
887 A151 50c multicolored .50 .50
888 A151 70c multicolored .70 .70
889 A151 $1 multicolored 1.00 1.00
890 A151 $1.10 multicolored 1.10 1.10
Nos. 886-890 (5) 3.60 3.60

End of World War II

Common Design Type

10c, Barbadians serving in the Middle East. 35c, Lancaster bomber. 55c, Spitfire fighter. $2.50, SS Davisian sunk off Barbados, July 10, 1940.

$2, Reverse of War Medal 1939-45.

Wmk. 373

1995, May 8 Litho. *Perf. 14*

891 CD351 10c multicolored .20 .20
892 CD351 35c multicolored .30 .30
893 CD351 55c multicolored .55 .55
894 CD351 $2.50 multicolored 2.50 2.50
Nos. 891-894 (4) 3.55 3.55

Souvenir Sheet

895 CD352 $2 multicolored 2.50 2.50

Combermere School, 300th Anniv. — A152

Designs: 5c, Scouting, Combermere 1st Barbados, 1912. 20c, Violin, sheet music. 35c, Cricket, Sir Frank Worrell, vert. 90c, Frank Collymore, #553. $3, Landscape.

Wmk. 373

1995, July 25 Litho. *Perf. 14*

896 A152 5c multicolored .20 .20
897 A152 20c multicolored .20 .20
898 A152 35c multicolored .35 .35
899 A152 $3 multicolored 3.00 3.00
Nos. 896-899 (4) 3.75 3.75

Souvenir Sheet

900 Sheet of 5, #896-899, 900a 4.50 4.50
a. A152 90c multicolored .90 .90

UN, 50th Anniv.

Common Design Type

Designs: 30c, Douglas C-124 Globemaster, Korea 1950-53. 45c, Royal Navy Sea King helicopter. $1.40, Wessex helicopter, UNFICYP, Cyprus 1964. $2, Gazelle helicopter, UNFICYP, Cyprus 1964.

Wmk. 373

1995, Oct. 24 Litho. *Perf. 14*

901 CD353 30c multicolored .30 .30
902 CD353 45c multicolored .45 .45
903 CD353 $1.40 multicolored 1.40 1.40
904 CD353 $2 multicolored 2.00 2.00
Nos. 901-904 (4) 4.15 4.15

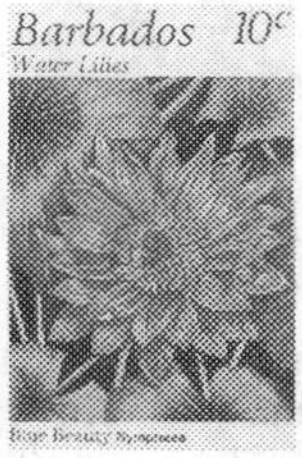

Water Lilies — A153

Wmk. 373

1995, Dec. 19 Litho. *Perf. 14*

905 A153 10c Blue beauty .20 .20
906 A153 65c White water lily .65 .65
907 A153 70c Sacred lotus .70 .70
908 A153 $3 Water hyacinth 3.00 3.00
Nos. 905-908 (4) 4.55 4.55

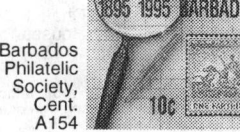

Barbados Philatelic Society, Cent. A154

Magnifiying glass, tongs, and: 10c, #70. 55c, #109. $1.10, #148. $1.40, #192.

Wmk. 373

1996, Jan. 30 Litho. *Perf. 14*

909 A154 10c multicolored .20 .20
910 A154 55c multicolored .55 .55
911 A154 $1.10 multicolored 1.10 1.10
912 A154 $1.40 multicolored 1.40 1.40
Nos. 909-912 (4) 3.25 3.25

A155

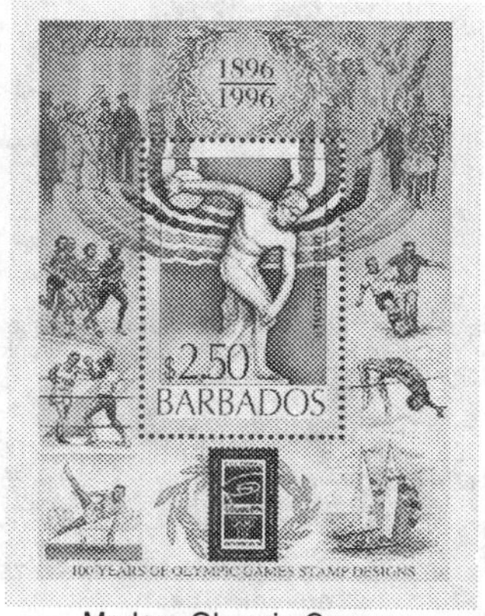

Modern Olympic Games, Cent. — A156

1996, Apr. 2 Litho. *Perf. 14*

913 A155 20c Soccer .20 .20
914 A155 30c Relay race .30 .30
915 A155 55c Basketball .55 .55
916 A155 $3 Rhythmic gymnastics 3.00 3.00
Nos. 913-916 (4) 4.05 4.05

Souvenir Sheet

917 A156 $2.50 Discus thrower 2.50 2.50

Olymphilex '96 (No. 917).

CAPEX '96 A157

Transportation links with Canada: 10c, Canadian Airlines DC10. 90c, Air Canada Boeing 767. $1, Air Canada 320 Airbus. $1.40, Canadian Airlines Boeing 767.

Wmk. 373

1996, June 7 Litho. *Perf. 14*

918 A157 10c multicolored .20 .20
919 A157 90c multicolored .90 .90
920 A157 $1 multicolored 1.00 1.00
921 A157 $1.40 multicolored 1.40 1.40
Nos. 918-921 (4) 3.50 3.50

Chattel Houses A158

House features: 35c, Shed roof, lattice work. 70c, Pedimented porch, carved wooden trim. $1.10, Decorative, elegant porch. $2, Hip roof, bell pelmet window hoods.

1996, June 7

922 A158 35c multicolored .35 .35
923 A158 70c multicolored .70 .70
924 A158 $1.10 multicolored 1.10 1.10
925 A158 $2 multicolored 2.00 2.00
Nos. 922-925 (4) 4.15 4.15

Christmas A159

Children's paintings: 10c, Going to Church on Christmas morning. 30c, The Tuk Band. 55c, Caroling on Christmas. $2.50, Decorated houses.

Wmk. 373

1996, Nov. 12 Litho. *Perf. 14½*

926 A159 10c multicolored .20 .20
927 A159 30c multicolored .30 .30
928 A159 55c multicolored .55 .55
929 A159 $2.50 multicolored 2.50 2.50
Nos. 926-929 (4) 3.55 3.55

UNICEF, 50th anniv.

Hong Kong '97 — A160

Dogs: 10c, Doberman pinscher. 30c, German shepherd. 90c, Japanese akita. $3, Irish red setter.

Perf. 14x14½

1997, Feb. 12 Litho. Wmk. 373

930 A160 10c multicolored .20 .20
931 A160 30c multicolored .30 .30
932 A160 90c multicolored .90 .90
933 A160 $3 multicolored 3.00 3.00
Nos. 930-933 (4) 4.40 4.40

Visit of US Pres. Clinton to Barbados, May 1997 A161

35c, Barbados flag, arms. 90c, US flag, arms.

1997, May 9 Litho. *Perf. 14*

934 A161 35c multicolored .35 .35
935 A161 90c multicolored .90 .90
a. Pair, #934-935 1.25 1.25

Issued in sheets of 8 stamps + 2 labels.

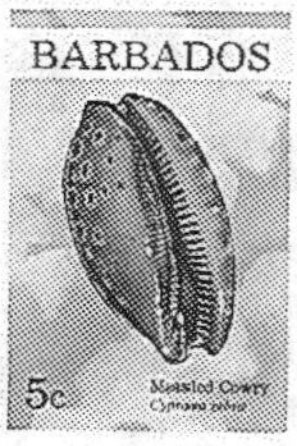

Shells — A162

Designs: 5c, Measled cowry. 35c, Trumpet triton. 90c, Scotch bonnet. $2, West Indian murex.

$2.50, Sea bottom with miscellaneous shells.

1997, July 29 Litho. *Perf. 14*

936 A162 5c multicolored .20 .20
937 A162 35c multicolored .35 .35
938 A162 90c multicolored .90 .90
939 A162 $2 multicolored 1.90 1.90
Nos. 936-939 (4) 3.35 3.35

Souvenir Sheet

940 A162 $2.50 multicolored 2.40 2.40

Public Library, 150th Anniv. A163

Designs: 10c, Lucas manuscripts. 30c, Storytelling to children. 70c, Bookmobile. $3, Information technology.

1997, Oct. 1 Litho. *Perf. 14*

941 A163 10c multicolored .20 .20
942 A163 30c multicolored .30 .30
943 A163 70c multicolored .70 .70
944 A163 $3 multicolored 3.10 3.10
Nos. 941-944 (4) 4.30 4.30

Fruit — A164

1997, Dec. 16 Litho. *Perf. 14½*

945 A164 35c Barbados cherry .35 .35
946 A164 40c Sugar apple .40 .40
947 A164 $1.15 Soursop 1.10 1.10
948 A164 $1.70 Papaya 1.60 1.60
Nos. 945-948 (4) 3.45 3.45

Souvenir Sheet

Sir Grantley Adams, Birth Cent. — A165

a, Natl. Arms. b, Grantley Adams. c, Natl. flag.

1998, Apr. 27 Litho. *Perf. 13*

949 A165 $1 Sheet of 3, #a.-c. 3.00 3.00

Diana, Princess of Wales (1961-97)

Common Design Type of 1998

Portraits wearing: a, Blue hat. b, Red suit jacket. c, Tiara. d, Black and white.

1998, May *Perf. 14½x14*

950 CD355 $1.15 Sheet of 4, #a.-d. 6.50 6.50

Organization of American States, 50th Anniv. — A166

Designs: 15c, Beach during storm, beach during sunny day. $1, Dancers in native costumes. $2.50, Judge reading at podium, statue of justice.

1998, June 30 Litho. *Perf. 14*

951 A166 15c multicolored .20 .20
952 A166 $1 multicolored .95 .95
953 A166 $2.50 multicolored 2.50 2.50
Nos. 951-953 (3) 3.65 3.65

University of West Indies, 50th Anniv. A167

1998, July 20 *Perf. 14½*

954 A167 40c Frank Worrell Hall .40 .40
955 A167 $1.15 Graduation 1.10 1.10
956 A167 $1.40 Plaque, hummingbird 1.40 1.40
957 A167 $1.75 Quadrangle 1.75 1.75
Nos. 954-957 (4) 4.65 4.65

Tourism A168

1998, Dec. 1 Litho. *Perf. 14*

958 A168 10c Catamaran, vert. .20 .20
959 A168 45c Jolly Roger .45 .45
960 A168 70c Atlantis submarine .70 .70
961 A168 $2 MV Harbor Master, vert. 2.00 2.00
Nos. 958-961 (4) 3.35 3.35

Australia '99, World Stamp Expo — A169

Illustration reduced.

1999, Mar. 19 Litho. *Perf. 14*

962 A169 $4 Sailboat 3.50 3.50

Piping Plover A170

World Wildlife Fund: 10c, Juvenile in shallow water. 45c, Female with eggs. 50c, Fledglings in nest, male, female. 70c, Male.

1999, Apr. 27 Litho. *Perf. 14*

963 A170 10c multicolored .20 .20
964 A170 45c multicolored .45 .45
965 A170 50c multicolored .50 .50
966 A170 70c multicolored .70 .70
Nos. 963-966 (4) 1.85 1.85

1st Manned Moon Landing, 30th Anniv.

Common Design Type

Designs: 40c, Astronaut training. 45c, First stage separation. $1.15, Lunar module. $1.40, Docking with service module.

$2.50, Looking at earth from moon.

Perf. 14x13¾

1999, July 20 Litho. Wmk. 384

967 CD357 40c multicolored .40 .40
968 CD357 45c multicolored .45 .45
969 CD357 $1.15 multicolored 1.10 1.10
970 CD357 $1.40 multicolored 1.40 1.40
Nos. 967-970 (4) 3.35 3.35

Souvenir Sheet

Perf. 14

971 CD357 $2.50 multicolored 2.50 2.50

No. 971 contains one 40mm circular stamp.

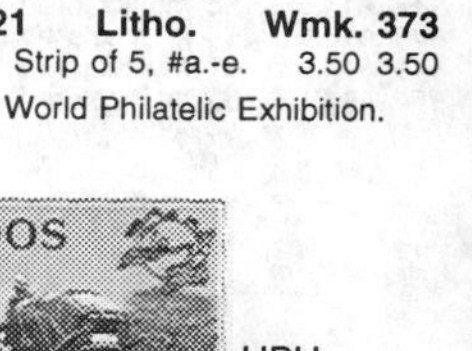

Rabbits A171

Designs: a, Rabbit running. b, Rabbit profile. c, Rabbit nursing young. d, Two rabbits leaping. e, Two rabbits at rest.

Perf. 14x14½

1999, Aug. 21 Litho. Wmk. 373

972 A171 70c Strip of 5, #a.-e. 3.50 3.50

China 1999 World Philatelic Exhibition.

UPU, 125th Anniv. A172

1999, Oct. 11 Litho. *Perf. 14*

973 A172 10c Mail coach .20 .20
974 A172 45c Mail van .45 .45
975 A172 $1.75 Airplane 1.75 1.75
976 A172 $2 Computers 2.00 2.00
Nos. 973-976 (4) 4.40 4.40

SEMI-POSTAL STAMPS

No. 73 Surcharged in Red

Kingston Relief Fund. 1d.

Perf. 14

1907, Jan. 25 Typo. Wmk. 2

B1	A8	1p on 2p sl & org	1.75	*2.50*
a.		No period after 1d	15.00	*17.50*
b.		Inverted surcharge	1.75	*2.50*
c.		Inverted surcharge, no period after 1d	15.00	*17.50*
d.		Double surcharge	750.00	
e.		Dbl. surch., both invtd.	750.00	

Catalogue values for unused stamps in this section, from this point to the end of the section, are for Never Hinged items.

No. 406 Surcharged

28c + 4c

ST. VINCENT RELIEF FUND

1979, May 29 Photo. Wmk. 314

B2	A56	28c + 4c on 35c multi	.30	.30

The surtax was for victims of the eruption of Mt. Soufrière.

POSTAGE DUE STAMPS

Catalogue values for unused stamps in this section are for Never Hinged items.

D1

1934-47 Typo. Wmk. 4 *Perf. 14*

J1	D1	½p green ('35)	.75	.75
J2	D1	1p black	1.40	1.40
J3	D1	3p dk car rose ('47)	22.50	22.50
		Nos. J1-J3 (3)	24.65	24.65

A 2nd die of the 1p was introduced in 1947.

1950

J4	D1	1c green	.20	.20
J5	D1	2c black	.40	.40
J6	D1	6c carmine rose	1.50	*1.75*
		Nos. J4-J6 (3)	2.10	*2.35*

Values are for 1953 chalky paper printing.

Wmk. 4a (error)

J4a	D1	1c green	140.00
J5a	D1	2c black	190.00
J6a	D1	6c carmine rose	110.00
		Nos. J4a-J6a (3)	440.00

1965, Aug. 3 Wmk. 314 *Perf. 14*

J7	D1	1c green	.30	.30
J8	D1	2c black	.35	.35
J9	D1	6c carmine rose	.65	.65
a.		Wmk. sideways, perf. 14x13½ ('74)	2.25	2.25
		Nos. J7-J9 (3)	1.30	1.30

Issued: No. J9a, 2/4/74.

Wmk. 314 Sideways

1974, Dec. 4 *Perf. 13x13½*

J8b	D1	2c	1.50	1.50
J9b	D1	6c	1.50	1.50

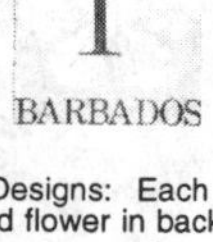

D2

Designs: Each stamp shows different stylized flower in background.

Perf. 13½x14

1976, May 12 Litho. Wmk. 373

J10	D2	1c brt pink & mag	.20	.20
J11	D2	2c lt & dk vio blue	.20	.20
J12	D2	5c yellow & brown	.20	.20
J13	D2	10c lilac & purple	.20	.20
J14	D2	25c yel green & dk grn	.25	.25
J15	D2	$1 rose & red	.90	.90
		Nos. J10-J15 (6)	1.95	1.95

1985, July *Perf. 15x14*

J10a	D2	1c	.20	.20
J11a	D2	2c	.20	.20
J12a	D2	5c	.20	.20
J13a	D2	10c	.20	.20
J14a	D2	25c	.25	.25
		Nos. J10a-J14a (5)	1.05	1.05

WAR TAX STAMP

No. 118 Overprinted **WAR TAX**

1917 Wmk. 3 *Perf. 14*

MR1	A12	1p carmine	.20	.20
a.		Imperf., pair	*4,000.*	

BARBUDA

bär-ˈbüd-ə

LOCATION — Northernmost of the Leeward Islands, West Indies
GOVT. — Dependency of Antigua
AREA — 63 sq. mi.
POP. — 1,500 (1995 est.)
See Antigua.

12 Pence = 1 Shilling

Catalogue values for unused stamps in this country are for Never Hinged items, beginning with Scott 12 in the regular postage section, and Scott B1 in the semi-postal section.

Watermark

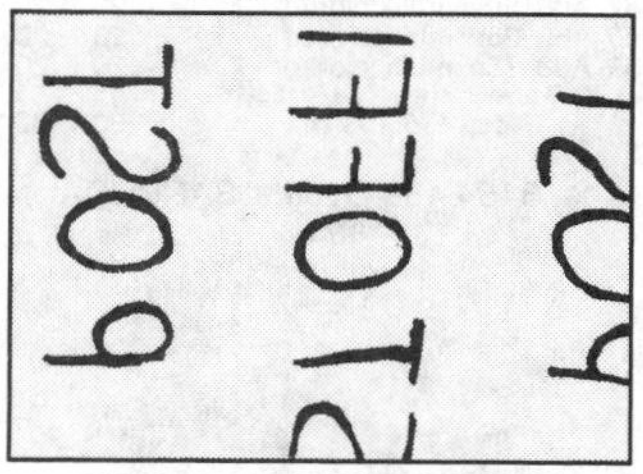

Wmk. 380- "POST OFFICE"

Leeward Islands Stamps and Types of 1912-22 Overprinted in Black or Red

BARBUDA

Die II

For description of dies I and II, see back of this section of the Catalogue.

1922, July 13 Wmk. 4 *Perf. 14*

1	A5	½p green	1.50	*4.50*
2	A5	1p rose red	1.50	*4.50*
3	A5	2p gray	1.60	*4.00*
4	A5	2½p ultramarine	1.60	*4.50*
5	A5	6p vio & red vio	4.00	*10.00*
6	A5	2sh vio & ultra, *bl*	15.00	*30.00*
7	A5	3sh green & violet	32.50	*50.00*
8	A5	4sh blk & scar (R)	35.00	*50.00*

Wmk. 3

9	A5	3p violet, *yel*	1.50	*4.75*
10	A5	1sh blk, *emer* (R)	3.25	*4.75*
11	A5	5sh grn & red, *yel*	95.00	*125.00*
		Nos. 1-11 (11)	192.45	*292.00*

Catalogue values for unused stamps in this section, from this point to the end of the section, are for Never Hinged items.

Map — B1

Fish — B2

1968-70 Litho. Unwmk. *Perf. 14*

12	B1	½c blk, salmon pink & red brn	.20	.20
13	B1	1c blk, org & brt org	.20	.20
14	B1	2c blk, brt pink & brt rose	.20	.20
15	B1	3c blk, yel & org yel	.20	.20
16	B1	4c blk, lt grn & brt grn	.20	.20
17	B1	5c blk, bl grn & brt bl grn	.20	.20
18	B1	6c blk, lt lil & red lil	.20	.20
19	B1	10c blk, lt bl & dk bl	.20	.20
20	B1	15c blk, dl grn & grn	.20	.20
21	B2	20c Great barracuda	.75	*1.25*
22	B2	25c Great amberjack	.30	.25
23	B2	35c French angelfish	.40	.40
24	B2	50c Porkfish	.55	.55
25	B2	75c Striped parrotfish	.80	.80
26	B2	$1 Longspine squirrelfish	1.10	1.10
27	B2	$2.50 Catalufa	2.75	2.75
28	B2	$5 Blue chromis	5.00	*6.00*
		Nos. 12-28 (17)	13.45	14.90

Issued: ½c-15c, 11/19/68; 20c, 7/22/70; 25c-75c, 2/5/69; others, 3/6/69.

For surcharge see No. 80.

1968 Summer Olympics, Mexico City — B3

Designs: 25c, Running, Aztec calendar stone. 35c, High jumping, Aztec statue. 75c, Yachting, Aztec lion mask. $1, Soccer, Aztec carved stone.

1968, Dec. 20

29	B3	25c multicolored	.20	.20
30	B3	35c multicolored	.30	.25
31	B3	75c multicolored	.50	.40
		Nos. 29-31 (3)	1.00	.85

Souvenir Sheet

32	B3	$1 multicolored	2.00	2.00

The Ascension, by Orcagna — B4

1969, Mar. 24

33	B4	25c blue & black	.20	.20
34	B4	35c dp carmine & blk	.20	.20
35	B4	75c violet & black	.25	.25
		Nos. 33-35 (3)	.65	.65

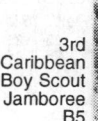

Easter.

3rd Caribbean Boy Scout Jamboree B5

1969, Aug. 7

36	B5	25c Flag ceremony	.45	.45
37	B5	35c Campfire	.60	.60
38	B5	75c Rowing	.75	.75
		Nos. 36-38 (3)	1.80	1.80

The Sistine Madonna, by Raphael — B6

1969, Oct. 20

39	B6	½c multicolored	.20	.20
40	B6	25c multicolored	.20	.20
41	B6	35c multicolored	.20	.20
42	B6	75c multicolored	.25	.25
		Nos. 39-42 (4)	.85	.85

Christmas.

English Monarchs — B7

#43, William I. #44, William II. #45, Henry I. #46, Stephen. #47, Henry II. #48, Richard I. #49, John. #50, Henry III. #51, Edward I. #52, Edward II. #53, Edward III. #54, Richard II. #55, Henry IV. #56, Henry V. #57, Henry VI. #58, Edward IV. #59, Edward V. #60, Richard III. #61, Henry VII. #62, Henry VIII. #63, Edward VI. #64, Lady Jane Grey. #65, Mary I. #66, Elizabeth I. #67, James I. #68, Charles I. #69, Charles II. #70, James II. #71, William III. #72, Mary II. #73, Anne. #74, George I. #75, George II. #76, George III. #77, George IV. #78, William IV. #79, Victoria.

1970-71 *Perf. 14½x14*

43-79	B7	35c Set of 37	3.25	3.25

Issued: 1970, #43, 2/16; #44, 3/2; #45, 3/16; #46, 4/4; #47, 4/15; #48, 5/1; #49, 5/15; #50, 6/1; #51, 6/15; #52, 7/1; #53, 7/15; #54, 8/1; #55, 8/15; #56, 9/1; #57, 9/15; #58, 10/1; #59, 10/15; #60, 11/2; #61, 11/16; #62, 12/1; #63, 12/15.

1971: #64, 1/2; #65, 1/15; #66, 2/1; #67, 2/15; #68, 3/1; #69, 3/15; #70, 4/1; #71, 4/15; #72, 5/1; #73, 5/15; #74, 6/1; #75, 6/15; #76, 7/1; #77, 7/15; #78, 8/2; #79, 8/16.

See Nos. 622-627 for other Monarchs.

No. 12 Surcharged

20c

1970, Feb. 26 *Perf. 14*

80	B1	20c on 1/2c multicolored	.20	.20

Easter — B8

1970, Mar. 16

81	B8	25c Carrying Cross	.20	.20
82	B8	35c Descent from cross	.20	.20
83	B8	75c Crucifixion	.25	.25
a.		Strip of 3, #81-83	.70	.70

Charles Dickens B9

1970, July 10

84 B9 20c Oliver Twist .20 .20
85 B9 75c Old Curiosity Shop .30 .30

Christmas — B10

Designs: 20c, Madonna of the Meadow, by Giovanni Bellini. 50c, Madonna, Child and Angels from Wilton Diptych. 75c, Nativity, by Piero della Francesca.

1970, Oct. 15

86 B10 20c multicolored .20 .20
87 B10 50c multicolored .20 .20
88 B10 75c multicolored .20 .20
Nos. 86-88 (3) .60 .60

British Red Cross, Cent. B11

1970, Dec. 21

89 B11 20c Patient in wheelchair, vert. .20 *.25*
90 B11 35c shown .30 *.35*
91 B11 75c Child care .50 *.60*
Nos. 89-91 (3) 1.00 *1.20*

Easter — B12

Details from the Mond Crucifixion, by Raphael.

1971, Apr. 7

92 B12 35c Angel .20 *.25*
93 B12 50c Crucifixion .25 *.30*
94 B12 75c Angel, diff. .30 *.40*
a. Strip of 3, #92-94 1.00 *1.00*

Martello Tower B13

1971, May 10

95 B13 20c shown .20 .20
96 B13 25c Sailboats .20 .20
97 B13 50c Hotel bungalows .20 .20
98 B13 75c Government House, mystery stone .20 .20
Nos. 95-98 (4) .80 .80

Christmas — B14

Paintings: ½c, The Granduca Madonna, by Raphael. 35c, The Ansidei Madonna, by Raphael. 50c, The Virgin and Child, by Botticelli. 75c, The Madonna of the Trees, by Bellini.

1971, Oct. 4

99 B14 ½c multicolored .20 .20
100 B14 35c multicolored .20 .20
101 B14 50c multicolored .25 .25
102 B14 75c multicolored .30 .30
Nos. 99-102 (4) .95 .95

A set of four stamps for Durer (20c, 35c, 50c, 75c) was not authorized.

All stamps are types of Antigua or overprinted on stamps of Antigua unless otherwise specified. Many of the "BARBUDA" overprints are vertical.

Nos. 321-322 Ovptd. "BARBUDA"

1973, Nov. 14 ***Perf. 13½***

103 A65 35c multicolored 1.50 1.50
104 A65 $2 multicolored 7.00 7.00

Nos. 313-315a Ovptd. in Red "BARBUDA"

1973, Nov. 26 ***Perf. 13½x14***

105 A63 20c multicolored .20 .20
106 A63 35c multicolored .20 .20
107 A63 75c multicolored .30 .30
Nos. 105-107 (3) .70 .70

Souvenir Sheet

108 Sheet of 4, #105-107, 108a 3.00 3.00
a. A63 5c multicolored

Carnival, 1973.

Nos. 307, 309, 311, 311a Ovptd. "BARBUDA"

Perf. 14x13½

1973, Nov. 26 **Wmk. 314**

109 A53 ½c multicolored .20 .20
110 A53 20c multicolored .20 .20
111 A53 75c multicolored .45 .45
Nos. 109-111 (3) .85 .85

Souvenir Sheet

112 Sheet of 5, #109-111, 112a-112b + label 3.25 3.25
a. A53 10c multicolored
b. A53 35c multicolored

Nos. 241a, 242-243, 244a, 245-248, 249a, 250-254, 255a, 256, 256a, 257 Ovptd. "BARBUDA"

Wmk. 314 Sideways, Upright

1973-74 ***Perf. 14***

113 A51 ½c multicolored .20 .20
114 A51 1c multicolored .20 .20
115 A51 2c multicolored .20 .20
116 A51 3c multicolored .20 .20
117 A51 4c multicolored .20 .20
118 A51 5c multicolored .20 .20
119 A51 6c multicolored .20 .20
120 A51 10c multicolored .20 .20
121 A51 15c multicolored .25 .25
122 A51 20c multicolored .25 .25
123 A51 25c multicolored .30 .30
124 A51 35c multicolored .40 .40
125 A51 50c multicolored .50 .50
126 A51 75c multicolored .50 .50
127 A51 $1 multicolored .55 .55
128 A51 $2.50 multicolored 1.25 1.25
a. Wmk. upright 9.25 9.25
129 A51 $5 multicolored 1.90 1.90
Nos. 113-129 (17) 7.50 7.50

Issue dates: ½c, 3c, 15c, $1, $2.50, Feb. 18, 1974. Others, Nov. 26.

Nos. 316-320a Ovptd. in Silver or Red "BARBUDA"

Perf. 14½

1973, Dec. 11 **Photo.** **Unwmk.**

130 A64 3c multicolored .20 .20
131 A64 5c multicolored .20 .20
132 A64 20c multicolored .20 .20
133 A64 35c multicolored (R) .25 .25
134 A64 $1 multicolored (R) .30 .30
Nos. 130-134 (5) 1.15 1.15

Souvenir Sheet

135 Sheet of 5 + label 7.50 7.50
a. A64 35c multicolored (S)
b. A64 $1 multicolored (S)

No. 135 contains Nos. 130-132, 135a-135b.

Nos. 323-324a Ovptd. "BARBUDA"

1973, Dec. 16 **Litho.** ***Perf. 13½***

136 A65 35c multicolored .25 .25
137 A65 $2 multicolored 1.25 1.25
a. Souvenir sheet of 2, #136-137 6.00 6.00

Nos. 325-328 Ovptd. "BARBUDA"

1974, Feb. 18 **Wmk. 314**

138 A66 5c multicolored .20 .20
139 A66 20c multicolored .20 .20
140 A66 35c multicolored .20 .20
141 A66 75c multicolored .30 .30
Nos. 138-141 (4) .90 .90

Nos. 329-333 Ovptd. "BARBUDA"

1974, May 1 ***Perf. 14x13½***

142 A53 ½c multicolored .20 .20
143 A53 10c multicolored .20 .20
144 A53 20c multicolored .25 .25
145 A53 35c multicolored .35 .35
146 A53 75c multicolored .60 .60
Nos. 142-146 (5) 1.60 1.60

No. 333a exists with overprint.

Nos. 334-340 Ovptd. Type "a" or "b" and No. 340 "BARBUDA" in Red

BARBUDA
15 SEPT.
1874 G.P.U.
a

BARBUDA
13 JULY 1922
b

1974, July 15 **Unwmk.** ***Perf. 14½***

Se-tenant Pairs Overprinted Type "a" on Left Stamp, Type "b" on Right Stamp

148 A67 ½c multicolored .20 .20
149 A67 1c multicolored .20 .20
150 A67 2c multicolored .20 .20
151 A67 5c multicolored .40 .40
152 A67 20c multicolored 1.25 1.25
153 A67 35c multicolored 2.25 2.25
154 A67 $1 multicolored 6.50 6.50
Nos. 148-154 (7) 11.00 11.00

Souvenir Sheet

Perf. 13

155 Sheet of 7 + label 7.00 7.00
a. A67 ½c multicolored .20 .20
b. A67 1c multicolored .20 .20
c. A67 2c multicolored .20 .20
d. A67 5c multicolored .20 .20
e. A67 20c multicolored 1.00 1.00
f. A67 35c multicolored 1.50 2.00
g. A67 $1 multicolored 3.50 3.50

UPU, cent.

Nos. 341-344a Ovptd. "BARBUDA"

1974, Aug. 14 **Wmk. 314** ***Perf. 14***

156 A68 5c multicolored .20 .20
157 A68 20c multicolored .20 .20
158 A68 35c multicolored .20 .20
159 A68 75c multicolored .20 .20
a. Souvenir sheet of 4, #156-159 1.25 1.25
Nos. 156-159 (4) .80 .80

Nos. 345-348a Ovptd. "BARBUDA" and

World Cup Soccer Championships — B16

Various soccer plays.

1974, Sept. 2 **Unwmk.** ***Perf. 15, 14***

160 A69 5c multicolored .20 .20
161 A69 35c multicolored .20 .20
162 B16 35c multicolored .20 .20
163 A69 75c multicolored .20 .20
164 A69 $1 multicolored .25 .25
a. Souv. sheet of 4, #160-161, 163-164 + 2 labels, perf. 13½ 2.25 2.25
165 B16 $1.20 multicolored .25 .25
166 B16 $2.50 multicolored .45 .45
a. Souv. sheet of 3, #162, 165-166 2.00 2.00
Nos. 160-166 (7) 1.75 1.75

UPU, Cent. — B17

1974, Sept. 30 ***Perf. 14x13½***

167 B17 35c Ship letter, 1833 .20 .20
168 B17 $1.20 #1, 2 on FDC .25 .25
169 B17 $2.50 Airplane, map .50 .50
a. Souvenir sheet of 3, #167-169 2.50 2.50
Nos. 167-169 (3) .95 .95

Greater Amberjack B18

1974-75 ***Perf. 14x14½, 14½x14***

170 B18 ½c Oleander, rose bay .20 .20
171 B18 1c Blue petrea .20 .20
172 B18 2c Poinsettia .20 .20
173 B18 3c Cassia tree .20 .20
174 B18 4c shown .20 .20
175 B18 5c Holy Trinity School .20 .20
176 B18 6c Snorkeling .20 .20
177 B18 10c Pilgrim Holiness Church .20 .20
178 B18 15c New Cottage Hospital .20 .20
179 B18 20c Post Office & Treasury .20 .20
180 B18 25c Island jetty & boats .20 .20
181 B18 35c Martello Tower .28 .30

Size: 39x25mm

Perf. 14

182 B18 50c Warden's House .40 .40
183 B18 75c Inter-island air service .60 .60
184 B18 $1 Tortoise .80 .80

Size: 45x29mm

Perf. 13½x14

185 B18 $2.50 Spiny lobster 2.00 2.00
186 B18 $5 Frigate birds 4.00 4.00
a. Perf. 14x15

Size: 34x47mm

187 B18 $10 Hibiscus 8.00 8.00
Nos. 170-187 (18) 18.28 18.30

Nos. 170-173, 180, 187 vert.

Issued: 4c, 5c, 6c, 10c, 15c, 20c, 25c, 35c, 75c, 10/15/74; ½c, 1c, 2c, 3c, 50c, $1, $2.50, #186, 1/6/75; #186a, 7/24/75; $10, 9/19/75.

For overprints see Nos. 213-214.

Nos. 349-352a Ovptd. "BARBUDA" in Red and

Winston Churchill, Birth Cent. — B19

1974 ***Perf. 14½, 13½x14***

188 A70 5c multicolored .20 .20
189 B19 5c Making broadcast .20 .20
190 A70 35c multicolored .35 .35
191 B19 35c Portrait .20 .20
192 A70 75c multicolored .75 .75
193 B19 75c Painting .30 .30
194 A70 $1 multicolored 1.00 1.00
a. Souv. sheet of 4, #188, 190, 192, 194 5.00 5.00
195 B19 $1 Victory sign .40 .40
a. Souv. sheet of 4, #189, 191, 193, 195 2.50 2.50
Nos. 188-195 (8) 3.40 3.40

Issue dates: Nos. 188, 190, 192, 194, Oct. 15, others, Nov. 20. For overprints see Nos. 213-214.

Nos. 353-360a Ovptd. "BARBUDA"

1974, Nov. 25 ***Perf. 14½***

196 A71 ½c multicolored .20 .20
197 A71 1c multicolored .20 .20
198 A71 2c multicolored .20 .20
199 A71 3c multicolored .20 .20
200 A71 5c multicolored .20 .20
201 A71 20c multicolored .20 .20
202 A71 35c multicolored .20 .20
203 A71 75c multicolored .20 .20
a. Souv. sheet of 4, #200-203, perf. 13½ 1.25 1.25
Nos. 196-203 (8) 1.60 1.60

Nos. 369-373a Ovptd. "BARBUDA"

1975, Mar. 17

204 A72 5c multicolored .20 .20
205 A72 15c multicolored .30 .30
206 A72 35c multicolored .50 .50
207 A72 50c multicolored .75 .75

208 A72 $1 multicolored 1.25 1.25
a. Souv. sheet of 5, #204-208 + label, perf. 13½x14 3.50 3.50
Nos. 204-208 (5) 3.00 3.00

Stamps from No. 208a are 43x28mm.

Battle of the Saints B20

1975, May 30 ***Perf. 13½x14***
209 B20 35c shown .75 .75
210 B20 50c Two ships 1.25 1.25
211 B20 75c Ships firing 1.50 1.50
212 B20 95c Sailors abandoning ship 2.00 2.00
Nos. 209-212 (4) 5.50 5.50

Barbuda No. 186a Ovptd.

a

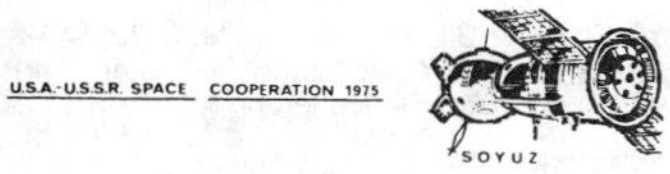

b

1975, July 2 ***Perf. 14x15***
213 B18 (a) $5 multicolored 4.00 4.00
214 B18 (b) $5 multicolored 4.00 4.00

Overprint "a" is in 1st and 3rd vertical rows, "b" 2nd and 4th. The 5th row has no overprint. This can be collected se-tenant either as Nos. 213, 214 or 213, 214 and 186a.

Military Uniforms — B21

Designs: 35c, Officer of 65th Foot, 1763. 50c, Grenadier, 27th Foot, 1701-1710. 75c, Officer of 21st Foot, 1793-1796. 95c, Officer, Royal Regiment of Artillery, 1800.

1975, Sept. 17 ***Perf. 14***
215 B21 35c multicolored .50 .50
216 B21 50c multicolored .75 .75
217 B21 75c multicolored 1.25 1.25
218 B21 95c multicolored 1.50 1.50
Nos. 215-218 (4) 4.00 4.00

Barbuda Nos. 189, 191, 193, 195 Ovptd.
"30th ANNIVERSARY / UNITED NATIONS / 1945 - 1975"

1975, Oct. 24 ***Perf. 13½x14***
219 B19 5c multicolored .20 .20
220 B19 35c multicolored .20 .20
221 B19 75c multicolored .25 .25
222 B19 $1 multicolored .35 .35
Nos. 219-222 (4) 1.00 1.00

Nos. 394-401a Ovptd. "BARBUDA"

1975, Nov. 17 ***Perf. 14***
223 A77 ½c multicolored .20 .20
224 A77 1c multicolored .20 .20
225 A77 2c multicolored .20 .20
226 A77 3c multicolored .20 .20
227 A77 5c multicolored .20 .20
228 A77 10c multicolored .20 .20
229 A77 35c multicolored .20 .20
230 A77 $2 multicolored .20 .20
a. Souvenir sheet of 4, #227-230 2.50 2.50
Nos. 223-230 (8) 1.60 1.60

Nos. 402-404 Ovptd. "BARBUDA"

1975, Dec. 15 ***Perf. 14***
231 A78 5c multicolored 1.10 1.10
232 A78 35c multicolored 2.25 2.25
233 A78 $2 multicolored 4.00 4.00
Nos. 231-233 (3) 7.35 7.35

American Revolution, Bicent. B22

Details from Surrender of Cornwallis at Yorktown, by Trumbull: No. 234a, British officers. b, Gen. Benjamin Lincoln. c, Washington, Allied officers.

The Battle of Princeton: No. 235a, Infantry. b, Battle. c, Cannon fire.

Surrender of Burgoyne at Saratoga by Trumbull: No. 236a, Mounted officer. b, Washington, Burgoyne. c, American officers.

Signing the Declaration of Independence, by Trumbull: No. 237a, Delegates to Continental Congress. b, Adams, Sherman, Livingston, Jefferson and Franklin. c, Hancock, Thomson, Read, Dickinson, and Rutledge. Strips of 3 have continuous designs.

1976, Mar. 8 ***Perf. 13½x13***
234 B22 15c Strip of 3, #a.-c. .30 .30
235 B22 35c Strip of 3, #a.-c. 1.00 1.00
d. Souvenir sheet, #234-235 2.00 2.00
236 B22 $1 Strip of 3, #a.-c. 1.50 1.50
237 B22 $2 Strip of 3, #a.-c. 2.50 2.50
d. Souvenir sheet, #236-237 10.00 10.00

See Nos. 244-247.

Birds B23

1976, June 30 ***Perf. 13½x14***
238 B23 35c Bananaquits 1.25 .75
239 B23 50c Blue-hooded euphonia 1.60 1.00
240 B23 75c Royal tern 1.60 1.00
241 B23 95c Killdeer 2.25 1.10
242 B23 $1.25 Glossy cowbird 2.25 1.10
243 B23 $2 Purple gallinule 2.75 1.25
Nos. 238-243 (6) 11.70 6.20

Barbuda #234-237 With Inscription Added at Top Across the Three Stamps in Blue
"H.M. Queen Elizabeth" "Royal Visit 6th July 1976" "H.R.H. Duke of Edinburgh"

1976, Aug. 12 ***Perf. 13½x14***
Size: 38x31mm
244 B22 15c Strip of 3, #a.-c. .30 .30
245 B22 35c Strip of 3, #a.-c. .50 .50
d. Souvenir sheet of 2, #244-245 1.10 1.10
246 B22 $1 Strip of 3, #a.-c. .75 .75
247 B22 $2 Strip of 3, #a.-c. 1.25 1.25
d. Souvenir sheet, #246-247 7.00 7.00

Nos. 244-247 are perforated on outside edges; imperf. vertically within.

Nos. 448-452 Ovptd. "BARBUDA"

1976, Dec. 2 ***Perf. 14***
248 A85 8c multicolored .20 .20
249 A85 10c multicolored .20 .20
250 A85 15c multicolored .20 .20
251 A85 50c multicolored .20 .20
252 A85 $1 multicolored .20 .20
Nos. 248-252 (5) 1.00 1.00

Nos. 431-437 Ovptd. "BARBUDA"

1976, Dec. 28 ***Perf. 15***
253 A82 ½c yellow & multi .20 .20
254 A82 1c purple & multi .20 .20
255 A82 2c emerald & multi .20 .20
256 A82 15c brt blue & multi .20 .20
257 A82 30c olive & multi .20 .20
258 A82 $1 orange & multi .20 .20
259 A82 $2 red & multi .30 .30
a. Souv. sheet of 4, #256-259, perf. 13½ 3.00 3.00
Nos. 253-259 (7) 1.50 1.50

Telephone, Cent. — B24

1977, Jan. 31 ***Perf. 14***
260 B24 75c shown .20 .20
261 B24 $1.25 Satellite dish, television .30 .30
262 B24 $2 Satellites in earth orbit .50 .50
a. Souv. sheet of 3, #260-262, perf. 15 2.50 2.50
Nos. 260-262 (3) 1.00 1.00

Coronation of Queen Elizabeth II, 25th Anniv. B25

Designs: Nos. 263a, St. Margaret's Church, Westminster. b, Westminster Abbey entrance. c, Westminster Abbey.

Nos. 264a, Riders on horseback. b, Coronation coach. c, Team of horses. Strips of 3 have continuous designs.

1977, Feb. 7 ***Perf. 13½x13***
263 B25 75c Strip of 3, #a.-c. .50 .50
264 B25 $1.25 Strip of 3, #a.-c. .75 .75

Souvenir Sheet

265 B25 Sheet of 6 1.75 1.75

Nos. 263a-264c se-tenant with labels. No. 265 contains Nos. 263a-264c with silver borders.

Nos. 405-422 Ovptd. "BARBUDA"

1977, Apr. 4 ***Perf. 15***
266 A79 ½c multicolored .20 .20
267 A79 1c multicolored .30 .20
268 A79 2c multicolored .30 .20
269 A79 3c multicolored .30 .20
270 A79 4c multicolored .30 .20
271 A79 5c multicolored .30 .20
272 A79 6c multicolored .30 .20
273 A79 10c multicolored .30 .20
274 A79 15c multicolored .30 .20
275 A79 20c multicolored .30 .25
276 A79 25c multicolored .30 .25
277 A79 35c multicolored .35 .30
278 A79 50c multicolored .40 .40
279 A79 75c multicolored .40 .40
280 A79 $1 multicolored .50 .50

Perf. 13½x14
281 A80 $2.50 multicolored 1.25 1.25
282 A80 $5 multicolored 2.25 2.25
283 A80 $10 multicolored 4.00 4.00
Nos. 266-283 (18) 12.35 11.40

For overprints see Nos. 506-516.

Nos. 459-464 Ovptd. "BARBUDA"

1977, Apr. 4 ***Perf. 13½x14, 12***
284 A87 10c multicolored .20 .20
285 A87 30c multicolored .25 .25
286 A87 50c multicolored .30 .30
287 A87 90c multicolored .50 .50
288 A87 $2.50 multicolored 1.00 1.00
Nos. 284-288 (5) 2.25 2.25

Souvenir Sheet

289 A87 $5 multicolored 3.00 3.00

A booklet of self-adhesive stamps contains one pane of six rouletted and die cut 50c stamps in design of 90c (silver overprint), and one pane of one die cut $5 (gold overprint) in changed colors. Panes have marginal inscriptions.

For overprints see Nos. 312-317.

Nos. 465-471a Ovptd. "BARBUDA"

1977, June 13 ***Perf. 14***
290 A88 ½c multicolored .20 .20
291 A88 1c multicolored .20 .20
292 A88 2c multicolored .20 .20
293 A88 10c multicolored .20 .20
294 A88 30c multicolroed .45 .45
295 A88 50c multicolored .75 .75
296 A88 $2 multicolored 2.00 2.00
a. Souvenir sheet of 3, #294-296 4.00 4.00
Nos. 290-296 (7) 4.00 4.00

Overprint is slightly smaller on No. 296a.

Nos. 472-476a Ovptd. "BARBUDA"

1977, Aug. 12
297 A89 10c multicolored .20 .20
298 A89 30c multicolored .25 .25
299 A89 50c multicolored .40 .40
300 A89 90c multicolored .45 .45
301 A89 $1 multicolored .50 .50
a. Souvenir sheet of 4, #298-301 2.00 2.00
Nos. 297-301 (5) 1.80 1.80

Royal Visit B26

1977, Oct. 27 ***Perf. 14½***
302 B26 50c Royal yacht Britannia .25 .25
303 B26 $1.50 Jubliee emblem .40 .40
304 B26 $2.50 Flags .60 .60
a. Souvenir sheet of 3, #302-304 2.00 2.00
Nos. 302-304 (3) 1.25 1.25

Nos. 483-489 Ovptd. "BARBUDA"

1977, Nov. 15 ***Perf. 14***
305 A90 ½c multicolored .20 .20
306 A90 1c multicolored .20 .20
307 A90 2c multicolored .20 .20
308 A90 8c multicolored .20 .20
309 A90 10c multicolored .20 .20
310 A90 25c multicolored .20 .20
311 A90 $2 multicolored .30 .30
a. Souvenir sheet of 4, #308-311 2.00 2.00
Nos. 305-311 (7) 1.50 1.50

Nos. 477-482 Ovptd. "BARBUDA" in Black

1977, Dec. 20 ***Perf. 12***
312 A87 10c multicolored .20 .20
313 A87 30c multicolored .20 .20
314 A87 50c multicolored .30 .30
315 A87 90c multicolored .50 .50
316 A87 $2.50 multicolored .75 .75
Nos. 312-316 (5) 1.95 1.95

Nos. 312-316 exist with blue overprint.

1977, Nov. 28 ***Perf. 13½x14***
312a A87 10c multicolored .20 .20
313a A87 30c multicolored .30 .30
314a A87 50c multicolored .40 .40
315a A87 90c multicolored .50 .50
316a A87 $2.50 multicolored .75 .75
Nos. 312a-316a (5) 2.15 2.15

Souvenir Sheet

317 A87 $5 multicolored 3.75 3.75

Overprint of Nos. 312a-316a differs from that on Nos. 312-316.

Anniversaries — B27

First navigable airships, 75th anniv: No. 318a, Zeppelin LZ1. b, German Naval airship L31. c, Graf Zeppelin. d, Gondola on military airship.

Soviet space program, 20th anniv: No. 319a, Sputnik, 1957. b, Vostok rocket, 1961. c, Voskhod rocket, 1964. d, Space walk, 1965.

Lindbergh's Atlantic crossing, 50th anniv: No. 320a, Fueling for flight. b, New York take-off. c, Spirit of St. Louis. d, Welcome in England.

Coronation of Queen Elizabeth II, 25th anniv: No. 321a, Lion of England. b, Unicorn of Scotland. c, Yale of Beaufort. d, Falcon of Plantagenets.

Rubens, 400th birth anniv: No. 322a, Two lions. b, Daniel in the Lion's Den. c, Two lions lying down. d, Lion at Daniel's feet. Block of 4 has continuous design.

1977, Dec. 29 ***Perf. 14½x14***
318 B27 75c Block of 4, #a.-d. 1.25 1.25
319 B27 95c Block of 4, #a.-d. 1.50 1.50
320 B27 $1.25 Block of 4, #a.-d. 1.60 1.60
321 B27 $2 Block of 4, #a.-d. 2.50 2.50
322 B27 $5 Block of 4, #a.-d. 5.00 5.00
e. Min. sheet, #318-322 + 4 labels 12.00 12.00
Nos. 318-322 (5) 11.85 11.85

Nos. 490-494a Ovptd. "BARBUDA"

1978, Feb. 15 ***Perf. 13x13½***
323 A91 10c multicolored .20 .20
324 A91 15c multicolored .20 .20
325 A91 50c multicolored .25 .25
326 A91 90c multicolored .35 .35
327 A91 $2 multicolored .50 .50
a. Souv. sheet of 4, #324-327, perf. 14 2.00 2.00
Nos. 323-327 (5) 1.50 1.50

Pieta, by Michelangelo — B28

Works by Michelangelo: 95c, Holy Family. $1.25, Libyan Sibyl. $2, The Flood.

1978, Mar. 23 *Perf. 13½x14*

328 B28 75c multicolored .25 .25
329 B28 95c multicolored .30 .30
330 B28 $1.25 multicolored .40 .40
331 B28 $2 multicolored .60 .60
a. Souvenir sheet of 4, #328-331 2.50 2.50
Nos. 328-331 (4) 1.55 1.55

Nos. 495-502 Ovptd. "BARBUDA"

1978, Mar. 23 *Perf. 14*

332 A92 ½c multicolored .20 .20
333 A92 1c multicolored .20 .20
334 A92 2c multicolored .20 .20
335 A92 10c multicolored .20 .20
336 A92 50c multicolored .35 .35
337 A92 90c multicolored .40 .40
338 A92 $2 multicolored 1.00 1.00
Nos. 332-338 (7) 2.55 2.55

Souvenir Sheet

339 A92 $2.50 multicolored 1.75 1.75

Nos. 503-507 Ovptd. "BARBUDA"

1978, May 22 *Perf. 14½*

340 A93 10c multicolored .20 .20
341 A93 50c multicolored .40 .40
342 A93 90c multicolored .70 .70
343 A93 $2 multicolored 1.40 1.40
Nos. 340-343 (4) 2.70 2.70

Souvenir Sheet

344 A93 $2.50 multicolored 2.50 2.50

Coronation of Queen Elizabeth II, 25th Anniv. — B29

Crowns: No. 345a, St. Edward's. b, Imperial State. No. 346a, Queen Mary's. b, Queen Mother's. No. 347a, Queen Consort's. b, Queen Victoria's.

1978, June 2 *Perf. 15*

Miniature Sheets of Two Each Plus Two Labels

345 B29 75c Sheet of 4 1.00 1.00
346 B29 $1.50 Sheet of 4 1.50 1.50
347 B29 $2.50 Sheet of 4 2.50 2.50

Souvenir Sheet

Perf. 14½

348 B29 Sheet of 6, #345a-347b 2.50 2.50

Nos. 508-514 Ovptd. in Black or Deep Rose Lilac "BARBUDA"

1978 *Perf. 14*

349 A94 10c multicolored .20 .20
350 A94 30c multicolored .20 .20
351 A94 50c multicolored .25 .25
352 A94 90c multicolored .40 .40
353 A94 $2.50 multicolored .95 .95
Nos. 349-353 (5) 2.00 2.00

Souvenir Sheet

354 A94 $5 multicolored 2.00 2.00

Self-adhesive

355 Souvenir booklet
a. A95 Bklt. pane, 3 each 25c and 50c, die cut, rouletted (DRL) 2.00 2.00
b. A95 $5 Bklt. pane of 1, die cut 5.00 5.00

Issue dates: #349-354. June 2, #355, Oct. 12.

Nos. 515-518 Ovptd. "BARBUDA"

1978, Sept. 12 *Perf. 15*

356 A96 10c multicolored .20 .20
357 A96 15c multicolored .20 .20
358 A96 $3 multicolored 2.25 2.25
Nos. 356-358 (3) 2.65 2.65

Souvenir Sheet

359 Sheet of 4 2.50 2.50
a. A96 25c multicolored .20 .20
b. A96 30c multicolored .25 .25
c. A96 50c multicolored .40 .40
d. A96 $2 multicolored 1.50 1.50

Nos. 519-523 Ovptd. "BARBUDA"

1978, Nov. 20 *Perf. 14*

360 A97 25c multicolored .25 .25
361 A97 50c multicolored .50 .50
362 A97 90c multicolored .95 .95
363 A97 $2 multicolored 2.25 2.25
Nos. 360-363 (4) 3.95 3.95

Souvenir Sheet

364 A97 $2.50 multicolored 3.00 3.00

Flora and Fauna B30

1978, Nov. 20 *Perf. 15*

365 B30 25c Blackbar soldierfish .50 .50
366 B30 50c Painted lady 1.00 1.00
367 B30 75c Dwarf poinciana 1.50 1.50
368 B30 95c Zebra butterfly 1.90 1.90
369 B30 $1.25 Bougainvillea 2.50 2.50
Nos. 365-369 (5) 7.40 7.40

Nos. 524-527 Ovptd. in Silver "BARBUDA"

1978, Nov. 20 *Perf. 14*

370 A98 8c multicolored .20 .20
371 A98 25c multicolored .20 .20
372 A98 $2 multicolored 1.10 1.10
Nos. 370-372 (3) 1.50 1.50

Souvenir Sheet

373 A98 $4 multicolored 3.00 3.00

Events and Annivs. B31

Designs: 75c, 1978 World Cup Soccer Championships, vert. 95c, Wright Brothers 1st powered flight, 75th anniv. $1.25, First Trans-Atlantic balloon flight, Aug. 1978. $2, Coronation of Elizabeth II, 25th anniv., vert.

1978, Dec. 20 *Perf. 14*

374 B31 75c multicolored .40 .40
375 B31 95c multicolored .50 .50
376 B31 $1.25 multicolored .75 .75
377 B31 $2 multicolored 1.00 1.00
a. Souv. sheet of 4, #374-377, imperf. 6.00 6.00
Nos. 374-377 (4) 2.65 2.65

No. 377a has simulated perfs.

Nos. 528-532 Ovptd. in Bright Blue "BARBUDA" and

Sir Rowland Hill, Death Cent. B32

1979, Apr. 4

378 A99 25c multicolored .20 .20
379 A99 50c multicolored .35 .35
380 B32 75c Sir Rowland Hill, vert. .40 .40
381 B32 95c Mail coach, 1840 .50 .50
382 A99 $1 multicolored .65 .65
383 B32 $1.25 London's first pillar box, 1855 .70 .70
384 B32 $2 St. Martin's Post Office, London, vert. 1.10 1.10
a. Souvenir sheet of 4, #380-381, 383-384, imperf. 2.75 2.75
385 A99 $2 multicolored 1.40 1.40
Nos. 378-385 (8) 5.30 5.30

Souvenir Sheet

386 A99 $2.50 multicolored 2.00 2.00

No. 384a has simulated perfs.

For overprints see Nos. 423-426.

Nos. 533-536 Ovptd. "BARBUDA"

1979, Apr. 16

387 A100 10c multicolored .20 .20
388 A100 50c multicolored .30 .30
389 A100 $4 multicolored 1.50 1.50
Nos. 387-389 (3) 2.00 2.00

Souvenir Sheet

390 A100 $2.50 multicolored 1.90 1.90

Intl. Civil Aviation Organization, 30th Anniv. — B33

1979, May 24 *Perf. 13½x14*

391 B33 75c Passengers leaving 747 .40 .40
392 B33 95c Air traffic controllers .50 .50
393 B33 $1.25 Plane on runway .60 .60
a. Block of 3, #391-393 + label 1.75 1.75

Nos. 537-541 Ovptd. "BARBUDA"

1979, May 24 *Perf. 14*

394 A101 25c multicolored .30 .30
395 A101 50c multicolored .50 .50
396 A101 90c multicolored 1.00 1.00
397 A101 $2 multicolored 1.75 1.75
Nos. 394-397 (4) 3.55 3.55

Souvenir Sheet

398 A101 $5 multicolored 3.00 3.00

Nos. 542-546 Ovptd. "BARBUDA"

1979, Aug. 1 *Perf. 14½*

399 A102 30c multicolored .25 .25
400 A102 50c multicolored .40 .40
401 A102 90c multicolored .70 .70
402 A102 $3 multicolored 2.50 2.50
Nos. 399-402 (4) 3.85 3.85

Souvenir Sheet

403 A102 $2.50 multicolored 2.50 2.50

Nos. 547-551 Ovptd. "BARBUDA"

1979, Aug. 1 *Perf. 14*

404 A103 25c multicolored .20 .20
405 A103 50c multicolored .40 .40
406 A103 90c multicolored .65 .65
407 A103 $3 multicolored 2.25 2.25
Nos. 404-407 (4) 3.50 3.50

Souvenir Sheet

408 A103 $2.50 multicolored 2.75 2.75

Intl. Year of the Child — B34

Details of the Christ Child from various paintings by Durer: 25c, 1512. 50c, 1516. 75c, 1526. $1.25, 1502.

1979, Sept. 24 *Perf. 14x13½*

409 B34 25c multicolored .20 .20
410 B34 50c multicolored .30 .30
411 B34 75c multicolored .40 .40
412 B34 $1.25 multicolored .60 .60
a. Souvenir sheet of 4, #409-412 2.25 2.25
Nos. 409-412 (4) 1.50 1.50

Nos. 552-556 Ovptd. "BARBUDA"

1979, Nov. 21 *Perf. 14*

413 A104 8c multicolored .20 .20
414 A104 25c multicolored .20 .20
415 A104 50c multicolored .30 .30
416 A104 $4 multicolored 2.00 2.00
Nos. 413-416 (4) 2.70 2.70

Souvenir Sheet

Perf. 12x12½

417 A104 $3 multicolored 2.00 2.00

Nos. 557-561 Ovptd. "BARBUDA"

1980, Mar. 18

418 A105 10c multicolored .20 .20
419 A105 25c multicolroed .20 .20
420 A105 $1 multicolored .50 .50
421 A105 $2 multicolored 1.00 1.00
Nos. 418-421 (4) 1.90 1.90

Souvenir Sheet

422 A105 $3 multicolored 2.00 2.00

Nos. 571A-571D Overprinted "BARBUDA" in Dark Blue

1980, May 6 *Perf. 12*

423 A99 25c multicolored .20 .20
424 A99 50c multicolored .40 .40
425 A99 $1 multicolored .75 .75
426 A99 $2 multicolored 1.65 1.65
Nos. 423-426 (4) 3.00 3.00

First Moon Landing, 10th Anniv. — B35

1980, May 21 *Perf. 13½x14*

427 B35 75c Crew badge .40 .40
428 B35 95c Plaque left on moon .60 .60
429 B35 $1.25 Lunar, command modules .75 .75
430 B35 $2 Lunar module 1.25 1.25
a. Souvenir sheet of 4, #427-430 3.00 3.00
Nos. 427-430 (4) 3.00 3.00

American Widgeon B36

1980, June 16 *Perf. 14½x14*

431 B36 1c shown .55 .40
432 B36 2c Snowy plover .55 .40
433 B36 4c Rose-breasted grosbeak .65 .40
434 B36 6c Mangrove cuckoo .65 .40
435 B36 10c Adelaide's warbler .65 .40
436 B36 15c Scaly-breasted thrasher .65 .40
437 B36 20c Yellow-crowned night heron .75 .40
438 B36 25c Bridled quail dove .75 .40
439 B36 35c Carib grackle .75 .40
440 B36 50c Northern pintail .75 .40
441 B36 75c Black-whiskered vireo .75 .45
442 B36 $1 Blue-winged teal 1.10 .75

Perf. 14x14½

443 B36 $1.50 Green-throated carib 1.40 1.00
444 B36 $2 Red-necked pigeon 2.00 1.40
445 B36 $2.50 Stolid flycatcher 2.75 1.60
446 B36 $5 Yellow-bellied sapsucker 3.25 3.25
447 B36 $7.50 Caribbean elaenia 4.75 4.75
448 B36 $10 Great egret 6.50 6.50
Nos. 431-448 (18) 29.20 23.70

Nos. 443-448 vert.

Nos. 572-578 Ovptd. "BARBUDA"

1980, July 29 *Perf. 13½x14, 14x13½*

449 A106a 10c multicolored .20 .20
450 A106a 30c multicolored .20 .20
451 A106a 50c multicolored .35 .35
452 A106a 90c multicolored .50 .50
453 A106a $1 multicolored .50 .50
454 A106a $4 multicolored 2.25 2.25
Nos. 449-454 (6) 4.00 4.00

Souvenir Sheet

Perf. 14

455 A106a $5 multicolored 3.50 3.50

Nos. 579-583 Ovptd. "BARBUDA"

1980, Sept. 8 *Perf. 14*

456 A107 30c multicolored .20 .20
457 A107 50c multicolored .35 .35
458 A107 90c multicolored .60 .60
459 A107 $3 multicolored 1.75 1.75
Nos. 456-459 (4) 2.90 2.90

Souvenir Sheet

460 A107 $5 multicolored 3.50 3.50

Nos. 584-586 Optd. "BARBUDA"

1980, Oct. 6

461 A108 10c multicolored .25 .25
462 A108 $2.50 multicolored 1.75 1.75

Souvenir Sheet

Perf. 12

463 A108 $3 multicolored 2.75 2.75

Nos. 587-591 Ovptd. "BARBUDA"

1980, Dec. 8 *Perf. 14*

464 A109 10c multicolored 1.50 .75
465 A109 30c multicolored 2.00 1.00
466 A109 $1 multicolored 3.25 1.75
467 A109 $2 multicolored 3.50 3.50
Nos. 464-467 (4) 10.25 7.00

Souvenir Sheet

468 A109 $2.50 multicolored 5.00 5.00

Nos. 602-606 Ovptd. "BARBUDA"

1981, Jan. 26

469 A111 25c multicolored 1.00 .25
470 A111 50c multicolored 1.25 .35
471 A111 90c multicolored 1.75 .50
472 A111 $3 multicolored 3.25 1.00
Nos. 469-472 (4) 7.25 2.10

Souvenir Sheet

473 A111 $2.50 multicolored 3.50 3.50

Famous Women — B37

1981, Mar. 9 *Perf. 14x13½*

474 B37 50c Florence Nightingale .25 .25
475 B37 90c Marie Curie .45 .45
476 B37 $1 Amy Johnson .55 .55
477 B37 $4 Eleanor Roosevelt 1.75 1.75
Nos. 474-477 (4) 3.00 3.00

Walt Disney Characters at Sea — B38

1981, May 15 *Perf. 13½x14*

478 B38 10c Goofy 1.25 .35
479 B38 20c Donald Duck 1.50 .45
480 B38 25c Mickey Mouse 1.90 .65
481 B38 30c Goofy fishing 1.90 .75
482 B38 35c Goofy sailing 1.90 .75
483 B38 40c Mickey fishing 2.10 1.00
484 B38 75c Donald Duck boating 2.25 1.25
485 B38 $1 Minnie Mouse 2.50 1.75
486 B38 $2 Chip 'n Dale 4.00 2.50
Nos. 478-486 (9) 19.30 9.45

Souvenir Sheet

487 B38 $2.50 Donald Duck, diff. 20.00 20.00

Nos. 618-622 Ovptd. "BARBUDA"

1981, June 9 *Perf. 14*

488 A112 10c multicolored .20 .20
489 A112 50c multicolored .50 .50
490 A112 90c multicolored 1.00 1.00
491 A112 $4 multicolored 2.75 2.75
Nos. 488-491 (4) 4.45 4.45

Souvenir Sheet

Perf. 14x14½

492 A112 $5 multicolored 6.00 6.00

Miniature Sheets

Royal Wedding — B39

Designs: $1, Buckingham Palace. $1.50, Caernarvon Castle. $4, Highgrove House.

1981, July 27 *Perf. 11x11½*

493 B39 Sheet of 6 8.00 8.00
494 B39 Sheet of 6 8.00 8.00
495 B39 Sheet of 6 8.00 8.00

Souvenir Sheet

Perf. 11½x11

496 B39 $5 St. Paul's Cathedral, vert. 2.25 2.25

Sheets of 6 contain two of each denomination. Stamps of same denomination have continuous design. For surcharges see Nos. 592-594.

Common Design Types pictured following the introduction.

Nos. 623-627 Ovptd. in Black or Silver "BARBUDA"

1981, Aug. 14 *Perf. 14*

497 CD331 25c multicolored .20 .20
498 CD331 50c multicolored .30 .30
499 CD331 $4 multicolored 2.00 2.00
Nos. 497-499 (3) 2.50 2.50

Souvenir Sheet

500 CD331 $5 multicolored 2.75 2.75

Self-adhesive

501 CD331 Booklet 15.00 15.00
a. Pane of 6 (2x25c, 2x$1, 2x$2), Charles, die cut, rouletted (S) 8.00 8.00
b. Pane of 1, $5 Couple, die cut (S) 6.50 6.50

Issued: #497-500, Aug. 24; #501, Oct. 12.
For surcharge see No. B1.

Intl. Year of the Disabled B40

1981, Sept. 14 *Perf. 14*

502 B40 50c Travel .35 .35
503 B40 90c Braille, sign language .65 .65
504 B40 $1 Helping hands .70 .70
505 B40 $4 Mobility aids 1.75 1.75
Nos. 502-505 (4) 3.45 3.45

Nos. 607-617 Ovptd. "BARBUDA"

1981, Nov. 1 *Perf. 15*

506 A79 6c multicolored .20 .20
507 A79 10c multicolored .20 .20
508 A79 20c multicolored .20 .20
509 A79 25c multicolored .25 .20
510 A79 35c multicolored .40 .30
511 A79 50c multicolored .50 .40
512 A79 75c multicolored .75 .60
513 A79 $1 multicolored 1.00 .75

Perf. 13½x14

514 A80 $2.50 multicolored 2.50 1.90
515 A80 $5 multicolored 5.00 3.75
516 A80 $10 multicolored 9.50 7.50
Nos. 506-516 (11) 20.50 16.00

Nos. 628-632 Ovptd. "BARBUDA"

1981, Dec. 14 *Perf. 15*

517 A113 10c multicolored .20 .20
518 A113 50c multicolored .50 .50
519 A113 90c multicolored .90 .90
520 A113 $2.50 multicolored 2.50 2.50
Nos. 517-520 (4) 4.10 4.10

Souvenir Sheet

521 A113 $5 multicolored 4.00 4.00

Nos. 643-647 Ovptd. "BARBUDA"

1981, Dec. 14

522 A116 10c multicolored .20 .20
523 A116 50c multicolored .55 .55
524 A116 90c multicolored 1.00 1.00
525 A116 $2 multicolored 2.25 2.25
Nos. 522-525 (4) 4.00 4.00

Souvenir Sheet

526 A116 $4 multicolored 3.00 3.00

Nos. 638-642 Ovptd. in Black or Silver "BARBUDA"

1981, Dec. 22

527 A115 8c multi .20 .20
528 A115 30c multi .20 .20
529 A115 $1 multi (S) .60 .60
530 A115 $3 multi 2.00 2.00
Nos. 527-530 (4) 3.00 3.00

Souvenir Sheet

531 A115 $5 multi 3.50 3.50

Birth of Prince William — B41

Various portraits.

1982, June 21 **Wmk. 380** *Perf. 14*

532 B41 $1 buff & multi .60 .60
533 B41 $2.50 lt pink & multi 1.50 1.50
534 B41 $5 lt lilac & multi 3.00 3.00
Nos. 532-534 (3) 5.10 5.10

Souvenir Sheet

535 B41 $5 Couple 4.00 4.00

See Nos. 540-543.

The overprint on stamps of Antigua, from here on, read "BARBUDA MAIL" in one or two lines.

#672-675 Ovptd. in Black or Silver

Perf. 14½x14

1982, Oct. 12 **Unwmk.**

536 CD332 90c multi .65 .65
537 CD332 $1 multi (S) .75 .75
538 CD332 $4 multi (S) 3.00 3.00
Nos. 536-538 (3) 4.40 4.40

Souvenir Sheet

539 CD332 $5 multi 3.50 3.50

Barbuda Nos. 532-535 Inscribed "Twenty First Birthday Greetings to H.R.H. The Princess of Wales"

Various portraits.

Perf. 14x14½

1982, July 1 **Wmk. 380**

540 B41 $1 lt grn & multi .60 .60
541 B41 $2.50 pale salmon & multi 1.50 1.50
542 B41 $5 lt bl & multi 3.00 3.00
Nos. 540-542 (3) 5.10 5.10

Souvenir Sheet

543 B41 $4 Couple 3.50 3.50

#663-666 Ovptd. in Black or Silver

Perf. 14½x14

1982, Aug. 30 **Unwmk.**

544 CD332 90c multi .75 .75
545 CD332 $1 multi (S) .85 .85
546 CD332 $4 multi 3.25 3.25
Nos. 544-546 (3) 4.85 4.85

Souvenir Sheet

547 CD332 $5 multi 4.50 4.50

Nos. 676-683 Overprinted

1982, Dec. 6 *Perf. 15*

551 A121 10c multicolored .20 .20
552 A121 25c multicolored .25 .25
553 A121 45c multicolored .35 .35
554 A121 60c multicolored .55 .55
555 A121 $1 multicolored .90 .90
556 A121 $3 multicolored 2.75 2.75
Nos. 551-556 (6) 5.00 5.00

Souvenir Sheets

557 A121 $4 on #682 3.25 3.25
558 A121 $4 on #683 3.25 3.25

Nos. 684-688 Overprinted

1982, Dec. 6 *Perf. 14*

559 A122 10c multicolored .20 .20
560 A122 30c multicolored .25 .25
561 A122 $1 multicolored .75 .75
562 A122 $4 multicolored 3.00 3.00
Nos. 559-562 (4) 4.20 4.20

Souvenir Sheet

563 A122 $5 multicolored 3.75 3.75

Nos. 689-693 Overprinted

1983, Mar. 14 *Perf. 14½*

564 A123 45c multicolored .30 .30
565 A123 50c multicolored .40 .40
566 A123 60c multicolored .45 .45
567 A123 $4 multicolored 3.00 3.00
Nos. 564-567 (4) 4.15 4.15

Souvenir Sheet

568 A123 $5 multicolored 3.75 3.75

Nos. 694-697 Overprinted

1983, Mar. 14 *Perf. 14*

569 A124 25c multicolored .25 .25
570 A124 45c multicolored .40 .40
571 A124 60c multicolored .55 .55
572 A124 $3 multicolored 2.75 2.75
Nos. 569-572 (4) 3.95 3.95

Nos. 698-702 Overprinted

1983, Apr. 12

573 A125 15c multicolored .20 .20
574 A125 50c multicolored .50 .50
575 A125 60c multicolored .55 .55
576 A125 $3 multicolored 3.00 3.00
Nos. 573-576 (4) 4.25 4.25

Souvenir Sheet

577 A125 $5 multicolored 4.00 4.00

First Manned Balloon Flight, Bicent. — B43

1983, June 13

578 B43 $1 Vincenzo Lunardi, 1785 1.00 1.00
579 B43 $1.50 Montgolfier brothers, 1783 1.50 1.50
580 B43 $2.50 Blanchard & Jeffries, 1785 2.50 2.50
Nos. 578-580 (3) 5.00 5.00

Souvenir Sheet

581 B43 $5 Graf Zeppelin, 1928 3.75 3.75

Nos. 703-707 Overprinted

1983, July 4 *Perf. 15*

582 A126 15c multicolored .20 .20
583 A126 50c multicolored .45 .45
584 A126 60c multicolored .55 .55
585 A126 $3 multicolored 2.75 2.75
Nos. 582-585 (4) 3.95 3.95

Souvenir Sheet

586 A126 $5 multicolored 4.50 4.50

Nos. 726-730 Overprinted

1983, Sept. 12

587 A128 30c multicolored .25 .25
588 A128 50c multicolored .45 .45
589 A128 60c multicolored .50 .50
590 A128 $4 multicolored 3.50 3.50
Nos. 587-590 (4) 4.70 4.70

Souvenir Sheet

591 A128 $5 multicolored 4.50 4.50

Barbuda Nos. 493-495 Surcharged 45c on $1, 50c on $1.50, or 60c on $4

1983, Oct. 21 *Perf. 11½x11*

592 Sheet of 6 11.00 11.00
593 Sheet of 6 11.00 11.00
594 Sheet of 6 11.00 11.00

Nos. 708-725 Overprinted

1983, Oct. 28 *Perf. 14*

595 A127 1c multicolored .20 .20
596 A127 2c multicolored .20 .20
597 A127 3c multicolored .20 .20
598 A127 5c multicolored .20 .20
599 A127 10c multicolored .20 .20
600 A127 15c multicolored .20 .20
601 A127 20c multicolored .20 .20
602 A127 25c multicolored .20 .20
603 A127 30c multicolored .25 .25

604 A127 40c multicolored .35 .35
605 A127 45c multicolored .35 .35
606 A127 50c multicolored .45 .45
607 A127 60c multicolored .50 .50
608 A127 $1 multicolored .85 .85
609 A127 $2 multicolored 1.75 1.75
610 A127 $2.50 multicolored 2.25 2.25
611 A127 $5 multicolored 4.25 4.25
612 A127 $10 multicolored 8.00 8.00
Nos. 595-612 (18) 20.60 20.60

Nos. 731-735 Overprinted

1983, Oct. 28 ***Perf. 14***
613 A129 10c multicolored .20 .20
614 A129 30c multicolored .20 .20
615 A129 $1 multicolored .75 .75
616 A129 $4 multicolored 3.00 3.00
Nos. 613-616 (4) 4.15 4.15

Souvenir Sheet

617 A129 $5 multicolored 3.75 3.75

#736-739 Ovptd. in Black or Silver

1983, Dec. 14 ***Perf. 14***
618 A130 15c multicolored (S) .20 .20
619 A130 50c multicolored (S) .45 .45
620 A130 60c multicolored .50 .50
621 A130 $3 multicolored 2.75 2.75
Nos. 618-621 (4) 3.90 3.90

Members of Royal Family — B44

1984, Feb. 14 ***Perf. 14½x14***
622 B44 $1 Edward VII 1.00 1.00
623 B44 $1 George V 1.00 1.00
624 B44 $1 George VI 1.00 1.00
625 B44 $1 Elizabeth II 1.00 1.00
626 B44 $1 Prince Charles 1.00 1.00
627 B44 $1 Prince William 1.00 1.00
Nos. 622-627 (6) 6.00 6.00

Nos. 740-744 Overprinted and

1984 Summer Olympics, Los Angeles B45

1984 ***Perf. 15, 13½ (B45)***
628 A131 25c multicolored .20 .20
629 A131 50c multicolored .40 .40
630 A131 90c multicolored .45 .45
631 B45 $1.50 Olympic Stadium, Athens 1.10 1.10
632 B45 $2.50 Olympic Stadium, Los Angeles 1.90 1.90
633 A131 $3 multicolored 2.50 2.50
634 B45 $5 Torch bearer 4.00 4.00
a. Souv. sheet of 1, perf. 15 4.00 4.00
Nos. 628-634 (7) 10.55 10.55

Souvenir Sheet

635 A131 $5 multicolored 4.00 4.00

Issue dates: A131, Apr. 26, B45, July 27.

Nos. 755-759 Overprinted

1984, July 12 ***Perf. 15***
636 A133 15c multicolored .20 .20
637 A133 50c multicolored .45 .45
638 A133 60c multicolored .55 .55
639 A133 $3 multicolored 2.75 2.75
Nos. 636-639 (4) 3.95 3.95

Souvenir Sheet

640 A133 $5 multicolored 4.25 4.25

Nos. 745-749 Overprinted

1984, July 12
641 A132 45c multicolored .40 .40
642 A132 50c multicolored .45 .45
643 A132 60c multicolored .50 .50
644 A132 $4 multicolored 3.50 3.50
Nos. 641-644 (4) 4.85 4.85

Souvenir Sheet

645 A132 $5 multicolored 4.50 4.50

#760-767 Ovptd. in Black or Silver

1984, Oct. 1 ***Perf. 14***
646 A134 10c multicolored (S) .20 .20
647 A134 20c multicolored .20 .20
648 A134 30c multicolored .25 .25
649 A134 40c multicolored .30 .30
650 A134 90c multicolored (S) .70 .70
651 A134 $1.10 multicolored (S) .90 .90
652 A134 $1.50 multicolored (S) 1.25 1.25
653 A134 $2 multicolored 1.60 1.60
Nos. 646-653 (8) 5.40 5.40

Nos. 768-772 Overprinted

1984, Oct. 1
654 A135 40c multicolored .35 .35
655 A135 50c multicolored .40 .40
656 A135 60c multicolored .50 .50
657 A135 $3 multicolored 2.75 2.75
Nos. 654-657 (4) 4.00 4.00

Souvenir Sheet

658 A135 $5 multicolored 4.25 4.25

Nos. 773-778 Overprinted

1984, Nov. 21 ***Perf. 15***
659 A136 40c multicolored .40 .40
660 A136 50c multicolored .50 .50
661 A136 60c multicolored .60 .60
662 A136 $2 multicolored 2.00 2.00
663 A136 $3 multicolored 3.00 3.00
Nos. 659-663 (5) 6.50 6.50

Souvenir Sheet

664 A136 $5 multicolored 5.00 5.00

Nos. 782-791 Overprinted in Silver

1984 ***Perf. 15***
665 A137a 15c multicolored .20 .20
666 A137a 25c multicolored .20 .20
667 A137a 50c multicolored .40 .40
668 A137a 60c multicolored .50 .50
669 A137a 70c multicolored .55 .55
670 A137a 90c multiocolored .75 .75
671 A137a $3 multicolored 2.50 2.50
672 A137a $4 multicolored 3.25 3.25
Nos. 665-672 (8) 8.35 8.35

Souvenir Sheets

673 A137a $5 #790 4.50 4.50
674 A137a $5 #791, horiz. 4.50 4.50

Issue dates: Correggio, Nov. 21; Degas, Nov. 30.

Nos. 779-781 Overprinted

1984, Nov. 30
675 A137 $1 multicolored .80 .80
676 A137 $5 multicolored 4.00 4.00

Souvenir Sheet

677 A137 $5 multicolored 4.50 4.50

Nos. 819-827 Overprinted

1985, Feb. 18
678 A139 60c multicolored .45 .45
679 A139 60c multicolored .45 .45
680 A139 60c multicolored .45 .45
681 A139 60c multicolored .45 .45
682 A139 $1 multicolored .75 .75
683 A139 $1 multicolored .75 .75
684 A139 $1 multicolored .75 .75
685 A139 $1 multicolored .75 .75
Nos. 678-685 (8) 4.80 4.80

Souvenir Sheet

686 A139 $5 multicolored 4.50 4.50

Queen Mother (Lady Elizabeth Bowes-Lyon), 1907 — B46

1985, Feb. 26 ***Perf. 14x14½***
687 B46 15c shown .20 .20
688 B46 45c Duchess of York, 1926 .35 .35
689 B46 50c Coronation, 1937 .40 .40
690 B46 60c Queen Mother .50 .50
691 B46 90c Wearing tiara .70 .70
692 B46 $2 Wearing blue hat 1.60 1.60
693 B46 $3 With children 2.50 2.50
Nos. 687-693 (7) 6.25 6.25

For overprints see Nos. 724-728, 733, 735.

Nos. 828-834 Overprinted

1985, May 10 ***Perf. 15***
694 A140 25c multicolored .20 .20
695 A140 30c multicolored .25 .25
696 A140 50c multicolored .40 .40
697 A140 90c multicolored .70 .70
698 A140 $1 multicolored .80 .80
699 A140 $3 multicolored 2.50 2.50
Nos. 694-699 (6) 4.85 4.85

Souvenir Sheet

700 A140 $5 multicolored 4.00 4.00

Audubon, Birth Bicentenary B47

1985, Apr. 4 ***Perf. 14***
701 B47 45c Roseate tern .40 .40
702 B47 50c Mangrove cuckoo .45 .45
703 B47 60c Yellow-crowned night heron .55 .55
704 B47 $5 Brown pelican 4.50 4.50
Nos. 701-704 (4) 5.90 5.90

Nos. 845-849, 910-913 Ovptd. in Black or Silver

1985-86 ***Perf. 15, 12½x12***
705 A143 60c on #910 (S) .50 .50
706 A143 90c on #845 .70 .70
707 A143 90c on #911 (S) .70 .70
708 A143 $1 on #846 .80 .80
709 A143 $1.50 on #847 1.25 1.25
710 A143 $1.50 on #912 1.25 1.25
711 A143 $3 on #848 2.50 2.50
712 A143 $3 on #913 2.50 2.50
Nos. 705-712 (8) 10.20 10.20

Souvenir Sheet

713 A143 $5 on #849 4.50 4.50

Issue dates: Nos. 706, 708-709, 711, 713, July 18, 1985. Others, Dec. 1986.

Nos. 850-854 Overprinted

1985, July 18 ***Perf. 14***
714 A144 25c multicolored .25 .25
715 A144 60c multicolored .50 .50
716 A144 95c multicolored .80 .80
717 A144 $4 multicolored 3.50 3.50
Nos. 714-717 (4) 5.05 5.05

Souvenir Sheet

718 A144 $5 multicolored 4.50 4.50

Nos. 840-844 Overprinted

1985, Aug. 2
719 A142 10c multicolored .20 .20
720 A142 30c multicolored .30 .30
721 A142 60c multicolored .50 .50
722 A142 $4 multicolored 3.75 3.75
Nos. 719-722 (4) 4.75 4.75

Souvenir Sheet

723 A142 $5 multicolored 4.50 4.50

Barbuda Nos. 687-693 Ovptd. "4TH AUG 1900-1985" and Antigua Nos. 866A-870 Ovptd. "BARBUDA / MAIL" in Silver or Black

Perf. 14, 12x12½ (#729, 731, 736)

1985-86
724 B46 15c multi .20 .20
725 B46 45c multi .35 .35
726 B46 50c multi .40 .40
727 B46 60c multi .50 .50
728 B46 90c multi .70 .70
729 A148 90c multi .70 .70
730 A148 $1 multi (S) .80 .80
731 A148 $1 like #730 .80 .80
732 A148 $1.50 multi (S) 1.25 1.25
733 B46 $2 multi 1.60 1.60
734 A148 $2.50 multi 2.00 2.00
735 B46 $3 multi 2.50 2.50
736 A148 $3 multi 2.50 2.50
Nos. 724-736 (13) 14.30 14.30

Souvenir Sheet

737 A148 $5 multi 4.50 4.50

Queen Mother's 85th birthday.
Issue dates: 15c, 45c, 50c, 60c, No. 728, $2, No. 735, Aug. 2. No. 730, $1.50, $2.50, Nov. 8. Others, Dec. 1986. Nos. 729, 731, 736 issued in sheets of 5 plus label.

Nos. 835-839 Overprinted

1985, Aug. 30 ***Perf. 15***
738 A141 15c multicolored .20 .20
739 A141 50c multicolored .40 .40
740 A141 60c multicolored .45 .45
741 A141 $3 multicolored 2.50 2.50
Nos. 738-741 (4) 3.55 3.55

Souvenir Sheet

742 A141 $5 multicolored 4.00 4.00

Nos. 855-859 Overprinted

1985, Aug. 30 ***Perf. 14***
743 A145 30c multicolored .25 .25
744 A145 90c multicolored .70 .70
745 A145 $1.50 multicolored 1.25 1.25
746 A145 $3 multicolored 2.50 2.50
Nos. 743-746 (4) 4.70 4.70

Souvenir Sheet

747 A145 $5 multicolored 4.25 4.25

Nos. 860-861 Overprinted

1985, Nov. 25 ***Perf. 14***
748 A146 $2 yellow green 1.60 1.60

Souvenir Sheet

749 A146 $5 deep brown 4.00 4.00

#871-875 Ovptd. in Black or Silver

1985, Nov. 25
750 A149 15c multi (S) .20 .20
751 A149 45c multi .40 .40
752 A149 60c multi .55 .55
753 A149 $3 multi (S) 3.00 3.00
Nos. 750-753 (4) 4.15 4.15

Souvenir Sheet

754 A149 $5 multi 4.50 4.50

Nos. 862-866 Overprinted

1986, Feb. 17
755 A147 25c multicolored .20 .20
756 A147 50c multicolored .40 .40
757 A147 60c multicolored .50 .50
758 A147 $3 multicolored 2.50 2.50
Nos. 755-758 (4) 3.60 3.60

Souvenir Sheet

759 A147 $5 multicolored 4.00 4.00

Nos. 886-889 Overprinted

1986, Feb. 17 ***Perf. 14½***
760 A152 60c multicolored .50 .50
761 A152 $1 multicolored .80 .80
762 A152 $4 multicolored 3.25 3.25
Nos. 760-762 (3) 4.55 4.55

Souvenir Sheet

763 A152 $5 multicolored 4.00 4.00

Nos. 876-880 Overprinted

1986, Mar. 10 ***Perf. 14***
764 A150 25c multicolored .20 .20
765 A150 50c multicolored .40 .40
766 A150 $1 multicolored .80 .80
767 A140 $3 multicolored 2.50 2.50
Nos. 764-767 (4) 3.90 3.90

Souvenir Sheet

768 A150 $5 multicolored 4.00 4.00

Nos. 881-885 Overprinted

1986, Mar. 10 ***Perf. 14***
769 A151 15c multicolored .20 .20
770 A151 45c multicolored .35 .35
771 A151 60c multicolored .50 .50
772 A151 $3 multicolored 2.50 2.50
Nos. 769-772 (4) 3.55 3.55

Souvenir Sheet

773 A151 $5 multicolored 4.00 4.00

Nos. 905-909 Overprinted

1986, Apr. 4 ***Perf. 15***
774 A156 10c multicolored .20 .20
775 A156 25c multicolored .20 .20
776 A156 60c multicolored .50 .50
777 A156 $4 multicolored 3.25 3.25
Nos. 774-777 (4) 4.15 4.15

Souvenir Sheet

778 A156 $5 multicolored 4.00 4.00

B48

1986, Apr. 21
779 B48 $1 Shaking hands .80 .80
780 B48 $2 Talking with woman 1.60 1.60
781 B48 $2.50 With officer 2.00 2.00
Nos. 779-781 (3) 4.40 4.40

Souvenir Sheet

Perf. 13½x14

782 B48 $5 Portraits 4.00 4.00

No. 782 contains one 34x27mm stamp.

Nos. 925-928 Overprinted in Silver or Black

1986, Aug. 12

783 CD339 60c multi .50 .50
784 CD339 $1 multi .80 .80
785 CD339 $4 multi 3.25 3.25
Nos. 783-785 (3) 4.55 4.55

Souvenir Sheet

786 CD339 $5 multi (Bk) 4.00 4.00

Nos. 920-924 Overprinted and

Halley's Comet B49

1986 ***Perf. 14, 15 (B49)***

787 A158 5c multicolored .20 .20
788 A158 10c multicolored .20 .20
789 A158 60c multicolored .50 .50
790 B49 $1 shown .85 .85
791 B49 $2.50 Early telescope, dish antenna, vert. 2.00 2.00
792 A158 $4 multicolored 3.25 3.25
793 B49 $5 World map, comet 4.00 4.00
Nos. 787-793 (7) 11.00 11.00

Souvenir Sheet

794 A159 $5 multicolored 4.00 4.00

Issued: #790-791, 793, 7/10; others, 9/22.

Nos. 901-904 Overprinted

1986, Aug. 12 ***Perf. 13½x14***

795 A155 40c multicolored .30 .30
796 A155 $1 multicolored .80 .80
797 A155 $3 multicolored 2.50 2.50
Nos. 795-797 (3) 3.60 3.60

Souvenir Sheet

Perf. 14x13½

798 A155 $5 multicolored 4.00 4.00

Nos. 915-919 Overprinted

1986, Aug. 28 ***Perf. 14***

799 A157 30c multicolored .25 .25
800 A157 60c multicolored .50 .50
801 A157 $1 multicolored .80 .80
802 A157 $4 multicolored 3.25 3.25
Nos. 799-802 (4) 4.80 4.80

Souvenir Sheet

803 A157 $5 multicolored 4.00 4.00

See Nos. 848-851.

Nos. 934-938 Overprinted

1986, Aug. 28 Litho. ***Perf. 15***

804 A161 25c multicolored .20 .20
805 A161 50c multicolored .40 .40
806 A161 $1 multicolored .80 .80
807 A161 $3 multicolored 2.50 2.50
Nos. 804-807 (4) 3.90 3.90

Souvenir Sheet

808 A161 $5 multicolored 4.00 4.00

Nos. 939-942 Ovptd. in Silver

1986, Sept. 22 ***Perf. 14***

809 CD340 45c multicolored .40 .40
810 CD340 60c multicolored .60 .60
811 CD340 $4 multicolored 4.00 4.00
Nos. 809-811 (3) 5.00 5.00

Souvenir Sheet

812 CD340 $5 multicolored 5.00 5.00

Nos. 943-947 Overprinted in Silver or Black

1986, Nov. 10 ***Perf. 15***

813 A162 15c multicolored .20 .20
814 A162 45c multicolored .30 .30
815 A162 60c multicolored .45 .45
816 A162 $3 multicolored 2.25 2.25
Nos. 813-816 (4) 3.20 3.20

Souvenir Sheet

817 A162 $5 multi (Bk) 4.00 4.00

Nos. 948-957 Overprinted

1986, Nov. 10

818 A163 10c multicolored .20 .20
819 A163 15c multicolored .20 .20
820 A163 50c multicolored .40 .40
821 A163 60c multicolored .45 .45
822 A163 70c multicolored .50 .50
823 A163 $1 multicolored .75 .75
824 A163 $3 multicolored 2.25 2.25
825 A163 $4 multicolored 3.00 3.00
Nos. 818-825 (8) 7.75 7.75

Souvenir Sheets

826 A163 $4 multicolored 3.25 3.25
827 A163 $5 multicolored 4.00 4.00

Nos. 958-962 Overprinted

1986, Nov. 28

828 A164 10c multicolored .20 .20
829 A164 50c multicolored .40 .40
830 A164 $1 multicolored .75 .75
831 A164 $4 multicolored 3.00 3.00
Nos. 828-831 (4) 4.35 4.35

Souvenir Sheet

832 A164 $5 multicolored 4.00 4.00

Nos. 929-933 Overprinted

1987, Jan. 12 ***Perf. 14***

833 A160 30c multicolored .30 .30
834 A160 60c multicolored .55 .55
835 A160 $1 multicolored .90 .90
836 A160 $3 multicolored 2.75 2.75
Nos. 833-836 (4) 4.50 4.50

Souvenir Sheet

837 A160 $5 multicolored 4.00 4.00

Nos. 968-972A Overprinted

1987, Jan. 12

838 A165 10c multicolored .20 .20
839 A165 15c multicolored .20 .20
840 A165 50c multicolored .40 .40
841 A165 60c multicolored .50 .50
842 A165 70c multicolored .55 .55
843 A165 $1 multicolored .80 .80
844 A165 $3 multicolored 2.50 2.50
845 A165 $4 multicolored 3.25 3.25
Nos. 838-845 (8) 8.40 8.40

Souvenir Sheets

846 A165 $5 multi (#972) 4.00 4.00
847 A165 $5 multi (#972A) 4.00 4.00

Automobile, cent.

Nos. 963-966 Overprinted

1987, Mar. 10

848 A157 30c multicolored .25 .25
849 A157 60c multicolored .45 .45
850 A157 $1 multicolored .75 .75
851 A157 $4 multicolored 3.00 3.00
Nos. 848-851 (4) 4.45 4.45

See Nos. 799-802.

Nos. 1000-1004 Overprinted

1987, Apr. 23 ***Perf. 15***

852 A170 30c multicolored .25 .25
853 A170 60c multicolored .45 .45
854 A170 $1 multicolored .75 .75
855 A170 $3 multicolored 2.25 2.25
Nos. 852-855 (4) 3.70 3.70

Souvenir Sheet

856 A171 $5 multicolored 5.00 5.00

Nos. 1005-1014 Overprinted

1987, July 1 ***Perf. 14***

857 A172 15c multicolored .20 .20
858 A173 30c multicolored .25 .25
859 A172 40c multicolored .30 .30
860 A173 50c multicolored .40 .40
861 A172 60c multicolored .45 .45
862 A172 $1 multicolored .75 .75
863 A173 $2 multicolored 1.50 1.50
864 A173 $3 multicolored 2.25 2.25
Nos. 857-864 (8) 6.10 6.10

Souvenir Sheets

865 A172 $5 multicolored 4.00 4.00
866 A173 $5 multicolored 4.00 4.00

Nos. 1025-1034 Overprinted

1987, July 28 ***Perf. 15***

867 A175 10c multicolored .20 .20
868 A175 15c multicolored .20 .20
869 A175 30c multicolored .25 .25
870 A175 50c multicolored .40 .40
871 A175 60c multicolored .50 .50
872 A175 70c multicolored .55 .55
873 A175 90c multicolored .70 .70
874 A175 $1.50 multicolored 1.25 1.25
875 A175 $2 multicolored 1.60 1.60
876 A175 $3 multicolored 2.25 2.25
Nos. 867-876 (10) 7.90 7.90

Marine Life B50

1987, July 28

877 B50 5c Shore crab .20 .20
878 B50 10c Sea cucumber .20 .20
879 B50 15c Stop light parrotfish .20 .20
880 B50 25c Banded coral shrimp .20 .20
881 B50 35c Spotted drum .25 .25
882 B50 60c Thorny star-fish .45 .45
883 B50 75c Atlantic trumpet triton .55 .55
884 B50 90c Feather-star, yellow beaker sponge .65 .65
885 B50 $1 Blue gorgonian, vert. .75 .75
886 B50 $1.25 Slender filefish, vert. .90 .90
887 B50 $5 Barred hamlet, vert. 3.75 3.75
888 B50 $7.50 Fairy basslet, vert. 5.50 5.50
889 B50 $10 Fire coral, butterfly fish, vert. 7.50 7.50
Nos. 877-889 (13) 21.10 21.10

For surcharges see Nos. 1133-1134.

#1048-1052 Ovptd. in Silver or Black

1987, Oct. 12 ***Perf. 14***

890 A178 10c multicolored .20 .20
891 A178 60c multicolored .50 .50
892 A178 $1 multicolored .80 .80
893 A178 $3 multicolored 2.25 2.25
Nos. 890-893 (4) 3.75 3.75

Souvenir Sheet

894 A178 $5 multi (Bk) 4.00 4.00

1988 Summer Olympics, Seoul.

#990-999 Ovptd. in Black or Silver

1987, Oct. 12 ***Perf. 13½x14***

895 A169 10c multicolored .20 .20
896 A169 30c multicolored .25 .25
897 A169 40c multicolored .30 .30
898 A169 60c multicolored .50 .50
899 A169 90c multicolored .70 .70
900 A169 $1 multicolored (S) .80 .80
901 A169 $3 multicolored 2.25 2.25
902 A169 $4 multicolored 3.00 3.00
Nos. 895-902 (8) 8.00 8.00

Size: 110x95mm

Imperf

903 A169 $5 multicolored 4.00 4.00
904 A169 $5 multicolored (S) 4.00 4.00

#1015-1024 Ovptd. in Silver or Black

1987, Nov. 5 ***Perf. 14***

905 A174 15c multicolored .20 .20
906 A174 30c multicolored .25 .25
907 A174 45c multicolored .35 .35
908 A174 50c multicolored (Bk) .40 .40
909 A174 60c multicolored .50 .50
910 A174 90c multicolored .70 .70
911 A174 $1 multicolored .80 .80
912 A174 $2 multicolored 1.60 1.60
913 A174 $3 multicolored (Bk) 2.25 2.25
914 A174 $5 multicolored 4.00 4.00
Nos. 905-914 (10) 11.05 11.05

#1040-1047 Ovptd. in Black or Silver

1987, Nov. 5

915 A177 15c multicolored .45 .30
916 A177 30c multicolored 1.00 .60
917 A177 45c multicolored .50 .40
918 A177 50c multicolored .55 .45
919 A177 60c multicolored 1.50 1.00
920 A177 $1 multicolored 1.00 .75
921 A177 $2 multicolored 1.50 1.25
922 A177 $3 multicolored (S) 3.50 3.00
Nos. 915-922 (8) 10.00 7.75

Nos. 1035-1039 Overprinted

1987, Dec. 8

923 A176 30c multicolored .25 .25
924 A176 60c multicolored .50 .50
925 A176 $1 multicolored .80 .80
926 A176 $3 multicolored 2.25 2.25
Nos. 923-926 (4) 3.80 3.80

Souvenir Sheet

927 A176 $5 multicolored 4.00 4.00

Nos. 1063-1067 Overprinted

1988, Jan. 12

928 A181 45c multicolored .30 .30
929 A181 60c multicolored .45 .45
930 A181 $1 multicolored .75 .75
931 A181 $4 multicolored 3.00 3.00
Nos. 928-931 (4) 4.50 4.50

Souvenir Sheet

932 A181 $5 multicolored 4.00 4.00

Nos. 1083-1091 Overprinted

1988, Mar. 25

933 A184 25c multicolored .20 .20
934 A184 30c multicolored .25 .25
935 A184 40c multicolored .30 .30
936 A184 45c multicolored .35 .35
937 A184 50c multicolored .40 .40
938 A184 60c multicolored .50 .50
939 A184 $1 multicolored .80 .80
940 A184 $2 multicolored 1.60 1.60
Nos. 933-940 (8) 4.40 4.40

Souvenir Sheet

941 A184 $5 multicolored 4.00 4.00

Nos. 1058-1062 Ovptd. in Silver

1988, May 6

942 A180 15c multicolored .20 .20
943 A180 45c multicolored .35 .35
944 A180 60c multicolored .50 .50
945 A180 $4 multicolored 3.25 3.25
Nos. 942-945 (4) 4.30 4.30

Souvenir Sheet

946 A180 $5 multicolored 4.00 4.00

Nos. 1068-1072 Overprinted

1988, July 4

947 A182 25c multicolored .20 .20
948 A182 60c multicolored .50 .50
949 A182 $2 multicolored 1.60 1.60
950 A182 $3 multicolored 2.25 2.25
Nos. 947-950 (4) 4.55 4.55

Souvenir Sheet

951 A182 $5 multicolored 4.00 4.00

Nos. 1073-1082 Overprinted

1988, July 4

952 A183 10c multicolored .20 .20
953 A183 15c multicolored .20 .20
954 A183 50c multicolored .40 .40
955 A183 60c multicolored .50 .50
956 A183 70c multicolored .55 .55
957 A183 $1 multicolored .80 .80
958 A183 $3 multicolored 2.25 2.25
959 A183 $4 multicolored 3.25 3.25
Nos. 952-959 (8) 8.15 8.15

Souvenir Sheets

960 A183 $5 multi (#1081) 4.00 4.00
961 A183 $5 multi (#1082) 4.00 4.00

Nos. 1092-1101 Overprinted

1988, July 25

962 A185 10c multicolored .20 .20
963 A185 30c multicolored .25 .25
964 A185 45c multicolored .40 .40
965 A185 60c multicolored .55 .55
966 A185 90c multicolored .75 .75
967 A185 $1 multicolored .85 .85
968 A185 $3 multicolored 2.50 2.50
969 A185 $4 multicolored 3.50 3.50
Nos. 962-969 (8) 9.00 9.00

Souvenir Sheets

970 A185 $5 multi (#1100) 4.00 4.00
971 A185 $5 multi (#1101) 4.00 4.00

Nos. 1102-1111 Overprinted

1988, July 25 ***Perf. 13½x14***

972 A187 30c multicolored .25 .25
973 A187 40c multicolored .30 .30
974 A187 45c multicolored .35 .35
975 A187 50c multicolored .40 .40
976 A187 $1 multicolored .80 .80
977 A187 $2 multicolored 1.60 1.60
978 A187 $3 multicolored 2.25 2.25
979 A187 $4 multicolored 3.25 3.25
Nos. 972-979 (8) 9.20 9.20

Souvenir Sheets

980 A187 $5 multi (#1110) 4.00 4.00
981 A187 $5 multi (#1111) 4.00 4.00

Nos. 1053-1057 Overprinted

1988, Aug. 25 ***Perf. 15***

982 A179 10c multicolored .20 .20
983 A179 60c multicolored .45 .45
984 A179 $1 multicolored .75 .75
985 A179 $3 multicolored 2.25 2.25
Nos. 982-985 (4) 3.65 3.65

Souvenir Sheet

986 A179 $5 multicolored 4.00 4.00

Nos. 1112-1116 Overprinted

1988, Aug. 25

987 A188 30c multicolored .25 .25
988 A188 60c multicolored .50 .50
989 A188 $1 multicolored .80 .80
990 A188 $3 multicolored 2.25 2.25
Nos. 987-990 (4) 3.80 3.80

Souvenir Sheet

991 A188 $5 multicolored 4.00 4.00

Nos. 1127-1136 Overprinted

1988, Sept. 16 ***Perf. 14***

992 A190 10c multicolored .20 .20
993 A190 30c multicolored .25 .25
994 A190 50c multicolored .40 .40
995 A190 90c multicolored .60 .60
996 A190 $1 multicolored .75 .75
997 A190 $2 multicolored 1.60 1.60
998 A190 $3 multicolored 2.25 2.25
999 A190 $4 multicolored 3.00 3.00
Nos. 992-999 (8) 9.05 9.05

Souvenir Sheets

1000 A191 $5 multi (#1135) 4.00 4.00
1001 A191 $5 multi (#1136) 4.00 4.00

Nos. 1140-1144 Overprinted

1988, Sept. 16

1002 A192 40c multicolored .30 .30
1003 A192 60c multicolored .50 .50
1004 A192 $1 multicolored .80 .80
1005 A192 $3 multicolored 2.25 2.25
Nos. 1002-1005 (4) 3.85 3.85

Souvenir Sheet

1006 A192 $5 multicolored 4.00 4.00

Nos. 1145-1162 Overprinted

1988-90

1007 A193 1c multicolored .20 .20
1008 A193 2c multicolored .20 .20
1009 A193 3c multicolored .20 .20
1010 A193 5c multicolored .20 .20
1011 A193 10c multicolored .20 .20
1012 A193 15c multicolored .20 .20
1013 A193 20c multicolored .20 .20
1014 A193 25c multicolored .20 .20
1015 A193 30c multicolored .25 .25
1016 A193 40c multicolored .30 .30
1017 A193 45c multicolored .35 .35
1018 A193 50c multicolored .40 .40
1019 A193 60c multicolored .50 .50
1020 A193 $1 multicolored .80 .80
1021 A193 $2 multicolored 1.60 1.60
1022 A193 $2.50 multicolored 2.00 2.00
1023 A193 $5 multicolored 4.00 4.00
1024 A193 $10 multicolored 8.00 8.00
1025 A193 $20 multi ('90) 16.00 16.00
Nos. 1007-1025 (19) 35.80 35.80

Issue dates: $20, May 4, others Dec. 8.

Nos. 1162A-1167 Overprinted

1989, Apr. 28

1026 A194 1c multicolored .20 .20
1027 A194 2c multicolored .20 .20
1028 A194 3c multicolored .20 .20
1029 A194 4c multicolored .20 .20
1030 A194 30c multicolored .25 .25
1031 A194 60c multicolored .50 .50
1032 A194 $1 multicolored .80 .80
1033 A194 $4 multicolored 3.25 3.25
Nos. 1026-1033 (8) 5.60 5.60

Souvenir Sheet

1034 A194 $5 multicolored 4.00 4.00

Nos. 1175-1176 Overprinted

1989, May 24

1035 A196 $1.50 Strip of 4, #a.-d. 4.75 4.75

Souvenir Sheet

1036 A196 $6 multicolored 4.75 4.75

Nos. 1177-1186 Overprinted

1989, May 29

1037 A197 10c multicolored .20 .20
1038 A197 30c multicolored .35 .35
1039 A197 40c multicolored .50 .50
1040 A197 60c multicolored .70 .70
1041 A197 $1 multicolored 1.25 1.25
1042 A197 $2 multicolored 2.25 2.25
1043 A197 $3 multicolored 3.50 3.50
1044 A197 $4 multicolored 4.75 4.75
Nos. 1037-1044 (8) 13.50 13.50

Souvenir Sheets

1045 A197 $7 multi (#1185) 5.50 5.50
1046 A197 $7 multi (#1186) 5.50 5.50

Nos. 1187-1196 Overprinted

1989, Sept. 18

1047 A198 25c multicolored .20 .20
1048 A198 45c multicolored .30 .30
1049 A198 50c multicolored .40 .40
1050 A198 60c multicolored .45 .45
1051 A198 75c multicolored .55 .55
1052 A198 90c multicolored .65 .65
1053 A198 $3 multicolored 2.25 2.25
1054 A198 $4 multicolored 3.00 3.00
Nos. 1047-1054 (8) 7.80 7.80

Souvenir Sheets

1055 A198 $6 multi (#1195) 4.50 4.50
1056 A198 $6 multi (#1196) 4.50 4.50

Nos. 1197-1206 Overprinted

1989, Dec. 14 ***Perf. 14x13½***

1057 A199 25c multicolored .20 .20
1058 A199 45c multicolored .30 .30
1059 A199 50c multicolored .40 .40
1060 A199 60c multicolored .45 .45
1061 A199 $1 multicolored .75 .75
1062 A199 $2 multicolored 1.50 1.50
1063 A199 $3 multicolored 2.25 2.25
1064 A199 $4 multicolored 3.00 3.00
Nos. 1057-1064 (8) 8.85 8.85

Souvenir Sheets

1065 A199 $5 multi (#1205) 3.75 3.75
1066 A199 $5 multi (#1206) 3.75 3.75

Nos. 1217-1222 Overprinted

1989, Dec. 20 ***Perf. 14***

1067 A201 15c multicolored .20 .20
1068 A201 25c multicolored .20 .20
1069 A201 $1 multicolored .75 .75
1070 A201 $4 multicolored 3.00 3.00
Nos. 1067-1070 (4) 4.15 4.15

Souvenir Sheets

1071 A201 $5 multi (#1221) 3.75 3.75
1072 A201 $5 multi (#1222) 3.75 3.75

Nos. 1264-1273 Overprinted

1989, Dec. 20

1073 A208 10c multicolored .20 .20
1074 A208 25c multicolored .20 .20
1075 A208 30c multicolored .25 .25
1076 A208 50c multicolored .40 .40
1077 A208 60c multicolored .45 .45
1078 A208 70c multicolored .50 .50
1079 A208 $4 multicolored 3.00 3.00
1080 A208 $5 multicolored 3.75 3.75
Nos. 1073-1080 (8) 8.75 8.75

Souvenir Sheets

1081 A208 $5 multi (#1272) 3.75 3.75
1082 A208 $5 multi (#1273) 3.75 3.75

Nos. 1223-1232 Overprinted

1990, Feb. 21

1083 A202 10c multicolored .20 .20
1084 A202 25c multicolored .20 .20
1085 A202 50c multicolored .40 .40
1086 A202 60c multicolored .45 .45
1087 A202 75c multicolored .55 .55
1088 A202 $1 multicolored .75 .75
1089 A202 $3 multicolored 2.25 2.25
1090 A202 $4 multicolored 3.00 3.00
Nos. 1083-1090 (8) 7.80 7.80

Souvenir Sheets

1091 A202 $6 multi (#1231) 4.50 4.50
1092 A202 $6 multi (#1232) 4.50 4.50

Nos. 1233-1237 Overprinted

1990, Mar. 30

1093 A203 25c multicolored .20 .20
1094 A203 45c multicolored .30 .30
1095 A203 60c multicolored .45 .45
1096 A203 $4 multicolored 3.00 3.00
Nos. 1093-1096 (4) 3.95 3.95

Souvenir Sheet

1097 A203 $5 multicolored 3.75 3.75

Nos. 1258-1262 Overprinted

1990, Mar. 30

1098 A206 10c multicolored .20 .20
1099 A206 45c multicolored .30 .30
1100 A206 $1 multicolored .75 .75
1101 A206 $4 multicolored 3.00 3.00
Nos. 1098-1101 (4) 4.25 4.25

Souvenir Sheet

1102 A206 $5 multicolored 3.75 3.75

Nos. 1275-1284 Overprinted

1990, June 6

1103 A210 10c multicolored .20 .20
1104 A210 20c multicolored .20 .20
1105 A210 25c multicolored .20 .20
1106 A210 45c multicolored .30 .30
1107 A210 60c multicolored .45 .45
1108 A210 $2 multicolored 1.50 1.50
1109 A210 $3 multicolored 2.25 2.25
1110 A210 $4 multicolored 3.00 3.00
Nos. 1103-1110 (8) 8.10 8.10

Souvenir Sheets

1111 A210 $5 multi (#1283) 3.75 3.75
1112 A210 $5 multi (#1284) 3.75 3.75

Nos. 1285-1294 Overprinted

1990, July 12

1113 A211 15c multicolored .20 .20
1114 A211 45c multicolored .30 .30
1115 A211 50c multicolored .40 .40
1116 A211 60c multicolored .45 .45
1117 A211 $1 multicolored .75 .75
1118 A211 $2 multicolored 1.50 1.50
1119 A211 $3 multicolored 2.25 2.25
1120 A211 $5 multicolored 3.75 3.75
Nos. 1113-1120 (8) 9.60 9.60

Souvenir Sheets

1121 A211 $6 multi (#1293) 4.50 4.50
1122 A211 $6 multi (#1294) 4.50 4.50

Nos. 1295-1304 Overprinted

1990, Aug. 14

1123 A212 10c multicolored .20 .20
1124 A212 15c multicolored .20 .20
1125 A212 50c multicolored .40 .40
1126 A212 60c multicolored .45 .45
1127 A212 $1 multicolored .75 .75
1128 A212 $2 multicolored 1.50 1.50
1129 A212 $3 multicolored 2.25 2.25
1130 A212 $4 multicolored 3.00 3.00
Nos. 1123-1130 (8) 8.75 8.75

Souvenir Sheets

1131 A212 $5 multi (#1303) 3.75 3.75
1132 A212 $5 multi (#1304) 3.75 3.75

Barbuda Nos. 888-889 Surcharged "1st Anniversary / Hurricane Hugo / 16th September, 1989-1990"

1990, Sept. 17 ***Perf. 15***

1133 A50 $5 on $7.50 3.75 3.75
1134 A50 $7.50 on $10 5.50 5.50

Nos. 1324-1328 Overprinted

1990, Oct. 12 ***Perf. 14***

1135 A217 15c multicolored .20 .20
1136 A217 35c multicolored .30 .30
1137 A217 75c multicolored .55 .55
1138 A217 $3 multicolored 2.25 2.25
Nos. 1135-1138 (4) 3.30 3.30

Souvenir Sheet

1139 A217 $6 multicolored 4.50 4.50

No. 1313 Ovptd. in Silver Miniature Sheet

1990, Dec. 14

1140 A215 45c Sheet of 20, #a.-t. 6.75 6.75

Nos. 1360-1369 Overprinted

Perf. 14x13½, 13½x14

1990, Dec. 14

1141 A221 25c multicolored .20 .20
1142 A221 30c multicolored .25 .25
1143 A221 40c multicolored .30 .30
1144 A221 60c multicolored .45 .45
1145 A221 $1 multicolored .75 .75
1146 A221 $2 multicolored 1.50 1.50
1147 A221 $4 multicolored 3.00 3.00
1148 A221 $5 multicolored 3.75 3.75
Nos. 1141-1148 (8) 10.20 10.20

Souvenir Sheets

1149 A221 $6 multi (#1368) 4.50 4.50
1150 A221 $6 multi (#1369) 4.50 4.50

Nos. 1305-1308 Overprinted

1991, Feb. 4 ***Perf. 15x14***

1151 A213 45c green .35 .35
1152 A213 60c bright rose .45 .45
1153 A213 $5 bright ultra 3.75 3.75
Nos. 1151-1153 (3) 4.55 4.55

Souvenir Sheet

1154 A213 $6 black 4.50 4.50

Nos. 1309-1312 Overprinted

1991, Feb. 4 ***Perf. 13½***

1155 A214 50c red & deep grn .40 .40
1156 A214 75c red & vio brn .60 .60
1157 A214 $4 red & brt ultra 3.00 3.00
Nos. 1155-1157 (3) 4.00 4.00

Souvenir Sheet

1158 A214 $6 red & black 4.50 4.50

Birds — B52

1991, Mar. 25 **Litho.** ***Perf. 14***

1164 B52 60c Troupial .45 .45
1168 B52 $2 Christmas bird 1.50 1.50
1169 B52 $4 Rose-breasted grosbeak 3.00 3.00
1171 B52 $7 Stolid flycatcher 5.25 5.25
Nos. 1164-1171 (4) 10.20 10.20

This is an expanding set. Numbers will change.

Nos. 1329-1333 Overprinted

1991, Apr. 23 **Litho.** ***Perf. 14***

1173 A218 50c multicolored .40 .40
1174 A218 75c multicolored .55 .55
1175 A218 $1 multicolored .75 .75
1176 A218 $5 multicolored 3.75 3.75
Nos. 1173-1176 (4) 5.45 5.45

Souvenir Sheet

1177 A218 $6 multicolored 4.50 4.50

Nos. 1350-1359 Overprinted

1991, Apr. 23

1178 A220 10c multicolored .20 .20
1179 A220 25c multicolored .20 .20
1180 A220 50c multicolored .40 .40
1181 A220 60c multicolored .45 .45
1182 A220 $1 multicolored .75 .75
1183 A220 $2 multicolored 1.50 1.50
1184 A220 $3 multicolored 2.25 2.25
1185 A220 $4 multicolored 3.00 3.00
Nos. 1178-1185 (8) 8.75 8.75

Souvenir Sheets

1186 A220 $6 multi (#1358) 4.50 4.50
1187 A220 $6 multi (#1359) 4.50 4.50

Nos. 1370-1379 Overprinted

1991, June 21 ***Perf. 14x13½***

1188 A222 25c multicolored .20 .20
1189 A222 45c multicolored .35 .35
1190 A222 50c multicolored .40 .40
1191 A222 60c multicolored .45 .45
1192 A222 $1 multicolored .75 .75
1193 A222 $2 multicolored 1.50 1.50
1194 A222 $3 multicolored 2.25 2.25
1195 A222 $4 multicolored 3.00 3.00
Nos. 1188-1195 (8) 8.90 8.90

Souvenir Sheets

1196 A222 $6 multi (#1378) 4.50 4.50
1197 A222 $6 multi (#1379) 4.50 4.50

Nos. 1380-1390 Overprinted

1991, July 25 **Litho.** ***Perf. 14***

1198 A223 10c multicolored .20 .20
1199 A223 15c multicolored .20 .20
1200 A223 25c multicolored .20 .20
1201 A223 45c multicolored .35 .35
1202 A223 50c multicolored .40 .40
1203 A223 $1 multicolored .75 .75
1204 A223 $2 multicolored 1.50 1.50
1205 A223 $4 multicolored 3.00 3.00
1206 A223 $5 multicolored 3.75 3.75
Nos. 1198-1206 (9) 10.35 10.35

Souvenir Sheets

1207 A223 $6 multi (#1389) 4.50 4.50
1208 A223 $6 multi (#1390) 4.50 4.50

Nos. 1411-1420 Overprinted

1991, Aug. 26 **Litho.** ***Perf. 14***

1209 A226 10c multicolored .20 .20
1210 A226 15c multicolored .20 .20
1211 A226 45c multicolored .35 .35
1212 A226 60c multicolored .45 .45
1213 A226 $1 multicolored .75 .75
1214 A226 $2 multicolored 1.50 1.50
1215 A226 $4 multicolored 3.00 3.00
1216 A226 $5 multicolored 3.75 3.75
Nos. 1209-1216 (8) 10.20 10.20

Souvenir Sheets

1217 A226 $6 multi (#1419) 4.50 4.50
1218 A226 $6 multi (#1420) 4.50 4.50

Nos. 1401-1410 Overprinted

1991, Oct. 18

1219 A225 10c multicolored .20 .20
1220 A225 35c multicolored .25 .25
1221 A225 50c multicolored .40 .40
1222 A225 75c multicolored .55 .55
1223 A225 $1 multicolored .75 .75
1224 A225 $2 multicolored 1.50 1.50
1225 A225 $4 multicolored 3.00 3.00
1226 A225 $5 multicolored 3.75 3.75
Nos. 1219-1226 (8) 10.40 10.40

Souvenir Sheets

1227 A225 $6 multi (#1409) 4.50 4.50
1228 A225 $6 multi (#1410) 4.50 4.50

Nos. 1446-1455 Overprinted

1991, Nov. 18

1229 CD347 10c multicolored .20 .20
1230 CD347 15c multicolored .20 .20
1231 CD347 20c multicolored .20 .20
1232 CD347 40c multicolored .30 .30
1233 CD347 $1 multicolored .85 .85
1234 CD347 $2 multicolored 1.50 1.50
1235 CD347 $4 multicolored 3.00 3.00
1236 CD347 $5 multicolored 3.75 3.75
Nos. 1229-1236 (8) 10.00 10.00

Souvenir Sheets

1237 CD347 $4 multi (#1454) 3.00 3.00
1238 CD347 $4 multi (#1455) 3.00 3.00

Nos. 1503-1510 Overprinted

1991, Dec. 24 ***Perf. 12***

1239 A238 10c multicolored .20 .20
1240 A238 30c multicolored .25 .25
1241 A238 40c multicolored .30 .30
1242 A238 60c multicolored .45 .45
1243 A238 $1 multicolored .80 .80
1244 A238 $3 multicolored 2.25 2.25
1245 A238 $4 multicolored 3.00 3.00
1246 A238 $5 multicolored 3.75 3.75
Nos. 1239-1246 (8) 11.00 11.00

Nos. 1421-1435 Overprinted

1992, Feb. 20 ***Perf. 13½***

1249 A227 5c multicolored .20 .20
1250 A227 10c multicolored .20 .20
1251 A227 15c multicolored .20 .20
1252 A227 25c multicolored .20 .20
1253 A227 30c multicolored .25 .25
1254 A227 40c multicolored .30 .30
1255 A227 50c multicolored .40 .40
1256 A227 75c multicolored .55 .55

1257 A227 $2 multicolored 1.50 1.50
1258 A227 $3 multicolored 2.25 2.25
1259 A227 $4 multicolored 3.00 3.00
1260 A227 $5 multicolored 3.75 3.75
Nos. 1249-1260 (12) 12.80 12.80

Size: 102x76mm

Imperf

1261 A227 $5 multi (#1433) 3.75 3.75
1262 A227 $5 multi (#1434) 3.75 3.75
1263 A227 $6 multi 4.50 4.50

Nos. 1476-1483 Overprinted

1992, Apr. 7 Litho. *Perf. 14*

1264 A231 10c multi .20 .20
1265 A231 15c multi, vert. .20 .20
1266 A231 45c multi, vert. .35 .35
1267 A231 60c multi, vert. .45 .45
1268 A231 $1 multi .75 .75
1269 A231 $2 multi 1.50 1.50
1270 A231 $4 multi 3.00 3.00
1271 A231 $5 multi, vert. 3.75 3.75
Nos. 1264-1271 (8) 10.20 10.20

Nos. 1484-1485 Overprinted

1992, Apr. 7 Litho. *Perf. 14*

Souvenir Sheets

1272 A231 $6 multi (#1484) 5.00 5.00
1273 A231 $6 multi (#1485) 5.00 5.00

Nos. 1551-1560 Overprinted

1992, Apr. 16 Litho. *Perf. 14x13½*

1274 A242 10c multicolored .20 .20
1275 A242 15c multicolored .20 .20
1276 A242 30c multicolored .25 .25
1277 A242 40c multicolored .35 .35
1278 A242 $1 multicolored .85 .85
1279 A242 $2 multicolored 1.60 1.60
1280 A242 $4 multicolored 3.25 3.25
1281 A242 $5 multicolored 4.25 4.25
Nos. 1274-1281 (8) 10.95 10.95

Souvenir Sheets

1282 A242 $6 multi (#1559) 5.00 5.00
1283 A242 $6 multi (#1560) 5.00 5.00

Nos. 1489-1492 Overprinted

1992, June 19 Litho. *Perf. 14*

1284 A234 75c multi .55 .55
1285 A234 $2 multi, vert. 1.50 1.50
1286 A234 $3.50 multi 2.75 2.75
Nos. 1284-1286 (3) 4.80 4.80

Souvenir Sheet

1287 A234 $5 multi, vert. 4.25 4.25

Nos. 1493-1494 Overprinted

1992, June 19

1288 A235 $1.50 multi 1.10 1.10
1289 A235 $4 multi 3.00 3.00

Nos. 1495-1496 Overprinted

1992, June 19

1290 A236 $2 multi 1.50 1.50
1291 A236 $2.50 multi, vert. 1.90 1.90

Nos. 1499-1502 Overprinted

1992, June 19

1292 A237 25c multicolored .20 .20
1293 A237 $2 multicolored 1.50 1.50
1294 A237 $3 multicolored 2.25 2.25
1295 A237 $4 multicolored 3.50 3.50
Nos. 1292-1295 (4) 7.45 7.45

Nos. 1571-1578 Overprinted

1992, Oct. 12 Litho. *Perf. 14*

1296 A244 15c multicolored .20 .20
1297 A244 30c multicolored .25 .25
1298 A244 40c multicolored .30 .30
1299 A244 $1 multicolored .75 .75
1300 A244 $2 multicolored 1.50 1.50
1301 A244 $4 multicolored 3.00 3.00
Nos. 1296-1301 (6) 6.00 6.00

Souvenir Sheets

1302 A244 $6 multicolored 4.50 4.50
1303 A244 $6 multicolored 4.50 4.50

Nos. 1599-1600 Overprinted

1992, Oct. 12 *Perf. 14½*

1304 A247 $1 multicolored .75 .75
1305 A247 $2 multicolored 1.50 1.50

Nos. 1513-1518 Overprinted

1992, Nov. 3 *Perf. 14*

1306 CD348 10c multicolored .20 .20
1307 CD348 30c multicolored .25 .25
1308 CD348 $1 multicolored .80 .80
1309 CD348 $5 multicolored 3.75 3.75
Nos. 1306-1309 (4) 5.00 5.00

Souvenir Sheets

1310 CD348 $6 multi (#1517) 4.50 4.50
1311 CD348 $6 multi (#1518) 4.50 4.50

Nos. 1541-1550 Ovptd. "BARBUDA / MAIL"

1992, Dec. 8

1312 A241 10c multicolored .20 .20
1313 A241 15c multicolored .20 .20
1314 A241 30c multicolored .25 .25
1315 A241 50c multicolored .40 .40
1316 A241 $1 multicolored .75 .75
1317 A241 $2 multicolored 1.50 1.50
1318 A241 $4 multicolored 3.00 3.00
1319 A241 $5 multicolored 3.75 3.75
Nos. 1312-1319 (8) 10.05 10.05

Souvenir Sheets

1320 A241 $6 multi (#1549) 5.50 5.50
1321 A241 $6 multi (#1550) 5.50 5.50

Nos. 1609-1618 Ovptd. "BARBUDA MAIL"

1992, Dec. 8 Litho. *Perf. 13½x14*

1322 A251 10c multicolored .20 .20
1323 A251 25c multicolored .20 .20
1324 A251 30c multicolored .25 .25
1325 A251 40c multicolored .30 .30
1326 A251 60c multicolored .45 .45
1327 A251 $1 multicolored .75 .75
1328 A251 $4 multicolored 3.00 3.00
1329 A251 $5 multicolored 3.75 3.75
Nos. 1322-1329 (8) 8.90 8.90

Souvenir Sheets

1330 A251 $6 multi (#1616) 5.50 5.50
1331 A251 $6 multi (#1617) 5.50 5.50

No. 1601 Ovptd. "BARBUDA MAIL"

1992 Litho. *Perf. 14*

Souvenir Sheet

1332 A248 $6 multicolored 4.50 4.50

Nos. 1519-1528 Ovptd.

1993, Jan. 25 Litho. *Perf. 14*

1333 A239 10c multicolored .20 .20
1334 A239 15c multicolored .20 .20
1335 A239 30c multicolored .30 .30
1336 A239 40c multicolored .35 .35
1337 A239 $1 multicolored .90 .90
1338 A239 $2 multicolored 1.75 1.75
1339 A239 $4 multicolored 3.50 3.50
1340 A239 $5 multicolored 4.50 4.50
Nos. 1332-1339 (8) 11.70 11.70

Souvenir Sheets

1341 A239 $6 multi (#1527) 5.50 5.50
1342 A239 $6 multi (#1528) 5.50 5.50

Nos. 1561-1570 Ovptd.

1993, Mar. 22 Litho. *Perf. 13*

1343 A243 10c multicolored .20 .20
1344 A243 15c multicolored .20 .20
1345 A243 30c multicolored .25 .25
1346 A243 40c multicolored .30 .30
1347 A243 $1 multicolored .80 .80
1348 A243 $2 multicolored 1.50 1.50
1349 A243 $4 multicolored 3.00 3.00
1350 A243 $5 multicolored 3.75 3.75
Nos. 1343-1350 (8) 10.00 10.00

Imperf

Size: 120x95mm

1351 A243 $6 multi (#1569) 5.50 5.50
1352 A243 $6 multi (#1570) 5.50 5.50

Nos. 1589-1598 Ovptd.

1993, May 10 Litho. *Perf. 14*

1353 A246 10c multicolored .20 .20
1354 A246 25c multicolored .20 .20
1355 A246 45c multicolored .35 .35
1356 A246 60c multicolored .45 .45
1357 A246 $1 multicolored .75 .75
1358 A246 $2 multicolored 1.50 1.50
1359 A246 $4 multicolored 3.00 3.00
1360 A246 $5 multicolored 3.75 3.75
Nos. 1353-1360 (8) 10.20 10.20

Souvenir Sheets

1361 A246 $6 multi (#1597) 5.50 5.50
1362 A246 $6 multi (#1598) 5.50 5.50

Nos. 1603-1608 Ovptd.

1993, June 29 Litho. *Perf. 14*

1363 A250 10c multicolored .20 .20
1364 A250 25c multicolored .25 .25
1365 A250 30c multicolored .30 .30
1366 A250 40c multicolored .35 .35
1367 A250 60c multicolored .55 .55
1368 A250 $1 multicolored .90 .90
1369 A250 $4 multicolored 3.50 3.50
1370 A250 $5 multicolored 4.50 4.50
Nos. 1363-1370 (8) 10.55 10.55

Souvenir Sheets

1371 A250 $6 multi (#1607) 5.50 5.50
1372 A250 $6 multi (#1608) 5.50 5.50

Nos. 1619-1632 Ovptd.

1993, Aug. 16 Litho. *Perf. 14*

1373 A252 10c multicolored .20 .20
1374 A252 40c multicolored .30 .30
1375 A253 45c multicolored .35 .35
1376 A252 75c multicolored .60 .60
1377 A252 $1 multicolored .75 .75
1378 A252 $1.50 multicolored 1.10 1.10
1379 A252 $2 multicolored 1.50 1.50
1380 A253 $2 multi (#1626) 1.50 1.50
1381 A253 $2 multi (#1627) 1.50 1.50
1382 A252 $2.25 multicolored 1.75 1.75
1383 A252 $3 multicolored 2.25 2.25
1384 A252 $4 multi (#1630) 3.00 3.00
1385 A252 $4 multi (#1631) 3.00 3.00
1386 A252 $6 multicolored 4.50 4.50
Nos. 1373-1386 (14) 22.30 22.30

Numbers have been reserved for four souvenir sheets in this set.

Nos. 1650-1659 Ovptd.

1993, Sept. 21 Litho. *Perf. 14*

1391 A256 15c multicolored .20 .20
1392 A256 25c multicolored .20 .20
1393 A256 30c multicolored .25 .25
1394 A256 40c multicolored .35 .35
1395 A256 $1 multicolored .75 .75
1396 A256 $2 multicolored 1.50 1.50
1397 A256 $4 multicolored 3.00 3.00
1398 A256 $5 multicolored 3.75 3.75
Nos. 1391-1398 (8) 10.00 10.00

Souvenir Sheets

1399 A256 $6 multi (#1658) 6.50 6.50
1400 A256 $6 multi (#1659) 6.50 6.50

No. 1660 Ovptd.

1993, Nov. 11 Litho. *Perf. 14*

1401 A257 $1 Sheet of 12, #a.-l. 9.00 9.00

Numbers have been reserved for two souvenir sheets in this set.

Nos. 1697-1710 Ovptd.

1994, Mar. 3 Litho. *Perf. 14*

1404-1415 A267 $2 Set of 12 18.00 18.00

Souvenir Sheets

1416-1417 A267 $6 each 4.50 4.50

Nos. 1676-1678 Ovptd.

1994, Apr. 21 Litho. *Perf. 14*

1418 A260 40c multicolored .30 .30
1419 A260 $3 multicolored 2.25 2.25

Souvenir Sheet

1420 A260 $6 multicolored 4.50 4.50

Nos. 1679-1682 Ovptd.

1994, Apr. 21

1421-1423 A261 Set of 3 4.50 4.50

Souvenir Sheet

1424 A261 $6 multicolored 4.50 4.50

Nos. 1683-1685 Ovptd.

1994, Apr. 21

1425 A262 40c multicolored .30 .30
1426 A262 $4 multicolored 3.25 3.25

Souvenir Sheet

1427 A262 $5 multicolored 3.75 3.75

Nos. 1686-1688 Ovptd.

1994, Apr. 21

1428 A263 30c multicolored .25 .25
1429 A263 $4 multicolored 3.25 3.25

Souvenir Sheet

1430 A263 $6 multicolored 4.50 4.50

Nos. 1692-1693 Ovptd.

1994, Apr. 21

1431 A265 $5 multicolored 4.00 4.00

Souvenir Sheet

1432 A265 $6 multicolored 4.50 4.50

Nos. 1694-1696 Ovptd.

1994, Apr. 21

1433 A266 15c multicolored .20 .20
1434 A266 $5 multicolored 4.00 4.00

Souvenir Sheet

1435 A266 $6 multicolored 4.50 4.50

Nos. 1732-1735 Ovptd.

1994, Apr. 21

1436-1439 A270 Set of 4 1.10 1.10

Nos. 1711-1720 Ovptd.

1994, June 15

1440-1446 A268 Set of 7 12.00 12.00

Souvenir Sheets

1447-1449 A268 $6 each 4.50 4.50

Nos. 1736-1741 Ovptd.

1994, June 15

1450-1453 A271 30c Set of 4 7.25 7.25

Souvenir Sheets

1454-1455 A271 $6 each 4.50 4.50

Nos. 1689-1691 Ovptd.

1994, Sept. 21 Litho. *Perf. 14*

1456 A264 $1 multicolored .75 .75
1457 A264 $3 multicolored 2.25 2.25

Souvenir Sheet

1458 A264 $6 multicolored 4.50 4.50

Nos. 1786-1795 Ovptd.

1994, Sept. 21 Litho. *Perf. 14*

1459-1466 A279 Set of 8 10.00 10.00

Souvenir Sheets

1467-1468 A279 $6 each 4.50 4.50

Nos. 1776-1779 Ovptd.

1994, Nov. 3 Litho. *Perf. 14*

1469 A277 $1.50 multi (#1776) 9.00 9.00
1470 A277 $1.50 multi (#1777) 9.00 9.00

Souvenir Sheets

1471 A277 $1.50 multi (#1778) 1.10 1.10
1472 A277 $1.50 multi (#1779) 1.10 1.10

Nos. 1835-1842 Ovptd.

1995, Jan. 12 Litho. *Perf. 14*

1473-1478 A291 Set of 6 8.50 8.50

Souvenir Sheets

1479 A291 $6 multi (#1841) 4.50 4.50
1480 A291 $6 multi (#1842) 4.50 4.50

Nos. 1857-1866 Ovptd.

1995, Jan. 12 Litho. *Perf. 14*

1481-1488 A295 Set of 8 6.75 6.75

Souvenir Sheets

Perf. 13½x14

1489 A295 $6 multi (#1865) 4.50 4.50
1490 A295 $6 multi (#1866) 4.50 4.50

Nos. 1829-1834 Ovptd.

1996, Feb. 14 Litho. *Perf. 14*

1491 A290 75c multi (#1829) 5.50 5.50
1492 A290 75c multi (#1830) 5.50 5.50
1493 A290 75c multi (#1831) 5.50 5.50

Souvenir Sheets

1494 A290 $6 multi (#1832) 5.50 5.50
1495 A290 $6 multi (#1833) 5.50 5.50
1496 A290 $6 multi (#1834) 5.50 5.50

Nos. 1867-1881 Ovptd.

1995 Litho. *Perf. 14½x14*

1497 A296 15c multi (#1867) .20 .20
1498 A296 25c multi (#1868) .20 .20
1499 A296 35c multi (#1869) .30 .30
1500 A296 40c multi (#1870) .35 .35
1501 A296 45c multi (#1871) .40 .40
1502 A296 60c multi (#1872) .55 .55
1503 A296 65c multi (#1873) .60 .60
1504 A296 70c multi (#1873) .65 .65
1505 A296 75c multi (#1874) .70 .70
1506 A296 90c multi (#1875) .80 .80
1507 A296 $1.20 multi (#1876) 1.10 1.10
1508 A296 $2 multi (#1877) 1.75 1.75
1509 A296 $5 multi (#1878) 4.50 4.50
1510 A296 $10 multi (#1879) 9.00 9.00
1511 A296 $20 multi (#1880) 18.00 18.00
Nos. 1497-1511 (15) 39.10 39.10

Nos. 1806-1808 Ovptd.

1996, Jan. 22 Litho. *Perf. 14*

1512 A281 50c Sheet of 9, #a.-i. 3.50 3.50

Souvenir Sheets

1513 A281 $6 multi (#1807) 4.50 4.50
1514 A281 $6 multi (#1808) 4.50 4.50

Nos. 1949-1956 Ovptd.

1996, Jan. 22 *Perf. 13½x14*

1515-1520 A314 Set of 6 6.75 6.75

Souvenir Sheets

1521 A314 $5 multi (#1955) 3.75 3.75
1522 A314 $6 multi (#1956) 4.50 4.50

Nos. 1810-1813 Ovptd.

1995, Sept. 29 Litho. *Perf. 14*

1546-1548 A283 Set of 3 4.00 4.00

Souvenir Sheet

1549 A283 $6 multi (on #1813) 5.50 5.50

End of World War II, 50th Anniv. — B53

Design: German bombers over St. Paul's Cathedral, London.

1995, Nov. 13 Litho. *Perf. 13*
1550 B53 $8 multicolored 6.00 6.00

For overprints and surcharges see #1639, B3.

Queen Elizabeth, the Queen Mother, 95th Birthday
B54

1995, Nov. 20
1551 B54 $7.50 multicolored 5.50 5.50

For overprints and surcharges see #1638, B2.

United Nations, 50th Anniv. — B55

1995, Nov. 27
1552 B55 $8 New York City 6.00 6.00

For surcharge see #B4.

Nos. 1848, 1851, 1854-1856 Ovptd.

1996, Feb. 14 Litho. *Perf. 14*
1553 A294 15c multi (#1848) .20 .20
1554 A294 $1 multi (#1851) .75 .75
1555 A294 $4 multi (#1854) 3.00 3.00
Nos. 1553-1555 (3) 3.95 3.95

Souvenir Sheets
1556 A294 $6 multi (#1855) 4.50 4.50
1557 A294 $6 multi (#1856) 4.50 4.50

Nos. 1882-1890 Ovptd.

1996, June 13 Litho. *Perf. 14*
1558-1563 A297 Set of 6 7.50 7.50
1564 A297 75c Sheet of 12, #a.-l. 8.25 8.25

Souvenir Sheets
1565 A297 $6 multi (#1889) 5.50 5.50
1566 A297 $6 multi (#1890) 5.50 5.50

Nos. 1891-1898 Ovptd.

1996, July 16 Litho. *Perf. 14*
1567-1572 A298 Set of 6 7.00 7.00

Souvenir Sheets
1573 A298 $6 multi (#1897) 5.00 5.00
1574 A298 $6 multi (#1898) 5.00 5.00

Nos. 1930-1933 Ovptd.

1996, Sept. 10
1575-1576 A310 Strip of 3, #a.-c., each 3.00 3.00

Souvenir Sheets
1577 A310 $6 multi (#1932) 5.00 5.00
1578 A310 $6 multi (#1933) 5.00 5.00

Nos. 1945-1948 Ovptd.

1996, Oct. 25 Litho. *Perf. 14*
1579 A313 $1 Sheet of 9, #a.-i. (#1945) 8.00 8.00
1580 A313 $1 Sheet of 9, #a.-i. (#1946) 8.00 8.00

Souvenir Sheets
1581 A313 $6 multi (#1947) 5.25 5.25
1582 A313 $6 multi (#1948) 5.25 5.25

Nos. 2001-2002 Ovptd.

1996, Nov. 14 *Perf. 13½x14*
1583 A323 $2 Strip of 3, #a.-c. 5.25 5.25

Souvenir Sheet
1584 A323 $6 multicolored 5.25 5.25

Nos. 2018-2025 Ovptd.

1997, Jan. 28 Litho. *Perf. 13½x14*
1585-1590 A328 Set of 6 6.50 6.50

Souvenir Sheets
1591 A328 $6 multi (#2024) 5.50 5.50
1592 A328 $6 multi (#2025) 5.50 5.50

Nos. 1905-1906 Ovptd.

1997, Feb. 24 *Perf. 14*
1593 A301 Strip of 3, #a.-c. 2.50 2.50

Souvenir Sheet
1594 A301 $6 multicolored 5.50 5.50

Nos. 1907-1908 Ovptd.

1997, Feb. 24
1595 A302 $5 multicolored 4.50 4.50

Souvenir Sheet
1596 A302 $6 multicolored 5.50 5.50

Nos. 1899-1902 Ovptd.
Sheets of 6 or 8 + Label

1997, Apr. 4 Litho. *Perf. 14*
1597 A299 $1.20 #a.-f. 6.50 6.50
1598 A299 $1.20 #a.-h. 8.50 8.50

Souvenir Sheets
1599 A299 $3 multicolored 2.75 2.75
1600 A299 $6 multicolored 5.50 5.50

Nos. 1903-1904 Ovptd.

1997 Litho. *Perf. 14*
1601 A300 Strip of 3, #a.-c. 2.50 2.50

Souvenir Sheet
1602 A300 $6 multicolored 5.50 5.50

Nos. 1909-1910 Ovptd.

1997 *Perf. 13½x14*
1603 A303 $1.50 Strip or block of 4, #a.-d. 5.50 5.50

Souvenir Sheet
1604 A303 $6 multicolored 5.50 5.50

Nos. 1913-1917 Ovptd.

1997 Litho. *Perf. 14*
1605-1608 A305 Set of 4 5.00 5.00

Souvenir Sheet
1609 A305 $6 multicolored 5.50 5.50

Nos. 1918-1919 Ovptd.

1997
1610 A306 45c Sheet of 12, #a.-l. 4.75 4.75

Souvenir Sheet
1611 A306 $6 multicolored 5.50 5.50

Nos. 1928-1929 Ovptd.

1997
1612 A309 75c Sheet of 12, #a.-l. 8.00 8.00

Souvenir Sheet
1613 A309 $6 multicolored 5.50 5.50

Nos. 1934-1942 Ovptd.

1997, May 30 Litho. *Perf. 14*
1614-1619 A311 Set of 6 7.50 7.50

Sheet of 9
1620 A311 $1.20 #a.-i. 8.25 8.25

Souvenir Sheets
1621 A311 $6 multi (#1941) 4.50 4.50
1621A A311 $6 multi (#1942) 4.50 4.50

Nos. 1911-1912 Ovptd.

1997 Litho. *Perf. 14*
1622 A304 75c Sheet of 12, #a.-l. 8.00 8.00

Souvenir Sheet
1623 A304 $6 multicolored 5.50 5.50

Nos. 1943-1944 Ovptd.

1997
1624 A312 75c Sheet of 12, #a.-l. 8.00 8.00

Souvenir Sheet
1625 A312 $6 multicolored 5.50 5.50

Nos. 1967-1970 Ovptd.

1997
1626-1627 A317 75c Strips of 4, #a.-d., each 2.75 2.75

Souvenir Sheets
1628 A317 $6 multi (#1969) 5.50 5.50
1629 A317 $6 multi (#1970) 5.50 5.50

Nos. 1970A-1974 Ovptd.

1997, Nov. 3 Litho. *Perf. 14*
1629A-1629F A318 Set of 6 2.50 2.50

Sheets of 6
1629G A318 $1.20 #k.-p. (#1971) 5.50 5.50
1629H A318 $1.50 #q.-v. (#1972) 6.75 6.75

Souvenir Sheets
1629I A318 $6 multi (#1973) 4.50 4.50
1629J A318 $6 multi (#1974) 4.50 4.50

Nos. 2111-2118 Ovptd.

1997 Litho. *Perf. 14*
1630-1635 A345 Set of 6 5.25 5.25

Souvenir Sheets
1636 A345 $6 multi (#2117) 4.50 4.50
1637 A345 $6 multi (#2118) 4.50 4.50

Nos. 2069-2070 Ovptd.

1997, Nov. 3 Litho. *Perf. 14*

Sheet of 6
1637A A337 $1 #c.-h. (#2069) 4.50 4.50

Souvenir Sheet
1637B A337 $6 multi (#2070) 4.50 4.50

Nos. 1550-1551 Ovptd. in Gold
"Golden Wedding of
H.M. Queen Elizabeth II
and H.R.H. Prince Phillip
1947-1997"

1997, July 25 Litho. *Perf. 13*
1638 B54 $7.50 on #1551 5.50 5.50
1639 B53 $8 on #1550 6.00 6.00

Nos. 1983-1986 Ovptd.

1998 Litho. *Perf. 14*
1640 A320 75c Vert. strip, #a.-d. (#1983) 2.75 2.75
1641 A320 75c Vert. strip, #a.-d. (#1984) 2.75 2.75

Souvenir Sheets
1643 A320 $5 multicolored 4.50 4.50
1644 A320 $6 multicolored 5.50 5.50

Nos. 2003-2004 Ovptd.

1998 Litho. *Perf. 14*
1645 A324 60c Block of 4, #a.-d. 2.00 2.00

Souvenir Sheet
1646 A324 $6 multi 5.25 5.25

Nos. 2094-2102 Ovptd.

1998
1647-1652 A342 Set of 6 5.75 5.75
1653 A342 $1 Sheet of 8 + label 6.75 6.75

Souvenir Sheets
1654 A342 $6 multi (#2101) 5.25 5.25
1655 A342 $6 multi (#2102) 5.25 5.25

Nos. 2005-2008 Ovptd.

1998 Litho. *Perf. 14*
1656-1658 A325 Set of 3 2.50 2.50

Souvenir Sheet
1659 A325 $6 multicolored 5.25 5.25

Nos. 2009-2012 Ovptd.

1998
1660-1662 A326 Set of 3 2.50 2.50

Souvenir Sheet
1663 A326 $6 multicolored 5.25 5.25

Nos. 2119-2122 Ovptd.

1998 Litho. *Perf. 14*

Sheets of 6
1664 A346 $1.65 #a.-f. (#2119) 8.50 8.50
1665 A346 $1.65 #a.-f. (#2120) 8.50 8.50

Souvenir Sheets
1666 A346 $6 multi (#2121) 5.25 5.25
1667 A346 $6 multi (#2122) 5.25 5.25

Nos. 2037-2038 Ovptd.

1998 Litho. *Perf. 14*

Sheet of 9
1668 A330 $1 #a.-i. (#2037) 7.75 7.75

Souvenir Sheet
1669 A330 $6 multi (#2038) 5.25 5.25

Nos. 2063-2064 Ovtpd.

1998

Sheet of 9
1670 A334 $1 #a.-i. (#2063) 7.75 7.75

Souvenir Sheet
1671 A334 $6 multi (#2064) 5.25 5.25

Nos. 2039-2047 Ovptd.

1998 Litho. *Perf. 14*
1672-1675 A331 Set of 4 4.75 4.75

Sheets of 9
1676 A331 $1.10 #a.-i. (#2043) 8.50 8.50
1677 A331 $1.10 #a.-i. (#2044) 8.50 8.50

Souvenir Sheets
1678-1680 A331 $6 each (#2045-2047) 5.25 5.25

Nos. 2140-2148 Ovptd.

1998
1681-1688 A349 Set of 8 6.50 6.50

Souvenir Sheet
1689 A349 $6 multi (#2148) 5.25 5.25

Nos. 2211-2219 Ovptd.

1998
1690-1696 A366 Set of 7 5.00 5.00

Souvenir Sheets
1697 A366 $6 multi (#2218) 5.25 5.25
1698 A366 $6 multi (#2219) 5.25 5.25

Nos. 2058-2062 Ovptd.

1998 Litho. *Perf. 14*

Sheets of 6
1699 A333 $1.20 #a.-f. (#2058) 5.50 5.50
1700 A333 $1.65 #a.-f. (#2059) 7.50 7.50

Souvenir Sheets
1701-1703 A333 $6 each (#2060-2062) 4.50 4.50

Nos. 2067-2068 Ovptd.

1999 Litho. *Perf. 14*
1704 A336 $1.75 Sheet of 3, #a.-c. 5.50 5.50

Souvenir Sheet
1705 A336 $6 multi (#2068) 6.50 6.50

Nos. 2071-2072 Ovptd.

1999 *Perf. 13½x14*
1706 A338 $1.75 Sheet of 3, #a.-c. 4.25 4.25

Souvenir Sheet
1707 A338 $6 multi (#2072) 4.75 4.75

Nos. 2084-2093 Ovptd.

1999 Litho. *Perf. 14*
1708-1713 A341 Set of 6 4.25 4.25

Sheets of 8
1714 A341 $1.65 #a.-h. (#2090) 5.00 5.00
1715 A341 $1.65 #a.-h.,(#2091) 5.00 5.00

Souvenir Sheets
1716-1717 A341 $6 each (#2092-2093) 4.50 4.50

Nos. 2065-2066 Ovptd.

1999 Litho. *Perf. 14*
1718 A335 $1.75 multicolored 1.40 1.40

Souvenir Sheet
1719 A335 $6 multicolored 4.75 4.75

Nos. 2075-2083 Ovptd.

1999
1720-1725 A340 Set of 6 4.00 4.00

Sheet of 6
1726 A340 $1.75 #a.-f. 8.00 8.00

Souvenir Sheets
1727 A340 $6 multi (#2082) 4.50 4.50
1728 A340 $6 multi (#2083) 4.50 4.50

No. 2184 Ovptd.

1999
1729 A358 $1.20 multicolored .90 .90

SEMI-POSTAL STAMP

Catalogue values for unused stamps in this section are for Never Hinged items.

Barbuda No. 501 Crudely Surcharged

S. Atlantic Fund + 50c

1982, June 28

Self-Adhesive
B1 CD331 Booklet 16.00

Nos. 1550-1552 Surcharged "HURRICANE RELIEF" in Silver

1995, Nov. Litho. *Perf. 13*

B2	B54	$7.50 +$1 on #1551	6.25	6.25
B3	B53	$8 +$1 on #1550	6.75	6.75
B4	B55	$8 +$1 on #1552	6.75	6.75
		Nos. B2-B4 (3)	19.75	19.75

BASUTOLAND

bə-ˈsü-tə-ˌland

LOCATION — An enclave in the state of South Africa
GOVT. — Former British Crown Colony
AREA — 11,716 sq. mi.
POP. — 733,000 (est. 1964)
CAPITAL — Maseru

The Colony, a former independent native state, was annexed to the Cape Colony in 1871. In 1883 control was transferred directly to the British Crown. Stamps of the Cape of Good Hope were used from 1871 to 1910 and those of the Union of South Africa from 1910 to 1933. Basutoland became the independent state of Lesotho on Oct. 4, 1966.

12 Pence = 1 Shilling
100 Cents = 1 Rand (1961)

Catalogue values for unused stamps in this country are for Never Hinged items, beginning with Scott 29 in the regular postage section and Scott J1 in the postage due section.

George V
A1

George VI
A2

Crocodile and River Scene

Perf. 12½

1933, Dec. 1 Engr. Wmk. 4

1	A1	½p emerald	.20	.60
2	A1	1p carmine	.30	.20
3	A1	2p red violet	.50	1.10
4	A1	3p ultra	.50	1.75
5	A1	4p slate	1.75	2.50
6	A1	6p yellow	2.25	2.50
7	A1	1sh red orange	3.50	5.25
8	A1	2sh6p dk brown	18.00	22.50
9	A1	5sh violet	35.00	50.00
10	A1	10sh olive green	100.00	125.00
		Nos. 1-10 (10)	162.00	211.40

Common Design Types pictured following the introduction.

Silver Jubilee Issue
Common Design Type

1935, May 4 *Perf. 13½x14*

11	CD301	1p car & blue	.30	.30
12	CD301	2p gray blk & ultra	.65	2.00
13	CD301	3p blue & brown	3.25	3.25
14	CD301	6p brt vio & indigo	8.70	6.50
		Nos. 11-14 (4)	8.70	12.05
		Set, never hinged	15.00	

Coronation Issue
Common Design Type

1937, May 12 *Perf. 13½x14*

15	CD302	1p carmine	.25	.20
16	CD302	2p rose violet	.40	.30
17	CD302	3p bright ultra	.50	.40
		Nos. 15-17 (3)	1.15	.90
		Set, never hinged	2.00	

1938, Apr. 1 *Perf. 12½*

18	A2	½p emerald	.30	.30
19	A2	1p rose car	.30	.20
20	A2	1½p light blue	.30	.20
21	A2	2p rose lilac	.30	.30
22	A2	3p ultra	.35	.35
23	A2	4p gray	.45	1.25
24	A2	6p yel ocher	.55	.65
25	A2	1sh red orange	.75	.90
26	A2	2sh6p black brown	2.75	2.75
27	A2	5sh violet	11.00	11.00
28	A2	10sh olive green	15.00	17.00
		Nos. 18-28 (11)	32.05	34.90
		Set, never hinged	60.00	

Catalogue values for unused stamps in this section, from this point to the end of the section, are for Never Hinged items.

Peace Issue

South Africa Nos. 100-102 Overprinted **Basutoland**

Basic stamps inscribed alternately in English and Afrikaans.

1945, Dec. 3 Wmk. 201 *Perf. 14*

29	A42	1p rose pink & choc, pair	.25	.25
a.		Single, English	.20	.20
b.		Single, Afrikaans	.20	.20
30	A43	2p vio & slate blue, pair	.30	.30
a.		Single, English	.20	.20
b.		Single, Afrikaans	.20	.20
31	A43	3p ultra & dp ultra, pair	.45	.45
a.		Single, English	.20	.20
b.		Single, Afrikaans	.20	.20
		Nos. 29-31 (3)	1.00	1.00

King George VI — A3

King George VI and Queen Elizabeth A4

Princess Margaret Rose and Princess Elizabeth A5

Royal British Family — A6

Perf. 12½

1947, Feb. 17 Wmk. 4 Engr.

35	A3	1p red	.20	.20
36	A4	2p green	.20	.20
37	A5	3p ultra	.20	.20
38	A6	1sh dark violet	.25	.25
		Nos. 35-38 (4)	.85	.85

Visit of the British Royal Family, Mar. 11-12, 1947.

Silver Wedding Issue
Common Design Types

1948, Dec. 1 Photo. *Perf. 14x14½*

39	CD304	1½p brt ultra	.20	

Engr.; Name Typo.

Perf. 11½

40	CD305	10sh dk brown olive	40.00	32.00

UPU Issue
Common Design Types

Engr.; Name Typo. on 3p, 6p

Perf. 13½, 11x11½

1949, Oct. 10 Wmk. 4

41	CD306	1½p blue	.30	.30
42	CD307	3p indigo	.75	.65
43	CD308	6p orange yel	1.25	.90
44	CD309	1sh red brown	1.40	1.10
		Nos. 41-44 (4)	3.70	2.95

Coronation Issue
Common Design Type

1953, June 3 Engr. *Perf. 13½x13*

45	CD312	2p red violet & black	.40	.40

Qiloane Hill — A7

Shearing Angora Goats — A8

Designs: 1p, Orange River. 2p, Mosotho horseman. 3p, Basuto household. 4½p, Maletsunyane falls. 6p, Herdboy with lesiba. 1sh, Pastoral scene. 1sh3p, Plane at Lancers Gap. 2sh6p, Old Fort Leribe. 5sh, Mission cave house.

1954, Oct. 18 Wmk. 4 *Perf. 13½*

46	A7	½p dk brown & gray	.20	.20
47	A7	1p dp grn & gray blk	.20	.20
48	A7	2p org & dp blue	.30	.25
49	A7	3p car & ol green	.35	.30
50	A7	4½p dp blue & ind	.80	.65
51	A7	6p dk grn & org brn	.75	.60
52	A7	1sh rose vio & dk ol green	1.40	1.10
53	A7	1sh3p aqua & brown	1.75	1.40
54	A7	2sh6p lilac rose & dp ultra	6.25	5.00
55	A7	5sh dp car & black	9.00	7.50
56	A8	10sh dp cl & black	19.00	15.00
		Nos. 46-56 (11)	40.00	32.20

See Nos. 72-82, 87-91. For surcharges see Nos. 57, 61-71.

No. 48 Surcharged ½d.

1959, Aug. 1

57	A7	½p on 2p org & dp blue	.25	.25

Chief Moshoeshoe (Moshesh) — A9

Designs: 1sh, Council chamber. 1sh3p, Mosotho on horseback.

Perf. 13x13½

1959, Dec. 15 Wmk. 314

58	A9	3p lt yel, grn & blk	.20	.20
59	A9	1sh green & pink	.35	.35
60	A9	1sh3p orange & ultra	.60	.60
		Nos. 58-60 (3)	1.15	1.15

Institution of the Basutoland National Council.

Nos. 46-56 Surcharged with New Value

2½c (I) 2½c (II) 3½c (I) 3½c (II)
5c (I) 5c (II) 10c (I) 10c (II)
12½c (I) 12½c (II)
25c (I) 25c (II) 25c (III)
50c (I) 50c (II) R1 (I) R1 (II) R1 (III)

1961, Feb. 14 Wmk. 4 *Perf. 13½*

61	A7	½c on ½p dk brn & gray	.20	.20
a.		Double surcharge	250.00	
62	A7	1c on 1p dp grn & gray blk	.20	.20
63	A7	2c on 2p org & dp bl	.20	.20
a.		Inverted surcharge	125.00	
64	A7	2½c on 3p (II)	.20	.20
a.		Type I	.20	.20
b.		Inverted surcharge (II)	1,750.	1,000.
65	A7	3½c on 4½p (I)	.20	.20
a.		Type II	4.50	4.50
66	A7	5c on 6p (II)	.20	.20
a.		Type I	.20	.20
67	A7	10c on 1sh (I)	.20	.20
a.		Type II	40.00	40.00
68	A7	12½c on 1sh3p (II)	.35	.35
a.		Type I	.65	.65
69	A7	25c on 2sh6p (I)	.65	.65
a.		Type II	12.00	12.00
b.		Type III	.65	.65
70	A7	50c on 5sh (II)	1.40	1.40
a.		Type I	2.25	2.25
71	A8	1r on 10sh (III)	2.75	2.75
a.		Type I	12.00	12.00
b.		Type II	12.00	12.00
		Nos. 61-71 (11)	6.55	6.55

Surcharge types on Nos. 64-71 are numbered chronologically.

Types of 1954
Value in Cents and Rands

Designs: ½c, Qiloane Hill. 1c, Orange River. 2c, Mosotho horseman. 2½c, Basuto household. 3½c, Maletsunyane Falls. 5c, Herdboy with lesiba. 10c, Pastoral scene. 12½c, Plane at Lancers Gap. 25c, Old Fort Leribe. 50c, Mission cave house. 1r, Shearing Angora goats.

1961-63 Wmk. 4 Engr. *Perf. 13½*

72	A7	½c dk brn & gray ('62)	.20	.20
73	A7	1c dp grn & gray blk ('62)	.20	.20
74	A7	2c org & dp bl ('62)	.20	.20
75	A7	2½c car & ol grn	.45	.20
76	A7	3½c dp bl & ind ('62)	.40	.20
77	A7	5c dk grn & org brn ('62)	.60	.30
78	A7	10c rose vio & dk ol ('62)	.95	.40
79	A7	12½c aqua & brn ('62)	1.25	.55
80	A7	25c lilac rose & dp ultra ('62)	2.25	1.00
81	A7	50c dp car & blk ('62)	9.00	4.00

Perf. 11½

82	A8	1r dp cl & blk ('63)	15.00	6.50
		Nos. 72-82 (11)	30.50	13.75

See Nos. 87-91. For overprints on stamps and types see Lesotho Nos. 5-14, 20a.

Freedom from Hunger Issue
Common Design Type

Perf. 14x14½

1963, June 4 Photo. Wmk. 314

83	CD314	12½c lilac	.50	.40

Red Cross Centenary Issue
Common Design Type

1963, Sept. 2 Litho. *Perf. 13*

84	CD315	2½c black & red	.20	.20
85	CD315	12½c ultra & red	.70	.70

Queen Type of 1961-63

1964 Engr. *Perf. 13½*

87	A7	1c grn & gray blk	.20	.20
88	A7	2½c car & ol green	.30	.20
89	A7	5c dk green & org brn	.70	.60
90	A7	12½c aqua & brown	1.50	1.40
91	A7	50c dp car & black	6.00	4.75
		Nos. 87-91 (5)	8.70	7.15

Mosotho Woman and Child — A10

Designs: 3½c, Maseru border post. 5c, Mountains. 12½c, Legislative Building.

Perf. 14x13½

1965, May 10 Photo. Wmk. 314

97	A10	2½c ultra & multi	.20	.20
98	A10	3½c blue & bister	.20	.20
99	A10	5c blue & ocher	.20	.20
100	A10	12½c lt blue, blk & buff	.40	.40
		Nos. 97-100 (4)	1.00	1.00

Attainment of self-government.

ITU Issue
Common Design Type

1965, May 17 Litho. *Perf. 11x11½*

101	CD317	1c ver & red lilac	.20	.20
102	CD317	20c grnsh bl & org brn	.85	.65

Intl. Cooperation Year Issue
Common Design Type

1965, Oct. 25 Wmk. 314 ***Perf. 14½***
103 CD318 ½c blue grn & cl .20 .20
104 CD318 12½c lt vio & green .90 .70

Churchill Memorial Issue
Common Design Type

1966, Jan. 24 Photo. ***Perf. 14***
Design in Black, Gold and Carmine Rose
105 CD319 1c bright blue .20 .20
106 CD319 2½c green .20 .20
107 CD319 10c brown .50 .50
108 CD319 22½c violet 1.25 1.25
Nos. 105-108 (4) 2.15 2.15

POSTAGE DUE STAMPS

Catalogue values for all unused stamps in this section are for Never Hinged items.

D1

1933-38 Wmk. 4 Typo. ***Perf. 14***
J1 D1 1p dark red ('38) .40 *1.00*
a. 1p dark carmine 1.00 *1.50*
b. Wmk. 4a (error) 67.50
J2 D1 2p lt violet .30 *1.00*
a. Wmk. 4a (error) 67.50

Nos. J1-J2 valued on chalky paper.
For surcharge see No. J7.

Coat of Arms — D2

1956, Dec. 1
J3 D2 1p carmine .35 .25
J4 D2 2p dark purple .35 .25

Nos. J2-J4 Surcharged with New Value

1961
J5 D2 1c on 1p carmine .20 .20
J6 D2 1c on 2p dk purple .20 .20
J7 D1 5c on 2p lt violet 3.00 3.00
a. Wmk. 4a (error) 275.00
J8 D2 5c on 2p dark pur ("5" 7½mm high) .20 .20
a. "5" 3½mm high 17.50 *25.00*
Nos. J5-J8 (4) 3.60 3.60

Value in Cents

1964 Wmk. 314 ***Perf. 14***
J9 D2 1c carmine *2.25 2.25*
J10 D2 5c dark purple *2.25 2.25*

For overprints see Lesotho Nos. J1-J2.

OFFICIAL STAMPS

Nos. 1-3 and 6 Overprinted "OFFICIAL"

1934 Wmk. 4 Engr. ***Perf. 12½***
O1 A1 ½p emerald *4,000. 4,000.*
O2 A1 1p carmine *1,100. 1,750.*
O3 A1 2p red violet *1,750. 1,000.*
O4 A1 6p yellow *4,000. 2,250.*

Counterfeits exist.

BATUM

LOCATION — A seaport on the Black Sea

Batum is the capital of Adzhar, a territory which, in 1921, became an autonomous republic of the Georgian Soviet Socialist Republic.

Stamps of Batum were issued under the administration of British forces which occupied Batum and environs between December, 1918, and July, 1920, following the Treaty of Versailles.

100 Kopecks = 1 Ruble

Counterfeits exist of Nos. 1-65.

Basic Russian Designs

A8

A11

A14

A15

A19

A1

1919 Unwmk. Litho. ***Imperf.***
1 A1 5k green .55 .55
2 A1 10k ultramarine .55 .55
3 A1 50k yellow .35 *.45*
4 A1 1r red brown .50 *.60*
5 A1 3r violet 1.90 *3.25*
6 A1 5r brown 3.00 *5.25*
Nos. 1-6 (6) 6.85 *10.65*

For overprints and surcharges see #13-20, 51-65.

Russian Stamps of 1909-17 Surcharged

БАТУМ. ОБ.
Руб 10 Руб.

1919 On Stamps of 1917
7 A14 10r on 1k orange 25.00 *27.50*
8 A14 10r on 3r red 12.00 *16.00*

On Stamp of 1909-12
Perf. 14x14½
9 A14 10r on 5k claret 250.00 250.00

On Stamp of 1917
10 A14 10r on 10k on 7k light blue 200.00 200.00
Nos. 7-10 (4) 487.00 493.50

Russian Stamps of 1909-13 Surcharged

БАТУМ. ОБ.
Коп 35 Коп.

1919
11 A15 35k on 4k carmine *1,650.*
12 A19 35k on 4k dull red *6,500.*

This surcharge was intended for postal cards. A few cards which bore adhesive stamps were also surcharged.

Values are for stamps off card and without gum.

Type of 1919 Issue Overprinted

BRITISH
OCCUPATION

1919 Unwmk. ***Imperf.***
13 A1 5k green 1.25 *1.75*
14 A1 10k dark blue 1.25 *1.75*
15 A1 25k orange 1.25 *1.75*
16 A1 1r pale blue .90 *1.25*
17 A1 2r salmon pink .40 *.55*
18 A1 3r violet .40 *.55*
19 A1 5r brown .40 *.55*
a. "CCUPATION" *190.00 190.00*
20 A1 7r dull red 1.25 *1.75*
Nos. 13-20 (8) 7.10 *9.90*

Russian Stamps of 1909-17 Surcharged in Various Colors:

БАТУМ ОБЛАС.
Р 10 Р.
BRITISH
OCCUPATION
10r & 50r

БАТУМЪ
BRITISH
Р. 15 Р.
OCCUPATION
ОБЛ.
15r

On Stamps of 1917

1919-20 ***Imperf.***
21 A14 10r on 3k red 25.00 22.50
22 A14 15r on 1k org (R) 50.00 45.00
23 A14 15r on 1k org (Bk) 75.00 65.00
24 A14 15r on 1k org (V) 50.00 45.00
25 A14 50r on 1k org 300.00 275.00
26 A14 50r on 2k green 350.00 350.00

On Stamps of 1909-17
Perf. 14x14½
27 A14 50r on 2k green 350.00 350.00
28 A14 50r on 3k red 500.00 500.00
29 A15 50r on 4k car 350.00 350.00
30 A14 50r on 5k claret 350.00 350.00
31 A15 50r on 10k dk blue (R) 850.00 850.00
32 A11 50r on 15k red brn & blue 325.00 325.00

Surcharged

БАТУМ.ОБЛ.
Р.25Р.
BRITISH
OCCUPATION

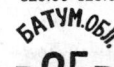

On Stamps of 1909-17
33 A14 25r on 5k cl (Bk) 50.00 50.00
34 A14 25r on 5k cl (Bl) 50.00 50.00
35 A14 25r on 10k on 7k lt blue (Bk) 75.00 75.00
36 A14 25r on 10k on 7k lt blue (Bl) 45.00 45.00
37 A11 25r on 20k on 14k bl & rose (Bk) 75.00 75.00
38 A11 25r on 20k on 14k bl & rose (Bl) 40.00 40.00
39 A11 25r on 25k grn & gray vio (Bk) 100.00 100.00
40 A11 25r on 25k grn & gray vio (Bl) 100.00 100.00
41 A8 25r on 50k vio & green (Bk) 45.00 45.00
42 A8 25r on 50k vio & green (Bl) 47.50 47.50
43 A14 50r on 2k green 65.00 65.00
44 A14 50r on 3k red 65.00 65.00
45 A15 50r on 4k car 100.00 100.00
46 A14 50r on 5k claret 100.00 100.00

On Stamps of 1917
Imperf
47 A14 50r on 2k green 150.00 150.00
48 A14 50r on 3k red 250.00 250.00
49 A14 50r on 5k claret *600.00 600.00*

On Stamp of 1913
Perf. 13½
50 A19 50r on 4k dull red (Bl) 75.00 75.00

Nos. 3, 13 and 15 Surcharged in Black or Blue:

РУБ 25 ПЕЙ

25 РУБ. 25

R. 50 R.
BRITISH
OCCUPATION
РУБ.

1920 ***Imperf.***
51 A1 25r on 5k green 24.00 24.00
52 A1 25r on 5k grn (Bl) 30.00 30.00
53 A1 25r on 25k orange 17.00 17.00
54 A1 25r on 25k org (Bl) *65.00 65.00*
55 A1 50r on 50k yellow 15.00 15.00
56 A1 50r on 50k yel (Bl) *60.00 60.00*
Nos. 51-56 (6) *211.00 211.00*

The surcharges on Nos. 21-56 inclusive are handstamped and are known double, inverted, etc.

Tree Type of 1919 Overprinted Like Nos. 13-20

1920
57 A1 1r orange brown .60 *.90*
58 A1 2r gray blue .60 *.90*
59 A1 3r rose .60 *.90*
60 A1 5r black brown .60 *.90*
61 A1 7r yellow .60 *.90*
62 A1 10r dark green .60 *.90*
63 A1 15r violet .75 *1.25*
64 A1 25r vermilion .75 *1.25*
65 A1 50r dark blue .90 *1.90*
Nos. 57-65 (9) 6.00 *9.80*

The variety "BPITISH" occurs on #57-65.

BECHUANALAND

ˌbech-ˈwä-nə-ˌland

(British Bechuanaland)

LOCATION — Southern Africa
GOVT. — A British Crown Colony, annexed in 1895 to the Cape of Good Hope Colony which became a province in the Union of South Africa.
AREA — 51,424 sq. mi.
POP. — 84,210 (1904)
CAPITAL — Mafeking

12 Pence = 1 Shilling
20 Shillings = 1 Pound

Watermarks

Wmk. 29- Orb

Wmk. 14- VR in Italics

Cape of Good Hope Stamps of 1871-85 Overprinted

British
Bechuanaland

1886 Wmk. 1 ***Perf. 14***
Black Overprint
1 A6 4p blue 50.00 *55.00*

Wmk. 2
Black Overprint
3 A6 3p claret 30.00 30.00

Red Overprint
4 A6 ½p black 10.00 10.00
a. Double overprint in red & blk 850.00

Wmk. Anchor (16)
Black Overprint
5 A6 ½p black 6.00 *10.00*
a. "ritish" 1,800. *1,800.*
b. Double overprint 2,500.
6 A6 1p rose 8.00 6.50
b. "ritish" 1,800. *1,600.*
7 A6 2p bister 22.50 10.00
a. "ritish" 4,500. *4,500.*
b. Double overprint 1,500.
8 A3 6p violet 60.00 32.50
9 A3 1sh green 215.00 125.00
a. "ritish" *10,000. 8,000.*

There is no period after Bechuanaland in the genuine stamps.

Black Ovpt. on Great Britain #111

BRITISH

BECHUANALAND

1887 **Wmk. 30**
10 A54 ½p vermilion .60 *1.00*
a. Double overprint 2,250.

For overprints see Bechuanaland Protectorate Nos. 51-53.

A1

A2

A3

1887 Typo. Wmk. 29

Country Name in Black

11 A1 1p lilac 12.00 4.75
12 A1 2p lilac 30.00 20.00
13 A1 3p lilac 3.25 4.75
14 A1 4p lilac 35.00 5.50
15 A1 6p lilac 40.00 18.00

Wmk. 14

16 A2 1sh green 30.00 5.00
17 A2 2sh green 45.00 30.00
18 A2 2sh6p green 55.00 40.00
19 A2 5sh green 90.00 90.00
20 A2 10sh green 190.00 225.00

Wmk. 29

21 A3 £1 lilac 900. 800.
22 A3 £5 lilac 2,750. 1,400.
Pen cancellation 165.

The corner designs and central oval differs on No. 22.

For overprints see Bechuanaland Protectorate Nos. 54-58, 60-66. For surcharges see Nos. 23-28, 30, Cape of Good Hope No. 171.

Nos. 11-12, 14-16 Surcharged 1d.

1888

Country Name in Black

Black Surcharge

23 A1 1p on 1p lilac 7.00 5.00
a. Double surcharge
24 A1 6p on 6p lilac 90.00 22.50

Red Surcharge

25 A1 2p on 2p lilac 12.50 3.00
a. "2" with curved tail 190.00 150.00
26 A1 4p on 4p lilac 150.00 200.00

Green Surcharge

27 A1 2p on 2p lilac 2,750.

Blue Surcharge

27A A1 6p on 6p lilac 4,500.

Wmk. 14

Black Surcharge

28 A2 1sh on 1sh green 85.00 47.50

British

Bechuanaland

No. 29

One Half-Penny

No. 30

Green Ovpt. on Cape of Good Hope #41

1889 Wmk. 16

29 A4 ½p black 4.75 13.00

Vertical overprint, double overprints one inverted or double, and varieties such as "British" omitted probably are from printers waste.

Wmk. 29

Black Surcharge on No. 13

30 A1 ½p on 3p lilac & blk 125.00 135.00

Cape of Good Hope Nos. 43-44 Overprinted in Black

British Bechuanaland.

1891 Wmk. 16

31 A4 1p rose 10.00 9.50
a. Horiz. pair, one without overprint 1,500.
b. "British" omitted — 575.00
c. "Bechuanaland" omitted 850.00
32 A4 2p bister 3.00 3.00
a. Without period 200.00

See Nos. 38-39.

Stamps of Great Britain Overprinted in Black

BRITISH BECHUANALAND

1891-94 Wmk. 30

33 A40 1p lilac 5.00 1.00
34 A56 2p green & car 3.00 2.50
35 A59 4p brown & green 2.50 .75
36 A62 6p violet, *rose* 2.50 1.75
37 A65 1sh green ('94) 11.00 13.00
Nos. 33-37 (5) 24.00 19.00

For surcharges see Cape of Good Hope Nos. 172, 176-177.

Cape of Good Hope Nos. 43-44 Overprinted Like Nos. 31-32 but Reading Down

1893-95 Wmk. 16

38 A6 1p rose 2.50 2.75
a. No dots over the "i's" of "British" 80.00 80.00
b. "British" omitted 650.00
c. As "a," reading up 750.00
d. Pair, one without overprint
39 A6 2p bister ('95) 4.75 2.75
a. Double overprint 900.00 900.00
b. No dots over the "i's" of "British" 125.00 125.00
c. "British" omitted 350.00 325.00
d. As "b," reading up

Cape of Good Hope No. 42 Overprinted

BRITISH

BECHUANALAND

"BECHUANALAND" 16mm Long Overprint Lines 13mm Apart

1897

40 A6 ½p light green 2.50 5.00

"BECHUANALAND" 15mm Long Overprint Lines 10½mm Apart

41 A6 ½p light green 10.00 27.50

"BECHUANALAND" 15mm Long Overprint Lines 13½mm Apart

42 A6 ½p light green 17.50 45.00
Nos. 40-42 (3) 30.00 77.50

BECHUANALAND PROTECTORATE

ˌbech-ˈwä-nə-ˌland prə-ˈtek-t(ə-)rət

LOCATION — In central South Africa, north of the Republic of South Africa, east of South-West Africa and bounded on the north and east by Angola and Southern Rhodesia

GOVT. — British Protectorate

AREA — 222,000 sq. mi.

POP. — 540,400 (1964)

Bechuanaland Protectorate became the independent republic of Botswana, Sept. 30, 1966.

12 Pence = 1 Shilling
20 Shillings = 1 Pound
100 Cents = 1 Rand (1961)

Catalogue values for unused stamps in this country are for Never Hinged items, beginning with Scott 137 in the regular postage section and Scott J7 in the postage due section.

Additional Overprint in Black on Bechuanaland No. 10

Protectorate a

Protectorate b

Protectorate c

1888-90 Wmk. 30 *Perf. 14*

51 A54(a) ½p vermilion 110.00 150.00
a. Double overprint 575.00
52 A54(b) ½p vermilion ('89) 2.50 16.00
a. Double overprint 300.00
53 A54(c) ½p vermilion 90.00 100.00
a. Inverted overprint 65.00 80.00
b. Double overprint 85.00 95.00
c. As "a," double 600.00 600.00

For surcharge see No. 68.

Bechuanaland Nos. 16-20 Overprinted Type "b" in Black

Wmk. 14

Country Name in Black

54 A2 1sh green 55.00 50.00
a. First "o" omitted 3,250. 3,000.
55 A2 2sh green 475.00 625.00
a. First "o" omitted 5,750. 4,250.
56 A2 2sh6p green 500.00 625.00
a. First "o" omitted 6,000. 4,500.
57 A2 5sh green 1,100. 1,500.
a. First "o" omitted 6,750. 6,000.
58 A2 10sh green 3,250. 4,000.
a. First "o" omitted 12,000.

Bechuanaland Nos. 11-15 Overprinted Type "b" and Surcharged in Black

1888 Wmk. 29

Country Name in Black

60 A1 1p on 1p lilac 5.50 10.00
a. Short "1" 275.00 300.00
61 A1 2p on 2p lilac 17.50 15.00
a. "2" with curved tail 300.00 300.00
63 A1 3p on 3p lilac 80.00 110.00
64 A1 4p on 4p lilac 175.00 175.00
a. Small "4" 2,500. 2,250.
65 A1 6p on 6p lilac 50.00 40.00

In #60 the "1" is 2½mm high; in #60a, 2mm.

Value Surcharged in Red

66 A1 4p on 4p lilac 50.00 42.50

Cape of Good Hope Type of 1886 Overprinted in Green

Bechuanaland

Protectorate.

1889 Wmk. 16

67 A6 ½p black 3.75 20.00
a. Double overprint 400.00 475.00
b. "Bechuanaland" omitted 600.00 600.00

Black Surcharge on Bechuanaland Protectorate No. 52

Wmk. 30

68 A54 4p on ½p ver 15.00 3.00
a. Inverted surcharge 4,500.

Stamps of Great Britain 1881-87, Overprinted in Black

BECHUANALAND PROTECTORATE

1897, Oct.

69 A54 ½p vermilion 1.00 1.00
70 A40 1p lilac 3.50 .50
71 A56 2p green & car 2.00 4.00
72 A58 3p violet, *yel* 5.00 7.50
73 A59 4p brown & green 10.00 10.00
74 A62 6p violet, *rose* 17.50 10.50
Nos. 69-74 (6) 39.00 33.50

For surcharges see Cape of Good Hope Nos. 167-170, 173-175.

Same on Great Britain No. 125

1902, Feb. 25

75 A54 ½p blue green 1.50 1.25

Stamps of Great Britain, 1902, Overprinted in Black

BECHUANALAND PROTECTORATE

1904-12

76 A66 ½p gray green ('06) 3.50 3.50
77 A66 1p car ('05) 4.75 1.25
78 A66 2½p ultra 6.25 5.75
79 A74 1sh scar & grn ('12) 12.00 15.00
Nos. 76-79 (4) 26.50 25.50

Same on Great Britain No. 143

1908

80 A66 ½p pale yel green 2.00 3.00

Transvaal No. 274 Overprinted

Bechuanaland

Protectorate

1910 Wmk. 3

81 A27 6p brn org & blk 180.00 210.00

This stamp was issued for fiscal use, although it is known postally used.

Great Britain No. 154 Overprinted Like Nos. 76-79

1912, Sept. Wmk. 30 *Perf. 15x14*

82 A81 1p scarlet 1.10 1.00

Great Britain Stamps of 1912-13 Overprinted Like Nos. 76-79

Wmk. Crown and GvR (33)

1914-24

83 A82 ½p green .95 1.25
84 A83 1p scarlet 2.50 .30
85 A84 1½p red brn ('20) 1.50 2.00
86 A85 2p orange (I) 2.25 2.25
a. 2p orange (II) ('24) 30.00 3.50
87 A86 2½p ultra 2.50 10.00
88 A87 3p bluish violet 4.75 11.00
89 A88 4p slate green 5.25 9.50
90 A89 6p dull violet 5.75 11.00
91 A90 1sh bister 6.50 12.00
Nos. 83-91 (9) 31.95 59.30

The dies of No. 86 are the same as in Great Britain 1912-13 issue.

Overprinted BECHUANALAND PROTECTORATE

Wmk. 34 *Perf. 11x12*

92 A91 2sh6p dk brown 100.00 140.00
a. 2sh6p light brown ('16) 125.00 140.00
93 A91 5sh rose car 150.00 200.00
a. 5sh carmine ('20) 200.00 250.00

Nos. 92, 93 were printed by Waterlow Bros. & Layton; Nos. 92a, 93a were printed by Thomas De La Rue & Co.

Same Overprint On Retouched Stamps of 1919

1920-23

94 A91 2sh6p gray brown 100.00 125.00
95 A91 5sh car rose 140.00 165.00

Great Britain Stamps of 1924 Overprinted like Nos. 76-79

Wmk. Crown and Block GvR Multiple (35)

1925-26 *Perf. 15x14*

96 A82 ½p green 1.00 1.60
97 A83 1p scarlet 1.25 1.60
99 A85 2p deep org (II) 2.50 2.25
101 A87 3p violet 3.25 6.50
102 A88 4p slate green 4.00 12.00
103 A89 6p dull violet 5.25 16.00
104 A90 1sh bister 14.00 21.00
Nos. 96-104 (7) 31.25 60.95

George V A11

George VI, Cattle and Baobab Tree A12

Perf. 12½

1932, Dec. 12 Engr. Wmk. 4

105 A11 ½p green .50 .35
106 A11 1p carmine .50 .35
107 A11 2p red brown .50 .45
108 A11 3p ultra 1.00 1.00
109 A11 4p orange 1.00 2.00
110 A11 6p red violet 2.50 1.25
111 A11 1sh blk & ol grn 5.00 5.00
112 A11 2sh black & org 22.50 25.00
113 A11 2sh6p black & car 17.50 20.00
114 A11 3sh black & red vio 25.00 27.50
115 A11 5sh black & ultra 35.00 40.00
116 A11 10sh blk & red brown 85.00 95.00
Nos. 105-116 (12) 196.00 217.90

Common Design Types pictured following the introduction.

Silver Jubilee Issue
Common Design Type

1935, May 4 *Perf. 11x12*
117 CD301 1p car & blue .25 *.35*
118 CD301 2p black & ultra .90 .90
119 CD301 3p ultra & brown 1.10 1.10
120 CD301 6p brown vio & ind 2.50 1.75
Nos. 117-120 (4) 4.75 4.10

Coronation Issue
Common Design Type

1937, May 12 *Perf. 13½x14*
121 CD302 1p carmine .20 .20
122 CD302 2p brown .20 .20
123 CD302 3p bright ultra .25 .25
Nos. 121-123 (3) .65 .65
Set, never hinged 1.50

1938, Apr. 1 *Perf. 12½*
124 A12 ½p green 1.25 *2.00*
125 A12 1p rose car .25 *.35*
126 A12 1½p light blue .25 *.60*
127 A12 2p brown .25 *.35*
128 A12 3p ultra .25 *1.25*
129 A12 4p orange .90 *2.00*
130 A12 6p rose violet 1.90 *2.25*
131 A12 1sh blk & ol grn 1.90 *2.50*
133 A12 2sh6p black & car 8.75 *7.50*
135 A12 5sh black & ultra 19.00 7.50
136 A12 10sh black & brn 8.75 *14.50*
Nos. 124-136 (11) 43.45 *40.80*
Set, never hinged 67.50

Catalogue values for unused stamps in this section, from this point to the end of the section, are for Never Hinged items.

Peace Issue

South Africa Nos. 100-102 Overprinted **Bechuanaland**

Basic stamps inscribed alternately in English and Afrikaans.

1945, Dec. 3 **Wmk. 201** *Perf. 14*
137 A42 1p rose pink & choc, pair .30 .30
a. Single, English .20 .20
b. Single, Afrikaans .20 .20
138 A43 2p vio & slate blue, pair .40 .40
a. Single, English .20 .20
b. Single, Afrikaans .20 .20
139 A43 3p ultra & dp ultra, pair .50 .50
a. Single, English .25 .25
b. Single, Afrikaans .25 .25
Nos. 137-139 (3) 1.20 1.20

World War II victory of the Allies.

Royal Visit Issue
Types of Basutoland, 1947
Perf. 12½

1947, Feb. 17 **Wmk. 4** **Engr.**
143 A3 1p red .20 .20
144 A4 2p green .20 .20
145 A5 3p ultra .20 .20
146 A6 1sh dark violet .30 .30
Nos. 143-146 (4) .90 .90

Visit of the British Royal Family, Apr. 17, 1947.

Silver Wedding Issue
Common Design Types

1948, Dec. 1 **Photo.** *Perf. 14x14½*
147 CD304 1½p brt ultra .20 .20

Engr.; Name Typo.
Perf. 11½x11
148 CD305 10sh gray black 24.00 *30.00*

UPU Issue
Common Design Types
Engr.; Name Typo. on 3p and 6p

1949, Oct. 10 *Perf. 13½, 11x11½*
149 CD306 1½p blue .25 .25
150 CD307 3p indigo .35 .35
151 CD308 6p red lilac .80 .80
152 CD309 1sh olive 1.50 1.50
Nos. 149-152 (4) 2.90 2.90

Coronation Issue
Common Design Type

1953, June 3 **Engr.** *Perf. 13½x13*
153 CD312 2p brown & black .30 .30

Elizabeth II
A13

Victoria, Elizabeth II and Water Hole
A14

1955-58 *Perf. 13x13½*
154 A13 ½p green .25 .25
155 A13 1p rose car .25 .25
156 A13 2p brown .25 .25
157 A13 3p ultra .35 .35
158 A13 4p orange ('58) *4.25* *4.25*
159 A13 4½p indigo 1.25 1.25
160 A13 6p rose violet .80 .80
161 A13 1sh blk & ol grn 1.50 1.50
162 A13 1sh3p blk & rose vio 2.00 *6.50*
163 A13 2sh6p black & car 5.50 *10.50*
164 A13 5sh black & ultra 10.50 *16.00*
165 A13 10sh black & brn 24.00 *30.00*
Nos. 154-165 (12) 50.90 *71.90*

For surcharges see Nos. 169-179.

Perf. 14½x14
1960, Jan. 21 **Photo.** **Wmk. 314**
166 A14 1p brown & black .20 .20
167 A14 3p car rose & black .20 .20
168 A14 6p ultra & black .30 .30
Nos. 166-168 (3) .70 .70

Proclamation of the Protectorate, 75th anniv.

Nos. 155-165 Surcharged

1c 1c 3½c 3½c 3½c
I II I II III

5c 5c R1 R1
I II I II

Perf. 13x13½
1961, Feb. 14 **Wmk. 4** **Engr.**
169 1c on 1p (I) .20 .20
a. Type II .20 .20
170 2c on 2p .20 .20
171 2½c on 2p .20 .20
a. Pair, one without surcharge 700.00
172 2½c on 3p .90 .90
173 3½c on 4p (III) .20 .20
a. Type I .50 .50
b. Type II 1.60 1.60
174 5c on 6p (II) .25 .25
a. Type I .75 .75
175 10c on 1sh .30 .30
a. Pair, one without surcharge 700.00
176 12½c on 1sh3p ("12½c" 11¼mm wide) .55 .55
a. "12½c" 12¼mm wide .75 .75
177 25c on 2sh6p .90 .90
178 50c on 5sh 1.90 1.90
179 1r on 10sh (II, "R1" at lower center) 4.50 4.50
a. Type II, "R1" at lower left 6.50 6.50
b. Type I 300.00 110.00
Nos. 169-179 (11) 10.10 10.10

Nos. 173a and 173b are found in the same sheet; each comes with "3½c" in both wide and narrow settings.

Surcharge types are numbered chronologically.

African Golden Oriole — A15

Baobab Tree — A16

Designs: 2c, African hoopoe. 2½c, Scarlet-chested sunbird. 3½c, Cape widow bird (Yellow bishop). 5c, Swallow-tailed bee-eater. 7½c, Gray hornbill. 10c, Red-headed weaver. 12½c, Brown-hooded kingfisher. 20c, Woman musician. 35c, Woman grinding corn. 50c, Bechuana ox. 1r, Lion. 2r, Police camel patrol.

Perf. 14x14½, 14½x14
1961, Oct. 2 **Photo.** **Wmk. 314**
180 A15 1c lilac, blk & yel .20 .20
181 A15 2c pale ol, blk & org .20 .20
182 A15 2½c bis, blk, grn & dp car .25 .20
183 A15 3½c pink, blk & yel .35 .25
184 A15 5c dl org, blk, grn & bl .45 .30
185 A15 7½c yel grn, blk, red & brn .65 .40
186 A15 10c aqua & multi .80 .50
187 A15 12½c gray, yel, red & blue 1.10 .55
188 A15 20c gray & brn 1.40 1.10
189 A16 25c yel & dk brn 2.50 1.40
190 A15 35c dp org & ultra 2.75 1.75
191 A16 50c lt ol grn & sep 4.00 2.75
192 A15 1r ocher & black 8.25 5.25
193 A15 2r blue & brn 16.00 10.50
Nos. 180-193 (14) 38.90 25.35

Freedom from Hunger Issue
Common Design Type

1963, June 4 *Perf. 14x14½*
194 CD314 12½c green .50 .50

Red Cross Centenary Issue
Common Design Type

1963, Sept. 2 **Litho.** *Perf. 13*
195 CD315 2½c black & red .20 .20
196 CD315 12½c ultra & red .80 .80

Shakespeare Issue
Common Design Type

1964, Apr. 23 **Photo.** *Perf. 14x14½*
197 CD316 12½c red brown .30 .30

Notwani River Dam, Gaberones Water Supply — A17

Wmk. 314
1965, Mar. 1 **Photo.** *Perf. 14½*
198 A17 2½c dark red & gold .20 .20
199 A17 5c deep ultra & gold .20 .20
200 A17 12½c brown & gold .30 .30
201 A17 25c emerald & gold .55 .55
Nos. 198-201 (4) 1.25 1.25

Internal self-government, Mar. 1, 1965.

ITU Issue
Common Design Type
Perf. 11x11½

1965, May 17 **Litho.** **Wmk. 314**
202 CD317 2½c ver & dl yel .20 .20
203 CD317 12½c red lil & pale brn .70 .70

Intl. Cooperation Year Issue
Common Design Type

1965, Oct. 25 *Perf. 14½*
204 CD318 1c bl grn & claret .20 .20
205 CD318 12½c lt vio & grn .75 .75

Churchill Memorial Issue
Common Design Type

1966, Jan. 24 **Photo.** *Perf. 14*
Design in Black, Gold and Carmine Rose
206 CD319 1c bright blue .20 .20
207 CD319 2½c green .20 .20
208 CD319 12½c brown .75 .75
209 CD319 20c violet 1.10 1.10
Nos. 206-209 (4) 2.25 2.25

Haslar Smoke Generator — A18

Wmk. 314
1966, June 1 **Photo.** *Perf. 14½*
210 A18 2½c shown .20 .20
211 A18 5c Bugler .20 .20
212 A18 15c Gun site .40 .40
213 A18 35c Regimental cap badge .85 .85
Nos. 210-213 (4) 1.65 1.65

25th anniv. of the Bechuanaland Pioneers and Gunners.

POSTAGE DUE STAMPS

Postage Due Stamps of Great Britain Overprinted BECHUANALAND PROTECTORATE

On Stamp of 1914-22
1926 **Wmk. 33** *Perf. 14x14½*
J1 D1 1p carmine 3.75 *40.00*

On Stamps of 1924-30
Wmk. 35
J2 D1 ½p emerald 3.75 *40.00*

Overprinted BECHUANALAND PROTECTORATE
J3 D1 2p black brown 7.25 *80.00*
Nos. J1-J3 (3) 14.75
Set, never hinged 30.00

D2

1932 **Wmk. 4** **Typo.** *Perf. 14½*
J4 D2 ½p olive green 6.00 *21.00*
J5 D2 1p carmine rose 6.00 *7.00*
J6 D2 2p dull violet 8.00 *24.00*
Nos. J4-J6 (3) 20.00 *52.00*
Set, never hinged 30.00

Catalogue values for unused stamps in this section, from this point to the end of the section, are for Never Hinged items.

Nos. J4-J6 Surcharged

2c 2c
I II

1961, Feb. 14
J7 D2 1c on 1p car rose (II) .20 .20
a. Type I .30 .30
b. Double surcharge (II) 140.00
J8 D2 2c on 2p dull vio (II) .25 .25
a. Type I .35 .35
J9 D2 5c on ½p ol green (I) .50 .50
Nos. J7-J9 (3) .95 .95

Nos. J7, J7a, J8 and J8a are on chalky paper. Nos. J7 and J8 printed on ordinary paper sell for much more.

Denominations in Cents
1961 **Wmk. 4** *Perf. 14*
J10 D2 1c carmine rose .20 .20
J11 D2 2c dull violet .20 .20
J12 D2 5c olive green .40 *1.25*
Nos. J10-J12 (3) .80 *1.65*

BELARUS

ˌbē-lə-ˈrüs

(Byelorussia)

(White Russia)

LOCATION — Eastern Europe, bounded by Russia, Latvia, Lithuania and Poland
GOVT. — Independent republic, member of the Commonwealth of Independent States
AREA — 80,134 sq. mi.
POP. — 10,401,784 (1999 est.)
CAPITAL — Minsk

With the breakup of the Soviet Union on Dec. 26, 1991, Belarus and ten former Soviet republics established the Commonwealth of Independent States.

100 Kopecks = 1 Ruble

Catalogue values for all unused stamps in this country are for Never Hinged items.

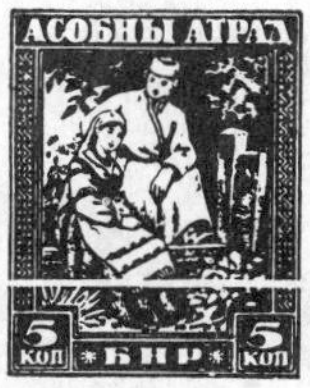

Five denominations, perf and imperf, of this design produced in 1920 were not put in use and were probably propaganda labels. They are common. Numerous forgeries exist.

Cross of Ephrosinia of Polotsk — A1

1992, Mar. 20 Litho. *Perf. 12x12½*

1 A1 1r multicolored .30 .20

For surcharge see No. 230.

R.R. Schurma (1892-1978), Composer A2

1992, Apr. 10 Photo. *Perf. 12x11½*

2 A2 20k blue & black .25 .20

For surcharge see No. 203.

Arms of Polotsk — A3

Designs: No. 13, Stag jumping fence. No. 14, Man's head, sword.

1992-94 Photo. *Perf. 12x11½*

11 A3 2r shown .20 .20

Perf. 12x12½

12 A3 25r Minsk .20 .20
13 A3 700r Grodno .20 .20
14 A3 700r Vitebsk .20 .20
Nos. 11-14 (4) .80 .80

Issued: 2r, 6/9/92; 25r, 11/11/93; #13, 14, 10/17/94.

This is an expanding set. Numbers will change if necessary.

Belarus stamps can be mounted in the annual Scott Belarus supplement.

National Symbols — A4

Designs: No. 15, Natl. arms. No. 16, Map, flag.

1992, Aug. 31 Litho. *Perf. 12x12½*

15 A4 5r black, red & yellow .20 .20
16 A4 5r multicolored .25 .20

For surcharges see Nos. 55-58, 61-64.

No. 1 Overprinted

1000 — ГОДЗЕ БЕЛАРУСКАЙ ПРАВАСЛАЎНАЙ ЦАРКВЫ

Cross of Ephrosinia of Polotsk — A5

A5 illustration reduced.

1992, Sept. 25 Litho. *Perf. 12x12½*

17 A1 1r on #1 multi .20 .20

Souvenir Sheet

Perf. 12

18 A5 5r multicolored .25 .25

Orthodox Church in Belarus, 1000th anniv. No. 18, imperf, was issued Feb. 15, 1993.

For surcharges see Nos. 59-60, 65-66.

Buildings A6

Designs: No. 19, Church of Boris Gleb, Grodno, 12th cent. No. 20, World Castle, 16th cent. No. 21, Nyasvizh Castle, 16th-19th cent. No. 22, Kamyanets Tower, 12th-13th cent, vert. No. 23, Church of Ephrosinia of Polotsk, 12th cent., vert. No. 24, Calvinist Church, Zaslaw, 16th cent., vert.

1992, Oct. 15 Litho. *Perf. 12*

19 A6 2r multicolored .20 .20
20 A6 2r multicolored .20 .20
21 A6 2r multicolored .20 .20
22 A6 2r multicolored .20 .20
23 A6 2r multicolored .20 .20
24 A6 2r multicolored .20 .20
Nos. 19-24 (6) 1.20 1.20

Centuries of construction are in Roman numerals.

Natl. Arms — A7

1992-94 Litho. *Perf. 12x12½*

25 A7 30k light blue .20 .20
26 A7 45k olive green .20 .20
27 A7 50k green .20 .20
28 A7 1r brown .20 .20
29 A7 2r red brown .20 .20
30 A7 3r org yellow .20 .20
31 A7 5r blue .20 .20
32 A7 10r red .20 .20
33 A7 15r violet .25 .25
34 A7 25r yellow green .40 .40
35 A7 50r bright pink .20 .20
36 A7 100r henna brown .25 .25
37 A7 150r plum .40 .40
38 A7 200r blue green .20 .20
39 A7 300r salmon pink .20 .20
40 A7 600r light lilac .20 .20
40A A7 1000r rose carmine .25 .25
40B A7 3000r gray blue .50 .50
Nos. 25-40B (18) 4.45 4.45

Issued: 30k, 45k, 50k, 11/10; 1r-3r, 10r, 1/4/93; 5r, 15r, 25r, 2/9/93; 50r, 100r, 150r, 6/16/93; 200r-3,000r, 12/28/94; others, 1992.

For surcharges see Nos. 141-142, 211A-212.

Ceramics — A8

Designs: No. 41, Pitcher and bowl. No. 42, Four pieces on tree branches. No. 43, Two large pitchers. No. 44, One large pitcher.

1992, Dec. 24 Litho. *Perf. 11½*

41 A8 1r multicolored .20 .20
42 A8 1r multicolored .20 .20
43 A8 1r multicolored .20 .20
44 A8 1r multicolored .20 .20
Nos. 41-44 (4) .80 .80

M. I. Garetzky (1893-1938), Writer — A9

1993, June 22 Photo. *Perf. 12x11½*

45 A9 50r magenta .30 .30

Straw Figures A10

Designs: 5r, Chickens. 10r, Child, mother, vert. 15r, Woman, vert. 25r, Man with scythe, woman with rake, vert.

Perf. 12x11½, 11½x12

1993, Apr. 22 Litho.

47 A10 5r multicolored .20 .20
48 A10 10r multicolored .25 .20
49 A10 15r multicolored .25 .20
50 A10 25r multicolored .30 .20
Nos. 47-50 (4) 1.00 .80

First World Congress of White Russians — A11

1993, July 8 Litho. *Perf. 12*

51 A11 50r multicolored 1.25 1.25

Europa — A12

Paintings by Chagall: No. 52, Promenade, vert. No. 53, Man Over Vitebsk. 2500r, Allegory.

1993, Oct. 12 Litho. *Perf. 14*

52 A12 1500r multicolored 3.00 3.00
53 A12 1500r multicolored 3.00 3.00
a. Pair, #52-53 6.00 6.00

Souvenir Sheet

54 A12 2500r multicolored 45.00 45.00

Nos. 15-16, 18 Surcharged

XVII ЗІМОВЫЯ АЛІМПІЙСКІЯ ГУЛЬНІ · ЛІЛЕХАМЕР, НАРВЕГІЯ, 1994

1500
a

WINTER PRE-OLYMPICS GAMES LILLEHAMMER, NORWAY

1500
b

Size and location of surcharge varies.

1993, Oct. 15 Litho. *Perf. 12x12½*

55 A4(a) 1500r on 5r #15 3.50 3.50
56 A4(b) 1500r on 5r #15 3.50 3.50
a. Pair, #55-56 7.00 7.00
57 A4(a) 1500r on 5r #16 3.50 3.50
58 A4(b) 1500r on 5r #16 3.50 3.50
a. Pair, #57-58 7.00 7.00
Nos. 55-58 (4) 14.00 14.00

Souvenir Sheets

Perf. 12

59 A5(a) 1500r on 5r #18 3.50 3.50
60 A5(b) 1500r on 5r #18 3.50 3.50

No. 59 exists imperf. The status of No. 60 is in question.

Nos. 15-16, 18 Surcharged

ЧЭМПІЯНАТ СВЕТУ ПА ФУТБОЛУ, ЗША. 1994

1500
c

WORLD CUP USA 94

1500
d

Size and location of surcharge varies.

1993, Oct. 15 Litho. *Perf. 12x12½*

61 A4(c) 1500r on 5r #15 3.50 3.50
62 A4(d) 1500r on 5r #15 3.50 3.50
a. Pair, #61-62 7.00 7.00

63 A4(c) 1500r on 5r #16 *3.50 3.50*
64 A4(d) 1500r on 5r #16 *3.50 3.50*
a. Pair, #63-64 *7.00 7.00*
Nos. 61-64 (4) 14.00 14.00

Souvenir Sheets
Perf. 12

65 A5(c) 1500r on 5r #18 *3.50 3.50*
66 A5(d) 1500r on 5r #18 *3.50 3.50*

The status of Nos. 65-66 are in question.

Stansilavski Church A13

1993, Nov. 24 Litho. *Perf. 12*
67 A13 150r multicolored .35 .35

For surcharge see No. 242.

Famous People — A14

Designs: 50r, Kastus Kalinovsky, led 1863 independence movement. No. 69, Prince Rogvold of Polotsk, map of Polotsk. No. 70, Princess Rogneda, daughter of Rogvold, fortress. 100r, Statue of Simon Budny (1530-93), writer and printer, vert.

1993 *Perf. 12x12½, 12½x12*
68 A14 50r multicolored .20 .20
69 A14 75r multicolored .20 .20
70 A14 75r multicolored .20 .20
71 A14 100r multicolored .35 .35
Nos. 68-71 (4) .95 .95

Issued: 50r, 12/29; 75r, 12/30; 100r, 12/31.

Nos. 27, 29, 30 Surcharged

15.00

1994, Feb. 1 Photo. *Perf. 12x12½*
72 A7 15r on 30k light green .20 .20
73 A7 25r on 45k olive green .20 .20
74 A7 50r on 50k green .20 .20
Nos. 72-74 (3) .60 .60

Birds A15

1994, Jan. 19 Litho. *Perf. 11½*
75 A15 20r Aguila chrysaetos .20 .20
76 A15 40r Cygnus olor .20 .20
77 A15 40r Alcedo atthis .20 .20
a. Block of 3, #75-77 + label .60 .60

See Nos. 87-89.

Six World Wildlife Fund labels with 1000r denominations depicting 3 different animals and 3 different birds exist. They were not valid for postage.

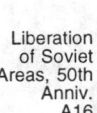

Liberation of Soviet Areas, 50th Anniv. A16

Battle maps and: a, Katyusha rockets, liberation of Russia. b, Fighter planes, liberation of Ukraine. c, Combined offensive, liberation of Belarus.

1994, July 3 Litho. *Perf. 12*
78 A16 500r Block of 3 + label .45 .45

See Russia No. 6213, Ukraine No. 195.

1994 Winter Olympics, Lillehammer — A17

1994, Aug. 30 Litho. *Perf. 12x12½*
79 A17 1000r Speed skating .20 .20
80 A17 1000r Women's figure skating .20 .20
81 A17 1000r Hockey .20 .20
82 A17 1000r Cross-country skiing .20 .20
83 A17 1000r Biathlon .20 .20
Nos. 79-83 (5) 1.00 1.00

Painters — A18

Designs: No. 84, Farmer, oxen in field, by Ferdinand Rushchyts. No. 85, Knight on horseback, by Jasev Drazdovich. No. 86, Couple walking up path, by Petra Sergievich. Illustration reduced

1994, July 18 Litho. *Perf. 12*
84 A18 300r multicolored .20 .20
85 A18 300r multicolored .20 .20
86 A18 300r multicolored .20 .20
Nos. 84-86 (3) .60 .60

For overprint see No. 127.

Bird Type of 1994

1994, Sept. 30 *Perf. 11½*
87 A15 300r like #75 .20 .20
88 A15 400r like #76 .20 .20
89 A15 400r like #77 .20 .20
Nos. 87-89 (3) .60 .60

Ilya Yefimovich Repin (1844-1930), Ukrainian Painter — A19

Designs: #90, Self-portrait. #91, Repin Museum.

1994, Oct. 31 Litho. *Perf. 12x12½*
90 A19 1000r multicolored .40 .30
91 A19 1000r multicolored .40 .30
a. Pair, #90-91 .80 .60

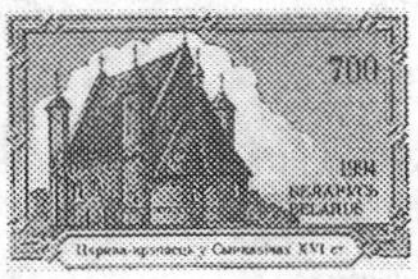

Churches A20

Designs: No. 92, Sacred Consolidated Church, Sinkavitsch, 16th cent. No. 93, Sts. Peter and Paul Cathedral, Gomel, 19th cent.

1994, Oct. 20 Litho. *Perf. 12*
92 A20 700r multicolored .20 .20
93 A20 700r multicolored .20 .20

Kosciuszko Uprising, Bicent. (in 1994) A21

Battle scene and: No. 94, Tomasz Vaishetcki (1754-1816). No. 95, Jakov Jasinski (1761-94). No. 96, Tadeusz Kosziuszko (1746-1817). No. 97, Mikhail K. Aginski (1765-1833).

1995, Jan. 11 *Perf. 12½x12*
94 A21 600r multicolored .20 .20
95 A21 600r multicolored .20 .20
96 A21 1000r multicolored .30 .30
97 A21 1000r multicolored .30 .30
Nos. 94-97 (4) 1.00 1.00

End of World War II, 50th Anniv. — A22

1995, May 4 Litho. *Perf. 13½*
98 A22 180r multicolored .20 .20
99 A22 600r multicolored .20 .20

A23

A24

1995, May 7 *Perf. 14*
100 A23 600r A Popov .20 .20

Radio, cent. Exists imperf.

1995-96 Litho. *Perf. 13x14*
102 A24 180r olive brown & red .20 .20
103 A24 200r gray green & bister .20 .20
105 A24 280r green & blue .20 .20
109 A24 600r plum & bister .20 .20
Nos. 102-109 (4) .80 .80

No. 102 exists imperf.

Issued: 180r, 5/10/95; 280r, 5/18/95; 600r, 8/29/95; 200r, 1/30/96.

This is an expanding set. Numbers may change.

Ivan Chersky (1845-92), Geographer A25

1995, May 15 Litho. *Perf. 13½x14*
113 A25 600r multicolored .20 .20

Exists imperf.

A26

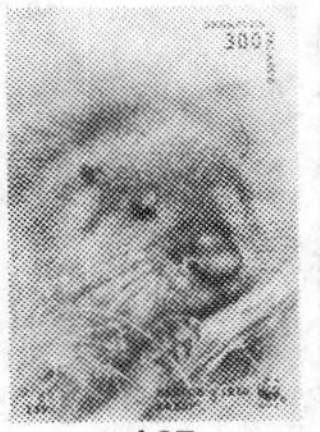

A27

Traditional Costumes: 600r, Woman wearing shawl, coat, ankle length skirt, man with long coat. 1200r, Woman wearing shawl & apron holding child, man wearing vest, knickers.

1995, July 13 Litho. *Perf. 14½x14*
114 A26 180r multicolored .20 .20
115 A26 600r multicolored .20 .20
116 A26 1200r multicolored .25 .25
Nos. 114-116 (3) .65 .65

See Nos. 164-167, 214-216.

1995, July 20 *Perf. 12*

World Wildlife Fund: Various pictures of a beaver.

117 A27 300r multi .20 .20
118 A27 450r multi .20 .20
119 A27 450r multi, horiz. .30 .20
120 A27 800r multi, horiz. .30 .20
Nos. 117-120 (4) 1.00 .80

A28

A29

1995, Aug. 29 Litho. *Perf. 14*
121 A28 600r Book Fair .20 .20

Exists imperf.

1995, Oct. 3 Litho. *Perf. 14*
122 A29 600r Natl. arms .20 .20
123 A29 600r Flag .20 .20

New national symbols. Exist imperf.

UN, 50th Anniv. — A30

1995, Oct. 24 Litho. *Perf. 13½x14*
124 A30 600r bister, black & blue .20 .20

Exists imperf.

Churches A31

Designs: No. 125, Mstislav, 17th-19th cent. No. 126, Kamai, 17th cent.

1995, Nov. 21 *Perf. 14*
125 A31 600r multicolored .20 .20
126 A31 600r multicolored .20 .20

No. 84 Ovptd. **1995 125 год з дня нараджэння**

1995, Dec. 27 Litho. *Perf. 12*
127 A18 300r multicolored .20 .20

P. V. Sukhi (1895-1975), Airplane Designer A32

1995, Dec. 27 *Perf. 13½*
128 A32 600r multicolored .20 .20

Wildlife A33

Designs: 1000r, Lynx lynx. No. 130, Capreolus capreolus, vert. No. 131, Ursus arctos. 3000r, Alces alces, vert. 5000r, Bison bonasus.
10,000r, Cervus elaphus, vert.

1995-96 Litho. *Perf. 14*

129 A33 1000r multicolored .25 .25
130 A33 2000r multicolored .35 .40
131 A33 2000r multicolored .40 .40
132 A33 3000r multicolored .75 .65
133 A33 5000r multicolored 1.25 1.10
Nos. 129-133 (5) 3.00 2.80

Souvenir Sheet

Imperf

134 A33 10,000r multicolored 2.00 1.75

Issued: #129-133, 2/6/96; #134, 12/29/95.

Famous People — A34

Designs: 600r, L. Sapega (1557-1633), statesman. 1200r, K. Semyanovitch (1600-51), military scholar. 1800r, S. Polotzki (1629-80), writer. Illustration reduced.

1995, Dec. 30 Litho. *Perf. 12*

135 A34 600r multicolored .20 .20
136 A34 1200r multicolored .30 .30
137 A34 1800r multicolored .45 .45
Nos. 135-137 (3) .95 .95

Miniature Sheet

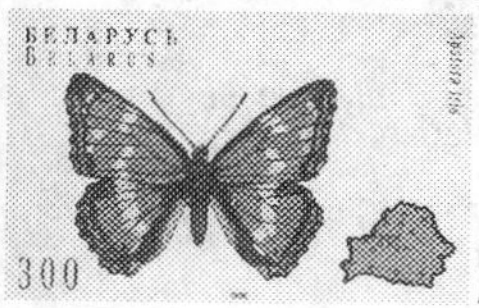

Butterflies A35

Designs: No. 138a, Apatura iris. b, Lopinga achine. c, Callimorpha dominula. d, Catocala fraxini. e, Papilio machaon. f, Parnassius apollo. g, Ammobiota hebe. h, Colias palaeno.
No. 139, Proserpinus proserpina. No. 140, Vacciniina optilete.

1996, Mar. 29 Litho. *Perf. 14*

138 A35 300r Sheet of 8, #a.-h. 10.00 10.00

Souvenir Sheets

139-140 A35 1000r each 4.00 4.00

Inscribed 1995.

Nos. 28, 34 Surcharged in Green or Red

B

1996 Litho. *Perf. 12x12½*

141 A7 (B) on 1r #28 (G) .20 .20
142 A7 (A) on 25r #34 (R) .20 .20

Nos. 141-142 were valued at 200r and 400r, respectively, on day of issue. Issued: No. 141, 2/28/96. No. 142, 3/13/96.

Souvenir Sheet

Beaver — A36

Illustration reduced.

1996, Mar. 26 Litho. *Perf. 12½x12*

143 A36 1200r multicolored .35 .35

Kondrat Krapiva (1896-1991), Writer — A37

1996, Mar. 5 Litho. *Perf. 14x14½*

144 A37 1000r multicolored .35 .35

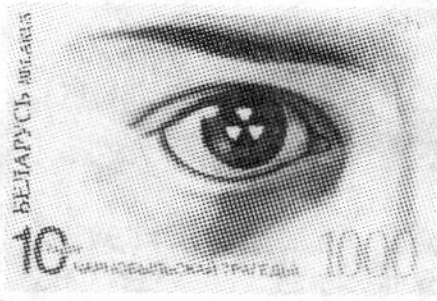

Chernobyl Disaster, 10th Anniv. A38

Radiation symbol and: a, Eye. b, Leaf showing contamination. c, Boarded-up window.

1996, Apr. 10 Litho. *Perf. 14*

145 A38 1000r Block of 3, #a.-c. + label .50 .50

Coat of Arms — A39

1996, May 6 Litho. *Perf. 13½*

146 A39 100r blue & black .20 .20
147 A39 500r green & black .20 .20
148 A39 600r vermilion & black .20 .20
149 A39 1000r orange & black .20 .20
150 A39 1500r dp lilac rose & blk .25 .25
151 A39 1800r violet & black .30 .30
152 A39 2200r rose violet & black .40 .40
153 A39 3300r yellow & black .50 .50
154 A39 5000r green blue & blk .75 .75
155 A39 10,000r apple green & blk 1.50 1.50
156 A39 30,000r brown & black 4.50 4.50
157 A39 50,000r red brown & blk 7.50 7.50
Nos. 146-157 (12) 16.50 16.50

See Nos. 182, 196-201.

Agreement with Russia — A40

1996, June 14 *Perf. 13½x14*

158 A40 1500r multicolored .30 .30

1996 Summer Olympic Games, Atlanta A41

1996, July 15 Litho. *Perf. 14*

159 A41 3000r Rhythmic gymnastics .25 .25
160 A41 3000r Discus .25 .25
161 A41 3000r Wrestling .25 .25
162 A41 3000r Weight lifting .25 .25
Nos. 159-162 (4) 1.00 1.00

Souvenir Sheet

Imperf

163 A41 5000r Shooting, vert. 1.00 1.00

No. 163 has simulated perforations.

Regional Costume Type of 1995

Couples in traditional 19th cent. costumes: 1800r, Kapilska-Kletzky region. 2200r, David-Gorodok-Turai region. 3300r, Kobrin region. 5000r, Naralyan region.

1996, Aug. 13 Litho. *Perf. 14*

164 A26 1800r multicolored .20 .20
165 A26 2200r multicolored .25 .25
166 A26 3300r multicolored .40 .40
Nos. 164-166 (3) .85 .85

Souvenir Sheet

Imperf

167 A26 5000r multicolored 1.00 1.00

Medicinal Plants — A42

No. 168, Sanguisorba officinaus. No. 169, Acorus calamus. 2200r, Potentilla erecta. 3300r, Frangula alnus. 5000r, Menyanthes trifoliata.

1996, Aug. 15 *Perf. 14x13½*

168 A42 1500r multicolored .25 .25
169 A42 1500r multicolored .25 .25
170 A42 2200r multicolored .40 .40
171 A42 3300r multicolored .60 .60
Nos. 168-171 (4) 1.50 1.50

Souvenir Sheet

Imperf

172 A42 5000r multicolored 1.00 1.00

Birds A44

No. 173: a, Ardea cinerea. b, Ciconia nigra. c, Phalacrocorax carbo. d, Ciconia ciconia. e, Larus ridibundus. f, Gallinago gallinago. g, Chlidonias leucopterus. h, Remiz pendulinus. i, Botaurus stellaris. j, Fulica atra. k, Ixobrychus minutus. l, Alcedo atthts.
No. 174: a, Anas crecca. b, Anas strepera. c, Anas acuta. d, Anas platyrhynchos. e, Aythya marila. f, Clangula hyemalis. g, Anas clypeata. h, Anas querquedula. i, Anas penelope. j, Arthya nyroca. k, Bucephala clangula. l, Mergus merganser. m, Mergus albellus. n, Aythya fuligula. o, Mergus serrator. p, Aythya ferina.
No. 175, Aythya ferina, diff. No. 176, Gallinago gallinago, diff.

1996, Sept. 10 Litho. *Perf. 14*

173 A44 400r Sheet of 12, #a.-l. 6.00 6.00
174 A44 400r Sheet of 16, #a.-p. 8.00 8.00

Souvenir Sheets

175-176 A44 1000r each 4.00 4.00

Grammar Book, 1596 — A45

1996, Sept. 19 Litho. *Perf. 14x13½*

177 A45 1500r multicolored .30 .30

Churches A46

1996, Sept. 24 *Perf. 14x14½*

178 A46 3300r Pinsk .50 .50
179 A46 3300r Mogilev, 17th cent. .50 .50

Mikola Shchakatskin (1896-1940), Art Critic — A47

1996, Oct. 16

180 A47 2000r multicolored .35 .35

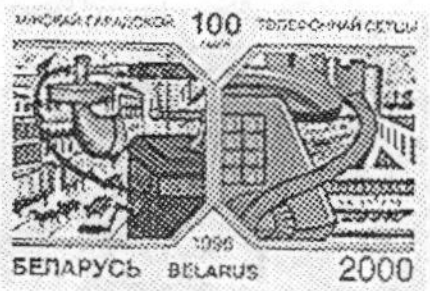

Minsk Telephone Station, Cent. — A48

1996, Nov. 14

181 A48 2000r multicolored .35 .35

Natl. Arms Type of 1996

1996, Nov. 21 Litho. *Perf. 13½x14*

182 A39 200r gray green & black .20 .20

Pres. Aleksandr G. Lukashenka, Natl. Flag — A49

1996, Dec. 6 Litho. *Perf. 13½*

183 A49 2500r multicolored .50 .50

Famous Men — A50

Designs: No. 184, Kyril Turovski (1130-81), Bishop of Turov. No. 185, Mikola Gusovski (1470-1533), writer. No. 186, Mikolaj Radziwil (1515-65), chancellor of Lithuania.

1996, Dec. 17 *Perf. 13½*

184 A50 3000r multicolored .40 .40
185 A50 3000r multicolored .40 .40
186 A50 3000r multicolored .40 .40
Nos. 184-186 (3) 1.20 1.20

New Year — A51

1500r, Christmas tree, buildings in Minsk.

1996, Dec. 21 *Perf. 14*

187 A51 1500r multicolored .30 .30
188 A51 2000r multicolored, vert. .40 .40

Natl. Museum of Art, Minsk — A52

Icons: No. 189, Madonna and Child, Smolensk, 16th cent. No. 190, Paraskeva, 16th cent. No. 191, Ilya, 17th cent. No. 192, Three saints, 18th cent.

5000r, Birth of Christ, by Peter Yacijevitsch, 1649.

1996, Dec. 26 *Perf. 13½*

189 A52 3500r multicolored .50 .50
190 A52 3500r multicolored .50 .50
191 A52 3500r multicolored .50 .50
192 A52 3500r multicolored .50 .50
Nos. 189-192 (4) 2.00 2.00

Souvenir Sheet

Imperf

193 A46 5000r multicolored .75 .75

Georgi K. Zhukov (1896-1974), Soviet Marshal A53

1997, Jan. 3 *Perf. 13½*

194 A53 2000r multicolored .35 .35

Kupala Natl. Theater, Minsk — A54

1997, Jan. 3 *Perf. 13½x14*

195 A54 3500r multicolored .55 .55

Coat of Arms Type of 1996

1997 Litho. *Perf. 13½x14*

196 A39 400r lt brown & black .20 .20
197 A39 800r dull blue & black .20 .20
198 A39 1500r brt blue & black .45 .45
199 A39 2000r apple green & black .60 .60
200 A39 2500r dk blue & black
201 A39 3000r brown & black .45 .45

Issued: 400r, 2000r, 1/9; 1500r, 1/16; 800r, 2500r, 3000r, 9/22.

V.K. Byalynitsky-Birulya (1872-1957), Painter — A55

1997, Feb. 26 *Perf. 14*

202 A55 2000r multicolored .60 .60

No. 2 Surcharged in Gray

3500
1997
105 гадоў з дня нараджэння

1997, Mar. 10 Photo. *Perf. 12x11½*

203 A2 3500r on 20k blue & black 1.00 1.00

Fish — A56

2000r, Salmo trutta. 3000r, Vimba vimba. #206, Thymallus thymallus. #207, Barbus barbus.

5000r, Acipenser ruthenus.

1997, Apr. 10 Litho. *Perf. 13½x14*

204 A56 2000r multicolored .60 .60
205 A56 3000r multicolored .90 .90
206 A56 4500r multicolored 1.25 1.25
207 A56 4500r multicolored 1.25 1.25
Nos. 204-207 (4) 4.00 4.00

Souvenir Sheet

208 A56 5000r multicolored 1.40 1.40

Intl. Conference on Sustainable Development of Countries with Economies in Transition — A57

Designs: 3000r, Earth with "SOS" formed in atmosphere. 4500r, Hand above flora and fauna.

1997, Apr. 16 *Perf. 14x14½*

209 A57 3000r multicolored .85 .85
210 A57 4500r multicolored 1.25 1.25
a. Pair, #209-210 + label 2.20 2.20

Entry into UPU, 50th Anniv. — A58

1997, May 13 *Perf. 14½x14*

211 A58 3000r multicolored .90 .90

Nos. 28-29 Surcharged in Violet Blue

100
1997

1997 Litho. *Perf. 12x12½*

211A A7 100r on 1r brown 5.00 5.00
212 A7 100r on 2r red brown .20 .20

Issued: 2r, 5/22.

World War II Liberation Day, July 3 — A59

1997, June 26 *Perf. 14½x14*

213 A59 3000r multicolored .90 .90

Traditional Costume Type of 1995

Men and women in 19th cent. costumes, regions: 2000r, Dzisna. 3000r, Navagrudak. 4500r, Byhau.

1997, July 10

214 A26 2000r multicolored .55 .55
215 A26 3000r multicolored .85 .85
216 A26 4500r multicolored 1.25 1.25
Nos. 214-216 (3) 2.65 2.65

Book Printing in Belarus, 480th Anniv. — A60

#217, Text, Vilnius period. #218, Text, Prague period. 4000r, F. Skorina (1488-1535), Polatsk period. 7500r, F. Skorina, Krakow period.

1997, Sept. 7 *Perf. 13½*

217 A60 3000r shown .85 .85
218 A60 3000r gray, black & red .85 .85
219 A60 4000r gray, black & red 1.10 1.10
220 A60 7500r gray, black & red 2.00 2.00
Nos. 217-220 (4) 4.80 4.80

Pinsk Jesuit College A61

1997, Sept. 13 *Perf. 14x14½*

221 A61 3000r multicolored .85 .85

National Library, 75th Anniv. A62

1997, Sept. 15

222 A62 3000r multicolored .90 .90

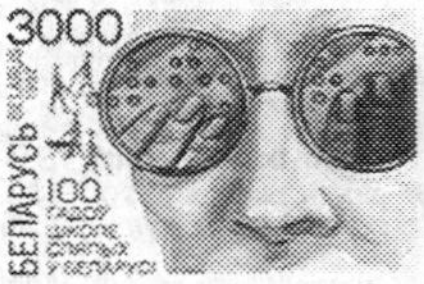

Belarus School for the Blind, Cent. A63

1997, Sept. 28 Litho. *Perf. 14x14¼*

223 A63 3000r multicolored .45 .45

Intl. Children's Day — A64

1997, Sept. 28 Litho. *Perf. 14x14½*

224 A64 3000r multicolored .85 .85

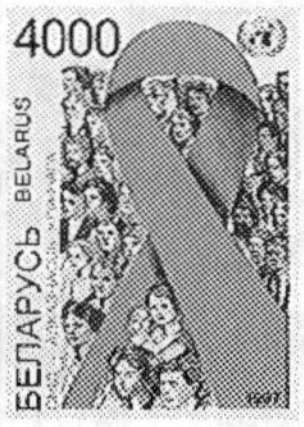

Fight Against AIDS — A65

1997, Oct. 14 *Perf. 14½x14*

225 A65 4000r multicolored 1.10 1.10

Farm Tractors A66

3300r, Belarus "1221." 4400r, First wheel tractor, 1953. #228, Belarus "952." #229, Belarus "680."

1997, Oct. 16 *Perf. 14x14½*

226 A66 3300r multicolored 1.00 1.00
227 A66 4400r multicolored 1.25 1.25
228 A66 7500r multicolored 2.00 2.00
229 A66 7500r multicolored 2.00 2.00
a. Sheet, 2 each, #226-229 + label 13.00 13.00
Nos. 226-229 (4) 6.25 6.25

No. 1 Surcharged

3000

1997, Dec. 8 Litho. *Perf. 12x12½*

230 A1 3000r on 1r multi .45 .45

Holiday Greetings A68

1997, Dec. 23 Litho. *Perf. 14x14¼*

231 A68 1400r New Year .20 .20
232 A68 4400r Christmas .50 .50

1998 Winter Olympic Games, Nagano — A69

Designs: a, 2000r, Cross country skiing. b, 3300r, Ice hockey. c, 4400r, Biathlon. d, 7500r, Freestyle skiing.

1998, Feb. 3 Litho. *Perf. 13½*

233 A69 Block of 4, #a.-d. 2.50

P.M. Mascherov (1918-80), Author A70

1998, Feb. 12 Litho. *Perf. 13½*

234 A70 2500r multicolored .30 .30

Minsk Automobile Plant — A71

Dump trucks: 1400r, 1947 MAZ-205. 2000r, 1968 MAZ-503B. 3000r, 1977 MAZ-5549. 4400r, 1985 MAZ-5551. 7500r, 1994 MAZ-5516.

1998, Apr. 23 Litho. *Perf. 13½*

235 A71 1400r multicolored .20 .20
236 A71 2000r multicolored .25 .25
237 A71 3000r multicolored .40 .40
238 A71 4400r multicolored .55 .55
239 A71 7500r multicolored .95 .95
a. Souvenir sheet, #235-239 + label 2.50 2.50
Nos. 235-239 (5) 2.35 2.35

A72

A73

1998, May 5 Litho. *Perf. 14*

240 A72 15,000r multicolored 1.00 1.00

Europa. Town of Nesvizh, 775th Anniv.

1998, May 20 Litho. *Perf. 14*

241 A73 8600r multicolored 1.10 1.10

Adam Mickiewicz (1798-1855), poet.

No. 67 Surcharged in Silver with Post Horn, New Value and Cyrillic Text

1998, May 22 *Perf. 12*

242 A13 8600r on 150r multi 1.10 1.10

St. Petersburt-Mahilyou Post Route, 225th anniv.

A74

A75

Songbirds from Red Book of Belarus: 1500r, Luscinia svecica. 3200r, Remiz pendulinus. 3800r, Acrocephalus paludicola. 5300r, Locustella luscinioides. 8600r, Parus cyanus.

1998, May 29 *Perf. 14*

243	A74	1500r multicolored	.20	.20
244	A74	3200r multicolored	.40	.40
245	A74	3800r multicolored	.50	.50
246	A74	5300r multicolored	.65	.65
247	A74	8600r multicolored	1.10	1.10
a.		Sheet of 2 each #243-247	5.75	5.75
		Nos. 243-247 (5)	2.85	2.85

1998 *Perf. 13½x14*

Mills, Musical Instruments: 100r, Water-powered mill. 200r, Windmill. 500r, Stork. 1000r, Ox. 2000r, Kalyady Star. 3200r, Dulcimer. 5000r, Church. 5300r, Hurdy-gurdy. 10,000r, Flaming wheel.

248	A75	100r green & black	.20	.20
249	A75	200r brown & black	.20	.20
250	A75	500r bl, lt blu & blk	.20	.20
251	A75	1000r grn, lt grn & blk	.20	.20
252	A75	2000r bl, lt bl & blk	.20	.20
253	A75	3200r apple green & black	*1.00*	*1.00*
254	A75	5000r bl, lt bl & blk	.20	.20
255	A75	5300r bister, black & buff	*1.75*	*1.75*
256	A75	10,000r org, lt org & blk	.30	.30
		Nos. 248-256 (9)	*4.25*	*4.25*

Issued: 100r, 200r, 7/1; 3200r, 5300r, 6/23; 2000r, 10,000r, 8/5;

This is an expanding set. Numbers may change.

Belarussian Auto Works (BelAZ), 50th Anniv. — A76

Designs: 1500r, Front end loader.

Large quarry truck models: 3200r, #75131. 3800r, #75303. 5300r, #75483. 8600r, #755.

1998, Aug. 12 *Perf. 14x14½*

259	A76	1500r multicolored	.20	.20
260	A76	3200r multicolored	.20	.20
261	A76	3800r multicolored	.20	.20
262	A76	5300r multicolored	.20	.20
263	A76	8600r multicolored	.20	.20
a.		Sheet of 5, #259-263 + label	.80	.80

A77

A78

Mushrooms: 2500r, Morchella esculenta. 3800r, Morchella conica. 4600r, Macrolepiota rhacodes. 5800r, Marcrolepiota procera. 9400r, Coprinus comatus.

1998, Sept. 10 *Perf. 14*

264	A77	2500r multicolored	.20	.20
265	A77	3800r multicolored	.20	.20
266	A77	4600r multicolored	.20	.20
267	A77	5800r multicolored	.20	.20
268	A77	9400r multicolored	.25	.25
		Nos. 264-268 (5)	1.05	1.05

1998, Oct. 6 *Perf. 13½*

Wooden Sculptures: 3400r, Naversha, 12-13th cent. 3800r, Archangel Michael, 1470-1480. 5800r, Prophet Zacharias, 1642-1646. 9400r, Madonna and Child, 16th cent.

269	A78	3400r multicolored	.20	.20
270	A78	3800r multicolored	.20	.20
271	A78	5800r multicolored	.20	.20
272	A78	9400r multicolored	.25	.25
		Nos. 269-272 (4)	.85	.85

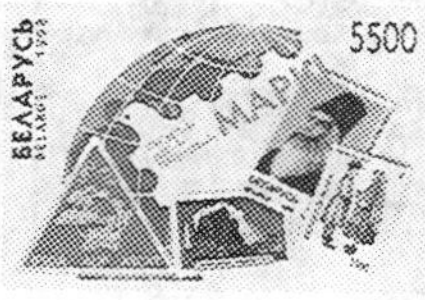
World Stamp Day — A79

1998, Oct. 9 *Perf. 14x14½*

273 A79 5500r multicolored .20 .20

Paintings from Natl. Art Museum — A80

3000r, "Kalozha" (church), by V.K. Tsvirko (1913-93). 3500r, "Corner Living Room," by S.U. Zhukovsky (1875-1944). 5000r, "Winter Dream," by V.K. Byalynitsky-Birulay (1872-1967). 5500r, "Portrait of a Girl," by I.I. Alyashkevich (1777-1830). 10,000r, "Woman with a Bowl of Fruit," by I.F. Hrutski (1810-85).

1998, Oct. 20 *Perf. 13½*

274	A80	3000r multi	.20	.20
275	A80	3500r multi	.20	.20
276	A80	5000r multi	.20	.20
277	A80	5500r multi, vert.	.20	.20
278	A80	10,000r multi, vert.	.30	.20
		Nos. 274-278 (5)	1.10	1.00

A81

A82

1998, Nov. 25 *Perf. 14½x14*

279 A81 7100r multicolored .20 .20

Universal Declaration of Human Rights, 50th anniv.

1998, Nov. 30

Christmas and New Year: No. 280, Girl wearing short yellow coat, rabbit, log cabin. No. 281, Rabbit, girl wearing long fur-trimmed pink coat, hat.

280	A82	5500r multicolored	.20	.20
281	A82	5500r multicolored	.20	.20
a.		Pair, #280-281	.20	.20

Europa — A98

Nature Reserves: No. 304, Berezina, 1925. No. 305, Belovezhskaya Forest, 1939.

1999, Apr. 27 Litho. *Perf. 13½*

304	A98	150,000r multicolored	1.25	1.25
305	A98	150,000r multicolored	1.25	1.25

BELGIAN CONGO

'bel-jən 'käŋ-ˌgō

LOCATION — Central Africa
GOVT. — Belgian colony
AREA — 902,082 sq. mi. (estimated)
POP. — 12,660,000 (1956)
CAPITAL — Léopoldville

Congo was an independent state, founded by Leopold II of Belgium, until 1908 when it was annexed to Belgium as a colony. In 1960 it became the independent Republic of the Congo. See Congo Democratic Republic and Zaire.

100 Centimes = 1 Franc

Catalogue values for unused stamps in this country are for Never Hinged items, beginning with Scott 187 in the regular postage section, Scott B32 in the semi-postal section, Scott C17 in the airpost section, and Scott J8 in the postage due section.

Independent State

King Leopold II
A1 A2 A3

1886 Unwmk. Typo. *Perf. 15*

1	A1	5c green	8.00	*22.50*
2	A1	10c rose	4.00	*5.00*
3	A2	25c blue	42.50	35.00
4	A3	50c olive green	6.50	6.50
5	A1	5fr lilac	340.00	275.00
a.		Perf. 14	850.00	
b.		5fr deep lilac	750.00	475.00

Counterfeits exist.

For surcharge see No. Q1.

King Leopold II — A4

1887-94

6	A4	5c grn ('89)	.75	.75
7	A4	10c rose ('89)	1.25	1.25
8	A4	25c blue ('89)	1.25	1.25
9	A4	50c reddish brown	45.00	21.00
10	A4	50c gray ('94)	2.50	*16.00*
11	A4	5fr violet	900.00	375.00
12	A4	5fr gray ('92)	110.00	95.00
13	A4	10fr buff ('91)	400.00	275.00

The 25fr and 50fr in gray were not issued. Values, each $20.

Counterfeits exist of Nos. 10-13, 25fr and 50fr, unused, used, genuine stamps with faked cancels and counterfeit stamps with genuine cancels.

For surcharges see Nos. Q3-Q6.

Port Matadi — A5

River Scene on the Congo, Stanley Falls — A6

Inkissi Falls — A7

Railroad Bridge on M'pozo River — A8

Hunting Elephants A9

Bangala Chief and Wife — A10

1894-1901 Engr. *Perf. 12½ to 15*

14	A5	5c pale bl & blk	12.50	12.50
15	A5	5c red brn & blk ('95)	3.25	1.40
16	A5	5c grn & blk ('00)	1.75	.50
17	A6	10c red brn & blk	12.50	12.50
18	A6	10c grnsh bl & blk ('95)	1.50	1.25
a.		Center inverted	1,900.	2,250.
19	A6	10c car & blk ('00)	3.00	.75
20	A7	25c yel org & blk	3.25	2.25
21	A7	25c lt bl & blk ('00)	3.00	1.25
22	A8	50c grn & blk	1.25	1.25
23	A8	50c ol & blk ('00)	3.00	.75
24	A9	1fr lilac & blk	20.00	11.00
a.		1fr rose lilac & black	225.00	22.50
25	A9	1fr car & blk ('01)	200.00	5.00
26	A10	5fr lake & blk	40.00	25.00
a.		5fr carmine rose & black	85.00	35.00
		Nos. 14-26 (13)	305.00	75.40

For overprints see Nos. 31-32, 34, 36-37, 39.

Climbing Oil Palms — A11

Congo Canoe — A12

1896

27	A11	15c ocher & blk	3.25	.50
28	A12	40c bluish grn & blk	3.25	2.50

For overprints see Nos. 33, 35.

Congo Village — A13

River Steamer on the Congo — A14

1898

29	A13	3.50fr red & blk	140.00	80.00
a.		Perf. 14x12	350.00	225.00
30	A14	10fr yel grn & blk	90.00	24.00
a.		Center inverted	25,000.	
b.		Perf. 12	525.00	22.50
c.		Perf. 12x14	325.00	—
		As "c," pen canceled		14.00

For overprints see Nos. 38, 40.

Belgian Congo

Overprinted **CONGO BELGE**

1908

31	A5	5c green & blk	7.00	7.00
a.		Handstamped	2.50	1.75
32	A6	10c carmine & blk	12.00	12.00
a.		Handstamped	2.50	1.75
33	A11	15c ocher & blk	7.00	7.00
a.		Handstamped	5.50	3.50
34	A7	25c lt blue & blk	3.75	2.50
a.		Handstamped	7.00	3.50
c.		Double overprint (#34)	190.00	
35	A12	40c bluish grn & blk	2.25	2.25
a.		Handstamped	7.00	5.50
36	A8	50c olive & blk	4.00	2.25
a.		Handstamped	3.75	3.00
b.		Inverted overprint (#36)	500.00	
37	A9	1fr carmine & blk	19.00	2.25
a.		Handstamped	25.00	7.00
38	A13	3.50fr red & blk	25.00	20.00
a.		Handstamped	160.00	110.00
39	A10	5fr carmine & blk	40.00	24.00
a.		Handstamped	60.00	40.00
40	A14	10fr yel grn & blk	85.00	20.00
a.		Perf. 14	225.00	—
b.		Handstamped	125.00	45.00
c.		Handstamped, perf. 14	275.00	225.00
		Nos. 31-40 (10)	205.00	99.25

Most of the above handstamps are also found inverted and double.

Values for handstamped overprints are for those applied locally.

Counterfeits of the handstamped overprints exist.

Port Matadi — A15

River Scene on the Congo, Stanley Falls — A16

Climbing Oil Palms — A17

Railroad Bridge on M'pozo River — A18

1909 *Perf. 14*

41	A15	5c green & blk	.75	.75
42	A16	10c carmine & blk	.75	.50
43	A17	15c ocher & blk	25.00	15.00
44	A18	50c olive & blk	3.00	2.50
		Nos. 41-44 (4)	29.50	18.75

Port Matadi — A19

River Scene on the Congo, Stanley Falls — A20

Climbing Oil Palms — A21

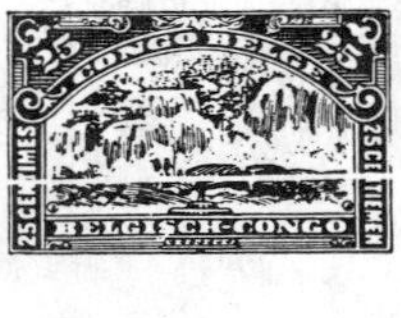

Inkissi Falls — A22

Congo Canoe — A23

Railroad Bridge on M'pozo River — A24

Hunting Elephants A25

Congo Village — A26

Bangala Chief and Wife — A27

River Steamer on the Congo — A28

1910-15 Engr. *Perf. 14, 15*

45	A19	5c green & blk	.75	.20
46	A20	10c carmine & blk	.40	.20
47	A21	15c ocher & blk	.40	.20
48	A21	15c grn & blk ('15)	.20	.20
a.		Booklet pane of 10	14.00	
49	A22	25c blue & blk	1.50	.30
50	A23	40c bluish grn & blk	2.00	1.75
51	A23	40c brn red & blk ('15)	3.75	1.75
52	A24	50c olive & blk	3.00	1.50
53	A24	50c brn lake & blk ('15)	6.00	1.75
54	A25	1fr carmine & blk	2.75	2.10
55	A25	1fr ol bis & blk ('15)	2.00	.65
56	A26	3fr red & blk	15.00	10.00
57	A27	5fr carmine & blk	17.00	14.00
58	A27	5fr ocher & blk ('15)	1.50	.65
59	A28	10fr green & blk	16.00	12.50
		Nos. 45-59 (15)	72.25	47.75

Nos. 48, 51, 53, 55 and 58 exist imperforate.

For overprints and surcharges see Nos. 64-76, 81-86, B5-B9.

Port Matadi — A29

Stanley Falls, Congo River — A30

Inkissi Falls — A31

TEN CENTIMES.

Type I - Large white space at top of picture and two small white spots at lower edge. Vignette does not fill frame.

Type II - Vignette completely fills frame.

1915

60	A29	5c green & blk	.20	.20
a.		Booklet pane of 10	7.50	
61	A30	10c car & blk (II)	.20	.20
a.		10c carmine & black (I)	.20	.20
d.		Booklet pane of 10 (II)	14.00	
62	A31	25c blue & blk	.85	.25
a.		Booklet pane of 10	65.00	
		Nos. 60-62 (3)	1.25	.65

Nos. 60 to 62 exist imperforate.

For surcharges see Nos. 77-80, 87, B1-B4.

Stamps of 1910 Issue Surcharged in Red or Black

10c 10c

1921

64	A23	5c on 40c bluish grn & blk (R)	.25	.25
65	A19	10c on 5c grn & blk (R)	.25	.25
66	A24	15c on 50c ol & blk (R)	.25	.25
67	A21	25c on 15c ocher & blk (R)	1.50	1.00
68	A20	30c on 10c car & blk	.35	.35
69	A22	50c on 25c bl & blk (R)	1.40	.90
		Nos. 64-69 (6)	4.00	3.00

The position of the new value and the bars varies on Nos. 64 to 69.

Overprinted **1921**

1921

70	A25	1fr carmine & blk	.75	.75
a.		Double overprint	20.00	
71	A26	3fr red & blk	2.50	2.50
72	A27	5fr carmine & blk	4.75	4.75
73	A28	10fr green & blk (R)	4.25	2.50
		Nos. 70-73 (4)	12.25	10.50

Belgian Surcharges

Nos. 51, 53, 60-62 Surcharged in Black or Red **·10c**

1922

74	A24	5c on 50c	.35	.30
75	A29	10c on 5c (R)	.35	.25
76	A23	25c on 40c (R)	2.00	.30
77	A30	30c on 10c (II)	.20	.20
a.		30c on 10c (I)	.20	.20
b.		Double surcharge	4.75	4.75
78	A31	50c on 25c (R)	.40	.25
		Nos. 74-78 (5)	3.30	1.30

No. 74 has the surcharge at each side.

Congo Surcharges

Nos. 60, 51 Surcharged in Red or Black:

10 c.

a

25 c.

b

1922

80	A29	10c on 5c (R)	.55	.55
a.		Inverted surcharge	17.50	17.50
b.		Double surcharge	4.75	
c.		Double surch., one invtd.	40.00	
d.		Pair, one without surcharge	42.50	
e.		On No. 45	125.00	125.00
81	A23	25c on 40c	.70	.35
a.		Inverted surcharge	17.50	17.50
b.		Double surcharge	5.50	
c.		"25c" double		
d.		25c on 5c, No. 60	100.00	100.00

Nos. 55, 58 Surcharged with vertical bars over original values **10 c.**

1922

84	A25	10c on 1fr (R)	.55	.55
a.		Double surcharge	14.00	
b.		Inverted surcharge	17.50	17.50
85	A27	25c on 5fr	1.50	1.50

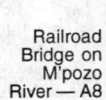

Nos. 68, 77 Handstamped **0,25**

86	A20	25c on 30c on 10c	7.00	*8.50*
87	A30	25c on 30c on 10c (II)	7.00	*8.50*

Nos. 86-87 exist with handstamp surcharge inverted.

Counterfeit handstamped surcharges exist.

Ubangi Woman — A32

Watusi Cattle — A44

Designs: 10c, Baluba woman. 15c, Babuende woman. No. 90, 40c, 1.25fr, 1.50fr, 1.75fr, Ubangi man. 25c, Basketmaking. 30c, 35c, Nos. 101, 102, Carving wood. 50c, Archer. Nos. 92, 100, Weaving. 1fr, Making pottery. 3fr, Working rubber. 5fr, Making palm oil. 10fr, African elephant.

1923-27 Engr. *Perf. 12*

88	A32	5c yellow	.20	.20
89	A32	10c green	.20	.20
90	A32	15c olive brn	.20	.20
91	A32	20c olive grn ('24)	.20	.20
92	A44	20c green ('26)	.20	.20
93	A44	25c red brown	.25	.20
94	A44	30c rose red ('24)	.45	.45
95	A44	30c olive grn ('25)	.20	.20
96	A44	35c green ('27)	.45	.35
97	A32	40c violet ('25)	.20	.20
98	A44	50c gray blue	.25	.20
99	A44	50c buff ('25)	.30	.20
100	A44	75c red orange	.25	.20
101	A44	75c gray bl ('25)	.40	.25
102	A44	75c salmon red ('26)	.20	.20
103	A44	1fr bister brn	.55	.20
104	A44	1fr dl blue ('25)	.35	.20
105	A44	1fr rose red ('27)	.85	.20
106	A32	1.25fr dl blue ('26)	.30	.20
107	A32	1.50fr dl blue ('26)	.30	.20
108	A32	1.75fr dl blue ('27)	3.75	3.25
109	A44	3fr gray brn ('24)	4.00	2.25
110	A44	5fr gray ('24)	10.00	4.75
111	A44	10fr gray blk ('24)	17.50	8.50

1925-26

112	A44	45c dk vio ('26)	.40	.25
113	A44	60c carmine rose	.40	.20
		Nos. 88-113 (26)	42.35	23.65

For surcharges see Nos. 114, 136-138, 157.

No. 107 Surcharged **1.75**

1927, June 14

114	A32	1.75fr on 1.50fr dl bl	.30	.20

Sir Henry Morton Stanley — A45

1928, June 30 *Perf. 14*

115	A45	5c gray blk	.20	.20
116	A45	10c dp violet	.20	.20
117	A45	20c orange red	.35	.25
118	A45	35c green	1.00	.75
119	A45	40c red brown	.40	.20
120	A45	60c black brn	.40	.20
121	A45	1fr carmine	.40	.20
122	A45	1.60fr dk gray	4.00	3.25
123	A45	1.75fr dp blue	1.60	.80
124	A45	2fr dk brown	1.10	.30
125	A45	2.75fr red violet	4.50	.45
126	A45	3.50fr rose lake	1.40	.75
127	A45	5fr slate grn	1.10	.30
128	A45	10fr violet blue	1.60	.75
129	A45	20fr claret	6.75	2.25
		Nos. 115-129 (15)	25.00	10.85

Sir Henry M. Stanley (1841-1904), explorer.

Nos. 118, 121-123, 125-126 Surcharged in Red, Blue or Black

1F25

1931, Jan. 15

130	A45	40c on 35c	.50	.40
131	A45	1.25fr on 1fr (Bl)	.40	.20
132	A45	2fr on 1.60fr	.80	.30
133	A45	2fr on 1.75fr	.75	.30
134	A45	3.25fr on 2.75fr (Bk)	2.25	2.00
135	A45	3.25fr on 3.25fr (Bk)	3.00	2.10

Nos. 96, 108, 112 Surcharged in Red

50c

Perf. 12½, 12

136	A44	40c on 35c grn	3.25	3.00
137	A44	50c on 45c dk vio	2.00	1.10

Surcharged **2**

138	A32	2(fr) on 1.75fr dl bl	8.50	7.50
		Nos. 130-138 (9)	21.45	16.90

View of Sankuru River — A46

Flute Players — A50

Designs: 15c, Kivu Kraal. 20c, Sankuru River rapids. 25c, Uele hut. 50c, Musicians of Lake Leopold II. 60c, Batetelas drummers. 75c, Mangbetu woman. 1fr, Domesticated elephant of Api. 1.25fr, Mangbetu chief. 1.50fr, 2fr, Village of Mondimbi. 2.50fr, 3.25fr, Okapi. 4fr, Canoes at Stanleyville. 5fr, Woman preparing cassava. 10fr, Baluba chief. 20fr, Young woman of Irumu.

1931-37 Engr. *Perf. 11½*

139	A46	10c gray brn ('32)	.20	.20
140	A46	15c gray ('32)	.20	.20
141	A46	20c brn lil ('32)	.20	.20
142	A46	25c dp blue ('32)	.20	.20
143	A50	40c dp grn ('32)	.20	.20
144	A46	50c violet ('32)	.20	.20
b.		Booklet pane of 8	6.25	
145	A50	60c vio brn ('32)	.20	.20
146	A50	75c rose ('32)	.20	.20
b.		Booklet pane of 8	1.25	
147	A50	1fr rose red ('32)	.20	.20
148	A50	1.25fr red brown	.20	.20
b.		Booklet pane of 8	1.25	
149	A46	1.50fr dk ol gray ('37)	.20	.20
b.		Booklet pane of 8	6.00	
150	A46	2fr ultra ('32)	.20	.20
151	A46	2.50fr dp blue ('37)	.30	.20
b.		Booklet pane of 8	8.50	
152	A46	3.25fr gray blk ('32)	.45	.30
153	A46	4fr dl vio ('32)	.20	.20
154	A50	5fr dp vio ('32)	.50	.25
155	A50	10fr red ('32)	.50	.40
156	A50	20fr blk brn ('32)	1.50	1.25
		Nos. 139-156 (18)	5.85	5.00

No. 109 Surcharged in Red **3F25**

1932, Mar. 15 *Perf. 12*

157	A44	3.25fr on 3fr gray brn	2.75	2.25

King Albert Memorial Issue

King Albert — A62

1934, May 7 Photo. *Perf. 11½*

158	A62	1.50fr black	.65	.35

Leopold I, Leopold II, Albert I, Leopold III A63

1935, Aug. 15 Engr. *Perf. 12½x12*

159	A63	50c green	.65	.50
160	A63	1.25fr dk carmine	.65	.20
161	A63	1.50fr brown vio	.65	.20
162	A63	2.40fr brown org	2.00	2.00
163	A63	2.50fr lt blue	2.00	.90
164	A63	4fr brt violet	2.00	1.25
165	A63	5fr black brn	2.00	1.50
		Nos. 159-165 (7)	9.95	6.55

Founding of Congo Free State, 50th anniv.

For surcharges see Nos. B21-B22.

Molindi River A64

Bamboos A65

Suza River — A66

Rutshuru River — A67

Karisimbi A68

Mitumba Forest — A69

1937-38 Photo. *Perf. 11½*

166	A64	5c purple & blk	.20	.20
167	A65	90c car & brn	.40	.30
168	A66	1.50fr dp red brn & blk	.20	.20
169	A67	2.40fr ol blk & brn	.20	.20
170	A68	2.50fr dp ultra & blk	.30	.20
171	A69	4.50fr dk grn & brn	.30	.20
172	A69	4.50fr car & sep	.20	.20
		Nos. 166-172 (7)	1.80	1.50

National Parks.

No. 172 was issued in sheets of four measuring 140x111mm. It was sold by subscription, the subscription closing Oct. 20, 1937. Value, $1.60.

Nos. 166-171 were issued Mar. 1, 1938.

See No. B26. For surcharges see Nos. 184, 186.

King Albert Memorial, Leopoldville — A70

1941, Feb. 7 Litho. *Perf. 11*

173	A70	10c lt gray	.20	.20
174	A70	15c brown vio	.25	.20
175	A70	25c lt blue	.30	.20
176	A70	50c lt violet	.25	.20
177	A70	75c rose pink	.95	.30
178	A70	1.25fr gray	.30	.20
179	A70	1.75fr orange	.95	.45
180	A70	2.50fr carmine	.65	.20
181	A70	2.75fr vio blue	.95	.60
182	A70	5fr lt olive grn	4.00	1.50
183	A70	10fr rose red	2.75	1.75
		Nos. 173-183 (11)	11.55	5.80

Exist imperforate.

For surcharge see No. 185.

Nos. 168, 179, 169 Surcharged in Blue or Black

5 c.

75 c.

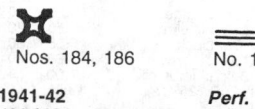

Nos. 184, 186 — No. 185

1941-42 *Perf. 11½, 11*

184	A66	5c on 1.50fr (Bl)	.20	.20
a.		Inverted surcharge	14.00	14.00
185	A70	75c on 1.75fr ('42)	.35	.35
a.		Inverted surcharge	14.00	14.00
186	A67	2.50(fr) on 2.40fr ('42)	.85	.70
a.		Double surcharge	27.50	27.50
b.		Inverted surcharge	14.00	14.00
		Nos. 184-186 (3)	1.40	1.25

Catalogue values for unused stamps in this section, from this point to the end of the section, are for Never Hinged items.

Oil Palms

A71 A72

Congo Woman — A73

Askari — A75

Leopard A74

Okapi — A76

Inscribed "Congo Belge Belgisch Congo"

1942, May 23 Engr. *Perf. 12½*

187 A71 5c red .20 .20
188 A72 10c olive grn .20 .20
189 A72 15c brown car .20 .20
190 A72 20c dp ultra .20 .20
191 A72 25c brown vio .20 .20
192 A72 30c blue .20 .20
193 A72 50c dp green .20 .20
194 A72 60c chestnut .20 .20
195 A73 75c dl lil & blk .20 .20
196 A73 1fr dk brn & blk .20 .20
197 A73 1.25fr rose red & blk .20 .20
198 A74 1.75fr dk gray brn .75 .35
199 A74 2fr ocher .75 .20
200 A74 2.50fr carmine .75 .20
201 A75 3.50fr dk ol grn .35 .20
202 A75 5fr orange .70 .20
203 A75 6fr brt ultra .50 .20
204 A75 7fr black .60 .20
205 A75 10fr dp brown .75 .20
206 A76 20fr plum & blk 8.00 .65
Nos. 187-206 (20) 15.35 4.60

Same Inscribed "Belgisch Congo Congo Belge"

207 A72 10c olive grn .20 .20
208 A72 15c brown car .20 .20
209 A72 20c dp ultra .20 .20
210 A72 25c brown vio .20 .20
211 A72 30c blue .20 .20
212 A72 50c dp green .20 .20
213 A72 60c chestnut .20 .20
214 A73 75c dl lil & blk .20 .20
215 A73 1fr dk brn & blk .20 .20
216 A73 1.25fr rose red & blk .20 .20
217 A74 1.75fr dk gray brn .75 .35
218 A74 2fr ocher .75 .20
219 A74 2.50fr carmine .75 .20
220 A75 3.50fr dk ol grn .30 .20
221 A75 5fr orange .55 .20
222 A75 6fr brt ultra .55 .20
223 A75 7fr black .55 .20
224 A75 10fr dp brown .65 .20
225 A76 20fr plum & blk 7.00 .65
Nos. 207-225 (19) 13.85 4.40

Miniature sheets of Nos. 193, 194, 197, 200, 211, 214, 217 and 219 were printed in 1944 by the Belgian Government in London and given to the Belgian political review, Message, which distributed them to its subscribers, one a month. Value per sheet, about $12.50.

Remainders of these eight miniature sheets received marginal overprints in various colors in 1950, specifying a surtax of 100fr per sheet and paying tribute to the UPU. These sheets, together with four of Ruanda-Urundi, were sold by the Committee of Cultural Works (and not at post offices) in sets of 12 for 1,217.15 francs. Set value, about $325.

Nos. 187-227 imperforate had no franking value.

For surcharges see Nos. B34-B37.

Congo Woman — A77

Askari — A78

1943, Jan. 1

226 A77 50fr ultra & blk 6.50 .40
227 A78 100fr car & blk 7.50 .60

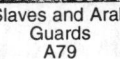

Slaves and Arab Guards A79

Auguste Lambermont A80

Design: 10fr, Leopold II.

Perf. 13x11½, 12½x12

1947 Engr. Unwmk.

228 A79 1.25fr black brown .25 .20
229 A80 3.50fr dark blue .40 .20
230 A80 10fr red orange .75 .20
Nos. 228-230 (3) 1.40 .60

50th anniv. of the abolition of slavery in Belgian Congo. See Nos. 261-262.

Baluba Carving of Former King — A82

Carved Figures and Masks of Baluba Tribe: 10c, 50c, 2fr, "Ndoha," figure of tribal king. 15c, 70c, 1.20fr, 2.50fr, "Tshimanyi," an idol. 20c, 75c, 1.60fr, 3.50fr, "Buangakokoma," statue of kneeling beggar. 25c, 1fr, 2.40fr, 5fr, "Mbuta," sacred double cup, carved with two faces, Man and Woman. 40c, 1.25fr, 6fr, 8fr, "Ngadimuashi," female mask. 1.50fr, 3fr, 10fr, 50fr, "Buadi-Muadi," mask with squared features. 6.50fr, 20fr, 100fr, "Mbowa," executioner's mask with buffalo horns.

1947-50 *Perf. 12½*

231 A82 10c dp org ('48) .20 .20
232 A82 15c ultra ('48) .20 .20
233 A82 20c brt bl ('48) .20 .20
234 A82 25c rose car ('48) .20 .20
235 A82 40c violet ('48) .20 .20
236 A82 50c olive brn .20 .20
237 A82 70c yel grn ('48) .20 .20
238 A82 75c magenta ('48) .20 .20
239 A82 1fr yel org & dk vio 1.50 .20
240 A82 1.20fr gray & brn ('50) .20 .20
241 A82 1.25fr lt bl grn & mag ('48) .30 .20
242 A82 1.50fr ol & mag ('50) 14.00 1.10
243 A82 1.60fr bl gray & brt bl ('50) .40 .20
244 A82 2fr org & mag ('48) .20 .20
245 A82 2.40fr bl grn & dk grn ('50) .30 .20
246 A82 2.50fr brn red & bl grn .30 .20
247 A82 3fr lt ultra & ind ('49) 4.25 .20
248 A82 3.50fr lt bl & blk ('48) 3.50 .20
249 A82 5fr bis & mag ('48) 1.25 .20
250 A82 6fr brn org & ind ('48) 1.40 .20
251 A82 6.50fr red org & red brn ('49) 1.90 .20
252 A82 8fr gray bl & dk grn ('50) 1.25 .20
253 A82 10fr pale vio & red brn ('48) 4.00 .20
254 A82 20fr red org & vio brn ('48) 1.90 .20
255 A82 50fr dp org & blk ('48) 3.75 .20
256 A82 100fr crim & blk brn ('48) 4.00 .30
Nos. 231-256 (26) 46.00 6.20

Railroad Train and Map — A83

1948, July 1 Unwmk. *Perf. 13½*

257 A83 2.50fr dp bl & grn 1.00 .20

50th anniv. of railway service in the Congo.

Globe and Ship A84

1949, Nov. 21 *Perf. 11½*

Granite Paper

258 A84 4fr violet blue .85 .20

75th anniv. of the UPU.

Allegorical Figure and Map — A85

1950, Aug. 12 *Perf. 12x12½*

259 A85 3fr blue & indigo 1.75 .20
260 A85 6.50fr car rose & blk brn 2.00 .25

Establishment of Katanga Province, 50th anniv.

Portrait Type of 1947

1.50fr, Cardinal Lavigerie. 3fr, Baron Dhanis.

Perf. 12½x12

1951, June 25 Unwmk.

261 A80 1.50fr purple 2.00 .25
262 A80 3fr black brown 2.00 .20

Littonia — A86

St. Francis Xavier — A86a

1952-53 Photo. *Perf. 11½*

Granite Paper

Flowers in Natural Colors

Size: 21x25½mm

263 A86 10c Dissotis .20 .20
264 A86 15c Protea .20 .20
265 A86 20c Vellozia .20 .20
266 A86 25c shown .20 .20
267 A86 40c Ipomoea .20 .20
268 A86 50c Angraecum .20 .20
269 A86 60c Euphorbia .20 .20
270 A86 75c Ochna .20 .20
271 A86 1fr Hibiscus .20 .20
272 A86 1.25fr Protea ('53) .65 .45
273 A86 1.50fr Schrizoglossum .20 .20
274 A86 2fr Ansellia .25 .20
275 A86 3fr Costus .25 .20
276 A86 4fr Nymphaea .30 .20
277 A86 5fr Thunbergia .45 .20
278 A86 6.50fr Thonningia .55 .20
279 A86 7fr Gerbera .55 .20
280 A86 8fr Gloriosa ('53) .90 .20
281 A86 10fr Silene ('53) 1.60 .20
282 A86 20fr Aristolochia 1.40 .20

Size: 22x32mm

283 A86 50fr Eulophia ('53) 7.00 .45
284 A86 100fr Crytosepalum ('53) 11.00 1.00
Nos. 263-284 (22) 26.90 5.70

Nos. 264, 269 and 270 with additional surcharges are varieties of Congo Democratic Republic Nos. 324, 327 and 328.

1953, Jan. 5 Engr. *Perf. 12½x13*

285 A86a 1.50fr ultra & gray blk .75 .30

400th death anniv. of St. Francis Xavier.

Canoe on Lake Kivu — A87

1953, Jan. 5 *Perf. 14*

286 A87 3fr car & blk 1.25 .20
287 A87 7fr dp bl & brn org 1.25 .25

Issued to publicize the Kivu Festival, 1953.

Royal Colonial Institute Jubilee Medal A88

Design: 6.50fr, Same with altered background and transposed inscriptions.

1954, Dec. 27 Photo. *Perf. 13½*

288 A88 4.50fr indigo & gray 1.10 .30
289 A88 6.50fr dk grn & brn .90 .20

25th anniv. of the founding of the Belgian Royal Colonial Institute.

King Baudouin and Tropical Scene A89

Designs: King and various views.

Inscribed "Congo Belge-Belgisch Congo"

Engr.; Portrait Photo.

1955, Feb. 15 Unwmk. *Perf. 11½*

Portrait in Black

290 A89 1.50fr rose car .70 .25
291 A89 3fr green .25 .20
292 A89 4.50fr ultra .30 .20
293 A89 6.50fr dp claret .55 .20

Inscribed "Belgisch Congo-Congo Belge"

294 A89 1.50fr rose car .30 .20
295 A89 3fr green .25 .20
296 A89 4.50fr ultra .30 .20
297 A89 6.50fr deep claret .55 .20
Nos. 290-297 (8) 3.20 1.65

Map of Africa and Emblem of Royal Touring Club — A90

1955, July 26 Engr. *Perf. 11½*

Inscription in French

298 A90 6.50fr vio blue 3.25 .25

Inscription in Flemish

299 A90 6.50fr vio blue 3.25 .25

5th International Congress of African Tourism, Elisabethville, July 26-Aug. 4. Nos. 298-299 printed in alternate rows.

Kings of Belgium A91

1958, July 1 Unwmk. *Perf. 12½*

300 A91 1fr rose vio .25 .20
301 A91 1.50fr ultra .25 .20
302 A91 3fr rose car .25 .20
303 A91 5fr green .70 .30
304 A91 6.50fr brn red .45 .20
305 A91 10fr dl vio .65 .20
Nos. 300-305 (6) 2.55 1.30

Belgium's annexation of Congo, 50th anniv.

Roan Antelope A92

Black Buffaloes A93

Animals: 20c, White rhinoceros. 40c, Giraffe. 50c, Thick-tailed bushbaby. 1fr, Gorilla. 2fr, Black-and-white colobus (monkey). 3fr, Elephants. 5fr, Okapis. 6.50fr, Impala. 8fr, Giant pangolin. 10fr, Eland and zebras.

1959, Oct. 15 Photo. *Perf. 11½*

Granite Paper

306	A92	10c bl & brn	.20	.20
307	A93	20c red org & slate	.20	.20
308	A92	40c brn & bl	.20	.20
309	A93	50c brt ultra, red & sep	.20	.20
310	A92	1fr brn, grn & blk	.20	.20
311	A93	1.50fr blk & org yel	.20	.20
312	A92	2fr crim, blk & brn	.20	.20
313	A93	3fr blk, gray & lil rose	.25	.20
314	A92	5fr brn, dk brn & brt grn	.40	.20
315	A93	6.50fr bl, brn & org yel	.45	.20
316	A92	8fr org brn, ol bis & lil	.50	.30
317	A93	10fr multi	.60	.20
		Nos. 306-317 (12)	3.60	2.50

Madonna and Child — A94

1959, Dec. 1 Unwmk. *Perf. 11½*

318	A94	50c golden brn, ocher & red brn	.20	.20
319	A94	1fr dk bl, pur & red brn	.20	.20
320	A94	2fr gray, brt bl & red brn	.20	.20
		Nos. 318-320 (3)	.60	.60

Map of Africa and Symbolic Honeycomb A95

1960, Feb. 19 Unwmk. *Perf. 11½*

Inscription in French

321	A95	3fr gray & red	.25	.20

Inscription in Flemish

322	A95	3fr gray & red	.25	.20

Commission for Technical Co-operation in Africa South of the Sahara (C. C. T. A.), 10th anniv.

SEMI-POSTAL STAMPS

Types of 1910-15 Issues Surcharged in Red **+ 10C**

1918, May 15 Unwmk. *Perf. 14, 15*

B1	A29	5c + 10c grn & bl	.20	*.20*
B2	A30	10c + 15c car & bl (l)	.20	*.20*
B3	A21	15c + 20c bl grn & bl	.20	*.20*
B4	A31	25c + 25c dp bl & pale bl	.20	*.25*
B5	A23	40c + 40c brn red & bl	.40	*.45*
B6	A24	50c + 50c brn lake & bl	.40	*.45*
B7	A25	1fr + 1fr ol bis & bl	2.00	*2.25*
B8	A27	5fr + 5fr ocher & bl	11.00	*17.50*
B9	A28	10fr + 10fr grn & bl	85.00	*150.00*
		Nos. B1-B9 (9)	99.60	*171.50*

The position of the cross and the added value varies on the different stamps.

Nos. B1-B9 exist imperforate.

SP1

Design: #B11 inscribed "Belgisch Congo."

1925, July 8 *Perf. 12½*

B10	SP1	25c + 25c carmine & blk	.20	*.25*
B11	SP1	25c + 25c carmine & blk	.20	*.25*
a.		Pair, Nos. B10-B11	.40	*.50*

Colonial campaigns in 1914-1918.

The surtax helped erect at Kinshasa a monument to those who died in World War I.

Nurse Weighing Child — SP3

First Aid Station SP5

20c+10c, Missionary & Child. 60c+30c, Congo hospital. 1fr+50c, Dispensary service. 1.75fr+75c, Convalescent area. 3.50fr+1.50fr, Instruction on bathing infant. 5fr+2.50fr, Operating room. 10fr+5fr, Students.

1930, Jan. 16 Engr. *Perf. 11½*

B12	SP3	10c + 5c ver	.55	.55
B13	SP3	20c + 10c dp brn	.70	.70
B14	SP5	35c + 15c dp grn	1.25	1.25
B15	SP5	60c + 30c dl vio	1.50	1.50
B16	SP3	1fr + 50c dk car	2.25	2.25
B17	SP5	1.75fr + 75c dp bl	4.25	4.50
B18	SP5	3.50fr + 1.50fr rose lake	8.50	8.50
B19	SP5	5fr + 2.50fr red brn	7.50	7.50
B20	SP5	10fr + 5fr gray blk	8.50	8.50
		Nos. B12-B20 (9)	35.00	35.25

The surtax was intended to aid welfare work among the natives, especially the children.

Nos. 161, 163 Surcharged "+50c" in Blue or Red

1936, May 15 *Perf. 12½x12*

B21	A63	1.50fr + 50c (Bl)	2.50	*3.00*
B22	A63	2.50fr + 50c (R)	2.00	2.00

Surtax was for the King Albert Memorial Fund.

Queen Astrid with Congolese Children — SP12

1936, Aug. 29 Photo. *Perf. 12½*

B23	SP12	1.25fr + 5c dark brown	.40	.35
B24	SP12	1.50fr + 10c dull rose	.40	.35
B25	SP12	2.50fr + 25c dark blue	.60	.60
		Nos. B23-B25 (3)	1.40	1.30

Issued in memory of Queen Astrid. The surtax was for the aid of the National League for Protection of Native Children.

National Park Type of 1937-38

Souvenir Sheet

1938, Oct. 3 *Perf. 11½*

Star in Yellow

B26		Sheet of 6	18.00	18.00
a.		A64 5c ultra & light brown	3.00	3.00
b.		A65 90c ultra & light brown	3.00	3.00
c.		A66 1.50fr ultra & light brown	3.00	3.00
d.		A67 2.40fr ultra & light brown	3.00	3.00
e.		A68 2.50fr ultra & light brown	3.00	3.00
f.		A69 4.50fr ultra & light brown	3.00	3.00

Intl. Tourist Cong. A surtax of 3.15fr was for the benefit of the Congo Tourist Service.

Marabou Storks and Vultures — SP14

Buffon's Kob — SP15

Designs: 1.50fr+1.50fr, Pygmy chimpanzees. 4.50fr+4.50fr, Dwarf crocodiles. 5fr+5fr, Lioness.

1939, June 6 Photo. *Perf. 14*

B27	SP14	1fr + 1fr dp claret	5.50	5.50
B28	SP15	1.25fr + 1.25fr car	5.50	5.50
B29	SP15	1.50fr + 1.50fr brt pur	7.50	7.50
B30	SP14	4.50fr + 4.50fr sl grn	5.50	5.50
B31	SP15	5fr + 5fr brown	6.00	6.00
		Nos. B27-B31 (5)	30.00	30.00

Surtax for the Leopoldville Zoological Gardens.

Sold in full sets by subscription.

Catalogue values for unused stamps in this section, from this point to the end of the section, are for Never Hinged items.

Lion of Belgium and Inscription "Belgium Shall Rise Again" — SP19

1942, Feb. 17 Engr. *Perf. 12½*

B32	SP19	10fr + 40fr brt grn	1.50	*1.75*
B33	SP19	10fr + 40fr vio bl	1.50	*1.75*

Nos. 193, 216, 198 and 220 Surcharged in Red

Au profit de la Croix Rouge + 50 Fr. Ten voordeele van het Roode Kruis
a

Ten voordeele van het Roode Kruis + 100 Fr. Au profit de la Croix Rouge
b

c
Au profit de la Croix Rouge + 100 Fr. Ten voordeele van het Roode Kruis

1945

B34	A72 (a)	50c + 50fr	2.00	*3.25*
B35	A73 (b)	1.25fr + 100fr	2.00	*3.25*
B36	A74 (c)	1.75fr + 100fr	2.00	*3.50*
B37	A75 (b)	3.50fr + 100fr	2.00	*3.50*
		Nos. B34-B37 (4)	8.00	*13.50*

The surtax was for the Red Cross.

Sold in full sets by subscription.

Mozart at Age 7 — SP20

Queen Elisabeth and Sonata by Mozart — SP21

Perf. 11½

1956, Oct. 10 Unwmk. Engr.

B38	SP20	4.50fr + 1.50fr brt lil	2.00	2.00
B39	SP21	6.50fr + 2.50fr ultra	3.00	3.00

200th anniv. of the birth of Wolfgang Amadeus Mozart.

The surtax was for the Pro-Mozart Committee.

Nurse and Children — SP22

Designs: 4.50fr+50c, Patient receiving injection. 6.50fr+40c, Patient being bandaged.

1957, Dec. 10 Photo. *Perf. 13x10½*

Cross in Carmine

B40	SP22	3fr + 50c dk bl	.90	.85
B41	SP22	4.50fr + 50c dk grn	.80	.75
B42	SP22	6.50fr + 50c red brn	1.00	.95
		Nos. B40-B42 (3)	2.70	2.55

The surtax was for the Red Cross.

High Jump SP23

1960, May 2 Unwmk. *Perf. 13½*

B43	SP23	50c + 25c shown	.20	*.25*
B44	SP23	1.50fr + 50c Hurdles	.20	*.25*
B45	SP23	2fr + 1fr Soccer	.20	*.30*
B46	SP23	3fr + 1.25fr Javelin	.75	*.90*
B47	SP23	6.50fr + 3.50fr Discus	1.00	*1.25*
		Nos. B43-B47 (5)	2.35	*2.95*

17th Olympic Games, Rome, Aug. 25-Sept. 11. The surtax was for the youth of Congo.

AIR POST STAMPS

Wharf on Congo River AP1

Congo "Country Store" AP2

View of Congo River AP3

Stronghold in the Interior — AP4

Unwmk.

1920, July 1 Engr. *Perf. 12*

C1	AP1	50c orange & blk	.20	.20
C2	AP2	1fr dull vio & blk	.20	.20
C3	AP3	2fr blue & blk	.50	.20
C4	AP4	5fr green & blk	.90	.40
		Nos. C1-C4 (4)	1.80	1.00

Kraal AP5

Porters on Safari
AP6

1930, Apr. 2

C5	AP5	15fr dk brn & blk	1.90	.75
C6	AP6	30fr brn vio & blk	2.25	.75

Fokker F VII over Congo — AP7

1934, Jan. 22 ***Perf. 13½x14***

C7	AP7	50c gray black	.20	.20
C8	AP7	1fr dk carmine	.20	.20
a.		Booklet pane of 8	5.25	
C9	AP7	1.50fr green	.20	.20
C10	AP7	3fr brown	.20	.20
C11	AP7	4.50fr brt ultra	.25	.20
a.		Booklet pane of 8	10.00	
C12	AP7	5fr red brown	.20	.20
C13	AP7	15fr brown vio	.40	.25
C14	AP7	30fr red orange	.70	.60
C15	AP7	50fr violet	2.00	.95
		Nos. C7-C15 (9)	4.35	3.00

The 1fr, 3fr, 4.50fr, 5fr, 15fr exist imperf.

No. C10 Surcharged in Blue with New Value and Bars

1936, Mar. 25

C16	AP7	3.50fr on 3fr brown	.20	.20

Catalogue values for unused stamps in this section, from this point to the end of the section, are for Never Hinged items.

No. C9 Surcharged in Black

50 c.

≡ ≡

1942, Apr. 27

C17	AP7	50c on 1.50fr green	.35	.20
a.		Inverted surcharge	6.50	6.50

POSTAGE DUE STAMPS

In 1908-23 regular postage stamps handstamped "TAXES" or "TAXE," usually boxed, were used in lieu of postage due stamps.

D1

1923-29(?) Typo. Unwmk. *Perf. 14*

J1	D1	5c black brown	.20	.20
J2	D1	10c rose red	.20	.20
J3	D1	15c violet	.20	.20
J4	D1	30c green	.25	.20
J5	D1	50c ultramarine	.30	.30
J6	D1	50c blue ('29)	.30	.30
J7	D1	1fr gray	.45	.25
		Nos. J1-J7 (7)	1.90	1.65

Catalogue values for unused stamps in this section, from this point to the end of the section, are for Never Hinged items.

D2

D3

1943 ***Perf. 14x14½***

J8	D2	10c olive green	.20	.20
J9	D2	20c dark ultra	.20	.20
J10	D2	50c green	.20	.20
J11	D2	1fr dark brown	.20	.20
J12	D2	2fr yellow orange	.20	.20
		Nos. J8-J12 (5)	1.00	1.00

1943 ***Perf. 12½***

J8a	D2	10c olive green	.30	.30
J9a	D2	20c dark ultramarine	.30	.30
J10a	D2	50c green	.30	.30
J11a	D2	1fr dark brown	.45	.45
J12a	D2	2fr yellow orange	.45	.45
		Nos. J8a-J12a (5)	1.80	1.80

1957 Engr. ***Perf. 11½***

J13	D3	10c olive brown	.20	.20
J14	D3	20c claret	.20	.20
J15	D3	50c green	.20	.20
J16	D3	1fr light blue	.30	.25
J17	D3	2fr vermilion	.40	.25
J18	D3	4fr purple	.60	.35
J19	D3	6fr violet blue	.75	.45
		Nos. J13-J19 (7)	2.65	1.90

PARCEL POST STAMPS

PP1

PP2

PP3

Handstamped Surcharges on Nos. 5, 11-12

1887-93 Unwmk. ***Perf. 15***

Blue-Black Surcharge

Q1	PP1	3.50fr on 5fr lilac	950.00	725.00

Black Surcharge

Q3	PP2	3.50fr on 5fr vio	850.00	500.00
Q4	PP3	3.50fr on 5fr vio ('88)	575.00	325.00
a.		Blue surcharge	625.00	375.00
Q6	PP3	3.50fr on 5fr gray ('93)	95.00	70.00

Nos. Q1, Q3-Q4, Q4a and Q6 are known with inverted surcharge, No. Q1 with double surcharge and No. Q6 in pair with unsurcharged stamp. These varieties sell for somewhat more than the normal surcharges.

Genuine stamps with counterfeit surcharges, counterfeit stamps with counterfeit surcharges, and both with counterfeit cancels exist.

BELGIUM

'bel-jəm

LOCATION — Western Europe, bordering the North Sea
GOVT. — Constitutional Monarchy
AREA — 11,778 sq. mi.
POP. — 10,192,264 (1998 est.)
CAPITAL — Brussels

100 Centimes = 1 Franc

Catalogue values for unused stamps in this country are for Never Hinged items, beginning with Scott 322 in the regular postage section, Scott B370 in the semi-postal section, Scott C8 in the airpost section, Scott CB1 in the airpost semi-postal section, Scott J40 in the postage due section, Scott M1 in the military stamp section, Scott O36 in the officials section, and Scott Q267 in the parcel post section.

Watermark

Wmk. 96 (No Frame)

King Leopold I
A1 A2

Wmk. Two "L's" Framed (96)

1849 Engr. ***Imperf.***

1	A1	10c brown	*2,250.*	75.00
a.		10c red brown	*3,500.*	475.00
b.		10c bister brown	*2,500.*	125.00
2	A1	20c blue	*2,750.*	57.50
a.		20c milky blue	*3,250.*	160.00
b.		20c greenish blue	*3,500.*	300.00

The reprints are on thick and thin wove and thick laid paper unwatermarked.

A pale blue shade exists that is often confused with the milky blue.

A souvenir sheet containing reproductions of the 10c, 20c and 40c of 1849-51 with black burelage on back was issued Oct. 17, 1949, for the cent. of the 1st Belgian stamps. It was sold at BEPITEC 1949, an intl. stamp exhib. at Brussels, and was not valid.

1849-50

3	A2	10c brown ('50)	*2,000.*	90.00
4	A2	20c blue ('50)	*1,750.*	52.50
5	A2	40c carmine rose	*1,650.*	425.00

Nos. 3-5 were printed on both thick and thin paper and sell for about the same prices.

Wmk. Two "L's" Without Frame (96)

1851-54

6	A2	10c brown	525.00	8.50
a.		Ribbed paper ('54)	900.00	50.00
7	A2	20c blue	550.00	8.00
a.		Ribbed paper ('54)	900.00	47.50
8	A2	40c car rose	*2,750.*	95.00
a.		Ribbed paper ('54)	*3,500.*	260.00

Nos. 6-8 were printed on both thin and thick paper and sell for about the same prices.

Nos. 6a, 7a, 8a must have regular and parallel ribs covering the whole stamp.

1858-61 **Unwmk.**

9	A2	1c green ('61)	*225.00*	125.00
10	A2	10c brown	375.00	7.50
11	A2	20c blue	400.00	7.50
12	A2	40c vermilion	*2,400.*	70.00

Nos. 9 and 13 were valid for postage on newspapers and printed matter only.

Nos. 10-12 were printed in two sizes: 21mm high (with a 16½mm high oval) and 22mm high (with a 17¼mm high oval). The 22mm high stamps were issued in 1861. The 21mm high stamps sell for more.

Reprints of Nos. 9 to 12 are on thin wove paper. The colors are brighter than those of the originals. They were made from the dies and show lines outside the stamps.

1863-65 ***Perf. 14½***

13	A2	1c green ('65)	35.00	25.00
14	A2	10c brown ('65)	47.50	3.25
15	A2	20c blue ('65)	50.00	3.25
16	A2	40c carmine rose ('65)	325.00	25.00
		Nos. 13-16 (4)	457.50	56.50

Values for Nos. 13-16 are for copies with perfs cutting into design.

Nos. 13-16 also come perf 12½ and 12½x13, which were issued in 1863. Values differ. See the Scott Classic Specialized Catalogue.

King Leopold I
A3 A3a

A4

A4a

A5

London Print

1865 Typo. ***Perf. 14***

17	A5	1fr pale violet	1,300.	110.00

Brussels Print
Thick or Thin Paper

1865-67 ***Perf. 15***

18	A3	10c slate ('67)	125.00	1.50
b.		Pair, imperf. between		—
19	A3a	20c blue ('67)	175.00	1.50
20	A4	30c brown ('67)	425.00	11.00
b.		Pair, imperf. between	*1,100.*	
21	A4a	40c rose ('67)	450.00	20.00
22	A5	1fr violet	1,200.	90.00

Nos. 18-22 also come perf. 14½x14, issued in 1865-66. Values differ. See the Scott Classic Specialized Catalogue. Nos. 18b and 20b are from the earlier printings.

The reprints are on thin paper, imperforate and ungummed.

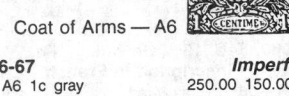

Coat of Arms — A6

1866-67 ***Imperf.***

23	A6	1c gray	250.00	150.00

Perf. 15, 14½x14

24	A6	1c gray	45.00	16.00
25	A6	2c blue ('67)	140.00	90.00
26	A6	5c brown	150.00	90.00
		Nos. 23-26 (4)	585.00	346.00

Nos. 23-26 were valid for postage on newspapers and printed matter only.

Values are for perf. 15 stamps. Values for 14½x14 differ. See the Scott Classic Specialized Catalogue.

Counterfeits exist.

Reprints of Nos. 24-26 are on thin paper, imperforate and with or without gum.

Imperf. varieties of 1869-1912 (between Nos. 28-105) are without gum.

A7 A8 A9

A10 A11 A12

King Leopold II
A13 A14 A15

1869-70 ***Perf. 15***

28	A7	1c green	6.50	.30
29	A7	2c ultra ('70)	20.00	1.50
30	A7	5c buff ('70)	45.00	.75
31	A7	8c lilac ('70)	80.00	50.00
32	A8	10c green	20.00	.40
33	A9	20c lt ultra ('70)	140.00	.90
34	A10	30c buff ('70)	75.00	4.00
35	A11	40c brt rose ('70)	110.00	6.00

36	A12	1fr dull lilac ('70)	350.00	17.00
a.		1fr rose lilac	350.00	20.00
		Nos. 28-36 (9)	846.50	80.85

The frames and inscriptions of Nos. 30, 31 and 42 differ slightly from the illustration.

Minor "broken letter" varieties exist on several values.

Nos. 28-30, 32-33, 35-38 also were printed in aniline colors. These are not valued separately.

See Nos. 40-43, 49-51, 55.

1875-78

37	A13	25c olive bister	135.00	1.25
a.		25c ocher	135.00	1.50
38	A14	50c gray	200.00	8.50
		Roller cancel		12.50
a.		50c gray black	325.00	55.00
b.		50c deep black	1,750.	225.00
39	A15	5fr dp red brown	1,500.	1,250.
		Roller cancel		575.00
a.		5fr pale brown ('78)	3,750.	1,250.
		Roller cancel		575.00

Dangerous counterfeits of No. 39 exist.

Printed in Aniline Colors

1881 **Perf. 14**

40	A7	1c gray green	20.00	.60
41	A7	2c lt ultra	17.50	2.50
42	A7	5c orange buff	57.50	1.10
a.		5c red orange	57.50	1.10
43	A8	10c gray green	30.00	.80
44	A13	25c olive bister	75.00	2.50
		Nos. 40-44 (5)	200.00	7.50

See note following No. 36.

A16

A17

A18

A19

1883

45	A16	10c carmine	27.50	2.50
46	A17	20c gray	150.00	7.75
47	A18	25c blue	260.00	35.00
		Roller cancel		15.00
48	A19	50c violet	260.00	35.00
		Roller cancel		15.00
		Nos. 45-48 (4)	697.50	80.25

A20

A21

A22

1884-85 **Perf. 14**

49	A7	1c olive green	13.50	.85
50	A7	1c gray	4.00	.30
51	A7	5c green	32.50	.40
52	A20	10c rose, *bluish*	10.00	.40
a.		Grayish paper	11.00	.50
c.		Yellowish paper	200.00	35.00
53	A21	25c blue, *pink* ('85)	11.00	.75
54	A22	1fr brown, *grnsh*	600.00	17.50

The frame and inscription of No. 51 differ slightly from the illustration.

See note after No. 36.

A23

A24

A25

A26

1886-91

55	A7	2c purple brn ('88)	12.50	1.50
56	A23	20c olive, *grnsh*	140.00	1.25
57	A24	35c vio brn, *brnsh* ('91)	18.00	3.00
58	A25	50c bister, *yelsh*	9.50	2.25
59	A26	2fr violet, *pale lil*	100.00	45.00
		Roller cancel		6.00
		Nos. 55-59 (5)	280.00	53.00

Values quoted for Nos. 60-107 are for stamps with label attached. Stamps without label sell for much less.

Coat of Arms
A27

King Leopold
A28

1893-1900

60	A27	1c gray	1.10	.20
61	A27	2c yellow	1.25	1.10
a.		Wmkd. coat of arms in sheet ('95)	—	—
62	A27	2c violet brn ('94)	1.60	.30
63	A27	2c red brown ('98)	3.25	.50
64	A27	5c yellow grn	7.75	.30
65	A28	10c orange brn	5.00	.30
66	A28	10c brt rose ('00)	3.50	.40
67	A28	20c olive green	22.50	.60
68	A28	25c ultra	20.00	.50
a.		No ball to "5" in upper left corner	32.50	12.50
69	A28	35c violet brn	25.00	1.50
a.		35c red brown	42.50	2.40
70	A28	50c bister	62.50	20.00
71	A28	50c gray ('97)	57.50	2.50
72	A28	1fr car, *lt grn*	75.00	20.00
73	A28	1fr orange ('00)	90.00	5.00
74	A28	2fr lilac, *rose*	90.00	70.00
75	A28	2fr lilac ('00)	150.00	13.50
		Nos. 60-75 (16)	615.95	136.70

Antwerp Exhibition Issue

Arms of Antwerp — A29

1894

76	A29	5c green, *rose*	4.75	3.25
77	A29	10c carmine, *bluish*	3.75	2.50
78	A29	25c blue, *rose*	1.00	1.00
		Nos. 76-78 (3)	9.50	6.75

Brussels Exhibition Issue

St. Michael and Satan
A30 A31

1896-97 **Perf. 14x14½**

79	A30	5c deep violet	1.00	.60
80	A31	10c orange brown	8.50	3.50
81	A31	10c lilac brown	.50	.35
		Nos. 79-81 (3)	10.00	4.45

A32

A33

A34

A35

A36

A37

A38

A39

Two types of 1c:

I - Periods after "Dimanche" and "Zondag" in label.

II - No period after "Dimanche." Period often missing after "Zondag."

1905-11 **Perf. 14**

82	A32	1c gray (I) ('07)	1.50	.20
a.		Type II ('08)	2.00	.60
83	A32	2c red brown ('07)	14.50	5.75
84	A32	5c green ('07)	11.50	.60
85	A33	10c dull rose	1.75	.60
86	A34	20c olive grn	26.00	1.00
87	A35	25c ultra	12.00	.85
a.		25c deep blue '11)	13.50	2.00
88	A36	35c red brn	25.00	1.75
89	A37	50c bluish gray	95.00	4.00
90	A38	1fr yellow orange	110.00	8.00
91	A39	2fr violet	75.00	22.50
		Bar cancellation		5.00
		Nos. 82-91 (10)	372.25	45.25

A40

A41

Lion of Belgium — A42

A43

King Albert I — A44

1912

92	A40	1c orange	.20	.20
93	A41	2c orange brn	.25	.45
94	A42	5c green	.20	.20
95	A43	10c red	.75	.40
96	A43	20c olive grn	16.00	4.00
97	A43	35c bister brn	1.00	.70
98	A43	40c green	16.00	14.50
99	A43	50c gray	1.00	.80
100	A43	1fr orange	4.00	3.00
101	A43	2fr violet	17.50	17.50
102	A44	5fr plum	80.00	25.00
		Nos. 92-102 (11)	136.90	66.75

Counterfeits exist of Nos. 97-102. Those of No. 102 are common.

For overprints see Nos. Q49-Q50, Q52, Q55-Q55A, Q57-Q60.

A45

1912-13

Larger Head

103	A45	10c red	.40	.20
a.		Without engraver's name	.20	.25
104	A45	20c olive grn ('13)	.40	.40
a.		Without engraver's name	2.00	2.00
105	A45	25c ultra	.25	.40
a.		With engraver's name	4.25	3.00
107	A45	40c green ('13)	.50	.60
		Nos. 103-107 (4)	1.55	1.60

For overprints see #Q51, Q53-Q54, Q56.

Albert I
A46

Cloth Hall of Ypres
A47

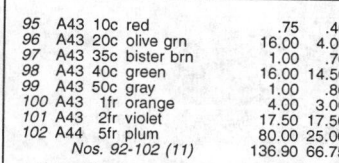

Bridge of Dinant — A48

Library of Louvain — A49

Scheldt River at Antwerp A50

Anti-slavery Campaign in the Congo — A51

King Albert I at Furnes A52

Kings of Belgium Leopold I, Albert I, Leopold II A53

1915-20 Typo. *Perf. 14, 14½*

108 A46 1c orange .20 .20
109 A46 2c chocolate .20 .20
110 A46 3c gray blk ('20) .30 .20
111 A46 5c green 1.00 .20
112 A46 10c carmine .90 .20
113 A46 15c purple 1.50 .20
114 A46 20c red violet 3.00 .20
115 A46 25c blue .50 .40

Engr.

116 A47 35c brown org & blk .50 .30
117 A48 40c green & black 1.00 .30
a. Vert. pair, imperf. btwn.
118 A49 50c car rose & blk 4.50 .30
119 A50 1fr violet 32.50 1.00
120 A51 2fr slate 21.00 2.00
121 A52 5fr dp blue 275.00 125.00
Telegraph or railroad cancel 55.00
122 A53 10fr brown 20.00 20.00
Nos. 108-122 (15) 362.10 150.70

Two types each of the 1c, 10c and 20c; three of the 2c and 15c; four of the 5c, differing in the top left corner.

See No. 138. For surcharges see Nos. B34-B47.

Perron of Liege (Fountain) A54

King Albert in Trench Helmet A55

1919 *Perf. 11½*

123 A54 25c deep blue 2.40 .35
a. Sheet of 10 *5,500. 5,750.*

Perf. 11, 11½, 11½x11, 11x11½

1919

Size: 18½x22mm

124 A55 1c lilac brn .20 .20
125 A55 2c olive .20 .20

Size: 22x26

126 A55 5c green .20 .20
127 A55 10c carmine, 22x26¾mm .25 .25
a. Size: 22½x26mm 1.00 .60
128 A55 15c gray vio, 22x26¾mm .30 .30
a. Size: 22½x26mm 2.40 .60
129 A55 20c olive blk 1.10 1.10
130 A55 25c deep blue 1.60 1.60
131 A55 35c bister brn 3.00 3.00
132 A55 40c red 5.00 5.00
133 A55 50c red brn 9.50 10.00
134 A55 1fr lt orange 40.00 40.00
135 A55 2fr violet 375.00 375.00

Size: 28x33½mm

136 A55 5fr car lake 100.00 100.00
137 A55 10fr claret 110.00 110.00
Nos. 124-137 (14) 646.35 646.85
Set, never hinged 1,143.

Type of 1915 Inscribed: "FRANK" instead of "FRANKEN"

1919, Dec. *Perf. 14, 15*

138 A52 5fr deep blue 1.75 1.25

Town Hall at Termonde — A56

1920 *Perf. 11½*

139 A56 65c claret & black, 27x22mm .75 .20
Never hinged 1.50
a. Center inverted *57,500.*
b. Size: 26¾x22½mm 5.75 2.40

For surcharge see No. 143.

Nos. B48-B50 Surcharged in Red or Black

20c X   20c X

1921 *Perf. 12*

140 SP6 20c on 5c + 5c (R) .60 .25
a. Inverted surcharge 525.00 525.00
Never hinged 1,000.
141 SP7 20c on 10c + 5c .40 .25
142 SP8 20c on 15c + 15c (R) .60 .25
a. Inverted surcharge 525.00 525.00
Never hinged 1,000.

No. 139 Surcharged in Red

55c   55c

143 A57 55c on 65c claret & blk 1.50 .35
a. Pair, one without surcharge 2.25 .85
Nos. 140-143 (4) 3.10 1.10
Set, never hinged 8.40

A58

A59

1922-27 Typo. *Perf. 14*

144 A58 1c orange .20 .20
145 A58 2c olive ('26) .20 .20
146 A58 3c fawn .20 .20
147 A58 5c gray .20 .20
148 A58 10c blue grn .20 .20
149 A58 15c plum ('23) .20 .20
150 A58 20c black brn .20 .20
151 A58 25c magenta .20 .20
a. 25c dull violet ('23) .50 .20
152 A58 30c vermilion .50 .20
153 A58 30c rose ('25) .35 .20
154 A58 35c red brown .35 .30
155 A58 35c blue grn ('27) .80 .35
156 A58 40c rose .50 .20
157 A58 50c bister ('25) .50 .20
158 A58 60c olive brn ('27) 3.00 .20
159 A58 1.25fr dp blue ('26) 1.10 1.10
160 A58 1.50fr brt blue ('26) 1.60 .40
161 A58 1.75fr ultra ('27) 1.25 .20
a. Tete beche pair 5.00 5.00
c. Bklt. pane of 4 + 2 labels 40.00
Nos. 144-161 (18) 11.55 4.95
Set, never hinged 27.00

See Nos. 185-190. For overprints and surcharges see Nos. 191-195, 197, B56, O1-O6.

Perf. 11, 11x11½, 11½, 11½x11, 11½x12, 11½x12½, 12½

1921-25 Engr.

162 A59 50c dull blue .30 .20
163 A59 75c scarlet ('22) .25 .25
164 A59 75c ultra ('24) .45 .20
165 A59 1fr black brn ('22) .80 .20
166 A59 1fr dk blue ('25) .60 .20
167 A59 2fr dk green ('22) .90 .25
168 A59 5fr brown vio ('23) 13.50 *15.00*
169 A59 10fr magenta ('22) 9.00 6.50
Nos. 162-169 (8) 25.80 *22.80*
Set, never hinged 50.00

No. 162 measures 18x20¾mm and was printed in sheets of 100.

Philatelic Exhibition Issues

1921, May 26 *Perf. 11½*

170 A59 50c dark blue 3.50 3.50
Never hinged 4.75
a. Sheet of 25 200.00 175.00
Never hinged 225.00

No. 170 measures 17½x21¼mm, was printed in sheets of 25 and sold at the Philatelic Exhibition at Brussels.

The sheet normally has pin holes and a cancellation-like marking in the margin. These are considered unused and the condition valued here.

Souvenir Sheet

1924, May 24 *Perf. 11½*

171 Sheet of 4 140.00 140.00
Never hinged 250.00
a. A59 5fr red brown 10.00 10.00
Never hinged 12.00

Sold only at the Intl. Phil. Exhib., Brussels. Sheet size: 130x145mm.

The sheet normally has pin holes and a cancellation-like marking in the margin. These are considered unused and the condition valued here.

Kings Leopold I and Albert I — A60

1925, June 1 *Perf. 14*

172 A60 10c dp green 7.25 *7.25*
173 A60 15c dull vio 3.75 *4.50*
174 A60 20c red brown 3.75 *4.50*
175 A60 25c grnsh black 3.75 *4.50*
176 A60 30c vermilion 3.75 *4.50*
177 A60 35c lt blue 3.75 *4.50*
178 A60 40c brnsh blk 3.75 *4.50*
179 A60 50c yellow brn 3.75 *4.50*
180 A60 75c dk blue 3.75 *4.50*
181 A60 1fr dk violet 6.50 6.50
182 A60 2fr ultra 4.00 4.00
183 A60 5fr blue blk 3.75 *4.50*
184 A60 10fr dp rose 6.50 *8.00*
Nos. 172-184 (13) 58.00 *66.25*
Set, never hinged 125.00

75th anniv. of Belgian postage stamps.

Nos. 172-184 were sold only in sets and only by The Administration of Posts, not at post offices.

A61

1926-27 Typo.

185 A61 75c dk violet .75 .70
186 A61 1fr pale yellow .60 .35
187 A61 1fr rose red ('27) 1.00 .20
a. Tete beche pair 7.50 4.50
c. Bklt. pane 4 + 2 labels 25.00
188 A61 2fr Prus blue 2.50 .45
189 A61 5fr emerald ('27) 27.50 1.60
190 A61 10fr dk brown ('27) 60.00 7.75
Nos. 185-190 (6) 92.35 11.05
Set, never hinged 250.00

For overprints and surcharge see Nos. 196, Q174-Q175.

Stamps of 1921-27 Surcharged in Carmine, Red or Blue

1F75

1927

191 A58 3c on 2c olive (C) .25 .20
192 A58 10c on 15c plum (R) .25 .20
193 A58 35c on 40c rose (Bl) .40 .20
194 A58 1.75fr on 1.50fr brt bl (C) 2.10 .80
Nos. 191-194 (4) 3.00 1.40
Set, never hinged 5.00

Nos. 153, 185 and 159 Surcharged in Black

BRUXELLES
1929
BRUSSEL
5c

1929, Jan. 1

195 A58 5c on 30c rose .20 .20
196 A61 5c on 75c dk violet .20 .20
197 A58 5c on 1.25fr dp blue .20 .20
Nos. 195-197 (3) .60 .60
Set, never hinged .75

The surcharge on Nos. 195-197 is a precancelation which alters the value of the stamp to which it is applied.

Values for precanceled stamps in unused column are for those which have not been through the post and have original gum. Values in second column are for postally used, gumless stamps.

A63

A64

1929-32 Typo. *Perf. 14*

198 A63 1c orange .20 .20
199 A63 2c emerald ('31) .45 .45
200 A63 3c red brown .20 .20
201 A63 5c slate .20 .20
c. Bklt. pane of 4 + 2 labels 8.25
202 A63 10c olive grn .20 .20
c. Bklt. pane of 4 + 2 labels 4.50
203 A63 20c brt violet 1.00 .25
204 A63 25c rose red .45 .20
c. Bklt. pane of 4 + 2 labels 8.25
205 A63 35c green .60 .20
c. Bklt. pane of 4 + 2 labels 9.75
206 A63 40c red vio ('30) .30 .20
c. Bklt. pane of 4 + 2 labels 9.75
207 A63 50c dp blue .45 .20
c. Bklt. pane of 4 + 2 labels 8.25
208 A63 60c rose ('30) 1.90 .20
c. Bklt. pane of 4 + 2 labels 30.00
209 A63 70c org brn ('30) 1.10 .20
c. Bklt. pane of 4 + 2 labels 22.50
210 A63 75c dk blue ('30) 2.00 .20
211 A63 75c dp brown ('32) 6.00 .20
b. Bklt. pane of 4 + 2 labels 100.00
Nos. 198-211 (14) 15.05 3.10
Set, never hinged 53.00

For overprints and surcharges see Nos. 225-226, 240-241, 254-256, 309, O7-O15.

Tete Beche Pairs

201a	A63	5c	.60	.60
202a	A63	10c	.30	.30
204a	A63	25c	1.75	1.75
205a	A63	35c	2.75	2.75
206a	A63	40c	2.75	2.75
207a	A63	50c	2.25	2.25
208a	A63	60c	8.00	7.50
209a	A63	70c	6.00	5.00
210a	A63	75c	9.00	8.50
211a	A63	75c	27.50	25.00
Nos. 201a-211a (10)			60.90	56.40
Set, never hinged			116.00	

Tete-beche gutter pairs also exist.

Perf. 14½, 14x14½

1929, Jan. 25 Engr.

212 A64 10fr dk brown 15.00 4.50
213 A64 20fr dk green 85.00 20.00
214 A64 50fr red violet 13.50 13.50
a. Perf. 14½ 37.50 40.00

215 A64 100fr brownish lake 13.50 13.50
a. Perf. 14½ 37.50 40.00
Nos. 212-215 (4) 127.00 51.50
Set, never hinged 275.00

Peter Paul Rubens A65

Zenobe Gramme A66

1930, Apr. 26 Photo. ***Perf. 12½x12***
216 A65 35c blue green .40 .20
217 A66 35c blue green .40 .20
Set, never hinged 2.10

No. 216 issued for the Antwerp Exhibition, No. 217 the Liege Exhibition.

Leopold I, by Jacques de Winne A67

Leopold II, by Joseph Lempoels A68

Design: 1.75fr, Albert I.

1930, July 1 Engr. ***Perf. 11½***
218 A67 60c brown violet .20 .20
219 A68 1fr carmine 1.10 1.10
220 A68 1.75fr dk blue 2.75 1.25
Nos. 218-220 (3) 4.05 2.55
Set, never hinged 10.00

Centenary of Belgian independence.
For overprints see Nos. 222-224.

Antwerp Exhibition Issue
Souvenir Sheet

Arms of Antwerp A70

1930, Aug. 9 ***Perf. 11½***
221 A70 4fr Sheet of 1 87.50 87.50
Never hinged 125.00

Size: 142x141mm. Inscription in lower margin "ATELIER DU TIMBRE-1930-ZEGELFABRIEK." Each purchaser of a ticket to the Antwerp Phil. Exhib., Aug. 9-15, was allowed to purchase one stamp. The ticket cost 6 francs.

The sheet normally has pin holes and a cancellation-like marking in the margin. These are considered unused and the condition valued here.

Nos. 218-220 Overprinted in Blue or Red

B.I.T.
OCT. 1930

1930, Oct.
222 A67 60c brown vio (Bl) 2.00 2.00
223 A68 1fr carmine (Bl) 8.25 7.75
224 A68 1.75fr dk blue (R) 14.50 14.50
Nos. 222-224 (3) 24.75 24.25
Set, never hinged 54.00

50th meeting of the administrative council of the Intl. Labor Bureau at Brussels.

The names of the painters and the initials of the engraver have been added at the foot of these stamps.

Stamps of 1929-30 Surcharged in Blue or Black:

BELGIQUE
1931
BELGIË
10c

≡2c≡

1931, Feb. 20 ***Perf. 14***
225 A63 2c on 3c red brown (Bl) .20 .20
226 A63 10c on 60c rose (Bk) .50 .20
Set, never hinged 3.75

The surcharge on No. 226 is a precancelation which alters the denomination. See note after No. 197.

King Albert
A71 A71a

1931, June 15 **Photo.**
227 A71 1fr brown carmine .50 .20
Never hinged 1.00

1932, June 1
228 A71a 75c bister brown 1.25 .20
Never hinged 5.00
a. Tete beche pair 6.75 6.75
Never hinged 17.50
c. Bklt. pane 4 + 2 labels 27.50

See No. 257. For overprint see No. O18.

A72

1931-32 **Engr.**
229 A72 1.25fr gray black .75 .50
230 A72 1.50fr brown vio 1.25 .50
231 A72 1.75fr dp blue .80 .15
232 A72 2fr red brown 1.10 .20
233 A72 2.45fr dp violet 1.90 .40
234 A72 2.50fr black brn ('32) 10.00 .50
235 A72 5fr dp green 18.00 1.10
236 A72 10fr claret 42.50 12.50
Nos. 229-236 (8) 76.30 15.85
Set, never hinged 250.00

Nos. 206 and 209 Surcharged as No. 226, but dated "1932"

1932, Jan. 1
240 A63 10c on 40c red vio 2.50 .30
241 A63 10c on 70c org brn 2.00 .20
Set, never hinged 13.50

See note after No. 197.

Gleaner A73

Mercury A74

1932, June 1 Typo. ***Perf. 13½x14***
245 A73 2c pale green .35 .35
246 A74 5c dp orange .20 .20
247 A73 10c olive grn .25 .20
a. Tete beche pair 4.00 4.00
c. Bklt. pane 4 + 2 labels 15.00
248 A74 20c brt violet 1.00 .20
249 A73 25c deep red .60 .20
a. Tete beche pair 3.50 3.50
c. Bklt. pane 4 + 2 labels 15.00
250 A74 35c dp green 2.40 .20
Nos. 245-250 (6) 4.80 1.35
Set, never hinged 15.30

For overprints see Nos. O16-O17.

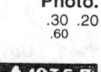

Auguste Piccard's Balloon — A75

1932, Nov. 26 Engr. ***Perf. 11½***
251 A75 75c red brown 3.50 .30
252 A75 1.75fr dk blue 13.50 2.10
253 A75 2.50fr dk violet 17.00 11.50
Nos. 251-253 (3) 34.00 13.90
Set, never hinged 94.50

Issued in commemoration of Prof. Auguste Piccard's two ascents to the stratosphere.

Nos. 206 and 209 Surcharged as No. 226, but dated "1933"

1933, Nov. ***Perf. 14***
254 A63 10c on 40c red vio 14.00 4.00
255 A63 10c on 70c org brn 12.50 1.50
Set, never hinged 65.00

No. 206 Surcharged as No. 226, but dated "1934"

1934, Feb.
256 A63 10c on 40c red vio 12.50 1.50
Never hinged 35.00

For Nos. 254 to 256 see note after No. 197.

Regummed copies of Nos. 254-256 abound.

King Albert Memorial Issue
Type of 1932 with Black Margins

1934, Mar. 10 **Photo.**
257 A71a 75c black .30 .20
Never hinged .60

Congo Pavilion — A76

Designs: 1fr, Brussels pavilion. 1.50fr, "Old Brussels." 1.75fr, Belgian pavilion.

1934, July 1 ***Perf. 14x13½***
258 A76 35c green .70 .30
259 A76 1fr dk carmine 1.25 .40
260 A76 1.50fr brown 5.00 .80
261 A76 1.75fr blue 5.00 .30
Nos. 258-261 (4) 11.95 1.80
Set, never hinged 43.75

Brussels Intl. Exhib. of 1935.

King Leopold III
A80 A81

1934-35 ***Perf. 13½x14***
262 A80 70c olive blk ('35) .35 .20
a. Tete beche pair 1.50 1.00
c. Bklt. pane 4 + 2 labels 6.25
263 A80 75c brown .65 .25

Perf. 14x13½
264 A81 1fr rose car ('35) 3.00 .35
Nos. 262-264 (3) 4.00 .80
Set, never hinged 10.25

For overprint see No. O19.

Coat of Arms — A82

1935-48 Typo. ***Perf. 14***
265 A82 2c green ('37) .20 .20
266 A82 5c orange .20 .20
267 A82 10c olive bister .20 .20
a. Tete beche pair .25 .25
b. Bklt. pane 4 + 2 labels 4.50
268 A82 15c dk violet .20 .20
269 A82 20c lilac .20 .20
270 A82 25c carmine rose .20 .20
a. Tete beche pair .30 .25
c. Bklt. pane 4 + 2 labels 4.50
271 A82 25c yel org ('46) .20 .20
272 A82 30c brown .20 .20
273 A82 35c green .20 .20
a. Tete beche pair .30 .25
c. Bklt. pane 4 + 2 labels 3.00
274 A82 40c red vio ('38) .20 .20
275 A82 50c blue .40 .20
276 A82 60c slate ('41) .20 .20
277 A82 65c red lilac ('46) .25 .20
278 A82 70c lt blue grn ('45) .25 .25
279 A82 75c lilac rose ('45) .25 .20
280 A82 80c green ('48) 3.50 .40
281 A82 90c dull vio ('46) .20 .20
282 A82 1fr red brown ('45) .20 .20
Nos. 265-282 (18) 7.25 3.85
Set, never hinged 15.00

Several stamps of type A82 exist in various shades.

Nos. 265, 361 were privately overprinted and surcharged "+10FR." by the Association Belgo-Americaine for the dedication of the Bastogne Memorial, July 16, 1950. The overprint is in six types.

See design O1. For overprints and surcharges see Nos. 312-313, 361-364, 390-394, O20-O22, O24, O26-O28, O33.

A83

A83a

Perf. 14, 14x13½, 11½
1936-51 **Photo.**
Size: 17½x21¾mm
283 A83 70c brown .30 .20
a. Tete beche pair .80 .80

c. Bklt. pane 4 + 2 labels 7.50

Size: 20¾x24mm

284 A83a 1fr rose car .30 .20
285 A83a 1.20fr dk brown ('51) .80 .20
286 A83a 1.50fr brt red vio ('43) .40 .30
287 A83a 1.75fr dp ultra ('43) .20 .20
288 A83a 1.75fr dk car ('50) .20 .20
289 A83a 2fr dk pur ('43) 1.00 1.00
290 A83a 2.25fr grnsh blk ('43) .25 .20
291 A83a 2.50fr org red ('51) 1.75 .30
292 A83a 3.25fr chestnut ('43) .20 .20
293 A83a 5fr dp green ('43) 1.00 .40
Nos. 283-293 (11) 6.40 3.40
Set, never hinged 16.65

Nos. 287-288, 290-291, 293 inscribed "Belgie-Belgique."

See designs A85, A91. For overprints and surcharges see #314, O23, O25, O29, O31, O34.

A84

A85

1936-51 Engr. *Perf. 14x13½*

294 A84 1.50fr rose lilac .60 .35
295 A84 1.75fr dull blue .20 .20
296 A84 2fr dull vio .40 .30
297 A84 2.25fr gray vio ('41) .25 .25
298 A84 2.45fr black 32.50 .70
299 A84 2.50fr ol blk ('40) 2.00 .25
300 A84 3.25fr org brn ('41) .30 .20
301 A84 5fr dull green 2.40 .50
302 A84 10fr vio brn .60 .20
a. 10fr light brown 1.00 .20
303 A84 20fr vermilion 1.00 .30

Perf. 11½

304 A84 3fr yel brn ('51) .55 .20
305 A84 4fr bl, *bluish* ('50) 1.50 .20
a. White paper 5.50 .20
306 A84 6fr brt rose car ('51) 2.75 .20
307 A84 10fr brn vio ('51) .55 .20
308 A84 20fr red ('51) 1.10 .20
Nos. 294-308 (15) 46.70 4.25
Set, never hinged 144.00

See No. 1159. For overprint and surcharges see Nos. 316-317, O32.

No. 206 Surcharged as No. 226, but dated "1937"

1937 Unwmk. *Perf. 14*

309 A63 10c on 40c red vio .20 .20
Never hinged .30

See note after No. 197.

1938-41 Photo. *Perf. 13½x14*

310 A85 75c olive gray .25 .20
a. Tete beche pair .75 .75
c. Bklt. pane 4 + 2 labels 6.75
311 A85 1fr rose pink ('41) .20 .20
a. Tete beche pair .25 .25
b. Booklet pane of 6 2.25
c. Bklt. pane 4 + 2 labels 2.25
Set, never hinged .75

For overprints and surcharges see Nos. 315, O25, O30, O35.

Nos. 272, 274, 283, 310, 299, 298 Surcharged in Blue, Black, Carmine or Red

= =

= 10 c = 10c.
a b

≡ 2F25
c

1938-42

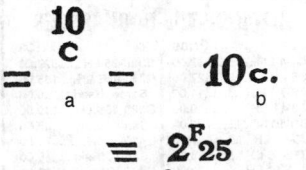

312 A82 (a) 10c on 30c (Bl) .20 .20
313 A82 (a) 10c on 40c (Bl) .20 .20
314 A83 (b) 10c on 70c (Bk) .20 .20
315 A85 (b) 50c on 75c (C) .20 .20
316 A84 (c) 2.25fr on 2.50fr (C) .45 .45
317 A84 (c) 2.50fr on 2.45fr (R) 11.00 .20
Nos. 312-317 (6) 12.25 1.45
Set, never hinged 26.55

Issue date: No. 317, Oct. 31, 1938.

Basilica and Bell Tower — A86

Water Exhibition Buildings — A87

Designs: 1.50fr, Albert Canal and Park. 1.75fr, Eygenbilsen Cut in Albert Canal.

1938, Oct. 31 *Perf. 14x13½, 13½x14*

318 A86 35c dk blue grn .20 .20
319 A87 1fr rose red .45 .30
320 A87 1.50fr vio brn 1.10 .60
321 A87 1.75fr ultra 1.25 .20
Nos. 318-321 (4) 3.00 1.30
Set, never hinged 10.80

Intl. Water Exhibition, Liège, 1939.

Catalogue values for unused stamps in this section, from this point to the end of the section, are for Never Hinged items.

Lion Rampant A90

Leopold III, Crown and V A91

1944 Unwmk. Photo. *Perf. 12½*

Inscribed: "Belgique-Belgie"

322 A90 5c chocolate .20 .20
323 A90 10c green .20 .20
324 A90 25c lt blue .20 .20
325 A90 35c brown .20 .20
326 A90 50c lt bl grn .20 .20
327 A90 75c purple .20 .20
328 A90 1fr vermilion .20 .20
329 A90 1.25fr chestnut .20 .20
330 A90 1.50fr orange .45 .40
331 A90 1.75fr brt ultra .20 .20
332 A90 2fr aqua 3.75 1.90
333 A90 2.75fr dp mag .20 .20
334 A90 3fr claret .75 .60
335 A90 3.50fr sl blk .75 .60
336 A90 5fr dk olive 6.75 4.75
337 A90 10fr black 1.25 1.10
Nos. 322-337 (16) 15.70 11.35

Inscribed: "Belgie-Belgique"

338 A90 5c chocolate .20 .20
339 A90 10c green .20 .20
340 A90 25c lt bl .20 .20
341 A90 35c brown .20 .20
342 A90 50c lt bl grn .20 .20
343 A90 75c purple .20 .20
344 A90 1fr vermilion .20 .20
345 A90 1.25fr chestnut .20 .20
346 A90 1.50fr orange .30 *.45*
347 A90 1.75fr brt ultra .20 .20
348 A90 2fr aqua 2.00 2.00
349 A90 2.75fr dp magenta .20 .20
350 A90 3fr claret .65 *.75*
351 A90 3.50fr slate blk .65 *.75*
352 A90 5fr dark olive 5.75 5.00
353 A90 10fr black 1.00 *1.25*
Nos. 338-353 (16) 12.35 12.20

1944-57 *Perf. 14x13½*

354 A91 1fr brt rose red .35 .20
355 A91 1.50fr magenta .50 .20
356 A91 1.75fr dp ultra .50 .55
357 A91 2fr dp vio 1.50 .20
358 A91 2.25fr grnsh blk .55 .65
359 A91 3.25fr chnt brn .75 .20
360 A91 5fr dk bl grn 3.00 .20
a. Perf. 11½ ('57) 75.00 .20
Nos. 354-360 (7) 7.15 2.20

Nos. 355, 357, 359 inscribed "Belgique-Belgie."

For surcharges see Nos. 365-367 and footnote following No. 367.

Stamps of 1935-41 Overprinted in Red

V

1944 *Perf. 14*

361 A82 2c pale green .20 .20
362 A82 15c indigo .20 .20
363 A82 20c brt violet .20 .20
364 A82 60c slate .25 .20
Nos. 361-364 (4) .85 .80

See note following No. 282.

Nos. 355, 357, and 360 Surcharged Typographically in Black or Carmine

−10%

1946 *Perf. 14x13½*

365 A91 On 1.50fr magenta .40 .20
366 A91 On 2fr dp vio (C) 1.50 .45
367 A91 On 5fr dk bl grn (C) 2.00 .30
Nos. 365-367 (3) 3.90 .95

To provide denominations created by a reduction in postal rates, the Government produced #365-367 by typographed surcharge. Also, each post office was authorized on May 20, 1946, to surcharge its stock of 1.50fr, 2fr and 5fr stamps "-10 percent." Hundreds of types and sizes of this surcharge exist, both hand-stamped and typographed. These include the "1,35," "1,80" and "4,50" applied at Ghislenghien.

M. S. Prince Baudouin — A92

2.25fr, S.S. Marie Henriette. 3.15fr, S.S. Diamant.

Perf. 14x13½, 13½x14

1946, June 15 Photo. Unwmk.

368 A92 1.35fr brt bluish grn .20 .20
369 A92 2.25fr slate green .30 .20
370 A92 3.15fr slate black .30 .20
Nos. 368-370 (3) .80 .60

Centenary of the steamship line between Ostend and Dover.

#368 exists in two sizes: 21¼x18¼mm and 21x17mm. #369-370 are 24½x20mm.

Capt. Adrien de Gerlache A95

Belgica and Explorers A96

1947, June *Perf. 14x13½, 11½*

371 A95 1.35fr crimson rose .45 .20
372 A96 2.25fr gray black 2.75 2.00

50th anniv. of Capt. Adrien de Gerlache's Antarctic Expedition.

Joseph A. F. Plateau — A97

1947, June *Perf. 14x13½*

373 A97 3.15fr deep blue .80 .20

Issued to mark the World Film and Fine Arts Festival, Brussels, June, 1947.

Chemical Industry A98

Industrial Arts A99

Agriculture — A100

Textile Industry — A102

Communications Center — A101

Iron Manufacture A103

Photogravure (#374-376, 378), Typographed (#377, 380), Engraved

1948 Unwmk. *Perf. 11½*

374 A98 60c blue grn .85 .20
375 A98 1.20fr brown 2.25 .20
376 A99 1.35fr red brown .85 .20
377 A100 1.75fr brt red 1.60 .20
378 A99 1.75fr dk gray grn 1.10 .20
379 A101 2.25fr gray blue 2.00 1.75
380 A100 2.50fr dk car rose 6.75 .20
381 A101 3fr brt red vio 9.00 .30
382 A102 3.15fr deep blue 2.00 .20
383 A102 4fr brt ultra 8.25 .20
384 A103 6fr blue green 13.00 .20
385 A103 6.30fr brt red vio 4.00 3.75
Nos. 374-385 (12) 51.65 7.60

See Nos. O42-O46.

Leopold I — A104

1949, July 1 Engr. *Perf. 14x13½*

386 A104 90c dk green 1.10 .55
387 A104 1.75fr brown .90 .20
388 A104 3fr red 3.50 3.00
389 A104 4fr deep blue 5.00 1.25
Nos. 386-389 (4) 10.50 5.00

Cent. of Belgium's 1st postage stamps. See note on souvenir sheet below No. 2.

Stamps of 1935-45 Precanceled and Surcharged in Black

I-I-49
31-XII-49
= 20c =

1949 *Perf. 14*

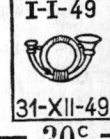

390 A82 5c on 15c dk vio .20 .20
391 A82 5c on 30c brown .20 .20
392 A82 5c on 40c red vio .20 .20
393 A82 20c on 70c lt bl grn .30 .35
394 A82 20c on 75c lil rose .20 .20

Similar Surcharge and Precancellation in Black on Nos. B455-B458

Perf. 14x13½

395 SP251 10c on #B455 3.50 3.00
396 SP251 40c on #B456 1.10 .85
397 SP251 80c on #B457 .65 .50
398 SP251 1.20fr on #B458 2.25 1.50
Nos. 390-398 (9) 8.60 7.00

See note after No. 197.

St. Mary Magdalene, from Painting by Gerard David — A105

1949, July 15 Photo. *Perf. 11*

399 A105 1.75fr dark brown .70 .35

Gerard David Exhibition at Bruges, 1949.

Allegory of UPU A106

1949, Oct. 1 Engr. *Perf. 11½*

400 A106 4fr deep blue 4.50 2.50

75th anniv. of the UPU.

Symbolical of Pension Fund A107

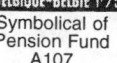

Lion Rampant A108

Perf. 11½

1950, May 1 Unwmk. Photo.

401 A107 1.75fr dark brown .50 .25

General Pension Fund founding, cent.

1951, Feb. 15 Engr. *Perf. 11½*

402 A108 20c blue .25 .20

1951-75 Typo. *Perf. 13½x14*

Size: 17½x21mm

403 A108 2c org brn ('60) .20 .20
404 A108 3c brt lil ('60) .20 .20
405 A108 5c pale violet .20 .20
406 A108 5c brt pink ('74) .20 .20
407 A108 10c red orange .20 .20
408 A108 15c brt pink ('59) .20 .20
409 A108 20c claret .20 .20
410 A108 25c green 1.75 .25
411 A108 25c lt bl grn ('66) .20 .20
412 A108 30c gray grn ('57) .20 .20
413 A108 40c brown olive .20 .20
414 A108 50c ultra .20 .20
a. 50c light blue .20 .20
415 A108 60c lilac rose .20 .20
416 A108 65c violet brn 12.50 .55
417 A108 75c bluish lilac .20 .20
418 A108 80c emerald .75 .20
419 A108 90c deep blue .75 .20
420 A108 1fr rose .20 .20
421 A108 2fr emerald ('73) .20 .20
422 A108 2.50fr brown ('70) .20 .20
423 A108 3fr brt pink ('70) .20 .20
424 A108 4fr brt rose lil ('74) .25 .20
425 A108 4.50fr blue ('74) .30 .20
426 A108 5fr brt lilac ('75) .30 .20

Size: 17x20½mm

427 A108 1.50fr dk sl grn ('69) .20 .20

Perf. 13½x13

428 A108 2fr emerald ('68) .20 .20

Photo. *Perf. 11½*

Size: 20½x24mm

429 A108 50c light blue ('61) .45 .20
430 A108 60c lilac rose ('66) 1.10 .70
431 A108 1fr carmine rose ('59) .20 .20

Perf. 13½x12½

Size: 17½x22mm

432 A108 50c lt blue ('75) .20 .20
a. Booklet pane of 4 (#432, 784 and 2 #785) + labels 1.00
b. Booklet pane of 4 (#432 and 3 #787) + labels 1.35
433 A108 1fr rose ('69) 2.00 .90
434 A108 2fr emerald ('72) .50 .30
e. Booklet pane of 6 (4 #434 + 2 #475) 5.50
f. Booklet pane of 5 (#434, 4 #476 + label) 8.00
Nos. 403-434 (32) 24.85 8.10

Counterfeits exist of No. 416. Nos. 429, 431 also issued in coils with black control number on back of every fifth stamp. Nos. 432-434 issued in booklet panes only. No. 432 has one straightedge, and stamps in the pane are tete-beche. Each pane has 2 labels showing Belgian postal emblem and a large selvage with postal code instructions.

Nos. 433-434 have 1 or 2 straight-edges. Panes have a large selvage with inscription or map of Belgium showing postal zones.

See designs A386, O5. For surcharges see Nos. 477-478, 563-567.

Francois de Tassis (Franz von Taxis) — A109

Portraits: 1.75fr, Jean-Baptiste of Thurn & Taxis. 2fr, Baron Leonard I. 2.50fr, Count Lamoral I. 3fr, Count Leonard II. 4fr, Count Lamoral II. 5fr, Prince Eugene Alexander. 5.75fr, Prince Anselme Francois. 8fr, Prince Alexander Ferdinand. 10fr, Prince Charles Anselme. 20fr, Prince Charles Alexander.

1952, May 14 Engr. *Perf. 11½*

Laid Paper

435 A109 80c olive grn .75 .30
436 A109 1.75fr red org .75 .30
437 A109 2fr violet brn 1.50 .40
438 A109 2.50fr carmine 2.25 1.65
439 A109 3fr olive bis 2.00 1.00
440 A109 4fr ultra 3.00 .85
441 A109 5fr red brn 4.00 1.75
442 A109 5.75fr blue vio 6.75 2.25
443 A109 8fr gray 12.50 2.75
444 A109 10fr rose vio 22.50 4.50
445 A109 20fr brown 60.00 22.50
Nos. 435-445,B514 (12) 291.00 213.25

13th UPU Cong., Brussels, 1952.

King Baudouin
A110 A111

1952-58 Engr. *Perf. 11½*

Size: 21x24mm

446 A110 1.50fr gray green .55 .20
447 A110 2fr crimson .40 .20
448 A110 4fr ultra 3.50 .20

Size: 24½x35mm

449 A110 50fr gray brn 1.75 .20
a. 50fr violet brown 35.00 .60
450 A110 100fr rose red ('58) 5.00 .25

1953-72 Photo. *Perf. 11½*

451 A111 1.50fr gray .25 .20
452 A111 2fr rose carmine 6.75 .20
453 A111 2fr green .25 .20
454 A111 2.50fr red brn ('57) .60 .20
a. 2.50fr orange brown ('70) .25 .20
455 A111 3fr rose lilac ('58) .40 .20
456 A111 3.50fr brt yel grn ('58) .75 .20
457 A111 4fr brt ultra .50 .20
458 A111 4.50fr dk red brn ('62) 3.00 .20
459 A111 5fr violet ('57) 1.25 .20
460 A111 6fr dp pink ('58) .75 .20
461 A111 6.50fr gray ('60) 62.50 15.00
462 A111 7fr blue ('60) .90 .20
463 A111 7.50fr grysh brn ('58) 47.50 14.00
464 A111 8fr bluish gray ('58) 1.25 .20
465 A111 8.50fr claret ('58) 15.00 .30
466 A111 9fr gray ('58) 47.50 .75
467 A111 12fr lt bl grn ('66) .90 .20
468 A111 30fr red org ('58) 5.50 .20

Redrawn

469 A111 2.50fr orange brn ('71) .35 .20
470 A111 4.50fr brown ('72) 2.25 .60
471 A111 7fr blue ('71) .60 .20

Perf. 13½x12½

Size: 17½x22mm

472 A111 1.50fr gray ('70) .60 .30
b. Bklt. pane of 10 6.50
c. Bklt. pane, 3 #472, 3 #475 15.00
473 A111 2.50fr org brn ('70) 9.00 6.25
h. Bklt. pane, 1 #473, 5 #475 16.00
474 A111 3fr lilac rose ('69) .60 .20
a. Bklt. pane of 5 + label 25.00
b. Bklt. pane, 2 #433, 6 #474 18.00
475 A111 3.50fr brt yel grn ('70) .60 .25
476 A111 4.50fr dull red brn ('72) .75 .45
Nos. 446-476 (31) 221.50 42.35

Nos. 451, 453, 454a, 455, 456, 458 also issued in coils with black control number on back of every fifth stamp. These coils, except for No. 451, are on luminescent paper.

On Nos. 469-471, the 2, 4 and 7 are 3mm high. The background around the head is white. On Nos. 454, 458, 462 the 2, 4 and 7 are 2½mm high and the background is tinted.

Nos. 472-476 issued in booklets only and have 1 or 2 straight-edges. All panes have a large selvage with inscription or map.

See designs M1, O3.

Luminescent Paper

Stamps issued on both ordinary and luminescent paper include: Nos. 307-308, 430-431, 449-451, 453-460, 462, 464, 467-468, 472, 643-644, 650-651, 837, Q385, Q410.

Stamps issued only on luminescent paper include: Nos. 433, 454a, 472b, 473-474, 649, 652-658, 664-670, 679-682, 688-690, 694-696, 698-703, 705-711, 713-726, 729-747, 751-754, 756-757, 759, 761-762, 764, 766, 769, 772, 774, 778, 789, 791-793, 795, 797-799, 801-807, 809-811, 814-818, 820-834, 836, 838-848.

See note after No. 857.

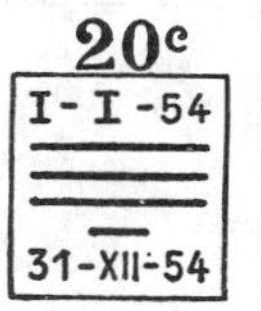

Nos. 416 and 419 Surcharged and Precanceled in Black

1954, Jan. 1 Unwmk. *Perf. 13½x14*

477 A108 20c on 65c vio brn 1.75 .30
478 A108 20c on 90c dp blue 1.75 .20

See note after No. 197.

Map and Rotary Emblem A112

Designs: 80c, Mermaid and Mercury holding emblem. 4fr, Rotary emblem and two globes.

1954, Sept. 10 Engr. *Perf. 11½*

479 A112 20c red .25 .20
480 A112 80c dark green .65 .30
481 A112 4fr ultra 1.40 .50
Nos. 479-481 (3) 2.30 1.00

5th regional conf. of Rotary Intl. at Ostend. No. 481 for Rotary 50th Anniv. (in 1955).

A souv. sheet containing one each, imperf., was sold for 500 francs. It was not valid for postage.

The Rabot and Begonia — A113

Designs: 2.50fr, The Oudeburg and azalea. 4fr, "Three Towers" and orchid.

1955, Feb. 15 Photo.

482 A113 80c brt carmine .85 .35
483 A113 2.50fr black brn 5.25 2.75
484 A113 4fr dk rose brn 5.00 .90
Nos. 482-484 (3) 11.10 4.00

Ghent Intl. Flower Exhibition, 1955.

Homage to Charles V as a Child, by Albrecht de Vriendt — A114

Charles V, by Titian — A115

4fr, Abdication of Charles V, by Louis Gallait.

1955, Mar. 25 Unwmk. *Perf. 11½*

485 A114 20c rose red .25 .20
486 A115 2fr dk gray green 1.90 .20
487 A114 4fr blue 5.00 1.25
Nos. 485-487 (3) 7.15 1.65

Charles V Exhibition, Ghent, 1955.

Emile Verhaeren, by Montald Constant — A116

1955, May 11 Engr.

488 A116 20c dark gray .20 .20

Birth cent. of Verhaeren, poet.

Allegory of Textile Manufacture A117

1955, May 11

489 A117 2fr violet brown 1.00 .20

2nd Intl. Textile Exhibition, Brussels, June 1955.

"The Foolish Virgin" by Rik Wouters A118

"Departure of Volunteers from Liege, 1830" by Charles Soubre A119

1955, June 10

490 A118 1.20fr olive green 1.10 1.10
491 A118 2fr violet 1.60 .20

3rd biennial exhibition of sculpture, Antwerp, June 11-Sept. 10, 1955.

1955, Sept. 10 Photo.

492 A119 20c grnsh slate .20 .20
493 A119 2fr chocolate .90 .20

Exhibition "The Romantic Movement in Liege Province," Sept. 10-Oct. 31, 1955; and 125th anniv. of Belgium's independence from the Netherlands.

Pelican Giving Blood to Young A120

Buildings of Tournai, Ghent and Antwerp A121

1956, Jan. 14 **Engr.**

494 A120 2fr brt carmine	.35	.20

Blood donor service of the Belgian Red Cross.

1956, July 14 **Photo.**

495 A121 2fr brt ultra	.30	.20

The Scheldt exhibition (Scaldis) at Tournai, Ghent and Antwerp, July-Sept. 1956.

Europa Issue

"Rebuilding Europe" — A122

1956, Sept. 15 **Engr.**

496 A122 2fr lt green	1.75	.20
497 A122 4fr purple	8.75	.70

Issued to symbolize the cooperation among the six countries comprising the Coal and Steel Community.

Train on Map of Belgium and Luxembourg A123

1956, Sept. 29

498 A123 2fr dark blue	.45	.20

Issued to mark the electrification of the Brussels-Luxembourg railroad.

Edouard Anseele A124

"The Atom" and Exposition Emblem A125

1956, Oct. 27

499 A124 20c violet brown	.20	.20

Cent. of the birth of Edouard Anseele, statesman, and in connection with an exhibition held in his honor at Ghent.

1957-58 **Unwmk.**

500 A125 2fr carmine rose	.25	.20
501 A125 2.50fr green ('58)	.40	.20
502 A125 4fr brt violet blue	.95	.20
503 A125 5fr claret ('58)	.85	.50
Nos. 500-503 (4)	2.45	1.10

1958 World's Fair at Brussels.

Emperor Maximilian I Receiving Letter — A126

1957, May 19

504 A126 2fr claret	.40	.20

Day of the Stamp, May 19, 1957.

Sikorsky S-58 Helicopter A127

1957, June 15

505 A127 4fr gray grn & brt bl	.80	.45

100,000th passenger carried by Sabena helicopter service, June 15, 1957.

Zeebrugge Harbor A128

1957, July 6

506 A128 2fr dark blue	.40	.20

50th anniv. of the completion of the port of Zeebrugge-Bruges.

Leopold I Entering Brussels, 1831 — A129

Leopold I Arriving at Belgian Border A130

1957, July 17 **Photo.**

507 A129 20c dk gray grn	.20	.20
508 A130 2fr lilac	.50	.20

126th anniv. of the arrival in Belgium of King Leopold I.

Boy Scout and Girl Scout Emblems A131

Design: 4fr, Robert Lord Baden-Powell, painted by David Jaggers, vert.

Perf. 11½

1957, July 29 **Unwmk.** **Engr.**

509 A131 80c gray	.25	.20
510 A131 4fr light green	1.00	.45

Cent. of the birth of Lord Baden-Powell, founder of the Boy Scout movement.

"Kneeling Woman" by Lehmbruck A132

"United Europe" A133

1957, Aug. 20 **Photo.**

511 A132 2.50fr dk blue grn	1.10	.85

4th Biennial Exposition of Sculpture, Antwerp, May 25-Sept. 15.

1957, Sept. 16 **Engr.** ***Perf. 11½***

512 A133 2fr dk violet brn	1.00	.20
513 A133 4fr dark blue	1.90	.45

Europa: United Europe for peace and prosperity.

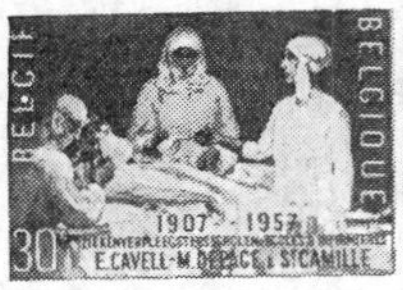

Queen Elisabeth Assisting at Operation, by Allard L'Olivier A134

Perf. 11½

1957, Nov. 23 **Unwmk.** **Engr.**

514 A134 30c rose lilac	.20	.20

50th anniv. of the founding of the Edith Cavell-Marie Depage and St. Camille schools of nursing.

Post Horn and Historic Postal Insignia A135

1958, Mar. 16 **Photo.** ***Perf. 11½***

515 A135 2.50fr gray	.25	.20

Postal Museum Day.

United Nations Issue

International Labor Organization A136

Allegory of UN — A137

Designs: 1fr, FAO. 2fr, World Bank. 2.50fr, UNESCO. 3fr, UN Pavilion. 5fr, ITU. 8fr, Intl. Monetary Fund. 11fr, WHO. 20fr, UPU.

Perf. 11½

1958, Apr. 17 **Unwmk.** **Engr.**

516 A136 50c gray	.90	*1.40*
517 A136 1fr claret	.30	*.45*
518 A137 1.50fr dp ultra	.30	*.45*
519 A137 2fr gray brown	.85	*1.25*
520 A136 2.50fr olive grn	.30	*.45*
521 A136 3fr grnsh blue	.85	*1.25*
522 A137 5fr rose lilac	.55	*.90*
523 A136 8fr red brown	1.00	*1.60*
524 A136 11fr dull lilac	1.25	*2.00*
525 A136 20fr car rose	1.60	*2.50*
Nos. 516-525,C15-C20 (16)	10.20	*14.70*

World's Fair, Brussels, Apr. 17-Oct. 19.

Postally valid only from the UN pavilion at the Brussels Fair. Proceeds went toward financing the UN exhibits.

Eugène Ysaye A138

1958, Sept. 1

526 A138 30c dk blue & plum	.20	.20

Ysaye (1858-1931), violinist, composer.

Common Design Types pictured in section at front of book.

Europa Issue, 1958

Common Design Type

1958, Sept. 13 **Photo.**

Size: 24½x35mm

527 CD1 2.50fr brt red & blue	.20	.20
528 CD1 5fr brt blue & red	.35	.35

Issued to show the European Postal Union at the service of European integration.

Infant and UN Emblem — A140

Charles V and Jean-Baptiste of Thurn and Taxis — A141

1958, Dec. 10 **Engr.**

529 A140 2.50fr blue gray	.30	.20

10th anniv. of the signing of the Universal Declaration of Human Rights.

1959, Mar. 15 **Unwmk.**

530 A141 2.50fr green	.35	.20

Issued for the Day of the Stamp. Design from painting by J.-E. van den Bussche.

NATO Emblem A142

City Hall, Audenarde A143

1959, Apr. 3 **Photo.** ***Perf. 11½***

531 A142 2.50fr dp red & dk bl	.45	.20
532 A142 5fr emerald & dk bl	1.25	*1.40*

10th anniv. of NATO. See No. 720.

1959, Aug. 17 **Engr.**

533 A143 2.50fr deep claret	.30	.20

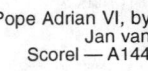

Pope Adrian VI, by Jan van Scorel — A144

1959, Aug. 31 *Perf. 11½*
534 A144 2.50fr dark red .20 .20
535 A144 5fr Prus blue .55 .55

500th anniv. of the birth of Pope Adrian VI.

Europa Issue, 1959
Common Design Type
1959, Sept. 19 **Photo.**
Size: 24x35½mm
536 CD2 2.50fr dark red .20 .20
537 CD2 5fr brt grnsh blue .45 .45

Boeing 707
A146

Engraved and Photogravure
1959, Dec. 1 *Perf. 11½*
538 A146 6fr dk bl gray & car 1.75 .80

Inauguration of jet flights by Sabena Airlines.

Countess of Taxis — A147

Indian Azalea — A148

1960, Mar. 21 **Engr.** *Perf. 11½*
539 A147 3fr dark blue .85 .20

Alexandrine de Rye, Countess of Taxis, Grand Mistress of the Netherlands Posts, 1628-1645, and day of the stamp, Mar. 21, 1960. The painting of the Countess is by Nicholas van der Eggermans.

1960, Mar. 28 **Unwmk.**
540 A148 40c shown .20 .20
541 A148 3fr Begonia .90 .20
542 A148 6fr Anthurium, bromelia 1.00 .90
Nos. 540-542 (3) 2.10 1.30

24th Ghent Intl. Flower Exhibition, Apr. 23-May 2, 1960.

Steel Workers, by Constantin Meunier — A149

Design: 3fr, The sower, field and dock workers, from "Monument to Labor," Brussels, by Constantin Meunier, horiz.

Engraved and Photogravure
1960, Apr. 30 *Perf. 11½*
543 A149 40c claret & brt red .20 .20
544 A149 3fr brown & brt red .85 .25

Socialist Party of Belgium, 75th anniv.

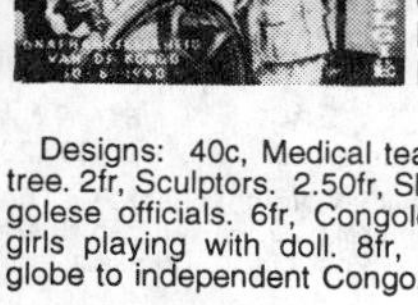

Congo River Boat Pilot — A150

Designs: 40c, Medical team. 1fr, Planting tree. 2fr, Sculptors. 2.50fr, Shot put. 3fr, Congolese officials. 6fr, Congolese and Belgian girls playing with doll. 8fr, Boy pointing on globe to independent Congo.

1960, June 30 **Photo.** *Perf. 11½*
Size: 35x24mm
545 A150 10c bright red .30 .20
546 A150 40c rose claret .45 .20
547 A150 1fr brt lilac .85 .75
548 A150 2fr gray green .95 .85
549 A150 2.50fr blue .85 .75
550 A150 3fr dk bl gray 1.00 .45

Size: 51x35mm
551 A150 6fr violet bl 3.00 1.90
552 A150 8fr dk brown 5.00 4.00
Nos. 545-552 (8) 12.40 9.10

Independence of Congo.

Europa Issue, 1960
Common Design Type
1960, Sept. 17
Size: 35x24½mm
553 CD3 3fr claret .60 .20
554 CD3 6fr gray 1.25 .40

Children Examining Stamp and Globe
A152

H. J. W. Frère-Orban
A153

1960, Oct. 1 **Photo.** *Perf. 11½*
555 A152 40c bister & blk + label .20 .20

Promoting stamp collecting among children.

Engraved and Photogravure
1960, Oct. 17 **Unwmk.**
Portrait in Brown
556 A153 10c orange yel .20 .20
557 A153 40c blue grn .20 .20
558 A153 1.50fr brt violet .70 .70
559 A153 3fr red 1.10 .20
Nos. 556-559 (4) 2.20 1.30

Centenary of Communal Credit Society.

King Baudouin and Queen Fabiola
A154

1960, Dec. 13 **Photo.** *Perf. 11½*
Portraits in Dark Brown
560 A154 40c green .20 .20
561 A154 3fr red lilac .30 .20
562 A154 6fr dull blue 1.25 .60
Nos. 560-562 (3) 1.75 1.00

Wedding of King Baudouin and Dona Fabiola de Mora y Aragon, Dec. 15, 1960.

Nos. 412, 414 Surcharged

1961-68 **Typo.** *Perf. 13½x14*
563 A108 15c on 30c gray grn .20 .20
564 A108 15c on 50c blue ('68) .20 .20
565 A108 20c on 30c gray grn .20 .20
Nos. 563-565 (3) .60 .60

No. 412 Surcharged and Precanceled

1961
566 A108 15c on 30c gray grn .90 .20
567 A108 20c on 30c gray grn 1.90 1.40

See note after No. 197.

Nicolaus Rockox, by Anthony Van Dyck — A155

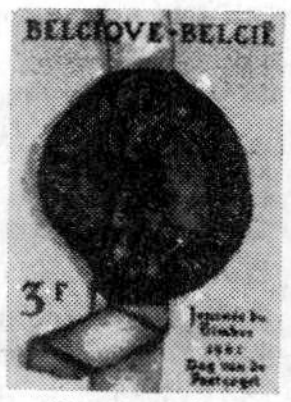

Seal of Jan Bode, Alderman of Antwerp, 1264 — A156

Engraved and Photogravure
1961, Mar. 18 *Perf. 11½*
568 A155 3fr bister, blk & brn .35 .20

400th anniv. of the birth of Nicolaus Rockox, mayor of Antwerp.

1961, Apr. 16 **Photo.**
569 A156 3fr buff & brown .35 .20

Issued for Stamp Day, April 16.

Senate Building, Brussels, Laurel and Sword
A157

Engraved and Photogravure
1961, Sept. 14 **Unwmk.** *Perf. 11½*
570 A157 3fr brn & Prus grn .30 .20
571 A157 6fr dk brn & dk car 2.75 1.00

50th Conference of the Interparliamentary Union, Brussels, Sept. 14-22.

Europa Issue, 1961
Common Design Type
1961, Sept. 16 **Photo.**
572 CD4 3fr yel grn & dk grn .25 .20
573 CD4 6fr org brn & blk .35 .25

Atomic Reactor Plant, BR2, Mol — A159

Designs: 3fr, Atomic Reactor BR3, vert. 6fr, Atomic Reactor plant BR3.

1961, Nov. 8 **Unwmk.** *Perf. 11½*
574 A159 40c dk blue grn .20 .20
575 A159 3fr red lilac .20 .20
576 A159 6fr bright blue .35 .25
Nos. 574-576 (3) .75 .65

Aatomic nuclear research center at Mol.

Horta Museum — A160

1962, Feb. 15 **Engr.**
577 A160 3fr red brown .25 .20

Baron Victor Horta (1861-1947), architect.

Postrider, 16th Century
A161

Engraved and Photogravure
1962, Mar. 25 *Perf. 11½*
Chalky Paper
578 A161 3fr brn & slate grn .30 .20

Stamp Day. See No. 677.

Gerard Mercator
A162

Bro. Alexis-Marie Gochet
A163

Engraved and Photogravure
1962, Apr. 14 **Unwmk.**
579 A162 3fr sepia & gray .30 .20

Mercator (Gerhard Kremer, 1512-1594), geographer and map maker.

1962, May 19 **Engr.** *Perf. 11½*
Portrait: 3fr, Canon Pierre-Joseph Triest.
580 A163 2fr dark blue .30 .20
581 A163 3fr golden brown .30 .20

Brother Alexis-Marie Gochet (1835-1910), geographer and educator, and Canon Pierre-Joseph Triest (1760-1836), educator and founder of hospitals and orphanages.

Europa Issue, 1962
Common Design Type
1962, Sept. 15 **Photo.**
582 CD5 3fr dp car, citron & blk .25 .20
583 CD5 6fr olive, citron & blk .35 .35

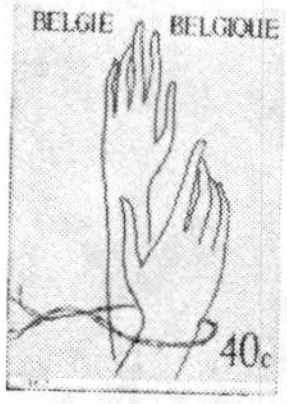

Hand with Barbed Wire and Freed Hand — A165

1962, Sept. 16 **Engr. & Photo.**
584 A165 40c lt blue & blk .20 .20

Issued in memory of concentration camp victims.

Adam, by Michelangelo, Broken Chain and UN Emblem
A166

1962, Nov. 24 *Perf. 11½*
585 A166 3fr gray & blk .25 .20
586 A166 6fr lt redsh brn & dk brn .40 .30

UN Declaration of Human Rights.

Henri Pirenne (1862-1935), Historian — A167

1963, Jan. 15 **Engr.**
587 A167 3fr ultramarine .35 .20

Swordsmen and Ghent Belfry
A168

Designs: 3fr, Modern fencers. 6fr, Arms of the Royal and Knightly Guild of St. Michael, vert.

Engraved and Photogravure

1963, Mar. 23 Unwmk. *Perf. 11½*

588 A168 1fr brn red & pale bl .20 .20
589 A168 3fr dk vio & yel grn .20 .20
590 A168 6fr gray, blk, red, bl & gold .30 .25
Nos. 588-590 (3) .70 .65

350th anniv. of the granting of a charter to the Ghent guild of fencers.

Stagecoach A169

1963, Apr. 7

591 A169 3fr gray & ocher .25 .20

Stamp Day. See No. 678.

Hotel des Postes, Paris, Stagecoach and Stamp, 1863 A170

Perf. 11½

1963, May 7 Unwmk. Engr.

592 A170 6fr dk brn, gray & yel grn .40 .35

Cent. of the 1st Intl. Postal Conf., Paris, 1863.

"Peace," Child in Rye Field — A171

1963, May 8 Engr. & Photo.

593 A171 3fr grn, blk, yel & brn .20 .20
594 A171 6fr buff, blk, brn & org .35 .25

May 8th Movement for Peace. (On May 8, 1945, World War II ended in Europe).

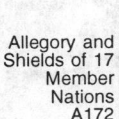

Allegory and Shields of 17 Member Nations A172

1963, June 13 Unwmk. *Perf. 11½*

595 A172 6fr blue & black .40 .30

10th anniversary of the Conference of European Transport Ministers.

Seal of Union of Belgian Towns — A173

1963, June 17

596 A173 6fr grn, red, blk & gold .40 .35

Intl. Union of Municipalities, 50th anniv.

Caravelle over Brussels National Airport A174

Photogravure and Engraved

1963, Sept. 1 Unwmk. *Perf. 11½*

597 A174 3fr green & gray .25 .20

40th anniversary of SABENA airline.

Europa Issue, 1963
Common Design Type

1963, Sept. 14 Photo.
Size: 35x24mm

598 CD6 3fr blk, dl red & lt brn .60 .20
599 CD6 6fr blk, lt bl & lt brn 1.60 .35

Jules Destrée A176

Design: No. 601, Henry Van de Velde.

Perf. 11½

1963, Nov. 16 Unwmk. Engr.

600 A176 1fr rose lilac .20 .20
601 A176 1fr green .20 .20

Jules Destrée (1863-1936), statesman and founder of the Royal Academy of French Language and Literature, and of Henry Van de Velde (1863-1957), architect.

No. 600 incorrectly inscribed "1864."

Development of the Mail, Bas-relief A177

1963, Nov. 23 Engr. & Photo.

602 A177 50c dl red, slate & blk .20 .20

50th anniversary of the establishment of postal checking service.

Dr. Armauer G. Hansen A178

Fight Against Leprosy: 2fr, Leprosarium. 5fr, Father Joseph Damien.

1964, Jan. 25 Unwmk. *Perf. 11½*

603 A178 1fr brown org & blk .20 .20
604 A178 2fr brown org & blk .20 .20
605 A178 5fr brown org & blk .25 .20
a. Souvenir sheet of 3, #603-605 1.90 1.90
Nos. 603-605 (3) .65 .60

No. 605a sold for 12fr.

Andreas Vesalius (1514-64), Anatomist — A179

Jules Boulvin (1855-1920), Mechanical Engineer A180

Design: 2fr, Henri Jaspar (1870-1939), statesman and lawyer.

Engraved and Photogravure

1964, Mar. 2 Unwmk. *Perf. 11½*

606 A179 50c pale grn & blk .20 .20
607 A180 1fr pale grn & blk .20 .20
608 A180 2fr pale grn & blk .20 .20
Nos. 606-608 (3) .60 .60

Postilion of Liege, 1830-40 — A181

1964, Apr. 5 Engr. *Perf. 11½*

609 A181 3fr black .20 .20

Issued for Stamp Day 1964.

Arms of Ostend A182

1964, May 16 Photo.

610 A182 3fr ultra, ver, gold & blk .20 .20

Millennium of Ostend.

Flame, Hammer and Globe — A183

1fr, "SI" and globe. 2fr, Flame over wavy lines.

1964, July 18 Unwmk. *Perf. 11½*

611 A183 50c dark blue & red .20 .20
612 A183 1fr dark blue & red .20 .20
613 A183 2fr dark blue & red .20 .20
Nos. 611-613 (3) .60 .60

Centenary of the First Socialist International, founded in London, Sept. 28, 1864.

Europa Issue, 1964
Common Design Type

1964, Sept. 12 Photo. *Perf. 11½*
Size: 24x35½mm

614 CD7 3fr yel grn, dk car & gray .25 .20
615 CD7 6fr car rose, yel grn & bl .40 .40

Benelux Issue

King Baudouin, Queen Juliana and Grand Duchess Charlotte — A185

1964, Oct. 12

616 A185 3fr olive, lt grn & mar .20 .20

20th anniv. of the customs union of Belgium, Netherlands and Luxembourg.

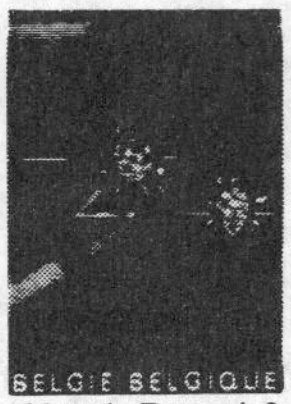

Hand, Round & Pear-shaped Diamonds A186

Symbols of Textile Industry A187

1965, Jan. 23 Unwmk. *Perf. 11½*

617 A186 2fr ultra, dp car & blk .20 .20

Diamond Exhibition "Diamantexpo," Antwerp, July 10-28, 1965.

1965, Jan. 25 Photo.

618 A187 1fr blue, red & blk .20 .20

Eighth textile industry exhibition "Textirama," Ghent, Jan. 29-Feb. 2, 1965.

Vriesia A188

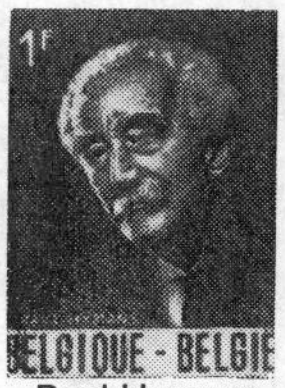

Paul Hymans A189

Designs: 2fr, Echinocactus. 3fr, Stapelia.

1965, Feb. 13 Engr. & Photo.

619 A188 1fr multicolored .20 .20
620 A188 2fr multicolored .20 .20
621 A188 3fr multicolored .20 .20
a. Souvenir sheet of 3, #619-621 1.75 1.75
Nos. 619-621 (3) .60 .60

25th Ghent International Flower Exhibition, Apr. 24-May 3, 1965.

No. 621a was issued Apr. 26 and sold for 20fr.

1965, Feb. 24 Engr. *Perf. 11½*

622 A189 1fr dull purple .20 .20

Paul Hymans (1865-1941), Belgian Foreign Minister and first president of the League of Nations.

Peter Paul Rubens A190

Sir Rowland Hill as Philatelist A191

Portraits: 2fr, Frans Snyders. 3fr, Adam van Noort. 6fr, Anthony Van Dyck. 8fr, Jacob Jordaens.

1965, Mar. 15 Photo. & Engr.
Portraits in Sepia

623 A190 1fr carmine rose .20 .20
624 A190 2fr blue green .20 .20
625 A190 3fr plum .20 .20
626 A190 6fr deep carmine .25 .20
627 A190 8fr dark blue .35 .35
Nos. 623-627 (5) 1.20 1.15

Issued to commemorate the founding of the General Savings and Pensions Bank.

1965, Mar. 27 Engr. *Perf. 11½*

628 A191 50c blue green .20 .20

Issued to publicize youth philately. The design is from a mural by J. E. Van den Bussche in the General Post Office, Brussels.

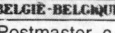

Postmaster, c. 1833 — A192

Staircase, Affligem Abbey — A194

Telephone, Globe and Teletype Paper — A193

1965, Apr. 26 Unwmk. *Perf. 11½*
629 A192 3fr emerald .20 .20

Issued for Stamp Day.

1965, May 8 Photo.
630 A193 2fr dull purple & blk .20 .20

Cent. of the ITU.

1965, May 27 Engr.
631 A194 1fr gray blue .20 .20

St. Jean Berchmans and his Birthplace A195

1965, May 27 Engr. & Photo.
632 A195 2fr dk brn & red brn .20 .20

Issued to honor St. Jean Berchmans (1599-1621), Jesuit "Saint of the Daily Life."

TOC H Lamp and Arms of Poperinge A196

Farmer with Tractor A197

1965, June 19 Photo. *Perf. 11½*
633 A196 3fr ol bis, blk & car .20 .20

50th anniv. of the founding of Talbot House in Poperinge, which served British soldiers in World War I, and where the TOC H Movement began (Christian Social Service; TOC H is army code for Poperinge Center).

Engraved and Photogravure

1965, July 17 Unwmk. *Perf. 11½*

Design: 3fr, Farmer with horse-drawn roller.

634 A197 50c bl, ol, bis brn & blk .20 .20
635 A197 3fr bl, ol grn, ol & blk .20 .20

75th anniv. of the Belgian Farmers' Association (Boerenbond).

Europa Issue, 1965

Common Design Type

1965, Sept. 25 *Perf. 11½*

Size: 35½x24mm

636 CD8 1fr dl rose & blk .20 .20
637 CD8 3fr grnsh gray & blk .20 .20

Leopold I A199

Joseph Lebeau A200

1965, Nov. 13 Engr.
638 A199 3fr sepia .20 .20
639 A199 6fr bright violet .25 .25

King Leopold I (1790-1865). The designs of the vignettes are similar to A4 and A5.

1965, Nov. 13 Photo.
640 A200 1fr multicolored .20 .20

Joseph Lebeau (1794-1865), Foreign Minister.

Tourist Issue

Grapes and Houses, Hoeilaart A201

Bridge and Castle, Huy A202

Designs: No. 643, British War Memorial, Ypres. No. 644, Castle Spontin. No. 645, City Hall, Louvain. No. 646, Ourthe Valley. No. 647, Romanesque Cathedral, gothic fountain, Nivalles. No. 648, Water mill, Kasterlee. No. 649, City Hall, Cloth Guild and Statue of Margarethe of Austria, Malines. No. 650, Town Hall, Lier. No. 651, Castle Bouillon. No. 652, Fountain and Kursaal Spa. No. 653, Windmill, Bokrijk. No. 654, Mountain road, Vielsalm. No. 655, View of Furnes. No. 656, City Hall and Belfry, Mons. No. 657, St. Martin's Church, Aalst. No. 658, Abbey and fountain, St. Hubert.

1965-71 Engr. *Perf. 11½*
641 A201 50c vio bl, lt bl & yel grn .20 .20
642 A202 50c sl grn, lt bl & red brn .20 .20
643 A202 1fr grn, lt bl, sal & brn .20 .20
644 A202 1fr ind, lt bl & ol .20 .20
645 A201 1fr brt rose lil, lt bl & blk .20 .20
646 A202 1fr blk, grnsh bl & ol .20 .20
647 A201 1.50fr sl, sky bl & bis .20 .20
648 A202 1.50fr blk, bl & ol .20 .20
649 A202 1.50fr dk bl & buff .20 .20
650 A201 2fr brn, lt bl & ind .20 .20
651 A202 2fr dk brn, grn & ocher .20 .20
652 A202 2fr bl, brt grn & blk .20 .20
653 A202 2fr blk, lt bl & yel .20 .20
654 A202 2fr blk, lt bl & yel grn .20 .20
655 A202 2fr car, lt bl & dk brn .20 .20
656 A201 2.50fr vio, buff & blk .20 .20
657 A201 2.50fr vio, lt bl, blk & ol .25 .20
658 A201 2.50fr vio bl & yel .25 .20
Nos. 641-658 (18) 3.70 3.60

Issued: #641-642, 11/13/65; #643-644, 7/15/67; #645-646, 12/16/68; #647-648, 7/6/70; #649, 656, 12/11/71; #650-651, 11/11/66; #652-653, 6/24/68; #654-655, 9/6/69; #657-658, 9/11/71.

Queen Elisabeth Type of Semi-Postal Issue, 1956

1965, Dec. 23 Photo. *Perf. 11½*
659 SP305 3fr dark gray .22 .20

Queen Elisabeth (1876-1965).

A dark frame has been added in design of No. 659; 1956 date has been changed to 1965; inscription in bottom panel is Koningin Elisabeth Reine Elisabeth 3F.

"Peace on Earth" A203

Arms of Pope Paul VI — A204

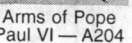

Rural Mailman, 19th Century — A205

Design: 1fr, "Looking toward a Better Future" (family, new buildings, sun and landscape).

1966, Feb. 12 Photo. *Perf. 11½*
660 A203 50c multicolored .20 .20
661 A203 1fr ocher, blk & bl .20 .20
662 A204 3fr gray, gold, car & blk .20 .20
Nos. 660-662 (3) .60 .60

75th anniv. of the encyclical by Pope Leo XIII "Rerum Novarum," which proclaimed the general principles for the organization of modern industrial society.

1966, Apr. 17 Photo. Unwmk.
663 A205 3fr blk, dl yel & pale lil .20 .20

Stamp Day. For overprint see No. 673.

Iguanodon, Natural Science Institute A206

Arend-Roland Comet, Observatory — A207

Designs: No. 665, Ancestral head and spiral pattern, Kasai; Central Africa Museum. No. 666, Snowflakes, Meteorological Institute. No. 667, Seal of Charles V, Royal Archives. No. 668, Medieval scholar, Royal Library. 8fr, Satellite and rocket, Space Aeronautics Institute.

1966, May 28 Engr. & Photo.
664 A206 1fr green & blk .20 .20
665 A206 2fr gray, blk & brn org .20 .20
666 A206 2fr blue, blk & yel .20 .20
667 A207 3fr dp rose, blk & gold .20 .20
668 A207 3fr multicolored .20 .20
669 A207 6fr ultra, yel & blk .25 .20
670 A207 8fr multicolored .30 .30
Nos. 664-670 (7) 1.55 1.50

National scientific heritage.

Atom Symbol and Retort — A208

August Kekulé, Benzene Ring — A209

Engraved and Photogravure

1966, July 9 Unwmk. *Perf. 11½*
671 A208 6fr gray, blk & red .30 .20

Issued to publicize the European chemical plant, EUROCHEMIC, at Mol.

1966, July 9
672 A209 3fr brt blue & blk .20 .20

August Friedrich Kekule (1829-96), chemistry professor at University of Ghent (1858-67).

No. 663 Overprinted with Red and Blue Emblem

1966, July 11 Photo.
673 A205 3fr multicolored .20 .20

19th Intl. P.T.T. Cong., Brussels, July 11-15.

Rik Wouters (1882-1916), Self-portrait — A210

1966, Sept. 6 Photo. *Perf. 11½*
674 A210 60c multicolored .20 .20

Europa Issue, 1966

Common Design Type

1966, Sept. 24 Engr. *Perf. 11½*

Size: 24x34mm

675 CD9 3fr brt green .20 .20
676 CD9 6fr brt rose lilac .30 .30

Types of 1962-1963 Overprinted in Black and Red

1966, Nov. 11 Engr. & Photo.
677 A161 60c sepia & grnsh gray .20 .20
678 A169 3fr sepia & pale bister .20 .20

75th anniv., Royal Fed. of Phil. Circles of Belgium. Overprint shows emblem of F.I.P.

Lions Emblem — A214

1967, Jan. 14 *Perf. 11½*
679 A214 3fr gray, blk & bl .20 .20
680 A214 6fr lt green, blk & vio .30 .20

Lions Club Intl., 50th anniv.

Pistol by Leonhard Cleuter A215

1967, Feb. 11 Photo.
681 A215 2fr dp car, blk & cream .20 .20

Fire Arms Museum in Liege.

International Tourist Year Emblem A216

1967, Feb. 11
682 A216 6fr ver, ultra & blk .30 .20

International Tourist Year, 1967.

Birches and Trientalis A217

Design: No. 684, Dunes, beach grass, privet and blue thistles.

1967, Mar. 11 Photo. *Perf. 11½*
683 A217 1fr multicolored .20 .20
684 A217 1fr multicolored .20 .20

Issued to publicize the nature preserves at Hautes Fagnes and Westhoek.

Paul E. Janson — A218

1967, Apr. 15 Engr. *Perf. 11½*
685 A218 10fr blue .35 .20

Issued in memory of Paul Emile Janson (1872-1944), lawyer and statesman.

Postilion A219

1967, Apr. 16 Photo. & Engr.
686 A219 3fr rose red & claret .20 .20

Issued for Stamp Day, 1967.

Inscribed: "FITCE"

1967, June 24 *Perf. 11½*
687 A219 10fr ultra, sep & emer .40 .30

Issued to commemorate the meeting of the Federation of Common Market Telecommunications Engineers, Brussels, July 3-8.

Europa Issue, 1967
Common Design Type

1967, May 2 Photo.
Size: 24x35mm
688 CD10 3fr blk, lt bl & red .20 .20
689 CD10 6fr blk, grnsh gray & yel .30 .30

Flax, Shuttle and Mills — A221

1967, June 3 Photo. *Perf. 11½*
690 A221 6fr tan & multi .30 .20

Belgian linen industry.

Old Kursaal, Ostend — A222

1967, June 3 Engr. & Photo.
691 A222 2fr dk brn, lt bl & yel .20 .20

700th anniversary of Ostend as a city.

A223

A224

Designs: #692, Caesar Crossing Rubicon, 15th Century Tapestry. #693, Emperor Maximilian Killing a Boar, 16th cent. tapestry.

1967, Sept. 2 Photo. *Perf. 11½*
692 A223 1fr multicolored .20 .20
693 A223 1fr multicolored .20 .20

Issued for the Charles Plisnier and Lodewijk de Raet Foundations.

Engraved and Photogravure

1967, Sept. 30 *Perf. 11½*

Arms of Universities: #694, Ghent. #695, Liege.

694 A224 3fr gray & multi .20 .20
695 A224 3fr gray & multi .20 .20

Universities of Ghent and Liège, 150th anniv.

Princess Margaret of York — A225

"Virga Jesse," Hasselt — A226

1967, Sept. 30 Photo.
696 A225 6fr multicolored .30 .25

British Week, Sept. 28-Oct. 2.

1967, Nov. 11 Engr. *Perf. 11½*
697 A226 1fr slate blue .20 .20

Christmas, 1967.

Hand Guarding Worker — A227

Military Mailman, 1916, by James Thiriar — A228

1968, Feb. 3 Photo. *Perf. 11½*
698 A227 3fr multicolored .20 .20

Issued to publicize industrial safety.

Engraved and Photogravure

1968, Mar. 17 *Perf. 11½*
699 A228 3fr sepia, lt bl & brn .20 .20

Issued for Stamp Day, 1968.

View of Grammont and Seal of Baudouin VI — A229

Stamp of 1866, No. 23 — A230

Historic Sites: 3fr, Theux-Franchimont fortress, sword and seal. 6fr, Neolithic cave and artifacts, Spiennes. 10fr, Roman oil lamp and St. Medard's Church, Wervik.

1968, Apr. 13 Photo. *Perf. 11½*
700 A229 2fr bl, blk, lil & rose .20 .20
701 A229 3fr orange, blk & car .20 .20
702 A229 6fr ultra, ind & bis .25 .20
703 A229 10fr tan, blk, yel & gray .35 .30
Nos. 700-703 (4) 1.00 .90

1968, Apr. 13 Engr. *Perf. 13*
704 A230 1fr black .20 .20

Centenary of the Malines Stamp Printery.

Europa Issue, 1968
Common Design Type

1968, Apr. 27 Photo. *Perf. 11½*
Size: 35x24mm
705 CD11 3fr dl grn, gold & blk .20 .20
706 CD11 6fr carmine, sil & blk .35 .25

St. Laurent Abbey, Liège A232

Designs: 3fr, Gothic Church, Lissweghe. No. 709. Barges in Zandvliet locks. No. 710, Ship in Neuzen lock, Ghent Canal. 10fr, Ronquieres canal ship lift.

Engraved and Photogravure

1968, Sept. 7 *Perf. 11½*
707 A232 2fr ultra, gray ol & sep .20 .20
708 A232 3fr ol bis, gray & sep .20 .20
709 A232 6fr ind, brt bl & sep .30 .20
710 A232 6fr black, grnsh bl & ol .25 .20
711 A232 10fr bister, brt bl & sep .50 .30
Nos. 707-711 (5) 1.45 1.10

No. 710 issued Dec. 14 for opening of lock at Neuzen, Netherlands.

Christmas Candle — A233

1968, Dec. 7 *Perf. 11½*
712 A233 1fr multicolored .20 .20

Christmas, 1968.

St. Albertus Magnus — A234

1969, Feb. 15 Engr. *Perf. 11½*
713 A234 2fr sepia .20 .20

The Church of St. Paul in Antwerp (16th century) was destroyed by fire in Apr. 1968.

Ruins of Aulne Abbey, Gozee A235

1969, Feb. 15 Engr. & Photo.
714 A235 3fr brt pink & blk .20 .20

Aulne Abbey was destroyed in 1794 during the French Revolution.

The Travelers, Roman Sculpture A236

Broodjes Chapel, Antwerp A237

1969, Mar. 15 Engr. *Perf. 11½*
715 A236 2fr violet brown .20 .20

2,000th anniversary of city of Arlon.

1969, Mar. 15 Engr. & Photo.
716 A237 3fr gray & blk .20 .20

150th anniv. of public education in Antwerp.

Post Office Train — A238

1969, Apr. 13 Photo. *Perf. 11½*
717 A238 3fr multicolored .20 .20

Issued for Stamp Day.

Europa Issue, 1969
Common Design Type

1969, Apr. 26
Size: 35x24mm
718 CD12 3fr lt grn, brn & blk .20 .20
719 CD12 6fr salmon, rose car & blk .30 .30

NATO Type of 1959 Redrawn and Dated "1949-1969"

1969, May 31 Photo. *Perf. 11½*
720 A142 6fr org brn & ultra .30 .30

20th anniv. of NATO. No. 720 inscribed Belgique-Belgie and OTAN-NAVO.

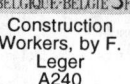

Construction Workers, by F. Leger A240

Bicyclist A241

1969, May 31
721 A240 3fr multicolored .20 .20

50th anniversary of the ILO.

1969, July 5 Photo. *Perf. 11½*
722 A241 6fr rose & multi .30 .25

World Bicycling Road Championships, Terlaemen to Zolder, Aug. 10.

Ribbon in Benelux Colors — A242

1969, Sept. 6 Photo. *Perf. 11½*
723 A242 3fr blk, red, ultra & yel .20 .20

25th anniv. of the signing of the customs union of Belgium, Netherlands and Luxembourg.

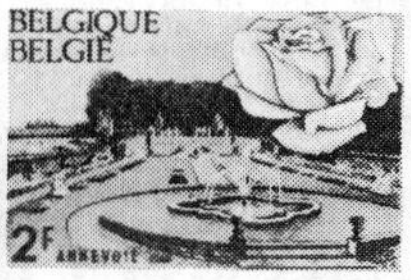
Annevoie Garden and Pascali Rose — A243

Design: No. 725, Lochristi Garden and begonia.

1969, Sept. 6
724 A243 2fr multicolored .20 .20
725 A243 2fr multicolored .20 .20

Armstrong, Collins, Aldrin and Map Showing Tranquillity Base — A245

1969, Sept. 20 Photo.
726 A245 6fr black .30 .25

See note after Algeria #427. See #B846.

Wounded Veteran A246

Mailman A247

1969, Oct. 11 Engr. *Perf. 11½*
727 A246 1fr blue gray .20 .20

Natl. war veterans' aid organization (O.N.I.G.). The design is similar to type SP10.

1969, Oct. 18 Photo.
728 A247 1fr deep rose & multi .20 .20

Issued to publicize youth philately. Design by Danielle Saintenoy, 14.

Kennedy Tunnel Under the Schelde, Antwerp A248

6fr, Three highways crossing near Loncin.

1969, Nov. 8 Engr. *Perf. 11½*
729 A248 3fr multicolored .25 .20
730 A248 6fr multicolored .30 .30

Issued to publicize the John F. Kennedy Tunnel under the Schelde and the Walloon auto route and interchange near Loncin.

Henry Carton de Wiart, by Gaston Geleyn — A249

1969, Nov. 8
731 A249 6fr sepia .30 .20

Count de Wiart (1869-1951), statesman.

The Census at Bethlehem (detail), by Peter Brueghel A250

1969, Dec. 13 Photo.
732 A250 1.50fr multicolored .20 .20

Christmas, 1969.

Symbols of Bank's Activity, 100fr Coin — A251

1969, Dec. 13 Engr. & Photo.
733 A251 3.50fr lt ultra, blk & sil .20 .20

50th anniv. of the Industrial Credit Bank (Societe nationale de credit a l'industrie).

Camellia A252

Beeches in Botanical Garden A253

1970, Jan. 31 Photo. *Perf. 11½*
734 A252 1.50fr shown .20 .20
735 A252 2.50fr Water lily .20 .20
736 A252 3.50fr Azalea .20 .20
a. Souvenir sheet of 3, #734-736 2.00 2.00
Nos. 734-736 (3) .60 .60

Ghent Int'l Flower Exhibition. No. 736a was issued Apr. 25 and sold for 25fr.

1970, Mar. 7 Engr. & Photo.
737 A253 3.50fr shown .20 .20
738 A253 7fr Birches .30 .30

European Nature Conservation Year.

Mailman A254

1970, Apr. 4 Photo.
739 A254 1.50fr multicolored .20 .20

Issued for Youth Stamp Day.

New UPU Headquarters and Monument, Bern — A255

1970, Apr. 12 Engr. & Photo.
740 A255 3.50fr grn & lt grn .30 .20

Opening of the new UPU Headquarters, Bern.

Europa Issue, 1970
Common Design Type

1970, May 1 Photo. *Perf. 11½*
Size: 35x24mm
741 CD13 3.50fr rose cl, yel & blk .20 .20
742 CD13 7fr ultra, pink & blk .40 .30

Cooperative Alliance Emblem — A257

1970, June 27 Photo. *Perf. 11½*
743 A257 7fr black & org .30 .20

Intl. Cooperative Alliance, 75th anniv.

Ship in Ghent Terneuzen Lock, Zelzate A258

Design: No. 745, Clock Tower, Virton, vert.

1970, June 27 Engr. & Photo.
744 A258 2.50fr indigo & lt bl .20 .20
745 A258 2.50fr dk pur & ocher .20 .20

King Baudouin — A259

1970-80 Engr. *Perf. 11½*
746 A259 1.75fr green ('71) .25 .20
747 A259 2.25fr gray grn ('72) .35 .20
748 A259 2.50fr gray grn ('74) .20 .20
749 A259 3fr emerald ('73) 3.00 2.00
750 A259 3.25fr violet brn ('75) .20 .20
751 A259 3.50fr orange brn .25 .20
752 A259 3.50fr brown ('71) .25 .20
753 A259 4fr blue ('72) .35 .20
754 A259 4.50fr brown ('72) .25 .20
755 A259 4.50fr grnsh bl ('74) .25 .20
756 A259 5fr lilac ('72) .25 .20
757 A259 6fr rose car ('72) .30 .20
758 A259 6.50fr vio blk ('74) .35 .20
759 A259 7fr ver ('71) .35 .20
760 A259 7.50fr brt pink ('75) .35 .20
761 A259 8fr black ('72) .35 .20
762 A259 9fr ol bis ('71) .60 .20
763 A259 9fr red brn ('80) .45 .20
764 A259 10fr rose car ('71) .50 .20
765 A259 11fr gray ('76) .50 .20
766 A259 12fr Prus bl ('72) .60 .20
767 A259 13fr slate ('75) .70 .20
768 A259 14fr gray grn ('76) .65 .20
769 A259 15fr lt vio ('71) .70 .20
770 A259 16fr green ('77) .70 .20
771 A259 17fr dull mag ('75) .80 .20
772 A259 18fr steel bl ('71) 1.00 .20
773 A259 18fr grnsh bl ('80) .90 .20
774 A259 20fr vio bl ('71) 1.00 .20
775 A259 22fr black ('74) 1.40 1.25
776 A259 22fr lt grn ('79) 1.10 .20
777 A259 25fr lilac ('75) 1.25 .20
778 A259 30fr ocher ('72) 1.50 .20
779 A259 35fr emer ('80) 1.50 .20
780 A259 40fr dk blue ('77) 2.00 .20
781 A259 45fr brown ('80) 2.25 .20

Perf. 12½x13½
Photo.
Size: 22x17mm
782 A259 3fr emerald ('73) 3.00 2.50
a. Booklet pane of 4 (#782 and 3 #783) + labels 10.00
783 A259 4fr blue ('73) .70 .60
784 A259 4.50fr grnsh bl ('75) .40 .30
785 A259 5fr lilac ('73) .25 .20
a. Booklet pane of 4 + labels 2.75
786 A259 6fr carmine ('78) .30 .20
787 A259 6.50fr dull pur ('75) .45 .20
788 A259 8fr gray ('78) .35 .20
Nos. 746-788 (43) 32.85 14.25

No. 751 issued Sept. 7, 1970, King Baudouin's 40th birthday, and is inscribed "1930-1970." Dates are omitted on other stamps of type A259.

Nos. 754, 756 also issued in coils in 1973 and Nos. 757, 761 in 1978, with black control number on back of every fifth stamp.

Nos. 782-788 issued in booklets only. Nos. 782, 784 have one straight-edge, Nos. 786, 788 have two. The rest have one or two. Stamps in the panes are tete-beche. Each pane has two labels showing Belgian Postal emblem with a large selvage with postal code instructions. Nos. 786, 788 not luminescent.

See designs M2, O4. See Nos. 432a, 432b, 977a, 977b.

UN Headquarters, NY — A260

Fair Emblem — A261

1970, Sept. 12 Engr. & Photo.
789 A260 7fr dk brn & Prus bl .30 .20

25th anniversary of the United Nations.

1970, Sept. 19
790 A261 1.50fr bister, org & brn .20 .20

Issued to publicize the 25th International Fair at Ghent, Sept. 12-27.

Queen Fabiola — A262

The Mason, by Georges Minne — A263

1970, Sept. 19
791 A262 3.50fr lt blue & blk .20 .20

Issued to publicize the Queen Fabiola Foundation for Mental Health.

1970, Oct. 17 ***Perf. 11½***
792 A263 3.50fr dull yel & sep .20 .20

50th anniv. of the National Housing Society.

Man, Woman and City — A264

1970, Oct. 17 **Photo.**
793 A264 2.50fr black & multi .20 .20

Social Security System, 25th anniv.

Madonna with the Grapes, by Jean Gossaert — A265

1970, Nov. 14 **Engr.** ***Perf. 11½***
794 A265 1.50fr dark brown .20 .20

Christmas 1970.

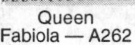

Arms of Eupen, Malmédy and Saint-Vith A266

Engraved and Photogravure

1970, Dec. 12 ***Perf. 11½***
795 A266 7fr sepia & dk brn .30 .20

The 50th anniversary of the return of the districts of Eupen, Malmédy and Saint-Vith.

Automatic Telephone A267

Touring Club Emblem A269

"Auto" A268

1971, Jan. 16 **Photo.** ***Perf. 11½***
796 A267 1.50fr multicolored .20 .20

Automatization of Belgian telephone system.

1971, Jan. 16
797 A268 2.50fr carmine & blk .20 .20

50th Automobile Show, Brussels, Jan. 19-31.

1971, Feb. 13
798 A269 3.50fr ultra & multi .20 .20

Belgian Touring Club, 75th anniversary.

Tournai Cathedral A270

1971, Feb. 13 **Engr.**
799 A270 7fr bright blue .30 .20

Cathedral of Tournai, 8th centenary.

"The Letter Box," by T. Lobrichon — A271

1971, Mar. 13 **Engr.** ***Perf. 11½***
800 A271 1.50fr dark brown .20 .20

Youth philately.

Albert I, Jules Destrée and Academy — A272

Engraved and Photogravure

1971, Apr. 17 ***Perf. 11½***
801 A272 7fr gray & blk .30 .20

50th anniversary of the founding of the Royal Academy of Language and French Literature.

Stamp Day — A273

1971, Apr. 25
802 A273 3.50fr Mailman .20 .20

Europa Issue, 1971

Common Design Type

1971, May 1 **Photo.**

Size: 35x24mm

803 CD14 3.50fr olive & blk .25 .20
804 CD14 7fr dk ol grn & blk .35 .20

Radar Ground Station A275

1971, May 15 **Photo.** ***Perf. 11½***
805 A275 7fr multicolored .30 .20

3rd World Telecommunications Day.

Antarctic Explorer, Ship and Penguins — A276

1971, June 19 **Photo.** ***Perf. 11½***
806 A276 10fr multicolored .50 .50

Tenth anniversary of the Antarctic Treaty pledging peaceful uses of and scientific cooperation in Antarctica.

A277

A278

1971, June 26 **Engr.** ***Perf. 11½***
807 A277 2.50fr Orval Abbey .20 .20

9th cent. of the Abbey of Notre Dame, Orval.

1971, June 26 **Engr. & Photo.**
808 A278 1.50fr vio bl & blk .20 .20

Georges Hubin (1863-1947), socialist leader and Minister of State.

Mr. and Mrs. Goliath, the Giants of Ath — A279

View of Ghent A280

1971, Aug. 7 **Photo.**
809 A279 2.50fr multicolored .20 .20

Engr.

810 A280 2.50fr gray brown .20 .20

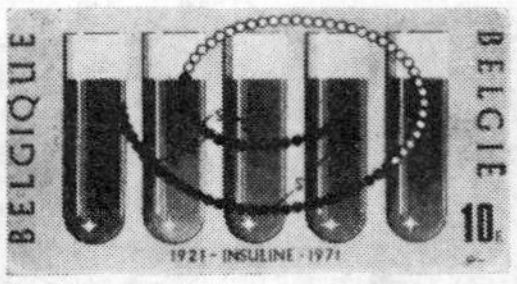

Test Tubes and Insulin Molecular Diagram — A281

1971, Aug. 7 **Photo.**
811 A281 10fr lt gray & multi .40 .30

50th anniversary of the discovery of insulin.

Family and "50" — A283

1971, Sept. 11 **Photo.**
812 A283 1.50fr green & multi .20 .20

Belgian Large Families League, 50th anniv.

Achaemenidaen Tomb, Buzpar, and Persian Coat of Arms — A284

Engraved and Photogravure

1971, Oct. 2 ***Perf. 11½***
813 A284 7fr multicolored .30 .20

2500th anniversary of the founding of the Persian empire by Cyrus the Great.

Dr. Jules Bordet A285

Flight into Egypt, Anonymous A286

Portrait: No. 815, Stijn Streuvels.

1971, Oct. 2 **Engr.**
814 A285 3.50fr slate green .20 .20
815 A285 3.50fr dark brown .20 .20

No. 814 honors Dr. Jules Bordet (1870-1945), serologist and immunologist; No. 815, Stijn Streuvels (1871-1945), novelist whose pen name was Frank Lateur.

1971, Nov. 13 **Photo.**
816 A286 1.50fr multicolored .20 .20

Christmas 1971.

Federation Emblem
A287

Book Year Emblem
A288

1971, Nov. 13
817 A287 3.50fr black, ultra & gold .20 .20

25th anniversary of the Federation of Belgian Industries (FIB).

1972, Feb. 19
818 A288 7fr bister, blk & bl .30 .20

International Book Year 1972.

Coins of Belgium and Luxembourg
A289

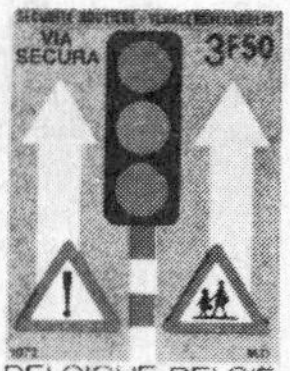

Traffic Signal and Road Signs
A290

1972, Feb. 19 **Engr. & Photo.**
819 A289 1.50fr orange, blk & sil .20 .20

Economic Union of Belgium and Luxembourg, 50th anniversary.

1972, Feb. 19 **Photo.**
820 A290 3.50fr blue & multi .20 .20

Via Secura (road safety), 25th anniversary.

Belgica '72 Emblem
A291

1972, Mar. 27
821 A291 3.50fr choc, bl & lil .20 .20

International Philatelic Exhibition, Brussels, June 24-July 9.

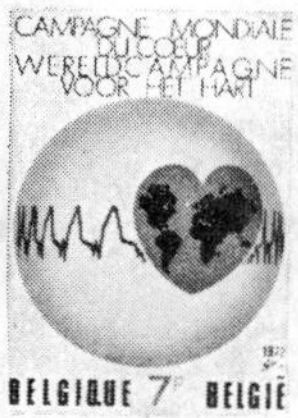

"Your Heart is your Health"
A292

Auguste Vermeylen
A293

1972, Mar. 27
822 A292 7fr blk, gray, red & bl .25 .20

World Health Day.

1972, Mar. 27
823 A293 2.50fr multicolored .20 .20

Centenary of the birth of Auguste Vermeylen (1872-1945), Flemish writer and educator. Portrait by Isidore Opsomer.

A294

A296

1972, Apr. 23
824 A294 3.50fr Astronaut on Moon .20 .20

Stamp Day 1972.

Europa Issue 1972
Common Design Type

1972, Apr. 29
Size: 24x35mm

825 CD15 3.50fr light blue & multi .20 .20
826 CD15 7fr rose & multi .40 .30

1972, May 13 **Photo.** ***Perf. 11½***
827 A296 2.50fr "Freedom of the Press" .20 .20

50th anniv. of the BELGA news information agency and 25th Congress of the Intl. Federation of Newspaper Editors (F.I.E.J.), Brussels, May 15-19.

Freight Cars with Automatic Coupling
A297

1972, June 3
828 A297 7fr blue & multi .30 .20

Intl. Railroad Union, 50th anniv.

View of Couvin — A298

No. 830, Aldeneik Church, Maaseik, vert.

1972, June 24 **Engr.** ***Perf. 13½x14***
829 A298 2.50fr bl, vio brn & sl grn .20 .20
830 A298 2.50fr dk brown & bl .20 .20

Beatrice, by Gustave de Smet
A299

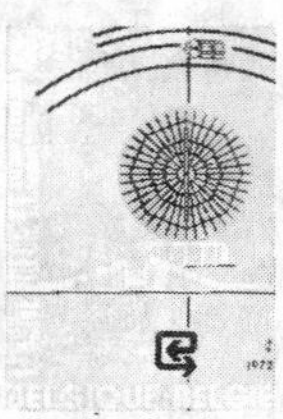

Radar Station, Intelsat 4
A300

1972, Sept. 9 **Photo.** ***Perf. 11½***
831 A299 3fr multicolored .20 .20

Youth philately.

1972, Sept. 16
832 A300 3.50fr lt bl, sil & blk .20 .20

Opening of the Lessive satellite earth station.

Frans Masereel, Self-portrait
A301

Adoration of the Kings, by Felix Timmermans
A302

1972, Oct. 21
833 A301 4.50fr lt olive & blk .20 .20

Frans Masereel (1889-1972), wood engraver.

1972, Nov. 11 **Photo.** ***Perf. 11½***
834 A302 3.50fr black & multi .20 .20

Christmas 1972.

Maria Theresa, Anonymous
A303

1972, Dec. 16 **Photo.** ***Perf. 11½***
835 A303 2fr multicolored .20 .20

200th anniversary of the Belgian Academy of Science, Literature and Art, founded by Empress Maria Theresa.

WMO Emblem, Meteorological Institute, Ukkel — A304

1973, Mar. 24 **Photo.** ***Perf. 11½***
836 A304 9fr blue & multi .40 .20

Cent. of intl. meteorological cooperation.

"Fire"
A305

Man and WHO Emblem
A306

1973, Mar. 24
837 A305 2fr multicolored .20 .20

Natl. industrial fire prevention campaign.

1973, Apr. 7
838 A306 8fr dk red, ocher & blk .30 .25

25th anniv. of WHO.

Europa Issue 1973
Common Design Type

1973, Apr. 28
Size: 35x24mm

839 CD16 4.50fr org brn, vio bl & yel .25 .20
840 CD16 8fr olive, dk bl & yel .55 .45

Thurn and Taxis Courier — A308

Arrows Circling Globe — A309

Engraved and Photogravure

1973, Apr. 28 ***Perf. 11½***
841 A308 4.50fr black & red brn .20 .20

Stamp Day.

1973, May 12 **Photo.**
842 A309 3.50fr dp ocher & multi .20 .20

5th International Telecommunications Day.

Workers' Sports Exhibition Poster, Ghent, 1913 — A310

1973, May 12
843 A310 4.50fr multicolored .20 .20

60th anniversary of the International Workers' Sports Movement.

Fair Emblem
A311

1973, May 12 **Photo.** ***Perf. 11½***
844 A311 4.50fr multicolored .20 .20

25th International Fair, Liege, May 12-27.

DC-10 and 1923 Biplane over Brussels Airport — A312

Design: 10fr, Tips biplane, 1908.

1973, May 19 **Engr. & Photo.**
845 A312 8fr gray bl, blk & ultra .30 .20
846 A312 10fr grn, lt bl & blk .45 .35

50th anniv. of SABENA, Belgian airline (8fr) and 25th anniv. of the "Vieilles Tiges" Belgian flying pioneers' society (10fr).

Adolphe Sax and Tenor Saxophone
A313

Fresco from Bathhouse, Ostend
A314

1973, Sept. 15 **Photo.**
847 A313 9fr green, blk & bl .40 .20

Adolphe Sax (1814-1894), inventor of saxophone.

1973, Sept. 15
848 A314 4.50fr multicolored .25 .20

Year of the Spa.

St. Nicholas Church, Eupen
A315

Charley, by Henri Evenepoel
A316

Designs: No. 850, Town Hall, Leau. No. 851, Aarshot Church. No. 852, Chiman Castle. No. 853, Gemmenich Border: Belgium, Germany, Netherlands. No. 854, St. Monan and church, Nassogne. No. 855, Church tower, Dottignes. No. 856, Grand-Place, Sint-Truiden.

1973-75 **Engr.** ***Perf. 13***

849	A315	2fr plum, sep & lt vio	.20	.20
850	A315	3fr black, lt bl & mar	.50	.20
851	A315	3fr brn blk & yel	.30	.20
852	A315	4fr grnsh blk & grnsh bl	.35	.20
853	A315	4fr grnsh blk & bl	.40	.20
854	A315	4fr grnsh blk & bl	.40	.20
855	A315	4.50fr multicolored	.50	.20
856	A315	5fr multicolored	.50	.20
	Nos. 849-856 (8)		3.15	1.60

Nos. 851, 855 not luminescent. Nos. 850, 852-854, 856 horiz.

1973, Oct. 13 **Photo.** ***Perf. 11½***
857 A316 3fr multicolored .20 .20

Youth philately.

Luminescent Paper
Starting with No. 858, all stamps are on luminescent paper unless otherwise noted.

Jean-Baptiste Moens
A317

1973, Oct. 13 **Engr. & Photo.**
858 A317 10fr gray & multi .40 .20

50th anniversary of the Belgian Stamp Dealers' Association. Printed in sheets of 12 stamps and 12 labels showing association emblem.

Adoration of the Shepherds, by Hugo van der Goes
A318

Louis Pierard, by M. I. Ianchelevici
A319

1973, Nov. 17 **Engr.** ***Perf. 11½***
859 A318 4fr blue .20 .20

Christmas 1973.

1973, Nov. 17 **Engr. & Photo.**
860 A319 4fr vermilion & buff .25 .20

Louis Pierard (1886-1952), journalist, member of Parliament.

Highway, Automobile Club Emblem
A320

1973, Nov. 17 **Photo.**
861 A320 5fr yellow & multi .25 .20

Flemish Automobile Club, 50th anniv.

Early Microphone, Emblem of Radio Belgium — A321

1973, Nov. 24 **Engr. & Photo.**
862 A321 4fr blue & black .20 .20

50th anniversary of Radio Belgium.

Felicien Rops, Self-portrait
A323

Engraved and Photogravure

1973, Dec. 8 ***Perf. 11½***
863 A323 7fr tan & black .30 .20

Felicien Rops (1833-1898), painter and engraver.

King Albert, (1875-1934)
A324

Sun, Bird, Flowers and Girl
A325

1974, Feb. 16 **Photo.** ***Perf. 11½***
864 A324 4fr Prus green & blk .25 .20

1974, Mar. 25 **Photo.** ***Perf. 11½***
865 A325 3fr violet & multi .20 .20

Protection of the environment.

NATO Emblem
A326

1974, Apr. 20 **Photo.** ***Perf. 11½***
866 A326 10fr dp to lt blue .45 .25

25th anniversary of the signing of the North Atlantic Treaty.

Hubert Krains — A327

"Destroyed City," by Ossip Zadkine — A328

1974, Apr. 27 **Engr. & Photo.**
867 A327 5fr black & gray .20 .20

Stamp Day.

Europa Issue 1974

1974, May 4

Design: 10fr, Solidarity, by Georges Minne.

868 A328 5fr black & red .25 .20
869 A328 10fr black & ultra .60 .30

Children
A329

1974, May 18 **Photo.** ***Perf. 11½***
870 A329 4fr lt blue & multi .20 .20

10th Lay Youth Festival.

Planetarium, Brussels
A330

Soleilmont Abbey Ruins — A331

Designs: 4fr, Pillory, Braine-le-Chateau. 7fr, Fountain, Ghent (procession symbolic of Chamber of Rhetoric). 10fr, Belfry, Bruges, vert.

Engr. and Photo.

1974, June 22 ***Perf. 11½***

871	A330	3fr sky blue & blk	.20	.20
872	A330	4fr lilac rose & blk	.20	.20
873	A331	5fr lt green & blk	.30	.20
874	A331	7fr dull yellow & blk	.35	.20
875	A330	10fr black, blue & brn	.45	.20
	Nos. 871-875 (5)		1.50	1.00

Historic buildings and monuments.

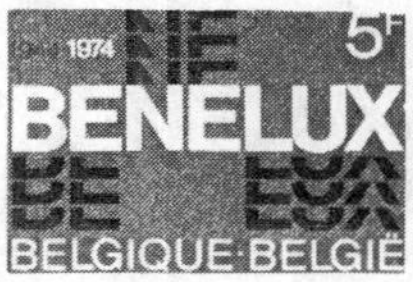

"BENELUX"
A332

1974, Sept. 7 **Photo.** ***Perf. 11½***
876 A332 5fr bl grn, dk grn & lt bl .25 .20

30th anniversary of the signing of the customs union of Belgium, Netherlands and Luxembourg.

Jan Vekemans, by Cornelis de Vos — A333

1974, Sept. 14
877 A333 3fr multicolored .20 .20

Youth philately.

Leon Tresignies, Willebroek Canal Bridge
A334

1974, Sept. 28 **Engr. & Photo.**
878 A334 4fr brn & ol grn .20 .20

60th death anniversary of Corporal Leon Tresignies (1886-1914), hero of World War I.

Montgomery Blair, UPU Emblem
A335

10fr, Heinrich von Stephan and UPU emblem.

1974, Oct. 5 ***Perf. 11½***
879 A335 5fr green & blk .20 .20
880 A335 10fr brick red & blk .40 .30

Centenary of Universal Postal Union.

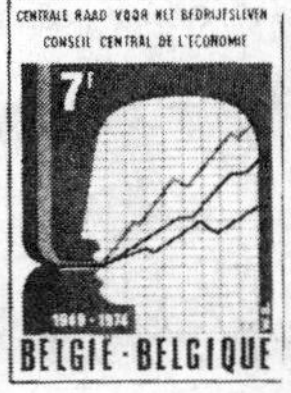

Symbolic Chart — A336

1974, Oct. 12 **Photo.** ***Perf. 11½***
881 A336 7fr multicolored .30 .20

Central Economic Council, 25th anniv.

Rotary Emblem
A337

1974, Oct. 19
882 A337 10fr multicolored .40 .20

Rotary International of Belgium.

A338

A341

Wild boar (regiment's emblem).

1974, Oct. 26
883 A338 3fr multicolored .20 .20

Granting of the colors to the Ardennes Chasseurs Regiment, 40th anniversary.

1974, Nov. 16 ***Perf. 11½***

Angel, by Van Eyck brothers.

884 A341 4fr rose lilac .20 .20

Christmas 1974. The Angel shown is from the triptyque "The Mystical Lamb" in the Saint-Bavon Cathedral, Ghent.

A342

A343

Adolphe Quetelet, by J. Odevaere.

1974, Dec. 14 **Engr. & Photo.**

885 A342 10fr black & buff .40 .20

Death centenary of Adolphe Quetelet (1796-1874), statistician, astronomer and Secretary of Royal Academy of Brussels.

1975, Feb. 15 **Photo.** ***Perf. 11½***

912 A343 6.50fr Themabelga emblem .30 .20

Themabelga, International Thematic Stamp Exhibition, Brussels, Dec. 13-21, 1975.

A344

A345

1975, Feb. 22

913 A344 4.50fr Neoregelia carolinae .25 .20

Photogravure and Engraved

914 A344 5fr Coltsfoot .25 .20
915 A344 6.50fr Azalea .30 .20
Nos. 913-915 (3) .80 .60

Ghent Intl. Flower Exhib., Apr. 26-May 5.

1975, Mar. 15 ***Perf. 11½***

School emblem, man Leading boy.

916 A345 4.50fr black & multi .20 .20

Centenary of the founding of the Charles Buls Normal School for Boys, Brussels.

Davids Foundation Emblem A346

1975, Mar. 22 **Photo.**

917 A346 5fr yellow & multi .25 .20

Centenary of the Davids Foundation, a Catholic organization for the promotion of Flemish through education and books.

King Albert (1875-1934) A347

Mailman, 1840, by James Thiriar A348

1975, Apr. 5 **Engr. & Photo.**

918 A347 10fr black & maroon .45 .25

1975, Apr. 19 **Engr.** ***Perf. 11½***

919 A348 6.50fr dull magenta .30 .20

Stamp Day 1975.

St. John, from Last Supper, by Bouts A349

Concentration Camp Symbols A350

Europa: 10fr, Woman's Head, detail from "Trial by Fire," by Dirk Bouts.

1975, Apr. 26 **Engr. & Photo.**

920 A349 6.50fr black, grn & blue .35 .20
921 A349 10fr black, ocher & red .60 .30

1975, May 3 **Photo.**

Design: "B" denoted political prisoners, "KG" prisoners of war.

922 A350 4.50fr multicolored .20 .20

Liberation of concentration camps, 30th anniv.

Hospice of St. John, Bruges A351

Church of St. Loup, Namur — A352

Design: 10fr, Martyrs' Square, Brussels.

1975, May 12 **Engr.** ***Perf. 11½***

926 A351 4.50fr deep rose lilac .25 .20
927 A352 5fr slate green .25 .20
928 A351 10fr bright blue .45 .30
Nos. 926-928 (3) .95 .70

European Architectural Heritage Year.

Library, Louvain University, Ryckmans and Cerfaux A355

1975, June 7 **Photo.** ***Perf. 11½***

931 A355 10fr dull blue & sepia .40 .20

25th anniversary of Louvain Bible Colloquium, founded by Professors Gonzague Ryckmans (1887-1969) and Lucien Cerfaux (1883-1968).

"Metamorphose" by Pol Mara — A356

Marie Popelin, Palace of Justice, Brussels — A357

1975, June 14

932 A356 7fr multicolored .30 .20

Queen Fabiola Mental Health Foundation.

1975, June 21 **Engr. & Photo.**

933 A357 6.50fr green & claret .30 .20

International Women's Year 1975. Marie Popelin (1846-1913), first Belgian woman doctor of law.

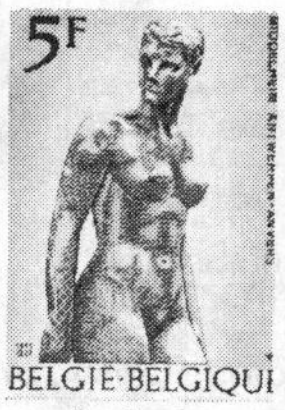

Assia, by Charles Despiau A358

Cornelia Vekemans, by Cornelis de Vos A359

1975, Sept. 6 ***Perf. 11½***

934 A358 5fr yellow grn & blk .25 .20

Middelheim Outdoor Museum, 25th anniv.

1975, Sept. 20 **Photo.**

935 A359 4.50fr multicolored .20 .20

Youth philately.

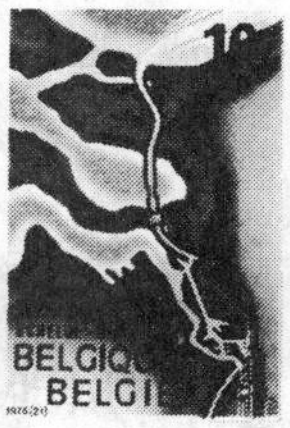
Map of Schelde-Rhine Canal — A360

1975, Sept. 20

936 A360 10fr multicolored .45 .25

Opening of connection between the Schelde and Rhine, Sept. 23, 1975.

National Bank, W. F. Orban, Founder A361

Photogravure and Engraved

1975, Oct. 11 ***Perf. 12½x13***

937 A361 25fr multicolored 1.00 .30

Natl. Bank of Belgium, 125th anniv.

Edmond Thieffry and Plane, 1925 — A362

1975, Oct. 18 ***Perf. 11½***

938 A362 7fr black & lilac .30 .20

First flight Brussels to Kinshasa, Congo, 50th anniversary.

"Seat of Wisdom" St. Peter's, Louvain — A363

1975, Nov. 8 ***Perf. 11½***

939 A363 6.50fr blue, blk & grn .30 .20

University of Louvain, 550th anniversary.

Angels, by Rogier van der Weyden A364

1975, Nov. 15

940 A364 5fr multicolored .25 .20

Christmas 1975.

Willemsfonds Emblem A365

American Bicentennial Emblem A366

1976, Feb. 21 **Photo.** ***Perf. 11½***

941 A365 5fr multicolored .25 .20

125th anniversary of the Willems Foundation, which supports Flemish language and literature.

1976, Mar. 13 **Photo.** ***Perf. 11½***

942 A366 14fr gold, red, bl & blk .60 .30

American Bicentennial. No. 942 printed checkerwise in sheets of 30 stamps and 30 gold and black labels which show medal with 1626 seal of New York. Black engraved inscription on labels commemorates arrival of first Walloon settlers in Nieu Nederland.

20-Cent Minimum Value

The minimum catalogue value is 20 cents. Separating se-tenant pieces into individual stamps does not increase the value of the stamps since demand for the separated stamps may be small.

Cardinal Mercier — A367

Symbolic of V.E.V. — A368

1976, Mar. 20 **Engr.**

943 A367 4.50fr brt rose lilac .20 .20

Desire Joseph Cardinal Mercier (1851-1926), professor at Louvain University, spiritual and patriotic leader during World War I, 50th death anniversary.

1976, Apr. 3 **Photo.** ***Perf. 11½***

944 A368 6.50fr multicolored .30 .20

Flemish Economic Organization (Vlaams Ekonomisch Verbond), 50th anniversary.

General Post Office, Brussels A369

1976, Apr. 24 **Engr.** ***Perf. 11½***

945 A369 6.50fr sepia .30 .20

Stamp Day.

Potter's Hands A370

Europa: 6.50fr, Basket maker, vert.

1976, May 8 **Photo.**

946 A370 6.50fr multicolored .45 .20

947 A370 14fr multicolored .65 .40

Truck on Road A371

1976, May 8

948 A371 14fr black, yel & red .65 .35

15th Intl. Road Union Cong., Brussels, May 9-13.

Queen Elisabeth (1876-1965) — A372

1976, May 24 ***Perf. 11½***

949 A372 14fr green .60 .30

Ardennes Draft Horses A373

1976, June 19

950 A373 5fr multicolored .25 .20

Ardennes Draft Horses Association, 50th anniversary.

Souvenir Sheets

King Baudouin — A374

1976, June 26

951	A374	Sheet of 3	2.50	.50
a.		4.50fr gray	.70	.70
b.		6.50fr ocher	.70	.70
c.		10fr brick red	.70	.70
952	A374	Sheet of 2	3.50	3.50
a.		20fr yellow green	.85	.85
b.		30fr Prussian blue	.85	.85

25th anniv. of the reign of King Baudouin. No. 951 sold for 30fr, No. 952 for 70fr. The surtax went to a new foundation for the improvement of living conditions in honor of the King.

Electric Train and Society Emblem — A375

1976, Sept. 11 **Photo.** ***Perf. 11½***

953 A375 6.50fr multi .30 .20

Natl. Belgian Railroad Soc., 50th anniv.

William of Nassau, Prince of Orange — A376

1976, Sept. 11 **Engr.**

954 A376 10fr slate green .40 .20

400th anniv. of the pacification of Ghent.

New Subway Train — A377

1976, Sept. 18 **Photo.**

955 A377 6.50fr multi .30 .20

Opening of first line of Brussels subway.

Young Musician, by W. C. Duyster — A378

1976, Oct. 2 **Photo.** ***Perf. 11½***

956 A378 4.50fr multi .20 .20

Young musicians and youth philately.

Charles Bernard — A379

St. Jerome in the Mountains, by Le Patinier — A380

Blind Leading the Blind, by Breughel the Elder A381

#958, Fernand Victor Toussaint van Boelaere.

1976, Oct. 16 **Engr.**

957	A379	5fr	violet	.20	.20
958	A379	5fr	red brn & sepia	.20	.20
959	A380	6.50fr	dark brown	.30	.20
960	A381	6.50fr	slate green	.30	.20
			Nos. 957-960 (4)	1.00	.80

Charles Bernard (1875-1961), French-speaking journalist; Toussaint van Boelaere (1875-1947), Flemish journalist; No. 959, Charles Plisnier Belgian-French Cultural Society. No. 960, Assoc. for Language Promotion.

Remouchamps Caves — A382

Hunnegem Priory, Gramont, and Madonna A383

Designs: No. 963, River Lys and St. Martin's Church. No. 964, Ham-sur-Heure Castle.

1976, Oct. 23 **Engr.** ***Perf. 13***

961	A382	4.50fr	multi	.20	.20
962	A383	4.50fr	multi	.20	.20
963	A383	5fr	multi	.25	.20
964	A383	5fr	multi	.25	.20
			Nos. 961-964 (4)	.90	.80

Tourism. #961-962 are not luminescent.

Nativity, by Master of Flemalle — A384

1976, Nov. 20 ***Perf. 11½***

965 A384 5fr violet .25 .20

Christmas 1976.

Rubens' Monogram — A385

1977, Feb. 12 **Photo. & Engr.**

966 A385 6.50fr lilac & blk .30 .20

Peter Paul Rubens (1577-1640), painter.

Heraldic Lion — A386

1977-85 **Typo.** ***Perf. 13½x14***

Size: 17x20mm

967	A386	50c	brn ('80)	.20	.20
a.			50c orange brown ('85)	.20	.20
968	A386	1fr	brt lil	.20	.20
a.			1fr bright rose lilac ('84)	.20	.20
969	A386	1.50fr	gray ('78)	.20	.20
970	A386	2fr	yel ('78)	.20	.20
970A	A386	2.50fr	yel grn ('81)	.20	.20
971	A386	2.75fr	Prus bl ('80)	.30	.20
972	A386	3fr	vio ('78)	.30	.20
a.			3fr dull violet ('84)	.20	.20
973	A386	4fr	red brn ('80)	.25	.20
a.			4fr rose brown ('85)	.25	.20
974	A386	4.50fr	lt ultra	.30	.20
975	A386	5fr	grn ('80)	.30	.20
a.			5fr emerald green ('84)	.20	.20
976	A386	6fr	dl red brn	.35	.20
a.			6fr light red brown ('85)	.35	.20
			Nos. 967-976 (11)	2.80	2.20

1978, Aug. **Photo.** ***Perf. 13½x12½***

Size: 17x22mm

Booklet Stamps

977	A386	1fr brt lilac	.20	.20
a.		Bklt. pane, #977-978, 2 #786	1.50	
b.		Bklt. pane, #977, 979, 2 #788	2.00	
978	A386	2fr yellow	.30	.30
979	A386	3fr violet	.50	.50
		Nos. 977-979 (3)	1.00	1.00

Each pane has 2 labels showing Belgian Postal emblem, also a large selvage with zip code instructions. No. 977-979 not luminescent.

See Nos. 1084-1088, design O5.

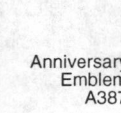

Anniversary Emblem A387

1977, Mar. 14 **Photo.** ***Perf. 11½***

982 A387 6.50fr sil & multi .30 .20

Royal Belgian Association of Civil and Agricultural Engineers, 50th anniversary.

Birds and Lions Emblem A388

1977, Mar. 28

983 A388 14fr multi .60 .30

Belgian District #112 of Lions Intl., 25th anniv.

Pillar Box, 1852 — A389

1977, Apr. 23 **Engr.**

984 A389 6.50fr slate green .45 .20

Stamp Day 1977.

Gileppe Dam, Jalhay A390

Europa: 14fr, War Memorial, Yser at Nieuport.

1977, May 7 Photo. *Perf. 11½*

985 A390 6.50fr multi .40 .20
986 A390 14fr multi .90 .20

Mars and Mercury Association Emblem — A391

1977, May 14

987 A391 5fr multi .25 .20

Mars and Mercury Association of Reserve and Retired Officers, 50th anniversary.

Prince de Hornes Coat of Arms A392

Conversion of St. Hubertus A394

Battle of the Golden Spur, from Oxford Chest A393

Design: 6.50fr, Froissart writing book.

1977, June 11 Engr. *Perf. 11½*

988 A392 4.50fr violet .30 .20
989 A393 5fr red .35 .20
990 A394 6.50fr dark brown .40 .25
991 A394 14fr slate green .75 .35
Nos. 988-991 (4) 1.80 1.00

300th anniv. of the Principality of Overijse (4.50fr); 675th anniv. of the Battle of the Golden Spur (5f); 600th anniv. of publication of 1st volume of the Chronicles of Jehan Froissart (6.50fr); 1250th anniv. of the death of St. Hubertus (14fr).

Rubens, Self-portrait — A395

1977, June 25 Photo.

992 A395 5fr multi .25 .20
a. Souvenir sheet of 3 1.25 .90

Peter Paul Rubens (1577-1640), painter. No. 992a sold for 20fr.

Open Book, from The Lamb of God, by Van Eyck Brothers — A396

1977, Sept. 3 Photo. *Perf. 11½*

993 A396 10fr multi .45 .25

Intl. Federation of Library Associations (IFLA), 50th Anniv. Congress, Brussels, Sept. 5-10.

Gymnast and Soccer Player — A397

Designs: 6.50fr, Fencers in wheelchairs, horiz. 10fr, Basketball players. 14fr, Hockey players.

1977, Sept. 10

994 A397 4.50fr multi .25 .20
995 A397 6.50fr multi .35 .20
996 A397 10fr multi .60 .20
997 A397 14fr multi .80 .30
Nos. 994-997 (4) 2.00 .90

Workers' Gymnastics and Sports Center, 50th anniversary (4.50fr); sport for the Handicapped (6.50fr); 20th European Basketball Championships (10fr); First World Hockey Cup (14fr).

Europalia 77 Emblem — A398

1977, Sept. 17

998 A398 5fr gray & multi .25 .20

5th Europalia Arts Festival, featuring German Federal Republic, Belgium, Oct.-Nov. 1977.

The Egg Farmer, by Gustave De Smet — A399

1977, Oct. 8 Engr. & Photo.

999 A399 4.50fr bister & blk .25 .20

Publicity for Belgian eggs.

Mother and Daughter with Album, by Constant Cap — A400

1977, Oct. 15 Engr.

1000 A400 4.50fr dark brown .25 .20

Youth Philately.

Bailiff's House, Gembloux — A401

Market Square, St. Nicholas A402

No. 1002, St. Aldegonde Church and Cultural Center. No. 1004, Statue and bridge, Liège.

1977, Oct. 22

1001 A401 4.50fr multi .25 .20
1002 A401 4.50fr multi .25 .20
1003 A402 5fr multi .25 .20
1004 A402 5fr multi .25 .20
Nos. 1001-1004 (4) 1.00 .80

Tourism. Nos. 1001-1004 not luminescent. See Nos. 1017-1018, 1037-1040.

Nativity, by Rogier van der Weyden — A403

1977, Nov. 11 Engr.

1005 A403 5fr rose red .30 .20

Christmas 1977.

Symbols of Transportation and Map — A404

Parliament of Europe, Strasbourg, and Emblem — A405

Campidoglio Palace, Rome, and Map — A406

Design: No. 1009, Paul-Henri Spaak and map of 19 European member countries.

1978, Mar. 18 Photo. *Perf. 11½*

1006 A404 10fr blue & multi .60 .20
1007 A405 10fr blue & multi 1.10 .20
1008 A406 14fr blue & multi .65 .55
1009 A406 14fr blue & multi .65 .55
Nos. 1006-1009 (4) 3.00 1.50

European Action: 25th anniversary of the European Transport Ministers' Conference; 1st general elections for European Parliament; 20th anniversary of the signing of the Treaty of Rome; Paul Henri Spaak (1899-1972), Belgian statesman who worked for the establishment of European Community.

Grimbergen Abbey — A407

1978, Apr. 1 Engr.

1010 A407 4.50fr red brown .25 .20

850th anniversary of the Premonstratensian Abbey at Grimbergen.

Emblem — A408

No. 39 with First Day Cancel — A409

1978, Apr. 8 Photo.

1011 A408 8fr multicolored .50 .20

Ostend Chamber of Commerce and Industry, 175th anniversary.

1978, Apr. 15

1012 A409 8fr multicolored .35 .20

Stamp Day.

Europa Issue

Pont des Trous, Tournai A410

8fr, Antwerp Cathedral, by Vaclav Hollar.

Photogravure and Engraved

1978, May 6 *Perf. 11½*

1013 A410 8fr multi, vert. .50 .20
1014 A410 14fr multi .75 .30

Virgin of Ghent, Porcelain Plaque A411

Paul Pastur Workers' University, Charleroi A412

1978, Sept. 16 Photo. *Perf. 11½*

1015 A411 6fr multicolored .40 .20
1016 A412 8fr multicolored .55 .20

Municipal education in Ghent, 150th anniversary; Paul Pastur Workers' University, Charleroi, 75th anniv. #1015-1016 are not luminescent.

Types of 1977 and

Tourist Guide, Brussels A413

#1017, Jonathas House, Enghien. #1018, View of Wetteren and couple in local costume. #1020, Prince Carnival, Eupen-St. Vith.

1978, Sept. 25 Photo. & Engr.

1017 A401 4.50fr multi .20 .20
1018 A402 4.50fr multi .20 .20
1019 A413 6fr multi .25 .20
1020 A413 6fr multi .25 .20
Nos. 1017-1020 (4) .90 .80

Tourism. #1017-1020 are not luminescent.

Emblem
A414

1978, Oct. 7 **Photo.**
1021 A414 8fr red & blk .35 .20

Royal Flemish Engineer's Organization, 50th anniversary.

Young Philatelist
A415

1978, Oct. 14 **Engr.** ***Perf. 11½***
1022 A415 4.50fr dk violet .25 .20

Youth philately.

Nativity, Notre Dame, Huy — A416

1978, Nov. 18 **Engr.** ***Perf. 11½***
1023 A416 6fr black .30 .20

Christmas 1978.

Tyll Eulenspiegel, Lay Action Emblem
A417

European Parliament Emblem
A418

1979, Mar. 3 **Photo.** ***Perf. 11½***
1024 A417 4.50fr multi .30 .20

10th anniversary of Lay Action Centers.

1979, Mar. 3
1025 A418 8fr multicolored .50 .20

European Parliament, first direct elections, June 7-10.

St. Michael Banishing Lucifer — A419

1979, Mar. 17 **Photo. & Engr.**
1026 A419 4.50fr rose red & blk .20 .20
1027 A419 8fr brt green & blk .30 .20

Millennium of Brussels.

NATO Emblem and Monument
A420

1979, Mar. 31 **Photo.**
1028 A420 3fr multicolored 1.75 .45

NATO, 30th anniv.

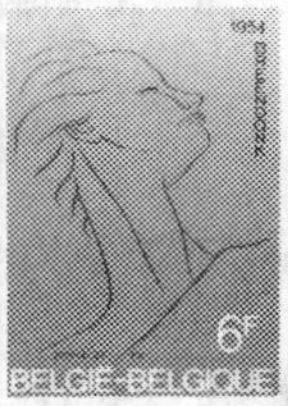

Prisoner's Head — A421

1979, Apr. 7 **Photo. & Engr.**
1029 A421 6fr orange & blk .25 .20

25th anniversary of the National Political Prisoners' Monument at Breendonk.

Belgium No. Q2 — A422

1979, Apr. 21 **Photo.** ***Perf. 11½***
1030 A422 8fr multicolored .50 .20

Stamp Day 1979.

Mail Coach and Truck
A423

Europa: 14fr, Chappe's heliograph, Intelsat satellite and dish antenna.

1979, Apr. 28 **Photo. & Engr.**
1031 A423 8fr multicolored .45 .20
1032 A423 14fr multicolored .90 .40

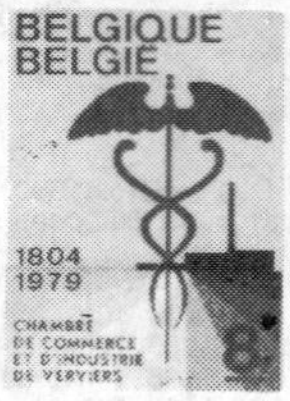

Chamber of Commerce Emblem — A424

1979, May 19 **Photo.** ***Perf. 11½***
1033 A424 8fr multicolored .35 .20

Verviers Chamber of Commerce and Industry, 175th anniversary.

"50" Emblem
A425

1979, June 9 **Photo.** ***Perf. 11½***
1034 A425 4.50fr gold & ultra .30 .20

Natl. Fund for Professional Credit, 50th anniv.

Merchants, Roman Bas-relief
A426

1979, June 9
1035 A426 10fr multicolored .60 .20

Belgian Chamber of Trade and Commerce, 50th anniversary.

"Tintin" as Philatelist
A427

1979, Sept. 29 **Photo.** ***Perf. 11½***
1036 A427 8fr multicolored 1.10 .20

Youth philately.

Tourism Types of 1977

Designs: No. 1037, Belfry, Thuin. No. 1038, Royal Museum of Central Africa, Tervuren. No. 1039, St. Nicholas Church and cattle, Ciney. No. 1040, St. John's Church and statue of Our Lady, Poperinge.

Perf. 11½ (A401), 13 (A402)

1979, Oct. 22 **Photo. & Engr.**
1037 A401 5fr multicolored .20 .20
1038 A402 5fr multicolored .20 .20
1039 A401 6fr multicolored .35 .20
1040 A402 6fr multicolored .35 .20
Nos. 1037-1040 (4) 1.10 .80

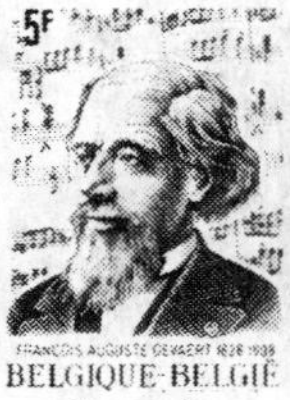

Francois Auguste Gevaert
A429

Piano, String Instruments
A430

Design: 6fr, Emmanuel Durlet.

1979, Nov. 3 ***Perf. 11½***
1041 A429 5fr brown .35 .20
1042 A429 6fr brown .40 .20
1043 A430 14fr brown .90 .35
Nos. 1041-1043 (3) 1.65 .75

Francois Auguste Gevaert (1828-1908), musicologist and composer; Emmanuel Durlet (1893-1977), pianist; Queen Elisabeth Musical Chapel Foundation, 40th anniv.

Virgin and Child, Notre Dame, Foy — A431

1979, Nov. 24 **Photo. & Engr.**
1044 A431 6fr lt grnsh blue .30 .20

Christmas 1979.

Independence, 150th Anniversary — A432

1980, Jan. 26 **Photo.** ***Perf. 11½***
1045 A432 9fr purple .40 .20

Frans van Cauwelaert
A433

Spring Flowers
A434

1980, Feb. 25 **Engr.**
1046 A433 5fr gray .25 .20

Frans van Cauwelaert (1880-1961), Minister of State.

1980, Mar. 10 **Photo.**
1047 A434 5fr shown .25 .20
1048 A434 6.50fr Summer flowers .30 .20
1049 A434 9fr Autumn flowers .45 .20
Nos. 1047-1049 (3) 1.00 .60

Ghent Flower Show, Apr. 19-27.

P.T.T., 50th Anniv.
A435

1980, Apr. 14 **Photo.** ***Perf. 11½***
1050 A435 10fr multicolored .45 .25

Belgium No. C4 — A436

1980, Apr. 21
1051 A436 9fr multicolored .50 .20

Stamp Day.

A437

A438

Europa: 9fr, St. Benedict, by Hans Memling. 14fr, Margaret of Austria (1480-1530).

1980, Apr. 28
1052 A437 9fr multicolored .45 .20
1053 A437 14fr multicolored .70 .25

1980, May 10 **Photo.** ***Perf. 11½***
1054 A438 5fr Palais des Nations, Brussels .25 .20

4th Interparliamentary Conference for European Cooperation and Security, Brussels, May 12-18.

Golden Carriage, 1780, Mons
A439

Tourism: #1056, Canal landscape, Damme.

1980, May 17
1055 A439 6.50fr multi .30 .20
1056 A439 6.50fr multi .30 .20

Souvenir Sheet

Royal Mint Theater, Brussels — A440

Photo. & Engr.

1980, May 31 — ***Perf. 11½***
1057 A440 50fr black 3.25 3.25

150th anniv. of independence. Sold for 75fr.

King Baudouin, 50th Birthday — A441

1980, Sept. 6 **Photo.** ***Perf. 11½***
1058 A441 9fr rose claret .40 .20

View of Chiny A442

Portal and Court, Diest — A443

1980 **Engr.** ***Perf. 13***
1059 A442 5fr multicolored .25 .20
1060 A443 5fr multicolored .25 .20

Tourism. Nos. 1059-1060 are not luminescent. Issue dates: No. 1059, Sept. 27; No. 1060, Dec. 13. See Nos. 1072-1075, 1120-1125.

Emblem of Belgian Heart League A444

1980, Oct. 4 **Photo.** ***Perf. 11½***
1061 A444 14fr blue & magenta .55 .25

Heart Week, Oct. 20-25.

Rodenbach Statue, Roulers — A445

1980, Oct. 11
1062 A445 9fr multicolored .40 .20

Albrecht Rodenbach (1856-1880), poet.

Youth Philately — A446

1980, Oct. 27 **Photo.** ***Perf. 11½***
1063 A446 5fr multicolored .25 .20

National Broadcasting Service, 50th Anniversary — A447

1980, Nov. 10
1064 A447 10fr gray & blk .45 .25

Garland and Nativity, by Daniel Seghers, 17th Century A448

1980, Nov. 17
1065 A448 6.50fr multicolored .40 .20

Christmas 1980.

Baron de Gerlache, by F.J. Navez — A449

Leopold I, By Geefs — A450

Design: 9fr, Baron de Stassart, by F.J. Navez.

1981, Mar. 16 **Photo.** ***Perf. 11½***
1066 A449 6fr multicolored .35 .20
1067 A449 9fr multicolored .55 .20

Photogravure and Engraved

1068 A450 50fr multicolored 3.00 .55

Sesquicentennial of Chamber of Deputies, Senate and Dynasty.

Europa Issue 1981

Tchantchès and Op-Signoorke, Puppets — A451

Photogravure and Engraved

1981, May 4 ***Perf. 11½***
1069 A451 9fr shown .40 .20
1070 A451 14fr d'Artagnan and Woltje .65 .35

Impression of M.A. de Cock (Founder of Post Museum) — A452

1981, May 18 **Photo.**
1071 A452 9fr multicolored .40 .20

Stamp Day.

Tourism Types of 1980

Designs: No. 1072, Virgin and Child statue, Our Lady's Church, Tongre-Notre Dame. No. 1073, Egmont Castle, Zottegem. No. 1074, Eau d'Heure River. No. 1075, Tongerlo Abbey, Antwerp.

1981, June 15 **Engr.** ***Perf. 11½***
1072 A442 6fr multi .35 .20
1073 A442 6fr multi .35 .20
1074 A443 6.50fr multi .35 .20
1075 A443 6.50fr multi .35 .20
Nos. 1072-1075 (4) 1.40 .80

Soccer Player A453

E. Remouchamps, Founder A454

1981, Sept. 5 **Photo.** ***Perf. 11½***
1076 A453 6fr multicolored .35 .20

Soccer in Belgium centenary; Royal Antwerp Soccer Club.

1981, Sept. 5 **Photo. & Engr.**
1077 A454 6.50fr multi .40 .20

Walloon Language and Literature Club 125th anniv.

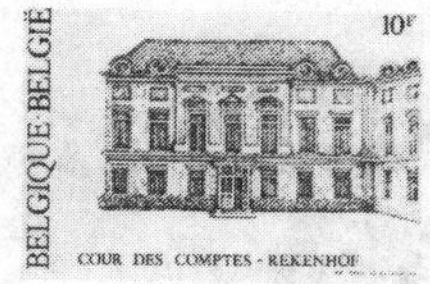

Audit Office Sesquicentennial — A455

1981, Sept. 12 **Engr.**
1078 A455 10fr tan & dk brn .60 .25

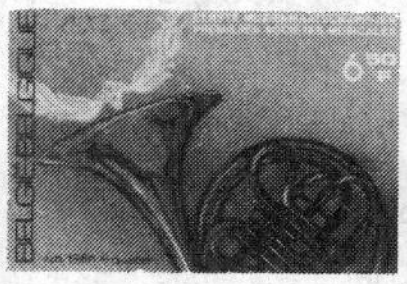

French Horn — A456

1981, Sept. 12 **Photo.**
1079 A456 6.50fr multi .40 .20

Vredekring (Peace Circle) Band of Antwerp centenary.

Souvenir Sheet

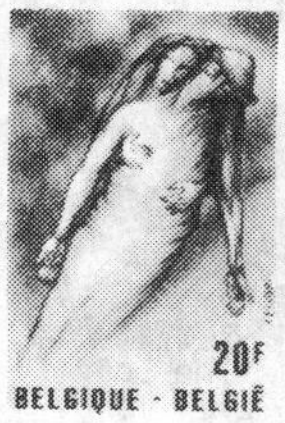

Pieta, by Ben Genaux — A457

1981, Sept. 19 **Photo.** ***Perf. 11½***
1080 A457 20fr multicolored 1.75 1.40

Mining disaster at Marcinelle, 25th anniv. Sold for 30fr.

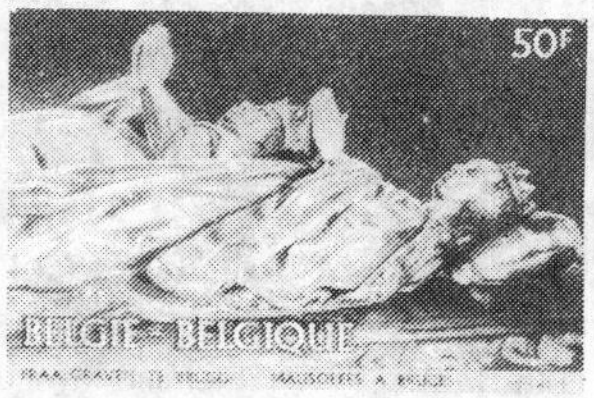

Mausoleum of Marie of Burgundy and Charles the Bold, Bruges — A458

1981, Oct. 10 **Photo. & Engr.**
1081 A458 50fr multi 2.75 .60

Youth Philately — A459

1981, Oct. 24 **Photo.**
1082 A459 6fr multi .30 .20

Type of 1977 and

A459a

A460

King Baudouin A460a

Photo. and Engr.; Photo.

1980-86 ***Perf. 13½x14, 11½***

1084	A386	65c brt rose	.20	.20
1085	A386	1fr on 5fr grn	.20	.20
1086	A386	7fr brt rose	.55	.20
1087	A386	8fr grnsh bl	.60	.20
1088	A386	9fr dl org	.55	.20
1089	A459a	10fr blue	.85	.20
1090	A459a	11fr dl red	.90	.20
1091	A459a	12fr grn	.90	.20
1092	A459a	13fr scar	.85	.20
1093	A459a	15fr red org	1.25	.20
1094	A459a	20fr dk bl	1.50	.30
1095	A459a	22fr lilac	1.60	.30
1096	A459a	23fr gray grn	1.00	.55
1097	A459a	30fr brown	2.25	.40
1098	A459a	40fr red org	2.50	.55
1099	A460	50fr lt grnsh bl & bl	3.25	.30
1100	A460a	50fr tan & dk brn	3.25	.60
1101	A460	65fr pale lil & blk	4.50	.90
1102	A460	100fr lt bis brn & dk bl	6.75	1.25
1103	A460a	100fr lt bl & dk bl	6.75	1.25
		Nos. 1084-1103 (20)	40.20	8.40

Issued: 65c, 4/14/80; 1fr, 5/3/82; 7fr, 5/17/82; 8fr, 5/9/83; 9fr, 2/11/85; 65fr, No. 1099, 1102, 11/5/81; 10fr, 11/15/82; 11fr, 4/5/83; 12fr, 1/23/84; 15fr, 22fr, 30fr, No. 1100, 3/26/84; 20fr, 40fr, No. 1103, 6/12/84; 23fr, 2/25/85; 13fr, 3/10/86. See Nos. 1231-1234.

Max Waller, Movement Founder
A461

The Spirit Drinkers, by Gustave van de Woestyne
A462

Fernand Severin, Poet, 50th Death Anniv. — A463

Jan van Ruusbroec, Flemish Mystic, 500th Birth Anniv. — A464

Thought and Man TV Series, 25th Anniv.
A465

Nativity, 16th Cent. Engraving
A466

1981, Nov. 7
1104 A461 6fr multi .30 .20
1105 A462 6.50fr multi .35 .20
1106 A463 9fr multi .50 .20
1107 A464 10fr multi .80 .25
1108 A465 14fr multi .75 .35
Nos. 1104-1108 (5) 2.70 1.20

La Jeune Belgique cultural movement cent. (6fr).

1981, Nov. 21
1109 A466 6.50fr multi .30 .20

Christmas 1981.

Royal Conservatory of Music Sesquicentennial — A467

Design: 9fr, Judiciary sesquicentennial.

1982, Jan. 25 Photo. *Perf. 11½*
1110 A467 6.50fr multi .30 .20
1111 A467 9fr multi .40 .20

A468

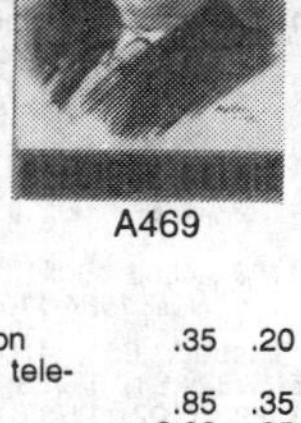

A469

1982, Mar. 1
1112 A468 6fr Cyclotron .35 .20
1113 A468 14fr Galaxy, telescope .85 .35
1114 A468 50fr Koch 3.00 .65
Nos. 1112-1114 (3) 4.20 1.20

Radio-isotope production, Natl. Radio-elements Institute, Fleurus (6fr); Royal Belgian Observatory (14fr); centenary of TB bacillus discovery (50fr).

1982, Apr. 17 Photo. *Perf. 11½*
1115 A469 6.50fr multi .30 .20

Joseph Lemaire (1882-1966), Minister of State.

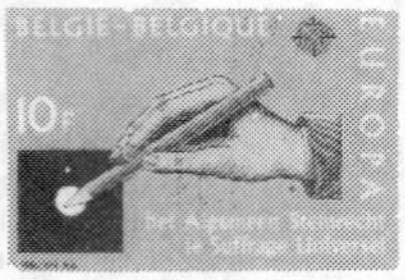

Europa 1982 — A470

1982, May 1
1116 A470 10fr Universal suffrage .50 .20
1117 A470 17fr Edict of Tolerance, 1781 .80 .40

Stamp Day — A471

1982, May 22 Photo. & Engr.
1118 A471 10fr multi .50 .20

67th World Esperanto Congress, Anvers
A472

1982, June 7 Photo. *Perf. 11½*
1119 A472 12fr Tower of Babel .60 .30

Tourism Type of 1980

Designs: No. 1120, Tower of Gosselies. No. 1121, Zwijveke Abbey, Dendermonde. No. 1122, Stavelot Abbey. No. 1123, Villers-la-Ville Abbey ruins. No. 1124, Geraardsbergen Abbey entrance. No. 1125, Beveren Pillory.

1982, June 21 Photo. & Engr.
1120 A443 7fr lt bl & blk .50 .20
1121 A443 7fr lt grn & blk .50 .20
1122 A442 7.50fr tan & dk brn .55 .25
1123 A442 7.50fr lt vio & pur .55 .25
1124 A443 7.50fr slate & blk .55 .25
1125 A443 7.50fr beige & blk .55 .25
Nos. 1120-1125 (6) 3.20 1.40

Self Portrait, by L.P. Boon (b. 1912)
A473

Abraham Hans, Writer (1882-1932)
A474

Designs: 10fr, Adoration of the Shepherds, by Hugo van der Goes (1440-1482). 12fr, The King on His Throne, carving by M. de Ghelderode (1898-1962). 17fr, Madonna and Child, by Pieter Paulus (1881-1959).

1982, Sept. 13 Photo. *Perf. 11½*
1126 A473 7fr multicolored .50 .20
1127 A473 10fr multicolored .60 .20
1128 A473 12fr multicolored .70 .35
1129 A473 17fr multicolored 1.00 .35
Nos. 1126-1129 (4) 2.80 1.10

1982, Sept. 27
1130 A474 17fr multicolored 1.10 .35

Youth Philately and Scouting
A475

1982, Oct. 2 Photo. *Perf. 11½*
1131 A475 7fr multicolored .50 .20

Grand Orient Lodge of Belgium Sesquicentennial
A476

1982, Oct. 16 Photo. & Engr.
1132 A476 10fr Man taking oath .60 .20

Cardinal Joseph Cardijn (1882-1967)
A477

1982, Nov. 13 Photo.
1133 A477 10fr multicolored .50 .20

St. Francis of Assisi (1182-1226) — A478

1982, Nov. 27
1134 A478 20fr multicolored .90 .30

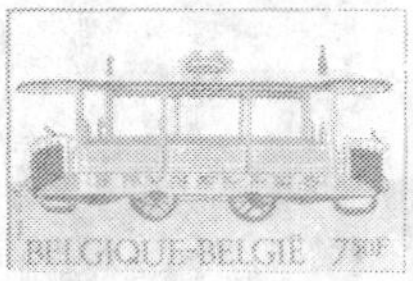

Horse-drawn Trolley
A479

1983, Feb. 12 Photo. *Perf. 11½*
1135 A479 7.50fr shown .40 .25
1136 A479 10fr Electric trolley .50 .20
1137 A479 50fr Trolley, diff. 2.50 .50
Nos. 1135-1137 (3) 3.40 .95

Intl. Fed. for Periodical Press, 24th World Congress, Brussels, May 11-13 — A480

1983, Mar. 19 Photo. *Perf. 11½*
1138 A480 20fr multicolored 1.00 .25

Homage to Women
A481

1983, Apr. 16
1139 A481 8fr Operator .45 .20
1140 A481 11fr Homemaker .55 .20
1141 A481 20fr Executive .95 .25
Nos. 1139-1141 (3) 1.95 .65

Stamp Day — A482

1983, Apr. 23
1142 A482 11fr multicolored .60 .20

Procession of the Precious Blood, Bruges
A483

1983, Apr. 30 Photo. *Perf. 11½*
1143 A483 8fr multi .60 .20

Europa 1983
A484

Paintings by P. Delvaux. 11fr vert.

1983, May 14
1144 A484 11fr Common Man .65 .20
1145 A484 20fr Night Train 1.25 .45

Manned Flight Bicentenary
A485

1983, June 11 Photo. *Perf. 11½*
1146 A485 11fr Balloon over city .65 .20
1147 A485 22fr Country 1.40 .45

Our Lady's Church, Hastiere
A486

1983, June 25
1148 A486 8fr shown .40 .20
1149 A486 8fr Landen .40 .20
1150 A486 8fr Park, Mouscron .40 .20
1151 A486 8fr Wijnendale Castle, Torhout .40 .20
Nos. 1148-1151 (4) 1.60 .80

Tineke Festival, Heule — A487

1983, Sept. 10 Photo.
1152 A487 8fr multi .40 .20

Enterprise Year Emblem
A488

1983, Sept. 24
1153 A488 11fr multicolored .55 .20

European year for small and medium-sized enterprises and craft industry.

Youth Philately — A489

1983, Oct. 10 Photo. *Perf. 11½*

1154 A489 8fr multicolored .40 .20

Belgian Exports A490

1983, Oct. 24 *Perf. 11½*

1155 A490 10fr Diamond industry .55 .20
1156 A490 10fr Metallurgy .55 .20
1157 A490 10fr Textile industry .55 .20
Nos. 1155-1157 (3) 1.65 .60

See Nos. 1161-1164.

A491

A492

1983, Nov. 7

1158 A491 20fr multicolored 1.00 .25

Hendrik Conscience, novelist (1812-1883).

Leopold III Type of 1936

1983, Dec. 12 Engr. *Perf. 12x11½*

1159 A84 11fr black .55 .20

Leopold III memorial (1901-1983), King 1934-1951.

Photogravure and Engraved

1984, Jan. 14 *Perf. 11½*

1160 A492 11fr multicolored .55 .20

Free University of Brussels, sesquicentennial.

Exports Type of 1983

1984, Jan. 28 Photo.

1161 A490 11fr Chemicals .55 .20
1162 A490 11fr Food .55 .20
1163 A490 11fr Transportation equipment .55 .20
1164 A490 11fr Technology .55 .20
Nos. 1161-1164 (4) 2.20 .80

A494

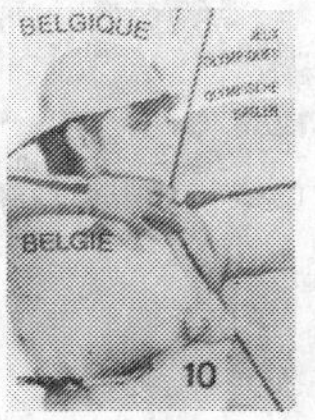

A495

1984, Feb. 11 Photo. & Engr.

1165 A494 8fr tan & dk brn .40 .20

50th death anniv. of King Albert I.

1984, Mar. 3 Photo.

Souvenir Sheet

1166 Sheet of 2 2.00 2.00
a. A495 10fr Archery .55 .55
b. A495 24fr Dressage 1.40 1.40

1984 Olympics. See Nos. B1029-B1030.

Family, Globe, Birds A496

St. John Bosco Canonization A497

1984, Mar. 24 Photo. *Perf. 11½*

1167 A496 12fr multicolored .60 .20

"Movement without a Name" peace org.

1984, Apr. 7

1168 A497 8fr multicolored .40 .20

Europa (1959-84) A498

1984, May 5 Photo. *Perf. 11½*

1169 A498 12fr black & red .75 .20
1170 A498 22fr black & ultra 1.40 .30

Stamp Day — A499

1984, May 19

1171 A499 12fr No. 52 .60 .20

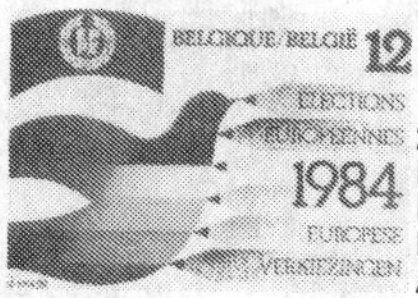

2nd European Parliament Elections A500

1984, May 26

1172 A500 12fr multicolored .60 .20

Royal Military School, 150th Anniv. — A501

1984, June 9 Photo. *Perf. 11½*

1173 A501 22fr Hat 1.10 .25

Notre-Dame de la Chappelle, Brussels A502

Churches: No. 1175, St. Martin's, Montignyle-Tilleul. No. 1176, Tielt, vert.

Perf. 11½x12, 12x11½

1984, June 23 Photo. & Engr.

1174 A502 10fr multicolored .55 .20
1175 A502 10fr multicolored .55 .20
1176 A502 10fr multicolored .55 .20
Nos. 1174-1176 (3) 1.65 .60

50th Anniv. of Chirojeugd (Christian Youth Movement) A503

1984, Sept. 15 Photo. *Perf. 11½*

1177 A503 10fr Emblem .50 .20

Affligem Abbey A504

1984, Oct. 6 Photo. & Engr.

1178 A504 8fr Averbode, vert. .40 .25
1179 A504 22fr Chimay, vert. 1.25 .25
1180 A504 24fr Rochefort, vert. 1.25 .40
1181 A504 50fr shown 2.50 .50
Nos. 1178-1181 (4) 5.40 1.40

Youth Philately A505

1984, Oct. 20 Photo.

1182 A505 8fr Postman smurf .45 .20

Arthur Meulemans (1884-1966), Composer — A506

1984, Nov. 17 Photo. & Engr.

1183 A506 12fr multi .60 .20

St. Norbert, 850th Death Anniv. — A507

Europalia '85 — A508

1985, Jan. 14 Photo. & Engr.

1184 A507 22fr sepia & beige 1.10 .30

1985, Jan. 21 Photo.

1185 A508 12fr Virgin of Louvain .65 .20

Belgian Assoc. of Professional Journalists, Cent. A509

1985, Feb. 11 Photo.

1186 A509 9fr multicolored .40 .20

Ghent Flower Festival, Orchids A510

Visit of Pope John Paul II A511

Photogravure and Engraved

1985, Mar. 18 *Perf. 11½*

1187 A510 12fr Vanda coerules .70 .20
1188 A510 12fr Phalaenopsis .70 .20
1189 A510 12fr Suphrolaelio cattlea riffe .70 .20
Nos. 1187-1189 (3) 2.10 .60

1985, Apr. 1 Photo.

1190 A511 12fr multicolored .60 .20

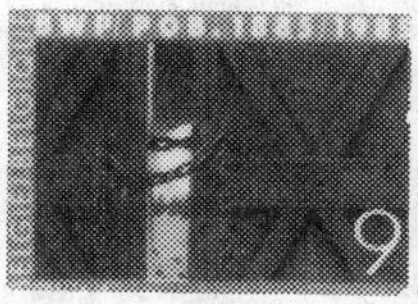

Belgian Worker's Party Cent. A512

1985, Apr. 15 Photo.

1191 A512 9fr Chained factory gate .40 .20
1192 A512 12fr Broken wall, red flag .60 .20

Jean de Bast (1883-1975), Engraver A513

1985, Apr. 22 Engr.

1193 A513 12fr blue black .60 .20

Stamp Day.

Public Transportation Year — A514

Design: 9fr, Steam tram locomotive Type 18, 1896. 12fr, Locomotive Elephant and tender, 1835. 23fr, Type 23 tank engine, 1904. 24fr, Type I Pacific locomotive, 1935. 50fr, Type 27 electric locomotive, 1975.

1985, May 6 Photo.

1194 A514 9fr multicolored .65 .20
1195 A514 12fr multicolored .85 .20
1196 A514 23fr multicolored 1.50 .35
1197 A514 24fr multicolored 1.90 .40
Nos. 1194-1197 (4) 4.90 1.15

Souvenir Sheet

1198 A514 50fr multicolored 4.50 3.75

Europa 1985 — A515

1985, May 13 Photo.

1199 A515 12fr Cesar Franck at organ, 1887 .80 .20
1200 A515 23fr Folk figures 1.50 .25

26th Navigation Congress, Brussels A516

1985, June 10 Photo. *Perf. 11½*

1201 A516 23fr Zeebruge Harbor 1.25 .25
1202 A516 23fr Projected lock at Strepy-Thieu 1.25 .25

St. Martin's Church, Marcinelle A517

Tourism: No. 1203, Church of the Assumption of Our Lady, Avernas-le-Baudouin, vert.

No. 1204, Church of the Old Beguinage, Tongres, vert. No. 1206, Private residence, Puyenbroeck.

1985, June 24 ***Perf. 11½***
1203 A517 12fr multicolored .60 .20
1204 A517 12fr multicolored .60 .20
1205 A517 12fr multicolored .60 .20
1206 A517 12fr multicolored .60 .20
Nos. 1203-1206 (4) 2.40 .80

Queen Astrid (1905-1935) A518

Baking Pies for the Mattetart of Geraardsbergen A519

1985, Sept. 2 ***Perf. 11½***
1207 A518 12fr brown .60 .20

1985, Sept. 16

Folk events: 24fr, Children dancing, centenary of the St. Lambert de Hermalle-Argenteau Le Rouges youth organization.

1208 A519 12fr multicolored .60 .20
1209 A519 24fr multicolored .95 .30

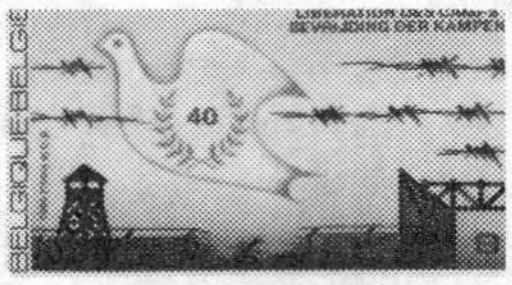

Liberation from German Occupation, 40th Anniv. — A520

Allegories: 9fr, Dove, liberation of concentration camps. 23fr, Battle of Ardennes. 24fr, Destroyer, liberation of the River Scheldt estuary.

1985, Sept. 30 **Photo.** ***Perf. 11½***
1210 A520 9fr multicolored .50 .25
1211 A520 23fr multicolored 1.25 .65
1212 A520 24fr multicolored 1.25 .70
Nos. 1210-1212 (3) 3.00 1.60

Ernest Claes (1885-1968), Author A521

1985, Oct. 7
1213 A521 9fr Portrait, book character .50 .25

Intl. Youth Year — A522

1985, Oct. 21
1214 A522 9fr Nude in repose, angel .50 .25

King Baudouin & Queen Fabiola, 25th Wedding Anniv. — A523

1985, Dec. 9
1215 A523 12fr multicolored .50 .40

Birds — A524

Photo. (50c-2fr, No. 1220, 4.50fr-6fr, No. 1229, 10fr), Typo. (Others)

1985-91 ***Perf. 11½***
1216 A524 50c Roitelet huppe .20 .20
1217 A524 1fr Pic Epechette .20 .20
1218 A524 2fr Moineau friquet .20 .20
1219 A524 3fr Gros bec .20 .20
1220 A524 3fr Bruant des roseax .25 .20
1221 A524 3.50fr Rouge gorge .20 .20
1222 A524 4fr Gorge bleue .25 .20
1223 A524 4.50fr Traquet Patre .35 .20
1224 A524 5fr Sittele tporche-pot .35 .20
1225 A524 6fr Bouvreuil .40 .20
1226 A524 7fr Mesange bleue .45 .20
1227 A524 8fr Martin-pechuer .45 .20
1228 A524 9fr Chardonneret .35 .20
1229 A524 9fr Grive musicienne .65 .20
1230 A524 10fr Pinson .65 .20
Nos. 1216-1230 (15) 5.15 3.00

Issued: 7fr, 9/7/87; 5fr, 6fr, 9/12/88; 4fr, 4/17/89; 2fr, 12/4/89; 1fr, 1/8/90; 10fr, 1/15/90; 50c, #1220, 1229, 9/30/91; others, 9/30/85.

See #1432-1447, 1627, 1641, 1645, 1651, 1660, 1676, 1696, 1700, 1702-1703, 1714-1715.

King Type of 1981

1986-90 **Photo.** ***Perf. 11½***
1231 A459a 14fr black .80 .20
1232 A459a 24fr dk grysh green 1.10 .85
1233 A459a 25fr blue black 1.40 .40
1234 A460a 200fr sage grn & dl gray grn 11.00 2.00
Nos. 1231-1234 (4) 14.30 3.45

Issued: 24fr, 4/7/86; 200fr, 11/3/86; 14fr, 1/15/90; 25fr, 2/19/90.

Congo Stamp Cent. — A525

1986, Jan. 27 **Photo.** ***Perf. 11½***
1236 A525 10fr Belgian Congo #3 .40 .20

See Zaire No. 1230.

Carnival Cities of Aalst and Binche A526

Folklore: masks, giants.

1986, Feb. 3
1237 A526 9fr Aalst Belfry .50 .20
1238 A526 12fr Binche Gilles .60 .20

Intl. Peace Year — A527

1986, Mar. 10
1239 A527 23fr Emblem, dove 1.25 .35

Stamp Day — A528

1986, Apr. 21 **Photo.** ***Perf. 11½***
1240 A528 13fr Artifacts .65 .40

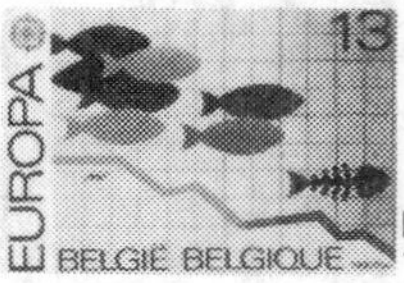

Europa 1986 — A529

1986, May 5
1241 A529 13fr Fish .65 .40
1242 A529 24fr Flora 1.40 .85

Dogs — A530

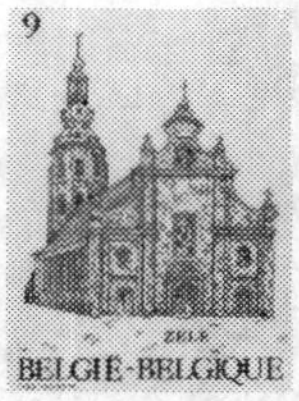

St. Ludger's Church, Zele — A531

1986, May 26 **Photo.** ***Perf. 11½***
1243 A530 9fr Malines sheepdog .65 .30
1244 A530 13fr Tervueren sheepdog .85 .45
1245 A530 24fr Groenendael sheepdog 1.60 .80
1246 A530 26fr Flemish cattle dog 1.60 .85
Nos. 1243-1246 (4) 4.70 2.40

1986, June 30 **Photo. & Engr.**

Designs: No. 1248, Waver Town Hall. No. 1249, Nederzwalm Canal, horiz. No. 1250, Chapel of Our Lady of the Dunes, Bredene. No. 1251, Licot Castle, Viroinval, horiz. No. 1252, Eynenbourg Castle, La Calamine, horiz.

1247 A531 9fr multicolored .60 .30
1248 A531 9fr multicolored .60 .30
1249 A531 13fr multicolored .80 .45
1250 A531 13fr multicolored .80 .45
1251 A531 13fr multicolored .80 .45
1252 A531 13fr multicolored .80 .45
Nos. 1247-1252 (6) 4.40 2.40

Youth Philately A532

1986, Sept. 1 **Photo.** ***Perf. 11½***
1253 A532 9fr dl ol grn, blk & dk red .50 .30

Cartoon Exhibition, Knokke.

Famous Men — A533

Designs: 9fr, Constant Permeke, painter, sculptor. 13fr, Baron Michel-Edmond de Selys Longchamps, scientist. 24fr, Felix Timmermans, writer. 26fr, Maurice Careme, poet.

1986, Sept. 29
1254 A533 9fr multicolored .50 .30
1255 A533 13fr multicolored .75 .45
1256 A533 24fr multicolored 1.40 .80
1257 A533 26fr multicolored 1.50 .90
Nos. 1254-1257 (4) 4.15 2.45

Royal Academy for Dutch Language and Literature, Cent. A534

1986, Oct. 6 **Engr.**
1258 A534 9fr dark blue .50 .30

Natl. Beer Industry A535

Perf. 12½x11½

1986, Oct. 13 **Photo.**
1259 A535 13fr Glass, barley, hops .70 .50

Provincial Law and Councils, 150th Anniv. A536

1986, Oct. 27 ***Perf. 11½***
1260 A536 13fr Stylized map .70 .50

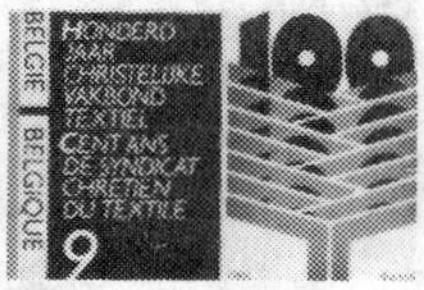

Christian Trade Union, Cent. A537

1986, Dec. 13 **Photo.** ***Perf. 11½***
1261 A537 9fr shown .45 .35
1262 A537 13fr design reversed .65 .50

Flanders Technology Intl. — A538

1987, Mar. 2 **Photo.**
1263 A538 13fr multi .70 .50

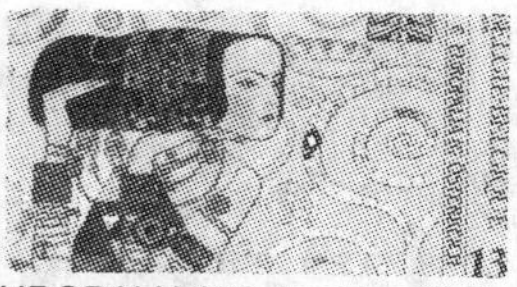

EUROPALIA '87, Austrian Cultural Events — A539

Design: Woman, detail of a fresco by Gustav Klimt, Palais Stoclet, Brussels.

1987, Apr. 4 Photo. *Perf. 11½*

1264 A539 13fr multicolored .70 .50

Stamp Day 1987 — A540

Portrait: Jakob Wiener (1815-1899), 1st engraver of Belgian stamps.

1987, Apr. 11 Photo. & Engr.

1265 A540 13fr lt greenish blue & sage grn .70 .50

Folklore A541

1987, Apr. 25 Photo.

1266 A541 9fr Penitents procession, Veurne .45 .35
1267 A541 13fr Play of John and Alice, Wavre .65 .50

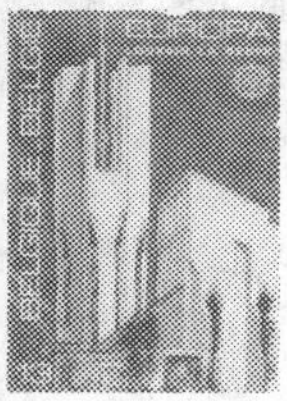

Europa 1987 — A542

Modern architecture: 13fr, Louvain-la-Neuve Church. 24fr, Regional Housing Assoc. Tower, St. Maartensdal at Louvain.

1987, May 9 Photo.

1268 A542 13fr multicolored .85 .55
1269 A542 24fr multicolored 1.50 1.00

Statue of Andre-Ernest Gretry (1741-1813), French Composer — A543

1987, May 23

1270 A543 24fr multicolored 1.50 1.00

Wallonie Royal Opera, Liege, 20th anniv.

Tourism — A544

Designs: No. 1271, Statues of Jan Breydel and Pieter de Conin, Bruges. No. 1272, Boondael Chapel, Brussels. No. 1273, Windmill, Keerbergen. No. 1274, St. Christopher's Church, Racour. No. 1275, Virelles Lake, Chimay.

1987, June 13

1271 A544 13fr multicolored 1.00 .55
1272 A544 13fr multicolored 1.00 .55
1273 A544 13fr multicolored 1.00 .55
1274 A544 13fr multicolored 1.00 .55
1275 A544 13fr multicolored 1.00 .55
Nos. 1271-1275 (5) 5.00 2.75

Royal Belgian Rowing Assoc., Cent. — A545

European Volleyball Championships A546

1987, Sept. 5

1276 A545 9fr multicolored .50 .40
1277 A546 13fr multicolored .75 .55

Foreign Trade Year — A547

1987, Sept. 12

1278 A547 13fr multi .75 .55

Belgian Social Reform, Cent. A548

1987, Sept. 19

1279 A548 26fr Leisure, by P. Paulus 1.40 1.10

Youth Philately A549

1987, Oct. 3

1280 A549 9fr multi .50 .40

Newspaper Centennials A550

1987, Dec. 12

1281 A550 9fr Le Soir .55 .40
1282 A550 9fr Hett Lattste Nieuws, vert. .55 .40

The Sea — A551

Designs: a, Lighthouse, trawler, rider and mount. b, Trawler, youths playing volleyball on beach. c, Cruise ship, sailboat, beach and cabana. d, Shore, birds.

1988, Feb. 6 Photo. *Perf. 11½*

1283 Strip of 4 + label 2.50 1.75
a.-d. A551 10fr any single .60 .45

No. 1283 has a continuous design.

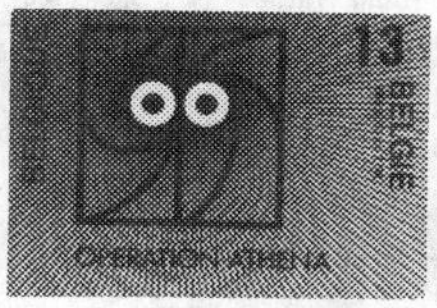

Dynamism of the Regions A552

1988, Mar. 5 Photo. *Perf. 11½*

1284 A552 13fr Operation Athena .80 .60
1285 A552 13fr Flanders Alive Campaign .80 .60

Stamp Day — A553

Europa 1988 — A554

Painting: 19th Cent. Postman, by James Thiriar.

1988, Apr. 16 Photo. & Engr.

1286 A553 13fr buff & sepia .80 .60

1988, May 9 Photo. *Perf. 11½*

Transport and communication.

1287 A554 13fr Satellite dish 1.10 .60
1288 A554 24fr Non-polluting combustion engine 1.90 1.10

Tourism A555

Designs: No. 1289, Romanesque watchtower, ca. 12th-13th cent., Amay, vert. No. 1290, Our Lady of Hanswijk Basilica, 988, Mechelen, vert. No. 1291, St. Sernin's Church, 16th cent., Waimes. No. 1292, Old Town Hall, 1637, and village water pump, 1761, Peer, vert. No. 1293, Our Lady of Bon-Secours Basilica, 1892, Peruwelz.

Photo. & Engr.

1988, June 20 *Perf. 11½*

1289 A555 9fr beige & blk .50 .40
1290 A555 9fr lt blue & blk .50 .40
1291 A555 9fr pale blue grn & blk .50 .40
1292 A555 13fr pale pink & blk .75 .55
1293 A555 13fr pale gray & blk .75 .55
Nos. 1289-1293 (5) 3.00 2.30

Our Lady of Hanswijk Basilica millennium (No. 1290); Waimes village, 1100th anniv. (No. 1291).

Jean Monnet (1888-1979), French Economist A556

Tapestry in the Hall of the Royal Academy of Medicine A557

1988, Sept. 12 *Perf. 11½*

1294 A556 13fr black .70 .50

1988, Sept. 17 Photo.

Academies building and: No. 1296, Lyre, quill pen, open book and atomic symbols.

1295 A557 9fr shown .50 .40
1296 A557 9fr multi .50 .40

Royal Academy of Medicine (#1295); Royal Academy of Science, Literature and Fine Arts (#1296).

Cultural Heritage A558

Artifacts: 9fr, Statue and mask in the Antwerp Ethnographical Museum. 13fr, Sarcophagus, St. Martin's Church, Trazegnies. 24fr, Church organ, Geraardsbergen. 26fr, Shrine, St. Hadelin's Church, Vise.

1988, Sept. 24

1297 A558 9fr multi .50 .40
1298 A558 13fr multi .70 .50
1299 A558 24fr multi 1.25 1.00
1300 A558 26fr multi 1.40 1.00
Nos. 1297-1300 (4) 3.85 2.90

Youth Philately A559

1988, Oct. 10

1301 A559 9fr multi .50 .40

Natl. Postal Savings Bank, 75th Anniv. A560

1988, Nov. 7

1302 A560 13fr multi .70 .50

Christmas 1988 and New Year 1989 A561

1988, Nov. 21

1303 A561 9fr Winter landscape .50 .40

Royal Mounted Guard, 50th Anniv. A562

1988, Dec. 12
1304 A562 13fr multi .75 .55

Printing Presses A563

9fr, J. Moretus I, Antwerp Museum, vert. 24fr, Stanhope, Printing Museum, Brussels, vert. 26fr, Litho Krause, Royal Museum, Mariemont.

1988, Dec. 19 **Engr.**
1305 A563 9fr bl blk & blk .50 .40
1306 A563 24fr dark red brn 1.40 1.10
1307 A563 26fr grn & slate grn 1.50 1.25
Nos. 1305-1307 (3) 3.40 2.75

Lace A564

1989, Mar. 20 **Photo.**
1308 A564 9fr Marche-en-Famenne .50 .40
1309 A564 13fr Brussels .70 .50
1310 A564 13fr Brugge .70 .50
Nos. 1308-1310 (3) 1.90 1.40

Stamp Day A565

1989, Apr. 24 **Photo. & Engr.**
1311 A565 13fr Mail coach, post chaise .75 .55

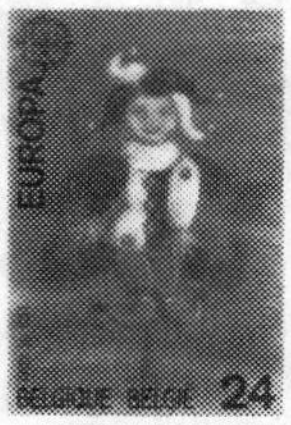

Europa 1989 — A566

Royal Academy of Fine Arts, Antwerp, 325th Anniv. — A567

Children's toys.

1989, May 8 **Photo.**
1312 A566 13fr Marbles, horiz. .75 .50
1313 A566 24fr Jumping-jack 1.40 1.00

1989, May 22 ***Perf. 11½***
1314 A567 13fr multi .75 .50

European Parliament 3rd Elections — A568

Illustration reduced.

1989, June 5 **Photo.**
1315 A568 13fr Brussels .75 .50

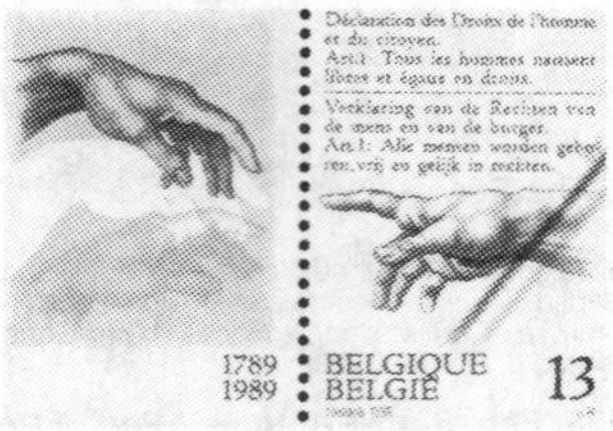

Declaration of Rights of Man and the Citizen, Bicent. — A569

1989, June 12 ***Perf. 11½***
1316 A569 13fr multi + label .75 .50

Tourism A570

Designs: No. 1317, St. Tillo's Church, Izegem. No. 1318, Logne Castle, Ferrieres. No. 1319, St. Laurentius's Church, Lokeren. No. 1320, Antoing Castle, Antoing. Nos. 1318-1320 vert.

1989, June 26 **Photo. & Engr.**
1317 A570 9fr shown .50 .40
1318 A570 9fr multi .50 .40
1319 A570 13fr multi .75 .50
1320 A570 13fr multi .75 .50
Nos. 1317-1320 (4) 2.50 1.80

Ducks — A571

1989, Sept. 4 **Photo.** ***Perf. 12***
Booklet Stamps
1321 A571 13fr Mallard (8a) 1.25 .50
1322 A571 13fr Winter teal (8b) 1.25 .50
1323 A571 13fr Shoveller (8c) 1.25 .50
1324 A571 13fr Pintail (8d) 1.25 .50
a. Bklt. pane of 4, #1321-1324 5.00

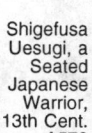

Shigefusa Uesugi, a Seated Japanese Warrior, 13th Cent. A572

1989, Sept. 18 ***Perf. 11½***
1325 A572 24fr multicolored 1.50 .50

Europalia.

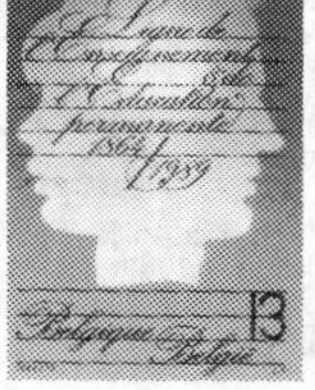

Education League, 125th Anniv. — A573

1989, Sept. 25
1326 A573 13fr multicolored .80 .20

Treaty of London, 150th Anniv. — A574

Mr. Nibbs — A575

1989, Oct. 2 **Photo.**
1327 A574 13fr Map of Limburg Provinces .80 .20

See Netherlands No. 750.

1989, Oct. 9 ***Perf. 11½***
1328 A575 9fr multicolored .60 .20

Youth philately promotion.

Christmas, New Year 1990 A576

1989, Nov. 20 **Photo.**
1329 A576 9fr Salvation Army band .60 .20

Fr. Damien (1840-89), Missionary, Molokai Is. Leper Colony, Hawaii A577

1989, Nov. 27 **Photo.**
1330 A577 24fr multicolored 1.50 .50

Father Adolf Daens — A578

1989, Dec. 11 **Photo. & Engr.**
1331 A578 9fr pale & dk grn .55 .20

The Young Post Rider, an Engraving by Albrecht Durer A579

Ghent Flower Festival A580

1990, Jan. 12 **Photo. & Engr.**
1332 A579 14fr buff & red blk .75 .55

Postal communications in Europe, 500th anniv.

See Austria No. 1486, Germany No. 1592, Berlin No. 9N584 and German Democratic Republic No. 2791.

1990, Mar. 3 **Photo.**
1333 A580 10fr *Iris florentina* .50 .40
1334 A580 14fr *Cattleya harrisoniana* .75 .55
1335 A580 14fr *Lilium bulbiferum* .75 .55
Nos. 1333-1335 (3) 2.00 1.50

Intl. Women's Day — A581

1990, Mar. 12 **Photo.** ***Perf. 11½***
1336 A581 25fr Emilienne Brunfaut 1.45 1.00

Wheelchair Basketball — A582

Sports.

1990, Mar. 19
1337 A582 10fr multicolored .60 .40
1338 A582 14fr multicolored .80 .60
1339 A582 25fr shown 1.40 1.00
Nos. 1337-1339 (3) 2.80 2.00

Special Olympics (10fr); and 1990 World Cup Soccer Championships, Italy (14fr).

Natl. Water Supply Soc., 75th Anniv. A583

1990, Apr. 2
1340 A583 14fr Water means life .80 .60

Postman Roulin, by Van Gogh — A584

1990, Apr. 9
1341 A584 14fr multicolored .80 .60

Stamp Day.

Labor Day, Cent. A585

1990, Apr. 30
1342 A585 25fr multicolored 1.40 1.00

Europa 1990 A586

Post offices.

1990, May 7 **Photo. & Engr.**
1343 A586 14fr Ostend 1 .80 .60
1344 A586 25fr Liege 1, vert. 1.40 1.00

18-Day Campaign, 1940 — A587

1990, May 14 Photo. *Perf. 11½*
1345 A587 14fr Lys Monument, Courtrai .80 .60

Resistance of German occupation.

Stamp Collecting Promotion Type of 1988
Souvenir Sheet

Various flowers from *Sixty Roses for a Queen*, by P.J. Redoute (1759-1840): a, *Rose tricolore*. b, Belle Rubaree. c, *Mycrophylla*. d, Amelie rose. e, Adelaide rose. f, Helene rose.

1990, June 2 Photo. & Engr.
1346 Sheet of 6 40.00 40.00
a.-c. SP487 14fr any single 1.40 1.40
d.-f. SP487 25fr any single 2.50 2.50

BELGICA '90, Brussels, June 2-10. sold for 220fr.

Battle of Waterloo, 1815 — A588

Design: Marshal Ney leading the French cavalry. (Illustration reduced).

1990, June 18 Photo.
1352 A588 25fr multi + label 1.60 1.10

Tourism A589

1990, July 9
1353 A589 10fr Antwerp .60 .45
1354 A589 10fr Dendermonde .60 .45
1355 A589 14fr Gerpinnes, vert. .80 .60
1356 A589 14fr Lommel .80 .60
1357 A589 14fr Watermael .80 .60
Nos. 1353-1357 (5) 3.60 2.70

A590

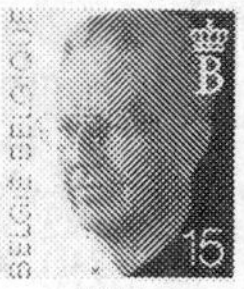

A590a

King Baudouin A590b

1990-92 Photo. *Perf. 11½*
1364 A590 14fr multicolored .80 .60
1365 A590a 15fr rose car .85 .65
1366 A590a 28fr blue green 1.75 1.25
1367 A590b 100fr slate green 6.00 1.50
Nos. 1364-1367 (4) 9.40 4.00

Issue dates: 14fr, Sept. 7; 15fr, Apr. 1; 28fr, Aug. 3, 1992; 100fr, Sept. 14, 1992.

Fish — A591

Designs: No. 1383, Perch (Perche). No. 1384, Minnow (Vairon). No. 1385, Bitterling (Bouviere). No. 1386, Stickleback (Epinoche).

1990, Sept. 8 *Perf. 12*
1383 A591 14fr multicolored 1.25 .60
1384 A591 14fr multicolored 1.25 .60
1385 A591 14fr multicolored 1.25 .60
1386 A591 14fr multicolored 1.25 .60
a. Bklt. pane of 4, #1383-1386 5.00

Youth Philately A592

1990, Oct. 13 *Perf. 11½*
1387 A592 10fr multicolored .60 .45

St. Bernard, 900th Birth Anniv. — A593

1990, Nov. 5 Photo & Engr.
1388 A593 25fr black & buff 1.50 1.10

Winter Scene by Jozef Lucas A594

1990, Nov. 12 Photo.
1389 A594 10fr .60 .40

Christmas.

Self-Portrait A595

Paintings by David Teniers (1610-1690).

1990, Dec. 3
1390 A595 10fr shown .60 .40
1391 A595 14fr Dancers .80 .60
1392 A595 25fr Bowlers 1.40 1.10
Nos. 1390-1392 (3) 2.80 2.10

A596

A597

Designs: 14fr, The Sower by Constantin Meunier (1831-1905). 25fr, Brabo Fountain by Jef Lambeaux (1852-1908).

Photo. & Engr.

1991, Mar. 18 *Perf. 11½*
1393 A596 14fr buff & blk .80 .60
1394 A596 25fr lt bl & dk bl 1.50 1.10

1991, Apr. 8 Photo. *Perf. 11½*
1395 A597 10fr Rhythmic gymnastics .65 .50
1396 A597 10fr Korfball .65 .50

No. 1395, European Youth Olympics. No. 1396, Korfball World Championships.

Stamp Printing Office, Mechlin — A598

1991, Apr. 22
1397 A598 14fr multicolored .90 .65

Stamp Day.

Liberal Trade Union, Cent. A599

1991, Apr. 29
1398 A599 25fr blue & lt blue 1.50 1.10

Europa A600

1991, May 6
1399 A600 14fr Olympus-1 satellite .90 .65
1400 A600 25fr Hermes space shuttle 1.50 1.10

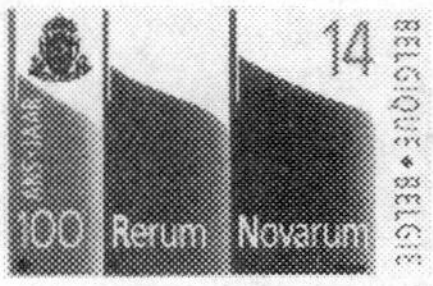

Rerum Novarum Encyclical, Cent. A601

1991, May 13 Photo. *Perf. 11½*
1401 A601 14fr multicolored .85 .65

Princess Isabel & Philip le Bon — A602

1991, May 27 Photo. *Perf. 11½*
1402 A602 14fr multicolored .85 .65

Europalia '91. See Portugal No. 1861.

Tourism A603

Designs: No. 1403, Neptune's Grotto, Couvin. No. 1404, Dieleghem Abbey, Jette. No. 1405, Town Hall, Niel, vert. No. 1406, Nature Reserve, Hautes Fagnes. No. 1407, Legend of giant Rolarius, Roeselare, vert.

1991, June 17 Photo. & Engr.
1403 A603 14fr multicolored .85 .65
1404 A603 14fr multicolored .85 .65
1405 A603 14fr multicolored .85 .65
1406 A603 14fr multicolored .85 .65
1407 A603 14fr multicolored .85 .65
Nos. 1403-1407 (5) 4.25 3.25

King Baudouin, Coronation, 40th Anniv. and 60th Birthday A604

1991, June 24 Photo.
1408 A604 14fr multicolored .85 .65

Royal Academy of Medicine, 150th Anniv. — A605

Photo. & Engr.

1991, Sept. 2 *Perf. 11½*
1409 A605 10fr multicolored .65 .50

The English Coast at Dover by Alfred W. Finch (1854-1930) A606

1991, Sept. 9 Photo.
1410 A606 25fr multicolored 1.50 1.10

See Finland Nos. 868-869.

Mushrooms — A607

1991, Sept. 16 Photo. *Perf. 12*
Booklet Stamps

1411 14fr Amanita phalloides (13A) 1.25 .65
1412 14fr Amanita rubescens (13B) 1.25 .65
1413 14fr Boletus erythropus (13C) 1.25 .65
1414 14fr Hygrocybe persistens (13D) 1.25 .65
a. Bklt. pane of 4, #1411-1414 5.00

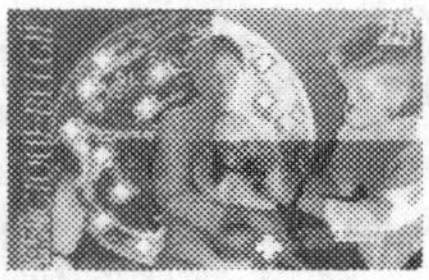

Doctors Without Borders A608

Design: No. 1415, Amnesty Intl.

1991, Sept. 23 *Perf. 11½*
1415 A608 25fr multicolored 1.50 1.10
1416 A608 25fr multicolored 1.50 1.10

Telecom '91 — A609

1991, Oct. 7 Photo. *Perf. 11½*
1417 A609 14fr multicolored .90 .70

6th World Forum and Exposition on Telecommunications, Geneva, Switzerland.

Youth Philately — A610

Cartoon characters: No. 1418, Blake and Mortimer, by Edgar P. Jacobs (16a). No. 1419, Cori the ship boy, by Bob De Moor (16b). No. 1420, Cities of the Fantastic, by Francois Schuiten (16c). No. 1421, Boule and Bill, by Jean Roba (16d).

1991, Oct. 14 *Perf. 12*
Booklet Stamps

1418 A610 14fr multicolored .90 .70
1419 A610 14fr multicolored .90 .70
1420 A610 14fr multicolored .90 .70
1421 A610 14fr multicolored .90 .70
a. Bklt. pane of 4, #1418-1421 3.60

Belgian Newspapers, Cent. — A611

1991, Nov. 4 Photo. *Perf. 11½*
1422 A611 10fr Gazet Van Antwerpen .65 .50
1423 A611 10fr Het Volk .65 .50

Icon of Madonna and Child, Chevetogne Abbey — A612

1991, Nov. 25 Photo. *Perf. 11½*
1424 A612 10fr multicolored .65 .50

Christmas.

Wolfgang Amadeus Mozart, Death Bicent. — A613

1991, Dec. 2 Photo. *Perf. 11½*
1425 A613 25fr multicolored 1.75 1.25

A614

A615

1992, Feb. 10 Photo. *Perf. 11½*
1426 A614 14fr Fire fighting .80 .60

1992, Feb. 24
1427 A615 14fr multicolored .80 .60

Belgian resistance in WWII.

Belgian Carpet Industry — A616

Antwerp Diamond Club, Cent. A617

Design: 14fr, Chef's hat, cutlery.

1992, Mar. 9
1428 A616 10fr multicolored .55 .40
1429 A616 14fr multicolored .80 .60
1430 A617 27fr multicolored 1.50 1.10
Nos. 1428-1430 (3) 2.85 2.10

Belgian Association of Master Chefs.

Expo '92, Seville A618

1992, Mar. 23
1431 A618 14fr multicolored .80 .60

Bird Type of 1985

1992-96 Photo. *Perf. 11½*

1432 A524 1fr Sizerin flamme .20 .20
1433 A524 2fr Merle noir .20 .20
1434 A524 2fr Grive mauvis .20 .20
1435 A524 4fr Gobe mouche noir .30 .25
1436 A524 4fr Bergeronette grise .25 .20
1437 A524 5fr Etourneau sansonnet .35 .20
1438 A524 5fr Hirondelle de cheminee .30 .20
1439 A524 5.50fr Geai des chenes .30 .25
1440 A524 6fr Cincle plongeur .35 .20
1441 A524 6.50fr Phragmite des jongs .45 .30
1442 A524 7fr Loriot .45 .20
1443 A524 8fr Mesange charbonniere .45 .20
1444 A524 10fr Verdier .60 .20
1445 A524 11fr Troglodyte mignon .65 .20
1446 A524 13fr Moineau domestique .70 .20
1446A A524 14fr Pouillot fitis .95 .25
1447 A524 16fr Jaseur boreal .90 .25
Nos. 1432-1447 (17) 7.60 3.70

Issued: 11fr, 4/1/92; 1fr, 2fr, 6fr, 8fr, 10fr, 6/92; 4fr, 5fr, 7fr, 9/7/92; 5.50fr, 9/27/93; 13fr, 16fr, 1/3/94; 6.50fr, 10/3/94; 14fr, 12/18/95; #1435A, 5/6/96; #1433A, 1434, 7/1/96.

Jean Van Noten (1903-1982), Stamp Designer — A619

Photo. & Engr.
1992, Apr. 13 *Perf. 11½*
1448 A619 15fr ver & black .90 .70

Stamp Day.

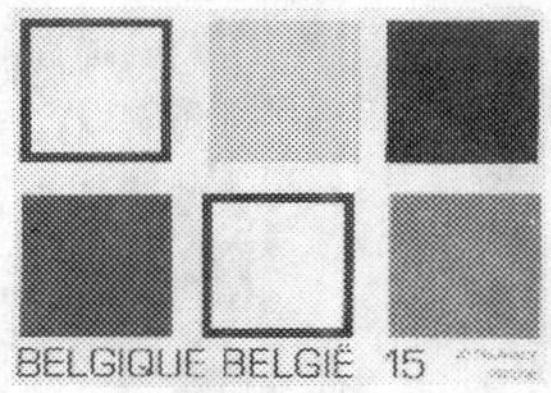

Abstract Painting by Jo Delahaut — A620

#1449, Witte Magie No. 6, by Roger Raveel.

1992, Apr. 27 Photo. *Perf. 11½*
1449 A620 15fr multi, vert. .85 .65
1450 A620 15fr multi .85 .65

Discovery of America, 500th Anniv. — A621

1992, May 4
1451 A621 15fr shown .85 .65
1452 A621 28fr 500, globe, astrolabe 1.60 1.25

Europa.

Fight Racism — A622

1992, May 18 Photo. *Perf. 11½*
1453 A622 15fr black, gray & pink .90 .70

Paintings from Orsay Museum, Paris — A623

Paintings by Belgian artists: 11fr, The Hamlet, by Jacob Smits. 15fr, The Bath, by Alfred Stevens. 30fr, The Man at the Helm, by Theo Van Rysselberghe.

1992, June 15 Photo. *Perf. 11½*
1454 A623 11fr multicolored .65 .50
1455 A623 15fr multicolored .90 .70
1456 A623 30fr multicolored 1.75 1.40
Nos. 1454-1456 (3) 3.30 2.60

Tourism — A624

Designs: No. 1457, Manneken Pis Fountain, Brussels. No. 1458, Landcommander Castle Alden Biesen, Bilzen, horiz. No. 1459, Building facade, Andenne. No. 1460, Fools' Monday Carnival, Renaix, horiz. No. 1461, Great Procession, Tournai, horiz.

Photo. & Engr.
1992, July 6 *Perf. 11½*
1457 A624 15fr multicolored .90 .70
1458 A624 15fr multicolored .90 .70
1459 A624 15fr multicolored .90 .70
1460 A624 15fr multicolored .90 .70
1461 A624 15fr multicolored .90 .70
Nos. 1457-1461 (5) 4.50 3.50

Village of Andenne, 1300th anniv. (#1459). Grand Procession of Tournai, 900th anniv. (#1461).

Animals — A625

1992, Sept. 7 Photo. *Perf. 12*
Booklet Stamps

1462 A625 15fr Polecat (13a) 1.10 .80
1463 A625 15fr Squirrel (13b) 1.10 .80
1464 A625 15fr Hedgehog (13c) 1.10 .80
1465 A625 15fr Dormouse (13d) 1.10 .80
a. Bklt. pane of 4, #1462-1465 4.50

Brabant Revolution — A626

Design: 15fr, Troops fighting and Henri Van der Noot, Jean Andre Van der Meersch, and Jean Francois Vonck, rebel leaders.

Photo. & Engr.

1992, Sept. 21 ***Perf. 11½***

1466 A626 15fr multicolored	.90	.70

Arms of Thurn and Taxis — A627

1992, Oct. 5 **Photo.** ***Perf. 11½***

1467 A627 15fr multicolored	.90	.70

Gaston Lagaffe, by Andre Franquin A628

1992, Oct. 12

1468 A628 15fr multicolored	.90	.70

Youth philately.

Single European Market — A629

1992, Oct. 26

1469 A629 15fr multicolored	.90	.70

Antwerp Zoo, 150th Anniv. — A630

1992, Nov. 16

1470 A630 15fr Okapi	.90	.70
1471 A630 30fr Tamarin	1.75	1.75

The Brussels Place Royale in Winter, by Luc De Decker A631

1992, Nov. 23

1472 A631 11fr multicolored	.70	.50

Christmas.

History A632

Designs: 11fr, Council of Leptines, 1250th anniv. 15fr, 28fr, Missale Romanum of Matthias Corvinus (Matyas Hunyadi, King of Hungary) (diff. details). 30fr, Battles of Neerwinden (1693, 1793).

1993, Mar. 15 **Photo.** ***Perf. 11½***

1473 A632 11fr multicolored	.65	.50
1474 A632 15fr multicolored	.90	.70
1475 A632 30fr multicolored	1.75	1.40
Nos. 1473-1475 (3)	3.30	2.60

Souvenir Sheet

1476 A632 28fr multicolored	1.75	1.25

Size of No. 1474, 80x28mm. No. 1476 contains one 55x40mm stamp.

See Hungary No. 3385-3386.

A633

A634

Antwerp, Cultural City of Europe A635

Designs: No. 1477, Panoramic view of Antwerp (illustration reduced). No. 1478, Antwerp Town Hall, designed by Cornelis Floris. No. 1479, Woman's Head and Warrior's Torso, by Jacob Jordaens. No. 1480, St. Job's Altar (detail), Schoonbroek. No. 1481, Angels on stained glass window, Mater Dei Chapel of Institut Marie-Josee, by Eugeen Yoors, vert.

1993, Mar. 22

1477 A633 15fr multicolored	.90	.70
1478 A634 15fr multicolored	.90	.70
1479 A635 15fr gray & multi	.90	.70
1480 A635 15fr green & multi	.90	.70
1481 A635 15fr blue & multi	.90	.70
Nos. 1477-1481 (5)	4.50	3.50

Antwerp '93.

Stamp Day — A636

1993, Apr. 5

1482 A636 15fr No. 74	.90	.70

Contemporary Paintings — A637

Europa: 15fr, Florence 1960, by Gaston Bertrand. 28fr, De Sjees, by Constant Permeke.

1993, Apr. 26 **Photo.** ***Perf. 11½***

1483 A637 15fr multicolored	.90	.70
1484 A637 28fr multicolored	1.75	1.40

Butterflies — A638

1993, May 10

1485 A638 15fr Vanessa atalanta	.90	.70
1486 A638 15fr Apatura iris	.90	.70
1487 A638 15fr Inachis io	.90	.70
1488 A638 15fr Aglais urticae	.90	.70
Nos. 1485-1488 (4)	3.60	2.80

Alumni Assoc. (UAE), Free University of Brussels, 150th Anniv. A639

1993, May 17

1489 A639 15fr blue & black	.90	.70

Europalia '93 — A640

1993, May 24

1490 A640 15fr Mayan statuette	.90	.70

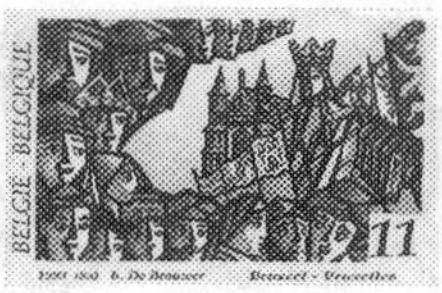

Folklore A641

Designs: 11fr, Ommegang Procession, Brussels. 15fr, Royal Moncrabeau Folk Group, Namur. 28fr, Stilt walkers of Merchtem, vert.

1993, June 7 **Photo.** ***Perf. 11½***

1491 A641 11fr multicolored	.65	.50
1492 A641 15fr multicolored	.90	.70
1493 A641 28fr multicolored	1.60	1.25
Nos. 1491-1493 (3)	3.15	2.45

Tourism A642

Castles: No. 1494, La Hulpe. No. 1495, Cortewalle (Beveren). No. 1496, Jehay. No. 1497, Arenberg (Heverlee), vert. No. 1498, Raeren.

Photo. & Engr.

1993, June 21 ***Perf. 11½***

1494 A642 15fr pale green & black	.90	.70
1495 A642 15fr pale lilac & black	.90	.70
1496 A642 15fr pale blue & black	.90	.70
1497 A642 15fr pale brown & black	.90	.70
1498 A642 15fr pale olive & black	.90	.70
Nos. 1494-1498 (5)	4.50	3.50

Intl. Triennial Exhibition of Tournai A643

1993, July 5 **Photo.** ***Perf. 11½***

1499 A643 15fr black, blue & red	.90	.70

Belgian Presidency of European Community Council A644

1993, Aug. 9 **Photo.** ***Perf. 11½***

1500 A644 15fr multicolored	.90	.70

Rene Magritte (1898-1967), Artist — A645

1993, Aug. 9

1501 A645 30fr multicolored	1.75	1.40

King Baudouin (1930-1993) — A646

1993, Aug. 17 **Photo.** ***Perf. 11½***

1502 A646 15fr black & gray	.90	.70

European House Cats — A647

1993, Sept. 6 Photo. *Perf. 12*

Booklet Stamps

1503 A647 15fr Brown & white (10a) .90 .70
1504 A647 15fr Black & white (10b) .90 .70
1505 A647 15fr Gray tabby (10c) .90 .70
1506 A647 15fr Calico (10d) .90 .70
a. Booklet pane of 4, #1503-1506 3.75

Publication of De Humani Corporis Fabrica, by Andreas Vesalius, 1543 — A648

1993, Oct. 4 Photo. *Perf. 11½*

1507 A648 15fr multicolored .90 .70

Air Hostess Natacha, by Francois Walthery — A649

1993, Oct. 18

1508 A649 15fr multicolored .85 .65

Youth philately.

Publication of "Faux Soir," 50th Anniv. — A650

1993, Nov. 8 Photo. *Perf. 11½*

1509 A650 11fr multicolored .60 .45

Notre-Dame de la Chapelle, Brussels A651

1993, Nov. 22 Photo. *Perf. 11½*

1510 A651 11fr multicolored .65 .50

Christmas, New Year.

Children, Future Decisionmakers — A652

1993, Dec. 13 Photo. *Perf. 11½*

1511 A652 15fr multicolored .90 .70

A653

A654

King Albert II

A655 A655a

1993-98 Photo. *Perf. 11½*

1519 A653 16fr lt gray & multi .95 .25
1520 A653 16fr lt & dk bl grn 1.00 .75
1521 A655 16fr multicolored 1.10 .80
1521A A655 16fr blue 1.10 .80
1521B A655 17fr blue 1.10 .80
1521C A655 18fr olive black 1.00 .75
1521D A655 19fr dp gray violet 1.40 1.00
1522 A653 20fr cream & brn 1.25 .30
1522A A655 20fr brown 1.10 .85
1523 A655 25fr sepia 1.40 1.00
1524 A655 28fr claret 1.90 1.40
1526 A653 30fr red lilac 1.60 .40
1526A A655 32fr violet blue 1.90 1.40
1527 A653 32fr cream & org brn 1.90 .50
1527A A655 34fr dark blue gray 2.00 1.50
1527B A655 36fr dark slate blue 2.20 1.60
1528 A653 40fr pink & car 2.50 .60
1529 A653 50fr green 3.00 .75
1530 A655 50fr green 3.25 2.50
1533 A654 100fr multicolored 6.25 4.75
1535 A654 200fr multicolored 14.00 3.50
Nos. 1519-1535 (21) 51.90 26.20

Coil Stamp

1536 A655a 19fr deep gray vio 1.25 .90

Issued: #1519, 12/15/93; #1520, 1/17/94; 30fr, 2/4/94; #1527, 3/7/94; 50fr, 4/18/94; #1522, 6/6/94; 40fr, 6/20/94; 100fr, 10/3/94; 200fr, 5/2/95; #1521, 6/6/96; #1521A, 1530, 28fr, 9/2/96; 17fr, 12/16/96; 34fr, 36fr, 2/10/97; 18fr, 4/7/97; #1521D, 7/7/97; 25fr, 4/20/98; #1536, 8/10/98; #1522A, 10/19/98; #1526a, 11/9/98.

This is an expanding set. Numbers will change.

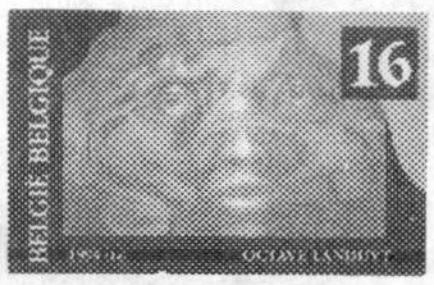

Paintings A656

Designs: No. 1537, The Malleable Darkness, by Octave Landuyt. No. 1538, Ma Toute Belle, by Serge Vandercam, vert.

1994, Jan. 31 Photo. *Perf. 11½*

1537 A656 16fr multicolored .90 .70
1538 A656 16fr multicolored .90 .70

Airplanes A657

13fr, Hanriot-Dupont HD-1. 15fr, Spad XIII. 30fr, Schreck FBA-H. 32fr, Stampe-Vertongen SV-4B.

1994, Feb. 28

1539 A657 13fr multicolored .70 .50
1540 A657 15fr multicolored .85 .65
1541 A657 30fr multicolored 1.60 1.25
1542 A657 32fr multicolored 1.75 1.40
Nos. 1539-1542 (4) 4.90 3.80

Daily Newspapers A658

Designs: No. 1543, "Le Jour-Le Courier," cent., vert. No. 1544, "La Wallonie," 75th anniv.

1994, Mar. 21 Photo. *Perf. 11½*

1543 A658 16fr multicolored .95 .70
1544 A658 16fr multicolored .95 .70

Fall of the Golden Calf (Detail), by Fernand Allard l'Olivier — A659

1994, Mar. 28

1545 A659 16fr multicolored .95 .70

Charter of Quaregnon, cent.

Stamp Day — A660

1994, Apr. 11 Photo. *Perf. 11½*

1546 A660 16fr No. 102 .95 .70

History A661

Scenes from Brabantse Yeesten, 15th cent. illuminated manuscript: 13fr, Reconciliation between John I and Arnold, squire of Wezemaal. 16fr, Tournament at wedding of John II and Margaret of York. 30fr, Battle of Woeringen.

1994, Apr. 25

1547 A661 13fr multicolored .75 .55
1548 A661 16fr multicolored .95 .70
1549 A661 30fr multicolored 1.75 1.25
Nos. 1547-1549 (3) 3.45 2.50

No. 1549 is 81x28mm.

Europa — A662

Designs: 16fr, Abbe Georges Lemaitre (1894-1966), proposed "big-bang" theory of origins of universe. 30fr, Gerardus Mercator (1512-94), cartographer, astronomer.

1994, May 9 Photo. *Perf. 11½*

1550 A662 16fr multicolored .95 .70
1551 A662 30fr multicolored 1.75 1.25

Papal Visit A663

#1552, Father Damien (1840-89). #1553, St. Mutien-Marie (1841-1917), Christian educator.

1994, May 16 *Perf. 11½x12*

1552 A663 16fr multicolored .95 .70
1553 A663 16fr multicolored .95 .70

Tourism A664

Churches: No. 1554, St. Peter's, Bertem. No. 1555, St. Bavo's, Kanegem, vert. No. 1556, Royal St. Mary's, Schaarbeek. No. 1557, St. Gery's, Aubechies. No. 1558, Sts. Peter and Paul, Saint-Severin, Condroz, vert.

1994, June 13 Photo. *Perf. 11½*

1554 A664 16fr multicolored .95 .70
1555 A664 16fr multicolored .95 .70
1556 A664 16fr multicolored .95 .70
1557 A664 16fr multicolored .95 .70
1558 A664 16fr multicolored .95 .70
Nos. 1554-1558 (5) 4.75 3.50

Guillaume Lekeu (1870-94), Composer A665

Design: No. 1560, Detail of painting by Hans Memling (c.1430-94).

1994, Aug. 16 Photo. *Perf. 11½*

1559 A665 16fr multicolored 1.10 .75
1560 A665 16fr multicolored 1.10 .75

Liberation of Belgium, 50th Anniv. — A666

Design: 16fr, General Crerar, Field Marshal Montgomery, Gen. Bradley, Belgium landscape. Illustration reduced.

1994, Sept. 5 Photo. *Perf. 11x11½*

1561 A666 16fr multicolored .95 .70

Wildflowers — A667

Designs: No. 1562, Caltha palustris. No. 1563, Cephalanthera damasonium. No. 1564, Calystegia soldanella. No. 1565, Epipactis helleborine.

1994, Sept. 26 Photo. *Perf. 12*

Booklet Stamps

1562 A667 16fr multi (14a) 1.10 .75
1563 A667 16fr multi (14b) 1.10 .75
1564 A667 16fr multi (14c) 1.10 .75
1565 A667 16fr multi (14d) 1.10 .75
a. Booklet pane of 4, #1562-1565 4.50

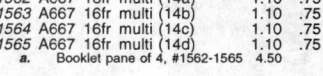

Cubitus the Dog, by Luc Dupanloup — A668

1994, Oct. 10 *Perf. 11½*

1566 A668 16fr multicolored 1.10 .75

Youth philately.

Georges Simenon (1903-89), Writer A669

Photo. & Engr.

1994, Oct. 17 ***Perf. 11½***

1567 A669 16fr multicolored	1.10	.75

See France No. 2443, Switzerland No. 948.

Christmas A670

1994, Dec. 5 **Photo.** ***Perf. 11½***

1568 A670 13fr multicolored	.85	.65

Anniversaries and Events — A671

Designs: No. 1569, August Vermeylen Fund, 50th anniv. No. 1570, Belgian Touring Club, cent. No. 1571, Assoc. of Belgian Enterprises, cent. No. 1572, Dept. of Social Security, 50th anniv.

1995, Feb. 13 **Photo.** ***Perf. 11½***

1569 A671 16fr multicolored	1.10	.75
1570 A671 16fr multicolored	1.10	.75
1571 A671 16fr multicolored	1.10	.75
1572 A671 16fr multicolored	1.10	.75
Nos. 1569-1572 (4)	4.40	3.00

Flowers of Ghent A672

1995, Mar. 6

1573 A672 13fr Hibiscus rosa-sinensis	.95	.70
1574 A672 16fr Rhododendron simsii	1.10	.75
1575 A672 30fr Fuchsia hybrida	2.25	1.60
Nos. 1573-1575 (3)	4.30	3.05

Games — A673

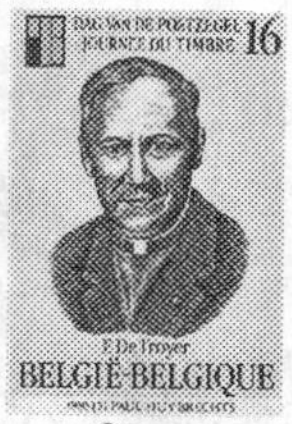

Stamp Day — A674

1995, Mar. 20

1576 A673 13fr Crossword puzzles	.95	.70
1577 A673 16fr Chess	1.10	.75
1578 A673 30fr Scrabble	2.25	1.60
1579 A673 34fr Cards	2.50	1.75
Nos. 1576-1579 (4)	6.80	4.80

1995, Apr. 10 **Photo. & Engr.**

1580 A674 16fr Frans de Troyer	1.10	.75

Peace & Freedom A675

Europa: 16fr, Broken barbed wire, prison guard tower. 30fr, Mushroom cloud, "Never again."

1995, Apr. 24 **Photo.** ***Perf. 11½***

1581 A675 16fr multicolored	1.10	.75
1582 A675 30fr multicolored	2.25	1.75

Liberation of concentration camps, 50th anniv. (#1581). Nuclear Non-Proliferation Treaty, 25th anniv. (#1582).

Battle of Fontenoy, 250th Anniv. — A676

Design: 16fr, Irish soldiers, Cross of Fontenoy.

1995, May 15 **Photo.** ***Perf. 11½***

1583 A676 16fr multicolored	1.10	.75

See Ireland No. 967.

UN, 50th Anniv. A677

1995, May 22 **Photo.** ***Perf. 11½***

1584 A677 16fr multicolored	1.10	.75

"Sauvagemont, Maransart," by Pierre Alechinsky — A678

No. 1586: "Telegram-style," by Pol Mara.

1995, June 6

1585 A678 16fr multicolored	1.10	.75
1586 A678 16fr multicolored	1.10	.75

Tourism A679

Architectural designs: No. 1587, Cauchie house, Brussels, by Paul Cauchie (1875-1952). No. 1588, De Viif Werelddelen, corner building, Antwerp, by Frans Smet-Verhas (1851-1925). No. 1589, House, Liege, by Paul Jaspar (1859-1945).

1995, June 26

1587 A679 16fr multicolored	1.10	.75
1588 A679 16fr multicolored	1.10	.75
1589 A679 16fr multicolored	1.10	.75
Nos. 1587-1589 (3)	3.30	2.25

Sailing Ships — A680

1995, Aug. 21 **Photo.** ***Perf. 12***

Booklet Stamps

1590 A680 16fr Mercator	1.10	.80
1591 A680 16fr Kruzenstern	1.10	.80
1592 A680 16fr Sagres II	1.10	.80
1593 A680 16fr Amerigo Vespucci	1.10	.80
a. Booklet pane of 4, #1590-1593	4.50	
Complete booklet, #1593a	4.50	

Classic Motorcycles A681

1995, Sept. 25 **Photo.** ***Perf. 11½***

1594 A681 13fr 1908 Minerva	.90	.65
1595 A681 16fr 1913 FN, vert.	1.10	.80
1596 A681 30fr 1929 La Mondiale	2.00	1.50
1597 A681 32fr 1937 Gillet, vert.	2.25	1.60
Nos. 1594-1597 (4)	6.25	4.55

Comic Character, Sammy, by Arthur Berckmans A682

1995, Oct. 9 **Photo.** ***Perf. 11½***

1598 A682 16fr multicolored	1.10	.80

Youth philately.

King's Day A683

Design: 16fr, King Albert II and Queen Paola.

1995, Nov. 15 **Photo.** ***Perf. 11½***

1599 A683 16fr multicolored	1.10	.80

A684

A685

Christmas: 13fr, Nativity scene from "Breviary," book of devotions, c. 1500.

1995, Nov. 20

1600 A684 13fr multicolored	.90	.70

1996, Mar. 4 **Photo.** ***Perf. 11½***

1601 A685 16fr multicolored	1.10	.80

Liberal Party, 150th anniv.

Portrait of Emile Mayrisch (1862-1928), by Théo Van Rysselberghe (1862-1926) A686

1996, Mar. 2

1602 A686 (A) multicolored	1.10	.80

No. 1602 was valued at 16fr on day of issue.

See Luxembourg No. 939.

Oscar Bonnevalle, Stamp Designer — A687

1996, Apr. 1

1603 A687 16fr multicolored	1.10	.80

Stamp Day.

Insects A688

Designs: No. 1604, Sympetrum sanguineum. No. 1605, Bombus terrestris. No. 1606, Lucanus cervus. No. 1607, Melolontha melolontha. No. 1608, Gryllus campestris. No. 1609, Coccinella septempunctata.

1996, Apr. 1 **Photo.** ***Perf. 12***

Booklet Stamps

1604 A688 16fr multicolored	1.10	.80
1605 A688 16fr multicolored	1.10	.80
1606 A688 16fr multicolored	1.10	.80
1607 A688 16fr multicolored	1.10	.80
1608 A688 16fr multicolored	1.10	.80
1609 A688 16fr multicolored	1.10	.80
a. Booklet pane, #1604-1609	6.60	
Complete booklet, #1609a	6.60	

Famous Women A689

Europa: 16fr, Yvonne Nevejean (1900-87), saved Jewish children during World War II. 30fr, Marie Gevers (1883-1975), poet.

1996, May 6 **Photo.** ***Perf. 11½***

1610 A689 16fr multicolored	1.10	.80
1611 A689 30fr multicolored	2.00	1.50

Tourism — A690

Architecture in Brussels — A691

Designs: No. 1612, Grotto of Han-Sur-Lesse, horiz. No. 1613, Village of Begijnendijk as separate community, bicent.

1996, June 10 Photo. *Perf. 11½*

1612 A690 16fr multicolored 1.10 .80
1613 A690 16fr multicolored 1.10 .80

1996, June 10

Designs: No. 1614, La Maison du Roi (Grand Place). No. 1615, Galeries Royales Saint-Hubert. No. 1616, Le Palais d'Egmont, Le Petit Sablon, horiz. No. 1617, Le Cinquantenaire, horiz.

1996, June 10

1614 A691 16fr multi (7a) 1.10 .80
1615 A691 16fr multi (7b) 1.10 .80
1616 A691 16fr multi (7c) 1.10 .80
1617 A691 16fr multi (7d) 1.10 .80
Nos. 1614-1617 (4) 4.40 3.20

Auto Races at Spa, Cent. A692

1996, July 1

1618 A692 16fr 1900 German 6CV 1.10 .80
1619 A692 16fr 1925 Alfa Romeo P2 1.10 .80
1620 A692 16fr 1939 Mercedes Benz W154 1.10 .80
1621 A692 16fr 1967 Ferrari 330P 1.10 .80
Nos. 1618-1621 (4) 4.40 3.20

Paintings of Historical Figures — A693

Portraits from town hall triptych, Zierikzee, Netherlands: No. 1622, Philip I, the Handsome (1478-1506). No. 1623, Juana of Castile, the Mad (1479-1555).

1996, Sept. 2 Photo. *Perf. 11½*

1622 A693 16fr multicolored 1.10 .80
1623 A693 16fr multicolored 1.10 .80

A694

A695

Paintings from National Gallery, London: 14fr, Reading Man, by Rogier Van Der Weyden (1399-1464). 16fr, Susanna Fourment, by Peter Paul Rubens (1577-1640). 30fr, A Man in a Turban, by Jan Van Eyck (1390-1441).

1996, Sept. 2

1624 A694 14fr multicolored .95 .70
1625 A694 16fr multicolored 1.10 .80
1626 A694 30fr multicolored 2.00 1.50
Nos. 1624-1626 (3) 4.05 3.00

Bird Type of 1985

1996, Oct. 7 Photo. *Perf. 11½*

1627 A524 6fr Tarin des aulnes .40 .30

1996, Oct. 7

Comic Character, Cloro, by Raymond Macherot.

1628 A695 16fr multicolored 1.10 .80

Youth Philately.

Almanac of Mons, by Fr. Charles Letellier, 150th Anniv. A696

1996, Oct. 7

1629 A696 16fr multicolored 1.10 .80

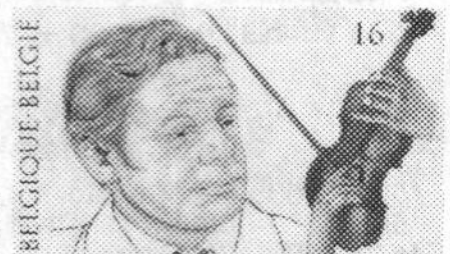

Music and Literature A697

Designs: No. 1630, Arthur Grumiaux (1921-86), violinist. No. 1631, Flor Peeters (1903-86), organist. No. 1632, Christian Dotremont (1922-79), poet, artist. No. 1633, Paul Van Ostaijen (1896-1928), writer.

Photo. & Engr.

1996, Oct. 28 *Perf. 11½*

1630 A697 16fr multicolored 1.10 .80
1631 A697 16fr multicolored 1.10 .80
1632 A697 16fr multicolored 1.10 .80
1633 A697 16fr multicolored 1.10 .80
Nos. 1630-1633 (4) 4.40 3.20

Christmas and New Year — A698

Scenes from Christmas Market: a, Decorated trees, rooftops. b, Lighted greeting signs. c, Church. d, Selling desert items. e, Selling Nativity scenes. f, Selling meat. g, Santa ringing bell. h, Man smoking pipe, people with presents. i, People shopping.

1996, Nov. 18 Photo. *Perf. 11½*

1634 A698 14fr Sheet of 9, #a.-i. 8.25 6.25

Catholic Faculty University, Mons, Cent. A699

1997, Jan. 20 Photo. *Perf. 11½*

1635 A699 17fr multicolored 1.10 .80

Opera at Theatre Royal de la Monnaie, Brussels — A700

#1636, Marie Sasse (1834-1907), soprano. #1637, Ernest Van Dijck (1861-1923), tenor. #1638, Hector Dufranne (1870-1951), baritone. #1639, Clara Clairbert (1899-1970), soprano.

1997, Feb. 10

1636 A700 17fr multicolored 1.00 .75
1637 A700 17fr multicolored 1.00 .75
1638 A700 17fr multicolored 1.00 .75
1639 A700 17fr multicolored 1.00 .75
Nos. 1636-1639 (4) 4.00 3.00

Eastern Cantons — A701

Illustration reduced.

1997, Feb. 10 Photo. *Perf. 11½*

1640 A701 17fr multicolored 1.00 .75

Bird Type of 1985

1997, Mar. 10

1641 A524 15fr Mesange boreale .90 .70

UN Peace-Keeping Forces — A702

1997, Mar. 10

1642 A702 17fr multicolored 1.00 .75

Stories and Legends A703

Europa: 17fr, "De Bokkenrijders" (The Goat Riders). 30fr, Jean de Berneau.

1997, Mar. 10 Photo. *Perf. 11½*

1643 A703 17fr multicolored 1.00 .75
1644 A703 30fr multicolored 1.75 1.25

Bird Type of 1985

1997, Apr. 7

Size: 35x25mm

1645 A524 150fr Ekster 8.50 6.25

Constant Spinoy (1924-93), Stamp Engraver — A704

1997, Apr. 7 Photo. & Engr.

1646 A704 17fr multicolored 1.00 .75

Stamp Day.

Intl. Flower Show, Liege A705

Paintings by Paul Delvaux (1897-1994) A706

1997, Apr. 21 Photo.

1647 A705 17fr multicolored 1.00 .75

1997, Apr. 21

Details or entire paintings: 15fr, Woman with garland of leaves in hair. 17fr, Nude, horiz. 32fr, Woman wearing hat, trolley.

1648 A706 15fr multicolored .85 .65
1649 A706 17fr multicolored 1.00 .75
1650 A706 32fr multicolored 1.75 1.40
Nos. 1648-1650 (3) 3.60 2.80

Bird Type of 1985

1997, May 7 Photo. *Perf. 11½*

1651 A524 3fr Alouette des champs .25 .20

Queen Paola, 60th Birthday A707

1997, May 26

1652 A707 17fr Belvedere Castle 1.00 .75

See Italy No. 2147.

Cartoon Character, "Jommeke," by Jef Nys — A708

1997, May 26

1653 A708 17fr multicolored 1.00 .75

A709

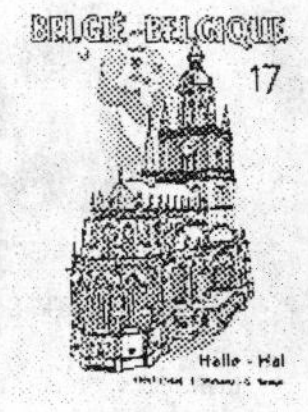

A710

Roses: No. 1654, Rosa damascena coccinea. No. 1655, Rosa sulfurea. No. 1656, Rosa centifolia.

1997, July 7 Photo. *Perf. 11½*

1654 A709 17fr multicolored 1.25 .90
1655 A709 17fr multicolored 1.25 .90
1656 A709 17fr multicolored 1.25 .90
Nos. 1654-1656 (3) 3.75 2.70

World Congress of Rose Societies.

1997, July 7 Photo. & Engr.

Churches: No. 1657, Basilica of St. Martin, Halle. No. 1658, Notre Dame Church, Laeken, horiz. No. 1659, Basilica of St. Martin, Liège.

1657 A710 17fr multicolored 1.25 .90
1658 A710 17fr multicolored 1.25 .90
1659 A710 17fr multicolored 1.25 .90
Nos. 1657-1659 (3) 3.75 2.70

Bird Type of 1985

1997, Sept. 1 Photo. *Perf. 11½*

1660 A525 7fr Bergeronnette printaniere .40 .30

Bees and Apiculture — A711

Designs: No. 1661, Queen, workers. No. 1662, Development of the larvae. No. 1663, Bee exiting cell. No. 1664, Bee collecting nectar. No. 1665, Two bees. No. 1666, Two bees on honeycomb.

1997, Sept. 1 Photo. *Perf. 12*

Booklet Stamps

1661 A711 17fr multicolored (15a) 1.00 .75
1662 A711 17fr multicolored (15b) 1.00 .75
1663 A711 17fr multicolored (15c) 1.00 .75
1664 A711 17fr multicolored (15d) 1.00 .75
1665 A711 17fr multicolored (15e) 1.00 .75
1666 A711 17fr multicolored (15f) 1.00 .75
a. Booklet pane of 6, #1661-1666 6.00
Complete booklet, #1666a 6.00

Craftsmen A712

1997, Sept. 1 ***Perf. 11½***

1667	A712	17fr	Stone cutter	.75	.60
1668	A712	17fr	Mason	.75	.60
1669	A712	17fr	Carpenter	.75	.60
1670	A712	17fr	Blacksmith	.75	.60
			Nos. 1667-1670 (4)	3.00	2.40

Antarctic Expedition by the Belgica, Cent. — A713

1997, Sept. 22 **Photo.** ***Perf. 11½***

1671 A713 17fr multicolored 1.00 .75

A714

A715

Royal Museum of Central Africa, Cent.: No. 1672, Mask, Shaba, Congo. No. 1673, Outside view of museum, horiz. 34fr, Dish Bearer sculpture, Buli area, Congo.

1997, Sept. 22 **Photo.** ***Perf. 11½***

1672	A714	17fr	multicolored	1.00	.75
1673	A714	17fr	multicolored	1.00	.75
1674	A714	34fr	multicolored	1.00	.75
			Nos. 1672-1674 (3)	3.00	2.25

No. 1673 is 25x73mm.

1997, Oct. 25 **Photo.** ***Perf. 11½***

Christmas: "Fairon," by Pierre Grahame.

1675 A715 15fr multicolored .90 .70

Bird Type of 1985

1997, Dec. 1 **Photo.** ***Perf. 11½***

1676 A524 15fr Mesange boreale, horiz. .90 .70

No. 1676 issued in coil rolls with every fifth stamp numbered on reverse.

Rhododendron A716

Serpentine Die Cut 13½ on 2 or 3 Sides

1997, Dec. 1

Booklet Stamp

Self-Adhesive

1677 A716 (17fr) multicolored 1.00 .75
a. Booklet pane of 10 10.00

By its nature, No. 1677a is a complete booklet. The peelable backing serves as a booklet cover.

"Thalys" High Speed Train — A717

1998, Jan. 19 **Photo.** ***Perf. 11½***

1678 A717 17fr multicolored 1.00 .75

Woman Suffrage in Belgium, 50th Anniv. — A718

1998, Jan. 19

1679 A718 17fr multicolored 1.00 .75

Norge (1898-1990), Writer — A719

Design: No. 1680, Gerard Walschap (1898-1989), poet, playwright.

1998, Feb. 16 **Photo.** ***Perf. 11½***

1680	A719	17fr	multicolored	.95	.70
1681	A719	17fr	multicolored	.95	.70

Paintings, by René Magritte (1898-1967) A720

#1682, "La Magie Noire (Black Magic),"nude woman. #1683, "La Corde Sensible (Heartstring)," cloud over champagne glass. #1684, "Le Chateau des Pyrenees (Castle of the Pyranees)," castle atop floating rock.

1998, Mar. 9 **Photo.** ***Perf. 11½***

1682	A720	17fr	multi, vert.	.95	.70
1683	A720	17fr	multi	.95	.70
1684	A720	17fr	multi, vert.	.95	.70
			Nos. 1682-1684 (3)	2.85	2.10

Belgian Artists — A721

Details or entire paintings: No. 1685, "La Foire aux Amours," by Félicien Rops (1833-98). No. 1686, "Hospitality for the Strangers," by Gustave van de Woestijne (1881-1947). No. 1687, Self-portrait, "The Man with the Beard," by Felix de Boeck (1898-1995). No. 1688, "Black Writing Mixed with Colors," by Karel Appel & Christian Cotremont of COBRA.

1998, Mar. 9 ***Perf. 12***

Booklet Stamps

1685	A721	17fr	multicolored	.95	.70
1686	A721	17fr	multicolored	.95	.70
1687	A721	17fr	multicolored	.95	.70
1688	A721	17fr	multicolored	.95	.70
a.			Booklet pane, #1685-1688	3.80	
			Complete booklet, #1688a	3.80	

Museum of Fine Arts, Ghent, bicent. (#1686). COBRA art movement of painters and poets, 50th anniv. (#1688).

Sabena Airlines, 75th Anniv. — A722

1998, Apr. 20 **Photo.** ***Perf. 11½***

1689 A722 17fr multicolored .95 .70

Belgian Stamp Dealers' Assoc., 75th Anniv. A723

1998, Apr. 20

1690 A723 17fr multicolored .95 .70

"The Return," by René Magritte (1898-1967) — A724

1998, Apr. 20

1691 A724 17fr multicolored .95 .70

See France No. 2637.

Wildlife A725

1998, Apr. 20

1692	A725	17fr	Vulpes vulpes	.95	.70
1693	A725	17fr	Cervus elaphus	.95	.70
1694	A725	17fr	Sus scrofa	.95	.70
1695	A725	17fr	Capreolus capreolus	.95	.70
			Nos. 1692-1695 (4)	3.80	2.80

Bird Type of 1985

1998, May 4 **Photo.** ***Perf. 11½***

1696 A524 1fr Mesange huppee .20 .20

Edmund Struyf (1911-96), Founder of Pro-Post, Assoc. for Promotion of Philately — A726

1998, May 4 **Photo. & Engr.**

1697 A726 17fr multicolored .95 .70

Stamp Day.

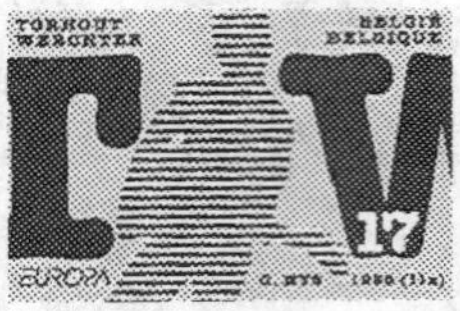

Natl. Festivals A727

1998, May 4 Photo. *Perf. 11½*

1698 A727 17fr Torhout & Werchter Rock Festival .95 .70
1699 A727 17fr Wallonia Festival .95 .70

Europa.

Bird Type of 1985

1998, July 6 Photo. *Perf. 11½*

1700 A524 7.50fr Pie-grieche grise .45 .35

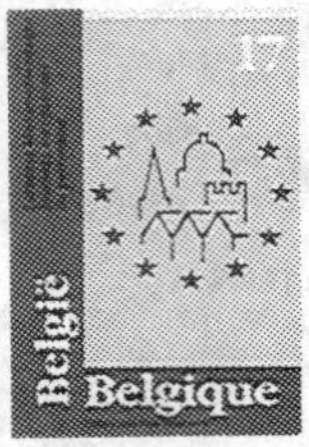

European Heritage Days — A728

Designs: a, Logo. b, Bourla Theatre, Antwerp. c, La Halle, Durbuy. d, Halletoren, Kortrijk. e, Louvain Town Hall. f, Perron, Liège. g, Royal Theatre, Namur. h, Aspremont-Lynden Castle, Rekem. i, Neo-Gothic kiosk, Sint-Niklaas. j, Chapelle Saint Vincent, Tournai. k, Villers-la-Ville Abbey. l, Saint Gilles Town Hall, Brussels.

1998, July 6

1701 A728 17fr Sheet of 12, #a.-l. 11.00 8.50

Bird Type of 1985

1998 Photo. *Perf. 11½*

1702 A524 9fr Pic vert .50 .40
1703 A524 10fr Turtle dove .60 .45

Issued: 9fr, 8/10; 10fr, 9/28/98.

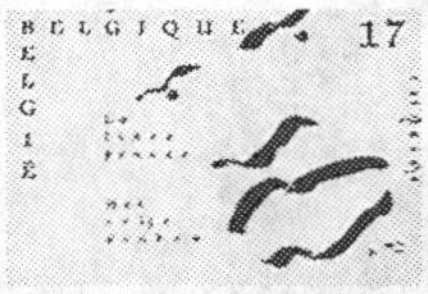

Free Thinking A729

1998, Aug. 10 Photo. *Perf. 11½*

1704 A729 17fr multicolored 1.00 .75

Philips van Marnix van Sint-Aldegonde (1540-98), Author — A730

1998, Aug. 10

1705 A730 17fr multicolored 1.00 .75

Mniszech Palace (Belgian Embassy), Warsaw, Bicent. — A731

Photo. & Engr.

1998, Sept. 28 *Perf. 11½*

1706 A731 17fr multicolored 1.00 .75

See Poland No. 3420.

Contemporary Belgium Films — A732

1998, Sept. 28 Photo.

1707 A732 17fr "Le Huitieme Jour" 1.00 .75
1708 A732 17fr "Daens" 1.00 .75

Cartoon Characters, "Chick Bill" and "Ric Hochet" — A733

1998, Oct. 19 Photo. *Perf. 11½*

1709 A733 17fr multicolored 1.00 .75

Youth philately.

Assoc. of Space Explorers, 14th World Congress, Brussels — A734

1998, Oct. 19

1710 A734 17fr multicolored 1.00 .75

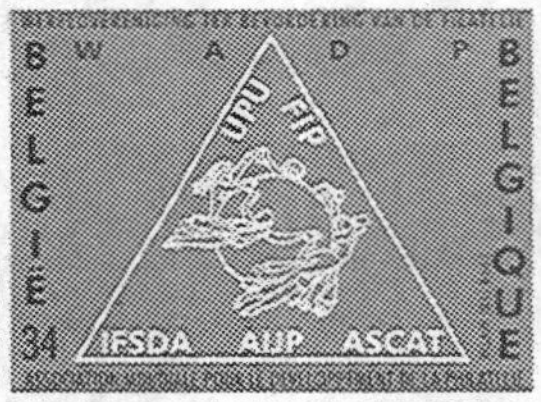

World Post Day A735

1998, Oct. 19 Photo. *Perf. 11½*

1711 A735 34fr blue & dark blue 2.00 1.50

World Assoc. for the Development of Philately.

FGTB-ABVV Trade Union, Cent. — A736

Center panel of triptych by Constant Draz (1875-)

1998, Nov. 9 Photo. *Perf. 11½*

1712 A736 17fr multicolored 1.00 .75

Christmas and New Year A737

1998, Nov. 9

1713 A737 (17fr) multicolored 1.00 .75

Bird Type of 1985

1998-99 Photo. *Perf. 11½*

1714 A524 16fr Mesange noire .85 .65
1715 A524 21fr Grive litorne, horiz. 1.10 .85

No. 1715 also issued in coils with number on reverse of every 5th stamp.

Issued: 16fr, 1/25/99; 21fr, 12/14/98.

A738

A739

Greetings Stamps: No. 1716, Burning candle burning. No. 1717, Stork carrying a heart. No. 1718, Wristwatch. No. 1719, Four leaf clover with one leaf a heart. No. 1720, Two doves. No. 1721, Heart with arrow through it. No. 1722, Heart-shaped head on woman. No. 1723, Heart-shaped head on man.

1999, Jan. 25 Photo. *Perf. 12*

Booklet Stamps

1716 A738 (17fr) multicolored 1.00 .75
1717 A738 (17fr) multicolored 1.00 .75
1718 A738 (17fr) multicolored 1.00 .75
1719 A738 (17fr) multicolored 1.00 .75
1720 A738 (17fr) multicolored 1.00 .75
1721 A738 (17fr) multicolored 1.00 .75
1722 A738 (17fr) multicolored 1.00 .75
1723 A738 (17fr) multicolored 1.00 .75
a. Booklet pane, #1716-1723 8.00
Complete booklet, #1723a 8.00

1999, Feb. 22 Photo. *Perf. 11½*

Owls.

1724 A739 17fr Tyto alba .90 .70
1725 A739 17fr Athene noctua .90 .70
1726 A739 17fr Strix aluco .90 .70
1727 A739 17fr Asio otus .90 .70
Nos. 1724-1727 (4) 3.60 2.80

NATO, 50th Anniv. A740

1999, Mar. 15

1728 A740 17fr Leopard tank .90 .70
1729 A740 17fr F16 fighter .90 .70
1730 A740 17fr Frigate Wandelaar .90 .70
1731 A740 17fr Hospital tent .90 .70
1732 A740 17fr General staff .90 .70
Nos. 1728-1732 (5) 4.50 3.50

UPU, 125th Anniv. A741

1999, Mar. 15

1733 A741 34fr multicolored 1.90 1.40

National Parks and Nature Reserves A742

Europa: No. 1734, De Bunt, near town of Hamme. No. 1735, Harchies-Hensies-Pommeroeul.

1999, Apr. 12

1734 A742 17fr multicolored .90 .70
1735 A742 17fr multicolored .90 .70

First Belgian Postage Stamps, 150th Anniv. A743

Photo. & Engr.

1999, Apr. 26 *Perf. 11½*

1736 A743 17fr No. 1	.95	.70
1737 A743 17fr No. 2	.95	.70
a. Pair, #1736-1737	1.80	1.40

Painting, "My Favorite Room," by James Ensor (1860-1949) — A744

Designs: No. 1739, Woman Eating Oysters, vert. 30fr, Triumph Over Death, vert. 32fr, Old Lady With Masks, vert.

1999, May 17 Photo. *Perf. 11½*

1738 A744 17fr multicolored	.95	.70
1739 A744 17fr multicolored	.95	.70
1740 A744 30fr multicolored	1.75	1.40
1741 A744 32fr multicolored	1.90	1.50
Nos. 1738-1741 (4)	5.55	4.30

See Israel No. 1365A.

Issued: No. 1738, 5/17; Nos. 1739-1741, 9/11.

King Albert and Queen Paola, 40th Wedding Anniv. — A747

1999, July 2 Photo. *Perf. 11½*

1747 A747 17fr multicolored	.95	.70

Nobel Laureates in Peace — A750

Designs: 17fr, Henri La Fontaine (1854-1943). 21fr, Auguste Beernaert (1829-1912).

Photo. & Engr.

1999, Sept. 30 *Perf. 11½*

1749 A750 17fr red & gold	.90	.70
1750 A750 21fr blue & gold	1.10	.85

See Sweden Nos. 2357-2358.

King Albert II — A751

1999 Photo. *Perf. 11¾x11½*

1752 A751 17fr multicolored	.90	.70

This is an expanding set. Numbers may change.

Youth Philately — A756

Comic strips: a, Corentin, by Paul Cuvelier (16a). b, Jerry Spring, by Jijé (16b). c, Gil Jourdan, by Maurice Tillieux (16c). d, La Patrouille des Castors, by Mitacq (16d). e, Entrance hall of Belgian Comic Strip Museum (16e). f, Hassan & Kadour, by Jacques Laudy (16f). g, Buck Danny, by Victor Hubinon (16g). h, Tif et Tondu, by Fernand Dineur (16h). i, Les Timour, by Sirius (16i).

1999, Oct. 2 Photo. *Perf. 11½*

1771 A756 17fr Sheet of 9, #a.-i.	7.75	6.00

SEMI-POSTAL STAMPS

Values quoted for Nos. B1-B24 are for stamps with label attached. Copies without label sell for one-tenth or less.

St. Martin of Tours Dividing His Cloak with a Beggar
SP1 SP2

Unwmk.

1910, June 1 Typo. *Perf. 14*

B1 SP1 1c gray	1.60	1.25
B2 SP1 2c purple brn	13.00	9.25
B3 SP1 5c peacock blue	3.50	2.50
B4 SP1 10c brown red	3.50	2.50
B5 SP2 1c gray green	3.50	2.50
B6 SP2 2c violet brn	10.00	7.25
B7 SP2 5c peacock blue	3.50	2.50
B8 SP2 10c carmine	3.50	2.50
Nos. B1-B8 (8)	42.10	30.25

Overprinted "1911" in Black

1911, Apr. 1

B9 SP1 1c gray	20.00	14.00
a. Inverted overprint		
B10 SP1 2c purple brn	50.00	45.00
B11 SP1 5c peacock blue	5.75	4.00
B12 SP1 10c brown red	5.75	4.00
B13 SP2 1c gray green	40.00	35.00
B14 SP2 2c violet brn	35.00	27.50
B15 SP2 5c peacock blue	5.75	4.00
B16 SP2 10c carmine	5.75	4.00
Nos. B9-B16 (8)	168.00	137.50

Overprinted "CHARLEROI-1911"

1911, June

B17 SP1 1c gray	5.00	5.00
B18 SP1 2c purple brn	17.00	17.00
B19 SP1 5c peacock blue	8.00	8.00
B20 SP1 10c brown red	7.50	7.50
B21 SP2 1c gray green	5.00	5.00
B22 SP2 2c violet brn	16.00	16.00
B23 SP2 5c peacock blue	6.75	6.75
B24 SP2 10c carmine	5.00	5.00
Nos. B17-B24 (8)	70.25	70.25

Nos. B1-B24 were sold at double face value, except the 10c denominations which were sold for 15c. The surtax benefited the national anti-tuberculosis organization.

SP3

Merode Monument — SP4 King Albert I — SP5

1914, Oct. 3 Litho.

B25 SP3 5c green & red	4.00	2.00
B26 SP3 10c red	.45	*.50*
B27 SP3 20c violet & red	12.00	12.00
Nos. B25-B27 (3)	16.45	14.50

Counterfeits of Nos. B25-B27 abound. Probably as many as 90% of the stamps on the market are counterfeits. Values are for genuine examples.

1914, Oct. 3

B28 SP4 5c green & red	4.50	*5.00*
B29 SP4 10c red	5.00	5.00
B30 SP4 20c violet & red	47.50	47.50
Nos. B28-B30 (3)	57.00	57.50

Counterfeits of Nos. B28-B30 abound. Probably as many as 90% of the stamps on the market are counterfeits. Values are for genuine examples.

1915, Jan. 1 *Perf. 12, 14*

B31 SP5 5c green & red	5.00	3.00
a. Perf. 12x14	16.00	12.00
B32 SP5 10c rose & red	20.00	6.00
B33 SP5 20c violet & red	25.00	14.00
a. Perf. 14x12	500.00	250.00
b. Perf. 12	50.00	32.50
Nos. B31-B33 (3)	50.00	23.00

Nos. B25-B33 were sold at double face value. The surtax benefited the Red Cross.

Types of Regular Issue of 1915 Surcharged in Red:

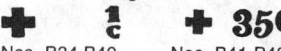

✚ 1/c ✚ 35c
Nos. B34-B40 Nos. B41-B43

✚ 1F
Nos. B44-B47

1918, Jan. 15 Typo. *Perf. 14*

B34 A46 1c + 1c dp orange	.50	.50
B35 A46 2c + 2c brown	.60	.60
B36 A46 5c + 5c blue grn	1.25	1.25
B37 A46 10c + 10c red	2.25	2.25
B38 A46 15c + 15c brt violet	3.25	3.25
B39 A46 20c + 20c plum	7.50	7.50
B40 A46 25c + 25c ultra	7.50	7.50
Engr.		
B41 A47 35c + 35c lt vio & blk	10.00	10.00
B42 A48 40c + 40c dull red & blk	10.00	10.00
B43 A49 50c + 50c turq blue & blk	12.00	12.00
B44 A50 1fr + 1fr bluish slate	35.00	35.00
B45 A51 2fr + 2fr dp gray grn	100.00	100.00
B46 A52 5fr + 5fr brown	250.00	250.00
B47 A53 10fr + 10fr dp blue	500.00	500.00
Nos. B34-B47 (14)	939.85	939.85

Discus Thrower — SP6 Racing Chariot — SP7

Runner — SP8

1920, May 20 Engr. *Perf. 12*

B48 SP6 5c + 5c dp green	1.40	1.40
B49 SP7 10c + 5c carmine	1.40	1.40
B50 SP8 15c + 15c dk brown	3.00	3.00
Nos. B48-B50 (3)	5.80	5.80

7th Olympic Games, 1920. Surtax benefited wounded soldiers. Exists imperf.

For surcharges see Nos. 140-142.

Allegory: Asking Alms from the Crown SP9 Wounded Veteran SP10

1922, May 20

B51 SP9 20c + 20c brown	1.40	1.40

1923, July 5

B52 SP10 20c + 20c slate gray	1.75	1.75

Surtax on #B51-B52 was to aid wounded veterans.

SP11 SP12

St. Martin, by Van Dyck
SP13 SP14

1925, Dec. 15 Typo. *Perf. 14*

B53 SP11 15c + 15c dull vio & red	.50	.20
B54 SP11 30c + 5c gray & red	.25	.20
B55 SP11 1fr + 10c chalky blue & red	1.25	1.40
Nos. B53-B55 (3)	2.00	1.80

Surtax for the Natl. Anti-Tuberculosis League.

1926, Feb. 10

B56 SP12 30c + 30c bluish grn (red surch.)	.50	.55
B57 SP13 1fr + 1fr lt blue	7.25	7.25
B58 SP14 1fr + 1fr lt blue	1.10	1.25
Nos. B56-B58 (3)	8.85	9.05

The surtax aided victims of the Meuse flood.

Lion and Cross of Lorraine SP15 Queen Elisabeth and King Albert SP16

1926, Dec. 6 Typo. *Perf. 14*

B59 SP15 5c + 5c dk brown	.25	.20
B60 SP15 20c + 5c red brown	.45	.40
B61 SP15 50c + 5c dull violet	.30	.20

Engr. *Perf. 11½*

B62 SP16 1.50fr + 25c dk blue	.75	.70
B63 SP16 5fr + 1fr rose red	6.50	6.00
Nos. B59-B63 (5)	8.25	7.50

Surtax was used to benefit tubercular war veterans.

Boat Adrift — SP17

1927, Dec. 15 Engr. Perf. 11½, 14

B64	SP17	25c + 10c dk brown	.70	.70
B65	SP17	35c + 10c yel grn	.70	.70
B66	SP17	60c + 10c dp violet	.60	.40
B67	SP17	1.75fr + 25c dk blue	1.50	*2.00*
B68	SP17	5fr + 1fr plum	4.50	*4.75*
		Nos. B64-B68 (5)	8.00	*8.55*

The surtax on these stamps was divided among several charitable associations.

Ogives of Orval Abbey — SP18

Monk Carving Capital of Column — SP19

Ruins of Orval Abbey SP20

Design: 60c+15c, 1.75fr+25c, 3fr+1fr, Countess Matilda recovering her ring.

1928, Sept. 15 Photo. Perf. 11½

B69	SP18	5c + 5c red & gold	.25	.30
B70	SP18	25c + 5c dk vio & gold	.45	.50

Engr.

B71	SP19	35c + 10c dp green	1.10	1.10
B72	SP19	60c + 15c red brown	1.60	1.60
B73	SP19	1.75fr + 25c dk blue	3.50	3.50
B74	SP19	2fr + 40c dp violet	13.00	13.00
B75	SP19	3fr + 1fr red	15.00	15.00

Perf. 14

B76	SP20	5fr + 5fr rose lake	15.00	15.00
B77	SP20	10fr + 10fr ol green	15.00	15.00
		Nos. B69-B77 (9)	64.90	65.00

Surtax for the restoration of the ruined Orval Abbey.

For overprints see Nos. B84-B92.

St. Waudru, Mons — SP22

St. Rombaut, Malines — SP23

Designs: 25c + 15c, Cathedral of Tournal. 60c + 15c, St. Bavon, Ghent. 1.75fr + 25c, St. Gudule, Brussels. 5fr + 5fr, Louvain Library.

1928, Dec. 1 Photo. Perf. 14, 11½

B78	SP22	5c + 5c carmine	.20	.20
B79	SP22	25c + 15c ol brn	.35	.40

Engr.

B80	SP23	35c + 10c dp green	1.25	1.25
B81	SP23	60c + 15c red brn	.50	.25
B82	SP23	1.75fr + 25c vio blue	8.50	7.00
B83	SP23	5fr + 5fr red vio	16.00	15.00
		Nos. B78-B83 (6)	26.80	24.10

The surtax was for anti-tuberculosis work.

Nos. B69-B77 with this overprint in blue or red were privately produced. They were for the laying of the 1st stone toward the restoration of the ruined Abbey of Orval. Forgeries of the overprint exist. Value, set, $650.

Waterfall at Coo — SP28

Bayard Rock, Dinant — SP29

Designs: 35c+10c, Menin Gate, Ypres. 60c+15c, Promenade d'Orleans, Spa. 1.75fr+25c, Antwerp Harbor. 5fr+5fr, Quai Vert, Bruges.

1929, Dec. 2 Engr. Perf. 11½

B93	SP28	5c + 5c red brown	.20	.25
B94	SP29	25c + 15c gray blk	.65	.60
B95	SP28	35c + 10c green	.80	.95
B96	SP28	60c + 15c rose lake	.55	.50
B97	SP28	1.75fr + 25c dp blue	4.50	4.50

Perf. 14

B98	SP29	5fr + 5fr dl vio	27.50	27.50
		Nos. B93-B98 (6)	34.20	34.30

Bornhem SP34

Beloeil SP35

Gaesbeek SP36

Designs: 25c + 15c, Wynendaele. 70c + 15c, Oydonck. 1fr + 25c, Ghent. 1.75fr + 25c, Bouillon.

1930, Dec. 1 Photo. Perf. 14

B99	SP34	10c + 5c violet	.25	*.30*
B100	SP34	25c + 15c olive brn	.60	.60

Engr.

B101	SP35	40c + 10c brown vio	.80	*1.00*
B102	SP35	70c + 15c gray blk	.55	.55
B103	SP35	1fr + 25c rose lake	3.50	3.50
B104	SP35	1.75fr + 25c dp blue	4.50	2.75
B105	SP36	5fr + 5fr gray grn	27.50	*32.50*
		Nos. B99-B105 (7)	37.70	*41.20*

Prince Leopold SP41

Queen Elisabeth SP42

Philatelic Exhibition Issue

Souvenir Sheet

1931, July 18 Photo. Perf. 14

B106	SP41	2.45fr + 55c car brn	140.00	140.00

Sold exclusively at the Brussels Phil. Exhib., July 18-21, 1931. Size: 122x159mm. Surtax for the Veterans' Relief Fund.

The sheet normally has pin holes and a cancellation-like marking in the margin. These are considered unused and the condition valued here.

1931, Dec. 1 Engr.

B107	SP42	10c + 5c red brown	.30	*.50*
B108	SP42	25c + 15c dk violet	1.10	*1.30*
B109	SP42	50c + 10c dk green	.95	*1.10*
B110	SP42	75c + 15c black brn	.90	.65
B111	SP42	1fr + 25c rose lake	6.75	6.00
B112	SP42	1.75fr + 25c ultra	4.75	4.00
B113	SP42	5fr + 5fr brown vio	55.00	55.00
		Nos. B107-B113 (7)	69.75	68.55

The surtax was for the National Anti-Tuberculosis League.

Désiré Cardinal Mercier SP43

Mercier Protecting Children and Aged at Malines SP44

Mercier as Professor at Louvain University — SP45

Mercier in Full Canonicals, Giving His Blessing SP46

1932, June 10 Photo. Perf. 14½x14

B114	SP43	10c + 10c dk violet	.40	*.60*
B115	SP43	50c + 30c brt violet	2.25	*2.50*
B116	SP43	75c + 25c olive brn	2.25	2.25
B117	SP43	1fr + 2fr brown red	6.00	6.00

Engr. Perf. 11½

B118	SP44	1.75fr + 75c dp blue	70.00	*82.50*
B119	SP45	2.50fr + 2.50fr dk brn	70.00	70.00
B120	SP44	3fr + 4.50fr dull grn	70.00	70.00
B121	SP45	5fr + 20fr vio brn	80.00	*82.50*
B122	SP46	10fr + 40fr brn lake	175.00	*210.00*
		Nos. B114-B122 (9)	475.90	*526.35*

Honoring Cardinal Mercier and to obtain funds to erect a monument to his memory.

Belgian Infantryman SP47

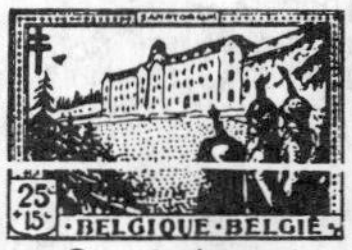

Sanatorium at Waterloo SP48

1932, Aug. 4 Perf. 14½x14

B123	SP47	75c + 3.25fr red brn	55.00	55.00
B124	SP47	1.75fr + 4.25fr dk blue	55.00	55.00

Honoring Belgian soldiers who fought in WWI and to obtain funds to erect a natl. monument to their glory.

1932, Dec. 1 Photo. Perf. 13½x14

B125	SP48	10c + 5c dk vio	.30	*.90*
B126	SP48	25c + 15c red vio	1.00	*1.25*
B127	SP48	50c + 10c red brn	1.00	*1.25*
B128	SP48	75c + 15c ol brn	1.00	.80
B129	SP48	1fr + 25c dp red	13.00	10.50
B130	SP48	1.75fr + 25c dp blue	10.50	9.25
B131	SP48	5fr + 5fr gray grn	85.00	*90.00*
		Nos. B125-B131 (7)	111.80	113.95

Surtax for the assistance of the Natl. Anti-Tuberculosis Society at Waterloo.

View of Old Abbey SP49

Ruins of Old Abbey — SP50

Count de Chiny Presenting First Abbey to Countess Matilda SP56

Restoration of Abbey in XVI and XVII Centuries SP57

Abbey in XVIII Century, Maria Theresa and Charles V — SP58

Madonna and Arms of Seven Abbeys SP60

Designs: 25c+15c, Guests, courtyard, 50c+25c, Transept. 75c+50c, Bell Tower. 1fr+1.25fr, Fountain. 1.25fr+1.75fr, Cloisters. 5fr+20fr, Duke of Brabant placing 1st stone of new abbey.

1933, Oct. 15 **Perf. 14**

B132 SP49 5c + 5c dull grn 35.00 40.00
B133 SP50 10c + 15c ol grn 32.50 35.00
B134 SP49 25c + 15c dk brn 32.50 35.00
B135 SP50 50c + 25c red brn 32.50 35.00
B136 SP50 75c + 50c dp grn 32.50 35.00
B137 SP50 1fr + 1.25fr cop red 32.50 35.00
B138 SP49 1.25fr + 1.75fr gray blk 32.50 35.00
B139 SP56 1.75fr + 2.75fr blue 37.50 40.00
B140 SP57 2fr + 3fr mag 37.50 40.00
B141 SP58 2.50fr + 5fr dull brn 37.50 40.00
B142 SP56 5fr + 20fr vio 40.00 40.00

Perf. 11½

B143 SP60 10fr + 40fr blue 225.00 225.00
Nos. B132-B143 (12) 607.50 635.00

The surtax was for a fund to aid in the restoration of Orval Abbey. Counterfeits exist.

"Tuberculosis Society" SP61

Peter Benoit SP62

1933, Dec. 1 **Engr.** **Perf. 14x13½**

B144 SP61 10c + 5c black .85 .85
B145 SP61 25c + 15c violet 3.00 3.00
B146 SP61 50c + 10c red brn 2.25 2.25
B147 SP61 75c + 15c blk brn 9.25 9.00
B148 SP61 1fr + 25c claret 10.50 10.50
B149 SP61 1.75fr + 25c vio bl 12.50 12.50
B150 SP61 5fr + 5fr lilac 115.00 115.00
Nos. B144-B150 (7) 153.35 153.10

The surtax was for anti-tuberculosis work.

1934, June 1 **Photo.**

B151 SP62 75c + 25c olive brn 5.50 5.50

The surtax was to raise funds for the Peter Benoit Memorial.

King Leopold III
SP63 SP64

1934, Sept. 15

B152 SP63 75c + 25c ol blk 18.00 17.00
a. Sheet of 20 750.00 750.00
B153 SP64 1fr + 25c red vio 17.00 16.00
a. Sheet of 20 750.00 750.00

The surtax aided the National War Veterans' Fund. Sold for 4.50fr a set at the Exhibition of War Postmarks 1914-18, held at Brussels by the Royal Philatelic Club of Veterans. The price included an exhibition ticket. Sold at Brussels post office Sept. 18-22. No. B152 printed in sheets of 20 (4x5) and 100 (10x10). No. B153 printed in sheets of 20 (4x5) and 150 (10x15).

1934, Sept. 24

B154 SP63 75c + 25c violet 1.25 1.25
B155 SP64 1fr + 25c red brn 7.00 7.00

The surtax aided the National War Veterans' Fund. No. B154 printed in sheets of 100 (10x10); No. B155 in sheets of 150 (10x15). These stamps remained in use one year.

Crusader SP65

1934, Nov. 17 **Engr.** **Perf. 13½x14**

Cross in Red

B156 SP65 10c + 5c black 1.25 1.25
B157 SP65 25c + 15c brown 1.75 1.75
B158 SP65 50c + 10c dull grn 1.75 1.75
B159 SP65 75c + 15c vio brn .85 .85
B160 SP65 1fr + 25c rose 8.50 8.50
B161 SP65 1.75fr + 25c ultra 7.50 7.50
B162 SP65 5fr + 5fr brn vio 105.00 105.00
Nos. B156-B162 (7) 126.60 126.60

The surtax was for anti-tuberculosis work.

Prince Baudouin, Princess Josephine and Prince Albert SP66

1935, Apr. 10 **Photo.**

B163 SP66 35c + 15c dk green .85 .75
B164 SP66 70c + 30c red brn .85 .60
B165 SP66 1.75fr + 50c dk blue 3.00 3.50
Nos. B163-B165 (3) 4.70 4.85

Surtax was for Child Welfare Society.

Stagecoach — SP67

Franz von Taxis — SP68

Queen Astrid — SP69

1935, Apr. 27

B166 SP67 10c + 10c ol blk .55 .65
B167 SP67 25c + 25c bis brn 1.90 1.75
B168 SP67 35c + 25c dk green 2.50 2.25
Nos. B166-B168 (3) 4.95 4.65

Printed in sheets of 10. Value, set of 3, $175.

Souvenir Sheet

1935, May 25 **Engr.** **Perf. 14**

B169 SP68 5fr + 5fr grnsh blk 125.00 125.00

Sheets measure 91½x117mm.

Nos. B166-B169 were issued for the Brussels Philatelic Exhibition (SITEB).

The sheet normally has pin holes and a cancellation-like marking in the margin. These are considered unused and the condition valued here.

1935 **Photo.** **Perf. 11½**

Borders in Black

B170 SP69 10c + 5c ol blk .20 .20
B171 SP69 25c + 15c brown .20 .30
B172 SP69 35c + 5c dk green .20 .25
B173 SP69 50c + 10c rose lil .65 .55
B174 SP69 70c + 5c gray blk .20 .20
B175 SP69 1fr + 25c red .90 .70
B176 SP69 1.75fr + 25c blue 2.00 1.50
B177 SP69 2.45fr + 55c dk vio 2.50 2.75
Nos. B170-B177 (8) 6.85 6.45

Queen Astrid Memorial issue. The surtax was divided among several charitable organizations.

Issued: #B174, 10/31; others, 12/1.

Borgerhout Philatelic Exhibition Issue

Souvenir Sheet

Town Hall, Borgerhout SP70

1936, Oct. 3

B178 SP70 70c + 30c pur brn 50.00 35.00

Sheet measures 115x126mm.

The sheet normally has pin holes and a cancellation-like marking in the margin. These are considered unused and the condition valued here.

Town Hall and Belfry of Charleroi SP71

Prince Baudouin SP72

Charleroi Youth Exhibition

Souvenir Sheet

1936, Oct. 18 **Engr.**

B179 SP71 2.45fr + 55c gray blue 42.50 40.00

Sheet measures 95x120mm.

The sheet normally has pin holes and a cancellation-like marking in the margin. These are considered unused and the condition valued here.

1936, Dec. 1 **Photo.** **Perf. 14x13½**

B180 SP72 10c + 5c dk brown .20 .20
B181 SP72 25c + 5c violet .20 .25
B182 SP72 35c + 5c dk green .20 .25
B183 SP72 50c + 5c vio brn .30 .35
B184 SP72 70c + 5c ol grn .20 .20
B185 SP72 1fr + 25c cerise .65 .45
B186 SP72 1.75fr + 25c ultra 1.10 .65
B187 SP72 2.45fr + 2.55fr vio rose 3.00 4.00
Nos. B180-B187 (8) 5.85 6.35

The surtax was for the assistance of the National Anti-Tuberculosis Society.

1937, Jan. 10

B188 SP72 2.45fr + 2.55fr slate 1.50 1.50

Intl. Stamp Day. Surtax for the benefit of the Brussels Postal Museum, the Royal Belgian Phil. Fed. and the Anti-Tuberculosis Soc.

Queen Astrid and Prince Baudouin SP73

Queen Mother Elisabeth SP74

1937, Apr. 15 **Perf. 11½**

B189 SP73 10c + 5c magenta .20 .20
B190 SP73 25c + 5c ol blk .20 .25
B191 SP73 35c + 5c dk grn .20 .25
B192 SP73 50c + 5c violet .50 .55
B193 SP73 70c + 5c slate .20 .30
B194 SP73 1fr + 25c dk car .65 .60
B195 SP73 1.75fr + 25c dp ultra 1.10 1.10
B196 SP73 2.45fr + 1.55fr dk brn 2.75 2.75
Nos. B189-B196 (8) 5.80 6.00

The surtax was to raise funds for Public Utility Works.

1937, Sept. 15 **Perf. 14x13½**

B197 SP74 70c + 5c int black .30 .30
B198 SP74 1.75fr + 25c brt ultra .70 .70

Souvenir Sheet

Perf. 11½

B199 Sheet of 4 26.00 15.00
a. SP74 1.50fr+2.50fr red brown 3.75 3.25
b. SP74 2.45fr+3.55fr red violet 3.25 2.00

Issued for the benefit of the Queen Elisabeth Music Foundation in connection with the Eugene Ysaye intl. competition.

No. B199 contains two se-tenant pairs of Nos. B199a and B199b. Size: 111x145mm. On sale one day, Sept. 15, at Brussels.

The sheet normally has pin holes and a cancellation-like marking in the margin. These are considered unused and the condition valued here.

Princess Josephine-Charlotte SP75

1937, Dec. 1 **Perf. 14x13½**

B200 SP75 10c + 5c sl grn .20 .20
B201 SP75 25c + 5c lt brn .20 .20
B202 SP75 35c + 5c yel grn .20 .20
B203 SP75 50c + 5c ol gray .40 .35
B204 SP75 70c + 5c brn red .20 .20
B205 SP75 1fr + 25c red .70 .55
B206 SP75 1.75fr + 25c vio bl .80 .70
B207 SP75 2.45fr + 2.55fr mag 3.25 3.50
Nos. B200-B207 (8) 5.95 5.90

King Albert Memorial Issue

Souvenir Sheet

King Albert Memorial — SP76

1938, Feb. 17 **Perf. 11½**

B208 SP76 2.45fr + 7.55fr brn vio 13.00 11.00

Dedication of the monument to King Albert.

The sheet normally has pin holes and a cancellation-like marking in the margin. These are considered unused and the condition valued here.

King Leopold III in Military Plane SP77

1938, Mar. 15

B209	SP77	10c + 5c car brn	.20	*.30*
B210	SP77	35c + 5c dp grn	.35	*.90*
B211	SP77	70c + 5c gray blk	.65	.50
B212	SP77	1.75fr + 25c ultra	1.50	1.40
B213	SP77	2.45fr + 2.55fr pur	3.50	3.00
		Nos. B209-B213 (5)	6.20	6.10

The surtax was for the benefit of the National Fund for Aeronautical Propaganda.

Basilica of Koekelberg SP78

Interior View of the Basilica of Koekelberg — SP79

1938, June 1 **Photo.**

B214	SP78	10c + 5c lt brn	.20	.20
B215	SP78	35c + 5c grn	.20	.20
B216	SP78	70c + 5c gray grn	.20	.20
B217	SP78	1fr + 25c car	.65	.55
B218	SP78	1.75fr + 25c ultra	.65	.65
B219	SP78	2.45fr + 2.55fr brn vio	2.75	*3.50*

Engr.

B220	SP79	5fr + 5fr dl grn	11.00	10.50
		Nos. B214-B220 (7)	15.65	15.80

Souvenir Sheet

1938, July 21 **Engr.** ***Perf. 14***

B221	SP79	5fr + 5fr lt vio	14.00	14.00

The surtax was for a fund to aid in completing the National Basilica of the Sacred Heart at Koekelberg.

Nos. B214, B216 and B218 are different views of the exterior of the Basilica.

The sheet normally has pin holes and a cancellation-like marking in the margin. These are considered unused and the condition valued here.

Stamps of 1938 Surcharged in Black:

40c

Nos. B222-B223

2Fr50 2Fr50

No. B224

1938, Nov. 10 ***Perf. 11½***

B222	SP78	40c on 35c+5c grn	.35	*.40*
B223	SP78	75c on 70c+5c gray grn	.50	*.60*
B224	SP78	2.50 +2.50fr on 2.45+2.55fr	4.50	*5.00*
		Nos. B222-B224 (3)	5.35	*6.00*

Prince Albert of Liege — SP81

1938, Dec. 10 **Photo.** ***Perf. 14x13½***

B225	SP81	10c + 5c brown	.20	.20
B226	SP81	30c + 5c magenta	.20	*.30*
B227	SP81	40c + 5c olive gray	.20	*.30*
B228	SP81	75c + 5c slate grn	.20	.20
B229	SP81	1fr + 25c dk car	.55	*.75*
B230	SP81	1.75fr + 25c ultra	.55	*.75*
B231	SP81	2.50fr + 2.50fr dp grn	3.50	*5.50*
B232	SP81	5fr + 5fr brn lake	11.00	8.50
		Nos. B225-B232 (8)	16.40	16.50

Henri Dunant SP82

Florence Nightingale SP83

Queen Mother Elisabeth and Royal Children — SP84

Queen Astrid — SP86

King Leopold and Royal Children SP85

Queen Mother Elisabeth and Wounded Soldier — SP87

1939, Apr. 1 **Photo.** ***Perf. 11½***

Cross in Carmine

B233	SP82	10c + 5c brn	.20	.20
B234	SP83	30c + 5c brn car	.30	.30
B235	SP84	40c + 5c ol gray	.20	*.30*
B236	SP85	75c + 5c slate blk	.40	.20
B237	SP84	1fr + 25c brt rose	1.90	1.10
B238	SP85	1.75fr + 25c brt ultra	.60	*.85*
B239	SP86	2.50fr + 2.50fr dl vio	1.25	*1.65*
B240	SP87	5fr + 5fr gray grn	4.25	*5.50*
		Nos. B233-B240 (8)	9.10	*10.10*

75th anniversary of the founding of the International Red Cross Society.

Rubens' House, Antwerp SP88

"Albert and Nicolas Rubens" — SP89

Arcade, Rubens' House SP90

"Helena Fourment and Her Children" SP91

Rubens and Isabelle Brandt SP92

Peter Paul Rubens — SP93

"The Velvet Hat" — SP94

"Descent from the Cross" SP95

1939, July 1

B241	SP88	10c + 5c brn	.20	.20
B242	SP89	40c + 5c brn car	.30	.30
B243	SP90	75c + 5c ol blk	.60	.50
B244	SP91	1fr + 25c rose	1.60	1.50
B245	SP92	1.50fr + 25c sep	1.60	1.50
B246	SP93	1.75fr + 25c dp ultra	2.25	1.60
B247	SP94	2.50fr + 2.50fr brt red vio	9.25	*10.50*
B248	SP95	5fr + 5fr slate gray	14.00	14.00
		Nos. B241-B248 (8)	29.80	30.10

Issued to honor Peter Paul Rubens. The surtax was used to restore Rubens' home in Antwerp.

"Martin van Nieuwenhove" by Hans Memling (1430?-1495), Flemish Painter — SP96

1939, July 1

B249	SP96	75c + 75c olive blk	2.75	2.75

Twelfth Century Monks at Work — SP97

Reconstructed Tower Seen through Cloister — SP98

Monks Laboring in the Fields SP99

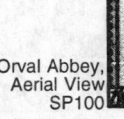

Orval Abbey, Aerial View SP100

Bishop Heylen of Namur, Madonna and Abbot General Smets of the Trappists — SP101

King Albert I and King Leopold III and Shrine — SP102

1939, July 20

B250	SP97	75c + 75c ol blk	2.50	2.75
B251	SP98	1fr + 1fr rose red	1.60	1.60
B252	SP99	1.50fr + 1.50fr dl brn	1.60	1.60
B253	SP100	1.75fr + 1.75fr saph	1.60	1.60
B254	SP101	2.50fr + 2.50fr brt red vio	7.25	6.50
B255	SP102	5fr + 5fr brn car	7.25	7.25
		Nos. B250-B255 (6)	21.80	21.30

The surtax was used for the restoration of the Abbey of Orval.

Bruges SP103

Furnes SP104

Belfries: 30c+5c, Thuin. 40c+5c, Lierre. 75c+5c, Mons. 1.75fr+25c, Namur. 2.50fr+2.50fr, Alost. 5fr+5fr, Tournai.

1939, Dec. 1 **Photo.** ***Perf. 14x13½***

B256	SP103	10c + 5c ol gray	.20	*.25*
B257	SP103	30c + 5c brn org	.25	*.35*
B258	SP103	40c + 5c brt red vio	.40	*.45*
B259	SP103	75c + 5c olive blk	.20	*.25*

Engr.

B260	SP104	1fr + 25c rose car	1.00	*1.25*
B261	SP104	1.75fr + 25c dk blue	1.00	*1.25*
B262	SP104	2.50fr + 2.50fr dp red brn	7.25	*8.00*
B263	SP104	5fr + 5fr purple	10.00	*11.00*
		Nos. B256-B263 (8)	20.30	*22.80*

Mons
SP111

Ghent
SP112

Coats of Arms: 40c+10c, Arel. 50c+10c, Bruges. 75c+15c, Namur. 1fr+25c, Hasselt. 1.75fr+50c, Brussels. 2.50fr+2.50fr, Antwerp. 5fr+5fr, Liege.

1940-41 Typo. *Perf. 14x13½*

B264	SP111	10c + 5c multi	.20	.20
B265	SP112	30c + 5c multi	.20	.20
B266	SP111	40c + 10c multi	.20	.20
B267	SP112	50c + 10c multi	.20	.20
B268	SP111	75c + 15c multi	.20	.20
B269	SP112	1fr + 25c multi	.30	.30
B270	SP111	1.75fr + 50c multi	.45	.40
B271	SP112	2.50fr + 2.50fr multi	1.25	1.25
B272	SP111	5fr + 5fr multi	1.50	1.50
		Nos. B264-B272 (9)	4.50	4.45

Nos. B264, B269-B272 issued in 1941. Surtax for winter relief. See No. B279.

Queen Elisabeth Music Chapel
SP120

Bust of Prince Albert of Liege — SP121

1940, Nov. Photo. *Perf. 11½*

B273	SP120	75c + 75c slate	1.25	1.25
B274	SP120	1fr + 1fr rose red	1.25	1.25
B275	SP121	1.50fr + 1.50fr Prus grn	1.25	1.25
B276	SP121	1.75fr + 1.75fr ultra	1.25	1.25
B277	SP120	2.50fr + 2.50fr brn org	2.50	2.50
B278	SP121	5fr + 5fr red vio	3.00	3.00
		Nos. B273-B278 (6)	10.50	10.50

The surtax was for the Queen Elisabeth Music Foundation. Nos. B273-B278 were not authorized for postal use, but were sold to advance subscribers either mint or canceled to order. See Nos. B317-B318.

Arms Types of 1940-41
Souvenir Sheets
Perf. 14x13½, Imperf.

1941, May Typo.

Cross and City Name in Carmine

Arms in Color of Stamp

B279		Sheet of 9	13.00	13.00
a.	SP111	10c + 5c slate	1.10	*1.25*
b.	SP112	30c + 5c emerald	1.10	*1.25*
c.	SP111	40c + 10c chocolate	1.10	*1.25*
d.	SP112	50c + 10c light violet	1.10	*1.25*
e.	SP111	75c + 15c dull purple	1.10	*1.25*
f.	SP112	1fr + 25c carmine	1.10	*1.25*
g.	SP111	1.75fr + 50c dull blue	1.10	*1.25*
h.	SP112	2.50fr + 2.50fr olive gray	1.10	*1.25*
i.	SP111	5fr + 5fr dull violet	4.00	*4.25*

The sheets measure 106x148mm. The surtax was used for relief work.

Painting
SP123

Sculpture
SP124

Monks Studying Plans of Orval Abbey — SP128

Designs: 40c+60c, 2fr+3.50fr, Monk carrying candle. 50c+65c, 1.75fr+2.50fr, Monk praying. 75c+1fr, 3fr+5fr, Two monks singing.

1941, June Photo. *Perf. 11½*

B281	SP123	10c + 15c brn org	.35	*.40*
B282	SP124	30c + 30c ol gray	.35	*.40*
B283	SP123	40c + 60c dp brn	.35	*.40*
B284	SP124	50c + 65c vio	.35	*.40*
B285	SP124	75c + 1fr brt red vio	.35	*.40*
B286	SP124	1fr + 1.50fr rose red	.35	*.40*
B287	SP123	1.25fr + 1.75fr dp yel grn	.35	*.40*
B288	SP123	1.75fr + 2.50fr dp ultra	.35	*.40*
B289	SP123	2fr + 3.50fr red vio	.35	*.40*
B290	SP124	2.50fr + 4.50fr dl red brn	.35	*.40*
B291	SP124	3fr + 5fr dk ol grn	.35	*.40*
B292	SP128	5fr + 10fr grnsh blk	1.25	1.25
		Nos. B281-B292 (12)	5.10	*5.65*

The surtax was used for the restoration of the Abbey of Orval.

Maria Theresa
SP129

Charles the Bold
SP130

Portraits (in various frames): 35c+5c, Charles of Lorraine. 50c+10c, Margaret of Parma. 60c+10c, Charles V. 1fr+15c, Johanna of Castile. 1.50fr+1fr, Philip the Good. 1.75fr+1.75fr, Margaret of Austria. 3.25fr+3.25fr, Archduke Albert. 5fr+5fr, Archduchess Isabella.

1941-42 Photo.

B293	SP129	10c + 5c ol blk	.20	.20
B294	SP129	35c + 5c dl grn	.20	.20
B295	SP129	50c + 10c brn	.20	.20
B296	SP129	60c + 10c pur	.20	.20
B297	SP129	1fr + 15c brt car rose	.20	.20
B298	SP129	1.50fr + 1fr red vio	.20	.20
B299	SP129	1.75fr + 1.75fr ryl bl	.20	.20
B300	SP130	2.25fr + 2.25fr dl red brn	.30	.30
B301	SP129	3.25fr + 3.25fr lt brn	.35	*.45*
B302	SP129	5fr + 5fr sl grn	.40	*.45*
		Nos. B293-B302 (10)	2.45	2.60

Souvenir Sheet

Archduke Albert and Archduchess Isabella — SP139

B302A	SP139	Sheet of 2 ('42)	6.00	6.00
b.		3.25fr+6.75fr turquoise blue	2.25	2.25
c.		5fr+10fr dark carmine	2.25	2.25

The surtax was for the benefit of National Social Service Work among soldiers' families.

Souvenir Sheets

Monks Studying Plans of Orval Abbey — SP140

1941, Oct. Photo. *Perf. 11½*

Inscribed "Belgie-Belgique"

B303	SP140	5fr + 15fr ultra	7.00	7.00

Inscribed "Belgique-Belgie"

Imperf

B304	SP140	5fr + 15fr ultra	7.00	7.00

Surtax for the restoration of Orval Abbey.

No. B304 exists perforated.

In 1942 these sheets were privately trimmed and overprinted "1142 1942" and ornament.

St. Martin Statue, Church of Dinant
SP141

Lennik, Saint-Quentin
SP142

St. Martin's Church, Saint-Trond
SP146

Statues of St. Martin: 50c+10c, 3.25fr+3.25fr, Beck, Limburg. 60c+10c, 2.25fr+2.25fr, Dave on the Meuse. 1.75fr+50c, Hal, Brabant.

1941-42 Photo. *Perf. 11½*

B305	SP141	10c + 5c chestnut	.20	.20
B306	SP142	35c + 5c dk bl grn	.20	.20
B307	SP142	50c + 10c violet	.20	.20
B308	SP142	60c + 10c dp brn	.20	.20
B309	SP142	1fr + 15c carmine	.20	.20
B310	SP141	1.50fr + 25c sl grn	.20	.20
B311	SP142	1.75fr + 50c dk ultra	.30	.30
B312	SP142	2.25fr + 2.25fr red vio	.30	.30
B313	SP142	3.25fr + 3.25fr brn vio	.30	.30
B314	SP146	5fr + 5fr dk ol grn	.45	.45
		Nos. B305-B314 (10)	2.55	2.55

Souvenir Sheets

Inscribed "Belgie-Belgique"

B315	SP146	5fr + 20fr vio brn ('42)	12.50	12.50

Inscribed "Belgique-Belgie"

B316	SP146	5fr + 20fr vio brn ('42)	12.50	12.50

In 1956, the Bureau Europeen de la Jeunesse et de l'Enfance privately overprinted Nos. B315-B316: "Congres Europeen de l'education 7-12 Mai 1956," in dark red and dark green respectively. A black bar obliterates "Winterhulp-Secours d'Hiver."

Souvenir Sheets

Queen Elisabeth Music Chapel
SP147

1941, Dec. 1 Photo. *Perf. 11½*

Inscribed "Belgique-Belgie"

B317	SP147	10fr + 15fr ol blk	4.50	4.00

Inscribed "Belgie-Belique"

B318	SP147	10fr + 15fr ol blk	4.50	4.00

The surtax was for the Queen Elisabeth Music Foundation. These sheets were perforated with the monogram of Queen Elisabeth in 1942.

In 1954 Nos. B317-B318 were overprinted to for the birth cent. of Edgar Tinel, composer. These overprinted sheets were not postally valid.

Jean Bollandus
SP148

Christophe Plantin
SP156

Designs: 35c+5c, Andreas Vesalius. 50c+10c, Simon Stevinus. 60c+10c, Jean Van Helmont. 1fr+15c, Rembert Dodoens. 1.75fr+50c, Gerardus Mercator. 3.25fr+3.25fr, Abraham Ortelius. 5fr+5fr, Justus Lipsius.

1942, May 15 Photo. *Perf. 14x13½*

B319	SP148	10c + 5c dl brn	.20	.20
B320	SP148	35c + 5c gray grn	.20	.20
B321	SP148	50c + 10c fawn	.20	.20
B322	SP148	60c + 10c grnsh blk	.20	.20

Engr.

B323	SP148	1fr + 15c brt rose	.20	.20
B324	SP148	1.75fr + 50c dl bl	.20	.20
B325	SP148	3.25fr + 3.25fr lil rose	.20	.20
B326	SP148	5fr + 5fr vio	.25	.25

Perf. 13½x14

B327	SP156	10fr + 30fr red org	.95	1.00
		Nos. B319-B327 (9)	2.60	2.65

The surtax was used to help fight tuberculosis.

No. B327 was sold by subscription at the Brussels Post Office, July 1-10, 1942.

Belgian Prisoner — SP158

1942, Oct. 1 *Perf. 11½*

B331	SP158	5fr + 45fr olive gray	5.50	5.50

The surtax was for prisoners of war. Value includes a brown inscribed label which alternates with the stamps in the sheet.

SP159

SP164

SP162

SP168

Various Statues of St. Martin.

1942-43

B332	SP159	10c + 5c org	.20	.20
B333	SP159	35c + 5c dk bl grn	.20	.20
B334	SP159	50c + 10c dp brn	.20	.20
B335	SP162	60c + 10c blk	.20	.20
B336	SP159	1fr + 15c brt rose	.20	.20
B337	SP164	1.50fr + 25c grnsh blk	.20	.20
B338	SP164	1.75fr + 50c dk bl	.20	.20
B339	SP162	2.25fr + 2.25fr brn	.30	.25
B340	SP162	3.25fr + 3.25fr brt red vio	.35	.30
B341	SP168	5fr + 10fr hn brn	.50	.45
B342	SP168	10fr + 20fr rose brn & vio brn ('43)	.65	.65

Inscribed "Belgique-Belgie"

B343	SP168	10fr + 20fr gldn brn & vio brn ('43)	.65	.65
		Nos. B332-B343 (12)	3.85	3.70

The surtax was for winter relief.

Issue dates: Nos. B332-B341, Nov. 12, 1942. Nos. B342-B343, Apr. 3, 1943.

Prisoners of War — SP170

#B345, 2 prisoners with package from home.

1943, May — Photo. — *Perf. 11½*

B344	SP170	1fr + 30fr ver	2.50	2.50
B345	SP170	1fr + 30fr brn rose	2.50	2.50

The surtax was used for prisoners of war.

Roof Tiler SP172

Coppersmith SP173

Statues in Petit Sablon Park, Brussels: 35c+5c, Blacksmith. 60c+10c, Gunsmith. 1fr+15c, Armsmith. 1.75fr+75c, Goldsmith. 3.25fr+3.25fr, Fishdealer. 5fr+25fr, Watchmaker.

1943, June 1

B346	SP172	10c + 5c chnt brn	.20	.20
B347	SP172	35c + 5c grn	.20	.20
B348	SP173	50c + 10c dk brn	.20	.20
B349	SP173	60c + 10c slate	.20	.20
B350	SP173	1fr + 15c dl rose brn	.20	.20
B351	SP173	1.75fr + 75c ultra	.20	.20
B352	SP173	3.25fr + 3.25fr brt red vio	.30	.40
B353	SP173	5fr + 25fr dk pur	.50	.55
		Nos. B346-B353 (8)	2.00	2.15

Surtax for the control of tuberculosis.

"O" — SP180

"ORVAL" — SP185

1943, Oct. 9

B354	SP180	50c + 1fr "O"	.50	.50
B355	SP180	60c + 1.90fr "R"	.30	.25
B356	SP180	1fr + 3fr "V"	.30	.25
B357	SP180	1.75fr + 5.25fr "A"	.30	.25
B358	SP180	3.25fr + 16.75fr "L"	.40	.40
B359	SP185	5fr + 30fr dp brn	.75	.75
		Nos. B354-B359 (6)	2.55	2.40

Surtax aided restoration of Orval Abbey.

St. Leonard Church, Leau SP186

St. Martin Church, Courtrai SP190

Basilica of St. Martin, Angre SP191

Notre Dame, Hal — SP193

St. Martin SP194

Designs: 35c+5c, St. Martin Church, Dion-le-Val. 50c+15c, St. Martin Church, Alost. 60c+20c, St. Martin Church, Liege. 3.25fr+11.75fr, St. Martin Church, Loppem. No. B369, St. Martin, beggar and Meuse landscape.

1943-44

B360	SP186	10c + 5c dp brn	.20	.20
B361	SP186	35c + 5c dk bl grn	.20	.20
B362	SP186	50c + 15c ol blk	.30	.30
B363	SP186	60c + 20c brt red vio	.30	.40
B364	SP190	1fr + 1fr rose brn	.40	.40
B365	SP191	1.75fr + 4.25fr dp ultra	.90	.60
B366	SP186	3.25fr + 11.75fr red lil	.90	.65
B367	SP193	5fr + 25fr dk bl	1.25	1.25
B368	SP194	10fr + 30fr gray grn ('44)	.90	.90
B369	SP194	10fr + 30fr blk brn ('44)	.90	.90
		Nos. B360-B369 (10)	6.25	5.80

Surtax for winter relief.

Catalogue values for unused stamps in this section, from this point to the end of the section, are for Never Hinged items.

"Daedalus and Icarus" SP196

Sir Anthony Van Dyck, Self-portrait SP200

Paintings by Van Dyck: 50c+2.50fr. "The Good Samaritan." 60c+3.40fr, Detail of "Christ Healing the Paralytic." 1fr+5fr, "Madonna and Child." 5fr+30fr, "St. Sebastian."

1944, Apr. 16 — Photo. — *Perf. 11½*

Crosses in Carmine

B370	SP196	35c + 1.65fr dk sl grn	.40	.30
B371	SP196	50c + 2.50fr grnsh blk	.40	.30
B372	SP196	60c + 3.40fr blk brn	.40	.30
B373	SP196	1fr + 5fr dk car	.60	.45
B374	SP200	1.75fr + 8.25fr int bl	.75	.60
B375	SP196	5fr + 30fr cop brn	.75	.60
		Nos. B370-B375 (6)	3.30	2.55

The surtax was for the Belgian Red Cross.

Jan van Eyck SP202

Godfrey of Bouillon SP203

Designs: 50c+25c, Jacob van Maerlant. 60c+40c, Jean Joses de Dinant. 1fr+50c, Jacob van Artevelde. 1.75fr+4.25fr, Charles Joseph de Ligne. 2.25fr+8.25fr, Andre Gretry. 3.25fr+11.25fr, Jan Moretus-Plantin. 5fr+35fr, Jan van Ruysbroeck.

1944, May 31

B376	SP202	10c + 15c dk pur	.40	.25
B377	SP203	35c + 15c green	.40	.25
B378	SP203	50c + 25c chnt brn	.40	.25
B379	SP203	60c + 40c ol blk	.40	.25
B380	SP203	1fr + 50c rose brn	.40	.25
B381	SP203	1.75fr + 4.25fr ultra	.40	.25
B382	SP203	2.25fr + 8.25fr grnsh blk	1.00	.55
B383	SP203	3.25fr + 11.25fr dk brn	.40	.25
B384	SP203	5fr + 35fr sl bl	.70	.70
		Nos. B376-B384 (9)	4.50	3.00

The surtax was for prisoners of war.

Sons of Aymon Astride Bayard SP211

Brabo Slaying the Giant Antigoon SP212

Till Eulenspiegel Singing to Nele SP214

Designs: 50c+10c, St. Hubert converted by stag with crucifix. 1fr+15fr, St. George slaying the dragon. 1.75fr+5.25fr, Genevieve of Brabant with son and roe-deer. 3.25fr+11.75fr, Tchantches wrestling with the Saracen. 5fr+25fr, St. Gertrude rescuing the knight with the cards.

1944, June 25

B385	SP211	10c + 5c choc	.20	.20
B386	SP212	35c + 5c dk bl grn	.20	.20
B387	SP211	50c + 10c dl vio	.20	.20
B388	SP214	60c + 10c blk brn	.20	.20
B389	SP214	1fr + 15c rose brn	.20	.20
B390	SP214	1.75fr + 5.25fr ultra	.20	*.30*
B391	SP211	3.25fr + 11.75fr grnsh blk	.35	*.50*
B392	SP211	5fr + 25fr dk bl	.45	*.70*
		Nos. B385-B392 (8)	2.00	*2.50*

The surtax was for the control of tuberculosis.

Nos. B385-B389 were overprinted "Breendonk+10fr." in 1946 by the Union Royale Philatelique for an exhibition at Brussels. They had no postal validity.

Union of the Flemish and Walloon Peoples in their Sorrow — SP219

Union in Reconstruction — SP220

Perf. 11½

1945, May 1 — Unwmk. — Photo.

B395	SP219	1fr + 30fr carmine	1.25	.90
B396	SP220	1¾fr + 30fr brt ultra	1.25	.90

1945, July 21

Size: 34½x23½mm

B397	SP219	1fr + 9fr scarlet	.25	.20
B398	SP220	1fr + 9fr car rose	.25	.20
		Nos. B395-B398 (4)	3.00	2.20

Surtax for the postal employees' relief fund.

Prisoner of War — SP221

Reunion SP222

Awaiting Execution SP223

Symbolical Figures "Recovery of Freedom" SP225

Design: 70c+30c, 3.50fr+3.50fr, Member of Resistance Movement.

1945, Sept. 10

B399	SP221	10c + 15c orange	.20	.20
B400	SP222	20c + 20c dp purple	.20	.20
B401	SP223	60c + 25c sepia	.20	.20
B402	SP221	70c + 30c dp yel grn	.20	.20
B403	SP221	75c + 50c org brn	.20	.20
B404	SP222	1fr + 75c brt bl grn	.25	.20
B405	SP223	1.50fr + 1fr brt red	.25	.20
B406	SP221	3.50fr + 3.50fr brt bl	1.10	1.00
B407	SP225	5fr + 40fr brown	.90	.90
		Nos. B399-B407 (9)	3.50	3.30

The surtax was for the benefit of prisoners of war, displaced persons, families of executed victims and members of the Resistance Movement.

Arms of West Flanders — SP226

Arms of Provinces: 20c+20c, Luxembourg. 60c+25c, East Flanders. 70c+30c, Namur. 75c+50c, Limburg. 1fr+75c, Hainaut. 1.50fr+1fr, Antwerp. 3.50fr+1.50fr, Liege. 5fr+45fr, Brabant.

1945, Dec. 1

B408	SP226	10c + 15c sl blk & sl gray	.20	.20
B409	SP226	20c + 20c rose car & rose	.20	.20
B410	SP226	60c + 25c dk brn & pale brn	.20	.20
B411	SP226	70c + 30c dk grn & lt grn	.20	.20
B412	SP226	75c + 50c org brn & pale org brn	.25	.20
B413	SP226	1fr + 75c pur & lt pur	.20	.20
B414	SP226	1.50fr + 1fr car & rose	.20	.20
B415	SP226	3.50fr + 1.50fr dp bl & gray bl	.30	.20
B416	SP226	5fr + 45fr dp mag & cerise	2.25	1.90
		Nos. B408-B416 (9)	4.00	3.50

The surtax was for tuberculosis prevention.

Father Joseph Damien — SP227

Father Damien Comforting Leper — SP229

Leper Colony, Molokai Island, Hawaii SP228

Symbols of Wisdom and Patriotism SP230

"In Memoriam" SP232

François Bovesse SP231

Emile Vandervelde SP233

Sower SP235

Vandervelde, Laborer and Family SP234

Perf. 11½

1946, July 15 Unwmk. Photo.

B417	SP227	65c + 75c dk blue	1.00	.65
B418	SP228	1.35fr + 2fr brown	1.00	.65
B419	SP229	1.75fr + 18fr rose brn	1.60	1.10

The surtax was for the erection of a museum in Louvain.

1946, July 15

B420	SP230	65c + 75c violet	1.00	.65
B421	SP231	1.35fr + 2fr dk org brn	1.40	.80
B422	SP232	1.75fr + 18fr car rose	1.90	1.10

The surtax was for the erection of a "House of the Fine Arts" at Namur.

1946, July 15

B423	SP233	65c + 75c dk sl grn	1.25	.65
B424	SP234	1.35fr + 2fr dk vio bl	1.40	.80
B425	SP235	1.75fr + 18fr dp car	1.90	1.10
		Nos. B417-B425 (9)	12.45	7.50

The surtax was for the Emile Vanderveide Institute, to promote social, economic and cultural activities.

For surcharges see Nos. CB4-CB12.

Pepin of Herstal SP236

Malines SP241

1fr+50c, Charlemagne. 1.50fr+1fr, Godfrey of Bouillon. 3.50fr+1.50fr, Robert of Jerusalem. #B430-B431, Baldwin of Constantinople.

1946, Sept. 15 Engr. ***Perf. 11½x11***

B426	SP236	75c + 25c green	.60	.35
B427	SP236	1fr + 50c violet	.90	.50
B428	SP236	1.50fr + 1fr plum	1.25	.65
B429	SP236	3.50fr + 1.50fr brt bl	1.50	.75
B430	SP236	5fr + 45fr red vio	12.00	7.00
B431	SP236	5fr + 45fr red org	15.00	7.75
		Nos. B426-B431 (6)	31.25	17.00

The surtax on Nos. B426-B429 was for the benefit of former prisoners of war, displaced persons, the families of executed patriots, and former members of the Resistance Movement.

The surtax on Nos. B430-B431 was divided among several welfare, national celebration and educational organizations.

Issue dates: Nos. B426-B429, Apr. 15; No. B430, Sept. 15; No. B431, Nov. 15.

See Nos. B437-B441, B465-B466, B472-B476.

1946, Dec. 2 ***Perf. 11½***

Coats of Arms: 90c+60c, Dinant. 1.35fr+1.15fr, Ostend. 3.15fr+1.85fr, Verviers. 4.50fr+45.50fr, Louvain.

B432	SP241	65c + 35c rose car	.50	.50
B433	SP241	90c + 60c lemon	.50	.50
B434	SP241	1.35fr + 1.15fr dp grn	.50	.50
B435	SP241	3.15fr + 1.85fr blue	1.50	1.25
B436	SP241	4.50fr + 45.50fr dk vio brn	13.00	12.00
		Nos. B432-B436 (5)	16.00	14.75

The surtax was for anti-tuberculosis work.

See Nos. B442-B446.

Type of 1946

Designs: 65c+35c, John II, Duke of Brabant. 90c+60c, Count Philip of Alsace. 1.35fr+1.15fr, William the Good. 3.15fr+1.85fr, Bishop Notger of Liege. 20fr+20fr, Philip the Noble.

1947, Sept. 25 Engr. ***Perf. 11½x11***

B437	SP236	65c + 35c Prus grn	.60	.50
B438	SP236	90c + 60c yel grn	1.00	.75
B439	SP236	1.35fr + 1.15fr car	1.40	1.10
B440	SP236	3.15fr + 1.85fr ultra	2.00	1.60
B441	SP236	20fr + 20fr red vio	52.50	42.50
		Nos. B437-B441 (5)	57.50	46.45

The surtax was for victims of World War II.

Arms Type of 1946 Dated "1947"

Coats of Arms: 65c+35c, Nivelles. 90c+60c, St. Trond. 1.35fr+1.15fr, Charleroi. 3.15fr+1.85fr, St. Nicolas. 20fr+20fr, Bouillon.

1947, Dec. 15 ***Perf. 11½***

B442	SP241	65c + 35c orange	.80	.65
B443	SP241	90c + 60c dp cl	.70	.65
B444	SP241	1.35fr + 1.15fr dk brn	1.00	.70
B445	SP241	3.15fr + 1.85fr dp bl	2.50	1.75
B446	SP241	20fr + 20fr dk grn	20.00	12.50
		Nos. B442-B446 (5)	25.00	16.25

The surtax was for anti-tuberculosis work.

St. Benedict and King Totila — SP247

Achel Abbey SP248

Designs: 3.15fr+2.85fr, St. Benedict, legislator and builder. 10fr+10fr, Death of St. Benedict.

1948, Apr. 5 **Photo.**

B447	SP247	65c + 65c red brn	1.25	.55
B448	SP248	1.35fr + 1.35fr gray	1.75	.55
B449	SP247	3.15fr + 2.85fr dp ultra	2.50	1.90
B450	SP247	10fr + 10fr brt red vio	12.50	10.00
		Nos. B447-B450 (4)	18.00	13.00

The surtax was to aid the Abbey of the Trappist Fathers at Achel.

St. Begga and Chevremont Castle — SP249

Chevremont Basilica and Convent SP250

Designs: 3.15fr+2.85fr, Madonna of Chevremont and Chapel. 10fr+10fr, Madonna of Mt. Carmel.

1948, Apr. 5 **Unwmk.**

B451	SP249	65c + 65c bl grn	1.00	.55
B452	SP250	1.35fr + 1.35fr dk car rose	1.60	.55
B453	SP249	3.15fr + 2.85fr dp bl	2.25	1.90
B454	SP249	10fr + 10fr dp brn	12.00	10.00
		Nos. B451-B454 (4)	16.85	13.00

The surtax was to aid the Basilica of the Carmelite Fathers of Chèvremont.

Anseele Monument Showing French Inscription — SP251

90c+60c, View of Ghent. 1.35fr+1.15fr, Van Artevelde monument, Ghent. 3.15fr+1.85fr. Anseele Monument, Flemish inscription.

1948, June 21 ***Perf. 14x13½***

B455	SP251	65c + 35c rose red	2.75	1.10
B456	SP251	90c + 60c gray	3.50	1.90
B457	SP251	1.35fr + 1.15fr hn brn	2.25	1.50
B458	SP251	3.15fr + 1.85fr brt bl	8.50	5.00
a.		Souv. sheet of 4, #B455-B458	140.00	55.00
		Nos. B455-B458 (4)	17.00	9.50

Issued to honor Edouard Anseele, statesman, founder of the Belgian Socialist Party.

No. B458a sold for 50fr.

For surcharges see Nos. 395-398.

Statue "The Unloader" SP252

Underground Fighter SP253

1948, Sept. 4 ***Perf. 11½x11***

B460	SP252	10fr + 10fr gray grn	35.00	19.00
B461	SP253	10fr + 10fr red brn	20.00	11.00

The surtax was used toward erection of monuments at Antwerp and Liege.

Portrait Type of 1946 and

Double Barred Cross — SP254

Designs: 4fr+3.25fr, Isabella of Austria. 20fr+20fr, Archduke Albert of Austria.

1948, Dec. 15 Photo. ***Perf. 13½x14***

B462	SP254	20c + 5c dk sl grn	.50	.20
B463	SP254	1.20fr + 30c magenta	1.25	.70
B464	SP254	1.75fr + 25c red	1.75	.60

Engr. ***Perf. 11½x11***

B465	SP236	4fr + 3.25fr ultra	9.50	6.50
B466	SP236	20fr + 20fr Prus grn	42.50	30.00
		Nos. B462-B466 (5)	55.50	38.00

The surtax was divided among several charities.

Souvenir Sheets

Rogier van der Weyden Paintings — SP255

Paintings by van der Weyden (No. B466A): 90c, Virgin and Child. 1.75fr, Christ on the Cross. 4fr, Mary Magdalene.

Paintings by Jordaens (No. B466B): 90c, Woman Reading. 1.75fr, The Flutist. 4fr, Old Woman Reading Letter.

1949, Apr. 1 Photo. ***Perf. 11½***

B466A	SP255	Sheet of 3	125.00	110.00
c.		90c deep brown	37.50	32.50
d.		1.75fr deep rose lilac	37.50	32.50
e.		4fr dark violet blue	37.50	32.50
B466B	SP255	Sheet of 3	125.00	110.00
f.		90c dark violet	37.50	32.50
g.		1.75fr red	37.50	32.50
h.		4fr blue	37.50	32.50

The surtax went to various cultural and philanthropic organizations. Sheets sold for 50fr each.

Gum on Nos. B466A-B466B is irregularly applied.

Guido Gezelle — SP256

1949, Nov. 15 Photo. ***Perf. 14x13½***

B467	SP256	1.75fr + 75c dk Prus grn	2.50	1.75

50th anniversary of the death of Guido Gezelle, poet. The surtax was for the Guido Gezelle Museum, Bruges.

Portrait Type of 1946 and

Arnica — SP257

Designs: 65c+10c, Sand grass. 90c+10c, Wood myrtle. 1.20fr+30c, Field poppy. 1.75fr+25c, Philip the Good. 3fr+1.50fr, Charles V. 4fr+2fr, Maria-Christina. 6fr+3fr, Charles of Lorraine. 8fr+4fr, Maria-Theresa.

1949, Dec. 20 Typo. ***Perf. 13½x14***

B468	SP257	20c + 5c multi	.50	.50
B469	SP257	65c + 10c multi	1.25	1.10
B470	SP257	90c + 10c multi	2.00	1.50
B471	SP257	1.20fr + 30c multi	2.50	1.75

Engr. ***Perf. 11½x11***

B472	SP236	1.75fr + 25c red org	1.40	.80
B473	SP236	3fr + 1.50fr dp claret	10.00	6.75
B474	SP236	4fr + 2fr ultra	10.00	8.00
B475	SP236	6fr + 3fr choc	16.00	11.00
B476	SP236	8fr + 4fr dl grn	16.00	8.75
		Nos. B468-B476 (9)	59.65	40.15

The surtax was apportioned among several welfare organizations.

Arms of Belgium and Great Britain SP258

British Memorial SP260

Design: 2.50fr+50c, British tanks at Hertain.

Perf. 13½x14, 11½

1950, Mar. 15 **Engr.**

B477	SP258	80c + 20c green	1.50	1.00
B478	SP258	2.50fr + 50c red	5.00	3.75
B479	SP260	4fr + 2fr dp bl	9.25	6.25
		Nos. B477-B479 (3)	15.75	11.00

6th anniv. of the liberation of Belgian territory by the British army.

Hurdling SP261

Relay Race SP262

Designs: 90c+10c, Javelin throwing. 4fr+2fr, Pole vault. 8fr+4fr, Foot race.

Perf. 14x13½, 13½x14

1950, July 1 Engr. Unwmk.

B480	SP261	20c + 5c brt grn	.90	.75
B481	SP261	90c + 10c vio brn	3.75	1.90
B482	SP262	1.75fr + 25c car	4.50	1.90
a.		Souvenir sheet of 1	55.00	42.50
B483	SP261	4fr + 2fr lt bl	35.00	19.00
B484	SP261	8fr + 4fr dp grn	40.00	24.00
		Nos. B480-B484 (5)	84.15	47.55

Issued to publicize the European Athletic Games, Brussels, August 1950.

The margins of No. B482a were trimmed in April, 1951, and an overprint ("25 Francs pour le Fonds Sportif-25e Foire Internationale Bruxelles") was added in red in French and in black in Flemish by a private committee. These pairs of altered sheets were sold at the Brussels Fair.

Gentian SP263

Sijsele Sanatorium SP264

Tombeek Sanatorium — SP265

Designs: 65c+10c, Cotton Grass. 90c+10c, Foxglove. 1.20fr+30c, Limonia. 4fr+2fr, Jauche Sanatorium.

1950, Dec. 20 Typo. ***Perf. 14x13½***

B485	SP263	20c + 5c multi	.80	.40
B486	SP263	65c + 10c multi	1.50	.80
B487	SP263	90c + 10c multi	1.60	1.10
B488	SP263	1.20fr + 30c multi	2.75	2.25

Perf. 11½

Engr.

Cross in Red

B489	SP264	1.75fr + 25c car	2.50	1.40
B490	SP264	4fr + 2fr blue	13.00	7.00
B491	SP265	8fr + 4fr bl grn	21.00	15.00
		Nos. B485-B491 (7)	43.15	27.95

The surtax was for tuberculosis prevention and other charitable purposes.

Chemist — SP266

Allegory of Peace — SP268

Colonial Instructor and Class SP267

1951, Mar. 27 Unwmk.

B492	SP266	80c + 20c grn	1.40	1.00
B493	SP267	2.50fr + 50c vio brn	9.50	5.00
B494	SP268	4fr + 2fr dp bl	10.50	6.00
		Nos. B492-B494 (3)	21.40	12.00

Surtax for the reconstruction fund of the UNESCO.

Monument to Political Prisoners SP269

Fort of Breendonk SP270

8fr+4fr, Monument: profile of figure on pedestal.

1951, Aug. 20 Photo. ***Perf. 11½***

B495	SP269	1.75fr + 25c blk brn	2.50	1.75
B496	SP270	4fr + 2fr bl & sl gray	17.00	14.00
B497	SP269	8fr + 4fr dk bl grn	22.50	17.00
		Nos. B495-B497 (3)	42.00	32.75

The surtax was for the erection of a national monument.

Queen Elisabeth — SP271

1951, Sept. 22

B498	SP271	90c + 10c grnsh gray	1.75	.75
B499	SP271	1.75fr + 25c plum	2.25	1.50
B500	SP271	3fr + 1fr green	21.00	9.25
B501	SP271	4fr + 2fr gray bl	24.00	12.00
B502	SP271	8fr + 4fr sepia	30.00	14.00
		Nos. B498-B502 (5)	79.00	37.50

The surtax was for the Queen Elisabeth Medical Foundation.

Cross, Sun Rays and Dragon SP272

Beersel Castle SP273

Horst Castle — SP274

Castles: 4fr+2fr, Lavaux St. Anne. 8fr+4fr, Veves.

1951, Dec. 17 Engr. Unwmk.

B503	SP272	20c + 5c red	.25	.20
B504	SP272	65c + 10c dp ultra	.85	.60
B505	SP272	90c + 10c sepia	.90	.80
B506	SP272	1.20fr + 30c rose vio	1.25	.90
B507	SP273	1.75fr + 75c red brn	1.75	1.50
B508	SP274	3fr + 1fr yel grn	12.00	7.50
B509	SP273	4fr + 2fr blue	14.00	8.50
B510	SP274	8fr + 4fr gray	19.00	11.00
		Nos. B503-B510 (8)	50.00	31.00

The surtax was for anti-tuberculosis work.

See Nos. B523-B526, B547-B550.

Main Altar SP275

Basilica of the Sacred Heart Koekelberg SP276

Procession Bearing Relics of St. Albert of Louvain — SP277

1952, Mar. 1 Photo. *Perf. 11½*

B511 SP275 1.75fr + 25c blk brn 1.50 1.25
B512 SP276 4fr + 2fr indigo 11.00 7.50

Engr.

B513 SP277 8fr + 4fr vio brn 15.00 9.25
a. Souvenir sheet, #B511-B513 250.00 125.00
Nos. B511-B513 (3) 27.50 18.00

25th anniv. of the Cardinalate of J. E. Van Roey, Primate of Belgium. The surtax was for the Basilica. No. B513a sold for 30fr.

Beaulieu Castle, Malines SP278

August Vermeylen SP279

1952, May 14 Engr.

Laid Paper

B514 SP278 40fr + 10fr lt grnsh bl 175.00 175.00

Issued on the occasion of the 13th Universal Postal Union Congress, Brussels, 1952.

Perf. 11½

1952, Oct. 24 Unwmk. Photo.

Portraits: 80c+40c, Karel Van de Woestijne. 90c+45c, Charles de Coster. 1.75fr+75c, M. Maeterlinck. 4fr+2fr, Emile Verhaeren. 8fr+4fr, Hendrik Conscience.

B515 SP279 65c + 30c purple 1.75 .90
B516 SP279 80c + 40c dk grn 3.75 1.10
B517 SP279 90c + 45c sepia 2.75 1.25
B518 SP279 1.75fr + 75c cer 3.75 1.75
B519 SP279 4fr + 2fr bl vio 30.00 19.00
B520 SP279 8fr + 4fr dk brn 30.00 21.00
Nos. B515-B520 (6) 72.00 45.00

1952, Nov. 15

4fr, Emile Verhaeren. 8fr, Hendrik Conscience.

B521 SP279 4fr (+ 9fr) blue 100.00 67.50
B522 SP279 8fr (+ 9fr) dk car rose 100.00 67.50

On Nos. B521-B522, the denomination is repeated at either side of the stamp. The surtax is expressed on se-tenant labels bearing quotations of Verhaeren (in French) and Conscience (in Flemish). Value is for stamp with label.

A 9-line black overprint was privately applied to these labels: "Conference Internationale de la Musique Bruxelles UNESCO International Music Conference Brussels 1953"

Type of 1951 Dated "1952," and

Arms of Malmédy — SP281

Castle Ruins, Burgreuland SP282

Designs: 4fr+2fr, Vesdre Dam, Eupen. 8fr+4fr, St. Vitus, patron saint of Saint-Vith.

1952, Dec. 15 Engr.

B523 SP272 20c + 5c red brn .40 .40
B524 SP272 80c + 20c green .85 .60
B525 SP272 1.20fr + 30c lil rose 1.75 1.00
B526 SP272 1.50fr + 50c ol brn 1.75 1.00
B527 SP281 2fr + 75c carmine 3.25 2.25
B528 SP282 3fr + 1.50fr choc 14.00 8.75
B529 SP281 4fr + 2fr blue 12.00 8.00
B530 SP281 8fr + 4fr vio brn 21.00 11.00
Nos. B523-B530 (8) 55.00 33.00

The surtax on Nos. B523-B530 was for anti-tuberculosis and other charitable works.

Walthère Dewé SP283

Princess Josephine-Charlotte SP284

1953, Feb. 16 Photo.

B531 SP283 2fr + 1fr brn car 3.25 1.75

The surtax was for the construction of a memorial to Walthère Dewé, Underground leader in World War II.

1953, Mar. 14 Cross in Red

B532 SP284 80c + 20c ol grn 1.25 .70
B533 SP284 1.20fr + 30c brown 1.75 .80
B534 SP284 2fr + 50c rose lake 1.25 1.25
a. Booklet pane of 8 80.00 65.00
B535 SP284 2.50fr + 50c crimson 14.00 6.75
B536 SP284 4fr + 1fr brt blue 9.25 5.25
B537 SP284 5fr + 2fr sl grn 11.00 6.75
Nos. B532-B537 (6) 38.50 21.50

The surtax was for the Belgian Red Cross.

The selvage of No. B534a is inscribed in French. Value for selvage inscribed in Dutch, $150.

Boats at Dock SP285

Bridge and Citadel, Namur SP286

Allegory SP287

Designs: 1.20fr+30c, Bridge at Bouillon. 2fr+50c, Antwerp waterfront. 4fr+2fr, Wharf at Ghent. 8fr+4fr, Meuse River at Freyr.

1953, June 22 Unwmk. *Perf. 11½*

B538 SP285 80c + 20c green 1.00 .85
B539 SP285 1.20fr + 30c redsh brn 1.75 1.60
B540 SP285 2fr + 50c sepia 2.25 2.00
B541 SP286 2.50fr + 50c dp mag 11.00 8.50
B542 SP286 4fr + 2fr vio bl 16.00 8.50
B543 SP286 8fr + 4fr gray blk 20.00 8.50
Nos. B538-B543 (6) 52.00 29.95

The surtax was used to promote tourism in the Ardenne-Meuse region and for various cultural works.

1953, Oct. 26 Engr.

B544 SP287 80c + 20c green 3.50 2.50
B545 SP287 2.50fr + 1fr rose car 32.50 24.00
B546 SP287 4fr + 1.50fr blue 37.50 30.00
Nos. B544-B546 (3) 73.50 56.50

The surtax was for the European Bureau of Childhood and Youth.

Type of 1951 Dated "1953," and

Ernest Malvoz — SP288

Robert Koch SP289

Portraits: 3fr+1.50fr, Carlo Forlanini. 4fr+2fr, Leon Charles Albert Calmette.

1953, Dec. 15

B547 SP272 20c + 5c blue .50 .45
B548 SP272 80c + 20c rose vio 1.00 .60
B549 SP272 1.20fr + 30c choc 1.25 .80
B550 SP272 1.50fr + 50c dk gray 1.75 1.00
B551 SP288 2fr + 75c dk grn 3.00 1.60
B552 SP288 3fr + 1.50fr dk red 13.00 8.50
B553 SP288 4fr + 2fr ultra 11.00 7.00
B554 SP289 8fr + 4fr choc 17.50 10.00
Nos. B547-B554 (8) 49.00 29.95

The surtax was for anti-tuberculosis and other charitable works.

King Albert I Statue — SP290

Albert I Monument, Namur SP291

Design: 9fr+4.50fr, Cliffs of Marche-les-Dames.

1954, Feb. 17 Photo.

B555 SP290 2fr + 50c chnt brn 2.50 1.75
B556 SP291 4fr + 2fr blue 15.00 11.00
B557 SP290 9fr + 4.50fr ol blk 22.50 12.00
Nos. B555-B557 (3) 40.00 24.75

20th anniv. of the death of King Albert I. The surtax aided in the erection of the monument pictured on #B556.

Political Prisoners' Monument — SP292

Camp and Fort, Breendonk SP293

Design: 9fr+4.50fr, Political prisoners' monument (profile).

1954, Apr. 1 Unwmk. *Perf. 11½*

B558 SP292 2fr + 1fr red 12.50 7.00
B559 SP293 4fr + 2fr dk brn 30.00 17.50
B560 SP292 9fr + 4.50fr ol grn 32.50 17.50
Nos. B558-B560 (3) 75.00 42.00

The surtax was used toward the creation of a monument to political prisoners.

Gatehouse and Gateway SP294

Nuns in Courtyard — SP295

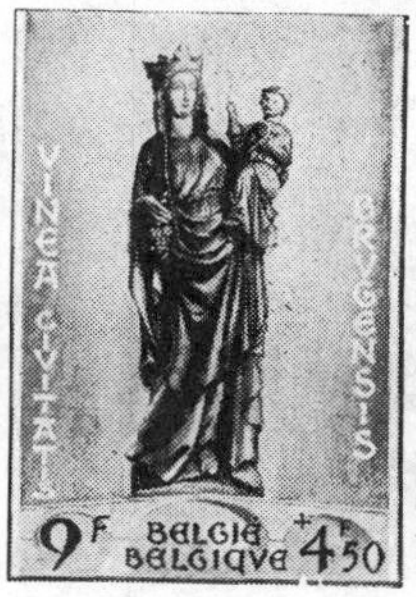
Our Lady of the Vine SP296

Designs: 2fr+1fr, Swans in stream. 7fr+3.50fr Nuns at well. 8fr+4fr, Statue above door.

1954, May 15

B561 SP294 80c + 20c dk bl grn 1.00 .75
B562 SP294 2fr + 1fr crimson 11.00 1.50
B563 SP295 4fr + 2fr violet 16.00 9.25
B564 SP295 7fr + 3.50fr lil rose 35.00 22.50
B565 SP295 8fr + 4fr brown 32.50 19.00
B566 SP296 9fr + 4.50fr gray bl 55.00 30.00
Nos. B561-B566 (6) 150.50 83.00

The surtax was for the Friends of the Beguinage of Bruges.

Child's Head SP297

"The Blind Man and the Paralytic," by Antoine Carte SP298

1954, Dec. 1 Engr.

B567 SP297 20c + 5c dk grn .50 .50
B568 SP297 80c + 20c dk gray 1.00 .85
B569 SP297 1.20fr + 30c org brn 1.50 1.00
B570 SP297 1.50fr + 50c purple 1.75 1.60
B571 SP298 2fr + 75c rose car 7.25 3.50
B572 SP298 4fr + 1fr brt blue 16.00 9.50
Nos. B567-B572 (6) 28.00 16.95

The surtax was for anti-tuberculosis work.

Ernest Solvay SP299

Jean-Jacques Dony — SP300

Portraits: 1.20fr+30c, Egide Walschaerts. 25fr+50c, Leo H. Baekeland. 3fr+1fr, Jean-Etienne Lenoir. 4fr+2fr, Emile Fourcault and Emile Gobbe.

Perf. 11½

1955, Oct. 22 Unwmk. Photo.

B573	SP299	20c + 5c brn & dk brn	.40	.35
B574	SP300	80c + 20c violet	1.00	.50
B575	SP299	1.20fr + 30c indigo	1.10	.65
B576	SP300	2fr + 50c dp car	4.00	2.50
B577	SP300	3fr + 1fr dk grn	12.50	6.25
B578	SP299	4fr + 2fr brown	12.50	6.25
		Nos. B573-B578 (6)	31.50	16.50

Issued in honor of Belgian scientists.
The surtax was for the benefit of various cultural organizations.

"The Joys of Spring" by E. Canneel SP301

Einar Holböll SP302

Portraits: 4fr+2fr, John D. Rockefeller. 8fr+4fr, Sir Robert W. Philip.

1955, Dec. 5 Unwmk. *Perf. 11½*

B579	SP301	20c + 5c red lilac	.70	.30
B580	SP301	80c + 20c green	1.00	.65
B581	SP301	1.20fr + 30c redsh brn	1.40	.80
B582	SP301	1.50fr + 50c vio bl	1.40	1.00
B583	SP302	2fr + 50c carmine	8.50	4.75
B584	SP302	4fr + 2fr ultra	17.50	10.00
B585	SP302	8fr + 4fr ol gray	21.00	12.50
		Nos. B579-B585 (7)	51.50	30.00

The surtax was for anti-tuberculosis work.

Palace of Charles of Lorraine — SP303

Queen Elisabeth and Sonata by Mozart — SP304

Design: 2fr+1fr, Mozart at age 7.

1956, Mar. 5 Engr.

B586	SP303	80c + 20c steel bl	1.00	1.00
B587	SP303	2fr + 1fr rose lake	4.25	3.00
B588	SP304	4fr + 2fr dull pur	6.75	3.75
		Nos. B586-B588 (3)	12.00	7.75

200th anniversary of the birth of Wolfgang Amadeus Mozart, composer.
The surtax was for the benefit of the Pro-Mozart Committee in Belgium.

Queen Elisabeth — SP305

1956, Aug. 16 Photo.

B589	SP305	80c + 20c slate grn	1.00	1.00
B590	SP305	2fr + 1fr deep plum	2.75	1.50
B591	SP305	4fr + 2fr brown	4.25	2.50
		Nos. B589-B591 (3)	8.00	5.00

Issued in honor of the 80th birthday of Queen Elisabeth. The surtax went to the Queen Elisabeth Foundation. See No. 659.

Ship with Cross SP306

Infant on Scales SP307

Rehabilitation SP308

Design: 4fr+2fr, X-Ray examination.

1956, Dec. 17 Engr.

B592	SP306	20c + 5c redsh brn	.35	.30
B593	SP306	80c + 20c green	.75	.60
B594	SP306	1.20fr + 30c dl lil	.90	.60
B595	SP306	1.5fr + 50c lt sl bl	.95	.90
B596	SP307	2fr + 50c ol grn	2.25	1.60
B597	SP307	4fr + 2fr dl pur	11.00	6.25
B598	SP308	8fr + 4fr dp car	11.00	7.25
		Nos. B592-B598 (7)	27.20	17.50

The surtax was for anti-tuberculosis work.

Charles Plisnier and Albrecht Rodenbach SP309

80c+20c, Emiel Vliebergh & Maurice Wilmotte. 1.20fr+30c, Paul Pastur & Julius Hoste. 2fr+50c, Lodewijk de Raet & Jules Destree. 3fr+1fr, Constantin Meunier & Constant Permeke. 4fr+2fr, Lieven Gevaert & Edouard Empain.

Perf. 11½

1957, June 8 Unwmk. Photo.

B599	SP309	20c + 5c brt vio	.40	.35
B600	SP309	80c + 20c lt red brn	.55	.35
B601	SP309	1.20f + 30c blk brn	.65	.60
B602	SP309	2fr + 50c claret	1.60	.95
B603	SP309	3fr + 1fr dk ol grn	2.25	1.75
B604	SP309	4fr + 2fr vio bl	3.25	2.50
		Nos. B599-B604 (6)	8.70	6.50

The surtax was for the benefit of various cultural organizations.

Dogs and Antarctic Camp SP310

1957, Oct. 18 Engr. *Perf. 11½*

B605	SP310	5fr + 2.50fr gray, org & vio brn	3.00	2.25
a.		Sheet of 4, #B605b	140.00	125.00
b.		Blue, slate & red brown	30.00	25.00

Surtax for Belgian Antarctic Expedition, 1957-58.

Gen. Patton's Grave and Flag SP311

Gen. George S. Patton, Jr. — SP312

Designs: 2.50fr+50c, Memorial, Bastogne. 3fr+1fr, Gen. Patton decorating Brig. Gen. Anthony C. McAuliffe. 6fr+3fr, Tanks of 1918 and 1944.

1957, Oct. 28 Photo.

Size: 36x25mm, 25x36mm

B606	SP311	1fr + 50c dk gray	1.25	.85
B607	SP311	2.50fr + 50c ol grn	1.75	1.50
B608	SP311	3fr + 1fr red brn	2.75	1.60
B609	SP312	5fr + 2.50fr grysh bl	6.25	5.00

Size: 53x35mm

B610	SP311	6fr + 3fr pale brn car	10.00	6.00
		Nos. B606-B610 (5)	22.00	14.95

The surtax was for the General Patton Memorial Committee and Patriotic Societies.

Adolphe Max — SP313

1957, Nov. 10 Engr.

B611	SP313	2.50fr + 1fr ultra	1.25	.75

18th anniversary of the death of Adolphe Max, mayor of Brussels. The surtax was for the national "Adolphe Max" fund.

"Chinels," Fosses SP314

"Op Signoorken," Malines SP315

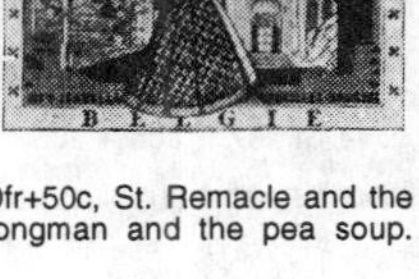

Infanta Isabella Shooting Crossbow SP316

Legends: 1.50fr+50c, St. Remacle and the wolf. 2fr+1fr, Longman and the pea soup. 5fr+2fr, The Virgin with Inkwell, vert. 6fr+2.50fr, "Gilles" (clowns), Binche.

1957, Dec. 14 Engr. & Photo.

B612	SP314	30c + 20c	.20	.30
B613	SP315	1fr + 50c	.40	.30
B614	SP314	1.50fr + 50c	.80	.50
B615	SP315	2fr + 1fr	1.10	1.00
B616	SP316	2.50fr + 1fr	1.25	.90
B617	SP316	5fr + 2fr	3.25	2.25
B618	SP316	6fr + 2.50fr	4.50	3.25
		Nos. B612-B618 (7)	11.50	8.50

The surtax was for anti-tuberculosis work.
See Nos. B631-B637.

Benelux Gate SP317

Designs: 1fr+50c, Civil Engineering Pavilion. 1.50fr+50c, Ruanda-Urundi Pavilion. 2.50fr+1fr, Belgium 1900. 3fr+1.50fr, Atomium. 5fr+3fr, Telexpo Pavilion.

Perf. 11½

1958, Apr. 15 Unwmk. Engr.

Size: 35½x24½mm

B619	SP317	30c + 20c multi	.20	.20
B620	SP317	1fr + 50c multi	.20	.20
B621	SP317	1.50fr + 50c multi	.25	.25
B622	SP317	2.50fr + 1fr multi	.45	.45
B623	SP317	3fr + 1.50fr multi	.90	.50

Size: 49x33mm

B624	SP317	5fr + 3fr multi	1.10	.50
		Nos. B619-B624 (6)	3.10	2.10

World's Fair, Brussels, Apr. 17-Oct. 19.

Marguerite van Eyck by Jan van Eyck — SP318

Christ Carrying Cross, by Hieronymus Bosch SP319

Paintings: 1.50fr+50c, St. Donatien, Jan Gossart. 2.50fr+1fr, Self-portrait, Lambert Lombard. 3fr+1.50fr, The Rower, James Ensor. 5fr+3fr, Henriette, Henri Evenepoel.

1958, Oct. 30 Photo. *Perf. 11½*

Various Frames in Ocher and Brown

B625	SP318	30c + 20c dk ol grn	.25	.30
B626	SP319	1fr + 50c mar	.75	.70
B627	SP318	1.50fr + 50c vio bl	1.00	.75
B628	SP318	2.50fr + 1fr dk brn	2.00	1.25
B629	SP319	3fr + 1.50fr dl red	2.75	2.00
B630	SP318	5fr + 3fr brt bl	5.25	5.00
		Nos. B625-B630 (6)	12.00	10.00

The surtax was for the benefit of various cultural organizations.

Type of 1957

Legends: 40c+10c, Elizabeth, Countess of Hoogstraten. 1fr+50c, Jean de Nivelles. 1.50fr+50c, St. Evermare play, Russon. 2fr+1fr, The Penitents of Furnes. 2.50fr+1fr, Manger and "Pax." 5fr+2fr, Sambre-Meuse procession. 6fr+2.50fr, Our Lady of Peace and "Pax," vert.

Engraved and Photogravure

1958, Dec. 6 Unwmk. *Perf. 11½*

B631	SP314	40c + 10c ultra & brt grn	.30	.20
B632	SP315	1fr + 50c gray brn & org	.40	.30
B633	SP315	1.50fr + 50c cl & brt grn	.60	.35
B634	SP314	2fr + 1fr brn & red	.70	.50

B635	SP316	2.50fr + 1fr vio brn & bl grn	2.50	1.90
B636	SP316	5fr + 2fr cl & bl	3.75	3.00
B637	SP316	6fr + 2.50fr bl & rose red	4.75	4.50
		Nos. B631-B637 (7)	13.00	10.75

The surtax was for anti-tuberculosis work.

"Europe of the Heart" SP320

1959, Feb. 25 Photo. Unwmk.

B638	SP320	1fr + 50c red lilac	.55	.30
B639	SP320	2.50fr + 1fr dk green	.95	.90
B640	SP320	5fr + 2.50fr dp brn	1.25	1.10
		Nos. B638-B640 (3)	2.75	2.30

The surtax was for aid for displaced persons.

Allegory of Blood Transfusion SP321

Henri Dunant and Battlefield at Solferino — SP322

Design: 2.50fr+1fr, 3fr+1.50fr, Red Cross, broken sword and drop of blood, horiz.

1959, June 10 Photo. *Perf. 11½*

B641	SP321	40c + 10c	.60	.30
B642	SP321	1fr + 50c	1.10	.45
B643	SP321	1.50fr + 50c	1.40	.60
B644	SP321	2.50fr + 1fr	1.90	1.10
B645	SP321	3fr + 1.50fr	4.75	2.50
B646	SP322	5fr + 3fr	7.25	3.25
		Nos. B641-B646 (6)	17.00	8.20

Cent. of the Intl. Red Cross idea. Surtax for the Red Cross and patriotic organizations.

Philip the Good — SP323

Arms of Philip the Good SP324

Designs: 1fr+50c, Charles the Bold. 1.50fr+50c, Emperor Maximilian of Austria. 2.50fr+1fr, Philip the Fair. 3fr+1.50fr, Charles V. Portraits from miniatures by Simon Bening (c. 1483-1561).

1959, July 4 Engr.

B647	SP323	40c + 10c multi	.50	.35
B648	SP323	1fr + 50c multi	.80	.50
B649	SP323	1.50fr + 50c multi	.95	.75
B650	SP323	2.50fr + 1fr multi	1.25	1.40
B651	SP323	3fr + 1.50fr multi	3.25	3.00
B652	SP324	5fr + 3fr multi	5.25	4.00
		Nos. B647-B652 (6)	12.00	10.00

The surtax was for the Royal Library, Brussels.

Portraits show Grand Masters of the Order of the Golden Fleece.

Whale, Antwerp SP325

Carnival, Stavelot SP326

Designs: 1fr+50c, Dragon, Mons. 2fr+50c, Prince Carnival, Eupen. 3fr+1fr, Jester and cats, Ypres. 6fr+2fr, Holy Family, horiz. 7fr+3fr, Madonna, Liége, horiz.

Engraved and Photogravure

1959, Dec. 5 *Perf. 11½*

B653	SP325	40c + 10c cit, Prus bl & red	.45	.40
B654	SP325	1fr + 50c ol & grn	.75	.60
B655	SP325	2fr + 50c lt brn, org & cl	.50	.40
B656	SP326	2.50fr + 1fr gray, pur & ultra	.80	.60
B657	SP326	3fr + 1fr gray, mar & yel	1.75	1.25
B658	SP326	6fr + 2fr ol, brt bl & hn brn	3.25	2.50
B659	SP326	7fr + 3fr chlky bl & org yel	5.00	4.25
		Nos. B653-B659 (7)	12.50	10.00

The surtax was for anti-tuberculosis work.

Child Refugee — SP327

Designs: 3fr+1.50fr, Man. 6fr+3fr, Woman.

1960, Apr. 7 Engr.

B660	SP327	40c + 10c rose claret	.20	.20
B661	SP327	3fr + 1.50fr gray brn	.65	.50
B662	SP327	6fr + 3fr dk bl	1.60	1.10
a.		Souvenir sheet of 3	50.00	45.00
		Nos. B660-B662 (3)	2.45	1.80

World Refugee Year, July 1, 1959-June 30, 1960.

No. B662a contains Nos. B660-B662 with colors changed: 40c+10c, dull purple; 3fr+1.50fr, red brown; 6fr+3fr, henna brown.

Parachutists and Plane SP328

Designs: 2fr+50c, 2.50fr+1fr, Parachutists coming in for landing, vert 3fr+1fr, 6fr+2fr, Parachutist walking with parachute.

Photogravure and Engraved

1960, June 13 *Perf. 11½*

B663	40c + 10c lt ultra & blk	.20	.20
B664	1fr + 50c bl & blk	.85	.60
B665	2fr + 50c bl, blk & ol	2.75	1.25
B666	2.50fr + 1fr grnsh bl, blk & gray ol	3.00	2.00
B667	3fr + 1fr bl, blk & sl grn	3.00	2.00
B668	6fr + 2fr lt vio bl, blk & ol	6.25	4.00
	Nos. B663-B668 (6)	16.05	10.05

The surtax was for various patriotic and cultural organizations.

Mother and Child, Planes and Rainbow SP329

Designs: 40c+10c, Brussels Airport, planes and rainbow. 6fr+3fr, Rainbow connecting Congo and Belgium, and planes, vert

Perf. 11½

1960, Aug. 3 Unwmk. Photo.

Size: 35x24mm

B669	SP329	40c + 10c grnsh blue	.20	.20
B670	SP329	3fr + 1.50fr brt red	2.50	2.25

Size: 35x52mm

B671	SP329	6fr + 3fr violet	3.75	3.00
		Nos. B669-B671 (3)	6.45	5.45

The surtax was for refugees from Congo.

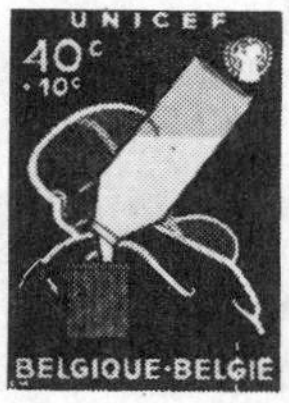

Infant, Milk Bottle and Mug — SP330

UNICEF: 1fr+50c, Nurse and children of 3 races. 2fr+50c, Refugee woman carrying gift clothes. 2.50fr+1fr, Negro nurse weighing infant. 3fr+1fr, Children of various races dancing. 6fr+2fr, Refugee boys.

Photogravure and Engraved

1960, Oct. 8 *Perf. 11½*

B672	SP330	40c + 10c gldn brn, yel & bl grn	.20	.20
B673	SP330	1fr + 50c ol gray, mar & slate	1.40	.75
B674	SP330	2fr + 50c vio, pale brn & brt grn	1.50	1.10
B675	SP330	2.50fr + 1fr dk red, sep & lt bl	1.75	1.40
B676	SP330	3fr + 1fr bl grn, red org & dl vio	.95	.85
B677	SP330	6fr + 2fr ultra, emer & brn	3.75	3.25
		Nos. B672-B677 (6)	9.55	7.55

Tapestry SP331

Belgian handicrafts: 1fr+50c, Cut crystal vases, vert. 2fr+50c, Lace, vert. 2.50fr+1fr, Metal plate & jug. 3fr+1fr, Diamonds. 6fr+2fr, Ceramics.

1960, Dec. 5 *Perf. 11½*

B678	40c + 10c bl, bis & brn	.20	.20
B679	1fr + 50c ind & org brn	1.10	1.00
B680	2fr + 50c dk red brn, blk & cit	2.00	1.50
B681	2.50fr + 1fr choc & yel	2.50	2.25
B682	3fr + 1fr org brn, blk & ultra	1.25	1.10
B683	6fr + 2fr dp blk & yel	5.00	4.00
	Nos. B678-B683 (6)	12.05	10.05

The surtax was for anti-tuberculosis work.

Jacob Kats and Abbe Nicolas Pietkin SP332

Portraits: 1fr+50c, Albert Mockel and J. F. Willems. 2fr+50c, Jan van Rijswijck and Xavier M. Neujean. 2.50fr+1fr, Joseph Demarteau and A. Van de Perre. 3fr+1fr, Canon Jan-Baptist David and Albert du Bois. 6fr+2fr, Henri Vieuxtemps and Willem de Mol.

1961, Apr. 22 Unwmk. *Perf. 11½*

Portraits in Gray Brown

B684	40c + 10c ver & mar	.20	.20
B685	1fr + 50c bis brn & mar	1.50	1.10
B686	2fr + 50c yel & crim	1.75	1.50
B687	2.50fr + 1fr pale cit & dk grn	2.75	1.50
B688	3fr + 1fr lt & dk bl	2.75	2.50
B689	6fr + 2fr lil & ultra	5.00	4.25
	Nos. B684-B689 (6)	13.95	11.05

The surtax was for the benefit of various cultural organizations.

White Rhinoceros SP333

Antonius Cardinal Perrenot de Granvelle SP334

Animals: 1fr+50c, Przewalski horses. 2fr+50c, Okapi. 2.50fr+1fr, Giraffe, horiz. 3fr+1fr, Lesser panda, horiz. 6fr+2fr, European elk, horiz.

Perf. 11½

1961, June 5 Unwmk. Photo.

B690	40c + 10c bis brn & dk brn	.20	.20
B691	1fr + 50c gray & brn	.90	.90
B692	2fr + 50c dp rose & blk	1.40	1.25
B693	2.50fr + 1fr red org & brn	1.10	1.10
B694	3fr + 1fr org & brn	1.00	1.00
B695	6fr + 2fr bl & bis brn	2.25	1.50
	Nos. B690-B695 (6)	6.85	5.95

The surtax was for various philanthropic organizations.

1961, July 29 Engr.

Designs: 3fr+1.50fr, Arms of Cardinal de Granvelle. 6fr+3fr, Tower and crosier, symbolic of collaboration between Malines and the Archbishopric.

B696	SP334	40c + 10c mag, car & brn	.20	.20
B697	SP334	3fr + 1.50fr multi	.65	.50
B698	SP334	6fr + 3fr mag pur & bis	1.25	1.10
		Nos. B696-B698 (3)	2.10	1.80

400th anniv. of Malines as an Archbishopric.

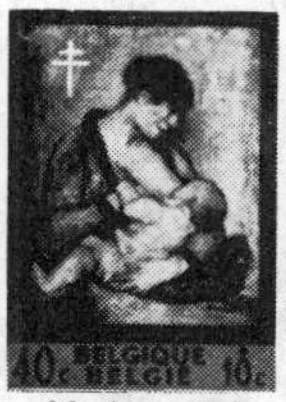

Mother and Child by Pierre Paulus SP335

Castle of the Counts of Male SP336

Plaintings: 1fr+50c, Mother Love, Francois-Joseph Navez. 2fr+50c, Motherhood, Constant Permeke. 2.50fr+1fr, Madonna and Child, Rogier van der Weyden. 3fr+1fr, Madonna with Apple, Hans Memling. 6fr+2fr, Madonna of the Forget-me-not, Peter Paul Rubens.

1961, Dec. 2 Photo. *Perf. 11½*
Gold Frame

B699	SP335	40c + 10c dp brn	.20	.20
B700	SP335	1fr + 50c brt bl	.40	.30
B701	SP335	2fr + 50c rose red	.60	.45
B702	SP335	2.50fr + 1fr magenta	.85	.75
B703	SP335	3fr + 1fr vio bl	1.00	.85
B704	SP335	6fr + 2fr dk sl grn	1.75	1.50
		Nos. B699-B704 (6)	4.80	4.05

The surtax was for anti-tuberculosis work.

1962, Mar. 12 Engr. *Perf. 11½*

Designs: 90c+10c, Royal library, horiz. 1fr+50c, Church of Our Lady, Tongres. 2fr+50c, Collegiate Church, Soignies, horiz. 2.50fr+1fr, Church of Our Lady, Malines. 3fr+1fr, St. Denis Abbey, Broqueroi. 6fr+2fr, Cloth Hall, Ypres, horiz.

B705	SP336	40c + 10c brt grn	.20	.20
B706	SP336	90c + 10c lil rose	.20	.20
B707	SP336	1fr + 50c dl vio	.40	.45
B708	SP336	2fr + 50c violet	.70	.60
B709	SP336	2.50fr + 1fr red brn	1.00	.85
B710	SP336	3fr + 1fr bl grn	1.00	.85
B711	SP336	6fr + 2fr car rose	1.50	1.40
		Nos. B705-B711 (7)	5.00	4.55

The surtax was for various cultural and philanthropic organizations.

Andean Cock of the Rock — SP337

Handicapped Child — SP338

Birds: 1fr+50c, Red lory. 2fr+50c, Guinea touraco. 2.50fr+1fr, Keel-billed toucan. 3fr+1fr, Great bird of paradise. 6fr+2fr, Congolese peacock.

Engraved and Photogravure
1962, June 23 Unwmk. *Perf. 11½*

B712	SP337	40c + 10c multi	.20	.20
B713	SP337	1fr + 50c multi	.45	.30
B714	SP337	2fr + 50c multi	.50	.40
B715	SP337	2.50fr + 1fr multi	.55	.45
B716	SP337	3fr + 1fr multi	1.10	.95
B717	SP337	6fr + 2fr multi	2.00	1.75
		Nos. B712-B717 (6)	4.80	4.05

The surtax was for various philanthropic organizations.

1962, Sept. 22 Photo.

Handicapped Children: 40c+10c, Reading Braille. 2fr+50c, Deaf-mute girl with earphones and electronic equipment, horiz. 2.50fr+1fr, Child with ball (cerebral palsy). 3fr+1fr, Girl with crutches (polio). 6fr+2fr, Sitting boys playing ball, horiz.

B718	SP338	40c + 10c choc	.20	.20
B719	SP338	1fr + 50c rose red	.30	.30
B720	SP338	2fr + 50c brt lil	.55	.60
B721	SP338	2.50fr + 1fr dl grn	.65	.65
B722	SP338	3fr + 1fr dk blue	.80	.80
B723	SP338	6fr + 2fr dk brn	1.50	1.25
		Nos. B718-B723 (6)	4.00	3.80

The surtax was for various institutions for handicapped children.

Queen Louise-Marie SP339

Belgian Queens: No. B725, like No. B724 with "ML" initials. 1fr+50c, Marie-Henriette. 2fr+1fr, Elisabeth. 3fr+1.50fr, Astrid. 8fr+2.50fr, Fabiola.

1962, Dec. 8 Photo. & Engr.
Gray, Black & Gold

B724	SP339	40c + 10c ("L")	.20	.20
B725	SP339	40c + 10c ("ML")	.20	.20
B726	SP339	1fr + 50c	.50	.50
B727	SP339	2fr + 1fr	.85	.85
B728	SP339	3fr + 1.50fr	.95	.85
B729	SP339	8fr + 2.50fr	1.40	1.00
		Nos. B724-B729 (6)	4.10	3.60

The surtax was for anti-tuberculosis work.

British War Memorial (Porte de Menin), Ypres SP340

1962, Dec. 26 Engr. *Perf. 11½*

B730	SP340	1fr + 50c multi	.50	.50

Millennium of the city of Ypres. Issued in sheets of eight.

Peace Bell Ringing over Globe SP341

The Sower by Brueghel SP342

Engraved and Photogravure
1963, Feb. 18 Unwmk. *Perf. 11½*

B731	3fr + 1.50fr blk, bl, org & grn	1.50	1.50
a.	Sheet of 4	7.25	7.25
B732	6fr + 3fr blk, brn & org	.75	.75

The surtax was for the installation of the Peace Bell (Bourdon de la Paix) at Koekelberg Basilica and for the benefit of various cultural organizations.

#B731 was issued in sheets of 4, #B732 in sheets of 30.

1963, Mar. 21 *Perf. 11½*

Designs: 3fr+1fr, The Harvest, by Brueghel, horiz. 6fr+2fr, "Bread," by Anton Carte, horiz.

B733	2fr + 1fr grn, ocher & blk	.20	.20
B734	3fr + 1fr red lil, ocher & blk	.40	.30
B735	6fr + 2fr red brn, cit & blk	.55	.50
	Nos. B733-B735 (3)	1.15	1.00

FAO "Freedom from Hunger" campaign.

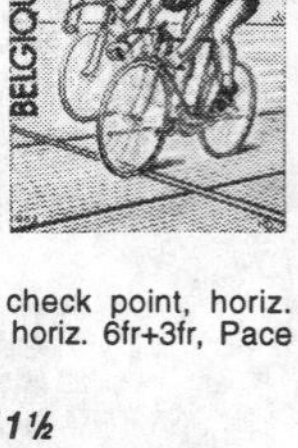

Speed Racing — SP343

2fr+1fr, Bicyclists at check point, horiz. 3fr+1.50fr, Team racing, horiz. 6fr+3fr, Pace setters.

Perf. 11½
1963, July 13 Unwmk. Engr.

B736	SP343	1fr + 50c multi	.20	.20
B737	SP343	2fr + 1fr bl, car, blk & ol gray	.20	.20
B738	SP343	3fr + 1.50fr multi	.35	.35
B739	SP343	6fr + 3fr multi	.50	.50
		Nos. B736-B739 (4)	1.25	1.25

80th anniversary of the founding of the Belgian Bicycle League. The surtax was for athletes at the 1964 Olympic Games.

Princess Paola with Princess Astrid — SP344

Prince Albert and Family — SP345

Designs: 40c+10c, Prince Philippe. 2fr+50c, Princess Astrid. 2.50fr+1fr, Princess Paola. 6fr+2fr, Prince Albert.

1963, Sept. 28 Photo.

B740	SP344	40c + 10c	.20	.20
B741	SP344	1fr + 50c	.35	.30
B742	SP344	2fr + 50c	.45	.40
B743	SP344	2.50fr + 1fr	.45	.40
B744	SP345	3fr + 1fr brn & multi	.45	.45
B745	SP345	3fr + 1fr yel grn & multi	1.50	1.40
a.		Booklet pane of 8	17.00	17.00
B746	SP344	6fr + 2fr	.90	.85
		Nos. B740-B746 (7)	4.30	4.00

Cent. of the Intl. Red Cross. No. B745 issued in booklet panes of 8, which are in two forms: French and Flemish inscriptions in top and bottom margins transposed. Value the same.

Daughter of Balthazar Gerbier, Painted by Rubens — SP346

Jesus, St. John and Cherubs by Rubens — SP347

Portraits (Rubens' sons): 1fr+40c, Nicolas, 2 yrs. old. 2fr+50c, Franz. 2.50fr+1fr, Nicolas, 6 yrs. old. 3fr+1fr, Albert.

Photogravure and Engraved
1963, Dec. 7 Unwmk. *Perf. 11½*

B747	SP346	50c + 10c	.20	.20
B748	SP346	1fr + 40c	.20	.20
B749	SP346	2fr + 50c	.20	.20
B750	SP346	2.50fr + 1fr	.45	.45
B751	SP346	3fr + 1fr	.35	.35
B752	SP347	6fr + 2fr	.45	.45
		Nos. B747-B752 (6)	1.85	1.85

The surtax was for anti-tuberculosis work. See No. B771.

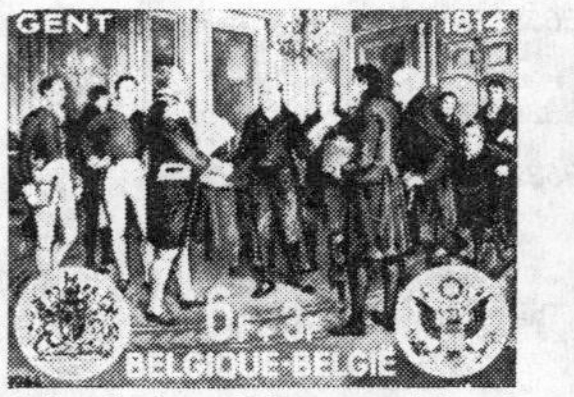

John Quincy Adams and Lord Gambier Signing Treaty of Ghent, by Amédée Forestier — SP348

1964, May 16 Photo. *Perf. 11½*

B753	SP348	6fr + 3fr dk blue	.75	.75

Signing of the Treaty of Ghent between the US and Great Britain, Dec. 24, 1814.

Philip van Marnix — SP349

Portraits: 3fr+1.50fr, Ida de Bure Calvin. 6fr+3fr, Jacob Jordaens.

1964, May 30 Engr.

B754	SP349	1fr + 50c blue gray	.20	.20
B755	SP349	3fr + 1.50fr rose pink	.25	.25
B756	SP349	6fr + 3fr redsh brn	.45	.45
		Nos. B754-B756 (3)	.90	.90

Issued to honor Protestantism in Belgium. The surtax was for the erection of a Protestant church.

Foot Soldier, 1918 SP350

Battle of Bastogne SP351

Designs: 2fr+1fr, Flag bearer, Guides Regiment, 1914. 3fr+1.50fr, Trumpeter of the Grenadiers and drummers, 1914.

1964, Aug. 1 Photo. *Perf. 11½*

B757	SP350	1fr + 50c multi	.20	.20
B758	SP350	2fr + 1fr multi	.25	.25
B759	SP350	3fr + 1.50fr multi	.25	.25
		Nos. B757-B759 (3)	.70	.70

50th anniversary of the German aggression against Belgium in 1914. The surtax aided patriotic undertakings.

1964, Aug. 1 Unwmk.

6fr+3fr, Liberation of the estuary of the Escaut.

B760	SP351	3fr + 1fr multi	.20	.20
B761	SP351	6fr + 3fr multi	.30	.30

Belgium's Resistance and liberation of World War II. The surtax was to help found an International Student Center at Antwerp and to aid cultural undertakings.

Souvenir Sheets

Rogier van der Weyden Paintings — SP352

Descent From the Cross — SP353

1964, Sept. 19 Photo. *Perf. 11½*

B762 SP352 Sheet of 3 2.25 2.25
- *a.* 1fr Philip the Good .50 .50
- *b.* 2fr Portrait of a Lady .50 .50
- *c.* 3fr Man with Arrow .50 .50

Engr.

B763 SP353 8fr red brown 2.25 2.25

Rogier van der Weyden (Roger de La Pasture, 1400-64). The surtax went to various cultural organizations. #B762 sold for 14fr, #B763 for 16fr.

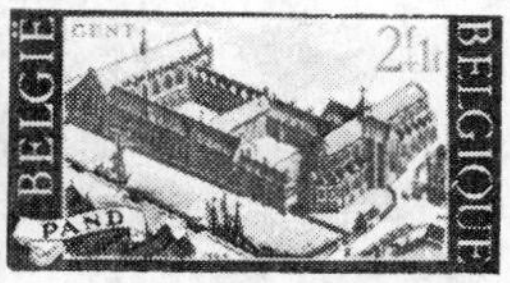

Ancient View of the Pand SP354

3fr+1fr, Present view of the Pand from Lys River.

1964, Oct. 10 Photo.

B764 SP354 2fr + 1fr blk, grnsh bl & ultra .40 .40
B765 SP354 3fr + 1fr lil rose, bl & dk brn .40 .40

The surtax was for the restoration of the Pand Dominican Abbey in Ghent.

Type of 1963 and

Child of Charles I, Painted by Van Dyck — SP355

Designs: 1fr+40c, William of Orange with his bride, by Van Dyck. 2fr+1fr, Portrait of a small boy with dogs by Erasmus Quellin and Jan Fyt. 3fr+1fr, Alexander Farnese by Antonio Moro. 4fr+2fr, William II, Prince of Orange by Van Dyck. 6fr+3fr, Artist's children by Cornelis De Vos.

1964, Dec. 5 Engr. *Perf. 11½*

B766 SP355 50c + 10c rose claret .20 .20
B767 SP355 1fr + 40c car rose .20 .20
B768 SP355 2fr + 1fr vio brn .20 .20
B769 SP355 3fr + 1fr gray .20 .20
B770 SP355 4fr + 2fr vio bl .25 .25
B771 SP347 6fr + 3fr brt pur .25 .25
Nos. B766-B771 (6) 1.30 1.30

The surtax was for anti-tuberculosis work.

Liberator, Shaking Prisoner's Hand, Concentration Camp — SP356

Designs: 1fr+50c, Prisoner's hand reaching for the sun. 3fr+1.50fr, Searchlights and tank breaking down barbed wire, horiz. 8fr+5fr, Rose growing amid the ruins, horiz.

Engraved and Photogravure

1965, May 8 Unwmk. *Perf. 11½*

B772 SP356 50c + 50c tan, blk & buff .20 .20
B773 SP356 1fr + 50c multi .20 .20
B774 SP356 3fr + 1.50fr dl lil & blk .25 .25
B775 SP356 8fr + 5fr multi .35 .35
Nos. B772-B775 (4) 1.00 1.00

20th anniv. of the liberation of the concentration camps for political prisoners and prisoners of war.

Stoclet House, Brussels SP357

Stoclet House: 6fr+3fr, Hall with marble foundation, vert. 8fr+4fr, View of house from garden.

1965, June 21

B776 SP357 3fr + 1fr slate & tan .25 .25
B777 SP357 6fr + 3fr sepia .30 .30
B778 SP357 8fr + 4fr vio brn & tan .45 .45
Nos. B776-B778 (3) 1.00 1.00

Austrian architect Josef Hoffmann (1870-1956), builder of the art nouveau residence of Adolphe Stoclet, engineer and financier.

Jackson's Chameleon SP358

Animals from Antwerp Zoo: 2fr+1fr, Common iguanas. 3fr+1.50fr, African monitor. 6fr+3fr, Komodo monitor. 8fr+4fr, Nile softshell turtle.

1965, Oct. 16 Photo. *Perf. 11½*

B779 SP358 1fr + 50c multi .20 .20
B780 SP358 2fr + 1fr multi .20 .20
B781 SP358 3fr + 1.50fr multi .25 .25
B782 SP358 6fr + 3fr multi .45 .45
Nos. B779-B782 (4) 1.10 1.10

Miniature Sheet

B783 SP358 8fr + 4fr multi 1.75 1.75

The surtax was for various cultural and philanthropic organizations. No. B783 contains one stamp, size: 52x35mm.

Boatmen's and Archers' Guild Halls SP359

Buildings on Grand-Place, Brussels: 1fr+40c, Brewers' Hall. 2fr+1fr, "King of Spain." 3fr+1.50fr, "Dukes of Brabant." 10fr+4.50fr, Tower of City Hall and St. Michael.

1965, Dec. 4 Engr. *Perf. 11½*

Size: 35x24mm

B784 SP359 50c + 10c ultra .20 .20
B785 SP359 1fr + 40c bl grn .20 .20
B786 SP359 2fr + 1fr rose claret .20 .20
B787 SP359 3fr + 1.50fr violet .20 .20

Size: 24x44mm

B788 SP359 10fr + 4.50fr sep & gray .30 .30
Nos. B784-B788 (5) 1.10 1.10

The surtax was for anti-tuberculosis work.

Souvenir Sheets

Queen Elisabeth — SP360

Design: No. B790, Types of 1931 and 1956.

1966, Apr. 16 Photo. *Perf. 11½*

B789 SP360 Sheet of 2 + label 1.50 1.50
- *a.* SP74 3fr dk brn & gray grn .60 .60
- *b.* SP87 3fr dk brn, yel grn & gold .60 .60

B790 SP360 Sheet of 2 + label 1.50 1.50
- *a.* SP42 3fr dk brn & dl bl .60 .60
- *b.* SP304 3fr dk brn & gray .60 .60

The surtax went to various cultural organizations.
Each sheet sold for 20fr.

Luminescent Paper was used in printing Nos. B789-B790, B801-B806, B808-B809, B811-B823, B825-B831, B833-B835, B837-B840, B842-B846, B848-B850, B852-B854, B856-B863, and from B865 onward unless otherwise noted. In many cases the low value of the set is not on luminescent paper. This will not be noted.

Diver — SP361

Design: 10fr+4fr, Swimmer at start.

1966, May 9 Engr.

B791 SP361 60c + 40c Prus grn, ol & org brn .20 .20
B792 SP361 10fr + 4fr ol grn, org brn & mag .40 .40

Issued to publicize the importance of swimming instruction.

Minorites' Convent, Liège — SP362

Designs: 1fr+50c, Val-Dieu Abbey, Aubel. 2fr+1fr, View and seal of Huy. 10fr+4.50fr, Statue of Ambiorix by Jules Bertin, and tower, Tongeren.

1966, Aug. 27 Engr. *Perf. 11½*

B793 SP362 60c + 40c multi .20 .20
B794 SP362 1fr + 50c multi .20 .20
B795 SP362 2fr + 1fr multi .20 .20
B796 SP362 10fr + 4.50fr multi .40 .40
Nos. B793-B796 (4) 1.00 1.00

The surtax was for various patriotic and cultural organizations.

Surveyor and Dog Team SP363

Designs: 3fr+1.50fr, Adrien de Gerlache and "Belgica." 6fr+3fr, Surveyor, weather balloon and ship. 10fr+5fr, Penguins and "Magga Dan" (ship used for 1964, 1965 and 1966 expeditions).

1966, Oct. 8 Engr. *Perf. 11½*

B797 SP363 1fr + 50c bl grn .20 .20
B798 SP363 3fr + 1.50fr pale vio .20 .20
B799 SP363 6fr + 3fr dk car .35 .35
Nos. B797-B799 (3) .75 .75

Souvenir Sheet

Engraved and Photogravure

B800 SP363 10fr + 5fr dk gray, sky bl & dk red .70 .70

Belgian Antarctic expeditions. #B800 contains one 52x35mm stamp.

Boy with Ball and Dog — SP364

Designs: 2fr+1fr, Girl skipping rope. 3fr+1.50fr, Girl and boy blowing soap bubbles. 6fr+3fr, Girl and boy rolling hoops, horiz. 8fr+3.50fr, Four children at play and cat, horiz.

1966, Dec. 3 *Perf. 11½*

B801 SP364 1fr + 1fr pink & blk .20 .20
B802 SP364 2fr + 1fr lt bluish grn & blk .20 .20
B803 SP364 3fr + 1.50fr lt vio & blk .20 .20
B804 SP364 6fr + 3fr pale sal & dk brn .25 .25
B805 SP364 8fr + 3.50fr lt yel grn & dk brn .30 .30
Nos. B801-B805 (5) 1.15 1.15

The surtax was for anti-tuberculosis work.

Souvenir Sheet

Refugees — SP365

Designs: 1fr, Boy receiving clothes. 2fr, Tibetan children. 3fr, African mother and children.

1967, Mar. 11 Photo. *Perf. 11½*

B806 SP365 Sheet of 3 1.25 1.25
- *a.* 1fr black & yellow .30 .30
- *b.* 2fr black & blue .30 .30
- *c.* 3fr black & orange .40 .40

Issued to help refugees around the world. Sheet has black border with Belgian P.T.T. and UN Refugee emblems. Sold for 20fr.

Robert Schuman SP366

Colonial Brotherhood Emblem SP368

Kongolo Memorial, Gentinnes SP367

1967, June 24 Engr. *Perf. 11½*
B807 SP366 2fr + 1fr gray blue .25 .25

Engraved and Photogravure
B808 SP367 5fr + 2fr brn & olive .30 .30
B809 SP368 10fr + 5fr multi .45 .35

Robert Schuman (1886-1963), French statesman, one of the founders of European Steel and Coal Community, 1st pres. of European Parliament (2fr+1fr); Kongolo Memorial, erected in memory of missionary and civilian victims in the Congo (5fr+2fr); a memorial for African Troops, Brussels (10fr+5fr).

Preaching Fool from "Praise of Folly" by Erasmus SP369

Erasmus, by Quentin Massys SP370

Designs: 2fr+1fr, Exhorting Fool from Praise of Folly. 5fr+2fr, Thomas More's Family, by Hans Holbein, horiz. 6fr+3fr, Pierre Gilles (Aegidius), by Quentin Massys.

Photogravure and Engraved (SP369); Photogravure (SP370)
1967, Sept. 2 Unwmk. *Perf. 11*
B810 SP369 1fr + 50c tan, blk, bl & car .20 .20
B811 SP369 2fr + 1fr tan, blk & car .20 .20
B812 SP370 3fr + 1.50fr multi .20 .20
B813 SP369 5fr + 2fr tan, blk & car .20 .20
B814 SP370 6fr + 3fr multi .25 .25
Nos. B810-B814 (5) 1.05 1.05

Issued to commemorate Erasmus (1466(?)-1536), Dutch scholar and his era.

Souvenir Sheet

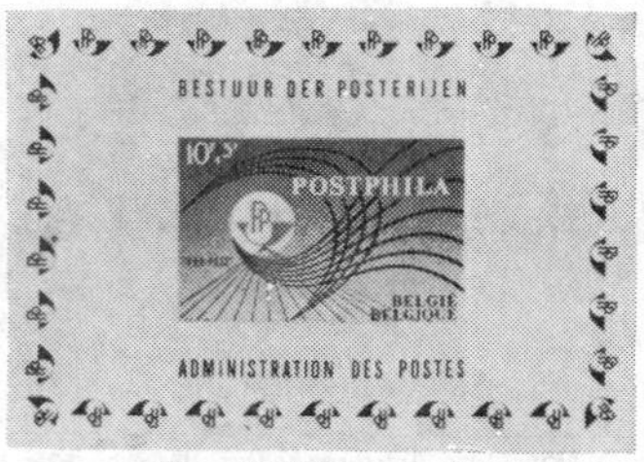

Pro-Post Association Emblem — SP371

Engraved and Photogravure
1967, Oct. 21 *Perf. 11½*
B815 SP371 10fr + 5fr multi .75 .75

Issued to publicize the POSTPHILA Philatelic Exhibition, Brussels, Oct. 21-29.

Detail from Brueghel's "Children's Games" — SP372

Designs: Various Children's Games. Singles of Nos. B816-B821 arranged in 2 rows of 3 show complete painting by Pieter Brueghel.

1967, Dec. 9 Photo. *Perf. 11½*
B816 SP372 1fr + 50c multi .20 .20
B817 SP372 2fr + 50c multi .20 .20
B818 SP372 3fr + 1fr multi .20 .20
B819 SP372 6fr + 3fr multi .30 .30
B820 SP372 10fr + 4fr multi .40 .40
B821 SP372 13fr + 6fr multi .60 .60
Nos. B816-B821 (6) 1.90 1.90

Queen Fabiola Holding Refugee Child from Congo — SP373

6fr+3fr, Queen Elisabeth & Dr. Depage.

1968, Apr. 27 Photo. *Perf. 11½*
Cross in Red
B822 SP373 6fr + 3fr sepia & gray .25 .25
B823 SP373 10fr + 5fr sepia & gray .45 .45

The surtax was for the Red Cross.

Woman Gymnast and Calendar Stone SP374

Yachting and "The Swimmer" by Andrien SP375

"Explosion" SP376

Designs: 2fr+1fr, Weight lifter and Mayan motif. 3fr+1.50fr, Hurdler, colossus of Tula and animal head from Kukulkan. 6fr+2fr, Bicyclists and Chichen Itza Temple.

Engraved and Photogravure
1968, May 27 *Perf. 11½*
B824 SP374 1fr + 50c multi .20 .20
B825 SP374 2fr + 1fr multi .20 .20
B826 SP374 3fr + 1.50fr multi .20 .20
B827 SP374 6fr + 2fr multi .25 .25

Photo.
B828 SP375 13fr + 5fr multi .50 .50
Nos. B824-B828 (5) 1.35 1.35

Issued to publicize the 19th Olympic Games, Mexico City, Oct. 12-27.

1968, June 22 Photo.
Designs (Paintings by Pol Mara): 12fr+5fr, "Fire." 13fr+5fr, "Tornado."

B829 SP376 10fr + 5fr multi .40 .40
B830 SP376 12fr + 5fr multi .65 .65
B831 SP376 13fr + 5fr multi .70 .70
Nos. B829-B831 (3) 1.75 1.75

The surtax was for disaster victims.

Undulate Triggerfish SP377

Tropical Fish: 3fr+1.50fr, Angelfish. 6fr+3fr, Turkeyfish (Pterois volitans). 10fr+5fr, Orange butterflyfish.

1968, Oct. 19 Engr. & Photo.
B832 SP377 1fr + 50c multi .20 .20
B833 SP377 3fr + 1.50fr multi .20 .20
B834 SP377 6fr + 3fr multi .30 .30
B835 SP377 10fr + 5fr multi .40 .40
Nos. B832-B835 (4) 1.10 1.10

King Albert and Queen Elisabeth Entering Brussels SP378

Tomb of the Unknown Soldier and Eternal Flame, Brussels — SP379

Designs: 1fr+50c, King Albert, Queen Elisabeth and Crown Prince Leopold on balcony, Bruges, vert. 6fr+3fr, King and Queen entering Liège.

1968, Nov. 9 Photo. *Perf. 11½*
B836 SP378 1fr + 50c multi .20 .20
B837 SP378 3fr + 1.50fr multi .20 .20
B838 SP378 6fr + 3fr multi .30 .30

Engraved and Photogravure
B839 SP379 10fr + 5fr multi .40 .40
Nos. B836-B839 (4) 1.10 1.10

50th anniv. of the victory in World War I.

Souvenir Sheet

The Painter and the Amateur, by Peter Brueghel — SP380

1969, May 10 Engr. *Perf. 11½*
B840 SP380 10fr + 5fr sepia 1.10 1.10

Issued to publicize the POSTPHILA 1969 Philatelic Exhibition, Brussels, May 10-18.

Huts, by Ivanka D. Pancheva, Bulgaria SP381

Msgr. Victor Scheppers SP382

Children's Drawings and UNICEF Emblem: 3fr+1.50fr, "My Art" (Santa Claus), by Claes Patric, Belgium. 6fr+3fr, "In the Sun" (young boy), by Helena Rejchlova, Czechoslovakia. 10fr+5fr, "Out for a Walk" by Phillis Sporn, US, horiz.

1969, May 31 Photo. *Perf. 11½*
B841 SP381 1fr + 50c multi .20 .20
B842 SP381 3fr + 1.50fr multi .20 .20
B843 SP381 6fr + 3fr multi .35 .35
B844 SP381 10fr + 5fr multi .50 .50
Nos. B841-B844 (4) 1.25 1.25

The surtax was for philanthropic purposes.

1969, July 5 Engr.
B845 SP382 6fr + 3fr rose claret .45 .45

Msgr. Victor Scheppers (1802-77), prison reformer and founder of the Brothers of Mechlin (Scheppers).

Moon Landing Type of 1969
Souvenir Sheet

Design: 20fr+10fr, Armstrong, Collins and Aldrin and moon with Tranquillity Base, vert.

1969, Sept. 20 Photo. *Perf. 11½*
B846 A245 20fr + 10fr indigo 3.00 3.00

See note after No. 726.

Heads from Alexander the Great Tapestry, 15th Century — SP383

Designs from Tapestries: 3fr+1.50fr, Fiddler from "The Feast," c. 1700. 10fr+4fr, Head of beggar from "The Healing of the Paralytic," 16th century.

1969, Sept. 20
B847 SP383 1fr + 50c multi .20 .20
B848 SP383 3fr + 1.50fr multi .20 .20
B849 SP383 10fr + 4fr multi .45 .45
Nos. B847-B849 (3) .85 .85

The surtax was for philanthropic purposes.

Bearded Antwerp Bantam SP384

1969, Nov. 8 Engr. & Photo.
B850 SP384 10fr + 5fr multi .70 .70

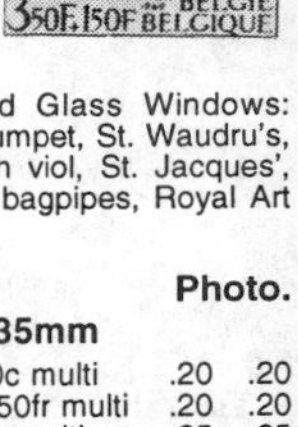

Angel Playing Lute — SP385

Designs from Stained Glass Windows: 1.50fr+50c, Angel with trumpet, St. Waudru's, Mons. 7fr+3fr, Angel with viol, St. Jacques', Liege. 9fr+4fr, King with bagpipes, Royal Art Museum, Brussels.

1969, Dec. 13 Photo.
Size: 24x35mm
B851 SP385 1.50fr + 50c multi .20 .20
B852 SP385 3.50fr + 1.50fr multi .20 .20
B853 SP385 7fr + 3fr multi .35 .35

Size: 35x52mm
B854 SP386 9fr + 4fr multi .50 .50
Nos. B851-B854 (4) 1.25 1.25

The surtax was for philanthropic purposes.

Farm and Windmill, Open-air Museum, Bokrijk SP386

Belgian Museums: 3.50fr+1.50fr, Stage Coach Inn, Courcelles. 7fr+3fr, "The Thresher of Trevires," Gallo-Roman sculpture, Gaumais Museum, Virton. 9fr+4fr, "The Sovereigns," by Henry Moore, Middelheim Museum, Antwerp.

Engraved and Photogravure

1970, May 30 ***Perf. 11½***

B855	SP386	1.50fr + 50c multi	.20	.20
B856	SP386	3.50fr + 1.50fr multi	.25	.25
B857	SP386	7fr + 3fr multi	.35	.35
B858	SP386	9fr + 4fr multi	.40	.40
		Nos. B855-B858 (4)	1.20	1.20

The surtax went to various culture organizations.

"Resistance" SP387

Design: 7fr+3fr, "Liberation of Camps." The designs were originally used as book covers.

1970, July 4 **Photo.** ***Perf. 11½***

B859	SP387	3.50fr + 1.50fr blk, gray grn & dp car	.20	.20
B860	SP387	7fr + 3fr blk, lil & dp car	.40	.40

Honoring the Resistance Movement and 25th anniv. of the liberation of concentration camps.

Fishing Rod and Reel SP388

Design: 9fr+4fr, Hockey stick and puck, vert.

1970, Sept. 19 **Engr. & Photo.**

B861	SP388	3.50fr + 1.50fr multi	.30	.30
B862	SP388	9fr + 4fr multi	.50	.50

Souvenir Sheet

Belgium Nos. 31, 36, 39 — SP389

1970, Oct. 10 ***Perf. 11½***

B863	SP389	Sheet of 3	4.75	4.75
a.		1.50fr + 50c black & dull lilac	1.40	1.40
b.		3.50fr + 1.50fr black & lilac	1.40	1.40
c.		9fr + 4fr black & red brown	1.40	1.40

BELGICA 72 International Philatelic Exhibition, Brussels, June 24-July 9.

Camille Huysmans (1871-1968) SP390

"Anxious City" (Detail) by Paul Delvaux SP391

Portraits: 3.50fr+1.50fr, Joseph Cardinal Cardijn (1882-1967). 7fr+3fr, Maria Baers (1883-1959). 9fr+4fr, Paul Pastur (1866-1938).

1970, Nov. 14 ***Perf. 11½***

Portraits in Sepia

B864	SP390	1.50fr + 50c car rose	.20	.20
B865	SP390	3.50fr + 1.50fr lilac	.20	.20
B866	SP390	7fr + 3fr green	.40	.40
B867	SP390	9fr + 4fr blue	.50	.50
		Nos. B864-B867 (4)	1.30	1.30

1970, Dec. 12 **Photo.**

7fr+3fr, "The Memory," by Rene Magritte.

B868	SP391	3.50fr + 1.50fr multi	.20	.20
B869	SP391	7fr + 3fr multi	.40	.40

Notre Dame du Vivier, Marche-les-Dames — SP392

7fr+3fr, Turnhout Beguinage and Beguine.

1971, Mar. 13 ***Perf. 11½***

B870	SP392	3.50fr + 1.50fr multi	.20	.20
B871	SP392	7fr + 3fr multi	.40	.40

The surtax was for philanthropic purposes.

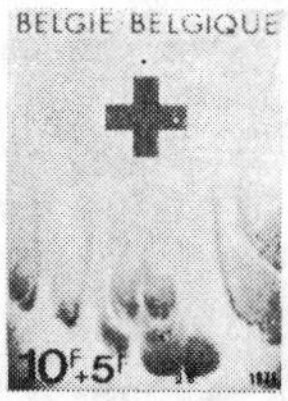

Red Cross — SP393

1971, May 22 **Photo.** ***Perf. 11½***

B872	SP393	10fr + 5fr crim & blk	.75	.75

Belgian Red Cross.

Discobolus and Munich Cathedral SP394

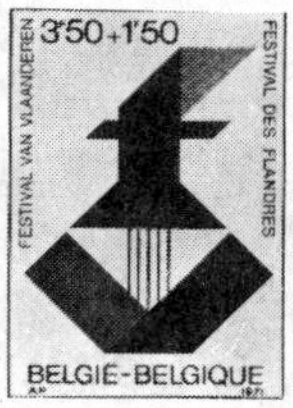

Festival of Flanders SP395

1971, June 19 **Engr. & Photo.**

B873	SP394	7fr + 3fr bl & blk	.40	.40

Publicity for the 20th Summer Olympic Games, Munich 1972.

1971, Sept. 11 **Photo.** ***Perf. 11½***

Design: 7fr+3fr, Wallonia Festival.

B874	SP395	3.50fr + 1.50fr multi	.20	.20
B875	SP395	7fr + 3fr multi	.40	.40

Attre Palace — SP396

Steen Palace, Elewijt — SP397

Design: 10fr+5fr, Royal Palace, Brussels.

1971, Oct. 23 **Engr.**

B876	SP396	3.50fr + 1.50fr sl grn	.30	.30
B877	SP397	7fr + 3fr red brn	.50	.50
B878	SP396	10fr + 5fr vio bl	.70	.70
		Nos. B876-B878 (3)	1.50	1.50

Surtax was for BELGICA 72, International Philatelic Exposition.

Ox Fly — SP398

Insects: 1.50fr+50c, Luna moth, vert. 7fr+3fr, Wasp, polistes gallicus. 9fr+4fr, Tiger beetle, vert.

1971, Dec. 11 **Photo.** ***Perf. 11½***

B879	SP398	1.50fr + 50c multi	.20	.20
B880	SP398	3.50fr + 1.50fr multi	.20	.20
B881	SP398	7fr + 3fr multi	.40	.40
B882	SP398	9fr + 4fr multi	.60	.60
		Nos. B879-B882 (4)	1.40	1.40

Surtax was for philanthropic purposes.

Leopold I on #1 SP399

Epilepsy Emblem SP400

Designs: 2fr+1fr, Leopold I on No. 5. 2.50fr+1fr, Leopold II on No. 45. 3.50fr+1.50fr, Leopold II on No. 48. 6fr+3fr, Albert I on No. 135. 7fr+3fr, Albert I on No. 214. 10fr+5fr, Albert I on No. 231. 15fr+7.50fr, Leopold III on No. 290. 20fr+10fr, King Baudouin on No. 718.

Engraved and Photogravure

1972, June 24 ***Perf. 11½***

B883	SP399	1.50fr + 50c	.20	.20
B884	SP399	2fr + 1fr	.20	.20
B885	SP399	2.50 + 1fr	.20	.20
B886	SP399	3.50fr + 1.50fr	.30	.30
B887	SP399	6fr + 3fr	.50	.50
B888	SP399	7fr + 3fr	.70	.70
B889	SP399	10fr + 5fr	.90	.90
B890	SP399	15fr + 7fr	1.10	1.10
B891	SP399	20fr + 10fr	2.00	2.00
		Nos. B883-B891 (9)	6.10	6.10

Belgica 72, Intl. Philatelic Exhibition, Brussels, June 24-July 9. Nos. B883-B891 issued in sheets of 10 and of 20 (2 tete beche sheets with gutter between). Sold in complete sets.

1972, Sept. 9 **Photo.** ***Perf. 11½***

B892	SP400	10fr + 5fr multi	.55	.55

The surtax was for the William Lennox Center for epilepsy research and treatment.

Gray Lag Goose — SP401

Designs: 4.50fr+2fr, Lapwing. 8fr+4fr, Stork. 9fr+4.50fr, Kestrel, horiz.

1972, Dec. 16 **Photo.** ***Perf. 11½***

B893	SP401	2fr + 1fr multi	.25	.25
B894	SP401	4.50fr + 2fr multi	.30	.30
B895	SP401	8fr + 4fr multi	.60	.60
B896	SP401	9fr + 4.50fr multi	.60	.60
		Nos. B893-B896 (4)	1.75	1.75

Bijloke Abbey, Ghent — SP402

Designs: 4.50fr+2fr, St. Ursmer Collegiate Church, Lobbes. 8fr+4fr, Park Abbey, Heverle. 9fr+4.50fr, Abbey, Floreffe.

1973, Mar. 24 **Engr.** ***Perf. 11½***

B897	SP402	2fr + 1fr slate grn	.20	.20
B898	SP402	4.50fr + 2fr brown	.25	.25
B899	SP402	8fr + 4fr rose lil	.50	.50
B900	SP402	9fr + 4.50fr brt bl	.60	.60
		Nos. B897-B900 (4)	1.55	1.55

Basketball SP403

1973, Apr. 7 **Photo. & Engr.**

B901	SP403	10fr + 5fr multi	.60	.60

First World Basketball Championships of the Handicapped, Bruges, Apr. 16-21.

Dirk Martens' Printing Press SP404

Lady Talbot, by Petrus Christus SP405

Hadrian and Marcus Aurelius Coins SP406

Council of Malines, by Coussaert — SP407

Designs: 3.50fr+1.50fr, Head of Amon and Tutankhamen's cartouche. 10fr+5fr, Three-master of Ostend Merchant Company.

Photogravure and Engraved; Photogravure (#B906)

1973, June 23 — ***Perf. 11½***

B902 SP404 2fr + 1fr multi .20 .20
B903 SP404 3.50fr + 1.50fr multi .20 .20
B904 SP405 4.50fr + 2fr multi .20 .20
B905 SP406 8fr + 4fr multi .60 .60
B906 SP407 9fr + 4.50fr multi .85 .85
B907 SP407 10fr + 5fr multi 1.50 1.50
Nos. B902-B907 (6) 3.55 3.55

500th anniv. of 1st book printed in Belgium (#B902); 50th anniv. of Queen Elisabeth Egyptological Foundation (#B903); 500th anniv. of death of painter Petrus Christus (#B904); Discovery of Roman treasure at Luttre-Liberchies (#B905); 500th anniv. of Great Council of Malines (#B906); 250th anniv. of the Ostend Merchant Company (#B907).

No. B902 is not luminescent.

Queen of Hearts SP408

Symbol of Blood Donations SP409

Old Playing Cards: #B909, King of Clubs. #B910, Jack of Diamonds. #B911, King of Spades.

1973, Dec. 8 **Photo.** ***Perf. 11½***

B908 SP408 5fr + 2.50fr multi .40 .40
B909 SP408 5fr + 2.50fr multi .40 .40
B910 SP408 5fr + 2.50fr multi .40 .40
B911 SP408 5fr + 2.50fr multi .40 .40
a. Block of 4, #B908-B911 1.60 1.60

Surtax was for philanthropic purposes.

1974, Feb. 23 **Photo.** ***Perf. 11½***

Design: 10fr+5fr, Traffic lights, Red Cross (symbolic of road accidents).

B912 SP409 4fr + 2fr multi .25 .25
B913 SP409 10fr + 5fr multi .55 .55

The Red Cross as blood collector and aid to accident victims.

Armand Jamar, Self-portrait SP410

Van Gogh, Self-portrait and House at Cuesmes SP411

Designs: 5fr+2.50fr, Anton Bergmann and view of Lierre. 7fr+3.50fr, Henri Vieuxtemps and view of Verviers. 10fr+5fr, James Ensor, self-portrait, and masks.

1974, Apr. 6 **Photo.** ***Perf. 11½***

Size: 24x35mm

B914 SP410 4fr + 2fr multi .25 .25
B915 SP410 5fr + 2.50fr multi .30 .30
B916 SP410 7fr + 3.50fr multi .40 .40

Size: 35x52mm

B917 SP410 10fr + 5fr multi .65 .65
Nos. B914-B917 (4) 1.60 1.60

1974, Sept. 21 **Photo.** ***Perf. 11½***

B918 SP411 10fr + 5fr multi .55 .55

Opening of Vincent van Gogh House at Cuesmes, where he worked as teacher.

> ***Buying Sets***
> *It is often less expensive to purchase complete sets than individual stamps that make up the set.*

Gentian — SP412

Spotted Cat's Ear — SP414

Badger SP413

Design: 7fr+3.50fr, Beetle.

1974, Dec. 8 **Photo.** ***Perf. 11½***

B919 SP412 4fr + 2fr multi .25 .25
B920 SP413 5fr + 2.50fr multi .30 .30
B921 SP413 7fr + 3.50fr multi .40 .40
B922 SP414 10fr + 5fr multi .60 .60
Nos. B919-B922 (4) 1.55 1.55

Pesaro Palace, Venice SP415

St. Bavon Abbey, Ghent SP416

Virgin and Child, by Michelangelo SP417

1975, Apr. 12 **Engr.** ***Perf. 11½***

B923 SP415 6.50fr + 2.50fr brn .35 .35
B924 SP416 10fr + 4.50 vio brn .60 .60
B925 SP417 15fr + 6.50fr brt bl .80 .80
Nos. B923-B925 (3) 1.75 1.75

Surtax was for various cultural organizations.

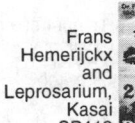

Frans Hemerijckx and Leprosarium, Kasai SP418

1975, Sept. 13 **Photo.** ***Perf. 11½***

B926 SP418 20fr + 10fr multi 1.40 1.40

Dr. Frans Hemerijckx (1902-1969), tropical medicine and leprosy expert.

Emile Moyson SP419

Beheading of St. Dympna SP420a

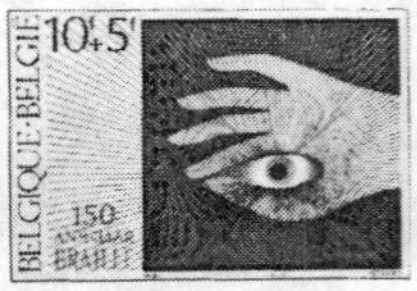

Hand Reading Braille SP420

6.50fr+3fr, Dr. Ferdinand Augustin Snellaert.

1975, Nov. 22 **Engr.** ***Perf. 11½***

B927 SP419 4.50fr + 2fr lilac .25 .25
B928 SP419 6.50fr + 3fr green .35 .35

Engraved and Photogravure

B929 SP420 10fr + 5fr multi .50 .50

Photo.

B930 SP420a 13fr + 6fr multi .70 .70
Nos. B927-B930 (4) 1.80 1.80

Emile Moyson (1838-1868), freedom fighter for the rights of Flemings and Walloons; Dr. Snellaert (1809-1872), physician and Flemish patriot; Louis Braille (1809-1852), sesquicentennial of invention of Braille system of writing for the blind; St. Dympna, patron saint of Geel, famous for treatment of mentally ill.

The Cheese Vendor — SP421

Designs (THEMABELGA Emblem and): No. B932, Potato vendor. No. B933, Basket carrier. No. B934, Shrimp fisherman with horse, horiz. No. B935, Knife grinder, horiz. No. B936, Milk vendor with dog cart, horiz.

1975, Dec. 13 **Engr. & Photo.**

B931 SP421 4.50fr + 1.50fr multi .20 .20
B932 SP421 6.50fr + 3fr multi .30 .30
B933 SP421 6.50fr + 3fr multi .30 .30
B934 SP421 10fr + 5fr multi .45 .45
B935 SP421 10fr + 5fr multi .45 .45
B936 SP421 30fr + 15fr multi 1.50 1.50
Nos. B931-B936 (6) 3.20 3.20

THEMABELGA Intl. Topical Philatelic Exhib., Brussels, Dec. 13-21. Issued in sheets of 10 (5x2).

Blackface Fund Collector — SP422

1976, Feb. 14 **Photo.** ***Perf. 11½***

B937 SP422 10fr + 5fr multi .55 .55

"Conservatoire Africain" philanthropic soc., cent., and to publicize the Princess Paola creches.

Swimming and Olympic Emblem SP423

Montreal Olympic Games Emblem and: 5fr+2fr, Running, vert. 6.50fr+2.50fr, Equestrian.

1976, Apr. 10 **Photo.** ***Perf. 11½***

B938 SP423 4.50fr + 1.50fr multi .20 .20
B939 SP423 5fr + 2fr multi .25 .25
B940 SP423 6.50fr + 2.50fr multi .45 .45
Nos. B938-B940 (3) .90 .90

21st Olympic Games, Montreal, Canada, July 17-Aug. 1.

Queen Elisabeth Playing Violin SP424

Perf. 11½

1976, May 1 **Engr.** **Photo.**

B941 SP424 14fr + 6fr blk & claret .95 .95

Queen Elisabeth International Music Competition, 25th anniversary.

Souvenir Sheet

Jan Olieslagers, Bleriot Monoplane, Aero Club Emblem — SP425

Engraved and Photogravure

1976, June 12 ***Perf. 11½***

B942 SP425 25fr + 10fr multi 2.25 2.25

Royal Belgian Aero Club, 75th anniversary, and Jan Olieslagers (1883-1942), aviation pioneer.

Adoration of the Shepherds (detail), by Rubens SP426

Dwarf, by Velazquez SP427

Rubens Paintings (Details): 4.50fr, Descent from the Cross. No. B945, The Virgin with the Parrot. No. B946, Adoration of the Kings. No. B947, Last Communion of St. Francis. 30fr+15fr, Virgin and Child.

1976, Sept. 4 **Photo.** ***Perf. 11½***

Size: 35x52mm

B943 SP426 4.50fr + 1.50fr multi .35 .35

Size: 24x35mm

B944 SP426 6.50fr + 3fr multi .55 .55
B945 SP426 6.50fr + 3fr multi .55 .55
B946 SP426 10fr + 5fr multi .85 .85
B947 SP426 10fr + 5fr multi .85 .85

Size: 35x52mm

B948 SP426 30fr + 15fr multi 1.75 1.75
Nos. B943-B948 (6) 4.90 4.90

Peter Paul Rubens (1577-1640), Flemish painter, 400th birth anniversary.

1976, Nov. 6 **Photo.** ***Perf. 11½***

B949 SP427 14fr + 6fr multi .80 .80

Surtax was for the National Association for the Mentally Handicapped.

Dr. Albert Hustin SP428

Red Cross and Rheumatism Year Emblem SP429

1977, Feb. 19 Photo. *Perf. 11½*

B950	SP428	6.50fr + 2.50 multi	.40	.40
B951	SP429	14fr + 7fr multi	.75	.75

Belgian Red Cross.

Bordet Atheneum, Empress Maria Theresa SP430

Conductor and Orchestra, by E. Tytgat SP431

Lucien Van Obbergh, Stage SP432

Humanistic Society Emblem SP433

Camille Lemonnier SP434

Design: No. B953, Marie-Therese College, Herve, and coat of arms.

1977, Mar. 21 Photo. *Perf. 11½*

B952	SP430	4.50fr + 1fr multi	.20	.20
B953	SP430	4.50fr + 1fr multi	.20	.20
B954	SP431	5fr + 2fr multi	.25	.25
B955	SP432	6.50fr + 2fr multi	.30	.30
B956	SP433	6.50fr + 2fr blk & red	.30	.30
		Engr.		
B957	SP434	10fr + 5fr slate bl	.50	.50
		Nos. B952-B957 (6)	1.75	1.75

Bicentenaries of the Jules Bordet Atheneum, Brussels, and the Marie-Therese College, Herve (#B952-B953); 50th anniv. of the Brussels Philharmonic Soc., and Artists' Union (#B954-B955): 25th anniv. of the Flemish Humanistic Organization (#B956); 75th anniv. of the French-speaking Belgian writers' organization (#957).

Young Soccer Players SP435

Albert-Edouard Janssen, Financier SP436

1977, Apr. 18 Photo.

B958	SP435	10fr + 5fr multi	.55	.55

30th Intl. Junior Soccer Tournament.

1977, Dec. 3 Engr. *Perf. 11½*

Famous Men: No. B960, Joseph Wauters (1875-1929), editor of Le Peuple, and newspaper. No. B961, Jean Capart (1877-1947), Egyptologist, and hieroglyph. No. B962, August de Boeck (1865-1937), composer, and score.

B959	SP436	5fr + 2.50fr brown	.30	.30
B960	SP436	5fr + 2.50fr red	.30	.30
B961	SP436	10fr + 5fr magenta	.55	.55
B962	SP436	10fr + 5fr blue gray	.55	.55
		Nos. B959-B962 (4)	1.70	1.70

Abandoned Child SP437

Checking Blood Pressure SP438

De Mick Sanatorium, Brasschaat — SP439

1978, Feb. 18 Photo. *Perf. 11½*

B963	SP437	4.50fr + 1.50fr multi	.20	.20
B964	SP438	6fr + 3fr multi	.40	.40
B965	SP439	10fr + 5fr multi	.60	.60
		Nos. B963-B965 (3)	1.20	1.20

Help for abandoned children (No. B963); fight against hypertension (No. B964); fight against tuberculosis (No. B965).

Actors and Theater SP440

Karel van de Woestijne SP441

Designs: No. B967, Harquebusier, Harquebusier Palace and coat of arms. 10fr+5fr, John of Austria and his signature.

Engraved and Photogravure

1978, June 17 *Perf. 11½*

B966	SP440	6fr + 3fr multi	.40	.40
B967	SP440	6fr + 3fr multi	.40	.40
		Engr.		
B968	SP441	8fr + 4fr black	.45	.45
B969	SP441	10fr + 5fr black	.55	.55
		Nos. B966-B969 (4)	1.80	1.80

Cent. of Royal Flemish Theater, Brussels (#B966); 400th anniv. of Harquebusiers' Guild of Vise, Liege (#967); Karel van de Woestijne (1878-1929), poet (#B968); 400th anniv. of signing of Perpetual Edict by John of Austria (#969).

Lake Placid '80 and Belgian Olympic Emblems — SP442

Designs (Moscow '80 Emblem and): 8fr+3.50fr, Kremlin Towers and Belgian Olympic Committee emblem. 7fr+3fr, Runners from Greek vase, Lake Placid '80 emblem and Olympic rings. 14fr+6fr, Olympic flame, Lake Placid '80 and Belgian emblems, Olympic rings.

1978, Nov. 4 Photo. *Perf. 11½*

B970	SP442	6fr + 2.50fr multi	.30	.30
B971	SP442	8fr + 3.50fr multi	.45	.45

Souvenir Sheet

B972		Sheet of 2	1.50	1.50
a.		SP442 7fr + 3fr multi	.55	.55
b.		SP442 14fr + 6fr multi	.90	.90

Surtax was for 1980 Olympic Games.

Great Synagogue, Brussels — SP443

Dancers SP444

Father Pire, African Village SP445

1978, Dec. 2 Engr. *Perf. 11½*

B973	SP443	6fr + 2fr sepia	.45	.45
		Photo.		
B974	SP444	8fr + 3fr multi	.35	.35
B975	SP445	14fr + 7fr multi	.65	.65
		Nos. B973-B975 (3)	1.45	1.45

Centenary of Great Synagogue of Brussels; Flemish Catholic Youth Action Organization, 50th anniversary; Nobel Peace Prize awarded to Father Dominique Pire for his "Heart Open to the World" movement, 20th anniversary.

Young People Giving First Aid SP446

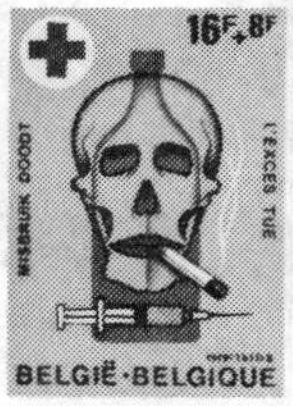

Skull with Bottle, Cigarette, Syringe SP447

1979, Feb. 10 Photo. *Perf. 11½*

B976	SP446	8fr + 3fr multi	.35	.35
B977	SP447	16fr + 8fr multi	.85	.85

Belgian Red Cross.

Beatrice Soetkens with Statue of Virgin Mary — SP448

Details from Tapestries, 1516-1518, Showing Legend of Our Lady of Sand: 8fr+3fr, Francois de Tassis accepting letter from Emperor Frederick III (beginning of postal service). 14fr+7fr, Arrival of statue, Francois de Tassis and Philip the Fair. No. B981, Statue carried in procession by future Emperor Charles V and his brother Ferdinand. No. B982, Ship carrying Beatrice Soetkens with statue to Brussels, horiz.

1979, May 5 Photo. *Perf. 11½*

B978	SP448	6fr + 2fr multi	.25	.25
B979	SP448	8fr + 3fr multi	.40	.40
B980	SP448	14fr + 7fr multi	.65	.65
B981	SP448	20fr + 10fr multi	1.10	1.10
		Nos. B978-B981 (4)	2.40	2.40

Souvenir Sheet

B982	SP448	20fr + 10fr multi	.90	.90

The surtax was for festivities in connection with the millennium of Brussels.

Notre Dame Abbey, Brussels SP449

Designs: 8fr+3fr, Beauvoorde Castle. 14fr+7fr, 1st issue of "Courrier de L'Escaut" and Barthelemy Dumortier, founder. 20fr+10fr, Shrine of St. Hermes, Renaix.

Engraved and Photogravure

1979, Sept. 15 *Perf. 11½*

B983	SP449	6fr + 2fr multi	.35	.35
B984	SP449	8fr + 3fr multi	.50	.50
B985	SP449	14fr + 7fr multi	.60	.60
B986	SP449	20fr + 10fr multi	1.10	1.10
		Nos. B983-B986 (4)	2.55	2.55

50th anniv. of restoration of Notre Dame de la Cambre Abbey; historic Beauvoorde Castle, 15th cent. sesquicentennial of the regional newspaper "Le Courrier de L'Escaut"; 850th anniv. of the consecration of the Collegiate Church of St. Hermes, Renaix.

Grand-Hornu Coal Mine SP450

1979, Oct. 22 Engr. *Perf. 11½*

B987	SP450	10fr + 5fr blk	.55	.55

Henry Heyman SP451

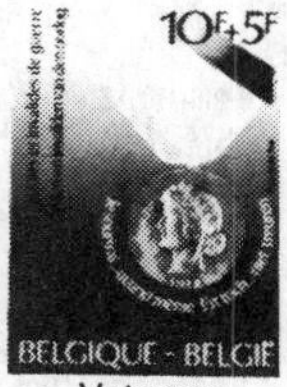

Veterans Organization Medal SP452

Boy and IYC Emblem SP453

1979, Dec. 8 Photo. *Perf. 11½*

B988	SP451	8fr + 3fr multi	.45	.45
B989	SP452	10fr + 5fr multi	.55	.55
B990	SP453	16fr + 8fr multi	.75	.75
		Nos. B988-B990 (3)	1.75	1.75

Henri Heyman (1879-1958), Minister of State; Disabled Veterans' Organization, 50th anniv.; Intl. Year of the Child.

Ivo Van Damme, Olympic Rings — SP454

1980, May 3 Photo. *Perf. 11½*

B991	SP454	20fr + 10fr multi	1.10	1.10

Ivo Van Damme (1954-1976), silver medalist, 800-meter race, Montreal Olympics, 1976. Surtax was for Van Damme Memorial Foundation.

Queen Louis-Marie, King Leopold I — SP455

150th Anniversary of Independence (Queens and Kings): 9fr+3fr, Marie Henriette. Leopold II. 14fr+6fr, Elisabeth, Albert I. 17fr+8fr, Astrid, Leopold III. 25fr+10fr, Fabiola, Baudouin.

Photogravure and Engraved

1980, May 31 *Perf. 11½*

B992	SP455	6.50 + 1.50fr multi	.30	.30
B993	SP455	9 + 3fr multi	.50	.50
B994	SP455	14 + 6fr multi	.70	.70
B995	SP455	17 + 8fr multi	1.00	1.00
B996	SP455	25 + 10fr multi	1.25	1.25
		Nos. B992-B996 (5)	3.75	3.75

Miner, by Constantine Meunier SP456

Seal of Bishop Notger, First Prince-Bishop — SP457

9fr+3fr, Brewer, 16th century, from St. Lambert's reliquary, vert. 25fr+10fr, Virgin and Child, 13th century, St. John's Collegiate Church, Liege.

1980, Sept. 13 Photo. *Perf. 11½*

B997	SP456	9 + 3fr multi	.35	.35
B998	SP456	17 + 6fr multi	.70	.70
B999	SP456	25 + 10fr multi	1.10	1.10
		Nos. B997-B999 (3)	2.15	2.15

Souvenir Sheet

B1000	SP457	20 + 10fr multi	1.25	1.25

Millennium of the Principality of Liege.

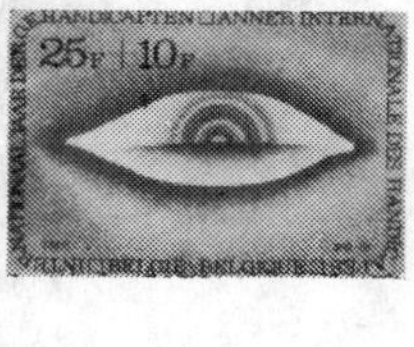

Visual and Oral Handicaps SP458

Intl. Year of the Disabled: 10fr+5fr, Cerebral handicap, vert.

1981, Feb. 9 Photo. *Perf. 11½*

B1001	SP458	10 + 5fr multi	.70	.70
B1002	SP458	25 + 10fr multi	1.60	1.60

Dove with Red Cross Carrying Globe SP459

Design: 10fr+5fr, Atomic model, vert.

1981, Apr. 6 Photo. *Perf. 11½*

B1003	SP459	10 + 5fr multi	.70	.70
B1004	SP459	25 + 10fr multi	1.60	1.60

Red Cross and: 15th Intl. Radiology Congress, Brussels, June 24-July 1 (#B1003); intl. disaster relief (#B1004).

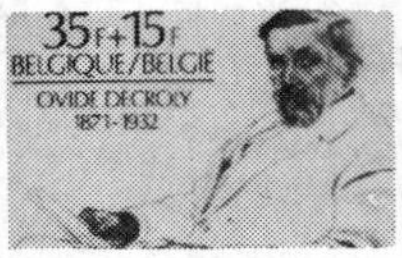

Ovide Decroly SP460

1981, June 1 Photo. *Perf. 11½*

B1005	SP460	35 + 15fr multi	2.00	2.00

Ovide Decroly (1871-1932), developer of educational psychology.

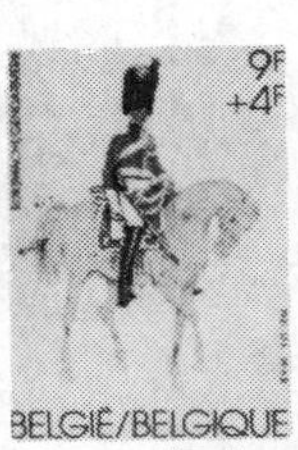

Mounted Police Officer — SP461

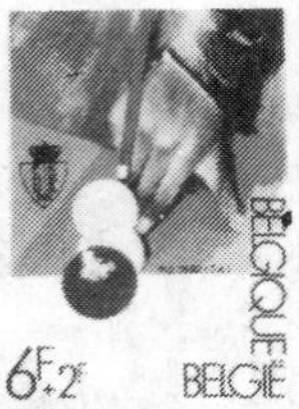

Billiards — SP462

Anniversaries: 9fr+4fr, Gendarmerie (State Police Force), 150th. 20fr+7fr, Carabineers Regiment, 150th. 40fr+20fr, Guides Regiment.

1981, Dec. 7 Photo. *Perf. 11½*

B1006	SP461	9 + 4fr multi	.60	.60
B1007	SP461	20 + 7fr multi	1.25	1.25
B1008	SP461	40 + 20fr multi	2.75	2.75
		Nos. B1006-B1008 (3)	4.60	4.60

1982, Mar. 29 Photo. *Perf. 11½*

B1009	SP462	6 + 2fr shown	.40	.40
B1010	SP462	9 + 4fr Cycling	.60	.60
B1011	SP462	10 + 5fr Soccer	.70	.70
B1012	SP462	50 + 14fr Yachting	3.00	3.00
		Nos. B1009-B1012 (4)	4.70	4.70

Souvenir Sheet

B1013	Sheet of 4	5.00	5.00
a.	SP462 25fr like #B1009	1.40	1.40
b.	SP462 25fr like #B1010	1.40	1.40
c.	SP462 25fr like #B1011	1.40	1.40
d.	SP462 25fr like #B1012	1.40	1.40

#B1013 shows designs in changed colors.

Christmas SP463

1982, Nov. 6

B1014	SP463	10 + 1fr multi	.60	.45

Surtax was for tuberculosis research.

Belgica '82 Intl. Stamp Exhibition, Brussels, Dec. 11-19 SP464

Messengers (Prints). Nos. B1016-B1018 vert.

Photogravure and Engraved

1982, Dec. 11 *Perf. 11½*

B1015	SP464	7 + 2fr multi	.40	.40
B1016	SP464	7.50 + 2.50fr multi	.45	.45
B1017	SP464	10 + 3fr multi	.55	.55
B1018	SP464	17 + 7fr multi	1.10	1.10
B1019	SP464	20 + 9fr multi	1.25	1.25
B1020	SP464	25 + 10fr multi	1.50	1.50
		Nos. B1015-B1020 (6)	5.25	5.25

Souvenir Sheet

B1021	SP464	50 + 25fr multi	6.00	6.00

No. B1021 contains one 48x37mm stamp.

50th Anniv. of Catholic Charities SP465

Mountain Climbing SP466

1983, Jan. 22 Photo. *Perf. 11½*

B1022	SP465	10 + 2fr multi	.65	.65

1983, Mar. 7 Photo.

B1023	SP466	12 + 3fr shown	.80	.80
B1024	SP466	20 + 5fr Hiking	1.25	1.25

Surtax was for Red Cross.

Madonna by Jef Wauters SP467

Rifles Uniform SP468

1983, Nov. 21 Photo. *Perf. 11½*

B1025	SP467	11 + 1fr multi	.60	.60

1983, Dec. 5 Photo. *Perf. 11½*

B1026	SP468	8 + 2fr shown	.50	.50
B1027	SP468	11 + 2fr Lancers uniform	.75	.75
B1028	SP468	50 + 12fr Grenadiers uniform	3.50	3.50
		Nos. B1026-B1028 (3)	4.75	4.75

Type of 1984

1984, Mar. 3 Photo. *Perf. 11½*

B1029	A495	8 + 2fr Judo, horiz.	.55	.55
B1030	A495	12 + 3fr Wind surfing	.85	.85

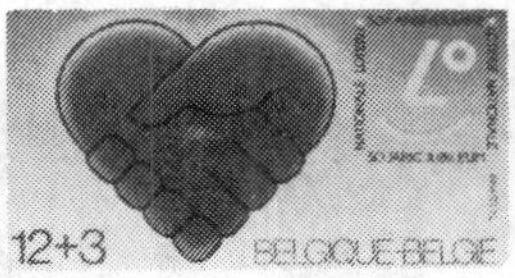

50th Anniv. of Natl. Lottery SP469

1984, Mar. 31 Photo. *Perf. 11½*

B1031	SP469	12 + 3fr multi	.75	.75

Brussels Modern Art Museum Opening SP470

Paintings: 8fr+2fr, Les Masques Singuliers, by James Ensor. 12fr+3fr, Empire des Lumieres, by Rene Magritte. 22fr+5fr, The End, by Jan Cox. 50fr+13fr, Rhythm No. 6, by Jo Delahaut.

1984, Sept. 1 Photo.

B1032	SP470	8 + 2fr multi	.60	.60
B1033	SP470	12 + 3fr multi	.90	.90
B1034	SP470	22 + 5fr multi	1.60	1.60
B1035	SP470	50 + 13fr multi	3.75	3.75
		Nos. B1032-B1035 (4)	6.85	6.85

Child with Parents — SP471

1984, Nov. 3 Photo.

B1036	SP471	10 + 2fr shown	.60	.60
B1037	SP471	12 + 3fr Siblings	.75	.75
B1038	SP471	15 + 3fr Merry-go-round	.85	.85
		Nos. B1036-B1038 (3)	2.20	2.20

Surtax was for children's programs.

Christmas 1984 SP472

1984, Dec. 1

B1039	SP472	12 + 1fr Three Kings	.75	.75

Belgian Red Cross Blood Transfusion Service, 50th Anniv. — SP473

1985, Mar. 4 Photo. *Perf. 11½*

B1040	SP473	9 + 2fr Tree	.60	.60
B1041	SP473	23 + 5fr Hearts	1.40	1.40

Surtax was for the Belgian Red Cross.

Solidarity SP474

Castles.

1985, Nov. 4 Photo. & Engr.

B1042	SP474	9 + 2fr Trazegnies	.60	.60
B1043	SP474	12 + 3fr Laarne	.80	.80
B1044	SP474	23 + 5fr Turnhout	1.40	1.40
B1045	SP474	50 + 12fr Colonster	3.50	3.50
		Nos. B1042-B1045 (4)	6.30	6.30

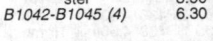

Christmas 1985, New Year 1986 — SP475

Painting: Miniature from the Book of Hours, by Jean duc de Berry.

1985, Nov. 25 Photo.

B1046	SP475	12 + 1fr multi	.70	.70

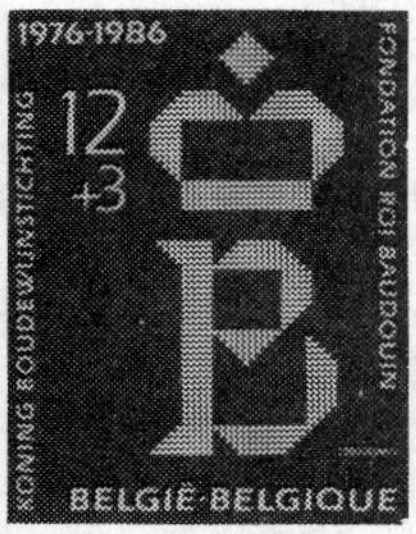

King Baudouin Foundation SP476

1986, Mar. 24 **Photo.**

B1047 SP476 12 + 3fr Emblem .80 .80

Surtax for the foundation.

Madonna SP477

Adoration of the Mystic Lamb, St. Bavon Cathedral Altarpiece, Ghent SP478

Paintings by Hubert van Eyck (c. 1370-1426).

1986, Apr. 5 **Photo.** ***Perf. 11½***

B1048 SP477 9 + 2fr shown .65 .65
B1049 SP477 13 + 3fr Christ in Majesty .95 .95
B1050 SP477 24 + 6fr St. John the Baptist 1.75 1.75
Nos. B1048-B1050 (3) 3.35 3.35

Souvenir Sheet

B1051 SP478 50 + 12fr multi 5.25 5.25

Surtax for cultural organizations.

Antique Automobiles SP479

1986, Nov. 3 **Photo.**

B1052 SP479 9 + 2fr Lenoir, 1863 .65 .65
B1053 SP479 13 + 3fr Pipe de Tourisme, 1911 .90 .90
B1054 SP479 24 + 6fr Minerva 22 HP, 1930 1.75 1.75
B1055 SP479 26 + 6fr FN 8 Cylinder, 1931 1.90 1.90
Nos. B1052-B1055 (4) 5.20 5.20

Christmas 1986, New Year 1987 SP480

1986, Nov. 24 **Photo.**

B1056 SP480 13 + 1fr Village in winter .75 .75

Natl. Red Cross — SP482

European Conservation Year — SP483

Nobel Prize winners for physiology (1938) and medicine (1974): No. B1058, Corneille Heymans (1892-1968). No. B1059, A. Claude (1899-1983).

Photogravure and Engraved

1987, Feb. 16 ***Perf. 11½***

B1058 SP482 13 + 3fr dk brn & red .90 .90
B1059 SP482 24 + 6fr dk brn & red 1.60 1.60

1987, Mar. 16 **Photo.**

B1060 SP483 9 + 2fr Bee orchid .60 .60
B1061 SP483 24 + 6fr Horseshoe bat 1.60 1.60
B1062 SP483 26 + 6fr Peregrine falcon 1.75 1.75
Nos. B1060-B1062 (3) 3.95 3.95

Castles — SP484

1987, Oct. 17 **Photo. & Engr.**

B1063 SP484 9 + 2fr Rixensart .60 .60
B1064 SP484 13 + 3fr Westerlo .90 .90
B1065 SP484 26 + 5fr Fallais 1.75 1.75
B1066 SP484 50 + 12fr Gaasbeek 3.50 3.50
Nos. B1063-B1066 (4) 6.75 6.75

Christmas 1987 — SP485

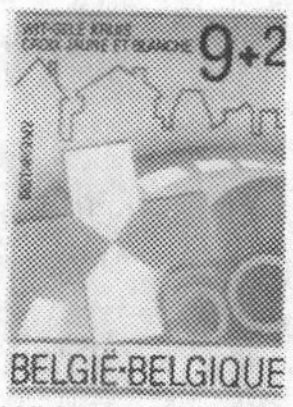

White and Yellow Cross of Belgium, 50th Anniv. — SP486

Painting: Holy Family, by Rev. Father Lens.

1987, Nov. 14 **Photo.**

B1067 SP485 13 + 1fr multi .85 .85

1987, Dec. 5

B1068 SP486 9 + 2fr multi .70 .70

Promote Philately — SP487

Various flowers from Sixty Roses for a Queen, by P. J. Redoute (1759-1840).

1988, Apr. 25 **Photo.** ***Perf. 11½***

B1069 SP487 13 + 3fr shown 1.00 1.00
B1070 SP487 24 + 6fr multi, diff. 1.75 1.75

Souvenir Sheet

B1071 SP487 50 + 12fr multi, diff. 3.75 3.75

See Nos. B1081-B1083, B1089-B1091, 1346.

1988 Summer Olympics, Seoul — SP488

1988, June 6 **Photo.** ***Perf. 11½***

B1072 SP488 9fr + 2fr Table tennis .65 .65
B1073 SP488 13fr + 3fr Cycling .95 .95

Souvenir Sheet

B1074 SP488 50fr + 12fr Marathon runners 3.70 3.70

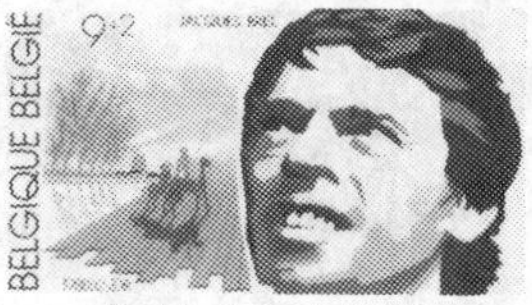

Solidarity — SP489

1988, Oct. 24 **Photo.** ***Perf. 12x11½***

B1075 SP489 9fr + 2fr Jacques Brel .60 .60
B1076 SP489 13fr + 3fr Jef Denyn .90 .90
B1077 SP489 26fr + 6fr Fr. Ferdinand Verbiest 1.75 1.75
Nos. B1075-B1077 (3) 3.25 3.25

Belgian Red Cross SP490

Paintings: No. B1078, *Crucifixion of Christ*, by Rogier van der Weyden (c. 1399-1464). No. B1079, *Virgin and Child*, by David (c. 1460-1523). B1089, *The Good Samaritan*, by Denis van Alsloot.

1989, Feb. 20 **Photo.** ***Perf. 11½***

B1078 SP490 9fr + 2fr multi .60 .60
B1079 SP490 13fr + 3fr multi .90 .90
B1080 SP490 24fr + 6fr multi 1.60 1.60
Nos. B1078-B1080 (3) 3.10 3.10

Stamp Collecting Promotion Type of 1988

Various flowers from *Sixty Roses for a Queen*, by P.J. Redoute (1759-1840) and inscriptions: No. B1081, "Centfeuille unique melee de rouge." No. B1082, "Bengale a grandes feuilles." No. B1083, Aeme vibere (tea roses).

1989, Apr. 17

B1081 SP487 13fr + 5fr multi 1.00 1.00
B1082 SP487 24fr + 6fr multi 1.60 1.60

Souvenir Sheet

B1083 SP487 50fr + 17fr multi 3.75 3.75

Solidarity SP491

Royal Greenhouses of Laeken.

1989, Oct. 23

B1084 SP491 9fr + 3fr Exterior .60 .60
B1085 SP491 13fr + 4fr Interior, vert. .85 .85
B1086 SP491 24fr + 5fr Dome exterior, vert. 1.40 1.40
B1087 SP491 26fr + 6fr Dome interior, vert. 1.50 1.50
Nos. B1084-B1087 (4) 4.35 4.35

Queen Elisabeth Chapelle Musicale, 50th Anniv. — SP492

1989, Nov. 6

B1088 SP492 24fr + 6fr G clef 1.50 1.50

Stamp Collecting Promotion Type of 1988

Various flowers from *Sixty Roses for a Queen*, by P.J. Redoute (1759-1840): No. B1089, *Bengale desprez*. No. B1090, *Bengale philippe*. No. B1091, *Maria leonida*.

1990, Feb. 5

B1089 SP487 14fr + 7fr multi 1.10 1.10
B1090 SP487 25fr + 12fr multi 2.00 2.00

Souvenir Sheet

B1091 SP487 50fr + 20fr multi 3.75 3.75

Youth and Music — SP493

Designs: 14fr+3fr, Beethoven and Lamoraal, Count of Egmont (1522-1568). 25fr+6fr, Joseph Cantre (1890-1957), drawing and sculpture.

1990, Oct. 6

B1092 SP493 10fr + 2fr multi .70 .70
B1093 SP493 14fr + 3fr multi 1.00 1.00
B1094 SP493 25fr + 6fr multi 1.75 1.75
Nos. B1092-B1094 (3) 3.45 3.45

King Baudouin & Queen Fabiola, 30th Wedding Anniv. — SP494

1990, Dec. 10

B1095 SP494 50fr +15fr multi 4.25 4.25

Belgian Red Cross SP495

Details from paintings: No. B1096, The Temptation of St. Anthony by Hieronymus Bosch. No. B1097, The Annunciation by Dirk Bouts.

1991, Feb. 25, **Photo.** ***Perf. 11½***

B1096 SP495 14fr +3fr multi 1.10 1.10
B1097 SP495 25fr +6fr multi 2.00 2.00

Belgian Film Personalities — SP496

Designs: 10fr+2fr, Charles Dekeukeleire (1905-1971), producer. 14fr+3fr, Jacques Ledoux (1921-1988), film conservationist. 25fr+6fr, Jacques Feyder (1899-1948), director.

1991, Oct. 28 Photo. *Perf. 11½*

B1098 SP496 10fr +2fr multi .75 .75
B1099 SP496 14fr +3fr multi 1.10 1.10
B1100 SP496 25fr +6fr multi 1.90 1.90
Nos. B1098-B1100 (3) 3.75 3.75

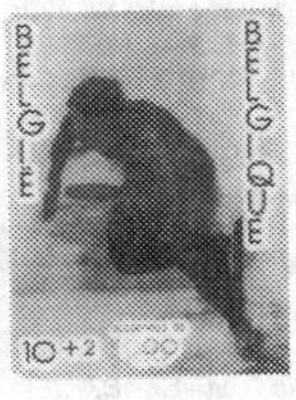

1992 Winter and Summer Olympics, Albertville and Barcelona — SP497

1992, Jan. 20 Photo. *Perf. 11½*

B1101 SP497 10fr +2fr Speed skating .75 .75
B1102 SP497 10fr +2fr Baseball .75 .75
B1103 SP497 14fr +3fr Women's tennis, horiz. 1.10 1.10
B1104 SP497 25fr +6fr Skeet shooting 1.90 1.90
Nos. B1101-B1104 (4) 4.50 4.50

Folk Legends SP498

11fr + 2fr, Proud Margaret. 15fr + 3fr, Gustine Maca & the Witches. 28fr + 6fr, Reynard the Fox.

1992, June 22 Photo. *Perf. 11½*

B1105 SP498 11fr +2fr multi .80 .80
B1106 SP498 15fr +3fr multi 1.10 1.10
B1107 SP498 28fr +6fr multi 2.00 2.00
Nos. B1105-B1107 (3) 3.90 3.90

Belgian Red Cross SP499

Paintings: 15fr + 3fr, Man with the Pointed Hat, by Adriaen Brouwer (1605-1638). 28fr + 7fr, Nereid and Triton, by Peter Paul Rubens, horiz.

1993, Feb. 15 Photo. *Perf. 11½*

B1108 SP499 15fr +3fr multi 1.10 1.10
B1109 SP499 28fr +7fr multi 2.10 2.10

Fight Against Cancer SP500

1993, Sept. 20 Photo. *Perf. 11½*

B1110 SP500 15fr +3fr multicolored 1.10 1.10

Intl. Olympic Committee, Cent. — SP501

#B1112, Soccer players. #B1113, Figure skater.

1994, Feb. 14 Photo. *Perf. 11½*

B1111 SP501 16fr +3fr multi 1.00 1.00
B1112 SP501 16fr +3fr multi 1.00 1.00
B1113 SP501 16fr +3fr multi 1.00 1.00
Nos. B1111-B1113 (3) 3.00 3.00

1994 World Cup Soccer Championships, Los Angeles (#B1112). 1994 Winter Olympics, Lillehammer, Norway (#B1113).

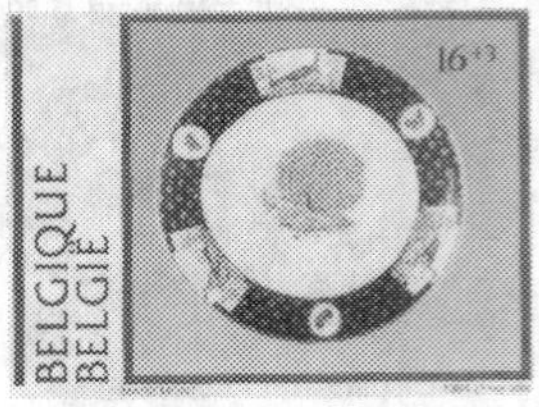

Porcelain — SP502

Designs: No. B1114, Tournai plate, Museum of Mariemont-Morlanweiz. No. B1115, Etterbeek cup, saucer, Municipal Museum, Louvain. 50fr+11fr, Delft earthenware jars, Pharmacy Museum of Maaseik.

1994, June 27 Photo. *Perf. 11½*

B1114 SP502 16fr +3fr multi 1.10 1.10
B1115 SP502 16fr +3fr multi 1.10 1.10

Souvenir Sheet

B1116 SP502 50fr +11fr multi 3.50 3.50

No. B1116 contains one 49x38mm stamp.

Solidarity SP503

Design: 16fr+3fr, Hearing-impaired person.

1994, Nov. 14 Photo. *Perf. 11½*

B1117 SP503 16fr +3fr multi 1.25 1.25

Museums — SP504

#B1118, Natl. Flax Museum, Kortrijk. #B1119, Natl. Water & Fountain Museum, Genval.

34fr+6fr, Intl. Carnival and Mask Museum, Binche.

1995, Jan. 30 Photo. *Perf. 11½*

B1118 SP504 16fr +3fr multi 1.25 1.25
B1119 SP504 16fr +3fr multi 1.25 1.25

Souvenir Sheet

B1120 SP504 34fr +6fr multi 2.75 2.75

Surtax for promotion of philately.

"Souvenir Sheets"

Beginning in 1995 items looking like souvenir sheets have appeared in the market. The 1995 one has the design used for No. B1120. The 1996 one has the design similar to the one used for No. B1128. The 1997 one has the design used for No. B1131. These have no postal value.

Royal Belgian Soccer Assoc., Cent. SP505

1995, Aug. 21 Photo. *Perf. 11½*

B1121 SP505 16fr +4fr multi 1.40 1.40

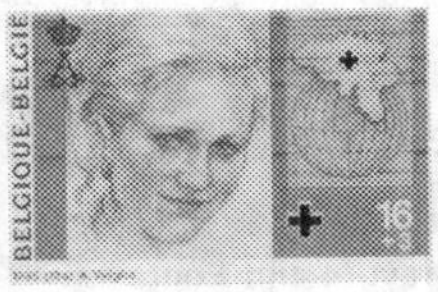

Belgian Red Cross SP506

Designs: No. B1122, Princess Astrid, chairwoman of Belgian Red Cross. No. B1123, Wilhelm C. Röntgen (1845-1923), discoverer of the X-ray. No. B1124, Louis Pasteur (1822-95), scientist.

1995, Sept. 11

B1122 SP506 16fr +3fr multi 1.25 1.25
B1123 SP506 16fr +3fr multi 1.25 1.25
B1124 SP506 16fr +3fr multi 1.25 1.25
Nos. B1122-B1124 (3) 3.75 3.75

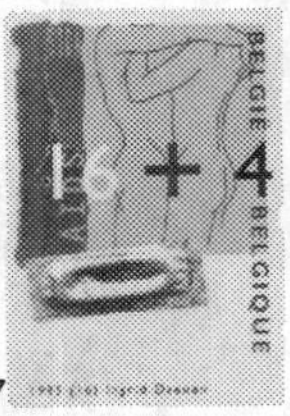

Solidarity — SP507

1995, Nov. 6 Photo. *Perf. 11½*

B1125 SP507 16fr +4fr multi 1.25 1.25

Surtax for fight against AIDS.

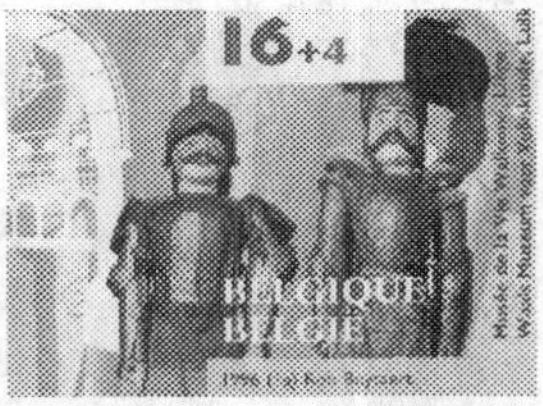

Museums — SP508

Designs: No. B1126, Museum of Walloon Life, Liège. No. B1127, Natl. Gin Museum, Hasselt.

34fr+6fr, Butchers' Guild Hall Museum, Antwerp.

1996, Feb. 19 Photo. *Perf. 11½*

B1126 SP508 16fr +4fr multi 1.25 1.25
B1127 SP508 16fr +4fr multi 1.25 1.25

Souvenir Sheet

B1128 SP508 34fr +6fr multi 2.50 2.50

Modern Olympic Games, Cent. SP509

1996, July 1 Photo. *Perf. 11½*

B1129 SP509 16fr +4fr Table tennis 1.25 1.25
B1130 SP509 16fr +4fr Swimming 1.25 1.25

Souvenir Sheet

B1131 SP509 34fr +6fr High jump 2.50 2.50

No. B1131 contains one 49x38mm stamp.

UNICEF, 50th Anniv. SP510

1996, Nov. 18 Photo. *Perf. 11½*

B1132 SP510 16fr +4fr multi 1.40 1.40

Museums SP511

#B1133, Deportation and Resistance Museum, Mechlin. #B1134, Iron Museum, Saint Hubert.

41fr+9fr, Horta Museum, Saint Gilles.

1997, Jan. 20 Photo. *Perf. 11½*

B1133 SP511 17fr +4fr multi 1.25 1.25
B1134 SP511 17fr +4fr multi 1.25 1.25

Souvenir Sheet

B1135 SP511 41fr +9fr multi 3.00 3.00

Surtax for "Pro-Post" association.

Judo — SP512 Solidarity — SP513

1997, May 5 Photo. *Perf. 11½*

B1136 SP512 17fr +4fr Men's (10a) 1.25 1.25
B1137 SP512 17fr +4fr Women's (10b) 1.25 1.25

Surtax for Belgian Olympic Committee.

1997, Oct. 25

B1138 SP513 17fr +4fr multi 1.25 1.25

Surtax for Multiple Sclerosis research.

King Leopold III — SP514

32fr+15fr, King Baudouin I. 50fr+25fr, King Albert II.

1998, Feb. 16 Engr. *Perf. 11½*

B1139 SP514 17fr +8fr dk grn 1.50 1.50
B1140 SP514 32fr +15fr dk brn blk 2.75 2.75

Souvenir Sheet

B1141 SP514 50fr +25fr dk vio brn 4.50 4.50

See Nos. B1146-B1148.

Sports SP515

1998, June 8 Photo. *Perf. 11½*

B1142 SP515 17fr +4fr Pelota 1.25 1.25
B1143 SP515 17fr +4fr Handball 1.25 1.25

Souvenir Sheet

B1144 SP515 30fr +7fr Soccer 2.00 2.00

1998 World Cup Soccer Championships, France (#B1144).

Assist the Blind — SP516

Photo. & Embossed

1998, Nov. 9 *Perf. 11½*

B1145 SP516 17fr +4fr multi 1.25 1.25

Face value is indicated in Braille.

Royalty Type of 1998

Designs: 17fr+8fr, King Albert I. 32fr+15fr, King Leopold II. 50fr+25fr, King Leopold I.

1999, Jan. 25 Engr. *Perf. 11½*

B1146 SP514 17fr +8fr deep green 1.50 1.50
B1147 SP514 32fr +15fr black 2.75 2.75

Souvenir Sheet

B1148 SP514 50fr +25fr deep brown 4.50 4.50

Motorcycles — SP517

1999, May 17 Photo. *Perf. 11½*

B1149 SP517 17fr +4fr Speed race 1.10 1.10
B1150 SP517 17fr +4fr Trial, vert. 1.10 1.10

Souvenir Sheet

B1151 SP517 30fr +7fr Motocross, vert. 2.00 2.00

AIR POST STAMPS

Fokker FVII/3m over Ostend AP1

Designs: 1.50fr, Plane over St. Hubert. 2fr, over Namur. 5fr, over Brussels.

Perf. 11½

1930, Apr. 30 Unwmk. Photo.

C1 AP1 50c blue .40 .40
C2 AP1 1.50fr black brn 2.25 2.50
C3 AP1 2fr deep green 2.00 .55
C4 AP1 5fr brown lake 1.75 .95
Nos. C1-C4 (4) 6.40 4.40
Set, never hinged 20.00

Exist imperf.

1930, Dec. 5

C5 AP1 5fr dark violet 30.00 30.00
Never hinged 50.00

Issued for use on a mail carrying flight from Brussels to Leopoldville, Belgian Congo, starting Dec. 7.

Exists imperf.

#C2, C4 Surcharged in Carmine or Blue

1Fr 1Fr

1935, May 23

C6 AP1 1fr on 1.50fr (C) .55 .40
C7 AP1 4fr on 5fr (Bl) 7.50 7.00
Set, never hinged 25.00

Catalogue values for unused stamps in this section, from this point to the end of the section, are for Never Hinged items.

DC-4 Skymaster, Sabena Airline AP5

1946, Apr. 20 Engr. *Perf. 11½*

C8 AP5 6fr blue .75 .25
C9 AP5 8.50fr violet brn 1.00 .35
C10 AP5 50fr yellow grn 5.00 .60
a. Perf. 12x11½ ('54) 325.00 1.00
C11 AP5 100fr gray 8.25 .80
a. Perf. 12x11½ ('54) 65.00 1.10
Nos. C8-C11 (4) 15.00 2.00

Evolution of Postal Transportation — AP6

1949, July 1

C12 AP6 50fr dark brown 42.50 15.00

Centenary of Belgian postage stamps.

Glider AP7

Design: 7fr, "Tipsy" plane.

1951, June 18 Photo. *Perf. 13½*

C12A Strip of 2 + label 70.00 60.00
b. AP7 6fr dark blue 25.00 17.50
c. AP7 7fr carmine rose 25.00 17.50

For the 50th anniv. of the Aero Club of Belgium. The strip sold for 50fr.

1951, July 25 *Perf. 13½*

C13 AP7 6fr sepia 4.50 .20
C14 AP7 7fr Prus green 3.50 .95

UN Types of Regular Issue, 1958

Designs: 5fr, ICAO. 6fr, World Meteorological Organization. 7.50fr, Protection of Refugees. 8fr, General Agreement on Tariffs and Trade. 9fr, UNICEF. 10fr, Atomic Energy Agency.

Perf. 11½

1958, Apr. 17 Unwmk. Engr.

C15 A137 5fr dull blue .25 .30
C16 A136 6fr yellow grn .30 .45
C17 A137 7.50fr lilac .30 .30
C18 A136 8fr sepia .30 .30
C19 A137 9fr carmine .40 .50
C20 A136 10fr redsh brown .75 .60
Nos. C15-C20 (6) 2.30 2.45

World's Fair, Brussels, Apr. 17-Oct. 19. See note after No. 476.

AIR POST SEMI-POSTAL STAMPS

Catalogue values for unused stamps in this section are for Never Hinged items.

American Soldier in Combat — SPAP1

Perf. 11x11½

1946, June 15 Unwmk. Engr.

CB1 SPAP1 17.50fr + 62.50fr dl brn 2.00 .90
CB2 SPAP1 17.50fr + 62.50fr dl gray grn 2.00 .90

Surtax for an American memorial at Bastogne.

An overprint, "Hommage a Roosevelt," was privately applied to Nos. CB1-CB2 in 1947 by the Association Belgo-Americaine.

In 1950 another private overprint was applied, in red, to Nos. CB1-CB2. It consists of "16-12-1944, 25-1-1945, Dedication July 16, 1950" and outlines of the American eagle emblem and the Bastogne Memorial. Similar overprints were applied to Nos. 265 and 345.

Flight Allegory SPAP2

1946, Sept. 7 *Perf. 11½*

CB3 SPAP2 2fr + 8fr brt vio .60 *1.00*

The surtax was for the benefit of aviation.

Nos. B417-B425 Surcharged in Various Arrangements in Red or Dark Blue

POSTE AERIENNE
LUCHTPOST
1F

LUCHTPOST
POSTE AERIENNE
2F + 1F +2F

Type I- Top line "POSTE AERIENNE"
Type II- Top line "LUCHTPOST"

1947, May 18 Photo. *Perf. 11½*

Type I

CB4 1fr + 2fr on #B417 (R) .60 *.90*
CB5 1.50fr + 2.50fr on #B418 .60 *.90*
CB6 2fr + 45fr on #B419 .60 *.90*
CB7 1fr + 2fr on #B420 (R) .60 *.90*
CB8 1.50fr + 2.50fr on #B421 .60 *.90*
CB9 2fr + 45fr on #B422 .60 *.90*
CB10 1fr + 2fr on #B423 (R) .60 *.90*
CB11 1.50fr + 2.50fr on #B424 (R) .60 *.90*
CB12 2fr + 45fr on #B425 .60 *.90*

Type II

CB4A 1fr + 2fr on #B417 (R) .60 *.90*
CB5A 1.50fr + 2.50fr on #B418 .60 *.90*
CB6A 2fr + 45fr on #B419 .60 *.90*
CB7A 1fr + 2fr on #B420 (R) .60 *.90*
CB8A 1.50fr + 2.50fr on #B421 .60 *.90*
CB9A 2fr + 45fr on #B422 .60 *.90*
CB10A 1fr + 2fr on #B423 (R) .60 *.90*
CB11A 1.50fr + 2.50fr on #B424 (R) .60 *.90*
CB12A 2fr + 45fr on #B425 .60 *.90*
Nos. CB4-CB12A (18) 10.80 *16.20*

Issued for CIPEX, NYC. In 1948 Nos. CB4-CB12 and CB4A-CB12A were punched with the letters "IMABA," and the inscription "Imaba du 21 au 29 aout 1948" was applied to the backs. Value $20.

Helicopter Leaving Airport SPAP3

1950, Aug. 7

CB13 SPAP3 7fr + 3fr blue 9.00 5.25

Surtax for the Natl. Aeronautical Committee.

SPECIAL DELIVERY STAMPS

From 1874 to 1903 certain hexagonal telegraph stamps were used as special delivery stamps.

Town Hall, Brussels — SD1

Eupen — SD2

2.35fr, Street in Ghent. 3.50fr, Bishop's Palace, Liege. 5.25fr, Notre Dame Cathedral, Antwerp.

1929 Unwmk. Photo. *Perf. 11½*

E1 SD1 1.75fr dark blue .80 .30
E2 SD1 2.35fr carmine 1.50 .45
E3 SD1 3.50fr dark violet 10.00 9.00
E4 SD1 5.25fr olive green 5.50 5.25

1931

E5 SD2 2.45fr dark green 11.00 2.50
Nos. E1-E5 (5) 28.80 17.50

No. E5 Surcharged in Red

2Fr 50

1932

E6 SD2 2.50fr on 2.45fr dk grn 9.00 1.25

POSTAGE DUE STAMPS

D1

D2

1870 Unwmk. Typo. *Perf. 15*

J1 D1 10c green 3.75 2.00
J2 D1 20c ultra, thin paper 30.00 3.75

In 1909 many bisects of Nos. J1-J2 were created. The 10c bisect used as 5c on piece sells for $3.50.

No. J2 was also printed on thicker paper and in aniline ink on thin paper.

1895-09 *Perf. 14*

J3	D2	5c yellow grn	.20	.20
J4	D2	10c orange brn	17.50	1.75
J5	D2	10c carmine ('00)	.20	.20
J6	D2	20c olive green	.20	.20
J7	D2	30c pale blue ('09)	.30	.25
J8	D2	50c yellow brn	17.50	5.00
J9	D2	50c gray ('00)	.75	.45
J10	D2	1fr carmine	20.00	11.50
J11	D2	1fr ocher ('00)	6.50	5.00
		Nos. J3-J11 (9)	63.15	24.55

1916 Redrawn

J12	D2	5c blue grn	25.00	7.00
J13	D2	10c carmine	42.50	11.00
J14	D2	20c dp gray grn	42.50	15.00
J15	D2	30c brt blue	6.00	5.00
J16	D2	50c gray	110.00	60.00
		Nos. J12-J16 (5)	226.00	98.00

In the redrawn stamps the lions have a heavy, colored outline. There is a thick vertical line at the outer edge of the design on each side.

D3

D4

1919 *Perf. 14*

J17	D3	5c green	.40	.50
J18	D3	10c carmine	.95	.40
J19	D3	20c gray green	7.25	1.25
J20	D3	30c bright blue	1.40	.40
J21	D3	50c gray	2.75	.50
		Nos. J17-J21 (5)	12.75	3.05

1922-32

J22	D4	5c dk gray	.20	.20
J23	D4	10c green	.20	.20
J24	D4	20c deep brown	.20	.20
J25	D4	30c ver ('24)	.65	.20
a.		30c rose red	1.00	.45
J26	D4	40c red brn ('25)	.25	.20
J27	D4	50c ultra	1.90	.20
J28	D4	70c red brn ('29)	.30	.20
J29	D4	1fr violet ('25)	.45	.20
J30	D4	1fr rose lilac ('32)	.55	.20
J31	D4	1.20fr ol grn ('29)	.65	.45
J32	D4	1.50fr ol grn ('32)	.65	.45
J33	D4	2fr violet ('29)	.75	.20
J34	D4	3.50fr dp blue ('29)	1.00	.25
		Nos. J22-J34 (13)	7.75	3.15

1934-46 *Perf. 14x13½*

J35	D4	35c green ('35)	.40	.45
J36	D4	50c slate	.20	.20
J37	D4	60c carmine ('38)	.40	.30
J38	D4	80c slate ('38)	.30	.20
J39	D4	1.40fr gray ('35)	.65	.45
J39A	D4	3fr org brn ('46)	1.50	.60
J39B	D4	7fr brt red vio ('46)	2.25	3.25
		Nos. J35-J39B (7)	5.70	5.45

See Nos. J54-J61.

Catalogue values for unused stamps in this section, from this point to the end of the section, are for Never Hinged items.

D5

D6

1945 Typo. *Perf. 12½*

Inscribed "TE BETALEN" at Top

J40	D5	10c gray olive	.20	.20
J41	D5	20c ultramarine	.20	.20
J42	D5	30c carmine	.20	.20
J43	D5	40c black violet	.20	.20
J44	D5	50c dl bl grn	.20	.20
J45	D5	1fr sepia	.20	.20
J46	D5	2fr red orange	.20	.20

Inscribed "A PAYER" at Top

J47	D5	10c gray olive	.20	.20
J48	D5	20c ultramarine	.20	.20
J49	D5	30c carmine	.20	.20
J50	D5	40c black vio	.20	.20
J51	D5	50c dl bl grn	.20	.20
J52	D5	1fr sepia	.20	.20
J53	D5	2fr red orange	.20	.20
		Nos. J40-J53 (14)	2.80	2.80

Type of 1922-32

1949-53 Typo. *Perf. 14x13½*

J54	D4	65c emerald	7.00	3.75
J55	D4	1.60fr lilac rose ('53)	14.00	6.50
J56	D4	1.80fr red	15.00	6.50
J57	D4	2.40fr gray lilac ('53)	9.00	4.00
J58	D4	4fr deep blue ('53)	11.00	.50
J59	D4	5fr red brown	3.50	.40
J60	D4	8fr lilac rose	7.25	3.75
J61	D4	10fr dark violet	7.25	3.75
		Nos. J54-J61 (8)	74.00	29.15

Numerals 6½mm or More High

1966-70 Photo.

J62	D6	1fr brt pink	.20	.20
J63	D6	2fr blue green	.20	.20
J64	D6	3fr blue	.20	.20
J65	D6	5fr purple	.25	.20
J66	D6	6fr bister brn	.40	.25
J67	D6	7fr red org ('70)	.45	.30
J68	D6	20fr slate grn	1.50	1.00
		Nos. J62-J68 (7)	3.20	2.35

Printed on various papers.

Numerals 4½-5½mm High

1985-87 Photo. *Perf. 14x13½*

J69	D6	1fr lilac rose	.20	.20
J70	D6	2fr dull blue grn	.20	.20
J71	D6	3fr greenish blue	.20	.20
J72	D6	4fr green	.20	.20
J73	D6	5fr lt violet	.25	.20
J74	D6	7fr brt orange	.35	.30
J75	D6	8fr pale gray	.40	.30
J76	D6	9fr rose lake	.45	.35
J77	D6	10fr lt red brown	.50	.40
J78	D6	20fr lt olive grn	1.10	1.10
		Nos. J69-J78 (10)	3.85	3.45

Printed on various papers.

Issue dates: 3fr, 4fr, 8fr-10fr, Mar. 25, 1985. 2fr, 20fr, 1986. 1fr, 5fr, 7fr, 1987.

This is an expanding set. Numbers will change again if necessary.

MILITARY STAMPS

Catalogue values for unused stamps in this section are for Never Hinged items.

King Baudouin
M1 M2

Unwmk.

1967, July 17 Photo. *Perf. 11*

M1	M1	1.50fr greenish gray	.25	.25

1971-75 Engr. *Perf. 11½*

M2	M2	1.75fr green	.50	.45
M3	M2	2.25fr gray green ('72)	.30	.30
M4	M2	2.50fr gray green ('74)	.20	.20
M5	M2	3.25fr vio brown ('75)	.25	.20
		Nos. M2-M5 (4)	1.25	1.15

#M1-M3 are luminescent, #M4-M5 are not.

MILITARY PARCEL POST STAMP

Type of Parcel Post Stamp of 1938 Surcharged with New Value and "M" in Blue.

1939 Unwmk. *Perf. 13½*

MQ1	PP19	3fr on 5.50fr copper red	.30	.20

OFFICIAL STAMPS

For franking the official correspondence of the Administration of the Belgian National Railways.

Counterfeits exist of Nos. O1-O25.

Regular Issue of 1921-27 Overprinted in Black

1929-30 Unwmk. *Perf. 14*

O1	A58	5c gray	.20	.20
O2	A58	10c blue green	.30	.40
O3	A58	35c blue green	.40	.30
O4	A58	60c olive green	.45	.30
O5	A58	1.50fr brt blue	8.00	6.25
O6	A58	1.75fr ultra ('30)	1.75	2.00
		Nos. O1-O6 (6)	11.10	9.45

Same Overprint, in Red or Black, on Regular Issues of 1929-30

1929-31

O7	A63	5c slate (R)	.25	.35
O8	A63	10c olive grn (R)	.50	.40
O9	A63	25c rose red (Bk)	1.50	.85
O10	A63	35c dp green (R)	1.75	.50
O11	A63	40c red vio (Bk)	1.25	.45
O12	A63	50c dp blue (R) ('31)	.80	.35
O13	A63	60c rose (Bk)	6.00	6.00
O14	A63	70c orange brn (Bk)	4.25	1.25
O15	A63	75c black vio (R) ('31)	4.00	.85
		Nos. O7-O15 (9)	20.30	11.00

Overprinted on Regular Issue of 1932

1932

O16	A73	10c olive grn (R)	.55	.60
O17	A74	35c dp green	9.00	.75
O18	A71a	75c bister brn (R)	1.50	.30
		Nos. O16-O18 (3)	11.05	1.65

Overprinted on No. 262 in Red

1935 *Perf. 13½x14*

O19	A80	70c olive black	2.75	.25

Regular Stamps of 1935-36 Overprinted in Red

1936-38 *Perf. 13½, 13½x14, 14*

O20	A82	10c olive bister	.20	.35
O21	A82	35c green	.25	.40
O22	A82	50c dark blue	.45	.35
O23	A83	70c brown	1.50	.65

Overprinted in Black or Red on Regular Issue of 1938

Perf. 13½x14

O24	A82	40c red violet (Bk)	.30	.35
O25	A85	75c olive gray (R)	.65	.30
		Nos. O20-O25 (6)	3.35	2.40

Regular Issues of 1935-41 Overprinted in Red or Dark Blue

1941-44 *Perf. 14, 14x13½, 13½x14*

O26	A82	10c olive bister	.20	.20
a.		Inverted overprint		40.00
O27	A82	40c red violet	.55	.75
O28	A82	50c dark blue	.20	.20
a.		Inverted overprint		
O29	A83a	1fr rose car (Bl)	.45	.35
O30	A85	1fr rose pink (Bl)	.20	.20
O31	A83a	2.25fr grnsh blk ('44)	.30	.50
O32	A84	2.25fr gray violet	.45	.70
		Nos. O26-O32 (7)	2.35	2.90

Nos. O21, O23 and O25 Surcharged with New Values in Black or Red

1942

O33	A82	10c on 35c green	.20	.35
O34	A83	50c on 70c brown	.20	.20
O35	A85	50c on 75c ol gray (R)	.20	.20
		Nos. O33-O35 (3)	.60	.75

Catalogue values for unused stamps in this section, from this point to the end of the section, are for Never Hinged items.

O1

O2

1946-48 Unwmk. *Perf. 14*

O36	O1	10c olive bister	.25	.20
O37	O1	20c brt violet	2.00	.50
O38	O1	50c dk blue	.25	.20
O39	O1	65c red lilac ('48)	3.25	.75
O40	O1	75c lilac rose	.25	.20
O41	O1	90c brown violet	4.25	.35
		Nos. O36-O41 (6)	10.25	2.20

Types A99, A101 and A102 with "B" Emblem Added to Design

1948 *Perf. 11½*

O42	A99	1.35fr red brown	4.25	.75
O43	A99	1.75fr dk gray green	4.75	.25
O44	A101	3fr brt red violet	25.00	3.50
O45	A102	3.15fr deep blue	11.00	7.00
O46	A102	4fr brt ultra	20.00	13.00
		Nos. O42-O46 (5)	65.00	24.50

1953-66 Typo. *Perf. 13½x14*

O47	O2	10c orange	.65	.20
O48	O2	20c red lilac	.80	.25
O49	O2	30c gray green ('58)	.80	.55
O50	O2	40c olive gray	.50	.20
O51	O2	50c light blue	.75	.20
O51A	O2	60c lilac rose ('66)	1.10	.55
O52	O2	65c red lilac	27.50	21.00
O53	O2	80c emerald	4.50	.70
O54	O2	90c deep blue	6.00	.85
O55	O2	1fr rose	.40	.20
		Nos. O47-O55 (10)	43.00	24.70

See Nos. O66, O68.

King Baudouin
O3 O4

1954-70 Photo. *Perf. 11½*

O56	O3	1.50fr gray	.30	.20
O57	O3	2fr rose red	37.50	.25
O58	O3	2fr blue grn ('59)	.30	.20
O59	O3	2.50fr red brown ('58)	27.50	.75
O60	O3	3fr red lilac ('58)	1.25	.20
O61	O3	3.50fr yel green ('70)	.75	.20
O62	O3	4fr brt blue	.90	.25
O63	O3	6fr car rose ('58)	1.50	.60
		Nos. O56-O63 (8)	70.00	2.65

Type of 1953-66 Redrawn

1970-75 Typo. *Perf. 13½x14*

O66	O2	1.50fr grnsh gray ('75)	.20	.20
O68	O2	2.50fr brown	.20	.20

1971-73 Engr. *Perf. 11½*

O71	O4	3.50fr org brn ('73)	.25	.25
O72	O4	4.50fr brown ('73)	.25	.25
O73	O4	7fr red	.40	.50
O74	O4	15fr violet	.75	.30
		Nos. O71-O74 (4)	1.65	1.30

Nos. O71-O74 are on luminescent paper.

1974-80

O75	O4	3fr yellow grn	1.50	1.00
O76	O4	4fr blue	1.50	.50
O77	O4	4.50fr grnsh bl ('75)	.30	.20
O78	O4	5fr lilac	.30	.20
O79	O4	6fr carmine ('78)	.35	.20
O80	O4	6.50fr black ('76)	.40	.35
O81	O4	8fr bluish blk ('78)	.50	.25
O82	O4	9fr lt red brn ('80)	.55	.25
O83	O4	10fr rose carmine	.60	.25
O84	O4	25fr lilac ('76)	1.50	.50
O85	O4	30fr org brn ('78)	1.75	.50
		Nos. O75-O85 (11)	9.25	4.20

Heraldic Lion — O5

1977-82 Typo. *Perf. 13½x14*

O87	O5	50c brown ('82)	.20	.20
O92	O5	1fr lilac ('82)	.20	.20
O94	O5	2fr orange ('82)	.20	.20
O95	O5	4fr red brown	.25	.20
O96	O5	5fr green ('80)	.25	.20
		Nos. O87-O96 (5)	1.10	1.00

NEWSPAPER STAMPS

Counterfeits exist of Nos. P1-P40.

Parcel Post Stamps of 1923-27 Overprinted

**JOURNAUX
DAGBLADEN
1928**

Perf. 14½x14, 14x14½

1928 Unwmk.

P1	PP12	10c vermilion	.25	.40
P2	PP12	20c turq blue	.25	.40
P3	PP12	40c olive grn	.25	.40
P4	PP12	60c orange	.70	.90
P5	PP12	70c dk brown	.45	.40
P6	PP12	80c violet	.60	.70
P7	PP12	90c slate	2.25	2.00
P8	PP13	1fr brt blue	.90	.60
a.		1fr ultramarine	12.00	5.00

P10 PP13 2fr olive grn 1.50 .60
P11 PP13 3fr orange red 1.60 .90
P12 PP13 4fr rose 2.25 1.10
P13 PP13 5fr violet 2.25 1.00
P14 PP13 6fr bister brn 4.50 1.75
P15 PP13 7fr orange 5.00 2.25
P16 PP13 8fr dk brown 6.00 2.75
P17 PP13 9fr red violet 10.00 3.00
P18 PP13 10fr blue green 9.00 2.75
P19 PP13 20fr magenta 15.00 7.00
Nos. P1-P8,P10-P19 (18) 62.75 28.90

Parcel Post Stamps of 1923-28 Overprinted **JOURNAUX DAGBLADEN**

1929-31
P20 PP12 10c vermilion .25 .20
P21 PP12 20c turq blue .25 .20
P22 PP12 40c olive green .30 .20
a. Inverted overprint
P23 PP12 60c orange .55 .35
P24 PP12 70c dk brown .55 .20
P25 PP12 80c violet .60 .25
P26 PP12 90c gray 2.00 1.00
P27 PP13 1fr ultra .60 .25
a. 1fr bright blue 4.00 2.50
P28 PP13 1.10fr org brn ('31) 6.25 1.40
P29 PP13 1.50fr gray vio ('31) 6.25 1.90
P30 PP13 2fr olive green 2.00 .25
P31 PP13 2.10fr sl gray ('31) 17.00 12.00
P32 PP13 3fr orange red 2.25 .45
P33 PP13 4fr rose 2.25 .70
P34 PP13 5fr violet 3.00 .55
P35 PP13 6fr bister brn 3.75 1.00
P36 PP13 7fr orange 3.75 1.00
P37 PP13 8fr dk brown 3.75 1.10
P38 PP13 9fr red violet 5.25 1.50
P39 PP13 10fr blue green 3.75 1.10
P40 PP13 20fr magenta 13.00 4.50
Nos. P20-P40 (21) 77.35 30.10

PARCEL POST AND RAILWAY STAMPS

Values for used Railway Stamps (Chemins de Fer) stamps are for copies with railway cancellations. Railway Stamps with postal cancellations sell for twice as much.

Coat of Arms — PP1

1879-82 Unwmk. Typo. *Perf. 14*
Q1 PP1 10c violet brown 57.50 5.75
Q2 PP1 20c blue 175.00 17.50
Q3 PP1 25c green ('81) 225.00 10.00
Q4 PP1 50c carmine 1,250. 10.00
Q5 PP1 80c yellow 1,300. 57.50
Q6 PP1 1fr gray ('82) 175.00 16.00

Used copies of Nos. Q1-Q6 with pinholes, a normal state, sell for approximately one third the values given.

Most of the stamps of 1882-1902 (Nos. Q7 to Q28) are without watermark. Twice in each sheet of 100 stamps they have one of three watermarks: (1) A winged wheel and "Chemins de Fer de l'Etat Belge," (2) Coat of Arms of Belgium and "Royaume de Belgique," (3) Larger Coat of Arms, without inscription.

PP2

1882-94 *Perf. 15½x14¼*
Q7 PP2 10c brown ('86) 20.00 1.50
Q8 PP2 15c gray ('94) 8.75 7.25
Q9 PP2 20c blue ('86) 65.00 7.00
a. 20c ultra ('90) 75.00 4.00
Q10 PP2 25c yel grn ('91) 72.50 4.25
a. 25c blue green ('87) 67.50 4.00
Q11 PP2 50c carmine 67.50 .75
Q12 PP2 80c brnsh buff 67.50 .80
Q13 PP2 80c lemon 75.00 1.60
Q14 PP2 1fr lavender 350.00 3.00
Q15 PP2 2fr yel buff ('94) 210.00 67.50

Counterfeits exist.

PP3

Name of engraver below frame

1895-97
Numerals in Black, except 1fr, 2fr
Q16 PP3 10c red brown ('96) 11.00 .60
Q17 PP3 15c gray 11.00 7.00
Q18 PP3 20c blue 17.50 1.00
Q19 PP3 25c green 17.50 1.25
Q20 PP3 50c carmine 25.00 .80
Q21 PP3 60c violet ('96) 50.00 1.00
Q22 PP3 80c ol yel ('96) 50.00 1.40
Q23 PP3 1fr lilac brown 175.00 3.00
Q24 PP3 2fr yel buff ('97) 200.00 15.00

Counterfeits exist.

1902
Numerals in Black
Q25 PP3 30c orange 21.00 2.00
Q26 PP3 40c green 26.00 1.75
Q27 PP3 70c blue 50.00 1.40
a. Numerals omitted 750.00
b. Numerals printed on reverse 750.00
Q28 PP3 90c red 65.00 1.60
Nos. Q25-CQ28 (4) 162.00 6.75

Winged Wheel — PP4

Without engraver's name

1902-14 *Perf. 15*
Q29 PP3 10c yel brn & slate .20 .20
Q30 PP3 15c slate & vio .20 .20
Q31 PP3 20c ultra & yel brn .20 .20
Q32 PP3 25c yel grn & red .20 .20
Q33 PP3 30c orange & bl grn .20 .20
Q34 PP3 35c bister & bl grn ('12) .35 .20
Q35 PP3 40c blue grn & vio .20 .20
Q36 PP3 50c pale rose & vio .20 .20
Q37 PP3 55c lilac brn & ultra ('14) .35 .20
Q38 PP3 60c violet & red .20 .20
Q39 PP3 70c blue & red .20 .20
Q40 PP3 80c lemon & vio brn .20 .20
Q41 PP3 90c red & yel grn .20 .20
Q42 PP4 1fr vio brn & org .20 .20
Q43 PP4 1.10fr rose & blk ('06) .20 .20
Q44 PP4 2fr ocher & bl grn .20 .20
Q45 PP4 3fr black & ultra .35 .20
Q46 PP4 4fr yel grn & red ('13) 1.25 .70
Q47 PP4 5fr org & bl grn ('13) .55 .55
Q48 PP4 10fr ol yel & brn vio ('13) .90 .55
Nos. Q29-Q48 (20) 6.55 5.20

Regular Issues of 1912-13 Handstamped in Violet

1915 *Perf. 14*
Q49 A42 5c green 165.00 165.00
Q50 A43 10c red 800.00 800.00
Q51 A45 10c red 175.00 175.00
a. With engraver's name 750.00 750.00
Q52 A43 20c olive grn *1,200. 1,200.*
Q53 A45 20c olive grn 200.00 200.00
a. With engraver's name 750.00 750.00
Q54 A45 25c ultra 200.00 200.00
a. With engraver's name 750.00 750.00
Q55 A43 35c bister brn 250.00 250.00
Q55A A43 40c green *1,750. 1,750.*
Q56 A45 40c green 250.00 250.00
Q57 A43 50c gray 250.00 250.00
Q58 A43 1fr orange 200.00 200.00
Q59 A43 2fr violet *1,650. 1,650.*
Q60 A44 5fr plum *3,500. 3,500.*

Excellent forgeries of this overprint exist.

PP5 PP6

1916 Litho. *Perf. 13½*
Q61 PP5 10c pale blue 1.10 .20
Q62 PP5 15c olive grn 1.40 .50
Q63 PP5 20c red 2.25 .50
Q64 PP5 25c lt brown 2.25 .50
Q65 PP5 30c lilac 1.40 .50
Q66 PP5 35c gray 1.40 .45
Q67 PP5 40c orange yel 3.00 1.50
Q68 PP5 50c bister 2.25 .45
Q69 PP5 55c brown 3.00 2.25
Q70 PP5 60c gray vio 2.25 .45
Q71 PP5 70c green 2.25 .45
Q72 PP5 80c red brown 2.25 .45
Q73 PP5 90c blue 2.25 .45
Q74 PP6 1fr gray 2.25 .45
Q75 PP6 1.10fr ultra *(Franken)* 27.50 21.00
Q76 PP6 2fr red 25.00 .45
Q77 PP6 3fr violet 25.00 .45
Q78 PP6 4fr emerald 45.00 1.50
Q79 PP6 5fr brown 45.00 3.00
Q80 PP6 10fr orange 45.00 1.50
Nos. Q61-Q80 (20) 241.80 37.00

Type of 1916 Inscribed "FRANK" instead of "FRANKEN"

1920
Q81 PP6 1.10fr ultra 2.00 .45

PP7 PP8

1920 *Perf. 14*
Q82 PP7 10c blue grn 1.75 .75
Q83 PP7 15c olive grn 1.75 1.10
Q84 PP7 20c red 1.75 .75
Q85 PP7 25c gray brn 2.50 .75
Q86 PP7 30c red vio 27.00 22.50
Q87 PP7 40c pale org 11.00 .75
Q88 PP7 50c bister 9.00 .75
Q89 PP7 55c pale brown 5.50 4.50
Q90 PP7 60c dk violet 10.00 .75
Q91 PP7 70c green 18.00 1.10
Q92 PP7 80c red brown 40.00 1.50
Q93 PP7 90c dull blue 10.00 .75
Q94 PP8 1fr gray 85.00 1.50
Q95 PP8 1.10fr ultra 26.00 2.00
Q96 PP8 1.20fr dk green 11.00 .75
Q97 PP8 1.40fr black brn 11.00 .75
Q98 PP8 2fr vermilion 110.00 1.25
Q99 PP8 3fr red vio 120.00 .85
Q100 PP8 4fr yel grn 120.00 .75
Q101 PP8 5fr bister brn 120.00 .75
Q102 PP8 10fr brown org 120.00 .75
Nos. Q82-Q102 (21) 861.25 45.30

PP9 PP10

Types PP7 and PP9 differ in the position of the wheel and the tablet above it.
Types PP8 and PP10 differ in the bars below "FR".
There are many other variations in the designs.

1920-21 Typo.
Q103 PP9 10c carmine .30 .20
Q104 PP9 15c yel grn .30 .20
Q105 PP9 20c blue grn .70 .20
Q106 PP9 25c ultra .65 .20
Q107 PP9 30c chocolate .85 .20
Q108 PP9 35c orange brn .90 .30
Q109 PP9 40c orange 1.10 .20
Q110 PP9 50c rose 1.10 .20
Q111 PP9 55c yel ('21) 4.50 3.25
Q112 PP9 60c dull rose 1.10 .20
Q113 PP9 70c emerald 3.00 .40
Q114 PP9 80c violet 2.25 .20
Q115 PP9 90c lemon 37.50 21.00
Q116 PP9 90c claret 4.50 .40
Q117 PP10 1fr buff 4.50 .35
Q118 PP10 1fr red brown 4.00 .30
Q119 PP10 1.10fr ultra 1.60 .45
Q120 PP10 1.20fr orange 6.25 .30
Q121 PP10 1.40fr yellow 10.00 1.75
Q122 PP10 1.60fr turq blue 18.00 .70
Q123 PP10 1.60fr emerald 40.00 .70
Q124 PP10 2fr pale rose 26.00 .30
Q125 PP10 3fr dp rose 24.00 .30
Q126 PP10 4fr emerald 24.00 .30
Q127 PP10 5fr lt violet 17.50 .30
Q128 PP10 10fr lemon 110.00 9.00
Q129 PP10 10fr dk brown 22.50 .30
Q130 PP10 15fr dp rose ('21) 22.50 .30
Q131 PP10 20fr dk blue ('21) 325.00 3.00
Nos. Q103-Q131 (29) 714.60 45.50

PP11

1922 Engr. *Perf. 11½*
Q132 PP11 2fr black 4.00 .20
Q133 PP11 3fr brown 37.50 .20
Q134 PP11 4fr green 9.00 .20
Q135 PP11 5r claret 9.00 .20
Q136 PP11 10fr yel brown 10.00 .20
Q137 PP11 15fr rose red 10.00 .25
Q138 PP11 20fr blue 67.50 .25
Nos. Q132-Q138 (7) 147.00 1.50

PP12

PP13

Perf. 14x13½, 13½x14
1923-40 Typo.
Q139 PP12 5c red brown .20 .25
Q140 PP12 10c vermilion .20 .20
Q141 PP12 15c ultra .20 .30
Q142 PP12 20c turq blue .20 .20
Q143 PP12 30c brn vio ('27) .20 .20
Q144 PP12 40c olive grn .20 .20
Q145 PP12 50c magenta ('27) .20 .20
Q146 PP12 60c orange .25 .20
Q147 PP12 70c dk brown ('24) .20 .20
Q148 PP12 80c violet .20 .20
Q149 PP12 90c slate ('27) 1.25 .20
Q150 PP13 1fr ultra .35 .20
Q151 PP13 1fr brt blue ('28) .55 .20
Q152 PP13 1.10fr orange 3.00 .30
Q153 PP13 1.50fr turq blue 3.25 .30
Q154 PP13 1.70fr dp brown ('31) .75 .60
Q155 PP13 1.80fr claret 4.25 .60
Q156 PP13 2fr olive grn ('24) .35 .20
Q157 PP13 2.10fr gray grn 7.50 .85
Q158 PP13 2.40fr dp violet 4.00 .85
Q159 PP13 2.70fr gray ('24) 12.00 .75
Q160 PP13 3fr orange red .45 .20
Q161 PP13 3.30fr brown ('24) 12.50 .75
Q162 PP13 4fr rose ('24) .55 .20
Q163 PP13 5fr violet ('24) .90 .20
Q163A PP13 5fr brn vio ('40) .45 .30
Q164 PP13 6fr bis brn ('27) .50 .20
Q165 PP13 7fr orange ('27) .90 .20
Q166 PP13 8fr dp brown ('27) .75 .20
Q167 PP13 9fr red vio ('27) 2.50 .20
Q168 PP13 10fr blue grn ('27) 1.10 .20
Q168A PP13 10fr black ('40) 4.00 3.75
Q169 PP13 20fr magenta ('27) 1.90 .20
Q170 PP13 30fr turq green ('31) 6.00 .40
Q171 PP13 40fr gray ('31) 55.00 .75
Q172 PP13 50fr bister ('27) 9.00 .30
Nos. Q139-Q172 (36) 135.80 15.25

See Nos. Q239-Q262. For overprints see Nos. Q216-Q238. Stamps overprinted "Bagages Reisgoed" are revenues.

No. Q158 Surcharged

2R30

1924

Green Surcharge

Q173 PP13 2.30fr on 2.40fr violet 3.00 .50
a. Inverted surcharge 57.50

Type of Regular Issue of 1926-27 Overprinted COLIS POSTAL POSTCOLLO

1928 ***Perf. 14***

Q174 A61 4fr buff 6.50 .90
Q175 A61 5fr bister 6.50 1.10
Set, never hinged 40.00

Central P.O., Brussels PP15

1929-30 Engr. ***Perf. 11½***

Q176 PP15 3fr black brn 1.40 .20
Q177 PP15 4fr gray 1.40 .20
Q178 PP15 5fr carmine 1.40 .20
Q179 PP15 6fr vio brn ('30) 22.50 25.00
Nos. Q176-Q179 (4) 26.70 25.60
Set, never hinged 100.00

No. Q179 Surcharged in Blue

X4 4X

1933

Q180 PP15 4(fr) on 6fr vio brn 25.00 .25
Never hinged 90.00

Modern Locomotive PP16

1934 Photo. ***Perf. 13½x14***

Q181 PP16 3fr dk green 10.00 2.50
Q182 PP16 4fr red violet 3.00 .20
Q183 PP16 5fr dp rose 9.50 .20
Nos. Q181-Q183 (3) 22.50 2.90
Set, never hinged 120.00

Modern Railroad Train — PP17

Old Railroad Train — PP18

1935 Engr. ***Perf. 14x13½, 13½x14***

Q184 PP17 10c rose car .30 .20
Q185 PP17 20c violet .35 .20
Q186 PP17 30c black brn .45 .30
Q187 PP17 40c dk blue .55 .20
Q188 PP17 50c orange red .55 .20
Q189 PP17 60c green .65 .20
Q190 PP17 70c ultra .70 .20
Q191 PP17 80c olive blk .65 .20
Q192 PP17 90c rose lake .85 .45
Q193 PP18 1fr brown vio .85 .20
Q194 PP18 2fr gray blk 2.00 .20
Q195 PP18 3fr red org 2.50 .20
Q196 PP18 4fr violet brn 3.00 .20
Q197 PP18 5fr plum 3.25 .20
Q198 PP18 6fr dp green 3.50 .20
Q199 PP18 7fr dp violet 17.00 .20
Q200 PP18 8fr olive blk 17.00 .20
Q201 PP18 9fr dk blue 17.00 .20
Q202 PP18 10fr car lake 17.00 .20
Q203 PP18 20fr green 90.00 .20
Q204 PP18 30fr violet 90.00 2.00
Q205 PP18 40fr black brn 90.00 2.50
Q206 PP18 50fr rose car 100.00 2.00
Q207 PP18 100fr ultra 250.00 45.00
Nos. Q184-Q207 (24) 708.15 55.85
Set, never hinged 1,750.

Centenary of Belgian State Railway.

Winged Wheel — PP19

Surcharge in Red or Blue

1938 Photo. ***Perf. 13½***

Q208 PP19 5fr on 3.50fr dk grn 6.50 .45
Q209 PP19 5fr on 4.50fr rose vio (Bl) .20 .20
Q210 PP19 6fr on 5.50fr cop red (Bl) .35 .20
a. Half used as 3fr on piece 1.50
Nos. Q208-Q210 (3) 7.05 .85
Set, never hinged 50.00

See Nos. MQ1, Q297-Q299.

Symbolizing Unity Achieved Through Railroads PP20

1939 Engr. ***Perf. 13½x14***

Q211 PP20 20c redsh brn 3.50 *3.75*
Q212 PP20 50c vio bl 3.50 *3.75*
Q213 PP20 2fr rose red 3.50 *3.75*
Q214 PP20 9fr slate grn 3.50 *3.75*
Q215 PP20 10fr dk vio 3.50 *3.75*
Nos. Q211-Q215 (5) 17.50 *18.75*
Set, never hinged 22.50

Railroad Exposition and Cong. held at Brussels.

Parcel Post Stamps of 1925-27 Overprinted in Blue or Carmine (B)

Perf. 14½x14, 14x14½

1940 **Unwmk.**

Q216 PP12 10c vermilion .20 .20
Q217 PP12 20c turq bl (C) .20 .20
Q218 PP12 30c brn vio .20 .20
Q219 PP12 40c ol grn (C) .20 .20
Q220 PP12 50c magenta .20 .20
Q221 PP12 60c orange .20 *.25*
Q222 PP12 70c dk brn .20 .20
Q223 PP12 80c vio (C) .20 .20
Q224 PP12 90c slate (C) .25 .25
Q225 PP13 1fr ultra (C) .25 .20
Q226 PP13 2fr ol grn (C) .25 .20
Q227 PP13 3fr org red .25 .20
Q228 PP13 4fr rose .25 .20
Q229 PP13 5fr vio (C) .25 .20
Q230 PP13 6fr bis brn .35 .25
Q231 PP13 7fr orange .35 .20
Q232 PP13 8fr dp brn .35 .20
Q233 PP13 9fr red vio .35 .20
Q234 PP13 10fr bl grn (C) .35 .25
Q235 PP13 20fr magenta .60 .25
Q236 PP13 30fr turq grn (C) 1.10 .75
Q237 PP13 40fr gray (C) 1.40 *2.00*
Q238 PP13 50fr bister 1.60 1.10
Nos. Q216-Q238 (23) 9.55 8.10
Set, never hinged 16.00

Types of 1923-40

1941

Q239 PP12 10c dl olive .20 .20
Q240 PP12 20c lt vio .20 .20
Q241 PP12 30c fawn .20 .20
Q242 PP12 40c dull blue .20 .20
Q243 PP12 50c lt grn .20 .20
Q244 PP12 60c gray .20 .20
Q245 PP12 70c chalky grn .20 .20
Q246 PP12 80c orange .20 .20
Q247 PP12 90c rose lilac .20 .20
Q248 PP13 1fr lt yel grn .20 .20
Q249 PP13 2fr vio brn .40 .20
Q250 PP13 3fr slate .45 .20
Q251 PP13 4fr dl olive .50 .20
Q252 PP13 5fr rose lilac .50 .20
Q253 PP13 5fr black .80 .30
Q254 PP13 6fr org ver .75 .30
Q255 PP13 7fr lilac .75 .20
Q256 PP13 8fr chalky grn .75 .20
Q257 PP13 9fr blue .90 .20
Q258 PP13 10fr rose lilac .90 .20
Q259 PP13 20fr milky blue 2.00 .20
Q260 PP13 30fr orange 4.50 .35
Q261 PP13 40fr rose 5.00 .35
Q262 PP13 50fr brt red vio 6.75 .20
Nos. Q239-Q262 (24) 26.95 5.30
Set, never hinged 90.00

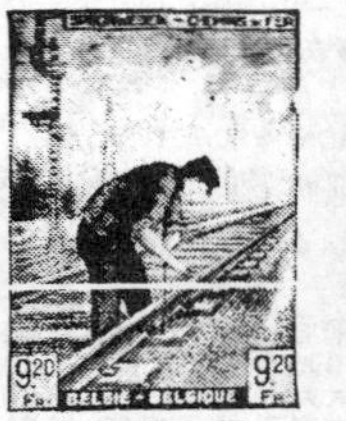

Adjusting Tie Plates — PP21

Engineer at Throttle — PP22

Freight Station Interior — PP23

Signal and Electric Train — PP24

1942 Engr. ***Perf. 14x13½***

Q263 PP21 9.20fr red org .60 *.85*
Q264 PP22 12.30fr dp grn .60 *.90*
Q265 PP23 14.30fr dk car .80 *1.25*

Perf. 11½

Q266 PP24 100fr ultra 20.00 17.00
Nos. Q263-Q266 (4) 22.00 20.00
Set, never hinged 25.00

Catalogue values for unused stamps in this section, from this point to the end of the section, are for Never Hinged items.

PP25

PP26

PP27

1945-46 Photo. Unwmk.

Q267 PP25 10c ol blk ('46) .30 .20
Q268 PP25 20c dp vio .30 .20
Q269 PP25 30c chnt brn ('46) .30 .20
Q270 PP25 40c dp bl ('46) .30 .20
Q271 PP25 50c peacock grn .30 .20
Q272 PP25 60c blk ('46) .30 .20
Q273 PP25 70c emer ('46) .45 .25
Q274 PP25 80c orange .75 .20
Q275 PP25 90c brn vio ('46) .30 .25
Q276 PP26 1fr bl grn ('46) .30 .20
Q277 PP26 2fr blk brn .30 .20
Q278 PP26 3fr grnsh blk ('46) 2.00 .20
Q279 PP26 4fr dark blue .45 .20
Q280 PP26 5fr sepia .45 .20
Q281 PP26 6fr dk ol grn ('46) 2.25 .20
Q282 PP26 7fr dk vio ('46) .75 .25
Q283 PP26 8fr red org .75 .20
Q284 PP26 9fr dp bl ('46) .90 .20
Q285 PP27 10fr dk red ('46) 3.25 .20
Q286 PP27 10fr sepia ('46) 1.60 .25
Q287 PP27 20fr dk yel grn ('46) .75 .20
Q288 PP27 30fr dp vio 1.00 .20
Q289 PP27 40fr rose pink .90 .20
Q290 PP27 50fr brt bl ('46) 12.00 .20
Nos. Q267-Q290 (24) 30.95 5.00

Mercury — PP28

1945-46 ***Perf. 13½x13***

Q291 PP28 3fr emer ('46) .25 .25
Q292 PP28 5fr ultra .20 .20
Q293 PP28 6fr red .20 .20

Inscribed "Belgique-Belgie"

Q294 PP28 3fr emer ('46) .25 .25
Q295 PP28 5fr ultra .20 .20
Q296 PP28 6fr red .20 .20
Nos. Q291-Q296 (6) 1.30 1.30

Winged Wheel Type of 1938 Carmine Surcharge

1946 ***Perf. 13½x14***

Q297 PP19 8fr on 5.50fr brn .65 .20
Q298 PP19 10fr on 5.50fr dk bl .75 .20
Q299 PP19 12fr on 5.50fr vio 1.10 .20
Nos. Q297-Q299 (3) 2.50 .60

Railway Crossing PP29

1947 Engr. ***Perf. 12½***

Q300 PP29 100fr dark green 7.00 .25

Crossbowman with Train — PP30

1947 Photo. ***Perf. 11½***

Q301 PP30 8fr dark olive brn 1.00 .20
Q302 PP30 10fr gray & blue 1.10 .25
Q303 PP30 12fr dark violet 1.60 .45
Nos. Q301-Q303 (3) 3.70 .90

Surcharged with New Value and Bars in Carmine

1948

Q304 PP30 9fr on 8fr 1.25 .20
Q305 PP30 11fr on 10fr 1.25 .25
Q306 PP30 13.50fr on 12fr 2.00 .25
Nos. Q304-Q306 (3) 4.50 .70

Delivery of Parcel PP31

1948

Q307 PP31 9fr chocolate 6.50 .20
Q308 PP31 11fr brown car 7.00 .20
Q309 PP31 13.50fr gray 10.50 .25
Nos. Q307-Q309 (3) 24.00 .65

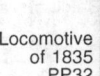

Locomotive of 1835 PP32

Various Locomotives.

Lathe Work in Frame Differs

1949 Engr. ***Perf. 12½***

Q310 PP32 ½fr dark brown .60 .20
Q311 PP32 1fr carmine rose .70 .20
Q312 PP32 2fr deep ultra .95 .20
Q313 PP32 3fr dp magenta 2.00 .20
Q314 PP32 4fr blue green 2.75 .20
Q315 PP32 5fr orange red 2.75 .20
Q316 PP32 6fr brown vio 3.00 .25
Q317 PP32 7fr yellow grn 4.00 .20
Q318 PP32 8fr grnsh blue 5.00 .20
Q319 PP32 9fr yellow brn 6.00 .25
Q320 PP32 10fr citron 7.25 .20
Q321 PP32 20fr orange 11.00 .20
Q322 PP32 30fr blue 15.00 .20
Q323 PP32 40fr lilac rose 21.00 .25
Q324 PP32 50fr violet 21.00 .30
Q325 PP32 100fr red 65.00 .25

Engraved; Center Typographed

Q326 PP32 10fr car rose & blk 9.00 .80
Nos. Q310-Q326 (17) 177.00 4.30

See No. Q337.

1949 **Engr.**

Design: Electric locomotive.

Q327 PP32 60fr black brown 20.00 .20

Opening of Charleroi-Brussels electric railway line, Oct. 15, 1949.

Mailing Parcel Post — PP33

Sorting PP34

Loading PP35

1950-52 ***Perf. 12, 12½***

Q328 PP33 11fr red orange 6.00 .20
Q329 PP33 12fr red vio ('51) 20.00 1.50
Q330 PP34 13fr dk blue grn 6.00 .20
Q331 PP34 15fr ultra ('51) 15.00 .30
Q332 PP35 16fr gray 6.00 .20
Q333 PP33 17fr brown ('52) 8.00 .20
Q334 PP35 18fr brt car ('51) 16.00 .45
Q335 PP35 20fr brn org ('52) 8.00 .20
Nos. Q328-Q335 (8) 85.00 3.25

For surcharges see Nos. Q338-Q340.

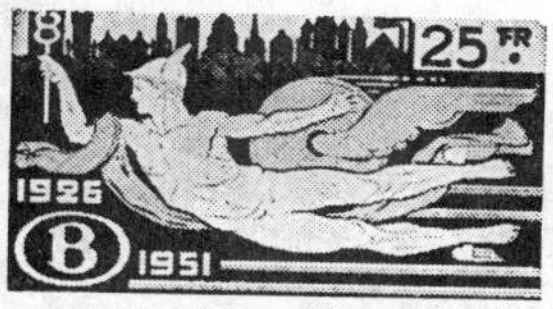

Mercury and Winged Wheel — PP36

1951

Q336 PP36 25fr dark blue 10.00 8.50

25th anniv. of the founding of the Natl. Soc. of Belgian Railroads.

Type of 1949

Design: Electric locomotive.

1952 **Unwmk.** ***Perf. 11½***

Q337 PP32 300fr red violet 150.00 .50

Nos. Q331, Q328 and Q334 Surcharged with New Value and "X" in Red, Blue or Green

1953 ***Perf. 12***

Q338 PP34 13fr on 15fr (R) 60.00 3.00
Q339 PP33 17fr on 11fr (Bl) 35.00 2.25
Q340 PP35 20fr on 18fr (G) 30.00 2.50
Nos. Q338-Q340 (3) 125.00 7.75

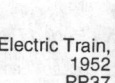

Electric Train, 1952 PP37

1953 **Engr.**

Q341 PP37 200fr dk yel grn & vio brn 250.00 4.00
Q342 PP37 200fr dk green 225.00 1.00

No. Q341 was issued to commemorate the opening of the railway link connecting Brussels North and South Stations, Oct. 4, 1952.

New North Station, Brussels — PP38

Chapelle Station, Brussels PP39

Designs: No. Q348, 15fr, Congress Station. 10fr, 20fr, 30fr, 40fr, 50fr, South Station. 100fr, 200fr, 300fr, Central Station.

1953-57 **Unwmk.** ***Perf. 11½***

Q343 PP38 1fr bister .30 .20
Q344 PP38 2fr slate .40 .20
Q345 PP38 3fr blue grn .60 .20
Q346 PP38 4fr orange .80 .20
Q347 PP38 5fr red brn .80 .20
Q348 PP38 5fr dk red brn 10.00 .25
Q349 PP38 6fr rose vio 1.10 .20
Q350 PP38 7fr brt green 1.10 .20
Q351 PP38 8fr rose red 1.40 .20
Q352 PP38 9fr brt grnsh bl 2.00 .20
Q353 PP38 10fr lt grn 2.25 .20
Q354 PP38 15fr dl red 13.00 .20
Q355 PP38 20fr blue 4.00 .20
Q356 PP38 30fr purple 6.25 .20
Q357 PP38 40fr brt purple 8.00 .20
Q358 PP38 50fr lilac rose 10.00 .20
Q359 PP39 60fr brt purple 20.00 .20
Q360 PP39 80fr brown vio 30.00 .20
Q361 PP39 100fr emerald 18.00 .20
Q361A PP39 200fr brt vio bl 95.00 1.60
Q361B PP39 300fr lilac rose 175.00 2.25
Nos. Q343-Q361B (21) 400.00 7.70

Issued: #Q347, 20fr, 30fr, 1953; 80fr, 1955; 200fr, 1956; 300fr, 1957; others, 1954.
See Nos. Q407, Q431-Q432.

Electric Train — PP40

Mercury and Winged Wheel — PP41

1954

Q362 PP40 13fr chocolate 14.00 .20
Q363 PP40 18fr dark blue 17.00 .20
Q364 PP40 21fr lilac rose 18.00 .45
Nos. Q362-Q364 (3) 49.00 .85

Nos. Q362-Q364 Surcharged with New Value and "X" in Blue, Red or Green

1956

Q365 PP40 14fr on 13fr (B) 8.00 .20
Q366 PP40 19fr on 18fr (R) 8.25 .25
Q367 PP40 22fr on 21fr (G) 8.75 .45
Nos. Q365-Q367 (3) 25.00 .90

1957 **Engr.** ***Perf. 11½***

Q368 PP41 14fr brt green 7.75 .20
Q369 PP41 19fr olive gray 8.00 .20
Q370 PP41 22fr carmine rose 8.75 .30
Nos. Q368-Q370 (3) 24.50 .70

Nos. Q369-Q370 Surcharged with New Value and "X" in Pink or Green

1959

Q371 PP41 20fr on 19fr (P) 22.50 .35
Q372 PP41 20fr on 22fr (G) 27.50 .55

Old North Station, Brussels PP42

1959 **Engr.** ***Perf. 11½***

Q373 PP42 20fr olive green 14.00 .20

See Nos. Q381, Q383. For surcharges see Nos. Q378, Q382, Q384.

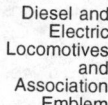

Diesel and Electric Locomotives and Association Emblem PP43

1960 **Unwmk.** ***Perf. 11½***

Q374 PP43 20fr red 42.50 30.00
Q375 PP43 50fr dark blue 42.50 30.00
Q376 PP43 60fr red lilac 42.50 30.00
Q377 PP43 70fr emerald 42.50 30.00
Nos. Q374-Q377 (4) 170.00 120.00

Intl. Assoc. of Railway Congresses, 75th anniv.

No. Q373 Surcharged with New Value and "X" in Red

1961

Q378 PP42 24fr on 20fr ol grn 65.00 .25

South Station, Brussels — PP44

1962 **Unwmk.** ***Perf. 11½***

Q379 PP44 24fr dull red 6.25 .25

No. Q379 Surcharged with New Value and "X" in Light Green

1963

Q380 PP44 26fr on 24fr dl red 6.50 .25

Type of 1959

Design: 26fr, Central Station, Antwerp.

1963 **Engr.** ***Perf. 11½***

Q381 PP42 26fr blue 6.25 1.75

No. Q381 Surcharged in Red

1964, Apr. 20

Q382 PP42 28fr on 26fr blue 6.25 .25

Type of 1959

Design: 28fr, St. Peter's Station, Ghent.

1965 **Engr.** ***Perf. 11½***

Q383 PP42 28fr red lilac 6.25 1.40

Nos. Q383 Surcharged with New Value and "X" in Green

1966

Q384 PP42 35fr on 28fr red lil 6.25 .20

Arlon Railroad Station PP45

Perf. 11½

1967, Aug. **Unwmk.** **Engr.**

Q385 PP45 25fr bister 10.00 .20
Q386 PP45 30fr blue green 5.00 .20
Q387 PP45 35fr deep blue 7.00 .35
Nos. Q385-Q387 (3) 22.00 .75

See #Q408. For surcharges see #Q410-Q412.

Electric Train — PP46

Designs: 2fr, 3fr, 4fr, 5fr, 6fr, 7fr, 8fr, 9fr, like 1fr. 10fr, 20fr, 30fr, 40fr, Train going right. 50fr, 60fr, 70fr, 80fr, 90fr, Train going left. 100fr, 200fr, 300fr, Diesel train.

1968-73 **Engr.** ***Perf. 11½***

Q388 PP46 1fr olive bis .20 .20
Q389 PP46 2fr slate .25 .20
Q390 PP46 3fr blue green .55 .20
Q391 PP46 4fr orange .55 .20
Q392 PP46 5fr brown .65 .20
Q393 PP46 6fr plum .55 .20
Q394 PP46 7fr brt green .65 .20
Q395 PP46 8fr carmine .80 .20
Q396 PP46 9fr blue 1.40 .20
Q397 PP46 10fr green 2.75 .20
Q398 PP46 20fr dk blue 1.60 .20
Q399 PP46 30fr dk purple 4.00 .20
Q400 PP46 40fr brt lilac 5.50 .20
Q401 PP46 50fr brt pink 6.75 .20
Q402 PP46 60fr brt violet 8.25 .30
Q402A PP46 70fr dp bister ('73) 6.75 .30
Q403 PP46 80fr dk brown 6.75 .20
Q403A PP46 90fr yel grn ('73) 5.50 .30
Q404 PP46 100fr emerald 11.00 .25
Q405 PP46 200fr violet blue 13.00 .50
Q406 PP46 300fr lilac rose 22.50 1.25
Nos. Q388-Q406 (21) 99.95 5.90

See No. Q409.

Types of 1953-68

Designs: 10fr, Congress Station, Brussels. 40fr, Arlon Station. 500fr, Electric train going left.

1968, June **Engr.** ***Perf. 11½***

Q407 PP38 10fr gray 1.50 .20
Q408 PP45 40fr vermilion 22.50 .20
Q409 PP46 500fr yellow 30.00 1.90
Nos. Q407-Q409 (3) 54.00 2.30

Nos. Q385, Q387 and Q408 Surcharged with New Value and "X"

1970, Dec.

Q410 PP45 37fr on 25fr bister 45.00 3.00
Q411 PP45 48fr on 35fr dp bl 13.00 5.00
Q412 PP45 53fr on 40fr ver 15.00 6.00
Nos. Q410-Q412 (3) 73.00 14.00

Ostend Station PP47

1971, Mar. **Engr.** ***Perf. 11½***

Q413 PP47 32fr bis & blk 2.50 2.25
Q414 PP47 37fr gray & blk 2.50 2.50
Q415 PP47 42fr bl & blk 4.00 3.00
Q416 PP47 44fr brt rose & blk 4.50 3.00
Q417 PP47 46fr vio & blk 4.50 3.00
Q418 PP47 50fr brick red & blk 5.25 3.25
Q419 PP47 52fr sep & blk 5.25 3.25
Q420 PP47 54fr yel grn & blk 5.75 3.25
Q421 PP47 61fr grnsh bl & blk 5.75 4.00
Nos. Q413-Q421 (9) 40.00 27.50

Nos. Q413-Q416, Q419-Q421 Surcharged with New Value and "X"

1971, Dec. 15

Denomination in Black

Q422 PP47 34fr on 32fr bister 2.00 .55
Q423 PP47 40fr on 37fr gray 2.50 .70
Q424 PP47 47fr on 44fr brt rose 2.75 .80
Q425 PP47 53fr on 42fr blue 3.25 .85
Q426 PP47 56fr on 52fr sepia 3.25 1.00
Q427 PP47 59fr on 54fr yel grn 3.25 1.00
Q428 PP47 66fr on 61fr grnsh blue 4.00 1.10
Nos. Q422-Q428 (7) 21.00 6.00

Track, Underpinning of Railroad Car and Emblems PP48

1972, Mar. **Photo.**

Q429	PP48	100fr emer, red & blk	10.00	1.10

Centenary of International Railroad Union.

Congress Emblem PP49

1974, Apr. **Photo.** ***Perf. 11½***

Q430	PP49	100fr yel, blk & red	8.00	1.25

4th International Symposium on Railroad Cybernetics, Washington, DC, Apr. 1974.

Type of 1953-1957

1975, June 1 **Engr.** ***Perf. 11½***

Q431	PP38	20fr emerald	1.75	.20
Q432	PP38	50fr blue	3.75	.55

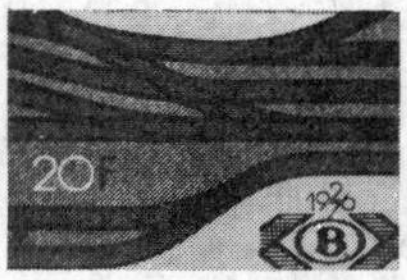

Railroad Tracks PP50

1976, June 10 **Photo.** ***Perf. 11½***

Q433	PP50	20fr ultra & multi	3.00	.20
Q434	PP50	50fr brt grn & multi	1.75	.50
Q435	PP50	100fr dp org & multi	4.00	1.00
Q436	PP50	150fr brt lil & multi	6.25	1.75
		Nos. Q433-Q436 (4)	15.00	3.45

Railroad Station — PP51

1977 **Photo.** ***Perf. 11½***

Q437	PP51	1000fr multi	45.00	*8.00*

Freight Car — PP52

Designs: 1fr-9fr, Freight car. 10fr-40fr, Hopper car. 50fr-90fr, Maintenance car. 100fr-500fr, Liquid fuel car.

1980, Dec. 16 **Engr.** ***Perf. 11½***

Q438	PP52	1fr bis brn & blk	.20	.20
Q439	PP52	2fr claret & blk	.20	.20
Q440	PP52	3fr brt bl & blk	.20	.20
Q441	PP52	4fr grnsh blk & blk	.20	.20
Q442	PP52	5fr sepia & blk	.20	.20
Q443	PP52	6fr dp org & blk	.35	.20
Q444	PP52	7fr purple & blk	.40	.20
Q445	PP52	8fr black	.40	.20
Q446	PP52	9fr green & blk	.45	.20
Q447	PP52	10fr yel bis & blk	.50	.20
Q448	PP52	20fr grnsh bl & blk	1.10	.20
Q449	PP52	30fr bister & blk	2.25	.35
Q450	PP52	40fr lt lil & blk	2.50	.40
Q451	PP52	50fr dk brn & blk	2.75	.55
Q452	PP52	60fr olive & blk	2.75	.70
Q453	PP52	70fr vio bl & blk	3.50	.75
Q454	PP52	80fr vio brn & blk	4.00	.85
Q455	PP52	90fr lil rose & blk	5.00	.95
Q456	PP52	100fr crim rose & blk	5.25	1.00
Q457	PP52	200fr brn & blk	10.00	2.00
Q458	PP52	300fr ol gray & blk	14.00	3.00
Q459	PP52	500fr dl pur & blk	25.00	5.25
		Nos. Q438-Q459 (22)	81.20	18.00

Train in Station PP53

Electric Locomotives PP54

1982 **Engr.** ***Perf. 11½***

Q460	PP53	10fr red & blk	1.75	.25
Q461	PP53	20fr green & blk	1.25	.50
Q462	PP53	50fr sepia & blk	4.25	.75
Q463	PP53	100fr blue & blk	7.25	2.75
		Nos. Q460-Q463 (4)	14.50	4.25

1985, May 3 **Photo.** ***Perf. 11½***

Q464	PP54	250fr BB-150	11.00	2.00
Q465	PP54	500fr BB-120	24.00	10.00

Stylized Castle, Gabled Station and Electric Rail Car — PP55

1987, Oct. 12 **Engr.** ***Perf. 11½***

Q466	PP55	10fr dk red & blk	.50	.40
Q467	PP55	20fr dk grn & blk	1.00	.75
Q468	PP55	50fr dk brn & blk	2.50	1.90
Q469	PP55	100fr dk lil & blk	5.25	3.75
Q470	PP55	150fr dark olive bister & blk	7.75	5.75
		Nos. Q466-Q470 (5)	17.00	12.55

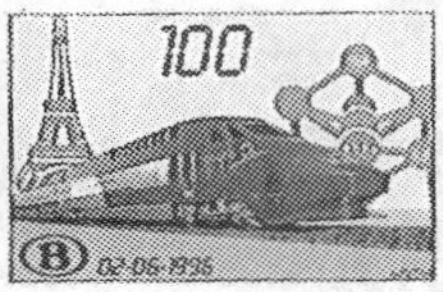

High Speed Trains PP56

1996, June 2 **Litho.** ***Perf. 11½***

Q471	PP56	100fr shown	6.00	4.50
Q472	PP56	300fr Train going left	18.50	13.50

Electric Trains PP57

Designs: 50fr, Passenger railcars. 100fr, End car. 200fr, Front car.

1997, Oct. 14 **Photo.** ***Perf. 11½***

Q473	PP57	50fr multicolored	2.75	2.10
Q474	PP57	100fr multicolored	5.50	4.25
Q475	PP57	200fr multicolored	11.00	8.50
		Nos. Q473-Q475 (3)	19.25	14.85

Electric Trains PP58

Designs: No. Q476, Eurostar (yellow & white train). No. Q477, Thalys (red & white train). 160fr, Eurostar, Thalys side by side.

1998 **Photo.** ***Perf. 11½***

Q476	PP58	80fr multicolored	4.75	3.50
Q477	PP58	80fr multicolored	4.75	3.50
Q478	PP58	160fr multicolored	9.50	7.25
		Nos. Q476-Q478 (3)	19.00	14.25

ISSUED UNDER GERMAN OCCUPATION

German Stamps of 1906-11 Surcharged

Belgien
3 Centimes

Nos. N1-N6

✱ 1Fr.25C. ✱

Belgien

Nos. N7-N9

Wmk. Lozenges (125)

1914-15 ***Perf. 14, 14½***

1	A16	3c on 3pf brown	.45	.20
2	A16	5c on 5pf green	.40	.20
3	A16	10c on 10pf car	.50	.20
4	A16	25c on 20pf ultra	.50	.25
5	A16	50c on 40pf lake & blk	2.50	1.25
6	A16	75c on 60pf mag	.90	*1.25*
7	A16	1fr on 80pf lake & blk, *rose*	2.50	1.75
8	A17	1fr25c on 1m car	20.00	12.50
9	A21	2fr50c on 2m gray bl	18.00	15.00
		Nos. N1-N9 (9)	45.75	32.60
		Set, never hinged	160.00	

German Stamps of 1906-18 Surcharged

Belgien **3 Cent.** Nos. N10-N21

Belgien **1F.** No. N22

✱ 1F.25Cent. ✱

Belgien

Nos. N23-N25

1916-18

10	A22	2c on 2pf drab	.25	.25
11	A16	3c on 3pf brn	.35	.25
12	A16	5c on 5pf grn	.35	.25
13	A22	8c on 7½pf org	.65	.35
14	A16	10c on 10pf car	.25	.25
15	A22	15c on 15pf yel brn	.65	.25
16	A22	15c on 15pf dk vio	.65	.45
17	A16	20c on 25pf org & blk, *yel*	.35	.35
18	A16	25c on 20pf ultra	.35	.25
a.		25c on 20pf blue	.40	.25
19	A16	40c on 30pf org & blk, *buff*	.40	.30
20	A16	50c on 40pf lake & blk	.35	.30
21	A16	75c on 60pf mag	1.00	*12.50*
22	A16	1fr on 80pf lake & blk, *rose*	2.00	*2.50*
23	A17	1fr25c on 1m car	2.00	2.00
24	A21	2fr50c on 2m gray bl	27.50	25.00
a.		2fr50c on 1m carmine (error)		*3,500.*
25	A20	6fr25c on 5m sl & car	40.00	37.50
		Nos. N10-N25 (16)	77.10	82.75
		Set, never hinged	145.00	

A similar series of stamps without "Belgien" was used in parts of Belgium and France while occupied by German forces. See France Nos. N15-N26.

BELIZE

bə-ˈlēz

LOCATION — Central America bordering on Caribbean Sea to east, Mexico to north, Guatemala to west
GOVT. — Independent state
AREA — 8,867 sq. mi.
POP. — 219,296 (1996 est.)
CAPITAL — Belmopan

Belize was known as British Honduras until 1973. The former British colony achieved independence in September 1981.

100 Cents = 1 Dollar

> **Catalogue values for all unused stamps in this country are for Never Hinged items.**

Fish-Animal Type of British Honduras Regular Issue 1968-72 Overprinted in Black on Silver Panel

☼ BELIZE ☼

Wmk. 314 (½c, 5c, $5), Unwmkd.

1973, June 1 **Litho.** ***Perf. 13x12½***

312	A37	½c multi (#235)	.20	.20
313	A37	1c multi (#214)	.20	.20
314	A37	2c multi (#215)	.20	.20
315	A37	3c multi (#216)	.20	.20
316	A37	4c multi (#217)	.20	.20
317	A37	5c multi (#238)	.20	.20
318	A37	10c multi (#219)	.20	.20
319	A37	15c multi (#220)	.20	.20
320	A37	25c multi (#221)	.30	.30
321	A37	50c multi (#222)	.50	.50
322	A37	$1 multi (#223)	.90	*1.25*
323	A37	$2 multi (#224)	2.00	*2.50*
324	A37	$5 multi (#240)	5.50	*7.00*
		Nos. 312-324 (13)	10.80	*13.15*

No. 315 with silver panel omitted exists canceled. Nos. 313 and 319 exist with silver panel double.

Common Design Types pictured following the introduction.

Princess Anne's Wedding Issue

Common Design Type

1973, Nov. 14 **Wmk. 314** ***Perf. 14***

325	CD325	26c blue grn & multi	.20	.25
326	CD325	50c ocher & multi	.35	*.50*

Crana — A50

1974, Jan. 1 **Litho.** ***Perf. 13½***

327	A50	½c shown	.20	.20
328	A50	1c Jewfish	.20	.20
329	A50	2c White-lipped peccary	.20	.20
330	A50	3c Grouper	.20	.20
331	A50	4c Collared anteater	.20	.20
332	A50	5c Bonefish	.20	.20
333	A50	10c Paca	.20	.20
334	A50	15c Dolphinfish	.20	.20
335	A50	25c Kinkajou	.25	.25
336	A50	50c Muttonfish	.55	.55
337	A50	$1 Tayra	1.00	1.00
338	A50	$2 Great barracudas	2.00	2.00
339	A50	$5 Mountain lion	5.25	5.25
		Nos. 327-339 (13)	10.65	10.65

Stag, Mayan Pottery A51

Designs: Mayan pottery decorations.

1974, May 1 ***Perf. 14½***

340	A51	3c shown	.20	.20
341	A51	6c Fire snake	.20	.20
342	A51	16c Mouse	.20	.20
343	A51	26c Eagle	.30	.30
344	A51	50c Parrot	.65	.65
		Nos. 340-344 (5)	1.55	1.55

Parides Arcas A52

Designs: Butterflies of Belize.

Wmk. 314 Sideways

1974-77 *Perf. 14*

345 A52 ½c shown .20 .20
346 A52 1c Thecla regalis .20 .20
347 A52 2c Colobura dirce .20 .20
348 A52 3c Catonephele numilia .20 .20
349 A52 4c Battus belus .20 .20
350 A52 5c Callicore patelina .35 .20
351 A52 10c Callicore astala .70 .35

Perf. 14x15; 14 (26, 35c)

352 A52 15c Nessaea aglaura .80 .50
a. Watermark upright ('75) .70 .40
353 A52 16c Prepona pseudojoiceyi .45 .25
354 A52 25c Papilio thoas 1.10 .65
a. Watermark upright ('77) .80 .45
355 A52 26c Hamadryas arethusa 7.00 *7.50*
356 A52 50c Thecla bathildis 2.25 1.25
a. Watermark upright ('77) 1.00 .60
357 A52 $1 Caligo uranus 2.25 1.25
358 A52 $2 Heliconius sapho 4.25 2.40
359 A52 $5 Eurytides philolaus 13.00 7.50
a. Watermark upright ('75) 11.00 6.00
360 A52 $10 Philaethria dido 21.00 12.00
Nos. 345-360 (16) 54.15 34.85

Issue dates: No. 355A, July 25, 1977; No. 360, Jan. 2, 1975; others Sept. 2, 1974.

For surcharges, see Nos. 380, 386. For overprint, see No. 395.

1975-78 **Wmk. 373**

345a A52 ½c multicolored .20 .20
347a A52 2c multi ('77) .20 .20
348a A52 3c multi ('77) .20 .20
349a A52 4c multi ('77) .25 .25
350a A52 5c multi ('77) .30 .30
351a A52 10c multicolored .65 .65
352b A52 15c multi ('77) .90 .90
354b A52 25c multi ('78) 1.25 1.25
355A A52 35c Parides arcas ('77) 2.00 2.00
Nos. 345a-355A (9) 5.95 5.95

For overprints and surcharges see Nos. 395-396, 424, 426-427.

Churchill and Coronation Coach of Queen Elizabeth II — A53

$1, Churchill & Williamsburg, VA Liberty Bell.

Wmk. 373

1974, Nov. 30 Litho. *Perf. 14*

363 A53 50c multicolored .20 .20
364 A53 $1 multicolored .35 .35

Sir Winston Churchill (1874-1965).

Mayan Urn — A54

Designs: Various Mayan vessels.

1975, June 2 Wmk. 314 *Perf. 14*

365 A54 3c lt green & multi .20 .20
366 A54 6c lt blue & multi .20 .20
367 A54 16c dull yel & multi .20 .20
368 A54 26c lilac & multi .30 .30
369 A54 50c lt brown & multi .65 .65
Nos. 365-369 (5) 1.55 1.55

Musicians A55

Christmas: 26c, Nativity (Thatched hut and children). 50c, Drummers, vert. $1, Map of Belize, star, fleeing family, vert.

Perf. 14x14½, 14½x14

1975, Nov. 17 Litho. Wmk. 314

370 A55 6c multicolored .20 .20
371 A55 26c multicolored .20 .20
372 A55 50c multicolored .25 .25
373 A55 $1 multicolored .55 .55
Nos. 370-373 (4) 1.20 1.20

William Wrigley, Jr., Sapodilla Tree A56

Bicentennial Emblem and: 35c, Charles Lindbergh and "Spirit of St. Louis." $1, John Lloyd Stephens and Mayan temple.

1976, Mar. 29 Wmk. 373 *Perf. 14½*

374 A56 10c multicolored .20 .20
375 A56 35c multicolored .25 .25
376 A56 $1 multicolored .65 .65
Nos. 374-376 (3) 1.10 1.10

American Bicentennial.

Bicycling A57

Wmk. 373

1976, July 17 Litho. *Perf. 14½*

377 A57 35c shown .20 .20
378 A57 45c Running .20 .20
379 A57 $1 Shooting .45 .45
Nos. 377-379 (3) .85 .85

21st Olympic Games, Montreal, Canada, July 17-Aug. 1.

No. 355 Surcharged with New Value and Bar

Wmk. 314

1976, Aug. 30 Litho. *Perf. 14*

380 A52 20c on 26c multi 1.40 1.40

Map of West Indies, Bats, Wicket and Ball A57a

Prudential Cup — A57b

Unwmk.

1976, Oct. 18 Litho. *Perf. 14*

381 A57a 35c lt blue & multi .45 .45
382 A57b $1 lilac rose & blk 1.25 1.25

World Cricket Cup, won by West Indies Team, 1975.

Royal Visit, 1975 A58

Designs: 35c, Rose window and Queen's head. $2, Queen surrounded by bishops.

1977, Feb. 7 Litho. *Perf. 13½x14*

383 A58 10c multicolored .20 .20
384 A58 35c multicolored .25 .25
385 A58 $2 multicolored 1.10 1.10
Nos. 383-385 (3) 1.55 1.55

25th anniv. of the reign of Elizabeth II.

No. 352 Surcharged with New Value and Bar

1977 Wmk. 314 *Perf. 14x15*

386 A52 5c on 15c multi .30 .30

The first setting has the "5c" close to the the right edge of the block (varies). The second, and more common, setting has about 7mm from the right edge to the "5c."

Red-capped Manakin — A59

Designs: Birds of Belize.

Wmk. 373

1977, Sept. 3 Litho. *Perf. 14½*

387 A59 8c shown .30 .20
388 A59 10c Hooded oriole .30 .20
389 A59 25c Blue-crowned motmot .90 .45
390 A59 35c Slaty-breasted tinamou 1.00 .60
391 A59 45c Ocellated turkey 1.50 .75
392 A59 $1 White hawk 3.00 1.75
a. Souvenir sheet of 6, #387-392 8.50 4.25
Nos. 387-392 (6) 7.00 3.95

See Nos. 398-403, 416-421, 500-501. For overprints and surcharges see No. 502.

Medical Laboratory A60

Design: $1, Mobile medical unit and children receiving treatment.

1977, Dec. 2 *Perf. 13½*

393 A60 35c multicolored .30 .30
394 A60 $1 multicolored .75 .75
a. Souvenir sheet of 2, #393-394 1.10 1.10

Pan American Health Org., 75th anniv.

Nos. 351 and 355A Overprinted in Gold: "BELIZE DEFENCE FORCE / 1ST JANUARY 1978"

Wmk. 314, 373

1978, Feb. 15 Litho. *Perf. 14*

395 A52 10c multicolored .20 .20
396 A52 35c multicolored .35 .35

Elizabeth II Coronation Anniversary Issue

Common Design Types

Souvenir Sheet

1978, Apr. 21 Unwmk. *Perf. 15*

397 Sheet of 6 1.25 1.25
a. CD326 75c White lion of Mortimer .20 .20
b. CD327 75c Elizabeth II .20 .20
c. CD328 75c Jaguar (Maya god) .20 .20

No. 397 contains 2 se-tenant strips of Nos. 397a-397c, separated by horizontal gutter with commemorative and descriptive inscriptions and showing central part of coronation procession with coach.

Bird Type of 1977

Wmk. 373

1978, July 31 Litho. *Perf. 14½*

398 A59 10c White-crowned parrot .40 .20
399 A59 25c Crimson-collared tanager .90 .45
400 A59 35c Citreoline trogon 1.00 .50
401 A59 45c Sungrebe 1.10 .60
402 A59 50c Muscovy duck 1.25 .65
403 A59 $1 King vulture 2.25 1.25
a. Souvenir sheet of 6, #398-403 9.50 4.00
Nos. 398-403 (6) 6.90 3.65

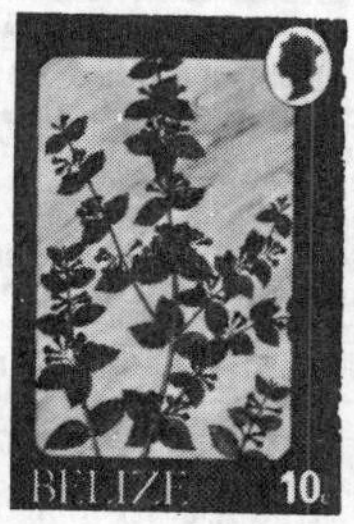

Russelia Sarmentosa A61

Wild Flowers and Ferns: 15c, Lygodium polymorphum. 35c, Heliconia aurantiaca. 45c, Adiantum tetraphyllum. 50c, Angelonia ciliaris. $1, Thelypteris obliterata.

1978, Oct. 16 Litho. *Perf. 14x13½*

404 A61 10c multicolored .20 .20
405 A61 15c multicolored .20 .20
406 A61 35c multicolored .40 .40
407 A61 45c multicolored .50 .50
408 A61 50c multicolored .55 .55
409 A61 $1 multicolored 1.10 1.10
Nos. 404-409 (6) 2.95 2.95

Christmas.

Internal Airmail Service, 1937 — A62

Mail Service: 10c, MV Heron, 1949. 35c, Dugout canoe on river, 1920. 45c, Stann Creek railroad, 1910. 50c, Mounted courier, 1882. $2, RMS Eagle, 1856, and "paid" cancel.

Perf. 13½x14

1979, Jan. 15 Litho. Wmk. 373

410 A62 5c multicolored .20 .20
411 A62 10c multicolored .20 .20
412 A62 35c multicolored .30 .30
413 A62 45c multicolored .40 .40
414 A62 50c multicolored .45 .45
415 A62 $2 multicolored 1.75 1.75
Nos. 410-415 (6) 3.30 3.30

Centenary of membership in UPU.

Bird Type of 1977

1979, Apr. 16 Unwmk. *Perf. 14½*

416 A59 10c Boat-billed heron .25 .25
417 A59 25c Gray-necked wood rail .70 .60
418 A59 35c Lineated woodpecker .85 .85
419 A59 45c Blue gray tanager 1.10 1.10
420 A59 50c Laughing falcon 1.25 1.25
421 A59 $1 Long-tailed hermit 2.50 2.50
a. Souvenir sheet of 6, #416-421 7.25 7.00
Nos. 416-421 (6) 6.65 6.55

Nos. 477, 354b, 595, 355A, 599, 651 Surcharged with New Value and Bar

10c $1.25

1979-83 Litho. *Perf. 14*

422 A67 10c on 15c multi .65 .65
423 A67 10c on 15c multi .65 .65
424 A52 10c on 25c multi *.65* .65
424A A67 10c on 35c multi
b. Round obliterator
425 A76 10c on 35c multi
426 A52 15c on 35c multi
427 A52 15c on 35c multi .30 .30
428 A76 $1.25 on $2 multi 2.00 2.00
429 A81 $1.25 on $2 multi 2.00 2.00

No. 422 has a square the width of the "10c" obliterating the old value. No. 423 has a rectangle that is wider than the "10c."

No. 424A has a square obliterator.

No. 426 has "15c" at top of stamp, No. 427 has "15c" at right of rectangle. Type differs.

No. 429 has rectangular obliterator with new value at top of stamp.

Many errors exist from printer's waste.

Issue dates: #426, Mar. 1979. #427, June, 1979. #424, Mar. 31, 1980. #422, Aug. 22, 1981. #423, Jan. 28, 1983. #425, Apr. 15, 1983. #428-429, June 9, 1983.

Used Stamps
Postally used copies are valued the same as unused. CTO's are of minimal value. Most used stamps from No. 430-679 exist CTO. Most of these appeared on the market after the contract was canceled and were not authorized. The cancellations are printed and the paper differs from the issued stamps.

Imperforate Stamps
Stamps from No. 430-679 exist imperforate in small quantities.

Queen Elizabeth II, 25th Anniv. of Coronation — A63

Designs: 25c, No. 439, Paslow Bldg., #397c. 50c, Parliament, London, #397a. 75c, Coronation coach. $1, Queen on horseback, vert. $2, Prince of Wales, vert. $3, Queen and Prince Philip, vert. $4, Queen Elizabeth II, portrait, vert. No. 437, St. Edward's Crown, vert. No. 438a, $5, Princess Anne on horseback, Montreal Olympics, vert. No. 438b, $10, Queen, Montreal Olympics, vert.

Unwmk.

1979, May 31 Litho. *Perf. 14*

430	A63	25c multicolored	.20
431	A63	50c multicolored	.45
432	A63	75c multicolored	.70
433	A63	$1 multicolored	.90
434	A63	$2 multicolored	1.75
435	A63	$3 multicolored	2.75
436	A63	$4 multicolored	3.75
437	A63	$5 multicolored	4.50
		Nos. 430-437 (8)	15.00

Souvenir Sheets

438	A63	Sheet of 2, #a.-b.	10.00
439	A63	$15 multicolored	10.00

Powered Flight, 75th Anniv. — A64

1979, July 30

440	A64	4c	Safety, 1909	
441	A64	25c	Boeing 707	
442	A64	50c	Concorde	
443	A64	75c	Handley Page W8b, 1922	
444	A64	$1	AVRO F, 1912	
445	A64	$1.50	Cody, 1910	
446	A64	$2	Triplane Roe II, 1909	
447	A64	$3	Santos-Dumont, 1906	
448	A64	$4	Wright Brothers Flyer, 1903	

Souvenir Sheets

Perf. 14½

449		Sheet of 2
a.		A64 $5 Dunne D.5, 1910
b.		A64 $5 Great Britain #581
450	A64	$10 Belize Airways Jet

Sir Rowland Hill, death cent., "75th anniv." of ICAO.

1980 Summer Olympics, Moscow — A65

1979, Oct. 10 *Perf. 14*

451	A65	25c	Handball	.20
452	A65	50c	Weight lifting	.45
453	A65	75c	Track	.70
454	A65	$1	Soccer	.90
455	A65	$2	Sailing	1.75
456	A65	$3	Swimming	2.75
457	A65	$4	Boxing	3.75
458	A65	$5	Cycling	4.50
			Nos. 451-458 (8)	15.00

Souvenir Sheets

Perf. 14½

459		Sheet of 2	12.00
a.		A65 $5 Track, diff.	4.00
b.		A65 $10 Boxing, diff.	8.00
460	A65	$15 Cycling, diff.	12.00

1980 Winter Olympics, Lake Placid — A66

1979, Dec. 4 *Perf. 14*

461	A66	25c	Torch	.20
462	A66	50c	Slalom skiing	.40
463	A66	75c	Figure skating	.65
464	A66	$1	Downhill skiing	.85
465	A66	$2	Speed skating	1.75
466	A66	$3	Cross country skiing	2.50
467	A66	$4	Biathlon	3.50
468	A66	$5	Olympic medals	4.25
			Nos. 461-468 (8)	14.10

Souvenir Sheets

Perf. 14½

469		Sheet of 2	12.00
a.		A66 $5 Torch bearers	4.00
b.		A66 $10 Medals, diff.	8.00
470	A66	$15 Torch, diff.	12.00

See Nos. 503-512.

Cypraea Zebra A67

1980, Jan. 7 Litho. *Perf. 14*

471	A67	1c	shown	.20	.20
472	A67	2c	Macrocallista maculata	.20	.20
473	A67	3c	Arca zebra, vert.	.20	.20
474	A67	4c	Chama macerophylla, vert.	.20	.20
475	A67	5c	Latirus cariniferus	.20	.20
476	A67	10c	Conus spurius, vert.	.20	.20
477	A67	15c	Murex cabritii, vert.	.20	.20
478	A67	20c	Atrina rigida	.25	.20
479	A67	25c	Chlamys imbricata, vert.	.30	.20
480	A67	35c	Conus granulatus	.40	.20
481	A67	45c	Tellina radiata, vert.	.55	.20
482	A67	50c	Leucozonia nassa	.60	.20
483	A67	85c	Tripterotyphis triangularis	1.00	.30
484	A67	$1	Strombus gigas, vert.	1.25	.35
485	A67	$2	Strombus gallus, vert.	2.50	.70
486	A67	$5	Fasciolaria tulipa	6.25	1.75
487	A67	$10	Arene cruentata	12.50	3.50
			Nos. 471-487 (17)	27.00	9.00

Souvenir Sheets

488	A67	Sheet of 2, 85c, $5	7.50	7.50
489	A67	Sheet of 2, $2, $10	15.00	17.50

Stamps in Nos. 488-489 have different color border and are of a slightly different size than the sheet stamps.

The 10c, 50c, 85c, $1 exist dated 1981.

For overprints and surcharges see Nos. 422-423, 424A, 572-589, 592-593.

Intl. Year of the Child — A68

Various children. No. 498a, Three children. No. 498b, Madonna and Child by Durer. No. 499, Children before Christmas tree.

1980, Mar. 15 Litho. *Perf. 14*

490	A68	25c	multicolored	.20
491	A68	50c	multicolored	.35
492	A68	75c	multicolored	.50
493	A68	$1	multicolored	.65
494	A68	$1.50	multicolored	1.00
495	A68	$2	multicolored	1.40
496	A68	$3	multicolored	2.00
497	A68	$4	multicolored	2.75
			Nos. 490-497 (8)	8.85

Souvenir Sheets

Perf. 13½

498	A68	$5 Sheet of 2, #a.-b.	6.00
499	A68	$10 multicolored	6.00

No. 498 contains two 35x54mm stamps. No. 499 contains one 73x110mm stamp.

Bird Type of 1977
Souvenir Sheets

1980, June 16 Unwmk. *Perf. 13½*

500	Sheet of 6	5.50	4.50
a.	A59 10c Jabiru	.20	.20
b.	A59 25c Barred antshrike	.50	.35
c.	A59 35c Royal flycatcher	.65	.50
d.	A59 45c White-necked puffbird	.75	.65
e.	A59 50c Ornate hawk-eagle	.85	.75
f.	A59 $1 Golden-masked tanager	1.90	1.50
g.	Sheet of 12	11.00	9.00
501	Sheet of 2	8.00	8.00
a.	A59 $2 Jabiru	3.00	3.00
b.	A59 $3 Golden-masked tanager	4.50	4.50

No. 500g contains 2 each Nos. 500a-500f with gutter between; inscribed "Protection of Environment" and "Wildlife Protection."

No. 500 Overprinted or Surcharged with Exhibition Emblem

1980, Oct. 3 Litho. *Perf. 13½*

502	Sheet of 6	4.00	4.00
a.	A59 10c multicolored	.20	.20
b.	A59 25c multicolored	.50	.50
c.	A59 35c multicolored	.65	.65
d.	A59 40c on 45c multi	.85	.85
e.	A59 40c on 50c multi	.85	.85
f.	A59 40c on $1 multi	.85	.85

ESPAMER '80 Stamp Exhibition, Madrid, Spain, Oct. 3-12.

1980 Winter Olympics, Lake Placid — A69

Events and winning country: 25c, Men's speed skating, US. 50c, Ice hockey, US. 75c, No. 512, Men's figure skating, Great Britain. $1, Alpine skiing, Austria. $1.50, Women's giant slalom, Germany. $2, Women's speed skating, Netherlands. $3, Cross country skiing, Sweden. $5, Men's giant slalom, Sweden. Nos. 511a ($5), 511b ($10), Speed skating, US.

1980, Aug. 20 Litho. *Perf. 14*

503	A69	25c	multicolored	.25
504	A69	50c	multicolored	.50
505	A69	75c	multicolored	.75
506	A69	$1	multicolored	.95
507	A69	$1.50	multicolored	1.50
508	A69	$2	multicolored	1.90
509	A69	$3	multicolored	3.00
510	A69	$5	multicolored	4.75
			Nos. 503-510 (8)	13.60

Souvenir Sheets

Perf. 14½

511	A69	Sheet of 2, #a.-b.	9.50
512	A69	$10 multicolored	9.50

Nos. 503-510 issued with se-tenant label.

Intl. Year of the Child — A70

Nos. 513-521: Scenes from Sleeping Beauty. $8, Detail from Paumgartner Family Altarpiece by Albrecht Durer.

1980, Nov. 24 *Perf. 14*

513	A70	35c	multicolored	.30
514	A70	40c	multicolored	.35
515	A70	50c	multicolored	.40
516	A70	75c	multicolored	.65
517	A70	$1	multicolored	.85
518	A70	$1.50	multicolored	1.25
519	A70	$3	multicolored	2.50
520	A70	$4	multicolored	3.50
			Nos. 513-520 (8)	9.80

Souvenir Sheets

Perf. 14½

521		Sheet of 2	9.50
a.		A70 $5 Marriage	4.25
b.		A70 $5 Couple on horseback	4.25
522	A70	$8 multicolored	7.50

Nos. 513-520 issued with se-tenent label.

Queen Mother Elizabeth, 80th Birthday A71

1980, Dec. 12

523	A71	$1 multicolored	1.00	1.00

Souvenir Sheet

Perf. 14½

524	A71	$5 multicolored

No. 524 contains one 46x31mm stamp.
No. 523 issued in sheet of 6.

Christmas A72

1980, Dec. 30 Litho. *Perf. 14*

525	A72	25c	Annunciation	.20
526	A72	50c	Bethlehem	.40
527	A72	75c	Holy Family	.65
528	A72	$1	Nativity	.85
529	A72	$1.50	Flight into Egypt	1.25
530	A72	$2	Shepards	1.60
531	A72	$3	With angel	2.50
532	A72	$4	Adoration	3.25
			Nos. 525-532 (8)	10.70

Souvenir Sheets

Perf. 14½

533 A72 $5 Nativity 5.00
534 A72 $10 Madonna & Child 10.00

Nos. 525-532 each issued in sheets of 20 + 10 labels. The 2nd and 5th vertical rows consist of labels.

Nos. 529, 532, 534 Surcharged

$2 ═══ WIPA 1981

1981, May 22

535 A72 $1 on $1.50 multi
536 A72 $2 on $4 multi

Souvenir Sheet

Perf. 14½

537 A72 $2 on $10 multi

Location of overprint and surcharge varies.

Intl. Rotary Club — A73

Designs: 25c, Paul P. Harris, founder. 50c, No. 546, Rotary, project emblem. $1, No. 545b, 75th anniv. emblem. $1.50 Diploma, horiz. $2, No. 545a, Project Hippocrates. $3, 75th anniv. project emblems, horiz. No. 544, Hands reach out, horiz.

1981, May 26 *Perf. 14*

538 A73 25c multicolored .25
539 A73 50c multicolored .50
540 A73 $1 multicolored .95
541 A73 $1.50 multicolored 1.40
542 A73 $2 multicolored 1.90
543 A73 $3 multicolored 2.75
544 A73 $5 multicolored 4.75
Nos. 538-544 (7) 12.50

Souvenir Sheets

Perf. 14½

545 Sheet of 2 18.00
a. A73 $5 multicolored 5.75
b. A73 $10 multicolored 12.00
546 A73 $10 multicolored 12.00

Originally scheduled to be issued Mar. 30, the set was postponed and issued without a 75c stamp. Supposedly some of the 75c were sold to the public.

For overprints and surcharges see Nos. 563-571, 590-591.

Royal Wedding of Prince Charles and Lady Diana — A74

1981, July 16 *Perf. 13½x14*

548 A74 50c Coat of Arms .20
549 A74 $1 Prince Charles .40
550 A74 $1.50 Couple .65

Size: 25x43mm

Perf. 13½

551 A74 50c like No. 548 .20
552 A74 $1 like No. 549 .40
553 A74 $1.50 like No. 550 .65
Nos. 548-553 (6) 2.50

Miniature Sheet

Perf. 14½

554 Sheet of 3, #554a-554c 5.00
a. A74 $3 like No. 550 1.60
b. A74 $3 like No. 548 1.60
c. A74 $3 like No. 549 1.60

Nos. 551-553 issued in sheets of 6 + 3 labels. No. 554 contains three 35x50mm stamps.

For overprints see Nos. 659-665.

1984 Olympics — A75

1981, Sept. 14 *Perf. 14*

555 A75 85c Track .75
556 A75 $1 Cycling .90
557 A75 $1.50 Boxing 1.40
558 A75 $2 Emblems 1.90
559 A75 $3 Baron Coubertin 2.75
560 A75 $5 Torch, emblems 4.50
Nos. 555-560 (6) 12.20

Souvenir Sheets

Perf. 13½

561 Sheet of 2 10.00
a. A75 $5 like No. 559 3.25
b. A75 $10 like No. 560 6.75

Perf. 14½

562 A75 $15 like No. 558 10.00

No. 561 contains two 35x54mm stamps. No. 562 contains one 46x68mm stamp.

Nos. 561-562 exist with gold background.

Nos. 538-546 Overprinted in Black or Gold

INDEPENDENCE
21 SEPT.,1981

1981, Sept. 21 *Perf. 14*

563 A73 25c multicolored (G)
564 A73 50c multicolored
565 A73 $1 multicolored
566 A73 $1.50 multicolored
567 A73 $2 multicolored (G)
568 A73 $3 multicolored
569 A73 $5 multicolored

Souvenir Sheets

Perf. 14½

570 A73 Sheet of 2, #a.-b. (G)
571 A73 $10 multicolored

Size of overprint varies.

Nos. 471-483, 485-489 Overprinted

Independence
21 Sept.,1981

1981, Sept. 21

572 A67 1c multicolored
573 A67 2c multicolored
574 A67 3c multicolored
575 A67 4c multicolored
576 A67 5c multicolored
577 A67 10c multicolored
578 A67 15c multicolored
579 A67 20c multicolored
580 A67 25c multicolored
581 A67 35c multicolored
582 A67 45c multicolored
583 A67 50c multicolored
584 A67 85c multicolored
585 A67 $2 multicolored
586 A67 $5 multicolored
587 A67 $10 multicolored

Souvenir Sheets

588 A67 Sheet of 2, #488
589 A67 Sheet of 2, #489

Size and style of overprint varies, italic on horiz. stamps, upright on vert. stamps and upright capitals on souvenir sheets.

The 10c is dated 1981. Less than 16 sheets dated 1980 were also overprinted.

Nos. 541, 545 Surcharged

$1 ═══ ESPAMER 81 13-22 NOV. BUENOS AIRES

1981, Nov. 13 *Perf. 14*

590 A73 $1 on $1.50 multi

Souvenir Sheet

Perf. 14½

591 Sheet of 2
a. A73 $1 on $5 multicolored
b. A73 $1 on $10 multicolored

Espamer '81.

Nos. 488, 489 Surcharged in Red

PHILATELIA'81 P 14 - 18 . XI . 1981 $1 ═══

1981, Nov. 14 *Perf. 14½*

Souvenir Sheets

592 Sheet of 2 2.50
a. A67 $1 on 85c
b. A67 $1 on $5
593 Sheet of 2 2.50
a. A67 $1 on $2
b. A67 $1 on $10

Independence — A76

1981-82 *Perf. 14*

594 A76 10c Flag
595 A76 35c Map, vert.
596 A76 50c Black orchid, vert.
597 A76 85c Tapir
598 A76 $1 Mahogany tree, vert.
599 A76 $2 Keel-billed toucan

Souvenir Sheet

Perf. 14½

600 A76 $5 like 10c

Issued: 50c-$2, 12/18; 10c, 35c, $5, 2/10/82.

For surcharges see Nos. 425, 428, 616.

1982 World Cup Soccer Championships, Spain — A77

1981, Dec. 28 *Perf. 14*

601 A77 10c Uruguay '30, '50 .20
602 A77 25c Italy '34, '38 .20
603 A77 50c Germany '54, '74 .40
604 A77 $1 Brazil '58, '62, '70 .75
605 A77 $1.50 Argentina '78 1.25
606 A77 $2 England '66 1.75
Nos. 601-606 (6) 4.55

Souvenir Sheets

Perf. 14½

607 A77 $2 Emblem 1.75
608 A77 $3 Player 2.50

No. 608 contains one 46x78mm stamp.

For surcharge see No. 617.

Sailing Ships — A78

1982, Mar. 15 *Perf. 14*

609 A78 10c Man of war, 19th cent.
610 A78 25c Madagascar, 1837
611 A78 35c Whitby, 1838
612 A78 50c China, 1838
613 A78 85c Swiftsure, 1850
614 A78 $2 Windsor Castle, 1857

Souvenir Sheet

Perf. 14½

615 A78 $5 19th cent. ships

Nos. 599 and 606 Surcharged

═══ $1 ESSEN 82

1982, Apr. 28

616 A76 $1 on $2 multi 2.25
617 A77 $1 on $2 multi 2.25

Essen '82 Philatelic Exhibition.

Princess of Wales, 21st Birthday — A79

Various portraits.

1982, May 20 *Perf. 13½x14*

618 A79 50c multicolored .25
619 A79 $1 multicolored .50
620 A79 $1.50 multicolored .75

Size: 25x42mm

Perf. 13½

621 A79 50c like No. 618 .25
622 A79 $1 like No. 619 .50
623 A79 $1.50 like No. 620 .75
Nos. 618-623 (6) 3.00

Souvenir Sheet

Stamp Size: 31x47mm

Perf. 14½

624 A79 $3 Sheet of 3, #a.-c. like #618-620 4.00

Nos. 618-620 also exist with gold borders, size: 30x45mm.

Overprinted in Silver

BIRTH OF H.R.H.
PRINCE
WILLIAM ARTHUR
PHILIP LOUIS
21ST JUNE 1982

1982, Oct. 21 *Perf. 13½x14*

628 A79 50c multicolored .40
629 A79 $1 multicolored .80
630 A79 $1.50 multicolored 1.25

Size: 25x42mm

Perf. 13½

631 A79 50c multicolored .40
632 A79 $1 multicolored .80
633 A79 $1.50 multicolored 1.25
Nos. 628-633 (6) 4.90

Souvenir Sheet

Perf. 14½

634 A79 $3 Sheet of 3, #a.-c. 8.50

Size of overprint varies. The overprint exists on the gold bordered stamps. No. 634 exists with a second type of overprint.

Boy Scouts — A80

1982, Aug. 31 *Perf. 14*

638 A80 10c Building camp fire .20
639 A80 25c Bird watching .35
640 A80 35c Playing guitar .50
641 A80 50c Hiking .75
642 A80 85c Flag, scouts 1.25
643 A80 $2 Salute 2.75
Nos. 638-643 (6) 5.80

Souvenir Sheets

Perf. 14½

644 A80 $2 Scout holding flag, vert. 4.00
645 A80 $3 Lord Baden Powell, vert. 6.00

Scouting, 75th anniv. and Lord Baden Powell, 125th birth anniv.

For overprints see Nos. 653-658.

Marine Life — A81

1982, Sept. 20 *Perf. 14*

646 A81 10c Gorgonia ventalina
647 A81 35c Carpilius corallinus
648 A81 50c Plexaura flexuosa
649 A81 85c Condylactis gigantea
650 A81 $1 Stenopus hispidus
651 A81 $2 Abudefduf saxatilis

Souvenir Sheet

Perf. 14½

652 A81 $5 Scyllarides aequinoctialis

For surcharge see No. 429.

Nos. 638-643 Ovptd. in Gold: BELGICA 82 INT. YEAR OF THE CHILD SIR ROWLAND HILL 1795 1879 Picasso CENTENARY OF BIRTH and Emblems

1982, Oct. 1 *Perf. 14*

653 A80 10c Building camp fire
654 A80 25c Bird watching
655 A80 35c Playing guitar
656 A80 50c Hiking
657 A80 85c Flag, scouts
658 A80 $2 Salute

Overprint is different on Nos. 654-655.

Sheets include labels with native Christmas themes.

Nos. 548-554 Overprinted in Gold Similar to Nos. 628-634

1982, Oct. 25 *Perf. 13½x14*

659 A74 50c Coat of Arms 1.40
660 A74 $1 Prince Charles 2.75
661 A74 $1.50 Couple 4.25

Size: 25x43mm

Perf. 13½

662 A74 50c like No. 659 1.40
663 A74 $1 like No. 660 2.75
664 A74 $1.50 like No. 661 4.25
Nos. 659-664 (6) 16.80

Miniature Sheet

Perf. 14½

665 Sheet of 3, #665a-665c 14.00
a. A74 $3 like No. 661 3.50
b. A74 $3 like No. 659 3.50
c. A74 $3 like No. 660 3.50

Nos. 662-664 issued in sheets of 6 plus 3 labels. No. 665 contains three 35x50mm stamps. Size and style of overprint varies.

Visit by Pope John Paul II A82

1983, Mar. 7 *Perf. 13½*

666 A82 50c Belize Cathedral 1.90

Souvenir Sheet

Perf. 14½

667 A82 $2.50 Pope John Paul II 4.75

No. 667 contains one 30x47mm stamp.
No. 666 issued in sheet of 6.

Commonwealth Day — A83

1983, Mar. 14 *Perf. 13½*

668 A83 35c Map, vert. .30
669 A83 50c Maya Stella .40
670 A83 85c Supreme Court Bldg. .80
671 A83 $2 University Center 2.00
Nos. 668-671 (4) 3.50

Issued in miniature sheets of 4. Other formats are suspect.

First Manned Flight, Bicent. — A84

1983, May 16 *Perf. 14*

672 A84 10c Flying boat, 1670 .20
673 A84 25c Flying machine, 1709 .20
674 A84 50c Airship Guyton de Morveau .30
675 A84 85c Dirigible .50
676 A84 $1 Clement Bayard .60
677 A84 $1.50 Great Britain R-34 .95
Nos. 672-677 (6) 2.75

Souvenir Sheets

Perf. 14½

678 A84 $3 Nassau Balloon 1.65
679 A84 $3 Montgolfier Brothers balloon, vert. 1.65

"Errors"

Many "errors," including imperforates, exist of Nos. 680-898. These unauthorized varieties were printed without the knowledge of the Belize postal service. There may be large quantities of them.

Mayan Monuments — A85

1983, Nov. 14 Litho. *Perf. 13½x14*

680 A85 10c Altun Ha .20 .20
681 A85 15c Xunantunich .20 .20
682 A85 75c Cerros .60 .60
683 A85 $2 Lamanai 1.40 1.40
Nos. 680-683 (4) 2.40 2.40

Souvenir Sheet

684 A85 $3 Xunantunich, diff. 2.75 2.75

World Communications Year — A86

1983, Nov. 28 *Perf. 14*

685 A86 10c Belmopan Earth Station .20 .20
686 A86 15c Telstar 2 .20 .20
687 A86 75c UPU monument .75 .75
688 A86 $2 Mail boat 2.00 2.00
Nos. 685-688 (4) 3.15 3.15

Jaguar, World Wildlife Fund Emblem A87

1983, Dec. 9

689 A87 5c Sitting .20 .20
690 A87 10c Standing .20 .20
691 A87 85c Swimming 1.10 1.10
692 A87 $1 Walking 1.40 1.40
Nos. 689-692 (4) 2.90 2.90

Souvenir Sheet

693 A87 $3 Sitting in tree 3.25 3.25

No. 693 contains one stamp 45x28mm.

Christmas — A88

Scenes from mass celebrated by Pope John Paul II during visit, Mar.

1983, Dec. 22

694 A88 10c multicolored .20 .20
695 A88 15c multicolored .20 .20
696 A88 75c multicolored .75 .75
697 A88 $2 multicolored 2.00 2.00
Nos. 694-697 (4) 3.15 3.15

Souvenir Sheet

698 A88 $3 multicolored 3.25 3.25

Foureye Butterflyfish — A89

1984, Feb. 27 *Perf. 15*

699 A89 1c shown .20 .20
700 A89 2c Cushion star .20 .20
701 A89 3c Flower coral .20 .20
702 A89 4c Fairy basslets .20 .20
703 A89 5c Spanish hogfish .20 .20
704 A89 6c Star-eyed hermit crab .20 .20
705 A89 10c Sea fans, fire sponge .20 .20
706 A89 15c Blueheads .20 .20
707 A89 25c Blue-striped grunt .25 .25
708 A89 50c Coral crab .50 .50
709 A89 60c Tube sponge .60 .60
710 A89 75c Brain coral .75 .75
711 A89 $1 Yellow-tail snapper 1.00 1.00
712 A89 $2 Common lettuce slug 2.00 2.00
713 A89 $5 Yellow damselfish 5.00 5.00
714 A89 $10 Rock beauty 10.00 10.00
Nos. 699-714 (16) 21.70 21.70

For overprints and surcharge see Nos. 715-716, 762A-762C, 922.

The 50c, 60c, 75c, $1 exist inscribed "1986."

1988, July *Perf. 13½*

705a A89 10c .20 .20
706a A89 15c .20 .20
707a A89 25c .25 .25
708a A89 50c .50 .50
709a A89 60c .60 .60
711a A89 $1 .95 .95
Nos. 705a-711a (6) 2.70 2.70

Nos. 705, 708 Overprinted: "VISIT OF THE LORD / ARCHBISHOP OF CANTERBURY / 8th-11th MARCH 1984"

1984, Mar. 8

715 A89 10c multicolored .20 .20
716 A89 50c multicolored .60 .60

1984 Summer Olympics — A90

1984, Apr. 30 *Perf. 13½x14*

717 A90 25c Shooting .25 .25
718 A90 75c Boxing .75 .75
719 A90 $1 Running 1.10 1.10
720 A90 $2 Bicycling 1.90 1.90
Nos. 717-720 (4) 4.00 4.00

Souvenir Sheet

721 A90 $3 Discus 2.25 2.25

1984 Summer Olympics A91

1984, Apr. 30 Litho. *Perf. 14½*

Booklet Stamps

722 A91 5c Running .20 .20
a. Booklet pane of 4 .30
723 A91 20c Javelin .25 .25
a. Booklet pane of 4 1.10
724 A91 25c Shot put .35 .35
a. Booklet pane of 4 1.50
725 A91 $2 Torch 2.50 2.50
a. Booklet pane of 4 10.50
Nos. 722-725 (4) 3.30 3.30

Ausipex '84 — A92

1984, Sept. 26 Litho. *Perf. 15*

726 A92 15c Br. Honduras #3 .20 .20
727 A92 30c Bath-Bristol mail coach, 1784 .30 .30
728 A92 65c Penny Black, Rowland Hill .65 .65
729 A92 75c Railroad Pier, Commerce Bight .75 .75

Perf. 14

730 A92 $2 Royal Exhibition Bldgs. 2.00 2.00
Nos. 726-730 (5) 3.90 3.90

Souvenir Sheet

731 A92 $3 Australia #132, Br. Hond. #3 3.00 3.00

House of Tudor, 500th Anniv. — A93

White-fronted Parrot — A94

1984, Oct. 15 *Perf. 14*

732 A93 50c Queen Victoria .35 .35
733 A93 50c Prince Albert .35 .35
a. Sheet of 4, 2 each, #732-733 1.50
734 A93 75c King George VI .55 .55
735 A93 75c Queen Elizabeth .55 .55
a. Sheet of 4, 2 each, #734-735 2.25

736 A93 $1 Prince Charles .75 .75
737 A93 $1 Princess Diana .75 .75
a. Sheet of 4, 2 each, #736-737 3.00
Nos. 732-737 (6) 3.30 3.30

Souvenir Sheet

738 Sheet of 2 2.00 2.00
a. A93 $1.50 Prince Philip 1.00 1.00
b. A93 $1.50 Queen Elizabeth II 1.00 1.00

1984, Nov. 1 ***Perf. 11***

Parrots: b, White-capped. c, Red-lored. d, Mealy. b, d, horiz.

739 Block of 4 4.00 4.00
a.-d. A94 $1 any single 1.00 1.00

Miniature Sheet

Perf. 14

740 A94 $3 Scarlet macaw 3.00 3.00

No. 740 contains one 48x32mm stamp.

Mayan Artifacts — A95

1984, Nov. 30 ***Perf. 15***

741 A95 25c Incense holder, 1450 .25 .25
742 A95 75c Cylindrical vase, 675 .75 .75
743 A95 $1 Tripod vase, 500 1.00 1.00
744 A95 $2 Kinich Ahau (sun god) 2.00 2.00
Nos. 741-744 (4) 4.00 4.00

Girl Guides 75th Anniv., Intl. Youth Year A96

1985, Mar. 15 **Litho.** ***Perf. 15***

745 A96 25c Gov.-Gen. Gordon .25 .25
746 A96 50c Camping .50 .50
747 A96 90c Map reading .90 .90
748 A96 $1.25 Students in laboratory 1.25 1.25
749 A96 $2 Lady Baden-Powell 2.00 2.00
Nos. 745-749 (5) 4.90 4.90

Each stamp shows the scouting and IYY emblems.
For overprints see Nos. 777-781.

Audubon Birth Bicentenary — A97

Illustrations by Audubon. 10c, 25c, 75c, $1, $5 vert.

Perf. 14, 15 ($1)

1985, May 30-1988 **Litho.**

750 A97 10c White-tailed kite .20 .20
751 A97 15c Cuvier's kinglet .20 .20
752 A97 25c Painted bunting .35 .35
752A A97 60c like #752 ('88)
753 A97 75c Belted kingfisher 1.00 1.00
754 A97 $1 Northern cardinal 1.40 1.40
755 A97 $3 Long-billed curlew 4.00 4.00
Nos. 750-752,753-755 (6) 7.15 7.15

Souvenir Sheet

Perf. 13½x14

756 A97 $5 Portrait of Audubon, 1826, by John Syme 5.00 5.00

No. 756 contains one 38x51mm stamp.

Queen Mother, 85th Birthday A98

Designs: 10c, The Queen Consort and Princess Elizabeth, 1928. 15c, Queen Mother, Elizabeth. 75c, Queen Mother waving a greeting. No. 760, Royal family photograph, christening of Prince Henry. $2, Holding the infant Prince Henry. No. 762, Queen Mother, diff.

1985, June 20

757 A98 10c shown .20 .20
758 A98 15c multicolored .20 .20
759 A98 75c multicolored .75 .75
760 A98 $5 multicolored 5.00 5.00
Nos. 757-760 (4) 6.15 6.15

Souvenir Sheets

761 A98 $2 multicolored 1.75 1.75
762 A98 $5 multicolored 4.25 4.25

Nos. 761-762 contain one 38x51mm stamp.
For overprints see Nos. 771-776.

Nos. 705-706, 708 Ovptd.: INAUGURATION OF NEW GOVERNMENT 21st. DECEMBER 1984

1985, June 24 ***Perf. 15***

762A A89 10c multicolored .30 .30
762B A89 15c multicolored .45 .45
762C A89 50c multicolored 1.25 1.25
Nos. 762A-762C (3) 2.00 2.00

Miniature Sheet

Commonwealth Stamp Omnibus, 50th Anniv. — A99

British Honduras Nos. 111-112, 127, 129, 143, 194, 307 and Belize Nos. 326, 385 and 397b on: a, George V and Queen Mary in an open carriage. b, George VI and Queen Consort Elizabeth crowned. c, Civilians celebrating the end of WWII. d, George VI and Queen Consort at mass service. e, Elizabeth II wearing robes of state and the imperial crown. f, Winston Churchill, WWII fighter planes. g, Bridal photograph of Elizabeth II and Prince Philip. h, Bridal photograph of Princess Anne and Capt. Mark Phillips. i, Elizabeth II. j, Imperial crown.

1985, July 25 ***Perf. 14½x14***

763 Sheet of 10 5.00 5.00
a.-j. A99 50c any single .50 .50

Souvenir Sheet

Perf. 14

764 A99 $5 Elizabeth II coronation photograph 5.00 5.00

No. 764 contains one 38x51mm stamp.
For overprints see Nos. 796-797.

British Post Office, 350th Anniv. A100

1985, Aug. 1 ***Perf. 15***

765 A100 10c Postboy, letters .20 .20
766 A100 15c Packet, privateer .20 .20
767 A100 25c Duke of Marlborough .25 .25
768 A100 75c Diana .75 .75
769 A100 $1 Falmouth P.O. packet 1.00 1.00
770 A100 $3 S. S. Conway 3.00 3.00
Nos. 765-770 (6) 5.40 5.40

Nos. 757-762 Ovptd. in Silver "COMMONWEALTH SUMMIT / CONFERENCE, BAHAMAS / 16th-22nd OCTOBER 1985"

1985, Sept. 5 **Litho.** ***Perf. 15***

771 A98 10c multicolored .20 .20
772 A98 15c multicolored .20 .20
773 A98 75c multicolored .75 .75
774 A98 $5 multicolored 5.00 5.00
Nos. 771-774 (4) 6.15 6.15

Souvenir Sheets

775 A98 $2 multicolored 1.90 1.90
776 A98 $5 multicolored 4.75 4.75

Nos. 745-749 Ovptd. "80th ANNIVERSARY OF / ROTARY INTERNATIONAL"

1985, Sept. 25 ***Perf. 15***

777 A96 25c multicolored .25 .25
778 A96 50c multicolored .50 .50
779 A96 90c multicolored .90 .90
780 A96 $1.25 multicolored 1.25 1.25
781 A96 $2 multicolored 2.00 2.00
Nos. 777-781 (5) 4.90 4.90

Royal Visit — A101

1985, Oct. 9 ***Perf. 15x14½***

782 A101 25c Royal and natl. flags .25 .25
783 A101 75c Elizabeth II .75 .75

Size: 81x38mm

784 A101 $4 Britannia 4.00 4.00
a. Strip of 3, #782-784 5.00
Nos. 782-784 (3) 5.00 5.00

Souvenir Sheet

Perf. 13½x14

785 A101 $5 Elizabeth II, diff. 5.00 5.00

No. 785 contains one 38x51mm stamp.

Disneyland, 30th Anniv. A102

Characters from "It's a Small World."

1985, Nov. 1 ***Perf. 11***

786 A102 1c Royal Canadian Mounted Police .20 .20
787 A102 2c American Indian .20 .20
788 A102 3c Inca of the Andes .20 .20
789 A102 4c Africa .20 .20
790 A102 5c Far East .20 .20
791 A102 6c Belize .20 .20
792 A102 50c Balkans .50 .50
793 A102 $1.50 Saudi Arabia 1.50 1.50
794 A102 $3 Japan 3.00 3.00
Nos. 786-794 (9) 6.20 6.20

Souvenir Sheet

Perf. 14

795 A102 $4 Montage 4.00 4.00

Christmas.

Nos. 763-764 Ovptd. "PRE 'WORLD CUP FOOTBALL' / MEXICO 1986"

1985, Dec. 20 ***Perf. 14½x14***

796 Sheet of 10 5.00 5.00
a.-j. A99 50c, any single .50 .50

Souvenir Sheet

797 A99 $5 multicolored 5.00 5.00

Women in Folk Costumes — A103

1986, Jan. 15 ***Perf. 15***

798 A103 5c India .20 .20
799 A103 10c Maya .20 .20
800 A103 15c Garifuna .20 .20
801 A103 25c Creole .30 .30
802 A103 50c China .65 .65
803 A103 75c Lebanon 1.00 1.00
804 A103 $1 Europe 1.25 1.25
805 A103 $2 South America 2.50 2.50
Nos. 798-805 (8) 6.30 6.30

Souvenir Sheet

Perf. 14

806 A103 $5 Maya, So. America 6.25 6.25

No. 806 contains one 38x51mm stamp.

Miniature Sheet

A104

Easter A105

Papal arms, crucifix and: a, Pius X. b, Benedict XV. c, Pius XI. d, Pius XII. e, John XXIII. f, Paul VI. g, John Paul I. h, John Paul II. No. 573, John Paul II saying mass in Belize.

1986, Apr. 15 **Litho.** ***Perf. 11***

807 Sheet of 8 + label 6.25 6.25
a.-h. A104 50c, any single .80 .80

Souvenir Sheet

Perf. 14

808 A105 $4 multi 6.50 6.50

No. 807 contains center label picturing the Vatican, and papal crest.

A106

Queen Elizabeth II, 60th Birthday A107

1986, Apr. 21 *Perf. 14*

809 Strip of 3 1.50 1.50
- ***a.*** A106 25c Age 2 .25 .25
- ***b.*** A106 50c Coronation .50 .50
- ***c.*** A106 75c Riding horse .75 .75

810 A106 $3 Wearing crown jewels 3.00 3.00

Souvenir Sheet

811 A107 $4 Portrait 3.25 3.25

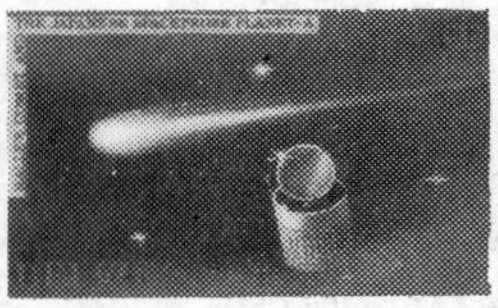

A108

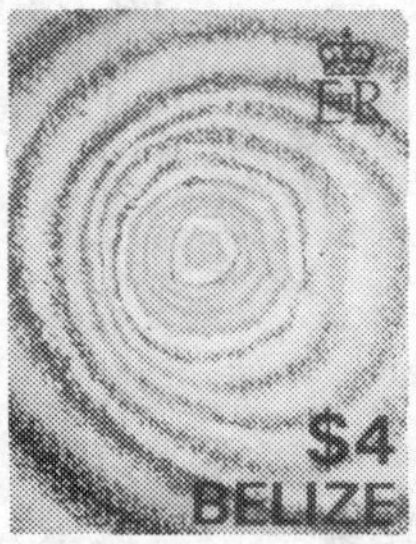

Halley's Comet
A109

1986, Apr. 30

812 Strip of 3 .75 .75
- ***a.*** A108 10c Planet-A probe .20 .20
- ***b.*** A108 15c Sighting, 1910 .20 .20
- ***c.*** A108 50c Giotto probe .50 .50

813 Strip of 3 3.75 3.75
- ***a.*** A108 75c Weather bureau .75 .75
- ***b.*** A108 $1 US space telescope, shuttle 1.00 1.00
- ***c.*** A108 $2 Edmond Halley 2.00 2.00

Souvenir Sheet

814 A109 $4 Computer graphics 4.00 4.00

Miniature Sheet

A110

US Presidents
A111

1986, May *Perf. 11*

815 Sheet of 6 + 3 labels 3.75 3.75
- ***a.*** A110 10c George Washington .20 .20
- ***b.*** A110 20c John Adams .20 .20
- ***c.*** A110 30c Thomas Jefferson .25 .25
- ***d.*** A110 50c James Madison .40 .40
- ***e.*** A110 $1.50 James Monroe 1.10 1.10
- ***f.*** A110 $2 John Quincy Adams 1.60 1.60

Souvenir Sheet

Perf. 14

816 A111 $4 Washington 4.00 4.00

No. 815 contains 3 center labels picturing the great seal of the US.

Issue dates: #815, May 5. #816, May 7.

A112

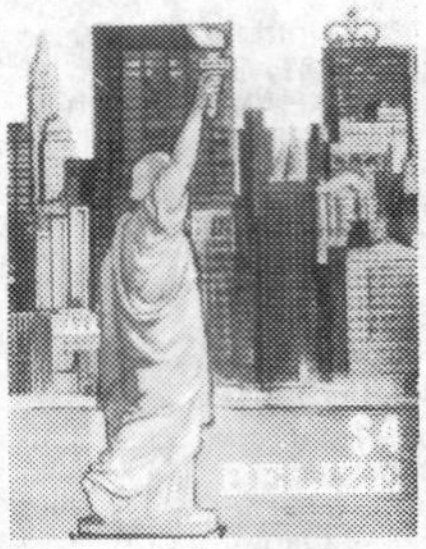

Statue of Liberty, Cent.
A113

Designs: 25c, Bartholdi, statue. 50c, Statue, US centennial celebration, Philadelphia, 1876. 75c, Statue close-up, flags, 1886 unveiling. $3, Flags, statue close-up. $4, Statue, New York City skyline.

1986, May 15 *Perf. 14*

817 Strip of 3 4.00 4.00
- ***a.*** A112 25c multicolored .25 .25
- ***b.*** A112 75c multicolored .75 .75
- ***c.*** A112 $3 multicolored 3.00 3.00

818 A112 50c multicolored .50 .50

Souvenir Sheet

819 A113 $4 multicolored 4.00 4.00

A114

AMERIPEX '86, Chicago, May 22-June 1 — A115

1986, May 22

820 Strip of 3 .75 .75
- ***a.*** A114 10c British Honduras No. 3 .20 .20
- ***b.*** A114 15c Stamp of 1981 .20 .20
- ***c.*** A114 50c US No. C3a .50 .50

821 Strip of 3 3.75 3.75
- ***a.*** A114 75c USS Constitution .75 .75
- ***b.*** A114 $1 Liberty Bell 1.00 1.00
- ***c.*** A114 $2 White House 2.00 2.00

Souvenir Sheet

822 A115 $4 Capitol Building 3.50 3.50

For overprints see Nos. 835-837.

1986 World Cup Soccer Championships, Mexico — A116

Designs: 25c, England vs. Brazil. 50c, Mexican player, Mayan statues. 75c, Belize players. $3, Aztec calendar stone, Mexico. $4, Flags composing soccer balls.

1986, June 16 Litho. *Perf. 11*

823 A116 25c multicolored .25 .25
824 A116 50c multicolored .50 .50
825 A116 75c multicolored .75 .75
826 A116 $3 multicolored 3.00 3.00
Nos. 823-826 (4) 4.50 4.50

Souvenir Sheet

Perf. 14

827 A116 $4 multicolored 4.00 4.00

Nos. 823-826 printed in sheets of 8 plus label picturing Azteca Stadium, 2 each value per sheet.

Nos. 823-827 Overprinted "ARGENTINA - /WINNERS 1986"

1986, Aug. 15

828 A116 25c multicolored .25 .25
829 A116 50c multicolored .50 .50
830 A116 75c multicolored .75 .75
831 A116 $3 multicolored 3.00 3.00
Nos. 828-831 (4) 4.50 4.50

Souvenir Sheet

832 A116 $4 multicolored 4.00 4.00

Wedding of Prince Andrew and Sarah Ferguson

A117 A118

1986, July 23 *Perf. 14x14½*

833 Strip of 3 3.25 3.25
- ***a.*** A117 25c Sarah .20 .20
- ***b.*** A117 75c Andrew .60 .60
- ***c.*** A117 $3 Couple 2.25 2.25

Souvenir Sheet

Perf. 14½

834 Sheet of 2 4.00 4.00
- ***a.*** A118 $1 Sarah, diff. 1.00 1.00
- ***b.*** A118 $3 Andrew, diff. 3.00 3.00

Size of No. 833c: 92x41mm.

Nos. 820-822 Ovptd. with STOCKHOLMIA '86 Emblems

1986, Aug. 28 Litho. *Perf. 14*

835 Strip of 3 .75 .75
- ***a.*** A114 10c multicolored .20 .20
- ***b.*** A114 15c multicolored .20 .20
- ***c.*** A114 50c multicolored .50 .50

836 Strip of 3 3.75 3.75
- ***a.*** A114 75c multicolored .75 .75
- ***b.*** A114 $1 multicolored 1.00 1.00
- ***c.*** A114 $2 multicolored 2.00 2.00

Souvenir Sheet

837 A115 $4 multicolored 4.00 4.00

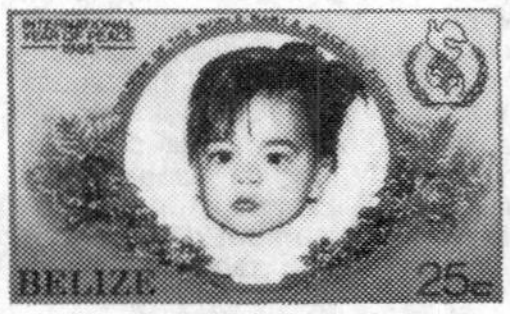

A119

Intl. Peace Year — A120

Children.

1986, Oct. 3 Litho. *Perf. 14*

838 A119 25c Infant .25 .25
839 A119 50c Caucasians .50 .50
840 A119 75c Oriental .75 .75
841 A119 $3 Indian, caucasian 3.00 3.00
Nos. 838-841 (4) 4.50 4.50

Souvenir Sheet

842 A120 $4 shown 4.00 4.00

Nos. 838-841 printed se-tenant in sheets of 8 (2 each) plus center label.

Fungi — A121 Toucans — A122

1986, Oct. 30 *Perf. 14*

843 A121 5c Amanita lilloi .20 .20
844 A122 10c Keel-billed toucan .20 .20
845 A121 20c Boletellus cubensis .30 .30
846 A122 25c Collared aracari .40 .40
847 A121 75c Psilocybe caerulescens 1.25 1.25
848 A122 $1 Emerald toucanet 1.50 1.50
849 A122 $1.25 Crimson-rumped toucan 1.75 1.75
850 A121 $2 Russula puiggarii 3.00 3.00
Nos. 843-850 (8) 8.60 8.60

Stamps of the same design printed in sheets of 8 plus center label picturing Audubon Society emblem.

Christmas
A123

Disney characters.

1986, Nov. 14 *Perf. 11*

851 Sheet of 9 6.50 6.50
- ***a.*** A123 2c Jose Carioca .20 .20
- ***b.*** A123 3c Carioca, Panchito, Donald .20 .20
- ***c.*** A123 4c Daisy .20 .20
- ***d.*** A123 5c Mickey, Minnie .20 .20
- ***e.*** A123 6c Carioca playing music .20 .20
- ***f.*** A123 50c Panchito, Donald .65 .65
- ***g.*** A123 65c Donald, Carioca .90 .90
- ***h.*** A123 $1.35 Donald 1.75 1.75
- ***i.*** A123 $2 Goofy 2.75 2.75

Souvenir Sheet

Perf. 14

852 A123 $4 Donald 6.00 6.00

A124

Marriage of Queen Elizabeth II and the Duke of Edinburgh, 40th Anniv. — A125

1987, Oct. 7 Litho. *Perf. 15*

853	A124	25c	Elizabeth, 1947	.20	.20
854	A124	75c	Couple, c. 1980	.55	.55
855	A124	$1	Elizabeth, 1986	.75	.75
856	A124	$4	Wearing robes of Order of the Garter	3.00	3.00
			Nos. 853-856 (4)	4.50	4.50

Souvenir Sheet

Perf. 14

857	A125	$6	shown	6.00	6.00

A126

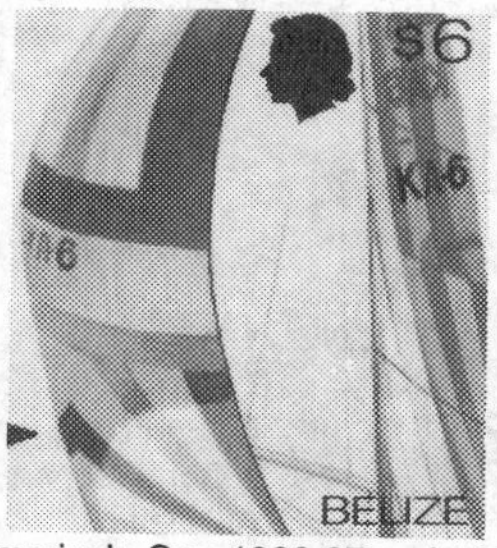

America's Cup 1986-87 — A127

Yachts that competed in the 1987 finals.

1987, Oct. 21 *Perf. 15*

858	A126	25c	America II	.25	.25
859	A126	75c	Stars and Stripes	.75	.75
860	A126	$1	Australia II	1.00	1.00
861	A126	$4	White Crusader	4.00	4.00
			Nos. 858-861 (4)	6.00	6.00

Souvenir Sheet

Perf. 14

862	A127	$6	Australia II sails	6.00	6.00

A128

Woodcarvings by Sir George Gabb (b. 1928) — A129

1987, Nov. 4 *Perf. 15*

863	A128	25c	Mother and Child	.20	.20
864	A128	75c	Standing Form	.60	.60
865	A128	$1	Love-Doves	.80	.80
866	A128	$4	Depiction of Music	3.25	3.25
			Nos. 863-866 (4)	4.85	4.85

Souvenir Sheet

Perf. 14

867	A129	$6	African Heritage	4.50	4.50

A130

Indigenous Primates — A131

1987, Nov. 11 *Perf. 15*

868	A130	25c	Black spider monkey	.25	.25
869	A130	75c	Male black howler	.75	.75
870	A130	$1	Spider monkeys	1.00	1.00
871	A130	$4	Howler monkeys	4.00	4.00
			Nos. 868-871 (4)	6.00	6.00

Souvenir Sheet

Perf. 14

872	A131	$6	Black spider, diff.	6.00	6.00

Natl. Girl Guides Movement, 50th Anniv. A132

Lady Olave Baden-Powell, Founder — A133

1987, Nov. 25 *Perf. 15*

873	A132	25c	Flag-bearers	.25	.25
874	A132	75c	Camping	.75	.75
875	A132	$1	On parade, camp	1.00	1.00
876	A132	$4	Olave Baden-Powell	4.00	4.00
			Nos. 873-876 (4)	6.00	6.00

Souvenir Sheet

Perf. 14

877	A133	$6	Lady Olave, diff.	6.00	6.00

Intl. Year of Shelter for the Homeless A134

1987, Dec. 3 *Perf. 15*

878	A134	25c	Tent dwellings	.25	.25
879	A134	75c	Urban slum	.75	.75
880	A134	$1	Tents, diff.	1.00	1.00
881	A134	$4	Construction	4.00	4.00
			Nos. 878-881 (4)	6.00	6.00

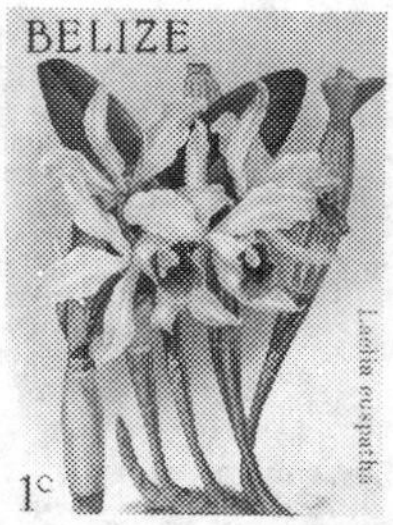

Orchids A135

Designs: Illustrations from Reichenbachia, published by Henry F. Sander in 1886.

1987, Dec. 16 Litho. *Perf. 14*

882	A135	1c	Laelia euspatha	.20	.20
883	A135	2c	Cattleya citrina	.20	.20
884	A135	3c	Masdevallia bachousiana	.20	.20
885	A135	4c	Cypripedium tautzianum	.20	.20
886	A135	5c	Trichopilia suavis alba	.20	.20
887	A135	6c	Odontoglossum hebraicum	.20	.20
888	A135	7c	Cattleya trianaei schroederiana	.20	.20
889	A135	10c	Saccolabium giganteum	.20	.20
890	A135	30c	Cattleya warscewiczii	.40	.40
891	A135	50c	Chysis bractescens	.65	.65
892	A135	70c	Cattleya rochellensis	.95	.95
893	A135	$1	Laelia elegans schilleriana	1.40	1.40
894	A135	$1.50	Laelia anceps percivaliana	2.00	2.00
895	A135	$3	Laelia gouldiana	4.00	4.00
			Nos. 882-895 (14)	11.00	11.00

Miniature Sheets

896	A135	$3	Odontoglossum roezlii	3.00	3.00
897	A135	$5	Cattleya dowiana aurea	5.00	5.00

Nos. 882-887 and 889-894 printed in blocks of six. Sheets of 14 contain 2 blocks of Nos. 882-887 plus 2 No. 888 and center label or 2 blocks of Nos. 889-894 plus center strip containing 2 No. 895 and center label. Center labels picture various illustrations from Reichenbachia.

Nos. 896, 897 contain one 44x51mm stamp.

Miniature Sheet

Easter — A136

Stations of the Cross (in sequential order): a, Jesus condemned to death. b, Carries the cross. c, Falls the first time. d, Meets his mother, Mary. e, Cyrenean takes up the cross. f, Veronica wipes Jesus's face. g, Falls the second time. h, Consoles the women of Jerusalem. i, Falls the third time. j, Stripped of his robes. k, Nailed to the cross. l, Dies. m, Taken down from the cross. n, Laid in the sepulcher.

1988, Mar. 21 *Perf. 14*

898		Sheet of 14 + label	5.75	5.75
a.-n.	A136	40c, any single	.40	.40

A $6 souvenir sheet was prepared but not issued.

1988 Summer Olympics, Seoul — A137

1988, Aug. 15 Litho. *Perf. 14*

899	A137	10c	Basketball	.20	.20
900	A137	25c	Volleyball	.25	.25
901	A137	60c	Table tennis	.60	.60
902	A137	75c	Diving	.75	.75
903	A137	$1	Judo	1.00	1.00
904	A137	$2	Field hockey	2.00	2.00
			Nos. 899-904 (6)	4.80	4.80

Souvenir Sheet

905	A137	$3	Women's gymnastics	3.00	3.00

Intl. Red Cross, 125th Anniv. A138

1988, Nov. 18 Litho. *Perf. 14*

906	A138	60c	Travelling nurse, 1912	.60	.60
907	A138	75c	Hospital ship, ambulance boat, 1937	.75	.75
908	A138	$1	Ambulance, 1956	1.00	1.00
909	A138	$2	Ambulance plane, 1940	2.00	2.00
			Nos. 906-909 (4)	4.35	4.35

Indigenous Small Animals A139

1989 Litho. Wmk. 384 *Perf. 14*

910	A139	10c	Gibnut (agouti)	.25	.25

Unwmk.

911	A139	25c	Four-eyed opossum, vert.	.65	.65
a.			Wmk. 384	.65	.65
912	A139	50c	Ant bear	1.40	1.40
913	A139	60c	like 10c	1.60	1.60
914	A139	75c	Antelope	2.00	2.00
915	A139	$2	Peccary	5.50	5.50
			Nos. 910-915 (6)	11.40	11.40

Issued: 10c, 7/23; #911a, 12/6; others, 2/24.

Moon Landing, 20th Anniv.

Common Design Type

Apollo 9: 25c, Command service and lunar modules docked in space. 50c, Command service module. 75c, Mission emblem. $1, First manned lunar module in space. $5, Apollo 11 command service module.

Perf. 14x13½

1989, July 20 Wmk. 384

Size of Nos. 680-681: 29x29mm

916	CD342	25c	multicolored	.20	.20
917	CD342	50c	multicolored	.45	.45
918	CD342	75c	multicolored	.65	.65
919	CD342	$1	multicolored	.90	.90
			Nos. 916-919 (4)	2.20	2.20

Souvenir Sheet

920	CD342	$5	multi	5.00	5.00

No. 920 Overprinted

WORLD STAMP EXPO '89™

United States Postal Service
Nov. 17 — 20 and
Nov. 24 — Dec. 3, 1989
Washington Convention Center
Washington, DC

1989, Nov. 17 *Perf. 14x13½*

921	CD342	$5	multicolored	5.00	5.00

World Stamp Expo '89.

No. 704 Surcharged

5c

1989, Nov. 15 *Perf. 15*
922 A89 5c on 6c multi 2.00

Christmas — A140 A141

Old churches.

Wmk. 384

1989, Dec. 13 Litho. *Perf. 14*
927 A140 10c Wesley .20 .20
928 A140 25c Baptist .25 .25
929 A140 60c St. John's Cathedral .60 .60
930 A140 75c St. Andrew's Presbyterian .75 .75
931 A140 $1 Holy Redeemer Cathedral 1.00 1.00
Nos. 927-931 (5) 2.80 2.80

Wmk. 373

1990, Mar. 1 Litho. *Perf. 14*

Birds and Butterfies: 5c, *Piranga leucoptera, Catonephele numilia* female. 10c, *Ramphastos sulfuratus, Nessaea aglaura.* 15c, *Fregata magnificens, Eurytides philolaus.* 25c, *Jabiru mycteria, Heliconius sapho.* 30c, *Ardea herodias, Colobura dirce.* 50c, *Icterus galbula, Hamadryas arethusia.* 60c, *Ara macao, Thecla regalis.* 75c, *Cyanerpes cyaneus, Callicore patelina.* $1, *Pulsatrix perspicillata, Caligo uranus.* $2, *Cyanocorax yncas, Philaethria dido.* $5, *Cathartes aura, Battus belus.* $10, *Pandion haliaetus, Papilio thoas.*

932 A141 5c multicolored .20 .20
933 A141 10c multicolored .20 .20
934 A141 15c multicolored .20 .20
935 A141 25c multicolored .25 .25
936 A141 30c multicolored .30 .30
937 A141 50c multicolored .50 .50
938 A141 60c multicolored .60 .60
939 A141 75c multicolored .75 .75
940 A141 $1 multicolored 1.00 1.00
941 A141 $2 multicolored 2.00 2.00
942 A141 $5 multicolored 5.00 5.00
943 A141 $10 multicolored 10.00 10.00
Nos. 932-943 (12) 21.00 21.00

The 10c exists inscribed "1993."
For overprints and surcharge see Nos. 944, 1021, 1030.

No. 940 Overprinted in Gold: "FIRST DOLLAR / COIN / 1990"

1990, Mar. 1
944 A141 $1 multicolored 1.00 1.00

Turtles A142

Wmk. 373

1990, Aug. 8 Litho. *Perf. 14*
945 A142 10c Green .20 .20
946 A142 25c Hawksbill .25 .25
947 A142 60c Loggerhead .60 .60
948 A142 75c Loggerhead, diff. .75 .75
949 A142 $1 Bocatora 1.00 1.00
950 A142 $2 Hicatee 2.00 2.00
Nos. 945-950 (6) 4.80 4.80

Battle of Britain, 50th Anniv. A143

Aircraft.

1990, Sept. 15 Wmk. 384 *Perf. 13½*
951 A143 10c Fairey Battle .20 .20
952 A143 25c Bristol Beaufort .25 .25
953 A143 60c Bristol Blenheim .60 .60
954 A143 75c Armstrong-Whitworth Whitley .75 .75
955 A143 $1 Vickers-Armstrong Wellington 1.00 1.00
956 A143 $2 Handley-Page Hampden 2.00 2.00
Nos. 951-956 (6) 4.80 4.80

Orchids — A144

1990, Nov. 1 Wmk. 384 *Perf. 14*
957 A144 25c Cattleya bowringiana .25 .25
958 A144 50c Rhyncholaelia digbyana .50 .50
959 A144 60c Sobralia macrantha .60 .60
960 A144 75c Chysis bractescens .75 .75
961 A144 $1 Vanilla planifolia 1.00 1.00
962 A144 $2 Epidendrum polyanthum 2.00 2.00
Nos. 957-962 (6) 5.10 5.10

Christmas.

Indigenous Fauna — A145

1991, Apr. 10
963 A145 25c Iguana .25 .25
964 A145 50c Crocodile .50 .50
965 A145 60c Manatee .60 .60
966 A145 75c Boa constrictor .75 .75
967 A145 $1 Tapir 1.00 1.00
968 A145 $2 Jaguar 2.00 2.00
Nos. 963-968 (6) 5.10 5.10

Elizabeth & Philip, Birthdays
Common Design Types

1991, June 17 ***Perf. 14½***
969 CD345 $1 multicolored 1.00 1.00
970 CD346 $1 multicolored 1.00 1.00
a. Pair, #969-970 + label 2.00 2.00

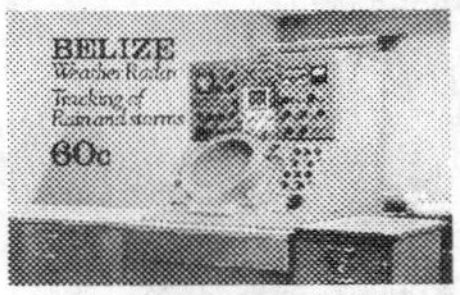

Hurricanes — A146

1991, July 31 Wmk. 373 *Perf. 14*
971 A146 60c Weather radar .60 .60
972 A146 75c Weather observation station .75 .75
973 A146 $1 Scene after hurricane 1.00 1.00
974 A146 $2 Hurricane Gilbert 2.00 2.00
Nos. 971-974 (4) 4.35 4.35

Independence, 10th Anniv. — A147

Famous Men: 25c, Thomas V. Ramos (1887-1955). 60c, Sir Isaiah Morter (1860-1924). 75c, Antonio Soberanis (1897-1975). $1, Santiago Ricalde (1920-1975).

1991, Sept. 4 Wmk. 384
975 A147 25c multicolored .30 .30
976 A147 60c multicolored .65 .65
977 A147 75c multicolored .80 .80
978 A147 $1 multicolored 1.10 1.10
Nos. 975-978 (4) 2.85 2.85

Folktales A148

Christmas.

Wmk. 373

1991, Nov. 6 Litho. *Perf. 14*
979 A148 25c Anansi .30 .30
980 A148 50c Jack-O-Lantern .55 .55
981 A148 60c Tata Duende, vert. .65 .65
982 A148 75c Xtabai .80 .80
983 A148 $1 Warrie Massa, vert. 1.10 1.10
984 A148 $2 Old Heg 2.25 2.25
Nos. 979-984 (6) 5.65 5.65

See Nos. 999-1002.

Orchids — A149

Easter: 25c, Gongora quinquenervis. 50c, Oncidium sphacelatum. 60c, Encyclia bractescens. 75c, Epidendrum ciliare. $1, Psygmorchis pusilla. $2, Galeandra batemanii.

1992, Apr. 1
985 A149 25c multicolored .30 .30
986 A149 50c multicolored .55 .55
987 A149 60c multicolored .65 .65
988 A149 75c multicolored .80 .80
989 A149 $1 multicolored 1.10 1.10
990 A149 $2 multicolored 2.25 2.25
Nos. 985-990 (6) 5.65 5.65

Famous Belizeans A150

Designs: 25c, Gwendolyn Lizarraga, MBE (1901-75). 60c, Rafael Fonseca, CMG, OBE (1921-78). 75c, Vivian Seay, MBE (1881-1971). $1, Samuel A. Haynes (1898-1971).

1992, Aug. 26 ***Perf. 13x12½***
991 A150 25c multicolored .30 .30
992 A150 60c multicolored .65 .65
993 A150 75c multicolored .80 .80
994 A150 $1 multicolored 1.10 1.10
Nos. 991-994 (4) 2.85 2.85

See Nos. 1013-1016.

Discovery of America, 500th Anniv. — A151

Mayan ruins, modern buildings: 25c, Xunantunich, National Assembly. 60c, Altun Ha, Supreme Court Building. 75c, Santa Rita, Tower Hill Sugar Factory. $5, Lamanai, The Citrus Company.

Perf. 13½x14

1992, Oct. 1 Litho. Wmk. 384
995 A151 25c multicolored .30 .30
996 A151 60c multicolored .65 .65
997 A151 75c multicolored .80 .80
998 A151 $5 multicolored 5.50 5.50
Nos. 995-998 (4) 7.25 7.25

Folklore Type of 1991

Christmas.

Perf. 13x12½

1992, Nov. 16 Litho. Wmk. 373
999 A148 25c Hashishi Pampi .25 .25
1000 A148 60c Cadejo .60 .60
1001 A148 $1 La Sucia, vert. 1.00 1.00
1002 A148 $5 Sisimito 5.00 5.00
Nos. 999-1002 (4) 6.85 6.85

Royal Air Force, 75th Anniv.
Common Design Type

Designs: 25c, Aerospatiale Puma. 50c, British Aerospace Harrier. 60c, DeHavilland Mosquito. 75c, Avro Lancaster. $1, Consolidated Liberator. $3, Short Stirling.

Wmk. 373

1993, Apr. 1 Litho. *Perf. 14*
1003 CD350 25c multicolored .25 .25
1004 CD350 50c multicolored .50 .50
1005 CD350 60c multicolored .65 .65
1006 CD350 75c multicolored .80 .80
1007 CD350 $1 multicolored 1.00 1.00
1008 CD350 $3 multicolored 3.25 3.25
Nos. 1003-1008 (6) 6.45 6.45

1993 World Orchid Conference, Glasgow — A152

Perf. 14½x14

1993, Apr. 24 Litho. Wmk. 384
1009 A152 25c Lycaste aromatica .30 .30
1010 A152 60c Sobralia decora .65 .65
1011 A152 $1 Maxillaria alba 1.10 1.10
1012 A152 $2 Brassavola nodosa 2.25 2.25
Nos. 1009-1012 (4) 4.30 4.30

Famous Belizeans Type of 1992

Designs: 25c, Herbert Watkin Beaumont (1880-1978). 60c, Dr. Selvyn Walford Young (1899-1977). 75c, Cleopatra White (1898-1987). $1, Dr. Karl Heusner (1872-1960).

Wmk. 384

1993, Aug. 11 Litho. *Perf. 14*
1013 A150 25c multicolored .30 .30
1014 A150 60c multicolored .65 .65
1015 A150 75c multicolored .85 .65
1016 A150 $1 multicolored 1.10 1.10
Nos. 1013-1016 (4) 2.90 2.70

Christmas A153

Wmk. 373

1993, Nov. 3 Litho. *Perf. 14*
1017 A153 25c Boom and chime band .30 .30
1018 A153 60c John Canoe dance .65 .65
1019 A153 75c Cortez dance .80 .80
1020 A153 $2 Maya Musical Group 2.25 2.25
Nos. 1017-1020 (4) 4.00 4.00

No. 940 Ovptd. with Hong Kong '94 Emblem

Wmk. 373

1994, Feb. 18 Litho. *Perf. 14*
1021 A141 $1 multicolored 1.10 1.10

Royal Visit — A154

Designs: 25c, Belize, United Kingdom Flags. 60c, Queen Elizabeth II wearing hat. 75c, Queen. $1, Queen, Prince Philip.

Perf. 14½x14

1994, Feb. 24 Litho. Wmk. 373

1022 A154 25c multicolored .30 .30
1023 A154 60c multicolored .65 .65
1024 A154 75c multicolored .80 .80
1025 A154 $1 multicolored 1.10 1.10
Nos. 1022-1025 (4) 2.85 2.85

Bats A155

Wmk. 384

1994, May 30 Litho. *Perf. 14*

1026 A155 25c Insect feeder .25 .25
1027 A155 60c Fruit feeder .60 .60
1028 A155 75c Fish feeder .75 .75
1029 A155 $2 Common vampire 2.00 2.00
Nos. 1026-1029 (4) 3.60 3.60

No. 939 Surcharged

Wmk. 373

1994, Aug. 18 Litho. *Perf. 14*

1030 A141 10c on 75c multi .20 .20

Christmas — A156

Orchids: 25c, Cycnoches chlorochilon. 60c, Brassavolas cucullata. 75c, Sobralia mucronata. $1, Nidema Boothii.

1994, Nov. 7 Wmk. 384

1031 A156 25c multicolored .25 .25
1032 A156 60c multicolored .60 .60
1033 A156 75c multicolored .75 .75
1034 A156 $1 multicolored 1.00 1.00
Nos. 1031-1034 (4) 2.60 2.60

For overprints see Nos. 1051-1054.

Insects A157

Wmk. 373

1995, Jan. 11 Litho. *Perf. 14*

1035 A157 5c Ground beetle .20 .20
1036 A157 10c Harlequin beetle .20 .20
1037 A157 15c Giant water bug .20 .20
1038 A157 25c Peanut-head bug .25 .25
1039 A157 30c Coconut weevil .30 .30
1040 A157 50c Mantis .50 .50
1041 A157 60c Tarantula wasp .60 .60
1042 A157 75c Rhinoceros beetle .75 .75
1043 A157 $1 Metallic wood borer 1.00 1.00
1044 A157 $2 Dobson fly 2.00 2.00
1045 A157 $5 Click beetle 5.00 5.00
1046 A157 $10 Long-horned beetle 10.00 10.00
Nos. 1035-1046 (12) 21.00 21.00

Nos. 1035-1046 exist inscribed "1996."
For overprints see Nos. 1063-1066.

End of World War II, 50th Anniv.
Common Design Type

Designs: 25c, War Memorial Cenotaph. 60c, Remembrance Sunday. 75c, British Honduras Forestry Unit. $1, Wellington Bomber.

Wmk. 373

1995, May 8 Litho. *Perf. 13½*

1047 CD351 25c multicolored .30 .30
1048 CD351 60c multicolored .65 .65
1049 CD351 75c multicolored .80 .80
1050 CD351 $1 multicolored 1.10 1.10
Nos. 1047-1050 (4) 2.85 2.85

Nos. 1031-1034 Ovptd. in Blue

1995, Sept. 1 Wmk. 384 *Perf. 14*

1051 A156 25c on No. 1031 .25 .25
1052 A156 60c on No. 1032 .60 .60
1053 A156 75c on No. 1033 .75 .75
1054 A156 $1 on No. 1034 1.00 1.00
Nos. 1051-1054 (4) 2.60 2.60

UN, 50th Anniv.
Common Design Type

Designs: 25c, M113 Light reconnaissance vehicle. 60c, Sultan, armored command vehicle. 75c, Leyland/DAF 8x4 "Drops" vehicle. $2, Warrior infantry combat vehicle.

Wmk. 384

1995, Oct. 24 Litho. *Perf. 14*

1055 CD353 25c multicolored .25 .25
1056 CD353 60c multicolored .60 .60
1057 CD353 75c multicolored .75 .75
1058 CD353 $2 multicolored 2.00 2.00
Nos. 1055-1058 (4) 3.60 3.60

Christmas — A158

Doves: 25c, Blue ground. 60c, White-fronted. 75c, Ruddy ground. $1, White-winged.

1995, Nov. 6 Wmk. 373

1059 A158 25c multicolored .25 .25
1060 A158 60c multicolored .60 .60
1061 A158 75c multicolored .75 .75
1062 A158 $1 multicolored 1.00 1.00
Nos. 1059-1062 (4) 2.60 2.60

Nos. 1037, 1039-1040, 1044 Ovptd.

Wmk. 373

1996, May 17 Litho. *Perf. 14*

1063 A157 15c on #1037 .20 .20
1064 A157 30c on #1039 .30 .30
1065 A157 50c on #1040 .50 .50
1066 A157 $2 on #1044 2.00 2.00
Nos. 1063-1066 (4) 3.00 3.00

CAPEX '96 A159

Trains: 25c, Unloading banana train onto freighter, Commerce Bight Pier. 60c, Engine No. 1, Stann Creek Station. 75c, Mahogany log train, Hunslet 0-6-0 Side Tank Engine No. 4. $3, LMS Jubilee Class 4-6-0 Locomotive No. 5602 "British Honduras."

Perf. 13½x13

1996, June 6 Litho. Wmk. 373

1067 A159 25c multicolored .25 .25
1068 A159 60c multicolored .60 .60
1069 A159 75c multicolored .75 .75
1070 A159 $3 multicolored 3.00 3.00
Nos. 1067-1070 (4) 4.60 4.60

Christmas — A160

Orchids: 25c, Epidendrum stamfordianum. 60c, Oncidium carthagenense. 75c, Oerstedella verrucosa. $1, Coryanthes speciosa.

Wmk. 373

1996, Nov. 6 Litho. *Perf. 14*

1071 A160 25c multicolored .25 .25
1072 A160 60c multicolored .60 .60
1073 A160 75c multicolored .75 .75
1074 A160 $1 multicolored 1.00 1.00
Nos. 1071-1074 (4) 2.60 2.60

Hong Kong '97 A161

Cattle: 25c, Red poll. 60c, Brahman. 75c, Longhorn. $1, Charbray.

Wmk. 373

1997, Feb. 12 Litho. *Perf. 14*

1075 A161 25c multicolored .30 .30
1076 A161 60c multicolored .70 .70
1077 A161 75c multicolored .85 .85
1078 A161 $1 multicolored 1.10 1.10
Nos. 1075-1078 (4) 2.95 2.95

Snakes — A162

Howler Monkeys — A163

25c, Coral snake. 60c, Green vine snake. 75c, Yellow-jawed tommygoff. $1, Speckled racer.

Wmk. 373

1997, May 28 Litho. *Perf. 14*

1079 A162 25c multicolored .30 .30
1080 A162 60c multicolored .65 .65
1081 A162 75c multicolored .80 .80
1082 A162 $1 multicolored 1.10 1.10
Nos. 1079-1082 (4) 2.85 2.85

Wmk. 373

1997, Aug. 13 Litho. *Perf. 14*

World Wildlife Fund: 10c, Adult male. 25c, Female feeding. 60c, Female with infant. 75c, Juvenile feeding.

1083 A163 10c multicolored .20 .20
1084 A163 25c multicolored .25 .25
1085 A163 60c multicolored .60 .60
1086 A163 75c multicolored .75 .75
Nos. 1083-1086 (4) 1.80 1.80

Christmas — A164

Orchids: 25c, Maxillaria elatior. 60c, Dimerandra emarginata. 75c, Macradenia brassavolae. $1, Ornithocephalus gladiatus.

Wmk. 373

1997, Nov. 21 Litho. *Perf. 14*

1087 A164 25c multicolored .25 .25
1088 A164 60c multicolored .65 .65
1089 A164 75c multicolored .80 .80
1090 A164 $1 multicolored 1.10 1.10
Nos. 1087-1090 (4) 2.80 2.80

Diana, Princess of Wales (1961-97)
Common Design Type

Designs: a, Up close portrait, smiling. b, Wearing evening dress. c, Up close portrait, serious. d, Holding bouquet of flowers.

Perf. 14½x14

1998, Mar. 31 Litho. Wmk. 373

1091 CD355 $1 Sheet of 4, #a.-d. 4.50 4.50

University of West Indies, 50th Anniv. A165

Wmk. 373

1998, July 22 Litho. *Perf. 13*

1092 A165 $1 multicolored 1.00 1.00

Organization of American States, 50th Anniv. A166

Designs: 25c, Children working computers, connecting high schools to the internet. $1, Map of Central America, Inter American Drug Abuse Control Commission.

1998, July 22

1093 A166 25c multicolored .25 .25
1094 A166 $1 multicolored 1.00 1.00

Battle of St. George's Cay, Bicent. A167

Views of Old Belize from St. George, vert: No. 1095, Woman, child beside small boat. No. 1096, Soldiers at dock, cannon. No. 1097, Cannon balls, cannon, boats in water.

25c, Bayman gun flats. 60c, Bayman sloops. 75c, Schooners. $1, HMS Merlin. $2, Spanish flagship.

1998, Aug. 5 *Perf. 13½*

1095 A167 10c multicolored .20 .20
1096 A167 10c multicolored .20 .20
1097 A167 10c multicolored .20 .20
a. Strip of 3, #1095-1097 .30 .30
1098 A167 25c multicolored .25 .25
1099 A167 60c multicolored .60 .60
1100 A167 75c multicolored .75 .75
1101 A167 $1 multicolored 1.00 1.00
1102 A167 $2 multicolored 2.00 2.00
Nos. 1095-1102 (8) 5.20 5.20

A168

A169

Christmas - Flowers: 25c, Brassia maculata. 60c, Encyclia radiata. 75c, Stanhopea ecornuta. $1, Isochilius carnosiflorus.

1998, Nov. 4 *Perf. 14*

1103 A168 25c multicolored .25 .25
1104 A168 60c multicolored .60 .60
1105 A168 75c multicolored .75 .75
1106 A168 $1 multicolored 1.00 1.00
Nos. 1103-1106 (4) 2.60 2.60

1999, Mar. 17 *Perf. 13*

Easter - Orchids: 10c, Eucharis grandiflora. 25c, Hippeastrum puniceum. 60c, Zephyranthes citrina. $1, Hymenocallis littoralis.

1107	A169	10c multicolored	.15	.15
1108	A169	25c multicolored	.25	.25
1109	A169	60c multicolored	.60	.60
1110	A169	$1 multicolored	1.00	1.00
		Nos. 1107-1110 (4)	2.00	2.00

UPU, 125th Anniv. A170

1999, Oct. 18 *Perf. 13¼*

1111	A170	25c Bicycle	.25	.25
1112	A170	60c Truck	.60	.60
1113	A170	75c Mailship "Dee"	.75	.75
1114	A170	$1 Airplane	1.00	1.00
		Nos. 1111-1114 (4)	2.60	2.60

Christmas A171

Designs: 25c, Holy Family with Jesus and St. John, by school of Peter Paul Rubens. 60c, The Holy Family with St. John, by unknown artist. 75c, Madonna with Child, St. John and Angel, by unknown artist. $1, Madonna with Child and St. John by Andrea del Salerno.

1999, Dec. 6 *Perf. 14*

1115	A171	25c multicolored	.25	.25
1116	A171	60c multicolored	.60	.60
1117	A171	75c multicolored	.75	.75
1118	A171	$1 multicolored	1.00	1.00
		Nos. 1115-1118 (4)	2.60	2.60

SEMI-POSTAL STAMPS

World Cup Soccer Championship — SP1

Designs: 20c+10c, 30c+15c, Scotland vs. New Zealand (diff.). 40c+20c, Kuwait vs. France. 60c+30c, Italy vs. Brazil. No. B5, France vs. Northern Ireland. $1.50+75c, Austria vs. Chile. No. B7, Italy vs. Germany, vert. $2+$1, England vs. France, vert.

1982, Dec. 10 **Litho.** *Perf. 14*

B1	SP1	20c +10c multi	.25	.25
B2	SP1	30c +15c multi	.35	.35
B3	SP1	40c +20c multi	.45	.45
B4	SP1	60c +30c multi	.75	.75
B5	SP1	$1 +50c multi	3.00	3.00
B6	SP1	$1.50 +75c multi	5.00	5.00
		Nos. B1-B6 (6)	9.80	9.80

Souvenir Sheets

Perf. 14½

B7	SP1	$1 +50c multi	3.50	3.50
B8	SP1	$2 +$1 multi	6.00	6.00

Nos. B7-B8 each contain one 50x70mm stamp.

POSTAGE DUE STAMPS

Numeral — D2

Each denomination has different border.

1976, July 1 **Litho.** **Wmk. 373**

J6	D2	1c green & red	.20	.20
J7	D2	2c violet & rose lil	.20	.20
J8	D2	5c ocher & brt grn	.20	.20
J9	D2	15c brown org & yel grn	.30	.30
J10	D2	25c slate grn & org	.50	.50
		Nos. J6-J10 (5)	1.40	1.40

CAYES OF BELIZE

Catalogue values for all unused stamps in this country are for Never Hinged items.

Spiny Lobster A1

Perf. 14½x14, 14x14½

1984, May 30 **Litho.** **Unwmk.**

1	A1	1c shown	.20	.20
2	A1	2c Blue crab	.20	.20
3	A1	5c Red-footed booby	.20	.20
4	A1	10c Brown pelican	.20	.20
5	A1	15c White-tailed deer	.20	.20
6	A1	25c Lighthouse, English Caye	.20	.20
7	A1	75c Spanish galleon, Santa Yaga, c. 1750	.55	.55
8	A1	$3 Map of Ambergris Caye, vert.	2.25	2.25
	a.	Souvenir booklet	7.50	
9	A1	$5 Jetty, windsurfers	3.75	3.75
		Nos. 1-9 (9)	7.75	7.75

No. 8a contains four panes. One has one $3 stamp, one has a block of four 25c stamps, two have blocks of four 75c stamps but different text. The stamps are larger than Nos. 6-8, have slightly different colors and are perf. 14½.

The $1 stamp was not issued. Eighteen sheets of 40 were sold for postage by accident.

Lloyd's List Issue

Common Design Type

1984, June 6 *Perf. 14½x14*

10	CD335	25c Queen Elizabeth 2	.20	.20
11	CD335	75c Lutine Bell	.55	.55
12	CD335	$1 Loss of the Fishburn	.75	.75
13	CD335	$2 Trafalgar Sword	1.50	1.50
		Nos. 10-13 (4)	3.00	3.00

1984 Summer Olympics, Los Angeles — A2

1984, Oct. 5 *Perf. 15*

14	A2	10c Yachting	.20	.20
15	A2	15c Windsurfing	.20	.20
16	A2	75c Swimming	.75	.75
17	A2	$2 Kayaking	2.00	2.00
		Nos. 14-17 (4)	3.15	3.15

No. 17 inscribed Canoeing.

First Cayes Stamps, 90th Anniv. A3

1984, Nov. 5

18	A3	10c 1895 cover	.20	.20
19	A3	15c Sydney Cuthbert	.20	.20
20	A3	75c Cuthbert's steam yacht	.55	.55
21	A3	$2 British Honduras #133	1.50	1.50
		Nos. 18-21 (4)	2.45	2.45

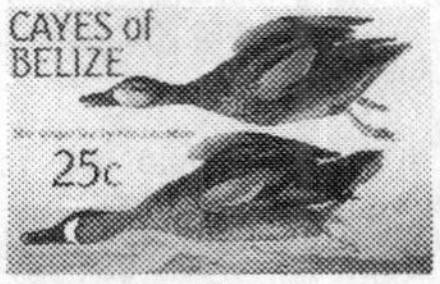

Audubon Birth Bicentenary — A4

Illustrations by Audubon.

1985, May 20 *Perf. 14*

22	A4	25c Blue-winged teal	.20	.20
23	A4	75c Semipalmated sandpiper	.55	.55
24	A4	$1 Yellow-crowned night heron, vert.	.75	.75
25	A4	$3 Common gallinule	2.25	2.25
		Nos. 22-25 (4)	3.75	3.75

Shipwrecks — A5

Designs: a, Oxford, c. 1675. b, Santa Yaga, 1780. c, No. 27, Comet, 1822. d, Yeldham, 1800.

1985, June 5 *Perf. 15*

26	A5	$1 Strip of 4+label, #a.-d.	4.00	4.00

Souvenir Sheet

Perf. 13½x14

27	A5	$5 multicolored	5.00	5.00

No. 27 contains one 38x51mm stamp. No. 26 has continuous design.

BENIN

bə-ˈnin

French Colony

LOCATION — West Coast of Africa
GOVT. — French Possession
AREA — 8,627 sq. mi.
POP. — 493,000 (approx.)
CAPITAL — Benin

In 1895 the French possessions known as Benin were incorporated into the colony of Dahomey and postage stamps of Dahomey superseded those of Benin. Dahomey took the name Benin when it became a republic in 1975.

100 Centimes = 1 Franc

Catalogue values for unused stamps in this country are for Never Hinged items, beginning with Scott 342 in the regular postage section, Scott C240 in the airpost section, Scott J44 in the postage due section, and Scott Q8 in the parcel post section.

Handstamped on Stamps of French Colonies **BÉNIN**

1892 **Unwmk.** *Perf. 14x13½*

Black Overprint

1	A9	1c blk, *bluish*	115.00	95.00
2	A9	2c brn, *buff*	85.00	72.50
3	A9	4c claret, *lav*	35.00	30.00
4	A9	5c grn, *grnsh*	13.00	12.00
5	A9	10c blk, *lavender*	57.50	45.00
6	A9	15c blue	20.00	8.00
7	A9	20c red, *grn*	160.00	150.00
8	A9	25c blk, *rose*	67.50	37.50
9	A9	30c brn, *yelsh*	140.00	100.00
10	A9	35c blk, *orange*	140.00	100.00
11	A9	40c red, *straw*	110.00	90.00
12	A9	75c car, *rose*	275.00	225.00
13	A9	1fr brnz grn, *straw*	300.00	275.00

Red Overprint

14	A9	15c blue	70.00	45.00

Blue Overprint

15	A9	5c grn, *grnsh*	1,750.	700.00
15A	A9	15c blue	1,750.	700.00

Nos. 1-13 all exist with overprint inverted, and several with it double. These sell for more (see the *Scott Classic Specialized Catalogue*). The overprints of Nos. 1-15A are of four types, three without accent mark on "E." They exist diagonal.

Counterfeits exist of Nos. 1-19.

Additional Surcharge in Red or Black **40**

1892

16	A9	01c on 5c grn, *grnsh*	225.	175.
	a.	Double surcharge	600.00	600.00
17	A9	40c on 15c blue	140.	60.
	a.	Double surcharge		2,500.
18	A9	75c on 15c blue	625.	425.
19	A9	75c on 15c bl (Bk)	2,500.	1,900.

Counterfeits exist.

Navigation and Commerce
A3 A4

1893 **Typo.** *Perf. 14x13½*

Name of Colony in Blue or Carmine

20	A3	1c blk, *bluish*	1.90	1.40
21	A3	2c brn, *buff*	2.25	1.75
22	A3	4c claret, *lav*	2.50	1.75
23	A3	5c grn, *grnsh*	3.25	2.00
24	A3	10c blk, *lavender*	3.25	2.40
25	A3	15c blue, quadrille paper	20.00	14.00
26	A3	20c red, *grn*	10.00	6.50
27	A3	25c blk, *rose*	27.50	16.00
28	A3	30c brn, *bis*	12.50	9.50
29	A3	40c red, *straw*	3.75	2.25
30	A3	50c car, *rose*	3.00	2.00
31	A3	75c vio, *org*	6.25	4.25
32	A3	1fr brnz grn, *straw*	42.50	35.00
		Nos. 20-32 (13)	138.65	98.80

Perf. 13½x14 stamps are counterfeits.

1894 *Perf. 14x13½*

33	A4	1c blk, *bluish*	2.00	1.40
34	A4	2c brn, *buff*	2.00	1.40
35	A4	4c claret, *lav*	2.00	1.40
36	A4	5c grn, *grnsh*	2.50	1.40
37	A4	10c blk, *lavender*	3.50	2.25
38	A4	15c bl, quadrille paper	4.50	2.25
39	A4	20c red, *grn*	4.50	3.50
40	A4	25c blk, *rose*	6.50	2.50
41	A4	30c brn, *bis*	4.00	2.50
42	A4	40c red, *straw*	11.00	7.00
43	A4	50c car, *rose*	15.00	7.50
44	A4	75c vio, *org*	9.50	8.00
45	A4	1fr brnz grn, *straw*	2.50	2.00
		Nos. 33-45 (13)	69.50	43.10

Perf. 13½x14 stamps are counterfeits.

PEOPLE'S REPUBLIC OF BENIN

LOCATION — West Coast of Africa
GOVT. — Republic.
AREA — 43,483 sq. mi.
POP. — 6,305,567 (1999 est.)
CAPITAL — Porto Novo (Cotonou is the seat of government)

The Republic of Dahomey proclaimed itself the People's Republic of

Benin on Nov. 30, 1975. See Dahomey for stamps issued before then.

Catalogue values for unused stamps in this section are for Never Hinged items.

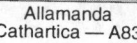

Allamanda Cathartica — A83

Flag Bearers, Arms of Benin — A84

Flowers: 35fr, Ixora coccinea. 45fr, Hibiscus, 60fr, Phaemeria magnifica.

Unwmk.

1975, Dec. 8 Photo. *Perf. 13*

342 A83 10fr lilac & multi .20 .20
343 A83 35fr gray & multi .25 .20
344 A83 45fr multi .35 .25
345 A83 60fr blue & multi .40 .30
Nos. 342-345 (4) 1.20 .95

For surcharges see Nos. 618, 719, 723, 788.

1976, Apr. 30 Litho. *Perf. 12*

Design: 60fr, Speaker, wall with "PRPB," flag and arms of Benin. 100fr, Flag and arms of Benin.

346 A84 50fr ocher & multi .30 .20
347 A84 60fr ocher & multi .30 .20
348 A84 100fr multi .55 .40
Nos. 346-348 (3) 1.15 .80

Proclamation of the People's Republic of Benin. Nov. 30, 1975.

A.G. Bell, Satellite and 1876 Telephone — A85

1976, July 9 Litho. *Perf. 13*

349 A985 200fr lilac, red & brn 1.10 .45

Centenary of first telephone call by Alexander Graham Bell, Mar. 10, 1876.

Dahomey Nos. 277-278 Surcharged

1976, July 19 Photo. *Perf. 12½x13*

350 A57 50fr on 1fr multi .30 .20
351 A57 60fr on 2fr multi .40 .20

For overprint and surcharge see Nos. 654A, 711.

African Jamboree, Nigeria 1976 — A86

1976, Aug. 16 Litho. *Perf. 12½x13*

352 A86 50fr Scouts Cooking .30 .20
353 A86 70fr Three scouts .40 .30

Blood Bank, Cotonou — A87

Designs: 50fr, Accident and first aid station. 60fr, Blood donation.

1976, Sept. 24 Litho. *Perf. 13*

354 A87 5fr multicolored .20 .20
355 A87 50fr multicolored .30 .20
356 A87 60fr multicolored .35 .25
Nos. 354-356 (3) .85 .65

National Blood Donors Day.

A88

A89

1976, Oct. 4 Litho. *Perf. 13x12½*

357 A88 20fr Manioc .20 .20
358 A88 50fr Corn .30 .20
359 A88 60fr Cacao .30 .20
360 A88 150fr Cotton .80 .60
Nos. 357-360 (4) 1.60 1.20

Natl. agricultural production campaign. For surcharge see No. 565.

1976, Oct. 25

361 A89 50fr Classroom .30 .20

Third anniversary of KPARO newspaper, used in local language studies.

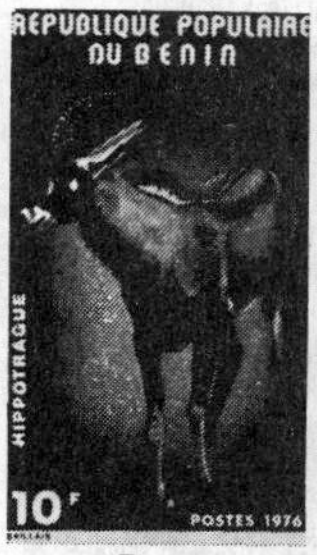

Roan Antelope — A90

Flags, Wall, Broken Chains — A91

Penhari National Park: 30fr, Buffalo. 50fr, Hippopotamus, horiz. 70fr, Lion.

1976, Nov. 8 Photo.

362 A90 10fr multicolored .20 .20
363 A90 30fr multicolored .20 .20
364 A90 50fr multicolored .30 .20
365 A90 70fr multicolored .40 .25
Nos. 362-365 (4) 1.10 .85

1976, Nov. 30 Litho. *Perf. 12½*

Design: 150fr, Corn, raised hands with weapons.

366 A91 40fr multicolored .20 .20
367 A91 150fr multicolored .80 .60

First anniversary of proclamation of the People's Republic of Benin.

Table Tennis, Map of Africa (Games' Emblem) — A92

Design: 50fr, Stadium, Cotonou.

1976, Dec. 26 Litho. *Perf. 13*

368 A92 10fr multi .20 .20
369 A92 50fr multi .30 .20

West African University Games, Cotonou, Dec. 26-31.

Europafrica Issue

Planes over Africa and Europe — A93

1977, May 13 Litho. *Perf. 13*

370 A93 200fr multi .70 .55

For surcharge see No. 590.

Snake — A94

1977, June 13 Litho. *Perf. 13x13½*

371 A94 2fr shown .20 .20
372 A94 3fr Tortoise .20 .20
373 A94 5fr Zebus .20 .20
374 A94 10fr Cats .20 .20
Nos. 371-374 (4) .80 .80

Patients at Clinic — A95

1977, Aug. 2 Litho. *Perf. 12½*

375 A95 100fr multi .60 .40

World Rheumatism Year.

Karate, Map of Africa — A96

Designs: 100fr, Javelin, map of Africa, Benin Flag, horiz. 150fr, Hurdles.

1977, Aug. 30 Litho. *Perf. 12½*

376 A96 90fr multi .35 .20
377 A96 100fr multi .45 .35
378 A96 150fr multi .60 .45
a. Souvenir sheet of 3, #376-378 2.00 2.00
Nos. 376-378 (3) 1.40 1.00

2nd West African Games, Lagos, Nigeria. For surcharge see No. 925.

Chairman Mao — A97

Lister and Vaporizer — A98

1977, Sept. 9 Litho. *Perf. 13x12½*

379 A97 100fr multicolored .50 .40

Mao Tse-tung (1893-1976), Chinese communist leader.

1977, Sept. 20 Engr. *Perf. 13*

Designs: 150fr, Scalpels and flames, symbols of antisepsis, and Red Cross.

380 A98 150fr multi .75 .60
381 A98 210fr multi 1.25 .80

Joseph Lister (1827-1912), surgeon, founder of antiseptic surgery.
For surcharges see Nos. 560, 566, 919.

Guelege Mask, Ethnographic Museum, Porto Novo — A99

Designs: 50fr, Jar, symbol of unity, emblem of King Ghezo, Historical Museum, Abomey, vert. 210fr, Abomey Museum.

1977, Oct. 17 *Perf. 13*

382 A99 50fr red & multi .30 .20
383 A99 60fr blk, bl & bister .35 .25
384 A99 210fr multi 1.25 .80
Nos. 382-384 (3) 1.90 1.25

For surcharge see Nos. 562, 920.

Atacora Falls — A100

Mother and Child, Owl of Wisdom — A101

Tourist Publicity: 60fr, Pile houses, Ganvie, horiz. 150fr, Round huts, Savalou.

1977, Oct. 24 Litho. *Perf. 12½*

385 A100 50fr multi .30 .25
386 A100 60fr multi .40 .25
387 A100 150fr multi 1.00 .70
a. Souvenir sheet of 3, #385-387 2.00 2.00
Nos. 385-387 (3) 1.70 1.20

Perf. 12½x13, 13x12½

1977, Dec. 3 Photo.

150fr, Chopping down magical tree, horiz.

388 A101 60fr multi .35 .25
389 A101 150fr multi .80 .60

Campaign against witchcraft.
For surcharge see No. 576.

Battle Scene — A102

1978, Jan. 16 Litho. *Perf. 12½*
390 A102 50fr multi .35 .20

Victory of people of Benin over imperialist forces.

Map, People and Houses of Benin — A103

1978, Feb. 1
391 A103 50fr multi .35 .20

General population and dwelling census.

Alexander Fleming, Microscope and Penicillin — A104

1978, Mar. 12 Litho. *Perf. 13*
392 A104 300fr multi 2.00 1.10

Alexnader Fleming (1881-1955), 50th anniversary of discovery of penicillin.

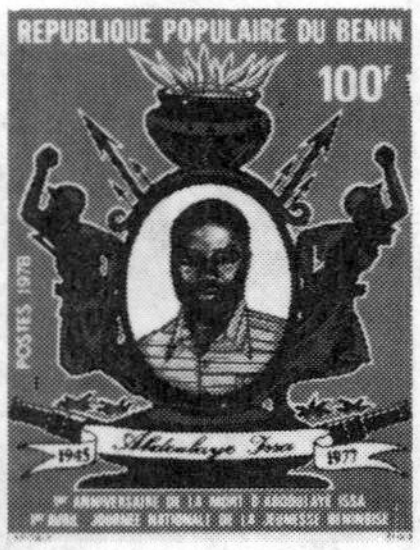

Abdoulaye Issa, Weapons and Fighters A105

1978, Apr. 1 *Perf. 12½x13*
393 A105 100fr red, blk & gold .65 .40

First anniversary of death of Abdoulaye Issa and National Day of Benin's Youth.

Ed Hadj Omar and Horseback Rider — A106

Design: 90fr, L'Almamy Samory Toure (1830-1900) and horseback riders.

1976, Apr. 10 *Perf. 13x12½*
394 A106 90fr red & multi .60 .35
395 A106 100fr multi .65 .40

African heroes of resistance against colonialism.

ITU Emblem, Satellite, Landscape — A107

1978, May 17 Litho. *Perf. 13*
396 A107 100fr multi .65 .40

10th World Telecommunications Day.

Soccer Player, Stadium, Argentina '78 Emblem — A108

Designs (Argentina '78 Emblem and): 300fr, Soccer players and ball, vert. 500fr, Soccer player, globe with ball on map.

1978, June 1 Litho. *Perf. 12½*
397 A108 200fr multi 1.50 .70
398 A108 300fr multi 2.00 1.10
399 A108 500fr multi 3.50 1.75
a. Souvenir sheet of 3 7.00 7.00
Nos. 397-399 (3) 7.00 3.55

11th World Cup Soccer Championship, Argentina, June 1-25. No. 399a contains 3 stamps similar to Nos. 397-399 in changed colors.
For surcharges see Nos. 591, 593, 595-596.

Nos. 397-399a Overprinted in Red Brown:
a. FINALE / ARGENTINE: 3 / HOLLANDE: 1
b. CHAMPION / 1978 / ARGENTINE
c. 3e BRESIL / 4e ITALIE

1978, June 25 Litho. *Perf. 12½*
400 A108 (a) 200fr multi 1.40 .75
401 A108 (b) 300fr multi 2.00 1.10
402 A108 (c) 500fr multi 3.50 1.75
a. Souvenir sheet of 3 7.00 7.00
Nos. 400-402 (3) 6.90 3.60

Argentina's victory in 1978 Soccer Championship.

Games' Flag over Africa, Basketball Players — A109

Designs: 60fr, Map of Africa, volleyball players. 80fr, Map of Benin, bicyclists.

1978, July 13 *Perf. 13x12½*
403 A109 50fr lt bl & multi .35 .20
404 A109 60fr ultra & multi .40 .25
405 A109 80fr multi .55 .35
a. Souvenir sheet of 3 1.40 1.40
Nos. 403-405 (3) 1.30 .80

3rd African Games, Algiers, July 13-28. No. 405a contains 3 stamps in changed colors similar to Nos. 403-405.

Martin Luther King, Jr. — A110

1978, July 30 *Perf. 12½*
406 A110 300fr multi 2.00 1.10

Martin Luther King, Jr. (1929-1968), American civil rights leader.
For surcharge see No. 592.

Kanna Taxi, Oueme A111

60fr Leatherworker & goods. 70fr, Drummer & tom-toms. 100fr, Metalworker & calabashes.

1978, Aug. 26
407 A111 50fr multi .35 .20
408 A111 60fr multi .40 .25
409 A111 70fr multi .45 .30
410 A111 100fr multi .65 .40
Nos. 407-410 (4) 1.85 1.15

Getting to know Benin through its provinces.

Map of Italy and Exhibition Poster — A112

1978, Aug. 26 Litho. *Perf. 13*
411 A112 200fr multi 1.40 .70

Riccione 1978 Philatelic Exhibition.
For overprint see No. 537.

Poultry Breeding — A113

1978 Oct. 5 Photo. *Perf. 12½x13*
412 A113 10fr Turkeys .20 .20
413 A113 20fr Ducks .20 .20
414 A113 50fr Chicken .35 .35
415 A113 60fr Guinea fowl .40 .40
Nos. 412-415 (4) 1.15 1.15

Royal Messenger, UPU Emblem A114

UPU Emblem and: 60fr, Boatsman, ship & car, vert. 90fr, Special messenger & plane, vert.

1978, Oct. 16 *Perf. 13x12½, 12½x13*
416 A114 50fr multi .35 .35
417 A114 60fr multi .40 .40
418 A114 90fr multi .60 .60
Nos. 416-418 (3) 1.35 1.35

Centenary of change of "General Postal Union" to "Universal Postal Union."
For surcharge see No. 1009.

Raoul Follereau A115

1978, Dec. 17 Litho. *Perf. 12½*
419 A115 200fr multi 1.75 1.75

Raoul Follereau (1903-1977), apostle to the lepers and educator of the blind.

IYC Emblem A116

Intl. Year of the Child: 20fr, Glove as balloon carrying childern. 50fr, Children of various races surrounding globe.

1979, Feb. 20 Litho. *Perf. 12x13*
420 A116 10fr multi .20 .20
421 A116 20fr multi .20 .20
422 A116 50fr multi .35 .35
Nos. 420-422 (3) .75 .75

Hydrangea — A117

Flowers: 25fr, Assangokan. 30fr, Geranium. 40fr, Water lilies, horiz.

Perf. 13x12½, 12½x13
1979, Feb. 28 Litho.
423 A117 20fr multi .20 .20
424 A117 25fr multi .20 .20
425 A117 30fr multi .20 .20
426 A117 40fr mutli .25 .25
Nos. 423-426 (4) .85 .85

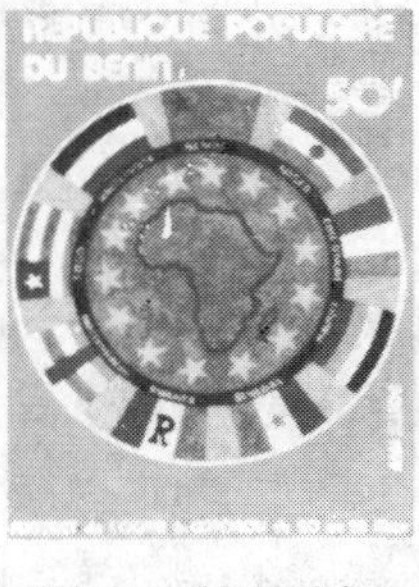

Emblem: Map of Africa and Members' Flags A118

60fr, Map of Benin & flags. 80fr, OCAM flag & map of Africa showing member states.

1979, Mar. 20 Litho. *Perf. 12x13*
427 A118 50fr multi .40 .40
428 A118 60fr multi .45 .45
429 A118 80fr multi .65 .65
Nos. 427-429 (3) 1.50 1.50

OCAM Summit Conf., Cotonou, Mar. 20-28.
For overprints see Nos. 434-436.

Tower, Waves, Satellite, ITU Emblem
A119

1979, May 17 **Litho.** ***Perf. 12½***
430 A119 50fr multi .40 .40

World Telecommunications Day.

Bank Building and Sculpture — A120

1979, May 26 **Litho.**
431 A120 50fr multi .35 .35

Opening of Headquarters of West African Savings Bank in Dakar.

Guelede Mask, Abomey Tapestry, Malaconotus Bird — A121

Design: 50fr, Jet, canoe, satellite, UPU and exhibition emblems.

1979, June 8 **Litho.** ***Perf. 13***
432 A121 15fr multi .20 .20

Engr.

433 A121 50fr multi .35 .35

Philexafrique II, Libreville, Gabon, June 8-17. Nos. 432, 433 each printed in sheets of 10 with 5 labels showing exhibition emblem.

Nos. 427-429 Overprinted: "26 au 28 juin 1979" and Dots

1979, June 26
434 A118 50fr multi .35 .35
435 A118 60fr multi .40 .40
436 A118 80fr multi .55 .55
Nos. 434-436 (3) 1.30 1.30

2nd OCAM Summit Conf., June 26-28.

Olympic Flame, and Emblems
A122

Pre-Olympic Year: 50fr, High jump.

1979, July 1 **Litho.**
437 A122 10fr multi .20 .20
438 A122 50fr multi .35 .35

Antelope
A123

Animals: 10fr, Giraffes, map of Benin, vert 20fr, Chimpanzee. 50fr, Elephants, map of Benin, vert.

1979, Oct. 1 **Litho.** ***Perf. 13***
439 A123 5fr multi .20 .20
440 A123 10fr multi .20 .20
441 A123 20fr multi .25 .25
442 A123 50fr multi .35 .30
Nos. 439-442 (4) 1.00 .95

Map of Africa, Emblem and Jet — A124

1979, Dec. 12 **Litho.** ***Perf. 12½***
443 A124 50fr multi .35 .35
444 A124 60fr multi .40 .40

ASECNA (Air Safety Board), 20th anniv.

Mail Services
A125

Design: 50fr, Post Office and headquarters, vert.

1979, Dec. 19 **Litho.** ***Perf. 13***
445 A125 50fr multi .35 .35
446 A125 60fr multi .40 .40

Office of Posts and Telecommunications, 20th anniversary.

Lenin and Globe
A126

1980, Apr. 22 **Litho.** ***Perf. 12½***
447 A126 50fr shown .25 .25
448 A126 150fr Lenin in library .75 .75

Lenin, 110th birth anniversary.

Monument to King Behanzin
A126a

Litho. & Embossed

1980, May 31 ***Perf. 12½***
448A A126a 1000fr gold & multi 5.50 5.50

For overprint see No. Q10A.

Cotonou Club Emlem
A127

Galileo, Astrolabe
A128

1980, Feb. 23 **Litho.** ***Perf. 12½***
449 A127 90fr shown .60 .60
450 A127 200fr Rotary emblem on globe, horiz. 1.40 1.40

Rotary International, 75th anniversary.
For surcharge see No. 915.

1980, Apr. 2
451 A128 100fr shown .45 .45
452 A128 100fr Copernicus, solar system .65 .65

Discovery of Pluto, 50th anniversary.

Abu Simbel, UNESCO Emblem — A129

1980, Apr. 15 ***Perf. 13***
453 A129 50fr Column, vert. .35 .35
454 A129 60fr Ramses II, vert. .40 .40
455 A129 150fr shown 1.00 1.00
Nos. 453-455 (3) 1.75 1.75

UNESCO campaign to save Nubian monuments, 20h anniversary.

Monument, Martyrs' Square, Cotonou
A130

Designs: Various monuments in Martyrs' Square. Cotonou. 60fr, 70fr, 100fr, horiz.

1980, May 2 ***Perf. 12½x13, 13x12½***
456 A130 50fr multi .35 .35
457 A130 60fr multi .40 .40
458 A130 70fr multi .45 .45
459 A130 100fr multi .65 .65
Nos. 456-459 (4) 1.85 1.85

For surcharge see No. 539.

Musical Instruments
A131

1980, May 20 ***Perf. 12½***
460 A131 5fr Assan, vert. .20 .20
461 A131 10fr Tinbo .20 .20
462 A131 15fr Tam-tam sato, vert. .20 .20
463 A131 20fr Kora .20 .20
464 A131 30fr Gangan .20 .20
465 A131 50fr Sinhoun .35 .35
Nos. 460-465 (6) 1.35 1.35

First Non-stop Flight, Paris-New York — A132

1980, June 2 **Litho.** ***Perf. 12½***
466 A132 90fr shown .60 .60
467 A132 100fr Dieudonne Coste, Maurice Bellonte .65 .65

For surcharge see No. 564.

Lunokhod I on the Moon — A133

1980, June 15 **Engr.** ***Perf. 13***
468 A133 90fr multi .60 .60

Lunokhod I Soviet unmanned moon mission, 10th anniv. See #C290. For surcharge see #C305.

Olympic Flame and Mischa, Moscow '80 Emblem — A134

1980, July 16 **Litho.** ***Perf. 12½***
469 A134 50fr shown .35 .35
470 A134 60fr Equestrian, vert. .40 .40
471 A134 70fr Judo .50 .50
472 A134 200fr Flag, sports, globe, vert. 1.40 1.40
473 A134 300fr Weight lifting, vert. 2.25 2.25
Nos. 469-473 (5) 4.90 4.90

22nd Summer Olympic Games, Moscow, July 19-Aug. 3.
For surcharges see Nos. 559, 561.

Telephone and Rising Sun — A135

World Telecommunications Day: 50fr, Farmer on telephone, vert.

1980, May 17 **Litho.** ***Perf. 12½***
474 A135 50fr multi .35 .35
475 A135 60fr multi .40 .40

Cotonou West African Community Village
A136

Designs: View of Cotonou.

1980, July 26 ***Perf. 13x13½***
476 A136 50fr multi .35 .35
477 A136 60fr multi .40 .40
478 A136 70fr multi .45 .45
Nos. 476-478 (3) 1.20 1.20

For surcharge see No. 540.

Agbadja Dancers — A137

Designs: Dancers and muscians.

1980, Aug. 1 ***Perf. 12½***

479 A137 30fr multi	.20	.20
480 A137 50fr multi	.35	.35
481 A137 66fr multi	.40	.40
Nos. 479-481 (3)	.95	.95

Fisherman A138

Philippines under Magnifier A139

Designs: 5fr, Throwing net. 15fr, Canoe and shore fishing. 20fr, Basket traps. 50fr, Hauling net. 60fr, River fishing. All horiz.

1980, Sept. 1

482 A138 5fr multi	.20	.20
483 A138 10fr multi	.20	.20
484 A138 15fr multi	.20	.20
485 A138 20fr multi	.20	.20
486 A138 50fr multi	.35	.35
487 A138 60fr multi	.40	.40
Nos. 482-487 (6)	1.55	1.55

For surcharge see No. 535.

Perf. 13x13½, 13x½x13

1980, Sept. 27

World Tourism Conference, Manila, Sept. 27: 60fr, Emblem on flag, hand pointing to Manila on globe, horiz.

488 A139 50fr multi	.35	.35
489 A139 60fr multi	.40	.40

For surcharge see No. 557.

A140

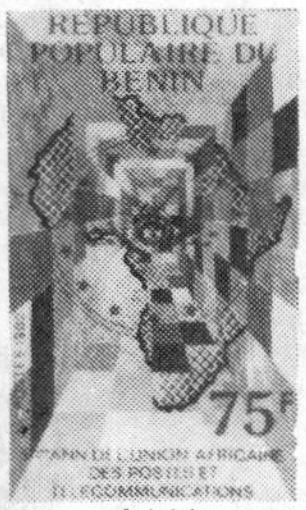

A141

1980, Oct. 1 ***Perf. 12½***

490 A140 40fr Othreis materna	.25	.25
491 A140 50fr Othreis fullonia	.35	.35
492 A140 200fr Oryctes sp.	1.40	1.40
Nos. 490-492 (3)	2.00	2.00

1980, Oct. 24 **Photo.** ***Perf. 13½***

493 A141 75fr multi	.50	.50

African Postal Union, 5th Anniv.

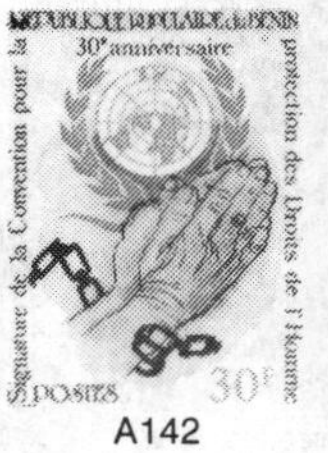

A142

A143

1980, Nov. 4 ***Perf. 12½x13***

494 A142 30fr shown	.25	.25
495 A142 50fr Freed prisoner	.35	.35
496 A142 60fr Man holding torch	.40	.40
Nos. 494-496 (3)	1.00	1.00

Declaration of human rights, 30th anniv.

1980, Dec. 1 **Litho.** ***Perf. 13***

Self-portrait, by Vincent van Gogh, 1888.

497 A143 100fr shown	.75	.75
498 A143 300fr Facteur Roulin	2.25	2.25

Vincent van Gogh (1853-1890), artist.
For surcharge see No. 579.

Offenbach and Scene from Orpheus in the Underworld — A144

1980, Dec. 15 **Engr.**

499 A144 50fr shown	.40	.40
500 A144 60fr Paris Life	.45	.45

Jacques Offenbach (1819-1880), composer.

Kepler and Satellites — A145

1980, Dec. 20

501 A145 50fr Kepler, diagram, vert.	.35	.35
502 A145 60fr shown	.40	.40

Johannes Kepler (1571-1630), astronomer.

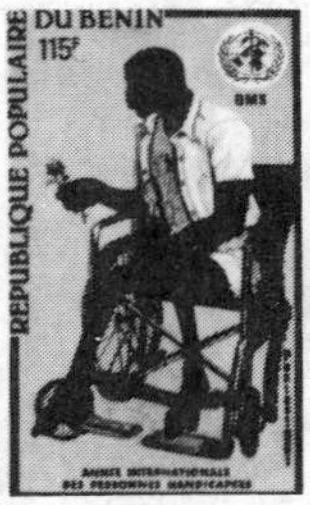

Intl. Year of the Disabled — A146

1981, Apr. 10 **Litho.** ***Perf. 12½***

503 A146 115fr multi	.75	.75

For surcharge see No. 582.

20th Anniv. of Manned Space Flight — A147

1981, May 30 ***Perf. 13***

504 A147 500fr multi	3.50	3.50

For surcharges see Nos. 580, 790.

13th World Telecommunications Day — A148

1981, May 30 **Litho.** ***Perf. 12½***

505 A148 115fr multi	.75	.75

For surcharge see No. 583.

Amaryllis A149

1981, June 20 ***Perf. 12½***

506 A149 10fr shown	.20	.20
507 A149 20fr Eischornia crassipes, vert.	.25	.25
508 A149 80fr Parkia biglobosa, vert.	.55	.55
Nos. 506-508 (3)	1.00	1.00

For surcharge see No. 542.

Benin Sheraton Hotel A150

1981, July

509 A150 100fr multi	.65	.65

For surcharge see No. 541.

Guinea Pig — A151

1981, July 31 ***Perf. 13x13½***

510 A151 5fr shown	.20	.20
511 A151 60fr Cat	.40	.40
512 A151 80fr Dogs	.55	.55
Nos. 510-512 (3)	1.15	1.15

For surcharges see Nos. 536, 543, 563.

World UPU Day — A152

1981, Oct. 9 **Engr.** ***Perf. 13***

513 A152 100fr red brn & blk	.65	.65

> *The Scott editorial staff regrettably cannot accept requests to identify, authenticate or appraise stamps and postal markings.*

25th Intl. Letter Writing Week, Oct. 6-12 — A153

1981, Oct. 15

514 A153 100fr dk bl & pur	.65	.65

For surcharge see No. 558.

West African Economic Community A154

1981, Nov. 20 **Litho.** ***Perf. 12½***

515 A154 60fr multi	.40	.40

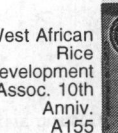

West African Rice Development Assoc. 10th Anniv. A155

1981, Dec. 10 ***Perf. 13x13½***

516 A155 60fr multi	.40	.40

TB Bacillus Centenary A156

1982, Mar. 1 **Litho.** ***Perf. 13***

517 A156 115fr multi	1.25	1.25

For surcharge see No. 584.

West African Economic Community, 5th Summit Conference A157

1982, May 27 ***Perf. 12½***

518 A157 60fr multi	.40	.40

1982 World Cup — A158

1982, June 1 ***Perf. 13***

519 A158 90fr Players	.65	.65
520 A158 300fr Flags on leg	2.25	2.25

For overprints and surcharges see #523-524, 594, 789.

France No. B349 Magnified, Map of France — A159

1982, June 11

521 A159 90fr multi .60 .60

For surcharge see No. 916.

PHILEXFRANCE '82 Stamp Exhibition, Paris, June 11-21.

George Washington — A160

1982, Mar. 10 Litho. *Perf. 14*

522 A160 200fr Washington, flag, map 1.00 1.00

For surcharge see No. 577.

Nos. 519-520 Overprinted with Finalists Names

1982, Aug. 16 *Perf. 12½*

523 A158 90fr multi .60 .60
524 A158 300fr multi 2.00 2.00

Italy's victory in 1982 World Cup.
For surcharge see No. 811.

Bluethroat A161

1982, Sept. 1 *Perf. 14x14½, 14½x14*

525 A161 5fr Daoelo gigas, vert. .20 .20
526 A161 10fr shown .20 .20
527 A161 15fr Swallow, vert. .20 .20
528 A161 20fr Kingfisher, weaver bird, vert. .20 .20
529 A161 30fr Great sedge warbler .25 .25
530 A161 60fr Common warbler .50 .50
531 A161 80fr Owl, vert. .65 .65
532 A161 100fr Cockatoo, vert. .80 .80
Nos. 525-532 (8) 3.00 3.00

ITU Plenipotentiaries Conference, Nairobi, Sept. — A162

1982, Sept. 26 *Perf. 13*

533 A162 200fr Map 1.00 1.00

For surcharge see No. 585.

13th World UPU Day — A163

1982, Oct. 9 Engr. *Perf. 13*

534 A163 100fr Monument .65 .65

Nos. 482, 510, 411 Overprinted in Red or Blue:
#535 "Croix Rouge / 8 Mai 1982"
#536 "UAPT 1982"
#537 "RICCONE 1982"

Perf. 13, 12½, 13x13½

1982, Nov. Litho.

535 A138 60fr on 5fr multi .40 .40
536 A151 60fr on 5fr multi .40 .40
537 A112 200fr multi (Bl) 1.40 1.40
Nos. 535-537 (3) 2.20 2.20

Visit of French Pres. Francois Mitterand A164

1983, Jan. 15 Litho. *Perf. 12½x13*

538 A164 90fr multi .60 .60

For surcharge see No. 917.

Nos. 458, 476, 508-509, 512 Surcharged

Perf. 13x12½, 13x13½, 12½

1983 Litho.

539 A130 60fr on 70fr multi .40 .40
540 A136 60fr on 50fr multi .40 .40
541 A150 60fr on 100fr multi .40 .40
542 A149 75fr on 80fr multi .50 .50
543 A151 75fr on 80fr multi .50 .50
Nos. 539-543 (5) 2.20 2.20

Seme Oil Rig — A165

1983, Apr. 28 Litho. *Perf. 13x12½*

544 A165 125fr multi .80 .80

World Communications Year — A166

1983, May 17 Litho. *Perf. 13*

545 A166 185fr multi 1.00 1.00

For surcharge see No. 898.

Riccione '83, Stamp Show — A167

1983, Aug. 27 Litho. *Perf. 13*

546 A167 500fr multi 3.25 3.25

For surcharge see No. 922.

Benin Red Cross, 20th Anniv. A168

1983, Sept. 5 Photo. *Perf. 13*

547 A168 105fr multi .70 .70

For surcharge see No. 581.

Handicrafts A169

Designs: 75fr, Handcarved lion chairs and table. 90fr, Natural tree table and stools. 200fr, Monkeys holding jar.

1983, Sept. 18 Litho. *Perf. 13*

548 A169 75fr multi .40 .40
549 A169 90fr multi .50 .50
550 A169 200fr multi 1.10 1.10
Nos. 548-550 (3) 2.00 2.00

For surcharge see No. 578.

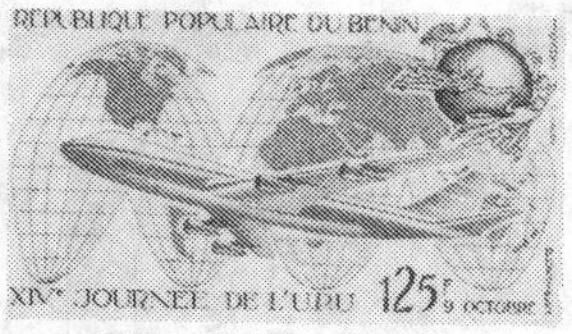

14th UPU Day — A170

1983, Oct. 9 Engr. *Perf. 13*

551 A170 125fr multi .80 .80

For surcharge see No. 575.

Religious Movements A171

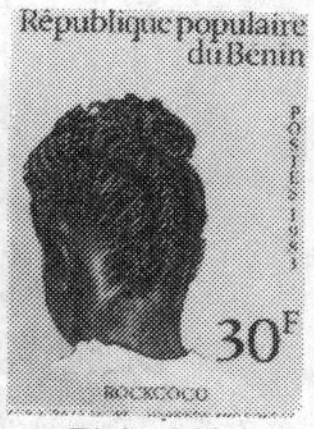

Plaited Hair Styles A172

1983, Oct. 31 Litho. *Perf. 14x15*

552 A171 75fr Zangbeto .35 .35
553 A171 75fr Egoun .35 .35

1983, Nov. 14

554 A172 30fr Rockcoco .25 .25
555 A172 75fr Serpent .35 .35
556 A172 90fr Songas .40 .40
Nos. 554-556 (3) 1.00 1.00

Stamps of 1976-81 Surcharged

1983, Nov.

557 A139 5fr on 50fr #488 .20 .20
558 A153 10fr on 100fr #514 .20 .20
559 A134 15fr on 200fr #472 .20 .20
560 A98 15fr on 210fr #381 .20 .20
561 A134 25fr on 70fr #471 .20 .20
562 A99 25fr on 210fr #384 .20 .20
563 A151 75fr on 5fr #510 .35 .35
564 A132 75fr on 100fr #467 .35 .35
565 A88 75fr on 150fr #360 .35 .35
566 A98 75fr on 150fr #380 .35 .35
Nos. 557-566 (10) 2.60 2.60

Alfred Nobel (1833-96) A173

1983, Dec. 19 Litho. *Perf. 15x14*

567 A173 300fr multi 1.40 1.40

For surcharge see No. 923.

Council of Unity — A174

1984, May 29 Litho. *Perf. 12*

568 A174 75fr multi .35 .35
569 A174 90fr multi .40 .40

For surcharge see No. 918.

1984 UPU Congress A175

1984, June 18 Litho. *Perf. 13*

570 A175 90fr multi .40 .40

Abomey Calavi Earth Station A176

1984, June 29 Litho. *Perf. 12½x13*

571 A176 75fr Satellite dish .35 .35

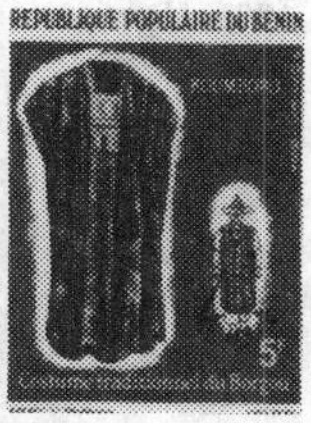

Traditional Costumes — A177

1984, July 2 Litho. *Perf. 13½x13*

572 A177 5fr Koumboro .20 .20
573 A177 10fr Taka .20 .20
574 A177 20fr Toko .20 .20
Set value .20 .20

Nos. 389, 498, 503-505, 517, 522, 533, 547, 550 and 551 Surcharged

1984, Sept.

575 A170 5fr on 125fr #551 .20 .20
576 A101 5fr on 150fr #389 .20 .20
577 A160 10fr on 200fr #522 .20 .20
578 A169 10fr on 200fr #550 .20 .20
579 A143 15fr on 300fr #498 .20 .20
580 A147 40fr on 500fr #504 .25 .25
581 A168 75fr on 105fr #547 .35 .35
582 A146 75fr on 115fr #503 .35 .35
583 A148 75fr on 115fr #505 .35 .35
584 A156 75fr on 115fr #517 .35 .35
585 A162 75fr on 200fr #533 .35 .35
Nos. 575-585 (11) 3.00 3.00

World Food Day A178

Dinosaurs A179

1984, Oct. 16 Litho. *Perf. 12½*

586 A178 100fr Malnourished child .30 .30

1984, Dec. 14 Litho. *Perf. 13½*

587 A179 75fr Anatosaurus		.25	.25
588 A179 90fr Brontosaurus		.25	.25

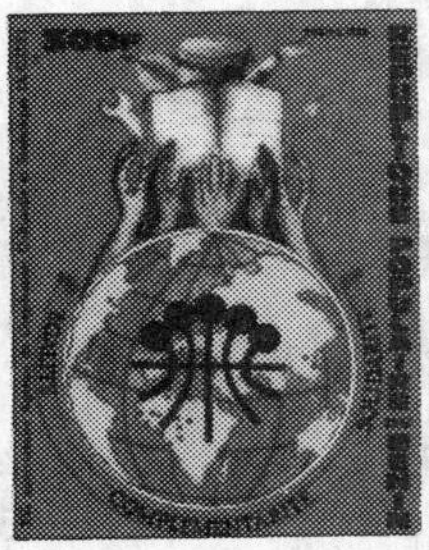

Cultural & Technical Cooperation Agency, 15th Anniv. A180

1985, Mar 20 Litho. *Perf. 13*

589 A180 300fr Emblem, globe, hands, book	.90	.90

Stamps of 1977-82 Surcharged

1985, Mar.

590 A93 75fr on 200fr No. 370	.20	.20
591 A108 75fr on 200fr No. 397	.20	.20
592 A110 75fr on 300fr No. 406	.20	.20
593 A108 75fr on 300fr No. 398	.20	.20
594 A158 90fr on 300fr No. 520	.25	.25
595 A108 90fr on 500fr No. 399	.25	.25
596 A108 90fr on 500fr No. 402	.25	.25
Nos. 590-596 (7)	1.55	1.55

End of World War II, 40th Anniv. — A180a

1985, May Litho. *Perf. 12*

596A A180a 100fr multicolored

Traditional Dances A181

1985, June 1 Litho. *Perf. 15x14½*

597 A181 75fr Teke, Borgou Tribe	.20	.20
598 A181 100fr Tipen'ti, L'Atacora Tribe	.30	.30

Intl. Youth Year — A182

1985, July 16 *Perf. 13½*

599 A182 150fr multi	.45	.45

1986 World Cup Soccer Championships, Mexico — A183

1985, July 22 *Perf. 13x12½*

600 A183 200fr multi	.60	.60

Beginning with Scott 601, Benin again surcharged stamps of Dahomey with a variety of surcharges. While the listings that follow contain more than 80 surcharged stamps, the Scott editors still need to examine more than 60 other stamps, in order to list all of those that are currently known to exist.

The size and location of the surcharge varies from stamp to stamp. The type face used in the surcharge may also vary from issue to issue.

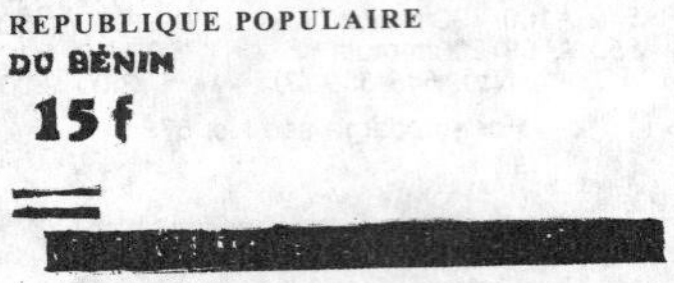

a

b

c

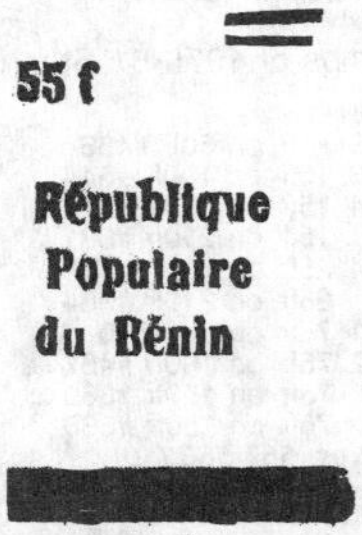

d

e

f

g h

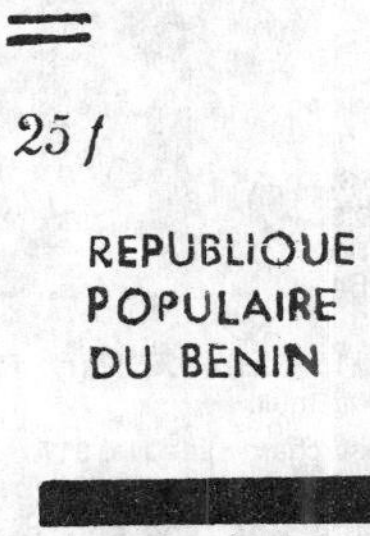

i

j

Dahomey No. 336 Surcharged with Black Bars and New Value

1985, Aug. *Perf. 12½*

601 A78(a) 15fr on 40fr multi	.20	.20

ASECNA Airlines, 25th Anniv. — A184

1985, Sept. 16 *Perf. 13*

602 A184 150fr multi	.45	.45

UN 40th Anniv. A185

1985, Oct. 24 *Perf. 12½*

603 A185 250fr multi	.90	.90

Benin UN membership, 25th anniv.

ITALIA'85, Rome A186

1985, Oct. 25 *Perf. 13½*

604 A186 200fr multi	.75	.75

PHILEXAFRICA '85, Lome — A187

1985, Nov. 16 *Perf. 13*

605 A187 250fr #569, labor emblem	.90	.90
606 A187 250fr #C252, Gabon #366, magnified stamp	.90	.90
a. Pair, Nos. 605-606 + label	1.80	1.80

Audubon Birth Bicent. A188

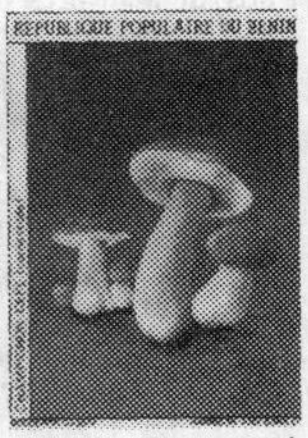

Mushrooms and Toadstools A189

1985, Oct. 17 Litho. *Perf. 14x15*

607 A188 150fr Skua gull	.55	.55
608 A188 300fr Oyster catcher	1.10	1.10

1985, Oct. 17

609 A189 35fr Boletus edible	.20	.20
610 A189 40fr Amanite phalloide	.20	.20
611 A189 100fr Brown chanterelle	.40	.40
Nos. 609-611 (3)	.80	.80

Dahomey Nos. 282, 292, Benin No. 343 Surcharged

1986, Mar. Photo.

612 A83(b) 75fr on 35fr #343	.25	.25
613 A57(c) 90fr on 70fr #282	.35	.35
614 A60(b) 90fr on 140fr #292	.40	.40
Nos. 612-614 (3)	1.00	1.00

African Parliamentary Union, 10th Anniv. — A190

1986, May 8 Litho. *Perf. 13x12½*

615 A190 100fr multi	.40	.40

9th Conference, Cotonou, May 8-10.

Halley's Comet — A191

1986, May 30 *Perf. 12½x12*

616 A191 250fr multi	.75	.75

For surcharge see No. 809.

Dahomey No. 283, Benin No. 344 Surcharged

Engraved, Photogravure

1986, June *Perf. 13*

617 A58(b) 100fr on 40fr #283	.40	.40
618 A83(b) 150fr on 45fr #344	.55	.55

1986 World Cup Soccer Championships, Mexico — A192

1986, June 29 **Litho.**

619 A192 500fr multi 1.75 1.75

For surcharge see No. 792.

Fight against Desert Encroachment — A193

1986, July 16 ***Perf. 13½***

620 A193 150fr multi .55 .55

King Behanzin A194

Amazon A194a

1986-88 **Engr.** ***Perf. 13***

621	A194	40fr black	.20	.20
622	A194a	100fr brt blue	.40	.40
623	A194	125fr maroon	.60	.60
624	A194a	150fr violet	.60	.60
625	A194	190fr dark ultra	.90	.90
627	A194	220fr dark grn	1.00	1.00
		Nos. 621-627 (6)	3.70	3.70

Issued: 100fr, 150fr, 8/1; others, 10/1/88.
See No. 636. For surcharge see No. 787.

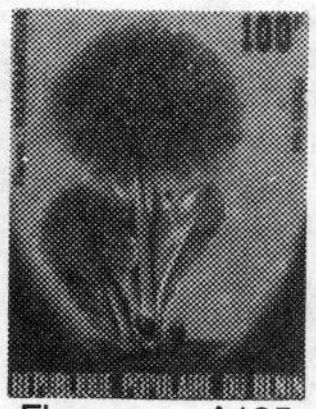

Flowers — A195

Butterflies — A196

Perf. 13x12½, 12½x13

1986, Sept. 1 **Litho.**

631 A195 100fr Haemanthus .40 .40
632 A195 205fr Hemerocalle, horiz. .90 .90

1986, Sept. 15

#633, Day peacock, little tortoiseshell, morio. #634, Aurora, machaon and fair lady.

633 A196 150fr multi .60 .60
634 A196 150fr multi .60 .60

Dahomey Nos. 290, 307 Overprinted

1985, Oct. 15

Perfs. & Printing Methods as Before

634A A67(b) 50fr on #307
634B A60(d) 150fr on 100fr #290

Statue of Liberty, Cent. — A197

King Behanzin — A198

1986, Oct. 28 **Litho.** ***Perf. 12½***

635 A197 250fr multi .90 .90

1986, Oct. 30 ***Perf. 13½***

636 A198 440fr multi 1.60 1.60

Behanzin, leader of resistance movement against French occupation (1886-1894).
For surcharge see No. 921.

Brazilian Cultural Week, Cotonou — A200

1987, Jan. 17 ***Perf. 12½***

638 A200 150fr multi .90 .90

Rotary Intl. District 910 Conference, Cotonou, Apr. 23-25 A201

1987, Apr. 23 **Litho.** ***Perf. 13½***

639 A201 300fr Center for the Blind, Cotonou 1.75 1.75

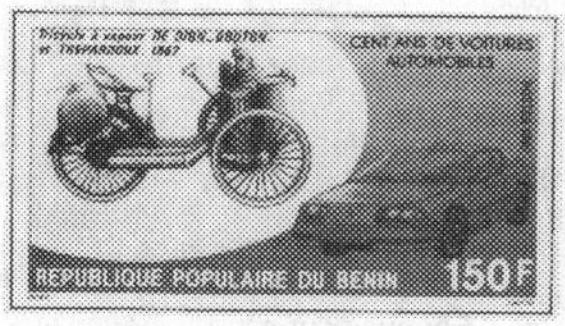

Automobile Cent. — A202

Modern car and: 150fr, Steam tricycle, by De Dion-Bouton and Trepardoux, 1887. 300fr, Gas-driven Victoria, by Daimler, 1886.

1987, July 1 ***Perf. 12½***

640 A202 150fr multi .90 .90
641 A202 300fr multi 1.75 1.75

For surcharge see No. 679B.

Snake Temple Baptism — A203

1987, July 20 ***Perf. 13½***

642 A203 100fr multi .55 .55

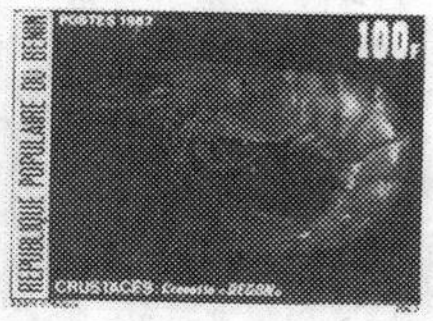

Shellfish A204

1987, July 24 ***Perf. 12½***

643 A204 100fr crayfish .55 .55
644 A204 150fr crab .90 .90

G. Hansen, R. Follerau — A205

1987, Sept. 4 ***Perf. 13***

645 A205 200fr Cure Leprosy 1.10 1.10

Beginning of Benin Revolution, 15th Anniv. — A205a

1987, Oct. 28 **Litho.** ***Perf. 12x12½***

645A A205a 100fr multicolored

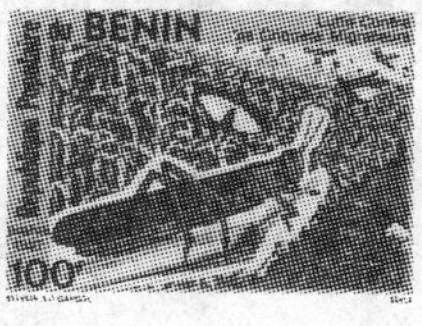

Locust Control A206

1987, Dec. 7 **Litho.** ***Perf. 12½x13***

646 A206 100fr multi .70 .70

Christmas 1987 A207

1987, Dec. 21 ***Perf. 13***

647 A207 150fr multi 1.10 1.10

Dahomey Nos. 268, 284 Ovptd. or Surchd.

1987 **Engr.** ***Perf. 13***

647A A58(b) 15fr on 100fr #284
647B A53(b) 40fr on #268

See Nos. C362, C369.

Intl. Red Cross and Red Crescent Organizations, 125th Anniv. — A208

1988, May 25 **Litho.** ***Perf. 13½***

648 A208 200fr multi 1.25 1.25

A209

A210

1988, July 11 ***Perf. 12½***

649 A209 200fr multi 1.25 1.25

Martin Luther King, Jr. (1929-68), American civil rights leader.

1988, May 25 **Litho.** ***Perf. 13½***

650 A210 125fr multi .90 .90

Organization of African Unity, 25th anniv.

WHO, 40th Anniv. — A211

1988, Sept. 1 **Litho.** ***Perf. 13x12½***

651 A211 175fr multi 1.10 1.10

Alma Ata Declaration, 10th anniv.; Health Care for All on Earth by the Year 2000.
For surcharge see No. 786.

Ganvie Lake Village A212

1988, Sept. 4 ***Perf. 13½***

652 A212 125fr shown .85 .85
653 A212 190fr Boatman, village, diff. 1.25 1.25

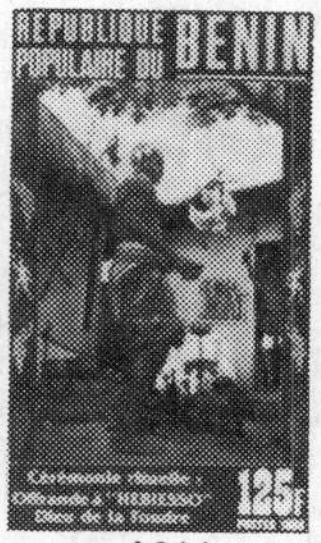

A213

A214

1988, Aug. 14 ***Perf. 12½***

654 A213 125fr multi .90 .90

1st Benin Scout Jamboree, Aug. 12-19.

Benin No. 351, Dahomey Nos. 296, 328 Surcharged

1988

Printing Method & Perfs as Before

654A A57(d) 10fr on 60fr on 2fr #351
654B A62(d) 10fr on 65fr #296
654E A74(d) 150fr on 200fr #328

1988, Dec. 30 Litho. *Perf. 13*

Ritual Offering to Hebiesso, God of Thunder and Lightning.

655 A214 125fr multicolored .80 .80

Dahomey Nos. 161, 247, 302, 333, 339, 341 Surcharged

1988 Photo. *Perf. 12½x13*

655A A19(d) 5fr on 3fr #161
655C A82(d) 30fr on 150fr #341
655D A76(d) 25fr on 100fr #333
655E A45(b) 50fr on 45fr #247
655F A81(d) 55fr on 200fr #339
655G A65(b) 65fr on 85fr #302

These are part of a set of 10. Another set of 19 surcharges also is known to exist. The editors need to see the rest of these stamps before listings can be created.

Rural Development Council, 30th Anniv. — A214a

1989, May 29 Litho. *Perf. 15x14*

655K A214a 75fr multicolored

World Wildlife Fund — A216

Roseate terns, *Sterna dougalli.*

1989, Jan. 30 Litho. *Perf. 13*

657 A216 10fr Three terns .20 .20
658 A216 15fr Feeding on fish .20 .20
659 A216 50fr Perched .30 .30
660 A216 125fr In flight .80 .80
Nos. 657-660 (4) 1.50 1.50

Eiffel Tower Cent. — A217

1989, Apr. 24 Litho. *Perf. 13x12½*

661 A217 190fr multi 1.10 1.10

PHILEXFRANCE '89, French Revolution Bicent. — A218

Design: Bastille, emblems, Declaration of Human Rights and Citizenship, France No. B252-B253.

1989, July 7 *Perf. 13*

662 A218 190fr multicolored 1.10 1.10

Electric Corp. of Benin, 20th Anniv. A219

1989, Oct. Litho. *Perf. 12½x13*

663 A219 125fr multicolored .80 .80

Fish A220

1989, Sept. 22 *Perf. 13½*

664 A220 125fr Lote .80 .80
665 A220 190fr Pike, salmon 1.25 1.25

Death of King Glele, Cent. — A221

1989, Dec. 16 Litho. *Perf. 13½*

666 A221 190fr multicolored 1.25 1.25

Christmas A222

1989, Dec. 25 *Perf. 13*

667 A222 200fr Holy family 1.40 1.40

Benin Posts & Telecommunications, Cent. — A223

1990, Jan. 1 *Perf. 13½*

668 A223 125fr multicolored .80 .80

Fruits and Flora A224

1990, Jan. 23 Litho. *Perf. 11½*

669 A224 60fr Oranges .40 .40
670 A224 190fr Kaufmann Tulips, vert. 1.40 1.40
671 A224 250fr Cashews, vert. 1.75 1.75
Nos. 669-671 (3) 3.55 3.55

Dated 1989.

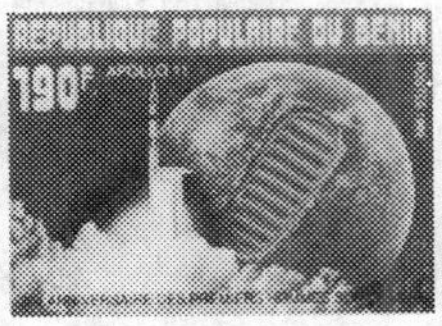

Moon Landing, 20th Anniv. A225

1990, Jan. 23

672 A225 190fr multicolored 1.40 1.40

Dated 1989.

World Cup Soccer Championships, Italy — A226

1990, June 8 Litho. *Perf. 12½*

673 A226 125fr shown 1.00 1.00
674 A226 190fr Character trademark, vert. 1.50 1.50

For overprint see No. 676.

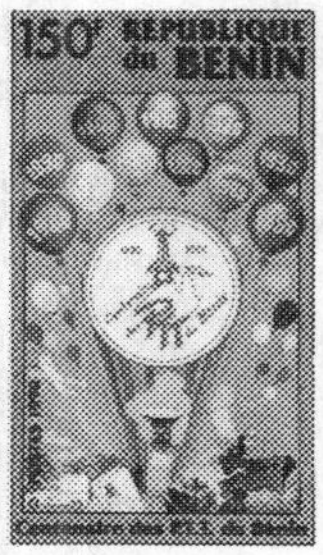

Post, Telephone & Telegraph Administration in Benin, Cent. — A227

1990, July 1 *Perf. 13*

675 A227 150fr multicolored 1.25 1.25

No. 673 Ovptd. **FINALE R.F.A. - ARGENTINE 1 - 0**

1990 Litho. *Perf. 12½*

676 A226 125fr multicolored 1.00 1.00

Charles de Gaulle (1890-1970) A228

1990, Nov. 22 Litho. *Perf. 13*

677 A228 190fr multicolored 1.50 1.50

See No. 689.

Galileo Probe and Jupiter A229

1990, Dec. 1

678 A229 100fr multicolored .75 .75

For overprint see No. 681.

A230

1990, Dec. 25 Litho. *Perf. 12½x13*

679 A230 200fr multicolored 1.75 1.75

Christmas.

Benin No. 641 Surcharged

1990

Perf. & Printing Method as Before

679B A202(e) 190fr on 300fr #641

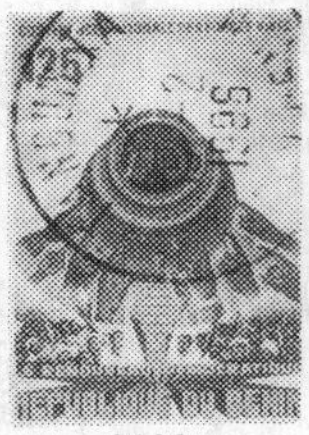

A230a

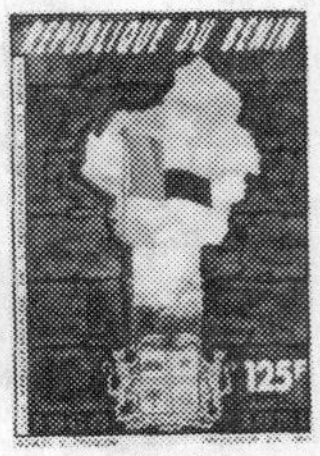

A231

1990 Litho. *Perf. 11½x12*

679C A230a 125fr multicolored

National People's Congress.

1991, Sept. 3 Litho. *Perf. 13½*

680 A231 125fr multicolored 1.00 1.00

Independence, 31st anniv.

No. 678 Ovptd. in Red **"Riccione 91"**

1991 *Perf. 13*

681 A229 100fr multicolored .85 .85

French Open Tennis Championships, Cent. — A232

1991 *Perf. 13½*
682 A232 125fr multicolored 1.00 1.00

African Tourism Year — A233

1991
683 A233 190fr multicolored 1.60 1.60

Christmas A234

1991, Dec. 2 **Litho.** *Perf. 13½*
684 A234 125fr multicolored 1.00 1.00

Dancer of Guelede — A235

Wolfgang Amadeus Mozart, Death Bicent. — A236

1991, Dec. 2
685 A235 190fr multicolored 1.60 1.60

1991, Dec. 2
686 A236 1000fr multicolored 8.50 8.50

For surcharge see No. 793.

Discovery of America, 500th Anniv. A237

Design: 1000fr, Columbus coming ashore, horiz.

1992, Apr. 24 **Litho.** *Perf. 13*
687 A237 500fr blk, blue & brn 3.75 3.75
688 A237 1000fr multicolored 7.50 7.50
a. Souvenir sheet of 2, #687-688 11.25 11.25

De Gaulle Type of 1990

1992 **Litho.** *Perf. 13*
689 A228 300fr like #677 2.25 2.25

Intl. Conference on Nutrition, Rome — A238

1992, Dec. 5 **Litho.** *Perf. 13*
690 A238 190fr multicolored 1.60 1.60

Dahomey Nos. 160, 266, 303, 311, 327, 334, 338, C161 Surcharged or Overprinted (#690A)

1992
Perfs. & Printing Methods as Before
690A A66(e) 5fr on #303
690E A80(f) 35fr on #338
690F A19(e) 125fr on 2fr #160
690G AP54(f) 125fr on 65fr #C161
690H A77(f) 125fr on 65fr #334 (G)
690I CD137(e) 125fr on 100fr #311
690J A52(f) 190fr on 45fr #266
690K A74(f) 125fr on 100fr #327

Visit of Pope John Paul II, Feb. 3-5 — A239

Ouidah 92, First Festival of Voodoo Culture — A240

1993, Feb. 3 **Litho.** *Perf. 13x12½*
691 A239 190fr multicolored 1.50 1.50

1993, Feb. 8 *Perf. 13½*
692 A240 125fr multicolored 1.00 1.00

Well of Possotome, Eurystome A241

1993, May 25 **Litho.** *Perf. 12½*
693 A241 125fr multicolored 1.00 1.00

OAU, 30th Anniv. A242

1993, June 7 **Litho.** *Perf. 13½*
694 A242 125fr multicolored 1.00 1.00

John F. Kennedy — A243

1993, June 24 *Perf. 13*
695 A243 190fr shown 1.50 1.50
696 A243 190fr Martin Luther King, vert. 1.50 1.50

Assassinations of Kennedy, 30th anniv. (#695), and King, 25th anniv. (#696).

Dahomey Nos. 161, 173, 175, 277, 335 Overprinted or Surcharged

1993
Perfs. & Printing Methods as Before
697 A21(e) 5fr on #175
700 A19(f) 10fr on 3fr #161
701 A77(f) 10fr on 100fr #335
703 A57(f) 20fr on 1fr #277
704 A21(f) 25fr on 1fr #173

Benin Nos. 343, 345, 350, Dahomey Nos. 169, 226-227, 249, 276, 295, 283, 319, 333 Surcharged or Overprinted (#711, 713)

1994-95
707 A38(f) 5fr on 1fr #226
709 A71(f) 25fr on #319
711 A57(e) 50fr on 1fr #350
712 A58(e) 80fr on 40fr #283
713 A76(g) 100fr on #333
715 A38(f) 135fr on 3fr #227
718 A62(e) 135fr on 30fr #295
719 A83(g) 135fr on 35fr #343
720 A56(h) 135fr on 40fr multi
722 A20(e) 135fr on 60fr #169
723 A83(g) 135fr on 60fr #345
725 A45(e) 200fr on 100fr #249

UNESCO Conference on The Slave Route — A244

1994 **Litho.** *Perf. 13x13½*
729 A244 200fr multicolored
730 A244 300fr multicolored

The editors would like to see the 135fr value in this set, for which a number has been reserved.

Intl. Year of the Family A246

1994 **Litho.** *Perf. 12½*
732 A246 200fr multicolored

1994 World Cup Soccer Championships, US — A247

1994 **Litho.** *Perf. 13x13½*
733 A247 300fr multicolored

1996 Summer Olympics, Atlanta A248

Perf. 12½x13, 13x12½

1995, Apr. 30 **Litho.**
734 A248 45fr Water polo .45 .45
735 A248 50fr Javelin .50 .50
736 A248 75fr Weight lifting .75 .75
737 A248 100fr Tennis 1.00 1.00
738 A248 135fr Baseball 1.40 1.40
739 A248 200fr Synchronized swimming 2.00 2.00
Nos. 734-739 (6) 6.10 6.10

Souvenir Sheet

740 A248 300fr Diving *4.50 4.50*

Nos. 735-740 are vert. No. 740 contains one 32x40mm stamp.

Dogs A249

1995, Aug. 23 **Litho.** *Perf. 12½*
741 A249 40fr German shepherd .35 .35
742 A249 50fr Beagle .50 .50
743 A249 75fr Great dane .75 .75
744 A249 100fr Boxer 1.00 1.00
745 A249 135fr Pointer 1.40 1.40
746 A249 200fr Fox terrier 2.00 2.00
Nos. 741-746 (6) 6.00 6.00

Souvenir Sheet

747 A249 300fr Schnauzer *6.50 6.50*

Ships A250

Designs: 40fr, Steam driven paddle boat, 1788. 50fr, Paddle steamer Charlotte, 1802. 75fr, Transatlantic steamship, Citta de Catania. 100fr, Hovercraft Mountbatten SR-N4. 135fr, QE II. 200fr, Japanese experimental atomic energy ship, Mutsu-NEF. 300fr, Paddle-steamer Savannah, 1819.

1995, May 20
748 A250 40fr multicolored .35 .35
749 A250 50fr multicolored .50 .50
750 A250 75fr multicolored .75 .75
751 A250 100fr multicolored 1.00 1.00
752 A250 135fr multicolored 1.40 1.40
753 A250 200fr multicolored 2.00 2.00
Nos. 748-753 (6) 6.00 6.00

Souvenir Sheet

754 A250 300fr multicolored *4.50 4.50*

No. 754 contains one 40x32mm stamp.

Primates — A251

1995, June 30
755 A251 50fr Pan troglodytes .50 .50
756 A251 75fr Mandrillus sphinx .75 .75
757 A251 100fr Colobus 1.00 1.00
758 A251 135fr Macaca sylvanus 1.40 1.40
759 A251 200fr Comopithecus hamadryas 2.00 2.00
Nos. 755-759 (5) 5.65 5.65

Souvenir Sheet

760 A251 300fr Papio cynocephalus 4.50 4.50

No. 760 contains one 32x40mm stamp.

Domestic Cats A252

1995, July 30 Litho. *Perf. 12½x13*

761 A252 40fr Shorthair tabby .35 .35
762 A252 50fr Ruddy red .50 .50
763 A252 75fr White longhair .75 .75
764 A252 100fr Seal color point 1.00 1.00
765 A252 135fr Tabby point 1.40 1.40
766 A252 200fr Black shorthair 2.00 2.00
Nos. 761-766 (6) 6.00 6.00

Souvenir Sheet

767 A252 300fr Cat in basket 4.50 4.50

No. 767 contains one 40x32mm stamp.

Flowers — A253

Designs: 40fr, Dracunculus vulgaris. 50fr, Narcissus watieri. 75fr, Amaryllis belladonna. 100fr, Nymphaea capensis. 135fr, Chrysanthemum carinatum. 200fr, Iris tingitana.

1995, Oct. 15 Litho. *Perf. 12½*

768 A253 40fr multicolored .40 .40
769 A253 50fr multicolored .55 .55
770 A253 75fr multicolored .80 .80
771 A253 100fr multicolored 1.10 1.10
772 A253 135fr multicolored 1.40 1.40
773 A253 200fr multicolored 2.25 2.25
Nos. 768-773 (6) 6.50 6.50

Wild Animals A254

Designs: 50fr, Panthera leo. 75fr, Syncerus caffer. 100fr, Pan troglodytes. 135fr, Aepyceros melampus. 200fr, Geosciurus inaurus.
300fr, Loxodonta, vert.

Perf. 13x12½, 12½x13

1995, Sept. 20

774 A254 50fr multicolored .55 .55
775 A254 75fr multicolored .80 .80
776 A254 100fr multicolored 1.10 1.10
777 A254 135fr multicolored 1.50 1.50
778 A254 200fr multicolored 2.25 2.25
Nos. 774-778 (5) 6.20 6.20

Souvenir Sheet

779 A254 300fr multicolored 4.75 4.75

Nos. 774-777 are vert. No. 779 contains one 32x40mm stamp.

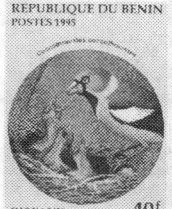

Birds Feeding Their Chicks — A255

Designs: 40fr, Cocothraustes cocothraustes. 50fr, Streptopelia chinensis. 75fr, Falco peregrinus. 100fr, Dendroica fusca. 135fr, Larus ridibundus. 200fr, Pelecanus onocrotalus.

1995, Aug. 28 *Perf. 12½x13*

780 A255 40fr multicolored .40 .40
781 A255 50fr multicolored .55 .55
782 A255 75fr multicolored .80 .80
783 A255 100fr multicolored 1.10 1.10
784 A255 135fr multicolored 1.40 1.40
785 A255 200fr multicolored 2.25 2.25
Nos. 780-785 (6) 6.50 6.50

Benin Nos. 344, 504, 520, 619, 627, 651, 686 and Dahomey No. 291 Surcharged

1994-95

Printing Method and Perfs as Before

786 A211 25fr on 175fr #651
787 A194 50fr on 220fr #627
788 A83(h) 150fr on 45fr #344
789 A158 150fr on 90fr #520
790 A147 150fr on 500fr #504
791 A60(f) 200fr on 135fr #291
792 A192 200fr on 500fr #619
793 A236 250fr on 1000fr #686

Natl. Arms — A256

1995 Litho. *Perf. 12½*

793A A256 135fr yellow & multi 1.30 1.30
793B A256 150fr yel grn & multi 1.45 1.45
794 A256 200fr multicolored

See Nos. 948-951.

Orchids — A257

Designs: 40fr, Angraecum sesquipedale. 50fr, Polystachya virginea. 75fr, Disa uniflora. 100fr, Ansellia africana. 135fr, Angraecum eichlerianum. 200fr, Jumellea confusa.

1995, Nov. 10 Litho. *Perf. 12½*

795 A257 40fr multicolored .40 .40
796 A257 50fr multicolored .50 .50
797 A257 75fr multicolored .75 .75
798 A257 100fr multicolored 1.00 1.00
799 A257 135fr multicolored 1.35 1.35
800 A257 200fr multicolored 2.00 2.00
Nos. 795-800 (6) 6.00 6.00

Butterflies A258

Designs: 40fr, Graphium policenes. 50fr, Vanessa atalanta. 75fr, Polymmatus icarus. 100fr, Danaus chrysipus. 135fr, Cynthia cardui. 200fr, Argus celbulina.
1000fr, Charaxes jasius.

1996, Mar. 10

801 A258 40fr multicolored .35 .35
802 A258 50fr multicolored .50 .50
803 A258 75fr multicolored .75 .75
804 A258 100fr multicolored 1.00 1.00
805 A258 135fr multicolored 1.40 1.40
806 A258 200fr multicolored 2.00 2.00
Nos. 801-806 (6) 6.00 6.00

Souvenir Sheet

807 A258 1000fr multicolored 6.00 6.00

CHINA '96, Beijing A259

Designs: a, 40fr, Dancer in traditional Chinese costume. b, 50fr, Exhibition emblem. c, 75fr, Water lily. d, 100fr, Temple of Heaven.

1996, Apr. 8

808 A259 Block of 4, #a.-d. 5.00 5.00

Benin Nos. 523, 616 and Dahomey No. 306 Surcharged or Overprinted (#810)

1996?

Perfs. & Printing Methods as Before

809 A191 5fr on 250fr #616
810 A67(g) 35fr on #306
811 A158 150fr on 90fr #523

15th Lions Intl. District Convention — A260

1996 Litho. *Perf. 12½*

811A A260 100fr multicolored .45 .45
811B A260 135fr green & multi 1.40 1.40
812 A260 150fr yellow & multi 1.50 1.50
813 A260 200fr red & multi 2.00 2.00
Nos. 811A-813 (4) 5.35 5.35

Issued: #811A, 12/27; others, 5/2.

La Francoponie Conference A261

1995, Dec. 2 Litho. *Perf. 12½*

814 A261 150fr pink & multi 1.25 1.25
815 A261 200fr blue & multi 1.75 1.75

Cats — A262

1995, Nov. 2 Litho. *Perf. 13*

816 A262 40fr Lynx lynx .40 .40
817 A262 50fr Felis concolor .50 .50
818 A262 75fr Acinonyx jubatus .70 .70
819 A262 100fr Panthera pardus .95 .95
820 A262 135fr Panthera tigris 1.25 1.25
821 A262 200fr Panthera leo 1.90 1.90
Nos. 816-821 (6) 5.70 5.70

1998 World Cup Soccer Championships, France — A263

Various soccer players.

1996, Feb. 10 Litho. *Perf. 13*

822 A263 40fr multicolored .35 .35
823 A263 50fr multicolored .50 .50
824 A263 75fr multicolored .75 .75
825 A263 100fr multicolored 1.00 1.00
826 A263 135fr multicolored 1.40 1.40
827 A263 200fr multicolored 2.00 2.00
Nos. 822-827 (6) 6.00 6.00

Souvenir Sheet

Perf. 12½

828 A263 1000fr multicolored 6.00 6.00

No. 828 contains one 32x40mm stamp.

1996 Summer Olympic Games, Atlanta — A264

1996, Jan. 28 Litho. *Perf. 13*

829 A264 40fr Diving .35 .35
830 A264 50fr Tennis .50 .50
831 A264 75fr Running .75 .75
832 A264 100fr Gymnastics 1.00 1.00
833 A264 135fr Weight lifting 1.40 1.40
834 A264 200fr Shooting 2.00 2.00
Nos. 829-834 (6) 6.00 6.00

Souvenir Sheet

835 A264 1000fr Water polo 6.00 6.00

No. 835 contains one 32x40mm stamp.

Christmas Paintings — A265

Entire paintings or details: 40fr, Holy Family Under the Oak Tree, by Raphael. 50fr, The Holy Family, by Raphael. 75fr, St. John the Baptist as a Child, by Murillo. 100fr, The Virgin of Balances, by Leonardo da Vinci. 135fr, The Virgin and the Infant, by Gerard David. 200fr, Adoration of the Magi, by Juan Batista Mayno.
1000fr, Rest on the Flight into Egypt, by Murillo.

1996, May 5 Litho. *Perf. 13*

836 A265 40fr multicolored .40 .40
837 A265 50fr multicolored .55 .55
838 A265 75fr multicolored .80 .80
839 A265 100fr multicolored 1.00 1.00
840 A265 135fr multicolored 1.40 1.40
841 A265 200fr multicolored 2.10 2.10
Nos. 836-841 (6) 6.25 6.25

Souvenir Sheet

842 A265 1000fr multicolored 6.25 6.25

No. 842 contains one 40x32mm stamp.

Wild Cats — A266

Designs: 40fr, Leptailurus serval. 50fr, Profelis temmincki. 75fr, Leopardus pardalis. 100fr, Lynx rufus. 135fr, Prionailurus bengalensis. 200fr, Felis euphtilura.
1000fr, Neofelis nebulosa.

1996, June 10 Litho. *Perf. 12x12½*

843 A266 40fr multicolored .40 .40
844 A266 50fr multicolored .55 .55
845 A266 75fr multicolored .80 .80
846 A266 100fr multicolored 1.00 1.00

847 A266 135fr multicolored 1.40 1.40
848 A266 200fr multicolored 2.10 2.10
Nos. 843-848 (6) 6.25 6.25

Souvenir Sheet

Perf. 12½

849 A266 1000fr multicolored *6.25 6.25*

No. 849 contains one 32x40mm stamp.

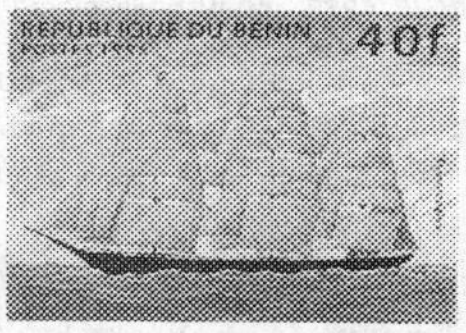

Sailing Ships A267

1996, May 27 ***Perf. 13x12½***

850 A267 40fr Thermopylae .40 .40
851 A267 50fr 5-masted bark .55 .55
852 A267 75fr Nightingale .80 .80
853 A267 100fr Opium clipper 1.00 1.00
854 A267 135fr The Torrens 1.40 1.40
855 A267 200fr English clipper 2.10 2.10
Nos. 850-855 (6) 6.25 6.25

Souvenir Sheet

Perf. 13

856 A267 1000fr Opium clipper, diff. *6.25 6.25*

No. 856 contains one 32x40mm stamp.

Olymphilex '96 — A268

1996, July 2 ***Perf. 13***

857 A268 40fr Running .40 .40
858 A268 50fr Kayaking .55 .55
859 A268 75fr Gymnastics .80 .80
860 A268 100fr Soccer 1.00 1.00
861 A268 135fr Tennis 1.40 1.40
862 A268 200fr Baseball 2.00 2.00
Nos. 857-862 (6) 6.15 6.15

Souvenir Sheet

863 A268 1000fr Basketball *6.25 6.25*

No. 863 contains one 32x40mm stamp.

Modern Olympic Games, Cent. — A269

a, 40fr, Gold medal, woman hurdler. b, 50fr, Runner, Olympic flame. c, 75fr, Pierre de Coubertin, map of US. d, 100fr, Map of US, "1996."

1996, June 20

864 A269 Block of 4, #a.-d. *5.25 5.25*

No. 864 is a continuous design.

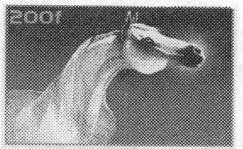

Horses A270

Various horses.

1996, Aug. 10 Litho. ***Perf. 13***

865 A270 40fr multi, vert. .35 .35
866 A270 50fr multi, vert. .50 .50
867 A270 75fr multi, vert. .75 .75
868 A270 100fr multi, vert. 1.00 1.00
869 A270 135fr multi, vert. 1.40 1.40
870 A270 200fr multicolored 2.00 2.00
Nos. 865-870 (6) 6.00 6.00

Flowering Cacti — A271

40fr, Parodia subterranea. 50fr, Astrophytum senile. 75fr, Echinocereus melanocentrus. 100fr, Turbinicarpus kinkerianus. 135fr, Astrophytum capricorne. 200fr, Nelloydia grandiflora.

1996, July 25

871 A271 40fr multicolored .35 .35
872 A271 50fr multicolored .50 .50
873 A271 75fr multicolored .75 .75
874 A271 100fr multicolored 1.00 1.00
875 A271 135fr multicolored 1.40 1.40
876 A271 200fr multicolored 2.00 2.00
Nos. 871-876 (6) 6.00 6.00

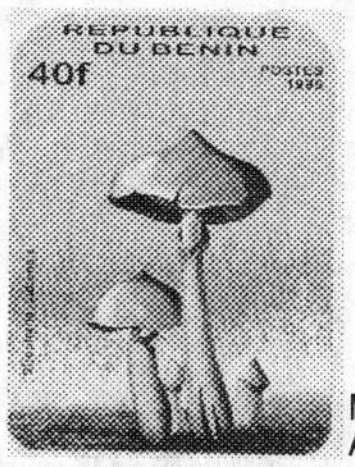

Mushrooms A272

Designs: 40fr, Stropharia cubensis. 50fr, Psilocybe zapotecorum. 75fr, Psilocybe mexicana. 100fr, Conocybe siligineoides. 135fr, Psilocybe caerulescens mazatecorum. 200fr, Psilocybe caerulescens nigripes.
1000fr, Psilocybe aztecorum, horiz.

1996, Sept. 30

877 A272 40fr multicolored .35 .35
878 A272 50fr multicolored .50 .50
879 A272 75fr multicolored .75 .75
880 A272 100fr multicolored 1.00 1.00
881 A272 135fr multicolored 1.40 1.40
882 A272 200fr multicolored 2.00 2.00
Nos. 877-882 (6) 6.00 6.00

Souvenir Sheet

Perf. 12½

883 A272 1000fr multicolored *6.00 6.00*

No. 883 contains one 40x32mm stamp.

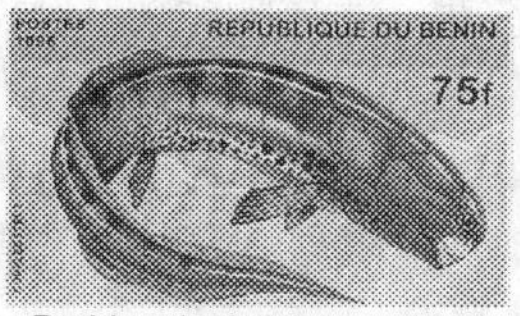

Prehistoric Animals — A273

1996, Aug. 30 ***Perf. 12½***

884 A273 40fr Longisquama, vert. .35 .35
885 A273 50fr Dimophodon, vert. .50 .50
886 A273 75fr Dunkleosteus .75 .75
887 A273 100fr Eryops 1.00 1.00
888 A273 135fr Peloneustes 1.40 1.40
889 A273 200fr Deinonychus 2.00 2.00
Nos. 884-889 (6) 6.00 6.00

Birds — A274

Designs: 40fr, Campephilus principalis. 50fr, Picathartes oreas. 75fr, Strigops habroptilus. 100fr, Amazona vittata. 135fr, Nipponia nippon. 200fr, Gymnogyps californianus.
1000fr, Paradisea rudolphi.

1996, Sept. 10

890 A274 40fr multicolored .35 .35
891 A274 50fr multicolored .50 .50
892 A274 75fr multicolored .75 .75
893 A274 100fr multicolored 1.00 1.00
894 A274 135fr multicolored 1.40 1.40
895 A274 200fr multicolored 2.00 2.00
Nos. 890-895 (6) 6.00 6.00

Souvenir Sheet

896 A274 1000fr multicolored *6.00 6.00*

No. 896 contains one 32x40mm stamp.

Dahomey No. 235 Overprinted
Benin No. 545 Surcharged

199?

Perfs. & Printing Methods as Before

897 A40(e) 30fr on #235
898 A166 75fr on 185fr #545

Dahomey Nos. 208, 239-241, 257-258, 261, 269, 274, 283, 320, 326, 334-336, 337 Surcharged or Overprinted (#899)

1996?

Perfs. & Printing Methods as Before

899 A77(f) 100fr on #335
900 A79(e) 125fr on 150fr #337
901 A77(h) 135fr on 65fr #334
902 A42(e) 150fr on 30fr #239
903 A43(h) 150fr on 30fr #241
904 A48(h) 150fr on 30fr #257
905 A50(h) 150fr on 30fr #261
906 CD132(h) 150fr on 40fr #269
907 A58(h) 150fr on 40fr #283
908 A71(e) 150fr on 40fr #320
909 A74(e) 150fr on 40fr #326
910 A78(e) 150fr on 40fr #336
911 A32(e) 150fr on 50fr #208
912 A42(e) 150fr on 70fr #240
913 A48(h) 150fr on 70fr #258
914 A55(h) 150fr on 200fr #274

Benin Nos. 381, 384, 449, 521, 538, 546, 567, 569, 636, Surcharged

1996?

Perfs. & Printing Methods as Before

915 A127 10fr on 90fr #449
916 A159 10fr on 90fr #521
917 A164 10fr on 90fr #538
918 A174 10fr on 90fr #569
919 A98 40fr on 210fr #381
920 A99 40fr on 210fr #384
921 A198 75fr on 440fr #636
922 A167 100fr on 500fr #546
923 A173 125r on 300fr #567

Obliterator on No. 922 has either one or two bars. Pairs of No. 922 exist with each stamp having a different obliterator.

Benin No. 376 Surcharged

1995

Perfs. & Printing Methods as Before

925 A96 10fr on 90fr #376

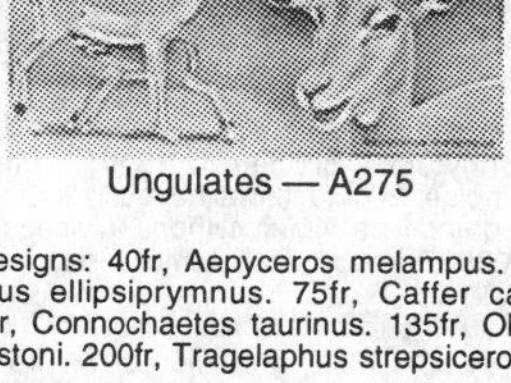

Ungulates — A275

Designs: 40fr, Aepyceros melampus. 50fr, Kobus ellipsiprymnus. 75fr, Caffer caffer. 100fr, Connochaetes taurinus. 135fr, Okapia johnstoni. 200fr, Tragelaphus strepsiceros.

1996, Oct. 15 Litho. ***Perf. 12½x12***

930 A275 40fr multicolored .35 .35
931 A275 50fr multicolored .50 .50
932 A275 75fr multicolored .75 .75
933 A275 100fr multicolored 1.00 1.00
934 A275 135fr multicolored 1.40 1.40
935 A275 200fr multicolored 2.00 2.00
Nos. 930-935 (6) 6.00 6.00

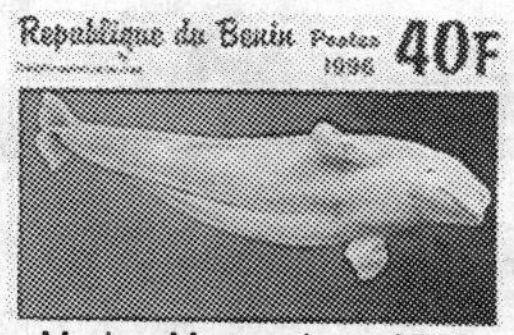

Marine Mammals — A276

Designs: 40fr, Delphinapterus leucas. 50fr, Tursiops truncatus. 75fr, Belaenoptera musculus. 100fr, Eubalaena australis. 135fr, Gramphidelphis griseus. 200fr, Orcinus orca.

1996, Nov. 5 ***Perf. 13***

936 A276 40fr multicolored .35 .35
937 A276 50fr multicolored .50 .50
938 A276 75fr multicolored .75 .75
939 A276 100fr multicolored 1.00 1.00
940 A276 135fr multicolored 1.40 1.40
941 A276 200fr multicolored 2.00 2.00
Nos. 936-941 (6) 6.00 6.00

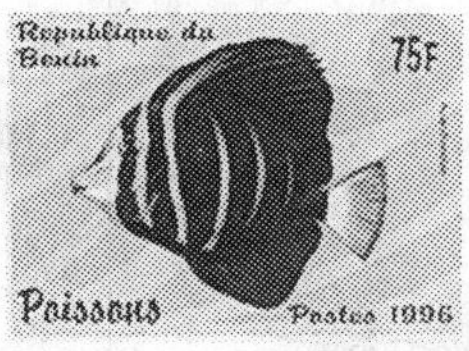

Fish A277

1996, Dec. 4 Litho. ***Perf. 12½***

942 A277 50fr Pomacanthidae, vert. .50 .50
943 A277 75fr Acanthuridae .75 .75
944 A277 100fr Carangidae 1.00 1.00
945 A277 135fr Chaetodontidae 1.40 1.40
946 A277 200fr Chaetodontidae, diff. 2.00 2.00
Nos. 942-946 (5) 5.65 5.65

Souvenir Sheet

947 A277 1000fr Scaridae *6.00 6.00*

No. 947 contains one 40x32mm stamp.

Coat of Arms Type of 1995

1996-97 ***Perf. 12½***

948 A256 100fr multicolored .45 .45
949 A256 135fr lt yellow & multi .55 .55
950 A256 150fr lt blue green & multi .60 .60
951 A256 200fr lt orange & multi .85 .85
Nos. 949-951 (3) 2.00 2.00

Issued: 100fr, 12/27/96; 135fr, 150fr, 200fr, 5/15/97.

Military Uniforms — A278

Regiments of European infantry: 135fr, Grenadier, Glassenapp. 150fr, Officer, Von Groben. 200fr, Musketeer, Comte Dohna. 270fr, Bombardier. 300fr, Gendarme. 400fr, Dragoon, Mollendorf.
1000fr, Soldiers, flag, horses, vert.

1997, Feb. 20

952 A278 135fr multicolored .55 .55
953 A278 150fr multicolored .60 .60
954 A278 200fr multicolored .80 .80
955 A278 270fr multicolored 1.10 1.10
956 A278 300fr multicolored 1.25 1.25
957 A278 400fr multicolored 1.60 1.60
Nos. 952-957 (6) 5.90 5.90

Souvenir Sheet

Perf. 13

958 A278 1000fr multicolored 4.00 4.00

No. 958 contains one 32x40mm stamp.

Trains
A279

135fr, Steam turbine, Reid Maclead, 1920. 150fr, Experimental high speed, 1935. 200fr, Renard Argent, 1935. 270fr, Class No. 21-C-6, 1941. 300fr, Diesel, 1960. 400fr, Diesel, 1960, diff.
1000fr, Coronation Scot, 1937.

1997, Mar. 26 Litho. *Perf. 13*

959	A279	135fr multicolored	.50	.50
960	A279	150fr multicolored	.55	.55
961	A279	200fr multicolored	.75	.75
962	A279	270fr multicolored	1.00	1.00
963	A279	300fr multicolored	1.10	1.10
964	A279	400fr multicolored	1.50	1.50
		Nos. 959-964 (6)	5.40	5.40

Souvenir Sheet

965 A279 1000fr multicolored 3.75 3.75

No. 965 contains one 40x32mm stamp.

1998 World Cup Soccer Championship, France — A280

Various soccer plays.

1997, Apr. 9 *Perf. 12½x13*

966 A280	135fr multicolored	.50	.50
967 A280	150fr multicolored	.55	.55
968 A280	200fr multicolored	.75	.75
969 A280	270fr multicolored	1.00	1.00
970 A280	300fr multi, horiz.	1.10	1.10
971 A280	400fr multi, horiz.	1.50	1.50
	Nos. 966-971 (6)	5.40	5.40

Souvenir Sheet

972 A280 1000fr multicolored 3.75 3.75

No. 972 contains one 40x32mm stamp.

Orchids — A281

Phalaenopsis: 135fr, Penetrate. 150fr, Golden sands. 200fr, Sun spots. 270fr, Fuscata. 300fr, Christi floyd. 400fr, Cayanne.
1000fr, Janet kuhn.

1997, June 9 Litho. *Perf. 12½x13*

973 A281	135fr multicolored	.50	.50
974 A281	150fr multicolored	.55	.55
975 A281	200fr multicolored	.70	.70
976 A281	270fr multicolored	1.00	1.00
977 A281	300fr multicolored	1.10	1.10
978 A281	400fr multicolored	1.40	1.40
	Nos. 973-978 (6)	5.25	5.25

Souvenir Sheet

Perf. 12½

979 A281 1000fr multicolored 3.60 3.60

No. 979 contains one 32x40mm stamp.

Dogs — A282

Designs: 135fr, Irish setter. 150fr, Saluki. 200fr, Doberman pinscher. 270fr, Siberian husky. 300fr, Basenji. 400fr, Boxer.
1000fr, Rhodesian ridgeback.

1997, May 30 *Perf. 13*

980 A282	135fr multicolored	.50	.50
981 A282	150fr multicolored	.55	.55
982 A282	200fr multicolored	.70	.70
983 A282	270fr multicolored	1.00	1.00
984 A282	300fr multicolored	1.10	1.10
985 A282	400fr multicolored	1.40	1.40
	Nos. 980-985 (6)	5.25	5.25

Souvenir Sheet

Perf. 12½

986 A282 1000fr multicolored 3.60 3.60

No. 986 contains one 32x40mm stamp.

Antique Automobiles — A283

1997, July 5 Litho. *Perf. 13x12½*

987 A283	135fr 1905 Buick	.45	.45
988 A283	150fr 1903 Ford	.50	.50
989 A283	200fr 1913 Stanley	.70	.70
990 A283	270fr 1911 Stoddar-Dayton	.90	.90
991 A283	300fr 1934 Cadillac	1.00	1.00
992 A283	400fr 1931 Cadillac	1.40	1.40
	Nos. 987-992 (6)	4.95	4.95

Souvenir Sheet

Perf. 13

993 A283 1000fr 1928 Ford 3.40 3.40

No. 993 contains one 40x32mm stamp.

Songbirds — A284

Designs: 135fr, Pyrrhula pyrrhula. 150fr, Carduelis spinus. 200fr, Turdus torquatus. 270fr, Parus cristatus. 300fr, Nucifraga caryocatactes. 400fr, Luscinia megarhynchos.
1000fr, Motacilla flava.

1997, July 30 *Perf. 13x12½*

994 A284	135fr multicolored	.45	.45
995 A284	150fr multicolored	.50	.50
996 A284	200fr multicolored	.70	.70
997 A284	270fr multicolored	.90	.90
998 A284	300fr multicolored	1.00	1.00
999 A284	400fr multicolored	1.40	1.40
	Nos. 994-999 (6)	4.95	4.95

Souvenir Sheet

Perf. 12½

1000 A284 1000fr multicolored 3.40 3.40

No. 1000 contains one 32x40mm stamp.

Flowering Cactus — A285

Designs: 135fr, Faucaria lupina. 150fr, Conophytum bilobun. 200fr, Lithops aucampiae. 270fr, Lithops helmutii. 300fr, Stapelia grandiflora. 400fr, Lithops fulviceps.
1000fr, Pleiospilos willowmorensis.

1997, Aug. 30 Litho. *Perf. 13x12½*

1001 A285	135fr multicolored	.45	.45
1002 A285	150fr multicolored	.50	.50
1003 A285	200fr multicolored	.70	.70
1004 A285	270fr multicolored	.90	.90
1005 A285	300fr multicolored	1.00	1.00
1006 A285	400fr multicolored	1.25	1.25
	Nos. 1001-1006 (6)	4.80	4.80

Souvenir Sheet

Perf. 12½

1007 A285 1000fr multicolored 3.40 3.40

No. 1007 contains one 32x40mm stamp.

Benin No. 418 Surcharged

1995

Perfs. & Printing Methods as Before

1009 A114 10fr on 90fr #418

Early Locomotives — A265

Designs: 135fr, Puffing Billy, 1813. 150fr, La Fusée, 1829. 200fr, Royal George, 1827. 270fr, Nouveauté, 1829. 300fr, Locomotion, 1825, vert. 400fr, Sans Pareil, 1829, vert.
1000fr, Trevithick locomotive.

1997, Dec. 3 Litho. *Perf. 13*

1022 A265	135fr multicolored	.45	.45
1023 A265	150fr multicolored	.50	.50
1024 A265	200fr multicolored	.70	.70
1025 A265	270fr multicolored	.95	.95
1026 A265	300fr multicolored	1.00	1.00
1027 A265	400fr multicolored	1.40	1.40
	Nos. 1022-1027 (6)	5.00	5.00

Souvenir Sheet

1028 A265 1000fr multicolored 3.50 3.50

No. 1028 contains one 40x32mm stamp.

Mushrooms
A266

Designs: 135fr, Amanita caesarea. 150fr, Cortinarius collinitus. 200fr, Amanita bisporigera. 270fr, Amanita rubescens. 300fr, Russula virescens. 400fr, Amanita inaurata.
1000fr, Amanita muscaria.

1997, Nov. 5 Litho. *Perf. 13*

1029 A266	135fr multicolored	.40	.40
1030 A266	150fr multicolored	.55	.55
1031 A266	200fr multicolored	.70	.70
1032 A266	270fr multicolored	.95	.95
1033 A266	300fr multicolored	1.00	1.00
1034 A266	400fr multicolored	1.40	1.40
	Nos. 1029-1034 (6)	5.00	5.00

Souvenir Sheet

1035 A266 1000fr multicolored 3.50 3.50

No. 1035 contains one 32x40mm stamp.

Assoc. of African Petroleum Producers, 10th Anniv. — A267

1997, Oct. 20 Litho. *Perf. 13*

1036 A267	135fr green & multi		
1037 A267	200fr orange & multi		
1038 A267	300fr blue & multi		
1039 A267	500fr yellow & multi	1.75	1.75

Old Sailing Vessels — A268

Designs: 135fr, Egyptian. 150fr, Greek. 200fr, Assyrian-Phoenician. 270fr, Roman. 300fr, Norman. 400fr, Mediterranean.
1000fr, English.

1997, Sept. 10 Litho. *Perf. 12½*

1040 A268	135fr multicolored	.50	.50
1041 A268	150fr multicolored	.55	.55
1042 A268	200fr multicolored	.75	.75
1043 A268	270fr multicolored	1.00	1.00
1044 A268	300fr multicolored	1.10	1.10
1045 A268	400fr multicolored	1.50	1.50
	Nos. 1040-1045 (6)	5.40	5.40

Souvenir Sheet

1046 A268 1000fr multicolored 3.75 3.75

No. 1046 contains one 32x40mm stamp.

Fish
A269

Designs: 135fr, Epinephelus fasciatus. 150fr, Apogon victoriae. 200fr, Scarus gibbus. 270fr, Pygoplites diacanthus. 300fr, Cirrhilabrus punctatus. 400fr, Cirrhitichthys oxycephalus.
1000fr, Bodianus bilunulatus.

1997, Sept. 15 Litho. *Perf. 12½*

1047 A269	135fr multicolored	.50	.50
1048 A269	150fr multicolored	.55	.55
1049 A269	200fr multicolored	.75	.75
1050 A269	270fr multicolored	1.00	1.00
1051 A269	300fr multicolored	1.10	1.10
1052 A269	400fr multicolored	1.50	1.50
	Nos. 1047-1052 (6)	5.40	5.40

Souvenir Sheet

Perf. 13

1053 A269 1000fr multicolored 3.75 3.75

No. 1053 contains one 40x32mm stamp.

Arabian Horse — A270

Various horses. Denominations and background colors: d, 135fr, green. e, 150fr, red brown. f, 200fr, yellow. g, 270fr, orange brown. h, 300fr, tan. i, 400fr, olive green.

1997, May 25 Litho. *Perf. 12½*

1053A A270	Pair, #d.-e.	1.00	1.00
1053B A270	Pair, #f.-g.	1.60	1.60
1053C A270	Pair, #h.-i.	2.50	2.50
	Nos. 1053A-1053C (3)	5.10	5.10

Souvenir Sheet

1054 A270 1000fr multicolored 3.50 3.50

Mushrooms
A271

Designs: 135fr, Tephrocybe carbonaria. 150fr, Suillus luteus. 200fr, Pleurotus ostreatus. 270fr, Hohenbuehelia geogenia. 300fr, Tylopilus felleus. 400fr, Lepiota leucothites.
1000fr, Gymnopilus junonius.

1998, Apr. 28 Litho. *Perf. 12½*

1055 A271 135fr multicolored .45 .45
1056 A271 150fr multicolored .50 .50
1057 A271 200fr multicolored .65 .65
1058 A271 270fr multicolored .90 .90
1059 A271 300fr multicolored 1.00 1.00
1060 A271 400fr multicolored 1.40 1.40
Nos. 1055-1060 (6) 4.90 4.90

Souvenir Sheet

1061 A271 1000fr multicolored 3.50 3.50

Fire Fighting Apparatus A272

Designs: 135fr, Philadelphia Double Deck, 1885. 150fr, Veteran, 1850. 200fr, Merry Weather, 1894. 270fr, Horse-drawn wagon, 19th cent. 300fr, 1948 Jeep. 400fr, Chevrolet 6400.

1000fr, 1952 American-La France-Foamite Corp.

1998, Apr. 30 Litho. *Perf. 12¾*

1062 A272 135fr multicolored .45 .45
1063 A272 150fr multicolored .50 .50
1064 A272 200fr multicolored .65 .65
1065 A272 270fr multicolored .90 .90
1066 A272 300fr multicolored 1.00 1.00
1067 A272 400fr multicolored 1.40 1.40
Nos. 1062-1067 (6) 4.90 4.90

Souvenir Sheet

1068 A272 1000fr multicolored 3.50 3.50

No. 1068 contains one 40x32mm stamp.

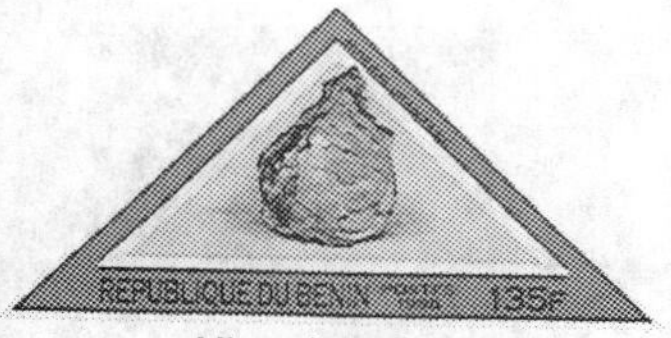

Minerals — A273

Designs: No. 1069a, 135fr, Uranifere. No. 1069b, 150fr, Quartz. No. 1070a, 200fr, Aragonite. No. 1070b, 270fr, Malachite. No. 1071a, 300fr, Turquoise. No. 1071b, 400fr, Corundum.

1000fr, Marble.

1998, June 5 Litho. *Perf. 12½*

1069 A273 Pair, #a.-b. 1.00 1.00
1070 A273 Pair, #a.-b. 1.60 1.60
1071 A273 Pair, #a.-b. 2.50 2.50
Nos. 1069-1071 (3) 5.10 5.10

Souvenir Sheet

1072 A273 1000fr multicolored 3.50 3.50

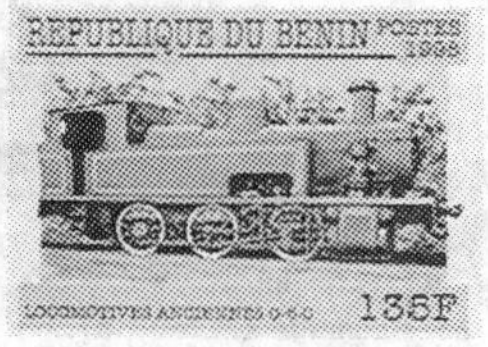

Locomotives — A273a

Designs: 135fr, Red 0-6-0. 150fr, 0-4-4. 200fr, Brown 0-6-0. 270fr, Purple 0-6-0. 300fr, Blue 0-6-0. 400fr, "Helvetia" 0-6-0.

1000fr, "Shelby Steel" 0-6-0.

1998, June 30 Litho. *Perf. 12¾*

1073 A273a 135fr multicolored .45 .45
1074 A273a 150fr multicolored .50 .50
1075 A273a 200fr multicolored .65 .65
1076 A273a 270fr multicolored .90 .90
1077 A273a 300fr multicolored 1.00 1.00
1078 A273a 400fr multicolored 1.40 1.40
Nos. 1073-1078 (6) 4.90 4.90

Souvenir Sheet

Perf. 13

1079 A273a 1000fr multicolored 3.50 3.50

No. 1079 contains one 40x32mm stamp.

Diana, Princess of Wales (1961-97) — A274

Various portraits: a, 135fr. b, 150fr. c, 200fr. d, 270fr. e, 300fr. f, 400fr. g, 500fr. h, 600fr. i, 700fr.

1998, July 10 Litho. *Perf. 12½*

1083 A274 Sheet of 9, #a.-i. 11.50 11.50

Dahomey No. 302 Surcharged

1997?

Perfs. & Printing Method as Before

1084 A65(h) 35fr on 85fr #302

Python Regius A276

Various views of python: a, 135fr. b, 150fr. c, 200fr. d, 2000fr.

1999, Apr. 27 Litho. *Perf. 13*

1086 A276 Strip of 4, #a.-d. 8.75 8.75

World Wildlife Fund.

Cats A278

135fr, Abyssinian. 150fr, Striped shorthair. 200fr, Siamese. 270fr, Red striped cat. 300fr, Gray cat with black stripes. 400fr, Manx.

1000fr, Cat with orange, black and white fur.

Perf. 12¼x12½, 12½x12¼

1998, Aug. 10 Litho.

1094 A278 135fr multi, vert. .45 .45
1095 A278 150fr multi, vert. .50 .50
1096 A278 200fr multi, vert. .65 .65
1097 A278 270fr multi .90 .90
1098 A278 300fr multi 1.00 1.00
1099 A278 400fr multi 1.25 1.25
Nos. 1094-1099 (6) 4.75 4.75

Souvenir Sheet

Perf. 13

1100 A278 1000fr multicolored 3.25 3.25

No. 1100 contains one 40x32mm stamp.

AIR POST STAMPS

PEOPLE'S REPUBLIC

Catalogue values for unused stamps in this section are for Never Hinged items.

Nativity, by Aert van Leyden — AP84

Christmas: 85fr, Adoration of the Kings, by Rubens, vert. 140fr, Adoration of the Shepherds, by Charles Lebrun. 300fr, The Virgin with the Blue Diadem, by Raphael, vert.

1975, Dec. 19 Litho. *Perf. 13*

C240 AP84 40fr gold & multi .20 .20
C241 AP84 85fr gold & multi .40 .20
C242 AP84 140fr gold & multi .60 .25
C243 AP84 300fr gold & multi 1.40 .65
Nos. C240-C243 (4) 2.60 1.30

For surcharges see Nos. C362, C367, C407.

Slalom, Innsbruck Olympic Emblem — AP85

Innsbruck Olympic Games Emblem and: 150fr, Bobsledding, vert. 300fr, Figure skating, pairs.

1976, June 28 Litho. *Perf. 12½*

C244 AP85 60fr multi .25 .20
C245 AP85 150fr multi .65 .25
C246 AP85 300fr multi 1.25 .55
Nos. C244-C246 (3) 2.15 1.00

12th Winter Olympic Games, Innsbruck, Austria, Feb. 4-15.

Dahomey Nos. C263-C265 Overprinted or Surcharged: "POPULAIRE / DU BENIN" and Bars

1976, July 4 Engr. *Perf. 13*

C247 AP86 135fr multi .55 .25
C248 AP86 210fr on 300fr multi .90 .35
C249 AP86 380fr on 500fr multi 1.50 .65
Nos. C247-C249 (3) 2.95 1.25

The overprint includes a bar covering "DU DAHOMEY" in shades of brown; "POPULAIRE DU BENIN" is blue on Nos. C247-C248, red on No. C249. The surcharge and bars over old value are blue on No. C248, red, brown on No. C249.

Long Jump AP86

Designs (Olympic Rings and): 150fr, Basketball, vert. 200fr, Hurdles.

1976, July 16 Photo. *Perf. 13*

C250 AP86 60fr multi .30 .20
C251 AP86 150fr multi .85 .30
C252 AP86 200fr multi 1.25 .45
a. Souv. sheet of 3, #C250-C252 3.00 3.00
Nos. C250-C252 (3) 2.40 .95

21st Olympic Games, Montreal, Canada, July 17-Aug 1.

Konrad Adenauer and Cologne Cathedral — AP87

Design: 90fr, Konrad Adenauer, vert.

1976, Aug. 27 Engr. *Perf. 13*

C253 AP87 90fr multi .60 .25
C254 AP87 250fr multi 1.75 .70

Konrad Adenauer (1876-1967), German Chancellor, birth centenary.

For surcharge see No. C289B.

Children's Heads and Flying Fish (Dahomey Type A32) — AP88

210fr, Lion cub's head and Benin type A3, vert.

1976, Sept. 13

C255 AP88 60fr Prus bl & vio bl .35 .20
C256 AP88 210fr multi 1.10 .45

JUVAROUEN 76, Intl. Youth Phil. Exhib., Rouen, France, Apr. 25-May 2.

For surcharge see No. C300.

Apollo 14 Emblem and Blast-off — AP89

Design: 270fr, Landing craft and man on moon.

1976, Oct. 18 Engr. *Perf. 13*

C257 AP89 130fr multi .45 .30
C258 AP89 270fr multi 1.00 .65

Apollo 14 Moon Mission, 5th anniversary.

For surcharges see Nos. C312, C454.

Annunciation, by Master of Jativa AP90

Christmas: 60fr, Nativity, by Gerard David. 270fr, Adoration of the Kings, Dutch School. 300fr, Flight into Egypt, by Gentile Fabriano, horiz.

1976, Dec. 20 Litho. *Perf. 12½*

C259 AP90 50fr gold & multi .25 .20
C260 AP90 60fr gold & multi .35 .20
C261 AP90 270fr gold & multi 1.50 .60
C262 AP90 300fr gold & multi 1.60 1.00
Nos. C259-C262 (4) 3.70 2.00

For surcharges see Nos. C310, C321, C484.

Gamblers and Lottery Emblem — AP91

1977, Mar. 13 Litho. *Perf. 13*

C263 AP91 50fr multi .25 .20

National lottery, 10th anniversary.

Sassenage Castle, Grenoble — AP92

1977, May 16 *Perf. 12½*

C264 AP92 200fr multi .80 .60

10th anniv. of Intl. French Language Council.

For surcharge see No. C334.

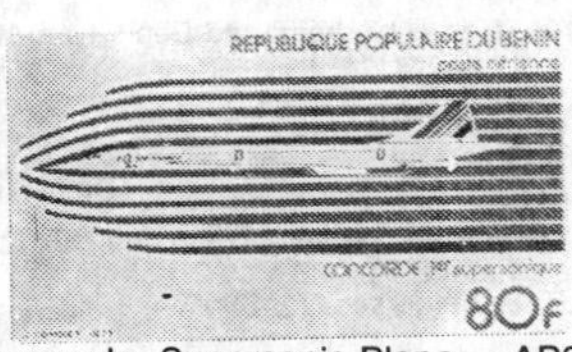

Concorde, Supersonic Plane — AP93

Designs: 150fr, Zeppelin. 300fr, Charles A. Lindbergh and Spirit of St. Louis. 500fr, Charles Nungesser and François Coli, French aviators lost over Atlantic, 1927.

1977, July 25 Engr. *Perf. 13*

C265 AP93 80fr ultra & red .40 .35
C266 AP93 150fr multi .80 .60
C267 AP93 300fr multi 1.60 1.25
C268 AP93 500fr multi 2.50 2.00
Nos. C265-C268 (4) 5.30 4.20

Aviation history.
For overprint and surcharges see Nos. C274, C316, C336.

Soccer Player — AP94

200fr, Soccer players and Games' emblem.

1977, July 28 Litho. *Perf. 12½x12*

C269 AP94 60fr multi .35 .20
C270 AP94 200fr multi 1.10 .80

World Soccer Cup elimination games.
For surcharges see Nos. C289A, C308.

Miss Haverfield, by Gainsborough — AP95

Designs: 150fr, Self-portrait, by Rubens. 200fr, Anguish, man's head by Da Vinci.

1977, Oct. 3 Engr. *Perf. 13*

C271 AP95 100fr sl grn & mar .55 .40
C272 AP95 150fr red brn & dk brn .80 .60
C273 AP95 200fr brn & red 1.10 .80
Nos. C271-C273 (3) 2.45 1.80

For surcharges see Nos. C309, C317.

No. C265 Overprinted: "1er VOL COMMERCIAL / 22.11.77 PARIS NEW-YORK"

1977, Nov. 22 Engr. *Perf. 13*

C274 AP93 80fr ultra & red .42 .35

Concorde, 1st commercial flight, Paris to NY.

Viking on Mars AP96

Designs: 150fr, Isaac Newton, apple globe, stars. 200fr, Vladimir M. Komarov, spacecraft and earth. 500fr, Dog Laika, rocket and space.

1977, Nov. 28 Engr. *Perf. 13*

C275 AP96 100fr multi .55 .40
C276 AP96 150fr multi .80 .60
C277 AP96 200fr multi 1.10 .80
C278 AP96 500fr multi 2.75 2.00
Nos. C275-C278 (4) 5.20 3.80

Operation Viking on Mars; Isaac Newton (1642-1727); 10th death anniv. of Russian cosmonaut Vladimir M. Komarov; 20th anniv. of 1st living creature in space.
For surcharges see Nos. C301, C314.

Monument, Red Star Place, Cotonou AP97

Lithographed; Gold Embossed

1977 Nov. 30 *Perf. 12½*

C279 AP97 500fr multi 1.75 1.10

Suzanne Fourment, by Rubens AP98

Design: 380fr, Nicholas Rubens, By Rubens.

1977, Dec. 12 Engr. *Perf. 13*

C280 AP98 200fr multi 1.10 .80
C281 AP98 380fr claret & ocher 2.00 1.40

For surcharges see Nos. C311, C313, C483.

Parthenon and UNESCO Emblem — AP99

Designs: 70fr, Acropolis and frieze showing Pan-Athenaic procession, vert. 250fr, Parthenon and frieze showing horsemen, vert.

1978, Sept. 22 Litho. *Perf. 12½x12*

C282 AP99 70fr multi .35 .20
C283 AP99 250fr multi 1.25 .80
C284 AP99 500fr multi 2.75 1.50
Nos. C282-C284 (3) 4.35 2.50

Save the Parthenon in Athens campaign.
For surcharge see No. C338.

Philexafrique II—Essen Issue
Common Design Types

Designs: No. C285, Buffalo and Dahomey #C33. No. C286, Wild ducks and Baden #1.

1978, Nov. 1 Litho. *Perf. 12½*

C285 CD138 100fr multi .65 .40
C286 CD139 100fr multi .65 .40
a. Pair, #C285-C286 1.30 1.00

Wilbur and Orville Wright and Flyer — AP100

1978, Dec. 28 Engr. *Perf. 13*

C287 AP100 500fr multi 3.50 2.00

75th anniversary of 1st powered flight.
For surcharge see No. C339.

Cook's Ships, Hawaii, World Map — AP101

Design: 50fr, Battle at Kowrowa.

1979, June 1 Engr. *Perf. 13*

C288 AP101 20fr multi .20 .20
C289 AP101 50fr multi .45 .45

Capt. James Cook (1728-1779), explorer.

No. C253, C269 Surcharged

1979

Perfs. & Printing Method as Before

C289A AP94 50fr on 60fr #C269
C289B AP87 50fr on 90fr multi

Lunokhod Type of 1980

1980, June 15 Engr. *Perf. 13*
Size: 27x48mm

C290 A133 210fr multi 1.40 1.40

For surcharges see Nos. C305, C450.

Soccer Players — AP102

1981, Mar. 31 Litho. *Perf. 13*

C291 AP102 200fr Ball, globe .90 .90
C292 AP102 500fr shown 2.50 2.50

ESPANA '82 World Soccer Cup eliminations.
For surcharges see Nos. C335, Q10B.

Prince Charles and Lady Diana, London Bridge — AP103

1981, July 29 Litho. *Perf. 12½*

C293 AP103 500fr multi 3.00 3.00

Royal wedding.
For surcharges see Nos. C323, C500.

Three Musicians, by Pablo Picasso (1881-1973) — AP104

Perf. 12½x13, 13x12½

1981, Nov. 2 Litho.

C294 AP104 300fr Dance, vert. 2.00 2.00
C295 AP104 500fr shown 3.50 3.50

For surcharges see Nos. C320, C340.

1300th Anniv. of Bulgaria — AP105

1981, Dec. 2 Litho. *Perf. 13*

C296 AP105 100fr multi .60 .60

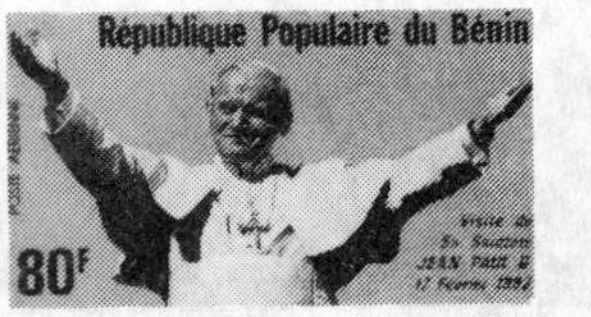

Visit of Pope John Paul II — AP106

1982, Feb. 17 Litho. *Perf. 13*

C297 AP106 80fr multi .55 .55

20th Anniv. of John Glenn's Flight — AP107

1982, Feb. 21 Litho. *Perf. 13*

C298 AP107 500fr multi 3.00 3.00

For surcharge see No. C315.

Scouting Year AP108

1982, June 1 *Perf. 12½*

C299 AP108 105fr multi .70 .70

For surcharge see No. C324.

Nos. C256, C275 Surcharged

1982, Nov. Engr. *Perf. 13*

C300 AP88 50fr on 210fr multi .35 .35
C301 AP96 50fr on 100fr multi .35 .35

Monet in Boat, by Claude Monet (1832-1883) — AP109

1982, Dec. 6 Litho. *Perf. 13x12½*
C302 AP109 300fr multi 2.00 2.00

For surcharge see No. C326.

Christmas 1982 AP110

Virgin and Child Paintings.

1982, Dec. 20 *Perf. 12½x13*
C303 AP110 200fr Matthias Grunewald 1.25 1.25
C304 AP110 300fr Correggio 1.75 1.75

For surcharges see Nos. C325, C337.

No. C290 Surcharged

1983 Engr. *Perf. 13*
C305 A133 75fr on 210fr multi .50 .50

Bangkok '83 Stamp Exhibition AP111

1983, Aug. 4 Photo. *Perf. 13*
C306 AP111 300fr multi 1.50 1.50

For surcharge see No. C322.

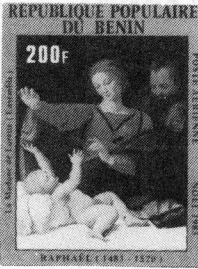

Christmas 1983 AP112

1983, Dec. 26 Litho. *Perf. 12½x13*
C307 AP112 200fr Loretto Madonna, by Raphael .65 .65

For surcharge see No. C319.

Types of 1976-82 Surcharged

1983, Nov.

C308	AP94	10fr on 200fr C270	.20	.20
C309	AP95	15fr on 200fr C273	.20	.20
C310	AP90	15fr on 270fr C261	.20	.20
C311	AP98	20fr on 200fr C280	.20	.20
C312	AP89	25fr on 270fr C258	.20	.20
C313	AP98	25fr on 380fr C281	.20	.20
C314	AP96	30fr on 200fr C277	.20	.20
C315	AP107	40fr on 500fr C298	.20	.20
C316	AP93	75fr on 150fr C266	.40	.40
C317	AP95	75fr on 150fr C272	.40	.40
		Nos. C308-C317 (10)	2.40	2.40

Summer Olympics — AP113

1984, July 16 Litho. *Perf. 13x13½*
C318 AP113 300fr Sam the Eagle, mascot 1.00 1.00

Nos. C262, C293-C294, C299, C302-C303, C306-C307 Surcharged

1984, Sept.

C319	AP112	15fr on 200fr multi	.20	.20
C320	AP104	15fr on 300fr multi	.20	.20
C321	AP90	25fr on 300fr multi	.20	.20
C322	AP111	25fr on 300fr multi	.20	.20
C323	AP103	40fr on 500fr multi	.20	.20
C324	AP108	75fr on 105fr multi	.25	.25
C325	AP110	90fr on 200fr multi	.30	.30
C326	AP109	90fr on 300fr multi	.30	.30
		Nos. C319-C326 (8)	1.85	1.85

Christmas 1984 AP114

1984, Dec. 17 Litho. *Perf. 12½x13*
C327 AP114 500fr Virgin and Child, by Murillo 1.50 1.50

For surcharge see No. C486

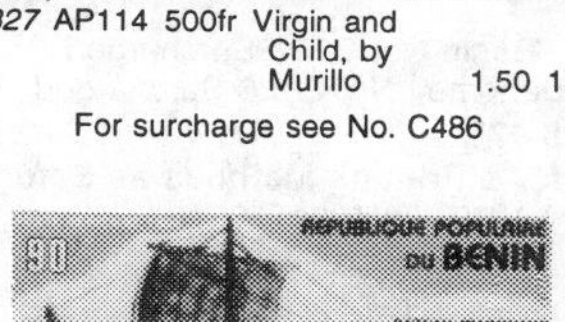

Ships — AP115

1984, Dec. 28 Litho. *Perf. 13*
C328 AP115 90fr Sidon merchant ship .30 .30
C329 AP115 125fr Wavertree, vert. .40 .40

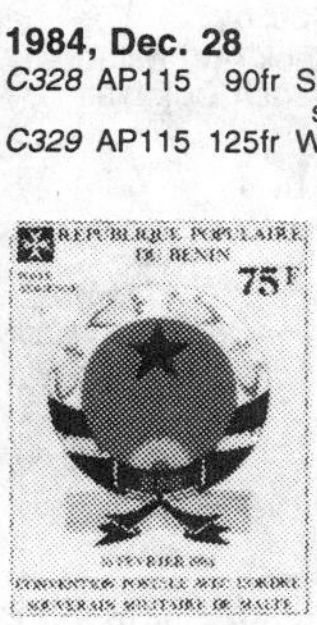

Benin-S.O.M. Postal Convention AP116

1985, Apr. 15 Litho. *Perf. 13½*
C330 AP116 75fr Benin arms .25 .25
C331 AP116 75fr Sovereign Order of Malta .25 .25
a. Pair, #C330-C331 .45 .45

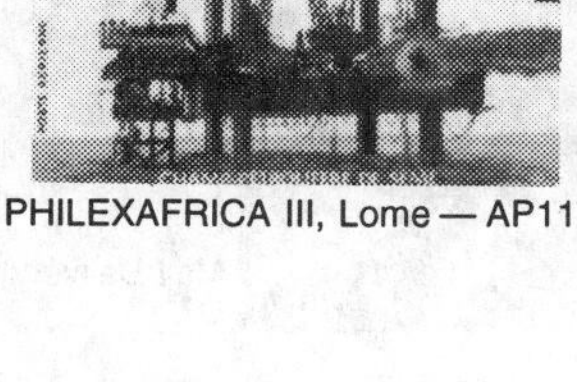

PHILEXAFRICA III, Lome — AP117

1985, June 24 *Perf. 13*
C332 AP117 200fr Oil platform .60 .60
C333 AP117 200fr Soccer players .60 .60
a. Pair, #C332-C333 + label 1.25 1.25

For surcharges see Nos. C485-C485A.

Stamps of 1977-82 Surcharged

1985, Mar.

C334	AP92	75fr on 200fr #C264	.20	.20
C335	AP102	75fr on 200fr #C291	.20	.20
C336	AP93	75fr on 300fr #C267	.20	.20
C337	AP110	75fr on 300fr #C304	.20	.20
C338	AP99	90fr on 500fr #C284	.25	.25
C339	AP100	90fr on 500fr #C287	.25	.25
C340	AP104	90fr on 500fr #C295	.25	.25
		Nos. C334-C340 (7)	1.55	1.55

Dahomey Stamps of 1971-75 Surcharged

1985, Aug.

C341	AP87(i)	25fr on 40fr #C266	.20	.20
C342	AP49(a)	40fr #C142	.20	.20
C343	AP56(i)	75fr on 85fr #C164	.20	.20
C344	AP60(a)	75fr on 100fr #C173	.20	.20
C345	AP64(i)	75fr on 125fr #C186	.20	.20
C346	AP56(i)	90fr on 20fr #C163	.25	.25
C347	A61(i)	90fr on 150fr #C153	.25	.25
C348	AP49(a)	90fr on 200fr #C143	.25	.25
C349	AP78(j)	90fr on 200fr #C237	.25	.25
C350	AP78(j)	150fr #C236	.45	.45
		Nos. C341-C350 (10)	2.45	2.45

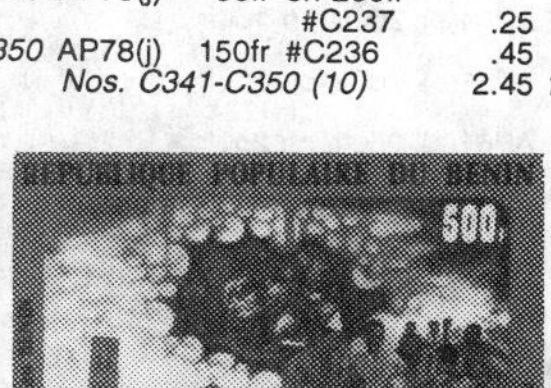

Christmas — AP118

1985, Dec. 20 Litho. *Perf. 13x12½*
C351 AP118 500fr multi 1.75 1.75

For surcharge see No. C449.

Dahomey Nos. C34-C37, C84, C131 Surcharged or Overprinted

1986 Photo. Perfs. as before

C352	AP33(b)	75fr on 70fr #C84	.25	.25
C353	AP14(b)	75fr on 100fr #C34	.25	.25
C354	AP15(b)	75fr on 200fr #C35	.25	.25
C355	AP15(b)	90fr on 250fr #C36	.35	.35
C356	AP45(b)	100fr #C131	.40	.40
C357	AP14(b)	150fr on 500fr #C37	.50	.50
		Nos. C352-C357 (6)	2.00	2.00

Issued: 75fr, 90fr, Mar; 100fr, 150fr, June.

Dahomey Nos. C82, C139, C141, C146 Surcharged

1986

Perfs. & Printing Methods as Before

C357A	AP33(d)	15fr on 45fr #C82
C357B	AP48(d)	25fr on 200fr #C141 (S)
C357D	AP48(d)	100fr on #C139
C357E	CD135(d)	100fr on #C146

Christmas — AP119

1986, Dec. 24 Litho. *Perf. 13x12½*
C358 AP119 300fr multi 1.25 1.25

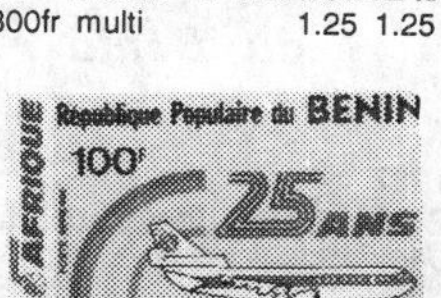

Air Africa, 25th Anniv. AP120

1986, Dec. 30 *Perf. 12½*
C359 AP120 100fr multi .40 .40

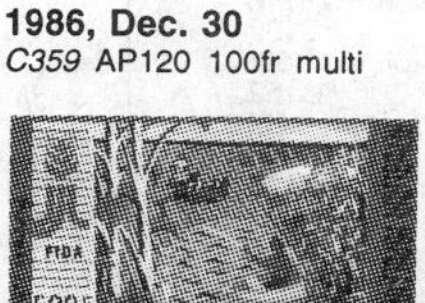

Intl. Agricultural Development Fund (FIDA), 10th Anniv. AP121

1987, Dec. 14 Litho. *Perf. 13½*
C360 AP121 500fr multi 3.50 3.50

Christmas — AP122

1988, Dec. 23 Litho. *Perf. 13x12½*
C361 AP122 500fr Adoration of the Magi, storyteller 3.25 3.25

No. C241 Surcharged

Rèpublique
Populaire
du Bénin

15 f

1989, Apr. 24 Litho. *Perf. 13*
C362 AP84(b) 15fr on 85fr multi .20 .20

The Scott Catalogue value is a retail value; that is, what you could expect to pay for the stamp in a grade of Very Fine. The value listed reflects recent actual dealer selling prices.

Dahomey Nos. C37, C53, C152, C156, C165, C175, C182, C234 Benin No. C242 Surcharged or Overprinted

[redacted]

République Populaire du Bénin

1987
Perfs. & Printing Methods as Before

C363 AP77 20fr on 250fr #C234
C364 AP48(b) 25fr on 150fr #C175 (S&B)
C365 AP63(b) 40fr on 15fr #C182
C366 AP48(b) 40fr on 100fr #C152
C367 AP84(b) 50fr on 140fr #C242
C368 AP14(b) 50fr on 500fr #C37
C369 AP22(b) 80fr on #C53
C370 AP56(b) 80fr on 150fr #C165
C373 AP52(b) 100fr on #C156

Dahomey Nos. C140, C144, C158, C166, C177, C185, C188 C191, C195, C207, C262 Surcharged

1988
Perfs. & Printing Methods as Before

C374 AP50(d) 10fr on 50fr #C144
C375 AP64(d) 10fr on 65fr #C185
C376 AP72(d) 15fr on 150fr #C207
C377 AP67(d) 25fr on 200fr #C191
C378 AP61(d) 40fr on 35fr #C195
C380 AP53(d) 70fr on 250fr #C158
C381 AP48(d) 100fr on #C140
C382 AP65(d) 100fr on #C188
C384 AP61(f) 125fr on #C177
C385 AP86(d) 125fr on 75fr #C262
C386 AP57(d) 150fr on 100fr #C166

Dahomey Nos. C181, C196, C208 Surcharged

1988
Perfs. & Printing Methods as Before

C388 AP61(d) 25fr on 100fr #C196
C390 AP62 40fr on 100fr #C181
C391 AP73(d) 40fr on 150fr #C208

Dahomey Nos. C108, C147-C148, C162, C167, C178, C187, C194

1992
Perfs. & Printing Methods as Before

C394 AP51(f) 70fr on #C148
C395 AP55(e) 100fr on #C162
C396 AP68(g) 100fr on #C194
C397 AP51(e) 125fr on 40fr #C147
C398 A52(f) 125fr on 70fr #C108
C400 AP64a(e) 125fr on 100fr #C187
C401 AP61(f) 190fr on 140fr #C178
C402 AP58(f) 190fr on 150fr #C167

Dahomey Nos. C145, C149-C150, C182, C189, C198, C257, C264-C265 Surcharged Benin No. C241 Surcharged

1993
Perfs. & Printing Methods as Before

C403 AP51(e) 5fr on 100fr #C149
C404 AP50(f) 10fr on 100fr #C145
C405 AP51(f) 20fr on 200fr #C150
C406 AP83(f) 20fr on 500fr #C257
C407 AP84(e) 25fr on 85fr #C241
C408 AP86(f) 25fr on 500fr #C265
C409 AP63(f) 30fr on 15fr #C182
C410 AP61(f) 30fr on 200fr #C198
C411 AP66(b) 35fr on #C189
C412 AP86(g) 300fr on #C264

Dahomey Nos. C14, C31, C34, C101, C110, C144, C151, C153, C155, C197, C222, C234, C250, C254, C256, C261, Benin C242 Surcharged or Overprinted

1994-95?
Perfs. & Printing Methods as Before

C414 AP52(e) 15fr on 40fr #C155
C415 AP83(f) 25fr on 200fr #C256
C417 AP49(g) 50fr on #C101
C418 AP48(g) 75fr on 40fr #C151
C419 AP4(g) 100fr on #C14
C421 AP50(g) 125fr on 50fr #C144
C422 AP75(e) 125fr on 65fr #C222
C425 AP21(f) 135fr on 45fr #C110
C430 AP81(f) 135fr on 250fr #C250
C432 AP84(f) 150fr on 140fr #C242
C433 A61(b) 150fr on #C153
C434 AP61(f) 150fr on #C197
C435 AP13(e) 200fr on 100fr #C31
C436 AP14(e) 200fr on 100fr #C34
C445 AP61(e) 200fr on 250fr #C234
C446 AP61(e) 200fr on 250fr #C254
C447 AP85(f) 300fr on #C261

Dahomey No. C37, Benin No. C351 Surcharged

1994-95
Printing Method and Perfs as Before

C448 AP14 150fr on 500fr #C37
C449 AP118 200fr on 500fr #C351

Benin No. C290 Surcharged
Dahomey Nos. C206, C257 Surcharged

1996?
Perfs. & Printing Methods as Before

C450 A133 40fr on 210fr #C290
C451 AP83(f) 200fr on 500fr #C257
C452 AP72(f) 1000fr on 150fr #C206

Dahomey No. C265 Surcharged
Benin Nos. C258, C292 Surcharged

1996?
Perfs. & Printing Methods as Before

C453 AP86(g) 25fr on 500fr #C265
C454 AP89 35fr on 270fr #C258
C455 AP102 100fr on 500fr #C292

Dahomey Nos. C61, C74, C85, C88, C94, C106, C109, C111, C113, C115, C120, C124-C125, C130, C135-C136, C138, C142-C143, C150, C157, C204-C205, C207-C208, C260, C263 Surcharged

1996?
Perfs. & Printing Methods as Before

C456 AP48(e) 70fr on 100fr #C138
C457 AP34(h) 150fr on #C88
C458 AP21(e) 150fr on #C115
C459 AP72(e) 150fr on #C207
C460 AP73(h) 150fr on #C208
C461 AP34(e) 150fr on 30fr #C85
C462 AP31(h) 150fr on 30fr #C74
C463 AP21(e) 150fr on 30fr #C109
C464 AP40(e) 150fr on 40fr on 30fr #C120
C465 AP47(e) 150fr on 40fr #C136
C466 AP49(e) 150fr on 40fr #C142
C467 CD128(h) 150fr on 50fr #C94
C468 AP38(h) 150fr on 50fr #C106
C469 AP71(e) 150fr on 50fr #C204
C470 AP54(h) 150fr on 70fr #C124
C471 CD124(h) 150fr on 100fr #C61
C472 AP21(e) 150fr on 100fr #C113
C473 AP53(h) 150fr on 100fr #C157
C474 AP84(h) 150fr on 100fr #C260
C475 AP21(h) 150fr on 110fr #C111
C476 AP44(h) 150fr on 110fr #C130
C477 AP54(h) 150fr on 120fr #C125
C478 AP86(g) 150fr on 135fr #C263
C479 AP46(h) 150fr on 200fr #C135
C480 AP49(e) 150fr on 200fr #C143
C481 AP51(h) 150fr on 200fr #C150
C482 AP71(e) 150fr on 200fr #C205

Benin Nos. C261, C281, C327, C332-C333 Surcharged
Dahomey No. C201 Surcharged

1996-97?
Perfs. & Printing Methods as Before

C483 AP98 30fr on 380fr #C281
C484 AP90 35fr on 270fr #C261
C485 AP117 125fr on 200fr #C332
C485A AP117 125fr on 200fr #C333
C486 AP114 200fr on 500fr #C327
C489 AP70(f) 150fr on 50fr #C201

Dahomey No. C250 Surcharged Type f

1997?
Perf. & Printing Method as Before

C509 AP81(f) 150fr on 250fr #C250

Benin No. C293 Surcharged
Dahomey No. C126 Surcharged

1995-97?
Perfs. & Printing Methods as Before

C500 AP103 150fr on 500fr #C293
C515 AP42(h) 35fr on 100fr on 200fr #C126

POSTAGE DUE STAMPS

French Colony

Handstamped in Black on Postage Due Stamps of French Colonies

BENIN

1894	**Unwmk.**		*Imperf.*	
J1 D1	5c black		120.00	45.00
J2 D1	10c black		120.00	45.00
J3 D1	20c black		120.00	45.00
J4 D1	30c black		120.00	45.00
	Nos. J1-J4 (4)		480.00	180.00

Nos. J1-J4 exist with overprint in various positions.

Catalogue values for unused stamps in this section are for Never Hinged items.

People's Republic

Pineapples
D6

Mail Delivery
D7

Designs: 20fr, Cashew, vert. 40fr, Oranges. 50fr, Akee. 80fr, Mail delivery by boat.

1978, Sept. 5	**Photo.**	*Perf. 13*	
J44 D6	10fr multi	.20	.20
J45 D6	20fr multi	.20	.20
J46 D6	40fr multi	.30	.20
J47 D6	50fr multi	.45	.25
	Engr.		
J48 D7	60fr multi	.30	.25
J49 D7	80fr multi	.45	.30
	Nos. J44-J49 (6)	1.90	1.40

PARCEL POST STAMPS

Catalogue values for unused stamps in this section are for Never Hinged items.

Nos. 448-448A, 459, 473, C292 Overprinted or Surcharged "Colis Postaux"

Perfs. and Printing Methods as Before

1982, Nov.				
Q8	A126	100fr on 150fr	.40	.20
Q9	A130	100fr multi	.40	.20
Q10	A134	300fr multi	1.25	.60
Q10A	A126a	1000fr multi	5.50	5.50
Q10B	AP102	5000fr on 500fr	27.50	27.50
		Nos. Q8-Q10B (5)	35.05	34.00

Dahomey No. C205 Surcharged

[redacted]

500 f

République Populaire du Bénin

colis postaux

1989	**Photo.**	*Perf. 12½x13*	
Q11 AP71	500fr on 200fr multi	3.25	3.25

BERMUDA

(ˌ)bər-ˈmyü-də

LOCATION — A group of about 150 small islands of which only 20 are inhabited, lying in the Atlantic Ocean about 580 miles southeast of Cape Hatteras.
GOVT. — British Crown Colony
AREA — 20.5 sq. mi.
POP. — 62,471 (1999 est.)
CAPITAL — Hamilton

Bermuda achieved internal self-government in 1968.

4 Farthings = 1 Penny
12 Pence = 1 Shilling
20 Shillings = 1 Pound
100 Cents = 1 Dollar (1970)

Catalogue values for unused stamps in this country are for Never Hinged items, beginning with Scott 131.

POSTMASTER STAMPS

PM1

1848-54 Unwmk. Imperf.

X1	PM1	1p blk, *bluish* (1848)	125,000.
a.		Dated 1849	135,000.
X2	PM1	1p red, *bluish* (1856)	175,000.
a.		Dated 1854	225,000.
X3	PM1	1p red (1853)	160,000.

PM2

1860

X4	PM2	(1p) red, *yellowish*	100,000.

Same inscribed "HAMILTON"

1861

X5	PM2	(1p) red, *bluish*	130,000.

Nos. X1-X3 were produced and used by Postmaster William B. Perot of Hamilton. No. X4 is attributed to Postmaster James H. Thies of St. George's.

Only a few of each stamp exist. Values reflect actual sales figures for stamps in the condition in which they are found.

GENERAL ISSUES

Values for unused stamps are for examples with original gum as defined in the catalogue introduction. Very fine examples of Nos. 1-1a, 2-15b will have perforations touching the design (or framelines where applicable) on at least one side due to the narrow spacing of the stamps on the plates. Stamps with perfs clear of the design on all four sides are scarce and will command higher prices.

Queen Victoria
A1 A2

A3

A4

A5

1865-74 Typo. Wmk. 1 Perf. 14

1	A1 1p rose red		100.00	3.00
b.	Imperf.		25,000.	17,500.
2	A2 2p blue ('66)		140.00	12.50
3	A3 3p buff ('73)		425.00	60.00
4	A4 6p brown lilac		1,200.	110.00
5	A4 6p lilac ('74)		22.50	17.50
6	A5 1sh green		175.00	35.00
	Nos. 1-6 (6)		2,062.	238.00

See Nos. 7-9, 19-21, 23, 25. For surcharges see Nos. 10-15.

No. 1b is a proof.

1882-1903 Perf. 14x12½

7	A3 3p buff	160.00	50.00
8	A4 6p violet ('03)	15.00	17.50
9	A5 1sh green ('94)	22.50	80.00
a.	Vert. strip of 3, perf. all around & imperf. btwn.	13,000.	
	Nos. 7-9 (3)	197.50	147.50

Handstamped Diagonally **THREE PENCE**

1874 Perf. 14

10	A5 3p on 1sh green	1,750.	950.

Handstamped Diagonally *THREE PENCE*

11	A1 3p on 1p rose	18,000.	7,500.
12	A5 3p on 1sh green	2,750.	900.
a.	"P" with top like "R"	2,250.	1,500.

No. 11 is stated to be an essay, but a few copies are known used. Nos. 10-12 are found with double or partly double surcharges.

Surcharged in Black **One Penny.**

1875

13	A2 1p on 2p blue	750.00	375.00
a.	Without period	15,000.	10,500.
14	A3 1p on 3p buff	450.00	350.00
15	A5 1p on 1sh green	450.00	300.00
a.	Inverted surcharge	—	30,000.
b.	Without period	15,000.	5,000.

A6 A7

1880 Wmk. 1

16	A6 ½p brown	1.75	2.75
17	A7 4p orange	15.00	2.50

See Nos. 18, 24.

A8 A9

1883-1904 Wmk. 2

18	A6 ½p dp gray grn ('93)	1.50	1.00
a.	½p green ('92)	2.00	2.00
19	A1 1p aniline car ('89)	6.00	.30
a.	1p dull rose	110.00	4.00
b.	1p rose red	60.00	2.25
c.	1p carmine rose ('86)	25.00	1.00
20	A2 2p blue ('86)	35.00	3.00
21	A2 2p brown purple ('98)	3.00	2.50
a.	2p aniline pur ('93)	8.50	4.00
22	A8 2½p ultra ('84)	6.00	.40
a.	2½p deep ultra	11.00	2.25
23	A3 3p gray ('86)	14.00	5.50
24	A7 4p brown org ('04)	24.00	60.00
25	A5 1sh ol bis ('93)	13.00	12.00
a.	1sh yellow brown	15.00	13.00
	Nos. 18-25 (8)	102.50	84.70

Black Surcharge

1901

26	A9 1f on 1sh gray	.40	.25

Dry Dock — A10

1902-03

28	A10 ½p gray grn & blk ('03)	8.25	2.50
29	A10 1p car rose & brown	7.50	.40
30	A10 3p ol grn & violet	1.75	3.75
	Nos. 28-30 (3)	17.50	6.65

1906-10 Wmk. 3

31	A10 ¼p pur & brn ('08)	1.10	1.25
32	A10 ½p gray grn & blk	11.50	1.65
33	A10 ½p green ('09)	7.00	2.25
34	A10 1p car rose & brn	14.00	.30
35	A10 1p carmine ('08)	13.00	.40
36	A10 2p orange & gray	5.75	5.75
37	A10 2½p blue & brown	10.00	13.00
38	A10 2½p ultra ('10)	9.50	9.50
39	A10 4p vio brn & blue ('09)	2.25	9.50
	Nos. 31-39 (9)	74.10	43.60

Caravel
A11

King George V
A12

1910-20 Engr. Perf. 14

40	A11 ¼p brown	.45	1.25
41	A11 ½p yel green	.90	.30
a.	½p dark green	3.00	1.40
42	A11 1p rose red (I)	7.00	.35
a.	1p carmine (I)	25.00	3.50
43	A11 2p gray	2.00	4.00
44	A11 2½p ultra (I)	2.25	.50
45	A11 3p violet, *yel*	1.40	5.00
46	A11 4p red, *yellow*	2.75	6.00
47	A11 6p claret	8.00	8.00
48	A11 1sh blk, *green*	4.00	5.00
a.	1sh black, *olive*	3.75	8.00

Typographed

Chalky Paper

49	A12 2sh ultra & dl vio, *bl* ('20)	14.00	32.50
50	A12 2sh6p red & blk, *bl*	18.00	42.50
51	A12 4sh car & black ('20)	40.00	70.00
52	A12 5sh red & grn, *yellow*	50.00	70.00
53	A12 10sh red & grn, *green*	140.00	125.00
54	A12 £1 black & vio, *red*	350.00	450.00
	Nos. 40-54 (15)	640.75	820.40

Types I of 1p and 2½p are illustrated above Nos. 81-97.

The 1p was printed from two plates, the 2nd of which, #42a, exists only in carmine on opaque paper with a bluish tinge. Compare #MR1 (as #42) and MR2 (as #42a).

Revenue cancellations are found on Nos. 52-54.

See Nos. 81-97.

Seal of the Colony and King George V
A13

1920-21 Wmk. 3 Ordinary Paper

55	A13 ¼p brown	.80	5.00
56	A13 ½p green	1.00	6.00
57	A13 2p gray	6.50	17.50

Chalky Paper

58	A13 3p vio & dl vio, *yel*	6.00	15.00
59	A13 4p red & blk, *yellow*	6.50	15.00
60	A13 1sh blk, *gray grn*	14.00	35.00

Ordinary Paper

Wmk. 4

67	A13 1p rose red	1.00	.60
68	A13 2½p ultra	5.50	8.00

Chalky Paper

69	A13 6p red vio & dl vio	12.50	35.00
	Nos. 55-60,67-69 (9)	53.80	137.10

Issued: 6p, Jan. 19, 1921; others, Nov. 11, 1920.

King George V — A14

1921, May 12 Engr.

71	A14 ¼p brown	.45	1.50
72	A14 ½p green	3.50	4.00
73	A14 1p carmine	2.50	1.00

Wmk. 3

74	A14 2p gray	6.00	10.00
75	A14 2½p ultra	6.00	4.00
76	A14 3p vio, *orange*	4.25	10.00
77	A14 4p scarlet, *org*	8.00	12.00
78	A14 6p claret	8.50	25.00
79	A14 1sh blk, *green*	16.00	30.00
	Nos. 71-79 (9)	55.20	97.50

Tercentenary of "Local Representative Institutions" (Nos. 55-79).

Types of 1910-20 Issue

Types of 1p: **1d** (I) **1d** (II) **1d** (III)

Types of 2½p: **2½d** (I) **2½d** (II)

1922-34 Wmk. 4

81	A11 ¼p brown ('28)	.30	.75
82	A11 ½p green	.20	.20
83	A11 1p car, III ('28)	7.50	.30
a.	1p carmine, II ('26)	8.00	.60
b.	1p carmine, I	8.00	.40
84	A11 1½p red brown ('34)	3.00	.30
85	A11 2p gray ('23)	1.00	1.00
86	A11 2½p ap grn ('23)	1.00	1.00
87	A11 2½p ultra, II ('32)	2.00	.35
a.	2½p ultra, I ('26)	1.75	.35
88	A11 3p ultra ('24)	14.00	20.00
89	A11 3p vio, *yellow* ('26)	.80	.60
90	A11 4p red, *yellow* ('24)	1.00	1.00
91	A11 6p claret ('24)	.80	.80
92	A11 1sh blk, *emer* ('27)	5.00	5.00
93	A11 1sh brn blk, *yel grn* ('34)	30.00	40.00

Chalky Paper

94	A12 2sh ultra & vio, *bl* ('27)	30.00	40.00
a.	2sh bl & dp vio, *dp bl* ('31)	35.00	40.00
95	A12 2sh 6p red & blk, *bl* ('27)	40.00	37.50
a.	2sh6p pale org ver & blk, *gray bl* ('30)	3,500.	2,250.
b.	2sh6p dp ver & blk, *deep blue* ('31)	55.00	60.00
96	A12 10sh red & grn, *emer* ('24)	150.00	175.00
a.	10sh dp red & pale grn, *dp emer* ('31)	150.00	175.00
97	A12 12sh 6p ocher & gray blk ('32)	300.00	350.00
	Nos. 81-97 (17)	586.60	673.80

Revenue cancellations are found on Nos. 94-97.

The 12sh6p with "Revenue" on both sides, was used postally from Feb. 1 to Apr., 1937. Copies with postal cancels in that time period are valued at three times No. 97.

Common Design Types pictured following the introduction.

Silver Jubilee Issue
Common Design Type

1935, May 6 ***Perf. 11x12***

100	CD301	1p car & dk bl	.20	.20
101	CD301	1½p blk & ultra	.45	.45
102	CD301	2½p ultra & brn	1.50	1.50
103	CD301	1sh brn vio & ind	6.00	*10.00*
		Nos. 100-103 (4)	8.15	*12.15*
		Set, never hinged	14.00	

Hamilton Harbor — A15

Yacht "Lucie" — A17

South Shore — A16

Grape Bay — A18

Typical Cottage A19

Scene at Par-la-Ville A20

1936-40 ***Perf. 12***

105	A15	½p blue green	.20	.20
106	A16	1p car & black	.30	.20
107	A16	1½p choc & black	.30	.20
108	A17	2p lt bl & blk	2.50	2.00
109	A17	2p brn blk & turq bl ('38)	22.50	8.00
109A	A17	2p red & ultra ('40)	.25	.20
110	A18	2½p dk bl & lt bl	.55	.35
111	A19	3p car & black	2.50	1.50
112	A20	6p vio & rose lake	.30	.20
113	A18	1sh deep green	5.50	5.00
114	A15	1sh6p brown	.50	.40
		Nos. 105-114 (11)	35.40	18.25
		Set, never hinged	50.00	

No. 108, blue border and black center.
No. 109, black border, blue center.

Coronation Issue
Common Design Type

1937, May 14 ***Perf. 13½x14***

115	CD302	1p carmine	.20	.20
116	CD302	1½p brown	.20	.20
117	CD302	2½p bright ultra	.50	.25
		Nos. 115-117 (3)	.90	.65
		Set, never hinged	1.50	

Hamilton Harbor — A21

Grape Bay — A22

St. David's Lighthouse A23

King George VI A25

Bermudian Water Scene and Yellow-billed Tropic Bird — A24

1938-51 **Wmk. 4** ***Perf. 12***

118	A21	1p red & black ('40)	.20	.20
a.		1p rose red & black	12.00	1.00
119	A21	1½p vio brn & blue	.50	.25
a.		1½p dl vio brn & bl ('43)	.20	.20
120	A22	2½p blue & lt bl	2.50	.75
120A	A22	2½p ol brn & lt bl ('41)	.30	.20
b.		2½p dk ol blk & pale blue ('43)	.30	.20
121	A23	3p car & blk	4.50	1.75
121A	A23	3p dp ultra & blk ('42)	.25	.20
c.		3p brt ultra & blk ('41)	.25	.20
121D	A24	7½p yel grn, bl & blk ('41)	1.25	1.00
122	A22	1sh green	1.00	.35

Typo.
Perf. 13

123	A25	2sh ultra & red vio, *bl* ('50)	6.00	4.00
a.		2sh ultra & vio, *bl*, perf. 14	5.00	3.50
b.		2sh ultra & dl vio, *bl* (mottled paper), perf. 14 ('42)	5.00	3.50
124	A25	2sh 6p red & blk, *bl*	8.00	6.00
a.		Perf. 14	8.00	3.50
125	A25	5sh red & grn, *yel*	10.00	7.50
a.		Perf. 14	13.00	7.50
126	A25	10sh red & grn, *grn* ('51)	20.00	14.00
a.		brn lake & grn, *grn*, perf. 14	175.00	200.00
b.		red & grn, *grn*, perf. 14 ('39)	40.00	40.00
127	A25	12sh 6p org & gray blk	55.00	50.00
a.		orange & gray, perf. 14	45.00	35.00
b.		yel & gray, perf. 14 ('47)	600.00	525.00
c.		brn orange & gray, perf. 14	300.00	300.00

Wmk. 3

128	A25	£1 blk & vio, *red* ('51)	35.00	30.00
a.		£1 blk & pur, *red*, perf. 14	190.00	100.00
b.		£1 blk & dk vio, *salmon*, perf. 14 ('42)	40.00	25.00
		Nos. 118-128 (14)	144.50	116.20
		Set, never hinged	220.00	

No. 127b is the so-called "lemon yellow" shade.

Revenue cancellations are found on Nos. 123-128. Copies with removed revenue cancellations and forged postmarks are abundant.

HALF
PENNY

No. 118a Surcharged in Black

X X

1940, Dec. 20 **Wmk. 4** ***Perf. 12***

129	A21	½p on 1p rose red & blk	.30	.30
		Never hinged	.50	

Catalogue values for unused stamps in this section, from this point to the end of the section, are for Never Hinged items.

Peace Issue
Common Design Type
Perf. 13½x14

1946, Nov. 6 **Engr.** **Wmk. 4**

131	CD303	1½p brown	.20	.20
132	CD303	3p deep blue	.30	.30

Silver Wedding Issue
Common Design Types

1948, Dec. 1 **Photo.** ***Perf. 14x14½***

133	CD304	1½p red brown	.20	.20

Engr.; Name Typo.
Perf. 11½x11

134	CD305	£1 rose carmine	47.50	35.00

Postmaster Stamp of 1848 A26

1949, Apr. 11 **Engr.** ***Perf. 13x13½***

135	A26	2½p dk brown & dp bl	.20	.20
136	A26	3p dp blue & black	.20	.20
137	A26	6p green & rose vio	.45	.45
		Nos. 135-137 (3)	.85	.85

No. 137 shows a different floral arrangement.
Bermuda's first postage stamp, cent.

UPU Issue
Common Design Types
Engr.; Name Typo.

1949, Oct. 10 ***Perf. 13½, 11x11½***

138	CD306	2½p slate	.55	.55
139	CD307	3p indigo	.70	.70
140	CD308	6p rose violet	1.10	1.10
141	CD309	1sh blue green	2.25	2.25
		Nos. 138-141 (4)	4.60	4.60

Coronation Issue
Common Design Type

1953, June 4 **Engr.** ***Perf. 13½x13***

142	CD312	1½p dk blue & blk	.40	.20

A27

Easter Lilies — A28

Designs: 1p, 4p, Perot stamp. 2p, Racing dinghy. 2½p, Sir George Somers and "Sea Venture." 3p, 1sh3p, Map. 4½p, 9p, "Sea Venture," boat, hog coin and Perot stamp. 6p, 8p, Yellow-billed tropic bird. 1sh, Hog coins. 2sh, Arms of St. George. 2sh6p, Warwick Fort. 5sh, Hog coin. 10sh, Earliest hog coin. £1, Arms of Bermuda.

1953-58 ***Perf. 13½x13, 13x13½***

143	A27	½p olive green	.20	.20
144	A27	1p rose red & blk	.20	.20
145	A28	1½p dull green	.20	.20
146	A27	2p red & ultra	.20	.20
147	A27	2½p carmine rose	.50	.20
148	A27	3p vio *(Sandy's)*	.45	.25
149	A27	3p violet *(Sandys)* ('57)	.55	.20
150	A27	4p dp ultra & blk	.25	.25
151	A27	4½p green	.60	.60
152	A27	6p dk bluish grn & blk	2.50	.30
153	A27	8p red & blk ('55)	.95	.35
154	A27	9p violet ('58)	2.00	.95
155	A27	1sh orange	.40	.20
156	A27	1sh3p blue *(Sandy's)*	2.00	.35
157	A27	1sh3p blue *(Sandys)* ('57)	4.00	.50
158	A27	2sh yellow brown	2.00	.65
159	A28	2sh6p scarlet	2.00	1.25
160	A27	5sh dp car rose	7.50	2.00
161	A27	10sh deep ultra	11.00	4.50

Engr. and Typo.

162	A27	£1 dp ol grn & multi	20.00	17.50
		Nos. 143-162 (20)	57.50	30.85

For overprints, see Nos. 164-167.

Type of 1953 Inscribed "ROYAL VISIT 1953"

Design: 6p, Yellow-billed tropic bird.

1953, Nov. 26 **Engr.**
163 A27 6p dk bluish grn & blk .40 .35

Visit of Queen Elizabeth II and the Duke of Edinburgh, 1953.

Nos. 148 and 156 Overprinted in Violet Blue or Red — **Three Power Talks December, 1953**

1953, Dec. 8 ***Perf. 13½x13***
164 A27 3p violet .20 .20
165 A27 1sh3p blue (R) .45 .40

Three Power Conference, Tucker's Town, December 1953.

Nos. 153 and 156 Overprinted in Black or Red — **50TH ANNIVERSARY U S – BERMUDA OCEAN RACE 1956**

1956, June 22
166 A27 8p red & black .25 .30
167 A27 1sh3p blue (R) .35 .50

Newport-Bermuda Yacht Race, 50th anniv.

Perot Post Office, Hamilton A29

Perf. 13½x13
1959, Jan. 1 **Engr.** **Wmk. 4**
168 A29 6p lilac & black .50 .30

Restoration and reopening of the post office operated at Hamilton by W. B. Perot in the mid-nineteenth century.

Arms of James I and Elizabeth II — A30

Engr. and Litho.
1959, July 29 **Wmk. 314** ***Perf. 13***
Coats of Arms in Blue, Yellow & Red
169 A30 1½p dark blue .20 .20
170 A30 3p gray .25 .30
171 A30 4p rose violet .30 .30
172 A30 8p violet gray .65 .65
173 A30 9p olive green .80 .80
174 A30 1sh3p orange brown 1.25 1.25
Nos. 169-174 (6) 3.45 3.50

350th anniv. of the shipwreck of the "Sea Venture" which resulted in the first permanent settlement of Bermuda.

The Old Rectory, St. George's, 1730 — A31

Designs: 2p, Church of St. Peter. 3p, Government House. 4p, Cathedral, Hamilton. 5p, No. 185A, H.M. Dockyard. 6p, Perot's Post Office, 1848. 8p, General Post Office, 1869. 9p, Library and Historical Society. 1sh, Christ Church, Warwick, 1719. 1sh3p, City Hall, Hamilton. 10p, No. 185, Bermuda Cottage, 1705. 2sh, Town of St. George. 2sh3p, Bermuda House, 1710. 2sh6p, Bermuda House, 18th century. 5sh, Colonial Secretariat, 1833. 10sh, Old Post Office, Somerset, 1890. £1, House of Assembly, 1815.

Wmk. 314 Upright
1962-65 **Photo.** ***Perf. 12½***
175 A31 1p org, lil & blk .20 .20
176 A31 2p sl, lt vio, grn & yel .20 .20
a. Light vio omitted 750.00 750.00
b. Green omitted 1,750.
d. Imperf., pair 1,250.
177 A31 3p lt bl & yel brn .20 .20
a. Yellow brown omitted 3,750.
178 A31 4p car rose & red brn .20 .20
179 A31 5p dk blue & pink .30 .30
180 A31 6p emer, lt & dk blue .20 .20
181 A31 8p grn, dp org & ultra .35 .30
182 A31 9p org brn & grnsh bl .30 .30
182A A31 10p brt vio & bister ('65) .65 .55
183 A31 1sh multicolored .40 .25
184 A31 1sh3p sl, lem & rose car .50 .25
185 A31 1sh6p brt vio & bis 2.75 2.25
186 A31 2sh brown & org 1.25 .85
187 A31 2sh3p brn & brt yel green 2.50 2.00
188 A31 2sh6p grn, yel & sep 1.50 1.10
189 A31 5sh choc & brt green 2.50 1.60
190 A31 10sh dl grn, buff & rose car 4.00 3.50
191 A31 £1 cit, bis, blk & orange 9.50 7.75
Nos. 175-191 (18) 27.50 22.00

See No. 252a. For surcharges see Nos. 238-254.

1966-69 **Wmk. 314 Sideways**
Unnamed Colors as in 1962-65 Issue
176c A31 2p ('69) 2.50 1.60
181a A31 8p ('67) 1.10 .90
182b A31 10p 1.40 1.10
183a A31 1sh ('67) 1.40 1.25
185A A31 1sh6p indigo & rose 2.50 3.00
186a A31 2sh ('67) 4.50 4.50
Nos. 176c-186a (6) 13.40 12.35

For surcharges see #239, 245-246, 248-249.

Freedom from Hunger Issue
Common Design Type
1963, June 4 ***Perf. 14x14½***
192 CD314 1sh3p sepia 2.75 2.25

Red Cross Centenary Issue
Common Design Type
Wmk. 314
1963, Sept. 2 **Litho.** ***Perf. 13***
193 CD315 3p black & red .50 .30
194 CD315 1sh3p ultra & red 5.50 3.00

Finn Boat — A32

Wmk. 314
1964, Sept. 28 **Photo.** ***Perf. 13½***
195 A32 3p blue, vio & red .30 .30

18th Olympic Games, Tokyo, Oct. 10-25.

ITU Issue
Common Design Type
Perf. 11x11½
1965, May 17 **Litho.** **Wmk. 314**
196 CD317 3p blue & emerald .40 .30
197 CD317 2sh yel & vio blue 3.50 3.50

Scout Badge and Royal Cipher A33

1965, July 24 **Photo.** ***Perf. 12½***
198 A33 2sh multicolored .85 .85

50th anniversary of Scouting in Bermuda.

Intl. Cooperation Year Issue
Common Design Type
1965, Oct. 25 **Litho.** ***Perf. 14½***
199 CD318 4p blue grn & cl .30 .30
200 CD318 2sh6p lt violet & grn 2.25 2.25

Churchill Memorial Issue
Common Design Type
1966, Jan. 24 **Photo.** ***Perf. 14***
Design in Black, Gold and Carmine Rose
201 CD319 3p bright blue .30 .20
202 CD319 6p green .65 .45
203 CD319 10p brown 1.25 1.00
204 CD319 1sh3p violet 2.50 2.00
Nos. 201-204 (4) 4.70 3.65

World Cup Soccer Issue
Common Design Type
1966, July 1 **Litho.** ***Perf. 14***
205 CD321 10p multicolored .65 .65
206 CD321 2sh6p multicolored 1.75 1.75

UNESCO Anniversary Issue
Common Design Type
1966, Dec. 1 **Litho.** ***Perf. 14***
207 CD323 4p "Education" .40 .40
208 CD323 1sh3p "Science" 1.50 1.50
209 CD323 2sh "Culture" 2.50 2.50
Nos. 207-209 (3) 4.40 4.40

Post Office, Hamilton A34

Wmk. 314
1967, June 23 **Photo.** ***Perf. 14½***
210 A34 3p vio blue & multi .20 .20
211 A34 1sh orange & multi .40 .40
212 A34 1sh6p green & multi .70 .70
213 A34 2sh6p red & multi 1.10 1.10
Nos. 210-213 (4) 2.40 2.40

Opening of the new GPO, Hamilton.

Cable Ship Mercury A35

Designs: 1sh, Map of Bermuda and Virgin Islands, telephone and microphone. 1sh6p, Radio tower, television set, telephone and cable. 2sh6p, Cable at sea bottom and ship.

1967, Sept. 14 **Photo.** **Wmk. 314**
214 A35 3p multicolored .20 .20
215 A35 1sh multicolored .40 .40
216 A35 1sh6p multicolored .70 .70
217 A35 2sh6p multicolored 1.10 1.10
Nos. 214-217 (4) 2.40 2.40

Completion of the Bermuda-Tortola, Virgin Islands, telephone link.

Human Rights Flame, Globe and Doves A36

1968, Feb. 1 **Litho.** ***Perf. 14x14½***
218 A36 3p indigo, lt grn & bl .20 .20
219 A36 1sh brown, lt bl & bl .45 .45
220 A36 1sh6p black, pink & blue .75 .75
221 A36 2sh6p green, yellow & bl .95 .95
Nos. 218-221 (4) 2.35 2.35

International Human Rights Year.

Mace A37

Design: 1sh6p, 2sh6p, House of Assembly, Bermuda; Parliament, London, and royal cipher.

1968, July 1 **Photo.** ***Perf. 14½***
222 A37 3p rose red & multi .20 .20
223 A37 1sh ultra & multi .45 .45
224 A37 1sh6p yellow & multi .75 .75
225 A37 2sh6p multicolored .95 .95
Nos. 222-225 (4) 2.35 2.35

New constitution.

Olympic Sports and Rings A38

1968, Sept. 24 **Wmk. 314** ***Perf. 12½***
226 A38 3p lilac & multi .20 .20
a. Rose brown omitted ("3d BERMUDA") 2,500.
227 A38 1sh multicolored .40 .35
228 A38 1sh6p multicolored .60 .60
229 A38 2sh6p multicolored 1.00 1.00
Nos. 226-229 (4) 2.20 2.15

19th Olympic Games, Mexico City, Oct. 12-27.

Girl Guides A39

Designs: 1sh, Like 3p. 1sh6p, 2sh6p, Girl Guides and arms of Bermuda.

1969, Feb. 17 **Litho.** ***Perf. 14***
230 A39 3p lilac & multi .20 .20
231 A39 1sh green & multi .35 .35
232 A39 1sh6p gray & multi .55 .55
233 A39 2sh6p red & multi 1.00 1.00
Nos. 230-233 (4) 2.10 2.10

Bermuda Girl Guides, 50th anniv.

Gold and Emerald Cross — A40

Design: 4p, 2sh, Different background.

Perf. 14½x14
1969, Sept. 29 **Photo.**
Cross in Yellow, Brown and Emerald
234 A40 4p violet .25 .25
235 A40 1sh3p green .75 .75
236 A40 2sh black 1.10 1.10
237 A40 2sh6p carmine rose 1.40 1.25
Nos. 234-237 (4) 3.50 3.35

Treasures salvaged off the coast of Bermuda. The cross shown is from the Tucker treasure from the 16th century Spanish galleon San Pedro.

Buildings Issue and Type of 1962-69 Surcharged with New Value and Bar in Black or Brown

1970, Feb. 6 **Wmk. 314** ***Perf. 12½***
238 A31 1c on 1p multi .20 .20
239 A31 2c on 2p multi .20 .20
a. Watermark upright 1.25 1.25
b. Light violet omitted 650.00
c. Pair, one without surch. 2,500.
240 A31 3c on 3p multi .20 .20
241 A31 4c on 4p multi (Br) .20 .20
242 A31 5c on 8p multi .20 .20
243 A31 6c on 6p multi .20 .20
244 A31 9c on 9p multi (Br) .25 .40
245 A31 10c on 10p multi .30 .50
246 A31 12c on 1sh multi .35 .60
247 A31 15c on 1sh3p multi .70 1.10

248	A31	18c on 1sh6p multi	.70	1.25
249	A31	24c on 2sh multi	.85	1.50
250	A31	30c on 2sh6p multi	1.00	1.90
251	A31	36c on 2sh3p multi	1.25	2.50
252	A31	60c on 5sh multi	2.00	3.75
a.		Surcharge omitted	600.00	
253	A31	$1.20 on 10sh multi	4.00	7.50
254	A31	$2.40 on £1 multi	8.00	15.00
		Nos. 238-254 (17)	20.60	37.20

Watermark upright on 1c, 3c to 9c and 36c; sideways on others. Watermark is sideways on No. 252a, upright on No. 189.

Spathiphyllum — A41

Flowers: 2c, Bottlebrush. 3c, Oleander, vert. 4c, Bermudiana. 5c, Poinsettia. 6c, Hibiscus. 9c, Cereus. 10c, Bougainvillea, vert. 12c, Jacaranda. 15c, Passion flower. 18c, Coralita. 24c, Morning glory. 30c, Tecoma. 36c, Angel's trumpet. 60c, Plumbago. $1.20, Bird of paradise. $2.40, Chalice cup.

Wmk. 314, Sideways on Horiz. Stamps

1970, July 6 *Perf. 14*

255	A41	1c lt green & multi	.20	.20
256	A41	2c pale bl & multi	.25	.20
257	A41	3c yellow & multi	.20	.20
258	A41	4c buff & multi	.20	.20
259	A41	5c pink & multi	.60	.25
a.		Imperf., pair	1,500.	
260	A41	6c orange & multi	.60	.30
261	A41	9c lt green & multi	.35	.20
262	A41	10c pale salmon & multi	.35	.20
263	A41	12c pale yellow & multi	1.60	.85
264	A41	15c buff & multi	1.40	.70
265	A41	18c pale salmon & multi	2.50	1.10
266	A41	24c pink & multi	1.60	.75
267	A41	30c plum & multi	1.60	.75
268	A41	36c dark gray & multi	2.50	1.10
269	A41	60c gray & multi	3.25	1.75
270	A41	$1.20 blue & multi	7.50	3.50
271	A41	$2.40 multicolored	15.00	8.25
		Nos. 255-271 (17)	39.70	20.50

See #322-328. For overprints see #288-291.

1974-76 **Wmk. 314 Upright**

259b	A41	5c multicolored	1.00	1.00
260a	A41	6c multicolored	2.25	2.25
263a	A41	12c multicolored	1.60	1.60
267a	A41	30c multicolored ('76)	3.00	3.00
		Nos. 259b-267a (4)	7.85	7.85

Issued: 30c, June 11; others, June 13.

1975-76 **Wmk. 373**

256a	A41	2c multicolored	1.00	1.00
260b	A41	6c multicolored	2.00	2.00

Issued: 2c, Dec. 8; 6c, June 11, 1976.

State House, St. George's, 1622-1815 A42

Designs: 15c, The Sessions House, Hamilton, 1893. 18c, First Assembly House, St. Peter's Church, St. George's. 24c, Temporary Assembly House, Hamilton, 1815-26.

1970, Oct. 12 **Litho.** *Perf. 14*

272	A42	4c multicolored	.20	.20
273	A42	15c multicolored	.45	.45
274	A42	18c multicolored	.65	.65
275	A42	24c multicolored	1.10	1.10
a.		Souvenir sheet of 4, #272-275	3.75	4.25
		Nos. 272-275 (4)	2.40	2.40

350th anniv. of Bermuda's Parliament.

Street in St. George's A43

"Keep Bermuda Beautiful": 15c, Horseshoe Bay. 18c, Gibb's Hill Lighthouse. 24c, View of Hamilton Harbor.

1971, Feb. 8 **Wmk. 314** *Perf. 14*

276	A43	4c multicolored	.25	.25
277	A43	15c multicolored	.70	.70
278	A43	18c multicolored	.90	.90
279	A43	24c multicolored	1.50	1.50
		Nos. 276-279 (4)	3.35	3.35

Building of "Deliverance" — A44

Designs: 15c, "Deliverance" and "Patience" arriving in Jamestown, Va., 1610, vert. 18c, Wreck of "Sea Venture," vert. 24c, "Deliverance" and "Patience" under sail, 1610.

1971, May 10 **Litho.** **Wmk. 314**

280	A44	4c multicolored	.40	.40
281	A44	15c brown & multi	1.40	1.40
282	A44	18c purple & multi	1.75	1.75
283	A44	24c blue & multi	2.50	2.50
		Nos. 280-283 (4)	6.05	6.05

Voyage of Sir George Somers to Jamestown, Va., from Bermuda, 1610.

Ocean View Golf Course A45

Golf Courses: 15c, Port Royal. 18c, Castle Harbour. 24c, Belmont.

1971, Nov. 1 *Perf. 13*

284	A45	4c multicolored	.20	.20
285	A45	15c multicolored	.65	.65
286	A45	18c multicolored	.75	.75
287	A45	24c multicolored	1.10	1.10
		Nos. 284-287 (4)	2.70	2.70

Golfing in Bermuda.

Nos. 258, 264-266 Overprinted: "HEATH-NIXON / DECEMBER 1971"

1971, Dec. 20 **Photo.** *Perf. 14*

288	A41	4c buff & multi	.20	.20
289	A41	15c buff & multi	.40	.40
290	A41	18c pale sal & multi	.50	.50
291	A41	24c pink & multi	.70	.70
		Nos. 288-291 (4)	1.80	1.80

Meeting of President Richard M. Nixon and Prime Minister Edward Heath of Great Britain, at Hamilton, Dec. 20-21, 1971.

Bonefish A46

1972, Aug. 7 **Litho.** *Perf. 13½x14*

292	A46	4c shown	.25	.25
293	A46	15c Wahoo	.75	.75
294	A46	18c Yellowfin tuna	.90	.90
295	A46	24c Greater amberjack	1.40	1.40
		Nos. 292-295 (4)	3.30	3.30

World fishing records.

Silver Wedding Issue, 1972
Common Design Type

Design: Queen Elizabeth II, Prince Philip, Admiralty oar and mace.

1972, Nov. 20 **Photo.** *Perf. 14x14½*

296	CD324	4c violet & multi	.20	.20
297	CD324	15c car rose & multi	.50	.50

Palmettos — A47

1973, Sept. 3 **Wmk. 314** *Perf. 14*

298	A47	4c shown	.25	.25
299	A47	15c Olivewood	.75	.75
a.		Brown (Queen's head, "15c") omitted	1,400.	
300	A47	18c Bermuda cedar	1.00	1.20
301	A47	24c Mahogany	1.25	1.25
		Nos. 298-301 (4)	3.25	3.45

Bermuda National Trust, and "Plant a Tree" campaign.

Princess Anne's Wedding Issue
Common Design Type

1973, Nov. 21 **Litho.**

302	CD325	15c lilac & multi	.35	.35
303	CD325	18c slate & multi	.45	.45

National Tennis Stadium, Pembroke, 1973 — A48

15c, Bermuda's 1st tennis court, Pembroke, 1873. 18c, Britain's 1st tennis court, Leamington Spa, 1872. 24c, 1t US tennis club, Staten Island, 1874.

1973, Dec. 17 **Wmk. 314**

304	A48	4c black & multi	.20	.20
305	A48	15c black & multi	.65	.65
306	A48	18c black & multi	.90	.90
307	A48	24c black & multi	1.25	1.25
		Nos. 304-307 (4)	3.00	3.00

Centenary of tennis in Bermuda.

Rotary Emblem, Weather Vane, City Hall, Hamilton A49

Rotary Emblem and: 17c, St. Peter's Church, St. George's. 20c, Somerset Drawbridge, Somerset. 25c, Map of Bermuda on globe, 1626.

1974, June 24 *Perf. 14*

308	A49	5c emerald & multi	.25	.25
309	A49	17c blue & multi	.75	.75
310	A49	20c yel org & multi	.85	.85
311	A49	25c lt violet & multi	1.10	1.10
		Nos. 308-311 (4)	2.95	2.95

50th anniv. of Rotary Intl. in Bermuda.

Jack of Clubs and a Good Bridge Hand — A50

Bermuda Bowl and: 17c, Queen of diamonds. 20c, King of hearts. 25c, Ace of spades.

1975, Jan. 27 **Litho.** **Wmk. 314**

312	A50	5c blue & multi	.25	.25
313	A50	17c dull yel & multi	.75	.75
314	A50	20c ver & multi	.80	.80
315	A50	25c lilac & multi	1.10	1.10
		Nos. 312-315 (4)	2.90	2.90

World Bridge Championship, Bermuda, Jan. 1975.

Queen Elizabeth II and Prince Philip — A51

Perf. 14x14½

1975, Feb. 17 **Photo.** **Wmk. 373**

316	A51	17c multicolored	.60	.60
317	A51	20c dk blue & multi	.80	.80

Royal Visit, Feb. 16-18, 1975.

British Cavalier Flying Boat, 1937 A52

Designs: 17c, U.S. Navy airship "Los Angeles," 1925, flying from Lakehurst, N.J. to Hamilton, Bermuda. 20c, Constellation over Kindley Field, 1946. 25c, Boeing 747 on tarmac, 1970.

1975, Apr. 28 **Litho.** *Perf. 14*

318	A52	5c lt green & multi	.40	.40
319	A52	17c lt ultra & multi	1.25	1.25
320	A52	20c multicolored	1.75	1.75
321	A52	25c rose lil & multi	2.00	2.00
a.		Souvenir sheet of 4, #318-321	6.00	7.50
		Nos. 318-321 (4)	5.40	5.40

Airmail service to Bermuda, 50th anniv.

Flower Type of 1970

1975, June 2 **Photo.** **Wmk. 314**

322	A41	17c Passion flower	1.25	1.25
323	A41	20c Coralita	1.25	1.25
324	A41	25c Morning glory	1.25	1.25
325	A41	40c Angel's trumpet	1.25	1.25
326	A41	$1 Plumbago	2.00	2.00
327	A41	$2 Bird-of-paradise flower	3.50	3.50
328	A41	$3 Chalice cup	6.00	6.00
		Nos. 322-328 (7)	16.50	16.50

Royal Magazine Break-in A54

Designs: 17c, Sympathizers rowing towards magazine. 20c, Loading gun powder barrels onto ships. 25c, Gun powder barrels on beach.

Perf. 13x13½

1975, Oct. 27 **Litho.** **Wmk. 373**

329	A54	5c multicolored	.25	.25
330	A54	17c multicolored	.75	.75
331	A54	20c multicolored	.85	.85
332	A54	25c multicolored	1.25	1.25
a.		Souv. sheet of 4, #329-332, perf. 14	4.00	5.00
		Nos. 329-332 (4)	3.10	3.10

Gunpowder Plot, 1775, American War of Independence.

Bermuda Biological Station A55

Designs: 5c, Launching of bathysphere from "Ready," vert. 20c, Sailing ship Challenger, 1873. 25c, Descent of Beebe's bathysphere, 1934, and marine life, vert.

1976, Mar. 29 **Litho.** *Perf. 14*

333	A55	5c multicolored	.30	.30
334	A55	17c multicolored	.70	.70
335	A55	20c multicolored	.85	.85
336	A55	25c multicolored	1.00	1.00
		Nos. 333-336 (4)	2.85	2.85

Bermuda Biological Station, 50th anniv.

Christian Radich, Norway
A56

Tall Ships: 12c, Juan Sebastian de Elcano, Spain. 17c, Eagle, US. 20c, Sir Winston Churchill, Great Britain. 40c, Kruzenshtern, USSR. $1, Cutty Sark (silver trophy).

1976, June 15 — Litho. — *Perf. 13*

337	A56	5c	lt green & multi	.30	.30
338	A56	12c	violet & multi	.55	.55
339	A56	17c	ultra & multi	.75	.75
340	A56	20c	blue & multi	1.00	1.00
341	A56	40c	yellow & multi	1.50	1.50
342	A56	$1	sl grn & multi	4.50	4.50
			Nos. 337-342 (6)	8.60	8.60

Trans-Atlantic Cutty Sark International Tall Ships Race, Plymouth, England-New York City (Operation Sail '76).

Silver Cup Trophy and Crossed Club Flags
A57

Designs: 17c, St. George's Cricket Club and emblem. 20c, Somerset Cricket Club and emblem. 25c, Cricket match.

1976, Aug. 16 — Wmk. 373 — *Perf. 14½*

343	A57	5c	multicolored	.25	.25
344	A57	17c	multicolored	.85	.85
345	A57	20c	multicolored	.95	.95
346	A57	25c	multicolored	1.40	1.40
			Nos. 343-346 (4)	3.45	3.45

St. George's and Somerset Cricket Club matches, 75th anniversary.

Queen's Visit to Bermuda, 1975 — A58

Designs: 20c, St. Edward's Crown. $1, Queen seated in Chair of Estate.

1977, Feb. 7 — Litho. — *Perf. 14x13½*

347	A58	5c	silver & multi	.20	.20
348	A58	20c	silver & multi	.55	.55
349	A58	$1	silver & multi	2.25	2.25
			Nos. 347-349 (3)	3.00	3.00

Reign of Queen Elizabeth II, 25th anniv.

Stockdale House, St. George's
A59

UPU Emblem and: 15c, Perot Post Office and Perot Stamp. 17c, St. George's Post Office, c. 1860. 20c, Old GPO, Hamilton, c. 1935. 40c, New GPO, Hamilton, 1967.

1977, June 20 — Litho. — *Perf. 13x13½*

350	A59	5c	multicolored	.20	.20
351	A59	15c	multicolored	.35	.35
352	A59	17c	multicolored	.40	.40
353	A59	20c	multicolored	.50	.50
354	A59	40c	multicolored	1.00	1.00
			Nos. 350-354 (5)	2.45	2.45

Bermuda's UPU membership, cent.

Sailing Ship, 17th Century, Approaching Castle Island — A60

Designs: 15c, King's pilot leaving 18th century naval ship at Murray's Anchorage. 17c, Pilot gigs racing to meet steamship, early 19th century. 20c, Harvest Queen, late 19th century. 40c, Pilot cutter and Queen Elizabeth II off St. David's Lighthouse.

Perf. 13½x14

1977, Sept. 26 — Wmk. 373

355	A60	5c	multicolored	.20	.20
356	A60	15c	multicolored	.40	.40
357	A60	17c	multicolored	.50	.50
358	A60	20c	multicolored	.65	.65
359	A60	40c	multicolored	1.25	1.25
			Nos. 355-359 (5)	3.00	3.00

Piloting in Bermuda waters.

Elizabeth II
A61

Designs: 8c, Great Seal of Elizabeth I. 50c, Great Seal of Elizabeth II.

1978, Aug. 28 — Litho. — *Perf. 14x13½*

360	A61	8c	gold & multi	.20	.20
361	A61	50c	gold & multi	.85	.85
362	A61	$1	gold & multi	1.60	1.60
			Nos. 360-362 (3)	2.65	2.65

25th anniv. of coronation of Elizabeth II.

White-tailed Tropicbird — A62

Perf. 14; 14x14½ (4c, 5c, $2, $3, $5)

1978-79 — Photo. — Wmk. 373

363	A62	3c	shown	.20	.20
364	A62	4c	White-eyed vireo	.20	.20
365	A62	5c	Eastern bluebird	.20	.20
366	A62	7c	Whistling tree frog	.20	.20
367	A62	8c	Cardinal	.20	.20
368	A62	10c	Spiny lobster	.20	.20
369	A62	12c	Land crab	.20	.20
370	A62	15c	Skink	.25	.25
371	A62	20c	Four-eyed butterflyfish	.35	.35
372	A62	25c	Red hind	.45	.45
a.			Greenish blue (background) omitted	450.00	
373	A62	30c	Monarch butterfly	.50	.50
374	A62	40c	Rock beauty	.70	.70
375	A62	50c	Banded butterflyfish	1.00	1.00
376	A62	$1	Blue angelfish	2.00	2.00
377	A62	$2	Humpback whale	4.25	4.25
378	A62	$3	Green turtle	6.25	6.25
379	A62	$5	Bermuda Petrel	10.50	10.50
			Nos. 363-379 (17)	27.65	27.65

Issued: 3c, 4c, 5c, 8c, $5, 1978; others, 1979.

For surcharge see No. 509.

Map of Bermuda, by George Somers, 1609 — A63

Old Maps of Bermuda: 15c, by John Seller, 1685. 20c, by Herman Moll, 1729, vert. 25c, by Desbruslins, 1740. 50c, by John Speed, 1626.

1979, May 14 — Litho. — *Perf. 13½*

380	A63	8c	multicolored	.20	.20
381	A63	15c	multicolored	.30	.30
382	A63	20c	multicolored	.40	.40
383	A63	25c	multicolored	.45	.45
384	A63	50c	multicolored	.95	.95
			Nos. 380-384 (5)	2.30	2.30

Bermuda Police Centenary — A64

Designs: 20c, Traffic direction, horiz. 25c, Water patrol, horiz. 50c, Motorbike and patrol car.

1979, Nov. 26 — Wmk. 373 — *Perf. 14*

385	A64	8c	multicolored	.20	.20
386	A64	20c	multicolored	.40	.40
387	A64	25c	multicolored	.50	.50
388	A64	50c	multicolored	1.00	1.00
			Nos. 385-388 (4)	2.10	2.10

Bermuda No. X1, Penny Black — A65

Bermuda #X1 and: 20c, Hill. 25c, "Paid 1" marking on cover. 50c, "Paid 1" marking.

1980, Feb. 25 — Litho. — *Perf. 13½x14*

389	A65	8c	multicolored	.20	.20
390	A65	20c	multicolored	.40	.40
391	A65	25c	multicolored	.50	.50
392	A65	50c	multicolored	1.00	1.00
			Nos. 389-392 (4)	2.10	2.10

Sir Rowland Hill (1795-1879), originator of penny postage.

Tristar-500, London 1980 Emblem — A66

1980, May 6 — Litho. — *Perf. 13x14*

393	A66	25c	shown	.35	.35
394	A66	50c	"Orduna," 1926	.70	.70
395	A66	$1	"Delta," 1856	1.50	1.50
396	A66	$2	"Lord Sidmouth," 1818	3.00	3.00
			Nos. 393-396 (4)	5.55	5.55

London 1980 Intl. Stamp Exhib., May 6-14.

Bermuda stamps can be mounted in the annually supplemented Scott Bermuda album.

Gina Swainson, Miss World, 1979-80, Arms of Bermuda — A67

1980, May 8 — *Perf. 14*

397	A67	8c	shown	.20	.20
398	A67	20c	After crowning ceremony	.35	.35
399	A67	50c	Welcome home party	.90	.90
400	A67	$1	In carriage	1.75	1.75
			Nos. 397-400 (4)	3.20	3.20

Queen Mother Elizabeth Birthday Issue

Common Design Type

1980, Aug. 4 — Wmk. 373 — *Perf. 14*

401	CD330	25c	multicolored	.45	.45

Camden, Prime Minister's House
A68

1980, Sept. 24 — Litho. — *Perf. 14*

402	A68	8c	View from satellite	.20	.20
403	A68	20c	shown	.40	.40
404	A68	25c	Princess Hotel, Hamilton	.50	.50
405	A68	50c	Government House	1.00	1.00
			Nos. 402-405 (4)	2.10	2.10

Commonwealth Finance Ministers Meeting, Bermuda, Sept.

18th Century Kitchen
A69

1981, May 21 — Wmk. 373 — *Perf. 14*

406	A69	8c	shown	.20	.20
407	A69	25c	Gathering Easter lilies	.40	.40
408	A69	30c	Fisherman	.50	.50
409	A69	40c	Stone cutting, 19th cent.	.70	.70
410	A69	50c	Onion shipping, 19th cent.	.85	.85
411	A69	$1	Ships, 17th cent.	1.75	1.75
			Nos. 406-411 (6)	4.40	4.40

Royal Wedding Issue

Common Design Type

1981, July 22 — Wmk. 373 — *Perf. 14*

412	CD331	30c	Bouquet	.50	.50
413	CD331	50c	Charles	.90	.90
414	CD331	$1	Couple	1.75	1.75
			Nos. 412-414 (3)	3.15	3.15

Girl Helping Blind Man Cross Street — A70

1981, Sept. 28 — Litho. — *Perf. 14*

415	A70	10c	shown	.20	.20
416	A70	25c	Kayaking, Paget Island	.50	.50
417	A70	30c	Mountain climbing, St. David's Island	.55	.55
418	A70	$1	Duke of Edinburgh	1.90	1.90
			Nos. 415-418 (4)	3.15	3.15

Duke of Edinburgh's Awards, 25th anniv.

Conus Species A71

1982, May 13 Wmk. 373 *Perf. 14*

419 A71 10c shown .20 .20
420 A71 25c Bursa finlayi .50 .50
421 A71 30c Sconsia striata .60 .60
422 A71 $1 Murex pterynotus lightbourni 1.90 1.90
Nos. 419-422 (4) 3.20 3.20

Bermuda Regiment A72

1982, June 17 Litho. Wmk. 373

423 A72 10c Color guard .20 .20
424 A72 25c Queen's birthday parade .40 .40
425 A72 30c Governor inspecting honor guard .60 .60
426 A72 40c Beating the retreat .80 .80
427 A72 50c Ceremonial gunners 1.00 1.00
428 A72 $1 Royal visit, 1975 2.00 2.00
Nos. 423-428 (6) 5.00 5.00

Southampton Fort — A73

1982, Nov. 18 Litho. Wmk. 373

429 A73 10c Charles Fort, vert. .20 .20
430 A73 25c Pembroks Fort, vert. .50 .50
431 A73 30c shown .60 .60
432 A73 $1 Smiths and Pagets Forts 1.90 1.90
Nos. 429-432 (4) 3.20 3.20

Arms of Sir Edwin Sandys (1561-1629) — A74

Fitted Dinghies — A75

Coats of Arms: 25c, Bermuda Company. 50c, William Herbert, 3rd Earl of Pembroke (1584-1630). $1, Sir George Somers (1554-1610).

1983, Apr. 14 Litho. *Perf. 13½*

433 A74 10c multicolored .20 .20
434 A74 25c multicolored .45 .45
435 A74 50c multicolored .90 .90
436 A74 $1 multicolored 1.75 1.75
Nos. 433-436 (4) 3.30 3.30

See Nos. 457-460, 474-477.

1983, July 21 Wmk. 373 *Perf. 14*

Old and modern boats.

437 A75 12c multicolored .25 .25
438 A75 30c multicolored .55 .55
439 A75 40c multicolored .70 .70
440 A75 $1 multicolored 1.75 1.75
Nos. 437-440 (4) 3.25 3.25

Manned Flight Bicentenary — A76

Designs: 12c, Curtiss Jenny, 1919 (first flight over Bermuda). 30c, Stinson Pilot Radio, 1930 (first completed US-Bermuda flight). 40c, Cavalier, 1937 (first scheduled passenger flight). $1, USS Los Angeles airship moored to USS Patoka, 1925.

1983, Oct. 13 Litho. *Perf. 14*

441 A76 12c multicolored .30 .30
442 A76 30c multicolored .65 .65
443 A76 40c multicolored .90 .90
444 A76 $1 multicolored 1.75 1.75
Nos. 441-444 (4) 3.60 3.60

Newspaper and Postal Services, 200th Anniv. — A77

1984, Jan. 26 Litho. *Perf. 14*

445 A77 12c Joseph Stockdale .25 .25
446 A77 30c First Newspaper .55 .55
447 A77 40c Stockdale's Postal Service, horiz. .70 .70
448 A77 $1 "Lady Hammond," horiz. 1.75 1.75
Nos. 445-448 (4) 3.25 3.25

375th Anniv. of Bermuda Settlement A78

Designs: 12c, Thomas Gates, George Somers. 30c, Jamestown, Virginia, US. 40c, Sea Venture shipwreck. $1, Fleet leaving Plymouth, England.

1984, May 3 Litho. Wmk. 373

449 A78 12c multicolored .25 .25
450 A78 30c multicolored .55 .55
451 A78 40c multicolored .70 .70
452 A78 $1 multicolored 1.75 1.75
a. Souv. sheet of 2, #450, 452 5.00 5.00
Nos. 449-452 (4) 3.25 3.25

1984 Summer Olympics A79

1984, July 19 Litho. *Perf. 14*

453 A79 12c Swimming, vert. .20 .20
454 A79 30c Track & field .50 .50
455 A79 40c Equestrian, vert. .65 .65
456 A79 $1 Sailing 1.60 1.60
Nos. 453-456 (4) 2.95 2.95

Arms Type of 1983

1984, Sept. 27 Litho. *Perf. 13½*

457 A74 12c Southampton .20 .20
458 A74 30c Smith .60 .60
459 A74 40c Devonshire .75 .75
460 A74 $1 St. George 1.60 1.60
Nos. 457-460 (4) 3.15 3.15

Architecture, Buttery — A80

1985, Jan. 24 Litho. *Perf. 13½x13*

461 A80 12c shown .35 .35
462 A80 30c Rooftops .75 .75
463 A80 40c Chimneys 1.00 1.00
464 A80 $1.50 Archway 3.50 3.50
Nos. 461-464 (4) 5.60 5.60

Audubon Birth Bicentenary — A81

1985, Mar. 21 Wmk. 373 *Perf. 14*

465 A81 12c Osprey, vert. .30 .30
466 A81 30c Yellow-crowned night heron, vert. .75 .75
467 A81 40c Great egret 1.00 1.00
468 A81 $1.50 Bluebird, vert. 3.50 3.50
Nos. 465-468 (4) 5.55 5.55

Queen Mother 85th Birthday Issue
Common Design Type

Designs: 12c, Queen Consort, 1937. 30c, With grandchildren, 80th birthday. 40c, At Clarence House, 83rd birthday. $1.50, Holding Prince Henry. No. 473, In coach with Prince Charles.

Perf. 14½x14

1985, June 7 Wmk. 384

469 CD336 12c gray, bl & blk .35 .35
470 CD336 30c multicolored .75 .75
471 CD336 40c multicolored 1.00 1.00
472 CD336 $1.50 multicolored 3.50 3.50
Nos. 469-472 (4) 5.60 5.60

Souvenir Sheet

473 CD336 $1 multicolored 4.50 4.50

Arms Type of 1983

Coats of Arms: 12c, James Hamilton, 2nd Marquess of Hamilton (1589-1625). 30c, William Paget, 4th Lord Paget (1572-1629). 40c, Robert Rich, 2nd Earl of Warwick (1587-1658). $1.50, Hamilton, 1957.

1985, Sept. 19 Litho. *Perf. 13½*

474 A74 12c multicolored .30 .30
475 A74 30c multicolored .75 .75
476 A74 40c multicolored 1.00 1.00
477 A74 $1.50 multicolored 3.75 3.75
Nos. 474-477 (4) 5.80 5.80

Halley's Comet A82

1985, Nov. 21 Wmk. 384 *Perf. 14½*

478 A82 15c Bermuda Archipelago .40 .40
479 A82 40c Nuremberg Chronicles, 1493 1.00 1.00
480 A82 50c Peter Apian woodcut, 1532 1.25 1.25
481 A82 $1.50 Painting by Samuel Scott (c.1702-72) 3.75 3.75
Nos. 478-481 (4) 6.40 6.40

Shipwrecks — A83

1986 Wmk. 384 *Perf. 14*

482 A83 3c Constellation, 1943 .20 .20
483 A83 5c Early Riser, 1876 .20 .20
484 A83 7c Madiana, 1903 .20 .20
485 A83 10c Curlew, 1856 .20 .20
486 A83 12c Warwick, 1619 .20 .20
487 A83 15c HMS Vixen, 1890 .30 .30
488 A83 20c San Pedro, 1594 .35 .35
489 A83 25c Alert, 1877 .50 .50
490 A83 40c North Carolina, 1880 .75 .75
491 A83 50c Mark Antonie, 1777 1.00 1.10
492 A83 60c Mary Celestia, 1864 1.10 1.10
493 A83 $1 L'Herminie, 1839 1.75 1.75
494 A83 $1.50 Caesar, 1818 2.75 2.75
495 A83 $2 Lord Amherst, 1778 3.50 3.50
496 A83 $3 Minerva, 1849 5.50 5.50
497 A83 $5 Caraquet, 1923 9.00 9.00
498 A83 $8 HMS Pallas, 1783 14.50 14.50
Nos. 482-498 (17) 42.00 42.10

Nos. 493, 495-496 exist inscribed "1989." Nos. 482, 488, "1990."

See #545-546. For surcharges see #598-600.

Inscribed "1992"

1992 Litho. Wmk. 373 *Perf. 14*

485a A83 10c .20 .20
487a A83 15c .30 .30
488a A83 20c .35 .35
489a A83 25c .45 .45
492a A83 60c 1.10 1.10
497a A83 $5 9.25 9.25
498a A83 $8 14.75 14.75
Nos. 485a-498a (7) 26.40 26.40

Queen Elizabeth II 60th Birthday
Common Design Type

Designs: 15c, Age 3. 40c, With the Earl of Rosebury, Oaks May Meeting, Epsom, 1954. 50c, With Prince Philip, state visit, 1979. 60c, At the British embassy in Paris, state visit, 1972. $1.50, Visiting Crown Agents' offices, 1983.

1986, Apr. 21 Wmk. 384 *Perf. 14½*

499 CD337 15c scar, blk & sil .25 .25
500 CD337 40c ultra & multi .65 .65
501 CD337 50c green & multi .80 .80
502 CD337 60c violet & multi .95 .95
503 CD337 $1.50 rose vio & multi 2.50 2.50
Nos. 499-503 (5) 5.15 5.15

AMERIPEX '86 — A84

1986, May 22 *Perf. 14*

504 A84 15c No. 452a .25 .25
505 A84 40c No. 307 .65 .65
506 A84 50c No. 441 .80 .80
507 A84 $1 No. 339 1.60 1.60
Nos. 504-507 (4) 3.30 3.30

Souvenir Sheet

508 A84 1.50 Statue of Liberty, S.S. Queen of Bermuda 4.50 4.50

Statue of Liberty, cent.

No. 378 Surcharged

Perf. 14x14½

1986, Dec. 4 Photo. Wmk. 373

509 A62 90c on $3 multi 3.00 3.00

Exists with double surcharge.

Transport Railway, c. 1931-1947 — A85

Wmk. 373

1987, Jan. 22 Litho. *Perf. 14*

510 A85 15c Front Street, c. 1940 .25 .25
511 A85 40c Springfield Trestle .65 .65
512 A85 50c No. 101, Bailey's Bay Sta. .80 .80
513 A85 $1.50 No. 31, ship Prince David 2.50 2.50
Nos. 510-513 (4) 4.20 4.20

Paintings by Winslow Homer (1836-1910) A86

1987, Apr. 30 *Perf. 14½*

514 A86 15c Bermuda Settlers, 1901 .30 .30
515 A86 30c Bermuda, 1900 .55 .55
516 A86 40c Bermuda Landscape, 1901 .75 .75

517 A86 50c Inland Water, 1901 .95 .95
518 A86 $1.50 Salt Kettle, 1899 3.00 3.00
Nos. 514-518 (5) 5.55 5.55

Booklet Stamps

519 A86 40c like 15c .65 .65
520 A86 40c like 30c .65 .65
521 A86 40c like No. 516 .65 .65
522 A86 40c like 50c .65 .65
523 A86 40c like $1.50 .65 .65
a. Bklt. pane, 2 each #519-523 6.50

Nos. 519-523 printed in strips of 5 within pane. "ER" at lower left.

Intl. Flights Inauguration — A87

1987, June 18 ***Perf. 14***

524 A87 15c Sikorsky S-42B, 1937 .50 .50
525 A87 40c Shorts S-23 Cavalier 1.40 1.40
526 A87 50c S-42B Bermuda Clipper 1.60 1.60
527 A87 $1.50 Cavalier, Bermuda Clipper 5.00 5.00
Nos. 524-527 (4) 8.50 8.50

Bermuda Telephone Company, Cent. — A88

1987, Oct. 1 Litho. Wmk. 384

528 A88 15c Telephone poles on wagon .25 .25
529 A88 40c Operators .70 .70
530 A88 50c Telephones .85 .85
531 A88 $1.50 Satellite, fiber optics, world 2.50 2.50
Nos. 528-531 (4) 4.30 4.30

Horse-drawn Commercial Vehicles — A89

1988, Mar. 3 Litho. ***Perf. 14***

532 A89 15c Mail wagon, c. 1869 .30 .30
533 A89 40c Open cart, c. 1823 .75 .75
534 A89 50c Closed cart, c. 1823 .95 .95
535 A89 $1.50 Two-wheel wagon, c. 1930 2.75 2.75
Nos. 532-535 (4) 4.75 4.75

Old Garden Roses — A90

1988, Apr. 21 Wmk. 373

536 A90 15c Old blush .25 .25
537 A90 30c Anna Olivier .50 .50
538 A90 40c Rosa chinensis semperflorens, vert. .70 .70
539 A90 50c Archduke Charles .90 .90
540 A90 $1.50 Rosa chinensis viridiflora, vert. 2.75 2.75
Nos. 536-540 (5) 5.10 5.10

See Nos. 561-575.

Lloyds of London, 300th Anniv.
Common Design Type

18c, Loss of the H.M.S. Lutine, 1799. 50c, Cable ship Sentinel. 60c, The Bermuda, Hamilton, 1931. $2, Valerian, lost during a hurricane, 1926.

1988, Oct. 13 Litho. Wmk. 384

541 CD341 18c multi .30 .30
542 CD341 50c multi, horiz. .90 .90
543 CD341 60c multi, horiz. 1.10 1.10
544 CD341 $2 multi 3.50 3.50
Nos. 541-544 (4) 5.80 5.80

Shipwreck Type of 1986

1988 Litho. Wmk. 384 ***Perf. 14***

545 A83 18c like 7c .35 .35
546 A83 70c like $1.50 1.40 1.40

Issue dates: 18c, Sept. 22; 70c, Oct. 27.

Military Uniforms — A91

18c, Devonshire Parish Militia, 1812. 50c, 71st Regiment Highlander, 1831-34. 60c, Cameron Highlander, 1942. $2, Troop of Horse, 1774.

1988, Nov. 10 Wmk. 373 ***Perf. 14½***

547 A91 18c multicolored .30 .30
548 A91 50c multicolored .85 .85
549 A91 60c multicolored 1.00 1.00
550 A91 $2 multicolored 3.50 3.50
Nos. 547-550 (4) 5.65 5.65

Ferry Service A92

1989 Litho. Wmk. 384 ***Perf. 14***

551 A92 18c Corona .30 .30
552 A92 50c Rowboat ferry .85 .85
553 A92 60c St. George's Ferry 1.00 1.00
554 A92 $2 Laconia 3.50 3.50
Nos. 551-554 (4) 5.65 5.65

Photography, Sesquicent. A93

Perf. 14x14½

1989, May 11 Litho. Wmk. 373

555 A93 18c Morgan's Is. .35 .35
556 A93 30c Front Street, Hamilton (cannon in square) .60 .60
557 A93 50c Front Street (seascape) 1.00 1.00
558 A93 60c Crow Lane, Hamilton Harbor 1.25 1.25
559 A93 70c Hamilton Harbor (shipbuilding) 1.40 1.40
560 A93 $1 Dockyard 2.00 2.00
Nos. 555-560 (6) 6.60 6.60

Old Garden Roses Type of 1988

1989, July 13 ***Perf. 14***

561 A90 18c Agrippina .35 .35
562 A90 30c Smith's Parish .60 .60
563 A90 50c Champney's pink cluster 1.00 1.00
564 A90 60c Rosette delizy 1.25 1.25
565 A90 $1.50 Rosa bracteata 3.00 3.00
Nos. 561-565 (5) 6.20 6.20

Nos. 561-562 vert.

Old Garden Roses Type of 1988 with Royal Cipher Instead of Queen's Silhouette

1989, July 13 Booklet Stamps

566 A90 50c like No. 562 1.00 1.00
567 A90 50c like No. 540 1.00 1.00
568 A90 50c like No. 561 1.00 1.00
569 A90 50c like No. 538 1.00 1.00
570 A90 50c like No. 563 1.00 1.00
571 A90 50c like No. 536 1.00 1.00
572 A90 50c like No. 564 1.00 1.00
573 A90 50c like No. 537 1.00 1.00
574 A90 50c like No. 565 1.00 1.00
575 A90 50c like No. 539 1.00 1.00
a. Bklt. pane of 10, #566-575 10.00

Bermuda Library, 150th Anniv. — A94

1989, Sept. 14 ***Perf. 13½x14***

576 A94 18c Hamilton Main Library .30 .30
577 A94 50c St. George's, The Old Rectory .85 .85
578 A94 60c Springfield, Somerset Library 1.00 1.00
579 A94 $2 Cabinet Building 3.50 3.50
Nos. 576-579 (4) 5.65 5.65

Commonwealth Postal Conference — A95

1989, Nov. 3 Wmk. 384 ***Perf. 14***

580 A95 18c No. 1 .30 .30
581 A95 50c No. 2 .85 .85
582 A95 60c Type A4 1.00 1.00
583 A95 $2 No. 6 3.50 3.50
Nos. 580-583 (4) 5.65 5.65

For overprints see Nos. 594-597.

Fairylands, Bermuda, c. 1890, by Ross Sterling Turner A96

Paintings: 50c, *Shinebone Alley, c. 1953,* by Ogden M. Pleissner. 60c, *Salt Kettle, 1916,* by Prosper Senate. $2, *St. George's, 1934,* by Jack Bush.

1990, Apr. 19

590 A96 18c multicolored .30 .30
591 A96 50c multicolored .85 .85
592 A96 60c multicolored 1.00 1.00
593 A96 $2 multicolored 3.50 3.50
Nos. 590-593 (4) 5.65 5.65

Nos. 580-583 Overprinted

1990, May 3

594 A95 18c multicolored .35 .35
595 A95 50c multicolored 1.00 1.00
596 A95 60c multicolored 1.25 1.25
597 A95 $2 multicolored 4.00 4.00
Nos. 594-597 (4) 6.60 6.60

Stamp World London '90.

Nos. 486, 491, 494 Surcharged

80c

1990, Aug. 13

598 A83 30c on 12c No. 486 .50 .50
599 A83 55c on 50c No. 491 1.00 1.00
600 A83 80c on $1.50 No. 494 1.50 1.50
Nos. 598-600 (3) 3.00 3.00

Nova Scotia-Bermuda Cable, Cent. — A97

1990, Oct. 18 Litho. Unwmk.

601 A97 20c Office .35 .35
602 A97 55c Cableship SS Westmeath 1.00 1.00
603 A97 70c Radio station, 1928 1.25 1.25
604 A97 $2 Cableship Sir Eric Sharp 3.50 3.50
Nos. 601-604 (4) 6.10 6.10

Nos. 601-602 with Added Inscription: "BUSH-MAJOR / 16 MARCH 1991"

1991, Mar. Unwmk. ***Perf. 14***

605 A97 20c like #601 .40 .40
606 A97 55c like #602 1.10 1.10

Carriages A98

Designs: 20c, Two-seat pony cart, c. 1805. 30c, Varnished rockaway, c. 1830. 55c, Vis-a-Vis Victoria, c. 1895. 70c, Semi-formal phaeton, c. 1900. 80c, Pony runabout, c. 1905. $1, Ladies' phaeton, c. 1910.

Perf. 14x14½

1991, Mar. 21 Litho. Wmk. 373

607 A98 20c green & multi .40 .40
608 A98 30c bl gray & multi .60 .60
609 A98 55c dk car & multi 1.10 1.10
610 A98 70c blue & multi 1.40 1.40
611 A98 80c yel org & multi 1.60 1.60
612 A98 $1 dk gray & multi 2.00 2.00
Nos. 607-612 (6) 7.10 7.10

Paintings A99

Designs: 20c, Bermuda by Prosper Senat, vert. 55c, Bermuda Cottage by Frank Allison. 70c, Old Maid's Lane by Jack Bush, vert. $2, St. George's by Ogden M. Pleissner.

Perf. 14x13½

1991, May 16 Litho. Wmk. 373

613 A99 20c multicolored .40 .40
614 A99 55c multicolored 1.10 1.10
615 A99 70c multicolored 1.40 1.40
616 A99 $2 multicolored 4.00 4.00
Nos. 613-616 (4) 6.90 6.90

Elizabeth & Philip, Birthdays
Common Design Types

1991, June 20 Wmk. 384 ***Perf. 14½***

617 CD346 55c multicolored 1.10 1.10
618 CD345 70c multicolored 1.40 1.40
a. Pair, #617-618 + label 2.50 2.50

Bermuda in World War II A100

Designs: 20c, Floating drydock. 55c, Kindley Air Field. 70c, Trans-atlantic air route, Boeing 314. $2, Censored trans-atlantic mail.

1991, Sept. 19 Wmk. 373 ***Perf. 14***

619 A100 20c multicolored .40 .40
620 A100 55c multicolored 1.10 1.10
621 A100 70c multicolored 1.40 1.40
622 A100 $2 multicolored 4.00 4.00
Nos. 619-622 (4) 6.90 6.90

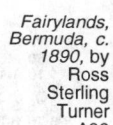

Queen Elizabeth II's Accession to the Throne, 40th Anniv.

Common Design Type

1992, Feb. 6

623 CD349 20c multicolored .40 .40
624 CD349 30c multicolored .60 .60
625 CD349 55c multicolored 1.10 1.10
626 CD349 70c multicolored 1.40 1.40
627 CD349 $1 multicolored 2.00 2.00
Nos. 623-627 (5) 5.50 5.50

Age of Exploration — A101

Artifacts: 25c, Rings, medallion. 35c, Ink wells. 60c, Gold pieces. 75c, Bishop button, crucifix. 85c, Pearl earrings and buttons. $1, 8-real coin, jug and measuring cups.

1992, July 23 ***Perf. 13½***

628 A101 25c multicolored .50 .50
629 A101 35c multicolored .70 .70
630 A101 60c multicolored 1.25 1.25
631 A101 75c multicolored 1.50 1.50
632 A101 85c multicolored 1.75 1.75
633 A101 $1 multicolored 2.00 2.00
Nos. 628-633 (6) 7.70 7.70

Stained Glass Windows — A102

Designs: 25c, Ship wreck. 60c, Birds in tree. 75c, St. Francis feeding bird. $2, Seashells.

1992, Sept. 24 ***Perf. 14***

634 A102 25c multicolored .50 .50
635 A102 60c multicolored 1.25 1.25
636 A102 75c multicolored 1.50 1.50
637 A102 $2 multicolored 4.00 4.00
Nos. 634-637 (4) 7.25 7.25

7th World Congress of Kennel Clubs — A103

Perf. 13½x14, 14x13½

1992, Nov. 12 Litho. Wmk. 373

638 A103 25c German shepherd .50 .50
639 A103 35c Irish setter .65 .65
640 A103 60c Whippet, vert. 1.10 1.10
641 A103 75c Border terrier, vert. 1.40 1.40
642 A103 85c Pomeranian, vert. 1.60 1.60
643 A103 $1 Schipperke, vert. 1.90 1.90
Nos. 638-643 (6) 7.15 7.15

Tourist Posters
A104 A105

1993, Feb. 25 Wmk. 373 ***Perf. 14***

644 A104 25c Cyclist, carriage, ship .50 .50
645 A105 60c Golf course 1.10 1.10
646 A105 75c Coastline 1.40 1.40
647 A104 $2 Dancers 3.75 3.75
Nos. 644-647 (4) 6.75 6.75

Royal Air Force, 75th Anniv.

Common Design Type

Designs: 25c, Consolidated Catalina. 60c, Supermarine Spitfire. 75c, Bristol Beaufighter. $2, Handley Page Halifax.

1993, Apr. 1

648 CD350 25c multicolored .50 .50
649 CD350 60c multicolored 1.10 1.10
650 CD350 75c multicolored 1.40 1.40
651 CD350 $2 multicolored 3.75 3.75
Nos. 648-651 (4) 6.75 6.75

Duchesse de Brabant Rose, Bee — A106

1993, Apr. 1 Wmk. 384

Booklet Stamps

652 A106 10c green & multi .20 .20
653 A106 25c violet & multi .50 .50
a. Booklet pane of 5 2.50
654 A106 50c sepia & multi 1.00 1.00
a. Booklet pane, 2 #652, 3 #654 3.50
655 A106 60c vermilion & multi 1.10 1.10
a. Booklet pane of 5 5.50
Nos. 652-655 (4) 2.80 2.80

Hamilton, Bicent. — A107

Designs: 25c, Modern skyline. 60c, Front Street, ships at left. 75c, Front Street, horse carts. $2, Hamilton Harbor, 1823.

Wmk. 373

1993, Sept. 16 Litho. ***Perf. 14½***

656 A107 25c multicolored .50 .50
657 A107 60c multicolored 1.10 1.10
658 A107 75c multicolored 1.40 1.40
659 A107 $2 multicolored 3.75 3.75
Nos. 656-659 (4) 6.75 6.75

Furness Lines — A108

Designs: 25c, Furness Liv-Aboard Bermuda cruises, vert. 60c, SS Queen of Bermuda entering port. 75c, SS Queen of Bermuda, SS Ocean Monarch. $2, Starlit night aboard ship, vert.

Perf. 15x14, 14x15

1994, Jan. 20 Litho. Wmk. 373

660 A108 25c multicolored .50 .50
661 A108 60c multicolored 1.10 1.10
662 A108 75c multicolored 1.40 1.40
663 A108 $2 multicolored 3.75 3.75
Nos. 660-663 (4) 6.75 6.75

Royal Visit — A109

25c, Queen Elizabeth II. 60c, Queen Elizabeth II, Duke of Edinburgh. 75c, Royal yacht Britannia.

Wmk. 373

1994, Mar. 9 Litho. ***Perf. 13½***

664 A109 25c multicolored .50 .50
665 A109 60c multicolored 1.10 1.10
666 A109 75c multicolored 1.50 1.50
Nos. 664-666 (3) 3.10 3.10

Flowering Fruits — A110

1994-95 Litho. Wmk. 373 ***Perf. 14***

668 A110 5c Peach .20 .20
669 A110 7c Fig .20 .20
670 A110 10c Calabash, vert .20 .20
671 A110 15c Natal plum .30 .30
672 A110 18c Locust & wild honey .35 .35
673 A110 20c Pomegranate .40 .40
674 A110 25c Mulberry, vert. .50 .50
675 A110 35c Grape, vert. .70 .70
676 A110 55c Orange, vert. 1.10 1.10
677 A110 60c Surinam cherry 1.25 1.25
678 A110 75c Loquat 1.50 1.50
679 A110 90c Sugar apple 1.75 1.75
680 A110 $1 Prickly pear, vert. 2.00 2.00
681 A110 $2 Paw paw 4.00 4.00
682 A110 $3 Bay grape 6.00 6.00
683 A110 $5 Banana, vert. 10.00 10.00
684 A110 $8 Lemon 16.00 16.00
Nos. 668-684 (17) 46.45 46.45

No. 672 exists dated "1996." Nos. 668, 671-674, 678-680 dated "1998."

Issued: 5c, 7c, 15c, 20c, $8, 7/14/94; 10c, 25c, 35c, 55c, $1, $5, 10/6/94; 18c, 60c, 75c, 90c, $2, $3, 3/23/95.

1996-98 Wmk. 384

668a A110 5c .20 .20
671a A110 15c .30 .30
672a A110 18c .35 .35
673a A110 20c .40 .40
674a A110 25c .50 .50
678a A110 75c 1.50 1.50
679a A110 90c 1.75 1.75
680a A110 $1 2.00 2.00
Nos. 668a-680a (8) 7.00 7.00

#672a exists dated "1998."

Issued: #668a, 671a, 673a-674a, 678a-680a, 9/1/98; #672a, 9/1/96.

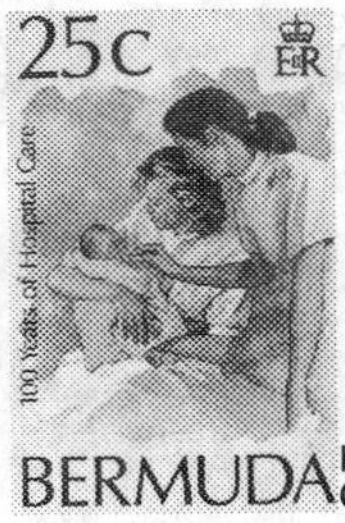

Hospital Care, Cent. — A111

1994, Sept. 15 ***Perf. 15x14***

685 A111 25c Child birth .50 .50
686 A111 60c Dialysis 1.10 1.10
687 A111 75c Emergency 1.50 1.50
688 A111 $2 Therapy 4.00 4.00
Nos. 685-688 (4) 7.10 7.10

Christmas — A112

1994, Nov. 10 ***Perf. 14x15***

689 A112 25c Gombey dancers .50 .50
690 A112 60c Carollers 1.10 1.10
691 A112 75c Marching band 1.50 1.50
692 A112 $2 Natl. dance group 4.00 4.00
Nos. 689-692 (4) 7.10 7.10

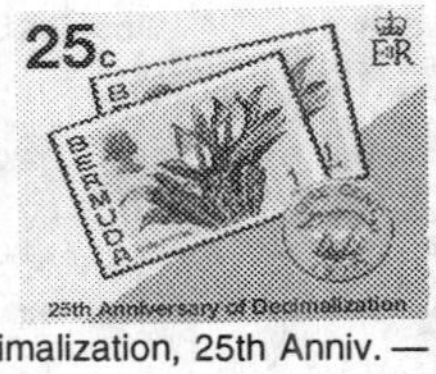

Decimalization, 25th Anniv. — A113

Stamps, 1970 coins: 25c, #255, one cent. 60c, #259, five cents. 75c, #262, ten cents. $2, #324, twenty-five cents.

Wmk. 373

1995, Feb. 6 Litho. ***Perf. 14***

693 A113 25c multicolored .50 .50
694 A113 60c multicolored 1.10 1.10
695 A113 75c multicolored 1.50 1.50
696 A113 $2 multicolored 4.00 4.00
Nos. 693-696 (4) 7.10 7.10

Outdoor Celebrations — A114

Perf. 14x15

1995, May 30 Litho. Wmk. 373

697 A114 25c Kite flying .50 .50
698 A114 60c Majorettes 1.10 1.10
699 A114 75c Portuguese dancers 1.50 1.50
700 A114 $2 Floral float 4.00 4.00
Nos. 697-700 (4) 7.10 7.10

Parliament, 375th Anniv. — A115

Designs: 25c, $1, Bermuda coat of arms.

Perf. 14x13½

1995, Nov. 3 Litho. Wmk. 373

701 A115 25c blue & multi .50 .50
702 A115 $1 green & multi 2.00 2.00

See No. 731.

Military Bases A116

Force insignia and: 20c, Ordnance Island Submarine Base. 25c, Royal Naval Dockyard. 60c, Fort Bell and Kindley Field. 75c, Darrell's Island. 90c, US Navy Operating Base. $1, Canadian Forces Station, Daniel's Head.

1995, Dec. 4 ***Perf. 14***

703 A116 20c multicolored .40 .40
704 A116 25c multicolored .50 .50
705 A116 60c multicolored 1.25 1.25
706 A116 75c multicolored 1.50 1.50
707 A116 90c multicolored 1.75 1.75
708 A116 $1 multicolored 2.00 2.00
Nos. 703-708 (6) 7.40 7.40

Modern Olympic Games, Cent. — A117

Wmk. 384

1996, May 21 Litho. ***Perf. 14***

709 A117 25c Track & field .50 .50
710 A117 30c Cycling .60 .60
711 A117 65c Sailing 1.25 1.25
712 A117 80c Equestrian 1.60 1.60
Nos. 709-712 (4) 3.95 3.95

CAPEX '96
A118

Methods of transportation: 25c, Sommerset Express, c. 1900. 60c, Bermuda Railway, 1930's. 75c, First bus, 1946. $2, Early sightseeing bus, c.1947.

Perf. 13½x14

1996, June 7 Litho. Wmk. 373

713 A118 25c multicolored	.50	.50
714 A118 60c multicolored	1.25	1.25
715 A118 75c multicolored	1.50	1.50
716 A118 $2 multicolored	4.00	4.00
Nos. 713-716 (4)	7.25	7.25

Panoramas of Hamilton and St. George's, by E. J. Holland, 1933
A119

Hamilton, looking across water from Bostock Hill: No. 717, Palm trees, Furness Line ship coming through Two Rock Passage. No. 718, House, buildings on other side. No. 719, Sailboats on water, Princess Hotel. No. 720, Island, Bermudiana Hotel, Cathedral. No. 721, Coral roads on hillside, city of Hamilton.

St. George's, looking across water from St. David's: No. 722, Island, harbor. No. 723, Sailboat, buildings along shore. No. 724, Sailboat, St. George's Hotel, buildings. No. 725, Hillside, ship. No. 726, Homes on hill top, passage out of harbor.

Perf. 14x14½

1996, May 21 Wmk. 373

Booklet Stamps

717 A119 60c multicolored	1.25	1.25
718 A119 60c multicolored	1.25	1.25
719 A119 60c multicolored	1.25	1.25
720 A119 60c multicolored	1.25	1.25
721 A119 60c multicolored	1.25	1.25
a. Strip of 5, #717-721	6.25	6.25
722 A119 60c multicolored	1.25	1.25
723 A119 60c multicolored	1.25	1.25
724 A119 60c multicolored	1.25	1.25
725 A119 60c multicolored	1.25	1.25
726 A119 60c multicolored	1.25	1.25
a. Strip of 5, #722-726	6.25	6.25
b. Booklet pane, #721a, 726a	12.50	
Complete booklet, #726b	12.50	

Lighthouses — A120

Designs: 30c, Hog Fish Beacon. 65c, Gibbs Hill Lighthouse. 80c, St. David's Lighthouse. $2, North Rock Beacon.

Perf. 14x13½

1996, Aug. 15 Litho. Wmk. 373

727 A120 30c multicolored	.60	.60
728 A120 65c multicolored	1.25	1.25
729 A120 80c multicolored	1.60	1.60
730 A120 $2 multicolored	4.00	4.00
Nos. 727-730 (4)	7.45	7.45

See Nos. 737-740.

Bermuda Coat of Arms Type of 1995 Inscribed "Commonwealth Finance Ministers Meeting"

Perf. 14x13½

1996, Sept. 24 Litho. Wmk. 373

731 A115 $1 red & multi	2.00	2.00

Queen Elizabeth II — A121

1996, Nov. 7

732 A121 $22 blue & org brn	44.00	44.00

Architectural Heritage — A122

Wmk. 384

1996, Nov. 28 Litho. *Perf. 14*

733 A122 30c Waterville	.60	.60
734 A122 65c Bridge House	1.25	1.25
735 A122 80c Fannie Fox's Cottage	1.60	1.60
736 A122 $2.50 Palmetto House	5.00	5.00
Nos. 733-736 (4)	8.45	8.45

Lighthouse Type of 1996 Redrawn

Wmk. 373

1997, Feb. 12 Litho. *Perf. 14*

737 A120 30c Like #727	.60	.60
738 A120 65c Like #728	1.25	1.25
739 A120 80c Like #729	1.60	1.60
740 A120 $2.50 Like #730	5.00	5.00
Nos. 737-740 (4)	8.45	8.45

Nos. 737-740 each have Hong Kong '97 emblem. No. 738 inscribed "Gibbs Hill Lighthouse c. 1900." No. 739 inscribed "St. David's Lighthouse c. 1900."

Birds
A123

Designs: 30c, White-tailed tropicbird. 60c, White-tailed tropicbird, adult, chick, vert. 80c, Cahow, adult, chick, vert. $2.50, Cahow.

Wmk. 384

1997, Apr. 17 Litho. *Perf. 14*

741 A123 30c multicolored	.60	.60
742 A123 60c multicolored	1.25	1.25
743 A123 80c multicolored	1.60	1.60
744 A123 $2.50 multicolored	5.00	5.00
Nos. 741-744 (4)	8.45	8.45

Queen Elizabeth II and Prince Philip, 50th Wedding Anniv.
A124

Perf. 14x14½

1997, Oct. 9 Litho. Wmk. 373

745 A124 30c Queen, crowd	.60	.60
746 A124 $2 Queen, Prince	4.00	4.00
a. Souvenir sheet of 2, #745-746	4.60	4.60

Education in Bermuda
A125

Designs: 30c, Man, children using blocks. 40c, Teacher, students with map. 60c, Boys holding sports trophy. 65c, Students in front of Berkeley Institute. 80c, Students working in lab. 90c, Students in graduation gowns.

Wmk. 384

1997, Dec. 18 Litho. *Perf. 14*

747 A125 30c multicolored	.60	.60
748 A125 40c multicolored	.80	.80
749 A125 60c multicolored	1.25	1.25
750 A125 65c multicolored	1.25	1.25
751 A125 80c multicolored	1.60	1.60
752 A125 90c multicolored	1.75	1.75
Nos. 747-752 (6)	7.25	7.25

Diana, Princess of Wales (1961-97)

Common Design Type

Various portraits: a. 30c. b, 40c. c, 65c. d, 80c.

Perf. 14x14½

1998, Mar. 31 Litho. Wmk. 373

753 CD355 Sheet of 4, #a.-d.	4.75	4.75

No. 753 sold for $2.15 + 25c, with surtax from international sales being donated to the Princess Diana Memorial Fund and surtax from national sales being donated to designated local charity.

Paintings of the Islands
A126

Designs: 30c, Fox's Cottage, St. David's. 40c, East Side, Somerset. 65c, Long Bay Road, Somerset. $2, Flatts Village.

1998, June 4 *Perf. 13½x14*

754 A126 30c multicolored	.60	.60
755 A126 40c multicolored	.80	.80
756 A126 65c multicolored	1.25	1.25
757 A126 $2 multicolored	4.00	4.00
Nos. 754-757 (4)	6.65	6.65

Hospitality for Tourists in Bermuda — A127

Designs: 25c, Carriage ride. 30c, Golfer at registration desk. 65c, Maid leaving flowers on hotel bed. 75c, Chefs preparing food. 80c, Waiter serving couple. 90c, Singer, bartender, guests.

Wmk. 384

1998, Sept. 24 Litho. *Perf. 14½*

758 A127 25c multicolored	.50	.50
759 A127 30c multicolored	.60	.60
760 A127 65c multicolored	1.25	1.25
761 A127 75c multicolored	1.50	1.50
762 A127 80c multicolored	1.60	1.60
763 A127 90c multicolored	1.75	1.75
Nos. 758-763 (6)	7.20	7.20

Bermuda's Botantical Gardens, Cent. — A128

Wmk. 373

1998, Oct. 15 Litho. *Perf. 14*

764 A128 30c Agave attenuata	.60	.60
765 A128 65c Bermuda palmetto tree	1.25	1.25
766 A128 $1 Banyan tree	2.00	2.00
767 A128 $2 Cedar tree	4.00	4.00
Nos. 764-767 (4)	7.85	7.85

Christmas
A129

Children's paintings: 25c, Lizard in Santa hat stringing Christmas lights, vert. 40c, Stairway, wreath on door.

Wmk. 373

1998, Nov. 26 Litho. *Perf. 14*

768 A129 25c multicolored	.50	.50
769 A129 40c multicolored	.75	.75

Beaches — A130

Wmk. 373

1999, Apr. 29 Litho. *Perf. 13½*

770 A130 30c Shelly Bay	.60	.60
771 A130 60c Catherine's Bay	1.25	1.25
772 A130 65c Jobson's Cove	1.25	1.25
773 A130 $2 Warwick Long Bay	4.00	4.00
Nos. 770-773 (4)	7.10	7.10

Common Design Type and:

First Manned Moon Landing, 30th Anniv.
A131

Wmk. 373

1999, July 20 Litho. *Perf. 13*

774 A131 30c Ground station	.60	.60
775 A131 60c Lift-off, vert.	1.25	1.25
776 A131 75c Aerial view of ground station	1.50	1.50
777 A131 $2 Moon walk, vert.	4.00	4.00
Nos. 774-777 (4)	7.35	7.35

Souvenir Sheet

Litho.

Wmk. *384Perf. 14*

778 CD357 65c Looking at earth from moon	1.25	1.25

No. 778 contains one 40mm circular stamp.

Mapmaking — A132

Wmk. 373

1999, Aug. 19 Litho. *Perf. 14*

779 A132 30c Somerset Is., theodolite	.60	.60
780 A132 65c 1901 street map	1.25	1.25
781 A132 80c Aerial photo, modern street map	1.60	1.60
782 A132 $1 Satellite, island	2.00	2.00
Nos. 779-782 (4)	5.45	5.45

Mail Boxes and Stamps — A133

Wmk. 373

1999, Oct. 5 Litho. *Perf. 14¼*

783 A133 30c Victoria era, #6	.60	.60
784 A133 75c George V era, #49	1.50	1.50
785 A133 95c George VI era, #121	1.90	1.90
786 A133 $1 Elizabeth II era, #142	2.00	2.00
Nos. 783-786 (4)	6.00	6.00

WAR TAX STAMPS

No. 42 Overprinted **WAR TAX**

1918		Wmk. 3	*Perf. 14*	
MR1	A11	1p rose red	.50	.40

No. 42a Overprinted **WAR TAX**

1920				
MR2	A11	1p carmine	.45	*.80*

BHUTAN

bü-ˈtän

LOCATION — Eastern Himalayas
GOVT. — Kingdom
AREA — 18,000 sq. mi.
POP. — 1,951,965(?) (1999 est.)
CAPITAL — Thimphu

100 Chetrum = 1 Ngultrum or Rupee

Catalogue values for all unused stamps in this country are for Never Hinged items.

Postal Runner — A1

Designs: 3ch, 70ch, Archer. 5ch, 1.30nu, Yak. 15ch, Map of Bhutan, portrait of Druk Gyalpo (Dragon King) Ugyen Wangchuk (1867-1902) and Paro Dzong (fortress-monastery). 33ch, Postal runner. All horiz. except 2ch and 33ch.

Perf. 14x14½, 14½x14

1962		Litho.		Unwmk.
1	A1	2ch red & gray	.20	.20
2	A1	3ch red & ultra	.20	.20
3	A1	5ch green & brown	.80	.80
4	A1	15ch red, blk & org yel	.20	.20
5	A1	33ch blue grn & lil	.20	.20
6	A1	70ch dp ultra & lt blue	.60	.60
7	A1	1.30nu blue & black	1.60	1.60
		Nos. 1-7 (7)	3.80	3.80

Nos. 1-7 were issued for inland use in April, 1962, and became valid for international mail on Oct. 10, 1962.

For overprint and surcharges see #42, 72-73.

Refugee Year Emblem and Arms of Bhutan A2

1962, Oct. 10			*Perf. 14½x14*	
8	A2	1nu dk blue & dk car rose	.65	.65
9	A2	2nu yel grn & red lilac	1.25	1.25

World Refugee Year. For surcharges see #68-69.

Equipment of Ancient Warrior — A3

Boy Filling Grain Box and Wheat Emblem — A4

1963		Unwmk.	*Perf. 14x14½*	
10	A3	33ch multicolored	.20	.20
11	A3	70ch multicolored	.40	.40
12	A3	1.30nu multicolored	.75	.75
		Nos. 10-12 (3)	1.35	1.35

Bhutan's membership in Colombo Plan.

1963, July 15			*Perf. 13½x14*	
13	A4	20ch lt blue, yel & red brn	.20	.20
14	A4	1.50nu rose lil, bl & red brn	.65	.65

FAO "Freedom from Hunger" campaign. For surcharge see No. 117M.

Masked Dancer — A5

Various Bhutanese Dancers (Five Designs; 2ch, 5ch, 20ch, 1nu, 1.30nu vert.)

1964, Apr. 16		*Perf. 14½x14, 14x14½*		
15	A5	2ch multicolored	.20	.20
16	A5	3ch multicolored	.20	.20
17	A5	5ch multicolored	.20	.20
18	A5	20ch multicolored	.20	.20
19	A5	33ch multicolored	.20	.20
20	A5	70ch multicolored	.20	.20
21	A5	1nu multicolored	.35	.35
22	A5	1.30nu multicolored	.40	.40
23	A5	2nu multicolored	.65	.65
		Nos. 15-23 (9)	2.60	2.60

For surcharges see Nos. 70-71, 74-75, 129A, 129G. For overprints see Nos. C1-C3, C11-C13.

Stone Throwing — A6

Sport: 5ch, 33ch, Boxing. 1nu, 3nu, Archery. 2nu, Soccer.

1964, Oct. 10		Litho.	*Perf. 14½*	
24	A6	2ch emerald & multi	.20	.20
25	A6	5ch orange & multi	.20	.20
26	A6	15ch brt citron & multi	.20	.20
27	A6	33ch rose lil & multi	.20	.20
28	A6	1nu multicolored	.40	.40
29	A6	2nu rose lilac & multi	.60	.60
30	A6	3nu lt blue & multi	.90	.90
		Nos. 24-30 (7)	2.70	2.70

18th Olympic Games, Tokyo, Oct. 10-25. See No. B4.

Nos. 24-30 exist imperf. Value $4.

Flags of the World at Half-mast — A7

1964, Nov. 22		Unwmk.	*Perf. 14½*	
		Flags in Original Colors		
31	A7	33ch steel gray	.20	.20
32	A7	1nu silver	.45	.45
33	A7	3nu gold	1.10	1.10
a.		Souv. sheet, perf. 13½ or imperf.	2.75	2.75
		Nos. 31-33 (3)	1.75	1.75

Issued in memory of those who died in the service of their country. Nos. 31-33 exist imperf.

No. 33a contains 2 stamps similar to Nos. 32-33.

For overprints see Nos. 44, 46.

Flowers — A8

1965, Jan. 6		Litho.	*Perf. 13*	
34	A8	2ch Primrose	.20	.20
35	A8	5ch Gentian	.20	.20
36	A8	15ch Primrose	.20	.20
37	A8	33ch Gentian	.20	.20
38	A8	50ch Rhododendron	.20	.20
39	A8	75ch Peony	.20	.20
40	A8	1nu Rhododendron	.20	.20
41	A8	2nu Peony	.40	.40
		Nos. 34-41 (8)	1.80	1.80

For overprints see Nos. 43, 45, C4-C5, C14-C15.

Nos. 5, 40, 32, 41 and 33 Overprinted: "WINSTON CHURCHILL 1874-1965"

1965, Feb. 27				
42	A1	33ch bl grn & lilac	.20	.20
43	A8	1nu pink, grn & dk gray	.40	.40
44	A7	1nu silver & multi	.40	.40
45	A8	2nu sepia, yel & grn	.75	.75
46	A7	3nu gold & multi	1.00	1.00
		Nos. 42-46 (5)	2.75	2.75

Issued in memory of Sir Winston Churchill (1874-1965), British statesman. The overprint is in three lines on Nos. 42-43 and 45; in two lines on Nos. 43 and 46.

Nos. 44 and 46 exist imperf. Value, both, $4.50.

Skyscraper, Pagoda and World's Fair Emblem — A9

Designs: 10ch, 2nu, Pieta by Michelangelo and statue of Khmer Buddha. 20ch, Skyline of NYC and Bhutanese village. 33ch, George Washington Bridge, NY, and foot bridge, Bhutan.

1965, Apr. 21		Litho.	*Perf. 14½*	
47	A9	1ch blue & multi	.20	.20
48	A9	10ch green & multi	.20	.20
49	A9	20ch rose lilac & multi	.20	.20
50	A9	33ch bister & multi	.20	.20
51	A9	1.50nu bister & multi	.50	.50
52	A9	2nu multicolored	.65	.65
a.		Souv. sheet, perf. 13½ or imperf.	2.75	2.75
		Nos. 47-52 (6)	1.95	1.95

Nos. 47-52 exist imperf.; value $3.50.

No. 52a contains two stamps similar to Nos. 51-52.

For overprints see #87-87B, C6-C10, C16-C20.

Telstar, Short-wave Radio and ITU Emblem — A10

Designs (ITU Emblem and): 2nu, Telstar and Morse key. 3nu, Syncom and ear phones.

1966, Mar. 2		Litho.	*Perf. 14½*	
53	A10	35ch multicolored	.20	.20
54	A10	2nu multicolored	.55	.55
55	A10	3nu multicolored	.75	.75
		Nos. 53-55 (3)	1.50	1.50

Cent. (in 1965) of the ITU. Souvenir sheets exist containing two stamps similar to Nos. 54-55, perf. 13½ and imperf. Value, 2 sheets, $5.

Leopard — A11

Animals: 1ch, 4nu, Asiatic black bear. 4ch, 2nu, Pigmy hog. 8ch, 75ch, Tiger. 10ch, 1.50nu, Dhole (Asiatic hunting dog). 1nu, 5nu, Takin (goat).

1966, Mar. 24		Litho.	*Perf. 13*	
56	A11	1ch yellow & blk	.20	.20
57	A11	2ch pale grn & blk	.20	.20
58	A11	4ch lt citron & blk	.20	.20
59	A11	8ch lt blue & blk	.20	.20
60	A11	10ch lt lilac & blk	.20	.20
61	A11	75ch lt yel grn & blk	.20	.20
62	A11	1nu lt green & blk	.50	.50
63	A11	1.50nu lt bl grn & blk	.40	.40
64	A11	2nu dull org & blk	.50	.50
65	A11	3nu bluish lil & blk	.75	.75
66	A11	4nu lt green & blk	1.00	1.00
67	A11	5nu pink & black	1.40	1.40
		Nos. 56-67 (12)	5.75	5.75

For surcharges see Nos. 115C, 115E, 115I, 117N, 117P, 129B, 129J.

Nos. 6-9, 20-23 Surcharged **10 CH**

1965(?)		*Perf. 14½x14, 14x14½*		
68	A2	5ch on 1nu	*26.00*	*26.00*
69	A2	5ch on 2nu	*26.00*	*26.00*
70	A5	10ch on 70ch	*4.25*	*4.25*
71	A5	10ch on 2nu	*4.25*	*4.25*
72	A1	15ch on 70ch	*6.25*	*6.25*
73	A1	15ch on 1.30nu	*6.25*	*6.25*
74	A5	20ch on 1nu	*8.25*	*8.25*
75	A5	20ch on 1.30nu	*8.25*	*8.25*
		Nos. 68-75 (8)	*89.50*	*89.50*

The surcharges on Nos. 68-69 contain two bars at left and right obliterating the denomination on both sides of the design. Four bars on Nos. 72-73.

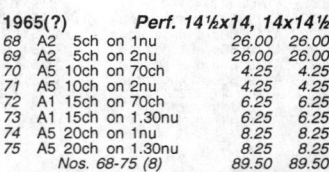

Simtokha Dzong A12

Tashichho Dzong — A13

Daga Dzong A14

Designs: 5ch, Rinpung Dzong. 50ch, Tongsa Dzong. 1nu, Lhuntsi Dzong.

Perf. 14½x14 (A12), 13½ (A13, A14)

1966-70				Photo.
76	A12	5ch orange brn ('67)	.20	.20
77	A13	10ch dk grn & rose vio ('68)	.20	.20
78	A12	15ch brown	.20	.20
79	A12	20ch green	.20	.20

80	A13	50ch blue grn ('68)	.25	.20
81	A14	75ch dk bl & ol gray ('70)	.25	.25
82	A14	1nu dk vio & vio bl ('70)	.40	.40
		Nos. 76-82 (7)	1.70	1.65

Sizes: 5ch, 15ch, 20ch, 37x20½mm. 10ch, 53½x28½mm. 50ch, 35½x25½mm.

King Jigme Wangchuk
A14a

Coins: 1.30nu, 3nu, 5nu, reverse.

Litho. & Embossed on Gold Foil

1966, July 8 Die Cut *Imperf.*

83	A14a	10ch green	.20	.20
83A	A14a	25ch green	.25	.25
83B	A14a	50ch green	.50	.50
83C	A14a	1nu red	1.00	1.00
83D	A14a	1.30nu red	1.15	1.15
83E	A14a	2nu red	1.80	1.80
83F	A14a	3nu red	2.60	2.60
83G	A14a	4nu red	3.75	3.75
83H	A14a	5nu red	4.50	4.50
		Nos. 83-83H (9)	15.75	15.75

See Nos. 98-98B.

Abominable Snowman — A14b

1966 Photo. *Perf. 13½*

84	A14b	1ch multicolored	.20	.20
84A	A14b	2ch multi, diff.	.20	.20
84B	A14b	3ch multi, diff.	.20	.20
84C	A14b	4ch multi, diff.	.20	.20
84D	A14b	5ch multi, diff.	.20	.20
84E	A14b	15ch like #84	.20	.20
84F	A14b	30ch like #84A	.20	.20
84G	A14b	40ch like #84B	.20	.20
84H	A14b	50ch like #84C	.20	.20
84I	A14b	1.25nu like #84D	.30	.30
84J	A14b	2.50nu like #84	.65	.65
84K	A14b	3nu like #84A	.75	.75
84L	A14b	5nu like #84B	1.25	1.25
84M	A14b	6nu like #84C	1.50	1.50
84N	A14b	7nu like #84D	1.75	1.75
		Nos. 84-84N (15)	8.00	8.00

Issue dates: 1ch, 2ch, 3ch, 4ch, 5ch, 15ch, 30ch, 40ch, 50ch, Oct. 12; others, Nov. 15. Exist imperf.

For overprints see Nos. 93-93G. For surcharges see Nos. 115D, 115K, 115O, 115P, 117I, 117S.

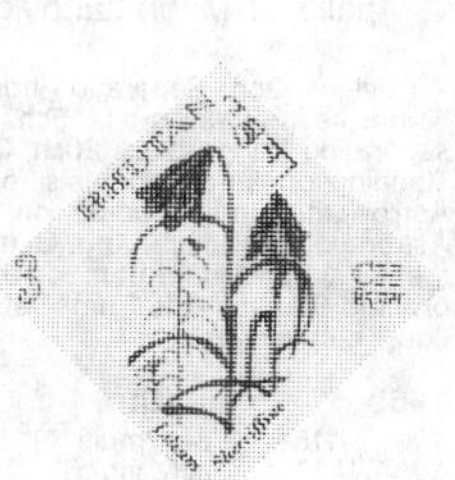

Flowers
A14c

Designs: 3ch, 50ch, Lilium sherriffiae. 5ch, 1nu, Meconopsis dhwoju. 7ch, 2.50nu, Rhododendron chaetomallum. 10ch, 4nu, Pleione hookeriana. 5nu, Rhododendron giganteum.

1967, Feb. 9 Litho. *Perf. 13*

85	A14c	3ch multicolored	.20	.20
85A	A14c	5ch multicolored	.20	.20
85B	A14c	7ch multicolored	.20	.20
85C	A14c	10ch multicolored	.20	.20

Gray Background

85D	A14c	50ch multicolored	.20	.20
85E	A14c	1nu multicolored	.30	.30
85F	A14c	2.50nu multicolored	.75	.75
85G	A14c	4nu multicolored	1.25	1.25
85H	A14c	5nu multicolored	1.50	1.50
		Nos. 85-85H (9)	4.80	4.80

For surcharges see Nos. 115F, 115L.

Boy Scouts — A14d

1967, Mar. 28 Photo. *Perf. 13½*

86	A14d	5ch Planting tree	.20	.20
86A	A14d	10ch Cooking	.20	.20
86B	A14d	15ch Mountain climbing	.20	.20

Emblem, Border in Gold

86C	A14d	50ch like #86	.20	.20
86D	A14d	1.25nu like #86A	.60	.60
86E	A14d	4nu like #86B	1.75	1.75
f.		Souv. sheet of 2, #86D, 86E	2.50	2.50
		Nos. 86-86E (6)	3.15	3.15

Exist imperf.

See Nos. 89-89E for overprints. For surcharges see Nos. 115G, 117J, 129K.

expo67

Perfs. as Before

1967, May 25 Litho.

87	A9	33ch on #50	.20	.20
87A	A9	1.50nu on #51	.45	.45
87B	A9	2nu on #52	.60	.60
c.		Souv. sheet of 2, on #52a	1.50	1.50
		Nos. 87-87B (3)	1.25	1.25

Nos. 87-87B exist imperf.

Airplanes — A14f

1967, June 26 Litho. *Perf. 13½*

88	A14f	45ch Lancaster	.20	.20
88A	A14f	2nu Spitfire	.45	.45
88B	A14f	4nu Hurricane	.95	.95
c.		Souv. sheet of 2, #88A, 88B	2.00	2.00
		Nos. 88-88B (3)	1.60	1.60

Churchill and Battle of Britain. Exist imperf. For surcharges see Nos. 117Q, 117T.

Nos. 86-86D, 86e Overprinted "WORLD JAMBOREE / IDAHO, U.S.A. / AUG. 1-9,/67"

1967, Aug. 8 Photo. *Perf. 13½*

89	A14d	5ch Planting tree	.20	.20
89A	A14d	10ch Cookout	.20	.20
89B	A14d	15ch Mountain climbing	.20	.20
89C	A14d	50ch like #89	.20	.20
89D	A14d	1.25nu like #89A	.60	.60
89E	A14d	4nu like #89B	1.90	1.90
f.		Souv. sheet of 2, #89D, 89E	2.75	2.75
		Nos. 89-89E (6)	3.30	3.30

No. 89f sold for 6.25nu. Exist imperf.

Girl Scouts — A14g

1967, Sept. 28 Photo. *Perf. 13½*

90	A14g	5ch Painting	.20	.20
90A	A14g	10ch Making music	.20	.20
90B	A14g	15ch Picking fruit	.20	.20

Emblem, Border in Gold

90C	A14g	1.50nu like #90	.30	.30
90D	A14g	2.50nu like #90A	.45	.45
90E	A14g	5nu like #90B	.90	.90
f.		Souv. sheet of 2, #90A, 90B	2.00	2.00
		Nos. 90-90E (6)	2.25	2.25

Exist imperf.

For surcharge see No. 266.

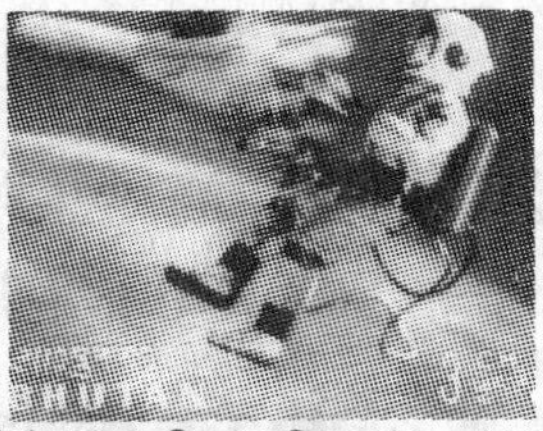

Astronaut, Space Capsule — A14h

Astronaut walking in space and: 5ch, 30ch, 4nu, Orbiter, Lunar modules docked. 7ch, 50ch, 5nu, Lunar module. 10ch, 1.25nu, 9nu, Other astronauts.

1967, Oct. 30 Litho. *Imperf.*

91	A14h	3ch multi	.20	.20
91A	A14h	5ch multi	.20	.20
91B	A14h	7ch multi	.20	.20
91C	A14h	10ch multi	.25	.25
m.		Souv. sheet of 4, #91-91C	.85	.85
91D	A14h	15ch multi	.35	.35
91E	A14h	30ch multi	.75	.75
91F	A14h	50ch multi	1.25	1.25
91G	A14h	1.25nu multi	3.00	3.00
n.		Souv. sheet of 4, #91D-91G	6.75	6.75
91H	A14h	2.50nu multi	1.75	1.75
91I	A14h	4nu multi	3.00	3.00
91J	A14h	5nu multi	3.75	3.75
91K	A14h	9nu multi	6.50	6.50
o.		Souv. sheet of 4, #91H-91K	20.00	20.00
		Nos. 91-91K (12)	21.20	21.20

Nos. 91H-91K are airmail. Simulated 3-dimensions using a plastic overlay.

For other space issues see types A15a, A15e.

Pheasants — A14i

Designs: 1ch, 2nu, Tragopan satyra. 2ch, 4nu, Lophophorus sclareti. 4ch, 5nu, Lophophorus impeyanus. 8ch, 7nu, Lophura leucomelana. 15ch, 9nu, Crossoptilon crossoptilon.

1968 Photo. *Perf. 13½*

92	A14i	1ch multicolored	.20	.20
92A	A14i	2ch multicolored	.20	.20
92B	A14i	4ch multicolored	.20	.20
92C	A14i	8ch multicolored	.20	.20
92D	A14i	15ch multicolored	.20	.20

Border in Gold

92E	A14i	2nu multicolored	.40	.40
92F	A14i	4nu multicolored	.80	.80
92G	A14i	5nu multicolored	1.00	1.00
92H	A14i	7nu multicolored	1.40	1.40
92I	A14i	9nu multicolored	1.90	1.90
		Nos. 92-92I (10)	6.50	6.50

Issue dates: 1ch, 2ch, 4ch, 8ch, 15ch, 2nu, 4nu, 7nu, Jan 20. 5nu, 9nu, Apr. 23.

Unauthorized imperfs. exist.

For surcharges see Nos. 115H, 117R, 117V, 129D, 129L.

Nos. 84G, 84I, 84K, 84M Ovptd. in Black on Silver

a

b

Perfs. as Before

1968, Feb. 16 Photo.

Overprint Type "a"

93	A14b	40ch on #84G	.20	.20
93A	A14b	1.25nu on #84I	.20	.20
93B	A14b	3nu on #84K	.50	.50
93C	A14b	6nu on #84M	1.00	1.00

Overprint Type "b"

93D	A14b	40ch on #84G	.20	.20
93E	A14b	1.25nu on #84I	.20	.20
93F	A14b	3nu on #84K	.50	.50
93G	A14b	6nu on #84M	1.00	1.00
		Nos. 93-93G (8)	3.80	3.80

Exist imperf.

Snow Lion — A14j

1968, Mar. 14 Photo. *Perf. 12½*

94	A14j	2ch Elephant	.20	.20
94A	A14j	3ch Garuda	.20	.20
94B	A14j	4ch Monastery Tiger	.20	.20
94C	A14j	5ch Wind Horse	.20	.20
94D	A14j	15ch Snow Lion	.20	.20
94E	A14j	20ch like #94	.20	.20
94F	A14j	30ch like #94A	.20	.20
94G	A14j	50ch like #94B	.20	.20
94H	A14j	1.25nu like #94C	.20	.20
94I	A14j	1.50nu like #94	.25	.25
94J	A14j	2nu like #94D	.35	.35
94K	A14j	2.50nu like #94A	.40	.40
94L	A14j	4nu like #94B	.65	.65
94M	A14j	5nu like #94C	.80	.80
94N	A14j	10nu like #94D	1.60	1.60
		Nos. 94-94N (15)	5.85	5.85

Nos. 94I, 94K-94N are airmail. All exist imperf.

For surcharges see Nos. 115, 115M, 115Q, 117-117E, 129C, C35-C36.

Butterflies — A14k

Designs: 15ch, Catagramma sorana. 50ch, Delias hyparete. 1.25nu, Anteos maerula. 2nu, Ornithoptera priamus urvilleanus. 3nu, Euploea mulciber. 4nu, Morpho rhetenor. 5nu, Papilio androgeous. 6nu, Troides magellanus.

1968, May 20 Litho. *Imperf.*

95	A14k	15ch multi	.20	.20
95A	A14k	50ch multi	.45	.45
95B	A14k	1.25nu multi	1.10	1.10

95C	A14k	2nu multi	1.75	1.75
h.		Souv. sheet of 4, #95-95C	3.50	3.50
95D	A14k	3nu multi	1.25	1.25
95E	A14k	4nu multi	1.60	1.60
95F	A14k	5nu multi	2.00	2.00
95G	A14k	6nu multi	2.50	2.50
i.		Souv. sheet of 4, #95D-95G	7.50	7.50
		Nos. 95-95G (8)	10.85	10.85

Souv. sheets issued Oct. 23. Nos. 95D-95G, 95i are airmail. Simulated 3-dimensions using a plastic overlay.

Paintings — A14m

1968 Litho. & Embossed *Imperf.*

96	A14m	2ch Van Gogh	.20	.20
96A	A14m	4ch Millet	.20	.20
96B	A14m	5ch Monet	.20	.20
96C	A14m	10ch Corot	.20	.20
p.		Souv. sheet of 4, #96-96C	.20	.20
96D	A14m	45ch like #96	.20	.20
96E	A14m	80ch like #96A	.35	.35
96F	A14m	1.05nu like #96B	.45	.45
96G	A14m	1.40nu like #96C	.60	.60
q.		Souv. sheet of 4, #96D-96G	1.60	1.60
96H	A14m	1.50nu like #96	.65	.65
96I	A14m	2nu like #96	.85	.85
96J	A14m	2.50nu like #96A	1.10	1.10
96K	A14m	3nu like #96A	1.25	1.25
96L	A14m	4nu like #96B	1.10	1.10
96M	A14m	5nu like #96C	1.40	1.40
r.		Souv. sheet of 4, #96I, 96K-96M	4.75	4.75
96N	A14m	6nu like #96B	1.75	1.75
96O	A14m	8nu like #96C	2.25	2.25
s.		Souv. sheet of 4, #96H, 96J, 96N-96O	6.00	6.00
		Nos. 96-96O (16)	12.75	12.75

Issue dates: Nos. 96-96G, 96I, 96K-96M, July 8. Nos. 96p, 96q, 96r, Aug. 5. Others, Aug. 28. Nos. 96H, 96J, 96N-96O are airmail.
See Nos. 114-114O, 144-144G.

Summer Olympics, Mexico, 1968
A14n

1968, Oct. 1 Photo. *Perf. 13½*

97	A14n	5ch Discus	.20	.20
97A	A14n	45ch Basketball	.20	.20
97B	A14n	60ch Javelin	.20	.20
97C	A14n	80ch Shooting	.20	.20
97D	A14n	1.05nu like #97	.20	.20
97E	A14n	2nu like #97B	.20	.20
97F	A14n	3nu like #97C	.35	.35
97G	A14n	5nu Soccer	.60	.60
h.		Souv. sheet of 2, #97D, 97G	2.25	2.25
		Nos. 97-97G (8)	2.15	2.15

Exist imperf.
For surcharges see Nos. 129E, B5-B7.

Coin Type of 1966 Overprinted

Embossed on Gold Foil

1968, Nov. 12 Die Cut *Imperf.*

98	A14a	15ch green	.20	.20
98A	A14a	33ch green	.25	.25
98B	A14a	9nu green	4.75	4.75
		Nos. 98-98B (3)	5.20	5.20

Human Rights Year.

Birds — A14p

Designs: 2ch, 20ch, 1.50nu, Crimson-winged laughing thrush. 3ch, 30ch, 2.50nu, Ward's trogon, vert. 4ch, 50ch, 4nu, Grey peacock-pheasant. 5ch, 1.25nu, 5nu, Rufous necked hornbill, vert. 15ch, 2nu, 10nu, Myzornis.

1968-69 Photo. *Perf. 12½*

99	A14p	2ch multicolored	.20	.20
99A	A14p	3ch multicolored	.20	.20
99B	A14p	4ch multicolored	.20	.20
99C	A14p	5ch multicolored	.20	.20
99D	A14p	15ch multicolored	.20	.20
99E	A14p	20ch multicolored	.20	.20
99F	A14p	30ch multicolored	.20	.20
99G	A14p	50ch multicolored	.20	.20
99H	A14p	1.25nu multicolored	.30	.30
99I	A14p	1.50nu multicolored	.35	.35
99J	A14p	2nu multicolored	.40	.40
99K	A14p	2.50nu multicolored	.50	.50
99L	A14p	4nu multicolored	.85	.85
99M	A14p	5nu multicolored	1.10	1.10
99N	A14p	10nu multicolored	2.00	2.00
		Nos. 99-99N (15)	7.10	7.10

Issue dates: 2ch, 3ch, 4ch, 5ch, 15ch, 30ch, 50ch, Dec. 7, 1968. 20ch, 1.25nu, 2nu, Dec. 28, 1968. Others, Jan. 29, 1969.
1.50nu, 2.50nu, 4nu, 5nu, 10nu are airmail.
Exist imperf.
For surcharges see Nos. 115A-115B, 115I, 115M, 115R, 117F-117G, 117K, 117O, 129H.

Fish
A14q

1969, Feb. 27 Litho. *Imperf.*

100	A14q	15ch multicolored	.80	.80
100A	A14q	20ch multi, diff.	1.00	1.00
100B	A14q	30ch multi, diff.	1.50	1.50
100C	A14q	5nu multi, diff.	2.00	2.00
100D	A14q	6nu multi, diff.	2.50	2.50
100E	A14q	7nu multi, diff.	3.00	3.00
f.		Souv. sheet of 4, #100B-100E	9.00	9.00
		Nos. 100-100E (6)	10.80	10.80

Nos. 100C-100E are airmail. Simulated 3-dimensions using a plastic overlay.

Insects — A14r

1969, Apr. 10 Litho. *Imperf.*

101	A14r	10ch multicolored	.20	.20
101A	A14r	75ch multi, diff.	.35	.35
101B	A14r	1.25nu multi, diff.	.60	.60
101C	A14r	2nu multi, diff.	1.00	1.00
h.		Souv. sheet of 4, #101-101C	3.75	3.75
101D	A14r	3nu multi, diff.	1.10	1.10
101E	A14r	4nu multi, diff.	1.50	1.50
101F	A14r	5nu multi, diff.	1.90	1.90
101G	A14r	6nu multi, diff.	2.25	2.25
i.		Souv. sheet of 4, #101D-101G	8.00	8.00
		Nos. 101-101G (8)	8.90	8.90

Nos. 101D-101G, 101i are airmail. Stamps from souvenir sheets have inscription at lower right. Simulated 3-dimensions using a plastic overlay.

Admission to UPU — A14s

Illustration reduced.

1969, May 2 Photo. *Perf. 13*

102	A14s	5ch multicolored	.20	.20
102A	A14s	10ch multicolored	.20	.20
102B	A14s	15ch multicolored	.20	.20
102C	A14s	45ch multicolored	.20	.20
102D	A14s	60ch multicolored	.20	.20
102E	A14s	1.05nu multicolored	.25	.25
102F	A14s	1.40nu multicolored	.35	.35
102G	A14s	4nu multicolored	1.00	1.00
		Nos. 102-102G (8)	2.60	2.60

Exist imperf.
For surcharges see #117H, 117L, 117U, 129.

History of Steel Making — A14t

Designs: 2ch, Pre-biblical. 5ch, Damascus sword. 15ch, 3nu, Saugus Mill. 45ch, Beehive coke ovens. 75ch, 4nu, Bessemer converter. 1.50nu, 5nu, Rolling mill. 1.75nu, Steel mill. 2nu, 6nu, Future applications.

Litho. on Steel Foil

1969, June 2 *Imperf.*

Without Gum

103	A14t	2ch multicolored	.20	.20
103A	A14t	5ch multicolored	.20	.20
103B	A14t	15ch multicolored	.20	.20
m.		Souv. sheet of 2, #103A-103B	.20	.20
103C	A14t	45ch multicolored	.20	.20
n.		Souv. sheet of 2, #103, 103C	.30	.30
103D	A14t	75ch multicolored	.20	.20
103E	A14t	1.50nu multicolored	.45	.45
103F	A14t	1.75nu multicolored	.50	.50
o.		Souv. sheet of 2, #103E-103F	2.25	2.25
103G	A14t	2nu multicolored	.60	.60
p.		Souv. sheet of 2, #103D, 103G	1.90	1.90
103H	A14t	3nu multicolored	.85	.85
103I	A14t	4nu multicolored	1.10	1.10
103J	A14t	5nu multicolored	1.40	1.40
q.		Souv. sheet of 2, #103I-103J	3.75	3.75
103K	A14t	6nu multicolored	1.60	1.60
r.		Souv. sheet of 2, #103H,103K	3.75	3.75
		Nos. 103-103K (12)	7.50	7.50

Nos. 103H-103K, 103q, 103r are airmail. Souv. sheets issued June 30.

Birds
A14u

1969, Aug. 5 Litho. *Imperf.*

104	A14u	15ch Owl	.20	.20
104A	A14u	50ch Red birds	.35	.35
104B	A14u	1.25nu Hawk	.95	.95
104C	A14u	2nu Penguin	1.50	1.50
h.		Souv. sheet of 4, #104-104C	3.25	3.25
104D	A14u	3nu Macaws	1.10	1.10
104E	A14u	4nu Bird of paradise	1.40	1.40
104F	A14u	5nu Duck	1.75	1.75
104G	A14u	6nu Pheasant	2.00	2.00
i.		Souv. sheet of 4, #104D-104G	6.75	6.75
		Nos. 104-104G (8)	9.25	9.25

Nos. 104D-104G, 104i are airmail. Simulated 3-dimensions using a plastic overlay. Souv. sheets issued Aug. 28.

Buddhist Prayer Banners — A14v

Litho. on Cloth

1969, Sep. 30 *Imperf.*

Self-adhesive

Sizes: 15ch, 75ch, 2nu, 57x57mm, 5nu, 6nu, 70x37mm

105	A14v	15ch multicolored	.20	.20
105A	A14v	75ch multi, diff.	.25	.25
105B	A14v	2nu multi, diff.	.70	.70
105C	A14v	5nu multi, diff.	1.75	1.75
105D	A14v	6nu multi, diff.	2.25	2.25
		Nos. 105-105D (5)	5.15	5.15

Souvenir Sheet

105E		Sheet of 3	5.00	5.00

No. 105E shows denominations of 75ch, 5nu, 6nu with design elements of Nos. 105A, 105C, 105D with gray frame. Exists perf. 13½.

Mahatma Gandhi — A15

1969, Oct. 2 Litho. *Perf. 13x13½*

106	A15	20ch light blue & brn	.20	.20
107	A15	2nu lemon & brn olive	.75	.75

Mohandas K. Gandhi (1869-1948), leader in India's struggle for independence.

Apollo 11 Moon Landing — A15a

Designs: 3ch, Separation from third stage. 5ch, Entering lunar orbit. 15ch, Lunar module separating from orbiter. 20ch, 3nu, Astronaut standing on lunar module's foot pad. 25ch, Astronaut, lunar module on moon. 45ch, Astronaut, flag. 50ch, 4nu, Setting up experiments. 1.75nu, Lunar module docking with orbiter. 5nu, Lift-off from Cape Canaveral. 6nu, Recovery at sea.

1969 Litho. *Imperf.*

108	A15a	3ch multi	.20	.20
108A	A15a	5ch multi	.20	.20
108B	A15a	15ch multi	.20	.20
108C	A15a	20ch multi	.25	.25
m.		Souv. sheet of 4, #108-108C	.60	.60
108D	A15a	25ch multi	.30	.30
108E	A15a	45ch multi	.50	.50
108F	A15a	50ch multi	.55	.55
108G	A15a	1.75nu multi	1.75	1.75
n.		Souv. sheet of 4, #108D-108G	4.00	4.00
108H	A15a	3nu multi	1.50	1.50
108I	A15a	4nu multi	2.00	2.00
108J	A15a	5nu multi	2.50	2.50
108K	A15a	6nu multi	3.00	3.00
o.		Souv. sheet of 4, #108H-108K	21.00	21.00
		Nos. 108-108K (12)	12.95	12.95

Issue dates: Nos. 108-108G, Nov. 3. Nos. 108H-108K, Nov. 20. Souv. sheets, Dec. 20.
Nos. 108H-108K, 108o are airmail. Simulated 3-dimensions using a plastic overlay.
"Aldrin" misspelled on No. 108o.

Paintings
A15b

1970, Jan. 19 Litho. *Imperf.*

109 A15b 5ch Clouet .20 .20
109A A15b 10ch van Eyck .20 .20
109B A15b 15ch David .20 .20
109C A15b 2.75nu Rubens 1.75 1.75
h. Souv. sheet of 4, #109-109C 2.50 2.50
109D A15b 3nu Homer 1.10 1.10
109E A15b 4nu Gentileschi 1.40 1.40
109F A15b 5nu Raphael 1.75 1.75
109G A15b 6nu Ghirlandaio 2.25 2.25
i. Souv. sheet of 4, #109D-109G 7.50 7.50
Nos. 109-109G (8) 8.85 8.85

Nos. 109D-109G, 109i are airmail. Simulated 3-dimensions using a plastic overlay. Souv. sheets issued Feb. 25.

Various Forms of Mail Transport, UPU Headquarters, Bern — A15c

1970, Feb. 27 Photo. *Perf. 13½*

110 A15c 3ch ol grn & gold .20 .20
111 A15c 10ch red brn & gold .20 .20
112 A15c 20ch Prus bl & gold .20 .20
113 A15c 2.50nu dp mag & gold .65 .65
Nos. 110-113 (4) 1.25 1.25

New Headquarters of Universal Postal Union, Bern, Switzerland.
Exist imperf. Value $5.
For surcharge see No. 129I.

Painting Type of 1968

Paintings of flowers.

Litho. & Embossed

1970, May 6 *Imperf.*

114 A14m 2ch Van Gogh .20 .20
114A A14m 3ch Redon .20 .20
114B A14m 5ch Kuroda .20 .20
114C A14m 10ch Renoir .20 .20
p. Souv. sheet of 4, #114-114C .20 .20
114D A14m 15ch Renoir, diff. .20 .20
114E A14m 75ch Monet .30 .30
114F A14m 80ch like #114 .20 .20
114G A14m 90ch like #114A .20 .20
114H A14m 1nu La Tour .40 .40
114I A14m 1.10nu like #114B .30 .30
114J A14m 1.40nu Oudot .60 .60
q. Souv. sheet of 4, #114D, 114E, 114H, 114J 1.90 1.90
114K A14m 1.40nu like #114C .35 .35
r. Souv. sheet of 4, #114F, 114G, 114I, 114K 1.25 1.25
114L A14m 1.60nu like #114D .40 .40
114M A14m 1.70nu like #114E .40 .40
114N A14m 3nu like #114H .75 .75
114O A14m 3.50nu like #114J .85 .85
s. Souv. sheet of 4, #114L-114O 2.75 2.75
Nos. 114-114O (16) 5.75 5.75

#114F-114G, 114I, 114K-114O are airmail.

Stamps of 1966-69 Surcharged

1970, June 19

115 A14j 20ch on 2nu, #94J *2.50 2.50*
115A A14p 20ch on 2nu, #99J *2.50 2.50*
115B A14p 20ch on 2.50nu, #99K *2.50 2.50*
115C A11 20ch on 3nu, #65 *2.50 2.50*
115D A14b 20ch on 3nu, #84K *2.50 2.50*
115E A11 20ch on 4nu, #66 *2.50 2.50*
115F A14c 20ch on 4nu, #85G *2.50 2.50*
115G A14d 20ch on 4nu, #86E *2.50 2.50*
115H A14i 20ch on 4nu, #92F *2.50 2.50*
115I A14p 20ch on 4nu, #99L *2.50 2.50*
115J A11 20ch on 5nu, #67 *2.50 2.50*
115K A14b 20ch on 5nu, #84L *2.50 2.50*
115L A14c 20ch on 5nu, #85H *2.50 2.50*
115M A14j 20ch on 5nu, #94M *2.50 2.50*
115N A14p 20ch on 5nu, #99M *2.50 2.50*
115O A14b 20ch on 6nu, #84M *2.50 2.50*
115P A14b 20ch on 7nu, #84N *2.50 2.50*
115Q A14j 20ch on 10nu, #94N *2.50 2.50*
115R A14p 20ch on 10nu, #99N *2.50 2.50*
Nos. 115-115R (19) *47.50 47.50*

Nos. 115B, 115I, 115M-115N, 115Q-115R are airmail.

Animals — A15d

1970, Oct. 15 Litho. *Imperf.*

116 A15d 5ch African elephant .20 .20
116A A15d 10ch Leopard .20 .20
116B A15d 20ch Ibex .25 .25
116C A15d 25ch Tiger .30 .30
116D A15d 30ch Abominable snowman .35 .35
116E A15d 40ch Water buffalo .50 .50
116F A15d 65ch Rhinoceros .80 .80
116G A15d 75ch Giant pandas .95 .95
116H A15d 85ch Snow leopard 1.10 1.10
116I A15d 2nu Young deer 1.50 1.50
116J A15d 3nu Wild boar, vert. 2.25 2.25
116K A15d 4nu Collared bear, vert. 3.00 3.00
116L A15d 5nu Takin 4.00 4.00
Nos. 116-116L (13) 15.40 15.40

Nos. 116I-116L are airmail. Simulated 3-dimensions using a plastic overlay.

Stamps of 1963-69 Surcharged

1970, Nov. 2

117 A14j 5ch on 30ch, #94F *.60 .60*
117A A14j 5ch on 50ch, #94G *.60 .60*
117B A14j 5ch on 1.25nu, #94H *.60 .60*
117C A14j 5ch on 1.50nu, #94I *.60 .60*
117D A14j 5ch on 2nu, #94J *.60 .60*
117E A14j 5ch on 2.50nu, #94K *.60 .60*
117F A14p 20ch on 30ch, #99F *2.50 2.50*
117G A14p 20ch on 50ch, #99G *2.50 2.50*
117H A14s 20ch on 1.05nu, #102E *2.50 2.50*
117I A14b 20ch on 1.25nu, #84I *2.50 2.50*
117J A14d 20ch on 1.25nu, #86D *2.50 2.50*
117K A14p 20ch on 1.25nu, #99H *2.50 2.50*
117L A14s 20ch on 1.40nu, #102F *2.50 2.50*
117M A4 20ch on 1.50nu, #14 *2.50 2.50*
117N A11 20ch on 1.50nu, #63 *2.50 2.50*
117O A14p 20ch on 1.50nu, #99I *2.50 2.50*
117P A11 20ch on 2nu, #64 *2.50 2.50*
117Q A14f 20ch on 2nu, #88A *2.50 2.50*
117R A14i 20ch on 2nu, #92E *2.50 2.50*
117S A14b 20ch on 2.50nu, #84J *2.50 2.50*
117T A14f 20ch on 4nu, #88B *2.50 2.50*
117U A14s 20ch on 4nu, #102G *2.50 2.50*
117V A14i 20ch on 7nu, #92H *2.50 2.50*
Nos. 117-117V (23) *46.10 46.10*

Nos. 117C, 117E, 117O are airmail.

Conquest of Space — A15e

Designs: 2ch, Jules Verne's "From the Earth to the Moon." 5ch, V-2 rocket. 15ch, Vostok. 25ch, Mariner 2. 30ch, Gemini 7. 50ch, Lift-off. 75ch, Edward White during space walk. 1.50nu, Apollo 13. 2nu, View of Earth from moon. 3nu, Another galaxy. 6nu, Moon, Earth, Sun, Mars, Jupiter. 7nu, Future space station.

1970 Litho. *Imperf.*

118 A15e 2ch multicolored .20 .20
118A A15e 5ch multicolored .20 .20
118B A15e 15ch multicolored .20 .20
118C A15e 25ch multicolored .20 .20
m. Souv. sheet of 4, #118-118C .60 .60
118D A15e 30ch multicolored .25 .25
118E A15e 50ch multicolored .35 .35
118F A15e 75ch multicolored .55 .55
118G A15e 1.50nu multicolored 1.10 1.10
n. Souv. sheet of 4, #118D-118G 3.75 3.75
118H A15e 2nu multicolored .65 .65
118I A15e 3nu multicolored 1.00 1.00
118J A15e 6nu multicolored 2.00 2.00
118K A15e 7nu multicolored 2.25 2.25
o. Souv. sheet of 4, #118H-118K 10.00 10.00
Nos. 118-118K (12) 8.95 8.95

Issue dates: Nos. 118-118G, Nov. 9. Nos. 118H-118K, Nov. 30. Souv. sheets, Dec. 18. Nos. 118H-118K are airmail. Simulated 3-dimensions using a plastic overlay.
See Nos. 127-127C. For surcharge see No. 129F.

Wangdiphodrang Dzong and Bridge — A15f

1971-72 Photo. *Perf. 13½*

119 A15f 2ch gray .20 .20
120 A15f 3ch deep red lilac .20 .20
121 A15f 4ch violet .20 .20
122 A15f 5ch dark green .20 .20
123 A15f 10ch orange brown .20 .20
124 A15f 15ch deep blue .20 .20
125 A15f 20ch deep plum .20 .20
Nos. 119-125 (7) 1.40 1.40

Issued: 5ch-20ch, Feb. 22. 2ch-4ch, Apr. 1972.

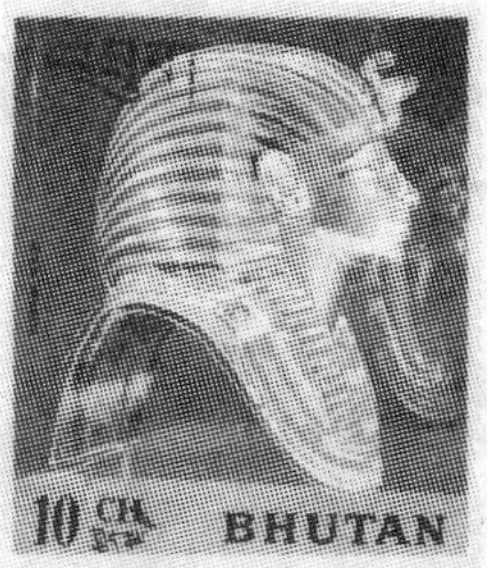

Funeral Mask of King Tutankhamen — A15g

History of Sculpture: 75ch, Winged Bull. 1.25nu, Head of Zeus. 2nu, She-wolf Suckling Romulus and Remus, horiz. 3nu, Head of Cicero. 4nu, Head of David, by Michaelangelo. 5nu, Age of Bronze, by Rodin. 6nu, Head of Woman, by Modigliani.

1971, Feb. 27 Litho. *Imperf.*
Self-adhesive

126 A15g 10ch multicolored .20 .20
126A A15g 75ch multicolored .35 .35
126B A15g 1.25nu multicolored .60 .60
126C A15g 2nu multicolored 1.00 1.00
h. Souv. sheet of 4, #126-126C 2.50 2.50
126D A15g 3nu multicolored .80 .80
126E A15g 4nu multicolored 1.10 1.10
126F A15g 5nu multicolored 1.40 1.40
126G A15g 6nu multicolored 1.60 1.60
i. Souv. sheet of 4, #126D-126G 5.50 5.50
Nos. 126-126G (8) 7.05 7.05

Stamps are plastic heat molded into three dimensions. Nos. 126D-126G are airmail.

Conquest of Space Type of 1970

Designs: 10ch, 2.50nu, Lunokhod 1. 1.70nu, 4nu, Apollo 15.

1971, Mar. 20 Litho. *Imperf.*

127 A15e 10ch multicolored .25 .25
127A A15e 1.70nu multicolored 1.00 1.00
127B A15e 2.50nu multicolored 1.50 1.50
127C A15e 4nu multicolored 2.25 2.25
d. Souv. sheet of 4, #127-127C 5.00 5.00
Nos. 127-127C (4) 5.00 5.00

Nos. 127B-127C are airmail. Simulated 3-dimensions using a plastic overlay.

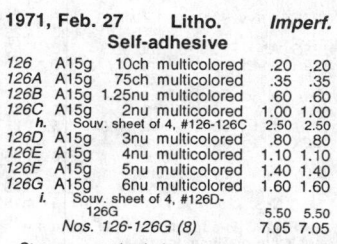

Antique Automobiles — A15h

1971 Litho. *Imperf.*

128 A15h 2ch Mercedes Benz, Germany .20 .20
128A A15h 5ch Ford, US .20 .20
128B A15h 10ch Alfa Romeo, Italy .20 .20
128C A15h 15ch Cord, US .20 .20
128D A15h 20ch Hispano Suiza, Spain .20 .20
128E A15h 30ch Invicta, Britain .20 .20
128F A15h 60ch Renault, France .20 .20
128G A15h 75ch Talbot, Britain .25 .25
128H A15h 85ch Mercer, US .30 .30
128I A15h 1nu Sunbeam, Britain .35 .35
128J A15h 1.20nu Austrian Daimler .40 .40
128K A15h 1.55nu Bugatti, Italy .55 .55
128L A15h 1.80nu Simplex, US .60 .60
128M A15h 2nu Amilcar, France .65 .65
128N A15h 2.50nu Bentley, Britain .85 .85
128O A15h 4nu Morris Garage, Britain .85 .85
128P A15h 6nu Duesenberg, US 1.10 1.10
128Q A15h 7nu Aston Martin, Britain 1.25 1.25
128R A15h 9nu Packard, US 1.60 1.60
128S A15h 10nu Rolls Royce, Britain 1.75 1.75
Nos. 128-128S (20) 11.90 11.90

Issue dates: Nos. 128-128F, May 20. Nos. 128G-128N, June 10. Nos. 128O-128S, July 5. Nos. 128O-128S are airmail. Simulated 3-dimensions using a plastic overlay.
"Romeo" misspelled.

Stamps of 1964-71 Surcharged

1971, July 1

129 A14s 55ch on 60ch, #102D .75 .75
129A A5 55ch on 1.30nu, #22 .40 .40
129B A11 55ch on 3nu, #65 .40 .40
129C A14j 55ch on 4nu, #94L .40 .40
129D A14i 55ch on 5nu, #92G .40 .40
129E A14n 90ch on 1.05nu, #97D 1.90 1.90

129F	A15e	90ch on 1.70nu, #127A	4.25	4.25
129G	A5	90ch on 2nu, #23	.40	.40
129H	A14p	90ch on 2nu, #99J	.75	.75
129I	A15c	90ch on 2.50nu, #113	1.10	1.10
129J	A11	90ch on 4nu, #66	.75	.75
129K	A14d	90ch on 4nu, #86E	1.90	1.90
129L	A14i	90ch on 9nu, #92I	.75	.75
		Nos. 129-129L (13)	14.15	14.15

No. 129C is airmail. No. 129F comes with lines 8mm or 18mm long.

UN Emblem and Bhutan Flag — A16

Designs (Bhutan Flag and): 10ch, UN Headquarters, NY. 20ch, Security Council Chamber and mural by Per Krohg. 3nu, General Assembly Hall.

1971, Sept. 21 Photo. *Perf. 13½*

130	A16	5ch gold, bl & multi	.20	.20
131	A16	10ch gold & multi	.20	.20
132	A16	20ch gold & multi	.20	.20
133	A16	3nu gold & multi	.60	.60
		Nos. 130-133,C21-C23 (7)	3.75	3.75

Bhutan's admission to the UN. Exist imperf.

For overprints see Nos. 140-143. For surcharge see No. 252.

Boy Scout Crossing Stream in Rope Sling — A17

Emblem & Boy Scouts: 20ch, 2nu, mountaineering. 50ch, 6nu, reading map. 75ch, as 10ch.

1971, Nov. 30 Litho. *Perf. 13½*

134	A17	10ch gold & multi	.20	.20
135	A17	20ch gold & multi	.20	.20
136	A17	50ch gold & multi	.20	.20
137	A17	75ch silver & multi	.20	.20
138	A17	2nu silver & multi	.40	.40
139	A17	6nu silver & multi	1.00	1.00
a.		Souv. sheet of 2, #138-139 + 2 labels	2.00	2.00
		Nos. 134-139 (6)	2.20	2.20

60th anniv. of the Boy Scouts. Exist imperf.

For overprint and surcharge see #253, 383.

Nos. 130-133 Overprinted in Gold

UNHCR
UNRWA
1971

1971, Dec. 23

140	A16	5ch gold & multi	.20	.20
141	A16	10ch gold & multi	.20	.20
142	A16	20ch gold & multi	.20	.20
143	A16	3nu gold & multi	.85	.85
		Nos. 140-143,C24-C26 (7)	5.45	5.45

World Refugee Year. Exist imperf.

The Bathing Girl by Renoir A17a

Designs: 20ch, A Bar at the Follies, by Monet, horiz. 90ch, Mona Lisa, by da Vinci. 1.70nu, Cart of Father Junier, by Rousseau, horiz. 2.50nu, The Gleaners, by Millet, horiz. 4.60nu, White Horse, by Gaugin. 5.40nu, The Dancing Lesson, by Degas. 6nu, After the Rain, by Gaillauman, horiz.

1972 Litho. & Embossed *Imperf.*

144	A17a	15ch multicolored	.30	.30
144A	A17a	20ch multicolored	.30	.30
144B	A17a	90ch multicolored	.35	.35
144C	A17a	1.70nu multicolored	.50	.50
144D	A17a	2.50nu multicolored	1.00	1.00
h.		Souv. sheet of 4, #144-144B, 144D	3.50	3.50
144E	A17a	4.60nu multicolored	1.40	1.40
144F	A17a	5.40nu multicolored	1.60	1.60
144G	A17a	6nu multicolored	1.90	1.90
i.		Souv. sheet of 4, #144C, 144E-144G	6.00	6.00
		Nos. 144-144G (8)	7.35	7.35

Issued: #144-144B, 144D, 1/29; others, 2/28.

Nos. 144C, 144E-144G are airmail.

Famous Men A17b

1972, Apr. 17 Litho. *Imperf.*

Self-adhesive

145	A17b	10ch John F. Kennedy	.20	.20
145A	A17b	15ch Gandhi	.20	.20
145B	A17b	55ch Churchill	.45	.45
145C	A17b	2nu De Gaulle	.50	.50
145D	A17b	6nu Pope John XVIII	1.50	1.50
145E	A17b	8nu Eisenhower	2.00	2.00
f.		Souv. sheet of 4, #145B-145E	5.00	5.00
		Nos. 145-145E (6)	4.85	4.85

Nos. 145C-145E are airmail. Stamps are plastic heat molded into three dimensions.

Book Year Emblem A17c

1972, May 15 Photo. *Perf. 13½x13*

146	A17c	2ch multicolored	.20	.20
146A	A17c	3ch multicolored	.20	.20
146B	A17c	5ch multicolored	.20	.20
146C	A17c	20ch multicolored	.20	.20
		Nos. 146-146C (4)	.80	.80

International Book Year.

1972 Summer Olympics, Munich A17d

1972, June 6 Photo. *Perf. 13½*

147	A17d	10ch Handball	.20	.20
147A	A17d	15ch Archery	.20	.20
147B	A17d	20ch Boxing	.20	.20
147C	A17d	30ch Discus	.20	.20
147D	A17d	35ch Javelin	.20	.20
147E	A17d	45ch Shooting	.20	.20
147F	A17d	1.35nu like #147A	.40	.40
147G	A17d	7nu like #147	1.90	1.90
h.		Souv. sheet of 3, #147D, 147F-147G	3.00	3.00
		Nos. 147-147G (8)	3.50	3.50

Nos. 147D, 147F-147G are airmail and have a gold border.

Exist imperf.

For overprint see No. 384.

Apollo 11 Type of 1969

Apollo 16: 15ch, Lift-off, vert. 20ch, Achieving lunar orbit. 90ch, Astronauts Young, Mattingly, Duke, vert. 1.70nu, Lunar module. 2.50nu, Walking on moon. 4.60nu, Gathering rock samples. 5.40nu, Apollo 16 on launch pad, vert. 6nu, Looking at earth, vert.

1972, Sept. 1 Litho. *Imperf.*

148	A15a	15ch multicolored	.20	.20
148A	A15a	20ch multicolored	.20	.20
148B	A15a	90ch multicolored	.20	.20
148C	A15a	1.70nu multicolored	.35	.35
148D	A15a	2.50nu multicolored	.50	.50
h.		Souv. sheet of 4, #148-148B, 148D	3.00	3.00
148E	A15a	4.60nu multicolored	.90	.90
148F	A15a	5.40nu multicolored	1.10	1.10
148G	A15a	6nu multicolored	1.25	1.25
i.		Souv. sheet of 4, #148C, 148E-148G	5.00	5.00
		Nos. 148-148G (8)	4.70	4.70

Nos. 148C, 148E-148G are airmail. Simulated 3-dimensions using a plastic overlay.

Dogs A17f

1972-73 Photo. *Perf. 13½*

149	A17f	2ch Pointer	.20	.20
149A	A17f	3ch Irish Setter	.20	.20
149B	A17f	5ch Lhasa Apso, vert	.20	.20
149C	A17f	10ch Dochi	.20	.20
149D	A17f	15ch Damci	.20	.20
149E	A17f	15ch Collie	.20	.20
149F	A17f	20ch Basset hound	.20	.20
149G	A17f	25ch Damci, diff	.20	.20
149H	A17f	30ch Fox terrier	.20	.20
149I	A17f	55ch Lhasa Apso, diff.	.20	.20
149J	A17f	99ch Boxer	.25	.25
149K	A17f	2.50nu St. Bernard	.55	.55
149L	A17f	4nu Cocker Spaniel	.90	.90
o.		Souv. sheet of 3, #149J-149L, perf. 14	3.00	3.00
149M	A17f	8nu Damci, diff.	1.90	1.90
p.		Souv. sheet of 2, #149I, 149M, perf. 14	3.25	3.25
		Nos. 149-149M (14)	5.60	5.60

Souvenir Sheet

Perf. 14

149N	A17f	18nu Poodle	5.00	5.00

Issue dates: Nos. 149B-149D, 149G, 149I, 149M, 149p, Oct. 5. Nos. 149-149A, 149E-149F, 149H, 149J-149L, 149o, Jan. 1, 1973. No. 149N, Jan. 15, 1973. No. 149N is airmail. All exist imperf.

For surcharges & overprints see #268-269, 385.

Roses — A17g

1973, Jan. 30 Photo. *Perf. 13½*

Scented Paper

150	A17g	15ch Wendy Cussons	.20	.20
150A	A17g	25ch Iceberg	.20	.20
150B	A17g	30ch Marchioness of Urquio	.20	.20
150C	A17g	3nu Pink parfait	.70	.70
150D	A17g	6nu Roslyn	1.40	1.40
150E	A17g	7nu Blue moon	1.60	1.60
f.		Souv. sheet of 2, #150D-150E	2.50	2.50
		Nos. 150-150E (6)	4.30	4.30

#150D-150E are airmail. Exist imperf.

Apollo 11 Type of 1969

Apollo 17: 10ch, Taking photographs on moon. 15ch, Setting up experiments. 55ch, Earth. 2nu, Driving lunar rover. 7nu, Satellite. 9nu, Astronauts Cernan, Evans, Schmitt.

1973, Feb. 28 Litho. *Imperf.*

Size: 50x49mm

151	A15a	10ch multicolored	.20	.20
151A	A15a	15ch multicolored	.20	.20
151B	A15a	55ch multicolored	.20	.20
151C	A15a	2nu multicolored	.70	.70
f.		Souv. sheet of 4, #151-151C	2.50	2.50
151D	A15a	7nu multicolored	2.25	2.25
151E	A15a	9nu multicolored	3.25	3.25
g.		Souv. sheet of 2, #151D-151E	10.00	10.00
		Nos. 151-151E (6)	6.80	6.80

Simulated 3-dimensions using a plastic overlay. Nos. 151D-151E are airmail. No. 151g is circular, 160mm in diameter.

Phonograph Records

A17h

Recordings: 10ch, Bhutanese History. 25ch, Royal Bhutan Anthem. 1.25nu, Bhutanese History (English). 3nu, Bhutanese History (Bhutanese), Folk Song #1. 7nu, Folk Song #1. 8nu, Folk Song #2. 9nu, History in English, Folk Songs #1 & 2.

1973, Apr. 15

Self-adhesive

Diameter: #152-152B, 152D-152E, 69mm, #152C, 152F, 100mm

152	A17h	10ch yel on red	*.70*	*.70*
152A	A17h	25ch gold on grn	*1.00*	*1.00*
152B	A17h	1.25nu sil on bl	*4.50*	*4.50*
152C	A17h	3nu sil on pur	*10.00*	*10.00*
152D	A17h	7nu sil on blk	*22.50*	*22.50*
152E	A17h	8nu red on white	*30.00*	*30.00*
152F	A17h	9nu blk on yel	*32.50*	*32.50*
		Nos. 152-152F (7)	*101.20*	*101.20*

Nos. 152C, 152F are airmail.

King Jigme Dorji Wangchuk (d. 1972) — A17i

Embossed on Gold Foil

1973, May 2 Die Cut *Imperf.*

153	A17i	10ch orange	.20	.20
153A	A17i	25ch red	.20	.20
153B	A17i	3nu green	.70	.70
153C	A17i	6nu blue	1.40	1.40
153D	A17i	8nu purple	1.90	1.90
e.		Souv. sheet of 2, #153C-153D	4.50	4.50
		Nos. 153-153D (5)	4.40	4.40

Nos. 153C-153D are airmail.

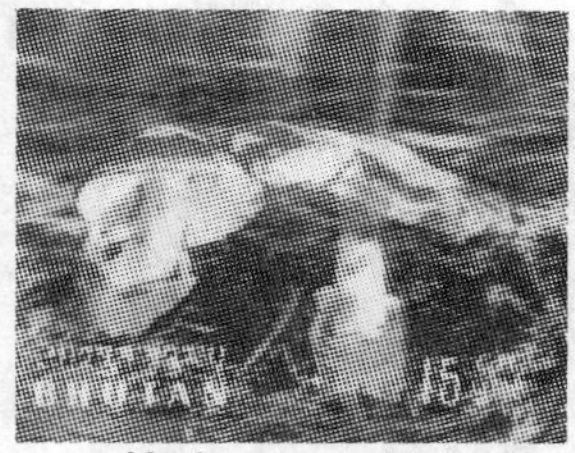

Mushrooms — A17j

Different mushrooms.

1973, Sept. 25 Litho. *Imperf.*

154	A17j	15ch multicolored	*.20*	*.20*
154A	A17j	25ch multicolored	*.20*	*.20*
154B	A17j	30ch multicolored	*.25*	*.25*
154C	A17j	3nu multicolored	*2.50*	*2.50*
f.		Souvenir sheet of 4, #154-154C	*15.00*	*15.00*
154D	A17j	6nu multicolored	*5.75*	*5.75*
154E	A17j	7nu multicolored	*6.75*	*6.75*
g.		Souvenir sheet of 2, #154D-154E	*35.00*	*35.00*
		Nos. 154-154E (6)	*15.65*	*15.65*

Simulated 3-dimensions using a plastic overlay. Nos. 154D-154E are airmail.

Bhutanese Mail Service — A17k

Designs: 5ch, 6nu, Letter carrier at mail box. 10ch, 5nu, Postmaster, letter carrier. 15ch, Sacking mail. 25ch, Mailtruck. 1.25nu, Sorting mail. 3nu, Hand-delivered mail.

1973, Nov. 14 Photo. *Perf. 13½*

155	A17k	5ch multicolored	.20	.20
155A	A17k	10ch multicolored	.20	.20
155B	A17k	15ch multicolored	.20	.20
155C	A17k	25ch multicolored	.20	.20
155D	A17k	1.25nu multicolored	.30	.30
155E	A17k	3nu multicolored	.65	.65
155F	A17k	5nu multicolored	1.10	1.10
155G	A17k	6nu multicolored	1.25	1.25
h.		Souv. sheet of 2, #155F-155G	6.00	6.00
		Nos. 155-155G (8)	4.10	4.10

Indipex '73. Nos. 155F-155G are airmail. All exist imperf.

For surcharges and overprint see Nos. 267, 382, C37-C38.

A set of 15 stamps plus souvenir sheet of 3 showing paintings with reading and writing themes was not authorized.

King Jigme Singye Wangchuk and Royal Crest — A18

Designs (King and): 25ch, 90ch, Flag of Bhutan. 1.25nu, Wheel with 8 good luck signs. 2nu, 4nu, Punakha Dzong, former winter capital. 3nu, 5nu, Crown. 5ch, same as 10ch.

1974, June 2 Litho. *Perf. 13½*

157	A18	10ch maroon & multi	.20	.20
158	A18	25ch gold & multi	.20	.20
159	A18	1.25nu multi	.35	.35
160	A18	2nu gold & multi	.55	.55
161	A18	3nu multi	.75	.75
		Nos. 157-161 (5)	2.05	2.05

Souvenir Sheets

Perf. 13½, Imperf.

162		Sheet of 2	2.75	2.75
a.		A18 5ch maroon & multi	.20	
b.		A18 5nu red orange & multi	2.50	
163		Sheet of 2	2.75	2.75
a.		A18 90ch gold & multi	.75	
b.		A18 4nu gold & multi	2.00	

Coronation of King Jigme Singye Wangchuk, June 2, 1974.

Mailman on Horseback A19

Old and New Locomotives A20

Designs (UPU Emblem, Carrier Pigeon and): 3ch, Sailing and steam ships. 4ch, Old biplane and jet. 25ch, Mail runner and jeep.

1974, Oct. 9 Litho. *Perf. 14½*

164	A19	1ch grn & multi	.20	.20
165	A20	2ch lilac & multi	.20	.20
166	A20	3ch ocher & multi	.20	.20
167	A20	4ch yel grn & multi	.20	.20
168	A20	25ch salmon & multi	.20	.20
		Nos. 164-168,C27-C29 (8)	2.15	2.15

Centenary of Universal Postal Union. Issued in sheets of 50 and sheets of 5 plus label with multicolored margin. Exist imperf.

Family and WPY Emblem — A21

1974, Dec. 17 *Perf. 13½*

169	A21	25ch bl & multi	.20	.20
170	A21	50ch org & multi	.20	.20
171	A21	90ch ver & multi	.30	.30
172	A21	2.50nu brn & multi	.75	.75
a.		Souvenir sheet, 10nu	2.25	2.25
		Nos. 169-172 (4)	1.45	1.45

For surcharge see No. 254.

Sephisa Chandra A22

Designs: Indigenous butterflies.

1975, Sept. 15 Litho. *Perf. 14½*

173	A22	1ch *shown*	.20	.20
174	A22	2ch *Lethe kansa*	.20	.20
175	A22	3ch *Neope bhadra*	.20	.20
176	A22	4ch *Euthalia duda*	.20	.20
177	A22	5ch *Vindula erota*	.20	.20
178	A22	10ch *Bhutanitis Lidderdale*	.20	.20
179	A22	3nu *Limenitis zayla*	.60	.60
180	A22	5nu *Delis thysbe*	1.40	1.40
		Nos. 173-180 (8)	3.20	3.20

Souvenir Sheet

Perf. 13

181	A22	10nu *Dabasa gyas*	2.50	2.50

For surcharges see Nos. 255-256.

Apollo and Apollo-Soyuz Emblem — A23

Design: No. 183, Soyuz and emblem.

1975, Dec. 1 Litho. *Perf. 14x13½*

182	A23	10nu multicolored	2.75	2.75
183	A23	10nu multicolored	2.75	2.75
a.		Souvenir sheet of 2, 15nu	7.00	7.00

Apollo Soyuz link-up in space, July 17. Nos. 182-183 printed se-tenant in sheets of 10. No. 183a contains two 15nu stamps similar to Nos 182-183. Exist imperf.

For surcharges see Nos. 257-258.

Jewelry A24

Designs: 2ch, Coffee pot, bell and sugar cup. 3ch, Container and drinking horn. 4ch, Pendants and box cover. 5ch, Painter. 15ch, Silversmith. 20ch, Wood carver with tools. 1.50nu, Mat maker. 5nu, 10nu, Printer.

1975, Dec. 17 *Perf. 14½*

184	A24	1ch multicolored	.20	.20
185	A24	2ch multicolored	.20	.20
186	A24	3ch multicolored	.20	.20
187	A24	4ch multicolored	.20	.20
188	A24	5ch multicolored	.20	.20
189	A24	15ch multicolored	.20	.20
190	A24	20ch multicolored	.20	.20
191	A24	1.50nu multicolored	.40	.40
192	A24	10nu multicolored	2.50	2.50
		Nos. 184-192 (9)	4.30	4.30

Souvenir Sheet

Perf. 13

193	A24	5nu multicolored	1.40	1.40

Handicrafts and craftsmen.

For surcharges see No. 259, 381.

King Jigme Singye Wangchuk A25

Designs: 25ch, 90ch, 1nu, 2nu, 4nu, like 15ch. 1.30nu, 3nu, 5nu, Coat of arms. Sizes (Diameter): 15ch, 1nu, 1.30nu, 38mm. 25ch, 2nu, 3nu, 49mm. 90ch, 4nu, 5nu, 63mm.

Lithographed, Embossed on Gold Foil

1975, Nov. 11 *Imperf.*

194	A25	15ch emerald	.20	.20
195	A25	25ch emerald	.20	.20
196	A25	90ch emerald	.35	.35
197	A25	1nu bright carmine	.40	.40
198	A25	1.30nu bright carmine	.45	.45
199	A25	2nu bright carmine	.65	.65
200	A25	3nu bright carmine	1.00	1.00
201	A25	4nu bright carmine	1.60	1.60
202	A25	5nu bright carmine	2.00	2.00
		Nos. 194-202 (9)	6.85	6.85

King Jigme Singye Wangchuk's 20th birthday.

Rhododendron Cinnabarinum — A28

Rhododendron: 2ch, Campanulatum. 3ch, Fortunei. 4ch, Red arboreum. 5ch, Pink arboreum. 1nu, Falconeri. 3nu, Hodgsonii. 5nu, Keysii. 10nu, Cinnabarinum.

1976, Feb. 15 Litho. *Perf. 15*

203	A28	1ch rose & multi	.20	.20
204	A28	2ch lt grn & multi	.20	.20
205	A28	3ch gray & multi	.20	.20
206	A28	4ch lil & multi	.20	.20
207	A28	5ch ol gray & multi	.20	.20
208	A28	1nu brn org & multi	.25	.20
209	A28	3nu ultra & multi	.75	.60
210	A28	5nu gray & multi	1.25	.90
		Nos. 203-210 (8)	3.25	2.70

Souvenir Sheet

Perf. 13½

211	A28	10nu multicolored	2.50	2.50

For surcharge see No. 260.

Slalom and Olympic Games Emblem — A29

Designs (Olympic Games Emblem and): 2ch, 4-men bobsled. 3ch, Ice hockey. 4ch, Cross-country skiing. 5ch, Figure skating, women's. 2nu, Downhill skiing. 4nu, Speed skating. 6nu, Ski jump. 10nu, Figure skating, pairs.

1976, Mar. 29 Litho. *Perf. 13½*

212	A29	1ch multicolored	.20	.20
213	A29	2ch multicolored	.20	.20
214	A29	3ch multicolored	.20	.20
215	A29	4ch multicolored	.20	.20
216	A29	5ch multicolored	.20	.20
217	A29	2nu multicolored	.40	.35
218	A29	4nu multicolored	.90	.75
219	A29	10nu multicolored	2.50	1.75
		Nos. 212-219 (8)	4.80	3.85

Souvenir Sheet

220	A29	6nu multicolored	1.50	1.50

12th Winter Olympic Games, Innsbruck, Austria, Feb. 4-15.

For surcharges see Nos. 261-262.

Ceremonial Masks — A29a

Various masks.

1976, Apr. 23 Litho. *Imperf.*

220A	A29a	5ch multicolored	.20	.20
220B	A29a	10ch multicolored	.20	.20
220C	A29a	15ch multicolored	.20	.20
220D	A29a	20ch multicolored	.20	.20
220E	A29a	25ch multi, horiz.	.20	.20
220F	A29a	30ch multi, horiz.	.20	.20
220G	A29a	35ch multi, horiz.	.20	.20
220H	A29a	1nu multi, horiz.	.45	.45
220I	A29a	2nu multi, horiz.	.90	.90

220J A29a 2.50nu multi, horiz. 1.10 1.10
220K A29a 3nu multi, horiz. 1.40 1.40
Nos. 220A-220K (11) 5.25 5.25

Souvenir Sheets

220L A29a 5nu like #220C 1.60 1.60
220M A29a 10nu like #220F 3.25 3.25

Simulated 3-dimensions using a plastic overlay. Nos. 220H-220M are airmail.

Sizes of stamps: No. 220L, 59x70mm, No. 220M, 69x57mm.

Orchid A30

Designs: Various flowers.

1976, May 29 Litho. *Perf. 14½*

221 A30 1ch multicolored .20 .20
222 A30 2ch multicolored .20 .20
223 A30 3ch multicolored .20 .20
224 A30 4ch multicolored .20 .20
225 A30 5ch multicolored .20 .20
226 A30 2nu multicolored .40 .30
227 A30 4nu multicolored .80 .60
228 A30 6nu multicolored 1.25 1.00
Nos. 221-228 (8) 3.45 2.90

Souvenir Sheet

Perf. 13½

229 A30 10nu multicolored 2.75 2.50

For surcharges see Nos. 263-264.

Double Carp Design A31

Designs: Various symbolic designs and Colombo Plan emblem.

1976, July 1 Litho. *Perf. 14½*

230 A31 3ch red & multi .20 .20
231 A31 4ch ver & multi .20 .20
232 A31 5ch multicolored .20 .20
233 A31 25ch bl & multi .20 .20
234 A31 1.25nu multicolored .35 .30
235 A31 2nu yel & multi .60 .50
236 A31 2.50nu vio & multi .75 .60
237 A31 3nu multicolored .90 .75
Nos. 230-237 (8) 3.40 2.95

Colombo Plan, 25th anniversary.

For surcharge see No. 265.

Bandaranaike Conference Hall — A32

1976, Aug. 16 Litho. *Perf. 13½*

238 A32 1.25nu multicolored .35 .25
239 A32 2.50nu multicolored .65 .45

5th Summit Conference of Non-aligned Countries, Colombo, Sri Lanka, Aug. 9-19.

Elizabeth II A33

Liberty Bell A34

Spirit of St. Louis — A35

Bhutanese Archer, Olympic Rings — A36

Designs: No. 242, Alexander Graham Bell. No. 245, LZ 3 Zeppelin docking, 1907. No. 246, Alfred B. Nobel.

1978, Nov. 15 Litho. *Perf. 14½*

240 A33 20nu multicolored 4.00 4.00
241 A34 20nu multicolored 4.00 4.00
242 A33 20nu multicolored 4.00 4.00
243 A35 20nu multicolored 4.00 4.00
244 A36 20nu multicolored 4.00 4.00
245 A35 20nu multicolored 4.00 4.00
246 A33 20nu multicolored 4.00 4.00
Nos. 240-246 (7) 28.00 28.00

25th anniv. of coronation of Elizabeth II; American Bicentennial; cent. of 1st telephone call by Alexander Graham Bell; Charles A. Lindbergh crossing the Atlantic, 50th anniv.; Olympic Games; 75th anniv. of the Zeppelin; 75th anniv. of Nobel Prize. Seven souvenir sheets exist, each 25nu, commemorating same events with different designs. Size: 103x80mm.

Issues of 1967-1976 Surcharged with New Value and Bars

Perforations and Printing as Before

1978

252 A16 25ch on 3nu (#133)
253 A17 25ch on 6nu (#139)
254 A21 25ch on 2.50nu (#172)
255 A22 25ch on 3nu (#179)
256 A22 25ch on 5nu (#180)
257 A23 25ch on 10nu (#182)
258 A23 25ch on 10nu (#183)
259 A24 25ch on 10nu (#192)
260 A28 25ch on 5nu (#210)
261 A29 25ch on 4nu (#218)
262 A29 25ch on 10nu (#219)
263 A30 25ch on 4nu (#227)
264 A30 25ch on 6nu (#228)
265 A31 25ch on 2.50nu (#236)
266 A14g 25ch on 5nu (#90E)
267 A17k 25ch on 3nu (#155E)
268 A17f 25ch on 4nu (#149L)
269 A17f 25ch on 8nu (#149M)
Nos. 252-269, C31-C38 (26) *80.00 80.00*

Mother and Child, IYC Emblem — A37

IYC Emblem and: 5nu, Mother and two children. 10nu, Boys with blackboards and stylus.

1979, June Litho. *Perf. 14x13½*

289 A37 2nu multicolored .50 .40
290 A37 5nu multicolored 1.40 1.00
291 A37 10nu multicolored 2.50 2.00
a. Souv. sheet of 3, #289-291 + label, perf. 15x13½ 4.25 3.25
Nos. 289-291 (3) 4.40 3.40

International Year of the Child.

For overprints see Nos. 761-763.

Conference Emblem and Dove — A38

Design: 10nu, Emblem and Bhutanese symbols.

1979, Sept. 3 Litho. *Perf. 14x13½*

292 A38 25ch multicolored .20 .20
293 A38 10nu multicolored 3.25 2.50

6th Non-Aligned Summit Conference, Havana, August 1979.

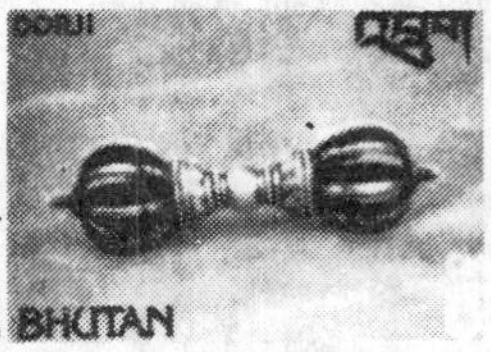

Silver Rattle, Dorji A39

Antiques: 10ch, Silver handell, Dilbu, vert. 15ch, Cylindrical jar, Jadum, vert. 25ch, Ornamental teapot, Jamjee. 1nu, Leather container, Kem, vert. 1.25nu, Brass teapot, Jamjee. 1.70nu, Vessel with elephant-head legs, Sangphor, vert. 2nu, Teapot with ornamental spout, Jamjee, vert. 3nu, Metal pot on claw-shaped feet, Yangtho, vert. 4nu, Dish inlaid with precious stones, Battha. 5nu, Metal circular flask, Chhap, vert.

1979, Dec. 17 Photo. *Perf. 14*

294 A39 5ch multicolored .20 .20
295 A39 10ch multicolored .20 .20
296 A39 15ch multicolored .20 .20
297 A39 25ch multicolored .20 .20
298 A39 1nu multicolored .45 .40
299 A39 1.25nu multicolored .50 .50
300 A39 1.70nu multicolored .70 .70
301 A39 2nu multicolored .90 .75
302 A39 3nu multicolored 1.25 1.10
303 A39 4nu multicolored 1.60 1.50
304 A39 5nu multicolored 2.25 1.90
Nos. 294-304 (11) 8.45 7.65

Hill, Rinpiang Dzong — A40

Hill Statue, Stamps of Bhutan and: 2nu, Dzong. 5nu, Ounsti Dzong. 10nu, Lingzi Dzong, Gt. Britain Type 81. 20nu, Rope bridge, Penny Black.

1980, May 6 Litho. *Perf. 14x13½*

305 A40 1nu multicolored .30 .25
306 A40 2nu multicolored .60 .50
307 A40 5nu multicolored 1.60 1.25
308 A40 10nu multicolored 3.00 2.50
Nos. 305-308 (4) 5.50 4.50

Souvenir Sheet

309 A40 20nu multicolored 5.75 4.25

Sir Rowland Hill (1795-1879), originator of penny postage.

Kichu Lhakhang Monastery, Phari — A41

Guru Padma Sambhava's Birthday: Monasteries.

1981, July 11 Litho. *Perf. 14*

310 A41 1nu Dungtse, Phari, vert .25 .20
311 A41 2nu shown .50 .40
312 A41 2.25nu Kurjey .65 .45
313 A41 3nu Tangu, Thimphu .75 .60
314 A41 4nu Cheri, Thimphu 1.00 .75
315 A41 5nu Chorten, Kora 1.50 1.00
316 A41 7nu Tak-Tsang, Phari, vert 2.00 1.50
Nos. 310-316 (7) 6.65 4.90

Prince Charles and Lady Diana — A42

Orange- bellied Chloropsis — A43

1981, Sept. 10 Litho. *Perf. 14½*

317 A42 1nu St. Paul's Cathedral .20 .20
318 A42 5nu like #317 1.00 .65
319 A42 20nu shown 4.00 2.50
320 A42 25nu like #319 4.50 3.50
Nos. 317-320 (4) 9.70 6.85

Souvenir Sheet

321 A42 20nu Wedding procession 5.00 4.00

Royal wedding. Nos. 318-319 issued in sheets of 5 plus label.

For surcharges see Nos. 471-475.

1982, Apr. 19 Litho. *Perf. 14*

322 A43 2nu shown .55 .40
323 A43 3nu Monal pheasant .80 .60
324 A43 5nu Ward's trogon 1.40 1.00
325 A43 10nu Mrs. Gould's sunbird 2.50 2.00
Nos. 322-325 (4) 5.25 4.00

Souvenir Sheet

326 A43 25nu Maroon oriole 7.00 5.00

1982 World Cup — A44

Designs: Various soccer players.

1982, June 25 Litho. *Perf. 14½x14*

327 A44 1nu multicolored .25 .20
328 A44 2nu multicolored .55 .40
329 A44 3nu multicolored .80 .60
330 A44 20nu multicolored 5.25 4.00
Nos. 327-330 (4) 6.85 5.20

Souvenir Sheets

331 A44 25nu multicolored 12.00 7.50

Nos. 331 have margins continuing design and listing finalists (Algeria, etc. or Hungary, etc.).

For surcharges see Nos. 481-485.

21st Birthday of Princess Diana — A45

1982, Aug.

332 A45 1nu St. James' Palace .25 .20
332A A45 10nu Diana, Charles 2.50 1.75

332B A45 15nu Windsor Castle 4.00 4.50
333 A45 25nu Wedding 6.50 4.50
Nos. 332-333 (4) 13.25 10.95

Souvenir Sheet

334 A45 20nu Diana 5.50 4.00

10nu-15nu issued only in sheets of 5 + label.
For overprints and surcharges see Nos. 361-363, 455-459, 476-480.

Scouting Year A46

1982, Aug. 23 Litho. *Perf. 14*

335 A46 3nu Baden-Powell, vert. .65 .50
336 A46 5nu Eating around fire 1.10 .85
337 A46 15nu Reading map 3.50 2.50
338 A46 20nu Pitching tents 4.50 3.50
Nos. 335-338 (4) 9.75 7.35

Souvenir Sheet

339 A46 25nu Mountain climbing 6.00 4.50

For surcharges see Nos. 450-454.

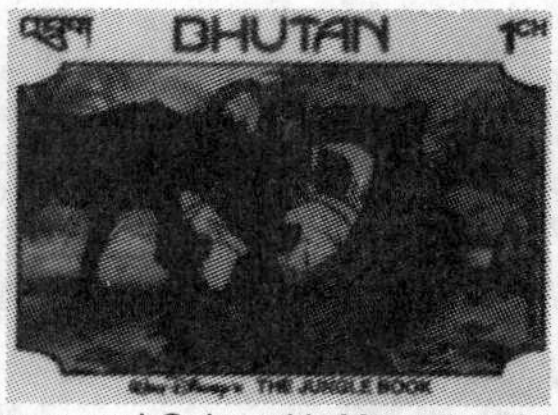

Rama and Cubs with Mowgli — A47

Scenes from Walt Disney's The Jungle Book.

1982, Sept. 1 *Perf. 11*

340 A47 1ch multicolored .20 .20
341 A47 2ch multicolored .20 .20
342 A47 3ch multicolored .20 .20
343 A47 4ch multicolored .20 .20
344 A47 5ch multicolored .20 .20
345 A47 10ch multicolored .20 .20
346 A47 30ch multicolored .20 .20
347 A47 2nu multicolored .50 .35
348 A47 20nu multicolored 5.50 4.25
Nos. 340-348 (9) 7.40 6.00

Souvenir Sheets

Perf. 13½

349 A47 20nu Baloo and Mowgli in forest 5.25 4.00
350 A47 20nu Baloo and Mowgli floating 5.25 4.00

George Washington Surveying A48

1982, Nov. 15 Litho. *Perf. 15*

351 A48 50ch shown .20 .20
352 A48 1nu FDR, Harvard .20 .20
353 A48 2nu Washington at Valley Forge .30 .25
354 A48 3nu FDR, family .50 .40
355 A48 4nu Washington, Battle of Monmouth .65 .50
356 A48 5nu FDR, White House .85 .65
357 A48 15nu Washington, Mt. Vernon 2.50 2.00
358 A48 20nu FDR, Churchill, Stalin 3.25 2.50
Nos. 351-358 (8) 8.45 6.70

Souvenir Sheets

359 A48 25nu Washington, vert. 4.25 3.25
360 A48 25nu FDR, vert. 4.25 3.25

Washington and Franklin D. Roosevelt.

Nos. 332-334 Overprinted: "ROYAL BABY / 21.6.82"

1982, Nov. 19 *Perf. 14½x14*

361 A45 1nu multicolored .25 .25
361A A45 10nu multicolored 2.50 1.75
361B A45 15nu multicolored 3.75 3.00
362 A45 25nu multicolored 6.25 4.75
Nos. 361-362 (4) 12.75 9.75

Souvenir Sheet

363 A45 20nu multicolored 5.25 4.25

Birth of Prince William of Wales, June 21.

500th Birth Anniv. of Raphael A51

Portraits.

1983, Mar. 23 *Perf. 13½*

375 A51 1nu Angelo Doni .25 .20
376 A51 4nu Maddalena Doni 1.00 .75
377 A51 5nu Baldassare Castiglione 1.25 .90
378 A51 20nu La Donna Velata 5.00 3.75
Nos. 375-378 (4) 7.50 5.60

Souvenir Sheets

379 A51 25nu Expulsion of Heliodorus 6.25 4.75
380 A51 25nu Mass of Bolsena 6.25 4.75

Nos. 184, 155F, 139, 184, 147G, 149M Surchd. or Ovptd.: "Druk Air"

1983, Feb. 11

381 A24 30ch on 1ch multi .20 .20
382 A17k 5nu multicolored 2.00 1.25
383 A17 6nu multicolored 2.25 1.50
384 A17d 7nu multicolored 2.50 1.50
385 A17f 8nu multicolored 2.50 1.75
Nos. 381-385 (5) 9.45 6.20

Druk Air Service inauguration. Overprint of 8nu all caps. Nos. 382, 384 air mail.

Manned Flight Bicentenary A52

1983, Aug. 15 Litho. *Perf. 15*

386 A52 50ch Dornier Wal .20 .20
387 A52 3nu Savoia-Marchetti S-66 .75 .55
388 A52 10nu Hawker Osprey 2.00 1.75
389 A52 20nu Ville de Paris 4.00 3.75
Nos. 386-389 (4) 6.95 6.25

Souvenir Sheet

390 A52 25nu Balloon Captif 5.00 3.75

Buddhist Symbols — A53

1983, Aug. 11 Litho. *Perf. 13½*

391 A53 25ch Sacred vase .20 .20
392 A53 50ch Five Sensory Symbols .20 .20
393 A53 2nu Seven Treasures .35 .30
394 A53 3nu Five Sensory Organs .60 .45
395 A53 8nu Five Fleshes 1.50 1.10
396 A53 9nu Sacrificial cake 1.75 1.25
a. Souv. sheet of 6, #391-396 4.50 3.50
Nos. 391-396 (6) 4.60 3.50

Size of Nos. 393, 396: 45x40mm.

World Communications Year (1983) — A54

Various Disney characters and history of communications.

1984, Apr. 10 Litho. *Perf. 14½x14*

397 A54 4ch multicolored .20 .20
398 A54 5ch multicolored .20 .20
399 A54 10ch multicolored .20 .20
400 A54 20ch multicolored .20 .20
401 A54 25ch multicolored .20 .20
402 A54 50ch multicolored .20 .20
403 A54 1nu multicolored .30 .25
404 A54 5nu multicolored 1.10 .95
405 A54 20nu multicolored 4.25 3.75
Nos. 397-405 (9) 6.85 6.15

Souvenir Sheets

Perf. 14x14½

406 A54 20nu Donald Duck on phone, horiz. 4.75 4.00
407 A54 20nu Mickey Mouse on TV 4.75 4.00

1984 Winter Olympics — A55

1984, June 16 *Perf. 14*

408 A55 50ch Skiing .20 .20
409 A55 1nu Cross-country skiing .25 .20
410 A55 3nu Speed skating .60 .45
411 A55 20nu Bobsledding 3.75 3.00
Nos. 408-411 (4) 4.80 3.85

Souvenir Sheet

412 A55 25nu Hockey 5.00 3.25

Golden Langur A56

Locomotives A57

1984, June 10 Litho. *Perf. 14½*

413 A56 50ch shown .20 .20
414 A56 1nu Group in tree, horiz. .20 .20
415 A56 2nu Family, horiz. .40 .30
416 A56 4nu Group walking .80 .60
Nos. 413-416 (4) 1.60 1.30

Souvenir Sheets

417 A56 20nu Snow leopard 4.00 2.00
418 A56 25nu Yak 4.00 2.00
419 A56 25nu Blue sheep, horiz. 4.00 2.00

1984, July 16

420 A57 50ch Sans Pareil, 1829 .20 .20
421 A57 1nu Planet, 1830 .20 .20
422 A57 3nu Experiment, 1832 .60 .45
423 A57 4nu Black Hawk, 1835 .80 .60
424 A57 5.50nu Jenny Lind, 1847 1.10 .85
425 A57 8nu Semmering-Bavaria, 1851 1.60 1.25
426 A57 10nu Great Northern #1, 1870 2.00 1.50
427 A57 25nu German Natl. Tinder, 1880 5.00 3.75
Nos. 420-427 (8) 11.50 8.80

Souvenir Sheets

428 A57 20nu Darjeeling Himalayan Railway, 1984 4.00 3.00
429 A57 20nu Sondermann Freight, 1896 4.00 3.00
430 A57 20nu Crampton's locomotive, 1846 4.00 3.00
431 A57 20nu Erzsebet, 1870 4.00 3.00

Nos. 424-427 horiz.

Classic Cars A58

1984, Aug. 29 Litho. *Perf. 14*

432 A58 50ch Riley Sprite, 1936 .20 .20
433 A58 1nu Lanchester, 1919 .20 .20
434 A58 3nu Itala, 1907 .65 .45
435 A58 4nu Morris Oxford Bullnose, 1913 .90 .60
436 A58 5.50nu Lagonda LG6, 1939 1.25 .85
437 A58 6nu Wolseley, 1903 1.40 .90
438 A58 8nu Buick Super, 1952 1.75 1.25
439 A58 20nu Maybach Zeppelin, 1933 4.50 3.00
Nos. 432-439 (8) 10.85 7.45

Souvenir Sheets

440 A58 25nu Simplex, 1912 2.50 1.50
441 A58 25nu Renault, 1901 2.50 1.50

For surcharges see Nos. 537-544.

Summer Olympic Games — A59

1984, Oct. 27 Litho.

442 A59 15ch Women's archery .20 .20
443 A59 25ch Men's archery .20 .20
444 A59 2nu Table tennis .40 .30
445 A59 2.25nu Basketball .45 .35
446 A59 5.50nu Boxing 1.10 .85
447 A59 6nu Running 1.25 .90
448 A59 8nu Tennis 1.60 1.25
Nos. 442-448 (7) 5.20 4.05

Souvenir Sheet

449 A59 25nu Archery 5.00 3.50

For overprints see Nos. 537-544.

Nos. 335-339 Surcharged with New Values and Bars in Black or Silver

1985 Litho. *Perf. 14*

450 A46 10nu on 3nu multi 2.00 1.50
451 A46 10nu on 5nu multi 2.00 1.50
452 A46 10nu on 15nu multi 2.00 1.50
453 A46 10nu on 20nu multi 2.00 1.50
Nos. 450-453 (4) 8.00 6.00

Souvenir Sheet

454 A46 20nu on 25nu multi 4.00 3.00

Nos. 332, 332A, 332B, 333-334 Surcharged with New Values and Bars

1985, Feb. 28

455 A45 5nu on 1nu multi 1.00 .70
456 A45 5nu on 10nu multi 1.00 .70
457 A45 5nu on 15nu multi 1.00 .70
458 A45 40nu on 25nu multi 8.00 5.25
Nos. 455-458 (4) 11.00 7.35

Souvenir Sheet

459 A45 25nu on 20nu multi 5.00 4.00

50th Anniv. of Donald Duck — A60

1984, Dec. 10 Litho. *Perf. 13½x14*
460 A60 4ch Magician Mickey .20 .20
461 A60 5ch Slide, Donald, Slide .20 .20
462 A60 10ch Donald's Golf Game .20 .20
463 A60 20ch Mr. Duck Steps Out .20 .20
464 A60 25ch Lion Around .20 .20
465 A60 50ch Alpine Climbers .20 .20
466 A60 1nu Flying Jalopy .20 .20
467 A60 5nu Frank Duck 1.10 .75
468 A60 20nu Good Scouts 4.50 3.25
Nos. 460-468 (9) 7.00 5.40

Souvenir Sheets
469 A60 20nu Three Caballeros 4.50 3.25
470 A60 20nu Sea Scouts 4.50 3.25

Nos. 317-321 Surcharged with New Values and Bars

1985, Feb. 28 Litho. *Perf. 14½*
471 A42 10nu on 1nu multi 2.00 1.50
472 A42 10nu on 5nu multi 2.00 1.50
473 A42 10nu on 20nu multi 2.00 1.50
474 A42 10nu on 25nu multi 2.00 1.50
Nos. 471-474 (4) 8.00 6.00

Souvenir Sheet
475 A42 30nu on 20nu multi 6.00 5.00

Nos. 361, 361A, 361B, 362-363 Surcharged with New Values and Bars

1985, Feb. 28 *Perf. 14½x14*
476 A45 5nu on 1nu multi .75 .75
477 A45 5nu on 10nu multi .75 .55
478 A45 5nu on 15nu multi .75 .55
479 A45 40nu on 25nu multi 7.50 5.50
Nos. 476-479 (4) 9.75 7.35

Souvenir Sheet
480 A45 25nu on 20nu multi 5.00 3.75

Nos. 327-331 Surcharged with New Values and Bars in Black or Silver

1985, June
481 A44 5nu on 1nu multi 1.50 1.10
482 A44 5nu on 2nu multi 1.50 1.10
483 A44 5nu on 3nu multi 1.50 1.10
484 A44 5nu on 20nu multi 1.50 1.10
Nos. 481-484 (4) 6.00 4.40

Souvenir Sheets
485 A44 20nu on 25nu multi 7.50 5.50

Mask Dance of the Judgement of Death — A61

1985, Apr. 27 *Perf. 13½*
486 A61 5ch Shinje Choegyel .20 .20
487 A61 35ch Raksh Lango .20 .20
488 A61 50ch Druelgo .20 .20
489 A61 2.50nu Pago .45 .35
490 A61 3nu Telgo .55 .40
491 A61 4nu Due Nakcung .75 .60
492 A61 5nu Lha Karpo .90 .70
a. Souv. sheet of 4, #486-487, 491-492 1.90 1.50
493 A61 5.50nu Nyalbum 1.00 .75
494 A61 6nu Khimda Pelkyi 1.10 .85
Nos. 486-494 (9) 5.35 4.25

For overprints see Nos. 764-772.

Monasteries A62

1984, Dec. 1 Litho. *Perf. 12*
495 A62 10ch Domkhar .20 .20
496 A62 25ch Shemgang .20 .20
497 A62 50ch Chapcha .20 .20
498 A62 1nu Tashigang .20 .20
499 A62 2nu Pungthang Chhug .30 .30
500 A62 5nu Dechhenphoda .70 .70
Nos. 495-500 (6) 1.80 1.80

Veteran's War Memorial Building, San Francisco A63

1985, Oct. 24 Litho. *Perf. 14*
502 A63 50ch Flags of Bhutan, UN, vert. .20 .20
503 A63 15nu Headquarters, NY, vert. 2.75 2.00
504 A63 20nu shown 3.75 2.75
Nos. 502-504 (3) 6.70 4.95

Souvenir Sheet
505 A63 25nu UN Human Rights Declaration 4.25 3.00

UN, 40th anniv.

Audubon Birth Bicentenary — A64

Illustrations of North American bird species by Audubon.

1985
506 A64 50ch Anas breweri .20 .20
507 A64 1nu Lagopus lagopus .20 .20
508 A64 2nu Charadrius montanus .35 .25
509 A64 3nu Cavia stellata .50 .40
510 A64 4nu Canachites canadensis .70 .50
511 A64 5nu Mergus cucullatus .85 .60
512 A64 15nu Olor buccinator 2.50 1.75
513 A64 20nu Bucephala clangula 3.50 2.50
Nos. 506-513 (8) 8.80 6.40

Souvenir Sheets
514 A64 25nu Accipiter striatus 3.75 2.25
515 A64 25nu Parus bicolor 3.75 2.25

Issue dates: Nos. 507, 510-511, 514 Nov. 15. Nos. 506, 508-509, 513, 515 Dec. 6.

A Tramp Abroad, by Mark Twain (1835-1910) A65

Walt Disney animated characters.

1985, Nov. 15
516 A65 50ch multicolored .20 .20
517 A65 2nu multicolored .35 .25
518 A65 5nu multicolored .85 .60
519 A65 9nu multicolored 1.50 1.10
520 A65 20nu multicolored 3.50 2.50
Nos. 516-520 (5) 6.40 4.65

Souvenir Sheet
521 A65 25nu Goofy, Mickey Mouse 5.00 3.50

Intl. Youth Year.
For overprints see Nos. 554, 556-557.

Rapunzel, by Jacob and Wilhelm Grimm A66

Walt Disney animated characters.

1985, Nov. 15
522 A66 1nu multicolored .20 .20
523 A66 4nu multicolored .70 .50
524 A66 7nu multicolored 1.25 .95
525 A66 8nu multicolored 1.40 1.00
526 A66 15nu multicolored 2.50 1.75
Nos. 522-526 (5) 6.05 4.40

Souvenir Sheet
527 A66 25nu multicolored 5.00 4.00

No. 525 printed in sheets of 8.
For overprints see Nos. 553, 555, 558.

First South Asian Regional Cooperation Summit, Dec. 7-8, Dacca, Bangladesh A67

1985, Dec. 8 *Perf. 14*
528 A67 50ch multicolored .20 .20
529 A67 5nu multicolored .85 .60

Seven Precious Attributes of the Universal King — A68

1986, Feb. 12 Litho. *Perf. 13x12½*
530 A68 30ch Wheel .20 .20
531 A68 50ch Gem .20 .20
532 A68 1.25nu Queen .20 .20
533 A68 2nu Minister .30 .30
534 A68 4nu Elephant .55 .55
535 A68 6nu Horse .85 .85
536 A68 8nu General 1.10 1.10
Nos. 530-536 (7) 3.40 3.40

Nos. 442-443, 445-449 Ovptd. with Medal, Winners' Names and Countries. No. 449 Ovptd. for Men's and Women's Events

1986, May 5 Litho. *Perf. 14*
537 A59 15ch Hyang Soon Seo, So. Korea .20 .20
538 A59 25ch Darrell Pace, US .20 .20
539 A59 2.25nu US .30 .30
540 A59 5.50nu Mark Breland, US .80 .80
541 A59 6nu Daley Thompson, Britain .85 .85
542 A59 8nu Stefan Edberg, Sweden 1.10 1.10
Nos. 537-542 (6) 3.45 3.45

Souvenir Sheets
543 A59 25nu Hyang Soon Seo 3.50 3.50
544 A59 25nu Darrel Pace 3.50 3.50

Kilkhor Mandalas, Deities — A69

Religious art: 10ch, 1nu, Phurpa, ritual dagger. 25ch, 3nu, Amitayus in wrath. 50ch, 5nu, Overpowering Deities. 75ch, 7nu, Great Wrathful One, Guru Rinpoche.

1986, June 17 *Perf. 13½*
545 A69 10ch multicolored .20 .20
546 A69 25ch multicolored .20 .20
547 A69 50ch multicolored .20 .20
548 A69 75ch multicolored .20 .20
549 A69 1nu multicolored .20 .20
550 A69 3nu multicolored .40 .40
551 A69 5nu multicolored .70 .70
552 A69 7nu multicolored 1.00 1.00
Nos. 545-552 (8) 3.10 3.10

Nos. 525, 519, 526, 520, 521 and 527 Ovptd. with AMERIPEX '86 Emblem

1986, June 16 Litho. *Perf. 14*
553 A66 8nu multi 1.40 1.00
554 A65 9nu multi 1.50 1.10
555 A66 15nu multi 2.50 1.75
556 A65 20nu multi 3.50 2.50
Nos. 553-556 (4) 8.90 6.35

Souvenir Sheets
557 A65 25nu #521 4.25 3.00
558 A66 25nu #527 4.25 3.00

A70

A71

Halley's Comet A72

Designs: 50ch, Babylonian tablet fragments, 2349 B.C. sighting. 1nu, 17th cent. print, A.D. 66 sighting. 2nu, French silhouette art, 1835 sighting. 3nu, Bayeux Tapestry, 1066 sighting. 4nu, Woodblock, 684 sighting. 5nu, Illustration from Bybel Printen, 1650. 15nu, 1456 Sighting, Cancer constellation. 20nu, Delft plate, 1910 sighting. No. 572, Comet over Himalayas. No. 573, Comet over domed temple Dug-gye Jong.

1986, Nov. 4 Litho. *Perf. 15*
564 A70 50ch multicolored .20 .20
565 A70 1nu multicolored .20 .20
566 A71 2nu multicolored .35 .30
567 A70 3nu multicolored .50 .35
568 A70 4nu multicolored .70 .50
569 A71 5nu multicolored .85 .65
570 A70 15nu multicolored 2.50 2.00
571 A70 20nu multicolored 3.50 2.50
Nos. 564-571 (8) 8.80 6.70

Souvenir Sheets
572 A72 25nu multicolored 4.25 3.00
573 A72 25nu multicolored 4.25 3.00

A73

Statue of Liberty, Cent. — A74

Statue and ships: 50ch, Mircea, Romania. 1nu, Shalom, Israel. 2nu, Leonardo da Vinci, Italy. 3nu, Libertad, Argentina. 4nu, France, France. 5nu, SS United States, US. 15nu, Queen Elizabeth II, England. 20nu, Europa, West Germany. No. 582, Statue. No. 583, Statue, World Trade Center.

1986, Nov. 4

574	A73	50ch	multicolored	.20	.20
575	A73	1nu	multicolored	.20	.20
576	A73	2nu	multicolored	.35	.30
577	A73	3nu	multicolored	.50	.35
578	A73	4nu	multicolored	.65	.50
579	A73	5nu	multicolored	.85	.65
580	A73	15nu	multicolored	2.50	1.90
581	A73	20nu	multicolored	3.50	2.50
			Nos. 574-581 (8)	8.75	6.60

Souvenir Sheets

582	A74	25nu	multicolored	4.25	3.00
583	A74	25nu	multi, diff.	4.25	3.00

Discovery of America, 500th Anniv. — A75

1987, May 25 Litho. *Perf. 14*

584	A75	20ch	Santa Maria	.40	.40
585	A75	25ch	Queen Isabella	.40	.40
586	A75	50ch	Ship, flying fish	.40	.40
587	A75	1nu	Columbus's coat of arms	.75	.60
588	A75	2nu	Christopher Columbus	1.40	1.00
589	A75	3nu	Landing in the New World	2.00	2.00
a.			Miniature sheet of 6, #584-589	5.00	5.00
			Nos. 584-589 (6)	5.35	4.80

Souvenir Sheets

590	A75	20ch	Pineapple		
591	A75	25ch	Indian hammock		
592	A75	50ch	Tobacco plant		
593	A75	1nu	Flamingo		
594	A75	2nu	Navigator, astrolabe, 15th cent.		
595	A75	3nu	Lizard		
596	A75	5nu	Iguana	1.25	.95

All stamps are vertical except those contained in Nos. 591, 595 and 596. Stamps from No. 589a have white background.

CAPEX '87 — A76

Locomotives.

1987, June 15

597	A76	50ch	Canadian Natl. U1-f	.20	.20
598	A76	1nu	Via Rail L.R.C.	.20	.20
599	A76	2nu	Canadian Natl. GM GF-30t	.35	.25
600	A76	3nu	Canadian Natl. 4-8-4	.50	.35
601	A76	8nu	Canadian Pacific 4-6-2	1.40	1.00
602	A76	10nu	Via Express passenger train	1.75	1.25
603	A76	15nu	Canadian Nat. Turbotrain	2.50	1.90
604	A76	20nu	Canadian Pacific Diesel-Electric Express	3.25	2.50
			Nos. 597-604 (8)	10.15	7.65

Souvenir Sheet

605	A76	25nu	Royal Hudson 4-6-4	4.25	3.00
606	A76	25nu	Canadian Natl. 4-8-4, diff.	4.25	3.00

Two Faces, Sculpture by Marc Chagall (1887-1984) A77

Paintings: 1nu, At the Barber's. 2nu, Old Jew with Torah. 3nu, Red Maternity. 4nu, Eve of Yom Kippur. 5nu, The Old Musician. 6nu, The Rabbi of Vitebsk. 7nu, Couple at Dusk. 9nu, The Artistes. 10nu, Moses Breaking the Tablets of the Law. 12nu, Bouquet with Flying Lovers. 20nu, In the Sky of the Opera. No. 619, Romeo and Juliet. No. 620, Magician of Paris. No. 621, Maternity. No. 622, The Carnival for Aleko: Scene II. No. 623, Visit to the Grandparents. No. 624, The Smolensk Newspaper. No. 625, The Concert. No. 626, Composition with Goat. No. 627, Still Life. No. 628. The Red Gateway. No. 629, Cow with Parasol. No. 630, Russian Village.

1987, Dec. 17 Litho. *Perf. 14*

607	A77	50ch	multicolored	.20	.20
608	A77	1nu	multicolored	.20	.20
609	A77	2nu	multicolored	.35	.25
610	A77	3nu	multicolored	.45	.35
611	A77	4nu	multicolored	.65	.45
612	A77	5nu	multicolored	.85	.60
613	A77	6nu	multicolored	.95	.70
614	A77	7nu	multicolored	1.10	.90
615	A77	9nu	multicolored	1.50	1.10
616	A77	10nu	multicolored	1.60	1.25
617	A77	12nu	multicolored	1.90	1.50
618	A77	20nu	multicolored	3.25	2.50

Size: 110x95mm

Imperf

619	A77	25nu	multicolored	4.00	3.00
620	A77	25nu	multicolored	4.00	3.00
621	A77	25nu	multicolored	4.00	3.00
622	A77	25nu	multicolored	4.00	3.00
623	A77	25nu	multicolored	4.00	3.00
624	A77	25nu	multicolored	4.00	3.00
625	A77	25nu	multicolored	4.00	3.00
626	A77	25nu	multicolored	4.00	3.00
627	A77	25nu	multicolored	4.00	3.00
628	A77	25nu	multicolored	4.00	3.00
629	A77	25nu	multicolored	4.00	3.00
630	A77	25nu	multicolored	4.00	3.00
			Nos. 607-630 (24)	61.00	46.00

1988 Winter Olympics, Calgary — A78

Emblem and Disney animated characters as competitors in Olympic events.

1988, Feb. 15 Litho. *Perf. 14*

631	A78	50ch	Slalom	.20	.20
632	A78	1nu	Downhill skiing	.20	.20
633	A78	2nu	Ice hockey	.30	.25
634	A78	4nu	Biathlon	.65	.50
635	A78	7nu	Speed skating	1.10	.85
636	A78	8nu	Figure skating	1.25	.95
637	A78	9nu	Figure skating, diff.	1.50	1.10
638	A78	20nu	Bobsled	3.25	2.50
			Nos. 631-638 (8)	8.45	6.55

Souvenir Sheets

639	A78	25nu	Ski jumping	4.00	4.00
640	A78	25nu	Ice dancing	4.00	4.00

Transportation Innovations — A79

1988, Mar. 31

641	A79	50ch	Pullman Pioneer, 1865	.20	.20
642	A79	1nu	Stephenson's Rocket, 1829	.20	.20
643	A79	2nu	Pierre L'Allement's Velocipede, 1866	.30	.25
644	A79	3nu	Benz Velocipede, 1886	.50	.35
645	A79	4nu	Volkswagen Beetle, c. 1960	.65	.50
646	A79	5nu	Natchez Vs. Robert E. Lee, 1870	.80	.60
647	A79	6nu	American La France, 1910	1.00	.75
648	A79	7nu	USS Constitution, 1787, vert.	1.10	.80
649	A79	9nu	Bell Rocket Belt, 1961, vert.	1.50	1.10
650	A79	10nu	Trevithick Locomotive, 1804	1.60	1.25
			Nos. 641-650 (10)	7.85	6.00

Souvenir Sheets

651	A79	25nu	Concorde jet	4.00	4.00
652	A79	25nu	Mallard, 1938, vert.	4.00	4.00
653	A79	25nu	Shinkansen	4.00	4.00
654	A79	25nu	TGV, 1981	4.00	4.00

1988 Summer Olympics, Seoul A80

7nu-20nu vert.

1989, Feb. 15 Litho.

655	A80	50ch	Women's gymnastics	.20	.20
656	A80	1nu	Tae kwon do	.20	.20
657	A80	2nu	Shot put	.30	.25
658	A80	4nu	Women's volleyball	.65	.50
659	A80	7nu	Basketball	1.10	.85
660	A80	8nu	Soccer	1.25	.95
661	A80	9nu	Women's high jump	1.50	1.10
662	A80	20nu	Running	3.25	2.50
			Nos. 655-662 (8)	8.45	6.55

Souvenir Sheets

663	A80	25nu	Archery, vert.	4.00	4.00
664	A80	25nu	Fencing	4.00	4.00

Paintings by Titian — A81

Designs: 50ch, *Gentleman with a Book.* 1nu, *Venus and Cupid, with a Lute Player.* 2nu, *Diana and Actaeon.* 3nu, *Cardinal Ippolito dei Medici.* 4nu, *Sleeping Venus.* 5nu, *Venus Risen from the Waves.* 6nu, *Worship of Venus.* 7nu, *Fete Champetre.* 10nu, *Perseus and Andromeda.* 15nu, *Danae.* 20nu, *Venus at the Mirror.* 25nu, *Venus and the Organ Player.* No. 677, *The Pardo Venus,* horiz. No. 678, *Venus and Cupid, with an Organist.* No. 679, *Miracle of the Irascible Son.* No. 680, *Diana and Callisto.* No. 681, *Saint John the Almsgiver.* No. 682, *Danae with the Shower of Gold,* horiz. No. 683, *Bacchus and Ariadne.* No. 684, *Venus Blindfolding Cupid.* No. 685, *Portrait of Laura Dianti.* No. 686, *Venus of Urbino.* No. 687, *Portrait of Johann Friedrich.* No. 688, *Mater Dolorosa with Raised Hands.*

Perf. 13½x14, 14x13½

1989, Feb. 15 Litho.

665	A81	50ch	multicolored	.20	.20
666	A81	1nu	multicolored	.20	.20
667	A81	2nu	multicolored	.30	.25
668	A81	3nu	multicolored	.50	.35
669	A81	4nu	multicolored	.65	.50
670	A81	5nu	multicolored	.80	.60
671	A81	6nu	multicolored	.90	.75
672	A81	7nu	multicolored	1.10	.85
673	A81	10nu	multicolored	1.60	1.25
674	A81	15nu	multicolored	2.50	1.75
675	A81	20nu	multicolored	3.25	2.50
676	A81	25nu	multicolored	4.00	3.00
			Nos. 665-676 (12)	16.00	12.20

Souvenir Sheets

677-688	A81	25nu	each	4.00	4.00

Mickey Mouse, 60th Anniv. (in 1988) — A82

Movie posters.

1989, June 20 Litho. *Perf. 13½x14*

689	A82	1ch	Mickey Mouse, 1930s	.20	.20
690	A82	2ch	*Barnyard Olympics,* 1932	.20	.20
691	A82	3ch	*Society Dog Show,* 1939	.20	.20
692	A82	4ch	*Fantasia,* 1980s re-release	.20	.20
693	A82	5ch	*The Mad Dog,* 1932	.20	.20
694	A82	10ch	*A Gentleman's Gentleman,* 1941	.20	.20
695	A82	50ch	*Symphony hour,* 1942	.20	.20
696	A82	10nu	*The Moose Hunt,* 1931	1.50	1.25
697	A82	15nu	*Wild Waves,* 1929	2.25	1.75
698	A82	20nu	*Mickey in Arabia,* 1932	3.00	2.50
699	A82	25nu	*Tugboat Mickey,* 1940	3.75	3.00
700	A82	30nu	*Building a Building,* 1933	4.25	3.50
			Nos. 689-700 (12)	16.15	13.40

Souvenir Sheets

701	A82	25nu	*The Mad Doctor,* 1933	4.00	4.00
702	A82	25nu	*The Meller Drammer,* 1933	4.00	4.00
703	A82	25nu	*Ye Olden Days,* 1933	4.00	4.00
704	A82	25nu	*Mickey's Good Deed,* 1932	4.00	4.00
705	A82	25nu	*Mickey's Pal Pluto,* 1933	4.00	4.00
706	A82	25nu	*Trader Mickey,* 1932	4.00	4.00
707	A82	25nu	*Touchdown Mickey,* 1932	4.00	4.00
708	A82	25nu	*Steamboat Willie,* 1928	4.00	4.00
709	A82	25nu	*The Whoopee Party,* 1932	4.00	4.00
710	A82	25nu	*Mickey's Nightmare,* 1932	4.00	4.00
711	A82	25nu	*The Klondike Kid,* 1932	4.00	4.00
712	A82	25nu	*The Wayward Canary,* 1932	4.00	4.00

Mushrooms — A83

1989, Aug. 22 Litho. *Perf. 14*

713	A83	50ch	*Tricholoma pardalotum*	.20	.20
714	A83	1nu	*Suillus placidus*	.20	.20
715	A83	2nu	*Boletus regius*	.30	.25
716	A83	3nu	*Gomphidius glutinosus*	.50	.35
717	A83	4nu	*Boletus calopus*	.65	.50
718	A83	5nu	*Suillus grevillei*	.80	.60
719	A83	6nu	*Boletus appendiculatus*	.90	.70
720	A83	7nu	*Lactarius torminosus*	1.10	.80
721	A83	10nu	*Macrolepiota rhacodes*	1.60	1.25
722	A83	15nu	*Amanita rubescens*	2.50	1.75
723	A83	20nu	*Amanita phalloides*	3.25	2.50
724	A83	25nu	*Amanita citrina*	4.00	3.00
			Nos. 713-724 (12)	16.00	12.10

Souvenir Sheets

725	A83	25nu	*Russula aurata*	4.00	4.00
726	A83	25nu	*Gyroporus castaneus*	4.00	4.00
727	A83	25nu	*Cantharellus cibarius*	4.00	4.00

728 A83 25nu *Boletus rhodoxanthus* 4.00 4.00
729 A83 25nu *Paxillus involutus* 4.00 4.00
730 A83 25nu *Gyroporus cyanescens* 4.00 4.00
731 A83 25nu *Lepista nuda* 4.00 4.00
732 A83 25nu *Dentinum repandum* 4.00 4.00
733 A83 25nu *Lepista saeva* 4.00 4.00
734 A83 25nu *Hydnum imbricatum* 4.00 4.00
735 A83 25nu *Xerocomus subtomentosus* 4.00 4.00
736 A83 25nu *Russula olivacea* 4.00 4.00

Intl. Maritime Organization, 30th Anniv. — A84

Ships: 50ch, Spanish galleon *La Reale*, 1680. 1 nu, Submersible *Turtle*, 1776. 2nu, *Charlote Dundas*, 1802. 3nu, *Great Eastern*, c. 1858. 4nu, HMS *Warrior*, 1862. 5nu, Mississippi steamer, 1884. 6nu, *Preussen*, 1902. 7nu, USS *Arizona*, 1915. 10nu, *Bluenose*, 1921. 15nu, Steam trawler, 1925. 20nu, American liberty ship, 1943. No. 748, S.S. *United States*, 1952. No. 749, Moran tug, c. 1950. No. 750, Sinking of the *Titanic*, 1912. No. 751, U-boat, c. 1942. No. 752, Japanese warship *Yamato*, 1944. No. 753, HMS *Dreadnought*. No. 754, S.S. *Normandie*, c. 1933, and a Chinese junk. No. 755, HMS *Victory*, 1805. No. 756, USS *Monitor*, 1862. No. 757, *Cutty Sark*, 1869. No. 758, USS *Constitution*. No. 759, HMS *Resolution*. No. 760, Chinese junk.

1989, Aug. 24 Litho. *Perf. 14*

737 A84 50ch multicolored .20 .20
738 A84 1nu multicolored .20 .20
739 A84 2nu multicolored .30 .25
740 A84 3nu multicolored .50 .35
741 A84 4nu multicolored .65 .50
742 A84 5nu multicolored .80 .60
743 A84 6nu multicolored .90 .70
744 A84 7nu multicolored 1.10 .80
745 A84 10nu multicolored 1.60 1.25
746 A84 15nu multicolored 2.50 1.75
747 A84 20nu multicolored 3.25 2.50
748 A84 25nu multicolored 4.00 3.00
Nos. 737-748 (12) 16.00 12.10

Souvenir Sheets

749-760 A84 25nu each 4.00 4.00

Nos. 289-291 Overprinted: WORLD / AIDS DAY

1988, Dec. 1 Litho. *Perf. 14x13½*

761 A37 2nu multicolored .45 .35
762 A37 5nu multicolored 1.10 .90
763 A37 10nu multicolored 2.25 1.75
Nos. 761-763 (3) 3.80 3.00

Nos. 486-494 Ovptd. in Silver: ASIA-PACIFIC EXPOSITION FUKUOKA '89

1989, Mar. 17 *Perf. 13½*

764 A61 5ch multicolored .20 .20
765 A61 35ch multicolored .20 .20
766 A61 50ch multicolored .20 .20
767 A61 2.50nu multicolored .40 .30
768 A61 3nu multicolored .50 .35
769 A61 4nu multicolored .65 .50
770 A61 5nu multicolored .80 .60
771 A61 5.50nu multicolored .90 .65
772 A61 6nu multicolored 1.00 .80
Nos. 764-772 (9) 4.85 3.80

This set exists overprinted in Japanese.

Chhukha Hydroelectric Project — A85

1988, Oct. 21 Litho. *Perf. 13½*

773 A85 50ch multicolored .20 .20

Jawaharlal Nehru (1889-1964), Indian Prime Minister A85a

1989, Nov. 14 Photo. *Perf. 14*

773A A85a 100ch olive brown .20 .20

Denomination is shown as 1.00ch in error.

Birds A86

Designs: 50ch, Larger goldenbacked woodpecker. 1nu, Black-naped monarch. 2nu, White-crested laughing thrush. 3nu, Bloodpheasant. 4nu, Blossom-headed parakeet. 5nu, Rosy minivet. 6nu, Chestnut-headed tit babbler. 7nu, Blue pitta. 10nu, Black-naped oriole. 15nu, Green magpie. 20nu, Indian three-toed kingfisher. No. 785, Ibisbill. No. 786, Great pied hornbill. No. 787, Himalayan redbreasted falconet. No. 788, Lammergeier. No. 789, Large racket-tailed drongo. No. 790, Fire-tailed sunbird. No. 791, Indian crested swift. No. 792, White-eared pheasant. No. 793, Satyr tragopan. No. 794, Wallcreeper. No. 795, Fairy bluebird. No. 796, Little spiderhunter. No. 797, Spotted forktail. Nos. 774-779 vert.

1989, Nov. 22 Litho. *Perf. 14*

774 A86 50ch multicolored .20 .20
775 A86 1nu multicolored .20 .20
776 A86 2nu multicolored .30 .25
777 A86 3nu multicolored .50 .35
778 A86 4nu multicolored .65 .50
779 A86 5nu multicolored .80 .60
780 A86 6nu multicolored .90 .70
781 A86 7nu multicolored 1.10 .80
782 A86 10nu multicolored 1.60 1.25
783 A86 15nu multicolored 2.50 1.75
784 A86 20nu multicolored 3.25 2.50
785 A86 25nu multicolored 4.00 3.00
Nos. 774-785 (12) 16.00 12.10

Souvenir Sheets

786-797 A86 25nu each 4.00 4.00

Steam Locomotives A87

Designs: 50ch, *Best Friend of Charleston*, 1830, US 1nu, Class U, 1949, France. 2nu, *Consolidation*, 1866, US. 3nu, *Luggage Engine*, 1843, Great Britain. 4nu, Class 60-3 Shay, 1913, US. 5nu, *John Bull*, 1831, US. 6nu, *Hercules*, 1837, US. 7nu, Eight-wheel tank engine, 1874, Great Britain. 10nu, *The Illinois*, 1852, US. 15nu, German State 4-6-4, 1935. 20nu, American Standard, 1865. No. 809, Class Ps-4, 1926, US. No. 810, *Puffing Billy*, 1814, Great Britain. No. 811, Stephenson's *Rocket*, 1829, Great Britain. No. 812, *Cumberland*, 1845, US, vert. No. 813, *John Stevens*, 1849, US, vert. No. 814, No. 22 Baldwin Locomotive Works, 1873, US, No. 815, *Ariel*, 1877, US. No. 816, 1899 *No. 1301* Webb Compound Engine, Great Britain. No. 817, 1893 *No. 999* Empire State Express, US. No. 818, 1923 Class K-36, US. No. 819, 1935 Class A4, Great Britain. No. 820, 1935 Class A, US. No. 821, 1943 Class P-1, US.

1990, Jan. 30

798 A87 50ch multi .20 .20
799 A87 1nu multi .20 .20
800 A87 2nu multi .30 .25
801 A87 3nu multi .50 .35
802 A87 4nu multi .65 .50
803 A87 5nu multi .80 .60
804 A87 6nu multi .90 .70
805 A87 7nu multi 1.10 .80
806 A87 10nu multi 1.60 1.25
807 A87 15nu multi 2.50 1.75
808 A87 20nu multi 3.25 2.50
809 A87 25nu multi 4.00 3.00
Nos. 798-809 (12) 16.00 12.10

Souvenir Sheets

810-821 A87 25nu each 4.00 4.00

Butterflies A88

1990, Jan. 30 Litho. *Perf. 14*

822 A88 50ch *Charaxes harmodius* .20 .20
823 A88 1nu *Prioneris thestylis* .20 .20
824 A88 2nu *Sephisa chandra* .30 .25
825 A88 3nu *Penthema usarda* .50 .35
826 A88 4nu *Troides aecus* .65 .50
827 A88 5nu *Polyura eudamippus* .80 .60
828 A88 6nu *Polyura dolon* .90 .70
829 A88 7nu *Neope bhadra* 1.10 .80
830 A88 10nu *Delias descombesi* 1.60 1.25
831 A88 15nu *Childreni childrena* 2.50 1.75
832 A88 20nu *Kallima inachus* 3.25 2.50
833 A88 25nu *Elymnias malelas* 4.00 3.00
Nos. 822-833 (12) 16.00 12.10

Souvenir Sheets

834 A88 25nu Red lacewing 4.00 4.00
835 A88 25nu Bhutan glory 4.00 4.00
836 A88 25nu Great eggfly 4.00 4.00
837 A88 25nu Kaiser-I-Hind 4.00 4.00
838 A88 25nu Chestnut tiger 4.00 4.00
839 A88 25nu Common map 4.00 4.00
840 A88 25nu Swallowtail 4.00 4.00
841 A88 25nu Jungle glory 4.00 4.00
842 A88 25nu Checkered swallowtail 4.00 4.00
843 A88 25nu Common birdwing 4.00 4.00
844 A88 25nu Blue banded peacock 4.00 4.00
845 A88 25nu Camberwell beauty 4.00 4.00

Nos. 822-824, 826-827, 830-831, 834-835, 844-845 are vert.

Paintings by Hiroshige A89

Designs: 10ch, Plum Estate, Kameido. 20ch, Yatsumi Bridge. 50ch, Ayase River and Kanegafuchi. 75ch, View of Shiba Coast. 1nu, Grandpa's Teahouse, Meguro. 2nu, Kameido Tenjin Shrine. 6nu, Yoroi Ferry, Koami-cho. 7nu, Sakasai Ferry. 10nu, Fukagawa Lumberyards. 15nu, Suido Bridge and Surugadai. 20nu, Meguro Drum Bridge and Sunset Hill. No. 857, Atagoshita and Yabu Lane. No. 858, Towboats Along the Yotsugi-dori Canal. No. 859, Minowa, Kanasugi, Mikawashima. No. 860, Horikiri Iris Garden. No. 861, Fukagawa Susaki and Jumantsubo. No. 862, Suijin Shrine and Massaki on the Sumida River. No. 863, New Year's Eve Foxfires at the Changing Tree, Oji. No. 864, Nihonbashi, Clearing After Snow. No. 865, View to the North from Asukayama. No. 866, Komakata Hall and Azuma Bridge. No. 867, The City Flourishing, Tanabata Festival. No. 868, Suruga-cho. No. 869, Sudden Shower over Shin-Ohashi Bridge and Atake.

1990, May 21 Litho. *Perf. 13½*

846 A89 10ch multicolored .20 .20
847 A89 20ch multicolored .20 .20
848 A89 50ch multicolored .20 .20
849 A89 75ch multicolored .20 .20
850 A89 1nu multicolored .20 .20
851 A89 2nu multicolored .30 .25
852 A89 6nu multicolored .95 .70
853 A89 7nu multicolored 1.10 .85
854 A89 10nu multicolored 1.60 1.25
855 A89 15nu multicolored 2.50 1.75
856 A89 20nu multicolored 3.25 2.50
857 A89 25nu multicolored 4.00 3.00
Nos. 846-857 (12) 14.70 11.30

Souvenir Sheets

858-869 A89 25nu each 4.00 3.00

Hirohito (1901-1989) and enthronement of Akihito as emperor of Japan.

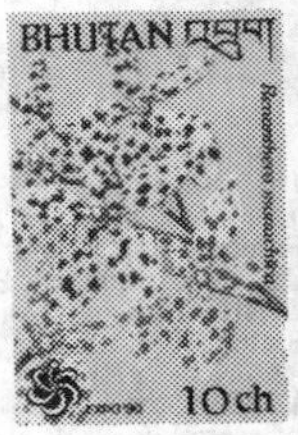

Orchids — A90

1990, Apr. 6 Litho. *Perf. 14*

870 A90 10ch *Renanthera monachica* .20 .20
871 A90 50ch *Vanda coerulea* .20 .20
872 A90 1nu *Phalaenopsis violacea* .20 .20
873 A90 2nu *Dendrobium nobile* .30 .25
874 A90 5nu *Vandopsis lissochiloides* .80 .60
875 A90 6nu *Paphiopedilum rothschildianum* .95 .70
876 A90 7nu *Phalaenopsis schilleriana* 1.10 .80
877 A90 9nu *Paphiopedilum insigne* 1.50 1.10
878 A90 10nu *Paphiopedilum bellatulum* 1.60 1.25
879 A90 20nu *Doritis pulcherrima* 3.25 2.50
880 A90 25nu *Cymbidium giganteum* 4.00 3.00
881 A90 35nu *Phalaenopsis mariae* 5.50 4.25
Nos. 870-881 (12) 19.60 15.05

Souvenir Sheets

882 A90 30nu *Vanda coerulescens* 4.75 4.75
883 A90 30nu *Vandopsis parishi* 4.75 4.75
884 A90 30nu *Dendrobium aphyllum* 4.75 4.75
885 A90 30nu *Phalaenopsis amabilis* 4.75 4.75
886 A90 30nu *Paphiopedilum haynaldianum* 4.75 4.75
887 A90 30nu *Dendrobium loddigesii* 4.75 4.75
888 A90 30nu *Vanda alpina* 4.75 4.75
889 A90 30nu *Phalaenopsis equestris* 4.75 4.75
890 A90 30nu *Vanda cristata* 4.75 4.75
891 A90 30nu *Phalaenopsis cornu cervi* 4.75 4.75
892 A90 30nu *Paphiopedilum niveum* 4.75 4.75
893 A90 30nu *Dendrobium margaritaceum* 4.75 4.75

EXPO '90 Intl. Garden and Greenery Exposition, Osaka, Apr. 1-Dec. 31.

G.P.O., Thimphu — A90a

1990, May 29 Photo. *Perf. 14*

893A A90a 1nu multicolored .20 .20

Penny Black, 150th Anniv. A90b

Penny Black and: 50ch, Bhutan #1. 1nu, Oldenburg #1. 2nu, Bergedorf #3. 4nu, German Democratic Republic #48. 5nu, Brunswick #1. 6nu, Basel #3L1. 8nu, Geneva #2L1. 10nu, Zurich #1L1. No. 902, France #3. 20nu, Vatican City #1. 25nu, Israel #1. No. 905, Japan #1.

Penny Black and: No. 906a, Mecklenburg-Schwerin #1. b, Mecklenburg-Strelitz #1. No. 907a, Germany #5, #9. b, Prussia #2. No. 908a, Hamburg #1. b, North German Confederation #1, #7. No. 909a, Baden #1. b, Wurttemberg #1. No. 910a, Heligoland #1. b, Hanover #1. No. 911a, Thurn & Taxis #3. b, Thurn & Taxis #42. No. 912a, Schleswig-Holstein #1. b, Lubeck #5. No. 913, Saxony #1. No. 914, Berlin #9N1. No. 915, No other stamp. No. 916, US #1. No. 917, Bavaria #1.

1990, Oct. 9 *Perf. 14*

894	A90b	50ch multicolored	.20	.20
895	A90b	1nu multicolored	.20	.20
896	A90b	2nu multicolored	.30	.25
897	A90b	4nu multicolored	.65	.50
898	A90b	5nu multicolored	.80	.60
899	A90b	6nu multicolored	1.00	.75
900	A90b	8nu multicolored	1.25	1.00
901	A90b	10nu multicolored	1.60	1.25
902	A90b	15nu multicolored	2.50	1.75
903	A90b	20nu multicolored	3.25	2.50
904	A90b	25nu multicolored	4.00	3.00
905	A90b	30nu multicolored	4.75	3.50
		Nos. 894-905 (12)	20.50	15.50

Souvenir Sheets

Sheets of 2 (#906-912) or 1

906-912 A90b	15nu each	4.75	4.75
913-917 A90b	30nu each	4.75	4.75

Stamp World London '90.

Giant Pandas A91

Tiger A92

Endangered wildlife of Asia.

1990 *Perf. 14*

918	A91	50ch multi, diff.	.20	.20
919	A91	1nu multi, diff.	.20	.20
920	A91	2nu multi, diff.	.30	.25
921	A91	3nu shown	.50	.35
922	A91	4nu multi, diff.	.65	.50
923	A92	5nu shown	.80	.60
924	A91	6nu multi, diff.	.90	.70
925	A91	7nu multi, diff.	1.10	.80
926	A92	10nu Elephant	1.60	1.25
927	A91	15nu multi, diff.	2.50	1.75
928	A92	20nu Barking deer	3.25	2.50
929	A92	25nu Snow leopard	4.00	3.00
		Nos. 918-929 (12)	16.00	12.10

Souvenir Sheets

930	A92	25nu Rhinoceros	4.00	4.00
931	A92	25nu Clouded leopard	4.00	4.00
932	A92	25nu Asiatic wild dog	4.00	4.00
933	A92	25nu Himalayan shou	4.00	4.00
934	A92	25nu Golden cat	4.00	4.00
935	A92	25nu Himalayan musk deer	4.00	4.00
936	A91	25nu multi, diff.	4.00	4.00
937	A92	25nu Asiatic black bear	4.00	4.00
938	A92	25nu Gaur	4.00	4.00
939	A92	25nu Pygmy hog	4.00	4.00
940	A92	25nu Wolf	4.00	4.00
941	A92	25nu Sloth bear	4.00	4.00

Nos. 919-920 and 927 vert.

Buddhist Musical Instruments — A93

1990, Sept. 29 Litho. *Perf. 13½x13*

942	A93	10ch Dungchen	.20	.20
943	A93	20ch Dungkar	.20	.20
944	A93	30ch Roim	.20	.20
945	A93	50ch Tinchag	.20	.20
946	A93	1nu Dradu & drilbu	.20	.20
947	A93	2nu Gya-ling	.30	.25
948	A93	2.50nu Nga	.40	.30
a.		Souv. sheet of 4, #943, 945, 947-948	.85	.65
949	A93	3.50nu Kang-dung	.55	.40
a.		Souv. sheet of 4, #942, 944, 946, 949	.85	.65
		Nos. 942-949 (8)	2.25	1.95

Year of the Girl Child — A94

1990, Dec. 8

950	A94	50ch shown	.20	.20
951	A94	20nu Young girl	3.25	2.50

Wonders of the World A95

Walt Disney characters viewing: 1ch, Temple of Artemis, Ephesus. 2ch, Statue of Zeus, Olympia. 3ch, Egyptian pyramids. 4ch, Lighthouse, Alexandria. 5ch, Mausoleum at Halicarnassus. 10ch, Colossus of Rhodes. 50ch, Hanging gardens of Babylon. 5nu, Mauna Loa volcano, Hawaii. 6nu, Carlsbad Caverns, New Mexico. 10nu, Rainbow Bridge, Utah. 15nu, Grand Canyon of the Colorado, Arizona. 20nu, Old Faithful geyser, Wyoming. 25nu, Giant sequoias, California. 30nu, Crater Lake and Wizard Island, Oregon. 5nu, 6nu, 10nu, 15nu, 20nu, 25nu, 30nu are horiz.

Walt Disney characters viewing: No. 966, Great Wall of China, horiz. No. 967, Mosque of St. Sophia, Istanbul, Turkey. No. 968, The Leaning Tower of Pisa, Italy. No. 969, Colosseum, Rome. No. 970, Stonehenge, England. No. 971, Catacombs of Alexandria, Egypt. No. 972, Porcelain Tower, Nanking, China, horiz. No. 973, The Panama Canal, horiz. No. 974, Golden Gate Bridge, San Francisco, horiz. No. 975, Sears Tower, Chicago, horiz. No. 976, Gateway Arch, St. Louis. No. 977, Alcan Highway, Alaska and Canada, horiz. No. 978, Hoover Dam, Nevada. No. 979, Empire State Building, New York.

1991, Feb. 2 Litho. *Perf. 14*

952	A95	1ch multicolored	.20	.20
953	A95	2ch multicolored	.20	.20
954	A95	3ch multicolored	.20	.20
955	A95	4ch multicolored	.20	.20
956	A95	5ch multicolored	.20	.20
957	A95	10ch multicolored	.20	.20
958	A95	50ch multicolored	.20	.20
959	A95	5nu multicolored	.80	.60
960	A95	6nu multicolored	.95	.70
961	A95	10nu multicolored	1.60	1.25
962	A95	15nu multicolored	2.50	1.75
963	A95	20nu multicolored	3.25	2.50
964	A95	25nu multicolored	4.00	3.00
965	A95	30nu multicolored	4.75	3.50
		Nos. 952-965 (14)	19.25	14.70

Souvenir Sheets

Perf. 14x13½, 13½x14

966-979 A95	25nu each	4.00	4.00

Peter Paul Rubens (1577-1640), Painter — A96

Entire paintings or different details from: 10ch, 5nu, 6nu, 10nu, No. 992, Atalanta and Meleager. 50ch, Fall of Phaethon. 1nu, No. 993, Feast of Venus Verticordia. 2nu, Achilles Slaying Hector. 3nu, No. 994, Arachne Punished by Minerva. 4nu, No. 995, Jupiter Receives Psyche on Olympus. 7nu, Venus in Vulcan's Furnace. 20nu, No. 996, Briseis Returned to Achilles. 30nu, No. 997, Mars and Rhea Sylvia. No. 998, Venus Shivering. No. 999, Ganymede and the Eagle. No. 1000, Origin of the Milky Way. No. 1001, Adonis and Venus. No. 1002, Hero and Leander. No. 1003, Fall of the Titans.

Nos. 994, 996-997, 1000-1003 are horiz.

1991, Feb. 2

980	A96	10ch multicolored	.20	.20
981	A96	50ch multicolored	.20	.20
982	A96	1nu multicolored	.20	.20
983	A96	2nu multicolored	.30	.20
984	A96	3nu multicolored	.50	.20
985	A96	4nu multicolored	.65	.20
986	A96	5nu multicolored	.80	.60
987	A96	6nu multicolored	.95	.70
988	A96	7nu multicolored	1.10	.85
989	A96	10nu multicolored	1.60	1.25
990	A96	20nu multicolored	3.25	2.50
991	A96	30nu multicolored	4.75	3.50
		Nos. 980-991 (12)	14.50	10.60

Souvenir Sheets

992-1003 A96	25nu each	4.00	4.00

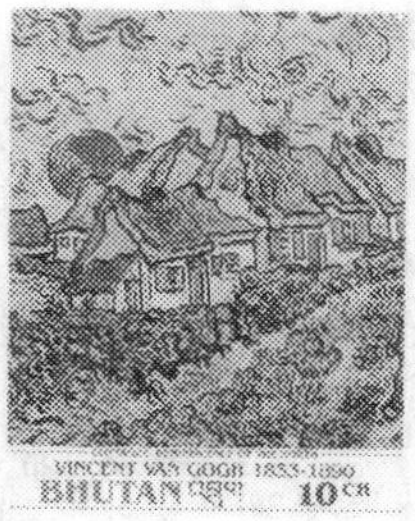

Vincent Van Gogh (1853-1890), Painter A97

Paintings: 10ch, Cottages, Reminiscence of the North. 50ch, Head of a Peasant Woman with Dark Cap. 1nu, Portrait of a Woman in Blue. 2nu, The Midwife. 8nu, Vase with Hollyhocks. 10nu, Portrait of a Man with a Skull Cap. 12nu, Agostina Segatori Sitting in the Cafe du Tambourin. 15nu, Vase with Daisies and Anemones. 18nu, Fritillaries in a Copper Vase. 20nu, Woman Sitting in the Grass. 25nu, On the Outskirts of Paris, horiz. 30nu, Chrysanthemums and Wild Flowers in a Vase.

No. 1016, Le Moulin de la Galette. No. 1017, Bowl with Sunflowers, Roses and Other Flowers, horiz. No. 1018, Poppies and Butterflies. No. 1019, Trees in the Garden of Saint-Paul Hospital. No. 1020, Le Moulin de Blute Fin. No. 1021, Le Moulin de la Galette, diff. No. 1022, Vase with Peonies. No. 1023, Vase with Zinnias. No. 1024, Fishing in the Spring, Pont de Clichy, horiz. No. 1025, Village Street in Auvers, horiz. No. 1026, Vase with Zinnias and Other Flowers, horiz. No. 2027, Vase with Red Poppies.

1991, July 22 Litho. *Perf. 13½*

1004	A97	10ch multicolored	.20	.20
1005	A97	50ch multicolored	.20	.20
1006	A97	1nu multicolored	.20	.20
1007	A97	2nu multicolored	.30	.20
1008	A97	8nu multicolored	1.25	1.00
1009	A97	10nu multicolored	1.60	1.25
1010	A97	12nu multicolored	2.00	1.50
1011	A97	15nu multicolored	2.50	1.75
1012	A97	18nu multicolored	3.00	2.25
1013	A97	20nu multicolored	3.25	2.50
1014	A97	25nu multicolored	4.00	3.00
1015	A97	30nu multicolored	4.75	3.50
		Nos. 1004-1015 (12)	23.25	17.55

Size: 76x102mm, 102x76mm

Imperf

1016-1027 A97	30nu each	4.75	4.75

History of World Cup Soccer — A98

Winning team pictures, plays or possible future site: 50ch, Uruguay, 1930. 1nu, Italy, 1934. 2nu, Italy, 1938. 3nu, Uruguay, 1950. 5nu, West Germany, 1954. 10nu, Brazil, 1958. 20nu, Brazil, 1962. 25nu, England, 1966. 29nu, Brazil, 1970. 30nu, West Germany, 1974. 31nu, Argentina, 1978. 32nu, Italy, 1982. 33nu, Argentina, 1986. 34nu, West Germany, 1990. 35nu, Los Angeles Coliseum, 1994.

Players: No. 1043, Claudio Caniggia, Argentina, vert. No. 1044, Salvatore Schillaci, Italy, vert. No. 1045, Roberto Baggio, Italy, vert. No. 1046, Peter Shilton, England, vert. No. 1047, Lothar Matthaus, West Germany, vert. No. 1048, Paul Gascoigne, England, vert.

1991, Aug. 1 Litho. *Perf. 13½*

1028	A98	50ch multicolored	.20	.20
1029	A98	1nu multicolored	.20	.20
1030	A98	2nu multicolored	.30	.20
1031	A98	3nu multicolored	.50	.20
1032	A98	5nu multicolored	.80	.60
1033	A98	10nu multicolored	1.60	1.25
1034	A98	20nu multicolored	3.25	2.50
1035	A98	25nu multicolored	4.00	3.00
1036	A98	29nu multicolored	4.75	3.50
1037	A98	30nu multicolored	4.75	3.50
1038	A98	31nu multicolored	5.00	3.75
1039	A98	32nu multicolored	5.25	4.00
1040	A98	33nu multicolored	5.50	4.00
1041	A98	34nu multicolored	5.50	4.25
1042	A98	35nu multicolored	5.75	4.25
		Nos. 1028-1042 (15)	47.35	35.40

Souvenir Sheets

1043-1048 A98	30nu each	4.75	4.75

Phila Nippon '91 — A99

1991, Nov. 16 *Perf. 13*

1049	A99	15nu multicolored	2.50	1.50

Education in Bhutan A100

1992, Mar. 5 Photo. *Perf. 13½*

1050	A100	1nu multicolored	.20	.20

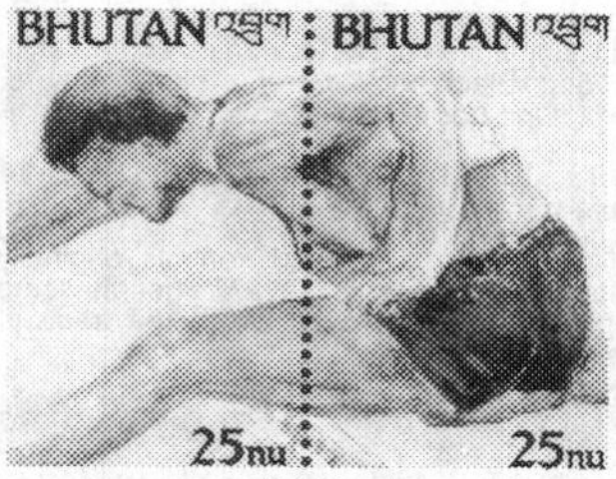

A101

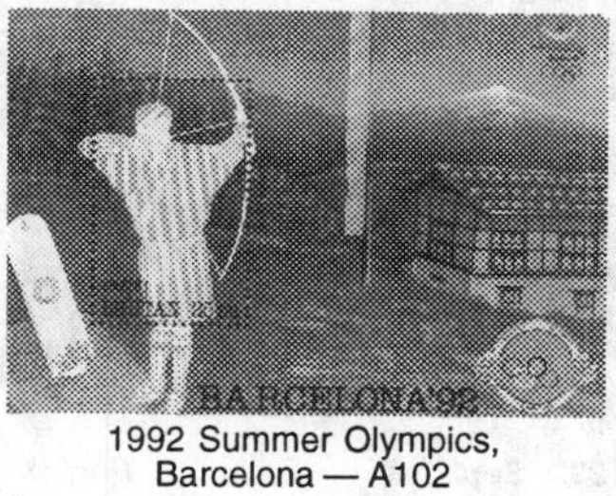

1992 Summer Olympics, Barcelona — A102

1992, July 24 Litho. *Perf. 12*

1051	A101	25nu Pair, #a.-b.	8.25	8.25

Souvenir Sheet

1052	A102	25nu Archer	4.00	4.00

German Reunification — A103

1992, Oct. 3 Litho. *Perf. 12*
1053 A103 25nu multicolored 2.00 2.00

Souvenir Sheet

1054 A103 25nu multicolored 2.00 2.00

Stamp from No. 1054 does not have white inscription or border.

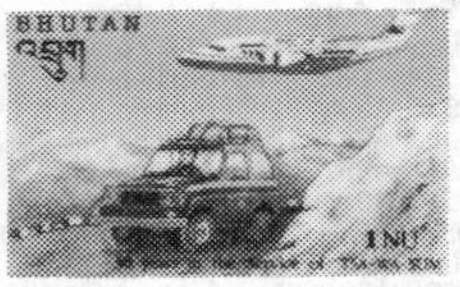

Bhutan Postal Service, 30th Anniv. A104

Designs: 1nu, Mail truck, plane. 3nu, Letter carrier approaching village. 5nu, Letter carrier emptying mail box.

1992, Oct. 9
1055 A104 1nu multicolored .20 .20
1056 A104 3nu multicolored .25 .25
1057 A104 5nu multicolored .40 .40
Nos. 1055-1057 (3) .85 .85

Environmental Protection — A105

Designs: a, 7nu, Red panda. b, 20nu, Takin. c, 15nu, Black-necked crane, blue poppy. d, 10nu, One-horned rhinoceros.

1993, July 1 Litho. *Perf. 14*
1058 A105 Sheet of 4, #b.-e.

No. 1058 was delayed from its originally scheduled release in 1992, although some copies were made available to the trade at that time.

A106

A107

1992, Sept. 18 *Perf. 12*
1059 A106 15nu Ship 1.25 1.25
1060 A106 20nu Portrait 1.60 1.60

Souvenir Sheet

1061 A106 25nu like #1060 2.00 2.00

Discovery of America, 500th anniv.
Stamp from No. 1061 does not have silver inscription or white border.

1992, Nov. 11 Litho. *Perf. 12*

Reign of King Jigme Singye Wangchuk, 20th Anniv.: a, 1nu, Man tilling field, factory. b, 5nu, Airplane. c, 10nu, House, well. d, 15nu, King.
20nu, People, flag, King, horiz.

1062 A107 Block of 4, #a.-d. 2.50 2.50

Souvenir Sheet

1063 A107 20nu multicolored 1.75 1.75

Intl. Volunteer Day — A108

Designs: a, 1.50nu, White inscription. b, 9nu, Green inscription. c, 15nu, Red inscription.

1992, Dec. 5 Litho. *Perf. 14*
1067 A108 Block of 4, #a.-c. + label 2.00 2.00

Medicinal Plants — A109

1993, Jan. 1 Litho. *Perf. 12*
1068 A109 1.50nu Meconopsis grandis prain .20 .20
1069 A109 7nu Meconopsis sp. .60 .60
1070 A109 10nu Meconopsis wallichii .80 .80
1071 A109 12nu Meconopsis horridula 1.00 1.00
1072 A109 20nu Meconopsis discigera 1.75 1.75
Nos. 1068-1072 (5) 4.35 4.35

Souvenir Sheet

1073 A109 25nu Meconopsis horridula, diff. 2.00 2.00

Miniature Sheet

Lunar New Year — A110

1993, Feb. 22 Litho. *Perf. 14*
1074 A110 25nu multicolored 2.00 2.00

No. 1074 Surcharged "TAIPEI '93" in Silver and Black

1993, Aug. 14 Litho. *Perf. 14*
1075 A110 30nu on 25nu 2.50 2.50

Door Gods — A112

Flowers — A113

1993, Dec. 17 Litho. *Perf. 12*
1091 A112 1.50nu Namtheo-Say .20 .20
1092 A112 5nu Pha-Ke-Po .50 .50
1093 A112 10nu Chen-Mi-Jang 1.00 1.00
1094 A112 15nu Yul-Khor-Sung 1.50 1.50
Nos. 1091-1094 (4) 3.20 3.20

1993, Jan. 1 *Perf. 13*

Designs: No. 1095a, 1nu, Rhododendron mucronatum. b, 1.5nu. Anemone rupicola. c, 2nu, Polemonium coeruleum. d, 2.5nu, Rosa marophylla. e, 4nu, Paraquilegia microphylla. f, 5nu, Aquilegia nivalis. g, 6nu, Geranium wallichianum. h, 7nu, Rhodendron campanulatum. i, 9nu, Viola suavis. j, 10nu, Cyananthus lobatus.
13nu, Red flower, horiz.

1095 A113 Strip of 10, #a.-j. 4.75 4.75

Souvenir Sheet

1096 A113 13nu multicolored 1.40 1.40

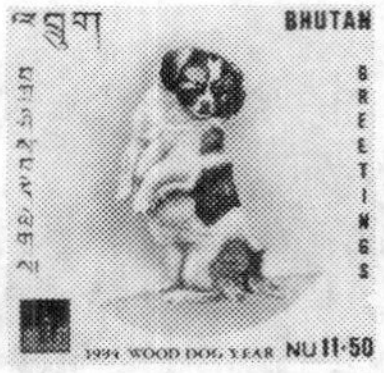

New Year 1994 (Year of the Dog) — A114

1994, Feb. 11 Litho. *Perf. 14*
1097 A114 11.50nu multicolored .80 .80

Souvenir Sheet

1098 A114 20nu like #1097 1.40 1.40

Hong Kong '94.

Stamp Cards — A115

Designs: 16nu, Tagtshang Monastery. 20nu, Map of Bhutan. Illustration reduced.

Rouletted 26 on 2 or 3 Sides

1994, Aug. 15 Litho.

Self-Adhesive

Cards of 6 + 6 labels

1099 A115 16nu #a.-f. 6.25 6.25
1100 A115 20nu #a.-f. 7.75 7.75

Individual stamps measure 70x9mm and have a card backing. Se-tenant labels inscribed "AIR MAIL."

Souvenir Sheet

First Manned Moon Landing, 25th Anniv. — A116

Designs: a, 30nu, Astronaut on moon. b, 36nu, Space shuttle, earth, moon. Illustration reduced.

1994, Nov. 11 Litho. *Perf. 14x14½*
1101 A116 Sheet of 2, #a.-b. 4.25 4.25

Nos. 1101a, 1101b have holographic images. Soaking in water may affect the holograms.

Souvenir Sheet

Victory Over Tibet-Mongol Army, 350th Anniv. — A117

Battle scene: a, Mounted officer. b, Hand to hand combat, soldiers in yellow or blue armor. c, Soldier on gray horse. d, Soldiers in red, drummer, horn player.

1994, Dec. 17 Litho. *Perf. 12½*

Granite Paper

1102 A117 15nu Sheet of 4, #a.-d. 4.00 4.00

Souvenir Sheet

Bridges A118

Designs: a, 15nu, Tower Bridge, London, cent. b, 16nu, Wangdue Bridge, Bhutan, 250th anniv.

1994, Nov. 11 *Perf. 12*
1103 A118 Sheet of 2, #a.-b. 2.00 2.00

1994 World Cup Soccer Championships, US — A119

1994, July 17 Litho. *Perf. 12*
1104 A119 15nu multicolored 1.00 1.00

Souvenir Sheet

World Tourism Year A120

Scenes of Bhutan: a, 1.50nu, Paro Valley. b, 5nu, Chorten Kora. c, 10nu, Thimphu Tshechu. d, 15nu, Wangdue Tshechu.

1995, Apr. 2 Litho. *Perf. 12*
1105 A120 Sheet of 4, #a.-d. 2.00 2.00

Miniature Sheet of 12

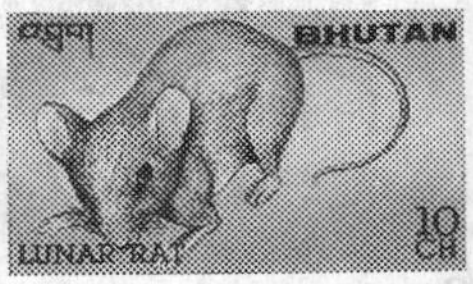

New Year 1995 (Year of the Boar) A121

Symbols of Chinese Lunar New Year: a, 10ch, Rat. b, 20ch, Ox. c, 30ch, Tiger. d, 40ch, Rabbit. e, 1nu, Dragon. f, 2nu, Snake. g, 3nu, Horse. h, 4nu, Sheep. i, 5nu, Monkey. j, 7nu, Rooster. k, 8nu, Dog. l, 9nu, Boar.
10nu, Wood Hog.

1995, Mar. 2
1106 A121 #a.-l. 2.50 2.50

Souvenir Sheet

1107 A121 10nu multicolored .65 .65

No. 1107 is a continuous design.

A122 A123

Flowers: 9nu, Pleione praecox. 10nu, Primula calderina. 16nu, Primula whitei. 18nu, Notholirion macrophyllum.

1995, May 2 Litho. *Perf. 12*

1108-1111 A122	Set of 4	3.50	3.50

1995, June 26 *Perf. 14*

UN, 50th Anniv.: a, 1.5nu, Human resources development. b, 9nu, Health & population. c, 10nu, Water & sanitation. d, 5nu, Transport & communications. e, 16nu, Forestry & environment. f, 18nu, Peace & security. g, 11.5nu, UN in Bhutan.

1112 A123	Strip of 7	4.75	4.75

Miniature Sheet of 6

Singapore '95 — A124

Birds: No. 1113a, 1nu, Himalayan pied kingfisher. b, 2nu, Blyth's tragopan. c, 3nu, Long-tailed minivet. d, 10nu, Red junglefowl. e, 15nu, Black-capped sibia. f, 20nu, Red-billed chough.
No. 1114, Black-neck crane.

1995, June 2 Litho. *Perf. 12*

1113 A124	#a.-f. + 3 labels	3.50	3.50

Souvenir Sheet

1114 A124	20nu multicolored	1.40	1.40

Traditional Crafts — A125

Designs: 1nu, Drying parchment. 2nu, Making tapestry. 3nu, Restoring archaeological finds. 10nu, Weaving textiles. 15nu, Sewing garments. No. 1120, 20nu, Carving wooden vessels.
No. 1121, Mosaic.

1995, Aug. 15 Litho. *Perf. 14*

1115-1120 A125	Set of 6	2.50	2.50

Souvenir Sheet

1121 A125	20nu multicolored	1.40	1.40

New Year 1996 (Year of the Rat) — A126

Designs: a, Monkey. b, Rat, fire. c, Dragon.

1996, Jan. 1 Litho. *Perf. 14*

1122 A126	10nu Sheet of 3, #a.-c.	2.00	2.00

Butterflies A127

Designs: a, 2nu, Blue pansy. b, 3nu, Blue peacock. c, 5nu, Great Mormon. d, 10nu, Frit-illary. e, 15nu, Blue duke. f, 25nu, Brown Gorgon.
No. 1124, Xanthomelas. No. 1124A, Fivebar swordtail.

1996, May 2 Litho. *Perf. 14*

1123 A127	Sheet of 6, #a.-f.	4.00	4.00

Souvenir Sheets

1124-1124A A127	30nu each	2.00	2.00

1996 Summer Olympic Games, Atlanta — A128

5nu, Silver 300n coin, soccer. 7nu, Silver 300n coin, basketball. 10nu, Gold 5s coin, judo.
15nu, Archery.

1996, June 15 Litho. *Perf. 14*

1125-1127 A128	Set of 3	1.50	1.50

Souvenir Sheet

1128 A128	15nu multicolored	1.00	1.00

Olymphilex '96.

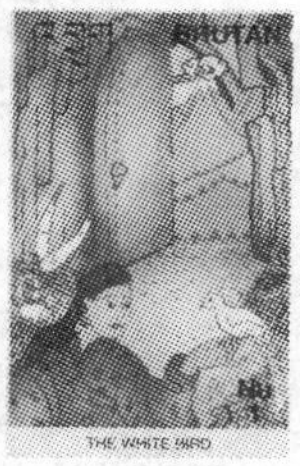

Folktales — A129

Designs: a, 1nu, The White Bird. b, 2nu, Sing Sing Lhamo and the Moon. c, 3nu, The Hoopoe. d, 5nu, The Cloud Fairies. e, 10nu, The Three Wishes. f, 20nu, The Abominable Snowman.

1996, Apr. 15 *Perf. 12*

1129 A129	Sheet of 6, #a.-f.	3.00	3.00

Souvenir Sheet

1130 A129	25nu like #1129d	1.75	1.75

Locomotives — A130

No. 1131: a, 0-6-4 Tank engine (Chile). b, First Pacific locomotive in Europe (France). c, 4-6-0 Passenger engine (Norway). d, Atlantic type express (Germany). e, 4-Cylinder 4-6-0 express (Belgium). f, Standard type "4" diesel-electric (England).
No. 1132: a, Standard 0-6-0 Goods engine (India). b, Main-line 1,900 horsepower diesel-electric (Finland). c, 0-8-0 Shunting tank engine (Russia). d, Alco "PA-1" diesel-electric (US). e, "C11" Class 2-6-4 branch passenger tank engine (Japan). f, "Settebello" deluxe high-speed electric train (Italy).
No. 1133, Class "KD" 0-6-0 Goods locomotive, 1900 (Sweden). No. 1134, Shinkansen "New Railway" series 200 (Japan).

1996, Nov. 25 Litho. *Perf. 14*

1131-1132 A130	20nu Sheets of 6, #a.-f., each	8.00	8.00

Souvenir Sheets

1133-1134 A130	70nu each	4.75	4.75

Penny Black — A131

Litho. & Embossed

1996, Dec. 17 *Perf. 13½*

1135 A131	140nu black & gold	9.50	9.50

A132 A133

Winter Olympic Medalists: 10nu, Vegard Ulvang, cross-country skiing, 1992. 15nu, Kristi Yamaguchi, figure skating, 1992. 25nu, Markus Wasmeier, giant slalom, 1994. 30nu, Georg Hackl, luge, 1992.
No. 1140: a, Andreas Ostler, 2-man bobsled, 1952. b, Wolfgang Hoppe, 4-man bobsled, 1984. c, Stein Eriksen, giant slalom, 1952. d, Alberto Tomba, giant slalom, 1988.
No. 1141, Henri Oreiller, downhill, 1948. No. 1142, Eduard Scherrer, 4-man bobsled, 1924.

1997, Jan. 1 *Perf. 14*

1136-1139 A132	Set of 4	5.50	5.50
1140 A132	15nu Strip of 4, #a.-d.	4.00	4.00

Souvenir Sheets

1141-1142 A132	70nu each	4.50	4.50

No. 1140 was issued in sheets of 8 stamps.

1997, Jan. 15 *Perf. 13*

Insects and Arachnids: a, 1ch, Apis laboriosa smith. b, 2ch, Neptunides polychromus. c, 3ch, Conocephalus maculctus. d, 4ch, Blattidae. e, 5ch, Dytiscus marginalis. f, 10ch, Dynastes hercules. g, 15ch, Hippodamia. h, 20ch, Sarcophaga haemorrhoidalis. i, 25ch, Lucanus cervus. j, 30ch, Caterpillar. k, 35ch, Lycia hirtaria. l, 40ch, Clytarlus pennatus. m, 45ch, Ephemera denica. n, 50ch, Gryllus campestris. o, 60ch, Deilephila elpenor. p, 65ch, Gerris. q, 70ch, Agrion splendens. r, 80ch, Tachyta nana. s, 90ch, Eurydema pulchra. t, 1nu, Hadrurus hirsutus. u, 1.50nu, Vespa germanica. v, 2nu, Pyrops. w, 2.50nu, Mantis religiosa. x, 3nu, Araneus diadematus. y, 3.50nu, Atrophaneura.
15nu, Melolontha.

1143 A133	Sheet of 25, #a.-y.	1.40	1.40

Souvenir Sheet

1144 A133	15nu multicolored	1.00	1.00

Hong Kong '97 — A134

Wildlife: a, Thalarctos maritiumus. b, Phascolarctos cinereus. c, Selenarcios thibelanus. d, Ailurus fulgens.
20nu, Ailuropoda melanoleuca.

1997, Feb. 1 Litho. *Perf. 14*

1145 A134	10nu Sheet of 4, #a.-d.	2.75	2.75

Souvenir Sheet

1146 A134	20nu multicolored	1.40	1.40

Signs of the Chinese Zodiac — A135

No. 1147: a, 1ch, Mouse. b, 2ch, Ox. c, 3ch, Tiger. d, 4ch, Rabbit. e, 5nu, Dragon. f, 6nu, Snake. g, 7nu, Horse. h, 8nu, Sheep. i, 90ch, Monkey. j, 10nu, Rooster. k, 11nu, Dog. l, 12nu, Pig.
20nu, Ox, diff.

1997, Feb. 8 Litho. *Perf. 14*

1147 A135	Sheet of 12, #a.-l. + label	4.00	4.00

Souvenir Sheet

1148 A135	20nu multicolored	1.40	1.40

Fauna A136

Cuon alpinus: No. 1149: a, Adult, hind legs off ground. b, Adult walking right. c, Mother nursing young. d, Two seated.
Endangered species: No. 1150: a, Lynx. b, Red panda. c, Takin. d, Musk deer. e, Snow leopard. f, Golden langur. g, Tiger. h, Muntjac. i, Marmot.
No. 1151, Pseudois nayaur. No. 1152, Ursus thibetanus.

1997, Apr. 24

1149 A136	10nu Block or strip of 4, #a.-d.	2.75	2.75
1150 A136	10nu Sheet of 9, #a.-i.	6.00	6.00

Souvenir Sheets

1151-1152 A136	70nu each	4.75	4.75

World Wildlife Fund (No. 1149).
No. 1149 issued in sheets of 12 stamps.

UNESCO, 50th Anniv. A137

No. 1153: a, Mount Hungshan, China. b, Mausoleum of first Qin Emperor, China. c, Imperial Bronze Dragon, China. d, Tikal Natl. Park, Guatemala. e, Evora, Portugal. f, Shirakami-Sanchi, Japan. g, Paris, France. h, Valley Below the Falls, Plitvice Lakes Natl. Park, Croatia.
Sites in Germany: No. 1154: a, Cathedral, Bamberg. b, Bamberg. c, St. Michael's Church, Hildesheim. d, Potsdam Palace. e, Potsdam Church. f, Lubeck. g, Quedlinberg. h, Benedictine Church, Lorsch.
No. 1155, Goslar, Germany, horiz. No. 1156, Cathedral, Comenzada, Portugal, horiz.

1997, May 15

Sheets of 8 + Label

1153 A137	10nu #a.-h.	5.50	5.50
1154 A137	15nu #a.-h.	8.00	8.00

Souvenir Sheets

1155-1156 A137	60nu each	4.00	4.00

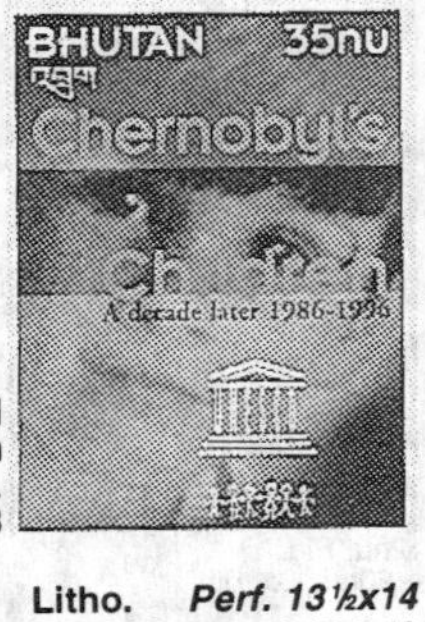

Chernobyl Disaster, 10th Anniv.
A138

1997, May 2 Litho. *Perf. 13½x14*

1157 A138 35nu UNESCO 2.40 2.40

Dogs — A139

Cats — A140

Designs: 10nu, Dalmatian. 15nu, Siberian husky. 20nu, Saluki. 25nu, Shar pei.

No. 1162: a, Dandie Dinmont terrier. b, Chinese crested. c, Norwich terrier. d, Basset hound. e, Cardigan welsh corgi. f, French bulldog.

60nu, Hovawart.

1997, July 15 *Perf. 14*

1158-1161 A139 Set of 4 4.75 4.75
1162 A139 20nu Sheet of 6, #a.-f. 8.00 8.00

Souvenir Sheet

1163 A139 60nu multicolored 4.00 4.00

1997, July 15

Designs: 10nu, Turkish angora. 15nu, Oriental shorthair. 20nu, British shorthair. 25nu, Burmese.

No. 1168: a, Japanese bobtail. b, Ceylon. c, Exotic. d, Rex. e, Ragdoll. f, Russian blue.

60nu, Tonkinese.

1164-1167 A140 Set of 4 4.75 4.75
1168 A140 15nu Sheet of 6, #a.-f. 6.00 6.00

Souvenir Sheet

1169 A140 60nu multicolored 4.25 4.25

1998 World Cup Soccer, France
A141

English players: 5nu, Pearce. 10nu, Gascoigne. 15nu, Beckham. 20nu, McManaman. 25nu, Adams. 30nu, Ince.

World Cup captains, horiz.: No. 1176: a, Maradona, Argentina, 1986. b, Alberto, Brazil, 1970. c, Dunga, Brazil, 1994. d, Moore, England, 1966. e, Fritzwalter, Germany, 1954. f, Matthaus, Germany, 1990. g, Beckenbauer, Germany, 1974. h, Passarella, Argentina, 1978.

Winning teams, horiz.: No. 1177: a, Italy, 1938. b, W. Germany, 1954. c, Uruguay, 1958. d, England, 1966. e, Argentina, 1978. f, Brazil, 1962. g, Italy, 1934. h, Brazil, 1970. i, Uruguay, 1930.

No. 1178, Philippe Albert, Belgium. No. 1179, Salvatore (Toto) Schillaci, Italy, horiz.

Perf. 13½x14, 14x13½

1997, Oct. 9 Litho.

1170-1175 A141 Set of 6 7.00 7.00

Sheets of 8 or 9

1176 A141 10nu #a.-h. + label 5.50 5.50
1177 A141 10nu #a.-i. 6.00 6.00

Souvenir Sheets

1178-1179 A141 35nu each 3.75 3.75

Friendship Between India and Bhutan
A142

3nu, Jawaharlal Nehru, King Jigme Dorji Wangchuk. 10nu, Rajiv Gandhi, King Jigme Singye Wangchuk.

20nu, Indian Pres. R. V. Venkataraman, King Jigme Singye Wangchuk.

1998 Litho. *Perf. 13x13½*

1180 A142 3nu multicolored .20 .20
1181 A142 10nu multicolored .80 .80

Souvenir Sheet

1182 A142 20nu multicolored 1.25 1.25

No. 1182 contains one 76x35mm stamp.

A143

A144

Indepex '97: No. 1183: a, 3nu, Buddha seated with legs crossed. b, 15nu, Buddha seated with legs down. c, 7nu, Gandhi with hands folded. d, 10nu, Gandhi.

No. 1184, Buddha. No. 1185, Gandhi holding staff.

1998 *Perf. 13½x13*

1183 A143 Sheet of 4, #a.-d. 2.10 2.10

Souvenir Sheets

1184-1185 A143 15nu each 1.25 1.25

India's independence, 50th anniv.

1998, Feb. 28 Litho. *Perf. 14*

New Year 1998 (Year of the Tiger): 3nu, Stylized tiger walking right.

Tigers: No. 1187: a, 5nu, Lying down. b, 15nu, Adult walking forward. c, 17nu, Cub walking over rocks.

20nu, Adult up close.

1186 A144 3nu multicolored .20 .20
1187 A144 Sheet of 4, #a.-c., #1186 2.40 2.40

Souvenir Sheet

1188 A144 20nu multicolored 1.25 1.25

WHO, 50th Anniv.
A145

1998, Apr. 7 Litho. *Perf. 13½*

1189 A145 3nu multicolored .20 .20
1190 A145 10nu multicolored .60 .60

Souvenir Sheet

Perf. 14

1191 A145 15nu Mother, child .90 .90

Safe Motherhood. No. 1191 contains one 35x35mm stamp.

Mother Teresa (1910-97)
A146

No. 1192: a, Portrait (shown). b, With Princess Diana. c, Holding child. d, Holding starving infant. e, Seated among nuns. f, Looking down at sick. g, With hands folded in prayer. h, With Pope John Paul II. i, Portrait, diff.

No. 1193: a, like #1192b. b, like #1192h.

1998, May 25 Litho. *Perf. 13½*

1192 A146 10nu Sheet of 9, #a.-i. 5.50 5.50

Souvenir Sheet

1193 A146 25nu Sheet of 2, #a.-b. 3.00 3.00

No. 1193 contains two 38x43mm stamps.

Birds — A147

No. 1194: a, 10ch, Red-billed chough. b, 30ch, Great hornbill. c, 50ch, Singing lark. d, 70ch, Chestnut-flanked white-eye. e, 90ch, Magpie-robin. f, 1nu, Mrs. Gould's sunbird. g, 2nu, Tailorbird. h, 3nu, Duck. i, 5nu, Spotted cuckoo. j, 7nu, Gold crest. k, 9nu, Common mynah. l, 10nu, Green cochoa.

15nu, Turtle dove.

1998, July 28 Litho. *Perf. 13*

1194 A147 Sheet of 12, #a.-l. 2.50 2.50

Souvenir Sheet

1195 A147 15nu multicolored .90 .90

No. 1195 contains one 40x30mm stamp.

New Year 1999 (Year of the Rabbit)
A148

1999, Jan. 1 Litho. *Perf. 13*

1196 A148 4nu White rabbit .25 .25
1197 A148 15nu Brown rabbit .90 .90

Souvenir Sheet

Perf. 13½

1198 A148 20nu Rabbit facing forward 1.25 1.25

No. 1198 contains one 35x35mm stamp.

King Jigme Singye Wangchuk, 25th Anniv. of Coronation — A149

Various portraits, background color - No. 1199: a, Blue. b, Yellow. c, Orange. d, Green.

No. 1200, Bright pink background.

1999, June 2 Litho. *Perf. 12¼*

1199 A149 25nu Sheet of 4, #a.-d. 5.00 5.00

Souvenir Sheet

1200 A149 25nu multicolored 1.25 1.25

Trains
A150

Designs: 5nu, Early German steam. 10nu, EID 711 electric. 20nu, Steam engine. 30nu, Trans Europe Express, Germany.

No. 1205: a, Bullet train, Japan, 1964. b, 2-D-2 Class 26, South Africa, 1953. c, Super Chief, US, 1946. d, Magleus Magnet, Japan, 1991. e, The Flying Scotsman, UK, 1922. f, Kodama Train, Japan, 1958. g, Blue Train, South Africa, 1969. h, Inter-City, Germany, 1960. i, High Speed ET 403, Germany, 1973. j, US Standard 4-4-0, 1855. k, Bayer Garratt, South Africa, 1954. l, Settebello train, Italy, 1953.

No. 1206: a, Diesel-electric, France. b, 6-4-4-6 Pennsylvania RR, US. c, 2-8-2 Steam, Germany. d, Amtrak, US. e, GS&W 2-2-2, Britain. f, Class P steam, Denmark. g, French electric. h, First Japanese locomotive. i, 2-8-2 Germany.

No. 1207: a, Pacific Class 01, Germany. b, Neptune Express, Germany. c, 4-4-0 Steam, Britain. d, Shovelnose streamliner, US. e, German electric. f, Early steam, Germany. g, Union Pacific, US. h, Borsig steam, Germany, 1881. i, Borsig 4-6-4, Germany.

No. 1208, Union Pacific electric locomotive E2 streamliner, US. No. 1209, Great Northern diesel electric streamliner, US.

1999, July 21 *Perf. 14*

1201-1204 A150 Set of 4 3.25 3.25

Sheets of 12 and 9

1205 A150 10nu Sheet of 12, #a.-l. 6.00 6.00
1206-1207 A150 15nu #a.-i., each 6.75 6.75

Souvenir Sheets

1208-1209 A150 80nu each 4.00 4.00

Paintings by Hokusai (1760-1849)
A151

Details or entire paintings - No. 1210: a, Suspension Bridge Between Hida and Etchu. b, Drawings of Women (partially nude). c, Exotic Beauty. d, The Poet Nakamaro in China. e, Drawings of Women (clothed). f, Chinese Poet in Snow.

No. 1211: a, Festive Dancers (with umbrella). b, Drawings of Women (holding book). c, Festive Dancers (man wearing checked pattern). d, Festive Dancers (person wearing black outfit). e, Drawings of Women (holding baby). f, Festive Dancers (woman with scarf tied under chin).

No. 1212, horiz.: a, Mount Fuji Seen Above Mist on the Tama River. b, Mount Fuji Seen from Shichirigahama. c, Sea Life (turtle). d, Sea Life (fish). e, Mount Fuji Reflected in a Lake. f, Mount Fuji Seen Through the Piers of Mannenbashi.

No. 1213, The Lotus Pedestal. No. 1214, Kushunoki Masashige. No. 1215, Peasants Leading Oxen.

1999, July 27 *Perf. 13½x14, 14x13½*

Sheets of 6

1210-1212 A151 15nu #a.-f., each 4.50 4.50

Souvenir Sheet

1213-1215 A151 80nu each 4.00 4.00

Souvenir Sheet

IBRA '99, Nuremberg
A152

a, 35nu, City view. b, 40nu, Show emblem.

1999, Apr. 27 Litho. *Perf. 13¾*

1216 A152 Sheet of 2, #a.-b. 3.50 3.50

Prehistoric Animals — A153

No. 1217: a, Pterodactylus, Brachiosaurus. b, Pteranodon. c, Anurognathus, Tyrannosaurus. d, Brachiosaurus. e, Corythosaurus. f, Iguanodon. g, Lesothosaurus. h, Allosaurus. i, Velociraptor. j, Triceratops. k, Stegosaurus. l, Compsognatus.

No. 1218: a, Tyrannosaurus, black inscriptions b, Dimorphodon. c, Diplodocus. d, Pterodaustro. e, Tyrannosaurus, white inscriptions. f, Edmontosaurus. g, Apatosaurus. h, Deinonychus. i, Hypsilophodon. j, Oviraptor. k, Stegosaurus, diff. l, Triceratops, diff.

No. 1219: a, Moeritherium. b, Platybelodon. c, Wooly mammoth. d, African elephant. e, Deinonychus, diff. f, Dimorphodon, diff. g, Archaeopteryx. h, Ring-necked pheasant.

No. 1220, Triceratops, vert. No. 1221, Pteranodon. No. 1222, Hoatzin, vert. No. 1223, Ichthyosaur, vert.

1999, Aug. 10 Litho. *Perf. 14*

Sheets of 12 and 8

1217-1218 A153 10nu a.-l., each 5.50 5.50
1219 A153 20nu a.-h. 7.50 7.50

Souvenir Sheets

1220-1223 A153 80nu each 3.75 3.75

No. 1221 is incorrectly inscribed "Triceratops" instead of "Pteranodon," and No. 1223 is "Present Day Dolphin" instead of "Ichthysoaur."

Fauna — A154

Designs: a, Musk deer. b, Takin. c, Blue sheep. d, Yak. e, Goral.

1999, Aug. 21 Litho. *Perf. 12¾*

1224 A154 20nu Sheet of 5, #a.-e. + label 4.75 4.75

Birds A155

No. 1225: a, Chestnut-bellied chlorophonia. b, Yellow-faced Amazon parrot. c, White ibis. d, Caique. e, Green jay. f, Tufted coquette. g, Common troupial. h, Purple gallinule. i, Copper-rumped hummingbird.

No. 1226: a, Common egret. b, Rufous-browed peppershrike. c, Glittering-throated emerald. d, Great kiskadee. e, Cuban green woodpecker. f, Scarlet ibis. g, Belted kingfisher. h, Barred antshrike. i, Caribbean parakeet.

No. 1227, vert.: a, Rufous-tailed jacamar. b, Scarlet macaw. c, Channel-billed toucan. d, Tricolored heron. e, St. Vincent parrot. f, Blue-crowned motmot. g, Horned screamer. h, Black-billed plover. i, Common meadowlark.

No. 1228, Toco toucan. No. 1229, Red-billed scythebill, vert. No. 1230, Military macaws, vert.

1999, Oct. 17 Litho. *Perf. 14*

Sheets of 9, #a.-i.

1225-1227 A155 15nu each 6.25 6.25

Souvenir Sheets

1228-1230 A155 80nu each 3.75 3.75

Butterflies — A156

Designs: 5nu, Sara orange tip. 10nu, Pipevine swallowtail. 15nu, Longwings. No. 1234, 20nu, Viceroy. 25nu, Silver-spotted skipper, vert. 30nu, Great spangled fritillary, vert. 35nu, Little copper.

No. 1238: a, Frosted skipper. b, Fiery skipper. c, Banded hairstreak. d, Clouded sulphur. e, Milberts tortoise shell. f, Eastern tailed blue.

No. 1239: a, Zebra swallowtail. b, Colorado hairstreak. c, Pink-edged sulphur. d, Fairy yellow. e, Red-spotted purple. f, Aphrodite.

No. 1240, Checkered white. No. 1241, Gray hairstreak, vert. No. 1242, Gulf fritillary, vert. No. 1243, Monarch, vert.

1999, Oct. 4 Litho. *Perf. 14*

1231-1237 A156 Set of 7 6.50 6.50

Sheets of 6

1238-1239 A156 20nu #a.-f., each 5.50 5.50

Souvenir Sheets

1240-1243 A156 80nu each 3.75 3.75

First Manned Moon Landing, 30th Anniv. — A157

No. 1244: a, Neil A. Armstrong (with name patch). b, Michael Collins. c, Edwin E. Aldrin, Jr. d, Command and service modules. e, Lunar module. f, Aldrin on Moon.

No. 1245: a, X-15 rocket. b, Gemini 8. c, Apollo 11 Saturn V rocket. d, Command and service modules (docked with lunar module). e, Lunar module (docked with command and service modules). f, Aldrin on lunar module ladder.

No. 1246: a, Yuri Gagarin. b, Alan B. Shepard, Jr. c, John H. Glenn, Jr. d, Valentina Tereshkova. e, Edward H. White II. f, Armstrong (no name patch).

No. 1247, Armstrong, diff. No. 1248, Apollo 11 splashdown. No. 1249, Gemini 8 docked with Agena rocket, horiz.

1999, Nov. 1 Litho. *Perf. 14*

Sheets of 6

1244-1246 A157 20nu #a.-f., each 5.50 5.50

Souvenir Sheets

1247-1249 A157 80nu each 3.75 3.75

No. 1249 contains one 57x42mm stamp.

Cats, Horses, Dogs A158

Cats: No. 1250, 5nu, Tortoiseshell. No. 1251, 5nu, Woman and cat. 10nu, Chinchilla Golden Longhair.

No. 1253: a, Russian Blue. b, Birman. c, Devon Rex. d, Pewter Longhair. e, Bombay. f, Sorrel Somali. g, Red Tabby Manx. h, Blue Smoke Longhair. i, Oriental Tabby Shorthair.

70nu, Norwegian Shorthair.

1999, Nov. 15 Litho. *Perf. 14*

1250-1252 A158 Set of 3 .90 .90

Sheet of 9

1253 A158 12nu #a.-i. 5.00 5.00

Souvenir Sheet

1254 A158 70nu multicolored 3.25 3.25

1999, Nov. 15

Horses: 15nu, Lipizzaner. 20nu, Andalusian.

No. 1257: a, Przewalski. b, Shetland. c, Dutch Gelderlander. d, Shire. e, Arabian. f, Boulonnais. g, Falabella. h, Orlov Trotter. i, Suffolk Punch.

70nu, Connemara.

1255-1256 A158 Set of 2 1.60 1.60

Sheet of 9

1257 A158 12nu #a.-i. 5.00 5.00

Souvenir Sheet

1258 A158 70nu multicolored 3.25 3.25

1999, Nov. 15

Dogs: 25nu, Weimaraner. 30nu, German Shepherd.

No. 1261: a, Australian Silky Terrier. b, Samoyed. c, Basset Bleu de Gascogne. d, Bernese Mountain Dog. e, Pug. f, Bergamasco. g, Basenji. h, Wetterhoun. i, Drever.

70nu, Labrador Retriever.

1259-1260 A158 Set of 2 1.60 1.60

Sheet of 9

1261 A158 12nu #a.-i. 5.00 5.00

Souvenir Sheet

1262 A158 70nu multicolored 3.25 3.25

Birds, Mushrooms A159

No. 1263: a, Crested lark. b, Ferruginous duck. c, Blood pheasant. d, Laughing thrush. e, Golden eagle. f, Siberian rubythroat.

No. 1264: a, Red-crested pochard. b, Satyr tragopan. c, Lammergeier vulture. d, Kalij pheasant. e, Great Indian hornbill. f, Stork.

No. 1265, a, Rufous-necked hornbill. b, Drongo. c, Himalayan monal pheasant. d, Black-necked crane. e, Little green bee-eater. f, Ibis.

No. 1266, Siberian rubythroat. No. 1267, Black-naped monarch. No. 1268, Mountain peacock pheasant.

1999, Dec. 17 *Perf. 13¾*

Sheets of 6

1263-1265 A159 20nu #a.-f., each 5.50 5.50

Souvenir Sheets

1266-1268 A159 100nu each 4.50 4.50

1999, Dec. 17

No. 1269: a, Boletus frostii. b, Morchella estculenta. c, Hypomyces lactifuorum. d, Polyporus auricularius. e, Cantahrellus lateritius. f, Volvariella pusilla.

No. 1270: a, Microglossum rufum. b, Lactarius hygrophoroides. c, Lactarius speciousus complex. d, Calostoma cinnabarina. e, Clitocybe clavipes. f, Microstoma floccosa.

No. 1271: a, Mutinus elegans. b, Pholiota squarrosoides. c, Coprinus quadrifudus. d, Clavulinopsis fusiformis. e, Spathularia velutipes. f, Ganoderma lucidum.

No. 1272, Pholiota aurivella. No. 1273, Ramaria grandis. No. 1274, Oudemansiella lucidum.

Sheets of 6

1269-1271 A159 20nu #a.-f., each 5.50 5.50

Souvenir Sheets

1272-1274 A159 100nu each 4.50 4.50

SEMI-POSTAL STAMPS

Nos. 10-12 Surcharged

+ 50 ch

Perf. 14x14½

1964, Mar. Litho. Unwmk.

B1 A3 33ch + 50ch multi 2.00 2.00
B2 A3 70ch + 50ch multi 2.00 2.00
B3 A3 1.30nu + 50ch multi 2.00 2.00
Nos. B1-B3 (3) 6.00 6.00

9th Winter Olympic Games, Innsbruck, Jan. 29-Feb. 9, 1964.

Olympic Games Type of Regular Issue, 1964
Souvenir Sheet

1964, Oct. 10 *Perf. 13½, Imperf.*

B4 A6 Sheet of 2 7.50 7.50
a. 1nu + 50ch Archery .90 .90
b. 2nu + 50ch Soccer 2.00 2.00

18th Olympic Games, Tokyo, Oct. 10-25.

Nos. 97, 97C, 97E Surcharged

FLOOD RELIEF

+ 5Ch

1968, Dec. 7 Photo. *Perf. 13½*

B5 A14n 5ch +5ch .20 .20
B6 A14n 80ch +25ch .35 .35
B7 A14n 2nu +50ch .85 .85
Nos. B5-B7 (3) 1.40 1.40

AIR POST STAMPS

Nos. 19-21, 38-39, 63-67 Ovptd.

a

b

Perfs. as Before

1967, Jan. 10 Litho.

Overprint "a"

C1 A5	33ch on #19	.20	.20
C2 A5	70ch on #20	.30	.30
C3 A5	1nu on #21	.40	.40
C4 A8	50ch on #38	.20	.20
C5 A8	75ch on #39	.30	.30
C6 A11	1.50nu on #63	.65	.65
C7 A11	2nu on #64	.85	.85
C8 A11	3nu on #65	1.25	1.25
C9 A11	4nu on #66	1.75	1.75
C10 A11	5nu on #67	2.25	2.25

Overprint "b"

C11 A5	33ch on #19	.20	.20
C12 A5	70ch on #20	.30	.30
C13 A5	1nu on #21	.40	.40
C14 A8	50ch on #38	.20	.20
C15 A8	75ch on #39	.30	.30
C16 A11	1.50nu on #63	.65	.65
C17 A11	2nu on #64	.85	.85
C18 A11	3nu on #65	1.25	1.25
C19 A11	4nu on #66	1.75	1.75
C20 A11	5nu on #67	2.25	2.25
Nos. C1-C20 (20)		16.30	16.30

UN Type of Regular Issue

Bhutan Flag and: 2.50nu, UN Headquarters, NYC. 5nu, Security Council Chamber and mural by Per Krohg. 6nu, General Assembly Hall.

1971, Sept. 21 Photo. *Perf. 13½*

C21 A16 2.50nu silver & multi .50 .50
C22 A16 5nu silver & multi .95 .95
C23 A16 6nu silver & multi 1.10 1.10
Nos. C21-C23 (3) 2.55 2.55

Bhutan's admission to the United Nations. Exist imperf.

Nos. C21-C23 Overprinted in Gold: "UNHCR / UNRWA / 1971" like Nos. 145-145C

1971, Dec. 23 Litho. *Perf. 13½*

C24 A16 2.50nu silver & multi .70 .70
C25 A16 5nu silver & multi 1.40 1.40
C26 A16 6nu silver & multi 1.90 1.90
Nos. C24-C26 (3) 4.00 4.00

World Refugee Year. Exist imperf.

UPU Types of 1974

UPU Emblem, Carrier Pigeon and: 1nu, Mail runner and jeep. 1.40nu, 10nu, Old and new locomotives. 2nu, Old biplane and jet.

1974, Oct. 9 Litho. *Perf. 14½*

C27 A19 1nu salmon & multi .25 .25
C28 A20 1.40nu lilac & multi .40 .40
C29 A20 2nu multicolored .50 .50
Nos. C27-C29 (3) 1.15 1.15

Souvenir Sheet
Perf. 13

C30	A20	10nu lilac & multi	2.75	2.75

Cent. of the UPU. Nos. C27-C29 were issued in sheets of 50 and sheets of 5 plus label with multicolored margin. Exist imperf.

Issues of 1968-1974 Surcharged 25ch and Bars

1978 — Perf. & Printing as Before

C31	A16	25ch on 5nu, #C22	1.25	1.25
C32	A16	25ch on 6nu, #C23	1.25	1.25
C33	A20	25ch on 1.40nu, #C28	1.25	1.25
C34	A20	25ch on 2nu, #C29	1.25	1.25
C35	A14j	25ch on 4nu, #94L	1.25	1.25
C36	A14j	25ch on 10nu, #94N	1.25	1.25
C37	A17k	25ch on 5nu, #154F	1.25	1.25
C38	A17k	25ch on 6nu, #154G	1.25	1.25
		Nos. C31-C38 (8)	10.00	10.00

BOLIVIA

bə-'li-vē-ə

LOCATION — Central South America, separated from the Pacific Ocean by Chile and Peru.
GOVT. — Republic
AREA — 424,165 sq. mi.
POP. — 7,949,933 (1998 est.)
CAPITAL — Sucre (La Paz is the actual seat of government).

100 Centavos = 1 Boliviano
100 Centavos = 1 Peso Boliviano (1963)
100 Centavos = 1 Boliviano (1987)

Catalogue values for unused stamps in this country are for Never Hinged items, beginning with Scott 308 in the regular postage section, Scott C112 in the airpost section, Scott RA5 in the postal tax section, and Scott RAC1 in airpost postal tax section.

On Feb. 21, 1863, the Bolivian Government decreed contracts for carrying the mails should be let to the highest bidder, the service to commence on the day the bid was accepted, and stamps used for the payment of postage. On Mar. 18, the contract was awarded to Sr. Justiniano Garcia and was in effect until Apr. 29, 1863, when it was rescinded. Stamps in the form illustrated above were prepared in denominations of ½, 1, 2 and 4 reales. All values exist in black and in blue. The blue are twice as scarce as the black. Value, black, $75 each.

It is said that used copies exist on covers, but the authenticity of these covers remains to be established.

Condor — A1

A2

A3

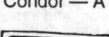

72 varieties of each of the 5c, 78 varieties of the 10c, 30 varieties of each of the 50c and 100c.

The plate of the 5c stamps was entirely reengraved 4 times and retouched at least 6 times. Various states of the plate have distinguishing characteristics, each of which is typical of most, though not all the stamps in a sheet. These characteristics (usually termed types) are found in the shading lines at the right side of the globe. a, vertical and diagonal lines. b, diagonal lines only. c, diagonal and horizontal with traces of vertical lines. d, diagonal and horizontal lines. e, horizontal lines only. f, no lines except the curved ones forming the outlines of the globe.

1867-68 — Unwmk. — Engr. — *Imperf.*

1	A1	5c yel grn, thin paper (a, b)	3.50	*4.50*
a.		5c blue green (a)	4.50	*14.00*
b.		5c deep green (a)	4.50	*14.00*
c.		5c ol grn, thick paper (a)	35.00	25.00
d.		5c yel grn, thick paper (a)	80.00	80.00
e.		5c yel grn, thick paper (b)	80.00	80.00
f.		5c blue green (b)	4.50	*14.00*
2	A1	5c green (d)	4.00	*7.00*
a.		5c green (c)	4.00	*7.00*
b.		5c green (e)	4.00	*7.00*
c.		5c green (f)	4.00	*7.00*
3	A1	5c vio ('68)	190.00	140.00
a.		5c rose lilac ('68)	190.00	140.00
		Revenue cancel		28.00
4	A3	10c brown	225.00	140.00
5	A2	50c orange	20.00	
6	A2	50c blue ('68)	*325.00*	
a.		50c dark blue ('68)	*325.00*	
		Revenue cancel		28.00
7	A3	100c blue	60.00	
		Revenue cancel		15.00
8	A3	100c green ('68)	140.00	
a.		100c pale blue grn ('68)	140.00	
		Revenue cancel		28.00

Used values are for postally canceled copies. Pen cancellations usually indicate that the stamps have been used fiscally and such stamps sell for about one-fifth as much as those with postal cancellations.

The 500c is an essay.

Reprints of Nos. 3,4, 6 and 8 are common. Value, $10 each. Reprints of Nos. 2 and 5 are scarcer. Value, $25 each.

Coat of Arms
A4 A5

1868-69 — *Perf. 12*

Nine Stars

10	A4	5c green	17.50	8.75
11	A4	10c vermilion	25.00	8.75
12	A4	50c blue	45.00	25.00
13	A4	100c orange	45.00	27.50
14	A4	500c black	475.00	375.00

Eleven Stars

15	A5	5c green	10.00	6.25
16	A5	10c vermilion	14.00	10.00
a.		Half used as 5c as cover		400.00
17	A5	50c blue	37.50	17.50
18	A5	100c dp orange	35.00	17.50
19	A5	500c black	*1,750.*	*1,750.*

See Nos. 26-27, 31-34.

Arms and "The Law" — A6

1878 — Various Frames — *Perf. 12*

20	A6	5c ultra	9.25	4.25
21	A6	10c orange	7.50	3.25
a.		Half used as 5c on cover		50.00
22	A6	20c green	22.50	4.25
a.		Half used as 10c on cover		160.00
23	A6	50c dull carmine	110.00	12.00
		Nos. 20-23 (4)	149.25	23.75

Numerals Upright
(11 Stars)-A7 (9 Stars)-A8

1887 — *Rouletted*

24	A7	1c rose	2.25	2.00
25	A7	2c violet	2.25	2.00
26	A5	5c blue	7.25	3.50
27	A5	10c orange	7.25	3.50
		Nos. 24-27 (4)	19.00	11.00

See No. 37.

1890 — *Perf. 12*

28	A8	1c rose	1.60	.80
29	A8	2c violet	4.25	2.00
30	A4	5c blue	3.00	.80
31	A4	10c orange	6.25	.95
32	A4	20c dk green	12.50	1.60
33	A4	50c red	6.25	1.60
34	A4	100c yellow	12.50	3.25
		Nos. 28-34 (7)	46.35	11.00

See Nos. 35-36, 38-39.

1893 — Litho. — *Perf. 11*

35	A8	1c rose	3.50	2.50
a.		Imperf. pair	35.00	
b.		Horiz. pair, imperf. vert.	20.00	
c.		Horiz. pair, imperf. btwn.	35.00	
36	A8	2c violet	3.50	2.50
a.		Block of 4 imperf. vert. and horiz. through center	50.00	
b.		Horiz. pair, imperf. btwn.	27.50	
37	A7	5c blue	6.00	2.50
a.		Vert. pair, imperf. horiz.	27.50	
b.		Horiz. pair, imperf. btwn.	35.00	
38	A8	10c orange	17.00	4.00
a.		Horiz. pair, imperf. btwn.	50.00	
39	A8	20c dark green	40.00	18.00
a.		Imperf. pair, vert. or horiz.	140.00	
b.		Pair, imperf. btwn., vert. or horiz.	140.00	
		Nos. 35-39 (5)	70.00	29.50

Coat of Arms — A9

1894 — Unwmk. — Engr. — *Perf. 14, 14½*

Thin Paper

40	A9	1c bister	1.00	.60
41	A9	2c red orange	1.00	.60
42	A9	5c green	1.00	.60
43	A9	10c yellow brn	1.00	.60
44	A9	20c dark blue	3.00	1.25
45	A9	50c claret	7.50	1.75
46	A9	100c brown rose	17.50	6.25
		Nos. 40-46 (7)	32.00	11.65

Stamps of type A9 on thick paper were surreptitiously printed in Paris on the order of an official and without government authorization. Some of these stamps were substituted for part of a shipment of stamps on thin paper, which had been printed in London on government order.

When the thick paper stamps reached Bolivia they were at first repudiated but afterwards were allowed to do postal duty. A large quantity of the thick paper stamps were fraudulently canceled in Paris with a cancellation of heavy bars forming an oval.

To be legitimate, copies of the thick paper stamps must have genuine cancellations of Bolivia. Value, on cover, each $125.

The 10c blue on thick paper is not known to have been issued.

Some copies of Nos. 40-46 show part of a papermakers' watermark "1011."

For overprints see Nos. 55-59.

President Tomas Frias — A10

President Jose M. Linares — A11

Pedro Domingo Murillo A12

Bernardo Monteagudo A13

Gen. Jose Ballivian A14

Gen. Antonio Jose de Sucre A15

Simon Bolivar — A16

Coat of Arms — A17

1897 — Litho. — *Perf. 12*

47	A10	1c pale yellow grn	1.25	.80
a.		Vert. pair, imperf. horiz.	50.00	
b.		Vert. pair, imperf. btwn.	50.00	
48	A11	2c red	1.75	1.40
49	A12	5c dk green	2.50	.80
a.		Horiz. pair, imperf. btwn.	50.00	
50	A13	10c brown vio	2.50	.80
a.		Vert. pair, imperf. btwn.	50.00	
51	A14	20c lake & blk	4.75	.95
a.		Imperf., pair		150.00
52	A15	50c orange	4.75	2.50
53	A16	1b Prus blue	4.75	*5.50*
54	A17	2b red, yel, grn & blk	37.50	*50.00*
		Nos. 47-54 (8)	59.75	*62.75*

Excellent forgeries of No. 54, perf and imperf, exist, some postally used.

Reprint of No. 53 has dot in numeral. Same value.

Nos. 40-44 Handstamped in Violet or Blue

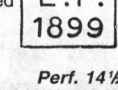

E.F.
1899

1899 — *Perf. 14½*

55	A9	1c yellow bis	13.00	13.00
56	A9	2c red orange	16.00	16.00
57	A9	5c green	10.50	10.50
58	A9	10c yellow brn	13.00	10.50
59	A9	20c dark blue	21.00	21.00
		Nos. 55-59 (5)	73.50	71.00

The handstamp is found inverted, double, etc. Values twice the listed amounts. Forgeries of this handstamp are plentiful. "E.F." stands for Estado Federal.

The 50c and 100c (Nos. 45-46) were overprinted at a later date in Brazil.

Antonio José de Sucre — A18

Perf. 11½, 12

1899 — Engr. — Thin Paper

62	A18	1c gray blue	2.50	.75
63	A18	2c brnsh red	1.75	.75
64	A18	5c dk green	6.00	1.50
65	A18	10c yellow org	2.50	1.25
66	A18	20c rose pink	3.00	.80
67	A18	50c bister brn	6.00	2.50
68	A18	1b gray violet	1.75	1.75
		Nos. 62-68 (7)	23.50	9.30

1901

69	A18	5c dark red	1.90	.60

Col. Adolfo Ballivian A19

Eliodoro Camacho A20

President Narciso Campero A21

Jose Ballivian A22

Gen. Andres Santa Cruz — A23

Coat of Arms — A24

1901-02 **Engr.**

No.	Type	Description	Unused	Used
70	A19	1c claret	.55	.20
71	A20	2c green	.55	.20
73	A21	5c scarlet	.55	.20
74	A22	10c blue	1.40	.20
75	A23	20c violet & blk	.80	.20
76	A24	2b brown	3.75	2.75
		Nos. 70-71,73-76 (6)	7.60	3.75

Nos. 73, 74 exist imperf. Value, pairs, each $50.

For surcharges see #95-96, 193.

1904 **Litho.**

No.	Type	Description	Unused	Used
77	A19	1c claret	2.25	.55

In No. 70 the panel above "CENTAVO" is shaded with continuous lines. In No. 77 the shading is of dots.

See Nos. 103-105, 107, 110.

Coat of Arms of Dept. of La Paz — A25

Murillo — A26

Jose Miguel Lanza — A27

Ismael Montes — A28

1909 **Litho.** ***Perf. 11***

No.	Type	Description	Unused	Used
78	A25	5c blue & blk	9.00	5.00
79	A26	10c green & blk	9.00	5.00
80	A27	20c orange & blk	9.00	5.00
81	A28	2b red & black	9.00	5.00
		Nos. 78-81 (4)	36.00	20.00

Centenary of Revolution of July, 1809.

Nos. 78-81 exist imperf. and tête bêche. Nos. 79-81 exist with center inverted.

Miguel Betanzos A29

Col. Ignacio Warnes A30

Murillo A31

Monteagudo A32

Esteban Arce — A33

Antonio Jose de Sucre — A34

Simon Bolivar A35

Manuel Belgrano A36

1909 **Dated 1809-1825** ***Perf. 11½***

No.	Type	Description	Unused	Used
82	A29	1c lt brown & blk	.55	.35
83	A30	2c green & blk	.55	.40
84	A31	5c red & blk	.55	.30
85	A32	10c dull bl & blk	.55	.30
86	A33	20c violet & blk	.65	.40
87	A34	50c olive bister & blk	1.00	.55
88	A35	1b gray brn & blk	1.00	.80
89	A36	2b chocolate & blk	1.60	1.10
		Nos. 82-89 (8)	6.45	4.20

War of Independence, 1809-1825.

Exist imperf. For surcharge see #97.

Warnes A37

Betanzos A38

Arce — A39

Dated 1910-1825

1910 ***Perf. 13x13½***

No.	Type	Description	Unused	Used
92	A37	5c green & black	.40	.20
a.		Imperf., pair	5.00	
93	A38	10c claret & indigo	.40	.20
a.		Imperf., pair	5.00	
94	A39	20c dull blue & indigo	.65	.40
a.		Imperf., pair	5.00	
		Nos. 92-94 (3)	1.45	.80

War of Independence.

Nos. 92-94 may be found with parts of a papermaker's watermark: "A I & Co/EXTRA STRONG/9303."

Both perf and imperf exist with inverted centers.

Nos. 71 and 75 Surcharged in Black

5 Centavos 1911

1911 ***Perf. 11½, 12***

No.	Type	Description	Unused	Used
95	A20	5c on 2c green	.45	.20
a.		Inverted surcharge	5.00	5.00
b.		Double surcharge	15.00	
c.		Period after "1911"	3.50	.80
d.		Blue surcharge	75.00	60.00
e.		Double dsurch., one invtd.	15.00	
96	A23	5c on 20c vio & blk	16.00	16.00
a.		Inverted surcharge	30.00	30.00
b.		Double surch., one invtd.	60.00	

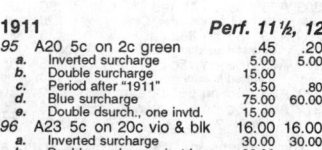

No. 83 Handstamp Surcharged in Green

20 CENTS 1911

No.	Type	Description	Unused	Used
97	A30	20c on 2c grn & blk		*1,100.*

This provisional was issued by local authorities at Villa Bella, a town on the Brazilian border. The 20c surcharge was applied after the stamp had been affixed to the cover. Excellent forgeries of No. 96-97 exist.

"Justice"

A40 A41

1912

Black or Dark Blue Overprint On Revenue Stamps

No.	Type	Description	Unused	Used
98	A40	2c green (Bk)	.35	.25
a.		Inverted overprint	5.00	
99	A41	10c ver (Bl)	1.10	.40
a.		Inverted overprint	5.00	

A42

A43

Red or Black Overprint

Engr.

No.	Type	Description	Unused	Used
100	A42	5c orange (R)	.55	.40
a.		Inverted overprint	5.00	
b.		Pair, one without overprint	12.50	
c.		Black overprint	50.00	

Red or Black Surcharge

No.	Type	Description	Unused	Used
101	A43	10c on 1c bl (R)	.55	.20
a.		Inverted surcharge	6.00	
b.		Double surcharge	6.00	
c.		Dbl. surcharge, one invtd.	7.50	
d.		Black surcharge	100.00	100.00
e.		As "d," inverted		
f.		As "d," double surcharge		
g.		Pair, one without black surch.	400.00	

Fakes of No. 101d are plentiful.

Revenue Stamp Surcharged "CORREOS / 10 Cts. / - 1917 -" in Red

1917 **Litho.**

No.	Type	Description	Unused	Used
102		10c on 1c blue	*6,000.*	*1,750.*

Design similar to type A43.

Excellent forgeries exist.

Types of 1901 and

Frias-A45 Sucre-A46 Bolivar-A47

1913 **Engr.** ***Perf. 12***

No.	Type	Description	Unused	Used
103	A19	1c car rose	.40	.25
104	A20	2c vermilion	.40	.20
105	A21	5c green	.45	.20
106	A45	8c yellow	.80	.50
107	A22	10c gray	.80	.25
108	A46	50c dull violet	1.50	.55
109	A47	1b slate blue	2.25	1.40
110	A24	2b black	4.50	2.75
		Nos. 103-110 (8)	11.10	6.10

No. 107, litho., was not regularly issued.

Nine values commemorating the Gui-qui-La Paz railroad were printed in 1915 but never issued. Typographed forgeries exist.

Monolith of Tiahuanacu A48

Mt. Potosí A49

Lake Titicaca — A50

Mt. Illimani — A51

Legislature Building — A53

FIVE CENTAVOS.

Type I - Numerals have background of vertical lines. Clouds formed of dots.

Type II - Numerals on white background. Clouds near the mountain formed of wavy lines.

1916-17 **Litho.** ***Perf. 11½***

No.	Type	Description	Unused	Used
111	A48	½c brown	.20	.20
a.		Horiz. pair, imperf. vert.	5.00	
112	A49	1c gray green	.20	.20
a.		Imperf., pair	2.00	
113	A50	2c car & blk	.25	.20
a.		Imperf., pair	2.00	
b.		Vert. pair, imperf. horiz.		
c.		Center inverted	12.50	11.25
d.		Imperf., center inverted	17.50	
114	A51	5c dk blue (I)	.50	.20
a.		Imperf., pair	2.00	
b.		Vert. pair, imperf. horiz.	3.50	
c.		Horiz. pair, imperf. vert.	3.50	
115	A51	5c dk blue (II)	.50	.20
a.		Imperf., pair	2.50	
116	A53	10c org & bl	1.00	.20
a.		Imperf., pair	3.50	
b.		No period after "Legislativo"	1.00	.20
c.		Center inverted	40.00	40.00
d.		Vertical pair, imperf. between	5.00	
		Nos. 111-116 (6)	2.65	1.20

For surcharges see Nos. 194-196.

Coat of Arms

A54 A55

Printed by the American Bank Note Co.

1919-20 **Engr.** ***Perf. 12***

No.	Type	Description	Unused	Used
118	A54	1c carmine	.25	.20
119	A54	2c dk violet	4.75	3.00
120	A54	5c dk green	.50	.20
121	A54	10c vermilion	.50	.20
122	A54	20c dk blue	1.50	.30
123	A54	22c lt blue	.90	.75
124	A54	24c purple	.60	.50
125	A54	50c orange	4.75	.60
126	A55	1b red brown	6.00	1.75
127	A55	2b black brn	9.00	4.50
		Nos. 118-127 (10)	28.75	12.00

Printed by Perkins, Bacon & Co., Ltd.

1923-27 **Re-engraved** ***Perf. 13½***

No.	Type	Description	Unused	Used
128	A54	1c carmine ('27)	.20	.20
129	A54	2c dk violet	.25	.20
130	A54	5c dp green	.80	.20
131	A54	10c vermilion	14.00	12.00
132	A54	20c slate blue	1.75	.20
135	A54	50c orange	2.75	.60
136	A55	1b red brown	.70	.30
137	A55	2b black brown	.50	.30
		Nos. 128-137 (8)	20.95	14.00

There are many differences in the designs of the two issues but they are too minute to be illustrated or described.

Nos. 128-137 exist imperf.

See Nos. 144-146, 173-177. For surcharges see Nos. 138-143, 160, 162, 181-186, 236-237.

Stamps of 1919-20 Surcharged in Blue, Black or Red

Habilitada 15 cts.

1924 ***Perf. 12***

No.	Type	Description	Unused	Used
138	A54	5c on 1c car (Bl)	.40	.20
a.		Inverted surcharge	5.00	5.00
b.		Double surcharge	5.00	5.00
139	A54	15c on 10c ver (Bk)	.70	.50
a.		Inverted surcharge	6.00	6.00
140	A54	15c on 22c lt bl (Bk)	.70	.30
a.		Inverted surcharge	5.25	5.25
b.		Double surcharge, one inverted		

No. 140 surcharged in red or blue probably are trial impressions. They appear jointly, and with black in blocks.

Same Surcharge on No. 131
Perf. 13½

142 A54 15c on 10c ver (Bk) .70 .25
a. Inverted surcharge 6.00 6.00

No. 121 Surcharged

Habilitada
15 cts.

Perf. 12

143 A54 15c on 10c ver (Bk) .90 .30
a. Inverted surcharge 6.00 6.00
b. Double surcharge 5.00 5.00
Nos. 138-143 (5) 3.40 1.55

Type of 1919-20 Issue
Printed by Waterlow & Sons
Second Re-engraving

1925 Unwmk. *Perf. 12½*

144 A54 5c deep green .80 .25
145 A54 15c ultra .80 .20
146 A54 20c dark blue .35 .20
Nos. 144-146 (3) 1.95 .65

These stamps may be identified by the perforation.

Miner — A56

Condor Looking Toward the Sea
A57

Designs: 2c, Sower. 5c, Torch of Eternal Freedom. 10c, National flower (kantuta). 15c, Pres. Bautista Saavedra. 50c, Liberty head. 1b, Archer on horse. 2b, Mercury. 5b, Gen. A. J. de Sucre.

1925 Engr. *Perf. 14*

150 A56 1c dark green .75
151 A56 2c rose .75
152 A56 5c red, *grn* .75 .35
153 A56 10c car, *yel* 1.25 .75
154 A56 15c red brown .50 .25
155 A57 25c ultra .50 .50
156 A56 50c dp violet .50 .50
157 A56 1b red 1.25 1.25
158 A57 2b orange 1.75 1.75
159 A56 5b black brn 2.00 2.00
Nos. 150-159 (10) 10.00

Cent. of the Republic. The 1c and 2c were not released for general use.
Nos. 150-159 exist imperf. Value, $60 each pair.
For surcharges see Nos. C59-C62.

Stamps of 1919-27 Surcharged in Blue, Black or Red

1927
5
CENTAVOS

1927

160 A54 5c on 1c car (Bl) 2.50 .90
a. Inverted surcharge 6.00 6.00
b. Black surcharge 22.50 22.50

Perf. 12

162 A54 10c on 24c pur (Bk) 2.50 1.50
a. Inverted surcharge 30.00 30.00
b. Red surcharge 22.50 22.50

Coat of Arms — A66

Printed by Waterlow & Sons

1927 Litho. *Perf. 13½*

165 A66 2c yellow .40 .20
166 A66 3c pink .50 .50
167 A66 4c red brown .40 .40
168 A66 20c lt ol grn .65 .20
169 A66 25c deep blue .65 .30
170 A66 30c violet .80 .80
171 A66 40c orange 1.50 1.25
172 A66 50c dp brown 1.50 .50
173 A55 1b red 1.75 1.25
174 A55 2b plum 2.50 2.50
175 A55 3b olive grn 2.50 2.50
176 A55 4b claret 4.00 3.50
177 A55 5b bister brn 4.75 4.00
Nos. 165-177 (13) 21.90 17.90

For overprints and surcharges see Nos. 178-180, 208, 211-212.

Type of 1927 Issue Overprinted

Octubre
1927

1927

178 A66 5c dark green .20 .20
179 A66 10c slate .45 .20
180 A66 15c carmine .65 .25
Nos. 178-180 (3) 1.30 .65

Exist with inverted overprint. Value $20 each.

Stamps of 1919-27 Surcharged

15 cts.
1928

1928 *Perf. 12, 12½, 13½*
Red Surcharge

181 A54 15c on 20c #122 9.00 9.00
182 A54 15c on 20c #132 9.00 9.00
a. Black surcharge 30.00
183 A54 15c on 20c #146 160.00 160.00

Black Surcharge

184 A54 15c on 24c #124 1.60 .90
a. Inverted surcharge 5.00 5.00
b. Blue surcharge 50.00
185 A54 15c on 50c #125 50.00 42.50
186 A54 15c on 50c #135 1.25 .70
Nos. 181-186 (6) 230.85 222.10

Condor
A67

Hernando Siles
A68

Map of Bolivia — A69

Printed by Perkins, Bacon & Co., Ltd.

1928 Engr. *Perf. 13½*

189 A67 5c green 1.50 .20
190 A68 10c slate .30 .20
191 A69 15c carmine lake .60 .20
Nos. 189-191 (3) 2.40 .60

Nos. 104, 111, 113, Surcharged in Various Colors

0.03
Centavos
R. S. 21-4
1930

1930 *Perf. 12, 11½*

193 A20 1c on 2c (Bl) .80 .80
a. "0.10" for "0.01" 12.50 12.50
194 A50 3c on 2c (Br) .80 .80
195 A48 25c on ½c (Bk) .80 .80
196 A50 25c on 2c (V) .80 .80
Nos. 193-196 (4) 3.20 3.20

The lines of the surcharges were spaced to fit the various shapes of the stamps. The surcharges exist inverted, double, etc.
Trial printings were made of the surcharges on #193 and 194 in black and on #196 in brown.

Mt. Potosi — A70

Mt. Illimani — A71

Eduardo Abaroa — A72

Map of Bolivia — A73

Sucre — A74

Bolivar — A75

1931 Engr. *Perf. 14*

197 A70 2c green 1.40 .50
198 A71 5c light blue 1.40 .20
199 A72 10c red orange 1.40 .20
200 A73 15c violet 1.40 .20
201 A73 35c carmine 2.00 .85
202 A73 45c orange 2.00 .75
203 A74 50c gray .55 .55
204 A75 1b brown .55 .55
Nos. 197-204 (8) 10.70 3.80

No. 198 exists imperf.
See #207, 241. For surcharges see #209-210.

Symbols of 1930 Revolution — A76

1931 Litho. *Perf. 11*

205 A76 15c scarlet 2.25 .40
a. Pair, imperf. between
206 A76 50c brt violet .70 .70
a. Pair, imperf. between 7.50

Revolution of June 25, 1930.
For surcharges see Nos. 239-240.

Map Type of 1931
Without Imprint

1932 Litho.

207 A73 15c violet 1.50 .35

Stamps of 1927-31 Surcharged

Habilitada
A 15 Cts.
D. S. 13-7-1933

1933 *Perf. 13½, 14*

208 A66 5c on 1b red .60 .35
a. Without period after "Cts" 1.25 1.25
209 A73 15c on 35c car .35 .35
a. Inverted surcharge 20.00
210 A73 15c on 45c orange .35 .35
a. Inverted surcharge 3.00 3.00
211 A66 15c on 50c dp brn 1.50 .30
212 A66 25c on 40c orange .60 .25
Nos. 208-212 (5) 3.40 1.60

The hyphens in "13-7-33" occur in three positions.

Coat of Arms — A77

1933 Engr. *Perf. 12*

213 A77 2c blue green .25 .20
214 A77 5c blue .25 .20
215 A77 10c red .45 .30
216 A77 15c deep violet .35 .20
217 A77 25c dark blue .65 .55
Nos. 213-217 (5) 1.95 1.45

For surcharges see Nos. 233-235, 238.

Mariano Baptista
A78

Map of Bolivia
A79

1935

218 A78 15c dull violet .45 .20

1935

219 A79 2c dark blue .20 .20
220 A79 3c yellow .20 .20
221 A79 5c vermilion .20 .20
222 A79 5c blue grn .35 .20
223 A79 10c black brn .35 .20
224 A79 15c deep rose .35 .20
225 A79 15c ultra .35 .20
226 A79 20c yellow grn .40 .20
227 A79 25c lt blue .40 .20
228 A79 30c deep rose .80 .55
229 A79 40c orange .80 .55
230 A79 50c gray violet .80 .25
231 A79 1b yellow .55 .35
232 A79 2b olive brown .80 .70
Nos. 219-232 (14) 6.55 4.20

Regular Stamps of 1925-33 Surcharged in Black

1937 *Perf. 11, 12, 13½*

233 A77 5c on 2c bl grn .25 .25
234 A77 15c on 25c dk bl .30 .30
235 A77 30c on 25c dk bl .50 .50
236 A55 45c on 1b red brn .60 .60
237 A55 1b on 2b plum .75 .75
a. "1" missing 7.50 7.50
238 A77 2b on 25c dk bl .75 .75

"Comunicaciones" on one line

239 A76 3b on 50c brt vio 1.25 1.25
a. "3" of value missing 6.00 6.00
240 A76 5b on 50c brt vio 1.25 1.25
Nos. 233-240 (8) 5.65 5.65

Exist inverted, double, etc.

Comuni-
caciones
D. S.
25-2-37
0.05

President Siles — A80

1937 Unwmk. *Perf. 14*

241 A80 1c yellow brown .30 .30

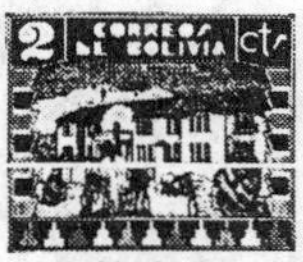

Native School — A81

Oil Wells — A82

Modern Factories
A83

Torch of Knowledge
A84

Map of the Sucre-Camiri R. R. — A85

Allegory of Free Education A86

Allegorical Figure of Learning A87

Symbols of Industry A88

Modern Agriculture A89

1938 Litho. *Perf. 10½, 11*

242	A81	2c	dull red	.40	.40
243	A82	10c	pink	.45	.25
244	A83	15c	yellow grn	.60	.30
245	A84	30c	yellow	.75	.35
246	A85	45c	rose red	1.40	.75
247	A86	60c	dk violet	1.10	.35
248	A87	75c	dull blue	1.50	.35
249	A88	1b	lt brown	2.25	.35
250	A89	2b	bister	2.00	.75
			Nos. 242-250 (9)	10.45	3.85

For surcharge see No. 314.

Llamas — A90

Vicuna — A91

Coat of Arms A92

Cocoi Herons A93

Chinchilla — A94

Toco Toucan — A95

Condor — A96

Jaguar — A97

1939, Jan. 21 *Perf. 10½, 11½x10½*

251	A90	2c	green	.40	.30
252	A90	4c	fawn	.40	.30
253	A90	5c	red violet	.40	.25
254	A91	10c	black	.60	.30
255	A91	15c	emerald	.60	.35
256	A91	20c	dk slate grn	.60	.25
257	A92	25c	lemon	.60	.25
258	A92	30c	dark blue	.60	.25
259	A93	40c	vermilion	1.40	.30
260	A93	45c	gray	1.40	.30
261	A94	60c	rose red	1.40	.55
262	A94	75c	slate blue	2.75	.55
263	A95	90c	orange	2.00	.55
264	A95	1b	blue	2.00	.55
265	A96	2b	rose lake	2.75	.55
266	A96	3b	dark violet	3.50	.80
267	A97	4b	brown org	4.00	1.10
268	A97	5b	gray brown	5.00	1.40
			Nos. 251-268 (18)	30.40	8.95

All but 20c exist imperf.

Imperf. counterfeits with altered designs exist of some values.

For surcharges see Nos. 315-317.

Flags of 21 American Republics A98

1940, Apr. Litho. *Perf. 10½*

269	A98	9b	multicolored	1.10	1.10

Pan American Union, 150th anniversary.

Statue of Murillo A99

Urns of Murillo and Sagarnaga A100

Dream of Murillo A101

Murillo A102

1941, Apr. 15

270	A99	10c	dull vio brn	.20	.20
271	A100	15c	lt green	.20	.20
a.			Imperf., pair	3.50	
b.			Double impression	6.00	
272	A101	45c	carmine rose	.20	.20
a.			Double impression	6.00	
273	A102	1.05b	dk ultra	.40	.20
			Nos. 270-273 (4)	1.00	.80

130th anniv. of the execution of Pedro Domingo Murillo (1759-1810), patriot.

For surcharge see No. 333.

First Stamp of Bolivia and 1941 Airmail Stamp — A103

1942, Oct. Litho. *Perf. 13½*

274	A103	5c	pink	.50	.50
275	A103	10c	orange	.50	.40
276	A103	20c	yellow grn	1.00	.65
277	A103	40c	carmine rose	1.25	.80
278	A103	90c	ultra	2.50	1.00
279	A103	1b	violet	3.00	1.60
280	A103	10b	olive bister	10.00	8.25
			Nos. 274-280 (7)	18.75	13.20

1st School Phil. Exposition held in La Paz, Oct., 1941.

Gen. Ballivian Leading Cavalry Charge, Battle of Ingavi — A104

1943 Photo. *Perf. 12½*

281	A104	2c	lt blue grn	.20	.20
282	A104	3c	orange	.20	.20
283	A104	25c	deep plum	.20	.20
284	A104	45c	ultra	.20	.20
285	A104	3b	scarlet	.40	.35
286	A104	4b	brt rose lilac	.55	.45
287	A104	5b	black brown	.80	.55
			Nos. 281-287 (7)	2.55	2.15

Souvenir Sheets

Perf. 13, Imperf.

288	A104	Sheet of 4	1.50	1.50
289	A104	Sheet of 3	4.50	4.50

Centenary of the Battle of Ingavi, 1841. No. 288 contains 4 stamps similar to Nos. 281-284, No. 289 three stamps similar to Nos. 285-287.

Potosi A107

Quechisla A108

Miner — A109

Dam A110

Mine Interior A111

Chaquiri Dam A112

Entrance to Pulacayo Mine A113

1943 Engr. *Perf. 12½*

290	A107	15c	red brown	.20	.20
291	A108	45c	vio blue	.20	.20
292	A109	1.25b	brt rose vio	.25	.30
293	A110	1.50b	emerald	.25	.30
294	A111	2b	brown blk	.30	.35
295	A112	2.10b	lt blue	.40	.45
296	A113	3b	red orange	.50	.55
			Nos. 290-296 (7)	2.10	2.35

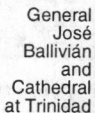

General José Ballivián and Cathedral at Trinidad A114

1943, Nov. 18

297	A114	5c	dk green & brn	.20	.20
298	A114	10c	dull pur & brn	.20	.20
299	A114	30c	rose red & brn	.20	.20
300	A114	45c	brt ultra & brn	.20	.25
301	A114	2.10b	dp org & brn	.30	.35
			Nos. 297-301,C91-C95 (10)	2.35	2.30

Department of Beni centenary.

"Honor, Work, Law" A115

"United for the Country" A116

1944 Litho. *Perf. 13½*

302	A115	20c	orange	.20	.20
303	A115	90c	ultra	.20	.20
304	A116	1b	brt red vio	.20	.20
305	A116	2.40b	dull brown	.20	.20

1945

306	A115	20c	green	.20	.20
307	A115	90c	dp rose	.20	.20
			Nos. 302-307,C96-C99 (10)	2.20	2.00

Nos. 302-307 were issued to commemorate the Revolution of Dec. 20, 1943.

Catalogue values for unused stamps in this section, from this point to the end of the section, are for Never Hinged items.

Leopold Benedetto Vincenti, Joseph Ignacio de Sanjines and Bars of Anthem A117

1946, Aug. 21 Litho. *Perf. 10½*

308	A117	5c	rose vio & blk	.20	.20
309	A117	10c	ultra & blk	.20	.20
310	A117	15c	blue grn & blk	.20	.20
311	A117	30c	vermilion & brn	.20	.20
a.			Souv. sheet of 1, imperf.	.65	.65
312	A117	90c	dk blue & brn	.20	.20
313	A117	2b	black & brn	.30	.20
a.			Souv. sheet of 1, imperf.	1.25	1.25
			Nos. 308-313 (6)	1.30	1.20

Cent. of the adoption of Bolivia's natl. anthem.

Nos. 311a and 313a sold for 4b over face.

Nos. 248 and 262 Surcharged in Carmine, Black or Orange

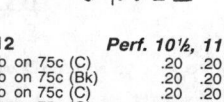

1947
Habilitada
Bs. 1.40

1947, Mar. 12 *Perf. 10½, 11*

314	A87	1.40b	on 75c (C)	.20	.20
315	A94	1.40b	on 75c (Bk)	.20	.20
316	A94	1.40b	on 75c (C)	.20	.20
317	A94	1.40b	on 75c (O)	.20	.20
			Nos. 314-317,C112 (5)	1.00	1.00

People Attacking Presidential Palace A118

Arms of Bolivia and Argentina A119

1947, Sept. Litho. *Perf. 13½*

318	A118	20c	blue grn	.20	.20
319	A118	50c	lilac rose	.20	.20
320	A118	1.40b	grnsh bl	.20	.20
321	A118	3.70b	dull org	.20	.20
322	A118	4b	violet	.20	.20
323	A118	10b	olive	.40	.25
			Nos. 318-323,C113-C117 (11)	2.40	2.25

1st anniv. of the Revolution of July 21, 1946. Exist imperf.

1947, Oct. 23

324	A119	1.40b	deep orange	.20	.20

Meeting of Presidents Enrique Hertzog of Bolivia and Juan D. Peron of Argentina at Yacuiba on Oct. 23, 1947. Exist imperf.

See No. C118.

Statue of Christ above La Paz — A120

2b, Child kneeling before cross of Golgotha. 3b, St. John Bosco. #328, Virgin of Copacabana. #329, Pope Pius XII blessing University of La Paz.

1948, Sept. 26 Unwmk. *Perf. 11½*

325	A120	1.40b blue & yel	.30	.20
326	A120	2b yel grn & sal	.40	.20
327	A120	3b green & gray	.65	.20
328	A120	5b violet & sal	.80	.25
329	A120	5b red brn & lt grn	1.10	.25
		Nos. 325-329,C119-C123 (10)	6.05	2.65

3rd Inter-American Cong. of Catholic Education.

Map and Emblem of Bolivia Auto Club — A125

Pres. Gregorio Pacheco, Map and Post Horn — A126

1948, Oct. 20

330 A125 5b indigo & salmon 1.50 .20

Intl. Automobile Races of South America, Sept.-Oct. 1948. See No. C124.

1950, Jan. 2 Litho. *Perf. 11½*

331	A126	1.40b violet blue	.20	.20
332	A126	4.20b red	.20	.20
		Nos. 331-332,C125-C127 (5)	1.00	1.00

75th anniv. of the UPU.

No. 273 Surcharged in Black

Bs.2.- Habilitada D.S.6·VII·50

1950 *Perf. 10½*

333 A102 2b on 1.05b dk ultra .20 .20

Crucifix and View of Potosi A127

Symbols of United Nations A128

Perf. 11½

1950, Sept. 14 Litho. Unwmk.

334	A127	20c violet	.20	.20
335	A127	30c dp orange	.20	.20
336	A127	50c lilac rose	.20	.20
337	A127	1b carmine	.20	.20
338	A127	2b blue	.30	.20
339	A127	6b chocolate	.25	.20
		Nos. 334-339 (6)	1.35	1.20

400th anniv. of the appearance of a crucifix at Potosi. Exist imperf.

1950, Oct. 24

340	A128	60c ultra	1.00	.20
341	A128	2b green	1.40	.22
		Nos. 340-341,C138-C139 (4)	3.55	.82

5th anniv. of the UN, Oct. 24, 1945.

Gate of the Sun and Llama A129

Church of San Francisco A130

40c, Avenue Camacho. 50c, Consistorial Palace. 1b, Legislative Palace. 1.40b, Communications Bldg. 2b, Arms. 3b, La Gasca ordering Mendoza to found La Paz. 5b, Capt. Alonso de Mendoza founding La Paz. 10b, Arms; portrait of Mendoza.

1951, Mar. Engr. *Perf. 12½*

Center in Black

342	A129	20c green	.20	.20
343	A130	30c dp orange	.20	.20
344	A129	40c bister brn	.20	.20
345	A129	50c dk red	.20	.20
346	A129	1b dp purple	.20	.20
347	A129	1.40b dk vio blue	.20	.20
348	A129	2b dp purple	.20	.20
349	A129	3b red lilac	.20	.20
	a.	Sheet, Nos. 345, 346, 348, 349	1.10	1.10
	b.	As "a," imperf.	1.10	1.10
350	A129	5b dk red	.25	.20
	a.	Sheet, Nos. 344, 347, 350	1.10	1.10
	b.	As "a," imperf.	1.10	1.10
351	A129	10b sepia	.50	.25
	a.	Sheet, Nos. 342, 343, 351	1.10	1.10
	b.	As "a," imperf.	1.10	1.10
		Nos. 342-351,C140-C149 (20)	5.55	5.25

400th anniv. of the founding of La Paz.
For surcharges see Nos. 393-402.

Boxing — A131

Perf. 12½

1951, July 1 Unwmk. Engr.

352	A131	20c shown	.20	.20
353	A131	50c Tennis	.20	.20
354	A131	1b Diving	.20	.20
355	A131	1.40b Soccer	.20	.20
356	A131	2b Skiing	.40	.30
357	A131	3b Handball	.80	.80
	a.	Sheet, Nos. 352, 353, 356, 357	2.25	1.75
	b.	As "a," imperf.	2.25	1.75
358	A131	4b Cycling	1.00	1.00
	a.	Sheet, Nos. 354, 355, 358	2.00	1.50
	b.	As "a," imperf.	2.00	1.50
		Nos. 352-358,C150-C156 (14)	8.25	6.25

The stamps were intended to commemorate the 5th athletic championship matches held at La Paz, October 1948.

Eagle and Flag of Bolivia — A132

1951, Nov. 5 Litho. *Perf. 11½*

Flag in Red, Yellow and Green.

359	A132	2b aqua	.20	.20
360	A132	3.50b ultra	.20	.20
361	A132	5b purple	.20	.20
362	A132	7.50b gray	.20	.20
363	A132	15b dp car	.25	.25
364	A132	30b sepia	.50	.50
		Nos. 359-364 (6)	1.55	1.55

Cent. of the adoption of Bolivia's natl. flag.

Eduardo Abaroa A133

Queen Isabella I A134

1952, Mar. *Perf. 11*

365	A133	80c dk carmine	.20	.20
366	A133	1b red orange	.20	.20
367	A133	2b emerald	.20	.20
368	A133	5b ultra	.25	.20
369	A133	10b lilac rose	.50	.20
370	A133	20b dk brown	.75	.65
		Nos. 365-370,C157-C162 (12)	5.10	4.45

73rd anniversary of the death of Eduardo Abaroa.

1952, July 16 Unwmk. *Perf. 13½*

371	A134	2b vio bl	.20	.20
372	A134	6.30b carmine	.20	.20
		Nos. 371-372,C163-C164 (4)	1.40	1.00

500th anniv. of the birth of Isabella I of Spain.

Columbus Lighthouse A135

1952, July 16 Litho.

373	A135	2b vio bl, *bl*	.20	.20
374	A135	5b car, *sal*	.50	.40
375	A135	9b emer, *grn*	.85	.60
		Nos. 373-375,C165-C168 (7)	2.55	2.00

Miner — A136

1953, Apr. 9

376	A136	2.50b vermilion	.20	.20
377	A136	8b violet	.20	.20

Nationalization of the mines.

Gualberto Villarroel, Victor Paz Estenssoro and Hernan Siles Zuazo A137

1953, Apr. 9 *Perf. 11½*

378	A137	50c rose lil	.20	.20
379	A137	1b brt rose	.20	.20
380	A137	2b vio bl	.20	.20
381	A137	3b lt grn	.20	.20
382	A137	4b yel org	.20	.20
383	A137	5b dl vio	.20	.20
		Nos. 378-383,C169-C175 (13)	2.85	2.60

Revolution of Apr. 9, 1952, 1st anniv.

Map of Bolivia and Cow's Head — A138

25b, 85b, Map and ear of wheat.

1954, Aug. 2 *Perf. 12x11½*

384	A138	5b car rose	.20	.20
385	A138	17b aqua	.20	.20
386	A138	25b chalky blue	.20	.20
387	A138	85b blk brn	.25	.20
		Nos. 384-387,C176-C181 (10)	3.05	2.10

Nos. 384-385 for the agrarian reform laws of 1953-54. Nos. 386-387 for the 1st National Congress of Agronomy. Exist imperf.

Oil Refinery A139

1955, Oct. 9 Unwmk. *Perf. 12x11½*

388	A139	10b ultra & lt ultra	.20	.20
389	A139	35b rose car & rose	.20	.20
390	A139	40b dk & lt yel grn	.20	.20
391	A139	50b red vio & lil rose	.20	.20
392	A139	80b brn & bis brn	.20	.20
		Nos. 388-392,C182-C186 (10)	3.50	3.25

Exist imperf.

Nos. 342-351, Surcharged with New Values and Bars in Ultramarine

1957, Feb. 14 Engr. *Perf. 12½*

Center in Black

393	A129	50b on 3b red lilac	.20	.20
394	A129	100b on 2b dp pur	.20	.20
395	A129	200b on 1b dp pur	.20	.20
396	A129	300b on 1.40b dk vio bl	.20	.20
397	A129	350b on 20c green	.20	.20
398	A129	400b on 40c bis brn	.20	.20
399	A130	600b on 30c dp org	.35	.20
400	A129	800b on 50c dk red	.40	.20
401	A129	1000b on 10b sepia	.40	.20
402	A129	2000b on 5b dk red	.65	.20
		Nos. 393-402 (10)	3.00	2.00

See Nos. C187-C196.

CEPAL Building, Santiago de Chile, and Meeting Hall in La Paz — A140

1957, May 15 Litho. *Perf. 13*

403	A140	150b gray & ultra	.20	.20
404	A140	350b bis brn & gray	.20	.20
405	A140	550b chlky bl & brn	.20	.20
406	A140	750b dp rose & grn	.30	.20
407	A140	900b grn & brn blk	.40	.20
		Nos. 403-407,C197-C201 (10)	5.10	3.60

7th session of the C. E. P. A. L. (Comision Economica para la America Latina de las Naciones Unidas), La Paz. Exist imperf.
For surcharges see Nos. 482-484,

Presidents Siles Zuazo and Aramburu A141

1957, Dec. 15 Unwmk. *Perf. 11½*

408	A141	50b red org	.20	.20
409	A141	350b blue	.25	.20
410	A141	1000b redsh brn	.50	.20
		Nos. 408-410,C202-C204 (6)	2.05	1.20

Opening of the Santa Cruz-Yacuiba Railroad and the meeting of the Presidents of Bolivia and Argentina. Exist imperf.
For surcharge see No. 699.

Flags of Bolivia and Mexico and Presidents Hernan Siles Zuazo and Adolfo Lopez Mateos A142

1960, Jan. 30 Litho. *Perf. 11½*

411	A142	350b olive	.20	.20
412	A142	600b red brown	.25	.25
413	A142	1500b black brown	.50	.50
		Nos. 411-413,C205-C207 (6)	3.10	2.25

Issued for an expected visit of Mexico's President Adolfo Lopez Mateos. On sale Jan. 30-Feb. 1, 1960.

Indians and Mt. Illimani A143

Refugee Children A144

1960, Mar. 26 **Unwmk.**

414 A143 500b olive bister .50 .20
415 A143 1000b blue .90 .30
416 A143 2000b brown 2.00 .50
417 A143 4000b green 3.75 2.50
Nos. 414-417,C208-C211 (8) 23.90 12.95

1960, Apr. 7 ***Perf. 11½***

418 A144 50b brown .20 .20
419 A144 350b claret .20 .20
420 A144 400b steel blue .20 .20
421 A144 1000b gray brown .50 .50
422 A144 3000b slate green 1.00 1.00
Nos. 418-422,C212-C216 (10) 4.40 4.35

Issued to publicize World Refugee Year, July 1, 1959-June 30, 1960.

For surcharges see Nos. 454-458, 529.

Jaime Laredo
A145

Rotary Emblem and Nurse with Children
A146

1960, Aug. 15 **Litho.** ***Perf. 11½***

423 A145 100b olive .20 .20
424 A145 350b deep rose .30 .25
425 A145 500b Prus green .40 .20
426 A145 1000b brown .50 .50
427 A145 1500b violet blue .90 .90
428 A145 5000b gray 3.00 3.00
Nos. 423-428,C217-C222 (12) 13.05 8.75

Issued to honor violinist Jaime Laredo.

For surcharge see No. 485.

1960, Nov. 19 ***Perf. 11½***

429 A146 350b multi .20 .20
430 A146 500b multi .25 .20
431 A146 600b multi .35 .35
432 A146 1000b multi .40 .20
Nos. 429-432,C223-C226 (8) 6.20 3.70

Issued for the Children's Hospital, sponsored by the Rotary Club of La Paz.

For surcharges see Nos. 486-487.

Designs from Gate of the Sun
A147 A148

Designs: Various prehistoric gods and ornaments from Tiahuanacu excavations.

1960, Dec. 16 ***Perf. 13x12, 12x13***

Gold Background

Surcharge in Black or Dark Red

Sizes: 21x23mm, 23x21mm

433 A147 50b on ½c red .45 .30
434 A147 100b on 1c red .35 .20
435 A147 200b on 2c blk .75 .35
436 A147 300b on 5c grn (DR) .25 .20
437 A147 350b on 10c grn .25 .75
438 A148 400b on 15c ind .35 .20
439 A148 500b on 20c red .35 .25
440 A148 500b on 50c red .40 .20
441 A148 600b on 22½c grn .45 .45
442 A148 600b on 60c vio .55 .50
443 A148 700b on 25c vio .70 .20
444 A148 700b on 1b grn 1.00 1.00
445 A148 800b on 30c red .60 .20
446 A148 900b on 40c grn .45 .20
447 A148 1000b on 2b bl .60 .50
448 A148 1800b on 3b gray 5.00 3.50

Perf. 11

Size: 49½x23mm

449 A148 4000b on 4b gray 30.00 25.00

Perf. 11x13½

Size: 49x53mm

450 A147 5000b on 5b gray 7.50 7.00
Nos. 433-450 (18) 50.00 41.00

Nos. 433-450 were not regularly issued without surcharge. Value, set $20.

The decree for Nos. 433-450 stipulated that 7 were for air mail (500b on 50c, 600b on 60c, 700b on 1b, 1000b, 1800b, 4000b and 5000b), but the overprinting failed to include "Aereo."

The 800b surcharge also exists on the 1c red and gold. This was not listed in the decree.

For surcharges see Nos. 528, 614.

Miguel de Cervantes
A149

Nuflo de Chaves
A150

1961, Nov. **Photo.** ***Perf. 13x12½***

451 A149 600b ocher & dl vio .40 .20

Cervantes' appointment as Chief Magistrate of La Paz. See No. C230.

1961, Nov. **Unwmk.**

452 A150 1500b dk bl, *buff* .75 .30

Founding of Santa Cruz de la Sierra, 400th anniv. See #468, C246. For surcharge see #533.

People below Eucharist Symbol
A151

Flowers
A152

1962, Mar. 19 **Litho.** ***Perf. 10½***

453 A151 1000b gray grn, red & yel .65 .35

4th Natl. Eucharistic Congress, Santa Cruz, 1961. See No. C231.

Nos. 418-422 Surcharged Horizontally with New Value and Bars or Greek Key Border Segment

1962, June ***Perf. 11½***

454 A144 600b on 50b brown .20 .20
455 A144 900b on 350b claret .25 .20
456 A144 1000b on 400b steel blue .30 .20
457 A144 2000b on 1000b gray brn .40 .25
458 A144 3500b on 3000b slate grn .65 .65
Nos. 454-458,C232-C236 (10) 5.20 4.60

Old value obliterated with two short bars on No. 454; four short bars on Nos. 455-456 and Greek key border on Nos. 457-458. The Greek key obliteration comes in two positions: two full "keys" on top, and one full and two half keys on top.

1962, June 28 **Litho.** ***Perf. 10½***

459 A152 200b Hibiscus .30 .20
460 A152 400b Bicolored vanda .45 .20
461 A152 600b Lily .75 .20
462 A152 1000b Orchid 1.00 .20
Nos. 459-462,C237-C240 (8) 7.50 3.45

Bolivia's Armed Forces
A153

Anti-Malaria Emblem
A154

1962, Sept. 5 ***Perf. 11½***

463 A153 400b Infantry .20 .20
464 A153 500b Cavalry .20 .20
465 A153 600b Artillery .20 .20
466 A153 2000b Engineers .50 .35
Nos. 463-466,C241-C244 (8) 4.10 2.35

1962, Oct. 4

467 A154 600b dk & lt vio & yel .25 .25

WHO drive to eradicate malaria. See #C245.

Portrait Type of 1961

Design: 600b, Alonso de Mendoza.

1962 **Photo.** ***Perf. 13x12½***

468 A150 600b rose vio, *bluish* .25 .20

Soccer and Flags — A155

Design: 1b, Goalkeeper catching ball, vert.

1963, Mar. 21 **Litho.** ***Perf. 11½***

Flags in National Colors

469 A155 60c gray .40 .40
470 A155 1b gray .60 .20

21st South American Soccer Championships. See Nos. C247-C248.

Globe and Wheat Emblem
A156

1963, Aug. 1 **Unwmk.** ***Perf. 11½***

471 A156 60c dk bl, bl & yel .25 .25

"Freedom from Hunger" campaign of the FAO. See No. C249.

Oil Derrick and Chart — A157

Designs: 60c, Map of Bolivia. 1b, Students.

1963, Dec. 21 **Litho.** ***Perf. 11½***

472 A157 10c green & dk brn .20 .20
473 A157 60c ocher & dk brn .25 .20
474 A157 1b dk blue, grn & yel .30 .20
Nos. 472-474,C251-C253 (6) 2.65 1.95

Revolution of Apr. 9, 1952, 10th anniv.

Flags of Bolivia and Peru — A158

1966, Aug. 10 **Wmk. 90** ***Perf. 13½***

Flags in National Colors

475 A158 10c black & tan .20 .20
476 A158 60c black & lt grn .20 .20
477 A158 1b black & gray .35 .35
478 A158 2b black & rose .50 .50
Nos. 475-478,C254-C257 (8) 2.95 2.95

Marshal Andrés Santa Cruz (1792-1865), president of Bolivia and of Peru-Bolivian Confederation.

Children — A159

Perf. 13½

1966, Dec. 16 **Unwmk.** **Litho.**

479 A159 30c ocher & sepia .20 .20

Issued to help poor children. See No. C258.

Map and Flag of Bolivia and Generals Ovando and Barrientos
A160

1966, Dec. 16 **Litho.** ***Perf. 13½***

Flag in Red, Yellow and Green

480 A160 60c violet brn & tan .30 .20
481 A160 1b dull grn & tan .45 .20

Issued to honor Generals Rene Barrientos Ortuno and Alfredo Ovando C., co-Presidents, 1965-66. See Nos. C259-C260.

Various Issues 1957-60 and Type A161 Surcharged with New Values and Bars

A161

1966, Dec. 21

On No. 403: "Centenario de la / Cruz Roja / Internacional"

482 A140 20c on 150b gray & ultra .20 .20

On Nos. 405-406: "Homenaje a la / Generala / J. Azurduy de / Padilla"

483 A140 30c on 550b chlky bl & brn .30 .20
484 A140 2.80b on 750b dp rose & grn .75 .50

On No. 424: "CL Aniversario / Heroinas Coronilla"

485 A145 60c on 350b dp rose .50 .20

Nos. 429-430 Surcharged

486 A146 1.60b on 350b multi .75 .50
487 A146 2.40b on 500b multi 1.00 .75

Revenue Stamps of 1946 surcharged with New Value, "X" and: "XXV Aniversario / Gobierno Busch"

488 A161 20c on 5b red .20 .20

Overprinted: "XX Aniversario / Gob. Villaroel"

489 A161 60c on 2b grn .30 .20

Overprinted: "Centenario do / Rurrenabaque"

490 A161 1b on 10b brn .50 .20

Overprinted: "XXV Aniversario / Dpto. Pando"

491 A161 1.60b on 50c vio .50 .20
Nos. 482-491,C261-C272 (22) 14.50 9.30

For surcharge see No. C272.

Sower
A162

"Macheteros"
A163

1967, Sept. 20 **Litho.** ***Perf. 13½x13***

492 A162 70c multicolored .35 .20

50th anniv. of Lions Intl. See #C273-C273a.

1968, June 24 ***Perf. 13½x13***

Designs (Folklore characters): 60c, Chunchos. 1b, Wiphala. 2b, Diablada.

493 A163 30c gray & multi .20 .20
494 A163 60c sky bl & multi .25 .25
495 A163 1b gray & multi .40 .20
496 A163 2b gray ol & multi .60 .20
Nos. 493-496,C274-C277 (8) 3.95 1.75

Issued to publicize the 9th Congress of the Postal Union of the Americas and Spain.

A souvenir sheet exists containing 4 imperf. stamps similar to #493-496. Size: 131x81½mm.

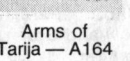

Arms of Tarija — A164

Pres. Gualberto Villaroel — A165

1968, Oct. 29 Litho. *Perf. 13½x13*

497 A164 20c pale sal & multi .20 .20
498 A164 30c gray & multi .20 .20
499 A164 40c dl yel & multi .20 .20
500 A164 60c lt yel grn & multi .20 .20
Nos. 497-500,C278-C281 (8) 3.30 2.60

Battle of Tablada sesquicentennial.

1968, Nov. 6 Unwmk.

501 A165 20c sepia & org .30 .20
502 A165 30c sepia & dl bl grn .30 .20
503 A165 40c sepia & dl rose .30 .20
504 A165 50c sepia & yel grn .30 .20
505 A165 1b sepia & ol bister .30 .20
Nos. 501-505 (5) 1.50 1.00

4th centenary of the founding of Cochabamba. See Nos. C282-C286.

ITU Emblem A166

1968, Dec. 3 Litho. *Perf. 13x13½*

506 A166 10c gray, blk & yel .20 .20
507 A166 60c org, blk & ol .40 .40

Cent. (in 1965) of the ITU. See Nos. C287-C288.

Polychrome Painted Clay Cup, Inca Period — A167

1968, Nov. 14 *Perf. 13½x13*

508 A167 20c dk bl grn & multi .20 .20
509 A167 60c vio bl & multi .35 .35

20th anniv. (in 1966) of UNESCO. See Nos. C289-C290.

John F. Kennedy — A168

Tennis Player — A169

1968, Nov. 22 *Perf. 13x13½*

510 A168 10c yel grn & blk .20 .20
511 A168 4b vio & blk 1.40 1.40

A souvenir sheet contains one imperf. stamp similar to No. 511. Green marginal inscription. Size: 131x81½mm.
See Nos. C291-C292.

1968, Dec. 10 *Perf. 13x13½*

512 A169 10c gray, blk & lt brn .25 .25
513 A169 20c yel, blk & lt brn .25 .25
514 A169 30c ultra, blk & lt brn .25 .25
Nos. 512-514 (3) .75 .75

32nd South American Tennis Championships, La Paz, 1965. See Nos. C293-C294.
A souvenir sheet exists containing 3 imperf. stamps similar to Nos. 512-514. Size: 131x81½mm.

Issue of 1863 — A170

1968, Dec. 23 Litho. *Perf. 13x13½*

515 A170 10c yel grn, brn & blk .35 .20
516 A170 30c lt bl, brn & blk .35 .35
517 A170 2b gray, brn & blk .35 .35
Nos. 515-517,C295-C297 (6) 3.55 3.40

Cent. of Bolivian postage stamps. See Nos. C295-C297.
A souvenir sheet exists containing 3 imperf. stamps similar to Nos. 515-517. Yellow green marginal inscription. Size: 131x81½mm.

Rifle Shooting A171

Sports: 50c, Equestrian. 60c, Canoeing.

1969, Oct. 29 Litho. *Perf. 13x13½*

518 A171 40c red brn, org & blk .40 .40
519 A171 50c emer, red & blk .40 .40
520 A171 60c bl, emer & blk .40 .40
Nos. 518-520,C299-C301 (6) 4.20 3.85

19th Olympic Games, Mexico City, 10/12-27/68.
A souvenir sheet exists containing 3 imperf. stamps similar to #518-520. Size: 130½x81mm.

Temenis Laothoe Violetta A172

Butterflies: 10c, Papilio crassus. 20c, Catagramma cynosura. 30c, Eunica eurota flora. 80c, Ituna phenarete.

1970, Apr. 24 Litho. *Perf. 13x13½*

521 A172 5c pale lil & multi .70 .70
522 A172 10c pink & multi 1.40 1.40
523 A172 20c gray & multi 1.40 1.40
524 A172 30c yel & multi 1.40 1.40
525 A172 80c multicolored 1.40 1.40
Nos. 521-525,C302-C306 (10) 20.20 20.20

A souvenir sheet exists containing 3 imperf. stamps similar to Nos. 521-523. Black marginal inscription. Size: 129½x80mm.

Boy Scout — A173

Design: 10c, Girl Scout planting rose bush.

1970, June 17 *Perf. 13½x13*

526 A173 5c multicolored .20 .20
527 A173 10c multicolored .20 .20

Issued to honor the Bolivian Scout movement. See Nos. C307-C308.

No. 437 Surcharged "EXFILCA 70 / $b. 0.30" and Two Bars in Red

1970, Dec. 6 Litho. *Perf. 13x12*

528 A147 30c on 350b on 10c .25 .25

EXFILCA 70, 2nd Interamerican Philatelic Exhib., Caracas, Venezuela, Nov. 27-Dec. 6.

Nos. 455 and 452 Surcharged in Black or Red

1970, Dec. Photo. *Perf. 11½*

529 A144 60c on 900b on 350b .25 .20
533 A150 1.20b on 1500b (R) .50 .20

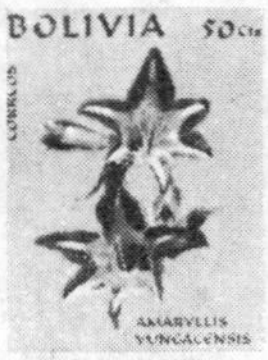

Amaryllis Yungacensis A174

Sica Sica Church, EXFILIMA Emblem A175

Bolivian Flowers: 30c, Amaryllis escobar uriae, horiz. 40c, Amaryllis evansae, horiz. 2b, Gymnocalycium chiquitanum.

Perf. 13x13½, 13½x13

1971, Aug. 9 Litho. Unwmk.

534 A174 30c gray & multi .30 .30
535 A174 40c multi .30 .30
536 A174 50c multi .35 .35
537 A174 2b multi 1.00 .60
Nos. 534-537,C310-C313 (8) 6.95 4.45

1971, Nov. 6 *Perf. 14x13½*

538 A175 20c red & multi .20 .20

EXFILIMA '71, 3rd Inter-American Philatelic Exhibition, Lima, Peru, Nov. 6-14.

A176

A177

Design: Pres. Hugo Banzer Suarez.

1972, Jan. 24 Litho. *Perf. 13½*

539 A176 1.20b blk & multi .50 .20

Bolivia's development, Aug. 19, 1971, to Jan. 24, 1972.

1972, Mar. 23 Litho. *Perf. 13½x13*

Folk Dances: 20c, Chiriwano de Achocalla. 40c, Rueda Chapaca. 60c, Kena-kena. 1b, Waca Thokori.

540 A177 20c red & multi .20 .20
541 A177 40c rose lil & multi .30 .25
542 A177 60c cream & multi .45 .20
543 A177 1b citron & multi .55 .25
Nos. 540-543,C314-C315 (6) 2.65 1.30

Madonna and Child by B. Bitti — A178

Tarija Cathedral, EXFILBRA Emblem — A179

Bolivian paintings: 10c, Nativity, by Melchor Perez de Holguin. 50c, Coronation of the Virgin, by G. M. Berrio. 70c, Harquebusier, anonymous. 80c, St. Peter of Alcantara, by Holguin.

1972 Litho. *Perf. 14x13½*

544 A178 10c gray & multi .20 .20
545 A178 50c sal & multi .25 .20
546 A178 70c lt grn & multi .35 .20
547 A178 80c buff & multi .40 .20
548 A178 1b multi .50 .20
Nos. 544-548,C316-C319 (9) 3.45 1.80

Issue dates: 1b, Aug. 17; others, Dec. 4.

1972, Aug. 26

549 A179 30c multi .20 .20

4th Inter-American Philatelic Exhibition, EXFILBRA, Rio de Janeiro, Brazil, Aug. 26-Sept. 2.

Echinocactus Notocactus A180

Designs: Various cacti.

1973, Aug. 6 Litho. *Perf. 13½*

550 A180 20c crim & multi .30 .25
551 A180 40c multi .30 .25
552 A180 50c multi .30 .20
553 A180 70c multi .30 .20
Nos. 550-553,C321-C323 (7) 2.70 1.55

Power Station, Santa Isabel A181

Designs: 20c, Tin industry. 90c, Bismuth industry. 1b, Natural gas plant.

1973, Nov. 26 Litho. *Perf. 13½*

554 A181 10c gray & multi .20 .20
555 A181 20c tan & multi .20 .20
556 A181 90c lt grn & multi .25 .20
557 A181 1b yel & multi .25 .20
Nos. 554-557,C324-C325 (6) 1.90 1.20

Bolivia's development.

Cattleya Nobilior — A182

Orchids: 50c, Zygopetalum bolivianum. 1b, Huntleya melagris.

1974, May 15 *Perf. 13½*

558 A182 20c gray & multi .40 .20
559 A182 50c lt bl & multi .40 .20
560 A182 1b cit & multi .40 .20
Nos. 558-560,C327-C330 (7) 7.70 2.15

For surcharge see No. 704.

UPU and Philatelic Exposition Emblems A183

1974, Oct. 9

561 A183 3.50b grn, blk & bl 1.00 .40

Centenary of Universal Postal Union: PRENFIL-UPU Philatelic Exhibition, Buenos Aires, Oct. 1-12; EXPO-UPU Philatelic Exhibition, Montevideo, Oct. 20-27.

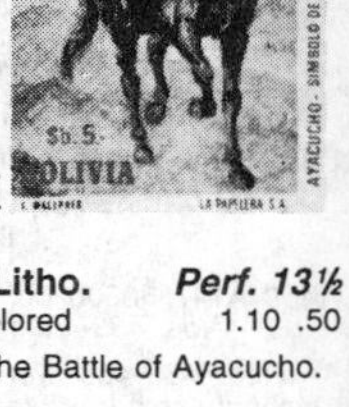

Gen. Sucre, by I. Wallpher — A184

1974, Dec. 9 Litho. *Perf. 13½*

562 A184 5b multicolored 1.10 .50

Sesquicentennial of the Battle of Ayacucho.

Lions Emblem and Steles
A185

1975, Mar. Litho. *Perf. 13½*
563 A185 30c red & multi .35 .35

Lions Intl. in Bolivia, 25th anniv.

España 75 Emblem
A186

1975, Mar.
564 A186 4.50b yel, red & blk .80 .35

Espana 75 International Philatelic Exhibition, Madrid, Apr. 4-13.

Emblem
A187

1975 Litho. *Perf. 13½*
565 A187 2.50b lil, blk & sil .65 .25

First meeting of Postal Ministers, Quito, Ecuador, March 1974, and for the Cartagena Agreement.

Pando Coat of Arms — A188

Designs: Departmental coats of arms.

1975, July 16 Litho. *Perf. 13½*
566 A188 20c shown .20 .20
567 A188 2b Chuquisaca .40 .40
568 A188 3b Cochabamba .50 .50
Nos. 566-568,C336-C341 (9) 4.25 4.25

Sesquicentennial of Republic of Bolivia.

Simón Bolívar — A189

Presidents and Statesmen of Bolivia: 30c, Victor Paz Estenssoro. 60c, Tomas Frias. 1b, Ismael Montes. 2.50b, Aniceto Arce. 7b, Bautista Saavedra. 10b, Jose Manuel Pando. 15b, Jose Maria Linares. 50b, Simon Bolivar.

1975 Litho. *Perf. 13½*

Size: 24x32mm

569 A189 30c multi .20 .20
569A A189 60c multi .20 .20
570 A189 1b multi .30 .30
571 A189 2.50b multi .50 .50
572 A189 7b multi 1.40 .50
573 A189 10b multi 2.00 .75
574 A189 15b multi 2.50 2.50

Size: 28x39mm

575 A189 50b multi 10.00 10.00
Nos. 569-575,C346-C353 (16) 36.10 31.20

Sesquicentennial of Republic of Bolivia.

"EXFIVIA 75"
A190

1975, Dec. 1 Litho. *Perf. 13½*
576 A190 3b multicolored .75 .60
a. Souvenir sheet 1.50 1.50

EXFIVIA 75, first Bolivian Philatelic Exposition. No. 576a contains one stamp similar to No. 576 with simulated perforations. Sold for 5b.

A191

A192

Chiang Kai-shek, flags of Bolivia and China.

1976, Apr. 4 Litho. *Perf. 13½*
577 A191 2.50b multi, red circle 1.00 1.00
578 A191 2.50b multi, bl circle 1.00 1.00

Pres. Chiang Kai-shek of China (1887-1975).
Erroneous red of sun's circle on Chinese flag of No. 577 was corrected on No. 578 with a dark blue overlay.

1976, Apr. Litho. *Perf. 13½*
579 A192 50c Naval insignia .40 .35

Navy anniversary.

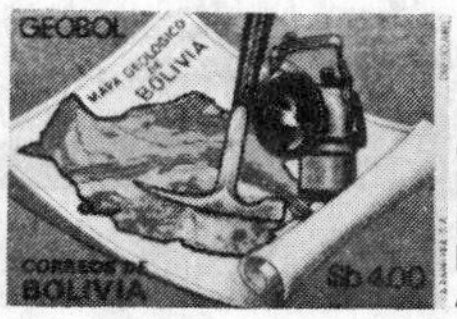

Geological Map, Pickax and Lamp
A193

1976, May
580 A193 4b multicolored .80 .60

Bolivian Geological Institute.

Lufthansa Jet, Bolivian and German Colors
A194

1976, May
581 A194 3b multicolored .80 .35

Lufthansa, 50th anniversary.

Boy Scout and Scout Emblem — A195

1976, May Litho. *Perf. 13½*
582 A195 1b multicolored .50 .50

Bolivian Boy Scouts, 60th anniversary.

Battle Scene, US Bicentennial Emblem — A196

1976, May 25
583 A196 4.50b bis & multi 1.40 .65

American Bicentennial.
A souvenir sheet contains one stamp similar to No. 583 with simulated perforations. Size: 130x80mm.

Family, Map of Bolivia
A197

Vicente Bernedo
A198

1976 *Perf. 13½*
584 A197 2.50b multicolored .50 .40

National Census 1976.

1976, Oct.
585 A198 1.50b multicolored .35 .30

Brother Vicente Bernedo de Potosi (1544-1619), missionary to the Indians.

Policeman with Dog, Rainbow over La Paz — A199

1976, Oct.
586 A199 2.50b multicolored .60 .60

Bolivian Police, 150 years of service.

Emblem, Bolivar and Sucre
A200

1976, Nov. 18 Litho. *Perf. 13½*
587 A200 1.50b multicolored .60 .60

Intl. Congress of Bolivarian Societies.

Pedro Poveda, View of La Paz — A201

1976, Dec.
588 A201 1.50b multicolored .35 .25

Pedro Poveda (1874-1936), educator.

A202

Boy and Girl — A203

1976, Dec. 17 *Perf. 10½*
594 A202 20c brown .30 .20
595 A202 1b ultra .45 .20
596 A202 1.50b green .75 .50
Nos. 594-596 (3) 1.50 .90

1977, Feb. 4 Litho. *Perf. 13½*
599 A203 50c multicolored .20 .20

Christmas 1976, and for 50th anniversary of the Inter-American Children's Institute.

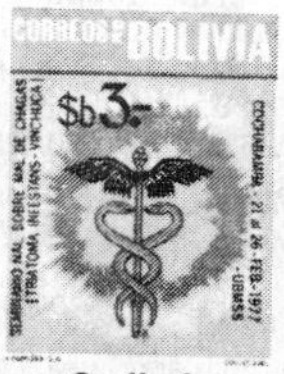

Staff of Aesculapius
A204

Supreme Court, La Paz
A205

1977, Mar. 18 Litho. *Perf. 13½x13*
600 A204 3b multicolored .75 .30

National Seminar on Chagas' disease, Cochabamba, Feb. 21-26.

1977, May 3

Designs: 4b, Manuel Maria Urcullu, first President of Supreme Court. 4.50b, Pantaleon Dalence, President 1883-1889.

601 A205 2.50b multi .30 .30
602 A205 4b multi .40 .20
603 A205 4.50b multi .50 .20
Nos. 601-603 (3) 1.20 .70

Sesquicentennial of Bolivian Supreme Court.

Newspaper Mastheads
A206

Map of Bolivia, Tower and Flag
A207

Designs: 2.50b, Alfredo Alexander and Hoy, horiz. 3b, Jose Carrasco and El Diario, horiz. 4b, Demetrio Canelas and Los Tiempos. 5.50b, Frontpage of Presencia.

1977, June Litho. *Perf. 13½*
604 A206 1.50b multi .25 .20
605 A206 2.50b multi .35 .30
606 A206 3b multi .40 .25
607 A206 4b multi .50 .35
608 A206 5.50b multi .65 .20
Nos. 604-608 (5) 2.15 1.30

Bolivian newspapers and their founders.

1977, June
609 A207 3b multi .50 .20

90th anniversary of Oruro Club.

Games' Poster
A208

Tin Miner and Emblem
A209

1977, Oct. 20 Litho. *Perf. 13½*
610 A208 5b blue & multi .75 .20

8th Bolivian Games, La Paz, Oct. 1977.

1977, Oct. 31 Litho. *Perf. 13*
611 A209 3b multicolored .60 .40

Bolivian Mining Corp., 25th anniv.

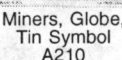

Miners, Globe, Tin Symbol A210

Map of Bolivia, Radio Masts A211

1977, Nov. 3
612 A210 6b silver & multi .80 .25

Intl. Tin Symposium, La Paz, Nov. 14-21.

1977, Nov. 11
613 A211 2.50b blue & multi .50 .35

Radio Bolivia, ASBORA, 50th anniversary.

No. 450 Surcharged with New Value, 3 Bars and "EXFIVIA-77"

1977, Nov. 25 Litho. *Perf. 11x13½*
614 A147 5b on 5000b on 5b 1.00 1.25

EXFIVIA '77 Philatelic Exhibition, Cochabamba.

Eye, Compass, Book of Law — A212

1978, May 3 Litho. *Perf. 13½x13*
615 A212 5b multi .65 .20

Audit Department, 50th anniversary.

Mt. Illimani — A213

Pre-Columbian Monolith — A214

Design: 1.50b, Mt. Cerro de Potosí.

Perf. 11x10½, 10½x11
1978, June 1 Litho.
616 A213 50c bl & Prus bl .20 .20
617 A214 1b brn & lemon .20 .20
618 A213 1.50b red & bl gray .35 .25
Nos. 616-618 (3) .75 .65

Andean Countries, Staff of Aesculapius A215

Map of Americas with Bolivia A216

1978, June 1 *Perf. 10½x11*
626 A215 2b org & blk .35 .20

Health Ministers of Andean Countries, 5th meeting.

1978, June 1
627 A216 2.50b dp ultra & red .35 .20

World Rheumatism Year.
For surcharges see Nos. 697, 972.

Central Bank Building — A217

Jesus and Children — A218

1978, July 26 Litho. *Perf. 13½*
628 A217 7b multi 1.00 .25

50th anniversary of Bank of Bolivia.

1979, Feb. 20 Litho. *Perf. 13½*
629 A218 8b multicolored .90 .20

International Year of the Child.

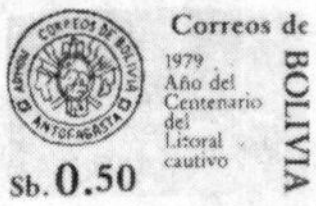

Antofagasta Cancel — A219

Eduardo Abaroa, Chain — A220

Designs: 1b, La Chimba cancel. 1.50b, Mejillones cancel. 5.50b, View of Antofagasta, horiz. 6.50b, Woman in chains, symbolizing captive province. 8b, Map of Antofagasta Province, 1876. 10b, Arms of province.

1979, Mar. 23 Litho. *Perf. 10½*
630 A219 50e buff & blk .30 .20
631 A219 1b pink & blk .50 .25
632 A219 1.50b pale grn & blk .50 .25

Perf. 13½
633 A220 5.50b multi .60 .25
634 A220 6.50b multi .80 .30
635 A220 7b multi .80 .30
636 A220 8b multi .90 .35
637 A220 10b multi 1.10 .35
Nos. 630-637 (8) 5.50 2.25

Loss of Antofagasta coastal area to Chile, cent.
For surcharge see No. 696.

Emblem and Map of Bolivia A221

Gymnast A222

1979, Mar. 26 *Perf. 13½x13*
638 A221 3b multicolored .75 .50

Radio Club of Bolivia.

Perf. 13x13½, 13½x13
1979, Mar. 27

6.50b, Runner and Games emblem, horiz.

639 A222 6.50b multi .80 .50
640 A222 10b multi 1.10 .25

Southern Cross Sports Games, Bolivia, Nov. 3-12, 1978.
A souvenir sheet contains 1 stamp similar to No. 640 with simulated perforations. Sold for 20b. Size: 80x130mm.
For surcharge see No. 965.

Bulgaria No. 1 — A223

EXFILMAR Emblem — A224

1979, Mar. 30 *Perf. 10½*
641 A223 2.50b multi .35 .25

PHILASERDICA '79 International Philatelic Exhibition, Sofia, Bulgaria, May 18-27.
For surcharge see No. 694.

1979, Apr. 2
642 A224 2b multi .20 .20

Bolivian Maritime Philatelic Exhibition, La Paz, Nov. 18-28.
For surcharge see No. 698.

OAS Emblem, Map of Bolivia — A226

1979, Oct. 22 Litho. *Perf. 14x13½*
644 A226 6b multi .75 .25

Organization of American States, 9th Congress, La Paz, Oct.-Nov.

Franz Tamayo — A227

Bolivian and Japanese Flags, Hospital — A228

UN Emblem and Meeting — A229

Radio Tower and Waves — A230

1979, Dec.
645 A227 2.80b blk & gray .35 .25
646 A228 5b multi .50 .35
648 A229 5b multi .50 .35
649 A230 6b multi .65 .25
Nos. 645-649 (4) 2.00 1.20

Franz Tamayo, lawyer, birth centenary; Japanese-Bolivian health care cooperation; CEPAL, 18th Congress, La Paz, Sept. 18-26; Bolivian National Radio, 50th anniversary.
For surcharge see No. 695.

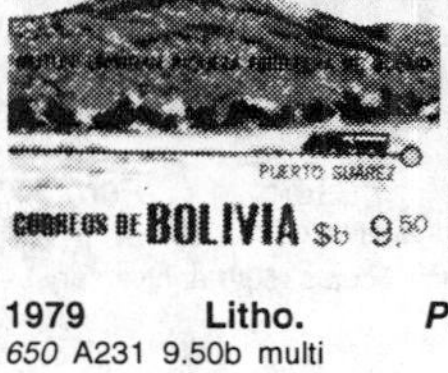

Puerto Suarez Iron Ore Deposits A231

1979 Litho. *Perf. 13½x14*
650 A231 9.50b multi 1.10 .50

Bolivia No. 19, EXFILMAR Emblem, Bolivian Flag A232

1980 Litho. *Perf. 13½*
651 A232 4b multi .55 .30

EXFILMAR, Bolivian Maritime Philatelic Exhibition, La Paz, Nov. 18-28, 1979.

Juana Azurduy on Horseback — A233

1980 Litho. *Perf. 14x13½*
652 A233 4b multi .55 .30

Juana Azurduy de Padilla, independence fighter, birth bicentenary.

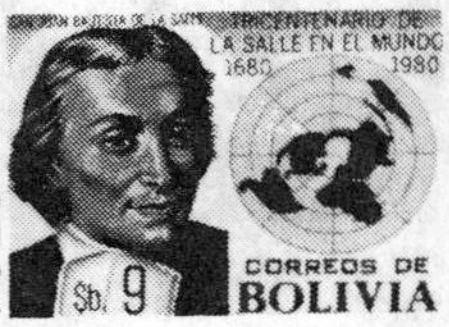

La Salle and World Map A234

1980 *Perf. 13½x14*
653 A234 9b multi 1.10 .60

St. Jean Baptiste de la Salle (1651-1719), educator.
For surcharge see No. 966.

"Victory" in Chariot, Madrid, Exhibition Emblem, Flags of Bolivia and Spain A235

1980, Oct. Litho. *Perf. 13½x14*
654 A235 14b multi 1.60 .75

ESPAMER '80 Stamp Exhibition, Madrid.

Map of South America, Flags of Argentina, Bolivia and Peru — A236

1980, Oct. *Perf. 14x13½*
655 A236 2b multi .25 .20

Ministers of Public Works and Transport of Argentina, Bolivia and Peru meeting.

Santa Cruz-Trinidad Railroad, Inauguration of Third Section — A237

1980, Oct.
656 A237 3b multi .35 .20

Flag on Provincial Map — A238

Parrots — A239

Perf. 14x13½, 13½x14

1981, May 11 **Litho.**
657 A238 1b Soldier, flag, map .20 .20
658 A238 3b Flag, map .35 .20
659 A238 40b shown 5.00 1.25
660 A238 50b Soldier, civilians, horiz. 6.00 1.25
Nos. 657-660 (4) 11.55 2.90

July 17 Revolution memorial.

1981, May 11 ***Perf. 14x13½***
661 A239 4b Ara macao .50 .30
662 A239 7b Ara chloroptera .80 .50
663 A239 8b Ara ararauna 1.00 .60
664 A239 9b Ara rubrogenys 1.10 .65
665 A239 10b Ara auricollis 1.10 .65
666 A239 12b Anodorynchus hyacinthinus 1.50 .75
667 A239 15b Ara militaris 1.75 1.00
668 A239 20b Ara severa 2.25 1.25
Nos. 661-668 (8) 10.00 5.70

Christmas 1981 — A240

1981, Dec. 7 **Litho.** ***Perf. 10½***
669 A240 1b Virgin and Child, vert. .20 .20
670 A240 2b Child, star .25 .20

American Airforces Commanders' 22nd Conference, Buenos Aires — A241

1982, Apr. 12 **Litho.** ***Perf. 13½***
671 A241 14b multi 1.60 .50

75th Anniv. of Cobija — A242

Simon Bolivar Birth Bicentenary (1983) — A243

1982, July 8 **Litho.** ***Perf. 13½***
672 A242 28b multi .40 .25

1982, July 12
673 A243 18b multi .25 .20

1983 World Telecommunications Day — A244

1982 World Cup — A245

1982, July 15
674 A244 26b Receiving station .40 .25

1982, July 21 ***Perf. 11***
675 A245 4b shown .20 .20
676 A245 100b Final Act, by Picasso 1.75 .95

For surcharge see No. 701.

Girl Playing Piano — A246

1982, July 25 ***Perf. 13½***
677 A246 16b Boy playing soccer, vert. .25 .20
678 A246 20b shown .35 .20

Bolivian-Chinese Agricultural Cooperation, 1972-1982 — A247

1982, Aug. 12
679 A247 30b multi .50 .25

First Bolivian-Japanese Gastroenterology Conference, La Paz, Jan. — A248

1982, Aug. 26
680 A248 22b multi .35 .25

A249

A250

1982, Aug. 31 **Litho.** ***Perf. 14x13½***
681 A249 19b Stamps .35 .20

10th Anniv. of Bolivian Philatelic Federation.

1982, Sept. 1
682 A250 20b tan & dk brown .30 .20

Pres. Hernando Siles, birth centenary.

Scouting Year — A251

Cochabamba Philatelic Center, 25th Anniv. — A252

1982, Sept. 3 ***Perf. 11***
683 A251 5b Baden-Powell .20 .20

For surcharge see No. 703.

1982, Sept. 14
684 A252 3b multicolored .20 .20

For surcharge see No. 700.

Cochabamba Superior Court of Justice Sesquicentennial — A253

1982 **Litho.** ***Perf. 13½***
685 A253 10b multicolored .20 .20

For surcharge see No. 970.

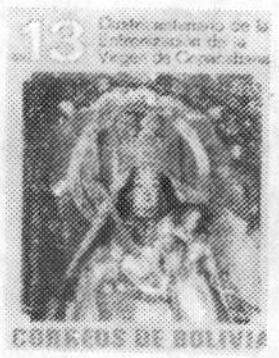

Enthronement of Virgin of Copacabana, 400th Anniv. — A254

Navy Day — A255

1982, Nov. 15 **Litho.** ***Perf. 13½***
686 A254 13b multicolored .25 .20

For surcharge see No. 971.

1982, Nov. 17
687 A255 14b Port Busch Naval Base .25 .20

A256

A257

1982, Nov. 19 ***Perf. 11***
688 A256 10b green & gray .20 .20

Christmas. For surcharge see No. 702.

1983, Feb. 13 **Litho.** ***Perf. 13½***
689 A257 50b multicolored .80 .40

10th Youth Soccer Championship, Jan. 22-Feb. 13.

EXFIVIA '83 Philatelic Exhibition A258

1983, Nov. 5 **Litho.** ***Perf. 13½***
690 A258 150b brown carmine 1.00 .50

Visit of Brazilian Pres. Joao Figueiredo, Feb. — A259

1984, Feb. 7 **Litho.** ***Perf. 13½x14***
691 A259 150b multicolored .40 .20

Simon Bolivar Entering La Paz, by Carmen Baptista A260

Paintings of Bolivar: 50b, Riding Horse, by Mulato Gil de Quesada, vert.

Perf. 14x13½, 13½x14

1984, Mar. 30
692 A260 50b multi .20 .20
693 A260 200b multi .55 .25

Types of 1957-79 Surcharged

$b. 60.-

No. 697

1984, Mar.
694 A223 40b on 2.50b #641 .20 .20
695 A227 40b on 2.80b #645 .20 .20
696 A219 60b on 1.50b #632 .20 .20
697 A216 60b on 2.50b #627 .20 .20
698 A224 100b on 2b #642 .30 .20
699 A141 200b on 350b #409 .60 .25
Nos. 694-699 (6) 1.70 1.25

See No. 972 for surcharge similar to No. 697.

Nos. 675, 683-684, 688, C328 Surcharged

1984, June 27 **Litho.** ***Perf. 11***
700 A252 500b on 3b #684 .75 .35
701 A245 1000b on 4b #675 1.50 .75
702 A256 2000b on 10b #688 3.00 1.25
703 A251 5000b on 5b #683 7.50 3.00

Perf. 13½
704 A182 10,000b on 3.80b #C328 10.00 6.00
Nos. 700-704 (5) 22.75 11.35

Road Safety Education A261

Jose Eustaquio Mendez, 200th Birth Anniv. A262

Cartoons.

1984, Sept. 7 **Litho.** ***Perf. 11***
705 A261 80b Jaywalker .20 .20
706 A261 120b Motorcycle policeman, ambulance .20 .20

Perf. 14x13½, 13½x14

1984, Sept. 19

Paintings: 300b, Birthplace, by Jorge Campos. 500b, Mendez Leading the Battle of La Tablada, by M. Villegas, horiz.

707 A262 300b multi .20 .20
708 A262 500b multi .20 .20

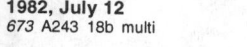

1983 World Cup Soccer Championships, Mexico — A263

Chasqui, Postal Runner — A264

Sponsoring shoe-manufacturers' trademarks and: 100b, 200b, Outline map of Bolivia, national colors. 600b, World map and soccer ball, horiz.

1984, Oct. 26 ***Perf. 11***

709 A263	100b multi	.20	.20
710 A263	200b multi	.20	.20
711 A263	600b multi	.20	.20
	Nos. 709-711 (3)	.60	.60

1985

712 A264	11000b vio bl	.25	.20

For surcharge see No. 962.

Intl. Year of Professional Education A265

Intl. Anti-Polio Campaign A266

1985, Apr. 25

713 A265	2000b Natl. Manual Crafts emblem	.20	.20

For surcharges see Nos. 721-722, 959.

1985, May 22

714 A266	20000b lt bl & vio	.25	.20

Endangered Wildlife — A267

1985, May 22

715 A267	23000b Altiplano boliviano	.20	.20
716 A267	25000b Sarcorhamphus gryphus	.25	.20
717 A267	30000b Blastocaros dichotomus	.30	.20
	Nos. 715-717 (3)	.75	.60

Nos. 716-717 vert.
For surcharge see No. 963.

Dona Vicenta Juaristi Eguino (b. 1785), Independence Heroine — A268

UN, 40th Anniv. — A269

1985, Oct. **Litho.** ***Perf. 13½***

718 A268	300000b multi	.20	.20

1985, Oct. 24 ***Perf. 11***

719 A269	1000000b bl & gold	.65	.30

For surcharge see No. 964.

A270

A271

1985, Nov.

720 A270	200000b multi	.20	.20

Soccer Team named "The Strongest," 75th anniv.

No. 713 Surcharged

1986 **Litho.** ***Perf. 11***

721 A265	200000b on 2000b	.25	.20
722 A265	5000000b on 2000b	5.25	2.50

1986

723 A271	300000 Emblems, vert.	.30	.20
724 A271	550000 Pique trademark, vert.	.60	.25
725 A271	1000000 Azteca Stadium	1.00	.50
726 A271	2500000 World cup, vert.	2.75	1.25
	Nos. 723-726 (4)	4.65	2.20

1986 World Cup Soccer Championships.
For surcharge see No. 961.

Intl. Youth Year
A272 A273

1986

727 A272	150000 brt car rose	.20	.20
728 A272	500000 bl grn	.55	.30
729 A273	3000000 multi	3.25	1.50
	Nos. 727-729 (3)	4.00	2.00

Inscribed 1985.
For surcharge see No. 958.

Alfonso Sobieta Viaduct, Carretera Quillacollo, Confital — A274

1986 ***Perf. 13½***

730 A274	400000 int bl & gray	.40	.20

Inter-American Development Bank, 25th anniv.

Admission of Bolivia to the UPU, Cent. — A275

Postal Workers Soc., 50th Anniv. — A276

1986, Apr. 3 ***Perf. 11***

731 A275	800000 multi	.85	.40

1986, Sept. 5

732 A276	2000000 brn & pale brn	2.10	1.00

For surcharge see No. 967.

Founding of Trinidad, 300th Anniv. A277

1986, May 25 ***Perf. 13½x14***

733 A277	1400000 Bull and Rider, by Vaca	1.50	.75

For surcharge see No. 960.

Bolivian Philatelic Federation, 15th Anniv. A278

1986, Nov. 28

734 A278	600000b No. 19	.60	.30

Death of a Priest, by Jose Antonio Zampa — A279

Intl. Peace Year — A280

1986, Nov. 21 ***Perf. 14x13½***

735 A279	400000b multi	.40	.20

1986, Sept. 16 ***Perf. 11***

736 A280	200000 yel grn & pale grn	.25	.20

Natl. Oil Corp. (YPBF), 50th Anniv. — A281

1986, Dec. 22 **Litho.** ***Perf. 11***

737 A281	1000000b multi	1.50	.50

A282

A283

Photograph of a Devil-mask Dancer, by Jimenez Cordero.

1987, Feb. 13 **Litho.** ***Perf. 14x13½***

738 A282	20c multi	.30	.20

February 10th Society, cent. (in 1985).

1987, Mar. 20 **Litho.** ***Perf. 14x13½***

739 A283	30c Crossed flags	.45	.25

State Visit of Richard von Weizsacker, Pres. of Germany, Mar. 20.

State Visit of King Juan Carlos of Spain, May 20 — A284

1987, May 20 ***Perf. 13½x14***

740 A284	60c Natl. arms	.90	.40

EXFIVIA '87 — A285

Mount Potosi, 18th cent. engraving.

1987, Oct. **Litho.** ***Perf. 13½***

741 A285	50c multi	.70	.35

See No. 750.

Wildlife Conservation A286

1987, Oct.

742 A286	20c Condor	.30	.20
743 A286	20c Tapir	.30	.20
744 A286	30c Vicuna	.45	.25
745 A286	30c Armadillo	.45	.25
746 A286	40c Spectacled bears	.60	.30
747 A286	60c Toucans	.90	.40
	Nos. 742-747 (6)	3.00	1.60

Wildlife in danger of extinction.

ESPAMER '87, La Coruna A287

1987, Oct. **Litho.** ***Perf. 14x13½***

748 A287	20c Nina, stern of Santa Maria	.30	.20
749 A287	20c Bow of Santa Maria, Pinta	.30	.20
a.	Pair, #748-749	.60	.25

No. 749a has a continuous design.

EXFIVIA Type of 1987

Photograph of Mt. Potosi by Jimenez Cordero.

1987, Aug. 5 **Litho.** ***Perf. 13½***

750 A285	40c multi	.60	.30

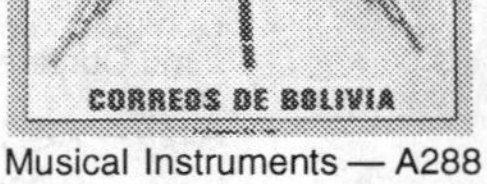

Musical Instruments — A288

1987, Dec. 3 ***Perf. 13½x14, 14x13½***

751 A288	50c Zampona and quena (wind instruments)	.70	.35
752 A288	1b Charango, vert.	1.40	.70

A289

State Visit of Pope John Paul II A290

Pontiff, religious architecture and art: No. 753, Cathedral of Kings, Beni. No. 754, Carabuco Church. No. 755, Tihuanacu Church. No. 756, St. Francis's Church, Sucre. No. 757, St. Joseph's of Chiquitos Church. 40c, Cobija Chapel, vert. No. 759, Jayu Kcota Church. No. 760, Cochabamba Cathedral, vert. 60c, St. Francis's Basilica, La Paz, vert. No. 762, Christ of Machaca Church. No. 763, St. Lawrence's Church, Potosi, vert. No. 764, *The Holy Family*, by Rubens, vert. No. 765, *The Virgin of Copacabana*, statue, vert. No. 766, Vallegrande Church. No. 767, Tarija Cathedral, vert. No. 768, Concepcion Church.

1988 Litho. *Perf. 13½x14, 14x13½*

753	A289	20c multi	.25	.20
754	A289	20c multi	.25	.20
755	A289	20c multi	.25	.20
756	A289	30c multi	.40	.20
757	A289	30c multi	.40	.20
758	A289	40c multi	.50	.25
759	A289	50c multi	.65	.30
760	A289	50c multi	.65	.30
761	A289	60c multi	.75	.35
762	A289	70c multi	.90	.35
763	A289	70c multi	.90	.35
764	A289	80c multi	1.00	.45
765	A289	80c multi	1.00	.45
766	A289	80c multi	1.00	.45
767	A289	1.30b multi	1.60	.75
768	A289	1.30b multi	1.60	.75
769	A290	1.50b shown	1.90	.90
		Nos. 753-769 (17)	14.00	6.65

Issue dates: 1.50b, May 9; others, Mar. 3.

Visit of Pres. Jose Sarney of Brazil A291

1988, Aug. 2 Litho. *Perf. 13½x14*
770 A291 50c multi .60 .30

St. John Bosco (1815-1888) — A292

1988, Aug. 16 *Perf. 13½*
771 A292 30c multi .40 .20

Bolivian Railways, Cent. A293

Design: 1b, Steam locomotive from the La Paz-Beni line, made by Marca Shy Ohio, Natl. Railway Museum, Sucre.

1988, Aug. 29
772 A293 1b multi 1.25 .60

Nataniel Aguirre (b. 1888), Author — A294

Department of Pando, 50th Anniv. — A295

1988, Sept. 14 Litho. *Perf. 13½*
773 A294 1b blk & beige 1.25 .60

1988, Sept. 26 *Perf. 13½*

Designs: 40c, *Columna Porvenir*, memorial to the Battle of Bahio. 60c, Siringuero rubber production (worker sapping latex from *Hevea brasiliensis*).

774 A295 40c multi .50 .25
775 A295 60c multi .70 .35

A296

A297

1988, Sept. 27
776 A296 1.50b multi 1.90 .90

1988 Summer Olympics, Seoul.

1988

Designs: 70c, Archbishop Bernardino de Cardenas (1579-1668). 80c, Mother Rosa Gattorno (1831-1900), founder of the Sisters of Santa Ana.

777 A297 70c multi .90 .45
778 A297 80c multi 1.00 .50

Issue dates: 70c, Oct. 20, 80c, Oct. 14.

Ministry of Transportation & Communications A298

1988, Oct. 24 Litho. *Perf. 14x13½*
779 A298 2b deep car, blk & pale olive grn 2.40 1.00

Army Communications, 50th Anniv. (in 1987) — A299

1988, Nov. 29 Litho. *Perf. 13½*
780 A299 70c multi .95 .45

Bolivian Automobile Club, 50th Anniv. — A300

1988, Dec. 29 Litho. *Perf. 13½*
781 A300 1.50b multi 1.50 .70

Flowering Plants and Emblems A301

Designs: 50c, Orchid, BULGARIA '89 emblem, vert. 60c, Kantuta blossoms, ITALIA '90 emblem. 70c, *Heliconia humilis*, Albertville '86 emblem, vert. 1b, Hoffmanseggia, Barcelona '92 Games emblem, vert. 2b, Puya raymondi, Seoul '88 Games and five-ring emblems, vert.

1989, Feb. 17 Litho. *Perf. 13½*

782	A301	50c multi	.60	.25
783	A301	60c multi	.70	.30
784	A301	70c multi	.80	.30
785	A301	1b multi	1.10	.45
786	A301	2b multi	2.25	.90
		Nos. 782-786 (5)	5.45	2.20

Radio FIDES, 50th Anniv. — A302

1989, Feb. 2
787 A302 80c multi .90 .40

Gold Quarto of 1852 A303

1989, Feb. 9 *Perf. 13½x14*
788 A303 1b multi 1.25 .50

French Revolution, Bicent. — A304

1989, June 23 Litho. *Perf. 14x13½*
789 A304 70c red, blk & blue .90 .35

Uyuni Township, Cent. — A305

1989, July 9 Litho. *Perf. 14x13½*
790 A305 30c blue, black & gray .40 .20

Noel Kempff Mercado Natl. Park, Santa Cruz — A306

Designs: 1.50b, Federico Ahlfeld Falls, Pauserna River. 3b, *Ozotoceros bezcarticus* (deer).

1989, Sept. 24 Litho. *Perf. 13½x14*
791 A306 1.50b multicolored 2.00 .75
792 A306 3b multicolored 4.00 1.50

UPAEP A306a

1989, Oct. 12 Litho. *Perf. 13½*
792A A306a 50c Metalworking .50 .20
792B A306a 1b Temple of Kalasasaya 1.00 .40

See Nos. 808-809

State Visit by Dr. Carlos Andres Perez, Pres. of Venezuela A306b

1989, Oct. 14
792C A306b 2b multi 2.00 .80

See Nos. 825-826, 832.

City of Potosi — A306c

1989, Nov. 10 Litho. *Perf. 13½*
792D A306c 60c Cobija Arch .75 .30
792E A306c 80c Mint .85 .40
f. Pair, #792D-792E 1.60 .70

Christmas A307

Paintings: 40c, *Andean Stillwaters*, by Arturo Borda. 60c, *The Virgin of the Roses*, anonymous. 80c, *The Conquistador*, by Jorge de la Reza. 1b, *Native Harmony*, by Juan Rimsa. 1.50b, *Woman with Jug*, by Cecilio Guzman de Rojas. 2b, *Bloom of Tenderness*, by Gil Imana. Nos. 794-798 vert.

Perf. 13½x14, 14x13½
1989, Dec. 18

793	A307	40c multicolored	.40	.20
794	A307	60c multicolored	.60	.25
795	A307	80c multicolored	.80	.30
796	A307	1b multicolored	1.00	.40
797	A307	1.50b multicolored	1.50	.60
798	A307	2b multicolored	2.00	.80
		Nos. 793-798 (6)	6.30	2.55

A308

A309

1990, Jan. 23 Litho. *Perf. 13½*
799 A308 80c multicolored .85 .35

Fight against drug abuse.

1990, May 13 *Perf. 14x13½*

Great Britain #1, Sir Rowland Hill & Bolivia #1

800 A309 4b multicolored 4.00 1.75

Penny Black, 150th anniv.

World Cup Soccer Championships, Italy — A310

1990, June 16 *Perf. 13½*
801 A310 2b Stadium, Milan 2.00 .80
802 A310 6b Game 6.00 2.40

Organization of American States, Cent. — A311

1990, Apr. 14
803 A311 80c dark bl & brt bl .80 .30

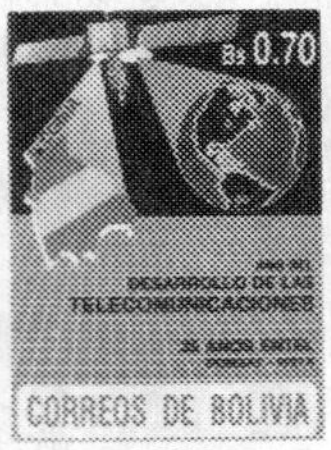

A312 A313

1990, Apr. 16
804 A312 1.20b multi 1.25 .60

1990 Litho. *Perf. 14x13½*
805 A313 70c Telecommunications .70 .55

National Chamber of Commerce, Cent. — A314

1990, June
806 A314 50c gold, blk & bl .60 .40

Cochabamba Social Club, Cent. — A315

1990, Sept. 14 Litho. *Perf. 13½*
807 A315 40c multicolored .40 .30

UPAEP Type of 1989

Perf. 13½x14, 14x13½

1990, Oct. 12 **Litho.**
808 A306a 80c Huts .75 .30
809 A306a 1b Mountains, lake, vert. .95 .40

A317 A318

1990, Oct. 19 *Perf. 14x13½*
810 A317 1.20b multicolored 1.00 .40

Magistrate's District of Larecaja, 400th Anniv.

1990, Oct. 12 *Perf. 14x13½*
811 A318 2b multicolored 1.75 .70

Discovery of America, 500th anniv. (in 1992).

German Reunification A319

1990, Nov. 19 Litho. *Perf. 14x13½*
812 A319 2b multicolored 1.75 .70

Visit of Carlos Salinas de Gortari, Pres. of Mexico — A320

Design: 80c, Visit of Rodrigo Borja Cevallos, Pres. of Ecuador.

1990, Dec. 13 Litho. *Perf. 13½*
813 A320 60c multicolored .75 .30
814 A320 80c multicolored .85 .40

4th Congress of the Andean Presidents A321

1990, Nov. 29 *Perf. 13½x14*
815 A321 1.50b multicolored 1.40 .55

Exfivia '90 A322

Christmas A323

1990, Dec. 9 *Perf. 13½*
816 A322 40c dk blue .40 .20

1990, Nov. 20 *Perf. 11*
817 A323 50c multicolored .45 .20

Express Mail Service A324

1990, Dec. 14 *Perf. 13½x14*
818 A324 1b multicolored .90 .35

Bolivian Radio Club, 50th Anniv. — A325

1991, Mar. 1 Litho. *Perf. 14x13½*
819 A325 2.40b multicolored 2.00 .80

End of Chaco War, 56th Anniv. A326

National Museums A327

Map of Heroes of Chaco Highway.

1991, June 14 Litho. *Perf. 14x13½*
820 A326 60c multicolored .55 .25

1991, June 13 *Perf. 13½*
821 A327 50c Archaeology .40 .20
822 A327 50c Art .40 .20
823 A327 1b Ethnology, Folklore .85 .35
a. Strip of 3, #821-823 1.70 .70

Espamer '91.

A328 A329

Our Lady of Peace, Metropolitan Cathedral.

1991, July 15 Litho. *Perf. 14x13½*
824 A328 1.20b multicolored 1.10 .45

Presidential State Visit Type of 1989

Jaime Paz Zamora, Pres. of Bolivia and: No. 825, Dr. Carlos Saul Menem, Pres. of Argentina. No. 826, Dr. Luis Alberto Lacalle, Pres. of Uruguay.

1991 *Perf. 13½x14*
825 A306b 1b multicolored .85 .35
826 A306b 1b multicolored .85 .35

Issue dates: #825, Aug. 5; #826, Aug. 12.

1991, May 31 *Perf. 13½*

Tremarctos ornatus.

827 A329 30c Adult, 2 cubs 1.10 .20
828 A329 30c Adult's head 1.10 .20
829 A329 30c Adult on tree limb 1.10 .20
830 A329 30c Adult, cubs on tree limb 1.10 .20
Nos. 827-830 (4) 4.40 .80

World Wildlife Fund.

A330 A331

1991, Aug. 21 Litho. *Perf. 14x13½*
831 A330 70c multicolored .70 .30

Bolivian Philatelic Federation, 20th anniv.

Presidential State Visit Type of 1989

Design: 50c, Jaime Paz Zamora, Pres. of Bolivia and Alberto Fujimori, Pres. of Peru.

1991, Aug. 29 *Perf. 13½x14*
832 A306b 50c multicolored .45 .20

1991, Nov. 19 Litho. *Perf. 14x13½*
833 A331 50c multicolored .45 .20

National census.

America Issue — A332

UPAEP emblem and: 60c, First Discovery of Chuquiago, 1535, by Arturo Reque M. 1.20c, Founding of the City of La Paz, 1548, by J. Rimsa, vert.

1991, Oct. 12 *Perf. 13½x14, 14x13½*
834 A332 60c multicolored .60 .25
835 A332 1.20b multicolored 1.10 .45

First National Grand Prix Auto and Motorcycle Race — A332a

1991, Sept. 5 Litho. *Perf. 14x13½*
835A A332a 50c multicolored .45 .20

ECOBOL, Postal Security System A333

1991, Sept. 9 *Perf. 13½x14*
836 A333 1.40b multicolored 1.40 .50

Simon Bolivar — A334

1992, Feb. 15 Litho. *Perf. 13½*
837 A334 1.20b buff, brn & org brn 1.10 .45

Exfilbo '92.

Scouting in Bolivia, 75th Anniv. (in 1990) and 1992 Andes Jamboree A335

1992, Jan. 13 *Perf. 13½x14*
838 A335 1.20b multicolored 1.10 .45

Dated 1991.

Christmas A336

Paintings: 2b, Landscape, by Daniel Pena y Sarmiento. 5b, Woman with Fruit, by Cecilio Guzman de Rojas. 15b, Native Mother, by Crespo Gastelu.

1991, Dec.19 **Litho.** *Perf. 13½*
839 A336 2b multicolored 1.50 .60
840 A336 5b multicolored 3.75 1.50
841 A336 15b multicolored 11.25 4.50
Nos. 839-841 (3) 16.50 6.60

Pacific Ocean Access Pact Between Bolivia and Peru A337

Designs: 1.20b, Pres. Zamora raising flag, vert. 1.50b, Pres. Jaime Paz Zamora of Bolivia and Pres. Alberto Fujimori, Peru. 1.80b, Shoreline of access zone near Ilo, Peru.

Perf. 14x13½, 13½x14
1992, Mar. 23
842 A337 1.20b multicolored .95 .40
843 A337 1.50b multicolored 1.10 .50
844 A337 1.80b multicolored 1.40 .55
Nos. 842-844 (3) 3.45 1.45

Expo '92, Seville A338

1992, Apr. 15 *Perf. 13½x14*
845 A338 30c multicolored .30 .20
846 A338 50c Columbus' ships .45 .20

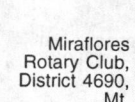

Miraflores Rotary Club, District 4690, Mt. Illimani — A339

1992, Apr. 30 **Litho.** *Perf. 13½*
847 A339 90c multicolored .70 .45

Prof. Elizardo Perez, Founder of Ayllu of Warisata School, Birth Cent. — A340

1992, June 6 **Litho.** *Perf. 13½*
848 A340 60c multicolored .50 .25

Government Palace, Sucre — A341

1992, July 10 **Litho.** *Perf. 13½x14*
849 A341 50c multicolored .40 .20

A342

A343

1992, Sept. 11 *Perf. 14x13½*
850 A342 50c multicolored .40 .20

Los Tiempos Newpaper, 25th anniv.

1992, Aug. 9 *Perf. 13½*

1.50b, Mario Martinez Guzman, tennis player.

851 A343 1.50b multicolored 1.10 .50

1992 Summer Olympics, Barcelona.

First Intl. Whitewater Canoe Regatta, Bermejo River — A343a

1992, Sept. 17 **Litho.** *Perf. 13½*
851A A343a 1.20b multicolored 1.10 .50

1994 World Cup Soccer Championships, US — A344

1992, Oct. 2 **Litho.** *Perf. 13½*
852 A344 1.20b multicolored 1.90 .75

Oruro Technical University, Cent. — A345

1992, Oct. 15 *Perf. 13½x14*
853 A345 50c multicolored .40 .20

Interamerican Institute for Agricultural Cooperation, 50th Anniv. — A346

1992, Oct. 7 *Perf. 13½*
854 A346 1.20b Chenopodium quinoa 1.10 .50

Discovery of America, 500th Anniv. A347

Paintings: 60c, Columbus departing from Palos, vert. 2b, Columbus with Caribbean natives.

1992, Oct. 1 *Perf. 14x13½, 13½x14*
855 A347 60c multicolored .40 .20
856 A347 2b multicolored 1.40 .60

Battle of Ingavi, 150th Anniv. (in 1991) A348

1992, Nov. 18 **Litho.** *Perf. 13½x14*
857 A348 1.20b sepia & black .95 .40

12th Bolivian Games, Cochabamba and Santa Cruz — A349

1992, Nov. 13
858 A349 2b multicolored 1.50 .60

Fauna, Events — A350

Event emblem and fauna: 20c, Beni Dept., sesquicentennial, caiman. 50c, Polska '93, paca. 1b, Bangkok '93, chinchilla. 2b, 1994 Winter Olympics, Lillehammer, Norway, ant-eater. 3b, Brandenburg Gate, jaguar. 4b, Brasiliana '93, hummingbird, vert. 5b, 1994 World Cup Soccer Championships, US, piranhas.

1992, Nov. 18 **Litho.** *Perf. 13½*
859 A350 20c multicolored .20 .20
860 A350 50c multicolored .35 .20
861 A350 1b multicolored .75 .30
862 A350 2b multicolored 1.50 .60
863 A350 3b multicolored 2.25 .90
864 A350 4b multicolored 3.00 1.25
865 A350 5b multicolored 3.75 1.50
Nos. 859-865 (7) 11.80 4.95

Christmas A350a

Designs: 1.20b, Man in canoe, star. 2.50b, Star over churches. 6b, Flowers, church, infant on hay.

1992, Dec. 1 **Litho.** *Perf. 13½*
865A A350a 1.20b multicolored .90 .35
865B A350a 2.50b multicolored 1.90 .75
865C A350a 6b multicolored 4.50 1.75
Nos. 865A-865C (3) 7.30 2.85

A351

A352

Nicolaus Copernicus (1473-1543), Polish Astronomer: 50c, Santa Ana Intl. astrometrical observatory, Tarija, horiz.

Perf. 13x13½, 13½x13
1993, Feb. 18 **Litho.**
866 A351 50c multicolored .40 .20
867 A351 2b black 1.50 .60

1993, Apr. 14 **Litho.** *Perf. 13½*
868 A352 60c multicolored .60 .25

Beatification of Mother Nazaria.

12th Bolivar Games A353

1993, Apr. 24 *Perf. 13½x14*
869 A353 2.30b multicolored 1.60 .65

Bolivia #C240, Brazil #3 — A354

1993, May 31
870 A354 2.30b multicolored 1.60 .65

First Brazilian Stamp, 150th anniv.

A355

A356

Eternal Father, by Gaspar de la Cueva.

1993, June 9 **Litho.** *Perf. 13½*
871 A355 1.80b multicolored 1.25 .50

1993, July 31 **Litho.** *Perf. 14x13½*
872 A356 50c Virgin of Urkupina .35 .20

City of Quillacollo, 400th anniv.

Pedro Domingo Murillo Industrial School — A357

1993, Aug. 4 *Perf. 13½*
873 A357 60c multicolored .40 .20

Butterflies A358

1993, June 4 *Perf. 13½x14*
874 A358 60c Archaeoprepona demophon .55 .20
875 A358 60c Morpho sp. .55 .20
876 A358 80c Papilio sp. .70 .25
877 A358 80c Historis odius .70 .25
878 A358 80c Euptoieta hegesia .70 .25
879 A358 1.80b Morpho deidamia 1.75 .55
880 A358 1.80b Papilio thoas 1.75 .55
881 A358 1.80b Danaus plexippus 1.75 .55
882 A358 2.30b Caligo sp. 2.00 .60
883 A358 2.30b Anaea marthesia 2.00 .60

884 A358 2.30b Rothschildia sp. 2.00 .60
885 A358 2.70b Heliconius sp. 2.25 .75
886 A358 2.70b Marpesia corinna 2.25 .75
887 A358 2.70b Prepona chromus 2.25 .75
888 A358 3.50b Heliconius sp., diff. 3.00 .95
889 A358 3.50b Siproeta epaphus 3.00 .95
a. Sheet of 16, #874-889 30.00 30.00
Nos. 874-889 (16) 27.20 8.75

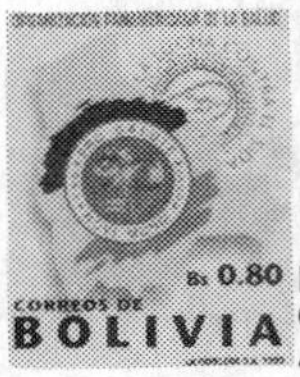

Pan-American Health Organization, 90th Anniv. — A359

1993, Oct. 13 Litho. *Perf. 13½*
890 A359 80c multicolored .55 .20

Archaeological Finds — A360

Location of cave paintings: No. 891, Oruro. No. 892, Santa Cruz, vert. No. 893, Beni, vert. No. 894, Chuquisaca, vert. No. 895, Chuquisaca. No. 896, Potosi. No. 897, La Paz, vert. No. 898, Tarija, vert. No. 899, Cochabamba.

1993, Sept. 28
891 A360 80c multicolored .55 .20
892 A360 80c multicolored .55 .20
893 A360 80c multicolored .55 .20
894 A360 80c multicolored .55 .20
895 A360 80c multicolored .55 .20
896 A360 80c multicolored .55 .20
897 A360 80c multicolored .55 .20
898 A360 80c multicolored .55 .20
899 A360 80c multicolored .55 .20
Nos. 891-899 (9) 4.95 1.80

America Issue — A361

1993, Oct. 9 Litho. *Perf. 13½*
900 A361 80c Saimiri sciereus .55 .20
901 A361 2.30b Felis pordalis 1.50 .60

Famous People A361a

Christmas A361b

Designs: 50c, Yolanda Bedregal, poet. 70c, Simon Martinic, President of Cochabamba Philatelic Center. 90c, Eugenio von Boeck, politician, President of Bolivian Philatelic Federation. 1b, Marina Nunez del Prado, sculptor.

1993, Nov. 17 Litho. *Perf. 11*
901A A361a 50c sepia .30 .20
901B A361a 70c sepia .45 .20
901C A361a 90c sepia .55 .25
901D A361a 1b sepia .60 .25
Nos. 901A-901D (4) 1.90 .90

1993, Dec. 8 *Perf. 14x13½*

Paintings: 2.30b, Adoration of the Shepherds, by Leonardo Flores. 3.50b, Virgin with Child and Saints, by unknown artist. 6b, Virgin of the Milk, by Melchor Perez de Holguin.

901E A361b 2.30b multicolored 1.40 .55
901F A361b 3.50b multicolored 2.25 .85
901G A361b 6b multicolored 3.75 1.50
Nos. 901E-901G (3) 7.40 2.90

Town of Riberalta, Cent. — A362

1994, Feb. 3 Litho. *Perf. 13½*
902 A362 2b multicolored 1.25 .60

World Population Day A363

1994, Feb. 17 Litho. *Perf. 13½*
903 A363 2.30b multicolored 1.50 .60

A364 A365

1994, Feb. 21 *Perf. 13½*
904 A364 2b buff & multi 1.25 .60
905 A364 2.30b multi 1.50 .60

Inauguration of Pres. Gonzalo Sanchez de Lozada.

1994, Mar. 22

1994 World Cup Soccer Championships, US: 80c, Mascot. 1.80b, Bolivia, Uruguay. 2.30b, Bolivia, Venezuela. No. 909, Part of Bolivian team, goalies in black. No. 910, Part of Bolivian team, diff. 2.70b, Bolivia, Ecuador. 3.50b, Bolivia, Brazil.

906 A365 80c multicolored .50 .20
907 A365 1.80b multicolored 1.10 .45
908 A365 2.30b multicolored 1.40 .55
909 A365 2.50b multicolored 1.50 .60
910 A365 2.50b multicolored 1.50 .60
a. Pair, #909-910 3.00 1.25
911 A365 2.70b multicolored 1.60 .65
912 A365 3.50b multicolored 2.25 .85
Nos. 906-912 (7) 9.85 3.90

SOS Children's Village, Bolivia — A366

1994, Apr. 12 Litho. *Perf. 13½*
913 A366 2.70b multicolored 1.60 .65

Catholic Archdiocese La Paz, 50th Anniv. — A367

Churches, priests: 1.80b, Church of San Pedro, Msgr. Jorge Manrique Hurtado. 2b, Archbishop Abel I. Antezana y Rojas, Church of the Sacred Heart of Mary, vert. 3.50b, Msgr. Luis Sainz Hinojosa, Church of Santo Domingo, vert.

1994, July 12 Litho. *Perf. 13½*
914 A367 1.80b multicolored 1.10 .45
915 A367 2b multicolored 1.25 .60
916 A367 3.50b multicolored 2.25 .85
Nos. 914-916 (3) 4.60 1.90

A368 A369

Design: 2b, Pres. Victor Paz Estenssoro.

1994, Oct. 2 Litho. *Perf. 13½*
917 A368 2b multicolored 1.25 .50

1994, Oct. 9
918 A369 1.80b No. 46 1.10 .45

Battle of Ft. Boqueron A370

Col. Manuel Marzana Oroza, battle scene.

1994, Oct. 6
919 A370 80c multicolored .50 .20

San Borja, 300th Anniv. — A371

1994, Oct. 14
920 A371 1.60b Erythrina fusca 1.00 .40

America Issue — A372

Old, new methods of postal transport: 1b, Streetcar, van. 5b, Airplane, ox cart.

1994, Oct. 12
921 A372 1b multicolored .65 .25
922 A372 5b multicolored 3.25 1.25

1994 Solar Eclipse A373

Environmental Protection A374

1994 Oct. 21
923 A373 3.50b multicolored 2.25 .85

1994, Sept. 21

Trees: 60c, Buddleja coriacea. 1.80b, Bertholletia exelsa. 2b, Schinus molle, horiz. 2.70b, Polylepis racemosa. 3, Tabebuia chrysantha. 3.50b, Erythrina falcata, horiz.

924 A374 60c multicolored .40 .20
925 A374 1.80b multicolored 1.10 .45
926 A374 2b multicolored 1.25 .50
927 A374 2.70b multicolored 1.60 .65
928 A374 3b multicolored 1.90 .75
929 A374 3.50b multicolored 2.25 .85
Nos. 924-929 (6) 8.50 3.40

Gen. Antonio Jose de Sucre (1795-1830) A375

1995, Jan. 25 Litho. *Perf. 13½*
930 A375 1.80b shown .75 .30
931 A375 3.50b diff. background 1.50 .60

A377 A378

1994, Nov. 25 Litho. *Perf. 13½*
933 A377 2b Tarija girl 1.10 .45
934 A377 5b High plateau child 2.75 .45
935 A377 20b Eastern girl 11.00 3.75
Nos. 933-935 (3) 14.85 4.65

Christmas.

1994, Nov. 28 Litho. *Perf. 13½*
936 A378 1.80b multicolored .90 .35

Pan-American Scout Jamboree, Cochabamba

Yacuma-Beni Province, Cent. — A379

Design: 1.90b, 2.90b, Cathedral of St. Anne.

1995, Apr. 21 Litho. *Perf. 13½*
937 A379 1.90b black & multi 1.25 .60
938 A379 2.90b blue & multi 1.75 .90

Franciscans at Copacabana Natl. Sanctuary, Cent. — A380

1995, May 2
939 A380 60c gray & multi .40 .15
940 A380 80c bister & multi .55 .20

A381 A382

1995 Litho. *Perf. 13½*
941 A381 2b multicolored 1.00 .40

Peace Between Bolivia and Paraguay. Dated 1994.

1995, July 25
942 A382 2.40b multicolored 1.25 .50

Andes Development Corporation (CAF), 25th anniv.

50th Anniv. of Publication of "Nationalism and the Colonial Age," by Carlos Montenegro (1904-53) A383

1995, Aug. 8
943 A383 1.20b pink & black .60 .25

A384 A385

1995, Sept. 26
944 A384 1b multicolored .50 .20

FAO, 50th anniv.

1995, Oct. 24 *Perf. 14½*
945 A385 2.90b multicolored 1.50 .60

UN, 50th anniv.

America Issue — A386

1995, Nov. 21 *Perf. 14*
946 A386 5b Condor 2.50 1.00
947 A386 5b Llamas 2.50 1.00
a. Pair, #946-947 5.00 2.00

ICAO, 50th Anniv. — A387

1995, Dec. 4 *Perf. 13½x13*
948 A387 50c multicolored .25 .20

Temple of Samaipata — A388

Archaeological finds and: a, 1.90b, Top of ruins. b, 1b, Top of ruins, diff. c, 2.40b, Lower excavation. d, 2b, Floor, tiers.

1995, Dec. 4 *Perf. 13x13½*
949 A388 Block of 4, #a.-d. 3.75 1.50

No. 949 is a continuous design.

Taquiña Brewery, Cent. — A389

1995, Dec. 8 *Perf. 14*
950 A389 1b multicolored .50 .20

Christmas A390

Paintings: 1.20b, The Annunciation, by Cima da Conegliano. 3b, The Nativity, by Hans Baldung. 3.50b, Adoration of the Magi, by Rogier van der Weyden.

1995, Dec. 15 *Perf. 14x13½*
951 A390 1.20b multicolored .60 .25
952 A390 3b multicolored 1.50 .60
953 A390 3.50b multicolored 1.75 .70
Nos. 951-953 (3) 3.85 1.55

Natl. Anthem, 150th Anniv. — A391

Designs: 1b, J.I. de Sanjines, lyricist. 2b, B. Vincenti, composer.

1995, Dec. 18 Litho. *Perf. 13½*
954 A391 1b multicolored .40 .20
955 A391 2b multicolored .80 .30
a. Pair, #954-955 1.20 .45

Decree to Abolish Abuse of Indian Labor, 50th Anniv. — A392

Designs: 1.90b, Modern representations of industry, Gov. Gualberto Villarroel. 2.90, Addressing labor policies, silhouettes of people rejoicing.

1996, Jan. 26 *Perf. 14*
956 A392 1.90b multicolored .75 .30
957 A392 2.90b multicolored 1.10 .45
a. Pair, #956-957 1.90 .75

Nos. 639, 653, 685-686, 712-713, 715, 719, 726, 729, 732-733, C332, C348 Surcharged

Bs. 0.50

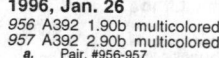

Perfs. and Printing Methods as Before

1996
958 A273 50c on 3,000,000b #729 .20 .20
959 A265 60c on 2000b #713 .25 .20
960 A277 60c on 1,400,000b #733 .25 .20
961 A271 1b on 2,500,000b #726 .40 .20
962 A264 1.50b on 11,000b #712 .60 .25
963 A267 2.50b on 23,000b #715 1.00 .40
964 A269 3b on 1,000,000b #719 1.10 .45
965 A222 3.50b on 6.50b #639 1.40 .55
966 A234 3.50b on 9b #653 1.40 .55
967 A276 3.50b on 2,000,000b #732 1.40 .55
968 AP67 3.80b on 3.80b #C332 1.50 .60
969 A189 20b on 3.80b #C348 8.00 3.25
970 A253 20b on 10b #685 8.00 3.25
971 A254 20b on 13b #686 8.00 3.25
Nos. 958-971 (14) 33.50 13.90

Size and location of surcharge varies.

Bs 0.60

No. 627 Surcharged

1996 Litho. *Perf. 10½*
972 A216 60c on 2.50b multicolored .40 .20

See No. 697 for similar surcharge.

10th Summit of the Chiefs of State and Government(Rio Group), Cochabamba A393

Designs: 2.50b, Stylized person. 3.50b, Stylized globe surrounded by lines.

1996, Sept. 4 *Perf. 14*
973 A393 2.50b multicolored 1.00 .40
974 A393 3.50b multicolored 1.40 .55

Anniversaries A394

50c, Natl. Bank of Bolivia, 125th anniv. 1b, Jose Joaquin de Lemoine (1776-1851), first postal administrator, vert.

1996, Dec. 8 Litho. *Perf. 13½*
975 A394 50c multicolored .20 .20
976 A394 1b multicolored .40 .20

Summit of the Americas to Sustain Development A395

CARE in Bolivia, 20th Anniv. A396

1996, Dec. 8 *Perf. 14x13½*
977 A395 2.50b brown & multi .95 .40
978 A395 5b black & multi 1.90 .75

1996, Dec. 19 *Perf. 13½*
979 A396 60c Family, horiz. .25 .20
980 A396 70c shown .25 .20

Natl. Symphony Orchestra, 50th Anniv. — A397

1996, Dec. 24
981 A397 1.50b shown .60 .25
982 A397 2b String instruments .75 .30
a. Pair, #981-982 1.40 .55

No. 982a is a continuous design.

Tourism in Oruro A398

Designs: 50c, Miners' Monument, vert. 60c, Folklore costume, vert. 1b, Virgin of Socavon, vert. 1.50b, Sajama mountains. 2.50b, Chipaya child, building, vert. 3b, Raul Shaw, "Moreno."

1997, Feb. 3 Litho. *Perf. 14½*
983 A398 50c multicolored .20 .20
984 A398 60c multicolored .25 .20
985 A398 1b multicolored .40 .20
986 A398 1.50b multicolored .60 .25
987 A398 2.50b multicolored .95 .40
988 A398 3b multicolored 1.10 .45
Nos. 983-988 (6) 3.50 1.70

Dated 1996.

Tourism in Chuquisaca — A399

Designs: 60c, La Glorieta. 1b, Governor's Palace, vert. No. 991, Dinosaur tracks. No. 992, House of Liberty. 2b, Tarabaqueno, vert. 3b, Statue of Juana Azurduy of Padilla, vert.

1997, Jan. 30 *Perf. 13½x14, 14x13½*
989 A399 60c multicolored .25 .20
990 A399 1b multicolored .40 .20
991 A399 1.50b multicolored .60 .25
992 A399 1.50b multicolored .60 .25
993 A399 2b multicolored .75 .30
994 A399 3b multicolored 1.10 .45
Nos. 989-994 (6) 3.70 1.65

Dated 1996.

Tourism in Tarija A400

Designs: 50c, House of Culture, Dorada, vert. 60c, Church of Entre Rios, vert. 80c, San Luis Falls. 1b, Monument to the Chaco War. 3b, Temple, Statue of the Virgin Mary, Chaguay. 20b, Eustaquio Mendez house, monument.

1997, Jan. 24 ***Perf. 14x13½, 13½x14***

995	A400	50c multicolored	.20	.20
996	A400	60c multicolored	.25	.20
997	A400	80c multicolored	.30	.20
998	A400	1b multicolored	.40	.20
999	A400	3b multicolored	1.10	.45
1000	A400	20b multicolored	7.75	3.00
		Nos. 995-1000 (6)	10.00	4.25

Dated 1996.

Visit of French Pres. Jacques Chirac A401

Design: Bolivian Pres. Gonzalo Sanchez de Lozada, Chirac.

1997, Mar. 15 ***Perf. 14***

1001	A401	4b multicolored	1.50	.60

Salesian Order in Bolivia, Cent. — A402

Designs: 1.50b, St. John Bosco (1815-88), church. 2b, Statue of St. John Bosco talking with boy, church.

1997, Apr. 29 **Litho.** ***Perf. 13½***

1002	A402	1.50b multicolored	.60	.25
1003	A402	2b multicolored	.75	.30

UNICEF, 50th Anniv. — A403

Children's drawings: 50c, Houses, children on playground. 90c, Child running, cactus, rock, lake. 1b, Boys, girls arm in arm across globe. 2.50b, Girl on swing, others in background.

1997

1004	A403	50c multicolored	.20	.20
1005	A403	90c multicolored	.35	.20
1006	A403	1b multicolored	.40	.20
1007	A403	2.50b multicolored	.95	.40
		Nos. 1004-1007 (4)	1.90	1.00

Department of La Paz — A404

Tourism: 50c, Mt. Chulumani, Las Yungas, vert. 80c, Inca monolith, vert. 1.50b, City, Mt. Illimani, vert. 2b, Gate of the Sun, Tiwanacu. 2.50b, Traditional dancers, vert. 10b, Virgin of Copacabana, reed boat.

1997, May 28 **Litho.** ***Perf. 13½***

1008	A404	50c multicolored	.20	.20
1009	A404	80c multicolored	.30	.20
1010	A404	1.50b multicolored	.60	.25
1011	A404	2b multicolored	.75	.30
1012	A404	2.50b multicolored	.95	.40
1013	A404	10b multicolored	3.75	1.50
		Nos. 1008-1013 (6)	6.55	2.85

1997 America Cup Soccer Championships, Bolivia — A405

1998 World Cup Soccer Championships, France — A406

1997, June 13

1014	A405	3b multicolored	1.25	.50
1015	A406	5b multicolored	1.90	.75

National Congress A407

1997, July 8 **Litho.** ***Perf. 13½***

1016	A407	1b multicolored	.40	.20

America Issue — A408

Women in traditional costumes: 5b, From valley region. 15b, From eastern Bolivia.

1997, July 14 **Litho.** ***Perf. 13½***

1017	A408	5b multicolored	1.90	.75
1018	A408	15b multicolored	5.75	2.25

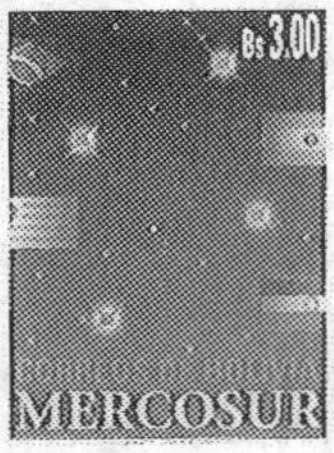

Mercosur (Common Market of Latin America) — A409

1997, Sept. 26

1019	A409	3b multicolored	1.10	.45

See Argentina #1975, Brazil #2646, Paraguay #2565, Uruguay #1681.

Christmas — A410

Paintings: 2b, Virgin del Cerro, by unknown artist. 5b, Virgin de la Leche, by unknown artist. 10b, The Holy Family, by Melchor Pérez de Holguin.

1997, Dec. 19 **Litho.** ***Perf. 13½***

1020	A410	2b multicolored	.75	.30
1021	A410	5b multicolored	1.75	.75
1022	A410	10b multicolored	3.50	1.50
		Nos. 1020-1022 (3)	6.00	2.55

Diana, Princess of Wales (1961-97) A411

1997, Dec. 29

1023	A411	2b Portrait, vert.	1.25	.50
1024	A411	3b In mine field	1.75	.75

Visit of Prime Minister of Spain A412

Hugo Banzer Suarez, Pres. of Bolivia and José Maria Aznar.

1998, Mar. 16

1025	A412	6b multicolored	3.25	1.25

Bolivian Society of Engineers, 75th Anniv. — A413

1998, Apr. 28

1026	A413	3.50b multicolored	1.25	.55

A414

A415

1998, Apr. 30 **Litho.** ***Perf. 13½***

1027	A414	5b multicolored	1.75	.75

Rotary Intl. in Bolivia, 70th anniv.

1998, July 9

Letter Carriers, 1942: 3b, Postman delivering mail to woman, vert.

1028	A415	3b multicolored	1.10	.45
1029	A415	4b multicolored	1.40	.60

America Issue.

Famous Men — A416

1.50b, Werner Guttentag Tichauer, bibliographer. 2b, Dr. Martin Cardenas Hermosa, botanist. 3.50b, Adrian Patiño Carpio, composer.

1998, July 10

1030	A416	1.50b brown	.55	.20
1031	A416	2b green, vert	.70	.30
1032	A416	3.50b black, vert	1.25	.50
		Nos. 1030-1032 (3)	2.50	1.00

Regions in Bolivia A417

Beni: 50c, Victoria regia. 1b, Callandria. 1.50b, White Tajibo tree, vert. 3.50b, Amazon mask. 5b, Nutrea. 7b, Tropical condor.

1998, Oct. 11 **Litho.** ***Perf. 13½***

1033	A417	50c black & multi	.20	.20
1034	A417	1b black & multi	.35	.20
1035	A417	1.50b black & multi	.55	.25
1036	A417	3.50b black & multi	1.25	.55
1037	A417	5b black & multi	1.75	.80
1038	A417	7b black & multi	2.50	1.10
		Nos. 1033-1038 (6)	6.60	3.10

Pando: 50c, Acre River. 1b, Sloth climbing bamboo tree, vert. 1.50b, Bahia Arroyo, vert. 4b, Boa. 5b, Family of capybaras. 7b, Houses, palm trees, vert.

1039	A417	50c green & multi	.20	.20
1040	A417	1b green & multi	.35	.20
1041	A417	1.50b green & multi	.55	.25
1042	A417	4b green & multi	1.40	.65
1043	A417	5b green & multi	1.75	.80
1044	A417	7b green & multi	2.50	1.10
		Nos. 1039-1044 (6)	6.75	3.20

Women of Bolivia — A418

First Lady Yolanda Prada de Banzer and: 1.50b, Women working in fields, making pottery, weaving. 2b, Women working on computer, standing at blackboard.

1998, Oct. 11

1045	A418	1.50b multicolored	.55	.25
1046	A418	2b multicolored	.70	.30
a.		Pair, #1045-1046	1.25	.55

America Issue.

City of La Paz, 450th Anniv. A419

1998, Oct. 14

1047	A419	2b Plaza de Laja Church	.70	.30

A420

A422

A421

1998, Nov. 6 Litho. ***Perf. 13½x13¾***
1048 A420 3.50b blue & yellow 1.25 .60

Organization of American States, 50th anniv.

1998, Nov. 12 ***Perf. 13¼x13½***
1049 A421 2b multicolored .70 .35

Bolivian Philatelic Federation, 25th anniv., Espamer '98, Buenos Aires.

Perf. 13¼x13½, 13½x13¼
1998, Nov. 26

Christmas: 2b, Child's drawing of church. 6b, Pope John Paul II. 7b, John Paul II, Mother Teresa.

1050 A422 2b multi, horiz. .70 .35
1051 A422 6b multi 2.00 .95
1052 A422 7b multi 2.40 1.25
Nos. 1050-1052 (3) 5.10 2.55

UPU, 125th Anniv. — A423

1999, Jan. 26 Litho. ***Perf. 13½***
1053 A423 3.50b multicolored 1.25 .60

AFC Soccer Club, 75th Anniv. — A424

1999, Apr. 22 Litho. ***Perf. 13½***
1054 A424 5b multicolored *4.25 2.25*

Geneva Convention and Bolivian Red Cross, 50th Anniv. — A425

1999, May 18
1055 A425 5b multicolored 1.90 .95

Bernardo Guarachi, First Bolivian to Reach Summit of Mt. Everest A426

1999, May 25
1056 A426 6b multicolored 2.25 1.10

Special Olympics of Bolivia, 30th Anniv. — A427

Designs: 2b, Medalists on podium. 2.50b, Winners of swimming event, running event.

1999
1057 A427 2b multicolored .75 .35
1058 A427 2.50b multicolored .90 .45

Japanese Immigration to Bolivia, Cent. — A428

Designs: 3b, Golden Pavilion, Kyoto. 6b, Sun setting across water, vert.

1999, June 3
1059 A428 3b multicolored 1.10 .55
1060 A428 6b multicolored 2.25 1.10

Bolivian Cinema, 100th Anniv. — A429

1999 Litho. ***Perf. 13½***
1061 A429 50c Hacia la Gloria, 1932-33 .20 .20
1062 A429 50c Jonas y la Ballena Rosada, 1995 .20 .20
1063 A429 1b Wara Wara, 1929 .35 .20
1064 A429 1b Vuelve Sebastiana, 1953 .35 .20
1065 A429 3b La Campaña del Chaco, 1933 .65 .30
1066 A429 3b La Vertiente, 1958 .65 .30
1067 A429 6b Yawar Mallku, 1969 2.00 .95
1068 A429 6b Mi Socio, 1982 2.00 .95
Nos. 1061-1068 (8) 6.40 3.30

SOS Children's Village, 50th Anniv. — A430

1999, July 8
1069 A430 3.50b multicolored 1.25 .60

Intl. Day Against Illegal Drugs A431

Perf. 13¼x13½
1999, June 26 Litho.
1070 A431 3.50b multicolored 1.25 .60

Completion of Bolivian-Brazilian Gas Pipeline — A432

Designs: 3b, Presidents of Bolivia and Brazil, map of pipeline. 6b, Presidents, gas flame.

1999, July 1 Litho. ***Perf. 13½***
1071 A432 3b multicolored 1.00 .50
1072 A432 6b multicolored 2.00 .95

La Paz Lions Club, 50th Anniv. — A433

1999 ***Perf. 13½x13¼***
1073 A433 3.50b multicolored 1.25 .60

Cochabamba Tourism — A434

50c, Mt. Tunari. 1b, Cochabamba Valley. 2b, Container from Omerque culture, idol from Pachamama culture. 3b, Totora. 5b, Composer Teofilo Vargas Candia. 6b, Statue of Jesus Christ.

1999 ***Perf. 13½x13¾, 13¾x13½***
1074 A434 50c multi .20 .20
1075 A434 1b multi .35 .20
1076 A434 2b multi, vert. .70 .35
1077 A434 3b multi 1.10 .55
1078 A434 5b multi, vert. 1.75 .85
1079 A434 6b multi, vert. 2.10 1.00
Nos. 1074-1079 (6) 6.20 3.15

AIR POST STAMPS

Aviation School
AP1 AP2

1924, Dec. Unwmk. Engr. ***Perf. 14***
C1 AP1 10c ver & blk .25 .30
a. Inverted center 800.00
C2 AP1 15c carmine & blk 1.50 .50
C3 AP1 25c dk bl & blk .60 .60
C4 AP1 50c orange & blk 1.50 1.25
C5 AP2 1b red brn & blk .90 .95
C6 AP2 2b blk brn & blk 1.75 1.75
C7 AP2 5b dk vio & blk 5.50 5.50
Nos. C1-C7 (7) 12.00 10.85

Natl. Aviation School establishment.
These stamps were available for ordinary postage. Nos. C1, C3, C5 and C6 exist imperforate. Proofs of the 2b with inverted center exist imperforate and privately perforated.
For overprints and surcharges see Nos. C11-C23, C56-C58.

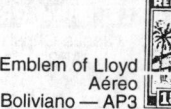

Emblem of Lloyd Aéreo Boliviano — AP3

1928 Litho. ***Perf. 11***
C8 AP3 15c green 1.00 1.00
a. Imperf., pair 50.00
C9 AP3 20c dark blue .25 .25
C10 AP3 35c red brown .60 .60
Nos. C8-C10 (3) 1.85 1.85

No. C8 exists imperf. between.
For surcharges see #C24-C26, C53-C55.

Graf Zeppelin Issues
Nos. C1-C5 Surcharged or Overprinted in Various Colors:

CORREO AEREO

R. S. 6-V-1930

5 Cts.

Nos. C11, C19

CORREO AEREO

R. S.

6-V- 1930

Nos. C12-C18, C20-C23

1930, May 6 ***Perf. 14***
C11 AP1 5c on 10c ver & blk (G) 9.50 9.50
C12 AP1 10c ver & blk (Bl) 9.50 9.50
C13 AP1 10c ver & blk (Br) 600.00 875.00
C14 AP1 15c car & blk (V) 9.50 9.50
C15 AP1 25c dk bl & blk (R) 9.50 9.50
C16 AP1 50c org & blk (Br) 9.50 9.50
C17 AP1 50c org & blk (R) 475.00 *600.00*
C18 AP2 1b red brn & blk (gold) 150.00 150.00

Experts consider the 50c with gold or silver overprint and 5c with black to be trial color proofs.
Nos. C11-C18 exist with the surcharges inverted, double, or double with one inverted, but the regularity of these varieties is questioned.
See notes following No. C23.

Surcharged or Overprinted in Bronze Inks of Various Colors

C19 AP1 5c on 10c ver & blk (G) 77.50 *80.00*
C20 AP1 10c ver & blk (Bl) 67.50 *67.50*
C21 AP1 15c car & blk (V) 77.50 *80.00*
C22 AP1 25c dk bl & blk (cop) 77.50 *80.00*
C23 AP2 1b red brn & blk (gold) 190.00 *200.00*
Nos. C19-C23 (5) 490.00 *507.50*

Flight of the airship Graf Zeppelin from Europe to Brazil and return via Lakehurst, NJ.
Nos. C19 to C23 were intended for use on postal matter forwarded by the Graf Zeppelin.
No. C18 was overprinted with light gold or gilt bronze ink. No. C23 was overprinted with deep gold bronze ink. Nos. C13 and C17 were overprinted with trial colors but were sold with the regular printings. The 5c on 10c is known surcharged in black and in blue.

Z 1930

No. C8-C10 Surcharged

Bs. 3.—

1930, May 6 ***Perf. 11***
C24 AP3 1.50b on 15c 25.00 25.00
a. Inverted surcharge 57.50 57.50
b. Comma instead of period after "1" 35.00 35.00
C25 AP3 3b on 20c 25.00 25.00
a. Inverted surcharge 62.50 62.50
b. Comma instead of period after "3" 40.00 40.00
C26 AP3 6b on 35c 37.50 *40.00*
a. Inverted surcharge 110.00 110.00
b. Comma instead of period after "6" 62.50 62.50
Nos. C24-C26 (3) 87.50 90.00

Airplane and Bullock Cart — AP6

Airplane and River Boat — AP7

1930, July 24 Litho. ***Perf. 14***
C27 AP6 5c dp violet 1.25 1.00
C28 AP7 15c red 1.25 1.00
C29 AP7 20c yellow .50 .45
C30 AP6 35c yellow grn .40 .25
C31 AP7 50c deep blue .40 .25
C32 AP6 1b lt brown .40 .25
C33 AP7 2b deep rose .40 .40
C34 AP6 3b slate 1.40 1.40
Nos. C27-C34 (8) 6.00 5.00

Nos. C27 to C34 exist imperforate.
For surcharge see No. C52.

Air Service Emblem AP8

1932, Sept. 16 ***Perf. 11***
C35 AP8 5c ultra .70 .55
C36 AP8 10c gray .45 .35
C37 AP8 15c dark rose .70 .55
C38 AP8 25c orange .70 .55
C39 AP8 30c green .60 .30

C40 AP8 50c violet .60 .35
C41 AP8 1b dk brown .60 .35
Nos. C35-C41 (7) 4.35 3.00

Map of Bolivia — AP9

1935, Feb. 1 Engr. *Perf. 12*

C42 AP9 5c brown red .20 .20
C43 AP9 10c dk green .20 .20
C44 AP9 20c dk violet .20 .20
C45 AP9 30c ultra .25 .20
C46 AP9 50c orange .30 .20
C47 AP9 1b bister brn .30 .25
C48 AP9 1½b yellow .60 .20
C49 AP9 2b carmine .60 .30
C50 AP9 5b green 1.10 .40
C51 AP9 10b dk brown 1.75 .75
Nos. C42-C51 (10) 5.50 2.90

Nos. C1, C4, C10, C30 Surcharged in Red (#C52-C56) or Green (#C57-C58) — c

Correo Aéreo
D. S. 25-2-37
0.05

1937, Oct. 6 *Perf. 11, 14*

C52 AP6 5c on 35c yel grn .40 .30
a. "Carreo" 12.50
b. Inverted surcharge
C53 AP3 20c on 35c red brn .50 .40
a. Inverted surcharge
C54 AP3 50c on 35c red brn 1.50 1.25
a. Inverted surcharge 17.50
C55 AP3 1b on 35c red brn 1.10 .65
a. Inverted surcharge
C56 AP1 2b on 50c org & blk 1.60 1.00
a. Inverted surcharge
C57 AP1 12b on 10c ver & blk 5.75 4.75
a. Inverted surcharge 22.50
C58 AP1 15b on 10c ver & blk 5.75 2.75
a. Inverted surcharge

Regular Postage Stamps of 1925 Surcharged in Green or Red — d

Correo
Aéreo
D. S.
25-2-37
Bs. 4.—

Perf. 14

C59 A56 (d) 3b on 50c dp vio (G) 1.10 1.00
C60 A56 (d) 4b on 1b red (G) 1.40 1.40
C61 A57 (c) 5b on 2b org (G) 1.90 1.60
a. Double surcharge 90.00
C62 A56 (d) 10b on 5b blk brn 4.50 3.25
a. Double surcharge 35.00
Nos. C52-C62 (11) 25.50 18.35

No. C59-C62 exist with inverted surcharge, No. C62a with black and black and red surcharges.

Courtyard of Potosi Mint — AP10

Miner — AP11

Emancipated Woman AP12

Pincers, Torch and Good Will Principles AP15

Airplane over Field — AP13

Airplanes and Liberty Monument AP14

Airplane over River AP16

Emblem of New Government AP17

Transport Planes over Map of Bolivia AP18

1938, May Litho. *Perf. 10½*

C63 AP10 20c deep rose .25 .25
C64 AP11 30c gray .25 .25
C65 AP12 40c yellow .25 .25
C66 AP13 50c yellow grn .50 .25
C67 AP14 60c dull blue .50 .25
C68 AP15 1b dull red .75 .25
C69 AP16 2b bister 1.25 .25
C70 AP17 3b lt brown 1.25 .25
C71 AP18 5b dk violet 1.90 .25
Nos. C63-C71 (9) 6.90 2.25

40c, 1b, 2b exist imperf.

Chalice — AP19

Virgin of Copacabana AP20

Jesus Christ AP21

Church of San Francisco, La Paz — AP22

St. Anthony of Padua — AP23

Perf. 13½, 10½

1939, July 19 Litho.

C72 AP19 5c dull violet .35 .35
a. Pair, imperf. between 30.00
C73 AP20 30c lt bl grn .30 .20
C74 AP21 45c violet bl .60 .20
a. Vertical pair, imperf. between 42.50
C75 AP22 60c carmine .40 .35
C76 AP23 75c vermilion .65 .60
C77 AP23 90c deep blue .45 .25
C78 AP22 2b dull brown .75 .25
C79 AP21 4b deep plum 1.00 .40
C80 AP20 5b lt blue 2.50 .25
C81 AP19 10b yellow 5.00 .25
Nos. C72-C81 (10) 12.00 3.10

2nd National Eucharistic Congress.
For surcharge see No. C112.

Plane over Lake Titicaca — AP24

Mt. Illimani and Condor — AP25

1941, Aug. 21 *Perf. 13½*

C82 AP24 10b dull green 3.25 .40
C83 AP24 20b light ultra 3.75 .65
C84 AP25 50b rose lilac 6.50 1.00
C85 AP25 100b olive bister 16.00 6.00
Nos. C82-C85 (4) 29.50 8.05

Counterfeits exist.

Liberty and Clasped Hands — AP26

1942, Nov. 12

C86 AP26 40c rose lake .25 .25
C87 AP26 50c ultra .25 .25
C88 AP26 1b orange brn 1.25 .75
C89 AP26 5b magenta .75 .25
a. Double impression
C90 AP26 10b dull brn vio 2.50 1.25
Nos. C86-C90 (5) 5.00 2.75

Conference of Chancellors, Jan. 15, 1942.

Ballivián Type of Regular Issue

General José Ballivián; old and modern transportation.

1943, Nov. 18 Engr. *Perf. 12½*

C91 A114 10c rose vio & brn .20 .20
C92 A114 20c emerald & brn .20 .20
C93 A114 30c rose car & brn .20 .20
C94 A114 3b blue & brn .25 .20
C95 A114 5b black & brn .40 .30
Nos. C91-C95 (5) 1.25 1.10

Condor and Sun Rising — AP28

Plane — AP29

1944, Sept. 19 Litho. *Perf. 13½*

C96 AP28 40c red violet .20 .20
C97 AP28 1b blue violet .20 .20
C98 AP29 1.50b yellow green .20 .20
C99 AP29 2.50b dk gray blue .40 .20
Nos. C96-C99 (4) 1.00 .80

Revolution of Dec. 20, 1943.

Map of Natl. Airways — AP30

Map of Bolivian Air Lines — AP31

1945, May 31 *Perf. 11*

C100 AP30 10c red .20 .20
a. Imperf., pair 9.00
C101 AP30 50c yellow .20 .20
a. Imperf., pair 27.50
C102 AP30 90c lt green .25 .20
a. Imperf., pair 30.00
C103 AP30 5b lt ultra .35 .20
C104 AP30 20b deep brown 1.00 .45
Nos. C100-C104 (5) 2.00 1.25

10th anniversary of first flight, La Paz to Tacha, Peru, by Panagra Airways.
For surcharges see Nos. C128-C129.

1945, Sept. 15 *Perf. 13½*

Centers in Red and Blue

C105 AP31 20c violet .20 .20
C106 AP31 30c orange brn .20 .20
C107 AP31 50c brt blue grn .20 .20
C108 AP31 90c brt violet .20 .20
C109 AP31 2b blue .20 .20
C110 AP31 3b magenta .20 .20
C111 AP31 4b olive bister .35 .20
Nos. C105-C111 (7) 1.55 1.40

Founding of Lloyd Aéreo Boliviano, 20th anniv.

Catalogue values for unused stamps in this section, from this point to the end of the section, are for Never Hinged items.

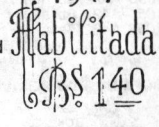

No. C76 Surcharged in Blue

1947
Habilitada
Bs. 1.40

1947, Mar. 23

C112 AP23 1.40b on 75c ver .20 .20
Nos. 314-317,C112 (5) 2.15 1.00

Mt. Illimani — AP32

L. A. B. Plane — AP35

1947, Sept. 15 Litho. *Perf. 11½*

C113 AP32 1b rose car .20 .20
C114 AP32 1.40b emerald .20 .20
C115 AP32 2.50b blue .20 .20
C116 AP32 3b dp orange .20 .20
C117 AP32 4b rose lilac .20 .20
Nos. C113-C117 (5) 1.00 1.00
Nos. 318-323,C113-C117 (11) 4.85 2.55

1st anniv. of the Revolution of July 21, 1946.
1.40b, 2.50b exist imperf.
For surcharge see No. C137.

Bolivia/Argentina Arms Type

1947, Oct. 23 *Perf. 13½*

C118 A119 2.90b ultra .25 .25
a. Imperf., pair 20.00
b. Perf. 10½ 5.00 4.00

Statue of Christ Type

Designs: 2.50b, Statue of Christ above La Paz. 3.70b, Child kneeling before cross. No. C121, St. John Bosco. No. C122, Virgin of Copacabana. 13.60b, Pope Plus XII blessing University of La Paz.

1948, Sept. 26 *Perf. 11½*

C119 A120 2.50b ver & yellow .45 .35
C120 A120 3.70b rose & cream .55 .35
C121 A120 4b rose lil & gray .55 .25
C122 A120 4b lt ultra & salmon .55 .20
C123 A120 13.60b ultra & lt grn .70 .40
Nos. C119-C123 (5) 2.80 1.55

Bolivia Auto Club Type

1948, Oct.

C124 A125 10b emerald & salmon 1.60 .20

Pacheco Type of Regular Issue

1950, Jan. 2 Unwmk.

C125 AP34 1.40b orange brown .20 .20
C126 AP34 2.50b orange .20 .20
C127 AP34 3.30b rose violet .20 .20
Nos. C125-C127 (3) .60 .60

75th anniv. of the UPU.

Nos. C100 and C104 Surcharged in Black

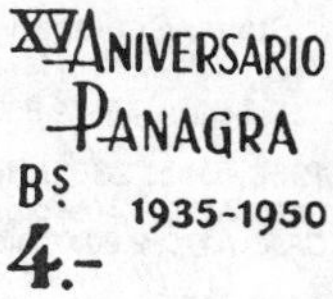

1950, May 31 *Perf. 11*
C128 AP30 4b on 10c red .20 .20
a. Inverted surcharge 17.50 17.50
C129 AP30 10b on 20b dp brn .30 .25
a. Inverted surcharge 17.50 17.50

Panagra air services in Bolivia, 15th anniv.

1950, Sept. 15 **Litho.** *Perf. 13½*
C130 AP35 20c red orange .20 .20
C131 AP35 30c purple .20 .20
C132 AP35 50c green .20 .20
C133 AP35 1b orange .20 .20
C134 AP35 3b ultra .25 .20
C135 AP35 15b carmine .50 .20
C136 AP35 50b chocolate 1.00 .35
Nos. C130-C136 (7) 2.55 1.55

25th anniv. of the founding of Lloyd Aero Boliviano. 30c, 50c, 15b exist imperforate.
No. C132 exists without imprint at bottom of stamp.

No. C116 Surcharged in Black

1950, Sept. 24 *Perf. 11½*
C137 AP32 1.40b on 3b dp orange .25 .25

1st anniv. of the ending of the Civil War of Aug. 24-Sept. 24, 1949.
Exists with inverted and double surcharge.

UN Type of Regular Issue

1950, Oct. 24 **Unwmk.**
C138 A128 3.60b crimson rose .50 .20
C139 A128 4.70b black brown .65 .20

La Paz Type of Regular Issue

20c, Gate of the Sun and llama. 30c, Church of Old Ssanfrancisco. 40c, Avenue Camacho. 50c, Consistorial Palace. 1b, Legislative Palace. 2b, Communications Bldg. 3b, Arms. 4b, La Gasca ordering Mendoza to found La Paz. 5b, Capt. Alonso de Mendoza founding La Paz. 10b, Arms; portrait of Mendoza.

1951, Mar. 1 **Engr.** *Perf. 12½*
Center in Black
C140 A129 20c carmine .20 .20
C141 A130 30c dk vio bl .20 .20
C142 A129 40c dark blue .20 .20
C143 A129 50c blue green .20 .20
C144 A129 1b red .20 .20
C145 A129 2b red orange .35 .35
C146 A129 3b deep blue .35 .35
C147 A129 4b vermilion .45 .45
a. Souvenir sheet of 4 1.00 1.00
b. As "a," imperf. 1.00 1.00
C148 A129 5b dark green .40 .40
a. Souvenir sheet of 3 1.00 1.00
b. As "a," imperf. 1.00 1.00
C149 A129 10b red brown .65 .65
a. Souvenir sheet of 3 1.00 1.00
b. As "a," imperf. 1.00 1.00
Nos. C140-C149 (10) 3.20 3.20
Nos. 342-351,C140-C149 (20) 13.20 10.35

#C147a-C147b contain #C143-C145, C147; #C148a-C148b contain #C142, C146, C148; #C149a-C149b contain #C140, C141, C149.
For surcharges see Nos. C187-C196.

Athletic Type of Regular Issue

20c, Horsemanship. 30c, Basketball. 50c, Fencing. 1b, Hurdling. 2.50b, Javelin throwing. 3b, Relay race. 5b, La Paz stadium.

1951, Aug. 23 **Unwmk.**
Center in Black
C150 A131 20c purple .20 .20
C151 A131 30c rose vio .30 .20
C152 A131 50c dp red org .50 .20
C153 A131 1b chocolate .50 .20
C154 A131 2.50b orange .75 .30
C155 A131 3b black brn 1.00 .75
a. Souvenir sheet of 3, #C153-C155 4.00 3.50
b. As "a," imperf. 4.00 4.00
C156 A131 5b red 2.00 1.50
a. Souv. sheet of 4, #C150-C152, C156 4.50 4.00
b. As "a," imperf. 4.50 4.50
Nos. C150-C156 (7) 5.25 3.35
Nos. 352-358,C150-C156 (10) 19.75 17.85

Eduardo Abaroa Type

Queen Isabella I — AP41

1952, Mar. 24 **Litho.** *Perf. 11*
C157 A133 70c rose red .20 .20
C158 A133 2b orange yel .20 .20
C159 A133 3b yellow green .25 .20
C160 A133 5b blue .25 .20
C161 A133 50b rose lilac 1.00 .90
C162 A133 100b gray black 1.10 1.10
a. Perf. 14 10.00
Nos. C157-C162 (6) 3.00 2.80

Queen Isabella I Type

1952, July 16 *Perf. 13½*
C163 A134 50b emerald .35 .25
C164 A134 100b brown .65 .35

Exist imperforate.

Columbus Lighthouse Type

1952, July 16
C165 A135 2b rose lilac, *salmon* .20 .20
C166 A135 3.70b blue grn, *bl* .20 .20
C167 A135 4.40b orange, *salmon* .20 .20
C168 A135 20b dk brn, *cream* .40 .20
Nos. C165-C168 (4) 1.00 .80

No. C168 exists imperforate.

Revolution Type and:

Soldiers — AP43

Perf. 13½ (AP43), 11½ (A137)

1953, Apr. 9 **Litho.**
C169 A137 3.70b chocolate .20 .20
C170 AP43 6b red violet .20 .20
C171 A137 9b brown rose .20 .20
C172 A137 10b aqua .20 .20
C173 A137 16b vermilion .20 .20
C174 AP43 22.50b dk brown .25 .20
C175 A137 40b gray .40 .20
Nos. C169-C175 (7) 1.65 1.40
Nos. C169-C175,378-383 (13) 2.85 2.60

Nos. C169-C170 and C174 exist imperf.

Map and Peasant Type and:

Pres. Victor Paz Estenssoro Embracing Indian — AP45

1954, Aug. 2 *Perf. 12x11½*
C176 AP45 20b orange brn .20 .20
C177 A138 27b brt pink .20 .20
C178 A138 30b red org .20 .20
C179 A138 45b violet brn .20 .20
C180 AP45 100b blue grn .40 .20
C181 A138 300b yellow grn 1.00 .30
Nos. C176-C181 (6) 2.20 1.30
Nos. C176-C181,384-387 (10) 3.05 2.10

AP45 for 3rd Inter-American Indian Cong. A138 agrarian reform laws of 1953-54.
Nos. C176-C180 exist imperf.
For surcharge see No. C261.

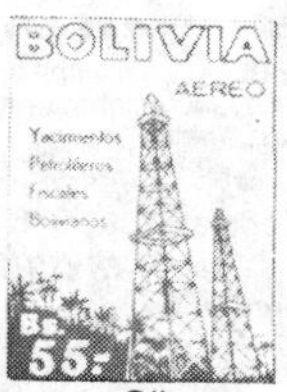

Oil Derricks — AP47

Map of South America and La Paz Arms — AP48

1955, Oct. 9 *Perf. 10½*
C182 AP47 55b dk & lt grnsh bl .20 .20
C183 AP47 70b dk gray & gray .20 .20
C184 AP47 90b dk & lt grn .20 .20

Perf. 13
C185 AP47 500b red lilac .65 .40
C186 AP47 1000b blk brn & fawn 1.25 1.25
Nos. C182-C186 (5) 2.50 2.25
Nos. C182-C186,388-392 (10) 3.50 3.25

For surcharge see No. C262.

Nos. C140-C149 Surcharged with New Values and Bars in Black or Carmine

1957 **Engr.** *Perf. 12½*
Center in Black
C187 A129 100b on 3b (C) .20 .20
C188 A129 200b on 2b .20 .20
C189 A129 500b on 4b .20 .20
C190 A129 600b on 1b .20 .20
C191 A129 700b on 20c .25 .20
C192 A129 800b on 40c (C) .35 .20
C193 A130 900b on 30c (C) .40 .20
C194 A129 1800b on 50c (C) .60 .25
C195 A129 3000b on 5b (C) 1.00 .45
C196 A129 5000b on 10b (C) 1.60 .75
Nos. C187-C196 (10) 5.00 2.85

See Nos. 393-402.

Unwmk.

1957, May 25 **Litho.** *Perf. 12*
C197 AP48 700b lilac & vio .35 .35
C198 AP48 1200b pale brn .40 .35
C199 AP48 1350b rose car .55 .50
C200 AP48 2700b blue grn 1.10 .65
C201 AP48 4000b violet bl 1.40 .75
Nos. C197-C201 (5) 3.80 2.60
Nos. C197-C201,403-407 (10) 5.10 3.60

Exist imperf.
For surcharges see Nos. C263-C265.

Type of Regular Issue, 1957

1957, Dec. 19 *Perf. 11½*
C202 A141 600b magenta .25 .20
C203 A141 700b violet blue .35 .20
C204 A141 900b pale green .50 .20
Nos. C202-C204 (3) 1.10 .60

Type of Regular Issue, 1960

1960, Jan. 30
C205 A142 400b rose claret .50 .30
C206 A142 800b slate blue .65 .40
C207 A142 2000b slate 1.00 .60
Nos. C205-C207 (3) 2.15 1.30

Gate of the Sun, Tiahuanacu AP49

Uprooted Oak Emblem AP50

1960, Mar. 26 **Litho.** *Perf. 11½*
C208 AP49 3000b gray 2.00 1.10
C209 AP49 5000b orange 3.00 1.10
C210 AP49 10,000b rose claret 4.75 2.75
C211 AP49 15,000b blue violet 7.00 4.50
Nos. C208-C211 (4) 16.75 9.45
Nos. C208-C211,414-417 (8) 23.90 12.95

1960, Apr. 7 *Perf. 11½*
C212 AP50 600b ultra .35 .35
C213 AP50 700b lt red brn .35 .35
C214 AP50 900b dk bl grn .35 .35
C215 AP50 1800b violet .60 .60
C216 AP50 2000b gray .65 .60
Nos. C212-C216 (5) 2.30 2.25
Nos. C212-C216,418-422 (10) 4.40 4.35

WRY, July 1, 1959-June 30, 1960.
No. C215 exists with "1961" overprint in dark carmine, but was not regularly issued in this form.

Jaime Laredo Type

Laredo facing left, Bolivia in color.

Perf. 11½

1960, Aug. 15 **Unwmk.** **Litho.**
C217 A145 600b rose vio .75 .45
C218 A145 700b ol gray .75 .25
C219 A145 800b vio brn .75 .25
C220 A145 900b dk bl 1.00 .25
C221 A145 1800b green 1.50 1.50
C222 A145 4000b dk gray 3.00 1.00
Nos. C217-C222 (6) 7.75 3.70

Issued to honor the violinist Jaime Laredo.
For surcharges see Nos. C266-C267.

Children's Hospital Type of 1960

1960, Nov. 21 *Perf. 11½*
C223 A146 600b multi .40 .25
C224 A146 1000b multi .60 .25
C225 A146 1800b multi 1.00 1.00
C226 A146 5000b multi 3.00 1.25
Nos. C223-C226 (4) 5.00 2.75

For surcharges see No. C268-C269.

Pres. Paz Estenssoro and Pres. Getulio Vargas of Brazil AP52

1960, Dec. 14 **Litho.** *Perf. 11½*
C227 AP52 1200b on 10b org & blk .70 .70

Exists with surcharge inverted.
No. C227 without surcharge was not regularly issued, although a decree authorizing its circulation was published. Value, $2.
Postally-used counterfeits of surcharge exist.

Pres. Paz Estenssoro and Pres. Frondizi of Argentina AP53

Design: 4000b, Flags of Bolivia and Argentina.

1961, May 23 *Perf. 10½*
C228 AP53 4000b brn, red, yel, grn & bl .75 .75
C229 AP53 6000b dk grn & blk 1.50 1.50

Visit of the President of Argentina, Dr. Arturo Frondizi, to Bolivia.
For surcharge see No. C309.

Miguel de Cervantes — AP54

1961, Oct. **Photo.** *Perf. 13*
C230 AP54 1400b pale grn & dk ol grn .60 .25

Cervantes' appointment as Chief Magistrate of La Paz. See No. 451.

Virgin of Cotoca and Symbol of Eucharist AP55

Planes and Parachutes AP56

1962, Mar. 19 **Litho.** *Perf. 10½*
C231 AP55 1400b brn, pink & yel .65 .35

4th Natl. Eucharistic Cong., Santa Cruz, 1961.

Nos. C212-C216 Surcharged Vertically with New Value and Greek Key Border

1962, June Unwmk. *Perf. 11½*

C232 AP50 1200b on 600b .55 .55
C233 AP50 1300b on 700b .50 .50
C234 AP50 1400b on 900b .55 .55
C235 AP50 2800b on 1,800b .90 .75
C236 AP50 3000b on 2,000b .90 .75
Nos. C232-C236 (5) 3.40 3.10

The overprinted segment of Greek key border on Nos. C232-C236 comes in two positions: two full "keys" on top, and one full and two half keys on top.

Flower Type of 1962

Flowers: 100b, 1800b, Cantua buxifolia. 800b, 10,000b, Cantua bicolor.

1962, June 28 Litho. *Perf. 10½*
Flowers in Natural Colors

C237 A152 100b dk bl .25 .20
C238 A152 800b green .50 .20
C239 A152 1800b violet 1.00 .50
a. Souvenir sheet of 3 7.50 6.00
C240 A152 10,000b dk bl 3.25 1.75
Nos. C237-C240 (4) 5.00 2.65

No. C239a contains 3 imperf. stamps similar to Nos. C237-C239, but with the 1,800b background color changed to dark violet blue.
For surcharges see Nos. C270-C271.

1962, Sept. 5 Litho. *Perf. 11½*

1200b, 5000b, Plane and oxcart. 2000b, Aerial photography (plane over South America).

Emblem in Red, Yellow & Green

C241 AP56 600b blk & bl .25 .20
C242 AP56 1200b multi .50 .20
C243 AP56 2000b multi .75 .35
C244 AP56 5000b multi 1.50 .65
Nos. C241-C244 (4) 3.00 1.40

Armed Forces of Bolivia.

Malaria Type of 1962

Design: Inscription around mosquito, laurel around globe.

1962, Oct. 4

C245 A154 2000b indigo, grn & yel .80 .50

Type of Regular Issue, 1961

Design: Pedro de la Gasca (1485-1567).

Perf. 13x12½
1962 Unwmk. Photo.

C246 A150 1200b brn, *yel* .35 .20

Condor, Soccer Ball and Flags AP57

Alliance for Progress Emblem AP58

1.80b, Map of Bolivia, soccer ball, goal and flags.

1963, Mar. 21 Litho. *Perf. 11½*

C247 AP57 1.40b multi 1.00 .65
C248 AP57 1.80b multi 1.00 1.00

21st South American Soccer Championships.

Freedom from Hunger Type

Design: Wheat, globe and wheat emblem.

1963, Aug. 1 Unwmk. *Perf. 11½*

C249 A156 1.20b dk grn, bl & yel .75 .75

1963, Nov. 15 *Perf. 11½*

C250 AP58 1.20b dl yel, ultra & grn .80 .75

2nd anniv. of the Alliance for Progress, which aims to stimulate economic growth and raise living standards in Latin America.

Type of Regular Issue, 1963

Designs: 1.20b, Ballot box and voters. 1.40b, Map and farmer breaking chain. 2.80b, Miners.

1963, Dec. 21 *Perf. 11½*

C251 A157 1.20b gray, dk brn & rose .40 .20
C252 A157 1.40b bister & grn .50 .25
C253 A157 2.80b slate & buff 1.00 .90
Nos. C251-C253 (3) 1.90 1.35

Andrés Santa Cruz — AP59

Perf. 13½
1966, Aug. 10 Wmk. 90 Litho.

C254 AP59 20c dp bl .20 .20
C255 AP59 60c dp grn .20 .20
C256 AP59 1.20b red brn .50 .50
C257 AP59 2.80b black .80 .80
Nos. C254-C257 (4) 1.70 1.70

Cent. (in 1965) of the death of Marshal Andrés Santa Cruz (1792-1865), pres. of Bolivia and of Peru-Bolivia Confederation.

Children Type of 1966

Design: 1.40b, Mother and children.

1966, Dec. 16 Unwmk. *Perf. 13½*

C258 A159 1.40b gray bl & blk 1.00 .40

Co-Presidents Type of Regular Issue

1966, Dec. 16 Litho. *Perf. 12½*
Flag in Red, Yellow and Green

C259 A160 2.80b gray & tan 1.40 1.00
C260 A160 10b sep & tan 1.60 .50
a. Souvenir sheet of 4 6.50 6.50

No. C260a contains 4 imperf. stamps similar to Nos. 480-481 and C259-C260. Dark green marginal inscription. Size: 135x82mm.

Various Issues 1954-62 Surcharged with New Values and Bars

1966, Dec. 21

On No. C177: "XII Aniversario / Reforma / Agraria"

C261 A138 10c on 27b .20 .20
a. Agraria/Agraria 10.00

On No. C182: "XXV / Aniversario Paz / del Chaco"

C262 AP47 10c on 55b .20 .20

On No. C199: "Centenario de / Tupiza"

C263 AP48 60c on 1350b .50 .20

On No. C200: "XXV / Aniversario / Automovil Club / Boliviano"

C264 AP48 2.80b on 2700b 2.00 1.60

On No. C201: "Centenario de la / Cruz Roja / Internacional"

C265 AP48 4b on 4000b 1.40 1.00

On No. C219: "CL Aniversario / Heroinas Coronilla"

C266 A145 1.20b on 800b .75 .50

On No. C222: "Centenario Himno / Paceño"

C267 A145 1.40b on 4,000b .75 .50

Nos. C224-C225 Surcharged

C268 A146 1.40b on 1,000b .60 .60
C269 A146 1.40b on 1,800b .60 .60

On Nos. C238-C239: "Aniversario / Centro Filatelico / Cochabamba"

C270 A152 1.20b on 800b 1.00 .25
C271 A152 1.20b on 1,800b 1.00 .25

Revenue Stamp of 1946 Surcharged with New Value "X" and: "XXV Aniversario / Dpto. Pando / Aéreo"

C272 A161 1.20b on 1b dk bl .50 .25
Nos. C261-C272 (12) 9.50 6.15

Lions Emblem and Pre-historic Sculptures AP60

1967, Sept. 20 Litho. *Perf. 13x13½*

C273 AP60 2b red & multi .80 .65
a. Souvenir sheet of 2 3.75 3.75

50th anniv. of Lions Intl. No. C273a contains 2 imperf. stamps similar to Nos. 492 and C273.

Folklore Type of Regular Issue

Designs (Folklore characters): 1.20p, Pujllay. 1.40p, Ujusiris. 2p, Morenada. 3p, Aukiaukis.

1968, June 24 *Perf. 13½x13*

C274 A163 1.20b lt yel grn & multi .35 .20
C275 A163 1.40b gray & multi .40 .20
C276 A163 2b dk ol bis & multi .75 .25
C277 A163 3b sky bl & multi 1.00 .25
Nos. C274-C277 (4) 2.50 .90

A souvenir sheet exists containing 4 imperf. stamps similar to Nos. C274-C277. Size: 131x81½mm.

Moto Mendez — AP61

1968, Oct. 29 Litho. *Perf. 13½x13*

C278 AP61 1b multi .35 .20
C279 AP61 1.20b multi .40 .35
C280 AP61 2b multi .75 .50
C281 AP61 4b multi 1.00 .75
Nos. C278-C281 (4) 2.50 1.80

Battle of Tablada sesquicentennial.

Pres. Gualberto Villaroel AP62

1968, Nov. 6 *Perf. 13x13½*

C282 AP62 1.40b org & blk .30 .25
C283 AP62 3b lt bl & blk .55 .30
C284 AP62 4b rose & blk .70 .40
C285 AP62 5b gray grn & blk .85 .55
C286 AP62 10b pale pur & blk 1.60 1.10
Nos. C282-C286 (5) 4.00 2.60

4th centenary of Cochabamba.

ITU Type of Regular Issue

1968, Dec. 3 Litho. *Perf. 13x13½*

C287 A166 1.20b gray, blk & yel .60 .30
C288 A166 1.40b bl, blk & gray ol .60 .20

UNESCO Emblem — AP63

1968, Nov. 14 *Perf. 13½x13*

C289 AP63 1.20b pale vio & blk .35 .35
C290 AP63 2.80b yel grn & blk .65 .65

20th anniv. (in 1966) of UNESCO.

Kennedy Type of Regular Issue

1968, Nov. 22 Unwmk.

C291 A168 1b grn & blk .25 .20
C292 A168 10b scar & blk 2.75 2.75

A souvenir sheet contains one imperf. stamp similar to No. C291. Dark violet marginal inscription. Size: 131x81½mm.

Tennis Type of Regular Issue

1968, Dec. 10 *Perf. 13x13½*

C293 A169 1.40b org, blk & lt brn .35 .35
C294 A169 2.80b sky bl, blk & lt brn .65 .65

A souvenir sheet exists containing one imperf. stamp similar to No. C293. Size: 131x81½mm.

Stamp Centenary Type of Regular Issue

Design: 1.40b, 2.80b, 3b, Bolivia No. 1.

1968, Dec. 23 Litho. *Perf. 13x13½*

C295 A170 1.40b org, grn & blk .50 .50
C296 A170 2.80b pale rose, grn & blk 1.00 1.00
C297 A170 3b lt vio, grn & blk 1.00 1.00
Nos. C295-C297 (3) 2.50 2.50

A souvenir sheet exists containing 3 imperf. stamps similar to Nos. C295-C297. Size: 131x81½mm.

Franklin D. Roosevelt — AP64

1969, Oct. 29 Litho. *Perf. 13½x13*

C298 AP64 5b brn, blk & buff 1.75 1.10

Olympic Type of Regular Issue

Sports: 1.20b, Woman runner, vert. 2.80b, Discus thrower, vert. 5b, Hurdler.

Perf. 13½x13, 13x13½
1969, Oct. 29 Litho.

C299 A171 1.20b yel grn, bis & blk .50 .40
C300 A171 2.80b red, org & blk 1.00 .75
C301 A171 5b bl, lt bl, red & blk 1.50 1.50
Nos. C299-C301 (3) 3.00 2.65

A souvenir sheet exists containing 3 imperf. stamps similar to Nos. C299-C301. Size: 130½x81mm.

Butterfly Type of Regular Issue

Butterflies: 1b, Metamorpha dido wernichei. 1.80b, Heliconius felix. 2.80b, Morpho casica. 3b, Papilio yuracares. 4b, Heliconius melitus.

1970, Apr. 24 Litho. *Perf. 13x13½*

C302 A172 1b sal & multi 1.40 1.40
C303 A172 1.80b lt bl & multi 2.00 2.00
C304 A172 2.80b multi 3.25 3.25
C305 A172 3b multi 3.25 3.25
C306 A172 4b multi 4.00 4.00
Nos. C302-C306 (5) 13.90 13.90

A souvenir sheet exists containing 3 imperf. stamps similar to Nos. C302-C304. Black marginal inscription. Size: 129½x80mm.

Scout Type of Regular Issue

Designs: 50c, Boy Scout building brick wall. 1.20b, Bolivian Boy Scout emblem.

1970, June 17 Litho. *Perf. 13½x13*

C307 A173 50c yel & multi .20 .20
C308 A173 1.20b multi .40 .40

No. C228 Surcharged

1970, Dec. Litho. *Perf. 10½*

C309 AP53 1.20b on 4000b multi .25 .20

Flower Type of Regular Issue

Bolivian Flowers: 1.20b, Amaryllis pseudopardina, horiz. 1.40b, Rebutia kruegeri. 2.80b, Lobivia pentlandii, horiz. 4b, Rebutia tunariensis.

Perf. 13x13½, 13½x13
1971, Aug. 9 Litho. Unwmk.

C310 A174 1.20b multi .70 .40
C311 A174 1.40b multi .80 .50
C312 A174 2.80b multi 1.50 .75
C313 A174 4b multi 2.00 1.25
Nos. C310-C313 (4) 5.00 2.90

Two souvenir sheets of 4 exist. One contains imperf. stamps similar to Nos. 534-535 and C310, C312. The other contains imperf. stamps similar to Nos. 536-537, C311, C313. Size: 130x80mm.

Folk Dance Type of Regular Issue

1972, Mar. 23 Litho. *Perf. 13½x13*

C314 A177 1.20b Kusillo .50 .20
C315 A177 1.40b Taquirari .65 .20

Two souvenir sheets of 3 exist. One contains imperf. stamps similar to Nos. 542-543, C314. The other contains imperf. stamps similar to Nos. 540-541, C315. Size: 80x129mm.

Painting Type of Regular Issue

Bolivian Paintings: 1.40b, Portrait of Chola Paceña, by Cecilio Guzman de Rojas. 1.50b, Adoration of the Kings, by G. Gamarra. 1.60b, Adoration of Pachamama (mountain), by A. Borda. 2b, The Kiss of the Idol, by Guzman de Rojas.

1972	**Litho.**	***Perf. 13½***	
C316 A178	1.40b multi	.40	.20
C317 A178	1.50b multi	.40	.20
C318 A178	1.60b multi	.40	.20
C319 A178	2b multi	.55	.20
Nos. C316-C319 (4)		1.75	.80

Two souvenir sheets of 2 exist. One contains imperf. stamps similar to Nos. 548 and C318. The other contains imperf. stamps similar to Nos. C317 and C319. Size: 129x80mm.

Issue dates: 1.40b, Dec. 4. Others, Aug. 17.

Bolivian Coat of Arms AP65

1972, Dec. 4		***Perf. 13½x14***	
C320 AP65	4b lt bl & multi	1.40	.50

Cactus Type of Regular Issue

Designs: Various cacti.

1973, Aug. 6	**Litho.**	***Perf. 13½***	
C321 A180	1.20b tan & multi	.35	.20
C322 A180	1.90b org & multi	.50	.20
C323 A180	2b multi	.65	.25
Nos. C321-C323 (3)		1.50	.65

Development Type of Regular Issue

1.40b, Highway 1Y4. 2b, Rail car on bridge.

1973, Nov. 26	**Litho.**	***Perf. 13½***	
C324 A181	1.40b salmon & multi	.40	.20
C325 A181	2b multi	.60	.20

Santos-Dumont and 14-Bis Plane — AP66

1973, July 20			
C326 AP66	1.40b yel & blk	.65	.35

Centenary of the birth of Alberto Santos-Dumont (1873-1932), Brazilian aviation pioneer.

Orchid Type of 1974

Orchids: 2.50b, Cattleya luteola, horiz. 3.80b, Stanhopaea. 4b, Catasetum, horiz. 5b, Maxillaria.

1974	**Litho.**	***Perf. 13½***	
C327 A182	2.50b multi	1.00	.25
C328 A182	3.80b rose & multi	1.50	.45
C329 A182	4b multi	1.50	.40
C330 A182	5b sal & multi	2.50	.45
Nos. C327-C330 (4)		6.50	1.55

Air Force Emblem, Plane over Map of Bolivia AP67

Designs: 3.80b, Plane over Andes. 4.50b, Triple decker and jet. 8b, Rafael Pabon and double decker. 15b, Jet and "50."

1974	**Litho.**	***Perf. 13x13½***	
C331 AP67	3b multi	.65	.25
C332 AP67	3.80b multi	1.00	.25
C333 AP67	4.50b multi	1.00	.25
C334 AP67	8b multi	1.60	.40
C335 AP67	15b multi	3.50	.50
Nos. C331-C335 (5)		7.75	1.65

Bolivian Air Force, 50th anniv. Exist imperf.

For surcharge see No. 968.

Coat of Arms Type of 1975

Designs: Departmental coats of arms.

1975, July 16	**Litho.**	***Perf. 13½***	
C336 A188	20c Beni	.20	.20
C337 A188	30c Tarija	.20	.20
C338 A188	50c Potosi	.25	.25
C339 A188	1b Oruro	.50	.50
C340 A188	2.50b Santa Cruz	1.00	1.00
C341 A188	3b La Paz	1.00	1.00
Nos. C336-C341 (6)		3.15	3.15

LAB Emblem AP68

Bolivia on Map of Americas AP69

Map of Bolivia, Plane and Kyllmann AP70

1975	**Litho.**	***Perf. 13½***	
C342 AP68	1b gold, bl & blk	.40	.40
C343 AP69	1.50b multi	.60	.60
C344 AP70	2b multi	.75	.75
Nos. C342-C344 (3)		1.75	1.75

Lloyd Aereo Boliviano, 50th anniversary, founded by Guillermo Kyllmann.

Bolivar, Presidents Perez and Banzer, and Flags AP71

1975, Aug. 4	**Litho.**	***Perf. 13½***	
C345 AP71	3b gold & multi	.75	.65

Visit of Pres. Carlos A. Perez of Venezuela.

Bolivar Type of 1975

Presidents and Statesmen of Bolivia: 50c, Rene Barrientos O. 2b, Francisco B. O'Connor. 3.80b, Gualberto Villarroel. 4.20b, German Busch. 4.50b, Hugo Banzer Suarez. 20b, José Ballivian. 30b, Andres de Santa Cruz. 40b, Antonio Jose de Sucre.

1975	**Litho.**	***Perf. 13½***	
Size: 24x33mm			
C346 A189	50c multi	.25	.25
C347 A189	2b multi	.50	.50
C348 A189	3.80b multi	.75	.75
C349 A189	4.20b multi	1.00	.75
Size: 28x39mm			
C350 A189	4.50b multi	1.00	.50
Size: 24x33mm			
C351 A189	20b multi	4.00	2.00
C352 A189	30b multi	5.00	5.00
C353 A189	40b multi	6.50	6.50
Nos. C346-C353 (8)		19.00	16.25

For surcharge see No. 969.

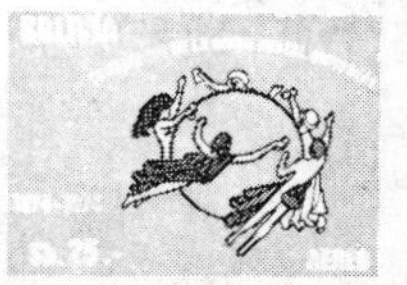

UPU Emblem AP72

1975, Dec. 7	**Litho.**	***Perf. 13½***	
C358 AP72	25b blue & multi	3.00	3.00

Cent. of UPU (in 1974).

POSTAGE DUE STAMPS

D1

1931	**Unwmk. Engr.**	***Perf. 14, 14½***	
J1 D1	5c ultra	1.10	*1.25*
J2 D1	10c red	1.10	*1.25*
J3 D1	15c yellow	1.75	*2.00*
J4 D1	30c deep green	1.75	*2.00*
J5 D1	40c deep violet	2.75	*3.25*
J6 D1	50c black brown	4.00	*4.50*
Nos. J1-J6 (6)		12.45	*14.25*

Symbol of Youth D2

Torch of Knowledge D3

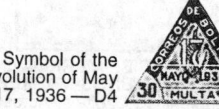

Symbol of the Revolution of May 17, 1936 — D4

1938	**Litho.**	***Perf. 11***	
J7 D2	5c deep rose	.50	.45
a.	Pair, imperf. between		
J8 D3	10c green	.50	.45
J9 D4	30c gray blue	.50	.45
Nos. J7-J9 (3)		1.50	1.35

POSTAL TAX STAMPS

Worker — PT1

Imprint: "LITO. UNIDAS LA PAZ."

Perf. 13½x10½, 10½, 13½

1939	**Litho.**	**Unwmk.**	
RA1 PT1	5c dull violet	.70	.20
a.	Double impression		

Redrawn

Imprint: "TALL. OFFSET LA PAZ."

1940		***Perf. 12x11, 11***	
RA2 PT1	5c violet	.60	.20
a.	Horizontal pair, imperf. between	2.00	
b.	Imperf. horiz., pair		

Tax of Nos. RA1-RA2 was for the Workers' Home Building Fund.

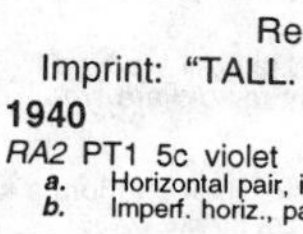

Communications Symbols — PT2

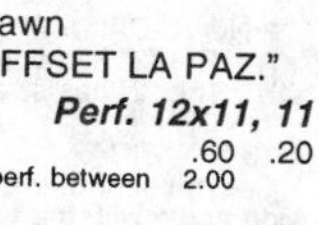

Condor, Envelope and Post Horn — PT3

Communication Symbols — PT4

Postman Blowing Horn — PT5

1944-45	**Litho.**	***Perf. 10½***	
RA3 PT2	10c salmon	.40	.20
RA4 PT2	10c blue ('45)	.40	.20

A 30c orange inscribed "Centenario de la Creacion del Departmento del Beni" was issued in 1946 and required to be affixed to all air and surface mail to and from the Department of Beni in addition to regular postage. Five higher denominations in the same scenic design were used for local revenue purposes.

Catalogue values for unused stamps in this section, from this point to the end of the section, are for Never Hinged items.

Type of 1944 Redrawn

1947-48	**Unwmk.**	***Perf. 10½***	
RA5 PT2	10c carmine	.40	.20
RA6 PT2	10c org yel ('48)	.35	.20
RA7 PT2	10c yel brn ('48)	.35	.20
RA8 PT2	10c emerald ('48)	.35	.20
Nos. RA5-RA8 (4)		1.45	.80

Post horn and envelope reduced in size.

1951-52			
RA9 PT3	20c deep orange	.40	.20
a.	Imperf., pair	20.00	
RA10 PT3	20c green ('52)	.50	.20
a.	Imperf., pair	20.00	
RA11 PT3	20c blue ('52)	.50	.20
a.	Imperf., pair	20.00	
Nos. RA9-RA11 (3)		1.40	.60

For surcharges see Nos. RA17-RA18.

1952-54	***Perf. 13½, 10½, 10½x12***		
RA12 PT4	50c green	.50	.20
RA13 PT4	50c carmine	.50	.20
RA14 PT4	3b green	.50	.20
RA15 PT4	3b olive bister	.50	.50
RA16 PT4	5b violet ('54)	.50	.50
Nos. RA12-RA16 (5)		2.50	1.60

For surcharges see Nos. RA21-RA22.

No. RA10 and Type of 1951-52 Surcharged with New Value in Black

1953		***Perf. 10½***	
RA17 PT3	50c on 20c green	.25	.20
RA18 PT3	50c on 20c red vio	.25	.20

1954-55	**Unwmk.**	***Perf. 10½***	
RA19 PT5	1b brown	.20	.20
RA20 PT5	1b car rose ('55)	.20	.20

Exist imperf.

Nos. RA15 and RA14 Surcharged in Black "Bs. 5.-/D. S./21-IV-55"

1955		***Perf. 10½, 10½x12***	
RA21 PT4	5b on 3b olive bister	.25	.20
RA22 PT4	5b on 3b green	.25	.20

Tax of Nos. RA3-RA22 was for the Communications Employees Fund.

No. RA21 is known with surcharge in thin type of different font and with comma added after "55."

Plane over Airport — PT6

Planes — PT7

Perf. 10½, 12, 13½

1955	**Unwmk.**	**Litho.**	
RA23 PT6	5b dp ultra	.25	.20
a.	Vertical pair imperf. between		
Perf. 11½			
RA24 PT7	10b light green	.20	.20

PT8

PT9

1955 Litho. *Perf. 10½*

RA25	PT8	5b red	7.50	7.50
a.		Imperf., pair	35.00	

Perf. 12

RA26	PT9	20b dark brown	.25	.20

Tax of Nos. RA23-RA26 was for the building of new airports.

General Alfredo Ovando and Three Men — PT10

1970, Sept. 26 Litho. *Perf. 13x13½*

RA27	PT10	20c black & red	.50	.20

See No. RAC1.

Pres. German Busch — PT11

1971, May 13 Litho. *Perf. 13x13½*

RA28	PT11	20c lilac & black	.50	.20

AIR POST POSTAL TAX STAMPS

Catalogue values for unused stamps in this section are for Never Hinged items.

Type of Postal Tax Issue

Design: 30c, General Ovando and oil well.

1970, Sept. 26 Litho. *Perf. 13x13½*

RAC1	PT10	30c blk & grn	.50	.20

Pres. Gualberto Villarroel, Refinery — PTAP1

1971, May 25 Litho. *Perf. 13x13½*

RAC2	PTAP1	30c lt bl & blk	.50	.20

Type of 1971 Inscribed: "XXV ANIVERSARIO DE SU GOBIERNO"

1975 Litho. *Perf. 13x13½*

RAC3	PTAP1	30c lt bl & blk	3.00	3.00

BOSNIA AND HERZEGOVINA

'bäz-nē-ə and ,hert-sə-gō-'vē-nə

LOCATION — Dalmatia and Serbia
GOVT. — Provinces of Turkey under Austro-Hungarian occupation, 1879-1908; provinces of Austria-Hungary 1908-1918
AREA — 19,768 sq. mi.
POP. — 2,000,000 (approx. 1918)
CAPITAL — Sarajevo

Following World War I Bosnia and Herzegovina united with the kingdoms of Montenegro and Serbia, and Croatia, Dalmatia and Slovenia, to form the Kingdom of Yugoslavia (See Yugoslavia.)

100 Novcica (Neukreuzer) = 1 Florin (Gulden)

100 Heller = 1 Krone (1900)

Watermark

Wmk. 91- BRIEF-MARKEN or (from 1890) ZEITUNGS-MARKEN in Double-lined Capitals, Across the Sheet

Coat of Arms — A1

Type I - The heraldic eaglets on the right side of the escutcheon are entirely blank. The eye of the lion is indicated by a very small dot, which sometimes fails to print.

Type II - There is a colored line across the lowest eaglet. A similar line sometimes appears on the middle eaglet. The eye of the lion is formed by a large dot which touches the outline of the head above it.

Type III - The eaglets and eye of the lion are similar to type I. Each tail feather of the large eagle has two lines of shading and the lowest feather does not touch the curved line below it. In types I and II there are several shading lines in these feathers, and the lowest feather touches the curved line.

Varieties of the Numerals

2 NOVCICA:
A - The "2" has curved tail. All are type I.
B - The "2" has straight tail. All are type II.

15 NOVCICA:
C - The serif of the "1" is short and forms a wide angle with the vertical stroke.
D - The serif of the "1" forms an acute angle with the vertical stroke.

The numerals of the 5n were retouched several times and show minor differences, especially in the flag.

Other Varieties

½ NOVCICA:
There is a black dot between the curved ends of the ornaments near the lower spandrels.
G - This dot touches the curve at its right. Stamps of this (1st) printing are litho.
H - This dot stands clear of the curved lines. Stamps of this (2nd) printing are typo.

10 NOVCICA:
Ten stamps in each sheet of type II show a small cross in the upper section of the right side of the escutcheon.

Perf. 9 to 13½ and Compound

1879-94 Litho. Wmk. 91

Type I

1	A1	½n blk (type II) ('94)	7.25	*15.00*
2	A1	1n gray	4.75	1.50
c.		1n gray lilac		1.50
4	A1	2n yellow	9.00	.90
5	A1	3n green	6.00	1.75
6	A1	5n rose red	10.00	.40
7	A1	10n blue	30.00	.75
8	A1	15n brown	32.50	4.50
9	A1	20n gray green ('93)	150.00	6.75
10	A1	25n violet	27.50	6.75
		Nos. 1-10 (9)	277.00	38.30

No. 2c was never issued. It is usually canceled by blue pencil marks and "mint" copies generally have been cleaned.

Perf. 10½ to 13 and Compound

1894-98 Typo.

Type II

1a	A1	½n black	10.00	*15.00*
2a	A1	1n gray	4.00	1.00
4a	A1	2n yellow	3.00	.55
5a	A1	3n green	4.00	1.25
6a	A1	5n rose red	55.00	.35
7a	A1	10n blue	5.50	.70
8a	A1	15n brown	4.75	3.25
9a	A1	20n gray green	6.75	3.50
10a	A1	25n violet	7.25	5.75
		Nos. 1a-10a (9)	100.25	31.35

Type III

6b	A1	5n rose red ('98)	1.50	.35

All the preceding stamps exist in various shades.

Nos. 1a to 10a were reprinted in 1911 in lighter colors, on very white paper and perf. 12½. Value, set $25.

A2

A3

Perf. 10½, 12½ and Compound

1900 Typo.

11	A2	1h gray black	.30	.20
12	A2	2h gray	.30	.20
13	A2	3h yellow	.30	.20
14	A2	5h green	.30	.20
15	A2	6h brown	.60	.20
16	A2	10h red	.25	.20
17	A2	20h rose	100.00	4.00
18	A2	25h blue	.85	.20
19	A2	30h bister brown	110.00	4.75
20	A2	40h orange	150.00	8.00
21	A2	50h red lilac	1.00	.35
22	A3	1k dark rose	1.25	.50
23	A3	2k ultra	1.50	1.25
24	A3	5k dull blue grn	3.75	3.75
		Nos. 11-24 (14)	370.40	24.00

All values of this issue except the 3h exist on ribbed paper.

Nos. 17, 19 and 20 were reprinted in 1911. The reprints are in lighter colors and on whiter paper than the originals. Reprints of Nos. 17 and 19 are perf. 10½ and those of No. 20 are perf. 12½. Value each $1.50.

Numerals in Black

1901-04 *Perf. 12½*

25	A2	20h pink ('02)	.55	.40
26	A2	30h bister brn ('03)	.55	.40
27	A2	35h blue	.75	.40
a.		35h ultramarine	*80.00*	4.75
28	A2	40h orange ('03)	1.00	.80
29	A2	45h grnsh blue ('04)	.65	.45
		Nos. 25-29 (5)	3.50	2.45

Nos. 11-16, 18, 21-29 exist imperf. Most of Nos. 11-29 exist perf. 6½; compound with 12½; part perf.; in pairs imperf. between. These were supplied only to some high-ranking officials and never sold at any P.O.

View of Deboj A4

The Carsija at Sarajevo — A5

Designs: 2h, View of Mostar. 3h, Pliva Gate, Jajce. 5h, Narenta Pass and Prenj River. 6h, Rama Valley. 10h, Vrbas Valley. 20h, Old Bridge, Mostar. 25h, Bey's Mosque, Sarajevo. 30h, Donkey post. 35h, Jezero and tourists' pavilion. 40h, Mail wagon. 45h, Bazaar at Sarajevo. 50h, Postal car. 2k, St. Luke's Campanile, Jajce. 5k, Emperor Franz Josef.

Perf. 6½, 9½, 10½ and 12½, also Compounds

1906 Engr. Unwmk.

30	A4	1h black	.20	.20
31	A4	2h violet	.20	.20
32	A4	3h olive	.20	.20
33	A4	5h dark green	.20	.20
34	A4	6h brown	.20	.20
a.		Perf. 13½	15.00	*18.00*
35	A4	10h carmine	.20	.20
36	A4	20h dark brown	.35	.20
a.		Perf. 13½	37.50	37.50
37	A4	25h deep blue	1.10	.75
38	A4	30h green	1.25	.30
39	A4	35h myrtle green	1.40	.30
40	A4	40h orange red	1.40	.30
41	A4	45h brown red	1.40	.90
42	A4	50h dull violet	1.50	.60
43	A5	1k maroon	3.75	1.25
44	A5	2k gray green	4.75	*6.00*
45	A5	5k dull blue	4.00	*4.50*
		Nos. 30-45 (16)	22.10	*16.30*

Nos. 30-45 exist imperf. Value, set $50 unused, $37.50 canceled.

For overprint and surcharges see #126, B1-B4.

Birthday Jubilee Issue

Designs of 1906 Issue, with "1830-1910" in Label at Bottom

1910 *Perf. 12½*

46	A4	1h black	.40	.20
47	A4	2h violet	.50	.20
48	A4	3h olive	.50	.20
49	A4	5h dark green	.55	.20
50	A4	6h orange brn	.55	.25
51	A4	10h carmine	.55	.20
52	A4	20h dark brown	1.25	1.25
53	A4	25h deep blue	2.50	2.50
54	A4	30h green	1.75	*2.00*
55	A4	35h myrtle grn	2.50	2.25
56	A4	40h orange red	2.50	*2.75*
57	A4	45h brown red	4.25	*4.75*
58	A4	50h dull violet	4.25	*5.00*
59	A5	1k maroon	4.25	*5.00*
60	A5	2k gray green	15.00	15.00
61	A5	5k dull blue	3.00	*3.25*
		Nos. 46-61 (16)	44.30	*45.00*

80th birthday of Emperor Franz Josef.

Scenic Type of 1906

Views: 12h, Jaice. 60h, Konjica. 72h, Vishegrad.

1912

62	A4	12h ultra	4.00	*4.25*
63	A4	60h dull blue	2.50	*3.75*
64	A4	72h carmine	12.00	*14.00*
		Nos. 62-64 (3)	18.50	*22.00*

Value, imperf. set, $75.

See Austria for similar designs inscribed "FELDPOST" instead of "MILITARPOST."

Emperor Franz Josef
A23 A24

A25

A26

1912-14

Various Frames

No.	Type	Description	Unused	Used
65	A23	1h olive green	.35	.20
66	A23	2h brt blue	.35	.20
67	A23	3h claret	.35	.20
68	A23	5h green	.35	.20
69	A23	6h dark gray	.35	.20
70	A23	10h rose car	.40	.20
71	A23	12h dp olive grn	1.10	.30
72	A23	20h orange brn	4.50	.20
73	A23	25h ultra	2.25	.20
74	A23	30h orange red	2.25	.20
75	A24	35h myrtle grn	2.25	.20
76	A24	40h dk violet	6.75	.20
77	A24	45h olive brn	3.00	.20
78	A24	50h slate blue	3.00	.20
79	A24	60h brown vio	2.75	.20
80	A24	72h dark blue	3.25	3.00
81	A25	1k brn vio, *straw*	12.50	.35
82	A25	2k dk gray, *bl*	7.25	.25
83	A26	3k carmine, *grn*	12.00	9.00
84	A26	5k dk vio, *gray*	22.50	20.00
85	A25	10k dk ultra, *gray* ('14)	82.50	70.00
		Nos. 65-85 (21)	170.00	105.70

Value, imperf. set, $450.

For overprints and surcharges see #127, B5-B8, Austria M1-M21.

A27

A28

1916-17 ***Perf. 12½***

No.	Type	Description	Unused	Used
86	A27	3h dark gray	.20	.20
87	A27	5h olive green	.25	.35
88	A27	6h violet	.30	.35
89	A27	10h bister	1.40	1.60
90	A27	12h blue gray	.45	.45
91	A27	15h car rose	.20	.20
92	A27	20h brown	.35	.45
93	A27	25h blue	.25	.35
94	A27	30h dark green	.25	.35
95	A27	40h vermilion	.25	.35
96	A27	50h green	.25	.35
97	A27	60h lake	.25	.35
98	A27	80h orange brn	1.25	.40
a.		Perf. 11½	3.50	3.00
99	A27	90h dark violet	.75	.50
a.		Perf. 11½	450.00	675.00
101	A28	2k claret, *straw*	.75	.75
102	A28	3k green, *bl*	1.90	3.25
103	A28	4k carmine, *grn*	5.75	7.25
104	A28	10k dp vio, *gray*	15.00	20.00
		Nos. 86-104 (18)	29.80	37.50

Value, imperf. set, $175.

For overprints see Nos. B11-B12.

Emperor Karl I
A29 A30

1917 ***Perf. 12½***

No.	Type	Description	Unused	Used
105	A29	3h olive gray	.20	.20
a.		Perf. 11½	75.00	75.00
b.		Perf. 12½x11½	13.00	21.00
106	A29	5h olive green	.20	.20
107	A29	6h violet	.30	.55
108	A29	10h orange brn	.20	.20
a.		Perf. 11½x12½	62.50	95.00
b.		Perf. 11½		
109	A29	12h blue	.50	.75
110	A29	15h brt rose	.20	.20
111	A29	20h red brown	.20	.20
112	A29	25h ultra	1.00	.50
113	A29	30h gray green	.25	.20
114	A29	40h olive bis	.25	.20
115	A29	50h dp green	.85	.50
116	A29	60h car rose	.85	.45
a.		Perf. 11½	15.00	21.00
117	A29	80h steel blue	.25	.25
118	A29	90h dull violet	1.00	1.40
119	A30	2k carmine, *straw*	.50	.45
120	A30	3k green, *bl*	13.00	16.00
121	A30	4k carmine, *grn*	5.25	7.25
122	A30	10k dp violet, *gray*	3.25	5.75
		Nos. 105-122 (18)	28.25	35.25

Value, imperf. set, $85.

Nos. 47 and 66 Overprinted in Red

1918

1918

No.	Type	Description	Unused	Used
126	A4	2h violet	.45	.50
b.		Inverted overprint	17.50	
d.		Double overprint	37.50	
f.		Double overprint, one inverted		
127	A23	2h bright blue	.50	.60
a.		Pair, one without overprint		
b.		Inverted overprint	15.00	
c.		Double overprint	15.00	
d.		Double overprint, one inverted		

Emperor Karl I — A31

1918 **Typo.** ***Perf. 12½, Imperf.***

No.	Type	Description	Unused	Used
128	A31	2h orange	9.00	
129	A31	3h dark green	9.00	
130	A31	5h lt green	9.00	
131	A31	6h blue green	9.00	
132	A31	10h brown	9.00	
133	A31	20h brick red	9.00	
134	A31	25h ultra	9.00	
135	A31	45h dk slate	9.00	
136	A31	50h lt bluish grn	9.00	
137	A31	60h blue violet	9.00	
138	A31	70h ocher	9.00	
139	A31	80h rose	9.00	
140	A31	90h violet brn	9.00	

Engr.

No.	Type	Description	Unused	Used
141	A30	1k ol grn, *grnsh*	2,250.	
		Nos. 128-140 (13)	117.00	

Nos. 128-141 were prepared for use in Bosnia and Herzegovina, but were not issued there. They were sold after the Armistice at the Vienna post office for a few days.

SEMI-POSTAL STAMPS

Nos. 33 and 35 Surcharged in Red

1914.
7 Heller

1914 **Unwmk.** ***Perf. 12½***

No.	Type	Description	Unused	Used
B1	A4	7h on 5h dk grn	.40	.40
B2	A4	12h on 10h car	.40	.40

Various minor varieties of the surcharge include "4" with open top, narrow "4" and wide "4."

Nos. B1-B2 exist with double and inverted surcharges. Value about $20 each.

Nos. 33 and 35 Surcharged in Red or Blue

1915.
7 Heller

1915 ***Perf. 12½***

No.	Type	Description	Unused	Used
B3	A4	7h on 5h (R)	9.50	9.00
a.		Perf. 9½	140.00	140.00
B4	A4	12h on 10h (Bl)	.30	.30

Nos. B3-B4 exist with double and inverted surcharges. Value about $18.50 each.

1915

Nos. 68 and 70 Surcharged in Red or Blue

7 Heller.

1915

No.	Type	Description	Unused	Used
B5	A23	7h on 5h (R)	.80	.75
a.		"1915" at top and bottom	35.00	37.50
B6	A23	12h on 10h (Bl)	1.40	1.50
a.		Surcharged "7 Heller."	35.00	37.50

Nos. B5-B6 are found in three types differing in length of surcharge lines:
I- date 18mm, denomination 14mm.
II- date 16mm, denomination 14mm.
III- date 18mm, denomination 16mm.

Nos. B5-B6 exist with double and inverted surcharges. Value $25 each.

Nos. B5a and B6a exist double and inverted.

1916.

Nos. 68 and 70 Surcharged in Red or Blue

7 Heller.

1916

No.	Type	Description	Unused	Used
B7	A23	7h on 5h (R)	.50	.65
B8	A23	12h on 10h (Bl)	.50	.65

Nos. B7-B8 exist with double and inverted surcharges. Value $12.50 each.

Wounded Soldier — SP1

Blind Soldier — SP2

1916 **Engr.**

No.	Type	Description	Unused	Used
B9	SP1	5h (+ 2h) green	.65	.60
B10	SP2	10h (+ 2h) magenta	1.00	.90

Nos. B9-B10 exist imperf. Value, set $27.50.

Nos. 89, 91 Overprinted

WITWEN- UND WAISENWOCHE
1917

1917

No.	Type	Description	Unused	Used
B11	A27	10h bister	.20	.20
B12	A27	15h carmine rose	.20	.20

Nos. B11-B12 exist imperf. Value set, $16.

Nos. B11-B12 exist with double and inverted overprint. Value $9 each.

Design for Memorial Church at Sarajevo SP3

Archduke Francis Ferdinand — SP4

Duchess Sophia and Archduke Francis Ferdinand SP5

1917 **Typo.** ***Perf. 11½, 12½***

No.	Type	Description	Unused	Used
B13	SP3	10h violet black	.20	.20
B14	SP4	15h claret	.20	.20
B15	SP5	40h deep blue	.20	.20
		Nos. B13-B15 (3)	.60	.60

Assassination of Archduke Ferdinand and Archduchess Sophia. Sold at a premium of 2h each which helped build a memorial church at Sarajevo.

Exist imperf. Value, set $2.50.

Blind Soldier — SP6

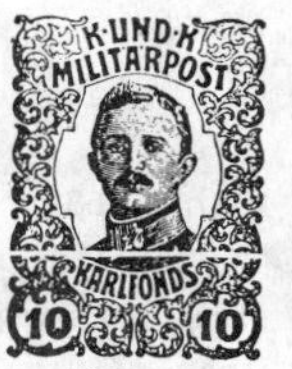
Emperor Karl I — SP8

Design: 15h, Wounded soldier.

1918 **Engr.** ***Perf. 12½***

No.	Type	Description	Unused	Used
B16	SP6	10h (+ 10h) grnsh bl	.60	.55
B17	SP6	15h (+ 10h) red brn	.60	.55

#B16-B17 exist imperf. Value, set $18.50.

1918 **Typo.** ***Perf. 12½x13***

Design: 15h, Empress Zita.

No.	Type	Description	Unused	Used
B18	SP8	10h gray green	.35	.45
B19	SP8	15h brown red	.35	.45
B20	SP8	40h violet	.35	.45
		Nos. B18-B20 (3)	1.05	1.35

Sold at a premium of 10h each which went to the "Karl's Fund."

#B18-B20 exist imperf. Value, set $22.50.

POSTAGE DUE STAMPS

D1

D2

Perf. 9½, 10½, 12½ and Compound

1904 **Unwmk.**

No.	Type	Description	Unused	Used
J1	D1	1h black, red & yel	.45	.20
J2	D1	2h black, red & yel	.45	.20
J3	D1	3h black, red & yel	.50	.20
J4	D1	4h black, red & yel	.50	.20
J5	D1	5h black, red & yel	.50	.20
J6	D1	6h black, red & yel	.20	.20
J7	D1	7h black, red & yel	2.75	2.50
J8	D1	8h black, red & yel	2.75	.50
J9	D1	10h black, red & yel	.65	.20
J10	D1	15h black, red & yel	.60	.20
J11	D1	20h black, red & yel	3.25	.20
J12	D1	50h black, red & yel	2.25	.20
J13	D1	200h black, red & grn	9.25	.70
		Nos. J1-J13 (13)	24.10	5.70

Value, imperf. set, $150.

For overprints see Western Ukraine Nos. 61-72.

1916-18 ***Perf. 12½***

No.	Type	Description	Unused	Used
J14	D2	2h red ('18)	.45	.55
J15	D2	4h red ('18)	.35	.40
J16	D2	5h red	.45	.55
J17	D2	6h red ('18)	.35	.40
J18	D2	10h red	.45	.55
J19	D2	15h red	3.25	4.00
J20	D2	20h red	.50	.60
J21	D2	25h red	1.40	1.75
J22	D2	30h red	1.10	1.40
J23	D2	40h red	8.75	10.00
J24	D2	50h red	26.00	32.50
J25	D2	1k dark blue	3.25	4.00
J26	D2	3k dark blue	14.50	17.50
		Nos. J14-J26 (13)	60.80	74.20

Nos. J25-J26 have colored numerals on a white tablet.

Value, imperf. set, $110.

For surcharges see Italy Nos. NJ1-NJ7.

NEWSPAPER STAMPS

Bosnian Girl — N1

1913 **Unwmk.** ***Imperf.***

No.	Type	Description	Unused	Used
P1	N1	2h ultra	.40	.40
P2	N1	6h violet	1.75	1.50
P3	N1	10h rose	1.75	1.50
P4	N1	20h green	2.10	1.90
		Nos. P1-P4 (4)	6.00	5.30

After Bosnia and Herzegovina became part of Yugoslavia stamps of type N1 perf., and imperf. copies surcharged with new values, were used as regular postage stamps. See Yugoslavia Nos. 1L21-1L22, 1L43-1L45.

SPECIAL HANDLING STAMPS

"Lightning" — SH1

1916	**Unwmk.**	**Engr.**	***Perf. 12½***	
QE1 SH1 2h vermilion			.20	.20
a. Perf. 11½x12½			250.00	250.00
QE2 SH1 5h deep green			.35	.35
a. Perf. 11½			13.00	13.00

For surcharges see Italy Nos. NE1-NE2.

BOSNIA AND HERZEGOVINA

'bäz-nē-ə and ˌhert-sə-gō-'vē-nə

LOCATION — Between Croatia and Yugoslavia.
GOVT. — Republic
CAPITAL — Sarajevo

Formerly part of Yugoslavia. Proclamation of independence in 1992 was followed by protracted civil war that was ended by the Dayton Peace Agreement of Nov. 21, 1995.

While Dinars were the official currency until 6/22/98, a currency pegged to the German mark was in use for some time prior to that. Stamps are denominated in pfennigs and marks in 11/97.

100 Paras = 1 Dinar
100 Fennig = 1 Mark (6/22/98)

Catalogue values for all unused stamps in this country are for Never Hinged items.

Muslim Government in Sarajevo

Natl. Arms — A50

Denominations: 100d, 500d, 1000d, 5000d, 10,000d, 20,000d, 50,000d.

1993, Oct. 27 **Litho.** ***Imperf.***

Booklet Stamps

200-206 A50 Set of 7 19.00 19.00

Nos. 200-206 each were available in bklts. of 50 (10 strips of 5).

1984 Winter Olympic Games, Sarajevo, 10th Anniv. — A51

#207, Games emblem. #208a, 100,000d, Four man bobsled. #208b, 200,000d, Hockey.

1994, Feb. 8

207 A51 50,000d org & blk 3.00 3.00

Souvenir Sheet

208 A51 Sheet of 2, #a.-b. 16.00 16.00

No. 208 contains 45x27mm stamps.

Souvenir Sheet

Bairam Festival A52

Various illustrations from Koran: a, 400d. b, 600d.

1995, May 12 ***Perf. 14***

209 A52 Sheet of 2, #a.-b. 8.50 8.50

Main Post Office, Sarajevo — A53

Designs: 10d, Facade. 20d, 30d, Demolished interior. 35d, 50d, Pre-civil war exterior. 100d, 200d, Post-war exterior.

1995, June 12

210-216 A53 Set of 7 8.50 8.50
216a Pane of 7 8.50 8.50

No. 216a sold unattached in booklet covers.

Bosnian History A54

Designs: 35d, Historical map, 10th-15th cent. 100d, Tomb, vert. 200d, Arms, Kotromanic Dynasty, vert. 300d, Charter by Ban Kulin, 1189.

1995, Aug. 12 ***Perf. 11½***

217-220 A54 Set of 4 12.00 12.00

Peace & Freedom, Europa A55

1995, Sept. 25

221 A55 200d multicolored 3.75 3.75

A56

A57

1995, Sept. 25

222 A56 100d multicolored 1.90 1.90

World Post Day.

1995, Oct. 12

Flowers: No. 223: a, 100d, Simphyandra hofmannii. b, 200d, Lilium bosniacum.

223 A57 Pair, #a.-b. 5.75 5.75

Fish — A58

No. 224: a, 200d, Aulopyge hugeli. b, 200d, Paraphoxinus alepidotus.

1995, Oct. 12

224 A58 Pair, #a.-b. 5.75 5.75

Children's Week A59

1995, Oct. 12

225 A59 100d multicolored 1.90 1.90

Electric Tram System, Sarajevo, Cent. A60

1995, Oct. 12

226 A60 200d multicolored 3.75 3.75

Bridges A61

Designs: 20d, Kozija, Sarajevo. 30d, Arslanagica, Trebinje. 35d, Latinska, Sarajevo. 50d, Old Bridge, Mostar. 100d, Visegrad.

1995, Dec. 12

227-231 A61 Set of 5 4.50 4.50

Christmas A62

Designs: 100d, Visiting friends. 200d, Madonna and Child, vert.

1995, Dec. 24

232-233 A62 Set of 2 5.75 5.75

A63

A64

Designs: 30d, Queen Jelena's tomb.

1995, Dec. 31

234 A63 30d multicolored .65 .65

1995, Dec. 31

Design: Husein Gradascevic (1802-33).

235 A64 35d multicolored .75 .75

Mirza Safvet Basagic (1870-1934) — A65

1995, Dec. 31

236 A65 100d multicolored 2.10 2.10

Religious Diversity A66

1995, Dec. 31

237 A66 35d multicolored .70 .70

Destruction of Olympic Stadium, Sarajevo A67

35d, Stadium, various skaters. 100d, Stadium ablaze, vert.

1995, Dec. 31

238-239 A67 Set of 2 2.50 2.50

Famous Women — A68

Europa: 80d, Bahrija Hadzic (1904-93), opera singer. 120d, Nasiha Hadzic (1932-95), writer.

1996, Apr. 15 ***Perf. 15***

240-241 A68 Set of 2 3.50 3.50

UNICEF, 50th Anniv. — A69

Designs: a, 50d, Child stepping on land mine. b, 150d, Child's handprint.

1996, Apr. 15 ***Perf. 11½***

242 A69 Pair, #a.-b. 3.50 3.50

Bobovac Castle — A70

Bairam Festival — A71

1996, May 5 ***Perf. 11½***

243 A70 35d multicolored .50 .50

1996, May 5 ***Perf. 14***

244 A71 80d multicolored 1.10 1.10

No. 244 was issued in sheets of 2.

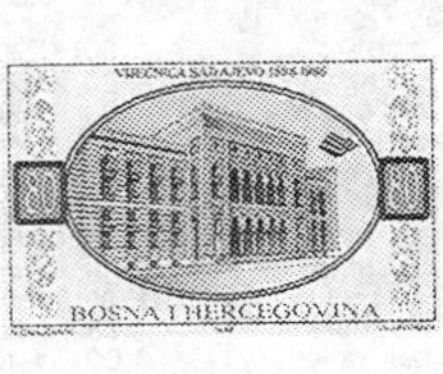

Sarajevo Town Hall, Cent. A72

1996, May 5 ***Perf. 11½***

245 A72 80d multicolored 1.10 1.10

Bosnian Journalists Assoc., Cent. A73

1996, May 5
246 A73 100d multicolored 1.40 1.40

Essen '96, Intl. Philatelic Expo A74

1996, May 25 ***Perf. 11½***
247 A74 200d multicolored 3.75 3.75

1996 Summer Olympic Games, Atlanta — A75

No. 248: a, 120d, Baron de Coubertin. b, 80d, Olympic Torch. c, 30d, Runners. d, 35d, Atlanta Games emblem.

1996, May 25
248 A75 Block of 4, #a.-d. 4.75 4.75

Background of No. 248 differs with location on sheet.

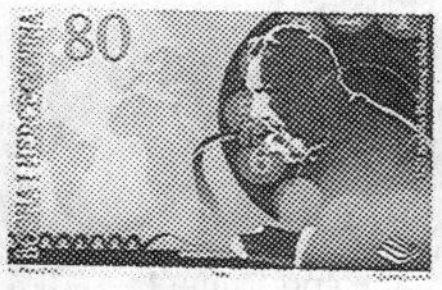

Alexander Graham Bell's Telephone, 120th Anniv. A76

1996, July 10 ***Perf. 11½***
249 A76 80d multicolored 1.40 1.40

Extension of Privleges to Dubrovnik by Ban Stepan II, 1333
A77

1996, July 10
250 A77 100d multicolored 1.75 1.75

Use of Mail Vans in Bosnia, Cent. A78

1996, July 10
251 A78 120d multicolored 2.10 2.10

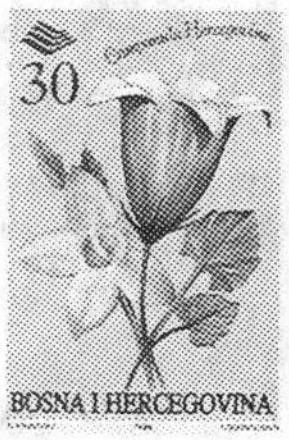

Flowers — A79

No. 252: a, 30d, Campanula hercegovina. b, 35d, Iris bosniaca.

1996, July 10
252 A79 Pair, #a.-b. 1.25 1.25

Printed checkerwise on the sheet.

Dogs A80

No. 253: a, 35d, Barak. b, 80d, Tornjak.

1996, July 10
253 A80 Pair, #a.-b. 2.00 2.00

Printed checkerwise on the sheet.

SOS Children's Village, Sarajevo — A81

1996, Sept. 1
254 A81 100d multicolored 1.75 1.75

A83

A84

Traditional costumes - No. 255: a, 50d, Moslem, Bjelasnice. b, 80d, Croatian. c, 100d, Moslem, Sarajevo.

Uniforms - No. 256: a, 35d, Bogomil soldier. b, 80d, Austro-Hungarian rifleman. c, 100d, Turkish light cavalry. d, 120d, Medieval Bosnian king.

1996, Sept. 20
255 A83 Strip of 3, #a.-c. + label 4.00 4.00
256 A84 Strip of 4, #a.-d. 6.00 6.00

Winter Festival, Sarajevo A85

1996, Nov. 25
257 A85 100d multicolored 1.75 1.75

Bosnia Day — A86

1996, Nov. 25
258 A86 120d Map, natl. arms 2.10 2.10

Christmas A87

1996, Dec. 21
259 A87 100d multicolored 1.75 1.75

Visit by Pope John Paul II — A88

1996, Dec. 21 ***Perf. 14***
260 A88 500d multicolored 8.00 8.00

Archaeological Finds — A89

Designs: 35d, Paleolithic rock carving, Badanj. 50d, Neolithic ceramic head, Butmir. 80d, Bronze age bird wagon, Glasinac.

Walls of Daorson, Illyria - No. 264: a, 100d, Walls, rock face at L. b, 120d, Low wall outside city wall.

1997, Mar. 31 ***Perf. 15***
261-263 A89 Set of 3 2.75 2.75

Souvenir Sheet

264 A89 Sheet of 2, #a.-b. 3.50 3.50

Children's Week — A90 Bairam Festival — A91

1997, Apr. 15 ***Perf. 11½***
265 A90 100d multicolored 1.60 1.60

1997, Apr. 15 ***Perf. 11½***
266 A91 200d Ferhad Pasha Mosque 3.25 3.25

A92

A93

1997, Apr. 25 ***Perf. 14***
267 A92 100d multicolored 1.60 1.60

Mujaga Komadina (1839-1925), mayor of Mostar.

1997, May 3 ***Perf. 11½***

Europa (Myths & Legends): 100d, Trojan warriors, map. 120d, Man on prayer mat, castle from The Miraculous Spring of Ajvatovica.

268-269 A93 Set of 2 3.50 3.50

Greenpeace, 25th Anniv. — A94

Rainbow Warrior, inscribed: a, 35d, Grace. b, 80d, Dorreboom. c, 100d, Beltra. d, 120d, Morgan.

1997, May 25
270 A94 Block or strip of 4, #a.-d. 5.25 5.25

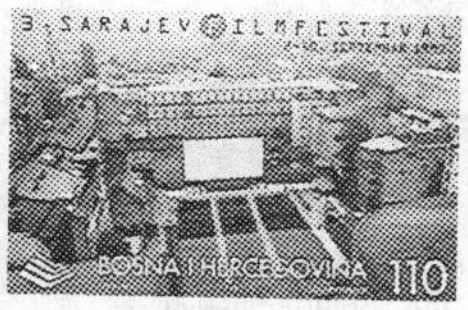

Third Intl. Film Festival, Sarajevo A95

1997, June 15
271 A95 110d multicolored 1.75 1.75

Mediterranean Games, Bari — A96

Designs: 40d, Games emblem. 130d, Boxing, basketball, kick boxing.

1997, June 15
272-273 A96 Set of 2 2.50 2.50

Discovery of Electrons, Cent. A97

1997, June 25
274 A97 40d multicolored .65 .65

Vasco da Gama's Voyage Around Africa, 500th Anniv. — A98

1997, June 25
275 A98 110d multicolored 1.75 1.75

Stamp Day — A99

1997, June 25
276 A99 130d multicolored 2.10 2.10

Railroads in Bosnia & Herzegovina, 125th Anniv. — A100

1997, June 25
277 A100 150d multicolored 2.25 2.25

Bosnia and Herzegovina stamps can be mounted in the Scott Bosnia and Herzegovina album.

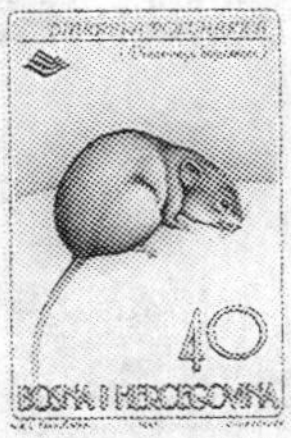

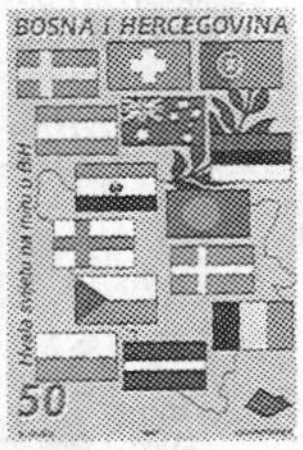

Fauna — A101 A102

No. 278: a, 40d, Dinaromys bogdanovi. b, 80d, Triturus alpestris.
No. 279: a, 40d, Oxytropis prenja. b, 110d, Dianthus freynii.

1997, Aug. 25

278 A101 Pair, #a.-b. 1.90 1.90
279 A101 Pair, #a.-b. 2.40 2.40

1997, Aug. 25

World Peace Day: a, 50d, Sweden, Switzerland, Australia & other flags. b, 60d, Flags, globe showing Europe, Africa. c, 70d, Flags, globe showing North & South America. d, 110d, US, UK, Canadian & other flags.

280 A102 Strip of 4, #a.-d. 4.50 4.50

Great Sarajevo Fire, 300th Anniv. — A103

1997, Sept. 15

281 A103 110d multicolored 1.75 1.75

Architecture — A104

Designs: 40d, House with attic. 50d, Tiled stove, door. 130d, Three-storied house.

1997, Sept. 15

282-284 A104 Set of 3 3.50 3.50

Italian Pioneer Corps Aid in Reconstruction of Sarajevo — A105

1997, Nov. 1 ***Perf. 14***

285 A105 1.40m multicolored 2.25 2.25

Famous Men A106

1.30m, Augustin Tin Ujevic (1891-1955), writer. 2m, Zaim Imamovic (1920-94), singer, vert.

1997, Nov. 1 ***Perf. 11½***

286-287 A106 Set of 2 5.25 5.25

Diana, Princess of Wales (1961-97) — A107

1997, Nov. 3 ***Perf. 14***

288 A107 2.50m multicolored 4.00 4.00

Gnijezdo, by Fikret Libovac A108

Sarajevo Library, by Nusret Pasic A109

1997, Nov. 6 ***Perf. 11½***

289-290 A108-A109 Set of 2 1.75 1.75

Samac-Sarajevo Railway, 50th Anniv. — A110

1997, Nov. 17 ***Perf. 14***

291 A110 35pf multicolored .55 .55

A111 A112

Religious Holidays: 50pf, Nativity Scene, Orthodox Christmas. No. 293, 1.10m, Wreath on door, Christmas. No. 294, 1.10m, Pupils before teacher, Hagada.

1997, Dec. 22 ***Perf. 11½***

292-294 A111 Set of 3 4.25 4.25

1998, Jan. 15 ***Perf. 14***

Designs: a, 35pf, Sports. b, 1m, Games emblem.

295 A112 Sheet of 2, #a.-b. 2.00 2.00

1998 Winter Olympic Games, Nagano.

Bairam Festival — A113

1998, Jan. 28

296 A113 1m Mosque fountain 1.50 1.50

Ahmed Muradbegovic (1898-1972), Writer — A114

1998, Mar. 20

297 A114 1.50m multicolored 2.25 2.25

Fortified Towns — A115

No. 298: a, 35pf, Zvornik. b, 70pf, Bihac. c, 1m, Pocitelj. d, 1.20m, Gradacac.

1998, Mar. 20

298 A115 Booklet pane of 4, #a.-d. 5.00 5.00
Complete booklet, #298 5.00

A116 A117

1998, May 5 ***Perf. 11½***

299 A116 1.10m multicolored 1.60 1.60

Intl. Theater Festival, Sarajevo, Europa.

1998, May 5

Former Presidents of Univ. of Arts and Science: 40pf, Branislav Durdev (1908-93). 70pf, Alojz Benac (1914-92). 1.30m, Edhem Camo (1909-96).

300-302 A117 Set of 3 3.50 3.50

A118 A119

Ciconia Ciconia - No. 303: a, 70pf, Three in water. b, 90pf, Two in flight. c, 1.10m, Two in nest. d, 1.30m, Adult, chicks.

1998, May 5

303 A118 Strip of 4, #a.-d. 4.00 4.00

1998, May 22

304 A119 2m Sheet with 2 labels 3.25 3.25

World Congress of Intl. League of Humanists, Sarajevo.

1998 World Cup Soccer Championships, France — A120

50pf, Soccer balls. 1m, Map, soccer ball. 1.50m, Asim Ferhatovic Hase (1934-87), soccer player.

1998, May 22 ***Perf. 14½***

305-307 A120 Set of 3 4.50 4.50

A121 A122

1998, July 20 ***Perf. 11½***

308 A121 1.10m multicolored 1.75 1.75

Sarajevo Tunnel, 5th anniv.

1998, July 30

Mushrooms: 50pf, Morchella esculenta. 80pf, Cantharellus cibarius. 1.10m, Boletus edulis. 1.35m, Amanita caesarea.

309-312 A122 Set of 4 6.00 6.00

Paris Subway A123

1998, Aug. 30

313 A123 2m violet blue & green 3.25 3.25

Henri Dunant — A124

1998, Sept. 14 ***Perf. 14***

314 A124 50f multicolored .75 .75

Intl. Red Cross fight against tuberculosis.

Cities — A125

1998, Sept. 24

315 A125 5pf Travnik .20 .20
316 A125 38pf Sarajevo .45 .45

Chess A126

Bosnian players - No. 317: a, 20pf, Woman at chess board. b, 40pf, Silver medal team, 31st Chess Olympiad. c, 60pf, Women's team, 32nd Chess Olympiad. d, 80pf, Men, Women's teams, 11th European Chess Championships.

1998, Sept. 24

317 A126 Sheet of 4, #a.-d. 3.25 3.25

A127

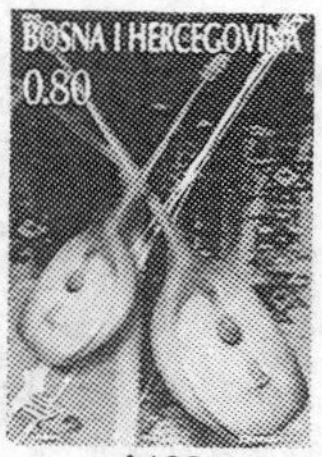

A128

1998, Oct. 9 *Perf. 11½*
318 A127 1m multicolored 1.60 1.60

World Post Day.

1998, Oct. 23
319 A128 80pf Musical instruments 1.40 1.40

Intl. Day of Disabled Persons A129

1998, Dec. 3
320 A129 1m multicolored 1.60 1.60

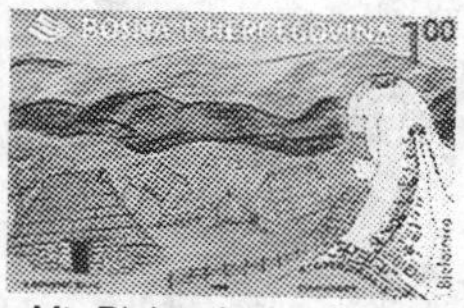

Mt. Bjelasnica — A130

1998, Dec. 3
321 A130 1m multicolored 1.60 1.60

Universal Declaration of Human Rights, 50th Anniv. A131

1998, Dec. 10 *Perf. 14½*
322 A131 1.35m multicolored 2.25 2.25

New Year A132

Christmas — A133

Designs: 1m, Child's drawing. 1.50m, Fr. Andeo Zvizdovic (1420?-98).

1998, Dec. 18 *Perf. 11½*
323-324 A132-A133 Set of 2 4.25 4.25

School Anniversaries — A134

Designs: No. 325, 40pf, First Sarajevo High School, 120th anniv. No. 326, 40pf, Sarajevo University, 50th anniv., vert.

1999, Apr. 22 **Litho.** *Perf. 11¾*
325-326 A134 Set of 2 1.10 1.10

Flora and Fauna A135

80pf, Pigeons. 1.10m, Knautia sarajevensis.

1999, Apr. 22 **Litho.** *Perf. 11¾*
327-328 A135 Set of 2 2.75 2.75

First Manned Moon Landing, 30th Anniv. — A136

1999, May 20 **Litho.** *Perf. 11¾*
329 A136 2m multicolored 3.00 3.00

Una River A137

1999, May 20
330 A137 2m multicolored 3.00 3.00

World Environmental Protection Day — A138

1999, June 15 **Litho.** *Perf. 11¾*
331 A138 80pf Buna River Wellspring 1.10 1.10

Philex France 99 — A139

1999, June 15
332 A139 2m multicolored 2.75 2.75

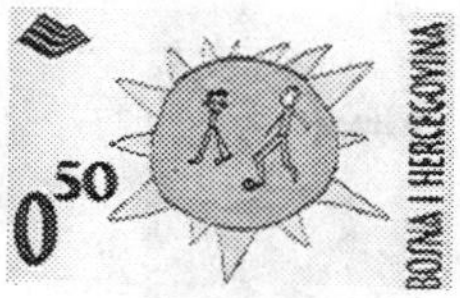

Special Olympics A140

1999, June 15
333 A140 50pf multicolored .70 .70

Bosnia & Herzegovina Postage Stamps, 120th Anniv. — A141

1999, July 1
334 A141 1m multicolored 1.00 1.00

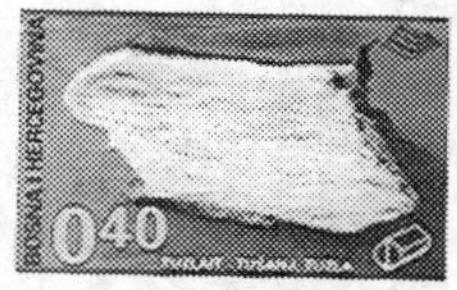

Minerals A143

Designs: 40pf, Tuzlite. 60pf, Siderite. 1.20m, Hijelofan. 1.80m, Quartz, vert.

1999, July 27 **Litho.** *Perf. 11¾*
336-339 A143 Set of 4 4.25 4.25

Dzuzovi Mehmed Pasha Sokolovic Koran Manuscript A144

1999, Sept. 23
340 A144 1.50m multicolored 1.60 1.60

Kursumli Medresa Library, Founded 1537 — A145

1999, Sept. 23
341 A145 1m multicolored 1.00 1.00

Radiology in Bosnia & Herzegovina, Cent. — A146

1999, Oct. 5
342 A146 90pf multicolored .95 .95

Handija Kasevljakovic (1888-1959), Historian — A147

1999, Oct. 5
343 A147 1.30m multicolored 1.40 1.40

25th European Chess Club Cup Finals — A148

1999 **Litho.** *Perf. 14*
344 A148 1.10m multicolored 1.10 1.10

Hvalov Zbornik, Book in Glagolitic Text — A149

1999 **Litho.** *Perf. 11¾*
345 A149 1.10m multicolored 1.10 1.10

BOSNIA AND HERZEGOVINA (CROAT ADMIN.)

Bosnian Croat Administration Located In Mostar
(Herceg Bosna)

100 Paras = 1 Dinar (1993)
100 Lipa = 1 Kuna (1994)

Catalogue values for all unused stamps in this country are for Never Hinged items.

A1

A2

1993, May 12 **Litho.** *Perf. 14*
1 A1 2000d multicolored 1.60 1.60

Our Lady of Peace Shrine, Medjugorje.

1993

Silvije Kranjcevic (1865-1908), poet: 500d, Waterfall, gate at Jajce. 1000d, Old bridge, Mostar, horiz.

2-4 A2 Set of 3 1.40 1.40

Issued: 200d, 5/20; 500d, 5/18; 1000d, 5/15.

Census in Bosnia & Herzegovina, 250th Anniv. — A3

1993, May 24
5 A3 100d Medieval gravestone .20 .20

Madonna of the Grand Duke, by Raphael — A4

1993, Dec. 3
6 A4 6000d multicolored 2.75 2.75
Christmas.

Paintings, by Gabrijel Jurkic (1886-1974) — A5

Europa: a, 3500d, Uplands in Bloom. b, 5000d, Wild Poppy.

1993, Dec. 6
7 A5 Pair, #a.-b. 6.75 6.75

Kravica Waterfalls A6

1993, Dec. 7
8 A6 3000d multicolored 1.50 1.50

Grand Duke Hrvoje Vukcic-Hrvatinic (1350-1416) — A7

1993, Dec. 8
9 A7 1500d multicolored .75 .75

Pleham Monastery A8

1993, Dec. 15
10 A8 2200d multicolored 1.00 1.00

Formation of Bosnian Croat Administration A9

1994, Feb. 10
11 A9 10,000d multicolored 4.25 4.25

Bronze Cross, Rama A10

1994, Nov. 28
12 A10 2.80k multicolored 1.25 1.25

Flora & Fauna — A11

a, 3.80k, Campanula hercegovina. b, 4k, Dog.

1994, Nov. 30
13 A11 Pair, #a.-b. 3.25 3.25

Hutovo Wetlands A12

1994, Dec. 2
14 A12 80 l multicolored .40 .40

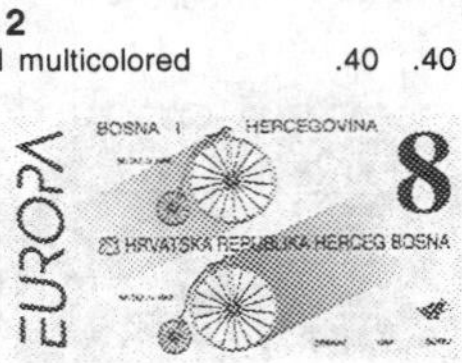

Europa A13

Transportation: a, 8k, Bicycles, 1885. b, 10k, 1901 Mercedes.

1994, Dec. 5
15 A13 Pair, #a.-b. 7.00 7.00

City of Ljubuski, 550th Anniv. — A14

1994, Dec. 8
16 A14 1k multicolored .45 .45

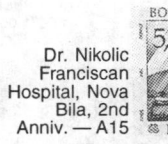

Dr. Nikolic Franciscan Hospital, Nova Bila, 2nd Anniv. — A15

1994, Dec. 12
17 A15 5k multicolored 2.25 2.25

UN, 50th Anniv. — A16

1995, Oct. 24 ***Rouletted***
Self-Adhesive
18 A16 1.50k Card of 10 6.75 6.75

Color ranges from pale pink at UL of card to dark rose at LR of card. Each stamp is numbered at LR.

Christmas — A17

1995, Dec. 4 ***Perf. 14***
19 A17 5.40k multicolored 2.25 2.25

Kraljeva Sutjeska Monastery A18

1995, Dec. 7
20 A18 3k multicolored 1.40 1.40

Cities — A19

Europa — A20

Monasteries: 2k, Srebrenica. 4k, Mostar.

1995
21-22 A19 Set of 2 2.50 2.50
Issued: 2k, 12/20; 4k, 12/12.

1995, Dec. 28
23 A20 6.50k multicolored 2.75 2.75

A21

Europa — A22

1996, June 24
24 A21 10k multicolored 4.25 4.25
a. Booklet pane of 4 17.00
Complete booklet, #24a 17.00

Apparitions at Medugorje, 15th anniv.

1996, July 20
25 A22 2.40k multicolored 1.00 1.00

Queen Katarina Kosaca Kotromanic.

A23

A24

1996, July 23
26 A23 1.40k multicolored .60 .60

Franciscan Monastery, Siroki Brijeg, 150th anniv.

1996, Aug. 14 ***Rouletted***
Self-Adhesive

Virgin Mary.

27 A24 2k multicolored .85 .85
a. Card of 10 8.50
28 A24 9k multicolored 3.75 3.75
a. Card of 5 + 5 labels 19.00

Numbers have been reserved for surcharges on Nos. 27-28. The editors would like to examine these stamps.

Christmas — A25

Europa — A26

1996, Dec. 8 **Litho.** ***Perf. 14***
31 A25 2.20k multicolored 1.00 1.00

1997, Apr. 4

Myths & legends: a, 2k, St. George slaying the dragon. b, 5k, Zeus coming to Europa disguised as a bull.

32 A26 Pair, #a.-b. 2.75 2.75
No. 32b is 39x34mm.

A27

A28

1997, Apr. 12
33 A27 3.60k multicolored 1.50 1.50
a. Pane of 4 6.00

Visit of Pope John Paul II.

1997, Apr. 20
34 A28 1.40k Samatorje Church .65 .65

Flora & Fauna — A29

Designs: 1k, Ardea purpurea. 2.40k, Symphyandra hofmannii.

1997
35-36 A29 Set of 2 1.60 1.60
Issued: 1k, 11/19. 2.40k, 11/17.

Christmas A30

1997, Dec. 1
37 A30 1.40k multicolored .65 .65

World Animated Film Festival A31

1998, Apr. 1
38 A31 6.50k multicolored 2.75 2.75
Europa.

Hercegovina, 550th Anniv. — A32

1998, Apr. 8

39 A32 2.30k multicolored 1.00 1.00

City of Livno, 1100th Anniv. — A33

1998, Apr. 9

40 A33 1.20k multicolored .50 .50

Sibiraea Croatica — A34

Gyps Fulvus — A35

1998, Nov. 9

41 A34 1.40k multicolored .60 .60

1998, Nov. 16

42 A35 2.40k multicolored 1.00 1.00

Christmas — A36

1998, Dec. 2

43 A36 5.40k multicolored 2.25 2.25

BOSNIA AND HERZEGOVINA (SERB ADMIN.)

Bosnian Serb Administration Located In Banja Luca (Republika Srpska)

100 Paras = 1 Dinar

Catalogue values for all unused stamps in this country are for Never Hinged items.

Stamps of Yugoslavia Surcharged

100 ═══
Република
Српска

1992, Oct. 26 Litho. ***Perf. 12½***

1	A559	5d on 10p #2004	.40	.40
2	A559	30d on 3d #2015	*125.00*	*125.00*
3	A559	50d on 40p #2007a, perf. 13½	1.00	1.00
a.		Thick bars in obliterator		
b.		on #2007, perf 12½	5.00	5.00
4	A559	60d on 20p #2005	1.25	1.25
5	A559	60d on 30p #2006	1.25	1.25
6	A559	100d on 1d #2013	2.00	2.00
7	A559	100d on 2d #2014a, perf. 13½	2.00	2.00
a.		on #2014, perf 12½		
8	A559	100d on 3d #2015	2.00	2.00
9	A621	300d on 5d #2017a, perf. 13½	6.00	6.00
a.		on #2017, perf 12½		
10	A620	500d on 50p #2008	10.00	10.00
11	A619	500d on 60p #2009	10.00	10.00
a.		on #2009 perf. 13½	*90.00*	*90.00*
		Nos. 1-11 (11)	*160.90*	*160.90*

Obliterator on Nos. 1, 3 and 9 has thin bars.

Musical Instrument — A1

Designs: 10d, 20d, 30d, 5000d, 6000d, 10,000d, Stringed instrument. 50d, 100d, 20,000d, 30,000d, Coat of arms, vert. 500d, 50,000d, Monastery.

1993 ***Perf. 13¼, 12½ (#19)***

12	A1	10d blk & org yel	.20	.20
13	A1	20d blk & blue	.30	.30
14	A1	30d blk & salmon	.45	.45
15	A1	50d blk & ver	.75	.75
16	A1	100d blk & ver	*1.50*	*1.50*
17	A1	500d blk & blue	*7.50*	*7.50*
18	A1	5000d blk & lilac	.20	.20
19	A1	6000d blk & yel	.20	.20
20	A1	10,000d blk & vio bl	.30	.30
a.		Perf. 12½		
21	A1	20,000d blk & ver	.60	.60
22	A1	30,000d blk & ver	.90	.90
23	A1	50,000d blk & lilac	1.50	1.50
		Nos. 12-23 (12)	14.40	*14.40*

Nos. 12-17 dated 1992, others dated 1993. Issued: Nos. 12-17, 1/11; others 6/8.

For surcharges see Nos. 24-26, 34-36, 41-45, F9

Nos. 15-16 Surcharged

референдум
7500 ═══
15-16. 05. '93.

1998, June 15

24	A1	7500d on 50d #15	2.00	2.00
25	A1	7500d on 100d #16	2.00	2.00
26	A1	9000d on 50d #15	2.75	2.75
		Nos. 24-26 (3)	6.75	6.75

Referendum, May 15-16, 1993.

A2

A3

1993, Aug. 16 ***Perf. 13¼***

Symbol of St. John, the Evangelist.

27 A2 (A) vermilion 1.00 1.00

1994, Jan. 9 ***Perf. 14***

28 A3 1d Icon of St. Stefan 8.00 8.00

King Peter I Karageorge A4

1994, May 28

29 A4 80p sepia 5.00 5.00

City of Banja Luka, 500th Anniv. A5

1994, July 18

30 A5 1.20d multicolored 5.00 5.00

Nos. 31-32 have been reserved for surcharges on Nos. 13, 21. The editors would like to examine these stamps.

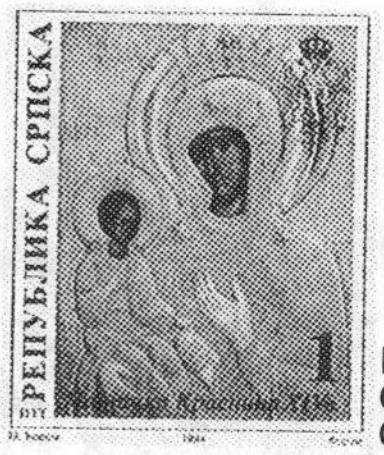

Madonna & Child, Cajnica Church — A6

1994, Sept. 1

33 A6 1d multicolored 5.00 5.00

Nos. 18, 20, 23 Surcharged

A
═══

1994, Nov. 1 ***Perf. 13¼***

34	A1	(A) on 5000d #18	1.75	1.75
35	A1	40p on 10,000d #20	1.75	1.75
a.		on #20a		
36	A1	2d on 50,000d #23	1.75	1.75
		Nos. 34-36,F9 (4)	7.00	7.00

No. 34 sold for 20p on day of issue.

Mostanica Monastery A7

Designs: 60p, Tavna Monastery, vert. 1.20d, Zitomislic Monastery, vert.

1994 ***Perf. 14***

37-39 A7 Set of 3 14.50 14.50

Issued: 60p, 11/11; 1d, 12/31; 1.20d, 12/28.

Flora & Fauna A8

No. 40: a, Shore lark. b, Dinaromys bogdanovi. c, Edraianthus niveus. d, Aquilegia dinarica.

1996, Mar. 1 ***Perf. 13¾***

40 A8 1.20d Block of 4, #a.-d. 7.00 7.00

Nos. 14-16, 19, 22 Surcharged

0,70
═══

1996, July 1 ***Perf. 13¼***

41	A1	70p on 30d #14	.60	.60
42	A1	1d on 100d #16	.80	.80
43	A1	2d on 30,000d #22	1.60	1.60
44	A1	3d on 50d #15	2.50	2.50

Perf. 12½

45	A1	5d on 6000d #19	4.50	4.50
		Nos. 41-45 (5)	10.00	10.00

Relay Station, Mt. Kozara — A9

1.20d, Drina River Bridge, Srbinje, horiz. 2d, Mt. Romanija relay station. 5d, Stolice relay station, Mt. Maljevica. 10d, Visegrad Bridge, horiz.

1996, Sept. 20 ***Perf. 14***

46	A9	(A) multicolored	.20	.20
47	A9	1.20d multicolored	.70	.70
48	A9	2d multicolored	1.25	1.25
49	A9	5d multicolored	3.00	3.00
50	A9	10d multicolored	6.00	6.00
		Nos. 46-50,F10 (6)	11.70	11.70

No. 46 sold for 30p on day of issue.

Church, Bashcharsi A10

1997, July 7 ***Perf. 13¾***

51 A10 2.50d multicolored 1.75 1.75

Mihailo Pupin (1848-1935), Electrical Engineer A11

1997, July 14

52 A11 2.50d multicolored 1.75 1.75

A12

A13

Flowers: No. 53, Oxytropis compestris. No. 54, Primula kitaibeliana. No. 55, Pedicularis hoermanniana. No. 56, Knautia sarajevensis.

1997, Sept. 12

53-56 A12 3.20d Set of 4 6.50 6.50

1997, Nov. 1 ***Perf. 13¾***

Famous Men: (A), Branko Copic (1915-85). 1.50d, Mesa Selimovic (1910-82). 3d, Aleksa Santic (1868-1924). 5d, Peter Kocic (1873-1916). 10d, Ivo Andric (1892-1975).

57	A13	(A) multicolored	.30	.30
58	A13	1.50d multicolored	.70	.70
59	A13	3d multicolored	1.40	1.40
60	A13	5d multicolored	2.25	2.25
61	A13	10d multicolored	4.50	4.50
		Nos. 57-61,F11 (6)	9.60	9.60

No. 57 for 60p on day of issue.

A14

Europa — A15

2.50d, Lutra lutra. 4.50d, Capreolus capreolus. 6.50d, Ursus arctos.

1997, Nov. 12

62-64 A14 Set of 3 7.25 7.25

1997, Nov. 12

Stories & legends: 2.50d, Two queens. 6.50d, Prince on horseback.

65-66 A15 Set of 2 6.25 6.25

Diana, Princess of Wales (1961-97) — A16

"Diana" in: a, Roman letters. b, Cyrillic letters.

1997, Dec. 22

67 A16 3.50d Pair, #a.-b. 13.00 13.00

1998 World Cup Soccer Championships, France — A17

Players, country flags - No. 68: a, Brazil. b, Morocco. c, Norway. d, Scotland. e, Italy. f, Chile. g, Austria. h, Cameroun.

No. 69: a, France. b, Saudi Arabia. c, Denmark. d, South Africa. e, Spain. f, Nigeria. g, Paraguay. h, Bulgaria.

No. 70: a, Netherlands. b, Belgium. c, Mexico. d, South Korea. e, Germany. f, US. g, Yugoslavia. h, Iran.

No. 71: a, Romania. b, England. c, Tunisia. d, Colombia. e, Argentina. f, Jamaica. g, Croatia. h, Japan.

1998, May 5

Sheets of 8 + label

68-71 A17 90p each 10.00 10.00

Europa — A18

Natl. festivals: No. 72, Instrument at R. No. 73, Instrument at L.

1998, June 9

72-73 A18 7.50d Set of 2 6.25 6.25

Icons, Chelandari Monastery A19

Various icons: 50p, 70p, 1.70d, 2d.

1998

74-77 A19 Set of 4 10.00 10.00

REGISTRATION STAMPS

No. 19 Surcharged **P**

1994, Nov. 1 Litho. *Perf. 13¼*

F9 A1 (P) on 6,000d #19 1.75 1.75

No. F9 sold for 40p on day of issue.

Relay Station Type of 1996

Kraljica relay station, Mt. Ozren.

1996, Sept. 20 *Perf. 14*

F10 A9 (R) multicolored .55 .55

No. F10 sold for 90p on day of issue.

Famous Men Type of 1997

1997, Nov. 1 *Perf. 13¾*

F11 A13 (R) Jovan Ducic (1871-1943) .45 .45

No. F11 sold for 90p on day of issue.

POSTAL TAX STAMPS

Robert Koch (1843-1910) PT1

Red Cross PT2

1997, Sept. 14 Litho. *Imperf.*

Self-Adhesive

RA1 PT1 15p red & blue 1.25 1.25

Obligatory on mail 9/14-21.

1998, May 5

Self-Adhesive

RA2 PT2 90p multicolored 1.50 1.50

Obligatory on mail 5/5-15.

Fight Against Tuberculosis PT3

1998, Sept. 14 *Perf. 10¾*

RA3 PT3 75p multicolored 1.50 1.50

Obligatory on mail 9/14-21.

BOTSWANA

bä-'swä-nə

LOCATION — In central South Africa, north of the Republic of South Africa, east of South-West Africa and bounded on the north and east by Angola and Zimbabwe.

GOVT. — Independent republic

AREA — 222,000 sq. mi.

POP. — 1,464,167 (1999 est.)

CAPITAL — Gaborone

The former Bechuanaland Protectorate became an independent republic, September 30, 1966, taking the name Botswana.

100 Cents = 1 Rand

100 Thebe = 1 Pula (1976)

Catalogue values for all unused stamps in this country are for Never Hinged items.

National Assembly Building A1

Designs: 5c, Abattoir, Lobatsi. 15c, Dakota plane. 35c, State House, Gaborone.

Unwmk.

1966, Sept. 30 Photo. *Perf. 14*

1 A1 2½c multicolored .20 .20

a. Imperf., pair *200.00*

2 A1 5c multicolored .20 .20

3 A1 15c multicolored .35 .35

4 A1 35c multicolored .75 .75

Nos. 1-4 (4) 1.50 1.50

Establishment of Republic of Botswana.

Bechuanaland Protectorate Nos. 180-193 Overprinted **REPUBLIC OF BOTSWANA**

Perf. 14x14½, 14½x14

1966, Sept. 30 Wmk. 314

5	A15	1c multicolored	.20	.20
6	A15	2c multicolored	.20	.20
7	A15	2½c multicolored	.20	.20
8	A15	3½c multicolored	.20	.20
9	A15	5c multicolored	.20	.20
10	A15	7½c multicolored	.20	.20
11	A15	10c multicolored	.25	.25
12	A15	12½c multicolored	1.25	.30
13	A15	20c gray & brown	1.25	.40
14	A15	25c yel & dk brn	.55	.55
15	A15	35c dp org & ultra	.70	.70
16	A15	50c lt ol grn & sep	1.75	1.25
17	A15	1r ocher & black	3.25	2.50
18	A15	2r blue & brown	7.00	*8.00*
		Nos. 5-18 (14)	17.20	*15.15*

European Golden Oriole — A2

Birds: 2c, African hoopoe. 3c, Groundscraper thrush. 4c, Blue waxbill. 5c, Secretary bird. 7c, Yellow-billed hornbill. 10c, Crimson-breasted shrike. 15c, Malachite kingfisher. 20c, Fish eagle. 25c, Gray lourie. 35c, Scimitar bill. 50c, Knob-billed duck. 1r, Crested barbet. 2r, Didrio cuckoo.

Perf. 14x14½

1967, Jan. 3 Photo. Unwmk.

19	A2	1c gray & multi	.20	.20
20	A2	2c lt blue & multi	.20	.20
21	A2	3c yel green & multi	.30	.20
22	A2	4c salmon & multi	.50	.25
23	A2	5c pink & multi	.50	.30
24	A2	7c slate & multi	.80	.45
25	A2	10c emerald & multi	1.00	.50
26	A2	15c lt green & multi	2.00	1.00
27	A2	20c ultra & multi	2.25	1.25
28	A2	25c green & multi	3.25	1.60
29	A2	35c multicolored	4.00	2.00
30	A2	50c dl yel & multi	6.00	3.00
31	A2	1r dl grn & multi	12.50	6.00
32	A2	2r org brn & multi	22.50	10.00
		Nos. 19-32 (14)	56.00	26.95

University Buildings and Graduates A3

1967, Apr. 7 *Perf. 14x14½*

33	A3	3c yel, sepia & dp blue	.20	.20
34	A3	7c blue, sepia & dp bl	.20	.20
35	A3	15c dull rose, sepia & dp bl	.20	.20
36	A3	35c lt vio, sepia & dp bl	.40	.40
		Nos. 33-36 (4)	1.00	1.00

1st conferment of degrees by the University of Botswana, Lesotho and Swaziland at Roma, Lesotho.

Chobe Bush Bucks A4

Designs: 7c, Sable antelopes. 35c, Fishing on the Chobe River.

1967, Oct. 2 Photo. *Perf. 14*

37	A4	3c multicolored	.20	.20
38	A4	7c multicolored	.25	.25
39	A4	35c multicolored	1.10	1.10
		Nos. 37-39 (3)	1.55	1.55

Publicity for Chobe Game Reserve.

Human Rights Flame and Arms of Botswana A5

Design elements rearranged on 15c, 25c.

1968, Apr. 8 Litho. *Perf. 13½x13*

40	A5	3c brown red & multi	.20	.20
41	A5	15c emerald & multi	.25	.20
42	A5	25c yellow & multi	.40	.30
		Nos. 40-42 (3)	.85	.70

International Human Rights Year.

Rock Painting — A6

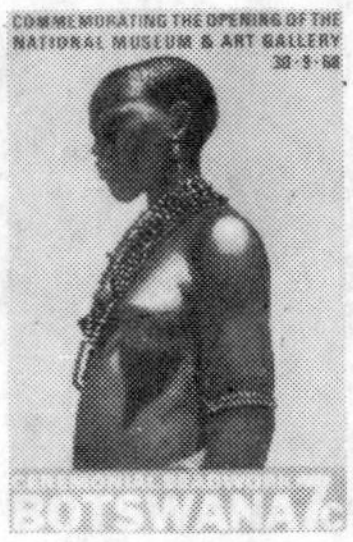

Girl Wearing Ceremonial Beads — A7

Designs: 10c, Baobab Trees, by Thomas Baines (34x25mm). 15c, National Museum and Art Gallery (71½x19mm).

Perf. 13x13½ (3c, 10c); Perf. 12½ (7c); Perf. 12½x13 (15c)

1968, Sept. 30 Litho.

43	A6	3c multicolored	.20	.20
44	A7	7c multicolored	.30	.30
45	A6	10c multicolored	.50	.50
46	A6	15c multicolored	1.00	1.00
a.		Souv. sheet of 4, #43-46, perf. 13½	2.25	*3.00*
		Nos. 43-46 (4)	2.00	2.00

Opening of the National Museum and Art Gallery, Gaborone, Sept. 30, 1968.

African Nativity Scene A8

1968, Nov. 11 Unwmk. *Perf. 13x14*

47	A8	1c car & multi	.20	.20
48	A8	2c brown & multi	.20	.20
49	A8	5c green & multi	.20	.20
50	A8	25c dp violet & multi	.55	.50
		Nos. 47-50 (4)	1.15	1.10

Christmas.

Boy Scout, Botswana Scout Emblem and Lion — A9

Botswana Boy Scout Emblem, Lion and: 15c, Boy Scouts cooking, vert. 25c, Boy Scouts around campfire.

1969, Aug. 21 Litho. *Perf. 13½*

51	A9	3c emerald & multi	.20	.20
52	A9	15c lt brown & multi	.85	.85
53	A9	25c dk brown & multi	1.50	1.50
		Nos. 51-53 (3)	2.55	2.55

22nd World Scouting Conf., Helsinki, Finland, Aug. 21-27.

Mother, Child and Star of Bethlehem A10

Diamond Treatment Plant, Orapa A11

1969, Nov. 6 *Perf. 14½x14*

54	A10	1c dk brn & lt blue	.20	.20
55	A10	2c dk brn & apple grn	.20	.20
56	A10	4c dk brn & dull yel	.20	.20
57	A10	35c dk brn & vio blue	.80	.80
a.		Souv. sheet of 4, #54-57, perf. 14½	1.40	1.00
		Nos. 54-57 (4)	1.40	1.40

Christmas.

Perf. 14½x14, 14x14½

1970, Mar. 23

Designs: 7c, Copper and nickel mining, Selebi-Pikwe. 10c, Copper and nickel mining and metal bars, Selebi-Pikwe, horiz. 35c, Orapa diamond mine and diamonds, horiz.

58	A11	3c multicolored	*.50*	*.25*
59	A11	7c multicolored	*1.10*	*.55*
60	A11	10c multicolored	*2.25*	*1.10*
61	A11	35c multicolored	*3.50*	*1.70*
		Nos. 58-61 (4)	7.35	*3.60*

Botswana development program.

Mr. Micawber and Charles Dickens A12

Charles Dickens (1812-70), English novelist and: 7c, Scrooge. 15c, Fagin. 25c, Bill Sykes.

1970, July 7 **Litho.** *Perf. 11*

62	A12	3c gray green & multi	.20	.20
63	A12	7c multicolored	.30	.30
64	A12	15c brown & multi	.60	.60
65	A12	25c dp violet & multi	1.00	1.00
a.		Souvenir sheet of 4, #62-65	4.50	4.50
		Nos. 62-65 (4)	2.10	2.10

UN Headquarters, Emblem — A13

1970, Oct. 24 **Litho.** *Perf. 11*

66	A13	15c ultra, red & silver	.70	.50

United Nations' 25th anniversary.

Toys A14

1970, Nov. 3 **Litho.** *Perf. 14*

67	A14	1c Crocodile	.20	.20
68	A14	2c Giraffe	.20	.20
69	A14	7c Elephant	.20	.20
70	A14	25c Rhinoceros	.75	.75
a.		Souvenir sheet of 4, #67-70	2.00	2.00
		Nos. 67-70 (4)	1.35	1.35

Christmas.

Sorghum A15

1971, Apr. 6 **Litho.** *Perf. 14*

71	A15	3c shown	.20	.20
72	A15	7c Millet	.20	.20
73	A15	10c Corn	.25	.25
74	A15	35c Peanuts	1.00	1.00
		Nos. 71-74 (4)	1.65	1.65

Ox Head and Botswana Map — A16

King Bringing Gift — A17

Map of Botswana and: 4c, Cogwheels and waves. 7c, Zebra rampant. 10c, Tusk and corn. 20c, Coat of arms of Botswana.

1971, Sept. 30 *Perf. 14½x14*

75	A16	3c yel grn, blk & brn	.20	.20
76	A16	4c lt blue, blk & bl	.20	.20
77	A16	7c orange & blk	.20	.20
78	A16	10c yellow & multi	.30	.30
79	A16	20c blue & multi	.60	.60
		Nos. 75-79 (5)	1.50	1.50

5th anniversary of independence.

1971, Nov. 11 *Perf. 14*

Christmas: 2c, King bringing gift. 7c, Kneeling King with gift. 20c, Three Kings and star.

80	A17	2c brt rose & multi	.20	.20
81	A17	3c lt blue & multi	.20	.20
82	A17	7c brt pink & multi	.20	.20
83	A17	20c vio blue & multi	.50	.50
a.		Souvenir sheet of 4, #80-83	1.50	1.50
		Nos. 80-83 (4)	1.10	1.10

Constellation Orion — A18

Night Sky over Botswana: 7c, Scorpio. 10c, Centaur. 20c, Southern Cross.

1972, Apr. 24 **Litho.** *Perf. 14*

84	A18	3c dp org, bl grn & blk	.35	.35
85	A18	7c org, blue & blk	.75	.75
86	A18	10c org, green & blk	1.10	1.10
87	A18	20c emer, vio bl & blk	2.25	2.25
		Nos. 84-87 (4)	4.45	4.45

Gubulawayo Cancel and Map of Trail — A19

Cross, Map of Botswana, Bells — A20

Sections of Mafeking-Gubulawayo Trail and: 4c, Bechuanaland Protectorate No. 65. 7c, Mail runners. 20c, Mafeking 638 killer cancellation.

1972, Aug. 21 *Perf. 13½x13*

88	A19	3c cream & multi	.20	.20
89	A19	4c cream & multi	.20	.20
90	A19	7c cream & multi	.45	.45
91	A19	20c cream & multi	1.50	1.50
a.		Souvenir sheet of 4	10.00	10.00
		Nos. 88-91 (4)	2.35	2.35

84th anniv. of Mafeking to Gubulawayo runner post. No. 91a contains one each of Nos. 88-91, arranged vertically to show map of trail. Compare with design A89.

1972, Nov. 6 **Litho.** *Perf. 14*

Cross, Map of Botswana and: 3c, Candle. 7c, Christmas tree. 20c, Star and holly.

92	A20	2c yellow & multi	.20	.20
93	A20	3c pale lilac & multi	.20	.20
94	A20	7c yel green & multi	.25	.25
95	A20	20c pink & multi	.60	.60
a.		Souvenir sheet of 4, #92-95	2.00	2.00
		Nos. 92-95 (4)	1.25	1.25

Christmas.

Chariot of the Sun, Trundholm, Denmark A21

WMO Emblem and: 3c, Thor, Norse thunder god, vert. 7c, Ymir, Icelandic frost giant, vert. 20c, Odin on 8-legged horse Sleipnir.

1973, Mar. 23 **Litho.** *Perf. 14*

96	A21	3c orange & multi	.20	.20
97	A21	4c yellow & multi	.25	.25
98	A21	7c ultra & multi	.45	.45
99	A21	20c gold & multi	1.25	1.25
		Nos. 96-99 (4)	2.15	2.15

Intl. meteorological cooperation, cent.

Livingstone and Boat on Lake Ngwami — A22

Design: 20c, Livingstone and his meeting with Henry Stanley.

1973, Sept. 10 **Litho.** *Perf. 13½x14*

100	A22	3c gray & multi	.20	.20
101	A22	20c yel green & multi	.95	.95

Dr. David Livingstone (1813-1873), medical missionary and explorer.

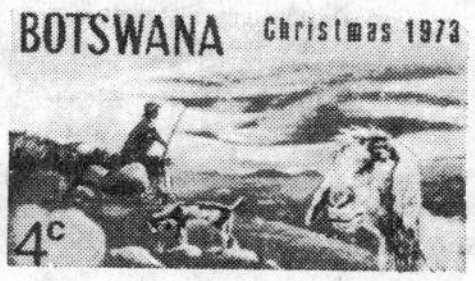

Shepherd and Flock A23

Christmas: 3c, Ass and foal, African huts, vert. 7c, African mother, child and star, vert. 20c, Tribal meeting (kgotla), symbolic of Wise Men.

1973, Nov. 12 **Litho.** *Perf. 14½*

102	A23	3c multicolored	.20	.20
103	A23	4c multicolored	.20	.20
104	A23	7c multicolored	.20	.20
105	A23	20c multicolored	.60	.60
		Nos. 102-105 (4)	1.20	1.20

Gaborone Campus, Botswana A24

Designs: 7c, Kwaluseni Campus, Swaziland. 20c, Roma Campus, Lesotho. 35c, Map and flags of Botswana, Swaziland and Lesotho.

1974, May 8 **Litho.** *Perf. 14*

106	A24	3c lt blue & multi	.20	.20
107	A24	7c yel green & multi	.20	.20
108	A24	20c yel green & multi	.20	.20
109	A24	35c brt blue & multi	.30	.30
		Nos. 106-109 (4)	.90	.90

10th anniversary of the University of Botswana, Lesotho and Swaziland.

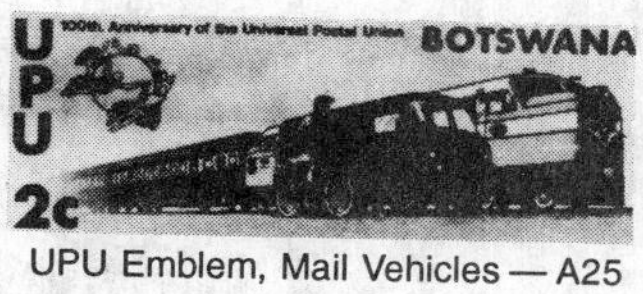

UPU Emblem, Mail Vehicles — A25

UPU Cent.: 3c, Post Office, Palapye, c. 1889. 7c, Bechuanaland police camel post, 1900. 20c, 1920 and 1974 planes.

1974, May 22 **Litho.** *Perf. 13½x14*

110	A25	2c car & multi	.25	.20
111	A25	3c green & multi	.40	.30
112	A25	7c brown & multi	1.00	.75
113	A25	20c blue & multi	3.00	2.25
		Nos. 110-113 (4)	4.65	3.50

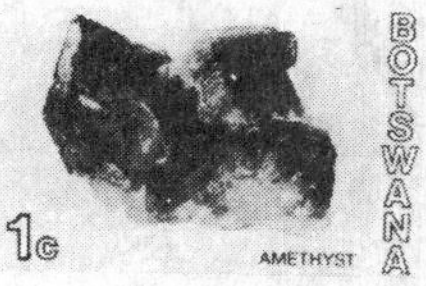

Amethyst A26

Minerals, precious and semiprecious stones.

1974, July 1 **Photo.** *Perf. 14x13*

114	A26	1c shown	.20	.20
115	A26	2c Agate	.20	.20
116	A26	3c Quartz	.25	.20
117	A26	4c Niccolite	.45	.35
118	A26	5c Moss agate	.55	.40
119	A26	7c Agate	.90	.60
120	A26	10c Stilbite	1.25	.85
121	A26	15c Moshaneng banded marble	2.00	1.25
122	A26	20c Gem diamonds	2.50	1.60
123	A26	25c Chrysotile	3.00	2.00
124	A26	35c Jasper	4.25	2.75
125	A26	50c Moss quartz	6.00	3.75
126	A26	1r Citrine	12.50	8.00
127	A26	2r Chalcopyrite	27.50	17.00
		Nos. 114-127 (14)	61.55	39.15

For surcharges see Nos. 155-168.

Stapelia Variegata — A27

Pres. Sir Seretse Khama — A28

Flowers of Botswana: 7c, Hibiscus lunarifolius. 15c, Ceratotheca triloba. 20c, Nerine laticoma.

1974, Nov. 4 **Litho.** *Perf. 14*

128	A27	2c multicolored	.20	.20
129	A27	7c multicolored	.50	.50
130	A27	15c multicolored	1.00	1.00
131	A27	20c multicolored	1.50	1.50
a.		Souvenir sheet of 4, #128-131	4.00	4.00
		Nos. 128-131 (4)	3.20	3.20

1975, Mar. 24 **Photo.** *Perf. 13½x13*

132	A28	4c olive & multi	.20	.20
133	A28	10c yellow & multi	.20	.20
134	A28	20c ultra & multi	.30	.30
135	A28	35c brown & multi	.50	.50
a.		Souvenir sheet of 4, #132-135	1.40	1.40
		Nos. 132-135 (4)	1.20	1.20

10th anniv. of self-government.

Ostrich and Rock Painting A29

Paintings and Animals: 10c, Rhinoceros. 25c, Hyena. 35c, Scorpion.

1975, June 23 **Litho.** *Perf. 14x14½*

136	A29	4c yel green & multi	.25	.25
137	A29	10c buff & multi	.75	.75
138	A29	25c blue & multi	1.75	1.75

139	A29	35c lilac & multi	2.75	2.75
a.		Souvenir sheet of 4, #136-139	9.00	9.00
		Nos. 136-139 (4)	5.50	5.50

Rock paintings from Tsodilo Hills.

Map of British Bechuanaland A30

Chiefs Sebele, Bathoen and Khama A31

Design: 10c, Khama the Great and antelope.

Perf. 14½x14, 14x14½

1975, Oct. 31 Litho.

140	A30	6c buff & multi	.25	.25
141	A30	10c rose & multi	.50	.50
142	A31	25c lt green & multi	1.25	1.25
		Nos. 140-142 (3)	2.00	2.00

Establishment of Protectorate, 90th anniv. (6c); Khama the Great (1828-1923), centenary of his accession as chief (10c); visit of the chiefs of the Bakwena, Bangwaketse and Bamangwato tribes to London, 80th anniv. (25c).

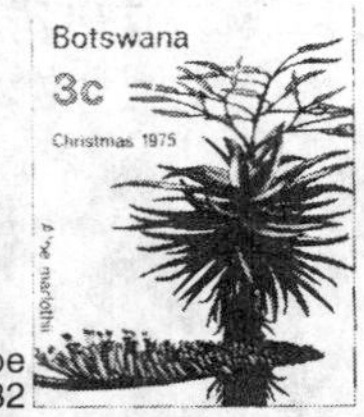

Aloe Marlothii — A32

Christmas: 10c, Aloe lutescens. 15c, Aloe zebrina. 25c, Aloe littoralis.

1975, Nov. 3 Litho. *Perf. 14½x14*

143	A32	3c multicolored	.25	.20
144	A32	10c multicolored	.75	.65
145	A32	15c multicolored	1.00	.90
146	A32	25c multicolored	2.00	1.75
		Nos. 143-146 (4)	4.00	3.50

Drum A33

Traditional Musical Instruments: 10c, Hand piano. 15c, Segankuru (violin). 25c, Kudu signal horn.

1976, Mar. 1 Litho. *Perf. 14*

147	A33	4c yellow & multi	.20	.20
148	A33	10c lilac & multi	.30	.30
149	A33	15c dull yel & multi	.50	.50
150	A33	25c lt blue & multi	.75	.75
		Nos. 147-150 (4)	1.75	1.75

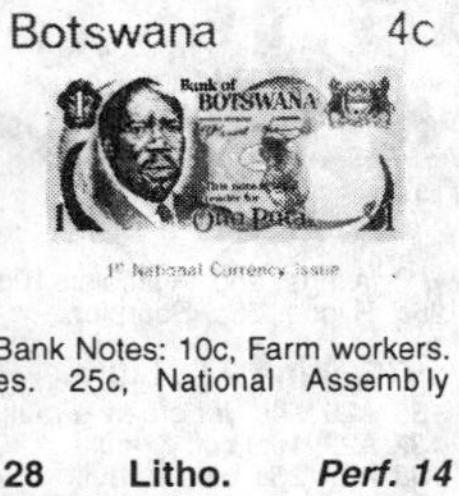

1-pula Bank Note with Seretse Khama A34

Reverse of Bank Notes: 10c, Farm workers. 15c, Antelopes. 25c, National Assembly building.

1976, June 28 Litho. *Perf. 14*

151	A34	4c rose & multi	.20	.20
152	A34	10c brt green & multi	.25	.25
153	A34	15c yel green & multi	.35	.35
154	A34	25c blue & multi	.65	.65
a.		Souvenir sheet of 4, #151-154	2.25	2.25
		Nos. 151-154 (4)	1.45	1.45

First national currency.

Nos. 114-127 Surcharged in Black or Gold

1976, Aug. 23 Photo. *Perf. 14x13*

155	A26	1t on 1c multi	.30	.20
156	A26	2t on 2c multi	.30	.20
157	A26	3t on 3c multi (G)	.30	.20
158	A26	4t on 4c multi	.60	.30
159	A26	5t on 5c multi	.75	.35
160	A26	7t on 7c multi	1.00	.50
161	A26	10t on 10c multi	1.50	.65
162	A26	15t on 15c multi (G)	2.50	1.00
163	A26	20t on 20c multi	3.00	1.50
164	A26	25t on 25c multi	4.00	1.75
165	A26	35t on 35c multi	5.00	2.00
166	A26	50t on 50c multi	6.00	2.50
167	A26	1p on 1r multi	12.50	6.50
168	A26	2p on 2r multi (G)	22.50	12.50
		Nos. 155-168 (14)	60.25	30.15

Cattle Industry A35

Designs: 10t, Antelope, tourism, vert. 15t, Schoolhouse and children, education. 25t, Rural weaving, vert. 35t, Mining industry, vert.

1976, Sept. 30 Litho. *Perf. 14x14½*

Textured Paper

169	A35	4t multicolored	.20	.20
170	A35	10t multicolored	.40	.40
171	A35	15t multicolored	.50	.50
172	A35	25t multicolored	.75	.75
173	A35	35t multicolored	1.00	1.00
		Nos. 169-173 (5)	2.85	2.85

10th anniversary of independence.

Colophospermum Mopane — A36

Trees: 4t, Baikiaea plurijuga. 10t, Sterculia rogersii. 25t, Acacia nilotica. 40t, Kigelia africana.

1976, Nov. 1 Litho. *Perf. 13*

174	A36	3t multicolored	.20	.20
175	A36	4t multicolored	.20	.20
176	A36	10t multicolored	.35	.35
177	A36	25t multicolored	.75	.75
178	A36	40t multicolored	1.25	1.25
		Nos. 174-178 (5)	2.75	2.75

Christmas.

Pres. Seretse Khama and Elizabeth II — A37

Designs: 25t, Coronation coach in procession. 40t, Recognition scene.

1977, Feb. 7 Litho. *Perf. 12*

179	A37	4t multicolored	.20	.20
180	A37	25t multicolored	.30	.30
181	A37	40t multicolored	.50	.50
		Nos. 179-181 (3)	1.00	1.00

Reign of Queen Elizabeth II, 25th anniv.

Clawless Otter A38

Wildlife Fund Emblem and: 4t, Serval. 10t, Bat-eared foxes. 25t, Pangolins. 40t, Brown hyena.

1977, June 6 Litho. *Perf. 14*

182	A38	3t multicolored	1.50	.50
183	A38	4t multicolored	2.00	1.00
184	A38	10t multicolored	4.00	1.75
185	A38	25t multicolored	10.00	4.00
186	A38	40t multicolored	20.00	9.00
		Nos. 182-186 (5)	37.50	16.25

Endangered wildlife.

Khama Memorial A39

Designs: 4t, Cwihaba Caves. 15t, Green's (expedition) tree. 20t, Mmajojo ruins. 25t, Ancient morabaraba board. 35t, Matsieng's footprints.

1977, Aug. 22 Litho. *Perf. 14*

187	A39	4t multicolored	.20	.20
188	A39	5t multicolored	.20	.20
189	A39	15t multicolored	.45	.45
190	A39	20t multicolored	.55	.55
191	A39	25t multicolored	.80	.80
192	A39	35t multicolored	1.10	1.10
a.		Souvenir sheet of 6, #187-192	3.50	3.50
		Nos. 187-192 (6)	3.30	3.30

Historical sites and national monuments.

Hypoxis itida — A40

Black Korhaan — A41

Lilies: 5t, Haemanthus magnificus. 10t, Boophane disticha. 25t, Vellozia retinervis. 40t, Ammocharis coranica.

1977, Oct. 31 Litho. *Perf. 14*

193	A40	3t sepia & multi	.20	.20
194	A40	5t gray & multi	.20	.20
195	A40	10t multicolored	.30	.30
196	A40	25t multicolored	.75	.75
197	A40	40t multicolored	1.25	1.25
		Nos. 193-197 (5)	2.70	2.70

Christmas.

1978, July 3 Photo. *Perf. 14*

Designs: Birds.

198	A41	1t shown	.20	.20
199	A41	2t Marabou storks	.20	.20
200	A41	3t Red-billed hoopoe	.20	.20
201	A41	4t Carmine bee-eaters	.20	.20
202	A41	5t African jacana	.20	.20
203	A41	7t Paradise flycatcher	.25	.20
204	A41	10t Bennett's woodpecker	.35	.25
205	A41	15t Red bishop	.50	.40
206	A41	20t Crowned plovers	.70	.50
207	A41	25t Giant kingfishers	.90	.65
208	A41	30t White-faced ducks	1.10	.75
209	A41	35t Green-backed heron	1.50	.90
210	A41	45t Black-headed herons	1.75	1.25
211	A41	50t Spotted eagle owl	2.00	1.50
212	A41	1p Gabar goshawk	3.75	2.50
213	A41	2p Martial eagle	7.50	5.00
214	A41	5p Saddlebill storks	15.00	10.00
		Nos. 198-214 (17)	36.30	24.90

For surcharges see Nos. 289-290.

Tawana Making Kaross (garment) A42

Designs: 5t, Map of Okavango Delta. 15t, Bushman collecting roots. 20t, Herero woman milking cow. 25t, Yei pulling mokoro (boat). 35t, Mbukushu fishing.

1978, Sept. 11 Litho. *Perf. 14*

Textured Paper

215	A42	4t multicolored	.20	.20
216	A42	5t multicolored	.20	.20
217	A42	15t multicolored	.20	.20
218	A42	20t multicolored	.30	.30
219	A42	25t multicolored	.40	.40
220	A42	35t multicolored	.50	.50
a.		Souvenir sheet of 6, #215-220	2.50	3.00
		Nos. 215-220 (6)	1.80	1.80

People of the Okavango Delta.

Caralluma Lutea — A43

Boy at Sip Well — A44

Flowers: 10t, Hoodia lugardii. 15t, Ipomoea transvaalensis. 25t, Ansellia gigantea.

1978, Nov. 6

221	A43	5t multicolored	.20	.20
222	A43	10t multicolored	.30	.30
223	A43	15t multicolored	.50	.50
224	A43	25t multicolored	.80	.80
		Nos. 221-224 (4)	1.80	1.80

Christmas.

1979, Feb. 12 Litho. *Perf. 14*

Water Development: 5t, Watering pit. 10t, Hand-dug well and goats. 25t, Windmill, well and cattle. 40t, Modern drilling rig.

225	A44	3t multicolored	.20	.20
226	A44	5t multicolored	.20	.20
227	A44	10t multicolored	.20	.20
228	A44	25t multicolored	.40	.40
229	A44	40t multicolored	.65	.65
		Nos. 225-229 (5)	1.65	1.65

Botswana Pot — A45

Handicrafts: 10t, Clay buffalo. 25t, Woven covered basket. 40t, Beaded bag.

1979, June 4 Litho. *Perf. 14*

230	A45	5t multicolored	.20	.20
231	A45	10t multicolored	.20	.20
232	A45	25t multicolored	.40	.40
233	A45	40t multicolored	.65	.65
a.		Souvenir sheet of 4, #230-233	1.60	1.60
		Nos. 230-233 (4)	1.45	1.45

Bechuanaland No. 6, Rowland Hill — A46

Sir Rowland Hill (1795-1879), originator of penny postage, and: 25t, Bechuanaland Protectorate No. 107. 45t, Botswana No. 20.

1979, Aug. 27 Litho. *Perf. 13½*

234	A46	5t rose & black	.20	.20
235	A46	25t multicolored	.35	.35
236	A46	45t multicolored	.60	.60
		Nos. 234-236 (3)	1.15	1.15

Children Playing A47

Design: 10t, Child playing with rag doll, and IYC emblem, vert.

1979, Sept. 24 *Perf. 14*

237 A47 5t multicolored .20 .20
238 A47 10t multicolored .25 .25

International Year of the Child.

Ximenia Caffra — A48

Christmas: 10t, Sclerocarya caffra. 15t, Hexalobus monopetalus. 25t, Ficus soldanella.

1979, Nov. 12 **Litho.** *Perf. 14*

239 A48 5t multicolored .20 .20
240 A48 10t multicolored .20 .20
241 A48 15t multicolored .30 .30
242 A48 25t multicolored .50 .50
Nos. 239-242 (4) 1.20 1.20

Flap-Necked Chameleon A49

1980, Mar. 3 **Litho.** *Perf. 14*

243 A49 5t shown .20 .20
244 A49 10t Leopard tortoise .20 .20
245 A49 25t Puff adder .45 .45
246 A49 40t White-throated monitor .75 .75
Nos. 243-246 (4) 1.60 1.60

Rock Breaking (Early Mining) — A50

1980, July 7 **Litho.** *Perf. 13½x14*

247 A50 5t shown .20 .20
248 A50 10t Ore hoisting .20 .20
249 A50 15t Ore transport .25 .25
250 A50 20t Ore crushing .35 .35
251 A50 25t Smelting .40 .40
252 A50 35t Tools, products .60 .60
Nos. 247-252 (6) 2.00 2.00

Chiwele and the Giant — A51

Folktales: 10t, Kgori Is Not Deceived. 30t, Nyambi's Wife and Crocodile. 45t, Clever Hare, horiz.

Perf. 14, 14½ (10t, 30t)

1980, Sept. 8

253 A51 5t multicolored .20 .20

Size: 28x36mm

254 A51 10t multicolored .20 .20
255 A51 30t multicolored .50 .50

Size: 44x26mm

256 A51 45t multicolored .80 .80
Nos. 253-256 (4) 1.70 1.70

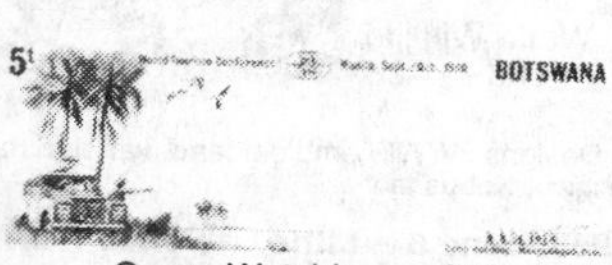

Game Watching — A52

1980, Oct. 6 **Litho.** *Perf. 14*

257 A52 5t multicolored .20 .20

World Tourism Conf., Manila, Sept. 27.

Acacia Gerrardii — A53

Christmas: Flowering Trees.

1980, Nov. 3 **Litho.** *Perf. 14*

258 A53 5t shown .20 .20
259 A53 10t Acacia nilotica .20 .20
260 A53 25t Acacia erubescens .30 .30
261 A53 40t Dichrostachys cinerea .45 .45
Nos. 258-261 (4) 1.15 1.15

Heinrich von Stephan, Bechuanaland Protectorate No. 150, Botswana No. 111 — A55

Design: 20t, Von Stephan, Bechuanaland Protectorate No. 151, Botswana No. 112.

1981, Jan. 7 *Perf. 14*

266 A55 6t multicolored .20 .20
267 A55 20t multicolored .45 .45

Von Stephan (1831-1897), founder of UPU.

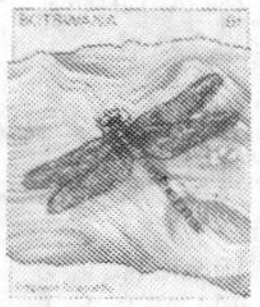

Emperor Dragonfly — A56

1981, Feb. 23 **Litho.** *Perf. 14*

268 A56 6t shown .20 .20
269 A56 7t Praying mantis .20 .20
270 A56 10t Elegant grasshopper .20 .20
271 A56 20t Dung beetle .25 .25
272 A56 30t Citrus swallowtail butterfly .40 .40
273 A56 45t Mopane worm .60 .60
a. Souv. sheet of 6, #268-273 2.00 2.00
Nos. 268-273 (6) 1.85 1.85

Blind Basket Weaver A57

1981, Apr. 4 **Litho.** *Perf. 14*

274 A57 6t Seamstress .20 .20
275 A57 20t shown .30 .30
276 A57 30t Carpenter .40 .40
Nos. 274-276 (3) .90 .90

International Year of the Disabled.

Woman Reading Letter (Literacy Campaign) — A58

1981, June 8

277 A58 6t shown .20 .20
278 A58 7t Man sending telegram .20 .20
279 A58 20t Boy, newspaper .25 .25
280 A58 30t Father and daughter reading .35 .35
Nos. 277-280 (4) 1.00 1.00

Pres. Seretse Khama and Flag — A59

First death anniv. of Pres. Khama: Portrait and local buildings.

1981, July 13

281 A59 6t multicolored .20 .20
282 A59 10t multicolored .20 .20
283 A59 30t multicolored .40 .40
284 A59 45t multicolored .60 .60
Nos. 281-284 (4) 1.40 1.40

Cattle in Agricultural Show — A60

1981, Sept. 21 **Litho.** *Perf. 14½*

285 A60 6t Plowing .20 .20
286 A60 20t shown .20 .20
287 A60 30t Meat Commission .35 .35
288 A60 45t Vaccine Institute .50 .50
Nos. 285-288 (4) 1.25 1.25

Nos. 209, 204 Surcharged in Black

1981, Sept. **Photo.** *Perf. 14*

289 A41 25t on 35t multicolored .30 .30
290 A41 30t on 10t multicolored .40 .40

Christmas — A61

Designs: Water lilies.

1981, Nov. 2 **Litho.**

291 A61 6t Nymphaea caerulea .20 .20
292 A61 10t Nymphoides indica .20 .20
293 A61 25t Nymphaea lotus .30 .30
294 A61 40t Ottelia kunenensis .50 .50
Nos. 291-294 (4) 1.20 1.20

Children's Drawings — A62

1982, Feb. 15 **Litho.** *Perf. 14½x14*

295 A62 6t Cattle .20 .20
296 A62 10t Kgotla meeting .20 .20
297 A62 30t Village .40 .40
298 A62 45t Huts .60 .60
Nos. 295-298 (4) 1.40 1.40

Traditional Houses — A63

1982, May 3 **Litho.** *Perf. 14*

299 A63 6t Common type .20 .20
300 A63 10t Kgatleng .20 .20
301 A63 30t Northeastern .40 .40
302 A63 45t Sarwa .60 .60
Nos. 299-302 (4) 1.40 1.40

Red-billed Teals — A64

Perf. 14x14½, 14½x14

1982, July 1 **Photo.**

303 A64 1t Masked weaver .20 .20
304 A64 2t Lesser double-collared sunbirds .20 .20
305 A64 3t White-fronted bee-eaters .20 .20
306 A64 4t Ostriches .20 .20
307 A64 5t Grey-headed gulls .30 .20
308 A64 6t Pygmy geese .40 .30
309 A64 7t Cattle egrets .50 .40
310 A64 8t Lanner falcon .60 .45
311 A64 10t Yellow-billed storks .75 .65
312 A64 15t shown 1.25 1.00
313 A64 20t Barn owls 1.50 1.25
314 A64 25t Hamerkops 2.00 1.40
315 A64 30t Stilts 2.25 1.60
316 A64 35t Blacksmith plovers 2.75 2.00
317 A64 45t Wattled plover 3.50 2.25
318 A64 50t Crowned guinea-fowl 3.75 2.75
319 A64 1p Cape vultures 8.00 5.50
320 A64 2p Augur bustards 15.00 11.00
Nos. 303-320 (18) 43.35 31.55

Nos. 303-311 vert.
For surcharges see Nos. 401-403.

Christmas — A65

Endangered Species — A67

A66

Designs: Mushrooms.

1982, Nov. 2 **Litho.** *Perf. 14½*

321 A65 7t Shaggy mane *.70 .70*
322 A65 15t Orange milk *1.50 1.50*
323 A65 35t Panther *3.50 3.50*
324 A65 50t King boletus *4.75 4.75*
Nos. 321-324 (4) *10.45 10.45*

1983, Mar. 14 **Litho.** *Perf. 14*

325 A66 7t Pres. Quett Masire .20 .20
326 A66 15t Dancers .20 .20
327 A66 35t Melbourne Conference Center .50 .50
328 A66 45t Heads of State meeting .60 .60

Commonwealth Day.

1983, Apr. 19 **Litho.** *Perf. 14x14½*

329 A67 7t Wattle crane .40 .20
330 A67 15t Aloe lutescens 1.10 .70
331 A67 35t Roan antelope 2.75 1.60
332 A67 50t Hyphaene ventricosa 3.50 2.00
Nos. 329-332 (4) 7.75 4.50

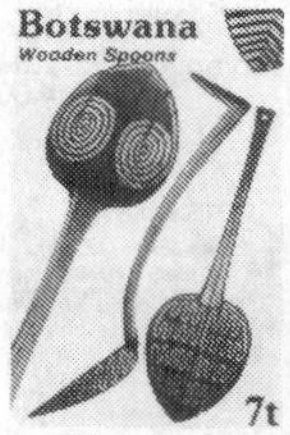

Wooden Spoons — A68

Christmas — A69

1983, July 20 **Litho.** *Perf. 14*

333 A68 7t shown .25 .20
334 A68 15t Jewelry .45 .35
335 A68 35t Ox-hide milk bag 1.10 .85
336 A68 50t Decorated knives 1.25 1.00
a. Souvenir sheet of 4, #333-336 6.00 5.00
Nos. 333-336 (4) 3.05 2.40

1983, Nov. 7 Litho. *Perf. 14½x14*

Designs: Dragonflies.

337 A69 6t Pantala flavescens .20 .20
338 A69 15t Anax imperator .30 .30
339 A69 25t Trithemis arteriosa .50 .50
340 A69 45t Chlorolestes elegans .90 .90
Nos. 337-340 (4) 1.90 1.90

Mining Industry — A70

1984, Mar. 19 Litho. *Perf. 14½*

341 A70 7t Diamonds .40 .20
342 A70 15t Lime 1.10 .65
343 A70 35t Copper, nickel, vert. 3.00 2.00
344 A70 50t Coal, vert. 3.50 2.50
Nos. 341-344 (4) 8.00 5.35

Traditional Transport A71

1984, June 16 Litho. *Perf. 14½x14*

345 A71 7t Man riding ox .20 .20
346 A71 25t Sled .40 .40
347 A71 35t Wagon .65 .65
348 A71 50t Cart .90 .90
Nos. 345-348 (4) 2.15 2.15

Intl. Civil Aviation Org., 40th Anniv. — A72

1984, Oct. 8 Litho. *Perf. 14x13½*

349 A72 7t Avro 504 .20 .20
350 A72 10t Westland Wessex .20 .20
351 A72 15t Junkers 52-3M .25 .25
352 A72 25t Dragon Rapide .40 .40
353 A72 35t DC-3 .60 .60
354 A72 50t F27 Fokker Friendship .80 .80
Nos. 349-354 (6) 2.45 2.45

Christmas A73

Butterflies.

1984, Nov. 5 Litho. *Perf. 14½x14*

355 A73 7t Papilio demodocus .40 .30
356 A73 25t Byblia acheloia 1.75 1.00
357 A73 35t Hypolimnas missipus 2.75 1.50
358 A73 50t Graphium taboranus 3.50 2.00
Nos. 355-358 (4) 8.40 4.80

Traditional & Exotic Foods — A74

Bechuanaland No. 4 — A75

1985, Mar. 18 Litho. *Perf. 14½*

359 A74 7t Man preparing seswaa .20 .20
360 A74 15t Woman preparing bogobe .20 .20
361 A74 25t Girl eating madilla .30 .30
362 A74 50t Woman collecting caterpillars .65 .65
a. Souvenir sheet of 4, #359-362 1.40 1.40
Nos. 359-362 (4) 1.35 1.35

Southern African Development Coordination Conference, 5th anniv.

1985, June 24

Postage stamp cent.: 15t, Bechuanaland Protectorate No. 72. 25t, Bechuanaland Protectorate No. 106. 35t, Bechuanaland No. 199, 50t, Botswana No. 1, horiz.

363 A75 7t multicolored .20 .20
364 A75 15t multicolored .20 .20
365 A75 25t multicolored .30 .30
366 A75 35t multicolored .40 .40
367 A75 50t multicolored .60 .60
Nos. 363-367 (5) 1.70 1.70

Police Centenary A76

7t, Bechuanaland Border Police, 1885-95. 10t, Bechuanaland Mounted Police, 1894-1902. 25t, Bechuanaland Protectorate Police, 1903-66. 50t, Botswana Motorcycle Police, 1966-85.

1985, Aug. 5 *Perf. 14½x14*

368 A76 7t multicolored .20 .20
369 A76 10t multicolored .20 .20
370 A76 25t multicolored .30 .30
371 A76 50t multicolored .60 .60
Nos. 368-371 (4) 1.30 1.30

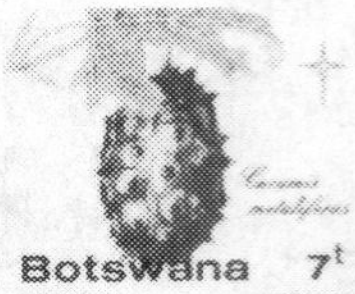

Edible Wild Cucumbers A77

1985, Nov. 4

372 A77 7t Cucumis metuliferus .20 .20
373 A77 15t Acanthosicyos naudinianus .20 .20
374 A77 25t Coccinia sessifolia .30 .30
375 A77 50t Momordica balsamina .60 .60
Nos. 372-375 (4) 1.30 1.30

Christmas.

Declaration of Protectorate, Cent. — A78

1985, Dec. 30 Litho. *Perf. 14x14½*

376 A78 7t Heads of state meet .20 .20
377 A78 15t Declaration reading, 1885 .20 .20
378 A78 25t Mackenzie and Khama .30 .30
379 A78 50t Map .60 .60
a. Souvenir sheet of 4, #376-379 1.25 1.25
Nos. 376-379 (4) 1.30 1.30

Halley's Comet — A79

1986, Mar. 24 *Perf. 14½x14*

380 A79 7t Comet over Serowe .20 .20
381 A79 15t Over Bobonong .20 .20
382 A79 35t Over Gomare swamps .40 .40
383 A79 50t Over Thamaga, Letlhakeng .60 .60
Nos. 380-383 (4) 1.40 1.40

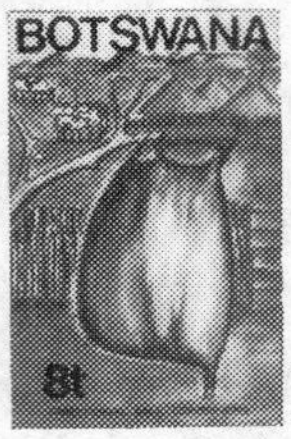

Milk Containers — A80

1986, June 23 *Perf. 14½*

384 A80 8t Leather bag .20 .20
385 A80 15t Ceramic pots .20 .20
386 A80 35t Wood pot .40 .40
387 A80 50t Woman, pots .60 .60
Nos. 384-387 (4) 1.40 1.40

Souvenir Sheet

Natl. Independence, 20th Anniv. — A81

Designs: a, Map of natl. parks and reserves. b, Morupule Power Station. c, Cattle, Kgalagadi. d, Natl. Assembly.

1986, Sept. 30 Litho. *Perf. 14½x14*

388 Sheet of 4 .90 .90
a.-d. A81 20t any single .25 .25

Flowers of the Okavango Swamps — A82

1986, Nov. 3 Litho. *Perf. 14x14½*

389 A82 8t Ludwigia stogonifera .20 .20
390 A82 15t Sopubia mannii .20 .20
391 A82 35t Commelina diffusa .40 .40
392 A82 50t Hibiscus diversifolius .55 .55
Nos. 389-392 (4) 1.35 1.35

Christmas.

Traditional Medicine A83

UN Child Survival Campaign A84

1987, Mar. 2 Litho. *Perf. 14½x14*

393 A83 8t Professional diviners .20 .20
394 A83 15t Lightning prevention .20 .20
395 A83 35t Rainmaker .45 .45
396 A83 50t Bloodletting .65 .65
Nos. 393-396 (4) 1.50 1.50

1987, June 1

397 A84 8t Oral rehydration therapy .20 .20
398 A84 15t Growth monitoring .20 .20
399 A84 35t Immunization .45 .45
400 A84 50t Breast-feeding .65 .65
Nos. 397-400 (4) 1.50 1.50

Nos. 308, 311 and 318 Surcharged

Perf. 14x14½,14½x14

1987, Apr. 1 Photo.

401 A64 3t on 6t No. 308 .20 .20
402 A64 5t on 10t No. 311 .20 .20
403 A64 20t on 50t No. 318 .30 .30
Nos. 401-403 (3) .70 .70

Wildlife Conservation — A85

1987, Aug. 3 *Perf. 14*

404 A85 1t Cape fox .20 .20
405 A85 2t Lechwe .20 .20
406 A85 3t Zebra .20 .20
407 A85 4t Duiker .20 .20
408 A85 5t Banded mongoose .20 .20
409 A85 6t Rusty-spotted genet .20 .20
410 A85 8t Hedgehog .20 .20
411 A85 10t Scrub hare .20 .20
412 A85 12t Hippopotamus .20 .20
413 A85 15t Suricate .20 .20
414 A85 20t Caracal .25 .20
415 A85 25t Steenbok .35 .30
416 A85 30t Gemsbok .45 .35
417 A85 35t Square-lipped rhino .50 .45
418 A85 40t Mountain reedbuck .60 .50
419 A85 50t Rock dassie .75 .60
420 A85 1p Giraffe 1.50 1.25
421 A85 2p Tsessebe 3.00 2.50
422 A85 3p Side-striped jackal 4.75 3.75
423 A85 5p Hartebeest 8.00 6.50
Nos. 404-423 (20) 22.15 18.40

For surcharges see Nos. 480-482, 506-509.

Wetland Grasses — A86

1987, Oct. 26 *Perf. 14x14½*

424 A86 8t Cyperus articulatus .20 .20
425 A86 15t Miscanthus junceus .20 .20
426 A86 30t Cyperus alopecuroides .35 .35
427 A86 1p Typha latifolia 1.25 1.25
a. Souvenir sheet of 4, #424-427 1.90 1.90
Nos. 424-427 (4) 2.00 2.00

Christmas, preservation of the Okavango and Kuando-Chobe River wetlands.

Early Cultivation Techniques A87

1988, Mar. 14 Litho. *Perf. 14½x14*

428 A87 8t Digging stick .20 .20
429 A87 15t Iron hoe .20 .20
430 A87 35t Wooden plow .40 .40
431 A87 50t Communal planting, Lesotla .60 .60
Nos. 428-431 (4) 1.40 1.40

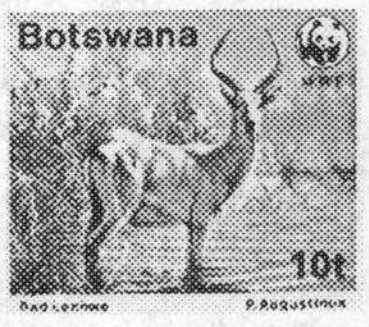

World Wildlife Fund — A88

Designs: WWF emblem and various red lechwe, Kobus leche.

1988, June 6 Litho. *Perf. 14½x14*

432 A88 10t Adult wading *.35 .35*
433 A88 15t Adult, sun *.50 .50*
434 A88 35t Cow, calf *1.10 1.10*
435 A88 75t Herd *2.50 1.75*
Nos. 432-435 (4) *4.45 3.70*

Runner Post, Cent. — A89

Routes and: 10t, Gubulawayo, Bechuanaland, cancellation dated Aug. 21 '88. 15t, Bechuanaland Protectorate No. 65. 30t, Pack traders. 60t, Mafeking killer cancel No. 638.

1988, Aug. 22 Litho. *Perf. 14½*

436 A89 10t multicolored .20 .20
437 A89 15t multicolored .20 .20
438 A89 30t multicolored .35 .35
439 A89 60t multicolored .65 .65
a. Souvenir sheet of 4, #436-439 1.25 1.25
Nos. 436-439 (4) 1.40 1.40

Printed in a continuous design picturing the Mafeking-Gubulawayo route and part of the Shoshong runner post route.

State Visit of Pope John Paul II, Sept. 13 — A90

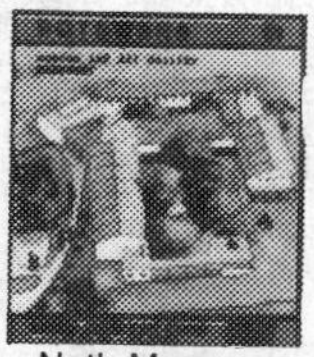

Natl. Museum and Art Gallery, Gaborone, 20th Anniv. — A91

1988, Sept. 13 Litho. *Perf. 14x14½*

440 A90 10t Map, portrait .20 .20
441 A90 15t Portrait .20 .20
442 A90 30t Map, portrait, diff. .35 .35
443 A90 80t Portrait, diff. .85 .85
Nos. 440-443 (4) 1.60 1.60

1988, Sept. 30 *Perf. 14½*

444 A91 8t Museum .20 .20
445 A91 15t Pottery, c. 400-1300 .20 .20
446 A91 30t Buffalo bellows .35 .35
447 A91 60t Children, mobile museum .70 .70
Nos. 444-447 (4) 1.45 1.45

A92

A93

Flowering plants of southeastern Botswana.

1988, Oct. 11 Litho. *Perf. 14x14½*

448 A92 8t Grewia flava .20 .20
449 A92 15t Cienfuegosia digitata .20 .20
450 A92 40t Solanum seaforthianum .40 .40
451 A92 75t Carissa bispinosa .80 .80
Nos. 448-451 (4) 1.60 1.60

Christmas.

1989, Mar. 13 Litho. *Perf. 14x14½*

Traditional grain storage.

452 A93 8t Sesigo basket granary .20 .20
453 A93 15t Letlole daga granary .20 .20
454 A93 30t Sefalana bisque granary .30 .30
455 A93 60t Serala granaries .60 .60
Nos. 452-455 (4) 1.30 1.30

Slaty Egrets A94

1989, July 5 *Perf. 15x14*

456 A94 8t Nesting .20 .20
457 A94 15t Young .45 .30
458 A94 30t Adult in flight .75 .60
459 A94 60t Two adults 1.60 1.40
a. Souvenir sheet of 4, #456-459 3.00 2.50
Nos. 456-459 (4) 3.00 2.50

Children's Drawings A95

1989, Sept. 4 *Perf. 14½x14, 14x14½*

460 A95 10t Ephraim Seeletso .20 .20
461 A95 15t Neelma Bhatia, vert. .20 .20
462 A95 30t Thabo Habana .30 .30
463 A95 1p Thabo Olesitse 1.00 1.00
Nos. 460-463 (4) 1.70 1.70

Star and Orchids — A96

1989, Oct. 30 Litho. *Perf. 14x14½*

464 A96 8t *Eulophia angolensis* .20 .20
465 A96 15t *Eulophia hereroensis* .25 .25
466 A96 30t *Eulophia speciosa* .50 .50
467 A96 60t *Eulophia petersii* 1.10 1.10
Nos. 464-467 (4) 2.05 2.05

Christmas.

Anniversaries — A97

8t, Bechuanaland Protectorate #201. 15t, Voter at ballot box. 30t, Map & flags of nations at SADCC conference. 60t, Great Britain #1.

1990, Mar. 5 Litho. *Perf. 14½*

468 A97 8t multicolored .20 .20
469 A97 15t multicolored .20 .20
470 A97 30t multicolored .30 .30
471 A97 60t multicolored .60 .60
Nos. 468-471 (4) 1.30 1.30

25th anniv. of self government (8t); 1st elections, 25th anniv. (15t); Southern African Development Coordination Conference (SADCC), 10th anniv. (30t); and Penny Black, 150th anniv. (60t).

Stamp World London '90 — A98

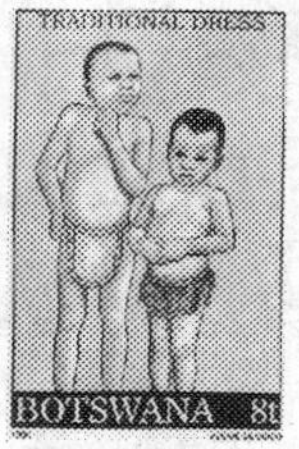

Traditional Dress — A99

Aspects of the telecommunications industry.

1990, May 3

472 A98 8t Training .20 .20
473 A98 15t Transmission .20 .20
474 A98 30t Public telephone .30 .30
475 A98 2p Testing circuitry 2.00 2.00
Nos. 472-475 (4) 2.70 2.70

1990, Aug. 1 Litho. *Perf. 14*

476 A99 8t Children .20 .20
477 A99 15t Young woman .20 .20
478 A99 30t Man .25 .25
479 A99 2p Adult woman 1.75 1.75
a. Souvenir sheet of 4, #476-479 2.50 2.50
Nos. 476-479 (4) 2.40 2.40

Nos. 404 and 412 Surcharged 10t

No. 409 Surcharged 20t

1990

480 A85 10t on 1t No. 404 .20 .20
481 A85 20t on 6t No. 409 .20 .20
482 A85 50t on 12t No. 412 .50 .50
Nos. 480-482 (3) .90 .90

Flowering Trees — A100

1990, Oct. 30 Litho. *Perf. 14*

483 A100 8t Acacia nigrescens .20 .20
484 A100 15t Peltophorum africanum .20 .20
485 A100 30t Burkea africana .25 .25
486 A100 2p Pterocarpus angolensis 1.75 1.75
Nos. 483-486 (4) 2.40 2.40

Christmas.

Natl. Road Safety Day A101

1990, Dec. 7 Litho. *Perf. 14½*

487 A101 8t Children playing on road .20 .20
488 A101 15t Accident .20 .20
489 A101 30t Livestock on road .35 .35
Nos. 487-489 (3) .75 .75

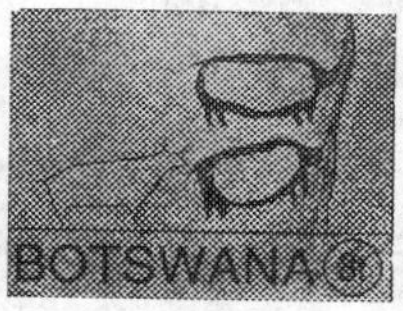

Petroglyphs A102

Various petroglyphs.

1991, Mar. 4 Litho. *Perf. 14x14½*

Textured Paper

490 A102 8t multicolored .20 .20
491 A102 15t multicolored .20 .20
492 A102 30t multicolored .30 .30
493 A102 2p multicolored 2.00 2.00
Nos. 490-493 (4) 2.70 2.70

Natl. Census — A103

1991, June 3 Litho. *Perf. 14*

494 A103 8t Children playing .20 .20

Perf. 14½

495 A103 15t Houses .20 .20

Perf. 14x14½

496 A103 30t Children in schoolyard .35 .35
497 A103 2p Children, hospital 2.40 2.40
Nos. 494-497 (4) 3.15 3.15

African Tourism Year A104

1991, Sept. 30 Litho. *Perf. 14*

498 A104 8t Tourists, elephants .20 .20
499 A104 15t Birds, crocodiles .20 .20
500 A104 35t Airplane, fish eagles .40 .40

Size 26x43mm

501 A104 2p Okavango Delta 2.40 2.40
Nos. 498-501 (4) 3.20 3.20

No. 501 incorporates designs of #498-500.

Christmas — A105

Seed pods: 8t, Harpagophytum procumbens. 15t, Tylosema esculentum. 30t, Abrus precatorius. 2p, Kigelia africana.

1991, Nov. 4 Litho. *Perf. 14*

502 A105 8t multicolored .20 .20
503 A105 15t multicolored .20 .20
504 A105 30t multicolored .30 .30
505 A105 2p multicolored 2.25 2.25
Nos. 502-505 (4) 2.95 2.95

Nos. 406, 409, & 412 Surcharged 8t

1992, Mar. 9 Litho. *Perf. 14*

506 A85 8t on 12t No. 412 .20 .20
507 A85 10t on 12t No. 412 .20 .20
508 A85 25t on 6t No. 409 .25 .25
509 A85 40t on 3t No. 406 .35 .35
Nos. 506-509 (4) 1.00 1.00

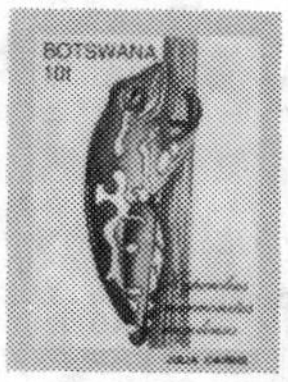

Climbing Frogs — A106

Designs: 8t, Cacosternum boettgeri, horiz. 10t, Hyperolius marmoratus angolensis. 40t, Bufo fenoulheti, horiz. 1p, Hyperolius.

Perf. 14½x14, 14x14½

1992, Mar. 23

510 A106 8t multicolored .20 .20
511 A106 10t multicolored .20 .20
512 A106 40t multicolored .40 .40
513 A106 1p multicolored .95 .95
Nos. 510-513 (4) 1.75 1.75

Botswana Railways A107

10t, Deluxe air-conditioned coaches. 25t, BD1 locomotive. 40t, Deluxe coach interio. 2p, Locomotive pulling air-conditioned coaches.

1992, June 29 Litho. *Perf. 14*

514 A107 10t multi .20 .20
515 A107 25t multi, vert. .20 .20
516 A107 40t multi, vert. .20 .20
517 A107 2p multi 1.00 1.00
a. Souv. sheet of 4, #514-517 + label 1.40 1.40
Nos. 514-517 (4) 1.60 1.60

Wild Animals A108

1992, Aug. 3 Litho. *Perf. 14½*

518 A108 1t Cheetah .20 .20
519 A108 2t Spring hares .20 .20
520 A108 4t Blackfooted cat .20 .20

521 A108	5t	Striped mouse	.20	.20
522 A108	10t	Oribi	.20	.20
523 A108	12t	Pangolin	.20	.20
524 A108	15t	Aardwolf	.20	.20
525 A108	20t	Warthog	.20	.20
526 A108	25t	Ground squirrels	.25	.25
527 A108	35t	Honey badger	.30	.30
528 A108	40t	Common mole rat	.35	.35
529 A108	45t	Wild dogs	.40	.40
530 A108	50t	Water mongoose	.45	.45
531 A108	80t	Klipspringer	.70	.70
532 A108	1p	Lesser bushbaby	.90	.90
533 A108	2p	Bushveld elephant shrew	1.75	1.75
534 A108	5p	Zorilla	4.50	4.50
535 A108	10p	Vervet monkey	9.00	9.00
		Nos. 518-535 (18)	20.20	20.20

For surcharges see Nos. 594A-597.

A109

Ferns — A110

1992, Aug. 7 ***Perf. 14x15***

536 A109	10t	Boxer	.20	.20
537 A109	50t	Four sprinters	.45	.45
538 A109	1p	Two boxers	.95	.95
539 A109	2p	Three runners	1.90	1.90
a.		Souvenir sheet of 4, #536-539	3.50	3.50
		Nos. 536-539 (4)	3.50	3.50

1992 Summer Olympics, Barcelona.

1992, Nov. 23 Litho. ***Perf. 14½***

540 A110	10t	Adiantum incisum	.20	.20
541 A110	25t	Actiniopteris radiata	.25	.25
542 A110	40t	Ceratopteris cornuta	.40	.40
543 A110	1.50p	Pellaea calomelanos	1.40	1.40
		Nos. 540-543 (4)	2.25	2.25

Christmas.

Organizations A111

10t, Lions Intl., conquering blindness. 15t, Red Cross Society. 25t, Ecumenical Decade, churches in solidarity with women. 35t, Round Table supporting the deaf. 40t, Rotary Intl. 50t, Botswana Christian Council.

1993, Mar. 29 Litho. ***Perf. 14***

544 A111	10t	multi, vert.	.20	.20
545 A111	15t	multi	.20	.20
546 A111	25t	multi, vert.	.20	.20
547 A111	35t	multi	.30	.30
548 A111	40t	multi, vert.	.40	.40
549 A111	50t	multi	.45	.45
		Nos. 544-549 (6)	1.75	1.75

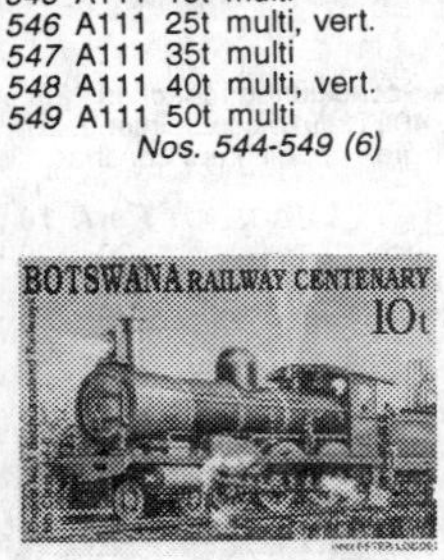

Botswana Railway, Cent. A112

Designs: 10t, Engine No. 1, 6th class 4-6-0, Bechuanaland Railways. 40t, Engine No. 317, 19th class 4-8-2. 50t, Engine No. 256, 12th class 4-8-2. 1.50p, Engine No. 71, 7th class 4-8-0, Rhodesia Railways.

1993, May 24 Litho. ***Perf. 15x14***

550 A112	10t	multicolored	.20	.20
551 A112	40t	multicolored	.40	.40
552 A112	50t	multicolored	.50	.50
553 A112	1.50p	multicolored	1.50	1.50
a.		Souvenir sheet of 4, #550-553	2.50	2.50
		Nos. 550-553 (4)	2.60	2.60

Eagles — A113

Christmas — A114

1993, Aug. 30 Litho. ***Perf. 14½***

554 A113	10t	Long crested eagle	.20	.20
555 A113	25t	Snake eagle	.50	.50
556 A113	50t	Bateleur eagle	1.00	1.00
557 A113	1.50p	Secretary bird	3.00	3.00
		Nos. 554-557 (4)	4.70	4.70

1993, Oct. 25 Litho. ***Perf. 14x14½***

558 A114	12t	Aloe zebrina	.20	.20
559 A114	25t	Croton megalobotrys	.20	.20
560 A114	50t	Boophane disticha	.45	.45
561 A114	1p	Euphorbia davyi	.90	.90
		Nos. 558-561 (4)	1.75	1.75

Traditional Children's Toys A115

1994, Mar. 28 Litho. ***Perf. 14½***

562 A115	10t	Mantadile	.20	.20
563 A115	40t	Dikgomo tsa mimopa	.30	.30
564 A115	50t	Sefuu-fuu	.40	.40
565 A115	1p	Mantlwane	.75	.75
		Nos. 562-565 (4)	1.65	1.65

ICAO, 50th Anniv. A116

Perf. 14½x14, 14x14½

1994, June 30 Litho.

566 A116	10t	Inside control tower	.20	.20
567 A116	25t	Fire engine	.25	.25
568 A116	40t	Baggage carts, vert.	.40	.40
569 A116	50t	Control tower, vert.	.50	.50
		Nos. 566-569 (4)	1.35	1.35

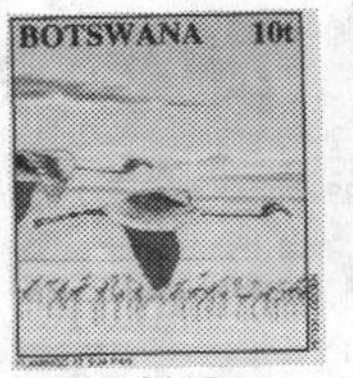

A117

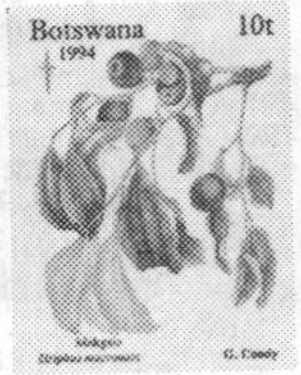

A118

Environmental Protection: 10t, Flamingos, Sua Pan, vert. 35t, Makgadikgadi Pan trees. 50t, Zebra, Makgadikgadi Palm trees, vert. 2p, Map of Makgadikgadi Pans.

1994, Aug. 30 Litho. ***Perf. 14***

570 A117	10t	multicolored	.20	.20
571 A117	35t	multicolored	.45	.45
572 A117	50t	multicolored	.65	.65
573 A117	2p	multicolored	2.50	2.50
		Nos. 570-573 (4)	3.80	3.80

1994, Oct. 24

Edible fruits: 10t, Ziziphus mucronata. 25t, Strychnos cocculoides. 40t, Bauhinia petersiana. 50t, Schinziphyton rautanei.

574 A118	10t	multicolored	.20	.20
575 A118	25t	multicolored	.20	.20
576 A118	40t	multicolored	.25	.25
577 A118	50t	multicolored	.35	.35
		Nos. 574-577 (4)	1.00	1.00

Christmas.

See Nos. 587-590.

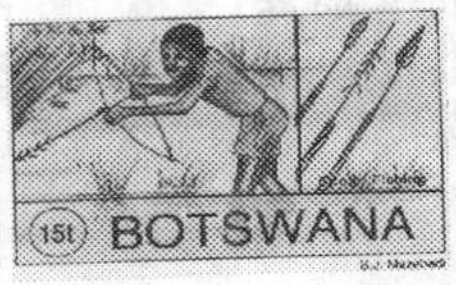

Traditional Fishing A119

1995, Apr. 3 Litho. ***Perf. 14***

578 A119	15t	Spear	.20	.20
579 A119	40t	Hook	.30	.30
580 A119	65t	Net	.50	.50
581 A119	80t	Basket	.60	.60
		Nos. 578-581 (4)	1.60	1.60

UN, 50th Anniv. — A120

1995, Oct. 16 Litho. ***Perf. 14***

582 A120	20t	FAO	.20	.20
583 A120	50t	World Food Program	.35	.35
584 A120	80t	Development Plan	.60	.60
585 A120	1p	UNICEF	.70	.70
		Nos. 582-585 (4)	1.85	1.85

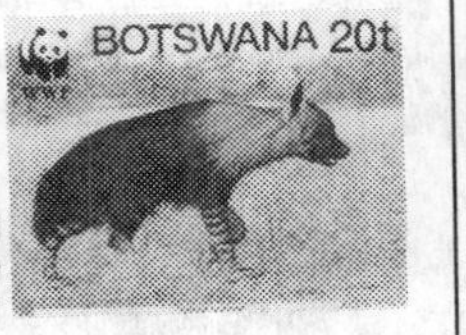

World Wildlife Fund — A121

Hyaena brunnea: a, 20t, Adult walking right. b, 50t, Two young. c, 80t, Adult finding eggs. d, 1p, Two young, adult resting.

1995, Nov. 6

586 A121		Strip of 4, #a.-d.	1.75	1.75

No. 586 was issued in miniature sheets of 4 each.

Christmas Type of 1994

1995, Nov. 27 Litho. ***Perf. 14***

587 A118	20t	Adenia glauca	.20	.20
588 A118	50t	Pterodiscus ngamicus	.35	.35
589 A118	80t	Sesamothamnus lugardii	.60	.60
590 A118	1p	Fockea multiflora	.70	.70
		Nos. 587-590 (4)	1.85	1.85

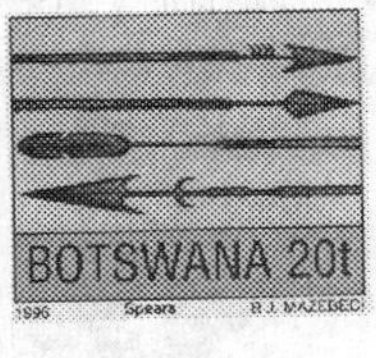

Traditional Weapons A122

1996, Mar. 25 Litho. ***Perf. 14***

591 A122	20t	Spears	.20	.20
592 A122	50t	Axes	.30	.30
593 A122	80t	Shield, knob-kerries	.50	.50
594 A122	1p	Knives, cases	.60	.60
		Nos. 591-594 (4)	1.60	1.60

No. 523 Surcharged 10t

Nos. 518-520 Surcharged 20t

1994-96 Litho. ***Perf. 14½***

594A A108	10t	multicolored	.20	.20
595 A108	20t	on 2t No. 519	.20	.20
596 A108	30t	on 1t No. 518	.20	.20
597 A108	70t	on 4t No. 520	.40	.40
		Nos. 595-597 (3)	.80	.80

Issued: #594, 8/1/94; others, 2/12/96.

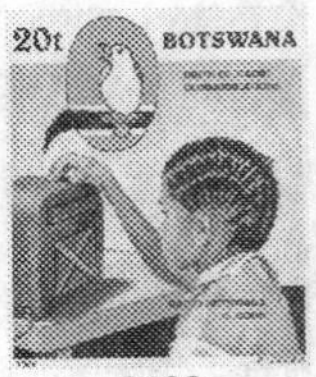

A123

A124

Radio, Cent.: 20t, Child listening to early radio. 50t, Mobile unit, transmitter. 80t, Local police. 1p, Radio Botswana at the Kgotila.

1996, June 3 Litho. ***Perf. 14***

598 A123	20t	multicolored	.20	.20
599 A123	50t	multicolored	.35	.35
600 A123	80t	multicolored	.60	.60
601 A123	1p	multicolored	.75	.75
		Nos. 598-601 (4)	1.90	1.90

1996, July 19 Litho. ***Perf. 14***

Modern Olympic Games, Cent.: 20t, Hand holding torch, laurel wreath, Olympic rings. 50t, Pierre de Coubertin. 80t, Map, flag of Botswana, athletes. 1p, Ruins of original Olympic Stadium, Olympia.

602 A124	20t	multicolored	.20	.20
603 A124	50t	multicolored	.35	.35
604 A124	80t	multicolored	.60	.60
605 A124	1p	multicolored	.75	.75
		Nos. 602-605 (4)	1.90	1.90

A125

A126

Worthy Causes: 20t, Family planning education, Welfare Association. 30t, Skills for the blind, Pudulogong Rehabilitation Center. 50t, Collection of seeds, Forestry Association. 70t, Secretarial class, YWCA. 80t, Day care center, Council of Women. 1p, SOS Children's Village, Tlokweng.

1996, Sept. 23 Litho. ***Perf. 14***

606 A125	20t	multicolored	.20	.20
607 A125	30t	multicolored	.25	.25
608 A125	50t	multicolored	.35	.35
609 A125	70t	multicolored	.55	.55
610 A125	80t	multicolored	.60	.60
611 A125	1p	multicolored	.75	.75
		Nos. 606-611 (6)	2.70	2.70

1996, Nov. 4 Litho. ***Perf. 14***

Adansonia Digitata

612 A126	20t	Leaf, flower	.20	.20
613 A126	50t	Fruit	.35	.35
614 A126	80t	Tree in leaf	.60	.60
615 A126	1p	Tree without leaves	.75	.75
		Nos. 612-615 (4)	1.90	1.90

Christmas.

Francistown, Cent. — A127

20t, Tati Hotel. 50t, Railway station. 80t, Company manager's house. 1p, Monarch Mine.

1997, Apr. 21 Litho. ***Perf. 14***

616 A127	20t	multicolored	.20	.20
617 A127	50t	multicolored	.30	.30
618 A127	80t	multicolored	.45	.45
619 A127	1p	multicolored	.55	.55
		Nos. 616-619 (4)	1.50	1.50

Birds — A128

5t, Pel's fishing owl. 10t, Gymnogene. 15t, Meyers parrot. 20t, Harlequin quail. 25t, Marico sunbird. 30t, Kurrichane thrush. 40t, Redheaded finch. 50t, Buffalo weaver. 60t, Sacred ibis. 70t, Cape shoveller. 80t, Greater honeyguide. 1p, Woodland kingfisher. 1.25p, Purple heron. 1.50p, Yellowbilled oxpecker. 2p, Shafttailed whydah. 2.50p, White stork. 5p, Ovambo sparrowhawk. 10p, Spotted crake.

1997, Aug. 4 Litho. *Perf. 13½*

620	A128	5t multi, vert.	.20	.20
621	A128	10t multi	.20	.20
622	A128	15t multi, vert.	.20	.20
623	A128	20t multi	.20	.20
624	A128	25t multi	.20	.20
625	A128	30t multi	.20	.20
626	A128	40t multi, vert.	.25	.25
627	A128	50t multi, vert.	.30	.30
628	A128	60t multi	.35	.35
629	A128	70t multi	.40	.40
630	A128	80t multi	.45	.45
631	A128	1p multi	.55	.55
632	A128	1.25p multi, vert.	.70	.70
633	A128	1.50p multi	.85	.85
634	A128	2p multi, vert.	1.10	1.10
635	A128	2.50p multi, vert.	1.40	1.40
636	A128	5p multi, vert.	2.75	2.75
637	A128	10p multi, vert.	5.50	5.50
		Nos. 620-637 (18)	15.80	15.80

Botswana Railway, Cent. — A129

Designs: 35t, Bechuanaland Rail, 1897. 50t, Elephants on the tracks. 80t, First locomotives in Bechuanaland, Cape of Good Hope 4-6-0. 1p, 4-6-4+4-6-4 Beyer Garratt. 2p, New BD3 locomotive. 2.50p, Fantuzzi Container Stacker.

1997, July 12 Litho. *Perf. 14x14½*

638	A129	35t multicolored	.20	.20
639	A129	50t multicolored	.30	.30
640	A129	80t multicolored	.50	.50
641	A129	1p multicolored	.60	.60
642	A129	2p multicolored	1.25	1.25
643	A129	2.50p multicolored	1.50	1.50
		Nos. 638-643 (6)	4.35	4.35

A130

A131

Queen Elizabeth II and Prince Philip, 50th Wedding Anniv.: No. 644, Prince in casual attire. No. 645, Queen wearing white & blue hat. No. 646, Queen with horse. No. 647, Prince with horse. No. 648, Prince, Queen. No. 649, Princess Ann in riding attire.

10p, Queen, Prince riding in open carriage.

Wmk. 373

1997, Sept. 22 Litho. *Perf. 13*

644	A130	35t multicolored	.20	.20
645	A130	35t multicolored	.20	.20
	a.	Pair, #644-645	.40	.40
646	A130	2p multicolored	1.25	1.25
647	A130	2p multicolored	1.25	1.25
	a.	Pair, #646-647	2.40	2.40
648	A130	2.50p multicolored	1.50	1.50
649	A130	2.50p multicolored	1.50	1.50
	a.	Pair, #648-649	3.00	3.00
		Nos. 644-649 (6)	5.90	5.90

Souvenir Sheet

650	A130	10p multicolored	6.00	6.00

1997, Nov. 10 Unwmk. *Perf. 14*

Christmas (Combretum):, 35t, Zeyheri. 1p, Apiculatum. 2p, Molle. 2.50p, Imberbe.

651	A131	35t multicolored	.20	.20
652	A131	1p multicolored	.60	.60
653	A131	2p multicolored	1.25	1.25
654	A131	2.50p multicolored	1.50	1.50
		Nos. 651-654 (4)	3.55	3.55

Tourism A132

1998, Mar. 23

655	A132	35t Baobab trees	.20	.20
656	A132	1p Crocodile	.55	.55
657	A132	2p Stalactites, vert.	1.10	1.10
658	A132	2.50p Tourists, vert.	1.40	1.40
		Nos. 655-658 (4)	3.25	3.25

Diana, Princess of Wales (1961-97)

Common Design Type

Portraits: 35t, #663a, Wearing red (without hat). 1p, #663b, Wearing red with hat. 2p, #663c, Wearing white (hand on face). #662, Greeting people.

1998, June 1 Wmk. 373 *Perf. 13*

659	CD355	35t multicolored	.20	.20
660	CD355	1p multicolored	.55	.55
661	CD355	2p multicolored	1.10	1.10
662	CD355	2.50p multicolored	1.40	1.40
		Nos. 659-662 (4)	3.25	3.25

Sheet of 4

663	CD355	2.50p #a.-c. + #662	5.50	5.50

A133

A134

Textiles: 35t, Tapestry of a village. 55t, Woman arranging materials on ground. 1p, Tapestry of African map, animals, huts, people. 2p, Woman seated at loom.

2.50p, Tapestry of elephants and trees, horiz.

Perf. 14x13½

1998, Sept. 28 Litho. Unwmk.

664	A133	35t multicolored	.20	.20
665	A133	55t multicolored	.30	.30
666	A133	1p multicolored	.55	.55
667	A133	2p multicolored	1.10	1.10
		Nos. 664-667 (4)	2.15	2.15

Souvenir Sheet

Perf. 13½

668	A133	2.50p multicolored	1.40	1.40

1998 Litho. *Perf. 13x13½*

Christmas - Berries: 35t, Ficus ingens. 55t, Ficus pygmaea. 1p, Ficus abutilifolia. 2.50p, Ficus sycomorus.

669	A134	35t multicolored	.20	.20
670	A134	55t multicolored	.30	.30
671	A134	1p multicolored	.55	.55
672	A134	2.50p multicolored	1.40	1.40
		Nos. 669-672 (4)	2.45	2.45

Tourism A135

Designs: 35t, Rock paintings. 55t, Salt pan. 1p. Rock paintings, diff, vert. 2p, Baobab tree, vert.

1999, May 24 Litho. *Perf. 13½x14*

673	A135	35t multicolored	.20	.20
674	A135	55t multicolored	.25	.25

Perf. 14x13½

675	A135	1p multicolored	.45	.45
676	A135	2p multicolored	.95	.95
		Nos. 673-676 (4)	1.85	1.85

UPU, 125th Anniv. A137

1999, Oct. 9 Litho. *Perf. 14¼*

678	A137	2p multicolored	.85	.85

Mpule Kwelagobe, Miss Universe 1999 A138

1999, Dec. 1 *Perf. 14½*

679	A138	35t With crown, vert.	.20	.20
680	A138	1p With headdress	.40	.40
681	A138	2p In swimsuit, vert.	.80	.80
682	A138	2.50p With Botswana sash	1.10	1.10
683	A138	15p With leopard	6.50	6.50
	a.	Souvenir sheet of 5, #679-683	9.00	9.00
		Nos. 679-683 (5)	9.00	9.00

POSTAGE DUE STAMPS

Bechuanaland Protectorate Nos. J10-J12 Overprinted: "REPUBLIC OF / BOTSWANA"

Perf. 14

1967, Mar. 1 Wmk. 4 Typo.

J1	D2	1c carmine rose	.20	*1.00*
J2	D2	2c dull violet	.25	*1.50*
J3	D2	5c olive green	.55	*2.00*
		Nos. J1-J3 (3)	1.00	*4.50*

Elephant D1

Zebra D2

Perf. 13½

1971, June 9 Litho. Unwmk.

J4	D1	1c carmine rose	1.00	*2.25*
J5	D1	2c violet blue	1.25	*3.00*
J6	D1	6c sepia	2.00	*5.00*
J7	D1	14c green	4.00	*7.00*
		Nos. J4-J7 (4)	8.25	*17.25*

1978 *Perf. 12½*

J8	D2	1t red orange & black	.70	.70
J9	D2	2t emerald & black	.70	.70
J10	D2	4t red & black	.70	.70
J11	D2	10t dark blue & black	.70	.70
J12	D2	16t brown & black	.70	.70
		Nos. J8-J12 (5)	3.50	*3.50*

1984 *Perf. 14½x14*

J8a	D2	1t	.60	*.60*
J9a	D2	2t	.60	*.60*
J10a	D2	4t	.60	*.60*
J11a	D2	10t	.60	*.60*
J12a	D2	16t	.60	*.60*
		Nos. J8a-J12a (5)	3.00	*3.00*

1989, Apr. 1 *Perf. 14½*

J8b	D2	1t	.20	.20
J9b	D2	2t	.20	.20
J10b	D2	4t	.20	.20
J11b	D2	10t	.20	.20
J12b	D2	16t	.45	.45
		Nos. J8b-J12b (5)	1.25	1.25

The design is the same size on the 1984 and 1989 issues, but the grass of Nos. J8b-J12b is lower and less defined than on previous issues. The paper is wider on the 1989 issue.

1994, Dec. 1 *Perf. 14*

J8c	D2	1t	.20	.20
J9c	D2	2t	.20	.20
J10c	D2	4t	.20	.20
J11c	D2	10t	.20	.20
J12c	D2	16t	.20	.20
		Nos. J8c-J12c (5)	1.00	1.00

See note after No. J12b.

BRAZIL

brə-'zil

Brasil (after 1918)

LOCATION — On the north and east coasts of South America, bordering on the Atlantic Ocean.
GOVT. — Republic
AREA — 3,286,000 sq. mi.
POP. — 157,070,163 (1996)
CAPITAL — Brasilia

Brazil was an independent empire from 1822 to 1889, when a constitution was adopted and the country became officially known as The United States of Brazil.

1000 Reis = 1 Milreis
100 Centavos = 1 Cruzeiro (1942)
100 Centavos = 1 Cruzado (1986)
100 Centavos = 1 Cruzeiro (1990)
(Cruzeiro Real 8/2/93-7/1/94)

Catalogue values for unused stamps in this country are for Never Hinged items, beginning with Scott 680 in the regular postage section, Scott B12 in the semi-postal section, Scott C66 in the airpost section, Scott RA2 in the postal tax section, and Scott RAB1 in the postal tax semi-postal section.

Values for unused stamps are for examples with original gum as defined in the catalogue introduction except for Nos. 1-38 and 42-52 which are valued without gum.

Watermarks

Wmk. 97- "CORREIO FEDERAL REPUBLICA DOS ESTADOS UNIDOS DO BRAZIL" in Sheet

Wmk. 98- "IMPOSTO DE CONSUMO REPUBLICA DOS ESTADOS UNIDOS DO BRAZIL" in Sheet

Wmk. 99- "CORREIO"

Wmk. 100- "CASA DA MOEDA" in Sheet

Because of the spacing of this watermark, a few stamps in each sheet may show no watermark.

Wmk. 101- Stars and CASA DA MOEDA

Wmk. 193- ESTADOS UNIDOS DO BRASIL

Wmk. 206- Star-framed CM, Multiple

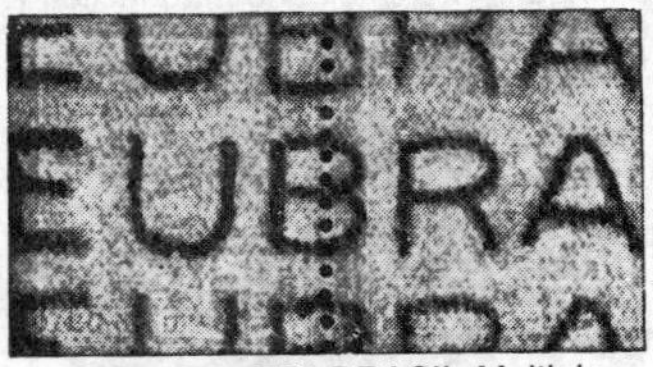

Wmk. 218- E U BRASIL Multiple, Letters 8mm High

Wmk. 221- ESTADOS UNIDOS DO BRASIL, Multiple, Letters 6mm High

Wmk. 222- CORREIO BRASIL and 5 Stars in Squared Circle

Wmk. 236- Coat of Arms in Sheet

Watermark (reduced illustration) covers 22 stamps in sheet.

Wmk. 245- Multiple "CASA DA MOEDA DO BRASIL" and Small Formee Cross

Wmk. 249- "CORREIO BRASIL" multiple

Wmk. 256- "CASA+DA+MOEDA+DO+BRAZIL" in 8mm Letters

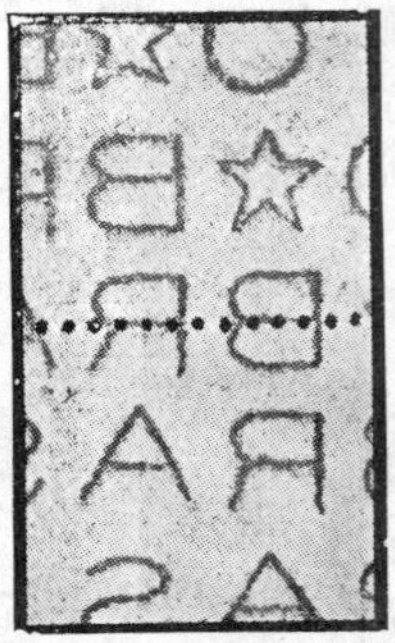

Wmk. 264- "*CORREIO*BRASIL*" Multiple, Letters 7mm High

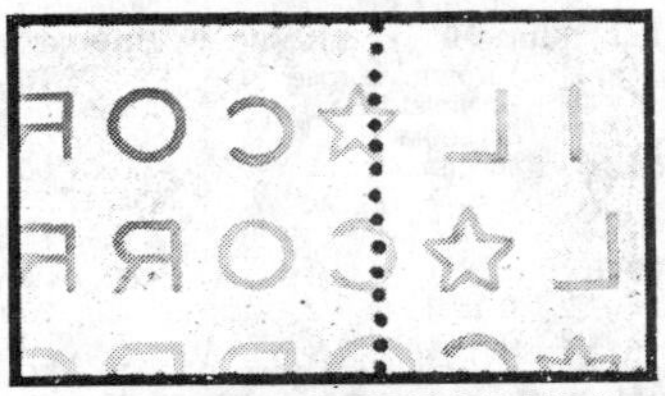

Wmk. 267- "*CORREIO*BRASIL*" Multiple in Small Letters 5mm High

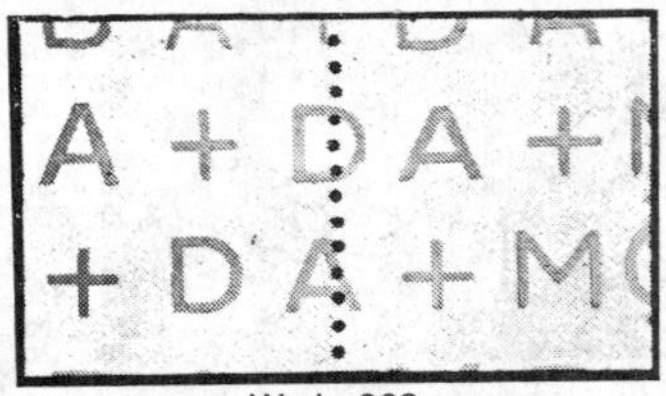

Wmk. 268- "CASA+DA+MOEDA+DO+BRASIL" in 6mm Letters

Wmk. 270- Wavy Lines and Seal

Wmk. 271- Wavy Lines

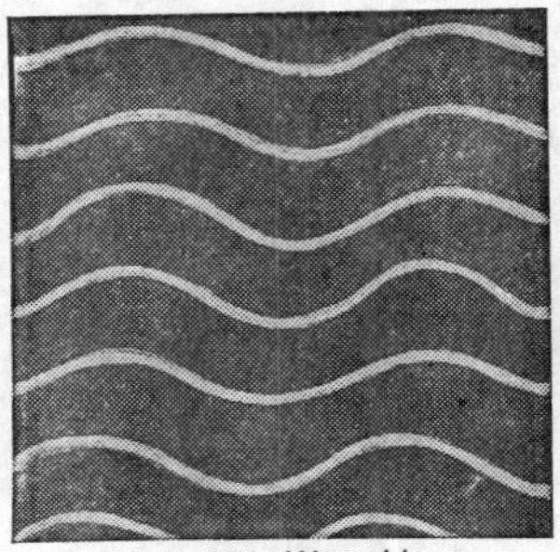

Wmk. 281- Wavy Lines

Issues of the Empire

A1

Grayish or Yellowish Paper
Fine Impressions

Unwmk.

1843, Aug. 1 **Engr.** ***Imperf.***

1	A1 30r black		3,000.	550.
c.	In pair with No. 2			*300,000.*
2	A1 60r black		600.	225.
3	A1 90r black		3,000.	1,200.

Nos. 1-3 were issued with gum, but very few unused examples retain even a trace of their original gum. Copies with original gum command substantial premiums.

Fine impressions are true black and have background lathework complete. Intermediate impressions are grayish black and have weaker lathework in the background. These sell for somewhat less than fine impressions. Worn impressions have white areas in the background surrounding the numerals due to plate wear affecting especially the lathework. These examples sell for somewhat less than intermediate impressions.

Most examples of Nos. 1-3 also exist on white paper, usually thin and somewhat translucent. Such examples are scarce and command premiums.

A2

A3

Grayish or Yellowish Paper

1844-46

7	A2	10r black	100.00	20.00
8	A2	30r black	125.00	30.00
9	A2	60r black	100.00	22.50
10	A2	90r black	750.00	100.00
11	A2	180r black	3,500.	1,300.
12	A2	300r black	5,250.	1,800.
13	A2	600r black	5,000.	2,000.

Nos. 8, 9 and 10 exist on thick paper and are considerably scarcer.

Grayish or Yellowish Paper

1850, Jan. 1

21	A3	10r black	25.00	*35.00*
22	A3	20r black	75.00	*100.00*
23	A3	30r black	10.00	3.00
24	A3	60r black	10.00	2.25
25	A3	90r black	80.00	11.50
26	A3	180r black	80.00	52.50
27	A3	300r black	325.00	60.00
28	A3	600r black	375.00	90.00

No. 22 used is generally found precanceled with a single horizontal line in pen or blue crayon. Value precanceled without gum, $75.

All values except the 90r were reprinted in 1910 on very thick paper.

1854

37	A3	10r blue	12.00	11.50
38	A3	30r blue	32.50	*50.00*

A4

1861

39	A4	280r red	140.00	100.00
40	A4	430r yellow	225.00	140.00

Nos. 39 and 40 have been reprinted on thick white paper with white gum. They are printed in aniline inks and the colors are brighter than those of the originals.

1866 ***Perf. 13½***

42	A3	10r blue	120.00	*150.00*
43	A3	20r black	900.00	400.00
44	A3	30r black	300.00	150.00
45	A3	30r blue	*675.00*	*750.00*
46	A3	60r black	120.00	25.00
47	A3	90r black	575.00	275.00
48	A3	180r black	600.00	275.00
49	A4	280r red	650.00	*675.00*
50	A3	300r black	750.00	400.00
51	A4	430r yellow	600.00	350.00
52	A3	600r black	575.00	240.00

Fraudulent perforations abound. Purchases should be accompanied by certificates of authenticity.

A 10r black is questioned.

A5

A6

A7

A8

A8a

A9

Emperor Dom Pedro — A9a

Thick or Thin White Wove Paper

1866, July 1 — ***Perf. 12***

53	A5	10r vermilion	12.00	5.00
54	A6	20r red lilac	20.00	3.00
a.		20r dull violet	65.00	25.00
56	A7	50r blue	30.00	2.50
57	A8	80r slate violet	75.00	5.00
58	A8a	100r blue green	30.00	1.50
a.		100r yellow green	30.00	1.50
59	A9	200r black	100.00	8.00
a.		Half used as 100r on cover		*1,500.*
60	A9a	500r orange	200.00	35.00
		Nos. 53-60 (7)	467.00	60.00

The 10r and 20r exist imperf. on both white and bluish paper. Some authorities consider them proofs.

Nos. 58 and 65 are found in three types.

Bluish Paper

53a	A5	10r	500.00	425.00
54b	A6	20r	160.00	24.00
56a	A7	50r	200.00	25.00
57a	A8	80r	240.00	27.50
58b	A8a	100r	800.00	115.00

1876-77 — ***Rouletted***

61	A5	10r vermilion ('77)	60.00	35.00
62	A6	20r red lilac ('77)	70.00	27.50
63	A7	50r blue ('77)	70.00	10.00
64	A8	80r violet ('77)	175.00	20.00
65	A8a	100r green	40.00	1.25
66	A9	200r black ('77)	80.00	7.50
a.		Half used as 100r on cover		*1,000.*
67	A9a	500r orange	190.00	40.00
		Nos. 61-67 (7)	685.00	141.25

A10

A11

A12

A13

A14

A15

A16

A17

A18

A19

A20

1878-79 — ***Rouletted***

68	A10	10r vermilion	12.00	3.00
69	A11	20r violet	15.00	2.50
70	A12	50r blue	24.00	2.00
71	A13	80r lake	27.50	10.00
72	A14	100r green	27.50	1.25
73	A15	200r black	140.00	17.50
a.		Half used as 100r on cover		*1,200.*
74	A16	260r dk brown	80.00	22.00
75	A18	300r bister	80.00	6.00
a.		One-third used as 100r on cover		*10,000.*
76	A19	700r red brown	160.00	85.00
77	A20	1000r gray lilac	190.00	37.50
a.		Half used as 500r on cover		*10,000.*
		Nos. 68-77 (10)	756.00	186.75

1878, Aug. 21 — ***Perf. 12***

78	A17	300r orange & grn	85.00	20.00

Nos. 68-78 exist imperforate.

A21

A22

A23

Small Heads
Laid Paper

Perf. 13, 13½ and Compound

1881, July 15

79	A21	50r blue	120.00	18.00
80	A22	100r olive green	500.00	30.00
81	A23	200r pale red brn	475.00	110.00
a.		Half used as 100r on cover		*1,750.*

On Nos. 79 and 80 the hair above the ear curves forward. On Nos. 83 and 88 it is drawn backward. On the stamps of the 1881 issue the beard is smaller than in the 1882-85 issues and fills less of the space between the neck and the frame at the left.

See No. 88.

A24

A25

A26

A27

Two types each of the 100 and 200 reis.

100 REIS:

Type I - Groundwork formed of diagonal crossed lines and horizontal lines.

Type II - Groundwork formed of diagonal crossed lines and vertical lines.

200 REIS:

Type I - Groundwork formed of diagonal and horizontal lines.

Type II - Groundwork formed of diagonal crossed lines.

Larger Heads
Laid Paper

Perf. 12½ to 14 and Compound

1882-84

82	A24	10r black	10.00	*20.00*
83	A25	100r ol grn, type I	35.00	3.00
a.		100r dark green, type I	37.50	3.00
b.		100r dark green, type II	200.00	12.00
84	A26	200r pale red brn, type I	85.00	22.50
a.		Half used as 100r on cover		*1,100.*
85	A27	200r pale rose, type II	45.00	4.50
a.		Diag. half used as 100r on cover		800.00
		Nos. 82-85 (4)	175.00	50.00

See No. 86.

A28

A29

A30

Three types of A29

Type I - Groundwork of horizontal lines.

Type II - Groundwork of diagonal crossed lines.

Type III - Groundwork solid.

Perf. 13, 13½, 14 and Compound

1884-85

86	A24	10r orange	2.50	2.00
87	A28	20r slate green	30.00	3.00
a.		20r olive green	30.00	3.00
b.		Half used as 10r on newspaper		*3,000.*
88	A21	50r bl, head larger	30.00	3.00
90	A29	100r lilac, type I	120.00	2.50
a.		100r lilac, type II	450.00	75.00
b.		100r lilac, type III	325.00	55.00
91	A30	100r lilac	180.00	4.00
		Nos. 86-91 (5)	362.50	14.50

A31

A32

Southern Cross
A33

Crown
A34

Perf. 13, 13½, 14 and Compound

1885

92	A31	100r lilac	100.00	2.50

Compare design A31 with A35.

1887

93	A32	50r chalky blue	27.50	4.00
94	A33	300r gray blue	200.00	25.00
95	A34	500r olive	110.00	12.00
		Nos. 93-95 (3)	337.50	41.00

A35

A36

Entrance to Bay of Rio de Janeiro — A37

1888

96	A35	100r lilac	60.00	1.50
a.		Imperf., pair	120.00	*160.00*
97	A36	700r violet	65.00	*100.00*
98	A37	1000r dull blue	250.00	100.00
		Nos. 96-98 (3)	375.00	*201.50*

Issues of the Republic

Southern Cross — A38

Wove Paper, Thin to Thick

Perf. 12½ to 14, 11 to 11½, and 12½ to 14x11 to 11½, Rough or Clean-Cut

Engraved; Typographed (#102)

1890-91

99	A38	20r gray green	2.00	1.50
a.		20r blue green	2.00	1.50
b.		20r emerald	16.00	6.00
100	A38	50r gray green	5.00	1.50
a.		50r olive green	12.00	6.00
b.		50r yellow green	12.00	6.00
c.		50r dark slate green	7.00	3.50
d.		Horiz. pair, imperf. btwn.		
101	A38	100r lilac rose	360.00	4.50
102	A38	100r red lil, redrawn	25.00	1.50
a.		Tete beche pair	*15,000.*	*16,500.*
103	A38	200r purple	8.00	1.50
a.		200r violet	10.00	2.00
b.		200r violet blue	22.50	3.00
104	A38	300r slate vio	150.00	25.00
a.		300r gray	75.00	8.50
b.		300r gray blue	85.00	8.50
c.		300r dark violet	75.00	5.00
105	A38	500r olive bister	17.50	8.00
a.		500r olive gray	17.50	10.00
106	A38	500r slate	17.50	12.00
107	A38	700r fawn	16.00	16.00
a.		700r chocolate	20.00	*22.50*
108	A38	1000r bister	15.00	3.00
a.		1000r yellow buff	30.00	7.50
		Nos. 99-108 (10)	616.00	74.50

The redrawn 100r may be distinguished by the absence of the curved lines of shading in the left side of the central oval. The pearls in the oval are not well aligned and there is less shading at right and left of "CORREIO" and "100 REIS."

A 100 reis stamp of type A38 but inscribed "BRAZIL" instead of "E. U. DO BRAZIL" was not placed in issue but postmarked copies are known. A reprint on thick paper was made in 1910.

No. 101 exists imperf., not regularly issued.

For surcharges see Nos. 151-158.

Liberty Head
A39 A40

Perf. 12½ to 14, 11 to 11½ and 12½ to 14x11 to 11½

1891, May 1 — **Typo.**

109	A39	100r blue & red	32.50	1.50
a.		Head inverted	100.00	90.00
b.		Tete beche pair	675.00	750.00
c.		100r ultra & red	32.50	1.50

Perf. 11, 11½, 13, 13½, 14 and Compound

1893, Jan. 18 — **Litho.**

111	A40	100r rose	75.00	1.75

Sugarloaf Mountain
A41 A41a

Liberty Head
A42 A42a

Hermes — A43

Perf. 11 to 11½, 12½ to 14 and 12½ to 14x11 to 11½

1894-97 — **Unwmk.**

112	A41	10r rose & blue	2.00	.75
113	A41a	10r rose & blue	2.00	.75
114	A41a	20r orange & bl	1.10	.35
115	A41a	50r dk blue & blue	8.00	1.25
116	A42	100r carmine & blk	4.00	.40
a.		Vert. pair, imperf. btwn.	100.00	
118	A42a	200r orange & blk	1.00	.40
a.		Imperf. horiz., pair	80.00	
b.		Vert. pair, imperf. btwn.	80.00	
119	A42a	300r green & blk	15.00	.60
120	A42a	500r blue & blk	25.00	1.75
121	A42a	700r lilac & blk	16.00	2.00
122	A43	1000r green & vio	55.00	1.75
124	A43	2000r blk & gray lil	65.00	15.00
		Nos. 112-124 (11)	194.10	25.00

The head of No. 116 exists in five types.

See Nos. 140-150A, 159-161, 166-171d.

Newspaper Stamps Surcharged:

100 **200**

1898 **1898**
100 **200**
a b

100
1898
100
c

Surcharged on 1889 Issue of type N1

1898 *Rouletted*

Green Surcharge

125 (b) 700r on 500r yel 6.75 10.00
126 (c) 1000r on 700r yel 32.50 27.50
a. Surcharged "700r" 675.00 775.00
127 (c) 2000r on 1000r yel 27.50 15.00
128 (c) 2000r on 1000r brn 20.00 6.00

Violet Surcharge

129 (a) 100r on 50r brn yel 2.00 *45.00*
130 (c) 100r on 50r brn yel 65.00 45.00
131 (c) 300r on 200r blk 3.50 1.25
a. Double surcharge 160.00 275.00

The surcharge on No. 130 is handstamped. The impression is blurred and lighter in color than on No. 129. The two surcharges differ most in the shapes and serifs of the figures "1."

Counterfeits exist of No. 126a.

Black Surcharge

132 (b) 200r on 100r violet 3.50 1.25
a. Double surcharge 80.00 *175.00*
b. Inverted surcharge 80.00 *175.00*
132C (b) 500r on 300r car 5.50 3.00
133 (b) 700r on 500r green 8.00 2.00

Blue Surcharge

134 (b) 500r on 300r car 6.50 5.50

Red Surcharge

135 (c) 1000r on 700r ultra 22.50 15.00
a. Inverted surcharge 200.00 200.00

Surcharged on 1890-94 Issues:

200
1898
d

1898
50 RÉIS 50
e

Perf. 11 to 14 and Compound

Black Surcharge

136 N3(e) 20r on 10r blue 3.00 6.00
137 N2(d) 200r on 100r red lilac 20.00 15.00
a. Double surcharge 225.00 250.00

Surcharge on No. 137 comes blue to deep black.

Blue Surcharge

138 N3(e) 50r on 20r green 8.00 10.00

Red Surcharge

139 N3(e) 100r on 50r green 18.00 20.00
a. Blue surcharge 12.50

The surcharge on Nos. 139 and 139a exists double, inverted, one missing, etc.

Types of 1894-97

1899

Perf. 5½-7 and 11-11½x5½-7

140 A41a 10r rose & bl 4.50 12.00
141 A41a 20r orange & bl 7.50 7.50
142 A41a 50r dk bl & lt bl 9.00 30.00
143 A42 100r carmine & blk 16.00 4.50
144 A42a 200r orange & blk 9.00 3.00
145 A42a 300r green & blk 60.00 7.50
Nos. 140-145 (6) 106.00 64.50

Perf. 8½-9½, 8½-9½x11-11½

146 A41a 10r rose & bl 4.50 3.00
147 A41a 20r orange & bl 15.00 3.00
147A A41a 50r dk bl & bl 125.00 30.00
148 A42 100r carmine & blk 30.00 1.50
149 A42a 200r orange & blk 15.00 1.00
150 A42a 300r green & blk 60.00 5.00
150A A43 1000r green & vio 125.00 12.50
Nos. 146-150A (7) 374.50 56.00

Nos. 140-150A are valued with perfs just cut into the design on one or two sides. Expect some irregularity of the perforations.

Issue of 1890-93 Surcharged in Violet or Magenta

1899
50 RÉIS

Perf. 11 to 11½, 12½ to 14 and Compound

1899, June 25

151 A38 50r on 20r gray grn 2.00 3.00
a. Double surcharge 125.00 125.00
152 A38 100r on 50r gray grn 2.00 3.00
b. Double surcharge 100.00 100.00
153 A38 300r on 200r pur 7.50 *12.00*
a. Double surcharge 250.00 250.00
b. Pair, one without surcharge 425.00 —
154 A38 500r on 300r ultra, perf. 13 18.00 7.50
a. 500r on 300r gray lilac 30.00 9.00
b. Pair, one without surcharge 425.00 *500.00*
c. 500r on 300r slate violet 37.50 15.00
155 A38 700r on 500r ol bis 24.00 6.00
a. Pair, one without surcharge 425.00 —
156 A38 1000r on 700r choc 17.50 6.00
157 A38 1000r on 700r fawn 17.50 6.00
a. Pair, one without surcharge 425.00 *500.00*
158 A38 2000r on 1000r yel buff 60.00 4.50
a. 2000r on 1000r bister 30.00 4.50
b. Pair, one without surcharge 425.00 *500.00*
Nos. 151-158 (8) 148.50 48.00

Types of 1894-97

Perf. 11, 11½, 13 and Compound

1900

159 A41a 50r green 10.00 .60
160 A42 100r rose 20.00 .30
a. Frame around inner oval 100.00 4.00
161 A42a 200r blue 12.00 .35
Nos. 159-161 (3) 42.00 1.25

Three types exist of No. 161, all of which have the frame around inner oval.

Cabral Arrives at Brazil — A44

Independence Proclaimed A45

"Emancipation of Slaves" — A46

Allegory, Republic of Brazil — A47

1900, Jan. 1 **Litho.** *Perf. 12½*

162 A44 100r red 5.50 4.50
a. Imperf., pair 400.00 500.00
163 A45 200r green & yel 5.50 4.50
164 A46 500r blue 5.50 4.50
165 A47 700r emerald 5.50 4.50
Nos. 162-165 (4) 22.00 18.00

Discovery of Brazil, 400th anniversary.

Types of 1894-97

Wmk. (97? or 98?)

1905 *Perf. 11, 11½*

166 A41a 10r rose & bl 5.75 4.00
167 A41a 20r orange & bl 10.00 2.00
168 A41a 50r green 20.00 3.00
169 A42 100r rose 27.50 1.00
170 A42a 200r dark blue 16.00 1.00
171 A42a 300r green & blk 55.00 2.00
Nos. 166-171 (6) 134.25 13.00

Positive identification of Wmk. 97 or 98 places stamp in specific watermark groups below.

Wmk. 97

166b A41a 10r rose & blue 30.00 16.00
167b A41a 20r orange & blue 30.00 8.00
168b A41a 50r green 55.00 8.00
169b A42 100r rose 200.00 30.00
170b A42a 200r dark blue 120.00 4.00
171b A42a 300r green & blk 375.00 30.00
171A A43 1000r green & vio 290.00 30.00
Nos. 166b-171A (7) 1,100. 126.00

Wmk. 98

166c A41a 10r rose & blue 40.00 40.00
167c A41a 20r orange & blue 80.00 20.00
168c A41a 50r green 160.00 30.00
169c A42 100r rose 80.00 4.00
170c A42a 200r dark blue 120.00 4.00
171d A42a 300r green & blk 290.00 30.00
Nos. 166c-171d (6) 770.00 128.00

Allegory, Pan-American Congress — A48

1906, July 23 **Litho.** **Unwmk.**

172 A48 100r carmine rose 30.00 30.00
173 A48 200r blue 75.00 10.00

Third Pan-American Congress.

Aristides Lobo — A48a

Benjamin Constant — A49

Pedro Alvares Cabral A50

Eduardo Wandenkolk A51

Manuel Deodoro da Fonseca — A52

Floriano Peixoto — A53

Prudente de Moraes — A54

Manuel Ferraz de Campos Salles — A55

Francisco de Paula Rodrigues Alves — A56

Liberty Head — A57

A58

A59

1906-16 **Engr.** *Perf. 12*

174 A48a 10r bluish slate .90 .20
175 A49 20r aniline vio .90 .20
176 A50 50r green .90 .20
a. Booklet pane of 6 ('08) 40.00 *120.00*
177 A51 100r anil rose 2.00 .20
a. Imperf. vert., coil ('16) 4.00 .35
b. Booklet pane of 6 ('08) 80.00 *120.00*
178 A52 200r blue 2.00 .20
a. Booklet pane of 6 ('08) 60.00 *120.00*
179 A52 200r ultra ('15) 2.00 .35
a. Imperf. vert., coil ('16) 2.00 .35
180 A53 300r gray blk 3.00 .65
181 A54 400r olive grn 30.00 2.00
182 A55 500r dk violet 6.00 .65
183 A54 600r olive grn ('10) 3.00 1.00
184 A56 700r red brown 6.00 3.00
185 A57 1000r vermilion 32.50 1.00
186 A58 2000r yellow grn 20.00 .65
187 A58 2000r Prus blue ('15) 10.00 1.00
188 A59 5000r carmine rose 8.00 2.00
Nos. 174-188 (15) 127.20 13.30

Allegorical Emblems: Liberty, Peace, Industry, etc. — A60

1908, July 14

189 A60 100r carmine 20.00 1.75

National Exhibition, Rio de Janeiro.

Emblems of Peace Between Brazil and Portugal A61

1908, July 14

190 A61 100r red 8.00 1.25

Opening of Brazilian ports to foreign commerce, cent. Medallions picture King Carlos I of Portugal and Pres. Affonso Penna of Brazil.

Bonifacio, Bolivar, Hidalgo, O'Higgins, San Martin, Washington — A62

1909

191 A62 200r deep blue 7.50 1.00

For surcharge see No. E1.

Nilo Peçanha — A63

Baron of Rio Branco — A64

1910, Nov. 15

192 A63 10,000r brown 8.00 2.00

1913-16

193 A64 1000r deep green 3.75 .35
194 A64 1000r slate ('16) 21.00 .65

Cabo Frio — A65

Perf. 11½

1915, Nov. 13 **Litho.** **Wmk. 99**

195 A65 100r dk grn, *yelsh* 4.00 3.50

Founding of the town of Cabo Frio, 300th anniversary.

Bay of Guajara — A66

1916, Jan. 5

196 A66 100r carmine 7.50 4.00

City of Belem, 300th anniversary.

Revolutionary Flag — A67

1917, Mar. 6

197	A67	100r deep blue	15.00	7.50

Revolution of Pernambuco, Mar. 6, 1817.

Rodrigues Alves — A68

Unwmk.

1917, Aug. 31 Engr. *Perf. 12*

198	A68	5000r red brown	60.00	10.00

Liberty Head
A69 A70

Perf. 12½, 13, 13x13½.

1918-20 Typo. Unwmk.

200	A69	10r orange brn	.50	.25
201	A69	20r slate	.50	.25
202	A69	25r ol gray ('20)	.50	.25
203	A69	50r green	27.50	3.25
204	A70	100r rose	1.75	.25
a.		Imperf., pair	—	
205	A70	300r red orange	19.00	3.25
206	A70	500r dull violet	19.00	3.25
		Nos. 200-206 (7)	68.75	10.75

1918-20 Wmk. 100

207	A69	10r red brown	6.00	1.75
a.		Imperf., pair	—	
207B	A69	20r slate	1.50	1.50
c.		Imperf., pair	—	
208	A69	25r ol gray ('20)	.75	.50
209	A69	50r green	1.50	.50
210	A70	100r rose	47.50	.50
a.		Imperf., pair	—	
211	A70	200r dull blue	6.00	.50
212	A70	300r orange	47.50	3.50
213	A70	500r dull violet	47.50	7.50
214	A70	600r orange	2.50	*7.50*
		Nos. 207-214 (9)	160.75	23.75

Because of the spacing of this watermark, a few stamps in each sheet may show no watermark.

"Education" — A72

1918 Engr. *Perf. 11½*

215	A72	1000r blue	6.00	.25
216	A72	2000r red brown	27.50	6.00
217	A72	5000r dark violet	7.50	6.00
		Nos. 215-217 (3)	41.00	12.25

Watermark note below No. 257 also applies to Nos. 215-217.

See Nos. 233-234, 283-285, 404, 406, 458, 460. For surcharge see No. C30.

Railroad
A73

"Industry"
A74

"Aviation"
A75

Mercury
A76

"Navigation" — A77

Perf. 13½x13, 13x13½

1920-22 Typo. Unwmk.

218	A73	10r red violet	.75	.40
219	A73	20r olive green	.75	.40
220	A74	25r brown violet	.50	.40
221	A74	50r blue green	.85	.40
222	A74	50r orange brn ('22)	1.40	.40
223	A75	100r rose red	2.75	.40
224	A75	100r orange ('22)	7.50	.40
225	A75	150r violet ('21)	1.40	.40
226	A75	200r blue	4.50	.40
227	A75	200r rose red ('22)	8.00	.40
228	A76	300r olive gray	12.50	.50
229	A76	400r dull blue ('22)	22.50	3.50
230	A76	500r red brown	17.50	.50
		Nos. 218-230 (13)	80.90	8.50

See Nos. 236-257, 265-266, 268-271, 273-274, 276-281, 302-311, 316-322, 326-340, 357-358, 431-434, 436-441, 461-463B, 467-470, 472-474, 488-490, 492-494. For surcharges see Nos. 356-358, 376-377.

Perf. 11, 11½

Engr. Wmk. 100

231	A77	600r red orange	2.00	.35
232	A77	1000r claret	5.00	.25
a.		Perf. 8½	37.50	7.50
233	A72	2000r dull violet	20.00	.75
234	A72	5000r brown	16.00	9.00
		Nos. 231-234 (4)	43.00	10.35

Nos. 233 and 234 are inscribed "BRASIL CORREIO." Watermark note below No. 257 also applies to Nos. 231-234.

See No. 282.

King Albert of Belgium and President Epitacio Pessoa
A78

1920, Sept. 19 Engr. *Perf. 11½x11*

235	A78	100r dull red	.65	.65

Visit of the King and Queen of Belgium.

Types of 1920-22 Issue

Perf. 13x13½, 13x12½

1922-29 Typo. Wmk. 100

236	A73	10r red violet	.30	.20
237	A73	20r olive green	.30	.20
238	A75	20r gray violet ('29)	.30	.20
239	A74	25r brown violet	.35	.20
240	A74	50r blue grn	*3.25*	*35.00*
241	A74	50r org brn ('23)	.45	.35
a.		Booklet pane of 6		
242	A75	100r rose red	22.50	.40
243	A75	100r orange ('26)	.50	.20
a.		Booklet pane of 6		
244	A75	100r turq grn ('28)	.35	.20
245	A75	150r violet	2.50	.20
246	A75	200r blue	300.00	12.50
247	A75	200r rose red	.40	.20
a.		Booklet pane of 6		
248	A75	200r ol grn ('28)	2.50	3.00
249	A76	300r olive gray	1.90	.25
a.		Booklet pane of 6		
250	A76	300r rose red ('29)	.35	.25
251	A76	400r blue	1.90	.20
252	A76	400r orange ('29)	.75	.60
253	A76	500r red brown	7.50	.50
a.		Booklet pane of 6		
254	A76	500r ultra ('29)	8.50	.20
255	A76	600r brn org ('29)	7.50	3.00
256	A76	700r dull vio ('29)	7.50	1.75
257	A76	1000r turq bl ('29)	9.50	.70
		Nos. 236-257 (22)	379.10	*60.30*

Because of the spacing of the watermark, a few stamps in each sheet show no watermark.

"Agriculture" — A79

1922 Unwmk. *Perf. 13x13½*

258	A79	40r orange brown	.50	.35
259	A79	80r grnsh blue	.35	*2.50*

See Nos. 263, 267, 275.

Declaration of Ypiranga — A80

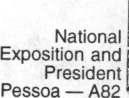

Dom Pedro I and Jose Bonifacio
A81

National Exposition and President Pessoa — A82

Unwmk.

1922, Sept. 7 Engr. *Perf. 14*

260	A80	100r ultra	5.00	.45
261	A81	200r red	6.00	.30
262	A82	300r green	6.00	.30
		Nos. 260-262 (3)	17.00	1.05

Cent. of independence and Natl. Exposition of 1922.

Agriculture Type of 1922

Perf. 13½x12

1923 Wmk. 100 Typo.

263	A79	40r orange brown	.60	*.60*

Brazilian Army Entering Bahia — A83

Unwmk.

1923, July 12 Litho. *Perf. 13*

264	A83	200r rose	7.50	5.00

Centenary of the taking of Bahia from the Portuguese.

Types of 1920-22 Issues

Perf. 13x13½

1924 Typo. Wmk. 193

265	A73	10r red violet	5.50	3.75
266	A73	20r olive green	6.00	3.75
267	A79	40r orange brown	4.25	.60
268	A74	50r orange brown	3.75	*18.00*
269	A75	100r orange	4.25	.35
270	A75	200r rose	6.00	.25
271	A76	400r blue	3.75	3.75
		Nos. 265-271 (7)	33.50	*30.45*

Arms of Equatorial Confederation, 1824 — A84

Unwmk.

1924, July 2 Litho. *Perf. 11*

272	A84	200r bl, blk, yel, & red	3.00	2.25
a.		Red omitted	275.00	275.00

Centenary of the Equatorial Confederation.

Types of 1920-22 Issues

Perf. 9½ to 13½ and Compound

1924-28 Typo. Wmk. 101

273	A73	10r red violet	.45	.30
274	A73	20r olive gray	.45	.30
275	A79	40r orange brn	.45	.30
276	A74	50r orange brn	.75	.30
277	A75	100r red orange	1.50	.30
278	A75	200r rose	.75	.30
279	A76	300r ol gray ('25)	7.00	1.00
280	A76	400r blue	4.00	.35
281	A76	500r red brown	9.00	.45

Engr.

282	A77	600r red orange ('26)	1.00	.30
283	A72	2000r dull vio ('26)	5.00	.30
284	A72	5000r brown ('26)	15.00	.70
285	A72	10,000r rose ('28)	17.50	.90
		Nos. 273-285 (13)	62.85	5.80

Nos. 283-285 are inscribed "BRASIL CORREIO."

Ruy Barbosa — A85

1925 Wmk. 100 *Perf. 11½*

286	A85	1000r claret	4.25	1.50

1926 Wmk. 101

287	A85	1000r claret	1.75	.35

"Justice" — A86

Scales of Justice and Map of Brazil — A87

Perf. 13½x13

1927, Aug. 11 Typo. Wmk. 206

288	A86	100r deep blue	.90	.50
289	A87	200r rose	.80	.35

Founding of the law courses, cent.

Liberty Holding Coffee Leaves — A88

1928, Mar. 5

290	A88	100r blue green	1.00	.60
291	A88	200r carmine	.65	.50
292	A88	300r olive black	5.00	.40
		Nos. 290-292 (3)	6.65	1.50

Introduction of the coffee tree in Brazil, bicent.

Official Stamps of 1919 Surcharged in Red or Black

700
Réis

Perf. 11, 11½

1928 Wmk. 100 Engr.

293	O3	700r on 500r orange	2.25	1.50
a.		Inverted surcharge	175.00	175.00
294	O3	1000r on 100r rose red (Bk)	1.50	.30
295	O3	2000r on 200r dull bl	2.25	.45
296	O3	5000r on 50r green	2.25	.55
297	O3	10,000r on 10r ol grn	11.00	.90
		Nos. 293-297 (5)	19.25	3.70

#293-297 were used for ordinary postage.

Stamps in the outer rows of the sheets are often without watermark.

Ruy Barbosa — A89

Perf. 9, 9½x11, 11, and Compound

1929 Wmk. 101

300	A89	5000r blue violet	12.50	.75

See #405, 459. For surcharge see #C29.

Types of 1920-21 Issue

Perf. 13½x12½

1929 Typo. Wmk. 218

302	A75	20r gray violet	.25	.20
303	A75	50r red brown	.25	.20
304	A75	100r turq green	.30	.20
305	A75	200r olive green	12.50	2.25
306	A76	300r rose red	.60	.20
307	A76	400r orange	.70	.25
308	A76	500r ultra	7.00	.45
309	A76	600r brown org	8.50	.60
310	A76	700r dp violet	2.25	.20
311	A76	1000r turq blue	4.00	.20
		Nos. 302-311 (10)	36.35	4.75

Wmk. 218 exists both in vertical alignment and in echelon.

Wmk. in echelon

302a	A75	20r	.25	.35
303a	A75	50r	80.00	27.50
306a	A76	300r	.65	.30
308a	A76	500r	110.00	15.00
311a	A76	1000r	6.50	6.50

Architectural Fantasies
A90 A91

Architectural Fantasy — A92

Perf. 13x13½

1930, June 20 **Wmk. 206**

312	A90	100r turq blue	1.25	.80
313	A91	200r olive gray	2.00	.70
314	A92	300r rose red	3.50	.80
		Nos. 312-314 (3)	6.75	2.30

Fourth Pan-American Congress of Architects and Exposition of Architecture.

Types of 1920-21 Issues

1930 **Wmk. 221** ***Perf. 13x12½***

316	A75	20r gray violet	.20	.20
317	A75	50r red brown	.20	.20
318	A75	100r turq blue	.25	.20
319	A75	200r olive green	3.00	.25
320	A76	300r rose red	.60	.25
321	A76	500r ultra	1.50	.25
322	A76	1000r turq blue	25.00	.70
		Nos. 316-322 (7)	30.75	2.05

Imperforates

Since 1930, imperforate or partly perforated sheets of nearly all commemorative and some definitive issues have become obtainable.

Types of 1920-29 Issue

Perf. 11, 13½x13, 13x12½

1931-34 **Typo.** **Wmk. 222**

326	A75	10r deep brown	.20	.20
327	A75	20r gray violet	.20	.20
328	A74	25r brn vio ('34)	.20	.60
330	A75	50r blue green	.20	.20
331	A75	50r red brown	.20	.20
332	A75	100r orange	.30	.20
334	A75	200r dp carmine	.45	.20
335	A76	300r olive green	.60	.20
336	A76	400r ultra	.85	.20
337	A76	500r red brown	3.50	.20
338	A76	600r brown org	3.50	.20
339	A76	700r deep violet	3.50	.20
340	A76	1000r turq blue	12.50	.20
		Nos. 326-340 (13)	26.20	3.00

Getulio Vargas and Joao Pessoa
A93

Vargas and Pessoa
A94

Oswaldo Aranha
A95 A96

Antonio Carlos
A97

Pessoa
A98

Vargas — A99

Unwmk.

1931, Apr. 29 **Litho.** ***Perf. 14***

342	A93	10r + 10r lt bl	.20	*4.50*
343	A93	20r + 20r yel brn	.20	*3.25*
344	A95	50r + 50r bl grn, red & yel	.20	.20
a.		Red missing at left	.90	.90
345	A93	100r + 50r orange	.30	.30
346	A93	200r + 100r green	.30	.30
347	A94	300r + 150r multi	.30	.30
348	A93	400r + 200r dp rose	1.00	.65
349	A93	500r + 250r dk blue	.70	.55
350	A93	600r + 300r brn vio	.50	*6.50*
351	A94	700r + 350r multi	.90	.55
352	A96	1000r + 500r brt grn, red & yel	2.00	.25
353	A97	2000r + 1000r gray blk & red	4.00	.55
354	A98	5000r + 2500r blk & red	17.50	4.50
355	A99	10000r + 5000r brt grn & yel	42.50	10.00
		Nos. 342-355 (14)	70.60	32.40

Revolution of Oct. 3, 1930. Prepared as semi-postal stamps, Nos. 342-355 were sold as ordinary postage stamps with stated surtax ignored.

Nos. 306, 320 and 250 Surcharged **1931 200 Réis**

Wmk. E U BRASIL Multiple (218)

1931, July 20 ***Perf. 13½x12½***

356	A76	200r on 300r rose red	.90	.90
a.		Wmk. in echelon	17.50	17.50
b.		Inverted surcharge	40.00	

Perf. 13x12½

Wmk. 221

357	A76	200r on 300r rose red	.30	.20
a.		Inverted surcharge	45.00	45.00

Perf. 13½x12½

Wmk. 100

358	A76	200r on 300r rose red	60.00	60.00

Map of South America Showing Meridian of Tordesillas
A100

Joao Ramalho and Tibiriça
A101

Martim Affonso de Souza
A102

King John III of Portugal
A103

Disembarkation of M. A. de Souza at Sao Vicente — A104

Wmk. 222

1932, June 3 **Typo.** ***Perf. 13***

359	A100	20r dk violet	.20	.20
360	A101	100r black	.35	.35
361	A102	200r purple	1.00	.25
362	A103	600r red brown	1.65	1.25

Engr.

Wmk. 101

Perf. 9½, 11, 9½x11

363	A104	700r ultra	2.50	1.75
		Nos. 359-363 (5)	5.70	3.80

1st colonization of Brazil at Sao Vicente, in 1532, under the hereditary captaincy of Martim Affonso de Souza.

Revolutionary Issue

Map of Brazil — A105

Soldier and Flag — A106

Allegory: Freedom, Justice, Equality — A107

Soldier's Head — A108

"LEX" and Sword
A109

Symbolical of Law and Order
A110

Symbolical of Justice
A111

Perf. 11½

1932, Sept. 13 **Litho.** **Unwmk.**

364	A105	100r brown org	.40	2.00
365	A106	200r dk carmine	.35	.70
366	A107	300r gray green	2.00	3.50
367	A108	400r dark blue	7.25	7.25
368	A105	500r black brown	7.25	7.25
369	A107	600r red	7.25	7.25
370	A106	700r violet	3.50	*7.25*
371	A108	1000r orange	1.75	*7.25*
372	A109	2000r dark brown	14.00	20.00
373	A110	5000r yellow grn	17.50	32.50
374	A111	10000r plum	20.00	37.50
		Nos. 364-374 (11)	81.25	132.45

Issued by the revolutionary forces in the state of Sao Paulo during the revolt of September, 1932. Subsequently the stamps were recognized by the Federal Government and placed in general use.

Excellent counterfeits of Nos. 373 and 374 exist. Counterfeit cancellations abound.

City of Vassouras and Illuminated Memorial — A112

Wmk. 222

1933, Jan. 15 **Typo.** ***Perf. 12***

375	A112	200r rose red	1.00	.90

City of Vassouras founding, cent.

Nos. 306, 320 Surcharged **200 RÉIS**

Perf. 13½x12½

1933, July 28 **Wmk. 218**

376	A76	200r on 300r rose red	.60	.60
a.		Wmk. 218 in echelon (No. 306a)	12.50	12.50
b.		Wmk. 100 (No. 250)	87.50	87.50

Perf. 13x12½

Wmk. 221

377	A76	200r on 300r rose red	.45	.45
a.		Inverted surcharge	35.00	
b.		Double surcharge	35.00	

Religious Symbols and Inscriptions — A113

Wmk. 222

1933, Sept. 3 **Typo.** ***Perf. 13***

378	A113	200r dark red	.90	.75

1st Natl. Eucharistic Congress in Brazil.

"Flag of the Race"
A114

1933, Aug. 18

379	A114	200r deep red	.90	.75

The raising of the "Flag of the Race" and the 441st anniv. of the sailing of Columbus from Palos, Spain, Aug. 3, 1492.

Republic Figure, Flags of Brazil and Argentina — A115

Wmk. 101

1933, Oct. 7 **Engr.** ***Perf. 11½***

380	A115	200r blue	.35	.25

Thick Laid Paper

Perf. 11, 11½

Wmk. 236

381	A115	400r green	.90	.80
382	A115	600r brt rose	3.00	3.25
383	A115	1000r lt violet	4.50	3.75
		Nos. 380-383 (4)	8.75	8.05

Visit of President Justo of the Argentina to Brazil, Oct. 2-7, 1933.

Allegory: "Faith and Energy" A116

Allegory of Flight A117

1933 Typo. Wmk. 222

384	A116	200r dark red	.25	.15
385	A116	200r dark violet	.30	.15

See Nos. 435, 471, 491.

Wmk. 236

1934, Apr. 15 Engr. *Perf. 12*

386	A117	200r blue	.50	.50

1st Natl. Aviation Congress at Sao Paulo.

A118

Wmk. 222

1934, May 12 Typo. *Perf. 11*

387	A118	200r dark olive	.30	.30
388	A118	400r carmine	1.50	1.50
389	A118	700r ultra	1.50	.90
390	A118	1000r orange	3.75	.60
		Nos. 387-390 (4)	7.05	3.30

7th Intl. Fair at Rio de Janeiro.

Christ of Corcovado — A119

1934, Oct. 20

392	A119	300r dark red	1.90	1.90
a.		Tete beche pair	6.00	7.25
393	A119	700r ultra	8.00	5.00
a.		Tete beche pair	19.00	22.50

Visit of Eugenio Cardinal Pacelli, later Pope Pius XII, to Brazil.

The three printings of Nos. 392-393, distinguishable by shades, sell for different prices.

José de Anchieta A120

Thick Laid Paper

Perf. 11, 12

1934, Nov. 8 Wmk. 236

394	A120	200r yellow brown	.55	.15
395	A120	300r violet	.45	.25
396	A120	700r blue	1.75	1.40
397	A120	1000r lt green	3.50	.55
		Nos. 394-397 (4)	6.25	2.35

Jose de Anchieta, S.J. (1534-1597), Portuguese missionary and "father of Brazilian literature."

"Brazil" and "Uruguay"
A121 A122

Wmk. 222

1935, Jan. 8 Typo. *Perf. 11*

398	A121	200r orange	.65	.40
399	A122	300r yellow	.80	.50
400	A122	700r ultra	3.25	3.25
401	A121	1000r dk violet	8.00	4.00
		Nos. 398-401 (4)	12.70	8.15

Visit of President Terra of Uruguay.

View of Town of Igarassu A123

1935, July 1

402	A123	200r maroon & brn	.85	.45
403	A123	300r vio & olive brn	.85	.35

Captaincy of Pernambuco founding, 400th anniv.

Types of 1918-29
Thick Laid Paper

Perf. 9½, 11, 12, 12x11

1934-36 Engr. Wmk. 236

404	A72	2000r violet	3.75	.40
405	A89	5000r blue vio ('36)	11.00	.50
406	A72	10000r claret ('36)	8.75	.75
		Nos. 404-406 (3)	23.50	1.65

No. 404 is inscribed "BRASIL CORREIO."

Revolutionist — A124

Bento Gonçalves da Silva — A125

Duke of Caxias A126

1935, Sept. 20 *Perf. 11, 12*

407	A124	200r black	.55	.45
408	A124	300r rose lake	.55	.35
409	A125	700r dull blue	2.25	2.25
410	A126	1000r light violet	2.50	1.40
		Nos. 407-410 (4)	5.85	4.45

Centenary of the "Ragged" Revolution.

Federal District Coat of Arms A127

Wmk. 222

1935, Oct. 19 Typo. *Perf. 11*

411	A127	200r blue	2.25	2.25

8th Intl. Sample Fair held at Rio de Janeiro.

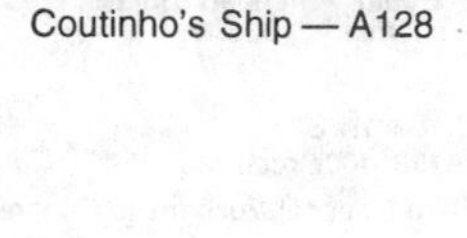

Coutinho's Ship — A128

Arms of Fernandes Coutinho — A129

1935, Oct. 25

412	A128	300r maroon	2.25	1.00
413	A129	700r turq blue	3.25	2.00

400th anniversary of the establishment of the first Portuguese colony at Espirito Santo by Vasco Fernandes Coutinho.

Gavea, Rock near Rio de Janeiro A130

1935, Oct. 12 Wmk. 245 *Perf. 11*

414	A130	300r brown & vio	1.75	1.50
415	A130	300r blk & turq bl	1.75	1.50
416	A130	300r Prus bl & ultra	1.75	1.50
417	A130	300r crimson & blk	1.75	1.50
		Nos. 414-417 (4)	7.00	6.00

"Child's Day," Oct. 12.

Viscount of Cairu — A131

Perf. 11, 12x11

1936, Jan. 20 Engr. Wmk. 236

418	A131	1200r violet	6.00	2.75

Jose da Silva Lisboa, Viscount of Cairu (1756-1835).

View of Cametá A132

1936, Feb. 26 *Perf. 11, 12*

419	A132	200r brown orange	1.25	1.00
420	A132	300r green	1.25	.80

300th anniversary of the founding of the city of Cameta, Dec. 24, 1635.

Coining Press A133

Thick Laid Paper

1936, Mar. 24 *Perf. 11*

421	A133	300r pur brn, *cr*	1.25	.90

1st Numismatic Cong. at Sao Paulo, Mar., 1936.

Carlos Gomes A134

"Il Guarany" — A135

Thick Laid Paper

1936, July 11 *Perf. 11, 11x12*

422	A134	300r dull rose	.50	.35
423	A134	300r black brown	.50	.35
424	A135	700r ocher	2.00	.90
425	A135	700r blue	1.75	.90
		Nos. 422-425 (4)	4.75	2.50

100th anniversary of the birth of Antonio Carlos Gomes, who composed the opera "Il Guarany."

Scales of Justice — A136

Wmk. 222

1936, July 4 Typo. *Perf. 11*

426	A136	300r rose	1.25	.45

First National Judicial Congress.

Federal District Coat of Arms A137

1936, Nov. 13 Typo. Wmk. 249

427	A137	200r rose red	.75	.45

Ninth International Sample Fair held at Rio de Janeiro.

Eucharistic Congress Seal — A138

1936, Dec. 17 Wmk. 245 *Perf. 11½*

428	A138	300r grn, yel, bl & blk	.70	.45

2nd Natl. Eucharistic Congress in Brazil.

Botafogo Bay — A139

Thick Laid Paper

Wmk. 236

1937, Jan. 2 Engr. *Perf. 11*

429	A139	700r blue	.75	.45
430	A139	700r black	.75	.45

Birth cent. of Francisco Pereira Passos, engineer who planned the modern city of Rio de Janeiro.

Types of 1920-21, 1933

Perf. 11, 11½ and Compound

1936-37 Typo. Wmk. 249

431	A75	10r deep brown	.20	.20
432	A75	20r dull violet	.20	.20
433	A75	50r blue green	.20	.20
434	A75	100r orange	.25	.20
435	A116	200r dk violet	.45	.20
436	A76	300r olive green	.25	.20
437	A76	400r ultra	.45	.20
438	A76	500r lt brown	.70	.20
439	A76	600r brn org ('37)	1.50	.20
440	A76	700r deep violet	2.75	.20
441	A76	1000r turq blue	3.00	.20
		Nos. 431-441 (11)	9.95	2.20

Massed Flags and Star of Esperanto A140

1937, Jan. 19

442 A140 300r green 1.00 .50

Ninth Brazilian Esperanto Congress.

Bay of Rio de Janeiro A141

1937, June 9 Unwmk. *Perf. 12½*

443 A141 300r orange red & blk .50 .50
444 A141 700r blue & dk brn 1.25 .50

2nd South American Radio Communication Conf. held in Rio, June 7-19.

Globe — A142

Perf. 11, 12

1937, Sept. 4 Wmk. 249

445 A142 300r green .85 .50

50th anniversary of Esperanto.

Monroe Palace, Rio de Janeiro A143

Botanical Garden, Rio de Janeiro A144

1937, Sept. 30 Unwmk. *Perf. 12½*

446 A143 200r lt brn & bl .50 .35
447 A144 300r org & ol grn .50 .35
448 A143 2000r grn & cerise 3.75 5.50
449 A144 10000r lake & indigo 32.50 27.50
Nos. 446-449 (4) 37.25 33.70

Brig. Gen. Jose da Silva Paes — A145

Eagle and Shield — A146

1937, Oct. 11 Wmk. 249 *Perf. 11½*

450 A145 300r blue .75 .30

Bicentenary of Rio Grande do Sul.

1937, Dec. 2 Typo. *Perf. 11*

451 A146 400r dark blue .75 .30

150th anniversary of the US Constitution.

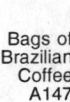

Bags of Brazilian Coffee A147

Frame Engraved, Center Typographed

1938, Jan. 17 Unwmk. *Perf. 12½*

452 A147 1200r multicolored 3.00 .40

Arms of Olinda A148

Perf. 11, 11x11½

1938, Jan. 24 Engr. Wmk. 249

453 A148 400r violet .50 .25

4th cent. of the founding of the city of Olinda.

Independence Memorial, Ypiranga — A149

1938, Jan. 24 Typo. *Perf. 11*

454 A149 400r brown olive .60 .25

Proclamation of Brazil's independence by Dom Pedro, Sept. 7, 1822.

Iguaçu Falls — A150

Perf. 12½

1938, Jan. 10 Unwmk. Engr.

455 A150 1000r sepia & yel brn 1.50 .75
456 A150 5000r ol blk & grn 17.00 7.50

Couto de Magalhaes — A151

Perf. 11, 11x11½

1938, Mar. 17 Wmk. 249

457 A151 400r dull green .50 .25

General Couto de Magalhaes (1837-1898), statesman, soldier, explorer, writer, developer.

Types of 1918-38

Perf. 11, 12x11, 12x11½, 12

1938 Engr. Wmk. 249

458 A72 2000r blue violet 6.50 .20
459 A89 5000r violet blue 24.00 .50
a. 5000r deep blue 20.00 .50
460 A72 10000r rose lake 27.50 1.00
Nos. 458-460 (3) 58.00 1.70

No. 458 is inscribed "BRASIL CORREIO."

Types of 1920-22

1938 Wmk. 245 Typo. *Perf. 11*

461 A75 50r blue green .50 .75
462 A75 100r orange .50 .75
463 A76 300r olive green .50 .20
463A A76 400r ultra 100.00 35.00
463B A76 500r red brown .50 *10.00*
Nos. 461-463B (5) 102.00 46.70

National Archives Building A152

1938, May 20 Wmk. 249

464 A152 400r brown .40 .25

Centenary of National Archives.

Souvenir Sheets

Sir Rowland Hill A153

1938, Oct. 22 *Imperf.*

465 A153 Sheet of 10 12.50 12.50
a. 400r dull green, single stamp .75 .75

Brazilian Intl. Philatelic Exposition (Brapex).

Issued in sheets measuring 106x118mm. A few perforated sheets exist.

President Vargas A154

1938, Nov. 10 *Perf. 11*

Without Gum

466 A154 Sheet of 10 5.00 8.50
a. 400r slate blue, single stamp .40 .40

Constitution of Brazil, set up by President Vargas, Nov. 10, 1937. Size: 113x135½mm.

Types of 1920-33

1939 Typo. Wmk. 256 *Perf. 11*

467 A75 10r red brown .30 .25
468 A75 20r dull violet .30 .20
469 A75 50r blue green .30 .20
470 A75 100r yellow org .45 .20
471 A116 200r dk violet .55 .20
472 A76 400r ultra 1.00 .20
473 A76 600r dull orange 1.00 .20
474 A76 1000r turq blue 7.00 .20
Nos. 467-474 (8) 10.90 1.65

View of Rio de Janeiro — A155

View of Santos — A156

1939, June 14 Engr. Wmk. 249

475 A155 1200r dull violet 1.25 .25

1939, Aug. 23

476 A156 400r dull blue .40 .20

Centenary of founding of Santos.

Chalice Vine and Blossoms A157

Eucharistic Congress Seal A158

1939, Aug. 23

477 A157 400r green 1.00 .25

1st South American Botanical Congress held in January, 1938.

1939, Sept. 3

478 A158 400r rose red .40 .20

Third National Eucharistic Congress.

Duke of Caxias, Army Patron — A159

1939, Sept. 12 Photo. *Rouletted*

479 A159 400r deep ultra .40 .25

Issued for Soldiers' Day.

A159a

A159b

A159d

A159c

Designs: 400r, George Washington. 800r, Emperor Pedro II. 1200r, Grover Cleveland. 1600r, Statue of Friendship, given by US.

Unwmk.

1939, Oct. 7 Engr. *Perf. 12*

480 A159a 400r yellow orange .40 .25
481 A159b 800r dark green .25 .20
482 A159c 1200r rose car .50 .20
483 A159d 1600r dark blue .50 .25
Nos. 480-483 (4) 1.65 .90

New York World's Fair.

Benjamin Constant A160

Fonseca on Horseback A161

Manuel Deodoro da Fonseca and President Vargas — A162

Wmk. 249

1939, Nov. 15 Photo. *Rouletted*

484 A160 400r deep green .30 .20
485 A162 1200r chocolate .75 .30

Engr. *Perf. 11*

486 A161 800r gray black .45 .30
Nos. 484-486 (3) 1.50 .80

50th anniv. of the Proclamation of the Republic.

President Roosevelt, President Vargas and Map of the Americas
A163

1940, Apr. 14

487	A163	400r slate blue	.70	.40

Pan American Union, 50th anniversary.

Types of 1920-33

1940-41 Typo. Wmk. 264 *Perf. 11*

488	A75	10r red brown	.20	.25
489	A75	20r dull violet	.25	.25
489A	A75	50r blue grn ('41)	.85	*1.25*
490	A75	100r yellow org	1.00	.20
491	A116	200r violet	.75	.20
492	A76	400r ultra	4.50	.20
493	A76	600r dull orange	4.50	.20
494	A76	1000r turq blue	11.00	.20
		Nos. 488-494 (8)	23.05	*2.75*

Map of Brazil — A164

1940, Sept. 7 Engr.

495	A164	400r carmine	.40	.20
a.		Unwmkd.	50.00	30.00

9th Brazilian Congress of Geography held at Florianopolis.

Victoria Regia Water Lily — A165

President Vargas — A166

Relief Map of Brazil — A167

1940, Oct. 30 Wmk. 249 *Perf. 11*
Without Gum

496	A165	1000r dull violet	.85	.85
a.		Sheet of 10	8.50	*25.00*
497	A166	5000r red	6.75	5.00
a.		Sheet of 10	72.50	*110.00*
498	A167	10,000r slate blue	7.50	2.50
a.		Sheet of 10	100.00	110.00
		Nos. 496-498 (3)	15.10	8.35

New York World's Fair.

All three sheets exist unwatermarked and also with papermaker's watermark of large globe and "AMERICA BANK" in sheet. A few imperforate sheets also exist.

Joaquim Machado de Assis — A168

Pioneers and Buildings of Porto Alegre — A169

1940, Nov. 1

499	A168	400r black	.50	.20

Birth centenary of Joaquim Maria Machado de Assis, poet and novelist.

1940, Nov. 2 Wmk. 264

500	A169	400r green	.40	.20

Colonization of Porto Alegre, bicent.

Proclamation of King John IV of Portugal — A173

1940, Dec. 1 Wmk. 249

501	A173	1200r blue black	1.00	.25

800th anniv. of Portuguese independence and 300th anniv. of the restoration of the monarchy.

No. 501 was also printed on paper with papermaker's watermark of large globe and "AMERICA BANK." Unwatermarked copies are from these sheets.

Brazilian Flags and Head of Liberty — A175

Wmk. 256
1940, Dec. 18 Engr. *Perf. 11*

502	A175	400r dull violet	.50	.20
b.		Unwmkd.	40.00	40.00

Wmk. 245

502A	A175	400r dull violet	40.00	40.00

10th anniv. of the inauguration of President Vargas.

Calendar Sheet and Inscription "Day of the Fifth General Census of Brazil" — A176

Wmk. 256
1941, Jan. 14 Typo. *Perf. 11*

503	A176	400r blue & red	.40	.20

Wmk. 245

504	A176	400r blue & red	3.00	.80

Fifth general census of Brazil.

King Alfonso Henriques
A177

Father Antonio Vieira
A178

Salvador Corrêia de Sa e Benevides — A179

President Carmona of Portugal and President Vargas
A180

Wmk. 264
1940-41 Photo. *Rouletted*

504A	A177	200r pink	.20	.20
505	A178	400r ultra	.20	.20
506	A179	800r brt violet	.25	.20
506A	A180	5400r slate grn	1.65	.70

Wmk. 249

507	A177	200r pink	5.25	3.25
507A	A178	400r ultra	25.00	8.50
508	A180	5400r slate grn	2.50	1.25
		Nos. 504A-508 (7)	35.05	14.30

Portuguese Independence, 800th anniv.

For surcharge and overprint see Nos. C45, C47.

Jose de Anchieta
A181

Amador Bueno
A182

Wmk. 264
1941, Aug. 1 Engr. *Perf. 11*

509	A181	1000r gray violet	1.00	.50

Society of Jesus, 400th anniversary.

1941, Oct. 20 *Perf. 11½*

510	A182	400r black	.50	.30

300th anniv. of the acclamation of Amador Bueno (1572-1648) as king of Sao Paulo.

Air Force Emblem
A183

1941, Oct. 20 *Perf. 11*

511	A183	5400r slate green	3.00	2.00

Issued in connection with Aviation Week, as propaganda for the Brazilian Air Force.

Petroleum
A184

Agriculture
A185

Steel Industry
A186

Commerce
A187

Marshal Peixoto — A188

Count of Porto Alegre — A189

Admiral J. A. C. Maurity — A190

"Armed Forces" — A191

Vargas — A192

1941-42 Wmk. 264 Typo. *Perf. 11*

512	A184	10r yellow brn	.20	.20
513	A184	20r olive grn	.20	.20
514	A184	50r olive bis	.20	.20
515	A184	100r blue grn	.20	.20
516	A185	200r brown org	.45	.20
517	A185	300r lilac rose	.25	.20
518	A185	400r grnsh blue	.65	.20
519	A185	500r salmon	.30	.20
520	A186	600r violet	.65	.20
521	A186	700r brt rose	.30	.20
522	A186	1000r gray	1.75	.20
523	A186	1200r dl blue	3.00	.20
524	A187	2000r gray vio	2.50	.20

Engr.

525	A188	5000r blue	5.50	.20
526	A189	10,000r rose red	7.00	.20
527	A190	20,000r dp brown	7.00	.35
528	A191	50,000r red ('42)	27.50	21.00
529	A192	100,000r blue ('42)	.60	*9.00*
		Nos. 512-529 (18)	58.25	33.35

Nos. 512 to 527 and later issues come on thick or thin paper. The stamps on both papers also exist with three vertical green lines printed on the back, a control mark.

See Nos. 541-587, 592-593, 656-670.

Bernardino de Campos
A193

Prudente de Morais
A194

1942, May 25

533	A193	1000r red	1.25	.40
534	A194	1200r blue	3.00	.25

100th anniversary of the birth of Bernardino de Campos and Prudente de Morais, lawyers and statesmen of Brazil.

Head of Indo-Brazilian Bull — A195

1942, May 1 Wmk. 264 *Perf. 11½*

535	A195	200r blue	.45	.25
536	A195	400r orange brn	.45	.25
a.		Wmk. 267	45.00	45.00

2nd Agriculture and Livestock Show of Central Brazil held at Uberaba.

Outline of Brazil and Torch of Knowledge
A196

Map of Brazil Showing Goiania
A197

Wmk. 264

1942, July 5 Typo. *Perf. 11*

537 A196 400r orange brn .30 .25

8th Brazilian Congress of Education.

1942, July 5

538 A197 400r lt violet .40 .30

Founding of Goiania city.

Seal of Congress
A198

1942, Sept. 20 Wmk. 264

539 A198 400r olive bister .25 .20
a. Wmk. 267 25.00 12.50

4th Natl. Eucharistic Cong. at Sao Paulo.

Types of 1941-42

1942-47 Wmk. 245 *Perf. 11*

541	A184	20r olive green	.20	.40
542	A184	50r olive bister	.20	.20
543	A184	100r blue grn	.40	.40
544	A185	200r brown org	.65	.50
545	A185	400r grnsh blue	.40	.20
546	A186	600r lt violet	3.00	.20
547	A186	700r brt rose	.35	.80
548	A186	1200r dl blue	1.25	.20
549	A187	2000r gray vio ('47)	9.00	9.00
		Engr.		
550	A188	5000r blue	10.00	.40
551	A189	10,000r rose red	6.00	1.50
552	A190	20,000r dp brn ('47)	4.50	.45
553	A192	100,000r blue	3.50	8.00
		Nos. 541-553 (13)	39.45	22.25

Types of 1941-42

1941-47 Typo. Wmk. 268 *Perf. 11*

554	A184	20r olive grn	.20	.20
555	A184	50r ol bis ('47)	.55	.55
556	A184	100r bl grn ('43)	.20	.20
557	A185	200r brn org ('43)	.20	.20
558	A185	300r lilac rose ('43)	.20	.20
559	A185	400r grnsh bl ('42)	.30	.20
560	A185	500r salmon ('43)	.20	.20
561	A186	600r violet	.60	.20
562	A186	700r brt rose ('45)	.35	*1.75*
563	A186	1000r gray	.65	.20
564	A186	1200r dp blue ('44)	.85	.20
565	A187	2000r gray vio ('43)	3.00	.20
		Engr.		
566	A188	5000r blue ('43)	4.25	.20
567	A189	10,000r rose red ('43)	8.50	.40
568	A190	20,000r dp brn ('42)	19.00	.45
569	A191	50,000r red ('42)	21.00	3.00
a.		50,000r dark brown red ('47)	15.00	8.50
570	A192	100,000r blue	.55	.55
		Nos. 554-570 (17)	60.60	8.90

Types of 1941-42

1942-47 Typo. Wmk. 267

573	A184	20r ol grn ('43)	.20	.20
574	A184	50r ol bis ('43)	.20	.20
575	A184	100r bl grn ('43)	.20	.20
576	A185	200r brn org ('43)	.25	.25
577	A185	400r grnsh blue	.25	.20
578	A185	500r sal ('43)	70.00	10.00
579	A186	600r violet ('43)	.45	.30
580	A186	700r brt rose ('47)	.35	*3.50*
581	A186	1000r gray ('44)	2.10	.20
582	A186	1200r dl bl	2.50	.20
583	A187	2000r gray vio	2.50	.20
		Engr.		
584	A188	5000r blue	4.25	.20
585	A189	10,000r rose red ('44)	7.00	.60
586	A190	20,000r dp brn ('45)	8.50	.45
587	A191	50,000r red ('43)	25.00	5.25
		Nos. 573-587 (15)	123.75	21.95

1942 Typo. Wmk. 249

592 A184 100r bl grn 4.00 2.50
593 A186 600r violet 4.00 .80

Map Showing Amazon River — A199

1943, Mar. 19 Wmk. 267 *Perf. 11*

607 A199 40c orange brown .35 .35

Discovery of the Amazon River, 400th anniv.

Reproduction of Brazil Stamp of 1866 — A200

1943, Mar. 28 Wmk. 267

608 A200 40c violet .50 .25
a. Wmk. 268 *650.00*

Centenary of city of Petropolis.

Adaptation of 1843 "Bull's-eye"
A201

1943, Aug. 1 Engr. *Imperf.*

609 A201 30c black .45 .25
610 A201 60c black .55 .25
611 A201 90c black .45 .25
Nos. 609-611 (3) 1.45 .75

Cent. of the 1st postage stamp of Brazil. The 30c and 90c exist unwatermarked; values $25 and $65.

Souvenir Sheet

A202

Wmk. 281 Horizontally or Vertically

1943 Engr. *Imperf.*

Without Gum

612 A202 Sheet of 3 7.50 6.75
a. 30c black 1.90 1.90
b. 60c black 1.90 1.90
c. 90c black 1.90 1.90

Ubaldino do Amaral
A203

"Justice"
A204

Perf. 11, 12

1943, Aug. 27 Typo. Wmk. 264

613 A203 40c dull slate green .40 .20
a. Wmk. 267 20.00 15.00

Birth centenary of Ubaldino do Amaral, banker and statesman.

1943, Aug. 30 Wmk. 267

614 A204 2cr bright rose .70 .40

Centenary of Institute of Brazilian Lawyers.

Indo-Brazilian Bull — A205

1943, Aug. 30 Engr.

615 A205 40c dk red brn .70 .40

9th Livestock Show at Bahia.

José Barbosa Rodrigues
A206

1943, Nov. 13 Typo.

616 A206 40c bluish grn .40 .20

Birth cent. of Jose Barbosa Rodrigues, botanist.

Charity Hospital, Santos
A207

1943, Nov. 7 Engr.

617 A207 1cr blue .40 .30

400th anniv. of Charity Hospital, Santos.

Pedro Americo de Figueirido e Melo (1843-1905), Artist-hero and Statesman — A208

Wmk. 267

1943, Dec. 16 Typo. *Perf. 11*

618 A208 40c brown orange .20 .20

Gen. A. E. Gomes Carneiro
A209

1944, Feb. 9 Engr.

619 A209 1.20cr rose .50 .35

50th anniversary of the Lapa siege.

Statue of Baron of Rio Branco — A210

1944, May 13 Typo.

620 A210 1cr blue .40 .25

Statue of the Baron of Rio Branco unveiling.

Duke of Caxias
A211

1944, May 13 Unwmk. *Perf. 12*

Granite Paper

621 A211 1.20cr bl grn & pale org .50 .30

Centenary of pacification of Sao Paulo and Minas Gerais in an independence movement in 1842.

YMCA Seal — A212

1944, June 7 Litho. *Perf. 11*

Granite Paper

622 A212 40c dp bl, car & yel .30 .20

Centenary of Young Men's Christian Assn.

Chamber of Commerce Rio Grande
A213

Wmk. 268

1944, Sept. 25 Engr. *Perf. 12*

623 A213 40c lt yellow brn .30 .25

Centenary of the Chamber of Commerce of Rio Grande.

Martim F. R. de Andrada
A214

1945, Jan. 30 *Perf. 11*

624 A214 40c blue .30 .25

Ccentenary of the death of Martim F. R. de Andrada, statesman.

Meeting of Duke of Caxias and David Canabarro
A215

1945, Mar. 19 **Photo.**
625 A215 40c ultra .30 .20

Pacification of Rio Grande do Sul, cent.

Globe and "Esperanto"
A216

1945, Apr. 16
626 A216 40c lt blue grn .50 .25

10th Esperanto Congress, Rio, Apr. 14-22.

Baron of Rio Branco's Bookplate — A217

1945, Apr. 20 **Wmk. 268** ***Perf. 11***
627 A217 40c violet .50 .25

Cent. of the birth of Jose Maria da Silva Paranhos, Baron of Rio Branco.

Tranquility
A218

Glory
A219

Victory
A220

Peace
A221

Cooperation
A222

Rouletted 7

1945, May 8 **Engr.** **Wmk. 268**
628 A218 20c dk rose vio .20 .20
629 A219 40c dk carmine .20 .20
630 A220 1cr dull orange .35 .30
631 A221 2cr steel blue .85 .45
632 A222 5cr green 1.65 .55
Nos. 628-632 (5) 3.25 1.70

Victory of the Allied Nations in Europe.
Nos. 628-632 exist on thin card, imperf. and unwatermarked.

Francisco Manoel da Silva (1795-1865), Composer (in 1831) of the National Anthem — A223

Wmk. 245

1945, May 30 **Typo.** ***Perf. 12***
633 A223 40c brt rose .45 .30
a. Wmk. 268 6.75 6.75

Bahia Institute of Geography and History
A224

1945, May 30 **Wmk. 268** ***Perf. 11***
634 A224 40c lt ultra .25 .20

50th anniv. of the founding of the Institute of Geography and History at Bahia.

Emblems of 5th Army and B.E.F.
A225 A226

US Flag and Shoulder Patches
A227

Brazilian Flag and Shoulder Patches
A228

Victory Symbol and Shoulder Patches — A229

1945, July 18 **Litho.**
635 A225 20c multicolored .20 .20
636 A226 40c multicolored .20 .20
637 A227 1cr multicolored .70 .40
638 A228 2cr multicolored 1.00 .60
639 A229 5cr multicolored 3.00 .70
Nos. 635-639 (5) 5.10 2.10

Honoring the Brazilian Expeditionary Force and the US 5th Army Battle against the Axis in Italy.

Radio Tower and Map — A230

1945, Sept. 3 **Engr.**
640 A230 1.20cr gray .45 .25

Third Inter-American Conference on Radio Communications.
No. 640 was reproduced on a souvenir card with blue background and inscriptions. Size: 145x161mm.

A 40c lilac stamp, picturing the International Bridge between Argentina and Brazil and portraits of Presidents Justo and Vargas, was prepared late in 1945. It was not issued, but later was sold, without postal value, to collectors. Value, 15 cents.

Admiral Luiz Felipe Saldanha da Gama (1846-1895)
A231

1946, Apr. 7
641 A231 40c gray black .25 .25

Princess Isabel d'Orleans-Braganca Birth Cent. — A232

1946, July 29 **Unwmk.**
642 A232 40c black .25 .25

Post Horn, V and Envelope — A233

Post Office, Rio de Janeiro
A234

Bay of Rio de Janeiro and Plane
A235

Wmk. 268

1946, Sept. 2 **Litho.** ***Perf. 11***
643 A233 40c blk & pale org .20 .20

Perf. 12½

Engr. **Unwmk.**

Center in Ultramarine

644 A234 2cr slate .50 .20
645 A234 5cr orange brn 2.50 .85
646 A234 10cr dk violet 2.75 .50

Center in Brown Orange

647 A235 1.30cr dk green .30 .35
648 A235 1.70cr car rose .30 .35
649 A235 2.20cr dp ultra .50 .50
Nos. 643-649 (7) 7.05 2.95

5th Postal Union Congress of the Americas and Spain.
No. 643 was reproduced on a souvenir card. Size: 188x239mm. Sold for 10cr.

Liberty — A236

Perf. 11x11½

1946, Sept. 18 **Wmk. 268**
650 A236 40c blk & gray .25 .20
a. Unwmkd. 150.00

Adoption of the Constitution of 1946.

Columbus Lighthouse, Dominican Republic
A237

1946, Sept. 14 **Litho.** ***Perf. 11***
651 A237 5cr Prus grn 4.00 1.50

Orchid
A238

Gen. A. E. Gomes Carneiro
A239

1946, Nov. 8 **Wmk. 268**
652 A238 40c ultra, red & yel .40 .30
a. Unwmkd. 55.00

4th National Exhibition of Orchids, Rio de Janeiro, November, 1946.

Perf. 10½x12

1946, Dec. 6 **Engr.** **Unwmk.**
653 A239 40c deep green .20 .20

Centenary of the birth of Gen. Antonio Ernesto Gomes Carneiro.

Brazilian Academy of Letters
A240

1946, Dec. 14 ***Perf. 11***
654 A240 40c blue .25 .20

50th anniv. of the foundation of the Brazilian Academy of Letters, Rio de Janeiro.

Antonio de Castro Alves (1847-1871), Poet — A241

1947, Mar. 14 **Litho.** **Wmk. 267**
655 A241 40c bluish green .20 .20

Types of 1941-42, Values in Centavos or Cruzeiros

1947-54 **Wmk. 267** **Typo.** ***Perf. 11***
656 A184 2c olive .20 .20
657 A184 5c yellow brn .20 .20
658 A184 10c green .20 .20
659 A185 20c brown org .20 .20
660 A185 30c dk lilac rose .60 .20
661 A185 40c blue .30 .20
b. Wmk. 268 800.00 60.00
661A A185 50c salmon .60 .20
662 A186 60c lt violet 1.00 .20
663 A186 70c brt rose ('54) .40 .20
664 A186 1cr gray 1.00 .20
665 A186 1.20cr dull blue 2.50 .20
a. Wmk. 268 11.00 9.00
666 A187 2cr gray violet 4.00 .20

Engr.

667 A188 5cr blue 7.50 .20
668 A189 10cr rose red 7.50 .20

Perf. 11, 13

669 A190 20cr deep brown 15.00 .75
670 A191 50cr red 30.00 .50
Nos. 656-670 (16) 71.20 4.05

The 5, 20, 50cr also exist with perf. 12-13.

Pres. Gonzalez Videla of Chile A242

1947, June 26 Unwmk. *Perf. 12x11*
671 A242 40c dk brown orange .20 .20

Visit of President Gabriel Gonzalez Videla of Chile, June 1947.

A souvenir folder contains four impressions of No. 671, and measures 6½x8¼ inches.

"Peace" and Western Hemisphere — A243

1947, Aug. 15 *Perf. 11x12*
672 A243 1.20cr blue .20 .20

Inter-American Defense Conference at Rio de Janeiro, August-September, 1947.

Pres. Harry S Truman, Map and Statue of Liberty A244

1947, Sept. 1 Typo. *Perf. 12x11*
673 A244 40c ultra .20 .20

Visit of US President Harry S Truman to Brazil, Sept. 1947.

Pres. Eurico Gaspar Dutra — A245

Mother and Child — A246

Wmk. 268

1947, Sept. 7 Engr. *Perf. 11*
674 A245 20c green .20 .20
675 A245 40c rose carmine .20 .20
676 A245 1.20cr deep blue .25 .20
Nos. 674-676 (3) .65 .60

The souvenir sheet containing Nos. 674-676 is listed as No. C73A. See No. 679.

1947, Oct. 10 Typo. Unwmk.
677 A246 40c brt ultra .20 .20

Issued to mark Child Care Week, 1947.

> ***20-Cent Minimum Value***
> *The minimum value for a single stamp is 20 cents. This value reflects the costs of handling inexpensive stamps.*

Arms of Belo Horizonte A247

Globe A248

1947, Dec. 12 Engr. Wmk. 267
678 A247 1.20cr rose carmine .30 .20

50th anniversary of the founding of the city of Belo Horizonte.

Dutra Type of 1947

1948 Engr. Wmk. 267
679 A245 20c green 1.50 1.50

> **Catalogue values for unused stamps in this section, from this point to the end of the section, are for Never Hinged items.**

1948, July 10 Litho.
680 A248 40c dl grn & pale lil .35 .20

International Exposition of Industry and Commerce, Petropolis, 1948.

Arms of Paranagua A249

Child Reading Book A250

1948, July 29
681 A249 5cr bister brown 1.75 .50

300th anniversary of the founding of the city of Paranagua, July 29, 1648.

1948, Aug. 1
682 A250 40c green .25 .20

National Education Campaign.

No. 682 was reproduced on a souvenir card. Size: 124x157mm.

Tiradentes A251

Symbolical of Cancer Eradication A252

1948, Nov. 12
683 A251 40c brown orange .25 .20

200th anniversary of the birth of Joaquim José da Silva Xavier (Tiradentes).

1948, Dec. 14
684 A252 40c claret .25 .25

Anti-cancer publicity.

Adult Student A253

1949, Jan. 3 Wmk. 267 *Perf. 12x11*
685 A253 60c red vio & pink .25 .20

Campaign for adult education.

"Battle of Guararapes," by Vitor Meireles — A254

1949, Feb. 15 *Perf. 11½x12*
686 A254 60c lt blue .95 .60

2nd Battle of Guararapes, 300th anniv.

Church of Sao Francisco de Paula A255

Manuel de Nobrega A256

Perf. 11x12

1949, Mar. 8 Unwmk. Engr.
687 A255 60c dark brown .20 .20
a. Souvenir sheet 30.00 30.00

Bicentenary of city of Ouro Fino, state of Minas Gerais.

No. 687a contains one imperf. stamp similar to No. 687, with dates in lower margin. Size: 70x89mm.

1949, Mar. 29 *Imperf.*
688 A256 60c violet .25 .25

Founding of the City of Salvador, 400th anniv.

Emblem of Brazilian Air Force and Plane A257

1949, June 18
689 A257 60c blue violet .25 .25

Issued to honor the Brazilian Air Force.

Star and Angel — A258

1949 Wmk. 267 Litho. *Perf. 11x12*
690 A258 60c pink .20 .20

1st Ecclesiastical Cong., Salvador, Bahia.

Globe A259

1949, Oct. 31 Typo. *Perf. 12x11*
691 A259 1.50cr blue .25 .20

75th anniv. of the UPU.

Ruy Barbosa A260

Unwmk.

1949, Dec. 14 Engr. *Perf. 12*
692 A260 1.20cr rose carmine .65 .30

Centenary of birth of Ruy Barbosa.

Joaquim Cardinal Arcoverde A. Cavalcanti, Birth Centenary — A261

Perf. 11x12

1950, Feb. 27 Litho. Wmk. 267
693 A261 60c rose .25 .20

Grapes and Factory A262

1950, Mar. 15 *Perf. 12x11*
694 A262 60c rose lake .25 .20

75th anniversary of Italian immigration to the state of Rio Grande do Sul.

Virgin of the Globe — A263

Globe and Soccer Players — A264

1950, May 31 *Perf. 11x12*
695 A263 60c blk & lt bl .25 .20

Establishment in Brazil of the Daughters of Charity of St. Vincent de Paul, cent.

1950, June 24
696 A264 60c ultra, bl & gray .85 .50

4th World Soccer Championship.

Symbolical of Brazilian Population Growth A265

1950, July 10 Typo. *Perf. 12x11*
697 A265 60c rose lake .25 .20

Issued to publicize the 6th Brazilian census.

Dr. Oswaldo Cruz — A266

1950, Aug. 23 Litho. *Perf. 11x12*

698 A266 60c orange brown .25 .20

5th International Congress of Microbiology.

View of Blumenau and Itajai River A267

Perf. 12x11

1950, Sept. 9 Wmk. 267

699 A267 60c bright pink .25 .20

Centenary of the founding of Blumenau.

Amazonas Theater, Manaus A268

1950, Sept. 27

700 A268 60c light brn red .20 .20

Centenary of Amazonas Province.

Arms of Juiz de Fora — A269

1950, Oct. 24 *Perf. 11x12*

701 A269 60c carmine .25 .25

Centenary of the founding of Juiz de Fora.

Post Office at Recife A270

1951, Jan. 10 Typo. *Perf. 12x11*

702 A270 60c carmine .20 .20

703 A270 1.20cr carmine .30 .20

Opening of the new building of the Pernambuco Post Office.

Arms of Joinville — A271

Jean-Baptiste de La Salle — A272

1951, Mar. 9 *Perf. 11x12*

704 A271 60c orange brown .25 .20

Centenary of the founding of Joinville.

1951, Apr. 30 Litho.

705 A272 60c blue .25 .20

Birth of Jean-Baptiste de La Salle, 300th anniv.

Heart and Flowers A273

Sylvio Romero A274

1951, May 13 Engr.

706 A273 60c deep plum .25 .20

Mother's Day, May 14, 1951.

1951, Apr. 21 Litho.

707 A274 60c dl vio brn .20 .20

Romero (1851-1914), poet and author.

Joao Caetano, Stage and Masks A275

1951, July 9 *Perf. 12x11*

708 A275 60c lt gray bl .25 .20

1st Brazilian Theater Cong., Rio, July 9-13, 1951.

Orville A. Derby — A276

First Mass Celebrated in Brazil — A277

1951, July 23 *Perf. 11x12*

709 A276 2cr slate .35 .35

Centenary of the birth (in New York State) of Orville A. Derby, geologist.

1951, July 25

710 A277 60c dl brn & buff .20 .20

4th Inter-American Congress on Catholic Education, Rio de Janeiro, 1951.

Euclides Pinto Martins A278

1951, Aug. 16 *Perf. 12x11*

711 A278 3.80cr brn & citron 1.50 .35

1st flight from NYC to Rio, 29th anniv.

Monastery of the Rock A279

1951, Sept. 8

712 A279 60c dl brn & cream .20 .20

Founding of Vitoria, 4th centenary.

Santos-Dumont and Model Plane Contest A280

Dirigible and Eiffel Tower A281

Perf. 11x12

1951, Oct. 19 Wmk. 267 Litho.

713 A280 60c salmon & dk brn .42 .35

Unwmk. Engr.

714 A281 3.80cr dk pur 1.25 .40

Week of the Wing and 50th anniv. of Santos-Dumont's flight around the Eiffel Tower.

In December 1951, Nos. 713 and 714 were privately overprinted: "Exposicao Filatelica Regional Distrito Federal 15-XII-1951 23-XII-1951." These were attached to souvenir sheets bearing engraved facsimiles of Nos. 38, 49 and 51, which were sold by Clube Filatelico do Brasil to mark its 20th anniversary. The overprinted stamps on the sheets were canceled, but 530 "unused" sets were sold by the club.

Farmers and Ear of Wheat — A282

1951, Nov. 10 Litho. Wmk. 267

715 A282 60c dp grn & gray .25 .25

Festival of Grain at Bage, 1951.

Map and Open Bible A283

1951, Dec. 9 *Perf. 12x11*

716 A283 1.20cr brn org .50 .35

Issued to publicize the Day of the Bible.

Queen Isabella A284

Henrique Oswald A285

1952, Mar. 10 *Perf. 11x12*

717 A284 3.80cr lt bl .60 .30

500th anniversary of the birth of Queen Isabella I of Spain.

1952, Apr. 22

718 A285 60c brown .25 .20

Oswald (1852-1931), composer.

Vicente Licinio Cardoso A286

Map and Symbol of Labor A287

1952, May 2

719 A286 60c gray bl .25 .20

4th Brazilian Homeopathic Congress.

1952, Apr. 30

720 A287 1.50cr brnsh pink .25 .20

5th International Labor Organization Conference for American Countries.

Gen. Polidoro da Fonseca A288

Luiz de Albuquerque M. P. Caceres A289

Portraits: 5cr, Baron de Capanema. 10cr, Minister Eusebio de Queiros.

Unwmk.

1952, May 11 Engr. *Perf. 11*

721 A288 2.40cr lt car .35 .20

722 A288 5cr blue 2.25 .30

723 A288 10cr dk bl grn 2.25 .30

Nos. 721-723 (3) 4.85 .80

Centenary of telegraph in Brazil.

Perf. 11x12

1952, June 8 Litho. Wmk. 267

724 A289 1.20cr vio bl .25 .20

200th anniversary of the founding of the city of Mato Grosso.

Symbolizing the Glory of Sports A290

1952, July 21 *Perf. 12x11*

725 A290 1.20cr dp bl & bl .60 .40

Fluminense Soccer Club, 50th anniversary.

José Antonio Saraiva
A291

Emperor Dom Pedro
A292

1952, Aug. 16 *Perf. 11x12*

726 A291 60c lil rose .25 .20

Centenary of the founding of Terezina, capital of Piaui State.

1952, Sept. 3 **Wmk. 267**

727 A292 60c lt bl & blk .25 .20

Issued for Stamp Day and the 2nd Philatelic Exhibition of Sao Paulo.

Flag-encircled Globe — A293

1952, Oct. 24 *Perf. 13½*

728 A293 3.80cr blue .85 .50

Issued to publicize United Nations Day.

View of Sao Paulo, Sun and Compasses
A294

1952, Nov. 8 **Litho.** *Perf. 12x11*

729 A294 60c dl bl, yel & gray grn .25 .20

City Planning Day.

Father Diogo Antonio Feijo — A295

1952, Nov. 9 *Perf. 11x12*

730 A295 60c fawn .25 .20

Rodolpho Bernardelli and His "Christ and the Adultress"
A297

1952, Dec. 18 *Perf. 12x11*

732 A297 60c gray bl .25 .20

Bernardelli, sculptor and painter, birth cent.

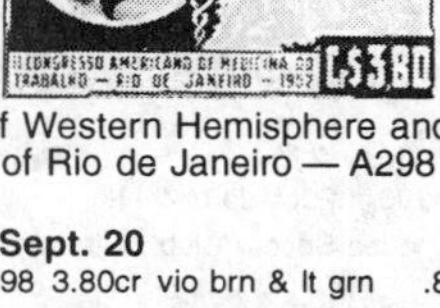

Map of Western Hemisphere and View of Rio de Janeiro — A298

1952, Sept. 20

733 A298 3.80cr vio brn & lt grn .80 .30

2nd Congress of American Industrial Medicine, Rio de Janeiro, 1952.

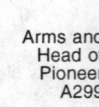

Arms and Head of Pioneer
A299

Coffee, Cotton and Sugar Cane — A300

Designs: 2.80cr, Jesuit monk planting tree. 3.80cr and 5.80cr, Spiral, symbolizing progress.

1953, Jan. 25 **Litho.** *Perf. 11*

734 A299 1.20cr ol brn & blk brn .52 .35
735 A300 2cr olive grn & yel 1.75 .35
736 A300 2.80cr red brn & dp org 1.20 .20
737 A300 3.80cr dk brn & yel grn 1.00 .20
738 A300 5.80cr int bl & yel grn .70 .20
Nos. 734-738 (5) 5.17 1.30

400th anniversary of Sao Paulo.

Used copies of No. 734 exist with design inverted.

Ledger and Winged Cap — A301

1953, Feb. 22 *Perf. 12x11*

739 A301 1.20cr dl brn & fawn .25 .20

6th Brazilian Accounting Congress.

Joao Ramalho — A302

Wmk. 264

1953, Apr. 8 **Engr.** *Perf. 11½*

740 A302 60c blue .25 .20

Founding of the city of Santo Andre, 4th cent.

Aarao Reis and Plan of Belo Horizonte
A303

1953, May 6 **Photo.**

741 A303 1.20cr red brn .25 .20

Aarao Leal de Carvalho Reis (1853-1936), civil engineer.

A304

A305

1953, May 16

742 A304 1.50cr Almirante Saldanha .40 .25

4th globe-circling voyage of the training ship Almirante Saldanha.

1953, July 5 **Photo.**

Joaquim Jose Rodrigues Torres, Viscount of Itaborai.

743 A305 1.20cr violet .20 .20

Centenary of the Bank of Brazil.

Lamp and Rio-Petropolis Highway — A306

1953, July 14

744 A306 1.20cr gray .25 .20

10th Intl. Congress of Nursing, Petropolis, 1953.

Bay of Rio de Janeiro
A307

1953, July 15

745 A307 3.80cr dk bl grn .40 .20

Issued to publicize the fourth World Congress of Baptist Youth, July 1953.

Arms of Jau and Map — A308

1953, Aug. 15 **Engr.**

746 A308 1.20cr purple .25 .20

Centenary of the city of Jau.

Ministry of Health and Education Building, Rio
A309

Maria Quiteria de Jesus Medeiros
A310

1953, Aug. 1

747 A309 1.20cr dp grn .25 .20

Day of the Stamp and the first Philatelic Exhibition of National Education.

1953, Aug. 21 **Photo.**

748 A310 60c vio bl .25 .20

Centenary of the death of Maria Quiteria de Jesus Medeiros (1792-1848), independence heroine.

Pres. Odria of Peru — A311

Duke of Caxias Leading his Troops — A312

1953, Aug. 25

749 A311 1.40cr rose brn .25 .20

Issued to publicize the visit of Gen. Manuel A. Odria, President of Peru, Aug. 25, 1953.

Engr. (60c, 5.80cr); Photo.

1953, Aug. 25

Designs: 1.20cr, Caxias' tomb. 1.70cr, 5.80cr, Portrait of Caxias. 3.80cr, Arms of Caxias.

750 A312 60c dp grn .30 .20
751 A312 1.20cr dp claret .40 .20
752 A312 1.70cr slate grn .40 .20
753 A312 3.80cr rose brn .65 .20
754 A312 5.80cr gray vio .65 .20
Nos. 750-754 (5) 2.40 1.00

150th anniversary of the birth of Luis Alves de Lima e Silva, Duke of Caxias.

Quill Pen, Map and Tree — A313

Horacio Hora — A314

1953, Sept. 12 **Photo.**

755 A313 60c ultra .25 .20

5th National Congress of Journalism.

1953, Sept. 17 **Litho.** **Wmk. 267**

756 A314 60c org & dp plum .25 .20

Horacio Pinto de Hora (1853-1890), painter.

Pres. Somoza of Nicaragua
A315

Auguste de Saint-Hilaire
A316

1953, Sept. 24 **Photo.** **Wmk. 264**

757 A315 1.40cr dk vio brn .25 .20

Issued to publicize the visit of Gen. Anastasio Somoza, president of Nicaragua.

1953, Sept. 30

758 A316 1.20cr dk brn car .25 .25

Centenary of the death of Auguste de Saint-Hilaire, explorer and botanist.

Jose Carlos do Patrocinio
A317

Clock Tower, Crato
A318

1953, Oct. 9 **Photo.**

759 A317 60c dk slate gray .25 .20

Jose Carlos do Patrocinio, (1853-1905), journalist and abolitionist.

1953, Oct. 17

760 A318 60c blue green .25 .20

Centenary of the city of Crato.

Joao Capistrano de Abreu
A319

Allegory: "Justice"
A320

1953, Oct. 23

761 A319 60c dull blue .20 .20
762 A319 5cr purple .85 .85

Joao Capistrano de Abreu (1853-1927), historian.

1953, Nov. 17

763 A320 60c indigo .25 .20
764 A320 1.20cr dp magenta .25 .20

50th anniv. of the Treaty of Petropolis.

Farm Worker in Wheat Field — A321

Teacher and Pupils — A322

1953, Nov. 29 **Photo.** ***Perf. 11½***

766 A321 60c dk green .25 .20

3rd Natl. Wheat Festival, Erechim, 1953.

1953, Dec. 14

767 A322 60c red .25 .25

First National Conference of Primary School Teachers, Salvador, 1953.

Zacarias de Gois e Vasconsellos
A323

Alexandre de Gusmao
A324

Design: 5cr, Porters with Trays of Coffee Beans.

1953-54 **Photo.**

768 A323 2cr org brn & blk, *buff* ('54) .65 .40
  a. White paper 1.75 .40
769 A323 5cr dp org & blk 1.25 .40

Centenary of the state of Parana.

1954, Jan. 13

770 A324 1.20cr brn vio .25 .20

Gusmao (1695-1753), statesman, diplomat and writer.

Symbolical of Sao Paulo's Growth — A325

Arms and View of Sao Paulo
A326

Designs: 2cr, Priest, settler and Indian. 2.80cr, José de Anchieta.

1954, Jan. 25 ***Perf. 11½x11***

771 A325 1.20cr dk vio brn .75 .50
  a. Buff paper 1.75 1.00

Engr.

772 A325 2cr lilac rose 1.05 .60
773 A325 2.80cr pur gray 1.05 1.00

Perf. 11x11½

774 A326 3.80cr dl grn 1.25 .50
  a. Buff paper 2.25 2.00
775 A326 5.80cr dl red 1.25 .60
  a. Buff paper 5.00 .75
Nos. 771-775 (5) 5.35 3.20

400th anniversary of Sao Paulo.

J. Fernandes Vieira, A. Vidal de Negreiros, A. F. Camarao and H. Dias
A327

Perf. 11x11½

1954, Feb. 18 **Photo.** **Unwmk.**

776 A327 1.20cr ultra .25 .25

300th anniversary of the recovery of Pernambuco from the Dutch.

Sao Paulo and Minerva
A328

1954, Feb. 24

777 A328 1.50cr dp plum .25 .25

10th International Congress of Scientific Organizations, Sao Paulo, 1954.

Stylized Grapes, Jug and Map
A329

Monument of the Immigrants
A330

1954, Feb. 27 **Photo.** ***Perf. 11½x11***

778 A329 40c dp claret .25 .20

Grape Festival, Rio Grande do Sul.

1954, Feb. 28

779 A330 60c dp vio bl .25 .20

Unveiling of the Monument to the Immigrants of Caxias do Sul.

First Brazilian Locomotive
A331

Perf. 11x11½

1954, Apr. 30 **Unwmk.**

781 A331 40c carmine .25 .20

Centenary of the first railroad engine built in Brazil.

Pres. Chamoun of Lebanon — A332

1954, May 12 **Photo.** ***Perf. 11½x11***

782 A332 1.50cr maroon .25 .25

Visit of Pres. Camille Chamoun of Lebanon.

Sao Jose College, Rio de Janeiro
A333

J. B. Champagnat Marcelin
A334

Apolonia Pinto
A335

1954, June 6 ***Perf. 11x11½, 11½x11***

783 A333 60c purple .20 .20
784 A334 120cr vio blue .22 .20

50th anniversary of the founding of the Marist Brothers in Brazil.

1954, June 21 **Photo.**

785 A335 1.20cr bright green .20 .20

Apolonia Pinto (1854-1937), actress.

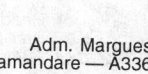

Adm. Margues Tamandare — A336

Portraits: 2c, 5c, 10c, Admiral Margues Tamandare. 20c, 30c, 40c, Oswaldo Cruz. 50c, 60c, 90c, Joaquim Murtinho. 1cr, 1.50cr, 2cr, Duke of Caxias. 5cr, 10cr, Ruy Barbosa. 20cr, 50cr, Jose Bonifacio.

1954-60 **Wmk. 267** ***Perf. 11x11½***

786 A336 2c vio blue .20 .20
787 A336 5c org red .20 .20
788 A336 10c brt green .20 .20
789 A336 20c magenta .20 .20
790 A336 30c dk gray grn .20 .20
791 A336 40c rose red .35 .20
792 A336 50c violet .25 .20
793 A336 60c gray grn .20 .20
794 A336 90c orange ('55) .35 .20
795 A336 1cr brown .20 .20
796 A336 1.50cr blue .20 .20
  a. Wmk. 264 16.00 8.00
797 A336 2cr dk bl grn ('56) .45 .20
798 A336 5cr rose lil ('56) .35 .20
799 A336 10cr lt grn ('60) .90 .20
800 A336 20cr crim rose ('59) .90 .20
801 A336 50cr ultra ('59) 5.50 .20
Nos. 786-801 (16) 10.65 3.20

See Nos. 890, 930-933.

Boy Scout Waving Flag (Statue)
A337

Baltasar Fernandes, Explorer
A338

1954, Aug. 2 **Unwmk.** ***Perf. 11½x11***

802 A337 1.20cr vio bl .40 .25

Intl. Boy Scout Encampment, Sao Paulo.

1954, Aug. 15

803 A338 60c dk red .25 .25

300th anniversary of city of Sorocaba.

Adeodato Giovanni Cardinal Piazza
A339

Our Lady of Aparecida, Map of Brazil
A340

1954, Sept. 2

804 A339 4.20cr red org .50 .35

Visit of Adeodato Cardinal Piazza, papal legate to Brazil.

1954

Design: 1.20cr, Virgin standing on globe.

805 A340 60c claret .30 .30
806 A340 1.20cr vio bl .40 .30

No. 805 was issued for the 1st Cong. of Brazil's Patron Saint (Our Lady of Aparecida); No. 806, the cent. of the proclamation of the dogma of the Immaculate Conception. Both stamps also for the Marian Year.

Issue dates: 60c, Sept. 6; 1.20cr, Sept. 8.

Benjamin Constant and Hand Reading Braille
A341

1954, Sept. 27 Photo. Unwmk.
807 A341 60c dk grn .25 .20

Centenary of the founding of the Benjamin Constant Institute.

River Battle of Riachuelo
A342

Admiral F. M. Barroso
A343

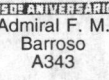

Dr. Christian F. S. Hahnemann
A344

1954, Oct. 6 *Perf. 11x11½, 11½x11*
808 A342 40c redsh brown .30 .20
809 A343 60c purple .20 .20

Admiral Francisco Manoel Barroso da Silva (1804-82).

1954, Oct. 8 *Perf. 11½x11*
810 A344 2.70cr dk green .30 .25

1st World Cong. of Homeopathic Medicine.

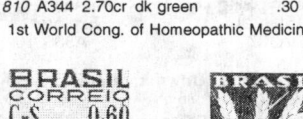

Nizia Floresta
A345

Ears of Wheat
A346

1954, Oct. 12
811 A345 60c lilac rose .25 .20

Reburial of the remains of Nizia Floresta (Dio Nizia Pinto Lisboa), writer and educator.

1954, Oct. 22
812 A346 60c olive green .20 .20

4th National Wheat Festival, Carazinho.

Basketball Player and Ball-Globe
A347

Allegory of the Spring Games
A348

1954, Oct. 23 Photo.
813 A347 1.40cr orange red .30 .30

Issued to publicize the second World Basketball Championship Matches, 1954.

Perf. 11½x11

1954, Nov. 6 Wmk. 267
814 A348 60c red brown .25 .20

Issued to publicize the 6th Spring Games.

San Francisco Hydroelectric Plant — A349

1955, Jan. 15 *Perf. 11x11½*
815 A349 60c brown org .20 .20

Issued to publicize the inauguration of the San Francisco Hydroelectric Plant.

Itutinga Hydroelectric Plant — A350

1955, Feb. 3
816 A350 40c blue .20 .20

Issued to publicize the inauguration of the Itutinga Hydroelectric Plant at Lavras.

Rotary Emblem and Bay of Rio de Janeiro — A351

1955, Feb. 23 *Perf. 12x11½*
817 A351 2.70cr slate gray & blk .85 .25

Rotary International, 50th anniversary.

Fausto Cardoso Palace
A352

1955, Mar. 17 *Perf. 11x11½*
818 A352 40c henna brown .25 .25

Centenary of Aracaju.

Aviation Symbols
A353

1955, Mar. 13 Photo. *Perf. 11½*
819 A353 60c dark gray green .20 .20

Issued to publicize the third National Aviation Congress at Sao Paulo, Mar. 6-13.

Arms of Botucatu
A354

1955, Apr. 14
820 A354 60c orange brn .20 .20
821 A354 1.20cr brt green .25 .20

Centenary of Botucatu.

Young Racers at Starting Line — A355

Perf. 11½

1955, Apr. 30 Photo. Unwmk.
823 A355 60c orange brn .25 .20

5th Children's Games.

Marshal Hermes da Fonseca
A356

Congress Altar, Sail and Sugarloaf Mountain
A357

1955, May 12 Wmk. 267
824 A356 60c purple .20 .20

Marshal Hermes da Fonseca, birth cent.

Engraved; Photogravure (2.70cr)

1955, July 17 Unwmk. *Perf. 11½*

Designs: 2.70cr, St. Pascoal. 4.20cr, Aloisi Benedetto Cardinal Masella.

Granite Paper

825 A357 1.40cr green .20 .20
826 A357 2.70cr deep claret .25 .20
827 A357 4.20cr blue .30 .20
Nos. 825-827 (3) .75 .60

36th World Eucharistic Cong. in Rio de Janeiro.

Girl Gymnasts
A358

1955, Nov. 12 Engr.

Granite Paper

828 A358 60c rose lilac .20 .20

Issued to publicize the 7th Spring Games.

José B. Monteiro Lobato, Author
A359

1955, Dec. 8

Granite Paper

829 A359 40c dark green .20 .20

Adolfo Lutz — A360

Lt. Col. Vilagran Cabrita — A361

1955, Dec. 18

Granite Paper

830 A360 60c dk green .20 .20

Centenary of the birth of Adolfo Lutz, public health pioneer.

1955, Dec. 22 Photo. Wmk. 267
831 A361 60c violet blue .20 .20

First Battalion of Engineers, cent.

Salto Grande Hydroelectric Dam — A362

1956, Jan. 15 Unwmk. *Perf. 11½*

Granite Paper

832 A362 60c brick red .20 .20

Arms of Mococa — A363

"G" and Globe — A364

Wmk. 256

1956, Apr. 17 Photo. *Perf. 11½*
833 A363 60c brick red .20 .20

Centenary of Mococa, Sao Paulo.

1956, Apr. 14 Unwmk.

Granite Paper

834 A364 1.20cr violet blue .20 .20

18th Intl. Geographic Cong., Rio, Aug. 1956.

Girls' Foot Race
A365

1956, Apr. 28 Photo.

Granite Paper

835 A365 2.50cr brt blue .30 .20

6th Children's Games.

Plane over Map of Brazil — A366

1956, June 12 Wmk. 267 *Perf. 11½*
836 A366 3.30cr brt vio bl .40 .20

National Airmail Service, 25th anniv.

Fireman Rescuing Child
A367

1956, July 2 Wmk. 264
837 A367 2.50cr crimson .40 .25
a. Buff paper 2.25 2.00

Centenary of the Fire Brigade.

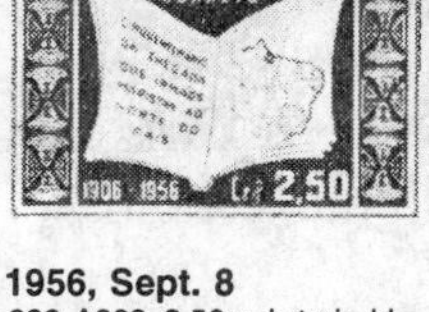

Map of Brazil and Open Book
A368

1956, Sept. 8 Wmk. 267
838 A368 2.50cr brt vio bl .30 .20

50th anniversary of the arrival of the Marist Brothers in Northern Brazil.

Church and Monument, Franca — A369

1956, Sept. 7 **Engr.**
839 A369 2.50cr dk blue .30 .20

Centenary of city of Franca, Sao Paulo.

Woman Hurdler A370

1956, Sept. 22 **Photo.** **Unwmk.**
Granite Paper
840 A370 2.50cr dk car .40 .20

Issued to publicize the 8th Spring Games.

Forest and Map of Brazil — A371

1956, Sept. 30 **Wmk. 267** ***Perf. 11½***
841 A371 2.50cr dk green .25 .20

Issued to publicize education in forestry.

Baron da Bocaina A372

1956, Oct. 8 **Engr.** **Wmk. 268**
842 A372 2.50cr reddish brown .25 .20

Centenary of the birth of Baron da Bocaina, who introduced the special delivery mail system to Brazil.

Marbleized Paper

Paper with a distinct wavy-line or marbleized watermark (which Brazilians call *marmorizado* paper) has been found on many stamps of Brazil, 1956-68, including Nos. 843-845, 847, 851-854, 858-858A, 864, 878, 880, 882, 884, 886-887, 896, 909, 918, 920-921, 925-928, 936-939, 949, 955-958, 960, 962-964, 978-979, 983, 985-987, 997-998, 1002-1003, 1005, 1009-1012, 1017, 1024, 1026, 1055, 1075, 1078, 1082, C82, C82a, C83-C87, C96, C99, C109.

Quantities are much less than those of stamps on regular paper.

Panama Stamp Showing Pres. Juscelino Kubitschek — A373

1956, Oct. 12 **Photo.** **Wmk. 267**
843 A373 3.30cr green & blk .40 .20

Issued on America Day, Oct. 12, to commemorate the meeting of the Presidents and the Pan-American Conference at Panama City, July 21-22.

Symbolical of Steel Production A374

Wmk. 267
1957, Jan. 31 **Photo.** ***Perf. 11½***
844 A374 2.50cr chocolate .25 .20

2nd expansion of the National Steel Company at Volta Redonda.

Joaquim E. Gomes da Silva — A375

1957, Mar. 1 **Photo.** **Unwmk.**
Granite Paper
845 A375 2.50cr dk bl grn .25 .20

Centenary of the birth (in 1856) of Joaquim E. Gomes da Silva.

Allan Kardec A376

Wmk. 268
1957, Apr. 18 **Engr.** ***Perf. 11½***
846 A376 2.50cr dk brown .25 .20

Issued in honor of Allan Kardec, pen name of Leon Hippolyto Denizard Rivail, and for the centenary of the publication of his "Codification of Spiritism."

Boy Gymnast A377

1957, Apr. 27 **Photo.** **Unwmk.**
Granite Paper
847 A377 2.50cr lake .50 .25

7th Children's Games.

Pres. Craveiro Lopes — A378

Stamp of 1932 — A379

1957, June 7 **Engr.** **Wmk. 267**
848 A378 6.50cr blue .40 .20

Visit of Gen. Francisco Higino Craveiro Lopes, President of Portugal.

1957, July 9 **Photo.**
849 A379 2.50cr rose .25 .20

25th anniv. of the movement for a constitution.

St. Antonio Monastery, Pernambuco A380

1957, Aug. 24 **Engr.** **Wmk. 267**
850 A380 2.50cr deep magenta .25 .20

300th anniv. of the emancipation of the Franciscan province of St. Antonio in Pernambuco State.

Volleyball A381

Basketball A382

1957, Sept. 28 **Photo.** ***Perf. 11½***
851 A381 2.50cr dull org red .45 .25

Issued for the 9th Spring Games.

1957, Oct. 12
852 A382 3.30cr org & brt grn .45 .25

2nd Women's International Basketball Championship, Rio de Janeiro.

Count of Pinhal and Sao Carlos A383

1957, Nov. 4 **Wmk. 267** ***Perf. 11½***
853 A383 2.50cr rose .30 .25

Centenary of the city of Sao Carlos and honoring the Count of Pinhal, its founder.

Auguste Comte — A384

1957, Nov. 15
854 A384 2.50cr dk red brn .25 .20

Centenary of the death of Auguste Comte, French mathematician and philosopher.

Radio Station A385

1957, Dec. 10 **Wmk. 268**
855 A385 2.50cr dk green .20 .20

Opening of Sarapui Central Radio Station.

Admiral Tamandare and Warship A386

Design: 3.30cr, Aircraft carrier.

1957-58 **Photo.**
856 A386 2.50cr light blue .25 .20
Engr.
857 A386 3.30cr green ('58) .30 .20

150th anniversary of the birth of Admiral Joaquin Marques de Tamandare, founder of the Brazilian navy.

Coffee Plant and Symbolic "R" — A387

Wmk. 267
1957-58 **Photo.** ***Perf. 11½***
858 A387 2.50cr magenta .50 .35
Unwmk.
Granite Paper
858A A387 2.50cr magenta ('58) .45 .35

Centenary (in 1956) of the city of Ribeirao Preto in Sao Paulo state.

Dom John VI — A388

1958, Jan. 28 **Engr.** **Wmk. 268**
859 A388 2.50cr magenta .35 .25

150th anniversary of the opening of the ports of Brazil to foreign trade.

Bugler A389

1958, Mar. 18 **Wmk. 267**
860 A389 2.50cr red .35 .25

Brazilian Marine Corps, 150th anniv.

Station at Rio and Locomotive of 1858 — A390

Court House — A391

Wmk. 267
1958, Mar. 29 **Photo.** ***Perf. 11½***
861 A390 2.50cr red brn .35 .25

Central Railroad of Brazil, cent.

1958, Apr. 1 **Engr.** **Wmk. 256**
862 A391 2.50cr green .25 .20

150th anniv. of the Military Superior Court.

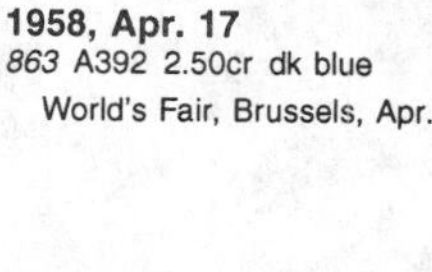

Emblem and Brazilian Pavilion A392

1958, Apr. 17 **Wmk. 267**
863 A392 2.50cr dk blue .25 .25

World's Fair, Brussels, Apr. 17-Oct. 19.

High Jump — A393

1958, Apr. 20 Photo. Unwmk.
Granite Paper

864 A393 2.50cr crimson rose .25 .20

8th Children's Games.

Marshal Mariano da Silva Rondon A394

1958, Apr. 19 Engr. Wmk. 267

865 A394 2.50cr magenta .25 .20

Issued to honor Marshal Mariano da Silva Rondon and the "Day of the Indian."

Hydroelectric Station A395

1958, Apr. 28 Wmk. 267 *Perf. 11½*

866 A395 2.50cr magenta .25 .20

Opening of Sao Paulo State power plant.

National Printing Plant — A396

1958, May 22 Photo.

867 A396 2.50cr redsh brn .20 .20

150th anniversary of the founding of the National Printing Plant.

Marshal Osorio — A397

1958, May 24

868 A397 2.50cr brt violet .20 .20

150th anniversary of the birth of Marshal Manoel Luiz Osorio.

Pres. Ramon Villeda Morales A398

Fountain A399

1958, June 7 Engr. *Perf. 11½*

869 A398 6.50cr dk green 1.25 .75
  a. Wmk. 268 5.00 2.00

Visit of Pres. Ramon Villeda Morales of Honduras.

1958, June 13

870 A399 2.50cr dk green .25 .20

Botanical Garden, Rio de Janeiro, 150th anniv.

Symbols of Agriculture A400

Prophet Joel A401

1958, June 18 Photo.

871 A400 2.50cr rose carmine .25 .20

50th anniv. of Japanese immigration to Brazil.

1958, June 21 Engr.

872 A401 2.50cr dk blue .25 .20

Bicentenary of the Cathedral of Bom Jesus at Matosinhos.

Stylized Globe A402

1958, July 10 Photo.

873 A402 2.50cr dk brown .20 .20

Intl. Investment Conference, Belo Horizonte.

Julio Bueno Brandao — A403

1958, Aug. 1 Wmk. 268 *Perf. 11½*

874 A403 2.50cr red brown .25 .20

Centenary of the birth of Julio Bueno Brandao, President of Minas Gerais.

Palacio Tiradentes (House of Congress) A404

1958, July 24 Engr.

875 A404 2.50cr sepia .25 .20

47th Interparliamentary Conference, Rio de Janeiro, July 24-Aug. 1.

Presidential Palace, Brasilia A405

1958, Aug. 8 Photo. Wmk. 267

876 A405 2.50cr ultra .20 .20

Issued to publicize the construction of Brazil's new capital, Brasilia.

Freighters A406

1958, Aug. 22

877 A406 2.50cr blue .25 .20

Brazilian merchant marine.

Joaquim Caetano da Silva — A407

1958, Sept. 2 Unwmk.
Granite Paper

878 A407 2.50cr redsh brn .25 .20

Joaquim Caetano da Silva, scientist & historian.

Giovanni Gronchi A408

Archers A409

1958, Sept. 4 Engr. Wmk. 268

879 A408 7cr dk blue .50 .20

Visit of Italy's President Giovanni Gronchi to Brazil.

Perf. 11½
1958, Sept. 21 Photo. Unwmk.
Granite Paper

880 A409 2.50cr red org .35 .20

Issued to publicize the 10th Spring Games.

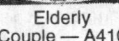

Elderly Couple — A410

Machado de Assis — A411

1958, Sept. 27 Wmk. 267

881 A410 2.50cr magenta .25 .20

Day of the Old People, Sept. 27.

1958, Sept. 28 Unwmk.

882 A411 2.50cr red brn .25 .20

50th anniversary of the death of Joaquim Maria Machado de Assis, writer.

Pres. Vargas and Oil Derrick A412

1958, Oct. 6 Wmk. 268

883 A412 2.50cr blue .25 .20

5th anniv. of Pres. Getulio D. Vargas' oil law.

Globe — A413

Gen. Lauro Sodré — A414

Wmk. 267
1958, Nov. 14 Photo. *Perf. 11½*

884 A413 2.50cr blue .30 .20

7th Inter-American Congress of Municipalities.

1958, Nov. 15 Engr.

885 A414 3.30cr green .25 .20

Cent. of the birth of Gen. Lauro Sodré.

UN Emblem A415

Soccer Player A416

1958, Dec. 26 Photo. *Perf. 11½*

886 A415 2.50cr brt blue .20 .20

10th anniv. of the signing of the Universal Declaration of Human Rights.

1959, Jan. 20

887 A416 3.30cr emer & red brn .40 .20

World Soccer Championships of 1958.

Railroad Track and Map A417

Pres. Sukarno of Indonesia A418

1959, Apr. Wmk. 267 *Perf. 11½*

888 A417 2.50cr dp orange .25 .20

Centenary of the linking of Patos and Campina Grande by railroad.

1959, May 20

889 A418 2.50cr blue .25 .20

Visit of President Sukarno of Indonesia.

Dom John VI — A419

Boy Polo Players — A420

Perf. 10½x11½
1959, June 12 Wmk. 267

890 A419 2.50cr crimson .25 .20

1959, June 13 *Perf. 11½*

891 A420 2.50cr orange brn .25 .20

9th Children's Games.

Loading Freighter A421

Organ and Emblem A422

1959, July 10
892 A421 2.50cr dk green .25 .20

Issued to honor the merchant marine.

1959, July 16 **Photo.**
893 A422 3.30cr magenta .25 .20

Bicentenary of the Carmelite Order in Brazil.

Joachim Silverio de Souza — A423

Symbolic Road — A424

1959, July 20 ***Perf. 11½***
894 A423 2.50cr red brown .25 .20

Birth centenary of Joachim Silverio de Souza, first bishop of Diamantina, Minas Gerais.

1959, Sept. 27 **Wmk. 267**
895 A424 3.30cr bl grn & ultra .25 .20

11th International Roadbuilding Congress.

Woman Athlete — A425

1959, Oct. 4
896 A425 2.50cr lilac rose .25 .20

11th Spring Games.

Map of Parana A426

1959, Sept. 27
897 A426 2.50cr dk green .25 .20

Founding of Londrina, Parana, 25th anniv.

Globe and Snipes A427

Cross of Lusitania A428

1959, Oct. 22 ***Perf. 11½***
898 A427 6.50cr dull grn .20 .20

World Championship of Snipe Class Sailboats, Porto Alegre, won by Brazilian yachtsmen.

1959, Oct. 24 **Engr.**
899 A428 6.50cr dull blue .20 .20

4th Intl. Conf. on Brazilian-Portuguese Studies, University of Bahia, Aug. 10-20.

Factory Entrance and Order of Southern Cross — A429

Corcovado Christ, Globe and Southern Cross — A430

1959, Nov. 19 **Photo.**
900 A429 3.30cr orange red .20 .20

Pres. Vargas Gunpowder Factory, 50th anniv.

1959, Nov. 26 ***Perf. 11½***
901 A430 2.50cr blue .20 .20

Universal Thanksgiving Day.

Burning Bush — A431

1959, Dec. 24 **Wmk. 267**
902 A431 3.30cr lt grn .20 .20

Centenary of Presbyterian work in Brazil.

Piraja da Silva and Schistosoma Mansoni A432

1959, Dec. 28
903 A432 2.50cr rose violet .20 .20

25th anniv. of the discovery and identification of schistosoma mansoni, a parasite of the fluke family, by Dr. Piraja da Silva.

Luiz de Matos A433

1960, Jan. 3 **Photo.**
904 A433 3.30cr red brown .20 .20

Birth centenary of Luiz de Matos.

Zamenhof A434

Adél Pinto A435

1960, Mar. 10 **Wmk. 267** ***Perf. 11½***
905 A434 6.50cr emerald .20 .20

Lazarus Ludwig Zamenhof (1859-1917), Polish oculist who invented Esperanto in 1887.

1960, Mar. 19 **Engr.** **Wmk. 268**
906 A435 11.50cr rose red .20 .20

Centenary of the birth of Adél Pinto, civil engineer and railroad expert.

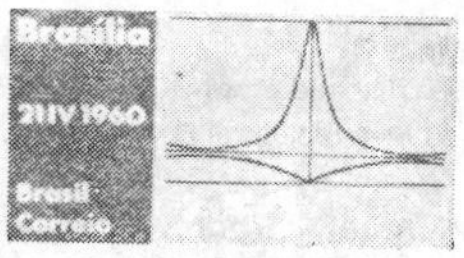

Presidential Palace, Colonnade — A436

Design: 27cr, Plan of Brasilia (like #C98).

Perf. 11x11½

1960 **Photo.** **Wmk. 267**
907 A436 2.50cr brt green .20 .20

Size: 105x46½mm

908 A436 27cr salmon .60 .60
Nos. 907-908,C95-C98 (6) 2.15 1.60

No. 907 for the inauguration of Brazil's new capital, Brasilia, Apr. 21, 1960.

No. 908 for the birthday of Pres. Juscelino Kubitschek and has a 27cr in design of No. C98, flanked by the chief design features of Nos. 907, C95-C97, with Kubitschek signature below. Issued in sheets of 4 with wide horizontal gutter.

Issued: 2.50cr, 4/21; 27cr, 9/12.

Grain, Coffee, Cotton and Cacao A437

Paulo de Frontin A438

Perf. 11½x11

1960, July 28 **Wmk. 267**
909 A437 2.50cr brown .20 .20

Centenary of Ministry of Agriculture.

1960, Oct. 12 **Wmk. 268**
910 A438 2.50cr orange red .20 .20

Cent. of the birth of Paulo de Frontin, engineer.

Woman Athlete Holding Torch — A439

1960, Oct. 18 ***Perf. 11½x11***
911 A439 2.50cr blue grn .20 .20

12th Spring Games.

Volleyball and Net A440

Locomotive Wheels A441

Perf. 11½x11

1960, Nov. 12 **Wmk. 268**
912 A440 11cr blue .20 .20

International Volleyball Championships.

1960, Oct. 15 ***Perf. 11½x11***
913 A441 2.50cr ultra .20 .20

10th Pan-American Railroad Congress.

Symbols of Flight A442

1960, Dec. 16 **Photo.** ***Perf. 11½***
914 A442 2.50cr brn & yel .20 .20

Intl. Fair of Industry and Commerce, Rio.

Emperor Haile Selassie — A443

1961, Jan. 31 ***Perf. 11½x11***
915 A443 2.50cr dk brown .20 .20

Visit of Emperor Haile Selassie of Ethiopia to Brazil, Dec. 1960.

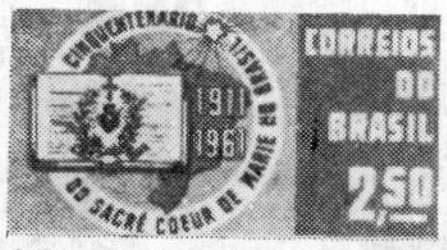

Map of Brazil, Open Book and Sacred Heart Emblem A444

Perf. 11x11½

1961, Mar. 13 **Wmk. 268**
916 A444 2.50cr blue .20 .20

50th anniv. of the operation in Brazil of the Order of the Blessed Heart of Mary.

Map of Guanabara A445

1961, Mar. 27 **Wmk. 267**
917 A445 7.50cr org brn .20 .20

Promulgation of the constitution of the state of Guanabara.

Arms of Agulhas Negras A446

Brazil and Senegal Linked on Map A447

Design: 3.30cr, Dress helmet and sword.

Perf. 11½x11

1961, Apr. 23 **Wmk. 267**

918 A446 2.50cr green .20 .20
919 A446 3.30cr rose car .20 .20

Sesquicentennial of the Agulhas Negras Military Academy.

1961, Apr. 28 **Photo.**

920 A447 27cr ultra .25 .20

Issued to commemorate the visit of Afonso Arinos, Brazilian foreign minister, to Senegal to attend its independence ceremonies.

View of Ouro Preto, 1711 A448

1961, June 6 ***Perf. 11x11½***

921 A448 1cr orange .20 .20

250th anniversary of Ouro Preto.

War Arsenal A449

1961, June 20 **Wmk. 256**

924 A449 5cr dk red brn .25 .20

150th anniv. of the War Arsenal, Rio de Janeiro.

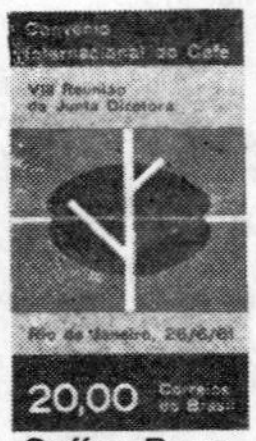

Coffee Bean and Branch A450

Rabindranath Tagore A451

Perf. 11½x11

1961, June 26 **Wmk. 267**

925 A450 20cr redsh brn .80 .25

8th Directorial Committee meeting of the Intl. Coffee Convention, Rio, June 26.

1961, July 28 **Photo.** **Wmk. 267**

926 A451 10cr rose car .20 .20

Rabindranath Tagore, Indian poet, birth cent.

Stamp of 1861 and Map of English Channel A452

Design: 20cr, 430r stamp of 1861 and map of Netherlands.

1961, Aug. 1 ***Perf. 11x11½***

927 A452 10cr rose .75 .20
928 A452 20cr salmon pink 2.00 .30

Centenary of 1861 stamp issue.

Portrait Type of 1954-60
Designs as Before

1961 **Wmk. 268** ***Perf. 11x11½***

930	A336	1cr brown	.80	.50
931	A336	2cr dk bl grn	1.25	.50
932	A336	5cr red lilac	3.75	.30
933	A336	10cr emerald	7.25	.30
		Nos. 930-933 (4)	13.05	1.60

1cr, 5cr and 10cr have patterned background.

Sun, Clouds, Rain and Weather Symbols — A453

Dedo de Deus Peak — A454

1962, Mar. 23 ***Perf. 11½x11***

936 A453 10cr red brown .75 .30

World Meteorological Day, Mar. 23.

1962, Apr. 14 **Photo.** **Wmk. 267**

937 A454 8cr emerald .20 .25

50th anniversary of the climbing of Dedo de Deus (Finger of God) peak.

Dr. Gaspar Vianna and Leishmania Protozoa A455

1962, Apr. 24 ***Perf. 11x11½***

938 A455 8cr blue .25 .20

Discovery by Gaspar Oliveiro Vianna (1885-1914) of a cure for leishmaniasis, 50th anniv.

Henrique Dias A456

1962, June 18 **Wmk. 267**

939 A456 10cr dk vio brn .30 .20

300th anniversary of the death of Henrique Dias, Negro military leader who fought against the Dutch and Spaniards.

Millimeter Gauge A457

Sailboats, Snipe Class A458

1962, June 26 ***Perf. 11½x11***

940 A457 100cr car rose .35 .20

Centenary of the introduction of the metric system in Brazil.

1962, July 21 **Photo.** **Wmk. 267**

941 A458 8cr Prus grn .20 .20

Issued to commemorate the 13th Brazilian championships for Snipe Class sailing.

Julio Mesquita A459

1962, Aug. 18 ***Perf. 11x11½***

942 A459 8cr dull brown .20 .20

Centenary of the birth of Julio Mesquita, journalist and founder of a Sao Paulo newspaper.

Empress Leopoldina — A460

1962, Sept. 7 ***Perf. 11½x11***

943 A460 8cr rose claret .20 .20

140th anniversary of independence.

Buildings, Brasilia A461

Perf. 11x11½

1962, Oct. 24 **Wmk. 267**

944 A461 10cr orange .30 .20

51st Interparliamentary Conf., Brasilia.

Pouring Ladle — A462

1962, Oct. 26 ***Perf. 11½x11***

945 A462 8cr orange .20 .20

Inauguration of the Usiminas State Iron and Steel Foundry at Belo Horizonte, Minas Gerais.

UPAE Emblem A463

1962, Nov. 19 ***Perf. 11x11½***

946 A463 8cr bright magenta .20 .20

Founding of the Postal Union of the Americas and Spain, UPAE, 50th anniv.

Chimney and Cogwheel Forming "10" — A464

1962, Nov. 26 ***Perf. 11½x11***

947 A464 10cr lt blue grn .20 .20

Natl. Economic and Development Bank, 10th anniv.

Quintino Bocaiuva A465

Soccer Player and Globe A466

Perf. 11½x11

1962, Dec. 27 **Photo.** **Wmk. 267**

948 A465 8cr brown org .20 .20

Bocaiuva, journalist, 50th death anniv.

1963, Jan. 14

949 A466 10cr blue grn .40 .20

World Soccer Championship of 1962.

Carrier Pigeon A467

1963, Jan. **Unwmk.** **Litho.** ***Perf. 14***

950 A467 8cr yel, dk bl, red & grn .20 .20

Souvenir Sheet

Imperf

951 A467 100cr yel, dk bl, red & grn 1.25 *3.00*

300 years of Brazilian postal service.
Issue dates: 8cr, Jan. 25; 100cr, Jan. 31.

Severino Neiva — A468

Perf. 10½x11½

1963, Jan. 31 **Photo.** **Wmk. 267**

952 A468 8cr brt vio .20 .20

Radar Tracking Station and Rockets A469

"Cross of Unity" A470

Perf. 11½x11

1963, Mar. 15 **Wmk. 268**

953 A469 21cr lt ultra .20 .20

Issued to publicize the International Aeronautics and Space Exhibition, Sao Paulo.

1963 **Wmk. 267** ***Perf. 11½x11***

954 A470 8cr red lilac .20 .20

Vatican II, the 21st Ecumenical Council of the Roman Catholic Church.

"ABC" in Geometric Form A471

Basketball Player A472

1963, Apr. 22 Photo. Wmk. 267
955 A471 8cr brt bl & lt bl .20 .20

Education Week, Apr. 22-27, 3-year alphabetization program.

1963, May 15
956 A472 8cr dp lilac rose .20 .20

4th International Basketball Championships, Rio de Janeiro, May 10-25, 1963.

Games Emblem A473

"OEA" and Map of the Americas A474

1963, May 22 ***Perf. 11½x11***
957 A473 10cr car rose .30 .20

4th Pan American Games, Sao Paulo.

1963, June 6
958 A474 10cr org & dp org .30 .20

15th anniversary of the charter of the Organization of American States.

José Bonifacio de Andrada — A475

1963, June 13
959 A475 8cr dk brown .20 .20

Bicentenary of the birth of José Bonifacio de Andrada e Silva, statesman.

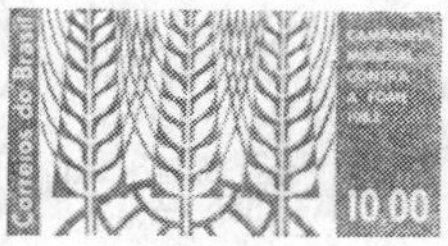

Wheat A476

Perf. 11x11½

1963, June 19 Photo. Wmk. 267
960 A476 10cr blue .30 .20

FAO "Freedom from Hunger" campaign.

Centenary Emblem A477

Joao Caetano A478

1963, Aug. 19 ***Perf. 11½x11***
961 A477 8cr yel org & red .25 .20

Centenary of International Red Cross.

1963, Aug. 24 ***Perf. 11½x11***
962 A478 8cr slate .20 .20

Death centenary of Joao Caetano, actor.

Symbols of Agriculture, Industry and Atomic Energy A479

Hammer Thrower A480

1963, Aug. 28
963 A479 10cr car rose .25 .20

Atomic Development Law, 1st anniv.

1963, Sept. 13
964 A480 10cr gray .40 .20

Intl. College Students' Games, Porto Alegre.

Marshal Tito — A481

Compass Rose, Map of Brazil and View of Rio — A482

1963, Sept. 19
965 A481 80cr sepia .35 .30

Visit of Marshal Tito of Yugoslavia.

1963, Sept. 20
966 A482 8cr lt blue grn .20 .20

8th International Leprology Congress.

Oil Derrick and Storage Tank A483

1963, Oct. 3 ***Perf. 11x11½***
967 A483 8cr dk slate grn .20 .20

10th anniv. of Petrobras, the natl. oil company.

"Spring Games" A484

1963, Nov. 5 Photo. Wmk. 267
968 A484 8cr yel & org .20 .20

1963 Spring Games.

Dr. Borges de Medeiros (1863-1962), Governor of Rio Grande do Sul — A485

1963, Nov. 29 ***Perf. 11½x11***
969 A485 8cr red brown .20 .20

Sao Joao del Rei A486

1963, Dec. 8 ***Perf. 11x11½***
970 A486 8cr violet blue .20 .20

250th anniversary of Sao Joao del Rei.

Dr. Alvaro Alvim A487

1963, Dec. 19
971 A487 8cr dk gray .20 .20

Alvaro Alvim (1863-1928), X-ray specialist and martyr of science.

Viscount de Mauá A488

Mandacaru Cactus and Emblem A489

1963, Dec. 28 ***Perf. 11½x11***
972 A488 8cr rose car .20 .20

Sesquicentennial of the birth of Viscount de Mauá, founder of first Brazilian railroad.

1964, Jan. 23 Photo. Wmk. 267
973 A489 8cr dull green .20 .20

Bank of Northeast Brazil, 10th anniv.

Coelho Netto — A490

Lauro Müller — A491

1964, Feb. 21 ***Perf. 11½x11***
974 A490 8cr brt violet .20 .20

Birth centenary of Coelho Netto, writer.

1964, Mar. 8 Wmk. 267
975 A491 8cr dp orange .20 .20

Lauro Siverino Müller, politician and member of the Brazilian Academy of Letters, birth cent.

Child Holding Spoon A492

1964, Mar. 25 ***Perf. 11x11½***
976 A492 8cr yel brn & yel .20 .20

Issued for "School Meals Week."

Chalice Rock A493

Allan Kardec A494

1964, Apr. 9 Engr. ***Perf. 11½x11***
977 A493 80cr red orange .20 .20

Issued for tourist publicity.

1964, Apr. 18 Photo.
978 A494 30cr slate green .45 .20

Cent. of "O Evangelho" (Gospel) of the codification of Spiritism.

Heinrich Lübke — A495

Pope John XXIII — A496

Perf. 11½x11

1964, May 8 Photo. Wmk. 267
979 A495 100cr red brown .60 .20

Visit of President Heinrich Lübke of Germany.

1964, June 29 Wmk. 267
980 A496 20cr dk car rose .20 .20
a. Unwmkd. .20 .20

Issued in memory of Pope John XXIII.

Pres. Senghor of Senegal — A497

1964, Sept. 19 **Wmk. 267**
981 A497 20cr dk brown .25 .20

Visit of Leopold Sedar Senghor, President of Senegal.

Botafogo Bay and Sugarloaf Mountain A498

Designs: 100cr, Church of Our Lady of the Rock, vert. 200cr, Copacabana beach.

Perf. 11x11½, 11½x11

1964-65 **Photo.**

983	A498	15cr org & bl		.30	.25
984	A498	100cr brt grn & red brn, *yel*		.20	.20
985	A498	200cr black & red		1.75	.30
a.		Souvenir sheet of 3 ('65)		4.75	4.00
		Nos. 983-985 (3)		2.25	.75

4th cent. of Rio de Janeiro.

No. 985a contains three imperf. stamps similar to Nos. 983-985, but printed in brown. Sold for 320cr. Issued Dec. 30, 1965.

A souvenir card containing one lithographed facsimile of No. 984, imperf., exists, but has no franking value. Size: 100x125mm. Sold by P.O. for 250cr.

Pres. Charles de Gaulle A499

Pres. John F. Kennedy A500

1964, Oct. 13 ***Perf. 11½x11***
986 A499 100cr orange brn .35 .20

Visit of Charles de Gaulle, President of France, Oct. 13-15.

1964, Oct. 24 **Photo.** **Wmk. 267**
987 A500 100cr slate .20 .20

"Prophet" by Lisboa — A501

1964, Nov. 18 ***Perf. 11½x11***
988 A501 10cr slate .20 .20

150th death anniv. of the sculptor Antonio Francisco Lisboa, "O Aleijadinho" (The Cripple).

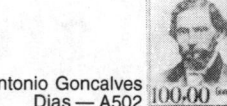

Antonio Goncalves Dias — A502

Designs: 30cr, Euclides da Cunha. 50cr, Prof. Angelo Moreira da Costa Lima. 200cr, Tiradentes. 500cr, Dom Pedro I. 1000cr, Dom Pedro II.

1965-66 **Wmk. 267** ***Perf. 11x11½***

989	A502	30cr brt bluish grn ('66)	2.00	.25
989A	A502	50cr dull brn ('66)	1.50	.20
990	A502	100cr blue	.60	.20
991	A502	200cr brown org	2.00	.20
992	A502	500cr red brown	6.00	.50
992A	A502	1000cr sl bl ('66)	10.00	.50
		Nos. 989-992A (6)	22.10	1.85

Statue of St. Sebastian, Guanataro Bay — A503

The Arches A504

Design: 35cr, Estacio de Sa (1520-67), founder of Rio de Janeiro.

1965 **Photo.** ***Perf. 11½***
Size: 24x37mm
993 A503 30cr bl & rose red .30 .20

Lithographed and Engraved
Perf. 11x11½
994 A504 30cr lt bl & blk .30 .20

Photo. ***Perf. 11½***
Size: 21x39mm

995	A503	35cr blk & org	.20	.25
a.		Souvenir sheet of 3	3.25	4.00
		Nos. 993-995 (3)	.80	.65

4th cent. of Rio de Janeiro. Issue dates: No. 993, Mar. 5. No. 994, Nov. 30. No. 995, July 28. No. 995a, Dec. 30.

No. 995a contains three imperf. stamps similar to Nos. 993-995, but printed in deep orange. Size: 130x79mm. Sold for 100cr.

Sword and Cross — A505

1965, Apr. 15 **Wmk. 267** ***Perf. 11½***
996 A505 120cr gray .30 .20

1st anniv. of the democratic revolution.

Vital Brazil — A506

Shah of Iran — A507

1965, Apr. 28 **Wmk. 267** ***Perf. 11½***
997 A506 120cr deep orange .30 .20

Centenary of birth of Vital Brazil, M.D.

A souvenir card containing one impression similar to No. 997, imperf., exists, printed in dull plum. Sold by P.O. for 250cr. Size: 114x180mm.

1965, May 5 **Photo.**
998 A507 120cr rose claret .25 .20

Issued to commemorate the visit of Shah Mohammed Riza Pahlavi of Iran.

Marshal Mariano da Silva Rondon A508

Lions' Emblem A509

1965, May 7 **Engr.**
999 A508 30cr claret .25 .20

Marshal Mariano da Silva Rondon (1865-1958), explorer and expert on Indians.

1965, May 14 **Photo.**
1000 A509 35cr pale vio & blk .20 .20

12th convention of the Lions Clubs of Brazil, Rio de Janeiro, May 11-16.

ITU Emblem, Old and New Communication Equipment — A510

1965, May 21 ***Perf. 11½***
1001 A510 120cr yellow & grn .30 .20

Centenary of the ITU.

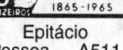

Epitácio Pessoa — A511

Statue of Admiral Barroso — A512

1965, May 23 **Photo.**
1002 A511 35cr blue gray .20 .20

Epitácio da Silva Pessoa (1865-1942), jurist, president of Brazil, 1919-22.

1965, June 11
1003 A512 30cr blue .25 .20

Cent. of the naval battle of Riachuelo.

A souvenir card containing one lithographed facsimile of No. 1003, imperf., exists. Size: 100x139½mm.

José de Alencar and Indian Princess — A513

1965, June 24 ***Perf. 11½x11***
1004 A513 30cr deep plum .25 .20

Centenary of the publication of "Iracema" by Joséde Alencar.

A souvenir card containing one lithographed facsimile of No. 1004, printed in rose red and imperf., exists. Size: 100x141½mm.

Winston Churchill A514

1965, June 25 ***Perf. 11x11½***
1005 A514 200cr slate .50 .25

Scout Jamboree Emblem — A515

1965, July 17 **Photo.**
1006 A515 30cr dull bl grn .30 .20

1st Pan-American Boy Scout Jamboree, Fundao Island, Rio de Janeiro, July 15-25.

ICY Emblem A516

1965, Aug. 25 **Wmk. 267** ***Perf. 11½***
1007 A516 120cr dl bl & blk .25 .20

International Cooperation Year, 1965.

Leoncio Correias A517

Emblem A518

1965, Sept. 1 ***Perf. 11½x11***
1008 A517 35cr slate grn .25 .20

Leoncio Correias, poet, birth cent.

1965, Sept. 4
1009 A518 30cr brt rose .20 .20

Issued to publicize the Eighth Biennial Fine Arts Exhibition, Sao Paulo, Nov.-Dec., 1965.

Pres. Saragat of Italy — A519

1965, Sept. 11 **Photo.** **Wmk. 267**
1010 A519 100cr slate grn, *pink* .25 .20

Visit of Pres. Giuseppe Saragat of Italy.

Grand Duke and Duchess of Luxembourg — A520

1965, Sept. 17 ***Perf. 11x11½***
1011 A520 100cr brn olive .25 .20

Visit of Grand Duke Jean and Grand Duchess Josephine Charlotte of Luxembourg.

Biplane — A521

1965, Oct. 8 **Photo.** ***Perf. 11½x11***
1012 A521 35cr ultra .20 .20

3rd Aviation Week Philatelic Exhibition, Rio.
A souvenir card carries one impression of this 35cr, imperf. Size: 102x140mm. Sold for 100cr.

Flags of OAS Members A522

1965, Nov. 17 ***Perf. 11x11½***
1013 A522 100cr brt bl & blk .25 .20

2nd meeting of OAS Foreign Ministers, Rio.

King Baudouin and Queen Fabiola of Belgium A523

1965, Nov. 18
1014 A523 100cr gray .25 .20

Visit of King and Queen of Belgium.

"Coffee Beans" — A524

Perf. 11½x11
1965, Dec. 21 **Photo.** **Wmk. 267**
1015 A524 30cr brown .30 .20

Brazilian coffee publicity.

Conveyor and Loading Crane A525

1966, Apr. 1 ***Perf. 11x11½***
1016 A525 110cr tan & dk sl grn .25 .20

Opening of the new terminal of the Rio Doce Iron Ore Company at Tubarao.

Pouring Ladle and Steel Beam A526

Prof. de Rocha Dissecting Cadaver A527

Perf. 11½x11
1966, Apr. 16 **Photo.** **Wmk. 267**
1017 A526 30cr blk, *dp org* .25 .20

25th anniv. of the National Steel Company (nationalization of the steel industry).

1966, Apr. 26
1018 A527 30cr brt bluish grn .40 .20

50th anniv. of the discovery and description of Rickettsia prowazeki, the cause of typhus fever, by Prof. Henrique de Rocha Lima.

Battle of Tuiuti A528

Perf. 11x11½
1966, May 24 **Photo.** **Wmk. 267**
1019 A528 30cr gray grn .30 .20

Centenary of the Battle of Tuiuti.

Symbolic Water Cycle — A529

Pres. Shazar of Israel — A530

1966, July 1 ***Perf. 11½x11***
1020 A529 100cr lt brn & bl .25 .20

Hydrological Decade (UNESCO), 1965-74.

1966, July 18 **Photo.** **Wmk. 267**
1021 A530 100cr ultra .30 .20

Visit of Pres. Zalman Shazar of Israel.

Imperial Academy of Fine Arts A531

Perf. 11x11½
1966, Aug. 12 **Engr.** **Wmk. 267**
1022 A531 100cr red brown .60 .20

150th anniversary of French art mission.

Military Service Emblem A532

1966, Sept. 6 **Photo.** ***Perf. 11x11½***
1023 A532 30cr yel, ultra & grn .25 .20
a. With commemorative border 3.50 3.00

New Military Service Law.
No. 1023a issued in sheets of 4. It carries at left a 30cr, design A532, in deeper tones of yellow and ultramarine, Wmk. 264. Without gum. Sold for 100cr.

Ruben Dario — A533

Perf. 11½x11
1966, Sept. 20 **Photo.** **Wmk. 267**
1024 A533 100cr brt rose lilac .25 .20

Ruben Dario (pen name of Felix Ruben Garcia Sarmiento (1867-1916), Nicaraguan poet, newspaper correspondent and diplomat.

Ceramic Candlestick from Santarém — A534

1966, Oct. 6 ***Perf. 11x11½***
1025 A534 30cr dk brn, *salmon* .25 .20

Centenary of Goeldi Museum at Belem.

Arms of Santa Cruz — A535

Perf. 11½x11
1966, Oct. 15 **Photo.** **Wmk. 267**
1026 A535 30cr slate grn .25 .20

1st Natl. Tobacco Exposition, Santa Cruz.

UNESCO Emblem A536

1966, Oct. 24 **Engr.** ***Perf. 11½***
1027 A536 120cr black .75 .25
a. With commemorative border 6.00 6.00

20th anniv. of UNESCO. No. 1027a issued in sheets of 4. It carries at right a design similar to No. 1027. Unwatermarked granite paper, without gum. Sold for 150cr.

Captain Antonio Correia Pinto and Map of Lages — A537

Cross of Lusitania and Southern Cross — A538

Perf. 11½x11
1966, Nov. 22 **Photo.** **Wmk. 267**
1028 A537 30cr salmon pink .25 .20

Arrival of Capt. Antonio Correia Pinto, cent.

1966, Dec. 4 ***Perf. 11½***
1029 A538 100cr blue green .30 .20

LUBRAPEX 1966 philatelic exhibition at the National Museum of Fine Arts, Rio.

Madonna and Child — A539

A540

Perf. 11½x11
1966, Dec. **Photo.** **Wmk. 267**
1030 A539 30cr blue green .25 .20

Perf. 11½
1031 A540 35cr salmon & ultra .20 .20
a. 150cr salmon & ultra 2.50 3.00

Christmas 1966.
No. 1031a measures 46x103mm and is printed in sheets of 4. It is inscribed "Pax Hominibus" (but not "Brasil Correio") and carries the Madonna shown on No. 1031. Issued without gum.
Issued: 30cr, 12/8; 35cr, 12/22; 150cr, 12/28.

Arms of Laguna A541

1967, Jan. 4 **Engr.** ***Perf. 11x11½***
1032 A541 60cr sepia .20 .20

Centenary of the Post and Telegraph Agency of Laguna, Santa Catarina.

Railroad Bridge A542

1967, Feb. 16 **Photo.** **Wmk. 267**
1033 A542 50cr deep orange .45 .20

Centenary of the Santos-Jundiai railroad.

Black Madonna of Czestochowa, Polish Eagle and Cross — A543

1967, Mar. 12 ***Perf. 11x11½***
1034 A543 50cr yel, bl & rose red .35 .20

Adoption of Christianity in Poland, 1,000th anniv.

Research Rocket A544

Anita Garibaldi A545

1967, Mar. 23 *Perf. 11½x11*
1035 A544 50cr blk & brt bl .60 .30

World Meteorological Day, March 23.

Perf. 11x11½
1967-69 Photo. Wmk. 267

Portraits: 1c, Mother Joana Angelica. 2c, Marilia de Dirceu. 3c, Dr. Rita Lobato. 6c, Ana Neri. 10c, Darcy Vargas.

1036	A545 1c dp ultra	.20	.20
1037	A545 2c red brn	.20	.20
1038	A545 3c brt grn	.20	.20
1039	A545 5c black	.35	.20
1040	A545 6c brown	.35	.20
1041	A545 10c dk slate grn	1.10	.30
	Nos. 1036-1041 (6)	2.40	1.30

Issued: 1c, May 3; 2c, Aug. 14; 3c, June 7; 5c, Apr. 14; 6c, May 14, 1967; 10c, June 18, 1969.

VARIG Airlines A546

Madonna and Child, by Robert Feruzzi A548

Lions Emblem and Globes A547

1967, May 8 *Perf. 11½x11*
1046 A546 6c brt bl & blk .30 .25

40th anniversary of VARIG Airlines.

1967, May 9 Engr. *Perf. 11x11½*
1047 A547 6c green .30 .25
a. Souvenir sheet 2.50 *3.00*

50th anniv. of Lions Intl. No. 1047a contains one imperf. stamp similar to No. 1047. Sold for 15c.

1967, May 14 Photo. *Perf. 11½x11*
1048 A548 5c violet .25 .20
a. 15c Souvenir sheet 2.25 *2.25*

Mother's Day. No. 1048a contains one 15c imperf. stamp in design of No. 1048.

Prince Akihito and Princess Michiko A549

1967, May 25 *Perf. 11x11½*
1049 A549 10c black & pink .30 .20

Visit to Brazil of Crown Prince Akihito and Princess Michiko of Japan.

Carrier Pigeon and Radar Screen A550

Brother Vicente do Salvador A551

Perf. 11½x11
1967, June 20 Photo. Wmk. 267
1050 A550 10c sl & brt pink .25 .20

Issued to commemorate the opening of the Communications Ministry in Brasilia.

1967, June 28 Engr.
1051 A551 5c brown .25 .20

400th birth anniv. of Brother Vicente do Salvador (1564-1636), founder of Franciscan convent in Rio de Janeiro, and historian.

Boy, Girl and 4-S Emblem A552

1967, July 12 Photo. *Perf. 11½*
1052 A552 5c green & blk .25 .20

National 4-S (4-H) Day.

Möbius Strip A553

1967, July 21 *Perf. 11x11½*
1053 A553 5c brt bl & blk .25 .20

6th Brazilian Mathematical Congress.

Fish A554

1967, Aug. 1 *Perf. 11½*
1054 A554 5c slate .30 .20

Bicentenary of city of Piracicaba.

Golden Rose and Papal Arms — A555

1967, Aug. 15
1055 A555 20c mag & yel 1.00 .40

Offering of a golden rose by Pope Paul VI to the Virgin Mary of Fatima (Our Lady of Peace), Patroness of Brazil.

General Sampaio A556

King Olaf of Norway A557

1967, Aug. 25 Engr. *Perf. 11½x11*
1056 A556 5c blue .25 .20

Issued to honor General Antonio de Sampaio, hero of the Battle of Tutui.

1967, Sept. 8 Photo.
1057 A557 10c brown org .25 .20

Visit of King Olaf of Norway.

Sun over Sugar Loaf, Botafogo Bay A558

Nilo Peçanha A559

Photogravure and Embossed
1967, Sept. 25 Wmk. 267 *Perf. 11½*
1058 A558 10c blk & dp org .25 .20

22nd meeting of the Intl. Monetary Fund, Intl. Bank for Reconstruction and Development, Intl. Financial Corporation and Intl. Development Assoc.

Perf. 11½x11
1967, Oct. 1 Photo. Wmk. 267
1059 A559 5c brown violet .25 .20

Peçanha (1867-1924), Pres. of Brazil 1909-10.

Virgin of the Apparition and Basilica of Aparecida A560

Cockerel, Festival Emblem A561

1967, Oct. 11 *Perf. 11½*
1060 A560 5c ultra & dl yel .30 .20
a. Souvenir sheet of 2 3.25 *3.25*

250th anniv. of the discovery of the statue of Our Lady of the Apparition, now in the National Basilica of the Apparition at Aparecida do Norte.

No. 1060a contains imperf. 5c and 10c stamps similar to No. 1060. Issued Dec. 27, 1967, for Christmas.

Engraved and Photogravure
1967, Oct. 16 *Perf. 11½x11*
1061 A561 20c black & multi .50 .40

Second International Folksong Festival.

Balloon, Plane and Rocket A562

Perf. 11x11½
1967, Oct. 18 Photo. Unwmk.
1062 A562 10c blue .50 .30
a. 15c souvenir sheet 4.50 *4.50*

Week of the Wing, Oct. 18-23. No. 1062a contains one imperf. 15c stamp similar to No. 1062 and was issued Oct. 23.

Pres. Arthur Bernardes — A563

Portraits of Brazilian Presidents: 20c, Campos Salles. 50c, Wenceslau Pereira Gomes Braz. 1cr, Washington Pereira de Souza Luiz. 2cr, Castello Branco.

Perf. 11x11½
1967-68 Photo. Wmk. 267

1063	A563 10c blue	.25	.20
1064	A563 20c dk red brn	.75	.20
	Engr.		
1065	A563 50c black ('68)	3.75	.30
1066	A563 1cr lil rose ('68)	6.00	.30
1067	A563 2cr emerald ('68)	1.10	.30
	Nos. 1063-1067 (5)	11.85	1.30

Carnival of Rio — A564

Ships, Anchor and Sailor — A565

1967, Nov. 22 *Perf. 11½x11*
1070 A564 10c lem, ultra & pink .30 .20
a. 15c souvenir sheet 3.50 *4.50*

Issued for International Tourist Year, 1967. No. 1070a contains a 15c imperf. stamp in design of No. 1070. Issued Nov. 24.

1967, Dec. 6
1071 A565 10c ultra .30 .25

Issued for Navy Week.

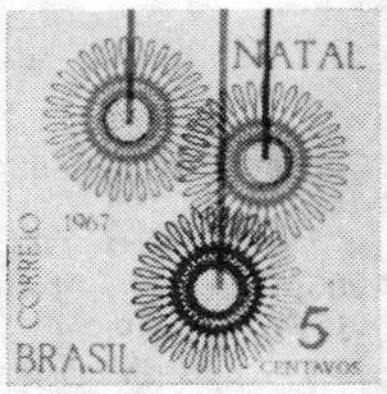
Christmas Decorations A566

1967, Dec. 8 *Perf. 11½*
1072 A566 5c car, yel & bl .25 .20

Christmas 1967.

Olavo Bilac, Planes, Tank and Aircraft Carrier A567

Perf. 11x11½
1967, Dec. 16 Photo. Wmk. 267
1073 A567 5c brt blue & yel .30 .20

Issued for Reservists' Day and to honor Olavo Bilac, sponsor of compulsory military service.

Rodrigues de Carvalho — A568

1967, Dec. 18 Engr. *Perf. 11½x11*

1074 A568 10c green .25 .20

Cent. of the birth of Rodrigues de Carvalho, poet and lawyer.

Orlando Rangel A569

1968, Feb. 29 Photo. *Perf. 11x11½*

1075 A569 5c lt grnsh bl & blk .35 .25

Orlando de Fonseca Rangel, pioneer of pharmaceutical industry in Brazil, birth cent.

Virgin of Paranagua and Diver A570

Map of Brazil Showing Manaus A571

1968, Mar. 9 *Perf. 11½x11*

1076 A570 10c dk sl grn & brt yel grn .35 .25

250th anniversary of the first underwater explorations at Paranagua.

1968, Mar. 13 Photo. Wmk. 267

1077 A571 10c yel, grn & red .35 .25

Free port of Manaus on the Amazon River.

Human Rights Flame A572

Paul Harris and Rotary Emblem A573

1968, Mar. 21 *Perf. 11½x11*

1078 A572 10c blue & salmon .35 .25

International Human Rights Year.

1968, Apr. 19 Litho. Unwmk.
Without Gum

1079 A573 20c grn & org brn 1.25 .70

Paul Percy Harris (1868-1947), founder of Rotary International.

Pedro Alvares Cabral and his Fleet — A574

Design: 20c, First Mass celebrated in Brazil.

1968 Without Gum *Perf. 11½*

1080 A574 10c multicolored .55 .45
1081 A574 20c multicolored .80 .60

500th anniversary of the birth of Pedro Alvares Cabral, navigator, who took possession of Brazil for Portugal.

Issue dates: 10c, Apr. 22; 20c, July 11.

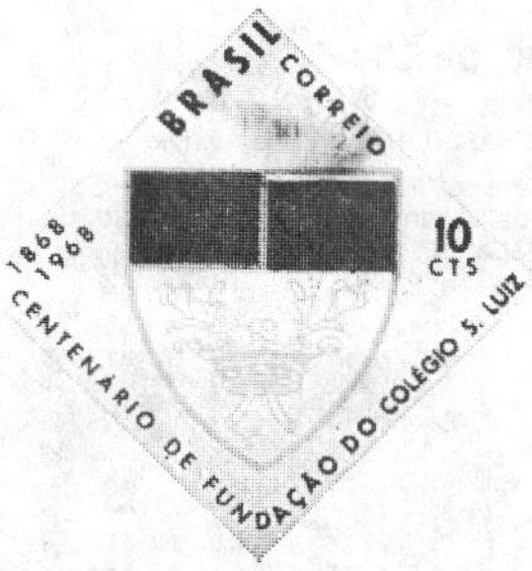

College Arms — A575

1968, Apr. 22 Photo. Wmk. 267

1082 A575 10c vio bl, red & gold .55 .35

Centenary of St. Luiz College, Sao Paulo.

Motherhood, by Henrique Bernardeli A576

1968, May 12 Litho. Unwmk.
Without Gum

1083 A576 5c multicolored .35 .25

Issued for Mother's Day.

Harpy Eagle A577

Photogravure and Engraved

1968, May 28 Wmk. 267

1084 A577 20c brt bl & blk 1.50 .50

Sesquicentennial of National Museum.

Brazilian and Japanese Women — A578

1968, June 28 Litho. Unwmk.
Without Gum

1085 A578 10c yellow & multi .60 .40

Issued to commemorate the inauguration of Varig's direct Brazil-Japan airline.

Horse Race A579

Perf. 11x11½

1968, July 16 Litho. Unwmk.
Without Gum

1086 A579 10c multicolored .35 .25

Centenary of the Jockey Club of Brazil.

Musician Wren A580

Designs: 10c, Red-crested cardinal, vert. 50c, Royal flycatcher, vert.

Perf. 11½x11, 11x11½

1968-69 Engr. Wmk. in Sheet
Without Gum

1087 A580 10c multi ('69) .45 .30
1088 A580 20c multicolored .75 .30
1089 A580 50c multicolored 1.00 .55
Nos. 1087-1089 (3) 2.20 1.15

Some stamps in each sheet of Nos. 1087-1089 show parts of a two-line papermaker's watermark: "WESTERPOST / INDUSTRIA BRASILEIRA" with diamond-shaped emblem between last two words. Entire watermark appears in one sheet margin.

Issue dates: 10c, Aug. 20, 1969. 20c, July 19, 1968. 50c, Aug. 2, 1968.

Mailbox and Envelope A581

Photogravure and Engraved

1968, Aug. 1 Wmk. 267 *Perf. 11*

1091 A581 5c citron, blk & grn .20 .20

Stamp Day, 1968 and for 125th anniv. of the 1st Brazilian postage stamps.

Emilio Luiz Mallet A582

Map of South America A583

Perf. 11½x11

1968, Aug. 25 Engr. Wmk. 267

1092 A582 10c pale purple .20 .20

Issued to honor Marshal Emilio Luiz Mallet, Baron of Itapevi, patron of the marines.

1968, Sept. 5 Photo.

1093 A583 10c deep orange .20 .20

Visit of President Eduardo Frei of Chile.

Seal of Portuguese Literary School — A584

Photogravure and Engraved

1968, Sept. 10 *Perf. 11½*

1094 A584 5c pink & grn .20 .20

Centenary of Portuguese Literary School.

Map of Brazil and Telex Tape A585

1968, Sept. Photo. *Perf. 11x11½*

1095 A585 20c citron & brt grn .50 .25

Linking of 25 Brazilian cities by teletype.

Soldiers' Heads on Medal — A586

Perf. 11½x11

1968, Sept. 24 Litho. Unwmk.
Without Gum

1096 A586 5c blue & gray .20 .25

8th American Armed Forces Conference.

Clef, Notes and Sugarloaf Mountain A587

1968, Sept. 30 *Perf. 11½*
Without Gum

1097 A587 6c blk, yel & red .50 .30

Third International Folksong Festival.

Catalytic Cracking Plant — A588

1968, Oct. 4
Without Gum
1098 A588 6c blue & multi .50 .40

Petrobras, the natl. oil company, 15th anniv.

Child Protection A589

Whimsical Girl — A590

Design: 5c, School boy walking toward the sun.

Perf. 11½x11, 11x11½
1968, Oct. 16 Litho. Unwmk.
Without Gum

1099 A590	5c gray & lt bl	.30	.30
1100 A589	10c brt bl, dk red & blk	.40	.25
1101 A590	20c multicolored	.50	.25
	Nos. 1099-1101 (3)	1.20	.80

22nd anniv. of UNICEF.

Children with Books A591

1968, Oct. 23 ***Perf. 11x11½***
Without Gum
1102 A591 5c multicolored .25 .25

Issued to publicize Book Week.

UN Emblem and Flags — A592

1968, Oct. 24 ***Perf. 11½x11***
Without Gum
1103 A592 20c black & multi .45 .25

20th anniv. of WHO.

Jean Baptiste Debret, Self-portrait — A593

Perf. 11x11½
1968, Oct. 30 Litho. Unwmk.
Without Gum
1104 A593 10c dk gray & pale yel .35 .25

Jean Baptiste Debret, (1768-1848), French painter who worked in Brazil (1816-31). Design includes his "Burden Bearer."

Queen Elizabeth II A594

1968, Nov. 4 ***Perf. 11½***
Without Gum
1105 A594 70c lt bl & multi 1.75 1.00

Visit of Queen Elizabeth II of Great Britain.

Francisco Braga — A595

Perf. 11½x11
1968, Nov. 19 Wmk. 267
1106 A595 5c dull red brn .40 .25

Cent. of the birth of Antonio Francisco Braga, composer of the Hymn of the Flag.

Brazilian Flag — A596

1968, Nov. 19 Unwmk. ***Perf. 11½***
Without Gum
1107 A596 10c multicolored .40 .30

Issued for Flag Day.

Clasped Hands and Globe A597

Perf. 11x11½
1968, Nov. 25 Typo. Unwmk.
Without Gum
1108 A597 5c multicolored .25 .25

Issued for Voluntary Blood Donor's Day.

Old Locomotive — A598

1968, Nov. 28 Litho. ***Perf. 11½***
Without Gum
1109 A598 5c multicolored 1.00 .50

Centenary of the Sao Paulo Railroad.

Bell — A599

Francisco Caldas, Jr. — A600

Design: 6c, Santa Claus and boy.

1968 Without Gum ***Perf. 11½x11***

1110 A599	5c multicolored	.30	.25
1111 A599	6c multicolored	.30	.25

Christmas 1968.
Issue dates: 5c, Dec. 12; 6c, Dec. 20.

1968, Dec. 13
Without Gum
1112 A600 10c crimson & blk .20 .20

Cent. of the birth of Francisco Caldas, Jr., journalist and founder of Correio de Povo, newspaper.

Map of Brazil, War Memorial and Reservists' Emblem — A601

Perf. 11x11½
1968, Dec. 16 Photo. Wmk. 267
1113 A601 5c bl grn & org brn .30 .20

Issued for Reservists' Day.

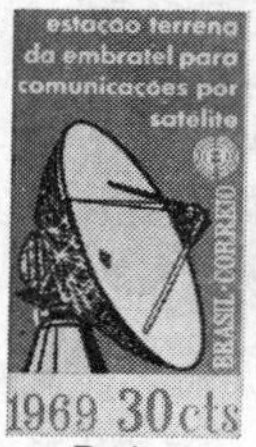

Radar Antenna A602

Viscount of Rio Branco A603

Perf. 11½x11
1969, Feb. 28 Litho. Unwmk.
Without Gum
1114 A602 30c ultra, lt bl & blk .70 .55

Inauguration of EMBRATEL, satellite communications ground station bringing US television to Brazil via Telstar.

1969, Mar. 16
Without Gum
1115 A603 5c black & buff .25 .25

José Maria da Silva Paranhos, Viscount of Rio Branco (1819-1880), statesman.

St. Gabriel — A604

1969, Mar. 24
Without Gum
1116 A604 5c multicolored .40 .25

Issued to honor St. Gabriel as patron saint of telecommunications.

Shoemaker's Last and Globe — A605

Perf. 11x11½
1969, Mar. 29 Litho. Unwmk.
Without Gum
1117 A605 5c multicolored .25 .25

4th Intl. Shoe Fair, Novo Hamburgo.

Allan Kardec A606

1969, Mar. 31 Photo. Wmk. 267
1118 A606 5c brt grn & org brn .25 .25

Allan Kardec (pen name of Leon Hippolyto Denizard Rivail, 1803-1869), French physician and spiritist.

Men of 3 Races and Arms of Cuiabá A607

1969, Apr. 8 Litho. Unwmk.
Without Gum
1119 A607 5c black & multi .25 .25

250th anniversary of the founding of Cuiabá, capital of Matto Grosso.

State Mint — A608

1969, Apr. 11 ***Perf. 11½***
Without Gum
1120 A608 5c olive bister & org .45 .35

Opening of the state money printing plant.

Brazilian Stamps and Emblem A609

Perf. 11x11½
1969, Apr. 30 Litho. Unwmk.
Without Gum
1121 A609 5c multicolored .25 .25

Sao Paulo Philatelic Society, 50th anniv.

St. Anne, Baroque Statue — A610

1969, May 8 ***Perf. 11½***

Without Gum

1122 A610 5c lemon & multi .50 .40

Issued for Mother's Day.

ILO Emblem A611

Perf. 11x11½

1969, May 13 Photo. Wmk. 267

1123 A611 5c dp rose red & gold .25 .20

50th anniv. of the ILO.

Diving Platform and Swimming Pool — A612

Mother and Child at Window — A613

Lithographed and Photogravure

Perf. 11½x11

1969, June 13 Unwmk.

Without Gum

1124 A612 20c bis brn, blk & bl grn .55 .40

40th anniversary of the Cearense Water Sports Club, Fortaleza.

1969 Litho. *Perf. 11½*

Designs: 20c, Modern sculpture by Felicia Leirner. 50c, "The Sun Sets in Brasilia," by Danilo di Prete. 1cr, Angelfish, painting by Aldemir Martins.

Size: 24x36mm

1125 A613 10c orange & multi .55 .25

Size: 33x34mm

1126 A613 20c red & multi .55 .50

Size: 33x53mm

1127 A613 50c yellow & multi 1.90 1.25

Without Gum

1128 A613 1cr gray & multi 2.50 1.25

Nos. 1125-1128 (4) 5.50 3.25

Issued to publicize the 10th Biennial Art Exhibition, Sao Paulo, Sept.-Dec. 1969.

Angelfish A614

Fish — A615

Fish: 10c, Tetra. 15c, Piranha. No. 1130c, Megalamphodus megalopterus. 30c, Black tetra.

Wmk. 267

1969, July 21 Litho. *Perf. 11½*

1129 A614 20c multicolored .70 .40

Souvenir Sheet

1969, July 24 Unwmk. *Imperf.*

1130	A615 Sheet of 4	5.00	*5.00*
a.	10c yellow & multi	.90	.90
b.	15c bright blue & multi	.90	.90
c.	20c green & multi	.90	.90
d.	30c orange & multi	.90	.90

Issued to publicize the work of ACAPI, an organization devoted to the preservation and development of fish in Brazil.

No. 1130 contains 4 stamps, size: 38½x21mm.

L. O. Teles de Menezes A616

Mailman A617

Perf. 11½x11

1969, July 26 Photo. Wmk. 267

1131 A616 50c dp org & bl grn 1.25 1.00

Centenary of Spiritism press in Brazil.

1969, Aug. 1

1132 A617 30c blue 1.10 .90

Issued for Stamp Day.

Map of Brazil A618

Gen. Tasso Fragoso A620

Railroad Bridge A619

Perf. 11½

1969, Aug. 25 Unwmk. Litho.

Without Gum

1133 A618 10c lt ultra, grn & yel .25 .20

Perf. 11x11½

1134 A619 20c multicolored .80 .40

Perf. 11½x11

Engr. Wmk. 267

With Gum

1135 A620 20c green .80 .50

Nos. 1133-1135 (3) 1.85 1.10

No. 1133 honors the Army as guardian of security; No. 1134, as promoter of development. No. 1135 the birth centenary of Gen. Tasso Fragoso.

Jupia Dam, Parana River — A621

Perf. 11½

1969, Sept. 10 Litho. Unwmk.

Without Gum

1136 A621 20c lt blue & multi .35 .35

Inauguration of the Jupia Dam, part of the Urubupunga hydroelectric system serving Sao Paulo.

Gandhi and Spinning Wheel A622

1969, Oct. 2 *Perf. 11x11½*

1137 A622 20c yellow & blk .40 .30

Mohandas K. Gandhi (1869-1948), leader in India's fight for independence.

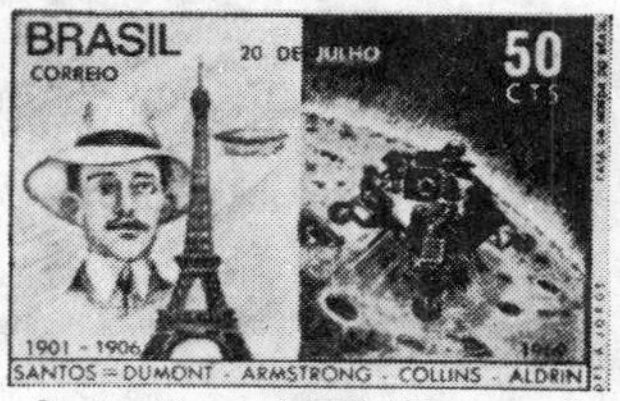

Santos Dumont, Eiffel Tower and Module Landing on Moon — A623

1969, Oct. 17 *Perf. 11½*

Without Gum

1138 A623 50c dk bl & multi 1.75 1.25

Man's first landing on the moon, July 20, 1969. See note after US No. C76.

Smelting Plant — A624

1969, Oct. 26 Unwmk. *Perf. 11½*

Without Gum

1139 A624 20c multicolored .45 .40

Expansion of Brazil's steel industry.

Steel Furnace A625

1969, Oct. 31 Litho.

Without Gum

1140 A625 10c yellow & multi .45 .40

25th anniversary of Acesita Steel Works.

Water Vendor, by J. B. Debret — A626

Design: 30c, Street Scene, by Debret.

1969-70

Without Gum

1141 A626 20c multicolored 1.25 .50

1141A A626 30c multicolored 1.25 1.00

Jean Baptiste Debret (1768-1848), painter.

Issued: 20c, Nov. 5, 1969; 30c, May 19, 1970.

Exhibition Emblem — A627

1969, Nov. 15 *Perf. 11½x11*

Without Gum

1142 A627 10c multicolored .35 .20

Issued to publicize the ABUEXPO 69 Philatelic Exposition, Sao Paulo, Nov. 15-23.

Plane — A628

1969, Nov. 23

Without Gum

1143 A628 50c multicolored 2.75 1.40

Issued to publicize the year of the expansion of the national aviation industry.

Pelé Scoring A629

1969-70

Without Gum

1144 A629 10c multicolored .40 .30

Souvenir Sheet

Imperf

1145 A629 75c multi ('70) 4.50 3.50

Issued to commemorate the 1,000th goal scored by Pele, Brazilian soccer player.

No. 1145 contains one imperf. stamp with simulated perforations.

Issued: 10c, Nov. 28, 1969; 75c, Jan. 23, 1970.

Madonna and Child from Villa Velha Monastery
A630

Perf. 11½

1969, Dec. Unwmk. Litho.

Without Gum

1146 A630 10c gold & multi .35 .20

Souvenir Sheet

Imperf

1147 A630 75c gold & multi 12.00 *15.00*

Christmas 1969.

No. 1147 has simulated perforations.

Issue dates: 10c, Dec. 8; 75c, Dec. 18.

Destroyer and Submarine
A631

Perf. 11x11½

1969, Dec. 9 Engr. Wmk. 267

1148 A631 5c bluish gray .40 .25

Issued for Navy Day.

Dr. Herman Blumenau
A632

1969, Dec. 26 ***Perf. 11½***

1149 A632 20c gray grn .85 .40

Dr. Herman Blumenau (1819-1899), founder of Blumenau, Santa Catarina State.

Carnival Scene — A633

Sugarloaf Mountain, Mask, Confetti and Streamers
A634

Designs: 5c, Jumping boy and 2 women, vert. 20c, Clowns. 50c, Drummer.

1969-70 Litho. Unwmk.

Without Gum

1150 A633 5c multicolored .40 .30
1151 A633 10c multicolored .40 .30
1152 A633 20c multicolored .50 .40
1153 A634 30c multicolored 3.00 3.00
1154 A634 50c multicolored 2.75 2.50
Nos. 1150-1154 (5) 7.05 6.50

Carico Carnival, Rio de Janeiro.

Issue dates: Nos. 1150-1152, Dec. 29, 1969. Nos. 1153-1154, Feb. 5, 1970.

Opening Bars of "Il Guarani" with Antonio Carlos Gomes Conducting
A635

1970, Mar. 19 Litho. ***Perf. 11½***

Without Gum

1155 A635 20c blk, yel, gray & brn .60 .40

Centenar y of the opera Il Guarani, by Antonio Carlos Gomes.

Church of Penha
A636

1970, Apr. 6 Unwmk. ***Perf. 11½***

Without Gum

1156 A636 20c black & multi .30 .20

400th anniversary of the Church of Penha, State of Espirito Santo.

Assembly Building
A637

10th anniv. of Brasilia: 50c, Reflecting Pool. 1cr, Presidential Palace.

1970, Apr. 21

Without Gum

1157 A637 20c multicolored .90 .70
1158 A637 50c multicolored 2.25 1.75
1159 A637 1cr multicolored 2.25 1.75
Nos. 1157-1159 (3) 5.40 4.20

Symbolic Water Design
A638

1970, May 5 Unwmk. ***Perf. 11½***

Without Gum

1161 A638 50c multicolored 2.50 3.00

Issued to publicize the Rondon Project for the development of the Amazon River basin.

Marshal Manoel Luiz Osorio and Osorio Arms — A639

1970, May 8

Without Gum

1162 A639 20c multicolored 1.50 1.00

Issued to commemorate the inauguration of the Marshal Osorio Historical Park.

Madonna, from San Antonio Monastery, Rio de Janeiro
A640

Detail from Brasilia Cathedral
A641

1970, May 10

Without Gum

1163 A640 20c multicolored .40 .40

Issued for Mother's Day.

1970, May 27 Engr. Wmk. 267

1164 A641 20c lt yellow grn .25 .25

8th National Eucharistic Congress, Brasilia.

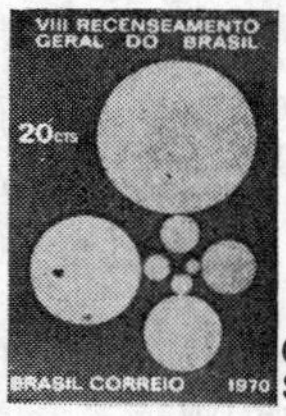

Census Symbol — A642

Perf. 11½

1970, June 22 Unwmk. Litho.

Without Gum

1165 A642 20c green & yel .60 .60

Issued to publicize the 8th general census.

Soccer Cup, Maps of Brazil and Mexico
A643

Swedish Flag and Player Holding Rimet Cup — A644

Designs: 2cr, Chilean flag and soccer. 3cr, Mexican flag and soccer.

1970

Without Gum

1166 A643 50c blk, lt bl & gold .90 .90
1167 A644 1cr pink & multi 2.75 1.50
1168 A644 2cr gray & multi 5.25 1.50
1169 A644 3cr multicolored 4.50 1.00
Nos. 1166-1169 (4) 13.40 4.90

9th World Soccer Championships for the Jules Rimet Cup, Mexico City, May 30-June 21. No. 1166 honors Brazil's victory.

Issued: #1166, June 24; #1167-1169, Aug. 4.

Corcovado Christ and Map of South America
A645

1970, July 18

Without Gum

1170 A645 50c brn, dk red & bl 2.50 2.50

6th World Cong. of Marist Brothers' Alumni.

Pandia Calogeras, Minister of War — A646

Perf. 11½x11

1970, Aug. 25 Photo. Unwmk.

1171 A646 20c blue green .50 .50

Brazilian Military Emblems and Map
A647

Perf. 11x11½

1970, Sept. 8 Litho. Unwmk.

Without Gum

1172 A647 20c gray & multi .50 .50

25th anniv. of victory in World War II.

Annunciation (Brazilian Primitive Painting)
A648

1970, Sept. 29 ***Perf. 11½***

Without Gum

1173 A648 20c multicolored 1.25 1.00

Issued for St. Gabriel's (patron saint of communications) Day.

Boy in Library
A649

UN Emblem
A650

1970, Oct. 23

Without Gum

1174 A649 20c multicolored 1.25 1.00

Issued to publicize Book Week.

1970, Oct. 24

Without Gum

1175 A650 50c dk bl, lt bl & sil 1.25 1.25

25th anniversary of the United Nations.

Rio de Janeiro, 1820 — A651

Designs: 50c, LUBRAPEX 70 emblem. 1cr, Rio de Janeiro with Sugar Loaf Mountain, 1970. No. 1179, like 20c.

1970, Oct.

Without Gum

1176	A651	20c multicolored	1.75	1.00
1177	A651	50c yel brn & blk	3.50	2.00
1178	A651	1cr multicolored	3.50	3.75
		Nos. 1176-1178 (3)	8.75	6.75

Souvenir Sheet

Imperf

1179	A651	1cr multicolored	11.00	*17.00*

LUBRAPEX 70, 3rd Portuguese-Brazilian Phil. Exhib., Rio de Janeiro, Oct. 24-31.

Issued: #1176-1178, Oct. 27; #1179, Oct. 31.

Holy Family by Candido Portinari A652

1970, Dec. Litho. *Perf. 11½*

Without Gum

1180	A652	50c multicolored	1.50	1.50

Souvenir Sheet

Imperf

1181	A652	1cr multicolored	15.00	*24.00*

Christmas 1970. No. 1181 contains one stamp with simulated perforations.

Issue dates: 50c, Dec. 1; 1cr, Dec. 8.

Battleship A653

CIH Emblem A654

1970, Dec. 11 Litho. *Perf. 11½*

Without Gum

1182	A653	20c multicolored	1.25	.75

Navy Day.

1971, Mar. 28 Litho. *Perf. 11½*

Without Gum

1183	A654	50c black & red	1.50	1.75

3rd Inter-American Housing Congress, Mar. 27-Apr. 3.

Links Around Globe — A655

1971, Mar. 31 Litho. *Perf. 12½x11*

Without Gum

1184	A655	20c grn, yel, blk & red	.65	.50

Intl. year against racial discrimination.

Morpho Melacheilus — A656

Design: 1cr, Papilio thoas brasiliensis.

Perf. 11x11½

1971, Apr. 28 Litho. Unwmk.

Without Gum

1185	A656	20c multicolored	1.25	.60
1186	A656	1cr multicolored	5.50	3.25

Madonna and Child — A657

1971, May 9 Litho. *Perf. 11½*

Without Gum

1187	A657	20c multicolored	.85	.40

Mother's Day, 1971.

Basketball A658

1971, May 19

Without Gum

1188	A658	70c multicolored	1.50	1.00

6th World Women's Basketball Championship.

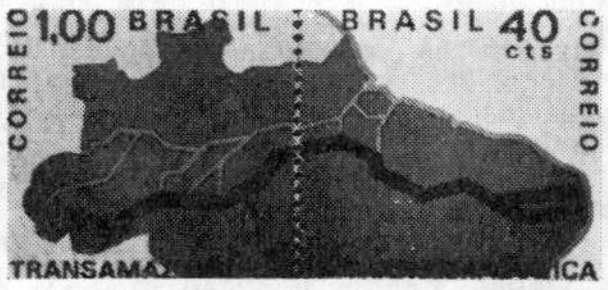

Map of Trans-Amazon Highway
A660 A659

Perf. 11½

1971, July 1 Unwmk. Litho.

Without Gum

1189	A659	40c multicolored	5.50	2.75
1190	A660	1cr multicolored	5.50	5.50
a.		Pair, #1189-1190	11.00	11.00

Trans-Amazon Highway. No. 1190a printed in sheets of 28 (4x7). Horizontal rows contain 2 No. 1190a with a label between. Each label carries different inscription.

Man's Head, by Victor Mairelles de Lima — A661

Stamp Day: 1cr, Arab Violinist, by Pedro Américo.

1971, Aug. 1

Without Gum

1191	A661	40c pink & multi	1.25	.80
1192	A661	1cr gray & multi	3.25	1.65

Duke of Caxias and Map of Brazil — A662

1971, Aug. 23 Photo.

1193	A662	20c yel grn & red brn	.50	.60

Army Week.

Anita Garibaldi — A663

1971, Aug. 30 Litho.

Without Gum

1194	A663	20c multicolored	.40	.40

Anita Garibaldi (1821-1849), heroine in liberation of Brazil.

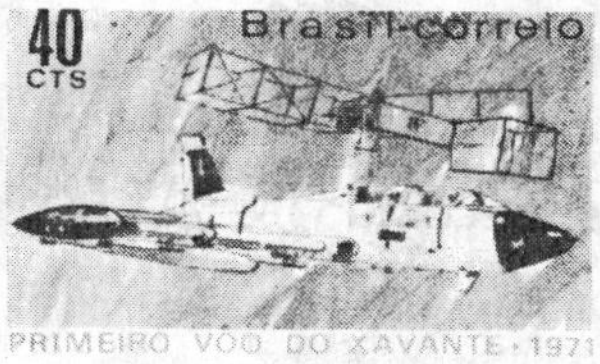

Xavante Jet and Santos Dumont's Plane, 1910 — A664

1971, Sept. 6

Without Gum

1195	A664	40c yellow & multi	1.40	.75

First flight of Xavante jet plane.

Flags and Map of Central American Nations — A665

"71" in French Flag Colors — A666

1971, Sept. 15

Without Gum

1196	A665	40c ocher & multi	1.25	.60

Sesquicentennial of the independence of Central American nations.

1971, Sept. 16

Without Gum

1197	A666	1.30cr ultra & multi	1.25	1.10

French Exhibition.

Black Mother, by Lucilio de Albuquerque A667

Archangel Gabriel A668

1971, Sept. 28

Without Gum

1198	A667	40c multicolored	.60	.50

Centenary of law guaranteeing personal freedom starting at birth.

1971, Sept. 29 *Perf. 11½x11*

Without Gum

1199	A668	40c multicolored	.75	.65

St. Gabriel's Day.

Bridge over River — A669

Children's Drawings: 35c, People crossing bridge. 60c, Woman with hat.

1971, Oct. 25 *Perf. 11½*

Without Gum

1200	A669	35c pink, bl & blk	.55	.45
1201	A669	45c black & multi	1.40	.45
1202	A669	60c olive & multi	.55	.45
		Nos. 1200-1202 (3)	2.50	1.35

Children's Day.

Werkhäuserii Superba — A670

1971, Nov. 16

Without Gum

1203	A670	40c blue & multi	2.00	1.00

In memory of Carlos Werkhauser, botanist.

Greek Key Pattern "25" — A671

Design: 40c, like 20c but inscribed "sesc / servicio social / do comercio."

1971, Dec. 3

Without Gum

1204	A671	20c black & blue	1.25	1.00
1205	A671	40c black & org	1.25	1.00
a.		Pair, #1204-1205	2.50	2.50

25th anniversary of SENAC (national apprenticeship system) and SESC (commercial social service).

Gunboat A672

1971, Dec. 8 *Perf. 11*

Without Gum

1206 A672 20c blue & multi .85 .50

Navy Day.

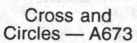

Cross and Circles — A673

Washing of Bonfim Church, Salvador, Bahia — A674

1971, Dec. 11

1207 A673 20c car & blue .40 .40
1208 A673 75c silver & gray .80 *3.00*
1209 A673 1.30cr blk, yel, grn & bl 4.75 2.50
Nos. 1207-1209 (3) 5.95 *5.90*

Christmas 1971.

1972, Feb. 18 Litho. *Perf. 11½x11*

Designs: 40c, Grape Festival, Rio Grande do Sul. 75c, Festival of the Virgin of Nazareth, Belém. 1.30cr, Winter Arts Festival, Ouro Preto.

Without Gum

1210 A674 20c silver & multi 1.50 .75
1211 A674 40c silver & multi 2.75 .75
1212 A674 75c silver & multi 2.75 3.00
1213 A674 1.30cr silver & multi 6.00 3.00
Nos. 1210-1213 (4) 13.00 7.50

Pres. Lanusse and Flag of Argentina A675

1972, Mar. 13 *Perf. 11x11½*

Without Gum

1214 A675 40c blue & multi 2.00 2.50

Visit of Lt. Gen. Alejandro Agustin Lanusse, president of Argentina.

Presidents Castello Branco, Costa e Silva and Garrastazu Medici A676

1972, Mar. 29

Without Gum

1215 A676 20c emerald & multi 1.25 .60

Anniversary of 1964 revolution.

Post Office Emblem — A677

Perf. 11½x11

1972, Apr. 10 Photo. Unwmk.

1216 A677 20c red brown 2.00 .20

No. 1216 is luminescent.

Pres. Thomas and Portuguese Flag — A678

1972, Apr. 22 Litho. *Perf. 11*

Without Gum

1217 A678 75c ol brn & multi 1.75 1.75

Visit of Pres. Americo Thomas of Portugal to Brazil, Apr. 22-27.

Soil Research (CPRM) A679

1972, May 3 *Perf. 11½*

Without Gum

1218 A679 20c shown 1.50 .50
1219 A679 40c Offshore oil rig 3.50 .85
1220 A679 75c Hydroelectric dam 1.50 1.75
1221 A679 1.30cr Iron ore production 3.50 1.40
Nos. 1218-1221 (4) 10.00 4.50

Industrial development. Stamps are inscribed with names of industrial firms. See Nos. 1228-1229.

Souvenir Sheet

Poster for Modern Art Week 1922 A680

1972, May 5

1222 A680 1cr black & car 26.00 26.00

50th anniversary of Modern Art Week.

Mailman, Map of Brazil and Letters A681

Designs: 45c, "Telecommunications", vert. 60c, Tropospheric scatter system. 70c, Road map of Brazil and worker.

1972, May 26

Without Gum

1223 A681 35c blue & multi 1.25 .40
1224 A681 45c silver & multi 1.50 1.50
1225 A681 60c black & multi 1.50 1.25
1226 A681 70c multicolored 1.75 1.25
Nos. 1223-1226 (4) 6.00 4.40

Unification of communications in Brazil.

Development Type and

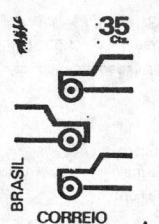

Automobiles — A682

Perf. 11x11½, 11½x11

1972, June 21 Photo.

1227 A682 35c shown 1.00 .50

Litho.

1228 A679 45c Ships 1.00 .60
1229 A679 70c Ingots 1.00 .40
Nos. 1227-1229 (3) 3.00 1.50

Industrial development. The 35c is luminescent.

Soccer — A683

Designs: 75c, Folk music. 1.30cr, Plastic arts.

Perf. 11½x11

1972, July 7 Photo. Unwmk.

1230 A683 20c black & yel 1.00 .50
1231 A683 75c black & ver 2.00 3.50
1232 A683 1.30cr black & ultra 4.00 3.50
Nos. 1230-1232 (3) 7.00 7.50

150th anniversary of independence. No. 1230 publicizes the 1972 sports tournament, a part of independence celebrations. Luminescent.

Souvenir Sheet

Shout of Independence, by Pedro Americo de Figueiredo e Melo — A684

1972, July 19 Litho. *Perf. 11½*

Without Gum

1233 A684 1cr multicolored 4.00 *9.00*

4th Inter-American Philatelic Exhibition, EXFILBRA, Rio de Janeiro, Aug 26-Sept. 2.

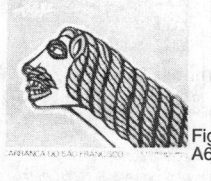

Figurehead A685

Brazilian folklore: 60c, Gauchos dancing fandango. 75c, Acrobats (capoeira). 1.15cr, Karajá (ceramic) doll. 1.30cr, Mock bullfight (bumba meu boi).

1972, Aug. 6

Without Gum

1234 A685 45c multicolored .85 .35
1235 A685 60c orange & multi 1.65 1.50
1236 A685 75c gray & multi .30 .30
1237 A685 1.15cr multicolored .55 .55
1238 A685 1.30cr yellow & multi 5.00 2.00
Nos. 1234-1238 (5) 8.35 4.70

Map of Brazil, by Diego Homem, 1568 — A686

Designs: 1cr, Map of Americas, by Nicholas Visscher, 1652. 2cr, Map of Americas, by Lopo Homem, 1519.

1972, Aug. 26 Litho. *Perf. 11½*

Without Gum

1239 A686 70c multicolored .50 .50
1240 A686 1cr multicolored 9.00 1.00
1241 A686 2cr multicolored 4.50 1.50
Nos. 1239-1241 (3) 14.00 3.00

4th Inter-American Philatelic Exhibition, EXFILBRA, Rio de Janeiro, Aug. 26-Sept. 2.

Dom Pedro Proclaimed Emperor, by Jean Baptiste Debret A687

Designs: 30c, Founding of Brazil (people with imperial flag), vert. 1cr, Coronation of Emperor Dom Pedro, vert. 2cr, Dom Pedro commemorative medal. 3.50cr, Independence Monument, Ipiranga.

1972, Sept. 4 Litho. *Perf. 11½x11*

1242 A687 30c yellow & grn 1.25 1.25
1243 A687 70c pink & rose lil 1.25 .80
1244 A687 1cr buff & red brn 8.00 1.25
1245 A687 2cr pale yel & blk 4.00 1.25
1246 A687 3.50cr gray & blk 7.25 4.00
Nos. 1242-1246 (5) 21.75 8.55

Sesquicentennial of independence.

Souvenir Sheet

"Automobile Race" — A688

1972, Nov. 14 *Perf. 11½*

1247 A688 2cr multicolored 10.00 15.00

Emerson Fittipaldi, Brazilian world racing champion.

Numeral and Post Office Emblem — A689

Möbius Strip A689a

Perf. 11½x11

1972-75 Unwmk. Photo.

1248 A689 5c orange .35 .20
a. Wmk. 267 .20 .20
1249 A689 10c brown ('73) .20 .20
a. Wmk. 267 4.00 .20
1250 A689 15c brt blue ('75) .20 .20
1251 A689 20c ultra .35 .20
1252 A689 25c sepia ('75) .25 .20
1253 A689 30c dp carmine .40 .20
1254 A689 40c dk grn ('73) .20 .20
1255 A689 50c olive .30 .20
1256 A689 70c red lilac ('75) .30 .20

Engr. *Perf. 11½*

1257 A689a 1cr lilac ('74) .45 .20
1258 A689a 2cr grnsh bl ('74) .65 .20
1259 A689a 4cr org & vio ('75) 1.40 .20
1260 A689a 5cr brn, car & buff ('74) 2.00 .20
1261 A689a 10cr grn, blk & buff ('74) 4.50 .30
Nos. 1248-1261 (14) 11.55 2.90

The 5cr and 10cr have beige lithographed multiple Post Office emblem underprint.

Nos. 1248-1261 are luminescent. Nos. 1248a and 1249a are not.

Hand Writing "Mobral" A690

20c, Multiracial group and population growth curve. 1cr, People and hands holding house. 2cr, People, industrial scene and upward arrow.

1972, Nov. 28 Litho. *Perf. 11½*
Without Gum

1262 A690 10c black & multi .20 *.50*
1263 A690 20c black & multi 1.00 .75
1264 A690 1cr black & multi 8.75 .30
1265 A690 2cr black & multi 2.00 .75
Nos. 1262-1265 (4) 11.95 2.30

Publicity for: "Mobral" literacy campaign (10c); Centenary of census (20c); Housing and retirement fund (1cr); Growth of gross national product (2cr).

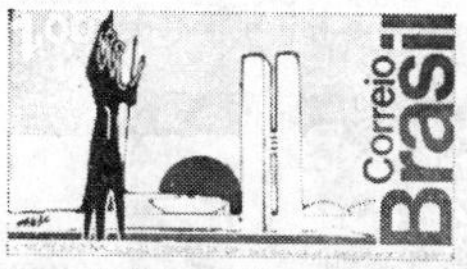

Congress Building, Brasilia, by Oscar Niemeyer, and "Os Guerreiros," by Bruno Giorgi — A691

1972, Dec. 4
Without Gum

1266 A691 1cr blue, blk & org 10.00 6.00

Meeting of Natl. Cong., Brasilia, Dec. 4-8.

Holy Family (Clay Figurines) A692

Retirement Plan A693

1972, Dec. 13 Photo. *Perf. 11½x11*

1267 A692 20c ocher & blk .85 .50

Christmas 1972. Luminescent.

Perf. 11½x11, 11x11½
1972, Dec. 20 Litho.

#1269, School children and traffic lights, horiz. 70c, Dr. Oswaldo Cruz with Red Cross, caricature. 2cr, Produce, fish and cattle, horiz.

Without Gum

1268 A693 10c blk, bl & dl org .50 .50
1269 A693 10c orange & multi 1.00 1.00
1270 A693 70c blk, red & brn 9.00 3.75
1271 A693 2cr green & multi 15.00 6.50
Nos. 1268-1271 (4) 25.50 11.75

Publicity for: Agricultural workers' assistance program (No. 1268); highway and transportation development (No. 1269); centenary of the birth of Dr. Oswaldo Cruz (1872-1917), Director of Public Health Institute (70c); agricultural and cattle export (2cr). Nos. 1268-1271 are luminescent.

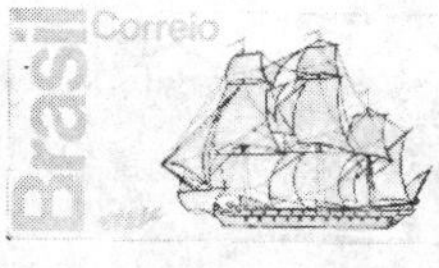

Sailing Ship, Navy A694

Designs: 10c, Monument, Brazilian Expeditionary Force. No. 1274, Plumed helmet, Army. No. 1275, Rocket, Air Force.

Lithographed and Engraved
1972, Dec. 28 *Perf. 11x11½*
Without Gum

1272 A694 10c brn, dk brn & blk 1.50 1.10
1273 A694 30c lt ultra, grn & blk 1.50 1.10
1274 A694 30c yel grn, bl grn & blk 1.50 1.10
1275 A694 30c lilac, mar & blk 1.50 1.10
a. Block of 4, #1272-1275 6.00 5.00

Armed Forces Day.

Rotary Emblem and Cogwheels A695

Perf. 11½
1973, Mar. 21 Litho. Unwmk.

1276 A695 1cr ultra, grnsh bl & yel 1.75 1.50

Rotary International serving Brazil 50 years.

Swimming A696

#1278, Gymnastics. #1279, Volleyball, vert.

1973 Photo. *Perf. 11x11½, 11½x11*

1277 A696 40c brt bl & red brn .35 .35
1278 A696 40c green & org brn 2.75 .70
1279 A696 40c violet & org brn .70 .70
Nos. 1277-1279 (3) 3.80 1.75

Issue dates: No. 1277, Apr. 19; No. 1278, May 22; No. 1279, Oct. 15.

Flag of Paraguay A697

Perf. 11½
1973, Apr. 27 Litho. Unwmk.

1280 A697 70c multicolored 1.75 1.25

Visit of Pres. Alfredo Stroessner of Paraguay, Apr. 25-27.

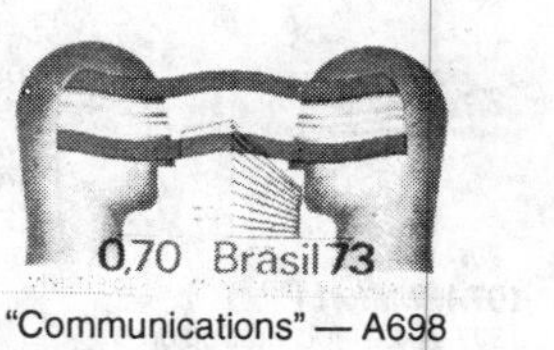

"Communications" — A698

1cr, Neptune, map of South America and Africa.

1973, May 5 *Perf. 11x11½*

1281 A698 70c multicolored .80 .70
1282 A698 1cr multicolored 4.25 3.00

Inauguration of the Ministry of Communications Building, Brasilia (70c); and of the first underwater telephone cable between South America and Europe, Bracan 1 (1cr).

Congress Emblem — A699

1973, May 19 *Perf. 11½x11*

1283 A699 1cr orange & pur 4.00 3.00

24th Congress of the International Chamber of Commerce, Rio de Janeiro, May 19-26.

Swallowtailed Manakin — A700

Birds: No. 1285, Orange-backed oriole. No. 1286, Brazilian ruby (hummingbird).

1973 Litho. *Perf. 11x11½*

1284 A700 20c multicolored .50 .20
1285 A700 20c multicolored .50 .20
1286 A700 20c multicolored .50 .20
Nos. 1284-1286 (3) 1.50 .60

Issue dates: No. 1284, May 26; No. 1285, June 6; No. 1286, June 19.

Tourists A701

1973, June 28 Litho. *Perf. 11x11½*

1287 A701 70c multicolored .90 .85

National Tourism Year.

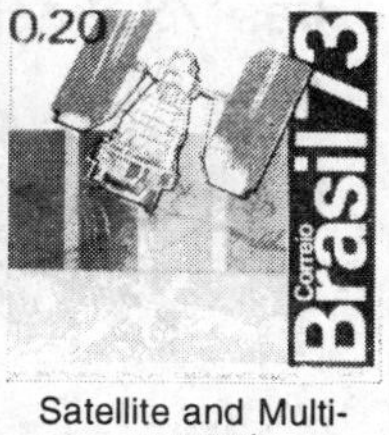

Conference at Itu — A702

Satellite and Multispectral Image — A703

1973 *Perf. 11½x11*

1288 A702 20c shown .50 .35
1289 A702 20c Decorated wagon .50 .35
1290 A702 20c Indian .50 .35
1291 A702 20c Graciosa Road .50 .35
Nos. 1288-1291 (4) 2.00 1.40

Centenary of the Itu Convention (1288); sesquicentennial of the July 2 episode (1289); 400th anniversary of the founding of Niteroi (1290); centenary of Graciosa Road (1291).
Issue dates: #1291, July 29; others July 2.

1973, July 11 *Perf. 11½*

Designs: 70c, Official opening of Engineering School, 1913. 1cr, Möbius strips and "IMPA."

1292 A703 20c black & multi .25 .40
1293 A703 70c dk blue & multi 2.25 1.00
1294 A703 1cr lilac & multi 3.00 1.00
Nos. 1292-1294 (3) 5.50 2.40

Institute for Space Research (20c); School of Engineering, Itajubá, 60th anniversary (70c); Institute for Pure and Applied Mathematics (1cr).

Santos-Dumont and 14-Bis Plane — A704

Designs (Santos-Dumont and): 70c, No. 6 Balloon and Eiffel Tower. 2cr Demoiselle plane.

Lithographed and Engraved
1973, July 20 *Perf. 11x11½*

1295 A704 20c lt grn, brt grn & brn .75 .25
1296 A704 70c yel, rose red & brn 1.75 1.25
1297 A704 2cr bl, vio bl & brn 1.75 1.25
Nos. 1295-1297 (3) 4.25 2.75

Centenary of the birth of Alberto Santos-Dumont (1873-1932), aviation pioneer.

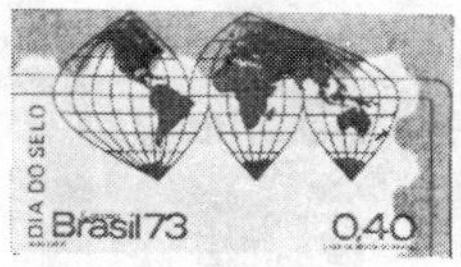

Mercator Map A705

No. 1299, Same, red border on top and at left.

Photogravure and Engraved
1973, Aug. 1 Wmk. 267

1298 A705 40c red & black 2.50 1.50
1299 A705 40c red & black 2.10 2.10
a. Block of 4 21.00 15.00

Stamp Day. Nos. 1298-1299 are printed se-tenant horizontally and tête bêche vertically in sheets of 55. Blocks of 4 have red border all around.

Gonçalves Dias (1823-1864), Poet — A706

Perf. 11½x11
1973, Aug. 10 Wmk. 267

1300 A706 40c violet & blk .70 .40

Souvenir Sheet

Copernicus and Sun — A707

Perf. 11x11½
1973, Aug. 15 Litho. Unwmk.

1301 A707 1cr multicolored 4.00 5.00

500th anniversary of the birth of Nicolaus Copernicus (1473-1543), Polish astronomer.

Values quoted in this catalogue are for stamps graded Very Fine and with no faults. An illustrated guide to grade is provided in the "Catalogue Information" section of the Introduction.

Folklore Festival Banner — A708

1973, Aug. 22 ***Perf. 11½***
1302 A708 40c ultra & multi .75 .50

Folklore Day, Aug. 22.

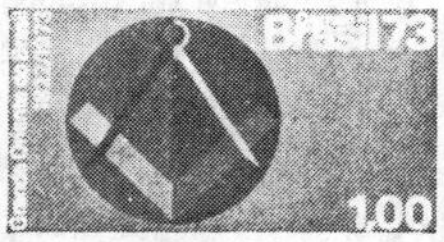

Masonic Emblem A709

1973, Aug. 24 Photo. ***Perf. 11x11½***
1303 A709 1cr Prus blue 3.00 2.00

Free Masons of Brazil, 1822-1973.

Nature Protection A710

#1305, Fire protection. #1306, Aviation safety. #1307, Safeguarding cultural heritage.

1973, Sept. 20 Litho. ***Perf. 11x11½***
1304 A710 40c brt grn & multi .75 .40
1305 A710 40c dk blue & multi .75 .40
1306 A710 40c lt blue & multi .75 .40
1307 A710 40c pink & multi .75 .40
Nos. 1304-1307 (4) 3.00 1.60

Souvenir Sheet

St. Gabriel and Proclamation of Pope Paul VI — A711

Lithographed and Engraved
1973, Sept. 29 Unwmk. ***Perf. 11½***
1308 A711 1cr bister & blk 7.50 *10.00*

1st National Exhibition of Religious Philately, Rio de Janeiro, Sept. 29-Oct. 6.

St. Teresa — A712

Photogravure and Engraved
Perf. 11½x11
1973, Sept. 30 **Wmk. 267**
1309 A712 2cr dk org & brn 3.50 2.50

St. Teresa of Lisieux, the Little Flower (1873-1897), Carmelite nun.

Monteiro Lobato and Emily A713

Perf. 11½
1973, Oct. 12 Litho. Unwmk.
1310 A713 40c shown .80 .50
1311 A713 40c Aunt Nastacia .80 .50
1312 A713 40c Snubnose, Peter and Rhino .80 .50
1313 A713 40c Viscount de Sabugosa .80 .50
1314 A713 40c Dona Benta .80 .50
a. Block of 5 + label 4.00 4.00

Monteiro Lobato, author of children's books.

Soapstone Sculpture of Isaiah (detail) — A714

Baroque Art in Brazil: No. 1316, Arabesque, gilded wood carving, horiz. 70c, Father José Mauricio Nuñes Garcia and music score. 1cr, Church door, Salvador, Bahia. 2cr, Angels, church ceiling painting by Manoel da Costa Athayde, horiz.

1973, Nov. 5
1315 A714 40c multicolored .30 .30
1316 A714 40c multicolored .30 .30
1317 A714 70c multicolored 1.50 1.40
1318 A714 1cr multicolored 9.00 3.00
1319 A714 2cr multicolored 4.00 3.00
Nos. 1315-1319 (5) 15.10 8.00

Old and New Telephones — A715

1973, Nov. 28 ***Perf. 11x11½***
1320 A715 40c multicolored .35 .30

50th anniv. of Brazilian Telephone Co.

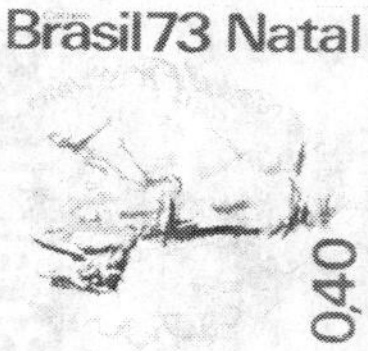

Symbolic Angel — A716

1973, Nov. 30 ***Perf. 11½***
1321 A716 40c ver & multi .35 .30

Christmas 1973.

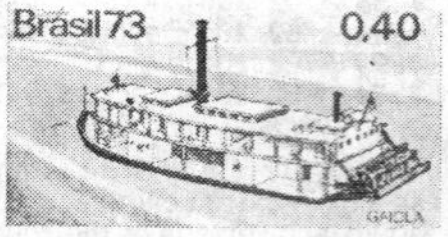

River Boats A717

1973, Nov. 30 Litho. ***Perf. 11x11½***
1322 A717 40c "Gaiola" .35 .35
1323 A717 70c "Regatao" 1.05 1.05
1324 A717 1cr "Jangada" 4.50 3.00
1325 A717 2cr "Saveiro" 4.25 3.00
Nos. 1322-1325 (4) 10.15 7.40

Nos. 1322-1325 are luminescent.

Scales of Justice — A718

1973, Dec. 5 ***Perf. 11½***
1326 A718 40c magenta & vio .50 .32

To honor the High Federal Court, created in 1891. Luminescent.

José Placido de Castro A719

Scarlet Ibis and Victoria Regia A720

Lithographed and Engraved
Perf. 11½x11
1973, Dec. 12 **Wmk. 267**
1327 A719 40c lilac rose & blk .60 .35

Centenary of the birth of Jose Placido de Castro, liberator of the State of Acre.

Perf. 11½x11
1973, Dec. 28 Litho. Unwmk.

Designs: 70c, Jaguar and spathodea campanulata. 1cr, Scarlet macaw and carnauba palm. 2cr, Rhea and coral tree.

1328 A720 40c brown & multi .80 .50
1329 A720 70c brown & multi 2.25 1.50
1330 A720 1cr bister & multi 3.50 .40
1331 A720 2cr bister & multi 6.25 3.50
Nos. 1328-1331 (4) 12.80 5.90

Nos. 1328-1331 are luminescent.

Saci Perere, Mocking Goblin — A721

Characters from Brazilian Legends: 80c, Zumbi, last chief of rebellious slaves. 1cr, Chico Rei, African king. 1.30cr, Little Black Boy of the Pasture. 2.50cr, Iara, Queen of the Waters.

Perf. 11½x11
1974, Feb. 28 Litho. Unwmk.
Size: 21x39mm
1332 A721 40c multicolored .35 .25
1333 A721 80c multicolored .70 .60
1334 A721 1cr multicolored 1.65 .45

Perf. 11½
Size: 32½x33mm
1335 A721 1.30cr multicolored 2.50 .85
1336 A721 2.50cr multicolored 10.50 2.50
Nos. 1332-1336 (5) 15.70 4.65

Nos. 1332-1336 are luminescent.

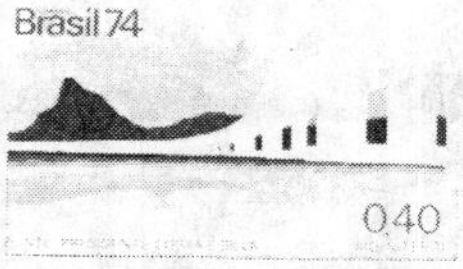

Pres. Costa e Silva Bridge A722

1974, Mar. 11
1337 A722 40c multicolored .60 .30

Inauguration of the Pres. Costa e Silva Bridge, Rio Niteroi, connecting Rio de Janeiro and Guanabara State.

"The Press" A723

1974, Mar. 25 ***Perf. 11½***
1338 A723 40c shown .50 .30
1339 A723 40c "Radio" .25 .25
1340 A723 40c "Television" .40 .30
Nos. 1338-1340 (3) 1.15 .85

Communications Commemorations: No. 1338, bicentenary of first Brazilian newspaper, published in London by Hipolito da Costa; No. 1339, founding of the Radio Sociedade do Rio de Janeiro by Roquette Pinto; No. 1340, installation of first Brazilian television station by Assis Chateaubriand. Luminescent.

"Reconstruction" — A724

1974, Mar. 31
1341 A724 40c multicolored .70 .45

10 years of progress. Luminescent.

Corcovado Christ, Marconi, Colors of Brazil and Italy — A725

1974, Apr. 25 Litho. ***Perf. 11½***
1342 A725 2.50cr multi 6.00 3.00

Guglielmo Marconi (1874-1937), Italian physicist and inventor. Luminescent.

Stamp Printing Press, Stamp Designing A726

1974, May 6
1343 A726 80c multicolored 1.00 .50

Brazilian mint.

World Map, Indian, Caucasian and Black Men — A727

World Map and: #1345, Brazilians. #1346, Cabin & German horseback rider. #1347, Italian farm wagon. #1348, Japanese woman & torii.

1974, May 3 **Unwmk.**
1344 A727 40c multicolored .30 .30
1345 A727 40c multicolored .20 .20
1346 A727 2.50cr multicolored 3.25 1.50
1347 A727 2.50cr multicolored 4.75 1.50
1348 A727 2.50cr multicolored 1.25 .85
Nos. 1344-1348 (5) 9.75 4.35

Ethnic and migration influences in Brazil.

Sandstone Cliffs, Sete Cidades National Park — A728

Tourist publicity: 80c, Ruins of Cathedral of Sao Miguel das Missões.

Lithographed and Engraved

1974, June 8 ***Perf. 11x11½***

1349 A728 40c multicolored .75 .50
1350 A728 80c multicolored .75 .50

Souvenir Sheet

Soccer — A729

1974, June 20 Litho. ***Perf. 11½***

1351 A729 2.50cr multi 3.50 *6.00*

World Cup Soccer Championship, Munich, June 13-July 7.

Church and College, Caraça A730

1974, July 6 Litho. ***Perf. 11x11½***

1352 A730 40c multicolored .45 .30

College (Seminary) of Caraça, bicent.

Wave on Television Screen A731

1974, July 15 ***Perf. 11½***

1353 A731 40c black & blue .30 .40

TELEBRAS, Third Brazilian Congress of Telecommunications, Brasilia, July 15-20.

Fernao Dias Paes — A732

1974, July 21 ***Perf. 11½***

1354 A732 20c green & multi .30 .30

3rd centenary of the expedition led by Fernao Dias Paes exploring Minas Gerais and the passage from South to North in Brazil.

Mexican Flag — A733

1974, July 24 Litho. ***Perf. 11½***

1355 A733 80c multicolored 2.25 1.10

Visit of Pres. Luis Echeverria Alvares of Mexico, July 24-29.

Flags of Brazil and Germany A734

1974, Aug. 5 ***Perf. 11x11½***

1356 A734 40c multicolored .50 .50

World Cup Soccer Championship, 1974, victory of German Federal Republic.

Souvenir Sheet

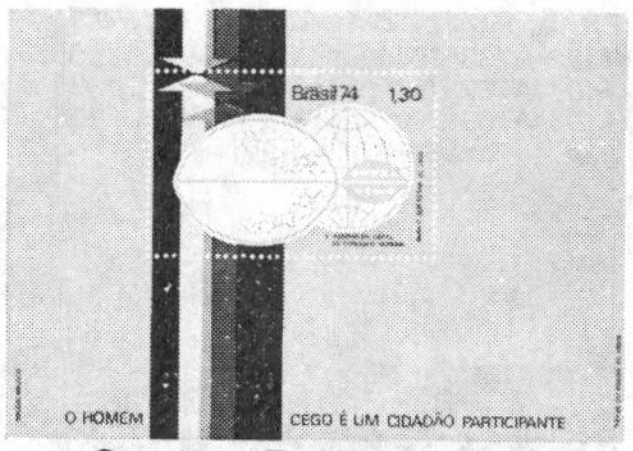

Congress Emblem — A735

1974, Aug. 7 ***Perf. 11½***

1357 A735 1.30cr multi .85 *1.75*

5th World Assembly of the World Council for the Welfare of the Blind, Sao Paulo, Aug. 7-16. Stamp and margin inscribed in Braille with name of Assembly.

Raul Pederneiras (1874-1953, Journalist, Professor of Law and Fine Arts), Caricature by J. Carlos — A736

Lithographed and Engraved

1974, Aug. 15 ***Perf. 11½x11***

1358 A736 40c buff, blk & ocher .30 .40

Society Emblem and Landscape A737

1974, Aug. 19 Litho. ***Perf. 11x11½***

1359 A737 1.30cr multi 1.25 .90

13th Congress of the International Union of Building and Savings Societies.

Souvenir Sheet

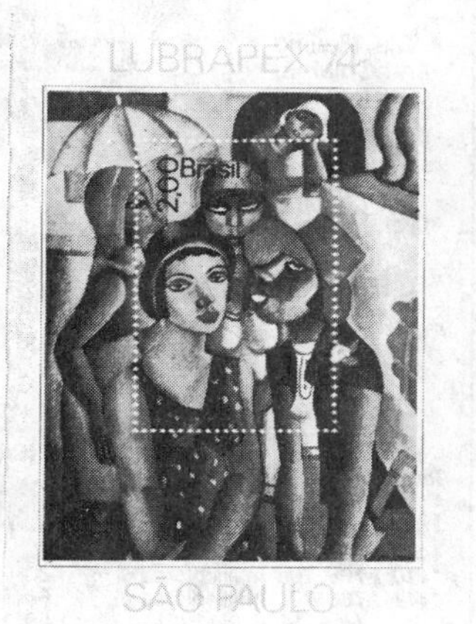

Five Women, by Di Cavalcanti — A738

1974, Aug. 26 Litho. ***Perf. 11½***

1360 A738 2cr multicolored 2.50 *6.00*

LUBRAPEX 74, 5th Portuguese-Brazilian Phil. Exhib., Sao Paulo, Nov. 26-Dec. 4.

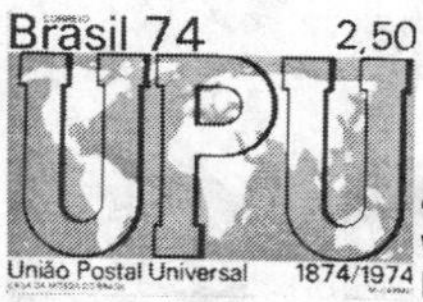

"UPU" and World Map — A739

1974, Oct. 9 Litho. ***Perf. 11½***

1361 A739 2.50cr blk & brt bl 4.50 1.75

Centenary of Universal Postal Union.

Hammock (Antillean Arawak Culture) A740

Bilro Lace — A741

Singer of "Cord" Verses — A742

Ceramic Figure by Master Vitalino — A743

1974, Oct. 16 Litho. ***Perf. 11½***

1362 A740 50c deep rose lilac 2.00 .40
1363 A741 50c lt & dk blue 2.50 .40
1364 A742 50c yel & red brn .60 .40
1365 A743 50c brt yel & dk brn .75 .40
Nos. 1362-1365 (4) 5.85 1.60

Popular Brazilian crafts.

Branch of Coffee A744

1974, Oct. 27 Unwmk. ***Perf. 11***

1366 A744 50c multicolored 1.00 .60

Centenary of city of Campinas.

Hornless Tabapua A745

Animals of Brazil: 1.30cr, Creole horse. 2.50cr, Brazilian mastiff.

1974, Nov. 10 ***Perf. 11½***

1367 A745 80c multi 1.10 .75
1368 A745 1.30cr multi 1.10 .75
1369 A745 2.50cr multi 7.75 2.50
Nos. 1367-1369 (3) 9.95 4.00

Christmas — A746

1974, Nov. 18 ***Perf. 11½x11***

1370 A746 50c Angel .70 .30

Solteira Island Hydroelectric Dam — A747

1974, Nov. 11 ***Perf. 11½***

1371 A747 50c black & yellow 1.40 .50

Inauguration of the Solteira Island Hydroelectric Dam over Parana River.

The Girls, by Carlos Reis — A748

1974, Nov. 26

1372 A748 1.30cr multi .70 .50

LUBRAPEX 74, 5th Portuguese-Brazilian Phil. Exhib., Sao Paulo, Nov. 26-Dec. 4.

Youths, Judge, Scales A749

1974, Dec. 20 Litho. ***Perf. 11½***

1373 A749 90c yel, red & bl .30 .35

Juvenile Court of Brazil, 50th anniversary.

Long Distance Runner — A750

1974, Dec. 23

1374 A750 3.30cr multi .75 .75

Sao Silvestre long distance running, 50th anniversary.

News Vendor, 1875, Masthead, 1975 — A751

1975, Jan. 4

1375 A751 50c multicolored 1.25 .75

Newspaper "O Estado de S. Paulo," cent.

Sao Paulo Industrial Park A752

Designs: 1.40cr, Natural rubber industry, Acre. 4.50cr, Manganese mining, Amapá.

1975, Jan. 24 Litho. *Perf. 11x11½*

1376 A752	50c vio bl & yel	1.25	.40
1377 A752	1.40cr yellow & brn	.60	.40
1378 A752	4.50cr yellow & blk	6.00	.40
	Nos. 1376-1378 (3)	7.85	1.20

Economic development.

Fort of the Holy Cross A753

Colonial forts: No. 1380, Fort of the Three Kings. No. 1381, Fort of Monteserrat. 90c, Fort of Our Lady of Help.

Litho. & Engr.

1975, Mar. 14 *Perf. 11½*

1379 A753	50c yel & red brn	.25	.20
1380 A753	50c yel & red brn	.40	.20
1381 A753	50c yel & red brn	.80	.20
1382 A753	90c yel & red brn	.25	.20
	Nos. 1379-1382 (4)	1.70	.80

House on Stilts, Amazon Region A754

Designs: 50c, Modern houses and plan of Brasilia. 1.40cr, Indian hut, Rondonia. 3.30cr, German-style cottage (Enxaimel), Santa Catarina.

1975, Apr. 18 Litho. *Perf. 11½*

1383 A754	50c yel & multi	1.25	2.25
1384 A754	50c yel & multi	8.50	6.25
a.	Pair, #1383-1384	10.00	8.50
1385 A754	1cr yel & multi	.85	.25
1386 A754	1.40cr yel & multi	1.75	2.50
1387 A754	1.40cr yel & multi	.50	.85
a.	Pair, #1386-1387	2.25	3.50
1388 A754	3.30cr yel & multi	.75	1.25
1389 A754	3.30cr yel & multi	3.50	4.00
a.	Pair, #1388-1380	4.25	5.25
	Nos. 1383-1389 (7)	17.10	17.35

Brazilian architecture. Nos. 1383, 1386, 1388 have yellow strip at right side, others at left.

Astronotus Ocellatus A755

Designs: Brazilian fresh-water fish.

1975, May 2 Litho. *Perf. 11½*

1390 A755	50c *shown*	1.40	.40
1391 A755	50c *Colomesus psitacus*	.25	.25
1392 A755	50c *Phallocerus caudimaculatus*	.25	.40
1393 A755	50c *Symphysodon discus*	.48	.50
	Nos. 1390-1393 (4)	2.38	1.55

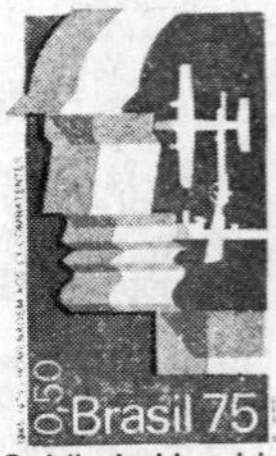

Soldier's Head in Brazil's Colors, Plane, Rifle and Ship — A756

Brazilian Otter — A757

1975, May 8 *Perf. 11½x11*

1394 A756	50c vio bl & multi	.35	.30

In honor of the veterans of World War II, on the 30th anniversary of victory.

1975, June 17 Litho. *Perf. 11½*

Nature protection: 70c, Brazilian pines, horiz. 3.30cr, Marsh cayman, horiz.

1395 A757	70c bl, grn & blk	1.05	.50
1396 A757	1cr multi	1.05	1.00
1397 A757	3.30cr multi	.90	.75
	Nos. 1395-1397 (3)	3.00	2.25

Petroglyphs, Stone of Ingá — A758

Marjoara Vase, Pará — A759

Vinctifer Comptoni, Petrified Fish — A760

1975, July 8 Litho. *Perf. 11½*

1398 A758	70c multicolored	.55	.40
1399 A759	1cr multicolored	.35	.40
1400 A760	1cr multicolored	.35	.40
	Nos. 1398-1400 (3)	1.25	1.20

Archaeological discoveries.

Immaculate Conception, Franciscan Monastery, Vitoria — A761

Post and Telegraph Ministry — A762

1975, July 15

1401 A761	3.30cr blue & multi	.95	.95

Holy Year 1975 and 300th anniv. of establishment of the Franciscan Province in Southern Brazil.

1975, Aug. 8 Engr. *Perf. 11½*

1402 A762	70c dk carmine	.70	.30

Stamp Day 1975.

Sword Dance, Minas Gerais A763

Folk Dances: No. 1404, Umbrella Dance, Pernambuco. No. 1405, Warrior's Dance, Alagoas.

1975, Aug. 22 Litho. *Perf. 11½*

1403 A763	70c gray & multi	.35	.35
1404 A763	70c pink & multi	.35	.35
1405 A763	70c yellow & multi	.35	.35
	Nos. 1403-1405 (3)	1.05	1.05

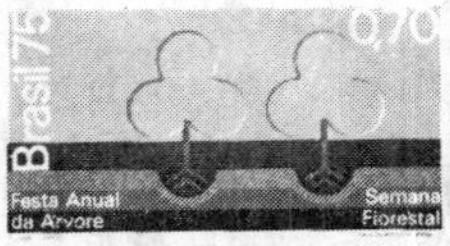

Trees A764

1975, Sept. 15 *Perf. 11x11½*

1406 A764	70c multicolored	.30	.25

Annual Tree Festival.

Globe, Radar and Satellite — A765

1975, Sept. 16 *Perf. 11½*

1407 A765	3.30cr multi	.70	.75

Inauguration of 2nd antenna of Tangua Earth Station, Rio de Janeiro State.

Woman Holding Flowers and Globe A766

1975, Sept. 23

1408 A766	3.30cr multi	1.00	1.00

International Women's Year 1975.

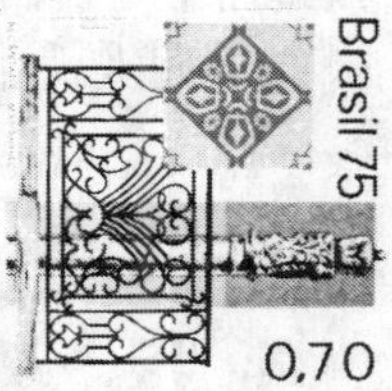

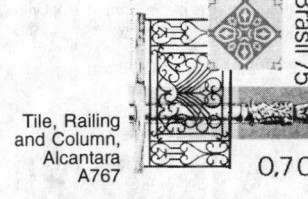

Tile, Railing and Column, Alcantara A767

Cross and Monastery, Sao Cristovao — A768

Historic cities: No. 1411, Jug and Clock Tower, Goiás, vert.

1975, Sept. 27 Litho. *Perf. 11½*

1409 A767	70c multicolored	.30	.45
1410 A768	70c multicolored	.60	.45
1411 A768	70c multicolored	.60	.45
	Nos. 1409-1411 (3)	1.50	1.35

"Books teach how to live" — A769

1975, Oct. 23 Litho. *Perf. 11½*

1412 A769	70c multicolored	.25	.30

Day of the Book.

ASTA Congress Emblem A770

1975, Oct. 27 *Perf. 11x11½*

1413 A770	70c multicolored	.25	.30

American Society of Travel Agents, 45th World Congress, Rio, Oct. 27-Nov. 1.

Angels — A771

1975, Nov. 11

1414 A771	70c red & brown	.25	.20

Christmas 1975.

Map of Americas, Waves — A772

Dom Pedro II — A773

1975, Nov. 19 *Perf. 11½x12*

1415 A772	5.20cr gray & multi	2.75	2.00

2nd Interamerican Conference of Telecommunications (CITEL), Rio, Nov. 19-27.

1975, Dec. 2 Engr. *Perf. 12*

1416 A773	70c violet brown	.75	.45

Dom Pedro II (1825-1891), emperor of Brazil, birth sesquicentennial.

People and Cross A774

1975, Nov. 27 Litho. *Perf. 11x11½*

1417 A774	70c lt bl & dp bl	.50	.65

National Day of Thanksgiving.

Guarapari Beach, Espirito Santo A775

Tourist Publicity: #1419, Salt Stone beach, Piaui. #1420, Cliffs, Rio Grande Do Sul.

1975, Dec. 19 Litho. *Perf. 11½*

1418 A775	70c multicolored	.30	.30
1419 A775	70c multicolored	.30	.30
1420 A775	70c multicolored	.30	.30
	Nos. 1418-1420 (3)	.90	.90

Triple Jump, Games Emblem A776

1975, Dec. 22 ***Perf. 11x11½***
1421 A776 1.60cr bl grn & blk .25 .35

Triple jump world record by Joao Carlos de Oliveira in 7th Pan-American Games, Mexico City, Oct. 12-26.

UN Emblem and Headquarters — A777

1975, Dec. 29 ***Perf. 11½***
1422 A777 1.30cr dp bl & vio bl .25 .30

United Nations, 30th anniversary.

Light Bulbs, House and Sun A778

Energy conservation: No. 1424, Gasoline drops, car and sun.

1976, Jan. 16
1423 A778 70c multicolored .30 .20
1424 A778 70c multicolored .30 .20

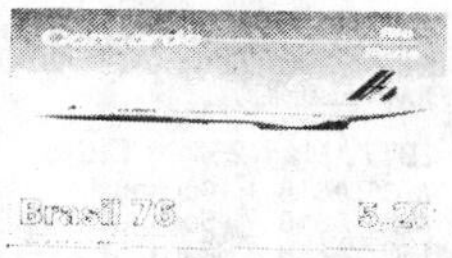

Concorde A779

1976, Jan. 21 **Litho.** ***Perf. 11x11½***
1425 A779 5.20cr bluish black .50 .35

First commercial flight of supersonic jet Concorde from Paris to Rio, Jan. 21.

Souvenir Sheet

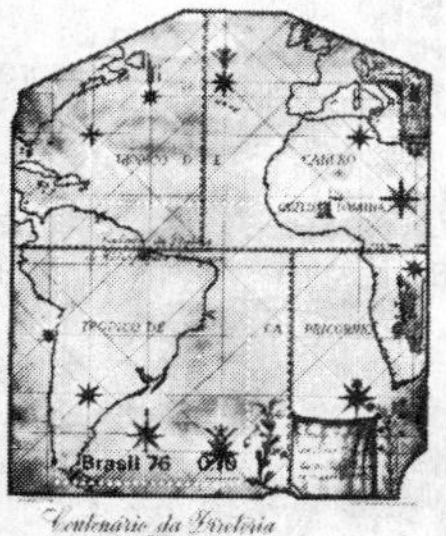

Nautical Map of South Atlantic, 1776 A780

1976, Feb. 2 ***Perf. 11½***
1426 A780 70c salmon & multi .85 *1.50*

Centenary of the Naval Hydrographic and Navigation Institute.

Telephone Lines, 1876 Telephone A781

1976, Mar. 10 **Litho.** ***Perf. 11x11½***
1427 A781 5.20cr orange & blue .65 .50

Centenary of first telephone call by Alexander Graham Bell, March 10, 1876.

Eye and Exclamation Point — A782

Kaiapo Body Painting — A783

1976, Apr. 7 **Litho.** ***Perf. 11½x11***
1428 A782 1cr vio red brn & brn .50 *.75*

World Health Day: "Foresight prevents blindness."

1976, Apr. 19 **Litho.** ***Perf. 11½***

Designs: No. 1430, Bakairi ceremonial mask. No. 1431, Karajá feather headdress.

1429 A783 1cr light violet & multi .20 .20
1430 A783 1cr light violet & multi .20 .20
1431 A783 1cr light violet & multi .20 .20
Nos. 1429-1431 (3) .60 .60

Preservation of indigenous culture.

Itamaraty Palace, Brasilia A784

1976, Apr. 20
1432 A784 1cr multicolored .60 .60

Diplomats' Day. Itamaraty Palace, designed by Oscar Niemeyer, houses the Ministry of Foreign Affairs.

Watering Can over Stones, by José Tarcisio A785

Fingers and Ribbons, by Pietrina Checcacci A786

1976, May 14 **Litho.** ***Perf. 11½***
1433 A785 1cr multi .25 .20
1434 A786 1.60cr multi .25 .20

Modern Brazilian art.

Basketball A787

Orchid A788

Designs (Olympic Rings and): 1.40cr, Yachting. 5.20cr, Judo.

1976, May 21 **Litho.** ***Perf. 11½***
1435 A787 1cr emerald & blk .20 .20
1436 A787 1.40cr dk blue & blk .20 .20
1437 A787 5.20cr orange & blk .65 .50
Nos. 1435-1437 (3) 1.05 .90

21st Olympic Games, Montreal, Canada, July 17-Aug. 1.

1976, June 4 ***Perf. 11½x11***

Nature protection: No. 1439, Golden-faced lion monkey.

1438 A788 1cr multicolored .25 .20
1439 A788 1cr multicolored .25 .20

Film Camera, Brazilian Colors — A789

1976, June 19
1440 A789 1cr vio bl, brt grn & yel .20 .25

Brazilian film industry.

Bahia Woman — A790

Designs: 10c, Oxcart driver, horiz. 20c, Raft fishermen, horiz. 30c, Rubber plantation worker. 40c, Cowboy, horiz. 50c, Gaucho. 80c, Gold panner. 1cr, Banana plantation worker. 1.10cr, Grape harvester. 1.30cr, Coffee picker. 1.80cr, Farmer gathering wax palms. 2cr, Potter. 5cr, Sugar cane cutter. 7cr, Salt mine worker. 10cr, Fisherman. 15cr, Coconut seller. 20cr, Lacemaker.

Perf. 11½x11, 11x11½

1976-78 **Photo.**
1441 A790 10c red brown ('77) .20 .20
1442 A790 15c brown .25 .30
1443 A790 20c violet blue .20 .20
1444 A790 30c lilac rose .20 .20
1445 A790 40c orange ('77) .20 .20
1446 A790 50c citron .20 .20
1447 A790 80c slate green .40 .20
1448 A790 1cr black .20 .20
1449 A790 1.10cr magenta ('77) .20 .20
1450 A790 1.30cr red ('77) .20 .20
1451 A790 1.80cr dk vio bl ('78) .20 .20

Engr.
1452 A790 2cr brown ('77) .25 .20
1453 A790 5cr dk pur ('77) .50 .20
1454 A790 7cr violet 1.50 .20
1455 A790 10cr yel grn ('77) .55 .20
1456 A790 15cr gray grn ('78) 1.40 .20
1457 A790 20cr blue 1.40 .20
Nos. 1441-1457 (17) 8.05 3.50

See Nos. 1653-1657.

Hyphessobrycon Innesi — A791

Designs: Brazilian fresh-water fish.

1976, July 12 **Litho.** ***Perf. 11x11½***
1460 A791 1cr *shown* .40 .40
1461 A791 1cr *Copeina arnoldi* .40 .40
1462 A791 1cr *Prochilodus insignis* .40 .40
1463 A791 1cr *Crenicichla lepidota* .40 .40
1464 A791 1cr *Ageneiosus* .40 .40
1465 A791 1cr *Corydoras reticulatus* .40 .40
a. Block of 6, #1460-1465 2.50 2.50

Santa Marta Lighthouse A792

1976, July 29 **Engr.** ***Perf. 12x11½***
1466 A792 1cr blue .20 .30

300th anniversary of the city of Laguna.

Children on Magic Carpet A793

1976, Aug. 1 **Litho.** ***Perf. 11½x12***
1467 A793 1cr multicolored .20 .20

Stamp Day.

Nurse's Lamp and Head A794

1976, Aug. 12 **Litho.** ***Perf. 11½***
1468 A794 1cr multicolored .20 .20

Brazilian Nurses' Assoc., 50th anniv.

Puppet, Soldier — A795

Winner's Medal — A796

Designs: 1.30cr, Girl's head. 1.60cr, Hand with puppet head on each finger, horiz.

1976, Aug. 20
1469 A795 1cr multi .20 .20
1470 A795 1.30cr multi .20 .20
1471 A795 1.60cr multi .20 .20
Nos. 1469-1471 (3) .60 .60

Mamulengo puppet show.

1976, Aug. 21
1472 A796 5.20cr multi .70 .50

27th International Military Athletic Championships, Rio de Janeiro, Aug. 21-28.

Family Protection — A797

1976, Sept. 12
1473 A797 1cr lt & dk blue .20 .20

National organizations SENAC and SESC helping commercial employees to improve their living standard, both commercially and socially.

Dying Tree — A798

1976, Sept. 20 Litho. *Perf. 11½*

1474 A798 1cr gray & multi .20 .20

Protection of the environment.

Atom Symbol, Electron Orbits A799

1976, Sept. 21

1475 A799 5.20cr multi .70 .50

20th General Conference of the International Atomic Energy Agency, Rio de Janeiro, Sept. 21-29.

Train in Tunnel A800

1976, Sept. 26

1476 A800 1.60cr multi .25 .25

Sao Paulo subway, 1st in Brazil.

St. Francis and Birds A801

1976, Oct. 4

1477 A801 5.20cr multi .60 .40

St. Francis of Assisi, 750th death anniv.

Ouro Preto School of Mining — A802

1976, Oct. 12 Engr. *Perf. 12x11½*

1478 A802 1cr dk vio .40 .50

Ouro Preto School of Mining, centenary.

Three Kings — A803

Designs: Children's drawings.

1976, Nov. 4 Litho. *Perf. 11½*

1479 A803 80c shown .30 .30

1480 A803 80c Santa Claus on donkey .30 .30

1481 A803 80c Virgin and Child and Angels .30 .30

1482 A803 80c Angels with candle .30 .30

1483 A803 80c Nativity .30 .30

a. Strip of 5, #1479-1483 1.40 1.40

Christmas 1976.

Souvenir Sheet

30,000 Reis Banknote — A804

1976, Nov. 5 Litho. *Perf. 11½*

1484 A804 80c multicolored .40 *1.50*

Opening of 1000th branch of Bank of Brazil, Barra do Bugres, Mato Grosso.

Virgin of Monte Serrat, by Friar Agostinho A805

St. Joseph, 18th Century Wood Sculpture — A806

Designs: 5.60cr, The Dance, by Rodolfo Bernadelli, 19th century. 6.50cr, The Caravel, by Bruno Giorgi, 20th century abstract sculpture.

1976, Nov. 5

1485 A805 80c multi .20 .20

1486 A806 5cr multi .65 .40

1487 A805 5.60cr multi .65 .40

1488 A806 6.50cr multi .65 .40

Nos. 1485-1488 (4) 2.15 1.40

Development of Brazilian sculpture.

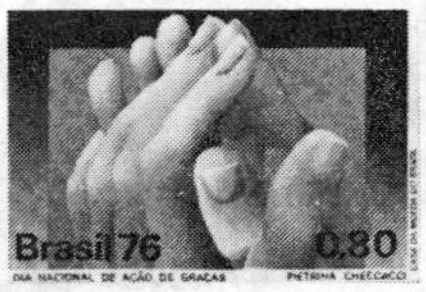

Praying Hands A807

1976, Nov. 25

1489 A807 80c multicolored .25 .25

National Day of Thanksgiving.

Sailor, 1840 — A808

Design: 2cr, Marine's uniform, 1808.

1976, Dec. 13 Litho. *Perf. 11½x11*

1490 A808 80c multicolored .25 .25

1491 A808 2cr multicolored .30 .25

Brazilian Navy.

"Natural Resources and Development" — A809

1976, Dec. 17 *Perf. 11½*

1492 A809 80c multicolored .20 .20

Brazilian Bureau of Standards, founded 1940.

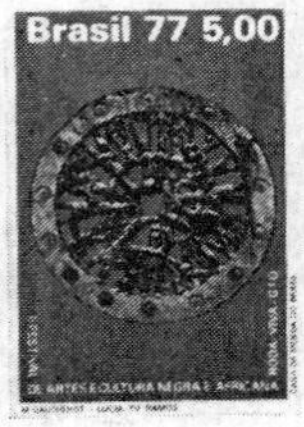

Wheel of Life — A810

Designs: 5.60cr, Beggar, sculpture by Agnaldo dos Santos. 6.50cr, Benin mask.

1977, Jan. 14

1493 A810 5cr multi .55 .35

1494 A810 5.60cr multi .55 .35

1495 A810 6.50cr multi 1.10 .35

Nos. 1493-1495 (3) 2.20 1.05

FESTAC '77, 2nd World Black and African Festival, Lagos, Nigeria, Jan. 15-Feb. 12.

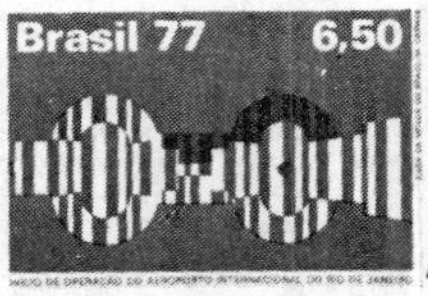

A811

1977, Jan. 20 Litho. *Perf. 11½*

1496 A811 6.50cr bl & yel grn .85 .65

Rio de Janeiro International Airport.

Seminar Emblem with Map of Americas A812

Salicylate, Microphoto A813

1977, Feb. 6

1497 A812 1.10cr gray, vio bl & bl .35 .20

6th Inter-American Budget Seminar.

1977, Apr. 10 Litho. *Perf. 11½*

1498 A813 1.10cr multi .20 .20

International Rheumatism Year.

Lions International Emblem A814

1977, Apr. 16

1499 A814 1.10cr multi .20 .20

25th anniv. of Brazilian Lions Intl.

Heitor Villa Lobos A815

1977, Apr. 26 *Perf. 11x11½*

1500 A815 1.10cr shown .20 .20

1501 A815 1.10cr Chiquinha Gonzaga .20 .20

1502 A815 1.10cr Noel Rosa .20 .20

Nos. 1500-1502 (3) .60 .60

Brazilian composers.

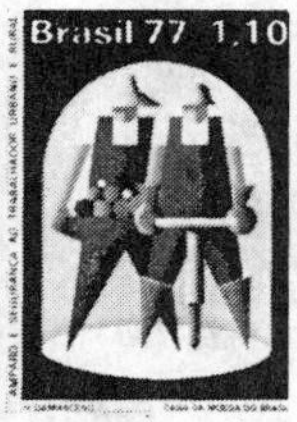

Farmer and Worker — A816

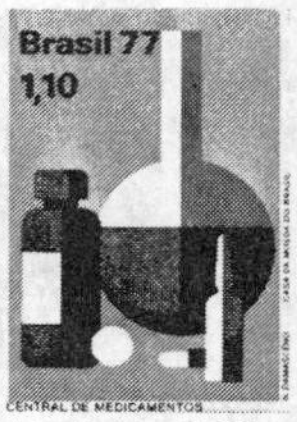

Medicine Bottles and Flask — A817

1977, May 8 Litho. *Perf. 11½*

1503 A816 1.10cr grn & multi .20 .20

1504 A817 1.10cr lt & dk grn .20 .20

Support and security for rural and urban workers (No. 1503) and establishment in 1971 of Medicine Distribution Center (CEME) for low-cost medicines (No. 1504).

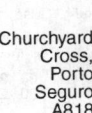

Churchyard Cross, Porto Seguro A818

Views, Porto Seguro: 5cr, Beach and boats. 5.60cr, Our Lady of Pena Chapel. 6.50cr, Town Hall.

1977, May 25 Litho. *Perf. 11½*

1505 A818 1.10cr multi .20 .20

1506 A818 5cr multi 1.40 .35

1507 A818 5.60cr multi .55 .45

1508 A818 6.50cr multi .80 .55

Nos. 1505-1508 (4) 2.95 1.55

Cent. of Brazil's membership in UPU.

Diario de Porto Alegre A819

1977, June 1

1509 A819 1.10cr multi .20 .20

Diario de Porto Alegre, newspaper, 150th anniv.

Blue Whale A820

1977, June 3

1510 A820 1.30cr multi .20 .20

Protection of marine life.

"Life and Development" A821

1977, June 20

1511 A821 1.30cr multi .20 .20

National Development Bank, 25th anniversary.

Train Leaving Tunnel — A822

1977, July 8 Engr. *Perf. 11½*

1512 A822 1.30cr black .20 .20

Centenary of Sao Paulo-Rio de Janeiro railroad.

Vasum Cassiforme A823

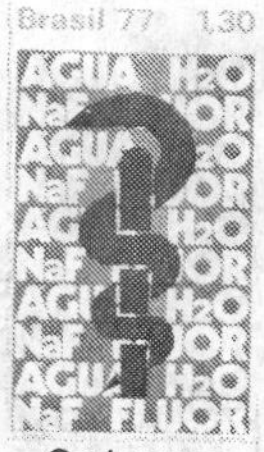

Caduceus, Formulas for Water and Fluoride A824

Sea Shells: No. 1514, Strombus goliath. No. 1515, Murex tenuivaricosus.

1977, July 14 Litho.

1513 A823 1.30cr blue & multi	.20	.20
1514 A823 1.30cr brown & multi	.20	.20
1515 A823 1.30cr green & multi	.20	.20
Nos. 1513-1515 (3)	.60	.60

1977, July 15 *Perf. 11½x11*

1516 A824 1.30cr multi .20 .20

3rd Intl. Odontology Congress, Rio, July 15-21.

Masonic Emblem, Map of Brazil — A825

"Stamps Don't Sink or Lose their Way" — A826

1977, July 18 *Perf. 11½*

1517 A825 1.30cr bl, lt bl & blk .20 .20

50th anniversary of the founding of the Brazilian Grand Masonic Lodge.

1977, Aug. 1

1518 A826 1.30cr multi .20 .20

Stamp Day 1977.

Dom Pedro's Proclamation — A827

Horses and Bulls — A828

1977, Aug. 11 Litho. *Perf. 11½*

1519 A827 1.30cr multi .20 .20

150th anniversary of Brazilian Law School.

Perf. 11½x11, 11x11½

1977, Aug. 20 Litho.

Brazilian folklore: No. 1521, King on horseback. No. 1522, Joust, horiz.

1520 A828 1.30cr ocher & multi	.20	.20
1521 A828 1.30cr blue & multi	.20	.20
1522 A828 1.30cr yel & multi	.20	.20
Nos. 1520-1522 (3)	.60	.60

2000-reis Doubloon A829

Brazilian Colonial Coins: No. 1524, 640r pataca. No. 1525, 20r copper "vintem."

1977, Aug. 31 *Perf. 11½*

1523 A829 1.30cr vio bl & multi	.20	.20
1524 A829 1.30cr dk red & multi	.20	.20
1525 A829 1.30cr yel & multi	.20	.20
Nos. 1523-1525 (3)	.60	.60

Pinwheel A830

Neoregelia Carolinae A831

1977, Sept. 1

1526 A830 1.30cr multi .20 .20

National Week.

1977, Sept. 21 Litho. *Perf. 11½*

1527 A831 1.30cr multi .20 .20

Nature preservation.

Pen, Pencil, Letters — A832

1977, Oct. 15 Litho. *Perf. 11½*

1528 A832 1.30cr multi .20 .20

Primary education, sesquicentennial.

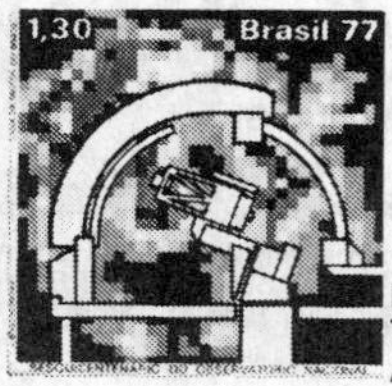

Dome and Telescope A833

1977, Oct. 15

1529 A833 1.30cr multi .20 .20

National Astrophysics Observatory, Brasópolis, sesquicentennial.

"Jahu" Hydroplane (Savoia Marchetti S-55) A834

Design: No. 1531, PAX, dirigible.

1977, Oct. 17

1530 A834 1.30cr multi	.25	.25
1531 A834 1.30cr multi	.25	.25

50th anniv. of crossing of South Atlantic by Joao Ribeiro de Barros, Genoa-Sao Paulo (#1530) and 75th anniv. of the PAX airship (#1531).

A835

A836

1977, Oct. 24

1532 A835 1.30cr Il'Guarani .20 .20

Book Day and to honor Jose Martiniano de Alencar, writer, jurist.

1977, Nov. 5 Litho. *Perf. 11½*

1533 A836 1.30cr Waves .20 .20

Amateur Radio Operators' Day.

Nativity A837

Christmas (folk art): 2cr, Annunciation. 5cr, Nativity.

1977, Nov. 10

1534 A837 1.30cr bister & multi	.25	.20
1535 A837 2cr bister & multi	.30	.20
1536 A837 5cr bister & multi	.65	.25
Nos. 1534-1536 (3)	1.20	.65

A838

A839

1977, Nov. 19

1537 A838 1.30cr Emerald	.20	.20
1538 A838 1.30cr Topaz	.20	.20
1539 A838 1.30cr Aquamarine	.20	.20
Nos. 1537-1539 (3)	.60	.60

PORTUCALE 77, 2nd International Topical Exhibition, Porto, Nov. 19-20.

1977, Nov. 24 Litho. *Perf. 11½*

1540 A839 1.30cr Angel, cornucopia .20 .20

National Thanksgiving Day.

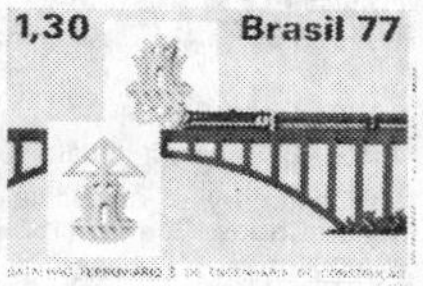

Army's Railroad Construction Battalion A840

Civilian services of armed forces: No. 1542, Navy's Amazon flotilla. No. 1543, Air Force's postal service (plane).

1977, Dec. 5

1541 A840 1.30cr multi	.20	.20
1542 A840 1.30cr multi	.20	.20
1543 A840 1.30cr multi	.20	.20
Nos. 1541-1543 (3)	.60	.60

Varig Emblem, Jet A841

1977, Dec. *Perf. 11x11½*

1544 A841 1.30cr bl & blk .20 .20

50th anniversary of Varig Airline.

Sts. Cosme and Damiao Church, Igaracu — A842

Woman Holding Sheaf — A843

Brazilian Architecture: 7.50cr, St. Bento Monastery Church, Rio de Janeiro. 8.50cr, Church of St. Francis of Assisi, Ouro Preto. 9.50cr, St. Anthony Convent Church, Joao Pessoa.

1977, Dec. 8

1545 A842 2.70cr multi	.30	.20
1546 A842 7.50cr multi	.90	.35
1547 A842 8.50cr multi	.90	.40
1548 A842 9.50cr multi	1.25	.45
Nos. 1545-1548 (4)	3.35	1.40

1977, Dec. 19 *Perf. 11½*

1549 A843 1.30cr multi .20 .20

Brazilian diplomacy.

Soccer Ball and Foot — A844

Designs: No. 1551, Soccer ball in net. No. 1552, Symbolic soccer player.

1978, Mar. 1 Litho. *Perf. 11½*

1550 A844 1.80cr multi	.30	.20
1551 A844 1.80cr multi	.30	.20
1552 A844 1.80cr multi	.30	.20
Nos. 1550-1552 (3)	.90	.60

11th World Cup Soccer Championship, Argentina, June 1-25.

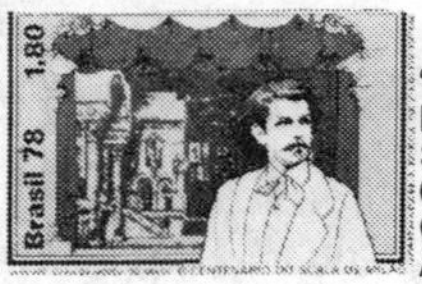

"La Fosca" on La Scala Stage and Carlos Gomes
A845

1978, Feb. 9

1553 A845 1.80cr multi .20 .20

Bicentenary of La Scala in Milan, and to honor Carlos Gomes (1836-1893), Brazilian composer.

Symbols of Postal Mechanization — A846

1978, Mar. 15 Litho. ***Perf. 11½***

1554 A846 1.80cr multi .20 .20

Opening of Postal Staff College.

Hypertension Chart — A847

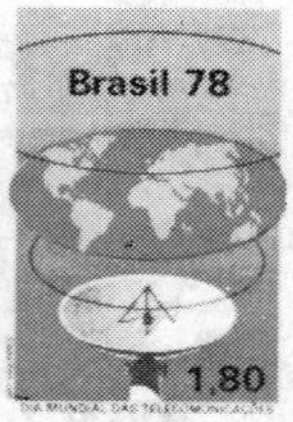

Waves from Antenna Uniting World — A848

1978, Apr. 4

1555 A847 1.80cr multi .20 .20

World Health Day, fight against hypertension.

1978, May 17 Litho. ***Perf. 12x11½***

1556 A848 1.80cr multi .20 .20

10th World Telecommunications Day.

Brazilian Canary
A849

Birds: 8.50cr, Cotinga. 9.50cr, Tanager fastuosa.

1978, June 5 ***Perf. 11½x12***

1557 A849 7.50cr multi 1.00 .75
1558 A849 8.50cr multi 1.00 .80
1559 A849 9.50cr multi 1.00 1.00
Nos. 1557-1559 (3) 3.00 2.55

Inocencio Serzedelo Correa and Manuel Francisco Correa, 1893
A850

1978, June 20 Litho. ***Perf. 11x11½***

1560 A850 1.80cr multi .20 .20

85th anniversary of Union Court of Audit.

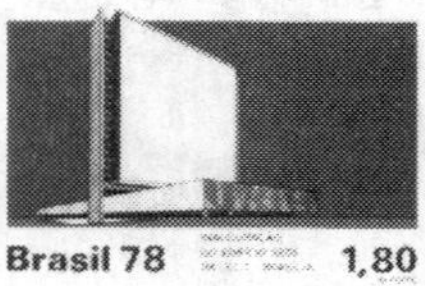

Post and Telegraph Building
A851

1978, June 22 ***Perf. 11½***

1561 A851 1.80cr multi .20 .25

Souvenir Sheet

Imperf

1562 A851 7.50cr multi .75 1.50

Inauguration of Post and Telegraph Building (ECT), Brasilia, and for BRAPEX, 3rd Brazilian Philatelic Exhibition, Brasilia, June 23-28 (No. 1562).

Ernesto Geisel, President of Brazil — A852

1978, June 22 Engr. ***Perf. 11½***

1563 A852 1.80cr dull green .20 .20

Savoia-Marchetti S-64, Map of South Atlantic — A853

1978, July 3 Litho.

1564 A853 1.80cr multi .20 .20

50th anniv. of 1st crossing of South Atlantic by Carlos del Prete and Arturo Ferrarin.

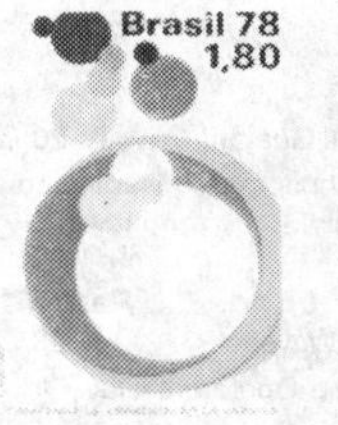

Symbolic of Smallpox Eradication
A854

Brazil No. 68
A855

1978, July 25

1565 A854 1.80cr multi .20 .20

Eradication of smallpox.

1978, Aug. 1

1566 A855 1.80cr multi .20 .20

Stamp Day, centenary of the "Barba Branca" (white beard) issue.

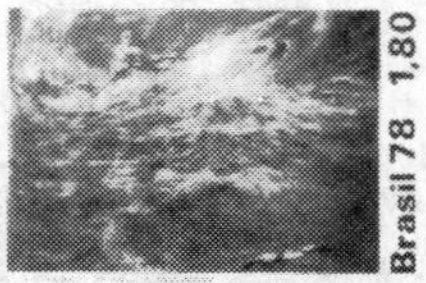

Stormy Sea, by Seelinger
A856

1978, Aug. 4

1567 A856 1.80cr multi .20 .20

Helios Seelinger, painter, birth centenary.

Guitar Players
A857

Musicians and Instruments: No. 1569, Flutes. No. 1570, Percussion instruments.

1978, Aug. 22 Litho. ***Perf. 11½***

1568 A857 1.80cr multi .20 .20
1569 A857 1.80cr multi .20 .20
1570 A857 1.80cr multi .20 .20
Nos. 1568-1570 (3) .60 .60

Children at Play
A858

1978, Sept. 1 Litho. ***Perf. 11½***

1571 A858 1.80cr multi .20 .20

National Week.

Collegiate Church
A859

1978, Sept. 6 Engr.

1572 A859 1.80cr red brn .20 .20

Restoration of patio of Collegiate Church, Sao Paulo.

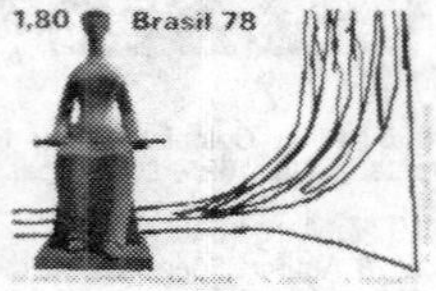

Justice by A. Geschiatti
A860

1978, Sept. 18 Litho.

1573 A860 1.80cr blk & olive .20 .20

Federal Supreme Court, sesquicentennial.

Iguacu Falls — A861

Design: No. 1575, Yellow ipecac.

1978, Sept. 21

1574 A861 1.80cr multi .20 .20
1575 A861 1.80cr multi .20 .20

Iguacu National Park.

Stages of Intelsat Satellite
A862

1978, Oct. 9 Litho. ***Perf. 11½***

1576 A862 1.80cr multi .20 .20

Flag of Order of Christ
A863

Brazilian Flags: No. 1578, Principality of Brazil. No. 1579, United Kingdom. No. 1580, Imperial Brazil. No. 1581, National flag (current).

1978, Oct. 13

1577 A863 1.80cr multi .65 .55
1578 A863 1.80cr multi .65 .55
1579 A863 1.80cr multi .65 .55
1580 A863 8.50cr multi .65 .55
1581 A863 8.50cr multi .65 .55
a. Block of 5, #1577-1581 + label 4.00 6.50
Nos. 1577-1581 (5) 3.25 2.75

7th LUBRAPEX Philatelic Exhibition, Porto Alegre.

Mail Street Car
A864

Mail Transportation: No. 1583, Overland mail truck. No. 1584, Mail delivery truck. 7.50cr. Railroad mail car. 8.50cr, Mail coach. 9.50cr, Post riders.

1978, Oct. 21 ***Perf. 11x11½***

1582 A864 1.80cr multi .50 .40
1583 A864 1.80cr multi .50 .40
1584 A864 1.80cr multi .50 .40
1585 A864 7.50cr multi .50 .40
1586 A864 8.50cr multi .50 .40
1587 A864 9.50cr multi .50 .50
a. Block of 6, #1582-1587 3.00 3.00

18th UPU Congress, Rio de Janeiro, 1979.

Gaucho Herding Cattle, and Cactus — A865

1978, Oct. 23 ***Perf. 11½x11***

1588 A865 1.80cr multi .20 .20

Joao Guimaraes Rosa, poet and diplomat, 70th birthday.

St. Anthony's Hill, by Nicholas A. Taunay
A866

Landscape Paintings: No. 1590, Castle Hill, by Victor Meirelles. No. 1591, View of Sabara, by Alberto da Veiga Guignard. No. 1592, View of Pernambuco, by Frans Post.

1978, Nov. 6 Litho. ***Perf. 11½***

1589 A866 1.80cr multi .20 .20
1590 A866 1.80cr multi .20 .20
1591 A866 1.80cr multi .20 .20
1592 A866 1.80cr multi .20 .20
Nos. 1589-1592 (4) .80 .80

Angel with Harp — A867

Christmas: No. 1594, Angel with lute. No. 1595, Angel with oboe.

1978, Nov. 10

1593 A867 1.80cr multi .20 .20
1594 A867 1.80cr multi .20 .20
1595 A867 1.80cr multi .20 .20
Nos. 1593-1595 (3) .60 .60

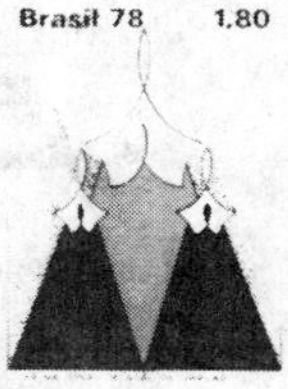

Symbolic Candles — A868

1978, Nov. 23
1596 A868 1.80cr blk, gold & car .20 .20

National Thanksgiving Day.

Red Crosses and Activities A869

1978, Dec. 5 Litho. *Perf. 11x11½*
1597 A869 1.80cr blk & red .20 .20

70th anniversary of Brazilian Red Cross.

Paz Theater, Belem — A870

12cr, José de Alencar Theater, Portaleza. 12.50cr, Municipal Theater, Rio de Janeiro.

1978, Dec. 6 *Perf. 11½*
1598 A870 10.50cr multi .70 .25
1599 A870 12cr multi .70 .25
1600 A870 12.50cr multi .70 .25
Nos. 1598-1600 (3) 2.10 .75

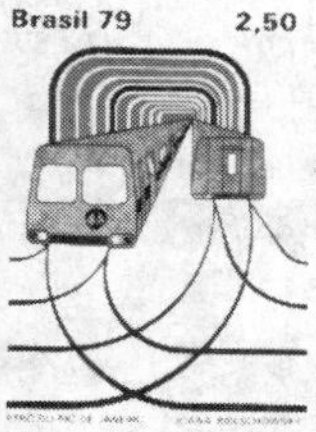

Subway Trains — A871

1979, Mar. 5 Litho. *Perf. 11½*
1601 A871 2.50cr multi .20 .20

Inauguration of Rio subway system.

Old and New Post Offices A872

Designs: No. 1603, Old and new mail boxes. No. 1604, Manual and automatic mail sorting. No. 1605, Old and new planes. No. 1606, Telegraph and telex machine. No. 1607, Mailmen's uniforms.

1979, Mar. 20 Litho. *Perf. 11x11½*
1602 A872 2.50cr multi .25 .20
1603 A872 2.50cr multi .25 .20
1604 A872 2.50cr multi .25 .20
1605 A872 2.50cr multi .25 .20
1606 A872 2.50cr multi .25 .20
1607 A872 2.50cr multi .25 .20
a. Block of 6, #1602-1607 1.50 1.50

10th anniv. of the new Post and Telegraph Dept., and 18th Universal Postal Union Cong., Rio de Janeiro, Sept.-Oct., 1979.

O'Day 23 Class Yacht A873

Yachts and Stamp Outlines: 10.50cr, Penguin Class. 12cr, Hobie Cat Class. 12.50cr, Snipe Class.

1979, Apr. 18 Litho. *Perf. 11x11½*
1608 A873 2.50cr multi .30 .25
1609 A873 10.50cr multi .55 .45
1610 A873 12cr multi .55 .35
1611 A873 12.50cr multi .75 .35
Nos. 1608-1611 (4) 2.15 1.40

Brasiliana '79, 3rd World Thematic Stamp Exhibition, Sao Conrado, Sept. 15-23.

Children, IYC Emblem — A874

1979, May 30 Litho. *Perf. 11½*
1612 A874 2.50cr multi .25 .20

Intl. Year of the Child & Children's Book Day.

Giant Water Lily — A875

12cr, Amazon manatee. 12.50cr, Arrau (turtle).

1979, June 5 Litho. *Perf. 11½*
1613 A875 10.50cr multi .70 .50
1614 A875 12cr multi .90 .60
1615 A875 12.50cr multi .90 .60
Nos. 1613-1615 (3) 2.50 1.70

Amazon National Park, nature conservation.

Bank Emblem A876

1979, June 7
1616 A876 2.50cr multi .20 .20

Northwest Bank of Brazil, 25th anniversary.

Physician Tending Patient 15th Cent. Woodcut A877

1979, June 30
1617 A877 2.50cr multi .20 .20

Natl. Academy of Medicine, 50th anniv.

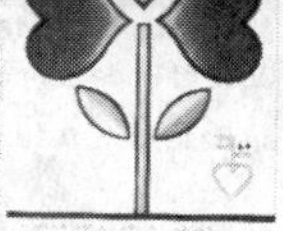

Flower made of Hearts — A878

1979, July 8 Litho. *Perf. 11½*
1618 A878 2.50cr multi .20 .20

35th Brazilian Cardiology Congress.

Souvenir Sheet

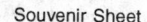

Hotel Nacional, Rio de Janeiro A879

1979, July 16
1619 A879 12.50cr multi .75 1.50

Brasiliana '79 comprising 1st Inter-American Exhibition of Classical Philately and 3rd World Topical Exhibition, Rio de Janeiro, Sept. 15-23.

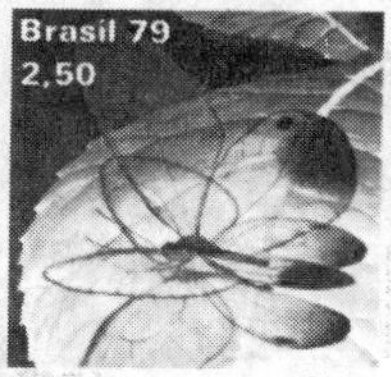

Cithaerias Aurora A880

Moths: 10.50cr, Evenus regalis. 12cr, Caligo eurilochus. 12.50cr, Diaethria clymena janeira.

1979, Aug. 1
1620 A880 2.50cr multi .20 .20
1621 A880 10.50cr multi .60 .40
1622 A880 12cr multi .70 .50
1623 A880 12.50cr multi .70 .50
Nos. 1620-1623 (4) 2.20 1.60

Stamp Day 1979.

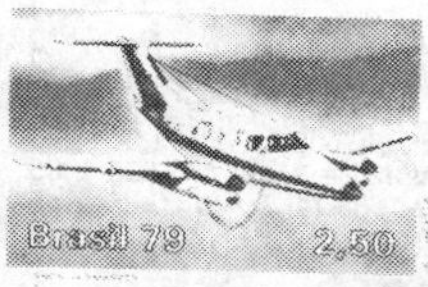

EMB-121 Xingo A881

1979, Aug. 19 Litho. *Perf. 11½*
1624 A881 2.50cr vio blue .20 .20

Embraer, Brazilian aircraft comp., 10th anniv.

A882

A883

Natl. emblem over landscape.

1979, Sept. 12
1625 A882 3.20cr multi .20 .20

National Week.

1979, Sept. 8 Litho. *Perf. 11½*
1626 A883 2.50cr multi .20 .20

Statue of Our Lady of the Apparition, 75th anniversary of coronation.

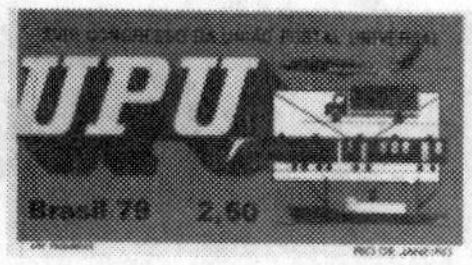

"UPU," Envelope and Mail Transport A884

"UPU" and: No. 1628, Post Office emblems. 10.50cr, Globe. 12cr, Flags of Brazil and UN. 12.50cr, UPU emblem.

1979, Sept. 12 *Perf. 11x11½*
1627 A884 2.50cr multi .20 .20
1628 A884 2.50cr multi .20 .20
1629 A884 10.50cr multi .50 .50
1630 A884 12cr multi .70 .70
1631 A884 12.50cr multi .70 .70
Nos. 1627-1631 (5) 2.30 2.30

18th UPU Cong., Rio, Sept.-Oct. 1979.

Pyramid Fountain, Rio de Janeiro — A885

Fountains: 10.50cr, Facade, Marilia, Ouro Preto, horiz. 12cr, Boa Vista, Recife.

Perf. 12x11½, 11½x12
1979, Sept. 15
1632 A885 2.50cr multi .20 .20
1633 A885 10.50cr multi .50 .50
1634 A885 12cr multi .60 .60
Nos. 1632-1634 (3) 1.30 1.30

Brasiliana '79, 1st Interamerican Exhibition of Classical Philately.

Church of the Glory — A886

Landscapes by Leandro Joaquim: 12cr, Fishing on Guanabara Bay. 12.50cr, Boqueirao Lake and Carioca Arches.

1979, Sept. 15 *Perf. 11½*
1635 A886 2.50cr multi .20 .20
1636 A886 12cr multi .60 .60
1637 A886 12.50cr multi .60 .60
Nos. 1635-1637 (3) 1.40 1.40

Brasiliana '79, 3rd World Topical Exhibition, Sao Conrado, Sept. 15-23.

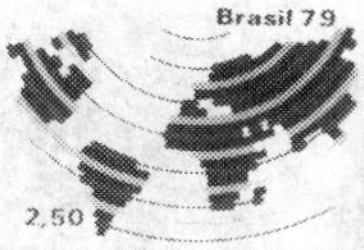

World Map — A887

1979, Sept. 20
1638 A887 2.50cr multi .20 .20

3rd World Telecommunications Exhibition, Geneva, Sept. 20-26.

"UPU" and UPU Emblem — A888

1979, Oct. 9 Litho. *Perf. 11½x11*
1639 A888 2.50cr multi .20 .20
1640 A888 10.50cr multi .55 .55
1641 A888 12cr multi .65 .65
1642 A888 12.50cr multi .65 .65
Nos. 1639-1642 (4) 2.05 2.05

Universal Postal Union Day.

IYC Emblem, Feather Toy A889

IYC Emblem and Toys: No. 1644, Bumble bee, ragdoll. No. 1645, Flower, top. No. 1646, Wooden acrobat.

1979, Oct. 12 ***Perf. 11½***

1643 A889 2.50cr multi .25 .20
1644 A889 3.20cr multi .25 .25
1645 A889 3.20cr multi .25 .25
1646 A889 3.20cr multi .25 .25
Nos. 1643-1646 (4) 1.00 .95

International Year of the Child.

Adoration of the Kings — A890

Christmas 1979: No. 1648, Nativity. No. 1649 Jesus and the Elders in the Temple.

1979, Nov. 12 Litho. ***Perf. 11½***

1647 A890 3.20cr multi .20 .20
1648 A890 3.20cr multi .20 .20
1649 A890 3.20cr multi .20 .20
Nos. 1647-1649 (3) .60 .60

Souvenir Sheet

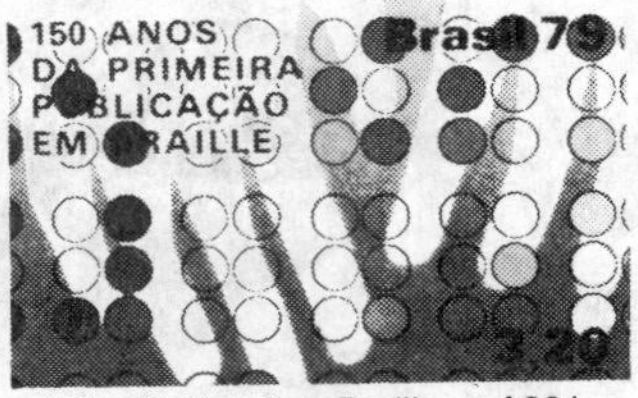

Hands Reading Braille — A891

Lithographed and Embossed

1979, Nov. 20. ***Perf. 11½***

1650 A891 3.20cr multi .50 1.25

Publication of Braille script, 150th anniversary. Margin shows extension of stamp design with Braille printed and embossed.

Wheat Harvester A892

Steel Mill A893

1979, Nov. 22

1651 A892 3.20cr multi .20 .20

Thanksgiving 1979.

1979, Nov. 23

1652 A893 3.20cr multi .20 .20

COSIPA Steelworks, Sao Paulo, 25th anniversary.

Type of 1976

Designs: 70c, Women grinding coconuts. 2.50cr, Basket weaver. 3.20cr, River boatman. 21cr, Harvesting ramie (China grass). 27cr, Man leading pack mule. 3.20cr, 27cr, horiz.

Photogravure, Engraved (21cr)

1979 ***Perf. 11x11½, 11½x11***

1653 A790 70c gray green .20 .20
1654 A790 2.50cr sepia .20 .20
1655 A790 3.20cr blue .20 .20
1656 A790 21cr purple .38 .20
1657 A790 27cr sepia .45 .20
Nos. 1653-1657 (5) 1.43 1.00

A894

Designs: 2cr, Coconuts. 3cr, Mangoes. 4cr, Corn. 5cr, Onions. 7cr, Oranges. 10cr, Maracuja. 12cr, Pineapple. 15cr, Bananas. 17cr, Guarana. 20cr, Sugar cane. 24cr, Beekeeping. 30cr, Silkworm. 34cr, Cacao. 38cr, Coffee. 42cr, Soybeans. 45cr, Mandioca. 50cr, Wheat. 57cr, Peanuts. 66cr, Grapes. 100cr, Cashews. 140cr, Tomatoes. 200cr, Mamona. 500cr, Cotton.

1980-83 Photo. ***Perf. 11½x11***

1658 A894 2cr yel brn ('82) .20 .20
1659 A894 3cr red ('82) .20 .20
1660 A894 4cr orange .20 .20
1661 A894 5cr dk pur ('82) .20 .20
1662 A894 7cr org ('81) .20 .20
1663 A894 10cr bl grn ('82) .20 .20
1664 A894 12cr dk grn ('81) .20 .20
1665 A894 15cr gldn brn ('83) .20 .20
1666 A894 17cr brn org ('82) .25 .20
1667 A894 20cr olive ('82) .25 .20
1668 A894 24cr bis ('82) .20 .20
1669 A894 30cr blk ('82) .20 .20
1670 A894 34cr brown .35 .20
1671 A894 38cr red ('83) .20 .20
1672 A894 42cr green 5.75 .50
1673 A894 45cr sepia ('83) .55 .20
1674 A894 50cr yel org ('82) .20 .20
1675 A894 57cr brn ('83) .20 .20
1676 A894 66cr pur ('81) 3.75 .20
1677 A894 100cr dk red brn ('81) 2.25 .20
1678 A894 140cr red ('82) 2.75 .20

Engr.

1678A A894 200cr grn ('82) 2.75 .20
1679 A894 500cr brn ('82) 5.75 .20
Nos. 1658-1679 (23) 27.00 4.90

See Nos. 1934-1941.

Plant Inside Raindrop — A896

Light Bulb Containing: 17cr+7cr, Sun. 20cr+8cr, Windmill. 21cr+9cr, Dam.

1980, Jan. 2 Litho. ***Perf. 12***

1680 A896 3.20cr multi .20 .20
1681 A896 24cr (17 + 7) 1.25 .65
1682 A896 28cr (20 + 8) 1.50 .75
1683 A896 30cr (21 + 9) 2.25 .85
Nos. 1680-1683 (4) 5.20 2.45

Anthracite Industry A897

1980, Mar. 19 Litho. ***Perf. 11½***

1684 A897 4cr multi .20 .20

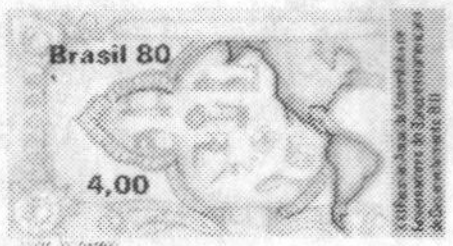

Map of Americas, Symbols of Development — A898

1980, Apr. 14 Litho. ***Perf. 11x11½***

1685 A898 4cr multi .20 .20

21st Assembly of Inter-American Development Bank Governors, Rio, Apr. 14-16.

Tapirape Mask, Mato Grosso A899

1980, Apr. 18 ***Perf. 11½***

1686 A899 4cr shown .20 .20
1687 A899 4cr Tukuna mask, Amazonas, vert. .20 .20
1688 A899 4cr Kanela mask, Maranhao, vert. .20 .20
Nos. 1686-1688 (3) .60 .60

Brazilian Television, 30th Anniversary A900

1980, May 5 Litho. ***Perf. 11½***

1689 A900 4cr multicolored .20 .20

Duke of Caxias, by Miranda A901

The Worker, by Candido Partinari A902

1980, May 7

1690 A901 4cr multicolored .20 .20

Duke of Caxias, death centenary.

1980, May 18

Paintings: 28cr, Mademoiselle Pogany, by Constantin Brancusi. 30cr, The Glass of Water, by Francisco Aurelio de Figueiredo.

1691 A902 24cr multi 1.10 .55
1692 A902 28cr multi 1.10 .55
1693 A902 30cr multi 1.65 .55
Nos. 1691-1693 (3) 3.85 1.65

Graf Zeppelin, 50th Anniversary of Atlantic Crossing A903

1980, June Litho. ***Perf. 11x11½***

1694 A903 4cr multicolored .20 .20

Pope John Paul II, St. Peter's, Rome, Congress Emblem A904

Pope, Emblem and Brazilian Churches: No. 1696, Fortaleza, vert. 24cr, Apericida 28cr, Rio de Janeiro. 30cr, Brasilia.

1980, June 24 ***Perf. 12***

1695 A904 4cr multi .20 .20
1696 A904 4cr multi .20 .20
1697 A904 24cr multi .90 .40
1698 A904 28cr multi .90 .40
1699 A904 30cr multi 1.75 .40
Nos. 1695-1699 (5) 3.95 1.60

Visit of Pope John Paul II to Brazil, June 30-July 12; 10th National Eucharistic Congress, Fortaleza, July 9-16.

1st Airmail Flight across the South Atlantic, 50th Anniv. A905

1980, June Litho. ***Perf. 11x11½***

1700 A905 4cr multicolored .20 .20

Souvenir Sheet

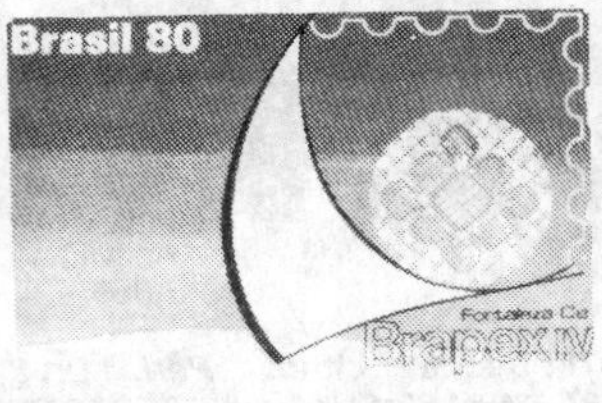

Yacht Sail, Exhibition Emblem — A906

1980, June ***Perf. 11½***

1701 A906 30cr multi 1.00 1.50

Brapex IV Stamp Exhib., Fortaleza, June 13-21.

Rowing, Moscow '80 Emblem A907

1980, June 30

1702 A907 4cr shown .20 .20
1703 A907 4cr Target shooting .20 .20
1704 A907 4cr Bicycling .20 .20
Nos. 1702-1704 (3) .60 .60

22nd Summer Olympic Games, Moscow, July 19-Aug. 3.

Rondon Community Works Project A908

1980, July 11

1705 A908 4cr multicolored .20 .20

Helen Keller and Anne Sullivan A909

1980, July 28

1706 A909 4cr multicolored .20 .20

Helen Keller (1880-1968), blind deaf writer and lecturer taught by Anne Sullivan (1867-1936).

Souvenir Sheet

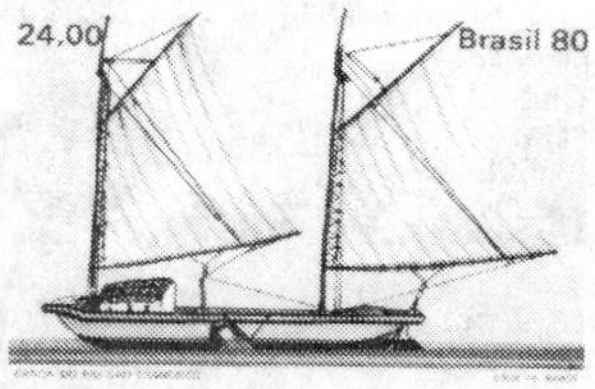

São Francisco River Canoe — A910

1980, Aug. 1 Litho. *Perf. 11½*
1707 A910 24cr multi 1.00 1.50

Stamp Day.

Microscope, Red Cross, Insects, Brick and Tile Houses — A911

1980, Aug. 5 *Perf. 11½x11*
1708 A911 4cr multi .25 .20

National Health Day.

Brazilian Postal Administration, 15th Anniversary — A912

1980, Sept. 16 Litho. *Perf. 12*
1709 A912 5cr multi .25 .20

Souvenir Sheet

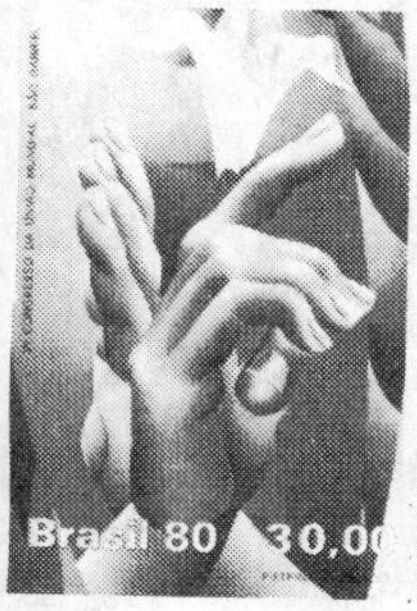

St. Gabriel World Union, 6th Congress A913

1980, Sept. 29 *Perf. 11½x12*
1710 A913 30cr multi 1.00 1.50

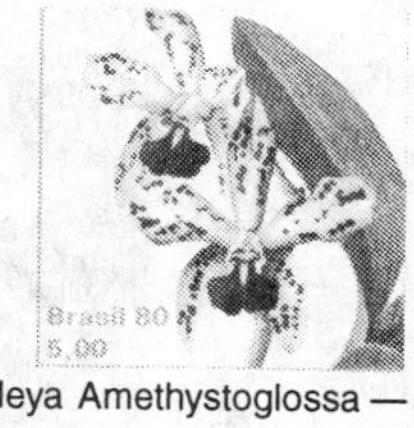

Cattleya Amethystoglossa — A914

1980, Oct. 3 *Perf. 11½*

1711	A914	5cr *shown*	.20	.20
1712	A914	5cr *Laelia cinnabarina*	.20	.20
1713	A914	24cr *Zygopetalum crinitum*	1.10	.60
1714	A914	28cr *Laelia tenebrosa*	1.10	.60
		Nos. 1711-1714 (4)	2.60	1.60

Espamer 80, American-European Philatelic Exhibition, Madrid, Oct. 3-12.

Amazona Braziliensis A915

Captain Rodrigo, Hero of Erico Verissimo's "O Continento" A916

Parrots: No. 1716, Amazona Vinacea. No. 1717, Touit melanonota. No. 1718, Amazona pretrei.

1980, Oct. 18 Litho. *Perf. 12*

1715	A915	5cr multi	.20	.20
1716	A915	5cr multi	.20	.20
1717	A915	28cr multi	1.10	.60
1718	A915	28cr multi	1.10	.60
		Nos. 1715-1718 (4)	2.60	1.60

Lubrapex '80 Stamp Exhib., Lisbon, Oct. 18-26.

1980, Oct. 23
1719 A916 5cr multi .25 .20

Book Day.

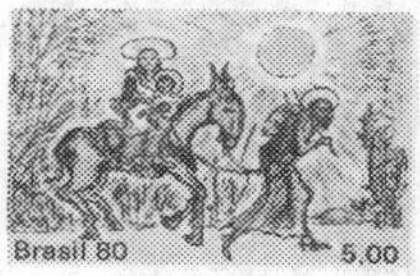

Flight into Egypt A917

1980, Nov. 5
1720 A917 5cr multi .25 .20

Christmas 1980.

Sound Waves and Oscillator Screen A918

1980, Nov. 7
1721 A918 5cr multi .25 .20

Telebras Research Center inauguration.

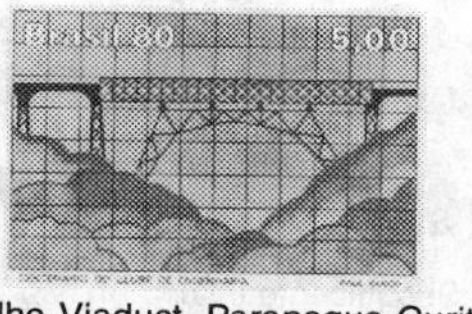

Carvalho Viaduct, Paranagua-Curitiba Railroad — A919

1980, Nov. 10
1722 A919 5cr multi .25 .20

Engineering Club centenary.

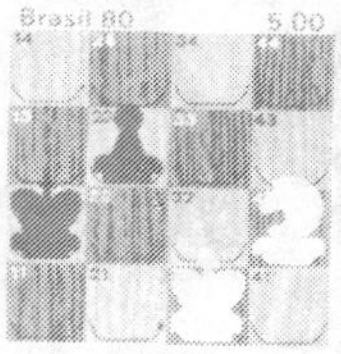

A920

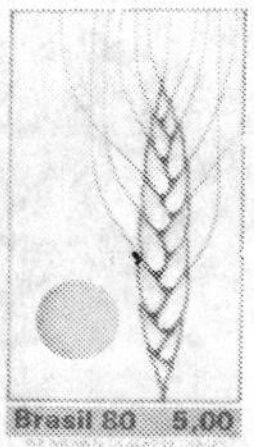

A921

1980, Nov. 18 Litho. *Perf. 11½*
1723 A920 5cr Portable chess board .25 .50

Postal chess contest.

1980, Nov. 27 *Perf. 11½x11*
1724 A921 5cr Sun, wheat .25 .40

Thanksgiving 1980

Father Anchieta Writing "Virgin Mary, Mother of God" on Sand of Iperoig Beach — A922

1980, Dec. 8 *Perf. 12*
1725 A922 5cr multi .25 .20

Christ Carrying Cross, By O Aleijadinho A923

Antonio Francisco Lisboa (O Aleijadinho), 250th Birth Anniv.: Paintings of the life of Christ: a, Mount of Olives. b, Arrest in the Garden. c, Flagellation. d, Crown of Thorns. f, Crucifixion.

1980, Dec. 29

1726	Block of 6	1.65	1.65
a.-f.	A923 5cr any single	.25	.20

Agricultural Productivity — A924

1981, Jan. 2 Litho. *Perf. 11x11½*

1727	A924	30cr shown	1.25	.35
1728	A924	35cr Domestic markets	1.10	.35
1729	A924	40cr Exports	1.10	.35
		Nos. 1727-1729 (3)	3.45	1.05

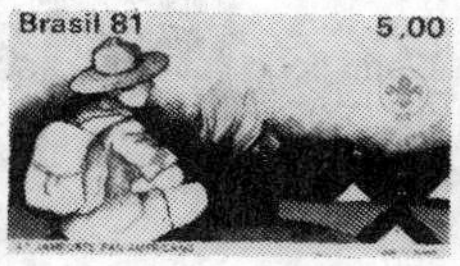

Boy Scout and Campfire A925

1981, Jan. 22 Litho. *Perf. 11x11½*

1730	A925	5cr shown	.25	.20
1731	A925	5cr Scouts cooking	.25	.20
1732	A925	5cr Scout, tents	.25	.20
		Nos. 1730-1732 (3)	.75	.60

4th Pan-American Scout Jamboree.

Souvenir Sheet

Mailman, 1930 — A926

1981, Mar. 11 Litho. *Perf. 11*

1733	Sheet of 3	4.00	4.00
a.	A926 30cr shown	1.00	1.00
b.	A926 35cr Mailman, 1981	1.00	1.00
c.	A926 40cr Telegram messenger, 1930	1.00	1.00

Dept. of Posts & Telegraphs, 50th anniv.

Souvenir Sheet

The Hunter and the Jaguar, by Felix Taunay (1795-1881) A927

1981, Apr. 10 Litho. *Perf. 11*
1734 A927 30cr multi 1.00 *2.00*

Lima Barreto and Rio de Janeiro, 1900 A928

1981, May 13 Litho. *Perf. 11½*
1735 A928 7cr multi .25 .20

Lima Barreto, writer, birth centenary.

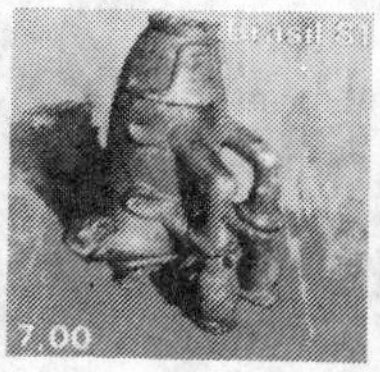

Maraca Indian Funerary Urn — A929

1981, May 18

1736	A929	7cr shown	.25	.20
1737	A929	7cr Marajoara triangular jug	.25	.20
1738	A929	7cr Tupi-Guarani bowl	.25	.20
		Nos. 1736-1738 (3)	.75	.60

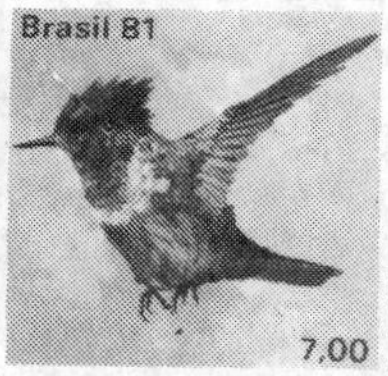

Lophornis Magnifica A930

Designs: Hummingbirds.

1981, May 22 *Perf. 11½*

1739	A930	7cr shown	.30	.20
1740	A930	7cr Phaethornis pretrei	.30	.20
1741	A930	7cr Chrysolampis mosquitus	.30	.20
1742	A930	7cr Heliactin cornuta	.30	.20
		Nos. 1739-1742 (4)	1.20	.80

Rotary Emblem and Faces — A931

1981, May 31

1743	A931	7cr Emblem, hands	.20	.20
1744	A931	35cr shown	1.00	.80

72nd Convention of Rotary Intl., Sao Paulo.

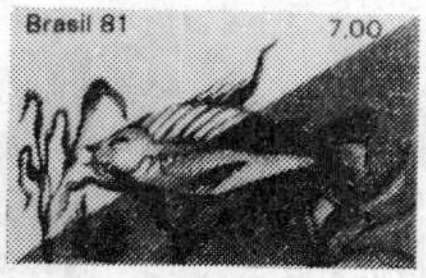

Environmental Protection — A932

1981, June 5 ***Perf. 12***

1745 A932 7cr shown .25 .20
1746 A932 7cr Forest .25 .20
1747 A932 7cr Clouds (air) .25 .20
1748 A932 7cr Village (soil) .25 .20
a. Block of 4, #1745-1748 1.00 1.00

Biplane, 1931 (Airmail Service, 50th Anniv.) A933

1981, June 10 ***Perf. 11½***

1749 A933 7cr multi .25 .20

Madeira-Mamore Railroad, 50th Anniv. of Nationalization — A934

1981, July 10 Litho. ***Perf. 11x11½***

1750 A934 7cr multi .25 .20

66th Intl. Esperanto Congress, Brasilia A935

1981, July 26 ***Perf. 12***

1751 A935 7cr green & blk .25 .20

No. 79 A936

1981, Aug. 1

1752 A936 50cr shown 1.40 .30
1753 A936 55cr No. 80 1.40 .30
1754 A936 60cr No. 81 1.40 .30
Nos. 1752-1754 (3) 4.20 .90

Stamp Day; cent. of "small head" stamps.

Institute of Military Engineering, 50th Anniv. A937

1981, Aug. 11 Litho. ***Perf. 11½***

1755 A937 12cr multi .25 .20

Reisado Dancers A938

1981, Aug. 22

1756 A938 50cr Dancers, diff. .80 .25
1757 A938 55cr Sailors .80 .25
1758 A938 60cr shown .80 .20
Nos. 1756-1758 (3) 2.40 .70

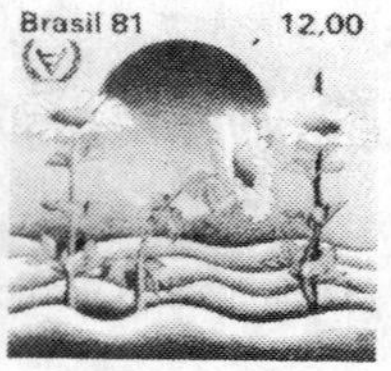

Intl. Year of the Disabled A939

1981, Sept. 17 Litho. ***Perf. 11½***

1759 A939 12cr multi .25 .20

Flowers of the Central Plateau A940

1981, Sept. 21 Litho. ***Perf. 12***

1760 A940 12cr Palicourea rigida .25 .20
1761 A940 12cr Dalechampia caperonioides .25 .20
1762 A940 12cr Cassia clausseni, vert. .25 .20
1763 A940 12cr Eremanthus sphaerocephalus, vert. .25 .20
Nos. 1760-1763 (4) 1.00 .80

Virgin of Nazareth Statue — A941

Christ the Redeemer Statue, Rio de Janeiro, 50th Anniv. — A942

1981, Oct. 10 Litho. ***Perf. 12***

1764 A941 12cr multi .25 .20

Candle Festival of Nazareth, Belem.

1981, Oct. 12

1765 A942 12cr multi .25 .20

World Food Day — A943

1981, Oct. 16

1766 A943 12c multi .25 .20

75th Anniv. of Santos-Dumont's First Flight — A944

1981, Oct. 23 Litho. ***Perf. 12***

1767 A944 60cr multi 1.00 .35

Father José de Santa Rita Durao, Titlepage of his Epic Poem Caramuru, Diego Alvares Correia (Character) A945

1981, Oct. 29

1768 A945 12cr multi .25 .20

Caramuru publication cent.; World Book Day.

Christmas 1981 — A946

Designs: Creches and figurines.

1981, Nov. 10 Litho. ***Perf. 12***

1769 A946 12cr multi .20 .20
1770 A946 50cr multi 1.25 .25
1771 A946 55cr multi, vert. 1.25 .25
1772 A946 60cr multi, vert. 1.25 .30
Nos. 1769-1772 (4) 3.95 1.00

State Flags A947

Designs: a, Alagoas. b, Bahia. c, Federal District. d, Pernambuco. e, Sergipe.

1981, Nov. 19

1773 Block of 5 + label 1.25 1.25
a.-e. A947 12cr, any single .20 .20

Label shows arms of Brazil.
See #1830, 1892, 1962, 2037, 2249.

Thanksgiving 1981 — A948

1981, Nov. 26 Litho. ***Perf. 11½***

1776 A948 12cr multi .25 .20

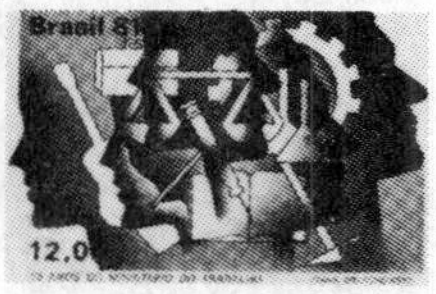

Ministry of Labor, 50th Anniv. A949

1981, Nov. 26

1777 A949 12cr multi .20 .20

School of Engineering, Itajuba — A950

1981, Nov. 30 ***Perf. 11x11½***

1778 A950 15cr lt grn & pur .35 .20

Theodomiro C. Santiago, founder, birth centenary.

Sao Paulo State Police Sesquicentennial A951

1981, Dec. 15 Litho. ***Perf. 12***

1779 A951 12cr Policeman with saxophone .20 .20
1780 A951 12cr Mounted policemen .20 .20

Army Library Centenary A952

1981, Dec. 17

1781 A952 12cr multi .20 .20

Souvenir Sheet

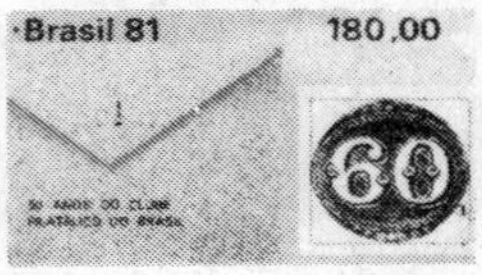

Philatelic Club of Brazil, 50th Anniv. A953

1981, Dec. 18 ***Perf. 11***

1782 A953 180cr multi 4.50 *4.50*

Brigadier Eduardo Gomes A954

1982, Jan. 20 Litho. ***Perf. 11x11½***

1783 A954 12cr blue & blk .30 .20

Birth Centenary of Henrique Lage, Industrialist — A956

1982, Mar. 14 Litho. ***Perf. 11½***

1785 A956 17cr multi .50 .20

1982 World Cup Soccer — A957

TB Bacillus Cent. — A958

Designs: Various soccer players.

1982, Mar. 19

1786 A957 75cr multi .75 .25
1787 A957 80cr multi .75 .30
1788 A957 85cr multi .75 .30
Nos. 1786-1788 (3) 2.25 .85

Souvenir Sheet

Imperf

1789 Sheet of 3 3.00 *6.00*
a. A957 100cr like #1786 1.00
b. A957 100cr like #1787 1.00
c. A957 100cr like #1788 1.00

1982, Mar. 24 ***Perf. 12***

1790 A958 90cr Microscope, lung 1.25 .80
1791 A958 100cr Lung, pills 1.25 .90
a. Pair, #1790-1791 2.50 2.00

Souvenir Sheet

A959

1982, Apr. 17 Litho. ***Perf. 11***

1792 Sheet of 3 3.50 3.25
a. A959 75cr Laelia Purpurata 1.00 .50
b. A959 80cr Oncidium flexuosum 1.00 .50
c. A959 85cr Cleistes revoluta 1.25 .55

BRAPEX V Stamp Exhibition, Blumenau.

Oil Drilling Centenary A960

1982, Apr. 18 ***Perf. 11½***
1793 A960 17cr multi .25 .20

400th Birth Anniv. of St. Vincent de Paul — A961

1982, Apr. 24 Litho. ***Perf. 11½***
1794 A961 17cr multi .25 .20

Seven Steps of Guaira (Waterfalls) A962

1982, Apr. 29
1795 A962 17cr Fifth Fall .20 .20
1796 A962 21cr Seventh Fall .30 .20

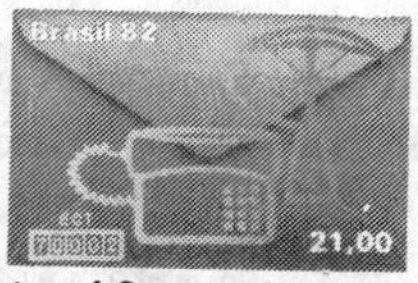

Ministry of Communications, 15th Anniv. — A963

1982, May 15
1797 A963 21cr multi .25 .20

Museology Course, Natl. Historical Museum, 50th Anniv. A964

1982, May 18
1798 A964 17cr blk & sal pink .20 .20

Vale de Rio Doce Mining Co. — A965

1982, June 1
1799 A965 17cr Gears .25 .20

Martin Afonso de Souza Reading Charter to Settlers A966

1982, June 3 Litho. ***Perf. 11½***
1800 A966 17cr multi .25 .20

Town of Sao Vincente, 450th anniv.

Armadillo A967

1982, June 4
1801 A967 17cr shown .55 .20
1802 A967 21cr Wolves .55 .20
1803 A967 30cr Deer 1.65 .25
Nos. 1801-1803 (3) 2.75 .65

Film Strip and Award A968

1982, June 19
1804 A968 17cr multi .25 .20

20th anniv. of Golden Palm award for The Promise Keeper, Cannes Film Festival.

Souvenir Sheet

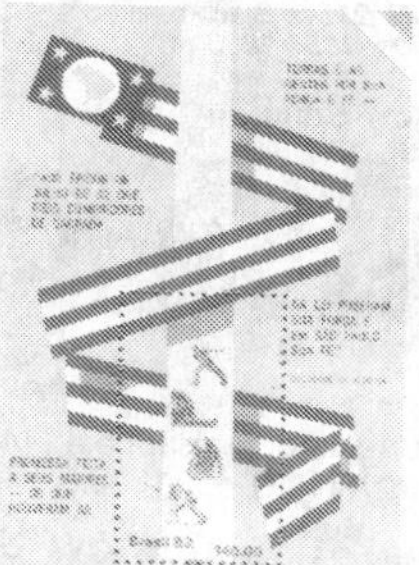

50th Anniv. of Constitutionalist Revolution — A969

1982, July 9 Litho. ***Perf. 11***
1805 A969 140cr multi 1.75 1.75

Church of Our Lady of O'Sabara — A970

St. Francis of Assisi, 800th Birth Anniv. — A971

Baroque Architecture, Minas Gerais State: No. 1807, Church of Our Lady of the Rosary, Diamantina. No. 1808, Town Square, Mariana.

1982, July 16 ***Perf. 11½***
1806 A970 17cr multi .25 .20
1807 A970 17cr multi, horiz. .25 .20
1808 A970 17cr multi, horiz. .25 .20
Nos. 1806-1808 (3) .75 .60

1982, July 24
1809 A971 21cr multi .20 .20

Stamp Day and Centenary of Pedro II "Large Head" Stamps A972

1982, Aug. 1
1810 A972 21cr No. 82 .25 .20

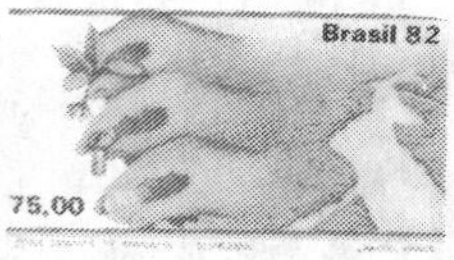

Port of Manaus Free Trade Zone A973

1982, Aug. 15 ***Perf. 11x11½***
1811 A973 75cr multi .65 .35

Scouting Year — A974

1982, Aug. 21 Litho. ***Perf. 11***
1812 Sheet of 2 2.75 *3.75*
a. A974 85cr Baden-Powell 1.00 *1.10*
b. A974 185cr Scout 1.65 *2.00*

Orixas Folk Costumes of African Origin — A975

1982, Aug. 21 ***Perf. 11½***
1813 A975 20cr Iemanja .20 .20
1814 A975 20cr Xango .20 .20
1815 A975 20cr Oxumare .20 .20
Nos. 1813-1815 (3) .60 .60

10th Anniv. of Central Bank of Brazil Currency Museum A976

1982, Aug. 31
1816 A976 25cr 12-florin coin, 1645, obverse and reverse .25 .20
1817 A976 25cr Emperor Pedro's 6.40-reis coronation coin, 1822 .25 .20

National Week — A977

1982, Sept. 1
1818 A977 25cr Don Pedro proclaiming independence .38 .25

A978 A979

1982, Oct. 4
1819 A978 85cr Portrait 1.00 .60

St. Theresa of Avila (1515-1582).

1982, Oct. 15 Litho. ***Perf. 11½x11***
1820 A979 75cr Instruments .65 .40
1821 A979 80cr Dancers .65 .40
1822 A979 85cr Musicians .70 .40
a. Souvenir sheet of 3, #1820-1822, perf. 11 2.75 *2.75*
Nos. 1820-1822 (3) 2.00 1.20

Lubrapex '82, 4th Portuguese-Brazilian Stamp Exhibition. Stamps in No. 1822a are without "LUBRAPEX 82."

Aviation Industry Day — A980

1982, Oct. 17 ***Perf. 12***
1823 A980 24cr Embraer EMB-312 trainer plane .25 .20

Bastos Tigre, Poet, Birth Centenary, and "Saudade" Text A981

1982, Oct. 29
1824 A981 24cr multi .25 .20

Book Day.

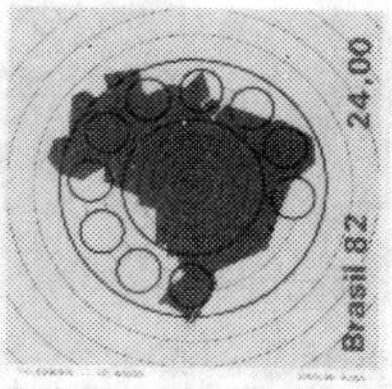

10th Anniv. of Brazilian Telecommunications Co. — A982

1982, Nov. 9 Litho. ***Perf. 11½***
1825 A982 24cr multi .25 .20

Christmas 1982 — A983

Children's Drawings.

1982, Nov. 10
1826 A983 24cr Nativity .25 .20
1827 A983 24cr Angels .25 .20
1828 A983 30cr Nativity, diff. .30 .45
1829 A983 30cr Flight into Egypt .30 .45
Nos. 1826-1829 (4) 1.10 1.30

State Flags Type of 1981

Designs: a, Ceara. b, Espirito Santo. c, Paraiba. d, Grande de Norte. e, Rondonia.

1982, Nov. 19
1830 Block of 5 + label 5.25 5.25
a.-e. A947 24cr any single 1.00 .20

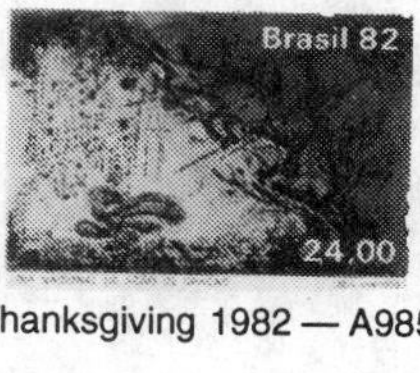

Thanksgiving 1982 — A985

1982, Nov. 25
1835 A985 24cr multi .25 .20

Homage to the Deaf — A986

1982, Dec. 1

1836 A986 24cr multi .25 .20

Naval Academy Bicentenary A987

Training Ships.

1982, Dec. 14

1837 A987 24cr Brazil .35 .20
1838 A987 24cr Benjamin Constant .35 .20
1839 A987 24cr Almirante Saldanha .35 .20
Nos. 1837-1839 (3) 1.05 .60

Souvenir Sheet

No. 12 — A988

1982, Dec. 18 **Litho.** ***Perf. 11***

1840 A988 200cr multi 4.00 *5.00*

BRASILIANA '83 Intl. Stamp Exhibition, Rio de Janeiro, July 29-Aug. 7.

Brasiliana '83 Carnival A989

1983, Feb. 9 **Litho.** ***Perf. 11½***

1841 A989 24cr Samba drummers .20 .20
1842 A989 130cr Street parade 1.40 .50
1843 A989 140cr Dancer 1.40 .50
1844 A989 150cr Male dancer 1.40 .55
Nos. 1841-1844 (4) 4.40 1.75

Antarctic Expedition A990

1983, Feb. 20 **Litho.** ***Perf. 11½***

1845 A990 150cr Support ship Barano de Teffe 2.00 .55

50th Anniv. of Women's Rights — A991

1983, Mar. 8

1846 A991 130cr multi 1.25 .50

Itaipu Hydroelectric Power Station Opening — A992

1983, Mar. **Litho.** ***Perf. 12***

1847 A992 140cr multi 1.90 .40

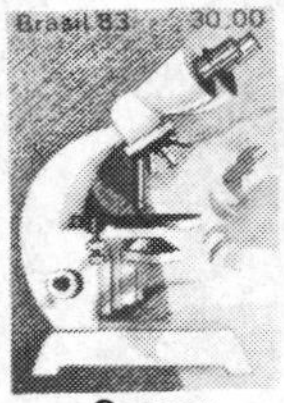

Cancer Prevention A993

Martin Luther (1483-1546) A994

30cr, Microscope. 38cr, Antonio Prudente, Paulista Cancer Assoc. founder, Camargo Hospital.

1983, Apr. 18

1848 A993 30cr multi .30 .20
1849 A993 38cr multi .30 .20
a. Pair, #1848-1849 .65 .35

1983, Apr. 18

1850 A994 150cr pale grn & blk 1.25 .50

Agricultural Research A995

1983, Apr. 26 **Litho.** ***Perf. 11½***

1851 A995 30cr Chestnut tree .20 .20
1852 A995 30cr Genetic research .20 .20
1853 A995 38cr Tropical soy beans .25 .20
Nos. 1851-1853 (3) .65 .60

Father Rogerio Neuhaus (1863-1934), Centenary of Ordination — A996

1983, May 3 ***Perf. 11½x11***

1854 A996 30cr multi .25 .20

30th Anniv. of Customs Cooperation Council — A997

1983, May 5 ***Perf. 11x11½***

1855 A997 30cr multi .25 .20

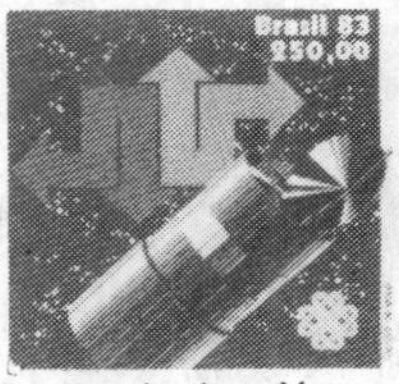

World Communications Year — A998

1983, May 17 **Litho.** ***Perf. 11½***

1856 A998 250cr multi 1.50 .45

Toucans A999

1983, May 21

1857 A999 30cr Tucanucu .20 .20
1858 A999 185cr White-breasted 1.25 .40
1859 A999 205cr Green-beaked 1.25 .40
1860 A999 215cr Black-beaked 1.25 .45
Nos. 1857-1860 (4) 3.95 1.45

Souvenir Sheet

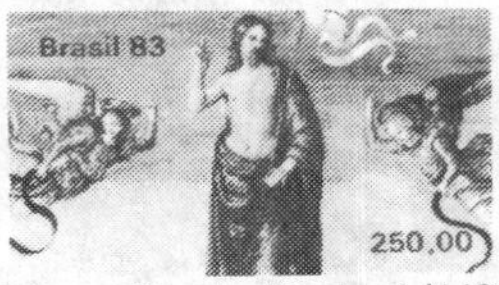

Resurrection, by Raphael (1483-1517) — A1000

1983, May 25 ***Perf. 11***

1861 A1000 250cr multi 2.50 *3.00*

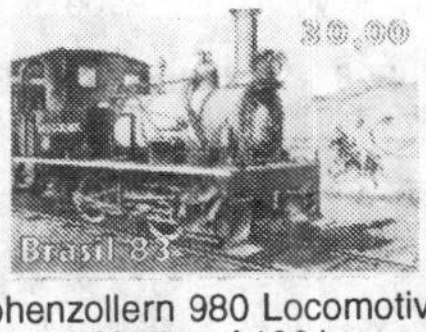

Hohenzollern 980 Locomotive, 1875 — A1001

Various locomotives.

1983, June 12 **Litho.** ***Perf. 11½***

1862 A1001 30cr shown .25 .20
1863 A1001 30cr Baldwin #1, 1881 .25 .20
1864 A1001 38cr Fowler #1, 1872 .30 .20
Nos. 1862-1864 (3) .80 .60

9th Women's Basketball World Championship A1002

1983, July 24 **Litho.** ***Perf. 11½x11***

1865 A1002 30cr Players, front view .20 .20
1866 A1002 30cr Players, rear view .20 .20

Simon Bolivar (1783-1830) A1003

1983, July 24 ***Perf. 12***

1867 A1003 30cr multi .20 .20

Children's Polio and Measles Vaccination Campaign A1004

1983, July 25

1868 A1004 30cr Girl, measles .20 .20
1869 A1004 30cr Boy, polio .20 .20

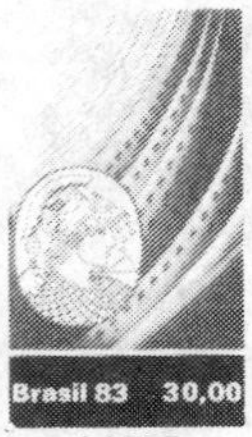

A1005

A1006

1983, July 28 ***Perf. 11½x11***

1870 A1005 30cr Minerva (goddess of wisdom), computer tape .20 .20

20th Anniv. of Master's program in engineering.

1983, July 29 **Engr.**

Guanabara Bay.

1871 A1006 185cr No. 1 1.50 .40
1872 A1006 205cr No. 2 1.50 .40
1873 A1006 215cr No. 3 1.50 .45
Nos. 1871-1873 (3) 4.50 1.25

Souvenir Sheet

Perf. 11

1874 Sheet of 3 8.00 *10.00*
a. A1006 185cr No. 1 2.00 *3.00*
b. A1006 205cr No. 2 2.00 *3.00*
c. A1006 215cr No. 3 2.00 *3.00*

BRASILIANA '83 Intl. Stamp Show, Rio de Janeiro, July 29-Aug. 7.

Stamps in No. 1874 have unframed denomination at bottom of the stamps. The background scene is enlarged to cover all 3 stamps in a continuous design.

Souvenir Sheet

The First Mass in Brazil, by Vitor Meireles (1833-1903) A1007

1983, Aug. 18 ***Perf. 11***

1875 A1007 250cr multi 3.00 1.50

EMB-120 Brasilia Passenger Plane A1008

1983, Aug. 19 ***Perf. 12***

1876 A1008 30cr multi .25 .20

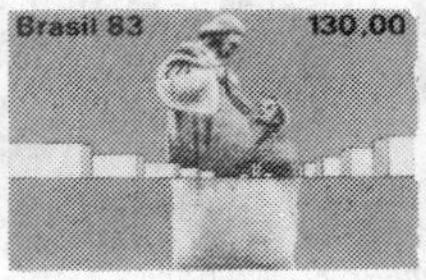

Vision of Don Bosco Centenary A1009

1983, Aug. 30

1877 A1009 130cr multi .75 .25

Independence Week — A1010

1983, Sept. 1 Litho. *Perf. 11½*
1878 A1010 50cr multi .25 .20

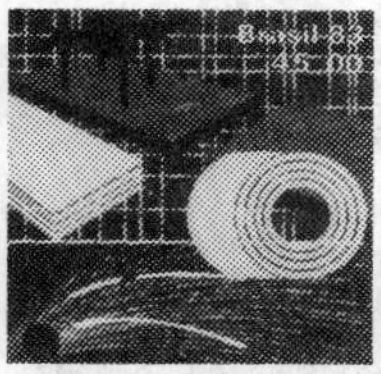

National Steel Corp., 10th Anniv. A1011

1983, Sept. 17 Litho. *Perf. 11½*
1879 A1011 45cr multi .25 .20

Cactus A1012

1983, Sept. 12 Litho. *Perf. 11½*
1880 A1012 45cr Pilosocereus gounellei .30 .20
1881 A1012 45cr Melocactus bahiensis .30 .20
1882 A1012 57cr Cereus jamacaru .40 .20
Nos. 1880-1882 (3) 1.00 .60

1st National Eucharistic Congress — A1013

1983, Oct. 12 Litho. *Perf. 11½*
1883 A1013 45cr multi .25 .20

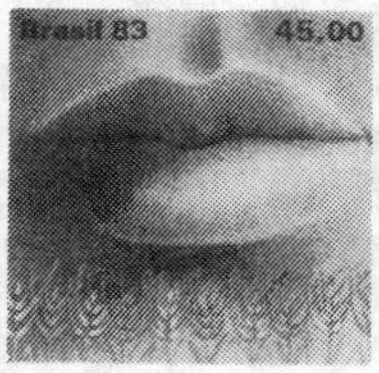

World Food Program A1014

1983, Oct. 14 Litho. *Perf. 11½*
1884 A1014 45cr Mouth, grain .30 .20
1885 A1014 57cr Fish, sailboat .40 .20

Souvenir Sheet

Louis Breguet, Death Centenary — A1015

1983, Oct. 27 Litho. *Perf. 11*
1886 A1015 376cr Telegraph transmitter 4.25 1.50

Christmas 1983 A1016

17th-18th Cent. Statues: 45cr, Our Lady of the Angels. 315cr, Our Lady of the Parturition. 335cr, Our Lady of Joy. 345cr, Our Lady of the Presentation.

1983, Nov. 10 Litho. *Perf. 11½*
1887 A1016 45cr multi .25 .20
1888 A1016 315cr multi 1.65 .60
1889 A1016 335cr multi 1.65 .65
1890 A1016 345cr multi 1.65 .70
Nos. 1887-1890 (4) 5.20 2.15

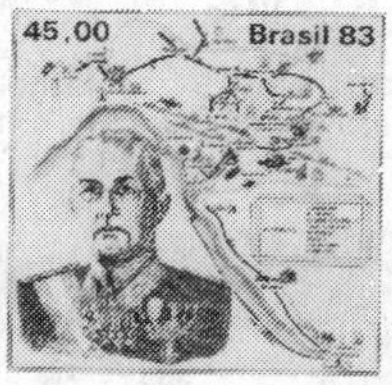

Marshal Mascarenhas Birth Centenary A1017

1983, Nov. 13 Litho. *Perf. 11½*
1891 A1017 45cr Battle sites .20 .20

Commander of Brazilian Expeditionary Force in Italy.

State Flags Type of 1981

Designs: a, Amazonas. b, Goias. c, Rio. d, Mato Grosso Do Sol. e, Parana.

1983, Nov. 17 Litho. *Perf. 11½*
1892 Block of 5 + label 3.00 3.00
a.-e. A947 45cr any single .50 .20

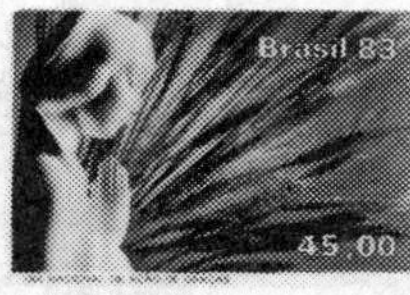

Thanksgiving — A1018

1983, Nov. 24 Litho. *Perf. 12*
1896 A1018 45cr Madonna, wheat .35 .20

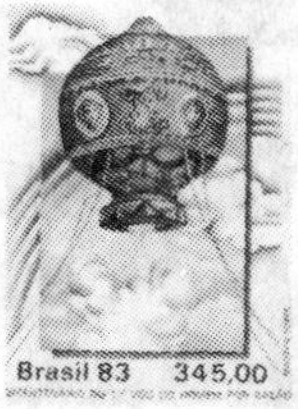

Manned Flight Bicentenary A1019

1983, Dec. 15 Litho. *Perf. 12*
1897 A1019 345cr Montgolfiere balloon, 1783 5.00 .50

Ethnic Groups A1020

1984, Jan. 20 Litho. *Perf. 12*
1898 A1020 45cr multi .20 .20

50th anniv. of publication of Masters and Slaves, sociological study by Gilberto Freyre.

Centenary of Crystal Palace, Petropolis A1021

1984, Feb. 2
1899 A1021 45cr multi .20 .20

Souvenir Sheet

Flags (Sculpture with 40 Figures), by Victor Brecheret (b. 1894) — A1022

1984, Feb. 22 Litho. *Perf. 11*
1900 A1022 805cr multi 1.50 1.00

Naval Museum Centenary A1023

1984, Mar. 23 Litho. *Perf. 11½*
1901 A1023 620cr Figurehead, frigate, 1847 .85 .50

Slavery Abolition Centenary A1024

1984, Mar. 25
1902 A1024 585cr Broken chain, raft .85 .55
1903 A1024 610cr Freed slave .90 .60

Souvenir Sheet

Visit of King Carl XVI Gustaf of Sweden A1025

1984, Apr. 2 *Perf. 11*
1904 A1025 2105cr multi 3.50 2.50

1984 Summer Olympics A1026

1984, Apr. 13 *Perf. 11½*
1905 A1026 65cr Long jump .20 .20
1906 A1026 65cr 100-meter race .20 .20
1907 A1026 65cr Relay race .20 .20
1908 A1026 585cr Pole vault .80 .65
1909 A1026 610cr High jump .85 .70
1910 A1026 620cr Hurdles .90 .80
a. Block of 6, #1905-1910 3.00 3.00

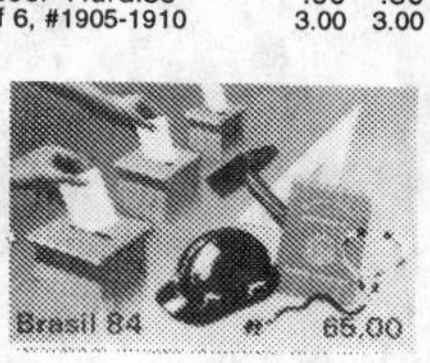

Voters Casting Ballots, Symbols of Labor A1027

Pres. Getulio Vargas Birth Centenary: Symbols of Development.

1984, Apr. 19 Litho. *Perf. 11½*
1911 A1027 65cr shown .20 .20
1912 A1027 65cr Oil rig, blast furnace .20 .20
1913 A1027 65cr High-tension towers .20 .20
Nos. 1911-1913 (3) .60 .60

Columbus, Espana '84 Emblem — A1028

1984, Apr. 27
1914 A1028 65cr Pedro Cabral .20 .20
1915 A1028 610cr shown 1.25 .70

Map of Americas, Heads — A1029

Lubrapex '84 — A1030

1984, May 7 Litho. *Perf. 11½*
1916 A1029 65cr multi .20 .20

Pan-American Association of Finance and Guarantees, 8th Assembly.

1984, May 8 *Perf. 11½x11*

18th Century Paintings, Mariana Cathedral.

1917 A1030 65cr Hunting scene .20 .20
1918 A1030 585cr Pastoral scene .75 .40
1919 A1030 610cr People under umbrellas .80 .50
1920 A1030 620cr Elephants .85 .50
Nos. 1917-1920 (4) 2.60 1.60

Souvenir Sheet

Intl. Fedn. of Soccer Associations, 80th Anniv. — A1031

1984, May 21 *Perf. 11*
1921 A1031 2115cr Globe 3.50 1.75

Matto Grosso Lowland Fauna A1032

1984, June 5 Litho. *Perf. 11½*
1922 Strip of 3 .60 .30
a. A1032 65cr Deer .20 .20
b. A1032 65cr Jaguar .20 .20
c. A1032 80cr Alligator .20 .20

First Letter Mailed in Brazil, by Guido Mondin — A1033

1984, June 8 *Perf. 12x11½*
1923 A1033 65cr multi .20 .20

Postal Union of Americas and Spain, first anniv. of new headquarters.

Brazil-Germany Air Service, 50th Anniv.
A1034 A1035

1984, June 19

1924 A1034 610cr Dornier-Wal seaplane 1.00 .70
1925 A1035 620cr Steamer Westfalen 1.05 .70
a. Pair, #1924-1925 2.05 1.50

Woolly Spider Monkey, World Wildlife Fund Emblem — A1036

1984, July 6 ***Perf. 11½***

1926 A1036 65cr Mother, baby .50 .20
1927 A1036 80cr Monkey .30 .20

Agriculture Type of 1980

Designs: 65cr, Rubber tree. 80cr, Brazil nuts. 120cr, Rice. 150cr, Eucalyptus. 300cr, Pinha da Parana. 800cr, Carnauba. 1000cr, Babacu. 2000cr, Sunflower.

Photogravure (65, 80, 120, 150cr), Engraved

1984-85 ***Perf. 11x11½***

1934 A894 65cr lilac .20 .20
1935 A894 80cr brn red .25 .20
1936 A894 120cr dk sl bl .35 .20
1937 A894 150cr green .20 .20
1938 A894 300cr rose mag .50 .20
1939 A894 800cr grnsh bl 1.40 .20
1940 A894 1000cr lemon 1.40 .20
1941 A894 2000cr yel org ('85) .75 .25
Nos. 1934-1941 (8) 5.05 1.65

Marajo Isld. Buffalo A1037

1984, July 9 Litho. ***Perf. 12***

1942 Strip of 3 .50 .30
a. A1037 65cr Approaching stream .20 .20
b. A1037 65cr Standing on bank .20 .20
c. A1037 80cr Drinking .20 .20

Continuous design.

Banco Economico Sesquicentenary — A1038

1984, July 13 ***Perf. 11½***

1943 A1038 65cr Bank, coins .20 .20

Historic Railway Stations A1039

1984, July 23 Litho. ***Perf. 11½***

1944 A1039 65cr Japeri .20 .20
1945 A1039 65cr Luz, vert. .20 .20
1946 A1039 80cr Sao Joao del Rei .20 .20
Nos. 1944-1946 (3) .60 .60

A1040 A1041

1984, Aug. 13 ***Perf. 11***

Souvenir Sheet

1947 A1040 585cr Girl scout 1.40 1.00

Girl Scouts in Brazil, 65th anniv.

1984, Aug. 21 Litho. ***Perf. 11½***

1948 A1041 65cr Couple sheltered from rain .20 .20

Housing project bank, 20th anniv.

Independence Week — A1042

Children's Drawings.

1984, Sept. 3

1949 A1042 100cr Explorer & ship .20 .20
1950 A1042 100cr Sailing ships .20 .20
1951 A1042 100cr "BRASIL" mural .20 .20
1952 A1042 100cr Children under rainbow .20 .20
Nos. 1949-1952 (4) .80 .80

Rio de Janeiro Chamber of Commerce Sesquicentenary — A1043

1984, Sept. 10

1953 A1043 100cr Monument, worker silhouette .20 .20

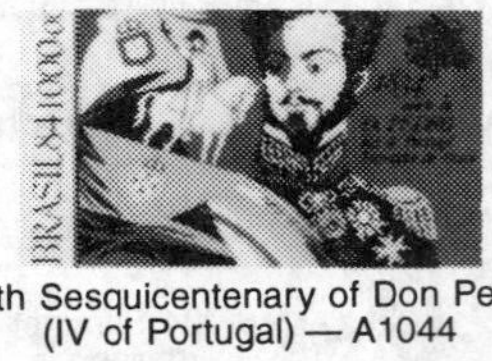

Death Sesquicentenary of Don Pedro I (IV of Portugal) — A1044

1984, Sept. 23 ***Perf. 12x11½***

1954 A1044 1000cr Portrait 1.50 1.10

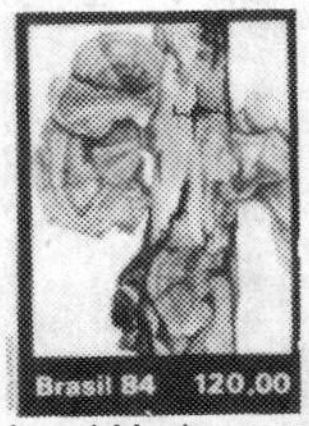

Local Mushrooms A1045 Book Day A1046

1984, Oct. 22 ***Perf. 11½***

1955 A1045 120cr Pycnoporus sanguineus .20 .20
1956 A1045 1050cr Calvatia sp 1.10 1.25
1957 A1045 1080cr Pleurotus sp, horiz. 1.20 1.30
Nos. 1955-1957 (3) 2.50 2.75

1984, Oct. 23 ***Perf. 11½***

1958 A1046 120cr Girl in open book .20 .20

New State Mint Opening — A1047

1984, Nov. 1

1959 A1047 120cr multi .20 .20

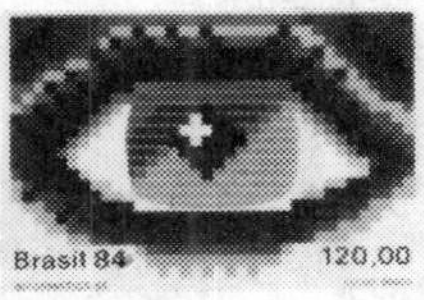

Informatics Fair & Congress A1048

1984, Nov. 5 Litho. ***Perf. 12***

1960 A1048 120cr Eye, computer terminal .20 .20

Org. of American States, 14th Assembly — A1049

1984, Nov. 14

1961 A1049 120cr Emblem, flags .20 .20

State Flags Type of 1981

Designs: a, Maranhaio. b, Mato Grosso. c, Minas Gerais. d, Piaui. e, Santa Catarina.

1984, Nov. 19 ***Perf. 11½***

1962 Block of 5 + label 1.00 1.00
a.-e. A947 120cr, any single .20 .20

Thanksgiving 1984 — A1051

1984, Nov. 22

1963 A1051 120cr Bell tower, Brasilia .20 .20

Christmas 1984 A1052

Paintings: No. 1964, Nativity, by Djanira. No. 1965, Virgin and Child, by Glauco Rodrigues. No. 1966, Flight into Egypt, by Paul Garfunkel. No. 1967, Nativity, by Di Cavalcanti.

1984, Dec. 3 Litho. ***Perf. 12***

1964 A1052 120cr multi .20 .20
1965 A1052 120cr multi .20 .20
1966 A1052 1050cr multi .85 .40
1967 A1052 1080cr multi .85 .40
Nos. 1964-1967 (4) 2.10 1.20

40th Anniv., International Civil Aviation Organization — A1053

1984, Dec. 7 Litho. ***Perf. 12***

1968 A1053 120cr Aircraft, Earth globe .20 .20

25th Anniv., North-Eastern Development — A1054

1984, Dec. 14 Litho. ***Perf. 12***

1969 A1054 120cr Farmer, field .20 .20

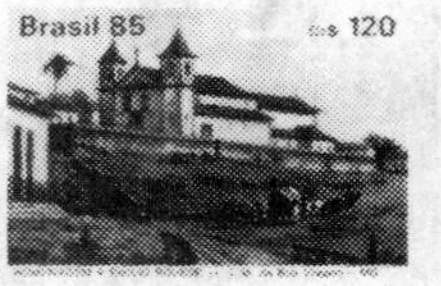

Emilio Rouede A1055

Painting: Church of the Virgin of Safe Travels, by Rouede.

1985, Jan. 22 Litho. ***Perf. 12***

1970 A1055 120cr multi .20 .20

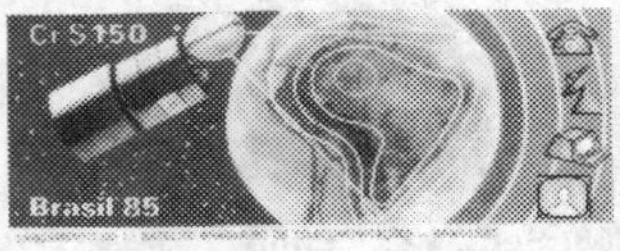

BRASILSAT — A1056

1985, Feb. 8 Litho. ***Perf. 11½x12***

1971 A1056 150cr Satellite, Brazil .20 .20

Metropolitan Railways — A1057

1985, Mar. 2 Litho. ***Perf. 11x11½***

1972 A1057 200cr Passenger trains .20 .20

Brasilia Botanical Gardens A1058

1985, Mar. 8 Litho. ***Perf. 11½x12***

1973 A1058 200cr Caryocar brasiliense .20 .20

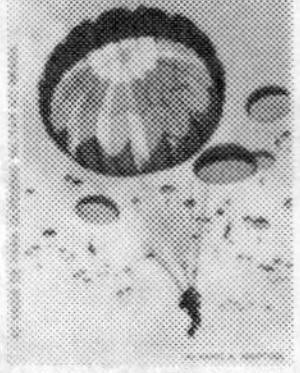

40th Anniv., Brazilian Paratroops — A1059

1985, Mar. 8 Litho. ***Perf. 11½x12***

1974 A1059 200cr Parachute drop .20 .20

Natl. Climate Awareness Program — A1060

1985, Mar. 18 Litho. ***Perf. 11½x12***

1975 A1060 500cr multi .20 .20

Pure Bred Horses
A1061

1985, Mar. 19 Litho. *Perf. 12*

1976 A1061 1000cr Campolina .40 .25
1977 A1061 1500cr Marajoara .70 .35
1978 A1061 1500cr Mangalarga marchador .70 .35
Nos. 1976-1978 (3) 1.80 .95

Ouro Preto — A1062

1985, Apr. 18 Litho. *Perf. 11½x12*

1979 A1062 220cr shown .20 .20
1980 A1062 220cr St. Miguel des Missoes .20 .20
1981 A1062 220cr Olinda .20 .20
Nos. 1979-1981 (3) .60 .60

Polivolume, by Mary Vieira — A1063

1985, Apr. 20 Litho.

1982 A1063 220cr multi .20 .20

Rio Branco Inst., 40th anniv.

Natl. Capital, Brasilia, 25th Anniv. — A1064

1985, Apr. 22 Litho.

1983 A1064 220cr Natl. Theater, acoustic shell .20 .20
1984 A1064 220cr Catetinho Palace, JK Memorial .20 .20

A1065

A1065a

1985-86 Photo. *Perf. 11½*

1985 A1065 50cr lake .20 .20
1986 A1065 100cr dp vio .20 .20
1987 A1065 150cr violet .20 .20
1988 A1065 200cr ultra .20 .20
1989 A1065 220cr green .20 .20
1990 A1065 300cr royal bl .20 .20
1991 A1065 500cr olive blk .30 .25
1992 A1065a 1000cr brn ol ('86) .20 .20
1993 A1065a 2000cr brt grn ('86) .35 .25
1994 A1065a 3000cr dl vio .40 .30
1995 A1065a 5000cr brown .60 .45
Nos. 1985-1995 (11) 3.05 2.65

Marshal Rondon, 120th Birth Anniv.
A1066

1985, May 5 *Perf. 11x11½*

1996 A1066 220cr multi .20 .20

Educator, protector of the Indians, building superintendent of telegraph lines.

Candido Fontoura (1885-1974)
A1067

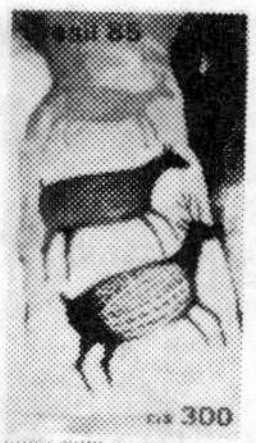

Brapex VI
A1068

1985, May 14 *Perf. 12x11½*

1997 A1067 220cr multi .20 .20

Pioneer of the Brazilian pharmaceutical industry.

1985, May 18 *Perf. 11½x11*

Cave paintings: No. 1998, Deer, Cerca Grande. No. 1999, Lizards, Lapa do Caboclo. No. 2000, Running deer, Grande Abrigo de Santana do Riacho.

1998 A1068 300cr multi .20 .20
1999 A1068 300cr multi .20 .20
2000 A1068 2000cr multi .75 .50
a. Souvenir sheet of 3, #1998-2000, perf. 10½x11 1.00 1.00
Nos. 1998-2000 (3) 1.15 .90

Wildlife Conservation
A1069

Birds in Marinho dos Abrolhos National Park.

1985, June 5 *Perf. 11½x12*

2001 A1069 220cr Fregata magnificens .20 .20
2002 A1069 220cr Sula dactylatra .20 .20
2003 A1069 220cr Anous stolidus .20 .20
2004 A1069 2000cr Pluvialis squatarola .60 .25
Nos. 2001-2004 (4) 1.20 .85

A1070

A1071

1985, June 11 *Perf. 12x11½*

2005 A1070 220cr Mother breastfeeding infant .20 .20
2006 A1070 220cr Hand, eyedropper, children .20 .20
a. Pair, #2005-2006 .25 .20

UN infant survival campaign.

1985, June 22 Litho. *Perf. 11½x11*

Helicopter rescue, search ship, diver.

2007 A1071 220cr multi .20 .20

Sea Search & Rescue.

Souvenir Sheet

World Cup Soccer, Mexico, 1986
A1072

1985, June 23 *Perf. 11*

2008 A1072 2000cr Player dribbling, World Cup 4.00 .85

Intl. Youth Year
A1073

11th Natl. Eucharistic Congress
A1074

1985, June 28 *Perf. 12*

2009 A1073 220cr Circle of children .20 .20

1985, July 16 *Perf. 12x11½*

2010 A1074 2000cr Mosaic, Priest raising host .55 .40

Director Humberto Mauro, Scene from Sangue Mineiro, 1929 — A1075

1985, July 27

2011 A1075 300cr multi .20 .20

Cataguases Studios, 60th anniv.

Escola e Sacro Museum, Convent St. Anthony, Joao Pessoa, Paraiba
A1076

1985, Aug. 5 *Perf. 11½x12*

2012 A1076 330cr multi .20 .20

Paraiba State 400th anniv.

Inconfidencia Museum — A1077

Cabanagem Insurrection, 150th Anniv. — A1078

1985, Aug. 11 *Perf. 12x11½*

2013 A1077 300cr shown .20 .20
2014 A1077 300cr Museum of History & Diplomacy .20 .20

1985, Aug. 14

Design: Revolutionary, detail from an oil painting by Guido Mondin.

2015 A1078 330cr multi .20 .20

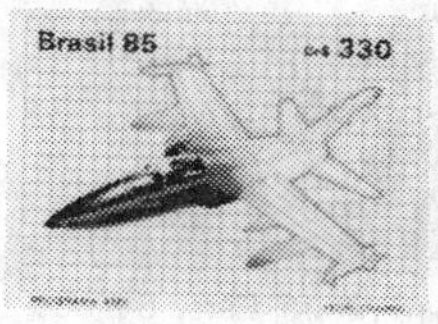

AMX Subsonic Air Force Fighter Plane
A1079

1985, Aug. 19 *Perf. 11½x12*

2016 A1079 330cr multi .20 .20

AMX Project, joint program with Italy.

16th-17th Century Military Uniforms — A1080

1985, Aug. 26 *Perf. 12x11½*

2017 A1080 300cr Captain, cross-bowman .20 .20
2018 A1080 300cr Harquebusier, sergeant .20 .20
2019 A1080 300cr Musketeer, pikeman .20 .20
2020 A1080 300cr Fusilier, pikeman .20 .20
Nos. 2017-2020 (4) .80 .80

Farrouphilha Insurrection, 150th Anniv. — A1081

Design: Bento Goncalves and insurrectionist cavalry on Southern battlefields, detail of an oil painting by Guido Mondin.

1985, Sept. 20 *Perf. 11½x12*

2021 A1081 330cr multi .20 .20

Aparados da Serra National Park
A1082

1985, Sept. 23

2022 A1082 3100cr Ravine .65 .50
2023 A1082 3320cr Mountains .70 .55
2024 A1082 3480cr Forest, waterfall .75 .60
Nos. 2022-2024 (3) 2.10 1.65

President-elect Tancredo Neves — A1083

Design: Portrait, Natl. Congress, Alvorada Palace, Federal Supreme Court.

1985, Oct. 10 Litho. *Perf. 11x11½*

2025 A1083 330cr multi .20 .20

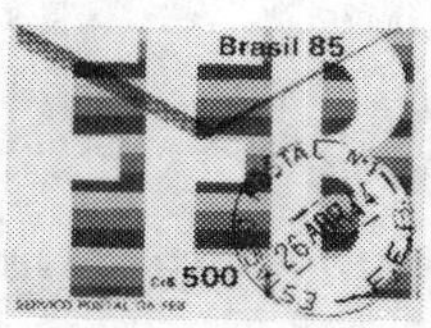

FEB, Postmark
A1084

1985, Oct. 10 *Perf. 11½x12*

2026 A1084 500cr multi .20 .20

Brazilian Expeditionary Force Postal Service, 41st anniv.

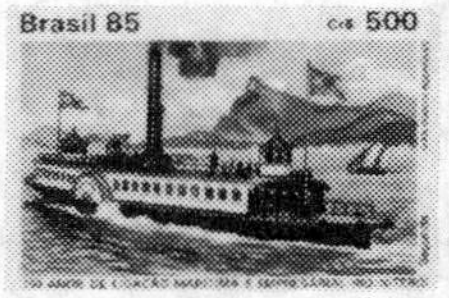

Rio de Janeiro-Niteroi Ferry Service, 150th Anniv. — A1085

1985, Oct. 14 ***Perf. 11½x12***

2027 A1085 500cr Segunda .20 .20
2028 A1085 500cr Terceira .20 .20
2029 A1085 500cr Especuladora .20 .20
2030 A1085 500cr Urca .20 .20
Nos. 2027-2030 (4) .80 .80

Muniz M-7 Inaugural Flight, 50th Anniv. — A1086

1985, Oct. 22

2031 A1086 500cr multi .20 .20

UN 40th Anniv. A1087

Natl. Press System A1088

1985, Oct. 24 ***Perf. 11½x11***

2032 A1087 500cr multi .20 .20

1985, Nov. 7

2033 A1088 500cr Newspaper masthead, reader .20 .20

Diario de Pernambuco, newspaper, 160th anniv.

Christmas 1985 A1089

1985, Nov. 11 ***Perf. 11½x12***

2034 A1089 500cr Christ in Manger .20 .20
2035 A1089 500cr Adoration of the Magi .20 .20
2036 A1089 500cr Flight to Egypt .20 .20
Nos. 2034-2036 (3) .60 .60

State Flags Type of 1981

a, Para. b, Rio Grande do Sul. c, Acre. d, Sao Paulo.

1985, Nov. 19 ***Perf. 12***

2037 Block of 4 .80 .60
a.-d. A947 500cr, any single .20 .20

Thanksgiving Day — A1091

1985, Nov. 28 ***Perf. 12x11½***

2038 A1091 500cr Child gathering wheat .20 .20

Economic Development of Serra dos Carajas Region A1092

1985, Dec. 11 Litho. ***Perf. 11½x12***

2039 A1092 500cr multi .20 .20

Fr. Bartholomeu Lourenco de Gusmao (1685-1724), Inventor, the Aerostat A1093

1985, Dec. 19 Litho. ***Perf. 11x11½***

2040 A1093 500cr multi .20 .20

A1094

A1095

The Trees, by Da Costa E Silva (b. 1885), poet.

1985, Dec. 20 Litho. ***Perf. 12x11½***

2041 A1094 500cr multi .20 .20

1986, Mar. 3 Litho. ***Perf. 11***

Souvenir Sheet

2042 A1095 10000cr multi 2.25 2.00

1986 World Cup Soccer Championships, Mexico. LUBRAPEX '86, philatelic exhibition.

Halley's Comet — A1096

1986, Apr. 11 Litho. ***Perf. 11½x12***

2043 A1096 50c multi .20 .20

Commander Ferraz Antarctic Station, 2nd Anniv. A1097

1986, Apr. 25

2044 A1097 50c multi .20 .20

Labor Day A1098

Maternity, by Henrique Bernardelli (1858-1936) A1099

1986, May 1 Litho. ***Perf. 12x11½***

2045 A1098 50c multi .20 .20

1986, May 8

2046 A1099 50c multi .20 .20

Amnesty Intl., 25th Anniv. A1100

1986, May 28 Litho. ***Perf. 11½x12***

2047 A1100 50c multi .20 .20

Butterflies A1101

1985, June 5 ***Perf. 12x11½***

2048 A1101 50c Pyrrhopyge rufi-cauda .20 .20
2049 A1101 50c Prepona eugenes diluta .20 .20
2050 A1101 50c Pierriballia mandel molione .20 .20
Nos. 2048-2050 (3) .60 .60

Score from Opera "Il Guarani" and Antonio Carlos Gomes (1836-1896), Composer A1102

1986, July 11 ***Perf. 11½x12***

2051 A1102 50c multi .20 .20

Natl. Accident Prevention Campaign — A1103

Stamp Day — A1104

1986, July 30 Litho. ***Perf. 11½x11***

2052 A1103 50c Lineman .20 .20

Souvenir Sheet

1986, Aug. 1 ***Perf. 11***

2053 A1104 5cz No. 53 .85 .35

Brazilian Phil. Soc., 75th anniv., and Dom Pedro II issue, Nos. 53-60, 120th anniv.

Architecture A1105

Famous Men A1106

Designs: 10c, House of Garcia D'Avila, Nazare de Mata, Bahia. 20c, Church of Our Lady of the Assumption, Anchieta Village. 50c, Fort Reis Magos, Natal. 1cz, Pilgrim's Column, Alcantara Village, 1648. 2cz, Cloisters, St. Francis Convent, Olinda. 5cz, St. Anthony's Chapel, Sao Roque. 10cz, St. Lawrence of the Indians Church, Niteroi. 20cz, Principe da Beiro Fort, Mato Dentro. 50cz, Jesus of Matozinhos Church, vert. 100cz, Church of our Lady of Sorrow, Campanha. 200cz, Casa dos Contos, Ouro Preto. 500cz, Antiga Alfandega, Belem, Para.

Perf. 11½x11, 11x11½

1986-88 **Photo.**

2055 A1105 10c sage grn .20 .20
2057 A1105 20c brt blue .20 .20
2059 A1105 50c orange .20 .20
2064 A1105 1cz golden brn .20 .20
2065 A1105 2cz dull rose .25 .20
a. Litho., perf. 13 ('88) .20 .20
2067 A1105 5cz lt olive grn .60 .45
a. Litho., perf. 13 ('88) .20 .20
2068 A1105 10cz slate blue .50 .35
2069 A1105 20cz lt red brn .75 .60
2070 A1105 50cz brn org 2.25 1.75
2071 A1105 100cz dull grn 2.70 2.00
2072 A1105 200cz deep blue 2.50 1.85
2073 A1105 500cz dull red brn 1.30 1.00
Nos. 2055-2073 (12) 11.65 9.00

Issued: 10c, 8/11; 20c, 12/8; 50c, 8/19; 1cz, 11/19; 2cz, 11/9; 5cz, 12/30; 10cz, 6/2/87; 20cz, 50cz, 9/18/87; 100cz, 12/21/87; 200cz, 5/9/88; 500cz, 11/22/88.

This is an expanding set. Numbers will change if necessary.

1986 ***Perf. 12x11½, 11½x12***

Designs: No. 2074, Juscelino Kubitschek de Oliveira, president 1956-61, and Alvorado Palace, Brasilia. No. 2075, Octavio Mangabeira, statesman, and Itamaraty Palace, Rio de Janeiro, horiz.

2074 A1106 50c multi .20 .20
2075 A1106 50c multi .20 .20

Issue dates: #2074, Aug. 21. #2075, Aug. 27.

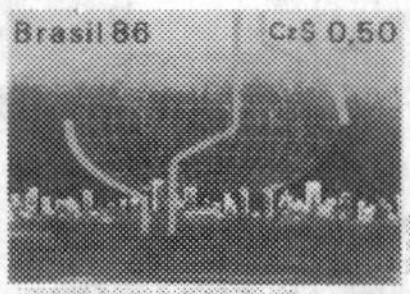

World Gastroenterology Congress, Sao Paulo — A1107

1986, Sept. 7 ***Perf. 11½x12***

2076 A1107 50c multi .20 .20

Federal Broadcasting System, 50th Anniv. — A1108

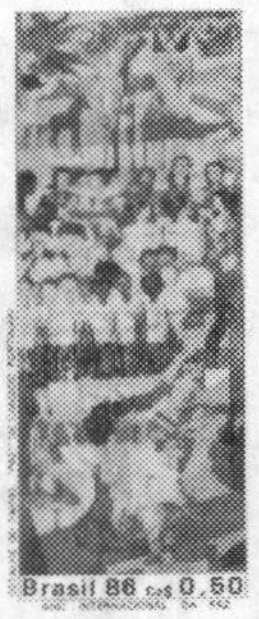

Intl. Peace Year — A1109

1986, Sept. 15 ***Perf. 12x11½***

2077 A1108 50c multi .20 .20

1986, Sept. 16

Painting (detail): War and Peace, by Candido Portinari.

2078 A1109 50c multi .20 .20

Ernesto Simoes Filho (b. 1886), Publisher of A Tarde A1110

1986, Oct. 4 Litho. ***Perf. 11½x12***

2079 A1110 50c multi .20 .20

Famous Men — A1111

Federal Savings Bank, 125th Anniv. — A1112

Designs: No. 2080, Title page from manuscript, c. 1683-94, by Gregorio Mattose e Guerra (b. 1636), author. No. 2081, Manuel Bandeira (1886-1968), poet, text from I'll Go Back to Pasargada.

1986, Oct. 29 ***Perf. 11½x11***
2080 A1111 50c lake & beige .20 .20
2081 A1111 50c lake & dl grn .20 .20

1986, Nov. 4 ***Perf. 12x11½***
2082 A1112 50c multi .20 .20

Flowering Plants A1113

Glauber Rocha, Film Industry Pioneer A1114

Perf. 12x11½, 11½x12
1986, Sept. 23
2083 A1113 50c Urera mitis .20 .20
2084 A1113 6.50cz Couroupita guyanensis .52 .40
2085 A1113 6.90cz Bauhinia variegata, horiz. .55 .40
Nos. 2083-2085 (3) 1.27 1.00

1986, Nov. 20 ***Perf. 12x11½***
2086 A1114 50c multi .20 .20

LUBRAPEX '86 — A1115

Cordel Folk Tales: No. 2087, Romance of the Mysterious Peacock. No. 2088, History of the Empress Porcina.

1986, Nov. 21 ***Perf. 11x12***
2087 A1115 6.90cz multi .45 .35
2088 A1115 6.90cz multi .45 .35
a. Souvenir sheet of 2, #2087-2088, perf. 11 1.10 .85

Christmas A1116

Birds: 50c, And Christ child. 6.50cz, And tree. 7.30cz, Eating fruit.

1986, Nov. 10 ***Perf. 11½x12***
2089 A1116 50c multi .20 .20
2090 A1116 6.50cz multi .65 .50
2091 A1116 7.30cz multi .75 .60
Nos. 2089-2091 (3) 1.60 1.30

Military Uniforms, c. 1930 — A1117

Bartolomeu de Gusmao Airport, 50th Anniv. — A1118

Designs: No. 2092, Navy lieutenant commander, dreadnought Minas Gerais. No. 2093, Army flight lieutenant, WACO S.C.O. biplane, Fortaleza Airport.

1986, Dec. 15 ***Perf. 12x11½***
2092 A1117 50c multi .20 .20
2093 A1117 50c multi .20 .20

Fortaleza Air Base, 50th anniv. (No. 2093).

1986, Dec. 26
2094 A1118 1cz multi .20 .20

Heitor Villa Lobos (1887-1959), Conductor — A1119

1987, Mar. 5 **Litho.** ***Perf. 12x11½***
2095 A1119 1.50cz multi .20 .20

Natl. Air Force C-130 Transport Plane, Flag, the Antarctic — A1120

1987, Mar. 9 ***Perf. 11x11½***
2096 A1120 1cz multi .20 .20

Antarctic Project.

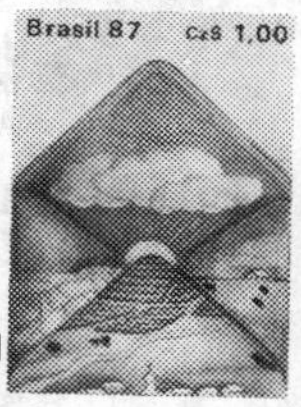

Special Mail Services — A1121

1987, Mar. 20 ***Perf. 12x11½***
2097 A1121 1cz Rural delivery .20 .20
2098 A1121 1cz Intl. express .20 .20

TELECOM '87, Geneva A1122

1987, May 5 ***Perf. 11½x12***
2099 A1122 2cz Brazilsat, wave, globe .20 .20

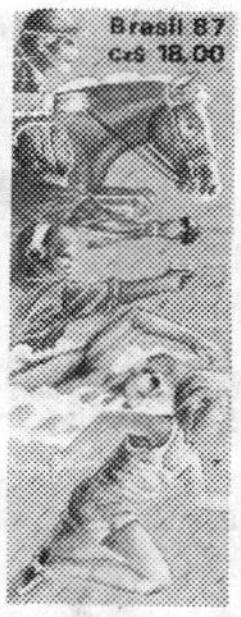

10th Pan American Games, Indianapolis, Aug. 7-25 — A1123

1987, May 20 ***Perf. 12x11½***
2100 A1123 18cz multi 1.00 .75

Natl. Fine Arts Museum, 150th Anniv A1124

1987, Jan. 13 ***Perf. 11½x12***
2101 A1124 1cz multi .20 .20

Marine Conservation — A1125

1987, June 5
2102 A1125 2cz Eubalaena australis .20 .20
2103 A1125 2cz Eretmochelys imbricata .20 .20

Federal Court of Appeal, 40th Anniv. A1126

1987, June 15
2104 A1126 2cz multi .20 .20

Military Club, Cent. — A1127

1987, June 26 ***Perf. 12x11½***
2105 A1127 3cz multi .20 .20

Agriculture Institute of Campinas, Cent. A1128

1987, June 27 ***Perf. 11½x12***
2106 A1128 2cz multi .20 .20

Entomological Society, 50th Anniv. — A1129

1987, July 17
2107 A1129 3cz Zoolea lopiceps .20 .20
2108 A1129 3cz Fulgora servillei .20 .20

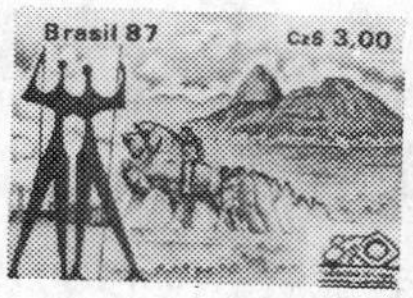

Natl. Tourism Year A1130

Designs: No. 2109, Monuments and Sugarloaf Mountain, Rio de Janeiro. No. 2110, Colonial church, sailboats, parrot, cashews.

1987, Aug. 4
2109 A1130 3cz multi .20 .20
2110 A1130 3cz multi .20 .20

Royal Portuguese Cabinet of Literature, 150th Anniv. — A1131

1987, Aug. 27 ***Perf. 12x11½***
2111 A1131 30cz ver & brt grn 1.10 .85

Sport Club Intl. — A1132

Championship soccer clubs, Brazil's Gold Cup: b, Sao Paulo. c, Guarani. d, Regatas do Flamengo.

1987, Aug. 29 ***Perf. 11½x12***
2112 Block of 4 .60 .40
a.-d. A1132 3cz any single .20 .20

St. Francis Convent, 400th Anniv. A1133

1987, Oct. 4
2113 A1133 4cz multi .20 .20

Jose Americo de Almeida, Author A1134

Design: Characters from romance novel, "A Bagaceira," 1928, and portrait of author.

1987, Oct. 23 **Litho.** ***Perf. 11x11½***
2114 A1134 4cz multi .20 .20

Spanish Galleons Anchored in Recife Port, 1537 A1135

1987, Nov. 12 **Litho.** ***Perf. 11½x12***
2115 A1135 5cz Harbor entrance .20 .20

Recife City, 450th anniv.

Thanksgiving
A1136

1987, Nov. 26 *Perf. 12x11½*
2116 A1136 5cz multi .20 .20

Christmas 1987
A1137

1987, Nov. 30 *Perf. 11½x12*
2117 A1137 6cz Shepherd and flock .20 .20
2118 A1137 6cz Christmas pageant .20 .20
2119 A1137 6cz Six angels .20 .20
Nos. 2117-2119 (3) .60 .60

Pedro II College, 150th Anniv. — A1138

Gold pen Emperor Pedro II used to sign edict establishing the school, and Senator Bernardo Pereira de Vasconcellos, founder.

1987, Dec. 2
2120 A1138 6cz multi .20 .20

Natl. Orchid Growers' Soc., 50th Anniv.
A1139

1987, Dec. 3
2121 A1139 6cz Laelia lobata veitch .20 .20
2122 A1139 6cz Cattleya guttata lindley .20 .20

Marian Year — A1140

Statue of Our Lady and Basilica at Fatima, Portugal.

1987, Dec. 20 *Perf. 12x11½*
2123 A1140 50cz multi 1.10 .85

Exhibit of the Statue of Our Lady of Fatima in Brazil.

Descriptive Treatise of Brazil, by Gabriel S. de Sousa, 400th Anniv.
A1141

1987, Dec. 21 **Litho.** *Perf. 11x11½*
2124 A1141 7cz multi .20 .20

Natl. Archives, 150th Anniv.
A1142

Design: Text from illuminated Gregorian canticle and computer terminal.

1988, Jan. 5 *Perf. 11½x12*
2125 A1142 7cz multi .20 .20

Opening of Brazilian Ports to Ships of Friendly Nations, 180th Anniv.
A1143

1988, Jan. 28 *Perf. 11x11½*
2126 A1143 7cz multi .25 .20

Souvenir Sheet

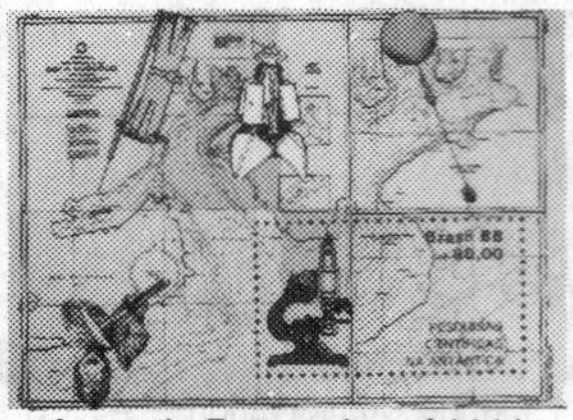
Antarctic Research — A1144

1988, Feb. 9 **Litho.** *Perf. 11*
2127 A1144 80cz multi 2.00 2.00

Energy Resources
A1145

1988, Mar. 15 **Litho.** *Perf. 12x11½*
2128 A1145 14cz Electricity .25 .20
2129 A1145 14cz Fossil fuels .25 .20

Souvenir Sheet

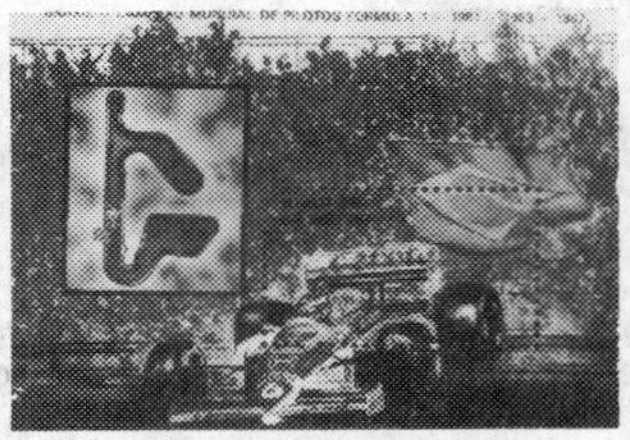
Brazilians as Formula 1 World Champions in 1981, 1983, 1987 — A1146

1988, Mar. 30 *Perf. 11*
2130 A1146 300cz multi 4.50 4.50

Jose Bonifacio, Armorial and Masonic Emblems — A1147

1988, Apr. 6 *Perf. 12x11½*
2131 A1147 20cz multi .30 .25

Jose Bonifacio de Andrada e Silva (c. 1763-1838), geologist and prime minister under Pedro I who supported the movement for independence from Portugal and was exiled for opposing the emperor's advisors.

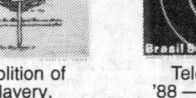

Abolition of Slavery, Cent. — A1148

Telecom '88 — A1149

Designs: 20cz, Declaration and quill pen. 50cz, Slave ship and maps of African coastline and slave trade route between Africa and South America.

1988, May 12 **Litho.** *Perf. 12x11½*
2132 A1148 20cz multi .25 .20
2133 A1148 50cz multi .65 .50

1988, May 16 *Perf. 11½x11*
2134 A1149 50cz multi .60 .45

Jesus of Matosinhos Sanctuary
A1150

1988, May 16 *Perf. 11½x12*
2135 A1150 20cz shown .25 .20
2136 A1150 50cz Pilot plan of Brazilia .60 .45
2137 A1150 100cz Salvador historic district 1.20 .90
Nos. 2135-2137 (3) 2.05 1.55

LUBRAPEX '88. World heritage list.

Japanese Immigrants in Brazil, 80th Anniv. — A1151

1988, June 18 **Litho.** *Perf. 11½x11*
2138 A1151 100cz multi .75 .55

A1152

A1153

1988, July 1 **Photo.** *Perf. 13*
2139 A1152 (A) brt blue .25 .20

No. 2139 met the first class domestic letter postage rate (28cz).
See Nos. 2201, 2218.

1988, July 14 **Litho.** *Perf. 12x11½*
2140 A1153 20cz Judo .25 .20

1988 Summer Olympics, Seoul.

Wildlife Conservation — A1154

1988, July 24 *Perf. 11½x12*
2141 A1154 20cz Myrmecophaga tridactyla .20 .20
2142 A1154 50cz Chaetomys subspinosus .30 .25
2143 A1154 100cz Speothos venaticus .65 .50
Nos. 2141-2143 (3) 1.15 .95

Souvenir Sheet

The Motherland, 1919 by Pedro Bruno — A1155

1988, Aug. 1 **Litho.** *Perf. 11*
2144 A1155 250cz multi 1.50 1.50

Stamp Day, BRASILIANA '89.

Natl. Confederation of Industries, 50th Anniv. — A1156

1988, Aug. 12 *Perf. 11½x12*
2145 A1156 50cz multi .25 .20

Soccer Clubs
A1157

No. 2146, Recife, Pernambuco. No. 2147, Coritiba, Parana. 100cz, Gremio, Porto Alegre, Rio Grande do Sul. 200cz, Fluminense, Rio de Janeiro.

1988, Sept. 29 *Perf. 11½x12*
2146 A1157 50cz multi .20 .20
2147 A1157 50cz multi .20 .20
2148 A1157 100cz multi .30 .25
2149 A1157 200cz multi .60 .50
a. Block of 4, #2146-2149 1.25 .95

Poems, 1888
A1158

Portraits and text: 50cz, *O Ateneu*, by Raul Pompeia. 100cz, *Poesias*, by Olavo Bilac.

1988, Oct. 28 *Perf. 11x11½*
2150 A1158 50cz multi .20 .20
2151 A1158 100cz multi .25 .20

Souvenir Sheet

1988 Democratic Constitution for the Union of the People and the State — A1159

1988, Oct. 5 Litho. *Perf. 11*
2152 A1159 550cz Government building 2.40 2.40

Origami Art — A1160

1988, Nov. 11 Litho. *Perf. 11½x12*
2153 A1160 50cz Abbey, nuns .20 .20
2154 A1160 100cz Nativity .25 .20
2155 A1160 200cz Santa Claus, presents .50 .40
Nos. 2153-2155 (3) .95 .80

Christmas.

ARBRAFEX Philatelic Exhibition of Argentina and Brazil A1161

1988, Nov. 26
2156 A1161 400cz multi .85 .65

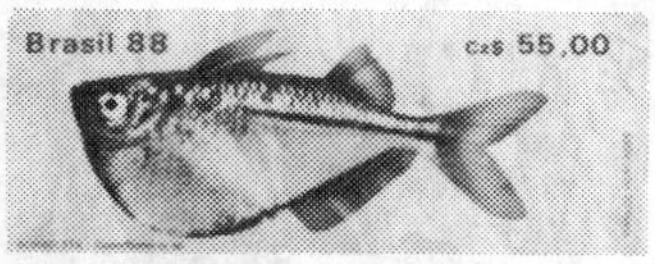

Fresh-water Fish — A1162

Designs: a, *Gasteropelecus*. b, *Osteoglossum ferreirai*. c, *Moenkhausia*. d, *Xavantei*. e, *Ancistrus hoplogenys*. f, *Brochis splendens*. Se-tenant in a continuous design.
Illustration reduced.

1988, Nov. 29 Litho. *Perf. 11½x12*
2157 Block of 6 .90 .70
a.-f. A1162 55cz any single .20 .20

Souvenir Sheet

BRAPEX '88, Ecological Preservation — A1163

1988, Dec. 10 *Perf. 11*
2158 Sheet of 3 1.80 1.80
a. A1163 100cz Parrot .25 .25
b. A1163 250cz Plant .60 .60
c. A1163 400cz Pelican .95 .95

Satellite Dishes A1164

Performing Arts A1165

1988, Dec. 20 *Perf. 12x11½*
2159 A1164 70cz multi .20 .20

Ansat 10-Earth satellite station communication.

1988, Dec. 21
2160 A1165 70cz multi .20 .20

Court of Justice, Bahia, 380th Anniv. A1166

1989, Mar. 10 Litho. *Perf. 11½x12*
2161 A1166 25c multi .40 .30

Public Library Year — A1167

1989, Mar. 13 *Perf. 11½*
2162 A1167 25c Library, Bahia, 1811 .40 .30

Brazilian Post & Telegraph Enterprise, 20th Anniv. A1168

Intl. and domestic postal services: a, Facsimile transmission (Post-Grama). b, Express mail (EMS). c, Parcel post (Sedex). d, Postal savings (CEFPostal).

1989, Mar. 20 *Perf. 11½x12*
2163 Block of 4 1.65 1.25
a.-d. A1168 25c any single .40 .30

Souvenir Sheet

Ayrton Senna, 1988 Formula 1 World Champion — A1169

1989, Mar. 23
2164 A1169 2cz multi 4.00 4.00

Environmental Conservation A1170

1989, Apr. 6 Litho. *Perf. 12x11½*
2165 A1170 25c multi .35 .25

Mineira Inconfidencia Independence Movement, Bicent. — A1171

Designs: a, Pyramid, hand. b, Figure of a man, houses. c, Destruction of houses.

1989, Apr. 21 *Perf. 11½x12*
2166 Strip of 3 1.30 .95
a.-b. A1171 30c any single .40 .30
c. A1171 40c multi .50 .40

First rebellion against Portuguese dominion.

Military School, Rio de Janeiro, Cent. A1172

1989, May 6 Litho. *Perf. 11½x12*
2167 A1172 50c multi .50 .40

Flowering Plants A1173

1989, June 5 *Perf. 11½x12, 12x11½*
2168 A1173 50c *Pavonia alnifolia* .60 .45
2169 A1173 1cz *Worsleya rayneri* 1.25 .90
2170 A1173 1.50cz *Heliconia farinosa* 1.75 1.40
Nos. 2168-2170 (3) 3.60 2.75

Nos. 2169-2170 vert.

Barreto and Recife Law School, Pedro II Square A1174

1989, June 7 *Perf. 11x11½*
2171 A1174 50c multi .65 .50

Tobias Barreto (b. 1839), advocate of Germanization of Brazil.

Cultura Broadcasting System, 20th Anniv. — A1175

1989, June 27 Litho. *Perf. 11½x12*
2172 A1175 50c multi .60 .45

Aviation A1176

1989, July 7
2173 A1176 50c Ultra-light aircraft .50 .40
2174 A1176 1.50cz Eiffel Tower, *Demoiselle* 1.65 1.10

Flight of Santos-Dumont's *Demoiselle*, 80th anniv (1.50cz).

Indigenous Flora — A1177

1989 Photo. *Perf. 11x11½, 11½x11*
2176 A1177 10c *Dichorisandra*, vert. .20 .20
2177 A1177 20c *Quiabentia zehnteri* .25 .20
2178 A1177 50c *Bougainvillea glabra* .50 .40
2179 A1177 1cz *Impatiens species* 1.00 .80
2180 A1177 2cz *Chorisia crispiflora* .25 .20
2181 A1177 5cz *Hibiscus trilineatus* .60 .45
Nos. 2176-2181 (6) 2.80 2.25

Issued: 10c, July 4; 20c, June 21; 50c, June 26; 1cz, June 19; 2cz, 5cz, Dec. 4.
No. 2181 vert.
See Nos. 2259-2273.

Souvenir Sheet

Largo da Carioca, by Nicolas Antoine Taunay — A1179

1989, July 7 Litho. *Perf. 11*
2197 A1179 3cz multi 3.00 3.00

PHILEXFRANCE '89, French revolution bicent.

Cut and Uncut Gemstones A1180

1989, July 12 Litho. *Perf. 12x11½*
2198 A1180 50c Tourmaline .40 .30
2199 A1180 1.50cz Amethyst 1.20 .90

Souvenir Sheet

Paco Imperial, Rio de Janeiro, and Map — A1181

1989, July 28 ***Perf. 11***
2200 A1181 5cz multi 3.75 3.75

BRASILANA '89.

Type of 1988 Redrawn

1989, July 26 Photo. ***Perf. 13***
Size: 17x21mm
2201 A1152 (A) org & brt blue .20 .20

Size of type and postal emblem are smaller on No. 2201; "1e PORTE" is at lower left.
No. 2201 met the first class domestic letter postage rate (cz).

Pernambuco Commercial Assoc., 150th Anniv. — A1182

1989, Aug. 1 Litho. ***Perf. 11½x12***
2202 A1182 50c multi .40 .30

Photography, 150th Anniv. — A1183

1989, Aug. 14
2203 A1183 1.50cz multi 1.10 .85

1st Hydroelecric Power Station in South America, Marmelos-o, Cent. — A1184

1989, Sept. 5 Litho. ***Perf. 11½x12***
2204 A1184 50c multi .35 .25

Conchs Endemic to the Brazilian Coast A1185

1989, Sept. 8
2205 A1185 50c *Voluta ebraea* .30 .25
2206 A1185 1cz *Morum matthewsi* .60 .45
2207 A1185 1.50cz *Agaronia travassosi* .90 .65
Nos. 2205-2207 (3) 1.80 1.35

Wildlife conservation.

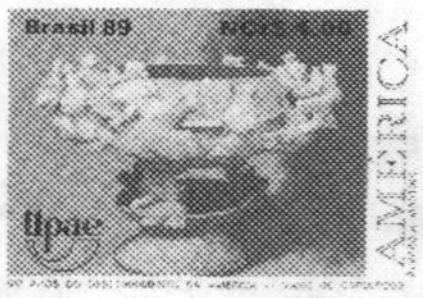

America Issue A1186

UPAE emblem and pre-Columbian stone carvings: 1cz, Muiraquita ritual statue, vert. 4cz, Ceramic brazier under three-footed votive urn.

Perf. 12x11½, 11½x12
1989, Oct. 12 Litho.
2208 A1186 1cz multicolored .50 .35
2209 A1186 4cz shown 1.85 1.40

Discovery of America 500th anniv. (in 1992).

A1187

A1188

Hologram and: a. *Lemons,* by Danilo di Prete. b. *O Indio E A Suacuapara,* by sculptor Victor Brecheret. c. Francisco Matarazzo.

1989, Oct. 14 ***Perf. 11***
Souvenir Sheet
2210 Sheet of 3 3.75 3.75
a. A1187 2cz multicolored .70 .70
b. A1187 3cz multicolored 1.10 1.10
c. A1187 5cz multicolored 1.75 1.75

Sao Paulo 20th intl. art biennial.

1989, Oct. 26 ***Perf. 11½x11***

Writers, residences and quotes: No. 2211, Casimiro de Abreu (b. 1839). No. 2212, Cora Coralina (b. 1889). No. 2213, Joaquim Machado de Assis (b. 1839).

2211 A1188 1cz shown .55 .40
2212 A1188 1cz multicolored .55 .40
2213 A1188 1cz multicolored .55 .40
Nos. 2211-2213 (3) 1.65 1.20

Federal Police Department, 25th Anniv. A1189

1989, Nov. 9 ***Perf. 11½x12***
2214 A1189 1cz multicolored .25 .20

Christmas A1190

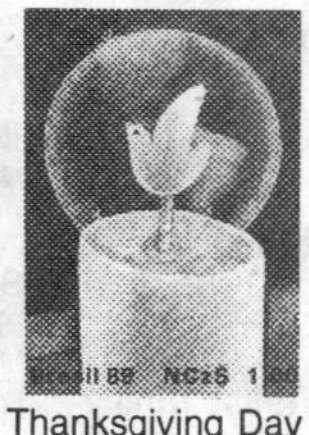

Thanksgiving Day A1191

1989, Nov. 10 ***Perf. 12x11½***
2215 A1190 70c Heralding angel .20 .20
2216 A1190 1cz Holy family .25 .20

1989, Nov. 23
2217 A1191 1cz multicolored .25 .20

Type of 1988 Redrawn

1989, Nov. 6 Photo. ***Perf. 13x13½***
Size: 22x26mm
2218 A1152 (B) org & dark red 2.00 1.50

Size of type and postal emblem are smaller on No. 2218; "1e PORTE" is at lower left.
No. 2218 met the first class intl. letter postage rate, initially at 9cz.

Souvenir Sheet

Proclamation of the Republic, Cent. — A1192

1989, Nov. 19 Litho. ***Perf. 11***
2225 A1192 15cz multicolored 4.50 4.50

Bahia Sports Club, 58th Anniv. A1193

1989, Nov. 30 ***Perf. 11½x12***
2226 A1193 50c Soccer .20 .20

Yellow Man, by Anita Malfatti (b. 1889) — A1194

1989, Dec. 2 ***Perf. 12x11½***
2227 A1194 1cz multicolored .25 .20

Bahia State Public Archives, Cent. — A1195

1990, Jan. 16 Litho. ***Perf. 11½x12***
2228 A1195 2cz multicolored .30 .20

Brazilian Botanical Soc., 40th Anniv. A1196

1990, Jan. 21
2229 A1196 2cz Sabia, Caatinga .25 .20
2230 A1196 13cz Pau, Brazil 1.40 1.10

Churches A1197

Designs: 2cz, St. John the Baptist Cathedral, Santa Cruz do Sul, vert. 3cz, Our Lady of Victory Church, Oeiras. 5cz, Our Lady of the Rosary Church, Ouro Preto, vert.

1990, Feb. 5 ***Perf. 12x11½, 11½x12***
2231 A1197 2cz multicolored .20 .20
2232 A1197 3cz multicolored .25 .20
2233 A1197 5cz multicolored .40 .30
Nos. 2231-2233 (3) .85 .70

Lloyd's of London in Brazil, Cent. A1198

1990, Feb. 19 Litho. ***Perf. 11½x12***
2234 A1198 3cz multicolored .20 .20

Souvenir Sheet

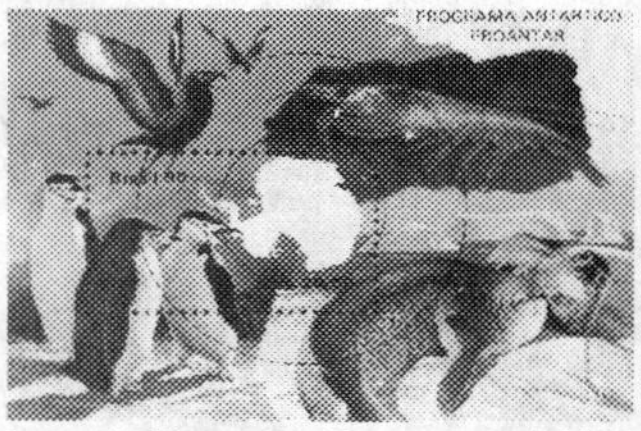

Antarctic Research Program — A1199

1990, Feb. 22 Litho. ***Perf. 11***
2235 A1199 20cz Fauna, map 1.55 1.55

Vasco da Gama Soccer Club A1200

1990, Mar. 5
2236 A1200 10cz multicolored .50 .40

Lindolfo Collor (b. 1890), Syndicated Columnist, and Labor Monument A1201

1990, Mar. 7
2237 A1201 20cz multicolored .95 .70

A1202

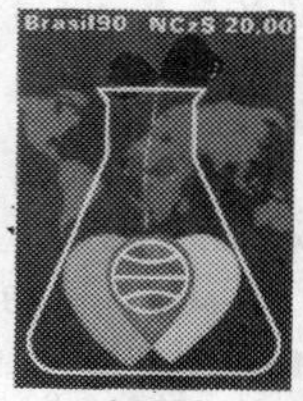

A1203

Pres. Jose Sarney.

1990, Mar. 8 ***Perf. 12x11½***
2238 A1202 20cz chalky blue .95 .70

1990, Apr. 6 ***Perf. 12x11½***
2239 A1203 20cz multicolored .70 .50

AIDS prevention.

Souvenir Sheet

Penny Black, 150th Anniv. — A1204

Designs: 20cr, Dom Pedro, Brazil No. 1. 100cr, Queen Victoria, Great Britain No. 1.

1990, May 3 Litho. *Perf. 11*

2240 A1204 Sheet of 2 2.35 1.75
- *a.* 20cr multicolored
- *b.* 100cr multicolored

Central Bank, 25th Anniv. A1205

1990, Mar. 30 Litho. *Perf. 11½x12*

2241 A1205 20cr multicolored .70 .50

Amazon River Postal Network, 21st Anniv. A1207

1990, Apr. 20 *Perf. 11x11½*

2243 A1207 20cr multicolored .70 .50

Souvenir Sheet

World Cup Soccer Championships, Italy — A1208

1990, May 12 Litho. *Perf. 12x11½*

2244 A1208 120cr multicolored 3.00 3.00

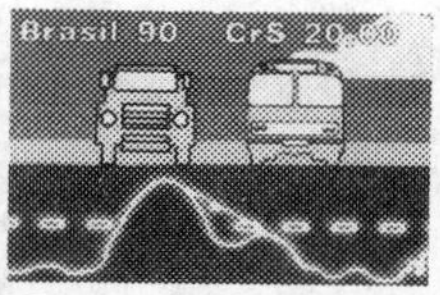

22nd Congress of the Intl. Union of Highway Transportation — A1209

1990. May 14 *Perf. 11½x12*

2245 A1209 20cr multicolored .65 .50
2246 A1209 80cr multicolored 3.00 2.25
- *a.* Pair, #2245-2246 3.75 2.75

No. 2246a has a continuous design.

Imperial Crown, 18th Cent. — A1210

Designs: No. 2248, Our Lady of Immaculate Conception, 18th cent.

1990, May 18 *Perf. 12x11½*

2247 A1210 20cr shown .70 .50
2248 A1210 20cr multicolored .70 .50

Imperial Museum, 50th anniv.(No. 2247). Mission Museum, 50th anniv. (No. 2248).

State Flags Type of 1981

1990, May 20 *Perf. 11½x12*

2249 A947 20cr Tocantins .70 .50

Army Geographical Service, Cent. — A1212

1990, May 30 *Perf. 11x11½*

2250 A1212 20cr multicolored .70 .50

Film Personalities — A1213

1990, June 19 *Perf. 11½x12*

2251 A1213 25cr Adhemar Gonzaga .80 .60
2252 A1213 25cr Carmen Miranda .80 .60
2253 A1213 25cr Carmen Santos .80 .60
2254 A1213 25cr Oscarito .80 .60
- *a.* Block of 4, #2251-2254 3.20 2.40

France-Brazil House, Rio de Janeiro — A1214

1990, July 14 Litho. *Perf. 11½x11*

2255 A1214 50cr multicolored 1.50 1.10

See France No. 2226.

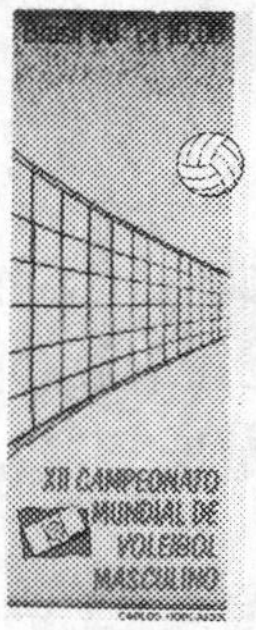

World Men's Volleyball Chmpships. A1215

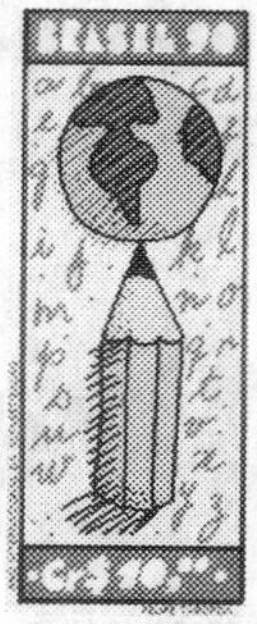

Intl. Literacy Year A1217

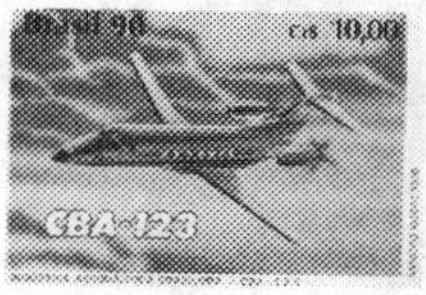

CBA 123 A1216

1990, July 28 Litho. *Perf. 12x11½*

2256 A1215 10cr multicolored .30 .25

1990, July 30 *Perf. 11½x12*

2257 A1216 10cr multicolored .30 .25

1990, Aug. 22 *Perf. 12x11½*

2258 A1217 10cr multicolored .30 .25

Flora Type of 1989

Perf. 11x11½, 11½x11

1989-93 Photo.

Design A1177

2259 1cr like #2179 .20 .20
2260 2cr like #2180 .20 .20
2261 5cr like #2181 .20 .20
2262 10cr Tibouchina granulosa .20 .20
2263 20cr Cassia macranthera .20 .20
2264 50cr Clitoria fairchildiana .30 .20
2265 50cr Tibouchina mutabilis .35 .35
2266 100cr Erythrina cristagalli, perf. 13 .55 .30
2267 200cr Jacaranda mimosifolia 1.10 .55
2268 500cr Caesalpinia peltophoroides 2.75 1.40
2269 1000cr Pachira aquatica .20 .20
2270 2000cr Hibiscus pernambucensis .20 .20
2271 5000cr Triplaris surinamensis .85 .85
2272 10,000cr Tabebuia heptaphylla 1.65 1.65
2273 20,000cr Erythrina speciosa 2.25 2.25
Nos. 2259-2273 (15) 11.20 8.95

Issued: 1cr, 11/8/90; 2cr, 11/12/90; 5cr, 11/16/90; #2264, 6/1/89; 10cr, 4/18/90; 20cr, 5/4/90; 100cr, 8/24/90; 200cr, 6/16/91; 500cr, 5/14/91; 1000cr, 9/2/92; 2000cr, 9/8/92; 5000cr, 10/16/92; 10,000cr, 11/16/92; 20,000cr, 4/25/93; #2265, 10/20/93.

Granbery Instutute, Cent. A1218

1990, Sept. 8 Litho. *Perf. 11½x12*

2279 A1218 13cr multicolored .40 .30

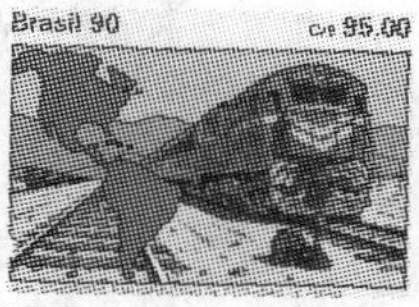

18th Panamerican Railroad Congress — A1219

1990, Sept. 9

2280 A1219 95cr multicolored 2.00 1.50

Embratel, 25th Anniv. — A1220

1990, Sept. 21

2281 A1220 13cr multicolored .40 .30

LUBRAPEX '90 — A1221

Statues by Ceschiatti and Giorgi (No. 2283).

1990, Sept. 22

2282 A1221 25cr As Banhistas .60 .45
2283 A1221 25cr Os Candangos .60 .45
2284 A1221 100cr Evangelista Sao Joao 1.25 .90
2285 A1221 100cr A Justica 1.25 .90
- *a.* Block of 4, #2282-2285 4.00 3.00
- *b.* Souv. sheet of 4, #2282-2285 6.00 6.00

Praia Do Sul Wildlife Reserve A1222

1990, Oct. 12

2286 A1222 15cr Flowers .45 .30
2287 A1222 105cr Shoreline 2.60 1.80
- *a.* Pair, #2286-2287 3.05 2.10

Discovery of America, 500th anniv. (in 1992).

Natl. Library, 180th Anniv. A1223

Writers: No. 2289, Guilherme de Almeida (1890-1969). No. 2290, Oswald de Andrade (1890-1954).

1990, Oct. 29 Litho. *Perf. 11x11½*

2288 A1223 15cr multicolored .40 .30
2289 A1223 15cr multicolored .40 .30
2290 A1223 15cr multicolored .40 .30
Nos. 2288-2290 (3) 1.20 .90

Natl. Tax Court, Cent. A1224

1990, Nov. 7 Litho. *Perf. 11½x12*

2291 A1224 15cr multicolored .40 .30

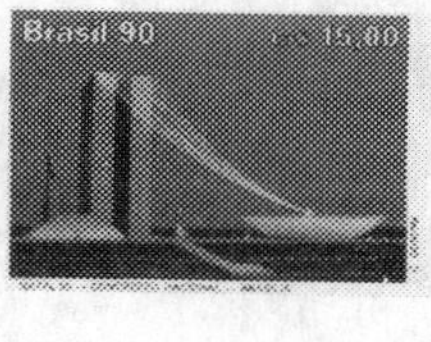

Christmas A1225

Architecture of Brasilia: No. 2292, National Congress. No. 2293, Television tower.

1990, Nov. 20

2292 A1225 15cr multicolored .40 .30
2293 A1225 15cr multicolored .40 .30

A1226

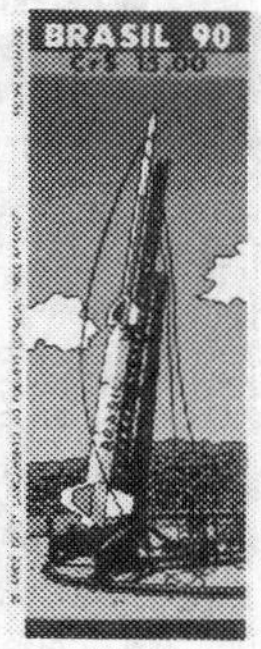

A1227

1990, Dec. 13 Litho. *Perf. 12x11½*

2294 A1226 15cr multicolored .20 .20

Organization of American States, cent.

1990, Dec. 14

2295 A1227 15cr multicolored .20 .20

First Flight of Nike Apache Missile, 25th anniv.

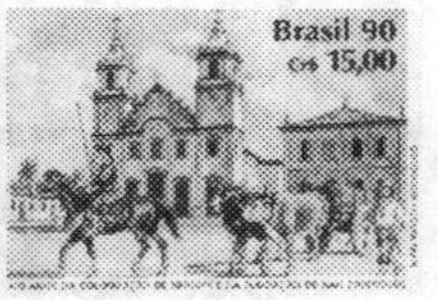

Colonization of Sergipe, Founding of Sao Cristovao, 400th Anniv.
A1228

1990, Dec. 18 Litho. ***Perf. 11½x12***
2296 A1228 15cr multicolored .20 .20

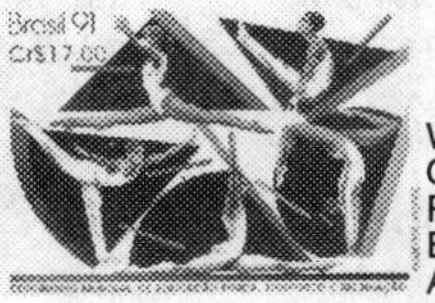

World Congress of Physical Education
A1229

1991, Jan. 7 ***Perf. 11½x12***
2297 A1229 17cr multicolored .20 .20

Rock in Rio II — A1230

1991, Jan. 9 ***Perf. 12x11½***
2298 A1230 25cr Cazuza .20 .20
2299 A1230 185cr Raul Seixas 1.65 1.00
a. Pair, #2298-2299 2.00 1.10

Printed in sheets of 12.

Ministry of Aviation, 50th Anniv.
A1231

1991, Jan. 20 ***Perf. 11x11½***
2300 A1231 17cr multicolored .20 .20

A1232 A1233

Carnivals.

1991, Feb. 8 Litho. ***Perf. 12x11½***
2301 A1232 25cr Olinda .25 .20
2302 A1232 30cr Salvador .25 .20
2303 A1232 280cr Rio de Janeiro 2.50 2.00
Nos. 2301-2303 (3) 3.00 2.40

1991, Feb. 20
2304 A1233 300cr multicolored 3.00 2.25

Visit by Pres. Collor to Antarctica.

Hang Gliding World Championships — A1234

1991, Feb. 24 ***Perf. 11½x12***
2305 A1234 36cr multicolored .35 .30

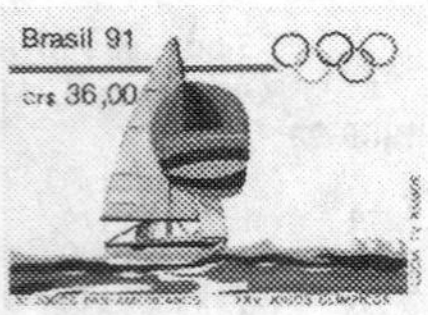

11th Pan American Games, 25th Summer Olympics
A1235

1991, Mar. 30 Litho. ***Perf. 11½x12***
2306 A1235 36cr Sailing .30 .25
2307 A1235 36cr Rowing .30 .25
2308 A1235 300cr Swimming 2.50 1.90
a. Block of 3, #2306-2308 + label 3.25 2.50

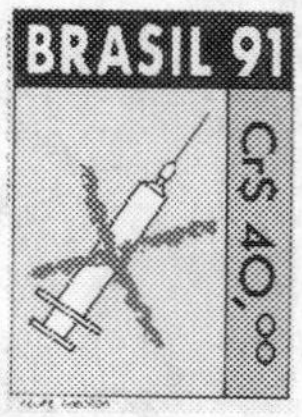

Fight Against Drugs
A1236

Yanomami Indian Culture
A1237

1991, Apr. 7 Litho. ***Perf. 12x11½***
2309 A1236 40cr Drugs .35 .30
2310 A1236 40cr Alcohol .35 .30
2311 A1236 40cr Smoking .35 .30
Nos. 2309-2311 (3) 1.05 .90

1991, Apr. 19 ***Perf. 11½x11, 11x11½***
2312 A1237 40cr shown .35 .30
2313 A1237 400cr Indian, horiz. 3.50 2.75

Journal of Brazil, Cent.
A1238

1991, Apr. 8 Litho. ***Perf. 11x11½***
2314 A1238 40cr multicolored .35 .30

Neochen Jubata (Orinoco Goose) — A1239

1991, June 5 Litho. ***Perf. 12x11½***
2315 A1239 45cr multi .30 .25

UN Conference on Development.

Snakes & Dinosaurs
A1240

1991, June 6 ***Perf. 11½x12***
2316 A1240 45cr Bothrops jararaca .30 .25
2317 A1240 45cr Corallus caninus .30 .25
a. Pair, #2316-2317 .60 .50
2318 A1240 45cr Teropods .30 .25
2319 A1240 350cr Sauropods 2.10 1.60
a. Pair, #2318-2319 2.40 1.85
Nos. 2316-2319 (4) 3.00 2.35

Flag of Brazil — A1241

1991, June 10 Photo. ***Perf. 13x13½***
2320 A1241 A multicolored .25 .20

Valued at domestic letter rate (cr) on day of issue.
Exists with inscription at lower right. Same value.

Fire Pumper
A1242

1991, July 2 Litho. ***Perf. 11½x12***
2321 A1242 45cr multicolored .30 .25

Tourism
A1243

Map location and: 45cr, Painted stones, Roraima. 350cr, Dedo de Deus Mountain, Rio De Janeiro.

1991, July 6 ***Perf. 11x11½***
2322 A1243 45cr multicolored .28 .20
2323 A1243 350cr multicolored 2.00 1.50

Labor Laws, 50th Anniv.
A1244

1991, Aug. 11 ***Perf. 11½x12***
2324 A1244 45cr multicolored .30 .25

Leonardo Mota, Birth Cent.
A1245

1991, Aug. 22
2325 A1245 45cr buff, blk & red .30 .25

Folklore Festival.

Jose Basilio da Gama (1741-1795), Poet
A1246

Designs: No. 2327, Fagundes Varela (b. 1841), poet. No. 2328, Jackson de Figueiredo (b. 1891), writer.

1991, Aug. 29
2326 A1246 45cr multicolored .25 .20
2327 A1246 50cr multicolored .30 .25
2328 A1246 50cr multicolored .30 .25
Nos. 2326-2328 (3) .85 .70

12th Natl. Eucharistic Congress — A1247

1991, Oct. 6 Litho. ***Perf. 12x11½***
2329 A1247 50cr Pope John Paul II .20 .20
2330 A1247 400cr Map, crosses 1.40 1.05
a. Pair, #2329-2330 1.60 1.20

Visit by Pope John Paul II.

First Brazilian Constitution, Cent.
A1248

1991, Oct. 7 ***Perf. 11½x12***
2331 A1248 50cr multicolored .20 .20

Telecom '91 — A1249

1991, Oct. 8 ***Perf. 12x11½***
2332 A1249 50cr multicolored .20 .20

Sixth World Forum and Exposition on Telecommunications, Geneva, Switzerland.

America Issue
A1250

UPAEP emblem and explorers: 50cr, Ferdinand Magellan (c. 1480-1521). 400cr, Francisco de Orellana (c. 1490-c. 1546).

1991, Oct. 12 ***Perf. 11½x12***
2333 A1250 50cr multicolored .20 .20
2334 A1250 400cr multicolored 1.40 1.05

Discovery of America, 500th anniv. (in 1992).

A1251 A1252

BRAPEX VIII (Orchids and Hummingbirds): 50cr, Colibri serrirostris, cattleya warneri. No. 2336, Chlorostilbon aureoventris, rodriguezia venusta. No. 2337, Clytolaema rubricauda, zygopetalum intermedium. No. 2338a, 50cr, Colibri serrirostris. b, 50cr, Chlorostilbon aureoventris. c, 500cr, Clytolaema rubricauda.

1991, Oct. 29 Litho. ***Perf. 12x11½***
2335 A1251 50cr multicolored .20 .20
2336 A1251 65cr multicolored .20 .20
2337 A1251 65cr multicolored .20 .20
Nos. 2335-2337 (3) .60 .60

Souvenir Sheet

2338 A1251 Sheet of 3, #a.-c. 2.20 1.65

1991, Oct. 29 Litho. *Perf. 11½x11*

2339 A1252 400cr multicolored .90 .65

Lasar Segall, artist, birth cent.

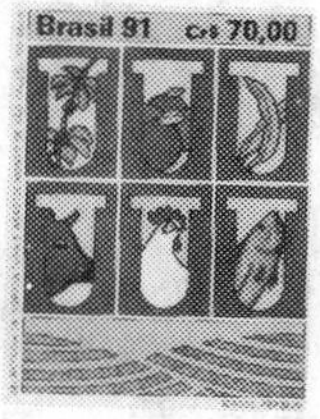

Bureau of Agriculture and Provision of Sao Paulo, Cent. — A1253

1991, Nov. 11 *Perf. 12x11½*

2340 A1253 70cr multicolored .20 .20

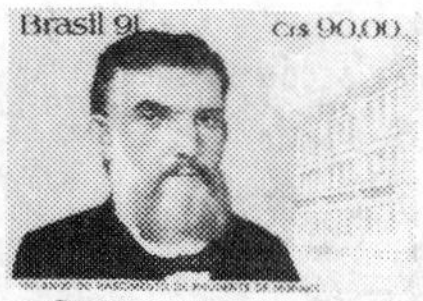

First Civilian Presidents, Birth Sesquicentennials — A1254

1991, Nov. 14 *Perf. 11½x12*

2341 A1254 70cr Manuel de Campos Salles .20 .20

2342 A1254 90cr Prudente de Moraes Barros .25 .20

a. Pair, #2341-2342 .45 .35

Christmas A1255

Thanksgiving A1256

1991, Nov. 20 *Perf. 12x11½*

2343 A1255 70cr multicolored .20 .20

1991, Nov. 28

2344 A1256 70cr multicolored .20 .20

Military Police A1257

1991, Dec. 1 *Perf. 11½x12*

2345 A1257 80cr multicolored .25 .20

Souvenir Sheet

Emperor Dom Pedro (1825-1891) — A1258

a, 80cr, Older age. b, 800cr, Wearing crown.

Litho. & Engr.

1991, Nov. 29 *Perf. 11*

2346 A1258 Sheet of 2, #a.-b. 2.50 2.50

BRASILIANA 93.

Churches — A1259

Designs: No. 2347, Presbyterian Church, Rio de Janeiro. No. 2348, First Baptist Church, Niteroi.

1992, Jan. 12 Litho. *Perf. 12x11½*

2347 A1259 250cr multicolored .30 .25

2348 A1259 250cr multicolored .30 .25

1992 Summer Olympics, Barcelona A1260

Medalists in shooting, Antwerp, 1920: 300cr, Afranio Costa, silver. 2500cr, Guihlherme Paraense, gold.

1992, Jan. 28 *Perf. 11½x12*

2349 A1260 300cr multicolored .30 .25

2350 A1260 2500cr multicolored 2.75 2.00

Port of Santos, Cent. A1261

1992, Feb. 3 Litho. *Perf. 11½*

2351 A1261 300cr multicolored .45 .35

Fauna of Fernando de Noronha Island A1262

1992, Feb. 25 Litho. *Perf. 11½x12*

2352 A1262 400cr White-tailed tropicbirds .40 .30

2353 A1262 2500cr Dolphins 2.50 1.75

Earth Summit, Rio de Janeiro.

Yellow Amaryllis — A1263

1992, Feb. 27 Photo. *Perf. 13½*

2354 A1263 (A) multicolored .25 .20

No. 2354 met the second class domestic letter postage rate of 265cr on date of issue.

ARBRAFEX '92, Argentina-Brazil Philatelic Exhibition — A1264

Designs: No. 2355, Gaucho throwing bola at rhea. No. 2356, Man playing accordion, couple dancing. No. 2357, Couple in horse-drawn cart, woman. 1000cr, Gaucho throwing lasso at steer.

No. 2358c, 250cr, like #2356. d, 500cr, like #2355. e, 1500cr, like #2358.

1992, Mar. 20 Litho. *Perf. 11½x12*

2355 A1264 250cr multicolored .20 .20

2356 A1264 250cr multicolored .20 .20

2357 A1264 250cr multicolored .20 .20

2358 A1264 1000cr multicolored .60 .60

a. Block of 4, Nos. 2355-2358 1.05 1.05

Souvenir Sheet

2358B A1264 Sheet of 4, #2357, 2358c-2358e 1.05 1.05

1992 Summer Olympics, Barcelona A1265

1992, Apr. 3 *Perf. 12x11½*

2359 A1265 300cr multicolored .20 .20

Discovery of America, 500th Anniv. A1266

1992, Apr. 24 *Perf. 11½x12*

2360 A1266 500cr Columbus' fleet .30 .30

2361 A1266 3500cr Columbus, map 2.10 2.10

a. Pair, #2360-2361 2.40 2.40

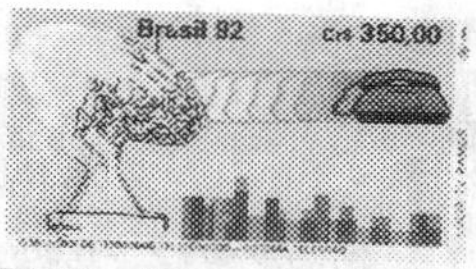

Telebras Telecommunications System — A1267

1992, May 5 *Perf. 11x11½*

2362 A1267 350cr multicolored .20 .20

Installation of 10 million telephones.

Langsdorff Expedition to Brazil, 170th Anniv. A1268

Designs: No. 2363, Aime-Adrien Taunay, natives. No. 2364, Johann Moritz Rugendas, monkey . No. 2365, Hercule Florence, flowering plant. 3000cr, Gregory Ivanovitch Langsdorff, map.

1992, June 2 *Perf. 11½x12*

2363 A1268 500cr multicolored .25 .25

2364 A1268 500cr multicolored .25 .25

2365 A1268 500cr multicolored .25 .25

2366 A1268 3000cr multicolored 1.50 1.50

Nos. 2363-2366 (4) 2.25 2.25

UN Conf. on Environmental Development, Rio.

UN Conference on Environmental Development, Rio de Janeiro — A1269

Globe and: No. 2367, Flags of Sweden and Brazil. No. 2368, City, grain, mountain and tree. 3000cr, Map of Brazil, parrot, orchid.

1992, June 3 Litho. *Perf. 11x11½*

2367 A1269 450cr multicolored .20 .20

2368 A1269 450cr multicolored .20 .20

2369 A1269 3000cr multicolored 1.50 1.50

Nos. 2367-2369 (3) 1.90 1.90

Ecology A1270

Designs: No. 2370, Flowers, waterfall, and butterflies. No. 2371, Butterflies, canoe, and hummingbirds. No. 2372, Boy taking pictures of tropical birds. No. 2373, Armadillo, girl picking fruit.

1992, June 4 *Perf. 11½x12*

2370 A1270 500cr multicolored .25 .25

2371 A1270 500cr multicolored .25 .25

2372 A1270 500cr multicolored .25 .25

2373 A1270 500cr multicolored .25 .25

a. Strip of 4, #2370-2373 1.00 1.00

UN Conf. on Environmental Development, Rio.

Floral Paintings by Margaret Mee — A1271

1992, June 5 *Perf. 12x11½*

2374 A1271 600cr Nidularium innocentii .35 .35

2375 A1271 600cr Canistrum exiguum .35 .35

2376 A1271 700cr Canistrum cyathiforme .40 .40

2377 A1271 700cr Nidularium rubens .40 .40

Nos. 2374-2377 (4) 1.50 1.50

UN Conf. on Environmental Development, Rio.

Souvenir Sheet

Joaquim Jose da Silva Xavier (1748-1792), Patriot — A1272

Litho. & Engr.

1992, Apr. 21 *Perf. 11*

2378 A1272 3500cr multicolored 2.10 2.10

Souvenir Sheet

Expedition of Alexandre Rodrigues Ferreira, Bicent. A1273

Designs: a, 500cr, Sailing ships, gray and green hulls. b, 1000cr, Sailing ships, red hulls. c, 2500cr, Sailing ship at shore.

1992, May 9 Litho. *Perf. 11½x12*
2379 A1273 Sheet of 3, #a.-c. 2.40 2.40

Lubrapex '92.

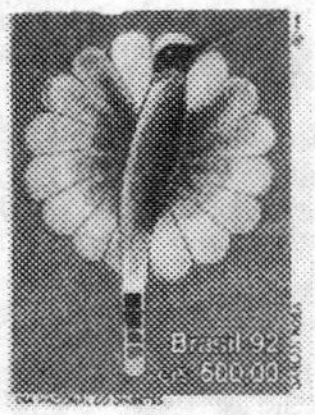

A1274

A1275

1992, June 5 Litho. *Perf. 12x11½*
2380 A1274 600cr Hummingbird .25 .25

Diabetes Day.

1992, July 13 Litho. *Perf. 11½x11*
2381 A1275 550cr multicolored .25 .25

Volunteer firemen of Joinville.

A1276

A1277

Serra da Capivara National Park: No. 2382, Leopard, animals, map of park. No. 2383, Canyon, map of Brazil.

1992, July 17 *Perf. 12x11½*
2382 A1276 550cr multicolored .25 .25
2383 A1276 550cr multicolored .25 .25
a. Pair, #2382-2383 .45 .45

1992, July 24
2384 A1277 550cr multicolored .25 .25

Financing for studies and projects.

Natl. Service for Industrial Training, 50th Anniv. — A1278

1992, Aug. 5 *Perf. 11½x12*
2385 A1278 650cr multicolored .35 .35

Fortresses A1279

1992, Aug. 19 Litho. *Perf. 11½x12*
2386 A1279 650cr Santa Cruz .30 .30
2387 A1279 3000cr Santo Antonio 1.25 1.25

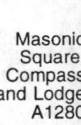

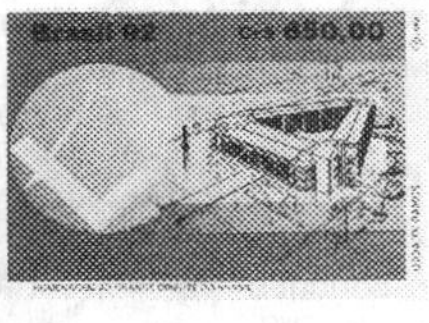

Masonic Square, Compass and Lodge A1280

1992, Aug. 20
2388 A1280 650cr multicolored .30 .30

Brazilian Assistance Legion, 50th Anniv. A1281

Hospital of Medicine and Orthopedics A1282

1992, Aug. 28 *Perf. 12x11½*
2389 A1281 650cr multicolored .30 .30

1992, Sept. 11
2390 A1282 800cr multicolored .30 .30

Merry Christmas A1283

1992, Nov. 20 *Perf. 11½*
2391 A1283 (1) multicolored .25 .25

No. 2391 met the first class domestic letter postage rate of 1090cr on day of issue.

Writers A1284

#2392, Graciliano Ramos (1892-1953), vert.
#2393, Menotti del Picchia (1892-1988), vert.
1000cr, Assis Chateaubriand (1892-1968).

Perf. 12x11½, 11½x12
1992, Oct. 29 Litho.
2392 A1284 900cr multicolored .25 .25
2393 A1284 900cr multicolored .25 .25
2394 A1284 1000cr multicolored .30 .30

Expedition of Luis Cruls, Cent. A1285

1992, Nov. 11 *Perf. 11½x12*
2395 A1285 900cr multicolored .25 25

Brazillian Program for Quality and Productivity A1286

1992, Nov. 12
2396 A1286 1200cr multicolored .30 .30

Souvenir Sheet

Tourism Year in the Americas — A1287

Designs: a, 1200cr, Mountains, coastline. b, 9000cr, Sugarloaf Mt., aerial tram, Rio de Janeiro.

1992, Nov. 18 Litho. *Perf. 11½x12*
2397 A1287 Sheet of 2, #a.-b. 2.00 2.00

Brasiliana '93.

Sister Irma Dulce A1288

1993, Mar. 13 Litho. *Perf. 11½x12*
2398 A1288 3500cr multicolored .35 .35

Souvenir Sheet

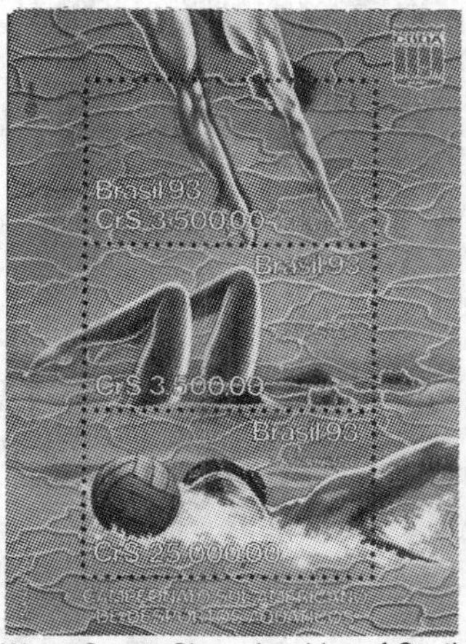

Water Sports Championships of South America — A1289

Designs: a, 3500cr, Diver. b, 3500cr, Synchronized swimmers. c, 25,000cr, Water polo.

1993, Mar. 21 Litho. *Perf. 11*
2399 A1289 Sheet of 3, #a.-c. 2.75 2.75

Curitiba, 300th Anniv. A1290

1993, Mar. 29
2400 A1290 4500cr multicolored .40 .40

Health and Preservation of Life — A1291

Pedro Americo, 150th Birth Anniv. — A1292

Red Cross emblem and: No. 2401, Bleeding heart, flowers. No. 2402, Cancer symbol, breast. No. 2403, Brain waves, rainbow emerging from head.

1993, Apr. 7 Litho. *Perf. 12x11½*
2401 A1291 4500cr multicolored .30 .30
2402 A1291 4500cr multicolored .30 .30
2403 A1291 4500cr multicolored .30 .30
a. Strip of 3, #2401-2403 .90 .90

1993, Apr. 29 *Perf. 12x11½, 11½x12*

Paintings: 5500cr, A Study of Love, 1883. No. 2405, David and Abizag, 1879, horiz. No. 2406, Seated Nude, 1882.

2404 A1292 5500cr multi .25 .25
2405 A1292 36,000cr multi 1.65 1.65
2406 A1292 36,000cr multi 1.65 1.65
Nos. 2404-2406 (3) 3.55 3.55

Natl. Flag — A1292a

1993, May 26 Litho. *Die Cut*
Self-adhesive
2407 A1292a A multicolored .35 .35

No. 2407 valued at first class domestic letter rate of 9570cr on day of issue.

Beetles A1293

1993, June 5 Litho. *Perf. 11½x12*
2408 A1293 8000cr Dynastes hercules .35 .35
2409 A1293 55,000cr Batus barbicornis 2.25 2.25

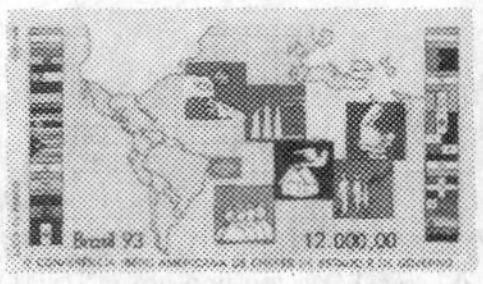

3rd Iberian-American Conference of Chiefs of State and Heads of Government, Salvador — A1294

1993, July 15 Litho. *Perf. 11x11½*
2410 A1294 12,000cr multi .20 .20

1st Brazilian Postage Stamps, 150th Anniv. — A1295

Litho. & Engr.

1993, July 30 ***Perf. 12x11½***

2411 A1295 30,000cr No. 1 .30 .30
2412 A1295 60,000cr No. 2 .60 .60
2413 A1295 90,000cr No. 3 .90 .90
a. Souvenir sheet of 3, #2411-2413, wmk. 268 2.00 2.00
Nos. 2411-2413 (3) 1.80 1.80

No. 2413a sold for 200,000cr.

Union of Portuguese Speaking Capitals A1296

a, 15,000cr, Brasilia. b, 71,000cr, Rio de Janiero.

1993, July 30 Litho. ***Perf. 11½x12***

2414 A1296 Pair, #a.-b. .90 .90

No. 2414 printed in continuous design.

Monica & Friends, by Mauricio de Sousa A1297

Monica, Cebolinha, Cascao, Magali, and Bidu: a, Engraving die. b, Reading proclamation, king, No. 1. c, Writing and sending letter, No. 2. d, Receiving letter, No. 3.

1993, Aug. 1

2415 A1297 (1) Strip of 4, #a.-d. .85 .85

First Brazilian postage stamps, 150th anniv. Nos. 2415a-2415d paid the first class rate (9600cr)on day of issue.

Brazilian Post, 330th Anniv. A1298

Postal buildings: a, Imperial Post Office, Rio de Janeiro. b, Petropolis. c, Central office, Rio de Janeiro. d, Niteroi.

1993, Aug. 3 Litho. ***Perf. 11½x12***

2416 A1298 20,000cr Block of 4, #a.-d. .45 .45

Brazilian Engineering Schools — A1299

Designs: No. 2417, School of Engineering, Federal University, Rio de Janeiro. No. 2418, Polytechnical School, University of Sao Paulo.

1993, Aug. 24 Litho. ***Perf. 11x11½***

2417 A1299 17cr multicolored .30 .30
2418 A1299 17cr multicolored .30 .30

Preservation of Sambaquis Archaelogical Sites — A1300

1993, Sept. 19 ***Perf. 12x11½***

2419 A1300 17cr Two artifacts .25 .25
2420 A1300 17cr Six artifacts .25 .25

Ulysses Guimaraes, Natl. Congress — A1301

1993, Oct. 6 Litho. ***Perf. 11x11½***

2421 A1301 22cr multicolored .30 .30

A1302

A1303

1993, Oct. 8 Litho. ***Perf. 12x11½***

2422 A1302 22cr multicolored .30 .30

Virgin of Nazare Religious Festival, bicent.

1993, Oct. 13 Litho. ***Perf. 11½x11***

Endangered birds (America Issue): 22cr, Anodorhynchus hyacinthinus, anodorhynchus glaucus, anodorhynchus leari. 130cr, Cyanopsitta spixii.

2423 A1303 22cr multicolored .25 .25
2424 A1303 130cr multicolored 1.40 1.40

Composers A1304

A1307

1993, Oct. 19 Litho. ***Perf. 12x11½***

2425 A1304 22cr Vinicius de Moraes .20 .20
2426 A1304 22cr Pixinguinha .20 .20

1993, Oct. 29 Litho. ***Perf. 12x11½***

Poets: No. 2427, Mario de Andrade (1893-1945). No. 2428, Alceu Amoroso Lima (Tristao de Athayde) (1893-1983). No. 2429, Gilka Machado (1893-1980).

2427 A1307 30cr multicolored .30 .30
2428 A1307 30cr multicolored .30 .30
2429 A1307 30cr multicolored .30 .30
Nos. 2427-2429 (3) .90 .90

Natl. Book Day.

Brazil-Portugal Treaty of Consultation and Friendship, 40th Anniv. — A1308

1993, Nov. 3 Litho. ***Perf. 11½x12***

2430 A1308 30cr multicolored .30 .30

See Portugal No. 1980.

Image of the Republic A1309

Photo. & Engr.

1993, Nov. 3 ***Perf. 13***

2431 A1309 (B) multicolored 2.50 2.50

Valued at first class international letter rate (178.70 cr) on day of issue.

2nd Intl. Biennial of Comic Strips A1310

Cartoon drawings: No. 2432, Nho-Quim. No. 2433, Benjamin. No. 2434, Lamparina. No. 2435, Reco-Reco, Bolao, Azeitona.

1993, Nov. 11 Litho. ***Perf. 11½x12***

2432 A1310 (1) multicolored .40 .40
2433 A1310 (1) multicolored .40 .40
2434 A1310 (1) multicolored .40 .40
2435 A1310 (1) multicolored .40 .40
a. Block of 4, #2432-2435 1.75 1.75

Valued at first class domestic letter rate (30.20 cr) on day of issue.

Launching of First Brazilian-Built Submarine — A1311

1993, Nov. 18 ***Perf. 11½***

2436 A1311 240cr multicolored 1.75 1.75

Christmas A1312

1993, Nov. 20

2437 A1312 (1) multicolored .45 .45

Valued at first class domestic letter rate (30.20 cr) on day of issue.

First Fighter Group, 50th Anniv. A1313

1993, Dec. 18 Litho. ***Perf. 11½***

2438 A1313 42cr multicolored .35 .35

Convent of Merces, 340th Anniv. A1314

1994, Jan. 31 Litho. ***Perf. 11½x12***

2439 A1314 58cr multicolored .30 .30

Mae Menininha of Gantois, Birth Cent. — A1315

1994, Feb. 10 Litho. ***Perf. 11x11½***

2440 A1315 80cr multicolored .40 .40

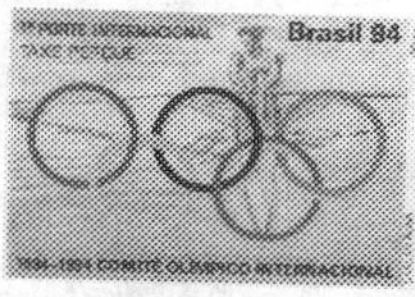

Intl. Olympic Committee, Cent. A1316

1994, Feb. 17 ***Perf. 11½x12***

2441 A1316 (1) multicolored 2.25 2.25

No. 2441 valued at first class international letter rate (446.30 cr) on day of issue.

Natl. Flag — A1317

1994, Jan. 31 Litho. ***Die Cut***

Self-Adhesive

2442 A1317 (1) multicolored .40 .40

No. 2442 valued at first class domestic letter rate (55.90 cr) on day of issue.

Birds — A1318

Image of the Republic — A1318a

1994 Photo. ***Perf. 11x11½***

2443 A1318 10cr Notiochelidon cyanoleuca .20 .20
2444 A1318 20cr Buteo magnirostris .20 .20
2445 A1318 50cr Turdus rufiventris .20 .20
2446 A1318 100cr Columbina talpacoti .20 .20
2447 A1318 200cr Vanellus chilensis .20 .20
2448 A1318 500cr Zonotrichia capensis .50 .50
Nos. 2443-2448 (6) 1.50 1.50

Issued: 10cr, 3/17/94. 20cr, 3/9/94. 50cr, 3/1/94. 100cr, 200cr, 4/4/94. 500cr, 4/13/94.

See Nos. 2484-2494.

1994, May 10 Litho.

Self-Adhesive

Die Cut

2449 A1318a (1) blue .25 .25
2450 A1318a (3) claret .40 .40

Size: 25x35mm

Perf. 12x11½

2451 A1318a (4) green .80 .80
2452 A1318a (5) henna brown 1.50 1.50
Nos. 2449-2452 (4) 2.95 2.95

Nos. 2449, 2450, 2451, 2452 valued 131.37cr, 321.14cr, 452.52cr 905.05cr on day of issue.

Prince Henry the Navigator (1394-1460) — A1319

1994, Mar. 4 Litho. *Perf. 11½x12*

2463 A1319	635cr multicolored	2.25	2.25

See Macao No. 719, Portugal No. 1987.

America Issue A1320

Postal vehicles: 110cr, Bicycle, country scene. 635cr, Motorcycle, city scene.

1994, Mar. 18

2464 A1320	110cr multicolored	.20	.20
2465 A1320	635cr multicolored	1.10	1.10

Father Cicero Romao Batista, 150th Birth Anniv. A1321

1994, Mar. 24 *Perf. 11x11½*

2466 A1321	(1) multicolored	.35	.35

No. 2466 valued at first class domestic letter rate (98.80 cr) on day of issue.

Albert Sabin, Campaign Against Polio A1322

1994, Apr. 7 *Perf. 11½x12*

2467 A1322	160cr multicolored	.30	.30

Carlos Castello Branco, Journalist A1323

1994, Apr. 14

2468 A1323	160cr multicolored	.30	.30

Karl Friedrich Phillip von Martius, Naturalist A1324

Flowers: No. 2469, Euterpe oleracea. No. 2470, Jacaranda paucifoliolata. No. 2471, Barbacernia tomentosa.

1994, Apr. 24 *Perf. 12x11½*

2469 A1324	(1) multicolored	.35	.35
2470 A1324	(1) multicolored	.35	.35
2471 A1324	(1) multicolored	2.00	2.00
	Nos. 2469-2471 (3)	2.70	2.70

Nos. 2469-2470 were valued at first class domestic letter rate (144 cr) on day of issue. No. 2471 valued at first class intl. letter rate (860 cr) on day of issue.

Monkeys — A1326

No. 2474, Leontopithecus rosalia. No. 2475, Saguinus imperator. No. 2476, Saguinus bicolor.

1994, May 24

2474 A1326	(1) multicolored	.35	.35
2475 A1326	(1) multicolored	.35	.35
2476 A1326	(1) multicolored	.35	.35
	Nos. 2474-2476 (3)	1.05	1.05

Nos. 2474-2476 were valued at first class domestic letter rate (207.03 cr) on day of issue.

1994 World Cup Soccer Championships, US — A1327

1994, May 19 *Perf. 11½x12*

2477 A1327	(1) multicolored	2.00	2.00

No. 2477 was valued at first class intl. rate (1378.32 cr) on day of issue.
Soccer in Brazil, cent.

Souvenir Sheet

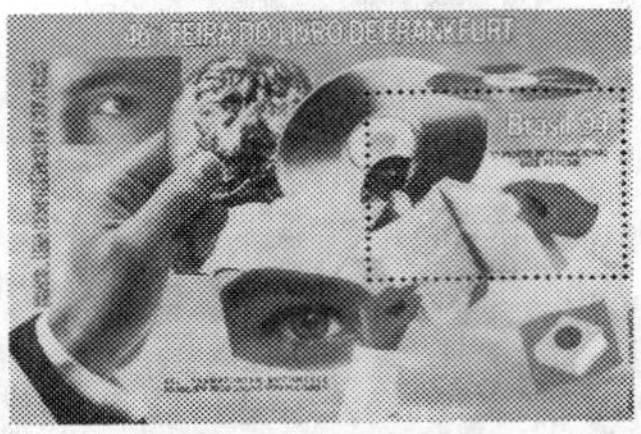

46th Frankfurt Intl. Book Fair — A1328

Illustration reduced.

1994, May 27

2478 A1328	(1) multicolored	2.00	2.00

No. 2478 was valued at first class intl. rate (1523.83 cr) on day of issue.

Natl. Literacy Program — A1329

Designs: No. 2479, Pencil, buildings. No. 2480, Pencil, people on television, people watching. No. 2481, Classroom, pencil. No. 2482, Pencils crossed over fingerprint, map of Brazil.

1994, June 3 Litho. *Perf. 12x11½*

2479 A1329	(1) multicolored	.30	.30
2480 A1329	(1) multicolored	.30	.30
2481 A1329	(1) multicolored	.30	.30
2482 A1329	(1) multicolored	.30	.30
	Nos. 2479-2482 (4)	1.20	1.20

Nos. 2479-2482 were valued at first class domestic letter rate (233.05 cr) on day of issue.

Souvenir Sheet

Treaty of Tordesillas, 500th Anniv. — A1330

1994, June 7

2483 A1330	(1) multicolored	2.25	2.25

No. 2483 was valued at first class intl. letter rate (1689.02 cr) on day of issue.

Bird Type of 1994 and

A1330a

Perf. 11x11½, 13 (15c), 12½13 (22c, (22c)

1994-98 Photo.

2484 A1318	1c	like No. 2443	.20	.20
2485 A1318	2c	like No. 2444	.20	.20
2486 A1318	5c	like No. 2445	.20	.20
2487 A1318	10c	like No. 2446	.20	.20
2488 A1330a	15c	Sicaris flaveola	.35	.35
2489 A1318	20c	like No. 2447	.40	.40
2490 A1318	22c	Tyrannus savana	.50	.50
2491 A1318	50c	like No. 2448	1.00	1.00
2494 A1318	1r	Furnarius rufus	2.25	2.25
		Nos. 2484-2494 (9)	5.30	5.30

Size: 21x26mm

Self-Adhesive

Serpentine Die Cut

2498 A1330a	22c	Myiozetetes similis	.50	.50
2499 A1330a	(22c)	Volatinia jacarina	.50	.50

No. 2499 is inscribed "1o PORTE NATIONAL" and was valued at 22c on day of issue.

Issued: 1c, 2c, 5c, 20c, 20c, 50c, 1r, 7/1/94; 11/16/95; #2490, 10/13/97; #2498, 2/16/98; #2499, 7/22/97.

This is an expanding set. Numbers may change.

Prominent Brazilians A1331

Designs: No. 2504, Edgard Santos (1894-1962), surgeon, educator. No. 2505, Oswaldo Aranha (1894-1960), politician. No. 2507, Otto Lara Resende (1922-92), writer, educator.

1994, July 5 Litho. *Perf. 11½x12*

2504 A1331	(1) multicolored	.30	.30
2505 A1331	(1) multicolored	.30	.30
2506 A1331	(1) multicolored	.30	.30
	Nos. 2504-2506 (3)	.90	.90

Nos. 2504-2506 were valued at first class domestic letter rate (12c) on day of issue.

A1332 A1333

1994, July 15 *Perf. 12x11½*

2507 A1332	12c multicolored	.30	.30

Petrobras, 40th anniv.

Litho. & Engr.

1994, July 26 *Perf. 11½*

2508 A1333	12c multicolored	.30	.30

Brazilian State Mint, 300th anniv.

Campaign Against Famine & Misery A1334

1994, July 27 Litho. *Perf. 11½x12*

2509 A1334	(1) Fish	.30	.30
2510 A1334	(1) Bread	.30	.30

Nos. 2509-2510 were valued at first class domestic letter rate (12c) on day of issue.

Institute of Brazilian Lawyers, 150th Anniv. A1335

1994, Aug. 11

2511 A1335	12c multicolored	.30	.30

Intl. Year of the Family A1336

1994, Aug. 16 *Perf. 11½*

2512 A1336	84c multicolored	2.00	2.00

Maternity Hospital of Sao Paulo, Cent. A1337

1994, Aug. 26 *Perf. 11½x12*

2513 A1337	12c multicolored	.30	.30

Vincente Celestino (1894-1968), Singer A1338

1994, Sept. 12

2514 A1338	12c multicolored	.30	.30

"Contos da Carochinha," First Brazilian Children's Book, Cent. A1339

Fairy tales: a, Joao e Maria (Hansel & Gretel). b, Dona Baratinha. c, Puss 'n Boots. d, Tom Thumb.

1994, Oct. 5 Litho. *Perf. 11½x12*

2515	Block of 4	4.75	4.75
a.-b.	A1339 12c any single	.30	.30
c.-d.	A1339 84c any single	2.00	2.00

Brazilian Literature A1340

Portraits: No. 2516, Tomas Antonio Gonzaga (1744-1809?), poet. No. 2517, Fernando de Azevedo (1894-1974), author.

1994, Oct. 5 *Perf. 11½*

2516	A1340 12c multicolored	.30	.30
2517	A1340 12c multicolored	.30	.30

St. Clare of Assisi (1194-1253) A1341

1994, Oct. 19 *Perf. 12x11½*

2518	A1341 12c multicolored	.30	.30

Ayrton Senna (1960-1994), Race Car Driver — A1342

Designs: a, McClaren Formula 1 race car, Brazilian flag. b, Fans, Senna. c, Flags, race cars, Senna.

1994, Oct. 24 *Perf. 11½x12*

2519	Triptych	2.75	2.75
a.-b.	A1342 12c any single	.30	.30
c.	A1342 84c multicolored	2.00	2.00

Institute of History & Geography of Sao Paulo, Cent. A1343

1994, Nov. 1

2520	A1343 12c multicolored	.30	.30

Popular Music A1344

Designs: No. 2521, Music from "The Sea," by Dorival Caymmi. No. 2522, Adoniran Barbosa (1910-82), samba composer.

1994, Nov. 5 *Perf. 11½*

2521	A1344 12c multicolored	.30	.30
2522	A1344 12c multicolored	.30	.30

Christmas A1345

Folk characters: No. 2523: a, Boy wearing Santa coat, pot on head. b, Worm in apple. c, Man, animals singing. d, Shoe on tree stump, man with pipe holding pen.

1994, Dec. 1 Litho. *Perf. 11½*

2523	Block of 4	2.75	2.75
a.	A1345 84c multicolored	1.90	1.90
b.-d.	A1345 12c any single	.30	.30
e.	Booklet pane, #2523 + 4 labels	*5.50*	
	Complete booklet, #2523a	*5.50*	

Souvenir Sheet

Brazil, 1994 World Cup Soccer Champions — A1346

Illustration reduced.

1994, Dec. 5 *Perf. 12x11½*

2524	A1346 2.14r multicolored	5.00	5.00

Louis Pasteur (1822-95) A1347

1995, Feb. 19 Litho. *Perf. 11½x12*

2525	A1347 84c multicolored	2.00	2.00

Historical Events A1348

Designs: No. 2526, Capture of Monte Castello, 50th anniv. No. 2527, End of the Farroupilha Revolution, 150th anniv.

1995, Feb. 21

2526	A1348 12c multicolored	.30	.30
2527	A1348 12c multicolored	.30	.30

Pres. Itamar Franco A1349

FAO, 50th Anniv. A1350

1995, Mar. 22 Litho. *Perf. 12x11½*

2528	A1349 12c multicolored	.30	.30

1995, Apr. 3 *Perf. 11½x11*

2529	A1350 84c multicolored	2.00	2.00

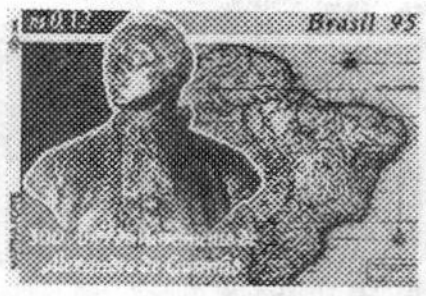

Famous Men A1351

#2530, Alexandre de Gusmao (1695-1753), diplomat. #2531, Francisco Brandao, Viscount of Jequitinhonha (1794-1870), lawyer, abolitionist. 15c, Jose da Silva Paranhos, Jr., Baron of Rio Branco (1845-1912), politician, diplomat.

1995, Apr. 28 *Perf. 11½x12*

2530	A1351 12c multicolored	.30	.30
2531	A1351 12c multicolored	.30	.30
2532	A1351 15c multicolored	.35	.35
	Nos. 2530-2532 (3)	.95	.95

Radio, Cent. A1352

Design: Guglielmo Marconi (1874-1937), transmitting equipment.

1995, May 5 Litho. *Perf. 11½x12*

2533	A1352 84c multicolored	2.00	2.00

Friendship Between Brazil & Japan A1353

1995, May 29

2534	A1353 84c multicolored	2.00	2.00

Endangered Birds — A1354

1995, June 5 *Perf. 12x11½*

2535	A1354 12c Tinamus solitarius	.30	.30
2536	A1354 12c Mitu mitu	.30	.30

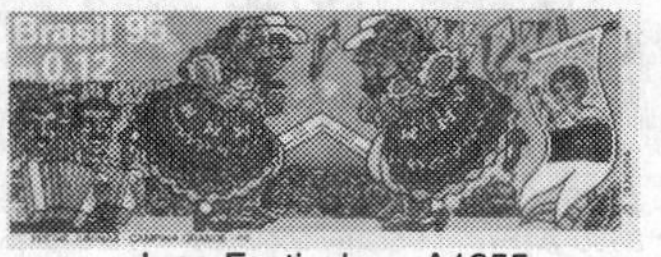

June Festivals — A1355

Designs: No. 2537, Couples dancing at Campina Grande, "Greatest St. John's Party of the World." No. 2538, Bride, bridegroom, festivities, Caruaru.

1995, June 11 *Perf. 11½x12*

2537	A1355 12c multicolored	.30	.30
2538	A1355 12c multicolored	.30	.30

St. Anthony of Padua (1195-1231) — A1356

1995, June 13

2539	A1356 84c multicolored	2.00	2.00

See Portugal No. 2054.

Souvenir Sheet

Motion Picture, Cent. — A1357

Design: Louis and Auguste Lumiere, camera.

1995, June 21

2540	A1357 2.14r multicolored	4.75	4.75

New Currency, The Real, 1st Anniv. — A1358

Volleyball, Cent. — A1359

1995, July 1 Litho. *Perf. 12x11½*

2541	A1358 12c multicolored	.30	.30

1995, July 8

2542	A1359 15c multicolored	.35	.35

Dinosaurs A1360

1995, July 23 *Perf. 11½x12*

2543	A1360 15c Angaturama limai	.35	.35
2544	A1360 1.50r Titanosaurus	3.25	3.25

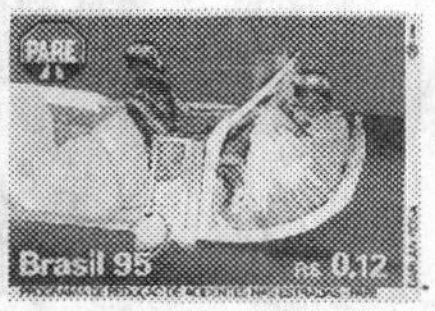

Traffic Safety Program A1361

Designs: 12c, Test dummy without seat belt hitting windshield. 71c, Auto hitting alcoholic beverage glass.

1995, July 25

2545	A1361 12c multicolored	.30	.30
2546	A1361 71c multicolored	1.65	1.65

Souvenir Sheet

Roberto Burle Marx, Botanist — A1362

Designs: a, 15c, Calathea burle-marxii. b, 15c, Vellozia burle-marxii. c, 1.50r, Heliconia aemygdiana. Illustration reduced.

1995, Aug. 4 Litho. ***Perf. 12x11½***

2547 A1362 Sheet of 3, #a.-c. 4.50 4.50

Singapore '95.

Parachute Infantry Brigade, 50th Anniv. — A1363

1995, Aug. 23

2548 A1363 15c multicolored .35 .35

Paulista Museum, Cent. A1364

1995, Sept. 5 ***Perf. 11½***

2549 A1364 15c multicolored .35 .35

Lighthouses A1365

1995, Sept. 28

2550 A1365 15c Olinda .35 .35
2551 A1365 15c Sao Joao .35 .35
2552 A1365 15c Santo Antonio da Barra .35 .35
Nos. 2550-2552 (3) 1.05 1.05

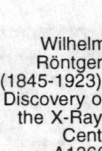

Wilhelm Röntgen (1845-1923), Discovery of the X-Ray, Cent. A1366

1995, Sept. 30

2553 A1366 84c multicolored 2.00 2.00

Lubrapex '95, 15th Brazilian-Portuguese Philatelic Exhibition — A1367

Wildlife scene along Tiete River: 15c, #2556a, Bird, otter with fish. 84c, #2556b, Birds, river boat.

1995, Sept. 30 ***Perf. 12x11½***

2554 A1367 15c multicolored .35 .35
2555 A1367 84c multicolored 2.00 2.00

Souvenir Sheet

2556 A1367 1.50r Sheet of 2, #a.-b. 6.50 6.50

No. 2556 is a continuous design.

Flamengo Regatta Soccer Club A1368

1995, Oct. 6 ***Perf. 11x11½***

2557 A1368 15c multicolored .35 .35

America Issue A1369

Outdoor scenes: 15c, Trees, mushrooms, alligator, lake. 84c, Black-neck swans on lake, false swans in air.

1995, Oct. 12 Litho. ***Perf. 11½x12***

2558 A1369 15c multicolored .35 .35
2559 A1369 84c multicolored 2.00 2.00
a. Pair, #2558-2559 2.35 2.35

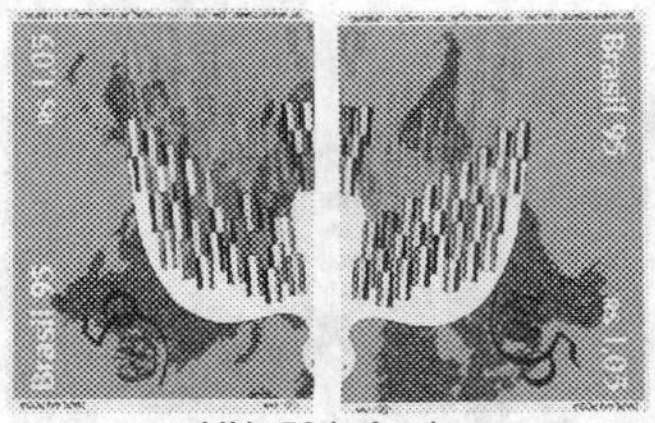

UN, 50th Anniv.
A1370 A1371

1995, Oct. 24 ***Perf. 12x11½***

2560 A1370 1.05r multicolored 2.25 2.25
2561 A1371 1.05r multicolored 2.25 2.25
a. Pair, No. 2560-2561 4.50 4.50

Writers — A1372

Designs: No. 2562, Eca de Queiroz (1845-90), village. No. 2563, Rubem Braga (1913-90), beach, Rio de Janeiro. 23c, Carlos Drummond de Andrade (1902-87), letters.

1995, Oct. 27 ***Perf. 12x11***

2562 A1372 15c multicolored .35 .35
2563 A1372 15c multicolored .35 .35
2564 A1372 23c multicolored .50 .50
Nos. 2562-2564 (3) 1.20 1.20

Souvenir Sheet

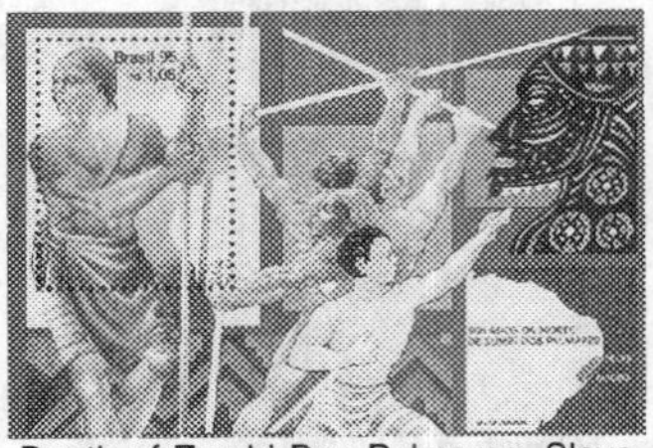

Death of Zumbi Dos Palmares, Slave Resistance Leader, 300th Anniv. — A1373

Illustration reduced.

1995, Nov. 20 ***Perf. 12x11½***

2565 A1373 1.05r multicolored 2.25 2.25

2nd World Short Course Swimming Championships — A1374

Four swimmers performing different strokes: a, Freestyle. b, Backstroke. c, Butterfly. d, Breaststroke.

1995, Nov. 30 ***Perf. 11½x12***

2566 A1374 23c Block of 4, #a.-d. 2.00 2.00

Christmas A1375

Designs: a, 23c, Cherub looking right, stars. b, 15c, Cherub looking left, stars.

1995, Dec. 1 ***Perf. 11½***

2567 A1375 Pair, #a.-b.+2 labels .85 .85

Botafogo Soccer and Regatta Club A1376

1995, Dec. 8 ***Perf. 11x11½***

2568 A1376 15c multicolored .35 .35

Diário de Pernambuco Newspaper, 170th Anniv. — A1377

1995, Dec. 14 Litho. ***Perf. 12x11½***

2569 A1377 23c multicolored .50 .50

Souvenir Sheet

Amazon Theatre, Cent. — A1378

Illustration reduced.

1996, Feb. 27

2570 A1378 1.23r multicolored 2.50 2.50

Francisco Prestes Maia, Politician, Birth Cent. A1379

1996, Mar. 19 ***Perf. 11½x12***

2571 A1379 18c multicolored .40 .40

Irineu Bornhausen, Governor of Santa Catarina, Birth Cent. — A1380

1996, Mar. 25 ***Perf. 11x11½***

2572 A1380 27c multicolored .55 .55

Paintings — A1381

Designs: No. 2573, Boat with Little Flags and Birds, by Alfredo Volpi. No. 2574, Ouro Preto Landscape, by Alberto da Veiga Guignard.

1996, Apr. 15 ***Perf. 12x11½***

2573 A1381 15c multicolored .30 .30
2574 A1381 15c multicolored .30 .30

UNICEF, 50th Anniv. A1382

1996, Apr. 16 ***Perf. 11½***

2575 A1382 23c multicolored .50 .50

Portuguese Discovery of Brazil, 500th Anniv. (in 2000) — A1383

1996, Apr. 22 ***Perf. 12x11½***

2576 A1383 1.05r multicolored 2.10 2.10

See No. 2626.

Israel Pinheiro da Silva, Politician, Business Entrepeneur, Birth Cent. A1384

1996, Apr. 23 ***Perf. 11½x12***

2577 A1384 18c multicolored .40 .40

Tourism — A1385

#2578, Amazon River. #2579, Swampland area. #2580, Sail boat, northeastern states. #2581, Sugarloaf, Guanabara Bay. #2582, Iguacu Falls.

1996, Apr. 24 ***Die Cut***

Self-Adhesive

2578 A1385 23c multicolored .50 .50
2579 A1385 23c multicolored .50 .50
2580 A1385 23c multicolored .50 .50
2581 A1385 23c multicolored .50 .50
2582 A1385 23c multicolored .50 .50
a. Strip of 5, #2578-2582 2.50

Hummingbirds — A1386

Espamer '96: 15c, Topaza pella. 1.05r, Stephano xis lalandi. 1.15r, Eupetomena macroura.

1996, May 4 **Litho.** ***Perf. 11½***

2583 A1386 15c multicolored .35 .35
2584 A1386 1.05r multicolored 2.40 2.40
2585 A1386 1.15r multicolored 2.60 2.60
Nos. 2583-2585 (3) 5.35 5.35

1996 Summer Olympic Games, Atlanta A1387

1996, May 21

2586 A1387 18c Marathon .40 .40
2587 A1387 23c Gymnastics .50 .50
2588 A1387 1.05r Swimming 2.40 2.40
2589 A1387 1.05r Beach volley-ball 2.40 2.40
Nos. 2586-2589 (4) 5.70 5.70

Souvenir Sheet

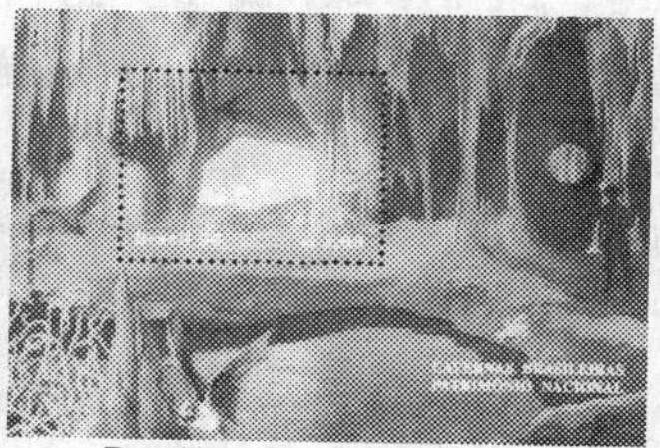

Brazilian Caverns — A1388

Illustration reduced.

1996, June 5 ***Perf. 11½x12***

2590 A1388 2.68r multicolored 6.25 6.25

Americas Telecom '96 — A1389

1996, June 10 ***Perf. 11½***

2591 A1389 1.05r multicolored 2.40 2.40

Souvenir Sheet

World Day to Fight Desertification — A1390

Illustration reduced.

1996, June 17 ***Perf. 12x11½***

2592 A1390 1.23r multicolored 2.80 2.80

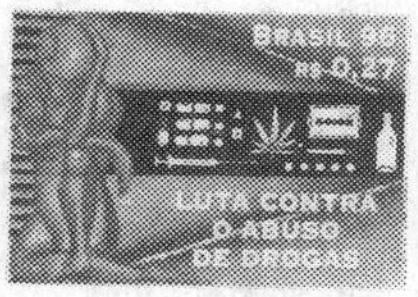

Fight Against Drug Abuse A1391

1996, June 26 ***Perf. 11½x12***

2593 A1391 27c multicolored .65 .65

Year of Education A1392

1996, July 10 ***Perf. 12x11½***

2594 A1392 23c multicolored .55 .55

Princess Isabel, 150th Birth Anniv. A1393

1996, July 29 ***Perf. 11½x12***

2595 A1393 18c multicolored .40 .40

Carlos Gomes (1836-96), Composer A1394

1996, Sept. 16 ***Perf. 11½***

2596 A1394 50c multicolored 1.25 1.25

15th World Orchid Conference A1395

#2597, Promenaea stapelioides. #2598, Cattleya eldorado. #2599, Cattleya loddigesii.

1996, Sept. 17

2597 A1395 15c multicolored .35 .35
2598 A1395 15c multicolored .35 .35
2599 A1395 15c multicolored .35 .35
Nos. 2597-2599 (3) 1.05 1.05

Apparition of Virgin Mary at La Salette, 150th Anniv. A1396

1996, Sept. 19

2600 A1396 1r multicolored 2.30 2.30

Souvenir Sheet

Popular Legends A1397

Designs: a, 23c, "Cuca" walking from house. b, 1.05r, "Boitatá," snake of life. c, 1.15r, "Caipora," defender of ecology.

1996, Sept. 28 ***Perf. 11x10½***

2601 A1397 Sheet of 3, #a.-c. 5.60 5.60

BRAPEX '96.

23rd Sao Paulo Intl. Biennial Exhibition A1398

Designs: a, Marilyn Monroe by Andy Warhol, vert. b, The Scream, by Edvard Munch, vert. c, Abstract, by Louise Bourgeois, vert. d, Woman Drawing, by Pablo Picasso.

1996, Oct. 5 ***Perf. 12x11½***

2602 A1398 55c Block of 4, #a.-d. 5.00 5.00

Traditional Costumes A1400

America issue: 50c, Man dressed as cowboy. 1r, Woman dressed in baiana clothes.

1996, Oct. 12 **Litho.** ***Perf. 11½***

2604 A1400 50c multicolored 1.15 1.15
2605 A1400 1r multicolored 2.30 2.30

Christmas A1401

José Carlos (1884-1950), Carcicaturist A1402

1996, Nov. 4 **Litho.** ***Perf. 12x11½***

2606 A1401 1st multicolored .60 .60

No. 2606 was valued at 23c on day of issue.

1996, Nov. 22

2607 A1402 1st multicolored .60 .60

No. 2607 was valued at 23c on day of issue.

Tourism — A1403

#2608, Ipiranga Monument, Sao Paulo. #2607, Hercílio Luz Bridge, Florianópolis. #2608, Natl. Congress Building, Brasília. #2609, Pelourinho, Salvador. #2610, Ver-o-Peso Market, Belém.

Serpentine Die Cut

1996, Dec. 9 **Photo.**

Self-Adhesive

2608 A1403 1st multicolored .75 .75
2609 A1403 1st multicolored .75 .75
2610 A1403 1st multicolored .75 .75
2611 A1403 1st multicolored .75 .75
2612 A1403 1st multicolored .75 .75
a. Strip of 5, #2608-2612 3.75

Nos. 2608-2612 are inscribed "1o PORTE NACIONAL," and were valued 23c on day of issue. Selvage surrounding each stamp in #2612a is rouletted.

Rio de Janeiro, Candidate for 2004 Summer Olympic Games A1404

1997, Jan. 17 **Litho.** ***Perf. 11½***

2613 A1404 1st multicolored 2.25 2.25

No. 2613 is inscribed "1o PORTE INTERNACIONAL" and was valued at 1.05r on day of issue.

The Postman A1405

1997, Jan. 25

2614 A1405 1st multicolored .85 .85

America issue. No. 2614 is inscribed "1o PORTE NACIONAL" and was valued at 23c on day of issue.

Antonio de Castro Alves (1847-71), Poet — A1406

1997, Mar. 14

2615 A1406 15c multicolored .35 .35

Marquis of Tamandaré, Naval Officer, Death Cent. — A1407

1997, Mar. 19 ***Perf. 11x11½***

2616 A1407 23c multicolored .50 .50

Stamp Design Contest Winner A1408

1997, Mar. 20 ***Perf. 11½x12***

2617 A1408 15c "Joy Joy" .35 .35

World Day of Water — A1409

1997, Mar. 22 ***Perf. 12x11½***

2618 A1409 1.05r multicolored 2.10 2.10

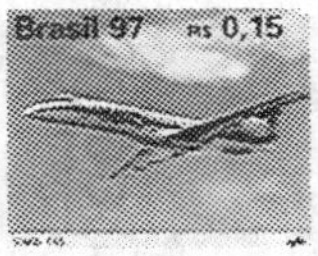

Brazilian Airplanes A1410

Designs: No. 2619, EMB-145. No. 2620, AMX. No. 2621, EMB-312 H Super Tucano. No. 2622, EMB-120 Brasilia. No. 2623, EMB-312 Tucano.

1997, Mar. 27 Litho. ***Die Cut***

Self-Adhesive

2619 A1410 15c multicolored .25 .25
2620 A1410 15c multicolored .25 .25
2621 A1410 15c multicolored .25 .25
2622 A1410 15c multicolored .25 .25
2623 A1410 15c multicolored .25 .25
a. Strip of 5, #2619-2623 1.25

Campaign Against AIDS — A1411

1997, Apr. 7 Litho. ***Perf. 12x11½***

2624 A1411 23c multicolored .50 .50

Souvenir Sheet

Indian Culture — A1412

Weapons of the Xingu Indians.
Illustration reduced.

1997, Apr. 16 ***Perf. 11x11½***

2625 A1412 1.15r multicolored 2.25 2.25

Portuguese Discovery of Brazil, 500th Anniv. Type of 1996

1997, Apr. 22 ***Perf. 12x11½***

2626 A1383 1.05r like #2576 2.10 2.20

No. 2576 has green background and blue in lower right corner. No. 2626 has those colors reversed and is inscribed "BRASIL 97" at top.

Pixinguinha (1897-1973), Composer, Musician — A1413

1997, Apr. 23

2627 A1413 15c multicolored .35 .35

Souvenir Sheet

Brazilian Claim to Trindade Island, Cent. — A1414

Illustration reduced.

1997, May 7 ***Perf. 11½x11***

2628 A1414 1.23r multicolored 2.50 2.50

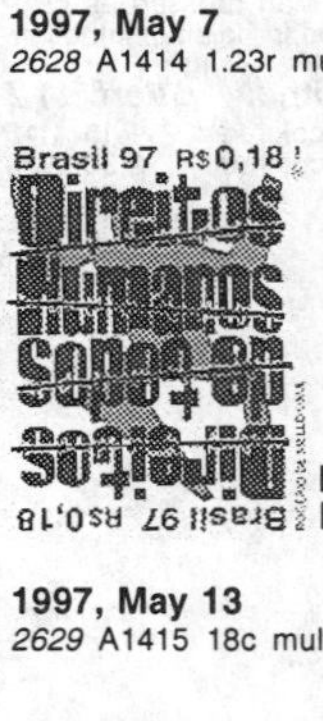

Human Rights — A1415

1997, May 13 ***Perf. 12x11½***

2629 A1415 18c multicolored .45 .45

Souvenir Sheet

Brazilian Antarctic Program — A1416

1997, May 13

2630 A1416 2.68r multicolored 5.50 5.50

Fruits and Nuts — A1417

1997-98 Litho. ***Serpentine Die Cut***

Self-Adhesive

2631 A1417 1c Oranges .20 .20
2632 A1417 2c Bananas .20 .20
2633 A1417 5c Papayas .20 .20
2634 A1417 10c Pineapple, vert. .20 .20
2635 A1417 20c Cashews, vert. .40 .40
2636 A1417 20c Sugar apple, vert. .40 .40
2636A A1417 22c Grapes .40 .40
2636B A1417 (22c) Watermelon .45 .45
2636C A1417 51c Coconuts, vert. 1.00 1.00
2636D A1417 80c Apples 1.40 1.40
2636E A1417 82c Lemons, vert. 1.60 1.60
2636F A1417 1r Strawberries, vert. 2.00 2.00
Nos. 2631-2636F (12) 8.45 8.45

Issued: #2636B, 5/28/97; #2631, 6/97; #2632, 2634, 2635, 7/97; #2633, 8/97; #2636F, 8/3/97; #2636A, 10/3/97; #2636, 2636C-2636E, 1/15/98.

No. 2636B is inscribed "1o PORTE NATIONAL" and was valued at 22c on day of issue.

This is an expanding set. Numbers may change.

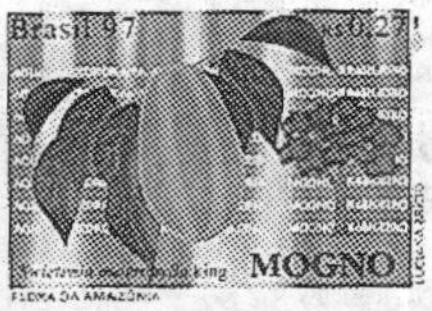

A1418

Amazon Flora and Fauna — A1419

Designs: No. 2637, Swietenia macropylla. No. 2638, Arapaima gigas.

1997, June 5 Litho. ***Perf. 11½x12***

2637 A1418 27c multicolored .55 .55
2638 A1419 27c multicolored .55 .55

Fr. José de Anchieta (1534-97), Missionary in Brazil — A1420

Design: No. 2640, Fr. António Vieira (1608-97), missionary in Brazil, diplomat.

1997, June 9 ***Perf. 12***

2639 A1420 1.05r multicolored 2.10 2.10
2640 A1420 1.05r multicolored 2.10 2.10

See Portugal Nos. 2168-2169.

Tourism A1421

Designs: No. 2641, Parnaíba River Delta. No. 2642, Lencóis Maranhenses Park.

1997, June 20 ***Perf. 11½x12***

2641 A1421 1st multicolored 2.10 2.10
2642 A1421 1st multicolored 2.10 2.10

Nos. 2641-2642 are inscribed "1o PORTE INTERNACIONAL TAXE PERCUE" and were each valued at on day of issue.

Brazilian Academy of Literature, Cent. A1422

1997, July 20

2643 A1422 22c multicolored .50 .50

Emiliano de Cavalcanti (1897-1976), Painter A1423

1997, Sept. 16 Litho. ***Perf. 11½***

2644 A1423 31c multicolored .65 .65

2nd World Meeting of the Pope with Families, Rio de Janeiro A1424

1997, Sept. 22 ***Perf. 11½x12***

2645 A1424 1.20r multicolored 2.50 2.50

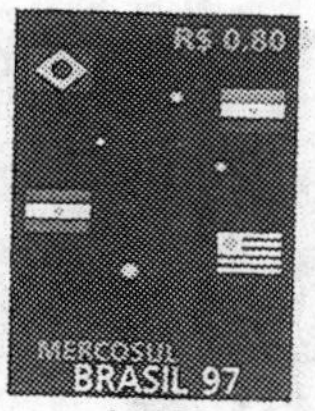

A1425

A1426

1997, Sept. 26 ***Perf. 12x11½***
2646 A1425 80c multicolored 1.60 1.60

MERCOSUR (Common Market of Latin America). See Argentina #1975, Bolivia #1019, Paraguay #2565, Uruguay #1681.

1997, Sept. 27
2647 A1426 22c multicolored .45 .45

End of Canudos War, cent.

Integration of MERCOSUR Communications by Telebras, 25th Anniv. — A1427

1997, Oct. 6 ***Perf. 11½***
2648 A1427 80c multicolored 1.60 1.60

Composers — A1428

#2649, Oscar Lorenzo Fernandez (1897-1948). #2650, Francisco Mignone (1897-1986).

1997, Oct. 7 ***Perf. 11x11½***
2649 A1428 22c multicolored .45 .45
2650 A1428 22c multicolored .45 .45

Marist Brothers Presence in Brazil, Cent. A1429

1997, Oct. 22
2651 A1429 22c multicolored .45 .45

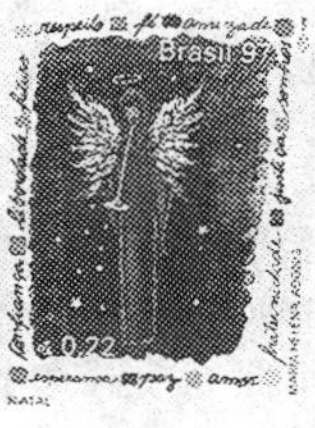

Christmas A1430

1997, Nov. 5 ***Perf. 12x11½***
2652 A1430 22c multicolored .45 .45

Education and Citzenship A1431

1997, Dec. 10 ***Perf. 11x11½***
2653 A1431 31c blue & yellow .65 .65

City of Belo Horizonte, Cent. A1432

1997, Dec. 12 ***Perf. 11½x12***
2654 A1432 31c multicolored .65 .65

Citzenship A1433

Map of Brazil and: No. 2655, Education, stack of books. No. 2656, Employment, worker's papers. No. 2657, Agriculture, oranges. No. 2658, Health, stethoscope, vert. No. 2659, Culture, clapboard with musical notes, artist's paint brush, vert.

1997, Dec. 20 ***Die Cut***

Self-Adhesive Booklet Stamps

2655 A1433 22c multicolored .45 .45
2656 A1433 22c multicolored .45 .45
2657 A1433 22c multicolored .45 .45
2658 A1433 22c multicolored .45 .45
2659 A1433 22c multicolored .45 .45
a. Booklet pane, 2 each #2655-2659 4.50

The peelable paper backing of No. 2659a serves as a booklet cover.

Gems — A1434

1998, Jan. 22 ***Perf. 12x11½***
2660 A1434 22c Alexandrite .45 .45
2661 A1434 22c Cat's eye chrysoberyl .45 .45
2662 A1434 22c Indicolite .45 .45
a. Strip of 3, #2660-2662 1.40 1.40

Famous Brazilian Women A1435

America Issue: No. 2663, Elis Regina, singer. No. 2664, Clementia de Jesus, singer. No. 2665, Dulcina de Moraes, actress. No. 2666, Clarice Lispector, writer.

1998, Mar. 11 ***Perf. 11½***
2663 A1435 22c multicolored .45 .45
2664 A1435 22c multicolored .45 .45
2665 A1435 22c multicolored .45 .45
2666 A1435 22c multicolored .45 .45
a. Block of 4, #2663-2666 1.80 1.80

Education A1436

1998, Mar. 19 ***Perf. 12x11½***
2667 A1436 31c Children at desks .65 .65
2668 A1436 31c Teacher at blackboard .65 .65
a. Pair, #2667-2668 1.30 1.30

Cruz e Sousa (1861-98), Poet A1437

1998, Mar. 19 Litho. ***Perf. 11½x12***
2669 A1437 36c multicolored .65 .65

Discovery of Brazil, 500th Anniv. — A1438

#2670, 1519 map showing natives, vegetation, fauna. #2671, Caravel from Cabral's fleet.

1998, Apr. 22 ***Perf. 12x11½***
2670 A1438 1.05r multicolored 1.75 1.75
2671 A1438 1.05r multicolored 1.75 1.75
a. Pair, #2670-2671 3.50 3.50

Volunteer Work A1439

Designs: a, Caring for sick man. b, Caring for sick child. c, Fighting forest fire. c, Child's hand holding adult's finger.

1998, May 5 ***Perf. 11½x12***
2672 A1439 31c Block of 4, #a.-d. 2.25 2.25

Brazilian Circus — A1440

Piolin the clown: a, Looking through circle. b, Standing in ring. c, With outside of tent to the left. d, With inside of tent to the right.

1998, May 18 ***Perf. 12x11½***
2673 A1440 31c Block of 4, #a.-d. 2.25 2.25

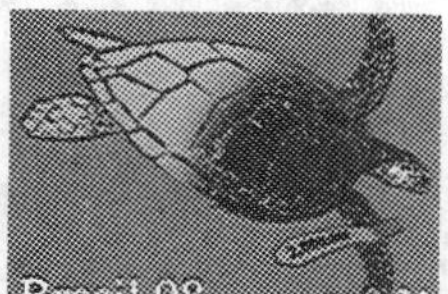

Intl. Year of the Ocean A1441

Pictures, drawings of marine life: a, Turtle. b, Tail fin of whale. c, Barracuda. d, Jellyfish, school of fish. e, School of fish, diver. f, Dolphins. g, Yellow round fish. h, Two whales. i, Two black-striped butterfly fish. j, Orange & yellow fish. k, Manatee. l, Yellow-striped fish. m, Blue & yellow fish. n, Several striped fish. o, Fish with wing-like fins. p, Manta ray. q, Two fish swimming in opposite directions. r, Long, thin fish, coral. s, Moray eel. t, Yellow & black butterfly fish, coral. u, Starfish, fish. v, Crab, coral. w, Black & orange fish, coral. x, Sea horse, coral.

1998, May 22 ***Perf. 11½x12***

Sheet of 24

2674 A1441 31c #a.-x. 12.50 12.50

Expo '98.

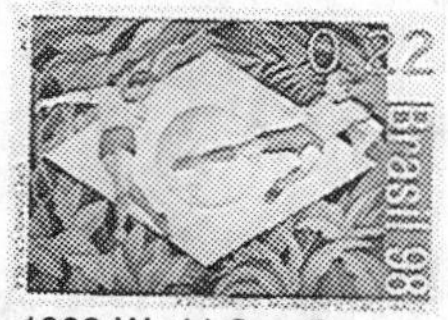

1998 World Cup Soccer Championships, France — A1442

Stylized paintings, by: a, Gregorio Gruber. b, Mario Gruber. c, Maciej Babinski. d, Cildo Meireles, vert. e, Claudio Tozzi, vert. f, Antonio Henrique Amaral, vert. g, Jose Roberto Aguilar. h, Nelson Leirner. i, Wesley Duke Lee. j, Mauricio Nogueira Lima. k, Zelio Alves Pinto, vert. l, Aldemir Martins, vert. m, Ivald Granato. n, Carlos Vergara. o, Joao Camara, vert. p, Roberto Magalhaes, vert. q, Guto Lacaz, vert. r, Glauco Rodrigues, vert. s, Leda Catunda. t, Tomoshige Kusuno. u, Jose Zaragoza. v, Luiz Zerbine, vert. w, Antonio Peticov, vert. x, Marcia Grostein, vert.

1998, May 28 ***Perf. 11½x12, 12x11½***
2675 A1442 22c Sheet of 24, #a.-x. 9.00 9.00

Feijoada, Traditional Cuisine A1443

1998, June 1 ***Perf. 11½***
2676 A1443 31c multicolored .55 .55

Preservation of Flora and Fauna — A1444

Designs: No. 2677, Araucaria angustifolia. No. 2678, Cyanocorax caeruleus.

1998, June 5 ***Perf. 11½x12***
2677 A1444 22c multicolored .40 .40
2678 A1444 22c multicolored .40 .40
a. Pair, #2677-2678 .80 .80

Launching of Submarine Tapajó A1445

1998, June 5
2679 A1445 51c multicolored .90 .90

Luiz de Queiroz (1849-98), Founder of Agricultural School A1446

1998, June 6 ***Perf. 11½***
2680 A1446 36c multicolored .65 .65

Benedictine Monastery, Sao Paulo, 400th Anniv. A1447

1998, July 10 Litho. ***Perf. 11½x12***
2681 A1447 22c multicolored .25 .25

Alberto Santos-Dumont (1873-1932), Aviation Pioneer — A1448

Designs: No. 2682, Balloon "Brazil." No. 2683, Dirigible Nr. 1, Santos-Dumont at controls.

1998, July 18

2682 A1448 31c multicolored .35 .35
2683 A1448 31c multicolored .35 .35
a. Pair, #2682-2683 .70 .70

Brazilian Cinema, Cent. (in 1997) A1449

Designs: a, Guanabara Bay, by Lumière, 1897. b, Taciana Reiss in "Limite," by Mário Peixoto, 1931. c, Actors in (Chanchada)," from "A Dupla do Barulho," by Carlos Manga, 1953. d, Films produced by Vera Cruz pictures, caricature of Mazzaropi from "The Dream Factory." e, Glauber Rocha's "New Cinema". f, International film festival awards won by Brazilian films.

1998, July 24 ***Perf. 11½***

2684 A1449 31c Block of 6, #a.-f. 2.00 2.00

Rodrigo Melo Franco de Andrade (1898-1969) — A1450

Church of Our Lady of the Rosary, Ouro Preto.

1998, Aug. 17 ***Perf. 11x11½***

2685 A1450 51c multicolored .60 .60

Luís da Camara Cascudo (1898-1986), Writer — A1451

1998, Aug. 22

2686 A1451 22c multicolored .25 .25

42nd Aeronautical Pentathlon World Championship A1452

Stylized designs: a, Fencing. b, Running. c, Swimming. d, Shooting. e, Basketball.

1998, Aug. 22 ***Perf. 12x11½***

2687 A1452 22c Strip of 5, #a.-e. 1.25 1.25

Mercosur — A1453

Design: Missionary Cross, ruins of the Church of Sao Migeul das Missoes.

1998, Sept. 17 ***Perf. 11½x12***

2688 A1453 80c multicolored .90 .90

24th Sao Paulo Art Biennial A1454

a, Biennial emblem, by José Leonilson. b, Tapuia Dance, by Albert von Eckhout. c, The Schoolboy, by Vincent van Gogh. d, Portrait of Michel Leiris, by Francis Bacon. e, The King's Museum, by René Magritte. f, Urutu, by Tarsila do Amaral. g, Facade with Arcs, Circle and Fascia, by Alfredo Volpi. h, The Raft of the Medusa, by Asger Jorn.

1998, Sept. 22

2689 A1454 31c Block of 8, #a.-h. 2.00 2.00

Nos. 2689b, 2689h have horiz. designs placed vert. on stamps.

Child and Citizenship Stamp Design Contest Winner A1455

1998, Oct. 9

2690 A1455 22c multicolored .25 .25

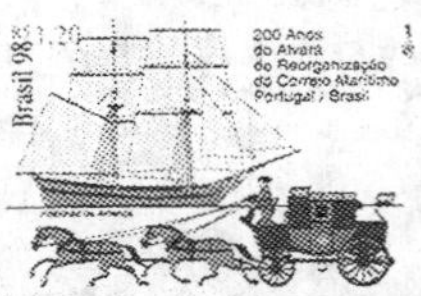

Reorganization of Maritime Mail from Portugal to Brazil, Bicent. — A1456

1998, Oct. 9

2691 A1456 1.20r multicolored 1.25 1.25

See Portugal Nos. 2271-2272.

Dom Pedro I (1798-1834) A1457

1998, Oct. 13 ***Perf. 11½***

2692 A1457 22c multicolored .25 .25

Frisco's Mango Refreshment Promotional Stamp — A1458

Serpentine Die Cut

1998, Oct. 15 **Photo.**

Self-Adhesive

2693 A1458 36c multicolored .40 .40

No. 2693 is valid on all mail, but must be used on mail entries to Frisco on Faustao's Truck raffle.

Flowers A1459

Designs: a, Solanum lycocarpum. b, Cattleya walkeriana. c, Kielmeyera coriacea.

1998, Oct. 23 **Litho.** ***Perf. 11½***

2694 A1459 31c Strip of 3, #a.-c. 1.00 1.00

Humanitarians — A1460

Designs: a, Mother Teresa (1910-97). b, Friar Galvao (1739-1822). c, Herbert José de Souza "Betinho" (b. 1935). d, Friar Damiao (1898-1997).

1998, Oct. 25

2695 A1460 31c Block of 4, #a.-d. 1.40 1.40

Natl. Telecommunications Agency (ANATEL) — A1461

Design: Sergio Motta, former Minister of Communications, ANATEL headquarters, Brasilia.

1998, Nov. 5 ***Perf. 12x11½***

2696 A1461 31c multicolored .35 .35

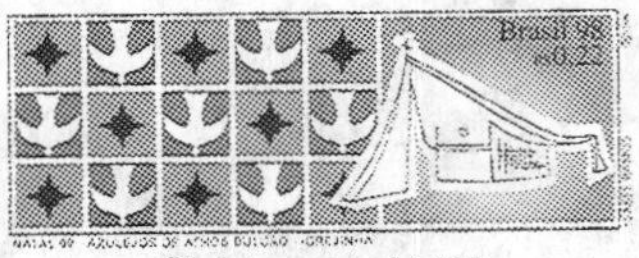

Christmas — A1462

Design: Athos Bulcao's tiles, Church of Our Lady of Fatima, Brasilia, outline of sanctuary.

1998, Nov. 19 ***Perf. 11½x12***

2697 A1462 22c multicolored .25 .25

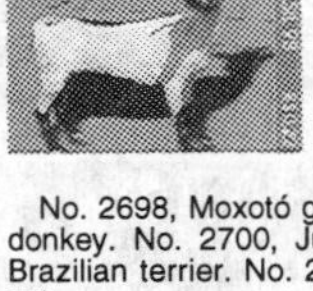

Domestic Animals — A1463

No. 2698, Moxotó goat. No. 2699, Brazilian donkey. No. 2700, Junqueira ox. No. 2701, Brazilian terrier. No. 2702, Brazilian shorthair cat.

1998, Nov. 20 ***Die Cut***

Booklet Stamps

Self-Adhesive

2698 A1463 22c multi .25 .25
2699 A1463 22c multi .25 .25
2700 A1463 22c multi .25 .25
2701 A1463 22c multi, vert. .25 .25
2702 A1463 22c multi, vert. .25 .25
a. Booklet pane, 2 each #2698-2702 2.50

No. 2702a is a complete booklet.

Universal Declaration of Human Rights, 50th Anniv. — A1464

1998, Dec. 9 ***Perf. 12x11½***

2703 A1464 1.20r multicolored 1.25 1.25

Natal, 400th Anniv. A1465

Perf. 11x11½, 11½x11

1999, Jan. 6 **Litho.**

2704 A1465 31c Wise Men's Fortress .35 .35
2705 A1435 31c Mother Luiza Lighthouse, vert. .35 .35

Program for Evaluating Resources in Brazil's Exclusive Economic Zone — A1466

No. 2706: a, Satellite, St. Peter and St. Paul Archpelago. b, Bird on buoy. c, Fishing boat. d, Sea turtle. e, Dolphin. f, Diver.

1999, Mar. 5 ***Perf. 11½x12***

2706 A1466 31c Block of 6, #a.-f. 2.00 2.00

Australia '99 World Stamp Expo.

UPU, 125th Anniv. A1467

No. 2707: a, Stamp vending machines from 1940s and 1998. b, Vending machines, 1906, 1998. c, Collection boxes, 1870, 1973. d, Federal Government's 1998 Quality Award.

1999, Mar. 19 ***Perf. 11½***

2707 A1467 31c Block of 4, #a.-d. 1.40 1.40

Reorganization of Brazilian Posts and Telegraphs, 30th anniv.

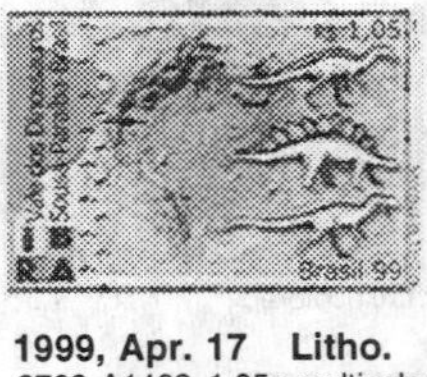

Dinosaurs' Valley A1469

1999, Apr. 17 **Litho.** ***Perf. 11½x12***

2709 A1469 1.05r multicolored 1.10 1.10

Fort of Santo Amaro da Barra Grande — A1470

1999, Apr. 21 **Litho.** ***Perf. 11½x12***

2710 A1470 22c multicolored .25 .25

6th Air Transportation Squadron, 30th Anniv. — A1472

1999, May 12 Litho. *Perf. 11x11½*
2712 A1472 51c multicolored .55 .55

Holy Spirit Feast, Planaltina — A1473

1999, May 21 *Perf. 12x11½*
2713 A1473 22c multicolored .25 .25

Historical and Cultural Heritage A1474

Views of cities: a, Ouro Preto. b, Olinda. c, Sao Luís.

1999, June 2 *Perf. 11½x11*
2714 A1474 1.05r Sheet of 3, #a.-c. 3.25 3.25

PhilexFrance '99, World Philatelic Exhibition.

Sao Paolo State Institute for Technological Research, Cent. — A1475

1999, June 24 Litho. *Perf. 11½x12*
2715 A1475 36c multicolored .40 .40

Flight of Alberto Santos-Dumont's Dirigible No. 3, Cent. — A1476

1999, July 20
2716 A1476 1.20r multicolored 1.40 1.40

Forest Fire Prevention A1477

a, Anteater. b, Flower. c, Leaf. d, Burnt trunk.

Serpentine Die Cut 6
1999, Aug. 1 Litho.
Self-Adhesive

2717 Block of 4 2.10
a.-d. A1477 51c Any single .50 .50

No. 2717 is printed on recycled paper impregnated with burnt wood odor.

Souvenir Sheet

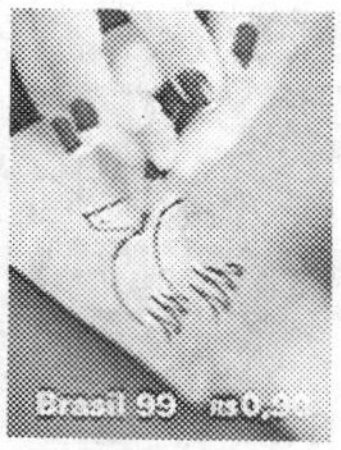

America Issue, A New Millennium Without Arms — A1478

Designs: a, Hands of adult and child drawing dove. b, Overturned tank.

1999, Aug. 6 Litho. *Perf. 12x11½*
2718 A1478 90c Sheet of 2, #a.-b. 1.90 1.90

Issued with rouletted tab at right showing Universal Product Code.

Political Amnesty, 20th Anniv. — A1479

1999, Aug. 18
2719 A1479 22c multicolored .25 .25

Famous Brazilians — A1480

Designs: 22c, Joaquim Nabuco (1849-1910), politician and diplomat. 31c, Ruy Barbosa (1849-1923), politician and justice for International Court.

1999, Aug. 19 Litho. *Perf. 11½x12*
2720 A1480 22c multicolored .25 .25
2721 A1480 31c multicolored .35 .35

Fish — A1481

Designs: a, 22c, Salminus maxillosus. b, 31c, Brycon microlepsus. c, 36c, Acestrorhynchus pantaneiro. d, 51c, Hyphessobrycon eques. e, 80c, Rineloricaria. f, 90c, Leporinus macrocephalus. g, 1.05r, Abramites. h, 1.20r, Ancistrus.

1999, Aug. 20 Litho. *Perf. 11½x12*
2722 A1481 Sheet of 8, #a.-h. 5.50 5.50

China 1999 World Philatelic Exhibition. No. 2722h has a holographic image. Soaking in water may affect hologram.

SEMI-POSTAL STAMPS

In 1980 three stamps that were intended to be semi-postals were issued as postage stamps at the total combined face value. See Nos. 1681-1683.

National Philatelic Exhibition Issue

SP1

Wmk. Coat of Arms in Sheet (236)
1934, Sept. 16 Engr. *Imperf.*
Thick Paper

B1 SP1 200r + 100r dp claret 1.00 *2.00*
B2 SP1 300r + 100r ver 1.00 *2.00*
B3 SP1 700r + 100r brt bl 6.00 *17.50*
B4 SP1 1000r + 100r blk 6.00 *17.50*
Nos. B1-B4 (4) 14.00 *39.00*

The surtax was to help defray the expenses of the exhibition. Issued in sheets of 60, inscr ibed "EXPOSICA O FILATELICA NACIONAL."

Red Cross Nurse and Soldier SP2

Wmk. 222
1935, Sept. 19 Typo. *Perf. 11*
B5 SP2 200r + 100r pur & red 1.25 1.25
B6 SP2 300r + 100r ol brn & red 1.25 .90
B7 SP2 700r + 100r turq bl & red 8.00 7.00
Nos. B5-B7 (3) 10.50 9.15

3rd Pan-American Red Cross Conf. Exist imperf.

Three Wise Men and Star of Bethlehem SP3

Angel and Child SP4

Southern Cross and Child — SP5

Mother and Child — SP6

Wmk. 249
1939, Dec. 20 Litho. *Perf. 10½*
B8 SP3 100r + 100r chlky bl & bl blk .75 .75
a. Horiz. or vert. pair, imperf. between 35.00
B9 SP4 200r + 100r brt grnsh bl 1.00 1.00
a. Horizontal pair, imperf. between 35.00
B10 SP5 400r + 200r ol grn & ol .80 .50
B11 SP6 1200r + 400r crim & brn red 3.25 1.50
a. Vertical pair, imperf. between 35.00
Nos. B8-B11 (4) 5.80 3.75

Surtax for charitable institutions.
For surcharges see Nos. C55-C59.

Catalogue values for unused stamps in this section, from this point to the end of the section, are for Never Hinged items.

Children and Citzenship — SP7

Designs: a, Cutouts of children forming pyramid. b, Man and woman's hands holding onto girl. c, Children going into school. d, Pregnant woman in front of house. e, Children flying paper doves. f, Parent working in garden, child writing letters, doves. g, Breastfeeding. h, Father holding birth certificate, mother holding infant. i, Disabled child on wheelchair ramp. j, Mother, father with sick child. k, Stylized child, pencil, letters. l, Hands above and below pregnant woman. m, Two families of different races. n, Small child playing large guitar. o, People looking to baby on pedestal. p, Children, book, "Statute of Children and Adolescent."

1997, Nov. 20 Litho. *Perf. 12x11½*
B12 Sheet of 16 9.60 9.60
a.-p. SP7 22c +8c any single .60 .60

Surcharge for Natl. Fund for Children and Adolescents.

AIR POST STAMPS

Nos. O14-O29 Surcharged

SERVIÇO AEREO 200 Rs.

1927, Dec. 28 Unwmk. *Perf. 12*
C1 O2 50r on 10r .35 .35
a. Inverted surcharge 325.00
b. Top ornaments missing 75.00
C2 O2 200r on 1000r 2.25 2.75
a. Double surcharge 325.00
C3 O2 200r on 2000r 1.40 4.75
a. Double surcharge 750.00
b. Double surcharge, one inverted 750.00
C4 O2 200r on 5000r 1.50 1.00
a. Double surcharge 325.00 —
b. Double surcharge, one inverted 350.00
c. Triple surcharge 450.00
C5 O2 300r on 500r 1.50 2.00
C6 O2 300r on 600r .75 .90
b. Pair, one without surch. —
C6A O2 500r on 10r 325.00 375.00
C7 O2 500r on 50r 1.50 .65
a. Double surcharge 300.00 —
C8 O2 1000r on 20r 1.00 .35
a. Double surcharge 300.00 —
C9 O2 2000r on 100r 2.25 1.40
a. Pair, one without surcharge —
b. Double surcharge 300.00
C10 O2 2000r on 200r 2.75 1.40
C11 O2 2000r on 10,000r 2.25 .50
C12 O2 5000r on 20,000r 7.50 3.00
C13 O2 5000r on 50,000r 7.50 3.00
C14 O2 5000r on 100,000r 25.00 30.00
C15 O2 10,000r on 500,000r 27.50 22.50
C16 O2 10,000r on 1,000,000r 25.00 25.00
Nos. C1-C6,C7-C16 (16) 110.00 99.55

Nos. C1, C1b, C7, C8 and C9 have small diamonds printed over the numerals in the upper corners.

Monument to de Gusmao — AP1

Santos-Dumont's Airship — AP2

Augusto Severo's Airship "Pax" — AP3

Santos-Dumont's Biplane "14 Bis" — AP4

Ribeiro de Barros's Seaplane "Jahu" — AP5

Perf. 11, 12½x13, 13x13½

1929 Typo. Wmk. 206

C17 AP1 50r blue grn .35 .20
C18 AP2 200r red 1.40 .20
C19 AP3 300r brt blue 1.75 .20
C20 AP4 500r red violet 2.50 .20
C21 AP5 1000r orange brn 9.00 .40
Nos. C17-C21 (5) 15.00 1.20

See #C32-C36. For surcharges see #C26-C27.

Bartholomeu de Gusmao AP6

Augusto Severo AP7

Alberto Santos-Dumont — AP8

Perf. 9, 11 and Compound

1929-30 Engr. Wmk. 101

C22 AP6 2000r lt green ('30) 7.50 .35
C23 AP7 5000r carmine 7.50 1.25
C24 AP8 10,000r olive grn 7.50 1.40
Nos. C22-C24 (3) 22.50 3.00

Nos. C23-C24 exist imperf.
See Nos. C37, C40.

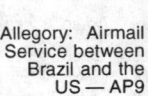

Allegory: Airmail Service between Brazil and the US — AP9

1929 Typo. Wmk. 206

C25 AP9 3000r violet 10.00 1.75

Exists imperf. See Nos. C38, C41. For surcharge see No. C28.

Nos. C18-C19 Surcharged in Blue or Red **ZEPPELIN 2$500**

1931, Aug. 16 ***Perf. 12½x13½***

C26 AP2 2500r on 200r (Bl) 25.00 25.00
C27 AP3 5000r on 300r (R) 30.00 30.00

No. C25 Surcharged **2.500 REIS**

1931, Sept. 2 ***Perf. 11***

C28 AP9 2500r on 3000r vio 27.50 *27.50*
a. Inverted surcharge 160.00 —
b. Surch. on front and back 160.00

Regular Issues of 1928-29 Surcharged **ZEPPELIN 3$500**

1932, May Wmk. 101 ***Perf. 11, 11½***

C29 A89 3500r on 5000r gray lil 20.00 20.00
C30 A72 7000r on 10,000r rose 20.00 20.00
b. Horiz. pair, imperf. between *750.00*

Imperforates

Since 1933, imperforate or partly perforated sheets of nearly all of the airmail issues have become available.

Flag and Airplane — AP10

Wmk. 222

1933, June 7 Typo. ***Perf. 11***

C31 AP10 3500r grn, yel & dk bl 5.00 2.00

See Nos. C39, C42.

1934 Wmk. 222

C32 AP1 50r blue grn 1.75 1.75
C33 AP2 200r red 2.25 .65
C34 AP3 300r brt blue 5.50 1.90
C35 AP4 500r red violet 2.25 .65
C36 AP5 1000r orange brn 7.50 .65
Nos. C32-C36 (5) 19.25 5.60

1934 Wmk. 236 Engr. ***Perf. 12x11***

Thick Laid Paper

C37 AP6 2000r lt green 4.50 1.50

Types of 1929, 1933

Perf. 11, 11½, 12

1937-40 Typo. Wmk. 249

C38 AP9 3000r violet 17.50 1.75
C39 AP10 3500r grn, yel & dk bl 3.00 1.50

Engr.

C40 AP7 5000r ver ('40) 4.00 .75
Nos. C38-C40 (3) 24.50 4.00

Watermark note after #501 also applies to #C40.

Types of 1929-33

Perf. 11, 11½x12

1939-40 Typo. Wmk. 256

C41 AP9 3000r violet 1.25 .60
C42 AP10 3500r bl, dl grn & yel ('40) .90 .50

Map of the Western Hemisphere Showing Brazil AP11

1941, Jan. 14 Engr. ***Perf. 11***

C43 AP11 1200r dark brown 2.50 .65

5th general census of Brazil.

No. 506A Overprinted in Carmine **AÉREO "10 Nov." 937-941**

1941, Nov. 10 Wmk. 264 ***Rouletted***

C45 A180 5400r slate grn 2.50 1.25
a. Overprint inverted 140.00

President Varges' new constitution, 4th anniv.

Nos. 506A and 508 Surcharged in Black **AÉREO "10 Nov." 937-942 Cr.$ 5,40**

1942, Nov. 10 Wmk. 264

C47 A180 5.40cr on 5400r sl grn 2.50 1.90
a. Wmk. 249 80.00 80.00
b. Surcharge inverted 60.00 75.00

President Vargas' new constitution, 5th anniv.
The status of No. C47a is questioned.

Southern Cross and Arms of Paraguay AP12

Wmk. 270

1943, May 11 Engr. ***Perf. 12½***

C48 AP12 1.20cr lt gray blue 1.75 1.00

Issued in commemoration of the visit of President Higinio Morinigo of Paraguay.

Map of South America — AP13

1943, June 30 Wmk. 271 ***Perf. 12½***

C49 AP13 1.20cr multi 1.75 .75

Visit of President Penaranda of Bolivia.

Numeral of Value AP14

1943, Aug. 7

C50 AP14 1cr blk & dull yel 2.00 1.50
a. Double impression 30.00
C51 AP14 2cr blk & pale grn 2.75 1.50
a. Double impression 40.00
C52 AP14 5cr blk & pink 3.25 2.00
Nos. C50-C52 (3) 8.00 5.00

Centenary of Brazil's first postage stamps.

Souvenir Sheet

AP15

Without Gum ***Imperf.***

C53 AP15 Sheet of 3 35.00 35.00
a. 1cr black & dull yellow 10.00 10.00
b. 2cr black & pale green 10.00 10.00
c. 5cr black & pink 10.00 10.00

100th anniv. of the 1st postage stamps of Brazil and the 2nd Phil. Exposition (Brapex). Printed in panes of 6 sheets, perforated 12½ between. Each sheet is perforated on two or three sides. Size approximately 155x155mm.

Law Book — AP16

1943, Aug. 13 ***Perf. 12½***

C54 AP16 1.20cr rose & lil rose .50 .30

2nd Inter-American Conf. of Lawyers.

AÉREO

No. B10 Surcharged in Red, Carmine or Black **20 Cts.**

1944, Jan. 3 Wmk. 249 ***Perf. 10½***

C55 SP5 20c on 400r+200r (R) .85 .65
C56 SP5 40c on 400r+200r (Bk) 1.25 .65
C57 SP5 60c on 400r+200r (C) 1.25 .45
C58 SP5 1cr on 400r+200r (Bk) 1.75 .65
C59 SP5 1.20cr on 400r+200r (C) 2.25 .45
Nos. C55-C59 (5) 7.35 2.85

No. C59 is known with surcharge in black but its status is questioned.

Bartholomeu de Gusmao and the "Aerostat" — AP17

Wmk. 268

1944, Oct. 23 Engr. ***Perf. 12***

C60 AP17 1.20cr rose carmine .35 .20

Week of the Wing.

L. L. Zamenhof AP18

1945, Apr. 16 Litho. ***Perf. 11***

C61 AP18 1.20cr dull brown .35 .25

Esperanto Congress held in Rio, Apr. 14-22.

Map of South America AP19

Baron of Rio Branco AP20

1945, Apr. 20

C62 AP19 1.20cr gray brown .35 .25
C63 AP20 5cr rose lilac .95 .40

Centenary of the birth of José Maria de Silva Paranhos, Baron of Rio Branco.

Dove and Flags of American Republics AP21

Perf. 12x11

1947, Aug. 15 Engr. Unwmk.

C64 AP21 2.20cr dk blue green .30 .25

Inter-American Defense Conference at Rio de Janeiro August-September, 1947.

Santos-Dumont Monument, St. Cloud, France — AP22

Bay of Rio de Janeiro and Rotary Emblem — AP23

1947, Nov. 15 Typo. *Perf. 11x12*

C65 AP22 1.20cr org brn & ol .30 .25

Issued to commemorate the Week of the Wing and to honor the Santos-Dumont monument which was destroyed in World War II.

Catalogue values for unused stamps in this section, from this point to the end of the section, are for Never Hinged items.

1948, May 16 Engr. *Perf. 11*

C66 AP23 1.20cr deep claret .50 .40
C67 AP23 3.80cr dull violet 1.00 .40

39th convention of Rotary Intl., Rio.

Hotel Quitandinha, Petropolis AP24

1948, July 10 Litho. Wmk. 267

C68 AP24 1.20cr org brn .25 .25
C69 AP24 3.80cr violet .50 .30

International Exposition of Industry and Commerce, Petropolis, 1948.

Musician and Singers AP25

1948, Aug. 13 Engr. Unwmk.

C70 AP25 1.20cr blue .30 .20

National School of Music, cent.

Luis Batlle Berres AP26

1948, Sept. 2 Typo.

C71 AP26 1.70cr blue .20 .20

Visit of President Luis Batlle Berres of Uruguay, September, 1948.

Merino Ram — AP27

Perf. 12x11

1948, Oct. 10 Wmk. 267

C72 AP27 1.20cr dp orange .50 .30

Intl. Livestock Exposition at Bagé.

Eucharistic Congress Seal — AP28

Unwmk.

1948, Oct. 23 Engr. *Perf. 11*

C73 AP28 1.20cr dk car rose .30 .30

5th Natl. Eucharistic Cong., Porto Alegre, Oct. 24-31.

Souvenir Sheet

AP28a

1948, Dec. 14 Engr. *Imperf.*
Without Gum

C73A AP28a Sheet of 3 50.00 65.00

No. C73A contains one each of Nos. 674-676. Issued in honor of President Eurico Gasper Dutra and the armed forces. Exists both with and without number on back. Measures 130x75mm.

Church of Prazeres, Guararapes — AP29

Perf. 11½x12

1949, Feb. 15 Litho. Wmk. 267

C74 AP29 1.20cr pink 1.50 .75

Second Battle of Guararapes, 300th anniv.

Thomé de Souza Meeting Indians — AP30

Perf. 11x12

1949, Mar. 29 Engr. Unwmk.

C75 AP30 1.20cr blue .20 .20

Founding of the City of Salvador, 400th anniv.

A souvenir folder, issued with No. C75, has an engraved 20cr red brown postage stamp portraying John III printed on it, and a copy of No. C75 affixed to it and postmarked. Paper is laid, and size of folder front is 100x150mm. Value, $5.

Franklin D. Roosevelt AP31

1949, May 20 Unwmk. *Imperf.*

C76 AP31 3.80cr deep blue .60 .60
a. Souvenir sheet 12.00 15.00

No. C76a measures 85x110mm, with deep blue inscriptions in upper and lower margins. It also exists with papermaker's watermark.

Joaquim Nabuco (1849-1910), Lawyer and Writer — AP32

1949, Aug. 30 *Perf. 12*

C77 AP32 3.80cr rose lilac .40 .30
a. Wmk. 256, imperf. 25.00

Maracaná Stadium AP33

Soccer Player and Flag — AP34

Perf. 11x12, 12x11

1950, June 24 Litho. Wmk. 267

C78 AP33 1.20cr ultra & salmon .95 .40
C79 AP34 5.80cr bl, yel grn & yel 2.75 .50

4th World Soccer Championship, Rio.

AP35

AP36

Symbolical of Brazilian population growth.

1950, July 10 *Perf. 12x11*

C80 AP35 1.20cr red brown .30 .20

Issued to publicize the 6th Brazilian census.

1956, Sept. 8 Engr. *Perf. 11½*

Design: J. B. Marcelino Champagnat.

C81 AP36 3.30cr rose lilac .30 .20

50th anniversary of the arrival of the Marist Brothers in Northern Brazil.

Santos-Dumont's 1906 Plane — AP37

1956 Photo.

C82	AP37	3cr dk blue grn	.85	.30
C83	AP37	3.30cr brt ultra	.20	.20
C84	AP37	4cr dp claret	.40	.20
C85	AP37	6.50cr red brown	.20	.20
C86	AP37	11.50cr orange red	.85	.35
		Nos. C82-C86 (5)	2.50	1.25

Souvenir Sheet

C86A AP37 Sheet of 4 6.00 6.00
b. 3cr dark carmine 1.50 .90

1st flight by Santos-Dumont, 50th anniv. Issued: #C86A, 10/14; others 10/16.

Lord Baden-Powell AP38

1957, Aug. 1 Unwmk.
Granite Paper

C87 AP38 3.30cr deep red lilac .25 .20

Centenary of the birth of Lord Baden-Powell, founder of the Boy Scouts.

UN Emblem, Soldier and Map of Suez Canal Area AP39

Wmk. 267

1957, Oct. 24 Engr. *Perf. 11½*

C88 AP39 3.30cr dark blue .25 .20

Brazilian contingent of the UN Emergency Force.

Basketball Player — AP40

1959, May 30 Photo. *Perf. 11½*

C89 AP40 3.30cr brt red brn & bl .25 .20

Brazil's victory in the World Basketball Championships of 1959.

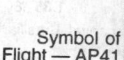

Symbol of Flight — AP41

1959, Oct. 21 Wmk. 267

C90 AP41 3.30cr deep ultra .20 .20

Issued to publicize Week of the Wing.

Caravelle AP42

1959, Dec. 18 *Perf. 11½*

C91 AP42 6.50cr ultra .20 .20

Inauguration of Brazilian jet flights.

20-Cent Minimum Value
The minimum catalogue value is 20 cents. Separating se-tenant pieces into individual stamps does not increase the value of the stamps since demand for the separated stamps may be small.

Pres. Adolfo Lopez Mateos
AP43

Pres. Dwight D. Eisenhower
AP44

1960, Jan. 19 Photo. Wmk. 267
C92 AP43 6.50cr brown .20 .20

Issued to commemorate the visit of President Adolfo Lopez Mateos of Mexico.

1960, Feb. 23 ***Perf. 11½***
C93 AP44 6.50cr deep orange .20 .20

Visit of Pres. Dwight D. Eisenhower.

World Refugee Year Emblem
AP45

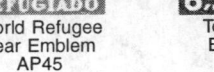

Tower at Brasilia
AP46

1960, Apr. 7 Wmk. 268
C94 AP45 6.50cr blue .20 .20

WRY, July 1, 1959-June 30, 1960.

Type of Regular Issue and AP46

Designs: 3.30cr, Square of the Three Entities. 4cr, Cathedral. 11.50cr, Plan of Brasilia.

Perf. 11x11½, 11½x11
1960, Apr. 21 Photo. Wmk. 267
C95 A436 3.30cr violet .20 .20
C96 A436 4cr blue .75 .20
C97 AP46 6.50cr rose carmine .20 .20
C98 A436 11.50cr brown .20 .20
Nos. C95-C98 (4) 1.35 .80

Inauguration of Brazil's new capital, Brasilia, Apr. 21, 1960.

Chrismon and Oil Lamp
AP47

1960, May 16 ***Perf. 11x11½***
C99 AP47 3.30cr lilac rose .20 .20

7th Natl. Eucharistic Congress at Curitiba.

Cross, Sugarloaf Mountain and Emblem
AP48

1960, July 1 Wmk. 267
C100 AP48 6.50cr brt blue .20 .20

10th Cong. of the World Baptist Alliance, Rio.

Boy Scout — AP49

Caravel — AP50

1960, July 23 ***Perf. 11½x11***
C101 AP49 3.30cr orange ver .20 .20

Boy Scouts of Brazil, 50th anniversary.

1960, Aug. 5 Engr. Wmk. 268
C102 AP50 6.50cr black .20 .20

Prince Henry the Navigator, 500th birth anniv.

Maria E. Bueno
AP51

1960, Dec. 15 Photo. ***Perf. 11x11½***
C103 AP51 60cr pale brown .20 .20

Victory at Wimbledon of Maria E. Bueno, women's singles tennis champion.

War Memorial, Sugarloaf Mountain and Allied Flags
AP52

1960, Dec. 22 Wmk. 268
C104 AP52 3.30cr lilac rose .20 .20

Reburial of Brazilian servicemen of WW II.

Power Line and Map
AP53

Malaria Eradication Emblem
AP54

1961, Jan. 20 ***Perf. 11½x11***
C105 AP53 3.30cr lilac rose .20 .20

Inauguration of Three Marias Dam and hydroelectric station in Minas Gerais.

1962, May 24 Wmk. 267 Engr.
C106 AP54 21cr blue .20 .20

WHO drive to eradicate malaria.

F. A. de Varnhagen — AP55

1966, Feb. 17 Photo. Wmk. 267
C107 AP55 45cr red brown .20 .20

Francisco Adolfo de Varnhagen, Viscount of Porto Seguro (1816-1878), historian and diplomat.

Map of the Americas and Alliance for Progress Emblem
AP56

1966, Mar. 14 ***Perf. 11x11½***
C108 AP56 120cr grnsh bl & vio bl .40 .20

5th anniv. of the Alliance for Progress.
A souvenir card contains one impression of No. C108, imperf. Size: 113x160mm.

Nun and Globe
AP57

Face of Jesus from Shroud of Turin
AP58

1966, Mar. 25 Photo. ***Perf. 11½x11***
C109 AP57 35cr violet .20 .20

Centenary of the arrival of the teaching Sisters of St. Dorothea.

1966, June 3 Photo. Wmk. 267
C110 AP58 45cr brown org .20 .20

Issued to commemorate Vatican II, the 21st Ecumenical Council of the Roman Catholic Church, Oct. 11, 1962-Dec. 8, 1965.
A souvenir card contains one impression of No. C110, imperf. Size: 100x39mm.

Admiral Mariz e Barros
AP59

"Youth" by Eliseu Visconti
AP60

1966, June 13 Photo. Wmk. 267
C111 AP59 35cr red brown .20 .20

Death centenary of Admiral Antonio Carlos Mariz e Barros, who died in the Battle of Itaperu.

1966, July 31 ***Perf. 11½x11***
C112 AP60 120cr red brown .40 .20

Birth centenary of Eliseu Visconti, painter.

SPECIAL DELIVERY STAMPS

No. 191 Surcharged **1000 REIS EXPRESSO**

1930 Unwmk. ***Perf. 12***
E1 A62 1000r on 200r dp blue 4.00 1.75
a. Inverted surcharge 500.00

POSTAGE DUE STAMPS

D1

D2

1889 Unwmk. Typo. ***Rouletted***
J1 D1 10r carmine 2.00 1.40
J2 D1 20r carmine 2.75 2.00
J3 D1 50r carmine 5.00 4.00
J4 D1 100r carmine 2.00 1.40
J5 D1 200r carmine 55.00 15.00
J6 D1 300r carmine 6.00 8.00
J7 D1 500r carmine 6.00 8.00
J8 D1 700r carmine 10.00 14.00
J9 D1 1000r carmine 10.00 10.00
Nos. J1-J9 (9) 98.75 63.80

Counterfeits are common.

1890
J10 D1 10r orange .60 .30
J11 D1 20r ultra .60 .30
J12 D1 50r olive 1.25 .30
J13 D1 200r magenta 6.00 .60
J14 D1 300r blue green 3.00 1.50
J15 D1 500r slate 4.00 3.00
J16 D1 700r purple 4.50 7.50
J17 D1 1000r dk violet 5.50 5.00
Nos. J10-J17 (8) 25.45 18.50

Perf. 11 to 11½, 12½ to 14 and Compound
1895-1901
J18 D2 10r dk blue ('01) 2.00 1.25
J19 D2 20r yellow grn 8.00 3.00
J20 D2 50r yellow grn ('01) 10.00 5.50
J21 D2 100r brick red 6.25 1.25
J22 D2 200r violet 6.00 .60
a. 200r gray lilac ('98) 12.00 2.00
J23 D2 300r dull blue 3.50 2.25
J24 D2 2000r brown 12.00 12.00
Nos. J18-J24 (7) 47.75 25.85

1906 Wmk. 97
J25 D2 100r brick red 8.00 3.00

Wmk. (97? or 98?)
J26 D2 200r violet 7.50 1.25
a. Wmk. 97 275.00 85.00
b. Wmk. 98 12.50 50.00

D3

D4

1906-10 Unwmk. Engr. ***Perf. 12***
J28 D3 10r slate .20 .20
J29 D3 20r brt violet .20 .20
J30 D3 50r dk green .25 .20
J31 D3 100r carmine 1.75 .60
J32 D3 200r dp blue 1.00 .30
J33 D3 300r gray blk .40 .60
J34 D3 400r olive grn 1.00 .90
J35 D3 500r dk violet 35.00 35.00
J36 D3 600r violet ('10) 1.25 *3.00*
J37 D3 700r red brown 30.00 30.00
J38 D3 1000r red 1.50 *3.00*
J39 D3 2000r green 4.75 5.50
J40 D3 5000r choc ('10) 1.50 *14.00*
Nos. J28-J40 (13) 78.80 93.50

Perf. 12½, 11, 11x10½
1919-23 Typo.
J41 D4 5r red brown .20 .25
J42 D4 10r violet .25 .25
J43 D4 20r olive gray .20 .20
J44 D4 50r green ('23) .20 .20
J45 D4 100r red 1.10 1.00
J46 D4 200r blue 5.25 1.50
J47 D4 400r brown ('23) 1.40 1.25
Nos. J41-J47 (7) 8.60 4.65

Perf. 12½, 12½x13½
1924-35 Wmk. 100
J48 D4 5r red brown .25 .20
J49 D4 100r red .75 .30
J50 D4 200r slate bl ('29) 1.00 .50
J51 D4 400r dp brn ('29) 1.50 1.00
J52 D4 600r dk vio ('29) 1.75 1.10
J53 D4 600r orange ('35) .75 .50
Nos. J48-J53 (6) 6.00 3.60

1924 Wmk. 193 ***Perf. 11x10½***
J54 D4 100r red 45.00 45.00
J55 D4 200r slate blue 5.50 5.50

Perf. 11x10½, 13x13½

1925-27 **Wmk. 101**

J56	D4	20r olive gray	.20	.20
J57	D4	100r red	1.05	.30
J58	D4	200r slate blue	3.25	.35
J59	D4	400r brown	1.75	1.25
J60	D4	600r dk violet	4.25	2.50
		Nos. J56-J60 (5)	10.50	4.60

Wmk. E U BRASIL Multiple (218)

1929-30 ***Perf. 12½x13½***

J61	D4	100r light red	.25	.20
J62	D4	200r blue black	.40	.25
J63	D4	400r brown	.40	.25
J64	D4	1000r myrtle green	.75	.50
		Nos. J61-J64 (4)	1.80	1.20

Perf. 11, 12½x13, 13

1931-36 **Wmk. 222**

J65	D4	10r lt violet ('35)	.20	.20
J66	D4	20r black ('33)	.20	.20
J67	D4	50r blue grn ('35)	.25	.20
J68	D4	100r rose red ('35)	.25	.20
J69	D4	200r sl blue ('35)	.40	.30
J70	D4	400r blk brn ('35)	2.00	2.00
J71	D4	600r dk violet	.35	.20
J72	D4	1000r myrtle grn	.50	.35
J73	D4	2000r brown ('36)	.80	.80
J74	D4	5000r indigo ('36)	1.25	1.00
		Nos. J65-J74 (10)	6.20	5.45

1938 **Wmk. 249** ***Perf. 11***

J75	D4	200r slate blue	2.00	.75

1940 **Typo.** **Wmk. 256**

J76	D4	10r light violet	.50	.50
J77	D4	20r black	.50	.50
J79	D4	100r rose red	.50	.50
J80	D4	200r myrtle green	.50	.50
		Nos. J76-J80 (4)	2.00	2.00

1942 **Wmk. 264**

J81	D4	10r lt violet	.20	.20
J82	D4	20r olive blk	.20	.20
J83	D4	50r lt blue grn	.20	.20
J84	D4	100r vermilion	.40	.30
J85	D4	200r gray blue	.40	.30
J86	D4	400r claret	.40	.30
J87	D4	600r rose vio	.30	.20
J88	D4	1000r dk bl grn	.30	.20
J89	D4	2000r dp yel brn	.75	.50
J90	D4	5000r indigo	.40	.30
		Nos. J81-J90 (10)	3.55	2.70

1949 **Wmk. 268**

J91	D4	10c pale rose lilac	4.00	3.25
J92	D4	20r black	25.00	25.00

No. J92 exists in shades of gray ranging to gray olive.

OFFICIAL STAMPS

Pres. Affonso Penna — O1

Pres. Hermes da Fonseca — O2

Unwmk.

1906, Nov. 15 **Engr.** ***Perf. 12***

O1	O1	10r org & grn	.75	.30
O2	O1	20r org & grn	.90	.30
O3	O1	50r org & grn	1.50	.30
O4	O1	100r org & grn	.75	.30
O5	O1	200r org & grn	.90	.30
O6	O1	300r org & grn	2.75	.60
O7	O1	400r org & grn	6.00	1.75
O8	O1	500r org & grn	3.00	1.25
O9	O1	700r org & grn	4.50	3.00
O10	O1	1000r org & grn	4.50	1.25
O11	O1	2000r org & grn	5.00	2.25
O12	O1	5000r org & grn	10.00	.50
O13	O1	10,000r org & grn	10.00	1.25
		Nos. O1-O13 (13)	50.55	13.35

The portrait is the same but the frame differs for each denomination of this issue.

1913, Nov. 15

Center in Black

O14	O2	10r gray	.35	.50
O15	O2	20r ol grn	.35	.50
O16	O2	50r gray	.35	.50
O17	O2	100r ver	1.05	.35
O18	O2	200r blue	2.00	.35
O19	O2	500r orange	3.00	.65
O20	O2	600r violet	3.50	2.75
O21	O2	1000r blk brn	4.25	1.25
O22	O2	2000r red brn	6.50	1.25
O23	O2	5000r brown	7.50	3.00
O24	O2	10,000r black	15.00	7.50
O25	O2	20,000r blue	27.50	27.50
O26	O2	50,000r green	50.00	55.00
O27	O2	100,000r org red	175.00	200.00
O28	O2	500,000r brown	300.00	325.00
O29	O2	1,000,000r dk brn	325.00	350.00
		Nos. O14-O29 (16)	921.05	976.10

The portrait is the same on all denominations of this series but there are eight types of the frame.

Pres. Wenceslau Braz — O3

Perf. 11, 11½

1919, Apr. 11 **Wmk. 100**

O30	O3	10r olive green	.40	2.00
O31	O3	50r green	1.00	1.25
O32	O3	100r rose red	2.00	.85
O33	O3	200r dull blue	2.75	.85
O34	O3	500r orange	7.50	14.00
		Nos. O30-O34 (5)	13.65	18.95

The official decree called for eleven stamps in this series but only five were issued.

For surcharges see Nos. 293-297.

NEWSPAPER STAMPS

N1

Rouletted

1889, Feb. 1 **Unwmk.** **Litho.**

P1	N1	10r yellow	3.00	3.00
	a.	Pair, imperf. between	125.00	145.00
P2	N1	20r yellow	6.00	7.50
P3	N1	50r yellow	10.00	6.00
P4	N1	100r yellow	3.75	3.00
P5	N1	200r yellow	3.00	1.50
P6	N1	300r yellow	3.00	1.50
P7	N1	500r yellow	20.00	8.00
P8	N1	700r yellow	3.00	10.00
P9	N1	1000r yellow	3.00	10.00
		Nos. P1-P9 (9)	54.75	50.50

For surcharges see Nos. 125-127.

1889, May 1

P10	N1	10r olive	2.00	.50
P11	N1	20r green	2.00	.50
P12	N1	50r brn yel	2.75	1.00
P13	N1	100r violet	3.00	2.00
	a.	100r deep violet	6.50	15.00
	b.	100r lilac	12.00	10.00
P14	N1	200r black	3.00	2.00
P15	N1	300r carmine	12.00	10.00
P16	N1	500r green	50.00	50.00
P17	N1	700r pale blue	25.00	30.00
	a.	100r ultramarine	65.00	75.00
	b.	100r cobalt	400.00	425.00
P18	N1	1000r brown	12.00	15.00
		Nos. P10-P18 (9)	111.75	111.00

For surcharges see Nos. 128-135.

N2

N3

White Wove Paper Thin to Thick

Perf. 11 to 11½, 12½ to 14 and 12½ to 14x11 to 11½

1890 **Typo.**

P19	N2	10r blue	14.00	10.00
	a.	10r ultramarine	14.00	10.00
P20	N2	20r emerald	40.00	15.00
P21	N2	100r violet	16.00	14.00
		Nos. P19-P21 (3)	70.00	39.00

For surcharge see No. 137.

1890-93

P22	N3	10r ultramarine	3.00	3.00
	a.	10r blue	7.50	4.00
P23	N3	10r ultra, *buff*	3.00	3.00
P24	N3	20r green	10.00	3.00
	a.	20r emerald	10.00	3.00
P25	N3	50r yel grn ('93)	17.50	10.00
		Nos. P22-P25 (4)	33.50	19.00

For surcharges see Nos. 136, 138-139.

POSTAL TAX STAMPS

Icarus from the Santos-Dumont Monument at St. Cloud, France — PT1

Perf. 13½x12½, 11

1933, Oct. 1 **Typo.** **Wmk. 222**

RA1	PT1	100r deep brown	.65	.25

Honoring the Brazilian aviator, Santos-Dumont. Its use was obligatory as a tax on all correspondence sent to countries in South America, the US and Spain. Its use on correspondence to other countries was optional. The funds obtained were used for the construction of airports throughout Brazil.

Catalogue values for unused stamps in this section, from this point to the end of the section, are for Never Hinged items.

Father Joseph Damien and Children PT2

Perf. 12x11

1952, Nov. 24 **Litho.** **Wmk. 267**

RA2	PT2	10c yellow brown	.25	.20

1953, Nov. 30

RA3	PT2	10c yellow green	.25	.20

Father Bento Dias Pacheco PT3

Eunice Weaver PT4

1954, Nov. 22 **Photo.** ***Perf. 11½***

RA4	PT3	10c violet blue	.20	.20

1955-69, Nov. 24

RA5	PT3	10c dk car rose	.20	.20
RA6	PT3	10c org red ('57)	.20	.20
RA7	PT3	10c dp emer ('58)	.20	.20
RA8	PT3	10c red lilac ('61)	.20	.20
RA9	PT3	10c choc ('62)	.20	.20
RA10	PT3	10c slate ('63)	.20	.20
RA11	PT3	2cr dp mag ('64)	.20	.20
RA12	PT3	2cr violet ('65)	.20	.20
RA13	PT3	2cr orange ('66)	.20	.20
RA14	PT3	5c brt yel grn ('68)	1.25	.75
RA15	PT3	5c deep plum ('69)	.50	.25

Issued: 11/25, #RA14; 11/28, #RA15; others, 11/24.

1971-73, Nov. 24

RA16	PT4	10c slate green	1.00	.40
RA17	PT4	10c brt rose lil ('73)	.20	.20

Father Nicodemos PT5

Father Vicente Borgard (1888-1977) PT6

1975, Nov. 24 **Litho.** **Unwmk.**

RA18	PT5	10c sepia	.20	.20

1983, Nov. 24 **Photo.** ***Perf. 11½***

RA19	PT6	10cr brown	.60	.60

Father Bento Dias Pacheco PT7

Father Santiago Uchoa PT8

1984, Nov. 24 **Photo.** ***Perf. 11½***

RA20	PT7	30cr deep blue	.20	.20

1985, Nov. 24 **Litho.**

RA21	PT7	100cr lake	.20	.20

1986, Nov. 24 **Litho.**

RA22	PT7	10c gray brown	.20	.20

1987, Nov. 24 **Photo.**

RA23	PT7	30c sage green	.20	.20

1988, Nov. 24 **Litho.**

RA24	PT8	1.30cz dull red brn	.20	.20

See Nos. RA29-RA30.

Fr. Joseph Damien — PT9

1989-92 **Photo.** ***Perf. 11½***

RA25	PT9	2c deep lilac rose	.20	.20
RA26	PT9	50c blue	.20	.20

Perf. 12½

RA27	PT9	3cr green	.20	.20
RA28	PT9	30cr brown	.20	.20
		Nos. RA25-RA28 (4)	.80	.80

Issued: 2c, Nov. 24; 50c, Nov. 24, 1990; 3cr, Nov. 24, 1991; 30cr, Nov. 24, 1992.

Father Santiago Uchoa Type of 1988

1993, Nov. 24 **Photo.** ***Perf. 12½***

RA29	PT8	50c blue	.20	.20

1994, Nov. 24

RA30	PT8	1c dull lake	.20	.20

The tax was for the care and treatment of lepers.

Use of #RA2-RA30 was required for one week.

POSTAL TAX SEMI-POSTAL STAMP

Catalogue values for unused stamps in this section are for Never Hinged items.

Icarus — PTSP1

Wmk. 267

1947, Nov. 15 **Typo.** ***Perf. 11***

RAB1	PTSP1	40c + 10c brt red	.35	.20
	a.	Pair, imperf. between	*350.00*	

Aviation Week, November 15-22, 1947, and compulsory on all domestic correspondence during that week.

BRITISH ANTARCTIC TERRITORY

'bri-tish (,)ant-'ärk-tik 'ter-ə-,tōr-ē

LOCATION — South Atlantic Ocean between 20-80 degrees longitude and south of 60 degrees latitude

GOVT. — British territory

POP. — About 300 scientific staff at research stations.

This territory includes Graham Land (Palmer Peninsula), South Shetland

Islands and South Orkney Islands. Formerly part of Falkland Islands Dependency.

12 Pence = 1 Shilling
20 Shillings = 1 Pound
100 Pence = 1 Pound (1971)

Catalogue values for all unused stamps in this country are for Never Hinged items.

M. V. Kista Dan — A1

Designs: 1p, Skiers hauling load. 1½p, Muskeg (tractor). 2p, Skiers. 2½p, Beaver seaplane. 3p, R.R.S. John Biscoe. 4p, Camp scene. 6p, H.M.S. Protector. 9p, Dog sled. 1sh, Otter ski-plane. 2sh, Huskies and aurora australis. 2sh6p, Helicopter. 5sh, Snocat (truck). 10sh, R.R.S. Shackleton. £1, Map of Antarctica.

Perf. 11x11½

1963, Feb. 1 Engr. Wmk. 314

1	A1	½p dark blue	.20	.20
2	A1	1p brown	.20	.20
3	A1	1½p plum & red	.20	.20
4	A1	2p rose violet	.30	.20
5	A1	2½p dull green	.35	.25
6	A1	3p Prus blue	.40	.35
7	A1	4p sepia	.50	.40
8	A1	6p dk blue & olive	.80	.70
9	A1	9p olive	1.00	.80
10	A1	1sh steel blue	1.30	1.10
11	A1	2sh dl vio & bis	6.75	5.50
12	A1	2sh6p blue	7.50	6.25
13	A1	5sh rose red & org	14.50	14.00
14	A1	10sh grn & vio bl	35.00	32.50
15	A1	£1 black & blue	85.00	67.50
		Nos. 1-15 (15)	154.00	130.15

See No. 24. For surcharges see Nos. 25-38.

Common Design Types pictured following the introduction.

Churchill Memorial Issue
Common Design Type

1966, Jan. 24 Photo. *Perf. 14*

16	CD319	½p bright blue	.40	.30
17	CD319	1p green	1.60	.70
18	CD319	1sh brown	16.00	15.00
19	CD319	2sh violet	21.00	16.00
		Nos. 16-19 (4)	39.00	32.00

Lemaire Channel, Iceberg and Adelie Penguins A2

Designs: 6p, Weather sonde and operator. 1sh, Muskeg (tractor) pulling tent equipment. 2sh, Surveyors with theodolite.

1969, Feb. 6 Litho.

20	A2	3½p blue, vio bl & blk	.90	.85
21	A2	6p emer, blk & dp org	1.60	1.50
22	A2	1sh ultra, blk & ver	2.75	2.75
23	A2	2sh grnsh bl, blk & ocher	5.50	5.50
		Nos. 20-23 (4)	10.75	10.60

25 years of continuous scientific work in the Antarctic.

Type of 1963

Design: £1, H.M.S. Endurance and helicopter.

1969, Dec. 1 Engr. *Perf. 11x11½*

24	A1	£1 black & rose red	125.00	125.00

Nos. 1-14 Surcharged in Decimal Currency; Three Bars Overprinted

1971, Feb. 15 Wmk. 314

25	A1	½p on ½p	.20	.20
26	A1	1p on 1p	.20	.20
27	A1	1½p on 1½p	.30	.25
28	A1	2p on 2p	.30	.30
29	A1	2½p on 2½p	.35	.40
30	A1	3p on 3p	.65	.55
31	A1	4p on 4p	.95	.90
32	A1	5p on 6p	1.25	1.10
33	A1	6p on 9p	1.60	1.40
34	A1	7½p on 1sh	2.00	1.90
35	A1	10p on 2sh	4.75	4.00
36	A1	15p on 2sh6p	14.00	12.00
37	A1	25p on 5sh	27.50	24.00
38	A1	50p on 10sh	62.50	60.00
		Nos. 25-38 (14)	116.55	107.20

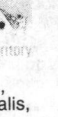

Map of Antarctica, Aurora Australis, Explorers A3

Capt. Cook and "Resolution" A4

Map of Antarctica, Aurora Australis and: 4p, Sea gulls. 5p, Seals. 10p, Penguins.

Litho. & Engr.

1971, June 23 *Perf. 14x13*

39	A3	1½p multicolored	3.25	1.25
40	A3	4p multicolored	6.00	4.00
41	A3	5p multicolored	8.00	6.00
42	A3	10p multicolored	13.00	10.00
		Nos. 39-42 (4)	30.25	21.25

10th anniv. of the Antarctic Treaty pledging peaceful uses of and scientific cooperation in Antarctica.

Silver Wedding Issue, 1972
Common Design Type

Design: Queen Elizabeth II, Prince Philip, seals and emperor penguins.

1972, Dec. 13 Photo. *Perf. 14x14½*

43	CD324	5p rose brn & multi	2.00	2.00
44	CD324	10p olive & multi	4.00	4.00

Wmk. 373

1975-80 Litho. *Perf. 14½*

Polar Explorers and their Crafts: 1p, Thaddeus von Bellingshausen and "Vostok." 1½p, James Weddell and "Jane." 2p, John Biscoe and "Tula." 2½p, J. S. C. Dumont d'Urville and "Astrolabe." 3p, James Clark Ross and "Erebus." 4p, C. A. Larsen and "Jason." 5p, Adrien de Gerlache and "Belgica." 6p, Otto Nordenskjöld and "Antarctic." 7½p, W. S. Bruce and "Scotia." 10p, Jean-Baptiste Charcot and "Pourquoi Pas?" 15p, Ernest Shackleton and "Endurance." 25p, Hubert Wilkins and airplane "San Francisco." 50p, Lincoln Ellsworth and airplane "Polar Star." £1, John Rymill and "Penola."

45	A4	½p multi	.20	.20
46	A4	1p multi ('78)	.20	.20
47	A4	1½p multi ('78)	.20	.20
48	A4	2p multi ('79)	.20	.20
49	A4	2½p multi ('79)	.20	.20
50	A4	3p multi ('79)	.20	.20
52	A4	5p multi ('79)	.30	.30
55	A4	10p multi ('79)	.65	.65
56	A4	15p multi ('79)	1.00	1.00
57	A4	25p multi ('79)	1.60	1.60
58	A4	50p multi ('79)	3.25	3.25
59	A4	£1 multi ('78)	5.25	5.25
		Nos. 45-59 (12)	13.25	13.25

1973, Feb. 14 Wmk. 314

45a	A4	½p multi	*1.75*	*1.75*
46a	A4	1p multi	*2.00*	*2.10*
47a	A4	1½p multi	*3.50*	*3.50*
48a	A4	2p multi	.25	.20
49a	A4	2½p multi	.30	.20
50a	A4	3p multi	.30	.20
51a	A4	4p multi	.30	.20
52a	A4	5p multi	.40	.30
53a	A4	6p multi	.40	.30
54a	A4	7½p multi	.55	.50
55a	A4	10p multi	1.00	.55
56a	A4	15p multi	1.75	1.00
57a	A4	25p multi	2.00	1.50
58a	A4	50p multi	4.00	3.00
59a	A4	£1 multi	12.00	11.00
		Nos. 45a-59a (15)	30.50	26.30

1980 Wmk. 373 *Perf. 12*

51	A4	4p multi	.30	.30
53	A4	6p multi	.40	.40
54	A4	7½p multi	.50	.50
55b	A4	10p multi	.65	.65
56b	A4	15p multi	.70	.70
57b	A4	25p multi	1.25	1.25
58b	A4	50p multi	2.50	2.50
59b	A4	£1 multi	5.00	5.00
		Nos. 51-59b (8)	11.30	11.30

Princess Anne's Wedding Issue
Common Design Type

1973, Nov. 14 Wmk. 314 *Perf. 14*

60	CD325	5p ocher & multi	.30	.30
61	CD325	15p blue grn & multi	.80	.80

Wedding of Princess Anne and Capt. Mark Phillips, Nov. 14, 1973.

Churchill and Map of Churchill Peninsula A5

Design: 15p, Churchill and "Trepassey" of Operation Tabarin, 1943.

1974, Nov. 30 Litho. *Perf. 14*

62	A5	5p multicolored	1.25	.80
63	A5	15p multicolored	2.50	2.50
a.		Souvenir sheet of 2, #62-63	6.75	4.50

Sir Winston Churchill (1874-1965).

Humpback Whale — A6

Wmk. 373

1977, Jan. 4 Litho. *Perf. 14*

64	A6	2p Sperm whale	2.25	1.00
65	A6	8p Fin whale	2.75	1.50
66	A6	11p shown	5.50	3.00
67	A6	25p Blue whale	6.50	4.50
		Nos. 64-67 (4)	17.00	10.00

Conservation of whales.

Prince Philip in Antarctica, 1956-57 — A7

Designs: 11p, Coronation oath. 33p, Queen before taking oath.

1977, Feb. 7 *Perf. 13½x14*

68	A7	6p multicolored	.35	.35
69	A7	11p multicolored	.65	.65
70	A7	33p multicolored	2.00	2.00
		Nos. 68-70 (3)	3.00	3.00

25th anniv. of the reign of Elizabeth II.

Elizabeth II Coronation Anniversary Issue
Common Design Types
Souvenir Sheet
Unwmk.

1978, June 2 Litho. *Perf. 15*

71		Sheet of 6	5.00	5.00
a.		CD326 25p Black bull of Clarence	.75	.75
b.		CD327 25p Elizabeth II	.75	.75
c.		CD328 25p Emperor penguin	.75	.75

No. 71 contains 2 se-tenant strips of Nos. 71a-71c, separated by horizontal gutter with commemorative and descriptive inscriptions and showing central part of coronation procession with coach.

Macaroni Penguins — A8

Perf. 13½x14

1979, Jan. 14 Litho. Wmk. 373

72	A8	3p shown	*6.25*	*2.00*
73	A8	8p Gentoo	*1.60*	*1.00*
74	A8	11p Adelie	*1.40*	*1.25*
75	A8	25p Emperor	*3.50*	*1.50*
		Nos. 72-75 (4)	*12.75*	*5.75*

John Barrow, Tula, Society Emblem A9

Royal Geographical Society Sesquicentennial (Past Presidents and Expedition Scenes): 7p, Clement Markham 11p, Lord Curzon. 15p, William Goodenough. 22p, James Wordie. 30p, Raymond Priestley.

Wmk. 373

1980, Dec. 1 Litho. *Perf. 13½*

76	A9	3p multicolored	.20	.20
77	A9	7p multicolored	.20	.20
78	A9	11p multicolored	.30	.30
79	A9	15p multicolored	.50	.50
80	A9	22p multicolored	.75	.75
81	A9	30p multicolored	.95	.95
		Nos. 76-81 (6)	2.90	2.90

20th Anniv. of Antarctic Treaty — A10

1981, Dec. 1 *Perf. 13½x14*

82	A10	10p Map	.25	.25
83	A10	13p Conservation research	.40	.40
84	A10	25p Satellite image mapping	.70	.70
85	A10	26p Global geophysics	.75	.75
		Nos. 82-85 (4)	2.10	2.10

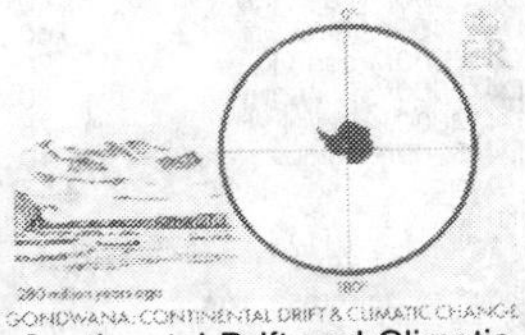

Continental Drift and Climatic Change — A11

1982, Mar. 8 Litho. *Perf. 13½x14*

86	A11	3p Land, water	.20	.20
87	A11	6p Shrubs	.20	.20
88	A11	10p Dinosaur	.35	.35
89	A11	13p Volcano	.40	.40
90	A11	25p Trees	.75	.75
91	A11	26p Penguins	.85	.85
		Nos. 86-91 (6)	2.75	2.75

Princess Diana Issue
Common Design Type

1982, July 1 Litho. *Perf. 14½x14*

92	CD333	5p Arms	.20	.20
93	CD333	17p Diana, by Bryan Organ	.55	.55
94	CD333	37p Wedding	1.25	1.25
95	CD333	50p Portrait	1.60	1.60
		Nos. 92-95 (4)	3.60	3.60

10th Anniv. of Convention for Conservation of Antarctic Seals — A12

1982, Nov. Litho.

96	A12	5p shown	.20	.20
97	A12	10p Weddell seals	.30	.30
98	A12	13p Elephant seals	.40	.40
99	A12	17p Fur seals	.55	.55
100	A12	25p Ross seal	.55	.55
101	A12	34p Crabeater seals	1.10	1.10
		Nos. 96-101 (6)	3.10	3.10

Corethron Criophilum A13

1984, Mar. 15 Litho. *Perf. 14*

102 A13 1p shown .20 .20
103 A13 2p Desmonema gaudichaudi .20 .20
104 A13 3p Tomopteris carpenteri .20 .20
105 A13 4p Pareuchaeta antarctica .20 .20
106 A13 5p Antarctomysis maxima .20 .20
107 A13 6p Antarcturus signiensis .20 .20
108 A13 7p Serolis comuta .20 .20
109 A13 8p Parathemisto gaudichaudii .25 .25
110 A13 9p Bovallia gigantea .30 .30
110A A13 10p Euphausia superba .35 .35
111 A13 15p Colossendeis australis .50 .50
112 A13 20p Todarodes sagittatus .65 .65
113 A13 25p Notothenia neglecta .85 .85
114 A13 50p Chaenocephalus aceratus 1.60 1.60
115 A13 £1 Lobodon carcinophagus 3.25 3.25
116 A13 £3 Antarctic marine food chain 8.25 8.25
Nos. 102-116 (16) 17.40 17.40

Manned Flight Bicentenary — A14

1983, Dec. 17 Wmk. 373

117 A14 5p De Havilland Twin Otter .20 .20
118 A14 13p De Havilland Single Otter .35 .35
119 A14 17p Consolidated Canso .55 .55
120 A14 50p Lockheed Vega 1.60 1.60
Nos. 117-120 (4) 2.70 2.70

British-Graham Land Expedition, 1934-1937 — A15

Designs: 7p, M. Y. Penola in Stella Creek. 22p, Northern base, Winter Island. 27p, D. H. Fox Moth at southern base, Barry Island. 54p, Dog team near Ablation Point, George VI Sound.

1985, Mar. 23 Litho. *Perf. 14½*

121 A15 7p multicolored .20 .20
122 A15 22p multicolored .55 .55
123 A15 27p multicolored .65 .65
124 A15 54p multicolored 1.40 1.40
Nos. 121-124 (4) 2.80 2.80

A16

A17

Naturalists, fauna and flora: 7p, Robert McCormick (1800-1890), Catharacta Skua Maccormicki. 22p, Sir Joseph Dalton Hooker (1817-1911), Deschampsea antarctica. 27p, Jean Rene C. Quoy (1790-1869), Lagenorhynchus cruciger. 54p, James Weddell (1787-1834), Leptonychotes weddelli.

1985, Nov. 4 Litho. *Perf. 14½*

125 A16 7p multicolored .25 .25
126 A16 22p multicolored .85 .85
127 A16 27p multicolored 1.00 1.00
128 A16 54p multicolored 2.00 2.00
Nos. 125-128 (4) 4.10 4.10

1986, Jan. 6 Wmk. 373 *Perf. 14*

Halley's comet.

129 A17 7p Edmond Halley .30 .30
130 A17 22p Halley Station .95 .95
131 A17 27p Trajectory, 1531 1.25 1.25
132 A17 54p Giotto space probe 2.50 2.50
Nos. 129-132 (4) 5.00 5.00

Intl. Glaciological Society, 50th Anniv. — A18

Different snowflakes.

1986, Dec. 6 Wmk. 384 *Perf. 14½*

133 A18 10p dp blue & lt bl .30 .30
134 A18 24p blue grn & lt bl grn .70 .70
135 A18 29p dp rose lil & lt lil .85 .85
136 A18 58p dp vio & pale vio blue 1.75 1.75
Nos. 133-136 (4) 3.60 3.60

Capt. Robert Falcon Scott, CVO RN (1868-1912) A19

Designs: 24p, The Discovery at Hut Point, 1902-1904. 29p, Cape Evans Hut, 1911-1913. 58p, South Pole, 1912.

1987, Mar. 19 Litho. Wmk. 373

137 A19 10p multicolored .30 .30
138 A19 24p multicolored .70 .70
139 A19 29p multicolored .85 .85
140 A19 58p multicolored 1.75 1.75
Nos. 137-140 (4) 3.60 3.60

Intl. Geophysical Year, 30th Anniv. A20

Commonwealth Trans-Antarctic Expedition A21

1987, Dec. 25 Wmk. 384

141 A20 10p Emblem .40 .40
142 A20 24p Port Lockroy .90 .90
143 A20 29p Argentine Islands 1.10 1.10
144 A20 58p Halley Bay 2.25 2.25
Nos. 141-144 (4) 4.65 4.65

1988, Mar. 19 *Perf. 14*

145 A21 10p Aurora over South Ice .35 .35
146 A21 24p Otter aircraft .80 .80
147 A21 29p Seismic ice-depth sounding .95 .95
148 A21 58p Sno-cat over crevasse 1.90 1.90
Nos. 145-148 (4) 4.00 4.00

Lichens A22

1989, Mar. 25 Wmk. 373

149 A22 10p Xanthoria elegans .40 .40
150 A22 24p Usnea aurantiacoatra 1.00 1.00
151 A22 29p Cladonia chlorophaea 1.25 1.25
152 A22 58p Umbilicaria antarctica 2.50 2.50
Nos. 149-152 (4) 5.15 5.15

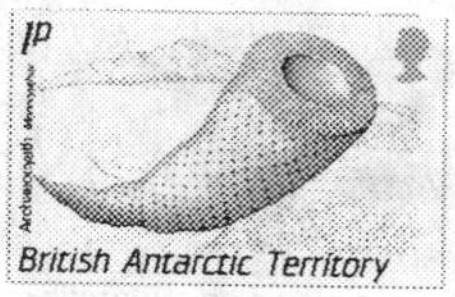

Fossils A23

1990, Apr. 2 Litho. Wmk. 384

153 A23 1p Archaeocyath .20 .20
154 A23 2p Brachiopod .20 .20
155 A23 3p Trilobite *(Triplagnostus)* .20 .20
156 A23 4p Trilobite *(Lyriaspis)* .20 .20
157 A23 5p Gymnosperm .20 .20
158 A23 6p Fern .20 .20
159 A23 7p Belemnite .20 .20
160 A23 8p Ammonite *(Sanmartinoceras)* .20 .20
161 A23 9p Bivalve *(Pinna)* .25 .25
162 A23 10p Bivalve *(Aucellina)* .30 .30
163 A23 20p Bivalve *(Trigonia)* .60 .60
164 A23 25p Gastropod .70 .70
165 A23 50p Ammonite *(Ainoceras)* 1.40 1.40
166 A23 £1 Ammonite *(Gunnarites)* 2.75 2.75
167 A23 £3 Crayfish 8.00 8.00
Nos. 153-167 (15) 15.60 15.60

Queen Mother, 90th Birthday

Common Design Types

1990, Aug. 4 Wmk. 384 *Perf. 14x15*

170 CD343 26p Wedding portrait, 1923 .90 .90

Perf. 14½

171 CD344 £1 Family portrait, 1940 3.25 3.25

Age of Dinosaurs A24

1991, Mar. 27 Wmk. 373 *Perf. 14*

172 A24 12p Late Cretaceous forest .75 .75
173 A24 26p Hypsilophodont dinosaur 1.50 1.50
174 A24 31p Frilled shark 1.90 1.90
175 A24 62p Mosasaur, plesiosaur 3.50 3.50
Nos. 172-175 (4) 7.65 7.65

Antarctic Ozone Hole A25

1991, Mar. 30 *Perf. 14½x14*

176 A25 12p Launching weather balloon .40 .40
177 A25 26p Measuring ozone .95 .95
178 A25 31p Ozone hole over Antarctica 1.25 1.25
179 A25 62p Airplane, chemical studies 2.40 2.40
Nos. 176-179 (4) 5.00 5.00

Antarctic Treaty, 30th Anniv. — A26

1991, June 24 *Perf. 14½*

180 A26 12p Dry valley .40 .40
181 A26 26p Mapping ice sheet .95 .95
182 A26 31p BIOMASS emblem 1.25 1.25
183 A26 62p Ross seal 2.40 2.40
Nos. 180-183 (4) 5.00 5.00

Royal Research Ship James Clark Ross — A27

Designs: 12p, HMS Erebus and Terror in Antarctic by John W. Carmichael. 26p, Launch of RRS James Clark Ross. 62p, Scientific research.

1991, Dec. 10 *Perf. 14x14½*

184 A27 12p multicolored .40 .40
185 A27 26p multicolored .95 .95
186 A27 31p shown 1.25 1.25
187 A27 62p multicolored 2.40 2.40
Nos. 184-187 (4) 5.00 5.00

Inscribed in Blue

200th Anniversary M. Faraday 1791-1867

1991, Dec. 24

188 A27 12p like #184 .40 .40
189 A27 26p like #185 .95 .95
190 A27 31p like #186 1.25 1.25
191 A27 62p like #187 2.40 2.40
Nos. 188-191 (4) 5.00 5.00

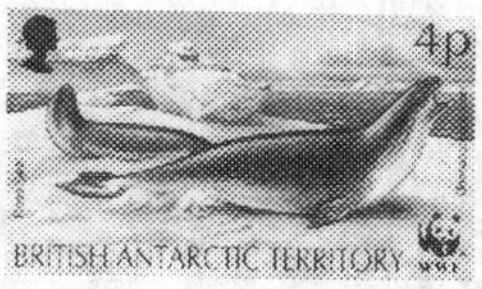

Seals and Penguins A28

1992, Oct. 20 *Perf. 13½*

192 A28 4p Ross seal .20 .20
193 A28 5p Adelie penguin .20 .20
194 A28 7p Weddell seal .30 .30
195 A28 29p Emperor penguin 1.25 1.25
196 A28 34p Crabeater seal 1.50 1.50
197 A28 68p Chinstrap penguin 3.00 3.00
Nos. 192-197 (6) 6.45 6.45

World Wildlife Fund.

Lower Atmospheric Phenomena A29

Perf. 14x14½

1992, Dec. 22 Litho. Wmk. 373

198 A29 14p Sun pillar at Faraday .50 .50
199 A29 29p Halo with iceberg 1.10 1.10
200 A29 34p Lee wave cloud 1.25 1.25
201 A29 68p Nacreous clouds 2.50 2.50
Nos. 198-201 (4) 5.35 5.35

Research Ships A30

Wmk. 373

1993, Dec. 13 Litho. *Perf. 14*

202 A30 1p SS Fitzroy .20 .20
203 A30 2p HMS William Scoresby .20 .20
204 A30 3p SS Eagle .20 .20
205 A30 4p MV Trepassey .20 .20
206 A30 5p RRS John Biscoe (I) .20 .20
207 A30 10p MV Norsel .30 .30
208 A30 20p HMS Protector .55 .55
209 A30 30p MV Oluf Sven .85 .85
210 A30 50p RRS John Biscoe (II), RRS Shackleton 1.40 1.40
a. Souvenir sheet of 1 1.75 1.75
211 A30 £1 MV Tottan 2.75 2.75
a. Souvenir sheet of 1 3.50 3.50
212 A30 £3 MV Perla Dan 8.50 8.50
213 A30 £5 HMS Endurance (I) 14.00 14.00
Nos. 202-213 (12) 29.35 29.35

No. 210a for Hong Kong '97. Issued 2/3/97.

No. 211a for return of Hong Kong to China. Issued 7/1/97.

Operation Taberin, 50th Anniv. — A31

Designs: 15p, Bransfield House and Post Office, Port Lockroy. 31p, Survey team, Hope Bay. 36p, Dog team, Hope Bay. 72p, SS Fitzroy, HMS William Scoresby at sea.

Wmk. 373

1994, Mar. 19 Litho. *Perf. 14*

214	A31	15p multicolored	.45	.45
215	A31	31p multicolored	.90	.90
216	A31	36p multicolored	1.10	1.10
217	A31	72p multicolored	2.25	2.25
		Nos. 214-217 (4)	4.70	4.70

Old and New Transportation — A32

Designs: 15p, Huskies. 24p, DeHavilland DHC-2 Turbo Beaver, British Antarctic Survey. 31p, Dogs, cargo being taken from aircraft. 36p, DHC-6 Twin Otter, sled team. 62p, DHC-6 in flight. 72p, DHC-6 taxiing down runway.

1994, Mar. 21

218	A32	15p multicolored	.45	.45
219	A32	24p multicolored	.70	.70
220	A32	31p multicolored	.90	.90
221	A32	36p multicolored	1.10	1.10
222	A32	62p multicolored	1.75	1.75
223	A32	72p multicolored	2.25	2.25
		Nos. 218-223 (6)	7.15	7.15

Ovptd. with Hong Kong '94 Emblem

1994, Feb. 18

224	A32	15p on #218	.45	.45
225	A32	24p on #219	.70	.70
226	A32	31p on #220	.90	.90
227	A32	36p on #221	1.10	1.10
228	A32	62p on #222	1.75	1.75
229	A32	72p on #223	2.25	2.25
		Nos. 224-229 (6)	7.15	7.15

Antarctic Food Chain A33

a, Crabeater seals. b, Blue whale. c, Wandering albatross. d, Mackeral icefish. e, Krill. f, Squid.

1994, Nov. 29

230	A33	35p Sheet of 6	6.50	6.50

Geological Structures A34

Designs: 17p, Hauberg Mountains, folded sedimentary rocks. 35p, Arrowsmith Peninsula, dikes cross-cutting granite. 40p, Colbert Mountains, columnar jointing in volcanic rocks. 76p, Succession Cliffs, flat-lying sedimentary rocks.

Perf. 14x14½

1995, Nov. 28 Litho. Wmk. 373

231	A34	17p multicolored	.55	.55
232	A34	35p multicolored	1.10	1.10
233	A34	40p multicolored	1.25	1.25
234	A34	76p multicolored	2.50	2.50
		Nos. 231-234 (4)	5.40	5.40

Scientific Committee on Antarctic Research (SCAR) — A35

Designs: 17p, World map showing SCAR member countries. 35p, Earth sciences. 40p, Atmospheric sciences. 76p, Life sciences. £1, Cambridge, August 1996.

Wmk. 384

1996, Mar. 23 Litho. *Perf. 14*

235	A35	17p multicolored	.55	.55
236	A35	35p multicolored	1.10	1.10
237	A35	40p multicolored	1.25	1.25
238	A35	76p multicolored	2.50	2.50
		Nos. 235-238 (4)	5.40	5.40

Souvenir Sheet

239	A35	£1 multicolored	3.25	3.25

Queen Elizabeth II, 70th Birthday

Common Design Type

Various portraits of Queen: 17p, Pink outfit. 35p, In formal dress, tiara. 40p, Blue outfit. 76p, Red coat.

Wmk. 384

1996, Nov. 25 Litho. *Perf. 14½*

240	CD354	17p multicolored	.60	.60
241	CD354	35p multicolored	1.10	1.10
242	CD354	40p multicolored	1.40	1.40
243	CD354	76p multicolored	2.50	2.50
		Nos. 240-243 (4)	5.60	5.60

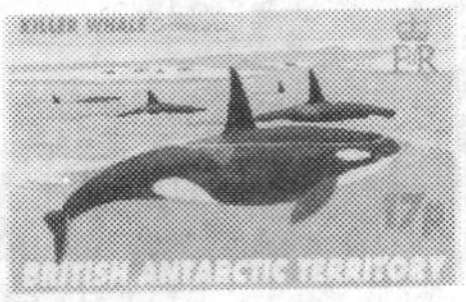

Whales A36

Wmk. 373

1996, Nov. 25 Litho. *Perf. 14*

244	A36	17p Killer whale	.60	.60
245	A36	35p Sperm whale	1.10	1.10
246	A36	40p Minke whale	1.40	1.40
247	A36	76p Blue whale	2.50	2.50
		Nos. 244-247 (4)	5.60	5.60

Souvenir Sheet

248	A36	£1 Humpback whale	3.50	3.50

Christmas — A37

Penguins in snow: 17p, Sledding. 35p, Caroling. 40p, Throwing snowballs. 76p, Ice skating.

Wmk. 384

1997, Dec. 22 Litho. *Perf. 14½*

249	A37	17p multicolored	.55	.55
250	A37	35p multicolored	1.10	1.10
251	A37	40p multicolored	1.40	1.40
252	A37	76p multicolored	2.40	2.40
		Nos. 249-252 (4)	5.45	5.45

History of Mapping — A38

Maps of Antarctic and: 16p, Surveyor looking through theodolite, 1902-03. 30p, Cartographer, 1949. 35p, Man using radar rangefinder, 1964. 40p, Satellite, 1981. 65p, Tripod, hand held remote control device, 1993.

Wmk. 373

1998, Mar. 19 Litho. *Perf. 14*

253	A38	16p multicolored	.55	.55
254	A38	30p multicolored	1.00	1.00
255	A38	35p multicolored	1.25	1.25
256	A38	40p multicolored	1.40	1.40
257	A38	65p multicolored	2.25	2.25
		Nos. 253-257 (5)	6.45	6.45

Diana, Princess of Wales (1961-97)

Common Design Type

Designs: a, Wearing sun glasses. b, In white top. c, Up close. d, Wearing blue-green blazer.

1998, Mar. 31 *Perf. 14½x14*

258	CD355	35p Sheet of 4, #a.-c.	5.25	5.25

No. 258 sold for £1.40 + 20p, with surtax and 50% of profit from total sales being donated to the Princess Diana Memorial Fund.

Antarctic Clothing Through the Ages — A39

Man outfitted for cold weather: 30p, Holding shovel, sailing ship, 1843. 35p, With dog, sailing ship, 1900. 40p, With sketch pad, tripod, dog, steamer ship, 1943. 65p, Wearing red suit, penguins, ship, 1998.

Perf. 14½x14

1998, Nov. 30 Litho. Wmk. 373

259	A39	30p multicolored	1.00	1.00
260	A39	35p multicolored	1.10	1.10
261	A39	40p multicolored	1.25	1.25
262	A39	65p multicolored	2.10	2.10
		Nos. 259-262 (4)	5.45	5.45

Birds A40

Designs: 1p, Sheathbill. 2p, Antarctic prion. 5p, Adelie penguin. 10p, Emperor penguin. 20p, Antarctic tern. 30p, Black bellied storm petrel. 35p, Antarctic fulmar. 40p, Blue eyed shag. 50p, McCormick's skua. £1, Kelp gull. £3, Wilson's storm petrel. £5, Brown skua.

1998 *Perf. 14*

263	A40	1p multicolored	.20	.20
264	A40	2p multicolored	.20	.20
265	A40	5p multicolored	.20	.20
266	A40	10p multicolored	.35	.35
267	A40	20p multicolored	.65	.65
268	A40	30p multicolored	1.00	1.00
269	A40	35p multicolored	1.10	1.10
270	A40	40p multicolored	1.25	1.25
271	A40	50p multicolored	1.60	1.60
272	A40	£1 multicolored	3.25	3.25
273	A40	£3 multicolored	10.00	10.00
274	A40	£5 multicolored	16.00	16.00
		Nos. 263-274 (12)	35.80	35.80

Fish — A41

Wmk. 373

1999, Nov. 14 Litho. *Perf. 13½*

275	A41	10p Mackerel icefish	.35	.35
276	A41	20p Toothfish	.65	.65
277	A41	25p Borch	.80	.80
278	A41	50p Marbled notothen	1.60	1.60
279	A41	80p Bernach	2.60	2.60
		Nos. 275-279 (5)	6.00	6.00

British Antarctic Territory stamps can be mounted in the annually supplemented Scott British Antarctic Territories album.

SEMI-POSTAL STAMPS

Antarctic Heritage SP1

Designs: 17p+3p, Capt. James Cook, HMS Resolution. 35p+15p, Sir James Clark Ross, HMS Erebus, HMS Terror. 40p+10p, Capt. Robert Falcon Scott. 76p+4p, Sir Ernest Shackleton, HMS Endurance trapped in ice.

Wmk. 384

1994, Nov. 23 Litho. *Perf. 14½*

B1	SP1	17p + 3p multi	.65	.65
B2	SP1	35p + 15p multi	1.50	1.50
B3	SP1	40p + 10p multi	1.50	1.50
B4	SP1	76p + 4p multi	2.50	2.50
		Nos. B1-B4 (4)	6.15	6.15

Surtax for United Kingdom Antarctic Heritage Trust.

BRITISH CENTRAL AFRICA

'bri-tish 'sen-trəl 'a-fri-kə

LOCATION — Central Africa, on the west shore of Lake Nyassa
GOVT. — Former British territory, under charter to the British South Africa Company
AREA — 37,800 sq. mi.
POP. — 1,639,329
CAPITAL — Zomba

In 1907 the name was changed to Nyasaland Protectorate, and stamps so inscribed replaced those of British Central Africa.

12 Pence = 1 Shilling
20 Shillings = 1 Pound

Rhodesia Nos. 2, 4-19 Overprinted in Black **B.C.A.**

1891-95 Unwmk. *Perf. 14*

1	A1	1p black	2.50	2.50
2	A2	2p gray green & ver	2.50	2.50
3	A2	4p red brn & blk	2.00	*3.00*
4	A1	6p ultramarine	45.00	24.00
5	A1	6p dark blue	5.00	*7.50*
6	A2	8p rose & blue	12.00	*25.00*
7	A1	1sh bis brown	11.00	10.00
8	A1	2sh vermilion	20.00	*40.00*
9	A1	2sh6p gray lilac	45.00	*55.00*
10	A2	3sh brn & grn ('95)	45.00	*50.00*
11	A2	4sh gray & ver ('93)	45.00	*65.00*
12	A1	5sh yellow	45.00	*55.00*
13	A1	10sh green	90.00	*120.00*
14	A3	£1 blue	600.00	*650.00*
15	A3	£2 rose red	800.00	*800.00*
16	A3	£5 yel green	1,600.	*1,700.*
17	A3	£10 red brown	*3,000.*	*3,000.*
		Nos. 1-13 (13)	370.00	*459.50*

High values with fiscal cancellation are fairly common and can be purchased at a small fraction of the above values. This applies to subsequent issues also.

For surcharge see No. 20.

Rhodesia Nos. 13-14 Surcharged in Black **B.C.A. THREE SHILLINGS.**

1892-93

18	A2	3sh on 4sh gray & ver ('93)	275.00	275.00
19	A1	4sh on 5sh yellow	65.00	*75.00*

No. 2 Surcharged in Black, with Bar **ONE PENNY.**

1895

20	A2	1p on 2p	7.50	*20.00*
	a.	Double surcharge	*3,000.*	*2,000.*

A double surcharge, without period after "Penny," and measuring 16mm instead of 18mm, is from a trial printing.

Coat of Arms of the Protectorate
A4 A5

1895 Unwmk. Typo. *Perf. 14*

21 A4 1p black 7.50 5.00
22 A4 2p green & black 12.50 10.00
23 A4 4p org & black 25.00 22.50
24 A4 6p ultra & black 37.50 7.50
25 A4 1sh rose & black 42.50 19.00
26 A5 2sh6p vio & black 110.00 *125.00*
27 A5 3sh yel & black 70.00 42.50
28 A5 5sh olive & blk 90.00 90.00
29 A5 £1 org & black 650.00 375.00
30 A5 £10 ver & black *3,250.* *2,750.*
31 A5 £25 bl grn & blk *5,750.* *6,000.*
Nos. 21-28 (8) 395.00 321.50

1896 Wmk. 2

32 A4 1p black 4.50 4.50
33 A4 2p green & black 12.00 5.75
34 A4 4p org brown & blk 14.00 *16.00*
35 A4 6p ultra & black 15.00 8.00
36 A4 1sh rose & black 16.00 9.00

Wmk. 1 Sideways

37 A5 2sh6p vio rose & blk 75.00 *90.00*
38 A5 3sh yel & black 55.00 40.00
39 A5 5sh olive & blk 80.00 *95.00*
40 A5 £1 blue & blk 675.00 475.00
41 A5 £10 ver & blk *3,750.* *2,250.*
42 A5 £25 bl grn & blk *9,500.* *9,500.*
Nos. 32-39 (8) 271.50 *268.25*

A6 A7

1897-1901 Wmk. 2

43 A6 1p ultra & black 1.00 .60
44 A6 1p rose & violet ('01) 1.25 .90
45 A6 2p yel & black 1.50 .70
46 A6 4p car rose & blk 4.50 2.50
47 A6 4p ol grn & vio ('01) 5.00 *6.00*
48 A6 6p green & black 27.50 4.00
49 A6 6p red brn & vio ('01) 4.00 3.75
50 A6 1sh gray lilac & blk 7.50 6.25

Wmk. 1

51 A7 2sh6p ultra & blk 32.50 *35.00*
52 A7 3sh gray grn & blk 150.00 *175.00*
53 A7 4sh car rose & blk 60.00 60.00
54 A7 10sh olive & black 75.00 *90.00*
55 A7 £1 dp vio & blk 225.00 140.00
56 A7 £10 orange & black *3,500.* *1,600.*
Nos. 43-54 (12) 369.75 *384.70*

No. 52 Surcharged in Red — ONE PENNY

1897

57 A7 1p on 3s 5.00 *7.50*
a. "PNNEY" 1,500.
b. "PENN" 900.00
c. Double surcharge 750.00 600.00

A8

1898, Mar. 11 Unwmk. *Imperf.*

58 A8 1p ver & ultra 1,500. 50.00
a. Center inverted *10,000.*
b. Double oval
c. Pair, one without oval *6,500.*
d. Pair with three ovals
e. Initials of P.M. General on back *450.00*

Perf. 12

59 A8 1p ver & blue 1,750. 15.00

There are two settings of Nos. 58-59, with 30 types of each.

No. 58 issued without gum.

King Edward VII
A9 A10

1903-04 Wmk. 2

60 A9 1p car & black 3.75 .75
61 A9 2p vio & dull vio 3.00 2.50
62 A9 4p blk & gray green 2.25 *5.75*
63 A9 6p org brn & blk 2.25 *4.50*
64 A9 1sh pale blue & blk ('04) 2.25 *4.00*

Wmk. 1

65 A10 2sh6p gray green 27.50 *35.00*
66 A10 4sh vio & dl vio 47.50 *70.00*
67 A10 10sh blk & gray green 62.50 *125.00*
68 A10 £1 scar & blk 175.00 135.00
69 A10 £10 ultra & blk *3,500.* *2,750.*
Nos. 60-68 (9) 326.00 *382.50*

1907 Wmk. 3

70 A9 1p car & black 2.00 .90
71 A9 2p vio & dull vio *7,250.*
72 A9 4p blk & gray grn *7,250.*
73 A9 6p org brn & blk 25.00 *32.50*

Nos. 71-72 were not issued.

British Central Africa stamps were replaced by those of Nyasaland Protectorate in 1908.

BRITISH EAST AFRICA

'bri-tish 'ēst 'a-fri-kə

LOCATION — Formerly included all of the territory in East Africa under British control.

Postage stamps were issued by the British East Africa Company in 1896. Later the territory administered by this company was incorporated in the East Africa and Uganda Protectorate which, together with Kenya, became officially designated Kenya Colony.

16 Annas = 1 Rupee

Queen Victoria
A1 A2 A3

1890 Wmk. 30 *Perf. 14*

1 A1 ½a on 1p lilac 300.00 200.00
2 A2 1a on 2p grn & car rose 400.00 250.00
3 A3 4a on 5p lilac & bl 450.00 275.00

Sun and Crown Symbolical of "Light and Liberty"
A4 A5

1890-94 Unwmk. Litho. *Perf. 14*

14 A4 ½a bister brown 1.00 *2.75*
b. ½a deep brown 1.00 *2.50*
c. As "b," horiz. pair, imperf. btwn. *1,500.* 750.00
d. As "b," vert. pair, imperf. btwn. 750.00 475.00
15 A4 1a blue green 1.00 1.00
16 A4 2a vermilion 2.50 1.50
17 A4 2½a black, *yel* ('91) 3.50 3.00
b. Vert. pair, imperf. btwn. 600.00 400.00
c. Horiz. pair, imperf. btwn. 800.00 500.00
18 A4 3a black, *red* ('91) 1.25 *1.40*
b. Horiz. pair, imperf. btwn. 600.00 400.00
c. Vert. pair, imperf. btwn. 450.00 350.00
19 A4 4a yellow brown 2.50 2.25
20 A4 4½a brown vio ('91) 2.50 *3.25*
b. 4½a gray violet ('91) 25.00 7.25
c. Horiz. pair, imperf. btwn. 1,250. 1,250.
d. Vert. pair, imperf. btwn. 675.00 450.00
21 A4 5a black, *blue* ('94) 1.10 *1.75*
22 A4 7½a black ('94) 1.10 *1.75*
23 A4 8a blue 5.50 *7.50*
24 A4 8a gray 250.00 *325.00*
25 A4 1r rose 6.00 *7.50*
26 A4 1r gray 225.00 225.00
27 A5 2r brick red 10.00 8.00
28 A5 3r gray violet 7.50 6.25
29 A5 4r ultra 12.00 *12.50*
30 A5 5r gray green 30.00 25.00
Nos. 14-30 (17) 562.45 *635.40*

Some of the paper used for this issue had a papermaker's watermark and parts of it often can be seen on the stamps.

Values for Nos. 14c, 14d, 17b, 17c, 18b, 18c, 20c, 20d, unused, are for copies with little or no original gum. Stamps with natural straight edges are almost as common as fully perforated stamps from the early printings of Nos. 14-30, and for all printings of the rupee values. Values about the same.

For surcharges and overprints see Nos. 31-53.

1890-91 *Imperf.*

Values for Pairs except No. 19b.

14a A4 ½a bister brown 600. 350.
14e A4 ½a deep brown 650. 400.
15a A4 1a blue green 800. 475.
16a A4 2a vermilion 1,200. 550.
17a A4 2½a black, *yellow* 750. 400.
18a A4 3a black, *red* 725. 600.
19a A4 4a yel brown 1,400. 600.
19b A4 4a gray 1,400. 1,400.
20a A4 4½a dull violet 1,100. 525.
23a A4 8a blue 1,800. 600.
25a A4 1r rose 2,400. 625.

A6 A7

Handstamped Surcharges

1891 *Perf. 14*

31 A6 ½a on 2a ver ("A.D.") 2,750. 900.00
a. Double surcharge *3,250.*
32 A6 1a on 4a yel brn ("A.B.") 6,000. 1,300.

Nos. 31-32 are initialed in manuscript "A.D." or "A.B." See note below No. 35.

Manuscript Surcharges

1891-95

33 A6 ½a on 2a ver ("A.B.") 3,000. 675.00
a. "½ Annas" ("A.B.") 1,200.
b. Initialed "A.D." 1,000.
c. "½ Annas" ("A.D.") 1,600.
34 A6 ½a on 3a blk, *red* ("T.E.C.R.") 200.00 50.00
b. Initialed "A.B." 2,400. 1,100.
34A A6 1a on 3a blk, *red* ("V.H.M.") 3,000. 1,200.
c. Initialed "T.E.C.R." 3,000. 1,500.
35 A6 1a on 4a yel brn ("A.B.") 2,750. 950.00

The manuscript initials on Nos. 31-35, given in parentheses, stand for Andrew Dick, Archibald Brown, Victor H. Mackenzie (1891) and T.E. C. Remington (1895).

Printed Surcharges

1894

36 A7 5a on 8a blue 52.50 *72.50*
37 A7 7½a on 1r rose 52.50 *72.50*

Stamps of 1890-94 Handstamped in Black — BRITISH EAST AFRICA

1895

38 A4 ½a deep brown 60.00 20.00
39 A4 1a blue green 70.00 65.00
40 A4 2a vermilion 125.00 90.00
41 A4 2½a black, *yellow* 110.00 45.00
42 A4 3a black, *red* 42.50 37.50
43 A4 4a yel brown 37.50 37.50
44 A4 4½a gray violet 125.00 85.00
a. 4½a brown violet 750.00 650.00
45 A4 5a black, *blue* 140.00 87.50
b. Inverted overprint *2,000.*
46 A4 7½a black 95.00 80.00
47 A4 8a blue 80.00 75.00
b. Inverted overprint *2,000.*
48 A4 1r rose 45.00 *47.50*
49 A5 2r brick red 250.00 175.00
50 A5 3r gray violet 140.00 125.00
b. Inverted overprint
51 A5 4r ultra 125.00 125.00
52 A5 5r gray green 325.00 *350.00*
Nos. 38-52 (15) 1,770. 1,445.

Double Overprints

38a A4 ½a 350. 350.
39a A4 1a 350. 350.
40a A4 2a 400. 400.
41a A4 2½a 400. 350.
43a A4 4a 375. 375.
44b A4 4½a gray violet 475. 450.
44c A4 4½a brown violet 1,500. 1,400.
45a A4 5a 700. 650.
46a A4 7½a 450. 450.
47a A4 8a 475. 475.
48a A4 1r 425. 425.
50a A5 3r 750. 750.
51a A5 4r 750. 750.
52a A5 5r 1,100. 1,100.

Surcharged in Red — 2½

1895

53 A4 2½a on 4½a gray vio 90.00 55.00
a. Double overprint (#44b) 700.00 700.00

Stamps of India 1874-95 Overprinted or Surcharged — British East Africa

2½ 2½ 2½
a b c

1895 Wmk. Star (39)

54 A17 ½a green 3.50 *4.00*
55 A19 1a maroon 3.50 3.50
56 A20 1a6p bister brn 3.50 3.00
57 A21 2a ultra 3.50 2.25
58 A28 2a6p green 5.00 2.75
59 A20(a) 2½a on 1a6p bis brown 40.00 27.50
a. "½" without fraction line 70.00
d. As "a," "1" of "½" invtd. 750.00 600.00
62 A22 3a orange 7.00 *7.50*
63 A23 4a olive green 25.00 16.00
64 A25 8a red violet 25.00 *32.50*
a. 8a red lilac 45.00 *50.00*
65 A26 12a vio, *red* 18.00 *22.50*
66 A27 1r gray 55.00 47.50
67 A29 1r car & grn 32.50 *55.00*
a. Dbl. ovpt., one sideways 350.00 *550.00*
68 A30 2r bis & rose 45.00 *75.00*
69 A30 3r grn & brn 55.00 *85.00*
70 A30 5r vio & ultra 80.00 *120.00*
a. Double overprint 1,800.

Wmk. Elephant's Head (38)

71 A14 6a bister 21.00 *30.00*
Nos. 54-59,62-71 (16) 422.50 *534.00*

Varieties of the overprint include: "Britlsh," "Brltish," "Bpitish" and "Biitish" for "British", "Afrlca" for "Africa"; "Eas" and "Easa" for "East."

No. 59 is surcharged in bright red; surcharges in brown red were prepared for the UPU, but not regularly issued as stamps. See note following No. 93.

Queen Victoria and British Lions — A8

1896-1903 Engr. Wmk. 2 *Perf. 14*

72 A8 ½a yel green .80 .70
73 A8 1a carmine 2.50 .40
a. 1a red 2.50 .40
74 A8 1a dp rose ('03) 27.50 3.25
75 A8 2a chocolate 3.75 3.25
76 A8 2½a dark blue 4.75 1.00
77 A8 3a gray 2.50 *4.50*
78 A8 4a deep green 5.00 2.50
79 A8 4½a orange 4.00 *8.00*
80 A8 5a dk ocher 6.00 3.50
81 A8 7½a lilac 4.50 *16.00*
82 A8 8a olive gray 2.25 *4.00*
83 A8 1r ultra 25.00 17.00
a. 1r pale blue 25.00 17.50
84 A8 2r red orange 42.50 22.50
85 A8 3r deep violet 42.50 22.50

86 A8 4r lake 42.50 42.50
87 A8 5r dark brown 42.50 35.00
Nos. 72-87 (16) 258.55 186.60

Zanzibar Nos. 38-40, 44-46 Overprinted in Black

British
East
Africa

1897 Wmk. Rosette (71)

88 A2 ½a yel grn & red 37.50 37.50
89 A2 1a indigo & red 75.00 75.00
90 A2 2a red brn & red 27.50 18.00
91 A2 4½a org & red 37.50 22.50
92 A2 5a bister & red 37.50 27.50
93 A2 7½a lilac & red 42.50 30.00
a. Ovptd. on front and back
Nos. 88-93 (6) 257.50 210.50

The 1a with red overprint, which includes a period after "Africa", was sent to the UPU, but never placed in use. Nos. 88, 90-93 and 95-100 also exist with period (in black) in sets sent to the UPU. Some experts consider these essays.

Black Ovpt. on Zanzibar #39, 42 New Value Surcharged in Red

1897

95 A2(a) 2½a on 1a 75.00 50.00
a. Black overprint double 6,500.
b. "2" over "1" for "½" 1,200.
96 A2(b) 2½a on 1a 140.00 90.00
97 A2(c) 2½a on 1a 85.00 55.00
98 A2(a) 2½a on 3a 65.00 45.00
a. "2" over "1" for "½" 1,200.
99 A2(b) 2½a on 3a 125.00 85.00
100 A2(c) 2½a on 3a 75.00 50.00
Nos. 95-100 (6) 565.00 375.00

A10

1898 Wmk. 1 Engr.

102 A10 1r gray blue 27.50 17.50
a. 1r ultra 125.00 100.00
103 A10 2r orange 42.50 *45.00*
104 A10 3r dk violet 42.50 *60.00*
105 A10 4r carmine 125.00 *150.00*
106 A10 5r black brown 110.00 *150.00*
107 A10 10r bister 160.00 *225.00*
108 A10 20r yel green 575.00 *1,000.*
109 A10 50r lilac 1,900. *2,750.*
Nos. 102-107 (6) 507.50 *647.50*

The stamps of this country were superseded in 1904 by the stamps of East Africa and Uganda Protectorate.

BRITISH GUIANA

'bri-tish gē-'a-nə, -'ä-nə

LOCATION — On the northeast coast of South America
GOVT. — Former British Crown Colony
AREA — 83,000 sq. mi.
POP. — 628,000 (estimated 1964)
CAPITAL — Georgetown

British Guiana became the independent state of Guyana May 26, 1966.

100 Cents = 1 Dollar

Catalogue values for unused stamps in this country are for Never Hinged items, beginning with Scott 242 in the regular postage section and Scott J1 in the postage due section.

Values for unused stamps are for copies with original gum except for Nos. 6-12 and 35-53, which are valued without gum. Very fine examples of all stamps from No. 6 on will have four clear margins. Inferior copies sell at much reduced prices, depending on the condition of the individual specimen.

A1

1850-51 Typeset Unwmk. *Imperf.*

1 A1 2c blk, *pale rose,* cut to shape ('51) *70,000.*
2 A1 4c black, *orange* *20,000.*
Cut to shape *3,500.*
a. 4c black, *yellow* *27,500.*
Cut to shape *4,000.*
3 A1 4c blk, *yellow* (pelure) *37,500.*
Cut to shape *4,000.*
4 A1 8c black, *green* *13,000.*
Cut to shape *2,500.*
5 A1 12c black, *blue* *5,250.*
Cut to shape *1,900.*
a. 12c black, *pale blue* *11,000.*
Cut to shape *3,000.*
b. 12c black, *indigo* *13,000.*
Cut to shape *3,000.*
c. "1" of "12" omitted —

These stamps were initialed before use by the Deputy Postmaster General or by one of the clerks of the Colonial Postoffice at Georgetown. The following initials are found:—E. T. E. D(alton); E. D. W(ight); G. B. S(mith); H. A. K(illikelley); W. H. L(ortimer). As these stamps are type-set there are several types of each value.

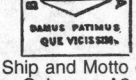

Ship and Motto of Colony — A2

Seal of the Colony — A3

1852 Litho.

6 A2 1c black, *magenta* *10,000.* *5,250.*
7 A2 4c black, *blue* *15,000.* *5,750.*

Both 1c and 4c are found in two types. Copies with paper cracked or rubbed sell for much less.

Some copies are initialed E. D. W(ight).

The reprints are on thicker paper and the colors are brighter. They are perforated 12½ and imperforate. Value $15 each.

1853-59 *Imperf.*

Without Line above Value

8 A3 1c vermilion 4,500. 1,150.

Copies in reddish brown probably are proofs.

Full or Partial White Line Above Value

9 A3 1c red 2,750. 950.
10 A3 4c blue 1,100. 450.
a. 4c dark blue 1,375. 525.
b. 4c pale blue 1,000. 375.

On No. 9, "ONE CENT" varies from 11 to 13mm in width.

No. 10 Retouched; White Line above Value Removed

11 A3 4c blue 1,650. 600.
a. 4c dark blue 2,000. 650.
b. 4c pale blue 1,600. 650.

Reprints of Nos. 8 and 10 are on thin paper, perf. 12½ or imperf. The 1c is orange red, the 4c sky blue.

1860

Numerals in Corners Framed

12 A3 4c blue 3,250. 450.

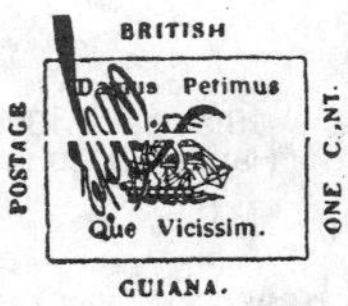

A4

1856 Typeset *Imperf.*

13 A4 1c black, *magenta* —
14 A4 4c black, *magenta* *7,500.*
a. 4c black, *rose carmine* *10,500.*
15 A4 4c black, *blue* *45,000.*
16 A4 4c black, *blue, paper colored through* *60,000.*

These stamps were initialed before being issued and the following initials are found:—E. T. E. D.; E. D. W.; W. H. L.; C. A. W. No. 13 is unique.

A5

Wide space between value and "Cents"

1860-61 Litho. *Perf. 12*

Thick Paper

17 A5 1c brown red ('61) 350.00 85.00
18 A5 1c pink 1,100. 165.00
19 A5 2c orange 150.00 37.50
20 A5 8c rose 300.00 45.00
21 A5 12c gray 350.00 30.00
a. 12c lilac 450.00 40.00
22 A5 24c green 950.00 75.00

All denominations of type A5 above four cents are expressed in Roman numerals.

Bisects and trisects are found on covers. These were not officially authorized.

The reprints of the 1c pink are perforated 12½; the other values have not been reprinted.

Thin Paper

1862-65

23 A5 1c brown 400.00 175.00
24 A5 1c black 100.00 45.00
25 A5 2c orange 80.00 30.00
26 A5 8c rose 110.00 45.00
27 A5 12c lilac 125.00 25.00
28 A5 24c green 750.00 85.00

Perf. 12½ and 13

29 A5 1c black 50.00 25.00
30 A5 2c orange 75.00 22.50
31 A5 8c rose 225.00 75.00
32 A5 12c lilac 475.00 110.00
33 A5 24c green 550.00 75.00

Medium Paper

33A A5 1c black 50.00 25.00
33B A5 2c orange 70.00 20.00
33C A5 8c pink 145.00 50.00
33D A5 12c lilac ('65) 425.00 90.00
33E A5 24c green 160.00 60.00
f. 24c deep green 325.00 80.00

Perf. 10

34 A5 12c gray lilac 400.00 65.00

Imperfs. are proofs. See Nos. 44-62.

A6

A7

A8

A9

A10

A11

1862 Typeset *Rouletted*

35 A6 1c black, *rose* *1,650.* *350.*
Unsigned *200.*
36 A7 1c black, *rose* *2,000.* *450.*
Unsigned *200.*
37 A8 1c black, *rose* *3,500.* *575.*
Unsigned *400.*
38 A6 2c black, *yellow* *1,600.* *275.*
Unsigned *350.*
39 A7 2c black, *yellow* *2,250.* *350.*
Unsigned *400.*
40 A8 2c black, *yellow* *3,250.* *575.*
Unsigned *600.*
41 A9 4c black, *blue* *2,000.* *475.*
Unsigned *375.*
42 A10 4c black, *blue* *3,500.* *1,450.*
Unsigned *600.*
a. Without inner lines *2,000.* *475.*
As "a," unsigned *350.*
43 A11 4c black, *blue* *1,750.* *400.*
Unsigned *350.*

Nos. 35-43 were typeset, there being 24 types of each value. They were initialed before use "R. M. Ac. R. G.," being the initials of Robert Mather, Acting Receiver General.

The initials are in black on the 1c and in red on the 2c. An alkali was used on the 4c stamps, which, destroying the color of the paper, caused the initials to appear to be written in white.

Uninitialed stamps are remainders, few sheets having been found.

Specimens with roulette on all sides are valued higher.

Narrow space between value and "Cents"

1860 Thick Paper Litho. *Perf. 12*

44 A5 4c blue 275.00 50.00
c. 4c deep blue 375.00 75.00

Thin Paper

44A A5 4c blue 75.00 20.00

Perf. 12½ and 13

44B A5 4c blue 75.00 22.50

Medium Paper

1863-68 *Perf. 12½ and 13*

45 A5 1c black ('66) 30.00 16.00
46 A5 2c orange 30.00 5.00
47 A5 4c blue ('64) 65.00 12.50
48 A5 8c rose ('68) 140.00 17.50
49 A5 12c lilac ('67) 375.00 22.50
Nos. 45-49 (5) 640.00 73.50

1866 *Perf. 10*

50 A5 1c black 8.00 4.00
51 A5 2c orange 17.50 2.50
52 A5 4c blue 75.00 7.00
a. Half used as 2c on cover 4,000.
53 A5 8c rose 110.00 13.00
a. Diagonal half used as 4c on cover —
54 A5 12c lilac 125.00 12.00
a. Third used as 4c on cover —
Nos. 50-54 (5) 335.50 38.50

1875 *Perf. 15*

58 A5 1c black 35.00 7.50
59 A5 2c orange 150.00 8.50
60 A5 4c blue 225.00 70.00
61 A5 8c rose 250.00 75.00
62 A5 12c lilac 525.00 47.50
Nos. 58-62 (5) 1,185. 208.50

Seal of Colony
A12 A13

1863 *Perf. 12*

63 A12 24c yellow green 125.00 12.50
a. 24c green 250.00 22.50

Perf. 12½ to 13

64 A12 6c blue 100.00 40.00
65 A12 24c green 125.00 10.00
66 A12 48c deep red 150.00 45.00
a. 48c rose 250.00 45.00
Nos. 63-66 (4) 500.00 107.50

1866 *Perf. 10*

67 A12 6c blue 100.00 22.50
a. 6c ultramarine 125.00 32.50
68 A12 24c yellow green 150.00 8.00
a. 24c green 190.00 10.00
69 A12 48c rose red 275.00 25.00
Nos. 67-69 (3) 525.00 55.50

For surcharges see Nos. 83-92.

1875 *Perf. 15*

70 A12 6c ultra 375.00 80.00
71 A12 24c yellow green 525.00 35.00
a. 24c deep green 650.00 55.00

1876 Typo. Wmk. 1 *Perf. 14*

72 A13 1c slate 2.50 1.50
a. Perf. 14x12½ 190.00
73 A13 2c orange 30.00 2.00
74 A13 4c ultra 110.00 7.00
a. Perf. 12½ 1,300. 200.00
75 A13 6c chocolate 70.00 7.50
76 A13 8c rose 90.00 1.90
77 A13 12c lilac 50.00 3.50
78 A13 24c green 60.00 5.00
79 A13 48c red brown 110.00 17.50
80 A13 96c bister 475.00 250.00
Nos. 72-80 (9) 997.50 295.90

See Nos. 107-111. For surcharges see Nos. 93-95, 98-101.

Stamps Surcharged by Brush-like Pen Lines

Surcharge Types:
Type a - Two horiz. lines.
Type b - Two lines, one horiz., one vert.
Type c - Three lines, two horiz., one vert.
Type d - One horiz. line.

On Nos. 75 and 67

1878 *Perf. 10, 14*

82 A13(a) (1c) on 6c choc 37.50 32.50
83 A12(b) (1c) on 6c blue 140.00 65.00
84 A13(b) (1c) on 6c choc 175.00 85.00

On Nos. O3, O8-O10

85 A13(c) (1c) on 4c ultra 175.00 85.00
a. Type b 2,500.
86 A13(c) (1c) on 6c choc 200.00 80.00
87 A5(c) (2c) on 8c rose *750.00* 175.00
88A A13(b) (2c) on 8c rose 250.00 90.00

On Nos. O1, O3, O6-O7

89 A5(d) (1c) on 1c blk 150.00 75.00
89A A5(d) (2c) on 8c rose
90 A13(d) (1c) on 1c sl 125.00 50.00
91 A13(d) (2c) on 2c org 250.00 60.00

The provisional values of Nos. 82 to 91 were established by various official decrees. The horizontal lines crossed out the old value, "OFFICIAL," or both.

Nos. 69 and 80 Surcharged with New Values in Black

No. 92

No. 93

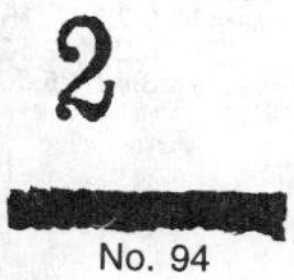
No. 94

No. 95

1881

92 A12 1c on 48c red 32.50 5.00
93 A13 1c on 96c bister 4.25 *5.00*
94 A13 2c on 96c bister 4.25 *8.50*
95 A13 2c on 96c bister 45.00 *50.00*
Nos. 92-95 (4) 86.00 *68.50*

Unissued Official Stamps Surcharged with New Values

A24

No. 96

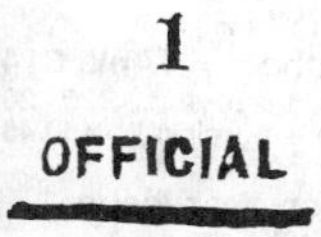
No. 97

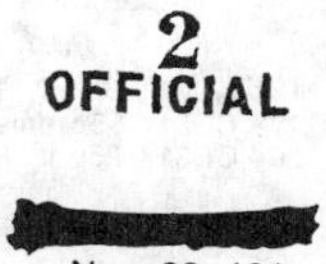
Nos. 99, 101

No. 102

1881

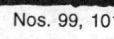

96 A13 1c on 12c lilac 110.00 65.00
97 A13 1c on 48c red brn 125.00 90.00
98 A24 2c on 12c lilac 325.00 225.00
99 A13 2c on 12c lilac 60.00 25.00
a. "2" inverted
b. "2" double *700.00* 475.00
100 A24 2c on 24c green 575.00 575.00
101 A13 2c on 24c green 70.00 37.50
a. "2" inverted
d. Double surcharge 750.00
102 A13 2c on 24c green 200.00 125.00

A27

Typeset

ONE AND TWO CENTS.
Type I - Ship with three masts.
Type II - Brig with two masts.

"SPECIMEN"

Perforated Diagonally across Stamp

1882 **Unwmk.** *Perf. 12*

103 A27 1c black, *lil rose*, I 35.00 30.00
a. Without "Specimen" *325.00 275.00*
104 A27 1c black, *lil rose*, II 35.00 30.00
a. Without "Specimen" *325.00 275.00*
105 A27 2c black, *yel*, I 50.00 40.00
a. Without "Specimen" *325.00 325.00*
b. Diagonal half used as 1c on cover
106 A27 2c black, *yel*, II 50.00 42.50
a. Without "Specimen" *325.00 325.00*
Nos. 103-106 (4) 170.00 142.50

Nos. 103-106 were typeset, 12 to a sheet, and, to prevent fraud on the government, the word *"Specimen"* was perforated across them before they were issued. There were 2 settings of the 1c and 3 settings of the 2c, thus there are 24 types of the former and 36 of the latter.

Type of 1876

1882 **Typo.** **Wmk. 2** *Perf. 14*

107 A13 1c slate 7.00 .35
108 A13 2c orange 20.00 .45
a. "2 CENTS" double —
109 A13 4c ultra 80.00 7.00
110 A13 6c brown 6.00 8.00
111 A13 8c rose 80.00 1.40
Nos. 107-111 (5) 193.00 17.20

A28

A29

4 CENTS and $4
Type I - Figure "4" is 3mm high.
Type II - Figure "4" is 3½mm high.
6 CENTS
Type I - Top of "6" is flat.
Type II - Top of "6" turns downward.

"INLAND REVENUE" Overprint and Surcharged in Black

1889

112 A28 1c lilac 1.60 .70
113 A28 2c lilac 1.40 .45
114 A28 3c lilac 1.00 .45
115 A28 4c lilac, I 3.00 .45
116 A28 4c lilac, II 21.00 14.00
117 A28 6c lilac, I 20.00 5.00
118 A28 6c lilac, II 3.00 3.00
119 A28 8c lilac 1.75 .80
120 A28 10c lilac 6.00 2.00
121 A28 20c lilac 16.00 10.00
122 A28 40c lilac 20.00 15.00
123 A28 72c lilac 32.50 32.50
124 A28 $1 green 400.00 400.00
125 A28 $2 green 175.00 175.00
126 A28 $3 green 110.00 110.00
127 A28 $4 green, I 375.00 375.00
127A A28 $4 green, II 900.00 900.00
128 A28 $5 green 225.00 200.00
Nos. 112-128 (18) 2,312. 2,244.

For surcharges see Nos.129, 148-151B.

No. 113 Surcharged "2" in Red

1889

129 A29 2c on 2c lilac .80 .40

Inverted and double surcharges of "2" were privately made.

A30

A31

1889-1903 **Typo.**

130 A30 1c lilac & gray 1.75 1.00
131 A30 1c green ('90) .50 .20
131A A30 1c gray grn ('00) 3.25 1.75
132 A30 2c lilac & org 1.50 .20
133 A30 2c lil & rose ('00) 3.25 .25
134 A30 2c vio & blk, *red* ('01) 1.10 .90
135 A30 4c lilac & ultra 4.00 1.25
a. 4c lilac & blue 12.00 2.00
136 A30 5c ultra ('91) 2.75 .25
137 A30 6c lilac & mar 6.00 6.00
a. 6c lilac & brown 30.00 8.50
138 A30 6c gray blk & ultra ('02) 6.00 *10.00*
139 A30 8c lilac & rose 8.00 .75
140 A30 8c lil & blk ('90) 3.00 2.25
141 A30 12c lilac & vio 8.00 1.75
142 A30 24c lilac & grn 7.00 2.25
143 A30 48c lilac & ver 15.00 8.50
144 A30 48c dk gray & lil brn ('01) 27.50 27.50
a. 48c gray & purple brown 50.00 35.00
145 A30 60c gray grn & car ('03) 60.00 *65.00*
146 A30 72c lil & org brn 25.00 *30.00*
a. 72c lilac & yellow brown 70.00 *75.00*
147 A30 96c lilac & carmine 70.00 *75.00*
a. 96c lilac & rose 75.00 *80.00*
Nos. 130-147 (19) 253.60 *234.80*

Stamps of the 1889-1903 issue with pen or revenue cancellation sell for a small fraction of the above quotations.
See Nos. 160-177.

Red Surcharge

1890

148 A31 1c on $1 grn & blk 1.00 .40
a. Double surcharge *80.00 80.00*
149 A31 1c on $2 grn & blk .55 .55
a. Double surcharge *80.00 80.00*
150 A31 1c on $3 grn & blk 1.50 1.25
a. Double surcharge *90.00 90.00*
151 A31 1c on $4 grn & blk, type I 2.00 *5.00*
a. Double surcharge *80.00*
151B A31 1c on $4 grn & blk, type II 10.00 *22.50*
c. Double surcharge
Nos. 148-151B (5) 15.05 *29.70*

Mt. Roraima
A32

Kaieteur (Old Man's) Falls — A33

1898 **Wmk. 1** **Engr.**

152 A32 1c car & gray blk 2.75 .90
153 A33 2c indigo & brn 6.00 1.00
a. Horiz. pair, imperf. between 4,500.
b. 2c blue & brown 15.00 1.50
154 A32 5c brown & grn 25.00 5.00
155 A33 10c red & blue blk 14.00 *20.00*
156 A32 15c blue & red brn 22.50 15.00
Nos. 152-156 (5) 70.25 41.90

60th anniv. of Queen Victoria's accession to the throne.

Nos. 154-156 Surcharged in Black **TWO CENTS.**

1899

157 A32 2c on 5c brn & grn 2.00 1.60
a. Without period 60.00 60.00
158 A33 2c on 10c red & bl black 1.00 *1.50*
a. "GENTS" 55.00 *75.00*
b. Inverted surcharge *300.00 350.00*
c. Without period 22.50 *45.00*
159 A32 2c on 15c bl & red brown 1.50 1.50
a. Without period 50.00 *55.00*
b. Double surcharge *425.00 525.00*
c. Inverted surcharge 300.00 *350.00*
Nos. 157-159 (3) 4.50 4.60

There are many slight errors in the setting of this surcharge, such as: small "E" in "CENTS"; no period and narrow "C"; comma between "T" and "S"; dash between "TWO" and "CENTS"; comma between "N" and "T."

Ship Type of 1889-1903

1905-10 **Wmk. 3**

Chalky Paper

160 A30 1c gray green 1.50 .30
a. 1c blue green, ordinary paper ('10) 3.50 1.50
b. Booklet pane of 6
161 A30 2c vio & blk, *red* 2.50 .20
162 A30 4c lilac & ultra 12.00 8.50
163 A30 5c lil & blue, *bl* 7.75 3.75
164 A30 6c gray black & ultra 14.00 *20.00*
165 A30 12c lilac & vio 17.50 *27.50*
166 A30 24c lil & grn ('06) 3.50 *4.25*
167 A30 48c gray & vio brn 11.00 *17.50*
168 A30 60c gray grn & car rose 12.50 *55.00*
169 A30 72c lil & org brn ('07) 32.50 *60.00*
170 A30 96c blk & red, *yel* ('06) 35.00 *42.50*
Nos. 160-170 (11) 149.75 *239.50*

The 2c-60c exist on ordinary paper.

A34

George V — A35

Black Overprint

171 A34 $2.40 grn & vio *190.00 190.00*

Ship Type of 1889-1903
Ordinary Paper

TWO CENTS
Type I - Only the upper right corner of the flag touches the mast.
Type II - The entire right side of the flag touches the mast.

1907

172 A30 2c red, type I 3.75 .30
b. 2c red, type II 1.00 .25
174 A30 4c brown & vio 3.25 1.60
175 A30 5c blue 5.00 .70
176 A30 6c gray & black 12.50 5.00
177 A30 12c orange & vio 5.50 5.00
Nos. 172-177 (5) 30.00 12.60

1913-16 *Perf. 14*

178 A35 1c green 1.75 .20
179 A35 2c scarlet .85 .20
a. 2c carmine .65 .20
180 A35 4c brn & red vio 1.10 .40
181 A35 5c ultra 1.10 .45
182 A35 6c gray & black 1.10 .95
183 A35 12c org & vio 1.50 1.50

Chalky Paper

184 A35 24c dl vio & grn 2.50 2.50
185 A35 48c blk & vio brn 6.00 6.00
186 A35 60c grn & car 13.00 *19.00*
187 A35 72c dl vio & org brn 24.00 *30.00*

Surface Colored Paper

188 A35 96c blk & red, *yel* 24.00 *30.00*

Paper Colored Through

189 A35 96c blk & red, *yel* ('16) 17.00 *21.00*
Nos. 178-189 (12) 93.90 *112.20*

The 72c and late printings of the 2c and 5c are from redrawn dies. The ruled lines behind the value are thin and faint, making the tablet appear lighter than before. The shading lines in other parts of the stamps are also lighter.

1921-27 **Wmk. 4**

191 A35 1c green 1.75 .25
192 A35 2c rose red 1.50 .20
193 A35 2c dp vio ('23) .90 .20
194 A35 4c brn & vio 2.00 .20
195 A35 6c ultra 1.60 .25
196 A35 12c org & vio 1.60 1.40

Chalky Paper

197 A35 24c dl vio & grn 2.75 2.75
198 A35 48c blk & vio brn ('26) 7.50 2.75
199 A35 60c grn & car ('26) 7.50 *25.00*
200 A35 72c dl vio & brn org 9.00 *22.50*
201 A35 96c blk & red, *yel* ('27) 12.50 *20.00*
Nos. 191-201 (11) 48.60 *75.50*

Plowing a Rice Field — A36

Indian Shooting Fish — A37

Kaieteur Falls — A38

Georgetown, Public Buildings — A39

1931, July 21 **Engr.** *Perf. 12½*

205 A36 1c blue green 1.25 .50
206 A37 2c dk brown 1.25 .45
207 A38 4c car rose 2.75 1.75

208 A39 6c ultra 2.25 *2.50*
209 A38 $1 violet 24.00 *30.00*
Nos. 205-209 (5) 31.50 *35.20*

Cent. of the union of Berbice, Demerara and Essequibo to form the Colony of British Guiana.

A40

A41

Gold Mining — A42

Shooting Logs over Falls — A44

Kaieteur Falls — A43

Stabroek Market — A45

Sugar Cane in Punts — A46

Forest Road — A47

Victoria Regia Lilies — A48

Mt. Roraima — A49

Sir Walter Raleigh and Son — A50

Botanical Gardens — A51

1934, Oct. 1 ***Perf. 12½***
210 A40 1c green .40 .25
211 A41 2c brown .75 .20
212 A42 3c carmine .30 .20
b. Perf. 12½x13½ ('43) .30 .20
c. Perf. 13x13½ ('49) .30 .20
213 A43 4c vio black 1.50 .50
a. Vert. pair, imperf. horiz. — *8,000.*
214 A44 6c dp ultra 2.00 1.75
215 A45 12c orange .20 .20
a. Perf. 13½x13 ('51) .20 *.40*
216 A46 24c rose violet 3.00 1.75
217 A47 48c black 10.50 9.25
218 A43 50c green 12.00 *15.00*
219 A48 60c brown 21.00 *24.00*
220 A49 72c rose violet 1.25 1.00
221 A50 96c black 20.00 *25.00*
222 A51 $1 violet 25.00 22.50
Nos. 210-222 (13) 97.90 *101.60*

See Nos. 236, 238, 240.

Common Design Types pictured following the introduction.

Silver Jubilee Issue
Common Design Type

1935, May 6 ***Perf. 13½x14***
223 CD301 2c gray blk & ultra .20 .20
224 CD301 6c blue & brown .85 .40
225 CD301 12c indigo & grn 1.40 1.00
226 CD301 24c brt vio & ind 3.25 3.25
Nos. 223-226 (4) 5.70 4.85

Coronation Issue
Common Design Type

1937, May 12 ***Perf. 13½x14***
227 CD302 2c brown .20 .20
228 CD302 4c gray black .20 .20
229 CD302 6c bright ultra .20 .20
Nos. 227-229 (3) .60 .60

A52

A53

A54

A56

A55

A57

A58

Victoria Regia Lilies and Jacanas — A59

1938-52 Engr. Wmk. 4 ***Perf. 12½***
230 A52 1c green .20 .20
b. Perf. 14x13 ('49) .20 *.65*
231 A53 2c violet blk, perf. 13x14 ('49) .20 .20
b. Perf. 12½ .45 .20
232 A54 4c black & rose, perf. 13x14 ('52) .35 .20
a. Perf. 12½ .55 .20
c. Vert. pair, imperf. between 6,500. 6,000.
233 A55 6c deep ultra, perf. 13x14 ('49) .20 .20
a. Perf. 12½ .30 .20
234 A56 24c deep green .95 .20
a. Wmk. upright 20.00 8.75
235 A53 36c purple 1.40 .20
a. Perf. 13x14 ('51) 1.90 .25
236 A47 48c orange yel .45 .35
a. Perf. 14x13 ('51) 1.10 1.10
237 A57 60c brown 8.50 3.00
238 A50 96c brown vio 1.90 *2.25*
a. Perf. 12½x13½ ('44) 3.00 *3.50*
239 A58 $1 deep violet 7.75 .30
a. Perf. 14x13 ('51) 225.00 *300.00*
240 A49 $2 rose vio ('45) 3.25 *11.00*
a. Perf. 14x13 ('50) 6.00 *11.00*
241 A59 $3 orange brn ('45) 19.00 *21.00*
a. Perf. 14x13 ('52) 17.50 *37.50*
Nos. 230-241 (12) 44.15 *39.10*

The watermark on No. 234 is sideways.

Catalogue values for unused stamps in this section, from this point to the end of the section, are for Never Hinged items.

Peace Issue
Common Design Type

1946, Oct. 21 ***Perf. 13½x14***
242 CD303 3c carmine .20 .20
243 CD303 6c deep blue .20 .20

Silver Wedding Issue
Common Design Types

1948, Dec. 20 Photo. ***Perf. 14x14½***
244 CD304 3c scarlet .20 .20

Engr.
Perf. 11½x11
245 CD305 $3 orange brown 11.00 *17.00*

UPU Issue
Common Design Types
Engr.; Name Typo. on 6c and 12c
Perf. 13½, 11x11½

1949, Oct. 10 **Wmk. 4**
246 CD306 4c rose carmine .35 .20
247 CD307 6c indigo .55 .55
248 CD308 12c orange .70 .70
249 CD309 24c blue green 1.40 1.40
Nos. 246-249 (4) 3.00 2.85

University Issue
Common Design Types

1951, Feb. 16 Engr. ***Perf. 14x14½***
250 CD310 3c carmine & black .30 .20
251 CD311 6c dp ultra & black .40 .40

Coronation Issue
Common Design Type

1953, June 2 ***Perf. 13½x13***
252 CD312 4c carmine & black .20 .20

G. P. O., Georgetown — A60

Indian Shooting Fish — A61

Designs: 2c, Botanical gardens. 3c, Victoria regia lilies and jacanas. 5c, Map. 6c, Rice combine. 8c, Sugar cane entering factory. 12c, Felling greenheart tree. 24c, Bauxite mining. 36c, Mt. Roraima. 48c, Kaieteur Falls. 72c, Arapaima (fish). $1, Toucan. $2, Dredging gold. $5, Coat of Arms.

Engr., Center Litho. on $1
Perf. 12½x13, 13

1954, Dec. 1 **Wmk. 4**
253 A60 1c black .20 .20
254 A60 2c dark green .20 .20
255 A60 3c red brn & ol 2.50 .20
256 A61 4c violet .20 .20
257 A60 5c black & red .25 .20
258 A60 6c yellow green .20 .20
259 A60 8c ultramarine .20 .20
260 A61 12c brown & black .50 .30
261 A60 24c orange & black 3.50 .20
262 A60 36c black & rose 1.25 .45
263 A61 48c red brn & ultra .60 .35
264 A61 72c emerald & rose 9.50 2.00
265 A60 $1 blk, yel, grn & sal 10.00 1.90
266 A60 $2 magenta 10.00 3.25
267 A61 $5 black & ultra 10.50 *12.00*
Nos. 253-267 (15) 49.60 21.85

See Nos. 279-287.

Clasped Hands — A62

Perf. 14½x14
1961, Oct. 23 Photo. Wmk. 314
268 A62 5c sal pink & brown .20 .20
269 A62 6c lt blue grn & brown .20 .20
270 A62 30c lt orange & brown .40 .40
Nos. 268-270 (3) .80 .80

Fourth annual History and Culture Week.

Freedom from Hunger Issue
Common Design Type

1963, June 4 ***Perf. 14x14½***
271 CD314 20c lilac .45 .45

Red Cross Centenary Issue
Common Design Type
Wmk. 314

1963, Sept. 2 Litho. ***Perf. 13***
272 CD315 5c black & red .20 .20
273 CD315 20c ultra & red .65 .65

Queen Types of 1954
Engr.; Center Litho. on $1
Perf. 12½x13, 13

1963-65 **Wmk. 314**
279 A60 3c red brn & ol ('65) 4.75 4.75
280 A60 5c black & red ('64) .20 .20
281 A61 12c brown & blk ('64) .20 .20
282 A60 24c orange & black 1.50 .20
283 A60 36c black & rose .50 .20
284 A61 48c red brn & ultra 1.00 *2.00*
285 A61 72c emerald & rose 3.25 *16.00*
286 A60 $1 blk, yel, grn & sal 5.75 .75
287 A60 $2 magenta 6.25 *12.50*
Nos. 279-287 (9) 23.40 *36.80*

Weight Lifter A63

1964, Oct. 1 Photo. ***Perf. 13x13½***
290 A63 5c orange .20 .20
291 A63 8c blue .20 .20
292 A63 25c carmine rose .40 .40
Nos. 290-292 (3) .80 .80

18th Olympic Games, Tokyo, Oct. 10-25.

ITU Issue
Common Design Type
Perf. 11x11½

1965, May 17 Litho. Wmk. 314
293 CD317 5c emerald & olive .20 .20
294 CD317 25c lt blue & brt pink .45 .45

Intl. Cooperation Year Issue
Common Design Type

1965, Oct. 25 Wmk. 314 ***Perf. 14½***
295 CD318 5c blue grn & claret .20 .20
296 CD318 25c lt vio & green .50 .50

Winston Churchill and St. George's Cathedral, Georgetown — A64

1966, Jan. 24 Photo. ***Perf. 14x14½***
297 A64 5c multicolored .20 .20
298 A64 25c dp blue, blk & gold .60 .50

Sir Winston Leonard Spencer Churchill (1874-1965), statesman and WWII leader.

Royal Visit Issue
Common Design Type

1966, Feb. 4 Litho. ***Perf. 11x12***
299 CD320 3c violet blue .25 .20
300 CD320 25c dark car rose 1.40 1.10

POSTAGE DUE STAMPS

Catalogue values for unused stamps in this section are for Never Hinged items.

D1

Perf. 13½x14

1940-52 Typo. Wmk. 4

J1 D1 1c green 1.25 1.25
a. Wmk. 4a (error) 40.00
J2 D1 2c black 1.25 1.25
a. Wmk. 4a (error) 35.00
J3 D1 4c ultra ('52) .80 *1.50*
a. Wmk. 4a (error) 35.00
J4 D1 12c carmine 3.50 *7.50*
Nos. J1-J4 (4) 6.80 *11.50*

The 2c and 12c are on chalky paper as well as ordinary paper.

WAR TAX STAMP

Regular Issue No. 179 Overprinted **War Tax**

1918, Jan. 4 Wmk. 3 ***Perf. 14***

MR1 A35 2c scarlet .20 .20

OFFICIAL STAMPS

Counterfeit overprints exist.

No. 50 Overprinted in Red **OFFICIAL**

1875 Unwmk. ***Perf. 10***

O1 A5 1c black 40.00 16.00
a. Horiz. pair, imperf btwn. —

Nos. 51, 53-54, 68 Overprinted in Black **OFFICIAL**

O2 A5 2c orange 140.00 16.00
O3 A5 8c rose 375.00 125.00
O4 A5 12c lilac 1,400. 550.00
O5 A12 24c green 850.00 275.00

For surcharges see Nos. 87, 89, 89A, 96, 102.

Nos. 72-76 Overprinted "OFFICIAL" Similar to #O2-O5

1877 Wmk. 1 ***Perf. 14***

O6 A13 1c slate 225.00 95.00
a. Vert. pair, imperf btwn. —
O7 A13 2c orange 90.00 16.00
O8 A13 4c ultramarine 100.00 35.00
O9 A13 6c chocolate 2,750. 625.00
O10 A13 8c rose 2,250. 500.00

The type A13 12c lilac, 24c green and 48c red brown overprinted "OFFICIAL" were never placed in use. A few copies of the 12c and 24c have been seen but the 48c is only known surcharged with new value for provisional use in 1881.

See #97-101. For surcharges see #85-86, 88A, 90-91.

BRITISH HONDURAS

'bri-tish hän-'dur-əs

LOCATION — Central America bordering on Caribbean on east, Mexico on north and Guatemala on west.
GOVT. — British Crown Colony
AREA — 8,867 sq. mi.
POP. — 130,000 (est. 1972)
CAPITAL — Belmopan

Before British Honduras became a colony (subordinate to Jamaica) in 1862, it was a settlement under British influence. In 1884 it became an independent colony. In 1973 the colony changed its name to Belize.

12 Pence = 1 Shilling
100 Cents = 1 Dollar (1888)

Catalogue values for unused stamps in this country are for Never Hinged items, beginning with Scott 127 in the regular postage section, Scott J1 in the postage due section.

Values for unused stamps are for examples with original gum as defined in the catalogue introduction. Very fine examples of Nos. 1-37 will have perforations touching the design on at least one side due to the narrow spacing of the stamps on the plates. Stamps with perfs clear of the design on all four sides are extremely scarce and will command higher prices.

Queen Victoria — A1

1866 Unwmk. Typo. ***Perf. 14***

1 A1 1p pale blue 50.00 50.00
a. Horiz. pair, imperf. btwn.
2 A1 6p rose 250.00 100.00
3 A1 1sh green 250.00 100.00
Nos. 1-3 (3) 550.00 250.00

The 6p and 1sh were printed only in a sheet with the 1p. The 1sh is known in se-tenant gutter pairs with the 1p and the 6p.

1872 Wmk. 1 ***Perf. 12½***

4 A1 1p blue 60.00 18.00
5 A1 3p brown 100.00 70.00
6 A1 6p rose 190.00 30.00
7 A1 1sh green 225.00 22.50
a. Horiz. pair, imperf. btwn. 12,500.
Nos. 4-7 (4) 575.00 140.50

For surcharges see Nos. 18-19. No. 7a is unique and has faults.

1877-79 ***Perf. 14***

8 A1 1p blue 50.00 14.00
a. Horiz. strip of 3, imperf. btwn. 4,500.
9 A1 3p brown 85.00 17.50
10 A1 4p violet ('79) 125.00 12.50
11 A1 6p rose ('78) 300.00 175.00
12 A1 1sh green 225.00 12.50
Nos. 8-12 (5) 785.00 231.50

For surcharges see Nos. 20-21, 29.

1882-87 Wmk. 2

13 A1 1p blue ('84) 40.00 18.00
14 A1 1p rose ('84) 20.00 12.50
a. Diag. half used as ½p on cover
15 A1 4p violet 70.00 4.00
16 A1 6p yellow ('85) 250.00 175.00
17 A1 1sh gray ('87) 250.00 150.00
Nos. 13-17 (5) 630.00 359.50

For surcharges see Nos. 22-26, 28-35.

Stamps of 1872-87 Surcharged in Black **2 CENTS**

1888 Wmk. 1 ***Perf. 12½***

18 A1 2c on 6p rose 120.00 100.00
19 A1 3c on 3p brown 10,000. 5,250.

Perf. 14

20 A1 2c on 6p rose 70.00 65.00
a. Diagonal half used as 1c on cover 225.00
b. Double surcharge 1,300. 1,300.
c. "2" with curved tail 850.00 850.00
21 A1 3c on 3p brown 60.00 55.00

Wmk. 2

22 A1 2c on 1p rose 9.00 *17.50*
a. Diagonal half used as 1c on cover 250.00
b. Double surcharge 1,000. 950.00
c. Inverted surcharge 1,300. 1,250.
23 A1 10c on 4p violet 35.00 15.00
a. Inverted surcharge —
24 A1 20c on 6p yellow 27.50 *30.00*
25 A1 50c on 1sh gray 350.00 *500.00*

No. 25 with Additional Surcharge in Red or Black **TWO**

26 A1 2c (R) on 50c on 1sh gray 40.00 *75.00*
a. "TWO" in black 8,750. 8,500.
b. "TWO" double (Blk + R) 8,750. 8,000.
c. Diagonal half used as 1c on cover 325.00

Stamps of 1872-87 Surcharged in Black

c **2 CENTS**

1888-89

28 A1 2c on 1p rose .50 *1.25*
a. Diagonal half used as 1c on cover 110.00
29 A1 3c on 3p brown 1.25 *1.50*
30 A1 10c on 4p violet 2.50 *1.75*
31 A1 20c on 6p yel ('89) 10.00 *15.00*
32 A1 50c on 1sh gray 20.00 *50.00*
Nos. 28-32 (5) 34.25 *69.50*

For other examples of this surcharge see Nos. 36, 47. For overprint see No. 51.

No. 30 with Additional Surcharge in Black or Red **6**

1891

33 A1 6c (Blk) on 10c on 4p 1.00 *3.75*
a. "6" and bar inverted 3,000. 900.
b. "6" only inverted 3,000.
34 A1 6c (R) on 10c on 4p .75 *2.50*
a. "6" and bar inverted 500. 500.
b. "6" only inverted 3,000.

Stamps similar to No. 33 but with "SIX" instead of "6," both with and without bar, were prepared but not regularly issued.

See No. 37.

No. 29 with Additional Surcharge in Black **FIVE**

35 A1 5c on 3c on 3p brown 1.50 *3.25*
a. Double surcharge of "Five" and bar 200.00 *250.00*

Black Surcharge, Type "c"

36 A1 6c on 3p blue 1.50 *7.50*

No. 36 with Additional Surcharge like Nos. 33-34 in Red

1891

37 A1 15c (R) on 6c on 3p blue 7.50 *20.00*
a. Double surcharge

A8

A9

1891-98 Wmk. 2 ***Perf. 14***

38 A8 1c green 1.00 1.00
39 A8 2c carmine rose 1.00 .25
40 A8 3c brown 3.75 1.50
41 A8 5c ultra ('95) 12.50 .90
42 A8 6c ultramarine 3.50 1.00
43 A8 10c vio & grn ('95) 8.50 8.50
44 A8 12c vio & green 3.50 2.50
45 A8 24c yellow & blue 6.00 *12.50*
46 A8 25c red brn & grn ('98) 30.00 *60.00*
Nos. 38-46 (9) 69.75 *88.15*

Numeral tablet on Nos. 43-46 has lined background with colorless value and "c."

For overprints see Nos. 48-50.

Type of 1866 Surcharged Type "c"

1892

47 A1 1c on 1p green .30 *.80*

Regular Issue Overprinted REVENUE in Black

1899

48 A8 5c ultramarine 4.50 2.25
a. "BEVENUE" 70.00 *80.00*
49 A8 10c lilac & green 3.50 *11.00*
a. "BEVENUE" 190.00 *225.00*
50 A8 25c red brn & grn 3.00 *25.00*
a. "BEVENUE" 140.00 *140.00*
51 A1 50c on 1sh gray (No. 32) 140.00 *275.00*
a. "BEVENUE" 2,750. 2,750.
Nos. 48-51 (4) 151.00 *313.25*

The overprint is found in two lengths: 12mm (43 to the pane) and 11mm (17 to the pane). The "U" is found in both a tall, narrow type and the more common small type.

1899-1901

52 A9 5c gray blk & ultra, *bl* ('00) 7.50 1.50
53 A9 10c vio & grn ('01) 6.50 *6.50*
54 A9 50c grn & car rose 16.00 *37.50*
55 A9 $1 grn & car rose 35.00 *60.00*
56 A9 $2 green & ultra 55.00 *75.00*
57 A9 $5 green & black 225.00 *275.00*
Nos. 52-57 (6) 345.00 *455.50*

Numeral tablet on Nos. 53-54 has lined background with colorless value and "c."

King Edward VII — A10

1902-04 Typo. Wmk. 2

58 A10 1c gray grn & grn ('04) 4.00 *12.50*
59 A10 2c vio & blk, *red* 2.00 .35
60 A10 5c gray blk & ultra, *blue* 3.00 .80
61 A10 20c dl vio & vio ('04) 5.00 *12.00*
Nos. 58-61 (4) 14.00 *25.65*

1904-06 Chalky Paper Wmk. 3

62 A10 1c green .30 *.50*
63 A10 2c vio & blk, *red* 1.25 .20
64 A10 5c blk & ultra, *bl* ('05) 1.75 .30
65 A10 10c vio & grn ('06) 4.00 *9.00*
67 A10 25c vio & org ('06) 6.00 *25.00*
68 A10 50c grn & car rose ('06) 10.00 *35.00*
69 A10 $1 grn & car rose ('06) 25.00 *50.00*
70 A10 $2 grn & ultra ('06) 55.00 *100.00*
71 A10 $5 grn & blk ('06) 190.00 *225.00*
Nos. 62-71 (9) 293.30 *445.00*

The 1c and 2c exist also on ordinary paper.

1909

Ordinary Paper

72 A10 2c carmine 3.00 .25
73 A10 5c ultramarine 3.00 .25

1911

74 A10 25c black, *green* 6.00 *27.50*

Numeral tablet on #61, 65-68, 74 has lined background with colorless value and "c."

King George V
A11 A12

1913-17 Wmk. 3 ***Perf. 14***

75 A11 1c green 1.00 .40
76 A11 2c scarlet 1.10 .30
a. 2c carmine .90 .95
77 A11 3c orange ('17) .45 .20
78 A11 5c ultra 2.25 1.25

Chalky Paper

79 A12 10c dl vio & ol grn 2.50 *5.00*
80 A12 25c blk, *gray grn* 3.75 *7.50*
a. 25c black, *emerald* 2.50 *12.50*
b. 25c blk, *bl grn, olive back* 3.25 *6.00*
81 A12 50c vio & ultra, *bl* 4.50 *9.00*
82 A11 $1 black & scar 8.00 *17.50*
83 A11 $2 grn & dull vio 32.50 *37.50*
84 A11 $5 vio & blk, *red* 225.00 *250.00*
Nos. 75-84 (10) 281.05 *328.65*

See No. 91. For overprints see Nos. MR2-MR5.

With Moire Overprint in Violet

1915

85 A11 1c green 1.50 *7.50*
86 A11 2c carmine 1.10 *2.00*
87 A11 5c ultramarine .75 *3.25*
Nos. 85-87 (3) 3.35 *12.75*

For overprint see No. MR1.

Peace Commemorative Issue

Seal of Colony and George V — A13

1921, Apr. 28 **Engr.**
89 A13 2c carmine 2.50 1.00

Similar to A13 but without "Peace Peace"

1922 **Wmk. 4**
90 A13 4c dark gray 2.75 .95

Type of 1913-17

1921 **Typo.** **Wmk. 4**
91 A11 1c green 2.00 *5.00*

A14

1922-33 **Typo.** **Wmk. 4**

92	A14	1c green ('29)	.80	*1.10*
93	A14	2c dark brown	.35	.20
94	A14	2c rose red ('27)	.85	.70
95	A14	3c orange ('33)	3.50	1.00
96	A14	4c gray ('29)	1.25	.25
97	A14	5c ultramarine	1.00	.20

Chalky Paper

98	A14	10c olive grn & lil	1.25	.35
99	A14	25c black, *emerald*	1.50	*4.00*
100	A14	50c ultra & vio, *bl*	4.00	*9.00*
101	A14	$1 scarlet & blk	6.50	*12.50*
102	A14	$2 red vio & grn	22.50	*50.00*

Wmk. 3

103	A14	25c black, *emerald*	4.25	*17.50*
104	A14	$5 blk & vio, *red*	200.00	*190.00*
		Nos. 92-104 (13)	247.75	*286.80*

For surcharges see Nos. B1-B5.

Common Design Types pictured following the introduction.

Silver Jubilee Issue
Common Design Type
Perf. 11x12

1935, May 6 **Engr.** **Wmk. 4**

108	CD301	3c black & ultra	.65	.60
109	CD301	4c indigo & grn	1.10	*1.40*
110	CD301	5c ultra & brn	2.00	2.00
111	CD301	25c brn vio & ind	4.00	*6.00*
		Nos. 108-111 (4)	7.75	*10.00*
		Set, never hinged	12.00	

Coronation Issue
Common Design Type

1937, May 12 ***Perf. 13½x14***

112	CD302	3c deep orange	.20	.20
113	CD302	4c gray black	.25	.20
114	CD302	5c bright ultra	.25	.35
		Nos. 112-114 (3)	.70	.75
		Set, never hinged	1.75	

Mayan Figures A15

Chicle Tapping — A16

Cohune Palm — A17

Local Products A18

Grapefruit Industry A19

Mahogany Logs in River — A20

Sergeant's Cay — A21

Dory — A22

Chicle Industry A23

Court House, Belize — A24

Mahogany Cutting — A25

Seal of Colony — A26

1938 ***Perf. 11x11½, 11½x11***

115	A15	1c green & violet	.20	*.70*
116	A16	2c car & black	.20	*.70*
a.		Perf. 12 ('47)	1.10	.75
117	A17	3c brown & dk vio	.20	*.50*
118	A18	4c green & black	.20	*.50*
119	A19	5c slate bl & red vio	.35	.30
120	A20	10c brown & yel grn	.45	*.50*
121	A21	15c blue & brown	.65	.50
122	A22	25c green & ultra	1.10	.85
123	A23	50c dk vio & blk	7.00	2.50
124	A24	$1 ol green & car	12.50	5.25
125	A25	$2 rose lake & ind	14.00	13.00
126	A26	$5 brn & carmine	13.00	*19.00*
		Nos. 115-126 (12)	49.85	*44.30*
		Set, never hinged	70.00	

Issued: 3c-5c, 1/10; 1c, 2c, 10c-50c, 2/14; $1-$5, 2/28.

Catalogue values for unused stamps in this section, from this point to the end of the section, are for Never Hinged items.

Peace Issue
Common Design Type
Perf. 13½x14

1946, Sept. 9 **Engr.** **Wmk. 4**

127	CD303	3c brown	.20	.20
128	CD303	5c deep blue	.20	.20

Silver Wedding Issue
Common Design Types

1948, Oct. 1 **Photo.** ***Perf. 14x14½***
129 CD304 4c dark green .20 .20

Engraved; Name Typographed
Perf. 11½x11
130 CD305 $5 light brown 22.50 *25.00*

St. George's Cay — A27

H.M.S. Merlin — A28

1949, Jan. 10 **Engr.** ***Perf. 12½***

131	A27	1c green & ultra	.20	.20
132	A27	3c yel brn & dp blue	.20	.20
133	A27	4c purple & brn ol	.30	.30
134	A28	5c dk blue & brown	.30	.30
135	A28	10c vio brn & blue grn	.50	.50
136	A28	15c ultra & emerald	.90	.90
		Nos. 131-136 (6)	2.40	2.40

Battle of St. George's Cay, 150th anniv.

UPU Issue
Common Design Types
Perf. 13½, 11x11½

1949, Oct. 10 **Engr.** **Wmk. 4**

137	CD306	4c blue green	.35	.35
138	CD307	5c indigo	.55	.55
139	CD308	10c chocolate	.90	.90
140	CD309	25c blue	1.50	1.50
		Nos. 137-140 (4)	3.30	3.30

University Issue
Common Design Types

1951, Feb. 16 **Engr.** ***Perf. 14x14½***

141	CD310	3c choc & purple	.35	.35
142	CD311	10c choc & green	.65	.65

Coronation Issue
Common Design Type

1953, June 2 ***Perf. 13½x13***
143 CD312 4c dk green & black .40 .40

Arms — A29

Maya — A30

Designs: 2c, Tapir. 3c, Legislative Council Chamber and mace. 4c, Pine industry. 5c, Spiny lobster. 10c, Stanley Field Airport. 15c, Mayan frieze. 25c, Blue butterfly. $1, Armadillo. $2, Hawkesworth Bridge. $5, Pine Ridge orchid.

1953-57 **Engr.** ***Perf. 13½***

144	A29	1c gray blk & green	.25	.20
145	A29	2c gray blk & brn, perf. 14 ('57)	.25	.20
a.		Perf. 13½	.35	.30
146	A29	3c mag & rose lil, perf. 14 ('57)	.25	.20
a.		Perf. 13½	.25	.20
147	A29	4c grn & dk brn	.25	.20
148	A29	5c car & ol brn, perf. 14 ('57)	.25	.20
a.		Perf. 13½	.50	.45
149	A29	10c ultra & bl gray	.25	.20
150	A29	15c vio & yel grn	.30	*.35*
151	A29	25c brown & ultra	3.75	1.75
152	A30	50c purple & brown	4.25	1.60
153	A29	$1 red brn & sl bl	4.25	3.50
154	A29	$2 gray & car	6.00	4.00
155	A30	$5 blue gray & pur	26.00	15.00
		Nos. 144-155 (12)	46.05	27.40

Issued: 5c, 5/15; 2c, 3c, 9/18, perf. 13½, 9/2.
For overprints see Nos. 159-166.

View of Belize, 1842 — A31

Designs: 10c, Public seals, 1860 and 1960. 15c, Tamarind Tree, Newtown Barracks.

Perf. 11½x11

1960, July 1 **Wmk. 314**

156	A31	2c green	.20	.20
157	A31	10c carmine	.25	.25
158	A31	15c blue	.45	.45
		Nos. 156-158 (3)	.90	.90

Cent. of the establishment of a local PO.

Nos. 145-146 and 149-150 Overprinted: "NEW CONSTITUTION/1960"

1961, Mar. 1 **Wmk. 4** ***Perf. 14, 13***

159	A29	2c gray black & brn	.20	.20
160	A29	3c mag & rose lilac	.20	.20
161	A29	10c ultra & blue gray	.35	.25
162	A29	15c violet & yel green	.50	.35
		Nos. 159-162 (4)	1.25	1.00

Nos. 144, 149, 151 and 152 Overprinted: "HURRICANE/HATTIE"

1962, Jan. 15 ***Perf. 13***

163	A29	1c gray black & green	.20	.20
164	A29	10c ultra & blue gray	.20	.20
165	A29	25c brown & ultra	.30	.30
166	A30	50c purple & brown	.70	.70
		Nos. 163-166 (4)	1.40	1.40

Hurricane Hattie struck Belize, Oct. 31, 1961.

Great Curassow A32

Birds: 2c, Red-legged honeycreeper. 3c, American jacana. 4c, Great kiskadee. 5c, Scarlet-rumped tanager. 10c, Scarlet macaw. 15c, Massena trogon. 25c, Redfooted booby. 50c, Keel-billed toucan. $1, Magnificent frigate bird. $2, Rufoustailed jacamar. $5, Montezuma oropendola.

Perf. 14x14½

1962, Apr. 2 **Photo.** **Wmk. 314**

Birds in Natural Colors; Black Inscriptions

167	A32	1c yellow	.90	.70
168	A32	2c gray	1.40	.20
a.		Green omitted	175.00	
169	A32	3c lt yel green	1.40	.85
a.		Dark grn (legs) omitted	250.00	
170	A32	4c lt gray	2.75	1.25
171	A32	5c buff	1.60	.20
172	A32	10c beige	1.90	.20
a.		Blue omitted	225.00	
173	A32	15c pale lemon	.90	.30
174	A32	25c bluish gray & pink	3.50	.25
175	A32	50c pale blue	5.00	.35
b.		Blue (beak & claw) omitted		
176	A32	$1 blue	7.75	.70
177	A32	$2 pale gray	8.25	2.50
178	A32	$5 light blue	24.00	12.50
		Nos. 167-178 (12)	59.35	20.00

For overprints see Nos. 182-186, 195-199.

1967 **Wmk. 314 Sideways**

Colors as 1962 Issue

167a	A32	1c	.20	.20
168b	A32	2c	.20	.20
170a	A32	4c	.30	.25
171a	A32	5c	.55	.30
172b	A32	10c	.80	.65
173a	A32	15c	1.10	.90
175a	A32	50c	4.25	3.50
		Nos. 167a-175a (7)	7.40	6.00

Issued: 1c, 4c, 5c, 50c, 2/16; 2c, 10c, 15c, 11/28.

Freedom from Hunger Issue
Common Design Type

1963, June 4 ***Perf. 14x14½***
179 CD314 22c green .85 .85

Red Cross Centenary Issue
Common Design Type
Wmk. 314

1963, Sept. 2 **Litho.** ***Perf. 13***

180	CD315	4c black & red	.20	.20
181	CD315	22c ultra & red	1.40	1.40

Nos. 167, 169, 170, 172 and 174 Overprinted: "SELF GOVERNMENT / 1964"

1964 Photo. *Perf. 14x14½*

182 A32 1c multicolored .20 .20
a. Yellow omitted 125.00
183 A32 3c multicolored .20 .20
184 A32 4c multicolored .20 .20
185 A32 10c multicolored .35 .30
186 A32 25c multicolored .65 .55
Nos. 182-186 (5) 1.60 1.45

Attainment of self-government.

ITU Issue
Common Design Type
Perf. 11x11½

1965, May 17 Litho. Wmk. 314

187 CD317 2c ver & green .20 .20
188 CD317 50c yel & red lilac 1.00 1.00

Intl. Cooperation Year Issue
Common Design Type

1965, Oct. 25 *Perf. 14½*

189 CD318 1c bl grn & claret .20 .20
190 CD318 22c lt violet & green .75 .75

Churchill Memorial Issue
Common Design Type

1966, Jan. 24 Photo. *Perf. 14*
Design in Black, Gold and Carmine Rose

191 CD319 1c bright blue .20 .20
192 CD319 4c green .20 .20
193 CD319 22c brown .70 .70
194 CD319 25c violet .90 .90
Nos. 191-194 (4) 2.00 2.00

Bird Type of 1962 Overprinted: "DEDICATION OF SITE / NEW CAPITAL / 9th OCTOBER 1965"

Wmk. 314 Sideways

1966, July 1 *Perf. 14x14½*

195 A32 1c multicolored .20 .20
196 A32 3c multicolored .25 .20
197 A32 4c multicolored .25 .20
198 A32 10c multicolored .30 .25
199 A32 25c multicolored .50 .50
Nos. 195-199 (5) 1.50 1.35

Citrus Grove — A33

10c, Half Moon Cay & Lighthouse Reef. 22c, Hidden Valley Falls & Mountain Pine Ridge. 25c, Xunantunich Mayan ruins in Cayo district.

Perf. 14x14½

1966, Oct. 1 Photo. Wmk. 314

200 A33 5c multicolored .20 .20
201 A33 10c multicolored .20 .20
202 A33 22c multicolored .25 .25
203 A33 25c multicolored .35 .35
Nos. 200-203 (4) 1.00 1.00

1st British Honduras stamp issue, cent.

International Tourist Year — A34

1967, Dec. 4 *Perf. 12½*

204 A34 5c Sailfish .20 .20
205 A34 10c Deer .20 .20
206 A34 22c Jaguar .35 .35
207 A34 25c Tarpon .45 .45
Nos. 204-207 (4) 1.20 1.20

Schomburgkia Tibicinis — A35

Belizean Patriots' Memorial, Belize City, and Human Rights Flame — A36

Orchids: 10c, Maxillaria tenuifolia. 22c, Bletia purpurea. 25c, Sobralia macrantha.

Inscribed: "20th Anniversary of E.C.L.A."

Perf. 14½x14

1968, Apr. 16 Photo. Wmk. 314

208 A35 5c violet & multi .20 .20
209 A35 10c green & multi .20 .20
210 A35 22c multicolored .35 .35
211 A35 25c olive & multi .50 .50
Nos. 208-211 (4) 1.25 1.25

20th anniv. of the Economic Commission for Latin America. See #226-229, 255-258.

Perf. 13x13½

1968, July 15 Litho. Wmk. 314

Design: 50c, Mayan motif stele, monument at new capital site and Human Rights flame.

212 A36 22c multicolored .30 .30
213 A36 50c multicolored .70 .70

International Human Rights Year.

Jewfish A37

Designs: 2c, White-lipped peccary. 3c, Grouper (sea bass). 4c, Collared anteater. 5c, Bonefish. 10c, Paca. 15c, Dolphinfish. 25c, Kinkajou. 50c, Yellow-and-green-banded muttonfish. $1, Tayra. $2, Great barracudas. $5, Mountain lion.

Perf. 13x12½

1968, Oct. 15 Litho. Unwmk.

214 A37 1c yellow & multi .20 .20
215 A37 2c brt yel & multi .20 .20
216 A37 3c pink & multi .20 .20
217 A37 4c brt grn & multi .20 .20
218 A37 5c brick red & multi .20 .20
219 A37 10c lilac & multi .20 .20
220 A37 15c org yel & multi .25 .20
221 A37 25c multicolored .45 .40
222 A37 50c bl grn & multi .95 .85
223 A37 $1 ocher & multi 1.90 1.75
224 A37 $2 violet & multi 3.75 3.50
225 A37 $5 ultra & multi 8.25 7.50
Nos. 214-225 (12) 16.75 15.40

See Nos. 234-240, Belize 327-339.
For overprints see Nos. 251-254, 281-282.

Orchid Type of 1968
Inscribed "Orchids of Belize"

Designs: 5c, Rhyncholaetia digbyana. 10c, Cattleya bowringiana. 22c, Lycaste cochleatum. 25c, Coryanthes speciosum.

Perf. 14½x14

1969, Apr. 9 Photo. Wmk. 314

226 A35 5c Prus blue & multi .20 .20
227 A35 10c olive bis & multi .30 .30
228 A35 22c yellow grn & multi .70 .70
229 A35 25c violet blue & multi .80 .80
Nos. 226-229 (4) 2.00 2.00

British Honduras stamps can be mounted in the Scott British Honduras album.

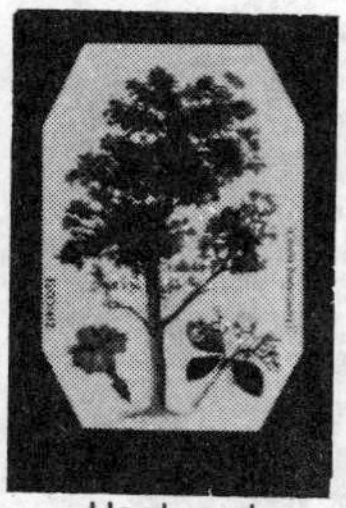
Hardwood Trees — A38

Virgin and Child, by Giovanni Bellini — A39

1969, Sept. 1 Litho. *Perf. 14*

230 A38 5c Ziricote .20 .20
231 A38 10c Rosewood .20 .20
232 A38 22c Mayflower .30 .30
233 A38 25c Mahogany .40 .40
Nos. 230-233 (4) 1.10 1.10

Timber industry of British Honduras. Issued in sheets of 9 (3x3) on simulated wood background.

Fish-Animal Type of 1968

Designs: ½c, Crana (fish). Others as before.

Wmk. 314 Sideways (½c, 2c, $5), Upright (3c, 5c, 10c)

1969-72 Litho. *Perf. 13x12½*

234 A37 ½c vio bl, yel & blk .20 .20
235 A37 ½c citron, blk & bl ('71) .70 *1.00*
236 A37 2c brt yel, blk & grn ('72) 3.00 3.00
237 A37 3c pink & multi ('72) 1.00 *1.60*
a. Wmk. sideways ('72) 3.00 3.00
238 A37 5c brick red & multi ('72) 1.00 *1.60*
239 A37 10c lilac & multi ('72) 1.00 *1.60*
a. Wmk. sideways ('72) 3.50 3.50
240 A37 $5 ultra & multi ('70) 9.00 9.00
Nos. 234-240 (7) 15.90 18.00

For overprints see Nos. 251-252.

1969, Oct. 1 Litho. *Perf. 14*

Christmas: 22c, 25c, Adoration of the Kings, by Veronese.

247 A39 5c multicolored .20 .20
248 A39 15c dp orange & multi .20 .20
249 A39 22c lilac rose & multi .40 .40
250 A39 25c emerald & multi .50 .50
Nos. 247-250 (4) 1.30 1.30

Nos. 238-239 and Type of 1968 Overprinted "POPULATION/ CENSUS 1970"

Wmk. 314 Sideways

1970, Feb. 2 Photo. *Perf. 13x12½*

251 A37 5c brick red & multi .20 .20
252 A37 10c lilac & multi .20 .20
253 A37 15c org yel & multi .25 .25
254 A37 25c multicolored .35 .35
Nos. 251-254 (4) 1.00 1.00

Orchid Type of 1968
Inscribed: "Orchids of Belize"

Wmk. 314

1970, Apr. 2 Litho. *Perf. 14*

255 A35 5c Black .20 .20
256 A35 15c White butterfly .35 .35
257 A35 22c Swan .50 .50
258 A35 25c Butterfly .60 .60
Nos. 255-258 (4) 1.65 1.65

Santa Maria Tree and Wood (Calophyllum Brasiliense) A40

Nativity, by Arthur Hughes A41

Hardwood Trees and Woods: 15c, Nargusta (terminalia amazonia). 22c, Cedar (cedrela mexicana). 25c, Sapodilla (achras sapota).

1970, Sept. 7 *Perf. 14*

259 A40 5c multicolored .20 .20
260 A40 15c multicolored .30 .30
261 A40 22c multicolored .45 .45
262 A40 25c multicolored .45 .45
Nos. 259-262 (4) 1.40 1.40

1970, Nov. 2 *Perf. 14*

Christmas: 5c, 15c, 50c, Mystic Nativity, by Botticelli.

263 A41 ½c black & multi .20 .20
264 A41 5c brown & multi .20 .20
265 A41 10c multicolored .20 .20
266 A41 15c slate bl & multi .25 .25
267 A41 22c dk green & multi .40 .40
268 A41 50c black & multi .85 .85
Nos. 263-268 (6) 2.10 2.10

Legislative Assembly House A42

Designs: 5c, View of South Side of Belize. 10c, Government Plaza, Belmopan. 22c, Magistrates' Court. 25c, Police Headquarters. 50c, New General Post Office.

1971, Jan. 30 Litho. *Perf. 13½x14*
Size: 59x22mm

269 A42 5c multicolored .20 .20
270 A42 10c multicolored .20 .20

Size: 37x21½mm

271 A42 15c multicolored .20 .20
272 A42 22c multicolored .30 .30
273 A42 25c multicolored .40 .40
274 A42 50c multicolored .70 .70
Nos. 269-274 (6) 2.00 2.00

New capital at Belmopan.

Tabebuia Chrysantha — A43

Flowers: 5c, 22c, Hymenocallis littoralis. 10c, 25c, Hippeastrum equestre. 15c, like ½c.

1971, Mar. 27 Litho. *Perf. 14*

275 A43 ½c vio blue & multi .20 .20
276 A43 5c olive & multi .20 .20
277 A43 10c violet & multi .20 .20
278 A43 15c multicolored .30 .30
279 A43 22c multicolored .45 .45
280 A43 25c lt brown & multi .55 .55
Nos. 275-280 (6) 1.90 1.90

Easter.

Type of 1968 Overprinted: "RACIAL EQUALITY / YEAR—1971"

Perf. 13x12½

1971, June 14 Litho. Wmk. 314

281 A37 10c lilac & multi .20 .20
282 A37 50c blue green & multi .70 .70

Intl. year against racial discrimination.

Tubroos (Enterolobium Cyclocarpum) A44

Hardwood Trees of Belize: 15c, Yemeri (Vochysia hondurensis). 26c, Billyweb (Sweetia panamensis). 50c, Logwood (Haematoxylum campechiaum).

1971, Aug. 16 *Perf. 14*
Queen's Head in Silver

283 A44 5c green, brn & blk .20 .20
284 A44 15c multicolored .50 .50
285 A44 26c multicolored .80 .80
286 A44 50c multicolored 1.50 1.50
a. Souvenir sheet of 4, #283-286 5.25 5.25
Nos. 283-286 (4) 3.00 3.00

Verrazano-Narrows Bridge, New York, and Quebec Bridge, Canada — A45

Bridges of the World: ½c, Hawksworth Bridge connecting San Ignacio and Santa Helena and Belcan Bridge, Belize, Br. Honduras. 26c, London Bridge in 1871, and at Lake Havasu City, Ariz., in 1971. 50c, Belize-Mexico Bridge and Belize Swing Bridge.

1971, Sept. 23 **Litho.**

287	A45	½c multicolored	.20	.20
288	A45	5c multicolored	.20	.20
289	A45	26c multicolored	.50	.50
290	A45	50c multicolored	1.10	1.10
		Nos. 287-290 (4)	2.00	2.00

Petrae Volubis — A46

Seated Jade Figure — A47

Wild Flowers: 15c, Vochysia hondurensis. 26c, Tabebuia pentaphylla. 50c, Erythrina americana.

1972, Feb. 28
Flowers in Natural Colors; Black Inscriptions

292	A46	6c lilac & yellow	.20	.20
293	A46	15c lt blue & pale grn	.35	.35
294	A46	26c pink & lt blue	.65	.65
295	A46	50c orange & lt grn	1.25	1.25
		Nos. 292-295 (4)	2.45	2.45

Easter.

Perf. 14x13½, 13½x14
1972, May 22 **Unwmk.**

Mayan Carved Jade, 4th-8th centuries: 6c, Dancing priest. 16c, Sun god's head, horiz. 26c, Priest on throne and sun god's head. 50c, Figure and mask.

296	A47	3c rose red & multi	.20	.20
297	A47	6c vio bl & multi	.20	.20
298	A47	16c brown & multi	.25	.25
299	A47	26c ol grn & multi	.40	.40
300	A47	50c purple & multi	.85	.85
		Nos. 296-300 (5)	1.90	1.90

Black inscription with details of designs on back of stamps.

Banak (Virola Koschnyi) — A48

Hardwood Trees of Belize: 5c, Quamwood (Schizolobium parahybum). 16c, Waika chewstick (Symphonia globulifera). 26c, Mammee-apple (Mammea americana). 50c, My lady (Aspidosperma megalocarpon).

1972, Aug. 21 Wmk. 314 *Perf. 14*
Queen's Head in Gold

301	A48	3c brt pink & multi	.20	.20
302	A48	5c gray & multi	.20	.20
303	A48	16c green & multi	.30	.30
304	A48	26c lemon & multi	.50	.50
305	A48	50c lt violet & multi	.90	.90
		Nos. 301-305 (5)	2.10	2.10

Silver Wedding Issue, 1972
Common Design Type

Design: Queen Elizabeth II, Prince Philip and Belize orchids.

1972, Nov. 20 Photo. *Perf. 14x14½*

306	CD324	26c slate grn & multi	.40	.40
307	CD324	50c violet & multi	.75	.75

Baron Bliss Day A49

Festivals of Belize: 10c, Labor Day boat race. 26c, Carib Settlement Day dance. 50c, Pan American Day parade.

1973, Mar. 9 Litho. *Perf. 14½*

308	A49	3c dull blue & black	.20	.20
309	A49	10c red & multi	.20	.20
310	A49	26c ver & multi	.40	.40
311	A49	50c black & multi	.75	.75
		Nos. 308-311 (4)	1.55	1.55

SEMI-POSTAL STAMPS

Regular Issue of 1921-29 Surcharged in Black or Red — BELIZE RELIEF FUND PLUS 3 CENTS

1932 Wmk. 4 *Perf. 14*

B1	A14	1c + 1c green	1.50	*4.75*
B2	A14	2c + 2c rose red	1.50	*4.75*
B3	A14	3c + 3c orange	2.50	*6.25*
B4	A14	4c + 4c gray (R)	3.25	*9.50*
B5	A14	5c + 5c ultra	5.00	*16.00*
		Nos. B1-B5 (5)	13.75	*41.25*

The surtax was for a fund to aid sufferers from the destruction of the city of Belize by a hurricane in Sept. 1931.

POSTAGE DUE STAMPS

Catalogue values for unused stamps in this section are for Never Hinged items.

D1

1923 Typo. Wmk. 4 *Perf. 14*

J1	D1	1c black	.90	*5.00*
J2	D1	2c black	1.10	*4.00*
J3	D1	4c black	3.00	*10.00*
		Nos. J1-J3 (3)	5.00	*19.00*

Nos. J1-J3 were re-issued on chalky paper in 1956.

Perf. 13½x13, 13½x14
1965-72 **Wmk. 314**

J4	D1	2c black ('72)	1.50	*3.00*
J5	D1	4c black	1.00	*3.50*

WAR TAX STAMPS

Nos. 85, 75 and 77 Overprinted WAR

1916-17 Wmk. 3 *Perf. 14*
With Moire Overprint

MR1	A11	1c green	.20	*.35*
a.		"WAR" inverted	250.00	*250.00*

Without Moire Overprint

MR2	A11	1c green ('17)	.25	*.75*
MR3	A11	3c orange ('17)	.75	.75
a.		Double overprint	450.00	*450.00*
		Nos. MR1-MR3 (3)	1.20	*1.85*

Nos. 75 and 77 Overprinted WAR

1918

MR4	A11	1c green	.20	*.25*
MR5	A11	3c orange	.20	*.50*

BRITISH INDIAN OCEAN TERRITORY

'bri-tish 'in-dēən 'ō-chən 'ter-ə-ˌtōr-ē

LOCATION — Indian Ocean
GOVT. — British Dependency
POP. — 0

B.I.O.T. was established Nov. 8, 1965. This island group lies 1,180 miles north of Mauritius. It consisted of Chagos Archipelago (chief island: Diego Garcia), Aldabra, Farquhar and Des Roches Islands until June 23, 1976, when the last three named islands were returned to Seychelles.

There is no permanent population on the islands. There are military personel located there.

100 Cents = 1 Rupee
100 Pence = 1 Pound (1990)

Catalogue values for all unused stamps in this country are for Never Hinged items.

Seychelles Nos. 198-202, 204-212 Overprinted B.I.O.T.

Perf. 14½x14, 14x14½
1968, Jan. 17 Photo. Wmk. 314
Size: 24x31, 31x24mm

1	A17	5c multicolored	.20	.20
2	A17	10c multicolored	.20	.20
3	A17	15c multicolored	.20	.20
4	A17	20c multicolored	.20	.20
5	A17	25c multicolored	.20	.20
6	A18	40c multicolored	.25	.30
7	A18	45c multicolored	.30	.30
8	A17	50c multicolored	.30	.35
9	A17	75c multicolored	.35	.35
10	A18	1r multicolored	1.00	1.00
11	A18	1.50r multicolored	1.60	1.75
12	A18	2.25r multicolored	3.00	3.00
13	A18	3.50r multicolored	4.50	4.50
14	A18	5r multicolored	10.00	10.50

Perf. 13x14
Size: 22½x39mm

15	A17	10r multicolored	20.00	21.00
		Nos. 1-15 (15)	42.30	44.05

Lascar A1

Marine Fauna: 10c, Hammerhead shark, vert. 15c, Tiger shark. 20c, Sooty eagle ray. 25c, Butterflyfish, vert. 30c, Robber crab. 40c, Green carangue. 45c, Needlefish, vert. 50c, Barracuda. 60c, Spotted pebble crab. 75c, Parrotfish. 85c, Rainbow runner (fish). 1r, Giant hermit crab. 1.50r, Humphead. 2.25r, Rock cod. 3.50r, Black marlin. 5r, Whale shark, vert. 10r, Lionfish.

Perf. 14x13½, 13½x14; 14 (30c, 60c, 85c)
1968-73 Litho. Wmk. 314

16	A1	5c multicolored	.40	.40
a.		Wmk. upright ('73)	.65	.65
17	A1	10c multicolored	.20	.20
18	A1	15c multicolored	.20	.20
19	A1	20c multicolored	.20	.20
20	A1	25c multicolored	.35	.35
21	A1	30c multi ('70)	.40	.40
22	A1	40c multicolored	.35	.35
23	A1	45c multicolored	2.75	2.75
24	A1	50c multicolored	.35	.35
25	A1	60c multi ('70)	.80	.80
26	A1	75c multicolored	4.00	4.00
27	A1	85c multi ('70)	1.75	1.75
28	A1	1r multicolored	1.40	1.40
29	A1	1.50r multicolored	1.75	1.75
30	A1	2.25r multicolored	14.00	14.00
31	A1	3.50r multicolored	4.00	4.00
32	A1	5r multicolored	6.00	6.00
33	A1	10r multicolored	17.00	17.00
		Nos. 16-33 (18)	55.90	55.90

No. 16 has watermark sideways.

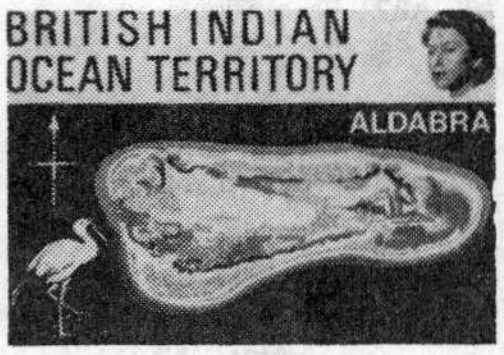

Aldabra Atoll and Sacred Ibis A2

1969, July 10 Litho. *Perf. 13½x13*

34	A2	2.25r vio blue & multi	2.25	1.60

Outrigger Canoe — A3

Designs: 75c, Beaching canoe. 1r, Merchant ship Nordvaer. 1.50r, Yacht, Isle of Farquhar.

Perf. 13½x14
1969, Dec. 15 Litho. Wmk. 314

35	A3	45c multicolored	.45	*.40*
36	A3	75c multicolored	.85	*.75*
37	A3	1r multicolored	1.25	*1.10*
38	A3	1.50r multicolored	2.25	*1.75*
		Nos. 35-38 (4)	4.80	*4.00*

Giant Land Tortoise — A4

Designs: 75c, Aldabra lily. 1r, Aldabra tree snail. 1.50r, Dimorphic egrets.

1971, Feb. 1 Litho. Wmk. 314

39	A4	45c multicolored	2.00	1.10
40	A4	75c multicolored	2.50	1.60
41	A4	1r multicolored	5.00	3.25
42	A4	1.50r multicolored	6.50	4.25
		Nos. 39-42 (4)	16.00	10.20

Aldabra Nature Reserve.

Society Coat of Arms and Flightless Rail — A5

1971, June 30 Litho. *Perf. 13½*

43	A5	3.50r multicolored	10.00	7.00

Opening of Royal Society Research Station at Aldabra.

Acropora Formosa A6

Corals: 60c, Goniastrea pectinata. 1r, Fungia fungites. 1.75r, Tubipora musica.

1972, Mar. 1

44	A6	40c blue & multi	.90	.90
45	A6	60c brt pink & multi	1.60	1.60
46	A6	1r blue & multi	3.25	3.25
47	A6	1.75r brt pink & multi	7.25	7.25
		Nos. 44-47 (4)	13.00	13.00

Common Design Types pictured following the introduction.

Silver Wedding Issue, 1972

Common Design Type

Design: Queen Elizabeth II, Prince Philip, flightless rail and sacred ibis.

1972, Nov. 20 Photo. *Perf. 14x14½*

48 CD324	95c multicolored	1.10	.50
49 CD324	1.50r violet & multi	1.50	.75

Crucifixion, 17th Century — A7

Upsidedown Jellyfish — A8

Paintings, Ethiopian Manuscripts, 17th Century: 75c, 1.50r, Joseph and Nicodemus burying Jesus. 1r, Like 45c.

1973, Apr. 9 Litho. *Perf. 14*

50 A7	45c buff & multi	.30	.20
51 A7	75c buff & multi	.45	.35
52 A7	1r buff & multi	.65	.40
53 A7	1.50r buff & multi	1.10	.70
a.	Souvenir sheet of 4, #50-53	3.50	2.75
	Nos. 50-53 (4)	2.50	1.65

Easter.

1973, Nov. 12 Litho. Wmk. 314

54 A8	50c shown	1.40	1.00
55 A8	1r Butterflies	2.25	1.50
56 A8	1.50r Spider	3.75	2.50
	Nos. 54-56 (3)	7.40	5.00

Nordvaer and July 14, 1969 Cancel — A9

Design: 2.50r, Nordvaer offshore and cancel.

1974, July 14

57 A9	85c multicolored	.80	.55
58 A9	2.50r multicolored	2.10	1.50

Nordvaer traveling post office, 5th anniv.

Terebra Maculata and Terebra Subulata — A10

Sea Shells: 75c, Turbo marmoratus. 1r, Drupa rubusidaeus. 1.50r, Cassis rufa.

1974, Nov. 12 Litho. *Perf. 13½x14*

59 A10	45c multicolored	.90	.70
60 A10	75c multicolored	1.40	1.25
61 A10	1r multicolored	2.25	1.75
62 A10	1.50r multicolored	4.00	3.00
	Nos. 59-62 (4)	8.55	6.70

British Indian Ocean Territory stamps can be mounted in the Scott British Africa album and the British Indian Ocean supplement.

Aldabra Drongo — A11

Grewia Salicifolia — A12

Birds: 10c, Malagasy coucal. 20c, Red-headed forest fody. 25c, Fairy tern. 30c, Crested tern. 40c, Brown booby. 50c, Noddy tern. 60c, Gray heron. 65c, Blue-faced booby. 95c, Malagasy white-eye. 1r, Green-backed heron. 1.75r, Lesser frigate bird. 3.50r, White-tailed tropic bird. 5r, Souimanga sunbird. 10r, Malagasy turtledove. Nos. 69, 71-77 horiz.

1975, Feb. 28 Wmk. 314 *Perf. 14*

63 A11	5c buff & multi	.20	*.20*
64 A11	10c lt ultra & multi	.20	*.20*
65 A11	20c dp yel & multi	.20	*.20*
66 A11	25c ultra & multi	.25	*.20*
67 A11	30c dl yel & multi	.35	*.30*
68 A11	40c bis & multi	.45	*.40*
69 A11	50c lt blue & multi	.50	*.45*
70 A11	60c yel & multi	.55	*.50*
71 A11	65c yel grn & multi	.65	*.60*
72 A11	95c citron & multi	.80	*.75*
73 A11	1r bister & multi	1.00	*.95*
74 A11	1.75r yel & multi	2.00	*1.90*
75 A11	3.50r blue & multi	4.00	*3.75*
76 A11	5r pale sal & multi	6.50	*6.25*
77 A11	10r brt yel & multi	10.00	*9.50*
	Nos. 63-77 (15)	27.65	*26.15*

1975, July 10 Litho. Wmk. 314

Native Plants: 65c, Cassia aldabrensis. 1r, Hypoestes aldabrensis. 1.60r, Euphorbia pyrifolia.

78 A12	50c multicolored	.35	.35
79 A12	65c multicolored	.50	.50
80 A12	1r multicolored	.75	.75
81 A12	1.60r multicolored	1.25	1.25
	Nos. 78-81 (4)	2.85	2.85

Nature protection.

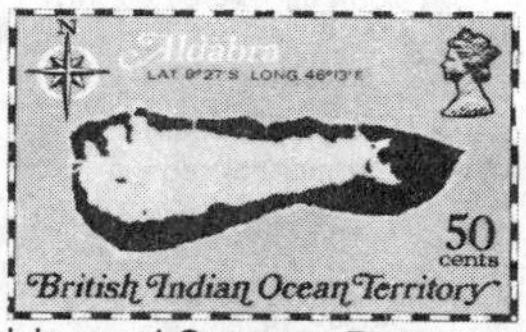

Aldabra and Compass Rose — A13

Maps of Islands: 1r, Desroches. 1.50r, Farquhar. 2r, Diego Garcia.

1975, Nov. 8 Litho. *Perf. 13½x14*

82 A13	50c blk, blue & grn	.30	.25
83 A13	1r green & multi	.65	.50
84 A13	1.50r blk, ultra & grn	1.00	.70
85 A13	2r blk, lilac & grn	1.40	1.00
a.	Souvenir sheet of 4, #82-85	7.50	7.50
	Nos. 82-85 (4)	3.35	2.45

British Indian Ocean Territory, 10th anniv.

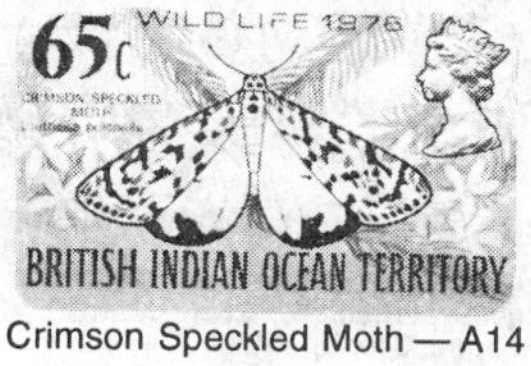

Crimson Speckled Moth — A14

Insects: 1.20r, Dysdercus fasciatus. 1.50r, Sphex torridus. 2r, Oryctes rhinoceros.

1976, Mar. 22 Litho. Wmk. 373

86 A14	65c multicolored	.45	.40
87 A14	1.20r multicolored	.70	.65
88 A14	1.50r multicolored	1.00	.90
89 A14	2r multicolored	1.50	1.40
	Nos. 86-89 (4)	3.65	3.35

Exhibition Emblem and No. 37 — A15

1990, May 3 Wmk. 373 *Perf. 14*

90 A15	15p No. 62	.75	.65
91 A15	20p No. 89	1.00	.90
92 A15	34p No. 85	1.90	1.50
93 A15	54p shown	3.50	2.75
	Nos. 90-93 (4)	7.15	5.80

Stamp World London '90.

Birds — A16

1990, May 3 Wmk. 384 *Perf. 14*

94 A16	15p White-tailed tropic birds	.45	.45
95 A16	20p Turtle doves	.70	.70
96 A16	24p Greater frigate birds	.75	.75
97 A16	30p Little green herons	1.00	1.00
98 A16	34p Greater sand plovers	1.10	1.10
99 A16	41p Crab plovers	1.40	1.40
100 A16	45p Crested terns	1.60	1.60
101 A16	54p Lesser crested terns	1.75	1.75
102 A16	62p Fairy terns	2.00	2.00
103 A16	71p Red-footed boobies	2.25	2.25
104 A16	80p Indian mynahs	2.75	2.75
105 A16	£1 Madagascar fodies	3.25	3.25
	Nos. 94-105 (12)	19.00	19.00

For overprints see Nos. 145-146.

Queen Mother, 90th Birthday

Common Design Types

Designs: 24p, Lady Elizabeth Bowes-Lyon, 1923. £1, Queen, Princesses Elizabeth & Margaret, 1940.

1990, Aug. 4 Wmk. 384 *Perf. 14x15*

106 CD343	24p multicolored	1.25	1.10

Perf. 14½

107 CD344	£1 brown & black	5.00	4.50

British Indian Ocean Territory, 25th Anniv. — A17

1990, Nov. 8 Litho. *Perf. 14*

108 A17	20p Flag	.90	.80
109 A17	24p Coat of arms	1.25	1.10

Souvenir Sheet

110 A17	£1 Map	5.00	5.00

Govt. Services A18

Wmk. 373

1991, June 3 Litho. *Perf. 14*

111 A18	20p Postal service	.70	.70
112 A18	24p Royal Marines	.85	.85
113 A18	34p Police station, officers	1.25	1.25
114 A18	54p Customs service	1.90	1.90
	Nos. 111-114 (4)	4.70	4.70

Visiting Ships A19

1991, Nov. 8

115 A19	20p Survey ship Experiment, 1786	.70	.70
116 A19	24p US Brig Pickering, 1819	.90	.90
117 A19	34p SMS Emden, 1914	1.25	1.25
118 A19	54p HMS Edinburgh, 1988	1.90	1.90
	Nos. 115-118 (4)	4.75	4.75

Queen Elizabeth II's Accession to the Throne, 40th Anniv.

Common Design Type

Wmk. 373

1992, Feb. 6 Litho. *Perf. 14*

119 CD349	15p multicolored	.55	.50
120 CD349	20p multicolored	.75	.70
121 CD349	24p multicolored	1.00	.90
122 CD349	34p multicolored	1.50	1.25
123 CD349	54p multicolored	2.25	2.00
	Nos. 119-123 (5)	6.05	5.35

Aircraft A20

Wmk. 384

1992, Oct. 23 Litho. *Perf. 14*

124 A20	20p Catalina	.90	.80
125 A20	24p Nimrod	1.25	1.00
126 A20	34p P-3 Orion	1.75	1.50
127 A20	54p B-52	3.00	2.50
	Nos. 124-127 (4)	6.90	5.80

Christmas — A21

Paintings: 5p, The Mystical Marriage of St. Cathrin, by Correggio. 24p, Madonna and Child by unknown artist. 34p, Madonna and Child by unknown artist, diff. 54p, The Birth of Jesus, by Kaspar Jele.

1992, Nov. 27 *Perf. 14½*

128 A21	5p multicolored	.25	.20
129 A21	24p multicolored	.90	.80
130 A21	34p multicolored	1.25	1.10
131 A21	54p multicolored	2.00	1.90
	Nos. 128-131 (4)	4.40	4.00

Coconut Crab A22

Wmk. 384

1993, Mar. 3 Litho. *Perf. 14*

132 A22	10p Crab, coconut	*1.10*	*1.10*
133 A22	10p Large crab	*1.10*	*1.10*
134 A22	10p Two crabs	*1.10*	*1.10*
135 A22	15p Crab on tree trunk	*1.75*	*1.75*
	Nos. 132-135 (4)	*5.05*	*5.05*

World Wildlife Fund.

Royal Air Force, 75th Anniv.
Common Design Type

#136, Vickers Virginia. 24p, Bristol Bulldog. 34p, Short Sunderland. 54p, Bristol Blenheim IV.
#140: a, Douglas Dakota. b, Gloster Javelin. c, Blackburn Beverley. d, Vickers VC10.

1993, Apr. 1 **Wmk. 373**
136 CD350 20p multicolored .75 .65
137 CD350 24p multicolored .85 .75
138 CD350 34p multicolored 1.25 1.10
139 CD350 54p multicolored 1.75 1.50
Nos. 136-139 (4) 4.60 4.00

Souvenir Sheet
140 CD350 20p Sheet of 4, #a.-d. 3.00 2.75

Flowers — A23

Christmas: 20p, Stachytarpheta urticifolia. 24p, Ipomea pes-caprae. 34p, Sida pusilla. 54p, Catharanthus roseus.

Wmk. 373
1993, Nov. 22 **Litho.** ***Perf. 14½***
141-144 A23 Set of 4 3.75 3.75

Nos. 96, 105 Ovptd. with Hong Kong '94 Emblem

Wmk. 384
1994, Feb. 18 **Litho.** ***Perf. 14***
145 A16 24p multicolored .65 .65
146 A16 £1 multicolored 2.75 2.75

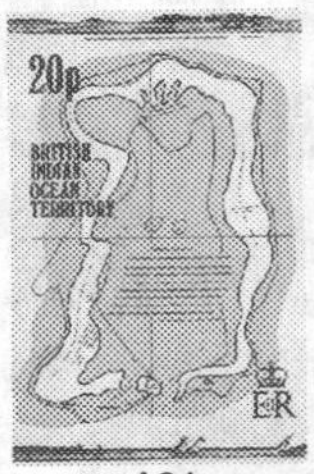

A24

Butterflies — A25

18th Cent. Maps and Charts: a, 20p, Sketch of Diego Garcia. b, 24p, Plan of harbor, Chagos Island or Diego Garcia, by Lt. Archibald Blair. c, 34p, Chart of Chagos Archipelago, by Lt. Blair. d, 44p, Plan of part of Chagos Island or Diego Garcia, from survey made by the Drake. e, 54p, Plan of Chagos Island or Diego Garcia, by M. Aa Fontaine.

1994, June 1 **Wmk. 373**
147 A24 Strip of 5, #a.-e. 5.25 5.25

1994, Aug. 16 **Wmk. 384**
148 A25 24p Junonia villida 1.10 1.10
149 A25 30p Petrelaea dana 1.40 1.40
150 A25 56p Hypolimnas misippus 2.50 2.50
Nos. 148-150 (3) 5.00 5.00

Sharks A26

1994, Nov. 1 **Wmk. 373**
151 A26 15p Nurse .45 .45
152 A26 20p Silver tip .60 .60
153 A26 24p Black tip reef .75 .75
154 A26 30p Oceanic white tip .95 .95
155 A26 35p Black tip 1.10 1.10
156 A26 41p Smooth hammerhead 1.25 1.25
157 A26 46p Lemon 1.40 1.40
158 A26 55p White tip reef 1.75 1.75
159 A26 65p Tiger 2.00 2.00
a. Souvenir sheet of 1 2.00 2.00
160 A26 74p Indian sand tiger 2.25 2.25
a. Souvenir sheet of 1 2.25 2.25
161 A26 80p Great hammerhead 2.50 2.50
162 A26 £1 Great white 3.00 3.00
Nos. 151-162 (12) 18.00 18.00

No. 159a for Hong Kong '97. Issued 2/3/97.
No. 160a for return of Hong Kong to China. Issued 7/1/97.

End of World War II, 50th Anniv.
Common Design Types

20p, War graves, memorial cross, Diego Garcia. 24p, 6-inch naval gun, Cannon Point. 30p, Sunderland flying boat, 230 Squadron. 56p, HMIS Clive.
£1, Reverse of War Medal 1939-45.

Wmk. 373
1995, May 8 **Litho.** ***Perf. 14***
163 CD351 20p multicolored .50 .50
164 CD351 24p multicolored .65 .65
165 CD351 30p multicolored .80 .80
166 CD351 56p multicolored 1.50 1.50
Nos. 163-166 (4) 3.45 3.45

Souvenir Sheet
167 CD352 £1 multicolored 2.75 2.75

Game Fish A27

1995, Oct. 6 **Wmk. 384**
168 A27 20p Dolphinfish .60 .60
169 A27 24p Sailfish .75 .75
170 A27 30p Wahoo .90 .90
171 A27 56p Striped marlin 1.75 1.75
Nos. 168-171 (4) 4.00 4.00

Sea Shells — A28

20p, Terebra crenulata. 24p, Bursa bufonia. 30p, Nassarius papillosus. 56p, Lopha cristagalli.

1996, Jan. 8 **Wmk. 373** ***Perf. 14***
172 A28 20p multicolored .60 .60
173 A28 24p multicolored .75 .75
174 A28 30p multicolored .90 .90
175 A28 56p multicolored 1.75 1.75
Nos. 172-175 (4) 4.00 4.00

Queen Elizabeth II, 70th Birthday
Common Design Type

Various portraits of Queen, scenes of British Indian Ocean Territory: 20p, View to north from south end of lagoon. 24p, Manager's House, Peros Banhos. 30p, Wireless station, Peros Banhos. 56p, Sunset scene.
£1, Wearing crown, formal dress.

Perf. 14x14½
1996, Apr. 22 **Wmk. 384**
176 CD354 20p multicolored .65 .65
177 CD354 24p multicolored .80 .80
178 CD354 30p multicolored 1.00 1.00
179 CD354 56p multicolored 1.75 1.75
Nos. 176-179 (4) 4.20 4.20

Souvenir Sheet
180 CD354 £1 multicolored 3.25 3.25

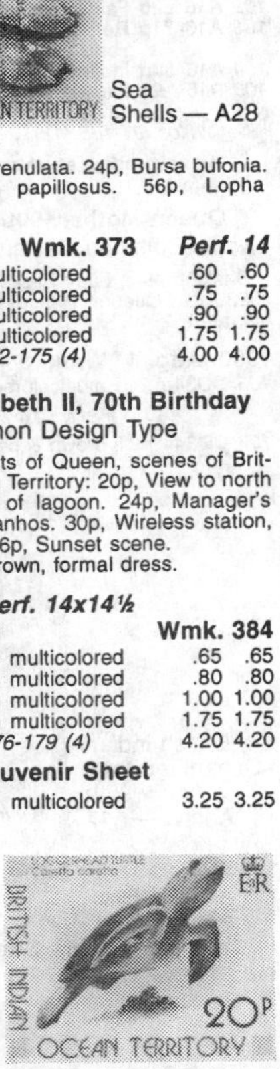

Turtles A29

1996, Sept. 2 **Wmk. 373**
181 A29 20p Loggerhead .60 .60
182 A29 24p Leatherback .75 .75
183 A29 30p Hawksbill .90 .90
184 A29 56p Green 1.75 1.75
Nos. 181-184 (4) 4.00 4.00

Uniforms — A30

Designs: 20p, British representative. 24p, Royal Marine officer. 30p, Royal Marine in camouflage. 56p, Police dog handler, female police officer.

1996, Dec. ***Perf. 14***
185 A30 20p multicolored .65 .65
186 A30 24p multicolored .80 .80
187 A30 30p multicolored 1.00 1.00
188 A30 56p multicolored 1.90 1.90
Nos. 185-188 (4) 4.35 4.35

Queen Elizabeth II and Prince Philip, 50th Wedding Anniv. — A31

#189, Queen up close. #190, 4-horse team fording river. #191, Queen riding in open carriage. #192, Prince Philip up close. #193, Prince driving 4-horse team, Prince, Queen near jeep. #194, Queen on horseback, castle in distance.
£1.50, Queen, Prince riding in open carriage.

1997, July 10 ***Perf. 14½x14***
189 A31 20p multicolored .65 .65
190 A31 20p multicolored .65 .65
a. Pair, #189-190 1.30 1.30
191 A31 24p multicolored .80 .80
192 A31 24p multicolored .80 .80
a. Pair, #191-192 1.60 1.60
193 A31 30p multicolored 1.00 1.00
194 A31 30p multicolored 1.00 1.00
a. Pair, #193-194 2.00 2.00
Nos. 189-194 (6) 4.90 4.90

Souvenir Sheet
195 A31 £1.50 multicolored 5.00 5.00

Ocean Wave '97, Naval Exercise A32

Designs: a, HMS Richmond, HMS Beaver. b, HMS Illustrious. c, HMS Beaver. d, RFA Sir Percivale, HMY Britannia, HMS Beaver. e, HMY Britannia. f, HMS Richmond, HMS Beaver, HMS Gloucester. g, HMS Richmond. h, HMS Illustrious (aerial view). i, HMS Sheffield. j, RFA Diligence, HMS Trenchant. k, HMS Illustrious, RFA Fort George, HMS Gloucester. l, HMS Richmond, HMS Beaver, HMS Gloucester.

1997, Dec. 1 **Litho.** ***Perf. 14x14½***
196 A32 24p Sheet of 12, #a.-l. 9.25 9.25

Diana, Princess of Wales (1961-97)
Common Design Type

Various portraits: a, 26p, shown. b, 26p, Close-up. c, 34p. d, 60p.

1998, Mar. 31 ***Perf. 14½x14***
197 CD355 Sheet of 4, #a.-d. 5.50 5.50

No. 197 sold for £1.46 + 20p, with surtax and 50% of profits from total sale being donated to the Princess Diana Memorial Fund.

Royal Air Force, 80th Anniv.
Common Design Type of 1993 Re-inscribed

Designs: 26p, Blackburn Iris, 1930-34. 34p, Gloster Gamecock, 1926-33. 60p, North American Sabre F86, 1953-56. 80p, Avro Lincoln, 1945-55.
No. 202: a, Sopwith Baby, 1915-19. b, Martinsyde Elephant, 1916-19. c, De Havilland Tiger Moth, 1932-55. d, North American Mustang III, 1943-47.

1998, Apr. 1 **Wmk. 384** ***Perf. 14***
198 CD350 26p multicolored .85 .85
199 CD350 34p multicolored 1.10 1.10
200 CD350 60p multicolored 2.00 2.00
201 CD350 80p multicolored 2.75 2.75
Nos. 198-201 (4) 6.70 6.70

Souvenir Sheet
202 CD350 34p Sheet of 4, #a.-d. 4.50 4.50

Intl. Year of the Ocean — A33

Dolphins and whales: No. 203, Striped dolphin. No. 204, Bryde's whale. No. 205, Pilot whale. No. 206, Spinner dolphin.

Wmk. 373
1998, Dec. 7 **Litho.** ***Perf. 14***
203 A33 26p multicolored .85 .85
204 A33 26p multicolored .85 .85
205 A33 34p multicolored 1.10 1.10
206 A33 34p multicolored 1.10 1.10
Nos. 203-206 (4) 3.90 3.90

Sailing Ships — A34

2p, Bark "Westminster," 1837. 15p, "Sao Cristovao," Spain, 1589. 20p, Clipper ship "Sea Witch," US, 1849. 26p, HMS "Royal George," 1778. 34p, Clipper ship "Cutty Sark," 1883. 60p, British East India Co. ship "Mentor," 1789. 80p, HM brig "Trinculo," 1809. £1, Paddle steamer "Enterprise," 1825. £1.15, Privateer "Confiance," France, 1800. £2, British East India Co. ship "Kent," 1820.

Wmk. 373
1999, Feb. 1 **Litho.** ***Perf. 14***
207 A34 2p multicolored .20 .20
208 A34 15p multicolored .50 .50
209 A34 20p multicolored .65 .65
210 A34 26p multicolored .85 .85
211 A34 34p multicolored 1.10 1.10
212 A34 60p multicolored 1.90 1.90
213 A34 80p multicolored 2.50 2.50
214 A34 £1 multicolored 3.25 3.25
215 A34 £1.15 multicolored 3.75 3.75
216 A34 £2 multicolored 6.50 6.50
Nos. 207-216 (10) 21.20 21.20

Tea Race, 1872 — A35

a, Cutty Sark (up close). b, Thermopylae (in distance).

Wmk. 384
1999, Mar. 19 **Litho.** ***Perf. 14***
217 A35 60p Sheet of 2, #a.-b. 3.75 3.75

Australia '99 World Stamp Expo.

BRUNEI

'brü-,nī

LOCATION — On the northwest coast of Borneo
GOVT. — Independent state
AREA — 2,226 sq. mi.
POP. — 322,982 (1999 est.)
CAPITAL — Bandar Seri Begawan

Brunei became a British protectorate in 1888. A treaty between the sultan and the British Government in 1979 provided for independence in 1983.

100 Cents (Sen) = 1 Dollar

Catalogue values for unused stamps in this country are for Never Hinged items, beginning with Scott 62.

Watermark

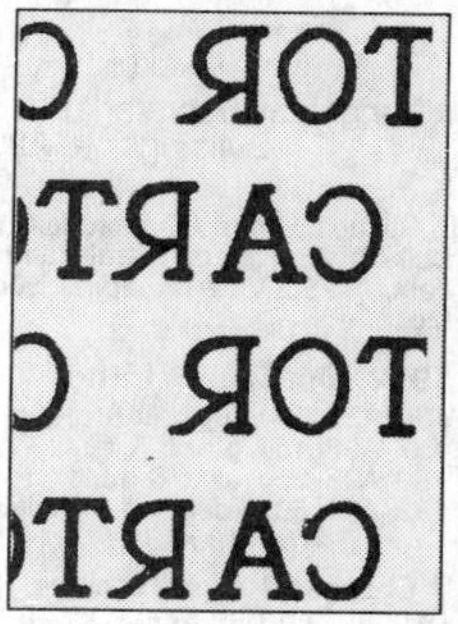

Wmk. 385 - CARTOR

Labuan Stamps of 1902-03 Overprinted or Surcharged in Red:

BRUNEI.

BRUNEI. **TWO CENTS.**

1906 Unwmk. *Perf. 12 to 16*

1 A38 1c violet & blk 22.50 *45.00*
a. Black overprint 2,000. *2,750.*
2 A38 2c on 3c brn & blk 1.50 *7.50*
a. "BRUNEI." double 4,250. *3,000.*
b. "TWO CENTS." double 9,500.
3 A38 2c on 8c org & blk 25.00 *70.00*
a. "TWO CENTS." double 8,250.
b. "TWO CENTS." omitted, in pair with normal 9,250.
4 A38 3c brown & blk 25.00 *70.00*
5 A38 4c on 12c yel & black 2.00 *5.00*
6 A38 5c on 16c org brn & green 37.50 *60.00*
7 A38 8c orange & blk 8.00 *25.00*
8 A38 10c on 16c org brn & green 6.50 *18.00*
9 A38 25c on 16c org brn & green 90.00 *125.00*
10 A38 30c on 16c org brn & green 85.00 *125.00*
11 A38 50c on 16c org brn & green 85.00 *125.00*
12 A38 $1 on 8c org & blk 85.00 *125.00*
Nos. 1-12 (12) 473.00 *800.50*

The 25c surcharge reads: "25 CENTS."

Scene on Brunei River — A1

Two Types of 1908 1c, 3c:
Type I - Dots form bottom line of water shading. (Double plate.)
Type II - Dots removed. (Single plate.)

1907-21 Engr. Wmk. 3 *Perf. 14*

13 A1 1c yel green & blk 1.50 *2.75*
14 A1 1c green (II) ('08) .40 .40
a. Type I ('19) .60 *1.50*
15 A1 2c red & black 1.50 *3.00*
16 A1 2c brn & blk ('11) .60 *1.40*
17 A1 3c red brn & blk 12.50 *15.00*
18 A1 3c car (I) ('08) .85 *1.50*
a. Type II ('17) 12.50 *17.50*
19 A1 4c lilac & blk 5.00 *9.00*
20 A1 4c claret ('12) 4.00 .50
21 A1 5c ultra & blk 37.50 *50.00*
22 A1 5c org & blk ('08) 3.50 *4.00*
23 A1 5c orange ('16) 1.75 *2.25*
24 A1 8c orange & blk 5.50 *20.00*
25 A1 8c blue ('08) 4.25 6.25
26 A1 8c ultra ('16) 2.00 *2.25*
27 A1 10c dk green & blk 9.00 *15.00*
28 A1 10c violet, *yel* ('12) 1.00 *1.25*
29 A1 25c yel brn & blue 19.00 *30.00*
30 A1 25c violet ('12) 1.90 *4.00*
31 A1 30c black & pur 19.00 *30.00*
32 A1 30c org & red vio ('12) 6.50 *12.50*
33 A1 50c brown & grn 19.00 *30.00*
34 A1 50c blk, *grn* ('12) 19.00 *30.00*
35 A1 50c blk, *grnsh bl* ('21) 5.50 *13.50*
36 A1 $1 slate & red 62.50 *75.00*
37 A1 $1 red & blk, *bl* ('12) 25.00 *50.00*
38 A1 $5 lake, *grn* ('08) 67.50 *125.00*
39 A1 $25 blk, *red* ('08) 450.00 *450.00*
Nos. 13-38 (26) 335.75 *534.55*

Used value for No. 39 is for CTO. CTOs dated before Dec. 1941 cost more.

Stamps of 1908-21 Overprinted in Black: "MALAYA-BORNEO EXHIBITION, 1922" in Four Lines

1922

14b A1 1c green 2.25 *17.00*
16a A1 2c brown & black 5.00 *21.00*
18b A1 3c carmine 6.75 *30.00*
20a A1 4c claret 5.25 *35.00*
23a A1 5c orange 10.00 *45.00*
28a A1 10c violet, *yellow* 8.75 *45.00*
30a A1 25c violet 19.00 *67.50*
35a A1 50c greenish blue 60.00 *125.00*
37a A1 $1 red & black, *blue* 92.50 *160.00*
Nos. 14b-37a (9) 209.50 *545.50*

Industrial fair, Singapore, Mar. 31-Apr. 15.

Type of 1907 Issue

1924-37 Wmk. 4

43 A1 1c black ('26) .20 *.30*
44 A1 2c deep brown .70 *2.75*
45 A1 2c green ('33) .25 *.25*
46 A1 3c green .70 *3.75*
47 A1 4c claret brown 1.90 .65
48 A1 4c orange ('29) .50 .40
49 A1 5c orange .65 *.75*
50 A1 5c lt gray ('31) 3.50 *5.75*
51 A1 5c brown ('33) 1.75 .20
52 A1 8c ultra ('27) 2.50 *4.25*
53 A1 8c gray ('33) 2.75 .45
54 A1 10c violet, *yel* ('37) 6.25 *15.00*
55 A1 25c dk violet ('31) 4.00 *9.00*
56 A1 30c org & red vio ('31) 4.75 *12.50*
57 A1 50c black, *grn* ('31) 6.00 *10.50*
58 A1 $1 red & blk, *bl* ('31) 25.00 *55.00*
Nos. 43-58 (16) 61.40 *121.50*

For overprints see Nos. N1-N20.

Dwellings in Town of Brunei — A2

1924-31

59 A2 6c black 3.50 *8.25*
60 A2 6c red ('31) 2.75 *9.00*
61 A2 12c blue 5.00 *7.50*
Nos. 59-61 (3) 11.25 *24.75*

See note after Nos. N1-N19.

Catalogue values for unused stamps in this section, from this point to the end of the section, are for Never Hinged items.

Types of 1907-24

1947-51 Engr. *Perf. 14*

62 A1 1c brown .20 .20
63 A1 2c gray .20 .20
a. Perf. 14½x13½ ('50) *1.75* *2.50*
64 A2 3c dark green .35 .35
65 A1 5c deep orange .20 .20
a. Perf. 14½x13½ ('50) *7.25* *9.00*
66 A2 6c gray black 1.75 1.75
67 A1 8c scarlet .20 .20
a. Perf. 13 ('51) .20 .20
68 A1 10c violet .20 .20
a. Perf. 14½x13½ ('50) *1.75* *3.00*
69 A1 15c brt ultra 3.75 3.75
70 A1 25c red violet .35 .35
a. Perf. 14½x13½ ('51) .60 *1.25*
71 A1 30c dp org & gray blk .45 .45
a. Perf. 14½x13½ ('51) .55 *1.25*
72 A1 50c black .45 .45
a. Perf. 13 ('50) 3.50 *12.00*
73 A1 $1 scar & gray blk 1.25 1.25
74 A1 $5 red org & grn ('48) 15.00 *15.00*
75 A1 $10 dp claret & gray blk ('48) 30.00 *42.50*
Nos. 62-75 (14) 54.35 *66.85*

Sultan Ahmed and Pile Dwellings A3

1949, Sept. 22 Wmk. 4 *Perf. 13*

76 A3 8c car & black 1.60 1.60
77 A3 25c red orange & pur 1.60 1.60
78 A3 50c blue & black 2.00 2.00
Nos. 76-78 (3) 5.20 5.20

25th anniv. of the reign of Sultan Ahmed Tajudin Akhazul Khair Wad-din.

Common Design Types pictured following the introduction.

UPU Issue

Common Design Types

Engr.; Name Typo. on 15c and 25c

1949, Oct. 10 *Perf. 13½, 11x11½*

79 CD306 8c rose car .50 .50
80 CD307 15c indigo .75 .75
81 CD308 25c red lilac 1.25 1.25
82 CD309 50c slate 2.50 2.50
Nos. 79-82 (4) 5.00 5.00

Sultan Omar Ali Saifuddin — A4

River Kampong A5

Perf. 13½x13

1952, Mar. 1 Engr. Wmk. 4

Center in Black

83 A4 1c black .20 .20
84 A4 2c red orange .20 .20
85 A4 3c red brown .20 .20
86 A4 4c green .20 .20
87 A4 6c gray .25 .20
88 A4 8c carmine .30 .20
89 A4 10c olive brown .30 .20
90 A4 12c violet .35 .20
91 A4 15c blue .50 .20
92 A4 25c purple .75 .25
93 A4 50c ultramarine 1.10 .30

Perf. 13

94 A5 $1 dull green 3.00 .60
95 A5 $2 red 4.50 1.50
96 A5 $5 deep plum 15.00 5.00
Nos. 83-96 (14) 26.85 9.45

See Nos. 101-114.

Mosque and Sultan Omar — A6

1958, Sept. 24 Wmk. 314 *Perf. 13*

Center in Black

97 A6 8c dull green .25 *.30*
98 A6 15c carmine rose .30 .25
99 A6 35c rose violet .50 *.75*
Nos. 97-99 (3) 1.05 *1.30*

Opening of the Brunei Mosque.

Freedom from Hunger Issue

Common Design Type with Portrait of Sultan Omar

1963, June 4 Photo. *Perf. 14x14½*

100 CD314 12c sepia 1.50 1.50

Types of 1952

Wmk. 314 Upright

1964-70 Engr. *Perf. 13½x13*

Center in Black

101 A4 1c black .20 .20
102 A4 2c red orange .20 .20
103 A4 3c red brown .20 .20
104 A4 4c green .20 .20
105 A4 6c black .25 .20
106 A4 8c dk carmine .45 .20
107 A4 10c olive brown .35 .25
108 A4 12c violet .55 .30
109 A4 15c blue .60 .35
110 A4 25c purple 1.25 .40
111 A4 50c ultramarine 2.50 1.50

Perf. 13

112 A5 $1 dull green ('68) 4.75 3.00
113 A5 $2 red ('70) 16.00 10.00
114 A5 $5 deep plum ('70) 32.50 25.00
Nos. 101-114 (14) 60.00 42.00

Nos. 101-112 were reissued in 1968-70 on whiter, glazed paper; the $2 and $5 are only on this paper.

Wmk. 314 Sideways

1972-73 *Perf. 13½x13*

Center in Black

102a A4 2c red orange .35 .35
103a A4 3c red brown .40 .40
104a A4 4c green .50 .50
105a A4 6c black .85 .85
106a A4 8c dark carmine 1.10 1.10
107a A4 10c olive brown 1.50 1.50
108a A4 12c violet 1.75 1.75
109a A4 15c blue 3.00 3.00
Nos. 102a-109a (8) 9.45 9.45

The stamps with watermark sideways are on the whiter, glazed paper.

Issue dates: 2c, 8c, May 9, 1973, others, Nov. 17, 1972.

The following six sets are Common Design Types but with the portrait of Sultan Omar.

ITU Issue

Perf. 11x11½

1965, May 17 Litho. Wmk. 314

116 CD317 4c red lil & org brn .20 .20
117 CD317 75c orange & emer 1.40 1.40

Intl. Cooperation Year Issue

1965, Oct. 25 *Perf. 14½*

118 CD318 4c blue grn & claret .20 .20
119 CD318 15c lt violet & grn .70 .70

Churchill Memorial Issue

1966, Jan. 24 Photo. *Perf. 14*

120 CD319 3c multicolored .25 .20
121 CD319 10c multicolored .65 .35
122 CD319 15c multicolored 1.00 .60
123 CD319 75c multicolored 3.50 2.50
Nos. 120-123 (4) 5.40 3.65

World Cup Soccer Issue

1966, July 4 Litho. *Perf. 14*

124 CD321 4c multicolored .20 .20
125 CD321 75c multicolored 1.25 1.25

WHO Headquarters Issue

1966, Sept. 20 Litho. *Perf. 14*

126 CD322 12c multicolored .25 .20
127 CD322 25c multicolored .75 .75

UNESCO Anniversary Issue

1966, Dec. 1 Litho. Wmk. 314

128 CD323 4c "Education" .20 .20
129 CD323 15c "Science" .45 .45
130 CD323 75c "Culture" 2.25 2.25
Nos. 128-130 (3) 2.90 2.90

State Religious Building and Sultan Hassanal Bolkiah — A7

1967, Dec. 19 Photo. *Perf. 12½*

131 A7 4c violet & multi .20 .20
132 A7 10c red & multi .20 .20
133 A7 25c orange & multi .35 .35
134 A7 50c lt violet & multi .65 .65
Nos. 131-134 (4) 1.40 1.40

A three-stamp set (12c, 25c, 50c) showing views of the new Language and Communications Headquarters was prepared and announced for release in April, 1968. The Crown Agents distributed sample sets, but the stamps were not issued. Later, Nos. 144-146 were issued instead.

Sultan Hassanal Bolkiah, Brunei Mosque and Flags — A8

Sultan Hassanal Bolkiah Installation: 12c, Sultan, Mosque and flags, horiz.

Perf. 13x14, 14x13

1968, July 9 Photo. Unwmk.

135 A8 4c green & multi	.20	.20
136 A8 12c dp bister & multi	.30	.30
137 A8 25c violet & multi	.75	.75
Nos. 135-137 (3)	1.25	1.25

Sultan Hassanal Bolkiah A9

Wmk. 314

1968, July 15 Litho. *Perf. 12*

138 A9 4c multicolored	.20	.20
139 A9 12c multicolored	.20	.20
140 A9 25c multicolored	.40	*.50*
Nos. 138-140 (3)	.80	*.90*

Sultan Hassanal Bolkiah's birthday.

Coronation of Sultan Hassanal Bolkiah, Aug. 1, 1968 — A10

1968, Aug. 1 Photo. *Perf. 14½x14*

141 A10 4c Prus blue & multi	.20	.20
142 A10 12c rose lilac & multi	.25	.25
143 A10 25c multicolored	.55	.55
Nos. 141-143 (3)	1.00	1.00

A11

Hall of Language and Culture — A12

Perf. 13½, 12½x13½ (A12)

1968, Sept. 29 Photo. Wmk. 314

144 A11 10c blue grn & multi	.20	*.25*
145 A12 15c ocher & multi	.20	*.30*
146 A12 30c ultra & multi	.45	*.75*
Nos. 144-146 (3)	.85	*1.30*

Opening of the Hall of Language and Culture and of the Broadcasting and Information Department Building. Nos. 144-146 are overprinted "1968" and 4 bars over the 1967 date. They were not issued without this overprint.

Human Rights Flame and Struggling Man — A13

Unwmk.

1968, Dec. 16 Litho. *Perf. 14*

147 A13 12c green, yel & blk	.20	.20
148 A13 25c ultra, yel & blk	.35	.35
149 A13 75c dk plum, yel & blk	.90	.90
Nos. 147-149 (3)	1.45	1.45

International Human Rights Year.

Sultan and WHO Emblem A14

1968, Dec. 19 Litho. *Perf. 14*

150 A14 4c lt blue, org & blk	.20	.20
151 A14 15c brt purple, org & blk	.25	.25
152 A14 25c olive, org & blk	.40	.40
Nos. 150-152 (3)	.85	.85

20th anniv. of the WHO.

Sultan Hassanal Bolkiah, Pengiran Shahbandar and Oil Rig — A15

Perf. 14x13

1969, July 10 Photo. Wmk. 314

153 A15 12c green & multi	.20	.20
154 A15 40c dk rose brn & multi	.60	.60
155 A15 50c violet & multi	.75	.75
Nos. 153-155 (3)	1.55	1.55

Installation of Pengiran Shahbandar as Second Minister (Di-Galong Sahibol Mal).

Royal Assembly Hall and Council Chamber — A16

Design: 50c, Front view of buildings.

Unwmk.

1969, Sept. 23 Litho. *Perf. 15*

156 A16 12c multicolored	.20	.20
157 A16 25c multicolored	.35	.35
158 A16 50c violet & pink	.65	.65
Nos. 156-158 (3)	1.20	1.20

Opening of the Royal Assembly Hall and Council Chamber.

Youth Center — A17

1969, Dec. 20 Litho. Wmk. 314

159 A17 6c lt org, blk & dull vio	.20	.20
160 A17 10c cit, blk & dl Prus grn	.20	.20
161 A17 30c yel green, blk & brn	.45	.45
Nos. 159-161 (3)	.85	.85

Opening of Youth Center, Mar. 15, 1969.

Helicopter and Emblem — A18

Designs: 10c, Soldier and emblem, vert. 75c, Patrol boat and emblem.

1971, May 31 Litho. *Perf. 14*

162 A18 10c green & multi	.40	.20
163 A18 15c Prus blue & multi	.45	.25
164 A18 75c lt ultra & multi	2.75	1.75
Nos. 162-164 (3)	3.60	2.20

10th anniv. of Royal Brunei Malay Reg.

50th Anniv. of the Royal Brunei Police Force — A19

1971, Aug. 14 *Perf. 14½*

165 A19 10c Superintendent	.40	.25
166 A19 15c Constable	.50	.30
167 A19 50c Traffic policeman	2.25	1.60
Nos. 165-167 (3)	3.15	2.15

Sultan, Heir Apparent and View of Brunei — A20

Portraits and: 25c, View of Brunei with Mosque. 50c, Mosque and banner.

1971, Aug. 27 Litho. Wmk. 314

168 A20 15c multicolored	.40	.25
169 A20 25c multicolored	.75	.55
170 A20 50c multicolored	1.40	1.10
Nos. 168-170 (3)	2.55	1.90

Installation of Sultan Hassanal Bolkiah's brother Muda Omar Ali Saifuddin as heir apparent (Perdana Wazir).

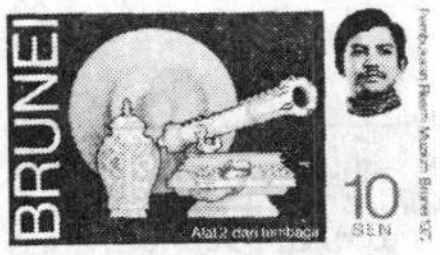

Brass and Copper Goods A21

Designs: 12c, Basketware. 15c, Leather goods. 25c, Silverware. 50c, Brunei Museum.

1972, Feb. 29 *Perf. 13½x14*

Size: 37x21mm

Portrait in Black

171 A21 10c brn, sal & yel grn	.20	.20
172 A21 12c org, yel & green	.20	.20
173 A21 15c dk grn, emer & org	.25	.25
174 A21 25c brown, org & slate	.70	.60

Size: 58x21mm

175 A21 50c dull blue & multi	1.50	1.10
Nos. 171-175 (5)	2.85	2.35

Opening of Brunei Museum.

Queen Elizabeth II, Sultan and View — A22

Queen Elizabeth II, Sultan Hassanal Bolkiah and: 15c, View of Brunei. 25c, Mosque and barge. 50c, Royal Assembly Hall.

1972, Feb. 29 Photo. *Perf. 13x13½*

176 A22 10c lt brown & multi	.25	.20
177 A22 15c lt blue & multi	.35	.30
178 A22 25c lt green & multi	.70	.60
179 A22 50c dull purple & multi	2.00	2.00
Nos. 176-179 (4)	3.30	3.10

Visit of Queen Elizabeth II, Feb. 29.

Bangunan Secretariat (Government Buildings) — A23

Sultans Omar Ali Saifuddin and Hassanal Bolkiah: 15c, Istana Darul Hana (Sultan's residence). 25c, View of capital. 50c, View of new Mosque.

1972, Oct. 4 Litho. *Perf. 13½*

180 A23 10c org, blk & green	.20	.20
181 A23 15c green & multi	.30	.30
182 A23 25c ultra & multi	.50	.50
183 A23 50c rose red & multi	1.00	1.00
Nos. 180-183 (4)	2.00	2.00

Change of capital's name from Brunei to Bandar Seri Begawan, Oct. 4, 1970.

Beverley Plane Landing — A24

Design: 25c, Blackburn Beverley plane dropping supplies by parachute, vert.

Perf. 14x13½, 13½x14

1972, Nov. 15 Litho.

184 A24 25c blue & multi	1.60	1.60
185 A24 75c ultra & multi	4.00	4.00

Opening of Royal Air Force Museum, Hendon, London.

Silver Wedding Issue, 1972

Common Design Type

Design: Queen Elizabeth II, Prince Philip; girl and boy with traditional gifts.

1972, Nov. 20 Photo. *Perf. 14x14½*

186 CD324 12c multi	.40	.20
187 CD324 75c multi	1.25	1.25

INTERPOL Emblem and Headquarters, Paris — A25

Design: 50c, similar to 25c.

1973, Sept. 7 Litho. *Perf. 14x14½*

188 A25 25c emerald & multi	.75	.75
189 A25 50c multicolored	1.50	1.50

50th anniv. of Intl. Criminal Police Org. (INTERPOL).

Princess Anne and Mark Phillips — A26

1973, Nov. 14 Litho. *Perf. 13½*
190 A26 25c vio blue & multi .20 .20
191 A26 50c red lilac & multi .40 .40

Wedding of Princess Anne and Capt. Mark Phillips, Nov. 14, 1973.

Churchill Painting Outdoors A27

Sultan Hassanal Bolkiah A28

Design: 50c, Churchill making "V" sign.

Perf. 14x13½
1973, Dec. 31 Litho. Wmk. 314
192 A27 12c car rose & multi .20 .20
193 A27 50c dk green & multi .55 .55

Winston Churchill Memorial Exhibition.

Wmk. 314 Sideways
1974, July 15 Photo. *Perf. 13x15*
194 A28 4c blue grn & multi .20 .20
195 A28 5c dull blue & multi .20 .20
196 A28 6c olive grn & multi .20 .20
197 A28 10c lt violet & multi .20 .20
b. Watermark upright ('76) .20 .20
198 A28 15c brown & multi .20 .20
199 A28 20c buff & multi .20 .20
b. Watermark upright ('76) .20 .20
200 A28 25c olive & multi .20 .20
b. Watermark upright ('76) .20 .20
201 A28 30c multicolored .25 .20
202 A28 35c gray & multi .25 .25
203 A28 40c multicolored .30 .30
204 A28 50c yel brn & multi .40 .35
205 A28 75c multicolored .60 .50
206 A28 $1 dull org & multi .75 .65
207 A28 $2 multicolored 1.60 1.40
208 A28 $5 silver & multi 3.50 3.25
209 A28 $10 gold & multi 8.25 8.25
Nos. 194-209 (16) 17.30 16.55

Issue date: Nos. 197b-200b, Apr. 12.

1975, Aug. 13 Wmk. 373
194a A28 4c .20 .20
195a A28 5c .20 .20
196a A28 6c .20 .20
197a A28 10c .20 .20
198a A28 15c .20 .20
199a A28 20c .20 .20
200a A28 25c .20 .20
201a A28 30c .25 .25
202a A28 35c .30 .30
203a A28 40c .35 .35
204a A28 50c .40 .40
205a A28 75c .60 .60
206a A28 $1 .80 .80
207a A28 $2 1.60 1.60
208a A28 $5 4.00 4.00
209a A28 $10 8.00 8.00
Nos. 194a-209a (16) 17.70 17.70

For surcharge see No. 225.

Brunei Airport A29

Design: 75c, Sultan Hassanal Bolkiah in uniform and jet over airport.

Perf. 14x14½, 12½x13 (75c)
1974, July 18 Litho. Wmk. 314
Size: 44x28mm
215 A29 50c multicolored 1.00 1.00
Size: 47x36mm
216 A29 75c multicolored 1.40 1.40

Opening of Brunei Airport.

UPU Emblem A30

1974, Oct. 28 *Perf. 14½*
217 A30 12c orange & multi .20 .20
218 A30 50c blue & multi .50 .50
219 A30 75c emerald & multi .75 .75
Nos. 217-219 (3) 1.45 1.45

Centenary of Universal Postal Union.

Winston Churchill A31

Design: 75c, Churchill smoking cigar.

1974, Nov. 30 Wmk. 373 *Perf. 14*
220 A31 12c vio blue, blue & gold .20 .20
221 A31 75c dk green, black & gold .90 .90

Sir Winston Churchill (1874-1965).

Boeing 737 Planes at Airport A32

Designs: 35c, Boeing 737 over Bandar Seri Begawan Mosque. 75c, Boeing 737 in flight. All planes with crest of Royal Brunei Airlines.

Perf. 12½x12
1975, May 14 Unwmk.
222 A32 12c multicolored .30 .25
223 A32 35c multicolored 1.00 .75
224 A32 75c multicolored 2.00 2.00
Nos. 222-224 (3) 3.30 3.00

Inauguration of Royal Brunei Airlines.

10
sen

No. 196a Surcharged in Silver

Perf. 13x15
1976, Aug. 16 Photo. Wmk. 373
225 A28 10c on 6c multicolored .25 .25

British Royal Coat of Arms — A33

20c, Imperial State Crown. 75c, Elizabeth II.

Wmk. 373
1977, June 7 Litho. *Perf. 14*
226 A33 10c dk blue & multi .20 .20
227 A33 20c purple & multi .20 .20
228 A33 75c yellow & multi .60 .60
Nos. 226-228 (3) 1.00 1.00

25th anniv. of the reign of Elizabeth II.

Coronation of Elizabeth II A34

20c, Elizabeth II with coronation regalia. 75c, Departure from Westminster Abbey (coach).

1978, June 2 Litho. *Perf. 13½x13*
229 A34 10c multicolored .20 .20
230 A34 20c multicolored .20 .20
231 A34 75c multicolored .60 .60
Nos. 229-231 (3) 1.00 1.00

25th anniv. of coronation of Elizabeth II.

Sultan's Coat of Arms — A35

Struggling Man, Human Rights Flame — A36

Coronation of Sultan Hassanal Bolkiah, 10th Anniv.: 20c, Ceremony. 75c, Royal crown.

1978, Aug. 1 Wmk. 373 *Perf. 12*
232 A35 10c multicolored .20 .20
233 A35 20c multicolored .25 .20
234 A35 75c multicolored .90 .75
a. Souvenir sheet of 3, #232-234 8.50 6.00
Nos. 232-234 (3) 1.35 1.15

1978, Dec. 10 Litho. *Perf. 14*
235 A36 10c red, black & yel .20 .20
236 A36 20c violet, black & yel .20 .20
237 A36 75c olive, black & yel .60 .60
Nos. 235-237 (3) 1.00 1.00

Universal Declaration of Human Rights, 30th anniversary.

Children and IYC Emblem A37

1979, June 30 Wmk. 373 *Perf. 14*
238 A37 10c shown .20 .20
239 A37 $1 IYC emblem .90 .90

Telisai Earth Satellite Station A38

Designs: 20c, Radar screen and satellite. 75c, Cameraman, telex operator, telephone.

1979, Sept. 23 Litho. *Perf. 14½x14*
240 A38 10c multicolored .20 .20
241 A38 20c multicolored .20 .20
242 A38 75c multicolored .75 .75
Nos. 240-242 (3) 1.15 1.15

Hajeer Emblem — A39

1979, Nov. 21
243 A39 10c multicolored .20 .20
244 A39 20c multicolored .20 .20
245 A39 75c multicolored .75 .75
a. Souvenir sheet of 3, #243-245 2.50 2.50
Nos. 243-245 (3) 1.15 1.15

Hegira, 1400th anniversary.

A40

A41

1980 Litho. *Perf. 14*
246 A40 10c Installation ceremony .20 .20
247 A40 10c Ceremony, diff. .20 .20
248 A40 75c Jefri Bolkiah .60 .60
249 A40 75c Sufri Bolkiah .60 .60
Nos. 246-249 (4) 1.60 1.60

Installation of Jefri Bolkiah and Sufri Bolkiah as Wizars (Ministers of State for Royalty) 1st anniv. Issue dates: Nos. 246, 248, Nov. 8; others, Dec. 6.

1981, Jan. 19 Litho. *Perf. 12x11½*
255 A41 10c Umbrella .20 .20
256 A41 15c Dagger, shield .20 .20
257 A41 20c Spears .25 .25
258 A41 30c Gold pouch .35 .35
Size: 22½x40mm
Perf. 14x13½
259 A41 50c Headdress .60 .60
a. Souvenir sheet of 5, #255-259 2.25 2.25
Nos. 255-259 (5) 1.60 1.60

A42

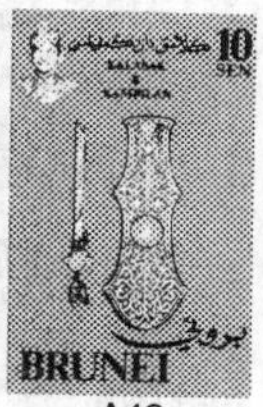

A43

1981, May 17 Litho. *Perf. 13x13½*
260 A42 10c car rose & black .20 .20
261 A42 75c dp violet & black .75 .75

13th World Telecommunications Day.

Perf. 12½x12, 12 (75c)
1981, July 15 Litho.
Deep Rose Lilac Background
262 A43 10c Dagger, case .20 .20
263 A43 15c Rifle, powder pouch .20 .20
264 A43 20c Spears .20 .20
265 A43 30c Sword, tunic, shield .30 .30
266 A43 50c Horns .50 .50
Size: 28½x45mm
267 A43 75c Gold bowl, table .75 .75
Nos. 262-267 (6) 2.15 2.15

See Nos. 278-289.

Royal Wedding Issue
Common Design Type
1981, July 29 *Perf. 14*
268 CD331 10c Bouquet .20 .20
269 CD331 $1 Charles .65 .65
270 CD331 $2 Couple 1.25 1.25
Nos. 268-270 (3) 2.10 2.10

World Food Day — A44

Intl. Year of the Disabled — A45

1981, Oct. 16 Litho. *Perf. 12*
271 A44 10c Fishermen .20 .20
272 A44 $1 Produce .80 .80

1981, Dec. 16 Wmk. 373 *Perf. 12*

273 A45 10c Blind man .20 .20
274 A45 20c Sign language .20 .20
275 A45 75c Man in wheelchair .60 .60
Nos. 273-275 (3) 1.00 1.00

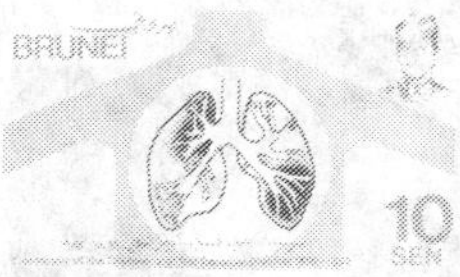

TB Bacillus Centenary A46

1982, Mar. 24 *Perf. 12, 13½ (75c)*

276 A46 10c Lungs .20 .20
277 A46 75c Bacillus, microscope .60 .60

Type of 1981

1982, May 31 Litho. *Perf. 12½x12*

Deep Magenta Background

278 A43 10c shown .20 .20
279 A43 15c Pedestal urn .20 .20
280 A43 20c Silver bowl .20 .20
281 A43 30c Candle .30 .30
282 A43 50c Gold pipe .50 .50

Size: 28x44mm

Perf. 13½

283 A43 75c Silver pointer .75 .75
Nos. 278-283 (6) 2.15 2.15

1982, July 15 Litho. *Perf. 12½x12*

Violet Background

284 A43 10c Urn .20 .20
285 A43 15c Crossed banners .20 .20
286 A43 20c Golden fan .20 .20
287 A43 30c Lid .30 .30
288 A43 50c Sword, sheath .50 .50

Size: 28x44mm

Perf. 12

289 A43 75c Golden chalice pole .75 .75
Nos. 284-289 (6) 2.15 2.15

A47

1983, Mar. 14 Litho. *Perf. 13½*

290 A47 10c Flag .20 .20
291 A47 20c Natl. palace .20 .20
292 A47 75c Oil drilling .75 .75
293 A47 $2 Sultan Bolkiah 2.00 2.00
a. Block of 4, #290-293 3.00 3.00

Commonwealth Day.

World Communications Year — A48

1983, July 15 Litho. *Perf. 13½*

294 A48 10c Mail delivery .20 .20
295 A48 75c Typewriter, phone .80 .80
296 A48 $2 Dish antenna, satellite, TV 2.00 2.00
Nos. 294-296 (3) 3.00 3.00

Opening of Hassanal Bolkiah National Stadium — A49

1983, Sept. 23 Litho. *Perf. 12*

297 A49 10c Soccer, vert. .20 .20
298 A49 75c Runners, vert. 1.00 1.00
299 A49 $1 shown 1.25 1.25
Nos. 297-299 (3) 2.45 2.45

Size, Nos. 297-298: 26x33mm.

Fishing Industry — A50

1983, Sept. 23 Litho. *Perf. 13½*

300 A50 10c Shrimp, lobster .20 .20
301 A50 50c Pacific jacks .60 .60
302 A50 75c Parrotfish, flatfish .90 .90
303 A50 $1 Tuna 1.25 1.25
Nos. 300-303 (4) 2.95 2.95

State Assembly Building A51

Map of Southeast Asia, Flag — A52

Sultan Hassanal Bolkiah — A53

1984, Jan. 1 Litho. *Perf. 13*

304 A51 10c shown .20 .20
305 A51 20c State Secretariat building .25 .25
306 A51 35c New Law Court .40 .40
307 A51 50c Liquid natural gas well .60 .60
308 A51 75c Omar Ali Saifuddin Mosque .90 .90
309 A51 $1 Sultan's Palace 1.25 1.25
310 A52 $3 shown 3.75 3.75
a. Souvenir sheet of 7, #304-310 7.25 7.25
Nos. 304-310 (7) 7.35 7.35

Souvenir Sheets

311 Sheet of 4, Constitution signing, 1959 1.25 1.25
a.-d. A53 25c any single .25 .25
312 Sheet of 4, Brunei U.K. Friendship Agreement, 1979 1.25 1.25
a.-d. A53 25c any single .25 .25

Forestry Resources — A54

1984, Apr. 21 Litho. *Perf. 13½*

313 A54 10c Forests, enrichment planting .20 .20
314 A54 50c Irrigation canal .65 .65
315 A54 75c Recreation forest .90 .90
316 A54 $1 Wildlife 1.25 1.25
Nos. 313-316 (4) 3.00 3.00

Philakorea 1984 — A55

Litho. & Engr.

1984, Oct. 22 *Perf. 13*

317 A55 10c No. 93 .20 .20
a. Souvenir sheet of 1 .20 .20
318 A55 75c No. 27 .90 .90
a. Souvenir sheet of 1 .90 .90
319 A55 $2 1895 local stamp 2.50 2.50
a. Souvenir sheet of 1 2.50 2.50
Nos. 317-319 (3) 3.60 3.60

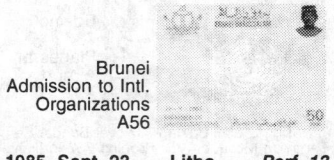

Brunei Admission to Intl. Organizations A56

1985, Sept. 23 Litho. *Perf. 13*

320 A56 50c UN .45 .45
321 A56 50c Commonwealth .45 .45
322 A56 50c ASEAN .45 .45
323 A56 50c OIC .45 .45
a. Souv. sheet of 4, #320-323 + label 2.00 2.00
Nos. 320-323 (4) 1.80 1.80

Intl. Youth Year — A57

1985, Oct. 17 *Perf. 12*

324 A57 10c shown .20 .20
325 A57 75c Industry, education .55 .55
326 A57 $1 Public Service .70 .70
Nos. 324-326 (3) 1.45 1.45

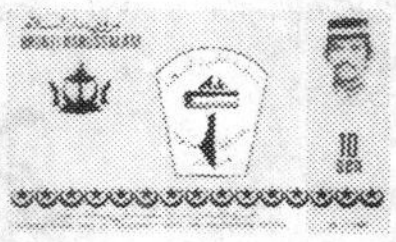

Intl. Day of Solidarity with the Palestinian People — A58

1985, Nov. 29 *Perf. 12x12½*

327 A58 10c lt blue & multi .20 .20
328 A58 50c pink & multi .55 .55
329 A58 $1 lt green & multi 1.10 1.10
Nos. 327-329 (3) 1.85 1.85

Natl. Scout Jamboree, Dec. 14-20 — A59

Sultan Hassanal Bolkiah — A60

1985, Dec. 14 *Perf. 13½*

330 A59 10c Scout handshake .20 .20
331 A59 20c Semaphore .20 .20
332 A59 $2 Jamboree emblem 1.75 1.75
Nos. 330-332 (3) 2.15 2.15

1985-86 Wmk. 233 *Perf. 13½x14½*

333 A60 10c multi .20 .20
334 A60 15c multi .20 .20
335 A60 20c multi .20 .20
336 A60 25c multi .25 .25
337 A60 35c multi ('86) .30 .30
338 A60 40c multi ('86) .35 .35
339 A60 50c multi ('86) .45 .45
340 A60 75c multi ('86) .70 .70

Size: 35x42mm

Perf. 14

341 A60 $1 multi ('86) .90 .90
342 A60 $2 multi ('86) 1.75 1.75
343 A60 $5 multi ('86) 4.50 4.50
344 A60 $10 multi ('86) 9.00 9.00
Nos. 333-344 (12) 18.80 18.80

Issued: #333-336, Dec. 23; #337-340, Jan. 15; #341-343, Feb. 23; #344, Mar. 29.

Admission to Intl. Organizations A61

Wmk. Cartor (385)

1986, Apr. 30 Litho. *Perf. 13*

345 A61 50c WMO .45 .45
346 A61 50c ITU .45 .45
347 A61 50c UPU .45 .45
348 A61 50c ICAO .45 .45
a. Souv. sheet of 4, #345-348 + label 1.80 1.80
Nos. 345-348 (4) 1.80 1.80

Royal Brunei Armed Forces, 25th Anniv. A62

1986, May 31 Unwmk. *Perf. 13½*

349 Strip of 4 1.40 1.40
a. A62 10c In combat .20 .20
b. A62 20c Communications .20 .20
c. A62 50c Air and sea defense .45 .45
d. A62 75c On parade, Royal Palace .70 .70

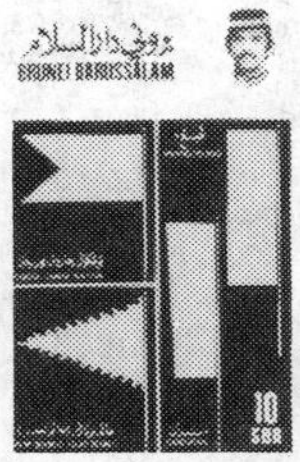

Royal Ensigns — A63

#350, Tunggul charok buritan, Pisang-pisang, Alam bernaga, Sandaran. #351, Dadap, Tunggul kawan, Ambal, Payong ubor-ubor, Sapu-sapu ayeng and Rawai lidah. #352, Ula-ula besar, Payong haram, Sumbu layang. #353, Payong ubor-ubor tiga ringkat and Payong tinggi. #354, Panji-panji, Chogan istiadat, Chogan ugama. #355, Lambang duli yang maha mulia and Mahligai.

1986 Litho. *Perf. 12½*

350 A63 10c multicolored .20 .20
351 A63 10c multicolored .20 .20
352 A63 75c multicolored .70 .70
353 A63 75c multicolored .70 .70
354 A63 $2 multicolored 1.75 1.75
355 A63 $2 multicolored 1.75 1.75
Nos. 350-355 (6) 5.30 5.30

Intl. Peace Year — A64

1986, Oct. 24 Litho. *Perf. 12*

356 A64 50c Peace doves .50 .50
357 A64 75c Hands .70 .70
358 A64 $1 Peace symbols .90 .90
Nos. 356-358 (3) 2.10 2.10

Natl. Anti-Drug Campaign Posters — A65

Brass Artifacts — A66

1987, Mar. 15 **Litho.** ***Perf. 12***

359 A65 10c Jail .20 .20
360 A65 75c Noose .65 .65
361 A65 $1 Execution .90 .90
Nos. 359-361 (3) 1.75 1.75

1987, July 15

362 A66 50c Kiri (kettle) .45 .45
363 A66 50c Langguai (bowl) .45 .45
364 A66 50c Badil (cannon) .45 .45
365 A66 50c Pelita (lamp) .45 .45
Nos. 362-365 (4) 1.80 1.80

See Nos. 388-391.

Dewan Bahasa Dan Pustaka, 25th Anniv. — A67

Illustration reduced.

1987, Sept. 29 ***Perf. 13½x13***

366 A67 Strip of 3 1.75 1.75
a. 10c multicolored .20 .20
b. 50c multicolored .30 .30
c. $2 multicolored 1.25 1.25

Language and Literature Bureau.

ASEAN, 20th Anniv. — A68

1987, Aug. 8 **Litho.** ***Perf. 14x13½***

367 A68 20c Map .20 .20
368 A68 50c Year dates .45 .45
369 A68 $1 Flags, emblem .90 .90
Nos. 367-369 (3) 1.55 1.55

World Food Day A70

Fruit: a, Artocarpus odoratissima. b, Canarium odontophyllum mig. c, Litsea garciae. d, Mangifera foetida lour.

1987, Oct. 31 ***Perf. 12½***

370 Strip of 4 1.90 1.90
a.-d. A70 50c any single .45 .45

See Nos. 374, 405, 423, 457-460.

Intl. Year of Shelter for the Homeless A71

Various houses.

1987, Nov. 28 **Litho.** ***Perf. 13***

371 A71 50c multi .50 .50
372 A71 75c multi, diff. .70 .70
373 A71 $1 multi, diff. .95 .95
Nos. 371-373 (3) 2.15 2.15

Fruit Type of 1987
Without FAO Emblem, Dated 1988

Fruit: a, Durio. b, Durio oxleyanus. c, Durio graveolens (cross section at L). d, Durio graveolens (cross section at R).

1988, Jan. 30 **Litho.** ***Perf. 12***

374 Strip of 4 2.00 2.00
a.-d. A70 50c, any single .50 .50

Opening of Malay Technology Museum — A72

1988, Feb. 29 ***Perf. 12½x12***

375 A72 10c Wooden lathe .20 .20
376 A72 75c Water wheel, buffalo .80 .80
377 A72 $1 Bird caller in blind 1.00 1.00
Nos. 375-377 (3) 2.00 2.00

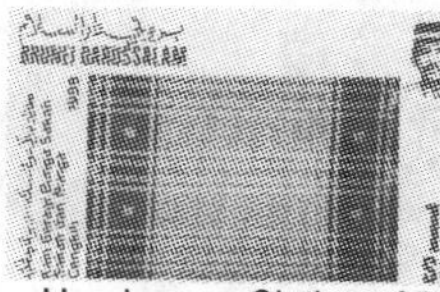

Handwoven Cloth — A73

Designs: 10c, Kain Beragi Bunga Sakah-Sakah Dan Bunga Cengkih. 20c, Kain Jong Sarat. 25c, Kain Si Pugut. 40c, Kain Si Pugut Bunga Berlapis. 75c, Kain Si Lobang Bangsi Bunga Belitang Kipas.

1988, Apr. 30 **Litho.** ***Perf. 12***

378 A73 10c multicolored .20 .20
379 A73 20c org brown & blk .20 .20
380 A73 25c multicolored .25 .25
381 A73 40c multicolored .40 .40
382 A73 75c multicolored .75 .75
a. Souvenir sheet of 5, #378-382 + label 1.75 1.75
Nos. 378-382 (5) 1.80 1.80

1988, Sept. 29 **Litho.** ***Perf. 12***

Designs: 10c, Kain Beragi. 20c, Kain Bertabur. 25c, Kain Sukma Indra. 40c, Kain Si Pugut Bunga Bersusup. 75c, Kain Beragi Si Lobang Bangsi Bunga Cendera Kesuma.

383 A73 10c multicolored .20 .20
384 A73 20c multicolored .20 .20
385 A73 25c multicolored .25 .25
386 A73 40c multicolored .40 .40
387 A73 75c multicolored .75 .75
a. Souvenir sheet of 5, #383-387 1.75 1.75
Nos. 383-387 (5) 1.80 1.80

Brass Artifacts Type of 1987

1988, June 30 **Litho.** ***Perf. 12***

388 A66 50c Celapa (repousse box) .50 .50
389 A66 50c Gangsa (footed plate) .50 .50
390 A66 50c Periok (lidded pot) .50 .50
391 A66 50c Lampong (candlestick) .50 .50
Nos. 388-391 (4) 2.00 2.00

Coronation of Sultan Hassanal Bolkiah, 20th Anniv. — A74

1988, Aug. 1 **Litho.** ***Perf. 14***

392 A74 20c shown .25 .25
393 A74 75c Reading from the Koran .75 .75

Size: 26x62mm
Perf. 12½x13

394 A74 $2 In full regalia 2.00 2.00
a. Souvenir sheet of 3, #392-394 3.00 3.00
Nos. 392-394 (3) 3.00 3.00

Eradicate Malaria, WHO 40th Anniv. — A75

1988, Dec. 17 **Litho.** ***Perf. 14x13½***

395 A75 25c Mosquito .25 .25
396 A75 35c Extermination .35 .35
397 A75 $2 Microscope, infected blood cells 2.10 2.10
Nos. 395-397 (3) 2.70 2.70

Natl. Day — A76

1989, Feb. 23 **Litho.** ***Perf. 12***
Size of 60c: 22x54½mm

398 A76 20c Sultan Bolkiah, officials .20 .20
399 A76 30c Honor guard .30 .30
400 A76 60c Fireworks, palace, vert. .60 .60
401 A76 $2 Religious ceremony 2.00 2.00
a. Souvenir sheet of 4, #398-401 3.25 3.25
Nos. 398-401 (4) 3.10 3.10

Independence from Britain, 5th anniv.

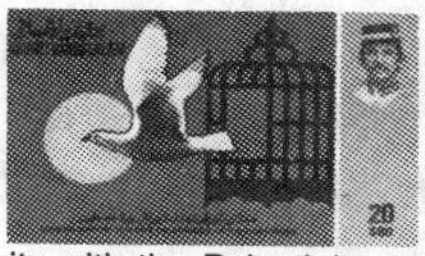

Solidarity with the Palestinians — A77

1989, Apr. 1 **Litho.** ***Perf. 13½***

402 A77 20c shown .25 .25
403 A77 75c Map, flag .75 .75
404 A77 $1 Dome of the Rock 1.00 1.00
Nos. 402-404 (3) 2.00 2.00

Fruit Type of 1987
Without FAO Emblem, Dated 1989

Designs: a, Daemonorops fissa. b, Eleiodoxa conferia. c, Salacca zalacca. d, Calamus ornatus.

1989, Oct. 31 **Litho.** ***Perf. 12***

405 Strip of 4 2.50 2.50
a.-d. A70 60c any single .80 .80

Oil and Gas Industry, 60th Anniv. A79

1989, Dec. 28 ***Perf. 13½***

406 A79 20c Drill .25 .25
407 A79 60c Tanker .65 .65
408 A79 90c Refinery 1.00 1.00
409 A79 $1 Rail transport 1.10 1.10
410 A79 $2 Offshore rig 2.25 2.25
Nos. 406-410 (5) 5.25 5.25

Brunei Museum, 25th Anniv. A80

1990, Jan. 1 **Litho.** ***Perf. 12x12½***

411 A80 30c Exhibits .30 .30
412 A80 60c Official opening, 1965 .60 .60
413 A80 $1 Museum exterior 1.00 1.00
Nos. 411-413 (3) 1.90 1.90

Intl. Literacy Year A81

1990, July 15 **Litho.** ***Perf. 12x12½***

414 A81 15c multicolored .20 .20
415 A81 90c multicolored .95 .95
416 A81 $1 multicolored 1.10 1.10
Nos. 414-416 (3) 2.25 2.25

Tarsier — A82

Fight Against AIDS — A83

1990, Sept. 29 **Litho.** ***Perf. 12***

417 A82 20c shown .25 .25
418 A82 60c Eating leaves .75 .75
419 A82 90c Climbing tree 1.00 1.00
Nos. 417-419 (3) 2.00 2.00

1990, Dec. 1 **Litho.** ***Perf. 13***

420 A83 20c shown .25 .25
421 A83 30c AIDS transmission .35 .35
422 A83 90c Tombstone, skulls 1.00 1.00
Nos. 420-422 (3) 1.60 1.60

Fruit Type of 1987
Without FAO Emblem, Dated 1990

Fruit: a, Willoughbea (uncut core). b, Willoughbea (core cut in half). c, Willoughbea angustifolia.

1990, Dec. 31 ***Perf. 12½***

423 Strip of 3 2.10 2.10
a.-c. A70 60c any single .70 .70

Proboscis Monkey — A84

1991, Mar. 30 **Litho.** ***Perf. 13½x14***

424 A84 15c shown .20 .20
425 A84 20c Head, facing .25 .25
426 A84 50c Sitting on branch .60 .60
427 A84 60c Adult with young .70 .70
Nos. 424-427 (4) 1.75 1.75

Teacher's Day A85

Design: 90c, Teacher at blackboard.

1991, Sept. 23 **Litho.** ***Perf. 13½x14***

428 A85 60c multicolored .70 .70
429 A85 90c multicolored 1.10 1.10

Brunei Beauty A86

1991, Oct. 1 **Litho.** ***Perf. 13***

430 A86 30c Three immature .35 .35
431 A86 60c Female .70 .70
432 A86 $1 Adult male 1.25 1.25
Nos. 430-432 (3) 2.30 2.30

Happy Family Campaign — A87

1991, Nov. 30 Litho. *Perf. 13*

433 A87 20c Family, graduating son .25 .25
434 A87 60c Mothers, children .65 .65
435 A87 90c Adults, children, heart 1.10 1.10
Nos. 433-435 (3) 2.00 2.00

World Health Day — A88

1992, Apr. 7 Litho. *Perf. 13*

436 A88 20c multicolored .25 .25
437 A88 50c multi, diff. .60 .60

Size: 48x28mm

438 A88 75c multi, diff. .90 .90
Nos. 436-438 (3) 1.75 1.75

Brunei-Singapore and Brunei-Malaysia-Philippines Fiber Optic Submarine Cables — A89

1992, Apr. 28 Litho. *Perf. 12*

439 A89 20c Map .25 .25
440 A89 30c Diagram .35 .35
441 A89 90c Submarine cable 1.10 1.10
Nos. 439-441 (3) 1.70 1.70

Visit ASEAN Year A90

Designs: a, 20c, Sculptures. b, 60c, Judo exhibition. c, $1, Sculptures, diff.

1992, June 30 Litho. *Perf. 13½x14*

442 A90 Strip of 3, #a.-c. 2.00 2.00

ASEAN, 25th Anniv. — A91

A92

1992, Aug. 8 Litho. *Perf. 14*

443 A91 20c shown .25 .25
444 A91 60c Building .65 .65
445 A91 90c Views of member states 1.10 1.10
Nos. 443-445 (3) 2.00 2.00

1992, Oct. 5 *Perf. 14x13½*

Sultan in various forms of dress and: No. 446a, Coronation procession. b, Airport. c, New Law Court, Sultan's Palace. d, Ship and Brunei University. e, Mosque, buildings.

446 A92 25c Strip of 5, #a.-e. 1.50 1.50

Sultan Hassanal Bolkiah's Accession to the Throne, 25th Anniv.

Birds — A93

Designs: No. 447, Crested wood partridge, vert. No. 448, Long-tailed parakeet, vert. No. 449, Chestnut-breasted malkoha. No. 450, Asian paradise flycatcher, vert. No. 451, Magpie robin, vert. No. 452, White-rumped shama. No. 453, Great argus pheasant, vert. No. 454, Malay lorikeet, vert. No. 455, Black and red broadbill, vert.

Perf. 14x13½, 13½x14

1992-93 Litho.

447 A93 30c multicolored .40 .40
448 A93 30c multicolored .40 .40
449 A93 30c multicolored .40 .40
450 A93 60c multicolored .75 .75
451 A93 60c multicolored .75 .75
452 A93 60c multicolored .75 .75
453 A93 $1 multicolored 1.25 1.25
454 A93 $1 multicolored 1.25 1.25
455 A93 $1 multicolored 1.25 1.25
Nos. 447-455 (9) 7.20 7.20

Issued: #447, 450, 453, 12/30/92; #448, 451, 454, 1/27/93; others, 5/3/93.

Natl. Day, 10th Anniv. — A94

10th anniv. emblem and: a, 10c, Natl. flag. b, 20c, Hands supporting inscription. c, 30c, Natl. day emblems, 1985-93. d, 60c, Emblem with star, crossed swords.

1994, June 16 Litho. *Perf. 13*

456 A94 Strip of 4, #a.-d. 1.50 1.50

Fruit Type of 1987
Without FAO Emblem, Dated 1994

Designs: No. 457, Nephelium mutabile. No. 458, Nephelium xerospermoides. No. 459, Nephelium spp. No. 460, Nephelium macrophyllum.

1994, Aug. 8 Litho. *Perf. 13½x13*

457 A70 60c multicolored .75 .75
458 A70 60c multicolored .75 .75
459 A70 60c multicolored .75 .75
460 A70 60c multicolored .75 .75
Nos. 457-460 (4) 3.00 3.00

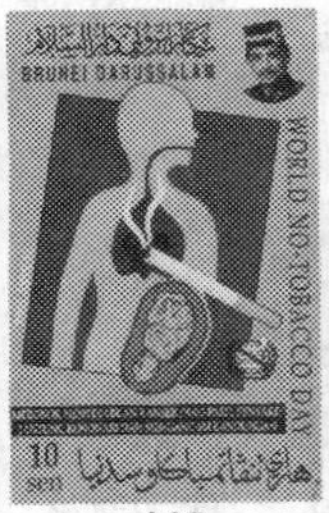

A95

A96

World Stop Smoking Day: 10c, Cigarette, lung, fetus over human figure. 15c, People throwing away tobacco, cigarettes, pipe. $2, Arms around world crushing out cigarettes.

1994, Sept. 1 Litho. *Perf. 13½x13*

461 A95 10c multicolored .20 .20
462 A95 15c multicolored .20 .20
463 A95 $2 multicolored 2.50 2.50
Nos. 461-463 (3) 2.90 2.90

1994, Oct. 7 *Perf. 13½*

Girl Guides in Brunei, 40th anniv.: a, Leader. b, Girl receiving award. c, Girl reading. d, Girls in various costumes. e, Girls camping out.

464 A96 40c Strip of 5, #a.-e. 2.50 2.50

Royal Brunei Airlines, 20th Anniv. — A97

Airplanes: 10c, Twin-engine propeller. 20c, Passenger jet attached to tow bar. $1, Passenger jet in air.

1994, Nov. 18 Litho. *Perf. 13½*

465 A97 10c multicolored .20 .20
466 A97 20c multicolored .30 .30
467 A97 $1 multicolored 1.25 1.25
Nos. 465-467 (3) 1.75 1.75

Intl. Day Against Drug Abuse — A98

Healthy people wearing traditional costumes: 20c, 60c, $1.

1994, Dec. 30 Litho. *Perf. 13½*

468 A98 Strip of 3, #a.-c. 2.25 2.25

No. 468 is a continuous design.

City of Bandar Seri Begawan, 25th Anniv. A100

Aerial view of city: 30c, In 1970. 50c, In 1980, with details of significant buildings. $1, In 1990.

1995, Oct. 4 Litho. *Perf. 13½*

481 A100 30c multicolored .40 .40
482 A100 50c multicolored .70 .70
483 A100 $1 multicolored 1.40 1.40
Nos. 481-483 (3) 2.50 2.50

A101

A102

UN headquarters: 20c, Delegates in General Assembly. 60c, Security Council. 90c, Exterior.

1995, Oct. 24 *Perf. 14½x14*

484 A101 20c multicolored .30 .30
485 A101 60c multicolored .85 .85

Size: 27x44mm

486 A101 90c multicolored 1.25 1.25
Nos. 484-486 (3) 2.40 2.40

UN, 50th anniv.

1995, Oct. 28 *Perf. 13x13½*

University of Brunei, 10th Anniv.: 30c, Students in classroom. 50c, Campus buildings. 90c, Sultan in procession.

487 A102 30c multicolored .40 .40
488 A102 50c multicolored .70 .70
489 A102 90c multicolored 1.25 1.25
Nos. 487-489 (3) 2.35 2.35

A103

A104

Royal Brunei Police, 25th Anniv.: 25c, Policemen in various uniforms. 50c, Various tasks performed by police. 75c, Sultan reviewing police.

1996, Feb. 10 Litho. *Perf. 13½x13*

490 A103 25c multicolored .35 .35
491 A103 50c multicolored .75 .75
492 A103 75c multicolored 1.10 1.10
Nos. 490-492 (3) 2.20 2.20

1996, May 17 Litho. *Perf. 13½*

World Telecommunications Day: 20c, Cartoon telephone, cordless telephone. 35c, Globe, telephone dial surrounded by communication devices. $1, Signals transmitting from earth, people communicating.

493 A104 20c multicolored .30 .30
494 A104 35c multicolored .50 .50
495 A104 $1 multicolored 1.40 1.40
Nos. 493-495 (3) 2.20 2.20

A105

A106

Sultan: No. 496, Among people, in black attire. No. 497, Waving, in yellow attire. No. 498, In blue shirt. No. 499, Among people, wearing cream-colored robe.

$1, Hand raised in yellow attire.

1996, July 15 Litho. *Perf. 13*

496 A105 50c multicolored .75 .75
497 A105 50c multicolored .75 .75
498 A105 50c multicolored .75 .75
499 A105 50c multicolored .75 .75
Nos. 496-499 (4) 3.00 3.00

Souvenir Sheet

500 A105 $1 multicolored 1.40 1.40

Sultan Paduka Seri Baginda, 50th birthday.
A souvenir sheet of five $50 stamps exists.

1996, Nov. 11 Litho. *Perf. 13½*

Terns.

501 A106 20c Black-naped tern .30 .30
502 A106 30c Roseate tern .45 .45
503 A106 $1 Bridle tern 1.40 1.40
Nos. 501-503 (3) 2.15 2.15

No. 502 is spelled "Roslate" on stamp.

Sultan Hassanal Bolkiah
A107 A108

Perf. 14x13½

1996, Oct. 9 Litho. Wmk. 387

Background Color

504	A107	10c yellow green	.20	.20
505	A107	15c pale pink	.20	.20
506	A107	20c lilac pink	.30	.30
507	A107	30c salmon	.45	.45
508	A107	50c yellow	.75	.75
509	A107	60c pale green	.85	.85
510	A107	75c blue	1.10	1.10
511	A107	90c lilac	1.25	1.25
512	A108	$1 pink	1.40	1.40
513	A108	$2 orange yellow	3.00	3.00
514	A108	$5 light blue	7.25	7.25
515	A108	$10 bright yellow	14.50	14.50
		Nos. 504-515 (12)	31.25	31.25

Flowers
A109

1997, May 29 Litho. *Perf. 12*

516	A109	20c Acanthus ebracteatus	.30	.30
517	A109	30c Lumnitzera littorea	.45	.45
518	A109	$1 Nypa fruticans	1.40	1.40
		Nos. 516-518 (3)	2.15	2.15

Marine Life
A110

Designs: No. 519, Bohadschia argus. No. 520, Oxycomanthus bennetti. No. 521, Heterocentrotus mammillatus. No. 522, Linckia laevigata.

1997, Dec. 15 Litho. *Perf. 12*

519	A110	60c multicolored	.85	.85
520	A110	60c multicolored	.85	.85
521	A110	60c multicolored	.85	.85
522	A110	60c multicolored	.85	.85
		Nos. 519-522 (4)	3.40	3.40

Asian and Pacific Decade of Disabled Persons (1993-2002)
A111

Designs: 20c, Silhouettes of people, hands finger spelling "Brunei," children. 50c, Fireworks over city, blind people participating in arts, crafts, music. $1, Handicapped people playing sports.

1998, Mar. 31 Litho. *Perf. 13x13½*

523	A111	20c multicolored	.25	.25
524	A111	50c multicolored	.65	.65
525	A111	$1 multicolored	1.25	1.25
		Nos. 523-525 (3)	2.15	2.15

ASEAN, 30th Anniv. — A112

Designs: No. 526, Night scene of Sultan's Palace, buildings, map of Brunei. No. 527, Flags of ASEAN nations. No. 528, Daytime scenes of Sultan's Palace, transportation methods, buildings in Brunei.

1998, Aug. 8 Litho. *Perf. 13½*

526	A112	30c multicolored	.40	.40
527	A112	30c multicolored	.40	.40
528	A112	30c multicolored	.40	.40
		Nos. 526-528 (3)	1.20	1.20

Sultan Hassanal Bolkiah, 30th Anniv. of Coronation — A113

Designs: 60c, In procession, saluting, on throne. 90c, Sultan Omar Ali Saifuddin standing, Sultan Hassanal Bolkiah on throne. $1, Procession.

1998, Aug. 1 Litho. *Perf. 12*

529	A113	60c multicolored	.65	.65
530	A113	90c multicolored	1.10	1.10
531	A113	$1 multicolored	1.25	1.25
a.		Souvenir sheet, #529-531	3.00	3.00
		Nos. 529-531 (3)	3.00	3.00

A114 A115

Investiture of Crown Prince Al-Muhtadee Billah: $1, Signing document. $2, Formal portrait. $3, Arms of the Crown Prince.

1998, Aug. 10

532	A114	$1 multicolored	1.25	1.25
533	A114	$2 multicolored	2.50	2.50
534	A114	$3 multicolored	3.50	3.50
a.		Souvenir sheet, #532-534	7.25	7.25
		Nos. 532-534 (3)	7.25	7.25

1998, Sept. 29 *Perf. 13x13½*

30c, Hands clasped, woman, man. 60c, Dollar sign over book, arrows, "7.45AM." 90c, Silhouettes of people seated at table, standing, scales.

535	A115	30c multicolored	.35	.35
536	A115	60c multicolored	.70	.70
537	A115	90c multicolored	1.10	1.10
		Nos. 535-537 (3)	2.15	2.15

Civil Sevice Day, 5th anniv.

Kingfishers — A116

A117

1998, Nov. 11 Litho. *Perf. 13½x13*

538	A116	20c Blue-eared	.25	.25
539	A116	30c Common	.35	.35
540	A116	60c White-collared	.75	.75
541	A116	$1 Stork-billed	1.25	1.25
		Nos. 538-541 (4)	2.60	2.60

1999, Feb. 23 Litho. *Perf. 13*

National Day, 15th Anniv.: 20c, Boat docks, residential area. 60c, Methods of communications. 90c, Buildings, roadways, tower, oil rig.

542	A117	20c multicolored	.25	.25
543	A117	60c multicolored	.75	.75
544	A117	90c multicolored	1.10	1.10
a.		Souvenir sheet, #542-544	2.25	2.25
		Nos. 542-544 (3)	2.10	2.10

20th Sea Games, 1999 — A119

No. 549: a, Field hockey, cycling. b, Basketball, soccer. c, Tennis, track and field. d, Billiards. e, Bowling.

No. 550: a, Shooting. b, Golf, squash. c, Boxing. d, Kick fighting, badminton, ping pong. e, Swimming, rowing.

$1, Shooting, tennis, running, soccer, cycling, basketball.

1999, Aug. 7 Litho. *Perf. 14¼*

Strips of 5, #a.-e.

549-550	A119	20c each	2.40	2.40

Souvenir Sheet

551	A119	$1 multicolored	1.25	1.25

No. 551 contains one 35x35mm stamp.

UPU, 125th Anniv. — A120

20c, Handshake, globe, letters. 30c, Emblems of UPU, Brunei Post. 75c, Postal workers & services.

1999, Oct. 9 Litho. *Perf. 14*

552	A120	20c multicolored	.25	.25
553	A120	30c multicolored	.35	.35
554	A120	75c multicolored	.90	.90
		Nos. 552-554 (3)	1.50	1.50

OCCUPATION STAMPS

Issued under Japanese Occupation

Stamps and Types of 1908-37 Handstamped in Violet, Red Violet, Blue or Red

大日本帝国政府

Perf. 14, 14x11½ (#N7)

1942-44 Wmk. 4

N1	A1	1c black	6.50	*11.00*
N2	A1	2c green	65.00	*100.00*
N3	A1	2c dull orange	3.50	*6.00*
N4	A1	3c green	27.50	*65.00*
N5	A1	4c orange	5.00	*14.00*
N6	A1	5c brown	5.50	*14.00*
N7	A2	6c slate gray	65.00	*140.00*
N8	A2	6c red	650.00	500.00
N9	A1	8c gray (RV)	650.00	*825.00*
N10	A2	8c carmine	5.00	*10.00*
N11	A1	10c violet, *yel*	10.00	*17.50*
N12	A2	12c blue	10.00	*17.50*
N13	A2	15c ultra	10.00	*17.50*
N14	A1	25c dk violet	22.50	*65.00*
N15	A1	30c org & red vio	110.00	*275.00*
N16	A1	50c blk, *green*	35.00	*80.00*
N17	A1	$1 red & blk, *bl*	60.00	*100.00*

Wmk. 3

N18	A1	$5 lake, *green*	800.	750.
N19	A1	$25 black, *red*	1,400.	*1,500.*

Overprints vary in shade. Nos. N3, N7, N10 and N13 without overprint are not believed to have been regularly issued.

大日本

No. 43 Surcharged in Red

参弗

帝国郵便

1944 Wmk. 4 *Perf. 14*

N20	A1	$3 on 1c black	*3,250.*	*3,250.*
a.		On No. N1	*3,250.*	*3,250.*

BULGARIA

ˌbəl-ˈgar-ē-ə

LOCATION — Southeastern Europe bordering on the Black Sea on the east and the Danube River on the north

GOVT. — Republic

AREA — 42,855 sq. mi.

POP. — 8,194,772 (1999 est.)

CAPITAL — Sofia

In 1885 Bulgaria, then a principality under the suzerainty of the Sultan of Turkey, was joined by Eastern Rumelia. Independence from Turkey was obtained in 1908.

100 Centimes = 1 Franc
100 Stotinki = 1 Lev (1881)

Catalogue values for unused stamps in this country are for Never Hinged items, beginning with Scott 293 in the regular postage section, Scott B1 in the semi-postal section, Scott C15 in the airpost section, Scott CB1 in the airpost semi-postal section, Scott E1 in the special delivery section, Scott J47 in the postage due section, Scott O1 in the officials section, and Scott Q1 in the parcel post section.

Watermarks

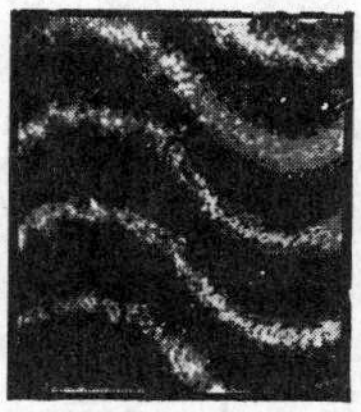

Wmk. 145- Wavy Lines

The Scott Catalogue value is a retail value; that is, what you could expect to pay for the stamp in a grade of Very Fine. The value listed reflects recent actual dealer selling prices.

Wmk. 168- Wavy Lines and EZGV in Cyrillic

Wmk. 275- Entwined Curved Lines

Lion of Bulgaria

A1 A2 A3

Perf. 14½x15

1879, June 1 Wmk. 168 Typo.

Laid Paper

1	A1	5c black & orange	65.00	18.00
2	A1	10c black & green	250.00	60.00
3	A1	25c black & violet	175.00	15.00
a.		Imperf.		
4	A1	50c black & blue	250.00	50.00
5	A2	1fr black & red	50.00	17.50

1881, June 10

6	A3	3s red & silver	12.50	2.50
7	A3	5s black & orange	15.00	2.50
a.		Background inverted		*1,750.*
8	A3	10s black & green	65.00	6.50
9	A3	15s dp car red & green	60.00	6.50
10	A3	25s black & violet	250.00	30.00
11	A3	30s blue & fawn	17.50	6.50

1882, Dec. 4

12	A3	3s orange & yellow	1.00	.50
a.		Background inverted	*2,750.*	*1,400.*
13	A3	5s green & pale green	6.00	.50
a.		5s rose & pale rose (error)	*1,600.*	*1,300.*
14	A3	10s rose & pale rose	8.00	.75
15	A3	15s red vio & pale lil	6.00	.40
16	A3	25s blue & pale blue	6.00	.50
17	A3	30s violet & green	6.00	.75
18	A3	50s blue & pink	6.00	.75
		Nos. 12-18 (7)	39.00	4.15

See Nos. 207-210, 286.

A4 A5

Surcharged in Black, Carmine or Vermilion

1884, May 1

Typo. Surcharge

19	A4	3s on 10s rose (Bk)	95.00	30.00
20	A4	5s on 30s blue & fawn (C)	95.00	45.00
20A	A4	5s on 30s bl & fawn (Bk)	*1,750.*	*1,750.*
21	A5	15s on 25s blue (C)	140.00	40.00

On some values the surcharge may be found inverted or double.

1885, June

Litho. Surcharge

21B	A4	3s on 10s rose (Bk)	45.00	27.50
21C	A4	5s on 30s bl & fawn (V)	50.00	35.00
21D	A5	15s on 25s blue (V)	70.00	45.00
22	A5	50s on 1fr blk & red (Bk)	190.00	125.00

Forgeries of Nos. 19-22 are plentiful.

Word below left star in oval has 5 letters — A6

Third letter below left star is "A" — A7

1885, May 25

23	A6	1s gray vio & pale gray	12.00	5.00
24	A7	2s sl grn & pale gray	12.00	4.00

Word below left star has 4 letters — A8

Third letter below left star is "b" with cross-bar in upper half — A9

A10

1886-87

25	A8	1s gray vio & pale gray	1.00	.20
26	A9	2s sl grn & pale gray	1.00	.20
27	A10	1 l black & red ('87)	27.50	3.00
		Nos. 25-27 (3)	29.50	3.40

For surcharge see No. 40.

A11

Perf. 10½, 11, 11½, 13, 13½

1889 Wove Paper Unwmk.

28	A11	1s lilac	.20	.20
29	A11	2s gray	.60	.20
30	A11	3s bister brown	.40	.20
31	A11	5s yellow green	.25	.20
a.		Vert. pair, imperf. btwn.		
32	A11	10s rose	1.10	.20
33	A11	15s orange	.60	.20
34	A11	25s blue	1.00	.20
35	A11	30s dk brown	8.75	.20
36	A11	50s green	.60	.30
37	A11	1 l orange red	.50	.40
		Nos. 28-37 (10)	14.00	2.30

The 10s orange is a proof.

Nos. 28-34 exist imperforate. Value, set $225.

See Nos. 39, 41-42. For overprints and surcharges see Nos. 38, 55-56, 77-81, 113.

No. 35 Surcharged in Black **15**

1892, Jan. 26

38	A11	15s on 30s brn	10.00	1.00
a.		Inverted surcharge	*70.00*	*52.50*

1894 *Perf. 10½, 11, 11½*

Pelure Paper

39	A11	10s red	7.00	.50
a.		Imperf.	*57.50*	

No. 26 Surcharged in Red **01**

Wmk. Wavy Lines (168)

1895, Oct. 25 *Perf. 14½x15*

Laid Paper

40	A9	1s on 2s	.75	.20
a.		Inverted surcharge	6.00	5.00
b.		Double surcharge	*62.50*	*62.50*
c.		Pair, one without surcharge	*125.00*	*125.00*

This surcharge on No. 24 is a proof.

Wmk. Coat of Arms in the Sheet

1896, Apr. 30 *Perf. 11½, 13*

Wove Paper

41	A11	2 l rose & pale rose	2.00	1.50
42	A11	3 l black & buff	3.50	3.00

Coat of Arms — A14

Cherry Wood Cannon — A15

1896, Feb. 2 *Perf. 13*

43	A14	1s blue green	.30	.20
44	A14	5s dark blue	.30	.20
45	A14	15s purple	.50	.20
46	A14	25s red	4.75	.85
		Nos. 43-46 (4)	5.85	1.45

Baptism of Prince Boris.

Examples of Nos. 41-46 from sheet edges show no watermark.

Nos. 43, 45-46 were also printed on rough unwatermarked paper.

1901, Apr. 20 Litho. Unwmk.

53	A15	5s carmine	1.25	.90
54	A15	15s yellow green	1.25	.90

Insurrection of Independence in April, 1876, 25th anniversary.

Exist imperf. Forgeries exist.

Nos. 30 and 36 Surcharged in Black **5**

1901, Mar. 24 Typo.

55	A11	5s on 3s bister brn	1.75	.75
a.		Inverted surcharge	42.50	42.50
b.		Pair, one without surcharge	*70.00*	*70.00*
56	A11	10s on 50s green	2.25	.75
a.		Inverted surcharge	50.00	50.00
b.		Pair, one without surcharge	*70.00*	*70.00*

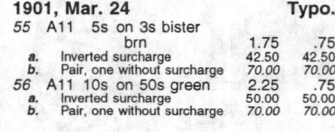

Tsar Ferdinand A17

Fighting at Shipka Pass A18

ONE LEV:

Type I - The numerals in the upper corners have, at the top, a sloping serif on the left side and a short straight serif on the right.

Type II - The numerals in the upper corners are of ordinary shape without the serif at the right.

1901-05 Typo. *Perf. 12½*

57	A17	1s vio & gray blk	.20	.20
58	A17	2s brnz grn & ind	.20	.20
a.		Imperf.		
59	A17	3s orange & ind	.20	.20
60	A17	5s emerald & brn	2.25	.20
61	A17	10s rose & blk	1.50	.20
62	A17	15s claret & gray blk	.65	.20
63	A17	25s blue & blk	.65	.20
64	A17	30s bis & gray blk	15.00	.20
65	A17	50s dk blue & brn	.80	.20
66	A17	1 l red org & brnz grn, type I	2.00	.20
67	A17	1 l brn red & brnz grn, II ('05)	45.00	1.75
68	A17	2 l carmine & blk	4.00	.85
69	A17	3 l slate & red brn	5.00	1.90
		Nos. 57-69 (13)	77.45	6.50

For surcharges see Nos. 73, 83-85, 87-88.

1902, Aug. 29 Litho. *Perf. 11½*

70	A18	5s lake	1.00	.35
71	A18	10s blue green	1.00	.35
72	A18	15s blue	5.25	1.60
		Nos. 70-72 (3)	7.25	2.30

Battle of Shipka Pass, 1877.

Imperf. copies are proofs.

Excellent forgeries of Nos. 70 to 72 exist.

No. 62 Surcharged in Black **10**

1903, Oct. 1 *Perf. 12½*

73	A17	10s on 15s	5.00	.35
a.		Inverted surcharge	*57.50*	*50.00*
b.		Double surcharge	*57.50*	*50.00*
c.		Pair, one without surcharge	*100.00*	*100.00*
d.		10s on 10s rose & black	*275.00*	*275.00*

Ferdinand in 1887 and 1907 A19

1907, Aug. 12 Litho. *Perf. 11½*

74	A19	5s deep green	9.00	.90
75	A19	10s red brown	16.00	.90
76	A19	25s deep blue	24.00	1.75
		Nos. 74-76 (3)	49.00	3.55

Accession to the throne of Ferdinand I, 20th anniversary.

Nos. 74-76 imperf. are proofs. Nos. 74-76 exist in pairs imperforate between.

Stamps of 1889 Overprinted **1909**

1909

77	A11	1s lilac	1.00	.50
a.		Inverted overprint	21.00	17.50
b.		Double overprint, one inverted	25.00	25.00
78	A11	5s yellow green	1.00	.50
a.		Inverted overprint	25.00	25.00
b.		Double overprint	25.00	25.00

With Additional Surcharge **5** or **10**

79	A11	5s on 30s brown (Bk)	1.50	.20
a.		"5" double		
b.		"1990" for "1909"	*700.00*	*550.00*
80	A11	10s on 15s org (Bk)	1.50	.40
a.		Inverted surcharge	17.50	17.50
b.		"1909" omitted	*27.50*	*27.50*
81	A11	10s on 50s dk grn (R)	1.50	.40
a.		"1990" for "1909"	100.00	100.00
b.		Black surcharge	52.50	52.50

Nos. 62 & 64 Surcharged with Value Only

83	A17	5s on 15s (Bl)	1.75	.60
a.		Inverted surcharge	21.00	21.00
84	A17	10s on 15s (Bl)	4.50	.40
a.		Inverted surcharge	21.00	21.00
85	A17	25s on 30s (R)	5.75	.90
a.		Double surcharge	70.00	70.00
b.		"2" of "25" omitted	87.50	87.50
c.		Blue surcharge	*275.00*	*175.00*

1910

Nos. 59 and 62 Surcharged in Blue **5**

1910, Oct.

87	A17	1s on 3s	3.50	.75
a.		"1910" omitted	21.00	
88	A17	5s on 15s	1.50	.50

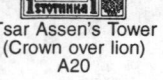

Tsar Assen's Tower (Crown over lion) A20

Tsar Ferdinand A21

City of Trnovo
A22

Tsar Ferdinand
A23

Ferdinand
A24

Isker River
A25

Ferdinand
A26

Rila Monastery (Crown at UR)
A27

Tsar and Princes — A28

Ferdinand in Robes of Ancient Tsars — A29

Monastery of Holy Trinity — A30

View of Varna — A31

1911, Feb. 14 Engr. *Perf. 12*

89	A20	1s myrtle green	.20	.20
90	A21	2s car & blk	.20	.20
91	A22	3s lake & blk	.40	.20
92	A23	5s green & blk	1.00	.20
93	A24	10s dp red & blk	1.40	.20
94	A25	15s brown bister	2.50	.20
95	A26	25s ultra & blk	.50	.20
96	A27	30s blue & blk	6.75	.20
97	A28	50s ocher & blk	16.00	.25
a.		Center inverted		*2,250.*
98	A29	1 l chocolate	6.00	.30
99	A30	2 l dull pur & blk	1.60	.90
100	A31	3 l blue vio & blk	6.75	3.00
		Nos. 89-100 (12)	43.30	6.05

See Nos. 114-120, 161-162. For overprints and surcharges see Nos. 104-112, 188, B8, Greece N167-N178, N182-N187, Thrace 16-21, Romania 2N1-2N4.

Tsar Ferdinand — A32

1912, Aug. 2 Typo. *Perf. 12½*

101	A32	5s olive green	2.25	.70
a.		5s pale green	*275.00*	*125.00*
102	A32	10s claret	3.50	1.50
103	A32	25s slate	5.00	1.75
		Nos. 101-103 (3)	10.75	3.95

25th year of reign of Tsar Ferdinand.

Nos. 89-95 Overprinted in Various Colors

ОСВОБ. ВОЙНА

1912-1913

1913, Aug. 6 Engr.

104	A20	1s myrtle grn (C)	.20	.20
105	A21	2s car & blk (Bl)	.20	.20
107	A22	3s lake & blk (Bl Bk)	.20	.20
108	A23	5s grn & blk (R)	.20	.20
109	A24	10s dp red & blk (Bk)	.30	.20
110	A25	15s brown bis (G)	.55	.25
111	A26	25s ultra & blk (R)	2.75	.40
		Nos. 104-111 (7)	4.40	1.65

Victory over the Turks in Balkan War of 1912-1913.

No. 95 Surcharged in Red

10 СТ.

1915, July 6

112	A26	10s on 25s	.50	.20

No. 28 Surcharged in Green

3 СТОТИНКИ

113	A11	3s on 1s lilac	3.50	4.50

Types of 1911 Re-engraved

1915, Nov. 7 *Perf. 11½, 14*

114	A20	1s dk bl grn	.20	.20
115	A23	5s grn & brn vio	1.40	.20
116	A24	10s red brn & brnsh blk	.25	.20
117	A25	15s olive green	.25	.20
118	A26	25s indigo & blk	.25	.20
119	A27	30s ol grn & red brn	.25	.20
120	A29	1 l dark brown	.30	.30
		Nos. 114-120 (7)	2.90	1.50

Widths: No. 114 is 19½mm; No. 89, 18½mm. No. 118 is 19¼mm; No. 95, 18¼mm. No. 120 is 20mm; No. 98, 19mm. The re-engraved stamps also differ from the 1911 issue in many details of design. Nos. 114-120 exist imperforate.

The 5s and 10s exist perf. 14x11½.

For Nos. 114-116 and 118 overprinted with Cyrillic characters and "1916-1917," see Romania Nos. 2N1-2N4.

Coat of Arms — A33

Peasant and Bullock — A34

Soldier and Mt. Sonichka A35

View of Nish A36

Town and Lake Okhrida — A37

Demir-Kapiya (Iron Gate) — A37a

View of Gevgeli — A38

Perf. 11½, 12½x13, 13x12½

1917-19 Typo.

122	A33	5s green	.30	.20
123	A34	15s slate	.20	.20
124	A35	25s blue	.20	.20
125	A36	30s orange	.20	.20
126	A37	50s violet	.50	.30
126A	A37a	2 l brn org ('19)	.50	.35
127	A38	3 l claret	.80	.75
		Nos. 122-127 (7)	2.70	2.20

Liberation of Macedonia. A 1 l dark green was prepared but not issued. Value $1.65.

For surcharges see Nos. B9-B10, B12.

View of Veles — A39

Monastery of St. Clement at Okhrida — A40

1918 *Perf. 13x14*

128	A39	1s gray	.20	.20
129	A40	5s green	.20	.20

Tsar Ferdinand A41

Plowing with Oxen A42

1918, July 1 *Perf. 12½x13*

130	A41	1s dark green	.20	.20
131	A41	2s dark brown	.20	.20
132	A41	3s indigo	.30	.20
133	A41	10s brown red	.30	.20
		Nos. 130-133 (4)	1.00	.80

Ferdinand's accession to the throne, 30th anniv.

1919 *Perf. 13½x13*

134	A42	1s gray	.20	.20

Sobranye Palace — A43

Tsar Boris III — A44

1919 *Perf. 11½x12, 12x11½*

135	A43	1s black	.20	.20
137	A43	2s olive green	.20	.20

For surcharges see Nos. 186, B1.

1919, Oct. 3

138	A44	3s orange brn	.20	.20
139	A44	5s green	.20	.20
140	A44	10s rose red	.20	.20
141	A44	15s violet	.20	.20
142	A44	25s deep blue	.20	.20
143	A44	30s chocolate	.20	.20
144	A44	50s yellow brn	.20	.20
		Nos. 138-144 (7)	1.40	1.40

1st anniv. of enthronement of Tsar Boris III.

Nos. 135-144 exist imperforate.

For surcharges see Nos. 187, B2-B7.

Birthplace of Vazov at Sopot and Cherrywood Cannon A47

"The Bear Fighter"-a Character from "Under the Yoke" — A48

Ivan Vazov in 1870 and 1920 — A49

Vazov — A50

The Monk Paisii — A52

Homes of Vazov at Plovdiv and Sofia — A51

1920, Oct. 20 Photo. *Perf. 11½*

147	A47	30s brown red	.20	.20
148	A48	50s dark green	.20	.20
149	A49	1 l drab	.25	.30
150	A50	2 l light brown	.60	.60
151	A51	3 l black violet	.95	.65
152	A52	5 l deep blue	1.10	.80
		Nos. 147-152 (6)	3.30	2.75

70th birthday of Ivan Vazov (1850-1921), Bulgarian poet and novelist.

Several values of this series exist imperforate and in pairs imperforate between.

Tsar Ferdinand
A53 A54

Mt. Shar — A55

Bridge over Vardar River — A56

View of Ohrid — A57

Perf. 13x14, 14x13

1921, June 11 Typo.

153	A53	10s claret	.20	.20
154	A54	10s claret	.20	.20
155	A55	10s claret	.20	.20
156	A56	10s rose lilac	.20	.20
157	A57	20s blue	.30	.20
		Nos. 153-157 (5)	1.10	1.00

Nos. 153-157 were intended to be issued in 1915 to commemorate the liberation of Macedonia. They were not put in use until 1921. A 50s violet was prepared but never placed in use. Value $1.75.

View of Sofia — A58

"The Liberator," Monument to Alexander II A59

Monastery at Shipka Pass — A62

Tsar Boris III — A63

Harvesting Grain — A64

Tsar Assen's Tower (No crown over lion) — A65

Rila Monastery (Rosette at upper right) — A66

1921-23 Engr. *Perf. 12*

158	A58	10s blue gray	.20	.20
159	A59	20s deep green	.20	.20
160	A63	25s blue grn ('22)	.20	.20
161	A22	50s orange	.20	.20
162	A22	50s dk blue ('23)	2.50	2.50
163	A62	75s dull vio	.20	.20
164	A62	75s dp blue ('23)	.30	.20
165	A63	1 l carmine	.30	.20
166	A63	1 l dp blue ('22)	.30	.20
167	A64	2 l brown	.30	.20
168	A65	3 l brown vio	.40	.20
169	A66	5 l lt blue	2.50	.30
170	A63	10 l violet brn	6.75	1.10
		Nos. 158-170 (13)	14.35	5.90

For surcharge see No. 189.

Bourchier in Bulgarian Costume A67

James David Bourchier A68

View of Rila Monastery A69

1921, Dec. 31

171	A67	10s red orange	.20	.20
172	A67	20s orange	.20	.20
173	A68	30s dp gray	.20	.20
174	A68	50s bluish gray	.20	.20
175	A68	1 l dull vio	.20	.20
176	A69	1½ l olive grn	.20	.20
177	A69	2 l deep green	.20	.20
178	A69	3 l Prus blue	.45	.20
179	A69	5 l red brown	.85	.35
		Nos. 171-179 (9)	2.70	1.95

Death of James D. Bourchier, Balkan correspondent of the London Times.

For surcharges see Nos. B13-B16.

Postage Due Stamps of 1919-22 Surcharged

a **10 СТОТИНКИ**

1924

182	D6	10s on 20s yellow	.20	.20
183	D6	20s on 5s gray grn	.20	.20
a.		20s on 5s emerald	7.00	7.00
184	D6	20s on 10s violet	.20	.20
185	D6	20s on 30s orange	.20	.20
		Nos. 182-185 (4)	.80	.80

Nos. 182 to 185 were used for ordinary postage.

Regular Issues of 1919-23 Surcharged in Blue or Red:

1 ЛЕВЪ b

3 ЛЕВА c

186	A43 (a)	10s on 1s black (R)	.20	.20
187	A44 (b)	1 l on 5s emer (Bl)	.20	.20
188	A22 (c)	3 l on 50s dk bl (R)	.20	.20
189	A63 (b)	6 l on 1 l car (Bl)	.60	.20
		Nos. 186-189 (4)	1.20	.80

The surcharge of No. 188 comes in three types: normal, thick and thin.

#182, 184-189 exist with inverted surcharge.

Lion of Bulgaria A70 A71

Tsar Boris III — A72

New Sofia Cathedral — A73

Harvesting A74

1925 Typo. *Perf. 13, 11½*

191	A70	10s red & bl, *pink*	.20	.20
192	A70	15s car & org, *blue*	.20	.20
193	A70	30s blk & buff	.20	.20
a.		Cliche of 15s in plate of 30s		
194	A71	50s choc, *green*	.20	.20
195	A72	1 l dull green	.50	.20
196	A73	2 l dk grn & buff	1.10	.20
197	A74	4 l lake & yellow	1.10	.20
		Nos. 191-197 (7)	3.50	1.40

Several values of this series exist imperforate and in pairs imperforate between.

See #199, 201. For overprint see #C2.

Cathedral of Sveta Nedelya, Sofia, Ruined by Bomb — A75

1926 *Perf. 11½*

198	A75	50s gray black	.20	.20

A76

A77

Type A72 Re-engraved. (Shoulder at left does not touch frame)

1926

199	A76	1 l gray	.45	.20
a.		1 l green	.45	.20
201	A76	2 l olive brown	.50	.20

Center Embossed

202	A77	6 l dp bl & pale lemon	1.10	.20
203	A77	10 l brn blk & brn org	4.00	.75
		Nos. 199-203 (4)	6.05	1.35

For overprints see Nos. C1, C3-C4.

Christo Botev — A78

Tsar Boris III — A79

1926, June 2

204	A78	1 l olive green	.30	.20
205	A78	2 l slate violet	.90	.20
206	A78	4 l red brown	.90	.35
		Nos. 204-206 (3)	2.10	.75

Botev (1847-76), Bulgarian revolutionary, poet.

Lion Type of 1881

1927-29 *Perf. 13*

207	A3	10s dk red & drab	.20	.20
208	A3	15s blk & org ('29)	.20	.20
209	A3	30s dk bl & bis brn ('28)	.20	.20
a.		30s indigo & buff	.20	.20
210	A3	50s blk & rose red ('28)	.20	.20
		Nos. 207-210 (4)	.80	.80

1928, Oct. 3 *Perf. 11½*

211	A79	1 l olive green	.90	.20
212	A79	2 l deep brown	1.00	.20

St. Clement A80

Konstantin Miladinov A81

George S. Rakovski A82

Drenovo Monastery A83

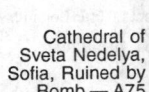

Paisii — A84

Tsar Simeon — A85

Lyuben Karavelov A86

Vassil Levski A87

Georgi Benkovski A88

Tsar Alexander II A89

1929, May 12

213	A80	10s dk violet	.20	.20
214	A81	15s violet brn	.20	.20
215	A82	30s red	.20	.20
216	A83	50s olive grn	.25	.20
217	A84	1 l orange brn	.60	.20
218	A85	2 l dk blue	.70	.20
219	A86	3 l dull green	1.50	.45
220	A87	4 l olive brown	2.50	.25
221	A88	5 l brown	1.50	.35
222	A89	6 l Prus green	2.25	.90
		Nos. 213-222 (10)	9.90	3.15

Millenary of Tsar Simeon and 50th anniv. of the liberation of Bulgaria from the Turks.

Royal Wedding Issue

Tsar Boris and Fiancee, Princess Giovanna A90

Queen Ioanna and Tsar Boris — A91

1930, Nov. 12 *Perf. 11½*

223	A90	1 l green	.25	.25
224	A91	2 l dull violet	.25	.30
225	A90	4 l rose red	.25	.30
226	A91	6 l dark blue	.25	.40
		Nos. 223-226 (4)	1.00	1.25

Fifty-five copies of a miniature sheet incorporating one each of Nos. 223-226 were printed and given to royal, governmental and diplomatic personages.

Tsar Boris III

A92 A93

Perf. 11½, 12x11½, 13

1931-37 Unwmk.

227	A92	1 l blue green	.25	.20
228	A92	2 l carmine	.40	.20
229	A92	4 l red org ('34)	.75	.20
230	A92	4 l yel org ('37)	.20	.20
231	A92	6 l deep blue	.70	.20
232	A92	7 l dp bl ('37)	.20	.20
233	A92	10 l slate blk	8.75	.70
234	A92	12 l lt brown	.40	.20
235	A92	14 l lt brn ('37)	.30	.25
236	A93	20 l claret & org brn	1.00	.45
		Nos. 227-236 (10)	12.95	2.80

Nos. 230-233 and 235 have outer bars at top and bottom as shown on cut A92; Nos. 227-229 and 234 are without outer bars.

See Nos. 251, 279-280, 287. For surcharge see No. 252.

Balkan Games Issues

Gymnast A95

Soccer — A96

Riding — A97

Swimmer A100

"Victory" A101

Designs: 6 l, Fencing. 10 l, Bicycle race.

1931, Sept. 18 — ***Perf. 11½***

237 A95	1 l lt green	1.75	.50
238 A96	2 l garnet	1.75	.50
239 A97	4 l carmine	4.00	.75
240 A95	6 l Prus blue	7.50	1.25
241 A95	10 l red org	20.00	3.75
242 A100	12 l dk blue	65.00	7.50
243 A101	50 l olive brn	60.00	22.50
	Nos. 237-243 (7)	160.00	36.75

1933, Jan. 5

244 A95	1 l blue grn	1.25	.95
245 A96	2 l blue	2.00	.95
246 A97	4 l brn vio	2.75	1.10
247 A95	6 l brt rose	5.00	1.60
248 A95	10 l olive brn	27.50	9.00
249 A100	12 l orange	60.00	18.00
250 A101	50 l red brown	110.00	82.50
	Nos. 244-250 (7)	208.50	114.10

Nos. 244-250 were sold only at the philatelic agency.

Boris Type of 1931
Outer Bars at Top and Bottom Removed

1933 — ***Perf. 13***

251 A92 6 l deep blue .80 .20

Type of 1931 Surcharged in Blue **2**

1934

252 A92 2 (l) on 3 l ol brn 4.00 .25

Soldier Defending Shipka Pass A102

Shipka Battle Memorial A103

Color-Bearer A104

Veteran of the War of Liberation, 1878 A105

Widow and Orphans — A106

Perf. 10½, 11½

1934, Aug. 26 — **Wmk. 145**

253 A102	1 l green	.45	.40
254 A103	2 l pale red	.45	.25
255 A104	3 l bister brn	1.40	1.25
256 A105	4 l dk carmine	1.25	.60
257 A104	7 l dk blue	2.25	2.00
258 A106	14 l plum	6.00	5.75
	Nos. 253-258 (6)	11.80	10.25

Shipka Pass Battle memorial unveiling.

An unwatermarked miniature sheet incorporating one each of Nos. 253-258 was put on sale in 1938 in five cities at a price of 8,000 leva. Printing: 100 sheets.

1934, Sept. 21

259 A102	1 l bright green	.45	.40
260 A103	2 l dull orange	.45	.25
261 A104	3 l yellow	1.40	1.25
262 A105	4 l rose	1.25	.60
263 A104	7 l blue	2.25	2.00
264 A106	14 l olive bister	6.00	5.75
	Nos. 259-264 (6)	11.80	10.25

An unwatermarked miniature sheet incorporating one each of Nos. 259-263 was issued.

Velcho A. Djamjiyata A108

Capt. G. S. Mamarchev A109

1935, May 5 — ***Perf. 11½***

265 A108 1 l deep blue .95 .25
266 A109 2 l maroon .95 .30

Bulgarian uprising against the Turks, cent.

Soccer Game — A110

Cathedral of Alexander Nevski — A111

Soccer Team A112

Symbolical of Victory A113

Player and Trophy — A114

The Trophy — A115

1935, June 14

267 A110	1 l green	1.10	.90
268 A111	2 l blue gray	2.50	1.40
269 A112	4 l crimson	4.00	2.00
270 A113	7 l brt blue	7.75	2.50
271 A114	14 l orange	7.75	3.25
272 A115	50 l lilac brn	60.00	52.50
	Nos. 267-272 (6)	83.10	62.55

5th Balkan Soccer Tournament.

Gymnast on Parallel Bars — A116

Youth in "Yunak" Costume — A117

Girl in "Yunak" Costume A118

Pole Vaulting A119

Stadium, Sofia — A120

Yunak Emblem — A121

1935, July 10

273 A116	1 l green	2.00	1.10
274 A117	2 l lt blue	2.75	1.10
275 A118	4 l carmine	5.50	2.25
276 A119	7 l dk blue	5.50	3.00
277 A120	14 l dk brown	5.50	3.00
278 A121	50 l red	65.00	42.50
	Nos. 273-278 (6)	86.25	52.95

8th tournament of the Yunak Gymnastic Organization at Sofia, July 12-14.

Boris Type of 1931

1935 — **Wmk. 145** — ***Perf. 12½, 13***

279 A92 1 l green .30 .20
280 A92 2 l carmine 20.00 .20

Janos Hunyadi A122

King Ladislas Varnenchik A123

Varna Memorial — A124

King Ladislas III — A125

Battle of Varna, 1444 — A126

1935, Aug. 4 — ***Perf. 10½, 11½***

281 A122	1 l brown org	1.10	.75
282 A123	2 l maroon	1.10	.75
283 A124	4 l vermilion	5.50	3.75
284 A125	7 l dull blue	2.50	1.25
285 A126	14 l green	2.50	1.25
	Nos. 281-285 (5)	12.70	7.75

Battle of Varna, and the death of the Polish King, Ladislas Varnenchik (1424-44).

Lion Type of 1881

1935 — **Wmk. 145** — ***Perf. 13***

286 A3 10s dk red & drab .70 .20

Boris Type of 1933
Outer Bars at Top and Bottom Removed

1935

287 A92 6 l gray blue .60 .20

Dimitr Monument A127

Haji Dimitr A128

Haji Dimitr and Stefan Karaja A129

Taking the Oath — A130

Birthplace of Dimitr — A131

1935, Oct. 1 — **Unwmk.** — ***Perf. 11½***

288 A127	1 l green	1.25	.35
289 A128	2 l brown	1.75	.70
290 A129	4 l car rose	3.50	2.50
291 A130	7 l blue	4.50	3.50
292 A131	14 l orange	4.50	3.50
	Nos. 288-292 (5)	15.50	10.55

67th anniv. of the death of the Bulgarian patriots, Haji Dimitr and Stefan Karaja.

Catalogue values for unused stamps in this section, from this point to the end of the section, are for Never Hinged items.

A132

A133

1936-39 — ***Perf. 13x12½, 13***

293 A132	10s red org ('37)	.20	.20
294 A132	15s emerald	.20	.20
295 A133	30s maroon	.20	.20
296 A133	30s yel brn ('37)	.20	.20
297 A133	30s Prus bl ('37)	.20	.20
298 A133	50s ultra	.20	.20
299 A133	50s dk car ('37)	.20	.20
300 A133	50s slate grn ('39)	.20	.20
	Nos. 293-300 (8)	1.60	1.60

Meteorological Station, Mt. Moussalla
A134

Peasant Girl
A135

Town of Nessebr
A136

1936, Aug. 16 Photo. *Perf. 11½*

301 A134	1 l purple		1.40	.65
302 A135	2 l ultra		1.40	.60
303 A136	7 l dark blue		3.75	1.50
	Nos. 301-303 (3)		6.55	2.75

4th Geographical & Ethnographical Cong., Sofia, Aug. 1936.

Sts. Cyril and Methodius
A137

Displaying the Bible to the People
A138

1937, June 2

304 A137	1 l dk green	.25	.20
305 A137	2 l dk plum	.25	.20
306 A138	4 l vermilion	.45	.25
307 A137	7 l dk blue	1.75	1.10
308 A138	14 l rose red	1.75	1.10
	Nos. 304-308 (5)	4.45	2.85

Millennium of Cyrillic alphabet.

Princess Marie Louise — A139

Tsar Boris III — A140

1937, Oct. 3

310 A139	1 l yellow green	.35	.20
311 A139	2 l brown red	.25	.20
312 A139	4 l scarlet	.35	.20
	Nos. 310-312 (3)	.95	.60

Issued in honor of Princess Marie Louise.

1937, Oct. 3

313 A140	2 l brown red	.35	.20

19th anniv. of the accession of Tsar Boris III to the throne. See No. B11.

National Products Issue

Peasants Bundling Wheat
A141

Sunflower
A142

Wheat — A143

Chickens and Eggs — A144

Cluster of Grapes — A145

Rose and Perfume Flask — A146

Strawberries
A147

Girl Carrying Grape Clusters
A148

Rose — A149

Tobacco Leaves — A150

1938 *Perf. 13*

316 A141	10s	orange	.20	.20
317 A141	10s	red org	.20	.20
318 A142	15s	brt rose	.30	.20
319 A142	15s	deep plum	.30	.20
320 A143	30s	golden brn	.20	.20
321 A143	30s	copper brn	.20	.20
322 A144	50s	black	.20	.20
323 A144	50s	indigo	.20	.20
324 A145	1 l	yel grn	.65	.20
325 A145	1 l	green	.65	.20
326 A146	2 l	rose pink	.60	.20
327 A146	2 l	rose brn	.60	.20
328 A147	3 l	dp red lil	1.25	.20
329 A147	3 l	brn lake	1.25	.20
330 A148	4 l	plum	.80	.20
331 A148	4 l	golden brn	.80	.20
332 A149	7 l	vio blue	1.50	.55
333 A149	7 l	dp blue	1.50	.55
334 A150	14 l	dk brown	2.25	.90
335 A150	14 l	red brn	2.25	.90
		Nos. 316-335 (20)	15.90	6.10

Several values of this series exist imperforate.

Crown Prince Simeon
A151 A153

Designs: 2 l, Same portrait as 1 l, value at lower left. 14 l, similar to 4 l, but no wreath.

1938, June 16

336 A151	1 l brt green	.20	.20
337 A151	2 l rose pink	.20	.20
338 A153	4 l dp orange	.20	.20
339 A151	7 l ultra	.80	.40
340 A153	14 l dp brown	.80	.40
	Nos. 336-340 (5)	2.20	1.40

First birthday of Prince Simeon.

Tsar Boris III
A155 A156

Various Portraits of Tsar.

1938, Oct. 3

341 A155	1 l lt green	.20	.20
342 A156	2 l rose brown	.60	.20
343 A156	4 l golden brn	.20	.20
344 A156	7 l brt ultra	.30	.25
345 A156	14 l deep red lilac	.35	.25
	Nos. 341-345 (5)	1.65	1.10

Reign of Tsar Boris III, 20th anniv.

Early Locomotive
A160

Designs: 2 l, Modern locomotive. 4 l, Train crossing bridge. 7 l, Tsar Boris in cab.

1939, Apr. 26

346 A160	1 l yel green	.20	.20
347 A160	2 l copper brn	.20	.20
348 A160	4 l red orange	1.40	.20
349 A160	7 l dark blue	3.25	.85
	Nos. 346-349 (4)	5.05	1.45

50th anniv. of Bulgarian State Railways.

Post Horns and Arrows — A164

Central Post Office, Sofia — A165

1939, May 14 Typo.

350 A164	1 l yellow grn	.20	.20
351 A165	2 l brt carmine	.25	.20

Establishment of the postal system, 60th anniv.

Gymnast on Bar
A166

Yunak Emblem
A167

Discus Thrower
A168

Athletic Dancer
A169

Weight Lifter — A170

1939, July 7 Photo.

352 A166	1 l yel grn & pale grn	.35	.20
353 A167	2 l brt rose	.35	.20
354 A168	4 l brn & gldn brn	.50	.25
355 A169	7 l dk bl & bl	1.25	.60
356 A170	14 l plum & rose vio	5.50	2.75
	Nos. 352-356 (5)	7.95	4.00

9th tournament of the Yunak Gymnastic Organization at Sofia, July 4-8.

Tsar Boris III — A171

Bulgaria's First Stamp — A172

1940-41 Typo.

356A A171	1 l dl grn ('41)	.80	.20
357 A171	2 l brt crimson	.20	.20

1940, May 19 Photo. *Perf. 13*

20 l, Similar design, scroll dated "1840-1940."

358 A172	10 l olive black	1.25	.85
359 A172	20 l indigo	1.25	.85

Cent. of 1st postage stamp. Exist imperf.

Peasant Couple and Tsar Boris — A174

Flags over Wheat Field and Tsar Boris — A175

Tsar Boris and Map of Dobrudja
A176

1940, Sept. 20

360 A174	1 l slate green	.20	.20
361 A175	2 l rose red	.20	.20
362 A176	4 l dark brown	.20	.20
363 A176	7 l dark blue	.60	.30
	Nos. 360-363 (4)	1.20	.90

Return of Dobrudja from Romania.

Fruit
A177

Bees and Flowers
A178

Plowing
A179

Shepherd and Sheep
A180

Tsar Boris III — A181

Perf. 10, 10½x11½, 11½, 13

1940-44 Typo. Unwmk.

364	A177	10s red orange	.20	.20
365	A178	15s blue	.20	.20
366	A179	30s olive brn ('41)	.20	.20
367	A180	50s violet	.20	.20
368	A181	1 l brt green	.20	.20
369	A181	2 l rose car	.20	.20
370	A181	4 l red orange	.20	.20
371	A181	6 l red vio ('44)	.30	.20
372	A181	7 l blue	.30	.20
373	A181	10 l blue grn ('41)	.30	.20
		Nos. 364-373 (10)	2.30	2.00

See Nos. 373A-377, 440. For overprints see Nos. 455-463, C31-C32.

1940-41 Wmk. 145 *Perf. 13*

373A	A180	50s violet ('41)	.20	.20
374	A181	1 l brt grn	.20	.20
375	A181	2 l rose car	.20	.20
376	A181	7 l dull blue	.45	.20
377	A181	10 l blue green	.65	.20
		Nos. 373A-377 (5)	1.70	1.00

Watermarked vertically or horizontally.

P. R. Slaveikov A182

Sofronii, Bishop of Vratza A183

Saint Ivan Rilski — A184

Martin S. Drinov — A185

Monk Khrabr — A186

Kolio Ficheto — A187

1940, Sept. 23 Photo. Unwmk.

378	A182	1 l brt bl grn	.20	.20
379	A183	2 l brt carmine	.20	.20
380	A184	3 l dp red brn	.20	.20
381	A185	4 l red orange	.20	.20
382	A186	7 l deep blue	1.00	.60
383	A187	10 l dp red brn	1.50	.85
		Nos. 378-383 (6)	3.30	2.25

Liberation of Bulgaria from the Turks in 1878.

Johannes Gutenberg A188

N. Karastoyanov, 1st Bulgarian Printer A189

1940, Dec. 16

384	A188	1 l slate green	.20	.20
385	A189	2 l orange brown	.20	.20

500th anniv. of the invention of the printing press and 100th anniv. of the 1st Bulgarian printing press.

Christo Botev — A190

Monument to Botev — A192

Botev with his Insurgent Band — A191

1941, May 3

386	A190	1 l dark blue green	.20	.20
387	A191	2 l crimson rose	.20	.20
388	A192	3 l dark brown	.65	.30
		Nos. 386-388 (3)	1.05	.70

Christo Botev, patriot and poet.

Palace of Justice, Sofia — A193

20 l, Workers' hospital. 50 l, National Bank.

1941-43 Engr. *Perf. 11½*

389	A193	14 l lt gray brn ('43)	.20	.20
390	A193	20 l gray grn ('43)	.40	.20
391	A193	50 l lt bl gray	1.90	1.25
		Nos. 389-391 (3)	2.50	1.65

Macedonian Woman A196

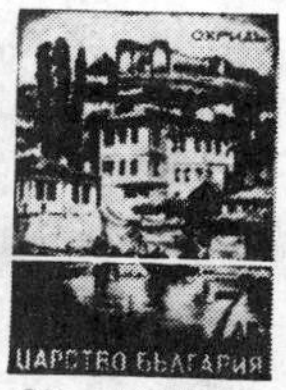
City of Okhrida A200

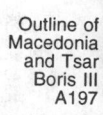

Outline of Macedonia and Tsar Boris III A197

View of Aegean Sea — A198

Poganovski Monastery A199

1941, Oct. 3 Photo. *Perf. 13*

392	A196	1 l slate grn	.20	.20
393	A197	2 l crimson	.20	.20
394	A198	2 l red org	.20	.20
395	A199	4 l org brn	.20	.20
396	A200	7 l dp gray bl	.40	.30
		Nos. 392-396 (5)	1.20	1.10

Issued to commemorate the acquisition of Macedonian territory from neighboring countries.

Peasant Working in a Field — A201

Designs: 15s, Plowing. 30s, Apiary. 50s, Women harvesting fruit. 3 l, Shepherd and sheep. 5 l, Inspecting cattle.

1941-44

397	A201	10s dk violet	.20	.20
398	A201	10s dk blue	.20	.20
399	A201	15s Prus blue	.20	.20
400	A201	15s dk ol brn	.20	.20
401	A201	30s red orange	.20	.20
402	A201	30s dk slate grn	.20	.20
403	A201	50s blue vio	.20	.20
404	A201	50s red lilac	.20	.20
405	A201	3 l henna brn	.40	.25
406	A201	3 l dk brn ('44)	1.40	1.10
407	A201	5 l sepia	.50	.50
408	A201	5 l vio bl ('44)	1.40	1.10
		Nos. 397-408 (12)	5.30	4.55

Girls Singing A207

Boys in Camp A208

Raising Flag A209

Folk Dancers A211

Camp Scene — A210

1942, June 1 Photo.

409	A207	1 l dk bl grn	.20	.20
410	A208	2 l scarlet	.20	.20
411	A209	4 l olive gray	.20	.20
412	A210	7 l deep blue	.20	.20
413	A211	14 l fawn	.30	.25
		Nos. 409-413 (5)	1.10	1.05

National "Work and Joy" movement.

Wounded Soldier — A212

Soldier's Farewell — A213

4 l, Aiding wounded soldier. 7 l, Widow & orphans at grave. 14 l, Tomb of Unknown Soldier. 20 l, Queen Ioanna visiting wounded.

1942, Sept. 7

414	A212	1 l slate grn	.20	.20
415	A213	2 l brt rose	.20	.20
416	A213	4 l yel org	.20	.20
417	A213	7 l dark blue	.20	.20
418	A213	14 l brown	.20	.20
419	A213	20 l olive blk	.25	.20
		Nos. 414-419 (6)	1.25	1.20

Issued to aid war victims. No. 419 was printed in sheets of 50, alternating with 50 labels.

Legend of Kubrat — A218

Cavalry Charge — A219

Designs: 30s, Rider of Madara. 50s, Christening of Boris I. 1 l, School, St. Naum. 2 l, Crowning of Tsar Simeon by Boris I. 3 l, Golden era of Bulgarian literature. 4 l, Sentencing of the Bogomil Basil. 5 l, Proclamation of 2nd Bulgarian Empire. 7 l, Ivan Assen II at Trebizond. 10 l, Deporting the Patriarch Jeftimi. 14 l, Wandering minstrel. 20 l, Monk Paisii. 30 l, Monument, Shipka Pass.

1942, Oct. 12

420	A218	10s bluish blk	.20	.20
421	A219	15s Prus grn	.20	.20
422	A219	30s dk rose vio	.20	.20
423	A219	50s indigo	.20	.20
424	A219	1 l slate grn	.20	.20
425	A219	2 l crimson	.20	.20
426	A219	3 l brown	.20	.20
427	A219	4 l orange	.20	.20
428	A219	5 l grnsh blk	.20	.20
429	A219	7 l dk blue	.20	.20
430	A219	10 l brown blk	.20	.20
431	A219	14 l olive blk	.20	.20
432	A219	20 l henna brn	.40	.30
433	A219	30 l black	.70	.40
		Nos. 420-433 (14)	3.50	3.10

Tsar Boris III — A234

Designs: Various portraits of Tsar.

Perf. 13, Imperf.

1944, Feb. 28 Photo. Wmk. 275

Frames in Black

434	A234	1 l olive grn	.20	.20
435	A234	2 l red brown	.20	.20
436	A234	4 l brown	.20	.20
437	A234	5 l gray vio	.30	.20
438	A234	7 l slate blue	.30	.20
		Nos. 434-438 (5)	1.20	1.00

Tsar Boris III (1894-1943).

Tsar Simeon II — A239

Perf. 11½, 13

1944, June 12 Typo. Unwmk.

439	A239	3 l red orange	.25	.20

Shepherd Type of 1940

1944

440	A180	50s yellow green	.20	.20

Parcel Post Stamps of 1944 Overprinted in Black or Orange

ВСИЧКО ЗА ФРОНТА

1945, Jan. 25 *Perf. 11½*

448	PP5	1 l dk carmine	.20	.20
449	PP5	7 l rose lilac	.20	.20
450	PP5	20 l org brn	.20	.20
451	PP5	30 l dk brn car	.20	.20
452	PP5	50 l red orange	.25	.20
453	PP5	100 l blue (O)	.60	.20

Overprint reads: "Everything for the Front."

No. 448 with Additional Surcharge of New Value in Black

454	PP5	4 l on 1 l dk car	.20	.20
		Nos. 448-454 (7)	1.85	1.40

Nos. 368 to 370 Overprinted in Black

СЪБИРАЙТЕ
СТАРО
ЖЕЛЪЗО

1945, Mar. 15 *Perf. 11½, 13*

455	A181	1 l brt green	.25	.20
456	A181	2 l rose carmine	.40	.20
457	A181	4 l red orange	.60	.20

Overprint reads: "Collect old iron."

Overprinted in Black

СЪБИРАЙТЕ
ХАРТИЕНИ
ОТПАДЪЦИ

458	A181	1 l brt green	.25	.20
459	A181	2 l rose carmine	.40	.20
460	A181	4 l red orange	.60	.20

Overprint reads: "Collect discarded paper."

Overprinted in Black

СЪБИРАЙТЕ
ВСЪКАКВИ
ПАРЦАЛИ

461	A181	1 l brt green	.25	.20
462	A181	2 l rose carmine	.40	.20
463	A181	4 l red orange	.60	.20
		Nos. 455-463 (9)	3.75	1.80

Overprint reads: "Collect all kinds of rags."

Oak Tree — A245

Imperf., Perf. 11½.

1945 **Litho.** **Unwmk.**

464	A245	4 l vermilion	.20	.20
465	A245	10 l blue	.20	.20

Imperf

466	A245	50 l brown lake	.20	.20
		Nos. 464-466 (3)	.60	.60

Slav Congress, Sofia, March, 1945.

A246

A247

A248

A249

A251

A252

A253

A254

2 l and 4 l:
Type I. Large crown close to coat of arms.
Type II. Smaller crown standing high.

1945-46 **Photo.** ***Perf. 13***

469	A246	30s yellow grn	.20	.20
470	A247	50s peacock grn	.20	.20
471	A248	1 l dk green	.20	.20
472	A249	2 l choc (I)	.20	.20
a.		Type II	.20	.20
473	A249	4 l dk blue (I)	.20	.20
a.		Type II	.20	.20
475	A251	5 l red violet	.20	.20
476	A251	9 l slate gray	.20	.20
477	A252	10 l Prus blue	.20	.20
478	A253	15 l brown	.20	.20
479	A254	20 l carmine	.20	.20
480	A254	20 l gray blk	.20	.20
		Nos. 469-480 (11)	2.20	2.20

Breaking Chain — A255

1 Lev Coin — A256

Water Wheel — A257

Coin and Symbols of Agriculture and Industry — A258

Unwmk.

1945, June 4 **Litho.** ***Imperf.***

Laid Paper

481	A255	50 l brn red, *pink*	.20	.20
482	A255	50 l org, *pink*	.20	.20
483	A256	100 l gray bl, *pink*	.20	.20
484	A256	100 l brn, *pink*	.20	.20
485	A257	150 l dk ol gray, *pink*	.35	.20
486	A257	150 l dl car, *pink*	.35	.20
487	A258	200 l dp bl, *pink*	.50	.30
488	A258	200 l ol grn, *pink*	.50	.30
		Nos. 481-488 (8)	2.50	1.80

Souvenir Sheets

489		Sheet of 4	3.00	1.75
a.	A255	50 l violet blue	.30	.20
b.	A256	100 l violet blue	.30	.20
c.	A257	150 l violet blue	.30	.20
d.	A258	200 l violet blue	.30	.20
490		Sheet of 4	3.00	1.75
a.	A255	50 l brown orange	.30	.20
b.	A256	100 l brown orange	.30	.20
c.	A257	150 l brown orange	.30	.20
d.	A258	200 l brown orange	.30	.20

Publicizing Bulgaria's Liberty Loan.

Olive Branch — A260

1945, Sept. 1 **Typo.** ***Perf. 13***

491	A260	10 l org brn & yel grn	.20	.20
492	A260	50 l dull red & dp grn	.25	.20

Victory of Allied Nations, World War II.

September 9, 1944 — A261

Numeral, Broken Chain — A262

1945, Sept. 7

493	A261	1 l gray green	.20	.20
494	A261	4 l deep blue	.20	.20
495	A261	5 l rose lilac	.20	.20
496	A262	10 l lt blue	.20	.20
497	A262	20 l brt car	.20	.20
498	A261	50 l brt bl grn	.40	.20
499	A261	100 l orange brn	.50	.35
		Nos. 493-499 (7)	1.90	1.55

1st anniv. of Bulgaria's liberation.

Old Postal Savings Emblem A263

Child Putting Coin in Bank A265

First Bulgarian Postal Savings Stamp — A264

Postal Savings Building, Sofia — A266

1946, Apr. 12

500	A263	4 l brown org	.20	.20
501	A264	10 l dk olive	.20	.20
502	A265	20 l ultra	.20	.20
503	A266	50 l slate gray	.50	.50
		Nos. 500-503 (4)	1.10	1.10

50th anniv. of Bulgarian Postal Savings.

Refugee Children A267

Nurse Assisting Wounded Soldier A269

Wounded Soldier — A268

Design: 35 l, 100 l, Red Cross hospital train.

1946, Apr. 4

Cross in Carmine

504	A267	2 l dk olive	.20	.20
505	A268	4 l violet	.20	.20
506	A267	10 l plum	.20	.20
507	A268	20 l ultra	.20	.20
508	A269	30 l brown org	.20	.20
509	A268	35 l gray blk	.20	.20
510	A269	50 l violet brn	.25	.20
511	A268	100 l gray brn	.70	.60
		Nos. 504-511 (8)	2.15	2.00

See Nos. 553-560.

Advancing Troops A271

Grenade Thrower A272

Attacking Planes — A274

Designs: 5 l, Horse-drawn cannon. 9 l, Engineers building pontoon bridge. 10 l, 30 l, Cavalry charge. 40 l, Horse-drawn supply column. 50 l, Motor transport column. 60 l, Infantry, tanks and planes.

1946, Aug. 9 **Typo.** **Unwmk.**

512	A271	2 l dk red vio	.20	.20
513	A272	4 l dk gray	.20	.20
514	A271	5 l dk org red	.20	.20
515	A274	6 l black brn	.20	.20
516	A271	9 l rose lilac	.20	.20
517	A271	10 l dp violet	.20	.20
518	A271	20 l dp blue	.25	.20
519	A271	30 l red org	.25	.20
520	A271	40 l dk ol bis	.30	.20
521	A271	50 l dk green	.30	.20
522	A271	60 l red brown	.40	.30
		Nos. 512-522 (11)	2.70	2.30

Bulgaria's participation in World War II.

Arms of Russia and Bulgaria A279

Lion Rampant A280

1946, May 23

523	A279	4 l red orange	.20	.20
525	A279	20 l turq green	.25	.20

Congress of the Bulgarian-Soviet Association, May 1946. The 4 l exists in dk car rose and 20 l in blue, value, set $7.

1946, May 25 ***Imperf.***

526	A280	20 l blue	.30	.25

Day of the Postage Stamp, May 26, 1946.

Alekandr Stamboliski A281

Flags of Albania, Romania, Bulgaria and Yugoslavia A282

1946, June 13 ***Perf. 12***

527	A281	100 l red orange	4.00	1.90

23rd anniversary of the death of Alekandr Stamboliski, agrarian leader.

1946, July 6 ***Perf. 11½***

528	A282	100 l black brown	.75	.50

1946 Balkan Games.

Sheet of 100 arranged so that all stamps are tete beche vert. and horiz., except 2 center rows in left pane which provide 10 vert. pairs that are not tete beche vert.

St. Ivan Rilski — A283

A286

A284

A285

Views of Rila Monastery
A287

1946, Aug. 26

529	A283	1 l	red brown	.20	.20
530	A284	4 l	black brn	.20	.20
531	A285	10 l	dk green	.20	.20
532	A286	20 l	dp blue	.20	.20
533	A287	50 l	dk red	.80	.50
			Nos. 529-533 (5)	1.60	1.30

Millenary of Rila Monastery.

People's Republic

A288

1946, Sept. 15 **Typo.**

534	A288	4 l	brown lake	.20	.20
535	A288	20 l	dull blue	.20	.20
536	A288	50 l	olive bister	.20	.20
			Nos. 534-536 (3)	.60	.60

No. 535 is inscribed "BULGARIA" in Latin characters.

Referendum of Sept. 8, 1946, resulting in the establishment of the Bulgarian People's Republic.

Partisan Army
A289

Snipers
A290

Soldiers: Past and Present — A291

Design: 30 l, Partisans advancing.

1946, Dec. 2

537	A289	1 l	violet brn	.20	.20
538	A290	4 l	dull grn	.20	.20
539	A291	5 l	chocolate	.20	.20
540	A290	10 l	crimson	.20	.20
541	A289	20 l	ultra	.25	.20
542	A290	30 l	olive bister	.25	.20
543	A291	50 l	black	.30	.25
			Nos. 537-543 (7)	1.60	1.45

Relief Worker and Children
A294

Child with Gift Parcels
A295

Waiting for Food Distribution
A296

Mother and Child
A297

1946, Dec. 30

545	A294	1 l	dk vio brn	.20	.20
546	A295	4 l	brt red	.20	.20
547	A295	9 l	olive bis	.20	.20
548	A294	10 l	slate gray	.20	.20
549	A296	20 l	ultra	.20	.20
550	A297	30 l	dp brn org	.20	.20
551	A296	40 l	maroon	.20	.20
552	A294	50 l	peacock grn	.30	.30
			Nos. 545-552 (8)	1.70	1.70

"Bulgaria" is in Latin characters on No. 548.

Red Cross Types of 1946

1947, Jan. 31

Cross in Carmine

553	A267	2 l	olive bister	.20	.20
554	A268	4 l	olive black	.20	.20
555	A267	10 l	blue grn	.20	.20
556	A268	20 l	brt blue	.20	.20
557	A269	30 l	yellow grn	.30	.25
558	A268	35 l	grnsh gray	.30	.25
559	A269	50 l	henna brn	.50	.35
560	A268	100 l	dark blue	.70	.50
			Nos. 553-560 (8)	2.60	2.15

Laurel Branch, Allied and Bulgarian Emblems — A298

Dove of Peace — A299

1947, Feb. 28

561	A298	4 l	olive	.20	.20
562	A299	10 l	brown red	.20	.20
563	A299	20 l	deep blue	.20	.20
			Nos. 561-563 (3)	.60	.60

Return to peace at the close of World War II. "Bulgaria" in Latin characters on No. 563.

A302

Guerrilla Fighters
A303 A304

1947, Jan. 21 ***Perf. 11½***

567	A302	10 l	choc & brn org	.30	.20
568	A303	20 l	dk bl & bl	.30	.20
569	A304	70 l	dp claret & rose	18.00	8.00
			Nos. 567-569 (3)	18.60	8.40

Issued to honor the anti-fascists.

Hydroelectric Station — A305

Miner
A306

Symbols of Industry
A307

Tractor — A308

1947, Aug. 6

570	A305	4 l	olive green	.20	.20
571	A306	9 l	red brown	.20	.20
572	A307	20 l	deep blue	.20	.20
573	A308	40 l	olive brown	.40	.30
			Nos. 570-573 (4)	1.00	.90

Exhibition Building
A309

Former Home of Alphonse de Lamartine
A310

Symbols of Agriculture and Horticulture — A311

Perf. 11x11½, 11½x11

1947, Aug. 31 **Litho.** **Unwmk.**

574	A309	4 l	scarlet	.20	.20
575	A310	9 l	brown lake	.20	.20
576	A311	20 l	brt ultra	.20	.20
			Nos. 574-576 (3)	.60	.60

Plovdiv Intl. Fair, 1947. See No. C54.

Basil Evstatiev Aprilov — A312

1947, Oct. 19 **Photo.** ***Perf. 11***

577	A312	40 l	brt ultra	.35	.20

Cent. of the death of Basil Evstatiev Aprilov, educator and historian. See No. 603.

Bicycle Race — A313

Basketball
A314

Chess
A315

Balkan Games: 20 l, Soccer players. 60 l, Four flags of participating nations.

1947, Sept. 29 **Typo.** ***Perf. 11½***

578	A313	2 l	plum	.20	.20
579	A314	4 l	dk olive grn	.20	.20
580	A315	9 l	orange brn	.40	.20
581	A315	20 l	brt ultra	.80	.20
582	A315	60 l	violet brn	1.60	.75
			Nos. 578-582 (5)	3.20	1.55

People's Theater, Sofia
A316

National Assembly
A317

Central Post Office, Sofia
A318

Presidential Mansion
A319

1947-48 **Typo.** ***Perf. 12½***

583	A316	50s	yellow grn	.20	.20
584	A317	50s	yellow grn	.20	.20
585	A318	1 l	green	.20	.20
586	A319	1 l	green	.20	.20
587	A316	2 l	brown lake	.20	.20
588	A317	2 l	lt brown	.20	.20
589	A316	4 l	deep blue	.20	.20
590	A317	4 l	deep blue	.20	.20
591	A316	9 l	carmine	.35	.20
592	A317	20 l	deep blue	.75	.30
			Nos. 583-592 (10)	2.70	2.10

On Nos. 583-592 inscription reads "Bulgarian Republic." No. 592 is inscribed in Latin characters.

Redrawn

НАРОДНА

added to inscription

593	A318	1 l	green	.20	.20
594	A318	2 l	brown lake	.20	.20
595	A318	4 l	deep blue	.20	.20
			Nos. 593-595 (3)	.60	.60

Cyrillic inscription beneath design on Nos. 593-595 reads "Bulgarian People's Republic."

Geno Kirov — A320

Actors' Portraits: 1 l, Zlatina Nedeva. 2 l, Ivan Popov. 3 l, Athanas Kirchev. 4 l, Elena Snejina. 5 l, Stoyan Bachvarov.

Perf. 10½

1947, Dec. 8 **Unwmk.** **Litho.**

596	A320	50s	bister brn	.20	.20
597	A320	1 l	lt blue grn	.20	.20
598	A320	2 l	slate green	.20	.20
599	A320	3 l	dp blue	.20	.20
600	A320	4 l	scarlet	.20	.20
601	A320	5 l	red brown	.20	.20
			Nos. 596-601,B22-B26 (11)	2.50	2.30

National Theater, 50th anniversary.

Merchant Ship "Fatherland" — A321

1947, Dec. 19

602	A321	50 l	Prus bl, *cream*	.45	.20

B. E. Aprilov
A322

Worker
A323

1948, Feb. 19 *Perf. 11*

603	A322	4 l brn car, *cream*	.20	.20

Centenary of the death of Basil Evstatiev Aprilov, educator and historian.

1948, Feb. 29 Photo. *Perf. 11½x12*

604	A323	4 l dp blue, *cream*	.20	.20

2nd Bulgarian Workers' Congress.

Self-education
A324

Accordion Player
A325

Factory Recess
A326

Girl Throwing Basketball
A327

1948, Mar. 31 **Photo.**

605	A324	4 l red	.20	.20
606	A325	20 l deep blue	.20	.20
607	A326	40 l dull green	.20	.20
608	A327	60 l brown	.60	.35
		Nos. 605-608 (4)	1.20	.95

Nicholas Vaptzarov — A328

Portraits: 9 l, P. K. Iavorov. 15 l, Christo Smirnenski. 20 l, Ivan Vazov. 45 l, P. R. Slaveikov.

1948, May 18 **Litho.** *Perf. 11*

Cream Paper

611	A328	4 l brt ver	.20	.20
612	A328	9 l lt brown	.20	.20
613	A328	15 l claret	.20	.20
614	A328	20 l deep blue	.20	.20
615	A328	45 l green	.30	.30
		Nos. 611-615 (5)	1.10	1.10

Soviet Soldier
A329

Civilians Offering Gifts to Soldiers
A330

Designs: 20 l, Soldiers, 1878 and 1944. 60 l, Stalin and Spasski Tower.

1948, July 5 **Photo.**

Cream Paper

616	A329	4 l brown org	.20	.20
617	A330	10 l olive grn	.20	.20
618	A330	20 l dp blue	.20	.20
619	A329	60 l olive brn	.40	.35
		Nos. 616-619 (4)	1.00	.95

The Soviet Army.

Demeter Blagoev
A331

Monument to Bishop Andrey
A332

9 l, Gabriel Genov. 60 l, Marching youths.

1948, Sept. 6 **Litho.**

Cream Paper

620	A331	4 l dk brown	.20	.20
621	A331	9 l brown org	.20	.20
622	A332	20 l dp blue	.20	.20
623	A332	60 l brown	.50	.40
		Nos. 620-623 (4)	1.10	1.00

No. 623 is inscribed in Cyrillic characters.
Natl. Insurrection of 1923, 25th anniv.

Christo Smirnenski
A333

Battle of Grivitza, 1877
A334

1948, Oct. 2 **Photo.** *Perf. 11½*

Cream Paper

624	A333	4 l blue	.20	.20
625	A333	16 l red brown	.20	.20

Christo Smirnenski, poet, 1898-1923.

1948, Nov. 1

626	A334	20 l blue	.20	.20
		Nos. 626,C56-C57 (3)	.95	.70

Romanian-Bulgarian friendship.

Bath, Gorna Banya
A335

Bath, Bankya
A336

Mineral Bath, Sofia
A337

Maliovitza
A338

1948-49 **Typo.** *Perf. 12½*

627	A335	2 l red brown	.20	.20
628	A336	3 l red orange	.20	.20
629	A337	4 l deep blue	.20	.20
630	A338	5 l violet brown	.20	.20
631	A336	10 l red violet	.20	.20
632	A338	15 l olive grn ('49)	.20	.20
633	A335	20 l deep blue	.75	.20
		Nos. 627-633 (7)	1.95	1.40

Latin characters on No. 633. See No. 653.

Emblem of the Republic — A339

1948-50

634	A339	50s red orange	.20	.20
634A	A339	50s org brn ('50)	.20	.20
635	A339	1 l green	.20	.20
636	A339	9 l black	.20	.20
		Nos. 634-636 (4)	.80	.80

Botev's Birthplace, Kalofer — A340

Christo Botev — A341

Designs: 9 l, Steamer "Radetzky." 15 l, Kalofer village. 20 l, Botev in uniform. 40 l, Botev's mother. 50 l, Pen, pistol and wreath.

Perf. 11x11½, 11½

1948, Dec. 21 **Photo.**

Cream Paper

638	A340	1 l dk green	.20	.20
639	A341	4 l violet brn	.20	.20
640	A340	9 l violet	.20	.20
641	A340	15 l brown	.20	.20
642	A341	20 l blue	.20	.20
643	A340	40 l red brown	.25	.20
644	A341	50 l olive blk	.35	.25
		Nos. 638-644 (7)	1.60	1.45

Botev, Bulgarian natl. poet, birth cent.

Lenin — A342

Lenin Speaking — A343

1949, Jan. 24 **Unwmk.** *Perf. 11½*

Cream Paper

645	A342	4 l brown	.20	.20
646	A343	20 l brown red	.30	.20

25th anniversary of the death of Lenin.

Road Construction
A344

Designs: 5 l, Tunnel construction. 9 l, Locomotive. 10 l, Textile worker. 20 l, Female tractor driver. 40 l, Workers in truck.

1949, Apr. 6 *Perf. 10½*

Inscribed: "CHM"

Cream Paper

647	A344	4 l dark red	.20	.20
648	A344	5 l dark brown	.20	.20
649	A344	9 l dk slate grn	.25	.20
650	A344	10 l violet	.25	.20
651	A344	20 l dull blue	.60	.40
652	A344	40 l brown	.95	.55
		Nos. 647-652 (6)	2.45	1.75

Issued to honor the Workers' Cultural Brigade.

Type of 1948
Redrawn
Country Name and "POSTA" in Latin Characters

1949 **Typo.** *Perf. 12½*

653	A337	20 l deep blue	.55	.20

Miner — A345

1949 *Perf. 11x11½*

654	A345	4 l dark blue	.20	.20

A347

Prime Minister George Dimitrov, 1882-1949 — A348

1949, July 10 **Photo.**

656	A347	4 l red brown	.25	.20
657	A348	20 l dark blue	.50	.20

Power Station
A349

Grain Towers
A350

Farm Machinery
A351

Tractor Parade
A352

Agriculture and Industry
A353

1949, Aug. 5 *Perf. 11½x11, 11x11½*

658	A349	4 l olive green	.20	.20
659	A350	9 l dark red	.20	.20
660	A351	15 l purple	.20	.20
661	A352	20 l blue	.55	.40
662	A353	50 l orange brn	1.75	.85
		Nos. 658-662 (5)	2.90	1.85

Bulgaria's Five Year Plan.

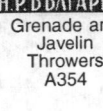

Grenade and Javelin Throwers
A354

Hurdlers
A355

Motorcycle and Tractor
A356

Boy and Girl Athletes
A357

1949, Sept. 5

663	A354	4 l	brown orange	.30	.20
664	A355	9 l	olive green	.60	.25
665	A356	20 l	violet blue	1.25	.65
666	A357	50 l	red brown	3.00	1.25
	Nos. 663-666 (4)			5.15	2.35

Frontier Guards
A358 A359

1949, Oct. 31

667	A358	4 l	chestnut brn	.20	.20
668	A359	20 l	gray blue	.60	.25

See No. C60.

George Dimitrov
A360

Allegory of Labor
A361

Laborers of Both Sexes — A362

Workers and Flags of Bulgaria and Russia — A363

Perf. 11½

1949, Dec. 13 Photo. Unwmk.

669	A360	4 l	orange brn	.20	.20
670	A361	9 l	purple	.20	.20
671	A362	20 l	dull blue	.30	.25
672	A363	50 l	red	.65	.45
	Nos. 669-672 (4)			1.35	1.10

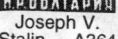

Joseph V. Stalin — A364

Stalin and Dove — A365

1949, Dec. 21

673	A364	4 l	deep orange	.20	.20
674	A365	40 l	rose brown	.60	.30

70th anniv. of the birth of Joseph V. Stalin.

Kharalamby Stoyanov — A366

Communications Strikers — A368

Railway Strikers — A367

1950, Feb. 15

675	A366	4 l	yellow brown	.20	.20
676	A367	20 l	violet blue	.25	.20
677	A368	60 l	brown olive	.60	.40
	Nos. 675-677 (3)			1.05	.80

30th anniv. (in 1949) of the General Railway and Postal Employees' Strike of 1919.

Miner — A369

Locomotive — A370

Shipbuilding
A371

Tractor
A372

Stalin Central Heating Plant
A374

Textile Worker
A375

Farm Machinery
A373

1950-51 ***Perf. 11½, 13***

678	A369	1 l	olive	.20	.20
679	A370	2 l	gray blk	.20	.20
680	A371	3 l	gray blue	.20	.20
681	A372	4 l	dk blue grn	1.75	.50
682	A373	5 l	henna brn	.40	.20
682A	A373	9 l	gray blk ('51)	.20	.20
683	A374	10 l	dp plum ('51)	.30	.20
684	A375	15 l	dk car ('51)	.40	.20
685	A375	20 l	dk blue ('51)	.70	.40
	Nos. 678-685 (9)			4.35	2.30

No. 685 is inscribed in Latin characters.

See Nos. 750-751A.

Vassil Kolarov (1877-1950) — A377

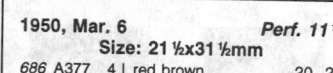

1950, Mar. 6 ***Perf. 11½***

Size: 21½x31½mm

686	A377	4 l	red brown	.20	.20

Size: 27x39½mm

687	A377	20 l	violet blue	.25	.25

No. 687 has altered frame and is inscribed in Latin characters.

Stanislav Dospevski, Self-portrait
A378

King Kaloyan and Desislava
A379

Plowman Resting, by Christo Stanchev
A380

Statue of Dimtcho Debelianov, by Ivan Lazarov
A381

"Harvest," by V. Dimitrov
A382

Design: 9 l, Nikolai Pavlovich, self-portrait.

1950, Apr. 15 ***Perf. 11½***

688	A378	1 l	dk olive grn	.30	.20
689	A379	4 l	dk red	.90	.25
690	A378	9 l	chocolate	.90	.25
691	A380	15 l	brown	1.50	.25
692	A380	20 l	deep blue	2.00	.80
693	A381	40 l	red brown	2.75	1.25
694	A382	60 l	deep orange	4.00	1.60
	Nos. 688-694 (7)			12.35	4.60

Latin characters on No. 692.

Ivan Vazov (1850-1921), Poet and Birthplace
A383

1950, June 26

695	A383	4 l	olive green	.20	.20

Road Building — A384

Men of Three Races and "Stalin" Flag — A385

Perf. 11½x11, 11x11½

1950, Sept. 19

696	A384	4 l	brown red	.20	.20
697	A385	20 l	violet blue	.30	.20

2nd National Peace Conference.

Molotov, Kolarov, Stalin and Dimitrov — A386

Spasski Tower and Flags — A387

Russian and Bulgarian Women
A388

Loading Russian Ship
A389

Perf. 11½

1950, Oct. 10 Unwmk. Photo.

698	A386	4 l	brown	.20	.20
699	A387	9 l	rose carmine	.20	.20
700	A388	20 l	gray blue	.20	.20
701	A389	50 l	dk grnsh blue	1.10	.45
	Nos. 698-701 (4)			1.70	1.05

2nd anniversary of the Soviet-Bulgarian treaty of mutual assistance.

St. Constantine Sanatorium — A390

2 l, 10 l, Children at seashore. 5 l, Rest home.

1950 **Typo.**

702	A390	1 l	dark green	.20	.20
703	A390	2 l	carmine	.20	.20
704	A390	5 l	deep orange	.20	.20
705	A390	10 l	deep blue	.40	.25
	Nos. 702-705 (4)			1.00	.85

Originally prepared in 1945 as "Sunday Delivery Stamps," this issue was released for ordinary postage in 1950.

Runners — A393

1950, Aug. 21 Photo. ***Perf. 11***

706	A393	4 l	shown	.20	.20
707	A393	9 l	Cycling	.20	.20
708	A393	20 l	Shot put	.20	.20
709	A393	40 l	Volleyball	.40	.40
	Nos. 706-709 (4)			1.00	1.00

Marshal Fedor I. Tolbukhin
A394

Natives Greeting Tolbukhin
A395

Perf. 11½x11, 11x11½

1950, Dec. 10 Photo. Unwmk.

710	A394	4 l	claret	.20	.20
711	A395	20 l	dk blue	.35	.20

The return of Dobrich and part of the province of Dobruja from Romania to Bulgaria.

Dimitrov's Birthplace A396

George Dimitrov
A397 A398

Various Portraits, Inscribed:

Г.ДИМИТРОВ

Design: 2 l, Dimitrov Museum, Sofia.

1950, July 2 *Perf. 10½*

712	A396	50s olive grn	.20	.20
713	A397	50s brown	.20	.20
714	A397	1 l redsh brn	.25	.20
715	A396	2 l gray	.25	.20
716	A397	4 l claret	.40	.20
717	A397	9 l red brown	.60	.25
718	A398	10 l brown red	.65	.35
719	A396	15 l olive gray	.65	.35
720	A396	20 l dark blue	1.75	.55
		Nos. 712-720,C61 (10)	7.95	3.60

1st anniversary of the death of George Dimitrov, statesman. No. 720 is inscribed in Latin characters.

A. S. Popov — A400

1951, Feb. 10

722	A400	4 l red brown	.20	.20
723	A400	20 l dark blue	.55	.20

No. 723 is inscribed in Latin characters.

Arms of Bulgaria
A401 A402

1950 Unwmk. Typo. *Perf. 13*

724	A401	2 l dk brown	.20	.20
725	A401	3 l rose	.20	.20
726	A402	5 l carmine	.20	.20
727	A402	9 l aqua	.20	.20
		Nos. 724-727 (4)	.80	.80

Nos. 724-727 were prepared in 1947 for official use but were issued as regular postage stamps Oct. 1, 1950.

Heroes Chankova, Antonov-Malchik, Dimitrov and Dimitrova — A403

Stanke Dimitrov-Marek A404

George Kirkov A405

George Dimitrov at Leipzig — A406

Natcho Ivanov and Avr. Stoyanov — A407

9 l, Anton Ivanov. 15 l, Christo Michailov.

1951, Mar. 25 Photo. *Perf. 11½*

728	A403	1 l red violet	.20	.20
729	A404	2 l dk red brn	.20	.20
730	A405	4 l car rose	.20	.20
731	A405	9 l orange brn	.45	.20
732	A405	15 l olive brn	.80	.25
733	A406	20 l dark blue	1.10	.55
734	A407	50 l olive gray	2.50	.90
		Nos. 728-734 (7)	5.45	2.50

First Bulgarian Tractor A408

First Steam Roller A409

First Truck — A410

Bulgarian Embroidery — A411

15 l, Carpet. 20 l, Tobacco & roses. 40 l, Fruits.

Perf. 11x10½

1951, Mar. 30 Photo. Unwmk.

735	A408	1 l olive brn	.20	.20
736	A409	2 l violet	.30	.20
737	A410	4 l red brown	.50	.20
738	A411	9 l purple	.70	.20
739	A409	15 l deep plum	1.00	.30
740	A411	20 l violet blue	1.50	.30
741	A410	40 l deep green	2.50	.65

Perf. 13

Size: 23x18½mm

742	A408	1 l purple	.20	.20
743	A409	2 l Prus green	.28	.20
744	A410	4 l red brown	.28	.20
		Nos. 735-744 (10)	7.46	2.65

See Nos. 894, 973. For surcharge see No. 973.

Turkish Attack on Mt. Zlee Dol A412

Designs: 4 l, Georgi Benkovski speaking to rebels. 9 l, Cherrywood cannon of 1876 and Russian cavalry, 1945. 20 l, Rebel, 1876 and partisan, 1944. 40 l, Benkovski and Dimitrov.

1951, May 3 *Perf. 10½*

Cream Paper

745	A412	1 l redsh brown	.20	.20
746	A412	4 l dark green	.20	.20
747	A412	9 l violet brown	.50	.30
748	A412	20 l deep blue	.65	.50
749	A412	40 l dark red	1.00	.70
		Nos. 745-749 (5)	2.55	1.90

75th anniv. of the "April" revolution.

Industrial Types of 1950

1951 *Perf. 13*

750	A369	1 l violet	.20	.20
751	A370	2 l dk brown	.20	.20
751A	A372	4 l dk yel grn	.75	.20
		Nos. 750-751A (3)	1.15	.60

Demeter Blagoev Addressing 1891 Congress at Busludja — A413

1951 Photo. *Perf. 11*

752	A413	1 l purple	.25	.20
753	A413	4 l dark green	.35	.20
754	A413	9 l deep claret	.60	.30
		Nos. 752-754 (3)	1.20	.70

60th anniversary of the first Congress of the Bulgarian Social-Democratic Party.
See Nos. 1174-1176.

Day Nursery A414

Designs: 4 l, Model building construction. 9 l, Playground. 20 l, Children's town.

1951, Oct. 10 Unwmk.

755	A414	1 l brown	.20	.20
756	A414	4 l deep plum	.20	.20
757	A414	9 l blue green	.60	.25
758	A414	20 l deep blue	1.00	.55
		Nos. 755-758 (4)	2.00	1.20

Children's Day, Sept. 25, 1951.

Order of Labor
A415 A416

1952, Feb. 1 *Perf. 13*

Reverse of Medal

759	A415	1 l red brown	.20	.20
760	A415	4 l blue green	.20	.20
761	A415	9 l dark blue	.30	.20

Obverse of Medal

762	A416	1 l carmine	.20	.20
763	A416	4 l green	.20	.20
764	A416	9 l purple	.30	.20
		Nos. 759-764 (6)	1.40	1.20

No. 764 has numeral at lower left and different background.

Workers and Symbols of Industry — A417

Design: 4 l, Flags, Dimitrov, Chervenkov.

1951, Dec. 29 *Perf. 11*

Inscribed: "16 XII 1951"

765	A417	1 l olive black	.20	.20
766	A417	4 l chocolate	.20	.20

Third Congress of Bulgarian General Workers' Professional Union.

Dimitrov and Chemical Works — A418

George Dimitrov and V. Chervenkov — A419

Portrait: 80s, Dimitrov.

Unwmk.

1952, June 18 Photo. *Perf. 11*

767	A418	16s brown	.35	.25
768	A419	44s brown carmine	.50	.25
769	A418	80s brt blue	1.10	.50
		Nos. 767-769 (3)	1.95	1.00

70th anniv. of the birth of George Dimitrov.

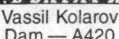

Vassil Kolarov Dam — A420

Republika Power Station — A421

1952, May 16 *Perf. 13*

770	A420	4s dark green	.20	.20
771	A420	12s purple	.20	.20
772	A420	16s red brown	.20	.20
773	A420	44s rose brown	.50	.20
774	A420	80s brt blue	1.60	.20
		Nos. 770-774 (5)	2.70	1.00

No. 774 is inscribed in Latin characters.

1952, June 30 *Perf. 13, Pin Perf.*

775	A421	16s dark brown	.20	.20
776	A421	44s magenta	.75	.20

Nikolai I. Vapzarov — A422

Designs: Various portraits.

1952, July 23 *Perf. 10½*

777	A422	16s rose brown	.20	.20
778	A422	44s dk red brn	.65	.20
779	A422	80s dk olive brn	1.40	.50
		Nos. 777-779 (3)	2.25	.90

10th anniversary of the death of Nikolai I. Vapzarov, poet and revolutionary.

Dimitrov and Youth Conference — A423

Designs: 16s, Resistance movement incident. 44s, Frontier guards and industrial scene. 80s, George Dimitrov and young workers.

1952, Sept. 1 — *Perf. 11x11½*

780	A423	2s brown carmine	.20	.20
781	A423	16s purple	.20	.20
782	A423	44s dark green	.50	.30
783	A423	80s dark brown	1.10	.60
		Nos. 780-783 (4)	2.00	1.30

40th anniv. of the founding conference of the Union of Social Democratic Youth.

Assault on the Winter Palace — A424

Designs: 8s, Volga-Don Canal. 16s, Symbols of world peace. 44s, Lenin and Stalin. 80s, Himlay hydroelectric station.

Perf. 11½

1952, Nov. 6 — **Unwmk.** — **Photo.**

Dated: "1917-1952"

784	A424	4s red brown	.20	.20
785	A424	8s dark green	.20	.20
786	A424	16s dark blue	.20	.20
787	A424	44s brown	.30	.20
788	A424	80s olive brown	.75	.35
		Nos. 784-788 (5)	1.65	1.15

35th anniv. of the Russian revolution.

Vassil Levski — A425

Design: 44s, Levski and comrades.

1953, Feb. 19 — *Perf. 11*

Cream Paper

789	A425	16s brown	.20	.20
790	A425	44s brown blk	.25	.20

80th anniv. of the death of Levski, patriot.

Ferrying Artillery and Troops into Battle A426

Soldier A427

Mother and Children A428

Designs: 44s, Victorious soldiers. 80s, Soldier welcomed. 1 l, Monuments.

1953, Mar. 3 — *Perf. 10½*

791	A426	8s Prus green	.20	.20
792	A427	16s dp brown	.25	.20
793	A426	44s dk slate grn	.40	.20
794	A426	80s dull red brn	.85	.20
795	A426	1 l black	1.10	.30
		Nos. 791-795 (5)	2.80	1.10

Bulgaria's independence from Turkey, 75th anniv.

1953, Mar. 9

796	A428	16s slate green	.20	.20
797	A428	16s bright blue	.20	.20

Women's Day.

Woodcarvings at Rila Monastery

A429 A430

Designs: 12s, 16s, 28s, Woodcarvings, Rila Monastery. 44s, Carved Ceilings, Trnovo. 80s, 1 l, 4 l, Carvings, Pasardjik.

1953 — **Unwmk.** — **Photo.** — *Perf. 13*

798	A429	2s gray brown	.20	.20
799	A430	8s dk slate grn	.20	.20
800	A430	12s brown	.20	.20
801	A430	16s rose lake	.25	.20
802	A429	28s dk olive grn	.30	.20
803	A430	44s dk brown	.50	.20
804	A430	80s ultra	.85	.20
805	A430	1 l violet blue	1.75	.25
806	A430	4 l rose lake	3.50	.90
		Nos. 798-806 (9)	7.75	2.55

For surcharge see No. 1204.

Karl Marx A431

"Das Kapital" A432

1953, Apr. 30 — *Perf. 10½*

807	A431	16s bright blue	.20	.20
808	A432	44s deep brown	.30	.20

70th anniversary of the death of Karl Marx.

Labor Day Parade — A433

Joseph V. Stalin — A434

1953, Apr. 30 — *Perf. 13*

809	A433	16s brown red	.20	.20

Labor Day, May 1, 1953.

1953, May 23 — *Perf. 13x13½*

810	A434	16s dark gray	.20	.20
811	A434	16s dark brown	.20	.20

Death of Joseph V. Stalin, Mar. 5, 1953.

Georgi Delchev A435

Battle Scene A436

Peasants Attacking Turkish Troops — A437

1953, Aug. 8 — *Perf. 13*

812	A435	16s dark brown	.20	.20
813	A436	44s purple	.30	.20
814	A437	1 l deep claret	.45	.20
		Nos. 812-814 (3)	.95	.60

50th anniv. of the Ilinden Revolt (#812, 814) and the Preobrazhene Revolt (#813).

Soldier and Rebels — A438

44s, Soldier guarding industrial construction.

1953, Sept. 18

815	A438	16s deep claret	.20	.20
816	A438	44s greenish blue	.35	.20

Army Day.

George Dimitrov and Vassil Kolarov A439

Demeter Blagoev A440

Designs: 16s, Citizens in revolt. 44s, Attack.

1953, Sept. 22

817	A439	8s olive gray	.20	.20
818	A439	16s dk red brn	.20	.20
819	A439	44s cerise	.45	.20
		Nos. 817-819 (3)	.85	.60

September Revolution, 30th anniversary.

1953, Sept. 21

Portraits: 44s, G. Dimitrov and D. Blagoev.

820	A440	16s brown	.25	.20
821	A440	44s red brown	.40	.20

50th anniversary of the formation of the Social Democratic Party.

Railway Viaduct — A441

Pouring Molten Metal — A442

Designs: 16s, Welder and storage tanks. 80s, Harvesting machine.

1953, Oct. 17

826	A441	8s brt blue	.20	.20
827	A441	16s grnsh blk	.20	.20
828	A442	44s brown red	.30	.20
829	A441	80s orange	.45	.30
		Nos. 826-829 (4)	1.15	.90

Month of Bulgarian-Russian friendship.

Belladonna A443

Kolarov Library, Sofia A444

Medicinal Flowers: 4s, Jimson weed. 8s, Sage. 12s, Dog rose. 16s, Gentian. 20s, Poppy. 28s, Peppermint. 40s, Bear grass. 44s, Coltsfoot. 80s, Cowslip. 1 l, Dandelion. 2 l, Foxglove.

1953 — **Unwmk.** — **Photo.** — *Perf. 13*

White or Cream Paper

830	A443	2s dull blue	.20	.20
831	A443	4s brown org	.20	.20
832	A443	8s blue grn	.20	.20
833	A443	12s brown org	.20	.20
834	A443	12s blue grn	.20	.20
835	A443	16s violet blue	.20	.20
836	A443	16s dp red brn	.20	.20
837	A443	20s car rose	.20	.20
838	A443	28s dk gray grn	.30	.20
839	A443	40s dark blue	.35	.20
840	A443	44s brown	.35	.20
841	A443	80s yellow brn	.60	.35
842	A443	1 l henna brn	2.25	.50
843	A443	2 l purple	3.75	1.25
a.		Souvenir sheet	27.50	20.00
		Nos. 830-843 (14)	9.20	4.30

No. 843a contains 12 stamps, one of each denomination above, printed in dark green. Size: 161x172mm. Sold for 6 leva.

1953, Dec. 16

854	A444	44s brown	.25	.20

75th anniversary of the founding of the Kolarov Library, Sofia.

Singer and Accordionist A445

Lenin and Stalin A446

1953, Dec. 26

855	A445	16s shown	.20	.20
856	A445	44s Dancers	.20	.20

1954, Mar. 13

Designs: 44s, Lenin statue. 80s, Lenin mausoleum, Moscow. 1 l, Lenin.

Cream Paper

857	A446	16s brown	.20	.20
858	A446	44s rose brown	.25	.20
859	A446	80s blue	.40	.20
860	A446	1 l dp olive grn	.60	.25
		Nos. 857-860 (4)	1.45	.85

30th anniversary of the death of Lenin.

Demeter Blagoev and Followers A447

Design: 44s, Blagoev at desk.

1954, Apr. 28

Cream Paper

861	A447	16s dp red brn	.20	.20
862	A447	44s black brn	.30	.20

30th anniv. of the death of Demeter Blagoev.

George Dimitrov A448

Dimitrov and Refinery A449

1954, June 11

863	A448	44s lake, *cream*	.25	.20
864	A449	80s brown, *cream*	.65	.20

5th anniv. of the death of George Dimitrov.

Train Leaving Tunnel — A450

1954, July 30

865	A450	44s dk grn, *cream*	.60	.20
866	A450	44s blk brn, *cream*	.60	.20

Day of the Railroads, Aug. 1, 1954.

Miner at Work — A451

1954, Aug. 19

867	A451	44s grnsh blk, *cream*	.20	.20

Miners' Day.

Academy of Science — A452

1954, Oct. 27

868	A452	80s black, *cream*	.55	.20

85th anniversary of the foundation of the Bulgarian Academy of Science.

Horsemanship A454

16s, 44s, 2 l, vert.

1954, Dec. 21

869	A454	16s Gymnastics	.50	.20
870	A454	44s Wrestling	.60	.20
871	A454	80s shown	1.25	.55
872	A454	2 l Skiing	3.00	1.60
		Nos. 869-872 (4)	5.35	2.55

Welcoming Liberators A455

Soldier's Return A456

Designs: 28s, Refinery. 44s, Dimitrov and Workers. 80s, Girl and boy. 1 l, George Dimitrov.

1954, Oct. 4

Cream Paper

873	A455	12s brown car	.20	.20
874	A456	16s dp carmine	.20	.20
875	A455	28s indigo	.20	.20
876	A455	44s redsh brn	.20	.20
877	A456	80s deep blue	.55	.25
878	A456	1 l dark green	.55	.25
		Nos. 873-878 (6)	1.90	1.30

10th anniversary of Bulgaria's liberation.

Recreation at Workers' Rest Home A457

Metal Worker and Furnace A458

Portraits: 80s, Dimitrov, Blagoev, and Kirkov.

Unwmk.

1954, Dec. 28 Photo. *Perf. 13*

Cream Paper

879	A457	16s dark green	.20	.20
880	A458	44s brown orange	.20	.20
881	A457	80s dp violet blue	.40	.20
		Nos. 879-881 (3)	.80	.60

50th anniversary of Bulgaria's trade union movement.

Geese — A459

Designs: 4s, Chickens. 12s, Hogs. 16s, Sheep. 28s, Telephone building. 44s, Communist party headquarters. 80s, Apartment buildings. 1 l, St. Kiradgieff Mills.

1955-56

882	A459	2s dk blue grn	.20	.20
883	A459	4s olive green	.30	.20
884	A459	12s dk red brn	.40	.20
885	A459	16s brown orange	.65	.20
886	A459	28s violet blue	.30	.20
887	A459	44s lil red, *cream*	.60	.20
a.		44s brown red	4.50	.20
888	A459	80s dk red brown	.75	.20
889	A459	1 l dk blue green	1.50	.20
		Nos. 882-889 (8)	4.70	1.60

Issued: #887, 4/20/56; others, 2/19/55.

Textile Worker — A460

Mother and Child — A461

Design: 16s, Woman feeding calf.

1955, Mar. 5

890	A460	12s dark brown	.20	.20
891	A460	16s dark green	.20	.20
892	A461	44s dk car rose	.50	.20
893	A461	44s blue	.50	.20
		Nos. 890-893 (4)	1.40	.80

Women's Day, Mar. 8, 1955.

No. 744 Surcharged in Blue

1955, Mar. 8 *Perf. 13*

894	A410	16s on 4 l red brown	.45	.20

May Day Demonstration of Workers A462

Sts. Cyril and Methodius A463

Design: 44s, Three workers and globe.

1955, Apr. 23 Photo.

895	A462	16s car rose	.20	.20
896	A462	44s blue	.30	.20

Labor Day, May 1, 1955.

1955, May 21

Designs: 8s, Paisii Hilendarski. 16s, Nicolas Karastoyanov's printing press. 28s, Christo Botev. 44s, Ivan Vazov. 80s, Demeter Blagoev and socialist papers. 2 l, Blagoev printing plant, Sofia.

Cream Paper

897	A463	4s deep blue	.20	.20
898	A463	8s olive	.20	.20
899	A463	16s black	.20	.20
900	A463	28s henna brn	.20	.20
901	A463	44s brown	.30	.20
902	A463	80s rose red	.50	.20
903	A463	2 l black	1.50	.40
		Nos. 897-903 (7)	3.10	1.60

Creation of the Cyrillic alphabet, 1100th anniv. Latin lettering at bottom on #901-903.

Sergei Rumyantzev A464

Mother and Children A465

Portraits: 16s, Christo Jassenov. 44s, Geo Milev.

1955, June 30 Unwmk. *Perf. 13*

Cream Paper

904	A464	12s orange brn	.20	.20
905	A464	16s lt brown	.20	.20
906	A464	44s grnsh blk	.40	.20
		Nos. 904-906 (3)	.80	.60

30th anniv. of the deaths of Sergei Rumyanchev, Christo Jassenov and Geo Milev. Latin lettering at bottom of No. 906.

1955, July 30

907	A465	44s brn car, *cream*	.30	.20

World Congress of Mothers in Lausanne, 1955.

Young People of Three Races — A466

Friedrich Engels and Book — A467

1955, July 30

908	A466	44s blue, *cream*	.30	.20

5th World Festival of Youth in Warsaw, July 31-Aug. 14.

1955, July 30

909	A467	44s brown	.30	.20

60th anniv. of the death of Friedrich Engels.

Entrance to Fair, 1892 — A468

Statuary Group at Fair, 1955 — A469

Designs: 44s, "Fruit of our Land." 80s, Woman holding Fair emblem.

1955, Aug. 31

Cream Paper

910	A468	4s deep brown	.20	.20
911	A469	16s dk car rose	.20	.20
912	A468	44s olive blk	.20	.20
913	A469	80s deep blue	.45	.20
		Nos. 910-913 (4)	1.05	.80

16th International Plovdiv Fair. Latin lettering on Nos. 912-913.

Friedrich von Schiller — A470

Portraits: 44s, Adam Mickiewicz. 60s, Hans Christian Andersen. 80s, Baron de Montesquieu. 1 l, Miguel de Cervantes. 2 l, Walt Whitman.

1955, Oct. 31

Cream Paper

914	A470	16s brown	.20	.20
915	A470	44s brown red	.40	.20
916	A470	60s Prus blue	.60	.20
917	A470	80s black	.60	.20
918	A470	1 l rose violet	1.40	.30
919	A470	2 l olive green	1.90	.50
		Nos. 914-919 (6)	5.10	1.60

Various anniversaries of famous writers. Nos. 918 and 919 are issued in sheets alternating with labels without franking value. The labels show title pages for Leaves of Grass and Don Quixote in English and Spanish, respectively. Latin lettering on #915-919.

Karl Marx Industrial Plant — A471

Friendship Monument A472

I. V. Michurin A473

Designs: 4s, Alekandr Stamboliski Dam. 16s, Bridge over Danube. 1 l, Vladimir V. Mayakovsky.

1955, Dec. 1 Unwmk.

920	A471	2s slate blk	.20	.20
921	A471	4s deep blue	.20	.20
922	A471	16s dk blue grn	.20	.20
923	A472	44s red brown	.20	.20
924	A473	80s dark green	.25	.20
925	A473	1 l gray blk	.40	.20
		Nos. 920-925 (6)	1.45	1.20

Russian-Bulgarian friendship.

Library Seal — A474

Krusto Pishurka — A475

Portrait: 44s, Bacho Kiro.

1956, Feb. 10 *Perf. 11x10½*

926	A474	12s car lake, *cream*	.20	.20
927	A475	16s dp brn, *cream*	.20	.20
928	A475	44s slate blk, *cream*	.25	.20
		Nos. 926-928 (3)	.65	.60

100th anniversary of the National Library. Latin lettering at bottom of No. 928.

Canceled to Order

Beginning about 1956, some issues were sold in sheets canceled to order. Values in second column when much less than unused are for "CTO" copies. Postally used stamps are valued at slightly less than, or the same as, unused.

Quinces A476

Cherrywood Cannon A477

Designs: 8s, Pears. 16s, Apples. 44s, Grapes.

1956 Photo. *Perf. 13*
929 A476 4s carmine .75 .20
930 A476 8s blue green .30 .20
931 A476 16s lilac rose .80 .20
932 A476 44s deep violet .80 .20
Nos. 929-932 (4) 2.65 .80

Latin lettering on #932. See #964-967. For surcharge see #1364.

1956, Apr. 28 *Perf. 11x10½*
933 A477 16s shown .20 .20
934 A477 44s Cavalry attack .25 .20

April Uprising against Turkish rule, 80th anniv.

Demeter Blagoev (1856-1924), Writer, Birthplace
A478

Cherries
A479

1956, May 30 *Perf. 11*
935 A478 44s Prus blue .25 .20

1956 Unwmk. *Perf. 13*
936 A479 2s shown .20 .20
937 A479 12s Plums .20 .20
938 A479 28s Peaches .20 .20
939 A479 80s Strawberries .55 .20
Nos. 936-939 (4) 1.15 .80

Latin lettering on No. 939.

Gymnastics
A480

Pole Vaulting
A481

Designs: 12s, Discus throw. 44s, Soccer, 80s, Basketball. 1 l, Boxing.

Perf. 11x10½, 10½x11
1956, Aug. 29
940 A480 4s brt ultra .20 .20
941 A480 12s brick red .20 .20
942 A481 16s yellow brn .30 .20
943 A481 44s dark green .50 .25
944 A480 80s dark red brn 1.00 .50
945 A481 1 l deep magenta 1.60 .65
Nos. 940-945 (6) 3.80 2.00

Latin lettering on Nos. 943-945.
16th Olympic Games at Melbourne, Nov. 22-Dec. 8, 1956.

Tobacco, Rose and Distillery
A482

People's Theater
A483

1956, Sept. 1 *Perf. 13*
946 A482 44s deep carmine .40 .20
947 A482 44s olive green .40 .20

17th International Plovdiv Fair.

1956, Nov. 16 Unwmk.

Design: 44s, Dobri Woinikoff and Sawa Dobroplodni, dramatists.

948 A483 16s dull red brown .20 .20
949 A483 44s dark blue green .25 .20

Bulgarian Theater centenary.

Benjamin Franklin
A484

Cyclists, Palms and Pyramids
A485

Portraits: 20s, Rembrandt. 40s, Mozart. 44s, Heinrich Heine. 60s, Shaw. 80s, Dostoevski. 1 l, Ibsen. 2 l, Pierre Curie.

1956, Dec. 29
950 A484 16s dark olive grn .20 .20
951 A484 20s brown .20 .20
952 A484 40s dark car rose .20 .20
953 A484 44s dark violet brn .25 .20
954 A484 60s dark slate .30 .20
955 A484 80s dark brown .45 .20
956 A484 1 l bluish grn .80 .30
957 A484 2 l Prus green 1.75 .50
Nos. 950-957 (8) 4.15 2.00

Great personalities of the world.

1957, Mar. 6 Photo. *Perf. 10½*
958 A485 80s henna brown .50 .25
959 A485 80s Prus green .50 .25

Fourth Egyptian bicycle race.

Woman Technician
A486

"New Times" Review
A487

Designs: 16s, Woman and children. 44s, Woman feeding chickens.

1957, Mar. 8
960 A486 12s deep blue .20 .20
961 A486 16s henna brown .20 .20
962 A486 44s slate green .30 .20
Nos. 960-962 (3) .70 .60

Women's Day. Latin lettering on 44s.

1957, Mar. 8 Unwmk.
963 A487 16s deep carmine .20 .20

60th anniversary of the founding of the "New Times" review.

Fruit Type of 1956.

4s, Quinces. 8s, Pears. 16s, Apples. 44s, Grapes.

1957 Photo. *Perf. 13*
964 A476 4s yellow green .20 .20
965 A476 8s brown orange .20 .20
966 A476 16s rose red .20 .20
967 A476 44s orange yellow .40 .20
Nos. 964-967 (4) 1.00 .80

Latin lettering on #967. For surcharge see #1364.

Sts. Cyril and Methodius
A488

Basketball
A489

1957, May 22 *Perf. 11*
968 A488 44s olive grn & buff .50 .20

Centenary of the first public veneration of Sts. Cyril and Methodius, inventors of the Cyrillic alphabet.

1957, June 20 Photo. *Perf. 10½x11*
969 A489 44s dark green .95 .30

10th European Basketball Championship at Sofia.

Dancer and Spasski Tower, Moscow — A490

1957, July 18 *Perf. 13*
970 A490 44s blue .30 .20

Sixth World Youth Festival in Moscow.

George Dimitrov (1882-1949) — A491

1957, July 18
971 A491 44s deep carmine .50 .20

Vassil Levski — A492

1957, July 18 *Perf. 11*
972 A492 44s grnsh black .30 .20

120th anniversary of the birth of Vassil Levski, patriot and national hero.

No. 742 Surcharged in Carmine

1957 Unwmk. *Perf. 13*
973 A408 16s on 1 l purple .20 .20

Trnovo and Lazarus L. Zamenhof
A493

1957, July 27
974 A493 44s slate green .50 .20

50th anniv. of the Bulgarian Esperanto Society and the 70th anniv. of Esperanto.
For surcharge see No. 1235.

Bulgarian Veteran of 1877 War and Russian Soldier — A494

Design: 44s, Battle of Shipka Pass.

1957, Aug. 13
975 A494 16s dk blue grn .20 .20
976 A494 44s brown .30 .20

80th anniversary of Bulgaria's liberation from the Turks. Latin lettering on No. 976.

Woman Planting Tree — A495

Red Deer in Forest — A496

Designs: 16s, Dam, lake and forest. 44s, Plane over forest. 80s, Fields on edge of forest.

1957, Sept. 16 Photo. *Perf. 13*
977 A495 2s deep green .20 .20
978 A496 12s dark brown .20 .20
979 A496 16s Prus blue .20 .20
980 A496 44s Prus green .25 .20
981 A496 80s yellow green .40 .20
Nos. 977-981 (5) 1.25 1.00

Latin lettering on Nos. 980 and 981.

Lenin — A497

Designs: 16s, Cruiser "Aurora." 44s, Dove over map of communist area. 60s, Revolutionaries and banners. 80s, Oil refinery.

1957, Oct. 29 *Perf. 11*
982 A497 12s chocolate .20 .20
983 A497 16s Prus green .30 .20
984 A497 44s deep blue .65 .20
985 A497 60s dk car rose .75 .20
986 A497 80s dark green 1.25 .25
Nos. 982-986 (5) 3.15 1.05

40th anniv. of the Communist Revolution.
Latin lettering on Nos. 984-985.

Globes
A498

1957, Oct. 4 *Perf. 13*
987 A498 44s Prus blue .30 .20

4th Intl. Trade Union Cong., Leipzig, Oct. 4-15.

Vassil Kolarov Hotel
A499

Bulgarian Health Resorts: 4s, Skis and Pirin Mountains. 8s, Old house at Koprivspitsa. 12s, Rest home at Velingrad. 44s, Momin-Prochod Hotel. 60s, Nesebr Hotel, shoreline and peninsula. 80s, Varna beach scene. 1 l, Hotel at Varna.

1958 Photo. *Perf. 13*
988 A499 4s blue .20 .20
989 A499 8s orange brn .20 .20
990 A499 12s dk green .20 .20
991 A499 16s green .20 .20
992 A499 44s dk blue grn .20 .20
993 A499 60s deep blue .20 .20
994 A499 80s fawn .30 .20
995 A499 1 l dk red brn .35 .20
Nos. 988-995 (8) 1.85 1.60

Latin lettering on 44s, 60s, 80s, and 1 l.
Issue dates: #991-994, Jan. 20; others, July 5.
For surcharges see Nos. 1200, 1436.

Mikhail I. Glinka — A500

Portraits: 16s, Jan A. Komensky (Comenius). 40s, Carl von Linné. 44s, William Blake. 60s, Carlo Goldoni. 80s, Auguste Comte.

1957, Dec. 30

996 A500 12s dark brown .20 .20
997 A500 16s dark green .20 .20
998 A500 40s Prus blue .20 .20
999 A500 44s maroon .20 .20
1000 A500 60s orange brown .75 .20
1001 A500 80s deep plum 2.50 .90
Nos. 996-1001 (6) 4.05 1.90

Famous men of other countries. Latin lettering on Nos. 999-1001.

Young Couple, Flag, Dimitrov A501

People's Front Salute A502

1957, Dec. 28 ***Perf. 11***

1002 A501 16s carmine rose .20 .20

10th anniversary of Dimitrov's Union of the People's Youth.

1957, Dec. 28

1003 A502 16s dk violet brn .20 .20

15th anniversary of the People's Front.

Hare A503

12s, Red deer (doe), vert. 16s, Red deer (stag). 44s, Chamois. 80s, Brown bear. 1 l, Wild boar.

Perf. 10½

1958, Apr. 5 **Unwmk.** **Photo.**

1004 A503 2s lt & dk ol grn .20 .20
1005 A503 12s sl grn & red brn .20 .20
1006 A503 16s bluish grn & dk red brn .20 .20
1007 A503 44s blue & brown .25 .20
1008 A503 80s bis & dk brn .75 .25
1009 A503 1 l stl bl & dk brn 1.00 .25
Nos. 1004-1009 (6) 2.60 1.30

Value, imperf. set $4.

Marx and Lenin A504

Designs: 16s, Marchers and flags. 44s, Lenin blast furnaces.

1958, July 2 ***Perf. 11***

1010 A504 12s dark brown .20 .20
1011 A504 16s dark carmine .20 .20
1012 A504 44s dark blue .85 .20
Nos. 1010-1012 (3) 1.25 .60

Bulgarian Communist Party, 7th Congress.

Wrestlers — A505

1958, June 20 ***Perf. 10½***

1013 A505 60s dk carmine rose .65 .35
1014 A505 80s deep brown 1.10 .55

World Wrestling Championship, Sofia.

Chessmen and Globe A506

Perf. 10½

1958, July 18 **Unwmk.** **Photo.**

1015 A506 80s grn & yel grn 2.50 .80

5th World Students' Chess Games, Varna.

Conference Emblem A507

1958, Sept. 24

1016 A507 44s blue .40 .20

World Trade Union Conference of Working Youth, Prague, July 14-20.

Swimmer A508

1958 Students' Games: 28s, Dancer, vert. 44s, Volleyball, vert.

1958, Sept. 19 ***Perf. 11x10½***

1017 A508 16s bright blue .20 .20
1018 A508 28s brown orange .25 .20
1019 A508 44s bright green .30 .20
Nos. 1017-1019 (3) .75 .60

Onions — A509

Vegetables: 12s, Garlic. 16s, Peppers. 44s, Tomatoes. 80s, Cucumbers. 1 l, Eggplant.

1958, Sept. 20 ***Perf. 13***

1020 A509 2s orange brown .20 .20
1021 A509 12s Prus blue .20 .20
1022 A509 16s dark green .20 .20
1023 A509 44s deep carmine .20 .20
1024 A509 80s deep green .40 .20
1025 A509 1 l brt purple .60 .20
Nos. 1020-1025 (6) 1.80 1.20

Value, imperf. set $4.

See No. 1072. For surcharge see No. 1201.

Plovdiv Fair Building A510

1958, Sept. 14 **Unwmk.** ***Perf. 11***

1026 A510 44s deep carmine .40 .20

18th International Plovdiv Fair.

Attack — A511

Design: 44s, Fighter dragging wounded man.

1958, Sept. 23 **Photo.** ***Perf. 11***

1027 A511 16s orange ver .20 .20
1028 A511 44s lake .35 .20

35th anniv. of the September Revolution.

Emblem, Brussels Fair — A512

1958, Oct. 13 ***Perf. 11***

1029 A512 1 l blk & brt blue 5.00 1.25

Brussels World's Fair, Apr. 17-Oct. 19. Exists imperf.

Runner at Finish Line — A513

Woman Throwing Javelin A514

60s, High jumper. 80s, Hurdler. 4 l, Shot putter.

1958, Nov. 30

1030 A513 16s red brn, *pnksh* .35 .20
1031 A514 44s olive, *yelsh* .35 .20
1032 A514 60s dk bl, *bluish* .65 .20
1033 A514 80s dp grn, *grnsh* .90 .20
1034 A513 4 l dp rose cl, *pnksh* 5.75 1.40
Nos. 1030-1034 (5) 8.00 2.20

1958 Balkan Games.

Latin lettering on Nos. 1032-1033.

Christo Smirnenski A515

1958, Dec. 22

1035 A515 16s dark carmine .20 .20

Christo Smirnenski (1898-1923), poet.

Girls Harvesting — A516

Girl Tending Calves A517

Designs: 16s, Boy and girl laborers. 40s, Boy pushing wheelbarrow. 44s, Headquarters building.

1959, Nov. 29 **Photo.**

1036 A516 8s dk olive green .20 .20
1037 A517 12s redsh brown .20 .20
1038 A516 16s violet brown .20 .20
1039 A517 40s Prus blue .20 .20
1040 A516 44s deep carmine .60 .20
Nos. 1036-1040 (5) 1.40 1.00

4th Congress of Dimitrov's Union of People's Youth.

UNESCO Building, Paris A518

1959, Mar. 28 **Unwmk.** ***Perf. 11***

1041 A518 2 l dp red lilac, *cream* 1.25 1.00

Opening of UNESCO Headquarters, Paris, Nov. 3, 1958. Value imperf. $2.50

Skier — A519

Soccer Players — A520

1959, Mar. 28 ***Perf. 11***

1042 A519 1 l blue, *cream* .90 .50

Forty years of skiing in Bulgaria.

1959, Mar. 25

1043 A520 2 l chestnut, *cream* 1.25 .65

1959 European Youth Soccer Championship.

Russian Soldiers Installing Telegraph Wires — A521

First Bulgarian Postal Coach A522

Designs: 60s, Stamp of 1879. 80s, First Bulgarian automobile. 1 l, Television tower. 2 l, Strike of railroad and postal workers, 1919.

1959, May 4

1044 A521 12s dk grn & cit .20 .20
1045 A522 16s deep plum .20 .20
1046 A521 60s dk brn & yel .30 .20
1047 A522 80s hn brn & sal .45 .20
1048 A521 1 l blue .60 .20
1049 A522 2 l dk red brown 1.60 .80
Nos. 1044-1049 (6) 3.35 1.80

80th anniv. of the Bulgarian post. Latin lettering on Nos. 1046-1049.

Two imperf. souvenir sheets exist with olive borders and inscriptions. One contains one copy of No. 1046 in black & ocher, and measures 92x121mm. The other sheet contains one copy each of Nos. 1044-1045 and 1047-1048 in changed colors: 12s, olive green & ocher; 16s, deep claret & ocher; 80s, dark red

& ocher; 1 l, olive & ocher. Each sheet sold for 5 leva. Value, each $22.50.

Great Tits
A523

Birds: 8s, Hoopoe. 16s, Great spotted woodpecker, vert. 45s, Gray partridge, vert. 60s, Rock partridge. 80s, European cuckoo.

1959, June 30 **Photo.**

1050	A523	2s olive & sl grn	.20	.20
1051	A523	8s dp orange & blk	.20	.20
1052	A523	16s chestnut & dk brn	.25	.20
1053	A523	45s brown & blk	.30	.20
1054	A523	60s dp blue & gray	.65	.20
1055	A523	80s dp bl grn & gray	1.10	.20
		Nos. 1050-1055 (6)	2.70	1.20

Bagpiper — A524

Designs: 12s, Acrobats. 16s, Girls exercising with hoops. 20s, Male dancers. 80s, Ballet dancers. 1 l, Ceramic pitcher. 16s, 20s, 80s are horizontal.

1959, Aug. 29 **Unwmk.** ***Perf. 11***

Surface-colored Paper

1056	A524	4s dk olive	.20	.20
1057	A524	12s scarlet	.20	.20
1058	A524	16s maroon	.20	.20
1059	A524	20s dk blue	.25	.20
1060	A524	80s brt green	.50	.25
1061	A524	1 l brown org	.95	.40
		Nos. 1056-1061 (6)	2.30	1.45

7th International Youth Festival, Vienna. Latin inscriptions on Nos. 1060-1061.

Partisans in Truck
A525

Designs: 16s, Partisans and soldiers shaking hands. 45s, Refinery. 60s, Tanks. 80s, Harvester. 1.25 l, Children with flag, vert.

1959, Sept. 8

1062	A525	12s red & Prus grn	.20	.20
1063	A525	16s red & dk pur	.20	.20
1064	A525	45s red & int bl	.20	.20
1065	A525	60s red & ol grn	.20	.20
1066	A525	80s red & brn	.25	.20
1067	A525	1.25 l red & dp brn	.65	.40
		Nos. 1062-1067 (6)	1.70	1.40

15th anniversary of Bulgarian liberation.

Soccer
A526

1959, Oct. 10 **Unwmk.** ***Perf. 11***

1068 A526 1.25 l dp green, *yel* 3.50 2.00

50 years of Bulgarian soccer.

Set exists imperf. in changed colors. Value $7.50 unused, $4 canceled.

Batak Defenders
A527

1959, Aug. 8

1069 A527 16s deep claret .20 .20

300th anniv. of the settlement of Batak.

Post Horn and Letter — A528

Bird-shaped Lyre — A529

Design: 1.25 l, Dove and letter.

1959, Nov. 23

1070	A528	45s emerald & blk	.30	.20
1071	A528	1.25 l lt blue, red & blk	.50	.20

Intl. Letter Writing Week Oct. 5-11.

Type of 1958 Surcharged "45 CT." in Dark Blue

Design: Tomatoes.

1959 **Photo.** ***Perf. 13***

1072 A509 45s on 44s scarlet .55 .20

1960, Feb. 23 **Unwmk.** ***Perf. 10½***

1073	A529	80s shown	.40	.20
1074	A529	1.25 l Lyre	.70	.20

50th anniv. of Bulgaria's State Opera.

N. I. Vapzarov
A530

Parachute and Radio Tower
A531

1959, Dec. 14 ***Perf. 11***

1075 A530 80s yel grn & red brn .35 .20

Vapzarov, poet and patriot, 50th birth anniv.

1959, Dec. 3 **Photo.**

1076 A531 1.25 l dp grnsh bl & yel 1.25 .45

3rd Cong. of Voluntary Participants in Defense.

Cotton Picker — A532

Harvester Combine — A533

Designs: 2s, Kindergarten. 4s, Woman doctor and child. 10s, Woman milking cow. 12s, Woman holding tobacco leaves. 15s, Woman working loom. 16s, Stalin textile mill, Dimitrovgrad. 25s, Rural electrification. 28s, Woman picking sunflowers. 40s, "Cold-well" hydroelectric dam. 45s, Miner. 60s, Foundry worker. 80s. Woman harvesting grapes. 1 l, Worker and peasant with cogwheel. 1.25 l, Industrial worker. 2 l, Party leader.

1959-61 **Photo.** ***Perf. 13***

1077	A533	2s brown org ('60)	.20	.20
1077A	A532	4s gldn brn ('61)	.20	.20
1078	A532	5s dk green	.20	.20
1079	A533	10s red brn ('61)	.20	.20
1080	A532	12s red brown	.20	.20
1081	A532	15s red lil ('60)	.20	.20
1082	A533	16s dp vio ('60)	.20	.20
1083	A533	20s orange	.20	.20
1084	A532	25s brt blue ('60)	.20	.20
1085	A532	28s brt green	.20	.20
1086	A533	40s brt grnsh bl	.30	.20
1087	A532	45s choc ('60)	.25	.20
1088	A533	60s scarlet	.40	.20
1089	A532	80s ol ('60)	.50	.20
1090	A532	1 l maroon	.50	.20
1090A	A533	1.25 l dull bl ('61)	1.75	.30
1091	A532	2 l dp car ('60)	1.10	.25
		Nos. 1077-1091 (17)	6.80	3.55

Early completion of the 5-year plan (in 1959).

For surcharges see Nos. 1192-1199, 1202-1203.

L. L. Zamenhof
A534

Path of Lunik 3
A535

1959, Dec. 5 **Unwmk.** ***Perf. 11***

1092 A534 1.25 l dk grn & yel grn .75 .40

Lazarus Ludwig Zamenhof (1859-1917), inventor of Esperanto.

1960, Mar. 28 ***Perf. 11***

1093 A535 1.25 l Prus bl & brt yel 3.50 1.90

Flight of Lunik 3 around moon. Value, imperf. $5

Skier
A536

1960, Apr. 15 **Litho.**

1094 A536 2 l ultra, blk & brn .95 .35

8th Winter Olympics, Squaw Valley, CA, Feb. 18-29. Value, imperf. $2 unused, $1 canceled.

Vela Blagoeva — A537

Portraits: 28s, Anna Maimunkova. 45s, Vela Piskova. 60s, Rosa Luxemburg. 80s, Klara Zetkin. 1.25 l, N. K. Krupskaya.

1960, Apr. 27 **Photo.** ***Perf. 11***

1095	A537	16s rose & red brn	.20	.20
1096	A537	28s citron & olive	.20	.20
1097	A537	45s ol grn & sl grn	.20	.20
1098	A537	60s lt bl & Prus bl	.20	.20
1099	A537	80s red org & dp brn	.35	.20
1100	A537	1.25 l dull yel & olive	.60	.20
		Nos. 1095-1100 (6)	1.75	1.20

International Women's Day, Mar. 8, 1960.

Lenin — A538

1960, May 12

1101	A538	16s shown	.50	.20
1102	A538	45s Lenin sitting	1.10	.20

90th anniversary of the birth of Lenin.

A539

A541

1960, June 3 ***Perf. 11***

1103 A539 1.25 l yel & slate grn .85 .35

Seventh European Women's Basketball championships.

1960, June 29 **Litho.**

1105	A541	16s Parachutist	.55	.30
1106	A541	1.25 l Parachutes	1.50	.45

5th International Parachute Championships.

Yellow Gentian — A542

Flowers: 5s, Tulips. 25s, Turk's-cap lily. 45s, Rhododendron. 60s, Lady's-slipper. 80s, Violets.

1960, July 27 **Photo.** ***Perf. 11***

1107	A542	2s beige, grn & yel	.20	.20
1108	A542	5s yel grn, grn & car rose	.20	.20
1109	A542	25s pink, grn & org	.20	.20
1110	A542	45s pale lil, grn & rose lil	.35	.20
1111	A542	60s yel, grn & org	.75	.20
1112	A542	80s gray, grn & vio bl	.90	.25
		Nos. 1107-1112 (6)	2.60	1.25

Soccer
A543

Sports: 12s, Wrestling. 16s, Weight lifting. 45s, Woman gymnast. 80s, Canoeing. 2 l, Runner.

1960, Aug. 29 **Unwmk.** ***Perf. 11***

Athletes' Figures in Pink

1113	A543	8s brown	.25	.20
1114	A543	12s violet	.25	.20
1115	A543	16s Prus blue	.25	.20
1116	A543	45s deep plum	.25	.20
1117	A543	80s blue	.50	.20
1118	A543	2 l deep green	1.75	.35
		Nos. 1113-1118 (6)	3.25	1.35

17th Olympic Games, Rome, Aug. 25-Sept. 11.

Value, set imperf. in changed colors, $3.50.

Globes
A544

Unwmk.

1960, Oct. 12 **Photo.** ***Perf. 11***

1125 A544 1.25 l blue & ultra .50 .20

15th anniversary of the World Federation of Trade Unions.

Alexander Popov — A545

1960, Oct. 12
1126 A545 90s blue & blk .75 .20

Centenary of the birth of Alexander Popov, radio pioneer.

Bicyclists A546

1960, Sept. 22
1127 A546 1 l yel, red org & blk .90 .45

The 10th Tour of Bulgaria Bicycle Race.

Jaroslav Vésin — A547

1960, Nov. 22 Unwmk. *Perf. 11*
1128 A547 1 l brt citron & ol grn 2.75 .65

Birth centenary of Jaroslav Vesin, painter.

UN Headquarters A548

Costume of Kyustendil A549

1961, Jan. 14 Photo. *Perf. 11*
1129 A548 1 l brown & yel 1.00 .45
a. Souvenir sheet 4.00 2.75

15th anniv. of the UN. #1129 sold for 2 l.
Value, imperf. $3.50.
No. 1129a sold for 2.50 l and contains one copy of No. 1129, imperf, in dark olive and pink.

1961, Jan. 28

Designs (Regional Costumes): 16s, Pleven. 28s, Sliven. 45s, Sofia. 60s, Rhodope. 80s, Karnobat.

1130 A549 12s salmon, sl grn & yel .20 .20
1131 A549 16s pale lil, brn vio & buff .20 .20
1132 A549 28s pale grn, sl grn & rose .20 .20
1133 A549 45s blue & red .30 .20
1134 A549 60s grnsh bl, Prus bl & yel .50 .20
1135 A549 80s yel, sl grn & pink .60 .25
Nos. 1130-1135 (6) 2.00 1.25

Theodor Tiro (Fresco) A550

Designs: 60s, Boyana Church. 1.25 l, Duchess of Dessislava (fresco).

1961, Jan. 28 Photo.
1136 A550 60s yel grn, blk & grn .50 .20
1137 A550 80s yel, sl grn & org .50 .20
1138 A550 1.25 l yel grn, hn brn & buff 1.00 .25
Nos. 1136-1138 (3) 2.00 .65

700th anniv. of murals in Boyana Church.

Clock Tower, Vratsa — A551

Wooden Jug — A552

Designs: 12s, Clock tower, Bansko. 20s, Anguchev House, Mogilitsa. 28s, Oslekov House, Koprivspitsa, horiz. 40s, Pasha's house. Melnik, horiz. 45s, Lion sculpture. 60s, Man on horseback, Madara. 80s, Fresco, Bratchkovo monastery. 1 l, Tsar Assen coin.

1961, Feb. 25 Unwmk. *Perf. 11*
Denomination and Stars in Vermilion
1139 A551 8s olive grn .20 .20
1140 A551 12s lt violet .20 .20
1141 A552 16s dk red brn .20 .20
1142 A551 20s brt blue .20 .20
1143 A551 28s grnsh blue .20 .20
1144 A551 40s red brown .20 .20
1145 A552 45s olive gray .20 .20
1146 A552 60s slate .30 .20
1147 A552 80s dk olive gray .55 .20
1148 A552 1 l green .70 .20
Nos. 1139-1148 (10) 2.95 2.00

Capercaillie A553

Birds: 4s, Dalmatian pelican. 16s, Ring-necked pheasant. 80s, Great bustard. 1 l, Lammergeier. 2 l, Hazel hen.

1961, Mar. 31
1149 A553 2s blk, sal & Prus grn .20 .20
1150 A553 4s blk, yel grn & org .20 .20
1151 A553 16s brn, lt grn & org .20 .20
1152 A553 80s brn, bluish grn & yel .35 .20
1153 A553 1 l blk, lt bl & yel .65 .20
1154 A553 2 l brn, bl & yel 1.60 .55
Nos. 1149-1153 (5) 1.60 1.00

Radio Tower and Winged Anchor A554

1961, Apr. 1 Unwmk. *Perf. 11*
1155 A554 80s brt green & blk .45 .20

50th anniv. of the Transport Workers' Union.

T. G. Shevchenko A555

Water Polo A556

1961, Apr. 27
1156 A555 1 l olive & blk 2.50 .65

Centenary of the death of Taras G. Shevchenko, Ukrainian poet.

1961, May 15

Designs: 5s, Tennis. 16s, Fencing. 45s, Throwing the discus. 1.25 l, Sports Palace. 2 l, Basketball. 5 l, Sports Palace, different view. 5s, 16s, 45s and 1.25 l, are horizontal.

Black Inscriptions
1157 A556 4s lt ultra .20 .20
1158 A556 5s orange ver .20 .20
1159 A556 16s olive grn .20 .20
1160 A556 45s dull blue .20 .20
1161 A556 1.25 l yellow brn .60 .20
1162 A556 2 l lilac .85 .40
Nos. 1157-1162 (6) 2.25 1.40

Souvenir Sheet
Imperf
1163 A556 5 l yel grn, dl bl & yel 7.50 6.50

1961 World University Games, Sofia, Aug. 26-Sept. 3.
Value, Nos. 1157-1162 in changed colors, imperf. $4.50.

Monk Seal A557

Black Sea Fauna: 12s, Jellyfish. 16s, Dolphin. 45s, Black Sea sea horse, vert. 1 l, Starred sturgeon. 1.25 l, Thornback ray.

1961, June 19 *Perf. 11*
1164 A557 2s green & blk .20 .20
1165 A557 12s Prus grn & pink .20 .20
1166 A557 16s ultra & vio bl .20 .20
1167 A557 45s lt blue & brn .30 .20
1168 A557 1 l yel grn & Prus grn .65 .20
1169 A557 1.25 l lt vio bl & red brn 1.10 .35
Nos. 1164-1169 (6) 2.65 1.35

Hikers — A558

Designs: 4s, "Sredetz" hostel, horiz. 16s, Tents. 1.25 l, Mountain climber.

1961, Aug. 25 Litho. *Perf. 11*
1170 A558 4s yel grn, yel & blk .20 .20
1171 A558 12s lt bl, cr & blk .20 .20
1172 A558 16s green, cr & blk .20 .20
1173 A558 1.25 l bister, cr & blk .45 .20
Nos. 1170-1173 (4) 1.05 .80

"Know Your Country" campaign.

Demeter Blagoev Addressing 1891 Congress at Busludja — A559

1961, Aug. 5 Photo.
1174 A559 45s dk red & buff .20 .20
1175 A559 80s blue & pink .30 .20
1176 A559 2 l dk brn & pale citron .75 .25
Nos. 1174-1176 (3) 1.25 .65

70th anniversary of the first Congress of the Bulgarian Social-Democratic Party.

The Golden Girl — A560

Fairy Tales: 8s, The Living Water. 12s, The Golden Apple. 16s, Krali-Marko, hero. 45s, Samovila-Vila, Witch. 80s, Tom Thumb.

1961, Oct. 10 Unwmk. *Perf. 11*
1177 A560 2s blue, blk & org .20 .20
1178 A560 8s rose lil, blk & gray .25 .20
1179 A560 12s bl grn, blk & pink .25 .20
1180 A560 16s red, blk, bl & gray .40 .20
1181 A560 45s ol grn, blk & pink .75 .25
1182 A560 80s ocher, blk & dk car 1.10 .30
Nos. 1177-1182 (6) 2.95 1.35

Caesar's Mushroom A561

Miladinov Brothers and Title Page A562

Designs: Various mushrooms.

1961, Dec. 20 Photo. *Perf. 11*
Denominations in Black
1183 A561 2s lemon & red .20 .20
1184 A561 4s ol grn & red brn .20 .20
1185 A561 12s bister & red brn .20 .20
1186 A561 16s lilac & red brn .20 .20
1187 A561 45s car rose & yel .20 .20
1188 A561 80s brn org & sepia .20 .20
1189 A561 1.25 l vio & dk brn .40 .20
1190 A561 2 l org brn & brn .70 .40
Nos. 1183-1190 (8) 2.30 1.80

Value, denomination in dark grn, imperf. set $5 unused, $1.75 canceled.

1961, Dec. 21 Unwmk. *Perf. 10½*
1191 A562 1.25 l olive & blk .60 .20

Publication of "Collected Folksongs" by the Brothers Miladinov, Dimitri and Konstantin, cent.

Nos. 1079-1085, 1087, 992, 1023, 1090-1091 and 806 Surcharged with New Value in Black, Red or Violet

1962, Jan. 1
1192 A533 1s on 10s red brown .20 .20
1193 A532 1s on 12s red brown .20 .20
1194 A532 2s on 15s red lilac .20 .20
1195 A533 2s on 16s dp vio (R) .20 .20
1196 A533 2s on 20s orange .20 .20
a. "2 CT." on 2 lines .20 .20
1197 A532 3s on 25s brt bl (R) .20 .20
a. Black surcharge 6.00 4.00
1198 A532 3s on 28s brt grn (R) .20 .20
1199 A532 5s on 45s chocolate .20 .20
1200 A499 5s on 44s dk bl grn (R) .20 .20
1201 A509 5s on 44s dp car (V) .20 .20
1202 A532 10s on 1 l maroon .25 .20
1203 A532 20s on 2 l dp car .70 .25
1204 A430 40s on 4 l rose lake (V) 1.50 .50
Nos. 1192-1204 (13) 4.45 2.95

Freighter "Varna" A563

Designs: 5s, Tanker "Komsomoletz." 20s, Liner "G. Dimitrov."

1962, Mar. 1 Photo. *Perf. 10½*
1205 A563 1s lt grn & brt bl .20 .20
1206 A563 5s lt blue & grn .20 .20
1207 A563 20s gray bl & grnsh bl .70 .20
Nos. 1205-1207 (3) 1.10 .60

Dimitrov Working as Printer — A564

Roses — A565

13s, Griffin, emblem of state printing works.

1962, Mar. 19 **Unwmk.**
1208 A564 2s ver, blk & yel .20 .20
1209 A564 13s red org, blk & yel .40 .20

80th anniversary (in 1961) of the George Dimitrov state printing works.

1962, Mar. 28
Various Roses in Natural Colors
1210 A565 1s deep violet .20 .20
1211 A565 2s salmon & dk car .20 .20
1212 A565 3s gray & car .20 .20
1213 A565 4s dark green .20 .20
1214 A565 5s ultra .25 .20
1215 A565 6s bluish grn & dk car .50 .20
1216 A565 8s citron & car 1.10 .20
1217 A565 13s blue 2.25 .60
Nos. 1210-1217 (8) 4.90 2.00

For overprint and surcharges see Nos. 1281-1283.

Malaria Eradication Emblem and Mosquito A566

Design: 20s, Malaria eradication emblem.

1962, Apr. 19
1218 A566 5s org brn, yel & blk .40 .20
1219 A566 20s emerald, yel & blk .85 .35

WHO drive to eradicate malaria.

Value, imperf. $2.50 unused, $1.50 canceled.

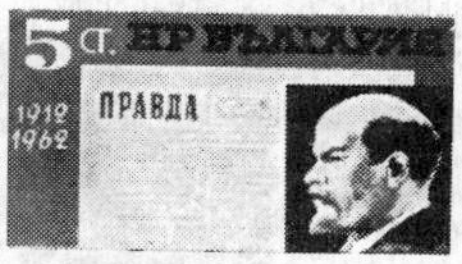

Lenin and First Issue of Pravda A567

1962, May 4 **Unwmk.** ***Perf. 10***
1220 A567 5s deep rose & slate .50 .20

50th anniversary of Pravda, Russian newspaper founded by Lenin.

Blackboard and Book — A568

1962, May 21 **Photo.**
1221 A568 5s Prus bl, blk & yel .25 .20

The 1962 Teachers' Congress.

Soccer Player and Globe A569

1962, May 26 ***Perf. 10½***
1222 A569 13s brt grn, blk & lt brn .65 .25

World Soccer Championship, Chile, May 30-June 17. Value, imperf. in changed colors, $2.50 unused, $1.65 canceled.

George Dimitrov A570

1962, June 18 **Photo.**
1223 A570 2s dark green .20 .20
1224 A570 5s turq blue .40 .20

80th anniv. of the birth of George Dimitrov (1882-1949), communist leader and premier of the Bulgarian Peoples' Republic.

Bishop — A571

1962, July 7 **Unwmk.** ***Perf. 10½***
1225 A571 1s shown .20 .20
1226 A571 2s Rook .20 .20
1227 A571 3s Queen .20 .20
1228 A571 13s Knight .65 .25
1229 A571 20s Pawn 1.10 .40
Nos. 1225-1229 (5) 2.35 1.25

15th Chess Olympics, Varna. Nos. 1225-1229 were also issued imperf. in changed colors.

An imperf. souvenir sheet contains one 20s horizontal stamp showing five chessmen. Size: 75x66mm.

Rila Mountain A572

Designs: 2s, Pirin mountain. 6s, Nesebr, Black Sea. 8s, Danube. 13s, Vidin Castle. 1 l, Rhodope mountain.

1962-63 ***Perf. 13***
1230 A572 1s dk blue grn .20 .20
1231 A572 2s blue .20 .20
1232 A572 6s grnsh blue .20 .20
1233 A572 8c lilac .20 .20
1234 A572 13s yellow grn .40 .20
1234A A572 1 l dp green ('63) 3.25 .30
Nos. 1230-1234A (6) 4.45 1.30

No. 974 Surcharged in Red

XXXV КОНГРЕС
1962

13 =

1962, July 14 ***Perf. 13***
1235 A493 13s on 44s slate grn 2.25 .80

25th Bulgarian Esperanto Congress, Burgas, July 14-16.

Girl and Festival Emblem A573

Design: 5s, Festival emblem.

1962, Aug. 18 **Photo.** ***Perf. 10½***
1236 A573 5s green, lt bl & pink .20 .20
1237 A573 13s lilac, lt bl & gray .35 .20

8th Youth Festival for Peace and Friendship, Helsinki, July 28-Aug. 6, 1962.

Parnassius Apollo — A574

1962, Sept. 13
Various Butterflies in Natural Colors
1238 A574 1s pale cit & dk grn .20 .20
1239 A574 2s rose & brown .20 .20
1240 A574 3s buff & red brn .20 .20
1241 A574 4s gray & brown .20 .20
1242 A574 5s lt gray & brn .20 .20
1243 A574 6s gray & black .20 .20
1244 A574 10s pale grn & blk 1.25 .25
1245 A574 13s buff & red brn 1.90 .40
Nos. 1238-1245 (8) 4.35 1.85

Planting Machine A575

2s, Electric locomotive. 3s, Blast furnace. 13s, Blagoev and Dimitrov and Communist flag.

1962, Nov. 1 ***Perf. 11½***
1246 A575 1s bl grn & dk ol grn .20 .20
1247 A575 2s bl & Prus bl .20 .20
1248 A575 3s carmine & brn .20 .20
1249 A575 13s plum, red & blk .55 .20
Nos. 1246-1249 (4) 1.15 .80

Bulgarian Communist Party, 8th Congress.

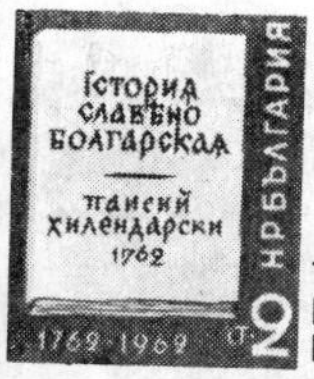

Title Page of "Slav-Bulgarian History" — A576

Paisii Hilendarski Writing History — A577

1962, Dec. 8 **Unwmk.** ***Perf. 10½***
1250 A576 2s olive grn & blk .20 .20
1251 A577 5s brown org & blk .20 .20

200th anniv. of "Slav-Bulgarian History."

Aleco Konstantinov (1863-1897), Writer — A578

1963, Mar. 5 **Photo.** ***Perf. 11½***
1252 A578 5s red, grn & blk .25 .20

Printed with alternating red brown and black label showing Bai Ganu, hero from Konstantinov's books.

A579

Sofia University — A580

Designs: No. 1255, Levski Stadium, Sofia. No. 1256, Arch, Nissaria. No. 1257, Parachutist.

1963, Feb. 20 **Unwmk.** ***Perf. 10***
1253 A579 1s brown red .20 .20
1254 A580 1s red brown .20 .20
1255 A580 1s blue green .20 .20
1256 A580 1s dark green .20 .20
1257 A580 1s brt blue .20 .20
Nos. 1253-1257 (5) 1.00 1.00

Vassil Levski — A581

Boy, Girl and Dimitrov — A582

1963, Apr. 11 **Photo.**
1258 A581 13s grnsh blue & buff .75 .25

90th anniversary of the death of Vassil Levski, revolutionary leader in the fight for liberation from the Turks.

1963, Apr. 25 **Unwmk.** ***Perf. 11½***

13s, Girl with book & boy with hammer.

1259 A582 2s org, ver, red brn & blk .20 .20
1260 A582 13s bluish grn, brn & blk .40 .20

10th Congress of Dimitrov's Union of the People's Youth.

Red Squirrel A583

Sun Coast Promenade A584

2s, Hedgehog. 3s, European polecat. 5s, Pine marten. 13s, Badger. 20s, Otter. 2s, 3s, 13s, horiz.

1963, Apr. 30
Red Numerals
1261 A583 1s grn & brn, *grnsh* .20 .20
1262 A583 2s grn & blk, *yel* .20 .20
1263 A583 3s grn & brn, *bis* .20 .20
1264 A583 5s vio & red brn, *lil* .20 .20
1265 A583 13s red brn & blk, *pink* .80 .20
1266 A583 20s blk & brn, *blue* 1.25 .20
Nos. 1261-1266 (6) 2.85 1.20

1963, Mar. 12 **Unwmk.** ***Perf. 13***

Black Sea Resorts: 2s, 3s, 13s, Views of Gold Sand. 5s, 20s, Sun Coast.

1267 A584 1s blue .20 .20
1268 A584 2s vermilion .25 .20
1269 A584 2s car rose .40 .20
1270 A584 3s ocher .20 .20
1271 A584 5s lilac .20 .20
1272 A584 13s blue green .50 .20
1273 A584 20s green .95 .20
Nos. 1267-1273 (7) 2.70 1.40

Freestyle Wrestling A585

Design: 20s, Freestyle wrestling, horiz.

1963, May 31 ***Perf. 11½***
1274 A585 5s yel bister & blk .20 .20
1275 A585 20s org brn & blk .80 .20

15th International Freestyle Wrestling Competitions, Sofia.

"Women for Peace" A586

1963, June 24 Unwmk. *Perf. 11½*

1276 A586 20s blue & blk .60 .20

World Congress of Women, Moscow, June 24-29.

Esperanto Emblem and Arms of Sofia — A587

Moon, Earth and Lunik 4 — A588

1963, June 29 Photo.

1277 A587 13s multicolored .60 .20

48th World Esperanto Congress, Sofia, Aug. 3-10.

1963, July 22

2s, Radar equipment. 3s, Satellites and moon.

1278 A588 1s ultra .20 .20
1279 A588 2s red lilac .20 .20
1280 A588 3s greenish blue .20 .20
Nos. 1278-1280 (3) .60 .60

Russia's rocket to the moon, Apr. 2, 1963.

MOSTRA EUROPEISTICA·1963
13
RICCIONE

Nos. 1211-1212 and 1215 Overprinted or Surcharged in Green, Ultramarine or Black

1963, Aug. 31 *Perf. 10½*

1281 A565 2s (G) .25 .20
1282 A565 5s on 3s (U) .40 .20
1283 A565 13s on 6s .70 .25
Nos. 1281-1283 (3) 1.35 .65

Intl. Stamp Fair, Riccione, Aug. 31.

Women's Relay Race A589

Designs: 2s, Hammer thrower. 3s, Women's long jump. 5s, Men's high jump. 13s, Discus thrower.

Perf. 11½

1963, Sept. 13 Photo. Unwmk.

Flags in National Colors

1284 A589 1s slate green .20 .20
1285 A589 2s purple .20 .20
1286 A589 3s Prus blue .20 .20
1287 A589 5s maroon .45 .30
1288 A589 13s chestnut brn 1.60 1.25
Nos. 1284-1288 (5) 2.65 2.15

Balkan Games. A multicolored, 50s, imperf. souvenir sheet shows design of women's relay race. Size: 74x70mm.

"Slav-Bulgarian History" — A590

1963, Sept. 19 *Perf. 10½*

1289 A590 5s salmon pink, slate & yel .20 .20

5th International Slavic Congress.

Revolutionists A591

Christo Smirnenski A592

1963, Sept. 22 *Perf. 11½*

1290 A591 2s brt red & blk .20 .20

40th anniversary of the September Revolution.

1963, Oct. 28 *Perf. 10½*

1291 A592 13s pale lilac & indigo .45 .20

Christo Smirnenski, poet, 65th birth anniv.

Columbine A593

Horses A594

1963, Oct. 9 Photo. *Perf. 11½*

1292 A593 1s shown .20 .20
1293 A593 2s Edelweiss .20 .20
1294 A593 3s Primrose .20 .20
1295 A593 5s Water lily .20 .20
1296 A593 6s Tulips .20 .20
1297 A593 8s Larkspur .30 .20
1298 A593 10s Alpine clematis .70 .20
1299 A593 13s Anemone 1.25 .25
Nos. 1292-1299 (8) 3.25 1.65

1963, Dec. 28 Unwmk. *Perf. 10½*

Designs: 2s, Charioteer and chariot. 3s, Trumpeters. 5s, Woman carrying tray with food. 13s, Man holding bowl. 20s, Woman in armchair. Designs are from a Thracian tomb at Kazanlik.

1300 A594 1s gray, org & dk red .20 .20
1301 A594 2s gray, ocher & pur .20 .20
1302 A594 3s gray, dl yel & sl grn .20 .20
1303 A594 5s pale grn, ocher & brn .20 .20
1304 A594 13s pale grn, bis & blk .40 .20
1305 A594 20s pale grn, org & dk car .75 .30
Nos. 1300-1305 (6) 1.95 1.30

World Map and Emblem A595

Designs: 2s, Blood transfusion. 3s, Nurse bandaging injured wrist. 5s, Red Cross nurse. 13s, Henri Dunant.

1964, Jan. 27 *Perf. 10½*

1306 A595 1s lem, blk & red .20 .20
1307 A595 2s ultra, blk & red .20 .20
1308 A595 3s gray, sl, blk & red .20 .20
1309 A595 5s brt bl, blk & red .20 .20
1310 A595 13s org yel, blk & red .40 .20
Nos. 1306-1310 (5) 1.20 1.00

Centenary of International Red Cross.

Speed Skating A596

Sports: 2s, 50s, Women's figure skating. 3s, Cross-country skiing. 5s, Ski jump. 10s, Ice hockey goalkeeper. 13s, Ice hockey players.

1964, Feb. 21 Unwmk. *Perf. 10½*

1311 A596 1s grnsh bl, ind & ocher .20 .20
1312 A596 2s brt pink, ol grn & dk sl grn .20 .20
1313 A596 3s dl grn, dk grn & brn .20 .20
1314 A596 5s bl, blk & yel brn .20 .20
1315 A596 10s gray, org & blk .40 .20
1316 A596 13s lil, blk & lil rose .70 .30
Nos. 1311-1316 (6) 1.90 1.30

Miniature Sheet

Imperf

1317 A596 50s gray, Prus grn & pink 3.75 3.00

9th Winter Olympic Games, Innsbruck, Jan. 29-Feb. 9, 1964.

Mask of Nobleman, 2nd Century — A597

2s, Thracian horseman. 3s, Ceramic jug. 5s, Clasp & belt. 6s, Copper kettle. 8s, Angel. 10s, Lioness. 13s, Scrub woman, contemporary sculpture.

1964, Mar. 14 Photo. *Perf. 10½*

Gray Frame

1318 A597 1s dp green & red .20 .20
1319 A597 2s ol gray & red .20 .20
1320 A597 3s bister & red .20 .20
1321 A597 5s indigo & red .20 .20
1322 A597 6s org brn & red .25 .20
1323 A597 8s brn red & red .40 .20
1324 A597 10s olive & red .40 .20
1325 A597 13s gray ol & red .65 .25
Nos. 1318-1325 (8) 2.50 1.65

2,500 years of Bulgarian art.

"The Unborn Maid" A598

Fairy Tales: 2s, Grandfather's Glove. 3s, The Big Turnip. 5s, The Wolf and the Seven Kids. 8s, Cunning Peter. 13s, The Wheat Cake.

1964, Apr. 17 Unwmk. *Perf. 10½*

1326 A598 1s bl grn, red & org brn .20 .20
1327 A598 2s ultra, ocher & blk .20 .20
1328 A598 3s cit, red & blk .20 .20
1329 A598 5s dp rose, brn & blk .20 .20
1330 A598 8s yel grn, red & blk .20 .20
1331 A598 13s lt vio bl, grn & blk .70 .20
Nos. 1326-1331 (6) 1.70 1.20

Ascalaphus Otomanus A599

Insects: 2s, Nemoptera coa., vert. 3s, Saga natalia (grasshopper). 5s, Rosalia alpina, vert. 13s, Anisoplia austriaca, vert. 20s, Scolia flavitrons.

1964, May 16 Photo. *Perf. 11½*

1332 A599 1s brn org, yel & blk .20 .20
1333 A599 2s dl bl grn, bis & blk .20 .20
1334 A599 3s gray, grn & blk .20 .20
1335 A599 5s lt ol grn, blk & vio .20 .20
1336 A599 13s vio, bis & blk .55 .20
1337 A599 20s gray bl, yel & blk .85 .30
Nos. 1332-1337 (6) 2.20 1.30

Soccer — A600

Designs: 13s, Women's volleyball. 60s, Map of Europe and European Women's Volleyball Championship Cup (rectangular, size: 60x69mm).

1964, June 8 Unwmk. *Perf. 11½*

1338 A600 2s bl, dk bl, ocher & red .20 .20
1339 A600 13s bl, dk bl, ocher & red .50 .25

Miniature Sheet

Imperf

1340 A600 60s ultra, ocher, red & gray 3.00 2.25

Levski Physical Culture Assoc., 50th anniv.

Peter Beron and Title Page of Primer A601

1964, June 22 *Perf. 11½*

1341 A601 20s red brn & dk brn, *grysh* 1.00 .60

140th anniversary of the publication of the first Bulgarian primer.

Robert Stephenson's "Rocket" Locomotive, 1825 — A602

Designs: 2s, Modern steam locomotive. 3s, Diesel locomotive. 5s, Electric locomotive. 8s, Freight train on bridge. 13s, Diesel locomotive and tunnel.

1964, July 1 Photo. *Perf. 11½*

1342 A602 1s multicolored .20 .20
1343 A602 2s multicolored .20 .20
1344 A602 3s multicolored .20 .20
1345 A602 5s multicolored .20 .20
1346 A602 8s multicolored .30 .20
1347 A602 13s multicolored .80 .20
Nos. 1342-1347 (6) 1.90 1.20

German Shepherd A603

1964, Aug. 22 Photo.

1348 A603 1s shown .20 .20
1349 A603 2s Setter .20 .20
1350 A603 3s Poodle .20 .20
1351 A603 4s Pomeranian .20 .20
1352 A603 5s St. Bernard .20 .20
1353 A603 6s Terrier .25 .20

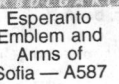

1354 A603 10s Pointer 1.40 .25
1355 A603 13s Dachshund 2.75 .40
Nos. 1348-1355 (8) 5.40 1.85

Partisans — A604

Designs: 2s, People welcoming Soviet army. 3s, Russian aid to Bulgaria. 4s, Blast furnace, Kremikovski. 5s, Combine. 6s, Peace demonstration. 8s, Sentry. 13s, Demeter Blagoev and George Dimitrov.

1964, Sept. 9 Unwmk. *Perf. 11½*
Flag in Red

1356 A604 1s lt & dp ultra .20 .20
1357 A604 2s ol bis & dp ol .20 .20
1358 A604 3s rose lil & mar .20 .20
1359 A604 4s lt vio & vio .20 .20
1360 A604 5s org & red brn .20 .20
1361 A604 6s bl & dp bl .20 .20
1362 A604 8s lt grn & grn .20 .20
1363 A604 13s fawn & red brn .40 .20
Nos. 1356-1363 (8) 1.80 1.60

20th anniv. of People's Government of Bulgaria.

No. 967 Surcharged

М М панаир
ПЛОВДИВ - 1964
ST 20

1964, Sept. 13 *Perf. 13*
1364 A476 20s on 44s org yel 1.00 .35

International Plovdiv Fair.

Gymnast on Parallel Bars A606

Vratcata Mountain Road A607

Sports: 2s, Long jump. 3s, Woman diver. 5s, Soccer. 13s, Women's volleyball. 20s, Wrestling.

1964, Oct. 10 *Perf. 11½*

1366 A606 1s pale grn, grn & red .20 .20
1367 A606 2s pale vio, vio bl & red .20 .20
1368 A606 3s bl grn, brn & red .20 .20
1369 A606 5s pink, pur & red .20 .20
1370 A606 13s bl, Prus grn & red .50 .20
1371 A606 20s yel, grn & red .90 .25
Nos. 1366-1371 (6) 2.20 1.25

18th Olympic Games, Tokyo, Oct. 10-25. See No. B27.

1964, Oct. 26 Photo. *Perf. 12½x13*

Bulgarian Views: 2s, Ritlite mountain road. 3s, Pines, Malovica peak. 4s, Pobitite rocks. 5s, Erkupria. 6s, Rhodope mountain road.

1372 A607 1s dk slate grn .20 .20
1373 A607 2s brown .20 .20
1374 A607 3s grnsh blue .20 .20
1375 A607 4s dk red brn .20 .20
1376 A607 5s deep green .20 .20
1377 A607 6s blue violet .30 .20
Nos. 1372-1377 (6) 1.30 1.20

Mail Coach, Plane and Rocket A608

1964, Oct. 3 Unwmk. *Perf. 11½*
1378 A608 20s greenish blue 1.25 .50

First national stamp exhibition, Sofia, Oct. 3-18. Issued in sheets of 12 stamps and 12 labels (woman's head and inscription, 5x5) arranged around one central label showing stylized bird design.

Students Holding Book — A609

1964, Dec. 30 Photo.
1379 A609 13s lt blue & blk .45 .20

8th Intl. Students' Congress, Sofia.

500-Year-Old Walnut Tree at Golemo Drenovo A610

Designs: Various old trees.

1964, Dec. 28

1380 A610 1s blk, buff & cl brn .20 .20
1381 A610 2s blk, pink & dp cl .20 .20
1382 A610 3s blk, yel & dk brn .20 .20
1383 A610 4s blk, lt bl & Prus bl .20 .20
1384 A610 10s blk, pale grn & grn .25 .20
1385 A610 13s blk, pale bis & dk ol grn .40 .20
Nos. 1380-1385 (6) 1.45 1.20

Soldiers' Monument A611

1965, Jan. 1 Unwmk.
1386 A611 2s red & black .20 .20

Bulgarian-Soviet friendship.

Olympic Medal Inscribed "Olympic Glory" — A612

1965, Jan. 27 Photo. *Perf. 11½*
1387 A612 20s org brn, gold & blk .60 .20

Bulgarian victories in the 1964 Olympic Games.

"Victory Over Fascism" A613

Design: 13s, "Fight for Peace" (dove and globe).

1965, Apr. 16 *Perf. 11½*
1388 A613 5s gray, blk & ol bis .20 .20
1389 A613 13s gray, blk & blue .25 .20

Victory over Fascism, May 9, 1945, 20th anniv.

Vladimir M. Komarov and Section of Globe — A614

Designs: 2s, Konstantin Feoktistov. 5s, Boris B. Yegorov. 13s, Komarov, Feoktistov and Yegorov. 20s, Spaceship Voskhod.

1965, Feb. 15 Photo.

1390 A614 1s pale lil & dk bl .20 .20
1391 A614 2s lt bl, ind & dl vio .20 .20
1392 A614 5s pale grn, grn & ol grn .20 .20
1393 A614 13s pale pink, dp rose & mar .40 .20
1394 A614 20s lt bl, vio bl, grnsh bl & yel .75 20
Nos. 1390-1394 (5) 1.77 1.00

Russian 3-man space flight, Oct. 12-13, 1964.

Imperfs. in changed colors. Four low values se-tenant. Value, set $2 unused, $1 canceled.

Bullfinch — A615

Birds: 2s, European golden oriole. 3s, Common rock thrush. 5s, Barn swallow. 8s, European roller. 10s, European goldfinch. 13s, Rosy pastor starling. 20s, Nightingale.

1965, Apr. 20 Unwmk. *Perf. 11½*
Birds in Natural Colors

1395 A615 1s blue green .20 .20
1396 A615 2s rose lilac .20 .20
1397 A615 3s rose .20 .20
1398 A615 5s brt blue .20 .20
1399 A615 8s citron .30 .20
1400 A615 10s gray 1.10 .20
1401 A615 13s lt vio blue 1.10 .20
1402 A615 20s emerald 2.25 .35
Nos. 1395-1402 (8) 5.55 1.75

Black Sea Fish — A616

1965, June 10 Photo. *Perf. 11½*
Gray Frames

1403 A616 1s Sting ray .20 .20
1404 A616 2s Belted bonito .20 .20
1405 A616 3s Hogfish .20 .20
1406 A616 5s Gurnard .20 .20
1407 A616 10s Scad .75 .20
1408 A616 13s Turbot 1.10 .25
Nos. 1403-1408 (6) 2.65 1.25

Plane, Bus, Train, Ship and Whale — A617

1965, Apr. 30
1409 A617 13s multicolored .45 .20

4th Intl. Conf. of Transport, Dock and Fishery Workers, Sofia, May 10-14.

ITU Emblem and Communications Symbols — A618

1965, May 17
1410 A618 20s multicolored .65 .30

Centenary of the ITU.

Col. Pavel Belyayev and Lt. Col. Alexei Leonov — A619

Design: 20s, Leonov floating in space.

1965, May 20 Unwmk.
1411 A619 2s gray, dull bl & dk brn .20 .20
1412 A619 20s multicolored 1.00 .45

Space flight of Voskhod 2 and the first man floating in space, Lt. Col. Alexei Leonov.

ICY Emblem — A620

1965, May 15 Photo.
1413 A620 20s orange, olive & blk .65 .20

International Cooperation Year, 1965.

Corn A621

Marx and Lenin A622

1965, Apr. 1 *Perf. 12½x13*

1414 A621 1s shown .20 .20
1415 A621 2s Wheat .20 .20
1416 A621 3s Sunflowers .20 .20
1417 A621 4s Sugar beet .20 .20
1418 A621 5s Clover .20 .20
1419 A621 10s Cotton .40 .20
1420 A621 13s Tobacco .60 .20
Nos. 1414-1420 (7) 2.00 1.40

1965, June *Perf. 10½*
1421 A622 13s red & dk brn .65 .20

6th Conference of Postal Ministers of Communist Countries, Peking, June 21-July 15.

Film and UNESCO Emblem
A623

1965, June 30

1422	A623	13s dp bl, blk & lt gray	.50	.20

Balkan Film Festival, Varna.

Ballerina — A624

1965, July 10 **Photo.**

1423	A624	5s dp lil rose & blk	.60	.25

2nd Intl. Ballet Competition, Varna.

Map of Balkan Peninsula and Dove with Letter — A625

Col. Pavel Belyayev and Lt. Col. Alexei Leonov — A626

2s, Sailboat and modern buildings. 3s, Fish and plants. 13s, Symbolic sun and rocket. 40s, Map of Balkan Peninsula and dove with letter (like 1s).

1965 ***Perf. 10½***

1424	A625	1s sil, dp ultra & yel	.20	.20
1425	A625	2s sil, pur & yel	.20	.20
1426	A625	3s gold, grn & yel	.20	.20
1427	A625	13s gold, hn brn & yel	.55	.50
1428	A626	20s sil, bl & brn	.70	.55
		Nos. 1424-1428 (5)	1.85	1.65

Miniature Sheet

Imperf

1429	A625	40s gold & brt bl	1.75	1.00

Balkanphila 1965 Philatelic Exhibition, Varna, Aug. 7-15, and visit of Russian astronauts Belyayev and Leonov.

Value, No. 1428 imperf. in changed colors, 90 cents.

Issued: 20s, 40s, 8/7; others, 7/23.

Woman Gymnast — A627

Designs: 2s, Woman gymnast on parallel bars. 3s, Weight lifter. 5s, Automobile and chart. 10s, Women basketball players. 13s, Automobile and map of rally.

1965, Aug. 14 ***Perf. 10½***

1430	A627	1s crim, brn & blk	.20	.20
1431	A627	2s rose vio, dp cl & blk	.20	.20
1432	A627	3s dp car, brn & blk	.20	.20
1433	A627	5s fawn, red brn & blk	.25	.20
1434	A627	10s dp lil rose, dp cl & blk	.50	.20
1435	A627	13s lilac, claret & blk	.65	.20
		Nos. 1430-1435 (6)	2.00	1.20

Sports events in Bulgaria during May-June, 1965.

No. 989 Surcharged

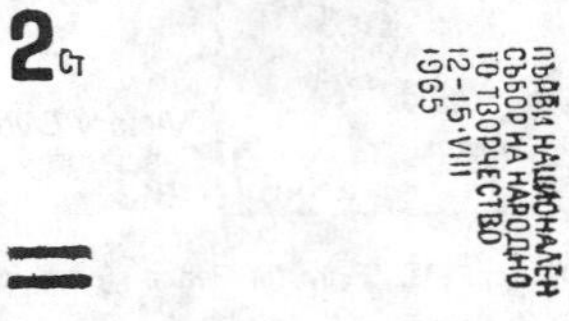

1965, Aug. 12 ***Perf. 13***

1436	A499	2s on 8s orange brn	.75	.25

1st Natl. Folklore Competition, Aug. 12-15.

Escaping Prisoners
A628

Fruit
A629

1965, July 23 ***Perf. 10½***

1437	A628	2s slate	.20	.20

40th anniversary of the escape of political prisoners from Bolshevik Island.

1965, July 1 ***Perf. 13***

1438	A629	1s Apples	.20	.20
1439	A629	2s Grapes	.20	.20
1440	A629	3s Pears	.20	.20
1441	A629	4s Peaches	.20	.20
1442	A629	5s Strawberries	.20	.20
1443	A629	6s Walnuts	.30	.20
		Nos. 1438-1443 (6)	1.30	1.20

Horsemanship — A630

1965, Sept. 30 **Unwmk.** ***Perf. 10½***

1444	A630	1s Dressage	.20	.20
1445	A630	2s Three-day test	.20	.20
1446	A630	3s Jumping	.20	.20
1447	A630	5s Race	.20	.20
1448	A630	10s Steeplechase	.75	.20
1449	A630	13s Hurdle race	1.40	.30
		Nos. 1444-1449 (6)	2.95	1.30

See No. B28.

Smiling Children — A631

Designs: 2s, Two girl Pioneers. 3s, Bugler. 5s, Pioneer with model plane. 8s, Two singing girls in national costume. 13s, Running boy.

1965, Oct. 24 **Photo.**

1450	A631	1s dk bl grn & yel grn	.20	.20
1451	A631	2s vio & deep rose	.20	.20
1452	A631	3s olive & lemon	.20	.20
1453	A631	5s dp blue & bister	.20	.20
1454	A631	8s olive bister & org	.30	.20
1455	A631	13s rose car & vio	.65	.25
		Nos. 1450-1455 (6)	1.75	1.25

Dimitrov Pioneer Organization.

U-52 Plane over Trnovo
A632

Designs: 2c, 1L-14 over Plovdiv. 3s, Mi-4 Helicopter over Dimitrovgrad. 5s, Tu-104 over Ruse. 13s, IL-18 over Varna. 20s, Tu-114 over Sofia.

1965, Nov. 25 ***Perf. 10½***

1456	A632	1s gray, blue & red	.20	.20
1457	A632	2s gray, lilac & red	.20	.20
1458	A632	3s gray, grnsh bl & red	.20	.20
1459	A632	5s gray, orange & red	.20	.20
1460	A632	13s gray, bister & red	.70	.20
1461	A632	20s gray, lt grn & red	1.00	.30
		Nos. 1456-1461 (6)	2.50	1.30

Development of Bulgarian Civil Air Transport.

IQSY Emblem, and Earth Radiation Zones
A633

Designs (IQSY Emblem and): 2s, Sun with corona. 13s, Solar eclipse.

1965, Dec. 15 **Photo.** ***Perf. 10½***

1462	A633	1s grn, yel & ultra	.20	.20
1463	A633	2s yel, red lil & red	.20	.20
1464	A633	13s bl, yel & blk	.30	.20
		Nos. 1462-1464 (3)	.70	.60

International Quiet Sun Year, 1964-65.

"North and South Bulgaria"
A634

"Martenitsa" Emblem
A635

1965, Dec. 6

1465	A634	13s brt yel grn & blk	.50	.25

Union of North and South Bulgaria, cent.

1966, Jan. 10 **Photo.** ***Perf. 10½***

"Spring" in Folklore: 2s, Drummer. 3s, Bird ornaments. 5s, Dancer "Lazarka." 8s, Vase with flowers. 13s, Bagpiper.

1466	A635	1s rose lil, vio bl & gray	.20	.20
1467	A635	2s gray, blk & crim	.20	.20
1468	A635	3s red, vio & gray	.20	.20
1469	A635	5s lil, blk & crimson	.20	.20
1470	A635	8s rose lil, brn & pur	.25	.20
1471	A635	13s bl, blk & rose lilac	.50	.20
		Nos. 1466-1471 (6)	1.55	1.20

Church of St. John the Baptist, Nessebr
A636

Designs: 1s, Christ, fresco from Bojana Church. 2s, Ikon "Destruction of Idols," horiz. 3s, Bratchkovo Monastery. 4s, Zemen Monastery, horiz. 13s, Nativity, ikon from Arbanassi. 20s, Ikon "Virgin and Child," 1342.

1966, Feb. 25 **Litho.** ***Perf. 11½***

1472	A636	1s gray & multi	*3.50*	*1.25*
1473	A636	2s gray & multi	.25	.20
1474	A636	3s multicolored	.25	.20
1475	A636	4s multicolored	.25	.20
1476	A636	5s multicolored	.25	.20
1477	A636	13s gray & multi	.50	.20
1478	A636	20s multicolored	.95	.35
		Nos. 1472-1478 (7)	*5.95*	*2.60*

2,500 years of art in Bulgaria.

Georgi Benkovski and T. Kableshkov — A637

1s, Proclamation of April Uprising, Koprivstitsa. 3s, Dedication of flag, Panaguriste. 5s, V. Petleshkov, Z. Dyustabanov. 10s, Botev landing at Kozlodui. 13s, P. Volov, Ilarion Dragostinov.

1966, Mar. 3 **Photo.** ***Perf. 10½***

Center in Black

1479	A637	1s red brn & gold	.20	.20
1480	A637	2s brt red & gold	.20	.20
1481	A637	3s ol grn & gold	.20	.20
1482	A637	5s steel bl & gold	.20	.20
1483	A637	10s brt rose lil & gold	.20	.20
1484	A637	13s lt vio & gold	.50	.20
		Nos. 1479-1484 (6)	1.50	1.20

April Uprising against the Turks, 90th anniv.

Sofia Zoo Animals
A638

1966, May 23 **Litho.**

1485	A638	1s Elephant	.20	.20
1486	A638	2s Tiger	.20	.20
1487	A638	3s Chimpanzee	.20	.20
1488	A638	4s Siberian ibex	.20	.20
1489	A638	5s Polar bear	.25	.20
1490	A638	8s Lion	.25	.20
1491	A638	13s Bison	.80	.20
1492	A638	20s Kangaroo	1.50	.30
		Nos. 1485-1492 (8)	3.60	1.70

WHO Headquarters, Geneva — A639

1966, May 3 **Photo.**

1493	A639	13s deep blue & silver	.60	.25

Inauguration of the WHO Headquarters, Geneva.

Worker
A640

1966, May 9 **Photo.** ***Perf. 10½***

1494	A640	20s gray & rose	.65	.20

Sixth Trade Union Congress.

Yantra River Bridge, Biela — A641

#1496, Maritsa River Bridge, Svilengrad. #1497, Fountain, Samokov. #1498, Ruins of Fort, Kaskovo. 8s, Old Fort, Ruse. 13s, House, Gabrovo.

1966, Feb. 10 **Photo.** ***Perf. 13***

1495	A641	1s Prus blue	.20	.20
1496	A641	1s brt green	.20	.20
1497	A641	2s olive green	.20	.20
1498	A641	2s dk red brown	.20	.20
1499	A641	8s red brown	.25	.20
1500	A641	13s dark blue	.40	.20
		Nos. 1495-1500 (6)	1.45	1.20

Souvenir Sheet

Moon Allegory — A642

1966, Apr. 29 ***Imperf.***

1501 A642 60s blk, plum & sil 2.50 1.25

1st Russian soft landing on the moon by Luna 9, Feb. 3, 1966.

Steamer Radetzky and Bugler A643

1966, May 28 ***Perf. 10½***

1502 A643 2s multicolored .20 .20

90th anniv. of the participation of the Danube steamer Radetzky in the uprising against the Turks.

Standard Bearer Nicola Simov-Kuruto A644

1966, May 30

1503 A644 5s bister, green & olive .25 .20

Hero of the Turkish War.

UNESCO Emblem — A645

1966, June 8

1504 A645 20s gold, blk & ver .60 .20

20th anniv. of UNESCO.

Youth Federation Badge — A646

1966, June 6 **Photo.** ***Perf. 10½***

1505 A646 13s silver, bl & blk .40 .20

7th Assembly of the Intl. Youth Federation.

Soccer — A647

Various soccer scenes. 50s, Jules Rimet Cup.

1966, June 27

1506 A647 1s gray, yel brn & blk .20 .20
1507 A647 2s gray, crim & blk .20 .20
1508 A647 5s gray, ol bis & blk .20 .20
1509 A647 13s gray, ultra & blk .35 .20
1510 A647 20s gray, Prus bl & blk .60 .20
Nos. 1506-1510 (5) 1.55 1.00

Miniature Sheet

Imperf

1511 A647 50s gray, dp lil rose & gold 2.25 1.50

World Soccer Cup Championship, Wembley, England, July 11-30. Size of No. 1511: 60x64mm.

Woman Javelin Thrower — A648

Designs: No. 1513, Runner. No. 1514, Young man and woman carrying banners, vert.

1966 **Photo.** ***Perf. 10½***

1512 A648 2s grn, yel & ver .20 .20
1513 A648 13s dp grn, yel & sal pink .40 .20
1514 A648 13s bl, lt bl & salmon .40 .20
Nos. 1512-1514 (3) 1.00 .60

Nos. 1512-1513: 3rd Spartacist Games; issued Aug. 10. No. 1514: 3rd congress of the Bulgarian Youth Federation; issued May 25.

Wrestlers Nicolas Petrov and Dan Kolov — A649

1966, July 29

1515 A649 13s bis brn, dk brn & lt ol grn .40 .20

3rd International Wrestling Championships.

Map of Balkan Countries, Globe and UNESCO Emblem — A650

1966, Aug. 26 ***Perf. 10½x11½***

1516 A650 13s ultra, lt grn & pink .40 .20

First Congress of Balkanologists.

Children with Building Blocks A651

2s, Bunny & teddy bear with book. 3s, Children as astronauts. 13s, Children with pails & shovel.

1966, Sept. 1 ***Perf. 10½***

1517 A651 1s dk car, org & blk .20 .20
1518 A651 2s emerald, blk & red brn .20 .20
1519 A651 3s ultra, org & blk .20 .20
1520 A651 13s blue, rose & blk .60 .20
Nos. 1517-1520 (4) 1.20 .80

Children's Day.

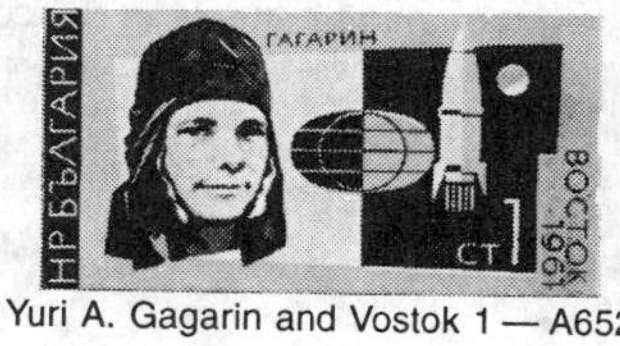

Yuri A. Gagarin and Vostok 1 — A652

Designs: 2s, Gherman S. Titov, Vostok 2. 3s, Andrian G. Nikolayev, Pavel R. Popovich, Vostoks 3 & 4. 5s, Valentina Tereshkova, Valeri Bykovski, Vostoks 5 & 6. 8s, Vladimir M. Komarov, Boris B. Yegorov, Konstantin Feoktistov, Voskhod 1. 13s, Pavel Belyayev, Alexei Leonov, Voskhod 2.

Perf. 11½x11

1966, Sept. 29 **Photo.**

1521 A652 1s slate & gray .20 .20
1522 A652 2s plum & gray .20 .20
1523 A652 3s yel brn & gray .20 .20
1524 A652 5s brn red & gray .20 .20
1525 A652 8s ultra & gray .20 .20
1526 A652 13s Prus bl & gray .50 .20
Nos. 1521-1526,B29 (7) 2.50 1.55

Russian space explorations.

St. Clement, 14th Century Wood Sculpture — A653

1966, Oct. 27 **Photo.** ***Perf. 11½x11***

1527 A653 5s red, buff & brown .20 .20

1050th anniversary of the birth of St. Clement of Ochrida.

Metodi Shatorov A654

Portraits: 3s, Vladimir Trichkov. 5s, Valcho Ivanov. 10s, Raiko Daskalov. 13s, General Vladimir Zaimov.

1966, Nov. 8 ***Perf. 11x11½***

Gold Frame, Black Denomination

1528 A654 2s crimson & bl vio .20 .20
1529 A654 3s magenta & blk .20 .20
1530 A654 5s car rose & dk bl .20 .20
1531 A654 10s orange & olive .30 .20
1532 A654 13s red & brown .40 .20
Nos. 1529-1532 (4) 1.10 .80

Fighters against fascism.

George Dimitrov — A655

Steel Worker — A656

1966, Nov. 14 **Photo.** ***Perf. 11½x11***

1533 A655 2s magenta & blk .20 .20
1534 A656 20s fawn, gray & blk .70 .20

Bulgarian Communist Party, 9th Congress.

Deer's Head Drinking Cup A667

Gold Treasure: 2s, 6s, 10s, Various Amazon's head jugs. 3s, Ram's head cup. 5s, Circular plate. 8s, Deer's head cup. 13s, Amphora. 20s, Ram drinking horn.

1966, Nov. 28 ***Perf. 12x11½***

Vessels in Gold and Brown; Black Inscriptions

1535 A667 1s gray & violet .20 .20
1536 A667 2s gray & green .20 .20
1537 A667 3s gray & dk bl .20 .20
1538 A667 5s gray & red brn .20 .20
1539 A667 6s gray & Prus bl .20 .20
1540 A667 8s gray & brn ol .85 .20
1541 A667 10s gray & sepia .85 .20
1542 A667 13s gray & dk vio bl .85 .30
1543 A667 20s gray & vio brn .95 .30
Nos. 1535-1543 (9) 4.50 2.00

The gold treasure from the 4th century B.C. was found near Panagyurishte in 1949.

Tourist House, Bansko — A668

Tourist Houses: No. 1545, Belogradchik. No. 1546, Triavna. 20s, Rila.

1966, Nov. 29 **Photo.** ***Perf. 11x11½***

1544 A668 1s dark blue .20 .20
1545 A668 2s dark green .20 .20
1546 A668 2s brown red .20 .20
1547 A668 20s lilac .40 .20
Nos. 1544-1547 (4) 1.00 .80

Decorated Tree — A669

Design: 13s, Jug with bird design.

1966, Dec. 12 ***Perf. 11***

1548 A669 2s grn, pink & gold .20 .20
1549 A669 13s brn lake, rose, emer & gold .40 .20

New Year, 1967.

Pencho Slavikov, Author — A670

Dahlia — A671

Portraits: 2s, Dimcho Debeljanov, author. 3s, P. H. Todorov, author. 5s, Dimitri Dobrovich, painter. 8s, Ivan Markvichka, painter. 13s, Ilya Bezhkov, painter.

1966, Dec. 15 ***Perf. 10½x11***

1550 A670 1s blue, olive & org .20 .20
1551 A670 2s orange, brn & gray .20 .20
1552 A670 3s olive, bl & org .20 .20
1553 A670 5s gray, red brn & org .20 .20
1554 A670 8s lilac, dk gray & bl .30 .20
1555 A670 13s blue, vio & lil .40 .20
Nos. 1550-1555 (6) 1.50 1.20

1966, Dec. 29

Flowers: No. 1557, Clematis. No. 1558, Foxglove. No. 1559, Narcissus. 3s, Snowdrop. 5s, Petunia. 13s, Tiger lily. 20s, Bellflower.

Flowers in Natural Colors

1556 A671 1s gray & lt brn .20 .20
1557 A671 1s gray & dull bl .20 .20
1558 A671 2s gray & dull lil .20 .20
1559 A671 2s gray & brown .20 .20
1560 A671 3s gray & dk grn .20 .20
1561 A671 5s gray & dp ultra .25 .20
1562 A671 13s gray & brown .60 .20
1563 A671 20s gray & ultra .95 .20
Nos. 1556-1563 (8) 2.80 1.60

Ringnecked Pheasant — A672

Game: 2s, Rock partridge. 3s, Gray partridge. 5s, Hare. 8s, Roe deer. 13s, Red deer.

1967, Jan. 28 *Perf. 11x10½*

1564 A672 1s lt ultra, dk brn & ocher .20 .20
1565 A672 2s pale yel grn & dk grn .20 .20
1566 A672 3s lt bl, blk & cr .20 .20
1567 A672 5s lt grn & blk .20 .20
1568 A672 8s pale bl, dk brn & ocher .70 .20
1569 A672 13s bl & dk brn 1.25 .25
Nos. 1564-1569 (6) 2.75 1.25

Bulgaria No. 1, 1879 — A673

Thracian Coin, 6th Century, B.C. — A674

1967, Feb. 4 **Photo.** *Perf. 10½*

1570 A673 10s emerald, blk & yel .75 .25

Bulgarian Philatelic Union, 10th Congress.

1967, Mar. 30 *Perf. 11½x11*

Coins: 2s, Macedonian tetradrachma, 2nd cent. B.C. 3s, Tetradrachma of Odessus, 2nd cent. B.C. 5s, Philip II of Macedonia, 4th cent., B.C. 13s, Thracian King Seuthus VII, 4th cent., B.C., obverse and reverse. 20s, Apollonian coin, 5th cent., B.C., obverse and reverse.

Size: 25x25mm

1571 A674 1s brn, blk & sil .20 .20
1572 A674 2s red lil, blk & sil .20 .20
1573 A674 3s grn, blk & sil .20 .20
1574 A674 5s brn org, blk & sil .20 .20

Size: 37½x25mm

1575 A674 13s brt bl, blk & brnz .70 .25
1576 A674 20s vio, blk & sil 1.25 .45
Nos. 1571-1576 (6) 2.75 1.50

Partisans Listening to Radio — A675

Design: 20s, George Dimitrov addressing crowd and Bulgarian flag.

1967, Apr. 20 *Perf. 11x11½*

1577 A675 1s red, gold, buff & sl grn .20 .20
1578 A675 20s red, gold, dl red, grn & blk .55 .20

25th anniversary of the Union of Patriotic Front Organizations.

Nikolas Kofardjiev A676

Portraits: 2s, Petko Napetov. 5s, Petko D. Petkov. 10s, Emil Markov. 13s, Traitcho Kostov.

1967, Apr. 24 *Perf. 11½x11*

1579 A676 1s brn red, gray & blk .20 .20
1580 A676 2s ol grn, gray & blk .20 .20
1581 A676 5s brn, gray & blk .20 .20
1582 A676 10s dp bl, gray & blk .20 .20
1583 A676 13s mag, gray & blk .40 .20
Nos. 1579-1583 (5) 1.20 1.00

Fighters against fascism.

Symbolic Flower and Flame — A677

1967, May 18 **Photo.** *Perf. 11x11½*

1584 A677 13s gold, yel & lt grn .45 .20

First Cultural Congress, May 18-19.

Gold Sand Beach and ITY Emblem A678

20s, Hotel, Pamporovo. 40s, Nessebr Church.

1967, June 12 **Photo.** *Perf. 11x11½*

1585 A678 13s ultra, yel & blk .30 .20
1586 A678 20s Prus bl, blk & buff .40 .20
1587 A678 40s brt grn, blk & ocher 1.00 .30
Nos. 1585-1587 (3) 1.70 .70

International Tourist Year, 1967.

Angora Cat — A679

Cats: 2s, Siamese, horiz. 3s, Abyssinian. 5s, Black European. 13s, Persian, horiz. 20s, Striped domestic.

Perf. 11½x11, 11x11½

1967, June 19

1588 A679 1s dl vio, dk brn & buff .20 .20
1589 A679 2s ol, sl & brt bl .20 .20
1590 A679 3s dull blue & brn .20 .20
1591 A679 5s grn, blk & yel .20 .20
1592 A679 13s dl red brn, sl & org .90 .20
1593 A679 20s gray grn, brn & buff 1.60 .25
Nos. 1588-1593 (6) 3.30 1.25

Scene from Opera "The Master of Boyana" by K. Iliev — A680

Songbird on Keyboard — A681

1967, June 19

1594 A680 5s gray, vio bl & dp car .40 .20
1595 A681 13s gray, dp car & dk bl 1.10 .20

3rd Intl. Competition for Young Opera Singers.

George Kirkov (1867-1919), Revolutionist — A682

1967, June 24 *Perf. 11x11½*

1596 A682 2s rose red & dk brn .20 .20

Symbolic Tree and Stars — A683

1967, July 28 **Photo.** *Perf. 11½x11*

1597 A683 13s dp bl, car & blk .30 .20

11th Congress of Dimitrov's Union of the People's Youth.

Roses and Distillery A684

Designs: No. 1599, Chick and incubator. No. 1600, Cucumbers and hothouse. No. 1601, Lamb and sheep farm. 3s, Sunflower and oil mill. 4s, Pigs and pig farm. 5s, Hops and hop farm. 6s, Corn and irrigation system. 8s, Grapes and Bolgar tractor. 10s, Apples and cultivated tree. 13s, Bees and honey. 20s, Bee, blossoms and beehives.

1967 *Perf. 11x11½*

1598 A684 1s multicolored .20 .20
1599 A684 1s dk car, yel & blk .20 .20
1600 A684 2s vio, lt grn & blk .20 .20
1601 A684 2s brt grn, gray & blk .20 .20
1602 A684 3s yel grn, yel & blk .20 .20
1603 A684 4s brt pur, yel & blk .20 .20
1604 A684 5s ol bis, yel grn & blk .20 .20
1605 A684 6s ol, brt grn & blk .20 .20
1606 A684 8s grn, bis & blk .20 .20
1607 A684 10s multicolored .25 .20
1608 A684 13s grn, bis brn & blk .40 .20
1609 A684 20s grnsh bl, brt pink & blk .55 .20
Nos. 1598-1609 (12) 3.00 2.40

Issue dates: Nos. 1598-1601, 1607, 1609, July 15; Nos. 1602-1606, 1608, July 24.

Map of Communist Countries, Spasski Tower A685

2s, Lenin speaking to soldiers. 3s, Fighting at Wlodaja, 1918. 5s, Marx, Engels & Lenin. 13s, Oil refinery. 20s, Molniya communication satellite.

1967, Aug. 25 *Perf. 11*

1610 A685 1s multicolored .20 .20
1611 A685 2s magenta & olive .20 .20
1612 A685 3s magenta & dull vio .20 .20
1613 A685 5s magenta & red .20 .20
1614 A685 13s magenta & ultra .25 .20
1615 A685 20s magenta & blue .45 .20
Nos. 1610-1615 (6) 1.50 1.20

50th anniv. of the Russian October Revolution.

Rod, "Fish" and Varna — A686

1967, Aug. 29 **Photo.** *Perf. 11*

1616 A686 10s multicolored .35 .20

7th World Angling Championships, Varna.

Skiers and Winter Olympics' Emblem — A687

Sports and Emblem: 2s, Ski jump. 3s, Biathlon. 5s, Ice hockey. 13s, Figure skating couple.

1967, Sept. 20 **Photo.** *Perf. 11*

1617 A687 1s dk bl grn, red & blk .20 .20
1618 A687 2s ultra, blk & ol .20 .20
1619 A687 3s vio brn, bl & blk .20 .20
1620 A687 5s green, yel & blk .20 .20
1621 A687 13s vio bl, blk & buff .35 .20
Nos. 1617-1621,B31 (6) 2.25 1.30

10th Winter Olympic Games, Grenoble, France, Feb. 6-18, 1968.

Mountain Peaks — A688

1967, Sept. 25 **Engr.** *Perf. 11½*

1622 A688 1s Bogdan .20 .20
1623 A688 2s Czerny .20 .20
1624 A688 3s Ruen, vert. .20 .20
1625 A688 5s Persenk .20 .20
1626 A688 10s Botev .20 .20
1627 A688 13s Rila, vert. .25 .20
1628 A688 20s Vihren .55 .20
Nos. 1622-1628 (7) 1.80 1.40

George Rakovski A689

1967, Oct. 20 **Photo.** *Perf. 11*

1629 A689 13s yellow grn & blk .40 .20

Centenary of the death of George Rakovski, revolutionary against Turkish rule.

Yuri A. Gagarin, Valentina Tereshkova and Alexei Leonov — A690

Designs: 2s, Lt. Col. John H. Glenn, Jr., and Maj. Edward H. White. 5s, Earth and Molniya 1. 10s, Gemini 6 and 7. 13s, Luna 13 moon probe. 20s, Gemini 10 and Agena rocket.

1967, Nov. 25

1630 A690 1s Prus bl, blk & yel .20 .20
1631 A690 2s dl bl, blk & dl yel .20 .20
1632 A690 5s vio bl, grnsh bl & blk .20 .20
1633 A690 10s dk bl, blk & red .35 .20

1634 A690 13s grnsh bl, brt yel & blk .55 .20
1635 A690 20s dl bl, blk & red .75 .20
Nos. 1630-1635 (6) 2.25 1.20

Achievements in space exploration.

Various Views of Trnovo — A691

1967, Dec. 5 Photo. *Perf. 11*

1636 A691 1s multicolored .20 .20
1637 A691 2s multicolored .20 .20
1638 A691 3s multicolored .20 .20
1639 A691 5s multicolored .20 .20
1640 A691 13s multicolored .30 .20
1641 A691 20s multicolored .50 .20
Nos. 1636-1641 (6) 1.60 1.20

Restoration of the ancient capital Veliko Trnovo.

Ratchenitza Folk Dance, by Ivan Markvichka — A692

1967, Dec. 9

1642 A692 20s gold & gray green 1.00 .80

Belgo-Bulgarian Philatelic Exposition, Brussels, Dec. 9-10. Printed in sheets of 8 stamps and 8 labels.

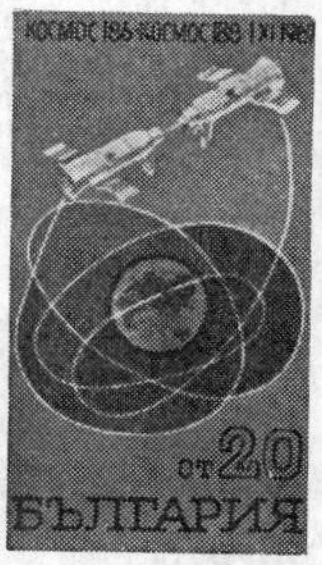

Cosmos 186 and 188 Docking — A693

40s, Venus 4 and orbits around Venus, horiz.

1968, Jan.

1643 A693 20s vio, gray & pink .55 .20
1644 A693 40s multicolored 1.00 .25

Docking maneuvers of the Russian spaceships Cosmos 186 and Cosmos 188, Nov. 1, 1967, and the flight to Venus of Venus 4, June 12-Nov. 18, 1967.

Crossing the Danube, by Orenburgski — A694

Paintings: 2s, Flag of Samara, by J. Veschin, vert. 3s, Battle of Pleven by Orenburgski. 13s, Battle of Orlovo Gnezdo, by N. Popov, vert. 20s, Welcome for Russian Soldiers, by D. Gudienov.

1968, Jan. 25 Photo. *Perf. 11*

1645 A694 1s gold & dk green .20 .20
1646 A694 2s gold & dk blue .20 .20
1647 A694 3s gold & chocolate .20 .20
1648 A694 13s gold & dk vio .30 .20
1649 A694 20s gold & Prus grn .50 .20
Nos. 1645-1649 (5) 1.40 1.00

90th anniv. of the liberation from Turkey.

Shepherds, by Zlatyn Boyadjiev — A695

Paintings: 2s, Wedding dance, by V. Dimitrov, vert. 3s, Partisans' Song, by Ilya Petrov. 5s, Portrait of Anna Penchovich, by Nikolai Pavlovich, vert. 13s, Self-portrait, by Zachary Zograf, vert. 20s, View of Old Plovdiv, by T. Lavrenov. 60s, St. Clement of Ochrida, by A. Mitov.

1967, Dec. Litho. *Perf. 11½*

Size: 45x38mm, 38x45mm

1650 A695 1s gray & multi .20 .20
1651 A695 2s gray & multi .20 .20

Size: 55x35mm

1652 A695 3s gray & multi .25 .20

Size: 38x45mm, 45x38mm

1653 A695 5s gray & multi .40 .20
1654 A695 13s gray & multi .90 .25
1655 A695 20s gray & multi 1.25 .40
Nos. 1650-1655 (6) 3.20 1.45

Miniature Sheet

Size: 65x84mm

Imperf

1656 A695 60s multicolored 3.25 1.90

Marx Statue, Sofia — A696

Maxim Gorky — A697

1968, Feb. 20 Photo. *Perf. 11*

1657 A696 13s black & red .35 .20

150th anniversary of birth of Karl Marx.

1968, Feb. 20

1658 A697 13s ver & grnsh blk .40 .20

Maxim Gorky (1868-1936), Russian writer.

Folk Dancers — A698

Designs: 5s, Runners. 13s, Doves. 20s, Festival poster, (head, flowers and birds). 40s, Globe and Bulgaria No. 1 under magnifying glass.

1968, Mar. 20

1659 A698 2s multicolored .20 .20
1660 A698 5s multicolored .20 .20
1661 A698 13s multicolored .25 .20
1662 A698 20s multicolored .50 .20
1663 A698 40s multicolored 1.10 .40
Nos. 1659-1663 (5) 2.25 1.20

9th Youth Festival for Peace and Friendship, Sofia, July 28-Aug. 6.

Bellflower — A699

1968, Apr. 25 *Perf. 11*

1664 A699 1s shown .20 .20
1665 A699 2s Gentian .20 .20
1666 A699 3s Crocus .20 .20
1667 A699 5s Iris .20 .20
1668 A699 10s Dog-tooth violet .20 .20
1669 A699 13s Sempervivum .70 .20
1670 A699 20s Dictamnus .95 .25
Nos. 1664-1670 (7) 2.65 1.45

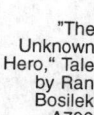

"The Unknown Hero," Tale by Ran Bosilek A700

Design: 20s, The Witch and the Young Man (Hans Christian Andersen fairy tale.)

1968, Apr. 25 Photo. *Perf. 10½*

1671 A700 13s black & multi .35 .20
1672 A700 20s black & multi .50 .20

Bulgarian-Danish Philatelic Exhibition.

Memorial Church, Shipka — A701

Show Jumping — A702

1968, May 3

1673 A701 13s multicolored .60 .20

Bulgarian Stamp Exhibition in Berlin.

1968, June 24 Photo. *Perf. 10½*

Olympic Rings and: 1s, Gymnast on bar. 3s, Fencer. 10s, Boxer. 13s, Woman discus thrower.

1674 A702 1s red & black .20 .20
1675 A702 2s gray, blk & rose brn .20 .20
1676 A702 3s magenta, gray & blk .20 .20
1677 A702 10s grnsh bl, blk & lem .20 .20
1678 A702 13s vio bl, gray & pink .55 .20
Nos. 1674-1678,B33 (6) 2.35 1.30

19th Olympic Games, Mexico City, Oct. 12-27.

Battle of Buzluja A703

Design: 13s, Haji Dimitr and Stefan Karaja.

1968, July 1

1679 A703 2s silver & red brn .20 .20
1680 A703 13s gold & sl grn .30 .20

Centenary of the death of the patriots Haji Dimitr and Stefan Karaja.

Lakes of Smolian A704

Sofia Zoo, Cent. A705

Bulgarian Scenes: 2s, Ropotamo Lake. 3s, Erma-Idreloto mountain pass. 8s, Isker River dam. 10s, Slanchev Breg (sailing ship). 13s, Cape Caliacra. 40s, Old houses, Sozopol. 2 l, Chudnite Skali ("Strange Mountains").

1968 Photo. *Perf. 13*

1681 A704 1s Prus green .20 .20
1682 A704 2s dark green .20 .20
1683 A704 3s dark brown .20 .20
1684 A704 8s olive green .20 .20
1685 A704 10s redsh brown .20 .20
1686 A704 13s dk olive grn .25 .20
1687 A704 40s Prus blue .60 .25
1688 A704 2 l sepia 3.75 .85
Nos. 1681-1688 (8) 5.60 2.30

1968, July 29 *Perf. 10½*

1689 A705 1s Cinereous vulture .20 .20
1690 A705 2s Crowned crane .20 .20
1691 A705 3s Zebra .25 .20
1692 A705 5s Cheetah .40 .20
1693 A705 13s Indian python .70 .20
1694 A705 20s African crocodile 1.25 .30
Nos. 1689-1694 (6) 3.00 1.30

Human Rights Flame — A706

1968, July 8

1695 A706 20s dp blue & gold .60 .20

International Human Rights Year, 1968.

Congress Hall, Varna, and Emblem A707

1968, Sept. 17 Photo. *Perf. 10½*

1696 A707 20s bister, grn & red .50 .20

56th International Dental Congress, Varna.

Flying Swans — A708

Rose A709

Stag Beetle A710

Designs: 2s, Jug. 20s, Five Viking ships.

1968 Photo. *Perf. 10½*

1697 A709 2s green & ocher .75 .50
1698 A708 5s dp blue & gray .75 .50
1699 A709 13s dp plum & lil rose .75 .50
a. Pair, #1698, 1699 + label 1.50 1.00
1700 A708 20s dp vio & gray .75 .50
a. Pair, #1697, 1700 + label 1.50 1.00
Nos. 1697-1700 (4) 3.00 2.00

Cooperation with the Scandinavian countries.

Issued: 5s, 13s, Sept. 12; 2s, 20s, Nov. 22.

Perf. 12½x13, 13x12½

1968, Aug. 26

#1702, Ground beetle (Procer us scabrosus). #1703, Ground beetle (Calosoma sycophania). #1704, Scarab beetle, horiz. #1705, Saturnid moth, horiz.

1701	A710	1s brown olive	.20	.20
1702	A710	1s dark blue	.20	.20
1703	A710	1s dark green	.20	.20
1704	A710	1s orange brown	.20	.20
1705	A710	1s magenta	.20	.20
		Nos. 1701-1705 (5)	1.00	1.00

Turks Fighting Insurgents, 1688 — A711

1968, Aug. 22 *Perf. 10½*

1706	A711	13s multicolored	.45	.20

280th anniv ersar y of the Tchipro vtzi insurrection.

Christo Smirnenski (1898-1923), Poet — A712

1968, Sept. 28 **Litho.** *Perf. 10½*

1707	A712	13s gold, red org & blk	.40	.20

Dalmatian Pelican A713

Birds: 2s, Little egret. 3s, Crested grebe. 5s, Common tern. 13s, European spoonbill. 20s, Glossy ibis.

1968, Oct. 28 **Photo.**

1708	A713	1s silver & multi	.20	.20
1709	A713	2s silver & multi	.20	.20
1710	A713	3s silver & multi	.20	.20
1711	A713	5s silver & multi	.20	.20
1712	A713	13s silver & multi	.50	.20
1713	A713	20s silver & multi	1.10	.30
		Nos. 1708-1713 (6)	2.40	1.30

Srebirna wild life reservation.

Carrier Pigeon A714

1968, Oct. 19

1714	A714	20s emerald	.70	.25
a.		Sheet of 4 + labels	5.00	1.60

2nd Natl. Stamp Exhib. in Sofia, Oct. 25-Nov. 15. No. 1714a contains 4 No. 1714 and 5 labels.

Values quoted in this catalogue are for stamps graded Very Fine and with no faults. An illustrated guide to grade is provided in the "Catalogue Information" section of the Introduction.

Man and Woman from Lovetch A715

Regional Costumes: 1s, Silistra. 3s, Jambol. 13s, Chirpan. 20s, Razgrad. 40s, Ihtiman.

1968, Nov. 20 **Litho.** *Perf. 13½*

1715	A715	1s dp org & multi	.20	.20
1716	A715	2s Prus bl & multi	.20	.20
1717	A715	3s multicolored	.20	.20
1718	A715	13s multicolored	.30	.20
1719	A715	20s multicolored	.55	.25
1720	A715	40s green & multi	1.40	.45
		Nos. 1715-1720 (6)	2.85	1.50

St. Arsenius A716

10th cent. Murals & Icons: 2s, Procession with relics of St. Ivan Rilsky, horiz. 3s, St. Michael Torturing the Soul of the Rich Man. 13s, St. Ivan Rilski. 20s, St. John. 40s, St. George. 1 l, Procession meeting relics of St. Ivan Rilsky, horiz.

Perf. 11½x12½, 12½x11½

1968, Nov. 25 **Photo.**

1721	A716	1s gold & multi	.20	.20
1722	A716	2s gold & multi	.20	.20
1723	A716	3s gold & multi	.20	.20
1724	A716	13s gold & multi	.40	.20
1725	A716	20s gold & multi	.95	.30
1726	A716	40s gold & multi	1.40	.60
		Nos. 1721-1726 (6)	3.35	1.70

Souvenir Sheet

Imperf

1727	A716	1 l gold & multi	3.75	2.75

Millenium of Rila Monastery. No. 1727 also: Sofia 1969 Intl. Phil. Exhib., May 31-June 8, 1969. No. 1727 contains one stamp, size: 57x51mm.

Medlar A717

Herbs: No. 1729, Camomile. 2s, Lily-of-the-valley. 3s, Belladonna. 5s, Mallow. 10s, Buttercup. 13s, Poppies. 20s, Thyme.

1969, Jan. 2 **Litho.** *Perf. 10½*

1728	A717	1s black, grn & org red	.20	.20
1729	A717	1s black, grn & yel	.20	.20
1730	A717	2s black, emer & grn	.20	.20
1731	A717	3s black & multi	.20	.20
1732	A717	5s black & multi	.20	.20
1733	A717	10s black, grn & yel	.20	.20
1734	A717	13s black & multi	.30	.20
1735	A717	20s black, lil & grn	.65	.20
		Nos. 1728-1735 (8)	2.15	1.60

Silkworms and Spindles A718

Designs: 2s, Silkworm, cocoons and pattern. 3s, Cocoons and spinning wheel. 5s, Cocoons, woof-and-warp diagram. 13s, Silk moth, Cocoon and spinning frame. 20s, Silk moth, eggs and shuttle.

1969, Jan. 30 **Photo.** *Perf. 10½*

1736	A718	1s bl, grn, sl & blk	.20	.20
1737	A718	2s dp car, sil & blk	.20	.20
1738	A718	3s Prus bl, sil & blk	.20	.20
1739	A718	5s pur, ver, sil & blk	.20	.20
1740	A718	13s red lil, ocher, sil & blk	.25	.20
1741	A718	20s grn, org, sil & blk	.45	.20
		Nos. 1736-1741 (6)	1.50	1.20

Bulgarian silk industry.

Attack and Capture of Emperor Nicephorus A719

Sts. Cyril and Methodius, Mural, Troian Monastery A720

Designs (Manasses Chronicle): No. 1742, Death of Ivan Asen. 3s, Khan Kroum feasting after victory. No. 1748, Invasion of Bulgaria by Prince Sviatoslav of Kiev. No. 1750, Russian invasion and campaigns of Emperor John I Zimisces, c. 972 A.D. 40s, Tsar Ivan Alexander, Jesus and Constantine Manasses.

Horizontal designs: No. 1743, Kings Nebuchadnezzar, Balthazar, Darius and Cyrus. No. 1745, Kings Cambyses, Gyges and Darius. 5s, King David and Tsar Ivan Alexander. No. 1749, Persecution of Byzantine army after battle of July 26, 811. No. 1751, Christening of Bulgarian Tsar Boris, 865. 60s, Arrival of Tsar Simeon in Constantinople and his succeeding surprise attack on that city.

1969 **Photo.** *Perf. 14x13½, 13½x14*

1742	A719	1s multicolored	.20	.20
1743	A719	1s multicolored	.20	.20
1744	A719	2s multicolored	.20	.20
1745	A719	2s multicolored	.20	.20
1746	A719	3s multicolored	.20	.20
1747	A719	5s multicolored	.20	.20
1748	A719	13s multicolored	.40	.20
1749	A719	13s multicolored	.40	.20
1750	A719	20s multicolored	.80	.20
1751	A719	20s multicolored	.80	.20
1752	A719	40s multicolored	1.25	.40
1753	A719	60s multicolored	2.25	.40
		Nos. 1742-1753 (12)	7.10	2.80

1969, Mar. 23

1754	A720	28s gold & multi	.75	.45

Post Horn — A721

Designs: 13s, Bulgaria Nos. 1 and 534. 20s, Street fighting at Stackata, 1919.

1969, Apr. 15 **Photo.** *Perf. 10½*

1755	A721	2s green & yel	.20	.20
1756	A721	13s multicolored	.40	.20
1757	A721	20s dk bl & lt bl	.50	.20
		Nos. 1755-1757 (3)	1.10	.60

Bulgarian postal administration, 90th anniv.

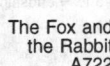

The Fox and the Rabbit A722

Children's Drawings: 2s, Boy reading to wolf and fox. 13s, Two birds and cat singing together.

1969, Apr. 21

1758	A722	1s emer, org & blk	.20	.20
1759	A722	2s org, lt bl & blk	.20	.20
1760	A722	13s lt bl, ol & blk	.40	.20
		Nos. 1758-1760 (3)	.80	.60

Issued for Children's Week.

ILO Emblem — A723

1969, Apr. 28

1761	A723	13s dull grn & blk	.30	.20

50th anniv. of the ILO.

St. George and SOFIA 69 Emblem A724

Designs: 2s, Virgin Mary and St. John Bogoslov. 3s, Archangel Michael. 5s, Three Saints. 8s, Jesus Christ. 13s, Sts. George and Dimitrie. 20s, Christ, the Almighty. 40s, St. Dimitr ie. 60s, The 40 Mar tyrs. 80s, The Transfiguration.

1969, Apr. 30 *Perf. 11x12*

1762	A724	1s gold & multi	.20	.20
1763	A724	2s gold & multi	.20	.20
1764	A724	3s gold & multi	.20	.20
1765	A724	5s gold & multi	.20	.20
1766	A724	8s gold & multi	.20	.20
1767	A724	13s gold & multi	.30	.20
1768	A724	20s gold & multi	.65	.25
1769	A724	40s gold & multi	1.40	.40
a.		Sheet of 4	5.75	5.00
1770	A724	60s gold & multi	1.75	.85
1771	A724	80s gold & multi	2.75	1.00
		Nos. 1762-1771 (10)	7.85	3.70

Old Bulgarian art from the National Art Gallery. No. 1769a contains 4 of No. 1769 with center gutter showing Alexander Nevski Shrine. See note on SOFIA 69 after Nos. C112-C120.

St. Cyril Preaching A725

Design: 28s, St. Cyril and followers.

1969, June 20 **Litho.** *Perf. 10½*

1772	A725	2s sil, grn & red	.20	.20
1773	A725	28s sil, dk bl & red	.75	.25

St. Cyril (827-869), apostle to the Slavs, inventor of Cyrillic alphabet. Issued in sheets of 25 with se-tenant labels; Cyrillic inscription on label of 2s, Glagolitic inscription on label of 28s.

St. Sophia Church — A726

Sofia Through the Ages: 1s, Roman coin with inscription "Ulpia Serdica." 2s, Roman coin with Aesculapius Temple. 4s, Bojana Church. 5s, Sobranic Parliament. 13s, Vasov National Theater. 20s, Alexander Nevski Shrine. 40s, Clement Ochrida University. 1 l, Coat of arms.

1969, May 25 ***Perf. 13x12½***

1774	A726	1s gold & blue	.20	.20
1775	A726	2s gold & ol grn	.20	.20
1776	A726	3s gold & red brn	.20	.20
1777	A726	4s gold & purple	.20	.20
1778	A726	5s gold & plum	.20	.20
1779	A726	13s gold & brt grn	.30	.20
1780	A726	20s gold & vio bl	.45	.20
1781	A726	40s gold & dp car	1.10	.25
		Nos. 1774-1781 (8)	2.85	1.65

Souvenir Sheet

Imperf

1782	A726	1 l grn, gold & red	2.25	2.00

Historic Sofia in connection with the International Philatelic Exhibition, Sofia, May 31-June 8.

#1782 contains one 43½x43½mm stamp. Emblems of 8 preceding philatelic exhibitions in metallic ink in margin; gold inscription.

No. 1782 was overprinted in green "IBRA 73" and various symbols, and released May 4, 1973, for the Munich Philatelic Exhibition. The overprint also exists in gray.

St. George A727

1969, June 9 **Litho.** ***Perf. 11½***

1783	A727	40s sil, blk & pale rose	1.25	.50

38th FIP Congress, June 9-11.

Hand Planting Sapling A728

1969, Apr. 28 **Photo.** ***Perf. 11***

1784	A728	2s ol grn, blk & lilac	.20	.20

25 years of the reforestation campaign.

Partisans A729

Designs: 2s, Combine harvester. 3s, Dam. 5s, Flutist and singers. 13s, Factory. 20s, Lenin, Dimitrov, Russian and Bulgarian flags.

1969, Sept. 9

1785	A729	1s blk, pur & org	.20	.20
1786	A729	2s blk, ol bis & org	.20	.20
1787	A729	3s blk, bl grn & org	.20	.20
1788	A729	5s blk, brn red & org	.20	.20
1789	A729	13s blk, bl & org	.30	.20
1790	A729	20s blk, brn & org	.50	.20
		Nos. 1785-1790 (6)	1.60	1.20

25th anniversary of People's Republic.

Women Gymnasts A730

1969, Sept. **Photo.** ***Perf. 11***

1791	A730	2s shown	.20	.20
1792	A730	20s Wrestlers	.40	.25

Third National Spartakiad.

Tchanko Bakalov Tcherkovski, Poet. Birth Cent. — A731

1969, Sept.

1793	A731	13s multicolored	.35	.20

Woman Gymnast A732

Designs: 2s, Two women with hoops. 3s, Woman with hoop. 5s, Two women with spheres.

1969, Oct.

Gymnasts in Light Gray

1794	A732	1s green & dk blue	.20	.20
1795	A732	2s blue & dk blue	.20	.20
1796	A732	3s emer & sl grn	.20	.20
1797	A732	5s orange & pur	.20	.20
		Nos. 1794-1797,B35-B36 (6)	1.90	1.30

World Championships for Artistic Gymnastics, Varna.

The Priest Rilski, by Zachary Zograf — A733

Paintings from the National Art Gallery. 2s, Woman at Window, by Vasil Stoilov. 3s, Workers at Rest, by Nenko Balkanski, horiz. 4s, Woman Dressing (Nude), by Ivan Nenov. 5s, Portrait of a Woman, by N. Pavlovich. 13s, Falstaff, by Duzunov Kr. Sarafov. No. 1804, Portrait of a Woman, by N. Mihajlov, horiz. No. 1805, Workers at Mealtime, by Stojan Sotirov, horiz. 40s, Self-portrait, by Tcheno Togorov.

Perf. 11½x12, 12x11½

1969, Nov. 10

1798	A733	1s gold & multi	.20	.20
1799	A733	2s gold & multi	.20	.20
1800	A733	3s gold & multi	.20	.20
1801	A733	4s gold & multi	.20	.20
1802	A733	5s gold & multi	.20	.20
1803	A733	13s gold & multi	.30	.20
1804	A733	20s gold & multi	.70	.25
1805	A733	20s gold & multi	.70	.25
1806	A733	40s gold & multi	1.40	.60
		Nos. 1798-1806 (9)	4.10	2.30

Roman Bronze Wolf A734

Design: 2s, Roman statue of woman, found at Silistra, vert.

1969, Oct. **Photo.** ***Perf. 11***

1807	A734	2s sil, ultra & gray	.20	.20
1808	A734	13s sil, dk grn & gray	.40	.20

City of Silistra's 1,800th anniversary.

Worker and Factory — A735

1969 ***Perf. 13***

1809	A735	6s ultra & blk	.20	.20

25th anniversary of the factory militia.

European Hake — A736

Designs: No. 1811, Deep-sea fishing trawler. Fish: 2s, Atlantic horse mackerel. 3s, Pilchard. 5s, Dentex macrophthalmus. 10s, Chub mackerel. 13s, Otolithes macrognathus. 20s, Lichia vadigo.

1969 ***Perf. 11***

1810	A736	1s ol grn & blk	.20	.20
1811	A736	1s ultra, ind & gray	.20	.20
1812	A736	2s lilac & blk	.20	.20
1813	A736	3s vio bl & blk	.20	.20
1814	A736	5s rose cl, pink & blk	.25	.20
1815	A736	10s gray & blk	.50	.20
1816	A736	13s ver, sal & blk	.70	.20
1817	A736	20s ocher & black	1.25	.20
		Nos. 1810-1817 (8)	3.50	1.60

Marin Drinov A737

1969, Nov. 10 **Litho.** ***Perf. 11***

1818	A737	20s black & red org	.35	.20

Centenary of the Bulgarian Academy of Science, founded by Marin Drinov.

Trapeze Artists A738

Pavel Bania Sanatorium A739

Circus Performers: 2s, Jugglers. 3s, Jugglers with loops. 5s, Juggler and bear on bicycle. 13s, Woman and performing horse. 20s, Musical clowns.

1969 **Photo.** ***Perf. 11***

1819	A738	1s dk blue & multi	.20	.20
1820	A738	2s dk green & multi	.20	.20
1821	A738	3s dk violet & multi	.20	.20
1822	A738	5s multicolored	.20	.20
1823	A738	13s multicolored	.30	.20
1824	A738	20s multicolored	.55	.20
		Nos. 1819-1824 (6)	1.65	1.20

1969, Dec. **Photo.** ***Perf. 10½-14***

Health Resorts: 5s, Chisar Sanatorium. 6s, Kotel Children's Sanatorium. 20s, Narechen Polyclinic.

1825	A739	2s blue	.20	.20
1826	A739	5s ultra	.20	.20
1827	A739	6s green	.20	.20
1828	A739	20s emerald	.30	.20
		Nos. 1825-1828 (4)	.90	.80

G. S. Shonin, V. N. Kubasov and Spacecraft — A740

Designs: 2s, A. V. Filipchenko, V. N. Volkov, V. V. Gorbatko and spacecraft. 3s, Vladimir A. Shatalov, Alexei S. Yeliseyev and spacecraft. 28s, Three spacecraft in orbit.

1970, Jan. **Photo.** ***Perf. 11***

1829	A740	1s rose car, ol grn & blk	.20	.20
1830	A740	2s bl, dl cl & blk	.20	.20
1831	A740	3s grnsh bl, vio & blk	.20	.20
1832	A740	28s vio bl, lil rose & lt bl	.70	.20
		Nos. 1829-1832 (4)	1.30	.80

Russian space flights of Soyuz 6, 7 and 8, Oct. 11-13, 1969.

Khan Krum and Defeat of Emperor Nicephorus, 811 — A741

Bulgarian History: 1s, Khan Asparuch and Bulgars crossing the Danube (679). 3s, Conversion of Prince Boris to Christianity, 865. 5s, Tsar Simeon and battle of Akhelo, 917. 8s, Tsar Samuel defeating the Byzantines, 976. 10s, Tsar Kaloyan defeating Emperor Baldwin, 1205. 13s, Tsar Ivan Assen II defeating Greek King Theodore Komnine, 1230. 20s, Coronation of Tsar Ivailo, 1277.

1970, Feb. ***Perf. 10½***

1833	A741	1s gold & multi	.20	.20
1834	A741	2s gold & multi	.20	.20
1835	A741	3s gold & multi	.20	.20
1836	A741	5s gold & multi	.20	.20
1837	A741	8s gold & multi	.20	.20
1838	A741	10s gold & multi	.30	.20
1839	A741	13s gold & multi	.40	.20
1840	A741	20s gold & multi	.70	.20
		Nos. 1833-1840 (8)	2.40	1.60

See Nos. 2126-2133.

Bulgarian Pavilion, EXPO '70 — A742

1970 ***Perf. 12½***

1841	A742	20s brown, sil & org	.75	.50

EXPO '70 International Exposition, Osaka, Japan, Mar. 15-Sept. 13, 1970.

Soccer A743

Designs: Various views of soccer game.

1970, Mar. 4 **Photo.** ***Perf. 12½***

1842	A743	1s blue & multi	.20	.20
1843	A743	2s rose car & multi	.20	.20
1844	A743	3s ultra & multi	.20	.20
1845	A743	5s green & multi	.20	.20
1846	A743	20s emerald & multi	.55	.20
1847	A743	40s red & multi	1.25	.30
		Nos. 1842-1847 (6)	2.60	1.30

9th World Soccer Championships for the Jules Rimet Cup, Mexico City, May 30-June 21, 1970. See No. B37.

Lenin (1870-1924)
A744

1970, Apr. 22

1848 A744 2s shown .20 .20
1849 A744 13s Portrait .30 .20
1850 A744 20s Writing .70 .20
Nos. 1848-1850 (3) 1.20 .60

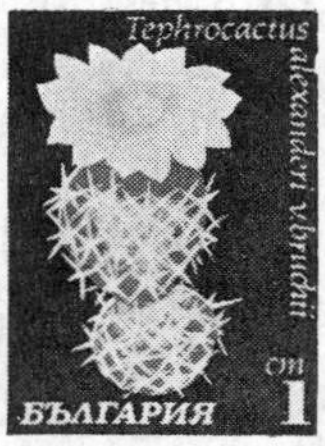

Tephrocactus Alexanderi V. Bruchii — A745

Cacti: 2s, Opuntia drummondii. 3s, Hatiora cilindrica. 5s, Gymnocalycium vatteri. 8s, Heliantho cereus grandiflorus. 10s, Neochilenia andreaeana. 13s, Peireskia vargasii v. longispina. 20s, Neobesseya rosiflora.

1970 Photo. *Perf. 12½*

1851 A745 1s multicolored .20 .20
1852 A745 2s dk green & multi .20 .20
1853 A745 3s multicolored .20 .20
1854 A745 5s blue & multi .20 .20
1855 A745 8s brown & multi .30 .20
1856 A745 10s vio bl & multi 1.00 .20
1857 A745 13s brn red & multi 1.00 .20
1858 A745 20s purple & multi 1.40 .30
Nos. 1851-1858 (8) 4.50 1.70

Rose — A746

Designs: Various Roses.

1970, June 8 Litho. *Perf. 13½*

1859 A746 1s gray & multi .20 .20
1860 A746 2s gray & multi .20 .20
1861 A746 3s gray & multi .20 .20
1862 A746 4s gray & multi .20 .20
1863 A746 5s gray & multi .20 .20
1864 A746 13s gray & multi .20 .20
1865 A746 20s gray & multi 1.10 .25
1866 A746 28s gray & multi 1.90 .40
Nos. 1859-1866 (8) 4.20 1.85

Gold Bowl — A747

Designs: Various bowls and art objects from Gold Treasure of Thrace.

1970, June 15 Photo. *Perf. 12½*

1867 A747 1s blk, bl & gold .20 .20
1868 A747 2s blk, lt vio & gold .20 .20
1869 A747 3s blk, ver & gold .20 .20
1870 A747 5s blk, yel grn & gold .20 .20
1871 A747 13s blk, org & gold .70 .20
1872 A747 20s blk, lil & gold .85 .20
Nos. 1867-1872 (6) 2.35 1.20

EXPO Emblem, Rose and Bulgarian Woman — A748

Designs (EXPO Emblem and): 2s, Three women. 3s, Woman and fruit. 28s, Dancers. 40s, Mt. Fuji and pavilions.

1970, June 20

1873 A748 1s gold & multi .20 .20
1874 A748 2s gold & multi .20 .20
1875 A748 3s gold & multi .20 .20
1876 A748 28s gold & multi .70 .25
Nos. 1873-1876 (4) 1.30 .85

Miniature Sheet

Imperf

1877 A748 40s gold & multi 1.00 .60

EXPO '70 International Exposition, Osaka, Japan, Mar. 15-Sept. 13. No. 1877 contains one stamp with simulated perforations.

Ivan Vasov
A749

1970, Aug. 1 Photo. *Perf. 12½*

1878 A749 13s violet blue .40 .20

120th anniv. of the birth of Ivan Vasov, author.

UN Emblem — A750

1970, Aug. 1

1879 A750 20s Prus bl & gold .50 .20

25th anniversary of the United Nations.

George Dimitrov
A751

Retriever
A752

1970, Aug.

1880 A751 20s blk, gold & org .60 .20

BZNC (Bulgarian Communist Party), 70th anniv.

1970 Photo. *Perf. 12½*

Dogs: 1s, Golden retriever, horiz. 3s, Great Dane. 4s, Boxer. 5s, Cocker spaniel. 13s, Doberman pinscher. 20s, Scottish terrier. 28s, Russian greyhound, horiz.

1881 A752 1s multicolored .20 .20
1882 A752 2s multicolored .20 .20
1883 A752 3s multicolored .20 .20
1884 A752 4s multicolored .20 .20
1885 A752 5s multicolored .20 .20
1886 A752 13s multicolored .50 .20
1887 A752 20s multicolored 1.10 .25
1888 A752 28s multicolored 1.60 .30
Nos. 1881-1888 (8) 4.20 1.75

Volleyball — A753

Designs: No. 1890, Two women players. No. 1891, Woman player. No. 1892, Man player.

1970, Sept. Photo. *Perf. 12½*

1889 A753 2s dk red brn, bl & blk .20 .20
1890 A753 2s ultra, org & blk .20 .20
1891 A753 20s Prus bl, yel & blk .50 .20
1892 A753 20s grn, yel & blk .50 .20
Nos. 1889-1892 (4) 1.40 .80

World Volleyball Championships.

Enrico Caruso and "I Pagliacci" by Ruggiero Leoncavallo — A754

Opera Singers and Operas: 2s, Christina Morfova and "The Bartered Bride" by Bedrich Smetana. 3s, Peter Reitchev and "Tosca" by Giacomo Puccini. 10s, Svetana Tabakova and "The Flying Dutchman" by Richard Wagner. 13s, Katia Popova and "The Masters" by Paroshkev Hadjev. 20s, Feodor Chaliapin and "Boris Godunov" by Modest Musorgski.

1970, Oct. 15 Photo. *Perf. 14*

1893 A754 1s black & multi .20 .20
1894 A754 2s black & multi .20 .20
1895 A754 3s black & multi .20 .20
1896 A754 10s black & multi .20 .20
1897 A754 13s black & multi .30 .20
1898 A754 20s black & multi 1.00 .25
Nos. 1893-1898 (6) 2.10 1.25

Honoring opera singers in their best roles.

Ivan Assen II Coin — A755

Coins from 14th Century with Ruler's Portrait: 2s, Theodor Svetoslav. 3s, Mikhail Chichman. 13s, Ivan Alexander and Mikhail Assen. 20s, Ivan Sratsimir. 28s, Ivan Chichman (initials).

1970, Nov. *Perf. 12½*

1899 A755 1s buff & multi .20 .20
1900 A755 2s gray & multi .20 .20
1901 A755 3s multicolored .20 .20
1902 A755 13s multicolored .25 .20
1903 A755 20s lt blue & multi .60 .20
1904 A755 28s multicolored .85 .25
Nos. 1899-1904 (6) 2.30 1.25

Fire Protection
A756

1970 Litho. *Perf. 12½*

1905 A756 1s Fireman .20 .20
1906 A756 3s Fire engine .20 .20

Bicyclists
A757

Congress Emblem
A758

1970 Photo.

1907 A757 20s grn, yel & pink .50 .20

20th Bulgarian bicycle race.

1970

1908 A758 13s gold & multi .35 .20

7th World Congress of Sociology, Varna, Sept. 14-19.

Ludwig van Beethoven — A759

Friedrich Engels — A760

1970

1909 A759 28s lil rose & dk bl .90 .40

Beethoven (1770-1827), composer.

1970 Photo. *Perf. 12½*

1910 A760 13s ver, tan & brn .30 .20

Friedrich Engels (1820-1895), German socialist, collaborator of Karl Marx.

Miniature Sheets

Luna 16
A761

Russian moon mission: 80s, Lunokhod 1, unmanned vehicle on moon, horiz.

1970 Photo. *Imperf.*

1911 A761 80s plum, sil, blk & bl 2.00 2.00
1912 A761 1 l vio bl, sil & red 4.00 2.75

No. 1911, Lunokhod 1, Nov. 10-17. No. 1912, Luna 16 mission, Sept. 12-24.
Issue dates: 80s, Dec. 18; 1 l, Nov. 10.

Snowflake
A762

1970, Dec. 15 Photo. *Perf. 12½x13*

1913 A762 2s ultra & multi .20 .20

New Year 1971.

Birds and Flowers A763

Folk Art: 2s, Bird and flowers. 3s, Flying birds. 5s, Birds and flowers. 13s, Sun. 20s, Tulips and pansies.

1971, Jan. 25 ***Perf. 12½x13½***

1914 A763 1s multicolored .20 .20
1915 A763 2s multicolored .20 .20
1916 A763 3s multicolored .20 .20
1917 A763 5s multicolored .20 .20
1918 A763 13s multicolored .20 .20
1919 A763 20s multicolored .55 .20
Nos. 1914-1919 (6) 1.55 1.20

Spring 1971.

Girl, by Zeko Spiridonov A764

Modern Bulgarian Sculpture: 2s, Third Class (people looking through train window), by Ivan Funev. 3s, Bust of Elin Pelin, by Marko Markov. 13s, Bust of Nina, by Andrej Nikolov. 20s, Monument to P. K. Yavorov (kneeling woman), by Ivan Lazarov. 28s, Engineer, by Ivan Funev. 1 l, Refugees, by Sekul Krimov, horiz.

1971, Feb. ***Perf. 12½***

1920 A764 1s gold & vio .20 .20
1921 A764 2s gold & dk ol grn .20 .20
1922 A764 3s gold & rose brn .20 .20
1923 A764 13s gold & dk grn .30 .20
1924 A764 20s gold & red brn .50 .20
1925 A764 28s gold & dk brn .80 .20
Nos. 1920-1925 (6) 2.20 1.20

Souvenir Sheet

Imperf

1926 A764 1 l gold, dk brn & buff 2.00 1.75

Runner A765

Design: 20s, Woman putting the shot.

1971, Mar. 13 Photo. ***Perf. 12½x13***

1927 A765 2s brown & multi .20 .20
1928 A765 20s dp grn, org & blk .90 .25

2nd European Indoor Track and Field Championships.

Bulgarian Secondary School, Bolgrad — A766

Educators: 20s, Dimiter Mitev, Prince Bogoridi and Sava Radoulov.

1971, Mar. 16 ***Perf. 12½***

1929 A766 2s silver, brn & grn .20 .20
1930 A766 20s silver, brn & vio .50 .20

First Bulgarian secondary school, 1858, in Bolgrad, USSR.

Communards — A767

1971, Mar. 18 Photo. ***Perf. 12½x13***

1931 A767 20s rose magenta & blk .50 .20

Centenary of the Paris Commune.

Dimitrov Facing Goering, Quotation, FIR Emblem A768

1971, Apr. 11 ***Perf. 12½***

1932 A768 2s grn, gold, blk & red .20 .20
1933 A768 13s plum, gold, blk & red .70 .20

Intl. Fed. of Resistance Fighters (FIR), 20th anniv.

George S. Rakovski (1821-1867), Revolutionary Against Turkish Rule — A769

1971, Apr. 14

1934 A769 13s olive & blk brn .30 .20

Edelweiss Hotel, Borovets A770

Designs: 2s, Panorama Hotel, Pamporovo. 4s, Boats at Albena, Black Sea. 8s, Boats at Rousalka. 10s, Shtastlivetsa Hotel, Mt. Vitosha.

1971 ***Perf. 13***

1935 A770 1s brt green .20 .20
1936 A770 2s olive gray .20 .20
1937 A770 4s brt blue .20 .20
1938 A770 8s blue .20 .20
1939 A770 10s bluish green .25 .20
Nos. 1935-1939 (5) 1.05 1.00

Technological Progress — A771

Designs: 1s, Mason with banner, vert. 13s, Two men and doves, vert.

1971, Apr. 20 Photo. ***Perf. 12½***

1940 A771 1s gold & multi .20 .20
1941 A771 2s gray blue & multi .20 .20
1942 A771 13s lt green & multi .50 .20
Nos. 1940-1942 (3) .90 .60

10th Cong. of Bulgarian Communist Party.

Panayot Pipkov and Anthem A772

1971, May 20

1943 A772 13s sil, blk & brt grn .45 .20

Panayot Pipkov, composer, birth cent.

Mammoth A773

Prehistoric Animals: 2s, Bear, vert. 3s, Hipparion (horse). 13s, Platybelodon. 20s, Dinotherium, vert. 28s, Saber-tooth tiger.

1971, May 29 ***Perf. 12½***

1944 A773 1s dull bl & multi .20 .20
1945 A773 2s lilac & multi .20 .20
1946 A773 3s multicolored .20 .20
1947 A773 13s multicolored .50 .20
1948 A773 20s dp grn & multi .80 .20
1949 A773 28s multicolored 1.40 .30
Nos. 1944-1949 (6) 3.30 1.30

Khan Asparuch Crossing Danube, 679 A.D., by Boris Angelushev — A774

Historical Paintings: 3s, Reception at Trnovo, by Ilya Petrov. 5s, Chevartov's Troops at Benkovsky, by P. Morozov. 8s, Russian Gen. Gurko and People in Sofia, 1878, by D. Gudjenko. 28s, People Greeting Red Army, by S. Venov.

1971, Mar. 6 ***Perf. 13½x14***

1950 A774 2s gold & multi .20 .20
1951 A774 3s gold & multi .20 .20
1952 A774 5s gold & multi .20 .20
1953 A774 8s gold & multi .30 .20
a. Souv. sheet of 4, #1950-1953 1.00 .50
1954 A774 28s gold & multi 2.75 .85
Nos. 1950-1954 (5) 3.65 1.65

In 1973, No. 1953a was surcharged 1 lev and overprinted "Visitez la Bulgarie," airline initials and emblems, and, on the 5s stamp, "Par Avion."

Freed Black, White and Yellow Men — A775

1971, May 20 Photo. ***Perf. 12½***

1955 A775 13s blue, blk & yel .35 .20

Intl. Year against Racial Discrimination.

Map of Europe, Championship Emblem — A776

"XXX" Supporting Barbell — A777

1971, June 19

1956 A776 2s lt blue & multi .20 .20
1957 A777 13s yellow & multi .60 .20

30th European Weight Lifting Championships, Sofia, June 19-27.

Facade, Old House, Koprivnica A778

Designs: Decorated facades of various old houses in Koprivnica.

1971, July 10 Photo. ***Perf. 12½***

1958 A778 1s green & multi .20 .20
1959 A778 2s brown & multi .20 .20
1960 A778 6s violet & multi .20 .20
1961 A778 13s dk red & multi .40 .20
Nos. 1958-1961 (4) 1.00 .80

Frontier Guard and German Shepherd A779

1971, July 31 ***Perf. 13***

1962 A779 2s green & ol grn .20 .20

25th anniversary of the Frontier Guards.

Congress of Busludja, Bas-relief — A780

1971, July 31 ***Perf. 12½***

1963 A780 2s dk red & ol grn .20 .20

80th anniversary of the first Congress of the Bulgarian Social Democratic party.

Young Woman, by Ivan Nenov — A781

Paintings: 2s, Lazarova in Evening Gown, by Stefan Ivanov. 3s, Performer in Dress Suit, by Kyril Zonev. 13s, Portrait of a Woman, by Detchko Uzunov. 20s, Woman from Kalotina, by Vladimir Dimitrov. 40s, Gorjanin (Mountain Man), by Stoyan Venev.

1971, Aug. 2 ***Perf. 14x13½***

1964 A781 1s green & multi .20 .20
1965 A781 2s green & multi .20 .20
1966 A781 3s green & multi .20 .20
1967 A781 13s green & multi .40 .20
1968 A781 20s green & multi .75 .30
1969 A781 40s green & multi 1.60 .45
Nos. 1964-1969 (6) 3.35 1.55

National Art Gallery.

Wrestlers A782

Designs: 13s, Wrestlers.

1971, Aug. 27 *Perf. 12½*

1970 A782 2s green, blk & bl .20 .20
1971 A782 13s red org, blk & bl .50 .20

European Wrestling Championships.

Young Workers A783

Post Horn Emblem A784

1971 **Photo.** *Perf. 13*

1972 A783 2s dark blue .20 .20

25th anniv. of the Young People's Brigade.

1971, Sept. 15 *Perf. 12½*

1973 A784 20s dp green & gold .45 .20

8th meeting of postal administrations of socialist countries, Varna.

FEBS Waves Emblem — A785

1971, Sept. 20

1974 A785 13s black, red & mar .50 .20

7th Congress of European Biochemical Association (FEBS), Varna.

Statue of Republic — A786

Design: 13s, Bulgarian flag.

1971, Sept. 20 *Perf. 13x12½*

1975 A786 2s gold, yel & dk red .20 .20
1976 A786 13s gold, grn & red .40 .20

Bulgarian People's Republic, 25th anniv.

Cross Country Skiing and Winter Olympics Emblem A787

Sport and Winter Olympics Emblem: 2s, Downhill skiing. 3s, Ski jump and skiing. 4s, Women's figure skating. 13s, Ice hockey. 28s, Slalom skiing. 1 l, Torch and stadium.

1971, Sept. 25 *Perf. 12½*

1977 A787 1s dk green & multi .20 .20
1978 A787 2s vio blue & multi .20 .20
1979 A787 3s ultra & multi .20 .20
1980 A787 4s dp plum & multi .20 .20
1981 A787 13s dk blue & multi .40 .20
1982 A787 28s multicolored .90 .35
Nos. 1977-1982 (6) 2.10 1.35

Miniature Sheet

Imperf

1983 A787 1 l multicolored 3.50 1.60

11th Winter Olympic Games, Sapporo, Japan, Feb. 3-13, 1972.

Factory, Botevgrad A788

Industrial Buildings: 2s, Petro-chemical works, Pleven, vert. 10s, Chemical works, Vratsa. 13s, Maritsa-Istok Power Station, Dimitrovgrad. 40s, Electronics works, Sofia.

1971 **Photo.** *Perf. 13*

1984 A788 1s violet .20 .20
1985 A788 2s orange .20 .20
1986 A788 10s deep purple .20 .20
1987 A788 13s lilac rose .25 .20
1988 A788 40s deep brown .70 .20
Nos. 1984-1988 (5) 1.55 1.00

UNESCO Emblem A789

1971, Nov. 4 *Perf. 12½*

1989 A789 20s lt bl, blk, gold & red .45 .20

25th anniv. of UNESCO.

Soccer Player, by Kyril Zonev (1896-1971) A790

Paintings by Kyril Zonev: 2s, Landscape, horiz. 3s, Self-portrait. 13s, Lilies. 20s, Landscape, horiz. 40s, Portrait of a Young Woman.

1971, Nov. 10 *Perf. 11x12*

1990 A790 1s gold & multi .20 .20
1991 A790 2s gold & multi .20 .20
1992 A790 3s gold & multi .20 .20
1993 A790 13s gold & multi .25 .20
1994 A790 20s gold & multi .85 .25
1995 A790 40s gold & multi 1.25 .35
Nos. 1990-1995 (6) 2.95 1.40

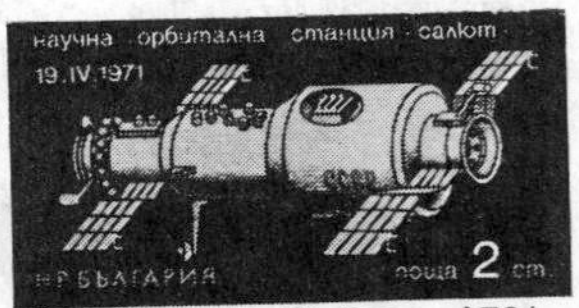

Salyut Space Station — A791

Astronauts Dobrovolsky, Volkov and Patsayev — A792

Designs: 13s, Soyuz 11 space transport. 40s, Salyut and Soyuz 11 joined.

1971, Dec. 20 *Perf. 12½*

1996 A791 2s dk grn, yel & red .20 .20
1997 A791 13s multicolored .25 .20
1998 A791 40s dk blue & multi 1.25 .40
Nos. 1996-1998 (3) 1.70 .80

Souvenir Sheet

Imperf

1999 A792 80s multicolored 2.00 1.50

Salyut-Soyuz 11 space mission, and in memory of the Russian astronauts Lt. Col. Georgi T. Dobrovolsky, Vladislav N. Volkov and Victor I. Patsayev, who died during the Soyuz 11 space mission, June 6-30, 1971.

Oil Tanker Vihren A793

1972, Jan. 8 **Photo.** *Perf. 12½*

2000 A793 18s lil rose, vio & blk .75 .25

Bulgarian shipbuilding industry.

Goce Delchev A794

Portraits: 5s, Jan Sandanski. 13s, Damjan Gruev.

1972, Jan. 21 **Photo.** *Perf. 12½*

2001 A794 2s brick red & blk .20 .20
2002 A794 5s green & blk .20 .20
2003 A794 13s lemon & blk .35 .20
Nos. 2001-2003 (3) .75 .60

Centenary of the births of Bulgarian patriots Delchev (1872-1903) and Sandanski, and of Macedonian Gruev (1871-1906).

Gymnast with Ball, Medals — A795

Designs: 18s, Gymnast with hoop, and medals. 70s, Gymnasts with hoops, and medals.

1972, Feb. 10

2004 A795 13s multicolored .40 .20
2005 A795 18s multicolored .55 .20

Miniature Sheet

Imperf

2006 A795 70s multicolored 2.25 2.00

5th World Women's Gymnastic Championships, Havana, Cuba.

View of Melnik, by Petar Mladenov — A796

Paintings from National Art Gallery: 2s, Plower, by Pencho Georgiev. 3s, Funeral, by Alexander Djendov. 13s, Husband and Wife, by Vladimir Dimitrov. 20s, Nursing Mother, by Nenko Balkanski. 40s, Paisii Hilendarski Writing History, by Koio Denchev.

1972, Feb. 20 *Perf. 13½x14*

2007 A796 1s green & multi .20 .20
2008 A796 2s green & multi .20 .20
2009 A796 3s green & multi .20 .20
2010 A796 13s green & multi .40 .20
2011 A796 20s green & multi .75 .20
2012 A796 40s green & multi 1.25 .35
Nos. 2007-2012 (6) 3.00 1.35

Paintings from National Art Gallery.

Worker — A797

1972, Mar. 7 *Perf. 12½*

2013 A797 13s silver & multi .20 .20

7th Bulgarian Trade Union Congress.

Singing Harvesters A798

Designs: Paintings by Vladimir Dimitrov.

Perf. 11½x12, 12x11½

1972, Mar. 31

2014 A798 1s shown .20 .20
2015 A798 2s Harvester .20 .20
2016 A798 3s Women Diggers .20 .20
2017 A798 13s Fabric Dyers .35 .20
2018 A798 20s "My Mother" .70 .20
2019 A798 40s Self-portrait 1.40 .30
Nos. 2014-2019 (6) 3.05 1.30

Vladimir Dimitrov, painter, 90th birth anniv.

"Your Heart is your Health" — A799

St. Mark's Basilica and Wave — A800

1972, Apr. 30 *Perf. 12½*

2020 A799 13s red, blk & grn .70 .30

World Health Day.

1972, May 6 *Perf. 13x12½*

Design: 13s, Ca' D'Oro and wave.

2021 A800 2s ol grn, bl grn & lt bl .20 .20
2022 A800 13s red brn, vio & lt grn .50 .20

UNESCO campaign to save Venice.

Dimitrov in Print Shop, 1901 — A801

Designs: Life of George Dimitrov.

1972, May 8 **Photo.** *Perf. 12½*

2023 A801 1s shown .20 .20
2024 A801 2s Dimitrov as leader of 1923 uprising .20 .20
2025 A801 3s Leipzig trial, 1933 .20 .20
2026 A801 5s As Communist functionary, 1935 .20 .20
2027 A801 13s As leader and teacher, 1948 .20 .20
2028 A801 18s Addressing youth rally, 1948 .40 .20
2029 A801 28s With Pioneers, 1948 .65 .20

2030 A801 40s Mausoleum 1.00 .30
2031 A801 80s Portrait 2.75 .45
a. Souvenir sheet 4.25 2.50
Nos. 2023-2031 (9) 5.80 2.15

90th anniversary of the birth of George Dimitrov (1882-1949), communist leader.

No. 2031a contains one imperf. stamp similar to No. 2031, but in different colors.

Value, No. 2031 imperf. in slightly changed colors, $5.

Paisii Hilendarski — A802

Design: 2s, Flame and quotation.

1972, May 12

2032 A802 2s gold, grn & brn .20 .20
2033 A802 13s gold, grn & brn .50 .20

Paisii Hilendarski (1722-1798), monk, writer of Bulgarian-Slavic history.

Canoeing, Motion and Olympic Emblems — A803

Designs (Motion and Olympic emblems and): 2s, Gymnastics. 3s, Swimming, women's. 13s, Volleyball. 18s, Jumping. 40s, Wrestling. 80s, Stadium and sports.

1972, June 25

Figures of Athletes in Silver & Black

2034 A803 1s lt blue & multi .20 .20
2035 A803 2s orange & multi .20 .20
2036 A803 3s multicolored .20 .20
2037 A803 13s yellow & multi .20 .20
2038 A803 18s multicolored .40 .20
2039 A803 40s pink & multi 1.25 .30
Nos. 2034-2039 (6) 2.45 1.30

Miniature Sheet

Imperf

Size: 62x60mm

2040 A803 80s gold, ver & yel 1.75 1.00

20th Olympic Games, Munich, Aug. 26-Sept. 11.

Angel Kunchev A804

1972, June 30 Photo. ***Perf. 12½***

2041 A804 2s magenta, dk pur & gold .20 .20

Centenary of the death of Angel Kunchev, patriot and revolutionist.

Zlatni Pyassatsi — A805

1972, Sept. 16

2042 A805 1s shown .20 .20
2043 A805 2s Drouzhba .20 .20
2044 A805 3s Slunchev Bryag .20 .20
2045 A805 13s Primorsko .20 .20
2046 A805 28s Roussalka .60 .25
2047 A805 40s Albena .85 .30
Nos. 2042-2047 (6) 2.25 1.35

Bulgarian Black Sea resorts.

Bronze Medal, Olympic Emblems, Canoeing A806

Olympic Emblems and: 2s, Silver medal, broad jump. 3s, Gold medal, boxing. 18s, Gold medal, wrestling. 40s, Gold medal, weight lifting.

1972, Sept. 29

2048 A806 1s Prus bl & multi .20 .20
2049 A806 2s dk green & multi .20 .20
2050 A806 3s orange brn & multi .20 .20
2051 A806 18s olive & multi .50 .20
2052 A806 40s multicolored 1.00 .40
Nos. 2048-2052 (5) 2.10 1.20

Bulgarian victories in 20th Olympic Games. For overprint see No. 2066.

Stoj Dimitrov — A807

Resistance Fighters: 2s, Cvetko Radoinov. 3s, Bogdan Stivrodski. 5s, Mirko Laiev. 13s, Nedelyo Nikolov.

1972, Oct. 30 Photo. ***Perf. 12½x13***

2053 A807 1s olive & multi .20 .20
2054 A807 2s multicolored .20 .20
2055 A807 3s multicolored .20 .20
2056 A807 5s multicolored .20 .20
2057 A807 13s multicolored .30 .20
Nos. 2053-2057 (5) 1.10 1.00

"50 Years USSR" A808

1972, Nov. 3 Photo. ***Perf. 12½x13***

2058 A808 13s gold, red & yellow .35 .20

50th anniversary of Soviet Union.

Turk's-cap Lily — A809

Protected Plants: 2s, Gentian. 3s, Sea daffodil. 4s, Globe flower. 18s, Primrose. 23s, Pulsatilla vernalis. 40s, Snake's-head.

1972, Nov. 25 ***Perf. 12½***

Flowers in Natural Colors

2059 A809 1s olive bister .20 .20
2060 A809 2s olive bister .20 .20
2061 A809 3s olive bister .20 .20
2062 A809 4s olive bister .20 .20
2063 A809 18s olive bister .30 .20
2064 A809 23s olive bister .75 .20
2065 A809 40s olive bister 1.40 .35
Nos. 2059-2065 (7) 3.25 1.55

No. 2052 Overprinted in Red СВЕТОВЕН ПЪРВЕНЕЦ

1972, Nov. 27

2066 A806 40s multicolored .95 .25

Bulgarian weight lifting Olympic gold medalists.

Dobri Chintulov — A810

1972, Nov. 28 Photo. ***Perf. 12½***

2067 A810 2s gray, dk & lt grn .20 .20

Dobri Chintulov, writer, 150th birth anniversary.

Forehead Band — A811

Designs (14th-19th Century Jewelry): 2s, Belt buckles. 3s, Amulet. 8s, Pendant. 23s, Earrings. 40s, Necklace.

1972, Dec. 27 Engr. ***Perf. 14x13½***

2068 A811 1s red brn & blk .20 .20
2069 A811 2s emerald & blk .20 .20
2070 A811 3s Prus bl & blk .20 .20
2071 A811 8s dk red & blk .20 .20
2072 A811 23s red org & multi .50 .20
2073 A811 40s violet & blk 1.10 .40
Nos. 2068-2073 (6) 2.40 1.40

Skin Divers A812

Designs: 2s, Shelf-1 underwater house and divers. 18s, Diving bell and diver, vert. 40s, Elevation balloon and divers, vert.

1973, Jan. 24 Photo. ***Perf. 12½***

2074 A812 1s lt bl, blk & yel .20 .20
2075 A812 2s blk, bl & org yel .20 .20
2076 A812 18s blk, Prus bl & dl org .40 .20
2077 A812 40s blk, ultra & bister .95 .30
Nos. 2074-2077 (4) 1.75 .90

Bulgarian deep-sea research in the Black Sea.

A souvenir sheet of four contains imperf. 20s stamps in designs of Nos. 2074-2077 with colors changed. Sold for 1 l. Value $3.50 unused, $3 canceled.

Execution of Levski, by Boris Angelushev A813

Design: 20s, Vassil Levski, by Georgi Danchev.

1973, Feb. 19 ***Perf. 13x12½***

2078 A813 2s dull rose & Prus grn .20 .20
2079 A813 20s dull grn & brn .90 .20

Centenary of the death of Vassil Levski (1837-1873), patriot, executed by the Turks.

Kukersky Mask, Elhovo Region A814

Nicolaus Copernicus A815

Kukersky Masks at pre-Spring Festival: 2s, Breznik. 3s, Hissar. 13s, Radomir. 20s, Karnobat. 40s, Pernik.

1973, Feb. 26 ***Perf. 12½***

2080 A814 1s dp rose & multi .20 .20
2081 A814 2s emerald & multi .20 .20
2082 A814 3s violet & multi .20 .20
2083 A814 13s multicolored .35 .20
2084 A814 20s multicolored .40 .20
2085 A814 40s multicolored 2.25 1.10
Nos. 2080-2085 (6) 3.60 2.10

1973, Mar. 21 Photo. ***Perf. 12½***

2086 A815 28s ocher, blk & claret 1.25 .60

500th anniversary of the birth of Nicolaus Copernicus (1473-1543), Polish astronomer.

Vietnamese Worker and Rainbow — A816

1973, Apr. 16

2087 A816 18s lt blue & multi .35 .20

Peace in Viet Nam.

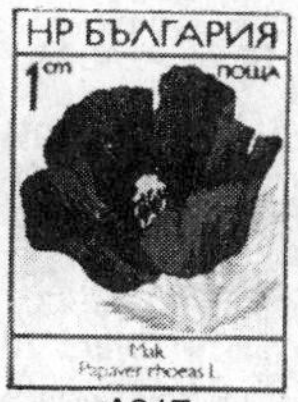

A817

A818

Wild flowers.

1973, May Photo. ***Perf. 13***

2088 A817 1s Poppy .20 .20
2089 A817 2s Daisy .20 .20
2090 A817 3s Peony .20 .20
2091 A817 13s Centaury .25 .20
2092 A817 18s Corn cockle 2.75 1.10
2093 A817 28s Ranunculus .60 .25
Nos. 2088-2093 (6) 4.20 2.15

1973, June 2

2094 A818 2s pale grn, buff & brn .20 .20
2095 A818 18s pale brn, gray & grn .65 .40

Christo Botev (1848-1876), poet.

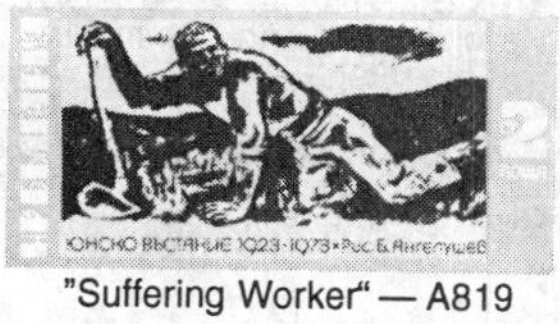

"Suffering Worker" — A819

Design: 1s, Asen Halachev and revolutionists.

1973, June 6 Photo. *Perf. 13*

2096	A819	1s gold, red & blk	.20	.20
2097	A819	2s gold, org & dk brn	.20	.20

50th anniversary of Pleven uprising.

Muskrat A820

Perf. 12½x13, 13x12½

1973, June 29 Litho.

2098	A820	1s shown	.20	.20
2099	A820	2s Racoon	.20	.20
2100	A820	3s Mouflon, vert.	.20	.20
2101	A820	12s Fallow deer, vert.	.25	.20
2102	A820	18s European bison	.50	.20
2103	A820	40s Elk	2.50	1.00
		Nos. 2098-2103 (6)	3.85	2.00

Aleksandr Stamboliski — A821

1973, June 14 Photo. *Perf. 12½*

2104	A821	18s dp brown & org	.35	.20
a.		18s orange	2.50	.75

Aleksandr Stamboliski (1879-1923), leader of Peasants' Party and premier.

Trade Union Emblem — A822

Stylized Sun, Olympic Rings — A823

1973, Aug. 27 Photo. *Perf. 12½*

2105	A822	2s yellow & multi	.20	.20

8th Congress of World Federation of Trade Unions, Varna, Oct. 15-22.

1973, Aug. 29 *Perf. 13*

28s, Emblem of Bulgarian Olympic Committee & Olympic rings. 80s, Soccer, emblems of Innsbruck & Montreal 1976 Games, horiz.

2106	A823	13s multicolored	.70	.30
2107	A823	28s multicolored	1.25	.40

Souvenir Sheet

2108	A823	80s multicolored	3.25	1.75

Olympic Congress, Varna. No. 2108 contains one stamp. It also exists imperf.; also with violet margin, imperf.

Revolutionists with Communist Flag — A824

Designs: 5s, Revolutionists on flatcar blocking train. 13s, Raising Communist flag, vert. 18s, George Dimitrov and Vassil Kolarov.

1973, Sept. 22 Photo. *Perf. 12½*

2109	A824	2s magenta & multi	.20	.20
2110	A824	5s magenta & multi	.20	.20
2111	A824	13s magenta & multi	.30	.20
2112	A824	18s magenta & multi	.85	.30
		Nos. 2109-2112 (4)	1.55	.90

50th anniv. of the September Revolution.

Warrior Saint A825

Murals from Boyana Church: 1s, Tsar Kaloyan and 2s, his wife Dessislava. 5s, "St. Wystratti." 10s, Tsar Constantine Assen. 13s, Deacon Laurentius. 18s, Virgin Mary. 20s, St. Ephraim. 28s, Jesus. 80s, Jesus in the Temple, horiz.

1973, Sept. 24

2113	A825	1s gold & multi	.20	.20
2114	A825	2s gold & multi	.20	.20
2115	A825	3s gold & multi	.20	.20
2116	A825	5s gold & multi	.20	.20
2117	A825	10s gold & multi	.35	.20
2118	A825	13s gold & multi	.45	.20
2119	A825	18s gold & multi	.70	.20
2120	A825	20s gold & multi	.95	.20
2121	A825	28s gold & multi	3.50	.35
		Nos. 2113-2121 (9)	6.75	1.95

Miniature Sheet

Imperf

2122	A825	80s gold & multi	3.75	2.25

No. 2122 contains one stamp with simulated perforations.

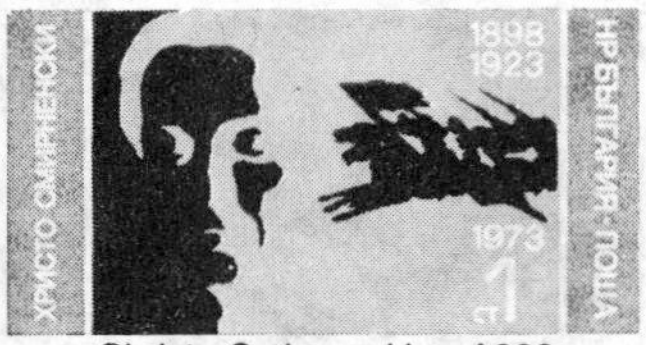

Christo Smirnenski — A826

1973, Sept. 29 Photo. *Perf. 12½*

2123	A826	1s multicolored	.20	.20
2124	A826	2s vio blue & multi	.20	.20

Christo Smirnenski (1898-1923), poet.

Human Rights Flame — A827

1973, Oct. 10

2125	A827	13s dk blue, red & gold	.30	.20

Universal Declaration of Human Rights, 25th anniv.

Type of 1970

History of Bulgaria: 1s, Tsar Theodor Svetoslav receiving Byzantine envoys. 2s, Tsar Mihail Shishman's army in battle with Byzantines. 3s, Tsar Ivan Alexander's victory at Russocastro. 4s, Patriarch Euthimius at the defense of Turnovo. 5s, Tsar Ivan Shishman leading horsemen against the Turks. 13s, Momchil attacking Turks at Umour. 18s, Tsar Ivan Stratsimir meeting King Sigismund's crusaders. 28s, The Boyars Balik, Theodor and Dobrotitsa, meeting ship bringing envoys from Anne of Savoy.

1973, Oct. 23 *Perf. 13*

Silver and Black Vignettes

2126	A741	1s olive bister	.20	.20
2127	A741	2s Prus blue	.20	.20
2128	A741	3s lilac	.20	.20
2129	A741	4s green	.20	.20
2130	A741	5s violet	.20	.20
2131	A741	13s orange & brn	.25	.20
2132	A741	18s olive green	.40	.20
2133	A741	28s yel brn & brn	1.10	.50
		Nos. 2126-2133 (8)	2.75	1.90

Finn Class — A828

Sailboats: 2s, Flying Dutchman. 3s, Soling class. 13s, Tempest class. 20s, Class 470. 40s, Tornado class.

1973, Oct. 29 Litho. *Perf. 13*

2134	A828	1s ultra & multi	.20	.20
2135	A828	2s green & multi	.20	.20
2136	A828	3s dk blue & multi	.20	.20
2137	A828	13s dull vio & multi	.30	.20
2138	A828	20s gray bl & multi	.60	.30
2139	A828	40s dk blue & multi	2.50	2.00
		Nos. 2134-2139 (6)	4.00	3.10

Value, set imperf. in changed colors, $10.

Village, by Bencho Obreshkov — A829

Paintings: 2s, Mother and Child, by Stoyan Venev. 3s, Rest (woman), by Tsenko Boyadjiev. 13s, Flowers in Vase, by Sirak Skitnik. 18s, Meri Kuneva (portrait), by Ilya Petrov. 40s, Winter in Plovdiv, by Zlatyu Boyadjiev. 13s, 18s, 40s, vert.

Perf. 12½x12, 12x12½

1973, Nov. 10

2140	A829	1s gold & multi	.20	.20
2141	A829	2s gold & multi	.20	.20
2142	A829	3s gold & multi	.20	.20
2143	A829	13s gold & multi	.25	.20
2144	A829	18s gold & multi	.40	.20
2145	A829	40s gold & multi	2.25	.75
		Nos. 2140-2145 (6)	3.50	1.75

Souvenir Sheet

Paintings by Stanislav Dospevski: a, Domnica Lambreva. b, Self-portrait. Both vert.

2146		Sheet of 2	2.75	1.75
a.		A829 50s gold & multi	.70	.50
b.		A829 50s gold & multi	.70	.50

Bulgarian paintings. No. 2146 commemorates the 150th birth anniv. of Stanislav Dospevski.

Souvenir Sheet

Soccer A830

1973, Dec. 10 Photo. *Perf. 13*

2147	A830	28s multicolored	4.00	3.50

No. 2147 sold for 1 l. Exists overprinted for Argentina 78.

Angel and Ornaments A831

Designs: 1s, Attendant facing right. 2s, Passover table and lamb. 3s, Attendant facing left. 8s, Abraham and ornaments. 13s, Adam and Eve. 28s, Expulsion from Garden of Eden.

1974, Jan. 21 Photo. *Perf. 13*

2148	A831	1s fawn, yel & brn	.20	.20
2149	A831	2s fawn, yel & brn	.20	.20
2150	A831	3s fawn, yel & brn	.20	.20
a.		Strip of 3, #2148-2150	.25	.20
2151	A831	5s slate grn & yel	.20	.20
2152	A831	8s slate grn & yel	.20	.20
a.		Pair, #2151-2152	.30	.25
2153	A831	13s lt brown, yel & ol	.30	.25
2154	A831	28s lt brown, yel & ol	.50	.30
a.		Pair, #2153-2154	.80	.35
		Nos. 2148-2154 (7)	1.80	1.55

Woodcarvings from Rozhen Monastery, 19th century.

Lenin, by N. Mirtchev — A832

18s, Lenin visiting Workers, by W. A. Serov.

1974, Jan. 28 Litho. *Perf. 12½x12*

2155	A832	2s ocher & multi	.20	.20
2156	A832	18s ocher & multi	.50	.25

50th anniversary of the death of Lenin.

1974, Jan. 28

Demeter Blagoev at Rally, by G. Kowachev.

2157	A832	2s multicolored	.20	.20

50th anniversary of the death of Demeter Blagoev, founder of Bulgarian Communist Party.

Domestic Animals A833

1974, Feb. 1 Photo. *Perf. 13*

2158	A833	1s Sheep	.20	.20
2159	A833	2s Goat	.20	.20
2160	A833	3s Pig	.20	.20
2161	A833	5s Cow	.20	.20
2162	A833	13s Buffalo cow	.30	.20
2163	A833	20s Horse	.80	.30
		Nos. 2158-2163 (6)	1.90	1.30

Comecon Emblem A834

1974, Feb. 11 Photo. *Perf. 13*

2164	A834	13s silver & multi	.40	.20

25th anniversary of the Council of Mutual Economic Assistance.

Soccer — A835

Designs: Various soccer action scenes.

1974, Mar. Photo. *Perf. 13*

2165	A835	1s dull green & multi	.20	.20
2166	A835	2s brt green & multi	.20	.20
2167	A835	3s slate grn & multi	.20	.20
2168	A835	13s olive & multi	.20	.20
2169	A835	28s blue grn & multi	.65	.40
2170	A835	40s emerald & multi	1.50	.70
		Nos. 2165-2170 (6)	2.95	1.90

Souvenir Sheet

2171	A835	1 l green & multi	3.00	1.60

World Soccer Championship, Munich, June 13-July 7. No. 2171 exists imperf.

Salt Production A836

Children's Paintings: 1s, Cosmic Research for Peaceful Purposes. 3s, Fire Dancers. 28s, Russian-Bulgarian Friendship (train and children). 60s, Spring (birds).

1974, Apr. 15 Photo. *Perf. 13*

2172	A836	1s lilac & multi	.20	.20
2173	A836	2s lt green & multi	.20	.20
2174	A836	3s blue & multi	.20	.20
2175	A836	28s slate & multi	1.75	.95
		Nos. 2172-2175 (4)	2.35	1.55

Souvenir Sheet

Imperf

2176	A836	60s blue & multi	2.25	1.75

Third World Youth Philatelic Exhibition, Sofia, May 23-30. No. 2176 contains one stamp with simulated perforations.

Folk Singers — A837

Designs: 2s, Folk dancers (men). 3s, Bagpiper and drummer. 5s, Wrestlers. 13s, Runners (women). 18s, Gymnast.

1974, Apr. 25 *Perf. 13*

2178	A837	1s vermilion & multi	.20	.20
2179	A837	2s orange brn & multi	.20	.20
2180	A837	3s brn red & multi	.20	.20
2181	A837	5s blue & multi	.20	.20
2182	A837	13s ultra & multi	.75	.25
2183	A837	18s violet bl & multi	.40	.20
		Nos. 2178-2183 (6)	1.95	1.25

4th Amateur Arts and Sports Festival

Flowers A838

1974, May Photo. *Perf. 13*

2184	A838	1s Aster	.20	.20
2185	A838	2s Petunia	.20	.20
2186	A838	3s Fuchsia	.20	.20
2187	A838	18s Tulip	.30	.20
2188	A838	20s Carnation	.60	.25
2189	A838	28s Pansy	1.60	.55
		Nos. 2184-2189 (6)	3.10	1.60

Souvenir Sheet

2190	A838	80s Sunflower	1.75	.85

Automobiles and Emblems — A839

1974, May 15 Photo. *Perf. 13*

2191	A839	13s multicolored	.30	.20

International Automobile Federation (FIA) Spring Congress, Sofia, May 20-24.

Old and New Buildings, UNESCO Emblem A840

1974, June 15

2192	A840	18s multicolored	.30	.20

UNESCO Executive Council, 94th Session, Varna.

Postrider A841

Designs: 18s, First Bulgarian mail coach. 28s, UPU Monument, Bern.

1974, Aug. 5

2193	A841	2s ocher, blk & vio	.20	.20
2194	A841	18s ocher, blk & grn	.40	.20

Souvenir Sheet

2195	A841	28s ocher, blk & bl	2.00	1.50

UPU cent. No. 2195 exists imperf.

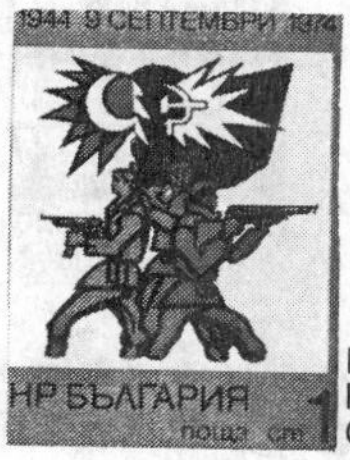

Pioneer and Komsomol Girl — A842

Designs: 2s, Pioneer and birds. 60s, Emblem with portrait of George Dimitrov.

1974, Aug. 12

2196	A842	1s green & multi	.20	.20
2197	A842	2s blue & multi	.20	.20

Souvenir Sheet

2198	A842	60s red & multi	1.60	1.10

30th anniversary of Dimitrov Pioneer Organization, Septemvrilche.

"Bulgarian Communist Party" — A843

Symbolic Designs: 2s, Russian liberators. 5s, Industrialization. 13s, Advanced agriculture and husbandry. 18s, Scientific and technical progress.

1974, Aug. 20

2199	A843	1s blue gray & multi	.20	.20
2200	A843	2s blue gray & multi	.20	.20
2201	A843	5s gray & multi	.20	.20
2202	A843	13s gray & multi	.25	.20
2203	A843	18s gray & multi	.35	.20
		Nos. 2199-2203 (5)	1.20	1.00

30th anniversary of the People's Republic.

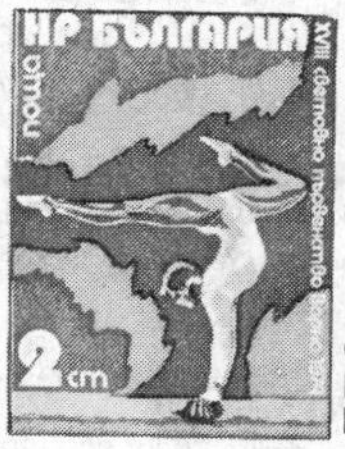

Gymnast on Parallel Bars — A844

Design: 13s, Gymnast on vaulting horse.

1974, Oct. 18 Photo. *Perf. 13*

2204	A844	2s multicolored	.20	.20
2205	A844	13s multicolored	.30	.20

18th Gymnastic Championships, Varna.

Souvenir Sheet

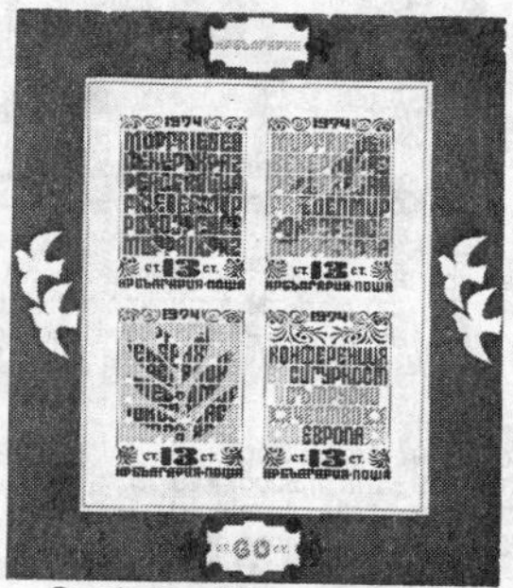

Symbols of Peace — A845

1974, Oct. 29 Photo. *Perf. 13*

2206	A845	Sheet of 4	2.50	1.10
a.		13s Doves	.20	.20
b.		13s Map of Europe	.20	.20
c.		13s Olive Branch	.20	.20
d.		13s Inscription	.20	.20

1974 European Peace Conference. "Peace" in various languages written on Nos. 2206a-2206c. Sold for 60s. Exists imperf.

Nib and Envelope — A846

1974, Nov. 20

2207	A846	2s yellow, blk & grn	.20	.20

Introduction of postal zone numbers.

Flowers A847

1974, Dec. 5

2208	A847	2s emerald & multi	.20	.20

St. Todor, Ceramic Icon A848

Fruit Tree Blossoms A849

Designs: 2s, Medallion, Veliko Turnovo. 3s, Carved capital. 5s, Silver bowl. 8s, Goblet. 13s, Lion's head finial. 18s, Gold plate with Cross. 28s, Breastplate with eagle.

1974, Dec. 18 Photo. *Perf. 13*

2209	A848	1s orange & multi	.20	.20
2210	A848	2s pink & multi	.20	.20
2211	A848	3s blue & multi	.20	.20
2212	A848	5s lt vio & multi	.20	.20
2213	A848	8s brown & multi	.20	.20
2214	A848	13s multicolored	.25	.20
2215	A848	18s red & multi	.30	.20
2216	A848	28s ultra & multi	1.00	.60
		Nos. 2209-2216 (8)	2.55	2.00

Art works from 9th-12th centuries.

1975, Jan. Photo. *Perf. 13*

2217	A849	1s Apricot	.20	.20
2218	A849	2s Apple	.20	.20
2219	A849	3s Cherry	.20	.20
2220	A849	19s Pear	.30	.20
2221	A849	28s Peach	.70	.20
		Nos. 2217-2221 (5)	1.60	1.00

Tree and Book A850

1975, Mar. 25 Photo. *Perf. 13*

2222	A850	2s gold & multi	.20	.20

Forestry High School, 50th anniversary.

Souvenir Sheet

Farmers' Activities (Woodcuts) — A851

1975, Mar. 25

2223	A851	Sheet of 4	.80	.50
a.		2s Farmer with ax and flag		
b.		5s Farmers on guard		
c.		13s Dancing couple		
d.		18s Woman picking fruit		

Bulgarian Agrarian Peoples Union, 75th anniv.

Michelangelo, Self-portrait A852

13s, Night, horiz. 18s, Day, horiz. Both designs after sculptures from Medici Tomb, Florence.

1975

2224 A852 2s plum & dk blue .20 .20
2225 A852 13s vio bl & plum .25 .20
2226 A852 18s brown & green .50 .20
Nos. 2224-2226 (3) .95 .60

Souvenir Sheet

2227 A852 2s olive & red 1.25 1.25

Michelangelo Buonarotti (1475-1564), Italian sculptor, painter and architect. No. 2227 issued to publicize ARPHILA 75 Intl. Phil. Exhib., Paris, June 6-16. Sheet sold for 60s. Issued: #2224-2226, 3/28; #2227, 3/31.

Souvenir Sheet

Spain No. 1 and España 75 Emblem A853

1975, Apr. 4

2228 A853 40s multicolored 3.75 3.00

Espana 75 International Philatelic Exhibition, Madrid, Apr. 4-13.

Gabrov Costume — A854

Regional Costumes: 3s, Trnsk. 5s, Vidin. 13s, Gocedelchev. 18s, Risen.

1975, Apr. Photo. *Perf. 13*

2229 A854 2s blue & multi .20 .20
2230 A854 3s emerald & multi .20 .20
2231 A854 5s orange & multi .20 .20
2232 A854 13s olive & multi .35 .20
2233 A854 18s multicolored .80 .25
Nos. 2229-2233 (5) 1.75 1.05

Red Star and Arrow — A855

Standard Kilogram and Meter — A856

Design: 13s, Dove and broken sword.

1975, May 9

2234 A855 2s red, blk & gold .20 .20
2235 A855 13s blue, blk & gold .30 .20

Victory over Fascism, 30th anniversary.

1975, May 9 *Perf. 13x13½*

2236 A856 13s silver, lil & blk .35 .20

Cent. of Intl, Meter Convention, Paris, 1875.

IWY Emblem, Woman's Head — A857

Ivan Vasov — A858

1975, May 20 Photo. *Perf. 13*

2237 A857 13s multicolored .35 .20

International Women's Year 1975.

1975, May

Design: 13s, Ivan Vasov, seated.

2238 A858 2s buff & multi .20 .20
2239 A858 13s gray & multi .30 .20

125th birth anniversary of Ivan Vasov.

Nikolov and Sava Kokarechkov — A859

Designs: 2s, Mitko Palaouzov and Ivan Vassilev. 5s, Nicolas Nakev and Stevtcho Kraychev. 13s, Ivanka Pachkoulova and Detelina Mintcheva.

1975, May 30

2240 A859 1s multicolored .20 .20
2241 A859 2s multicolored .20 .20
2242 A859 5s multicolored .20 .20
2243 A859 13s multicolored .28 .20
Nos. 2240-2243 (4) .88 .80

Teen-age resistance fighters, killed during World War II.

Mother Feeding Child, by John E. Millais — A861

Etchings: 2s, The Dead Daughter, by Goya. 3s, Reunion, by Beshkov. 13s, Seated Nude, by Renoir. 20s, Man in a Fur Hat, by Rembrandt. 40s, The Dream, by Daumier, horiz. 1 l, Temptation, by Dürer.

Photogravure and Engraved

1975, Aug. *Perf. 12x11½, 11½x12*

2248 A861 1s yel grn & multi .20 .20
2249 A861 2s orange & multi .20 .20
2250 A861 3s lilac & multi .20 .20
2251 A861 13s lt blue & multi .25 .20
2252 A861 20s ocher & multi .40 .20
2253 A861 40s rose & multi 1.10 .30
Nos. 2248-2253 (6) 2.35 1.30

Souvenir Sheet

2254 A861 1 l emerald & multi 2.00 1.25

World Graphics Exhibition.

Letter "Z" from 12th Century Manuscript A862

Initials from Illuminated Manuscripts: 2s, "B" from 17th cent. prayerbook. 3s, "V" from 16th cent. Bouhovo Gospel. 8s, "B" from 14th cent. Turnovo collection. 13s, "V" from Dobreisho's Gospel, 13th cent. 18s, "E" from 11th cent. Enina book of the Apostles.

1975, Aug. Litho. *Perf. 11½*

2255 A862 1s multicolored .20 .20
2256 A862 2s multicolored .20 .20
2257 A862 3s multicolored .20 .20
2258 A862 8s multicolored .20 .20
2259 A862 13s multicolored .25 .20
2260 A862 18s multicolored .65 .20
Nos. 2255-2260 (6) 1.70 1.20

Bulgarian art.

Whimsical Globe — A863

1975, Aug. Photo. *Perf. 13*

2261 A863 2s multicolored .20 .20

Festival of Humor and Satire.

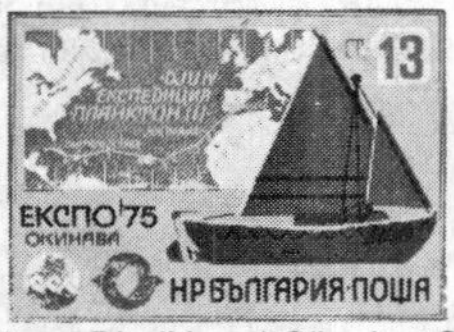

Lifeboat Dju IV and Gibraltar-Cuba Route — A864

1975, Aug. 5 Photo. *Perf. 13*

2262 A864 13s multicolored .25 .20

Oceanexpo 75, 1st Intl. Ocean Exhib., Okinawa, July 20, 1975-Jan. 18, 1976.

Sts. Cyril and Methodius A865

Sts. Constantine and Helena A866

St. Sophia Church, Sofia, Woodcut by V. Zahriev — A867

1975, Aug. 21

2263 A865 2s ver, yel & brn .20 .20
2264 A866 13s green, yel & brn .25 .20

Souvenir Sheet

2265 A867 50s orange & multi 1.25 .80

Balkanphila V, philatelic exhibition, Sofia, Sept. 27-Oct. 5.

Peace Dove and Map of Europe — A868

1975, Nov. Photo. *Perf. 13*

2266 A868 18s ultra, rose & yel .45 .25

European Security and Cooperation Conference, Helsinki, Finland, July 30-Aug. 1. No. 2266 printed in sheets of 5 stamps and 4 labels, arranged checkerwise.

Acherontia Atropos A869

Designs: Moths.

1975 Photo. *Perf. 13*

2267 A869 1s *shown* .20 .20
2268 A869 2s *Daphnis nerii* .20 .20
2269 A869 3s *Smerinthus ocellata* .20 .20
2270 A869 10s *Deilephila nicea* .20 .20
2271 A869 13s *Choerocampa elpenor* .25 .20
2272 A869 18s *Macroglossum fuciformis* .90 .25
Nos. 2267-2272 (6) 1.95 1.25

Soccer Player — A870

1975, Sept. 21

2273 A870 2s multicolored .20 .20

8th Inter-Toto (soccer pool) Soccer Championships, Varna.

Constantine's Rebellion Against the Turks, 1403 — A871

Designs (Woodcuts): 2s, Campaign of Vladislav III, 1443-1444. 3s, Battles of Turnovo, 1598 and 1686. 10s, Battle of Liprovsko, 1688. 13s, Guerrillas, 17th century. 18s, Return of exiled peasants.

1975, Nov. 27 Photo. *Perf. 13*

2274 A871 1s bister, grn & blk .20 .20
2275 A871 2s blue, car & blk .20 .20
2276 A871 3s yellow, lil & blk .20 .20
2277 A871 10s orange, grn & blk .20 .20
2278 A871 13s green, lil & blk .25 .20
2279 A871 18s pink, grn & blk .45 .20
Nos. 2274-2279 (6) 1.50 1.20

Bulgarian history.

Red Cross and First Aid — A872

Design: 13s, Red Cross and dove.

1975, Dec. 1

2280	A872	2s red brn, red & blk	.20	.20
2281	A872	13s bl grn, red & blk	.25	.20

90th anniversary of Bulgarian Red Cross.

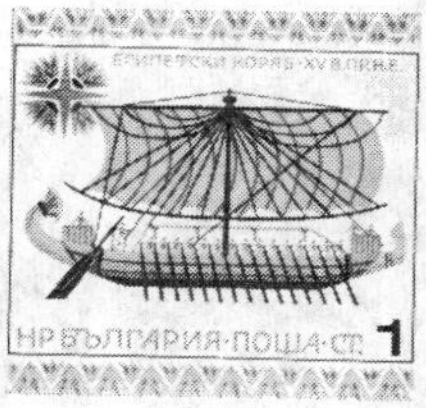

Egyptian Galley A873

Historic Ships: 2s, Phoenician galley. 3s, Greek trireme. 5s, Roman galley. 13s, Viking longship. 18s, Venetian galley.

1975, Dec. 15 Photo. *Perf. 13*

2282	A873	1s multicolored	.20	.20
2283	A873	2s multicolored	.20	.20
2284	A873	3s multicolored	.20	.20
2285	A873	5s multicolored	.20	.20
2286	A873	13s multicolored	.30	.20
2287	A873	18s multicolored	.60	.20
		Nos. 2282-2287 (6)	1.70	1.20

See Nos. 2431-2436, 2700-2705.

Souvenir Sheet

Ethnographical Museum, Plovdiv — A874

1975, Dec. 17

2288		Sheet of 3	4.50	2.50
a.		A874 80s green, yellow & dark brown	1.25	.65

European Architectural Heritage Year. No. 2288 contains 3 stamps and 3 labels showing stylized bird.

Dobri Hristov — A875

1975, Dec. *Perf. 13*

2289	A875	5s brt green, yel & brn	.20	.20

Dobri Hristov, musician, birth centenary.

United Nations Emblem — A876

1975, Dec.

2290	A876	13s gold, blk & mag	.20	.20

United Nations, 30th anniversary.

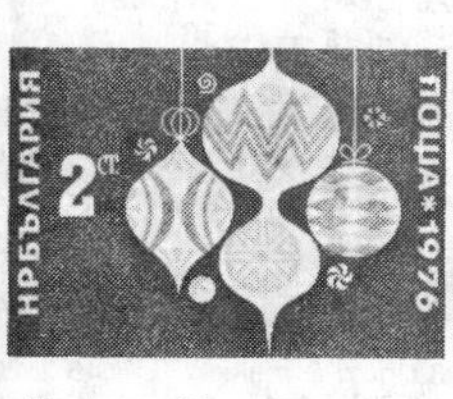

Glass Ornaments A877

Design: 13s, Peace dove, decorated ornament.

1975, Dec. 22 Photo. *Perf. 13*

2291	A877	2s brt violet & multi	.20	.20
2292	A877	13s gray & multi	.20	.20

New Year 1976.

Downhill Skiing — A878

Designs (Winter Olympic Games Emblem and): 2s, Cross country skier, vert. 3s, Ski jump. 13s, Biathlon, vert. 18s, Ice hockey, vert. 23s, Speed skating, vert. 80s, Figure skating, pair, vert.

1976, Jan. 30 *Perf. 13½*

2293	A878	1s silver & multi	.20	.20
2294	A878	2s silver & multi	.20	.20
2295	A878	3s silver & multi	.20	.20
2296	A878	13s silver & multi	.25	.20
2297	A878	18s silver & multi	.30	.20
2298	A878	23s silver & multi	.80	.30
		Nos. 2293-2298 (6)	1.95	1.30

Souvenir Sheet

2299	A878	80s silver & multi	1.60	1.10

12th Winter Olympic Games, Innsbruck, Austria, Feb. 4-15.

Electric Streetcar, Sofia, 1976 — A879

Design: 13s, Streetcar and trailer, 1901.

1976, Jan. 12 Photo. *Perf. 13½x13*

2300	A879	2s gray & multi	.20	.20
2301	A879	13s gray & multi	.40	.20

75th anniversary of Sofia streetcars.

Stylized Bird — A880

Designs: 5s, Dates "1976" and "1956" and star. 13s, Hammer and sickle. 50s, George Dimitrov.

1976, Mar. 1 *Perf. 13*

2302	A880	2s gold & multi	.20	.20
2303	A880	5s gold & multi	.20	.20
2304	A880	13s gold & multi	.25	.20
		Nos. 2302-2304 (3)	.65	.60

Souvenir Sheet

2305	A880	50s gold & multi	1.00	.45

11th Bulgarian Communist Party Congress.

A. G. Bell and Telephone, 1876 A881

1976, Mar. 10

2306	A881	18s dk brn, yel & ocher	.25	.20

Centenary of first telephone call by Alexander Graham Bell, Mar. 10, 1876.

Mute Swan — A882

Waterfowl: 2s, Ruddy shelduck. 3s, Common shelduck. 5s, Garganey teal. 13s, Mallard. 18s, Red-crested pochard.

1976, Mar. 27 Litho. *Perf. 11½*

2307	A882	1s vio bl & multi	.20	.20
2308	A882	2s yel grn & multi	.20	.20
2309	A882	3s blue & multi	.20	.20
2310	A882	5s multicolored	.25	.20
2311	A882	13s purple & multi	.65	.20
2312	A882	18s green & multi	.90	.20
		Nos. 2307-2312 (6)	2.40	1.20

Guerrillas — A883

Designs (Woodcuts by Stoev): 2s, Peasants with rifle and proclamation. 5s, Raina Knaginia with horse and guerrilla. 13s, Insurgents with cherrywood cannon.

1976, Apr. 5 Photo. *Perf. 13*

2313	A883	1s multicolored	.20	.20
2314	A883	2s multicolored	.20	.20
2315	A883	5s multicolored	.20	.20
2316	A883	13s multicolored	.25	.20
		Nos. 2313-2316 (4)	.85	.80

Centenary of uprising against Turkey.

Guard and Dog A884

13s, Men on horseback, observation tower.

1976, May 15

2317	A884	2s multicolored	.20	.20
2318	A884	13s multicolored	.20	.20

30th anniversary of Border Guards.

Construction Worker — A885

1976, May 20

2319	A885	2s multicolored	.20	.20

Young Workers Brigade, 30th anniversary.

Busludja, Bas-relief A886

AES Complex A887

Design: 5s, Memorial building.

1976, May 28 Photo. *Perf. 13*

2320	A886	2s green & multi	.20	.20
2321	A886	5s violet bl & multi	.20	.20

First Congress of Bulgarian Social Democratic Party, 85th anniversary.

1976, Apr. 7

Designs: 8s, Factory. 10s, Apartment houses. 13s, Refinery. 20s, Hydroelectric station.

2322	A887	5s green	.20	.20
2323	A887	8s maroon	.20	.20
2324	A887	10s green	.20	.20
2325	A887	13s violet	.30	.20
2326	A887	20s brt green	.40	.20
		Nos. 2322-2326 (5)	1.30	1.00

Five-year plan accomplishments.

Children Playing Around Table — A888

Kindergarten Children: 2s, with doll carriage & hobby horse. 5s, playing ball. 23s, in costume.

1976, June 15

2327	A888	1s green & multi	.20	.20
2328	A888	2s yellow & multi	.20	.20
2329	A888	5s lilac & multi	.20	.20
2330	A888	23s rose & multi	.40	.20
		Nos. 2327-2330 (4)	1.00	.80

Demeter Blagoev — A889

Christo Botev — A890

1976, May 28

2331	A889	13s bluish blk, red & gold	.25	.20

Demeter Blagoev (1856-1924), writer, political leader, 120th birth anniversary.

1976, May 25

2332	A890	13s ocher & slate grn	.25	.20

Christo Botev (1848-1876), poet, death centenary. Printed se-tenant with yellow green and ocher label, inscribed with poem.

Boxing, Montreal Olympic Emblem — A891

Belt Buckle — A892

Designs (Montreal Olympic Emblem): 1s, Wrestling, horiz. 3s, 1 l, Weight lifting. 13s, One-man kayak. 18s, Woman gymnast. 28s, Woman diver. 40s, Woman runner.

1976, June 25

2333	A891	1s orange & multi	.20	.20
2334	A891	2s multicolored	.20	.20
2335	A891	3s lilac & multi	.20	.20
2336	A891	13s multicolored	.20	.20
2337	A891	18s multicolored	.30	.20

2338 A891 28s blue & multi .40 .20
2339 A891 40s lemon & multi .75 .30
Nos. 2333-2339 (7) 2.25 1.50

Souvenir Sheet

2340 A891 1 l orange & multi 1.60 1.10

21st Olympic Games, Montreal, Canada, July 17-Aug. 1.

1976, July 30 Photo. *Perf. 13*

Thracian Art (8th-4th Centuries): 2s, Brooch. 3s, Mirror handle. 5s, Helmet cheek cover. 13s, Gold ornament. 18s, Lion's head (harness decoration). 20s, Knee guard. 28s, Jeweled pendant.

2341 A892 1s brown & multi .20 .20
2342 A892 2s blue & multi .20 .20
2343 A892 3s multicolored .20 .20
2344 A892 5s claret & multi .20 .20
2345 A892 13s purple & multi .25 .20
2346 A892 18s multicolored .30 .20
2347 A892 20s multicolored .40 .20
2348 A892 28s multicolored .60 .20
Nos. 2341-2348 (8) 2.35 1.60

Souvenir Sheet

Composite of Bulgarian Stamp Designs A893

1976, June 5

2349 A893 50s red & multi 1.60 .65

International Federation of Philately (F.I.P.), 50th anniversary and 12th Congress.

Partisans at Night, by Ilya Petrov — A894

Paintings: 5s, Old Town, by Tsanko Lavenov. 13s, Seated Woman, by Petrov, vert. 18s, Seated Boy, by Petrov, vert. 28s, Old Plovdiv, by Lavenov, vert. 80s, Ilya Petrov, self-portrait, vert.

1976, Aug. 11 Photo. *Perf. 14*

2350 A894 2s multicolored .20 .20
2351 A894 5s multicolored .20 .20
2352 A894 13s ultra & multi .30 .20
2353 A894 18s multicolored .45 .20
2354 A894 28s multicolored .65 .20
Nos. 2350-2354 (5) 1.80 1.00

Souvenir Sheet

2354A A894 80s multicolored 1.25 .95

Souvenir Sheet

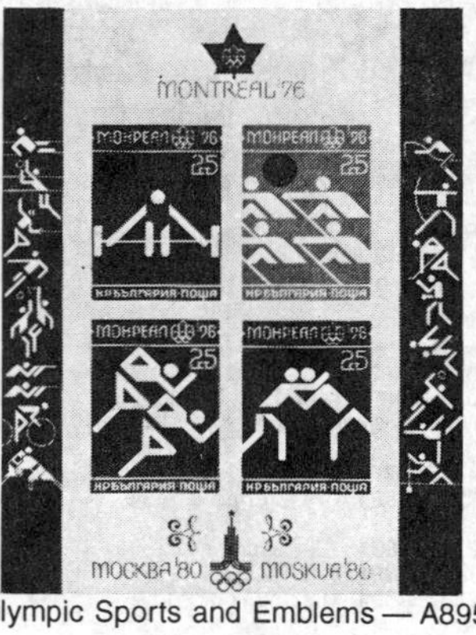

Olympic Sports and Emblems — A895

1976, Sept. 6 Photo. *Perf. 13*

2355 A895 Sheet of 4 1.60 1.00
a. 25s Weight Lifting .35 .20
b. 25s Rowing .35 .20
c. 25s Running .35 .20
d. 25s Wrestling .35 .20

Medalists, 21st Olympic Games, Montreal.

Souvenir Sheet

Fresco and UNESCO Emblem — A896

1976, Dec. 3

2356 A896 50s red & multi 1.25 .55

UNESCO, 30th anniv.

"The Pianist" by Jendov — A897

Fish and Hook — A898

Designs (Caricatures by Jendov): 5s, Imperialist "Trick or Treat." 13s, The Leader, 1931.

1976, Sept. 30 Photo. *Perf. 13*

2357 A897 2s green & multi .20 .20
2358 A897 5s purple & multi .20 .20
2359 A897 13s magenta & multi .30 .20
Nos. 2357-2359 (3) .70 .60

Alex Jendov (1901-1953), caricaturist.

1976, Sept. 21 Photo. *Perf. 13*

2360 A898 5s multicolored .20 .20

World Sport Fishing Congress, Varna.

St. Theodore A899

Frescoes: 3s, St. Paul. 5s, St. Joachim. 13s, Melchizedek. 19s, St. Porphyrius. 28s, Queen. 1 l, The Last Supper.

1976, Oct. 4 Litho. *Perf. 12x12½*

2361 A899 2s gold & multi .20 .20
2362 A899 3s gold & multi .20 .20
2363 A899 5s gold & multi .20 .20
2364 A899 13s gold & multi .30 .20
2365 A899 19s gold & multi .35 .20
2366 A899 28s gold & multi .65 .20
Nos. 2361-2366 (6) 1.90 1.20

Miniature Sheet

Perf. 12

2367 A899 1 l gold & multi 1.50 .95

Zemen Monastery frescoes, 14th cent.

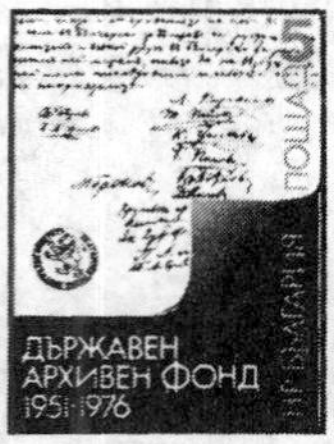

Document A900

1976, Oct. 5

2368 A900 5s multicolored .20 .20

State Archives, 25th anniversary.

Cinquefoil — A901

1976, Oct. 14 Photo. *Perf. 13*

2369 A901 1s Chestnut .20 .20
2370 A901 2s shown .20 .20
2371 A901 5s Holly .20 .20
2372 A901 8s Yew .20 .20
2373 A901 13s Daphne .30 .20
2374 A901 23s Judas tree .60 .20
Nos. 2369-2374 (6) 1.70 1.20

Dimitri Polianov — A902

1976, Nov. 19

2375 A902 2s dk purple & ocher .20 .20

Dimitri Polianov (1876-1953), poet.

Christo Botev, by Zlatyu Boyadjiev A903

Paintings: 2s, Partisan Carrying Cherrywood Cannon, by Ilya Petrov. 3s, "Necklace of Immortality" (man's portrait), by Detchko Uzunov. 13s, "April 1876," by Georgi Popoff. 18s, Partisans, by Stoyan Venev. 60s, The Oath, by Svetlin Ruseff.

1976, Dec. 8

2376 A903 1s bister & multi .20 .20
2377 A903 2s bister & multi .20 .20
2378 A903 3s bister & multi .20 .20
2379 A903 13s bister & multi .25 .20
2380 A903 18s bister & multi .35 .20
Nos. 2376-2380 (5) 1.20 1.00

Souvenir Sheet

Imperf

2381 A903 60s gold & multi .95 .55

Uprising against Turkish rule, centenary.

"Pollution" and Tree A904

Design: 18s, "Pollution" obscuring sun.

1976, Nov. 10 *Perf. 13*

2382 A904 2s ultra & multi .20 .20
2383 A904 18s blue & multi .30 .20

Protection of the environment.

Congress Emblem — A904a

Flags — A904b

1976, Nov. 28 Photo. *Perf. 13*

2384 A904a 2s multicolored .20 .20
2384A A904b 13s multicolored .25 .20

33rd BSIS Cong. (Bulgarian Socialist Party).

Tobacco Workers, by Stajkov A905

Paintings by Stajkov: 2s, View of Melnik. 13s, Shipbuilder.

1976, Dec. 16 Photo. *Perf. 13*

2385 A905 1s multicolored .20 .20
2386 A905 2s multicolored .20 .20
2387 A905 13s multicolored .30 .20
Nos. 2385-2387 (3) .70 .60

Veselin Stajkov (1906-1970), painter.

Snowflake — A906

1976, Dec. 20

2388 A906 2s silver & multi .20 .20

New Year 1977.

Zachary Stoyanov (1851-1889), Historian — A907

1976, Dec. 30

2389 A907 2s multicolored .20 .20

Bronze Coin of Septimus Severus — A908

Roman Coins: 2s, 13s, 18s, Bronze coins of Caracalla, diff. 23s, Copper coin of Diocletian.

1977, Jan. 28 Photo. *Perf. 13½x13*

2390 A908 1s gold & multi .20 .20
2391 A908 2s gold & multi .20 .20
2392 A908 13s gold & multi .20 .20
2393 A908 18s gold & multi .25 .20
2394 A908 23s gold & multi .45 .20
Nos. 2390-2394 (5) 1.30 1.00

Coins struck in Serdica (modern Sofia).

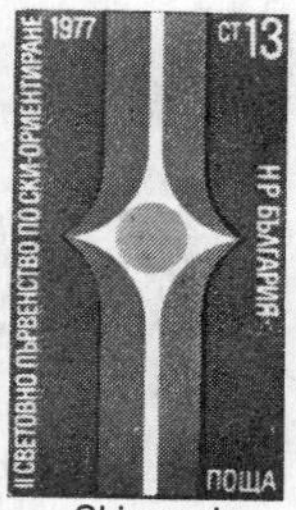

Skis and Compass
A909

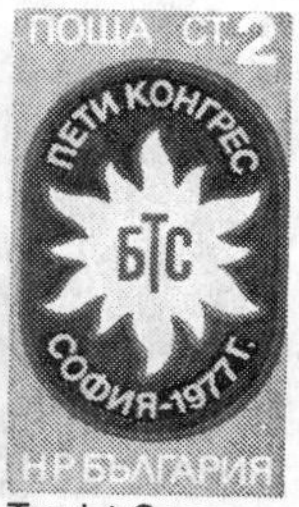

Tourist Congress Emblem
A910

1977, Feb. 14 ***Perf. 13***
2395 A909 13s ultra, red & lt bl .25 .20

2nd World Ski Orienteering Championships.

1977, Feb. 24 **Photo.** ***Perf. 13***
2396 A910 2s multicolored .20 .20

5th Congress of Bulgarian Tourist Organization.

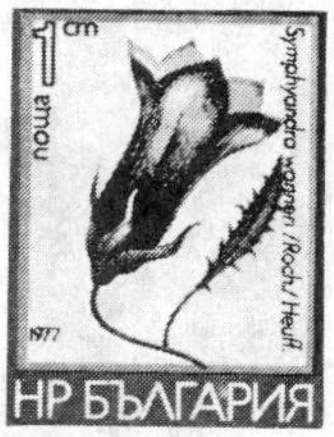

Bellflower — A911

Designs: Various bellflowers.

1977, Mar. 2

2397	A911	1s yellow & multi	.20	.20
2398	A911	2s rose & multi	.20	.20
2399	A911	3s lt blue & multi	.20	.20
2400	A911	13s multicolored	.30	.20
2401	A911	43s yellow & multi	1.10	.30
		Nos. 2397-2401 (5)	2.00	1.10

Vasil Kolarov — A912

Union Congress Emblem — A913

1977, Mar. 21 **Photo.** ***Perf. 13***
2402 A912 2s blue & black .20 .20

Vasil Kolarov (1877-1950), politician.

1977, Mar. 25
2403 A913 2s multicolored .20 .20

8th Bulgarian Trade Union Cong., Apr. 4-7.

Wolf
A914

Wild Animals: 2s, Red fox. 10s, Weasel. 13s, European wildcat. 23s, Jackal.

1977, May 16 **Litho.** ***Perf. 12½x12***

2404	A914	1s multicolored	.20	.20
2405	A914	2s multicolored	.20	.20
2406	A914	10s multicolored	.20	.20
2407	A914	13s multicolored	.35	.20
2408	A914	23s multicolored	.60	.20
		Nos. 2404-2408 (5)	1.55	1.00

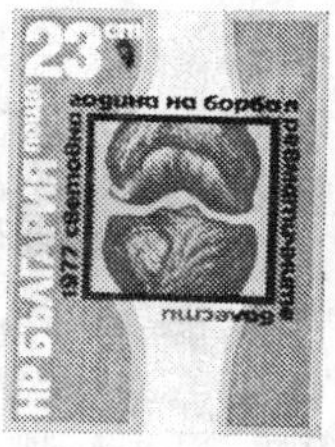

Diseased Knee — A915

1977, Mar. 31 **Photo.** ***Perf. 13***
2409 A915 23s multicolored .40 .15

World Rheumatism Year.

Writers' Congress Emblem
A916

1977, June 7
2410 A916 23s lt bl & yel grn .65 .20

International Writers Congress: "Peace, the Hope of the Planet." No. 2410 printed in sheets of 8 stamps and 4 labels with signatures of participating writers.

Old Testament Trinity, Sofia, 16th Century
A917

Icons: 1s, St. Nicholas, Nessebur, 13th cent. 3s, Annunciation, Royal Gates, Veliko Turnovo, 16th cent. 5s, Christ Enthroned, Nessebur, 17th cent. 13s, St. Nicholas, Elena, 18th cent. 23s, Presentation of the Virgin, Rila Monastery, 18th cent. 35s, Virgin and Child, Tryavna, 19th cent. 40s, St. Demetrius on Horseback, Provadia, 19th cent. 1 l, The 12 Holidays, Rila Monastery, 18th cent.

1977, May 10 **Photo.** ***Perf. 13***

2411	A917	1s black & multi	.20	.20
2412	A917	2s green & multi	.20	.20
2413	A917	3s brown & multi	.20	.20
2414	A917	5s blue & multi	.20	.20
2415	A917	13s olive & multi	.30	.20
2416	A917	23s maroon & multi	.50	.20
2417	A917	35s green & multi	.80	.25
2418	A917	40s dp ultra & multi	1.10	.40
		Nos. 2411-2418 (8)	3.50	1.85

Miniature Sheet

Imperf

2419 A917 1 l gold & multi 2.25 1.10

Bulgarian icons. See Nos. 2615-2619.

Souvenir Sheet

St. Cyril
A918

1977, June 7 **Photo.** ***Perf. 13***
2420 A918 1 l gold & multi 1.75 .90

1150th anniversary of the birth of St. Cyril (827-869), reputed inventor of Cyrillic alphabet.

Congress Emblem — A919

1977, May 9
2421 A919 2s red, gold & grn .20 .20

13th Komsomol Congress.

Newspaper Masthead — A920

1977, June 3 **Photo.** ***Perf. 13***
2422 A920 2s multicolored .20 .20

Cent. of Bulgarian daily press and 50th anniv. of Rabotnichesko Delo newspaper.

Patriotic Front Emblem — A921

Weight Lifting — A922

1977, May 26
2423 A921 2s gold & multi .20 .20

8th Congress of Patriotic Front.

1977, June 15
2424 A922 13s dp brown & multi .25 .20

European Youth Weight Lifting Championships, Sofia, June.

Women Basketball Players — A923

1977, June 15 ***Perf. 13***
2425 A923 23s multicolored .50 .20

7th European Women's Basketball Championships.

Wrestling — A924

Designs (Games Emblem and): 13s, Running. 23s, Basketball. 43s, Women's gymnastics.

1977, Apr. 15

2426	A924	2s multicolored	.20	.20
2427	A924	13s multicolored	.20	.20
2428	A924	23s multicolored	.40	.20
2429	A924	43s multicolored	.70	.25
		Nos. 2426-2429 (4)	1.50	.85

UNIVERSIADE '77, University Games, Sofia, Aug. 18-27.

TV Tower, Berlin — A925

1977, Aug. 12 **Litho.** ***Perf. 13***
2430 A925 25s blue & dk blue .50 .20

SOZPHILEX 77 Philatelic Exhibition, Berlin, Aug. 19-28.

Ship Type of 1975

Historic Ships: 1s, Hansa cog. 2s, Santa Maria, caravelle. 3s, Golden Hind, frigate. 12s, Santa Catherina, carrack. 13s, La Corone, galleon. 43s, Mediterranean galleass.

1977, Aug. 29 **Photo.** ***Perf. 13***

2431	A873	1s multicolored	.20	.20
2432	A873	2s multicolored	.20	.20
2433	A873	3s multicolored	.20	.20
2434	A873	12s multicolored	.25	.20
2435	A873	13s multicolored	.25	.20
2436	A873	43s multicolored	1.00	.25
		Nos. 2431-2436 (6)	2.10	1.25

Ivan Vasov National Theater
A926

Buildings, Sofia: 13s, Party Headquarters. 23s, House of the People's Army. 30s, Clement Ochrida University. 80s, National Gallery. 1 l, National Assembly.

1977, Aug. 30 **Photo.** ***Perf. 13***

2437	A926	12s red, *gray*	.20	.20
2438	A926	13s red brn, *gray*	.20	.20
2439	A926	23s blue, *gray*	.30	.20
2440	A926	30s olive, *gray*	.40	.20
2441	A926	80s violet, *gray*	1.10	.40
2442	A926	1 l claret, *gray*	1.40	.50
		Nos. 2437-2442 (6)	3.60	1.70

Map of Europe
A927

1977, June 10
2443 A927 23s brown, bl & grn .40 .20

21st Congress of the European Organization for Quality Control, Varna.

Union of Earth and Water, by Rubens
A928

Rubens Paintings: 23s, Venus and Adonis. 40s, Pastoral Scene (man and woman). 1 l, Portrait of a Lady in Waiting.

1977, Sept. 23 Litho. *Perf. 12*

2444	A928	13s gold & multi	.45	.20
2445	A928	23s gold & multi	.65	.20
2446	A928	40s gold & multi	1.10	.25
		Nos. 2444-2446 (3)	2.20	.65

Souvenir Sheet

2447	A928	1 l gold & multi	2.50	1.60

Peter Paul Rubens (1577-1640).

George Dimitrov A929

1977, June 17 Photo. *Perf. 13*

2448	A929	13s red & deep claret	.35	.20

George Dimitrov (1882-1947).

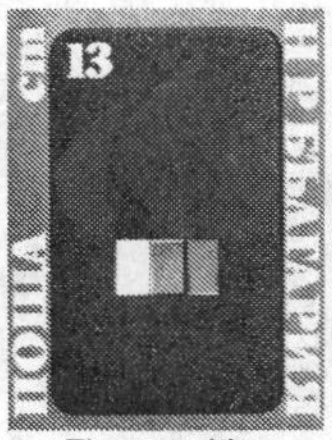

Flame with Star — A930

Smart Pete on Donkey, by Ilya Beshkov — A931

1977, May 17

2449	A930	13s gold & multi	.25	.20

3rd Bulgarian Culture Congress.

1977, May 19

2450	A931	2s multicolored	.20	.20

11th National Festival of Humor and Satire Gabrovo.

Elin Pelin — A932

Dr. Pirogov — A934

13th Canoe World Championships — A933

Albena, Black Sea A933a

Writers: 2s, Pelin (Dimitur Ivanov Stojanov, (1877-1949). 5s, Peju K. Jaworov (1878-1914).

Artists: 13s, Boris Angelushev (1902-1966), 23s, Ceno Todorov (Ceno Todorov Dikov, 1877-1953). Each printed with label showing scenes from authors' works or illustrations by the artists.

1977, Aug. 26 Photo. *Perf. 13*

2451	A932	2s gold & brown	.20	.20
2452	A932	5s gold & gray grn	.20	.20
2453	A932	13s gold & claret	.25	.20
2454	A932	23s gold & blue	.45	.20
		Nos. 2451-2454 (4)	1.10	.80

1977, Sept. 1 Photo. *Perf. 13*

2455	A933	2s shown	.20	.20
2456	A933	23s 2-man canoe	.40	.20

1977, Oct. 5 Photo. *Perf. 13*

2456A	A933a	35s shown	.65	.25
2456B	A933a	43s Rila Monastery	.80	.30

Sheet contains 4 each plus label.

1977, Oct. 14 Photo. *Perf. 13*

2457	A934	13s olive, ocher & brown	.25	.20

Centenary of visit by Russian physician N. J. Pirogov during war of liberation from Turkey.

Peace Decree, 1917 A935

Old Soldier with Grandchild A936

13s, Lenin, 1917. 23s, "1917" as a flame.

1977, Oct. 21

2458	A935	2s black, buff & red	.20	.20
2459	A935	13s multicolored	.25	.20
2460	A935	23s multicolored	.45	.20
		Nos. 2458-2460 (3)	.90	.60

60th anniv. of Russian October Revolution.

1977, Sept. 30

Designs (Festival Posters): 13s, "The Bugler." 23s, Liberation Monument, Sofia (detail). 25s, Samara flag.

2461	A936	2s multicolored	.20	.20
2462	A936	13s multicolored	.25	.20
2463	A936	23s multicolored	.40	.20
2464	A936	25s multicolored	.50	.25
		Nos. 2461-2464 (4)	1.35	.85

Liberation from Turkish rule, centenary.

Souvenir Sheet

Games' and Sports Emblems — A937

1977, Aug. 10 Photo. *Perf. 13½x13*

2465	A937	1 l multicolored	1.50	1.25

University Games '77, Sofia.

Conference Building — A938

1977, Sept. 12 *Perf. 13½*

2466	A938	23s multicolored	.40	.20

64th Interparliamentary Union Conference, Sofia.

Bulgarian Worker's Newspaper, Anniversaries A939

1977, Sept. 12 Photo. *Perf. 13*

2467	A939	2s yel grn, blk & red	.20	.20

Ornament A940

New Year 1978: 13s, Different ornament.

1977, Dec. 1

2468	A940	2s gold & multi	.20	.20
2469	A940	13s silver & multi	.25	.20

Railroad Bridge — A941

1977, Nov. 9

2470	A941	13s green, yel & gray	.30	.20

Transport Organization, 50th anniversary.

A942

A943

1977, Nov. 15

2471	A942	8s gold & vio brn	.20	.20

Petko Ratchev Slaveikov (1827-95), poet, birth sesquicentennial. No. 2471 printed in sheets of 8 stamps and 8 labels in 4 alternating vertical rows.

1978, Jan. 30 Photo. *Perf. 13*

Designs: 23s, Soccer player and Games' emblem. 50s, Soccer players.

2472	A943	13s multicolored	.25	.20
2473	A943	23s multicolored	.45	.20

Souvenir Sheet

2474	A943	50s ultra & multi	1.00	.85

11th World Cup Soccer Championship, Argentina, June 1-25.

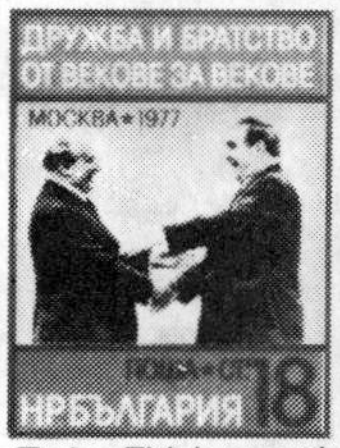

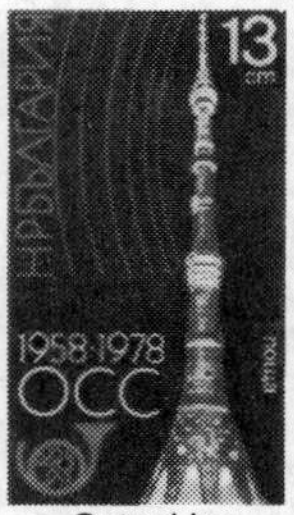

Todor Zhivkov and Leonid I. Brezhnev — A944

Ostankino Tower, Moscow, Bulgarian Post Emblem — A945

1977, Sept. 7 Photo. *Perf. 13*

2475	A944	18s gold, car & brn	.30	.20

Bulgarian-Soviet Friendship. No. 2475 issued in sheets of 3 stamps and 3 labels.

1978, Mar. 1

2476	A945	13s multicolored	.25	.20

20th anniversary of the Comecon Postal Organization (Council of Mutual Economic Assistance).

Leo Tolstoy A946

Shipka Pass Monument A947

5s, Fedor Dostoevski. 13s, Ivan Sergeevich Turgenev. 23s, Vasili Vasilievich Vershchagin. 25s, Giuseppe Garibaldi. 35s, Victor Hugo.

1978, Mar. 28 Photo. *Perf. 13*

2477	A946	2s yellow & dk grn	.20	.20
2478	A946	5s lemon & brown	.20	.20
2479	A946	13s tan & sl grn	.25	.20
2480	A946	23s gray & vio brn	.35	.20
2481	A946	25s yel grn & blk	.40	.20
2482	A946	35s lt bl & vio bl	.80	.40
		Nos. 2477-2482 (6)	2.20	1.40

Souvenir Sheet

2483	A947	50s multicolored	.80	.60

Bulgaria's liberation from Ottoman rule, cent.

Bulgarian and Russian Colors A948

1978, Mar. 18

2484	A948	2s multicolored	.20	.20

30th anniv. of Russo-Bulgarian co-operation.

Heart and WHO Emblem A949

1978, May 12

2485	A949	23s gray, red & org	.30	.20

World Health Day, fight against hypertension.

Goddess A950

Ceramics (2nd-4th Centuries) and Exhibition Emblem: 5s, Mask of bearded man. 13s, Vase. 23s, Vase. 35s, Head of Silenus. 53s, Cock.

1978, Apr. 26

2486	A950	2s green & multi	.20	.20
2487	A950	5s multicolored	.20	.20
2488	A950	13s multicolored	.25	.20
2489	A950	23s multicolored	.50	.20
2490	A950	35s multicolored	.75	.25
2491	A950	53s carmine & multi	1.25	.30
		Nos. 2486-2491 (6)	3.15	1.35

Philaserdica Philatelic Exhibition.

Nikolai Roerich, by Svyatoslav Roerich — A951

"Mind and Matter," by Andrei Nikolov — A952

1978, Apr. 5

2492	A951	8s multicolored	.20	.20
2493	A952	13s multicolored	.30	.20

Nikolai K. Roerich (1874-1947) and Andrei Nikolov (1878-1959), artists.

Bulgarian Flag and Red Star — A953

1978, Apr. 18

2494	A953	2s vio blue & multi	.20	.20

Bulgarian Communist Party Congress.

Young Man, by Albrecht Dürer A954

Paintings: 23s, Bathsheba at Fountain, by Rubens. 25s, Portrait of a Man, by Hans Holbein the Younger. 35s, Rembrandt and Saskia, by Rembrandt. 43s, Lady in Mourning, by Tintoretto. 60s, Old Man with Beard, by Rembrandt. 80s, Knight in Armor, by Van Dyck.

1978, June 19 Photo. *Perf. 13*

2495	A954	13s multicolored	.20	.20
2496	A954	23s multicolored	.30	.20
2497	A954	25s multicolored	.30	.20
2498	A954	35s multicolored	.45	.20
2499	A954	43s multicolored	.55	.20
2500	A954	60s multicolored	.85	.25
2501	A954	80s multicolored	1.10	.40
		Nos. 2495-2501 (7)	3.75	1.65

Dresden Art Gallery paintings.

Doves and Festival Emblem — A955

1978, May 31

2502	A955	13s multicolored	.25	.20

11th World Youth Festival, Havana, 7/28-8/5.

Fritillaria Stribrnyi — A956

Rare Flowers: 2s, Fritillaria drenovskyi. 3s, Lilium rhodopaeum. 13s, Tulipa urumoffii. 23s, Lilium jankae. 43s, Tulipa rhodopaea.

1978, June 27

2503	A956	1s multicolored	.20	.20
2504	A956	2s multicolored	.20	.20
2505	A956	3s multicolored	.20	.20
2506	A956	13s multicolored	.25	.20
2507	A956	23s multicolored	.45	.20
2508	A956	43s multicolored	.90	.30
		Nos. 2503-2508 (6)	2.20	1.30

Yacht Cor Caroli and Map of Voyage A957

1978, May 19 Photo. *Perf. 13*

2509	A957	23s multicolored	.50	.20

First Bulgarian around-the-world voyage, Capt. Georgi Georgiev, Dec. 20, 1976-Dec. 20, 1977.

Market, by Naiden Petkov — A958

Views of Sofia: 5s, Street, by Emil Stoichev. 13s, Street, by Boris Ivanov. 23s, Tolbukhin Boulevard, by Nikola Tanev. 35s, National Theater, by Nikola Petrov. 53s, Market, by Anton Mitov.

1978, Aug. 28 Litho. *Perf. 12½x12*

2510	A958	2s multicolored	.20	.20
2511	A958	5s multicolored	.20	.20
2512	A958	13s multicolored	.20	.20
2513	A958	23s multicolored	.30	.20
2514	A958	35s multicolored	.50	.20
2515	A958	53s multicolored	.85	.30
		Nos. 2510-2515 (6)	2.25	1.30

Miniature Sheet

Sleeping Venus, by Giorgione — A959

1978, Aug. 7 Photo. *Imperf.*

2516	A959	1 l multicolored	2.00	.85

View of Varna — A960

1978, July 13 Photo. *Perf. 13*

2517	A960	13s multicolored	.25	.20

63rd Esperanto Cong., Varna, July 29-Aug. 5.

Black Woodpecker A961

Woodpeckers: 2s, Syrian. 3s, Three-toed. 13s, Middle spotted. 23s, Lesser spotted. 43s, Green.

1978, Sept. 1

2518	A961	1s multicolored	.20	.20
2519	A961	2s multicolored	.20	.20
2520	A961	3s multicolored	.20	.20
2521	A961	13s multicolored	.25	.20
2522	A961	23s multicolored	.40	.20
2523	A961	43s multicolored	1.10	.25
		Nos. 2518-2523 (6)	2.35	1.25

"September 1923" — A962

1978, Sept. 5

2524	A962	2s red & brn	.25	.20

55th anniversary of September uprising.

Souvenir Sheet

National Theater, Sofia A963

Photogravure and Engraved

1978, Sept. 1 *Perf. 12x11½*

2525	Sheet of 4	2.50	1.00
a.	A963 40s shown	.60	.20
b.	A963 40s Festival Hall, Sofia	.60	.20
c.	A963 40s Charles Bridge, Prague	.60	.20
d.	A963 40s Belvedere Palace, Prague	.60	.20

PRAGA '78 and PHILASERDICA '79 Philatelic Exhibitions.

Black and White Hands, Human Rights Emblem — A964

1978, Oct. 3 Photo. *Perf. 13x13½*

2526	A964	13s multicolored	.25	.20

Anti-Apartheid Year.

Gotse Deltchev A965

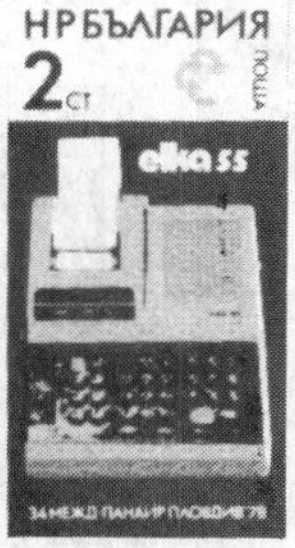

Bulgarian Calculator A966

1978, Aug. 1 Photo. *Perf. 13*

2527	A965	13s multicolored	.25	.20

Gotse Deltchev (1872-1903), patriot.

1978, Sept. 3

2528	A966	2s multicolored	.20	.20

International Sample Fair, Plovdiv.

Guerrillas — A967

1978, Aug. 1

2529	A967	5s blk & rose red	.20	.20

Ilinden and Preobrazhene revolts, 75th anniv.

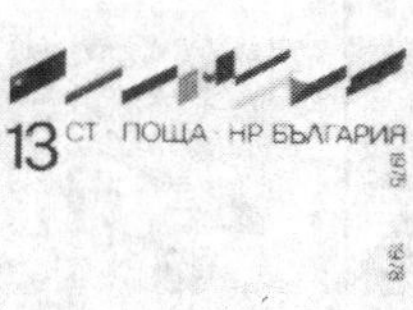

"Pipe Line" and Flags A968

1978, Oct. 3

2530	A968	13s multicolored	.25	.20

Construction of gas pipe line from Orenburg to Russian border.

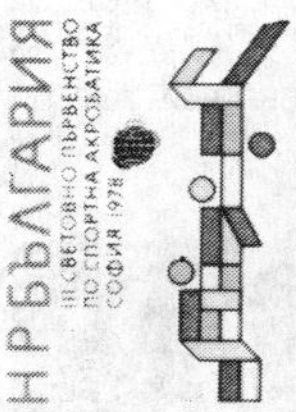

A969

A970

1978, Oct. 4 ***Perf. 13x13½***
2531 A969 13s Three acrobats .25 .20

3rd World Acrobatic Championships, Sofia, Oct. 6-8.

1978, Sept. 18 **Photo.** ***Perf. 13***
2532 A970 2s dp claret & ocher .20 .20

Christo G. Danov (1828-1911), 1st Bulgarian publisher. No. 2532 printed with se-tenant label showing early printing press.

Insurgents, by Todor Panajotov A971

1978, Sept. 20
2533 A971 2s multicolored .20 .20

Vladaja mutiny, 60th anniversary.

A972

A973

1978, Oct. 11 **Photo.** ***Perf. 13***
2534 A972 13s dk brn & org red .25 .20

Salvador Allende (1908-1973), president of Chile.

1978, Oct. 18
2535 A973 23s Human Rights flame .50 .20

Universal Declaration of Human Rights, 30th anniversary.

A974

A975

Burgarian Paintings: 1s, Levski and Matei Mitkaloto, by Kalina Tasseva. 2s, "Strength for my Arm" by Zlatyu Boyadjiev. 3s, Rumena, woman military leader, by Nikola Mirchev, horiz. 13s, Kolju Ficeto, by Elza Goeva. 23s, Family, National Revival Period, by Naiden Petkov.

Perf. 12x12½, 12½x12

1978, Oct. 25 **Litho.**

2536	A974	1s multicolored		.20	.20
2537	A974	2s multicolored		.20	.20
2538	A974	3s multicolored		.20	.20
2539	A974	13s multicolored		.25	.20
2540	A974	23s multicolored		.40	.20
		Nos. 2536-2540 (5)		1.25	1.00

1300th anniversary of Bulgaria (in 1981).

1978, Nov. 1 **Photo.** ***Perf. 13***

Designs: a, Tourism building, Plovdiv. b, Chrelo Tower, Rila Cloister.

Souvenir Sheet

2541	Sheet of 5 + label	4.00	2.00
a.	A975 43s multicolored	.70	.30
b.	A975 43s multicolored	.70	.30

Conservation of European architectural heritage. No. 2541 contains 3 No. 2541a & 2 No. 2541b.

Ferry, Map of Black Sea with Route A976

1978, Nov. 1 **Photo.** ***Perf. 13***
2542 A976 13s multicolored .25 .20

Opening of Ilychovsk-Varna Ferry.

Bird, from Marble Floor, St. Sofia Church — A977

1978, Nov. 20
2543 A977 5s multicolored .20 .20

3rd Bulgaria '78, National Philatelic Exhibition, Sofia. Printed se-tenant with label showing emblems of Bulgaria '78 and Philaserdica '79.

Initial, 13th Century Gospel — A978

Designs: 13s, St. Cyril, miniature, 1567. 23s, Book cover, 16th century. 80s, St. Methodius, miniature, 13th century.

1978, Dec. 15 **Photo.** ***Perf. 13***

2544	A978	2s multicolored	.20	.20
2545	A978	13s multicolored	.20	.20
2546	A978	23s multicolored	.35	.20
		Nos. 2544-2546 (3)	.75	.60

Souvenir Sheet

2547 A978 80s multicolored 1.25 1.00

Cent. of the Cyril and Methodius Natl. Library.

Bulgaria No. 53 A979

Bulgarian Stamps: 13s, #534. 23s, #968. 35s, #1176, vert. 53s, #1223, vert. 1 l, #1.

1978, Dec. 30

2548	A979	2s ol grn & red	.20	.20
2549	A979	13s ultra & rose car	.20	.20
2550	A979	23s rose lil & ol grn	.30	.20
2551	A979	35s brt bl & blk	.50	.20
2552	A979	53s ver & sl grn	.90	.30
		Nos. 2548-2552 (5)	2.10	1.10

Souvenir Sheet

2553 A979 1 l multicolored 1.50 1.25

Philaserdica '79, International Philatelic Exhibition, Sofia, May 18-27, 1979, and centenary of Bulgarian stamps. No. 2553 exists imperf. See Nos. 2560-2564.

St. Clement of Ochrida — A980

1978, Dec. 8
2554 A980 2s multicolored .20 .20

Clement of Ochrida University, 90th anniv.

Ballet Dancers A981

1978, Dec. 22
2555 A981 13s multicolored .30 .20

Bulgarian ballet, 50th anniversary.

Nikola Karastojanov A982

1978, Dec. 12
2556 A982 2s multicolored .20 .20

Nikola Karastojanov (1778-1874), printer. No. 2556 printed se-tenant with label showing printing press.

Christmas Tree Made of Birds — A983

1978, Dec. 22

2557	A983	2s shown	.20	.20
2558	A983	13s Post horn	.20	.20

New Year 1979.

COMECON Building, Moscow, Members' Flags — A984

1979, Jan. 25 **Photo.** ***Perf. 13***
2559 A984 13s multicolored .25 .20

Council for Mutual Economic Aid (COMECON), 30th anniversary.

Philaserdica Type of 1978
Designs as Before

1979, Jan. 30

2560	A979	2s brt bl & red	.20	.20
2561	A979	13s grn & dk car	.20	.20
2562	A979	23s org brn & multi	.30	.20
2563	A979	35s dl red & blk	.50	.25
2564	A979	53s vio & dk ol	.90	.35
		Nos. 2560-2564 (5)	2.10	1.20

Philaserdica '79.

Bank Building, Commemorative Coin — A985

1979, Feb. 13
2565 A985 2s yel, gray & silver .20 .20

Centenary of Bulgarian People's Bank.

Aleksandr Stamboliski A986

1979, Feb. 28
2566 A986 2s orange & dk brn .20 .20

Aleksandr Stamboliski (1879-1923), leader of peasant's party and premier.

Flower with Child's Face, IYC Emblem — A987

1979, Mar. 8
2568 A987 23s multicolored .40 .20

International Year of the Child.

Stylized Heads, World Association Emblem — A988

1979, Mar. 20
2569 A988 13s multicolored .25 .20

8th World Cong. for the Deaf, Varna, June 20-27.

"75" and Trade Union Emblem — A989

1979, Mar. 20
2570 A989 2s slate grn & org .20 .20

75th anniversary of Bulgarian Trade Unions.

Souvenir Sheet

Sculptures in Sofia — A990

Designs: 2s, Soviet Army Monument (detail). 5s, Mother and Child, Central Railroad Station. 13s, 23s, 25s, Bas-relief from Monument of the Liberators.

1979, Apr. 2 Photo. *Perf. 13*

2571 A990	Sheet of 5 + label	1.25	.60
a.	2s multicolored	.20	
b.	5s multicolored	.20	
c.	13s multicolored	.25	
d.	23s multicolored	.40	
e.	25s multicolored	.50	

Centenary of Sofia as capital.

Rocket Launch, Space Flight Emblems A991

Designs (Intercosmos and Bulgarian-USSR Flight Emblems and): 25s, Link-up, horiz. 35s, Parachute descent. 1 l, Globe, emblems and orbit, horiz.

1979, Apr. 11

2572 A991 12s multicolored	.20	.20
2573 A991 25s multicolored	.45	.20
2574 A991 35s multicolored	.60	.25
Nos. 2572-2574 (3)	1.25	.65

Souvenir Sheet

2575 A991 1 l multicolored	1.50	.75

1st Bulgarian cosmonaut on Russian space flight.

A slightly larger imperf. sheet similar to No. 2575 with control numbers at bottom and rockets at sides exists.

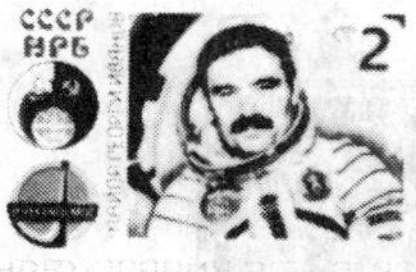

Nicolai Rukavishnikov — A992

Design: 13s, Rukavishnikov and Soviet cosmonaut Georgi Ivanov.

1979, May 14 Photo. *Perf. 13*

2576 A992 2s multicolored	.20	.20
2577 A992 13s multicolored	.30	.20

Col. Rukavishnikov, 1st Bulgarian astronaut.

Souvenir Sheet

Thracian Gold-leaf Collar — A993

1979, May 16

2578 A993 1 l multicolored	2.00	1.50

48th International Philatelic Federation Congress, Sofia, May 16-17.

Post Horn, Carrier Pigeon, Jet, Globes and UPU Emblem — A994

Designs (Post Horn, Globes and ITU Emblem): 5s, 1st Bulgarian and modern telephones. 13s, Morse key and teleprinter. 23s, Old radio transmitter and radio towers. 35s, Bulgarian TV tower and satellite. 50s, Ground receiving station

1979, May 8 *Perf. 13½x13*

2579 A994 2s multicolored	.20	.20
2580 A994 5s multicolored	.20	.20
2581 A994 13s multicolored	.20	.20
2582 A994 23s multicolored	.40	.20
2583 A994 35s multicolored	.60	.25
Nos. 2579-2583 (5)	1.60	1.05

Souvenir Sheet

Perf. 13

2584 A994 50s vio, blk & gray	1.00	.65

Intl. Telecommunications Day and cent. of Bulgarian Postal & Telegraph Services. Size of stamp in #2584: 39x28mm. #2584 exists imperf.

Hotel Vitosha-New Otani — A996

1979, May 20

2586 A996 2s ultra & pink	.20	.20

Philaserdica '79 Day.

Horseman Receiving Gifts, by Karellia and Boris Kuklievi — A997

1979, May 23

2587 A997 2s multicolored	.20	.20

Bulgarian-Russian Friendship Day.

A998

A999

Design: Man on Donkey, by Boris Angeloushev.

1979, May 23 Photo. *Perf. 13½*

2588 A998 2s multicolored	.20	.20

12th National Festival of Humor and Satire, Gabrovo.

Lithographed and Engraved

1979, May 31 *Perf. 14x13½*

Durer Engravings: 13s, Four Women. 23s, Three Peasants. 25s, The Cook and his Wife. 35s, Portrait of Helius Eobanus Hessus. 80s, Rhinoceros, horiz.

2589 A999 13s multicolored	.25	.20
2590 A999 23s multicolored	.40	.20
2591 A999 25s multicolored	.45	.20
2592 A999 35s multicolored	.65	.20
Nos. 2589-2592 (4)	1.75	.80

Souvenir Sheet

Imperf

2593 A999 80s multicolored	1.50	1.25

Albrecht Durer (1471-1528), German engraver and painter.

R. Todorov (1879-1916) A1000

Bulgarian Writers: No. 2595, Dimitri Dymov (1909-1966). No. 2596, S. A. Kostov (1879-1939).

1979, June 26 Photo. *Perf. 13*

2594 A1000 2s multicolored	.20	.20
2595 A1000 2s slate grn & yel grn	.20	.20
2596 A1000 2s dp claret & yel	.20	.20
Nos. 2594-2596 (3)	.60	.60

Nos. 2594-2596 each printed se-tenant with label showing title page or character from writer's work.

Moscow '80 Emblem, Runners A1001

Moscow '80 Emblem and: 13s, Pole vault, horiz. 25s, Discus. 35s, Hurdles, horiz. 43s, High jump, horiz. 1 l, Long jump.

1979, May 15 *Perf. 13*

2597 A1001 2s multicolored	.20	.20
2598 A1001 13s multicolored	.20	.20
2599 A1001 25s multicolored	.40	.20
2600 A1001 35s multicolored	.80	.25
2601 A1001 43s multicolored	1.00	.30
2602 A1001 1 l multicolored	2.25	.65
Nos. 2597-2602 (6)	4.85	1.80

Souvenir Sheet

2602A A1001 2 l multicolored	6.00	3.25

22nd Summer Olympic Games, Moscow, July 19-Aug. 3, 1980.

Rocket — A1002

5s, Flags of USSR and Bulgaria. 13s, "35."

1979, Sept. 4 Photo.

2603 A1002 2s multicolored	.20	.20
2604 A1002 5s multicolored	.20	.20
2605 A1002 13s multicolored	.20	.20
Nos. 2603-2605 (3)	.60	.60

35th anniversary of liberation.

Moscow '80 Emblem, Gymnast A1003

Moscow '80 Emblem & gymnasts. 13s horiz.

1979, July 31 Photo. *Perf. 13*

2606 A1003 2s multicolored	.20	.20
2607 A1003 13s multicolored	.20	.20
2608 A1003 25s multicolored	.50	.20
2609 A1003 35s multicolored	.75	.25
2610 A1003 43s multicolored	1.00	.25
2611 A1003 1 l multicolored	2.25	.80
Nos. 2606-2611 (6)	4.90	1.90

Souvenir Sheet

2612 A1003 2 l multicolored	6.00	3.25

22nd Summer Olympic Games, Moscow, July 19-Aug. 3, 1980.

A1004

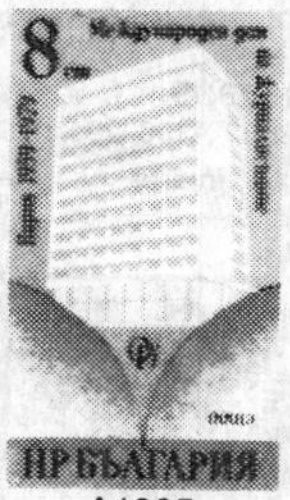

A1005

1979, July 8 Photo. *Perf. 13*

2613 A1004 13s ultra & blk	.20	.20

Theater Institute, 18th Congress.

1979, July 17

2614 A1005 8s multicolored	.20	.20

Journalists' Vacation House, Varna, 20th Anniv.

Icon Type of 1977

Virgin and Child by: 13s, 23s, Nesebar, 16th cent., diff. 35s, 43s, Sozopol, 16th cent., diff. 53s, Samokov, 19th cent. Inscribed 1979.

1979, Aug. 7 Litho. *Perf. 12½*

2615 A917 13s multicolored	.20	.20
2616 A917 23s multicolored	.35	.20
2617 A917 35s multicolored	.50	.20
2618 A917 43s multicolored	.60	.20
2619 A917 53s multicolored	.85	.25
Nos. 2615-2619 (5)	2.50	1.05

A1006

A1007

1979, Aug. 9 Photo. *Perf. 13x13½*
2620 A1006 2s Anton Besenschek .20 .20

Bulgarian stenography centenary.

1979, Aug. 28 ***Perf. 13***
2621 A1007 2s multicolored .20 .20

Bulgarian Alpine Club, 50th anniv.

Public Health Ordinance A1008

1979, Aug. 31 ***Perf. 13½***
2622 A1008 2s multicolored .20 .20

Public Health Service centenary. No. 2622 printed with label showing Dimitar Mollov, founder.

Isotope Measuring Device — A1009

1979, Sept. 8 ***Perf. 13½x13***
2623 A1009 2s multicolored .20 .20

International Sample Fair, Plovdiv.

Games' Emblem — A1010

1979, Sept. 20 ***Perf. 13***
2624 A1010 5s multicolored .20 .20

Universiada '79, World University Games, Mexico City, Sept.

Sofia Locomotive Sports Club, 50th Anniversary — A1011

1979, Oct. 2
2625 A1011 2s blue & org red .20 .20

Ljuben Karavelov (1837-1879), Poet and Freedom Fighter — A1012

1979, Oct. 4 Photo. *Perf. 13*
2626 A1012 2s blue & slate grn .20 .20

A1013

A1014

1979, Oct. 20

2627	A1013	2s	Biathlon	.20	.20
2628	A1013	13s	Speed skating	.25	.20
2629	A1013	23s	Downhill skiing	.40	.20
2630	A1013	43s	Luge	.75	.25
			Nos. 2627-2630 (4)	1.60	.85

Souvenir Sheet

Imperf

2631 A1013 1 l Slalom 1.75 1.10

13th Winter Olympic Games, Lake Placid, NY, Feb. 12-24.

1979, Oct. 31 ***Perf. 14***

Decko Uzunov, 80th Birthday: 12s, Apparition in Red. 13s, Woman from Thrace. 23s, Composition.

2632	A1014	12s	multicolored	.25	.20
2633	A1014	13s	multicolored	.25	.20
2634	A1014	23s	multicolored	.40	.20
			Nos. 2632-2634 (3)	.90	.60

Swimming, Moscow '80 Emblem A1016

1979, Nov. 30 Photo. *Perf. 13*

2636	A1016	2s	Two-man kayak, vert.	.20	.20
2637	A1016	13s	Swimming, vert.	.20	.20
2638	A1016	25s	shown	.40	.20
2639	A1016	35s	One-man kayak	.80	.20
2640	A1016	43s	Diving, vert	1.00	.40
2641	A1016	1 l	Diving, vert., diff.	2.25	.70
			Nos. 2636-2641 (6)	4.85	1.90

Souvenir Sheet

2642 A1016 2 l Water polo, vert. 6.00 3.25

22nd Summer Olympic Games, Moscow, July 19-Aug. 3, 1980.

Nikola Vapzarov A1017

1979, Dec. 7 Photo. *Perf. 13*
2643 A1017 2s claret & rose .20 .20

Vapzarov (1909-1942), poet and freedom fighter. No. 2643 printed with label showing smokestacks.

The First Socialists, by Bojan Petrov — A1018

Paintings: 13s, Demeter Blagoev Reading Newspaper, by Demeter Gjudshenov, 1892. 25s, Workers' Party March, by Sotir Sotirov, 1917. 35s, Dawn in Plovdiv, by Johann Leviev, vert.

Perf. 12½x12, 12x12½

1979, Dec. 10 Litho.

2644	A1018	2s	multicolored	.20	.20
2645	A1018	13s	multicolored	.25	.20
2646	A1018	25s	multicolored	.40	.20
2647	A1018	35s	multicolored	.55	.20
			Nos. 2644-2647 (4)	1.40	.80

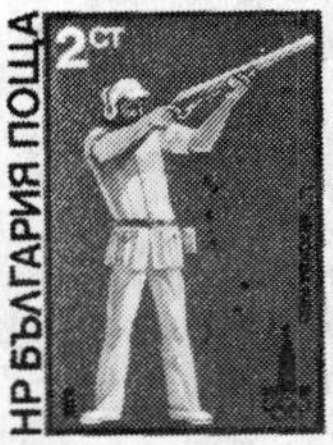

Sharpshooting, Moscow '80 Emblem — A1019

1979, Dec. 22 Photo. *Perf. 13*

2648	A1019	2s	shown	.20	.20
2649	A1019	13s	Judo, horiz.	.20	.20
2650	A1019	25s	Wrestling, horiz.	.40	.20
2651	A1019	35s	Archery	.80	.25
2652	A1019	43s	Fencing, horiz.	1.00	.50
2653	A1019	1 l	Fencing	2.25	.90
			Nos. 2648-2653 (6)	4.85	2.25

Souvenir Sheet

2654 A1019 2 l Boxing 6.00 4.00

Procession with Relics, 11th Century Fresco A1020

Frescoes of Sts. Cyril and Methodius, St. Clement's Basilica, Rome: 13s, Reception by Pope Hadrian II. 23s, Burial of Cyril the Philosopher, 18th century. 25s, St. Cyril. 35s, St. Methodius.

1979, Dec. 25

2655	A1020	2s	multicolored	.20	.20
2656	A1020	13s	multicolored	.25	.20
2657	A1020	23s	multicolored	.40	.20
2658	A1020	25s	multicolored	.45	.20
2659	A1020	35s	multicolored	.65	.20
			Nos. 2655-2659 (5)	1.95	1.00

Bulgarian Television Emblem A1021

1979, Dec. 29 ***Perf. 13½***
2660 A1021 5s violet bl & lt bl .20 .20

Bulgarian television, 25th anniversary. No. 2660 printed with label showing Sofia television tower.

Doves in Girl's Hair A1022

Design: 2s, Children's heads, mosaic, vert.

1979 ***Perf. 13***

2661	A1022	2s	multicolored	.20	.20
2662	A1022	13s	multicolored	.20	.20

International Year of the Child. Issue dates: 2s, July 17; 13s, Dec. 14.

Puppet on Horseback, IYC Emblem A1023

Thracian Rider, Votive Tablet, 3rd Century A1024

1980, Jan. 22 Photo. *Perf. 13*
2663 A1023 2s multicolored .20 .20

UNIMA, Intl. Puppet Theater Organization, 50th anniv. (1979); Intl. Year of the Child (1979).

1980, Jan. 29 Photo. *Perf. 13x13½*

National Archaeological Museum Centenary; 13s, Deines stele, 5th century B.C.

2664	A1024	2s	brown & gold	.20	.20
2665	A1024	13s	multicolored	.20	.20

Dimitrov Meeting Lenin in Moscow, by Alexander Poplilov A1026

1980, Mar. 28 ***Perf. 12x12½***
2667 A1026 13s multicolored .20 .20

Lenin, 110th birth anniversary.

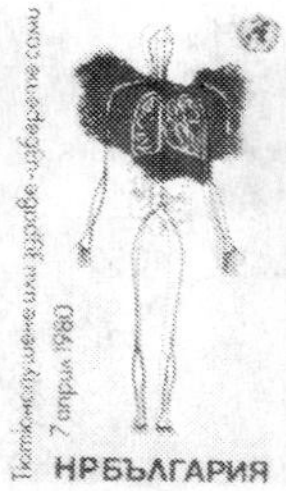

A1027

A1027a

Circulator y system, lungs enveloped in smoke.

1980, Apr. 7 *Perf. 13*

2668 A1027 5s multicolored .20 .20

World Health Day fight against cigarette smoking.

1980, Apr. 10 Photo. *Perf. 13*

2669	A1027a	2s	Basketball	.20	.20
2670	A1027a	13s	Soccer	.20	.20
2671	A1027a	25s	Hockey	.40	.20
2672	A1027a	35s	Cycling	.80	.20
2673	A1027a	43s	Handball	1.00	.40
2674	A1027a	1 l	Volleyball	2.25	.70
			Nos. 2669-2674 (6)	4.85	1.90

Souvenir Sheet

2675 A1027a 2 l Weightlifting 6.50 4.25

Souvenir Sheet

Intercosmos Emblem, Cosmonauts — A1028

1980, Apr. 22 *Perf. 12*

2676 A1028 50s multicolored 1.00 .45

Intercosmos cooperative space program.

Penio Penev (1930-1959), Poet — A1029

1980, Apr. 22 Photo. *Perf. 13*

2677 A1029 5s multicolored .20 .20

Se-tenant with label showing quote from author's work.

Penny Black — A1030

1980, Apr. 24 *Perf. 13*

2678 A1030 25s dark red & sepia .60 .45

London 1980 International Stamp Exhibition, May 6-14; printed se-tenant with label showing Rowland Hill between every two stamps.

Demeter H. Tchorbadjiiski, Self-portrait — A1031

1980, Apr. 29

2679 A1031 5s shown .20 .20

2680 A1031 13s "Our People" .20 .20

Nikolai Giaurov — A1032

Raising Red Flag Reichstag Building, Berlin — A1033

1980, Apr. 30

2681 A1032 5s multicolored .20 .20

Nikolai Giaurov (b. 1930), opera singer; printed se-tenant with label showing Boris Godunov.

1980, May 6 *Perf. 13x13½*

Armistice, 35th Anniversary: 13s, Soviet Army memorial, Berlin-Treptow.

2682 A1033 5s multicolored .20 .20

2683 A1033 13s multicolored .20 .20

Numeral — A1034

1979 *Perf. 14*

2684 A1034 2s ultra .20 .20

2685 A1034 5s rose car .20 .20

A1034a

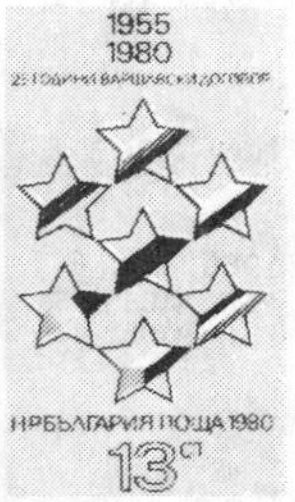

A1035

1980, May 12 Photo. *Perf. 13*

2685A A1034a 5s multicolored .20 .20

75th Anniv. of Teachers' Union.

1980, May 14 Photo. *Perf. 13*

2686 A1035 13s multicolored .20 .20

Warsaw Pact, 25th anniv.

A1036

A1037

Statues.

1980, June 10

2687	A1036	2s	multicolored	.20	.20
2688	A1036	13s	multicolored	.20	.20
2689	A1036	25s	multicolored	.40	.20
2690	A1036	35s	multicolored	.80	.30
2691	A1036	43s	multicolored	1.00	.60
2692	A1036	1 l	multicolored	2.25	1.10
			Nos. 2687-2692 (6)	4.85	2.60

Souvenir Sheet

2693 A1036 2 l multicolored 6.00 3.25

22nd Summer Olympic Games, Moscow, July 19-Aug. 3.

1980, Sept. Photo. *Perf. 13*

2694 A1037 13s multicolored .25 .20

10th Intl. Ballet Competition, Varna.

Hotel Europa, Sofia A1038

Hotels: No. 2696, Bulgaria, Burgas, vert. No. 2697, Plovdiv, Plovdiv. No. 2698, Riga, Russe, vert. No. 2699, Varna, Djuba.

1980, July 11

2695	A1038	23s	lt ultra & multi	.30	.20
2696	A1038	23s	orange & multi	.30	.20
2697	A1038	23s	gray & multi	.30	.20
2698	A1038	23s	blue & multi	.30	.20
2699	A1038	23s	yellow & multi	.30	.20
			Nos. 2695-2699 (5)	1.50	1.00

See No. 2766.

Ship Type of 1975

Ships of 16th, 17th Centuries: 5s, Christ of Lubeck, galleon. 8s, Roman galley. 13s, Eagle, Russian galleon. 23s, Mayflower. 35s, Maltese galley. 53s, Royal Louis, galleon.

1980, July 14

2700	A873	5s	multicolored	.20	.20
2701	A873	8s	multicolored	.20	.20
2702	A873	13s	multicolored	.25	.20
2703	A873	23s	multicolored	.45	.20
2704	A873	35s	multicolored	.70	.20
2705	A873	53s	multicolored	1.10	.35
			Nos. 2700-2705 (6)	2.90	1.35

Int'l Year of the Child, 1979 — A1040

Designs: Children's drawings and IYC emblem. 43s, Tower. 5s, 25s, 43s, vert.

1980 Litho. *Perf. 12½x12, 12x12½*

2708	A1040	3s	multicolored	.20	.20
2709	A1040	5s	multicolored	.20	.20
2710	A1040	8s	multicolored	.20	.20
2711	A1040	13s	multicolored	.20	.20
2712	A1040	25s	multicolored	.40	.20
2713	A1040	35s	multicolored	.50	.20
2714	A1040	43s	multicolored	.65	.20
			Nos. 2708-2714 (7)	2.35	1.40

Helicopter, Missile Transport, Tank — A1041

1980, Sept. 23 Photo. *Perf. 13*

2715	A1041	3s	shown	.20	.20
2716	A1041	5s	Jet, radar, rocket	.20	.20
2717	A1041	8s	Helicopter, ships	.20	.20
			Nos. 2715-2717 (3)	.60	.60

Bulgarian People's Army, 35th anniversary.

St. Anne, by Leonardo da Vinci A1042

Da Vinci Paintings: 8s, 13s, Annunciation (diff.). 25s, Adoration of the Kings. 35s, Lady with the Ermine. 50s, Mona Lisa.

1980, Nov.

2718	A1042	5s	multicolored	.20	.20
2719	A1042	8s	multicolored	.20	.20
2720	A1042	13s	multicolored	.20	.20
2721	A1042	25s	multicolored	.40	.20
2722	A1042	35s	multicolored	.55	.20
			Nos. 2718-2722 (5)	1.55	1.00

Souvenir Sheet

Imperf

2723 A1042 50s multicolored 1.00 .35

International Peace Conference, Sofia — A1043

1980, Sept. 4 Photo. *Perf. 13*

2724 A1043 25s multicolored .35 .20

Jordan Jowkov (1880-1937), Writer — A1044

1980, Sept. 19

2725 A1044 5s multicolored .20 .20

Se-tenant with label showing scene from Jowkov's work.

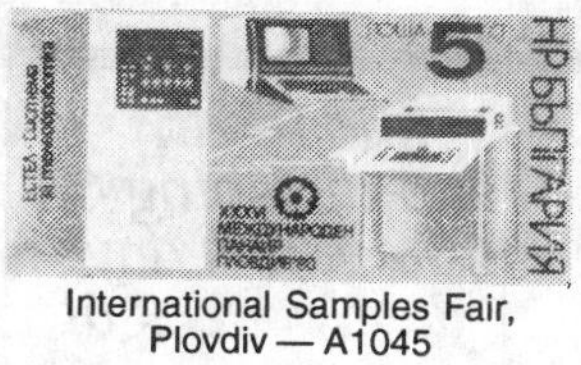

International Samples Fair, Plovdiv — A1045

1980, Sept. 24 *Perf. 13½x13*

2726 A1045 5s multicolored .20 .20

Blooming Cacti — A1045a

1980, Nov. 4 Photo. *Perf. 13*

2726A A1045a	5s multicolored	.20	.20
2726B A1045a	13s multicolored	.20	.20
2726C A1045a	25s multicolored	.42	.20
2726D A1045a	35s multicolored	.60	.25
2726E A1045a	53s multicolored	1.00	.30
Nos. 2726A-2726E (5)		2.42	1.15

Souvenir Sheet

25th Anniv. of Bulgarian UN Membership — A1045b

1980, Nov. 25

2726F A1045b 60s multicolored 2.25 2.00

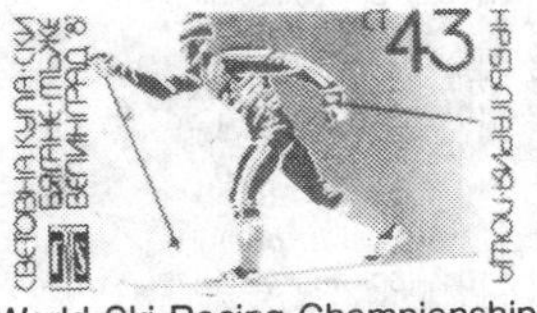

World Ski Racing Championship, Velingrad — A1046

1981, Jan. 17 Photo. *Perf. 13*

2727 A1046 43s multicolored .60 .25

Hawthorn A1047

Slalom A1048

Designs: Medicinal herbs.

1981, Jan.

2728 A1047	3s shown	.20	.20
2729 A1047	5s St. John's wort	.20	.20
2730 A1047	13s Common elder	.20	.20
2731 A1047	25s Blackberries	.40	.20
2732 A1047	35s Lime	.55	.20
2733 A1047	43s Wild briar	.65	.25
Nos. 2728-2733 (6)		2.20	1.25

1981, Feb. 27 Photo. *Perf. 13*

2734 A1048 43s multicolored .60 .25

Evian Alpine World Ski Cup Championship, Borovets.

Nuclear Traces, Research Institute — A1049

1981, Mar. 10 *Perf. 13½x13*

2735 A1049 13s gray & blk .20 .20

Nuclear Research Institute, Dubna, USSR, 25th anniversary.

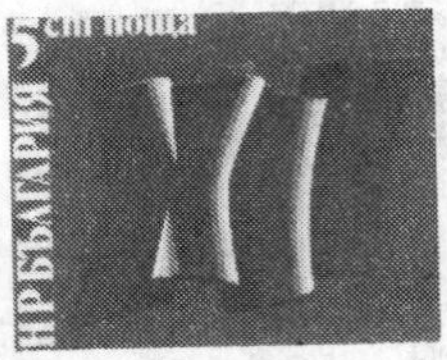

Congress Emblem A1050

1981, Mar. 12 *Perf. 13½*

2736 A1050	5s shown	.20	.20
2737 A1050	13s Stars	.20	.20
2738 A1050	23s Teletape	.35	.20
Nos. 2736-2738 (3)		.75	.60

Souvenir Sheet

2739 A1050 50s Demeter Blagoev, George Dimitrov .80 .50

12th Bulgarian Communist Party Congress. Nos. 2736-2738 each printed se-tenant with label.

Paintings by Zachary Zograf — A1050a

1981, Mar. 23 Photo. *Perf. 12x12½*

2739A A1050a	5s multicolored	.20	.20
2739B A1050a	13s multicolored	.25	.20
2739C A1050a	23s multicolored	.40	.20
2739D A1050a	25s multicolored	.50	.20
2739E A1050a	35s multicolored	.70	.20
Nos. 2739A-2739E (5)		2.05	1.00

Nos. 2739A-2739C are vert.

EXPO '81, Plovdiv A1050b

1981, Apr. 7

2739F A1050b	5s multicolored	.20	.20
2739G A1050b	8s multicolored	.20	.20
2739H A1050b	13s multicolored	.25	.20
2739J A1050b	25s multicolored	.45	.20
2739K A1050b	53s multicolored	1.00	.25
Nos. 2739F-2739K (5)		2.10	1.05

Centenary of Bulgarian Shipbuilding — A1050c

1981, Apr. 15 Photo. *Perf. 13*

2739L A1050c	35s Georgi Dimitrov, liner	.55	.20
2739M A1050c	43s 5th from RMS, freighter	.65	.25
2739N A1050c	53s Khan Asparuch, tanker	.80	.30
Nos. 2739L-2739N (3)		2.00	.75

Arabian Horse A1051

Various breeds.

1980, Nov. 27 Litho. *Perf. 12½x12*

2740 A1051	3s multicolored	.20	.20
2741 A1051	5s multicolored	.20	.20
2742 A1051	13s multicolored	.30	.20
2743 A1051	23s multicolored	.45	.20
2744 A1051	35s multicolored	.75	.20
Nos. 2740-2744 (5)		1.90	1.00

Vassil Stoin, Ethnologist, Birth Centenary — A1052

1980, Dec. 5 Photo. *Perf. 13½x13*

2745 A1052 5s multicolored .20 .20

12th Bulgarian Communist Party Congress — A1052a

1980, Dec. 26 Photo. *Perf. 13x13½*

2745A A1052a 5s Party symbols .20 .20

New Year A1053

1980, Dec. 8 *Perf. 13*

2746 A1053	5s shown	.20	.20
2747 A1053	13s Cup, date	.20	.20

Culture Palace, Sofia A1053a

1981, Mar. 13 Photo. *Perf. 13*

2747A A1053a 5s multicolored .20 .20

Vienna Hofburg Palace A1054

1981, May 15 Photo. *Perf. 13*

2748 A1054 35s multicolored .45 .20

WIPA 1981 Intl. Philatelic Exhibition, Vienna, May 22-31.

34th Farmers' Union Congress A1055

1981, May 18 *Perf. 13½*

2749 A1055	5s shown	.20	.20
2750 A1055	8s Flags	.20	.20
2751 A1055	13s Flags, diff.	.20	.20
Nos. 2749-2751 (3)		.60	.60

Wild Cat A1056

1981, May 27

2752 A1056	5s shown	.20	.20
2753 A1056	13s Boar	.25	.20
2754 A1056	23s Mouflon	.40	.20
2755 A1056	25s Mountain goat	.45	.20
2756 A1056	35s Stag	.60	.20
2757 A1056	53s Roe deer	1.00	.25
Nos. 2752-2757 (6)		2.90	1.25

Souvenir Sheet

Perf. 13½x13

2758 A1056 1 l Stag, diff. 1.60 .85

EXPO '81 Intl. Hunting Exhibition, Plovdiv. Nos. 2752-2757 each se-tenant with labels showing various hunting rifles. No. 2758 contains one stamp, size: 48½x39mm.

25th Anniv. of UNESCO Membership A1057

1981, June 11 *Perf. 13*

2759 A1057 13s multicolored .20 .20

Hotel Type of 1980

1981, July 13 Photo. *Perf. 13*

2766 A1038 23s Veliko Tirnovo Hotel .35 .20

Flying Figure, Sculpture by Velichko Minekov — A1059

Bulgarian Social Democratic Party Buzludja Congress, 90th Anniv. (Minkov Sculpture): 13s, Advancing Female Figure.

1981, July 16 *Perf. 13½*

2767 A1059	5s multicolored	.20	.20
2768 A1059	13s multicolored	.20	.20

Kukeri, by Georg Tschapkanov
A1060

Statistics Office Centenary
A1061

1981, May 28 **Photo.** ***Perf. 13***

2769 A1060 5s multicolored .20 .20

13th Natl. Festival of Humor and Satire.

1981, June 9

2770 A1061 5s multicolored .20 .20

Gold Dish
A1063

Designs: Goldsmiths' works, 7th-9th cent.

1981, July 21

2772	A1063	5s multicolored	.20	.20
2773	A1063	13s multicolored	.20	.20
2774	A1063	23s multicolored	.35	.25
2775	A1063	25s multicolored	.40	.25
2776	A1063	35s multicolored	.55	.35
2777	A1063	53s multicolored	.90	.40
		Nos. 2772-2777 (6)	2.60	1.65

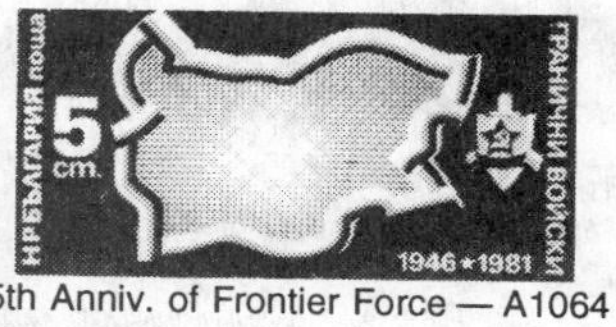

35th Anniv. of Frontier Force — A1064

1981, July 28 ***Perf. 13½x13***

2778 A1064 5s multicolored .20 .20

1300th Anniv. of First Bulgarian State — A1065

Designs: No. 2779, Sts. Cyril and Methodius. No. 2780, 9th cent. bas-relief. 8s, Floor plan, Round Church, Preslav, 10th cent. 12s, Four Evangelists of King Ivan Alexander, miniature, 1356. No. 2783, King Ivan Asen II memorial column. No. 2784, Warriors on horseback. 16s, April uprising, 1876. 23s, Russian liberators, Tirnovo. 25s, Social Democratic Party founding, 1891. 35s, September uprising, 1923. 41s, Fatherland Front. 43s, Prime Minister George Dimitrov, 5th Communist Party Congress, 1948. 50s, Lion, 10th cent. bas-relief. 53s, 10th Communist Party Congress. 55s, Kremikovski Metalurgical Plant. 1 l, Brezhnev, Gen. Todor Zhivkov.

1981, Aug. 10

2779	A1065	5s multicolored	.20	.20
2780	A1065	5s multicolored	.20	.20
2781	A1065	8s multicolored	.20	.20
2782	A1065	12s multicolored	.20	.20
2783	A1065	13s multicolored	.20	.20
2784	A1065	13s multicolored	.20	.20
2785	A1065	16s multicolored	.25	.20
2786	A1065	23s multicolored	.30	.20
2787	A1065	25s multicolored	.35	.20
2788	A1065	35s multicolored	.50	.20
2789	A1065	41s multicolored	.55	.25
2790	A1065	43s multicolored	.60	.25
2791	A1065	53s multicolored	.75	.30
2792	A1065	55s multicolored	.75	.30
		Nos. 2779-2792 (14)	5.25	3.10

Souvenir Sheets

2793	A1065	50s multicolored	.90	.55
2794	A1065	1 l multicolored	1.90	1.10

European Volleyball Championship
A1066

1981, Sept. 16 ***Perf. 13***

2795 A1066 13s multicolored .20 .20

Pegasus, Bronze Sculpture (Word Day) — A1067

World Food Day — A1068

1981, Oct. 2

2796 A1067 5s olive & cream .20 .20

1981, Oct. 16

2797 A1068 13s multicolored .20 .20

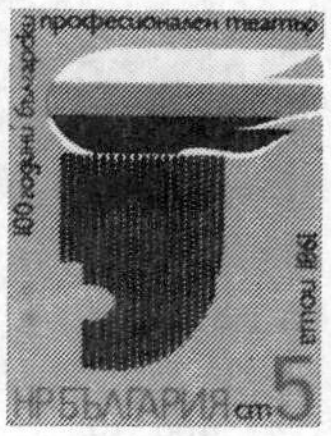

Professional Theater Centenary
A1069

1981, Oct. 30

2798 A1069 5s multicolored .20 .20

Anti-Apartheid Year — A1070

1981, Dec. 2

2799 A1070 5s multicolored .20 .20

Espana '82 World Cup Soccer — A1071

Designs: Various soccer players.

1981, Dec.

2800	A1071	5s multicolored	.20	.20
2801	A1071	13s multicolored	.25	.20
2802	A1071	43s multicolored	.70	.25
2803	A1071	53s multicolored	.95	.35
		Nos. 2800-2803 (4)	2.10	1.00

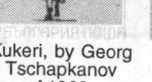

Heritage Day
A1072

1981, Nov. 21 **Photo.** ***Perf. 13***

2804 A1072 13s multicolored .20 .20

Souvenir Sheet

2804A A1072 60s multicolored 4.25 1.10

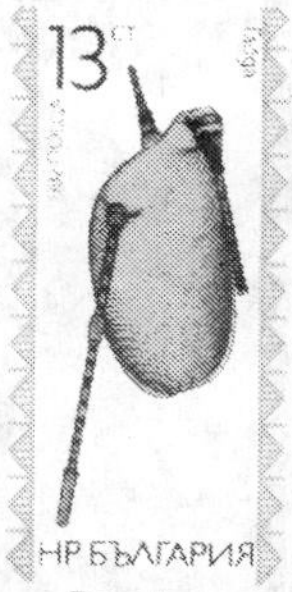

Bagpipe
A1073

Public Libraries and Reading Rooms, 125th Anniv
A1074

1982, Jan. 14

2805	A1073	13s shown	.20	.20
2806	A1073	25s Flutes	.40	.20
2807	A1073	30s Rebec	.50	.20
2808	A1073	35s Flute, recorder	.55	.25
2809	A1073	44s Mandolin	.75	.30
		Nos. 2805-2809 (5)	2.40	1.15

1982, Jan. 20

2810 A1074 5s dk grn .20 .20

Souvenir Sheet

Intl. Decade for Women (1975-1985) — A1075

1982, Mar. 8

2811 A1075 1 l multicolored 1.60 1.00

New Year 1982
A1076

1981, Dec. 22 **Photo.** ***Perf. 13***

2812	A1076	5s Ornament	.20	.20
2813	A1076	13s Ornament, diff.	.20	.20

The Sofia Plains, by Nicolas Petrov (1881-1916) — A1077

1982, Feb. 10 ***Perf. 12½***

2814	A1077	5s shown	.20	.20
2815	A1077	13s Girl Embroidering	.20	.20
2816	A1077	30s Fields of Peshtera	.50	.20
		Nos. 2814-2816 (3)	.90	.60

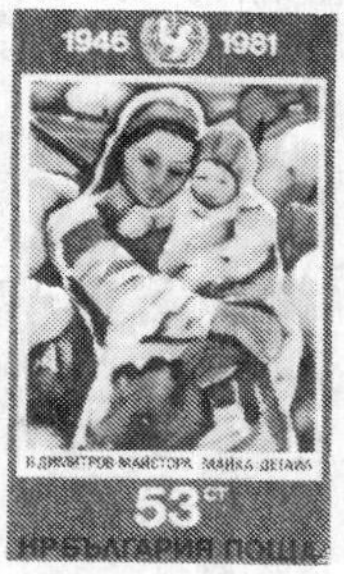

25th Anniv. of UNICEF (1981) — A1078

Mother and Child Paintings.

1982, Feb. 25 ***Perf. 14***

2817	A1078	53s Vladimir Dimitrov	.80	.30
2818	A1078	53s Basil Stoilov	.80	.30
2819	A1078	53s Ivan Milev	.80	.30
2820	A1078	53s Liliana Russeva	.80	.30
		Nos. 2817-2820 (4)	3.20	1.20

Figures, by Vladamir Dimitrov (1882-1961) — A1079

1982, Mar. 8 **Litho.**

2821	A1079	5s shown	.20	.20
2822	A1079	8s Landscape	.20	.20
2823	A1079	13s View of Istanbul	.25	.20
2824	A1079	25s Harvesters, vert.	.40	.20
2825	A1079	30s Woman in a Landscape, vert.	.50	.20
2826	A1079	35s Peasant Woman, vert.	.60	.25
		Nos. 2821-2826 (6)	2.15	1.25

Souvenir Sheet

2827 A1079 50s Self-portrait .80 .65

No. 2827 contains one stamp, size: 54x32mm.

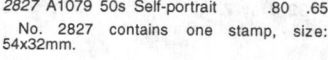

Trade Union Congress
A1080

1982, Apr. 8 **Photo.** ***Perf. 13½***

2828	A1080	5s Dimitrov reading union paper	.20	.20
2829	A1080	5s Culture Palace	.20	.20

#2828-2829 se-tenant with label showing text.

Marsh Snowdrop
A1081

Designs: Medicinal plants.

1982, Apr. 10 Photo. *Perf. 13*

2830 A1081	3s	shown	.20	.20
2831 A1081	5s	Chicory	.20	.20
2832 A1081	8s	Chamaenerium angustifolium	.20	.20
2833 A1081	13s	Solomon's seal	.25	.20
2834 A1081	25s	Violets	.50	.20
2835 A1081	35s	Centaury	.70	.25
		Nos. 2830-2835 (6)	2.05	1.25

Cosmonauts' Day — A1082

1982, Apr. 12 *Perf. 13½*

2836 A1082 13s Salyut-Soyuz link-up .20 .20

Se-tenant with label showing K.E. Tsiolkovsky (space pioneer).

Souvenir Sheet

SOZFILEX Stamp Exhibition — A1083

1982, May 7 *Perf. 13*

2837 A1083 50s Dimitrov, emblems .80 .45

14th Komsomol Congress (Youth Communists) — A1084

1982, May 25

2838 A1084 5s multicolored .20 .20

PHILEXFRANCE '82 Intl. Stamp Exhibition, Paris, June 11-21 — A1085

1982, May 28

2839 A1085 42s France #1, Bulgaria #1 .65 .25

19th Cent. Fresco
A1086

Designs: Various floral pattern frescoes.

1982, June 8 *Perf. 11½*

2840 A1086	5s	red & multi	.20	.20
2841 A1086	13s	green & multi	.25	.20
2842 A1086	25s	violet & multi	.40	.20
2843 A1086	30s	ol grn & multi	.50	.20
2844 A1086	42s	blue & multi	.75	.25
2845 A1086	60s	brown & multi	1.00	.40
		Nos. 2840-2845 (6)	3.10	1.45

Souvenir Sheet

George Dimitrov (1882-1949), First Prime Minister — A1087

1982, June 15 *Perf. 13*

2846 A1087 50s multicolored 1.00 .45

9th Congress of the National Front — A1088

1982, June 21 Photo. *Perf. 13*

2847 A1088 5s Dimitrov .20 .20

35th Anniv. of Balkan Bulgarian Airline
A1089

1982, June 28 *Perf. 13½x13*

2848 A1089 42s multicolored .65 .25

A1090

A1091

1982, July 15 *Perf. 13*

2849 A1090 13s multicolored .25 .20

Nuclear disarmament.

1982, July Photo. *Perf. 13*

2850 A1091 5s multicolored .20 .20
2851 A1091 13s multicolored .20 .20

Souvenir Sheet

2852 A1091 1 l multicolored 1.50 .75

Ludmila Zhivkova (b. 1942), artist.

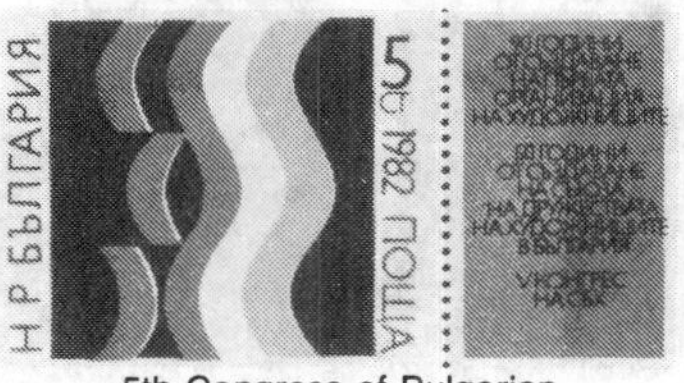

5th Congress of Bulgarian Painters — A1092

1982, July 27 *Perf. 13½*

2853 A1092 5s multicolored .20 .20

Se-tenant with label showing text.

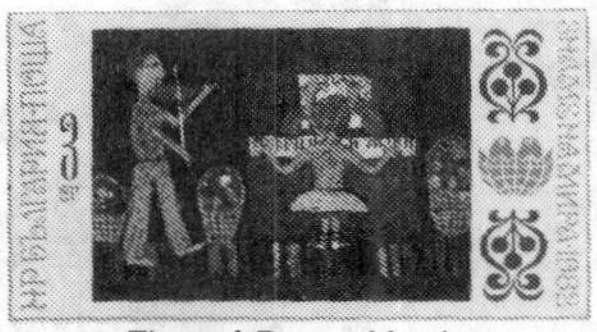

Flag of Peace Youth Assembly — A1093

Various children's drawings.

1982, Aug. 10 *Perf. 14*

2853A A1093	3s	multicolored	.20	.20
2853B A1093	5s	multicolored	.20	.20
2853C A1093	8s	multicolored	.20	.20
2853D A1093	13s	multicolored	.25	.20
		Nos. 2853A-2853D (4)	.85	.80

Souvenir Sheet

Perf. 14, Imperf.

2853E A1093 50s In balloon 3.00 .35

See Nos. 2864-2870, 3052-3058, 3321-3327.

10th Anniv. of UN Conference on Human Environment, Stockholm — A1093a

1982, Nov. 10 *Perf. 13*

2854 A1093a 13s dk blue & grn .20 .20

A1094

A1095

Designs: No. 2855, Park Hotel Moskva, Sofia. No. 2856, Tchernomore, Varna.

1982, Oct. 20 Photo. *Perf. 13*

2855 A1094 32s lt blue & multi .40 .20
2856 A1094 32s pink & multi .40 .20

1982, Nov. 4

2857 A1095 13s Cruiser Aurora, Sputnik II .20 .20

October Revolution, 65th anniv.

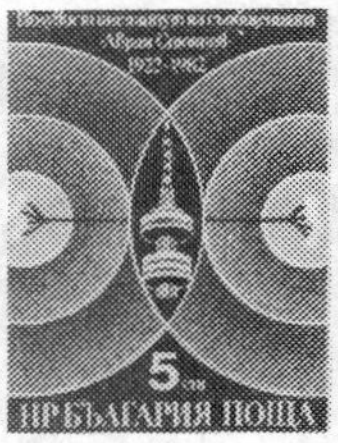

60th Anniv. of Institute of Communications
A1096

1982, Dec. 9

2858 A1096 5s ultra .20 .20

60th Anniv. of USSR
A1097

1982, Dec. 9

2859 A1097 13s multicolored .20 .20

The Piano, by Pablo Picasso (1881-1973)
A1098

Perf. 11½x12½

1982, Dec. 24 Litho.

2860 A1098	13s	shown	.20	.20
2861 A1098	30s	Portrait of Jacqueline	.40	.20
2862 A1098	42s	Maternity	.60	.25
		Nos. 2860-2862 (3)	1.20	.65

Souvenir Sheet

2863 A1098 1 l Self-portrait 2.50 .75

Children's Drawings Type of 1982

Various children's drawings. 8s, 13s, 50s vert.

1982, Dec. 28 *Perf. 14*

2864 A1093	3s	multicolored	.20	.20
2865 A1093	5s	multicolored	.20	.20
2866 A1093	8s	multicolored	.20	.20
2867 A1093	13s	multicolored	.20	.20
2868 A1093	25s	multicolored	.35	.20
2869 A1093	30s	multicolored	.40	.20
		Nos. 2864-2869 (6)	1.55	1.20

Souvenir Sheet

Perf. 14, Imperf.

2870 A1093 50s Shaking hands 2.50 .35

New Year
A1100

1982, Dec. 28 **Photo.** ***Perf. 13***

2872 A1100	5s multicolored		.20	.20
2873 A1100	13s multicolored		.20	.20

A1101

A1102

1982, Dec. 28

2874 A1101	25s Robert Koch	.40	.20
2875 A1101	30s Simon Bolivar	.40	.20
2876 A1101	30s Rabindranath Tagore (1861-1941)	.40	.20
	Nos. 2874-2876 (3)	1.20	.60

No. 2874 also for TB bacillus cent.

1983, Jan. 10 **Photo.** ***Perf. 13x13½***

2877 A1102	5s olive & brown	.20	.20

Vassil Levski (1837-73), revolutionary.

Universiade Games — A1103

1983, Feb. 15 ***Perf. 13***

2878 A1103	30s Downhill skiing	.35	.20

Fresh-water Fish — A1104

1983, Mar. 24 **Photo.** ***Perf. 13½x13***

2879 A1104	3s Pike	.20	.20
2880 A1104	5s Sturgeon	.20	.20
2881 A1104	13s Chub	.20	.20
2882 A1104	25s Perch	.40	.20
2883 A1104	30s Catfish	.40	.20
2884 A1104	42s Trout	.55	.25
	Nos. 2879-2884 (6)	1.95	1.25

Karl Marx (1818-1883)
A1105

1983, Apr. 5 ***Perf. 13x13½***

2885 A1105	13s multicolored	.20	.20

Jaroslav Hasek (1883-1923) — A1106

1983, Apr. 20 **Photo.** ***Perf. 13***

2886 A1106	13s multicolored	.20	.20

Martin Luther (1483-1546)
A1107

1983, May 10

2887 A1107	13s multicolored	.20	.20

55th Anniv. of Komsomol Youth Movement — A1108

1983, May 13

2888 A1108	5s "PMC"	.20	.20

A1109

A1111

National costumes.

1983, May 17 **Litho.** ***Perf. 14***

2889 A1109	5s Khaskovo	.20	.20
2890 A1109	8s Pernik	.20	.20
2891 A1109	13s Burgas	.20	.20
2892 A1109	25s Tolbukhin	.35	.20
2893 A1109	30s Blagoevgrad	.40	.20
2894 A1109	42s Topolovgrad	.50	.20
	Nos. 2889-2894 (6)	1.85	1.20

1983, May 20

6th Intl. Satire and Humor Biennial, Gabrovo: Old Man Feeding Chickens.

2900 A1111	5s multicolored	.20	.20

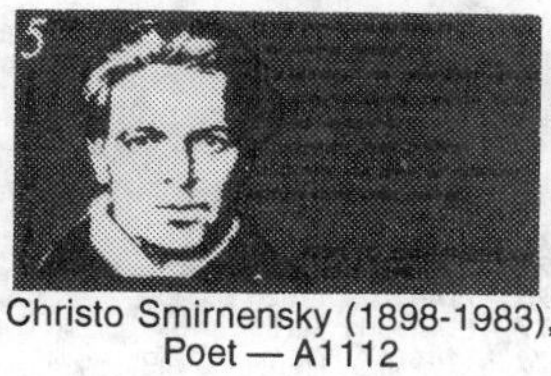

Christo Smirnensky (1898-1983), Poet — A1112

1983, May 25

2901 A1112	5s multicolored	.20	.20

17th Intl. Geodesists' Congress — A1113

1983, May 27

2902 A1113	30s Emblem	.45	.20

Interarch '83 Architecture Exhibition, Sofia — A1114

1983, June 6

2903 A1114	30s multicolored	.45	.20

8th European Chess Championships, Plovdiv — A1115

1983, June 20 **Photo.** ***Perf. 13***

2904 A1115	13s Chess pieces, map of Europe	.20	.20

Souvenir Sheet

BRASILIANA '83 Philatelic Exhibition — A1116

1983, June 24

2905 A1116	1 l Brazilian and Bulgarian stamps	1.50	.95

Social Democratic Party Congress of Russia, 80th Anniv.
A1118

Design: Lenin addressing congress.

1983, July 29 **Photo.** ***Perf. 13***

2907 A1118	5s multicolored	.20	.20

Ilinden-Preobrazhensky Insurrection, 80th Anniv. — A1119

1983, July 29

2908 A1119	5s Gun, dagger, book	.20	.20

Institute of Mining and Geology, Sofia, 30th Anniv. — A1120

1983, Aug. 10

2909 A1120	5s multicolored	.20	.20

60th Anniv. of September 1923 Uprising — A1121

1983, Aug. 19

2910 A1121	5s multicolored	.20	.20
2911 A1121	13s multicolored	.20	.20

Angora Cat
A1123

1983, Sept. 26 ***Perf. 13***

2917 A1123	5s shown	.20	.20
2918 A1123	13s Siamese	.25	.20
2919 A1123	20s Abyssinian, vert.	.40	.20
2920 A1123	25s Persian	.45	.20
2921 A1123	30s European, vert.	.55	.25
2922 A1123	42s Indochinese	.75	.30
	Nos. 2917-2922 (6)	2.60	1.35

Animated Film Festival — A1124

Perf. 14x13½

1983, Sept. 15 **Photo.**

2923 A1124	5s Articulation layout	.20	.20

Trevethick's Engine, 1804 — A1125

Locomotiv es: 13s, Blenkinsop's Prince Royal, 1810. 42s, Hedley's Puffing Billy, 1812. 60s, Adler (first German locomotive), 1835.

1983, Oct. 20 ***Perf. 13***

2924 A1125	5s multicolored	.20	.20
2925 A1125	13s multicolored	.30	.20
2926 A1125	42s multicolored	.95	.30
2927 A1125	60s multicolored	1.40	.40
	Nos. 2924-2927 (4)	2.85	1.10

See Nos. 2983-2987.

Souvenir Sheet

Liberation Monument, Plovdiv — A1126

1983, Nov. 4

2928	A1126	50s multicolored	.80	.60

Philatelic Federation, 90th anniv.

Sofia Opera, 75th Anniv. — A1127

Composers' Assoc., 50th Anniv. — A1128

1983, Dec. 2 ***Perf. 13x13½***

2929	A1127	5s Mask, lyre, laurel	.20	.20

1983, Dec. 5

Composers: 5s, Ioan Kukuzel (14th cent.) 8s, Atanasov. 13s, Petko Stainov. 20s, Veselin Stodiov. 25s, Liubomir Pipkov. 30s, Pancho Vladigerov. Se-tenant with labels showing compositions.

2930	A1128	5s multicolored	.20	.20
2931	A1128	8s multicolored	.20	.20
2932	A1128	13s multicolored	.20	.20
2933	A1128	20s multicolored	.30	.20
2934	A1128	25s multicolored	.40	.20
2935	A1128	30s multicolored	.50	.20
		Nos. 2930-2935 (6)	1.80	1.20

New Year 1984 A1129

1983, Dec. 10 ***Perf. 13***

2936	A1129	5s multicolored	.20	.20

Angelo Donni, by Raphael A1130

1983, Dec. 22 ***Perf. 14***

2937	A1130	5s shown	.20	.20
2938	A1130	13s Cardinal	.20	.20
2939	A1130	30s Baldassare Castiglioni	.45	.20
2940	A1130	42s Donna Belata	.70	.30
		Nos. 2937-2940 (4)	1.55	.90

Souvenir Sheet

2941	A1130	1 l Sistine Madonna	1.60	1.25

Bat, World Wildlife Emblem — A1131

Various bats and rodents.

1983, Dec. 30 ***Perf. 13***

2942	A1131	12s multicolored	.20	.20
2943	A1131	13s multicolored	.20	.20
2944	A1131	20s multicolored	.30	.20
2945	A1131	30s multicolored	.45	.25
2946	A1131	42s multicolored	.65	.30
		Nos. 2942-2946 (5)	1.80	1.15

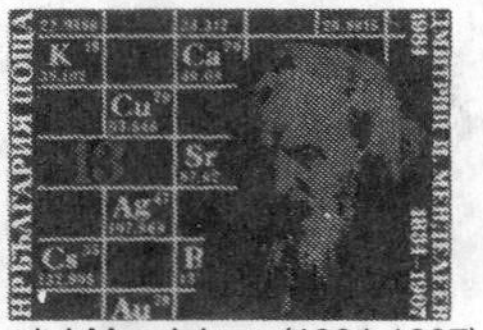

Dmitri Mendeleev (1834-1907), Russian Chemist — A1132

1984, Mar. 14

2947	A1132	13s multicolored	.25	.20

Ljuben Karavelov, Poet and Freedom Fighter, Birth Sesquicentenary A1133

1984, Jan. 31 ***Perf. 13x13½***

2948	A1133	5s multicolored	.20	.20

Tanker Gen. V.I. Zaimov A1137

1984, Mar. 22 ***Perf. 13½***

2959	A1137	5s shown	.20	.20
2960	A1137	13s Mesta	.20	.20
2961	A1137	25s Veleka	.40	.20
2962	A1137	32s Ferry	.50	.20
2963	A1137	42s Cargo ship Rossen	.70	.30
		Nos. 2959-2963 (5)	2.00	1.10

Souvenir Sheet

World Cup Soccer Commemorative of 1982, Spain No. 2281 — A1137a

1984, Apr. 18 Photo. ***Perf. 13x13½***

2963A	A1137a	2 l multicolored	3.00	2.50

ESPANA '84.

Dove with Letter over Globe — A1138

Berries — A1139

1984, Apr. 24 ***Perf. 13***

2964	A1138	5s multicolored	.20	.20

World Youth Stamp Exhibition, Pleven, Oct. 5-11.

1984, May 5

2965	A1139	5s Cherries	.20	.20
2966	A1139	8s Strawberries	.20	.20
2967	A1139	13s Blackberries	.20	.20
2968	A1139	20s Raspberries	.35	.20
2969	A1139	42s Currants	.70	.30
		Nos. 2965-2969 (5)	1.65	1.10

A1140

A1142

1984, May 23

2970	A1140	13s Athlete, doves	.20	.20

6th Republican Spartikiade games,

1984, June 12

2972	A1142	5s Folk singer, drum	.20	.20

6th amateur art festival.

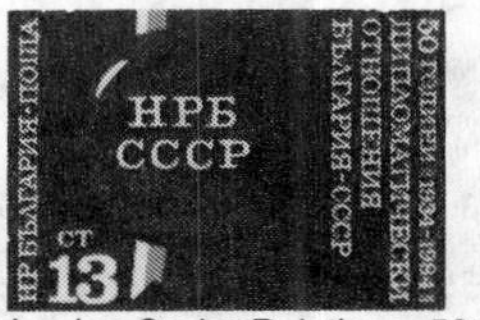

Bulgarian-Soviet Relations, 50th Anniv. — A1143

1984, June 27

2973	A1143	13s Initialed seal	.20	.20

Doves and Pigeons — A1144

1984, July 6 Litho. ***Perf. 14***

2974	A1144	5s Rock dove	.20	.20
2975	A1144	13s Stock dove	.20	.20
2976	A1144	20s Wood pigeon	.35	.20
2977	A1144	30s Turtle dove	.50	.20
2978	A1144	42s Domestic pigeon	.70	.30
		Nos. 2974-2978 (5)	1.95	1.10

1st Natl. Communist Party Congress, 60th Anniv. — A1145

1984, May 18 Photo. ***Perf. 13½x13***

2979	A1145	5s multicolored	.20	.20

Souvenir Sheet

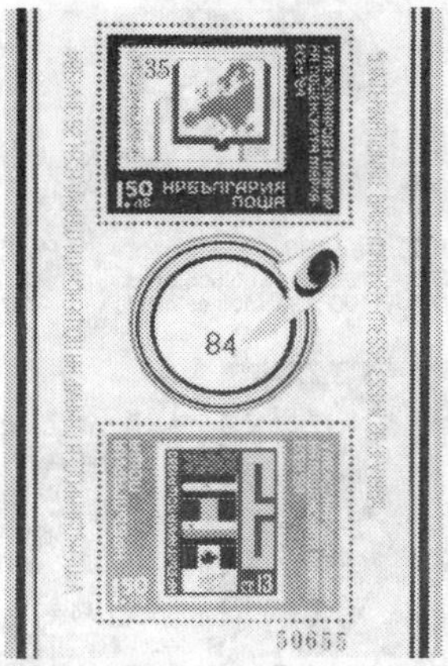

Intl. Stamp Exhibition, Essen, May 26-31 — A1146

Europa Conference stamps: No. 2980a, 1980. No. 2980b, 1981.

1984, May 22 ***Perf. 13x13½***

2980	A1146	Sheet of 2	*12.00*	*10.00*
a.-b.		1.50 l multi	*6.00*	*5.00*

Mount Everest — A1147

1984, May 31 ***Perf. 13***

2981	A1147	5s multicolored	.20	.20

1st Bulgarian Everest climbing expedition, Apr. 20-May 9.

Souvenir Sheet

UPU Congress, Hamburg — A1148

1984, June 11 ***Perf. 13½x13***

2982	A1148	3 l Sailing ship	*12.00*	*10.00*

Locomotives Type of 1983

1984, July 31 ***Perf. 13***

2983	A1125	13s Best Friend of Charleston, 1830, US	.25	.20
2984	A1125	25s Saxonia, 1836, Dresden	.40	.25
2985	A1125	30s Lafayette, 1837, US	.50	.30
2986	A1125	42s Borsig, 1841, Germany	.75	.40
2987	A1125	60s Philadelphia, 1843, Austria	1.10	.65
		Nos. 2983-2987 (5)	3.00	1.80

September 9 Revolution, 40th Anniv. — A1149

1984, Aug. 4

2988 A1149 5s K, production quality emblem .20 .20
2989 A1149 20s Victory Monument, Sofia .35 .20
2990 A1149 30s Star, "9" .55 .30
Nos. 2988-2990 (3) 1.10 .70

Paintings by Nenko Balkanski (1907-1977) — A1150

1984, Sept. 17 ***Perf. 14***

2991 A1150 5s Boy Playing Harmonica, vert. .20 .20
2992 A1150 30s A Paris Window, vert. .55 .30
2993 A1150 42s Double Portrait .80 .40
Nos. 2991-2993 (3) 1.55 .90

Souvenir Sheet

2994 A1150 1 l Self-portrait, vert. 1.75 1.25

MLADPOST '84 International Youth Stamp Exhibition, Pleven — A1151

Buildings in Pleven: 5s, Mausoleum to Russian soldiers, 1877-78 Russo-Turkish War. 13s, Panorama Building.

1984, Sept. 20 ***Perf. 13***

2995 A1151 5s multicolored .20 .20
2996 A1151 13s multicolored .30 .20

Septembrist Young Pioneers Org., 40th Anniv. — A1152

1984, Sept. 21 **Photo.** ***Perf. 13***

2997 A1152 5s multicolored .20 .20

Nikola Vapzarov A1153

1984, Oct. 2

2998 A1153 5s maroon & pale yel .20 .20

Natl. Soccer, 75th Anniv. A1154

1984, Oct. 3

2999 A1154 42s multicolored .75 .40

Souvenir Sheet

MLADPOST '84 — A1155

1984, Oct. 5 **Photo.** ***Perf. 13***

3000 A1155 50s multicolored 1.00 .50

Bridges and Maps — A1156

1984, Oct. 5 **Photo.** ***Perf. 13½x13***

3001 A1156 5s Devil's Bridge, Arda River .20 .20
3002 A1156 13s Koljo-Fitscheto, Bjala .25 .20
3003 A1156 30s Asparuchow, Warna .60 .30
3004 A1156 42s Bebresch Highway Bridge, Botevgrad .75 .40
Nos. 3001-3004 (4) 1.80 1.10

Intl. Olympic Committee, 90th Anniv. — A1158

1984, Oct. 24 **Photo.** ***Perf. 13***

3007 A1158 13s multicolored .25 .20

A1159

A1160

Pelecanus crispus.

1984, Nov. 2

3008 A1159 5s Adult, young .20 .20
3009 A1159 13s Two adults .30 .20
3010 A1159 20s Adult in water .40 .20
3011 A1159 32s In flight .65 .30
Nos. 3008-3011 (4) 1.55 .90

World Wildlife Fund.

1984, Nov. 2

3012 A1160 5s multicolored .20 .20

Anton Ivanov (1884-1942), labor leader.

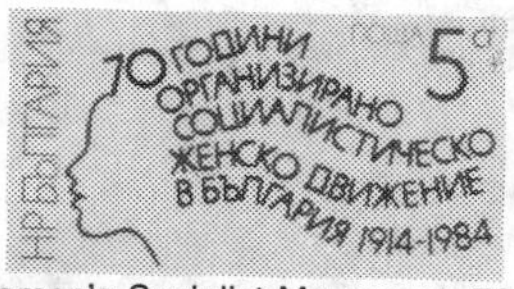

Women's Socialist Movement, 70th Anniv. — A1161

1984, Nov. 9

3013 A1161 5s multicolored .20 .20

Telecommunication Towers — A1162

1984, Nov. 23

3014 A1162 5s Snezhanka .20 .20
3015 A1162 1 l Orelek 1.90 1.00

Snowflakes, New Year 1985 — A1163

1984, Dec. 5

3016 A1163 5s Doves, posthorns .20 .20
3017 A1163 13s Doves, blossom .25 .20

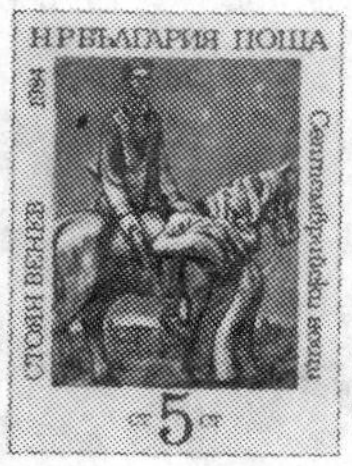

Paintings by Stoyan Venev (b. 1904) — A1164

1984, Dec. 10 **Litho.**

3018 A1164 5s September Nights .20 .20
3019 A1164 30s Man with Three Medals .50 .30
3020 A1164 42s The Best .70 .40
Nos. 3018-3020 (3) 1.40 .90

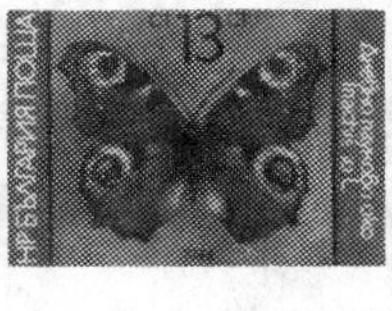

Butterflies A1165

1984, Dec. 14 ***Perf. 11½***

3021 A1165 13s Inachis io .25 .20
3022 A1165 25s Papilio machaon .40 .25
3023 A1165 30s Brintesia circe .50 .30
3024 A1165 42s Anthocaris cardamines .75 .40
3025 A1165 60s Vanessa atalanta 1.00 .60
Nos. 3021-3025 (5) 2.90 1.75

Souvenir Sheet

3026 A1165 1 l Limenitis populi 2.00 1.00

A1166

A1167

1984, Dec. 18 **Photo.** ***Perf. 13x13½***

3027 A1166 13s multicolored .25 .20

Cesar Augusto Sandino (1895-1934), Nicaraguan freedom fighter.

1984, Dec. 28 **Litho.** ***Perf. 14***

3028 A1167 5s The Three Graces .20 .20
3029 A1167 13s Cupid and the Graces .30 .20
3030 A1167 30s Original Sin .55 .30
3031 A1167 42s La Fornarina .80 .40
Nos. 3028-3031 (4) 1.85 1.10

Souvenir Sheet

3032 A1167 1 l Galatea 2.00 1.00

Raphael, 500th birth anniv. (1983).

Cruise Ship Sofia, Maiden Voyage — A1168

1984, Dec. 29 **Photo.** ***Perf. 13***

3033 A1168 13s blue, dk bl & yel .25 .20

Predators A1170

1985, Jan. 17

3035 A1170 13s Conepatus leuconotus .25 .20
3036 A1170 25s Prionodon linsang .40 .25
3037 A1170 30s Ictonix striatus .50 .30
3038 A1170 42s Hemigalus derbyanus .75 .40
3039 A1170 60s Galidictis fasciata 1.00 .60
Nos. 3035-3039 (5) 2.90 1.75

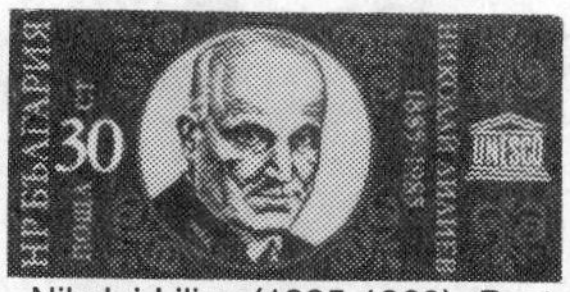

Nikolai Liliev (1885-1960), Poet, UNESCO Emblem — A1171

1985, Jan. 25

3040 A1171 30s multicolored .50 .30

Zviatko Radojnov (1895-1942), Labor Leader — A1172

1985, Jan. 29

3041 A1172 5s dk red & dk brn .20 .20

Dr. Assen Zlatarov (1885-1936), Chemist A1173

1985, Feb. 14

3042 A1173 5s multicolored .20 .20

Souvenir Sheet

Akademik, Research Vessel — A1174

1985, Mar. 1

3043 A1174 80s multicolored 1.25 .80

UNESCO Intl. Oceanographic Commission, 25th anniv.

Souvenir Sheet

Lenin — A1175

1985, Mar. 12

3044 A1175 50s multicolored .85 .50

A1176 A1177

1985, Mar. 19

3045 A1176 13s multicolored .25 .20

Warsaw Treaty Org., 30th anniv.

1985, Mar. 25

Composers.

3046 A1177 42s Bach .50 .30
3047 A1177 42s Mozart .50 .30
3048 A1177 42s Tchaikovsky .50 .30
3049 A1177 42s Mussorgsky .50 .30
3050 A1177 42s Verdi .50 .30
3051 A1177 42s Tenev .50 .30
Nos. 3046-3051 (6) 3.00 1.80

Children's Drawings Type of 1982

Inscribed 1985. Various children's drawings.

1985, Mar. 26 Litho. *Perf. 14*

3052 A1093 5s multicolored .20 .20
3053 A1093 8s multicolored .20 .20
3054 A1093 13s multicolored .20 .20
3055 A1093 20s multicolored .30 .20
3056 A1093 25s multicolored .40 .25
3057 A1093 30s multicolored .50 .30
Nos. 3052-3057 (6) 1.80 1.35

Souvenir Sheet

3058 A1093 50s Children dancing, vert. 1.00 .50

3rd Flag of Peace Intl. Assembly, Sofia. No. 3058 exists imperf. with blue control number, same value.

St. Methodius, 1100th Death Anniv. — A1179

1985, Apr. 6 Photo. *Perf. 13*

3059 A1179 13s multicolored .25 .20

Victory Parade, Moscow, 1945 A1180

13s, 11th Infantry on parade, Sofia. 30s, Soviet soldier, orphan. 50s, Soviet flag-raising, Berlin.

1985, Apr. 30 *Perf. 13½*

3060 A1180 5s multicolored .20 .20
3061 A1180 13s multicolored .25 .20
3062 A1180 30s multicolored .50 .30
Nos. 3060-3062 (3) .95 .70

Souvenir Sheet

Perf. 13

3063 A1180 50s multicolored 1.00 .50

Defeat of Nazi Germany, end of World War II, 40th anniv. Nos. 3060-3062 printed se-tenant with labels picturing Soviet (5s, 30s) and Bulgarian medals of honor.

7th Intl. Humor and Satire Biennial A1181

1985, Apr. 30 *Perf. 13½*

3064 A1181 13s yel, sage grn & red .25 .20

No. 3064 printed se-tenant with label picturing Gabrovo Cat emblem.

Intl. Youth Year — A1182

1985, May 21 *Perf. 13*

3065 A1182 13s multicolored .25 .20

Ivan Vasov (1850-1921), Poet — A1183

1985, May 30 *Perf. 13½*

3066 A1183 5s tan & sepia .20 .20

No. 3066 printed se-tenant with label picturing Vasov's birthplace in Sopot.

Soviet War Memorial, Haskovo City Arms A1184

1985, June 1 *Perf. 13*

3067 A1184 5s multicolored .20 .20

Haskovo millennium.

12th World Youth Festival, Moscow — A1185

1985, June 25

3068 A1185 13s multicolored .25 .20

Indira Gandhi (1917-1984), Prime Minister of India — A1186

1985, June 26

3069 A1186 30s org yel, sepia & ver .60 .30

Vasil Aprilov, Founder — A1187

1985, June 30

3070 A1187 5s multicolored .20 .20

1st secular school, Gabrovo, 150th anniv.

INTERSTENO '85 — A1188

1985, June 30

3071 A1188 13s multicolored .25 .20

Congress for the Intl. Union of Stenographers and Typists, Sofia.

Alexander Nevski Cathedral A1189

1985, July 9

3072 A1189 42s multicolored .80 .40

World Tourism Org., general assembly, Sofia.

UN, 40th Anniv. A1190

1985, July 16

3073 A1190 13s multicolored .25 .20

A1191 Roses — A1192

1985, July 16

3074 A1191 13s multicolored .25 .20

Admission of Bulgaria to UN, 30th anniv.

1985, July 20 Litho.

3075 A1192 5s Rosa damascena .20 .20
3076 A1192 13s Rosa trakijka .25 .20
3077 A1192 20s Rosa radiman .35 .20
3078 A1192 30s Rosa marista .50 .30
3079 A1192 42s Rosa valentina .75 .40
3080 A1192 60s Rosa maria 1.00 .60
a. Min. sheet of 6, #3075-3080 3.50 2.00
Nos. 3075-3080 (6) 3.05 1.90

Helsinki Conference, 10th Anniv. — A1193

1985, Aug. 1 **Photo.**
3081 A1193 13s multicolored .25 .20

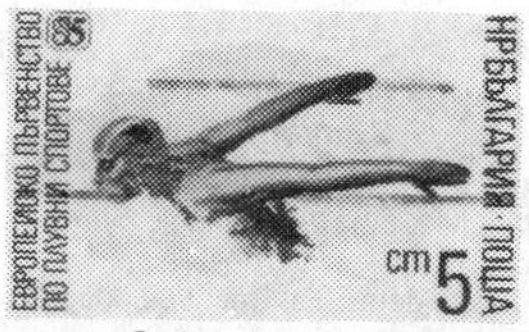

European Swimming Championships, Sofia — A1194

1985, Aug. 2 **Litho.** ***Perf. 12½***
3082 A1194 5s Butterfly stroke .20 .20
3083 A1194 13s Water polo, vert. .20 .20
3084 A1194 42s Diving, vert. .60 .35
3085 A1194 60s Synchronized swimming .75 .40
Nos. 3082-3085 (4) 1.75 1.15

The 60s exists with central design inverted.

Natl. Tourism Assoc., 90th Anniv. A1195

1985, Aug. 15 **Photo.** ***Perf. 13***
3086 A1195 5s multicolored .20 .20

1986 World Cup Soccer Championships, Mexico — A1196

Various soccer plays. Nos. 3087-3090 vert.

1985, Aug. 29 ***Perf. 13***
3087 A1196 5s multicolored .20 .20
3088 A1196 13s multicolored .20 .20
3089 A1196 30s multicolored .40 .20
3090 A1196 42s multicolored .50 .25
Nos. 3087-3090 (4) 1.30 .85

Souvenir Sheet

3091 A1196 1 l multicolored 1.25 .75

Union of Eastern Rumelia and Bulgaria, 1885 — A1197

1985, Aug. 29 ***Perf. 14x13½***
3092 A1197 5s multicolored .20 .20

Computer Design Portraits — A1198

1985, Sept. 23 ***Perf. 13***
3093 A1198 5s Boy .20 .20
3094 A1198 13s Youth .25 .20
3095 A1198 30s Cosmonaut .50 .30
Nos. 3093-3095 (3) .95 .70

Intl. Exhibition of the Works of Youth Inventors, Plovdiv.

St. John the Baptist Church, Nessebar A1199

Natl. restoration projects: 13s, Tyrant Hreljo Tower, Rila Monastery. 35s, Soldier, fresco, Ivanovo Rock Church. 42s, Archangel Gabriel, fresco, Bojana Church. 60s, Thracian Woman, fresco, Tomb of Kasanlak, 3rd century B.C. 1 l, The Horseman of Madara, bas-relief.

1985, Sept. 25 **Litho.** ***Perf. 12½***
3096 A1199 5s multicolored .20 .20
3097 A1199 13s multicolored .25 .20
3098 A1199 35s multicolored .60 .30
3099 A1199 42s multicolored .75 .40
3100 A1199 60s multicolored 1.10 .60
Nos. 3096-3100 (5) 2.90 1.70

Souvenir Sheet

Imperf

3101 A1199 1 l multicolored 1.75 1.00

UNESCO, 40th anniv.

Souvenir Sheet

Ludmila Zhishkova Cultural Palace, Sofia — A1200

1985, Oct. 8 ***Perf. 13***
3102 A1200 1 l multicolored 1.75 1.00

UNESCO 23rd General Assembly, Sofia.

Colosseum, Rome — A1201

1985, Oct. 15 **Photo.** ***Perf. 13½***
3103 A1201 42s multicolored .75 .40

ITALIA '85. No. 3103 printed se-tenant with label picturing the exhibition emblem.

Souvenir Sheet

Cultural Congress, Budapest — A1202

Designs: No. 3104a, St. Cyril, patron saint of Europe. No. 3104b, Map of Europe. No. 3104c, St. Methodius, patron saint of Europe.

Perf. 13, 13 Vert. (#3104b)

1985, Oct. 22 **Photo.**
3104 A1202 Sheet of 3 2.75 1.50
a.-c. 50s, any single .90 .50

Helsinki Congress, 10th anniv.

Flowers — A1203

1985, Oct. 22 **Photo.** ***Perf. 13x13½***
3105 A1203 5s Gladiolus hybridy .20 .20
3106 A1203 5s Iris germanica .20 .20
3107 A1203 5s Convolvulus tricolor .20 .20
Nos. 3105-3107 (3) .60 .60

See Nos. 3184-3186.

Historic Sailing Ships A1204

1985, Oct. 28 **Photo.** ***Perf. 13***
3108 A1204 5s Dutch .20 .20
3109 A1204 12s Sea Sovereign, Britain .25 .20
3110 A1204 20s Mediterranean .35 .20
3111 A1204 25s Royal Prince, Britain .45 .25
3112 A1204 42s Mediterranean .75 .40
3113 A1204 60s British battleship 1.10 .60
Nos. 3108-3113 (6) 3.10 1.85

Souvenir Sheet

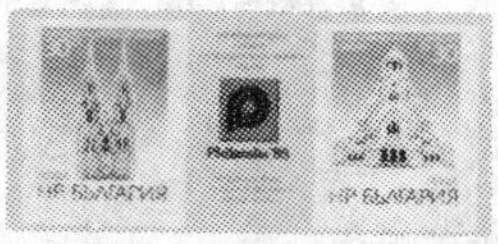

PHILATELIA '85, Cologne — A1205

Designs: a, Cologne Cathedral. b, Alexander Nevski Cathedral, Sofia.

1985, Nov. 4 ***Imperf.***
3114 A1205 Sheet of 2 1.25 .65
a.-b. 30s, any single .60 .30

Conspiracy to Liberate Bulgaria from Turkish Rule, 150th Anniv. — A1206

Freedom fighters and symbols: #3115, Georgi Stojkov Rakowski (1820-76). #3116, Batscho Kiro (1835-76). #3117, Sword, Bible & hands.

1985, Nov. 6 ***Perf. 13***
3115 A1206 5s multicolored .20 .20
3116 A1206 5s multicolored .20 .20
3117 A1206 13s multicolored .25 .20
Nos. 3115-3117 (3) .65 .60

Liberation from Byzantine Rule, 800th Anniv. A1207

Paintings: 5s, The Revolt 1185, by G. Bogdanov. 13s, The Revolt 1185, by Alexander Tersiev. 30s, Battle Near Klokotnitza, by B. Grigorov and M. Ganowski. 42s, Velika Tarnovo Town Wall, by Zanko Lawrenov. 1 l, St. Dimitriev Church, 12th cent.

1985, Nov. 15 **Litho.**
3118 A1207 5s multicolored .20 .20
3119 A1207 13s multicolored .25 .20
3120 A1207 30s multicolored .50 .30
3121 A1207 42s multicolored .75 .40
Nos. 3118-3121 (4) 1.70 1.10

Souvenir Sheet

Imperf

3122 A1207 1 l multicolored 2.00 1.00

Souvenir Sheet

BALKANPHILA '85 — A1208

1985, Nov. 29 **Photo.** ***Perf. 13***
3123 A1208 40s Dove, posthorn .75 .40

Intl. Post and Telecommunications Development Program — A1209

1985, Dec. 2
3124 A1209 13s multicolored .25 .20

Anton Popov (1915-1942), Freedom Fighter — A1210

1985, Dec. 11 **Photo.** ***Perf. 13***
3125 A1210 5s lake .20 .20

New Year 1986 A1211

1985, Dec. 11 Photo. *Perf. 13*
3126 A1211 5s Doves, snowflake .20 .20
3127 A1211 13s Doves .25 .20

Hunting Dogs and Prey — A1212

Designs: 5s, Pointer and partridge. 8s, Irish setter and pochard. 13s, English setter and mallard. 20s, Cocker spaniel and woodcock. 25s, German pointer and rabbit. 30s, Balkan hound and boar. 42s, Shorthaired dachshund and fox.

1985, Dec. 27 Litho. *Perf. 13x12½*
3128 A1212 5s multicolored .20 .20
3129 A1212 8s multicolored .20 .20
3130 A1212 13s multicolored .30 .20
3131 A1212 20s multicolored .40 .20
3132 A1212 25s multicolored .50 .25
3133 A1212 30s multicolored .60 .30
3134 A1212 42s multicolored .85 .40
Nos. 3128-3134 (7) 3.05 1.75

Intl. Year of the Handicapped — A1213

1985, Dec. 30 Photo. *Perf. 13*
3135 A1213 5s multicolored .20 .20

George Dimitrov (1882-1949) — A1214

1985, Dec. 30 Photo. *Perf. 13*
3136 A1214 13s brn lake .25 .20

7th Intl. Communist Congress, Moscow.

UN Child Survival Campaign — A1215

1986, Jan. 21 Photo. *Perf. 13*
3137 A1215 13s multicolored .25 .20

UNICEF, 40th anniv.

Demeter Blagoev (1856-1924) A1216

1986, Jan. 28 Photo. *Perf. 13*
3138 A1216 5s dk lake, car & dk red .20 .20

Intl. Peace Year A1217

1986, Jan. 31 *Perf. 13½*
3139 A1217 5s multicolored .20 .20

Orchids — A1218

1986, Feb. 12 Litho. *Perf. 13x12½*
3140 A1218 5s Dactylorhiza romana .20 .20
3141 A1218 13s Epipactis palustris .20 .20
3142 A1218 30s Ophrys cornuta .40 .30
3143 A1218 32s Limodorum abortivum .40 .30
3144 A1218 42s Cypripedium calceolus .50 .40
3145 A1218 60s Orchis papilionacea 1.00 .50
a. Min. sheet of 6, #3140-3145 3.00 1.50
Nos. 3140-3145 (6) 2.70 1.90

Hares and Rabbits A1219

1986, Feb. 24 *Perf. 12½x12*
3146 A1219 5s multicolored .20 .20
3147 A1219 25s multicolored .45 .25
3148 A1219 30s multicolored .55 .30
3149 A1219 32s multicolored .60 .30
3150 A1219 42s multicolored .75 .40
3151 A1219 60s multicolored 1.00 .60
Nos. 3146-3151 (6) 3.55 2.05

Bulgarian Eagle, Newspaper, 140th Anniv. — A1220

Front page of 1st issue & Ivan Bogorov, journalist.

1986, Feb. 2 Photo. *Perf. 13*
3152 A1220 5s multicolored .20 .20

Souvenir Sheet

Halley's Comet A1221

Comet's orbit in the Solar System: a, 1980. b, 1910-86. c, 1916-70. d, 1911.

1986, Mar. 7 *Perf. 13½x13*
3153 Sheet of 4 1.75 1.25
a.-d. A1221 25s, any single .40 .30

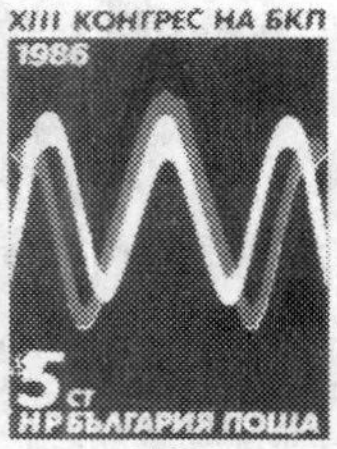

A1222 A1223

1986, Mar. 12 *Perf. 13x13½*
3154 A1222 5s dp bl & bl .20 .20

Vladimir Bachev (1935-1967), poet.

1986, Mar. 17 *Perf. 13*
3155 A1223 5s Wavy lines .20 .20
3156 A1223 8s Star .20 .20
3157 A1223 13s Worker .25 .20
Nos. 3155-3157 (3) .65 .60

Souvenir Sheet

Imperf

3158 A1223 50s Scaffold, flags .90 .50

13th Natl. Communist Party Congress.

Souvenir Sheet

1st Manned Space Flight, 25th Anniv. — A1224

Designs: a, Vostok I, 1961. b, Yuri Gagarin (1934-68), Russian cosmonaut.

1986, Mar. 28 *Perf. 13½x13*
3159 Sheet of 2 1.75 1.00
a.-b. A1224 50s, any single 1.00 .50

April Uprising against the Turks, 110th Anniv. — A1225

Monuments: 5s, 1876 Uprising monument, Panagjuriste. 13s, Christo Botev, Vraca.

1986, Mar. 30 *Perf. 13*
3160 A1225 5s multicolored .20 .20
3161 A1225 13s multicolored .25 .20

A1225a

Levsky-Spartak Sports Club, 75th Anniv. — A1226

1986 *Perf. 13*
3161A A1225a 5s multicolored .20 .20

Souvenir Sheet

Imperf

3162 A1226 50s Rhythmic gymnastics .80 .50

Issue dates: 5s, Dec. 50s, May 12.

A1227 A1228

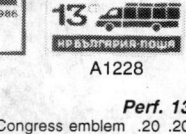

1986, May 19 *Perf. 13*
3163 A1227 5s Congress emblem .20 .20
3164 A1227 8s Emblem on globe .20 .20
3165 A1227 13s Flags .25 .20
Nos. 3163-3165 (3) .65 .60

35th Congress of Bulgarian farmers, Sofia.

1986, May 27 *Perf. 13x13½*
3166 A1228 13s multicolored .25 .20

Conference of Transport Ministers from Socialist Countries.

17th Intl. Book Fair, Sofia — A1229

1986, May 28
3167 A1229 13s blk, brt red & grysh blk .25 .20

1986 World Cup Soccer Championships, Mexico — A1230

Various soccer plays; attached labels picture Mexican landmarks.

1986, May 30 *Perf. 13½*
3168 A1230 5s multi, vert. .20 .20
3169 A1230 13s multicolored .25 .20
3170 A1230 20s multicolored .35 .20
3171 A1230 30s multicolored .55 .30
3172 A1230 42s multicolored .75 .40
3173 A1230 60s multi, vert. 1.10 .60
Nos. 3168-3173 (6) 3.20 1.90

Souvenir Sheet

Perf. 13

3174 A1230 1 l Azteca Stadium 1.75 1.00

Treasures of Preslav — A1231

Gold artifacts: 5s, Embossed brooch. 13s, Pendant with pearl cross, vert. 20s, Crystal and pearl pendant. 30s, Embossed shield. 42s, Pearl and enamel pendant, vert. 60s, Enamel shield.

1986, June 7 ***Perf. 13½x13, 13x13½***

3175	A1231	5s multicolored	.20	.20
3176	A1231	13s multicolored	.25	.20
3177	A1231	20s multicolored	.35	.20
3178	A1231	30s multicolored	.55	.30
3179	A1231	42s multicolored	.75	.40
3180	A1231	60s multicolored	1.00	.60
		Nos. 3175-3180 (6)	3.10	1.90

World Fencing Championships, Sofia, July 25-Aug. 3 — A1232

1986, July 25 **Photo.** ***Perf. 13***

3181	A1232	5s Head cut, lunge	.20	.20
3182	A1232	13s Touche	.25	.20
3183	A1232	25s Lunge, parry	.45	.25
		Nos. 3181-3183 (3)	.90	.65

Flower Type of 1985

1986, July 29 ***Perf. 13x13½***

3184	A1203	8s Ipomoea tricolor	.20	.20
3185	A1203	8s Anemone coronaria	.20	.20
3186	A1203	32s Lilium auratum	.55	.30
		Nos. 3184-3186 (3)	.95	.70

A1233

A1234

1986, Aug. 25

3187	A1233	42s sepia, sal brn & lake	.75	.40

STOCKHOLMIA '86. No. 3187 printed in sheets of 3 + 3 labels picturing folk art.

Miniature Sheet

Environmental Conservation: a, Ciconia ciconia. b, Nuphar lutea. c, Salamandra salamandra. d, Nymphaea alba.

1986, Aug. 25 **Litho.** ***Perf. 14***

3188		Sheet of 4 + label	2.00	1.00
a.-d.		A1234 30s any single	.50	.25

No. 3188 contains center label picturing the oldest oak tree in Bulgaria, Granit Village.

Natl. Arms, Building of the Sobranie — A1235

1986, Sept. 13 **Photo.** ***Perf. 13***

3189	A1235	5s Prus grn, yel grn & red	.20	.20

People's Republic of Bulgaria, 40th anniv.

15th Postal Union Congress — A1236

1986, Sept. 24

3190	A1236	13s multicolored	.25	.20

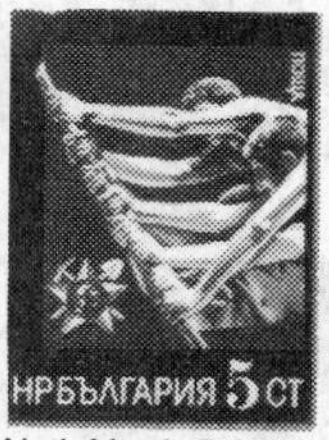

Natl. Youth Brigade Movement, 40th Anniv. A1237

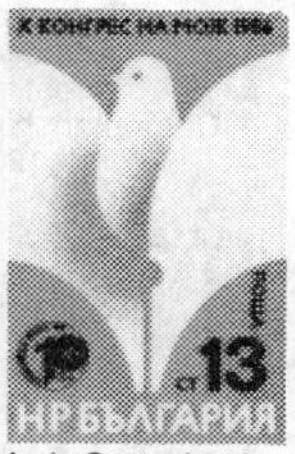

Intl. Organization of Journalists, 10th Congress A1238

1986, Oct. 4

3191	A1237	5s multicolored	.20	.20

1986, Oct. 13

3192	A1238	13s blue & dark blue	.25	.20

Sts. Cyril and Methodius, Disciples — A1239

1986, Oct. 23 ***Perf. 13½***

3193	A1239	13s dark brown & buff	.25	.20

Sts. Cyril and Methodius in Bulgaria, 1100th anniv. No. 3193 se-tenant with inscribed label.

Telephones in Bulgaria, Cent. — A1240

1986, Nov. 5 ***Perf. 13***

3194	A1240	5s multicolored	.20	.20

World Weight Lifting Championships — A1241

1986, Nov. 6

3195	A1241	13s multicolored	.25	.20

Ships A1242

1986, Nov. 20

3196	A1242	5s King of Prussia	.20	.20
3197	A1242	13s East Indiaman, 18th cent.	.25	.20
3198	A1242	25s Shebek, 18th cent.	.45	.25
3199	A1242	30s St Paul	.55	.30
3200	A1242	32s Topsail schooner, 18th cent.	.60	.30
3201	A1242	42s Victory	.80	.40
		Nos. 3196-3201 (6)	2.85	1.65

Souvenir Sheet

European Security and Cooperation Congress, Vienna — A1243

Various buildings and emblems: a, Bulgaria. b, Austria. c, Donau Park, UN.

Perf. 13, Imperf. x13 (#3202b)

1986, Nov. 27

3202		Sheet of 3	3.00	1.50
a.-c.		A1243 50s any single	1.00	.50

Exists imperf. bearing control number.

Rogozen Thracian Pitchers A1244

1986, Dec. 5 ***Perf. 13***

3203	A1244	10s Facing left	.20	.20
3204	A1244	10s Facing right	.20	.20

Union of Bulgarian Philatelists, 14th Congress. Nos. 3203-3204 printed se-tenant with labels picturing carved figures on pitchers in blocks of 4.

New Year 1987 A1245

1986, Dec. 9

3205	A1245	5s shown	.20	.20
3206	A1245	13s Snow flakes	.25	.20

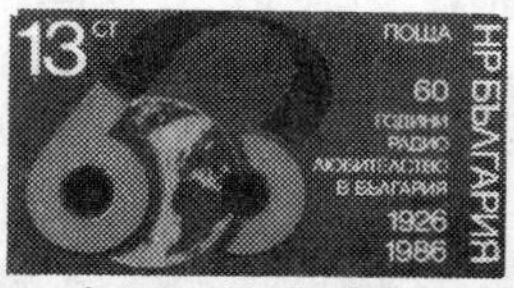

Home Amateur Radio Operators in Bulgaria, 60th Anniv. — A1246

1986, Dec. 10

3207	A1246	13s multicolored	.25	.20

Miniature Sheet

Paintings by Bulgarian Artists — A1247

Designs: a, Red Tree, by Danail Dechev (1891-1962). b, Troopers Confront Two Men, by Ilya Beshkov (1901-58). c, View of Melnik, by Veselin Stajkov (1906-70). d, View of Houses through Trees, by Kyril Zonev (1896-1961).

1986, Dec. 10 **Litho.** ***Perf. 14***

3208		Sheet of 4	2.25	1.10
a.-b.		A1247 25s any single	.50	.25
c.-d.		A1247 30s any single	.60	.30

Sofia Academy of Art, 90th anniv.

Augusto Cesar Sandino (1893-1934), Nicaraguan Revolutionary, and Flag — A1248

1986, Dec. 16 **Photo.** ***Perf. 13***

3209	A1248	13s multicolored	.25	.20

Sandinista movement in Nicaragua, 25th anniv.

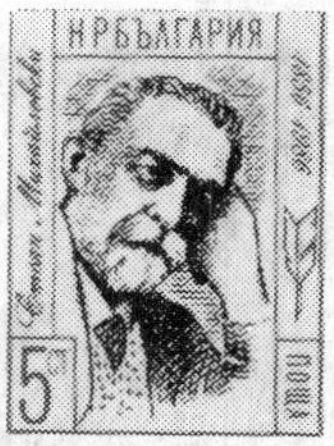

Smoyan Mihylovsky (b. 1856), Writer — A1249

Ran Bossilek (b. 1886) A1250

Title Page from Bulgarian Folk Songs of the Miladinov Brothers A1251

Annivs. and events: No. 3211, Pentcho Slaveyckov (b. 1861), writer. No. 3212, Nickola Atanassov (b. 1886), musician.

1986, Dec. 17

3210	A1249	5s multicolored	.20	.20
3211	A1249	5s multicolored	.20	.20
3212	A1249	8s multicolored	.20	.20
3213	A1250	8s multicolored	.20	.20
3214	A1251	10s multicolored	.20	.20
		Nos. 3210-3214 (5)	1.00	1.00

A1252

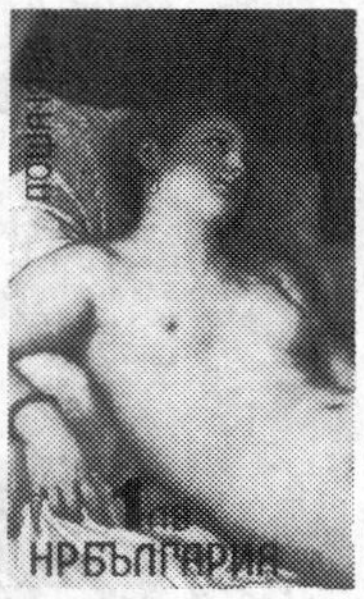

Paintings by Titian — A1253

Various portraits.

1986, Dec. 23 Litho. *Perf. 14*

3215	A1252	5s multicolored	.20	.20
3216	A1252	13s multicolored	.30	.20
3217	A1252	20s multicolored	.40	.20
3218	A1252	30s multicolored	.60	.30
3219	A1252	32s multicolored	.65	.30
3220	A1252	42s multicolored	.85	.40
a.		Min. sheet of 6, #3215-3220	3.00	1.50
		Nos. 3215-3220 (6)	3.00	1.60

Souvenir Sheet

3221	A1253	1 l multicolored	2.25	1.00

Rayko Daskalov (b. 1886), Politician A1254

1986, Dec. 23 Photo. *Perf. 13*

3222	A1254	5s deep claret	.20	.20

Sports Cars — A1255

1986, Dec. 30 Litho. *Perf. 13½*

3223	A1255	5s 1905 Fiat	.20	.20
3224	A1255	10s 1928 Bugatti	.20	.20
3225	A1255	25s 1936 Mercedes	.40	.25
3226	A1255	32s 1952 Ferrari	.50	.30
3227	A1255	40s 1985 Lotus	.60	.40
3228	A1255	42s 1986 McLaren	.65	.40
		Nos. 3223-3228 (6)	2.55	1.75

Varna Railway Inauguration, 120th Anniv. — A1257

1987, Jan. 19 Photo.

3229	A1257	5s multicolored	.20	.20

Dimcho Debelianov (1887-1916), Poet — A1258

1987, Jan. 20 Photo. *Perf. 13*

3230	A1258	5s blue, dull yel & dp blue	.20	.20

L.L. Zamenhof, Creator of Esperanto A1259

1987, Feb. 12

3231	A1259	13s multicolored	.20	.20

Mushrooms A1260

10th Natl. Trade Unions Congress A1261

1987, Feb. 6 Litho. *Perf. 11½*

3232	A1260	5s Amanita rubescens	.20	.20
3233	A1260	20s Boletus regius	.35	.25
3234	A1260	30s Leccinum aurantiacum	.50	.35
3235	A1260	32s Coprinus comatus	.55	.40
3236	A1260	40s Russula vesca	.75	.50
3237	A1260	60s Cantharellus cibarius	1.00	.60
a.		Min. sheet of 6, #3232-3237	5.00	
		Nos. 3232-3237 (6)	3.35	2.30

1987, Mar. 20 Photo. *Perf. 13*

3238	A1261	5s dark red & violet	.20	.20

Rogozen Thracian Treasure A1262

Embossed and gilded silver artifacts: 5s, Plate, Priestess Auge approaching Heracles. 8s, Pitcher, lioness attacking stag. 20s, Plate, floral pattern. 30s, Pitcher, warriors on horseback dueling. 32s, Urn, decorative pattern. 42s, Pitcher (not gilded), winged horses.

1987, Mar. 31

3239	A1262	5s multicolored	.20	.20
3240	A1262	8s multicolored	.20	.20
3241	A1262	20s multicolored	.45	.30
3242	A1262	30s multicolored	.70	.45
3243	A1262	32s multicolored	.75	.50
3244	A1262	42s multicolored	.90	.60
		Nos. 3239-3244 (6)	3.20	2.25

Miniature Sheet

Modern Architecture — A1263

Designs: a, Ludmila Zhivkova conf. center, Varna. b, Ministry of Foreign Affairs, Sofia. c, Interpred Building, Sofia. d, Hotel, Sandanski.

1987, Apr. 7 *Perf. 13½x13*

3245		Sheet of 4	3.00	1.90
a.-d.	A1263	30s any single	.75	.45

Exists imperf. with black control number.

European Freestyle Wrestling Championships A1264

1987, Apr. 22 *Perf. 13*

3246	A1264	5s multicolored	.20	.20
3247	A1264	13s multi, diff.	.40	.20

CAPEX '87, Toronto A1265

1987, Apr. 24

3248	A1265	42s multicolored	1.00	.40

10th Congress of the Natl. Front — A1266

1987, May 11

3249	A1266	5s multicolored	.20	.20

15th Communist Youth Congress — A1267

1987, May 13

3250	A1267	5s George Dimitrov	.20	.20

8th Intl. Humor and Satire Biennial, Gabrovo — A1268

1987, May 15 *Perf. 13x13½*

3251	A1268	13s multicolored	.35	.20

13th World Rhythmic Gymnastics Championships, Varna — A1269

Gymnasts.

1987, Aug. 5 Photo. *Perf. 13*

3252	A1269	5s Maria Gigova	.20	.20
3252A	A1269	8s Iliana Raeva	.20	.20
3252B	A1269	13s Anelia Ralenkova	.30	.20
3252C	A1269	25s Pilyana Georgieva	.55	.30
3252D	A1269	30s Lilia Ignatova	.65	.40
3252E	A1269	42s Bianca Panova	.90	.50
		Nos. 3252-3252E (6)	2.80	1.80

Souvenir Sheet

Perf. 13x13½

3252F	A1269	1 l Neshka Robeva, coach	2.25	1.50

Exists imperf. with black control number.

Vassil Kolarov — A1270

1987, June 3 *Perf. 13*

3253	A1270	5s dk red, yel & dk bl	.20	.20

Stela Blagoeva (b. 1887) — A1271

1987, June 4

3254	A1271	5s pink & sepia	.20	.20

Rabotnichesko Delo Newspaper, 60th Anniv. — A1272

1987, May 28

3255	A1272	5s black & lake	.20	.20

Deer A1273

1987, June 23 Litho.

3256	A1273	5s Capreolus capreolus, vert.	.20	.20
3257	A1273	10s Alces alces	.25	.20
3258	A1273	32s Dama dama, vert.	.75	.25
3259	A1273	40s Cervus nippon, vert.	1.10	.30

3260 A1273 42s Cervus elaphus 1.10 .30
3261 A1273 60s Rangifer tarandus, vert. 1.40 .45
a. Min. sheet of 6, #3256-3261, imperf. 5.50 2.75
Nos. 3256-3261 (6) 4.80 1.70

Vassil Levski (1837-73) A1274

Various portraits.

1987, June 19 **Photo.**
3262 A1274 5s red brn & dark grn .20 .20
3263 A1274 13s dark grn & red brn .35 .20

Namibia Day A1275

1987, July 8
3264 A1275 13s org, blk & dark red .30 .20

Georgi Kirkov (1867-1919), Revolutionary A1276

1987, July 17 ***Perf. 13x13½***
3265 A1276 5s claret & deep claret .20 .20

Bees and Plants — A1277

1987, July 29 **Litho.** ***Perf. 13***
3266 A1277 5s Phacelia tanacetifolia .20 .20
3267 A1277 10s Helianthus annuus .20 .20
3268 A1277 30s Robinia pseudoacacia .60 .35
3269 A1277 32s Lavandula vera .65 .40
3270 A1277 42s Tilia parvifolia .90 .50
3271 A1277 60s Onobrychis sativa 1.10 .70
a. Min. sheet of 6, #3266-3271 4.50 2.75
Nos. 3266-3271 (6) 3.65 2.35

BULGARIA '89 — A1278

1987, Sept. 3 ***Perf. 13½x13***
3272 A1278 13s No. 1 .40 .20

HAFNIA '87 — A1279

1987, Sept. 8 ***Perf. 13***
3273 A1279 42s multicolored 1.00 .60

No. 3273 issued in sheets of 3 plus 2 labels picturing emblems of the HAFNIA '87 and BULGARIA '89 exhibitions, and 1 label with background similar to Denmark Type A32 with castle instead of denomination.

Portrait of a Girl, by Stefan Ivanov — A1280

Paintings in the Sofia City Art Galler: 8s, Grape-gatherer, by Bencho Obreshkov. 20s, Portrait of a Lady with a Hat, by David Perets. 25s, Listeners of Marimba, by Kiril Tsonev. 32s, Boy with an Harmonica, by Nenko Balkanski. 60s, Rumyana, by Vasil Stoilov.

1987, Sept. 15 **Litho.** ***Perf. 14***
3274 A1280 5s shown .20 .20
3275 A1280 8s multicolored .20 .20
3276 A1280 20s multicolored .50 .30
3277 A1280 25s multicolored .60 .35
3278 A1280 32s multicolored .75 .45
3279 A1280 60s multicolored 1.25 .80
Nos. 3274-3279 (6) 3.50 2.30

Intl. Atomic Energy Agency, 30th Anniv. A1281

Perf. 13½x13
1987, Sept. 15 **Photo.**
3280 A1281 13s red, lt blue & emer .35 .20

Songbirds A1282

1987, Oct. 12 **Litho.** ***Perf. 12½x12***
3281 A1282 5s Troglodytes troglodytes .20 .20
3282 A1282 13s Emberiza citrinella .35 .20
3283 A1282 20s Sitta europaea .55 .25
3284 A1282 30s Turdus merula .80 .35
3285 A1282 42s Coccothraustes coccothraustes 1.10 .50
3286 A1282 60s Cinclus cinclus 1.50 .75
a. Min. sheet of 6, #3281-3286 5.00 2.25
Nos. 3281-3286 (6) 4.50 2.25

Balkan War, 75th Anniv. A1283

1987, Sept. 15 **Photo.** ***Perf. 13½***
3287 A1283 5s buff, blk & brt org .20 .20

Newspaper Anniversaries — A1283a

1987, Sept. 24 **Photo.** ***Perf. 13***
3287A A1283a 5s multicolored .20 .20

Rabotnik, 95th anniv., *Rabotnicheski Vstnik,* 90th anniv. and *Rabotnichesko Delo,* 60th anniv.

October Revolution, Russia, 70th Anniv. A1284

Lenin and: 5s, Revolutionar y. 13s, Cosmonaut.

1987, Oct. 27 **Photo.** ***Perf. 13***
3288 A1284 5s rose brn & red org .20 .20
3289 A1284 13s brt ultra & red org .35 .20

1988 Winter Olympics, Calgary — A1285

1987, Oct. 27 **Litho.** ***Perf. 13x13½***
3290 A1285 5s Biathlon .20 .20
3291 A1285 13s Slalom .40 .20
3292 A1285 30s Women's figure skating .85 .45
3293 A1285 42s 4-Man bobsled 1.10 .60
Nos. 3290-3293 (4) 2.55 1.45

Souvenir Sheet

3294 A1285 1 l Ice hockey 2.75 1.50

No. 3294 exists imperf.

Souvenir Sheet

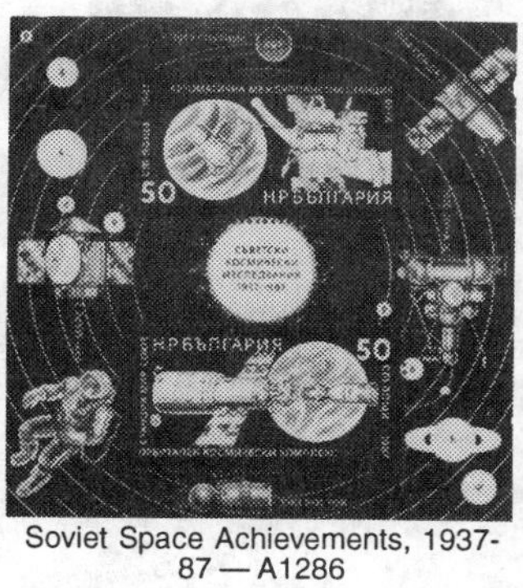

Soviet Space Achievements, 1937-87 — A1286

Designs: No. 3295a, Vega probe. No. 3295b, Mir-Soyuz Space Station.

1987, Dec. 24 **Photo.** ***Perf. 13½x13***
3295 A1286 Sheet of 2 2.75 1.50
a.-b. 50s any single 1.25 .75

Exists imperf.

New Year 1988 A1287

Sofia stamp exhibition emblem within folklore patterns.

1987, Dec. 25 ***Perf. 13***
3296 A1287 5s multicolored .20 .20
3297 A1287 13s multi, diff. .35 .20

Souvenir Sheet

European Security Conferences — A1288

Conferences held in Helsinki, 1973, and Vienna, 1987: a, Helsinki Conf. Center. b, Map of Europe. c, Vienna Conf. Center.

Perf. 13x13½ on 2 or 4 Sides
1987, Dec. 30
3298 Sheet of 3 4.00 3.00
a.-c. A1288 50s any single 1.50 .75

Exists imperf.

A1289

A1290

1988, Jan. 20
3299 A1289 5s multicolored .20 .20

Christo Kabaktchiev (b. 1878), party leader.

1988, Jan. 25 **Litho.** ***Perf. 12***

Marine flowers.

3300 A1290 5s Scilla bythynica .20 .20
3301 A1290 10s Geum rhodopaeum .20 .20
3302 A1290 13s Caltha polypetala .30 .20
3303 A1290 25s Nymphoides peltata .50 .30
3304 A1290 30s Cortusa matthioli .60 .40
3305 A1290 42s Stratiotes aloides .75 .50
a. Min. sheet of 6, #3300-3305 3.00 2.00
Nos. 3300-3305 (6) 2.55 1.80

Liberation of Bulgaria, 110th Anniv. A1291

1988, Feb. 15 **Photo.** ***Perf. 13***
3306 A1291 5s Officer, horse .20 .20
3307 A1291 13s Soldiers .35 .20

8th Intl. Civil Servants Congress, Sofia A1292

1988, Mar. 22 Photo. *Perf. 13*

3308 A1292 13s multicolored .30 .20

State Railways, Cent. — A1293

Locomotives: 5s, Jantra, 1888. 13s, Christo Botev, 1905. 25s, 0-10-1, 1918. 32s, 4-12-1 heavy duty, 1943. 42s, Diesel, 1964. 60s, Electric, 1979.

1988, Mar. 25 Litho. *Perf. 11*

3309 A1293 5s multicolored .20 .20
3310 A1293 13s multicolored .25 .20
3311 A1293 25s multicolored .50 .30
3312 A1293 32s multicolored .65 .35
3313 A1293 42s multicolored .80 .45
3314 A1293 60s multicolored 1.00 .60
a. Min. sheet of 6, #3309-3314 3.50 2.00
Nos. 3309-3314 (6) 3.40 2.10

Ivan Nedyalkov (1880-1925) A1294

Postal workers, heroes of socialism: 8s, Delcho Spasov (1918-43). 10s, Nikola Ganchev (1915-43). 13s, Ganka Stoyanova Rasheva (1921-44).

1988, Mar. 31 Photo. *Perf. 13½x13*

3315 A1294 5s buff & dark rose brn .20 .20
3316 A1294 8s pale ultra & violet blue .20 .20
3317 A1294 10s pale olive grn & olive grn .25 .20
3318 A1294 13s pale pink & lake .25 .20
Nos. 3315-3318 (4) .90 .80

Georgi Traikov (b. 1898), Statesman A1295

Intl. Red Cross and Red Crescent Organizations, 125th Annivs. A1296

1988, Apr. 8 Litho. *Perf. 13x13½*

3319 A1295 5s orange & brn .20 .20

1988, Apr. 26 Photo. *Perf. 13*

3320 A1296 13s multicolored .25 .20

Children's Drawings Type of 1982

Designs: 5s, Girl wearing a folk costume, vert. 8s, Painter at easel, vert. 13s, Children playing. 20s, Ringing bells for peace. 32s, Accordion player, vert. 42s, Cosmonaut, vert. 50s, Assembly emblem.

1988, Apr. 28 Litho. *Perf. 14*

3321 A1093 5s multicolored .20 .20
3322 A1093 8s multicolored .20 .20
3323 A1093 13s multicolored .30 .20
3324 A1093 20s multicolored .40 .25
3325 A1093 32s multicolored .65 .40
3326 A1093 42s multicolored .90 .50
Nos. 3321-3326 (6) 2.65 1.75

Souvenir Sheet

3327 A1093 50s multicolored 1.00 .60

4th Intl. Children's Assembly, Sofia. No. 3327 exists imperf.

Karl Marx A1297

1988, May 5 *Perf. 13*

3328 A1297 13s multicolored .30 .20

Birds — A1297a

1988, May 6 Litho. *Perf. 13x13½*

3328A A1297a 5s *Ciconia ciconia* .20 .20
3328B A1297a 5s *Larus argentatus* .20 .20
3328C A1297a 8s *Ardea cinerea* .20 .20
3328D A1297a 8s *Corvus corone cornix* .20 .20
3328E A1297a 10s *Accipiter gentillis* .25 .20
3328F A1297a 42s *Bubo bubo* .90 .50
Nos. 3328A-3328F (6) 1.95 1.50

Dated 1987.

Sofia Zoo, Cent. A1298

1988, May 20

3329 A1298 5s Loxodonta africana .20 .20
3330 A1298 13s Ceratotherium simum .25 .20
3331 A1298 25s Lycaon pictus .50 .30
3332 A1298 30s Pelecanus onocrotalus .65 .35
3333 A1298 32s Bucorvus abissinicus .70 .40
3334 A1298 42s Nyctea scandiaca .90 .55
a. Min. sheet of 6, #3329-3334 3.50 1.75
Nos. 3329-3334 (6) 3.20 2.00

FINLANDIA '88 — A1299

1988, June 7

3335 A1299 30s Finland No. 1 .70 .35

No. 3335 printed in miniature sheets of 3 plus 3 labels picturing skyline, SOFIA '89 and FINLANDIA '88 exhibition emblems.
Exists imperf.

2nd Joint USSR-Bulgaria Space Flight — A1300

1988, June 7

3336 A1300 5s shown .20 .20
3337 A1300 13s Rocket, globe .30 .20

EXPO '91, Plovdiv — A1301

1988, June 7 *Perf. 13½x13*

3338 A1301 13s multicolored .30 .20

1988 European Soccer Championships — A1302

1988, June 10 *Perf. 13*

3339 A1302 5s Corner kick .20 .20
3340 A1302 13s Heading the ball .25 .20
3341 A1302 30s Referee, player .55 .35
3342 A1302 42s Player holding trophy .85 .55
Nos. 3339-3342 (4) 1.85 1.30

Souvenir Sheet

3343 A1302 1 l Stadium 2.25 1.25

Paintings by Dechko Usunov (1899-1986) A1303

Designs: 5s, *Portrait of a Young Girl.* 13s, *Portrait of Maria Wassilewa.* 30s, *Self-portrait.*

1988, June 14 *Perf. 13x13½*

3344 A1303 5s multicolored .20 .20
3345 A1303 13s multicolored .30 .20
3346 A1303 30s multicolored .70 .35
Nos. 3344-3346 (3) 1.20 .75

Souvenir Sheet

1st Woman in Space, 25th Anniv. — A1304

1988, June 16 *Perf. 13½x13*

3347 A1304 1 l multicolored 2.50 1.50

Valentina Tereshkova's flight, June 16-19, 1963.

Kurdzhali Region Religious Art — A1305

Designs: 5s, *St. John the Baptist,* 1592. 8s, *St. George Slaying the Dragon,* 1841.

1988, June 27 *Perf. 13x13½*

3348 A1305 5s multicolored .20 .20
3349 A1305 8s multicolored .20 .20

1988 Summer Olympics, Seoul — A1306

1988, July 25 Litho. *Perf. 13*

3350 A1306 5s High jump .20 .20
3351 A1306 13s Weight lifting .30 .20
3352 A1306 30s Greco-Roman wrestling .65 .40
3353 A1306 42s Rhythmic gymnastics .90 .50
Nos. 3350-3353 (4) 2.05 1.30

Souvenir Sheet

3354 A1306 1 l Volleyball 2.50 1.25

No. 3354 exists imperf.

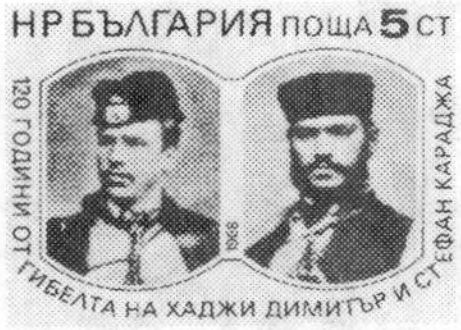

Dimitr and Karaja A1307

1988, July 25 Litho. *Perf. 13*

3355 A1307 5s blk, dark olive bister & grn .20 .20

120th anniv. of the deaths of Haji Dimitr and Stefan Karaja, patriots killed during the Balkan Wars.

Problems of Peace and Socialism, 30th Anniv. A1308

1988, July 26 Photo.

3356 A1308 13s multicolored .25 .20

Paintings in the Ludmila Zhivkova Art Gallery — A1309

Paintings: No. 3357, *Harbor, Algiers,* by Albermarke (1875-1947). No. 3358, *Portrait of Ermin David in the Studio,* by Jul Pasken (1885-1930). No. 3359, *Madonna with Child* and Sts. Sebastian and Roko, by Giovanni Rosso (1494-1540). No. 3360, *The Barren Tree*, by Roland Udo (1879-1982).

1988, July 27 Litho. *Perf. 14*

3357 A1309 30s multicolored	.65	.40
3358 A1309 30s multicolored	.65	.40
3359 A1309 30s multicolored	.65	.40
3360 A1309 30s multicolored	.65	.40
Nos. 3357-3360 (4)	2.60	1.60

St. Clement of Ohrid University, Sofia, 100th Anniv.
A1310

1988, Aug. 22 *Perf. 13*
3361 A1310 5s blk & pale yel .20 .20

PRAGA '88
A1311

1988, Aug. 22
3362 A1311 25s Czechoslovakia #2 in vermilion .60 .30

Printed in miniature sheets of 3 plus 3 labels pictur ing skyline, PRAGA '88 and SOFIA '89 exhibition emblems.
Exists imperf.

OLYMPHILEX '88 — A1312

1988, Sept. 1
3363 A1312 62s Korea No. 1 1.25 .75

Printed in miniature sheets of 3 plus 3 labels picturing skyline, OLYMPHILEX '88 and SOFIA '89 exhibition emblems.
Exists imperf.

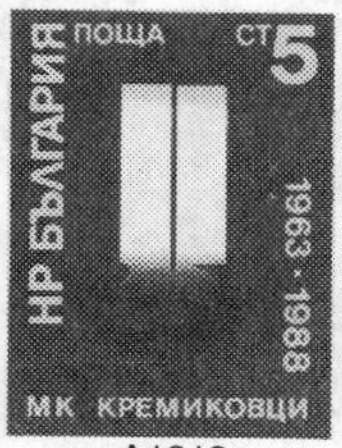

A1313

A1314

1988, Sept. 15
3364 A1313 5s deep blue, lt blue & red .20 .20

Kremikovtsi steel mill, 25th anniv.

1988, Sept. 16 *Perf. 13½x13*
3365 A1314 13s dark red & ultra .25 .20

80th Interparliamentary Conference.

Transportation Commission 80th Congress — A1315

1988, Oct. 17
3366 A1315 13s deep lil rose & blk .25 .20

Kurdzhali Region Artifacts — A1316

5s, Earthenware bowl, 13th-14th cent. 8s, Medieval fortification, Gorna Krepost Village, vert.

1988, Sept. 20 *Perf. 13*
3367 A1316 5s multicolored .20 .20
3368 A1316 8s multicolored .20 .20

Chiprovo Uprising, 300th Anniv. — A1317

1988, Sept. 23
3369 A1317 5s multicolored .20 .20

Bears
A1318

1988, Sept. 26 *Perf. 12½*

3370 A1318 5s *Ursus arctos*	.20	.20
3371 A1318 8s *Thalassarctos maritimus*	.20	.20
3372 A1318 13s *Melursus ursinus*	.30	.20
3373 A1318 20s *Helarctos malayanus*	.45	.25
3374 A1318 32s *Selenarctos thibetanus*	.70	.40
3375 A1318 42s *Tremarctos ornatus*	.95	.50
a. Min. sheet of 6, #3370-3375	3.00	1.50
Nos. 3370-3375 (6)	2.80	1.75

ECOFORUM for Peace — A1319

1988, Oct. 29 *Perf. 13*
3376 A1319 20s multicolored .50 .25

PLOVDIV '88
A1320

Design: Amphitheater ruins, PRAGA '88 and PLOVDIV '88 emblems.

1988, Nov. 2
3377 A1320 5s multicolored .20 .20

Exists in imperf. sheet of six.

Radio & Television Authority, 25th Anniv. — A1321

1988, Nov. 17 Litho. *Perf. 13*
3378 A1321 5s multicolored .20 .20

BULGARIA '89 — A1321a

1988, Nov. 22 Litho. *Perf. 13*
3379 A1321a 42s No. 1 1.10 .60

Printed in miniature sheets of 3+3 labels picturing exhib. emblem and conf. center.
Exists imperf.

Souvenir Sheet

Danube Cruise Excursion Industry, 40th Anniv. — A1321b

1988, Nov. 25 *Perf. 13½x13*

3380 Sheet of 2	4.75	2.75
a. A1321b 1 l *Russia*	2.50	1.40
b. A1321b 1 l *Aleksandr Stamboliski*	2.50	1.40

Traffic Safety
A1321c

1988, Nov. 28
3381 A1321c 5s multicolored .20 .20

New Year 1989 — A1321d

1988, Dec. 20 *Perf. 13*
3382 A1321d 5s shown .20 .20
3383 A1321d 13s multi, diff. .35 .25

Hotels in Winter
A1322

1988, Dec. 19 Litho. *Perf. 13½x13*

3384 A1322 5s shown	.20	.20
3385 A1322 8s multi, diff.	.20	.20
3386 A1322 13s multi, diff.	.30	.20
3387 A1322 30s multi, diff.	.70	.40
Nos. 3384-3387 (4)	1.40	1.00

Souvenir Sheet

Soviet Space Shuttle *Energija-Buran* — A1322a

1988, Dec. 28 *Perf. 13½x13*
3387A A1322a 1 l dark blue 2.75 1.50

BULGARIA '89 — A1322b

Traditional modes of postal conveyance.

1988, Dec. 29 *Perf. 13½x13*

3387B A1322b 25s Mail coach	.50	.30
3387C A1322b 25s Biplane	.50	.30
3387D A1322b 25s Truck	.50	.30
3387E A1322b 25s Steam packet	.50	.30
Nos. 3387B-3387E (4)	2.00	1.20

Philatelic Exhibitions
A1323

1989 Litho. *Perf. 13*
3388 A1322 42s France No. 1 1.00 .50
3389 A1322 62s India No. 200 1.50 .80

BULGARIA '89 and PHILEXFRANCE '89 (42s) or INDIA '89 (62s).
Nos. 3388-3389 each printed in sheets of 3 + 3 labels picturing skylines, BULGARIA '89 and PHILEXFRANCE or INDIA exhibition labels. Exist in sheets of 4 also. Exist imperf.
Issue dates: 42s, Feb. 23; 62s, Jan. 14.

Souvenir Sheet

Universiade Winter Games, Sofia — A1324

Designs: a, Downhill skiing. b, Ice hockey. c, Cross-country skiing. d, Speed skating.

1989, Jan. 30 Litho. *Imperf.*
Simulated Perforations

3390 Sheet of 4	2.25	1.25
a.-d. A1324 25s multicolored	.55	.30

No. 3390 exists imperf. without simulated perforations and containing black control number.

Humor and Satire Festival, Gabrovo
A1325

1989, Feb. 7 *Perf. 13½x13*
3391 A1325 13s Don Quixote .30 .20

Endangered Plant Species — A1326

1989, Feb. 22 ***Perf. 13x13½***

3392 A1326 5s *Ramonda serbica* .20 .20
3393 A1326 10s *Paeonia maskula* .20 .20
3394 A1326 25s *Viola perinensis* .50 .30
3395 A1326 30s *Dracunculus vulgaris* .60 .35
3396 A1326 42s *Tulipa splendens* .85 .50
3397 A1326 60s *Rindera umbellata* 1.25 .70
a. Min. sheet of 6, #3392-3397 4.00 2.50
Nos. 3392-3397 (6) 3.60 2.25

World Wildlife Fund A1327

Bats.

1989, Feb. 27 ***Perf. 13***

3398 A1327 5s *Nyctalus noctula* .20 .20
3399 A1327 13s *Rhinolophus ferrumequinum* .30 .20
3400 A1327 30s *Myotis myotis* .70 .35
3401 A1327 42s *Vespertilio murinus* 1.00 .50
a. Min. sheet of 4, #3398-3401 2.25 1.25
Nos. 3398-3401 (4) 2.20 1.25

Aleksandr Stamboliski (1879-1923), Premier — A1328

1989, Mar. 1 ***Perf. 13½x13***

3402 A1328 5s brt org & blk .20 .20

Souvenir Sheet

Soviet-Bulgarian Joint Space Flight, 10th Anniv. — A1329

Designs: a, Liftoff. b, Crew.

1989, Apr. 10 ***Perf. 13***

3403 A1329 Sheet of 2 2.25 1.25
a.-b. 50s any single 1.10 .60

Exists imperf.

Buying Sets
It is often less expensive to purchase complete sets than individual stamps that make up the set.

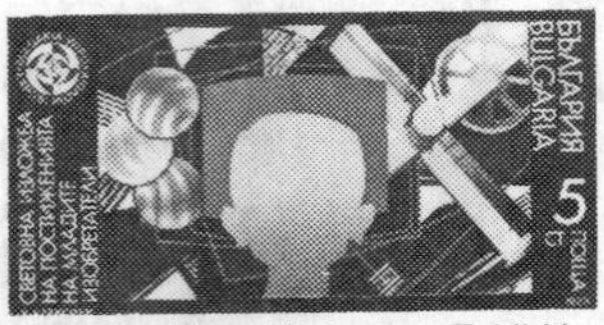

EXPO '91 Young Inventors Exhibition, Plovdiv — A1330

1989, Apr. 20 ***Perf. 13½x13***

3404 A1330 5s multicolored .20 .20

Petko Enev (b. 1889) A1331

Stanke Dimitrov Marek (b. 1889) — A1332

1989, Apr. 28 ***Perf. 13½x13, 13x13½***

3405 A1331 5s scarlet & black .20 .20
3406 A1332 5s scarlet & black .20 .20

Icons A1333

Photocopier A1334

Paintings by Bulgarian artists: No. 3407, Archangel Michael, by Dimiter Molerov. No. 3408, Mother and Child, by Toma Vishanov. No. 3409, St. John, by Vishanov. No. 3410, St. Dimitri, by Ivan Terziev.

1989, Apr. 28 ***Perf. 13x13½***

3407 A1333 30s multicolored .65 .35
3408 A1333 30s multicolored .65 .35
3409 A1333 30s multicolored .65 .35
3410 A1333 30s multicolored .65 .35
Nos. 3407-3410 (4) 2.60 1.40

Nos. 3408, 3410 exist in sheets of four. Nos. 3407-3410 exist in souvenir sheets of four and together in one sheet of four, imperf.

1989, May 5

3411 A1334 5s shown .20 .20
3412 A1334 8s Computer .20 .20
3413 A1334 35s Telephone .80 .45
3414 A1334 42s Dish receiver .90 .50
Nos. 3411-3414 (4) 2.10 1.35

Bulgarian Communications, 110th anniv. Nos. 3411-3413 exist in imperf. sheets of six.

Souvenir Sheet

58th FIP Congress — A1335

1989, May 22

3415 A1335 1 l Charioteer 2.00 1.00

Exists imperf.

1st Communist Party Congress in Bulgaria, 70th Anniv. — A1336

Famous Men — A1337

1989, June 15

3416 A1336 5s mar, blk & dk red .20 .20

1989

#3417, Ilya Blaskov. #3418, Sofronii, Bishop of Vratza. #3419, Vassil Aprilov (b. 1789), educator, historian. #3420, Christo Jassenov (1889-1925). 10s, Stoyan Zagorchinov (1889-1969).

3417 A1337 5s black & gray olive .20 .20
3418 A1337 5s blk, brn blk & pale green .20 .20
3419 A1337 8s lt blue, blk & vio blk .30 .20
3420 A1337 8s tan, blk & dark red brown .25 .20
3421 A1337 10s blk, pale pink & gray blue .30 .20
Nos. 3417-3421 (5) 1.25 1.00

Issued: #3417-3418, June 15; #3419, Aug. 1; #3420, Sept. 25; 10s, Aug. 5.

French Revolution, Bicent. — A1338

1989, June 26 ***Perf. 13½x13***

3422 A1338 13s Anniv. emblem .25 .20
3423 A1338 30s Jean-Paul Marat .60 .35
3424 A1338 42s Robespierre .85 .50
Nos. 3422-3424 (3) 1.70 1.05

7th Army Games A1339

1989, June 30 ***Perf. 13***

3425 A1339 5s Gymnast .20 .20
3426 A1339 13s Equestrian .30 .20
3427 A1339 30s Running .65 .40
3428 A1339 42s Shooting .95 .50
Nos. 3425-3428 (4) 2.10 1.30

22nd World Canoe and Kayak Championships, Plovdiv — A1340

1989, Aug. 11 **Litho.** ***Perf. 13***

3429 A1340 13s Woman paddling .30 .20
3430 A1340 30s Man rowing .60 .25

Photography, 150th Anniv. — A1341

1989, Aug. 29 ***Perf. 13½x13***

3431 A1341 42s blk, buff & yellow .85 .45

September 9 Revolution, 45th Anniv. — A1342

1989, Aug. 30 ***Perf. 13***

3432 A1342 5s Revolutionaries .20 .20
3433 A1342 8s Couple embracing .20 .20
3434 A1342 13s Faces in a crowd .25 .20
Nos. 3432-3434 (3) .65 .60

Natural History Museum, Cent. A1343

1989, Aug. 31

3435 A1343 13s multicolored .30 .20

Postal Workers Killed in World War II — A1343a

Designs: 5s, L.D. Dardjikov. 8s, I.B. Dobrev. 10s, N.P. Antonov.

1989, Sept. 22 **Litho.** ***Perf. 13***

3436 A1343a 5s multicolored .20 .20
3437 A1343a 8s multicolored .20 .20
3438 A1343a 13s multicolored .30 .20
Nos. 3436-3438 (3) .70 .60

12th Shipping Unions Congress (FIATA) — A1344

1989, Sept. 25 Litho. ***Perf. 13½x13***
3439 A1344 42s light blue & dark blue .85 .45

Jawaharlal Nehru, 1st Prime Minister of Independent India — A1346

1989, Oct. 10
3440 A1346 13s blk, pale yel & brn .30 .20

Souvenir Sheet

European Ecology Congress — A1347

1989, Oct. 12 ***Perf. 13***
3441 A1347 Sheet of 2 3.50 1.75
a. 50s multicolored 1.20 .60
b. 1 l multicolored 2.25 1.10

Snakes A1368

1989, Oct. 20 Litho. ***Perf. 13***
3491 A1368 5s *Eryx jaculus turcicus* .20 .20
3492 A1368 10s *Elaphe longissima* .25 .20
3493 A1368 25s *Elaphe situla* .55 .30
3494 A1368 30s *Elaphe quatuorlineata* .65 .35
3495 A1368 42s *Telescopus fallax* .90 .50
3496 A1368 60s *Coluber rubriceps* 1.25 .70
a. Min. sheet of 6, #3491-3496 4.00 2.00
Nos. 3491-3496 (6) 3.80 2.25

Intl. Youth Science Fair, Plovdiv, 1989 — A1369

1989, Nov. 4
3497 A1369 13s multicolored .25 .20

1990 World Soccer Championships, Italy — A1370

Various athletes: No. 3502a, Athletes facing right. No. 3502b, Athletes facing left.

1989, Dec. 1
3498 A1370 5s shown .20 .20
3499 A1370 13s multi, diff. .30 .20
3500 A1370 30s multi, diff. .70 .35
3501 A1370 42s multi, diff. 1.00 .50
Nos. 3498-3501 (4) 2.20 1.25

Souvenir Sheet

3502 Sheet of 2 2.25 1.10
a.-b. A1370 50s any single 1.10 .55

Air Sports A1371

1989, Dec. 8
3503 A1371 5s Glider planes .20 .20
3504 A1371 13s Hang glider .30 .20
3505 A1371 30s Sky diving .70 .35
3506 A1371 42s Three sky divers 1.00 .50
Nos. 3503-3506 (4) 2.20 1.25

82nd General conference of the FAI, Varna.

Traffic Safety A1372

1989, Dec. 12
3507 A1372 5s multicolored .20 .20

New Year 1990 — A1373

1989, Dec. 25 Litho. ***Perf. 13***
3508 A1373 5s Santa's sleigh .20 .20
3509 A1373 13s Snowman .30 .20

Cats A1374

Designs: No. 3510, Persian. No. 3511, Tiger. 8s, Tabby. No. 3513, Himalayan. No. 3514, Persian, diff. 13s, Siamese. Nos. 3511 and 3514-3515 vert.

Perf. 13½x13, 13x13½
1989, Dec. 26 Background Color
3510 A1374 5s gray .20 .20
3511 A1374 5s yellow .20 .20
3512 A1374 8s orange .20 .20
3513 A1374 10s blue .25 .20
3514 A1374 10s brown orange .25 .20
3515 A1374 13s red .30 .20
Nos. 3510-3515 (6) 1.40 1.20

Explorers and Their Ships — A1375

1990, Jan. 17 ***Perf. 13***
3516 A1375 5s Christopher Columbus .20 .20
3517 A1375 8s Vasco da Gama .20 .20
3518 A1375 13s Fernando Magellan .25 .20
3519 A1375 32s Sir Francis Drake .60 .35
3520 A1375 42s Henry Hudson .75 .50
3521 A1375 60s James Cook 1.00 .70
a. Min. sheet of 6, #3516-3521 3.50 1.75
Nos. 3516-3521 (6) 3.00 2.15

Natl. Esperanto Movement, Cent. — A1376

1990, Feb. 23 Litho. ***Perf. 13***
3522 A1376 10s multicolored .25 .20

Paintings by Foreign Artists in the Natl. Museum A1377

Artists: No. 3523, Suzanna Valadon (1867-1938). No. 3524, Maurice Brianchon (1899-1978). No. 3525, Moise Kisling (1891-1953). No. 3526, Giovanni Beltraffio (1467-1516).

1990, Mar. 23 ***Perf. 14***
3523 A1377 30s multicolored .65 .40
3524 A1377 30s multicolored .65 .40
3525 A1377 30s multicolored .65 .40
3526 A1377 30s multicolored .65 .40
Nos. 3523-3526 (4) 2.60 1.60

1990 World Soccer Championships, Italy — A1378

Various athletes.

1990, Mar. 26 ***Perf. 13***
3527 A1378 5s multicolored .20 .20
3528 A1378 13s multi, diff. .30 .20
3529 A1378 30s multi, diff. .70 .40
3530 A1378 42s multi, diff. .95 .50
Nos. 3527-3530 (4) 2.15 1.30

Souvenir Sheet

3531 Sheet of 2 2.25 1.25
a. A1378 50s Three players 1.10 .60
b. A1378 50s Two players 1.10 .60

Bavaria No. 1 A1379

1990, Apr. 6 Litho. ***Perf. 13***
3532 A1379 42s vermilion & blk 1.00 .50

ESSEN '90, Germany, Apr. 12-22. No. 3532 printed in sheets of 3 + 3 labels.

Souvenir Sheet

Penny Black, 150th Anniv. A1380

1990, Apr. 10
3533 Sheet of 2 2.25 1.25
a. A1380 50s Great Britain #1 1.10 .60
b. A1380 50s Sir Rowland Hill 1.10 .60

Cooperative Farming in Bulgaria, Cent. — A1381

1990, Apr. 17
3534 A1381 5s multicolored .20 .20

Dimitar Chorbadjiski-Chudomir (1890-1967) — A1382

1990, Apr. 24
3535 A1382 5s multicolored .20 .20

Labor Day, Cent. — A1383

1990, May 1 ***Perf. 13x13½***
3536 A1383 10s multicolored .25 .20

ITU, 125th Anniv. — A1384

1990, May 13 Litho. ***Perf. 13½x13***
3537 A1384 20s blue, red & black .45 .25

Belgium No. 1 A1385

1990, May 23 ***Perf. 13***

3538 A1385 30s multicolored .75 .40

Belgica '90. No. 3538 printed in sheets of 3 + 3 labels.

Lamartine (1790-1869), French Poet A1386

1990, June 15 ***Perf. 13½x13***

3539 A1386 20s multicolored .45 .25

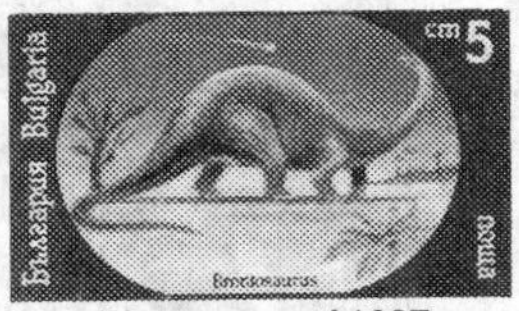

Dinosaurs — A1387

1990, June 19 ***Perf. 12½***

3540 A1387 5s Brontosaurus .20 .20
3541 A1387 8s Stegosaurus .20 .20
3542 A1387 13s Edaphosaurus .30 .20
3543 A1387 25s Rhamphorhynchus .60 .30
3544 A1387 32s Protoceratops .80 .40
3545 A1387 42s Triceratops 1.10 .55
a. Min. sheet of 6, #3540-3545 3.25 1.60
Nos. 3540-3545 (6) 3.20 1.85

1992 Summer Olympic Games, Barcelona — A1388

1990, July 13 ***Perf. 13½x13***

3546 A1388 5s Swimming .20 .20
3547 A1388 13s Handball .30 .20
3548 A1388 30s Hurdling .75 .40
3549 A1388 42s Cycling 1.10 .55
Nos. 3546-3549 (4) 2.35 1.35

Souvenir Sheet

3550 Sheet of 2 2.50 1.25
a. A1388 50s Tennis, forehand 1.25 .60
b. A1388 50s Tennis, backhand 1.25 .60

Butterflies A1389

1990, Aug. 8 **Litho.** ***Perf. 13***

3551 A1389 5s Zerynthia Polyxena .20 .20
3552 A1389 10s Panaxia quadripunctaria .25 .20
3553 A1389 20s Proserpinus proserpina .45 .25
3554 A1389 30s Hyles lineata .65 .35
3555 A1389 42s Thecla betulae .95 .55
3556 A1389 60s Euphydryas cynthia 1.25 .70
a. Min. sheet of 6, #3551-3556 4.00 2.10
Nos. 3551-3556 (6) 3.75 2.25

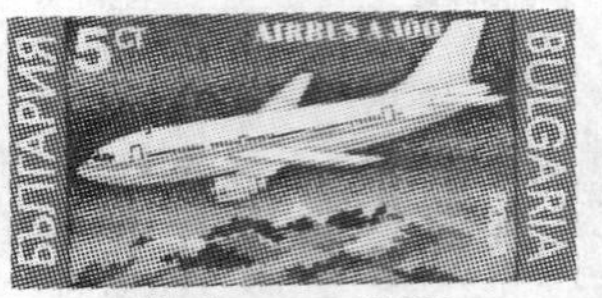

Airplanes — A1390

1990, Aug. 30 **Litho.** ***Perf. 13½x13***

3557 A1390 5s Airbus A-300 .20 .20
3558 A1390 10s Tu-204 .20 .20
3559 A1390 25s Concorde .30 .25
3560 A1390 30s DC-9 .40 .30
3561 A1390 42s Il-86 .55 .40
3562 A1390 60s Boeing 747 .75 .55
a. Min. sheet of 6, #3557-3562 3.00 2.00
Nos. 3557-3562 (6) 2.40 1.90

Exarch Joseph I (1840-1915), Religious Leader — A1391

1990, Sept. 27 ***Perf. 13***

3563 A1391 5s blk, pur & grn .20 .20

Intl. Traffic Safety Year A1392

1990, Oct. 9 **Litho.** ***Perf. 13***

3564 A1392 5s multicolored .20 .20

Olymphilex '90, Varna — A1393

1990, Oct. 16 ***Perf. 13x13½***

3565 A1393 5s Shot put .20 .20
3566 A1393 13s Discus .25 .20
3567 A1393 42s Hammer throw .90 .55
3568 A1393 60s Javelin 1.25 .70
a. Souv. sheet of 4, #3565-3568, imperf. *12.00* 1.50
Nos. 3565-3568 (4) 2.60 1.65

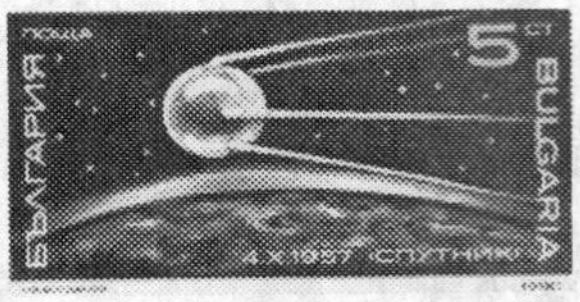

Space Exploration — A1394

Designs: 5s, Sputnik, 1957, USSR. 8s, Vostok, 1961, USSR. 10s, Voshkod 2, 1965, USSR. 20s, Apollo-Soyuz, 1975, US-USSR. 42s, Space Shuttle Columbia, 1981, US. 60s, Galileo, 1989-1996, US. 1 l, Apollo 11 Moon landing, 1969, US.

1990, Oct. 22 ***Perf. 13½x13***

3569 A1394 5s multicolored .20 .20
3570 A1394 8s multicolored .20 .20
3571 A1394 10s multicolored .20 .20
3572 A1394 20s multicolored .40 .25
3573 A1394 42s multicolored .90 .55
3574 A1394 60s multicolored 1.25 .70
Nos. 3569-3574 (6) 3.15 2.10

Souvenir Sheet

3575 A1394 1 l multicolored 2.75 1.50

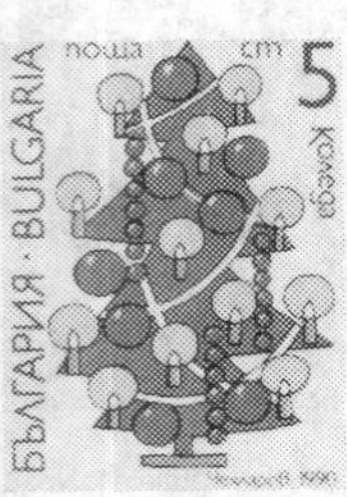

St. Clement of Okhrida A1395

Christmas A1396

1990, Nov. 29 **Litho.** ***Perf. 13***

3576 A1395 5s multicolored .20 .20

1990, Dec. 25 **Litho.** ***Perf. 13***

3577 A1396 5s Christmas tree .20 .20
3578 A1396 20s Santa Claus .40 .25

European Figure Skating Championships, Sofia — A1397

1991, Jan. 18 ***Perf. 13½x13***

3579 A1397 15s multicolored .35 .20

Farm Animals A1398

1991-92 ***Perf. 14x13½***

3581 A1398 20s Sheep .30 .20
3582 A1398 25s Goose .35 .20
3583 A1398 30s Hen, chicks .40 .20
3584 A1398 40s Horse .55 .25
3585 A1398 62s Goat .85 .30
3586 A1398 86s Sow 1.25 .50
3587 A1398 95s Goat .70 .30
3588 A1398 1 l Donkey 1.40 .40
3589 A1398 2 l Bull 2.75 .50
3590 A1398 5 l Turkey 7.00 1.25
3591 A1398 10 l Cow 14.00 1.75
Nos. 3581-3591 (11) 29.55 5.85

Issued: 20s, 25s, 40s, 86s, 1 l, Aug. 21; 10 l, Feb. 22; 95s, May 5, 1992; others, Feb. 11, 1991.

Mushrooms — A1399

1991, Mar. 19 ***Perf. 12½x13***

3597 A1399 5s Amanita phalloides .20 .20
3598 A1399 10s Amanita verna .20 .20
3599 A1399 20s Amanita pantherina .30 .20
3600 A1399 32s Amanita muscaria .50 .30
3601 A1399 42s Gyromitra esculenta .60 .35
3602 A1399 60s Boletus satanas .80 .50
a. Min. sheet of 6, #3597-3602 3.00 1.50
Nos. 3597-3602 (6) 2.60 1.75

French Impressionists A1400

Designs: 20s, Good Morning, by Gauguin. 43s, Madame Dobini, by Degas. 62s, Peasant Woman, by Pissarro. 67s, Woman with Black Hair, by Manet. 80s, Blue Vase, by Cezanne. 2 l, Jeanny Samari, by Renoir. 3 l, Self portrait, by Van Gogh.

1991, Apr. 1 ***Perf. 13***

3603 A1400 20s multicolored .25 .20
3604 A1400 43s multicolored .50 .40
3605 A1400 62s multicolored .70 .55
3606 A1400 67s multicolored .80 .60
3607 A1400 80s multicolored 1.00 .75
3608 A1400 2 l multicolored 2.25 1.75
Nos. 3603-3608 (6) 5.50 4.25

Miniature Sheet

3609 A1400 3 l multicolored 4.50 2.75

Swiss Confederation, 700th Anniv. — A1401

1991, Apr. 11

3610 A1401 62s multicolored .90 .55

Philatelic Review, Cent. — A1402

1991, May 7 **Litho.** ***Perf. 13***

3611 A1402 30s multicolored .45 .25

Europa — A1403

1991, May 10 ***Perf. 13x13½***

3612 A1403 43s Meteosat .70 .40
3613 A1403 62s Ariane rocket 1.00 .55

Horses — A1404

1991, May 21 ***Perf. 13x12½***

3614 A1404 5s Przewalski's horse .20 .20
3615 A1404 10s Tarpan .20 .20
3616 A1404 25s Arabian .35 .20
3617 A1404 35s Arabian .45 .30
3618 A1404 42s Shetland pony .55 .35

3619 A1404 60s Draft horse .80 .50
a. Min. sheet of 6, #3614-3619 3.00 1.50
Nos. 3614-3619 (6) 2.55 1.75

EXPO 91, Plovdiv — A1405

1991, June 6 Litho. *Perf. 13½x13*
3620 A1405 30s multicolored .45 .30

Wolfgang Amadeus Mozart A1406

1991, July 2 *Perf. 13*
3621 A1406 62s multicolored .95 .55

Space Shuttle Missions, 10th Anniv. A1407

1991, July 23 Litho. *Perf. 13*
3622 A1407 12s Columbia .20 .20
3623 A1407 32s Challenger .30 .20
3624 A1407 50s Discovery .40 .20
3625 A1407 86s Atlantis, vert. .75 .40
3626 A1407 1.50 l Buran, vert. 1.25 .60
3627 A1407 2 l Atlantis, diff., vert. 1.50 .75
Nos. 3622-3627 (6) 4.40 2.35

Souvenir Sheet

3628 A1407 3 l US shuttle, earth 4.00 2.00

1992 Winter Olympics, Albertville — A1408

1991, Aug. 7 Litho. *Perf. 13x13½*
3629 A1408 30s Luge .40 .30
3630 A1408 43s Slalom skiing .50 .40
3631 A1408 67s Ski jumping .85 .60
3632 A1408 2 l Biathlon 2.50 1.75
Nos. 3629-3632 (4) 4.25 3.05

Souvenir Sheet

3633 A1408 3 l Two-man bobsled 4.50 2.75

Sheraton Sofia Hotel Balkan A1409

1991, Sept. 6 Litho. *Perf. 13*
3634 A1409 62s multicolored 1.10 .55

Printed in sheets of 3 + 3 labels.

Dogs — A1410

1991, Oct. 11 *Perf. 13x13½*
3635 A1410 30s Japanese .25 .20
3636 A1410 43s Chihuahua .40 .20
3637 A1410 62s Pinscher .55 .30
3638 A1410 80s Yorkshire terrier .70 .35
3639 A1410 1 l Chinese .90 .45
3640 A1410 3 l Pug 2.50 1.25
a. Min. sheet of 6, #3635-3640 5.50 2.75
Nos. 3635-3640 (6) 5.30 2.75

Cologne '91, Intl. Philatelic Exhibition A1411

1991, Oct. 21 *Perf. 13*
3641 A1411 86s multicolored 1.50 .75

Printed in sheets of 3 + 3 labels.

Souvenir Sheet

Brandenburg Gate, Bicent. — A1412

1991, Oct. 23
3642 A1412 4 l multicolored 7.00 3.50

Exists imperf.

Phila Nippon '91 A1413

1991, Nov. 11
3643 A1413 62s Japan #1 1.10 .55

Printed in sheets of 3 + 3 labels.

Bulgarian Railroad, 125th Anniv. — A1414

1991, Nov. 30
3644 A1414 30s Locomotive .55 .30
3645 A1414 30s Passenger car .55 .30

Medicinal Plants A1415

Designs: 30s, Pulsatilla vernalis. 40s, Pulsatilla pratensis. 55s, Pulsatilla halleri. 60s, Aquilegia nigricans. 1 l, Hippophae rhamnoides. 2 l, Ribes nigrum.

1991, Nov. 20 Litho. *Perf. 13*
3646 A1415 30s +15s label .40 .20
3647 A1415 40s multicolored .35 .20
3648 A1415 55s multicolored .50 .25
3649 A1415 60s multicolored .55 .30
3650 A1415 1 l multicolored .90 .45
3651 A1415 2 l multicolored 1.75 .90
a. Min. sheet of 6, #3646-3651 4.50 2.50
Nos. 3646-3651 (6) 4.45 2.30

No. 3646 printed se-tenant with label. No. 3651a sold for 5 l, but does not contain the 15s label printed with No. 3646.

Basketball, Cent. A1416

1991, Dec. 6 *Perf. 13½x13*
3652 A1416 43s Ball below rim .50 .25
3653 A1416 62s Ball at rim .75 .40
3654 A1416 90s Ball in cylinder 1.10 .55
3655 A1416 1 l Ball in basket 1.25 .65
Nos. 3652-3655 (4) 3.60 1.85

El Greco, 450th Birth Anniv. — A1417

Paintings: 43s, Christ Carrying the Cross. 50s, Holy Family with St. Anne. 60s, St. John the Evangelist and St. John the Baptist. 62s, St. Andrew and St. Francis. 1 l, Holy Family with St. Mary Magdalene. 2 l, Cardinal Nino de Guevara. 3 l, Holy Family with St. Anne (detail).

1991, Dec. 13 *Perf. 13*
3656 A1417 43s multicolored .45 .25
3657 A1417 50s multicolored .55 .30
3658 A1417 60s multicolored .65 .35
3659 A1417 62s multicolored .70 .40
3660 A1417 1 l multicolored 1.10 .55
3661 A1417 2 l multicolored 2.00 1.00
Nos. 3656-3661 (6) 5.45 2.85

Souvenir Sheet

3662 A1417 3 l multicolored 4.00 2.00

No. 3662 contains one 43x53mm stamp.

Christmas — A1418

1991, Dec. 18
3663 A1418 30s Snowman, candle, bell, heart .55 .30
3664 A1418 62s Star, angel, flower, house, tree 1.10 .55

Marine Mammals — A1419

Designs: 30s, Phogophoca graenlandica. 43s, Orcinus orca. 62s, Odobenus rosmarus. 68s, Tursiops truncatus. 1 l, Monachus monachus. 2 l, Phocaena phocaena.

1991, Dec. 24
3665 A1419 30s multicolored .35 .20
3666 A1419 43s multicolored .50 .25
3667 A1419 62s multicolored .75 .40
3668 A1419 68s multicolored .80 .40
3669 A1419 1 l multicolored 1.25 .65
3670 A1419 2 l multicolored 2.50 1.25
a. Min. sheet of #3665-3670 6.25 3.25
Nos. 3665-3670 (6) 6.15 3.15

Settlement of Jews in Bulgaria, 500th Anniv. — A1420

1992, Mar. 5 Litho. *Perf. 13*
3671 A1420 1 l multicolored 1.75 .90

Gioacchino Rossini (1792-1868), Composer — A1421

1992, Mar. 11
3672 A1421 50s multicolored .90 .45

Plovdiv Fair, Cent. A1422

1992, Mar. 25
3673 A1422 1 l buff & black 1.75 .90

Fiat Croma — A1423

Automobiles.

1992, Mar. 26 *Perf. 13½x13*
3674 A1423 30s Volvo 740 .35 .20
3675 A1423 45s Ford Escort .55 .30
3676 A1423 50s shown .60 .30
3677 A1423 50s Mercedes 600 .60 .30
3678 A1423 1 l Peugeot 605 1.10 .55
3679 A1423 2 l BMW 316 1.75 .90
Nos. 3674-3679 (6) 4.95 2.55

Francisco de Orellana A1424

Explorers: No. 3681, Vespucci. No. 3682, Magellan. No. 3683, Gonzalo Jimenez de Quesada (1500-1579). 2 l, Drake. 3 l, Pedro de Valdivia (1500-1553). 4 l, Columbus.

1992, Apr. 22 Litho. *Perf. 13*
3680 A1424 50s multicolored .45 .25
3681 A1424 50s multicolored .45 .25
3682 A1424 1 l multicolored .90 .45
3683 A1424 1 l multicolored .90 .45

3684 A1424 2 l multicolored 1.75 .90
3685 A1424 3 l multicolored 2.70 1.40
Nos. 3680-3685 (6) 7.15 3.70

Souvenir Sheet

3686 A1424 4 l multicolored 3.50 1.75

Granada '92 A1425

1992, Apr. 23

3687 A1425 62s multicolored .55 .30

No. 3687 printed in sheets of 3 + 3 labels.

Discovery of America, 500th Anniv. A1426

1992, Apr. 24

3688 A1426 1 l Ships, map .90 .45
3689 A1426 2 l Columbus, ship 1.75 .90
a. Pair, #3688-3689 2.75 1.40

Europa.

SOS Children's Village A1427

1992, June 15 Litho. *Perf. 13*

3690 A1427 1 l multicolored .90 .45

1992 Summer Olympics, Barcelona — A1428

1992, July 15 *Perf. 13½x13*

3691 A1428 50s Swimming .45 .25
3692 A1428 50s Long jump .45 .25
3693 A1428 1 l High jump .90 .45
3694 A1428 3 l Gymnastics 2.70 1.40
Nos. 3691-3694 (4) 4.50 2.35

Souvenir Sheet

Perf. 13x13½

3695 A1428 4 l Torch, vert. 3.75 1.75

Motorcycles — A1429

Designs: 30s, 1902 Laurin & Klement. No. 3697, 1928 Puch 200 Luxus. No. 3698, 1931 Norton CS1. 70s, 1950 Harley Davidson. 1 l, 1986 Gilera SP 01. 2 l, 1990 BMW K1.

1992, July 30 *Perf. 13*

3696 A1429 30s multicolored .20 .20
3697 A1429 50s multicolored .30 .20
3698 A1429 50s multicolored .30 .20
3699 A1429 70s multicolored .40 .20
3700 A1429 1 l multicolored .60 .30
3701 A1429 2 l multicolored 1.25 .65
Nos. 3696-3701 (6) 3.05 1.75

Genoa '92 Intl. Philatelic Exhibition A1430

1992, Sept. 18 *Perf. 13*

3702 A1430 1 l multicolored .90 .45

This is a developing set. Numbers may change.

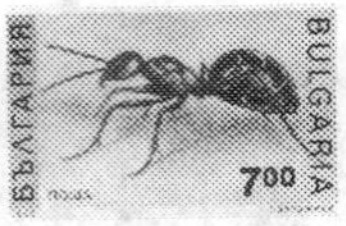

Insects — A1431

1992 Litho. *Perf. 14x13½*

3710 A1431 1 l Dragonfly .20
3711 A1431 2 l Mayfly .25
3712 A1431 3 l Locust .30
3713 A1431 4 l Stag beetle .45
3714 A1431 5 l Carrion beetle .55
3715 A1431 7 l Ant .75
3716 A1431 20 l Bee 2.25
3717 A1431 50 l Praying mantis 5.75
Nos. 3710-3717 (8) 10.50

Issued: 7, 20 l, 9/25; 3, 50 l, 11/30; 1, 2, 4, 5 l, 12/15/93.

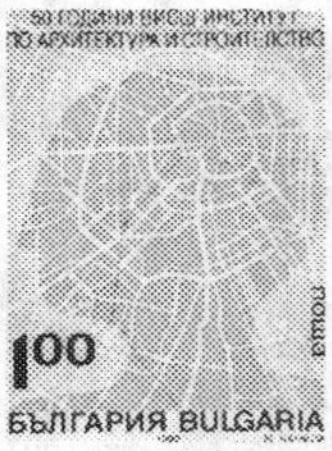

A1432

A1433

1992, Sept. 30 *Perf. 13*

3719 A1432 1 l blk, pink & rose .90 .45

Higher Institute of Architecture and Building, 50th anniv.

1992, Oct. 16 Litho. *Perf. 13*

Trees: No. 3720, Quercus mestensis. No. 3721, Aesculus hippocastanum. No. 3722, Quercus thracica. No. 3723, Pinus peuce. 2 l, Acer heldreichii. 3 l, Pyrus bulgarica.

3720 A1433 50s multicolored .30 .20
3721 A1433 50s multicolored .30 .20
3722 A1433 1 l multicolored .60 .30
3723 A1433 1 l multicolored .60 .30
3724 A1433 2 l multicolored 1.25 .65
3725 A1433 3 l multicolored 2.00 1.00
Nos. 3720-3725 (6) 5.05 2.65

Ethnographical Museum, Cent. — A1434

1992, Oct. 23

3726 A1434 1 l multicolored .90 .45

Tanker Bulgaria — A1435

1992, Oct. 30 Litho. *Perf. 13*

3727 A1435 30s Freighter Bulgaria .20 .20
3728 A1435 50s Castor .30 .20
3729 A1435 1 l Hero of Sevastopol .60 .30
3730 A1435 2 l shown 1.25 .65
3731 A1435 2 l Aleko Constantinov 1.25 .65
3732 A1435 3 l Varna 2.00 1.00
Nos. 3727-3732 (6) 5.60 3.00

Bulgarian Merchant Fleet, Cent.

Bulgaria, Member of the Council of Europe — A1436

1992, Nov. 6 Litho. *Perf. 13*

3733 A1436 7 l multicolored 6.25 3.00

Souvenir Sheet

4th World Congress of Popular Sports, Varna — A1437

1992, Nov. 17 Litho. *Perf. 13*

3734 A1437 4 l multicolored 4.00

Christmas A1438

1992, Dec. 1 *Perf. 13½x13*

3735 A1438 1 l Santa Claus .75
3736 A1438 7 l Madonna & Child 5.25

Wild Cats — A1439

1992, Dec. 18 Litho. *Perf. 13*

3737 A1439 50s Panthera pardus .25
3738 A1439 50s Acinonyx jubatus .25
3739 A1439 1 l Panthera onca .50
3740 A1439 2 l Panthera tigris 1.00
3741 A1439 2 l Felis concolor 1.00
3742 A1439 3 l Panthera leo 1.50
Nos. 3737-3742 (6) 4.50

Sports A1440

1992, Dec. 18

3743 A1440 50s Baseball .35
3744 A1440 50s Cricket .35
3745 A1440 1 l Polo .75
3746 A1440 1 l Harness racing .75
3747 A1440 2 l Field hockey 1.50
3748 A1440 3 l Football 2.25
Nos. 3743-3748 (6) 5.95

Owls A1441

1992, Dec. 23

3749 A1441 30s Aegolius funereus .20
3750 A1441 50s Strix aluco .25
3751 A1441 1 l Asio otus .50
3752 A1441 2 l Otus scops 1.00
3753 A1441 2 l Asio flammeus 1.00
3754 A1441 3 l Tyto alba 1.50
Nos. 3749-3754 (6) 4.45

Nos. 3749, 3751, 3753-3754 are vert.

Paintings Depicting History of Bulgaria A1442

Artists: 50s, Dimiter Gyudzhenov. 1 l, 3 l, Nikolai Pavlovich. 2 l, Dimiter Panchev. 4 l, Mito Ganovski.

1992, Dec. 28

3755 A1442 50s multicolored .40
3756 A1442 1 l multicolored .75
3757 A1442 2 l multicolored 1.50
3758 A1442 3 l multicolored 2.25
Nos. 3755-3758 (4) 4.90

Souvenir Sheet

3759 A1442 4 l multicolored, vert. 3.00

Archeological Museum, Cent. A1443

1993 World Biathlon Championships, Borovetz A1444

1993, Jan. 1 Litho. *Perf. 13x13½*

3760 A1443 1 l multicolored .75

1993, Feb. 5

3761 A1444 1 l Woman aiming rifle .75
3762 A1444 7 l Skiing 5.25

Neophit Rilski, Birth Bicent.
A1445

1993, Apr. 22 Litho. *Perf. 13½x13*

3763 A1445 1 l henna brn & ol bis *.75*

Contemporary Art — A1446

Europa: 3 l, Sculpture of centaur, by Georgi Chapkinov. 8 l, Painting of geometric forms, by D. Bujukliski.

1993, Apr. 29 *Perf. 13x13½*

3764 A1446 3 l multicolored 2.25
3765 A1446 8 l multicolored 6.00

Fish
A1447

1993, June 29 Litho. *Perf. 13*

3766 A1447 1 l C.a.j. bicaudatus .75
3767 A1447 2 l Mollienesia velifera 1.50
3768 A1447 3 l Aphyosemion bivittatum 2.25
3769 A1447 3 l Pterophyllum eimekei 2.25
3770 A1447 4 l Symphysodon discus 3.00
3771 A1447 8 l Trichogaster leeri 6.00
Nos. 3766-3771 (6) 15.75

Fruit — A1448

1993, July 8 *Perf. 13x13½*

3772 A1448 1 l Malus domestica .35
3773 A1448 2 l Pyrus sativa .70
3774 A1448 2 l Persica vulgaris .70
3775 A1448 3 l Cydonia oblonga 1.00
3776 A1448 5 l Punica granatum 1.75
3777 A1448 7 l Ficus carica 2.50
Nos. 3772-3777 (6) 7.00

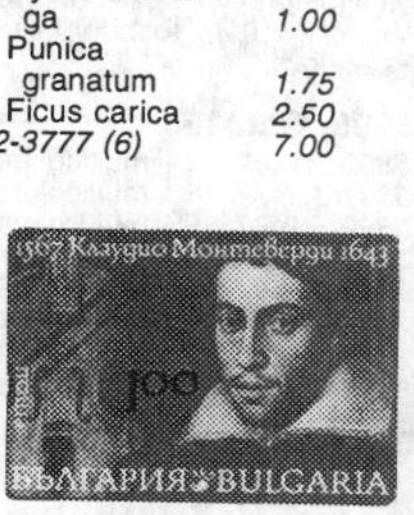

Claudio Monteverdi (1567-1643), Composer
A1449

1993, July 20 Litho. *Perf. 13½x13*

3778 A1449 1 l multicolored .75

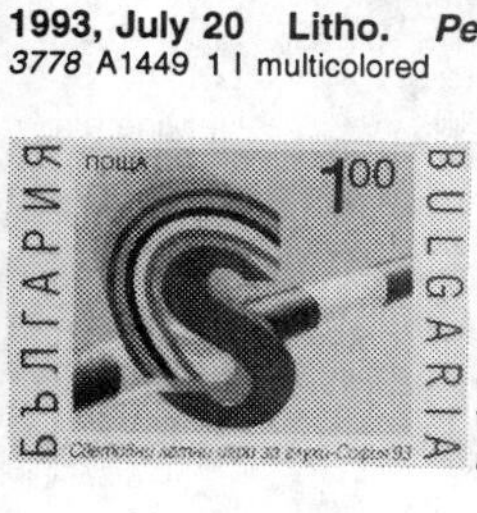

17th World Summer Games for the Deaf
A1450

1993, July 20 *Perf. 13*

3779 A1450 1 l shown .75
3780 A1450 2 l Swimming 1.50
3781 A1450 3 l Cycling 2.25
3782 A1450 4 l Tennis 3.00
Nos. 3779-3782 (4) 7.50

Souvenir Sheet

3783 A1450 5 l Soccer

Miniature Sheet

A1451

Council of Preslav, Cyrillic Alphabet in Bulgaria, 1100th Anniv.: a, Baptism of Christian convert. b, Tsar Boris I (852-889). c, Tsar Simeon (893-927). d, Battle between Bulgarians and Byzantines.

1993, Sept. 16 Litho. *Perf. 13½x13*

3784 A1451 5 l Sheet of 4, #a.-d. *3.50*

Alexander of Battenberg (1857-93), Prince of Bulgaria — A1452

1993, Sept. 23 *Perf. 13x13½*

3785 A1452 3 l multicolored .50

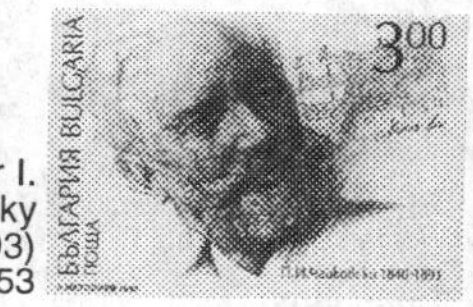

Peter I. Tchaikovsky (1840-93)
A1453

1993, Sept. 30 *Perf. 13½x13*

3786 A1453 3 l multicolored .50

Small Arms
A1454

Isaac Newton (1643-1725)
A1455

1993, Oct. 22 Litho. *Perf. 13½x14*

3787 A1454 1 l Crossbow, 16th cent. .20
3788 A1454 2 l Pistol, 18th cent. .35
3789 A1454 3 l Luger, 1908 .50
3790 A1454 3 l Pistol, 1873 .50
3791 A1454 5 l Rifle, 1938 .85
3792 A1454 7 l Kalashnikov, 1947 1.25
Nos. 3787-3792 (6) 3.65

1993, Oct. 29 *Perf. 13½x13*

3793 A1455 1 l multicolored .20

Organized Philately in Bulgaria, Cent.
A1456

1993, Nov. 16

3794 A1456 1 l multicolored .20

Ecology
A1457

1993, Nov. 17

3795 A1457 1 l shown .20
3796 A1457 7 l Ecology 1.25

Game Animals
A1458

1993, Nov. 25

3797 A1458 1 l Anas platrhynchos .20
3798 A1458 1 l Phasianus colchicus .20
3799 A1458 2 l Vulpes vulpes .35
3800 A1458 3 l Capreolus capreolus .50
3801 A1458 6 l Lepus europaeus 1.00
3802 A1458 8 l Sus scrofa 1.40
Nos. 3797-3802 (6) 3.65

Christmas
A1459

Signs of Zodiac on sundial: No. 3803a, Taurus, Gemini, Cancer. b, Libra, Virgo, Leo.
No. 3804a, Aquarius, Pisces, Aries. b, Capricorn, Sagittarius, Scorpio.

1993, Dec. 1

3803 A1459 1 l Pair, #a.-b. .35
3804 A1459 7 l Pair, #a.-b. 2.50

When placed together, Nos. 3803-3804 form a complete sundial.

Regional Folk Costumes for Men

A1460 A1461

1993, Dec. 16 Litho. *Perf. 13½x14*

3805 A1460 1 l Sofia .20
3806 A1461 1 l Plovdiv .20
3807 A1460 2 l Belogradchik .25
3808 A1460 3 l Shumen .30
3809 A1461 3 l Oryakhovitsa .30
3810 A1461 8 l Kurdzhali .90
Nos. 3805-3810 (6) 2.15

1994 Winter Olympics, Lillehammer
A1462

1994, Feb. 8 *Perf. 13*

3811 A1462 1 l Freestyle skiing .20
3812 A1462 2 l Speed skating .25
3813 A1462 3 l 2-Man luge .30
3814 A1462 4 l Hockey .45
Nos. 3811-3814 (4) 1.20

Souvenir Sheet

3815 A1462 5 l Downhill skiing .55

Nikolai Pavlovich (1835-94)
A1463

1994, Feb. 16 *Perf. 13½x13*

3816 A1463 3 l multicolored .30

Dinosaurs
A1464

1994, Apr. 27 Litho. *Perf. 13*

3817 A1464 2 l Plesiosaurus .20
3818 A1464 3 l Iguanodon .20
3819 A1464 3 l Archaeopteryx .20
3820 A1464 4 l Edmontonia .20
3821 A1464 5 l Styracosaurus .20
3822 A1464 7 l Tyrannosaurus Rex .30
Nos. 3817-3822 (6) 1.30

1994 World Cup Soccer Championships, US — A1465

Players in championships of : 3 l, Chile, 1962. 6 l, England, 1966. 7 l, Mexico, 1970. 9 l, West Germany, 1974. No. 3827a, Mexico, 1986, vert. b, US, 1994.

1994, Apr. 28

3823 A1465 3 l multicolored .20
3824 A1465 6 l multicolored .25
3825 A1465 7 l multicolored .30
3826 A1465 9 l multicolored .35
Nos. 3823-3826 (4) 1.10

Souvenir Sheet

3827 A1465 5 l Sheet of 2, #a.-b. .40

For No. 3827 with inscription reading up along the left margin, see No. 3851.

Europa
A1466

European Discoveries: 3 l, Axis of symmetry. 15 l, Electrocardiogram.

1994, Apr. 29 Litho. *Perf. 13½*

3828 A1466 3 l multicolored .20
3829 A1466 15 l multicolored .60

Boris Hristov (1914-93) — A1467

1994, May 18 Litho. *Perf. 13*

3830 A1467 3 l brown & bister .20

Cricetus Cricetus — A1468

Designs: 3 l, In nest. 7 l, Emerging from burrow. 10 l, Standing on hind legs. 15 l, Finding berry.

1994, Sept. 23 Litho. *Perf. 13*

3831	A1468	3 l	multicolored	.20
3832	A1468	7 l	multicolored	.30
3833	A1468	10 l	multicolored	.40
3834	A1468	15 l	multicolored	.60
			Nos. 3831-3834 (4)	1.50

World Wildlife Fund.

Space Program A1469

Intl. Olympic Committee, Cent. A1470

1994, Nov. 4 Litho. *Perf. 13*

3835 A1469 3 l multicolored .20

1994, Nov. 7

3836 A1470 3 l multicolored .20

Icons A1471

Christmas A1472

1994, Nov. 24 Litho. *Perf. 13x13½*

3837	A1471	2 l	Christ	.20
3838	A1471	3 l	Christ, the healer	.20
3839	A1471	5 l	Crucifixion	.20
3840	A1471	7 l	Archangel Michael	.25
3841	A1471	8 l	Sts. Cyril, Methodius	.25
3842	A1471	15 l	Madonna & Child	.45
			Nos. 3837-3842 (6)	1.55

1994, Dec. 1

3843	A1472	3 l	Ancient coin	.20
3844	A1472	15 l	Coin, diff.	1.00

Roses A1473

1994, Dec. 12 *Perf. 13*

Color of Rose

3845	A1473	2 l	yellow	.20
3846	A1473	3 l	rose red	.20
3847	A1473	5 l	white	.20
3848	A1473	7 l	salmon	.20
3849	A1473	10 l	carmine	.30
3850	A1473	15 l	orange & yellow	.40
			Nos. 3845-3850 (6)	1.50

Souvenir Sheet

No. 3827 with Additional Inscription in Left Sheet Margin

1994, Dec. 15 Litho. *Perf. 13*

3851 A1465 5 l Sheet of 2, #a.-b. .40

Trams A1474

1994, Dec. 29

3852	A1474	1 l	Model 1912	.20
3853	A1474	2 l	Model 1928	.20
3854	A1474	3 l	Model 1931	.20
3855	A1474	5 l	Model 1942	.20
3856	A1474	8 l	Model 1951	.25
3857	A1474	10 l	Model 1961	.30
			Nos. 3852-3857 (6)	1.35

Vassil Petleshkov (1845-76), Revolutionary A1475

1995, Feb. 27 Litho. *Perf. 13½x13*

3858 A1475 3 l multicolored .20

End of World War II, 50th Anniv. — A1476

Europa: 15 l, Dove holding olive branch standing on gun barrel.

1995, May 3 Litho. *Perf. 13*

3859	A1476	3 l	multicolored	.20
3860	A1476	15 l	multicolored	.45

Souvenir Sheet

Men's World Volleyball League, Cent. — A1477

Designs: a, 10 l, Player digging ball. b, 15 l, Player spiking ball, vert.

1995, May 25 Litho. *Perf. 13*

3861 A1477 Sheet of 2, #a.-b. .75

Souvenir Sheet

European Nature Conservation Year — A1478

Designs: a, 10 l, Pancratium maritimum. b, 15 l, Aquila heliaca. Illustration reduced.

1995, June 23 Litho. *Perf. 13*

3862 A1478 Sheet of 2, #a.-b. .75

Antarctic Wildlife — A1479

1 l, Euphausia superba. 2 l, Chaenocephalus. 3 l, Physeter catodon. 5 l, Leptonychotes weddelli. 8 l, Stercorarius skua. 10 l, Aptenodytes forsteri, vert.

1995, June 29

3863	A1479	1 l	multicolored	.20
3864	A1479	2 l	multicolored	.20
3865	A1479	3 l	multicolored	.20
3866	A1479	5 l	multicolored	.20
3867	A1479	8 l	multicolored	.25
3868	A1479	10 l	multicolored	.30
			Nos. 3863-3868 (6)	1.35

Stephan Stambolov (1854-95), Revolutionary Leader, Politician — A1480

1995, July 6 Litho. *Perf. 13*

3869 A1480 3 l multicolored .20

1996 Summer Olympics, Atlanta A1481

Designs: 3 l, Pole vault. 7 l, High jump. 10 l, Women's long jump. 15 l, Track.

1995, July 17

3870	A1481	3 l	multicolored	.20
3871	A1481	7 l	multicolored	.20
3872	A1481	10 l	multicolored	.30
3873	A1481	15 l	multicolored	.45
			Nos. 3870-3873 (4)	1.15

Legumes — A1482

1995, July 31

3874	A1482	2 l	Pisum sativum	.20
3875	A1482	3 l	Glicine	.20
3876	A1482	3 l	Cicer arietinum	.20
3877	A1482	4 l	Spinacia oleracea	.20
3878	A1482	5 l	Arachis hypogaea	.20
3879	A1482	15 l	Lens esculenta	.45
			Nos. 3874-3879 (6)	1.45

Organized Tourism in Bulgaria, Cent. — A1483

1995, Aug. 21 Litho. *Perf. 13*

3880 A1483 3 l multicolored .20

Vassil Zahariev (1895-1971), Graphic Artist — A1484

Designs: 2 l, Woodcut of a man. 3 l, Woodcut of building in valley. 5 l, Self-portrait. 10 l, Carving of two women.

1995, Sept. 4 Litho. *Perf. 13*

3881	A1484	2 l	multicolored	.20
3882	A1484	3 l	multicolored	.20
3883	A1484	5 l	multicolored	.20
3884	A1484	10 l	multicolored	.30
			Nos. 3881-3884 (4)	.90

UN, 50th Anniv. A1485

1995, Sept. 12

3885 A1485 3 l multicolored .20

Airplanes — A1486

1995, Sept. 26 Litho. *Perf. 13*

3886	A1486	3 l	PO-2	.20
3887	A1486	5 l	Li-2	.20
3888	A1486	7 l	JU52-3M	.20
3889	A1486	10 l	FV-58	.30
			Nos. 3886-3889 (4)	.90

Motion Pictures, Cent. — A1487

Designs: 2 l, Charlie Chaplin, Mickey Mouse. 3 l, Marilyn Monroe, Marlene Dietrich. 5 l, Humphrey Bogart. 8 l, Sophia Loren, Liza Minnelli. 10 l, Toshiro Mifune. 15 l, Katya Paskaleva.

1995, Oct. 16

3890	A1487	2 l	multicolored	.20
3891	A1487	3 l	multicolored	.20
3892	A1487	5 l	multicolored	.20
3893	A1487	8 l	multicolored	.25
3894	A1487	10 l	multicolored	.30
3895	A1487	15 l	multicolored	.45
			Nos. 3890-3895 (6)	1.60

Minerals A1488

1995, Nov. 20 Litho. *Perf. 13*

3896	A1488	1 l	Agate	.20
3897	A1488	2 l	Sphalerite	.20
3898	A1488	5 l	Calcite	.20
3899	A1488	7 l	Quartz	.20

3900 A1488 8 l Pyromorphite .25
3901 A1488 10 l Almandine .30
Nos. 3896-3901 (6) 1.35

Christmas A1489

1995, Dec. 8 Litho. *Perf. 13*

3902 A1489 3 l shown .20
3903 A1489 15 l Magi .45

Southern Fruit, by Cyril Tsonev (1896-1961) — A1490

1996, Jan. 25 Litho. *Perf. 13*

3904 A1490 3 l multicolored .20

Martin Luther (1483-1546) — A1491

1996, Feb. 5

3905 A1491 3 l multicolored .20

Historic Buildings A1492

Monasteries: 3 l, Preobragenie. 5 l, Arapovsky. 10 l, Drianovo. 20 l, Bachkovo. 25 l, Troyan. 40 l, Zografski.

1996, Feb. 28 *Perf. 14x13½*

3906 A1492 3 l green .20
3907 A1492 5 l red .20
3908 A1492 10 l blue .30
3909 A1492 20 l yellow orange .60
3910 A1492 25 l brown .75
3911 A1492 40 l purple 1.25
Nos. 3906-3911 (6) 3.30

5th Meeting of European Bank for Reconstruction and Development A1493

1996, Apr. 15 Litho. *Perf. 13*

3912 A1493 7 l shown .20
3913 A1493 30 l Building, diff. .50

Conifers A1494

Designs: 5 l, Taxus baccata. 8 l, Abies alba. 10 l, Picea abies. 20 l, Pinus silvestris. 25 l, Pinus heldreichii. 40 l, Juniperus excelsa.

1996, Apr. 23 *Perf. 13½x13*

3914 A1494 5 l multicolored .20
3915 A1494 8 l multicolored .20
3916 A1494 10 l multicolored .20
3917 A1494 20 l multicolored .30
3918 A1494 25 l multicolored .45
3919 A1494 40 l multicolored .65
Nos. 3914-3919 (6) 2.00

A1495

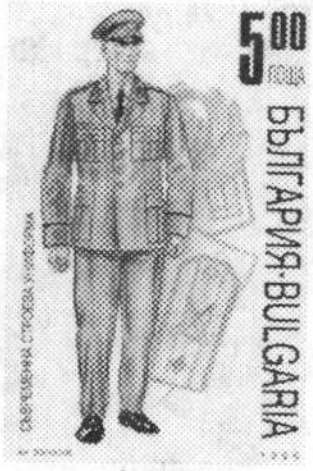

A1496

Designs: 10 l, People in distress. 40 l, Khristo Botev (1848-1876), poet, patriot, horiz.

1996, May 1 *Perf. 13*

3920 A1495 10 l multicolored .20
3921 A1495 40 l multicolored .65

April Uprising, death of Khristo Botev, 120th anniv.

1996, May 6

Uniforms: 5 l, Light brown dress uniform. 8 l, Brown combat, helmet. 10 l, Brown uniform, holding gun with fixed bayonet. 20 l, Early red, blue dress uniform. 25 l, Officer's early green dress uniform. 40 l, Soldier's green uniform.

1996, May 6

3922 A1496 5 l multicolored .20
3923 A1496 8 l multicolored .20
3924 A1496 10 l multicolored .20
3925 A1496 20 l multicolored .30
3926 A1496 25 l multicolored .45
3927 A1496 40 l multicolored .65
Nos. 3922-3927 (6) 2.00

Republic of Bulgaria, 50th Anniv. — A1497

1996, May 13 Litho. *Perf. 13½*

3928 A1497 10 l multicolored .20

Famous Women A1498

Europa: 10 l, Elisaveta Bagriana (1893-1990), poet. 40 l, Katia Popova (1924-66), opera singer.

1996, May 29 Litho. *Perf. 13*

3929 A1498 10 l multicolored .25
Complete booklet, 5 #3929 1.25
3930 A1498 40 l multicolored .95
Complete booklet, 5 #3930 4.75

A1499

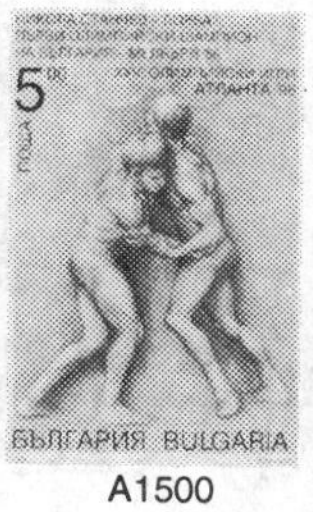

A1500

10 l, Soccer player. 15 l, Soccer player, diff.

1996, June 4

Souvenir Sheet

3931 A1499 Sheet of 2, #a.-b. .60

Euro '96, European Soccer Championships, Great Britain.

1996, July 4

3932 A1500 5 l Wrestling .20
3933 A1500 8 l Boxing .20
3934 A1500 10 l Women's shot put .25
3935 A1500 25 l Women sculling .60
Nos. 3932-3935 (4) 1.25

Souvenir Sheet

3936 A1500 15 l Pierre de Coubertin .35

1996 Summer Olympic Games, Atlanta. Olymphilex '96 (#3936).

Crabs A1501

Designs: 5 l, Gammarus arduus. 10 l, Asellus aquaticus. 12 l, Astacus astacus. 25 l, Palaemon serratus. 30 l, Cumella limicola. 40 l, Carcinus mediterraneus.

1996, July 30

3937 A1501 5 l multicolored .20
3938 A1501 10 l multicolored .25
3939 A1501 12 l multicolored .30
3940 A1501 25 l multicolored .60
3941 A1501 30 l multicolored .70
3942 A1501 40 l multicolored .95
Nos. 3937-3942 (6) 3.00

Francisco Goya (1746-1828) A1502

Entire paintings or details: 8 l, Young Woman with a Letter. 26 l, The Second of May, 1808. 40 l, Neighboring Women on a Balcony.

No. 3947: a, 10 l, The Clothed Maja. b, 15 l, The Naked Maja.

1996, July 9 Litho. *Perf. 13*

3943 A1502 5 l multicolored .20
3944 A1502 8 l multicolored .20
3945 A1502 26 l multicolored .65
3946 A1502 40 l multicolored 1.00
Nos. 3943-3946 (4) 2.05

Souvenir Sheet

Perf. 13½x13

3947 A1502 Sheet of 2, #a.-b. .60

No. 3947 contains two 54x29mm stamps.

Souvenir Sheet

St. John of Rila (876-946), Founder of Rila Monastery — A1503

1996, Sept. 3

3948 A1503 10 l multicolored .25

Bulgarian Renaissance Houses — A1504

Various multi-level houses.

1996, Sept. 12 Litho. *Perf. 14x13½*

Background Color

3949 A1504 10 l buff .20
3950 A1504 15 l orange yellow .20
3951 A1504 30 l yellow green .30
3952 A1504 50 l red lilac .45
3953 A1504 60 l apple green .55
3954 A1504 100 l green blue .95
Nos. 3949-3954 (6) 2.65

Steam Locomotives — A1505

1996, Sept. 24 *Perf. 13*

3955 A1505 5 l 1836 .20
3956 A1505 10 l 1847 .20
3957 A1505 12 l 1848 .20
3958 A1505 26 l 1876 .25
Nos. 3955-3958 (4) .85

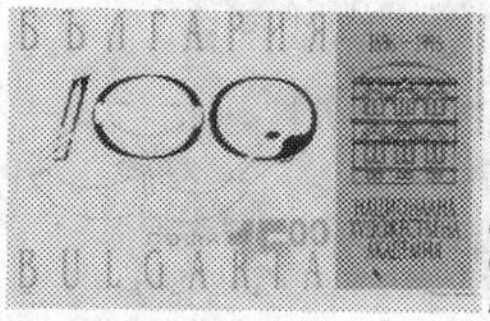

Natl. Gallery of Art, Cent. A1506

1996, Oct. 14 Litho. *Perf. 13*

3959 A1506 15 l multicolored .20

Defeat of Byzantine Army by Tsar Simeon, 1100th Anniv. — A1507

Designs: 10 l, Sword hilt, soldiers on horseback. 40 l, Sword blade, dagger, fallen soldiers.

1996, Oct. 21
3960 A1507 10 l multicolored .20
3961 A1507 40 l multicolored .35
a. Pair, #3960-3961 .50

No. 3961 is a continuous design.

UNICEF, 50th Anniv. — A1508

Children's drawings: 7 l, Diver, fish. 15 l, Circus performers. 20 l, Boy, artist's pallete. 60 l, Women seated at table.

1996, Nov. 18 Litho. *Perf. 13*
3962 A1508 7 l multicolored .20
3963 A1508 15 l multicolored .30
3964 A1508 20 l multicolored .40
3965 A1508 60 l multicolored 1.25
Nos. 3962-3965 (4) 2.15

A1509 A1510

1996, Nov. 26
3966 A1509 15 l Candles on tree .30
3967 A1509 60 l Church 1.25

Christmas.

1996, Dec. 11 Litho. *Perf. 13*

Painting of Old Bulgarian Town, by Tsanko Lavrenov (1896-1978).

3968 A1510 15 l multicolored .30

Puppies A1511

1997, Feb. 25 Litho. *Perf. 13*
3969 A1511 5 l Pointer .20
3970 A1511 7 l Chow chow .20
3971 A1511 25 l Carakachan dog .30
3972 A1511 50 l Basset hound .60
Nos. 3969-3972 (4) 1.30

Alexander Graham Bell (1847-1922) — A1512

1997, Mar. 10
3973 A1512 30 l multicolored .40

Ivan Milev (1897-1927), Painter A1513

Stories and Legends A1514

Paintings: 5 l, Boy drinking from jar. 15 l, Person with head bowed holding up hand. 30 l, Woman. 60 l, Woman carrying child.

1997, Mar. 20
3974 A1513 5 l multicolored .20
3975 A1513 15 l multicolored .20
3976 A1513 30 l multicolored .40
3977 A1513 60 l multicolored .80
Nos. 3974-3977 (4) 1.60

1997, Apr. 14

Europa: 120 l, "March" lady in folk costume, symbol of spring. 600 l, St. George.

3978 A1514 120 l multicolored 1.60
3979 A1514 600 l multicolored 7.75

Konstantin Kissimov (1897-1965), Actor — A1515

1997, Apr. 16
3980 A1515 120 l multicolored 1.60

A1516 A1517

1997, Apr. 21
3981 A1516 60 l multicolored .80

Heinrich von Stephan (1831-97).

1997, May 2 *Perf. 13½*

Historical Landmarks: 80 l, Nessebar. 200 l, Ivanovo Rock Churches. 300 l, Boyana Church. 500 l, Madara horseman. 600 l, Tomb of Sveshtari. 1000 l, Tomb of Kazanlak.

3982 A1517 80 l browm & multi 1.00
3983 A1517 200 l purple & multi 2.50
3984 A1517 300 l bister & multi 4.00
3985 A1517 500 l green & multi 6.50
3986 A1517 600 l yellow & multi 7.75
3987 A1517 1000 l orange & multi 13.00
Nos. 3982-3987 (6) 34.75

Composers — A1518

Designs: a, Gaetano Donizetti (1797-1848). b, Franz Schubert (1797-1828). c, Felix Mendelssohn (1809-1847). d, Johannes Brahms (1833-1897).

1997, May 29 Litho. *Perf. 13½x13*
3988 A1518 120 l Sheet of 4, #a.-d. 6.50

Plants in Bulgaria's Red Book — A1519

Designs: 80 l, Trifolium rubens. 100 l, Tulipa hageri. 120 l, Inula spiraeifolia. 200 l, Paeonia tenuifolia.

1997, June 24 *Perf. 13*
3989 A1519 80 l multicolored 1.00
3990 A1519 100 l multicolored 1.25
3991 A1519 120 l multicolored 1.60
3992 A1519 200 l multicolored 2.50
Nos. 3989-3992 (4) 6.35

A1520 A1521

1997, June 29 Litho. *Perf. 13*
3993 A1520 120 l multicolored 1.60

Civil aviation in Bulgaria, 50th anniv.

1997, July 3
3994 A1521 120 l multicolored 1.60

Evlogy Georgiev (1819-97), banker, philanthropist.

Sofia '97, Modern Pentathlon World Championship — A1522

Designs: 60 l, Equestrian cross-country, running. 80 l, Fencing, swimming. 100 l, Running, women's fencing. 120 l, Men's shooting, diving. 200 l, Equestrian jumping, women's shooting.

1997, July 25
3995 A1522 60 l multicolored .75
3996 A1522 80 l multicolored 1.00
3997 A1522 100 l multicolored 1.25
3998 A1522 120 l multicolored 1.60
3999 A1522 200 l multicolored 2.50
Nos. 3995-3999 (5) 7.10

City of Moscow, 850th Anniv. — A1523

1997, July 30
4000 A1523 120 l multicolored 1.60

No. 4000 is printed se-tenant with label for Moscow '97 Intl. Philatelic Exhibition.

Diesel Engine, Cent. A1524

1997, Sept. 8 Litho. *Perf. 13½x13*
4001 A1524 80 l Boat .20
4002 A1524 100 l Tractor .20
4003 A1524 120 l Truck .20
4004 A1524 200 l Forklift .30
Nos. 4001-4004 (4) .90

43rd General Assembly of Atlantic Club of Bulgaria — A1525

Designs: a, Goddess Tyche. b, Eagle on sphere. c, Building, lion statue, denomination UL. d, Building, denomination UR.

1997, Oct. 2 *Perf. 13*
4005 A1525 120 l Sheet of 4, #a.-d. .55

Miguel de Cervantes (1547-1616) — A1526

1997, Oct. 15
4006 A1526 120 l multicolored .20

Asen Raztsvetnikov (1897-1951), Poet, Writer — A1527

1997, Nov. 5
4007 A1528 120 l multicolored .20

Tsar Samuel (d. 1014), Ascension to Throne, 1000th Anniv. A1528

1997, Nov. 18 *Perf. 13½x13*
4008 A1528 120 l Inscription .20
4009 A1528 600 l Tsar, soldiers .85
a. Pair, #4008-4009 1.00

Christmas — A1529

Designs: 120 l, Snow-covered houses, stars inside shape of Christmas tree, animals. 600 l, Nativity scene.

1997, Dec. 8 *Perf. 13x13½*
4010 A1529 120 l multicolored .20
4011 A1529 600 l multicolored .85

1998 Winter Olympic Games, Nagano
A1530

Designs: 60 l, Speed skating. 80 l, Skiing. 120 l, Biathlon. 600 l, Pairs figure skating.

1997, Dec. 17 ***Perf. 13½x13***

4012 A1530 60 l multicolored *.20*
4013 A1530 80 l multicolored *.20*
4014 A1530 120 l multicolored *.20*
4015 A1530 600 l multicolored *.85*
Nos. 4012-4015 (4) *1.45*

For overprint see No. 4029.

Coat of Arms of Bulgaria
A1531

1997, Dec. 22 **Litho.** ***Perf. 13½x13***

4016 A1531 120 l multicolored *.35*

Souvenir Sheet

Bulgarian Space Program, 25th Anniv. — A1532

Illustration reduced.

1997, Dec. 22 ***Perf. 13***

4017 A1532 120 l multicolored *.35*

Christo Botev (1848-76), Revolutionary, Poet
A1533

Bertolt Brecht (1898-1956), Playwright
A1534

1998, Jan. 6 **Litho.** ***Perf. 13***

4018 A1533 120 l multicolored *.20*

1998, Feb. 10

4019 A1534 120 l multicolored *.20*

Bulgarian Telegraph Agency, Cent.
A1535

1998, Feb. 13

4020 A1535 120 l multicolored *.20*

Illustrations by Alexander Bozhinov (1878-1968)
A1536

Designs: a, Bird wearing bonnet. b, Black bird wearing hat. c, Grandfather Frost, children. d, Girl among flowers looking upward at rain.

1998, Feb. 24 ***Perf. 13½x13***

4021 A1536 120 l Sheet of 4, #a.-d. *.55*

A1537

Easter — A1538

1998, Feb. 27 ***Perf. 13***

4022 A1537 120 l Prince Alexander *.20*
4023 A1537 600 l Monument *.65*
a. Pair, #4022-4023 *.80*

Bulgarian independence from Turkey, 120th anniv.

1998, Mar. 27 **Litho.** ***Perf. 13***

4024 A1538 120 l multicolored *.20*

Bulgarian Olympic Committee, 75th Anniv. — A1539

1998, Mar. 30

4025 A1539 120 l multicolored *.20*

PHARE (Intl. Post and Telecommunications Program) — A1540

1998, Apr. 24 **Litho.** ***Perf. 13***

4026 A1540 120 l multicolored *.35*

National Days and Festivals — A1541

Europa: 120 l, Girls with flowers, "Enyovden." 600 l, Masked men with bells, "Kukery."

1998, Apr. 27

4027 A1541 120 l multicolored *.35*
4028 A1541 600 l multicolored *1.60*

No. 4014 Ovptd.

ПЪРВИ
ЗЛАТЕН МЕДАЛ
ЗА БЪЛГАРИЯ

Е. ДАФОВСКА

1998, Apr. 29 ***Perf. 13½x13***

4029 A1530 120 l multicolored *.35*

Dante and Virgil in Hell, by Eugene Delacroix (1798-1863) — A1542

1998, Apr. 30

4030 A1542 120 l multicolored *.35*

A1543

A1544

1998, May 15 ***Perf. 13***

4031 A1543 120 l multicolored *.20*

Soccer Team of Central Sports Club of the Army, 50th anniv.

1998, May 25

Cats: 60 l, European tabby. 80 l, Siamese. 120 l, Exotic shorthair. 600 l, Birman.

4032 A1544 60 l multicolored *.20*
4033 A1544 80 l multicolored *.20*
4034 A1544 120 l multicolored *.35*
4035 A1544 600 l multicolored *1.60*
Nos. 4032-4035 (4) *2.35*

Are You Jealous?, by Paul Gauguin (1848-1903) — A1545

1998, June 4

4036 A1545 120 l multicolored *.35*

Neophit Hylendarsky-Bozvely (1745-1848), Priest, Author — A1546

1998, June 4

4037 A1546 120 l multicolored *.35*

1998 World Cup Soccer Championships, France — A1547

Lion mascot with soccer ball, various stylized soccer plays.

1998, June 10

4038 A1547 60 l multicolored *.20*
4039 A1547 80 l multicolored *.20*
4040 A1547 120 l multicolored *.35*
4041 A1547 600 l multicolored *1.60*
Nos. 4038-4041 (4) *2.35*

Souvenir Sheet

4042 A1547 120 l Mascot, Eiffel Tower *.35*

A. Aleksandrov's Flight on Mir, 10th Anniv. — A1548

1998, June 17 **Litho.** ***Perf. 13***

4043 A1548 120 l multicolored *.20*

Lisbon '98
A1549

Designs: a, Map showing route around Cape of Good Hope, Vasco da Gama (1460-1524). b, Sailing ship, map of Africa.

1998, June 23

4044 A1549 600 l Sheet of 2, #a.-b. + 2 labels *1.40*

Helicopters — A1550

Designs: 80 l, Focke Wulf FW61, 1937. 100 l, Sikorsky R-4, 1943. 120 l, Mil Mi-12 (V-12), 1970. 200 l, McDonnell-Douglas MD-900, 1995.

1998, July 7 **Litho.** ***Perf. 13***

4045 A1550 80 l multicolored *.20 .20*
4046 A1550 100 l multicolored *.25 .25*
4047 A1550 120 l multicolored *.30 .30*
4048 A1550 200 l multicolored *.45 .45*
Nos. 4045-4048 (4) *1.20 1.20*

Souvenir Sheet

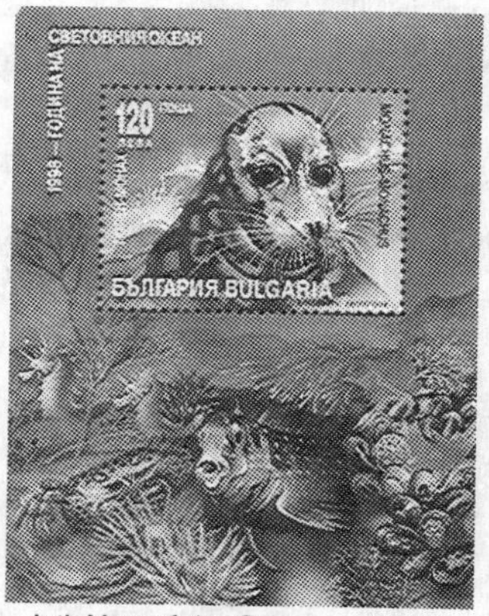

Intl. Year of the Ocean — A1551

Monachus monachus. Illustration reduced.

1998, July 14 **Litho.** ***Perf. 13***

4049 A1551 120 l multicolored *.30 .30*

Dimitr Talev (1898-1966), Writer — A1552

1998, Sept. 14

4050 A1552 180 l multicolored .20 .20

A1553

A1554

1998, Sept. 22

4051 A1553 180 l multicolored .20 .20

Declaration of Bulgarian Independence, 90th anniv.

1998, Sept. 24

Butterflies, flowers: 60 l, Limenitis redukta, ligularia sibirica. 180 l, Vanessa cardui, anthemis macrantha. 200 l, Vanessa atalanta, trachelium jacquinii. 600 l, Anthocharis gruneri, geranium tuberosum.

4052 A1554 60 l multicolored .20 .20
4053 A1554 180 l multicolored .20 .20
4054 A1554 200 l multicolored .25 .25
4055 A1554 600 l multicolored .75 .75
Nos. 4052-4055 (4) 1.40 1.40

Christo Smirnenski (1898-1923), Poet — A1555

1998, Sept. 29

4056 A1555 180 l multicolored .20 .20

Universal Declaration of Human Rights, 50th Anniv. — A1556

1998, Oct. 26 Litho. *Perf. 13*

4057 A1556 180 l multicolored .20 .20

Giordano Bruno (1548-1600), Philosopher — A1557

1998, Oct. 26

4058 A1557 180 l multicolored .20 .20

Greetings Stamps A1558

#4059, Man diving through flaming heart, "I Love You." #4060, Baby emerging from chalice, "Happy Birthday." #4061, Grape vine, bird, wine coming from vat, "Happy Holiday." #4062, Waiter carrying tray with glass & ttle of wine, "Happy Name Day."

1998, Nov. 11

4059 A1558 180 l multi .20 .20
4060 A1558 180 l multi, vert. .20 .20
4061 A1558 180 l multi, vert. .20 .20
4062 A1558 180 l multi, vert. .20 .20
Nos. 4059-4062 (4) .80 .80

Christmas A1559

1998, Dec. 2 Litho. *Perf. 13½x13*

4063 A1559 180 l multicolored .20 .20

Ivan Geshov (1849-1924), Finance Minister — A1560

1999, Feb. 8 Litho. *Perf. 13*

4064 A1560 180 l multicolored .20 .20

Third Bulgarian State, 120th Anniv. — A1561

Designs: a, Reflection of National Assembly. b, Men, paper, Council of Ministers. c, Scales of Justice, Supreme Court of Appeal. d, Coins, Bulgarian Natl. Bank. e, Soldiers, Bulgarian Army. f, Lion, lightpost, Sofia, capital of Bulgaria.

1999, Feb. 10

4065 A1561 180 l Sheet of 6, #a.-f. 1.25 1.25

Bulgarian Culture and Art — A1562

180 l, Georgy Karakashev (1899-1970), set designer. 200 l, Bencho Obreshkov (1899-1970), artist. 300 l, Assen Naydenov (1899-1995), conductor. 600 l, Pancho Vladiguerov (1899-1978), composer.

1999, Mar. 12 Litho. *Perf. 13*

4066 A1562 180 l multicolored .20 .20
4067 A1562 200 l multicolored .25 .25
4068 A1562 300 l multicolored .40 .40
4069 A1562 600 l multicolored .70 .70
Nos. 4066-4069 (4) 1.55 1.55

Bulgaria '99 — A1562a

Parrots: a, Trichoglossus haematodus. b, Platycercus eximius. c, Melopsittacus undulatus. d, Ara chloroptera.

1999, Mar. 15 Litho. *Perf. 13x13¼*
Sheet of 4

4069A A1562a 600 l #a.-d. 6.50 6.50

NATO, 50th Anniv. — A1563

1999, Mar. 29 Litho. *Perf. 13*

4070 A1563 180 l multicolored .20 .20

Easter A1564

1999, Apr. 1

4071 A1564 180 l multicolored .20 .20

National Parks and Nature Preserves — A1565

Europa: 180 l, Duck, pond, Ropotamo Preserve. 600 l, Ibex, waterfall, Central Balkan Natl. Park.

1999, Apr. 13 Litho. *Perf. 13*

4072 A1565 180 l multicolored .20 .20
4073 A1565 600 l multicolored .65 .65

IBRA '99, Intl. Philatelic Exhibition, Nuremberg — A1566

1999, Apr. 15

4074 A1566 600 l multicolored .65 .65

No. 4074 is divided in half by vert. simulated perfs. and was issued in sheets of 3 + 3 labels.

Council of Europe, 50th Anniv. — A1567

1999, May 5 Litho. *Perf. 13*

4075 A1567 180 l multicolored .20 .20

Foreign Culture and Art — A1567a

Designs: 180 l, Honoré de Balzac (1799-1850), novelist. 200 l, Johann Wolfgang von Goethe (1749-1832), poet. 250 l, Aleksandr Pushkin (1799-1837), poet. 600 l, Diego Velázquez (1599-1660), painter.

1999, May 18

4076 A1567a 180 l multicolored .20 .20
4077 A1567a 200 l multicolored .20 .20
4078 A1567a 300 l multicolored .30 .30
4078A A1567a 600 l multicolored .65 .65
Nos. 4076-4078A (4) 1.35 1.35

Bicycles — A1568

Designs: 180 l, Large front-wheeled bicycle, 1867. 200 l, Multi-gear bicycle. 300 l, BMX racing bike. 600 l, Mountain racing bike.

1999, June 1 Litho. *Perf. 13¼*

4079 A1568 180 l multicolored .20 .20
4080 A1568 200 l multicolored .20 .20
4081 A1568 300 l multicolored .35 .35
4082 A1568 600 l multicolored .65 .65
Nos. 4079-4082 (4) 1.40 1.40

Sts. Cyril and Methodius — A1569

Various paintings of Sts. Cyril and Methodius standing side by side with denomination at: a, UL. b, UR. c, LL. d, LR.

1999, June 15 Litho. *Perf. 13¼*

4083 A1569 600 l Sheet of 4, #a.-d. 2.75 2.75

Bulgaria '99, European Philatelic Exhibition.

Flowers A1570

a, Oxytropis urumovii. b, Campanula transsilvanica. c, Iris reichenbachii. d, Gentiana punctata.

1999, July 20

4084 A1570 60s Sheet of 4, #a.-d. 2.75 2.75

Bulgaria '99, European Philatelic Exhibition.

Mushrooms A1571

Designs: a, 10s, Russula virescens. b, 18s, Agaricus campestris. c, 20s, Hygrophorus russula. d, 60s, Lepista nuda.

1999, July 27

4085 A1571	Sheet of 4, #a.-d.	2.75	2.75

Souvenir Sheet

Total Solar Eclipse, Aug. 11, 1999 — A1572

Illustration reduced.

1999, Aug. 10 ***Perf. 13***

4086 A1572	20s multicolored	.50	.50

A1573

A1574

1999, Sept. 23 **Litho.** ***Perf. 13***

4087 A1573	18s multicolored	.20	.20

Organized agrarian movement in Bulgaria, 100th anniv.

Souvenir Sheet

1999, Oct. 5 ***Perf. 13x13½***

Lion (portion) and: a, No. J2. b, Dove and letter. c, Eastern hemisphere. d, Western hemisphere.

4088 A1574	60s Sheet of 4, #a.-d.	2.75	2.75

Bulgaria '99, UPU 125th anniv.

Birds, Eggs and Nests — A1575

8s, Lanius minor. 18s, Turdus viscivorus. 20s, Prunella modularis. 60s, Emberiza hortulana.

1999, Oct. 6 ***Perf. 13***

4089 A1575	8s multicolored	.20	.20
4090 A1575	18s multicolored	.20	.20
4091 A1575	20s multicolored	.20	.20
4092 A1575	60s multicolored	.70	.70
	Nos. 4089-4092 (4)	1.30	1.30

Endangered Turtles — A1576

10s, Testudo graeca. 18s, Emys orbicularis. 30s, Testudo hermanni. 60s, Mauremys caspica.

1999, Oct. 8 ***Perf. 13***

4093 A1576	10s multicolored	.20	.20
4094 A1576	18s multicolored	.20	.20
4095 A1576	30s multicolored	.35	.35
4096 A1576	60s multicolored	.65	.65
	Nos. 4093-4096 (4)	1.40	1.40

Olympic Sports A1577

1999, Oct. 10

4097 A1577	10s Boxing	.20	.20
4098 A1577	20s High jump	.20	.20
4099 A1577	30s Weight lifting	.35	.35
4100 A1577	60s Wrestling	.65	.65
	Nos. 4097-4100 (4)	1.40	1.40

Fountains — A1578

Fountains from: 1s, Sopotski Monastery. 10s, Koprivshchitsa. 18s, Sandanski. 20s, Karlovo.

1999 **Litho.** ***Perf. 13½x14***

Fountain Color

4101 A1578	1s bister	.20	.20
4103 A1578	10s brown	.20	.20
4104 A1578	18s light blue	.30	.30
4105 A1578	20s dark blue	.35	.35
	Nos. 4101-4105 (4)	1.05	1.05

This is an expanding set. Numbers may change.

SEMI-POSTAL STAMPS

Catalogue values for unused stamps in this section are for Never Hinged items.

Regular Issues of 1911-20 Surcharged:

ЗА НАШИТѢ ПЛѢННИЦИ
1
a

ЗА НАШИТѢ ПЛѢННИЦИ
5
b

ЗА НАШИТѢ ПЛѢННИЦИ
50
c

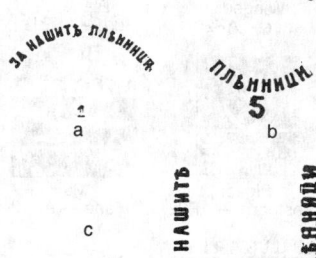

Perf. 11½x12, 12x11½

1920, June 20 **Unwmk.**

B1	A43 (a)	2s + 1s ol grn	.20	.20
B2	A44 (b)	5s + 2½s grn	.20	.20
B3	A44 (b)	10s + 5s rose	.20	.20
B4	A44 (b)	15s + 7½s vio	.20	.20
B5	A44 (b)	25s + 12½s dp bl	.20	.20
B6	A44 (b)	30s + 15s choc	.20	.20
B7	A44 (b)	50s + 25s yel brn	.20	.20
B8	A29 (c)	1 l + 50s dk brn	.20	.20
B9	A37a (a)	2 l + 1 l brn org	.25	.25
B10	A38 (a)	3 l + 1½ l claret	.55	.45
		Nos. B1-B10 (10)	2.40	2.30

Surtax aided ex-prisoners of war. Value, Nos. B1-B7 imperf., $7.75.

Tsar Boris Type of 1937
Souvenir Sheet

1937, Nov. 22 **Photo.** ***Imperf.***

B11 A140	2 l + 18 l ultra	4.50	2.50

19th anniv. of the accession of Tsar Boris III to the throne.

Stamps of 1917-21 Surcharged in Black

Наводнението
1939
1+1
лєва

1939, Oct. 22 ***Perf. 12½, 12***

B12 A34	1 l + 1 l on 15s slate	.20	.20
B13 A69	2 l + 1 l on 1½ l ol grn	.20	.20
B14 A69	4 l + 2 l on 2 l dp grn	.20	.20
B15 A69	7 l + 4 l on 3 l Prus bl	.50	.30
B16 A69	14 l + 7 l on 5 l red brn	.85	.50
	Nos. B12-B16 (5)	1.95	1.40

Surtax aided victims of the Sevlievo flood. The surcharge on #B13-B16 omits "leva."

Map of Bulgaria SP2

1947, June 6 **Typo.** ***Perf. 11½***

B17 SP2	20 l + 10 l dk brn red & grn	.45	.30

30th Jubilee Esperanto Cong., Sofia, 1947.

Postman SP3

Radio Towers SP6

#B19, Lineman. #B20, Telephone operators.

1947, Nov. 5

B18 SP3	4 l + 2 l ol brn	.20	.20
B19 SP3	10 l + 5 l brt red	.20	.20
B20 SP3	20 l + 10 l dp ultra	.20	.20
B21 SP6	40 l + 20 l choc	.70	.55
	Nos. B18-B21 (4)	1.30	1.15

Christo Ganchev — SP7

Actors' Portraits: 10 l+6 l, Adriana Budevska. 15 l+7 l, Vasil Kirkov. 20 l+15 l, Sava Ognianov. 30 l+20 l, Krostyu Sarafov.

1947, Dec. 8 **Litho.** ***Perf. 10½***

B22 SP7	9 l + 5 l Prus grn	.20	.20
B23 SP7	10 l + 6 l car lake	.20	.20
B24 SP7	15 l + 7 l rose vio	.20	.20
B25 SP7	20 l + 15 l ultra	.20	.20
B26 SP7	30 l + 20 l vio brn	.50	.30
	Nos. B22-B26 (5)	1.30	1.10

National Theater, 50th anniversary.

Souvenir Sheet

Olympic Emblem — SP8

1964, Oct. 10 **Litho.** ***Imperf.***

B27 SP8	40s + 20s bis, red & bl	2.75	1.40

18th Olympic Games, Tokyo, Oct. 10-25.

Horsemanship Type of 1965
Miniature Sheet

1965, Sept. 30 **Photo.** ***Imperf.***

B28 A630	40s + 20s Hurdle race	2.00	1.00

Space Exploration Type of 1966

Designs: 20s+10s, Yuri A. Gagarin, Alexei Leonov and Valentina Tereshkova. 30s+10s, Rocket and globe.

Perf. 11½x11

1966, Sept. 29 **Photo.**

B29 A652	20s + 10s pur & gray	1.00	.35

Miniature Sheet

B30 A652	30s + 10s gray, fawn & blk	2.00	.95

Winter Olympic Games Type of 1967

Sports and Emblem: 20s+10s, Slalom. 40s+10s, Figure skating couple.

1967, Sept. Photo. *Perf. 11*

B31 A687 20s + 10s multi 1.10 .30

Souvenir Sheet

Imperf

B32 A687 40s + 10s multi 2.00 .85

Type of Olympic Games Issue, 1968

Designs: 20s+10s, Rowing. 50s+10s, Stadium, Mexico City, and communications satellite.

1968, June 24 Photo. *Perf. 10½*

B33 A702 20s + 10s vio bl, gray & pink 1.00 .30

Miniature Sheet

Imperf

B34 A702 50s + 10s gray, blk & Prus bl 2.25 1.50

Sports Type of Regular Issue, 1969

Designs: 13s+5s, Woman with ball. 20s+10s, Acrobatic jump.

1969, Oct. Photo. *Perf. 11*

Gymnasts in Light Gray

B35 A732 13s + 5s brt rose & vio .40 .20
B36 A732 20s + 10s citron & bl grn .70 .30

Miniature Sheet

Soccer Ball SP9

1970, Mar. 4 Photo. *Imperf.*

B37 SP9 80s + 20s multi 2.25 1.40

9th World Soccer Championships for the Jules Rimet Cup, Mexico City, May 30-June 21, 1970.

Souvenir Sheet

Yuri A. Gagarin — SP10

1971, Apr. 12 Photo. *Imperf.*

B38 SP10 40s + 20s multi 2.00 1.10

10th anniversary of the first man in space.

SP11

SP12

Bulgarian lion, magnifying glass, stamp tongs

1971, July 10 Photo. *Perf. 12½*

B39 SP11 20s + 10s brn org, blk & gold .90 .40

11th Congress of Bulgarian Philatelists, Sofia, July, 1971.

1989, Nov. 10 Litho. *Perf. 13x13½*

Toys: a, Skateboarding. b, Doll, ball. c, Rope. d, Train set.

Souvenir Sheet

B40 Sheet of 4 2.75 1.40
a.-d. SP12 30s +15s any single .65 .35

For the benefit of the Children's Foundation.

AIR POST STAMPS

Regular Issues of 1925-26 Overprinted in Various Colors

1927-28 Unwmk. *Perf. 11½*

C1 A76 2 l ol (R) ('28) 1.10 .70
C2 A74 4 l lake & yel (Bl) 1.10 .70
C3 A77 10 l brn blk & brn org (G) ('28) 17.00 13.00

Overprinted Vertically and Surcharged with New Value

C4 A77 1 l on 6 l dp bl & pale lem (C) 1.10 .70
a. Inverted surcharge 325.00 275.00
b. Pair, one without surcharge 425.00
Nos. C1-C4 (4) 20.30 15.10

Nos. C2-C4 overprinted in changed colors were not issued, value set $10.50.

Dove Delivering Message AP1

Junkers Plane, Rila Monastery AP2

1931, Oct. 28 Typo.

C5 AP1 1 l dk green .20 .20
C6 AP1 2 l maroon .20 .20
C7 AP1 6 l dp blue .30 .20
C8 AP1 12 l carmine .30 .30
C9 AP1 20 l dk violet .65 .55
C10 AP1 30 l dp orange 1.10 1.25
C11 AP1 50 l orange brn 2.25 1.40
Nos. C5-C11 (7) 5.00 4.10

Counterfeits exist. See Nos. C15-C18.

1932, May 9

C12 AP2 18 l blue grn 14.00 11.00
C13 AP2 24 l dp red 14.00 11.00
C14 AP2 28 l ultra 14.00 11.00
Nos. C12-C14 (3) 42.00 33.00

Catalogue values for unused stamps in this section, from this point to the end of the section, are for Never Hinged items.

1938, Dec. 27

C15 AP1 1 l violet brown .25 .20
C16 AP1 2 l green .20 .20
C17 AP1 6 l deep rose .70 .30
C18 AP1 12 l peacock blue .85 .30
Nos. C15-C18 (4) 2.00 1.00

Counterfeits exist.

Mail Plane — AP3

Plane over Tsar Assen's Tower — AP4

Designs: 4 l, Plane over Bachkovski Monastery. 6 l, Bojurishte Airport, Sofia. 10 l, Plane, train and motorcycle. 12 l, Planes over Sofia Palace. 16 l, Plane over Pirin Valley. 19 l, Plane over Rila Monastery. 30 l, Plane and Swallow. 45 l, Plane over Sofia Cathedral. 70 l, Plane over Shipka Monument. 100 l, Plane and Royal Cipher.

1940, Jan. 15 Photo. *Perf. 13*

C19 AP3 1 l dk green .20 .20
C20 AP4 2 l crimson 1.10 .20
C21 AP4 4 l red orange .20 .20
C22 AP3 6 l dp blue .20 .20
C23 AP4 10 l dk brown .30 .20
C24 AP3 12 l dull brown .50 .20
C25 AP3 16 l brt bl vio .55 .25
C26 AP3 19 l sapphire .75 .30
C27 AP4 30 l rose lake 1.10 .50
C28 AP4 45 l gray violet 2.75 .95
C29 AP4 70 l rose pink 2.75 1.25
C30 AP4 100 l dp slate bl 9.00 3.75
Nos. C19-C30 (12) 19.40 8.20

Nos. 368 and 370 Overprinted in Black

1945, Jan. 26

C31 A181 1 l bright green .20 .20
C32 A181 4 l red orange .20 .20

A similar overprint on Nos. O4, O5, O7 and O8 was privately applied.

Type of Parcel Post Stamps of 1944 Surcharged or Overprinted in Various Colors

Imperf

C37 PP5 10 l on 100 l dl yel (Bl) .20 .20
C38 PP5 45 l on 100 l dl yel (C) .30 .20
C39 PP5 75 l on 100 l dl yel (G) .40 .25
C40 PP5 100 l dl yel (V) .70 .35
Nos. C37-C40 (4) 1.60 1.00

Plane and Sun — AP16

Pigeon with Letter — AP17

Plane, Letter — AP18

Wings, Posthorn — AP19

Winged Letter — AP20

Plane, Sun — AP21

Pigeon, Posthorn — AP22

Mail Plane — AP23

Conventionalized Figure Holding Pigeon — AP24

1946, July 15 Litho. *Perf. 13*

C41 AP16 1 l dull lilac .20 .20
C42 AP16 2 l slate gray .20 .20
C43 AP17 4 l violet blk .20 .20
C44 AP18 6 l blue .20 .20
C45 AP19 10 l turq green .20 .20
C46 AP19 12 l yellow brn .20 .20
C47 AP20 16 l rose violet .20 .20
C48 AP19 19 l carmine .20 .20
C49 AP21 30 l orange .20 .20
C50 AP22 45 l lt ol grn .20 .20
C51 AP22 75 l red brown .25 .20
C52 AP23 100 l slate blk .65 .25
C53 AP24 100 l red .65 .25
Nos. C41-C53 (13) 3.55 2.70

No. C47 exists imperf. Value $90.

People's Republic

Plane over Plovdiv AP25

1947, Aug. 31 Photo. *Imperf.*

C54 AP25 40 l dull olive grn .60 .50

Plovdiv International Fair, 1947.

Baldwin's Tower — AP26

1948, May 23 Litho. *Perf. 11½*

C55 AP26 50 l ol brn, *cr* .75 .60

Stamp Day and the 10th Congress of Bulgarian Philatelic Societies, June 1948.

Romanian and Bulgarian Parliament Buildings AP27

Romanian and Bulgarian Flags, Bridge over Danube AP28

1948, Nov. 3 Photo.

C56 AP27 40 l ol gray, *cr* .25 .20
C57 AP28 100 l red vio, *cr* .50 .30

Romanian-Bulgarian friendship.

Mausoleum of Pleven — AP29

1949, June 26

C58 AP29 50 l brown 2.00 1.25

7th Congress of Bulgarian Philatelic Associations, June 26-27, 1949.

Symbols of the UPU — AP30

Frontier Guard and Dog — AP31

1949, Oct. 10 *Perf. 11½*
C59 AP30 50 l violet blue 1.50 .75

75th anniv. of the UPU.

1949, Oct. 31
C60 AP31 60 l olive black 1.25 .90

Dimitrov Mausoleum AP32

1950, July 3 *Perf. 10½*
C61 AP32 40 l olive brown 3.00 1.10

1st anniv. of the death of George Dimitrov.

Belogradchic Rocks — AP33

Air View of Plovdiv Fair — AP34

Designs: 16s, Beach, Varna. 20s, Harvesting grain. 28s, Rila monastery. 44s, Studena dam. 60s, View of Dimitrovgrad. 80s, View of Trnovo. 1 l, University building, Sofia. 4 l, Partisans' Monument.

1954, Apr. 1 **Unwmk.** *Perf. 13*

C62	AP33	8s olive black		.20	.20
C63	AP34	12s rose brown		.20	.20
C64	AP33	16s brown		.20	.20
C65	AP33	20s brn red, *cream*		.20	.20
C66	AP33	28s dp bl, *cream*		.20	.20
C67	AP33	44s vio brn, *cream*		.20	.20
C68	AP33	60s red brn, *cream*		.25	.20
C69	AP34	80s dk grn, *cream*		.30	.20
C70	AP33	1 l dk bl grn, *cream*		1.25	.35
C71	AP34	4 l deep blue		3.00	.80
		Nos. C62-C71 (10)		6.00	2.75

Glider on Mountainside AP35

60s, Glider over airport. 80s, Three gliders.

1956, Oct. 15 **Photo.**

C72	AP35	44s brt blue	.20	.20
C73	AP35	60s purple	.30	.20
C74	AP35	80s dk blue grn	.50	.20
		Nos. C72-C74 (3)	1.00	.60

30th anniv. of glider flights in Bulgaria.

Passenger Plane — AP36

1957, May 21 **Unwmk.** *Perf. 13*
C75 AP36 80s deep blue .60 .30

10th anniv. of civil aviation in Bulgaria.

Sputnik 3 over Earth — AP37

1958, Nov. 28 *Perf. 11*
C76 AP37 80s brt grnsh blue 3.00 2.25

International Geophysical Year, 1957-58. Value, imperf. $7.50.

Lunik 1 Leaving Earth for Moon — AP38

1959, Feb. 28 *Perf. 10½*
C77 AP38 2 l brt blue & ocher 3.00 2.75

Launching of 1st man-made satellite to orbit moon. Value, imperf. in slightly different colors, $7.50 unused, $5.25 canceled.

Statue of Liberty and Tu-110 Airliner AP39

Perf. 10½
1959, Nov. 11 **Photo.** **Unwmk.**
C78 AP39 1 l violet bl & pink 1.75 1.50

Visit of Khrushchev to US. Value, imperf. $5.

Lunik 2 and Moon — AP40

1960, June 23 **Litho.** *Perf. 11*
C79 AP40 1.25 l blue, blk & yel 3.50 1.60

Russian rocket to the Moon, Sept. 12, 1959.

Sputnik 5 and Dogs Belka and Strelka — AP41

1961, Jan. 14 **Photo.** *Perf. 11*
C80 AP41 1.25 l brt grnsh bl & org 4.00 2.50

Russian rocket flight of Aug. 19, 1970.

Maj. Yuri A. Gagarin and Vostok 1 AP42

1961, Apr. 26 **Unwmk.**
C81 AP42 4 l grnsh bl, blk & red 2.50 1.50

First manned space flight, Apr. 12, 1961.

Soviet Space Dogs AP43

1961, June 28 *Perf. 11*
C82 AP43 2 l slate & dk car 2.00 1.00

Venus-bound Rocket — AP44

1961, June 28
C83 AP44 2 l brt bl, yel & org 4.00 2.50

Soviet launching of the Venus space probe, 2/12/61.

Maj. Gherman Titov — AP45

Design: 1.25 l, Spaceship Vostok 2.

1961, Nov. 20 **Photo.** *Perf. 11x10½*
C84 AP45 75s dk ol grn & gray grn 1.75 1.25
C85 AP45 1.25 l vio bl, lt bl & pink 2.25 1.75

1st manned space flight around the world, Maj. Gherman Titov of Russia, Aug. 6-7, 1961.

Iskar River Narrows AP46

Designs: 2s, Varna and sailboat. 3s, Melnik. 10s, Trnovo. 40s, Pirin mountains.

1962, Feb. 3 **Unwmk.** *Perf. 13*

C86	AP46	1s bl grn & gray bl	.20	.20
C87	AP46	2s blue & pink	.20	.20
C88	AP46	3s brown & ocher	.25	.20
C89	AP46	10s black & lemon	.45	.20
C90	AP46	40s dk green & green	1.10	.30
		Nos. C86-C90 (5)	2.20	1.10

Ilyushin Turboprop Airliner AP47

1962, Aug. 18 *Perf. 11*
C91 AP47 13s blue & black .60 .25

15th anniversary of TABSO airline.

Konstantin E. Tsiolkovsky and Rocket Launching — AP48

Design: 13s, Earth, moon and rocket on future flight to the moon.

1962, Sept. 24 *Perf. 11*
C92 AP48 5s dp green & gray 1.90 .85
C93 AP48 13s ultra & yellow 1.10 .35

13th meeting of the International Astronautical Federation.

Maj. Andrian G. Nikolayev — AP49

Designs: 2s, Lt. Col. Pavel R. Popovich. 40s, Vostoks 3 and 4 in orbit.

1962, Dec. 9 **Photo.** **Unwmk.**

C94	AP49	1s bl, sl grn & blk	.20	.20
C95	AP49	2s bl grn, grn & blk	.25	.20
C96	AP49	40s dk bl grn, pink & blk	1.60	.85
		Nos. C94-C96 (3)	2.05	1.25

First Russian group space flight of Vostoks 3 and 4, Aug. 12-15, 1962.

Spacecraft "Mars 1" Approaching Mars — AP50

Design: 13s, Rocket launching spacecraft, Earth, Moon and Mars.

1963, Feb. 25 **Unwmk.** *Perf. 11*
C97 AP50 5s multicolored .50 .30
C98 AP50 13s multicolored 1.00 .45

Launching of the Russian spacecraft "Mars 1," Nov. 1, 1962.

Lt. Col. Valeri F. Bykovski AP51

Designs: 2s, Lt. Valentina Tereshkova. 5s, Globe and trajectories.

1963, Aug. 26 **Unwmk.** *Perf. 11½*

C99	AP51	1s pale vio & Prus bl	.20	.20
C100	AP51	2s citron & red brn	.20	.20
C101	AP51	5s rose & dk red	.20	.20
		Nos. C99-C101 (3)	.60	.60

The space flights of Valeri Bykovski, June 14-19, and Valentina Tereshkova, first woman cosmonaut, June 16-19, 1963. An imperf. souvenir sheet contains one 50s stamp showing Spasski tower and globe in lilac and red brown. Light blue border with red brown inscription. Size: 77x67mm. Value $2.50. See No. CB3.

Nos. C99-C100 Surcharged in Magenta or Green

1964, Aug. 22
C102 AP51 10s on 1s (M) .30 .20
C103 AP51 20s on 2s .65 .25

International Space Exhibition in Riccione, Italy. Overprint in Italian on No. C103.

St. John's Monastery, Rila — AP52

13s, Notre Dame, Paris; French inscription.

1964, Dec. 22 Photo. *Perf. 11½*

C104	AP52	5s pale brn & blk	.20	.20
C105	AP52	13s lt ultra & sl bl	.65	.20

The philatelic exhibition at St. Ouen (Seine) organized by the Franco-Russian Philatelic Circle and philatelic organizations in various People's Democracies.

Paper Mill, Bukijovtz AP53

10s, Metal works, Plovdiv. 13s, Metal works, Kremikovtsi. 20s, Oil refinery, Stara-Zagora. 40s, Fertilizer plant, Stara-Zagora. 1 l, Rest home, Meded.

1964-68 Unwmk. *Perf. 13*

C106 AP53	8s grnsh blue	.20	.20
C107 AP53	10s red lilac	.20	.20
C108 AP53	13s brt violet	.25	.20
C109 AP53	20s slate blue	.70	.20
C110 AP53	40s dk olive grn	1.10	.20
C111 AP53	1 l red ('68)	1.90	.30
	Nos. C106-C111 (6)	4.35	1.30

Issue dates: 1 l, May 6. Others, Dec. 7.

Three-master AP54

Veliko Turnovo AP55

Means of Communication: 2s, Postal coach. 3s, Old steam locomotive. 5s, Early cars. 10s, Montgolfier balloon. 13s, Early plane. 20s, Jet planes. 40s, Rocket and satellites. 1 l, Postrider.

1969, Mar. 31 Photo. *Perf. 13x12½*

C112 AP54	1s gray & multi	.20	.20
C113 AP54	2s gray & multi	.20	.20
C114 AP54	3s gray & multi	.20	.20
C115 AP54	5s gray & multi	.20	.20
C116 AP54	10s gray & multi	.20	.20
C117 AP54	13s gray & multi	.25	.20
C118 AP54	20s gray & multi	.50	.25
C119 AP54	40s gray & multi	.90	.40
	Nos. C112-C119 (8)	2.65	1.85

Miniature Sheet

Imperf

C120 AP54	1 l gold & org	2.25	1.50

SOFIA 1969 Philatelic Exhibition, Sofia, May 31-June 8.

1973, July 30 Photo. *Perf. 13*

Designs: Historic buildings in various cities.

C121 AP55	2s shown	.20	.20
C122 AP55	13s Roussalka	.25	.20
C123 AP55	20s Plovdiv	1.50	.80
C124 AP55	28s Sofia	.65	.20
	Nos. C121-C124 (4)	2.60	1.40

Aleksei A. Leonov and Soyuz AP56

Designs: 18s, Thomas P. Stafford and Apollo. 28s, Apollo and Soyuz over earth. 1 l, Apollo Soyuz link-up.

1975, July 15

C125 AP56	13s blue & multi	.30	.20
C126 AP56	18s purple & multi	.40	.20
C127 AP56	28s multicolored	1.00	.30
	Nos. C125-C127 (3)	1.70	.70

Souvenir Sheet

C128 AP56	1 l violet & multi	2.00	1.25

Apollo Soyuz space test project (Russo-American cooperation), launching July 15; link-up July 17.

Balloon Over Plovdiv — AP57

1977, Sept. 3

C129 AP57	25s yellow, brn & red	.50	.20

Alexei Leonov Floating in Space — AP58

Designs: 25s, Mariner 6, US spacecraft. 35s, Venera 4, USSR Venus probe.

1977, Oct. 14 Photo. *Perf. 13½*

C130 AP58	12s multicolored	.20	.20
C131 AP58	25s multicolored	.40	.20
C132 AP58	35s multicolored	.60	.25
	Nos. C130-C132 (3)	1.20	.65

Space era, 20 years.

TU-154, Balkanair Emblem — AP59

1977 *Perf. 13*

C133 AP59	35s ultra & multi	.75	.35

30th anniv. of Bulgarian airline, Balkanair. Issued in sheets of 6 stamps + 3 labels (in lilac) with inscription and Balkanair emblem.

Baba Vida Fortress AP60

Design: 35s, Peace Bridge, connecting Rousse, Bulgaria, with Giurgiu, Romania.

1978 Photo. *Perf. 13*

C134 AP60	25s multicolored	.40	.40
C135 AP60	35s multicolored	.55	.55

The Danube, European Intercontinental Waterway. Issued in sheets containing 5 each of Nos. C134-C135 and 2 labels, one showing course of Danube, the other hydrofoil and fish.

Red Cross AP61

1978, Mar. Photo. *Perf. 13*

C136 AP61	25s multicolored	.50	.20

Centenary of Bulgarian Red Cross.

AP62

AP63

Clock towers.

1979, June 5 Litho. *Perf. 12x12½*

C137 AP62	13s Byalla Cherkva	.20	.20
C138 AP62	23s Botevgrad	.30	.20
C139 AP62	25s Pazardgick	.30	.20
C140 AP62	35s Grabovo	.40	.20
C141 AP62	53s Tryavna	.75	.30
	Nos. C137-C141 (5)	1.95	1.10

1980, Oct. 22 Photo. *Perf. 12x12½*

C142 AP62	13s Bjala	.20	.20
C143 AP62	23s Rasgrad	.35	.25
C144 AP62	25s Karnabat	.40	.20
C145 AP62	35s Serlievo	.50	.25
C146 AP62	53s Berkovitza	.80	.35
	Nos. C142-C146 (5)	2.25	1.25

1980

C147 AP63	13s shown	.20	.20
C148 AP63	25s Parachutist	.40	.20

15th World Parachute Championships, Kazanluk.

DWVY-1 Aircraft — AP64

1981, June 27 Litho. *Perf. 12½*

C149 AP64	5s shown	.20	.20
C150 AP64	12s LAS-7	.20	.20
C151 AP64	25s LAS-8	.40	.20
C152 AP64	35s DAR-1	.50	.20
C153 AP64	45s DAR-3	.70	.25
C154 AP64	55s DAR-9	.90	.30
	Nos. C149-C154 (6)	2.90	1.35

AP65

AP66

1983, June 28

C155	Sheet of 2	1.50	1.00
a.	AP65 50s Valentina Tereshkova	.75	.50
b.	AP65 50s Svetlana Savitskaya	.75	.50

Women in space, 20th anniv.

1983, July 20 Photo. *Perf. 13*

C156 AP66	5s TV tower, Tolbukhin	.20	.20
C157 AP66	13s Postwoman	.25	.20
C158 AP66	30s TV tower, Mt. Botev	.60	.30
a.	Strip of 3, #C156-C158	.95	.50

World Communications Year. Emblems of World Communications Year, Bulgarian Post, UPU and ITU on attached margins.

Souvenir Sheet

Geophysical Map of the Moon, Russia's Luna I, II and III Satellites — AP67

1984, Oct. 24 Photo. *Perf. 13*

C159 AP67	1 l multicolored	2.00	1.00

Conquest of Space.

Intl. Civil Aviation Org., 40th Anniv. — AP68

1984, Dec. 21 Photo. *Perf. 13*

C160 AP68	42s Balkan Airlines jet	.85	.40

Balkan Airlines — AP69

Design: Helicopter MU-8, passenger jet TU-154 and AN-21 transport plane.

1987, Aug. 25 Photo.

C161 AP69	25s multicolored	.75	.35

2nd Joint Soviet-Bulgarian Space Flight — AP70

Cosmonauts: A. Aleksandrov, A. Solovov and V. Savinich.

1989, June 7 Litho. *Perf. 13½x13*

C162 AP70	13s multicolored	.35	.20

AIR POST SEMI-POSTAL STAMPS

Catalogue values for unused stamps in this section are for Never Hinged items.

Statue of Liberty, Plane and Bridge SPAP1

Perf. 11½.

1947, May 24 Unwmk. Litho.

CB1 SPAP1	70 l + 30 l red brown	.95	.95

5th Philatelic Congress, Trnovo, and CIPEX, NYC, May, 1947.

Bulgarian Worker SPAP2

1948, Feb. 28 Photo. *Perf. 12x11½.*
CB2 SPAP2 60 l henna brn, *crean* .45 .35

2nd Bulgarian Workers' Congress, and sold by subscription only, at a premium of 16 l over face value.

Type of Air Post Stamps, 1963

Valeri Bykovski & Valentina Tereshkova.

1963, Aug. 26 Unwmk. *Perf. 11½*
CB3 AP51 20s + 10s pale bluish grn & dk grn 1.25 .45

See note after No. C101.

SPECIAL DELIVERY STAMPS

Catalogue values for unused stamps in this section are for Never Hinged items.

Postman on Bicycle — SD1

Mail Car — SD2

Postman on Motorcycle — SD3

1939 Unwmk. Photo. *Perf. 13*
E1 SD1 5 l deep blue .60 .20
E2 SD2 6 l copper brn .25 .20
E3 SD3 7 l golden brn .35 .20
E4 SD2 8 l red orange .60 .20
E5 SD1 20 l bright rose 1.25 .40
Nos. E1-E5 (5) 3.05 1.20

POSTAGE DUE STAMPS

D1

D2

Large Lozenge Perf. 5½ to 6½

1884 Typo. Unwmk.
J1 D1 5s orange 150.00 15.00
J2 D1 25s lake 75.00 10.00
J3 D1 50s blue 12.00 5.00
Nos. J1-J3 (3) 237.00 30.00

1886 *Imperf.*
J4 D1 5s orange 75.00 2.50
J5 D1 25s lake 120.00 2.50
J6 D1 50s blue 5.00 2.75
Nos. J4-J6 (3) 200.00 7.75

1887 *Perf. 11½*
J7 D1 5s orange 9.50 1.00
J8 D1 25s lake 9.50 1.00
J9 D1 50s blue 3.50 1.00
Nos. J7-J9 (3) 22.50 3.00

Same, Redrawn
24 horizontal lines of shading in upper part instead of 30 lines

1892 *Perf. 10½, 11½*
J10 D1 5s orange 7.50 1.25
J11 D1 25s lake 7.50 1.25

1893

Pelure Paper

J12 D2 5s orange 10.00 3.50

D3

D4

1895 *Imperf.*
J13 D3 30s on 50s blue 7.00 2.00

Perf. 10½, 11½
J14 D3 30s on 50s blue 7.00 2.00

Wmk. Coat of Arms in the Sheet

1896 *Perf. 13*
J15 D4 5s orange 3.00 .75
J16 D4 10s purple 2.00 .75
J17 D4 30s green 1.40 .45
Nos. J15-J17 (3) 6.40 1.95

Nos. J15-J17 are also known on unwatermarked paper from the edges of sheets.

In 1901 a cancellation, "T" in circle, was applied to Nos. 60-65 and used provisionally as postage dues.

D5

D6

1901-04 Unwmk. *Perf. 11½*
J19 D5 5s dl rose .20 .20
J20 D5 10s yel grn .40 .20
J21 D5 20s dl bl ('04) 3.25 .20
J22 D5 30s vio brn .35 .20
J23 D5 50s org ('02) 5.50 4.00
Nos. J19-J23 (5) 9.70 4.80

Nos. J19-J23 exist imperf. and in pairs imperf. between. Value, imperf., $250.

1915 Unwmk. *Perf. 11½*

Thin Semi-Transparent Paper

J24 D6 5s green .20 .20
J25 D6 10s purple .20 .20
J26 D6 20s dl rose .20 .20
J27 D6 30s dp org 1.10 .20
J28 D6 50s dp bl .35 .20
Nos. J24-J28 (5) 2.05 1.00

1919-21 *Perf. 11½, 12x11½*
J29 D6 5s emerald .20 .20
a. 5s gray green ('21) .30 .20
J30 D6 10s violet .20 .20
J31 D6 20s salmon .20 .20
a. 20s yellow .20 .20
J32 D6 30s orange .20 .20
a. 30s red orange ('21) .65 .65
J33 D6 50s blue .20 .20
J34 D6 1 l emerald ('21) .20 .20
J35 D6 2 l rose ('21) .20 .20
J36 D6 3 l brown org ('21) .30 .20
Nos. J29-J36 (8) 1.70 1.60

Stotinki values of the above series surcharged 10s or 20s were used as ordinary postage stamps. See Nos. 182-185.

The 1919 printings are on thicker white paper with clean-cut perforations, the 1921 printings on thicker grayish paper with rough perforations.

Most of this series exist imperforate and in pairs imperforate between.

Heraldic Lion — D7

1932, Aug. 15

Thin Paper

J37 D7 1 l olive bister .25 .20
J38 D7 2 l rose brown .25 .20
J39 D7 6 l brown violet .75 .35
Nos. J37-J39 (3) 1.25 .75

Lion of Trnovo — D8

National Arms — D9

1933, Apr. 10
J40 D8 20s dk brn .20 .20
J41 D8 40s dp bl .20 .20
J42 D8 80s car rose .20 .20
J43 D9 1 l org brn .25 .20
J44 D9 2 l olive .30 .25
J45 D9 6 l dl vio .20 .20
J46 D9 14 l ultra .25 .20
Nos. J40-J46 (7) 1.60 1.45

Catalogue values for unused stamps in this section, from this point to the end of the section, are for Never Hinged items.

National Arms — D10

1947, June Typo. *Perf. 10½*
J47 D10 1 l chocolate .20 .20
J48 D10 2 l deep claret .20 .20
J49 D10 8 l deep orange .20 .20
J50 D10 20 l blue .25 .20
Nos. J47-J50 (4) .85 .80

Arms of the People's Republic — D11

1951 *Perf. 11½x10½*
J51 D11 1 l chocolate .20 .20
J52 D11 2 l claret .20 .20
J53 D11 8 l red orange .25 .20
J54 D11 20 l deep blue .60 .30
Nos. J51-J54 (4) 1.25 .90

OFFICIAL STAMPS

Catalogue values for unused stamps in this section are for Never Hinged items.

Bulgarian Coat of Arms
O1 O2

1942 Unwmk. Typo. *Perf. 13*
O1 O1 10s yel grn .20 .20
O2 O1 30s red .20 .20
O3 O1 50s bister .20 .20
O4 O2 1 l vio bl .20 .20
O5 O2 2 l dk grn .20 .20
O6 O2 3 l lilac .20 .20
O7 O2 4 l rose .20 .20
O8 O2 5 l carmine .20 .20
Nos. O1-O8 (8) 1.60 1.60

1944 *Perf. 10½x11½*
O9 O2 1 l blue .20 .20
O10 O2 2 l brt red .20 .20

Lion Rampant
O3 O4

O5

1945 *Imperf.*
O11 O5 1 l pink .20 .20

Perf. 10½x11½, Imperf.
O12 O3 2 l blue green .20 .20
O13 O4 3 l bister brown .20 .20
O14 O4 4 l light ultra .20 .20
O15 O5 5 l brown lake .20 .20
Nos. O11-O15 (5) 1.00 1.00

In 1950, four stamps prepared for official use were issued as regular postage stamps. See Nos. 724-727.

PARCEL POST STAMPS

Catalogue values for unused stamps in this section are for Never Hinged items.

Weighing Packages PP1

Parcel Post PP2

Designs: 3 l, 8 l, 20 l, Parcel post truck. 4 l, 6 l, 10 l, Motorcycle.

Perf. 12½x13½, 13½x12½

1941-42 Photo. Unwmk.
Q1 PP1 1 l slate grn .20 .20
Q2 PP2 2 l crimson .20 .20
Q3 PP2 3 l dull brn .20 .20
Q4 PP2 4 l red org .20 .20
Q5 PP1 5 l deep blue .20 .20
Q6 PP1 5 l slate grn ('42) .20 .20
Q7 PP2 6 l red vio .20 .20
Q8 PP2 6 l henna brn ('42) .20 .20
Q9 PP1 7 l dark blue .20 .20
Q10 PP1 7 l dk brn ('42) .20 .20
Q11 PP2 8 l brt bl grn .20 .20
Q12 PP2 8 l green ('42) .20 .20
Q13 PP2 9 l olive gray .20 .20
Q14 PP2 9 l dp olive ('42) .20 .20
Q15 PP2 10 l orange .20 .20
Q16 PP2 20 l gray vio .40 .20
Q17 PP2 30 l dull blk .55 .20
Q18 PP2 30 l sepia ('42) .50 .20
Nos. Q1-Q18 (18) 4.45 3.60

Arms of Bulgaria — PP5

1944 Litho. *Imperf.*
Q21 PP5 1 l dk carmine .20 .20
Q22 PP5 3 l blue grn .20 .20
Q23 PP5 5 l dull bl grn .20 .20
Q24 PP5 7 l rose lilac .20 .20
Q25 PP5 10 l deep blue .20 .20
Q26 PP5 20 l orange brn .20 .20
Q27 PP5 30 l dk brn car .20 .20
Q28 PP5 50 l red orange .30 .20
Q29 PP5 100 l blue .50 .25
Nos. Q21-Q29 (9) 2.20 1.85

For overprints and surcharges see Nos. 448-454, C37-C40.

POSTAL TAX STAMPS

The use of stamps Nos. RA1 to RA18 was compulsory on letters, etc., to be delivered on Sundays and holidays. The money received from their sale was used toward maintaining a sanatorium for employees of the post, telegraph and telephone services.

View of Sanatorium PT1

Sanatorium, Peshtera PT2

1925-29 Unwmk. Typo. *Perf. 11½*

RA1	PT1	1 l blk, *grnsh bl*	2.75	.20
RA2	PT1	1 l chocolate ('26)	2.75	.20
RA3	PT1	1 l orange ('27)	3.00	.20
RA4	PT1	1 l pink ('28)	4.50	.20
RA5	PT1	1 l vio, *pnksh* ('29)	4.25	.20
RA6	PT2	2 l blue green	.35	.20
RA7	PT2	2 l violet ('27)	.35	.20
RA8	PT2	5 l deep blue	3.00	.80
RA9	PT2	5 l rose ('27)	3.75	.40
		Nos. RA1-RA9 (9)	24.70	2.60

St. Constantine Sanatorium PT3

1930-33

RA10	PT3	1 l red brn & ol grn	4.00	.20
RA11	PT3	1 l ol grn & yel ('31)	.50	.20
RA12	PT3	1 l red vio & ol brn ('33)	.50	.20
		Nos. RA10-RA12 (3)	5.00	.60

Trojan Rest Home — PT4

Sanatorium PT5

1935 Wmk. 145 *Perf. 11, 11½*

RA13	PT4	1 l choc & red org	.30	.20
RA14	PT4	1 l emer & indigo	.30	.20
RA15	PT5	5 l red brn & indigo	1.40	.35
		Nos. RA13-RA15 (3)	2.00	.75

St. Constantine Sanatorium PT6

2 l, Children at seashore. 5 l, Rest home.

1941 Unwmk. Photo. *Perf. 13*

RA16	PT6	1 l dark olive green	.20	.20
RA17	PT6	2 l red orange	.20	.20
RA18	PT6	5 l deep blue	.30	.20
		Nos. RA16-RA18 (3)	.70	.60

See Nos. 702-705 for same designs in smaller size issued as regular postage.

BURKINA FASO

bur-ˈkē-nə-ˈfä-sō

Upper Volta

LOCATION — Northwestern Africa, north of Ghana
GOVT. — Republic
AREA — 105,869 sq. mi.
POP. — 11,575,898 (1999 est.)
CAPITAL — Ouagadougou

In 1919 the French territory of Upper Volta was detached from the southern section of Upper Senegal and Niger and made a separate colony. In 1933 the colony was divided among its neighbors: French Sudan, Ivory Coast, and Niger Territory. The Republic of Upper Volta was proclaimed December 11, 1958; the name was changed to Burkina Faso on August 4, 1984.

100 Centimes = 1 Franc

Catalogue values for unused stamps in this country are for Never Hinged items, beginning with Scott 70 in the regular postage section, Scott B1 in the semi-postal section, Scott C1 in the air-post section, Scott J21 in the postage due section, and Scott O1 in the official section.

See French West Africa Nos. 67, 84 for additional stamps inscribed "Haute Volta" and "Afrique Occidentale Francaise."

Stamps and Types of Upper Senegal and Niger, 1914-17, Overprinted in Black or Red **HAUTE-VOLTA**

1920-28 Unwmk. *Perf. 13½x14*

1	A4	1c brn vio & vio	.20	.20
2	A4	2c gray & brn vio (R)	.20	.20
3	A4	4c blk & bl	.20	.20
4	A4	5c yel grn & bl grn	.60	.25
5	A4	5c ol brn & dk brn ('22)	.20	.20
6	A4	10c red org & rose	1.00	.50
7	A4	10c yel grn & bl grn ('22)	.20	.20
8	A4	10c claret & bl ('25)	.25	.25
a.		Overprint omitted	80.00	
9	A4	15c choc & org	.40	.30
10	A4	20c brn vio & blk (R)	.65	.55
11	A4	25c ultra & bl	.80	.50
12	A4	25c blk & bl grn ('22)	.45	.40
a.		Overprint omitted	65.00	
13	A4	30c ol brn & brn (R)	1.50	1.25
14	A4	30c red org & rose ('22)	.40	.35
15	A4	30c vio & brn red ('25)	.40	.35
16	A4	30c dl grn & bl grn ('27)	.70	.60
17	A4	35c car rose & vio	.45	.30
18	A4	40c gray & car rose	.45	.35
19	A4	45c bl & brn (R)	.35	.20
20	A4	50c blk & grn	1.75	1.25
21	A4	50c ultra & bl ('22)	.50	.50
22	A4	50c red org & bl ('25)	.60	.60
23	A4	60c org red ('26)	.20	.20
24	A4	65c bis & pale bl ('28)	.80	.60
25	A4	75c org & brn	.30	.30
26	A4	1fr brn & brn vio	.80	.70
27	A4	2fr grn & bl	1.25	.80
28	A4	5fr vio & blk (R)	2.50	2.25
		Nos. 1-28 (28)	18.10	14.35

No. 9 Surcharged in Various Colors **0,01 ≡ 0,01**

1922

29	A4	0,01c on 15c (Bk)	.40	.40
a.		Double surcharge	50.00	50.00
30	A4	0,02c on 15c (Bl)	.40	.40
31	A4	0,05c on 15c (R)	.40	.40
		Nos. 29-31 (3)	1.20	1.20

Type of 1920 Surcharged **60 = 60**

1922

32	A4	60c on 75c vio, *pnksh*	.35	.35

Stamps and Types of 1920 Surcharged with New Value and Bars

1924-27

33	A4	25c on 2fr grn & bl	.45	.45
34	A4	25c on 5fr vio & blk	.45	.45
35	A4	65c on 45c bl & brn ('25)	.50	.50
36	A4	85c on 75c org & brn ('25)	.70	.70
37	A4	90c on 75c brn red & sal pink ('27)	.70	.70
38	A4	1.25fr on 1fr dp bl & lt bl (R) ('26)	.45	.45
39	A4	1.50fr on 1fr dp bl & ultra ('27)	1.25	1.25
40	A4	3fr on 5fr dl red & brn org ('27)	1.60	1.60
41	A4	10fr on 5fr ol grn & lil rose ('27)	7.25	7.25
42	A4	20fr on 5fr org brn & vio ('27)	10.00	10.00
		Nos. 33-42 (10)	23.35	23.35

Hausa Chief — A5

Hausa Woman — A6

Hausa Warrior A7

1928 Typo. *Perf. 13½x14*

43	A5	1c indigo & grn	.20	.20
44	A5	2c brn & lil	.20	.20
45	A5	4c blk & yel	.20	.20
46	A5	5c indigo & gray bl	.20	.20
47	A5	10c indigo & pink	.50	.50
48	A5	15c brn & bl	.90	.90
49	A5	20c brn & grn	.90	.90
50	A6	25c brn & yel	1.10	1.10
51	A6	30c dp grn & grn	1.10	1.10
52	A6	40c blk & pink	1.10	1.10
53	A6	45c brn & blue	1.10	1.10
54	A6	50c blk & grn	1.10	1.10
55	A6	65c indigo & bl	1.60	1.60
56	A6	75c blk & lil	1.10	1.10
57	A6	90c brn red & lil	1.10	1.10

Perf. 14x13½

58	A7	1fr brn & grn	1.10	1.10
59	A7	1.10fr indigo & lil	1.10	1.10
60	A7	1.50fr ultra & grysh	1.75	1.75
61	A7	2fr blk & bl	2.25	2.25
62	A7	3fr brn & yel	2.25	2.25
63	A7	5fr brn & lil	2.25	2.25
64	A7	10fr blk & grn	9.00	9.00
65	A7	20fr blk & pink	13.00	13.00
		Nos. 43-65 (23)	45.10	45.10

Common Design Types pictured following the introduction.

Colonial Exposition Issue
Common Design Types

1931 Engr. *Perf. 12½*
Country Name Typo. in Black

66	CD70	40c dp grn	1.75	1.75
67	CD71	50c violet	2.00	2.00
68	CD72	90c red org	2.00	2.00
69	CD73	1.50fr dull blue	2.50	2.50
		Nos. 66-69 (4)	8.25	8.25

Catalogue values for unused stamps in this section, from this point to the end of the section, are for Never Hinged items.

Republic

President Ouezzin Coulibaly — A8

Deer Mask and Deer — A9

1959 Unwmk. Engr. *Perf. 13*

70	A8	25fr black & magenta	.25	.20

1st anniv. of the proclamation of the Republic; Ouezzin Coulibaly, Council President, who died in December, 1958.

Imperforates
Most Upper Volta stamps from 1959 onward exist imperforate in issued and trial colors, and also in small presentation sheets in issued colors.

1960

Animal Masks: 1fr, 2fr, 4fr, Wart hog. 5fr, 6fr, 8fr, Monkey. 10fr, 15fr, 20fr, Buffalo. 25fr, Coba (antelope). 30fr, 40fr, 50fr, Elephant. 60fr, 85fr, Secretary bird.

71	A9	30c rose & violet	.20	.20
72	A9	40c buff & dp claret	.20	.20
73	A9	50c bl grn & gray ol	.20	.20
74	A9	1fr red, blk & red brn	.20	.20
75	A9	2fr emer, yel grn & dk grn	.20	.20
76	A9	4fr bl, vio & ind	.20	.20
77	A9	5fr ol bis, red & brn	.20	.20
78	A9	6fr grnsh bl & vio brn	.20	.20
79	A9	8fr org & red brn	.20	.20
80	A9	10fr lt yel grn & plum	.20	.20
81	A9	15fr org, ultra & brn	.20	.20
82	A9	20fr green & ultra	.25	.20
83	A9	25fr bl, emer & dp claret	.25	.20
84	A9	30fr dk bl grn, blk & brn	.30	.20
85	A9	40fr ultra, ind & dk car	.40	.20
86	A9	50fr brt pink, brn & grn	.45	.20
87	A9	60fr org brn & bl	.55	.25
88	A9	85fr gray ol & dk bl	.80	.30
		Nos. 71-88 (18)	5.20	3.75

C.C.T.A. Issue
Common Design Type

1960 Engr. *Perf. 13*

89	CD106	25fr vio bl & slate	.35	.35

Emblem of the Entente — A9a

Pres. Maurice Yameogo — A10

1960 Photo. *Perf. 13x13½*

90	A9a	25fr multicolored	.40	.35

Council of the Entente.

1960, May 1 Engr. *Perf. 13*

91	A10	25fr dk vio brn & slate	.25	.20

Flag, Village and Couple — A11

1960, Aug. 5 Unwmk. *Perf. 13*

92	A11	25fr red brn, blk & red	.35	.25

Proclamation of independence, Aug. 5, 1960.

World Meteorological Organization Emblem — A12

1961, May 4
93 A12 25fr blk, bl & red .30 .25

First World Meteorological Day.

Arms of Republic — A13

1961, Dec. 8 Photo. *Perf. 12x12½*
94 A13 25fr multicolored .25 .25

The 1961 independence celebrations.

WMO Emblem, Weather Station and Sorghum Grain — A14

1962, Mar. 23 Unwmk. *Perf. 13*
95 A14 25fr dk bl, emer & brn .30 .25

UN 2nd World Meteorological Day, Mar. 23.

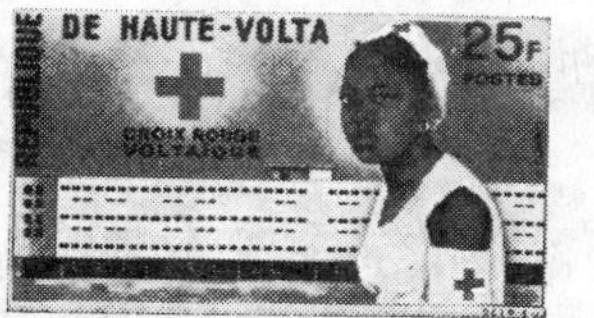
Hospital and Nurse — A15

1962, June 23 *Perf. 13x12*
96 A15 25fr multicolored .35 .35

Founding of Upper Volta Red Cross.

Buffalos at Water Hole — A16

Designs: 10fr, Lions, horiz. 15fr, Defassa waterbuck. 25fr, Arly reservation, horiz. 50fr, Diapaga reservation, horiz. 85fr, Buffon's kob.

Perf. 12½x12, 12x12½
1962, June 30 Engr.
97 A16 5fr sepia, bl & grn .20 .20
98 A16 10fr red brn, grn & yel .20 .20
99 A16 15fr sepia, grn & yel .25 .20
100 A16 25fr vio brn, bl & grn .45 .20
101 A16 50fr vio brn, bl & grn .80 .55
102 A16 85fr red brn, bl & grn 1.25 .80
Nos. 97-102 (6) 3.15 2.15

Abidjan Games Issue
Common Design Type

Designs: 20fr, Soccer. 25fr, Bicycling. 85fr, Boxing. All horiz.

1962, July 21 Photo. *Perf. 12½x12*
103 CD109 20fr multicolored .25 .20
104 CD109 25fr multicolored .30 .25
105 CD109 85fr multicolored .60 .40
Nos. 103-105 (3) 1.15 .85

African-Malgache Union Issue
Common Design Type

1962, Sept. 8 Unwmk.
106 CD110 30fr red, bluish grn & gold .70 .65

Weather Map and UN Emblem A17

1963, Mar. 23 *Perf. 12x12½*
107 A17 70fr multicolored .60 .45

3rd World Meteorological Day, Mar. 23.

Friendship Games, Dakar, Apr. 11-21 — A18

1963, Apr. 11 Engr. *Perf. 13*
108 A18 20fr Basketball .25 .20
109 A18 25fr Discus .25 .20
110 A18 50fr Judo .50 .25
Nos. 108-110 (3) 1.00 .65

Amaryllis A19

Flowers: 50c, Hibiscus. 1fr, Oldenlandia grandiflora. 1.50fr, Rose moss (portulaca). 2fr, Tobacco. 4fr, Morning glory. 5fr, Striga senegalensis. 6fr, Cowpea. 8fr, Lepidagathis heudelotiana. 10fr, Spurge. 25fr, Argyreia nervosa. 30fr, Rangoon creeper. 40fr, Water lily. 50fr, White plumeria. 60fr, Crotalaria retusa. 85fr, Hibiscus.

1963 Photo.
111 A19 50c multi, vert. .20 .20
112 A19 1fr multi, vert. .20 .20
113 A19 1.50fr multi, vert. .20 .20
114 A19 2fr multi, vert. .20 .20
115 A19 4fr multi, vert. .20 .20
116 A19 5fr multi, vert. .20 .20
117 A19 6fr multi, vert. .20 .20
118 A19 8fr multi, vert. .20 .20
119 A19 10fr multi, vert. .20 .20
120 A19 15fr multi .20 .20
121 A19 25fr multi .30 .20
122 A19 30fr multi .35 .20
123 A19 40fr multi .40 .30
124 A19 50fr multi .55 .40
125 A19 60fr multi .65 .45
126 A19 85fr multi .90 .55
Nos. 111-126 (16) 5.15 4.10

Centenary Emblem and Globe — A20

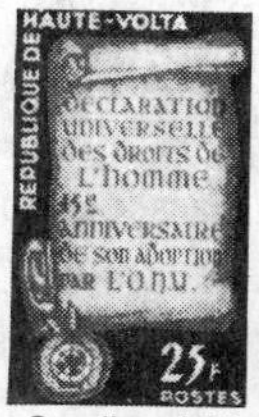
Scroll — A21

1963, Oct. 21 Unwmk. *Perf. 12*
127 A20 25fr multicolored .50 .40

Centenary of International Red Cross.

1963, Dec. 10 Photo. *Perf. 13x12½*
128 A21 25fr dp claret, gold & bl .30 .20

15th anniv. of the Universal Declaration of Human Rights.

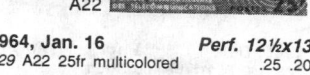

Sound Wave Patterns A22

1964, Jan. 16 *Perf. 12½x13*
129 A22 25fr multicolored .25 .20

Upper Volta's admission to the ITU.

Barograph and WMO Emblem A23

1964, Mar. 23 Engr. *Perf. 13*
130 A23 50fr dk car rose, grn & bl .55 .40

4th World Meteorological Day, Mar. 23.

World Connected by Letters and Carrier Pigeon — A24

60fr, World connected by letters and jet plane.

1964, Mar. 29 Photo. *Perf. 13x12*
131 A24 25fr gray brn & ultra .25 .20
132 A24 60fr gray brn & org .60 .40

Upper Volta's admission to the UPU.

IQSY Emblem and Seasonal Allegories — A25

1964, Aug. 17 Engr. *Perf. 13*
133 A25 30fr grn, ocher & car .35 .25

International Quiet Sun Year.

Cooperation Issue
Common Design Type

1964, Nov. 7 Unwmk. *Perf. 13*
134 CD119 70fr dl bl grn, dk brn & car .65 .40

Hotel Independance, Ouagadougou — A26

1964, Dec. 11 Litho. *Perf. 12½x13*
135 A26 25fr multicolored 1.00 .35

Pigmy Long-tailed Sunbird A27

Comoe Waterfall A28

1965, Mar. 1 Photo. *Perf. 13x12½*
Size: 22x36mm
136 A27 10fr shown .20 .20
137 A27 15fr Olive-bellied Sunbird .25 .20
138 A27 20fr Splendid Sunbird .40 .25
Nos. 136-138,C20 (4) 6.35 3.15

1965 Engr. *Perf. 13*

Design: 25fr, Great Waterfall of Banfora, horiz.

139 A28 5fr yel grn, bl & red brn .20 .20
140 A28 25fr dk red, brt bl & grn .25 .20
Nos. 139-140 (2) .45 .40

Soccer — A29

Abraham Lincoln — A30

Designs: 25fr, Boxing gloves and ring. 70fr, Tennis rackets, ball and net.

1965, July 15 Unwmk. *Perf. 13*
141 A29 15fr brn, red & dk grn .20 .20
142 A29 25fr pale org, bl & brn .30 .20
143 A29 70fr dk car & brt grn .60 .30
Nos. 141-143 (3) 1.10 .70

1st African Games, Brazzaville, July 18-25.

1965, Nov. 3 Photo. *Perf. 13x12½*
144 A30 50fr green & multi .50 .40

Centenary of death of Abraham Lincoln.

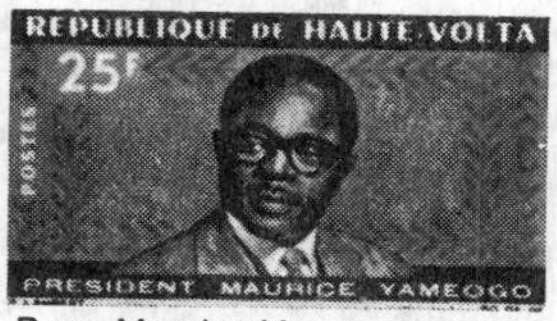

Pres. Maurice Yameogo — A31

1965, Dec. 11 Photo. *Perf. 13x12½*
145 A31 25fr multicolored .25 .20

Mantis A32

Wart Hog A33

Headdress A34

1966 *Perf. 13x12½, 12½x13*
146 A33 1fr Nemopistha imperatrix .20 .20
147 A33 2fr Ball python .20 .20
148 A32 3fr shown .20 .20
149 A32 4fr Grasshopper .20 .20
150 A33 5fr shown .20 .20
151 A32 6fr Scorpion .20 .20
152 A33 8fr Green monkey .20 .20
153 A32 10fr Dromedary .20 .20
154 A33 15fr Leopard .20 .20
155 A32 20fr Cape buffalo .25 .20
156 A33 25fr Hippopotamus .30 .20
157 A32 30fr Agama lizard .40 .20
158 A33 45fr Common puff adder .55 .25
159 A33 50fr Chameleon .60 .35
160 A33 60fr Ugada limbata .70 .40
161 A33 85fr Elephant .90 .50
Nos. 146-161 (16) 5.50 3.90

1966, Apr. 9 Photo. *Perf. 13x12½*

25fr, Plumed headdress. 60fr, Male dancer.

162 A34 20fr yel grn, choc & red .20 .20
163 A34 25fr multicolored .25 .20
164 A34 60fr org, dk brn & red .55 .35
Nos. 162-164 (3) 1.00 .75

Intl. Negro Arts Festival, Dakar, Senegal, 4/1-24.

Pô Church A35

Design: No. 166, Bobo-Dioulasso Mosque.

1966, Apr. 15 *Perf. 12½x13*

165 A35 25fr multicolored .25 .20
166 A35 25fr bl, cream & red brn .25 .20

The Red Cross Helping the World — A36

1966, June Photo. *Perf. 13x12½*

167 A36 25fr lemon, blk & car .25 .20

Issued to honor the Red Cross.

Boy Scouts in Camp A37

15fr, Two Scouts on a cliff exploring the country.

1966, June 15 *Perf. 12½x13*

168 A37 10fr multicolored .20 .20
169 A37 15fr blk, bis brn, & dl yel .20 .20

Issued to honor the Boy Scouts.

Cow Receiving Injection A38

1966, Aug. 16 Photo. *Perf. 12½x13*

170 A38 25fr yel, blk & blue .25 .20

Campaign against cattle plague.

Plowing with Donkey A39

Design: 30fr, Crop rotation, Kamboince Experimental Station.

Perf. 12½x13

1966, Sept. 15 Photo.

171 A39 25fr multicolored .25 .20
172 A39 30fr multicolored .25 .20

Natl. and rural education; 3rd anniv. of the Kamboince Experimental Station (No. 172).

UNESCO Emblem and Map of Africa A40

UNICEF Emblem and Children A41

1966, Dec. 10 Engr. *Perf. 13*

173 A40 50fr brt bl, blk & red .50 .25
174 A41 50fr dk vio, dp lil & dk red .50 .25

20th anniv. of UNESCO and of UNICEF.

Arms of Upper Volta — A42

Symbols of Agriculture, Industry, Men and Women — A43

1967, Jan. 2 Photo. *Perf. 12½x13*

175 A42 30fr multicolored .25 .20

Europafrica Issue

1967, Feb. 4 Photo. *Perf. 12½*

176 A43 60fr multicolored .50 .30

Scout Handclasp and Jamboree Emblem A44

5fr, Jamboree emblem and Scout holding hat.

1967, June 8 Photo. *Perf. 12½x13*

177 A44 5fr multicolored .20 .20
178 A44 20fr multicolored .55 .40

12th Boy Scout World Jamboree, Farragut State Park, Idaho, Aug. 1-9. See No. C41.

Bank Book and Hands with Coins — A45

1967, Aug. 22 Engr. *Perf. 13*

179 A45 30fr slate grn, ocher & olive .25 .20

National Savings Bank.

Mailman on Bicycle — A46

1967, Oct. 15 Engr. *Perf. 13*

180 A46 30fr dk bl, emer & brn .30 .20

Stamp Day.

Monetary Union Issue

Common Design Type

1967, Nov. 4 Engr. *Perf. 13*

181 CD125 30fr dk vio & dl bl .25 .20

View of Nizier — A47

Olympic Emblem and: 50fr, Les Deux-Alps, vert. 100fr, Ski lift and view of Villard-de-Lans.

1967, Nov. 28

182 A47 15fr brt bl, grn & brn .20 .20
183 A47 50fr brt bl & slate grn .45 .20
184 A47 100fr brt bl, grn & red .90 .45
Nos. 182-184 (3) 1.55 .85

10th Winter Olympic Games, Grenoble, France, Feb. 6-18, 1968.

White and Black Men Holding Human Rights Emblem A48

1968, Jan. 2 Photo. *Perf. 12½x13*

185 A48 20fr brt bl, gold & dp car .20 .20
186 A48 30fr grn, gold & dp car .30 .20

International Human Rights Year.

Administration School and Student — A49

1968, Feb. 2 Engr. *Perf. 13*

187 A49 30fr ol bis, Prus bl & brt grn .25 .20

National School of Administration.

WHO Emblem and Sick People A50

1968, Apr. 7 Engr. *Perf. 13*

188 A50 30fr ind, brt bl & car rose .30 .20
189 A50 50fr brt bl, sl grn & lt brn .45 .25

WHO, 20th anniversary.

Telephone Office, Bobo-Dioulasso — A51

Perf. 12½x12

1968, Sept. 30 Photo.

190 A51 30fr multicolored .30 .20

Opening of the automatic telephone office in Bobo-Dioulasso.

Weaver A52

1968, Oct. 30 Engr. *Perf. 13*

Size: 36x22mm

191 A52 30fr magenta, brn & ocher .30 .20

See No. C58.

Grain Pouring over World, Plower and FAO Emblem — A53

1969, Jan. 7 Engr. *Perf. 13*

192 A53 30fr slate, vio bl & maroon .25 .20

UNFAO world food program.

Automatic Looms and ILO Emblem A54

1969, Mar. 15 Engr. *Perf. 13*

193 A54 30fr brt grn, mar & indigo .25 .20

ILO, 50th anniversary.

Smith — A55

1969, Apr. 3 Engr. *Perf. 13*

Size: 36x22mm

194 A55 5fr magenta & blk .20 .20

See No. C64.

Blood Donor A56

1969, May 15 Engr. *Perf. 13*

195 A56 30fr blk, bl & car .25 .20

League of Red Cross Societies, 50th anniv.

Nile Pike — A57

Fish: 20fr, Nannocharax gobioides. 25fr, Hemigrammocharax polli. 55fr, Alestes luteus. 85fr, Micralestes voltae.

1969 Engr. *Perf. 13*

Size: 36x22mm

196 A57 20fr brt bl, brn & yel .30 .20
197 A57 25fr slate, brn & dk brn .30 .20
198 A57 30fr dk olive & blk .45 .25
199 A57 55fr dk grn, yel & ol .60 .40
200 A57 85fr slate brn & pink 1.25 .90
Nos. 196-200,C66-C67 (7) 5.20 2.95

Development Bank Issue

Common Design Type

1969, Sept. 10 Engr. *Perf. 13*

201 CD130 30fr sl grn, grn & ocher .25 .20

Millet — A58

Design: 30fr, Cotton.

1969, Oct. 30 Photo. *Perf. 12½x13*

202 A58 15fr dk brn, grn & yel .20 .20
203 A58 30fr dp claret & brt bl .30 .20

See Nos. C73-C74.

ASECNA Issue
Common Design Type

1969, Dec. 12 Engr. *Perf. 13*
204 CD132 100fr brown .80 .50

Niadale Mask — A59

Carvings from National Museum: 30fr, Niaga. 45fr, Man and woman, Iliu Bara. 80fr, Karan Weeba figurine.

1970, Mar. 5 Engr. *Perf. 13*
207 A59 10fr dk car rose, org & dk brn .20 .20
209 A59 30fr dk brn, brt vio & grnsh bl .25 .20
211 A59 45fr yel grn, brn & bl .30 .20
212 A59 80fr pur, rose lil & brn .60 .25
Nos. 207-212 (4) 1.35 .85

African Huts and European City — A60

1970, Apr. 25 Engr. *Perf. 13*
213 A60 30fr dk brn, red & bl .25 .20

Issued for Linked Cities' Day.

Mask for Nebwa Gnomo Dance A61

Designs: 8fr, Cauris dancers, vert. 20fr, Gourmantchés dancers, vert. 30fr, Larllé dancers.

1970, May 7 Photo. *Perf. 13*
214 A61 5fr lt brn, vio bl & blk .20 .20
215 A61 8fr org brn, car & blk .20 .20
216 A61 20fr dk brn, sl grn & ocher .20 .20
217 A61 30fr dp car, dk gray & brn .25 .20
Nos. 214-217 (4) .85 .80

Education Year Emblem, Open Book and Pupils A62

Design: 90fr, Education Year emblem, telecommunication and education symbols.

1970, May 14 *Perf. 12½x12*
218 A62 40fr black & multi .35 .20
219 A62 90fr olive & multi .65 .35

International Education Year.

UPU Headquarters Issue

Abraham Lincoln, UPU Headquarters and Emblem — A63

1970, May 20 Engr. *Perf. 13*
220 A63 30fr dk car rose, ind & red brn .30 .20
221 A63 60fr dk bl grn, vio & red brn .50 .25

See note after CD133, Common Design section.

Ship-building Industry A64

45fr, Chemical industry. 80fr, Electrical industry.

1970, June 15
222 A64 15fr brt pink, red brn & blk .20 .20
223 A64 45fr emerald, dp bl & blk .35 .20
224 A64 80fr red brn, claret & blk .65 .35
Nos. 222-224 (3) 1.20 .75

Hanover Fair.

Cattle Vaccination A65

1970, June 30 Photo. *Perf. 13*
225 A65 30fr Prus bl, yel & sepia .30 .20

National Veterinary College.

Vaccination and Red Cross — A66

1970, Aug. 28 Engr. *Perf. 12½x13*
226 A66 30fr chocolate & car .25 .20

Issued for the Upper Volta Red Cross. For surcharge see No. 252.

Europafrica Issue

Nurse with Child, by Frans Hals — A67

Paintings: 30fr, Courtyard of a House in Delft, by Pieter de Hooch. 150fr, Christina of Denmark, by Hans Holbein. 250fr, Courtyard of the Royal Palace at Innsbruck, Austria, by Albrecht Dürer.

1970, Sept. 25 Litho. *Perf. 13x14*
227 A67 25fr multicolored .25 .20
228 A67 30fr multicolored .35 .20
229 A67 150fr multicolored 1.40 .65
230 A67 250fr multicolored 2.00 1.00
Nos. 227-230 (4) 4.00 2.05

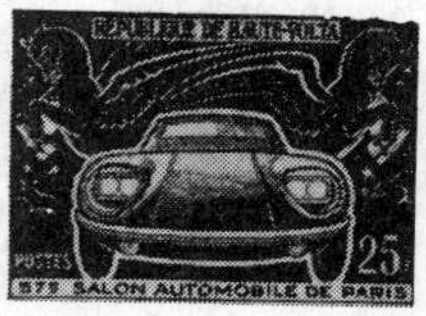

Citroen A68

Design: 40fr, Old and new Citroen cars.

1970, Oct. 16 Engr. *Perf. 13*
231 A68 25fr ol brn, mar & sl grn .25 .20
232 A68 40fr brt grn, plum & sl .40 .20

57th Paris Automobile Salon.

Professional Training Center A69

1970, Dec. 10 Engr. *Perf. 13*
233 A69 50fr grn, bis & brn .40 .20

Opening of Professional Training Center under joint sponsorship of Austria and Upper Volta.

Upper Volta Arms and Soaring Bird — A70

1970, Dec. 10 Photo.
234 A70 30fr lt blue & multi .25 .20

Tenth anniversary of independence, Dec. 11.

Political Maps of Africa — A71

1970, Dec. 14 Litho. *Perf. 13½*
235 A71 50fr multicolored .40 .20

10th anniv. of the declaration granting independence to colonial territories and countries.

Beingolo Hunting Horn — A72

Musical Instruments: 15fr, Mossi guitar, vert. 20fr, Gourounsi flutes, vert. 25fr, Lunga drums.

1971, Mar. 1 Engr. *Perf. 13*
236 A72 5fr blue, brn & car .20 .20
237 A72 15fr green, crim rose & brn .20 .20
238 A72 20fr car rose, bl & gray .20 .20
239 A72 25fr brt grn, red brn & ol gray .20 .20
Nos. 236-239 (4) .80 .80

Voltaphilex I, National Phil. Exhibition.

Four Races — A73

1971, Mar. 21 Engr. *Perf. 13*
240 A73 50fr rose cl, lt grn & dk brn .40 .25

Intl. year against racial discrimination.

Telephone and Globes A74

1971, May 17 Engr. *Perf. 13*
241 A74 50fr brn, gray & dk pur .40 .20

3rd World Telecommunications Day.

Cane Field Worker, Banfora Sugar Mill A75

Cotton and Voltex Mill Emblem A76

1971, June 24 Photo. *Perf. 13*
242 A75 10fr multicolored .20 .20
243 A76 35fr multicolored .25 .20

Industrial development.

Gonimbrasia Hecate A77

Butterflies and Moths: 2fr, Hamanumida daedalus. 3fr, Ophideres materna. 5fr, Danaus chrysippus. 40fr, Hypolimnas misippus. 45fr, Danaus petiverana.

1971, June 30
244 A77 1fr blue & multi .20 .20
245 A77 2fr lt lilac & multi .20 .20
246 A77 3fr multicolored .20 .20
247 A77 5fr gray & multi .20 .20
248 A77 40fr ocher & multi .60 .35
249 A77 45fr multicolored .80 .50
Nos. 244-249 (6) 2.20 1.65

Kabuki Actor — A78

Design: 40fr, African mask and Kabuki actor.

1971, Aug. 12 Photo. *Perf. 13*
250 A78 25fr multicolored .20 .20
251 A78 40fr multicolored .30 .20

Philatokyo 71, Philatelic Exposition, Tokyo, Apr. 19-29.

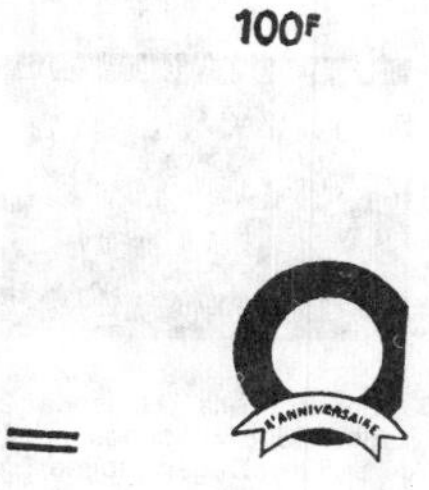

No. 226 Surcharged

1971 Engr. *Perf. 12½x13*
252 A66 100fr on 30fr choc & car .65 .40

10th anniversary of Upper Volta Red Cross.

Seed Preparation A79

Designs: 75fr, Old farmer with seed packet, vert. 100fr, Farmer in rice field.

1971, Sept. 30 **Photo.** ***Perf. 13***
253 A79 35fr ocher & multi .25 .20
254 A79 75fr lt blue & multi .50 .20
255 A79 100fr brown & multi .65 .35
Nos. 253-255 (3) 1.40 .75

National campaign for seed protection.

Outdoor Classroom A80

Design: 50fr, Mother learning to read.

1971, Oct. 14
256 A80 35fr multicolored .25 .20
257 A80 50fr multicolored .40 .20

Women's education.

Joseph Dakiri, Soldiers Driving Tractors — A81

Children and UNICEF Emblem — A84

Spraying Lake, Fly, Man Leading Blind Women A82

40fr, Dakiri & soldiers gathering harvest.

1971, Oct. 13 ***Perf. 12x12½***
258 A81 15fr blk, yel & red brn .20 .20
259 A81 40fr blue & multi .25 .20

Joseph Dakiri (1938-1971), inaugurator of the Army-Aid-to-Agriculture Program.

1971, Nov. 26 **Photo.** ***Perf. 13***
260 A82 40fr dk brn, yel & bl .25 .20

Drive against onchocerciasis, roundworm infestation.

For surcharge see No. 295.

1971, Dec. 11 ***Perf. 13***
262 A84 45fr red, bister & blk .35 .20

UNICEF, 25th anniv.

Peulh House A85

Upper Volta Houses: 20fr, Gourounsi house. 35fr, Mossi houses. 45fr, Bobo house, vert. 50fr, Dagari house, vert. 90fr, Bango house, interior.

Perf. 13x13½, 13½x13
1971-72 **Photo.**
263 A85 10fr ver & multi .20 .20
264 A85 20fr multicolored .20 .20
265 A85 35fr brt grn & multi .25 .20
266 A85 45fr multi ('72) .35 .20
267 A85 50fr multi ('72) .40 .20
268 A85 90fr multi ('72) .60 .35
Nos. 263-268 (6) 2.00 1.35

Town Halls of Bobo-Dioulasso and Chalons-sur-Marne — A86

1971, Dec. 23 ***Perf. 13x12½***
269 A86 40fr yellow & multi .25 .20

Kinship between the cities of Bobo-Dioulasso, Upper Volta, and Chalons-sur-Marne, France.

Louis Armstrong — A87

1972, May 17 ***Perf. 14x13***
270 A87 45fr multicolored .45 .25

Black musician. See No. C104.

Red Crescent, Cross and Lion Emblems A88

1972, June 23 ***Perf. 13x14***
271 A88 40fr yellow & multi .35 .20

World Red Cross Day. See No. C105.

Coiffure of Peulh Woman — A89

Designs: Various hair styles.

1972, July 23 **Litho.** ***Perf. 13***
272 A89 25fr blue & multi .20 .20
273 A89 35fr emerald & multi .25 .20
274 A89 75fr yellow & multi .45 .20
Nos. 272-274 (3) .90 .60

Classroom A90

Designs: 15fr, Clinic. 20fr, Factory. 35fr, Cattle. 40fr, Plowers. 85fr, Road building machinery.

1972, Oct. 30 **Engr.** ***Perf. 13***
275 A90 10fr sl grn, lt grn & choc .20 .20
276 A90 15fr brt grn, brn org & brn .20 .20
277 A90 20fr bl, lt brn & grn .20 .20
278 A90 35fr grn, brn & brt bl .20 .20
279 A90 40fr choc, pink & sl grn .25 .20
Nos. 275-279,C106 (6) 1.50 1.25

2nd Five-Year Plan.

West African Monetary Union Issue
Common Design Type

1972, Nov. 2
280 CD136 40fr brn, bl & gray .25 .20

Lottery Office and Emblem A91

1972, Nov. 6 **Litho.**
281 A91 35fr multicolored .25 .20

5th anniversary of National Lottery.

Domestic Animals — A92

1972, Dec. 4 **Litho.** ***Perf. 13½x12½***
282 A92 5fr Donkeys .20 .20
283 A92 10fr Geese .20 .20
284 A92 30fr Goats .20 .20
285 A92 50fr Cow .35 .20
286 A92 65fr Dromedaries .40 .20
Nos. 282-286 (5) 1.35 1.00

Mossi Woman's Hair Style, and Village — A93

1973, Jan. 24 **Engr.** ***Perf. 13***
287 A93 5fr slate grn, org & choc .20 .20
288 A93 40fr bl, org & chocolate .25 .20

Eugene A. Cernan and Lunar Module A94

65fr, Ronald E. Evans & splashdown. 100fr, Capsule, in orbit & interior, horiz. 150fr, Harrison H. Schmitt & lift-off. 200fr, Conference & moon-buggy. 500fr, Moon-buggy & capsule, horiz.

Perf. 12½x13½, 13½x12½
1973, Mar. 29 **Litho.**
289 A94 50fr multi .30 .20
290 A94 65fr multi .40 .20
291 A94 100fr multi .60 .30
292 A94 150fr multi .90 .45
293 A94 200fr multi 1.25 .60
Nos. 289-293 (5) 3.45 1.75

Souvenir Sheet

294 A94 500fr multi 3.50 1.60

Apollo 17 moon mission.

No. 260 Surcharged in Red

O. M. S.
25e Anniversaire
45F

1973, Apr. 7 **Photo.** ***Perf. 13***
295 A82 45fr on 40fr multi .25 .20

WHO, 25th anniversary.

Scout Bugler A95

1973, July 18 **Litho.** ***Perf. 12½x13***
296 A95 20fr multicolored .20 .20
Nos. 296,C160-C163 (5) 3.35 1.80

African Postal Union Issue
Common Design Type

1973, Sept. 12 **Engr.** ***Perf. 13***
297 CD137 100fr brt red, mag & dl yel .65 .25

Pres. Kennedy, Saturn 5 on Assembly Trailer A96

Pres. John F. Kennedy (1917-1963) and: 10fr, Atlas rocket carrying John H. Glenn. 30fr, Titan 2 rocket and Gemini 3 capsule.

1973, Sept. 12 **Litho.** ***Perf. 12½x13***
298 A96 5fr multicolored .20 .20
299 A96 10fr multicolored .20 .20
300 A96 30fr multicolored .20 .20
Nos. 298-300,C167-C168 (5) 4.00 2.25

Cross-examination — A97

Designs: 65fr, "Diamond Ede." 70fr, Forensic Institute. 150fr, Robbery scene.

1973, Sept. 15 ***Perf. 13x12½***
301 A97 50fr multicolored .30 .20
302 A97 65fr multicolored .40 .20
303 A97 70fr multicolored .40 .20
304 A97 150fr multicolored .90 .40
Nos. 301-304 (4) 2.00 1.00

Interpol, 50th anniversary. See No. C170.

Market Place, Ouagadougou — A98

40fr, Swimming pool, Hotel Independence.

1973, Sept. 30
305 A98 35fr multicolored .25 .20
306 A98 40fr multicolored .25 .20

Tourism. See Nos. C171-C172.

Protestant Church — A99

Design: 40fr, Ouahigouya Mosque.

1973, Sept. 28 ***Perf. 13x12½***

307 A99 35fr multicolored .25 .20
308 A99 40fr multicolored .25 .20

Houses of worship. See No. C173.

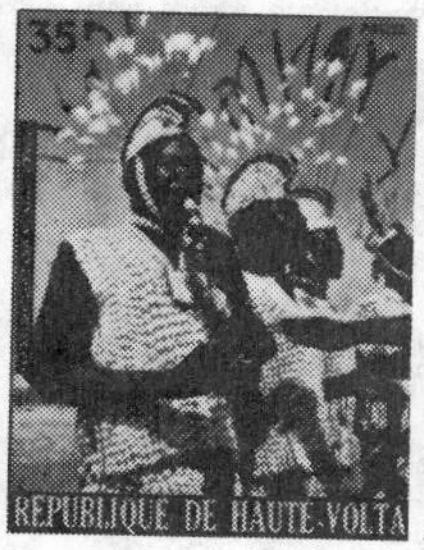

Kiembara Dancers A100

Design: 40fr, Dancers.

1973, Nov. 30 Litho. ***Perf. 12½x13***

309 A100 35fr multicolored .25 .20
310 A100 40fr multicolored .25 .20

Folklore. See Nos. C174-C175.

Yuri Gagarin and Aries — A101

Famous Men and their Zodiac Signs: 10fr, Lenin and Taurus. 20fr, John F. Kennedy, rocket and Gemini. 25fr, John H. Glenn, orbiting capsule and Cancer. 30fr, Napoleon and Leo. 50fr, Goethe and Virgo. 60fr, Pelé and Libra. 75fr, Charles de Gaulle and Scorpio. 100fr, Beethoven and Sagittarius. 175fr, Conrad Adenauer and Capricorn. 200fr, Edwin E. Aldrin, Jr. (Apollo XI) and Aquarius. 250fr, Lord Baden-Powell and Pisces.

1973, Dec. 15 Litho. ***Perf. 13x14***

311 A101 5fr multicolored .20 .20
312 A101 10fr multicolored .20 .20
313 A101 20fr multicolored .20 .20
314 A101 25fr multicolored .20 .20
315 A101 30fr multicolored .20 .20
316 A101 50fr multicolored .30 .20
317 A101 60fr multicolored .40 .20
318 A101 75fr multicolored .45 .20
319 A101 100fr multicolored .60 .30
320 A101 175fr multicolored 1.10 .55
321 A101 200fr multicolored 1.25 .55
322 A101 250fr multicolored 1.50 .70
Nos. 311-322 (12) 6.60 3.70

See Nos. C176-C178.

Rivera with Italian Flag and Championship '74 Emblem — A102

40fr, World Cup, soccer ball, World Championship '74 emblem & Pelé with Brazilian flag.

1974, Jan. 15 ***Perf. 13x12½***

323 A102 5fr multicolored .20 .20
324 A102 40fr multicolored .25 .20
Nos. 323-324,C179-C181 (5) 3.20 1.80

10th World Cup Soccer Championship, Munich, June 13-July 7.

Charles de Gaulle A103

40fr, De Gaulle memorial. 60fr, Pres. de Gaulle.

1974, Feb. 4 Litho. ***Perf. 12½x13***

325 A103 35fr multicolored .20 .20
326 A103 40fr multicolored .20 .20
327 A103 60fr multicolored .35 .20
  a. Strip of 3, Nos. 325-327 .75 .45
Nos. 325-327,C183 (4) 2.75 1.60

Gen. Charles de Gaulle (1890-1970), president of France. See #C184.

N'Dongo and Cameroun Flag — A104

World Cup, Emblems and: 20fr, Kolev and Bulgarian flag. 50fr, Keita and Mali flag.

1974, Mar. 19

328 A104 10fr multicolored .20 .20
329 A104 20fr multicolored .20 .20
330 A104 50fr multicolored .35 .20
Nos. 328-330,C185-C186 (5) 3.00 1.75

10th World Cup Soccer Championship, Munich, June 13-July 7.

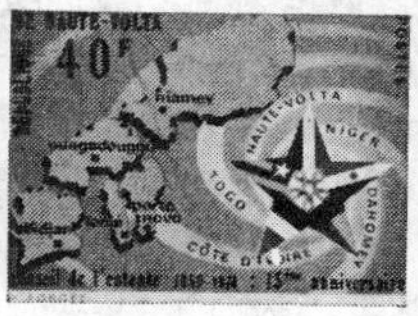

Map and Flags of Members A105

1974, May 29 Photo. ***Perf. 13x12½***

331 A105 40fr blue & multi .25 .20

15th anniversary of the Council of Accord.

UPU Emblem and Mail Coach — A106

1974, July 23 Litho. ***Perf. 13½***

332 A106 35fr shown .25 .20
333 A106 40fr Steamship .25 .20
334 A106 85fr Mailman .55 .30
Nos. 332-334,C189-C191 (6) 4.05 2.20

Universal Postal Union centenary.
For overprints see #339-341, C197-C200.

Soccer Game, Winner Italy, in France, 1938 — A107

World Cup, Game and Flags: 25fr, Uruguay, in Brazil, 1950. 50fr, East Germany, in Switzerland, 1954.

1974, Sept. 2 Litho. ***Perf. 13½***

335 A107 10fr multicolored .20 .20
336 A107 25fr multicolored .20 .20
337 A107 50fr multicolored .35 .20
Nos. 335-337,C193-C195 (6) 4.75 2.55

World Cup Soccer winners.

Map and Farm Woman — A108

1974, Oct. 2 Litho. ***Perf. 13x12½***

338 A108 35fr yellow & multi .20 .20

Kou Valley Development.

Nos. 332-334 Overprinted in Red "100e ANNIVERSAIRE DE L'UNION POSTALE UNIVERSELLE / 9 OCTOBRE 1974"

1974, Oct. 9

339 A106 35fr multicolored .25 .20
340 A106 40fr multicolored .25 .20
341 A106 85fr multicolored .55 .30
Nos. 339-341,C197-C199 (6) 5.05 2.70

Universal Postal Union centenary.

Flowers, by Pierre Bonnard A109

Flower Paintings by: 10fr, Jan Brueghel. 30fr, Jean van Os. 50fr, Van Brussel.

1974, Oct. 31 Litho. ***Perf. 12½x13***

342 A109 5fr multicolored .20 .20
343 A109 10fr multicolored .20 .20
344 A109 30fr multicolored .20 .20
345 A109 50fr multicolored .25 .20
Nos. 342-345,C201 (5) 2.85 1.80

Churchill as Officer of India Hussars — A110

Churchill: 75fr, As Secretary of State for Interior. 100fr, As pilot. 125fr, meeting with Roosevelt, 1941. 300fr, As painter. 450fr, and "HMS Resolution."

1975, Jan. 11 ***Perf. 13½***

346 A110 50fr multicolored .30 .20
347 A110 75fr multicolored .45 .20
348 A110 100fr multicolored .55 .30
349 A110 125fr multicolored .70 .40
350 A110 300fr multicolored 1.60 .80
Nos. 346-350 (5) 3.60 1.90

Souvenir Sheet

351 A110 450fr multicolored 2.50 1.25

Sir Winston Churchill, birth centenary.

US No. 619 and Minutemen — A111

US Stamps: 40fr, #118 and Proclamation of Independence. 75fr, #798 and Signing the Constitution. 100fr, #703 and Surrender at Yorktown. 200fr, #1003 and George Washington. 300fr, #644 and Surrender of Burgoyne at Saratoga. 500fr, #63, 68, 73, 157, 179, 228 and 1483a.

1975, Feb. 17 Litho. ***Perf. 11***

352 A111 35fr multicolored .20 .20
353 A111 40fr multicolored .25 .20
354 A111 75fr multicolored .40 .20
355 A111 100fr multicolored .55 .30
356 A111 200fr multicolored 1.25 .55
357 A111 300fr multicolored 1.60 .80
Nos. 352-357 (6) 4.25 2.25

Souvenir Sheet

Imperf

358 A111 500fr multicolored 3.00 1.50

American Bicentennial.

"Atlantic" No. 2670, 1904-12 — A112

Locomotives from Mulhouse, France, Railroad Museum: 25fr, No. 2029, 1882. 50fr, No. 2129, 1882.

1975, Feb. 28 Litho. ***Perf. 13x12½***

359 A112 15fr multicolored .20 .20
360 A112 25fr multicolored .20 .20
361 A112 50fr multicolored .35 .20
Nos. 359-361,C203-C204 (5) 2.80 1.60

French Flag and Renault Petit Duc, 1910 — A113

Flags and Old Cars: 30fr, US and Ford Model T, 1909. 35fr, Italy and Alfa Romeo "Le Mans," 1931.

1975, Apr. 6 ***Perf. 14x13½***

362 A113 10fr multicolored .20 .20
363 A113 30fr multicolored .20 .20
364 A113 35fr multicolored .25 .20
Nos. 362-364,C206-C207 (5) 3.05 1.75

Washington and Lafayette — A114

American Bicentennial: 40fr, Washington reviewing troops at Valley Forge. 50fr, Washington taking oath of office.

1975, May 6 Litho. *Perf. 14*

365 A114 30fr multicolored .20 .20
366 A114 40fr multicolored .25 .20
367 A114 50fr multicolored .35 .20
Nos. 365-367,C209-C210 (5) 4.20 2.25

Souvenir Sheet

367A A114 500fr multicolored 3.50 1.60

Schweitzer and Pelicans — A115

15fr, Albert Schweitzer and bateleur eagle.

1975, May 25 Litho. *Perf. 13½*

368 A115 5fr multicolored .20 .20
369 A115 15fr multicolored .20 .20
Nos. 368-369,C212-C214 (5) 4.05 2.10

Albert Schweitzer, birth centenary.

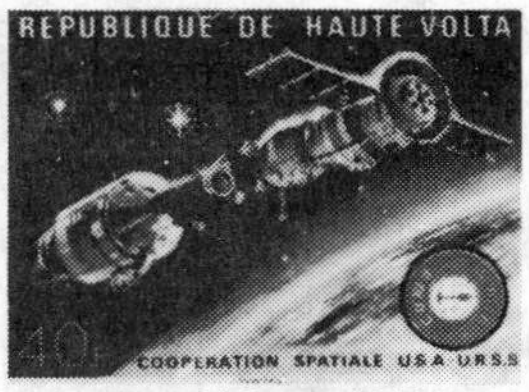

Apollo and Soyuz Orbiting Earth — A116

Design: 50fr, Apollo and Soyuz near link-up.

1975, July 18

370 A116 40fr multicolored .25 .20
371 A116 50fr multicolored .35 .20
Nos. 370-371,C216-C218 (5) 4.60 2.40

Apollo-Soyuz space test project, Russo-American cooperation, launched July 15, link-up July 17.

Maria Picasso Lopez, Artist's Mother A117

Paintings by Pablo Picasso (1881-1973): 60fr, Self-portrait. 90fr, First Communion.

1975, Aug. 7

372 A117 50fr multicolored .35 .20
373 A117 60fr multicolored .40 .20
374 A117 90fr multicolored .60 .30
Nos. 372-374,C220-C221 (5) 4.60 2.45

Expo '75 Emblem and Tanker, Idemitsu Maru — A118

Oceanographic Exposition, Okinawa: 25fr, Training ship, Kaio Maru. 45fr, Firefighting ship, Hiryu. 50fr, Battleship, Yamato. 60fr, Container ship, Kamakura Maru.

1975, Sept. 26 Litho. *Perf. 11*

375 A118 15fr multicolored .20 .20
376 A118 25fr multicolored .20 .20
377 A118 45fr multicolored .30 .20
377A A118 50fr multicolored .35 .20
378 A118 60fr multicolored .40 .20
Nos. 375-378,C223 (6) 2.20 1.40

Woman, Globe and IWY Emblem — A119

1975, Nov. 20 Photo. *Perf. 13*

379 A119 65fr multicolored .40 .25

International Women's Year.

Msgr. Joanny Thevenoud and Cathedral — A120

65fr, Father Guillaume Templier & Cathedral.

1975, Nov. 20 Engr. *Perf. 13x12½*

380 A120 55fr grn, blk & dl red .20 .20
381 A120 65fr blk, org & dl red .25 .20

75th anniv. of the Evangelization of Upper Volta.

Farmer's Hat, Hoe and Emblem A121

1975, Dec. 10 Photo. *Perf. 13x13½*

382 A121 15fr buff & multi .20 .20
383 A121 50fr lt green & multi .20 .20

Development of the Volta valleys.

Sledding and Olympic Emblem — A122

Innsbruck Background, Olympic Emblem and: 45fr, Figure skating. 85fr, Skiing.

1975, Dec. 16 Litho. *Perf. 13½*

384 A122 35fr multicolored .20 .20
385 A122 45fr multicolored .25 .20
386 A122 85fr multicolored .45 .25
Nos. 384-386,C225-C226 (5) 2.95 1.65

12th Winter Olympic Games, Innsbruck, Austria, Feb. 4-15, 1976.

Gymnast and Olympic Emblem — A123

1976, Mar. 17

387 A123 40fr shown .20 .20
388 A123 50fr Sailing .25 .20
389 A123 100fr Soccer .55 .30
Nos. 387-389,C228-C229 (5) 2.40 1.40

21st Olympic Games, Montreal, Canada, July 17-Aug. 1.

Olympic Emblem and Sprinters A124

Olympic Emblem and: 55fr, Equestrian. 75fr, Hurdles.

1976, Mar. 25 Litho. *Perf. 11*

390 A124 30fr multicolored .20 .20
391 A124 55fr multicolored .30 .20
392 A124 75fr multicolored .40 .20
Nos. 390-392,C231-C232 (5) 2.65 1.50

21st Olympic Games, Montreal.
For overprints see #420-422, C245-C247.

Blind Woman and Man — A125

1976, Apr. 7 Engr. *Perf. 13*

393 A125 75fr dk brn, grn & org .40 .25
394 A125 250fr dk brn, ocher & org 1.40 .80

Drive against onchocerciasis, roundworm infestation.

"Deutschland" over Friedrichshafen — A126

Airships: 40fr, "Victoria Louise" over sailing ships. 50fr, "Sachsen" over German countryside.

1976, May 11 Litho. *Perf. 11*

395 A126 10fr multicolored .70 .20
396 A126 40fr multicolored .25 .20
397 A126 50fr multicolored .35 .20
Nos. 395-397,C234-C236 (6) 5.30 2.60

75th anniversary of the Zeppelin.

Viking Lander and Probe on Mars — A127

Viking Mars project: 55fr, Viking orbiter in flight. 75fr, Titan rocket start for Mars, vert.

1976, June 24 *Perf. 13½*

398 A127 30fr multicolored .20 .20
399 A127 55fr multicolored .25 .20
400 A127 75fr multicolored .30 .20
Nos. 398-400,C238-C239 (5) 3.25 1.85

World Map, Arms of Upper Volta A128

Design: 100fr, World map, arms and dove.

1976, Aug. 19 Litho. *Perf. 12½*

401 A128 55fr brown & multi .25 .20
402 A128 100fr blue & multi .40 .30

5th Summit Conference of Non-aligned Countries, Colombo, Sri Lanka, Aug. 9-19.

Bicentennial, Interphil 76 Emblems and Washington at Battle of Trenton — A129

Design: 90fr, Bicentennial, Interphil 76 emblems and Seat of Government, Pennsylvania.

1976, Sept. 30 *Perf. 13½*

403 A129 60fr multicolored .40 .20
404 A129 90fr multicolored .55 .25
Nos. 403-404,C241-C243 (5) 4.95 2.45

American Bicentennial, Interphil 76, Philadelphia, Pa., May 29-June 6.

UPU and UN Emblems — A130

1976, Dec. 8 Engr. *Perf. 13*

405 A130 200fr red, olive & blue 1.00 .60

UN Postal Administration, 25th anniv.

Arms of Tenkodogo A131

Bronze Statuette A132

Coats of Arms: 20fr, 100fr, Ouagadougou.

1977, May 2 Litho. *Perf. 13*

406 A131 10fr multicolored .20 .20
407 A131 20fr multicolored .20 .20
408 A131 65fr multicolored .35 .25
409 A131 100fr multicolored .55 .35
Nos. 406-409 (4) 1.30 1.00

1977, June 13 Photo. *Perf. 13*

Design: 65fr, Woman with bowl, bronze.

410 A132 55fr multicolored .30 .20
411 A132 65fr multicolored .35 .20

#410-411 issued in sheets and coils with black control number on every 5th stamp.

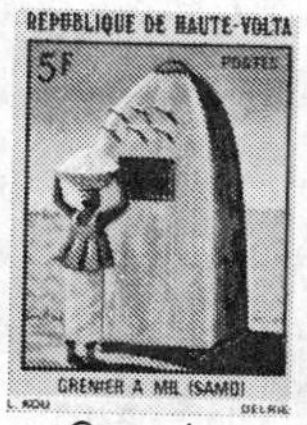

Granaries
A133

Handbags
A134

1977, June 20 Photo. *Perf. 13½x13*

412 A133 5fr Samo .20 .20
413 A133 35fr Boromo .20 .20
414 A133 45fr Banfora .25 .20
415 A133 55fr Mossi .30 .20
Nos. 412-415 (4) .95 .80

1977, June 20

416 A134 30fr Gouin .20 .20
417 A134 40fr Bissa .20 .20
418 A134 60fr Lobi .35 .20
419 A134 70fr Mossi .40 .25
Nos. 416-419 (4) 1.15 .85

Nos. 390-392 Overprinted in Gold:
a. VAINQUEUR 1976 / LASSE VIREN / FINLANDE
b. VAINQUEUR 1976 / ALWIN SCHOCKEMOHLE / R.F.A.
c. VAINQUEUR 1976 / JOHANNA SCHALLER / R.D.A.

1977, July 4 Litho. *Perf. 11*

420 A124 (a) 30fr multicolored .20 .20
421 A124 (b) 55fr multicolored .30 .20
422 A124 (c) 75fr multicolored .40 .20
Nos. 420-422,C245-C246 (5) 3.30 1.75

Winners, 21st Olympic Games.

Crinum Ornatum
A135

Haemanthus Multiflorus
A136

Hannoa Undulata — A137

Designs: Flowers, flowering branches and wild fruits. 175fr, 300fr, horiz.

1977 Litho. *Perf. 12½*

423 A137 2fr Cordia myxa .20 .20
424 A137 3fr Opilia celtidifolia .20 .20
425 A135 15fr shown .20 .20
426 A136 25fr shown .20 .20
427 A137 50fr shown .25 .20
428 A135 90fr Cochlospermum planchonii .45 .35
429 A135 125fr Clitoria ternatea .65 .50
430 A136 150fr Cassia alata .80 .60
431 A136 175fr Nauclea latifolia .90 .70
432 A136 300fr Bombax costatum 1.60 1.25
433 A135 400fr Eulophia cucullata 2.00 1.60
Nos. 423-433 (11) 7.45 6.00

Issued: 25fr, 150fr, 175fr, 300fr, Aug. 1; 2fr, 3fr, 50fr, Aug. 8; 15fr, 90fr, 125fr, 400fr, Aug. 23.

De Gaulle and Cross of Lorraine
A138

Designs: 200fr, King Baudouin of Belgium.

1977, Aug. 16 *Perf. 13½x14*

434 A138 100fr multicolored .55 .25
435 A138 200fr multicolored 1.10 .40

Elizabeth II
A139

Designs: 300fr, Elizabeth II taking salute. 500fr, Elizabeth II after Coronation.

1977, Aug. 16

436 A139 200fr multicolored .80 .30
437 A139 300fr multicolored 1.25 .50

Souvenir Sheet

438 A139 500fr multicolored 2.00 .90

25th anniv. of reign of Queen Elizabeth II.
For overprints see Nos. 478-480.

Lottery Tickets, Cars and Map of Upper Volta in Flag Colors — A140

1977, Sept. 16 Photo. *Perf. 13*

439 A140 55fr multicolored .30 .25

10th anniversary of National Lottery.

Selma Lagerlof, Literature — A141

Nobel Prize Winners: 65fr, Guglielmo Marconi, physics. 125fr, Bertrand Russell, literature. 200fr, Linus C. Pauling, chemistry. 300fr, Robert Koch, medicine. 500fr, Albert Schweitzer, peace.

1977, Sept. 22 Litho. *Perf. 13½*

440 A141 55fr multicolored .30 .20
441 A141 65fr multicolored .40 .20
442 A141 125fr multicolored .60 .25
443 A141 200fr multicolored 1.10 .40
444 A141 300fr multicolored 1.60 .65
Nos. 440-444 (5) 4.00 1.70

Souvenir Sheet

445 A141 500fr multicolored 2.50 1.20

The Three Graces, by Rubens
A142

Paintings by Peter Paul Rubens (1577-1640): 55fr, Heads of Black Men, horiz. 85fr, Bathsheba at the Fountain. 150fr, The Drunken Silenus. 200fr, 300fr, Life of Maria de Medicis, diff.

1977, Oct. 19 Litho. *Perf. 14*

446 A142 55fr multicolored .30 .20
447 A142 65fr multicolored .40 .20
448 A142 85fr multicolored .45 .25
449 A142 150fr multicolored .80 .40
450 A142 200fr multicolored 1.10 .45
451 A142 300fr multicolored 1.60 .60
Nos. 446-451 (6) 4.65 2.10

Lenin in His Office
A143

85fr, Lenin Monument, Kremlin. 200fr, Lenin with youth. 500fr, Lenin & Leonid Brezhnev.

1977, Oct. 28 Litho. *Perf. 12*

452 A143 10fr multicolored .20 .20
453 A143 85fr multicolored .45 .25
454 A143 200fr multicolored 1.10 .65
455 A143 500fr multicolored 2.50 1.60
Nos. 452-455 (4) 4.25 2.70

Russian October Revolution, 60th anniv.

Stadium and Brazil No. C79 — A144

Stadium and: 65fr, Brazil #1144. 125fr, Gt. Britain #458. 200fr, Chile #340. 300fr, Switzerland #350. 500fr, Germany #1147.

1977, Dec. 30 Litho. *Perf. 13½*

456 A144 55fr multicolored .30 .20
457 A144 65fr multicolored .40 .20
458 A144 125fr multicolored .60 .25
459 A144 200fr multicolored 1.10 .40
460 A144 300fr multicolored 1.60 .65
Nos. 456-460 (5) 4.00 1.70

Souvenir Sheet

461 A144 500fr multicolored 2.50 1.25

11th World Cup Soccer Championship, Argentina.
For overprints see Nos. 486-491.

Jean Mermoz and Seaplane — A145

History of Aviation: 75fr, Anthony H. G. Fokker. 85fr, Wiley Post. 90fr, Otto Lilienthal, vert. 100fr, Concorde. 500fr, Charles Lindbergh and "Spirit of St. Louis."

1978, Jan. 2 Litho. *Perf. 13½*

462 A145 65fr multicolored .35 .20
463 A145 75fr multicolored .40 .20
464 A145 85fr multicolored .45 .20
465 A145 90fr multicolored .50 .20
466 A145 100fr multicolored .55 .20
Nos. 462-466 (5) 2.25 1.00

Souvenir Sheet

467 A145 500fr multicolored 2.50 1.25

Crataeva Religiosa — A146

1978, Feb. 28 Litho. *Perf. 12½*

468 A146 55fr shown .30 .25
469 A146 75fr Fig tree .40 .30

Souvenir Sheet

Virgin and Child, by Rubens
A147

1978, May 24 Litho. *Perf. 13½x14*

470 A147 500fr multicolored 2.50 1.25

Peter Paul Rubens (1577-1640).

Antenna and ITU Emblem
A148

1978, May 30 *Perf. 13*

471 A148 65fr silver & multi .40 .20

10th World Telecommunications Day.

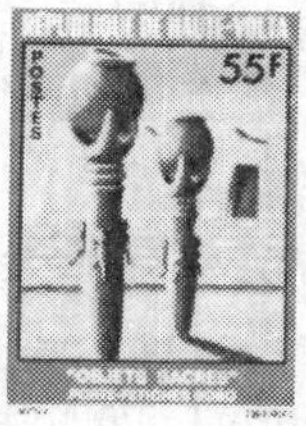

Fetish Gate of Bobo — A149

1978, July 10 Litho. *Perf. 13½*

472 A149 55fr shown .30 .20
473 A149 65fr Mossi fetish .40 .20

Capt. Cook and "Endeavour" — A150

Capt. James Cook (1728-1779) and: 85fr, Death on Hawaiian beach. 250fr, Navigational instruments. 350fr, "Resolution."

1978, Sept. 1 Litho. *Perf. 14½*

474 A150 65fr multicolored .40 .20
475 A150 85fr multicolored .45 .20
476 A150 250fr multicolored 1.40 .65
477 A150 350fr multicolored 1.90 .80
Nos. 474-477 (4) 4.15 1.85

Nos. 436-438 Overprinted Vertically in Silver: "ANNIVERSAIRE DU COURONNEMENT 1953-1978"

1978, Oct. 24 Litho. *Perf. 13½x14*

478 A139 200fr multicolored 1.10 .40
479 A139 300fr multicolored 1.60 .65

Souvenir Sheet

480 A139 500fr multicolored 2.50 1.25

25th anniversary of Coronation of Queen Elizabeth II. Overprint in 3 lines on 200fr, in 2 lines on 300fr and 500fr.

#478-480 exist with overprint in metallic red.

Trent Castle, by Dürer — A151

Paintings by Albrecht Durer (1471-1528): 150fr, Virgin and Child with St. Anne, vert. 250fr, Sts. George and Eustachius, vert. 350fr, Hans Holzschuher, vert.

Perf. 14x13½, 13½x14

1978, Nov. 20 Litho.

481 A151 65fr multicolored .40 .20
482 A151 150fr multicolored .80 .40
483 A151 250fr multicolored 1.40 .65
484 A151 350fr multicolored 1.90 .65
Nos. 481-484 (4) 4.50 1.90

Human Rights Emblem A152

1978, Dec. 10 Litho. *Perf. 12½*

485 A152 55fr multicolored .30 .20

Universal Declaration of Human Rights, 30th anniv.

Nos. 456-461 Overprinted in Silver
a, VAINQUEURS 1950 URUGUAY / 1978 / ARGENTINE
b, VAINQUEURS 1970 BRESIL / 1978 ARGENTINE
c, VAINQUEURS 1966 GRANDE BRETAGNE / 1978 ARGENTINE
d, VAINQUEURS / 1962 BRESIL / 1978 ARGENTINE
e, VAINQUEURS 1954 ALLEMAGNE (RFA) / 1978 ARGENTINE
f, VAINQUEURS 1974 ALLEMAGNE (RFA) / 1978 ARGENTINE

1979, Jan. 4 Litho. *Perf. 13½*

486 A144(a) 55fr multicolored .30 .20
487 A144(b) 65fr multicolored .40 .20
488 A144(c) 125fr multicolored .60 .25
489 A144(d) 200fr multicolored 1.10 .40
490 A144(e) 300fr multicolored 1.60 .65
Nos. 486-490 (5) 4.00 1.70

Souvenir Sheet

491 A144(f) 500fr multicolored 2.50 1.25

Winners, World Soccer Cup Championships 1950-1978.

Radio Station A153

Design: 65fr, Mail plane at airport.

1979, Mar. 30 Litho. *Perf. 12½*

492 A153 55fr multicolored .30 .20
493 A153 65fr multicolored .40 .20

Post and Telecommunications Org., 10th anniv.

Teacher and Pupils, IYC Emblem — A154

1979, Apr. 9 *Perf. 13½*

494 A154 75fr multicolored .40 .20

International Year of the Child.

Telecommunications A155

1979, May 17 Litho. *Perf. 13*

495 A155 70fr multicolored .45 .20

11th Telecommunications Day.

Basketmaker and Upper Volta No. 111 — A156

Design: No. 497, May of Upper Volta, Concorde, truck and UPU emblem.

1979, June 8 Photo.

496 A156 100fr multicolored .65 .35
497 A156 100fr multicolored .65 .35

Philexafrique II, Libreville, Gabon, June 8-17. Nos. 496, 497 each printed in sheets of 10 and 5 labels showing exhibition emblem.

Synodontis Voltae A157

Fresh-water Fish: 50fr, Micralestes comoensis. 85fr, Silurus.

1979, June 10 Litho. *Perf. 12½*

498 A157 20fr multicolored .20 .20
499 A157 50fr multicolored .35 .20
500 A157 85fr multicolored .55 .30
Nos. 498-500 (3) 1.10 .70

Rowland Hill, Train and Upper Volta No. 60 — A158

Sir Rowland Hill (1795-1879), originator of penny postage, Trains and Upper Volta Stamps: 165fr, #59. 200fr, #57. 300fr, #56. 500fr, #55.

1979, June Litho. *Perf. 13½*

501 A158 65fr multicolored .40 .20
502 A158 165fr multicolored 1.10 .55
503 A158 200fr multicolored 1.40 .65
504 A158 300fr multicolored 2.00 1.00
Nos. 501-504 (4) 4.90 2.40

Souvenir Sheet

505 A158 500fr multicolored 3.50 1.60

Wildlife Fund Emblem and Protected Animals — A159

1979, Aug. 30 Litho. *Perf. 14½*

506 A159 30fr Waterbuck .20 .20
507 A159 40fr Roan antelope .25 .20
508 A159 60fr Caracal .40 .20
509 A159 100fr African bush elephant .65 .35
510 A159 175fr Hartebeest 1.25 .55
511 A159 250fr Leopard 1.60 .80
Nos. 506-511 (6) 4.35 2.30

Adult Students and Teacher — A160

Design: 55fr, Man reading book, vert.

1979, Sept. 8 *Perf. 12½x13, 13x12½*

512 A160 55fr multicolored .40 .20
513 A160 250fr multicolored 1.60 .85

World Literacy Day.

Map of Upper Volta, Telephone Receiver and Lines, Telecom Emblem — A161

1979, Sept. 20 *Perf. 13x12½*

514 A161 200fr multicolored 1.40 .65

3rd World Telecommunications Exhibition, Geneva, Sept. 20-26.

King Vulture — A162

1979, Oct. 26 Litho. *Perf. 13*

515 A162 5fr shown .20 .20
516 A162 10fr Hoopoe .20 .20
517 A162 15fr Bald vulture .20 .20
518 A162 25fr Herons .20 .20
519 A162 35fr Ostrich .25 .20
520 A162 45fr Crowned crane .30 .20
521 A162 125fr Eagle .80 .40
Nos. 515-521 (7) 2.15 1.60

Control Tower, Emblem, Jet — A163

1979, Dec. 12 Photo. *Perf. 13x12½*

522 A163 65fr multicolored .45 .20

ASECNA (Air Safety Board), 20th anniv.

Central Bank of West African States — A164

1979, Dec. 28 Litho. *Perf. 12½*

523 A164 55fr multicolored .40 .20

Eugene Jamot, Map of Upper Volta, Tsetse Fly — A165

1979, Dec. 28 *Perf. 13x13½*

524 A165 55fr multicolored .40 .20

Eugene Jamot (1879-1937), discoverer of sleeping sickness cure.

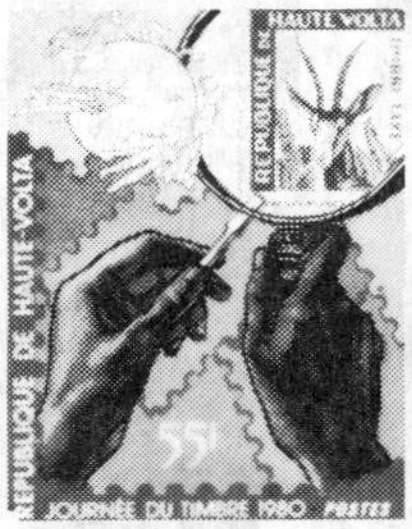

UPU Emblem, Upper Volta Type D4 under Magnifier A166

1980, Feb. 26 Litho. *Perf. 12½x13*

525 A166 55fr multicolored .40 .20

Stamp Day.

World Locomotive Speed Record, 25th Anniversary A167

1980, Mar. 30 Litho. *Perf. 12½*

526 A167 75fr multicolored .50 .25
527 A167 100fr multicolored .65 .35

Pres. Sangoule Lamizana, Pope John Paul II, Cardinal Pau Zoungrana, Map of Upper Volta — A168

1980, May 10 **Litho.** ***Perf. 12½***
528 A168 65fr shown .45 .20

Size: 21x36mm

529 A168 100fr Pope John Paul II .65 .35

Visit of Pope John Paul II to Upper Volta.

A169

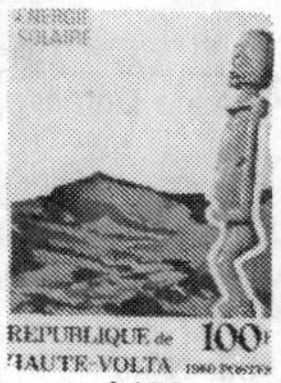
A170

1980, May 17 ***Perf. 13x12½***
530 A169 50fr multicolored .35 .20

12th World Telecommunications Day.

1980, June 12 **Litho.** ***Perf. 13***
531 A170 65fr Sun and earth .45 .20
532 A170 100fr Solar energy .65 .35

Downhill Skiing, Lake Placid '80 Emblem A171

1980, June 26 ***Perf. 14½***
533 A171 65fr shown .35 .20
534 A171 100fr Women's down-hill .50 .30
535 A171 200fr Figure skating 1.25 .50
536 A171 350fr Slalom, vert. 1.90 1.00
Nos. 533-536 (4) 4.00 2.00

Souvenir Sheet

537 A171 500fr Speed skating 3.50 1.60

12th Winter Olympic Game Winners, Lake Placid, NY, Feb. 12-24.

Map of Europe and Africa, Jet — A172

Hand Holding Back Sand Dune — A173

Europafrica Issue

1980, July 14 **Litho.** ***Perf. 13***
538 A172 100fr multicolored .65 .35

1980, July 18

Operation Green Sahel: 55fr, Hands holding seedlings.

539 A173 50fr multicolored .35 .20
540 A173 55fr multicolored .40 .20

Gourmantche Chief Initiation — A174

1980, Sept. 12 **Litho.** ***Perf. 14***
541 A174 30fr shown .20 .20
542 A174 55fr Moro Naba, Mossi Emperor .40 .20
543 A174 65fr Princess Guimbe Quattara, vert. .45 .20
Nos. 541-543 (3) 1.05 .60

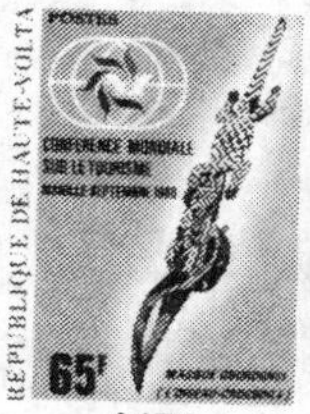
A175

A176

Gourounsi mask, conference emblem.

1980, Oct. 6 ***Perf. 13½x13***
544 A175 65fr multicolored .45 .20

World Tourism Conf., Manila, Sept. 27.

1980, Nov. 5 **Litho.** ***Perf. 12½***
545 A176 55fr Agriculture .40 .20
546 A176 65fr Transportation .45 .20
547 A176 75fr Dam, highway .50 .25
548 A176 100fr Industry .65 .35
Nos. 545-548 (4) 2.00 1.00

West African Economic Council, 5th anniv.

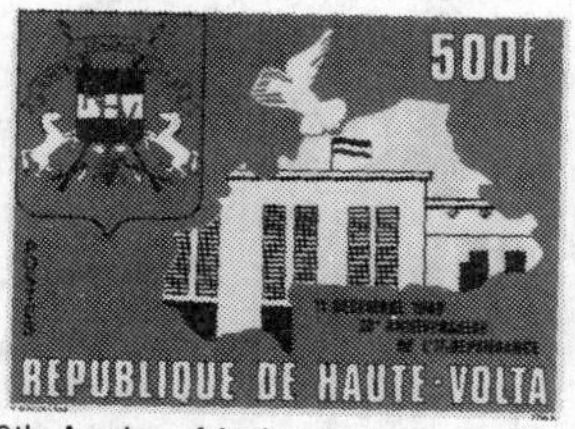
20th Anniv. of Independence — A177

1980, Dec. 11 ***Perf. 13***
549 A177 500fr multicolored 3.50 1.60

Madonna and Child, by Raphael — A178

West African Postal Union, 5th Anniv. — A179

Christmas: Paintings of Madonna and Child, by Raphael.

1980, Dec. 22 ***Perf. 12½***
550 A178 60fr multicolored .40 .20
551 A178 150fr multicolored 1.00 .50
552 A178 250fr multicolored 1.60 .80
Nos. 550-552 (3) 3.00 1.50

1980, Dec. 24 **Photo.** ***Perf. 13½***
553 A179 55fr multicolored .40 .20

Dung Beetle A180

Perf. 13x13½, 13½x13

1981, Mar. 10 **Litho.**
554 A180 5fr shown .20 .20
555 A180 10fr Crickets .20 .20
556 A180 15fr Termites .20 .20
557 A180 20fr Praying mantis, vert. .20 .20
558 A180 55fr Emperor moth .40 .25
559 A180 65fr Locust, vert. .45 .25
Nos. 554-559 (6) 1.65 1.30

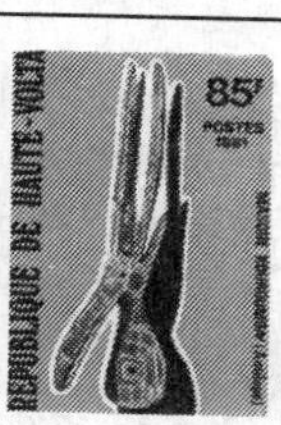
Antelope Mask, Kouroumba — A181

Designs: Various ceremonial masks.

1981, Mar. 20 **Litho.** ***Perf. 13***
560 A181 45fr multicolored .25 .20
561 A181 55fr multicolored .30 .20
562 A181 85fr multicolored .50 .25
563 A181 105fr multicolored .60 .35
Nos. 560-563 (4) 1.65 1.00

Notre Dame of Kologh' Naba College, 25th Anniv. A182

1981, Mar. 30
564 A182 55fr multicolored .30 .20

Heinrich von Stephan, UPU Founder, Birth Sesquicentennial — A183

1981, May 4 **Litho.** ***Perf. 13***
565 A183 65fr multicolored .35 .20

13th World Telecommunications Day — A184

1981, May 17 ***Perf. 13½x13***
566 A184 90fr multicolored .50 .25

Diesel Train, Abidjan-Niger Railroad A185

Designs: Trains.

1981, July 6 **Litho.** ***Perf. 13***
567 A185 25fr shown .20 .20
568 A185 30fr Gazelle .20 .20
569 A185 40fr Belier .25 .20
Nos. 567-569 (3) .65 .60

Tree Planting Month — A186

1981, July 15
570 A186 70fr multicolored .45 .25

Natl. Red Cross, 20th Anniv. A187

1981, July 31 ***Perf. 12½x13***
571 A187 70fr multicolored .45 .25

Intl. Year of the Disabled — A188

1981, Aug. 20 **Litho.** ***Perf. 13x12½***
572 A188 70fr multicolored .45 .25

View of Koudougou A189

1981, Sept. 3 **Litho.** ***Perf. 12½***
573 A189 35fr shown .25 .20
574 A189 45fr Toma .30 .20
575 A189 85fr Volta Noire .55 .30
Nos. 573-575 (3) 1.10 .70

World Food Day A190

1981, Oct. 16 ***Perf. 13***
576 A190 90fr multicolored .60 .30

Elephant A191

Designs: Various protected species.

1981, Oct. 21 **Photo.** ***Perf. 14***
577 A191 5fr multicolored .20 .20
578 A191 15fr multicolored .20 .20
579 A191 40fr multicolored .25 .20
580 A191 60fr multicolored .40 .20
581 A191 70fr multicolored .45 .20
Nos. 577-581 (5) 1.50 1.00

Fight Against Apartheid A192

Mangoes A193

1981, Dec. 9 **Litho.** ***Perf. 12½***
582 A192 90fr red orange .60 .30

Perf. 13x13½, 13½x13

1981, Dec. 15
583 A193 20fr Papayas, horiz. .20 .20
584 A193 35fr Fruits, vegetables, horiz. .25 .20
585 A193 75fr shown .50 .25
586 A193 90fr Melons, horiz. .60 .35
Nos. 583-586 (4) 1.55 1.00

Guinea Hen — A194

West African Rice Development Assoc., 10th Anniv. — A195

Designs: Breeding animals. 10fr, 25fr, 70fr, 250fr, 300fr horiz.

1981, Dec. 22 *Perf. 13*

587 A194 10fr Donkey .20 .20
588 A194 25fr Pig .20 .20
589 A194 70fr Cow .45 .25
590 A194 90fr shown .55 .30
591 A194 250fr Rabbit 1.60 .80
Nos. 587-591 (5) 3.00 1.75

Souvenir Sheet

592 A194 300fr Sheep 2.00 1.00

1981, Dec. 29

593 A195 90fr multicolored .60 .30

20th Anniv. of World Food Program — A196

1982, Jan. 18

594 A196 50fr multicolored .35 .20

Traditional Houses — A197

1982, Apr. 23 **Litho.** *Perf. 12½*

595 A197 30fr Morhonaba Palace, vert. .20 .20
596 A197 70fr Bobo .45 .25
597 A197 100fr Gourounsi .65 .35
598 A197 200fr Peulh 1.40 .65
599 A197 250fr Dagari 1.60 .80
Nos. 595-599 (5) 4.30 2.25

14th World Telecommunications Day — A198

1982, May 17

600 A198 125fr multicolored .85 .40

Water Lily — A199

25th Anniv. of Cultural Aid Fund — A201

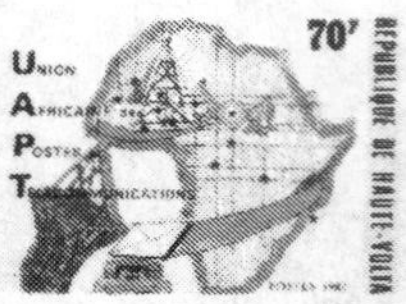

African Postal Union A200

1982, Sept. 22 *Perf. 13x12½*

601 A199 25fr shown .20 .20
602 A199 40fr Kapoks .20 .20
603 A199 70fr Frangipani .35 .20
604 A199 90fr Cochlospermum planchonii .60 .25
605 A199 100fr Cotton .50 .25
Nos. 601-605 (5) 1.85 1.10

1982, Oct. 7

606 A200 70fr multicolored .45 .25
607 A200 90fr multicolored .60 .30

1982, Nov. 10 *Perf. 12½x13*

608 A201 70fr multicolored .45 .25

Map, Hand Holding Grain, Steer Head A202

1982 *Perf. 12½*

609 A202 90fr multicolored .60 .30

Traditional Hairstyle A203

1983, Jan. **Litho.** *Perf. 12½*

610 A203 90fr lt green & multi .50 .25
611 A203 120fr lt blue & multi .70 .35
612 A203 170fr pink & multi .95 .50
Nos. 610-612 (3) 2.15 1.10

For overprints see Nos. 884-886.

8th Film Festival, Ouagadougou — A204

1983, Feb. 10 **Litho.** *Perf. 13x12½*

613 A204 90fr Scene .60 .30
614 A204 500fr Filmmaker Dumarou Ganda 3.50 1.60

UN Intl. Drinking Water and Sanitation Decade, 1981-90 — A205

1983, Apr. 21 **Litho.** *Perf. 13½x13*

615 A205 60fr Water drops .40 .20
616 A205 70fr Carrying water .45 .25

Manned Flight Bicentenary A206

Portraits and Balloons: 15fr, J.M. Montgolfier, 1783. 25fr, Etienne Montgolfier's balloon, 1783, Pilatre de Rozier. 70fr, Charles & Roberts flight, 1783, Jacques Charles. 90fr, Flight over English Channel, John Jeffries. 100fr, Testu-Brissy's horseback flight, Wilhemine Reichardt. 250fr, Andree's Spitzbergen flight, 1897, S.A. Andree. 300fr, Piccard's stratosphere flight, 1931, August Piccard.

1983, Apr. 15 **Litho.** *Perf. 13½*

617 A206 15fr multicolored .20 .20
618 A206 25fr multicolored .20 .20
619 A206 70fr multicolored .45 .25
620 A206 90fr multicolored .60 .30
621 A206 100fr multicolored .65 .35
622 A206 250fr multicolored 1.60 .80
Nos. 617-622 (6) 3.70 2.10

Souvenir Sheet

623 A206 300fr multicolored 2.00 1.00

No. 623 contains one stamp 38x47mm. Nos. 621-623 airmail.

World Communications Year — A207

1983, May 26 **Litho.** *Perf. 12½*

624 A207 30fr Man reading letter .20 .20
625 A207 35fr Like No. 624 .20 .20
626 A207 45fr Aircraft over stream .25 .20
627 A207 90fr Girl on telephone .50 .25
Nos. 624-627 (4) 1.15 .85

Fishing Resources A208

1983, July 28 **Litho.** *Perf. 13*

628 A208 20fr Synadontis gambiensis .20 .20
629 A208 30fr Palmotochromis .20 .20
630 A208 40fr Boy fishing, vert. .20 .20
631 A208 50fr Fishing with net .20 .20
632 A208 75fr Fishing with basket .20 .20
Nos. 628-632 (5) 1.00 1.00

Anti-deforestation — A209

1983, Sept. 13 **Litho.** *Perf. 13*

633 A209 10fr Planting saplings .20 .20
634 A209 50fr Tree nursery .20 .20
635 A209 100fr Prevent forest fires .35 .20
636 A209 150fr Woman cooking .50 .25
637 A209 200fr Prevent felling, vert. .65 .35
Nos. 633-637 (5) 1.90 1.20

Fresco Detail, by Raphael — A210

Paintings: 120fr, Self-portrait, by Pablo Picasso, 1901, vert. 185fr, Self-portrait at the palette, by Manet, 1878, vert. 350fr, Fresco Detail, diff., by Raphael. 500fr, Goethe, by George Oswald May, 1779, vert.

1983, Nov. **Litho.** *Perf. 13*

638 A210 120fr multicolored .40 .20
639 A210 185fr multicolored .60 .30
640 A210 300fr multicolored 1.00 .50
641 A210 350fr multicolored 1.25 .60
642 A210 500fr multicolored 1.60 .80
Nos. 638-642 (5) 4.85 2.40

25th Anniv. of the Republic A211

1983, Dec. 9 **Litho.** *Perf. 14*

643 A211 90fr Arms .30 .20
644 A211 500fr Family, flag 1.60 .80

A212

Scouting — A213

1984, May 29 **Litho.** *Perf. 12½*

645 A212 90fr multicolored .30 .20
646 A212 100fr multicolored .35 .20

Council of Unity, 25th anniv.

1984, June 15 **Litho.** *Perf. 13½*

647 A213 25fr Polystictus leoninus .20 .20
648 A213 185fr Pterocarpus Lucens .85 .45
649 A213 200fr Phlebopus colossus sudanicus 1.10 .50
650 A213 250fr Cosmos sulphureus 1.25 .60
651 A213 300fr Trametes versicolor 1.50 .80
652 A213 400fr Ganoderma lucidum 2.00 1.10
Nos. 647-652 (6) 6.90 3.65

Souvenir Sheet

653 A213 600fr Leucocoprinus cepaestipes 3.25 1.60

Nos. 651-653 are airmail. For overprints see Nos. 669-674.

Wildlife A214

Wildlife — A215

1984, July 19

654 A214 15fr Cheetah, four cubs .20 .20
655 A214 35fr Two adults .20 .20
656 A214 90fr One adult .35 .20
657 A214 120fr Cheetah, two cubs .50 .25
658 A214 300fr Baboons 1.25 .55
659 A214 400fr Vultures 1.50 .80
Nos. 654-659 (6) 4.00 2.20

Souvenir Sheet

660 A215 1000fr Antelopes 4.00 1.90

World Wildlife Fund (Nos. 654-567); Rotary Intl. (Nos. 658, 660); Natl. Boy Scouts (No. 659). Nos. 658-660 are airmail.

Sailing Ships and Locomotives — A216

1984, Aug. 14 ***Perf. 12½***

661 A216 20fr Maiden Queen .20 .20
662 A216 40fr CC 2400 ch .20 .20
663 A216 60fr Scawfell .25 .20
664 A216 100fr PO 1806 .40 .20
665 A216 120fr Harbinger .45 .25
666 A216 145fr Livingstone .55 .30
667 A216 400fr True Briton 1.50 .80
668 A216 450fr Pacific C51 1.60 .85
Nos. 661-668 (8) 5.15 3.00

Burkina Faso

Natl. Defense — A216a

Design: 120fr, Capt. Sankara, crowd, horiz.

1984, Nov. 21 Litho. ***Perf. 13½***

668A A216a 90fr multicolored
668B A216a 120fr multicolored

Nos. 647-652 Ovptd. with Two Bars and "BURKINA FASO"

1985, Mar. 5 Litho. ***Perf. 13½***

669 A213 25fr multicolored .20 .20
670 A213 185fr multicolored .55 .25
671 A213 200fr multicolored .60 .30
672 A213 250fr multicolored .75 .40
673 A213 300fr multicolored .90 .45
674 A213 400fr multicolored 1.25 .60
Nos. 669-674 (6) 4.25 2.20

A217

Designs: 5fr, 120fr, Flag. 15fr, 150fr, Natl. Arms, vert. 90fr, 185fr, Map.

1985, Mar. 8 Litho. ***Perf. 12½***

675 A217 5fr multicolored
676 A217 15fr multicolored
677 A217 90fr multicolored
678 A217 120fr multicolored
679 A217 150fr multicolored
680 A217 185fr multicolored

Nos. 678-680 are airmail.

1986 World Cup Soccer Championships, Mexico — A218

A219

Various soccer plays and Aztec artifacts.

1985, Apr. 20 Litho. ***Perf. 13***

681 A218 25fr multicolored .20 .20
682 A218 45fr multicolored .20 .20
683 A218 90fr multicolored .35 .20
684 A218 100fr multicolored .40 .20
685 A218 150fr multicolored .55 .25
686 A218 200fr multicolored .70 .40
687 A218 250fr multicolored .90 .45
Nos. 681-687 (7) 3.30 1.90

Souvenir Sheet

688 A219 500fr multicolored 1.90 1.25

Nos. 681-685 vert. No. 684-688 are airmail.

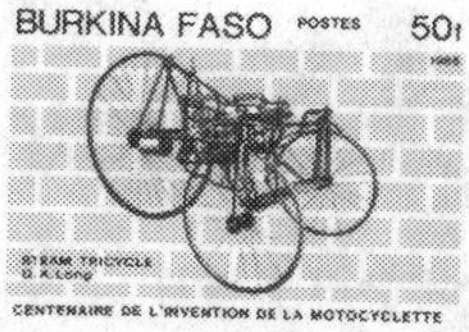

Motorcycle, Cent. — A220

1985, May 26

689 A220 50fr Steam tricycle, G.A. Long .20 .20
690 A220 75fr Pope .25 .20
691 A220 80fr Manet-90 .30 .20
692 A220 100fr Ducati .40 .20
693 A220 150fr Jawa .55 .30
694 A220 200fr Honda .70 .40
695 A220 250fr B.M.W. .90 .50
Nos. 689-695 (7) 3.30 2.00

Nos. 692-695 are airmail.

Reptiles A221

1985, June 20

696 A221 5fr Chamaeleon dilepis .20 .20
697 A221 15fr Agama stellio .20 .20
698 A221 35fr Lacerta Lepida .20 .20
699 A221 85fr Hiperolius marmoratus .30 .20
700 A221 100fr Echis leucogaster .40 .20
701 A221 150fr Kinixys erosa .55 .30
702 A221 250fr Python regius .90 .45
Nos. 696-702 (7) 2.75 1.75

#696-697 vert. #700-702 are airmail.

A222

Queen Mother, 85th Birthday A222a

1985, June 21 ***Perf. 13½***

703 A222 75fr On pony bobs .25 .20
704 A222 85fr Wedding, 1923 .25 .20
705 A222 500fr Holding infant Elizabeth, 1926 1.60 .80
706 A222 600fr Coronation of King George VI, 1937 1.90 .90
Nos. 703-706 (4) 4.00 2.10

Litho. & Embossed

Perf. 13¼

706A A222a 1500fr gold & multi

Souvenir Sheet

707 A222 1000fr Christening of Prince William, 1982 3.25 1.60

Nos. 705-707 are airmail.

Vintage Autos and Aircraft — A223

1985, June 21

708 A223 5fr Benz Victoria, 1893 .20 .20
709 A223 25fr Peugeot 174, 1927 .20 .20
710 A223 45fr Louis Bleriot .20 .20
711 A223 50fr Breguet 14 .20 .20
712 A223 500fr Bugatti Coupe Napoleon T41 Royale 1.90 .90
713 A223 500fr Airbus A300-P4 1.90 .90
714 A223 600fr Mercedes-Benz 540K, 1938 2.25 1.25
715 A223 600fr Airbus A300B 2.25 1.25
Nos. 708-715 (8) 9.10 5.10

Souvenir Sheet

716 A223 1000fr Louis Bleriot, Karl Benz 4.00 1.90

Automobile, cent. Nos. 712-716 are airmail.

Audubon Birth Bicent. A224

Illustrations of No. American bird species by Audubon and scouting trefoil.

1985, June 21

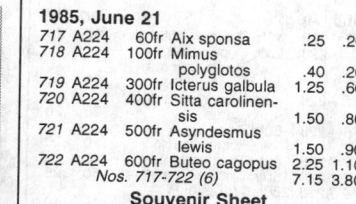

717 A224 60fr Aix sponsa .25 .20
718 A224 100fr Mimus polyglotos .40 .20
719 A224 300fr Icterus galbula 1.25 .60
720 A224 400fr Sitta carolinensis 1.50 .80
721 A224 500fr Asyndesmus lewis 1.50 .90
722 A224 600fr Buteo cagopus 2.25 1.10
Nos. 717-722 (6) 7.15 3.80

Souvenir Sheet

723 A224 1000fr Columba leucocephala 4.00 1.90

Nos. 721-723 are airmail.

ARGENTINA '85, Buenos Aires — A225

Various equestrians.

1985, July 5 ***Perf. 13***

724 A225 25fr Gaucho, piebald .20 .20
725 A225 45fr Horse and rider, Andes Mountains .20 .20
726 A225 90fr Rodeo .30 .20
727 A225 100fr Hunting gazelle .40 .20
728 A225 150fr Gauchos, 3 horses .55 .25
729 A225 200fr Rider beside mount .70 .35
730 A225 250fr Contest .90 .40
Nos. 724-730 (7) 3.25 1.80

Souvenir Sheet

731 A225 500fr Foal 1.90 .70

Nos. 727-731 are airmail.

Locomotives — A226

1985, July 23

732 A226 50fr 105-30 electric, tank wagon .20 .20
733 A226 75fr Diesel shunting locomotive .25 .20
734 A226 80fr Diesel locomotive .25 .20
735 A226 100fr Diesel railcar .35 .20
736 A226 150fr No. 6093 .50 .25
737 A226 200fr No. 105 diesel railcar .60 .35
738 A226 250fr Diesel, passenger car .75 .40
Nos. 732-738 (7) 2.90 1.80

Nos. 735-738 are airmail.

Artifacts — A227

Fungi — A228

1985, July 27 ***Perf. 13x12½***

739 A227 10fr 4-legged jar, Tikare .20 .20
740 A227 40fr Lidded pot with bird handles, P. Bazega .20 .20
741 A227 90fr Mother and child, bronze statue, Ouagadougou .35 .20
742 A227 120fr Drummer, bronze statue, Ouagadougou .40 .20
Nos. 739-742 (4) 1.15 .80

No. 742 is airmail.

1985, Aug. 8 *Perf. 13*

743 A228 15fr Philiota mutabilis .20 .20
744 A228 20fr Hypholoma (nematoloma) fasciculare .20 .20
745 A228 30fr Ixocomus granulatus .20 .20
746 A228 60fr Agaricus campestris .20 .20
747 A228 80fr Trachypus scaber .30 .20
748 A228 150fr Armillaria mellea .50 .25
749 A228 250fr Marasmius scorodonius .75 .40
Nos. 743-749 (7) 2.35 1.65

Nos. 748 is airmail.

ITALIA '85 — A228a

Paintings by Botticelli: 25fr, Virgin and Child. 45fr, Portrait of a Man. 90fr, Mars and Venus. 100fr, Birth of Venus. 150fr, Allegory of the Calumny. 200fr, Pallas and the Centaur. 250fr, Allegory of Spring. 500fr, The Virgin of Melagrana.

1985, Oct. 25 Litho. *Perf. 12½x13*

749A A228a 25fr multicolored .20 .20
749B A228a 45fr multicolored .25 .20
749C A228a 90fr multicolored .45 .25
749D A228a 100fr multicolored .50 .25
749E A228a 150fr multicolored .70 .40
749F A228a 200fr multicolored 1.00 .50
749G A228a 250fr multicolored 1.25 .60
Nos. 749A-749G (7) 4.35 2.40

Souvenir Sheet

749H A228a 500fr multicolored 2.50 1.25

No. 749D-749H are airmail.

Intl. Red Cross in Burkina Faso, 75th Anniv. A229

1985, Nov. 10

750 A229 40f Helicopter .20 .20
751 A229 85fr Ambulance .30 .20
752 A229 150fr Henri Dunant .60 .25
753 A229 250fr Physician, patient .90 .35
Nos. 750-753 (4) 2.00 1.00

Nos. 752-753 are vert. and airmail.

Child Survival — A230

1986, Jan. 6

754 A230 90fr Breast-feeding .50 .25

Dated 1985.

Dodo Carnival — A231

1986, Jan. 6 *Perf. 12½*

755 A231 20fr Three children, drummer .20 .20
756 A231 25fr Lion, 4 dancers .20 .20
757 A231 40fr Two dancers, two drummers .25 .20
758 A231 45fr Three dancers .25 .20
759 A231 90fr Zebra, ostrich, dancers .50 .25
760 A231 90fr Elephant, dancer .50 .25
Nos. 755-760 (6) 1.90 1.30

Dated 1985.

Christopher Columbus (1451-1506) — A232

Columbus: 250fr, At Court of King of Portugal, the Nina. 300fr, Using astrolable, the Santa Maria. 400fr, Imprisonment at Hispanola, 1500, the Santa Maria. 450fr, At San Salvador, 1492, the Pinta. 1000fr, Fleet departing Palos harbor, 1492.

1986, Feb. 10 *Perf. 13½*

761 A232 250fr multicolored 1.40 .70
762 A232 300fr multicolored 1.60 .80
763 A232 400fr multicolored 2.25 1.10
764 A232 450fr multicolored 2.50 1.25
Nos. 761-764 (4) 7.75 3.85

Souvenir Sheet

765 A232 1000fr multicolored 5.50 2.75

Nos. 764-765 are airmail. Dated 1985.

Railroad Construction — A233

1986, Feb. 10

766 A233 90fr Man, woman carrying rail .50 .25
767 A233 120fr Laying rails .65 .30
768 A233 185fr Diesel train on new tracks 1.00 .50
769 A233 500fr Adler locomotive, 1835 2.75 1.40
Nos. 766-769 (4) 4.90 2.45

Souvenir Sheet

770 A233 1000fr Electric train, Series 290 diesel 5.00 2.75

German Railways, sesquicentennial. Nos. 769-770 are airmail. Dated 1985.

Intl. Peace Year — A234

World Health by the Year 2000 — A235

1986, Oct. 10 Photo. *Perf. 12½x13*

771 A234 90fr blue 1.10 .55

1986, Aug. 8 Litho. *Perf. 13*

Designs: 100fr, Primary care medicine. 150fr, Mass inoculations.

772 A235 90fr multicolored .65 .30

Size: 26x30mm

Perf. 12½x13

773 A235 100fr multicolored .70 .30
774 A235 120fr multicolored .85 .40
Nos. 772-774 (3) 2.20 1.00

Insects — A236

World Post Day — A237

1986, Sept. 10 Litho. *Perf. 12½x13*

775 A236 15fr Phryneta aurocinta .20 .20
776 A236 20fr Sternocera interrupta .20 .20
777 A236 40fr Prosoprocera lactator .35 .20
778 A236 45fr Gonimbrasia hecate .40 .20
778A A236 85fr Charaxes epijasius .80 .35
Nos. 775-778A (5) 1.95 1.15

1986, Oct. 9 *Perf. 13*

779 A237 120fr multicolored .70 .35

UN Child Survival Campaign — A238

Designs: 30fr, Mother feeding child. 60fr, Adding medicines to food. 90fr, Nurse vaccinating child.

1986, Oct. 8 Litho. *Perf. 11½x12*

780 A238 30fr multicolored
781 A238 60fr multicolored
782 A238 90fr multicolored

No. 783 has been reserved for a 120fr stamp.

Mammals A239

Designs: 50fr, Warthog. 65fr, Hyena. 90fr, Antelope. 100fr, Gazelle. 120fr, Bushbuck. 145fr, Kudu. 500fr, Gazelle, diff.

1986, Nov. 3 Litho. *Perf. 13x12½*

784 A239 50fr multicolored
784A A239 65fr multicolored
784B A239 90fr multicolored
784C A239 100fr multicolored
784D A239 120fr multicolored
784E A239 145fr multicolored
784F A239 500fr multicolored

Traditional Dances — A240

Designs: 10fr, Namende. 25fr, Mouhoun. 90fr, Houet. 105fr, Seno. 120fr, Ganzourgou.

1986, Nov. 3 Litho. *Perf. 12½x13*

785 A240 10fr multicolored
785A A240 25fr multicolored
785B A240 90fr multicolored
785C A240 105fr multicolored
785D A240 120fr multicolored

Hairstyles A241

1986, Nov. 4 Litho. *Perf. 12½x13*

788 A241 35fr Peul .30 .20
789 A241 75fr Dafing .55 .30
790 A241 90fr Peul, diff. .70 .35
791 A241 120fr Mossi .95 .50
792 A241 185fr Peul, diff. 1.50 .75
Nos. 788-792 (5) 4.00 2.10

10th African Film Festival — A242

Intl Women's Day — A243

1987, Feb. 21 Litho. *Perf. 12x12½*

793 A242 90fr Maps, cameras
794 A242 120fr Jolson, cameramen
795 A242 185fr Charlie Chaplin

60th Anniv. of the film *The Jazz Singer* (120fr); 10th anniv. of the death of Charlie Chaplin (185fr).

1987, Mar. 8 *Perf. 13½*

796 A243 90fr multicolored

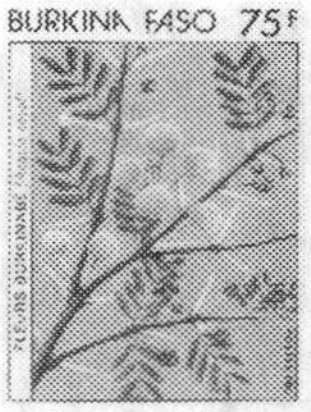

Flora — A244

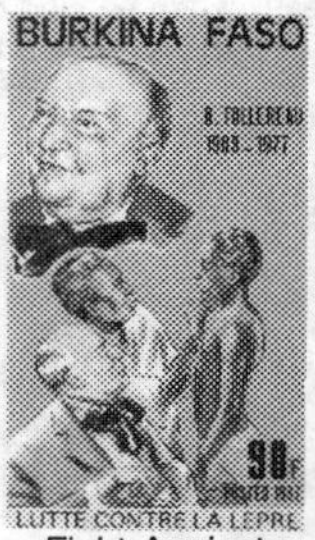

Fight Against Leprosy — A245

1987, June 6 Litho. *Perf. 12½x13*

797 A244 70fr Calotropis procera .50 .25
798 A244 75fr Acacia seyal .55 .25
799 A244 85fr Parkia biglobosa .60 .30
800 A244 90fr Sterospernum kunthianum .65 .30
801 A244 100fr Dichrostachys cinerea .70 .35
802 A244 300fr Combretum paniculatum 2.10 1.00
Nos. 797-802 (6) 5.10 2.45

1987, Aug. 6 *Perf. 13*

Raoul Follereau (1903-1977) and: 90fr, Doctors examining African youth. 100fr, Laboratory research. 120fr, Gerhard Hansen (1841-1912), microscope, bacillus under magnification. 300fr, Follereau embracing cured leper.

803 A245 90fr multicolored .60 .30
804 A245 100fr multicolored .70 .35
805 A245 120fr multicolored .85 .40
806 A245 300fr multicolored 2.10 1.00
Nos. 803-806 (4) 4.25 2.05

World Environment Day — A246

1987, Aug. 18 Litho. *Perf. 13x12½*

807 A246 90fr shown .70 .35
808 A246 145fr Emblem, huts 1.10 .55

Pre-Olympic Year — A247

1987, Aug. 31 *Perf. 12½*

809 A247 75fr High jump .55 .30
810 A247 85fr Tennis, vert. .60 .30
811 A247 90fr Ski jumping .70 .35
812 A247 100fr Soccer .75 .40
813 A247 145fr Running 1.10 .55
814 A247 350fr Pierre de Coubertin, tennis, vert. 2.60 1.25
Nos. 809-814 (6) 6.30 3.15

Pierre de Coubertin (1863-1937).

World Post Day — A248

1987, Oct. 5 Litho. *Perf. 12½x13*

815 A248 90fr multicolored

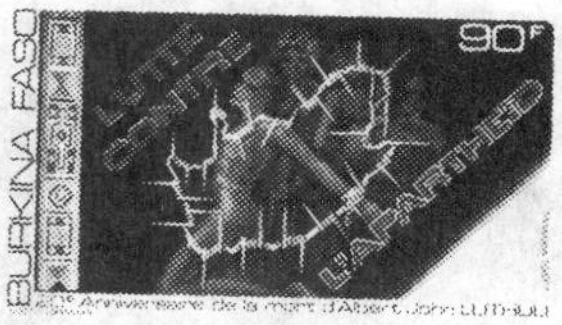

Fight Against Apartheid — A249

1987, Nov. 11 Litho. *Perf. 13*

816 A249 90fr shown 1.00 .50
817 A249 100fr Luthuli, book, 1962 1.10 .55

Albert John Luthuli (1898-1967), South African reformer, author and 1960 Nobel Peace Prize winner. No. 817 incorrectly inscribed "1899-1967."

Traditional Costumes — A250

1987, Dec. 4 Litho. *Perf. 11½x12*

818 A250 10fr Dagari
819 A250 30fr Peul
820 A250 90fr Mossi
821 A250 200fr Senoufo

No. 822 has been reserved for a 500fr stamp.

Traditional Musical Instruments A251

Perf. 12x11½, 11½x12

1987, Dec. 4 Litho.

823 A251 20fr Xylophone .20 .20
824 A251 25fr 3-Stringed lute, vert. .25 .20
825 A251 35fr Zither .30 .20
826 A251 90fr Conical drum .80 .40
827 A251 1000fr Calabash drum, vert. 8.50 4.25
Nos. 823-827 (5) 10.05 5.25

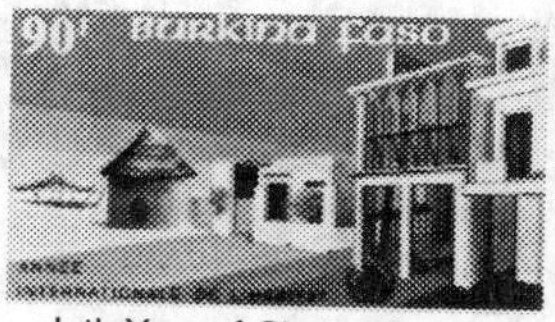

Intl. Year of Shelter for the Homeless — A252

1987, Dec. 4 Litho. *Perf. 13*

828 A252 90fr multicolored .65 .30

Five-year Natl. Development Plan — A253

1987, Dec. 15 *Perf. 13½*

829 A253 40fr Small businesses .30 .20
830 A253 55fr Agriculture .40 .20
831 A253 60fr Constructing schools .45 .25
832 A253 90fr Transportation and communications .65 .30
833 A253 100fr Literacy .75 .35
834 A253 120fr Animal husbandry .90 .45
Nos. 829-834 (6) 3.45 1.75

World Health Organization, 40th Anniv. — A254

1988, Mar. 31 Litho. *Perf. 12½x13*

835 A254 120fr multicolored .80 .40

1988 Summer Olympics, Seoul A255

1988, May 5 *Perf. 13x12½*

836 A255 30fr shown .20 .20
837 A255 160fr Torch, vert. 1.10 .50
838 A255 175fr Soccer 1.25 .60
839 A255 235fr Volleyball, vert. 1.50 .75
840 A255 450fr Basketball, vert. 2.90 1.50
Nos. 836-840 (5) 6.95 3.55

Souvenir Sheet

Perf. 12½x13

841 A255 500fr Runners 3.25 1.60

No. 841 contains one stamp, size: 40x52mm plus two labels.

Ritual Masks A256

1988, May 30 Litho. *Perf. 13*

842 A256 10fr Epervier, Houet .20 .20
843 A256 20fr Jeunes Filles, Oullo .20 .20
844 A256 30fr Bubale, Houet .20 .20
845 A256 40fr Forgeron, Mouhoun .30 .20
846 A256 120fr Nounouma, Ouri .80 .40
847 A256 175fr Chauve-souris, Ouri 1.25 .60
Nos. 842-847 (6) 2.95 1.80

Nos. 842-846 vert.

Handicrafts A257

1988, Aug. 22 Litho. *Perf. 13½*

848 A257 5fr Kieriebe ceramic pitcher, vert. .20 .20
849 A257 15fr Mossi basket .20 .20
850 A257 25fr Gurunsi chair .20 .20
851 A257 30fr Bissa basket .20 .20
852 A257 45fr Ougadougou leather box .35 .20
853 A257 85fr Ougadougou bronze statue, vert. .70 .35
854 A257 120fr Ougadougou leather valise .80 .40
Nos. 848-854 (7) 2.65 1.75

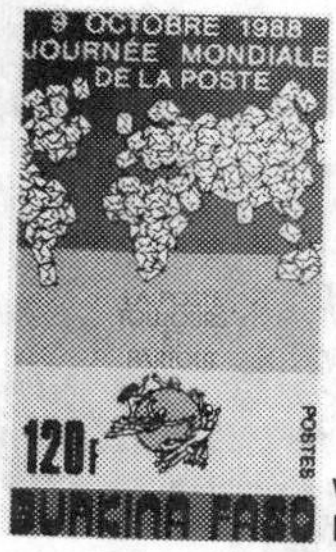

World Post Day — A258

1988, Oct. 9 Litho. *Perf. 13*

855 A258 120fr multicolored .80 .40

Aquatic Fauna — A259

1988, Oct. 31 *Perf. 12*

856 A259 70fr Angler martin .50 .25
857 A259 100fr Mormyrus rume .70 .35
858 A259 120fr Frog .80 .40
859 A259 160fr Duck 1.10 .55
Nos. 856-859 (4) 3.10 1.55

Civil Rights and Political Activists A260

Designs: 80fr, Mohammed Ali Jinnah (1876-1948), 1st Governor General of Pakistan. 120fr, Mahatma Gandhi (1869-1948), India. 160fr, John F. Kennedy. 235fr, Martin Luther King, Jr.

1988, Nov. 22 Litho. *Perf. 14*

860 A260 80fr multicolored .50 .25
861 A260 120fr multicolored .80 .40
862 A260 160fr multicolored 1.00 .50
863 A260 235fr multicolored 1.50 .75
Nos. 860-863 (4) 3.80 1.90

A261

A262

Christmas: Stained-glass windows.

1988, Dec. 2 *Perf. 12*

864 A261 120fr Adoration of the shepherds .80 .40
865 A261 160fr Adoration of the Magi 1.00 .50
866 A261 450fr Madonna and child 2.90 1.50
867 A261 1000fr Flight into Egypt 6.25 3.25
Nos. 864-867 (4) 10.95 5.65

1989, Feb. 25 Litho. *Perf. 14*

868 A262 75fr shown .20 .20
869 A262 500fr Ababacar Makharam 1.60 .80
870 A262 500fr Jean Tchissoukou 1.60 .80
871 A262 500fr Paulin Vieyra 1.60 .80
Nos. 868-871 (4) 5.00 2.60

Souvenir Sheet

872 Sheet of 3 9.00 4.50
a.-c. A262 500fr like #869-871, inscribed in gold 3.00 1.50

Panafrican Film Festival (FESPACO), 20th anniv. Nos. 869-872 are airmail.

World Fight Against AIDS A263

1989, Apr. 7 Litho. *Perf. 13*

873 A263 120fr multicolored .80 .40

Council for Rural Development, 30th Anniv. — A264

1989, May 3 Litho. *Perf. 15x14*

874 A264 75fr multicolored .50 .25

Parasitic Plants — A265

Legumes and cereals.

1989, Oct. 9 Litho. *Perf. 11½*

Granite Paper

875 A265 20fr *Striga generiodes* .20 .20
876 A265 50fr *Striga hermonthica* .30 .20
877 A265 235fr *Striga aspera* 1.50 .80
878 A265 450fr *Alectra vogelii* 3.00 1.50
Nos. 875-878 (4) 5.00 2.70

Dogs A266

1989, Oct. 9 *Perf. 15x14½*

879 A266 35fr Sahel .25 .20
880 A266 50fr Puppy .35 .20
881 A266 60fr Hunting dog .40 .20
882 A266 350fr Guard dog 2.25 1.10
Nos. 879-882 (4) 3.25 1.70

Solidarity with the Palestinian People — A267

1989, Nov. 15 *Perf. 13*
883 A267 120fr Monument, Place de la Palestine .80 .40

Nos. 610-612 Overprinted

BURKINA FASO

1988, Dec. 21 Litho. *Perf. 12½*
884 A203 90fr multicolored .60 .30
885 A203 120fr multicolored .85 .40
886 A203 170fr multicolored 1.25 .60
Nos. 884-886 (3) 2.70 1.30

Visit of Pope John Paul II A268

1990, Jan. 1 Litho. *Perf. 15x14*
887 A268 120fr Our Lady of Yagma .85 .40
888 A269 160fr Pope, crowd 1.25 .60

150th Anniv. of the Postage Stamp A269

1990, Mar. 20 Litho. *Perf. 15x14*
889 A269 120fr multicolored 1.00 .50

Souvenir Sheet

Perf. 14x15

890 A269 500fr Penny Black, ship 4.00 2.00

Stamp World London '90.

World Cup Soccer Championships, Italy — A270

1990, Apr. 26 Litho. *Perf. 11½*
891 A270 30fr multicolored .25 .20
892 A270 150fr multi, diff. 1.10 .55

Souvenir Sheet

893 A270 1000fr multi, horiz. 7.25 3.75

Intl. Literacy Year — A271

1990, July 10 Litho. *Perf. 13*
894 A271 40fr multicolored .30 .20
895 A271 130fr multicolored .90 .45

Mushrooms — A272

1990, May 17 Litho. *Perf. 11½*
896 A272 10fr Cantharellus cibarius .20 .20
897 A272 15fr Psalliota bispora .20 .20
898 A272 60fr Amanita caesarea .50 .25
899 A272 190fr Boletus badius 1.50 .75
a. Souv. sheet of 4, #896-899 2.25 1.10
Nos. 896-899 (4) 2.40 1.40

Intl. Exposition of Handicrafts — A273

1990, Sept. 25 Litho. *Perf. 13*
900 A273 35fr Masks, fans, vert. .30 .20
901 A273 45fr shown .40 .20
902 A273 270fr Rattan chair, vert. 2.50 1.25
Nos. 900-902 (3) 3.20 1.65

Gen. Charles de Gaulle (1890-1970) A274

1990, Nov. 22 Litho. *Perf. 13*
903 A274 200fr multicolored 1.75 .90

Minerals A275

1991, Feb. 4 Litho. *Perf. 15x14*
904 A275 20fr Quartz .20 .20
905 A275 50fr Granite .40 .20
906 A275 280fr Amphibolite 2.25 1.10
Nos. 904-906 (3) 2.85 1.50

African Film Festival A276

Fight Against Drugs A277

1991, Feb. 20 *Perf. 11½*
907 A276 150fr multicolored 1.25 .60

Souvenir Sheet

908 A276 1000fr Award 8.00 4.00

1991, Feb. 20
909 A277 130fr multicolored 1.00 .55

Samuel F.B. Morse (1791-1872), Inventor — A278

1991, May 17 Litho. *Perf. 13*
910 A278 200fr multicolored 1.60 .80

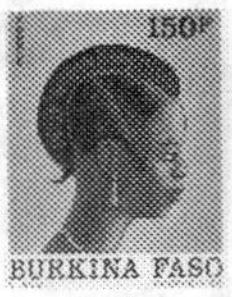

Native Girl — A279

Flowers — A280

1991-93 Litho. *Perf. 14½x15*
911 A279 5fr gray & multi .20 .20
912 A279 10fr yellow & multi .20 .20
913 A279 25fr lilac rose & multi .20 .20
914 A279 50fr red lilac & multi .30 .20
915 A279 130fr blue & multi 1.10 .55
916 A279 150fr multicolored 1.25 .60
920 A279 200fr multicolored 1.60 .80
922 A279 330fr orange & multi 2.75 1.40
Nos. 911-922 (8) 7.60 4.15

Issued: 150fr, 200fr, 6/20/91; 130fr, 330fr, 1/15/93; 5-50fr, 5/3/94.

This is an expanding set. Numbers may change.

1991, July 31 Litho. *Perf. 11½*
926 A280 5fr Grewia tenax .20 .20
927 A280 15fr Hymenocardia acide .20 .20
928 A280 60fr Cassia sieberiana, vert. .50 .25
929 A280 100fr Adenium obesum .80 .40
930 A280 300fr Mitragyna inermis 2.40 1.25
Nos. 926-930 (5) 4.10 2.30

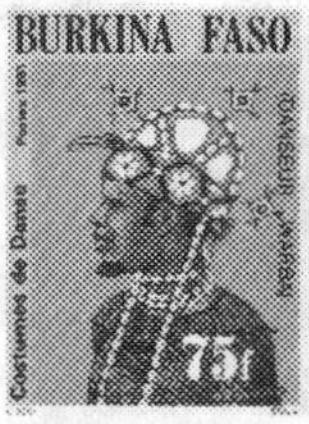

Traditional Dance Costumes A281

World Post Day A282

1991, Aug. 20 *Perf. 12½*
931 A281 75fr Warba .60 .30
932 A281 130fr Wiskamba 1.00 .50
933 A281 280fr Pa-zenin 2.25 1.10
Nos. 931-933 (3) 3.85 1.90

1991, Oct. 9 *Perf. 13½*
934 A282 130fr multicolored 1.00 .50

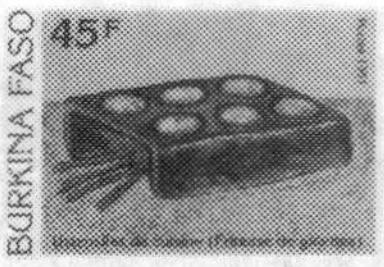

Cooking Utensils A283

1992, Jan. 8 Litho. *Perf. 11½*
935 A283 45fr Pancake fryer .35 .20
936 A283 130fr Cooking pot, vert. 1.00 .55
937 A283 310fr Mortar & pestle, vert. 2.40 1.25
938 A283 500fr Ladle, calabash 4.00 2.00
Nos. 935-938 (4) 7.75 4.00

1992 African Soccer Championships, Senegal — A284

1992, Jan. 17 *Perf. 13½*
939 A284 50fr Yousouf Fofana .40 .20
940 A284 100fr Francois-Jules Bocande .80 .40

Souvenir Sheet

Perf. 13x12½

941 A284 500fr Trophy 4.00 2.00

UN Decade For the Handicapped — A285

1992, Mar. 31 Litho. *Perf. 12½*
942 A285 100fr multicolored .85 .40

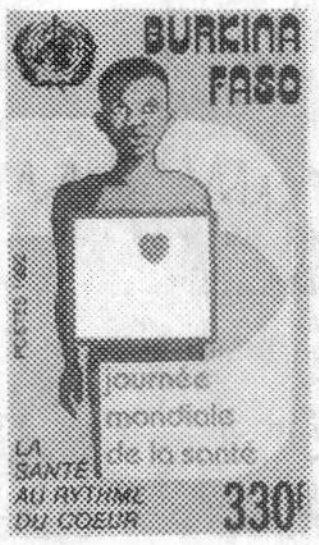

World Health Day — A286

1992, Apr. 7 *Perf. 13*
943 A286 330fr multicolored 2.75 1.40

Discovery of America, 500th Anniv. A287

1992, Aug. 12 Litho. *Perf. 12½*
944 A287 50fr Columbus, Santa Maria .40 .25
945 A287 150fr Ships, natives 1.25 .65

Souvenir Sheet

946 A287 350fr Map 3.00 1.50

Genoa '92. No. 946 contains one 52x31mm stamp.

A288

A289

Insects.

1992, Aug. 17 *Perf. 15x14*

947 A288 20fr Dysdercus voelkeri .20 .20
948 A288 40fr Rhizopertha dominica .35 .20
949 A288 85fr Orthetrum microstigma .75 .35
950 A288 500fr Apis mellifera 4.25 2.25
Nos. 947-950 (4) 5.55 3.00

1992, Dec. 21 **Litho.** *Perf. 11½*

Christmas: 10fr, Boy, creche. 130fr, Children decorating creche. 1000fr, Boy holding painting of Madonna and Child.

951 A289 10fr multicolored .20 .20
952 A289 130fr multicolored 1.00 .50
953 A289 1000fr multicolored 8.00 4.00
Nos. 951-953 (3) 9.20 4.70

Invention of the Diesel Engine, Cent. A290

1993, Jan. 25 **Litho.** *Perf. 11½*

954 A290 1000fr multicolored 8.00 4.00

The date of issue is in question.

Paris '94, Philatelic Exhibition A291

1993, July 15

955 A291 400fr multicolored 3.50 1.75
956 A291 650fr multi, diff. 5.50 2.75

African Film Festival A292

Birds A293

Designs: 250fr, Monument to the cinema. 750fr, M. Douta (1919-1991), comedian, horiz.

Perf. 11½x12, 12x11½

1993, Feb. 16 **Litho.**

957 A292 250fr multicolored 2.00 1.00
958 A292 750fr multicolored 6.00 3.00

1993, Mar. 31 *Perf. 11½x12*

100fr, Mycteria ibis. 200fr, Leptoptilos crumeniferus. 500fr, Ephippiorhynchus senegalensis.

959 A293 100fr multicolored .80 .40
960 A293 200fr multicolored 1.60 .80
961 A293 500fr multicolored 4.00 2.00
a. Souvenir sheet of 3, #959-961 9.50 4.75
Nos. 959-961 (3) 6.40 3.20

No. 961a sold for 1200fr.

1994 World Cup Soccer Championships, US — A294

1993, Apr. 8 *Perf. 15*

962 A294 500fr shown 4.00 2.00
963 A294 1000fr Players, US flag 8.00 4.00

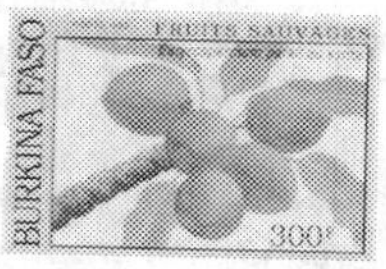
Fruit Trees — A295

150fr, Saba senegalensis, vert. 300fr, Butyrospermum parkii. 600fr, Adansonia digitata, vert.

1993, June 2 **Litho.** *Perf. 11½*

964 A295 150fr multicolored 1.25 .65
965 A295 300fr multicolored 2.50 1.25
966 A295 600fr multicolored 5.00 2.50
Nos. 964-966 (3) 8.75 4.40

Traditional Jewelry A296

1993, Sept. 25 **Litho.** *Perf. 11½*

967 A296 200fr Ring for hair 1.65 .85
968 A296 250fr Agate necklace, vert. 2.00 1.00
969 A296 500fr Bracelet 4.00 2.00
Nos. 967-969 (3) 7.65 3.85

Gazella Rufifrons A297

1993, Dec. 10 **Litho.** *Perf. 14½*

970 A297 30fr shown .25 .20
971 A297 40fr Two facing left .30 .20
972 A297 60fr Two standing .50 .25
973 A297 100fr Young gazelle .80 .35
a. Souvenir sheet, #970-973 3.25 1.60
Nos. 970-973 (4) 1.85 1.00

World Wildlife Fund (#970-973). No. 973a sold for 400fr.

Kingfishers — A298

1994, Mar. 8 **Litho.** *Perf. 11½*

974 A298 600fr Halcyon senegalensis 2.00 1.00
975 A298 1200fr Halcyon chelicuti 4.25 2.25

Souvenir Sheet

976 A298 2000fr Ceyx picta 7.00 3.50

1994 World Cup Soccer Championships, US — A299

1994, Mar. 28

977 A299 1000fr Players, US map 3.50 1.75
978 A299 1800fr Soccer ball, players 6.50 3.25
a. Souvenir sheet of 1 7.00 3.50

No. 978a sold for 2000fr.

First Manned Moon Landing, 25th Anniv. — A300

1994, July 15 **Litho.** *Perf. 11½*

979 A300 750fr Astronaut, flag 3.75 1.90
980 A300 750fr Lunar module, earth 3.75 1.90
a. Pair, #979-980 7.50 3.75

No. 980a is a continuous design.

First Stamp Exhibition, Paris, 1994 A301

1994, Apr. 28

981 A301 1500fr Dogs 7.75 3.75
a. Souvenir sheet of 1 7.75 3.75

Legumes — A302

Designs: 40fr, Hibiscus sabdariffa. 45fr, Solanum aethiopicum. 75fr, Solanum melongena. 100fr, Hibiscus esculentus.

1994 **Litho.** *Perf. 11½*

982 A302 40fr multicolored .20 .20
983 A302 45fr multicolored .25 .20
984 A302 75fr multicolored .40 .20
985 A302 100fr multicolored .50 .25
Nos. 982-985 (4) 1.35 .85

Intl. Olympic Committee, Cent. A303

Domestic Animals A304

1994, Oct. 10 *Perf. 15*

986 A303 320fr multicolored 1.60 .80

1994, Oct. 10 *Perf. 11½*

987 A304 150fr Pig, horiz. .75 .35
988 A304 1000fr Capra hircus 4.75 2.50
989 A304 1500fr Ovis aries, horiz. 7.25 3.75
Nos. 987-989 (3) 12.75 6.60

Elvis Presley (1935-77) A305

A305a

Portraits in feature films: 300fr, Loving You. 500fr, Jailhouse Rock. 1000fr, Blue Hawaii. 1500fr, Marilyn Monroe, Presley. 0

1995 **Litho.** *Perf. 13½*

990-992 A305 Set of 3 7.50 3.75

Souvenir Sheets

993 A305 1500fr multicolored 6.00 3.00

Litho. & Embossed

993A A305a 3000fr gold & multi

Nos. 990-992 exist in souvenir sheets of one. No. 993 contains one 51x42mm stamp with continuous design. No. 993A, exists in souvenir sheets of silver & multi with different designs in sheet margin.

Issued: No. 993A, 2/24/95.

See Nos. 1012-1015A.

Crocodile — A306

1995, Feb. 6 **Litho.** *Perf. 15x14½*

994 A306 10fr brown & multi .20 .20
995 A306 20fr lilac & multi .20 .20
996 A306 25fr olive brn & multi .20 .20
997 A306 30fr green & multi .20 .20
998 A306 40fr red brown & multi .20 .20
999 A306 50fr gray & multi .25 .20
1000 A306 75fr gray violet & multi .40 .20
1001 A306 100fr gray brown & multi .50 .25
1002 A306 150fr olive & multi .75 .40
1003 A306 175fr gray blue & multi .90 .45
1004 A306 250fr brown lake & multi 1.25 .65
1005 A306 400fr blue green & multi 2.00 1.00
Nos. 994-1005 (12) 7.05 4.15

World Tourism Organization, 20th Anniv. — A307

Designs: 150fr, Man riding donkey, vert. 350fr, Bobo-Dioulasso railroad station. 450fr, Grand Mosque, Bani. 650fr, Gazelle, map.

1995, Jan. 26 **Litho.** *Perf. 11½*

1006 A307 150fr multicolored .75 .40
1007 A307 350fr multicolored 1.75 .90
1008 A307 450fr multicolored 2.25 1.10
1009 A307 650fr multicolored 3.25 1.60
Nos. 1006-1009 (4) 8.00 4.00

FESPACO '95 — A308

Motion pictures: 150fr, "Rabi," Gaston Kabore. 250fr, "Tilai," Idrissa Ouedraogo.

1995 ***Perf. 13½***

1010 A308 150fr multicolored .80 .40
1011 A308 250fr multicolored 1.40 .70

Nos. 1010-1011 exist in souvenir sheets of one. Motion pictures, cent.

Stars of Motion Pictures Type of 1995

Marilyn Monroe in feature films: 400fr, The Joyful Parade. 650fr, The Village Tramp. 750fr, Niagara.
1500fr, The Seven Year Itch. 3000fr, Marilyn Monroe (1926-62).

1995 Litho. ***Perf. 13½***

1012-1014 A305 Set of 3 7.50 3.75

Souvenir Sheets

1015 A305 1500fr multicolored 6.00 3.00

Litho. & Embossed

1015A A305a 3000fr gold & multi

Nos. 1012-1014 exist in souvenir sheets of 1. No. 1015 contains one 42x51mm stamp with continuous design. No. 1015A exists in souvenir sheets of silver & multi with different designs in sheet margin.

Birds — A309

Designs: 450fr, Laniarius barbarus. 600fr, Estrilda bengala. 750fr, Euplectes afer.

1995, Apr. 5 Litho. ***Perf. 11½***

1016 A309 450fr multicolored 2.00 1.00
1017 A309 600fr multicolored 2.75 1.40
1018 A309 750fr multicolored 3.50 1.75
a. Souvenir sheet of 3, #1016-1018 9.00 4.50
Nos. 1016-1018 (3) 8.25 4.15

No. 1018a sold for 2000fr.

Reptiles A310

Designs: 450fr, Psammophis sibilans. 500fr, Eryx muelleri. 1500fr, Turtle.

1995, Dec. 31

1019 A310 450fr multicolored 2.00 1.00
1020 A310 500fr multicolored 2.25 1.10
1021 A310 1500fr multicolored 6.75 3.50
Nos. 1019-1021 (3) 11.00 5.60

1996 Summer Olympics, Atlanta — A311

Design: 3000fr, Tennis, diff.

1995, Sept. 20 Litho. ***Perf. 13½***

1022 A311 150fr Basketball .70 .35
1023 A311 250fr Baseball 1.25 .60
1024 A311 650fr Tennis 3.00 1.50
1025 A311 750fr Table tennis 3.50 1.75
a. Souv. sheet of 4, #1022-1025 8.50 4.25
Nos. 1022-1025 (4) 8.45 4.20

Souvenir Sheets

1026 A311 1500fr Equestrian event 7.00 7.00

Litho. & Embossed

1026A A311 3000fr gold & multi

No. 1026A also exists as a silver & multi souvenir sheet with different design in sheet margin. Both the gold & silver stamps also exist together in a souvenir sheet of 2.

Sports Figures A312

Ayrton Senna (1960-94), World Driving Champion A313

Designs: 300fr, Juan Manuel Fangio, race car driver, 1955 Mercedes W 196. 400fr, Andre Agassi, US tennis player. 500fr, Ayrton Senna (1960-94), race car driver, McLaren MP 4/6 Honda. 1000fr, Michael Schumacher, race car driver, 1995 Benetton B 195.
1500fr, Enzo Ferrari, 412 TR, F40.

1995, Sept. 20

1027 A312 300fr multi 2.25 1.10
1028 A312 400fr multi 3.25 1.60
1029 A312 500fr multi 4.00 2.00
1030 A312 1000fr multi 8.00 4.00
a. Souvenir sheet of 3, #1027, 1029-1030 14.50 7.25
Nos. 1027-1030 (4) 17.50 8.70

Souvenir Sheets

1031 A312 1500fr multicolored *7.00 3.50*

Litho. & Embossed

1032 A313 3000fr gold & multi

Nos. 1027-1030 exist in souvenir sheets of 1. No. 1031 contains one 55x48mm stamp.
No. 1032 also exists as a silver & multi souvenir sheet with different design in sheet margin. Both the gold and silver stamps also exist together in a souvenir sheet of 2.
For surcharge see No. 1078.

Souvenir Sheets

John Lennon (1940-1980) — A314

Designs: No. 1033, With guitar, circular pattern with name "LENNON," portrait. No. 1034, With guitar, emblem, portrait.

1995 Litho. & Embossed ***Perf. 13½***

1033 A314 3000fr gold & multi
1034 A314 3000fr gold & multi

Nos. 1033-1034 each exist in souvenir sheets of silver & multi. Souvenir sheets of one gold and one silver exist in same designs and one of each design.

1995 Boy Scout Jamboree, Holland A315

Mushrooms: 150fr, Russula nigricans. 250fr, Lepiota rhacodes. 300fr, Xerocomus subtomentos. 400fr, Boletus erythropus. 500fr, Russula sanguinea. 650fr, Amanita rubescens. 750fr, Amanita vaginata. 1000fr, Geastrum sessil.
No. 1043, Amanita muscaria. No. 1044, Morchella esculenta.

1996, Feb. 20 Litho. ***Perf. 13½***

1035-1042 A315 Set of 8 16.00 8.00
1041a Sheet of 4, #1035, 1037, 1040-1041 7.50 3.75
1042a Sheet of 4, #1036, 1038-1039, 1042 8.50 4.25

Souvenir Sheets

1043-1044 A315 1500fr each 6.00 3.00

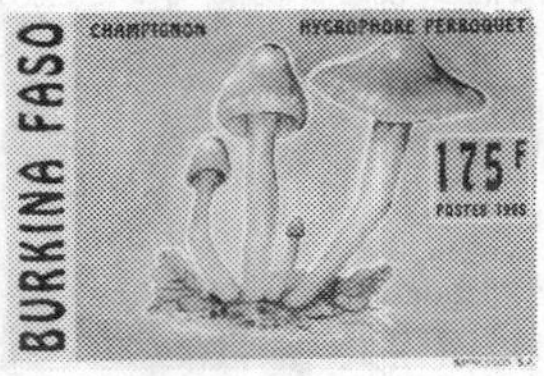

Mushrooms — A316

Designs: 175fr, Hygrophore perroquet. 250fr, Pleurote en huitre. 300fr, Pezize (oreille d'ane). 450fr, Clavaire jolie.

1996, Jan. 24

1045-1048 A316 Set of 4 4.50 2.25
1048a Souvenir sheet of 4, #1045-1048 4.50 2.25

#1045-1048 each exist in souvenir sheets of 1.

UN, 50th Anniv. — A317

Designs: 500fr, UN headquarters, New York. 1000fr, UN emblem, people, vert.

1995, Dec. 20 ***Perf. 11½***

1049 A317 500fr multicolored 2.75 1.25
1050 A317 1000fr multicolored 5.25 2.75

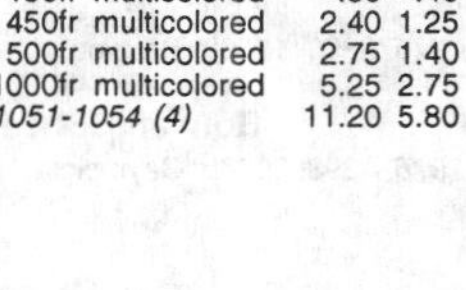

Christmas A318

Designs: 150fr, Christmas tree, children pointing to picture of nativity scene. 450fr, Yagma Grotto. 500fr, Flight into Egypt. 1000fr, Adoration of the Magi.

1995, Dec. 18

1051 A318 150fr multicolored .80 .40
1052 A318 450fr multicolored 2.40 1.25
1053 A318 500fr multicolored 2.75 1.40
1054 A318 1000fr multicolored 5.25 2.75
Nos. 1051-1054 (4) 11.20 5.80

Entertainers A319

Portraits: No. 1062, Elvis Presley, smiling. No. 1063, Presley, hand under chin. No. 1064, Stevie Wonder.

1996, May 14 Litho. ***Perf. 13½***

Souvenir Sheets

1062-1064 A319 1500fr multi, each 5.25 2.50

Numbers have been reserved for a set of 8 individual stamps released with these souvenir sheets.
Dated 1995.

Butterflies and Insects A320

Designs: 100fr, Epiphora bauhiniae, vert. 150fr, Kraussella amabile, vert. 175fr, Charaxes epijasius, vert. 250fr, Locusta migratoria.

1996 Litho. ***Perf. 13½***

1065 A320 100fr multicolored .45 .20
1066 A320 150fr multicolored .70 .35
1067 A320 175fr multicolored .80 .40
1068 A320 250fr multicolored 1.10 .60
Nos. 1065-1068 (4) 3.05 1.55

Two souvenir sheets containing Nos. 1065, 1067 and Nos. 1066, 1068, respectively, exist.

Butterflies A321

Designs: 150fr, Morpho rega. 250fr, Hypolymnas misippus. 450fr, Pseudacraea boisduvali. 600fr, Charaxes castor.
1500fr, Antanartia delius.

1996, June 28 Litho. ***Perf. 13½***

1069 A321 150fr multicolored .70 .35
1070 A321 250fr multicolored 1.10 .55
1071 A321 450fr multicolored 2.00 1.00
1072 A321 600fr multicolored 2.75 2.75
Nos. 1069-1072 (4) 6.55 4.65

Souvenir Sheet

1073 A321 1500fr multicolored 6.75 6.75
a. Ovptd. in sheet margin 6.25 6.25

Overprint in silver in sheet margin of No. 1073a contains Hong Kong '97 Exhibition emblem and two line inscription in Chinese. Issued in 1997.

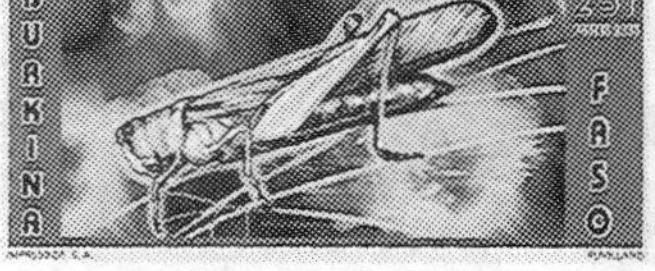

Insects — A321a

c, 25fr, Sauterelle. d, 75fr, Schistocerca gregaria. e, 300fr, Pardolata haasi. f, 400fr, Psammomys obesus.

1996, June 28 Litho. *Perf. 13½*

1073B A321a Strip of 4, #c.-f. 2.75 1.40

1998 World Cup Soccer Championships, France — A322

Various soccer plays.

1996 Litho. *Perf. 13*

1074	A322	50fr multi	.20	.20
1075	A322	150fr multi, vert.	.65	.25
1076	A322	250fr multi, vert.	1.10	.55
1077	A322	450fr multi, vert.	1.90	1.00
		Nos. 1074-1077 (4)	3.85	2.00

No. 1028 Ovptd. in Metallic Red

1996 Litho. *Perf. 13½*

1078 A312 400fr multicolored 1.60 .80

No. 1078 exists in souvenir sheet of 1.

Wild Cats — A323

Designs: 100fr, Panthera leo. 150fr, Acinonyx jubatus. 175fr, Lynx caracal. 250fr, Panthera pardus.

Illustration reduced.

1996 *Perf. 12½x12*

1079	A323	100fr multicolored	.40	.20
1080	A323	150fr multicolored	.55	.30
1081	A323	175fr multicolored	.65	.35
1082	A323	250fr multicolored	.95	.45
		Nos. 1079-1082 (4)	2.55	1.30

Orchids — A324

Various orchids.

1996, Aug. 30 Litho. *Perf. 12½x13*

1083	A324	100fr blue & multi	1.10	.55
1084	A324	175fr lilac & multi	1.90	.95
1085	A324	250fr orange & multi	2.75	1.25
1086	A324	300fr olive & multi	3.25	1.60
		Nos. 1083-1086 (4)	9.00	4.35

Birds A325

Designs: 500fr, Falco peregrinus. 750fr, Crossoptilon mantchuricum. 1000fr, Branta canadensis. 1500fr, Pelecanus crispus.

1996, June 25 *Perf. 12½x12*

1087	A325	500fr multicolored	*2.00*	*1.00*
1088	A325	750fr multicolored	*2.50*	*1.25*
1089	A325	1000fr multicolored	*3.75*	*1.90*
1090	A325	1500fr multicolored	*5.75*	*2.75*
		Nos. 1087-1090 (4)	*14.00*	*6.90*

#1087-1090 each printed se-tenant with labels.

Diana, Princess of Wales (1961-97) A325a

Various portraits, color of sheet margin: No. 1090A, blue. No. 1090K, deep pink.

No. 1090U, In yellow. No. 1090V, Wearing tiara.

1997 Litho. *Perf. 13½*

Sheets of 9

1090A	A325a	150fr #Ab.-Aj.	4.75	2.40
1090K	A325a	180fr #Kl.-Kt.	5.75	3.00

Souvenir Sheets

1090U-1090V A325a 2000fr each 7.25 3.50

Nos. 1090U-1090V each contain one 41x46mm stamp.

See Nos. 1126-1128.

A326

A327

Various portraits, color of sheet margin: No. 1091, Pale pink. No. 1092, Pale blue. No. 1093, Pale yellow.

No. 1094, In white dress, serving food to child (in sheet margin). No. 1095, Wearing wide-brimmed hat.

1998 Litho. *Perf. 14*

1091	A326	425fr Sheet of 6, #a.-f.	8.75	4.50
1092	A326	530fr Sheet of 6, #a.-f.	11.00	5.50
1093	A326	590fr Sheet of 6, #a.-f.	12.00	6.00

Souvenir Sheets

1094-1095 A326 1500fr each 5.00 2.50

Diana, Princess of Wales (1961-97).

1998 Litho. *Perf. 14*

1096 A327 260fr shown .60 .30

Souvenir Sheet

1097 A327 1500fr Portrait, diff. 5.00 2.50

Mother Teresa (1910-97). No. 1096 was issued in sheets of 6. Nos. 1096-1097 have birth date inscribed "1907."

Birds — A328

5fr, White-winged triller. 10fr, Golden sparrow. 100fr, American goldfinch. 170fr, Red-legged thrush. 260fr, Willow warbler. 425fr, Blue grosbeak.

No. 1104: a, Bank swallow. b, Kirtland's warbler. c, Long-tailed minivet. d, Blue-gray gnatcatcher. e, Reed-bunting. f, Black-collared apalis. g, American robin. h, Cape long-claw. i, Wood thrush.

No. 1105: a, Song sparrow. b, Dartford warbler. c, Eastern bluebird. d, Rock thrush. e, Northern mockingbird. f, Northern cardinal. g, Eurasian goldfinch. h, Varied thrush. i, Northern oriole.

No. 1106, Golden whistler. No. 1107, Barn swallow, horiz.

1998, Oct. 1 Litho. *Perf. 13½*

1098-1103 A328 Set of 6 3.50 1.75

Sheets of 9

1104	A328	260fr #a.-i.	8.25	4.00
1105	A328	425fr #a.-i.	14.00	7.00

Souvenir Sheets

1106-1107 A328 1500fr each 5.50 2.75

Butterflies and Moths — A329

No. 1108: a, Arctia caja. b, Nymphalis antiopa. c, Brahmaea wallichii. d, Issoria lathonia. e, Speyeria cybele. f, Vanessa virginiensis. g, Rothchildia orizaba. h, Cethosia hypsea. i, Marpesia petreus.

No. 1109: a, Agraulis vanillae. b, Junonia coenia. c, Danaus gilippus. d, Polygonia comma. e, Anthochar is cardamines. f, Heliconius aoede. g, Atlides halesus. h, Mesosemia croseus. i, Automeris io.

No. 1110, Papilio xuthus. No. 1111, Pterourus multicaudatus. No. 1112, Pterourus troilus. No. 1113, Papilio machaon.

1998, Oct. 25

Sheets of 9

1108	A329	170fr #a.-i.	5.25	2.75
1109	A329	530fr #a.-i.	16.00	8.00

Souvenir Sheets

1110-1113 A329 1500fr each 5.50 2.75

#1110-1113 each contain one 56x42mm stamp.

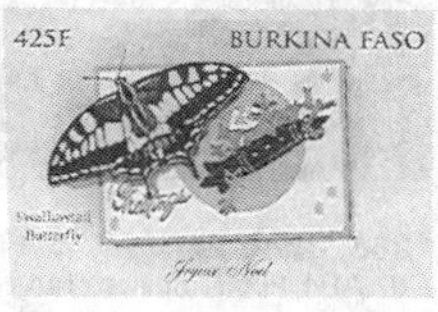

Christmas A330

Fauna, flora with Christmas items: 100fr, Tersina viridis, holly, vert. 170fr, Citherias menander, present, vert. 260fr, Chrysanthemum, reindeer, sleigh, vert. 425fr, Swallowtail butterfly, greeting card. 530fr, European bee eater, Santa Claus, snowman.

No. 1119, Anthemis tinctoria, sleigh. No. 1120, Papilio ulysses, greeting card.

1998, Dec. 1 Litho. *Perf. 14*

1114-1118 A330 Set of 5 5.50 2.75

Souvenir Sheets

1119-1120 A330 1500fr each 5.50 2.75

Trains A331

No. 1121: a, CDR No. 19, Ireland. b, EMD "F" Series Bo-Bo, US. c, Class 72000, France. d, Class AE 4/4 Bo-Bo, Switzerland. e, Class 277, Spain. f, ET 403 four car train, West Germany. g, Class EM2 Co-Co, UK. h, Europe Dutch Swiss Tee.

No. 1122: a, DF 4 East Wind IV Co-Co, China. b, Union Pacific Railroad, US. c, No. 3.641, Norway. d, Class GE 4/4 Bo-bo, Switzerland. e, Class GE Bo-Bo, South Africa. f, WDM-2 Co-Co, India. g, Kraus Mafeei Co-Co, US. h, RTG Four-car transit, France.

No. 1123, ETR 401 Pendolino, Italy. No. 1124, No. 12 Sarah Siddons, UK.

1998, Nov. 10

Sheets of 8

1121	A331	170fr #a.-h.	5.00	2.50
1122	A331	425fr #a.-h.	12.50	6.25

Souvenir Sheets

1123-1124 A331 1500fr each 5.50 2.75

Diana, Princess of Wales, Type of 1997

425fr, Diana in white blouse. 590fr, Diana with Pope John Paul II. No. 1127A: various portraits, color of sheet margin is violet.

1500fr, Diana speaking, American Red Cross emblem in sheet margin. 2000fr, Diana wearing Japanese kimono.

1997 Litho. *Perf. 13½*

1126	A325a	425fr multi	1.60	1.60
1127	A325a	590fr multi	2.25	1.10

Sheet of 9

1127A A325a 180fr #b.-j. 6.00 3.00

Souvenir Sheets

1127K	A325a	1500fr multi	5.50	2.75
1128	A325a	2000fr multi	7.50	3.75

No. 1127 was issued in sheets of 9. No. 1127K contains one 41x46mm stamp.

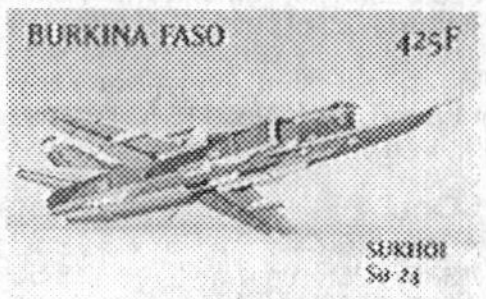

Airplanes — A332

No. 1129: a, Sukhoi Su-24. b, Yakovlev Yak-38. c, Tupolev Blackjack. d, Antonov An-26. e, Antonov An-22 Anteus. f, Antonov An-124.

1000fr, Ilyushin Il-76T.

1999, Sept. 8 Litho. *Perf. 14*

1129 A332 425fr Sheet of 6, #a.-f. 8.50 8.50

Souvenir Sheet

1130 A332 1000fr multicolored 3.25 3.25

No. 1130 contains one 57x43mm stamp.

Ships A333

No. 1131: a, Portland. b, Goethe. c, Fulton.

No. 1132: a, CSS Nashville. b, Cutty Sark. c, Brilliant. d, Eagle. e, Red Jacket. f, USS Columbia. g, HMS Rose. h, Resolution. i, 1000-ton paquebot. j, Mayflower.

No. 1133: a, USS Tennessee. b, HMS Alacrity. c, Bismarck. d, Yamoto. e, Aurora. f, Iowa class battleship. g, Liberty Ship. h, F209. i, Star. j, Big Eagle.

No. 1134, Batavia. No. 1135, Grand Voilier.

1999, Sept. 8

Sheets of 3 and 10

1131	A333	170fr #a.-c.	1.75	1.75
1132	A333	100fr #a.-j.	3.25	3.25
1133	A333	200fr #a.-j.	6.50	6.50

Souvenir Sheets

1134-1135 A333 1000fr each 3.25 3.25

Domesticated Animals — A334

Designs: 5fr, Tabby cat, vert. 10fr, Chinchilla. 20fr, Yorkshire terriers. 25fr, Cocker spaniels.

No. 1140, vert.: a, Afghan hound. b, Fox terrier. c, Pug. d, Dalmatian. e, Boston terrier. f, Cocker spaniel.

No. 1141: a, American wirehaired. b, Tabby. c, Blue Burmese. d, Abyssinian. e, Lilac Burmese. f, Siamese.

No. 1142, Persian. No. 1143, Japanese bobtail, vert. No. 1144, Labrador retriever, vert. No. 1145, Labrador retrievers, vert.

1999, Oct. 4
1136-1139 A334 Set of 4 .20 .20

Sheets of 6

1140 A334 260fr #a.-f. 5.25 5.25
1141 A334 530fr #a.-f. 10.50 10.50

Souvenir Sheets

1142-1145 A334 1000fr each 3.25 3.25

Domesticated Animals — A335

No. 1146 - Horses: a, Gelderlander. b, Trait lourd. c, Vladimir. d, Percheron. e, Sumba. f, Dartmoor.
No. 1147 - Dogs: a, French bulldog. b, Bernese. c, Griffon. d, King Charles spaniel. e, Spitz. f, Yorkshire terrier.
No. 1148 - Cats: a, American wirehaired. b, Japanese bobtail. c, Himalayan. d, LaPerm. e, Lilac Siamese colorpoint. f, Norwegian forest cat.
No. 1149, Shetland pony, vert. No. 1150, Basset hound, vert. No. 1151, Japanese bobtail, diff., vert.

1999, Oct. 4 **Sheets of 6**
1146 A335 170fr #a.-f. 3.50 3.50
1147 A335 425fr #a.-f. 8.50 8.50
1148 A335 590fr #a.-f. 11.50 11.50

Souvenir Sheets

1149-1151 A335 1000fr each 3.25 3.25

SEMI-POSTAL STAMPS

Catalogue values for unused stamps in this section are for Never Hinged items.

Anti-Malaria Issue
Common Design Type
Perf. 12½x12

1962, Apr. 7 **Engr.** **Unwmk.**
B1 CD108 25fr + 5fr red org .50 .50

Freedom from Hunger Issue
Common Design Type

1963, Mar. 21 ***Perf. 13***
B2 CD112 25fr + 5fr dk grn, bl & brn .50 .50

CAN '96 (African Nations) Soccer Championships — SP1

Designs: 150fr+25fr, Stallions, soccer ball. 250fr+25fr, Map of Africa, soccer player.

1996, Jan. 2 **Litho.** ***Perf. 11½***
B3 SP1 150fr +25fr multi .95 .45
a. Souvenir sheet of 1 2.75 1.40
B4 SP1 250fr +25fr multi 1.50 .75

No. B3a sold for 500fr.

AIR POST STAMPS

Catalogue values for unused stamps in this section are for Never Hinged items.

Plane over Map Showing Air Routes — AP1

Designs: 200fr, Plane at airport, Ouagadougou. 500fr, Champs Elysees, Ouagadougou.

Unwmk.

1961, Mar. 4 **Engr.** ***Perf. 13***
C1 AP1 100fr multicolored .85 .30
C2 AP1 200fr multicolored 1.60 .55
C3 AP1 500fr multicolored 4.00 1.50

Air Afrique Issue
Common Design Type

1962, Feb. 17
C4 CD107 25fr brt pink, dk pur & lt grn .30 .20

UN Emblem and Upper Volta Flag — AP2

Perf. 13½x12½

1962, Sept. 22 **Photo.**
C5 AP2 50fr multicolored .40 .25
C6 AP2 100fr multicolored .85 .50

Admission to UN, second anniversary.

Post Office, Ouagadougou — AP3

1962, Dec. 11 ***Perf. 13x12***
C7 AP3 100fr multicolored .75 .40

Jet Over Map AP4

1963, June 24
C8 AP4 200fr multicolored 1.60 .65

First jet flight, Ouagadougou to Paris. For surcharge see No. C10.

African Postal Union Issue
Common Design Type

1963, Sept. 8 **Unwmk.** ***Perf. 12½***
C9 CD114 85fr dp vio, ocher & red .70 .50

No. C8 Surcharged in Red

AIR AFRIQUE
19-11-63

50F

1963, Nov. 19 ***Perf. 13x12***
C10 AP4 50fr on 200fr multi .50 .40

See note after Mauritania No. C26.

Europafrica Issue
Common Design Type

50fr, Sunburst & Europe linked with Africa.

1964, Jan. 6 ***Perf. 12x13***
C11 CD116 50fr multicolored .75 .50

Ramses II, Abu Simbel — AP5

Greek Sculptures — AP6

1964, Mar. 8 **Engr.** ***Perf. 13***
C12 AP5 25fr dp green & choc .35 .30
C13 AP5 100fr brt bl & brn 1.40 1.25

UNESCO world campaign to save historic monuments of Nubia.

1964, July 1 **Unwmk.** ***Perf. 13***
C14 AP6 15fr Greek Portrait Head .20 .20
C15 AP6 25fr Seated boxer .25 .20
C16 AP6 85fr Victorious athlete .80 .60
C17 AP6 100fr Venus of Milo 1.10 .70
a. Min. sheet of 4, #C14-C17 3.50 3.50
Nos. C14-C17 (4) 2.35 1.70

18th Olympic Games, Tokyo, Oct. 10-25.

West African Gray Woodpecker AP7

President John F. Kennedy (1917-1963) AP8

1964, Oct. 1 **Engr.** ***Perf. 13***
C18 AP7 250fr multicolored 2.75 1.90

1964, Nov. 25 **Photo.** ***Perf. 12½***
C19 AP8 100fr orange, brn & lil .70 .70
a. Souvenir sheet of 4 4.50 4.50

Bird Type of Regular Issue, 1965

1965, Mar. 1 **Photo.** ***Perf. 13***
Size: 27x48mm
C20 A27 500fr Abyssinian roller 5.50 2.50

Earth and Sun — AP9

1965, Mar. 23 **Engr.**
C21 AP9 50fr multicolored .45 .20

5th World Meteorological Day.

Hughes Telegraph, ITU Emblem and Dial Telephone — AP10

1965, May 17 **Unwmk.** ***Perf. 13***
C22 AP10 100fr red, sl grn & bl grn .80 .40

ITU, centenary.

Intl. Cooperation Year — AP10a

1965, June 21 **Photo.** ***Perf. 13***
C23 AP10a 25fr multicolored .20 .20
C24 AP10a 100fr multicolored .55 .25
a. Min. sheet, 2 each #C23-C24 1.90 1.90

Sacred Sabou Crocodile — AP11

1965, Aug. 9 **Engr.** ***Perf. 13***
C25 AP11 60fr shown .60 .30
C26 AP11 85fr Lion, vert. .80 .40

Early Bird Satellite over Globe — AP12

Tiros Satellite and Weather Map — AP13

1965, Sept. 15 **Unwmk.** ***Perf. 13***
C27 AP12 30fr brt bl, brn & brn red .30 .20

Space communications.

1966, Mar. 23 **Engr.** ***Perf. 13***
C28 AP13 50fr dk car, brt bl & blk .40 .30

6th World Meteorological Day.

FR-1 Satellite over Ouagadougou Space Tracking Station — AP14

1966, Apr. 28 ***Perf. 13***
C29 AP14 250fr mag, ind & org brn 2.00 .90

Inauguration of WHO Headquarters, Geneva — AP15

1966, May 3 **Photo.**
C30 AP15 100fr yel, blk & bl .80 .45

Air Afrique Issue
Common Design Type

1966, Aug. 31 **Photo.** ***Perf. 13***
C31 CD123 25fr tan, blk & yel grn .30 .20

Sir Winston Churchill, British Lion and "V" Sign — AP16

1966, Nov. 5 **Engr.** ***Perf. 13***

C32 AP16 100fr slate grn & car rose 1.00 .55

Sir Winston Spencer Churchill (1874-1965), statesman and WWII leader.

Pope Paul VI, Peace Dove, UN General Assembly and Emblem — AP17

1966, Nov. 5

C33 AP17 100fr dk blue & pur 1.00 .55

Pope Paul's appeal for peace before the UN General Assembly, Oct. 4, 1965.

Blind Man and Lions Emblem — AP18

1967, Feb. 28 **Engr.** ***Perf. 13***

C34 AP18 100fr dk vio bl, brt bl & dk brn 1.40 .55

50th anniversary of Lions Intl.

UN Emblem and Rain over Landscape AP19

Diamant Rocket AP20

1967, Mar. 23 **Engr.** ***Perf. 13***

C35 AP19 50fr ultra, dk grn & bl grn .50 .25

7th World Meteorological Day.

1967, Apr. 18 **Engr.** ***Perf. 13***

French Spacecraft: 20fr, FR-1 satellite, horiz. 30fr, D1-C satellite. 100fr, D1-D satellite, horiz.

C36 AP20 5fr brt bl, sl grn & org .20 .20
C37 AP20 20fr lilac & slate blue .20 .20
C38 AP20 30fr red brn, brt bl & emer .30 .20
C39 AP20 100fr emer & dp claret .90 .40
Nos. C36-C39 (4) 1.60 1.00

For overprint see No. C69.

Albert Schweitzer (1875-1965), Medical Missionary and Organ Pipes — AP21

1967, May 12 **Engr.** ***Perf. 13***

C40 AP21 250fr claret & blk 1.75 .95

World Map and 1967 Jamboree Emblem — AP22

1967, June 8 **Photo.**

C41 AP22 100fr multicolored 1.00 .55

12th Boy Scout World Jamboree, Farragut State Park, Idaho, Aug. 1-9.

Madonna and Child, 15th Century AP23

Paintings: 20fr, Still life by Paul Gauguin. 50fr, Pietà, by Dick Bouts. 60fr, Anne of Cleves, by Hans Holbein the Younger. 90fr, The Money Lender and his Wife, by Quentin Massys (38x40mm). 100fr, Blessing of the Risen Christ, by Giovanni Bellini. 200fr, The Handcart, by Louis Le Nain, horiz. 250fr, The Four Evangelists, by Jacob Jordaens.

Perf. 12½x12, 12x12½, 13½ (90fr)

1967-68 **Photo.**

C42 AP23 20fr multi ('68) .25 .20
C43 AP23 30fr multicolored .30 .20
C44 AP23 50fr multicolored .50 .25
C45 AP23 60fr multi ('68) .60 .25
C46 AP23 90fr multi ('68) .85 .40
C47 AP23 100fr multicolored 1.00 .40
C48 AP23 200fr multi ('68) 2.00 .70
C49 AP23 250fr multicolored 2.75 1.00
Nos. C42-C49 (8) 8.25 3.40

See Nos. C70-C72.

African Postal Union Issue, 1967
Common Design Type

1967, Sept. 9 **Engr.** ***Perf. 13***

C50 CD124 100fr multicolored .80 .35

Caravelle "Ouagadougou" — AP24

1968, Feb. 29 **Engr.** ***Perf. 13***

C51 AP24 500fr bl, dp claret & blk 3.75 1.40

WMO Emblem, Sun, Rain, Wheat — AP25

1968, Mar. 23 **Engr.** ***Perf. 13***

C52 AP25 50fr dk red, ultra & gray grn .45 .25

8th World Meteorological Day.

Europafrica Issue

Clove Hitch — AP25a

1968, July 20 **Photo.** ***Perf. 13***

C53 AP25a 50fr yel bis, blk & dk red .40 .20

See note after Niger No. C89.

Vessel in Form of Acrobat with Bells, Colima Culture — AP26

Mexican Sculptures: 30fr, Ballplayer, Veracruz, vert. 60fr, Javelin thrower, Colima, vert. 100fr, Seated athlete with cape, Jalisco.

1968, Oct. 14 **Engr.** ***Perf. 13***

C54 AP26 10fr dk red, ocher & choc .20 .20
C55 AP26 30fr bl grn, brt grn & dk brn .25 .20
C56 AP26 60fr ultra, ol & mar .45 .25
C57 AP26 100fr brt grn, bl & mar .65 .35
Nos. C54-C57 (4) 1.55 1.00

19th Olympic Games, Mexico City, Oct. 12-27.

Artisan Type of Regular Issue

1968, Oct. 30 **Engr.** ***Perf. 13***
Size: 48x27mm

C58 A52 100fr Potter .70 .30

PHILEXAFRIQUE Issue

Too Late or The Letter, by Armand Cambon AP27

1968, Nov. 22 **Photo.** ***Perf. 12½***

C59 AP27 100fr multicolored 1.00 .75

PHILEXAFRIQUE, Phil. Exhib., Abidjan, Feb. 14-23, 1969. Printed with alternating rose claret label.

Albert John Luthuli — AP28

Design: No. C61, Mahatma Gandhi.

1968, Dec. 16 **Photo.** ***Perf. 12½***

C60 AP28 100fr dk grn, yel grn & blk .75 .40
C61 AP28 100fr dk grn, yel & blk .75 .40
a. Min. sheet, 2 each #C60-C61 3.00 3.00

Exponents of non-violence.

2nd PHILEXAFRIQUE Issue
Common Design Type

50fr, Upper Volta #59, dancers & musicians.

1969, Feb. 14 **Engr.** ***Perf. 13***

C62 CD128 50fr pur, bl car & brn .55 .55

Weather Sonde, WMO Emblem, Mule and Cattle in Irrigated Field — AP29

1969, Mar. 24 **Engr.** ***Perf. 13***

C63 AP29 100fr dk brn, brt bl & grn .90 .50

9th World Meteorological Day.

Artisan Type of Regular Issue

Design: 150fr, Basket weaver.

1969, Apr. 3 **Engr.** ***Perf. 13***
Size: 48x27mm

C64 A55 150fr brn, bl & blk 1.25 .60

Lions Emblem, Eye and Blind Man — AP30

1969, Apr. 30 **Photo.**

C65 AP30 250fr red & multi 2.50 1.00

12th Congress of District 403 of Lions Intl., Ouagadougou, May 2-3.

Fish Type of Regular Issue

Designs: 100fr, Phenacogrammus pabrensis. 150fr, Upside-down catfish.

1969 **Engr.** ***Perf. 13***
Size: 48x27mm

C66 A57 100fr slate, pur & yel .90 .40
C67 A57 150fr org brn, gray & slate 1.40 .60

Earth and Astronaut — AP31

Embossed on Gold Foil

1969 ***Die-cut Perf. 10½x10***
C68 AP31 1000fr gold 8.25 8.25

Apollo 8 mission, which put the first man into orbit around the moon, Dec. 21-27, 1968.

No. C39 Overprinted in red with Lunar Landing Module and: "L'HOMME SUR LA LUNE / JUILLET 1969 / APOLLO 11"

1969, July 25 **Engr.** ***Perf. 13***
C69 AP20 100fr emer & dp claret 2.25 1.90

See note after Mali No. C80.

Painting Type of 1967-68

Paintings: 50fr, Napoleon Crossing Great St. Bernard Pass, by Jacques Louis David. 150fr, Napoleon Awarding the First Cross of the Legion of Honor, by Jean-Baptiste Debret. 250fr, Napoleon Before Madrid, by Carle Vernet.

1969, Aug. 18 **Photo.** ***Perf. 12½x12***
C70 AP23 50fr carmine & multi .45 .35
C71 AP23 150fr violet & multi 1.10 .80
C72 AP23 250fr green & multi 2.25 1.40
Nos. C70-C72 (3) 3.80 2.55

Napoleon Bonaparte (1769-1821).

Agriculture Type of Regular Issue

1969, Oct. 30 **Photo.** ***Perf. 12½x13***
Size: 47½x27mm
C73 A58 100fr Peanuts .75 .28
C74 A58 200fr Rice 1.60 .55

AP32

AP33

Tree of Life, symbols of science, agriculture and industry.

1969, Nov. 21 **Photo.** ***Perf. 12x13***
C75 AP32 100fr multicolored .65 .35

See note after Mauritania No. C28.

1970, Apr. 22 **Photo.** ***Perf. 12½***

Designs: 20fr, Lenin. 100fr, Lenin Addressing Revolutionaries in Petrograd, by V. A. Serov, horiz.

C76 AP33 20fr ocher & brn .20 .20
C77 AP33 100fr blk, lt grn & red .65 .40

Lenin (1870-1924), Russian communist leader.

Pres. Roosevelt with Stamp Collection — AP34

Design: 10fr, Franklin Delano Roosevelt, vert.

1970, June 4 **Photo.** ***Perf. 12½***
C78 AP34 10fr dk brn, emer & red brn .20 .20
C79 AP34 200fr vio bl, gray & dk car 1.40 .45

Soccer Game and Jules Rimet Cup — AP35

100fr, Goalkeeper catching ball, globe.

1970, June 4 **Engr.** ***Perf. 13***
C80 AP35 40fr olive, brt grn & brn .40 .20
C81 AP35 100fr blk, lil, brn & grn .90 .40

9th World Soccer Championships for the Jules Rimet Cup, Mexico City, May 30-June 21, 1970.

EXPO Emblem, Monorail and "Cranes at the Seashore" AP36

UN Emblem, Dove and Star AP37

Design: 150fr, EXPO emblem, rocket, satellites and "Geisha."

1970, Aug. 7 **Photo.** ***Perf. 12½***
C82 AP36 50fr multicolored .35 .20
C83 AP36 150fr green & multi 1.00 .60

Issued to publicize EXPO '70 International Exhibition, Osaka, Japan, Mar. 15-Sept. 13.

1970, Oct. 2 **Engr.** ***Perf. 13***

Design: 250fr, UN emblem and doves, horiz.

C84 AP37 60fr dk bl, bl & grn .40 .20
C85 AP37 250fr dk red brn, vio bl & ol 1.60 .65

25th anniversary of the United Nations.

Holy Family — AP38

Silver Embossed

1970, Nov. 27 ***Die-Cut Perf. 10***
C86 AP38 300fr silver 2.50 2.50

Gold Embossed

C87 AP38 1000fr gold 9.00 9.00

Christmas.

Family and Upper Volta Flag — AP39

Gamal Abdel Nasser — AP41

UN "Key to a Free World" — AP40

Litho.; Gold Embossed

1970, Dec. 10 ***Perf. 12½***
C88 AP39 500fr gold, blk & red 2.50 1.50

10th anniversary of independence, Dec. 11.

1970, Dec. 14 **Engr.** ***Perf. 13***
C89 AP40 40fr red, bister & blue .35 .20

UN Declaration of Independence for Colonial Peoples, 10th anniv.

1971, Jan. 30 **Photo.** ***Perf. 12½***
C90 AP41 100fr green & multi .65 .30

Nasser (1918-1970), president of Egypt.

Herons, Egyptian Art, 1354 — AP42

250fr, Page from Koran, Egypt, 1368-1388.

1971, May 13 **Photo.** ***Perf. 13***
C91 AP42 100fr multi .55 .25
C92 AP42 250fr multi, vert. 1.40 .70

Olympic Rings and Various Sports — AP43

1971, June 10 **Engr.** ***Perf. 13***
C93 AP43 150fr vio bl & red 1.00 .60

Pre-Olympic Year.

Boy Scout and Buildings — AP44

1971, Aug. 12 **Photo.** ***Perf. 12½***
C94 AP44 45fr multicolored .35 .20

13th Boy Scout World Jamboree, Asagiri Plain, Japan, Aug. 2-10.

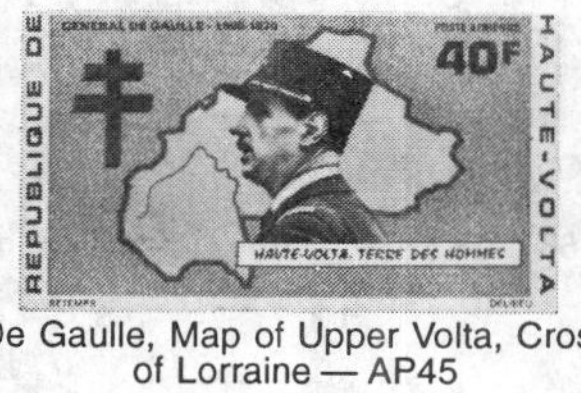

De Gaulle, Map of Upper Volta, Cross of Lorraine — AP45

Charles de Gaulle — AP46

1971, Nov. 9 **Photo.** ***Perf. 13x12***
C95 AP45 40fr lt brn, grn & blk .40 .35

Lithographed; Gold Embossed

Perf. 12½
C96 AP46 500fr gold & grn 4.00 3.75

Gen. Charles de Gaulle (1890-1970), president of France.

African Postal Union Issue, 1971

Common Design Type

Design: 100fr, Mossi dancer and UAMPT building, Brazzaville, Congo.

1971, Nov. 13 **Photo.** ***Perf. 13x13½***
C97 CD135 100fr bl & multi .65 .35

Gen. Sangoule Lamizana AP47

Kabuki Actor and Ice Hockey AP48

1971, Dec. 11 ***Perf. 12½***
C98 AP47 35fr sep, blk, gold & ultra .25 .20

Inauguration of 2nd Republic of Upper Volta.

1972, Feb. 15 **Engr.** ***Perf. 13***
C99 AP48 150fr red, bl & pur 1.00 .60

11th Winter Olympic Games, Sapporo, Japan, Feb. 3-13.

Music, by Pietro Longhi AP49

Design: 150fr, Gondolas and general view, by Ippolito Caffi, horiz.

1972, Feb. 28 **Photo.** ***Perf. 13***
C100 AP49 100fr gold & multi .65 .35
C101 AP49 150fr gold & multi 1.10 .40

UNESCO campaign to save Venice.

Running and Olympic Rings — AP50

Design: 200fr, Discus and Olympic rings.

1972, May 5 **Engr.** ***Perf. 13***

C102 AP50 65fr dp bl, brn & grn .35 .20
C103 AP50 200fr dp bl & brn 1.10 .35
a. Min. sheet of 2, #C102-C103 1.60 1.60

20th Olympic Games, Munich, Aug. 26-Sept. 10.

Musician Type of Regular Issue

Design: 500fr, Jimmy Smith and keyboard.

1972, May 17 **Photo.** ***Perf. 14x13***

C104 A87 500fr green & multi 4.00 1.90

Red Crescent Type of Regular Issue

1972, June 23 ***Perf. 13x14***

C105 A88 100fr yellow & multi .65 .25

2nd Plan Type of Regular Issue

Design: 85fr, Road building machinery.

1972, Oct. 30 **Engr.** ***Perf. 13***

C106 A90 85fr brick red, bl & blk .45 .25

Presidents Pompidou and Lamizana — AP51

Design: 250fr, Presidents Pompidou and Lamizana, different design.

1972, Nov. 20 **Photo.** ***Perf. 13***

Size: 48x37mm

C107 AP51 40fr gold & multi .45 .35

Photogravure; Gold Embossed

Size: 56x36mm

C108 AP51 250fr yel grn, dk grn & gold 2.50 2.50

Visit of Pres. Georges Pompidou of France, Nov. 1972.

Skeet-shooting, Scalzone, Italy — AP52

Gold-medal Winners: 40fr, Pentathlon, Peters, Great Britain. 45fr, Dressage, Meade, Great Britain. 50fr, Weight lifting, Talts, USSR. 60fr, Boxing, light-weight, Seales, US. 65fr, Fencing, Ragno-Lonzi, Italy. 75fr, Gymnastics, rings, Nakayama, Japan. 85fr, Gymnastics, Touritcheva, USSR. 90fr, 110m high hurdles, Milburn, US. 150fr, Judo, Kawaguchi, Japan. 200fr, Sailing, Finn class, Maury, France. 250fr, Swimming, Spitz, US (7 gold). 300fr, Women's high jump, Meyfarth, West Germany. 350fr, Field Hockey, West Germany. 400fr, Javelin, Wolfermann, West Germany. No. C124, Women's diving, King, US. No. C125, Cycling, Morelon, France. No. C126, Individual dressage, Linsenhoff, West Germany.

1972-73 **Litho.** ***Perf. 12½***

C109 AP52 35fr multi ('73) .20 .20
C110 AP52 40fr multicolored .20 .20
C111 AP52 45fr multi ('73) .25 .20
C112 AP52 50fr multi ('73) .25 .20
C113 AP52 60fr multi ('73) .30 .20
C114 AP52 65fr multicolored .35 .20
C115 AP52 75fr multi ('73) .40 .20
C116 AP52 85fr multicolored .40 .20
C117 AP52 90fr multi ('73) .45 .25
C118 AP52 150fr multi ('73) .80 .40
C119 AP52 200fr multicolored 1.10 .50
C120 AP52 250fr multi ('73) 1.40 .65
C121 AP52 300fr multicolored 1.60 .80
C122 AP52 350fr multi ('73) 1.90 .90
C123 AP52 400fr multi ('73) 2.00 1.10
Nos. C109-C123 (15) 11.60 6.20

Souvenir Sheets

C124 AP52 500fr multicolored 2.25 1.60
C125 AP52 500fr multi ('73) 2.25 1.60
C126 AP52 500fr multi ('73) 2.25 1.60

20th Olympic Games, Munich.

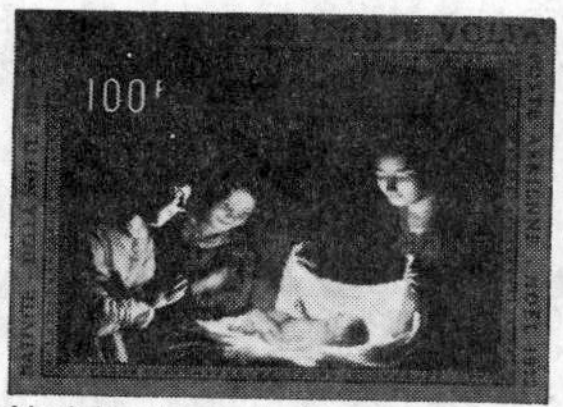

Nativity, by Della Notte — AP53

Christmas: 200fr, Adoration of the Kings, by Albrecht Dürer.

1972, Dec. 23 **Photo.** ***Perf. 13***

C127 AP53 100fr gold & multi .50 .25
C128 AP53 200fr gold & multi 1.10 .65

Madonna and Child, by Albrecht Dürer AP54

Christmas: 75fr, Virgin Mary, Child and St. John, by Joseph von Führich. 100fr, The Virgin of Grand Duc, by Raphael. 125fr, Holy Family, by David. 150fr, Madonna and Child, artist unknown. 400fr, Flight into Egypt, by Gentile da Fabriano, horiz.

1973, Mar. 22 **Litho.** ***Perf. 12½x13***

C129 AP54 50fr multi .35 .20
C130 AP54 75fr multi .50 .25
C131 AP54 100fr multi .65 .35
C132 AP54 125fr multi .80 .40
C133 AP54 150fr multi 1.00 .50
Nos. C129-C133 (5) 3.30 1.70

Souvenir Sheet

C134 AP54 400fr multi 2.50 1.40

Manned Lunar Buggy on Moon — AP55

Moon Exploration: 65fr, Lunakhod, Russian unmanned vehicle on moon. 100fr, Lunar module returning to orbiting Apollo capsule. 150fr, Apollo capsule in moon orbit. 200fr, Space walk. 250fr, Walk in Sea of Tranquillity.

1973, Apr. 30 **Litho.** ***Perf. 13x12½***

C135 AP55 50fr multi .35 .20
C136 AP55 65fr multi .40 .20
C137 AP55 100fr multi .65 .35
C138 AP55 150fr multi 1.00 .50
C139 AP55 200fr multi 1.40 .65
Nos. C135-C139 (5) 3.80 1.90

Souvenir Sheet

C140 AP55 250fr multi 1.60 .80

Giraffes AP56

African Wild Animals: 150fr, Elephants. 200fr, Leopard, horiz. 250fr, Lion, horiz. 300fr, Rhinoceros, horiz. 500fr, Crocodile, horiz.

Perf. 12½x13, 13x12½

1973, May 3 **Litho.**

C141 AP56 100fr multi .65 .35
C142 AP56 150fr multi 1.00 .50
C143 AP56 200fr multi 1.40 .65
C144 AP56 250fr multi 1.60 .80
C145 AP56 500fr multi 3.50 1.60
Nos. C141-C145 (5) 8.15 3.90

Souvenir Sheet

C146 AP56 300fr multi 2.00 1.00

Europafrica Issue

Girl Reading Letter, by Jan Vermeer AP57

Paintings: 65fr, Portrait of a Lady, by Roger van der Weyden. 100fr, Young Lady at her Toilette, by Titian. 150fr, Jane Seymour, by Hans Holbein. 200fr, Mrs. Williams, by John Hoppner. 250fr, Milkmaid, by Jean-Baptiste Greuze.

1973, June 7 **Litho.** ***Perf. 12½x13***

C147 AP57 50fr multi .35 .20
C148 AP57 65fr multi .40 .20
C149 AP57 100fr multi .65 .35
C150 AP57 150fr multi 1.00 .50
C151 AP57 200fr multi 1.40 .65
Nos. C147-C151 (5) 3.80 1.90

Souvenir Sheet

C152 AP57 250fr multi 1.60 .80

For overprint see No. C165-C166.

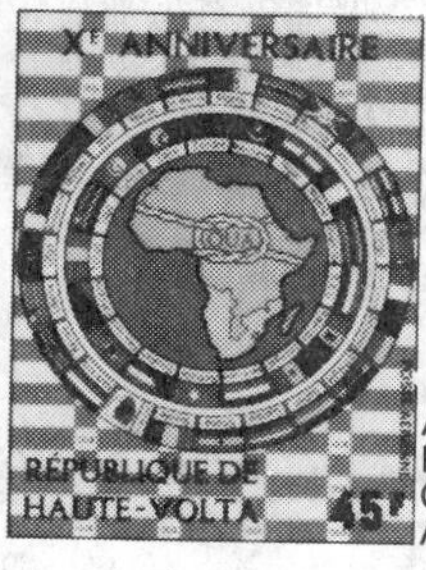

Africa Encircled by OAU Flags AP58

1973, June 7

C153 AP58 45fr multi .30 .20

10th anniv. of Org. for African Unity.

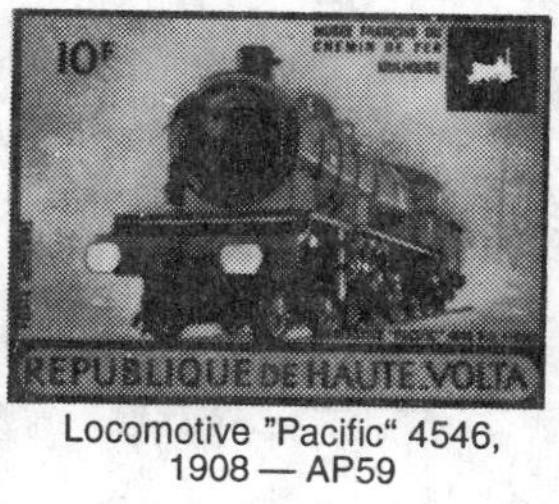

Locomotive "Pacific" 4546, 1908 — AP59

Locomotives from Railroad Museum, Mulhouse, France: 40fr, No. 242, 1927. 50fr, No. 2029, 1882. 150fr, No. 701, 1885-92. 250fr, "Coupe-Vent" No. C145, 1900. 350fr, Buddicomb No. 33, Paris to Rouen, 1884.

1973, June 30 ***Perf. 13x12½***

C154 AP59 10fr multi .20 .20
C155 AP59 40fr multi .25 .20
C156 AP59 50fr multi .35 .20
C157 AP59 150fr multi 1.00 .50
C158 AP59 250fr multi 1.60 .80
Nos. C154-C158 (5) 3.40 1.90

Souvenir Sheet

C159 AP59 350fr multi 2.25 1.25

Boy Scout Type of 1973

40fr, Flag signaling. 75fr, Skiing. 150fr, Cooking. 200fr, Hiking. 250fr, Studying stars.

1973, July 18 **Litho.** ***Perf. 12½x13***

C160 A95 40fr multi .25 .20
C161 A95 75fr multi .50 .25
C162 A95 150fr multi 1.00 .50
C163 A95 200fr multi 1.40 .65
Nos. C160-C163 (4) 3.15 1.60

Souvenir Sheet

C164 A95 250fr multi 1.60 .80

Nos. C148 and C150 Surcharged in Silver New Value and "SECHERESSE / SOLIDARITE AFRICAINE / ET INTERNATIONALE"

1973, Aug. 16

C165 AP57 100fr on 65fr multi .65 .35
C166 AP57 200fr on 150fr multi 1.40 .65

Drought relief.

Kennedy Type, 1973

John F. Kennedy and: 200fr, Firing Saturn 1 rocket, Apollo program. 300fr, First NASA manned space capsule. 400fr, Saturn 5 countdown.

1973, Sept. 12 **Litho.** ***Perf. 12½x13***

C167 A96 200fr multi 1.40 .65
C168 A96 300fr multi 2.00 1.00

Souvenir Sheet

C169 A96 400fr multi 2.50 1.40

10th death anniv. of Pres John F. Kennedy.

Interpol Type of 1973

Souvenir Sheet

Design: Victim in city street.

1973, Sept. 15 ***Perf. 13x12½***

C170 A97 300fr multi 2.00 1.00

Tourism Type of 1973

1973, Sept. 30

C171 A98 100fr Waterfalls .65 .35

Souvenir Sheet

C172 A98 275fr Elephant 1.90 .90

House of Worship Type of 1973

Cathedral of the Immaculate Conception.

1973, Sept. 28

C173 A99 200fr multi 1.40 .65

Folklore Type of 1973

100fr, 225fr, Bobo masked dancers, diff.

1973, Nov. 30 **Litho.** ***Perf. 12½x13***

C174 A100 100fr multi .65 .35
C175 A100 225fr multi 1.50 .70

Zodiac Type of 1973

Souvenir Sheets

Zodiacal Light and: #C176, 1st 4 signs of Zodiac. #C177, 2nd 4 signs. #C178, Last 4 signs.

1973, Dec. 15 ***Perf. 13x14***

C176 A101 250fr multi 1.60 .80
C177 A101 250fr multi 1.60 .80
C178 A101 250fr multi 1.60 .80

Nos. C176-C178 have multicolored margin showing night sky and portraits: No. C176, Louis Armstrong; No. C177, Mahatma Gandhi; No. C178, Martin Luther King.

Soccer Championship Type, 1974

Championship '74 emblem and: 75fr, Gento, Spanish flag. 100fr, Bereta, French flag. 250fr, Best, British flag. 400fr, Beckenbauer, West German flag.

1974, Jan. 15 Litho. ***Perf. 13x12½***

C179 A102 75fr multi .50 .25
C180 A102 100fr multi .65 .35
C181 A102 250fr multi 1.60 .80
Nos. C179-C181 (3) 2.75 1.40

Souvenir Sheet

C182 A102 400fr multi 2.50 1.40

De Gaulle Type, 1974

Designs: 300fr, De Gaulle and Concorde, horiz. 400fr, De Gaulle and French space shot.

Perf. 13x12½, 12½x13

1974, Feb. 4 Litho.

C183 A103 300fr multi 2.00 1.00

Souvenir Sheet

C184 A103 400fr multi 2.50 1.40

Soccer Cup Championship Type, 1974

World Cup, Emblems and: 150fr, Brindisis, Argentinian flag. No. C186, Kenko, Zaire flag. No. C187, Streich, East German flag. 400fr, Cruyff, Netherlands flag.

1974, Mar. 19 ***Perf. 12½x13***

C185 A104 150fr multi .75 .40
C186 A104 300fr multi 1.50 .75

Souvenir Sheets

C187 A104 300fr multi 1.50 .75
C188 A104 400fr multi 2.00 1.00

UPU Type, 1974

UPU Emblem and: 100fr, Dove carrying mail. 200fr, Air Afrique 707. 300fr, Dish antenna. 500fr, Telstar satellite.

1974, July 23 ***Perf. 13½***

C189 A106 100fr multi .50 .25
C190 A106 200fr multi 1.00 .50
C191 A106 300fr multi 1.50 .75
Nos. C189-C191 (3) 3.00 1.50

Souvenir Sheet

C192 A106 500fr multi 2.50 1.25

For overprint see No. C197-C200.

Soccer Cup Winners Type, 1974

World Cup, Game and Flags: 150fr, Brazil, in Sweden, 1958. 200fr, Brazil, in Chile, 1962. 250fr, Brazil, in Mexico, 1970. 450fr, England, in England, 1966.

1974, Sept. 2

C193 A107 150fr multi 1.00 .50
C194 A107 200fr multi 1.40 .65
C195 A107 250fr multi 1.60 .80
Nos. C193-C195 (3) 4.00 1.95

Souvenir Sheet

C196 A107 450fr multi 3.00 1.50

Nos. C189-C192 Overprinted in Red "100e ANNIVERSAIRE DE L'UNION POSTALE UNIVERSELLE / 9 OCTOBRE 1974"

1974, Oct. 9

C197 A106 100fr multi .60 .35
C198 A106 200fr multi 1.40 .65
C199 A106 300fr multi 2.00 1.00
Nos. C197-C199 (3) 4.00 2.00

Souvenir Sheet

C200 A106 500fr multi 3.00 1.40

Universal Postal Union, centenary.

Flower Type of 1974

Flower Paintings by: 300fr, Auguste Renoir. 400fr, Carl Brendt.

1974, Oct. 31 Litho. ***Perf. 12½x13***

C201 A109 300fr multi 2.00 1.00

Souvenir Sheet

C202 A109 400fr multi 2.50 1.40

Locomotive Type of 1975

Locomotives from Railroad Museum. Mulhouse, France: 100fr, Crampton No. 80, 1852. 200fr, No. 701, 1885-92. 300fr, "Forquenot," 1882.

1975, Feb. 28 Litho. ***Perf. 13x12½***

C203 A112 100fr multi .65 .35
C204 A112 200fr multi 1.40 .65

Souvenir Sheet

C205 A112 300fr multi 2.00 1.00

Old Cars Type, 1975

Flags and Old Cars: 150fr, Germany and Mercedes-Benz, 1929. 200fr, Germany and Maybach, 1936. 400fr, Great Britain and Rolls Royce Silver Ghost, 1910.

1975, Apr. 6 ***Perf. 14x13½***

C206 A113 150fr multi 1.00 .50
C207 A113 200fr multi 1.40 .65

Souvenir Sheet

C208 A113 400fr multi 2.50 1.40

American Bicentennial Type of 1975

200fr, Washington crossing Delaware. 300fr, Hessians Captured at Trenton.

1975, May 6 Litho. ***Perf. 14***

C209 A114 200fr multi 1.40 .65
C210 A114 300fr multi 2.00 1.00

Schweitzer Type of 1975

Albert Schweitzer and: 150fr, Toucan. 175fr, Vulturine guinea fowl. 200fr, King vulture. 450fr, Crested corythornis.

1975, May 25 Litho. ***Perf. 13½***

C212 A115 150fr multi 1.00 .50
C213 A115 175fr multi 1.25 .55
C214 A115 200fr multi 1.40 .65
Nos. C212-C214 (3) 3.65 1.70

Souvenir Sheet

C215 A115 450fr multi 3.00 1.50

Apollo Soyuz Type of 1975

Designs: 100fr, Apollo and Soyuz near linkup. 200fr, Cosmonauts Alexei Leonov and Valeri Kubasov. 300fr, Astronauts Donald K. Slayton, Vance Brand and Thomas P. Stafford. 500fr, Apollo Soyuz emblem, US and USSR flags.

1975, July 18 Litho. ***Perf. 13½***

C216 A116 100fr multi .60 .35
C217 A116 200fr multi 1.40 .65
C218 A116 300fr multi 2.00 1.00
Nos. C216-C218 (3) 4.00 2.00

Souvenir Sheet

C219 A116 500fr multi 3.50 1.60

Picasso Type of 1975

Picasso Paintings: 150fr, El Prado, horiz. 350fr, Couple in Patio. 400fr, Science and Charity.

1975, Aug. 7

C220 A117 150fr multi 1.00 .50
C221 A117 350fr multi 2.25 1.25

Souvenir Sheet

C222 A117 400fr multi 2.50 1.40

EXPO '75 Type of 1975

Expo '75 emblem and: 150fr, Passenger liner Asama Maru. 300fr, Future floating city Aquapolis.

1975, Sept. 26 Litho. ***Perf. 11***

C223 A118 150fr multi .75 .40

Souvenir Sheet

Perf. 13½

C224 A118 300fr multi 1.50 .75

Winter Olympic Games Type of 1975

Innsbruck Background, Olympic Emblem and: 100fr, Ice hockey. 200fr, Ski jump. 300fr, Speed skating.

1975, Dec. 15 ***Perf. 13½***

C225 A122 100fr multi .65 .35
C226 A122 200fr multi 1.40 .65

Souvenir Sheet

C227 A122 300fr multi 2.00 1.00

Olympic Games Type of 1976

Olympic Emblem and: 125fr, Heavyweight judo. 150fr, Weight lifting. 500fr, Sprint.

1976, Mar. 17 Litho. ***Perf. 13½***

C228 A123 125fr multi .65 .30
C229 A123 150fr multi .75 .40

Souvenir Sheet

C230 A123 500fr multi 2.50 1.25

Summer Olympic Games Type of 1976

Olympic emblem and: 150fr, Pole vault. 200fr, Gymnast on balance beam. 500fr, Two-man sculls.

1976, Mar. 25 ***Perf. 11***

C231 A124 150fr multi .75 .40
C232 A124 200fr multi 1.00 .50

Souvenir Sheet

C233 A124 500fr multi 2.50 1.25

For overprint see No. C245-C247.

Zeppelin Type of 1976

Airships: 100fr, Graf Zeppelin over Swiss Alps. 200fr, LZ-129 over city. 300fr, Graf Zeppelin. 500fr, Zeppelin over Bodensee.

1976, May 11

C234 A126 100fr multi .60 .35
C235 A126 200fr multi 1.40 .65
C236 A126 300fr multi 2.00 1.00
Nos. C234-C236 (3) 4.00 2.00

Souvenir Sheet

C237 A126 500fr multi 3.50 1.60

Viking Mars Type of 1976

Designs: 200fr, Viking lander assembly. 300fr, Viking orbiter in descent on Mars. 450fr, Viking in Mars orbit.

1976, June 24 Litho. ***Perf. 13½***

C238 A127 200fr multi 1.00 .50
C239 A127 300fr multi 1.50 .75

Souvenir Sheet

C240 A127 450fr multi 2.25 1.10

American Bicentennial Type of 1976

Bicentennial and Interphil '76 Emblems and: 100fr, Siege of Yorktown. 200fr, Battle of Cape St. Vincent. 300fr, Peter Francisco's bravery. 500fr, Surrender of the Hessians.

1976, Sept. 30 Litho. ***Perf. 13½***

C241 A129 100fr multi .60 .35
C242 A129 200fr multi 1.40 .65
C243 A129 300fr multi 2.00 1.00
Nos. C241-C243 (3) 4.00 2.00

Souvenir Sheet

C244 A129 500fr multi 3.50 1.60

Nos. C231-C233 Overprinted in Gold:
a. VAINQUEUR 1976 / TADEUSZ SLUSARSKI / POLOGNE
b. VAINQUEUR 1976 / NADIA COMANECI / ROUMANIE
c. VAINQUEUR 1976 / FRANK ET ALF HANSEN / NORVEGE

1976, July 4 Litho. ***Perf. 11***

C245 A124(a) 150fr multi 1.00 .50
C246 A124(b) 200fr multi 1.40 .65

Souvenir Sheet

C247 A124(c) 500fr multi 3.50 1.60

Winners, 21st Olympic Games.

UPU Emblem over Globe — AP60

1978, Aug. 8 Litho. ***Perf. 13***

C248 AP60 350fr multi 2.25 1.50

Congress of Paris, establishing UPU, cent.

Jules Verne, Apollo 11 Emblem, Footprint on Moon, Neil Armstrong — AP61

Space Conquest: 50fr, Yuri Gagarin and moon landing. 100fr, Montgolfier hot air balloon and memorial medal, 1783; Bleriot's monoplane, 1909.

1978, Sept. 27 Litho. ***Perf. 13x12½***

C249 AP61 50fr multi .35 .20
C250 AP61 60fr multi .40 .20
C251 AP61 100fr multi .65 .35
Nos. C249-C251 (3) 1.40 .75

Anti-Apartheid Year — AP62

1978, Oct. 12 Litho. ***Perf. 13***

C252 AP62 100fr blue & multi .65 .35

Philexafrique II-Essen Issue

Common Design Types

Designs: #C253, Hippopotamus and Upper Volta #C18. #C254, Hummingbird and Hanover #1.

1978, Nov. 1 Litho. ***Perf. 12½***

C253 CD138 100fr multi .65 .35
C254 CD139 100fr multi .65 .35

Nos. C253-C254 printed se-tenant.

Sun God Horus with Sun — AP63

Jules Verne and Balloon — AP64

300fr, Falcon with cartouches, UNESCO emblem.

1978, Dec. 4

C255 AP63 200fr multi 1.40 .65
C256 AP63 300fr multi 2.00 1.00

UNESCO Campaign to safeguard monuments at Philae.

1978, Dec. 10 Engr. ***Perf. 13***

C257 AP64 200fr multi 1.40 .65

Verne (1828-1905), science fiction writer.

Bicycling, Olympic Rings — AP65

Designs: Bicycling scenes.

1980 ***Perf. 14½***

C258 AP65 65fr multi .65 .30
C259 AP65 150fr multi, vert. 1.00 .50
C260 AP65 250fr multi 1.60 .80
C261 AP65 350fr multi 2.25 1.25
Nos. C258-C261 (4) 5.50 2.85

Souvenir Sheet

C262 AP65 500fr multi 3.50 1.60

22nd Summer Olympic Games, Moscow, July 19-Aug. 3.

Nos. C258-C262 Overprinted with Name of Winner and Country

1980, Nov. 22 Litho. ***Perf. 14½***

C263 AP65 65fr multi .40 .20
C264 AP65 150fr multi 1.00 .50
C265 AP65 250fr multi 1.60 .80
C266 AP65 350fr multi 2.25 1.25
Nos. C263-C266 (4) 5.25 2.75

Souvenir Sheet

C267 AP65 500fr multi 3.50 1.60

1982 World Cup — AP66

Designs: Various soccer players.

1982, June 22 Litho. *Perf. 13½*

C268 AP66 70fr multi .45 .25
C269 AP66 90fr multi .60 .30
C270 AP66 150fr multi 1.00 .45
C271 AP66 300fr multi 2.00 1.00
Nos. C268-C271 (4) 4.05 2.00

Souvenir Sheet

C272 AP66 500fr multi 3.50 1.60

Anniversaries and Events — AP67

1983, June Litho. *Perf. 13½*

C273 AP67 90fr Space Shuttle .30 .20
C274 AP67 120fr World Soccer Cup .40 .20
C275 AP67 300fr Cup, diff. 1.00 .50
C276 AP67 450fr Royal Wedding 1.50 .70
Nos. C273-C276 (4) 3.20 1.60

Souvenir Sheet

C277 AP67 500fr Prince Charles, Lady Diana 1.60 1.60

Pre-Olympics, 1984 Los Angeles — AP68

1983, Aug. 1 Litho. *Perf. 13*

C278 AP68 90fr Sailing .30 .20
C279 AP68 120fr Type 470 .40 .20
C280 AP68 300fr Wind surfing 1.00 .50
C281 AP68 400fr Wind surfing, diff. 1.40 .65
Nos. C278-C281 (4) 3.10 1.55

Souvenir Sheet

C282 AP68 500fr Soling Class, Wind surfing 1.60 1.60

Christmas AP69

Rubens Paintings.

1983 Litho. *Perf. 13*

C283 AP69 120fr Adoration of the Shepherds .40 .20
C284 AP69 350fr Virgin of the Garland 1.25 .60
C285 AP69 500fr Adoration of the Kings 1.60 .80
Nos. C283-C285 (3) 3.25 1.60

1984 Summer Olympics — AP70

1984, Mar. 26 Litho. *Perf. 12½*

C286 AP70 90fr Handball, vert. .30 .20
C287 AP70 120fr Volleyball, vert. .40 .20
C288 AP70 150fr Handball, diff. .50 .25
C289 AP70 250fr Basketball .80 .40
C290 AP70 300fr Soccer 1.00 .50
Nos. C286-C290 (5) 3.00 1.55

Souvenir Sheet

C291 AP70 500fr Volleyball, diff. 1.60 .80

Local Birds — AP71

1984, May 14 Litho. *Perf. 12½*

C292 AP71 90fr Phoenicopterus roseus .30 .20
C293 AP71 185fr Choriotis kori, vert. .60 .30
C294 AP71 200fr Buphagus erythrorhynchus, vert. .65 .35
C295 AP71 300fr Bucorvus leadbeateri 1.00 .50
Nos. C292-C295 (4) 2.55 1.35

AP72

Famous Men — AP73

Designs: 5fr, Houari Boumediene (1927-1978), president of Algeria 1965-78. 125fr, Gottlieb Daimler (1834-1900), German automotive pioneer, and 1886 Daimler. 250fr, Louis Bleriot (1872-1936), French aviator, first to fly the English Channel in a heavier-than-air craft. 300fr, Abraham Lincoln. 400fr, Henri Dunant (1828-1910), founder of the Red Cross. 450fr, Auguste Piccard (1884-1962), Swiss physicist, inventor of the bathyscaphe Trieste, 1948. 500fr, Robert Baden-Powell (1856-1941), founder of Boy Scouts. 600fr, Anatoli Karpov, Russian chess champion. 1000fr, Paul Harris (1868-1947), founder of Rotary Intl.

1984, May 21 Litho. *Perf. 13½*

C296 AP72 5fr multi .20 .20
C297 AP72 125fr multi .50 .25
C298 AP72 250fr multi 1.00 .50
C299 AP72 300fr multi 1.25 .60
C300 AP72 400fr multi 1.60 .80
C301 AP72 450fr multi 1.90 .90
C302 AP72 500fr multi 2.00 1.00
C303 AP72 600fr multi 2.25 1.25
Nos. C296-C303 (8) 10.70 5.50

Souvenir Sheet

C304 AP73 1000fr multi 4.00 2.00

No. C304 contains one 51x30mm stamp.

Burkina Faso

Butterflies — AP73a

1984, May 23 *Perf. 13½*

C305 AP73a 10fr Graphium pylades .20 .20
C306 AP73a 120fr Hypolimnas misippus .50 .25
C307 AP73a 400fr Danaus chrysippus 1.60 .80
C308 AP73a 450fr Papilio demodocus 1.90 .90
Nos. C305-C308 (4) 4.20 2.15

Philexafrica '85, Lome — AP74

1985, May 20 Litho. *Perf. 13*

C309 AP74 200fr Solar & wind energy .55 .25
C310 AP74 200fr Children .55 .25

Nos. C309-C310 se-tenant with center label picturing a map of Africa or the exhibition emblem.

PHILEXAFRICA '85, Lome — AP75

National development: No. C311, Youth. No. C312, Communications and transportation.

1985, Nov. 16 Litho. *Perf. 13*

C311 AP75 250fr multi .90 .45
C312 AP75 250fr multi .90 .45

Intl. Youth Year (No. C311). Nos. C311-C312 printed se-tenant with center label picturing PHILEXAFRICA '85 emblem or outline map of Africa.

French Revolution, Bicent. — AP76

Designs: 150fr, *Oath of the Tennis Court,* by David. 200fr, *Storming of the Bastille,* by Thevenin. 600fr, *Rouget de Lisle Singing La Marseillaise,* by Pils.
Illustration reduced.

1989, May 3 Litho. *Perf. 13*

C313 AP76 150fr multi .90 .45
C314 AP76 200fr multi 1.25 .60
C315 AP76 600fr multi 3.50 1.75
Nos. C313-C315 (3) 5.65 2.80

PHILEXFRANCE '89. Printed se-tenant with label containing the exhibition emblem.

POSTAGE DUE STAMPS

Postage Due Stamps of Upper Senegal and Niger, 1914, Overprinted in Black or Red **HAUTE-VOLTA**

1920 Unwmk. *Perf. 14x13½*

J1 D2 5c green .30 .30
J2 D2 10c rose .30 .30
J3 D2 15c gray .30 .30
J4 D2 20c brown (R) .40 .40
J5 D2 30c blue .45 .45
J6 D2 50c black (R) .65 .65
J7 D2 60c orange .65 .65
J8 D2 1fr violet .95 .95
Nos. J1-J8 (8) 4.00 4.00

Type of 1914 Issue Surcharged **2F.**

1927

J9 D2 2fr on 1fr lilac rose 2.25 2.25
J10 D2 3fr on 1fr orange brn 2.50 2.50

D3

Red-fronted Gazelle — D4

1928 Typo.

J11 D3 5c green .30 .30
J12 D3 10c rose .30 .30
J13 D3 15c dark gray .40 .40
J14 D3 20c dark brown .40 .40
J15 D3 30c dark blue .50 .50
J16 D3 50c black 1.75 1.75
J17 D3 60c orange 2.00 2.00
J18 D3 1fr dull violet 3.50 3.50
J19 D3 2fr lilac rose 6.00 6.00
J20 D3 3fr orange brn 6.50 6.50
Nos. J11-J20 (10) 21.65 21.65

Catalogue values for unused stamps in this section, from this point to the end of the section, are for Never Hinged items.

Republic

1962, Jan. 31 *Perf. 14x13½*

Denomination in Black

J21 D4 1fr bright blue .20 .20
J22 D4 2fr orange .20 .20
J23 D4 5fr brt vio blue .20 .20
J24 D4 10fr red lilac .20 .20
J25 D4 20fr emerald .45 .45
J26 D4 50fr rose red 1.10 1.10
Nos. J21-J26 (6) 2.35 2.35

OFFICIAL STAMPS

Catalogue values for unused stamps in this section are for Never Hinged items.

Elephant O1

Perf. 12½

1963, Feb. 1 Unwmk. Photo.

Center in Sepia

O1 O1 1fr red brown .20 .20
O2 O1 5fr yel green .20 .20
O3 O1 10fr deep vio .20 .20
O4 O1 15fr red org .25 .25
O5 O1 25fr brt rose lilac .35 .35
O6 O1 50fr brt green .55 .55
O7 O1 60fr brt red .70 .70
O8 O1 85fr dk slate grn 1.10 1.10
O9 O1 100fr brt blue 1.75 1.75
O10 O1 200fr bright rose 3.00 3.00
Nos. O1-O10 (10) 8.30 8.30

BURMA

'bər-mə

Myanmar

LOCATION — Bounded on the north by China; east by China, Laos and Thailand; south and west by the Bay of Bengal, Bangladesh and India.
GOVT. — Republic
AREA — 261,228 sq. mi.
POP. — 48,081,302 (1999 est.)
CAPITAL — Yangon (Rangoon)

Burma was part of India from 1826 until April 1, 1937, when it became a self-governing unit of the British Commonwealth and received a constitution. On January 4, 1948, Burma became an independent nation.

12 Pies = 1 Anna
16 Annas = 1 Rupee
100 Pyas = 1 Kyat (1953)

Catalogue values for unused stamps in this country are for Never Hinged items, beginning with Scott 35 in the regular postage section and Scott O28 in the official section.

Watermarks

Wmk. 254-Elephant Heads

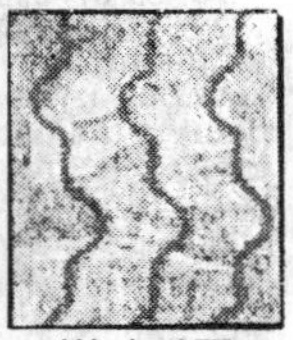

Wmk. 257-Curved Wavy Lines

Stamps of India 1926-36 Overprinted **BURMA**

1937, Apr. 1 Wmk. 196 *Perf. 14*

1	A46	3p slate	.20	.20
2	A71	½a green	.20	.20
3	A68	9p dark green	.20	.20
4	A72	1a dark brown	.20	.20
5	A49	2a ver (small die)	.20	.20
6	A57	2a6p buff	.20	.20
7	A51	3a carmine rose	.40	.20
8	A70	3a6p deep blue	.40	.20
9	A52	4a olive green	.45	.20
10	A53	6a bister	.40	.25
11	A54	8a red violet	.90	.20
12	A55	12a claret	1.50	.50

Overprinted **BURMA**

13	A56	1r green & brown	5.00	.75
14	A56	2r brn org & car rose	7.50	2.50
15	A56	5r dk violet & ultra	10.00	3.00
16	A56	10r car & green	27.50	6.00
17	A56	15r ol green & ultra	125.00	60.00
18	A56	25r blue & ocher	250.00	150.00
		Nos. 1-18 (18)	430.25	225.00

For overprints see #1N1-1N3, 1N25-1N26, 1N47.

King George VI
A1 A2

Royal Barge — A3

Elephant Moving Teak Log — A4

Farmer Plowing Rice Field — A5

Sailboat on Irrawaddy River — A6

Peacock — A7

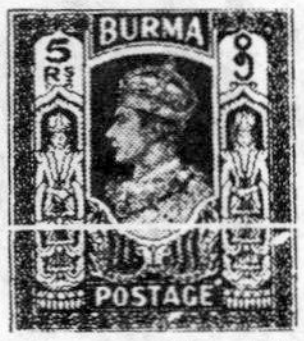

George VI — A8

Perf. 13½x14

1938-40 Litho. Wmk. 254

18A	A1	1p red orange ('40)	.85	.30
19	A1	3p violet	.20	.20
20	A1	6p ultramarine	.20	.20
21	A1	9p yel green	.55	.35
22	A2	1a brown violet	.20	.20
23	A2	1½a turquoise green	.20	.20
24	A2	2a carmine	.30	.20
		Perf. 13		
25	A3	2a6p rose lake	.80	.45
26	A4	3a dk violet	2.50	.50
27	A5	3a6p dp blue & brt bl	1.50	*2.75*
28	A2	4a slate blue, perf. 13½x14	.20	.20
29	A6	8a slate green	1.50	.20
		Perf. 13½		
30	A7	1r brt ultra & dk violet	2.25	.30
31	A7	2r dk vio & red brown	5.50	1.50
32	A8	5r car & dull vio	22.50	9.00
33	A8	10r gray grn & brn	45.00	35.00
		Nos. 18A-33 (16)	84.25	51.55
		Set, never hinged	110.00	

See Nos. 51-65. For overprints and surcharges see Nos. 34-50, O15-O27, 1N4-1N11, 1N28-1N30, 1N37-1N46, 1N48-1N49.

No. 25 Surcharged in Black

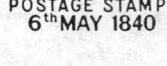

COMMEMORATION
POSTAGE STAMP
6th MAY 1840

ၥ ONE ANNA 1A

1940, May 6 *Perf. 13*

34	A3	1a on 2a6p rose lake	1.00	.80
		Never hinged	4.00	

Centenary of first postage stamp.

Catalogue values for unused stamps in this section, from this point to the end of the section, are for Never Hinged items.

Nos. 18A to 33 Overprinted in Black:

MILY ADMN
a

MILY ADMN
b

1945

35	A1(a)	1p red orange	.20	.20
36	A1(a)	3p violet	.20	.20
37	A1(a)	6p ultramarine	.20	.20
38	A1(a)	9p yel green	.20	.20
39	A2(a)	1a brown violet	.20	.20
40	A2(a)	1½a turq green	.20	.20
41	A2(a)	2a carmine	.20	.20
42	A3(b)	2a6p rose lake	.45	.45
43	A4(b)	3a dk violet	.75	.20
44	A5(b)	3a6p dp bl & brt bl	.20	.20
45	A2(a)	4a slate blue	.20	.20
46	A6(b)	8a slate green	.20	.20
47	A7(b)	1r brt ultra & dk violet	.30	.40
48	A7(b)	2r dk vio & red brown	.30	.75
49	A8(b)	5r car & dull vio	.70	.80
50	A8(b)	10r gray grn & brn	1.50	1.50
		Nos. 35-50 (16)	6.00	6.10

Types of 1938

Perf. 13½x14

1946, Jan. 1 Litho. Wmk. 254

51	A1	3p brown	.20	.20
52	A1	6p violet	.20	.20
53	A1	9p dull green	.20	.20
54	A2	1a deep blue	.20	.20
55	A2	1½a salmon	.20	.20
56	A2	2a rose lake	.20	.20
		Perf. 13		
57	A3	2a6p greenish blue	.25	.20
58	A4	3a blue violet	6.75	1.50
59	A5	3a6p ultra & gray blk	.20	.20
60	A2	4a rose lil, perf. 13½x14	.20	.20
61	A6	8a deep magenta	2.25	.20
		Perf. 13½		
62	A7	1r dp mag & dk vio	1.25	.25
63	A7	2r salmon & red brn	7.50	1.75
64	A8	5r red brn & dk grn	7.50	7.50
65	A8	10r dk vio & car	7.50	7.50
		Nos. 51-65 (15)	34.60	20.50

For overprints see Nos. 70-84, O28-O42.

Burmese Man — A9

Burmese Woman — A10

Mythological Chinze — A11

Elephant Hauling Teak — A12

1946, May 2 *Perf. 13*

66	A9	9p peacock green	.20	.20
67	A10	1½a brt violet	.20	.20
68	A11	2a carmine	.20	.20
69	A12	3a6p ultramarine	.20	.20
		Nos. 66-69 (4)	.80	.80

Victory of the Allied Nations in WWII.

Nos. 51-65 Overprinted in Black ကြားဖြတ် အစိုးရ။

1947, Oct. 1 *Perf. 13½x14, 13, 13½*

70	A1	3p brown	.45	.45
71	A1	6p violet	.20	*.25*
72	A1	9p dull green	.20	*.25*
a.		Inverted overprint	12.50	12.50
73	A2	1a deep blue	.20	*.25*
74	A2	1½a salmon	1.25	.20
75	A2	2a rose lake	.30	.20
76	A3	2a6p greenish bl	1.40	.75
77	A4	3a blue violet	2.50	1.25
78	A5	3a6p ultra & gray blk	.50	*.75*
79	A2	4a rose lilac	1.60	.25
80	A6	8a dp magenta	1.60	.70
81	A7	1r dp mag & dk vio	2.25	.30
82	A7	2r sal & red brn	2.50	2.50
83	A8	5r red brn & dk grn	3.50	*3.75*
84	A8	10r dk vio & car	3.50	*3.75*
		Nos. 70-84 (15)	21.95	*15.60*

The overprint is slightly larger on #76-78, 80-84. The Burmese characters read "Interim Government."

Other denominations are known with the overprint inverted or double.

Issues of the Republic

U Aung San Map and Chinze — A13

Martyrs' Memorial — A14

Perf. 12½x12

1948, Jan. 6 Litho. Unwmk.

85	A13	½a emerald	.20	.20
86	A13	1a deep rose	.20	.20
87	A13	2a carmine	.20	.20
88	A13	3½a blue	.20	.20
89	A13	8a lt chocolate	.20	.20
		Nos. 85-89 (5)	1.00	1.00

Attainment of independence, Jan. 4, 1948.

1948, July 19 Engr. *Perf. 14x13½*

90	A14	3p ultramarine	.20	.20
91	A14	6p green	.20	.20
92	A14	9p dp carmine	.20	.20
93	A14	1a purple	.20	.20
94	A14	2a lilac rose	.20	.20
95	A14	3½a dk slate green	.20	.20
96	A14	4a yel brown	.20	.20
97	A14	8a orange red	.20	.20
98	A14	12a claret	.20	.20
99	A14	1r blue green	.20	.20
100	A14	2r deep blue	.50	.35
101	A14	5r chocolate	1.25	.80
		Nos. 90-101 (12)	3.75	3.15

1st anniv. of the assassination of Burma's leaders in the fight for independence.

Ball Game (Chinlon) A15

Bell A16

Mythical Bird — A17

Rice Planting — A18

Throne — A19

Designs: 6p, Dancer. 9p, Musician. 3a, Spinning. 3a6p, Royal Palace. 4a, Cutting teak. 8a, Plowing rice field.

Perf. 12½ (A15-A17), 12x12½ (A18), 13 (A19)

1949, Jan. 4

102	A15	3p ultramarine	.20	.20
103	A15	6p green	.20	.20
104	A15	9p carmine	.20	.20
105	A16	1a red orange	.20	.20
106	A17	2a orange	.20	.20
107	A18	2a6p lilac rose	.20	.20
108	A18	3a purple	.20	.20
109	A18	3a6p dk slate grn	.20	.20
110	A16	4a chocolate	.20	.20
111	A18	8a carmine	.25	.20
112	A19	1r blue green	.40	.20
a.		Perf. 14		2.50
113	A19	2r deep blue	.90	.30
114	A19	5r chocolate	1.75	.70
115	A19	10r orange red	4.00	1.00
		Nos. 102-115 (14)	9.10	4.20

See Nos. 122-135, 139-152, O56-O67.

UPU Monument, Bern — A20

1949, Oct. 9 Unwmk. Perf. 13

116	A20	2a orange	.20	.20
117	A20	3½a olive grn	.20	.20
118	A20	6a lilac	.30	.20
119	A20	8a crimson	.40	.20
120	A20	12½a ultra	.50	.20
121	A20	1r blue green	.75	.50
		Nos. 116-121 (6)	2.35	1.50

75th anniv. of the UPU.

Types of 1949

Designs as before.

Perf. 13½x14, 14x13½, 13

1952-53 Litho. Wmk. 254

122	A15	3p brown orange	.20	.20
123	A15	6p deep plum	.20	.20
124	A15	9p blue	.20	.20
125	A16	1a violet bl	.20	.20
126	A17	2a green ('52)	.20	.20
127	A18	2a6p green	.20	.20
128	A18	3a sal pink ('52)	.20	.20
129	A18	3a6p brown orange	.20	.20
130	A16	4a vermilion	.20	.20
131	A18	8a lt blue ('52)	.20	.20
132	A19	1r rose violet	.25	.20
133	A19	2r yel green	.55	.25
134	A19	5r ultramarine	1.75	.85
135	A19	10r aquamarine	3.25	1.60
		Nos. 122-135 (14)	7.80	4.90

Map of Burma and Monument — A21

1953, Jan. 4 Perf. 14

136	A21	14p green	.20	.20

Perf. 13

Size: 36½x26mm

137	A21	20p salmon pink	.20	.20
138	A21	25p ultramarine	.20	.20

Fifth anniversary of independence.
For surcharge see No. 166.

Types of 1949

Designs: 2p, Dancer. 3p, Musician. 20p, Spinning. 25p, Royal Palace. 30p, Cutting teak. 50p, Plowing rice field.

1954, Jan. 4 *Perf. 14x13½, 13, 14*

139	A15	1p brown orange	.20	.20
140	A15	2p plum	.20	.20
141	A15	3p blue	.20	.20
142	A16	5p ultramarine	.20	.20
143	A18	10p yel green	.20	.20
144	A17	15p green	.20	.20
145	A18	20p vermilion	.20	.20
146	A18	25p lt red org	.20	.20
147	A16	30p vermilion	.20	.20
148	A18	50p blue	.25	.20
149	A19	1k rose violet	.50	.20
150	A19	2k green	1.00	.20
151	A19	5k ultramarine	2.75	.20
152	A19	10k light blue	5.00	.25
		Nos. 139-152 (14)	11.30	2.85

For overprints and surcharges see Nos. 163-165, 173-175, O68-O79, O80-O81, O83, O85, O87.

Peace Pagoda, Monks' Hostels and Meeting-cave — A22

Designs: 10p, Sangha (community) of Cambodia. 15p, Council meeting. 50p, Sangha of Thailand. 1k, Sangha of Ceylon. 2k, Sangha of Laos.

1954 Typo. Perf. 13

153	A22	10p deep blue	.20	.20
154	A22	15p deep claret	.20	.20
155	A22	35p dark brown	.20	.20
156	A22	50p green	.20	.20
157	A22	1k carmine	.30	.20
158	A22	2k violet	.60	.40
		Nos. 153-158 (6)	1.70	1.40

6th Buddhist Council, Rangoon, 1954-56.

Marble Markers of 5th Buddhist Council — A23

Designs: 40p, Thatbyinnyu Pagoda. 60p, Shwedagon Pagoda, Rangoon. 1.25k, Aerial View of 6th Buddhist Council, Yegu.

Perf. 11x11½

1956, May 24 Litho. Unwmk.

159	A23	20p blue & gray olive	.20	.20
160	A23	40p blue & brt yel grn	.20	.20
161	A23	60p green & lemon	.20	.20
162	A23	1.25k gray blue & yel	.30	.20
		Nos. 159-162 (4)	.90	.80

2500th anniv. of the Buddhist Era.

Nos. 146, 149-150 Surcharged or Overprinted

မန္တလေး-နှစ်တရာ

၁၂၂၁-၁၃၂၁

15 P ၁၅ပြား

Perf. 13, 14

1959, Nov. 9 Wmk. 254

163	A18	15p on 25p lt red org	.20	.20
164	A19	1k rose violet	.25	.20
165	A19	2k green	.55	.45
		Nos. 163-165 (3)	1.00	.85

Centenary of Mandalay, former capital.
The two lines of overprint are 4mm apart on No. 163; 7mm on Nos. 164-165.

No. 136 Surcharged: ၁၅ပြား

1961, June Perf. 14

166	A21	15p on 14p green	.30	.20

Children — A24

Unwmk.

1961, Dec. 11 Litho. Perf. 13

167	A24	15p claret & rose claret	.20	.20

15th anniversary of UNICEF.

Runner with Torch — A25

Soccer, Pole Vault and Shot Put — A26

Designs: 50p, Women runners. 1k, Hurdling, weight lifting, boxing, bicycling and swimming.

1961, Dec. 11 Photo. Perf. 14x13

168	A25	15p red & ultra	.20	.20
169	A26	25p dk green & ocher	.20	.20
170	A26	50p vio blue & pink	.20	.20
171	A25	1k brt green & yel	.35	.25
		Nos. 168-171 (4)	.95	.85

2nd South East Asia Peninsular Games, Rangoon.

Map and Flag of Burma — A27

Wmk. 254

1963, Mar. 2 Engr. Perf. 13

172	A27	15p red	.20	.20

First anniversary of new government.

Nos. 143 and 148 Overprinted in Violet or Red: "FREEDOM FROM HUNGER"

1963, Mar. 21 Litho.

173	A18	10p yel green (V)	.20	.20
174	A18	50p blue (R)	.20	.20

FAO "Freedom from Hunger" campaign.

No. 145 Overprinted

အလုပ်သမားနေ့
၁၉၆၃

1963, May 1

175	A18	20p vermilion	.20	.20

Issued for May Day.

White-browed Fantail — A28

Indian Roller — A29

Birds: 20p, Red-whiskered bulbul. 25p, Crested serpent eagle. 50p, Sarus crane. 1k, Malabar pied hornbill. 2k, Lineated kalij pheasant. 5k, Green peafowl.

Unwmk.

1964, Apr. 16 Photo. Perf. 13

Size: 25x21mm

176	A28	1p gray	.20	.20
177	A28	2p carmine rose	.20	.20
178	A28	3p blue green	.20	.20

Size: 22x26½mm

179	A29	5p violet blue	.20	.20
180	A29	10p orange brn	.20	.20
181	A29	15p olive	.20	.20

Size: 35x25mm

182	A28	20p rose & brn	.20	.20

Size: 27x36½mm, 36½x27mm

183	A29	25p yel & brown	.20	.20
184	A29	50p red, blk & gray	.50	.20
185	A29	1k gray, ind & yel	1.00	.20
186	A28	2k pale ol, ind & red	2.00	.30
187	A29	5k citron, dk bl & red	4.75	.65
		Nos. 176-187 (12)	9.85	2.95

See Nos. 197-208. For overprints see Nos. O82, O84, O86, O88-O93, O94-O115.

ITU Emblem, Old and New Communication Equipment A30

1965, May 17 Litho. Perf. 15

Size: 32x22mm

188	A30	20p bright pink	.20	.20

Perf. 13

Size: 34x24½mm

189	A30	50p dull green	.25	.25

Centenary of the ITU.

ICY Emblem A31

1965, July 1 Unwmk. Perf. 13

190	A31	5p violet blue	.20	.20
191	A31	10p brown orange	.20	.20
192	A31	15p olive	.20	.20
		Nos. 190-192 (3)	.60	.60

International Cooperation Year.

Rice Farmer — A32

Cogwheel and Hammer — A33

1966, Mar. 2

193	A32	15p multicolored	.20	.20

Issued for Farmers' Day.

1967, May 1 Litho. Unwmk.

194	A33	15p lt blue, yel & black	.20	.20

Issued for Labor Day, May 1.

Aung San, Tractor and Farmers A34

1968, Jan. 4 Unwmk. Perf. 13

195	A34	15p sky blue, black & ocher	.20	.20

20th anniversary of independence.

Largest Burmese Pearl — A35

1968, Mar. 4 Litho. *Perf. 13½x13*

196	A35	15p blue, ultra, gray & yel	.20	.20

Burmese pearl industry.

Bird Types of 1964 in Changed Sizes; Designs as Before

Unwmk.

1968, July 1 Photo. Perf. 14

Size: 21x17mm

197	A28	1p gray	.20	.20
198	A28	2p carmine rose	.20	.20
199	A28	3p blue green	.20	.20

Size: 23½x28mm

200	A29	5p violet blue	.20	.20
201	A29	10p orange brown	.20	.20
202	A29	15p olive	.20	.20

Size: 38½x21, 21x38½mm

203	A28	20p rose & brown	.20	.20
204	A29	25p yel & brown	.20	.20
205	A29	50p ver, blk, & gray	.30	.20
206	A29	1k gray, ind & yel	.65	.20
207	A28	2k dull cit, ind & red	1.40	.25
208	A29	5k yel, dk blue & red	3.25	.55
		Nos. 197-208 (12)	7.20	2.80

For overprints see Nos. O92-O102.

Wheat — A36

1969, Mar. 2 Litho. Perf. 13

209	A36	15p blue, emerald & yel	.20	.20

Issued for Peasant's Day.

ILO Emblem A37

1969, Oct. 29 Photo. Wmk. 254

210 A37 15p dk blue grn & gold .20 .20
211 A37 50p dp carmine & gold .20 .20

50th anniv. of the ILO.

Soccer — A38

Designs: 25p, Runner, horiz. 50p, Weight lifter. 1k, Women's volleyball.

Perf. 12½x13, 13x12½

1969, Dec. 1 Litho. Wmk. 254

212 A38 15p brt olive & multi .20 .20
213 A38 25p brown & multi .20 .20
214 A38 50p brt green & multi .25 .20
215 A38 1k blue, yel grn & blk .45 .30
Nos. 212-215 (4) 1.10 .90

5th South East Asia Peninsular Games, Rangoon.

Burmese Flags and Marching Soldiers — A39

1970, Mar. 27 ***Perf. 13***

216 A39 15p multicolored .20 .20

Issued for Armed Forces Day.

Solar System and UN Emblem A40

1970, June 26 Photo. Unwmk.

217 A40 15p lt ultra & multi .20 .20

25th anniversary of the United Nations.

Scroll, Marchers, Peacock Emblem A41

Designs: 25p, Students' boycott demonstration. 50p, Banner and marchers at Shwedagon Camp.

1970, Nov. 23 Litho. ***Perf. 13x13½***

218 A41 15p ultra & multi .20 .20
219 A41 25p multicolored .20 .20
220 A41 50p lt blue & multi .25 .20
Nos. 218-220 (3) .65 .60

50th National Day (Students' 1920 uprising).

Workers, Farmers, Technicians — A42

15p, Burmese of various races, & flags. 25p, Hands holding document. 50p, Red party flag.

1971, June 28 Litho. ***Perf. 13½***

221 A42 5p blue & multi .20 .20
222 A42 15p blue & multi .20 .20
223 A42 25p blue & multi .20 .20
224 A42 50p blue & multi .25 .20
a. Souvenir sheet of 4, #221-224 .45 .45
Nos. 221-224 (4) .85 .80

1st Congress of Burmese Socialist Program Party.

Child Drinking Milk — A43

UNICEF, 25th Anniv.: 50p, Marionettes.

1971, Dec. 11 ***Perf. 14½***

225 A43 15p lt ultra & multi .20 .20
226 A43 50p emerald & multi .30 .20

Aung San, Independence Monument, Pinlon — A44

Union Day, 25th Anniv.: 50p, Bogyoke Aung San and people in front of Independence Monument. 1k, Map of Burma with flag pointing to Pinlon, vert.

1972, Feb. 12 ***Perf. 14***

227 A44 15p ocher & multi .20 .20
228 A44 50p blue & multi .25 .20
229 A44 1k green, ultra & red .40 .20
Nos. 227-229 (3) .85 .60

Burmese and Double Star A45

1972 Litho. ***Perf. 14***

230 A45 15p bister & multi .20 .20

Revolutionary Council, 10th anniversary.

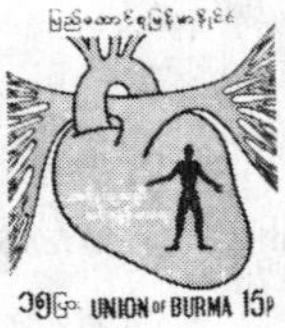

"Your Heart is your Health" — A46

1972, Apr. 7 ***Perf. 14x14½***

231 A46 15p yellow, red & black .20 .20

World Health Day.

Burmese of Various Ethnic Groups A47

1973, Feb. 12 Litho. ***Perf. 14***

232 A47 15p multicolored .20 .20

1973 census.

Casting Vote — A48

Natl. Referendum: 10p, Voters holding map of Burma. 15p, Farmer & soldier holding ballots.

Perf. 14x14½, 14½x14

1973, Dec. 15 Litho.

233 A48 5p deep org & black .20 .20
234 A48 10p blue & multi .20 .20
235 A48 15p blue & multi, vert. .20 .20
Nos. 233-235 (3) .60 .60

Open-air Meeting A49

Designs: 15p, Regional flags. 1k, Scales of justice and Burmese emblem.

1974, Mar. 2 Photo. ***Perf. 13***

Size: 80x26mm

236 A49 15p blue & multi .20 .20

Size: 37x25mm

237 A49 50p blue & multi .20 .20
238 A49 1k lt blue, bis & blk .40 .25
Nos. 236-238 (3) .80 .65

First meeting of People's Parliament.

Messenger Bird and UPU Emblem A50

UPU Cent.: 20p, Mother reading letter to child, vert. 50p, Simulated block of stamps, vert. 1k, Burmese doll, vert. 2k, Mailman delivering letter to family.

1974, May 22

239 A50 15p grn, lt grn & org .20 .20
240 A50 20p multicolored .20 .20
241 A50 50p green & multi .25 .20
242 A50 1k ultra & multi .50 .25
243 A50 2k blue & multi .95 .50
Nos. 239-243 (5) 2.10 1.35

Children A51

Man and Woman A52

Designs: 3p, Girl. 5p, 15p, Man and woman. 10p, Children (like 1p). 50p, Woman with fan. 1k, Seated woman. 5k, Drummer.

Perf. 13, 13x13½ (#248-251)

1974-78 Photo.

244 A51 1p rose & lilac rose .20 .20
245 A51 3p dk brown & pink .20 .20
246 A51 5p pink & violet .20 .20
246A A51 10p Prus blue ('76) .20 .20
247 A51 15p lt green & olive ('75) .20 .20
248 A52 20p lt blue & multi .20 .20
249 A52 50p ocher & multi .25 .20
250 A52 1k brt rose & multi .50 .30
251 A52 5k ol green & multi 2.00 1.40
Nos. 244-251 (9) 3.95 3.10

For different country names see Nos. 298-303.

IWY Emblem, Woman and Globe A53

IWY: 2k, Symbolic flower, globe and IWY emblem, vert.

1975, Dec. 15 Photo. ***Perf. 13½***

252 A53 50p green & black .20 .20
253 A53 2k black & blue .70 .50

Burmese with Raised Fists — A54

Constitution Day: 50p, Demonstrators with banners and emblem. 1k, People and map of Burma, emblem.

1976, Jan. 3 ***Perf. 14***

254 A54 20p blue & black .20 .20
255 A54 50p blue, blk & brn .25 .20

Size: 56x20mm

256 A54 1k blue & multi .45 .20
Nos. 254-256 (3) .90 .60

Students, Campaign Emblem A55

Abacus A56

Intl. Literacy Year: 50p, Campaign emblem. 1k, Emblem, book and globe.

1976, Sept. 8 Photo. ***Perf. 14***

257 A55 10p salmon & black .20 .20
258 A56 15p blue grn & multi .20 .20
259 A56 50p ultra, org & blk .25 .20
260 A55 1k multicolored .60 .30
Nos. 257-260 (4) 1.25 .90

Steam Locomotive A57

Diesel Train Emerging from Tunnel A58

Cent. of Burma's Railroad: 20p, Early train and oxcart. 25p, Old and new trains approaching station. 50p, Railroad bridge.

1977, May 1 ***Perf. 13½***

261 A57 15p multicolored .20 .20

Size: 38x26, 26x38mm

262 A57 20p multicolored .20 .20
263 A57 25p multicolored .20 .20
264 A57 50p multicolored .25 .20
265 A58 1k multicolored .50 .25
Nos. 261-265 (5) 1.35 1.05

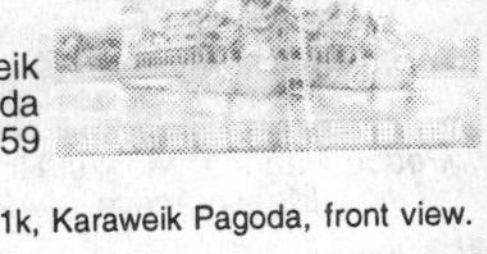

Karaweik Pagoda A59

Design: 1k, Karaweik Pagoda, front view.

1977

266 A59 50p light brown .20 .20

Size: 78x25mm

267 A59 1k multicolored .35 .25

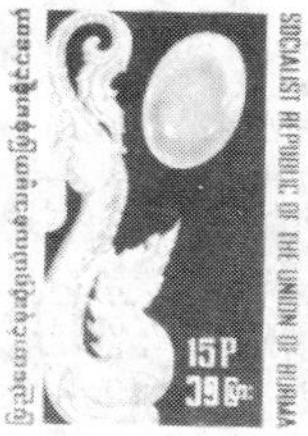

Jade Dragon — A60

Precious Jewelry: 20p, Gold bird with large pearl. 50p, Hand holding pearl necklace with pendant. 1k, Gold dragon, horiz.

1978 Photo. *Perf. 13*
268 A60 15p green & yel grn .20 .20
269 A60 20p multicolored .20 .20
270 A60 50p multicolored .30 .20

Size: 55x20mm
Perf. 14
271 A60 1k multicolored .50 .30
Nos. 268-271 (4) 1.20 .90

Satellite over Map of Asia — A61

1979, Feb., 12 Photo. *Perf. 13*
272 A61 25p multicolored .20 .20

IYC Emblem in Map of Burma — A62

Weather Balloon, WMO Emblem — A63

1979, Dec. Photo. *Perf. 13½*
273 A62 25p multicolored .20 .20
274 A62 50p multicolored .30 .20

International Year of the Child.

1980, Mar. 23 Photo. *Perf. 13½*
275 A63 25p shown .20 .20
276 A63 50p Weather satellite, cloud .30 .20

World Meteorological Day.

Weight Lifting, Olympic Rings A64

1980, Dec. Litho. *Perf. 14*
277 A64 20p shown .20 .20
278 A64 50p Boxing .20 .20
279 A64 1k Soccer .40 .25
Nos. 277-279 (3) .80 .65

22nd Summer Olympic Games, Moscow, July 19-Aug. 3.

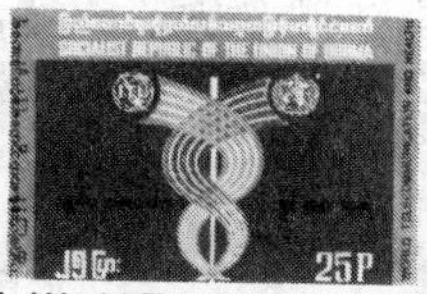

13th World Telecommunications Day — A65

1981, May 17 Photo. *Perf. 13½*
280 A65 25p orange & black .20 .20

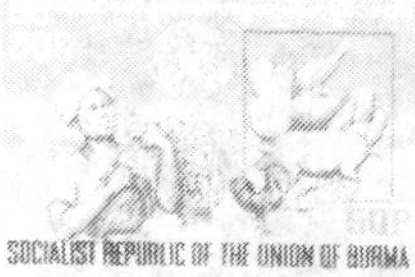

World Food Day — A66

1981, Oct. 16 Photo. *Perf. 13½*
281 A66 25p Livestock, produce .20 .20
282 A66 50p Farmer, rice, produce .20 .20
283 A66 1k Emblems .40 .25
Nos. 281-283 (3) .80 .65

Intl. Year of the Disabled A67

1981, Dec. 12
284 A67 25p multicolored .20 .20

World Communications Year — A68

1983, Sept. 15 Litho. *Perf. 14½x14*
285 A68 15p pale blue & black .20 .20
286 A68 25p dull lake & black .20 .20
287 A68 50p pale brn, blk & lake .30 .20
288 A68 1k buff, blk, beige & yel grn .60 .40
Nos. 285-288 (4) 1.30 1.00

Fish, Ship, Globe, FAO Emblem — A69

1983, Oct. 16 Photo. *Perf. 14x14½*
289 A69 15p brt blue, bister & blk .20 .20
290 A69 25p yel grn, pale org & blk .20 .20
291 A69 50p org, pale grn & blk .30 .20
292 A69 1k yel, ultra & black .60 .40
Nos. 289-292 (4) 1.30 1.00

World Food Day.

Stylized Trees, Hemispheres and Log — A70

1984, Oct. 16 *Perf. 14½x14*
293 A70 15p org, black & blue .20 .20
294 A70 25p pale yel, blk & lt vio .20 .20
295 A70 50p pale pink, blk & lt grn .30 .20
296 A70 1k yel, blk & lt rose vio .60 .40
Nos. 293-296 (4) 1.30 1.00

World Food Day.

Intl. Youth Year — A71

1985, Oct. 15 *Perf. 14x14½*
297 A71 15p multicolored .20 .20

Types of 1974
Inscribed: Union of Burma

1989 Photo. *Perf. 13½*
298 A51 15p olive & lt green .20 .20
299 A52 50p violet & brown .25 .25
300 A52 1k multicolored .55 .55
Nos. 298-300 (3) 1.00 1.00

Issued: 15p, June 26; 50p, June 12; 1k, Sept. 6.

Inscribed: Union of Myanmar

1990 Photo. *Perf. 13½*
301 A51 15p olive & lt green .20 .20
301A A51 20p
302 A52 50p violet & brown .25 .25
303 A52 1k multicolored .50 .50

Issued: 15p, May 26; 50p, May 12.

Fountain, Natl. Assembly Park — A74

Illustration reduced.

1990, May 27 Litho. *Perf. 14½x14*
304 A74 1k multicolored .50 .50

State Law and Order Restoration Council.

A75 A76

1990, Dec. 20 Litho. *Perf. 14x14½*
305 A75 2k multicolored .80 .80

UN Development Program, 40th anniv.

1991, Jan. 26
306 A76 50p Nawata ruby .30 .30

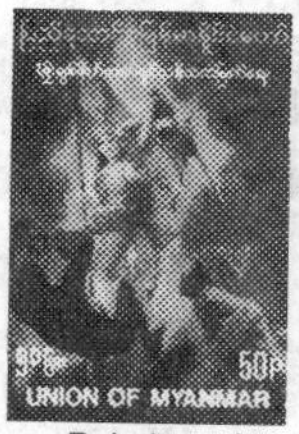

Painting of Freedom Fighters — A77

Bronze Statue — A78

1992, Jan. 4 Litho. *Perf. 14x14½*
307 A77 50p multicolored .20 .20
308 A78 2k multicolored .80 .80

A79 A80

1992, Apr. 10 Litho. *Perf. 14x14½*
309 A79 50p multicolored .50 .50

National Sports Festival.

1992, Dec. 1 Litho. *Perf. 14x14½*
310 A80 50p red .35 .35

World Campaign Against AIDS.

A81 Artifacts — A82

1992, Dec. 5 Litho. *Perf. 14x14½*
Background Color
311 A81 50p pink .20 .20
312 A81 1k yellow .40 .40
313 A81 3k orange 1.25 1.25
314 A81 5k green 2.00 2.00
Nos. 311-314 (4) 3.85 3.85

Intl. Conference on Nutrition, Rome.

1993, Sept. 1 Litho. *Perf. 14x14½*
315 A82 5k Bird 1.60 1.60
316 A82 10k shown 3.25 3.25

Natl. Assembly — A83

1993, Jan. 1 Litho. *Perf. 14x14½*
317 A83 50p multicolored .20 .20
318 A83 3k multicolored 1.00 1.00

Equestrian Festival A84

1993, Oct. 23 Litho. *Perf. 14½x14*
319 A84 3k multicolored 1.00 1.00

A85

A86

1994, June 5 Litho. *Perf. 14*

320 A85 4k multicolored 1.50 1.50

Environment day.

1994, Sept. 15 Litho. *Perf. 14*

321 A86 3k multicolored 1.25 1.25

Union of Solidarity & Development, 1st anniv.

Armed Forces, 50th Anniv. A87

1995, Mar. 27 Litho. *Perf. 14½x14*

322 A87 50p multicolored .25 .25

A88

A89

1995, June 26 Litho. *Perf. 14*

323 A88 2k multicolored .80 .80

Prevent drug abuse.

1995, Oct. 17 Litho. *Perf. 14x14½*

324 A89 50p multicolored .40 .40

Myanmar motion pictures, 60th anniv.

A90

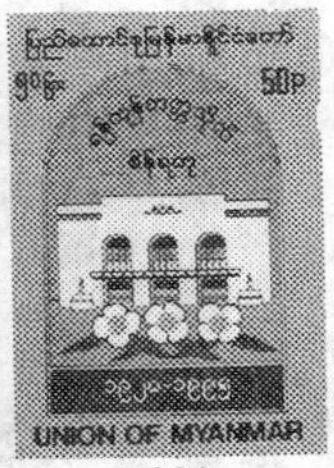

A91

1995, Oct. 24

325 A90 4k UN, 50th Anniv. 2.00 2.00

1995, Nov. 1

326 A91 50p pink & multi .25 .25
327 A91 2k green & multi 1.00 1.00

University of Yangon (Rangoon), 75th anniv.

Visit Myanmar Year — A92

Designs: 50p, Couple in boat on Inlay Lake with food bowl for Buddha, Buddhist monks. 4k, Decorated royal barge on Kandawgyi (Royal Lake), Yangoon. 5k, Royal moat, entrance of Yadanabon (Mandalay), vert.

Perf. 14½x14, 14x14½

1996, Mar. 1 Litho.

328 A92 50p multicolored .20 .20
329 A92 4k multicolored 1.75 1.75
330 A92 5k multicolored 2.25 2.25
Nos. 328-330 (3) 4.20 4.20

UNICEF, 50th Anniv. — A93

Stylized designs: 1k, Mother breastfeeding. 2k, Vaccinating child. 4k, Girls going to school.

1996, Dec. 11 Litho. *Perf. 14x14½*

331 A93 1k multicolored .40 .40
332 A93 2k multicolored .85 .85
333 A93 4k multicolored 1.75 1.75
Nos. 331-333 (3) 3.00 3.00

Intl. Letter Writing Week A94

Designs: 2k, Men in canoe. 5k, Stylized figures forming pyramid, flag, map, vert.

1996, Oct. 7 *Perf. 14½x14, 14x14½*

334 A94 2k multicolored .85 .85
335 A94 5k multicolored 2.00 2.00

A95

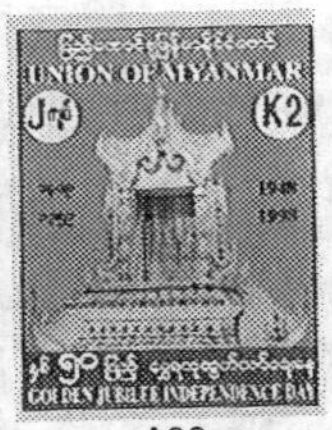

A96

1997, July 24 Litho. *Perf. 14x14½*

336 A95 1k blue & multi .40 .40
337 A95 2k yellow & multi .85 .85

Assoc. of Southeast Asian Nations (ASEAN), 30th anniv.

1998 Litho. *Perf. 14x14½*

338 A96 2k multicolored .90 .90

Independence, 50th anniv.

Musical Instruments — A97

1998 Photo. *Perf. 13¼*

339 A97 5k Xylophone 1.90 1.90
340 A97 10k Mon brass gongs 3.75 3.75
341 A97 20k Rakhine (drum) 7.75 7.75
342 A97 30k Harp 11.50 11.50
Nos. 339-342 (4) 24.90 24.90

Issued: 5k, 8/28/98. Numbers have been reserved for additional values in this set.

Decade of Disabled Persons (1993-2002) A98

1998 Litho. *Perf. 14*

345 A98 2k yellow & multi .75 .75
346 A98 5k apple green & multi 1.90 1.90

OFFICIAL STAMPS

BURMA

Stamps of India, 1926-34, Overprinted in Black

SERVICE

1937 Wmk. 196 *Perf. 14*

O1 A46 3p gray .40 .20
O2 A71 ½a green 2.25 .20
O3 A68 9p dark green 1.50 .40
O4 A72 1a dark brown 1.50 .25
O5 A49 2a vermilion 2.25 .55
O6 A57 2a6p buff 2.25 .90
O7 A52 4a olive grn 1.50 .90
O8 A53 6a bister 2.25 *3.50*
O9 A54 8a red violet 1.40 1.00
O10 A55 12a claret 1.40 *1.75*

BURMA

Overprinted

SERVICE

O11 A56 1r green & brown 11.00 3.25
O12 A56 2r buff & car rose 20.00 17.50
O13 A56 5r dk vio & ultra 47.50 32.50
O14 A56 10r car & green 140.00 *85.00*
Nos. O1-O14 (14) 235.20 *147.90*

For overprint see No. 1N27.

Regular Issue of 1938 Overprinted in Black **SERVICE**

Perf. 13½x14, 13, 13½

1939 Wmk. 254

O15 A1 3p violet .20 .20
O16 A1 6p ultramarine .20 .20
O17 A1 9p yel green 3.25 .20
O18 A2 1a brown violet .20 .20
O19 A2 1½a turquoise green 3.00 .20
O20 A2 2a carmine .80 .20
O21 A2 4a slate blue 3.50 .40

Overprinted **SERVICE**

O22 A3 2a6p rose lake 16.00 2.50
O23 A6 8a slate green 16.00 3.00
O24 A7 1r brt ultra & dk vio 25.00 3.00
O25 A7 2r dk vio & red brn 30.00 5.00
O26 A8 5r car & dull vio 27.50 *32.50*
O27 A8 10r gray grn & brn 80.00 42.50
Nos. O15-O27 (13) 205.65 90.10

For overprints see Nos. 1N12-1N16, 1N31-1N36, 1NO1.

Catalogue values for unused stamps in this section, from this point to the end of the section, are for Never Hinged items.

Nos. 51-56, 60 Overprinted Like Nos. O15-O21

1946 *Perf. 13½x14*

O28 A1 3p brown .20 .20
O29 A1 6p violet .20 .20
O30 A1 9p dull green .20 .20
O31 A2 1a deep blue .20 .20
O32 A2 1½a salmon .20 .20
O33 A2 2a rose lake .20 .20
O34 A2 4a rose lilac .20 .20

Nos. 57, 61-65 Ovptd. Like Nos. O22-O27

Perf. 13, 13½

O35 A3 2a6p greenish blue .20 .20
O38 A6 8a deep magenta .20 *1.50*
O39 A7 1r dp mag & dk vio .70 *2.25*
O40 A7 2r salmon & red brn 5.00 *20.00*
O41 A8 5r red brn & dk grn 10.00 *22.50*
O42 A8 10r dk violet & car 17.50 *35.00*
Nos. O28-O42 (13) 35.00 *82.85*

Nos. O28 to O42 Overprinted in Black အစိုးရကိစ္စ

1947

O43 A1 3p brown .20 .20
O44 A1 6p violet .20 .20
O45 A1 9p dull green .20 .20
O46 A2 1a deep blue .20 .20
O47 A2 1½a salmon .20 .20
O48 A2 2a rose lake .20 .20
O49 A3 2a6p greenish bl .20 .20
O50 A2 4a rose lilac 3.00 1.25
O51 A6 8a dp magenta 3.50 2.25
O52 A7 1r dp mag & dk vio 6.50 2.25
O53 A7 2r sal & red brn *12.50* *9.00*
O54 A8 5r red brn & dk grn *17.50* *17.50*
O55 A8 10r dk vio & car *25.00* *25.00*
Nos. O43-O55 (13) *69.40* *58.65*

The overprint is slightly larger on Nos. O49 and O51 to O55. The Burmese characters read "Interim Government."

Issues of the Republic

Nos. 102 to 106 and 109 to 115 Overprinted in Carmine or Black ကြားဖြတ် အစိုးရ။

a. Overprint 13mm long.
b. Overprint 15mm long.

1949 Unwmk. *Perf. 12½, 13*

O56 A15(a) 3p ultra (C) .20 .20
O57 A15(a) 6p green (C) .20 .20
O58 A15(a) 9p carmine .20 .20
O59 A16(a) 1a red orange .20 .20
O60 A17(a) 2a orange .20 .20
O61 A18(b) 3a6p dk sl grn (C) .20 .20
O62 A16(a) 4a chocolate .20 .20
O63 A18(b) 8a carmine .20 .20
O64 A19(b) 1r blue green (C) .35 .25
O65 A19(b) 2r dp blue (C) .65 .40
O66 A19(b) 5r chocolate 1.60 1.25
O67 A19(b) 10r orange red 3.25 2.50
Nos. O56-O67 (12) 7.45 6.00

Same Overprint in Black on Nos. 139-142, 144-152

Perf. 14x13½, 13, 14

1954-57 Wmk. 254

O68 A15(a) 1p brown org .20 .20
O69 A15(a) 2p plum .20 .20
O70 A15(a) 3p blue .20 .20
O71 A16(a) 5p ultra .20 .20
O72 A17(a) 15p green .20 .20
O72A A18(b) 20p ver ('57) .20 .20
O73 A18(b) 25p lt red org .20 .20
O74 A16(a) 30p vermilion .20 .20
O75 A18(b) 50p blue .20 .20
O76 A19(b) 1k rose violet .50 .20
O77 A19(b) 2k green .85 .20
O78 A19(b) 5k ultra 1.60 .35
O79 A19(b) 10k light blue 3.25 .45
Nos. O68-O79 (13) 8.00 3.00

No. 141 Ovptd. Service

1964 Litho. *Perf. 14*

O80 A15 3p blue *10.00* *7.00*

Nos. 139, 141-142, 144, 177-179, 181, 183 Ovptd. အစိုးရကိစ္စ

1964-65

Overprint: 11½mm

O81 A15 1p brown orange *3.00* .75
O82 A28 2p carmine rose ('65) *2.50* .60
O83 A15 3p blue *3.00* .75
O84 A28 3p blue green ('65) *2.50* .60
O85 A16 5p ultramarine *3.00* .75
O86 A28 5p violet blue ('65) *2.50* .60
O87 A17 15p green *3.00* .75
O88 A28 15p olive ('65) *2.50* .60
O89 A29 25p yel & brn ('65) *2.60* .60
Nos. O81-O89 (9) *24.60* 6.00

အစိုးရကိစ္စ #176-178 Ovptd.

အစိုးရကိစ္စ #181 Ovptd.

1966

Overprint: 15mm

O90 A28 1p black
O91 A28 2p carmine rose
O92 A28 3p blue green

Overprint: 12mm

O93 A28 15p olive

Nos. 176-179, 181-187 Overprinted in Black or Red

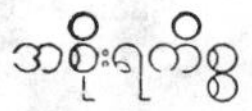

1967 Unwmk. Photo. *Perf. 13*

Overprint: 15mm

Size: 25x21mm

O94 A28 1p gray .20 .20
O95 A28 2p carmine rose .20 .20
O96 A28 3p blue green .20 .20

Size: 22x26½mm

O97 A29 5p violet blue .20 .20
O98 A29 15p olive .20 .20

Size: 35x25mm

O99 A28 20p rose & brown .20 .20

Size: 27x36½mm, 36½x27mm

O100 A29 25p yel & brown (R) .20 .20
O101 A29 50p red, blk & gray .25 .20
O102 A29 1k gray, ind & yel (R) .50 .20
O103 A28 2k pale ol, ind & red (R) 1.10 .30
O104 A29 5k cit, dk bl & red (R) 2.75 .65
Nos. O94-O104 (11) 6.00 2.75

Similar Overprint on Nos. 197-200, 202-208 in Black or Red

1968 Unwmk. *Perf. 14*

Size: 21x17mm

Overprint: 13mm

O105 A28 1p gray .20 .20
O106 A28 2p carmine rose .20 .20
O107 A28 3p blue green .20 .20

Size: 23½x28mm

Overprint: 15mm

O108 A29 5p violet blue .20 .20
O109 A29 15p olive .20 .20

Size: 38½x21mm, 21x38½mm

Overprint: 14mm

O110 A28 20p rose & brn .20 .20
O111 A29 25p yel & brown (R) .20 .20
O112 A29 50p ver, blk & gray .25 .20
O113 A29 1k gray, ind & yel (R) .50 .20
O114 A28 2k dl cit, ind & red (R) 1.10 .25
O115 A29 5k yel, dk bl & red (R) 2.75 .55
Nos. O105-O115 (11) 6.00 2.60

OCCUPATION STAMPS

Issued by Burma Independence Army (in conjunction with Japanese occupation officials)

Stamps of Burma, 1937-40, Overprinted in Blue, Black Blue, Black or Red

Henzada Issue

#1, 3, 5 Overprinted in Blue or Black

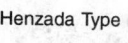

Henzada Type I

1942, May Wmk. 196 *Perf. 14*

1N1 A46 3p slate 5.00 *7.50*
1N2 A68 9p dark green 17.50 *25.00*
1N3 A49 2a vermilion 50.00 *75.00*

On 1938-40 George VI Issue

Perf. 13½x14

Wmk. 254

1N4 A1 1p red orange 150.00 *87.50*
1N5 A1 3p violet 17.50 *35.00*
1N6 A1 6p ultra 15.00 *30.00*
1N7 A1 9p yel green 200.00
1N8 A2 1a brown violet 5.00 *7.50*
1N9 A2 1½a turq green 12.50 *17.50*
1N10 A2 2a carmine 15.00 *17.50*
1N11 A2 4a slate blue 30.00 *37.50*

On Official Stamps of 1939

1N12 A1 3p violet 50.00 *62.50*
1N13 A1 6p ultra 45.00 *62.50*
1N14 A2 1½a turq green 65.00 *87.50*
1N15 A2 2a carmine 150.00 150.00
1N16 A2 4a slate blue 200.00 *250.00*

Authorities believe this overprint was officially applied only to postal stationery and that the adhesive stamps existing with it were not regularly issued. It has been called "Henzada Type II."

Myaungmya Issue

1937 George V Issue Overprinted in Black

Myaungmya Type I

1942, May Wmk. 196 *Perf. 14*

1N25 A68 9p dk green 50.00 *62.50*
1N26 A70 3a6p deep blue 25.00 *32.50*

On Official Stamp of 1937, No. O8

1N27 A53 6a bister 50.00 *62.50*

On 1938-40 George VI Issue

Perf. 13½x14

Wmk. 254

1N28 A1 9p yel green 100.00 *125.00*
1N29 A2 1a brown vio 175.00 *225.00*
1N30 A2 4a sl blue (blk ovpt. over red) 100.00 *125.00*

On Official Stamps of 1939

1N31 A1 3p violet 15.00 15.00
1N32 A1 6p ultra 7.50 *10.00*
1N33 A2 1a brown vio 7.50 *10.00*
1N34 A2 1½a turq green 400.00
1N35 A2 2a carmine 15.00 *20.00*
1N36 A2 4a slate blue 12.50 *17.50*

1938-40 George VI Issue Overprinted

Myaungmya Type II

1942, May

1N37 A1 3p violet 12.50 *20.00*
1N38 A1 6p ultra 25.00 *30.00*
1N39 A1 9p yel green 10.00 *15.00*
1N40 A2 1a brown vio 10.00 *12.50*
1N41 A2 2a carmine 15.00 *20.00*
1N42 A2 4a slate blue 15.00 *25.00*

Nos. 30-31 Overprinted

Myaungmya Type III

1N43 A7 1r brt ultra & dk vio 150.00
1N44 A7 2r dk vio & red brn 110.00

Pyapon Issue

No. 5 and 1938-40 George VI Issue Overprinted

1942, May

1N45 A1 6p ultra 75.00
1N46 A2 1a brown vio 65.00 50.00
1N47 A49 2a vermilion 75.00
1N48 A2 2a carmine 45.00 *62.50*
1N49 A2 4a slate blue 150.00 *200.00*
Nos. 1N45-1N49 (5) 410.00

Counterfeits of the peacock overprints exist.

OCCUPATION OFFICIAL STAMP

Myaungmya Issue

Burma No. O23 Overprinted in Black

1942, May Wmk. 254 *Perf. 13*

1NO1 A6 8a slate green 50.00 *62.50*

Overprint characters translate: "Office use." Two types of overprint differ mainly in base of peacock which is either 5mm or 8mm.

ISSUED UNDER JAPANESE OCCUPATION

Yano Seal — OS1

Wmk. ABSORBO DUPLICATOR and Outline of Elephant in Center of Sheet

Handstamped

1942, June 1 *Perf. 12x11*

Without Gum

2N1 OS1 1(a) vermilion 30.00 *37.50*

This stamp is the handstamped impression of the personal chop or seal of Shizuo Yano, chairman of the committee appointed to re-establish the Burmese postal system. It was prepared in Rangoon on paper captured from the Burma Government Offices. Not every stamp shows a portion of the watermark.

Farmer Plowing — OS2

Vertically Laid Paper

Without Gum

Wmk. ELEPHANT BRAND and Outline of Trumpeting Elephant Covering Several Stamps

1942, June 15 Litho. *Perf. 11x12*

2N2 OS2 1a scarlet 20.00 *25.00*

See illustration OS4.

Same, Surcharged with New Value

1942, Oct. 15

2N3 OS2 5c on 1a scarlet 12.50 10.50

Rice Harvest — A83

General Nogi — A84

Power Plant — A85

Admiral Togo — A86

Diamond Mountains, Korea — A89

Meiji Shrine, Tokyo — A90

Yomei Gate, Nikko — A91

Mount Fuji and Cherry Blossoms — A94

Torii of Miyajima Shrine — A96

Stamps of Japan, 1937-42, Handstamp Surcharged with New Value in Black

1942, Sept. Wmk. 257 *Perf. 13*

2N4 A83 ¼a on 1s fawn 12.50 *15.00*
2N5 A84 ½a on 2s crim 12.50 *15.00*
2N6 A85 ¾a on 3s green 20.00 20.00
2N7 A86 1a on 5s brn lake 17.50 *20.00*
2N8 A89 3a on 7s dp green 30.00 *32.50*
2N9 A86 4a on 4s dk green 22.50 *27.50*
a. 4a on 4s + 2s dk green (#B5) 75.00 *87.50*
2N10 A90 8a on 8s dk pur & pale vio 100.00 100.00
a. Red surcharge 140.00 *150.00*
2N11 A91 1r on 10s lake 12.50 *15.00*
2N12 A94 2r on 20s ultra 30.00 *35.00*
a. Red surcharge 37.50 37.50
2N13 A96 5r on 30s pck bl 10.00 10.00
a. Red surcharge 15.00 15.00
Nos. 2N4-2N13 (10) 267.50 *290.00*

Numerous double, inverted, etc., surcharges exist.

Re-surcharged in Black

1942, Oct. 15

2N14 A83 1c on ¼a on 1s 25.00 25.00
2N15 A84 2c on ½a on 2s 25.00 25.00
2N16 A85 3c on ¾a on 3s 30.00 *32.50*
a. "3C." in blue 75.00 *100.00*
2N17 A86 5c on 1a on 5s 40.00 40.00
a. "3C." in blue 125.00
2N18 A89 10c on 3a on 7s 45.00 45.00
2N19 A86 15c on 4a on 4s 10.50 10.50
2N20 A90 20c on 8a on 8s (#2N10) 110.00 90.00
a. On #2N10a 125.00 100.00
Nos. 2N14-2N20 (7) 285.50 268.00

No. 2N16a was issued in the Shan States.

Done locally, numerous different handstamps of each denomination can exist.

Stamps of Japan, 1937-42, Handstamp Surcharged with New Value in Black

1942, Oct. 15

2N21 A83 1c on 1s fawn 10.00 *12.50*
2N22 A84 2c on 2s crim 17.50 *20.00*
2N23 A85 3c on 3s green 20.00 *25.00*
a. "3C." in blue 75.00 *87.50*
2N24 A86 5c on 5s brn lake 20.00 *25.00*
a. "5C." in violet 87.50 *100.00*
2N25 A89 10c on 7s dp grn 25.00 *30.00*
2N26 A86 15c on 4s dk grn 10.00 *12.50*
2N27 A90 20c on 8s dk pur & pale vio 70.00 60.00
Nos. 2N21-2N27 (7) 172.50 *185.00*

Nos. 2N23a and 2N24a were issued in the Shan States.

Burma State Government Crest — OS3

Unwmk.

1943, Feb. 15 Litho. *Perf. 12*

Without Gum

2N29	OS3	5c carmine	10.00	*12.50*
a.		Imperf.	12.50	*15.00*

This stamp was intended to be used to cover the embossed George VI envelope stamp and generally was sold affixed to such envelopes. It is also known used on private envelopes.

Farmer Plowing — OS4

1943, Mar. Typo.

Without Gum

2N30	OS4	1c deep orange	1.00	1.00
2N31	OS4	2c yel green	1.00	*1.50*
2N32	OS4	3c blue	1.00	1.00
a.		Laid paper	10.00	10.00
2N33	OS4	5c carmine	.50	*.65*
a.		Small "5c"	3.00	*4.00*
b.		Imperf.		
2N34	OS4	10c violet brown	.75	*.90*
2N35	OS4	15c red violet	.25	.25
a.		Laid paper	10.00	
2N36	OS4	20c dull purple	.25	*.75*
2N37	OS4	30c blue green	.25	*.75*
		Nos. 2N30-2N37 (8)	5.00	*6.80*

Small "c" in Nos. 2N34 to 2N37.

Burmese Soldier Carving "Inde-pendence" OS5

Farmer Rejoicing OS6

Boy with Burmese Flag — OS7

Hyphen-hole Perf., Pin-Perf. x Hyphen-hole Perf.

1943, Aug. 1 Typo.

2N38	OS5	1c orange	1.00	*2.00*
a.		Perf. 11	3.50	*4.00*
2N39	OS6	3c blue	1.00	*2.00*
a.		Perf. 11	3.50	*4.00*
2N40	OS7	5c rose	1.00	*2.00*
a.		Perf. 11	3.50	*4.00*
		Nos. 2N38-2N40 (3)	3.00	*6.00*

Declaration of the independence of Burma by the Ba Maw government, Aug. 1, 1943.

Burmese Girl Carrying Water Jar — OS8

Elephant Carrying Teak Log — OS9

Watch Tower of Mandalay Palace — OS10

1943, Oct. 1 Litho. *Perf. 12½*

2N41	OS8	1c dp salmon	17.00	*10.00*
2N42	OS8	2c yel green	.60	*1.25*
2N43	OS8	3c violet	.60	*1.00*
2N44	OS9	5c rose	.65	*1.00*
2N45	OS9	10c blue	.80	.60
2N46	OS9	15c vermilion	.80	*1.00*
2N47	OS9	20c yel green	.80	*1.25*
2N48	OS9	30c brown	.80	*1.25*
2N49	OS10	1r vermilion	.35	*3.00*
2N50	OS10	2r violet	.35	*5.00*
		Nos. 2N41-2N50 (10)	22.75	*25.35*

No. 2N49 exists imperforate. Canceled to order copies of Nos. 2N42-2N50 same values as unused.

Bullock Cart — OS11

Shan Woman — OS12

1943, Oct. 1 *Perf. 12½*

2N51	OS11	1c brown	22.50	*35.00*
2N52	OS11	2c yel green	22.50	*35.00*
2N53	OS11	3c violet	20.00	*30.00*
2N54	OS11	5c ultra	4.50	*12.00*
2N55	OS12	10c blue	20.00	*35.00*
2N56	OS12	20c rose	22.50	*35.00*
2N57	OS12	30c brown	22.50	*35.00*
		Nos. 2N51-2N57 (7)	134.50	*217.00*

For use only in the Shan States. Perak No. N34 also used in Shan States. CTO's ½ used value.

ဗမာနိုင်ငံတော်

Surcharged in Black

၁ ဆင့်။

1944, Nov. 1

2N58	OS11	1c brown	4.00	*5.00*
2N59	OS11	2c yel green	.20	*1.25*
a.		Inverted surcharge	150.00	*200.00*
2N60	OS11	3c violet	2.50	*4.00*
2N61	OS11	5c ultra	1.25	1.50
2N62	OS12	10c blue	2.50	*3.50*
2N63	OS12	20c rose	.60	*1.50*
2N64	OS12	30c brown	.75	*1.50*
		Nos. 2N58-2N64 (7)	11.80	*18.25*

Top line of surcharge reads: "Bama naing ngan daw" (Burma State). Bottom line repeats denomination in Burmese. Surcharge applied when the Shan States came under Burmese government administration, Dec. 24, 1943. CTO's same value as unused.

BURUNDI

bu-'rün-dē

LOCATION — Central Africa, adjoining the ex-Belgian Congo Republic, Rwanda and Tanzania
GOVT. — Republic
AREA — 10,759 sq. mi.
POP. — 5,735,937 (1999 est.)
CAPITAL — Bujumbura

Burundi was established as an independent country on July 1, 1962. With Rwanda, it had been a UN trusteeship territory (Ruanda-Urundi) administered by Belgium. A military coup overthrew the monarchy November 28, 1966.

100 Centimes = 1 Franc

Catalogue values for all unused stamps in this country are for Never Hinged items.

Flower Issue of Ruanda-Urundi, 1953 Overprinted:

Royaume du

Burundi

Perf. 11½

1962, July 1 Unwmk. Photo.

Flowers in Natural Colors

1	A27	25c dk grn & dull org	.20	.20
2	A27	40c green & salmon	.20	.20
3	A27	60c blue grn & pink	.20	.20
4	A27	1.25fr dk green & blue	7.00	6.50
5	A27	1.50fr vio & apple grn	.30	.25
6	A27	5fr dp plum & lt bl grn	.40	.30
7	A27	7fr dk green & fawn	.85	.55
8	A27	10fr dp plum & pale ol	1.25	.80
		Nos. 1-8 (8)	10.40	9.00

Animal Issue of Ruanda-Urundi, 1959-61 with Similar Overprint or Surcharge in Black or Violet Blue

Size: 23x33mm, 33x23mm

9	A29	10c brn, crim & blk brn	.20	.20
10	A30	20c gray, ap grn & blk	.20	.20
11	A29	40c mag, blk & gray grn	.20	.20
12	A30	50c grn, org yel & brn	.20	.20
a.		Larger overprint and bar	.20	.20
13	A29	1fr brn, ultra & blk	.20	.20
14	A30	1.50fr blk, gray & org (VB)	.20	.20
15	A29	2fr grnsh bl, ind & brn	.20	.20
16	A30	3fr brn, dp car & blk	.20	.20
17	A30	3.50fr on 3fr brn, dp car & blk	.20	.20
18	A30	4fr on 10fr multi ("XX" 6mm wide)	.20	.20
a.		"XX" 4mm wide	.45	.45
19	A30	5fr multicolored	.20	.20
20	A30	6.50fr red, org yel & brn	.25	.20
21	A30	8fr bl, mag & blk	.30	.25
a.		Violet blue overprint	.65	.65
22	A30	10fr multicolored	.35	.30

Size: 45x26½mm

23	A30	20fr multicolored	.65	.65
24	A30	50fr multi (ovpt. bars 2mm wide)	1.25	1.10
a.		Overprint bars 4mm wide	1.90	1.10
		Nos. 9-24 (16)	5.00	4.70

On #12a, "Burundi" is 13mm long; bar is continuous line across sheet. On #12, "Burundi" is 10mm; bar is 29mm. #12a was issued in 1963.

Two types of overprint exist on 10c, 40c, 1fr and 2fr: I, "du" is below "me"; bar 22½mm. II, "du" below "oy"; bar 20mm.

The 50c and 3fr exist in two types, besides the larger 50c overprint listed as No. 12: I, "du" is closer to "Royaume" than to "Burundi"; bar is less than 29mm; wording is centered above bar. II, "du" is closer to "Burundi"; bar is more than 30mm; wording is off-center leftward.

King Mwami Mwambutsa IV and Royal Drummers — A1

Flag and Arms of Burundi — A2

Design: 2fr, 8fr, 50fr, Map of Burundi and King.

Unwmk.

1962, Sept. 27 Photo. *Perf. 14*

25	A1	50c dull rose car & dk brn	.20	.20
26	A2	1fr dk green, red & emer	.20	.20
27	A1	2fr brown ol & dk brn	.20	.20
28	A1	3fr vermilion & dk brn	.25	.20
29	A2	4fr Prus blue, red & emer	.20	.20
30	A1	8fr violet & dk brn	.30	.20
31	A1	10fr brt green & dk brn	.50	.20
32	A2	20fr brown, red & emer	1.25	.20
33	A1	50fr brt pink & dk brn	2.25	.40
		Nos. 25-33 (9)	5.35	2.00

Burundi's independence, July 1, 1962.

See #47-50. For overprints see #45-46, 51-52.

Ruanda-Urundi Nos. 151-152 Surcharged:

HOMMAGE A
DAG HAMMARSKJÖLD
3.50F
ROYAUME DU BURUNDI

Photogravure, Surcharge Engraved

1962, Oct. 31 *Perf. 11½*

Inscription in French

34	A31	3.50fr on 3fr ultra & red	.20	.20
35	A31	6.50fr on 3fr ultra & red	.20	.20
36	A31	10fr on 3fr ultra & red	.30	.25

Inscription in Flemish

37	A31	3.50fr on 3fr ultra & red	.20	.20
38	A31	6.50fr on 3fr ultra & red	.20	.20
39	A31	10fr on 3fr ultra & red	.30	.25
		Nos. 34-39 (6)	1.40	1.30

Dag Hammarskjold, Secretary General of the United Nations, 1953-61.

King Mwami Mwambutsa IV, Map of Burundi and Emblem — A3

1962, Dec. 10 Photo. *Perf. 14*

40	A3	8fr yel, bl grn & blk brn	.65	.20
41	A3	50fr gray grn, bl grn & blk brn	1.75	.35

WHO drive to eradicate malaria.

Stamps of type A3 without anti-malaria emblem are listed as Nos. 27, 30 and 33.

Sowing Seed over Africa — A4

1963, Mar. 21 *Perf. 14x13*

42	A4	4fr olive & dull pur	.20	.20
43	A4	8fr dp org & dull pur	.20	.20
44	A4	15fr emerald & dull pur	.20	.20
		Nos. 42-44 (3)	.60	.60

FAO "Freedom from Hunger" campaign.

Nos. 27 and 33 Overprinted in Dark Green

1963, June 19 Unwmk. *Perf. 14*

45	A1	2fr brn olive & dk brn	1.60	1.25
46	A1	50fr brt pink & dk brn	1.90	1.25

Conquest and peaceful use of outer space.

Types of 1962 Inscribed: "Premier Anniversaire" in Red or Magenta

1963, July 1 Photo.

47	A2	4fr olive, red & emer (R)	.20	.20
48	A1	8fr orange & dk brn (M)	.20	.20
49	A1	10fr lilac & dk brn (M)	.20	.20
50	A2	20fr gray, red & emer (R)	.40	.25
		Nos. 47-50 (4)	1.00	.85

First anniversary of independence.

Nos. 26 and 32 Surcharged in Brown

1963, Sept. 24 Unwmk. *Perf. 14*

51	A2	6.50fr on 1fr multi	.40	.20
52	A2	15fr on 20fr multi	.75	.25

Red Cross Flag over Globe with Map of Africa — A5

1963, Sept. 26 *Perf. 14x13*

53	A5	4fr emer, car & gray	.20	.20
54	A5	8fr brn ol, car & gray	.25	.20
55	A5	10fr blue, car & gray	.40	.20
56	A5	20fr lilac, car & gray	.75	.30
		Nos. 53-56 (4)	1.60	.90

Centenary of International Red Cross. See No. B7.

"1962", Arms of Burundi, UN and UNESCO Emblems — A6

UN Agency Emblems: 8fr, ITU. 10fr, World Meteorological Organization. 20fr, UPU. 50fr, FAO.

1963, Nov. 4 Unwmk. *Perf. 14*

57	A6	4fr yel, ol grn & blk	.20	.20
58	A6	8fr pale lil, Prus bl & blk	.20	.20
59	A6	10fr blue, lil & blk	.20	.20
60	A6	20fr yel grn, grn & blk	.35	.20
61	A6	50fr yel, red brn & blk	.90	.30
a.		Souvenir sheet of 2	3.00	3.00
		Nos. 57-61 (5)	1.85	1.10

1st anniv. of Burundi's admission to the UN. No. 61a contains two imperf. stamps with simulated perforations similar to Nos. 60-61. The 20fr stamp shows the FAO and the 50fr the WMO emblems.

UNESCO Emblem, Scales and Map — A7

Designs: 3.50fr, 6.50fr, Scroll, scales and "UNESCO." 10fr, 20fr, Abraham Lincoln, broken chain and scales.

1963, Dec. 10 Litho. *Perf. 14x13½*

62	A7	50c pink, lt bl & blk	.20	.20
63	A7	1.50fr org, lt bl & blk	.20	.20
64	A7	3.50fr fawn, lt grn & blk	.20	.20
65	A7	6.50fr lt vio, lt grn & blk	.20	.20
66	A7	10fr blue, bis & blk	.30	.20
67	A7	20fr pale brn, ocher, bl & blk	.60	.20
		Nos. 62-67 (6)	1.70	1.20

15th anniv. of the Universal Declaration of Human Rights and the cent. of the American Emancipation Proclamation (Nos. 66-67).

Ice Hockey — A8

Impala — A9

Designs: 3.50fr, Women's figure skating. 6.50fr, Torch. 10fr, Men's speed skating. 20fr, Slalom.

Unwmk.

1964, Jan. 25 Photo. *Perf. 14*

68	A8	50c olive, blk & gold	.20	.20
69	A8	3.50fr lt brown, blk & gold	.20	.20
70	A8	6.50fr pale gray, blk & gold	.40	.20
71	A8	10fr gray, blk & gold	.50	.20
72	A8	20fr tan, blk & gold	1.00	.30
		Nos. 68-72 (5)	2.30	1.10

Issued to publicize the 9th Winter Olympic Games, Innsbruck, Jan. 29-Feb. 9, 1964.

A souvenir sheet contains two stamps (10fr+5fr and 20fr+5fr) in tan, black and gold.

Canceled to Order

Starting about 1964, values in the used column are for "canceled to order" stamps. Postally used copies sell for much more.

Perf. 14x13, 13x14

1964, Feb. 10 Litho.

Animals: 1fr, 5fr, Hippopotam us, horiz. 1.50fr, 10fr, Giraffe. 2fr, 8fr, Cape buffalo, horiz. 3fr, 6.50fr, Zebra, horiz. 3.50fr, 15fr, Defassa waterbuck. 20fr, Cheetah. 50fr, Elephant. 100fr, Lion.

Size: 21½x35mm, 35x21½mm

73	A9	50c multi	.20	.20
74	A9	1fr multi	.20	.20
75	A9	1.50fr multi	.20	.20
76	A9	2fr multi	.20	.20
77	A9	3fr multi	.20	.20
78	A9	3.50fr multi	.20	.20

Size: 26x42mm, 42x26mm

79	A9	4fr multi	.25	.20
80	A9	5fr multi	.30	.20
81	A9	6.50fr multi	.35	.20
82	A9	8fr multi	.40	.20
83	A9	10fr multi	.50	.20
84	A9	15fr multi	.65	.20

Perf. 14

Size: 53x33mm

85	A9	20fr multi	.85	.20
86	A9	50fr multi	2.25	.30
87	A9	100fr multi	4.00	.65
		Nos. 73-87,C1-C7 (22)	13.50	5.15

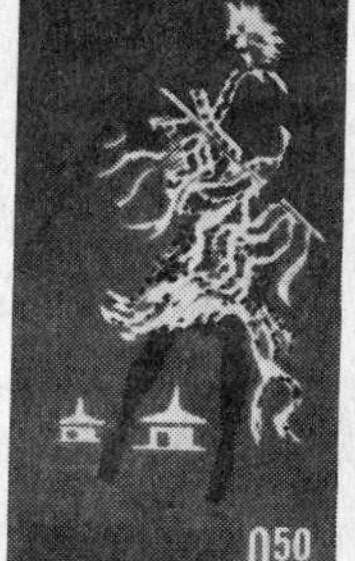

Burundi Dancer — A10

Designs: Various Dancers and Drummers.

Unwmk.

1964, Aug. 21 Litho. *Perf. 14*

Dancers Multicolored

88	A10	50c gold & emerald	.20	.20
89	A10	1fr gold & vio blue	.20	.20
90	A10	4fr gold & brt blue	.20	.20
91	A10	6.50fr gold & red	.20	.20
92	A10	10fr gold & brt blue	.30	.20
93	A10	15fr gold & emerald	.45	.20
94	A10	20fr gold & red	.65	.25
a.		Souvenir sheet of 3, #92-94	1.50	1.50
		Nos. 88-94 (7)	2.20	1.45

1965, Sept. 10

Dancers Multicolored

88a	A10	50c silver & emerald	.20	.20
89a	A10	1fr silver & violet blue	.20	.20
90a	A10	4fr silver & bright blue	.20	.20
91a	A10	6.50fr silver & red	.20	.20
92a	A10	10fr silver & bright blue	.20	.20
93a	A10	15fr silver & emerald	.20	.20
94b	A10	20fr silver & red	.30	.30
c.		Souvenir sheet of 3, #92a-94b	1.50	1.50
		Nos. 88a-94b (7)	1.50	1.50

New York World's Fair, 1964-65.

Pope Paul VI and King Mwami Mwambutsa IV — A11

22 Sainted Martyrs — A12

4fr, 14fr, Pope John XXIII and King Mwami.

1964, Nov. 12 Photo. *Perf. 12*

95	A11	50c brt bl, gold & red brn	.20	.20
96	A12	1fr mag, gold & slate	.20	.20
97	A11	4fr pale rose lil, gold & brn	.20	.20
98	A12	8fr red, gold & brn	.20	.20
99	A11	14fr lt grn, gold & brn	.40	.20
100	A11	20fr red brn, gold & grn	.65	.30
		Nos. 95-100 (6)	1.85	1.30

Canonization of 22 African martyrs, 10/18/64.

Shot Put A13

African Purple Gallinule A14

Sports: 1fr, Discus. 3fr, Swimming. 4fr, Running. 6.50fr, Javelin, woman. 8fr, Hurdling. 10fr, Broad jump. 14fr, Diving, woman. 18fr, High jump. 20fr, Vaulting.

3fr, 8fr, 10fr, 18fr, 20fr are horiz.

1964, Nov. 18 Litho. *Perf. 14*

101	A13	50c olive & multi	.20	.20
102	A13	1fr brt pink & multi	.20	.20
103	A13	3fr multi	.20	.20
104	A13	4fr multi	.20	.20
105	A13	6.50fr multi	.20	.20
106	A13	8fr lt bl & multi	.20	.20
107	A13	10fr multi	.20	.20
108	A13	14fr multi	.25	.20
109	A13	18fr bister & multi	.30	.20
110	A13	20fr gray & multi	.35	.20
		Nos. 101-110 (10)	2.30	2.00

18th Olympic Games, Tokyo, Oct. 10-25, 1964. See No. B8.

1965 Unwmk. *Perf. 14*

Birds: 1fr, 5fr, Little bee eater. 1.50fr, 6.50fr, Secretary bird. 2fr, 8fr, Yellow-billed stork. 3fr, 10fr, Congo peacock. 3.50fr, 15fr, African anhinga. 20fr, Saddle-billed stork. 50fr, Abyssinian ground hornbill. 100fr, Crowned crane.

Birds in Natural Colors

Size: 21x35mm

111	A14	50c tan, grn & blk	.20	.20
112	A14	1fr pink, mag & blk	.20	.20
113	A14	1.50fr blue & blk	.20	.20
114	A14	2fr yel grn, dk grn & blk	.20	.20
115	A14	3fr yellow, brn & blk	.20	.20
116	A14	3.50fr yel grn, dk grn & blk	.20	.20

Size: 26x43mm

117	A14	4fr tan, grn & blk	.20	.20
118	A14	5fr pink, mag & blk	.20	.20
119	A14	6.50fr blue & blk	.20	.20
120	A14	8fr yel grn, dk grn & blk	.20	.20
121	A14	10fr yel, brn & blk	.20	.20
122	A14	15fr yel grn, dk grn & blk	.35	.20

Size: 33x53mm

123	A14	20fr rose lilac & blk	.45	.30
124	A14	50fr yellow, brn & blk	1.25	.20
125	A14	100fr green, yel & blk	2.75	.40
		Nos. 111-125 (15)	7.00	3.30

Issue dates: Nos. 111-116, Mar. 31. Nos. 117-122, Apr. 16. Nos. 123-125, Apr. 30.

For overprints see #174-184, C35A-C35I.

Relay Satellite and Morse Key — A15

Designs: 3fr, Telstar and old telephone handpiece. 4fr, Relay satellite and old wall telephone. 6.50fr, Orbiting Geophysical Observatory and radar screen. 8fr, Telstar II and headphones. 10fr, Sputnik II and radar aerial. 14fr, Syncom and transmission aerial. 20fr, Interplanetary Explorer and tracking aerial.

1965, July 3 Litho. *Perf. 13*

126	A15	1fr multi	.20	.20
127	A15	3fr multi	.20	.20
128	A15	4fr multi	.20	.20
129	A15	6.50fr multi	.20	.20
130	A15	8fr multi	.20	.20
131	A15	10fr multi	.20	.20
132	A15	14fr multi	.25	.20
133	A15	20fr multi	.30	.20
		Nos. 126-133 (8)	1.75	1.60

Cent. of the ITU. Perf. and imperf. souv. sheets of 2 contain Nos. 131, 133. Size: 120x86mm. Value, both sheets, $7.50.

Globe and ICY Emblem — A16

Designs: 4fr, Map of Africa and UN development emblem. 8fr, Map of Asia and Colombo Plan emblem. 10fr, Globe and UN emblem. 18fr, Map of the Americas and Alliance for Progress emblem. 25fr, Map of Europe and EUROPA emblems. 40fr, Map of Outer Space and satellite with UN wreath.

1965, Oct. 1 Litho. *Perf. 13*

134	A16	1fr ol green & multi	.20	.20
135	A16	4fr dull blue & multi	.20	.20
136	A16	8fr pale yellow & multi	.20	.20
137	A16	10fr lilac & multi	.20	.20
138	A16	18fr salmon & multi	.25	.20
139	A16	25fr gray & multi	.50	.20

140	A16	40fr blue & multi	.75	.20
a.		Souvenir sheet of 3, #138-140	1.60	1.60
		Nos. 134-140 (7)	2.30	1.40

International Cooperation Year.

Protea
A17

Flowers: 1fr, 5fr, Crossandra. 1.50fr, 6.50fr, Ansellia. 2fr, 8fr, Thunbergia. 3fr, 10fr, Schizoglossum. 3.50fr, 15fr, Dissotis. 4fr, 20fr, Protea. 50fr, Gazania. 100fr, Hibiscus. 150fr, Markhamia.

1966 Unwmk. *Perf. 13½*

Size: 26x26mm

141	A17	50c multi	.20	.20
142	A17	1fr multi	.20	.20
143	A17	1.50fr multi	.20	.20
144	A17	2fr multi	.20	.20
145	A17	3fr multi	.20	.20
146	A17	3.50fr multi	.20	.20

Size: 31x31mm

147	A17	4fr multi	.20	.20
148	A17	5fr multi	.20	.20
149	A17	6.50fr multi	.20	.20
150	A17	8fr multi	.20	.20
151	A17	10fr multi	.20	.20
152	A17	15fr multi	.30	.20

Size: 39x39mm

153	A17	20fr multi	.40	.20
154	A17	50fr multi	1.00	.25
155	A17	100fr multi	1.90	.40
156	A17	150fr multi	2.75	.55
		Nos. 141-156,C17-C25 (25)	12.80	5.75

Issue dates: Nos. 141-147, Feb. 28; Nos. 148-153, May 18; Nos. 154-156, June 15.

For overprints see Nos. 159-173, C27-C35.

Souvenir Sheets

Allegory of Prosperity and Equality Tapestry by Peter Colfs — A18

1966, Nov. 4 Litho. *Perf. 13½*

157	A18	Sheet of 7 (1.50fr)	.65	.25
158	A18	Sheet of 7 (4fr)	1.60	.65

20th anniv. of UNESCO. Each sheet contains 6 stamps showing a reproduction of the Colfs tapestry from the lobby of the General Assembly Building, NYC, and one stamp with the UNESCO emblem plus a label. The labels on Nos. 157-158 and C26 are inscribed in French or English. The 3 sheets with French inscription have light blue marginal border. The 3 sheets with English inscription have pink border. See No. C26.

Republic

Nos. 141-152, 154-156 Overprinted

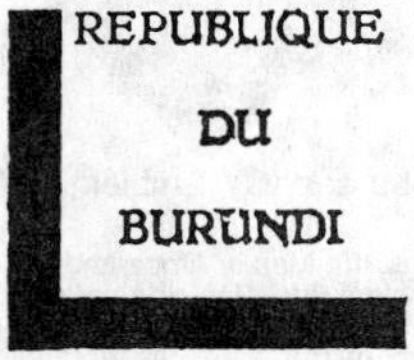

1967 Litho. *Perf. 13½*

Size: 26x26mm

159	A17	50c multi	.20	.20
160	A17	1fr multi	.20	.20
161	A17	1.50fr multi	.20	.20
162	A17	2fr multi	.20	.20
163	A17	3fr multi	.20	.20
164	A17	3.50fr multi	.20	.20

Size: 31x31mm

165	A17	4fr multi	.80	.30
166	A17	5fr multi	.20	.20
167	A17	6.50fr multi	.20	.20
168	A17	8fr multi	.25	.20
169	A17	10fr multi	.30	.20
170	A17	15fr multi	.40	.20

Size: 39x39mm

171	A17	50fr multi	3.75	1.25
172	A17	100fr multi	6.25	2.50
173	A17	150fr multi	5.00	2.25
		Nos. 159-173,C27-C35 (24)	29.65	11.80

Nos. 111, 113, 116, 118-125 Overprinted "REPUBLIQUE DU BURUNDI" and Horizontal Bar

1967 Litho. *Perf. 14*

Birds in Natural Colors

Size: 21x35mm

174	A14	50c multi	1.25	.65
175	A14	1.50fr blue & black	.20	.20
176	A14	3.50fr multi	.20	.20

Size: 26x43mm

177	A14	5fr multi	.20	.20
178	A14	6.50fr blue & black	.20	.20
179	A14	8fr multi	.20	.20
180	A14	10fr yel, brn & blk	.30	.20
181	A14	15fr multi	.65	.20

Size: 33x53mm

182	A14	20fr multi	2.00	.40
183	A14	50fr multi	4.00	1.40
184	A14	100fr multi	6.00	2.75
		Nos. 174-184 (11)	15.20	6.60

Haplochromis Multicolor — A19

Various Tropical Fish.

1967 Photo. *Perf. 13½*

Size: 42x19mm

186	A19	50c multi	.20	.20
187	A19	1fr multi	.20	.20
188	A19	1.50fr multi	.20	.20
189	A19	2fr multi	.20	.20
190	A19	3fr multi	.20	.20
191	A19	3.50fr multi	.20	.20

Size: 50x25mm

192	A19	4fr multi	.20	.20
193	A19	5fr multi	.20	.20
194	A19	6.50fr multi	.25	.20
195	A19	8fr multi	.30	.20
196	A19	10fr multi	.35	.20
197	A19	15fr multi	.50	.20

Size: 59x30mm

198	A19	20fr multi	.75	.20
199	A19	50fr multi	1.50	.20
200	A19	100fr multi	3.00	.30
201	A19	150fr multi	4.25	.45
		Nos. 186-201,C46-C54 (25)	21.00	5.46

Issue Dates: Nos. 186-191, Apr. 4; Nos. 192-197, Apr. 28; Nos. 198-201, May 18.

Ancestor Figures, Ivory Coast — A20

African Art: 1fr, Seat of Honor, Southeast Congo. 1.50fr, Antelope head, Aribinda Region. 2fr, Buffalo mask, Upper Volta. 4fr, Funeral figures, Southwest Ethiopia.

1967, June 5 Photo. *Perf. 13½*

202	A20	50c silver & multi	.20	.20
203	A20	1fr silver & multi	.20	.20
204	A20	1.50fr silver & multi	.20	.20
205	A20	2fr silver & multi	.20	.20
206	A20	4fr silver & multi	.20	.20
		Nos. 202-206,C36-C40 (10)	2.25	2.05

Scouts on Hiking Trip — A21

Designs: 1fr, Cooking at campfire. 1.50fr, Lord Baden-Powell. 2fr, Boy Scout and Cub Scout giving Scout sign. 4fr, First aid.

1967, Aug. 9 Photo. *Perf. 13½*

207	A21	50c silver & multi	.20	.20
208	A21	1fr silver & multi	.20	.20
209	A21	1.50fr silver & multi	.20	.20
210	A21	2fr silver & multi	.20	.20
211	A21	4fr silver & multi	.20	.20
		Nos. 207-211,C41-C45 (10)	2.85	2.00

60th anniv. of the Boy Scouts and the 12th Boy Scout World Jamboree, Farragut State Park, Idaho, Aug. 1-9.

The Gleaners, by Francois Millet A22

Paintings Exhibited at EXPO '67: 8fr, The Water Carrier of Seville, by Velazquez. 14fr, The Triumph of Neptune and Amphitrite, by Nicolas Poussin. 18fr, Acrobat Standing on a Ball, by Picasso. 25fr, Marguerite van Eyck, by Jan van Eyck. 40fr, St. Peter Denying Christ, by Rembrandt.

1967, Oct. 12 Photo. *Perf. 13½*

212	A22	4fr multi	.20	.20
213	A22	8fr multi	.20	.20
214	A22	14fr multi	.25	.20
215	A22	18fr multi	.30	.20
216	A22	25fr multi	.50	.20
217	A22	40fr multi	.75	.25
a.		Souvenir sheet of 2, #216-217	1.25	1.00
		Nos. 212-217 (6)	2.20	1.25

EXPO '67 International Exhibition, Montreal, Apr. 28-Oct. 27. Printed in sheets of 10 stamps and 2 labels inscribed in French or English. No. 217a exists imperf.

Place de la Revolution and Pres. Michel Micombero — A23

Designs: 5fr, President Michel Micombero and flag. 14fr, Formal garden and coat of arms. 20fr, Modern building and coat of arms.

1967, Nov. 23 *Perf. 13½*

218	A23	5fr multi	.20	.20
219	A23	14fr multi	.20	.20
220	A23	20fr multi	.30	.20
221	A23	30fr multi	.45	.25
		Nos. 218-221 (4)	1.15	.85

First anniversary of the Republic.

Madonna by Carlo Crivelli — A24

Designs: 1fr, Adoration of the Shepherds by Juan Bautista Mayno. 4fr, Holy Family by Anthony Van Dyck. 14fr, Nativity by Maitre de Moulins.

1967, Dec. 7 Photo. *Perf. 13½*

222	A24	1fr multi	.20	.20
223	A24	4fr multi	.20	.20
224	A24	14fr multi	.25	.20
225	A24	26fr multi	.60	.25
		Nos. 222-225 (4)	1.25	.85

Christmas 1967. Printed in sheets of 25 and one corner label inscribed "Noel 1967" and giving name of painting and painter.

Slalom — A25

10fr, Ice hockey. 14fr, Women's skating. 17fr, Bobsled. 26fr, Ski jump. 40fr, Speed skating. 60fr, Hand holding torch, and Winter Olympics emblem.

1968, Feb. 16 Photo. *Perf. 13½*

226	A25	5fr silver & multi	.20	.20
227	A25	10fr silver & multi	.20	.20
228	A25	14fr silver & multi	.25	.20
229	A25	17fr silver & multi	.30	.20
230	A25	26fr silver & multi	.50	.20
231	A25	40fr silver & multi	.75	.20
232	A25	60fr silver & multi	1.25	.20
		Nos. 226-232 (7)	3.45	1.40

Issued to publicize the 10th Winter Olympic Games, Grenoble, France, Feb. 6-18. Issued in sheets of 10 stamps and label.

The Lacemaker, by Vermeer A26

Paintings: 1.50fr, Portrait of a Young Man, by Botticelli. 2fr, Maja Vestida, by Goya, horiz.

1968, Mar. 29 Photo. *Perf. 13½*

233	A26	1.50fr gold & multi	.20	.20
234	A26	2fr gold & multi	.20	.20
235	A26	4fr gold & multi	.20	.20
		Nos. 233-235,C59-C61 (6)	1.95	1.20

Issued in sheets of 6.

Moon Probe — A27

Designs: 6fr, Russian astronaut walking in space. 8fr, Weather satellite. 10fr, American astronaut walking in space.

1968, May 15 Photo. *Perf. 13½*

Size: 35x35mm

236	A27	4fr silver & multi	.20	.20
237	A27	6fr silver & multi	.20	.20
238	A27	8fr silver & multi	.20	.20
239	A27	10fr silver & multi	.25	.20
		Nos. 236-239,C62-C65 (8)	2.55	1.60

Issued to publicize peaceful space explorations.

A souvenir sheet contains one 25fr stamp in Moon Probe design and one 40fr in Weather Satellite design. Stamp size: 41x41mm. Value $2. Sheet exists imperf. Price $3.

Salamis Aethiops — A28

Butterflies: 1fr, 5fr, Graphium ridleyanus. 1.50fr, 6.50fr, Cymothoe. 2fr, 8fr, Charaxes eupale. 3fr, 10fr, Papilio bromius. 3.50fr, 15fr, Teracolus annae. 20fr, Salamis aethiops. 50fr, Papilio zonobia. 100fr, Danais chrysippus. 150fr, Salamis temora.

1968

Size: 30x33½mm

240	A28	50c gold & multi	.20	.20
241	A28	1fr gold & multi	.20	.20
242	A28	1.50fr gold & multi	.20	.20
243	A28	2fr gold & multi	.20	.20
244	A28	3fr gold & multi	.20	.20
245	A28	3.50fr gold & multi	.20	.20

Size: 33½x37½mm

246	A28	4fr gold & multi	.20	.20
247	A28	5fr gold & multi	.20	.20
248	A28	6.50fr gold & multi	.55	.20
249	A28	8fr gold & multi	.65	.20
250	A28	10fr gold & multi	.75	.20
251	A28	15fr gold & multi	.90	.20

Size: 41x46mm

252	A28	20fr gold & multi	1.50	.20
253	A28	50fr gold & multi	3.00	.20
254	A28	100fr gold & multi	5.00	.30
255	A28	150fr gold & multi	7.50	.50
		Nos. 240-255,C66-C74 (25)	31.45	5.40

Issue dates: Nos. 240-245, June 7; Nos. 246-251, June 28. Nos. 252-255, July 19.

Women, Along the Manzanares, by Goya — A29

Paintings: 7fr, The Letter, by Pieter de Hooch. 11fr, Woman Reading a Letter, by Gerard Terborch. 14fr, Man Writing a Letter, by Gabriel Metsu.

1968, Sept. 30 Photo. *Perf. 13½*

256	A29	4fr multi	.20	.20
257	A29	7fr multi	.20	.20
258	A29	11fr multi	.20	.20
259	A29	14fr multi	.30	.20
		Nos. 256-259,C84-C87 (8)	2.90	1.60

International Letter Writing Week.

Soccer — A30

1968, Oct. 24

260	A30	4fr shown	.20	.20
261	A30	7fr Basketball	.20	.20
262	A30	13fr High jump	.20	.20
263	A30	24fr Relay race	.35	.20
264	A30	40fr Javelin	.60	.30
		Nos. 260-264,C88-C92 (10)	4.20	2.20

19th Olympic Games, Mexico City, Oct. 12-27. Printed in sheets of 8.

Virgin and Child, by Fra Filippo Lippi — A31

Paintings: 5fr, The Magnificat, by Sandro Botticelli. 6fr, Virgin and Child, by Albrecht Durer. 11fr, Madonna del Gran Duca, by Raphael.

1968, Nov. 26 Photo. *Perf. 13½*

265	A31	3fr multi	.20	.20
266	A31	5fr multi	.20	.20
267	A31	6fr multi	.20	.20
268	A31	11fr multi	.25	.20
a.		Souvenir sheet of 4, #265-268	1.00	1.00
		Nos. 265-268,C93-C96 (8)	2.00	1.60

Christmas 1968. For overprints see Nos. 272-275, C100-C103.

WHO Emblem and Map of Africa — A32

1969, Jan. 22

269	A32	5fr gold, dk grn & yel	.20	.20
270	A32	6fr gold, vio & ver	.20	.20
271	A32	11fr gold, pur & red lil	.25	.20
		Nos. 269-271 (3)	.65	.60

20th anniv. of WHO in Africa.

Nos. 265-268 Overprinted in Silver

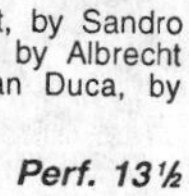

1969, Feb. 17 Photo. *Perf. 13½*

272	A31	3fr multi	.20	.20
273	A31	5fr multi	.20	.20
274	A31	6fr multi	.20	.20
275	A31	11fr multi	.22	.20
		Nos. 272-275,C100-C103 (8)	2.17	1.65

Man's 1st flight around the moon by the US spacecraft Apollo 8, Dec. 21-27, 1968.

Map of Africa, and CEPT Emblem — A33

Designs: 14fr, Plowing with tractor. 17fr, Teacher and pupil. 26fr, Maps of Europe and Africa and CEPT (Conference of European Postal and Telecommunications Administrations) emblem, horiz.

1969, Mar. 12 Photo. *Perf. 13*

276	A33	5fr multi	.20	.20
277	A33	14fr multi	.20	.20
278	A33	17fr multi	.25	.20
279	A33	26fr multi	.35	.20
		Nos. 276-279 (4)	1.00	.80

5th anniv. of the Yaounde (Cameroun) Agreement, creating the European and African-Malgache Economic Community.

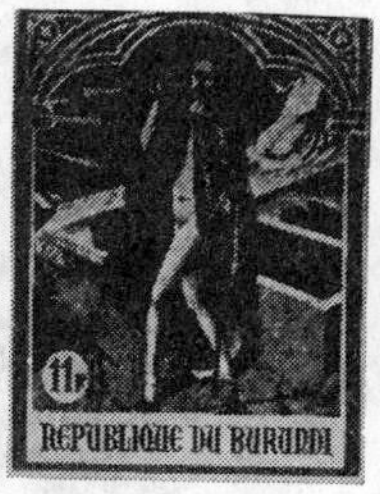

Resurrection, by Gaspard Isenmann A34

Paintings: 14fr, Resurrection by Antoine Caron. 17fr, Noli me Tangere, by Martin Schongauer. 26fr, Resurrection, by El Greco.

1969, Mar. 24

280	A34	11fr gold & multi	.20	.20
281	A34	14fr gold & multi	.20	.20
282	A34	17fr gold & multi	.25	.20
283	A34	26fr gold & multi	.35	.20
a.		Souvenir sheet of 4, #280-283	1.50	1.50
		Nos. 280-283 (4)	1.00	.80

Easter 1969.

Potter — A35

ITU Emblem and: 5fr, Farm workers. 7fr, Foundry worker. 10fr, Woman testing corn crop.

1969, May 17 Photo. *Perf. 13½*

284	A35	3fr multicolored	.20	.20
285	A35	5fr multicolored	.20	.20
286	A35	7fr multicolored	.20	.20
287	A35	10fr multicolored	.20	.20
		Nos. 284-287 (4)	.80	.80

50th anniv. of the ILO.

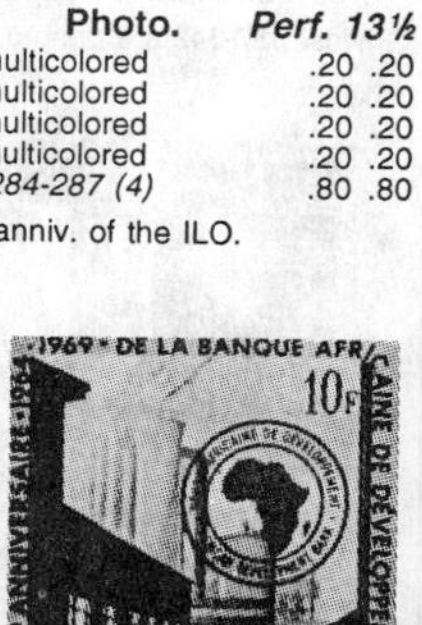

Industry and Bank's Emblem A36

Designs (African Development Bank Emblem and): 17fr, Communications. 30fr, Education. 50fr, Agriculture.

1969, July 29 Photo. *Perf. 13½*

288	A36	10fr gold & multi	.20	.20
289	A36	17fr gold & multi	.30	.20
290	A36	30fr gold & multi	.50	.20
291	A36	50fr gold & multi	.80	.25
a.		Souvenir sheet of 4, #288-291	1.90	1.90
		Nos. 288-291 (4)	1.80	.85

5th anniversary of the African Development Bank.

Girl Reading Letter, by Vermeer A37

Paintings: 7fr, Graziella (young woman), by Auguste Renoir. 14fr, Woman writing a letter, by Gerard Terborch. 26fr, Galileo Galilei, painter unknown. 40fr, Ludwig van Beethoven, painter unknown.

1969, Oct. 24 Photo. *Perf. 13½*

292	A37	4fr multicolored	.20	.20
293	A37	7fr multicolored	.20	.20
294	A37	14fr multicolored	.30	.20
295	A37	26fr multicolored	.55	.20
296	A37	40fr multicolored	.75	.20
a.		Souvenir sheet of 2, #295-296	1.75	1.75
		Nos. 292-296 (5)	2.00	1.00

Intl. Letter Writing Week, Oct. 7-13.

Rocket Launching A38

Moon Landing: 6.50fr, Rocket in space. 7fr, Separation of landing module from capsule. 14fr, 26fr, Landing module landing on moon. 17fr, Capsule in space. 40fr, Neil A. Armstrong leaving landing module. 50fr, Astronaut on moon.

1969, Nov. 6 Photo. *Perf. 13½*

297	A38	4fr blue & multi	.20	.20
298	A38	6.50fr vio blue & multi	.25	.20
299	A38	7fr vio blue & multi	.25	.20
300	A38	14fr black & multi	.35	.20
301	A38	17fr vio blue & multi	.55	.25
		Nos. 297-301,C104-C106 (8)	3.75	2.15

Souvenir Sheet

302		Sheet of 3	3.00	3.00
a.		A38 26fr multicolored	.50	.50
b.		A38 40fr multicolored	.75	.75
c.		A38 50fr multicolored	1.00	1.00

See note after Algeria No. 427.

Madonna and Child, by Rubens — A39

Paintings: 6fr, Madonna and Child with St. John, by Giulio Romano. 10fr, Magnificat Madonna, by Botticelli.

1969, Dec. 2 **Photo.**

303 A39 5fr gold & multi .20 .20
304 A39 6fr gold & multi .20 .20
305 A39 10fr gold & multi .25 .20
a. Souvenir sheet of 3, #303-305 .75 .75
Nos. 303-305,C107-C109 (6) 2.45 1.30

Christmas 1969.

Sternotomis Bohemani — A40

Designs: Various Beetles and Weevils.

1970 ***Perf. 13½***

Size: 39x28mm

306 A40 50c multicolored .20 .20
307 A40 1fr multicolored .20 .20
308 A40 1.50fr multicolored .20 .20
309 A40 2fr multicolored .20 .20
310 A40 3fr multicolored .20 .20
311 A40 3.50fr multicolored .20 .20

Size: 46x32mm

312 A40 4fr multicolored .20 .20
313 A40 5fr multicolored .20 .20
314 A40 6.50fr multicolored .20 .20
315 A40 8fr multicolored .20 .20
316 A40 10fr multicolored .25 .20
317 A40 15fr multicolored .40 .20

Size: 52x36mm

318 A40 20fr multicolored .50 .20
319 A40 50fr multicolored 1.00 .20
320 A40 100fr multicolored 1.90 .35
321 A40 150fr multicolored 2.75 .50
Nos. 306-321,C110-C118 (25) 19.80 5.75

Issue dates: Nos. 306-313, Jan. 20; Nos. 314-318, Feb. 17; Nos. 319-321, Apr. 3.

Jesus Condemned to Death — A41

Stations of the Cross, by Juan de Aranoa y Carredano: 1.50fr, Jesus carries His Cross. 2fr, Jesus falls the first time. 3fr, Jesus meets His mother. 3.50fr, Simon of Cyrene helps carry the cross. 4fr, Veronica wipes the face of Jesus. 5fr, Jesus falls the second time.

1970, Mar. 16 **Photo.** ***Perf. 13½***

322 A41 1fr gold & multi .20 .20
323 A41 1.50fr gold & multi .20 .20
324 A41 2fr gold & multi .20 .20
325 A41 3fr gold & multi .20 .20
326 A41 3.50fr gold & multi .20 .20
327 A41 4fr gold & multi .20 .20
328 A41 5fr gold & multi .20 .20
a. Souv. sheet of 7, #322-328 + label .60 .60
Nos. 322-328,C119-C125 (14) 3.60 2.90

Easter 1970.

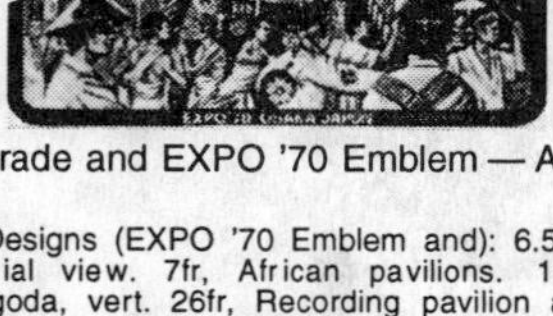

Parade and EXPO '70 Emblem — A42

Designs (EXPO '70 Emblem and): 6.50fr, Aerial view. 7fr, African pavilions. 14fr, Pagoda, vert. 26fr, Recording pavilion and pool. 40fr, Tower of the Sun, vert. 50fr, Flags of participating nations.

1970, May 5 **Photo.** ***Perf. 13½***

329 A42 4fr gold & multi .20 .20
330 A42 6.50fr gold & multi .20 .20
331 A42 7fr gold & multi .20 .20
332 A42 14fr gold & multi .25 .20
333 A42 26fr gold & multi .40 .20
334 A42 40fr gold & multi .55 .20
335 A42 50fr gold & multi .80 .20
Nos. 329-335 (7) 2.60 1.40

EXPO '70 Intl. Exhibition, Osaka, Japan, Mar. 15-Sept. 13, 1970. See No. C126.

White Rhinoceros — A43

Designs, FAUNA: Camel, dromedary, okapi, addax, Burundi cow (2 stamps of each animal in 2 different poses). MAP OF THE NILE: Delta and pyramids, dhow, cataract, Blue Nile and crowned crane, Victoria Nile and secretary bird, Lake Victoria and source of Nile on Mt. Gikizi.

1970, July 8 **Photo.** ***Perf. 13½***

336 Sheet of 18 7.00 1.50
a. A43 7fr any single .40 .20

Issued in sheets of 18 (3x6) stamps of different designs, to publicize the southernmost source of the Nile on Mt. Gikizi in Burundi. See No. C127.

Winter Wren, Firecrest, Skylark and Crested Lark — A44

Birds: 2fr, 3.50fr, 5fr, vert.; others horiz.

1970, Sept. 30 **Photo.** ***Perf. 13½***

Stamp Size: 44x33mm

337 A44 Block of 4 .60 .20
a. 2fr Northern shrike .20
b. 2fr European starling .20
c. 2fr Yellow wagtail .20
d. 2fr Bank swallow .20
338 A44 Block of 4 .90 .20
a. 3fr Winter wren .20
b. 3fr Firecrest .20
c. 3fr Skylark .20
d. 3fr Crested lark .20
339 A44 Block of 4 1.25 .20
a. 3.50fr Woodchat shrike .30
b. 3.50fr Common rock thrush .30
c. 3.50fr Black redstart .30
d. 3.50fr Ring ouzel .30
340 A44 Block of 4 1.50 .20
a. 4fr European Redstart .35
b. 4fr Hedge sparrow .35
c. 4fr Gray wagtail .35
d. 4fr Meadow pipit .35
341 A44 Block of 4 1.75 .20
a. 5fr Eurasian hoopoe .40
b. 5fr Pied flycatcher .40
c. 5fr Great reed warbler .40
d. 5fr Eurasian kingfisher .40
342 A44 Block of 4 2.00 .20
a. 6.50fr House martin .50
b. 6.50fr Sedge warbler .50
c. 6.50fr Fieldfare .50
d. 6.50fr European Golden oriole .50
Nos. 337-342,C132-C137 (12) 38.50 3.65

Nos. 337-342 are printed in sheets of16.

Library, UN Emblem — A45

Designs: 5fr, Students taking test, and emblem of University of Bujumbura. 7fr, Students in laboratory and emblem of Ecole Normale Superieure of Burundi. 10fr, Students with electron-microscope and Education Year emblem.

1970, Oct. 23

343 A45 3fr gold & multi .20 .20
344 A45 5fr gold & multi .20 .20
345 A45 7fr gold & multi .20 .20
346 A45 10fr gold & multi .20 .20
Nos. 343-346 (4) .80 .80

Issued for International Education Year.

Pres. and Mrs. Michel Micombero — A46

Designs: 7fr, Pres. Michel Micombero and Burundi flag. 11fr, Pres. Micombero and Revolution Memorial.

1970, Nov. 28 **Photo.** ***Perf. 13½***

347 A46 4fr gold & multi .20 .20
348 A46 7fr gold & multi .20 .20
349 A46 11fr gold & multi .20 .20
a. Souvenir sheet of 3 .50 .50
Nos. 347-349 (3) .60 .60

4th anniv. of independence. No. 349a contains 3 stamps similar to Nos. 347-349, but inscribed "Poste Aerienne." Exists imperf.
See Nos. C140-C142.

Lenin with Delegates A47

Designs (Lenin, Paintings): 5fr, addressing crowd. 6.50fr, with soldier and sailor. 15fr, speaking from balcony. 50fr, Portrait.

1970, Dec. 31 **Photo.** ***Perf. 13½***

Gold Frame

350 A47 3.50fr dk red brown .20 .20
351 A47 5fr dk red brown .20 .20
352 A47 6.50fr dk red brown .20 .20
353 A47 15fr dk red brown .30 .20
354 A47 50fr dk red brown 1.10 .20
Nos. 350-354 (5) 2.00 1.00

Lenin's birth centenary (1870-1924).

Lion — A48

1971, Mar. 19 **Photo.** ***Perf. 13½***

Size: 38x38mm

355 Strip of 4 .35 .20
a. A48 1fr Lion .20
b. A48 1fr Cape buffalo .20
c. A48 1fr Hippopotamus .20
d. A48 1fr Giraffe .20
356 Strip of 4 .40 .20
a. A48 2fr Hartebeest .20
b. A48 2fr Black rhinoceros .20
c. A48 2fr Zebra .20
d. A48 2fr Leopard .20
357 Strip of 4 .50 .20
a. A48 3fr Grant's gazelles .20
b. A48 3fr Cheetah .20
c. A48 3fr African white-backed vultures .20
d. A48 3fr Johnston's okapi .20
358 Strip of 4 .75 .20
a. A48 5fr Chimpanzee .20
b. A48 5fr Elephant .20
c. A48 5fr Spotted hyenas .20
d. A48 5fr Beisa .20
359 Strip of 4 1.00 .42
a. A48 6fr Gorilla .25
b. A48 6fr Gnu .25
c. A48 6fr Wart hog .25
d. A48 6fr Cape hunting dog .25
360 Strip of 4 2.00 .45
a. A48 11fr Sable antelope .50
b. A48 11fr Caracal lynx .50
c. A48 11fr Ostriches .50
d. A48 11fr Bongo .50
Nos. 355-360,C146-C151 (12) 24.25 3.62

For overprints and surcharges see Nos. C152, CB15-CB18.

The Resurrection, by Il Sodoma — A49

Paintings: 6fr, Resurrection, by Andrea del Castagno. 11fr, Noli me Tangere, by Correggio.

1971, Apr. 2

361 A49 3fr gold & multi .20 .20
362 A49 6fr gold & multi .20 .20
363 A49 11fr gold & multi .30 .20
a. Souvenir sheet of 3, #361-363 .60 .60
Nos. 361-363,C143-C145 (6) 1.45 1.20

Easter 1971. No. 363a exists imperf.

Young Venetian Woman, by Dürer — A50

Dürer Paintings: 11fr, Hieronymus Holzschuher. 14fr, Emperor Maximilian I. 17fr, Holy Family, from Paumgartner Altar. 26fr, Haller Madonna. 31fr, Self-portrait, 1498.

1971, Sept. 20

364 A50 6fr multicolored .20 .20
365 A50 11fr multicolored .25 .20
366 A50 14fr multicolored .40 .20
367 A50 17fr multicolored .45 .25
368 A50 26fr multicolored .65 .35
369 A50 31fr multicolored .80 .40
a. Souvenir sheet of 2, #368-369 1.60 1.60
Nos. 364-369 (6) 2.75 1.60

International Letter Writing Week. Albrecht Dürer (1471-1528), German painter and engraver. No. 369a exists imperf.

Nos. 364-369, 369a Overprinted in Black and Gold: "VIème CONGRES / DE L'INSTITUT INTERNATIONAL / DE DROIT D'EXPRESSION FRANCAISE"

1971, Oct. 8

370 A50 6fr multicolored .20 .20
371 A50 11fr multicolored .25 .20
372 A50 14fr multicolored .30 .20
373 A50 17fr multicolored .35 .20
374 A50 26fr multicolored .50 .20
375 A50 31fr multicolored .65 .20
a. Souvenir sheet of 2 1.25 1.25
Nos. 370-375 (6) 2.25 1.20

6th Congress of the Intl. Legal Institute of the French-speaking Area, Bujumbura, Aug. 10-19.

Madonna and Child, by Il Perugino — A51

Paintings of the Madonna and Child by: 5fr, Andrea del Sarto. 6fr, Luis de Morales.

1971, Nov. 2 Photo. *Perf. 13½*

376	A51	3fr dk green & multi	.20	.20
377	A51	5fr dk green & multi	.20	.20
378	A51	6fr dk green & multi	.20	.20
a.		Souvenir sheet of 3, #376-378	.40	.40
		Nos. 376-378,C153-C155 (6)	1.75	1.20

Christmas 1971. No. 378a exists imperf.
For surcharges see #B49-B51, CB19-CB21.

Lunar Orbiter — A52

Designs: 11fr, Vostok. 14fr, Luna 1. 17fr, Apollo 11 astronaut on moon. 26fr, Soyuz 11. 40fr, Lunar Rover (Apollo 15).

1972, Jan. 15

379	A52	6fr gold & multi	.20	.20
380	A52	11fr gold & multi	.25	.20
381	A52	14fr gold & multi	.30	.20
382	A52	17fr gold & multi	.40	.20
383	A52	26fr gold & multi	.40	.30
384	A52	40fr gold & multi	.60	.30
a.		Souvenir sheet of 6	2.25	2.25
		Nos. 379-384 (6)	2.15	1.40

Conquest of space. See No. C156.
No. 384a contains one each of Nos. 379-384 inscribed "APOLLO 16."

Slalom and Sapporo '72 Emblem — A53

Designs (Sapporo '72 Emblem and): 6fr, Figure skating, pairs. 11fr, Figure skating, women's. 14fr, Ski jump. 17fr, Ice hockey. 24fr, Speed skating, men's. 26fr, Snow scooter. 31fr, Downhill skiing. 50fr, Bobsledding.

1972, Feb. 3

385	A53	5fr silver & multi	.20	.20
386	A53	6fr silver & multi	.20	.20
387	A53	11fr silver & multi	.20	.20
388	A53	14fr silver & multi	.25	.20
389	A53	17fr silver & multi	.30	.20
390	A53	24fr silver & multi	.35	.20
391	A53	26fr silver & multi	.40	.20
392	A53	31fr silver & multi	.50	.20
393	A53	50fr silver & multi	.80	.20
		Nos. 385-393 (9)	3.20	1.80

11th Winter Olympic Games, Sapporo, Japan, Feb. 3-13. Printed in sheets of 12. See No. C157.
Issued: #385-390, Feb. 1; #391-393, Feb. 21.

Ecce Homo, by Quentin Massys — A54

Paintings: 6.50fr, Crucifixion, by Rubens. 10fr, Descent from the Cross, by Jacopo da Pontormo. 18fr, Pieta, by Ferdinand Gallegos. 27fr, Trinity, by El Greco.

1972, Mar. 20 Photo. *Perf. 13½*

394	A54	3.50fr gold & multi	.20	.20
395	A54	6.50fr gold & multi	.20	.20
396	A54	10fr gold & multi	.20	.20
397	A54	18fr gold & multi	.25	.20
398	A54	27fr gold & multi	.65	.20
a.		Souv. sheet of 5, #394-398 + label	1.50	1.25
		Nos. 394-398 (5)	1.50	1.00

Easter 1972. Printed in sheets of 8 with label. No. 398a exists imperf.

Gymnastics, Olympic Rings and "Motion" A55

1972, May 19

399	A55	5fr shown	.20	.20
400	A55	6fr Javelin	.20	.20
401	A55	11fr Fencing	.25	.20
402	A55	14fr Bicycling	.25	.20
403	A55	17fr Pole vault	.30	.20
		Nos. 399-403,C158-C161 (9)	3.05	1.80

Souvenir Sheet

404		Sheet of 2	1.75	1.25
a.		A55 31fr Discus	.45	.45
b.		A55 40fr Soccer	.60	.60

20th Olympic Games, Munich, Aug. 26-Sept. 11.

Prince Rwagasore, Pres. Micombero, Burundi Flag, Drummers A56

Designs: 7fr, Rwagasore, Micombero, flag, map of Africa, globe. 13fr, Micombero, flag, globe.

1972, Aug. 24 Photo. *Perf. 13½*

405	A56	5fr silver & multi	.20	.20
406	A56	7fr silver & multi	.20	.20
407	A56	13fr silver & multi	.25	.20
a.		Souvenir sheet of 3, #405-407	.50	
		Nos. 405-407,C162-C164 (6)	1.65	1.20

10th anniversary of independence.

Madonna and Child, by Andrea Solario — A57

Paintings of the Madonna and Child by: 10fr, Raphael. 15fr, Botticelli.

1972, Nov. 2

408	A57	5fr lt blue & multi	.20	.20
409	A57	10fr lt blue & multi	.20	.20
410	A57	15fr lt blue & multi	.25	.20
a.		Souvenir sheet of 3, #408-410	.50	
		Nos. 408-410,C165-C167 (6)	1.95	1.20

Christmas 1972. Sheets of 20 stamps + label.
For surcharges see #B56-B58, CB26-CB28.

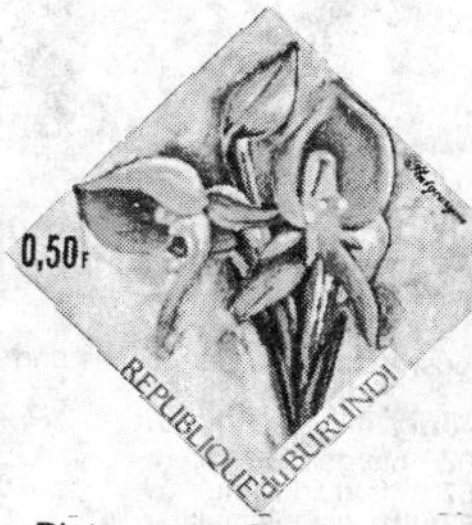

Platycoryne Crocea — A58

1972

Size: 33x33mm

411	A58	50c *shown*	.20	.20
412	A58	1fr *Cattleya trianaei*	.20	.20
413	A58	2fr *Eulophia cucullata*	.20	.20
414	A58	3fr *Cymbidium hamsey*	.20	.20
415	A58	4fr *Thelymitra pauciflora*	.20	.20
416	A58	5fr *Miltassia*	.20	.20
417	A58	6fr *Miltonia*	.20	.20

Size: 38x38mm

418	A58	7fr Like 50c	.20	.20
419	A58	8fr Like 1fr	.20	.20
420	A58	9fr Like 2fr	.20	.20
421	A58	10fr Like 3fr	.30	.20
		Nos. 411-421,C168-C174 (18)	11.05	3.60

Orchids. Issued: #411-417, 11/6; #418-421, 11/29.

Henry Morton Stanley — A59

Designs: 7fr, Porters, Stanley's expedition. 13fr, Stanley entering Ujiji.

1973, Mar. 19 Photo. *Perf. 13½*

422	A59	5fr gold & multi	.20	.20
423	A59	7fr gold & multi	.20	.20
424	A59	13fr gold & multi	.20	.20
		Nos. 422-424,C175-C177 (6)	1.55	1.20

Exploration of Africa by David Livingstone (1813-1873) and Henry Morton Stanley (John Rowlands; 1841-1904).

Crucifixion, by Roger van der Weyden — A60

Easter (Paintings): 5fr, Flagellation of Christ, by Caravaggio. 13fr, The Burial of Christ, by Raphael.

1973, Apr. 10

425	A60	5fr gold & multi	.20	.20
426	A60	7fr gold & multi	.20	.20
427	A60	13fr gold & multi	.20	.20
a.		Souvenir sheet of 3, #425-427	.60	.60
		Nos. 425-427,C178-C180 (6)	1.75	1.20

INTERPOL Emblem, Flag — A61

Design: 10fr, INTERPOL flag and emblem. 18fr, INTERPOL Headquarters and emblem.

1973, May 19 Photo. *Perf. 13½*

428	A61	5fr silver & multi	.20	.20
429	A61	10fr silver & multi	.20	.20
430	A61	18fr silver & multi	.30	.20
		Nos. 428-430,C181-C182 (5)	1.60	1.00

Intl. Criminal Police Organization, 50th anniv.

Signs of the Zodiac, Babylon — A62

Designs: 5fr, Greek and Roman gods representing planets. 7fr, Ptolemy (No. 433a) and Ptolemaic solar system. 13fr, Copernicus (No. 434a) and heliocentric system.
a, UL. b, UR. c, LL. d, LR.

1973, July 27 Photo. *Perf. 13½*

431	A62	3fr Block of 4, #a.-d.	.20	.20
432	A62	5fr Block of 4, #a.-d.	.25	.20
433	A62	7fr Block of 4, #a.-d.	.30	.20
434	A62	13fr Block of 4, #a.-d.	.75	.20
e.		Souvenir sheet of 4, #431-434	2.75	1.40
		Nos. 431-434,C183-C186 (8)	9.25	2.65

500th anniversary of the birth of Nicolaus Copernicus (1473-1543), Polish astronomer.

Flowers and Butterflies — A63

Designs: Each block of 4 contains 2 flower and 2 butterfly designs. The 1fr, 2fr, 5fr and 11fr have flower designs listed as "a" and "d" numbers, butterflies as "b" and "c" numbers; the arrangement is reversed for the 3fr and 6fr.

1973, Sept. 3 Photo. *Perf. 13*
Stamp Size: 34x41½mm

435 A63 Block of 4 .35 .20
a. 1fr *Protea cynaroides* .20 .20
b. 1fr *Precis octavia* .20 .20
c. 1fr *Epiphora bauhiniae* .20 .20
d. 1fr *Gazania longiscapa* .20 .20
436 A63 Block of 4 .35 .20
a. 2fr *Kniphofia* .20 .20
b. 2fr *Cymothoe coccinata* .20 .20
c. 2fr *Nudaurelia zambesina* .20 .20
d. 2fr *Freesia refracta* .20 .20
437 A63 Block of 4 .40 .20
a. 3fr *Calotis eupompe* .20 .20
b. 3fr *Narcissus* .20 .20
c. 3fr *Cineraria hybrida* .20 .20
d. 3fr *Cyrestis camillus* .20 .20
438 A63 Block of 4 .65 .20
a. 5fr *Iris tingitana* .20 .20
b. 5fr *Pappilio demodocus* .20 .20
c. 5fr *Catopsilia avelaneda* .20 .20
d. 5fr *Nerine sarniensis* .20 .20
439 A63 Block of 4 .80 .20
a. 6fr *Hypolimnas dexithea* .20 .20
b. 6fr *Zantedeschia tropicalis* .20 .20
c. 6fr *Sandersonia aurantiaca* .20 .20
d. 6fr *Drurya antimachus* .20 .20
440 A63 Block of 4 1.75 .25
a. 11fr *Nymphaea capensis* .40 .20
b. 11fr *Pandoriana pandora* .40 .20
c. 11fr *Precis orythia* .40 .20
d. 11fr *Pelargonium domestica* .40 .20
Nos. 435-440,C187-C192 (12) 34.80 4.45

Virgin and Child, by Giovanni Bellini — A64

Virgin and Child by: 10fr, Jan van Eyck. 15fr, Giovanni Boltraffio.

1973, Nov. 13 Photo. *Perf. 13*

441 A64 5fr gold & multi .20 .20
442 A64 10fr gold & multi .20 .20
443 A64 15fr gold & multi .25 .20
a. Souvenir sheet of 3, #441-443 .50 .50
Nos. 441-443,C193-C195 (6) 1.95 1.20

Christmas 1973.
For surcharges see #B59-B61, CB29-CB31.

Pietá, by Paolo Veronese — A65

Paintings: 10fr, Virgin and St. John, by van der Weyden. 18fr, Crucifixion, by van der Weyden. 27fr, Burial of Christ, by Titian. 40fr, Pietá, by El Greco.

1974, Apr. 19 Photo. *Perf. 14x13½*

444 A65 5fr gold & multi .20 .20
445 A65 10fr gold & multi .20 .20
446 A65 18fr gold & multi .30 .20
447 A65 27fr gold & multi .40 .20
448 A65 40fr gold & multi .65 .20
a. Souvenir sheet of 5, #444-448 1.60 1.60
Nos. 444-448 (5) 1.75 1.00

Easter 1974.

Fish — A66

1974, May 30 Photo. *Perf. 13*
Stamp Size: 35x35mm

449 A66 Block of 4 .30 .20
a. 1fr *Haplochromis multicolor* .20 .20
b. 1fr *Pantodon buchholzi* .20 .20
c. 1fr *Tropheus duboisi* .20 .20
d. 1fr *Distichodus sexfasciatus* .20 .20
450 A66 Block of 4 .30 .20
a. 2fr *Pelmatochromis kribensis* .20 .20
b. 2fr *Nannaethiops tritaeniatus* .20 .20
c. 2fr *Polycentropsis abbreviata* .20 .20
d. 2fr *Hemichromis bimaculatus* .20 .20
451 A66 Block of 4 .30 .20
a. 3fr *Ctenopoma acutirostre* .20 .20
b. 3fr *Synodontis angelicus* .20 .20
c. 3fr *Tilapia melanopleura* .20 .20
d. 3fr *Aphyosemion bivittatum* .20 .20
452 A66 Block of 4 .50 .20
a. 5fr *Monodactylus argenteus* .20 .20
b. 5fr *Zanclus canescens* .20 .20
c. 5fr *Pygoplites diacanthus* .20 .20
d. 5fr *Cephalopholis argus* .20 .20
453 A66 Block of 4 .60 .20
a. 6fr *Priacanthus arenatus* .20 .20
b. 6fr *Pomacanthus arcuatus* .20 .20
c. 6fr *Scarus guacamaia* .20 .20
d. 6fr *Zeus faber* .20 .20
454 A66 Block of 4 1.00 .20
a. 11fr *Lactophrys quadricornis* .20 .20
b. 11fr *Balistes vetula* .20 .20
c. 11fr *Acanthurus bahianus* .20 .20
d. 11fr *Holocanthus ciliaris* .20 .20
Nos. 449-454,C207-C212 (12) 18.75 2.85

Soccer and Cup A67

Designs: Various soccer scenes and cup.

1974, July 4 Photo. *Perf. 13*

455 A67 5fr gold & multi .20
456 A67 6fr gold & multi .20
457 A67 11fr gold & multi .20
458 A67 14fr gold & multi .25
459 A67 17fr gold & multi .25
a. Souvenir sheet of 3 1.40
Nos. 455-459,C196-C198 (8) 2.40

World Soccer Championship, Munich, June 13-July 7. No. 459a contains 3 stamps similar to Nos. C196-C198 without "Poste Aerienne."
Nos. 455-459 and 459a exist imperf.

Flags over UPU Headquarters, Bern — A68

#461, G.P.O., Bujumbura. #462, Mailmen ("11F" in UR). #463, Mailmen ("11F" in UL). #464, UPU emblem. #465, Means of transportation. #466, Pigeon over globe showing Burundi. #467, Swiss flag, pigeon over map showing Bern.

1974, July 23

460 A68 6fr gold & multi .20
461 A68 6fr gold & multi .20
462 A68 11fr gold & multi .30
463 A68 11fr gold & multi .30
464 A68 14fr gold & multi .40
465 A68 14fr gold & multi .40
466 A68 17fr gold & multi .45
467 A68 17fr gold & multi .50
a. Souvenir sheet of 8, #460-467 2.75
Nos. 460-467,C199-C206 (16) 10.05
Set, used 1.00

Cent. of UPU. Stamps of same denomination printed se-tenant (continuous design).

St. Ildefonso Writing Letter, by El Greco A69

Paintings: 11fr, Lady Sealing Letter, by Chardin. 14fr, Titus at Desk, by Rembrandt. 17fr, The Love Letter, by Vermeer. 26fr, The Merchant G. Gisze, by Holbein. 31fr, Portrait of Alexandre Lenoir, by David.

1974, Oct. 1 Photo. *Perf. 13*

468 A69 6fr gold & multi .20
469 A69 11fr gold & multi .20
470 A69 14fr gold & multi .25
471 A69 17fr gold & multi .25
472 A69 26fr gold & multi .40
473 A69 31fr gold & multi .45
a. Souvenir sheet of 2, #472-473 1.10
Nos. 468-473 (6) 1.75

International Letter Writing Week, Oct. 6-12. No. 473a exists imperf.

Virgin and Child, by Bernaert van Orley — A70

Paintings of the Virgin and Child: 10fr, by Hans Memling. 15fr, by Botticelli.

1974, Nov. 7 Photo. *Perf. 13*

474 A70 5fr gold & multi .20
475 A70 10fr gold & multi .20
476 A70 15fr gold & multi .25
a. Souvenir sheet of 3, #474-476 .50
Nos. 474-476,C213-C215 (6) 1.95

Christmas 1974. Sheets of 20 stamps and one label. No. 476a exists imperf.

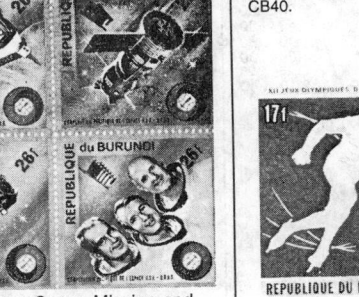

Apollo-Soyuz Space Mission and Emblem — A71

1975, July 10 Photo. *Perf. 13*

477 A71 Block of 4 .80
a. 26fr A.A. Leonov, V.N. Kubasov, Soviet flag .20
b. 26fr Soyuz and Soviet flag .20
c. 26fr Apollo and American flag .20
d. 26fr D.K. Slayton, V.D. Brand, T.P. Stafford, American flag .20
478 A71 Block of 4 1.25
a. 31fr Apollo-Soyuz link-up .30
b. 31fr Apollo, blast-off .30
c. 31fr Soyuz, blast-off .30
d. 31fr Kubasov, Leonov, Slayton, Brand, Stafford .30
Nos. 477-478,C216-C217 (4) 4.30

Apollo Soyuz space test project (Russo-American cooperation), launching July 15; link-up, July 17.

Addax A72

1975, July 31 Photo. *Perf. 13½*

479 Strip of 4 .20
a. A72 1fr shown .20
b. A72 1fr Roan antelope .20
c. A72 1fr Nyala .20
d. A72 1fr White rhinoceros .20
480 Strip of 4 .20
a. A72 2fr Mandrill .20
b. A72 2fr Eland .20
c. A72 2fr Salt's dik-dik .20
d. A72 2fr Thomson's gazelles .20
481 Strip of 4 .20
a. A72 3fr African small-clawed otter .20
b. A72 3fr Reed buck .20
c. A72 3fr Indian civet .20
d. A72 3fr Cape buffalo .20
482 Strip of 4 .35
a. A72 5fr White-tailed gnu .20
b. A72 5fr African wild asses .20
c. A72 5fr Black-and-white colobus monkey .20
d. A72 5fr Gerenuk .20
483 Strip of 4 .35
a. A72 6fr Dama gazelle .20
b. A72 6fr Black-backed jackal .20
c. A72 6fr Sitatungas .20
d. A72 6fr Zebra antelope .20
484 Strip of 4 .65
a. A72 11fr Fennec .20
b. A72 11fr Lesser kudus .20
c. A72 11fr Blesbok .20
d. A72 11fr Serval .20
Nos. 479-484,C218-C223 (12) 12.70

For overprints see Nos. C224-C227.

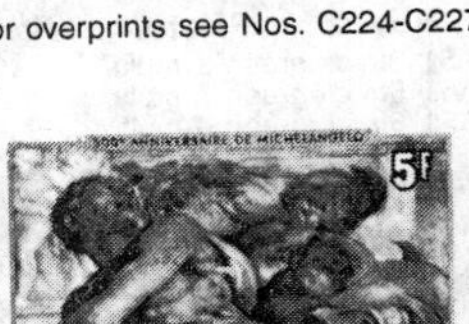
Jonah, by Michelangelo — A73

Designs: Paintings from Sistine Chapel.

1975, Dec. 3 Photo. *Perf. 13*

485 A73 5fr shown .20
486 A73 5fr Libyan Sybil .20
487 A73 13fr Prophet Isaiah .20
488 A73 13fr Delphic Sybil .20
489 A73 27fr Daniel .40
490 A73 27fr Cumaean Sybil .40
a. Souvenir sheet of 6, #485-490 2.00
Nos. 485-490,C228-C233 (12) 5.20

Michelangelo Buonarotti (1475-1564), Italian sculptor, painter and architect. Stamps of same denominations printed se-tenant in sheets of 18 stamps and 2 labels.
For surcharges see Nos. B65-B70, CB35-CB40.

Speed Skating A74

Basketball A75

Designs (Innsbruck Games Emblem and): 24fr, Figure skating, women's. 26fr, Two-man bobsled. 31fr, Cross-country skiing.

1976, Jan. 23 Photo. *Perf. 14x13½*

491 A74 17fr dp bl & multi .30
492 A74 24fr multi .45
493 A74 26fr multi .50
494 A74 31fr plum & multi .55
a. Souvenir sheet of 3, perf. 13½ 2.25
Nos. 491-494,C234-C236 (7) 3.70

12th Winter Olympic Games, Innsbruck, Austria, Feb. 4-15.
No. 494a contains stamps similar to #C234-C236, without "POSTE AERIENNE."

1976, May 3 Litho. *Perf. 13½*

Montreal Games Emblem and: #496, 499, 503b, Pole vault. #497, 500, 503d, Running. #498, 501, 503a, Soccer. #502, 503c, Basketball.

495 A75 14fr blue & multi .25
496 A75 14fr olive & multi .25
497 A75 17fr magenta & multi .30
498 A75 17fr vermilion & multi .30
499 A75 28fr olive & multi .50
500 A75 28fr magenta & multi .50
501 A75 40fr vermilion & multi .70
502 A75 40fr blue & multi .70
Nos. 495-502,C237-C242 (14) 7.20

Souvenir Sheet

503 Sheet of 4 1.60
a. A75 14fr red & multi .25
b. A75 17fr olive & multi .25
c. A75 28fr blue & multi .40
d. A75 40fr magenta & multi .60

21st Olympic Games, Montreal, Canada, July 17-Aug. 1. Stamps of same denomination printed se-tenant in sheets of 20.

Virgin and Child, by Dirk Bouts — A76

Virgin and Child by: 13fr, Giovanni Bellini. 27fr, Carlo Crivelli.

1976, Oct. 18 Photo. *Perf. 13½*

504 A76 5fr gold & multi .20
505 A76 13fr gold & multi .20
506 A76 27fr gold & multi .40
a. Souvenir sheet of 3, #504-506 .75
Nos. 504-506,C250-C252 (6) 2.10

Christmas 1976. Sheets of 20 stamps and descriptive label.
For surcharges see #B71-B73, CB41-CB43.

St. Veronica, by Rubens A77

Paintings by Rubens: 21fr, Christ on the Cross. 27fr, Descent from the Cross. 35fr, The Deposition.

1977, Apr. 5 Photo. *Perf. 13*

507 A77 10fr gold & multi .20
508 A77 21fr gold & multi .30
509 A77 27fr gold & multi .40
510 A77 35fr gold & multi .55
a. Souvenir sheet of 4 1.50
Nos. 507-510 (4) 1.45

Easter 1977. Sheets of 30 stamps and descriptive label. No. 510a contains 4 stamps similar to Nos. 507-510 inscribed "POSTE AERIENNE."

Alexander Graham Bell A78

Intelsat Satellite, Modern and Old Telephones A79

Designs: No. 513, Switchboard operator, c. 1910, and wall telephone. No. 514, Intelsat and radar. No. 515, A.G. Bell and first telephone. No. 516, Satellites around globe and videophone.

1977, May 17 Photo. *Perf. 13*

511 A78 10fr multi .20
512 A79 10fr multi .20
513 A78 17fr multi .20
514 A79 17fr multi .20
515 A78 26fr multi .25
516 A79 26fr multi .25
Nos. 511-516,C253-C256 (10) 2.20

Centenary of first telephone call by Alexander Graham Bell, Mar. 10, 1876. Stamps of same denomination printed se-tenant in sheets of 32.

Buffon's Kob — A80

1977, Aug. 22 Photo. *Perf. 14x14½*

517 Strip of 4 .40
a. A80 2fr shown .20
b. A80 2fr Marabous .20
c. A80 2fr Brindled gnu .20
d. A80 2fr River hog .20
518 Strip of 4 .60
a. A80 5fr Zebras .20
b. A80 5fr Shoebill .20
c. A80 5fr Striped hyenas .20
d. A80 5fr Chimpanzee .20
519 Strip of 4 1.00
a. A80 8fr Flamingos .25
b. A80 8fr Nile crocodiles .25
c. A80 8fr Green mamba .25
d. A80 8fr Greater kudus .25
520 Strip of 4 1.25
a. A80 11fr Hyrax .30
b. A80 11fr Cobra .30
c. A80 11fr Jackals .30
d. A80 11fr Verreaux's eagles .30
521 Strip of 4 2.50
a. A80 21fr Honey badger .60
b. A80 21fr Harnessed antelopes .60
c. A80 21fr Secretary bird .60
d. A80 21fr Klipspringer .60
522 Strip of 4 2.50
a. A80 27fr African big-eared fox .60
b. A80 27fr Elephants .60
c. A80 27fr Vulturine guineafowl .60
d. A80 27fr Impalas .60
Nos. 517-522,C258-C263 (12) 28.40

The Goose Girl, by Grimm — A81

Fairy Tales: 5fr, by Grimm Brothers. 11fr, by Aesop. 14fr, by Hans Christian Andersen. 17fr, by Jean de La Fontaine. 26fr, English fairy tales.

1977, Sept. 14 *Perf. 14*

523 Block of 4 .40
a. A81 5fr shown .20
b. A81 5fr The Two Wanderers .20
c. A81 5fr The Man of Iron .20
d. A81 5fr Snow White and Rose Red .20
524 Block of 4 .85
a. A81 11fr The Quarreling Cats .20
b. A81 11fr The Blind and the Lame .20
c. A81 11fr The Hermit and the Bear .20
d. A81 11fr The Fox and the Stork .20
525 Block of 4 1.00
a. A81 14fr The Princess and the Pea .25
b. A81 14fr The Old Tree Mother .25
c. A81 14fr The Ice Maiden .25
d. A81 14fr The Old House .25
526 Block of 4 1.25
a. A81 17fr The Oyster and the Suitors .30
b. A81 17fr The Wolf and the Lamb .30
c. A81 17fr Hen with the Golden Egg .30
d. A81 17fr The Wolf as Shepherd .30
527 Block of 4 2.00
a. A81 26fr Three Heads in the Well .50
b. A81 26fr Mother Goose .50
c. A81 26fr Jack and the Beanstalk .50
d. A81 26fr Alice in Wonderland .50
Nos. 523-527 (5) 5.50

Security Council Chamber, UN Nos. 28, 46, 37, C7 — A82

Designs (UN Stamps and): 8fr, UN General Assembly, interior. 21fr, UN Meeting Hall.

1977, Oct. 10 Photo. *Perf. 13½*

528 A82 Block of 4 .65
a. 8fr No. 25 .20
b. 8fr No. C5 .20
c. 8fr No. 23 .20
d. 8fr No. 2 .20
529 A82 Block of 4 .75
a. 10fr No. 28 .20
b. 10fr No. 46 .20
c. 10fr No. 37 .20
d. 10fr No. C7 .20
530 A82 Block of 4 1.50
a. 21fr No. 45 .35
b. 21fr No. 42 .35
c. 21fr No. 17 .35
d. 21fr No. 13 .35
e. Souvenir sheet of 3 .65
Nos. 528-530,C264-C266 (6) 10.05

25th anniv. (in 1976) of the UN Postal Administration. No. 530e contains 8fr in design of No. 529d, 10fr in design of No. 530b, 21fr in design of No. 528c.

Virgin and Child — A83

Designs: Paintings of the Virgin and Child.

1977, Oct. 31 Photo. *Perf. 14x13*

531 A83 5fr By Meliore Toscano .20
532 A83 13fr By J. Lombardos .20
533 A83 27fr By Emmanuel Tzanes, 1610-1680 .40
a. Souvenir sheet of 3, #531-533 .75
Nos. 531-533,C267-C269 (6) 2.20

Christmas 1977. Sheets of 24 stamps with descriptive label.
For surcharges see #B74-B76, CB44-CB46.

Cruiser Aurora, Russia Nos. 211, 303, 1252, 187 — A84

Russian Stamps and: 8fr, Kremlin, Moscow. 11fr, Pokrovski Cathedral, Moscow. 13fr, Labor Day parade, 1977 and 1980 Olympic Games emblem.

1977, Nov. 14 Photo. *Perf. 13*

534 A84 Block of 4 .40
a. 5fr No. 211 .20
b. 5fr No. 303 .20
c. 5fr No. 1252 .20
d. 5fr No. 187 .20
535 A84 Block of 4 .65
a. 8fr No. 856 .20
b. 8fr No. 1986 .20
c. 8fr No. 908 .20
d. 8fr No. 2551 .20
536 A84 Block of 4 .85
a. 11fr No. 3844b .20
b. 11fr No. 3452 .20
c. 11fr No. 3382 .20
d. 11fr No. 3837 .20
537 A84 Block of 4 1.00
a. 13fr No. 4446 .25
b. 13fr No. 3497 .25
c. 13fr No. 2926 .25
d. 13fr No. 2365 .25
Nos. 534-537 (4) 2.90

60th anniv. of Russian October Revolution.

Ship at Dock, Arms and Flag — A85

Burundi Arms and Flag and: 5fr, Men at lathes. 11fr, Male leopard dance. 14fr, Coffee harvest. 17fr, Government Palace.

1977, Nov. 25 Photo. *Perf. 13½*

538 A85 1fr sil & multi .20
539 A85 5fr sil & multi .20
540 A85 11fr sil & multi .20
541 A85 14fr sil & multi .20
542 A85 17fr sil & multi .20
Nos. 538-542 (5) 1.00

15th anniversary of independence.

A86 A87

Paintings of the Virgin and Child by: 13fr, Rubens. 17fr, Solario. 27fr, Tiepolo. 31fr, Gerard David. 40fr, Bellini.

1979, Feb. Photo. *Perf. 14x13*

543 A86 13fr multi .20
544 A86 17fr multi .25
545 A86 27fr multi .40
546 A86 31fr multi .50
547 A86 40fr multi .65
Nos. 543-547 (5) 2.00

Christmas 1978. See No. C270.

1979 Photo. *Perf. 13½x13*

548 A87 1fr *Abyssinian hornbill* .20
549 A87 2fr *Snakebird* .20
550 A87 3fr *Melittophagus pusillus* .20
551 A87 5fr *Flamingo* .20
552 A87 8fr *Afropavo congenis* .20
553 A87 10fr *Gallinule* .35
554 A87 20fr *Martial eagle* .65
555 A87 27fr *Ibis* .85
556 A87 50fr *Saddle-billed stork* 1.75
Nos. 548-556,C273-C281 (18) 13.45

Mother and Infant, IYC Emblem A88

IYC Emblem and: 20fr, Infant. 27fr, Girl with doll. 50fr, Children in Children's Village.

1979, July 19 Photo. *Perf. 14*

557 A88 10fr multi .20
558 A88 20fr multi .25
559 A88 27fr multi .30
560 A88 50fr multi .55
Nos. 557-560 (4) 1.30

Intl. Year of the Child. See No. B82.

A89 A90

Virgin and Child by: 20fr, del Garbo. 27fr, Giovanni Penni. 31fr, G. Romano. 50fr, Jacopo Bassano.

1979, Oct. 12

561 A89 20fr multi .30
562 A89 27fr multi .40
563 A89 31fr multi .50
564 A89 50fr multi .75
Nos. 561-564,B83-B86 (8) 3.95

Christmas 1979. See Nos. C271, CB48.

1979, Nov. 6

Designs: 20fr, Rowland Hill, Penny Black. Stamps of Burundi: 27fr, German East Africa Nos. 17, N17. 31fr, Nos. 4, 24. 40fr, Nos. 29, 294. 60fr, Heinrich von Stephan, Nos. 464-465.

565 A90 20fr multi .30
566 A90 27fr multi .40
567 A90 31fr multi .50
568 A90 40fr multi .60
569 A90 60fr multi .90
Nos. 565-569 (5) 2.70

Sir Rowland Hill (1795-1879), originator of penny postage. See No. C272.

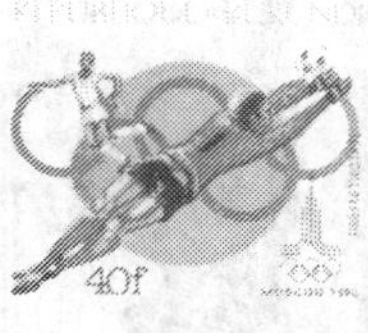

A91

1980, Oct. 24 Photo. *Perf. 13x13½*

570 A91 20fr 110-meter hurdles .40
571 A91 20fr Hurdles, Thomas Munkelt .40
572 A91 20fr Hurdles, R.D.A. .40
573 A91 30fr Discus .55
574 A91 30fr Discus, V. Rassh-chupkin .55
575 A91 30fr Discus, U.R.S.S. .55
576 A91 40fr Soccer, Tchecos-lovaquie .75
577 A91 40fr "Football" .75
578 A91 40fr shown .75
Nos. 570-578 (9) 5.10

22nd Summer Olympic Games, Moscow, July 19-Aug. 3. Stamps of same denomination se-tenant.
See No. C282.

Virgin and Child, by Mainardi — A92

Christmas 1980 (Paintings): 30fr, Holy Family, by Michelangelo. 40fr, Virgin and Child, by di Cosimo. 45fr, Holy Family, by Fra Bartolomeo.

1980, Dec. 12 Photo. *Perf. 13½x13*

579 A92 10fr multi .20
580 A92 30fr multi .30
581 A92 40fr multi .40
582 A92 45fr multi .45
Nos. 579-582,B87-B90 (8) 2.75

UPRONA Party National Congress, 1979 — A93

1980, Dec. 29 *Perf. 14x13½*

583 A93 10fr multi .20
584 A93 40fr multi .60
585 A93 45fr multi .65
Nos. 583-585 (3) 1.45

Johannes Kepler, Dish Antenna A94

1981, Feb. 12 *Perf. 14*

586 A94 10fr shown .20
587 A94 40fr Satellite .60
588 A94 45fr Satellite, diff. .65
a. Souvenir sheet of 3, #586-588 1.50
Nos. 586-588 (3) 1.45

350th death anniv. of Johannes Kepler and 1st earth satellite station in Burundi.

Lion A95

1983, Apr. 22 Photo. *Perf. 13*

589 A95 2fr shown
590 A95 3fr Giraffes
591 A95 5fr Rhinoceros
592 A95 10fr Water buffalo
593 A95 20fr Elephant
594 A95 25fr Hippopotamus
595 A95 30fr Zebra
596 A95 50fr Warthog
597 A95 60fr Oryx
598 A95 65fr Wild dog
599 A95 70fr Cheetah
600 A95 75fr Wildebeest
601 A95 85fr Hyena
Nos. 589-601 (13) *50.00*

Nos. 589-601 Overprinted in Silver with World Wildlife Fund Emblem

1983 Photo. *Perf. 13*

589a A95 2fr multi
590a A95 3fr multi
591a A95 5fr multi
592a A95 10fr multi
593a A95 20fr multi
594a A95 25fr multi
595a A95 30fr multi
596a A95 50fr multi
597a A95 60fr multi
598a A95 65fr multi
599a A95 70fr multi
600a A95 75fr multi
601a A95 85fr multi
Nos. 589a-601a (13) *600.00*

Apparently there is speculation in these two sets.

20th Anniv. of Independence, July 1, 1982 — A96

Flags, various arms, map or portrait.

1983 *Perf. 14*

602 A96 10fr multi .20
603 A96 25fr multi .40
604 A96 30fr multi .45
605 A96 50fr multi .75
606 A96 65fr multi 1.00
Nos. 602-606 (5) 2.80

Christmas 1983 — A97

Virgin and Child paintings: 10fr, by Luca Signorelli (1450-1523). 25fr, by Esteban Murillo (1617-1682). 30fr, by Carlo Crivelli (1430-1495). 50fr, by Nicolas Poussin (1594-1665).

1983, Oct. 3 Litho. *Perf. 14½x13½*

607 A97 10fr multi .20
608 A97 25fr multi .40
609 A97 30fr multi .45
610 A97 50fr multi .75
Nos. 607-610,B91-B94 (8) 3.65

See Nos. C285, CB50.

Butterflies — A98

1984, June 29 Photo. *Perf. 13*

611 A98 5fr Cymothoe coccinata .20
612 A98 5fr Papilio zalmoxis .20
613 A98 10fr Asterope pechueli .40
614 A98 10fr Papilio antimachus .40
615 A98 30fr Papilio hesperus 1.00
616 A98 30fr Bebearia mardania 1.00
617 A98 35fr Euphaedra neophron 1.25
618 A98 35fr Euphaedra perseis 1.25
619 A98 65fr Euphaedra imperialis 2.25
620 A98 65fr Pseudocraea striata 2.25
Nos. 611-620 (10) 10.20

Stamps of the same denomination printed horizontally se-tenant.
For surcharges see Nos. 654D-654E.

19th UPU Congress, Hamburg A99

UPU emblem and: 10fr, German East Africa, #17, N17. 30fr, #4, 24. 35fr, #294, 595. 65fr, Dr. Heinrich von Stephan, #464-465.

1984, July 14 Litho. *Perf. 13x13½*

621 A99 10fr multi .20
622 A99 30fr multi .45
623 A99 35fr multi .50
624 A99 65fr multi 1.00
Nos. 621-624 (4) 2.15

See No. C286.

1984 Summer Olympics — A100

Gold medalists: 10fr, Jesse Owens, US, track and field, Berlin, 1936. 30fr, Rafer Johnson, US, decathlon, 1960. 35fr, Bob Beamon, US, long jump, 1968. 65fr, Kipchoge Keino, Kenya, 3000-meter steeplechase, 1972.

1984, Aug. 6 *Perf. 13½x13*

625 A100 10fr multi .25
626 A100 30fr multi .70
627 A100 35fr multi .85
628 A100 65fr multi 1.50
Nos. 625-628 (4) 3.30

See No. C287.

Christmas 1984 — A101

Paintings: 10fr, Rest During the Flight into Egypt, by Murillo (1617-1682). 25fr, Virgin and Child, by R. del Garbo. 30fr, Virgin and Child, by Botticelli (1445-1510). 50fr, The Adoration of the Shepherds, by Giacomo da Bassano (1517-1592).

1984, Dec. 15 *Perf. 13½*

629 A101 10fr multi .20
630 A101 25fr multi .40
631 A101 30fr multi .45
632 A101 50fr multi .75
Nos. 629-632,B95-B98 (8) 3.65

See Nos. C288, CB51.

Flowers A102

1986, July 31 Photo. *Perf. 13x13½*

633 A102 2fr Thunbergia .20
634 A102 3fr Saintpaulia .20
635 A102 5fr Clivia .20
636 A102 10fr Cassia .20
637 A102 20fr Strelitzia .25
638 A102 35fr Gloriosa .55
Nos. 633-638,C289-C294 (12) 8.40

Intl. Peace Year — A103

1986, May 1 Litho. *Perf. 14*

639 A103 10fr Rockets as housing .20
640 A103 20fr Atom as flower .20
641 A103 30fr Handshake .25
642 A103 40fr Globe, chicks .35
a. Souvenir sheet of 4, #639-642 .90
Nos. 639-642 (4) 1.00

No. 642a exists imperf.

Great Lake Nations Economic Community (CEPGI), 10th Anniv. — A104

Outline maps of Lake Tanganyika, CEPGI emblem and: 5fr, Aviation. 10fr, Agriculture. 15fr, Industry. 25fr, Electrification. 35fr, Flags of Burundi, Rwanda and Zaire.

1986, May 1 Photo. *Perf. 13½x14½*

643 A104 5fr multi .20
644 A104 10fr multi .20
645 A104 15fr multi .20
646 A104 25fr multi .30
647 A104 35fr multi .45
a. Souv. sheet of 5, #643-647 + label 1.25
Nos. 643-647 (5) 1.35

Intl. Year of Shelter for the Homeless A105

1987, June Litho. *Perf. 14*

648 A105 10fr Hovel .30
649 A105 20fr Drain pipe shelter .55
650 A105 80fr Shoveling sand 2.15

651 A105 150fr Children, house model 4.00
a. Souvenir sheet of 4, #648-651 7.00
Nos. 648-651 (4) 7.00

A106

A107

1987(?) **Litho.** ***Perf. 14***
652 A106 5fr shown .20
653 A106 20fr Skull, lungs .30
654 A106 80fr Cigarette, face 1.25
Nos. 652-654 (3) 1.75

WHO Anti-smoking campaign.

Nos. 615-616 Surcharged **80f**

1989 **Photo.** ***Perf. 13***
654D A98 80fr on 30fr #615
654E A98 80fr on 30fr #616

Numbers have been reserved for additional values in this set.

1990 **Litho.** ***Perf. 14***
655 A107 5fr red lil & multi .20
656 A107 10fr blue & multi .25
657 A107 20fr gray & multi .50
658 A107 30fr ol grn & multi .70
659 A107 50fr brt blue & multi 1.25
660 A107 80fr grn bl & multi 2.00
a. Souv. sheet of 6, #655-660, perf. 13½ 4.75
Nos. 655-660 (6) 4.90

Visit of Pope John Paul II.

Animals A108

1991, Oct. 4 **Litho.** ***Perf. 14***
661 A108 5fr Hippopotamus .20
662 A108 10fr Chickens .20
663 A108 20fr Lion .30
664 A108 30fr Elephant .50
665 A108 50fr Guinea fowl .80
666 A108 80fr Crocodile 1.25
a. Souv. sheet of 6, #661-666, perf. 13½ 3.25
Nos. 661-666 (6) 3.25

No. 666a exists imperf.

Flowers — A108a

1992, June 2 **Litho.** ***Perf. 14***
666B A108a 15fr Impatiens petersiana .40
666C A108a 20fr Lachenalia aloides .50
666D A108a 30fr Nymphaea lotus .80
666E A108a 50fr Clivia miniata 1.25
f. Souvenir sheet of 4, #666B-666E, perf. 13½ 3.00
Nos. 666B-666E (4) 2.95

A109

Native Music and Dancing A110

Designs: 15fr, Native drummer. 30fr, Two dancers. 115fr, Drummers. 200fr, Five dancers.

1992, Apr. 2 **Litho.** ***Perf. 14***
667 A109 15fr multicolored .25
668 A109 30fr multicolored .50
669 A110 115fr multicolored 1.75
670 A110 200fr multicolored 3.00
a. Souvenir sheet 5.75
Nos. 667-670 (4) 5.50

No. 670a contains one each of Nos. 667-668, perf. 13x13½, and Nos. 669-670, perf. 13½x13.

Independence, 30th Anniv. — A111

Designs: 30fr, 140fr, People with flag. 85fr, 115fr, Natl. flag. 110fr, 200fr, Monument, vert. 120fr, 250fr, Map, vert.

1992, June 30 **Litho.** ***Perf. 15***
671 A111 30fr multicolored .35
672 A111 85fr multicolored 1.00
673 A111 110fr multicolored 1.25
674 A111 115fr multicolored 1.25
675 A111 120fr multicolored 1.40
676 A111 140fr multicolored 1.60
677 A111 200fr multicolored 2.25
678 A111 250fr multicolored 3.00
Nos. 671-678 (8) 12.10

Discovery of America, 500th Anniv. A112

Columbus' fleet, globe and: 200fr, Pre-Columbian artifacts. 400fr, Fruits and vegetables.

1992, Oct. 12 **Litho.** ***Perf. 15***
679 A112 200fr multicolored 3.00
680 A112 400fr multicolored 6.25

Felis Serval A113

1992, Oct. 16
681 A113 30fr shown .50
682 A113 130fr Two seated 2.00
683 A113 200fr One standing, one lying 3.10
684 A113 220fr Two faces 3.50
Nos. 681-684 (4) 9.10

World Wildlife Fund.

Mushrooms A114

1992 Summer Olympics, Barcelona A115

Designs: 10fr, Russula ingens. 15fr, Russula brunneorigida. 20fr, Amanita zambiana. 30fr, Russula subfistulosa. 75fr, 85fr, Russula meleagris. 100fr, Russula immaculata. 110fr, like #685. 115fr, like #686. 120fr, 130fr, Russula sejuncta. 250fr, Afroboletus luteolus.

1992-93 ***Perf. 11½x12***

Granite Paper

685 A114 10fr multicolored .20
686 A114 15fr multicolored .25
687 A114 20fr multicolored .30
688 A114 30fr multicolored .50
689 A114 75fr multicolored 1.10
690 A114 85fr multicolored 1.40
691 A114 100fr multicolored 1.50
691A A114 110fr multicolored 1.60
691B A114 115fr multicolored 1.75
692 A114 120fr multicolored 1.90
693 A114 130fr multicolored 2.00
694 A114 250fr multicolored 3.75
Nos. 685-694 (12) 16.25

Issued: 110fr, 115fr, 1993; others, 9/30/92.

1992, Nov. 6 ***Perf. 15***
695 A115 130fr Runners 2.00
696 A115 500fr Hurdler 7.75

A116

A116a

Christmas (Details of Adoration of the Kings, by Gentile da Fabriano): a, 100fr, Crowd, horses. b, 130fr, Kings. c, 250fr, Nativity scene.

1992, Dec. 7 **Litho.** ***Perf. 11½***
697 A116 Strip of 3, #a.-c. 5.25
d. Souvenir sheet of 3, #697a-697c 6.50

Nos. 697a-697c have white border. No. 697d has continuous design and sold for 580fr.

1992, Dec. 5 **Litho.** ***Perf. 15***

Designs: 200fr, Emblems. 220fr, Profile of person made from fruits and vegetables.

697E A116a 200fr multicolored 5.25
697F A116a 220fr multicolored 5.75

Intl. Conference on Nutrition, Rome.

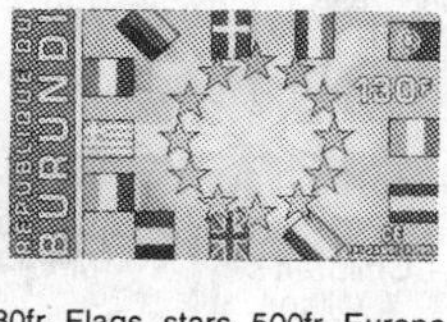

European Common Market A117

Designs: 130fr, Flags, stars. 500fr, Europe, Africa, clasped hands, stars.

1993, Mar. 29 **Litho.** ***Perf. 15***
698 A117 130fr multicolored 1.50
699 A117 500fr multicolored 5.75

1994 World Cup Soccer Championships, US — A118

Players, stadium, US flag and: 130fr, Statue of Liberty. 200fr, Golden Gate Bridge.

1993, July 5 **Litho.** ***Perf. 15***
700 A118 130fr multicolored 1.50
701 A118 200fr multicolored 2.25

Traditional Musical Instruments — A119

1993, Apr. 30 **Litho.** ***Perf. 15***
702 A119 200fr Indonongo 2.25
703 A119 220fr Ingoma 2.50
704 A119 250fr Ikembe 2.75
705 A119 300fr Umuduri 3.50
Nos. 702-705 (4) 11.00

A120

A121

1993, June 4 **Litho.** ***Perf. 11½***
706 A120 130fr Papilio bromius 1.50
707 A120 200fr Charaxes eupale 2.25
708 A120 250fr Cymothoe caenis 2.75
709 A120 300fr Graphium ridleyanus 3.50
a. Souvenir sheet of 4, #706-709 11.50
Nos. 706-709 (4) 10.00

No. 709a sold for 980fr.

1993, Dec. 9 ***Perf. 14***
710 A121 100fr Cattle 1.10
711 A121 120fr Sheep 1.40
712 A121 130fr Pigs 1.50
713 A121 250fr Goats 2.75
Nos. 710-713 (4) 6.75

Christmas A122

Rock Stars A123

Natives adoring Christ Child: a, 100fr, Woman carrying baby, two people kneeling. b, 130fr, With Christ Child. 250fr, c, Woman carrying baby, three other people.

1993, Dec. 10 ***Perf. 11½***
714 A122 Strip of 3, #a.-c. 5.00
d. Souvenir sheet of 3, #714a-714c 6.00

Nos. 714a-714c have white border. No. 714d has continuous design and sold for 580fr.

1994 **Litho.** ***Perf. 15***
715 A123 60fr Elvis Presley .65
716 A123 115fr Mick Jagger 1.25
717 A123 120fr John Lennon 1.25

718 A123 200fr Michael Jackson 2.25
a. Souvenir sheet, #715-718 6.50
Nos. 715-718 (4) 5.40

No. 718a sold for 600fr.

A124

A125

1994, Oct. 10 Litho. *Perf. 15*
719 A124 150fr multicolored 1.10

Intl. Olympic Committee, cent.

1994, Dec. 14 Photo. *Perf. 15*

Christmas (Madonna and Child): a, 115fr, Chinese. b, 120fr, Japanese. c, 250fr, Polish.

720 A125 Strip of 3, #a.-c. 5.00
d. Souvenir sheet of 1, #720c 2.75

A126

A127

115fr, FAO, 50th anniv. 120fr, UN, 50th anniv.

1995, Feb. 21 Litho. *Perf. 11½*
721 A126 115fr multicolored 1.25
722 A126 120fr multicolored 1.25

1995 Litho. *Perf. 11½*

Flowers: 15fr, Cassia didymobotrya. 20fr, Mitragyna rubrostipulosa. 30fr, Phytolacca dodecandra. 85fr, Acanthus pubescens. 100fr, Bulbophyllum comatum. 110fr, Angraecum evradianum. 115fr, Eulophia burundiensis. 120fr, Habenaria adolphii.

Granite Paper

723 A127 15fr multicolored .20
724 A127 20fr multicolored .20
725 A127 30fr multicolored .30
726 A127 85fr multicolored .80
727 A127 100fr multicolored .90
728 A127 110fr multicolored 1.00
729 A127 115fr multicolored 1.00
730 A127 120fr multicolored 1.10
Nos. 723-730 (8) 5.50

Transportation Methods — A128

30fr, Otraco bus. 115fr, Transintra semi truck. 120fr, Arnolac tugboat. 250fr, Air Burundi airplane.

1995, Nov. 16 Litho. *Perf. 11½*
731 A128 30fr multicolored .45
732 A128 115fr multicolored 1.75
733 A128 120fr multicolored 1.75
734 A128 250fr multicolored 3.50
Nos. 731-734 (4) 7.45

A129

A130

Christmas (African sculpture): a, 100fr, Boy with panga, basket on head. b, 130fr, Boy carrying sheaf of wheat. c, 250fr, Mother, children.

1995, Dec. 26 Litho. *Perf. 11½x12*
735 A129 Strip of 3, #a.-c. 2.25
d. Souvenir sheet of 3, #735a-735c 2.25

1996, June 28 Litho. *Perf. 14*

Athlete, national flag: 130fr, Venuste Niyongabo. 500fr, Arthemon Hatungimana.

736 A130 130fr multicolored .65
737 A130 500fr multicolored 2.50

1996 Summer Olympic Games, Atlanta.

Birds A131

Designs: 15fr, Hagedashia hagedash. 20fr, Alopochen aegyptiacus. 30fr, Haliaeetus vocifer. 120fr, Ardea goliath. 165fr, Balearica regulorum. 220fr, Actophilornis africana.

1996 Litho. *Perf. 14*
740 A131 15fr multicolored .20
741 A131 20fr multicolored .20
742 A131 30fr multicolored .30
743 A131 120fr multicolored 1.10
744 A131 165fr multicolored 1.60
745 A131 220fr multicolored 2.00
Nos. 740-745 (6) 5.40

Fish of Lake Tanganyika A132

Designs: 30fr, Julidochromis malieri. 115fr, Cyphotilapia frontosa. 120fr, Lamprologus brichardi. 250fr, Synodonis petricola.

1996, June 4 Litho. *Perf. 11¾x11½*
746 A132 30fr multicolored .20 .20
747 A132 115fr multicolored .40 .40
748 A132 120fr multicolored .40 .40
749 A132 250fr multicolored .85 .85
a. Souvenir sheet of 4, #746-749, perf. 11¾ 2.10 2.10
Nos. 746-749 (4) 1.85 1.85

No. 749a sold for 615fr.
Although ostensibly issued in 1996, this set was not available in the philatelic marketplace until 1999.

SOS Children's Village, 50th Anniv. A133

Designs: 100fr, Children in Village. 250fr, Children, flags. 270fr, Children around flagpole.

1998, Dec. 26 Litho. *Perf. 14*
750 A133 100fr multicolored .35 .35
751 A133 250fr multicolored .85 .85
752 A133 270fr multicolored .90 .90
Nos. 750-752 (3) 2.10 2.10

Christmas — A134

Various paintings of Madonna and Child.

1999, Jan. 19 *Perf. 11¾*

Frame color

753 A134 100fr green .35 .35
754 A134 130fr yellow brown .45 .45
755 A134 250fr rose .85 .85
a. Souvenir sheet of 3, #753-755 2.00 2.00
Nos. 753-755 (3) 1.65 1.65

Nos. 753-755 are dated "1996," "1997," and "1998," respectively.
No. 755a sold for 580fr.

Diana, Princess of Wales (1961-97) A135

Denominations: a, 100fr. b, 250fr. c, 300fr.

1999, Sept. 30 *Perf. 13¾*
756 A135 Sheet of 6, 2 each #a.-c. 4.50 4.50

SEMI-POSTAL STAMPS

Prince Louis Rwagasore — SP1

Prince and Stadium SP2

Design: 1.50fr+75c, 6.50fr+3fr, Prince and memorial monument.

Perf. 14x13, 13x14

1963, Feb. 15 Photo. Unwmk.
B1 SP1 50c + 25c brt vio .20 .20
B2 SP2 1fr + 50c red org & dk bl .20 .20
B3 SP2 1.50fr + 75c lem & dk vio .20 .20
B4 SP1 3.50fr + 1.50fr lil rose .20 .20
B5 SP2 5fr + 2fr rose pink & dk bl .20 .20
B6 SP2 6.50fr + 3fr gray ol & dk vio .20 .20
Nos. B1-B6 (6) 1.20 1.20

Issued in memory of Prince Louis Rwagasore (1932-61), son of King Mwami Mwambutsa IV and Prime Minister. The surtax was for the stadium and monument in his honor.

Red Cross Type of Regular Issue
Souvenir Sheet

1963, Sept. 26 Litho. *Imperf.*
B7 Sheet of 4 2.00 2.00
a. A5 4fr + 2fr fawn, red & black .30 .30
b. A5 8fr + 2fr green, red & black .40 .40
c. A5 10fr + 2fr gray, red & black .45 .45
d. A5 20fr + 2fr ultra, red & black .65 .65

Surtax for Red Cross work in Burundi.

Olympic Type of Regular Issue
Souvenir Sheet

Designs: 18fr+2fr, Hurdling, horiz. 20fr+5fr, Vaulting, horiz.

1964, Nov. 18 *Perf. 13½*
B8 Sheet of 2 3.00 2.75
a. A13 18fr + 2fr yel grn & multi 1.25 1.00
b. A13 20fr + 5fr brt pink & multi 1.25 1.00

Scientist with Microscope and Map of Burundi — SP3

Lithographed and Photogravure

1965, Jan. 28 Unwmk. *Perf. 14½*
B9 SP3 2fr + 50c multi .20 .20
B10 SP3 4fr + 1.50fr multi .20 .20
B11 SP3 5fr + 2.50fr multi .20 .20
B12 SP3 8fr + 3fr multi .25 .20
B13 SP3 10fr + 5fr multi .40 .20
Nos. B9-B13 (5) 1.25 1.00

Souvenir Sheet

Perf. 13x13½

B14 SP3 10fr + 10fr multi .85 .85

Issued for the fight against tuberculosis.

Coat of Arms, 10fr Coin, Reverse SP4

Designs (Coins of Various Denominations): 4fr+50c, 8fr+50c, 15fr+50c, 40fr+50c, King Mwambutsa IV, obverse.

Lithographed; Embossed on Gilt Foil

1965, Aug. 9 *Imperf.*

Diameter: 39mm

B15 SP4 2fr + 50c crimson & org .20 .20
B16 SP4 4fr + 50c ultra & ver .20 .20

Diameter: 45mm

B17 SP4 6fr + 50c org & gray .20 .20
B18 SP4 8fr + 50c bl & magenta .20 .20

Diameter: 56mm

B19 SP4 12fr + 50c lt grn & red lil .25 .25
B20 SP4 15fr + 50c yel grn & lt lil .30 .30

Diameter: 67mm

B21 SP4 25fr + 50c vio bl & buff .50 .50
B22 SP4 40fr + 50c brt pink & red brn .75 .75
Nos. B15-B22 (8) 2.60 2.60

Stamps are backed with patterned paper in blue, orange and pink engine-turned design.

Prince Louis Rwagasore and Pres. John F. Kennedy SP5

Designs: 4fr+1fr, 20fr+5fr, Prince Louis and memorial. 20fr+2fr, 40fr+5fr, Pres. John F. Kennedy and library shelves. 40fr+2fr, King Mwambutsa IV at Kennedy grave, Arlington, vert.

1966, Jan. 21 Photo. *Perf. 13½*

B23 SP5 4fr + 1fr gray bl & dk brn .20 .20
B24 SP5 10fr + 1fr pale grn, ind & brn .20 .20
B25 SP5 20fr + 2fr lil & dp grn .40 .20
B26 SP5 40fr + 2fr gray grn & dk brn .65 .20
Nos. B23-B26 (4) 1.45 .80

Souvenir Sheet

B27 Sheet of 2 1.50 1.00
a. SP5 20fr + 5fr gray blue & dk brn .50 .45
b. SP5 40fr + 5fr lilac & deep green .75 .50

Issued in memory of Prince Louis Rwagasore and President John F. Kennedy.

Republic

Winston Churchill and St. Paul's, London SP6

Designs: 15fr+2fr, Tower of London and Churchill. 20fr+3fr, Big Ben and Churchill.

1967, Mar. 23 Photo. *Perf. 13½*

B28 SP6 4fr + 1fr multi .20 .20
B29 SP6 15fr + 2fr multi .35 .20
B30 SP6 20fr + 3fr multi .45 .20
Nos. B28-B30 (3) 1.00 .60

Issued in memory of Sir Winston Churchill (1874-1965), statesman and World War II leader.

A souvenir sheet contains one airmail stamp, 50fr+5fr, with Churchill portrait centered. Size: 80x80mm. Exists perf. and imperf. Value, each sheet, $3.50.

Nos. B28-B30 Overprinted

1967, July 14 Photo. *Perf. 13½*

B31 SP6 4fr + 1fr multi .20 .20
B32 SP6 15fr + 2fr multi .40 .20
B33 SP6 20fr + 3fr multi .65 .30
Nos. B31-B33 (3) 1.25 .70

50th anniversary of Lions International. Exist with dates transposed.

The souvenir sheets described below No. B30 also received this Lions overprint. Value, each $3.50.

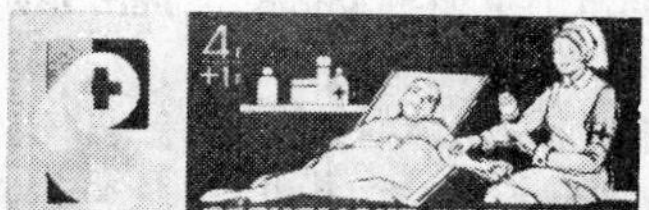

Blood Transfusion and Red Cross — SP7

Designs: 7fr+1fr, Stretcher bearers and wounded man. 11fr+1fr, Surgical team. 17fr+1fr, Nurses tending blood bank.

1969, June 26 Photo. *Perf. 13½*

B34 SP7 4fr + 1fr multi .20 .20
B35 SP7 7fr + 1fr multi .20 .20
B36 SP7 11fr + 1fr multi .30 .20
B37 SP7 17fr + 1fr multi .30 .20
Nos. B34-B37,CB9-CB11 (7) 2.60 1.40

League of Red Cross Societies, 50th anniv.

Pope Paul VI and Map of Africa — SP8

3fr+2fr, 17fr+2fr, Pope Paul VI. 10fr+2fr, Flag made of flags of African Nations. 14fr+2fr, View of St. Peter's, Rome. 40fr+2fr, 40fr+5fr, Martyrs of Uganda. 50fr+2fr, 50fr+5fr, Pope on Throne.

1969, Sept. 12 Photo. *Perf. 13½*

B38 SP8 3fr + 2fr multi, vert. .20 .20
B39 SP8 5fr + 2fr multi .20 .20
B40 SP8 10fr + 2fr multi .30 .20
B41 SP8 14fr + 2fr multi .40 .20
B42 SP8 17fr + 2fr multi, vert. .50 .20
B43 SP8 40fr + 2fr multi 1.00 .20
B44 SP8 50fr + 2fr multi 1.10 .20
Nos. B38-B44 (7) 3.70 1.40

Souvenir Sheet

B45 Sheet of 2 2.00 1.75
a. SP8 40fr + 5fr multi .90 .75
b. SP8 50fr + 5fr multi 1.00 .90

Visit of Pope Paul VI to Uganda, July 31-Aug. 2.

Virgin and Child, by Albrecht Dürer — SP9

Christmas (Paintings): 11fr+1fr, Madonna of the Eucharist, by Sandro Botticelli. 20fr+1fr, Holy Family, by El Greco.

1970, Dec. 14 Photo. *Perf. 13½*

Gold Frame

B46 SP9 6.50fr + 1fr multi .20 .20
B47 SP9 11fr + 1fr multi .25 .20
B48 SP9 20fr + 1fr multi .40 .20
a. Souvenir sheet of 3B46-B48 .90 .90
Nos. B46-B48,CB12-CB14 (6) 2.20 1.20

Nos. 376-378 Surcharged in Gold and Black

1971, Nov. 27

B49 A51 3fr + 1fr multi .20 .20
B50 A51 5fr + 1fr multi .20 .20
B51 A51 6fr + 1fr multi .20 .20
a. Souvenir sheet of 3 .55 .55
Nos. B49-B51,CB19-CB21 (6) 1.90 1.20

UNICEF, 25th anniv. #B51a contains 3 stamps similar to #B49-B51 with 2fr surtax each.

"La Polenta," by Pietro Longhi SP10

Designs: 3fr+1fr, Archangel Michael, Byzantine icon from St. Mark's 6fr+1fr, "Gossip," by Pietro Longhi. 11fr+1fr, "Diana's Bath," by Giovanni Batista Pittoni. All stamps inscribed UNESCO.

1971, Dec. 27

B52 SP10 3fr + 1fr gold & multi .20 .20
B53 SP10 5fr + 1fr gold & multi .20 .20
B54 SP10 6fr + 1fr gold & multi .20 .20
B55 SP10 11fr + 1fr gold & multi .30 .20
a. Souvenir sheet of 4 .75 .50
Nos. B52-B55,CB22-CB25 (8) 2.40 1.60

The surtax was for the UNESCO campaign to save the treasures of Venice. No. B55a contains 4 stamps similar to Nos. B52-B55, but with 2fr surtax. Sheet exists imperf.

Nos. 408-410 Surcharged "+1F" in Silver

1972, Dec. 12 Photo. *Perf. 13½*

B56 A57 5fr + 1fr multi .20 .20
B57 A57 10fr + 1fr multi .25 .20
B58 A57 15fr + 1fr multi .30 .20
a. Souvenir sheet of 3 .75 .70
Nos. B56-B58,CB26-CB28 (6) 2.10 1.20

Christmas 1972. No. B58a contains 3 stamps similar to Nos. B56-B58, but with 2fr surtax.

Nos. 441-443 Surcharged "+1F" in Silver

1973, Dec. 14 Photo. *Perf. 13*

B59 A64 5fr + 1fr multi .20 .20
B60 A64 10fr + 1fr multi .20 .20
B61 A64 15fr + 1fr multi .30 .20
a. Souvenir sheet of 3 .65 .65
Nos. B59-B61,CB29-CB31 (6) 2.00 1.20

Christmas 1973. No. B61a contains 3 stamps similar to Nos. B59-B61 with 2fr surtax each.

Christmas Type of 1974

1974, Dec. 2 Photo. *Perf. 13*

B62 A70 5fr + 1fr multi .20 .20
B63 A70 10fr + 1fr multi .20 .20
B64 A70 15fr + 1fr multi .30 .20
a. Souvenir sheet of 3 .75 .75
Nos. B62-B64,CB32-CB34 (6) 2.20 1.50

No. B64a contains 3 stamps similar to Nos. B62-B64 with 2fr surtax each.

Nos. 485-490 Surcharged "+ 1F" in Silver and Black

1975, Dec. 22 Photo. *Perf. 13*

B65 A73 5fr + 1fr #485 .20
B66 A73 5fr + 1fr #486 .20
B67 A73 13fr + 1fr #487 .30
B68 A73 13fr + 1fr #488 .30
B69 A73 27fr + 1fr #489 .50
B70 A73 27fr + 1fr #490 .50
a. Souvenir sheet of 6 2.50
Nos. B65-B70,CB35-CB40 (12) 5.30

Michelangelo Buonarroti (1475-1564), 500th birth anniversary. No. B70a contains 6 stamps similar to Nos. B65-B70 with 2fr surcharge each.

Nos. 504-506 Surcharged "+1f" in Silver and Black

1976, Nov. 25 Photo. *Perf. 13½*

B71 A76 5fr + 1fr multi .20
B72 A76 13fr + 1fr multi .25
B73 A76 27fr + 1fr multi .40
a. Souvenir sheet of 3 .85
Nos. B71-B73,CB41-CB43 (6) 2.25

Christmas 1976. No. B73a contains 3 stamps similar to Nos. B71-B73 with 2fr surtax each.

Nos. 531-533 Surcharged "+1fr" in Silver and Black

1977 Photo. *Perf. 14x13*

B74 A83 5fr + 1fr multi .20
B75 A83 13fr + 1fr multi .25
B76 A83 27fr + 1fr multi .40
a. Souvenir sheet of 3 .85
Nos. B74-B76,CB44-CB46 (6) 2.25

Christmas 1977. No. B76a contains 3 stamps similar to Nos. B74-B76 with 2fr surtax each.

Christmas Type of 1979

1979, Feb. Photo. *Perf. 14x13*

B77 A86 13fr + 1fr multi .25
B78 A86 17fr + 1fr multi .30
B79 A86 27fr + 1fr multi .40
B80 A86 31fr + 1fr multi .50
B81 A86 40fr + 1fr multi .60
Nos. B77-B81 (5) 2.05

IYC Type of 1979

1979, July 19 Photo. *Perf. 14*

B82 Sheet of 4 1.25 1.00
a. A88 10fr + 2fr like #557 .20 .20
b. A88 20fr + 2fr like #558 .25 .20
c. A88 27fr + 2fr like #559 .30 .20
d. A88 50fr + 2fr like #560 .55 .30

Christmas Type of 1979

1979, Dec. 10 Photo. *Perf. 13½*

B83 A89 20fr + 1fr like #561 .30
B84 A89 27fr + 1fr like #562 .40
B85 A89 31fr + 1fr like #563 .50
B86 A89 50fr + 1fr like #564 .80
Nos. B83-B86 (4) 2.00

Christmas Type of 1980

1981, Jan. 16 Photo. *Perf. 13½x13*

B87 A92 10fr + 1fr like #579 .20
B88 A92 30fr + 1fr like #580 .30
B89 A92 40fr + 1fr like #581 .40
B90 A92 50fr + 1fr like #582 .50
Nos. B87-B90 (4) 1.40

Christmas Type of 1983

1983, Nov. 2 Litho. *Perf. 14½x13½*

B91 A97 10fr + 1fr like #607 .20
B92 A97 25fr + 1fr like #608 .40
B93 A97 30fr + 1fr like #609 .50
B94 A97 50fr + 1fr like #610 .75
Nos. B91-B94 (4) 1.85

Christmas Type of 1984

1984, Dec. 15 *Perf. 13½*

B95 A101 10fr + 1fr like #629 .20
B96 A101 25fr + 1fr like #630 .40
B97 A101 30fr + 1fr like #631 .50
B98 A101 50fr + 1fr like #632 .75
Nos. B95-B98 (4) 1.85

Multi-party Elections, 1st Anniv.
SP11 SP12

Designs: 30fr+10fr, Pres. Buyoya handing Baton of Power to Pres. Ndadaye. 110fr+10fr, Pres. Ndadaye giving inauguration speech. 115fr+10fr, Arms, map of Burundi. 120fr+10fr, Warrior, flag of Burundi, trees, map of Burundi.

1994, Oct. 20 Litho. *Perf. 15*

B99 SP11 30fr +10fr multi .30
B100 SP11 110fr +10fr multi .90
B101 SP12 115fr +10fr multi .95
B102 SP12 120fr +10fr multi 1.00
Nos. B99-B102 (4) 3.15

AIR POST STAMPS

Animal Type of Regular Issue

6fr, Zebra. 8fr, Cape buffalo (bubalis). 10fr, Impala. 14fr, Hippopotamus. 15fr, Defassa waterbuck. 20fr, Cheetah. 50fr, Elephant.

Unwmk.

1964, July 2 Litho. *Perf. 14*

Size: 42x21mm, 21x42mm

C1 A9 6fr multi .20 .20
C2 A9 8fr multi .20 .20
C3 A9 10fr multi, vert. .25 .20
C4 A9 14fr multi .30 .20
C5 A9 15fr multi, vert. .30 .20

Size: 53x32½mm

C6 A9 20fr multi .40 .20
C7 A9 50fr multi 1.10 .40
Nos. C1-C7 (7) 2.75 1.60

Bird Type of Regular Issue

Birds: 6fr, Secretary bird. 8fr, African anhinga. 10fr, African peacock. 14fr, Bee eater. 15fr, Yellow-billed stork. 20fr, Saddle-billed stork. 50fr, Abyssinian ground hornbill. 75fr, Martial eagle. 130fr, Lesser flamingo.

1965, June 10 Litho. *Perf. 14*

Size: 26x43mm

C8 A14 6fr multi .20 .20
C9 A14 8fr multi .20 .20
C10 A14 10fr multi .20 .20
C11 A14 14fr multi .25 .20
C12 A14 15fr multi .30 .20

Size: 33x53mm

C13 A14 20fr multi .35 .20
C14 A14 50fr multi .90 .20
C15 A14 75fr multi 1.25 .25
C16 A14 130fr multi 2.25 .35
Nos. C8-C16 (9) 5.90 2.00

For overprints see Nos. C35A-C35I.

Flower Type of Regular Issue

Flowers: 6fr, Dissotis. 8fr, Crossandra. 10fr, Ansellia. 14fr, Thunbergia. 15fr, Schizoglossum. 20fr, Gazania. 50fr, Protea. 75fr, Hibiscus. 130fr, Markhamia.

1966, Oct. 10 Unwmk. *Perf. 13½*

Size: 31x31mm

C17	A17	6fr multi	.20	.20
C18	A17	8fr multi	.20	.20
C19	A17	10fr multi	.20	.20
C20	A17	14fr multi	.25	.20
C21	A17	15fr multi	.25	.20

Size: 39x39mm

C22	A17	20fr multi	.25	.20
C23	A17	50fr multi	.60	.20
C24	A17	75fr multi	.80	.25
C25	A17	130fr multi	1.50	.30
		Nos. C17-C25 (9)	4.25	1.95

For overprints see Nos. C27-C35.

Tapestry Type of Regular Issue
Souvenir Sheet

1966, Nov. 4 Unwmk. *Perf. 13½*

C26	A18	Sheet of 7 (14fr)	1.25	.65

See note after No. 158.

Republic
Nos. C17-C25 Overprinted

1967 Litho. *Perf. 13½*

Size: 31x31mm

C27	A17	6fr multi	.20	.20
C28	A17	8fr multi	.25	.20
C29	A17	10fr multi	.25	.20
C30	A17	14fr multi	.50	.20
C31	A17	15fr multi	.50	.20

Size: 39x39mm

C32	A17	20fr multi	.70	.20
C33	A17	50fr multi	1.90	.50
C34	A17	75fr multi	3.00	.50
C35	A17	130fr multi	4.00	1.10
		Nos. C27-C35 (9)	11.30	3.30

Nos. C8-C16 Overprinted "REPUBLIQUE / DU / BURUNDI" and Horizontal Bar

1967 Litho. *Perf. 14*

Size: 26x43mm

C35A	A14	6fr multi	*.20*
C35B	A14	8fr multi	*.20*
C35C	A14	10fr multi	*.20*
C35D	A14	14fr multi	*.30*
C35E	A14	15fr multi	*.50*

Size: 33x53mm

C35F	A14	20fr multi	*.75*
C35G	A14	50fr multi	*1.90*
C35H	A14	75fr multi	*3.00*
C35I	A14	130fr multi	*3.50*
		Nos. C35A-C35I (9)	*10.55*

African Art Type of Regular Issue

African Art: 10fr, Spirit of Bakutu figurine, Equatorial Africa. 14fr, Pearl throne of Sultan of the Bamum, Cameroun. 17fr, Bronze head of Mother Queen of Benin, Nigeria. 24fr, Statue of 109th Bakouba king, Kata-Mbula, Central Congo. 26fr, Baskets and lances, Burundi.

1967, June 5 Photo. *Perf. 13½*

C36	A20	10fr gold & multi	.20	.20
C37	A20	14fr gold & multi	.20	.20
C38	A20	17fr gold & multi	.20	.20
C39	A20	24fr gold & multi	.25	.20
C40	A20	26fr gold & multi	.40	.25
		Nos. C36-C40 (5)	1.25	1.05

Boy Scout Type of Regular Issue

10fr, Scouts on hiking trip. 14fr, Cooking at campfire. 17fr, Lord Baden-Powell. 24fr, Boy Scout & Cub Scout giving Scout sign. 26fr, First aid.

1967, Aug. 9 *Perf. 13½*

C41	A21	10fr gold & multi	.20	.20
C42	A21	14fr gold & multi	.25	.20
C43	A21	17fr gold & multi	.30	.20
C44	A21	24fr gold & multi	.40	.20
C45	A21	26fr gold & multi	.70	.20
		Nos. C41-C45 (5)	1.85	1.00

A souvenir sheet of 2 contains one each of Nos. C44-C45 and 2 labels in the designs of Nos. 208-209 with commemorative inscriptions was issued Jan. 8, 1968. Size: 100x100mm

Fish Type of Regular Issue

Designs: Various Tropical Fish

1967, Sept. 8 Photo. *Perf. 13½*

Size: 50x23mm

C46	A19	6fr multi	.20	.20
C47	A19	8fr multi	.20	.20
C48	A19	10fr multi	.30	.20
C49	A19	14fr multi	.40	.20
C50	A19	15fr multi	.40	.20

Size: 58x27mm

C51	A19	20fr multi	.50	.20
C52	A19	50fr multi	1.25	.20
C53	A19	75fr multi	2.00	.20
C54	A19	130fr multi	3.25	.25
		Nos. C46-C54 (9)	8.50	1.85

Boeing 707 of Air Congo and ITY Emblem — AP1

Designs: 14fr, Boeing 727 of Sabena over lake. 17fr, Vickers VC10 of East African Airways over lake. 26fr, Boeing 727 of Sabena over airport.

1967, Nov. 3 Photo. *Perf. 13*

C55	AP1	10fr blk, yel brn & sil	.20	.20
C56	AP1	14fr blk, org & sil	.20	.20
C57	AP1	17fr blk, brt bl & sil	.25	.20
C58	AP1	26fr blk, brt rose lil & sil	.35	.20
		Nos. C55-C58 (4)	1.00	.80

Opening of the jet airport at Bujumbura and for International Tourist Year, 1967.

Paintings Type of Regular Issue

Paintings: 17fr, Woman with Cat, by Renoir. 24fr, The Jewish Bride, by Rembrandt, horiz. 26fr, Pope Innocent X, by Velazquez.

1968, Mar. 29 Photo. *Perf. 13½*

C59	A26	17fr multi	.35	.20
C60	A26	24fr multi	.45	.20
C61	A26	26fr multi	.55	.20
		Nos. C59-C61 (3)	1.35	.60

Issued in sheets of 6.

Space Type of Regular Issue

Designs: 14fr, Moon Probe. 18fr, Russian astronaut walking in space. 25fr, Weather satellite. 40fr, American astronaut walking in space.

1968, May 15 Photo. *Perf. 13½*

Size: 41x41mm

C62	A27	14fr sil & multi	.25	.20
C63	A27	18fr sil & multi	.30	.20
C64	A27	25fr sil & multi	.45	.20
C65	A27	40fr sil & multi	.70	.20
		Nos. C62-C65 (4)	1.70	.80

Butterfly Type of Regular Issue

Butterflies: 6fr, Teracolus annae. 8fr, Graphium ridleyanus. 10fr, Cymothoe. 14fr, Charaxes eupale. 15fr, Papilio bromius. 20fr, Papilio zenobia. 50fr, Salamis aethiops. 75fr, Danais chrysippus. 130fr, Salamis temora.

1968, Sept. 9 Photo. *Perf. 13½*

Size: 38x42mm

C66	A28	6fr gold & multi	.20	.20
C67	A28	8fr gold & multi	.20	.20
C68	A28	10fr gold & multi	.35	.20
C69	A28	14fr gold & multi	.40	.20
C70	A28	15fr gold & multi	.50	.20

Size: 44x49mm

C71	A28	20fr gold & multi	.60	.20
C72	A28	50fr gold & multi	1.25	.20
C73	A28	75fr gold & multi	2.50	.20
C74	A28	130fr gold & multi	4.00	.20
		Nos. C66-C74 (9)	10.00	1.80

Painting Type of Regular Issue

Paintings: 17fr, The Letter, by Jean H. Fragonard. 26fr, Young Woman Reading Letter, by Jan Vermeer. 40fr, Lady Folding Letter, by Elisabeth Vigée-Lebrun. 50fr, Mademoiselle Lavergne, by Jean Etienne Liotard.

1968, Sept. 30 Photo. *Perf. 13½*

C84	A29	17fr multi	.25	.20
C85	A29	26fr multi	.45	.20
C86	A29	40fr multi	.60	.20
C87	A29	50fr multi	.70	.20
		Nos. C84-C87 (4)	2.00	.80

Olympic Games Type

1968, Oct. 24

C88	A30	10fr Shot put	.20	.20
C89	A30	17fr Running	.25	.20
C90	A30	26fr Hammer throw	.40	.20
C91	A30	50fr Hurdling	.70	.20
C92	A30	75fr Broad jump	1.10	.30
		Nos. C88-C92 (5)	2.65	1.10

Christmas Type of 1968

Paintings: 10fr, Virgin and Child, by Correggio. 14fr, Nativity, by Federigo Baroccio. 17fr, Holy Family, by El Greco. 26fr, Adoration of the Magi, by Maino.

1968, Nov. 26 Photo. *Perf. 13½*

C93	A31	10fr multi	.20	.20
C94	A31	14fr multi	.25	.20
C95	A31	17fr multi	.30	.20
C96	A31	26fr multi	.40	.20
a.		Souv. sheet of 4, #C93-C96	1.10	
		Nos. C93-C96 (4)	1.15	.80

For overprints see Nos. C100-C103.

Human Rights Flame, Hand and Globe — AP2

1969, Jan. 22

C97	AP2	10fr multi	.20	.20
C98	AP2	14fr multi	.25	.20
C99	AP2	26fr lil & multi	.40	.20
		Nos. C97-C99 (3)	.85	.60

International Human Rights Year, 1968.

Nos. C93-C96 Overprinted in Silver

1969, Feb. 17 Photo. *Perf. 13½*

C100	A31	10fr multi	.20	.20
C101	A31	14fr multi	.30	.20
C102	A31	17fr multi	.35	.20
C103	A31	26fr multi	.50	.25
		Nos. C100-C103 (4)	1.35	.85

Man's 1st flight around the moon by the US spacecraft Apollo 8, Dec. 21-27, 1968.

Moon Landing Type of 1969

Designs: 26fr, Neil A. Armstrong leaving landing module. 40fr, Astronaut on moon. 50fr, Splashdown in the Pacific.

1969, Nov. 6 Photo. *Perf. 13½*

C104	A38	26fr gold & multi	.50	.25
C105	A38	40fr gold & multi	.75	.40
C106	A38	50fr gold & multi	.90	.45
		Nos. C104-C106 (3)	2.15	1.10

Christmas Type of 1969

Paintings: 17fr, Madonna and Child, by Benvenuto da Garofalo. 26fr, Madonna and Child, by Jacopo Negretti. 50fr, Madonna and Child, by Il Giorgione. All horizontal.

1969, Dec. 2 Photo.

C107	A39	17fr gold & multi	.40	.20
C108	A39	26fr gold & multi	.50	.20
C109	A39	50fr gold & multi	.90	.30
a.		Souv. sheet of 3, #C107-C109	1.90	1.50
		Nos. C107-C109 (3)	1.80	.70

Insect Type of Regular Issue

Designs: Various Beetles and Weevils.

1970 *Perf. 13½*

Size: 46x32mm

C110	A40	6fr gold & multi	.20	.20
C111	A40	8fr gold & multi	.20	.20
C112	A40	10fr gold & multi	.20	.20
C113	A40	14fr gold & multi	.30	.20
C114	A40	15fr gold & multi	.35	.20

Size: 52x36mm

C115	A40	20fr gold & multi	1.00	.20
C116	A40	50fr gold & multi	2.00	.25
C117	A40	75fr gold & multi	3.00	.25
C118	A40	130fr gold & multi	3.75	.40
		Nos. C110-C118 (9)	11.00	2.10

Issued: #C110-C115, 1/20; $C116-C118, 2/27.

Easter Type of 1970

Stations of the Cross, by Juan de Aranoa y Carredano: 8fr, Jesus meets the women of Jerusalem. 10fr, Jesus falls a third time. 14fr, Jesus stripped. 15fr, Jesus nailed to the cross. 18fr, Jesus dies on the cross. 20fr, Descent from the cross. 50fr, Jesus laid in the tomb.

1970, Mar. 16 Photo. *Perf. 13½*

C119	A41	8fr gold & multi	.20	.20
C120	A41	10fr gold & multi	.20	.20
C121	A41	14fr gold & multi	.25	.20
C122	A41	15fr gold & multi	.25	.20
C123	A41	18fr gold & multi	.30	.20
C124	A41	20fr gold & multi	.30	.20
C125	A41	50fr gold & multi	.70	.30
a.		Souv. sheet of 7, #C119-C125 + label	2.25	1.75
		Nos. C119-C125 (7)	2.20	1.50

EXPO '70 Type of Regular Issue
Souvenir Sheet

Designs: 40fr, Tower of the Sun, vert. 50fr, Flags of participating nations, vert.

1970, May 5 Photo. *Perf. 13½*

C126		Sheet of 2	1.40	1.40
a.	A42	40fr multi	.50	.50
b.	A42	50fr multi	.60	.60

Rhinoceros Type of Regular Issue

FAUNA: Camel, dromedar y, okapi, rhinoceros, addax, Burundi cow (2 stamps of each animal in 2 different poses). MAP OF THE NILE: Delta and pyramids, dhow, cataract, Blue Nile and crowned crane, Victoria Nile and secretary bird, Lake Victoria and source of Nile on Mt. Gikizi.

1970, July 8 Photo. *Perf. 13½*

C127		Sheet of 18	5.25	
a.	A43	14fr any single	.30	.20

Issued in sheets of 18 (3x6) stamps of different designs, to publicize the southernmost source of the Nile on Mt. Gikizi in Burundi.

UN Emblem and Headquarters, NYC — AP3

25th Anniv. of the UN (UN Emblem and): 11fr, Security Council and mural by Per Krohg. 26fr, Pope Paul VI and U Thant. 40fr, Flags in front of UN Headquarters, NYC.

1970, Oct. 23 Photo. *Perf. 13½*

C128	AP3	7fr gold & multi	.20	.20
C129	AP3	11fr gold & multi	.20	.20
C130	AP3	26fr gold & multi	.40	.20
C131	AP3	40fr gold & multi	.60	.20
a.		Souvenir sheet of 2	1.10	.90
		Nos. C128-C131 (4)	1.40	.80

No. C131a contains 2 stamps similar to Nos. C130-C131 but without "Poste Aerienne." Exists imperf.

Bird Type of Regular Issue

8fr, 14fr, 30fr, vert.; 10fr, 20fr, 50fr, horiz.

1970 Photo. *Perf. 13½*

Stamp size: 52x44mm

C132	A44	Block of 4	2.00	.20
a.		8fr Northern shrike	.50	.20
b.		8fr European starling	.50	.20
c.		8fr Yellow wagtail	.50	.20
d.		8fr Bank swallow	.50	.20
C133	A44	Block of 4	2.50	.20
a.		10fr Winter wren	.60	.20
b.		10fr Firecrest	.60	.20
c.		10fr Skylark	.60	.20
d.		10fr Crested lark	.60	.20
C134	A44	Block of 4	3.00	.25
a.		14fr Woodchat shrike	.75	.20
b.		14fr Common rock thrush	.75	.20
c.		14fr Black redstart	.75	.20
d.		14fr Ring ouzel	.75	.20
C135	A44	Block of 4	5.00	.35
a.		20fr European redstart	1.25	.20
b.		20fr Hedge sparrow	1.25	.20
c.		20fr Gray wagtail	1.25	.20
d.		20fr Meadow pipit	1.25	.20
C136	A44	Block of 4	7.00	.55
a.		30fr Eurasian hoopoe	1.75	.20
b.		30fr Pied flycatcher	1.75	.20
c.		30fr Great reed warbler	1.75	.20
d.		30fr Eurasian kingfisher	1.75	.20

C137 A44 Block of 4 11.00 .90
a. 50fr House martin 2.75 .20
b. 50fr Sedge warbler 2.75 .20
c. 50fr Fieldfare 2.75 .20
d. 50fr European Golden oriole 2.75 .20
Nos. C132-C137 (6) 30.50 2.45

Queen Fabiola and King Baudouin of Belgium AP4

Designs: 20fr, Pres. Michel Micombero and King Baudouin. 40fr, Pres. Micombero and coats of arms of Burundi and Belgium.

1970, Nov. 28 Photo. *Perf. 13½*
C140 AP4 6fr multicolored .20 .20
C141 AP4 20fr multicolored .45 .20
C142 AP4 40fr multicolored .90 .30
a. Souvenir sheet of 3 1.50 1.50
Nos. C140-C142 (3) 1.55 .70

Visit of the King and Queen of Belgium. No. C142a contains 3 stamps similar to Nos. C140-C142, but without "Poste Aerienne." No. C142a exists imperf.

Easter Type of Regular Issue

Paintings of the Resurrection: 14fr, by Louis Borrassá. 17fr, Piero della Francesca. 26fr, Michel Wohlgemuth.

1971, Apr. 2 Photo. *Perf. 13½*
C143 A49 14fr gold & multi .20 .20
C144 A49 17fr gold & multi .25 .20
C145 A49 26fr gold & multi .30 .20
a. Souv. sheet of 3, #C143-C145 1.00 .75
Nos. C143-C145 (3) .75 .60

Easter 1971. No. C145a sheet exists imperf.

Animal Type of Regular Issue

1971 Photo. *Perf. 13½*
Size: 44x44mm
C146 Strip of 4 1.50 .20
a. A48 10fr Lion .35 .20
b. A48 10fr Cape buffalo .35 .20
c. A48 10fr Hippopotamus .35 .20
d. A48 10fr Giraffe .35 .20
C147 Strip of 4 2.25 .25
a. A48 14fr Hartebeest .55 .20
b. A48 14fr Black rhinoceros .55 .20
c. A48 14fr Zebra .55 .20
d. A48 14fr Leopard .55 .20
C148 Strip of 4 3.00 .25
a. A48 17fr Grant's gazelles .75 .20
b. A48 17fr Cheetah .75 .20
c. A48 17fr African white-backed vultures .75 .20
d. A48 17fr Johnston's okapi .75 .20
C149 Strip of 4 3.50 .35
a. A48 24fr Chimpanzee .85 .20
b. A48 24fr Elephant .85 .20
c. A48 24fr Spotted Hyenas .85 .20
d. A48 24fr Beisa .85 .20
C150 Strip of 4 4.00 .40
a. A48 26fr Gorilla 1.00 .20
b. A48 26fr Gnu 1.00 .20
c. A48 26fr Warthog 1.00 .20
d. A48 26fr Cape hunting dog 1.00 .20
C151 Strip of 4 5.00 .50
a. A48 31fr Sable antelope 1.25 .20
b. A48 31fr Caracal lynx 1.25 .20
c. A48 31fr Ostriches 1.25 .20
d. A48 31fr Bongo 1.25 .20
Nos. C146-C151 (6) 19.25 1.95

For overprint and surcharges see Nos. C152, CB15-C18.

No. C146 Overprinted in Gold and Black

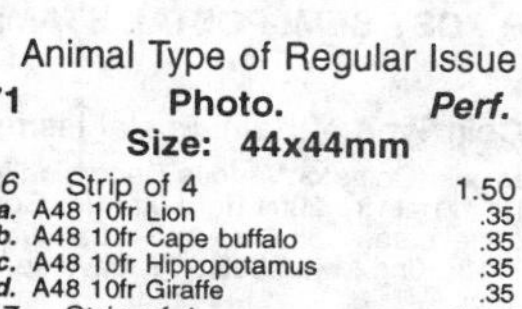

1971, July 20 Photo. *Perf. 13½*
C152 Strip of 4 .60 .20
a. A48 10fr Lion .20 .20
b. A48 10fr Cape buffalo .20 .20
c. A48 10fr Hippopotamus .20 .20
d. A48 10fr Giraffe .20 .20

Intl. Year Against Racial Discrimination.

Christmas Type of Regular Issue

Paintings of the Madonna and Child by: 14fr, Cima de Conegliano. 17fr, Fra Filippo Lippi. 31fr, Leonardo da Vinci.

1971, Nov. 2 Photo. *Perf. 13½*
C153 A51 14fr red & multi .30 .20
C154 A51 17fr red & multi .35 .20
C155 A51 31fr red & multi .50 .20
a. Souv. sheet of 3, #C153-C155 1.10 1.10
Nos. C153-C155 (3) 1.15 .60

Christmas 1971. No. C155a exists imperf. For surcharges see Nos. CB19-CB21.

Spacecraft Type of Regular Issue Souvenir Sheet

1972, Jan. 15 Photo. *Perf. 13½*
C156 Sheet of 6 1.50 1.00
a. A52 6fr Lunar Orbiter .20 .20
b. A52 11fr Vostok .20 .20
c. A52 14fr Luna I .20 .20
d. A52 17fr Apollo 11 astronaut on moon .25 .20
e. A52 26fr Soyuz 11 .35 .20
f. A52 40fr Lunar rover (Apollo 15) .50 .25

Sapporo '72 Type of Regular Issue Souvenir Sheet

Designs (Sapporo '72 Emblem and): 26fr, Snow scooter. 31fr, Downhill skiing. 50fr, Bobsledding.

1972, Feb. 3
C157 Sheet of 3 1.50 1.25
a. A53 26fr silver & multi .35 .25
b. A53 31fr silver & multi .40 .30
c. A53 50fr silver & multi .65 .40

No. C157 contains 3 stamps, arranged vertically.

Olympic Games Type of 1972

1972, July 24 Photo. *Perf. 13½*
C158 A55 24fr Weight lifting .35 .20
C159 A55 26fr Hurdles .40 .20
C160 A55 31fr Discus .50 .20
C161 A55 40fr Soccer .60 .20
Nos. C158-C161 (4) 1.85 .80

Independence Type of 1972

Designs: 15fr, Prince Rwagasore, Pres. Micombero, Burundi flag, drummers. 18fr, Rwagasore, Micombero, flag, map of Africa, globe. 27fr, Micombero, flag, globe.

1972, Aug. 24 Photo. *Perf. 13½*
C162 A56 15fr gold & multi .25 .20
C163 A56 18fr gold & multi .30 .20
C164 A56 27fr gold & multi .45 .20
a. Souv. sheet of 3, #C162-C164 1.10 1.10
Nos. C162-C164 (3) 1.00 .60

Christmas Type of 1972

Paintings of the Madonna and Child by: 18fr, Sebastiano Mainardi. 27fr, Hans Memling. 40fr, Lorenzo Lotto.

1972, Nov. 2 Photo. *Perf. 13½*
C165 A57 18fr dk car & multi .30 .20
C166 A57 27fr dk car & multi .40 .20
C167 A57 40fr dk car & multi .60 .20
a. Souv. sheet of 3, #C165-C167 1.40 1.40
Nos. C165-C167 (3) 1.30 .60

For surcharges see Nos. CB26-CB28.

Orchid Type of Regular Issue

1973, Jan. 18 Photo. *Perf. 13½*
Size: 38x38mm
C168 A58 13fr *Thelymitra pauciflora* .80 .20
C169 A58 14fr *Miltassia* .80 .20
C170 A58 15fr *Miltonia* .90 .20
C171 A58 18fr *Platycoryne crocea* 1.00 .20
C172 A58 20fr *Cattleya trinaei* 1.25 .20
C173 A58 27fr *Eulophia cucullata* 1.75 .20
C174 A58 36fr *Cymbidium hamsey* 2.25 .20
Nos. C168-C174 (7) 8.75 1.40

African Exploration Type of 1973

Designs: 15fr, Livingstone writing his diary. 18fr, "Dr. Livingstone, I presume." 27fr, Livingstone and Stanley discussing expedition.

1973, Mar. 19 Photo. *Perf. 13½*
C175 A59 15fr gold & multi .25 .20
C176 A59 18fr gold & multi .30 .20
C177 A59 27fr gold & multi .40 .20
a. Souv. sheet of 3 1.10 1.10
Nos. C175-C177 (3) .95 .60

#C177a contains 3 stamps similar to #C175-C177, but without "Poste Aerienne."

Easter Type of 1973

Paintings: 15fr, Christ at the Pillar, by Guido Reni. 18fr, Crucifixion, by Mathias Grunewald. 27fr, Descent from the Cross, by Caravaggio.

1973, Apr. 10
C178 A60 15fr gold & multi .30 .20
C179 A60 18fr gold & multi .35 .20
C180 A60 27fr gold & multi .50 .20
a. Souv. sheet of 3, #C178-C180 1.25 1.25
Nos. C178-C180 (3) 1.15 .60

INTERPOL Type of Regular Issue

Designs: 27fr, INTERPOL emblem and flag. 40fr, INTERPOL flag and emblem.

1973, May 19 Photo. *Perf. 13½*
C181 A61 27fr gold & multi .40 .20
C182 A61 40fr gold & multi .50 .20

Copernicus Type of Regular Issue

Designs: 15fr, Copernicus (C183a), Earth, Pluto, and Jupiter. 18fr, Copernicus (No. C184a), Venus, Saturn, Mars. 27fr, Copernicus (No. C185a), Uranus, Neptune, Mercury. 36fr, Earth and various spacecrafts.
a, UL. b, UR. c, LL. d, LR.

1973, July 27 Photo. *Perf. 13½*
C183 A62 15fr Block of 4, #a.-d. 1.40 .30
C184 A62 18fr Block of 4, #a.-d. 1.60 .35
C185 A62 27fr Block of 4, #a.-d. 2.00 .50
C186 A62 36fr Block of 4, #a.-d. 2.75 .70
e. Souv. sheet of 4, #C183-C186 7.00 7.00
Nos. C183-C186 (4) 7.75 1.85

Flower-Butterfly Type of 1973

Designs: Each block of 4 contains 2 flower and 2 butterfly designs. The 10fr, 14fr, 24fr and 31fr have flower designs listed as "a" and "d" numbers, butterflies as "b" and "c" numbers; the arrangement is reversed for the 17fr and 26fr.

1973, Sept. 28 Photo. *Perf. 13*
Stamp Size: 35x45mm
C187 A63 Block of 4 3.00 .40
a. 10fr *Protea cynaroides* .75 .20
b. 10fr *Precis octavia* .75 .20
c. 10fr *Epiphora bauhiniae* .75 .20
d. 10fr *Gazania longiscapa* .75 .20
C188 A63 Block of 4 4.00 .50
a. 14fr *Kniphofia* 1.00 .20
b. 14fr *Cymothoe coccinata* 1.00 .20
c. 14fr *Nudaurelia zambesina* 1.00 .20
d. 14fr *Freesia refracta* 1.00 .20
C189 A63 Block of 4 5.00 .60
a. 17fr *Calotis eupompe* 1.25 .20
b. 17fr *Narcissus* 1.25 .20
c. 17fr *Cineraria hybrida* 1.25 .20
d. 17fr *Cyrestis camillus* 1.25 .20
C190 A63 Block of 4 5.50 .50
a. 24fr *Iris tingitana* 1.25 .20
b. 24fr *Papilio demodocus* 1.25 .20
c. 24fr *Catopsilia avelaneda* 1.25 .20
d. 24fr *Nerine sarniensis* 1.25 .20
C191 A63 Block of 4 6.00 .55
a. 26fr *Hypolimnas dexithea* 1.50 .20
b. 26fr *Zantedeschia tropicalis* 1.50 .20
c. 26fr *Sandersonia aurantiaca* 1.50 .20
d. 26fr *Drurya antimachus* 1.50 .20
C192 A63 Block of 4 7.00 .65
a. 31fr *Nymphaea capensis* 1.75 .20
b. 31fr *Pandoriana pandora* 1.75 .20
c. 31fr *Precis orythia* 1.75 .20
d. 31fr *Pelargonium domestica* 1.75 .20
Nos. C187-C192 (6) 30.50 3.20

Christmas Type of 1973

Virgin and Child by: 18fr, Raphael. 27fr, Pietro Perugino. 40fr, Titian.

1973, Nov. 19
C193 A64 18fr gold & multi .30 .20
C194 A64 27fr gold & multi .40 .20
C195 A64 40fr gold & multi .60 .20
a. Souv. sheet of 3, #C193-C195 1.40 1.40
Nos. C193-C195 (3) 1.30 .60

For surcharges see Nos. CB239-CB31.

Soccer Type of Regular Issue

Designs: Various soccer scenes and cup.

1974, July 4 Photo. *Perf. 13*
C196 A67 20fr gold & multi .30
C197 A67 26fr gold & multi .40
C198 A67 40fr gold & multi .60
Nos. C196-C198 (3) 1.30

For souvenir sheet see No. 459a.

UPU Type of 1974

Designs: No. C199, Flags over UPU Headquarters, Bern. No. C200, G.P.O., Usumbura. No. C201, Mailmen ("26F" in UR). No. C202, Mailmen ("26F" in UL). No. C203, UPU emblem. No. C204, Means of transportation. No. C205, Pigeon over globe showing Burundi. No. C206, Swiss flag, pigeon over map showing Bern.

1974, July 23
C199 A68 24fr gold & multi .65
C200 A68 24fr gold & multi .65
C201 A68 26fr gold & multi .75
C202 A68 26fr gold & multi .75
C203 A68 31fr gold & multi 1.00
C204 A68 31fr gold & multi 1.00
C205 A68 40fr gold & multi 1.25
C206 A68 40fr gold & multi 1.25
a. Souv. sheet of 8, #C199-C206 7.50
Nos. C199-C206 (8) 7.30

Stamps of same denomination printed setenant (continuous design) in sheets of 40.

Fish Type of 1974

1974, Sept. 9 Photo. *Perf. 13*
Size: 35x35mm
C207 A66 Block of 4 1.50 .20
a. 10fr *Haplochromis multicolor* .35 .20
b. 10fr *Pantodon buchholzi* .35 .20
c. 10fr *Tropheus duboisi* .35 .20
d. 10fr *Distichodus sexfasciatus* .35 .20
C208 A66 Block of 4 1.75 .20
a. 14fr *Pelmatochromis kribensis* .40 .20
b. 14fr *Nannaethiops tritaeniatus* .40 .20
c. 14fr *Polycentropsis abbreviata* .40 .20
d. 14fr *Hemichromis bimaculatus* .40 .20
C209 A66 Block of 4 2.50 .20
a. 17fr *Ctenopoma acutirostre* .60 .20
b. 17fr *Synodontis angelicus* .60 .20
c. 17fr *Tilapia melanopleura* .60 .20
d. 17fr*Aphyosemion bivittatum* .60 .20
C210 A66 Block of 4 3.00 .30
a. 24fr *Monodactylus argenteus* .75 .20
b. 24fr *Zanclus canescens* .75 .20
c. 24fr *Pygoplites diacanthus* .75 .20
d. 24fr *Cephalopholis argus* .75 .20
C211 A66 Block of 4 3.00 .35
a. 26fr *Priacanthus arenatus* .75 .20
b. 26fr *Pomacanthus arcutus* .75 .20
c. 26fr *Scarus guacamaia* .75 .20
d. 26fr *Zeus faber* .75 .20
C212 A66 Block of 4 4.00 .40
a. 31fr *Lactophrys quadricornis* 1.00 .20
b. 31fr *Balistes vetula* 1.00 .20
c. 31fr *Acanthurus bahianus* 1.00 .20
d. 31fr *Holocanthus ciliaris* 1.00 .20
Nos. C207-C212 (6) 15.75 1.65

Christmas Type of 1974

Paintings of the Virgin and Child: 18fr, by Hans Memling. 27fr, by Filippino Lippi. 40fr, by Lorenzo di Gredi.

1974, Nov. 7 Photo. *Perf. 13*
C213 A70 18fr gold & multi .30 .25
C214 A70 27fr gold & multi .40 .30
C215 A70 40fr gold & multi .60 .45
a. Souv. sheet of 3, #C213-C215 1.50 1.50
Nos. C213-C215 (3) 1.30 1.00

Christmas 1974. Sheets of 20 stamps and one label. No. C215a exists imperf.

Apollo-Soyuz Type of 1975

1975, July 10 Photo. *Perf. 13*
C216 A71 Block of 4 1.00
a. 27fr A.A. Leonov, V.N. Kubasov, Soviet flag .25
b. 27fr Soyuz and Soviet flag .25
c. 27fr Apollo and American flag .25
d. 27fr Slayton, Brand, Stafford, American flag .25
C217 A71 Block of 4 1.25
a. 40fr Apollo-Soyuz link-up .30
b. 40fr Apollo, blast-off .30
c. 40fr Soyuz, blast-off .30
d. 40fr Kubasov, Leonov, Slayton, Brand, Stafford .30

Nos. C216-C217 are printed in sheets of 32 containing 8 blocks of 4.

Animal Type of 1975

1975, Sept. 17 Photo. *Perf. 13½*
C218 Strip of 4 1.00
a. A72 10fr Addax .25
b. A72 10fr Roan antelope .25
c. A72 10fr Nyala .25
d. A72 10fr White rhinoceros .25
C219 Strip of 4 1.25
a. A72 14fr Mandrill .30
b. A72 14fr Eland .30
c. A72 14fr Salt's dik-dik .30
d. A72 14fr Thomson's gazelles .30
C220 Strip of 4 1.50
a. A72 17fr African small-clawed otter .35
b. A72 17fr Reed buck .35
c. A72 17fr Indian civet .35
d. A72 17fr Cape buffalo .35
C221 Strip of 4 2.00
a. A72 24fr White-tailed gnu .50
b. A72 24fr African wild asses .50
c. A72 24fr Black-and-white colobus monkey .50
d. A72 24fr Gerenuk .50
C222 Strip of 4 2.25
a. A72 26fr Dama gazelle .55
b. A72 26fr Black-backed jackal .55
c. A72 26fr Sitatungas .55
d. A72 26fr Zebra antelope .55
C223 Strip of 4 2.75
a. A72 31fr Fennec .65
b. A72 31fr Lesser kudus .65
c. A72 31fr Blesbok .65
d. A72 31fr Serval .65
Nos. C218-C223 (6) 10.75

Nos. C218-C219 Overprinted in Black and Silver with IWY Emblem and: "ANNEE INTERNATIONALE / DE LA FEMME"

1975, Nov. 19 Photo. *Perf. 13½*
C224 Strip of 4 .60 .20
a. A72 10fr Addax .20 .20
b. A72 10fr Roan antelope .20 .20
c. A72 10fr Nyala .20 .20
d. A72 10fr White rhinoceros .20 .20

C225 Strip of 4 .80 .20
a. A72 14fr Mandrill .20 .20
b. A72 14fr Oryx .20 .20
c. A72 14fr Dik-dik .20 .20
d. A72 14fr Thomson's gazelles .20 .20

International Women's Year 1975.

Nos. C222-C223 Overprinted in Black and Silver with UN Emblem and:"30ème ANNIVERSAIRE DES/ NATIONS UNIES"

1975, Nov. 19
C226 Strip of 4 1.60 .30
a. A72 26fr Dama gazelle .40 .20
b. A72 26fr Wild dog .40 .20
c. A72 26fr Sitatungas .40 .20
d. A72 26fr Striped duiker .40 .20
C227 Strip of 4 1.90 .30
a. A72 31fr Fennec .45 .20
b. A72 31fr Lesser kudus .45 .20
c. A72 31fr Blesbok .45 .20
d. A72 31fr Serval .45 .20

United Nations, 30th anniversary.

Michelangelo Type of 1975

Designs: Paintings from Sistine Chapel.

1975, Dec. 3 Photo. *Perf. 13*
C228 A73 18fr Zachariah .35
C229 A73 18fr Joel .35
C230 A73 31fr Erythrean Sybil .65
C231 A73 31fr Prophet Ezekiel .65
C232 A73 40fr Persian Sybil .80
C233 A73 40fr Prophet Jeremiah .80
a. Souv. sheet of 6, #C228-C233 3.75
Nos. C228-C233 (6) 3.60

Stamps of same denominations printed se-tenant in sheets of 18 stamps and 2 labels.
For surcharges see Nos. CB35-CB40.

Olympic Games Type, 1976

Designs (Olympic Games Emblem and): 18fr, Ski jump. 36fr, Slalom. 50fr, Ice hockey.

1976, Jan. 23 Photo. *Perf. 14x13½*
C234 A74 18fr ol brn & multi .30
C235 A74 36fr grn & multi .70
C236 A74 50fr pur & multi .90
a. Souvenir sheet of 4 2.00
Nos. C234-C236 (3) 1.90

No. C236a contains 4 stamps similar to Nos. 491-494, perf. 13½, inscribed "POSTE AERIENNE."

Hurdles — AP5

Montreal Games Emblem and: #C238, C241, C243b, High jump. #C239, C242, C243a, Athlete on rings. #C240, C243c, Hurdles.

1976, May 3 Litho. *Perf. 13½*
C237 AP5 27fr grn & multi .40
C238 AP5 27fr dk bl & multi .40
C239 AP5 31fr ocher & multi .55
C240 AP5 31fr grn & multi .55
C241 AP5 50fr dk bl & multi .90
C242 AP5 50fr ocher & multi .90
Nos. C237-C242 (6) 3.70

Souvenir Sheet

C243 Sheet of 3 1.75
a. AP5 27fr ocher & multi .40
b. AP5 31fr dark blue & multi .45
c. AP5 50fr green & multi .75

21st Olympic Games, Montreal, Canada, July 17-Aug. 1. Stamps of same denomination printed se-tenant in sheets of 20.

Battle of Bunker Hill, by John Trumbull
AP6 AP7

Paintings: 26fr, Franklin, Jefferson and John Adams. 36fr, Declaration of Independence, by John Trumbull.

1976, July 16 Photo. *Perf. 13*
C244 AP6 18fr gold & multi .35
C245 AP7 18fr gold & multi .35
C246 AP6 26fr gold & multi .45
C247 AP7 26fr gold & multi .45
C248 AP6 36fr gold & multi .75
C249 AP7 36fr gold & multi .75
a. Souv. sheet of 6, #C244-C249 3.25
Nos. C244-C249 (6) 3.10

American Bicentennial. Stamps of same denomination printed se-tenant in sheets of 50.

Christmas Type of 1976

Paintings: 18fr, Virgin and Child with St. Anne, by Leonardo da Vinci. 31fr, Holy Family with Lamb, by Raphael. 40fr, Madonna of the Basket, by Correggio.

1976, Oct. 18 Photo. *Perf. 13½*
C250 A76 18fr gold & multi .25
C251 A76 31fr gold & multi .45
C252 A76 40fr gold & multi .60
a. Souv. sheet of 3, #C250-C252 1.40
Nos. C250-C252 (3) 1.30

Christmas 1976. Sheets of 20 stamps and descriptive label.
For surcharges see Nos. CB41-CB43.

A.G. Bell Type of 1977

Designs: 10fr, A.G. Bell and first telephone. Nos. C253, 17fr, A.G. Bell speaking into microphone. Nos. C254, C257e, Satellites around globe and videophone. No. C255, Switchboard operator, c.1910, and wall telephone. Nos. C256, 26fr, Intelsat satellite, modern and old telephones. No. C257c, Intelsat and radar.

1977, May 17 Photo. *Perf. 13*
C253 A78 18fr multi .20
C254 A79 18fr multi .20
C255 A78 36fr multi .25
C256 A79 36fr multi .25
C257 Sheet of 5 1.75 1.00
a. A78 10fr multi .20 .20
b. A78 17fr multi .25 .20
c. A79 18fr multi .25 .20
d. A79 26fr multi .40 .25
e. A79 36fr multi .50 .25

No. C257 contains 3 postage (10fr, 17fr, 26fr) and 2 air post stamps (18fr, 36fr).

Animal Type of 1977

1977, Aug. 22 Photo. *Perf. 14x14½*
C258 Strip of 4 1.00
a. A80 9fr Buffon's kob .25
b. A80 9fr Marabous .25
c. A80 9fr Brindled gnu .25
d. A80 9fr River hog .25
C259 Strip of 4 1.40
a. A80 13fr Zebras .35
b. A80 13fr Shoebill .35
c. A80 13fr Striped hyenas .35
d. A80 13fr Chimpanzee .35
C260 Strip of 4 2.75
a. A80 30fr Flamingos .70
b. A80 30fr Nile Crocodiles .70
c. A80 30fr Green mamba .70
d. A80 30fr Greater kudus .70
C261 Strip of 4 3.50
a. A80 35fr Hyrax .85
b. A80 35fr Cobra .85
c. A80 35fr Jackals .85
d. A80 35fr Verreaux's eagles .85
C262 Strip of 4 5.25
a. A80 54fr Honey badger 1.25
b. A80 54fr Harnessed antelopes 1.25
c. A80 54fr Secretary bird 1.25
d. A80 54fr Klipspringer 1.25
C263 Strip of 4 6.25
a. A80 70fr African big-eared fox 1.50
b. A80 70fr Elephants 1.50
c. A80 70fr Vulturine guineafowl 1.50
d. A80 70fr Impalas 1.50
Nos. C258-C263 (6) 20.15

UN Type of 1977

Designs (UN Stamps and): 24fr, UN buildings by night. 27fr, UN buildings and view of Manhattan. 35fr, UN buildings by day.

1977, Oct. 10 Photo. *Perf. 13½*
C264 A82 Block of 4 1.90
a. 24fr No. 77 .45
b. 24fr No. 78 .45
c. 24fr No. 40 .45
d. 24fr No. 32 .45
C265 A82 Block of 4 2.00
a. 27fr No. 50 .50
b. 27fr No. 21 .50
c. 27fr No. 30 .50
d. 27fr No. 44 .50
C266 A82 Block of 4 3.25
a. 35fr No. C6 .75
b. 35fr No. 105 .75
c. 35fr No. 4 .75
d. 35fr No. 1 .75
e. Souvenir sheet of 3 1.40
Nos. C264-C266 (3) 7.15

No. C266e contains 24fr in design of No. C265b, 27fr in design of No. C266a, 35fr in design of No. C264c.

Christmas Type of 1977

Designs: Paintings of the Virgin and Child.

1977, Oct. 31 Photo. *Perf. 14x13*
C267 A83 18fr Master of Moulins .30
C268 A83 31fr Workshop of Lorenzo de Credi .50
C269 A83 40fr Palma Vecchio .60
a. Souv. sheet of 3, #C267-C269 1.50
Nos. C267-C269 (3) 1.40

Sheets of 24 stamps and descriptive label.
For surcharges see Nos. CB44-CB46.

Christmas 1978 Type of 1979
Souvenir Sheet

1979, Feb. Photo. *Perf. 14x13½*
C270 Sheet of 5 2.00
a. A86 13fr like #543 .20
b. A86 17fr like #544 .25
c. A86 27fr like #545 .40
d. A86 31fr like #546 .50
e. A86 40fr like #547 .60

Christmas Type of 1979
Souvenir Sheet

1979, Oct. 12 *Perf. 13½*
C271 Sheet of 4 2.00 1.25
a. A89 20fr like #561 .30 .20
b. A89 27fr like #562 .40 .25
c. A89 31fr like #563 .50 .30
d. A89 50fr like #564 .75 .40

Hill Type of 1979
Souvenir Sheet

1979, Nov. 6
C272 Sheet of 5 3.50 1.75
a. A90 20fr like #565 .40 .20
b. A90 27fr like #566 .55 .25
c. A90 31fr like #567 .60 .30
d. A90 40fr like #568 .80 .35
e. A90 50fr like #569 1.00 .50

Sir Rowland Hill (1795-1879), originator of penny postage.

Bird Type of 1979

1979 Photo. *Perf. 13½x13*
C273 A87 6fr like #548 .20
C274 A87 13fr like #549 .40
C275 A87 18fr like #550 .55
C276 A87 26fr like #551 .75
C277 A87 31fr like #552 1.00
C278 A87 36fr like #553 1.10
C279 A87 40fr like #554 1.25
C280 A87 54fr like #555 1.60
C281 A87 70fr like #556 2.00
Nos. C273-C281 (9) 8.85

Olympic Type of 1980
Souvenir Sheet

1980, Oct. 24 Photo. *Perf. 13½*
C282 Sheet of 9 4.25
a. A91 20fr like #570 .30
b. A91 20fr like #571 .30
c. A91 20fr like #572 .30
d. A91 30fr like #573 .45
e. A91 30fr like #574 .45
f. A91 30fr like #575 .45
g. A91 40fr like #576 .60
h. A91 40fr like #577 .60
i. A91 40fr like #578 .60

22nd Summer Olympic Games, Moscow, July 19-Aug. 3.

Christmas Type of 1980
Souvenir Sheet

1980, Dec. 12 Photo. *Perf. 13½x13*
C283 Sheet of 4 1.90 1.40
a. A92 10fr like #579 .20 .20
b. A92 30fr like #580 .45 .30
c. A92 40fr like #581 .60 .40
d. A92 45fr like #582 .65 .45

UPRONA Type of 1980
Souvenir Sheet

1980, Dec. 29 *Perf. 14½x13½*
C284 Sheet of 3 1.50
a. A93 10fr like #583 .20
b. A93 40fr like #584 .60
c. A93 45fr like #585 .65

Christmas Type of 1983
Souvenir Sheet

1983, Oct. 3 Litho. *Perf. 14½x13½*
C285 Sheet of 4 1.75
a. A97 10fr like #607 .20
b. A97 25fr like #608 .40
c. A97 30fr like #609 .45
d. A97 50fr like #610 .75

UPU Congress Type of 1984
Souvenir Sheet

1984, July 14 *Perf. 13x13½*
C286 Sheet of 4 2.25
a. A99 10fr like #621 .20
b. A99 30fr like #622 .45
c. A99 35fr like #623 .50
d. A99 65fr like #624 1.00

Summer Olympics Type of 1984
Souvenir Sheet

1984, Aug. 6 *Perf. 13½x13*
C287 Sheet of 4 2.25
a. A100 10fr like #625 .20
b. A100 30fr like #626 .45
c. A100 35fr like #627 .50
d. A100 65fr like #628 1.00

Christmas Type of 1984
Souvenir Sheet

1984, Dec. 15 *Perf. 13½*
C288 Sheet of 4 1.75
a. A101 10fr like #629 .20
b. A101 25fr like #630 .40
c. A101 30fr like #631 .45
d. A101 50fr like #632 .75

Flower Type of 1986 with Dull Lilac Border

1986, July 31 Photo. *Perf. 13x13½*
C289 A102 70fr like #633 .80
C290 A102 75fr like #634 .90
C291 A102 80fr like #635 1.00
C292 A102 85fr like #636 1.10
C293 A102 100fr like #637 1.25
C294 A102 150fr like #638 1.75
Nos. C289-C294 (6) 6.80

Animals AP8

1992, June 2 Litho. *Perf. 14*
C298 AP8 100fr M. nemestrina 1.50
C299 AP8 115fr Equus grevyi 1.75
C300 AP8 200fr Long horn cattle 3.00
C301 AP8 220fr Pelecanus onocrotalus 3.50
a. Souvenir sheet of 4, #C298-C301, perf. 13½ 10.00
Nos. C298-C301 (4) 9.75

AIR POST SEMI-POSTAL STAMPS

Coin Type of Semi-Postal Issue

Designs (Coins of Various Denominations): 3fr+1fr, 11fr+1fr, 20fr+1fr, 50fr+1fr, Coat of Arms, reverse. 5fr+1fr, 14fr+1fr, 30fr+1fr, 100fr+1fr, King Mwambutsa IV, obverse.

Lithographed; Embossed on Gilt Foil

1965, Nov. 15 *Imperf.*

Diameter: 39mm

CB1 SP4 3fr + 1fr lt & dk vio .20 .20
CB2 SP4 5fr + 1fr pale grn & red .20 .20

Diameter: 45mm

CB3 SP4 11fr + 1fr org & lilac .25 .25
CB4 SP4 14fr + 1fr red & emer .30 .30

Diameter: 56mm

CB5 SP4 20fr + 1fr ultra & blk .40 .40
CB6 SP4 30fr + 1fr dp org & mar .60 .60

Diameter: 67mm

CB7 SP4 50fr + 1fr bl & vio bl 1.00 1.00
CB8 SP4 100fr + 1fr rose & dp cl 2.25 2.25
Nos. CB1-CB8 (8) 5.20 5.20

Stamps are backed with patterned paper in blue, orange, and pink engine-turned design.

Red Cross Type of Semi-Postal Issue

Designs: 26fr+3fr, Laboratory. 40fr+3fr, Ambulance and thatched huts. 50fr+3fr, Red Cross nurse with patient.

1969, June 26 Photo. *Perf. 13½*
CB9 SP7 26fr + 3fr multi .40 .20
CB10 SP7 40fr + 3fr multi .55 .20
CB11 SP7 50fr + 3fr multi .65 .20
Nos. CB9-CB11 (3) 1.60 .60

Perf. and imperf. souvenir sheets exist containing 3 stamps similar to Nos. CB9-CB11, but without "Poste Aerienne." Size: 90½x97mm

Christmas Type of Semi-Postal Issue

Paintings: 14fr+3fr, Virgin and Child, by Velázquez. 26fr+3fr, Holy Family, by Joos van Cleve. 40fr+3fr, Virgin and Child, by Rogier van der Weyden.

1970, Dec. 14 Photo. *Perf. 13½*

CB12 SP9 14fr + 3fr multi .25 .20
CB13 SP9 26fr + 3fr multi .45 .20
CB14 SP9 40fr + 3fr multi .65 .20
a. Souv. sheet of 3, #CB12-CB14 1.50 1.50
Nos. CB12-CB14 (3) 1.35 .60

No. C147 Surcharged in Gold and Black

+2F
UNESCO
LUTTE CONTRE
L'ANALPHABETISME

1971, Aug. 9 Photo. *Perf. 13½*

CB15 Strip of 4 .80 .20
a. A48 17fr+2fr Hartebeest .20 .20
b. A48 14fr+2fr Black rhinoceros .20 .20
c. A48 14fr+2fr Zebra .20 .20
d. A48 14fr+2fr Leopard .20 .20

UNESCO campaign against illiteracy.

No. C148 Surcharged in Gold and Black

+1F
AIDE INTERNATIONALE
AUX REFUGIES

1971, Aug. 9

CB16 Strip of 4 1.00 .20
a. A48 17fr+1fr Grant's gazelles .25 .20
b. A48 17fr+1fr Cheetah .25 .20
c. A48 17fr+1fr African white-backed vultures .25 .20
d. A48 17fr+1fr Johnston's okapi .25 .20

International help for refugees.

Nos. C150-C151 Surcharged in Black and Gold

a
+1F
75eme ANNIVERSAIRE DES
JEUX OLYMPIQUES MODERNES
(1896-1971)

b
+1F
JEUX PRE-OLYMPIQUES
MUNICH 1972

1971, Aug. 16

CB17 Strip of 4 2.25 .45
a. A48(a) 26fr+1fr Gorilla .55 .20
b. A48(a) 26fr+1fr Gnu .55 .20
c. A48(a) 26fr+1fr Warthog .55 .20
d. A48(a) 26fr+1fr Cape hunting dog .55 .20
CB18 Strip of 4 3.00 .60
a. A48(b) 31fr+1fr Sable antelope .75 .20
b. A48(b) 31fr+1fr Caracal lynx .75 .20
c. A48(b) 31fr+1fr Ostriches .75 .20
d. A48(b) 31fr+1fr Bongo .75 .20

75th anniv. of modern Olympic Games (#CB17); Olympic Games, Munich, 1972 (#CB18).

Nos. C153-C155 Surcharged

1971, Nov. 27 Photo. *Perf. 13½*

CB19 A51 14fr + 1fr multi .30 .20
CB20 A51 17fr + 1fr multi .40 .20
CB21 A51 31fr + 1fr multi .60 .20
Nos. CB19-CB21 (3) 1.30 .60

25th anniv. of UNICEF.

Casa D'Oro, Venice SPAP1

Views in Venice: 17fr+1fr, Doge's Palace. 24fr+1fr, Church of Sts. John and Paul. 31fr+1fr, Doge's Palace and Piazzetta at Feast of Ascension, by Canaletto.

1971, Dec. 27

CB22 SPAP1 10fr + 1fr multi .20 .20
CB23 SPAP1 17fr + 1fr multi .30 .20
CB24 SPAP1 24fr + 1fr multi .45 .20
CB25 SPAP1 31fr + 1fr multi .55 .20
a. Souvenir sheet of 4 1.50 1.50
Nos. CB22-CB25 (4) 1.50 .80

Surtax for the UNESCO campaign to save the treasures of Venice. No. CB25a contains 4 stamps similar to Nos. CB22-CB25, but with 2fr surtax.

Nos. C165-C167, C193-C195 Surcharged "+1F" in Silver

1972, Dec. 12 Photo. *Perf. 13½*

CB26 A57 18fr + 1fr multi .30 .20
CB27 A57 27fr + 1fr multi .45 .20
CB28 A57 40fr + 1fr multi .60 .20
a. Souvenir sheet of 3 1.50 1.50
Nos. CB26-CB28 (3) 1.35 .60

Christmas 1972. No. CB28a contains 3 stamps similar to Nos. CB26-CB28 but with 2fr surtax.

1973, Dec. 14 Photo. *Perf. 13*

CB29 A64 18fr + 1fr multi .30 .20
CB30 A64 27fr + 1fr multi .40 .20
CB31 A64 40fr + 1fr multi .60 .20
a. Souvenir sheet of 3 1.50 1.50
Nos. CB29-CB31 (3) 1.30 .60

Christmas 1973. No. CB31 contains 3 stamps similar to Nos. CB29-CB31 with 2fr surtax each.

Christmas Type of 1974

1974, Dec. 2 Photo. *Perf. 13*

CB32 A70 18fr + 1fr multi .30 .20
CB33 A70 27fr + 1fr multi .50 .30
CB34 A70 40fr + 1fr multi .70 .40
a. Souvenir sheet of 3 1.75 1.75
Nos. CB32-CB34 (3) 1.50 .90

Christmas 1974. No. CB34a contains 3 stamps similar to Nos. CB32-CB34 with 2fr surtax.

Nos. C228-C233 Surcharged "+ 1F" in Silver and Black

1975, Dec. 22 Photo. *Perf. 13*

CB35 A73 18fr + 1fr #C228 .35
CB36 A73 18fr + 1fr #C229 .35
CB37 A73 31fr + 1fr #C230 .55
CB38 A73 31fr + 1fr #C231 .55
CB39 A73 40fr + 1fr #C232 .75
CB40 A73 40fr + 1fr #C233 .75
a. Souvenir sheet of 6 4.25
Nos. CB35-CB40 (6) 3.30

Michelangelo Buonarroti (1475-1564). No. CB40a contains 6 stamps similar to Nos. CB35-CB40 with 2fr surtax each.

Nos. C250-C252 Surcharged "+1f" in Silver and Black

1976, Nov. 25 Photo. *Perf. 13½*

CB41 A76 18fr + 1fr multi .30
CB42 A76 31fr + 1fr multi .50
CB43 A76 40fr + 1fr multi .60
a. Souvenir sheet of 3 1.50
Nos. CB41-CB43 (3) 1.40

Christmas 1976. No. CB43a contains 3 stamps similar to Nos. CB41-CB43 with 2fr surtax each.

Nos. C267-C269 Surcharged "+1fr" in Silver and Black

1977 Photo. *Perf. 14x13*

CB44 A83 18fr + 1fr multi .30
CB45 A83 31fr + 1fr multi .50
CB46 A83 40fr + 1fr multi .60
a. Souvenir sheet of 3 1.50
Nos. CB44-CB46 (3) 1.40

Christmas 1977. No. CB46a contains 3 stamps similar to Nos. CB44-CB46 with 2fr surtax each.

Christmas 1978 Type
Souvenir Sheet

1979, Feb. Photo. *Perf. 14x13*

CB47 Sheet of 5 3.00
a. A86 13fr + 2fr multi .30
b. A86 17fr + 2fr multi .35
c. A86 27fr + 2fr multi .55
d. A86 31fr + 2fr multi .70
e. A86 40fr + 2fr multi .85

Christmas Type of 1979
Souvenir Sheet

1979, Dec. 10 Photo. *Perf. 13½*

CB48 Sheet of 4 2.75
a. A89 20fr + 2fr like #561 .45
b. A89 27fr + 2fr like #562 .55
c. A89 31fr + 2fr like #563 .70
d. A89 50fr + 2fr like #564 1.00

Christmas Type of 1980
Souvenir Sheet

1981, Jan. 16 Photo. *Perf. 13½x13*

CB49 Sheet of 4 2.50
a. A92 10fr + 2fr like #579 .20
b. A92 30fr + 2fr like #580 .55
c. A92 40fr + 2fr like #581 .75
d. A92 50fr + 2fr like #582 .90

Christmas Type of 1983
Souvenir Sheet

1983, Nov. 2 Litho. *Perf. 14½x13½*

CB50 Sheet of 4 1.90
a. A97 10fr + 2fr like #607 .20
b. A97 25fr + 2fr like #608 .40
c. A97 30fr + 2fr like #609 .50
d. A97 50fr + 2fr like #610 .75

Christmas Type of 1984
Souvenir Sheet

1984, Dec. 15 *Perf. 13½*

CB51 Sheet of 4 1.90
a. A101 10fr + 2fr like #629 .20
b. A101 25fr + 2fr like #630 .40
c. A101 30fr + 2fr like #631 .50
d. A101 50fr + 2fr like #632 1.00

BUSHIRE

bü-'shir

LOCATION — On Persian Gulf

Bushire is a Persian port which British troops occupied Aug. 8, 1915.

20 Chahis (or Shahis) = 1 Kran
10 Krans = 1 Toman

Watermark

Wmk. 161 - Lion

ISSUED UNDER BRITISH OCCUPATION

Basic Iranian Designs

Shah Ahmed — A32

Imperial Crown — A33

King Darius, Ahura-Mazda Overhead — A34

Ruins of Persepolis — A35

Iranian Stamps of 1911-13 Overprinted in Black

BUSHIRE
Under British
Occupation.

Perf. 11½, 11½x11
Typo. & Engr.

1915, Aug. 15 Unwmk.

N1 A32 1c green & org 27.50 27.50
N2 A32 2c red & sepia 27.50 27.50
N3 A32 3c gray brn & grn 30.00 27.50
N4 A32 5c brown & car 300.00 300.00
N5 A32 6c green & red brn 22.50 22.50
N6 A32 9c yel brn & vio 25.00 *27.50*
a. Double overprint
N7 A32 10c red & org brn 25.00 25.00
N8 A32 12c grn & ultra 32.50 32.50
N9 A32 1k ultra & car 45.00 27.50
a. Double overprint 5,250.
N10 A32 24c vio & grn 52.50 30.00
N11 A32 2k grn & red vio 175.00 140.00
N12 A32 3k vio & blk 150.00 *160.00*
N13 A32 5k red & ultra 87.50 82.50
N14 A32 10k ol bis & cl 80.00 80.00
Nos. N1-N14 (14) 1,080. 1,010.

Nos. N1-N14, except No. N4, exist without period after "Occupation." This variety sells for more.

Forged overprints exist of Nos. N1-N29.

The Bushire overprint exists on Iran No. 537 but is considered a forgery.

On Iranian Stamps of 1915

Perf. 11, 11½

1915, Sept. Wmk. 161

N15 A33 1c car & indigo 350. 350.
N16 A33 2c blue & car 4,750. *6,000.*
N17 A33 3c dk grn 350. *400.*
N18 A33 5c red 4,000. *4,250.*
N19 A33 6c ol grn & car 3,000. *3,500.*
N20 A33 9c yel brn & vio 500. *525.*
N21 A33 10c bl grn & yel brn 800. *900.*
N22 A33 12c ultra 950. *1,250.*
N23 A34 1k sil, yel brn & gray 350. *375.*
N24 A33 24c yel brn & dk brn 450. 400.
N25 A34 2k sil, bl & rose 300. 350.
N26 A34 3k sil, vio & brn 400. 425.
N27 A34 5k sil, brn & grn 450. 450.
a. Inverted overprint
N28 A35 1t gold, pur & blk 325. *375.*
N29 A35 3t gold, cl & red brn 2,500. *2,750.*

Persia resumed administration of Bushire post office Oct. 16, 1915.

Vol. 1 Number Additions, Deletions & Changes

United States

Number in 2000 Catalogue	Number in 2001 Catalogue
new	21a
73d	73f
73a	73a/73d
new	135b
new	375b
new	398a
restored	512a
new	632c
new	1039a
new	1040a, 1043a
1044b	1044d
new	1044b
new	1047a, 1049b
new	1284d
1330d	footnoted
new	1420b, 1431b
1576a	1576b
new	1683a
1689f	1689s
new	1689f
new	1841b, 1843d
1844d	1844e
1853a, 1853b	1853b, 1853c
1856a-1856d	1856b-1856e
1863a-1863c	1863d-1863f
1895a	1895d
1895b, 1895c	1895f, 1895g
1895d	1895e
1895e	1895b
new	1951e
new	2085b, 2104d
new	2170a
2171b	2171a
new	2171b
2175d	2175e
2194	2194b
new	2194, 2194d, 2194e
new	2209b
2225a, 2225b	2225b, 2225c
2280a	2280c
2280b	2280e
2280d	2280f
new	2418a
2464a	2464b
new	2491c, 2492g
new	2495Ab
new	2528c, 2528d
new	2539a, 2541a
new	2598b, 2599b
2624d, 2625d, 2626a	footnoted
2627d, 2628d, 2629a	footnoted
new	2629a
new	2704a
new	2799b, 2813b
new	2814b, 2814e
new	2868c, 2868d
new	2872b, 2872c, 2873b
new	2886b
new	2940a
new	3000w
new	3017a
new	3055a, 3060a
new	3116b, 3252c, 3257a
new	3265a-3265d
new	3281a
3320a	3320b

Air Post

new	C51b, C60b, C72d

Officials

new	O57Sd

Envelopes

new	U544e
new	U600b, U603a
new	U641c

Confederate States Of America

Number in 2000 Catalogue	Number in 2001 Catalogue
new	1AX1
new	2AXU1
new	3AX1
61X1	4AX1
new	5AXU1
U.S. 12XU1	6AXU1
footnoted	9X1
new	21XU3A, 21XU7
restored	30X2-30X3
new	39XU1
new	76XU1A
new	100XU2
new	122XU1
new	123XU1
new	124XU1
new	125XU1-125XU2
new	126XU1
new	127XU1-127XU2
new	128XU1
new	129XU1
new	130XU1
new	132XU1
new	133XU1
new	134XU1
new	135XU1-135XU2
new	136XU1
new	137XU1
new	138XU1
new	139XU1-139XU2
new	140XU1-140XU2
new	141X1
new	142XU1
new	143XU1

Danish West Indies

new	6a, 6b, 6c
new	8a, 10a

Ryukyu Islands

new	C11a

Algeria

new	15a, 20a

Andorra, Spanish

E3a	footnoted

Antigua

4c	deleted

Argentina

12b	12c

Ascension

214a	Tristan 208a

Australian States

New South Wales

94, 94a	switched

Queensland

125, 125a	switched
new	AR1-AR52

Tasmania

new	AR1-AR35

Victoria

47, 47b	switched
AR1-AR2	AR36-AR37
AR3	AR38
AR4	AR39
AR5-AR6	AR15-AR16
AR7-AR8	AR42-AR44
AR9	AR17
AR10-AR11	AR45-AR46
AR12	AR19
AR13-AR14	AR47-AR48
AR15-AR17	AR21-AR23
AR18-AR19	AR51-AR52
AR20	AR26
AR21	AR61
new	AR1-AR14, AR18
new	AR20, AR24-AR25
new	AR27-AR37
new	AR40-AR41
new	AR49-AR50
new	AR53-AR60
new	AR62-AR65

Western Australia

new	AR1-AR11

Australia

Number in 2000 Catalogue	Number in 2001 Catalogue
399b, 400a	footnoted
new	406b
2d	Classic only
new	2h, 5a, 8b
new	21d, 21e, 21f
new	40a
new	45a, 47a, 47b
new	48c, 51b
50,50a	switched
51a, 54a, 55a, 56b	Classic only
170, 170a	switched
1539Bc	1539Bh
1732a	1729a

Austria

22a	22b
new	22a, 24a
new	34e-37e

Bahamas

112a	deleted
126a, 127a	deleted

Bechuanaland

new	5b, 7b

Bechuanaland Protectorate

new	64a

Belarus

250A-250B	251-252
251-251A	253-254
252	255
258	256

Belgium

19a	deleted

Belize, Cayes of

new	8a

Benin

new	16a, 17a

Bermuda

new	X1a, X2a
1a	deleted
18	18a
new	18
new	22a
new	299a, 372a

Bolivia

footnoted	C147b-C149b
footnoted	C155b-C156b

Botswana

569A	594A

Brazil

107, 107a	switched

Brunei

new	2b

Bulgaria

3718-3718A	3716-3717

Dies of British Colonial Stamps

DIE A

DIE B

DIE A:

1. The lines in the groundwork vary in thickness and are not uniformly straight.
2. The seventh and eighth lines from the top, in the groundwork, converge where they meet the head.
3. There is a small dash in the upper part of the second jewel in the band of the crown.
4. The vertical color line in front of the throat stops at the sixth line of shading on the neck.

DIE B:

1. The lines in the groundwork are all thin and straight.
2. All the lines of the background are parallel.
3. There is no dash in the upper part of the second jewel in the band of the crown.
4. The vertical color line in front of the throat stops at the eighth line of shading on the neck.

DIE I

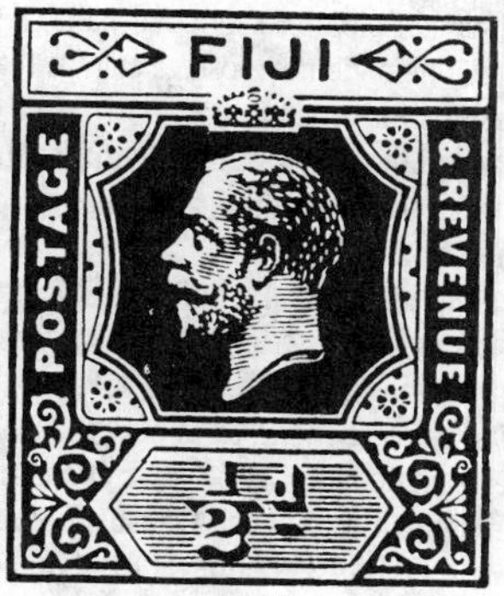

DIE II

DIE I:

1. The base of the crown is well below the level of the inner white line around the vignette.
2. The labels inscribed "POSTAGE" and "REVENUE" are cut square at the top.
3. There is a white "bud" on the outer side of the main stem of the curved ornaments in each lower corner.
4. The second (thick) line below the country name has the ends next to the crown cut diagonally.

DIE Ia.	DIE Ib.
1 as die II.	1 and 3 as die II.
2 and 3 as die I.	2 as die I.

DIE II:

1. The base of the crown is aligned with the underside of the white line around the vignette.
2. The labels curve inward at the top inner corners.
3. The "bud" has been removed from the outer curve of the ornaments in each corner.
4. The second line below the country name has the ends next to the crown cut vertically.

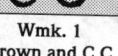

Wmk. 1
Crown and C C

Wmk. 2
Crown and C A

Wmk. 3
Multiple Crown and C A

Wmk. 4
Multiple Crown and Script C A

Wmk. 4a

Wmk. 314
St. Edward's Crown and C A Multiple

Wmk. 373

Wmk. 384

British Colonial and Crown Agents Watermarks

Watermarks 1 to 4, 314, 373, and 384, common to many British territories, are illustrated here to avoid duplication.

The letters "CC" of Wmk. 1 identify the paper as having been made for the use of the Crown Colonies, while the letters "CA" of the others stand for "Crown Agents." Both Wmks. 1 and 2 were used on stamps printed by De La Rue & Co.

Wmk. 3 was adopted in 1904; Wmk. 4 in 1921; Wmk. 314 in 1957; Wmk. 373 in 1974; and Wmk. 384 in 1985.

In Wmk. 4a, a non-matching crown of the general St. Edwards type (bulging on both sides at top) was substituted for one of the Wmk. 4 crowns which fell off the dandy roll. The non-matching crown occurs in 1950-52 printings in a horizontal row of crowns on certain regular stamps of Johore and Seychelles, and on various postage due stamps of Barbados, Basutoland, British Guiana, Gold Coast, Grenada, Northern Rhodesia, St. Lucia, Swaziland and Trinidad and Tobago. A variation of Wmk. 4a, with the non-matching crown in a horizontal row of crown-CA-crown, occurs on regular stamps of Bahamas, St. Kitts-Nevis and Singapore.

Wmk. 314 was intentionally used sideways, starting in 1966. When a stamp was issued with Wmk. 314 both upright and sideways, the sideways varieties usually are listed also – with minor numbers. In many of the later issues, Wmk. 314 is slightly visible.

Wmk. 373 is usually only faintly visible.

Illustrated Identifier

This section pictures stamps or parts of stamp designs that will help identify postage stamps that do not have English words on them.

Many of the symbols that identify stamps of countries are shown here as well as typical examples of their stamps.

See the Index and Identifier on the previous pages for stamps with inscriptions such as "sen," "posta," "Baja Porto," "Helvetia," "K.S.A.", etc.

Linn's Stamp Identifier is now available. The 144 pages include more 2,000 inscriptions and over 500 large stamp illustrations. Available from Linn's Stamp News, P.O. Box 29, Sidney, OH 45365-0029.

1. HEADS, PICTURES AND NUMERALS

GREAT BRITAIN

Great Britain stamps never show the country name, but, except for postage dues, show a picture of the reigning monarch.

Victoria

Edward VII

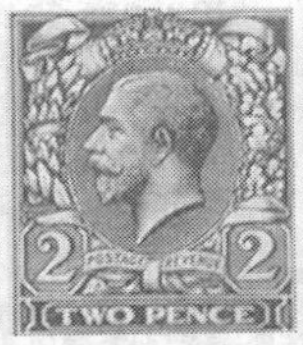

George V

Edward VIII

George VI

Elizabeth II

Some George VI and Elizabeth II stamps are surcharged in annas, new paisa or rupees. These are listed under Oman.

Silhouette (sometimes facing right, generally at the top of stamp)

The silhouette indicates this is a British stamp. It is not a U.S. stamp.

VICTORIA

Queen Victoria

INDIA

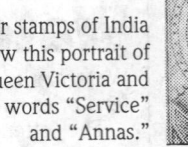

Other stamps of India show this portrait of Queen Victoria and the words "Service" and "Annas."

AUSTRIA

YUGOSLAVIA

(Also BOSNIA & HERZEGOVINA if imperf.)

BOSNIA & HERZEGOVINA

Denominations also appear in top corners instead of bottom corners.

HUNGARY

Another stamp has posthorn facing left

BRAZIL

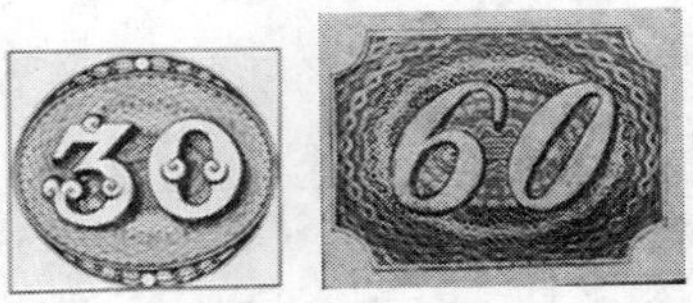

AUSTRALIA

Kangaroo and Emu

GERMANY

Mecklenburg-Vorpommern

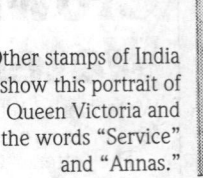

SWITZERLAND

2. ORIENTAL INSCRIPTIONS

CHINA

中 中

Any stamp with this one character is from China (Imperial, Republic or People's Republic). This character appears in a four-character overprint on stamps of Manchukuo. These stamps are local provisionals, which are unlisted. Other overprinted Manchukuo stamps show this character, but have more than four characters in the overprints. These are listed in People's Republic of China.

Some Chinese stamps show the Sun.

中華民國郵票

Most stamps of Republic of China show this series of characters.

Stamps with the China character and this character are from People's Republic of China. 人

中国人民邮政

Calligraphic form of People's Republic of China

Chinese stamps without China character

REPUBLIC OF CHINA

PEOPLE'S REPUBLIC OF CHINA

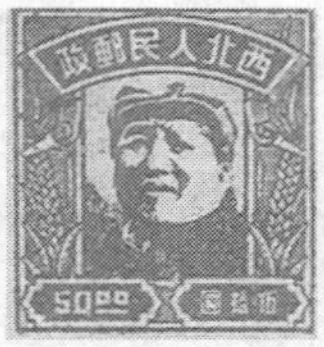

Mao Tse-tung

MANCHUKUO

Temple   Emperor Pu-Yi

政郵國   政郵國

The first 3 characters are common to many Manchukuo stamps.

國洲滿   國洲滿

The last 3 characters are common to other Manchukuo stamps.

Orchid Crest

Manchukuo stamp without these elements

JAPAN

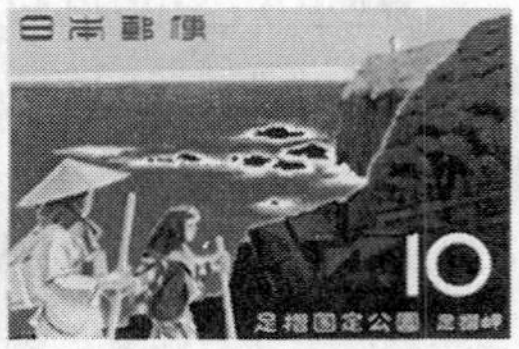

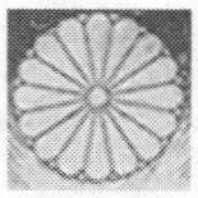

日本郵便

Chrysanthemum Crest   Country Name

Japanese stamps without these elements

The number of characters in the center and the design of dragons on the sides will vary.

RYUKYU ISLANDS

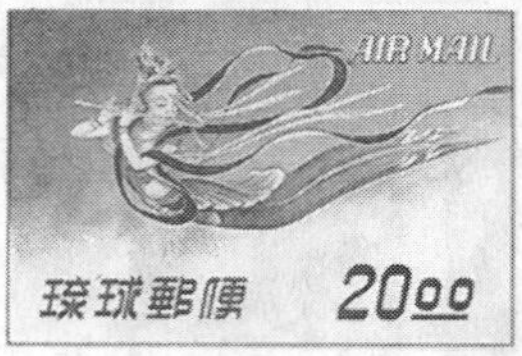

琉球郵便

Country Name

PHILIPPINES (Japanese Occupation)

比島郵便

Country Name

NORTH BORNEO (Japanese Occupation)

大日本帝國郵便   北ボルネオ

Indicates Japanese Occupation   Country Name

MALAYA (Japanese Occupation)

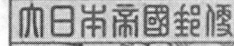

大日本帝國郵便   マライ

Indicates Japanese Occupation   Country Name

BURMA (Japanese Occupation)

大日本帝國郵便   シャン

Indicates Japanese Occupation   Country Name

Other Burma Japanese Occupation stamps without these elements

Burmese Script

KOREA

These two characters, in any order, are common to stamps from the Republic of Korea (South Korea) or the unlisted stamps of the People's Democratic Republic of Korea (North Korea).

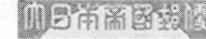

This series of four characters can be found on the stamps of both Koreas.

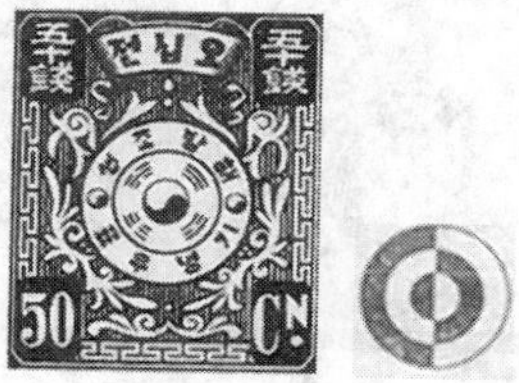

Yin Yang appears on some stamps.

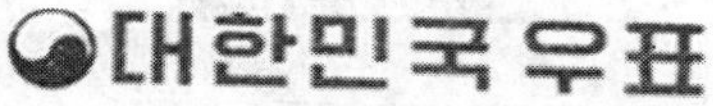

Indicates Republic of Korea (South Korea)

South Korean postage stamps issed after 1952 do not show currency expressed in Latin letters. Stamps wiith "HW," "HWAN," "WON," "WN," "W" or "W" with two lines through it, if not illustrated in listings of stamps before this date, are revenues. North Korean postage stamps do not have currency expressed in Latin letters.

THAILAND

Country Name

King Chulalongkorn

King Prajadhipok and Chao P'ya Chakri

3. CENTRAL AND EASTERN ASIAN INSCRIPTIONS

INDIA - FEUDATORY STATES

Alwar

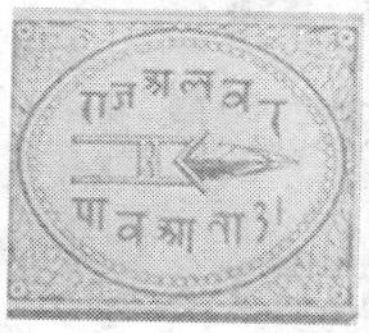

Bhor

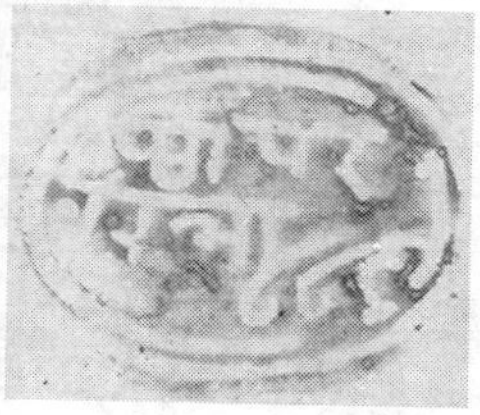

Bundi

Similar stamps come with different designs in corners and differently drawn daggers (at center of circle).

Dhar

Faridkot

Hyderabad

Similar stamps exist with straight line frame around stamp, and also with different central design which is inscribed "Postage" or "Post & Receipt."

Indore

Jhalawar

A similar stamp has the central figure in an oval.

Nandgaon

Nowanuggur

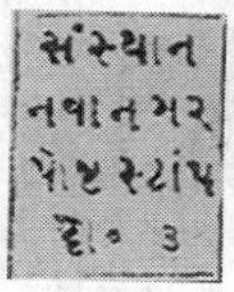

Poonch

Similar stamps exist in various sizes

Rajpeepla

Soruth

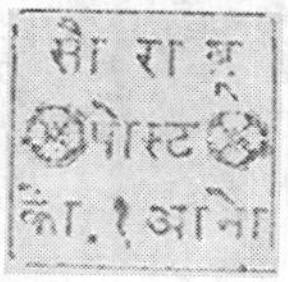

BANGLADESH

Country Name

NEPAL

Similar stamps are smaller, have squares in upper corners and have five or nine characters in central bottom panel.

TANNU TUVA

ISRAEL

GEORGIA

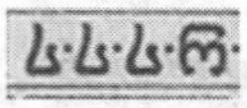

This inscription is found on other pictorial stamps.

Country Name

ARMENIA

The four characters are found somewhere on pictorial stamps. On some stamps only the middle two are found.

4. AFRICAN INSCRIPTIONS

ETHIOPIA

5. ARABIC INSCRIPTIONS

AFGHANISTAN

Many early Afghanistan stamps show Tiger's head, many of these have ornaments protruding from outer ring, others show inscriptions in black.

Arabic Script

Mosque Gate & Crossed Cannons
The four characters are found somewhere on pictorial stamps. On some stamps only the middle two are found.

BAHRAIN

EGYPT

Postage

INDIA - FEUDATORY STATES

Jammu & Kashmir

Text and thickness of ovals vary. Some stamps have flower devices in corners.

India-Hyderabad

IRAN

Country Name

Royal Crown

Lion with Sword

Symbol

IRAQ

JORDAN

LEBANON

Similar types have denominations at top and slightly different design.

LIBYA

Country Name in various styles

Other Libya stamps show Eagle and Shield (head facing either direction) or Red, White and Black Shield (with or without eagle in center).

SAUDI ARABIA

Tughra (Central design)

Palm Tree and Swords

SYRIA

THRACE

YEMEN

PAKISTAN

PAKISTAN - BAHAWALPUR

Country Name in top panel, star and crescent

TURKEY

Star & Crescent is a device found on many Turkish stamps, but is also found on stamps from other Arabic areas (see Pakistan-Bahawalpur)

Tughra (similar tughras can be found on stamps of Turkey in Asia, Afghanistan and Saudi Arabia)

Mohammed V

Mustafa Kemal

Plane, Star and Crescent

TURKEY IN ASIA

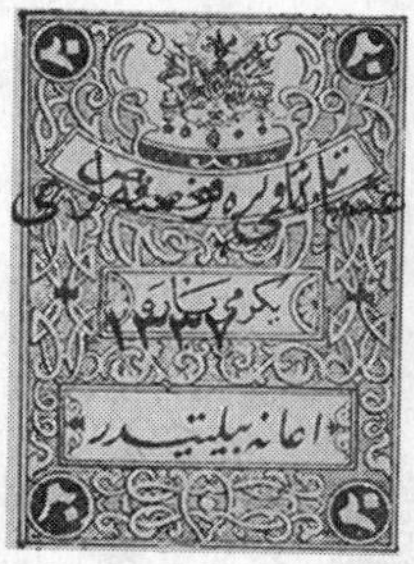

Other Turkey in Asia pictorials show star & crescent.
Other stamps show tughra shown under Turkey.

6. GREEK INSCRIPTIONS

GREECE

Country Name in various styles
(Some Crete stamps overprinted with the Greece country name are listed in Crete.)

Lepta

Drachma Drachmas Lepton

Abbreviated Country Name 

Other forms of Country Name

No country name

CRETE

Country Name

These words are on other stamps

Grosion

Crete stamps with a surcharge that have the year "1922" are listed under Greece.

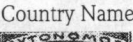

EPIRUS

Country Name

IONIAN IS.

7. CYRILLIC INSCRIPTIONS

RUSSIA

Postage Stamp

Imperial Eagle

Postage in various styles

Abbreviation for Kopeck

Abbreviation for Ruble

Russia

Abbreviation for Russian Soviet Federated Socialist Republic

RSFSR stamps were overprinted (see below)

Abbreviation for Union of Soviet Socialist Republics

This item is footnoted in Latvia

RUSSIA - Army of the North

"OKCA"

RUSSIA - Wenden

RUSSIAN OFFICES IN THE TURKISH EMPIRE

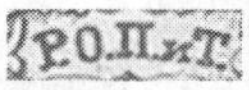

These letters appear on other stamps of the Russian offices.

The unoverprinted version of this stamp and a similar stamp were overprinted by various countries (see below).

ARMENIA

BELARUS

FAR EASTERN REPUBLIC

Country Name

SOUTH RUSSIA

Country Name

FINLAND

Circles and Dots on stamps similar to Imperial Russia issues

BATUM

Forms of Country Name

TRANSCAUCASIAN FEDERATED REPUBLICS

Abbreviation for Country Name

KAZAKHSTAN

ҚАЗАҚСТАН

Country Name

KYRGYZSTAN

КЫРГЫЗСТАН Country Name

ROMANIA

TADJIKISTAN

Country Name & Abbreviation

UKRAINE

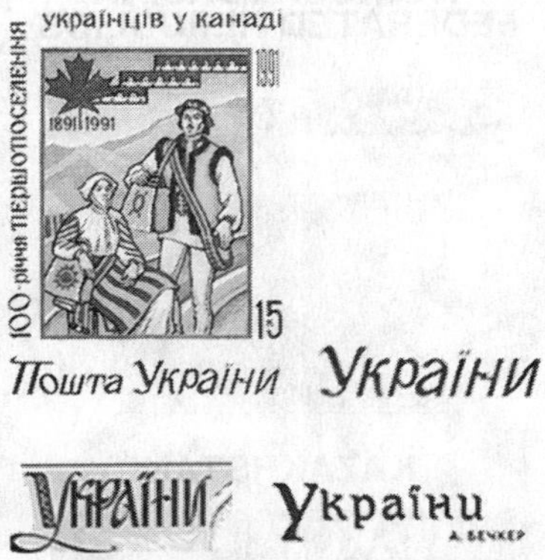

Country Name in various forms

The trident appears on many stamps, usually as an overprint.

Abbreviation for Ukrainian Soviet Socialist Republic

WESTERN UKRAINE

Abbreviation for Country Name

AZERBAIJAN

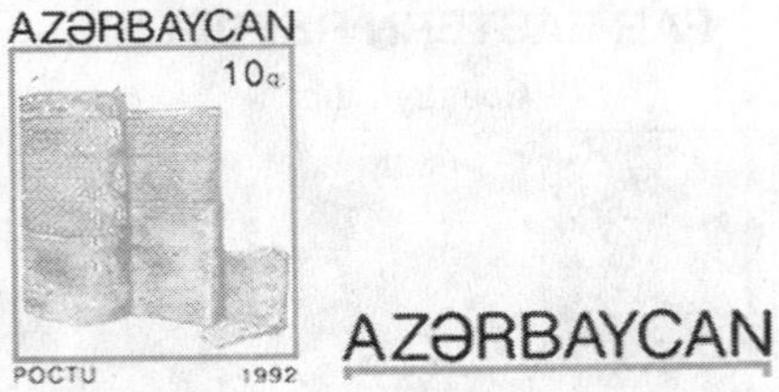

Country Name

Abbreviation for Azerbaijan Soviet Socialist Republic

MONTENEGRO

Country Name in various forms

Abbreviation for country name

No country name (A similar Montenegro stamp without country name has same vignette.)

SERBIA

Country Name in various forms

Abbreviation for country name

No country name

YUGOSLAVIA

Showing country name

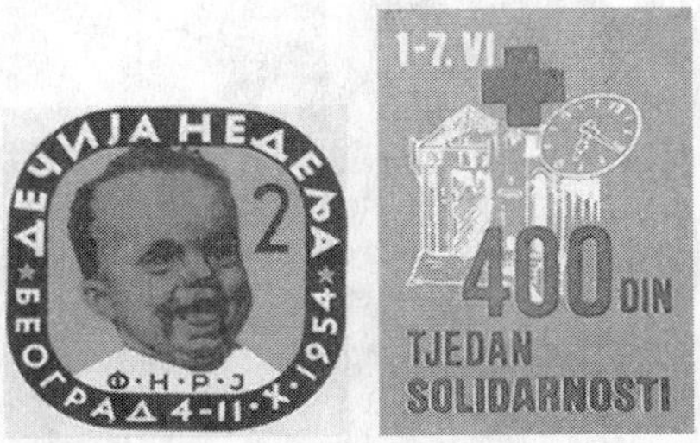

No Country Name

MACEDONIA

Country Name

Different form of Country Name

BULGARIA

Country Name   Postage

Stotinka

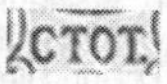

Stotinki (plural)   Abbreviation for Stotinki

Country Name in various forms and styles

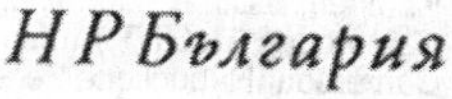

No country name

Abbreviation for Lev, leva

MONGOLIA

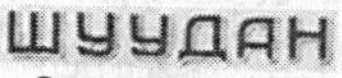

Country name in one word   Tugrik in Cyrillic

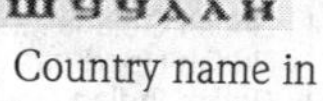

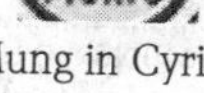

Country name in two words   Mung in Cyrillic

Mung in Mongolian

Tugrik in Mongolian

Arms

No Country Name

Index and Identifier

All page numbers shown are those in this Volume 1.
Postage stamps that do not have English words on them are shown in the Identifier which begins on page 942.

INDEX TO ADVERTISERS – 2001 VOLUME 1

2001
VOLUME 1
DEALER DIRECTORY
YELLOW PAGE LISTINGS

This section of your Scott Catalogue contains advertisements to help you conveniently find what you need, when you need it...!

Accessories

BROOKLYN GALLERY COIN & STAMP
8725 4th Avenue
Brooklyn, NY 11209
718-745-5701
718-745-2775 Fax
Web:http://www.brooklyngallery.com

Albums& Access.

THE KEEPING ROOM
P.O. Box 257
Trumbull, CT 06611-0257
203-372-8436

Antarctic

ANTARCTIC PHILATELIC EXCHANGE
1208A-280 Simco Street
Toronto, ON M5T 2Y5
Canada
416-593-7849
Email:jporter@interlog.com
Web:http://www.interlog.com/~jporter

Appraisals

CONNEXUS
P.O. Box 819
Snow Camp, NC 27349
336-376-8207 Telephone/Fax
Email:Connexus1@worldnet.att.net

RANDY SCHOLL STAMP CO.
Southhampton Square
7460 Jager Court
Cincinnati, OH 45230-4344
513-624-6800
513-624-6440 Fax

Appraisals

UNIQUE ESTATE APPRAISALS
1937 NE Broadway
Portland, OR 97232
503-287-4200 or 800-646-1147
Email: uea@stampsandcoins.com
Web:http://www.stampsandcoins.com

Approvals-Personalized WW & U.S.

THE KEEPING ROOM
P.O. Box 257
Trumbull, CT 06611-0257
203-372-8436

Approvals-Worldwide

ROSS WETREICH INC.
P.O. Box 1300
Valley Stream, NY 11582-1300
516-825-8974

Argentina-New Issues

VICTOR R. OSTOLAZA LTD.
P.O. Box 4664
Wayne, NJ 07474-4664
973-720-5884
Email:vroltd@worldnet.att.net

Asia

MICHAEL ROGERS, INC.
199 E. Welbourne Ave.
Winter Park, FL 32789
407-644-2290
407-645-4434 Fax
Web:http://www.michaelrogersinc.com

Asia

THE STAMP ACT
P.O. Box 1136
Belmont, CA 94002
650-592-3315
650-508-8104
Email:bchang@ix.netcom.com
Web:http://www.thestampact.com

Auction House

B TRADING CO.
114 Quail Street
Albany, NY 12206
518-465-3497 Telephone & Fax
Email:btradeco@wizvax.net
Web:http://www.wizvax.net/btradeco/

Auctions

CHARLES G. FIRBY AUCTIONS
6695 Highland Road
Suite 101
Waterford, MI 48327-1967
248-666-5333
248-666-5020 Fax
Email:Firbystamps@prodigy.net

DANIEL F. KELLEHER CO., INC
24 Farnsworth Street
Suite 605
Boston, MA 02210
617-443-0033
617-443-0789 Fax

Auctions

JACQUES C. SCHIFF JR., INC
195 Main Street
Ridgefield Park, NJ 07660
201-641-5566 from NYC 662-2777
201-641-5705 Fax

KUKSTIS AUCTIONS INC.
P.O. Box 130
Scituate, MA 02066
781-545-8494
Email:paulk@dreamcom.net
Web:http://www.kukstis.com

LAKESIDE PHILATELICS
3935 Lakeside Road
Penticton, BC V2A 8W1
CANADA
250-493-5239
250-493-3324 Fax
Email:greek@tnet.net
Web:http://vvv.com/~greek

SAM HOUSTON PHILATELICS
13310 Westheimer #150
Houston, TX 77077
281-493-6386
281-496-1445 Fax
Email:shduck@aol.com
Web:http://www.shauctions.com

STAMP CENTER / DUTCH COUNTRY AUCTIONS
4115 Concord Pike
Wilmington, DE 19803
302-478-8740
302-478-8779 Fax
Email:scdca@compuserve.com
Web:http://www.thestampcenter.com

Auctions

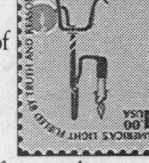

Auctions-Public

ALAN BLAIR STAMPS / AUCTIONS
5407 Lakeside Ave.
Suite 4
Richmond, VA 23228
800-689-5602 Telephone & Fax
Email:alanblair@prodigy.net

CEE-JAY STAMP AUCTIONS
775 Passaic Ave
West Caldwell, NJ 07006
800-360-2022
973-882-3499 Fax
Email:cfulmer@gregmanning.com

Austria

AMEEN STAMPS
8831 Long Point Road
Suite 204
Houston, TX 77055
713-468-0644
713-468-2420 Fax

COLONIAL STAMP COMPANY
5757 Wilshire Blvd. PH #8
Los Angeles, CA 90036
323-933-9435
323-939-9930 Fax
Email:gwh225@aol.com

GOTHIC STAMPS EUROPE
P.O. Box 399
Georgetown, CO 80444
303-832-4700
303-832-0959 Fax
Email:info@gothicstamps.com
Web:http://www.gothicstamps.com

JOSEPH EDER
P.O. Box 5517
Hamden, CT 06518
203-281-0742
203-230-2410 Fax
Email:jeder@nai.net

Bahamas

COLONIAL STAMP COMPANY
5757 Wilshire Blvd. PH #8
Los Angeles, CA 90036
323-933-9435
323-939-9930 Fax
Email:gwh225@aol.com

Bangkok

COLONIAL STAMP COMPANY
5757 Wilshire Blvd. PH #8
Los Angeles, CA 90036
323-933-9435
323-939-9930 Fax
Email:gwh225@aol.com

Barbados

COLONIAL STAMP COMPANY
5757 Wilshire Blvd. PH #8
Los Angeles, CA 90036
323-933-9435
323-939-9930 Fax
Email:gwh225@aol.com

Belgium

LEON FISCHER
P.O. Box 1338
Gracie Station
New York, NY 10028

Bosnia

DELAWARE VALLEY STAMP CO.
6173 Strasburg Rd.
Atglen, PA 19310
610-593-6684
610-593-8013 Fax
Email:devasco@epix.com

Brazil-New Issues

VICTOR R. OSTOLAZA LTD.
P.O. Box 4664
Wayne, NJ 07474-4664
973-720-5884
Email:vroltd@worldnet.att.net

British Colonies

EMPIRE STAMP CO.
P.O. Box 19248
Encino, CA 91416
818-880-6764
818-880-6864 Fax
Email:empirestamps@msn.com
Web:http://www.empirestamps.com

HUNT & COMPANY
3933 Spicewood Springs Road
Suite E-400
Austin, TX 78759
512-346-4830 or 800-458-5745
512-346-4984 Fax
Email:info@huntstamps.com
Web:http://www.huntstamps.com

British Comm.

BRITISH COMMONWEALTH STAMP CO.
P.O. Box 10218 S-5
Wilmington, NC 28404
910-256-0971 Fax
Email:bcstamp@stamp-mall.com
Web:http://www.stamp-mall.com/

JAY'S STAMP COMPANY
Box 28484
Dept S
Philadelphia, PA 19149
215-743-0207 Telephone & Fax
Email: JASC@Juno.com
Web:http://www.jaysco.com

British Comm.

METROPOLITAN STAMP CO
P.O. Box 1133
Chicago, IL 60690-1133
815-439-0142
815-439-0143 Fax

VICTORIA STAMP CO
P.O. Box 745
Ridgewood, NJ 07451
201-652-7283
201-612-0024 Fax

British Commonwealth

British Commonwealth

British E. Africa

COLONIAL STAMP COMPANY
5757 Wilshire Blvd. PH #8
Los Angeles, CA 90036
323-933-9435
323-939-9930 Fax
Email:gwh225@aol.com

Brunei

COLONIAL STAMP COMPANY
5757 Wilshire Blvd. PH #8
Los Angeles, CA 90036
323-933-9435
323-939-9930 Fax
Email:gwh225@aol.com

Burma

COLONIAL STAMP COMPANY
5757 Wilshire Blvd. PH #8
Los Angeles, CA 90036
323-933-9435
323-939-9930 Fax
Email:gwh225@aol.com

Bushire

COLONIAL STAMP COMPANY
5757 Wilshire Blvd. PH #8
Los Angeles, CA 90036
323-933-9435
323-939-9930 Fax
Email:gwh225@aol.com

Canada

LAKESIDE PHILATELICS
3935 Lakeside Road
Penticton, BC V2A 8W1
CANADA
250-493-5239
250-493-3324 Fax
Email:greek@tnet.net
Web:http://vvv.com/~greek

Canada-Duck Stamps

METROPOLITAN STAMP CO
P.O. Box 1133
Chicago, IL 60690-1133
815-439-0142
815-439-0143 Fax

Canada-Postal Bid Sales

BOW CITY PHILATELICS, LTD.
P.O. Box 6444 Central P.O.
Retail: 206 7th Ave SW
Suite 614
Calgary, AB T2P 2E1
CANADA
403-237-5828
403-264-5287 Fax
Email:bow.city@nucleus.com
Web:http://www.nucleus.com/~bowcity

Central America

GUY SHAW
P.O. Box 10025
Bakersfield, CA 93389
661-834-7135 Telephone/Fax
Email:Gsaw3@aol.com
Web:http://www.guyshaw.com

China

EXPERTS AND CONSULTANTS LTD.
Dr. Shiu - Hon Chan & K.L. Poon
P.O. Box 9840
General Post Office
Hong Kong
852-2519-6510 Fax

MICHAEL ROGERS, INC.
199 E. Welbourne Ave.
Winter Park, FL 32789
407-644-2290
407-645-4434 Fax
Web:http://www.michaelrogersinc.com

Classics-US Stamps & Covers

KUKSTIS AUCTIONS INC.
P.O. Box 130
Scituate, MA 02066
781-545-8494
Email:paulk@dreamcom.net
Web:http://www.kukstis.com

Collections

HUNT & COMPANY
3933 Spicewood Springs Road
Suite E-400
Austin, TX 78759
512-346-4830 or 800-458-5745
512-346-4984 Fax
Email:info@huntstamps.com
Web:http://www.huntstamps.com

Collections

Collections

QUALITY INVESTORS LTD.
P.O. Box 891
Middletown, NY 10940
914-343-2174
914-342-2597 Fax
Email:lrlm@poineeris.net

Conservation Stamps

SAM HOUSTON DUCK CO.
P.O. Box 820087
Houston,TX 77282
281-493-6386 or 800-231-5926
281-496-1445 Fax
Email:shduck@aol.com
Web:http://www.shduck.com

Czechoslovakia

SOCIETY FOR CZECHOSLOVAK PHILATELY, INC.
Tom Cossaboom
SCP Secretary
Box 25332
Scott Air Force Base, IL 62225
USA
Web:http://www.erols.com/sibpost

Disney

WONDERFUL WORLD OF STAMPS
P.O. Box 55, St Martin
Chomedey, Laval, PQ H7V 3P4
CANADA
450-687-0632
450-687-3143 Fax
Email:info@topicalsetc.com
Web:http://www.topicalsetc.com

Ducks

SAM HOUSTON DUCK CO.
P.O. Box 820087
Houston,TX 77282
281-493-6386 or 800-231-5926
281-496-1445 Fax
Email:shduck@aol.com
Web:http://www.shduck.com

Duck Stamps

MICHAEL JAFFE
P.O. Box 61484
Vancouver, WA 98666
360-695-6161or 800-782-6770
360-695-1616 Fax
mjaffe@brookmanstamps.com
Web:http://www.brookmanstamps.com

METROPOLITAN STAMP CO
P.O. Box 1133
Chicago, IL 60690-1133
815-439-0142
815-439-0143 Fax

TRENTON STAMP & COIN CO.
THOMAS DELUCA
Forest Glen Plaza
1804 Route 33
Hamilton Square, NJ 08690
800-446-8664
609-587-8664 Fax

Duck Stamps-Foreign

METROPOLITAN STAMP CO
P.O. Box 1133
Chicago, IL 60690-1133
815-439-0142
815-439-0143 Fax

Egypt

KAMAL SHALABY
3 Aly Basha Fahmy St.
Gleem, Alexandria
EGYPT
20-3-5880254 Telephone & Fax

Errors, Freaks & Oddities

SAM HOUSTON PHILATELICS
13310 Westheimer #150
Houston, TX 77077
281-493-6386
281-496-1445 Fax
Email:shduck@aol.com
Web:http://www.shauctions.com

STEVE CRIPPE, INC.
Box 236
Bothell, WA 98041-0236
425-487-2789
Email:stamp@stevecrippe.com
Web:http://www.stevecrippe.com

Exchange

ROBERT'S STAMP EXCHANGE /
ROBERT LEFRANCOIS
250 Skylane Dr.
Lake Geneva, WI 53147
626-248-8159

First Day Covers

ROSS WETREICH INC.
P.O. Box 1300
Valley Stream, NY 11582-1300
516-825-8974

France

JOSEPH EDER
P.O. Box 5517
Hamden, CT 06518
203-281-0742
203-230-2410 Fax
Email:jeder@nai.net

German Areas

JOSEPH EDER
P.O. Box 5517
Hamden, CT 06518
203-281-0742
203-230-2410 Fax
Email:jeder@nai.net

German Colonies

COLONIAL STAMP COMPANY
$1 million - photo price list, $5.00 (refundable against purchase)
5757 Wilshire Blvd. PH #8
Los Angeles, CA 90036
323-933-9435
323-939-9930 Fax
Email:gwh225@aol.com

Great Britain

COLONIAL STAMP COMPANY
5757 Wilshire Blvd. PH #8
Los Angeles, CA 90036
323-933-9435
323-939-9930 Fax
Email:gwh225@aol.com

NOVA PHILATELIC SALES
Box 161
Lakeside, NS B3T 1M6
CANADA
902-826-2165
902-826-1049 Fax
Email:novafil@ns.sympatico.ca

Imperial China

TREASURE HUNTERS LTD
GPO Box 11446
Hong Kong
852-2507-3773 or 852-2507-5770
852-2519-6820 Fax

Insurance

COLLECTIBLES INSURANCE AGENCY
P.O. Box 1200 SSC
Westminster, MD 21158
888-837-9537
410-876-9233 Fax
Email:collectinsure@pipeline.com
Web:http://www.collectinsure.com

Iran

MEHDI ESMAILI
P.O. Box 694
F.D.R. Station
New York, NY 10150-0694
718-520-1807
Email:info@mehdistamps.com
Web:http://www.mehdistamps.com

Korea

ALLKOR STAMP COMPANY
Box 1346
Port Washington, NY 11050
516-883-3296 Telephone & Fax

Latin America

GUY SHAW
P.O. Box 10025
Bakersfield, CA 93389
661-834-7135 Telephone/Fax
Email:Gsaw3@aol.com
Web:http://www.guyshaw.com

JUAN N. SIMONA
Ventas Filatelicas
Casilla de Correo #40-7311
Chillar Buenos Aires
Argentina
54-281-97281
Email:simonafilatelia@simon afilatelia.com.ar
Web:http://www.simonafilatelia.com.ar

Lots & Collections

BOB & MARTHA FRIEDMAN
624 Homestead Place
Joliet, IL 60435
815-725-6666
815-725-4134 Fax

DR. ROBERT FRIEDMAN & SONS
2029 West 75th Street
Woodridge, IL 60517
630-985-1515
630-985-1588 Fax

RANDY SCHOLL STAMP CO.
Southhampton Square
7460 Jager Court
Cincinnati, OH 45230-4344
513-624-6800
513-624-6440 Fax

Mail Bid Auctions

HUNT & COMPANY
3933 Spicewood Springs Road
Suite E-400
Austin, TX 78759
512-346-4830 or 800-458-5745
512-346-4984 Fax
Email:info@huntstamps.com
Web:http://www.huntstamps.com

Mail Bid Sales

COLLECTOR'S FEAST
GPO Box 4131
Melbourne Vic. 3001
Australia
61 3 9654 2770
61 3 9650 7748 Fax
Email:collectorsfeast@bigpond.com

DALE ENTERPRISES INC.
P.O. Box 539-C
Emmaus, PA 18049
610-433-3303
610-965-6089
Email:daleent@fast.net
Web:http://www.dalestamps.com

Mail Order

ALMAZ CO., DEPT. V4
P.O. Box 100-812
Vanderveer Station
Brooklyn, NY 11210
718-241-6360 Telephone & Fax

HUNT & COMPANY
3933 Spicewood Springs Road
Suite E-400
Austin, TX 78759
512-346-4830 or 800-458-5745
512-346-4984 Fax
Email:info@huntstamps.com
Web:http://www.huntstamps.com

SHARI'S STAMPS
104-3 Old Highway 40 #130
O'Fallon, MO 63366
800-382-3597
314-980-1552 Fax
Email:sharistmps@aol.com
Web:http://www.stampdealers.com/shari

Major Errors

SUBURBAN STAMP INC.
176 Worthington St.
Springfield, MA 01103
413-785-5348
413-746-3788 Fax

New Issues

DALE ENTERPRISES INC.
P.O. Box 539-C
Emmaus, PA 18049
610-433-3303
610-965-6089 Fax
Email:daleent@fast.net
Web:http://www.dalestamps.com

DAVIDSON'S STAMP SERVICE
P.O. Box 36355
Indianapolis, IN 46236-0355
317-826-2620
Email:davidson@in.net
Web:http://www.newstampissues.com

New Issues- Retail

BOMBAY PHILATELIC
P.O. Box 7719
Delray Beach, FL 33482
561-499-7990
561-499-7553 Fax
Email:sales@bombaystamps.com
Web:http://www.bombaystamps.com

New Issues- Wholesale

BOMBAY PHILATELIC
P.O. Box 7719
Delray Beach, FL 33482
561-499-7990
561-499-7553 Fax
Email:sales@bombaystamps.com
Web:http://www.bombaystamps.com

Officials

QUALITY INVESTORS LTD.
P.O. Box 891
Middletown, NY 10940
914-343-2174
914-342-2597 Fax
Email:lrlm@poineeris.net

Philatelic Literature

LEWIS KAUFMAN
P.O. Box 255
Kiamesha Lake, NY 12751
914-794-8013 Telephone/Fax
800-491-5453 Telephone/Fax
Email:mamet1@aol.com

PRC

GUANLUN HONG
P.O. Box 12623
Toledo, OH 43606
419-382-6096
419-382-0203 Fax
Email:guanlun@hotmail.com

Postal History

LEWIS KAUFMAN
P.O. Box 255
Kiamesha Lake, NY 12751
914-794-8013 Telephone/Fax
800-491-5453 Telephone/Fax
Email:mamet1@aol.com

Proofs & Essays

SUBURBAN STAMP CO.
176 Worthington St.
Springfield, MA 01103
413-785-5348
413-746-3788 Fax

Public Auctions

SUBURBAN STAMP INC.
176 Worthington St.
Springfield, MA 01103
413-785-5348
413-746-3788 Fax

Publications - Collector

AMERICAN PHILATELIC SOCIETY
Dept. TZ
P.O. Box 8000
State College, PA 16803
814-237-3803
814-237-6128 Fax
Email:flsente@stamps.org
Web:http://www.stamps.org

GLOBAL STAMP NEWS
P.O. Box 97
Sidney, OH 45365-0097
937-492-3183
937-492-6514 Fax
Email:global@bright.net

South America

GUY SHAW
P.O. Box 10025
Bakersfield, CA 93389
661-834-7135 Telephone/Fax
Email:Gsaw3@aol.com
Web:http://www.guyshaw.com

Stamps on the Internet

KUKSTIS AUCTIONS INC.
P.O. Box 130
Scituate, MA 02066
781-545-8494
Email:paulk@dreamcom.net
Web:http://www.kukstis.com

Stamp Shows

ATLANTIC COAST EXHIBITIONS
Division of Beach Philatelics
42 Baltimore Lane
Palm Coast, FL 32137-8850
904-445-4550
904-447-0811 Fax
Email:mrstamp2@aol.com
Web:http://www.beachphilatelics.com

New Issues

STAMP STORES

Arizona

AMERICAN STAMP & COIN CO.
7225 N. Oracle Rd., Suite 102
Tucson, AZ 85704
520-297-3456
Email:stamps@azstarnet.com

B.J.'S STAMPS
BARBARA J. JOHNSON
6342 W. Bell Road
Glendale, AZ 85308
623-878-2080
623-412-3456 Fax
Email:info@bjstamps.com
Web:http://www.bjstamps.com

MOLNAR'S STAMP & COIN SHOP
7118 E. Sahuaro Drive
Scottsdale, AZ 85254
602-948-9672 or 800-516-4850
602-948-8425 Fax
Email: molnar7118@aol.com

California

ASHTREE STAMP & COIN
2410 N. Blackstone
Fresno, CA 93703
559-227-7167

BROSIUS STAMP & COIN
2105 Main Street
Santa Monica, CA 90405
310-396-7480
310-396-7455 Fax

FISCHER-WOLK PHILATELICS
24771 "G" Alicia Parkway
Laguna Hills, CA 92653
949-837-2932

NATICK STAMPS & HOBBIES
405 S. Myrtle Ave.
Monrovia, CA 91016
626-305-7333
626-305-7335 Fax
Email:natickco@earthlink.net
Web:http://www.natickco.com

STANLEY M. PILLER
3351 Grand Ave.
Oakland, CA 94610
510-465-8290
510-465-7121 Fax
Email:stmpdlr@aol.com

Colorado

ACKLEY'S ROCKS & STAMPS
3230 N. Stone Avenue
Colorado Springs, CO 80907
719-633-1153

SHOWCASE STAMPS
3865 Wadsworth
Wheatridge, CO 80033
303-425-9252
303-425-7410 Fax

Connecticut

SILVER CITY COIN & STAMPS
41 Colony Street
Meriden, CT 06451
203-235-7634
203-237-4915 Fax

Florida

CORBIN STAMP & COIN, INC.
115-A East Brandon Blvd.
Brandon, FL 33511
813-651-3266

Florida

When visting
Central Florida
be sure to stop by.
Send 33¢ long
SASE for our
Monthly Newsletter
of stamps for sale!

WINTER PARK STAMP SHOP
Ranch Mall (17-92)
325 S. Orlando Avenue, Suite 1-2
Winter Park, FL 32789-3608
Phone 407-628-1120 • Fax 407-628-0091
1-800-845-1819
Mon. through Sat. 10 am-6 pm (4 miles North of Orlando)

Florida

HAUSER'S COIN & STAMPS
3425 South Florida Ave
Lakeland FL 33803
863-647-2052
863-644-5738 Fax
Email:hausercoin@aol.com
Web:http://www.coinsandgifts.com

INTERCONTINENTAL/RICARDO DEL CAMPO
7379 Coral Way
Miami, FL 33155-1402
305-264-4983
305-262-2919 Fax
Email:rdcstamp@worldnet.att.net

JERRY SIEGEL/STAMPS FOR COLLECTORS
501 Golden Isles Drive
Suite 206C
Hallandale, FL 33009
954-457-0422 Telephone/Fax
Email:dochallandale@telocity.com

ROBERT LEVINE STAMPS, INC
2219 South University Drive
Davie, FL 33324
954-473-1303
954-473-1305 Fax

SUN COAST STAMP CO.
3231 Gulf Gate Drive, Suite 102
Sarasota, FL 34231
941-921-9761 or 800-927-3351
941-921-1762 Fax
Email:suncoaststamp@aol.com

THE STAMP PLACE
576 First Ave North
St. Petersburg, FL 33701
727-894-4082

WINTER PARK STAMP SHOP
Ranch Mall (17-92)
325 S. Orlando Ave., Suite 1-2
Winter Park, FL 32789-3608
407-628-1120 or 800-845-1819
407-628-0091 Fax

Georgia

STAMPS UNLIMITED OF GEORGIA
133 Carnegie Way, Room 250
Atlanta, GA 30303
404-688-9161

Illinois

DON CLARK'S STAMPS
937 1/2 W. Galena Blvd.
Aurora, IL 60506
630-896-4606

DR. ROBERT FRIEDMAN & SONS
2029 West 75th Street
Woodridge, IL 60517
630-985-1515
630-985-1588 Fax

MARSHALL FIELD'S STAMP DEPT
111 N. State Street
Chicago, IL 60602
312-781-4237
Email:TRH200@aol.com

Indiana

J & J COINS AND STAMPS
7019 Calumet Ave. or
6526 Indianapolis Blvd.
Hammond, IN 46324
219-932-5818
219-845-2003 Fax

KNIGHT STAMP & COIN CO.
237 Main Street
Hobart, IN 46342
219-942-7529 or 800-634-2646
Email: knight@knightcoin.com
Web:http://www.knightcoin.com

Kentucky

COLLECTORS STAMPS LTD.
4012 DuPont Circle #313
Louisville, KY 40207
502-897-9045
Email:csl@aye.net

Maryland

BALTIMORE COIN & STAMP EXCHANGE
10194 Baltimore National Pike
Unit 104
Ellicott City, MD 21042
410-418-8282
410-418-4813 Fax

BULLDOG STAMP CO.
4641 Montgomery Ave.
Bethesda, MD 20814
301-654-1138

Massachusetts

FALMOUTH STAMP & COIN
11 Town Hall Square
Falmouth, MA 02540
508-548-7075 or 800-341-3701
Email:falstamp@capecod.net
Web:http://www.coinsandstamps.com

J & N FORTIER COIN, STAMPS & ANTIQUES
484 Main Street
Worcester, MA 01608
508-757-3657
508-852-8329 Fax

KAPPY'S COINS & STAMPS
534 Washington Street
Norwood, MA 02062
781-762-5552
781-762-3292 Fax

SUBURBAN STAMP INC.
176 Worthington St.
Springfield, MA 01103
413-785-5348
413-746-3788 Fax

Michigan

BIRMINGHAM COIN & JEWELRY
33802 Woodward
Birmingham, MI 48009
248-642-1234
248-642-4207 Fax

THE MOUSE AND SUCH
696 N. Mill Street
Plymouth, MI 48170
734-454-1515

Nebraska

TUVA ENTERPRISES
209 South 72nd Street
Omaha, NE 68114
402-397-9937

New Jersey

AALLSTAMPS
38 N. Main Street
P.O. Box 249
Milltown, NJ 08850
732-247-1093
732-247-1094 Fax
Email:mail@aallstamps.com
Web:http://www.aallstamps.com

A.D.A. STAMP CO., INC.
Store: 910 Boyd Street
Toms River, NJ 08753
P.O. Drawer J
Island Heights, NJ 08732
732-240-1131
732-240-2620 Fax

BERGEN STAMPS & COLLECTIBLES
717 American Legion Dr.
Teaneck, NJ 07666
201-836-8987

CHARLES STAMP SHOP
47 Old Post Road
Edison, NJ 08817
732-985-1071
732-819-0549
Email:cerratop@aol.com

STAMP STORES

New Jersey

RON RITZER STAMPS INC.
Millburn Mall
2933 Vauxhall Road
Vauxhall, NJ 07088
908-687-0007
908-687-0795 Fax
Email:ritzerstamps@mindspring.com

TRENTON STAMP & COIN CO.
THOMAS DELUCA
Forest Glen Plaza
1804 Route 33
Hamilton Square, NJ 08690
800-446-8664
609-587-8664 Fax

New York

CHAMPION STAMP CO., INC.
432 West 54th Street
New York, NY 10019
212-489-8130
212-581-8130 Fax

LINCOLN COIN & STAMP
33 West Tupper Street
Buffalo, NY 14202
716-856-1884
716-856-4727 Fax

THE FIFTH AVENUE STAMP GALLERY
460 West 34th Street
10th Floor
New York, NY 10001
212-629-7979
212-629-3350 Fax

Ohio

FEDERAL COIN INC. /ARCADE STAMP & COIN
P.O. Box 14579
405 Leader Building
Cleveland, OH 44114
216-861-1160
216-861-5960 Fax

HILLTOP STAMP SERVICE
P.O. Box 626
Wooster, OH 44691
330-262-5378
330-262-8907 Telephone & Fax
Email:hilltop@bright.net

JLF STAMP STORE
3041 E. Waterloo Road
Akron, OH 44312
330-628-8343

NEWARK STAMP COMPANY
49 North Fourth Street
Newark, OH 43055
740-349-7900

RANDY SCHOLL STAMP CO.
Southhampton Square
7460 Jager Court
Cincinnati, OH 45230-4344
513-624-6800
513-624-6440 Fax

THE LINK STAMP CO.
3461 E. Livingston Ave.
Columbus, OH 43227
614-237-4125 or 800-546-5726

Oregon

UNIQUE ESTATE APPRAISALS
1937 NE Broadway
Portland, OR 97232
503-287-4200 or 800-646-1147
Email: uea@stampsandcoins.com
Web:http://www.stampsandcoins.com

Pennsylvania

DAVE ALLEGO
648 Merchant Street
Ambridge, PA 15003
724-266-4237 Telephone & Fax

LARRY LEE STAMPS
322 S. Front Street
Greater Harrisburg Area
Wormleysburg, PA 17043
717-763-7605

PHILLY STAMP & COIN CO., INC.
1804 Chestnut Street
Philadelphia, PA 19103
215-563-7341
215-563-7382 Fax
Email:phillysc@netreach.net
Web:http://www.mrstamp.com

TREASURE HUNT COLLECTIBLE COINS & STAMPS
10925 Perry Hwy.
Suite 11
Wexford, PA 15090
724-934-7771 or 800-545-6604
Email:TRH200@aol.com

TREASURE HUNT COLLECTIBLE COINS & STAMPS
1687 Washington Road
Suite 200
Pittsburgh, PA 15228
412-851-9991 or 800-259-4727
Email:TRH200@aol.com

Rhode Island

PODRAT COIN EXCHANGE, INC
769 Hope Street
Providence, RI 02906
401-861-7640
401-272-3032 Fax
Email: kpodrat@aol.com

Tennessee

HERRON HILL, INC.
5007 Black Road
Suite 140
Memphis, TN 38117-4505
901-683-9644

Texas

DALLAS STAMP GALLERY
1002 North Central Expwy.
Suite 501
Richardson, TX 75080
972-669-4741
972-669-4742 Fax

HUNT & COMPANY
3933 Spicewood Springs Road
Suite E-400
Austin, TX 78759
512-346-4830 or 800-458-5745
512-346-4984 Fax
Email:info@huntstamps.com
Web:http://www.huntstamps.com

SAM HOUSTON PHILATELICS
13310 Westheimer #150
Houston, TX 77077
281-493-6386
281-496-1445 Fax
Email:shduck@aol.com
Web:http://www.shauctions.com

Virginia

KENNEDY'S STAMPS & COINS
7059 Brookfield Plaza
Springfield, VA 22150
703-569-7300
703-569-7644 Fax
Email:kenny@patriot.net

LATHEROW & CO . INC.
5054 Lee Hwy.
Arlington, VA 22207
703-538-2727
Email:TRH200@aol.com

PRINCE WILLIAM STAMP & COIN
14011-H St. Germain Drive
Centreville, VA 20121
703-830-4669

Washington

TACOMA MALL BLVD COIN & STAMP
5225 Tacoma Mall, Blvd. E101
Tacoma, WA 98409
253-472-9632
253-472-8948 Fax
Email:kfeldman01@sprynet.com
Web:http://www.tmbcoinandstamp.com

THE STAMP & COIN PLACE
1310 Commercial
Bellingham, WA 98225
360-676-8720
360-647-6947 Fax
Email:stmpcoin@az.com

THE STAMP & COIN SHOP
725 Pike Street #6
Seattle, WA 98101
206-624-1400
206-621-8975 Fax
Email:jkonrad@attglobal.net
Web:http://www.Stamp-Coin.com

Wisconsin

JIM LUKE'S STAMP & COIN
815 Jay Street
P.O. Box 1780
Manitowoc, WI 54221
920-682-2324

Supplies & Accessories

BEACH PHILATELICS
42 Baltimore Lane
Palm Coast, FL 32137-8850
904-445-4550
904-447-0811 Fax
Email:mrstamp2@aol.com
Web:http://www.beachphilatelics.com

Supplies -Mail Order

GOPHER SUPPLY
2525 Nevada Ave. North
Suite 102
Minneapolis, MN 55427
800-815-3868 or 612-525-1750
612-544-5683 Fax
Email:gopher@pclink.com
Web:http://www.gophersupply.com

Topicals

ERCOLE GLORIA
Piazza PIO XI
20123 Milan,
ITALY
39-028-04106
39-028-64217 Fax
Email:gloria@iol.it

WONDERFUL WORLD OF STAMPS
P.O. Box 55, St Martin
Chomedey, Laval, PQ H7V 3P4
CANADA
450-687-0632
450-687-3143 Fax
Email:info@topicalsetc.com
Web:http://www.topicalsetc.com

Topicals - Columbus

MR. COLUMBUS
Box 1492
Frankenmuth, MI 48734
Email: Columbus@tir.com

Topicals - Miscellaneous

BOMBAY PHILATELIC
P.O. Box 7719
Delray Beach, FL 33482
561-499-7990
561-499-7553 Fax
Email:sales@bombaystamps.com
Web:http://www.bombaystamps.com

Topicals

Topicals - Miscellaneous

MINI-ARTS
P.O. Box 457
Estherville, IA 51334
712-362-4710
Email:pmga@rconnect.com
Web:http://www.miniarts.com

Ukraine

MR VAL ZABIJAKA
P.O. Box 3711
Silver Springs, MD 20918
301-593-5316 Telephone/Fax
Email: bnm123@erols.com

United Nations

BEACH PHILATELICS
42 Baltimore Lane
Palm Coast, FL 32137-8850
904-445-4550
904-447-0811 Fax
Email:mrstamp2@aol.com
Web:http://www.beachphilatelics.com

United Nations - New Issues

VICTOR R. OSTOLAZA LTD.
P.O. Box 4664
Wayne, NJ 07474-4664
973-720-5884
Email:vroltd@worldnet.att.net

United States

BEACH PHILATELICS
42 Baltimore Lane
Palm Coast, FL 32137-8850
904-445-4550
904-447-0811 Fax
Email:mrstamp2@aol.com
Web:http://www.beachphilatelics.com

BOB & MARTHA FRIEDMAN
624 Homestead Place
Joliet, IL 60435
815-725-6666
815-725-4134 Fax

BROOKMAN STAMP CO.
P.O. Box 90
Vancouver, WA 98666
360-695-1391 or 888-545-4871
360-695-1616 Fax
Email:dave@brookmanstamps.com
Web:http://www.brookmanstamps.com

United States

DALE ENTERPRISES INC.
P.O. Box 539-C
Emmaus, PA 18049
610-433-3303
610-965-6089 Fax
Email:daleent@fast.net
Web:http://www.dalestamps.com

DR. ROBERT FRIEDMAN & SONS
2029 West 75th Street
Woodridge, IL 60517
630-985-1515
630-985-1588 Fax

GARY POSNER
1405 Avenue Z, PMB #535
Brooklyn, NY 11235
800-323-4279
718-241-2801 Fax

HUNT & COMPANY
3933 Spicewood Springs Road
Suite E-400
Austin, TX 78759
512-346-4830 or 800-458-5745
512-346-4984 Fax
Email:info@huntstamps.com
Web:http://www.huntstamps.com

QUALITY INVESTORS LTD.
P.O. Box 891
Middletown, NY 10940
914-343-2174
914-342-2597 Fax
Email:lrlm@poineeris.net

US - Booklet Panes

DALE ENTERPRISES INC.
P.O. Box 539-C
Emmaus, PA 18049
610-433-3303
610-965-6089 Fax
Email:daleent@fast.net
Web:http://www.dalestamps.com

LEWIS KAUFMAN
P.O. Box 255
Kiamesha Lake, NY 12751
914-794-8013 Telephone/Fax
800-491-5453 Telephone/Fax
Email:mamet1@aol.com

US - Classics

DALE ENTERPRISES INC.
P.O. Box 539-C
Emmaus, PA 18049
610-433-3303
610-965-6089 Fax
Email:daleent@fast.net
Web:http://www.dalestamps.com

US - Classics

GARY POSNER
1405 Avenue Z, PMB #535
Brooklyn, NY 11235
800-323-4279
718-241-2801 Fax

KUKSTIS AUCTIONS INC.
P.O. Box 130
Scituate, MA 02066
781-545-8494
Email:paulk@dreamcom.net
Web:http://www.kukstis.com

US - Classic Covers

KUKSTIS AUCTIONS INC.
P.O. Box 130
Scituate, MA 02066
781-545-8494
Email:paulk@dreamcom.net
Web:http://www.kukstis.com

US - Classics/ Modern

LEWIS KAUFMAN
P.O. Box 255
Kiamesha Lake, NY 12751
914-794-8013 Telephone/Fax
800-491-5453 Telephone/Fax
Email:mamet1@aol.com

SUBURBAN STAMP INC.
176 Worthington St.
Springfield, MA 01103
413-785-5348
413-746-3788 Fax

US - Duck Stamps

METROPOLITAN STAMP CO
P.O. Box 1133
Chicago, IL 60690-1133
815-439-0142
815-439-0143 Fax

US - Federal Duck Stamps

SAM HOUSTON DUCK CO.
P.O. Box 820087
Houston,TX 77282
281-493-6386 or 800-231-5926
281-496-1445 Fax
Email:shduck@aol.com
Web:http://www.shduck.com

United States

United States

US - State Duck Stamps

SAM HOUSTON DUCK CO.
P.O. Box 820087
Houston,TX 77282
281-493-6386 or 800-231-5926
281-496-1445 Fax
Email:shduck@aol.com
Web:http://www.shduck.com

US - EFOs

GARY POSNER
1405 Avenue Z, PMB #535
Brooklyn, NY 11235
800-323-4279
718-241-2801 Fax

US - Mint

HUNT & COMPANY
3933 Spicewood Springs Road
Suite E-400
Austin, TX 78759
512-346-4830 or 800-458-5745
512-346-4984 Fax
Email:info@huntstamps.com
Web:http://www.huntstamps.com

US - Plate Blocks

BEACH PHILATELICS
42 Baltimore Lane
Palm Coast, FL 32137-8850
904-445-4550
904-447-0811 Fax
Email:mrstamp2@aol.com
Web:http://www.beachphilatelics.com

US - Plate Blocks

GARY POSNER
1405 Avenue Z, PMB #535
Brooklyn, NY 11235
800-323-4279
718-241-2801 Fax

LEWIS KAUFMAN
P.O. Box 255
Kiamesha Lake, NY 12751
914-794-8013 Telephone/Fax
800-491-5453 Telephone/Fax
Email:mamet1@aol.com

US - Price Lists

DALE ENTERPRISES INC.
P.O. Box 539-C
Emmaus, PA 18049
610-433-3303
610-965-6089
Email:daleent@fast.net
Web:http://www.dalestamps.com

ROBERT E. BARKER
P.O. Box 888063
Dunwoody, GA 30356
770-395-1757
770-671-8918 Fax
Email:rebarker@rebarker.com

US - Rare Stamps

GARY POSNER
1405 Avenue Z, PMB #535
Brooklyn, NY 11235
800-323-4279
718-241-2801 Fax

US - Rare Stamps

KUKSTIS AUCTIONS INC.
P.O. Box 130
Scituate, MA 02066
781-545-8494
Email:paulk@dreamcom.net
Web:http://www.kukstis.com

US - Singles - Classic & Modern

BOB & MARTHA FRIEDMAN
624 Homestead Place
Joliet, IL 60435
815-725-6666
815-725-4134 Fax

US - Souvenir Cards

LEWIS KAUFMAN
P.O. Box 255
Kiamesha Lake, NY 12751
914-794-8013 Telephone/Fax
800-491-5453 Telephone/Fax
Email:mamet1@aol.com

US Souvenir Pages/Panels

LEWIS KAUFMAN
P.O. Box 255
Kiamesha Lake, NY 12751
914-794-8013 Telephone/Fax
800-491-5453 Telephone/Fax
Email:mamet1@aol.com

US - Stamps

GARY'S STAMPS & COINS
120 E. Broadway
Box 6011
Enid, OK 73701
580-233-0007

US - Transportation Coils

DALE ENTERPRISES INC.
P.O. Box 539-C
Emmaus, PA 18049
610-433-3303
610-965-6089 Fax
Email:daleent@fast.net
Web:http://www.dalestamps.com

US - Used

BOB & MARTHA FRIEDMAN
624 Homestead Place
Joliet, IL 60435
815-725-6666
815-725-4134 Fax

US - Want Lists

GARY POSNER
1405 Avenue Z, PMB #535
Brooklyn, NY 11235
800-323-4279
718-241-2801 Fax

United States

UNITED STATES & WORLDWIDE
ACCUMULATIONS, COLLECTIONS, ETC.

• BUYING •

PAYING HIGH PRICES SINCE 1955. WRITE TO US OR CALL FIRST TO DISCUSS YOUR HOLDINGS, PROMPT, CASH OFFERS AND PROMPT RETURNS SHOULD OUR OFFER BE DECLINED. WE WILL TRAVEL TO INSPECT LARGE HOLDINGS! ACT TODAY!

• SELLING •

EXCELLENT STOCK OF UNITED STATES AND WORLDWIDE MATERIAL! WRITE TO RECEIVE OUR FREE "FULL-OF-BARGAINS" PRICE LIST UNITED STATES or FOREIGN... (PLEASE INCLUDE 55¢ POSTAGE).

• ESTATE SERVICES •

INHERITED A COLLECTION AND FRUSTRATED WITH HOW TO DISPOSE OF THE STAMPS? LET ME HELP. REPUTABLE SERVICE SINCE 1955. OUT RIGHT PURCHASE, APPRAISALS, AND ADVISORY SERVICES AVAILABLE. CALL WITH CONFIDENCE.

CALL TOLL FREE 1-800-833-0217 (24 HOURS)
NO PRICELIST CALLS PLEASE

ROBERT E. BARKER

BOX 888244, ATLANTA, GA 30356
Phone/Fax • 770-395-1757 • 770-671-8918
Email:rebarker@rebarker.com
Website:www.rebarker.com

Vietnam

ALLKOR STAMP CO.
Box 1346
Port Washington, NY 11050
516-883-3296 Telephone & Fax

Want Lists

BROOKMAN INTERNATIONAL
P.O. Box 450
Vancouver, WA 98666
360-695-1391 or 800-545-4871
360-695-1616 Fax
Email:dave@brookmanstamps.com

CHARLES P. SCHWARTZ
P.O. Box 165
Mora, MN 55051
320-679-4705
Email:charlesp@ecenet.com

Want Lists- British Empire 1840-1935 German Col./Offices

COLONIAL STAMP COMPANY
5757 Wilshire Blvd. PH #8
Los Angeles, CA 90036
323-933-9435
323-939-9930 Fax
Email:gwh225@aol.com

Wanted - Estates

DALE ENTERPRISES INC.
P.O. Box 539-C
Emmaus, PA 18049
610-433-3303
610-965-6089 Fax
Email:daleent@fast.net
Web:http://www.dalestamps.com

FRED BOATWRIGHT
P.O. Box 695
Sullivan, MO 63080
573-860-4057 Telephone & Fax
Email:stampooh@fidnet.com

GARY POSNER
1405 Avenue Z, PMB #535
Brooklyn, NY 11235
800-323-4279
718-241-2801 Fax

Wanted To Buy

KUKSTIS AUCTIONS INC.
P.O. Box 130
Scituate, MA 02066
781-545-8494
Email:paulk@dreamcom.net
Web:http://www.kukstis.com

Wanted - US

GARY POSNER
1405 Avenue Z, PMB #535
Brooklyn, NY 11235
800-323-4279
718-241-2801 Fax

LEWIS KAUFMAN
P.O. Box 255
Kiamesha Lake, NY 12751
914-794-8013 Telephone/Fax
800-491-5453 Telephone/Fax
Email:mamet1@aol.com

Websites

KUKSTIS AUCTIONS INC.
P.O. Box 130
Scituate, MA 02066
781-545-8494
Email:paulk@dreamcom.net
Web:http://www.kukstis.com

MILLER'S STAMP SHOP
41 New London Turnpike
Uncasville, CT 06382
860-848-0468
860-848-1926 Fax
Email:millstamps@aol.com
Web:http://www.millerstamps.com

Wholesale - Collections

A.D.A. STAMP CO., INC.
Store:910 Boyd Street
Toms River, NJ 08753
P.O. Drawer J
Island Heights, NJ 08732
732-240-1131
732-240-2620 Fax

Wholesale -Supplies

JOHN VAN ALSTYNE STAMPS
1787 Tribute Rd., Suite J
Sacramento,CA 95815
916-565-0606 or 800-297-3929
916-565-0539 Fax
Email:sherjohn@softcom.net

Wholesale -US

GARY POSNER
1405 Avenue Z, PMB #535
Brooklyn, NY 11235
800-323-4279
718-241-2801 Fax

Worldwide

EDWARD J. MCKIM
1373 Isabelle
Memphis, TN 38122
901-327-8959

Worldwide-Collections

BOB & MARTHA FRIEDMAN
624 Homestead Place
Joliet, IL 60435
815-725-6666
815-725-4134 Fax

Worldwide-Romania

GEORGE ARGHIR, PHILATELISTS
Detunata Str. 17-27
P.O. Box 521
RO-3400 CLUJ-Napoca 9
Romania
40-64-414036 Telephone & Fax

Worldwide-Year Sets

BOMBAY PHILATELIC
P.O. Box 7719
Delray Beach, FL 33482
561-499-7990
561-499-7553 Fax
Email:sales@bombaystamps.com
Web:http://www.bombaystamps.com

WALLACE STAMPS
Box 82
Port Washington, NY 11050
516-883-5578

SCOTTMOUNTS

HOW TO ORDER THE RIGHT SIZE:
Pre-cut ScottMounts come in sizes labeled as stamp width by stamp height, measured in millimeters. Strips of mount material come in three different lengths: 215mm, 240mm and 265mm. The strip you should use is based on the height of the stamp you wish to mount.
ScottMounts are available with clear or black backs. Please indicate color choice when ordering.

Pre-Cut Single Mounts

Size	Description	# Mounts	Item	Price
40 x 25	U.S. Standard Commemorative–Horizontal	40	901	$2.75
25 x 40	U.S. Standard Commemorative–Vertical	40	902	2.75
25 x 22	U.S. Regular Issue–Horizontal	40	903	2.75
22 x 25	U.S. Regular Issue–Vertical	40	904	2.75
41 x 31	U.S. Semi–Jumbo–Horizontal	40	905	2.75
31 x 41	U.S. Semi–Jumbo–Vertical	40	906	2.75
50 x 31	U.S. Jumbo–Horizontal	40	907	2.75
31 x 50	U.S. Jumbo–Vertical	40	908	2.75
25 x 27	U.S. Famous Americans	40	909	2.75
33 x 27	United Nations	40	910	2.75
40 x 27	United Nations	40	911	2.75
67 x 25	PNC, Strips of Three	40	976	4.75
67 x 34	Pacific '97 Triangle	10	984	2.25
111 x 25	PNC, Strips of Five	25	985	4.75
51 x 36	U.S. Hunting Permit/Express Mail	40	986	4.75

Pre-Cut Plate Block, FDC & Postal Card Mounts

Size	Description	# Mounts	Item	Price
57 x 55	Regular Issue Plate Block	25	912	$4.75
73 x 63	Champions of Liberty	25	913	4.75
106 x 55	Rotary Press Standard Commemorative	20	914	4.75
105 x 57	Giori Press Standard Commemorative	20	915	4.75
165 x 94	First Day Cover	10	917	4.75
140 x 90	Postal Card Size	10	918	4.75

Strips 215mm Long

Size	Description	# Mounts	Item	Price
20	U.S. 19th Century/Horizontal Coil	22	919	$ 5.95
22	U.S. Early Air Mail	22	920	5.95
24	U.S., Canada, Great Britain	22	921	5.95
25	U.S. Comm. and Regular	22	922	5.95
27	U.S. Famous Americans	22	923	5.95
28	U.S. 19th Century	22	924	5.95
30	U.S. 19th Century	22	925	5.95
31	U.S. Jumbo and Semi-Jumbo	22	926	5.95
33	United Nations	22	927	5.95
36	U.S. Hunting Permit, Canada	15	928	5.95
39	U.S. Early 20th Century	15	929	5.95
41	U.S. Semi-Jumbo	15	930	5.95
	Multiple Assortment: one strip of each size 22-41 (Two 25mm strips)	12	931	5.95
44	U.S. Vertical Coil Pair	15	932	5.95
48	U.S. Farley, Gutter Pair	15	933	5.95
50	U.S. Jumbo	15	934	5.95
52	U.S. Standard Commemorative Block	15	935	5.95
55	U.S. Century of Progress	15	936	5.95
57	U.S. Famous Americans Block	15	937	5.95
61	U.S. Blocks, Israel Tab	15	938	5.95

Strips 240mm Long

Size	Description	# Mounts	Item	Price
63	U.S. Jumbo Commemorative–Horizontal Block	10	939	$6.75
66	Israel Tab Block	10	940	6.75
68	U.S. Farley, Gutter Pair & Souvenir Sheets	10	941	6.75
74	U.S. TIPEX Souvenir Sheet	10	942	6.75
80	U.S. Standard Commemorative–Vertical Block	10	943	6.75
82	U.S. Blocks of Four	10	944	6.75
84	Israel Tab Block/Mars Pathfinder	10	945	6.75
89	U.S. Postal Card Size	10	946	6.75

Strips 265mm Long

Size	Description	# Mounts	Item	Price
100	U.N. Margin Inscribed Block	7	947	6.75
120	Various Souvenir Sheets and Blocks	7	948	6.75
40	Standard Commemorative Vertical	10	949	$6.75
55	U.S. Regular Plate Block Strip 20	10	950	6.75
59	U.S. Double Issue Strip	10	951	6.75
70	U.S. Jumbo Com. Plate Block	10	952	9.75
91	Great Britain Souvenir Sheet/Norman Rockwell	10	953	9.75
105	U.S. Standard Plate Number Strip	10	954	9.75
107	Same as above–Wide Margin	10	955	9.75
111	U.S. Gravure-Intaglio Plate Number Strip	10	956	11.25
127	U.S. Jumbo Commemorative Plate Number Strip	10	957	13.75
137	Great Britain Coronation	10	958	14.50
158	U.S. Apollo-Soyuz Plate Number Strip	10	959	15.25
231	U.S. Full Post Office Pane Regular and Commemorative	5	961	14.25

Souvenir Sheets/Small Panes

Size	Description	# Mounts	Item	Price
111 x 25	PNC, Strips of Five	25	985	4.75
204 x 153	U.S. Bicent. White Plains	5	962	$ 6.95
187 x 144	U.N. Flag Sheet	10	963	12.25
160 x 200	New U.N., Israel Sheet	10	964	12.25
120 x 207	AMERIPEX President Sht.	4	965	4.75
229 x 131	World War II Commemorative Sheet	5	968	6.95
111 x 91	Columbian Souvenir Sheet	6	970	2.95
148 x 196	Apollo Moon Landing	4	972	5.95
129 x 122	U.S. Definitive Mini-Sheet	8	989	7.95
189 x 151	Chinese New Year	5	990	7.95
150 x 185	Dr. Davis/World Cup	5	991	7.95
198 x 151	Cherokee	5	992	7.95
198 x 187	Postal Museum	4	994	7.95
156 x 187	Sign Lang., Statehood	5	995	7.95
188 x 197	Country-Western	4	996	7.95
151 x 192	Olympic	5	997	7.95
174 x 185	Buffalo Soldiers	5	998	7.95
130 x 198	Silent Screen Stars	5	999	7.95
190 x 199	Leg. West, Civil, Comic	4	1000	7.95
178 x 181	Cranes	4	1001	7.95
183 x 212	Wonders of the Sea	3	1002	7.95
156 x 264	$14 Eagle	4	1003	7.95
159 x 270	$9.95 Moon Landing	4	1004	7.95
159 x 259	$2.90 Priority/$9.95 Express Mail	4	1005	7.95
223 x 187	Marilyn Monroe	3	1006	7.95
185 x 181	Challenger Shuttle	4	1007	7.95
152 x 228	Indian Dances/Antique Autos	5	1008	7.95
165 x 150	River Boat/Hanukkah	6	1009	7.95
275 x 200	Large Gutter Blocks/Aircraft/Dinosaurs	2	1010	7.95
161 x 160	Pacific '97 Triangle Block of 16	6	1011	7.95
174 x 130	Bugs Bunny	6	1012	7.95
196 x 158	Football Coaches	4	1013	7.95
184 x 184	American Dolls	4	1014	7.95
186 x 230	Classic Movie Monsters	3	1015	7.95
187 x 160	Trans-Mississippi Sheet	4	1016	7.95
192 x 230	Celebrate the Century	3	1017	7.95
156 x 204	Space Discovery	5	1018	7.95
192 x 209	American Ballet	5	1019	7.95
139 x 151	Christmas Wreaths	5	1020	7.95

Available from your favorite stamp dealer or direct from:

SCOTT®

P.O. Box 828 Sidney OH 45365-0828

For more information on Scott products visit our web site at:
www.scottonline.com

Colonies, Former Colonies, Offices, Territories Controlled by Parent States

Belgium

Belgian Congo
Ruanda-Urundi

Denmark

Danish West Indies
Faroe Islands
Greenland
Iceland

Finland

Aland Islands

France

COLONIES PAST AND PRESENT, CONTROLLED TERRITORIES

Afars & Issas, Territory of
Alaouites
Alexandretta
Algeria
Alsace & Lorraine
Anjouan
Annam & Tonkin
Benin
Cambodia (Khmer)
Cameroun
Castellorizo
Chad
Cilicia
Cochin China
Comoro Islands
Dahomey
Diego Suarez
Djibouti (Somali Coast)
Fezzan
French Congo
French Equatorial Africa
French Guiana
French Guinea
French India
French Morocco
French Polynesia (Oceania)
French Southern & Antarctic Territories
French Sudan
French West Africa
Gabon
Germany
Ghadames
Grand Comoro
Guadeloupe
Indo-China
Inini
Ivory Coast
Laos
Latakia
Lebanon
Madagascar
Martinique
Mauritania
Mayotte
Memel
Middle Congo
Moheli
New Caledonia
New Hebrides
Niger Territory
Nossi-Be
Obock
Reunion
Rouad, Ile
Ste.-Marie de Madagascar
St. Pierre & Miquelon
Senegal
Senegambia & Niger
Somali Coast
Syria
Tahiti
Togo
Tunisia
Ubangi-Shari
Upper Senegal & Niger
Upper Volta
Viet Nam
Wallis & Futuna Islands

POST OFFICES IN FOREIGN COUNTRIES

China
Crete
Egypt
Turkish Empire
Zanzibar

Germany

EARLY STATES

Baden
Bavaria
Bergedorf
Bremen
Brunswick
Hamburg
Hanover
Lubeck
Mecklenburg-Schwerin
Mecklenburg-Strelitz
Oldenburg
Prussia
Saxony
Schleswig-Holstein
Wurttemberg

FORMER COLONIES

Cameroun (Kamerun)
Caroline Islands
German East Africa
German New Guinea
German South-West Africa
Kiauchau
Mariana Islands
Marshall Islands
Samoa
Togo

Italy

EARLY STATES

Modena
Parma
Romagna
Roman States
Sardinia
Tuscany
Two Sicilies
  Naples
  Neapolitan Provinces
  Sicily

FORMER COLONIES, CONTROLLED TERRITORIES, OCCUPATION AREAS

Aegean Islands
  Calimno (Calino)
  Caso
  Cos (Coo)
  Karki (Carchi)
  Leros (Lero)
  Lipso
  Nisiros (Nisiro)
  Patmos (Patmo)
  Piscopi
  Rodi (Rhodes)
  Scarpanto
  Simi
  Stampalia
Castellorizo
Corfu
Cyrenaica
Eritrea
Ethiopia (Abyssinia)
Fiume
Ionian Islands
  Cephalonia
  Ithaca
  Paxos
Italian East Africa
Libya
Oltre Giuba
Saseno
Somalia (Italian Somaliland)
Tripolitania

POST OFFICES IN FOREIGN COUNTRIES

"ESTERO"*
Austria
China
  Peking
  Tientsin
Crete
Tripoli
Turkish Empire
  Constantinople
  Durazzo
  Janina
Jerusalem
Salonika
Scutari
Smyrna
Valona

*Stamps overprinted "ESTERO" were used in various parts of the world.

Netherlands

Aruba
Netherlands Antilles (Curacao)
Netherlands Indies
Netherlands New Guinea
Surinam (Dutch Guiana)

Portugal

COLONIES PAST AND PRESENT, CONTROLLED TERRITORIES

Angola
Angra
Azores
Cape Verde
Funchal
Horta
Inhambane
Kionga
Lourenco Marques
Macao
Madeira
Mozambique
Mozambique Co.
Nyassa
Ponta Delgada
Portuguese Africa
Portuguese Congo
Portuguese Guinea
Portuguese India
Quelimane
St. Thomas & Prince Islands
Tete
Timor
Zambezia

Russia

ALLIED TERRITORIES AND REPUBLICS, OCCUPATION AREAS

Armenia
Aunus (Olonets)
Azerbaijan
Batum
Estonia
Far Eastern Republic
Georgia
Karelia
Latvia
Lithuania
North Ingermanland
Ostland
Russian Turkestan
Siberia
South Russia
Tannu Tuva
Transcaucasian Fed. Republics
Ukraine
Wenden (Livonia)
Western Ukraine

Spain

COLONIES PAST AND PRESENT, CONTROLLED TERRITORIES

Aguera, La
Cape Juby
Cuba
Elobey, Annobon & Corisco
Fernando Po
Ifni
Mariana Islands
Philippines
Puerto Rico
Rio de Oro
Rio Muni
Spanish Guinea
Spanish Morocco
Spanish Sahara
Spanish West Africa

POST OFFICES IN FOREIGN COUNTRIES

Morocco
Tangier
Tetuan

British Commonwealth of Nations

Dominions, Colonies, Territories, Offices and Independent Members

Comprising stamps of the British Commonwealth and associated nations.

A strict observance of technicalities would bar some or all of the stamps listed under Burma, Ireland, Kuwait, Nepal, New Republic, Orange Free State, Samoa, South Africa, South-West Africa, Stellaland, Sudan, Swaziland, the two Transvaal Republics and others but these are included for the convenience of collectors.

1. Great Britain

Great Britain: Including England, Scotland, Wales and Northern Ireland.

2. The Dominions, Present and Past

AUSTRALIA

The Commonwealth of Australia was proclaimed on January 1, 1901. It consists of six former colonies as follows:

New South Wales
Queensland
South Australia
Victoria
Tasmania
Western Australia

Territories belonging to, or administered by Australia: Australian Antarctic Territory, Christmas Island, Cocos (Keeling) Islands, Nauru, New Guinea, Norfolk Island, Papua New Guinea.

CANADA

The Dominion of Canada was created by the British North America Act in 1867. The following provinces were former separate colonies and issued postage stamps:

British Columbia and Vancouver Island
New Brunswick
Newfoundland
Nova Scotia
Prince Edward Island

FIJI

The colony of Fiji became an independent nation with dominion status on Oct. 10, 1970.

GHANA

This state came into existence Mar. 6, 1957, with dominion status. It consists of the former colony of the Gold Coast and the Trusteeship Territory of Togoland. Ghana became a republic July 1, 1960.

INDIA

The Republic of India was inaugurated on January 26, 1950. It succeeded the Dominion of India which was proclaimed August 15, 1947, when the former Empire of India was divided into Pakistan and the Union of India. The Republic is composed of about 40 predominantly Hindu states of three classes: governor's provinces, chief commissioner's provinces and princely states. India also has various territories, such as the Andaman and Nicobar Islands.

The old Empire of India was a federation of British India and the native states. The more important princely states were autonomous. Of the more than 700 Indian states, these 43 are familiar names to philatelists because of their postage stamps.

CONVENTION STATES

Chamba
Faridkot
Gwalior
Jhind
Nabha
Patiala

NATIVE FEUDATORY STATES

Alwar
Bahawalpur
Bamra
Barwani
Bhopal
Bhor
Bijawar
Bundi
Bussahir
Charkhari
Cochin
Dhar
Duttia
Faridkot (1879-85)
Hyderabad
Idar
Indore
Jaipur
Jammu
Jammu and Kashmir
Jasdan
Jhalawar
Jhind (1875-76)
Kashmir
Kishangarh
Las Bela
Morvi
Nandgaon
Nowanuggur
Orchha
Poonch
Rajpeepla
Sirmur
Soruth
Travancore
Wadhwan

NEW ZEALAND

Became a dominion on September 26, 1907. The following islands and territories are, or have been, administered by New Zealand:

Aitutaki
Cook Islands (Rarotonga)
Niue
Penrhyn
Ross Dependency
Samoa (Western Samoa)
Tokelau Islands

PAKISTAN

The Republic of Pakistan was proclaimed March 23, 1956. It succeeded the Dominion which was proclaimed August 15, 1947. It is made up of all or part of several Moslem provinces and various districts of the former Empire of India, including Bahawalpur and Las Bela. Pakistan withdrew from the Commonwealth in 1972.

SOUTH AFRICA

Under the terms of the South African Act (1909) the self-governing colonies of Cape of Good Hope, Natal, Orange River Colony and Transvaal united on May 31, 1910, to form the Union of South Africa. It became an independent republic May 3, 1961.

Under the terms of the Treaty of Versailles, South-West Africa, formerly German South-West Africa, was mandated to the Union of South Africa.

SRI LANKA (CEYLON)

The Dominion of Ceylon was proclaimed February 4, 1948. The island had been a Crown Colony from 1802 until then. On May 22, 1972, Ceylon became the Republic of Sri Lanka.

3. Colonies, Past and Present; ControlledTerritory and Independent Members of the Commonwealth

Aden
Aitutaki
Antigua
Ascension
Bahamas
Bahrain
Bangladesh
Barbados
Barbuda
Basutoland
Batum
Bechuanaland
Bechuanaland Prot.
Belize
Bermuda
Botswana
British Antarctic Territory
British Central Africa
British Columbia and Vancouver Island
British East Africa
British Guiana

British Honduras
British Indian Ocean Territory
British New Guinea
British Solomon Islands
British Somaliland
Brunei
Burma
Bushire
Cameroons
Cape of Good Hope
Cayman Islands
Christmas Island
Cocos (Keeling) Islands
Cook Islands
Crete,
British Administration
Cyprus
Dominica
East Africa & Uganda
Protectorates
Egypt
Falkland Islands
Fiji
Gambia
German East Africa
Gibraltar
Gilbert Islands
Gilbert & Ellice Islands
Gold Coast
Grenada
Griqualand West
Guernsey
Guyana
Heligoland
Hong Kong
Indian Native States
(see India)
Ionian Islands
Jamaica
Jersey
Kenya
Kenya, Uganda & Tanzania
Kuwait
Labuan
Lagos
Leeward Islands
Lesotho
Madagascar
Malawi
Malaya
Federated Malay States
Johore
Kedah
Kelantan
Malacca
Negri Sembilan
Pahang
Penang
Perak
Perlis
Selangor
Singapore
Sungei Ujong
Trengganu
Malaysia
Maldive Islands
Malta
Man, Isle of
Mauritius
Mesopotamia
Montserrat
Muscat
Namibia
Natal
Nauru
Nevis
New Britain
New Brunswick
Newfoundland
New Guinea
New Hebrides
New Republic
New South Wales
Niger Coast Protectorate
Nigeria
Niue
Norfolk Island
North Borneo
Northern Nigeria
Northern Rhodesia
North West Pacific Islands
Nova Scotia
Nyasaland Protectorate
Oman
Orange River Colony
Palestine
Papua New Guinea
Penrhyn Island
Pitcairn Islands
Prince Edward Island
Queensland
Rhodesia
Rhodesia & Nyasaland
Ross Dependency
Sabah
St. Christopher
St. Helena
St. Kitts
St. Kitts-Nevis-Anguilla
St. Lucia
St. Vincent
Samoa
Sarawak
Seychelles
Sierra Leone
Solomon Islands
Somaliland Protectorate
South Arabia
South Australia
South Georgia
Southern Nigeria
Southern Rhodesia
South-West Africa
Stellaland
Straits Settlements
Sudan
Swaziland
Tanganyika
Tanzania
Tasmania
Tobago
Togo
Tokelau Islands
Tonga
Transvaal
Trinidad
Trinidad and Tobago
Tristan da Cunha
Trucial States
Turks and Caicos
Turks Islands
Tuvalu
Uganda
United Arab Emirates
Victoria
Virgin Islands
Western Australia
Zambia
Zanzibar
Zululand

POST OFFICES IN FOREIGN COUNTRIES

Africa
East Africa Forces
Middle East Forces
Bangkok
China
Morocco
Turkish Empire

Pronunciation Symbols

ə .... banana, collide, abut

ˈə, ˌə .... humdrum, abut

ᵊ .... immediately preceding \l\, \n\, \m\, \ŋ\, as in battle, mitten, eaten, and sometimes open \ˈō-pᵊm\, lock and key \-ᵊŋ-\; immediately following \l\, \m\, \r\, as often in French table, prisme, titre

ər .... further, merger, bird

ˈər-, ˈə-r .... as in two different pronunciations of hurry \ˈhər-ē, ˈhə-rē\

a .... mat, map, mad, gag, snap, patch

ā .... day, fade, date, aorta, drape, cape

ä .... bother, cot, and, with most American speakers, father, cart

ȧ .... father as pronounced by speakers who do not rhyme it with *bother*; French patte

au̇ .... now, loud, out

b .... baby, rib

ch .... chin, nature \ˈnā-chər\

d .... did, adder

e .... bet, bed, peck

ˈē, ˌē .... beat, nosebleed, evenly, easy

ē .... easy, mealy

f .... fifty, cuff

g .... go, big, gift

h .... hat, ahead

hw .... whale as pronounced by those who do not have the same pronunciation for both *whale* and *wail*

i .... tip, banish, active

ī .... site, side, buy, tripe

j .... job, gem, edge, join, judge

k .... kin, cook, ache

k̲ .... German ich, Buch; one pronunciation of loch

l .... lily, pool

m .... murmur, dim, nymph

n .... no, own

ⁿ .... indicates that a preceding vowel or diphthong is pronounced with the nasal passages open, as in French *un bon vin blanc* \œⁿ -bōⁿ -vaⁿ -bläⁿ\

ŋ .... sing \ˈsiŋ\, singer \ˈsiŋ-ər\, finger \ˈfiŋ-gər\, ink \ˈiŋk \

ō .... bone, know, beau

ȯ .... saw, all, gnaw, caught

œ .... French boeuf, German Hölle

œ̄ .... French feu, German Höhle

ȯi .... coin, destroy

p .... pepper, lip

r .... red, car, rarity

s .... source, less

sh .... as in shy, mission, machine, special (actually, this is a single sound, not two); with a hyphen between, two sounds as in *grasshopper* \ˈgras-ˌhä-pər\

t .... tie, attack, late, later, latter

th .... as in thin, ether (actually, this is a single sound, not two); with a hyphen between, two sounds as in *knighthood* \ˈnīt-ˌhu̇d\

t̲h̲ .... then, either, this (actually, this is a single sound, not two)

ü .... rule, youth, union \ˈyün-yən\, few \ˈfyü\

u̇ .... pull, wood, book, curable \ˈkyu̇r-ə-bəl\, fury \ˈfyu̇r-ē\

ue .... German füllen, hübsch

ue̅ .... French rue, German fühlen

v .... vivid, give

w .... we, away

y .... yard, young, cue \ˈkyü\, mute \ˈmyüt\, union \ˈyün-yən\

ʸ .... indicates that during the articulation of the sound represented by the preceding character the front of the tongue has substantially the position it has for the articulation of the first sound of *yard*, as in French *digne* \dēnʸ\

z .... zone, raise

zh .... as in vision, azure \ˈa-zhər\ (actually, this is a single sound, not two); with a hyphen between, two sounds as in *hogshead* \ˈhȯgz-ˌhed, ˈhägz-\

\ .... slant line used in pairs to mark the beginning and end of a transcription: \ˈpen\

ˈ .... mark preceding a syllable with primary (strongest) stress: \ˈpen-mən-ˌship\

ˌ .... mark preceding a syllable with secondary (medium) stress: \ˈpen-mən-ˌship\

\- .... mark of syllable division

( ) .... indicate that what is symbolized between is present in some utterances but not in others: *factory* \ˈfak-t(ə-)rē\

÷ .... indicates that many regard as unacceptable the pronunciation variant immediately following: *cupola* \ˈkyü-pə-lə, ÷-ˌlō\